CHAMBERS & PARTNERS

A GUIDE TO THE LEGAL PROFESSION

1998-99

NINTH EDITION

REENA SENGUPTA

Editor

Research audit by BMRB International

"It is our opinion that Chambers display a vigorous and professional methodological approach to their task… All their interviewers were considered to have displayed a high level of clarity, professionalism and objectivity, and to have been very thorough in the conduct of interviews."

Gailynn Nicks, Director of Business Markets,
British Market Research Bureau (July 1998)

Chambers & Partners Publishing
Saville House, 23 Long Lane, London EC1A 9HL
Tel: (0171) 606 1300
www.chambersandpartners.com

Orders to Biblios Distribution Services
Tel: (01403) 710 971

Published by Chambers & Partners Publishing
(a division of Orbach & Chambers Ltd)
Saville House, 23 Long Lane, London EC1A 9HL
Tel: (0171) 606 1300 Fax: (0171) 600 3191

Chambers & Partners Legal Recruitment: (0171) 606 8844

Copyright © Michael Chambers and Orbach & Chambers Ltd 1998
ISBN: 0-85514-108-5

Publisher: *Michael Chambers*

Editor: *Reena SenGupta*

Deputy Editor: *Jo Stafford*

Editorial Assistants: *Jackie Tilston, Lisa Carroll*

Senior researchers: *Caroline Walker, Jane Cozens, Robert Diepstraten,
Richard Freeland, Chris Hallatt Wells, Liz Speakman*

Production Manager: *Kerry Hall*

Database Manager: *Derek Wright*

Production Team: *John Crookes, Shannon Bruce, Ralph Davies*

Marketing Consultant: *Graham Seldon*

Database design & CD-Rom: *Chris Randle, Amethyst Logic*

Printed in England by Bath Press

Acknowledgements:
Our thanks to the thousands of lawyers who assisted our research team in identifying leading practitioners
in all the main areas of law, and to the many clients who recommended law firms. Thanks, too, to the
Chambers & Partners' recruitment consultants whose knowledge of solicitors
and law firms throughout the country was invaluable.

THE RESEARCH AUDIT

For information on the research audit

Gailynn Nicks
Director of Business Markets

BMRB International
Hadley House
79-81 Uxbridge Road
London W5 5SU

Tel: 0181-566-5000
Fax: 0181-840-1668
gailynn.nicks@bmrb.co.uk

BMRB International, the longest-established UK market research company and one of the five largest UK agencies, conducted an audit of the Chambers directory. It was carried out by BMRB's Business Markets division, which specialises in business-to-business research. Divisional director, Gailynn Nicks, who conducted the audit, has over 10 years' experience in research.

Research audit

IN JULY 1998, we carried out a thorough analysis of the Chambers and Partners' research process, from questionnaire and data gathering through to analysis and reporting. In addition we interviewed a number of research respondents (legal practitioners, clients and trade associations) to obtain their perspective on the research process.

Research methods

The first part of Chambers contains a guide to the legal profession which is based on a research programme conducted by a full-time research team of 9 lawyers in the first half of 1998. Sixty areas of law (Admin and Public, Advertising, and so on) were researched with the aim of providing an objective list of recommended legal practitioners (law firms, sets of chambers, and individual practitioners).

The Chambers database provides the sampling frame for the research. This is kept current by means of an interactive process whereby information is obtained not only through the research process but also through voluntary provision of information regarding changes by legal firms.

The research process consists of a number of data gathering exercises. In addition to a comprehensive programme of telephone interviews, written submissions are included. The research programme was conducted from January to June 1998.

In total 4228 interviews were conducted: 3903 with legal practitioners, and 325 with clients and other disinterested bodies.

In some areas, particularly where there are relatively few practitioners, such as Advertising and Marketing, a full census was attempted, and indeed a high percentage of practitioners were contacted. In other areas, such as Commercial Litigation, the interviews were conducted with a representative sample of practitioners.

The interviews were carried out by telephone, and they lasted, on average, 30 minutes. Telephone interviewing does have a number of key benefits, notably the elimination of regional bias, objectivity of findings, and efficiency of data gathering.

The interviews were conducted with senior personnel, usually heads of the relevant department and other key personnel in each area of law. Interviews were also held with selected client companies and with other relevant bodies or associations.

Validation of findings

Key to quality control is the validation of findings, to ensure that they are not biased by the researcher or by individual responses. Findings therefore were subject to the following checks:

- Weight of numbers, ie that there were sufficient respondents to form a representative sample.
- Checks against former years to identify trends and variations over time
- Investigation of dramatic changes or anomalies or contradictions within the findings through further interviews
- The team of researchers changes each year
- Internal decisions were made by teams to avoid personal bias
- The interactive nature of the process including the written submissions, provides several opportunities for errors to be identified.

The research team

The research team are all legal professionals, and are thus able to draw on their own experience and expertise when collecting and reporting data.

For each area of law, a team member or number of team members has responsibility for all data gathering, analysis, validation and reporting.

(Details of the research team are given on the following page.)

Gailynn Nicks, BMRB

THE RESEARCH TEAM

Jo Stafford (Deputy Editor)

Solicitor, admitted 1996. BA (Hons), PG Dip law. Read English at Nottingham University. Worked for a leading media firm in London, specialising in defamation. Researched the 1997-1998 Chambers Directory. Editor of the 1998 Student Edition of the Directory.

Jane Cozens

Solicitor, admitted 1989. B.Soc.Sci (Hons) Read Law and Psychology at Keele University. Practised commercial litigation at a City firm for three years. Head of litigation at an investment bank from 1992-1997. She had sole responsibility for the bank's in-house recoveries, property, and insolvency litigation.

Elizabeth Speakman

Solicitor, admitted 1987. BA (Hons). Read English at London University. Practised general litigation at the Hong Kong office of a major City firm before doing personal injury at a leading Bristol firm. Has also worked in Latin America and Spain.

Gordon McBain

Solicitor, admitted 1989. BA Hons. Read English at Girton College, Cambridge. Practised in London as an Assistant Solicitor in the company/commercial department of a leading Knightsbridge firm. Was a journalist on *Commercial Lawyer* from 1994 to 1996, and then became a researcher on the Chambers Directory.

Christopher Hallatt Wells

Solicitor, admitted 1994. BA (Hons). Read Law at Fitzwilliam College, Cambridge. Articled with leading City corporate practice. He then moved to another leading City firm in 1995 where he specialised in construction and PFI projects.

Robert Diepstraten

Solicitor, admitted 1986. LLB (Hons). Read Law at London School of Economics. Practised commercial and media law for nine years at a leading City firm. Specialist experience of litigation and dispute resolution. Clients included National Newspapers, TV companies, UK and overseas banks, and a foreign government.

Caroline Walker

Solicitor, admitted 1995. BA (Hons), PG Dip. Read Classics at Girton College, Cambridge. Qualified and practised both contentious and non-contentious employment law in a leading City firm.

Vanessa Robinson

Solicitor, qualified 1995. MA (Hons) in Art History at St. Andrews University. Worked for a medium-sized City firm. Has also worked in the arts and media as a marketing and commercial manager. Researcher on the 1997-1998 Chambers Directory.

Samantha Benitez

Solicitor, admitted 1994. LLB (Hons). Read Law at Cardiff University. Practised commercial litigation and professional negligence with a niche law firm in London.

Suraiya Haq

Solicitor, admitted 1994. Read Law at Warwick University. Articled with top Birmingham firm, where she specialised in commercial property. Practised commercial litigation at one of the national firms for two years.

Richard Freeland

Called to the Bar in 1997. Read History at University College London. Postgraduate Diploma in EC law at Kings College, London. Contributes articles on legal subjects to specialist publications.

Additional research

Matthew Scott
Called to The Bar in 1996;
BA (Hons) Jurisprudence (Oxon).

Lola Adewale
BSc (Hons); LLB; LPC

Rubindar Singh
L.L.B. (Hons); LPC

Carl Gorton
BA (Hons); CPE

CONTENTS

Leading firms and leading solicitors *(green pages)*   *(Full index overleaf)*

Solicitors' A – Z   797

FULL INDEX OF SPECIALIST AREAS

THE LAW FIRMS

AN INTRODUCTION

CHAMBERS & PARTNERS

LARGEST FIRMS (An index to these tables is on p.20)

(An index to these tables is on p.20)

NATIONWIDE : THE 50 LARGEST FIRMS BY TOTAL NO. OF SOLICITORS IN THE UK

		Ptnrs	Assts	Other Fee Earners	Total Sols			Ptnrs	Assts	Other Fee Earners	Total Sols
1	Clifford Chance	180	683	165	**863**	26	Masons	65	126	62	**191**
2	Eversheds	322	455	533	**777**	27	Clyde & Co	79	106	58	**185**
3	Linklaters	156	441	202	**597**	28	Davies Arnold Cooper	56	129	65	**185**
4	Dibb Lupton Alsop	222	360	285	**582**	29	Barlow Lyde & Gilbert	71	113	64	**184**
5	Allen & Overy	132	441	171	**573**	30	Rowe & Maw	70	113	68	**183**
6	Freshfields	132	384	175	**516**	31	Irwin Mitchell	75	104	261	**179**
7	Lovell White Durrant	129	321	198	**450**	32	Shoosmiths & Harrison	69	105	191	**174**
8	Cameron McKenna	149	271	155	**420**	33	Dundas & Wilson CS	56	115	45	**171**
9	Herbert Smith	121	288	183	**409**	34	Garretts	46	123	24	**169**
10	Simmons & Simmons	125	275	169	**400**	35	Osborne Clarke	50	118	41	**168**
11	Slaughter and May	91	270	119	**361**	36	Taylor Joynson Garrett	77	89	61	**166**
12	Nabarro Nathanson	111	237	85	**348**	37	Bevan Ashford	60	105	84	**165**
13	Norton Rose	95	249	139	**344**	38	Baker & McKenzie	55	110	67	**165**
14	Ashurst Morris Crisp	75	235	132	**310**	39	Thompsons	80	84	92	**164**
15	Hammond Suddards	87	215	223	**302**	40	Stephenson Harwood	60	95	51	**155**
16	Addleshaw Booth & Co	86	172	185	**258**	41	Lawrence Graham	77	77	57	**154**
17	Pinsent Curtis	124	130	123	**254**	42	Theodore Goddard	54	93	29	**147**
18	Denton Hall	92	137	98	**229**	43	Richards Butler	62	84	72	**146**
19	Wansbroughs Willey Hargrave	65	159	62	**224**	44	Burges Salmon	40	106	39	**146**
20	Wragge & Co	60	164	97	**224**	45	Bond Pearce	53	92	69	**145**
21	Berrymans Lace Mawer	83	118	68	**201**	46	Macfarlanes	51	88	62	**139**
22	Wilde Sapte	66	135	81	**201**	47	Morgan Bruce	59	78	34	**137**
23	Berwin Leighton	73	123	48	**196**	48	McGrigor Donald	48	85	42	**133**
24	Edge & Ellison	78	117	72	**195**	49	Field Fisher Waterhouse	58	71	54	**129**
25	S J Berwin & Co	73	120	78	**193**	50	Charles Russell	62	65	35	**127**

LONDON: THE 200 LARGEST FIRMS

The rankings in this table are determined by the number of solicitors working in this region. They are based on partner and assistant solicitor figures only: all other fee-earners are excluded.

		Ptnrs	Asst Solrs	Total No of Solicitors						Ptnrs	Asst Solrs	Total No of Solicitors			
				'98	'97	'96	'95					'98	'97	'96	'95
1	Clifford Chance	180	683	**863**	773	708	715	23	Stephenson Harwood	60	95	**155**	167	149	163
2	Linklaters	156	441	**597**	573	540	485	24	Lawrence Graham	77	77	**154**	133	118	114
3	Allen & Overy	132	441	**573**	493	422	413	25	Theodore Goddard	54	93	**147**	133	122	122
4	Freshfields	132	384	**516**	449	421	398	26	Richards Butler	62	84	**146**	132	131	125
5	Lovell White Durrant	129	321	**450**	403	346	387	27	Davies Arnold Cooper	48	93	**141**	120	111	113
6	Herbert Smith	121	288	**409**	369	326	296	28	Macfarlanes	51	88	**139**	126	119	110
7	Simmons & Simmons	125	275	**400**	353	344	321	29	Clyde & Co	58	75	**133**	109	121	123
8	Cameron McKenna	142	252	**394**	399	–	–	30	Masons	44	87	**131**	155	116	105
9	Slaughter and May	91	270	**361**	356	330	353	31	Field Fisher Waterhouse	58	71	**129**	98	92	79
10	Norton Rose	95	249	**344**	321	301	275	32	Titmuss Sainer Dechert	42	81	**123**	103	84	85
11	Ashurst Morris Crisp	75	235	**310**	280	238	223	33	Hammond Suddards	37	86	**123**	90	42	42
12	Nabarro Nathanson	86	169	**255**	237	266	262	34	Travers Smith Braithwaite	47	73	**120**	113	114	107
13	Denton Hall	87	120	**207**	215	213	180	35	Beachcroft Stanleys	42	77	**119**	112	95	82
14	Wilde Sapte	66	135	**201**	232	195	203	36	Ince & Co	54	58	**112**	102	102	84
15	Dibb Lupton Alsop	83	120	**203**	146	–	–	37	Reynolds Porter Chamberlain	42	68	**110**	95	108	101
16	Berwin Leighton	73	123	**196**	169	146	140	38	Charles Russell	52	55	**107**	86	68	62
17	S J Berwin & Co	73	120	**193**	113	141	118	39	D J Freeman	47	57	**104**	100	100	109
18	Eversheds	72	115	**187**	135	136	112	40	Gouldens	35	66	**101**	97	88	96
19	Barlow Lyde & Gilbert	71	113	**184**	189	144	137	41	Bird & Bird	39	59	**98**	86	78	73
20	Rowe & Maw	70	113	**183**	159	153	148	42	Trowers & Hamlins	41	51	**92**	78	70	73
21	Taylor Joynson Garrett	77	89	**166**	162	168	149	43	Holman, Fenwick & Willan	50	41	**91**	90	92	91
22	Baker & McKenzie	55	110	**165**	145	119	121	44	Withers	43	48	**91**	89	80	58

		Ptnrs	Asst Solrs	Total No of Solicitors '98	'97	'96	'95
45	Paisner & Co	44	47	**91**	87	77	77
46	Watson, Farley & Williams	35	54	**89**	78	85	121
47	Nicholson Graham & Jones	52	35	**87**	81	81	66
48	Olswang	33	52	**85**	69	48	41
49	Mishcon de Reya	32	50	**82**	73	58	58
50	Farrer & Co	39	42	**81**	76	71	65
51	Berrymans Lace Mawer	32	49	**81**	77	–	–
52	Kennedys	33	43	**76**	62	58	52
53	Manches & Co	32	41	**73**	72	66	66
54	Biddle	34	36	**70**	69	56	50
55	Speechly Bircham	40	27	**67**	73	57	56
56	Harbottle & Lewis	15	50	**65**	57	41	43
57	Sinclair Roche & Temperley	27	35	**62**	68	87	84
58	Weil, Gotshal & Manges	16	45	**61**	42	–	–
59	Radcliffes	36	22	**58**	62	65	70
60	Vizards	29	28	**57**	61	52	39
61	Lewis Silkin	25	32	**57**	63	63	57
62	Garretts	17	40	**57**	47	30	27
63	Bristows	19	37	**56**	60	68	66
64	Finers	35	20	**55**	46	47	36
65	Hill Taylor Dickinson	23	31	**54**	48	48	73
66	Pinsent Curtis	21	33	**54**	37	33	35
67	Wedlake Bell	27	26	**53**	51	56	56
68	Edward Lewis	20	32	**52**	46	46	37
69	Jeffrey Green Russell	26	25	**51**	43	40	36
70	Kroll, Rubin & Fionella LLP	10	40	**50**	–	–	–
71	Howard Kennedy	29	19	**48**	38	37	37
72	Wansbroughs Willey Hargrave	12	36	**48**	39	–	–
73	Kingsley Napley	32	15	**47**	42	38	34
74	Russell Jones & Walker	21	25	**46**	59	36	36
75	Edge & Ellison	17	28	**45**	32	32	24
76	Capsticks	16	29	**45**	45	37	27
77	Osborne Clarke	16	29	**45**	36	19	19
78	Fladgate Fielder	25	19	**44**	44	45	43
79	Le Brasseur J Tickle	21	23	**44**	35	28	37
80	Arnheim & Co	14	29	**43**	27	–	–
81	Warner Cranston	16	26	**42**	35	31	29
82	Russell-Cooke, Potter & Chapman	17	24	**41**	42	40	34
83	Salans Hertzfeld & Heilbronn HRK	10	30	**40**	–	–	–
84	Lee & Pembertons	21	18	**39**	34	33	31
85	Rosling King	15	24	**39**	39	39	29
86	Penningtons	17	21	**38**	37	45	41
87	Bircham & Co. (incorporating Dyson Bell Martin)	21	16	**37**	44	44	39
88	Campbell Hooper	18	19	**37**	32	25	25
89	Beaumont and Son	14	23	**37**	29	25	28
90	Bolt Burdon	10	27	**37**	31	–	–
91	Boodle Hatfield	21	14	**35**	35	35	39
92	Hobson Audley Hopkins & Wood	17	18	**35**	36	33	25
93	Kingsford Stacey Blackwell	16	19	**35**	22	22	20
94	Hodge Jones & Allen	13	22	**35**	30	23	20
95	Pritchard Englefield	21	13	**34**	34	45	40
96	Fisher Meredith	6	28	**34**	32	25	25
97	Constant & Constant	26	7	**33**	34	35	35
98	Winckworth & Pemberton (incorporating Sherwood & Co)	15	18	**33**	42	46	43
99	Fox Williams	13	20	**33**	26	25	22
100	The Simkins Partnership	22	10	**32**	41	38	40
101	LeBoeuf, Lamb, Greene & MacRae	8	24	**32**	28	–	–
102	Hextall Erskine	21	10	**31**	29	23	21
103	Druces & Attlee	15	16	**31**	33	24	24
104	E. Edwards Son & Noice	9	22	**31**	17	–	–
105	Tarlo Lyons	21	9	**30**	24	19	19
106	Edwin Coe	17	13	**30**	27	27	27
107	Sacker & Partners	15	15	**30**	23	20	–
108	Davenport Lyons	15	15	**30**	28	26	25
109	Sidley & Austin	8	22	**30**	30	20	20
110	White & Case	8	22	**30**	28	28	–
111	T.V. Edwards	5	25	**30**	30	31	31
112	Middleton Potts	18	11	**29**	30	29	30
113	Coudert Brothers	16	13	**29**	23	21	21
114	Fishburn Boxer	13	16	**29**	29	29	30
115	Rooks Rider	11	18	**29**	26	24	23
116	Hempsons	18	10	**28**	43	26	30
117	Payne Hicks Beach	18	10	**28**	25	24	25
118	Hamlin Slowe	21	6	**27**	26	25	24
119	Collyer-Bristow	17	10	**27**	27	26	26
120	Park Nelson	16	11	**27**	22	25	27
121	Goodman Derrick	14	13	**27**	24	24	24
122	Rakisons	11	16	**27**	22	19	22
123	Crockers Oswald Hickson	9	18	**27**	22	14	14
124	Prince Evans	7	20	**27**	30	30	–
125	Dawson & Co	17	9	**26**	25	23	23
126	Devonshires	16	10	**26**	24	23	20
127	Teacher Stern Selby	14	12	**26**	26	26	20
128	Cleary, Gottlieb, Steen & Hamilton	7	19	**26**	28	–	–
129	Amhurst Brown Colombotti	17	8	**25**	25	35	32
130	Bindman & Partners	15	10	**25**	21	20	16
131	Morgan Bruce	15	10	**25**	26	23	23
132	Bates, Wells & Braithwaite	13	12	**25**	22	21	20
133	Memery Crystal	10	15	**25**	23	21	20
134	Rowley Ashworth	9	16	**25**	26	45	17
135	Skadden, Arps, Slate, Meagher & Flom LLP	6	19	**25**	25	–	–
136	Sheridans	17	7	**24**	21	19	19
137	Stringer Saul	15	9	**24**	23	22	20
138	Lee Bolton & Lee	16	7	**23**	24	27	25
139	Rees & Freres	16	7	**23**	25	22	22
140	Maxwell Batley	15	8	**23**	31	21	20
141	Thomas Cooper & Stibbard	15	8	**23**	26	21	21
142	Leigh, Day & Co	12	11	**23**	20	16	16
143	Llewelyn Zietman	12	11	**23**	6	–	–
144	Barnett Alexander Chart	11	12	**23**	20	18	18
145	Morgan, Lewis & Bockius	9	14	**23**	13	12	–
146	David Levene & Co	6	17	**23**	18	–	–
147	William Sturges & Co	12	10	**22**	22	22	22
148	Holmes Hardingham	11	11	**22**	21	20	20
149	Covington & Burling	5	17	**22**	18	16	–
150	Marriott Harrison	14	7	**21**	22	24	24
151	Thompsons	13	8	**21**	25	51	–
152	Anthony Gold, Lerman & Muirhead	12	9	**21**	22	19	17
153	Palmer Cowen	10	11	**21**	21	19	–
154	McGrigor Donald	8	13	**21**	19	19	19
155	Peter Carter-Ruck and Partners	15	5	**20**	21	22	23
156	Royds Treadwell	14	6	**20**	21	22	16
157	Seddons	14	6	**20**	18	18	17
158	Glovers	11	9	**20**	19	17	16
159	Ross & Craig	9	11	**20**	20	–	–
160	Stewarts	8	12	**20**	22	18	18
161	Mayer Brown & Platt	7	13	**20**	20	20	–
162	Stephens Innocent	7	13	**20**	18	18	18
163	Townleys	5	15	**20**	12	9	–
164	Hickman & Rose	5	15	**20**	12	–	–
165	Lawrence Jones	15	4	**19**	18	17	19
166	Clintons	13	6	**19**	19	17	17

		Ptnrs	Asst Solrs	Total No of Solicitors '98	'97	'96	'95
167	Cumberland Ellis Peirs	12	7	**19**	16	18	18
168	Lane & Partners	12	7	**19**	18	17	17
169	Laytons	12	7	**19**	20	24	21
170	Sharpe Pritchard	11	8	**19**	24	19	19
171	Elborne Mitchell	11	8	**19**	24	34	35
172	Underwood & Co (incorporating Corbould Rigby & Co)	9	10	**19**	17	18	15
173	Orchard	8	11	**19**	15	–	–
174	Duthie Hart & Duthie	5	14	**19**	19	17	15
175	Jay Benning & Peltz	11	7	**18**	–	–	–
176	Peters & Peters	11	7	**18**	18	18	–
177	Magrath & Co	6	12	**18**	18	17	–
178	Osbornes	6	12	**18**	14	–	–
179	Brown & Wood	5	13	**18**	–	–	–
180	Kidd Rapinet	14	3	**17**	17	15	14
181	Gordon Dadds	11	6	**17**	19	14	19
182	Maples Teesdale	11	6	**17**	15	14	–
183	Winward Fearon	10	7	**17**	17	18	18
184	Bentleys, Stokes & Lowless	9	8	**17**	20	23	23
185	Stones Porter	9	8	**17**	21	23	21
186	Walker Martineau	9	8	**17**	17	19	28
187	Cartwright Cunningham Haselgrove & Co	6	11	**17**	14	15	18
188	J.B. Wheatley & Co	5	12	**17**	5	–	–
189	Jackson Parton	12	4	**16**	16	16	14
190	Hardwick Stallards	11	5	**16**	–	–	–
191	May, May & Merrimans	11	5	**16**	15	16	15
192	Reid Minty	11	5	**16**	16	–	–
193	More Fisher Brown	9	7	**16**	16	14	–
194	Thomas Eggar Church Adams	7	9	**16**	–	–	–
195	Latham & Watkins	6	10	**16**	8	9	–
196	Rosenblatt	6	10	**16**	16	–	–
197	Schilling & Lom and Partners	6	10	**16**	14	8	–
198	Irwin Mitchell	5	11	**16**	4	3	–
199	Hunters	11	4	**15**	16	14	14
200	Shaw and Croft	10	5	**15**	15	14	16

SOUTH EAST: THE 50 LARGEST FIRMS

The rankings in this table are determined by the number of solicitors working in this region. They are based on partner and assistant solicitor figures only: all other fee-earners are excluded.

		Ptnrs	Asst Solrs	Total No of Solicitors '98	'97	'96	'95
1	Blake Lapthorn *Fareham, Portsmouth, Southampton*	41	75	**116**	107	91	76
2	Cole & Cole *Oxford (2), Abingdon, Croydon, Reading, Witney*	35	43	**78**	62	68	63
3	Shoosmiths & Harrison *Banbury, Reading, Southampton*	21	52	**73**	67	65	65
4	Thomas Eggar Church Adams *Chichester, Horsham, Reigate, Worthing*	36	32	**68**	–	–	–
5	Cripps Harries Hall *Tunbridge Wells, Kent, Crowborough, Heathfield*	28	40	**68**	61	46	41
6	Pictons *St. Albans, Bedford, Central Milton Keynes, Hemel Hempstead, Luton, Stevenage, Watford*	34	32	**66**	59	68	55
7	Thomson Snell & Passmore *Tunbridge Wells, Maidstone, Tonbridge*	38	20	**58**	52	52	49
8	Donne Mileham & Haddock *Brighton, Crawley, East Grinstead, Lewes, Newhaven, Worthing*	33	24	**57**	52	46	41
9	Bond Pearce *Southampton (3)*	21	35	**56**	22	20	–
10	Clyde & Co *Guildford*	20	30	**50**	39	42	41
11	Hart Brown *Guildford (2), Cobham, Cranleigh, Farnham, Godalming, Woking*	17	32	**49**	45	41	41
12	Linnells *Oxford, Bicester, Central Milton Keynes, Newport Pagnell*	21	26	**47**	47	39	38
13	Coffin Mew & Clover *Portsmouth, Cosham, Fareham (2), Gosport, Havant, Southampton*	20	21	**41**	40	34	34
14	Blaser Mills Winter Taylors *High Wycombe (2), Aylesbury, Chesham, Harrow, Marlow, Princes Risborough, Rickmansworth*	18	23	**41**	41	–	–
15	Brachers *Maidstone*	18	22	**40**	38	34	31
16	Penningtons *Basingstoke, Godalming, Newbury*	20	17	**37**	42	40	41
17	Iliffes Booth Bennett *Uxbridge (3), Chesham, Ingatestone, Slough,*	17	20	**37**	37	33	35
18	Taylor Walton *Luton, Harpenden, Hemel Hempstead, St Albans*	17	18	**35**	30	25	24
19	Burstows *Crawley, Brighton, Horsham*	15	19	**34**	20	20	20
20	Clarks *Reading*	15	19	**34**	32	30	27
21	Barlows *Guildford, Chertsey, Godalming*	12	22	**34**	30	30	24
22	Pitmans *Reading*	13	20	**33**	35	28	27
23	Moore & Blatch *Southampton, Lymington, Milford-on-Sea*	15	17	**32**	25	25	22
24	Henmans *Oxford, Woodstock*	15	17	**32**	31	26	26
25	Stevens & Bolton *Guildford, Farnham*	15	17	**32**	25	–	–
26	Glanvilles *Portsmouth, Fareham, Havant, Newport, Waterlooville*	17	14	**31**	24	26	26
27	Paris Smith & Randall *Southampton*	14	17	**31**	15	28	23
28	Kidd Rapinet *Aylesbury, Basingstoke, Haslemere, High Wycombe, Maidenhead, Reading, Slough, Wendover*	23	6	**29**	29	32	32
29	Buss Murton *Tunbridge Wells, Cranbrook, Hawkhurst, Tenterden*	21	8	**29**	30	30	27
30	Boyes Turner & Burrows *Reading*	12	17	**29**	23	–	–
31	Nabarro Nathanson *Reading*	7	21	**28**	21	–	–
32	Manches & Co *Oxford*	14	13	**27**	19	15	–
33	Bower & Bailey *Oxford, Banbury, Witney*	12	15	**27**	27	19	–
34	Warner Goodman & Streat *Fareham, Parkgate, Portsmouth, Southampton, Waterlooville*	12	15	**27**	25	23	24
35	Matthew Arnold & Baldwin *Watford*	15	11	**26**	26	20	20
36	White & Bowker *Winchester, Eastleigh, Southampton*	14	12	**26**	26	27	27
37	Fennemores *Central Milton Keynes*	14	11	**25**	41	38	33

		Ptnrs	Asst Solrs	Total No of Solicitors '98	'97	'96	'95
38	**B.P. Collins & Co** Gerrards Cross, Beaconsfield, Chalfont St. Peter	14	11	**25**	25	19	–
39	**Marshall & Galpin** Oxford, Abingdon, Cowley, Summertown, Thame	11	14	**25**	25	24	22
40	**Garretts** Reading	5	20	**25**	19	19	–
41	**Sherwin Oliver** Portsmouth, Fareham	12	12	**24**	26	23	20
42	**Stanley Tee & Company** Bishop's Stortford, Braintree, Great Dunmow	12	11	**23**	23	18	–
43	**Turbervilles with Nelson Cuff** Uxbridge, Harrow, Hillingdon	10	13	**23**	20	–	–
44	**Darbys** Oxford	9	14	**23**	24	21	21
45	**Lamport Bassitt** Southampton	9	14	**23**	18	18	–
46	**Furley Page Fielding & Barton** Canterbury, Whitstable	16	6	**22**	22	20	20
47	**Hawkins Russell Jones** Hitchin, Hatfield, Stevenage, Welwyn Garden City	16	6	**22**	22	24	24
48	**Gepp & Sons** Chelmsford, Colchester	14	8	**22**	20	22	21
49	**T.G. Baynes & Sons** Bexleyheath, Dartford, Orpington, Sidcup, Welling	13	9	**22**	22	22	–
50	**Eric Robinson & Co** Southampton (6)	10	12	**22**	20	23	23

SOUTH WEST: THE 50 LARGEST FIRMS

The rankings in this table are determined by the number of solicitors working in this region. They are based on partner and assistant solicitor figures only: all other fee-earners are excluded.

		Ptnrs	Asst Solrs	Total No of Solicitors '98	'97	'96	'95
1	**Bevan Ashford** Bristol, Exeter, Plymouth, Taunton, Tiverton	54	92	**146**	133	120	101
2	**Burges Salmon** Bristol	40	106	**146**	122	107	94
3	**Osborne Clarke** Bristol	32	85	**117**	95	83	76
4	**Clarke Willmott & Clarke** Bristol, Bridgwater, Taunton (2), Yeovil	35	61	**96**	73	93	76
5	**Bond Pearce** Plymouth, Bristol, Exeter	32	57	**89**	82	100	104
6	**Wansbroughs Willey Hargrave** Bristol (2)	19	49	**68**	70	56	55
7	**Stephens & Scown** Exeter, Liskeard, St Austell, Truro	33	26	**59**	59	48	55
8	**Veale Wasbrough** Bristol	25	34	**59**	56	59	54
9	**Lyons Davidson** Bristol, Plymouth	16	34	**50**	40	40	40
10	**Lawrence Tucketts** Bristol	17	32	**49**	42	39	37
11	**Lester Aldridge** Bournemouth	29	19	**48**	50	43	56
12	**Battens (with Poole & Co)** Yeovil, Crewkerne, Dorchester, Shaftesbury, Sherborne, Taunton, Weymouth	25	21	**46**	44	41	32
13	**Cartwrights** Bristol	16	27	**43**	42	41	36
14	**Wolferstans** Plymouth, Bristol, Plympton, Plymstock, Taunton	26	16	**42**	37	34	39
15	**Foot & Bowden** Plymouth, Exeter	21	18	**39**	40	40	40
16	**Davies and Partners** Gloucester, Bristol	17	22	**39**	40	25	25
17	**Porter Dodson** Yeovil, Blandford Forum, Bridgwater, Langport, Sherborne, Sturminster Newton, Taunton, Wellington	25	13	**38**	38	29	–
18	**Woollcombe Beer Watts** Newton Abbot, Buckfastleigh, Chagford, Exeter, Torquay	21	14	**35**	31	33	32
19	**Tozers** Exeter, Dawlish, Newton Abbot, Paignton, Plymouth, Teignmouth, Torquay	18	14	**32**	31	25	29
20	**Townsends** Swindon	18	13	**31**	29	32	33
21	**Rickerby Watterson** Cheltenham	18	12	**30**	32	28	–
22	**Thrings & Long** Bath, Frome	12	18	**30**	26	19	28
23	**Anstey Sargent & Probert** Exeter (2), Budleigh Salterton	17	10	**27**	27	25	23
24	**Ford Simey Daw Roberts** Exeter, Exmouth, Sidmouth, Southernhay Gdns	16	10	**26**	26	25	21
25	**Wilsons Solicitors** Salisbury	14	12	**26**	26	25	25
26	**Burroughs Day** Bristol, Portishead	13	13	**26**	24	21	21
27	**Stones Cann & Hallett** Exeter (2), Okehampton	16	9	**25**	–	–	–
28	**Coles Miller** Poole (2), Bournemouth, Broadstone, West Moors, Wimborne	14	10	**24**	23	24	23
29	**Wiggin and Co** Cheltenham	11	13	**24**	23	22	19
30	**Trumps** Bristol	8	15	**23**	22	21	21
31	**Wards** Bristol, Axbridge, Bradley Stoke, Staple Hill, Weston-super-Mare, Worle	7	16	**23**	18	18	17
32	**Bishop Longbotham & Bagnall** Trowbridge, Bath, Bradford-on-Avon, Swindon	11	10	**21**	20	15	–
33	**Bretherton Price Elgoods** Cheltenham (3)	11	9	**20**	10	11	–
34	**Withy King** Bath, Trowbridge	11	9	**20**	18	16	–
35	**Metcalfes** Bristol	7	13	**20**	17	16	16
36	**Bobbetts Mackan** Bristol	5	15	**20**	20	15	–
37	**Turners** Bournemouth	15	4	**19**	19	16	16
38	**Steele Raymond** Bournemouth, Wimborne	12	7	**19**	19	23	20
39	**Crosse & Crosse** Exeter (2)	10	9	**19**	19	16	16
40	**Wansbroughs** Devizes, Melksham	10	9	**19**	17	22	22
41	**Kirby Simcox** Bristol (3), Thornbury	7	12	**19**	26	16	17
42	**Michelmores** Exeter	13	5	**18**	18	17	17
43	**Goughs** Calne, Chippenham, Corsham, Devizes, Melksham	12	6	**18**	17	17	17
44	**Nalder & Son** Truro (2), Camborne, Falmouth, Helston	12	6	**18**	16	17	15

		Ptnrs	Asst Solrs	Total No of Solicitors						Ptnrs	Asst Solrs	Total No of Solicitors			
				'98	'97	'96	'95					'98	'97	'96	'95
45	**Pardoes** *Bridgwater, Taunton, Newquay, St Austell*	10	8	**18**	21	18	–	48	**Slee Blackwell** *Barnstaple, Braunton, South Molton*	9	8	**17**	12	12	–
46	**Humphries Kirk** *Wareham, Bournemouth, Dorchester, Swanage, Upton*	8	10	**18**	19	14	–	49	**Eastleys** *Paignton, Brixham, Totnes*	8	9	**17**	18	13	–
47	**Laytons** *Bristol*	8	10	**18**	17	16	16	50	**Stone King** *Bath*	8	9	**17**	16	15	–

WALES: THE 10 LARGEST FIRMS

The rankings in this table are determined by the number of solicitors working in this region. They are based on partner and assistant solicitor figures only: all other fee-earners are excluded.

		Ptnrs	Asst Solrs	Total No of Solicitors						Ptnrs	Asst Solrs	Total No of Solicitors			
				'98	'97	'96	'95					'98	'97	'96	'95
1	**Morgan Bruce** *Cardiff, Newport, Swansea*	44	68	**112**	98	89	105	6	**Gamlins** *Rhyl, Colwyn Bay, Conwy, Flintshire, Llandudno, Rhos-on-Sea*	11	16	**27**	27	11	–
2	**Hugh James** *Cardiff, Bargoed, Blackwood, Merthyr Tydfil, Pontlottyn, Talbot Green, Treharris*	41	33	**74**	72	61	67	7	**Dolmans** *Cardiff (2)*	11	15	**26**	27	27	27
3	**Edwards Geldard** *Cardiff*	23	34	**57**	51	42	46	8	**Palser Grossman** *Cardiff Bay, Swansea*	13	12	**25**	28	23	–
4	**Eversheds** *Cardiff*	28	23	**51**	83	65•	95	9	**Douglas-Jones Mercer** *Swansea, Ammanford, Gorseinon, Morriston, Mumbles*	13	8	**21**	22	20	20
5	**Leo Abse & Cohen** *Cardiff*	7	41	**48**	43	43	36	10	**Loosemores** *Cardiff, Canton, Roath*	10	11	**21**	20	20	20

MIDLANDS: THE 50 LARGEST FIRMS

The rankings in this table are determined by the number of solicitors working in this region. They are based on partner and assistant solicitor figures only: all other fee-earners are excluded.

		Ptnrs	Asst Solrs	Total No of Solicitors						Ptnrs	Asst Solrs	Total No of Solicitors			
				'98	'97	'96	'95					'98	'97	'96	'95
1	**Wragge & Co** *Birmingham*	60	164	**224**	213	199	143	18	**Herbert Wilkes** *Birmingham (2)*	16	22	**38**	37	37	37
2	**Eversheds** *Birmingham, Derby, Nottingham*	55	105	**160**	183	175	173	19	**Lee Crowder** *Birmingham*	14	24	**38**	25	17	–
3	**Edge & Ellison** *Birmingham, Leicester*	61	89	**150**	161	154	149	20	**Knight & Sons** *Newcastle-under-Lyme*	17	20	**37**	34	28	28
4	**Pinsent Curtis** *Birmingham*	56	52	**108**	90	104	107	21	**Higgs & Sons** *Brierley Hill, Dudley, Kingswinford, Stourbridge*	20	15	**35**	34	33	33
5	**Freeth Cartwright Hunt Dickins** *Nottingham (2), Derby, Leicester*	45	59	**104**	109	77	62	22	**Irwin Mitchell** *Birmingham (2)*	13	22	**35**	35	15	–
6	**Shoosmiths & Harrison** *Northampton (3), Nottingham, Rugby*	48	53	**101**	92	86	78	23	**Hewitson Becke + Shaw** *Northampton*	15	19	**34**	33	28	27
7	**Browne Jacobson** *Nottingham*	32	56	**88**	80	74	64	24	**Toller Hales & Collcutt** *Northampton, Corby, Kettering, Wellingborough*	17	16	**33**	31	34	34
8	**Martineau Johnson** *Birmingham*	33	46	**79**	71	61	63	25	**The Lewington Partnership** *Birmingham*	7	26	**33**	28	26	–
9	**Dibb Lupton Alsop** *Birmingham*	25	46	**71**	53	36	–	26	**Flint, Bishop & Barnett** *Derby (4), Ashbourne, Belper, Matlock*	19	12	**31**	28	20	26
10	**Nelsons** *Nottingham, Derby*	23	38	**61**	56	50	45	27	**THM Tinsdills** *Stoke-on-Trent, Leek, Newcastle-under-Lyme, Tunstall*	16	14	**30**	27	25	25
11	**Harvey Ingram Owston** *Leicester, Oadby, Wigston*	26	24	**50**	44	49	28	28	**Wright Hassall & Co** *Leamington Spa*	19	10	**29**	25	26	21
12	**Shakespeares** *Birmingham*	17	32	**49**	44	36	46	29	**Manby & Steward** *Wolverhampton (2), Bridgnorth (2), Shropshire, Brierley Hill, Telford, Telford Town Centre*	14	15	**29**	27		
13	**Challinors Lyon Clark** *West Bromwich, Birmingham, Edgbaston, Smethwick, Wolverhampton*	21	22	**43**	42	31	–	30	**Roythorne & Co** *Spalding, Boston, Nottingham*	18	10	**28**	28	27	27
14	**Morton Fisher** *Kidderminster, Bewdley, Bromsgrove, Stourport-on-Severn, Worcester*	19	24	**43**	39	39	39	31	**Kent Jones and Done** *Stoke-on-Trent*	15	13	**28**	27	28	26
15	**Thompsons** *Birmingham, Nottingham, Stoke-on Trent*	14	27	**41**	33	–	–	32	**Grindeys** *Stoke on Trent (2), Longton, Tunstall*	13	14	**27**	26	27	22
16	**Gateley Wareing** *Birmingham, Leicester*	13	27	**40**	34	23	28	33	**Wansbroughs Willey Hargrave** *Birmingham*	7	20	**27**	23	22	–
17	**The Smith Partnership** *Derby (2), Burton-on-Trent, Longton, Swadlincote*	12	27	**39**	36	28	28	34	**Garretts** *Birmingham*	6	21	**27**	17	12	–

		Ptnrs	Asst Solrs	Total No of Solicitors '98	'97	'96	'95
35	**Marron Dodds** *Leicester (2)*	14	11	**25**	22	20	–
36	**Berryman & Co** *Nottingham*	14	11	**25**	23	–	–
37	**Hadens (formerly Haden Stretton Slater Miller)** *Walsall (2), Cannock (2), Darlaston (2), Hednesford (2), Lichfield*	16	8	**24**	28	25	25
38	**Foster Baxter Cooksey** *Wolverhampton, Telford, Willenhall*	15	8	**23**	22	20	22
39	**Chattertons** *Boston (2)*	9	14	**23**	12	16	–
40	**Putsmans** *Birmingham, West Bromwich*	14	8	**22**	22	19	–
41	**Willcox Lane Clutterbuck with Rees Edwards Maddox** *Birmingham*	13	9	**22**	17	15	–
42	**Tyndallwoods** *Birmingham (2)*	10	12	**22**	24	25	24
43	**Actons** *Nottingham*	10	12	**22**	20	20	–
44	**Warren & Allen** *Nottingham, Bingham, Ilkeston*	10	12	**22**	23	25	22
45	**R. Gwynne & Sons** *Wellington, Newport, Shrewsbury, Telford*	9	13	**22**	19	16	–
46	**Rees Page** *Wolverhampton (2), Bilston, Dudley*	15	6	**21**	22	22	22
47	**Trumans** *Nottingham, Grantham*	10	11	**21**	20	19	–
48	**McGrath & Co** *Birmingham*	7	14	**21**	21	17	–
49	**Thursfields** *Kidderminster, Stourport-on-Severn, Worcester*	13	7	**20**	20	17	–
50	**Hawley & Rodgers** *Loughborough, Leicester, Nottingham*	12	8	**20**	20	23	23

EAST ANGLIA: THE 20 LARGEST FIRMS

The rankings in this table are determined by the number of solicitors working in this region. They are based on partner and assistant solicitor figures only: all other fee-earners are excluded.

		Ptnrs	Asst Solrs	Total No of Solicitors '98	'97	'96	'95
1	**Mills & Reeve** *Cambridge, Norwich*	50	77	**127**	133	120	120
2	**Eversheds** *Ipswich, Norwich*	44	45	**89**	95	85	82
3	**Hewitson Becke + Shaw** *Cambridge, Peterborough*	29	20	**49**	46	50	46
4	**Taylor Vinters** *Cambridge*	22	21	**43**	38	46	46
5	**Ashton Graham** *Bury St. Edmunds, Ipswich*	17	20	**37**	–	–	–
6	**Greenwoods** *Peterborough*	17	14	**31**	33	32	28
7	**Prettys** *Ipswich*	15	16	**31**	26	27	34
8	**Leathes Prior** *Norwich, North Walsham*	17	13	**30**	28	27	27
9	**Birketts** *Ipswich*	20	9	**29**	39	37	33
10	**Hunt & Coombs** *Peterborough*	10	15	**25**	20	18	17
11	**Fosters** *Norwich, Bungay*	10	13	**23**	23	19	–
12	**Steele & Co** *Norwich, Diss, Thetford*	12	10	**22**	18	21	19
13	**Metcalfe Copeman & Pettefar** *Wisbech, King's Lynn, Peterborough, Thetford*	12	9	**21**	21	23	23
14	**Gotelee & Goldsmith** *Ipswich, Hadleigh*	10	11	**21**	21	22	20
15	**Hansell Stevenson** *Norwich*	8	13	**21**	16	20	20
16	**Ward Gethin** *King's Lynn, Hunstanton, Swaffham*	14	5	**19**	19	19	18
17	**Leeds Day** *Sandy, Biggleswade, Huntingdon, St. Ives, St. Neots*	11	8	**19**	19	19	–
18	**Buckle Mellows** *Peterborough, Whittlesey*	10	8	**18**	18	18	18
19	**Cunningham, John & Co** *Thetford, Bury St. Edmunds, Watton*	9	9	**18**	19	17	–
20	**Kenneth Bush** *King's Lynn (2), Norfolk, Swaffham*	13	4	**17**	–	–	–

NORTH WEST: THE 50 LARGEST FIRMS

The rankings in this table are determined by the number of solicitors working in this region. They are based on partner and assistant solicitor figures only: all other fee-earners are excluded.

		Ptnrs	Asst Solrs	Total No of Solicitors '98	'97	'96	'95
1	**Dibb Lupton Alsop** *Liverpool, Manchester*	53	91	**144**	104	–	–
2	**Addleshaw Booth & Co** *Manchester*	42	80	**122**	112	–	–
3	**Davies Wallis Foyster** *Liverpool, Manchester*	43	67	**110**	110	92	71
4	**Hill Dickinson** *Liverpool, Chester, Manchester*	60	49	**109**	109	80	60
5	**Halliwell Landau** *Manchester*	42	61	**103**	84	67	46
6	**Berrymans Lace Mawer** *Liverpool, Manchester*	43	58	**101**	81	–	–
7	**Weightmans** *Liverpool*	38	55	**93**	84	84	–
8	**Pannone & Partners** *Manchester*	45	33	**78**	62	51	44
9	**Eversheds** *Manchester*	28	46	**74**	68	53	38
10	**Hammond Suddards** *Manchester*	15	57	**72**	71	34	34
11	**Cobbetts** *Manchester, Wilmslow*	33	36	**69**	64	59	–
12	**Vaudreys** *Manchester*	14	47	**61**	61	53	46
13	**Forbes & Partners** *Blackburn (3), Accrington (2), Chorley, Clitheroe, Preston*	16	41	**57**	49	46	38

		Ptnrs	Asst Solrs	Total No of Solicitors			
				'98	'97	'96	'95
14	**Keogh Ritson** Bolton	20	33	**53**	47	47	41
15	**James Chapman & Co** Manchester	24	22	**46**	45	45	39
16	**Brabner Holden Banks Wilson** Liverpool, Preston	18	26	**44**	43	39	35
17	**Slater Heelis** Manchester, Sale	20	23	**43**	40	36	36
18	**Mace & Jones** Liverpool, Huyton, Knutsford	17	25	**42**	50	47	34
19	**Davies Arnold Cooper** Manchester	8	32	**40**	33	33	36
20	**J. Keith Park & Co** St. Helens, Toxteth	5	32	**37**	37	49	26
21	**Walker Smith & Way** Chester, Ellesmere Port	18	15	**33**	33	33	34
22	**Birchall Blackburn** Preston, Accrington, Chorley, Manchester, Whalley	12	21	**33**	17	21	21
23	**Farleys** Blackburn (2), Accrington (2), Burnley	10	23	**33**	30	19	19
24	**Hempsons** Manchester	7	26	**33**	27	25	–
25	**Stephensons** Leigh, Salford, St. Helens, Wigan	15	17	**32**	32	26	26
26	**Cuff Roberts** Liverpool	19	12	**31**	28	28	29
27	**Jones Maidment Wilson** Manchester, Altrincham	13	18	**31**	31	24	24
28	**Masons** Manchester	9	19	**28**	31	31	–
29	**Silverbeck Rymer** Liverpool	4	24	**28**	26	15	–
30	**Peter Rickson and Partners** Preston, Manchester	17	10	**27**	25	24	22
31	**Canter Levin & Berg** Liverpool (2), Kirkby, Skelmersdale, St. Helens	12	15	**27**	25	23	23
32	**Bullivant Jones & Company** Liverpool	10	17	**27**	24	27	27
33	**Wacks Caller** Manchester	12	14	**26**	22	22	23
34	**Linder Myers** Manchester, Openshaw, Salford (2)	10	16	**26**	21	–	–
35	**Elliott & Company** Manchester	10	16	**26**	23	25	38
36	**Ingham Clegg & Crowther** Preston, Blackpool, Cleveleys, Fleetwood, Knott End on Sea, Lancaster, Poulton-le-Fylde	13	12	**25**	25	25	26
37	**Russell & Russell** Bolton (2), Bury, Chester, Manchester	12	13	**25**	24	27	27
38	**Rowlands** Manchester, Droylsden, New Moston, Sale, Stockport, Urmston	11	14	**25**	25	26	40
39	**Kuit Steinart Levy** Manchester	15	9	**24**	20	17	–
40	**Fieldings Porter** Bolton (3), Blackburn	11	13	**24**	24	23	21
41	**Cartmell Shepherd** Carlisle, Brampton, Carlisle (Rosehill), Penrith	11	13	**24**	25	26	26
42	**George Davies & Co** Manchester, Wilmslow	14	9	**23**	22	17	–
43	**Betesh Fox & Co** Manchester	9	14	**23**	24	16	–
44	**Thompsons** Liverpool, Manchester	16	6	**22**	22	38	–
45	**Burton Copeland** Manchester	14	8	**22**	22	35	–
46	**Burnetts** Carlisle	16	5	**21**	22	22	22
47	**Whittles** Manchester	9	12	**21**	21	15	–
48	**Morecroft Urquhart** Liverpool (3), Crosby, Moreton, Wirral	14	6	**20**	22	21	21
49	**Chaffe Street** Manchester	14	6	**20**	16	15	–
50	**Aaron & Partners** Chester	10	10	**20**	18	20	18

NORTH EAST: THE 50 LARGEST FIRMS

The rankings in this table are determined by the number of solicitors working in this region. They are based on partner and assistant solicitor figures only: all other fee-earners are excluded.

		Ptnrs	Asst Solrs	Total No of Solicitors			
				'98	'97	'96	'95
1	**Eversheds** Leeds, Middlesbrough, Newcastle upon Tyne	89	117	**206**	186	179	178
2	**Dibb Lupton Alsop** Bradford, Leeds, Sheffield	61	103	**164**	113	12	–
3	**Addleshaw Booth & Co** Leeds	44	92	**136**	138	107	–
4	**Irwin Mitchell** Sheffield, Leeds	56	71	**127**	118	126	88
5	**Hammond Suddards** Leeds, Bradford	35	72	**107**	101	137	102
6	**Walker Morris** Leeds	30	75	**105**	99	81	76
7	**Dickinson Dees** Newcastle upon Tyne	46	56	**102**	82	73	67
8	**Pinsent Curtis** Leeds	47	45	**92**	71	79	89
9	**Wansbroughs Willey Hargrave** Leeds, Sheffield	23	44	**67**	75	63	54
10	**Nabarro Nathanson** Sheffield	18	47	**65**	66	74	45
11	**Ward Hadaway** Newcastle upon Tyne, South Shields	32	26	**58**	57	53	32
12	**Andrew M. Jackson & Co** Hull	23	24	**47**	43	44	44
13	**Gosschalks** Hull	25	21	**46**	41	37	32
14	**Rollit Farrell & Bladon** Hull, Beverley, Helmsley, York	28	15	**43**	43	45	45
15	**Watson Burton** Newcastle upon Tyne	20	22	**42**	35	41	41
16	**Ford & Warren** Leeds	12	29	**41**	41	40	31
17	**Lupton Fawcett** Leeds, Harrogate	14	25	**39**	29	31	31
18	**Garretts** Leeds	11	26	**37**	34	21	17
19	**Robert Muckle** Newcastle-upon-Tyne	12	24	**36**	35	27	31
20	**Attey Bower & Jones with Dibb and Clegg** Doncaster (2), Barnsley, Goldthorpe, Mexborough, Rotherham, Thorne, Wath	26	9	**35**	20	20	20
21	**Gordons Wright & Wright** Bradford, Bingley, Keighley	17	18	**35**	43	40	36
22	**Crutes** Newcastle-upon-Tyne, Middlesbrough, Sunderland	16	18	**34**	26	26	26
23	**Jacksons** Stockton-on-Tees, Newcastle Upon Tyne	18	15	**33**	35	36	36

		Ptnrs	Asst Solrs	Total No of Solicitors			
				'98	'97	'96	'95
24	**Philip Hamer & Co** Hull, Doncaster, Hessle, Leeds, Sheffield	6	26	**32**	31	29	24
25	**Hay & Kilner** Newcastle-upon-Tyne, Gosforth, Wallsend	23	8	**31**	29	29	29
26	**Tilly Bailey & Irvine** Hartlepool, Barnard Castle, Darlington, Stockton on Tees	14	17	**31**	32	24	20
27	**Hempsons** Harrogate	3	28	**31**	19	17	–
28	**Keeble Hawson Moorhouse** Sheffield, Leeds	22	8	**30**	24	25	17
29	**Thompsons** Leeds, Newcastle-upon-Tyne, Sheffield	16	11	**27**	29	39	–
30	**Howells** Sheffield (3)	11	16	**27**	28	29	29
31	**Read Hind Stewart** Leeds	14	11	**25**	24	22	22
32	**Ison Harrison & Co** Leeds, Chapeltown, Crossgates	8	17	**25**	23	19	20
33	**Lee & Priestley** Leeds (3), Bradford	15	9	**24**	19	17	–
34	**Wake Smith** Sheffield	12	10	**22**	21	18	18
35	**Brooke North** Leeds	14	7	**21**	19	14	–
36	**Graysons** Sheffield	12	9	**21**	18	16	16

		Ptnrs	Asst Solrs	Total No of Solicitors			
				'98	'97	'96	'95
37	**Taylor & Emmet** Sheffield (2)	11	10	**21**	23	19	19
38	**Punch Robson** Middlesbrough, Berwickhills, Stockton-on-Tees	13	6	**19**	20	20	20
39	**Harrowell Shaftoe** York (2), Haxby	11	8	**19**	17	17	15
40	**Oxley & Coward** Rotherham	10	9	**19**	14	17	–
41	**Wilkin Chapman** Grimsby, Immingham	9	10	**19**	19	20	18
42	**Denison Till** Leeds (2), York	14	4	**18**	20	20	20
43	**Godloves** Leeds (4), Beeston, Chapel Allerton, Garforth	12	6	**18**	17	16	16
44	**Bury & Walkers** Barnsley, Leeds, Wombwell	12	6	**18**	17	20	20
45	**Nelson & Co** Leeds (2), Headingley	9	9	**18**	18	17	–
46	**Stamp Jackson and Procter** Hull	8	10	**18**	19	19	19
47	**Hartley & Worstenholme** Castleford, Hemsworth, Pontefract	8	10	**18**	12	12	–
48	**Heptonstalls** Goole, Howden, Pontefract	6	12	**18**	18	14	–
49	**Archers** Stockton-on-Tees	9	8	**17**	15	12	–
50	**Grahame Stowe, Bateson** Leeds, Bramley, Halton, Meanwood, Wakefield	8	9	**17**	16	16	–

SCOTLAND: THE 50 LARGEST FIRMS

The rankings in this table are determined by the number of solicitors working in this region. They are based on partner and assistant solicitor figures only: all other fee-earners are excluded.

		Ptnrs	Asst Solrs	Total No of Solicitors			
				'98	'97	'96	'95
1	**Dundas & Wilson CS** Edinburgh, Glasgow (2)	53	112	**165**	163	107	99
2	**McGrigor Donald** Glasgow, Edinburgh	40	72	**112**	109	99	99
3	**Maclay Murray & Spens** Glasgow, Edinburgh	34	69	**103**	87	95	97
4	**Shepherd & Wedderburn WS** Edinburgh, Glasgow	30	60	**90**	83	75	69
5	**Brodies WS** Edinburgh	26	46	**72**	73	71	64
6	**MacRoberts** Glasgow, Edinburgh	25	47	**72**	58	50	43
7	**Tods Murray WS** Edinburgh	29	40	**69**	52	44	42
8	**Paull & Williamsons** Aberdeen (2), Edinburgh	29	30	**59**	51	47	47
9	**McClure Naismith** Glasgow, Edinburgh	17	41	**58**	58	61	62
10	**Ledingham Chalmers** Edinburgh, Aberdeen, Inverness	25	32	**57**	60	58	58
11	**Burness** Edinburgh, Glasgow	25	32	**57**	59	71	53
12	**Bird Semple** Glasgow, Edinburgh	17	39	**56**	49	38	38
13	**Anderson Strathern WS** Edinburgh (2), Haddington	26	27	**53**	53	56	56
14	**Biggart Baillie** Glasgow, Edinburgh	20	32	**52**	53	58	58
15	**Henderson Boyd Jackson WS** Edinburgh, Glasgow	20	29	**49**	39	31	23
16	**The Morton Fraser Partnership** Edinburgh	20	29	**49**	49	48	36

		Ptnrs	Asst Solrs	Total No of Solicitors			
				'98	'97	'96	'95
17	**Ross Harper & Murphy WS** Glasgow, Arden, Bellshill, East Kilbride, Glasgow Castlemilk, Glasgow Easterhouse, Glasgow Maryhill, Glasgow Shawlands, Hamilton, Rutherglen, Uddingston	16	31	**47**	47	43	63
18	**Fyfe Ireland WS** Edinburgh	12	30	**42**	33	27	27
19	**Thorntons WS** Dundee, Arbroath, Forfar, Perth	20	20	**40**	41	47	42
20	**Bishop and Robertson Chalmers** Glasgow, Edinburgh	19	21	**40**	38	38	38
21	**Stronachs** Aberdeen (4), Inverness, Inverurie	23	15	**38**	28	24	30
22	**Simpson & Marwick WS** Edinburgh, Aberdeen, Dundee, Glasgow	15	23	**38**	35	32	29
23	**Drummond Miller WS** Edinburgh, Bathgate, Dalkeith, Dunfermline, Glasgow, Kirkcaldy, Livingston, Musselburgh	20	16	**36**	36	34	34
24	**Balfour & Manson** Edinburgh	16	20	**36**	29	29	31
25	**Peterkins** Aberdeen, Banchory, Glasgow, Inverurie	23	10	**33**	32	32	32
26	**Alex Morison & Co WS** Edinburgh (3), Glasgow	16	16	**32**	32	27	27
27	**Wright, Johnston & Mackenzie** Glasgow, Edinburgh	12	20	**32**	32	37	28
28	**Brechin Tindal Oatts** Glasgow, Edinburgh	15	14	**29**	28	17	–
29	**Steedman Ramage WS** Edinburgh, Glasgow	13	15	**28**	26	27	28
30	**Semple Fraser WS** Glasgow, Edinburgh	13	14	**27**	24	23	19

		Ptnrs	Asst Solrs	Total No of Solicitors			
				'98	'97	'96	'95
31	**Blair & Bryden** *Greenock, Clydebank (3), Dumbarton, Dunoon, Port Glasgow*	15	12	**27**	23	21	28
32	**Bennett & Robertson** *Edinburgh (2), Glasgow*	12	15	**27**	24	23	24
33	**Archibald Campbell & Harley WS** *Edinburgh*	14	12	**26**	24	26	26
34	**Raeburn Christie & Co** *Aberdeen, Banchory, Ellon, Stonehaven*	12	14	**26**	26	26	26
35	**Robson McLean WS** *Edinburgh*	8	17	**25**	21	17	–
36	**Harper Macleod** *Glasgow*	10	14	**24**	21	18	–
37	**Miller Hendry** *Perth, Dundee*	15	8	**23**	23	21	21
38	**Aberdein Considine & Co** *Aberdeen (2), Aboyne, Ballater, Banchory, Culter, Dyce, Ellon, Inverurie, Peterhead, Torry*	13	10	**23**	22	29	29
39	**Blackadder Reid Johnston** *Dundee, Carnoustie, Kirriemuir, Monifieth*	13	9	**22**	28	28	30
40	**Russel & Aitken** *Denny, Edinburgh, Falkirk*	13	9	**22**	22	22	22

		Ptnrs	Asst Solrs	Total No of Solicitors			
				'98	'97	'96	'95
41	**Lindsays WS** *Edinburgh (3)*	12	10	**22**	22	22	28
42	**Iain Smith & Company** *Aberdeen (3), Stonehaven*	10	12	**22**	21	24	20
43	**Murray Beith Murray W.S.** *Edinburgh*	9	12	**21**	22	20	22
44	**Gillespie Macandrew WS** *Edinburgh*	9	11	**20**	20	19	19
45	**Golds** *Glasgow*	7	13	**20**	11	11	–
46	**Pagan Osborne** *Cupar, Anstruther, Dundee, St. Andrews*	12	7	**19**	18	16	–
47	**Borland Montgomerie Keyden** *Glasgow, Hamilton*	13	5	**18**	20	21	21
48	**Mitchells Roberton** *Glasgow*	12	6	**18**	18	18	–
49	**Digby Brown** *Glasgow, Dundee, Edinburgh*	10	8	**18**	16	8	–
50	**Ketchen & Stevens WS** *Edinburgh (3), Glasgow*	7	11	**18**	12	17	17

NORTHERN IRELAND: THE 10 LARGEST FIRMS

The rankings in this table are determined by the number of solicitors working in this region. They are based on partner and assistant solicitor figures only: all other fee-earners are excluded.

		Ptnrs	Asst Solrs	Total No of Solicitors			
				'98	'97	'96	'95
1	**McKinty & Wright** *Belfast*	11	12	**23**	23	22	20
2	**Cleaver Fulton & Rankin** *Belfast, Armagh*	11	12	**23**	23	24	23
3	**Carson & McDowell** *Belfast*	8	13	**21**	20	17	17
4	**L'Estrange & Brett** *Belfast*	9	10	**19**	18	18	16
5	**Elliott Duffy Garrett** *Belfast*	11	7	**18**	18	13	13

		Ptnrs	Asst Solrs	Total No of Solicitors			
				'98	'97	'96	'95
6	**C & H Jefferson** *Belfast*	8	10	**18**	18	17	17
7	**Wilson Nesbitt** *Belfast, Bangor, Holywood, Sleralne*	7	11	**18**	19	21	–
8	**Tughan & Co** *Belfast*	9	7	**16**	15	15	12
9	**Arthur Cox** *Belfast*	5	7	**12**	9	6	–
10	**Madden & Finucane** *Belfast*	4	8	**12**	12	8	–

INDEX TO LARGEST FIRMS TABLES

Payne Hicks Beach
London No.117
Penningtons
South East No.16, London No.86
Peter Carter-Ruck and Partners
London No.155
Peter Rickson and Partners
North West No.30
Peterkins
Scotland No.25
Peters & Peters
London No.176
Philip Hamer & Co
North East No.24
Pictons
South East No.6
Pinsent Curtis
Midlands No.4, North East No.8,
Nationwide No.17, London No.66
Pitmans
South East No.22
Porter Dodson
South West No.17
Prettys
East Anglia No.7
Prince Evans
London No.124
Pritchard Englefield
London No.95
Punch Robson
North East No.38
Putsmans
Midlands No.40
Radcliffes
London No.59
Raeburn Christie & Co
Scotland No.34
Rakisons
London No.122
Read Hind Stewart
North East No.31
Rees & Freres
London No.139
Rees Page
Midlands No.46
Reid Minty
London No.192
Reynolds Porter Chamberlain
London No.37
Richards Butler
London No.26, Nationwide No.43
Rickerby Watterson
South West No.21
Robert Muckle
North East No.19
Robson McLean WS
Scotland No.35
Rollit Farrell & Bladon
North East No.14
Rooks Rider
London No.115
Rosenblatt
London No.196
Rosling King
London No.85
Ross & Craig
London No.159
Ross Harper & Murphy WS
Scotland No.17
Rowe & Maw
London No.20, Nationwide No.30
Rowlands
North West No.38
Rowley Ashworth
London No.134
Royds Treadwell
London No.156
Roythorne & Co
Midlands No.30
Russel & Aitken
Scotland No.40

Russell & Russell
North West No.37
Russell Jones & Walker
London No.74
Russell-Cooke, Potter & Chapman
London No.82
Sacker & Partners
London No.107
Salans Hertzfeld & Heilbronn HRK
London No.83
Schilling & Lom and Partners
London No.197
Seddons
London No.157
Semple Fraser WS
Scotland No.30
Shakespeares
Midlands No.12
Sharpe Pritchard
London No.170
Shaw and Croft
London No.200
Shepherd & Wedderburn WS
Scotland No.4
Sheridans
London No.136
Sherwin Oliver
South East No.41
Shoosmiths & Harrison
South East No.3, Midlands No.6,
Nationwide No.32
Sidley & Austin
London No.109
Silverbeck Rymer
North West No.29
The Simkins Partnership
London No.100
Simmons & Simmons
London No.7,
Nationwide No.10
Simpson & Marwick WS
Scotland No.22
Sinclair Roche & Temperley
London No.57
Skadden, Arps, Slate, Meagher &
Flom LLP
London No.135
Slater Heelis
North West No.17
Slaughter and May
London No.9, Nationwide No.11
Slee Blackwell
South West No.48
The Smith Partnership
Midlands No.17
Speechly Bircham
London No.55
Stamp Jackson and Procter
North East No.46
Stanley Tee & Company
South East No.42
Steedman Ramage WS
Scotland No.29
Steele & Co
East Anglia No.12
Steele Raymond
South West No.37
Stephens & Scown
South West No.7
Stephens Innocent
London No.162
Stephenson Harwood
London No.23, Nationwide No.40
Stephensons
North West No.25
Stevens & Bolton
South East No.25
Stewarts
London No.160
Stone King
South West No.50

Stones Cann & Hallett
South West No.27
Stones Porter
London No.185
Stringer Saul
London No.137
Stronachs
Scotland No.21
T.V. Edwards
London No.111
Tarlo Lyons
London No.105
Taylor & Emmet
North East No.37
Taylor Joynson Garrett
London No.21, Nationwide No.36
Taylor Vinters
East Anglia No.4
Taylor Walton
South East No.18
Teacher Stern Selby
London No.127
Theodore Goddard
London No.25, Nationwide No.42
THM Tinsdills
Midlands No.27
Thomas Cooper & Stibbard
London No.141
Thomas Eggar Church Adams
South East No.4, London No.194
Thompsons
Midlands No.15, North East No.29,
Nationwide No.39, North West No.44,
London No.151
Thomson Snell & Passmore
South East No.7
Thorntons WS
Scotland No.19
Thrings & Long
South West No.22
Thursfields
Midlands No.49
Tilly Bailey & Irvine
North East No.26
Titmuss Sainer Dechert
London No.32
Tods Murray WS
Scotland No.7
Toller Hales & Collcutt
Midlands No.24
Townleys
London No.163
Townsends
South West No.20
Tozers
South West No.19
Travers Smith Braithwaite
London No.34
Trowers & Hamlins
London No.42
Trumans
Midlands No.47
Trumps
South West No.30
Tughan & Co
Northern Ireland No.8
Turbervilles with Nelson Cuff
South East No.43
Turners
South West No.40
Tyndallwoods
Midlands No.42
Underwood & Co (incorporating
Corbould Rigby &
London No.172
Vaudreys
North West No.12
Veale Wasbrough
South West No.8
Vizards
London No.60

Wacks Caller
North West No.33
Wake Smith
North East No.34
Walker Martineau
London No.186
Walker Morris
North East No.6
Walker Smith & Way
North West No.21
Wansbroughs
South West No.41
Wansbroughs Willey Hargrave
South West No.6, North East No.9,
Nationwide No.19, Midlands No.33,
London No.72
Ward Gethin
East Anglia No.16
Ward Hadaway
North East No.11
Wards
South West No.31
Warner Cranston
London No.81
Warner Goodman & Streat
South East No.34
Warren & Allen
Midlands No.44
Watson Burton
North East No.15
Watson, Farley & Williams
London No.46
Wedlake Bell
London No.67
Weightmans
North West No.7
Weil, Gotshal & Manges
London No.58
White & Bowker
South East No.36
White & Case
London No.110
Whittles
North West No.47
Wiggin and Co
South West No.29
Wilde Sapte
London No.14, Nationwide No.22
Wilkin Chapman
North East No.41
Willcox Lane Clutterbuck with Rees
Edwards Madd
Midlands No.41
William Sturges & Co
London No.147
Wilson Nesbitt
Northern Ireland No.7
Wilsons Solicitors
South West No.25
Winckworth & Pemberton
(incorporating Sherwood
London No.98
Winward Fearon
London No.183
Withers
London No.44
Withy King
South West No.34
Wolferstans
South West No.14
Woollcombe Beer Watts
South West No.18
Wragge & Co
Midlands No.1, Nationwide No.20
Wright Hassall & Co
Midlands No.28
Wright, Johnston & Mackenzie
Scotland No.27

REGIONAL REVIEW

KEY TO TERMS

There are 60 specialist areas or sections in *Chambers' Directory* in which a firm can be ranked. There are six 'bands' in which a firm can appear: bands 1-3 are classified as 'leading'; bands 4-6 are classified as 'highly regarded'. Fee income/profit figures when quoted are based on the *Commercial Lawyer* Fee Table of the 100 largest firms. Although the majority were supplied by the firms themselves, some of them were estimated.

NATIONWIDE

In our nationwide review this year, we have tightened the criteria for our definition of a national firm. To be truly nationwide, a firm needs to have offices in three or more regions including London and offer a broad range of legal services.

The five firms that fit this definition are Eversheds, Dibb Lupton Alsop, Hammond Suddards, Pinsent Curtis and Garretts/ Dundas & Wilson.

There are other firms which have a national presence such as Berrymans Lace Mawer, Wansbroughs Willey Hargrave, Davies Arnold Cooper and Masons but we have not included them in this review as their practices are focused on niche areas of specialisation – insurance and health-related litigation, for instance, or construction. (Each of these firms is written about in detail in the regional reviews).

FIRMS

Eversheds The biggest national firm with 12 offices in all the commercial centres. The past year has seen consolidation and further integration of the various offices into a national entity.

The best performing office across the board this year was undoubtedly Newcastle. Appearing for the first time in seven specialist areas of *Chambers*, they are showing the success of the Wilkinson Maughan merger. The integration of Leeds and Manchester into one cost centre is bearing fruit and both offices are benefitting from the closer co-operation. Manchester was recommended in two new sections, and was promoted in three (including banking). Leeds handled the Du Pont deal. Valued at £1.8bn, it stimulated immediate respect and consolidated Leeds position as the strongest Eversheds office overall. The weakest office is Bristol which went down in three sections this year.

The key development for the firm however has been the strengthening of the London office through the merger with Frere Cholmeley Bischoff. The London corporate practice was reinforced and moved up a band in our tables.

The firm as a whole is trying to get away from its image as a federation of firms, and plans are in place to make the network an integrated financial unit by the year 2000. A number of offices have specialist expertise in particular practice areas. This enables the firm to operate nationally integrated groups in these areas. Education is an example where ten of the firm's offices are ranked as leading firms in *Chambers*. The firm also achieved 6th place this year in our commercial property survey amongst clients and practitioners nationwide.

Conversely, there are centres of excellence where individual offices have expertise in a particular practice area. Leeds, for instance, in planning and local government work. Financially, fee income has expanded 16% and the firm has seen growth in commercial and property.

Dibb Lupton Alsop Despite recent marketing announcements that it is now a London firm with regional offices, the market still regards the heart of Dibb Lupton Alsop as being in the North. Both east and west of the Pennines, the firm is a dominant force in the local legal marketplace. The merger with Alsop Wilkinson has bedded down smoothly. Manchester has had a particularly good year, making up for Liverpool which dropped out of four specialist areas in *Chambers*. Litigation is a particular strength in the North West. Leeds – the firm's 'home town' – they also continued to do well. With back-up from offices in Sheffield and Bradford, Leeds achieved recommendations in more sections of *Chambers* than any other office.

Dibb Lupton Alsop should be pleased with its Birmingham office, which improved its reputation for corporate finance this year on the basis of some key lateral hires. It is showing the first signs of challenging the big four in Birmingham. In London, however, the office has some way to go before it is considered on a par with other firms in its size-bracket. Overseas, they have recently acquired the Eversheds Brussels office.

Of all the practice areas, insolvency showed the most improvement with four of

the firm's offices moving up a band in our tables. Financially, the firm's fee-income has increased an estimated 10%. Profit margins, however, are disappointingly low as the firm invests in new fee-earners. In the longer term, this key lateral hiring will pay off. They now have 72 leading individuals in *Chambers*.

Hammond Suddards Have retained much of the dynamic image that fuelled their expansion out of Yorkshire in the nineties. The firm's key offices (Leeds, Manchester and London) are all ranked in the core practice areas in *Chambers*.

The firm's cohesion is evinced by the number of practice areas in which the three key offices are ranked: commercial litigation, construction, insolvency, intellectual property, corporate finance, pensions and tax. Our research this year showed that the firm had the strongest London office out of all the national firms in terms of leaders in their field and reputation. This position may change next year with the merger between Eversheds and Frere Cholmeley.

There has been some change in the national corporate finance practice. The London office has benefited from the relocation of corporate head, Richard Burns, from Manchester. Overall Hammond's lawyers inspired distinctive views in the market. They are seen as hard-hitting but their practices in the 23 specialist areas in which they appear in *Chambers* also have a reputation for quality. (They have 37 recommended leaders in *Chambers*.) Although they are smaller in size than Dibb Lupton, their market profile is as high. Financially, this has been a successful year with fee-income increasing by 23%.

Pinsent Curtis Now the seventeenth largest firm in the UK, they are the fourth largest of the national firms. Despite recent upheavals in Leeds, the firm is consolidating its national reputation: fee income increased 16% this year and seven of its top clients are listed in the FTSE350.

Birmingham and Leeds are still the strongest offices, with Leeds ranked in 24 specialist areas in *Chambers* and Birmingham 25. London on the other hand appears only in four, but two of these are corporate finance and commercial litigation and the office contributes 20% of the firm's fee income.

In corporate finance, Alan Greenough moved from Birmingham to Leeds, and although this meant a slip in the rankings for Birmingham, the Leeds office has held steady. Both are rated in band two.

Projects/PFI work remains a particular strength of the firm despite last year's departure of Frank Suttie to Garretts. Both the Leeds and Birmingham offices are ranked in band one for their PFI work. Birmingham has an excellent public sector practice and continues to have top notch practices in local government and administrative and public law. Leeds has band one practices in employment and tax. Both Leeds and Birmingham have a nationally renowned niche employee benefits practice.

Dundas & Wilson/Garretts Always watched with interest, the UK legal arm of Andersens has had a mixed year. After the successful incorporation of leading Scottish firm Dundas & Wilson in September 1997, Andersens then entered into talks with Simmons & Simmons. These foundered, but AA then announced their negotiations with City firm Wilde Sapte and signed heads of agreement. Weeks later, the merger was called off.

Andersens needed a strong London firm to boost the network. Their London office is one of the weakest in the network and features in only two *Chambers* sections: computer/IT and travel. Garretts offices in London, Leeds, Manchester, Birmingham, Reading and Cambridge fare differently in our research. Leeds is the strongest. It was able to hire some heavyweight corporate players such as Sean Lippell from Pinsents. Of the 11 recommended leaders in *Chambers*, five of them are in the Leeds office. However, it will have to go some way before it can really break into the magic Leeds circle of the big six firms. In *Chambers*, it appears in six specialist areas – the most for any Garretts office. These include banking, corporate finance, commercial property and projects/PFI.

In Birmingham, they have not done as well as the other national newcomer Dibb Lupton Alsop and are only ranked in three specialist areas of *Chambers*: construction and corporate finance (which they enter anew) and pensions. Manchester appears in two sections of *Chambers* – corporate finance and banking, but it does have a leading practice in the latter. Cambridge appears in one section – corporate finance – a new core ranking for a new office. Reading does quite well and appears in three sections, IT, IP and corporate finance.

Overall, the firm has dropped out of five sections but has entered into three. All the offices are ranked in corporate finance, and three of the offices are ranked in computer/IT work. Significantly, Birmingham and Cambridge, the newer offices, are doing corporate transactions and being recognised as serious players.

The picture is very different in Scotland. This is the first of year of Dundas & Wilson's incorporation and the firm continues to hold the respected position it had pre-merger. Strengthened by the merger with Dorman Jeffrey, the firm continues to be pre-eminent in the Scottish market (see separate entry under Scotland Review). It appears in 31 specialist areas of *Chambers*, and is rated in band one in 12 sections including corporate finance, commercial property and commercial litigation.

The two firms remain separate partnerships under the rules of the English and Scottish Law Societies. However, they share the same management team and are moving toward being called Andersen Legal. The big difference between them is the share of their respective legal markets. Garretts will need a boost to be able to compare to Dundas & Wilson.

FIRMS
Regional Heavyweights

In this section, we have picked out three firms who do not qualify as national firms in terms of the number of their offices and their location, but do have national reputations. All three have stood out in our research this year as performing particularly well across the board. They have consistently inspired praise from other practitioners and clients in all the specialist areas in which they appear in *Chambers*. They are also firms that have done well in the *Commercial Lawyer* 100 and who have been proven to have flourishing businesses. (For more details of these practices, see under the respective regional reviews.)

REGIONAL HEAVYWEIGHTS 1998

WRAGGE & CO

ADDLESHAW BOOTH & CO

OSBORNE CLARK

Wragges Have long had a strategy for developing a national practice from a single office in Birmingham. Their outstanding financial performance over the past year, when fee-income rose 26%, is reflected in their pre-eminence in the Midlands. Their reputation for quality ensures that they often chosen as secondary regional advisers to some of the major corporates in property and litigation.

Addleshaw Booth & Co's Branding themselves 'the firm of the North' is a potent claim. The firm also has a national presence, and often features in our national surveys of The Times 1000 clients for property or commercial work. This year they came tenth in our national commercial property survey. Although competition in Leeds and Manchester is intensifying, Addleshaws still manage to be slightly ahead across the board.

Osborne Clarke We have included Osborne Clarke this year as a regional heavyweight. They have made more progress than any other regional firm in the South. Our research in every specialist area showed them to be a firm that was improving its profile. Part of this is down to marketing. But it also follows astute lateral hires and well-judged expansion. Opening an office in Reading in January is a good example of this. The office does not attempt to be full-service, but concentrates on a couple of core areas such as IT and corporate. In IT, it recruited ex-Frere Cholmeley Bischoff lawyer Russell Bowyer to head the Reading practice. In corporate, it will build on being panel solicitors to 3i. The new office, and the firm's ability to attract and keep senior quality lawyers makes Osborne Clarke one to watch.

LONDON REVIEW

Reviewed here are the top fifty firms in London by size

FIRMS (1-20 in size)

Clifford Chance Still the largest firm in London and the largest globally. Under challenge now from Linklaters' new European alliance of law firms, but they can play on the fact that organically they are the largest international firm. Do well across the board, but have suffered a set-back in corporate this year with the resignation of Peter Brooks, which was shown up in our written surveys and our telephone research. They have also lost the top slot in insolvency after the recent departmental upheavals. However, they maintain their position in banking and continue to make strides in international capital markets work, remaining at the cutting edge of securitisation. Other significant improvements are in the new-media field. They maintain a dominance in international projects. Overall the firm is ranked in 39 sections, and has a record 102 individuals ranked in the list. They have had their best year in terms of profits. Overall turnover was £370m (an increase of 22% on last year) and average individual profits per partner were £464,000.

Linklaters & Alliance Finally put their money on the table and announced in July 1998 that they have entered into an alliance with four other European firms, De Bandt (Belgium), De Brauw (Netherlands), Lagerlöf (Sweden), and Oppenhoff & Rädler (Germany). At a stroke, they become a serious pan-European law presence with the intention to implement a full merger within three years or so. This will obviously affect their rankings in all the internationally based sections. Over the past year they have continued to do well. Topping M&A league tables and bond tables in the finance sector, they have also stormed ahead in commercial property and are now undisputably the leading firm in this area. Ranked in 32 sections and with 78 individuals

Allen & Overy Banking is still at the heart of this City practice, but they are now beginning to make significant strides in corporate work, and are slowly moving up the rankings. They remain a highly profitable firm, in part because of their banking strength, but also because they combine their position at the forefront of modern legal practice with the internal cohesion of a successful professional partnership. In Europe they merged with Italian firm Brosio Casati e Associati on 1 January 1998. Overall they have increased their number of fee-earners by 350. Turnover this year was a record £220m and average profits per partner rose to £529,000. They appeared in 30 different sections in *Chambers* dominating all the finance-based sectors such

as international project finance and capital markets. Have 71 leaders in their field.

Freshfields One of the three leading corporate practices in London, they have had an all-round excellent year in every practice area. Turnover increased by 27% and average profits per partner have been estimated at £524,000. A firm that brings quality to everything they do. They merged with German firm Deringer in January 1998, and will be seeking to reinforce their international practice areas. In this year's *Chambers*, they were ranked in 29 sections overall and appeared top rated in ten of them. Have 78 leaders in their field.

Herbert Smith Still primarily known as the litigation firm. Their litigation strength takes them into a number of other areas and they are actually rated in 42 sections of *Chambers* overall. They also have an excellent showing of recommended individuals. A quality firm across all their practice areas, they are top rated in energy, PFI and insurance. They have seen their best ever year in corporate finance (ranked second in their size band).

Lovell White Durrant Are ranked in 39 different areas of law in *Chambers*, on a par with Clifford Chance, and fifth nationwide. They also have 65 recommended leaders in their field. What does this say about the practice? Out of the areas in which they are ranked, they achieve a top rating in insurance, European union/competition, intellectual property, pensions, parliamentary and the debt side of buy-outs. Of these areas, the most significant, perhaps, is the debt side of buy-outs which is linked to a good banking practice. On the corporate side, however, they are still lagging behind the other top City firms. Litigation continues to be a strength, and the firm has a number of quality individuals across the board. Turnover was up by 11%, and average profits per partner were estimated at £320,000.

Simmons & Simmons In their niche specialist areas, such as employment, IP, immigration, environment and recently telecoms, the firm has leading practices and excellent top-of-the-range practitioners. The challenge is to compete squarely against the top corporate, property and litigation practices in the City so that they can achieve their goal of being among the top five firms in the next millennium. No easy task. However, it would appear that they are taking some steps in this direction. Over the past year, they have set up an international securities unit that has achieved some significant deals; and have been instructed by six new investment banks. Ranked in 35 sections in *Chambers* this year, the

firm also had 44 leading individuals recommended.

Cameron McKenna One year post merger and it has very much been a case of 2+2=4. No surprises. The year has been spent consolidating the merger to produce a solid practice. The firm dominates in the expected sectors: insurance, professional negligence, product liability and health. On the projects side they have done particularly well in the electricity sector, and have a leading practice in non-contentious construction, largely due to star Ann Minogue. However, across the board, the projects practice still has some way to go to challenge for the very top slot. Overall the firm is rated in 31 areas of *Chambers*, with a niche leading practice in immigration. There are 47 recommended individuals at the firm, a relatively good showing, with particular stars in product liability and insurance.

Slaughter and May The quality of their individual lawyers and their client base make them a firm that is indisputably still at the top. Despite speculation about the wisdom of their international strategy, the firm does handle an enormous volume of cross-border transactions. They also market themselves quite actively internationally. They are ranked in 26 sections of *Chambers* this year, four as a band-one firm. They have 52 individuals recommended as leaders in their field. Picking out highlights of their year is a difficult task. Most of their corporate deals are significant, high profile transactions such as the Unilever/ICI merger. The firm will be moving to new purpose-built offices in three years time which will enable them to operate from the same building. What stands out about the firm is the sense of a seamless partnership which retains the spirit of a traditional law firm. Maybe this is why – out of the top three City corporate firms – their fees came in for the least criticism from clients.

They were perceived as offering value for money.

Norton Rose Have had a good year in *Chambers* this year which is reflected in their fee-income – up a remarkable 32.5%. They are top ranked in asset finance, including ship and aviation finance. In corporate and banking, they have been promoted in our tables. Over half of their work is international, although their presence in Hong Kong ended this year with the termination of their association with Johnson Stokes & Master. The dissolution of the Norton Rose M5 Group appears to have had no adverse impact. Overall the firm has 38 leaders in their field and was ranked in 30 practice areas.

Ashurst Morris Crisp Have an enviable reputation as a quality firm. They have a superb equity practice and continue to be the top international player in this field. This in turn gives them a stronger reputation in general corporate finance work than they probably deserve. In other areas, they have leading practices but only achieve a number one ranking in equity. Commercial property is a strength, as is project finance work and other related finance areas.

However, their banking team announced its move this year to Shearman & Sterling, and it remains to be seen how Ashursts realigns itself to deal with the departure. At the time of going to press, senior partner Andrew Soundy announced his retirement in April 1999. Overall, the firm has made significant (and costly) investments overseas in the two new offices in Singapore and Frankfurt, and upgrades in IT, so average profits have not increased on last year. The Paris office is strong and the firm reported a 20% increase in turnover. They were ranked in 25 sections in *Chambers* and have 43 leaders in their field.

Nabarro Nathanson Comments throughout our research this year indicated a firm not quite up to their usual standards. This is most evident in commercial property, traditionally the firm's core area, where they have slipped to second place behind Linklaters. Without their top ranking in property, the London office achieves a number one slot only in Local Government.

They have not seen the high increase in turnover of the other big firms, partly due to the closure of their Warsaw and Dubai offices. In London, they will be moving from the West End to a mid-town location. Out of their two UK offices Reading was top of the lists for IT, but Sheffield was perceived as a sleeping giant. Generally, the firm appeared in 36 practice areas, and had 42 leaders in their field.

Denton Hall Continue to be top ranked in two specialist areas: media and energy. Have a growing strength in project finance as a result of their energy expertise. Overall they are rated in 28 practice areas, and have a respectable 36 leading individuals. The quandary that faces them is how to increase profitability when growth is not focused around any of the core practice areas, such as corporate or property.

Wilde Sapte The year started out well, but has ended on a down note. The prospective merger with Andersens caused waves through the legal market when it was announced in February, and when it was aborted in June. Certainly, the asset finance practice has been hit by major defections to Allen & Overy. In addition the New York office has now closed and the future of the Paris office is uncertain following further partner defections. The firm now faces the task of rebuilding their own and market confidence. They still remain respected players in insolvency, banking and financial services. They have 18 leading individuals and are ranked in 18 sections overall.

Dibb Lupton Alsop The London office has grown by 57 fee-earners over the past year which makes them the 15th largest firm in London. In terms of size, they are therefore definitely a presence. In terms of *Chambers* ratings, the office is ranked in 16 sections, but only has leading practices in five. The most significant of these are the debt side of buy-outs (largely due to Mark Vickers), and computer/IT (David Barrett). They also have niche expertise in aviation, rail and yachts and have nine recommended leaders in their field. They have recently announced their intention to rebrand themselves as a London firm, and although they have a reasonable presence in corporate finance, commercial property and commercial litigation, they have a way to go.

Berwin Leighton Property forms the bedrock of the practice, although they do have a respectable corporate finance practice as well. Out of the 16 areas in which they are ranked in *Chambers*, they are top rated in planning and have a leading property litigation practice. Out of the 27 recommended individuals, there are four up and coming lawyers, and Laurie Heller makes it as one of the top five property lawyers nationwide (source: *Chambers* national property survey June 1998). The firm plays to its strengths which is shown in an increase in fee-income and profits – estimated at nearly 20% – and an increase in fee-earners.

Taylor Joynson Garrett Have set out to become major players in IP, IT, telecoms and corporate and have certainly achieved this

objective in intellectual property, where four of their 14 leading individuals are ranked. They have also achieved rankings in their other focus areas in *Chambers*. In corporate, nearly 30% of their client base has an international slant, and the firm can claim that they act for approximately 230 technology and life science companies. The firm is making steady progress in the realisation of their strategy. Fee-income was up 13% on last year.

S J Berwin Known for their dynamism and sometimes aggressive style, they have continued to do very well which is reflected in a 30% increase in their fee income. They have an excellent commercial property practice which competes with the big City firms. For their size they also do well in corporate finance. They are ranked in 18 sections overall and have leading practices in 11 of them. The firm also had 23 individuals recommended in *Chambers*, of which six are up and coming, and two are 'stars': David Shapiro in ADR and Patricia Thomas in planning.

Eversheds The major development for the London office was the merger with Frere Cholmeley Bischoff. The newly merged office is now ranked 19th in London by size. Not all of FCB decided to join Eversheds. The property, private client and media groups decided to set up a new firm called Forsters. Nevertheless Eversheds London has acquired reinforcement in two key areas: corporate finance and litigation. (In the latter area via ex-senior partner of FCB and leading litigator Alan Jenkins.) They have also acquired a top notch investment funds practice. Eversheds, London is now ranked in 19 sections overall and is top ranked in three: intellectual property, franchising and education. In each of these, the firm can boast some of the leading stars: Isabel Davies in IP, Martin Mendelsohn in franchising and John Hall in education. Internationally, Eversheds acquire an immediate European presence with offices in Paris, Brussels, Moscow, Copenhagen and Monaco.

Barlow Lyde & Gilbert The leading insurance and professional negligence firm, they are going from strength to strength in their core areas. They made some key lateral hires in general claims insurance in 1997 namely Sheila Simison who helps their insurance domination. Top rated in *Chambers* in both sections, the firm is also moving up our rankings in financial professional negligence and commercial litigation. As expected the majority of their leading individuals are recommended in insurance and professional negligence although the firm does have a related presence in aviation and shipping.

FIRMS: (21-50)

Rowe & Maw A respected general commercial practice, praised by clients for their professionalism. Not aggressive marketeers, they are nevertheless instructed by ten of the top 250 FTSE companies. They are ranked in 20 areas in *Chambers*. Out of these, they have leading practices in a variety of specialist areas but are top-ranked only in pensions (which represents 7% of the firm's turnover). They maintain their second tier ranking in corporate finance for their size, and do well in construction.

Baker & McKenzie Still have a strong reputation locally in the IT sector and have leading practices in IT, IP and employment law. Their focus areas are IT, banking & finance and corporate/commercial. In each of these areas they are exploiting their international network of offices. For example, having US securities lawyers based in London has helped the credibility of the capital markets' practice. (They recently topped a Privatisation International table with the number of deals completed worldwide). An issue for the firm is whether they are classified as a London firm or a US firm with a London branch. The nature of the partnership is such that each foreign office is a profit centre in its own right, and only 26% of the worldwide firm's turnover is produced by its North American offices. The question is can they create enough of a presence in their chosen core areas both nationally and internationally? Ranked in 17 sections of *Chambers* this year, with 20 leading individuals.

Stephenson Harwood Are ranked in 14 areas overall, but are best known for their shipping and corporate finance work. They are also top-ranked in white collar fraud and have a reasonable litigation practice. Have overall had a steady year with no significant change or upheaval. They have 15 recommended individuals, four of whom are ranked in shipping.

Theodore Goddard Have had a good year and seem to be making something of a come-back with fee-income up nearly 18%. With a new and younger management team, they have rejuvenated the partnership. Have done well in the finance-related areas, going up in asset and corporate finance. Acting in the Guinness/Grand Met merger was a significant milestone for the corporate department. Media work is still a key area and the firm has leading practices in film and music. Martin Kramer, their libel specialist, is doing good things and the firm moves up the rankings in defamation. Overall, they are ranked in 17 *Chambers* sections, and feature as a leading firm in six of them. Have 15 recommended individuals.

Richards Butler Are recommended in a mixed range of practice areas (16 in total) from shipping to media to corporate finance. As a firm they have a strong international emphasis in their work (largely because of their shipping practice) which can mean that their UK profile does not reflect the breadth and quality of the work they handle. They are top ranked in the niche areas of licensing, film finance and commodities.

Davies Arnold Cooper Insurance litigation is still the core strength of the firm, and is an area where they excel. As is to be expected, they are ranked in all the related areas in *Chambers* as a leading firm. Their professional negligence work in the construction sector has also given them a ranking in straight construction, and they have a ranked corporate finance practice. The Manchester office has performed well this year with growth in pensions and PFI work, and overall the firm has seen a respectable 17% increase in fee-income.

Macfarlanes A leading corporate practice that can compete in quality with the top ten City practices. As a result they are exceptionally profitable for their size and have carved a stable position for themselves in the legal market as a successful medium-sized firm, and second advisor to the major corporates. They are top ranked in five sections including corporate finance and trusts, and appear in a further 13. They have been prominent in PFI projects in the health sector and continue to have a large number of recommended lawyers in *Chambers* (25 in total).

Clyde & Co One of the leading specialist shipping firms with strength in the related areas of insurance, litigation and commodities. They also have a reasonable corporate finance department, and are top ranked in the road-transport sector. With fee-income showing a steady improvement, they continue to be successful in their niche.

Lawrence Graham Are a broad commercial practice with a thriving private client side. They have resisted the current trend to specialise in a limited number of core areas but their rankings in 19 *Chambers* sections are testimony to their stability as a generalist firm. The acquisition of Forsyte Saunders Kerman's commercial property department will strengthen an already good property practice and may compensate for the loss of some of Legal & General's property work. With a highly regarded corporate finance practice the firm saw a rise in total fee income of nearly 18%.

Masons The pre-eminent construction firm with offices in the North and now in Glasgow and Scotland. Their reputation for aggression seems to be mellowing as the firm successfully continues to develop its specialisms in IT and major projects.

Field Fisher Waterhouse Are ranked in a broad spread of areas in *Chambers* and, in a few niche areas, have star players, such as Mark Abell in franchising, Tony Ballard in media and telecoms, and Peter Stewart in travel. The merger with Allison & Humphreys has bedded down well and has given the firm a presence in telecommunications. Ranked in 24 specialist areas, the firm has had a measured increase in fee-income.

Titmuss Sainer Dechert Have an international presence via US firm Dechert Price & Rhoads which is reflected in their core areas of litigation, property and corporate. In the latter practice area, for example, they have a significant presence in the French market. In commercial property, they have one of the star property lawyers in the UK, Steven Fogel, who was nominated as one of the top five in the latest *Chambers* property survey. Ranked in 16 practice areas overall, they achieve a new ranking in the investment funds section of *Chambers* this year reflecting the establishment of their Financial Services and Investment Management Group. It consists of seven fee-earners and works as part of the Dechert Price team. Overall turnover has increased by 14%, and the firm is making steady progress.

Hammond Suddards The London office is best known for intellectual property, and in particular Larry Cohen, one of the leading IP practitioners in the country. However, the office has many other well-known leading names such as Brian Eagles – recommended in sports and media. Overall the office has 14 leaders in their field in *Chambers*, and it appears in 13 specialist areas. For its size, it is ranked in band one in corporate finance, giving the other London based firms with 1-125 fee earners stiff competition. It has a particular niche in film finance work. (See national firms for more details.)

Travers Smith Braithwaite Have had an excellent year and put last year's trauma with CWS behind them. The heart of the practice is corporate finance, which competes with the larger City firms. They also have highly regarded practices in financial services and related areas. Ranked in 12 specialist areas in *Chambers*, 15 of their lawyers were recommended to us as leaders in their field.

Beachcroft Stanleys Have a strong reputation in the health sector, and correspondingly appear in related sections in *Chambers* with top rankings in health care and defendant medical negligence. They also have a leading practice in the education sector acting mainly for institutions. Announced earlier in the year a potential merger with Wansbroughs Willey Hargrave, and Manchester firm Vaudreys. At time of going to press, the talks were still going on. If the merger does go ahead, it could make Beachcrofts the leading health sector firm.

Ince & Co Have been ranked as the top shipping practice in London for the last three years and are continuing to hold their position through star practitioners such as Richard Sayer, Peter Rogan and Richard Williams. They are also top ranked in insurance.

Reynolds Porter Chamberlain Have leading practices in professional negligence work in the construction, insurance and legal sectors. They also have a good reputation for commercial litigation and have a new ranking in defamation this year via the lateral hire of Liz Hartley from DJ Freeman. Have six leading individuals in *Chambers*, and appear in eight sections.

Charles Russell Have a considerable reputation as a private client firm with leading practices in trusts and personal tax, family and charity work. The hires made last year (in particular Norton Rose's private client group and four IP lawyers from Eversheds) have made their presence felt within the firm and fee-income has increased by 30% on last year. They also have a successful niche specialism in sports. Their Guildford office will be merging with a local Guildford firm Baldocks on 1 September 1998.

DJ Freeman Were one of the original firms to focus on core areas of practice and the results of this strategy now appear to be paying off. They are ranked in their focus areas of insurance, property and media/communications, and this year have improved their ranking in commercial litigation. They have 11 leading individuals and are rated in 12 sections in *Chambers*.

Gouldens A firm that is enormously successful in terms of fee-income and profitability. Strong emphasis is placed on their merit-based culture and on recruiting high quality staff. They have not lost an equity partner to another firm for at least two decades. They are a broadly based practice and for their size they have a leading corporate practice. They also have a niche specialism in environmental law. Have had their second best year financially although they only have six leaders in their field. Under new management now with Charters Macdonald-Brown as managing partner and Patrick Burgess as senior partner.

Bird & Bird Have a remarkably successful niche practice in IP, IT digital media and telecoms work and have top rankings in all these areas in *Chambers*. Most of their leading individuals are to be found in these sectors, and overall the firm can boast 16 leaders in their fields. This puts them on a par with much larger firms. They are true experts in their field and they also have a reputation in health care and medical negligence.

Trowers & Hamlins The leading housing associations practice in the UK. Interestingly, the firm has managed to "wedge out" from its niche and is now ranked in ten sections of *Chambers*. Most of their experts are ranked in housing associations although they also have a leading local government practice through Ian Doolittle. They will be moving to a new home in the city in Sceptre Court after 200 years in Lincoln's Inn.

Holman Fenwick & Willan One of the leading shipping firms, they are top-ranked in admiralty and also have good practices in insurance and litigation. They have had a steady year but no dramatic changes. They have 11 leaders in their field including star shipping lawyer Archie Bishop.

Withers Number one private client firm, with top ratings in agriculture, family and trusts and personal tax. They also have a respected niche banking practice acting for Italian banks. Have had a good year with a 25% increase in fee-income.

Paisner & Co Are ranked in ten sections in *Chambers*, and have 13 leading individuals in a variety of specialisms. They have notable lawyers in charities, food law and media, which ensures them leading rankings in these niche areas. When compared with other firms of their size, they achieve a second tier ranking in corporate finance. Overall fee income is up approximately 27% on last year.

Watson Farley & Williams Have achieved a top ranking practice on the finance side of shipping. Have been through some internal realignments recently but appear to be back on track. Their standing in this directory in asset finance, corporate tax and EU/competition work has improved and they have eight leaders in their field. Have recently acquired the Singapore office of Sinclair Roche & Temperley.

Nicholson Graham & Jones A general commercial City firm with highly regarded practices in litigation, corporate finance and commercial property. They have a niche specialism in the travel industry and have improved their standing in sports law. The acquisition of the Bristows construction team has promoted them in *Chambers'* construction section and the merger with Brecher & Co in 1995 has now firmly bedded down. The firm also has a leading trusts and personal tax department. They have ten leaders in their field.

Olswang One of the firms of the year. They have gone from being a small dynamic media practice to a successful medium-sized firm knocking on the doors of the big league players. Their success has come from being able to keep that dynamism and maintain quality lawyers. They have 15 recommended individuals in *Chambers* including star players such as libel lawyer Geraldine Proudler. Overall they are ranked in 13 sections (number one in media, defamation and corporate finance) and have seen a 26% increase in total fee-income. Olswang equity partners can earn as much as those in larger City firms which is partly due to an improved presence in the core areas of corporate and property and high quality clients.

Mishcon de Reya Have unfortunately been the focus of intense media attention this year for their handling of the Princess of Wales trust. It was not the sort of publicity that the firm welcomed and internally the firm seems under strain. Their best-known lawyer, Anthony Julius, became a consultant this year. Overall they appear in six *Chambers* sections, and have recommended individuals in family and media.

Berrymans Lace Mawer The London office of this now national firm is known for defendant personal injury work and professional negligence work in construction. It also has a niche specialism in yachts and road-carriage/commercial work. Nationally, it has offices in Manchester, Liverpool, Birmingham, Leeds and Southampton.

SOUTH EAST REVIEW

Bedfordshire, Berkshire, Buckinghamshire, East Sussex, Essex, Hampshire,
Hertfordshire, Kent, Isle of Wight, Oxfordshire, West Sussex

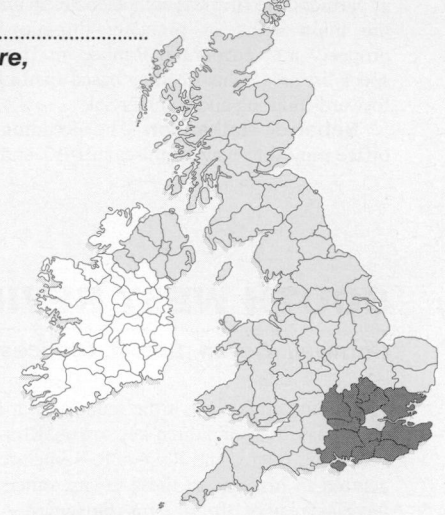

The South East as a region in *Chambers* comprises two centres of commercial activity – the Thames Valley and the counties of Surrey, Kent, Sussex and Hampshire with other south coast centres. It is not an integrated region as in other parts of the book, with firms rarely coming across each other. However, the region has good communication links to London and internationally, and the commercial firms see London as their main competition.

Here we discuss the ten largest firms in the region and then a selection of others in the Thames Valley.

Blake Lapthorn is still the leading firm in the South East overall, although competition is intensifying. Osborne Clarke opened a Reading office this year which was almost an overnight success; Bond Pearce are intensifying their presence with their merger with Southampton firm Hepherd Winstanley & Pugh and Thomas Eggar Verrall Bowles merged with Church Adams Tatham.

In general, most of the firms have enjoyed the benefits of the upturn in the economy, handling larger and better quality deals. However, there have been notable failures such as the dissolution of niche IP firm Dallas Brett in Oxford.

FIRMS

Blake Lapthorn A regional heavyweight that leads our tables in all the core areas – corporate, property and litigation. Litigation is a particular strength due in part to David Higham who is also outstanding in professional negligence work. (He acted in Barclays Bank v Dean Wilson and Others.) In all areas in which it was recommended, the firm was praised for its professionalism. The highlight in corporate this year was acting for Kerry Group plc in an acquisition from Dalgety plc, total deal value £335m. The firm also has a medical negligence and personal injury practice, and enters the trusts and personal tax section for the first time. Overall fee-income showed a steady increase this year of about 10%.

Cole & Cole Have offices in Reading and Oxford and have a broad commercial base with a nationally rated employment practice. The Reading office handles personal injury work, and most of the heavyweight commercial work is done out of Oxford. Their most notable move up the rankings this year came in corporate finance (now in the number one band) where the recruitment of Jonathan Loake from the now defunct Dallas Brett is making a difference. They also achieve a number one rating in family law and appear in a total of 15 different specialist areas.

Shoosmiths & Harrison In the South East they have offices in Banbury, Reading and Southampton. All three handle litigation-related work and have expertise in personal injury and debt collection. The Southampton office has a highly regarded commercial property practice.

Cripps Harries Hall Are trying to get away from their previous 'county' image, but are still best known as a private client firm. They are top rated in trusts and personal tax work, and have leading agriculture, bloodstock and family practices. In the last year they set up a new service called 'Private Office' – repackaging their private client services in association with Citibank. It offers an integrated package of competencies from investment management to pensions for high net-worth individuals. The firm is the largest in Kent, East Sussex and Surrey and continues to expand. They are rated in 16 specialist areas in *Chambers*, and also have a highly regarded litigation side.

Thomas Eggar Church Adams The result of the merger between private client firm Thomas Eggar Verrall Bowles and commercial firm Church Adams Tatham on 1 May 1998. The new firm has offices in Chichester, Horsham, Reigate, Worthing and London. It is too early to assess the impact of the merged firm. They are still top ranked in agriculture and trusts, and THESIS (TEVB's financial services business) now has more than 850 clients. The merger has reinforced both firms' highly regarded commercial property and litigation practices. Overall they are ranked in ten *Chambers* sections.

Thomson Snell & Passmore Are a leading private client firm, ranked in 11 specialist areas in *Chambers*. They are strong in litigation, and have leading practices in plaintiff medical negligence, personal injury and professional negligence. Have five leading individuals.

Donne Mileham & Haddock Are ranked in 21 specialist areas in *Chambers*, the highest in the region. Litigation is a key strength, and they are ranked number one in both commercial and property litigation. They have leading practices in corporate finance, but are also strong on the trusts and family side. With seven leaders in their field recommended on both the commercial and private client sides of legal practice, they are a broad and well-balanced practice.

Bond Pearce Have dramatically joined the ranks of the top ten largest firms in the South East. The merger with Hepherd Winstanley & Pugh has moved the firm from number 47 in size to number 9, doubling the number of fee-earners. The Southampton offices now have leading practices in corporate finance, shipping, personal injury and insolvency. Market perception is that the merged firm has brought together two first class practices. As a result of the merger, they achieve five new rankings in *Chambers*.

Clyde & Co The Guildford office of this leading London shipping firm is best known for insurance work. They also have a top notch reputation in the transport sector (road: carriage/commercial). With six recommended lawyers, they are a strong regional office.

Linnells Based in Oxford, the firm is ranked in eight specialist areas and has leading practices in family, partnership and immigration. The latter is a particular niche, and Philip Turpin their immigration lawyer has a national reputation. They are also notable for having two of the leading ADR specialists in the country, Jonathan Lloyd-Jones and Euan Temple.

Brachers Recommended in a number of specialist areas (14), this Maidstone practice has an outstanding reputation in agriculture and bloodstock work. Besides this niche, the firm also has leading specialisms in family, property litigation, defendant medical negligence and personal injury. For the first time this year, the firm makes an entry into the corporate finance tables, largely due to the efforts of newly ranked Stuart Butler-Gallie.

Clarks A first class commercial practice based in Reading. The firm is well-respected and liked by both competitors and clients. They act for three of the FTSE 250 companies, and have been promoted to the first band of leading firms in corporate finance. They also have a leading pensions practice and are active in the health care sector. Overall they are ranked in ten specialist areas.

Pitmans Are best known for their commercial property and planning expertise, but also have a leading regional corporate practice. With a number of ex-City lawyers as partners, the firm has competencies in all the main areas of practice: litigation, property and corporate. Ranked in five specialist areas, this Reading based firm is forward-thinking and commercial.

Nabarro Nathanson The Reading office moved to new premises in 1997 and consolidated its reputation for computer and IT work by hosting the Thames Valley IT Industry Awards. Ex-TKB partner and IT specialist Tony Bailes appears in the highest band in the region for both computer/IT and intellectual property. Another niche area for the firm is charities and the national team based in Reading is ranked in the highest band. The work has a commercial slant and the firm acts for 34 of the country's leading charities. They also have a corporate finance capability and service many Thames Valley clients.

SOUTH WEST REVIEW

Cornwall, Devon, Dorset, Gloucestershire, Somerset, Wiltshire

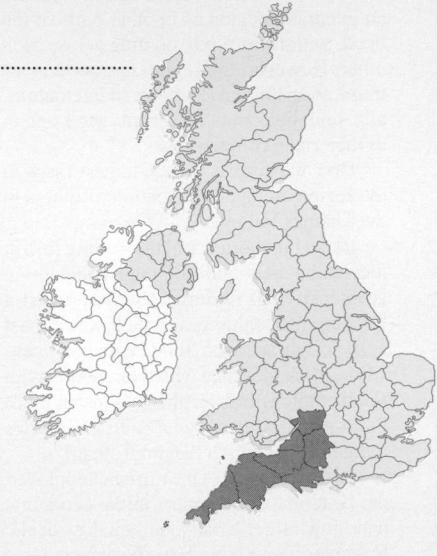

Commercial firms in the South West are based around three key towns, Bristol, Exeter and Plymouth. Some are centred in just one of these towns; others have a spread of offices across the region. A few have expanded out of the region, into London or the South East or internationally.

In Bristol, the two leading commercial firms are Burges Salmon and Osborne Clarke. The latter has taken an expansionist route out of the region, whilst Burges Salmon follows the 'single office handling national work' strategy. Both strategies are successful for the respective firms. With the demise of the Norton Rose M5 Group, this situation may change.

The legal competition has continued to intensify. Key big hitters have moved between rival firms, taking the reputation for a particular practice area with them. Bond Pearce has aggressively expanded across the South, and has finally opened a long awaited Bristol office.

Cameron McKenna has reinforced its Bristol office by moving down a corporate finance team from London. Clarke Willmott & Clarke have also consolidated their presence in Bristol, as a result of a firm-wide strategy designed to focus their strength in three key towns including Taunton and Yeovil. Much of the South West corporate work is handled by London firms. This expansion in the number of corporate players is seen as a positive development by other Bristol firms. It will boost Bristol's reputation as a legal centre.

We discuss here the top ten firms in the region and a couple of others who have performed especially well this year.

FIRMS

Bevan Ashford Have an excellent reputation in the health care sector. Their strong NHS client base is complemented by a public sector presence. The firm has a leading local government practice and is ranked in band one in administrative & public law and planning. Unsurprisingly their commercial litigation and property work is therefore skewed to serve these sectors. The firm has recently lost several senior lawyers such as corporate practitioners Patrick Graves and Paul Cooper to Osborne Clarke; previous head of their public sector group Malcolm Iley to Nabarro Nathanson; and PFI specialist Iain Fairbairn and some of his team to Masons. However, they are recovering from these losses. The firm still has a role in PFI, and has managed to hold its leading positions in the various public sector specialisms. More importantly, they recruited Veale Wasbrough's top corporate lawyers Stuart Whitfield and Nigel Campbell in July 1998 (actual start dates to be confirmed). This should go some way to restoring the firm's corporate profile in Bristol. The corporate group in Exeter on the other hand have done very well this year under Simon Rous.

The firm is the dominant defendant medical negligence firm in the South West and is still on the NHS Litigation Authority's panel which could mean a possible expansion into the Midlands. They move up the rankings in construction and commercial litigation. Ranked in 24 sections in *Chambers* overall, they have 14 recommended individuals.

Burges Salmon Best known nationally for their agricultural practice, they have leading regional practices in corporate, litigation and property. They have seven leading experts in agriculture work and are beginning to handle international instructions. In commercial property, they are thought to be the top practice, although the competition is getting more fierce. Another significant area of growth has been in the financial sector. They achieve an asset finance ranking for the first time and have a respected banking practice. Overall they are ranked in 30 specialist areas, achieving band one status in ten of them. Although they only have the Bristol office, they have a reputation for approaching matters with a national perspective, and there are plans to open a London office later in the year. Overall the firm has continued to expand, fee-income has increased by 21% and the firm shows no negative effect from the demise of the Norton Rose M5 Group.

Osborne Clarke Rebranded with a new corporate image 18 months ago in the shape of an orange puma. This image realistically reflects their continued aggressive expansion both in terms of new offices, and senior lateral hires. They opened in Reading this year, and have recently recruited top advertising and marketing lawyer Stephen Groom in London. Last year they made waves in the Bristol pool by recruiting corporate lawyers Paul Cooper and Patrick Graves from Bevan Ashford. All three of their UK offices, Bristol, Reading and London are well respected. In Bristol, they are undoubtedly the leading commercial practice. They are ranked in 29 specialist areas in *Chambers*, and appear in band one in nine of them including corporate finance, commercial litigation, banking and IP. The IT/IP and media groups across the firm are fast developing expertise. The firm has become a dynamic regional force which has enjoyed a 17.5% increase in turnover.

Clarke Willmott & Clarke With a new strategy that focuses on their Bristol, Taunton and Yeovil offices, the firm has ambitions to become the third commercial firm in Bristol. Over the last year, they have imported lawyers into their Bristol office and efforts to raise their profile there are paying off. They are beginning to establish themselves in corporate finance work and have a new recommended lawyer, Robert Hunt, in this area. Overall, they have four new leaders in their field in *Chambers*. They have a particular niche in planning work in Taunton and Bristol, and are top ranked in the region. Commercial property is also doing well.

Ranked in 15 specialist areas, the firm fee-income has grown by 10%.

Bond Pearce The demise of the Norton Rose M5 group has allowed the firm finally to open an office in Bristol in competition with fellow NRM5 group member, Burges Salmon. This will consolidate its reputation as a premier South West firm, already having powerful offices in Plymouth and Exeter. The recent merger with Hepherd Winstanley & Pugh has also given them a huge presence in the South East.

In the South West they have leading practices in corporate finance, commercial property and a band one ranking in commercial litigation. Their strength in the related contentious areas of defendant personal injury and professional negligence gives their litigation profile an insurance slant. This insurance strength, and their appointment as one of the Post Office's four national firms, is part of the rationale for their move into Bristol. Other specialist areas in which they achieve top ranking include employment, environment (where they have a niche in wind farms), planning, insolvency and trusts. Ranked in 20 sections overall in *Chambers* with 12 leaders in their field.

Wansbroughs Willey Hargrave The Bristol office is the largest of the national network. Its mix of practice areas deviates slightly from the usual blend of health and insurance litigation, and it is undoubtedly the strongest commercially. The office has an obvious dominance in the insurance and health sectors, but is ranked in 15 specialist sections of *Chambers,* some of which are non-health or insurance related.

Stephens & Scown Full service firm with offices in Devon and Cornwall. Their offices in Exeter and Truro are the best known. They appear in 14 specialist areas in *Chambers* and have six leaders in their field. They have a highly regarded corporate finance practice, acting in a deal for Terry Adams Ltd worth £105m, which was significant for the firm in both size and complexity. TAL, a waste disposal company, was purchased by South West Water. Perhaps unsurprisingly, Stephens & Scown were recommended as a new entry into our energy & utilities section, on the basis of their minerals and waste knowledge. Continue to have particular reputations in personal injury, family, admin & public and agriculture.

Veale Wasbrough Single office firm in Bristol, their client base has a strong public sector emphasis. They have a niche educational practice acting for independent schools. Their work for Bristol City Council on the harbourside development reinforced their leading commercial property, construction, and PFI practices. However the firm has been hit by a spate of significant defections: namely employment lawyer Chris Southam to Hammond Suddards in London, and more importantly corporate finance lawyers Stuart Whitfield and Nigel Campbell to Bevan Ashford. The firm still has David Bellew in corporate finance who with Stuart Whitfield was a recommended leader in his field this year. Overall the firm has a further 12 leading individuals, and was ranked in 21 specialist areas in *Chambers*.

Lyons Davidson Have offices in Bristol and Plymouth in the South West. Ranked in ten specialist areas in *Chambers*, they are highest ranked in personal injury – both defendant and plaintiff litigation with a reputation for motor accidents. They have a niche leading practice in health and safety. They are also improving their profile in environmental and planning largely due to the highly respected Kevin Gibbs who has individually been promoted in our tables. They are highly regarded in commercial property, acting for developers. They also make our tables in corporate and banking.

Lawrence Tucketts Have expanded over the last year to be in the top ten largest firms in the region. As a firm they are broad based and are rated for both commercial and private client work. Ranked in eleven specialist areas, they have leading practices in family and trusts and personal tax work. They are also well-known for their planning and environmental practice through high-flier Stephen Pasterfield.

Lester Aldridge The largest firm in Bournemouth, they are ranked in 20 sections and have seven leading individuals. This broad commercial firm also has a thriving private client side with leading practices in family and trusts and personal tax. In *Chambers*, they have leading practices in consumer finance, intellectual property and health and safety, although this latter expertise is derived from Richard Byrne's employment practice.

Cartwrights Have a single office in Bristol, and are known nationally for their top-notch licensing practice. Ranked in 14 specialist areas in *Chambers*, they also have a leading road transport practice dealing with regulatory matters. Their brewing, leisure and transport niches influence their practices in the core areas of corporate, property and litigation. In their dominant sectors, their reputation as an active and dynamic firm is increasing.

WALES REVIEW

In recent years Wales has benefitted from government grants which have attracted investment from British and foreign big business. Thanks in part to this growing commercial infrastructure, the big four legal firms in Wales – Eversheds, Morgan Bruce, Edwards Geldard and Hugh James – have generally had a good year, concentrating on the key areas of company/corporate finance, commercial property and litigation.

FIRMS

Eversheds The Cardiff office maintains its lead in traditional areas of expertise such as commercial property and education. It also dominates in a variety of other fields ranging from employment to trusts and personal tax. Overall the statistics are impressive: they are rated in band one in six sections including commercial property, insolvency, employment and administrative and public law. They appear in 30 sections overall. However, they have lost ground in corporate finance following the departures of Alan Whiteley (out of the profession) and Laurence James (to Palser Grossman). 11 of their lawyers were recommended to us as leaders in their field this year. (For further details on Eversheds see Nationwide firms).

Morgan Bruce The 1997 merger with Newport practice Guthrie Francis has helped to push the firm into the top band for corporate finance. The department's fee income has increased by over 40% in the last year, and they acted in the acquisition of GEC-Plessey Semiconductors by Mitel Corp of Canada. The firm leads the field in nine of the 26 sections in which they appear. The

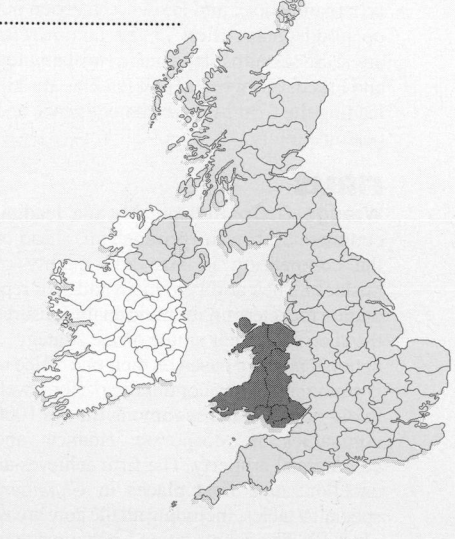

Swansea office is strong for commercial property, especially health trust work, and the firm continues to be ranked top in key areas such as commercial litigation and insolvency. They have 16 leading individuals in *Chambers* this year – five more than their nearest Welsh competitor.

Although recent years have seen **Edwards Geldard** expand into England, opening offices in Nottingham and Derby, Cardiff remains their largest office. The firm appears in 20 sections and is ranked top in corporate finance, commercial property and trusts. The corporate department has built up

a respected buy-in/buy-out practice and clients include Welsh Water. They also maintain their traditional strengths in administrative and public law, local government and planning, with Huw Williams consistently ranked number one in these areas. Licensing work continues with Bass as a major client. The Deeside (North Wales) office still services the Welsh Development Agency. Overall, eight of their lawyers were recommended to us as leaders in their field.

A steadily growing firm, **Hugh James** has a different emphasis from the other big Welsh practices. It has not sought to turn

itself into a corporate finance outfit. Instead it sticks to its strengths in litigation. The firm continues to reign supreme in commercial litigation, acting in the Welsh Rugby Union v Cardiff RFC case and defending Hoover in the ongoing 'free flights' litigation. It is also top ranked in property litigation, personal injury and professional negligence, with star litigator Michael Jefferies particularly praised for recent actions against accountants. They have nine leaders in their field in *Chambers*.

MIDLANDS REVIEW

Derbyshire, Hereford & Worcester, Leicestershire, Lincolnshire, Northamptonshire, Nottinghamshire, Shropshire, Staffordshire, Warwickshire

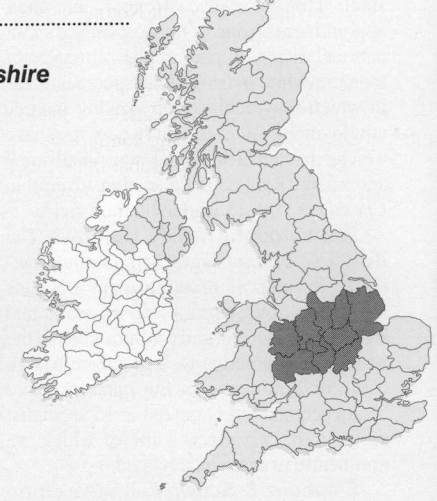

The last year has been one of changing fortunes for the top Midlands firms. Of the big four in Birmingham, Wragge & Co have managed to move ahead. They are followed by Pinsent Curtis who lead over Eversheds Birmingham by a slight edge. The most notable slippage was at Edge & Ellison who suffered defections and who are now trying to regain lost ground. The dynamic new pretender is Dibb Lupton Alsop who has picked off some key Edge & Ellison lawyers. They are steadily becoming more of a force.

The market is still tough for medium-sized firms in Birmingham. Martineau Johnson and Gateley Wareing stand out in this next tier of firms. After them come smaller firm Lee Crowder who are notable for their efforts to raise their profile in this market.

In the East Midlands, a different set of firms are vying for pre-eminence. Eversheds is here of course, and Browne Jacobson put up good competition in the commercial arena. Shoosmiths stand out in Northampton and Freeth Cartwright Hunt Dickins are still leading the field in medical negligence and personal injury.

FIRMS

Wragge & Co Indisputably the leading commercial firm in Birmingham, ahead of the competition in size and quality of business. Their ability to focus and their reputation for determination and quality ensures the success of their single office strategy: a national practice based on their one office in Birmingham. They continue to perform well in our national surveys among the top 1000 companies in corporate finance and commercial property. The firm achieves an excellent nine first places in *Chambers* specialist tables, including all the core areas, plus IP, IT, construction, pensions and

environment. They have 30 recommended lawyers, testament to the enduring quality of the firm. Their premier position in the Midlands is backed up by an outstanding year financially, which saw an increase in total fee income of 26%, much of this being in commercial and corporate finance. (See Regional Heavyweights)

Eversheds With offices in Birmingham, Nottingham and Derby, they are a strong presence in the region. All three offices have had a successful year, although Birmingham still has a way to go before it can challenge Wragges and Pinsent Curtis for the top slots in the core areas. They are ranked in 25 different specialist areas in *Chambers*, but only achieve four band one ratings: employment and pensions, insolvency and planning. The offices have a number of quality individuals, achieving 25 leaders in their field this year. (See Nationwide Review for more details)

Edge & Ellison Have had a troubled year, and are now trying to recover from the failure of merger talks with Pinsents, and the resignations of senior partner Digby Jones and corporate partner Chris Rawstron. Market perception was mixed about the firm. Some thought they were fading; others that they still had a solid base on which to rebuild their reputation. The new senior partner James Retallack obviously has the latter view. He may be just the man to steer the firm into clear waters. An ex-employment lawyer, he typifies the strengths of the firm, professional and sound. His determination is supported by our research. In *Chambers* this year they are still ranked in 28 specialist areas and have 24 leaders in their field. Although they only appear in the top band in four of these areas (food, property litigation, pensions and planning), they appear as a leading firm (band 2 or 3) in 15 others – which shows a solidity. Their London office increased its

fee-income by 25% which has gone a long way to maintaining the firm's overall fee-income levels despite the defections from Birmingham.

Pinsent Curtis In Birmingham, they pose Wragge's most serious competition. However, it is increasingly difficult to assess them as simply a regional office. Their practice is influenced by the needs of the national firm, such as the move of corporate finance head Alan Greenough to Leeds last year. This has meant that the profile of the Birmingham practice has slipped this year, and they are now rated in band two. However, they are still ranked in band one for commercial litigation and professional negligence. The office dominates in public sector work, and continues to develop its expertise in PFI projects for local authorities. Overall the office is ranked in 25 specialist areas and has 28 leaders in their field which includes two 'star' individuals: David Pett in employee benefits and Andrew Paton in professional negligence. (See Nationwide Review for more details)

Freeth Cartwright Hunt Dickins A litigation-biased firm based in the East Midlands. They are best known for their plaintiff medical negligence and personal injury work where they have band one rankings in *Chambers*. They also have a leading crime practice. Ranked in 20 sections overall, they have eight recommended lawyers. A year of consolidation has seen the firm complete two mergers: one with Bramleys in Nottingham and Barradales in Leicester.

Shoosmiths & Harrison A Northampton based firm which dominates commercial work in the area. It also has smaller offices in Nottingham and Rugby and offices in the South East. Despite a strategy which focuses outside the centres of fierce competition such as Birmingham, Shoosmiths has a highly regarded corporate finance practice which can handle quite complex work. They appear in nine specialist areas in *Chambers*.

Browne Jacobson Dominant in the East Midlands. Offices in Nottingham and London and an association in Paris. With insurance related services making up almost half of the practice, the firm has a band one ranking in professional negligence and acts for SIF. It also has leading commercial litigation and defendant personal injury practices. Has a highly regarded corporate finance practice locally, and has expanded this practice by 30% in the past year, handling higher value transactions. Overall the firm is ranked in 15 specialist areas and has eight recommended lawyers. They reported a growth in fee-income last year of 20%.

Martineau Johnson Broad based commercial firm with a band one trusts and personal tax practice. They are a single office firm in Birmingham, and appear in 17 specialist areas in *Chambers* with 13 leaders in their field. They have a thriving client base in the education sector (they now act for 17 universities) and a particularly strong litigation practice. Their IP practice has a contentious emphasis, and they have been promoted in our tables. Another area of promotion was insolvency following the lateral hire of Helen Readett from Edge & Ellison.

Dibb Lupton Alsop From the troubled Edge & Ellison they have recruited Chris Rawstron (which has given them a corporate presence) and Royston Tozer (recommended in fraud and food). They have made strides this year in gaining the critical mass necessary to become serious competitors for the top firms, although their property and litigation practices still have a way to go. They are ranked in 14 specialist areas in *Chambers*, and have band one practices in PFI and local government work. (See Nationwide Review for more details.)

Nelsons Are the tenth largest firm in the region, and have a leading general crime practice through leading lawyer Richard Nelson. Ranked in six sections overall, they have a strong private client side and a niche specialism in immigration. They also have a leading plaintiff personal injury practice.

Shakespeares An example of the difficulty of maintaining the middle ground in the Birmingham market. They appear in 13 specialist areas in *Chambers*, but fare better in the non-commercial sections such as education, housing associations and trusts and personal tax. They have held steady over the year and have ranked practices in commercial litigation and corporate finance.

Gateley Wareing Middle ranked finance practice based in Birmingham and Leicester. They have achieved a successful niche in corporate finance in MBO's and venture capital. They also have a leading insolvency practice (largely due to senior partner Brendan McGeever) and a highly regarded banking practice. Ranked in eight specialist areas overall, they have six leading lawyers. They are seen as a young dynamic firm whose reputation outstrips their actual size.

Lee Crowder A year after their move into the centre of Birmingham, their strategy is beginning to pay off in litigation and commercial property, although the jury is still out on corporate. The firm occupies the middle ground in Birmingham – no easy position. However, they appear to have the energy to make the move work and have a number of quality institutional clients including 3i. Their continued rankings in all the core areas in *Chambers* is evidence of their success.

Garretts Lurking at number 32 in size in the region, the Birmingham office makes its presence felt largely through its potential to become a major player in the future. (See under Nationwide Review for more details.)

EAST ANGLIA REVIEW

Cambridgeshire, Norfolk and Suffolk

Cambridge is a leading centre for hi-tech industries. Consequently the firms doing best in this region have strong IP and corporate practices. But there is still great demand for the more traditional agricultural and private client practices, owing largely to Newmarket's continued pre-eminence in the world of bloodstock.

FIRMS

Mills and Reeve A premier division firm with strength across the board. Profits have risen due to an increasing amount of commercial, NHS trust, education and agricultural work. They are top-ranked in 13 sections and feature in 25 sections overall. With a growing number of health sector, pharmaceutical and bio-tech clients, they have maintained their lead in the public and private healthcare fields. They are also regional market leaders in the related area of medical negligence and personal injury. Recently, they opened an office in Birmingham, a shrewd move capitalising on their high market profile. They also offer an excellent regional service in the core corporate areas, and are particularly strong in construction where they have a wide international client base. In IP they have improved their position – due in part to the arrival of Isabel Napper from Taylor Vinters. They have 29 recommended lawyers in *Chambers*.

Eversheds Have a strong commitment to the region. The Norwich office is long-established, the Ipswich office has moved to larger premises and they will establish a Cambridge office in November 1998 through the merger with local firm Palmer Wheeldon. The new Cambridge office will be reinforced by three existing Eversheds partners including Cornelius Medvei, head of the national property group, and corporate partner Anthony McGurk. The East Anglian offices appear in 26 sections and are top-ranked in eight of them. They have increased their profile in IP and remain

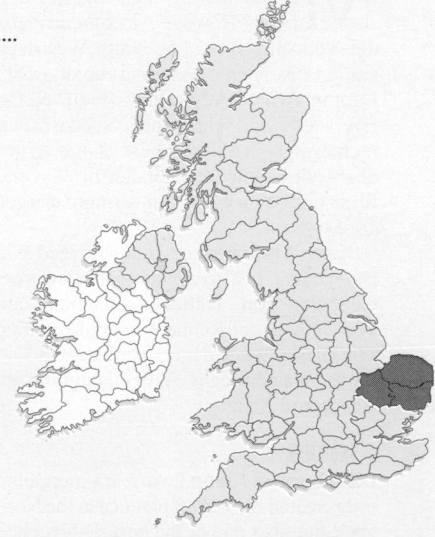

strong in both commercial and property litigation. In corporate finance, leaders Terry Gould and Andrew Croome have handled some substantial deals, helping to maintain the firm's top ranking in this field. They have 12 leading individuals overall in *Chambers*.

Hewitson Becke + Shaw This four-office firm has had a good year. Profits have risen sharply following a period of investment in IT and personnel. They have extended their international links, and this is reflected in a growing amount of work from the USA and Germany. The firm is ranked in 15 sections and achieves a top banding in trusts, employment, debt collection and IP. In the latter field, their impressive client list includes Nike and Microsoft Research Ltd. The firm remains committed to private client services, and the investment services unit now manages over £12m in client funds. They are also becoming a force in property litigation, acting among others for the Environment Agency. They have eight leaders in their field in *Chambers*.

Prettys This Ipswich firm divides its practice into business and personal law. On the business side, they are best known for commercial litigation, but also field a small corporate team. On the personal side, they have a strong trusts and personal tax department handling domestic and international probate matters, especially mixed UK and French estates. Building on their litigation expertise, they are also leaders in personal injury and medical negligence. They appear in 13 sections overall.

Greenwoods This Peterborough firm appears in 12 specialist areas in *Chambers*. Their strong litigation expertise has helped increase their profile in other commercial areas such as construction (where they have two leading individuals) and IP. They also have leading individuals in employment, corporate, IP and family. The firm has six leaders in their field in total in *Chambers*. It is ranked top in debt collection, acting for Railtrack and other substantial plcs and also has a leading licensing practice.

Taylor Vinters Have a mixed practice, featuring in 11 sections overall. In corporate finance, partner John Short has been advising the Bulgarian Government on corporate structures as well as overseeing the sale of major client Symbionics Group Ltd. With their office overlooking the Cambridge Science Park, the firm also places great emphasis on IP work, although they suffered a blow with the loss of Isabel Napper to Mills and Reeve. The firm does still achieve 10 leading individuals in *Chambers*. They have a leading private client department with a particular niche in bloodstock work.

Leathes Prior Best known for private client and legal aid work for plaintiffs. They have a leading plaintiff personal injury practice, and are strong in immigration and franchising. Other notable recommendations in *Chambers* are in banking where they have a strong litigious practice and act for Midland bank. Maintain a high regional profile in insolvency, continuing to act for local branches of the major accountancy firms. They are ranked in 11 sections and have four recommended leaders in *Chambers*.

Birketts The firm's main strength is commercial litigation where their work includes shipping and international trade disputes. They enter the construction tables for the first time and appear in eight sections overall.

Ashton Graham Will be the product of a merger on the 1st October 1998 between Bury St Edmunds firm Bankes Ashton and Ipswich practice Graham & Oldham. The new firm will have offices in Stowmarket and Felixstowe, giving a good regional spread. The merger of the two firms immediately catapults them into the top ten firms in East Anglia by size and they are now the fifth largest in the region. Bankes Ashton is recommended in four specialist areas in *Chambers* with their highest ranking in trusts and personal tax.

NORTH WEST REVIEW

Cheshire, Lancashire, Cumbria

Manchester has long been considered a less mature legal market than Leeds. However, since the arrival of the Yorkshire firms, the North West legal market has been developing rapidly. Dibb Lupton Alsop, Addleshaw Booth & Co, Eversheds and Hammond Suddards are increasingly handling most of the largest deals not handled by London firms. Other firms risk being edged out, so more mergers are expected.

Lace Mawer successfully merged with Berrymans last year, but talks between Cobbetts and Halliwell Landau, and Weightmans and Kennedys came to nothing. The latest projected merger is between Vaudreys, Wansbroughs Willey Hargrave and Beachcroft Stanleys.

FIRMS

Dibb Lupton Alsop Last year's merger not only created the largest practice in the North West but also one of the best. Dibbs either maintained or improved its rankings in all but one area (education), adding banking and property litigation to the list of specialisms where it is ranked in the first band. Overall Dibbs (we have treated Manchester and Liverpool as one unit) features in 14 sections and is ranked in first or second place in ten. Twenty-two individuals are listed as leaders, almost half of them in the top band.

The firm is doing especially well in property with Manchester alone acting on £1 billion worth of deals in 1997. Five individuals now make the leaders' list in property including two much praised 'up and comings,' Anita Weightman and Mark Beardwood. Litigation is another area where Dibbs excels. Liverpool received particular praise for being tough but fair. In corporate finance Dibbs has a high profile and respected practice and is ranked in second place after Addleshaws, the result of the strength of the latter rather than any weakness on Dibbs' part.

Addleshaw Booth & Co A dream merger. The market resoundingly approves of the newly combined practice which now acts for 36 of the FTSE 250 companies. In its first year, Addleshaw Booth & Co has been successful in more than half of the competitive tenders it has bid for. Manchester features in 21 specialist areas and ranks as a leader (first, second or third band) in 16 of them. Corporate finance has been a huge success and is undoubtedly the top practice in the North West. Five individuals are recommended as leaders but the real strength is the quality of the group as a whole. Addleshaws is in the first band for commercial property but this is an area where competition is fiercer – four other firms share the top slot. Other first places are banking, employment, intellectual property, pensions and PFI. Twenty-six individuals make the leaders' list, five in the first band.

Davies Wallis Foyster The third largest firm in the region, with offices in Liverpool and Manchester, DWF has a broad commer-

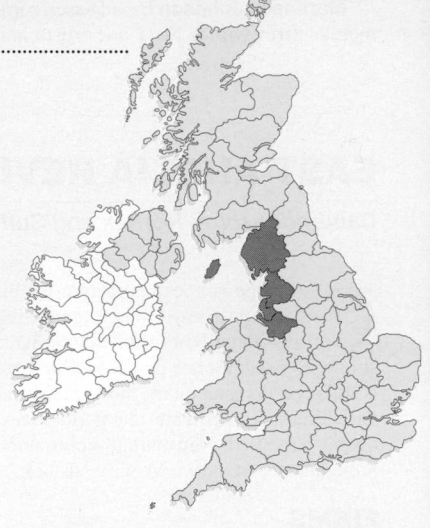

cial practice. It was recommended in 12 different specialist sections again this year, including the three core areas – corporate work, commercial litigation and commercial property – retaining its position as a leading firm for both commercial litigation and commercial property. DWF also enjoys leading firm status for licensing (it is one of the few English firms who handle work in Scotland) and defendant personal injury. It no longer appears in our construction and civil engineering section, but is newly listed for pensions. The firm experienced a solid 10.3% increase in turnover in the past year.

Hill Dickinson Also recommended in 12 sections of *Chambers* again this year, the firm has had a successful 12 months. £12.5m fee income last year has grown to £17.5m in 1997/98. Longstanding strengths in shipping and transport, medical negligence and personal injury have been maintained, and the firm also remains strong in commercial litigation. Merger in October 1997 with niche IP practice Philip Woods & Co of Stockport has propelled Hill Dickinson into our IP tables this year as a leading firm. Philip Woods is a recognised specialist. He and nine other individuals at the firm were recommended to us as leaders in their fields this year.

Berrymans Lace Mawer The merger last May of London, Southampton and Birmingham-based Berrymans, with Lace Mawer of Leeds, Manchester and Liverpool created a new national practice. Turnover for the firm as a whole reached £28m in 1997/98. The North West offices featured in eight different sections, their principal strengths continuing to be defendant personal injury work and trusts and tax (for which they appear in the top band). The firm is also ranked in the region for corporate work, commercial property and commercial litigation. With 24 more qualified staff this year BLM now ranks as the fifth largest firm in the North West.

Halliwell Landau Has continued its impressive expansion this year, adding a further 19 solicitors and recording a 23% increase in turnover. The firm is mentioned for a wide variety of specialisms (21 in all), appears in band one for four of them and is ranked as a leading firm for 11. It has moved into the top band for its IP work, leader Richard Boardman having recently joined the firm. It has also moved up from band three to two for banking, with Claire Shepherd joining the list of recommended specialists. Halliwell Landau is also making a mark in professional negligence and is newly ranked this year. In planning, commercial property and trusts and personal tax it has maintained its top band rankings.

Weightmans Merger talks with Kennedys came to naught when the latter firm took over the London offices of another Manchester practice, Elliott & Co. It is generally believed Weightmans will open in

Manchester in the near future and the firm is now reported to be in discussions with other possible merger partners, including Jacksons of Stockton. Its greatest strengths are professional negligence work, for which it retained band one ranking this year, and licensing where it is seen as the leading firm in Liverpool (Mark Owen is ranked as one of the top three licensing specialists in the north west). Weightmans also continues to be a leading defendant personal injury firm in the region and was ranked in a total of seven sections this year

Pannone & Partners The firm has had an encouraging 12 months, posting an impressive 19.46% increase in turnover. It appears in our construction and engineering tables for the first time this year, increasing its number of editorial mentions again, from 13 to 14. With 16 additional solicitors in 1997/98 it has also moved up from 11th to eighth largest firm in the region. Pannones has maintained its position as a top band personal injury firm and has also moved into the top band for medical negligence work this year. Janine Tobias who recently joined from Betesh Fox has given the firm a further boost in this area. She is one of four individuals recommended as leaders in medical negligence. Family law is another strength, and the firm moves up to join the leading firms for licensing work this year, thanks in no small part to the reputation of Anthony Lyons.

Eversheds The firm's presence in the region has strengthened further over the past 12 months. Its Manchester office features in 18 sections of the directory again this year, and has increased its band one rankings from four to seven. The firm has moved into band one for projects/PFI work and is particularly experienced in education and local authority PFIs. Its most impressive progress has probably been in banking work, where it also moves into band one. Nigel Dale received numerous recommendations for his work in this area. Eversheds is also a leading firm in the region for commercial litigation and for corporate work, with Edward Pysden the outstanding individual in the field. The firm had an impressive number of individuals ranked as leaders – 16 in all.

Hammond Suddards From a standing start in 1993 Hammond Suddards has become a premier league Manchester practice. Whilst Dibbs, Addleshaws and Eversheds have grown by around 10% this year, Hammond Suddards Manchester saw its turnover increase by 35% to £13.25 million. Although not yet full-service (many departments are run from London or Leeds and are staffed by a few assistants) its profile is improving and this year it is ranked in commercial property for the first time. Although not mentioned by any competitor, every Manchester-based surveyor recommended the firm (and Liam Buckley) as leaders in the region – having acted for P&O on the £300

million sale of the Arndale Centre it would be churlish to argue otherwise. The firm now features in 12 specialist areas and, with Addleshaws, is ranked in the first band for employment where Sue Nickson is the region's most respected practitioner. The one weakness is corporate finance where the firm has slipped following the relocations of Richard Burns to London and another partner to Leeds.

Cobbetts The 'last traditional firm in Manchester' is a common description applied to this long established and extremely reputable practice. In an age where competition between rival firms is intense, Cobbetts retains a reputation for old school charm and manners. Ranked in 14 specialist areas including banking, defamation and employment, its greatest strength is in property and related disciplines. Half the firm's turnover derives from commercial property and it retains its ranking in the top band. Other top placings are in property litigation, licensing and trusts. Eight individuals make the leaders tables. Despite strong showing in *Chambers*' tables, profits were not as good this year as last year.

Vaudreys At the time of going to press, the firm was in talks over a proposed merger with Wansbroughs Willey Hargrave, and possibly also Beachcroft Stanleys. Vaudreys would bring a healthy commercial property practice to any merger: now in band two, its ranking improved again this year. The firm also has a leading defendant personal injury practice which was widely praised in our research. The firm appears to be in good shape generally. In the past year turnover increased by 10.7%

James Chapman & Co Though only recommended in four sections, the firm is perceived as a leader in three of them. It moves up this year to join McCormicks of Leeds as one of the top two firms in the north for sports law (particularly football-related), and remains top ranked in the north west with Weightmans of Liverpool for professional negligence. It has also maintained its reputation for defendant personal injury work.

Brabner Holden Banks Wilson Based in Liverpool and Preston, Brabner Holden Banks Wilson has a solid commercial practice and appears in a total of eight sections this year. It is ranked for commercial property and commercial litigation, and has a steadily strengthening corporate practice, which moved up again (into band four) this year. Tony Harper is highly rated for acting for owner managed businesses. Brabner Holden also remains one of the top four firms in the region for trusts and personal tax, and continues to be a leading firm for housing associations work. In Lawrence Holden it possesses the outstanding housing associations specialist in the region. He is one of four individuals at the firm recommended as leaders in their field

Slater Heelis Another medium-sized firm with a good commercial practice in three key areas. It was recommended again this year for corporate and commercial litigation work and is particularly strong in commercial property. It also shows up as a leading firm in another three sections – banking, housing associations and insolvency (including directors disqualification). John Joyce and Egan Brooks were both recommended for their insolvency work.

Davies Arnold Cooper Turnover figures for the firm as a whole have increased by a healthy 17.1% and the Manchester office has performed well this year, reporting growth in its pensions and PFI practices in particular. It was recommended for seven different specialisms this year, remaining strongest (band two) for personal injury work. The firm remains highly regarded for construction work and Nigel Proctor was newly recommended for his expertise in this area.

NORTH EAST REVIEW

Durham, Northumberland, Yorkshire

Lawyers in other cities hate to admit it, but Leeds is firmly established as the second legal centre after London. No other regional centre can match its concentration of full-service law firms. The 'Big Six' are increasingly successful in their efforts to retain work in Yorkshire which in earlier years would have been referred to the City. The size and volume of corporate deals undertaken by Leeds firms increases every year – 1997 saw a £1.8 billion deal being handled by Eversheds from Leeds.

Another significant development is that competition, already fierce, is becoming still more ferocious. Addleshaw Booth & Co vigorously markets itself as the firm of the North and in previous years there was some weight behind its claim. Now its rivals, particularly Eversheds and Hammond Suddards and Dibb Lupton Alsop are rapidly catching up and even overtaking it in some key areas.

South Yorkshire is a smaller market place but is still home to some regionally important practices. Hull boasts a number of respected names, such as Gosschalks and Rollit Farrell & Bladon, with national profiles in niche areas. However it is Newcastle that is the other major legal hub in the region. Geographically and culturally Tyneside and Teesside are quite distinct from Leeds. The success of the Services Challenge, a scheme to encourage local businesses to use local lawyers, accountants and other professionals, is now acknowledged by the Yorkshire firms.

Bradford is too close to Leeds to be considered a separate legal market place.

FIRMS

Eversheds Nationally Eversheds has its critics but even the most vociferous respect the firms' North East offices. Leeds and Newcastle/Middlesbrough are treated separately in *Chambers*. Each could be (and was) a substantial and successful firm in its own right. This year Leeds acted on DuPonts' £1.8 billion acquisition of ICI's specialty chemical business. That deal was only one of 53 M&A transactions in 1997, up from 31 in 1996. Even if DuPont is ignored, the total aggregate value of deals in 1997 increased by 250%. If Dupont is included the increase is 600%. With the combined resources of Newcastle/Middlesbrough, Eversheds can argue to be at least the equal of any firm in the region. Either one or both of the offices appear in 39 sections, 13 more than any other firm. Thirty-seven individuals are mentioned, with nine being ranked in first place and two (Stephen Cirell and Chris Hilton) receiving the highest 'starred' ranking. Highly ranked in litigation (first band) and property (second band), the offices are best known for construction (where Newcastle is the firm's centre of excellence) and local government/PFI where the Leeds office is the leading practice in the UK. (See the Nationwide Review.)

Dibb Lupton Alsop However much Dibbs positions itself in the market place as a City firm with a national network, it is still regarded as the archetypal aggressively expansionist Leeds firm. Ranked in 20 sections in the North East, 15 in either first or second place, the firm has offices in Leeds, Sheffield and Bradford. The first places include corporate finance (46 deals in 1997 including the £193 million flotation of Newcastle United), litigation, and intellectual property. Commercial litigation has seen a 25% increase in fee earners this year, however this figure does not include other specialist litigation teams (there are eight). In total the firm has 14 partners and 61 fee earners working on specialist litigation. The firm's IP department continues to do well, this year acquiring Exxon Chemicals as a client. In property Dibbs is emerging from a brief period in the doldrums and noticeably increasing its share of the market. (See the Nationwide Review.)

Addleshaw Booth & Co It would be hard to conduct a survey of Northern firms that did not flatter Addleshaw Booth & Co. The Leeds office appears in 26 sections and is ranked in either first or second place in 17 of them. Eversheds may appear in more sections but Addleshaws is more consistent in its high rankings – the firm is alone in being ranked in the top band for the three key

specialisms (corporate finance, commercial property and litigation). During 1997 Addleshaws advised on over 300 deals, including four flotations and 50 buy-outs. In banking and financial services the firm also has the top slot, acting on 299 banking deals since 1 January 1997. A comment repeatedly made about the firm was that it is less personality led than others, with a greater emphasis on overall team strength. Despite this, 28 individuals are recommended, seven in the first band with one (Mark Chidley in banking) making the 'starred' band.

Irwin Mitchell Not one of the Leeds 'Big Six,' Irwin Mitchell is nevertheless a major player both in the North generally and increasingly in Leeds. Of the firms' four national offices, Sheffield continues to attract the most comment – the firm is the largest in South Yorkshire. Amongst the leading firms Irwin Mitchell has an unusual profile. Although recommended in 17 sections there is a heavy bias towards litigious practice areas (personal injury, medical negligence, commercial litigation, product liability, etc.). Similarly nine of the 11 individuals who were recommended are in litigious areas. It is also noticeable that two thirds of those ranked make the top band. Although the firm has been involved in some large corporate transactions (e.g. the £103 million buy-out of William Cook plc) and has three individuals mentioned, overall the firm has slipped one band. The perception is that the department is extremely good but constrained by its size.

Hammond Suddards People have vastly different experiences with Hammond Suddards. Some find them over-aggressive whilst others describe them as entirely commercial, constructive and helpful. It is almost as if interviewees were describing two different firms. What is not disputed is that Hammond Suddards is extremely successful. Leeds appears in seventeen sections and Bradford in one (debt collection), with seven first or second place rankings. Interestingly, Dibbs – not a firm noted for promoting competitors – ranked Hammond Suddards above itself for corporate finance, a strong recommendation indeed. Deals included Allied Colloids Group's £393 million acquisition of CPS Chemical Co Inc. It is also in the top band for commercial litigation where there are "lots of hungry young people" coming through. The picture is less rosy in commercial property but overall the firm is a leader in a broad range of specialisms. (See the Nationwide Review.)

Walker Morris The largest firm in Leeds not to have plans for national expansion. They are admired for their ability to build strong and lasting relationships with their clients. Walker Morris features in 19 sections, six in either band one or two. Whilst continuing to do well in many areas, including property (second band), insolvency (where it is the leading North East practice), commercial litigation (second band) and corporate tax (second band), the firm has a lower profile in the general corporate market this year and has slipped two places in corporate finance. 15 individuals were recommended in a variety of fields including intellectual property, planning, banking and sports law (in addition to those areas mentioned above).

Dickinson Dees The beneficiary of fierce regional loyalty, Dickinson Dees is the Newcastle practice that lawyers outside Tyneside are most likely to have heard of. It is the only Tyneside/Teesside firm that competes with the big boys in Leeds on anything like a level playing field. The firm features in 25 sections – three more than the combined total of Ward Hadaway, Watson Burton and Robert Muckle. Twenty individuals make the leaders' tables. Overall the firm has maintained or improved its rankings. The greatest jump is in projects/PFI where the firm moves

up to become a leader having closed the £86 million Carlisle Hospitals project.

Pinsent Curtis Alan Greenough's arrival from Birmingham has made a real difference to the firm's standing. A wave of defections last year cast doubts over Pinsent's corporate capability but the firm remains on its feet and is moving forward again. Notable deals include HSBC's £145 million private equity deal with AM Paper and SIG's £65 million sale of Architectural Products. Importantly there have been no new defections and the lower profile this year of some of the big names who left in 1997 may well be causing wry amusement in Park Square. With the benefit of John McMullen's national reputation the firm continues to lead the North in employment and employee benefits. It also remains in the top slot for PFI (closing the £96 million North Durham DGH project in March '98) and for tax where Pinsents beat the path that the other firms are now trying with varying degrees of success to follow. (See the Nationwide Review.)

Wansbroughs Willey Hargrave The bulk of Wansbroughs' work nationally is health care, defendant medical negligence and professional negligence. The Leeds and Sheffield offices rank in the top band for all three of these specialisms. Appearing in nine sections in total, they also feature in the related areas of personal injury, insurance and projects/PFI. Six individuals in the above fields were recommended and one individual features in the top band for employment law.

Nabarro Nathanson The northern outpost of the Nabarros empire, Sheffield leads the field in health & safety work. It is also known for its environment, energy and planning practices and appears in nine sections in total. The personal injury department maintains its strength, continuing to act for British Coal Corporation in respiratory disease litigation and gaining new clients from the loss adjuster sphere. Six individuals make the leaders' tables.

Ward Hadaway One of the largest firms in Tyneside, Ward Hadaway has a heavy bias towards property and litigation, with company and commercial constituting only 15% of the work load. Despite this, the firm is highly regarded for corporate work and is a favourite with accountants, having a good reputation for smaller MBOs. It has one of the leading agriculture & bloodstock practices in the North, with specialist Chris

Hewitt being ranked in the first band of leading individuals. Well placed in eleven sections overall, with a total of five individuals being recommended as leaders.

Andrew M. Jackson Whilst highly regarded for corporate, property and litigation the firm is best known for its work in niche areas. It is a leader in product liability (food), shipping, road transport and trusts & personal tax. In total the firm features in nine sections with five individuals making the leaders' tables.

Gosschalks Whilst best known nationally for licensing work, Gosschalks is also one of the largest practices in Hull. Senior partner, Les Green, retains his 'starred' ranking as one of the leading licensing specialists in the country. The firm as a whole appears in six sections, including property (where much of the work feeds off the licensing department's client list) and crime for which the firm is highly regarded.

Rollit Farrell & Bladon A long established firm (it was founded in 1841), Rollit Farrell & Bladon appears in more sections than any other Hull firm (it also has offices in Beverley, Helmsley and York). All four of the firm's departments (company/commercial, property, litigation and private client) are ranked, and overall the firm features in 11 sections. As a result RF&B is widely thought of as the leading firm on the Humber. The highest rankings are for agriculture & bloodstock, employment and housing associations for which it is a leading practice.

Garretts A rapidly growing practice. Without doubt the strongest office in the Garretts network. Since 1996 Garretts has increased its fee earners by 30% (to 40 professional staff) and seen turnover grow by 100%. The corporate department was described as "supremely sensible and practical" and in one 12 month period was involved in £500 million worth of deals. The firm has done particularly well in commercial property. Although not moving up a band it has raised its profile to the point where it is on the brink of becoming a leading property practice. Two of the property department's fee earners make the leaders' table (only one was listed last year). Overall Garretts appears in six sections with five individuals on the leaders list. Leeds is also the centre of the national PFI practice headed by Frank Suttie, who joined last year from Pinsent Curtis.

SCOTLAND REVIEW

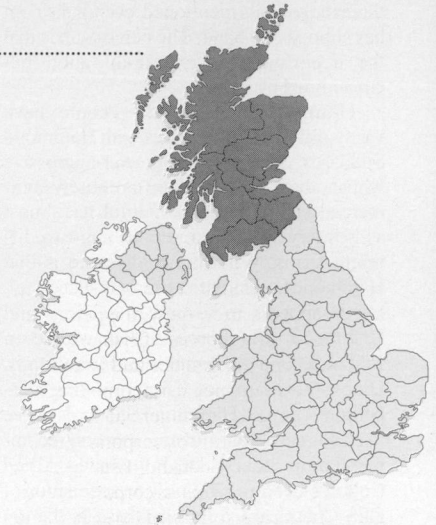

The Scottish legal market moved a step forward last year when its largest firm, Dundas & Wilson, merged with Dorman Jeffrey and became part of the Arthur Andersen network. So far none of the other large firms have been tempted down the same path. However, partner moves between firms, once a rarity in Scotland, have become relatively commonplace. Another development affecting the market has been devolution and the advent of the Scottish parliament. Firms have been establishing internal groups to identify opportunities which the new parliament will create for them.

Until recently Dundas & Wilson and McGrigor Donald used to be spoken of as the "big two" Scottish firms. Now, Dundas & Wilson have become comfortably the largest firm, but represent a different type of practice, while a "big three" group of independent firms is emerging – McGrigor Donald, Maclay Murray & Spens and Shepherd & Wedderburn. Together with D&W and Dickson Minto they have gained something of a stranglehold on the top flight corporate work in Scotland.

FIRMS

Dundas & Wilson CS The merger with Dorman Jeffrey created a 53 partner firm, easily the largest in Scotland. The new Dundas & Wilson has close links with Andersen's English law firm, Garretts, and is part of one of the largest networks of law firms worldwide. Ten partners left in 1997 following the decision to join forces with Andersens. Seven private client partners left to set up a new firm – Turcan Connell – and D&W are no longer ranked for trusts, charities, personal tax work, or agriculture this year. Head of litigation Alayne Swanson also left for Maclay Murray & Spens, unconvinced that, as part of the Andersen network, Dundas & Wilson would have a commitment to litigation. However, the firm has maintained its position in our tables this year as joint leader in commercial litigation in Scotland. It also gained a number of partners from Dorman Jeffrey, including corporate finance specialist Brian Dorman.

Overall the firm is ranked in 31 sections this year (down slightly from 34 last year, but still more than any other Scottish firm) and was in band one in 12 of them. It maintains band one ranking in the key areas of corporate finance, commercial litigation and commercial property. It has risen in the rankings for employment law and insolvency, and also has the highest number of leading individuals, 30 in all. (See national review for further details.)

McGrigor Donald Now the largest independent firm in Scotland following Dundas & Wilson's decision to join Arthur Andersen, they are reportedly the first Scottish firm to record annual turnover of more than £20m representing an increase of 10%. The firm has maintained its position in traditional areas of strength, with band one rankings in computer law/IT, IP, and the core areas of commercial litigation, and commercial property. It is also a leading firm for corporate finance. It features in 28 sections in all, up three from last year. The firm is newly included for partnership law, but its rankings have slipped a little in construction, projects/PFI and defamation. Once again 22 individuals were identified as leaders in their field. The firm has been focusing attention on growth outside Scotland. It now has seven partners and 20 other lawyers in its expanding London office. It has also formed a multi-disciplinary Scottish Parliament Group to respond to the opportunities for new work the parliament will create.

Maclay Murray & Spens Has shown impressive growth, with a total of 103 solicitors in 1998 compared to 87 last year, including five new partners and three associates. The firm's rankings have changed little. It appears in a total of 22 sections (one more than last year) and was newly mentioned for insurance work. They have one of only two dedicated IP practices in Scotland and one of the few dedicated property litigation practices. It maintains band one ranking for these specialists and for computer law/IT, trusts and personal tax and shipping (sharing most of the work in Scotland with Henderson Boyd Jackson). 22 individuals were recommended to us as leaders in their field. Fiona Nicholson was identified as the outstanding IP practitioner in Scotland this year. Leading commercial litigator Alayne Swanson joined from Dundas & Wilson.

Shepherd & Wedderburn WS The major development of the past year was the opening of an office in Glasgow with three partners and 22 staff. Also launched a new legal lobbying division, Saltire Parliamentary Consultants in January, to assist businesses wanting to influence the decisions of the Scottish parliament. Turnover increased by 15%.

They are ranked in 25 sections this year (down from 27 last year), with 18 individuals ranked as leaders. Has moved up into band 1 for aviation work, and maintained top band ranking in financial services, investment funds, housing associations and medical negligence. Continues to enjoy leading firm status in corporate finance, commercial litigation and commercial property work

(where it is seen as rapidly catching the top two firms). Has also strengthened its position in planning, administrative law, charities and professional negligence.

Brodies WS Appears in a total of 17 sections – one less than last year and there have been no major changes in the firm's rankings. Long-standing strengths in agriculture, trusts and personal tax, planning and environmental law have been maintained. The firm's ranking for employment law has gradually improved over the past couple of years, and it has now joined the leading practices, thanks in large part to the reputation of Joyce Cullen. It drops out of our corporate tax and financial services tables, but is newly ranked for administrative and public law. It is still the only Scottish firm with a specialism in franchising law.

MacRoberts The firm's impressive growth continues – last year's figure of 58 qualified staff has increased to 72. There is now a widespread perception that MacRoberts has put "clear blue water" between itself and its nearest rivals in construction law. (Although it is likely to face competition in the next couple of years from the new Masons office in Glasgow.) The firm is also joint top in PFI work and a band one firm for licensing. Other strengths include employment law, trusts and personal tax and intellectual property. However, it is no longer ranked for commercial litigation. Among the 14 lawyers recommended as leaders in their field was the versatile David Flint who appears in four different sections. Jim McGinn, who joined recently from Dickson Minto, was newly recommended this year for corporate work and will strengthen the department.

Tods Murray WS Another firm that has jumped up the rankings in terms of size (seventh largest this year, 12th last year). It maintains a strong profile, appearing in 16 different sections and with ten lawyers recommended as leaders. Tods Murray is a leading firm in both financial services and investment funds work, with Christopher Athanas, Martin Thurston Smith and David Dunsire all recommended. It remains the leading firm in the UK for timeshare work. The firm handles a substantial amount of commercial property work and appears in our property litigation section for the first time this year.

Paull & Williamsons Has moved up to 8th largest firm in Scotland from 13th last year, thanks to eight more qualified staff. Now marginally the largest Aberdeen-based firm ahead of Ledingham Chalmers. Has a broad commercial practice and is ranked in each of the three core areas (corporate, commercial property, commercial litigation). Seen as the top firm for corporate work in the North East of Scotland. Established an Oil and Gas Unit within its corporate department last year and is ranked for energy work for the first time this year. The firm's ranking for employment law improved again this year and it now appears in band two. Had eight individuals recommended as leaders.

McClure Naismith The firm appears in eight sections this year and remains strong in certain niche areas. It is one of the two Scottish firms (the other being McGrigor Donald) with a specialist consumer finance practice, based around the reputation of leader Frank Johnstone. Another niche specialism is health and safety, where the firm is again one of only two recommended in Scotland. It also has an excellent debt collection practice, one of the top two in Scotland, and leading employment law and PFI practices. The quality of the firm's banking work merited a higher ranking this year.

Ledingham Chalmers An Aberdeen-based firm with a strong oil and gas practice, which has moved up in our energy tables. Unusually for a Scottish firm it has foreign offices in Baku (Azerbaijan), Istanbul and the Falkland Islands, which facilitate its work in this area, and in shipping, corporate and

other matters. Has had a successful year: global turnover increased by 15% in 1997. The firm was ranked in seven sections of *Chambers* this year and earned a place in our housing associations tables for the first time. It is also ranked for corporate work and commercial property and has a strong private client practice.

Burness The firm has been shifting its focus to commercial areas of law, concentrating on the core areas of corporate work, commercial litigation and property, together with construction and PFI. In construction and PFI there is evidence that this policy is reaping dividends, with the firm's ranking improving in both areas. It is also a new entrant to our energy tables on the back of strong recommendations. In line with the shift in focus it has dropped out of our tables for charities, agriculture and bloodstock and trusts and personal tax. The firm's Edinburgh private client partners have joined Turcan & Connell and total numbers of qualified staff have gone down to 57, from 71 in 1996. Burness appears in 19 sections of this year's *Chambers* and had 14 lawyers recommended as leaders in their field. Following its opening of larger offices in Glasgow last year, the firm has recently moved to new offices in Edinburgh.

Bird Semple Has a broad commercial practice and is ranked in each of the key areas of corporate work, commercial litigation and property. Performing particularly well in commercial property, where it moves up from the highly regarded to leading firms bracket. The firm has also increased its numbers of qualified lawyers in the past year. Ranked in ten different sections this year. Enters our computer law/IT tables for the first time.

Henderson Boyd Jackson WS Arguably the Scottish firm making the most rapid progress of late. It has more than doubled in size over the past three years – with 54 qualified staff compared to just 23 in

1995. It is ranked in the three core areas – commercial litigation, commercial property and corporate work – and in nine sections in all. It was included in our corporate tables for the first time last year, and has moved up a band this year. The firm has also maintained band one rankings in three other important specialisms – housing association work, shipping (James Lowe and Duncan MacLean are both acknowledged leaders) and sports law. They are newly mentioned this year for administrative and public law. A firm that is clearly going places.

Anderson Strathern WS Has had a successful year and, where others have focused on purely commercial areas, remains committed to being a full service firm. Ranked for seven different specialisms this year (five last year), with new recommendations for personal injury, media and entertainment and housing association work. The media ranking owes much to the appointment in 1997 of Simon Brown, formerly Head of Corporate at Steedman Ramage. The firm has also moved up into band one for sports law with John Kerr's profile continuing to grow, and it continues to enjoy a national reputation for private client work and agriculture.

Biggart Baillie The past 18 months have seen the firm change its name, adopt a new corporate image and logo, appoint a new managing partner and move to new offices in Edinburgh. However, it has shrunk over the past few years in terms of numbers of qualified fee-earners. It now ranks 15th in terms of size, having formerly been one of the ten largest firms. It has a broad practice and is ranked in ten different areas this year. Handling the lion's share of the work for Scottish Power, Biggart Baillie has one of the strongest energy practices in the region, and is also one of the leading firms for defender personal injury. It has improved its rankings this year for professional negligence and commercial property work.

Top 100 law firms

These figures are taken from the August 1998 issue of Commercial Lawyer magazine. Most were supplied by the firms themselves, either officially or unofficially. A few, however, were estimated on the basis of journalists' research.

Total billings of the top 100 law firms in the last financial year (1997-98) were £4,313 million. Of this total, the top five firms by revenues – Clifford Chance, Linklaters, Allen & Overy, Freshfields, and Slaughter and May (the 'national firms' have not been included) – bill more than a quarter (28.5%). The top ten by revenues (which goes on to include Lovell White Durrant, Herbert Smith, Norton Rose, Cameron McKenna and Simmons & Simmons) bill 43%. Adding the large national firms would make the concentration at the top even more apparent.

The distinctiveness of the top five firms is shown in their average profits per equity partner: a remarkable £527,200 a year. Partner profits for the next five firms are much lower: they average £288,000 a year. The bottom thirty firms, by comparison, average £139,250.

Among the top five firms, revenues per fee-earner average £225,375 a year. These are high figures and seen alongside revenues per equity partner (£1,329,373) they provide the key to the firms' extraordinary profitability. There is no hint of commodity product here. The super-profits per partner are then a function of the leverage ratios between equity partners and fee-earners. In spite of the top firms' 'full-equity-no-salaried-partners' policies which create an abundance of equity partners, they manage to keep their ratios high (around 1 partner to 5 fee-earners). Hence their half-a-million pound profits.

Revenues per fee-earner among the bottom thirty firms (ranked by fee-income) fall to £95,072 a year. Interestingly, they are also low among the the 'national firms' such as Eversheds, Dibb Lupton and Garretts. Although these firms rank among the largest in the UK, they handle a substantial volume of commodity work. As a group, therefore, their revenues per fee-earner are down at £118,586 a year. Average profits per equity partner are kept up at £223,833 by maintaining a high leverage ratio of 1 : 7.4.

Firm	Fees 97-98	Equity partners	All fee-earners[1]	Leverage ratio[2]	Fees per fee-earner	Profits per equity partner	Profit ranking
Addleshaw Booth & Co	£43,289,000	76	432	1:4.7	£100,206	£150,000	72
Allen & Overy	£220,000,000	161	1109	1:5.9	£198,377	£529,000	2
Ashurst Morris Crisp	£85,300,000	84	384	1:3.6	£222,135	£305,000	16
Baker & McKenzie	£42,000,000	39	230	1:4.9	£182,609	£295,000	19
Barlow Lyde & Gilbert	£41,000,000	37	258	1:6.0	£158,915	£265,000	23
Beachcroft Stanleys	£22,900,000	36	186	1:4.2	£123,118	£173,000	63
Berrymans Lace Mawer	£28,000,000	38	308	1:7.1	£90,909	£188,000	55
S J Berwin & Co	£50,500,000	40	262	1:5.6	£192,748	£390,000	8
Berwin Leighton	£47,000,000	53	247	1:3.7	£190,283	£260,000	24
Bevan Ashford	£19,794,000	37	225	1:5.1	£87,973	£115,000	92
Biddle	£12,900,000	24	85	1:2.5	£151,765	£190,000	54
Bird & Bird	£20,700,000	16	127	1:6.9	£162,992	£337,000	12
Bond Pearce	£15,000,000	23	164	1:6.1	£91,463	£140,000	79
Browne Jacobson	£12,900,000	22	151	1:5.9	£85,430	£140,000	82
Burges Salmon	£17,500,000	29	185	1:5.4	£94,595	£150,000	73

1. 'All fee-earners' includes equity partners, trainees and other fee-earners.   2. Leverage is the ratio of equity partners to other fee-earners.

Firm	Fees 97-98	Equity partners	All fee-earners[1]	Leverage ratio[2]	Fees per fee-earner	Profits per equity partner	Profit ranking
Cameron McKenna	£102,000,000	122	708	1:4.8	£144,068	£245,000	27
Charles Russell	£21,300,000	37	157	1:3.2	£135,669	£161,000	68
Clarke Willmott & Clarke	£12,900,000	26	224	1:7.6	£57,589	£102,000	99
Clifford Chance	£370,000,000	271	1795	1:5.6	£206,128	£464,000	5
Clyde & Co	£52,000,000	54	295	1:4.5	£176,271	£260,000	25
Cobbetts	£9,700,000	23	90	1:2.9	£107,778	£122,000	90
Cole & Cole	£10,500,000	18	127	1:6.1	£82,677	£103,000	98
Cripps Harries Hall	£10,500,000	21	116	1:4.5	£90,517	£128,000	87
D J Freeman	£23,300,000	20	134	1:5.7	£173,881	£210,000	43
Davies Arnold Cooper	£37,060,000	32	282	1:7.8	£131,418	£231,000	34
Davies Wallis Foyster	£12,244,000	23	110	1:3.8	£111,309	£110,000	96
Denton Hall	£72,000,000	72	396	1:4.5	£181,818	£230,000	36
Dibb Lupton Alsop	£111,500,000	82	967	1:10.8	£115,305	£238,000	31
Dickinson Dees	£13,000,000	25	150	1:5.0	£86,667	£145,000	78
Edge & Ellison	£30,600,000	39	260	1:5.7	£117,692	£147,000	74
Edwards Geldard	£11,800,000	16	114	1:6.1	£103,509	£145,000	77
Eversheds	£145,000,000	186	1306	1:6.0	£111,026	£191,000	50
Farrer & Co	£14,850,000	22	106	1:3.8	£140,094	£168,000	65
Field Fisher Waterhouse	£22,700,000	31	141	1:3.5	£160,993	£208,000	44
Freeth Cartwright Hunt Dickins	£12,600,000	24	165	1:5.9	£76,364	£110,000	95
Freshfields	£232,000,000	186	957	1:4.1	£242,424	£524,000	3
Garretts	£48,000,000	52	315	1:5.1	£152,381	£175,000	62
Gouldens	£26,000,000	21	137	1:5.5	£189,781	£396,000	7
Halliwell Landau	£13,300,000	17	126	1:6.4	£105,556	£205,000	47
Hammond Suddards	£66,300,000	43	530	1:11.3	£125,094	£327,000	13
Harbottle & Lewis	£10,100,000	15	63	1:3.2	£160,317	£213,000	41
Herbert Smith	£114,000,000	100	693	1:5.9	£164,502	£315,000	15
Hewitson Becke + Shaw	£13,000,000	30	150	1:4.0	£86,667	£130,000	85
Hill Dickinson	£17,500,000	36	184	1:4.1	£95,109	£160,000	71
Holman, Fenwick & Willan	£33,400,000	41	168	1:3.1	£198,810	£206,000	45

1. 'All fee-earners' includes equity partners, trainees and other fee-earners.   2. Leverage is the ratio of equity partners to other fee-earners.

Firm	Fees 97-98	Equity partners	All fee-earners[1]	Leverage ratio[2]	Fees per fee-earner	Profits per equity partner	Profit ranking
Ince & Co	£31,000,000	35	160	1:3.6	£193,750	£215,000	40
Irwin Mitchell	£31,500,000	30	406	1:12.5	£77,586	£168,000	66
Kennedys	£16,500,000	21	160	1:6.6	£103,125	£160,000	69
Lawrence Graham	£30,600,000	37	196	1:4.3	£156,122	£245,000	26
Laytons	£7,200,000	15	89	1:4.9	£80,899	£105,000	97
Lewis Silkin	£1,1050,000	17	85	1:4.0	£130,000	£190,000	52
Linklaters	£259,000,000	201	1063	1:4.3	£243,650	£489,000	4
Lovell White Durrant	£145,000,000	142	781	1:4.5	£185,659	£320,000	14
Macfarlanes	£40,000,000	36	193	1:4.4	£207,254	£435,000	6
Maclay Murray & Spens	£17,500,000	40	200	1:4.0	£87,500	£140,000	80
MacRoberts	£7,900,000	16	82	1:4.1	£96,341	£184,000	59
Manches & Co	£17,565,000	31	108	1:2.5	£162,639	£129,000	86
Martineau Johnson	£10,350,000	22	110	1:4.0	£94,091	£145,000	75
Masons	£40,000,000	35	283	1:7.1	£141,343	£194,000	49
McClure Naismith	£7,600,000	15	78	1:4.2	£97,436	£140,000	81
McGrigor Donald	£20,600,000	26	176	1:5.8	£117,045	£190,000	51
Mills & Reeve	£17,200,000	42	168	1:3.0	£102,381	£122,000	89
Mishcon de Reya	£14,375,000	12	107	1:7.9	£134,346	£227,000	37
Morgan Bruce	£18,400,000	34	168	1:3.9	£109,524	£135,000	84
Nabarro Nathanson	£70,000,000	60	433	1:6.2	£161,663	£233,000	33
Nicholson Graham & Jones	£19,250,000	21	116	1:4.5	£165,948	£240,000	30
Norton Rose	£110,000,000	107	592	1:4.5	£185,811	£350,000	10
Olswang	£182,225,130	20	95	1:3.8	£191,816	£343,000	11
Osborne Clarke	£23,500,000	35	205	1:4.9	£114,634	£205,000	46
Paisner & Co	£18,800,000	31	116	1:2.7	£162,069	£201,000	48
Pannone & Partners	£9,200,000	26	124	1:3.8	£74,194	£112,000	94
Paull & Williamsons	£5,800,000	15	74	1:3.9	£78,378	£115,000	93
Penningtons	£13,000,000	20	123	1:5.2	£105,691	£88,000	100
Pinsent Curtis	£47,000,000	45	375	1:7.3	£125,333	£242,000	29

1. 'All fee-earners' includes equity partners, trainees and other fee-earners.   2. Leverage is the ratio of equity partners to other fee-earners.

Firm	Fees 97-98	Equity partners	All fee-earners[1]	Leverage ratio[2]	Fees per fee-earner	Profits per equity partner	Profit ranking
Reynolds Porter Chamberlain	£22,000,000	41	155	1:2.8	£141,935	£184,000	57
Richards Butler	£57,400,000	53	334	1:5.3	£171,856	£358,000	9
Rowe & Maw	£37,000,000	39	221	1:4.7	£167,421	£230,000	35
Shepherd & Wedderburn WS	£13,400,000	21	146	1:6.0	£91,781	£184,000	58
Shoosmiths & Harrison	£31,000,000	28	331	1:10.8	£93,656	£160,000	70
Simmons & Simmons	£102,000,000	120	729	1:5.1	£139,918	£210,000	42
Sinclair Roche & Temperley	£18,200,000	20	120	1:5.0	£151,667	£145,000	76
Slaughter and May	£150,000,000	107	538	1:4.0	£278,810	£630,000	1
Speechly Bircham	£14,240,000	23	96	1:3.2	£148,333	£166,000	67
Stephenson Harwood	£44,500,000	52	268	1:4.2	£166,045	£180,000	61
Taylor Joynson Garrett	£36,800,000	44	218	1:4.0	£168,807	£300,000	18
Theodore Goddard	£30,627,000	28	167	1:5.0	£183,395	£268,854	22
Thomas Eggar Church Adams	£13,000,000	30	120	1:3.0	£108,333	£124,000	88
Titmuss Sainer Dechert	£25,900,000	37	136	1:2.7	£190,441	£220,000	39
Tods Murray WS	£10,000,000	25	93	1:2.7	£107,527	£116,000	91
Travers Smith Braithwaite	£30,205,000	38	150	1:2.9	£201,367	£290,000	20
Trowers & Hamlins	£24,150,000	26	160	1:5.2	£150,938	£190,000	53
Vaudreys	£7,200,000	7	62	1:7.9	£116,129	£180,000	60
Walker Morris	£19,600,000	25	205	1:7.2	£95,610	£188,000	56
Wansbroughs Willey Hargrave	£28,200,000	39	268	1:5.9	£105,224	£170,000	64
Watson, Farley & Williams	£36,000,000	29	185	1:5.4	£194,595	£300,000	17
Weightmans	£15,500,000	20	168	1:7.4	£92,262	£135,000	83
Weil, Gotshal & Manges	£14,850,000	18	79	1:3.4	£187,975	£275,000	21
Wilde Sapte	£52,000,000	42	289	1:5.9	£179,931	£235,000	32
Withers	£19,500,000	24	125	1:4.2	£156,000	£243,000	28
Wragge & Co	£34,400,000	56	330	1:4.9	£104,242	£223,000	38

1. 'All fee-earners' includes equity partners, trainees and other fee-earners. 2. Leverage is the ratio of equity partners to other fee-earners.

INDEX TO THE AREAS IN WHICH EACH FIRM IS RANKED

Index to areas in which each firm is ranked

This index does not represent a full listing of the areas in which a firm might specialise, only those in which they were highly recommended. For the full coverage of a particular firm, please refer to the Solicitors' A–Z.

A

Aaron & Partners
Corporate Finance, Debt Collection, Energy, Planning, Property (Commercial), Transport

A S Law
Civil Liberties, Immigration

Abson Hall
Personal Injury

Actons
Insolvency

Adam Cochran
Agric, Licensing

Adams
Crime

Adams & Remers
Trusts

Addleshaw Booth & Co
Advising Lenders (UK wide), Agric, Asset Finance, Banking, Charities, Computer/IT, Construction, Corporate Finance, Debt Collection, Education, Employee Share Schemes, Employment, Environmental, EU, Family, Financial Services, Insolvency, IP, Lit (Commercial), Lit (Property), Pensions, Planning, Prof Neg, Projects, Property (Commercial), Sports, Tax (Corporate), Trusts

Adie Evans & Warner
Family

Agnew, Andress, Higgins
Personal Injury

Aitken Nairn WS
Debt Collection

Alan J. Baillie
Housing Associations

Alexander Harris
Med Neg, Personal Injury, Product Liability

Alexanders
Agric

Alexander Stone & Co
Charities, Property (Commercial)

Alex Morison & Co WS
Property (Commercial), Sports

Alistair Meldrum & Co
Crime

Allan Henderson Beecham and Peacock
Personal Injury

Allan Janes
Licensing

Allan McDougall & Co SSC
Personal Injury

Allen & Fraser
Licensing

Allen & Overy
Admin/Public, Advising Lenders (UK wide), Arbitration, Asset Finance, Banking, Capital Markets, Charities, Computer/IT, Construction, Corporate Finance, Corporate Finance: Debt, Corporate Finance: Equity, Employee Share Schemes, Employment, Energy, Environmental, EU, Financial Services, Fraud, Insolvency, Investment Funds, IP, Lit (Commercial), Partnership, Pensions, PFI, Planning, Projects, Property (Commercial), Tax (Corporate), Telecoms, Travel, Trusts

Allington Hughes
Church

Alsters
Planning, Sports

Amery-Parkes
Personal Injury

Andersen & Co
Housing Associations

Anderson Fyfe
Debt Collection, Housing Associations, Lit (Commercial)

Anderson MacArthur & Co
Agric

Andersons
Housing Associations

Anderson Strathern WS
Agric, Housing Associations, Lit (Commercial), Media & Ent, Personal Injury, Sports, Trusts

Andrew Bryce & Co
Environmental

Andrew Gregg & Co
Food, Licensing

Andrew M. Jackson & Co
Agric, Corporate Finance, Family, Food, Lit (Commercial), Property (Commercial), Shipping, Transport, Trusts

Andrew Keenan & Co
Crime

Anne Hall Dick & Co
Family

Ann L. Humphrey
VAT

Anstey Sargent & Probert
Computer/IT, Corporate Finance, Debt Collection, Insolvency, Lit (Commercial), Trusts

Anthony Collins Solicitors
Charities, Church, Housing Associations, Licensing, Lit (Property), Local Government, Med Neg

Anthony Gold, Lerman & Muirhead
Admin/Public, Family, Personal Injury

Archers
Family, Property (Commercial)

Archibald Campbell & Harley WS
Lit (Property), Planning, Property (Commercial)

Argles & Court
Licensing, Personal Injury

Armitage Sykes Hall Norton
Trusts

Arnheim & Co
Commodities, Investment Funds

Arnold Thomson
Agric

Arthur Cox
Asset Finance, Banking, Corporate Finance

Ashton Bond Gigg
Construction

Ashurst Morris Crisp
Banking, Capital Markets, Computer/IT, Construction, Corporate Finance, Corporate Finance: Debt, Corporate Finance: Equity, Employee Share Schemes, Energy, Environmental, EU, Insolvency, Insurance, Investment Funds, IP, Lit (Commercial), Lit (Property), Local Government, Media & Ent, PFI, Planning, Projects, Property (Commercial), Sports, Tax (Corporate), Telecoms

Askews
Family, Trusts

Attey Bower & Jones with Dibb and Clegg
Property (Commercial)

B

Babbington & Bray Solicitors Limited
Media & Ent

Babington & Croasdaile
Crime, Debt Collection, Family

Backhouses
Transport

Badhams Thompson
Agric

Baird & Company
Housing Associations

Baker & McKenzie
Banking, Capital Markets, Computer/IT, Construction, Corporate Finance, Customs, Employee Share Schemes, Employment, Energy, Environmental, EU, Immigration, IP, Lit (Commercial), Pensions, Projects, Telecoms

Baldocks
Family, Trusts

Balfour & Manson
Charities, Debt Collection, Family, Lit (Commercial), Med Neg, Personal Injury, Prof Neg

Band Hatton
Property (Commercial)

Bankes Ashton
Agric, Corporate Finance, Debt Collection, Trusts

Bannatyne, Kirkwood, France & Co
Defamation

Banners
Crime

Bannisters Solicitors
Personal Injury

Barbara Carter
Family

Barcan Woodward
Med Neg

Barker, Booth & Eastwood
Licensing, Property (Commercial)

Barker Gotelee
Agric, Transport

Barlow Lyde & Gilbert
Aviation, Construction, Environmental, Food, Insolvency, Insurance, Lit (Commercial), Personal Injury, Prof Neg, Shipping, Travel

Barlows
Charities, Lit (Commercial), Trusts

Barnett Alexander Chart
Corporate Finance, Local Government

Barnett Sampson
Admin/Public, Family

Barratt Goff & Tomlinson
Personal Injury

Barrie Ward & Julian Griffiths
Civil Liberties, Crime

Barry Shaw
Media & Ent

Bartram & Co
Immigration

Bates, Wells & Braithwaite
Admin/Public, Charities, Family, Immigration, Personal Injury

Battens (with Poole & Co)
Agric, Family, Personal Injury

T.G. Baynes & Sons
Personal Injury

Beachcroft Stanleys
Advertising & Marketing, Corporate Finance, Education, Employment, Energy, Health Care, Insurance, Lit (Commercial), Med Neg, Personal Injury, PFI

Beale and Company
Construction, Prof Neg

Beaumont and Son
Aviation

Bell Lamb & Joynson
Housing Associations

Bell Lax Litigation
Aviation, Lit (Commercial)

Bell & Scott WS
Charities, Media & Ent, Partnership

Belmores
Crime

Beltrami & Co
Crime

Bennett & Robertson
Debt Collection, Local Government, Sports

Bentleys, Stokes & Lowless
Shipping

Beor Wilson & Lloyd
Property (Commercial), Trusts

Berg & Co
Consumer Finance, Lit (Commercial)

Bermans
Debt Collection, Licensing, Property (Commercial)

Bernard Chill & Axtell
Crime

Berryman & Co
Crime, Fraud, Insurance

Berrymans Lace Mawer
Construction, Corporate Finance, Environmental, EU, Family, Insurance, Lit (Commercial), Personal Injury, Prof Neg, Property (Commercial), Shipping, Transport, Trusts

Berry Smith
Corporate Finance, Property (Commercial)

Berwin Leighton
Asset Finance, Banking, Capital Markets, Construction, Corporate Finance, Corporate Finance: Equity, Environmental, Insolvency, Lit (Commercial), Lit (Property), Local Government, Media & Ent, PFI, Planning, Prof Neg, Property (Commercial), Tax (Corporate)

S J Berwin & Co
Charities, Construction, Corporate Finance, Corporate Finance: Equity, Employment, Environmental, EU, Financial Services, Fraud, Investment Funds, Lit (Commercial), Lit (Property), Media & Ent, Parliamentary, PFI, Planning, Projects, Property (Commercial), Tax (Corporate), Travel

Betesh Fox & Co
Crime, Fraud, Personal Injury

Bevan Ashford
Admin/Public, Agric, Banking, Construction, Corporate Finance, Debt Collection, Defamation, Education, Employment, Environmental, Food, Health & Safety, Health Care, Housing Associations, IP, Licensing, Lit (Commercial), Lit (Property), Local Government, Med Neg, Personal Injury, Planning, Projects, Property (Commercial)

Bevirs
Agric
Beviss & Beckingsale
Agric, Licensing
Biddle
Corporate Finance, Defamation, Food, Insolvency, Licensing, Lit (Commercial), Media & Ent, Pensions
Biggart Baillie
Banking, Construction, Corporate Finance, Energy, Insolvency, Insurance, Lit (Commercial), Personal Injury, Prof Neg, Property (Commercial)
Bindman & Partners
Admin/Public, Civil Liberties, Crime, Defamation, Education, Employment, Family, Immigration, Med Neg
Bircham & Co. (incorporating Dyson Bell Martin)
Charities, Parliamentary, Trusts
Birch Cullimore
Agric, Charities, Church, Trusts
Bird & Bird
Computer/IT, Corporate Finance, Health Care, IP, Med Neg, Media & Ent, PFI, Sports, Telecoms
Bird Semple
Asset Finance, Computer/IT, Construction, Corporate Finance, Debt Collection, Defamation, Insolvency, Lit (Commercial), Lit (Property), Property (Commercial)
Birkett Long
Education
Birketts
Agric, Construction, Corporate Finance, Debt Collection, Insolvency, Lit (Commercial), Personal Injury, Property (Commercial)
B.M. Birnberg & Co
Civil Liberties, Crime, Immigration
Bishop Longbotham & Bagnall
Personal Injury
Bishop and Robertson Chalmers
Construction, Debt Collection, Employment, Environmental, Insolvency, Insurance, Lit (Commercial), Pensions, Prof Neg, Property (Commercial)
Blackadder Reid Johnston
Debt Collection, Employment, Licensing
Blackhurst Parker & Yates
Personal Injury, Transport
Blacks
Family
Blair Allison & Co
Family
Blair & Bryden
Crime
Blake Lapthorn
Charities, Construction, Corporate Finance, Debt Collection, Environmental, Fraud, Insolvency, Licensing, Lit (Commercial), Local Government, Med Neg, Personal Injury, Prof Neg, Property (Commercial), Tax (Corporate), Trusts
Blakesley Rice MacDonald
Family
Blandy & Blandy
Family, Licensing, Trusts
Blythe Liggins
Family, Financial Services, Trusts
Bobbetts Mackan
Crime, Fraud, Immigration, Lit (Property)
Bogue and McNulty
Crime
Bolt Burdon
Personal Injury
Bonar Mackenzie WS
Debt Collection

Bond Pearce
Agric, Banking, Construction, Corporate Finance, Debt Collection, Education, Employment, Energy, Environmental, Family, Insolvency, Insurance, Lit (Commercial), Lit (Property), Personal Injury, Planning, Prof Neg, Property (Commercial), Shipping, Transport, Trusts
Boodle Hatfield
Charities, Employment, Lit (Property), Property (Commercial), Trusts
Borland Montgomerie Keyden
Trusts
Bower Cotton
Lit (Commercial)
Boyce Hatton
Personal Injury, Property (Commercial)
Boyds
Property (Commercial), Trusts
Boyes Turner & Burrows
Computer/IT, Debt Collection, Insolvency, Med Neg, Personal Injury
B.P. Collins & Co
Corporate Finance, Property (Commercial), Trusts
Brabner Holden Banks Wilson
Charities, Corporate Finance, Defamation, Housing Associations, Lit (Commercial), Property (Commercial), Trusts
Braby & Waller (Debt Recovery Division of Irwin Mitchell Solicitors)
Debt Collection
Brachers
Agric, Corporate Finance, Debt Collection, Employment, Environmental, Family, Health Care, Licensing, Lit (Commercial), Lit (Property), Med Neg, Personal Injury, Planning, Trusts
Bradleys
Crime
Brechin Tindal Oatts
Debt Collection, Employment, Housing Associations, Prof Neg
Bremner Sons & Corlett
Property (Commercial)
Brendan Kearney Kelly & Co
Crime
Bretherton Price Elgoods
Property (Commercial)
Brethertons
Agric, Crime, Trusts
Brian Koffman & Co
Crime
Bridge McFarland Solicitors
Employment
Bridgewood Hopkinson & Wozny
Crime
Briffa & Co
IP
Bristows
Charities, Computer/IT, Environmental, EU, IP, Partnership
Brodies WS
Admin/Public, Agric, Banking, Corporate Finance, Debt Collection, Employment, Environmental, Franchising, Insolvency, Lit (Commercial), Lit (Property), Local Government, Personal Injury, Planning, Prof Neg, Property (Commercial), Trusts
Brooke North
Insolvency, Licensing, Lit (Commercial), Trusts
BrookStreet Des Roches
Charities, Property (Commercial)
R.M. Broudie & Co
Crime
Browell Smith & Goodyear
Personal Injury

Browne Jacobson
Admin/Public, Corporate Finance, Debt Collection, Employment, Environmental, Housing Associations, Insurance, IP, Lit (Commercial), Lit (Property), Local Government, Pensions, Personal Injury, Planning, Prof Neg
Brunton Miller
Licensing
Brutton & Co
Church
Buckle Mellows
Family, Personal Injury
Buller Jeffries
Insurance, Personal Injury
Bullivant Jones & Company
Licensing, Property (Commercial)
Bunkers
Insolvency
Burd Pearse
Trusts
Burges Salmon
Agric, Asset Finance, Banking, Charities, Computer/IT, Construction, Corporate Finance, Debt Collection, Employee Share Schemes, Employment, Environmental, EU, Family, Financial Services, Housing Associations, Insolvency, Investment Funds, IP, Lit (Commercial), Lit (Property), Partnership, Pensions, Planning, Prof Neg, Projects, Property (Commercial), Tax (Corporate), Transport, Trusts
Burley & Geach
Trusts
Burness
Admin/Public, Banking, Construction, Corporate Finance, Energy, Environmental, EU, Housing Associations, Insolvency, IP, Lit (Commercial), Lit (Property), Local Government, Pensions, Planning, Product Liability, Projects, Property (Commercial), Sports
Burnett & Reid
Agric, Family
Burnetts
Education, Family
Burnside Kemp Fraser
Employment, Personal Injury
Burroughs Day
Personal Injury
Burstows
Corporate Finance, Insolvency, Lit (Commercial), Lit (Property), Trusts
Burt Brill & Cardens
Lit (Commercial)
Burton Copeland
Crime, Fraud
Buss Murton
Family, Personal Injury, Travel, Trusts
Bywaters Topham Phillips Solicitors
Transport

C

Cadwalader, Wickersham & Taft
Insolvency
Cameron McKenna
Admin/Public, Advertising & Marketing, Arbitration, Asset Finance, Aviation, Banking, Construction, Corporate Finance, Corporate Finance: Equity, Employment, Energy, Environmental, EU, Financial Services, Fraud, Health & Safety, Health Care, Immigration, Insolvency, Insurance, IP, Lit (Commercial), Lit (Property), Pensions, Personal Injury, PFI, Planning, Product Liability, Prof Neg, Projects, Property (Commercial), Tax (Corporate)
Camerons
Church
Campbell Hooper
Agric, Immigration, Media & Ent
Campbell Smith WS
Education, Local Government, Trusts
Capsticks
Health Care, Med Neg
Carless Davies & Co
Transport
Carnson Morrow Graham
Family
Carrick Carr & Wright
Debt Collection
Carrick Read Insolvency
Insolvency
Carson & McDowell
Construction, Corporate Finance, Debt Collection, Employment, Insolvency, Lit (Commercial), Lit (Property), Personal Injury, Prof Neg, Property (Commercial), Trusts
Cartmell Shepherd
Agric, Corporate Finance, Property (Commercial)
Cartwright & Lewis
Personal Injury
Cartwrights
Aviation, Corporate Finance, Debt Collection, Employment, Fraud, Licensing, Lit (Commercial), Lit (Property), Personal Injury, Planning, Prof Neg, Property (Commercial), Transport, Trusts
Cartwrights Adams & Black
Licensing, Transport
Chadbourne & Parke
Projects
Chaffe Street
Asset Finance, Banking, Corporate Finance, Financial Services, Insolvency, Lit (Commercial), Property (Commercial)
Challinors Lyon Clark
Family, Licensing, Med Neg, Personal Injury
Chambers & Co
Franchising
Chapman Everatt
Personal Injury
Charles Lucas & Marshall
Charities
Charles Russell
Charities, Corporate Finance, Employment, Family, IP, Med Neg, Property (Commercial), Sports, Telecoms, Trusts
Charles Stansfield & Co
Transport
Chattertons
Agric
C & H Jefferson
Employment, Lit (Commercial), Personal Injury, Prof Neg
Christian Fisher
Civil Liberties, Crime
C & J Black
Property (Commercial), Trusts
Clairmonts
Travel

Claricoat Phillips
Charities

Clarke Willmott & Clarke
Admin/Public, Agric, Charities, Corporate Finance, Debt Collection, Environmental, Family, Insolvency, IP, Licensing, Lit (Commercial), Planning, Property (Commercial), Tax (Corporate), Trusts

Clark Holt
Computer/IT

Clark Ricketts
Aviation

Clarks
Construction, Corporate Finance, Debt Collection, Employment, Health Care, Lit (Commercial), Pensions, Planning, Property (Commercial), Trusts

Clarkson Wright & Jakes
Debt Collection, Employment, Partnership, Personal Injury

Claude Hornby & Cox
Crime, Fraud

Claytons
Church

Clayton Utz
Projects

Cleary, Gottlieb, Steen & Hamilton
Capital Markets, Projects

Cleaver Fulton & Rankin
Admin/Public, Construction, Corporate Finance, Debt Collection, Employment, EU, Insolvency, Lit (Commercial), Lit (Property), Prof Neg, Property (Commercial), Trusts

Clifford Chance
Admin/Public, Advertising & Marketing, Advising Lenders (UK wide), Arbitration, Asset Finance, Banking, Capital Markets, Commodities, Computer/IT, Construction, Corporate Finance, Corporate Finance: Debt, Corporate Finance: Equity, Defamation, Employee Share Schemes, Employment, Energy, Environmental, EU, Financial Services, Fraud, Insolvency, Insurance, Investment Funds, IP, Lit (Commercial), Lit (Property), Local Government, Media & Ent, Parliamentary, Pensions, PFI, Planning, Product Liability, Projects, Property (Commercial), Shipping, Tax (Corporate), Telecoms, Transport, Travel

Clintons
Media & Ent, Sports

Clyde & Co
Arbitration, Aviation, Commodities, Computer/IT, Corporate Finance, Debt Collection, Energy, Insolvency, Insurance, Lit (Commercial), Prof Neg, Shipping, Tax (Corporate), Transport

Cobbetts
Asset Finance, Banking, Charities, Corporate Finance, Debt Collection, Defamation, Employment, Licensing, Lit (Commercial), Lit (Property), Partnership, Planning, Property (Commercial), Trusts

Coffin Mew & Clover
Family, Housing Associations, Lit (Property), Property (Commercial)

Cole & Co
Crime

Cole & Cole
Agric, Construction, Corporate Finance, Debt Collection, Education, Employment, Family, Health Care, Insolvency, Licensing, Lit (Commercial), Med Neg, Personal Injury, Property (Commercial), Trusts

Colemans
Property (Commercial)

Colemans Solicitors
Franchising, Personal Injury

Collyer-Bristow
Family, IP, Sports, Trusts

Comerton & Hill
Debt Collection, Insolvency

Condies
Crime

Constant & Constant
Shipping

Coodes
Family, Trusts

Coole & Haddock
Asset Finance

Copleys
Crime

Corbett & Co
Construction

Coudert Brothers
Arbitration, Corporate Finance, Energy, Projects, Property (Commercial), Telecoms

Covington & Burling
Food

Cozens-Hardy & Jewson
Charities, Family, Trusts

Crane & Walton
Energy

Cranswick Watson
Family, Property (Commercial)

Crawford Owen
Property (Commercial)

Cripps Harries Hall
Agric, Charities, Construction, Corporate Finance, Debt Collection, Employment, Family, Housing Associations, Insolvency, Lit (Commercial), Lit (Property), Personal Injury, Prof Neg, Property (Commercial), Trusts

Crockers Oswald Hickson
Defamation

Croftons
Housing Associations

Crombie Wilkinson
Family

Crosse & Crosse
Crime, Licensing, Personal Injury

Crutes
Med Neg, Personal Injury, Prof Neg

Cuff Roberts
Charities, Debt Collection, Family, Insolvency, Lit (Commercial), Partnership, Property (Commercial)

Culbert and Martin
Employment

Cumberland Ellis Peirs
Trusts

Cunningham, John & Co
Med Neg, Personal Injury

Cunninghams
Crime

Cunningham Turner
Transport

Currey & Co
Trusts

D

Dale & Co Solicitors
Shipping

Darbys
Family, Immigration, Personal Injury

M C Darlington
Church

Darlington & Parkinson
Crime

Davenport Lyons
Defamation, Media & Ent

David Bigmore & Co
Franchising

E. David Brain & Co
Family

David Charnley & Co
Crime

David du Pré & Co
Family

David Gist & Co
Personal Injury

David Gray & Company
Civil Liberties, Crime, Immigration

David Levene & Co
Admin/Public, Education

David Price & Co
Defamation

Davidson Chalmers WS
Property (Commercial)

David Truex and Company
Family

Davies and Partners
Debt Collection, Financial Services, Lit (Commercial), Personal Injury, Planning, Property (Commercial)

Davies Arnold Cooper
Construction, Corporate Finance, Debt Collection, Defamation, Health Care, Insolvency, Insurance, Lit (Commercial), Pensions, Personal Injury, Planning, Product Liability, Prof Neg, Projects, Sports, Transport

Davies, Johnson & Co
Shipping

Davies Lavery
Personal Injury, Transport

Davies Wallis Foyster
Banking, Corporate Finance, Debt Collection, Employment, Insolvency, IP, Licensing, Lit (Commercial), Pensions, Personal Injury, Planning, Property (Commercial)

Davis Blank Furniss
Immigration

Dawbarns
Med Neg, Personal Injury

Dawson & Co
Agric, Family, Housing Associations, Trusts

Dawson Cornwell & Co
Family

Dean Wilson
Property (Commercial)

Deas Mallen Souter
Personal Injury

Debevoise & Plimpton
Projects, Telecoms

Deborah Mills Associates
Energy

Deighton Guedalla
Civil Liberties, Immigration

Denison Till
Agric, Church, Construction, Lit (Commercial), Property (Commercial)

Denton Hall
Admin/Public, Advertising & Marketing, Arbitration, Banking, Charities, Commodities, Computer/IT, Construction, Corporate Finance, Employment, Energy, Environmental, EU, Fraud, Insolvency, IP, Lit (Commercial), Lit (Property), Local Government, Media & Ent, PFI, Planning, Projects, Property (Commercial), Sports, Tax (Corporate), Telecoms, Transport, Travel

Devonshires
Advising Lenders (UK wide), Housing Associations

Dewar Hogan
Lit (Property)

Dewey Ballantine
Projects

S.J. Diamond & Son
Debt Collection, Personal Injury, Trusts

Dibb Lupton Alsop
Advertising & Marketing, Aviation, Banking, Computer/IT, Construction, Corporate Finance, Corporate Finance: Debt, Corporate Finance: Equity, Debt Collection, Education, Employment, Environmental, EU, Fraud, Insolvency, Insurance, IP, Licensing, Lit (Commercial), Lit (Property), Local Government, Media & Ent, Pensions, Personal Injury, Planning, Prof Neg, Projects, Property (Commercial), Shipping, Tax (Corporate), Transport

Dickinson Dees
Agric, Banking, Charities, Construction, Corporate Finance, Employment, Energy, Environmental, EU, Family, Financial Services, Health Care, Housing Associations, Insolvency, IP, Lit (Commercial), Lit (Property), Media & Ent, Pensions, Planning, Projects, Property (Commercial), Tax (Corporate), Transport, Trusts

Dickinson Manser
Debt Collection

Dickson Minto WS
Banking, Corporate Finance, Corporate Finance: Debt, Corporate Finance: Equity, Financial Services, Investment Funds, Property (Commercial)

Digby Brown
Personal Injury

Dixon, Coles & Gill
Church

D J Freeman
Corporate Finance, Defamation, Employment, Fraud, Insolvency, Insurance, Lit (Commercial), Lit (Property), Local Government, Media & Ent, Planning, Property (Commercial)

Dolmans
Insolvency, Lit (Commercial), Local Government, Personal Injury, Prof Neg, Property (Commercial)

Donald Rennie WS
Agric

Donns Solicitors
Personal Injury

Donnelly & Wall
Crime

Donne Mileham & Haddock
Church, Computer/IT, Corporate Finance, Debt Collection, Education, Employment, Environmental, Family, Fraud, Health Care, IP, Licensing, Lit (Commercial), Lit (Property), Personal Injury, Planning, Prof Neg, Property (Commercial), Shipping, Transport, Trusts

Douglas-Jones Mercer
Debt Collection, Personal Injury

Douglas & Partners
Crime

Douglas Wignall & Co
Travel

Dowse & Co
Crime

Druces & Attlee
Family, Lit (Property)

Drummond Miller WS
Family, Med Neg, Personal Injury, Trusts

Dukes Arnold Du Feu
Crime

Gordon Dadds
Family

Gordons Wright & Wright
Church, Corporate Finance, Employment, Family, Licensing, Lit (Commercial), Property (Commercial), Trusts

Gorna & Co
Housing Associations, Lit (Property), Property (Commercial), Sports

Gosschalks
Corporate Finance, Crime, Family, Licensing, Lit (Commercial), Property (Commercial)

Gotelee & Goldsmith
Admin/Public, Corporate Finance, Crime, Debt Collection, Local Government, Planning, Property (Commercial), Transport

Gouldens
Banking, Corporate Finance, Environmental, IP, Lit (Commercial), Planning, Property (Commercial), Trusts

Graeme Carmichael
Family

Grahame Stowe, Bateson
Crime, Family

Graham Evans & Partners
Crime, Personal Injury

Graham & Rosen
Family

Grant & Horton Marine Solicitors
Shipping

Granville-West
Family

Grays
Agric, Charities, Church, Education

Greathead & Whitelock
Agric

Green & Co
Family

Greene & Greene
Agric, Corporate Finance, Trusts

Greenland Houchen
Debt Collection, Property (Commercial), Sports

Greenwoods
Agric, Charities, Construction, Corporate Finance, Debt Collection, Employment, Family, IP, Licensing, Lit (Commercial), Personal Injury, Property (Commercial)

Gregory, Rowcliffe & Milners
Charities, Trusts

Griffith Smith
Charities, Environmental, Planning, Transport, Trusts

Grigor & Young
Agric, Licensing

Gross & Co.
Immigration

Gulbenkian Harris Andonian
Immigration

R. Gwynne & Sons
Agric, Trusts

H

Hacking Ashton
Construction

Hadens (formerly Haden Stretton Slater Miller)
Family

Hall & Haughey
Crime

Hallett & Co
Agric, Trusts

Hallinan, Blackburn, Gittings & Nott
Crime

Halliwell Landau
Banking, Charities, Computer/IT, Construction, Corporate Finance, Debt Collection, Employment, Financial Services, Franchising, Health & Safety, Insolvency, IP, Licensing, Lit (Commercial), Lit (Property), Pensions, Personal Injury, Planning, Prof Neg, Property (Commercial), Trusts

A. Halsall & Co
Housing Associations, Licensing

Hamilton Burns & Moore
Crime, Personal Injury

Hamlin Slowe
Lit (Commercial), Media & Ent, Property (Commercial)

Hammond Suddards
Banking, Computer/IT, Construction, Corporate Finance, Corporate Finance: Equity, Debt Collection, Employee Share Schemes, Employment, Environmental, Health & Safety, Insolvency, Insurance, IP, Lit (Commercial), Lit (Property), Media & Ent, Pensions, Personal Injury, Planning, Prof Neg, Property (Commercial), Sports, Tax (Corporate)

Hancock & Lawrence
Prof Neg, Property (Commercial)

Hansell Stevenson
Aviation

Harbottle & Lewis
Advertising & Marketing, Asset Finance, Aviation, Charities, Computer/IT, Corporate Finance, Defamation, Immigration, Lit (Commercial), Media & Ent, Sports

Harding Evans
Family

Harold Benjamin & Collins
Lit (Property), Property (Commercial)

Harper Macleod
Employment, Housing Associations, Licensing, Local Government, Property (Commercial), Sports

Harris & Cartwright
Personal Injury

Harris & Harris
Agric, Church

Harrison Bundey & Co.
Civil Liberties, Immigration

Harrison Curtis
Media & Ent

Harrison, Leitch & Logan
Personal Injury

Harrowell Shaftoe
Trusts

Hartfields
Prof Neg

Hart-Jackson & Hall
Media & Ent

Hartnell & Co
Family

Harvey Ingram Owston
Charities, Church, Corporate Finance, Housing Associations, Property (Commercial)

Hasties
Licensing

Hatch Brenner
Crime, Family

Hawkins Russell Jones
Property (Commercial), Transport

Hawley & Rodgers
Crime

Hay & Kilner
Construction, Employment, Family, Lit (Commercial), Med Neg, Personal Injury, Prof Neg

Hedleys
Travel

Hegarty & Co
Crime

Hempsons
Defamation, Health Care, Med Neg, Partnership

Henderson Boyd Jackson WS
Admin/Public, Corporate Finance, Debt Collection, Housing Associations, Lit (Commercial), Projects, Property (Commercial), Shipping, Sports

Henmans
Agric, Employment, Personal Injury, Trusts

Henry Hepworth
Defamation, IP, Media & Ent

Henry Hyams & Co
Crime, Family

Henry Milner & Co
Crime

Heptonstalls
Agric, Med Neg

Herbert Smith
Admin/Public, Arbitration, Asset Finance, Aviation, Banking, Capital Markets, Commodities, Computer/IT, Construction, Corporate Finance, Corporate Finance: Equity, Employee Share Schemes, Employment, Energy, Environmental, EU, Fraud, Health Care, Insolvency, Insurance, Investment Funds, IP, Lit (Commercial), Lit (Property), Local Government, Media & Ent, Partnership, Pensions, PFI, Planning, Prof Neg, Projects, Property (Commercial), Shipping, Sports, Tax (Corporate), Transport, Travel

Herbert Wilkes
Lit (Commercial), Trusts

Hewitson Becke + Shaw
Agric, Charities, Computer/IT, Construction, Corporate Finance, Debt Collection, Employment, Environmental, Insolvency, IP, Lit (Commercial), Lit (Property), Pensions, Personal Injury, Planning, Property (Commercial), Trusts

Hewitt & Gilpin
Debt Collection, Lit (Property), Property (Commercial), Trusts

Hextall Erskine
Insurance, Personal Injury, Prof Neg

Hickman & Rose
Crime

Higgs & Sons
Corporate Finance, Employment, Property (Commercial), Trusts

R. & J.M. Hill Brown & Co
Licensing

Hill Dickinson
Church, Construction, Insurance, IP, Lit (Commercial), Med Neg, Partnership, Personal Injury, Prof Neg, Property (Commercial), Shipping, Transport

Hill Taylor Dickinson
Commodities, Insurance, Shipping, Transport

Hobson Audley Hopkins & Wood
Corporate Finance, IP

G.L. Hockfield & Co
Housing Associations, Personal Injury

Hodge Jones & Allen
Crime, Employment, Family, Housing Associations, Personal Injury, Product Liability

Hollingworth Bissell
Transport

Holman, Fenwick & Willan
Arbitration, Commodities, Energy, EU, Insolvency, Insurance, Lit (Commercial), Prof Neg, Shipping

Holmes Hardingham
Commodities, Shipping, Transport

Hood Vores & Allwood
Trusts

Hooper & Wollen
Family, Trusts

Hornby, Baker Jones & Wood
Crime

Horwich Farrelly
Personal Injury

Howard Kennedy
Corporate Finance, Licensing, Lit (Commercial)

Howarth Goodman
Housing Associations

Howell & Co
Fraud

Howells
Civil Liberties, Crime, Immigration

Howes Percival
Agric, Corporate Finance, Debt Collection, Licensing, Lit (Commercial)

Hugh James
Church, Construction, Corporate Finance, Education, Family, Health & Safety, Housing Associations, Insolvency, Lit (Commercial), Lit (Property), Med Neg, Personal Injury, Prof Neg, Property (Commercial)

Humphreys & Co.
Insurance, IP

Humphries Kirk
Agric

Hunt & Coombs
Crime, Education, Family

Hunters
Charities, Family, Trusts

Hunton & Williams
Projects

Huttons
Crime, Fraud, Med Neg, Personal Injury

I

Iain Smith & Company
Corporate Finance, Family, Insolvency

Ian Downing
Family

Iliffes Booth Bennett
Charities, Family, Personal Injury, Trusts

Ince & Co
Arbitration, Commodities, Energy, Insurance, Lit (Commercial), Prof Neg, Shipping

Ironsides
Transport

Irwin Mitchell
Charities, Civil Liberties, Corporate Finance, Crime, Debt Collection, Employment, Family, Fraud, Housing Associations, Insolvency, Lit (Commercial), Med Neg, Personal Injury, Product Liability, Prof Neg, Projects, Property (Commercial), Trusts

Isadore Goldman
Insolvency

J

Jackson & Canter
Crime, Family, Immigration, Personal Injury

Jackson Parton
Shipping

Jacksons
Corporate Finance, Employment, Family, Insurance, Personal Injury, Property (Commercial)

Jack Thornley
Personal Injury

James & Co
Immigration

James Chapman & Co
Insurance, Personal Injury, Prof Neg, Sports

James & George Collie
Licensing, Trusts

James Kendall
Financial Services

Jameson & Hill
Planning

Jane Coker & Partners
Immigration

J.B. Wheatley & Co
Crime

Jeffrey Aitken Solicitors
Transport

Jeffrey Green Russell
Debt Collection, Fraud, Licensing, Lit (Commercial), Planning
Jeffreys & Powell
Agric
Jenkins & Hand
Housing Associations, Local Government
Jeremy Fear & Co
Transport
Joelson Wilson & Co
Licensing, Travel
John Batters & Co
Licensing
John Bowden Trainer & Co
Sports
John Boyle and Co
Crime
John Ford Solicitors
Education
John Gaunt & Partners
Licensing
John Hodge & Co
Med Neg
John McKee & Son
Debt Collection, Insolvency, Lit (Property), Personal Injury
John O'Neill & Co
Transport
John Pickering & Partners
Personal Injury
Johns Elliot
Construction, Corporate Finance, Employment, Family, Lit (Commercial), Lit (Property), Property (Commercial)
The Johnson Partnership
Crime
Johnsons
Corporate Finance, Defamation, Lit (Commercial), Personal Injury, Property (Commercial), Trusts
Johnston & Herron
Licensing
John Weston & Co
Shipping
Jonathan Stephens & Co
Agric
Jones & Cassidy
Employment
Jones Maidment Wilson
Crime, Family, Fraud, Med Neg, Property (Commercial), Trusts
Jones Myers Gordon
Family
Joy Merriam & Co
Crime
J.R. Jones
Crime
Julian Holy
Property (Commercial)

Kearney Sefton
Property (Commercial)
Keeble Hawson Moorhouse
Corporate Finance, Insolvency
Keene Marsland
Sports
J. Keith Park & Co
Immigration
Kelley, Drye & Warrens
Projects
Kemp & Co
Computer/IT
E. & L. Kennedy
Licensing
Kennedys
Construction, Insolvency, Insurance, Lit (Commercial), Personal Injury, Prof Neg
Kenneth Bush
Licensing
Kenneth Curtis & Co
Licensing
Kenneth Elliott & Rowe
Property (Commercial), Transport
Kent Jones and Done
Corporate Finance, Energy, Environmental, Lit (Commercial)

Keogh Ritson
Insurance, Personal Injury, Prof Neg
Kershaw Abbott
Partnership
Ketchen & Stevens WS
Trusts
Kidstons & Co
Debt Collection, Employment
Kieran & Co
Crime
Kimbell & Co
Corporate Finance
King & Gowdy
Insolvency
Kingsford Stacey Blackwell
Licensing, Lit (Commercial), Travel
Kingsley Napley
Crime, Family, Fraud, Immigration, Licensing, Med Neg, Partnership
Kirby Simcox
Personal Injury
Kirk Jackson
Construction
Kitsons
Property (Commercial)
Knights
Admin/Public, Agric, Defamation
Knight & Sons
Agric, Construction, Corporate Finance, Energy, Environmental, Insolvency, Licensing, Lit (Commercial), Planning, Property (Commercial)
Kuit Steinart Levy
Corporate Finance, IP, Property (Commercial)

Laceys
Property (Commercial)
Lamport Bassitt
Insolvency, Licensing, Lit (Commercial), Personal Injury, Trusts
Lane & Partners
Arbitration, Aviation, Lit (Commercial), Travel
Langley & Co
Employment
Langleys
Personal Injury
Lanyon Bowdler
Agric, Debt Collection, Family, Licensing, Lit (Property)
Larby Williams
Family
Latham & Watkins
Projects
Latimer Hinks
Agric, Trusts
Lawford & Co
Aviation, Education, Employment, Personal Injury
Lawford Kidd
Med Neg, Personal Injury
The Law Offices of Marcus J. O'Leary
Computer/IT, IP
Lawrence Graham
Admin/Public, Advertising & Marketing, Advising Lenders (UK wide), Charities, Corporate Finance, Energy, Environmental, Housing Associations, Insolvency, Investment Funds, Lit (Commercial), Lit (Property), Local Government, Personal Injury, PFI, Planning, Property (Commercial), Shipping, Sports, Trusts
Lawrence Tucketts
Corporate Finance, Debt Collection, Environmental, Family, Franchising, Insolvency, Lit (Commercial), Lit (Property), Planning, Property (Commercial), Trusts
Lawrence Wood
Lit (Property)

Lawson Coppock & Hart
IP
Laytons
Computer/IT, Construction, Corporate Finance, Insolvency, IP, Lit (Commercial), Property (Commercial)
Lea & Company
Media & Ent
Leathes Prior
Banking, Charities, Debt Collection, Employment, Franchising, Immigration, Insolvency, Media & Ent, Personal Injury, Planning, Property (Commercial)
LeBoeuf, Lamb, Greene & MacRae
Energy, Lit (Commercial)
Le Brasseur J Tickle
Health Care, Med Neg, Personal Injury
Ledingham Chalmers
Corporate Finance, Energy, Housing Associations, Licensing, Planning, Property (Commercial), Trusts
Lee Bolton & Lee
Charities, Church, Education
Lee Crowder
Corporate Finance, Housing Associations, Lit (Commercial), Property (Commercial), Trusts
Leeds Day
Church, Debt Collection
Lee & Pembertons
Agric, Charities, Trusts
Lees Lloyd Whitley
Debt Collection, Trusts
Lee & Thompson
Media & Ent
Lefevre Litigation
Personal Injury
Leigh, Day & Co
Admin/Public, Environmental, Med Neg, Personal Injury, Product Liability
Leo Abse & Cohen
Crime, Employment, Family, Fraud, Personal Injury
Leonard Gray
Family
Léonie Cowen & Associates
Local Government
Leslie Wolfson & Co
Property (Commercial)
Lester Aldridge
Advertising & Marketing, Asset Finance, Banking, Charities, Computer/IT, Consumer Finance, Corporate Finance, Debt Collection, Employment, Environmental, Family, Health & Safety, Insolvency, IP, Licensing, Lit (Commercial), Partnership, Planning, Prof Neg, Property (Commercial), Trusts
L'Estrange & Brett
Banking, Construction, Corporate Finance, Employment, Insolvency, Lit (Commercial), Lit (Property), Property (Commercial), Trusts
Levi & Co
Crime
Levison Meltzer Pigott
Family
Levy & McRae
Defamation, Franchising, Personal Injury
The Lewington Partnership
Employment, Health Care, Med Neg
Lewis Moore & Co.
Shipping
Lewis Silkin
Advertising & Marketing, Corporate Finance, Defamation, Employment, Housing Associations, Lit (Commercial)
Lightfoots
Prof Neg

Linder Myers
Med Neg, Personal Injury
Lindsay Roland
Product Liability
Lindsays WS
Admin/Public, Agric, Charities, Construction, Licensing
Linklaters
Arbitration, Asset Finance, Aviation, Banking, Capital Markets, Commodities, Computer/IT, Construction, Corporate Finance, Employee Share Schemes, Employment, Energy, Environmental, EU, Financial Services, Fraud, Insolvency, Insurance, Investment Funds, IP, Lit (Commercial), Lit (Property), Pensions, PFI, Planning, Projects, Property (Commercial), Tax (Corporate), Telecoms, Transport, Travel, Trusts
Linnells
Agric, Charities, Construction, Debt Collection, Family, Immigration, Partnership, Property (Commercial)
Linskills Solicitors
Crime
Linsley & Mortimer
Lit (Commercial), Personal Injury
Livingstone Browne
Crime
Llewelyn Zietman
IP
Lochners Technology Solicitors
IP
Lonsdales
Med Neg
Loosemores
Personal Injury
Loudons WS
Family
Lovell White Durrant
Admin/Public, Advertising & Marketing, Arbitration, Asset Finance, Banking, Capital Markets, Commodities, Computer/IT, Construction, Corporate Finance, Corporate Finance: Debt, Corporate Finance: Equity, Defamation, Employee Share Schemes, Employment, Energy, Environmental, EU, Financial Services, Fraud, Insolvency, Insurance, Investment Funds, IP, Lit (Commercial), Lit (Property), Media & Ent, Parliamentary, Partnership, Pensions, PFI, Planning, Product Liability, Prof Neg, Projects, Property (Commercial), Sports, Tax (Corporate), Telecoms, Travel
Loxleys
Licensing
Lucas & Wyllys
Crime
Lumb & Macgill
Crime
Lupton Fawcett
Corporate Finance, Debt Collection, Insolvency, IP, Licensing, Lit (Commercial), Personal Injury, Trusts
Lyons Davidson
Banking, Corporate Finance, Environmental, Health & Safety, Insurance, International Law, Lit (Commercial), Lit (Property), Personal Injury, Planning, Property (Commercial)

Mace & Jones
Employment, Partnership, Personal Injury

Macfarlanes
Advertising & Marketing, Agric, Banking, Charities, Church, Corporate Finance, Corporate Finance: Equity, Employment, Fraud, Health Care, Investment Funds, IP, Lit (Commercial), Lit (Property), Partnership, PFI, Planning, Property (Commercial), Tax (Corporate), Trusts

Mackay Simon
Employment

Mackinnons
Shipping

Mackintosh & Wylie
Licensing

Mackrell Turner Garrett
Lit (Commercial)

Maclay Murray & Spens
Aviation, Banking, Computer/IT, Construction, Corporate Finance, Employment, Environmental, EU, Financial Services, Housing Associations, Insolvency, Insurance, Investment Funds, IP, Lit (Commercial), Lit (Property), Pensions, Planning, Projects, Property (Commercial), Shipping, Tax (Corporate), Trusts

Macleod & MacCallum
Agric, Housing Associations

MacPhee & Partners
Agric

MacRoberts
Charities, Computer/IT, Construction, Corporate Finance, Employment, Energy, Environmental, EU, Insolvency, IP, Licensing, Prof Neg, Projects, Property (Corporate), Tax (Corporate), Trusts

Madden & Finucane
Admin/Public, Crime

Magrath & Co
Crime, Immigration

Maidments
Crime

Mainprice & Co
VAT

Maitland Walker
EU

Malcolm Lynch
Charities, Employee Share Schemes, Energy, Financial Services

Manby & Steward
Agric, Church, Property (Commercial)

Manches & Co
Advertising & Marketing, Charities, Computer/IT, Construction, Corporate Finance, Defamation, Education, Family, Housing Associations, Insurance, Lit (Commercial), Media & Ent, Property (Commercial)

Mander Hadley & Co
Charities

Maples Teesdale
Lit (Property)

Margaret Bennett
Family

Margraves
Agric

Marriott Harrison
Corporate Finance, Media & Ent

Marron Dodds
Crime, Planning

Marrons
Personal Injury

Marsden Huck
Education

Marshall & Galpin
Personal Injury, Trusts

Marsh, Ferriman & Cheale
Crime

Marsons Solicitors
Housing Associations

Martineau Johnson
Admin/Public, Agric, Banking, Charities, Church, Corporate Finance, Education, Employment, Energy, EU, Insolvency, IP, Lit (Commercial), Lit (Property), Planning, Property (Commercial), Trusts

Martin Prowel, Edwards & Davies
Crime, Family, Fraud

Mason Bond
Travel

Mason & Moore Dutton
Agric

Masons
Arbitration, Computer/IT, Construction, Energy, Environmental, Health & Safety, Lit (Property), Local Government, PFI, Planning, Projects, Trusts

Matthew Arnold & Baldwin
Debt Collection, Family, Lit (Commercial), Trusts

Matthew McCloy & Partners
Agric, Sports

Mattila Solicitors
Crime

Max Barford & Co
Crime, Family

Max Bitel, Greene
Sports

Max Gold & Co
Crime

Maxwell Batley
Lit (Property), Property (Commercial), Trusts

Maxwell Entwistle & Byrne
Med Neg

Maxwell MacLaurin
Employment

Maycock's
IP

Mayer Brown & Platt
Commodities, Projects

May, May & Merrimans
Agric, Trusts

Mayo & Perkins
Trusts

McArthur Stanton
Licensing

McCann & Greystoke
Licensing

McCash & Hunter
Agric

McClenahan Crossey & Co
Crime

McClure Naismith
Asset Finance, Banking, Consumer Finance, Corporate Finance, Debt Collection, Employment, Health & Safety, Planning, Projects

McCormacks
Crime

McCormicks
Crime, Fraud, Lit (Commercial), Media & Ent, Sports

McCourts
Crime

McGrath & Co
Immigration, Lit (Property)

McGrigor Donald
Admin/Public, Banking, Computer/IT, Construction, Consumer Finance, Corporate Finance, Debt Collection, Defamation, Employee Share Schemes, Employment, Energy, Environmental, EU, Financial Services, Insolvency, Insurance, Investment Funds, IP, Licensing, Lit (Commercial), Lit (Property), Media & Ent, Partnership, Pensions, Planning, Projects, Property (Commercial), Tax (Corporate)

McGuinness Finch
Planning, Property (Commercial)

McKay & Norwell WS
Crime

McKenzie Bell
Licensing

McKinty & Wright
Construction, Corporate Finance, Defamation, Lit (Commercial), Lit (Property), Personal Injury, Prof Neg, Property (Commercial)

McLellans
Licensing

McManus & Kearney
Insolvency

McMillan Kilpatrick S.S.C.
Trusts

McNeive
Media & Ent

Meade-King
Insolvency, Trusts

Memery Crystal
Corporate Finance, Fraud, Lit (Commercial), Sports

Merricks
Construction, Insurance, Personal Injury, Prof Neg

Merriman White
Property (Commercial)

Metcalfe Copeman & Pettefar
Personal Injury

Metcalfes
Personal Injury

Michael Hutchings
EU

Michael W. Halsall
Personal Injury

Michelmores
Charities, Church, Corporate Finance, Debt Collection, Education, Property (Commercial), Trusts

Middleton Potts
Arbitration, Commodities, Corporate Finance, Shipping

Middleweeks
Crime

Milbank, Tweed, Hadley & McCloy
Banking, Energy, Projects

Miles Preston & Co
Family

Millar Shearer & Black
Crime

Miller & Company
Family

Miller Gardner
Crime

Miller Hendry
Agric

Miller Samuel & Co
Debt Collection, Property (Commercial)

Mills & Co
Shipping

Mills & Reeve
Agric, Banking, Charities, Church, Construction, Corporate Finance, Education, Employment, Environmental, Family, Health Care, Insolvency, Insurance, IP, Licensing, Lit (Commercial), Lit (Property), Med Neg, Personal Injury, Planning, Prof Neg, Projects, Property (Commercial), Tax (Corporate), Trusts

Mills Selig
Construction, Corporate Finance, Defamation, Lit (Commercial), Property (Commercial)

Mincoffs
Licensing

Mishcon de Reya
Defamation, Family, Lit (Commercial), Media & Ent, Property (Commercial), Sports

Mitchells Roberton
Trusts

Monier-Williams & Boxalls
Partnership

H. Montlake & Co
Property (Commercial)

Moore & Blatch
Debt Collection, Planning, Property (Commercial), Transport, Trusts

Moorhead James
Sports

More & Co
Crime

Morecroft Urquhart
Family

More Fisher Brown
Commodities, Shipping

Morgan Bruce
Admin/Public, Banking, Computer/IT, Construction, Corporate Finance, Education, Employment, Environmental, EU, Family, Health Care, Housing Associations, Insolvency, IP, Licensing, Lit (Commercial), Lit (Property), Local Government, Med Neg, Media & Ent, Personal Injury, Planning, Prof Neg, Projects, Property (Commercial)

Morgan Jones & Pett
Med Neg

Morrison & Foerster
Telecoms

Morton Fisher
Agric, Family

The Morton Fraser Partnership
Asset Finance, Debt Collection, Employment, Environmental, Family, Licensing, Lit (Commercial), Property (Commercial), Trusts

Mowat Dean & Co WS
Family

Mullis & Peake
Licensing

Mundays
Corporate Finance, Debt Collection, EU, Franchising, Partnership

Munro & Noble
Agric

Murphy & O'Rawe
Personal Injury

Murray Beith Murray W.S.
Agric, Trusts

Murray & Co
Food

Myer Wolff & Manley
Crime

N

Nabarro Nathanson
Admin/Public, Banking, Charities, Computer/IT, Construction, Corporate Finance, Corporate Finance: Equity, Debt Collection, Employment, Energy, Environmental, Health & Safety, Insolvency, IP, Lit (Commercial), Lit (Property), Local Government, Partnership, Pensions, Personal Injury, PFI, Planning, Property (Commercial), Tax (Corporate)

Nalder & Son
Family, Licensing

Napier & Sons
Insolvency

Napthen Houghton Craven
Property (Commercial)

Nash & Co.
Family, Personal Injury

Needham & Grant
IP

Needham & James
Housing Associations, Property (Commercial)

Neil F. Jones & Co
Construction

Nelsons
Crime, Family, Fraud, Immigration, Licensing, Personal Injury

Ness Gallagher
Crime

Newsome Vaughan
Med Neg, Personal Injury

Nicholls & Co
Licensing

Nicholson Graham & Jones
Construction, Corporate Finance, Employee Share Schemes, Environmental, Insolvency, Lit (Commercial), Planning, Property (Commercial), Sports, Travel, Trusts

Russell-Cooke, Potter & Chapman
Crime, Family, Trusts
Russell Jones & Walker
Defamation, Employment, Family, Fraud, Med Neg, Personal Injury, Sports
Russell & Russell
Crime
Russells
Media & Ent
Russells Gibson McCaffrey
Family
Rustons & Lloyd
Agric

S

Sacker & Partners
Pensions
Salans Hertzfeld & Heilbronn HRK
Employment
Samuel Phillips & Co
Family, Immigration, Med Neg, Personal Injury
Sansbury Hill
Personal Injury
Saunders & Co
Crime
Schilling & Lom and Partners
Defamation, Media & Ent
Scrivenger Seabrook
Med Neg
Sean Redmond
Media & Ent
Searles
Media & Ent
Sears Tooth
Family
Seddons
Lit (Commercial)
Semple Fraser WS
Lit (Property), Property (Commercial)
Senior Calveley & Hardy
Agric
Shacklocks
Licensing
Shadbolt & Co
Construction, Corporate Finance
Shakespeares
Asset Finance, Charities, Corporate Finance, Debt Collection, Education, Employment, Housing Associations, Lit (Commercial), Med Neg, Personal Injury, Prof Neg, Travel, Trusts
Sharman & Trethewy
Agric
Sharpe Pritchard
Admin/Public, Local Government, Parliamentary
Shaw and Croft
Commodities, Shipping
Shean Dickson Merrick
Licensing
Shearman & Sterling
Banking, Capital Markets, Corporate Finance, Energy, Projects
Shepherd & Wedderburn WS
Admin/Public, Agric, Aviation, Banking, Charities, Corporate Finance, Employment, Energy, Financial Services, Housing Associations, Insolvency, Insurance, Investment Funds, IP, Lit (Commercial), Lit (Property), Local Government, Med Neg, Pensions, Personal Injury, Planning, Prof Neg, Projects, Property (Commercial), Trusts
Sheridans
Lit (Commercial), Media & Ent
Sherrards
Housing Associations
Sherwin Oliver
Insolvency, Property (Commercial)

Shoosmiths & Harrison
Banking, Corporate Finance, Debt Collection, Food, Insolvency, Lit (Commercial), Lit (Property), Personal Injury, Planning, Property (Commercial)
Short Richardson & Forth
Employment
Shulmans
Lit (Commercial)
Sidley & Austin
Banking, Capital Markets, Telecoms
Silks
Crime
Silverbeck Rymer
Personal Injury
Silver Savory Smith
Family
The Simkins Partnership
Advertising & Marketing, Commodities, Family, Media & Ent, Sports
Simmonds Church Smiles
Personal Injury, Trusts
Simmons & Simmons
Admin/Public, Arbitration, Banking, Capital Markets, Commodities, Computer/IT, Construction, Corporate Finance, Corporate Finance: Equity, Employment, Energy, Environmental, EU, Financial Services, Food, Fraud, Health & Safety, Health Care, Immigration, Insolvency, Investment Funds, IP, Lit (Commercial), Lit (Property), Pensions, PFI, Planning, Product Liability, Projects, Property (Commercial), Sports, Tax (Corporate), Telecoms, Transport, Travel, Trusts
Simons Muirhead & Burton
Civil Liberties, Crime, Defamation, Fraud, Immigration
Simpson & Marwick WS
Admin/Public, Aviation, Construction, Employment, Insurance, Lit (Commercial), Local Government, Med Neg, Personal Injury, Product Liability, Prof Neg
Simpson Thatcher & Bartlett
Capital Markets
Sinclair Roche & Temperley
Arbitration, Commodities, Corporate Finance, Lit (Commercial), Shipping
Sinclair Taylor & Martin
Charities
Singletons
Computer/IT
Sinton & Co
Family, Personal Injury
Sisman Nichols
Planning
S J Cornish
Prof Neg
Skadden, Arps, Slate, Meagher & Flom LLP
Banking, Corporate Finance, Energy, Projects, Telecoms
Slater Heelis
Banking, Corporate Finance, Housing Associations, Insolvency, Lit (Commercial), Property (Commercial)
Slaughter and May
Admin/Public, Asset Finance, Banking, Capital Markets, Computer/IT, Corporate Finance, Employee Share Schemes, Employment, Energy, Environmental, EU, Financial Services, Fraud, Insolvency, Insurance, Investment Funds, IP, Lit (Commercial), Partnership, Pensions, PFI, Planning, Projects, Property (Commercial), Tax (Corporate), Transport
Slee Blackwell
Agric, Partnership, Personal Injury
A.E. Smith & Son
Agric, Education, Trusts

Smith & Graham
Med Neg, Personal Injury
Smith Llewelyn Partnership
Med Neg
The Smith Partnership
Crime
Smyth Barkham
Trusts
Sparling Benham & Brough
Trusts
Speechly Bircham
Charities, Construction, Corporate Finance, Employment, Investment Funds, Lit (Property), Local Government, Property (Commercial), Trusts, VAT
Spicketts
Crime, Family
Spiro Grech & Co
Crime
Spraggon Stennett Brabyn
Media & Ent
Sprecher Grier
Debt Collection, Insolvency
Squire & Co
Prof Neg
Squire Sanders & Dempsey LLP
Projects, Telecoms
Staffurth & Bray
Trusts
Stamp Jackson and Procter
Med Neg, Personal Injury, Property (Commercial)
Stanley Tee & Company
Agric, Trusts
Statham Gill Davies
Media & Ent
Steedman Ramage WS
Construction, Corporate Finance, Environmental, IP, Lit (Property), Property (Commercial), Trusts
Steele & Co
Employment, Local Government, Planning, Trusts
Steele Raymond
Debt Collection, Education, Property (Commercial), Trusts
Stephen Rimmer & Co
Crime
Stephens Innocent
Admin/Public, Civil Liberties, Defamation, Personal Injury
Stephenson Flint & Holmes
Family
Stephenson Harwood
Banking, Corporate Finance, Employment, Environmental, Family, Fraud, Insolvency, Investment Funds, IP, Lit (Commercial), Lit (Property), Planning, Shipping, Travel
Stephens & Scown
Admin/Public, Agric, Banking, Corporate Finance, Crime, Debt Collection, Employment, Energy, Environmental, Family, Insolvency, Licensing, Lit (Commercial), Personal Injury, Planning
Stepien Lake Gilbert & Paling
Property (Commercial)
Stevens & Bolton
Corporate Finance, Debt Collection, Employment, Lit (Commercial), Property (Commercial), Trusts
Stewarts
Personal Injury
Stewart & Watson
Agric
Stockler Charity
Shipping
Stone King
Charities, Church, Education, Employment, Family
Stones Cann & Hallett
Agric, Construction, Family, Housing Associations, Licensing, Personal Injury, Sports, Travel, Trusts
Stronachs
Insolvency

Stuart Miller
Immigration
Sturtivant & Co
Immigration
Sugaré & Co
Crime
Sullivan & Cromwell
Banking, Capital Markets, Corporate Finance, Projects
Swepstone Walsh
Defamation, Licensing

T

Tallents Godfrey & Co
Agric, Charities
Tarlo Lyons
Computer/IT, Debt Collection, Media & Ent
Taylor Joynson Garrett
Arbitration, Banking, Computer/IT, Construction, Corporate Finance, Employment, Food, Franchising, Insolvency, IP, Lit (Commercial), Media & Ent, Planning, Projects, Telecoms, Trusts
Taylor Nichol
Civil Liberties, Crime, Immigration
Taylors
IP
Taylor Vinters
Agric, Charities, Corporate Finance, Employment, Insolvency, IP, Lit (Commercial), Personal Injury, Planning, Property (Commercial), Trusts
Taylor Walton
Lit (Commercial)
Tayntons
Personal Injury
Teacher Stern Selby
Admin/Public, Education, Property (Commercial)
Thanki Novy Taube
Crime
The Berkson Globe Partnership
Crime
Theodore Goddard
Admin/Public, Advertising & Marketing, Asset Finance, Banking, Computer/IT, Corporate Finance, Defamation, Employment, EU, Fraud, Lit (Commercial), Media & Ent, Planning, Product Liability, Sports, Tax (Corporate), Transport
The Stokes Partnership
Family
THM Tinsdills
Prof Neg
Thomas Cooper & Stibbard
Commodities, Shipping
Thomas Eggar Church Adams
Agric, Charities, Church, Corporate Finance, Education, Insolvency, Lit (Commercial), Lit (Property), Property (Commercial), Tax (Corporate), Trusts
Thompson & Jackson
Licensing
Thompsons
Employment, Family, Personal Injury
Thomson Snell & Passmore
Charities, Corporate Finance, Debt Collection, Family, Lit (Commercial), Lit (Property), Med Neg, Personal Injury, Prof Neg, Property (Commercial), Trusts
Thorntons WS
Agric, Corporate Finance, Licensing, Lit (Property), Property (Commercial)
Thrings & Long
Agric, Charities, Employment
Thursfields
Agric

BEST BUSINESS LAWYER 1998

BEST BUSINESS LAWYERS	
BERINGER Guy	Allen & Overy
BOARDMAN Nigel	Slaughter and May
MOTANI Habib	Clifford Chance
SALZ Anthony	Freshfields
CHEYNE David	Linklaters
CHILDS David	Clifford Chance
CLARK Tim	Slaughter and May
HALLY Paul	Shepherd & Wedderburn
HERRINGTON Timothy	Clifford Chance
JAMES Glen	Slaughter and May
JOHNS Michael	Ashurst Morris Crisp
RAWLINSON Mark	Freshfields
RICHARDS Philip	Freshfields
SHAW Michael	Herbert Smith
UNDERHILL William	Slaughter and May

Survey

To identify the 'Best Business Lawyers' questionnaires were sent to in-house lawyers and company secretaries at the UK's largest companies and institutions. Respondents were asked to recommend the lawyers who, in addition to pure legal skills, bring business acumen and innovative thinking to complex commercial problems.

In total we received two hundred and thirty seven recommendations.

All the lawyers who make the list of the top fifteen Best Business Lawyers are at major City firms with the notable exception of Paul Hally at Scottish firm, Shepherd & Wedderburn. Two thirds of the individuals who make the list are at just three firms: Slaughter and May, Clifford Chance and Freshfields.

The individuals are divided into two broad bands. Within the bands the ordering is alphabetical. Interestingly three individuals (Guy Beringer, Michael Shaw and Michael Johns) who make the Best Business Lawyers list are not included in the main body of the Guide as being specialists in a particular practice area. Of the rest ten are ranked for Corporate Finance, two for Insurance and Reinsurance, with others ranked for Capital Markets, Insolvency, Project Finance, Investment Funds and Financial Services. Several are ranked in two or more sections.

First Band

Guy Beringer (described as "a charming and sophisticated user friendly lawyer" who "responds rapidly to a changing situation") is the sole representative of Allen & Overy to make the list. Nigel Boardman

is the highest placed of the four Slaughter and May partners in the list and is head of the firm's corporate department. "Outstandingly able and effective," Boardman was also praised for his "great breadth of knowledge and experience" and for giving "creative, pragmatic advice." Habib Motani (Clifford Chance) is a leading individual in International Capital Markets and Derivatives. Anthony Salz, senior partner of Freshfields, is "undoubtedly one of the market leaders" and "a hands on, lead from the front lawyer."

Second Band

The "always diplomatic" David Cheyne of Linklaters is "simply excellent." With Nigel Boardman, Cheyne is ranked in the highest band in the Corporate Finance section of the Guide. David Childs (Clifford Chance) is "the epitome of a lawyer who is also a man of business." Head of CC's corporate practice area he is said to be "the firm's heavy hitter" and "razor sharp." Tim Clark (Slaughter and May) is "a serious operator who gets things done." Paul Hally is the only non City lawyer to make the list. A partner in Edinburgh firm Shepherd and Wedderburn, he appears in the Corporate Finance, Insolvency and Project Finance/PFI sections of the Guide. Unsurprisingly he is regarded as an "outstanding all-round practitioner." Timothy Herrington (Clifford Chance) is a "brilliant" and "statesman-like but approachable" partner who combines an in-depth knowledge of FSA with "wide commercial experience." He is ranked in the highest band for both Financial Services and Investment Funds. Glen James (Slaughter and May) is "a real guru" with "immense technical knowledge" but "never loses sight of the commercial objective." Michael Johns (Ashurst Morris Crisp) is "exceptionally commercially astute, inspires confidence and is a pleasure to work with or against." Mark Rawlinson (Freshfields) "combines practicality with great people skills." Philip Richards, also at Freshfields, enjoys a reputation for providing a top class service in both corporate finance and non-contentious insurance – "Philip always has a sensible take on things." Michael Shaw of Herbert Smith was described as "relentlessly sensible" with a "good feel and an eye for the right solution." Finally, William Underhill (Slaughter and May) is "always one of the first to be picked when you're choosing your team."

LAW FIRMS	Number of individuals recommended
Slaughter & May	20
Linklaters & Paines	12
Clifford Chance	11
Herbert Smith	11
Freshfields	9
Cameron McKenna	7
Ashurst Morris Crisp	6
Allen & Overy	5
Clyde & Co	4
Hammond Suddards	3
Norton Rose	3
Addleshaw Booth & Co	2
Beaumont & Sons	2
Bond Pearce	2
Garretts	2
Macfarlanes	2
More Fisher Brown	2
Rowe & Maw	2
Travers Smith Braithwaite	2
Wragge & Co	2

Table of Law Firms

The inner circle of City firms also dominate the table of firms with the most lawyers nominated overall. Whilst one hundrcd and forty six lawyers at forty nine firms were nominated we have restricted the table to firms with two or more nominated individuals.

Slaughter and May are by far the leading firm in terms of the number of individuals nominated, with almost twice as many as its nearest rivals. Placed in fourth place last year, its position in 1998 is perhaps a truer reflection of its actual profile and a testament to Slaughter's policy of "multispecialists," with partners undertaking a wider range of work than is usual compared to other City practices.

Last year's first placed firm, Linklaters, came second this year. Herbert Smith was again highly placed, coming joint third with Clifford Chance, supporting the firm's contention that it is on the verge of entering the upper echelons of the City hierarchy.

Clyde & Co (particularly known for shipping and insurance) is a new entrant to the list as are Beaumont and Son (the leading firm in aviation with the lion's share of insurance work it that industry, estimated to be at least 50% of the total market) and shipping firm More Fisher Brown.

Hammond Suddards and Garretts are the only national firms to be ranked. Wragge & Co, Bond Pearce and Addleshaw Booth & Co are the only regional practices to appear.

INTERNATIONAL

CHAMBERS & PARTNERS

INTERNATIONAL BRANCH OFFICES

Abu Dhabi
Richards Butler, Simmons & Simmons, Trowers & Hamlins

Albania
Allen & Overy

Argentina
Baker & McKenzie

Australia
Baker & McKenzie

Azerbaijan
Baker & McKenzie, Ledingham Chalmers

Bahrain
Norton Rose, Trowers & Hamlins

Belgium
Allen & Overy, Ashurst Morris Crisp, Baker & McKenzie, Beachcroft Stanleys, S J Berwin & Co, Berwin Leighton, Bird & Bird, Cameron McKenna, Clifford Chance, Denton Hall, Dibb Lupton Alsop, Dickinson Dees, Eversheds, Field Fisher Waterhouse, Freshfields, Gouldens, Hammond Suddards, Herbert Smith, Linklaters, Lovell White Durrant, Macfarlanes, Maclay Murray & Spens, Masons, McGrigor Donald, The Morton Fraser Partnership, Nabarro Nathanson, Norton Rose, Osborne Clarke, Paisner & Co, Pinsent Curtis, Richards Butler, Rowe & Maw, Simmons & Simmons, Slaughter and May, Stephenson Harwood, Taylor Joynson Garrett, Theodore Goddard, Titmuss Sainer Dechert, Wilde Sapte

Brazil
Baker & McKenzie, Beaumont and Son, Richards Butler

Canada
Baker & McKenzie

Chile
Baker & McKenzie

China
Allen & Overy, Baker & McKenzie, Clifford Chance, Denton Hall, Freshfields, Lovell White Durrant, Masons, Richards Butler, Simmons & Simmons, Sinclair Roche & Temperley, Stephenson Harwood

Columbia
Baker & McKenzie

Czech Republic
Allen & Overy, Baker & McKenzie, Cameron McKenna, Clifford Chance, Lovell White Durrant, Seddons

Denmark
Eversheds, Osborne Clarke, Watson, Farley & Williams

Dubai
Allen & Overy, Clifford Chance, Hill Taylor Dickinson, Malkins, Nabarro Nathanson, Trowers & Hamlins

Egypt
Baker & McKenzie, Fox & Gibbons

Eire
Masons

England & Wales
Bird Semple

Falkland Islands
Ledingham Chalmers

France
Allen & Overy, Ashurst Morris Crisp, Baker & McKenzie, Bannatyne, Kirkwood, France & Co, Browne Jacobson, Clifford Chance, Clyde & Co, Constant & Constant, Eversheds, Frere Cholmeley Bischoff, Freshfields, Herbert Smith, Holman, Fenwick & Willan, Linklaters, Lovell White Durrant, Nabarro Nathanson, Norton Rose, Osborne Clarke, Penningtons, Richards Butler, Simmons & Simmons, Slaughter and May, Titmuss Sainer Dechert, Vizards, Watson, Farley & Williams, Wilde Sapte, Withers

Germany
Allen & Overy, Ashurst Morris Crisp, Baker & McKenzie, S J Berwin & Co, Clifford Chance, Freshfields, Linklaters, Osborne Clarke

Gibraltar
Fox & Gibbons

Greece
Clyde & Co, Hill Taylor Dickinson, Holman, Fenwick & Willan, Ince & Co, Norton Rose, Richards Butler, Stephenson Harwood, Watson, Farley & Williams

Guernsey
Burness, Wedlake Bell

Hong Kong
Allen & Overy, Baker & McKenzie, Barlow Lyde & Gilbert, Bird & Bird, Cameron McKenna, Clifford Chance, Clyde & Co, Denton Hall, Dibb Lupton Alsop, Freshfields, Herbert Smith, Hill Taylor Dickinson, Holman, Fenwick & Willan, Ince & Co, Linklaters, Lovell White Durrant, Masons, Nabarro Nathanson, Norton Rose, Richards Butler, Simmons & Simmons, Sinclair Roche & Temperley, Slaughter and May, Stephenson Harwood, Wilde Sapte

Hungary
Allen & Overy, Baker & McKenzie, Cameron McKenna, Clifford Chance

India
Ashurst Morris Crisp

Italy
Allen & Overy, Amhurst Brown Colombotti, Baker & McKenzie, Clifford Chance, Frere Cholmeley Bischoff, Freshfields, Osborne Clarke, Simmons & Simmons

Japan
Allen & Overy, Ashurst Morris Crisp, Baker & McKenzie, Clifford Chance, Denton Hall, Freshfields, Linklaters, Lovell White Durrant, Slaughter and May, Wilde Sapte

Jersey
Gouldens

Kazakhstan
Baker & McKenzie, Cameron McKenna

Lithuania
Bishop and Robertson Chalmers

Mexico
Baker & McKenzie

Monaco
Eversheds, Frere Cholmeley Bischoff

Oman
Fox & Gibbons, Richards Butler, Trowers & Hamlins

Pakistan
Amhurst Brown Colombotti, Richards Butler

Poland
Allen & Overy, Amhurst Brown Colombotti, Baker & McKenzie, Cameron McKenna, Clifford Chance, Richards Butler

Portugal
Simmons & Simmons

Qatar
Richards Butler

Romania
Sinclair Roche & Temperley, Taylor Joynson Garrett

Russia
Allen & Overy, Baker & McKenzie, Cameron McKenna, Clifford Chance, Denton Hall, Eversheds, Frere Cholmeley Bischoff, Freshfields, Gouldens, Linklaters, Lovell White Durrant, Norton Rose, Watson, Farley & Williams

Saudi Arabia
Baker & McKenzie

Singapore
Allen & Overy, Ashurst Morris Crisp, Baker & McKenzie, Beaumont and Son, Clifford Chance, Clyde & Co, Denton Hall, Freshfields, Herbert Smith, Holman, Fenwick & Willan, Ince & Co, Linklaters, Lovell White Durrant, Masons, Norton Rose, Sinclair Roche & Temperley, Slaughter and May, Stephenson Harwood

Spain
Allen & Overy, Amhurst Brown Colombotti, Baker & McKenzie, Clifford Chance, Davies Arnold Cooper, Freshfields, Osborne Clarke, Stephenson Harwood

Sweden
Baker & McKenzie

Switzerland
Baker & McKenzie

Taiwan
Baker & McKenzie

Thailand
Baker & McKenzie, Clifford Chance, Freshfields, Linklaters

The Netherlands
Baker & McKenzie, Clifford Chance, Osborne Clarke

The Phillipines
Baker & McKenzie

Turkey
Fox & Gibbons, Ledingham Chalmers

Ukraine
Baker & McKenzie

United Arab Emirates
Berrymans Lace Mawer, Clyde & Co, Fox & Gibbons

USA
Allen & Overy, Baker & McKenzie, Bermans, Cameron McKenna, Clifford Chance, Collyer-Bristow, Denton Hall, Freshfields, Linklaters, Lovell White Durrant, Simmons & Simmons, Slaughter and May, Titmuss Sainer Dechert, Watson, Farley & Williams

Uzbekistan
Cameron McKenna

Venezuela
Baker & McKenzie, Clyde & Co

Vietnam
Baker & McKenzie, Clifford Chance, Freshfields, Lovell White Durrant, Sinclair Roche & Temperley

FOREIGN LAW FIRMS IN LONDON

Country of Origin and Firm Name	FEE-EARNERS London	World

EUROPE

Belgium

De Bandt, Van Hecke & Lagae (0171) 600 3607
2   165

A leading Belgian firm with offices in Brussels, Antwerp, New York, Prague, Warsaw and London.

Denmark

Abbott King & Troen (0171) 430 1709
16   3

Provides litigation, property commercial and EU-related services for corporate clients in the United Kingdom and Denmark.

Berning Schlüter Hald (0171) 236 2023
1   30

International transactions including banking and international arbitration and litigation.

Kromann & Münter (0171) 404 4825
1   97

Company/commercial, finance and banking.

Reumert & Partners (0171) 236 4406
2   45

Company/commercial, Banking and finance, leasing, shipping.

Eire

A & L Goodbody (0171) 929 2425
3   171

Mergers and acquisitions, corporate restructuring, banking and tax based financing, corporate finance, share and loan issues, Stock Exchange flotations, joint ventures, competition law, financial services, inward investment, ship and aircraft financing, corporate insolvency and examination, intellectual property, employment, commercial litigation, property, insurance and general corporate advice.

Matheson Ormsby Prentice (0171) 404 0998
3   80

Corporate (mergers and acquisitions, joint ventures, venture capital, MBOs), banking, financial services (fund management, structured finance), general (including property, litigation, private client).

McCann FitzGerald (0171) 621 1000
7   163

Company and commercial (including corporate finance, mergers and acquisitions, venture capital and employment), banking and financing (including asset finance, aviation, project finance, financial services, IFSC, securitisation and insolvency), investment in Ireland (including corporate and tax aspects), tax (corporation and income tax) and stamp duty.

Finland

Roschier-Holmberg & Waselius (0171) 929 0966
2   43

Largest Law firm in Finland. Banking and financial services, general corporate, mergers and acquisitions, litigation, tax.

France

Azéma Sells (0171) 836 7993
1

Jeantet & Associes (0171) 600 3608
1   120

Banking, corporate, financial law, labour law, competition, intellectual property, securities regulations, insurance (exclusively French law).

Salans Hertzfeld & Heilbronn HRK (0171) 509 6000
63   270

Mergers and acquisitions; corporate finance, banking; licensing, distribution, franchising; natural resources, oil and gas; intellectual property; litigation, arbitration; real estate, construction; communications; labour law; taxation; other commercial matters; with particular reference to the EU, France, Central/Eastern Europe and the CIS.

Germany

Beiten Burkhardt Mittl & Wegener (0171) 392 9100
6   154

Specialised areas: Cross-border mergers, acquisitions and joint ventures, corporate finance, corporate and commercial; media law.

Dabelstein & Passehl (0171) 702 4661
6   16

Shipping and marine insurance. Litigation-based law firm. Offices in Hamburg and London.

Hartwig (0171) 235 1504
5   0

Oppenhoff & Radler (0171) 600 3609
3   272

Corporate (mergers and acquisition, restructuring, German company law), commercial (distribution, agency, licensing), banking and finance (loans, bond issues, factoring, finance leasing, security over German assets, investment funds), tax law and tax planning.

Gibraltar

Marrache & Co (0171) 581 2161
3   18

Commercial law, banking and finance, shipping including ship finance, commercial and international litigation, employment, offshore work.

Italy

Carnelutti (0171) 626 6996 1
50

Chiomenti E. Associati Studio Legale (0171) 495 6430
6   80

Banking, corporate tax and general commercial.

Dobson & Pinci (0171) 628 8163
5   55

Corporate/commercial, banking, securities, privatisation, property, telecommunications, entertainment, construction, oil and gas, food industries.

Studio Legale Bisconti (0171) 383 5052
1   15

Mergers and acquisitions, general corporate work (mostly Italian law).

Studio Legale Sutti (0171) 409 1384
2   32

Commercial law (work includes commercial contracts, banking and financial, joint ventures, insolvency, international trade), intellectual property and competition, employment law and related matters.

Norway

Bugge, Arentz-Hansen & Rasmussen (0171) 236 0099
2   65

Corporate and commercial, banking and finance, financial regulations, Stock Exchange securities law, mergers and acquisitions, corporate taxation, shipping and maritime law.

Thommessen Krefting Greve Lund (0171) 404 4825
1   80

Company (mergers and acquisitions), financial services, finance (shipping).

Wikborg Rein & Co (0171) 236 4598
2   55

Shipping, sale and purchase, chartering, financing and insurance), company law (acquisitions in Norway), securities law (Norwegian regulations), energy (petroleum law, offshore contracts).

Spain

Diaz-Bastien & Truan (0171) 409 2018
1   18

Company/commercial (mergers and acquisitions, distribution agreements), real estate (commercial and large developments), entertainment (TV productions, film); intellectual property; private client, taxation; litigation.

Fernando Scornik Gerstein (0171) 839 1581
6   30

Private client, personal injury, company/commercial, litigation, probate and tax, property, immigration, conveyancing (Spanish law).

Hector Diaz & Co (0171) 489 8119
1   0

Private client.

Michael Soul & Associates (0171) 353 3358
2   17

Spanish law firm specialising in: company, commercial, tax and tax planning, commercial and residential conveyancing, inheritance and litigation and arbitration.

Uria & Menéndez (0171) 600 3610
2   85

Corporate (corporate finance, foreign investment in Spain), mergers and acquisitions (acquisition of Spanish companies by UK clients and vice-versa and joint ventures), financial and securities (issues of securities, investment funds, securities markets), banking syndicate loans, co-operation contracts), commercial (distribution, agency, free competition).

Country of Origin and Firm Name	FEE-EARNERS London	World

Sweden

Grundberg Mocatta (0171) 368 4100

8   2

Company/commercial, property, trusts, probate and conveyancing.

Hamilton & Co Advokatbyra HB (0171) 938 5408

1   32

Insolvency, general commercial law.

Lagerlöf & Leman (0171) 606 1715

4   120

Corporate/commercial, mergers and acquisitions, banking and finance, litigation, East-West trade.

Switzerland

Froriep Renggli (0171) 236 6000

3   36

Secretan Troyanov (0171) 404 1199

2   19

Swiss commercial law, banking, mergers and acquisitions, litigation, arbitration.

The Netherlands

De Brauw Blackstone Westbroek (0171) 600 1719

5   140

Banking and securities law (bonds issues, loan agreements); derivatives, programmes (debt insurance), share issues, Amsterdam Stock Exchange listings, corporate (mergers and acquisitions, joint ventures).

Nauta Dutilh (0171) 786 9100

4   425

One of the largest legal practices in continental Europe. The London office concentrates on Dutch and Netherlands Antilles corporate, financial and securities law.

Stibbe Simont Monahan Duhot (0171) 600 4400

4   400

Banking, corporate finance, project finance, leasing, capital markets, financial services, investment funds, mergers and acquisitions, joint ventures, taxation.

MIDDLE EAST & AFRICA

Egypt

Hameed & Mallassi Advocates Ltd (0171) 258 0636

3   0

Iran

Dr Anvari & Associates (0171) 724 9073

5   2

International trade contracts, banking and finance law, construction contracts and litigation, investment laws, insurance and shipping laws, oil and gas contracts and laws.

Israel

Zellermayer, Pelossof & Schiffer (0171) 629 1920

7   25

Business and corporate finance.

Saudi Arabia

Nader Law Offices (0171) 373 0975

2   19

Country of Origin and Firm Name	FEE-EARNERS London	World

South Africa

Bowman Gilfillan Hayman Godfrey (0171) 430 0888

2   85

Corporate finance, general commercial, tax planning, point ventures, acquisitions, investments in South Africa.

Maitland & Co (0171) 344 7500

9   250

International corporate, trust and tax planning, mergers and acquisitions, capital markets, shipping, commodities and trade law.

Mallinicks Attorneys (0171) 333 2700

8   35

Telecommunications, exchange control and investment, intellectual property, joint ventures in South Africa, immigration, private client services, litigation, arbitration.

Shepstone & Wylie (UK) (0171) 344 7600

9   250

Corporate, commercial, banking, asset finance, trade and maritime law.

NORTH AMERICA

Canada

Blake, Cassels & Graydon (0171) 680 4600

3   350

Mergers and acquisitions, capital markets (debt and equity), banking, corporate, commercial.

Borden DuMoulin Howard Gervais (0171) 929 2099

2   500

Email address: nletalik

resolution and mediation, international insolvency, and cross-border corporate and financial transactions.

Fasken Martineau (0171) 929 2894

1   375

Mergers and acquisitions, capital markets, insolvency, banking and projects finance, litigation, general corporate and commercial.

McCarthy Tétrault (0171) 353 2355

2   523

Euromarkets, corporate finance, international mining, oil and gas project work.

Ogilvy Renault (0171) 600 9005

2   292

Business law, business organisation, mergers and acquisitions, securities law, financing and financial services, banking and insolvency, alternative dispute resolution methods.

Osler Hoskin & Harcourt (0171) 606 0777

3   280

Firm of Canadian barristers and solicitors. The London office mainly undertakes business law, including mergers and acquisitions, capital markets, banking, finance and international securities.

Stikeman Elliott (0171) 378 0880

9   333

Mergers and acquisitions, privatisations, project finance, international bond advisory, banking securities, capital markets, private capital taxation.

Country of Origin and Firm Name	FEE-EARNERS London	World

Tory Tory DesLauriers & Binnington (0171) 831 8155

2   207

Euromarkets, corporate finance, banking and aircraft finance, commercial transactions (acting for financial institutions, governments and multinational corporations).

USA

Arnold & Porter (0171) 329 4329

1   –

See A-Z section for further details.

B.C. Toms & Co (0171) 638 7711

2   15

Ukrainian legal issues, oil and gas, general commercial transactions, investments in the Ukraine, 2 offices in Ukraine (Kiev and Odessa).

Bigham Englar Jones & Houston (0171) 283 9541

0   30

The London office acts as a liaison office for this American law firm.

Bingham Dana LLP (0171) 799 2646

3   0

International finance, tax planning and licences, joint ventures, cross-border acquisitions, equity investment, debt restructuring.

Bracewell & Patterson (0171) 355 3330

4   225

Energy and petrochemical industries.

Brobeck Hale & Dorr International (0171) 638 6688

13   750

Headquartered in New York, the firm has approximately 700 lawyers in the US and London. See A-Z section for further details.

Brown & Wood, a Multinational Partnership (0171) 778 1800

23   315

Corporate and securities, international tax, trusts and estate. See A-Z section for further details.

Bryan Cave (0171) 896 1900

7   534

Corporate and commercial, individual and corporate taxation, international litigation and arbitration.

Chadbourne & Parke (0171) 337 8000

8   –

See A-Z section for further details.

Cleary, Gottlieb, Steen & Hamilton (0171) 614 2200

33   547

A leading international firm engaged in the general practice of law in major cities around the world.

Coudert Brothers (0171) 203 2248

41   544

See A-Z section for further details.

Covington & Burling (0171) 495 5655

15   325

Specific areas of work include competition law, the regulation of food, drugs and other consumer products; technology licensing and legislation; EC regulation of intellectual property; international litigation and arbitration; acquisitions, mergers, licensing and other transactional matters; communications issues and pharmaceuticals. See A-Z section for further details.

Country of Origin and Firm Name	FEE-EARNERS London	World

Cravath, Swaine & Moore
(0171) 453 1000 — 12 — 442
General US corporate, financial and securities law practice.

Crowell & Moring (0171) 413 0011
— 4 — 220
Anti-trust, aviation, business crime, communications, construction, corporate finance, mergers and acquisitions, energy, environmental, government contracts, international employment, litigation, product liability and insurance.

Curtis, Mallet-Prevost, Colt & Mosle
(0171) 638 7957 — 4 — 200
International finance, corporate transactions, litigation and arbitration, international taxation, trusts and estates.

Davis Polk & Wardwell (0171) 418 1300
— 34 — 490
Securities, mergers and acquisition law, banking, corporate.

Debevoise & Plimpton (0171) 786 9000
— 12 — 324
An international firm specialising in capital markets, financings, telecommunications, privatisations mergers and acquisitions, investment funds, international arbitrations and commercial litigation. New York, Washington DC, Paris, Moscow and Hong Kong.

Dewey Ballantine (0171) 456 6000
— 25 — 515
See A-Z section for further details.

Diane Hinch (0171) 917 9680
— 1 — 0
US immigration and nationality law. See A-Z section for further details.

Dorsey & Whitney (0171) 588 0800
— 3 — 443
Corporate finance (asset securitisation, Eurobonds, other international securities, offerings, capital markets transactions), Mergers and Acquisitions, Joint Ventures, Contract Negotiation and Tax and Energy Law. (English and U.S. law).

Faegre Benson Hobson Audley
(0171) 450 4510 — 4 — 300
Corporate and commercial. See A-Z section for further details.

Fredrikson & Byron
(0171) 395 3110 — 1 — –

Fried, Frank, Harris, Shriver & Jacobson
(0171) 972 9600 — 8 — 493
Mergers and acquisitions, corporate finance, company and commercial.

Fulbright & Jaworski (0171) 629 1207
— 5 — 796
Middle East law and regulations, international arbitration, international project funding, corporate, commercial, tax.

Gibson Dunn & Crutcher (0171) 925 0440
— 7 — 700
Mergers, acquisitions and joint ventures, commercial transactions, corporate finance, international tax structuring.

Gottesman Jones & Partners
(0171) 203 5200 — 4 — 4
Tax (including US and international tax planning,), securities (including sales in Europe of securities of US issuers), joint ventures and investments in the US, venture capital, mergers and acquisitions, license and distribution agreements).

Graham & James (0171) 353 1840
— 1 — 391
Anti-trust, banking, bankruptcy and creditors' right, corporate and commercial, employee benefits and stock ownership plans, energy, entertainment, environmental, equipment leasing, estate planning, family, financial services, food and drug, healthcare, immigration, insurance, IP, international asset management, international trade and customs, labour and employment, arbitration, maritime, M&A, product liability, public finance, public utilities, property, real estate, securities, tax, telecommunications, transportation.

Hancock Rothert & Bunshoft
(0171) 220 7567 — 1 — 111
Insured (Lloyd's and London market companies, direct insurance/reinsurance, litigation and advice); environmental pollution, asbestos, directors' and officers' liability, lawyers', architects' and engineers' and brokers' errors and omissions, employment, maritime, construction and recreational liability.

Haythe & Curley (0171) 930 0061
— 1 — 80
Oil and gas (exploration and development), private client (international trusts), project finance.

Hogan & Hartson (0171) 815 1200
— 4 — 500
European based international corporate and commercial transactions, US-based corporate and securities matters, US regulatory counselling.

Holme Roberts & Owen LLP
(0171) 499 8776 — 4 — 185
The London office of Denver-based HRO serves clients in the cable television, telecommunications, beverages and professional sports industries.

J. Scott Brown & Associates
(0181) 300 4475 — 1 — 200

Jones, Day, Reavis & Pogue
(0171) 236 3939 — 27 — 1200
Corporate/M&A and securities, tax/structured finance, litigation and project finance. See A-Z section for further details.

Kilpatrick Stockton (0171) 321 0477
— 4 — 370
Company/commercial, securities (European offerings of securities by US issuers).

Kirkland & Ellis (0171) 816 8700
— 10 — 581
An international firm advising on arbitration, litigation, corporate finance and commercial matters.

Kroll, Rubin & Fionella LLP
(0171) 621 1142 — 5 — 100
Insurance and reinsurance.

Ladas & Parry (0171) 242 5566
— 5 — 75
Intellectual property, (patents, trademarks, copyright), licensing.

Latham & Watkins (0171) 374 4444
— 17 — 850
Project, corporate and aircraft financing, telecommunications. See A-Z section for further details.

Law Offices of Gary M. Ferman
(0171) 499 5702 — 1 — 1

LeBoeuf, Lamb, Greene & MacRae
(0171) 459 5000 — 32 — 600
Civil litigation, US, UK and EC insurance regulations, corporate finance, corporate, commercial, energy, project finance, marine, aviation, insolvency and banking regulation. See A-Z section for further details.

Loughran & Co (0171) 355 2051
— 7 — 7
General corporate and commercial law, tax planning, trusts and estates, arbitration.

Mayer Brown & Platt (0171) 246 6200
— 37 — 900
The London office opened in 1975, and engages in general US and English finance, corporate and securities work in the former Soviet Union. See A-Z section for further details.

Milbank, Tweed, Hadley & McCloy
(0171) 448 3000 — 16 — 400
Has acknowledged expertise in advising governments, lenders and sponsors in financing international infrastructure projects under English and New York law.

Morgan, Lewis & Bockius
(0171) 747 5500 — 27 — 1095
International and cross-border financing, tax planning, international and cross-border business transactions, mergers and acquisitions, international litigation. See A-Z section for further details.

O'Melveny & Myers (0171) 256 8451
— 5 — 580
Corporate finance, acquisition finance, capital markets, securitisation, structured finance.

Pepper, Hamilton & Scheetz
(0171) 628 1122 — 1 — 290
International practice providing the full range of general corporate and trade services.

Perkins Coie (0171) 369 9966
— 1 — 380
The firm has expertise in cross-border financial transactions, particularly projects finance and aircraft finance. It is also well known for its work in telecommunications, tax, environmental and natural resources issues.

Piper & Marbury (0171) 638 3833
— 2 — 0
Company law, general corporate work.

Rogers & Wells LLP (0171) 628 0101
— 20 — 400
Capital markets, securities, corporate, funds, banking, mergers and acquisitions, intellectual property, tax. See A-Z section for further details.

Country of Origin and Firm Name	FEE-EARNERS London	World

Sedgwick, Detert, Moran & Arnold
(0171) 929 1829   7   260
Directors and officers' liability, fidelity, professional indemnity, entertainment and property claims, arbitration. See A-Z section for further details.

Shearman & Sterling (0171) 920 9000
53   705
Corporate finance, mergers and acquisitions, privatisations, private finance and banking, oil and gas.

Shook Hardy & Bacon (0171) 821 5595
22   827
Product liability.

Sidley & Austin (0171) 360 3600
46   811
Banking and structured finance, asset securitisation, telecoms, IT, soft IP and media, taxation advice and property finance. See A-Z section for further details.

Simpson Thacher & Bartlett
(0171) 422 4000   13   500
Securities law, mergers and acquisitions, banking and project finance.

Skadden, Arps, Slate, Meagher & Flom LLP
(0171) 519 7000   28   1100
The London office is involved in financial transactions including mergers and acquisitions, project and lease financing, joint ventures, anti-trust and general corporate advice.

Squire Sanders & Dempsey LLP
(0171) 776 5200   6   400
International transactions, mergers and acquisitions, joint ventures, privatisations, corporate finance, capital markets, securities, infrastructure, project and asset financing, telecommunications, multimedia.

Sullivan & Cromwell (0171) 710 6500
31   475
Capital markets offerings with US participation, mergers and acquisitions, US litigation, US and European anti-trust law, and general corporate work.

Vinson & Elkins
(0171) 491 7236   8   560
International energy, project finance and development, general company and commercial.

Weil, Gotshal & Manges (0171) 903 1000
72   650
Banking, litigation and arbitration, capital markets, M&A, competition, derivatives, real estate, structured finance, securitisation, taxation, telecommunications and media, business reorganisation, employment law and ERISA, trade practices and regulatory law, trusts and estates. See A-Z section for further details.

White & Case (0171) 726 6361
30   700
A global law firm, established in 1901. It handles corporate, capital markets and other financial transactions, litigation, arbitration and tax advice in the world's primary financial and commercial centres. See A-Z section for further details.

Country of Origin and Firm Name	FEE-EARNERS London	World

Whitman Breed Abbott & Morgan
(0171) 839 3226   10   400
Pensions and probate.

Willkie Farr & Gallagher (0171) 696 9060
3   425
US flotations,(all varieties of stock exchange listings); venture capital (negotiated acquisitions of stake in start up companies), corporate (venture, LBO establishment, investment management arrangements).

Wilmer, Cutler & Pickering
(0171) 872 1000   14   300
An international firm, its London office is a multi-national partnership that advises on international transactions, international commercial arbitration, ADR, litigation, aviation and transport, telecommunications. See A-Z section for further details.

Wilson, Elser, Moskowitz, Edelman & Dicker
(0171) 623 6723   2   440
Reinsurance, insurance, coverage disputes, US defence litigation, directors and officer liability, creditors' rights, arbitration, insurance broker errors and omissions. See A-Z section for further details.

Winthrop, Stimson, Putnam & Roberts
(0171) 628 4931   3   300
Banking, securities, acquisitions.

PACIFIC RIM & ASIA

Australia

Blake Dawson Waldron (0171) 600 3030
3   560
Mergers and acquisitions, Stock Exchange Listings and rules, capital markets, banking and finance, taxation and stamp duty, joint ventures, foreign investment, intellectual property, communications, general corporate advice, anti-trust law, general commercial law.

Allens Arthur Robinson (0171) 248 6130
2   800
General corporate, banking, capital markets, Australian and Asian investment.

Corrs Chambers Westgarth
(0171) 929 4955   2   425
Mergers and acquisitions, capital markets, competition law, banking and finance, general corporate/commercial, taxation, intellectual property.

Mallesons Stephen Jaques
(0171) 982 0982   7   690
Mergers and acquisitions, foreign investment in Australia, banking and finance, international and domestic securities offerings, telecommunications law, general corporate/commercial, stamp duty and taxation, energy and resources law.

Minter Ellison (0171) 831 7871
5   728
Company/commercial, financial services, banking, corporate finance and international securities offerings, mergers and acquisitions, corporate tax, international work

Country of Origin and Firm Name	FEE-EARNERS London	World

India

Singhania & Co (0171) 828 3384
4   70
Corporate/commercial, intellectual property, securities, project finance, litigation, arbitration, full service law firm (Indian law specialists).

Brazil

Noronha-Advogados (0171) 581 5040
5   96
Business, international, administrative and banking law, taxation, mergers & acquisitions, litigation, oil, mining and energy law, labour law, environmental law, aviation and maritime law, trade law.

Pinheiro Neto-Advogados
(0171) 583 5060   2   160
General corporate, capital markets, international corporate finance, debt equity swaps, international contracts, tax, intellectual, property, entertainment, privatisations, maritime law, EC law.

Jamaica

Myers Fletcher & Gordon
(0171) 610 4433   5   60
Company and commercial, litigation, Privy Council agents, property, wills and probate both in the Carribean and UK.

Panama

Arias, Fabrega & Fabrega
(0171) 287 3277   2   10
Maritime, admiralty, banking, commercial, general corporate.

Arosemena Noriega & Contreras
(0171) 828 6313   1   12
Corporate (banks, industrial and manufacturing concerns, real estate investments), shipping (shipowners, ship charters, companies operating ships in international trade).

Morgan & Morgan (0171) 493 1978
2
Company and shipping law of Panama, Belize, BVI and Bahamas. Company and trust formation and administration, and ship and registration finance. Admiralty work at the Panama Canal.

Patton Moreno & Asvat (0171) 434 2024
2   8
Shipping (registration of vessels, legal assistance in respect of financial documents); commercial (incorporation of companies, legal advice on Panamanian companies).

Vallarino Vallarino & Rivera
(0171) 486 5324   1   5
The firm handles a wide range of legal work including administrative, commercial, corporate, labour law, admiralty and maritime law, banking, patents and trademarks, taxation, litigation, tourism investment, oil and gas law and arbitration.

INDEX TO SOLICITORS' PROFILES

CHAMBERS & PARTNERS

Leading Solicitors' Profiles Index

C

Chambers & Partners

SOLICITORS'
EDITORIAL

CHAMBERS & PARTNERS

ADMINISTRATIVE AND PUBLIC LAW

RESEARCH: In compiling the tables, we considered all the information available to us, paying particular regard to the market research carried out by our team of ten qualified lawyers. (The researchers' details are set out on page three.)

The rankings, therefore, reflect the opinion of the marketplace as revealed by systematic and objective research: see page four. (Our research is audited every year by the British Market Research Bureau.)

OVERVIEW: Administrative and public law covers advice to public bodies and challenges to decisions of public bodies by means of judicial review ("JR") or statutory appeals. Almost all practitioners commented that this section is uniquely diverse given that judicial review is a remedy which can be pursued against any public bodies in respect of decisions made by them. Significant legal developments affecting this practice area are the proposed incorporation of the European Convention on Human Rights into UK law and the proposed Freedom of Information Bill. In fact many JRs are already being founded on the rights to be established under the Human Rights Bill.

In London, Bindman & Partners move into the top band on their own following praise for the volume and quality of their high profile work. Outside London those firms with strong local authority practices tend to maintain that strength in administrative and public law work, while some niche practitioners such as Matthew Knight of Knights in Tunbridge Wells and Richard Buxton in Cambridge also fare well in our tables.

LEADING FIRMS • LONDON

BINDMAN & PARTNERS

LEIGH, DAY & CO
SHARPE PRITCHARD
TEACHER STERN SELBY

ALLEN & OVERY
BATES, WELLS & BRAITHWAITE
HERBERT SMITH
NABARRO NATHANSON

HIGHLY REGARDED FIRMS
LONDON

Clifford Chance
David Levene & Co
Lovell White Durrant
Rowe & Maw
Stephens Innocent
T.V. Edwards
Winstanley-Burgess

Anthony Gold, Lerman & Muirhead
Denton Hall
Lawrence Graham
Olswang
Theodore Goddard
Wilde Sapte
Winckworth & Pemberton

Barnett Sampson
Cameron McKenna
Eversheds
Simmons & Simmons
Slaughter and May
Travers Smith Braithwaite

LONDON

Bindman & Partners (6ptnrs/4assts) There is "no contest for the top position." Have an "excellent practice," best known for its civil liberties JR work. *Stephen Grosz* works virtually full-time on this kind of work, which is rare; he "understands the nuances of the area and approaches it in an intellectual manner." *Geoffrey Bindman* currently spends much of his time involved in the Hanratty case before the Criminal Cases Review Commission. **Clients/Work:** R v Lord Chancellor ex p Witham: successful challenge to Lord Chancellor's regulations removing provisions exempting people on income support from paying court fees. R v MoD ex p Perkins: a "gays in the military" case now referred to ECJ. Acting for Indonesia Human Rights Campaign, World Development Movement and Campaign Against Arms Trade in application for JR of Trade Secretary's refusal to revoke licences for export of arms to Indonesia.

Leigh Day & Co (2ptnrs/2assts) A "very talented" practice known for its group action and environmental work. *Martyn Day* "a talented and imaginative operator," has recently been involved in the Japanese prisoners of war case. *Richard Stein* is now a partner; he is "very very highly regarded and has a more laid back approach." **Clients/Work:** Successfully acting for Diane Blood in Court of Appeal (regarding use of dead husband's sperm). Acting in Re S, Court of Appeal decision that sectioning S and forcing caesarean section upon her was unlawful. Ex p Alliance against Birmingham Relief Road regarding access to information and attempt to prevent the road.

Sharpe Pritchard (4ptnrs/4assts) Known for acting "almost exclusively for respondents as agents" in education cases for local authorities. Handle a high volume of work. *Trevor Griffiths* handles administrative law and local authority work exclusively. **Clients/Work:** Have this year won challenges by six water authorities to decision by Director-General of Water Services not to exercise his discretion in respect of pre-payment water metres.

Teacher Stern Selby (2ptnrs/3assts) Handle a large number of judicial review cases in connection with their education

practice. *Jack Rabinowicz* is "the main person in the education area." **Clients/Work:** Court of Appeal case over whether provisions of Education Act 1986 can be backdated, appealed to House of Lords. Case regarding expression of education preferences by parents, won for applicant in Court of Appeal, appealed to House of Lords. Important case on exclusion from schools.

Allen & Overy (3ptnrs) Advise public bodies on their regulatory powers as well as commercial judicial review work. They have "a great repeat client in the Independent Television Commission" and therefore are best known in the field of broadcasting review. The team includes *Peter Watson*. **Clients/ Work:** Acting for the ITC in successfully defending claim brought by the Referendum Party re allocation of party political broadcasts during general election in May 1997. Advising Teesside Power Limited and Humber Power Limited in JR against Director General of Electricity Supply. Acting for Arts Council of England re JR proceedings relating to disbursement of National Lottery funding.

Bates Wells & Braithwaite Traditionally an applicants' practice, now also involved in commercial JRs. Head of Litigation *John Trotter* leads the team. **Clients/ Work:** Case of Beth Tandy: House of Lords landmark decision concerning performance by local authorities of obligations under statute and relevance of LA's financial state. Challenging Charity Commission on behalf of Arthur Scargill. Numerous skirmishes on behalf of ICSTIS (premium rate telephone service regulator).

Herbert Smith (7ptnrs/7assts) Known for their "excellent broad litigation practice" and judicial review experience. Act in statutory appeals for applicants, respondents and third parties across the whole ambit of commercial work as well as advising regulators on powers etc. *Andrew Lidbetter* is the key administrative and public law practitioner in the firm. **Clients/Work:** Acting for Sussex Police in R v The Chief Constable of Sussex ex p International Trader's Ferry Limited in House of Lords concerning policing of live animal exports. Successful defence in R v Panel of the Federation of Communication Services ex p Kubis. Acting for Northern Ireland Electricity plc in challenge to Director General of Electricity for Northern Ireland.

Nabarro Nathanson (4ptnrs/11assts) Handle advisory work for public sector clients. The team is settling down after the loss of Carl Hopkins to Lawrence Graham. *Malcolm Iley* has moved from Bevan Ashford to head the public sector team. *Ray Ambrose* is "a particularly good public lawyer." **Clients/ Work:** One of first "Best Value" outsourcings and commercial contracts for London Borough of Hackney. First PFI school, police station, NHS Trust projects. DTI procurement advice (national policy).

Clifford Chance (2ptnrs/5assts) A "high quality practice doing high quality work" in the commercial sphere, particularly in respect of financial and regulatory services disciplinary procedures. All lawyers in the team have advocacy experience arguing public law points in these tribunals. *Michael Smyth* is in the process of writing a book on the implications for business of the incorporation of the European Convention on

Human Rights. **Clients/Work:** Acting for four newspaper groups in wake of High Court decision to no longer permit blanket inspection of Writs. Acting for British investors petitioning Human Rights Court in Strasbourg claiming discriminatory treatment in French handling of investment development on Lake Geneva.

David Levene & Co (1ptnr/2assts) Team specialises in education, community care and health law judicial review cases for applicants. *David Ruebain* is an education specialist whose public law practice takes up 95% of his time. **Clients/Work:** R v LB Haringey ex p Norton: a community care case determining that in carrying out community care assessments regard must be had to a person's recreational needs. Commencing JR proceedings for severely disabled woman when therapy stopped by HA; HA recommended treatment before leave application.

T V Edwards (12assts) Generally known as a criminal practice. JR work is carried out within the housing, social welfare and welfare benefits departments. *Nicola Mackintosh* does mental health and community care work for applicants and is known as "a tenacious and effective litigator." **Clients/Work:** Successfully settled first case under Carers Recognition and Services Act 1995 for young and adult carers. Three High Court and five Court of Appeal hearings in JR challenging NHS Trust decision to close Beckford Hospital in Warminster – successful in Court of Appeal.

Freshfields (7ptnrs/10assts) Practice stems from specialist areas of environment, energy, insurance, anti-trust and sports law. *Paul Bowden* is an environmental litigator and handles 50% JR work. **Clients/Work:** Acting for joint liquidators of EMLICO to set aside leave granted to Kemper Re to bring JR proceedings in Bermuda; since appealed to Privy Council. Advising on JR proceedings for ScottishPower against Director General for Electricity Supply regarding electricity pricing.

Lovell White Durrant (6ptnrs/7assts) Handle both JR and advisory work for applicants and respondents. *Jennifer McDermott* is "a good and thoughtful lawyer." **Clients/Work:** British Steel plc: British Steel plc v Commissioners for Customs & Excise, Court of Appeal challenge to rule of procedural exclusivity. Kemper Reinsurance Company: challenge to decisions of Bermuda Government to allow EMLICO to redomesticate to Bermuda.

Rowe & Maw (1ptnr/5assts) Act in regulatory cases. *Tony Child* handles local government litigation for district auditors and NHS auditors. He is praised by competitors. **Clients/Work:** Acting for the Auditor in successfully resisting appeal by Dame Shirley Porter in Westminster Designated Sales Appeal ("Homes for Votes").

Obtaining leave for Ernst & Young's JR of Inland Revenue regarding tax treatment of limited liability partnerships.

Stephens Innocent Known more for their media practice than for JR, but still have a presence in this field. *Mark Stephens* is extremely high profile in other areas but currently "not seen on the circuit."

Winstanley-Burgess (3ptnrs/2assts) Known for its "great" immigration work, which accounts for about 50% of JR work time. Have also handled prison and criminal procedure cases during the last year. *David Burgess* is recommended.

Anthony Gold, Lerman & Muirhead (2ptnrs/2assts) Known for JR work in community care, immigration and housing. *Robin Levett* heads the team. **Clients/Work:** Concentrated on housing and property-related JR

Denton Hall (4ptnrs/4assts) Specialise in non-contentious public and administration law, ensuring that public sector bodies and their private sector partners act within their relevant powers. **Clients/Work:** Revision for MoD at Portland Harbour. Drafting public law elements for DBFO contracts. Advising Department of Environment on Local Government (Contracts) Bill.

Lawrence Graham (2ptnrs/3assts; 25ptnrs+assts from time to time) The firm's specialist field is urban regeneration and they also have expertise in housing law, charity law and major projects. *Carl Hopkins* moved from Nabarro Nathanson last year. **Clients/Work:** Acting as lead consultant preparing regeneration strategy and advising in implementation of highways CPO. Advising London First on LA and planning authority powers re new "Habitable Bridge" across Thames.

Olswang (2ptnrs/3assts) The public law practice deals mainly with JRs arising for their media industry clients. **Clients/Work:** JR of two decisions of the Advertising Standards Authority. JR of the Independent Television Commission.

Theodore Goddard (3ptnrs/3assts) Known mainly for their work for the Advertising Standards Authority. *Martin Kramer* is recommended. **Clients/Work:** Acting for regulatory clients including sporting and educactional bodies. Acting for foreign governments.

Wilde Sapte (2ptnrs/3assts) Former leader Richard Caird has left to work in-house. IP specialist *John Hull* does JR work more in the commercial and educational sphere, and with his background as a law lecturer at Exeter University, has a particular specialism in acting for universities. **Clients/Work:** Acting for a London-based University on two significant JR actions: one concerning challenges to decisions concerning falsification of research results.

Winckworth & Pemberton (12ptnrs/ 12assts) Work in the parliamentary, local government, educational and ecclesiastical spheres. Also advise the police service. **Clients/Work:** Advising national body concerned with auditing public sector expenditure. Advising police services on vires, constitutional, public and administrative law matters. Acting for Department of Transport in promotion of Channel Tunnel Rail Link Act.

Barnett Sampson (2ptnrs) Act for applicants in JRs concerning financial services as well as regulatory work and advice to local authorities. *Richard Barnett* maintains his leader status. **Clients/ Work:** Advising on a potential application for JR against the Investors Compensation Scheme.

Cameron McKenna (3ptnrs/6assts) Act for government departments, the Crown Estate, utility companies and local authorities in JR proceedings. Regularly assist in drafting of new legislation world-wide. **Clients/Work:** Acting for Camelot to judicially review the DPP. Review of decision by Northumbrian Water not to fluoridate. JR of local authority decisions in connection with planning applications.

Eversheds Handles JR proceedings and advisory work for public bodies, particularly educational establishments.

Simmons & Simmons (5ptnrs/9assts) Handle commercial JR and advisory work. Previous leader David Wilson left the firm last year. *Paul Mitchard* is a member of the Advisory Board of Commercial Judicial Review. **Clients/Work:** Advising Rhone-Poulenc Rorer Ltd on application for JR of decision of Medicines Control Agency to grant parallel export licences. Acting for group of oil licensees re Greenpeace's application for JR of DTI decision.

Slaughter and May (3ptnrs/4assts do this work from the commercial litigation department) Act in commercial JR cases. *Richard Grandison* leads the team. **Clients/ Work:** Advising in ex p Ross and ex p Tee on behalf of LAUTRO. Advising Associated British Ports in successfully resisting JR application of decision by SS for Transport to sell Ipswich Port Limited to ABP.

Travers Smith Braithwaite (2ptnrs/ 3assts) Handle commercial JR from within the commercial litigation department. *Jonathan Leslie*, head of the Administrative Law Group is recommended as a "straightforward, good litigator." **Clients/Work:** Acting for Redland Aggregates Ltd in 2 JRs involving challenges to decisions of Environment Agency. Challenge by Ulster Bank in Court of Appeal to powers of Inland Revenue.

LEADERS' PROFILES · LONDON

AMBROSE, Ray
Nabarro Nathanson, London
(0171) 518 3177
Specialisation: Local government and administrative law (powers and duties, statutory interpretation, capital controls, companies). Formerly at GLC and London Residuary Body. Recently advised on 'best value' housing management contract, football stadium development, other regeneration schemes (SRB and others), and partnership structures, Redbridge audit inquiry and transfer of UDC property to EP.
Prof. Memberships: Law Society.
Career: Qualified 1975; Head of Administrative Law and Parliamentary Branch GLC 1985/6; Deputy Director of Legal Services, London Residuary Body 1986-1990. Joined *Nabarro Nathanson* 1991.

BARNETT, Richard
Barnett Sampson, London (0171) 831 7181
Specialisation: Company Commercial, Commercial Litigation and Administrative Law. Media contributor on financial and regulatory law.
Career: Educated Christ College Finchley Grammar School, B.A. History, University of Warwick.
Personal: Married, 2 children. Keen sportsman, including tennis, skiing, cycling.

BINDMAN, Geoffrey
Bindman & Partners, London
(0171) 833 4433
See under Defamation, p. 278

BOWDEN, Paul
Freshfields, London (0171) 936 4000
See under Litigation (Commercial): 200+ Solicitors, p. 518

BURGESS, David C.W.
Winstanley-Burgess, London
(0171) 278 7911
See under Immigration & Nationality: Personal Immigration, p. 430

CHILD, Tony
Rowe & Maw, London (0171) 248 4282
See under Local Government, p. 552

DAY, Martyn
Leigh, Day & Co, London (0171) 650 1200
See under Environmental Law, p. 342

GRANDISON, Richard
Slaughter and May, London
(0171) 600 1200
See under Litigation (Commercial): 200+ Solicitors, p. 519

GRIFFITHS, Trevor
Sharpe Pritchard, London (0171) 405 4600
Partner specialising in judicial review, statutory and planning appeals.
Specialisation: Judicial review, statutory and planning appeals, including appellate court litigation of the High Court, costs awards and taxation of costs and environmental and planning injunction work. Has dealt with compulsory competitive tendering challenges, local government reorganisation challenges

and the recent challenge to the legality of the use of pre-payment budget water meters.
Career: Joined *Sharpe Pritchard* in 1982, qualified in 1984 and became a Partner in 1987.
Personal: Born 6th December 1957. Educated at Bishop Wordsworth School 1969-76 and U.W.I.S.T 1976-79. Recreations include golf and cricket. Lives in London.

GROSZ, Stephen
Bindman & Partners, London
(0171) 833 4433
Partner in Public Law and Litigation Department.
Specialisation: Specialises in public and administrative law handling applicant work on behalf of pressure groups and individuals in civil liberties and environmental cases including European Community law. Also handles respondent work on behalf of the Law Society and the Office for the Supervision of Solicitors. Major clients include Friends of the Earth, the World Development Movement (the Pergau Dam case) and Amnesty International. Frequently writes articles on public law.
Prof. Memberships: Administrative Law Bar Association, United Kingdom Environmental Law Association, Solicitors European Group, Executive Committee of Public Law Project and Governor of British Institute of Human Rights, Member of the Advisory Board of Judicial Review quarterly; Member of the Advisory Board of Education, Public Law & the Individual; Member of the Advisory Board of the Human Rights Incorporation Project.
Career: Qualified in 1978. Entire career spent at *Bindman & Partners*. Partner since 1981.

Personal: Born April 1953. Graduate in Law of Cambridge University and in European Law of Université Libre de Bruxelles.

HOPKINS, Carl W.V.

Lawrence Graham, London (0171) 395 4661
E-mail: 180845@msn.com and carl.hopkins@lawgram.com Partner in Public Law and Urban Regeneration.
Specialisation: Principal area of practice is public law including urban regeneration, advising local authorities city challenge projects and , formerly, development corporations on a wide range of subjects including legal consultancy, strategy, compulsory purchase, planning and litigation.
Prof. Memberships: British Urban Regeneration Association (Director); London Chamber of Commerce and Industry Policy Committee; Vision for London Executive Committee; Member London Planning Advisory Committee's London Office Trends Panel; Member RICS, Joseph Rowntree Foundation Experts Panel supervising research on private sector finance for urban regeneration. Honorary member Local Government Solicitors Group; formerly on 4 PPPPs (local Government) panel of specialist legal advisers on the private finance initiative; member of the Council of the Town and Country Planning Association; former Chairman of the CBI London Regional Council Strategy Group which prepared a business plan for London entitled "Succeeding Tomorrow" and, on behalf of the CBI, served on the Board of London Pride. Elected to the CBI London Regional Council 1989-1995; Honorary Adviser to the Civic Trust and member of the Executive Committee, Member Reform Club and Wales in London.
Career: Solicitor and administrator with Kent County Council, 1971-81. One year on secondment as acting Principal in the Department of the Environment with responsibilities including policy and administration of 5 New Towns and the Commission for New Towns 1979-80. Solicitor and Secretary to the Board of London Docklands Development Corporation 1981-87. Joined *Nabarro Nathanson* as a Partner in 1987-97, joined *Lawrence Graham* as Partner 1997.
Personal: Born 18th August 1945. Attended Haverfordwest and Milford Haven Grammar Schools 1956-63. Lives in Central London.

HULL, John

Wilde Sapte, London (0171) 246 7000
See under Intellectual Property, p. 480

ILEY, Malcolm

Nabarro Nathanson, London (0171) 493 9933
Partner specialising in public sector and local government. Head of Nabarro Nathanson's Public Sector Team
Specialisation: Main practice area is public law relating to local government, government departments and public sector powers generally. Experience in local authority outsourcings, asset transfer, regeneration, compulsory purchase, planning, education, competition and PFI, including the consideration of wider European involvement. Currently advising on one of the first "best value" partnership joint ventures. Clients have included London boroughs, district and county

councils, government departments, local authority related companies, higher and further education, LAWDAC, and urban development corporations. Currently involved in research concerning the proposed regional development agencies. Media advisor and broadcaster on public sector legal issues. Regular contributor to local government and regional press.
Career: Qualified in 1976. Began career in the private sector, transferred to local government and later became a senior lawyer with Leeds City Council. Appointed City Solicitor and Deputy Chief Executive for Plymouth City Council. Held other senior posts in Lancashire, Sussex and Norfolk. Joined *Nabarro Nathanson* in 1997 as a Partner.
Personal: Born 12 April 1950. College Governor. F.E. Governor, company director, director of environmental trust and Business in the Community.

KRAMER, Martin

Theodore Goddard, London (0171) 606 8855
Specialisation: Acts for both applicants and respondents. Has acted for newspaper publishers, pharmaceutical, biotechnology and television companies, pressure groups and a foreign government challenging decisions of local authorities, Secretaries of State, the Controller of the Patent Office, the Independent Television Commission and the Inland Revenue. Regulatory clients include advertising, sporting and educational bodies.
Prof. Memberships: Law Society.
Career: Main areas of practice are administrative and public law and media-related litigation. Qualified 1969. Partner 1978.

LESLIE, Jonathan

Travers Smith Braithwaite, London (0171) 248 9133 or 295 3000
Specialisation: Practice includes most areas of commercial litigation and arbitration, particularly for financial institutions, corporations and professional advisers; and judicial review in commercial cases.
Prof. Memberships: Fellow Chartered Institue of Arbitrators, The City of London Solicitors' Company.
Career: Qualified 1978. Partner, *Travers Smith Braithwaite*, 1984.
Personal: Educated Highgate School; Magdalen College, Oxford.

LEVETT, Robin

Anthony Gold, Lerman & Muirhead, London (0171) 940 4000
Partner in Property and Public Law Litigation Department.
Specialisation: Main.area of practice landlord and tenant and other property litigation; in particular leasehold residents associations work and disrepair and illegal eviction. Public law work includes judicial review usually housing based, with some education. Also deals with property related professional negligence claims.
Career: Qualified in 1983 and became partner in 1986; entire career with *Anthony Gold Lerman and Muirhead*.
Personal: Born 10 July 1958. Educated at Kings's School Rochester 1969-76, King's College, London 1977-80, and College of Law.

Leisure interests include IT, Fencing (late SE Region team captain), music and travel. Rotarian. Lives in Beckenham.

LIDBETTER, Andrew

Herbert Smith, London (0171) 374 8000
Specialisation: Specialist in public and administrative law and other contentious regulatory matters, particularly judicial review, statutory appeals, DTI investigations, other inquiries, disciplinary proceedings, local government and environmental cases. Also handles general commercial litigation. Clients include both applicants and regulators. Member of the advisory board of "JR" (Judicial Review) and frequently writes on public law.
Prof. Memberships: Administrative Law Bar Association.
Career: Qualified 1990.
Personal: Educated at Worcester College, Oxford (First class law degree and BCL).

MACKINTOSH, Nicola

T.V. Edwards, London (0171) 791 1050
Specialisation: Expert in Judicial Review proceedings relating to all aspects of Community Care, Health, Mental Health Law. Hospital and Day Centre closure cases undertaken on a regular basis. Co-ordinator of Community Care Practitioners' Group, and co-author of "Community Care Assessments" (second Edition, Pub. FT Law & Tax). Member of Editorial Board of Community Care Law Reports. Regular training sessions undertaken for health/ social care professionals and voluntary organisations. Major recent cases include the first case under the Carers (Recognition and Services) Act 1995 (Ex Parte Whittingham), prevention of closure of the "Beckford Centre" in Warminster, Wiltshire (Ex Parte Beck and Others), consultation cases involving the closure of residential care homes and withdrawal of health services (various).

MCDERMOTT, Jennifer

Lovell White Durrant, London (0171) 236 0066
Specialisation: Commercial litigation with specialisation in administrative law and media litigation, particularly including defamation, privacy, confidentiality and broadcasting regulatory matters. Extensive expertise in commercial judicial review having been involved in a number of high profile applications against and in conjunction with a wide variety of regulatory authorities. On the editorial board of Communications Law; contributes to publications such as the Press Gazette and PLC and speaks at conferences on both judicial review and media law.
Prof. Memberships: Member of the Media Society, the Royal Television Society, JUSTICE's public and administrative law panel and the Law Society.
Career: Qualified 1981 with *Lovell White & King*; partner of *Lovell White Durrant* 1989.

MITCHARD, Paul

Simmons & Simmons, London (0171) 628 2020
See under Litigation (Commercial): 200+ Solicitors, p. 520

RABINOWICZ, Jack

Teacher Stern Selby, London (0171) 242 3191
See under Education, p. 287

RUEBAIN, David
David Levene & Co, London
(0181) 881 7777
Head of Education and Disability Law
Department.
Specialisation: The Department specialises in all aspects of education law, health law, community care law and disability discrimination. He has published and taught extensively on education and disability law and is author of the Code of Practice on Admission, Exclusion and Reinstatement Appeals for Maintained Schools in England and Wales; co-author of the 1995 Disabled Persons' (Civil Rights) Bill; consultant editor to Disability Discrimination: Advising on the Law and Practice; author of Notes on the Disability Discrimination Act; co-author of Taking Action, a guide for parents of children with Special Educational Needs; an editorial board member of Disability and Society; and co-author of the Legal Action Group's Education and the Law.
Prof. Memberships: Trustee of the Disability Discrimination Act Representation and Advice Project, a trustee of the Disability Law Service, Vice Chair of the Rights Now Campaign, a member of the Law Society's Mental Health and Disability Sub-Committee, Vice Chair of Disability Equality in Education and a member of the Advisory Board of the Disablement Policy and Law Research Unit.

SMYTH, Michael T.
Clifford Chance, London (0171) 600 1000
Partner Contentious Business.
Specialisation: Extensive experience in all kinds of commercial disputes, but main area of practice is media litigation and public law.

Clients include public bodies, newspapers, book publishers, news agencies and film companies. Heads pre-publication unit providing advice on 24-hour basis. Publishes Media Law Review jointly with Periodical Publishers Association. Involved in a number of the leading judicial review cases in recent years and handles capital casework before the Privy Council and the United National Human Rights Committee in Geneva. Writes and lectures frequently on variety of legal issues.
Prof. Memberships: Law Society, City of London Solicitors' Company, Media Society, Administrative Law Bar Association, Royal Television Society. Admitted Hong Kong and Northern Ireland.
Career: Qualified 1982. Partner 1990.
Personal: Royal Belfast Academical Institution and Clare College, Cambridge (MA).

STEIN, Richard
Leigh, Day & Co, London (0171) 650 1200
Specialisation: Practice covers administrative and public law including environmental town planning and community care matters. Acts principally for campaigning and community groups and individuals in judicial reviews of local authorities and public authorities.
Co- Author of "Planning and Environmental Law" by Longmans. Acted in 'R v. HFEA exp Diane Blood, forced caesarian re S' and Save Our Railways anti-privatisation case.
Prof. Memberships: United Kingdom Environmental Law Association and Environmental Law Foundation.
Career: Called to the Bar 1982. Admitted solicitor 1994. Joined Leigh Day & Co 1993.
Personal: Born 15th December 1954.

STEPHENS, Mark H.
Stephens Innocent, London
(0171) 353 2000
Senior Partner.
Specialisation: Main areas of practice are libel, human rights, protecting freedom of expression and media law, acting in dozens of cases widely reported in the national media.
Career: Qualified in 1982.
Personal: Born 7th April 1957.

TROTTER, John M.
Bates, Wells & Braithwaite, London
(0171) 551 7777
Partner and Head of Litigation Department since 1976.
Specialisation: Administrative Law and Judicial Review for both Applicants and Respondents. Advises in particular regulatory bodies in various fields including telecommunications and accountancy. Lectures extensively.
Personal: Born 1948.

WATSON, Peter M.
Allen & Overy, London (0171) 330 3000
Specialisation: Deals with the full range of contentious commercial work in particular aviation, professional negligence, banking and finance, commercial fraud, judicial review and trade promotion issues.
Career: Assistant solicitor Allen & Overy 1981-86, seconded to Allen & Overy Dubai office 1984-86; partner Allen & Overy 1987.
Personal: BA Oxford University 1978. Born 1956.

THE SOUTH AND WALES

Bevan Ashford (Bristol) (2ptnrs/1assoc) Particular experience advising NHS Trusts and also advise quango and private sector clients. **Clients/Work:** Advising specialist learning disability trusts re health and social care issues. R v Wiltshire HA and others ex p Beck re proposed closure and sale of former hospital in Warminster. R v North East Devon Health Authority ex p Pow re closure of Winford Hospitals.

Eversheds (Cardiff) (7ptnrs/2assocs) Described as "highly competent," and active in this area stemming from their governmental work. *Eric Evans* co-ordinates work for public sector clients across the whole firm. **Clients/Work:** Advising local authority

on vires issues in bidding for WDA site. Advising National Museum of Wales (a charity) on status in disposing of land which may be subject of compulsory purchase. Advising public authority on claims by Lord of Manor that a major development interfered with manorial rights.

Morgan Bruce (Cardiff) A professional practice. Former leader Peter Burgess has left to work in-house. *Alun Cole* does public law and JR with a commercial contract bias. **Clients/Work:** Act for University of Wales and Housing Association Ombudsman.

Edwards Geldard (Cardiff) (1ptnr/1assoc) Practice is concentrated around planning and compulsory purchase work but the team including leader *Huw Williams* also advises on public sector compliance. **Clients/Work:** Advising on power to implement a system of groundwater control as part of Barrage project. Public law aspects of transfer of SS's responsibilities for urban investment grant to WDA. Public law aspects of aid package to LG Group of Korea.

Clarke Willmott & Clarke (Taunton) **Clients/Work:** Actions against MAFF re withdrawal of grant aid for prototype alternative energy project part funded by EEC. Successful challenge to Compulsory Purchase Order re land required to construct nuclear reactor at Hinkley Point. Applica-

tions for JR of planning decisions by local authorities and Secretary of State.

Knights (Tunbridge Wells) (1ptnr) Reputation for challenging and overturning local authority hunting bans. Gained new clients over the last year who have broadened their practice. *Matthew Knight*, senior partner, handles this work. **Clients/Work:** LB Hounslow tenant: challenge to proposal by Hounslow LBC to change tenancy agreement to forbid keeping licensed firearms on premises. Challenge to MoD on behalf of interested party over plans to revoke licence to local hunt to use land.

Stephens & Scown (Exeter) (1ptnr/1asst) Do a lot of advisory work for the National Farmer's Union. Also planning-related cases. *Peter Smith*, an associate, is the specialist. **Clients/Work:** Completion of House of Lords Judicial Review case re Environmental Protection Act 1990 on successful terms.

SEE PROFILES AT END OF THIS SECTION

MIDLANDS and EAST ANGLIA

Pinsent Curtis (Birmingham) (6ptnrs/ 3assts) Their client base has slightly changed since the urban development corporations ceased to exist in March 1998. However the firm now acts for the Commission for the New Towns and NHS Trust work is also significant. *Andrew Stacey* and *Martin White* are recommended. **Clients/ Work:** Judicial Review seeking to challenge rulings of coroner at major inquest concerning death in custody. London Luton Airport – £60m concession based financing scheme. Charitable/corporate structure advice to three Midlands local authorities.

Tyndallwoods (Birmingham) (2ptnrs/ 9assts) An applicants' firm. Former leader Madeleine Rees has now left practice and they have recently been joined by a solicitor from the Public Law Project. The remaining lawyers dealing with JR work are divided between the planning/environment, immigration and housing practices. *Phil Shiner* is newly recommended. **Clients/Work:** R v

Environment Agency ex p Leam: case concerning environmental protection duties of Environment Agency. R v Bolton MBC ex p Kirkman: case concerning environmental protection duties of local authorities. Fathi Saleh Salem v Secretary of State for Home Department, concerning entitlement of asylum seekers to welfare benefits.

Browne Jacobson (Nottingham) (4ptnrs/ 16assts) Do "a lot on the defence side" representing and advising local authorities, as well as police authorities, fire authorities. Also do the enforcement work for English Nature. **Clients/Work:** Representing public liability insurers of county councils involved at Tribunal of Inquiry into Social Services in N Wales. Representing English Nature in enforcement work including 3-week arbitration hearing relating to payments to maintain nature conservation interests. Acting for Garsington Opera and Leonard Ingrams in successful JR.

Gotelee & Goldsmith (Ipswich) (1ptnr/ 2assts) The firm's Managing Partner has over 25 years' experience in local authority law, which is his main practice. **Clients/Work:** Drafting agreements on accommodation for asylum seekers for consortium of inner London boroughs. JR of planning decision by Secretary of State for the Environment leading to quashing of decision on perversity grounds.

Martineau Johnson (Birmingham) (3ptnrs/3assts) Work from within the Education and Health Department and about 90% of the work is education-related. Clients are mainly national universities and further education colleges. **Clients/Work:** Publication of Higher Education and the Law – A Guide for Managers with chapters by

Martineau Johnson partners on Judicial Review etc. Acting for one of the final bidders in the Birmingham Schools PPP Project. Acting for a University in defending application by a student regarding degree examination results.

Richard Buxton (Cambridge) Sole practitioner *Richard Buxton* is an environmental specialist who has expertise in planning and environmental judicial review as well as in bringing cases against the local government ombudsman. He is "quite an authority." **Clients/ Work:** Judicially reviewing Cambridge City Council's administration of its trishaw licensing scheme. Two cases of JR of the Ombudsman; ex parte Turpin and ex parte Smith.

Freeth Cartwright Hunt Dickins (Nottingham) (1ptnr/2assts) Have gained a reputation for acting for applicants in education and personal injury matters, although they have handled no judicial review work in the last 12 months. *Richard Beverley* has a strong reputation. **Clients/Work:** Previously handled high profile judicial reviews against the Legal Aid Board in relation to flourosis and tobacco-related disease.

The NORTH

Eversheds (Leeds, Manchester) (3ptnrs/ 11assts) Main public sector client base is local government. Are still "a long way ahead for local authorities work; no one can dispute they have a strong practice." This depends to a large extent on the reputation and experience of leader *Stephen Cirell* who is himself ex-local

authority. **Clients/Work:** Developing partnership initiatives for public sector in fields of outsourcing, joint ventures and development.

Pinsent Curtis (Leeds) (10ptnrs/4assocs) Act for a range of public sector clients from number of government departments and NHS Trusts. **Clients/Work:** Department for Education and Employment "Welfare to Work" programme – drafting contract for rollout nationally. Advice on a wide range of public law matters to NHS Supplies Authority. Continuing advice to Trustees on Royal Armouries Project to Trustees.

Oxley & Coward (Rotherham) (1ptnr) The firm is "well-known for its health sector clients," and its judicial review experience is in that particular area.

Wansbroughs Willey Hargrave (Sheffield) (3ptnrs) Predominantly health sector related work. Commonly acting in JRs on issues such as care in the community, the closure of nursing homes and consent to treatment. **Clients/Work:** High profile Health and Safety investigations/ prosecutions. Successfully fought several limitation arguments. Appeal of a brain damage settlement where the plaintiff died days after the award.

SCOTLAND

Simpson & Marwick WS (Edinburgh) (1ptnr) A "highly regarded firm doing mainly court work for respondents." The firm has previously maintained the highest reputation on the basis of the amount of housing and licensing work done as agents for Glasgow City Council. However the council is now using Edinburgh City Council as agents for this work. It remains to be seen how much work the firm will have from remaining clients such as South and North Lanarkshire District Councils. *Catherine Shaw* does the work. **Clients/Work:** Housing JRs against Housing Benefit Review Board. Disputes with planners involving local authorities.

Burness (Edinburgh) (6ptnrs/5assts) Act for respondents. *Bruce Logan* who is the firm's court partner does this work.

Erskine MacAskill & Co (Edinburgh) (1ptnr/1asst) Acting as agents for law centres and West Coast solicitors. Most work is housing related or social security work, with immigration and mental health work also significant. **Clients/Work:** Kenneth Dowds: fatal accident inquiry into death in police custody. Gerald Rae: successful damages action against Strathclyde Police. Rena Mulvey: House of Lords decision on whether SS for Social Security can recover overpayment of benefit from sequestrated estate.

Shepherd & Wedderburn WS (Edinburgh) (1ptnr) Acts in an advisory capacity and in judicial review work. *Ian Macleod* is highly regarded as a court person.

Brodies (Edinburgh) (1ptnr) Have a newly-established Administrative Law and Judicial Review Group working alongside Local Authority Support Group. *William Holligan* is the specialist partner. **Clients/Work:** Acting for councils in contentious aspects of building and contractual matters.

Advising on vires of local authority schemes including transfer of CCTV operations to company set up for that purpose. Acting in judicial review cases on behalf of local authorities.

Henderson Boyd Jackson (Edinburgh) Newly recommended for work related to their immigration practice.

Lindsays WS (Edinburgh) (1ptnr/1asst) Recommended for their immigration practice. **Clients/Work:** Involved in handling judicial review petitions in Edinburgh Court of Session as agents for law firms throughout Scotland.

McGrigor Donald (Glasgow) (2ptnrs/ 2assts) **Clients/Work:** Dumfries and Galloway Council – public law advice on externalisation of homes for the elderly. East Ayrshire Council – new housing partnerships.

NORTHERN IRELAND

Cleaver Fulton & Rankin (Belfast) (1ptnr/ 1asst) Known for their judicial review work in the fields of planning and education. They act for a mixture of clients including environmental campaign groups, retail and energy clients. *Neil Faris* spends some 25% of his time on this kind of work. **Clients/Work:** Supermarket and advisory work.

Madden & Finucane (Belfast) (3ptnrs) Act for applicants in civil liberties cases against the police, the DPP and the prison service on issues arising for the criminal defence client base of the firm. Often called upon to advise their British equivalents. **Clients/ Work:** Cases against the Security Agency and the Northern Ireland Housing Executive.

LEADERS' PROFILES · REGIONS

BEVERLEY, Richard
Freeth Cartwright Hunt Dickins, Nottingham
(0115) 936 9369
See under Product Liability, p. 661

BUXTON, Richard
Richard Buxton, Cambridge (01223) 328933
See under Environmental Law, p. 349

CIRELL, Stephen
Eversheds, Leeds (0113) 243 0391
See under Local Government, p. 557

COLE, Alun
Morgan Bruce, Cardiff (01222) 385385
Partner in Public Law and Commercial Unit.
Specialisation: Principal area of practice is public law and commercial work for public bodies. Advises a wide range of public bodies on the scope of their powers and on the effective use of those powers. Undertakes major commercial work on their behalf (including PFI transactions, privatisations, contracting out and joint ventures) and advises on the implications/ opportunities presented by EU law. Undertakes corresponding transactional work for the private sector. Also deals with mainstream commercial work, with an emphasis on transactions with an international element. Clients in the public sector include health authorities, NHS Trusts, universities and FEC's, development agencies, executive agencies of government departments, local authorities, housing associations and a number of "quangos". Regular speaker at conferences and seminars.
Prof. Memberships: Law Society, Welsh Centre for International Affairs.
Career: Qualified in 1977. Senior Principal Legal Assistant at the Home Office 1977-85, then at the Welsh Office 1985-88. Joined *Morgan Bruce* in 1988.
Personal: Born 9th June 1951. Educated at the London School of Economics 1969-73 (LL.B and LL.M). Spare time activities include voluntary work, outdoor pursuits, sport and politics. Lives in Pontsticill, Mid Glamorgan.

EVANS, Eric
Eversheds, Cardiff (01222) 471147
See under Planning, p. 653

FARIS, Neil C.
Cleaver Fulton & Rankin, Belfast
(01232) 243141
Specialisation: Commercial Property with special emphasis on Environmental Law. Practice also covers issues of Administrative and Public Law and European Union/Competition Law with special reference to Northern Ireland.
Prof. Memberships: Member: UKELA, IAEL, Competition Working Party.
Career: Qualified in 1977 and Partner and Head Consultancy Department.
Personal: Born 1950, educated in Belfast and at Trinity College Dublin and University of Cambridge.

HOLLIGAN, William
Brodies WS, Edinburgh (0131) 228 3777
Specialisation: Partner in the litigation
department dealing mainly with commercial and
administrative law matters. Wide experience of
both having been involved in several judicial
review matters recently involving councils and
central government, and also European
administrative law. Contributor to Scots Law
Times on litigation matters. Convened a Law
Society course on the subject of Judicial Review
this year. Member of the Committee of the Law
Society dealing with the Scotland Bill. Part time
lecturer at Edinburgh University on civil court
practice. Solicitor Advocate. Qualified to
practice in South Australia.
Prof. Memberships: Writer to the Signet, Law
Society of Scotland.
Career: Education: University of Edinburgh
(LLB); Adelaide (LLM). Qualified 1981; Assistant
Solicitor *Brodies* 1981-85; Assistant Solicitor
and Partner *Finlaysons*, Adelaide, Australia
1985-91; Partner *Brodies* since 1992; Admitted
to practice South Australia.
Personal: Married, lives in Edinburgh.

KNIGHT, Matthew
Knights, Tunbridge Wells (01892) 537311
Senior Partner.
Specialisation: Main area of practice is judicial
review. Also handles defamation, crime,
trespass, commercial litigation, EU competition
law and advising on drafting of legislation.
Acted in Sawrij & Swalesmoor Mink Farm Ltd v.
Lynx & Others; in R v. Somerset County Council
ex parte Fewings, Leyland & Down and in British
Field Sports Society as Commissioners of HM
Customs & Excise . Author of various articles.
Prof. Memberships: Law Society.
Career: Qualified in 1982 after joining *Farrer &
Co.* in 1980. Worked at *Sinclair Roche &
Temperley* 1982-84, then at *Cripps Harries Hall*
1984-94, from 1986 as a Partner. Established
Knights in 1994.
Personal: Born 2nd April 1957. Attended
Eltham College 1970-76, Newcastle University
1976-79 and College of Law 1979-80. Leisure
interests include hunting, shooting and sailing.
Lives in London.

LOGAN, Bruce
Burness, Edinburgh (0131) 473 6000
Specialisation: Extensive experience in high
value commercial litigation and arbitration,
including Judicial Review. Construction and oil
industry disputes. Defamation. Represents

public bodies and newspaper and publishing
interests.

MACLEOD, D. Ian K.
Shepherd & Wedderburn WS, Edinburgh
(0131) 228 9900
See under Litigation (Commercial): 200+
Solicitors, p. 534

SHAW, Catherine
Simpson & Marwick WS, Edinburgh
(0131) 557 1545

SHINER, Phil
Tyndallwoods, Birmingham (0121) 243 3105
See under Environmental Law, p. 349

SMITH, Peter
Stephens & Scown, Exeter (01392) 210700
Specialisation: Agricultural litigation (including
Judicial Review applications for the NFU); C.T.T.
under Environmental Protection Act 1990.
Career: Five years with *Stephens & Scown* -
Exeter. Now a partner.

STACEY, Andrew J.
Pinsent Curtis, Birmingham (0121) 200 1050
Partner Litigation Department.
Specialisation: Judicial review. Specialises in
all aspects of local government related law with
emphasis on planning, highways, compulsory
purchase, environment and consumer
protection.
Career: 1972 Articled Dorset County Council.
Qualified 1974. 1974 Solicitor at Cheshire
County Council. 1977 Assistant County
Secretary Hertfordshire County Council.1982
Solicitor *Eager & Sons*, Horsham, 1984 Partner
Thomas Eggar & Son, Horsham. 1987 Solicitor
Pinsent & Co. (Birmingham). Partner in 1990.
Personal: Born 1950. Educated Sir Joseph
Williamsons Mathematical School, Rochester,
Kent and Bristol University (LLB). Interests
include sport, music, theatre.

WHITE, Martin
Pinsent Curtis, Birmingham (0121) 200 1050
Partner in Property Department. Head of
Planning and Environment. Member of Major
Projects Unit.
Specialisation: Handles planning and related
areas including environmental issues, with
emphasis on planning appeal work,
development plans, issues of planning gain,
Section 106 agreements and waste matters.
Has acted in appeals relating to major inward

investment, airports and business parks, for
local Planning Authorities and private sector
clients. Also handles local government and
public law generally. Involved generally in
advice given to local authorities. Involved with
substantial PFI projects. Author of articles,
speaker at conferences and seminars on
planning gain and environmental issues.
Prof. Memberships: Law Society (Member of
Planning Panel), Legal Associate of Royal Town
Planning Institute.
Career: Qualified in 1979. Articled at Solihull
Council 1977-79. Joined *Pinsent & Co.* in 1981.
Partner in 1987.
Personal: Born 1953. Attended Cambridge
University 1972-76; Newcastle Polytechnic
1976-77. Interests include drama and music.

WILLIAMS, Huw
Edwards Geldard, Cardiff (01222) 238239
Partner, Public Law.
Specialisation: Principal area of practice
encompasses public, planning and
environmental law. Has worked extensively
since 1987 on major urban renewal projects for
the Welsh Development Agency, Cardiff Bay
Development Corporation and local authorities,
including numerous compulsory purchase
orders, Parliamentary procedures relating to the
Cardiff Bay Barrage project and joint ventures.
Advice to both public and private interests on
planning law and related matters including
highways and utilities. Environmental
experience includes cases relating to water
pollution and contaminated land. Retained on a
number of Millennium projects including Wales
Millennium Centre and National Botanic Garden
of Wales. Other public bodies advised include
Cardiff University, National Library of Wales and
the Arts Council of Wales. Currently preparing
advice for clients on the inauguration of the
National Assembly for Wales.
Prof. Memberships: Law Society.
Career: Qualified 1978. Assistant Solicitor, Mid
Glamorgan County Council 1978-80, Senior
Assistant Solicitor 1980-84 and Principal
Assistant Solicitor (Environmental Services)
1984-87. Joined *Edwards Geldard* in 1987 and
became Partner in charge of Public Law in
1988.
Personal: Born 4th January 1954. Attended
Llanelli Grammar School 1965-72, then Jesus
College, Oxford 1972-75 (MA). Chairman, South
East Wales branch, The Oxford Society;
Member of the Advisory Committee, Centre for
Professional Legal Studies, Cardiff University;
Member of the Regional Committee of
Fairbridge. Leisure pursuits include skiing,
scuba diving, art history and architecture.

ADVERTISING AND MARKETING

See also Intellectual Property; Media & Entertainment; Sports Law

RESEARCH: Advertising and Marketing is such a small specialised area that our team were able to interview nearly all the practitioners active in the field. This was supplemented by interviews with in-house lawyers at advertising agencies and key individuals in advertising associations.

In compiling the tables, we considered all the information available to us, paying particular regard to the market research carried out by our team of ten qualified lawyers. (The researchers' details are set out on page three.) The rankings, therefore, reflect the opinion of the marketplace as revealed by systematic and objective research: see page four. (Our research is audited every year by the British Market Research Bureau.)

OVERVIEW: The work in this sector falls into two categories. 'Pure' advertising law revolves around copy clearance for advertising, marketing, PR and other media clients. General advertising law is advice to the same clients on all aspects of their corporate, employment and litigation affairs. Firms act for agencies or advertisers or both.

There is a major change at the top of the tables, with the star advertising lawyer, Stephen Groom, leaving Lewis Silkin and joining Osborne Clarke. This elevates Osborne Clarke to the second band of firms. Lewis Silkin remain in the top band for this year because they retain the experience of senior partner, Roger Alexander. There has been some movement in the lower bands, with Cameron McKenna, Edge & Ellison and Lawrence Graham joining Field Fisher Waterhouse in the top band of highly regarded firms.

Outside London, Mark Hill has moved from Garretts to Dibb Lupton Alsop in Leeds. Dibbs replaces Garretts in the tables as a result. The other three firms recommended offer more limited advertising expertise.

LEADING FIRMS · LONDON
- LEWIS SILKIN
- MACFARLANES
- OSBORNE CLARKE
- THE SIMKINS PARTNERSHIP

HIGHLY REGARDED FIRMS
- Cameron McKenna
- Edge & Ellison
- Field Fisher Waterhouse
- Lawrence Graham

- Beachcroft Stanleys
- Lovell White Durrant
- Manches & Co
- Theodore Goddard

- Clifford Chance
- Denton Hall
- Harbottle & Lewis
- Olswang
- Townleys

LONDON

Lewis Silkin (8ptnrs/9assts in the Marketing Services Law Group) Felt by some to be the "pre-eminent firm," particularly on "pure advertising" law. "They combine expertise with forceful marketing tactics" and have "knowledge across the whole advertising spectrum." However the departure of Stephen Groom to Osborne Clarke will be a blow to the firm and it remains to be seen whether they have the same profile next year without him. The "likeable" *Roger Alexander* is seen as more of a corporate lawyer, but "important in terms of client relationships." **Clients/Work:** Acted for Christine Walker in her high profile departure from Zenith and her setting up of a media buying operation with M&C Saatchi. Continue to act for Abbott Mead Vickers, in particular on a number of major acquisitions. Advised on the reorganisation of GGT following its acquisition of the BDDP group.

Macfarlanes (5ptnrs/9assts in the Advertising & Marketing Group) Have cornered the market with Lewis Silkin. "Particularly strong on the corporate side, but with a good across-the-board practice and lots of activity." *William King* ("impressive," "knowledgeable") and *Jeremy Courtenay-Stamp* ("commercial, sensible") are at the top of the field. **Clients/Work:** Advised KFC and Pizza Hut on their recent campaigns, including performers' contracts. Other clients include Pepsi, Walkers Crisps and Wrigleys and agencies such as Bates Dorland and Saatchi & Saatchi.

Osborne Clarke (4 ptnrs (two 100%, two 50%), 3assts in the corporate dept and 2 ptnrs (50%), 1 asst (100%) in the IP dept work in the advertising and marketing sector) Move dramatically up the tables due to the acquisition of the "bright and creative" *Stephen Groom* who "stands out at the top". Continually described as "innovative and proactive with a tremendous knowledge

base", he is "always looking at things from an advertising client's point of view". His arrival should consolidate the already solid practice developed by the "unassuming but authoritative" *Timothy Birt*. He has a corporate finance background and "a good grip on the sector." **Clients/Work:** Represented BBH in their merger with Leo Burnett. Acted for the management of Omnicom in their acquisition of the remaining MGM shares. Acted in the sale of Buchanan Communications to the WPP Group plc.

The Simkins Partnership (4ptnrs/2assts) All-round entertainment practice with two well-known advertising specialists: *Charles Swan* ("well-known," "stands out–but perhaps leaving more day to day work to his team") and *Vanessa Hall-Smith* ("increasingly impressive," "good depth of knowledge"). **Clients/Work:** Acted for Direct Line Financial Services Ltd in its successful application for an injunction against the ASA to prevent publication of an adjudication concerning a Direct Line ad.

Other clients include J Walter Thompson, BMP DDP, Bartle Bogle Hegarty and the IPA.

Cameron McKenna (6ptnrs/5assts – p/t) A solid team with expertise across the sector. Particular specialism in the advertising of medicinal and healthcare products. **Clients/Work:** Representing Procter & Gamble in its High Court action against Merck, Sharp and Dohme in which each party claimed the other was in breach of the industry code of practice. Acted on behalf of Mellors Reay & Partners to contract a well-known personality to appear in a television advertising campaign.

Edge & Ellison (3ptnrs/3assts handle general contracts and clearance; 2ptnrs/4assts handle M&A work in the advertising sector). **Clients/Work:** Act for WPP Group plc including agencies Ogilvy & Mather and J Walter Thompson. Signed up David Duchovny (X-files) to appear in Ford advertising and the Fat Slags (Viz) to appear in Lucozade advertising.

Field Fisher Waterhouse (1ptnr/2assts in the Advertising & Marketing Law Group). Richard Bagehot has retired but remains a consultant to the firm. *Hayley Stallard* ("charming," "good all-rounder") now heads the group and has moved up in our tables. **Clients/Work:** Acting for Avnet Inc (US company) in the leading "Webvertising" case with implications for the way the Internet is used to advertise products and services. Acting for the Music Gallery in its High Court Proceedings against Direct Line Insurance and the agency TBWA for using the Direct Line jingle in its advertising. Clients also include Kiss FM Radio and BBL Marketing Communications Ltd.

Lawrence Graham (7ptnrs/8assts undertake advertising and marketing work within the company and commercial department) *Andrew Dobson* ("old school style," "knows his stuff") has a high profile. **Clients/Work:** Advising on the sponsorship by British Telecom of the new Cardiff Arms Park Millennium Sports Stadium. Advising the direct selling industry on the impact of the Trading Schemes Regulations and two new Codes of Conduct. Other clients include

Option One, Black Cat and the Financial Times.

Beachcroft Stanleys (7ptnrs/7assts in the Advertising & Marketing Law Group) **Clients/Work:** Acting for DMB&B in national and European-wide campaigns for Texaco and Littlewoods Pools. Advising The Peoples Bank in its advertising and direct marketing campaign to capture a market share from High Street banks.

Lovell White Durrant (2ptnrs/6assts handle advertising and marketing – including internet, pan-European and cross brand campaigns) *Peter Watts* has worked in the sector for many years and has particularly focused on M&A work in the last 12 months. **Clients/Work:** Advised Interpublic on its acquisition of Ludgate Group Ltd, Complete Medical Group Ltd and Davis Baron Ltd. Negotiated contracts for the "Gold Blend couple." Advise Mars on their advertising and sponsorship.

Manches & Co ("Manches Media" consists of 5 ptnrs including *Ian Yonge* and 7assts) **Clients/Work:** Agency clients include Ammerati Puri Lintas, WWAV and Bates Dorland. Advertisers include Compaq and Woolwich plc.

Theodore Goddard (5ptnrs/6assts undertake advertising work in conjunction with other areas of practice) Assistant *Rafi Azim-Khan* ("hard worker," "clearly focusing on advertising in a big way,") has the highest profile. **Clients/Work:** Advice to two Hollywood companies on their UK sales promotion sponsorship deals. Copy clearance work for one of the world's largest brands. Advertising and promotion deal for the perfume of a leading opera singer.

Clifford Chance (5ptnrs and 10-15assts – none full-time) *Richard Thomas* ("bright and able") heads the public policy unit and co-ordinates the marketing & advertising group which acts primarily for advertisers rather than agencies. **Clients/Work:** Advised a top ITV advertiser when a competitor challenged the content of its television campaign. Advising a publishing company on copyright infringement issues over a comparative advertising campaign on TV.

Other clients include AT&T and the BBC.

Denton Hall (3ptnrs/2assts) Advertising work is combined with the general entertainment and sports practices. **Clients/Work:** Advising FA Premier League on renewal of sponsorship of The FA Carling Premiership for £36 million. Negotiating contracts with Cricket World Cup sponsors. Act for Dewe Rogerson Group Ltd.

Harbottle & Lewis (12 fee-earners: none full-time) Like Denton Hall, combine advertising with their strong entertainment practice. **Clients/Work:** Advice to 19 Management Group in relation to Spice Girls advertising and merchandising deals. Advised the shareholders of HHCL on the acquisition of HHCL by Chime Communications. Advised an internet service provider on co-branding deals on the internet.

Olswang (6ptnrs/6assts – none full-time) *Jonathan Goldstein* is known as a corporate lawyer with one particularly high profile advertising client. **Clients/Work:** Acted for M&C Saatchi in finalising the joint venture arrangements with Christine Walker (ex-Chief Executive of Zenith Media). Also acting for Walker Media.

Townleys Premier sports law practice with related sponsorship and personality marketing experience.

THE REGIONS

Dibb Lupton Alsop (Leeds) (1 ptnr) *Mark Hill* has recently moved from Garretts to

Dibbs, taking the advertising expertise with him. He works within the communications and technology department. **Clients/Work:** Advising major publisher on poster campaign to be run on key sites including London Underground. Clearance for European release of rock video. Review of sales promotion strategies for a leading publisher.

Edge & Ellison (Leicester) (1ptnr/1asst) **Clients/Work:** Sales promotion work and food industry clients.

Eversheds (Birmingham) (1ptnr/1asst (part-time)) **Clients/Work:** Advising Carlsberg-Tetley on the advertising aspects

of a concert at Wembley and its sponsorship of the England cricket team in the 1997 Ashes. Other clients include Victoria Wine and Page & Moy.

Lester Aldridge (Bournemouth) (1 ptnr, 1 asst) **Clients/Work:** Advise mainly on the advertising provisions under the Consumer Credit Act 1974. Advised the AA on direct marketing. Act for Bank of Ireland.

ALEXANDER, Roger
Lewis Silkin, London (0171) 227 8000
Partner in Corporate Department.
Specialisation: Advising companies in the
Marketing Services Industry in relation to
corporate finance, mergers, acquisitions,
flotations and high level employment issues
including share incentivisation schemes and
corporate governance. Acts for a raft of
companies in the sector, both public and
private, including some of the largest agency
groups; also advises industry bodies. Lectures
on issues and trends in the industry.
Prof. Memberships: Law Society, Solicitors
European Group, Society of Share Scheme
Practitioners.
Career: Qualified 1965. Partner at *Lewis Silkin*
1965. Head of Marketing Services Law Group
1990-92. Lead Partner since 1989.

AZIM-KHAN, Rafi
Theodore Goddard, London
(0171) 606 8855
Solicitor and member of *Theodore Goddard*'s
Media and Communications Group.
Specialisation: Specialises in advertising,
entertainment, intellectual property, internet and
commercial law. Has considerable experience
of advising both advertisers and agencies on
"clearance" of materials and IP, consumer,
media and marketing law and regulation both
above and below the line. Has advised on a
wide range of sales promotions, prize
competitions, lotteries, newspaper and
television promotions, related formats and
terms and conditions. Also has particular
experience of negotiating and drafting a wide
range of marketing, media, music, sports
sponsorship, performer, merchandising,
licensing and various other commercial
agreements. Lectures and writes regularly on
copyright, intellectual property, media,
marketing and various other related topics. Is
the firm's representative to the IPA's Advertising
Law Group.
Career: Qualified 1993. *Lewis Silkin*
1993-1995, *Cameron McKenna* 1995-1997,
when joined *Theodore Goddard*.
Personal: Born 14 April 1969. Educated at
Cranbrook College and at Queen Mary College,
University of London 1987 to 1990 (LLB Hons.
Studied IP at IP Law Unit). Keen sportsman and
enjoys travel, music and motor racing. Resides
London.

BIRT, Timothy D.
Osborne Clarke, London (0171) 634 1622
Partner in Corporate Department.
Specialisation: Corporate, with a bias towards
advising clients in marketing services, media
and retail sectors. Has been particularly active
in the new issues market over the last few
years. Although responsible for managing a
team of specialist solicitors, remains very
actively involved in transactions. Edits
Butterworths company law service, contributing
the section on structuring joint ventures and
owner-managed business.
Prof. Memberships: Law Society.
Career: Qualified in 1985. With *D.J. Freeman*
1983-87. Joined *Osborne Clarke* in 1987 and
became a Partner in 1988.

COURTENAY-STAMP, D. Jeremy
Macfarlanes, London (0171) 831 9222
Partner in Company, Commercial and Banking
Department.
Specialisation: Specialises in advertising and
marketing. Acting for 5 of the top 20 advertising
agencies, as well as a number of other above,
below and through the line agencies. Has
written articles and lectured extensively on this
subject. Also advises on all aspects of
commercial and intellectual property.
Prof. Memberships: City of London Law
Society. Member of Commercial Law sub-
committee.
Career: Qualified in 1986 while with
Macfarlanes. Became a Partner in 1992.

DOBSON, Andrew Charles
Lawrence Graham, London (0171) 379 0000
Partner in Litigation Department.
Specialisation: Specialises in all types of
commercial dispute resolution, including brand
protection and intellectual property. Advises the
Estate of Diana, Princess of Wales in such
matters. Also deals with commercial litigation,
arbitration and alternative dispute resolution
involving international cross border disputes of
all types. Was involved in the Court of Appeal
cases of 'New Bullas Trading (Fixed charge on
book debts), Credit Suisse v L.B'. 'Waltham
Forest' (enforceability of Local Authority
guarantee) and is taking the case of' Re Park
Air Services' to the House of Lords. (Disclaimer
of a lease).
Career: With *Macfarlanes* 1978-86. Qualified in
1980. Partner at *Knapp Fisher* 1986-87. Joined
Lawrence Graham as a Partner in 1987.
Personal: Born 20th February 1956. Educated
at Oundle School 1969-74 and St. Catharine's
College, Cambridge 1974-77. Sporting
enthusiast. Lives in Wandsworth.

GOLDSTEIN, Jonathan
Olswang, London (0171) 208 8888
Partner in Corporate Group.
Specialisation: Principal area of practice is
corporate finance, including mergers and
acquisitions and banking. Recent transactions
include flotations of Minerva plc and
Technoplast Industries Limited, work on the
Ginger acquisition of Virgin Radio and disposal
by Time-Warner of shareholding in Classic FM.
Clients in sector include advertising agencies,
advertisers, direct marketing agencies and
production companies. Acted for the three
amigos in high profile Saatchi litigation and
continues to act for M & C Saatchi Limited.
Career: Qualified in 1990. With *S.J. Berwin* &
Co 1990-1992. Joined *Olswang* in 1992.
Partner since 1994.
Personal: Born 30th March 1966. Educated at
Ilford County High School for Boys, and the
University of Manchester (LLB (Hons)). Lives in
London.

GROOM, Stephen
Lewis Silkin, London (0171) 227 8000
Specialisation: Partner in Media and
Marketing Communications Department.
Extensive experience of advising on libel,
copyright, passing off, trade marks, design
rights, lotteries and competitions. Cases have
included Williamson Music v National Express
coaches (an important musical copyright case).

Waterlow Publishers v Rose (directory
copyright) Sterling Winthrop v Scott (malicious
falsehood). Co-author of 'Advertising Law in
Europe and North America' and frequent
articles on intellectual property and marketing
communications. Regular speaker at
conferences.
Prof. Memberships: European Advertising
Lawyers' Association, The Advertising Law
Group, Solicitors European Group, Westminster
Law Society.
Career: Qualified 1975. Worked at *Oswald
Hickson Collier* 1973-82, becoming a Partner in
1977. Moved to *Macfarlanes* in 1982, then
Lewis Silkin from 1985, becoming a Partner
there in 1986.
Personal: Born 1st February 1951. Attended
Gravesend Upper School for Boys 1961-69,
St Edmund Hall, Oxford 1969-72, and
Lancaster Gate College of Law 1972-73.

HALL-SMITH, Vanessa
The Simkins Partnership, London
(0171) 631 1050
Partner in Advertising and Marketing
Department.
Specialisation: Principal area of practice is
advertising and marketing. Work includes copy
advice on TV, print and direct marketing
campaigns, agency/ client contracts, sales
promotion, data protection and multimedia
applications. Clients include advertising
agencies, advertisers, sales promotion and
direct marketing agencies and photographers.
Also handles employment-related immigration,
with focus on entertainment and leisure
industries. Contributing Editor to 'Butterworth's
Encyclopaedia of Forms and Precedents'
(Advertising Title). Speaks regularly on
advertising and marketing at conferences and
seminars.
Career: In practice at the Bar 1987-91.
Qualified as a Solicitor in 1993. Partner with *The
Simkins Partnership* since 1996.
Personal: Educated at Exeter University,
Johannes Gutenberg Universitat, Mainz,
Germany and the Universite d'Aix/ Marseille,
France. Lives in London.

HILL, Mark
Dibb Lupton Alsop, Leeds (0345) 262728
Leeds (0113) 241 2641 Partner in Media and
Communications Group.
Specialisation: Main areas of practice are
intellectual property and marketing and
advertising. Experience covers all aspects of
marketing and advertising work including: The
drafting of contracts between clients and
agents; branding and trade marks (including
full registered trade mark prosecution service);
sales promotion and advertising clearance
(including under relevant legal controls and self
regulatory codes of practice); comparative
advertising clearance and litigation/disputes; all
related intellectual property work including
copyright, trade marks, passing off ;
reputations (including libel): Trading Standards
issues (including labelling, trade descriptions
and price indications); direct marketing, direct
mail etc; anti-counterfeiting; sponsorship;
character and personality merchandising; and
full litigation service covering all aspects of the
sector. Recent experience includes:
Undertaking a major review of sales promotion

strategies for a leading UK publishing group; advising one of the UK's top FMCG brand owners on compliance with relevant labelling legislation; advising a major UK retail chain on TV advertising campaigns; and providing legal consultancy in relation to various high profile national campaigns including contentious knocking copy and parody ads for one of the U.K's leading publishing groups. Often speaks on advertising law issues and is interviewed and quoted in the press including in the specialist marketing press.

KING, William L.

Macfarlanes, London (0171) 831 9222
Specialisation: Copyright and trade mark law, particularly for ideas based businesses. Advertising and marketing law and regulation. Exploitation of publishers' rights, and merchandising of characters. Commissioning and distribution of television programme material.
Prof. Memberships: Law Society; City of London Solicitor's Company – Master 1996-97; City of London Law Society – President 1996-97. Advertising Association Working Party on EC Green Paper on Commercial Communications – Member.
Career: Cambridge (Trinity Hall). *Macfarlanes* 1970-date.

STALLARD, Hayley

Field Fisher Waterhouse, London
(0171) 481 4841
Specialisation: Main area of practice is intellectual property with almost exclusive emphasis on advertising, marketing, sponsorship, merchandising, endorsement and lotteries. Clients incude major advertisers such as Whitbread PLC, Codemasters Software Company, Evian/Volvic, Pizza Hut and Kiss FM, leading promotional agencies and trade organisations such as ISBA. Legal consultant editor to 'Essential Facts: Sales and Marketing' and author of second edition of 'Bagehot on Sponsorship, Merchandising and Endorsement' (published by Sweet and Maxwell). Regular speaker at conferences.
Prof. Memberships: Member of the European Sponsorship Consultants Association (ESCA); the British Association of Sport and Law (BASL); the Institute of Sports Sponsorship (ISS); the IPA's Advertising Law Group; and the Executive Committee/Intellectual Property Commission of the Association Internationale des Jeunes Avocats (AIJA).
Career: Qualified at *Winckworth and*

Pemberton, 1990, becoming a partner in January 1995. Joined *Field Fisher Waterhouse* in October 1996.

SWAN, Charles

The Simkins Partnership, London
(0171) 631 1050
Partner in Advertising and Marketing Department.
Specialisation: Main area of practice is advertising law, covering copy clearance, contracts, disputes, intellectual property and general advice to advertisers, their agencies and trade associations. Other area of expertise is copyright law, especially in relation to photographers and photo libraries. Co-author of Butterworth's 'Encyclopaedia of Forms and Precedents' (Advertising title), co-author of 'The ABC of UK Photographic Copyright', contributor to the IPA's 'Some suggested Provisions for Use in Agency/ Client Agreements' and author of numerous articles in legal and trade journals. Frequent speaker at advertising, publishing and photographic trade seminars.
Career: Qualified 1983. Articled at *Woodham Smith* 1981-83 before moving to the *Speechly Bircham* litigation department. Joined *The Simkins Partnership* in 1985 and became a Partner in 1990. General Secretary of Advertising Law International.
Personal: Born 1956. Attended Cambridge University 1975-78. Leisure interests include hill walking.

THOMAS, Richard

Clifford Chance, London (0171) 600 1000
Director, Public Policy Group since 1992.
Specialisation: Chairs *Clifford Chance*'s Marketing and Advertising Group, co-ordinating advisory, transactional and regulatory work undertaken for leading brand owners across a range of practice areas – intellectual property; media, computer and communications; commercial; contentious. Particular focus on dealing with all aspects of consumer law. More generally, deals with governmental activities across Whitehall, Westminister and Brussels.
Career: Qualified 1973. 1979-86 Legal Officer and Head of Public Affairs at National Consumer Council. 1989-92 Director of Consumer Affairs at Office of Fair Trading, responsible for all OFT's regulatory and policy work relating to consumer issues, including enforcement of Misleading Advertisements Regulations.
Personal: LL.B (Southampton) 1970. Member,

Lord Chancellors' Civil Justice Review (1985-8). Currently member Banking Ombudsman Council, Oftel Convergence Panel, ITC Advisory Committee and Direct Marketing Authority. Vice-President of Institute of Trading Standards.

WATTS, Peter

Lovell White Durrant, London (0171) 236 0066
Specialisation: Partner in the Commercial and Trading law practice area whose principal areas of work are marketing, advertising, sponsorship, co-branding and electronic communications. Advises both major UK and multi-national advertisers (eg. Mars) and leading advertising and sales promotions agencies including the Interpublic group and its member agencies such as McGann Gricksen. Experience includes development of many innovative sales promotional mechanics in addition to clearance both of campaigns and copy. Has also worked on sponsorship of major international sporting events as well as a range of Internet sites used for advertising. Has recently been involved in a number of contracted co-operative projects which draw together a range of leading contributors in a specially badged package. During the last year was also particularly active in M&A work in the industry.
Career: Qualified in 1989. Articled at *Lovell White Durrant*. Became a partner in 1998.
Personal: Born 1963. Leeds University 1982-85. Leisure interests include vegetarian cookery and cricket.

YONGE, Ian

Manches & Co, London (0171) 404 4433
Partner in Commercial Department.
Specialisation: Principal area of practice is advertising and marketing law including sales promotions. Emphasis on advising on copy and contracts for above and below the line with a speciality in financial advertising. Contributes articles to specialist journals and is currently working on a book on advertising law aimed at the lay reader. Lectures on financial advertising and regularly presents in-house client seminars.
Prof. Memberships: Law Society.
Career: Joined *Rubinstein Callingham Polden & Gale* in 1967, qualified in 1971 and became a Partner in 1980.
Personal: Born 18th January 1946. Attended Ealing Grammar 1959-64. Leisure pursuits include gardening, travel and reading. Lives in Haslemere.

AGRICULTURE & BLOODSTOCK

RESEARCH: Our team carried out extensive interviews with specialist practitioners and individuals in the agricultural industry and leading regulatory organisations.

In compiling the tables, we considered all the information available to us, paying particular regard to the market research carried out by our team of ten qualified lawyers. (The researchers' details are set out on page three.)

The rankings, therefore, reflect the opinion of the marketplace as revealed by systematic and objective research: see page four. (Our research is audited every year by the British Market Research Bureau.)

OVERVIEW: The work in this area is comprised of contentious and non-contentious matters. Most firms will cover both areas as they act for long-standing clients for whatever problem may arise. Some firms concentrate on non-contentious matters like land sale and purchase, estate management and tax planning. These are likely to be the firms with many landed estates as clients. Other firms concentrate on contentious work, where for instance a landlord/tenant arrangement is in dispute.

The leading firms tend to be those with a traditional, well-established specialist agricultural department. The others include large firms where the private client department deals with agricultural matters and smaller firms in agricultural areas whose main client base is the farming and property owning communities. Five leading firms across the country (Brachers, Dickinson Dees, Roythorne & Co, Taylor Vinters and Wilsons) have formed the group Agrilaw.

LEADING FIRMS · LONDON

- FARRER & CO
- MACFARLANES
- WITHERS

HIGHLY REGARDED FIRMS

- Badhams Thompson
- Campbell Hooper
- Dawson & Co
- Payne Hicks Beach

- Forsters
- Lee & Pembertons
- May, May & Merrimans

- Alexanders
- Titmuss Sainer Dechert
- Trowers & Hamlins

LONDON

Farrer & Co (4ptnrs – 50%/2assts) An established practice with a strong traditional landed estate following. *Christopher Jessel* is a "real specialist" who is accustomed to dealing with the traditional client. Ivor Dicker, who was highly regarded, has retired. *Simon Pring* is promoted from up and coming. **Clients/Work:** Handling charities and environmental trusts work in the last year, being involved in some significant purchases.

Macfarlanes (3ptnrs – 50%/5assts – 75%) Large firm with many institutional clients. *John Moore* is "well known" in agricultural circles. *John Hornby* retains his good reputation. **Clients/Work:** Concentration on non-contentious work with clients including pension funds (such as Abbey Life, AXA Sun Life and Boots) and landed estates (estate management, tax planning, etc.). Acted in the sale of the Hurdcott and Lotherton Estates and the purchase of a large forestry estate for CERN.

Withers (2ptnrs: 1f/t. 3assts: 1f/t. 2mgrs) *Andrew Lane* is the head of the team and has a "good reputation." Over the years the firm has built up a large client base. **Clients/Work:** For farms and over a hundred landed estates. Mainly non-contentious work including sales and purchases, farm business tenancies, options. In the last year acted in the sale of the Mount Prosperous Estate, acquisition of the Pusey estate (for Coutts Ltd) and the sale of the Warter Priory Estate for over £30m.

Badhams Thompson (2ptnrs: p/t. 1asst: p/t) *John Cousins* is well respected. **Clients/Work:** NFU panel. Acts for ADAS and insurance companies. Chiefly involved in contentious work, particularly professional indemnity claims and product liability. Involved in the judicial review of the European beef ban.

Campbell Hooper (1ptnr/1asst – p/t) Small but good team headed by *Alex Cuppage*. **Clients/Work:** Handles general agricultural work for landed estates and owner-managed businesses. Routinely involved in sales and purchases, quotas, tax and estate planning.

Dawson & Co (5ptnrs/2assts – p/t) "Prominent" in agriculture. **Clients/Work:** Recently involved in milk quota litigation in the European Court of Justice. Farm purchases and a substantial dispute regarding an agricultural holding in the West Country.

Payne Hicks Beach (3ptnrs, assistance from other departments) **Clients/Work:** Act for large land owning charities, companies and estates.

Forsters (2ptnrs/2consultants – p/t) Formerly the private client department at

LEADING INDIVIDUALS · LONDON

JESSEL Christopher Farrer & Co	
MOORE John Macfarlanes	
COUSINS John Badhams Thompson	
CUPPAGE Alex Campbell Hooper	
HORNBY John Macfarlanes	
LANE Andrew Withers	
PRING Simon Farrer & Co	

SEE PROFILES AT END OF THIS SECTION

Frere Cholmeley Bischoff. **Clients/Work:** Act for 30 traditional landed estates of over 1000 acres whom they advise on sales and purchases of farm businesses, tenancy and trust issues.

Lee & Pembertons (3ptnrs/1asst) **Clients/Work:** The property and private client departments deal with agricultural work, acting in sales and purchases, tax

planning and partnerships for clients including landed estates.

May, May & Merrimans (4ptnrs – 40%/1asst – 20%) **Clients/Work:** Main clients are land owning families and individuals. Planning and sales and purchase work is undertaken.

Alexanders (1ptnr – p/t) **Clients/Work:** Handle agricultural property and any related matters.

Titmuss Sainer Dechert (1ptnr/3assts) **Clients/Work:** Handle the acquisition, management and development of agricultural land for large estates.

Trowers & Hamlins (6fee-earners) **Clients/Work:** Work handled mainly by private client dept. Landlord and tenant matters are a speciality.

LEADERS' PROFILES · LONDON

COUSINS, J.T.
Badhams Thompson, London
(0171) 242 4154
Specialisation: Is the litigation adviser to several national agricultural bodies. Specialises in claims in tort and contract arising out of sale and purchase of equipment, livestock feed, seed, fertilizers and chemicals. Also specialises in professional indemnity and personal injury cases arising out of farming activities, including equestrian and field sports. Acts for Insurance Companies and private clients.
Prof. Memberships: Law Society and Holborn Law Society.
Career: Qualified in 1975 and became a Partner in 1978. Attended Cranbrook School 1963-1968. Mercersbury Academy USA 1968-1969. Cardiff University 1969-72.

CUPPAGE, Alex
Campbell Hooper, London (0171) 222 9070
Head of Private Client Department.
Specialisation: Principal areas of practice are agricultural estate and tax planning with particular emphasis on landlord and tenant, quotas, sales and purchases, tax and estate planning for farmers and farming companies. Additional specialisation is charity law. Regular lecturer.
Prof. Memberships: Law Society, S.T.E.P., Charities Law Association and CLA (Country Landowners Association)
Career: Qualified in 1973. Partner at *Whitley Hughes and Luscombe* (then *Donne Mileham and Haddock*) from 1976 to 1992. Joined *Campbell Hooper* as a Partner in January 1993.
Personal: Born 23rd June 1949. Educated at Ampleforth College 1962-67. Leisure interests include golf and holidays. Lives in Fletching, Sussex.

HORNBY, John H.
Macfarlanes, London (0171) 831 9222
Partner in Property Department.
Specialisation: Commercial work covering the leisure industry, agricultural law, housing and

residential work. Acts for investors, private estate landlords and working farmers. Has noted on a significant number of transactions involving hotels and golf courses. Recent and current work includes negotiations with Millennium Commission for funding an z80 million development – The Renaissance of Portsmouth Harbour and a substantial flow of sales and purchases of prime landed estates and farms and advising a national firm of land agents on agricultural and housing landlord and tenant matters. Author of 'Leasehold Enfranchisement- The New Proposals Put in Context' (1993).
Prof. Memberships: Law Society.
Career: Qualified in 1980 while with *Macfarlanes*. Became a Partner in 1987.

JESSEL, Christopher.R.
Farrer & Co, London (0171) 242 2022
Partner in Estates and Private Property Team.
Specialisation: Main area of practice covers rural estates, agriculture and manors. Acts on farms, common land and rural estate work generally including development sales with trust and personal advice. Also covers charity and constitutional work, establishing and advising charities on parliamentary and administrative law. Author of The Law of the Manor 1998 and numerous articles in professional and investment magazines. Lectures extensively in London and elsewhere.
Prof. Memberships: Law Society.
Career: Joined *Farrer & Co* in 1967. Qualified in 1970. Became a Partner in 1979.
Personal: Born 16th March 1945. Attended Bryanston School 1958-63, Balliol College, Oxford 1964-67. Leisure interests include archaeology. Lives in Guildford.

LANE, Andrew
Withers, London (0171) 936 1000
Partner and Head of Property Department.
Specialisation: Practice covers all types of agricultural property work including agricultural holdings law, estate management and sales

and acquisitions of farms and estates. Also advises on tax implications of property transactions; particularly Capital Gains Tax and VAT. Clients range from private individuals through family trusts and institutions to major plcs.
Prof. Memberships: Agricultural Law Association, Royal Agricultural Society of England.
Career: Was a full-time farmer between 1978 and 1987. Joined *Withers* in 1987 qualifying in 1992 and becoming a partner in 1994. Personal: Born 22nd January 1957. Educated Malvern College 1970-1974 Christ's College Cambridge 1975-1978. Lives near Salisbury, Wiltshire.

MOORE, John E.
Macfarlanes, London (0171) 831 9222
Partner in Property Development.
Specialisation: Has acted since qualification for Institutional Investors, including Insurance Companies and Pension Funds, in connection with the investment and development of land, and agricultural law. Represents tenants as well as landlords in relation to their agricultural holdings and Public Bodies (including NHS Trusts) in relation to agricultural tenancy rights on surplus land when considering developments and PFI proposals. Lectures on agricultural law.
Career: Joined *Macfarlanes* in 1970. Qualified 1973. Partner in 1979.

PRING, Simon J.
Farrer & Co, London (0171) 242 2022
Partner in the Estates and Private Property Team.
Specialisation: All aspects of property law with an emphasis on agricultural estates, charity land holding and VAT. Assistant Solicitor to the Duchy of Lancaster.
Prof. Memberships: Holborn Law Society.
Career: Blundell's School, Devon, Robinson College, Cambridge. Joined *Farrer & Co* 1986, Partner 1995.
Personal: Born 24 March 1964. Married. Lives in London. Leisure: country pursuits and golf.

SOUTH EAST

Brachers (6ptnrs – 50%/4assts – 50%) The firm has a specialist agricultural department with a long history that has enabled them to develop their expertise. *Douglas Horner* ("driven", "good communicator") is widely respected for his "across the board grasp" of agricultural law. Joined Agrilaw in 1997. **Clients/Work:** Act for small and large farmers and estate owners, dealing with contentious and non-contentious work

of all kinds. NFU panel. Compensation litigation before the Lands Tribunal and challenging the use of satellite imagery to monitor IACS.

Thomas Eggar Church Adams (4ptnrs: two 100% agriculture, two tax planning/4assts, two 100% agriculture, two tax planning) Well established agricultural firm, particularly recognised for its non-contentious work. *Richard Kyrke* is known as a real specialist. **Clients/Work:** Acts for many landed estates including Exbury Estates and

are on the NFU panel. Work includes sale and acquisition, quotas, farm business tenancies and farm animal protection as well as tax advice and general agricultural matters.

White & Bowker (3ptnrs/2assts – p/t) A smaller firm than Brachers or Thomas Eggar Church Adams but one that is "dedicated to" and "making a considered effort in" agriculture. *John Steel* is described as a "commanding figure" and "very focused." **Clients/Work:** NFU panel. Deal with tenancy issues, rights of way, environmental issues and planning appeals. Acts for farmers and landed estates.

Cole & Cole (1ptnr/2assts) Have a good reputation. *Christopher Findley* is considered excellent on partnership and tenancy matters. **Clients/Work:** NFU panel.

Cripps Harries Hall (2ptnrs/2assts) *John Mulcare* ("thorough") is a prominent lawyer in the field and was brought in from his own firm in 1996 to bolster the department. **Clients/Work:** NFU panel. Wealthy private

landowners. Landlord/tenant and quota to animal welfare and advice to water companies.

Stanley Tee & Company (6ptnrs – 30%; 3assts – 40%) One of the major firms in the area, being recognised in East Anglia as well as the South East. The private client department deals with agricultural work. **Clients/Work:** NFU panel. Active in farm sales, trusts and tax planning.

Hallett & Co (3ptnrs/1asst – p/t) **Clients/Work:** The firm are closely tied to the local farming community. Undertake a lot of quota work, along with general agricultural matters.

Knights (2ptnrs/1asst – p/t) The firm has a growing reputation mainly due to *Matthew Knight* ("an aggressive litigator"), who is new to our lists. **Clients/Work:** NFU panel. Litigation firm, with a particular speciality in field sports. Act for the Countryside Alliance and the Tenant Farmers Association.

Penningtons (3ptnrs/3assts) Said to have an increasing presence in the market. **Clients/Work:** NFU panel. Act for landed estates and charitable and private trusts. A lot of work revolves around the estates e.g. sale and purchase, options, boundary disputes and tax planning.

Pryce & Co (1ptnr – 80%/1asst – p/t) **Clients/ Work:** Deal with many land agents, especially Adkin. Clients include individual

farms, creameries, grain co-operatives and Parish Councils. Have done a lot of tax planning and planning agreement work in the last year.

Henmans (3ptnrs/2assts) **Clients/Work:** Work in 1997 included the disposal of potentially contaminated landfill sites, the de-merger of a large agricultural partnership as well as looking into development opportunities for farmland and granting options. Act for the Royal Agricultural Benevolent Institution, Sir Francis Dashwood and some Oxford colleges.

Linnells (2ptnrs) **Clients/Work:** Farmers, mainly in Oxfordshire. Quotas, land transactions. Act for financiers involved in farm business.

Sharman & Trethewy (2ptnrs (100%, 30%),1asst – 30%) **Clients/Work:** Large farmer client base in and around Bedfordshire, which has been growing in the last year.

SOUTH EAST BLOODSTOCK

There are only a few firms in the region which handle this work. **Matthew McCloy & Partners** work for stables, trainers and jockeys' associations. *Andrew Chalk* ("very competent") is the leading individual in the area. *Matthew McCloy* is active in racing and general sports law.

Cripps Harries Hall act for the British Horse Society, British Equestrian Federa-

tion, British Equestrian Trade Association and private individuals.

SOUTH WEST

Burges Salmon (11ptnrs – 6f/t/ 36assts – f/t and p/t) Described as "the best practice in the country", the firm is nationally recognised as leading the field. *Peter Williams* heads the department and is described as "very committed." Known more for their contentious work. *Andrew Densham* specialises in agricultural holdings and has a "formidable reputation", and deserves respect for his experience. *William Neville* is known for his quota work and has been called "very bright." *James Buxton, William Batstone, Della Evans* and *Alastair Morrison* are also recommended. **Clients/Work:** NFU panel. Major clients include CWS, United Milk Producers and the National Trust (Knipe v National Trust). Dealing with more and more international and national work.

Wilsons Solicitors (4ptnrs/9assts) A strong team who fully deserve to be among the leaders. *Peter Fitzgerald* ("land management expert") does a lot of work with heritage property. *Robert Swift* ("able" and "sensible") concentrates on farm sales and purchases. **Clients/ Work:** Many landed estates. Concentrates on non-contentious work. Involved in major farm sales and purchases and tax advice in 1997. Members of Agrilaw.

Clarke Willmott & Clarke (3ptnrs, with ptnrs &assts from other depts serving farm clients) Highly rated amongst competitors and independent organisations and is elevated in the rankings due to this. The three partners are members of CLA and ALA. **Clients/ Work:** NFU panel (recent national case involving European Grant 5b), large estates and farmers in the region. Particular

expertise in quota, planning and environmental matters.

Stephens & Scown (3ptnrs – 50%, 4assts – 50%) A substantial agricultural practice known for its expertise. Some of the partners are members of the ALA. **Clients/Work:** NFU panel. Estates and farmers in Devon, Cornwall and throughout the country. Work on a range of agricultural topics. Specialise in landlord/tenant, quota, property issues and environmental matters.

Thrings & Long (3ptnrs – f/t/2ptnrs 50%, 4assts) The team is felt to have a "good spread of knowledge." *Jonathan Cheal* has a high profile and a definite style. **Clients/Work:** NFU panel. Strong links with CLA and ALA. Extensive client base of landowners and farmers. Work covers property issues, quotas, planning, tax advice, landlord/tenant. Also the niche area of employment law relating to agricultural workers.

Battens (1ptnr/1asst) **Clients/ Work:** Mainly farmers in the Somerset, Dorset and Wiltshire regions. Handles partnership disputes in particular, as well as farm sales, quotas, landlord/tenant. Is looking to set up a mediation scheme.

Bond Pearce (3ptnrs/3assts) New to the lists and appear following recommendations. **Clients/Work:** Include the Agricultural Mortgage Corporation, agricultural receivers land owners and farmers. The emphasis is more on the insolvency and banking side.

Porter Dodson (2ptnrs – 75%/6assts – p/t) **Clients/Work:** NFU panel. Handle all types of agricultural matters from the various rural offices.

Bevan Ashford (3ptnrs – 80%;2consultants – 40%;3assts – 75%) Respected by their competitors. Their "milk quota work is very good." **Clients/Work:** NFU panel. Clients include landed estates and waste disposal authorities. Deal with non-contentious and contentious work e.g. quota work, arbitration and litigation, landlord/tenant. Court of appeal shooting rights case in 1997.

Every & Phillips (3ptnrs/2assts – p/t in one of the Honiton offices, other 5 offices deal with farming clients) Referred to as "a nice solid firm." **Clients/Work:** Based in a rural area, they have many agricultural clients. Work includes quotas, inheritance issues and property transactions.

Pardoes (2ptnrs/8assts) Described as "well established with trustworthy people." **Clients/Work:** NFU panel.

Peter, Peter & Wright (4ptnrs – 2f/t, 2p/t) **Clients/Work:** Farming clients. Handle freehold transactions, tax planning and quotas.

Stones Cann & Hallett (2ptnrs – 1 f/t, 1 p/t/2assts – p/t) Stones merged with Cann & Hallett in May and it is expected that the merger will enhance the agricultural work formerly done by Stones' private client department.

Bevirs (2ptnrs – 50%/2assts – 50%) Private client firm who have farming clients as opposed to a pure agricultural team. **Clients/ Work:** NFU panel.

Beviss & Beckingsale (1ptnr in Stroud office with other offices also handling agricultural work) **Clients/Work:** Acts for tenants or landlords, large estates and a range of other clients throughout the south west. Also handles some equine work.

Harris & Harris (2ptnrs/2assts) **Clients/ Work:** Have a reasonable spread of work.

Humphries Kirk (5ptnrs – 2 land law 20%, 3 agricultural litigation 40%) **Clients/ Work:** NFU panel. Specialise in contentious work. Involved in pollution issues, environmental agency work and cruelty to animals cases. Two of the partners are working farmers and one is a member of CLA.

Osborne Clarke (4ptnrs/4assts – p/t) The team was mentioned by competitors although this is not a core area for the firm. **Clients/Work:** Land owner clients. The four partners deal with property, tax, trusts and litigation.

Slee Blackwell (2ptnrs/1asst) **Clients/ Work:** Quota work, farm business tenancies, agricultural partnerships and environmental matters.

A.E. Smith & Son (2ptnrs/1asst – p/t) **Clients/Work:** NFU panel. Litigation, criminal defences for farmers, land transfers and tax planning.

Woollcombe Beer Watts (3ptnrs at Newton Abbot office/1ptnr at Chagford office) **Clients/Work:** Handle agricultural work for the local community.

WALES

Margraves (2ptnrs – 1f/t, 1p/t) *Clive Margrave-Jones* ("established" and "experienced") is an acknowledged expert. The firm was usually the first to be mentioned in this area. **Clients/Work:** Niche private client and agricultural practice. Acts for farmers and estates around Wales and England with a lot of the work being referred by land agents and other solicitors.

Edward Harris & Son (2ptnrs/3assts) *Edward Harris* has a good reputation and is known for his common land work. **Clients/ Work:** Handles all agricultural work in particular rights of way, tenancy issues, environmental issues and estate planning.

Jonathan Stephens & Co (1ptnr/1 asst) *Jonathan Stephens* is considered highly competent. **Clients/Work:** Act mainly for family owned farms. Client base extends throughout Wales and the West Country. Handles quota work along with general agricultural work.

Price & Son (2ptnrs – 50%/1 asst – 25%) Like Margraves, the firm is in a rural area and so does a lot of agricultural work. *David* and *Stephen Hill* are both well established, with David being known for his quota work.

Clients/Work: Contentious and non-contentious work for farmers and landowners.

Jeffreys & Powell (2ptnrs – 1 f/t, 1 p/t) Maintain a solid reputation in this field. **Clients/Work:** Handles a range of agricultural matters including commons work.

Ungoed Thomas & King (4ptnrs – 25%/1asst – 25 %) Based in a rural area and handle a good volume of work. The team "get the job done" and are particularly good on commons work. **Clients/Work:** Acts for land owners and farmers on a range of matters like quotas, succession and tenancy issues.

Gabb & Co (5ptnrs – p/t at the various offices in Wales) Described as big and efficient with a good reputation. **Clients/Work:**

Deals with a whole range of matters e.g. quotas, tenancy issues for farmers and land owners.

Greathead & Whitelock (4ptnrs/1 asst) Handle a lot of local work. **Clients/Work:** General practice.

MIDLANDS

LEADING FIRMS • MIDLANDS	
ROYTHORNE & CO Spalding	
WRIGHT HASSALL & CO Leamington Spa	
ARNOLD THOMSON Towcester	

HIGHLY REGARDED FIRMS	
Hewitson Becke + Shaw Northampton	
Knight & Sons Newcastle-under-Lyme	
Lanyon Bowdler Shrewsbury	
Morton Fisher Worcester	
Brethertons Rugby	
Chattertons Horncastle	
Gabb & Co Hereford	
R. Gwynne & Sons Wellington	
Manby & Steward Wolverhampton	
Martineau Johnson Birmingham	
Tallents Godfrey & Co Newark-on-Trent	
Thursfields Kidderminster	
Wace Morgan Shrewsbury	
Wilkin Chapman Louth	

Roythorne & Co (7ptnrs – 60%/4assts – 60%) Regional leaders with a national reputation. A good team of strong individuals. *Nigel Davis* has been a leading figure in agriculture for some time and *Graham Smith* "knows his stuff." *Alan Plummer* handles the litigation and has well respected litigious skills. *Miles Farren*, who came from the NFU, and *Jeanette Sharpe* also feature. **Clients/Work:** NFU Panel. Member of Agrilaw. Range of agricultural work for farming companies, landowners and farmers both inside the Midlands and around the country.

Wright Hassall & Co (1ptnr/2assts) Described as "very impressive." *Robin Ogg* is considered the "backbone of the firm's reputation" and is "good at what he does." **Clients/Work:** Farm business tenancies, sale of milk quotas.

Arnold Thomson (1ptnr/4assts) Small specialist agricultural practice. A "good straight firm." *Michael Thomson* ("brilliant", "easy to get on with") has developed the

firm's reputation. **Clients/Work:** Deal with all matters relating to land owners and farmers including litigation throughout England and Wales.

Hewitson Becke + Shaw (3ptnrs/ 1asst – p/t, backed up by the private client and litigation solicitors) Highly rated and with a good standing in the Midlands area. *Ian Barnett* is "sound." **Clients/Work:** Granting development options by landowners, farm partnerships, taxation, joint venture and share farming agreements.

Knight & Sons (6ptnrs – 20%) Produce work of "good quality" and are held in high esteem. **Clients/Work:** Concentrate on non-contentious work but undertake litigation when required. A range of work involving tax planning, partnerships, tenancy issues for clients such as ARC Ltd, Hepworth Minerals and Chemicals Ltd and landed estates.

Lanyon Bowdler (2ptnrs/2assts) Well respected, with a good reputation among competitors and individual organisations. **Clients/Work:** NFU Panel. Has in the last year acted in various farm sales and purchases, a multi-million pound restructuring and the case of Cork v Cork.

Morton Fisher (5ptnrs/2assts) The firm was recommended for its good tax planners and for *James Quinn* ("efficient," "knows his stuff"). **Clients/Work:** Rent reviews, quota work and general estates advice.

Brethertons (1ptnr/1asst) **Clients/Work:** Mainly non-contentious work. The firm has been doing a lot of work relating to development and options for farmers in the area.

Chattertons (1ptnr/1asst) **Clients/Work:** Acts mainly for local landowners.

Gabb & Co (1ptnr/1asst – p/t) **Clients/ Work:** Farming and land owner clients for whom they undertake a range of agricultural matters.

R. Gwynne & Sons (2ptnrs – f/t, p/t/3assts – p/t) **Clients/Work:** As well as dealing with general agricultural matters, one assistant is a member of the Association of Equine Lawyers.

Manby & Steward (2ptnrs/1asst – p/t)

Clients/Work: Now looking to concentrate on agriculture the firm deals with sales and purchases, trusts and settlements and partnerships. Clients are farmers and landed estates (including one national estate).

Martineau Johnson (Agriculture is handled in the private client dept consisting of 5ptnrs/2assts) Recently lost a senior partner but still thought of as easy to deal with and quick. **Clients/Work:** Property and estate related work e.g. estate management and tax planning for landed estates. Restructuring inherited farms.

Tallents Godfrey & Co (4ptnrs/1asst – p/t) On the NFU panel and considered competent. **Clients/Work:** As well as the NFU work the firm deals with property matters, tax planning and succession.

Thursfields (1ptnr 70%, with assistance from litigation and tax depts) Known for its work in Worcestershire. **Clients/Work:** General agricultural work for farmers and land owners. Also handles conservation matters, working with the Nature Conservatory Council for England (English Nature).

Wace Morgan (3ptnrs – 1f/t/1asst) **Clients/Work:** Acts for farming and estate clients in the region.

Wilkin Chapman (1ptnr – f/t/2assts p/t) **Clients/Work:** Clients range from small farmers to large estates. All types of work undertaken.

LEADING INDIVIDUALS MIDLANDS	
DAVIS Nigel Roythorne & Co	
SMITH Graham Roythorne & Co	
THOMSON Michael Arnold Thomson	
BARNETT Ian Hewitson Becke + Shaw	
OGG Robin Stuart Wright Hassall & Co	
PLUMMER Alan Roythorne & Co	
QUINN James Morton Fisher	
SHARPE Jeanette Roythorne & Co	

UP AND COMING	
FARREN Miles Roythorne & Co	

EAST ANGLIA

Mills & Reeve (9ptnrs/8assts) A traditional agricultural practice which has a "good team" and is the "best practice" in East Anglia. *William Barr* ("very astute", "good all-round practitioner") heads the team. *Matthew Arrowsmith-Brown* is "technically sound" and *Michael Aubrey* is an "extremely hard worker." **Clients/Work:** Clients range from farming families to food chain businesses, for which they undertake property work, litigation, tax planning, business advice and all agri-related work. Act for The Woodland Trust (a programme of acquisitions) and Sentry Farming Group Plc.

Barker Gotelee (4ptnrs – 1p/t/ 9assts) A large, well thought of, specialist agricultural team. *Richard Barker* ("knows his stuff") has a good reputation and is an expert in European matters. *Geoff Whittaker* ("switched on") is fairly new to the area but is "doing well." **Clients/Work:** NFU panel. A growing client base of landed estates and over 700 farmers. Also act for ADAS and the Meat and Livestock Commission. Land development, environmental, European and employment matters. Involved in a European action on nitrate vulnerable zones in 1997.

Eversheds (4ptnrs – p/t/1asst – f/t) The main agricultural department of this national firm has some "good people." **Clients/Work:** NFU panel. Over 400 farming and business clients including Norfolk County Council, Bernard Matthews plc and the Country Gentlemen's Association. All types of work undertaken from contentious to non-contentious.

Taylor Vinters (9ptnrs – 60%/6assts – 60%) A large team with strength in depth. *Jeanette Dennis* is "doing well" and *Adrian Horwood-Smart* is a "good lawyer." Have gone up the lists this year. **Clients/Work:** NFU panel. Act for Oxford and Cambridge colleges, Jockey Club Estates Ltd and Broadoak Farming Ltd as well as major landowners, farmers, and institutions. Members of Agrilaw.

Birketts (6ptnrs/6assts) *Angela Sydenham* (ex CLA advisor, "academically expert", "good on rights of way") is high profile in the area but there are doubts as to the strength in depth of the team. **Clients/Work:** NFU panel. In 1997 involved in a statutory and judicial review regarding a council's modification order and a public enquiry into rights of way.

Palmer Wheeldon (4ptnrs – 1 f/t, 3 p/t/ 4assts – p/t) *Jane Lichtenstein* is extremely well regarded ("knows her onions", "determined and aggressive") but it is felt that the firm is too small to be amongst the top bands of leaders. **Clients/ Work:** Concentration on contentious work and concerns partnerships, landlord/tenant disputes, rights of way (recent public enquiry) and environmental matters. Some work for colleges.

Bankes Ashton (2ptnrs/1asst) *David Wybar* ("good working knowledge", "pragmatic") is new to the lists and is the leading light in this well thought of firm. **Clients/ Work:** Handle general agricultural matters and get work from the NFU. They have initiated and sponsored a regional farm diversification award.

Greene & Greene (3ptnrs – 2 f/t/ 3assts – 1 f/t) Localised but well regarded. **Clients/ Work:** General work of a non-contentious nature for clients including landed estates in the Suffolk area.

Hewitson Becke + Shaw (3ptnrs/3assts; close links with the private client dept.) There are some doubts as to the commitment to agriculture but nevertheless a major firm in the region. **Clients/Work:** Particular expertise in farm and estate management, tax planning, pensions, sales and purchases. In the last year has acted in many sales and purchases for clients such as HR Philpot & Son (Holdings) Ltd and Chivers Farms Ltd.

Howes Percival (3ptnrs – 1 f/t/3assts – 1 f/t) A firm which is "good in the field." *Jeremy Heal* is "sensible" and "understands his law." **Clients/Work:** Include The Sandringham Estate, The Quilter Estate and the International League for the Protection of Horses.

Greenwoods (1ptnr/1asst – p/t, assistance from other depts) A major agricultural practice in Peterborough. **Clients/Work:** Act for farmers and estates. Handles any matters that arise for clients in the area.

Prettys (2ptnrs – 1 f/t/1asst) **Clients/ Work:** In the past year has worked on several large land deals, defended Environment Agency prosecutions for NFU members and given employment and landlord/ tenant advice to a major farming estate in Suffolk. Specialises in environmental matters, rights of way, contract and landlord/tenant. Retained by two Newmarket studs.

Rustons & Lloyd (3ptnrs – p/t/1asst) **Clients/Work:** Has a lot of estate and farming clients in the Fens and the rest of the country.

EAST ANGLIA BLOODSTOCK

There are three firms in the East Anglia area that have significant dealings with Bloodstock. **Edmondson Hall** is a niche practice with *Anna Hall* ("very personable") leading the non-contentious side and *Mark Edmondson* ("combative") leading the litigation. *Owen Tebbs* at **Rustons & Lloyd** is very experienced and is renowned for his tax work, sitting on tax committees for horse societies such as the Joint Horse & Pony Tax Committee. He heads a team of 4 partners and 3 assistants who also deal with buying and selling studs and stable-related matters (e.g. health and safety). **Taylor Vinters** provide assistance to the bloodstock and racing industry from multiple ownership advice to Jockey Club Inquiries. *Rachel Flynn* has a growing reputation and is a new addition to the lists.

NORTH WEST

Cartmell Shepherd (1ptnr/3assts) An "excellent, on the ball" practice. Renowned throughout the North, thanks mainly to the specialist skills of *Timothy Cartmell* ("intel-lectual"). Clients/Work: NFU Panel. A range of work with quotas, partnerships and tenancy issues included. Clients include North West Water, English Nature and landed estates.

Oglethorpe Sturton & Gillibrand (3ptnrs – 1 f/t, 2 pt/1asst – p/t) Well respected team with *Martin Gillibrand* noted for his ability in a breadth of matters. Clients/Work: NFU Panel. All types of work undertaken for farmers, commons right owners and landed estates.

Walker Smith & Way (3ptnrs/1asst – p/t) Known as a firm that handles work for tenants as opposed to landlords. *Peter Collins* heads the team. Clients/Work: Handle contentious and non-contentious work. Have dealt with a lot of landlord/tenant work and development opportunities in the past year.

Mason & Moore Dutton (2ptnrs – p/t) Well-established and handle a lot of work in Cheshire. Clients/Work: Farmer clients for whom it handles all matters e.g. quota work, tenancy issues (including contentious issues) and property transactions.

Birch Cullimore (3ptnrs/2assts – p/t) Respected firm which "does enough work to have established a reputation" in this field. Known as landlord's solicitors. Clients/Work: Have seen an increase in tax planning, tenancy issues and quota work. Handle contentious and non-contentious work.

Senior Calveley & Hardy (2ptnrs – p/t) Clients/Work: Handle all general matters for mainly small local farmers.

NORTH EAST

Dickinson Dees (3ptnrs) A "good, long-established practice" recognised as a leading firm in the region. *Hume Hargreave* is "highly experienced" and "knows the area." *Simon Kirkup* is "very involved" in agriculture. Clients/Work: Member of Agrilaw. Act for estate and farming clients across the North. Deal with both contentious and non-contentious work e.g. tenancy issues, partnerships, estate planning and management.

Ward Hadaway (5ptnrs: 1 f/t/2assts – p/t) *Chris Hewitt* ("deep knowledge and experience") is very involved and is well known in the community. He is particularly recommended for his quota and subsidy work. Clients/Work: Client base includes the Forestry Commission and the Central Association of Agricultural Valuers. Mineral work, tenancy issues, quotas and land planning are particular specialities.

Addleshaw Booth & Co (3ptnrs/6assts –/p/t) Known as a firm which acts for landlords as opposed to tenants. The team "know their way around" with *James Stone* ("highly competent") at the helm. Clients/Work: Work is of a commercial nature and has recently included a number of property transactions. Commission for the New Towns and English Partnerships are clients.

Eversheds (5ptnrs/2assts) The former Wilkinson Maughan team now working at Eversheds following the merger of the two firms. Clients/Work: NFU Panel. A range of work is undertaken locally and nationally. Clients include Newcastle University as well as farmers and land owners.

Rollit Farrell & Bladon (3ptnrs/1asst – p/t) Well-regarded team who "know their stuff." The leading firm in Hull. Clients/Work: Landed estate clients for whom it undertakes matters like estate and tax planning.

Andrew M. Jackson & Co (3ptnrs – 1 f/t, 2 p/t) Considered to be a very good firm but not quite on a par with the leaders in this area. Clients/Work: Has in the last year acted in the purchase of the Warter Priory Estate (over £30m), the Burton Pidsea Estate and Hepburn Farm.

Latimer Hinks (3ptnrs – p/t) A long-standing, "solid" firm which was rated by independent organisations. Clients/Work: NFU panel. Cover the whole remit of agricultural work with a lot of clients in what is a very rural area.

Denison Till (4ptnrs – 20%/1asst – 20%) Suffered from the loss of a well regarded member of the team but still well thought of. Clients/Work: A lot of the work is related to property transactions. Works for farmers and landed estates in the North Yorkshire area.

Ford & Warren (1ptnr/2assts) Produces "good quality work." Clients/Work: Works for landed estates dealing with succession, property, quotas, development.

Grays (3ptnrs – p/t) Clients/Work: Tenancy issues, sale and purchase, land disputes and diversification issues for land-owning clients.

Heptonstalls (1ptnr/3assts – 1 f/t, 2 pt) Recieved enough recommendations to be mentioned. Clients/Work: Has over 300 farming and land-owning clients. Handle all types of agricultural work.

Wilkin Chapman (1ptnr/2assts, plus involvement from other departments) The firm has a reputation for producing work of a high standard. Clients/Work: Undertake a range of work with particular expertise in tax and estate planning.

Wrigleys Well regarded firm with "decent private clients." Essentially a private client firm which acts for landed estates, farmers and charities. Clients/Work: Deal with estate and tax planning, tenancy issues and property transactions.

SCOTLAND

Brodies WS (4ptnrs/4assts from the Private Client Department) Although Michael Gascoigne has retired, the firm was still regarded as the top firm in the country. *Hew Dalrymple* is the main contact point for agricultural matters. **Clients/Work:** Property-based work with the firm employing surveyors to provide a one-stop shop for sales and purchases. Clients include landed estates for which estate planning, tax planning and any related matters are handled.

Anderson Strathern WS (5ptnrs – 3 f/t, 2 p/t/5assts) A large firm with an extensive client base. The firm has a national reputation. *Alasdair Fox* is a long-established expert and is widely recognised. **Clients/Work:** Handles a range of work including estate management, landord/tenant work, arbitrations, forestry and in the last year a high profile notice to quit case.

Thorntons WS (5ptnrs – 40%/2assts – 40%) A good team with strong individuals. Considered a major player in the north east of the country. **Clients/Work:** Handle all agricultural work including environmental and sports issues for landed estates, owner occupiers and farmers.

Turcan Connell WS (7ptnrs – 5 f/t, 2 p/t/ 14assts – 12 f/t, 2 p/t) The private client departments from Dundas & Wilson and Burness have come together to become Turcan Connell. *Robert Turcan* is the lead man for agriculture. *Malcolm Strang Steel* is picked out as "an important man on the agricultural scene." *Jonathan Robertson* and *Kenneth MacKay* are also highly thought of. **Clients/Work:** All types of work are undertaken including property, estate planning, environmental.

Turnbull, Simson & Sturrock WS (4ptnrs) The firm are doing "good work in the borders" and are well regarded throughout the country. *David Sturrock* is highly rated and *Denbeigh Kirkpatrick* ("sound chap") has "substantial knowledge." **Clients/Work:** Range of work, particularly property transactions.

Burnett & Reid (2ptnrs – 50%, 60%/ 2assts – 25%) Highly rated but not universally recognised outside the north east of Scotland. **Clients/Work:** The firm places a lot of emphasis on agricultural work, acting for estates, tenant farmers and agricultural co-operatives in the area.

Gillespie MacAndrew WS (3ptnrs/ 2assts – p/t) "Competent" and "quite prominent." **Clients/Work:** Deals with all aspects of agricultural work for clients throughout Scotland. Most of the clients are landlords or owner occupiers.

Grigor & Young (1ptnr) A small local firm with a good agricultural reputation, created by *William Mennie*.

Lindsays WS (1ptnr/1asst) Small firm with an established reputation. *Roy Shearer* is described as a "clever chap." **Clients/Work:** Handles succession, sales and purchases, tax planning, estate management and general agricultural work for landed estates.

Miller Hendry (2ptnrs – f/t, p/t/1asst) Described as "doing a lot of work well." **Clients/Work:** Forestry work, acting for Fountain Forestry Ltd. Estate purchasing (Glenfeshie, Dunlappie and Tullock in the last year) and work for local clients.

Donald Rennie WS (Sole practitioner) *Donald Rennie* is an acknowledged expert. His name "immediately springs to mind" in the context of agricultural law.

Tods Murray WS (7ptnrs – 2 f/t, 5 p/t/ 5assts) A big firm with a commercial reputation, but also have an increasing agricultural client base. **Clients/Work:** Forestry work and

work for over 180 land owners. Clients include the Forestry Commission, RSPB and the Royal Highland Society.

Munro & Noble (1 prtnr) **Clients/Work:** General agricultural work including crofting.

Murray Beith Murray WS (3ptnrs/2assts – p/t) Another major firm that are perhaps more commercially focused, but nevertheless handle agricultural matters. **Clients/ Work:** Act mainly for landlords in any issues that arise (contentious or non-contentious).

Paull & Williamsons (1ptnr – 50%/1asst – 90%, with assistance from other depts) **Clients/Work:** Act for estates with large numbers of farms on them. Deal with a range of agricultural issues. Have dealt with a major representation to the NFU on an IACS issue on behalf of a group of farmers.

Stewart & Watson (1ptnr – p/t, with help from other ptnrs) Perceived to be deeply involved in agricultural matters. **Clients/ Work:** Have an accredited specialist who deals mainly with agricultural sales and purchases and tenancy issues.

Adam Cochran (1ptnr – p/t) Known for acting in a lot of sales and purchases, especially milk quota sales.

McCash & Hunter (2ptnrs – p/t) Well regarded in the Perth area. Localised but do a good standard of work. New to the lists following many recommendations.

Shepherd & Wedderburn WS (1ptnr/ 2assts from the private client dept.) Large firm who undertake agricultural matters as part of the private client work. **Clients/Work:** General agricultural and forestry work e.g. tax planning, estate management and partnerships.

SCOTLAND CROFTING

LEADING FIRMS · SCOTLAND

ANDERSON MACARTHUR & CO Stornoway
MACLEOD & MACCALLUM Inverness
MACPHEE & PARTNERS Fort William
LINDSAYS WS Edinburgh

HIGHLY REGARDED FIRMS

Brodies WS Edinburgh

Derek Flyn, (Macleod & MacCallum) *Simon Fraser* (Anderson MacArthur & Co) and *Duncan MacPhee* (MacPhee & Partners) are the three acknowledged crofting experts. They each deal with a different area of Scotland. All three are accredited by the Law Society as specialists and are members of the Crofting Law Group. The two firms acting out of Edinburgh (Brodies WS and Lindsays WS) are involved by way of their landed estate clients. *Roy Shearer* also deserves a mention for his crofting work.

LEADING INDIVIDUALS
SCOTLAND

FLYN Derek Macleod & MacCallum
FRASER Simon Anderson MacArthur & Co
MACPHEE Duncan MacPhee & Partners
SHEARER Roy Lindsays WS

SEE PROFILES AT END OF THIS SECTION

LEADERS' PROFILES · REGIONS

ARROWSMITH-BROWN, Matthew R.
Mills & Reeve, Norwich +44 (0)1603 660155
Specialisation: Advisory farming businesses and families. Examples of particular issues covered last year are: two cooperative ventures for sharing irrigation rights and building water storage reservoirs; the tax and agricultural holdings implications of unravelling a family tenancy structure; substituting a long term FBT for a 1986 Act tenancy.
Prof. Memberships: Law Society; Agricultural Law Association; Royal Agricultural Society of England; Royal Norfolk Agricultural Association.
Career: Clifton College; University of York; articles and 2.5 years post qualification with *Slaughter and May* 1974-1979; *Mills and Reeve* 1979 to date; partner since 1981.
Personal: Brought up on Dartmoor Farm; married; two daughters (17 & 18); Driving fast cars.

AUBREY, Michael J.
Mills & Reeve, Cambridge
+44 (0)1223 364422
Partner in Agriculture Department
Specialisation: Practice covers all areas of agricultural property work and in particular corporate and institutional agriculture. Main areas of work include acquisition and disposal of agricultural and development land and estates, agricultural tenancies, minerals, share farming, contract farming and partnerships.
Prof. Memberships: Royal Forestry Society; Law Society;
Career: BSc (Hons) in Agricultural Economics from University of Newcastle Upon Tyne. Joined *Mills & Reeve* in 1989 and became a partner in 1997
Personal: Leisure interests include rugby, cricket and golf.

BARKER, Richard
Barker Gotelee, Ipswich (01473) 611211
Specialisation: Acting for landowners and farmers throughout the UK. Head of Agricultural team dealing with all aspects of agricultural law both UK and Community legislation and in addition town and country planning, waste management, taxation, employment, litigation both UK and ECJ. His particular expertise is EC legislation and lobbying. Frequent visits to EC Commission Brussels. Council member Suffolk Agricultural Association. Chairman Suffolk Professional European Committee. CLA branch and national Committees. Speaks nationally at seminars. Regularly involved in all aspects of media coverage.

Prof. Memberships: Qualified 1969. Since 1969 has acted for a wide range of landowners and farmers nationwide.
Personal: Born 1944. Interests: Hill walking and gardening.

BARNETT, Ian
Hewitson Becke + Shaw, Northampton (01604) 233233
Senior Partner. Agricultural Property Division.
Specialisation: Main area of practice is agriculture. Also deals with commercial property and charities.
Prof. Memberships: Northants Committee CLA.
Career: Qualified in 1965. Joined *Hewitson Becke & Shaw* in 1967, becoming a Partner in 1968 and Senior Partner in 1994.
Personal: Born in 1940. Educated at Repton School and Oxford University 1958-61 (MA). Undersheriff of Northamptonshire since 1973. Leisure interests include field sports, antiques, food and wine. Lives in East Haddon.

BARR, William D.W.
Mills & Reeve, Cambridge
+ 44(0) (01223) 64422
Partner in Agriculture Department.
Specialisation: Work covers farm tenancies and partnerships, share farming, quotas and farm taxation. Most recently he has been involved in food chain issues and reviewing the structures of farm businesses and co-operatives. Co-author of 'Farm Tenancies'. Lectures frequently and contributes the share farming section to 'Agricultural Law Tax & Finance' and agricultural articles to Solicitors Journal.
Prof. Memberships: Law Society, Agricultural Law Association, USA Agricultural Law Association.

BATSTONE, William
Burges Salmon, Bristol (0117) 939 2000

BUXTON, James
Burges Salmon, Bristol (0117) 939 2000

CARTMELL, Timothy H.
Cartmell Shepherd, Carlisle (01228) 531561
Partner in Agriculture Department.
Specialisation: Work covers agricultural quotas, Landlord & Tenant matters, Agricultural Land Tribunal work, arbitrations and litigation in the Courts. Also farming legal matters generally, partnerships and private client work.
Personal: Glenalmond College 1961-66, Christ's College, Cambridge 1966-69. Articled with *Walker Martineau* in London 1970-72.

CHALK, Andrew
Matthew McCloy & Partners, Newbury (01635) 551515
Specialisation: All aspects of legal work relating to bloodstock with clients including jockeys, trainers, owners, breeders, bloodstock agents and veterinary surgeons. Retained by the Jockeys Association of Great Britain and other high profile sporting organisations and individuals. Has a detailed knowledge of the horseracing industry and the Rules of Racing. Deals with disciplinary hearings (including drug related cases), the transfer of ownership of racehorses, sponsorship agreements, personal injury, veterinary negligence, property, libel and employment. Has acted in numerous celebrated racing cases including representation before the Disciplinary and licensing Committees of the Jockey Club.
Prof. Memberships: Law Society. Thoroughbred Breeders Association.
Personal: Born 30th July 1961. Educated at Nottingham University. Enjoys all sports particularly cricket, horseracing and rugby. Lives in Lambourn.

CHEAL, Jonathan
Thrings & Long, Bath (01225) 448494
Partner in Agriculture Department.
Specialisation: Main areas of practice are agricultural law and real property law. Work includes farm sales and purchases, landlord and tenant, partnerships, succession and wills, tax, quotas, town and country planning and farm buildings, rights of way, easements and housing of farm workers and has wide experience of public speaking, lectures and seminars.
Prof. Memberships: Previously Legal Adviser at Country Landowners Association Head Office in London, 1983-87. Currently a professional member of CLA, NFU and TFA. Sits on CLA Somerset Committee; approved panel AMC solicitors, Agricultural Law Association.
Career: Qualified in 1976. Articled in London and Sussex. Worked in Hong Kong 1976-82; CLA 1983-87. Joined *Thrings & Long* in 1987, becoming a Partner in 1989.
Personal: Born 30th June 1950.

COLLINS, Peter
Walker Smith & Way, Chester (01244) 357 400

DALRYMPLE, Hew D.K.
Brodies WS, Edinburgh (0131) 228 3777
Specialisation: Main areas of practice are in Agricultural Law, Mineral Law, Sporting Estates

and Private Client Work including Capital Tax Planning; major matters have included during the last year: Sale of Glenfeshie Estate; the Gold Mine Project at Tyndrum in Perthshire; advising farmers and Landowners generally; advising on the implications of proposed changes to the tax regime affecting "Conditionally exempt assets".
Prof. Memberships: Society of Her Majesty's Writers to the Signet.
Career: Edinburgh Academy; Edinburgh University; *Brodies WS* from 1975 to date.
Personal: Married to Deirdre MacNeill, QC., one son. Leisure interests include shooting, fishing, painting and sketching and travel.

DAVIS, Nigel R.
Roythorne & Co, Nottingham
(0115) 948 4555
Partner. Head of Agricultural Law Unit – Nottingham.
Specialisation: Agricultural law. Particularly, landlord and tenant disputes, arbitration and tribunal hearings, partnerships and EU interpretation – milk quota and livestock regimes. Accredited Mediator; contributor to Legal Network Television; author of numerous articles on agricultural law; considerable experience of lecturing and seminar presentations. Advisory work in Hungary (1993), consultancy on legal practice management in Lithuania via BESO.
Career: Qualified 1975. Joined *Roythorne & Co* in August 1996 as a Partner.
Personal: Born 1949.

DENNIS, Jeanette A.
Taylor Vinters, Cambridge (01223) 423444
Associate in Agriculture Department.
Specialisation: Principal area of practice is agriculture. Work includes sales and purchases of farms and land, tenancies (including Agricultural Holdings Act 1986, Agricultural Tenancies Act 1995 and short term business leases), crop loss claims and financial arrangements for farmers.
Prof. Memberships: Cambridge Young Solicitors, Cambridge Law Society.
Career: Joined *Taylor Vinters* in 1988 and qualified in 1990. Has specialised in agricultural law since qualification. National AgriLaw Lecturer.
Personal: Graduated from Hull University in 1987(LL.B).

DENSHAM, Andrew
Burges Salmon, Bristol (0117) 939 2000

EDMONDSON, Mark Andrew
Edmondson Hall, Newmarket
(01638) 560556
Head of Litigation.
Specialisation: All matters relating to the ownership of racehorses, veterinary negligence, building disputes, personal injury, debt recovery, libel, employment, mostly equine related. Equine Insurance Law and Jockey Club matters. Clients include Trainers, owners, breeders, jockeys, bloodstock agents, shipping companies, stud farmers and racing charities.
Prof. Memberships: Law Society, Thoroughbred Breeders Association (firm member). Equine Lawyers Association.

EVANS, D.E.
Burges Salmon, Bristol (0117) 939 2000

FARREN, Miles
Roythorne & Co, Nottingham (0115) 948 4555
Specialisation: Agricultural Law particularly contentious Landlord and Tenant matters; milk and other agri-commodity quotas; tax trusts, wills and estate planning; contentious probate and inheritance claims; Partnership creation and dissolution. Speaker at lectures and seminars on Agricultural Law.
Career: Former NFU Local Secretary in Shropshire; strong links with NFU. LLB (Hons) part time Staffordshire University; qualified 1994.
Personal: Shropshire born and bred; articled at *Lanyon Bowdler* in Shrewsbury . Born 12/1/56. Member of AgriLaw and the Agricultural Law Association.

FINDLEY, C.D.
Cole & Cole, Oxford (01865) 262600
Specialisation: All aspects of law including Agricultural Holdings and Arbitrations and Farm Business Tenancy legislation, advising Agricultural Estates on land and tax issues. Town & Country planning, experience includes Options and Sales of farm land and buildings for development, representation at Planning Appeals, Local Plan Inquiries and Judicial Review proceedings. Milk Quota and subsidy law CAP Reform. Extensive experience in creation and dissolution of Farming Partnerships and Companies. Advising on Mineral Extraction and Waste Disposal sites.
Prof. Memberships: Country Landowners Association (Oxfordshire Committee) and Legal & Parliamentary Sub-Committee member, Agricultural Law Association (Committee), National Farmers Union, Tenant Farmers Association.
Career: Qualified in 1979 Head of Agricultural Law Department at *Thomas Mallam* Oxford 1983-1993. Joined *Cole and Cole* as Partner and Head of Agricultural Law Department 1994.

FITZGERALD, Peter R.
Wilsons Solicitors, Salisbury (01722) 412412
See under Trusts & Personal Tax, p. 793

FLYN, Derek
Macleod & MacCallum, Inverness
(01463) 239393
Partner in general practice.
Specialisation: Main area of practice is crofting law, a peculiarly complex system of law with few specialist solicitors. Co-author of Butterworths 'Crofting Law' (1990). Crofting law adviser to Scottish Crofters Union, and a number of crofting landlords.
Prof. Memberships: Law Society of Scotland, Scottish Law Agents Society (Vice President).
Career: Qualified in 1975(LLB). Joined *Macleod & MacCallum* in 1975, becoming a Partner in 1978. Council Member of Scottish Law Agents Society since 1992; Sheriff Clerk Depute, Portree, Isle of Skye 1967-70.
Personal: Leisure interests include travel, walking, reading and writing.

FLYNN, Rachel
Taylor Vinters, Cambridge (01223) 423444
Specialisation: Prinicpal area of practice is bloodstock. First point of contact for the National Trainers Federation's Members under Assistance to Members Scheme. Receives referrals from British Horse society. Deals with

major bloodstock litigation, TBF Nomination Arbitration and Jockey Club Inquiries. Also syndicate and joint ownership agreements, southern hemisphere keep agreements etc. Amateur ladies rider, successful on first two rides in 1997. Rides out daily in Newmarket. Speaks at seminars and writes for trade press.
Prof. Memberships: Thoroughbread Breeders Association. Amateur Jockeys Association.
Career: Graduated from Durham University in 1991. Has specialised in bloodstock throughout career in law.

FOX, Alasdair
Anderson Strathern WS, Edinburgh
(0131) 220 2345
Specialisation: Head of Rural Department and Land Ventures with over twenty five years experience of all aspects of rural property law. Particular expertise in the areas of agricultural landlord and tenant law and agricultural arbitrations (acting principally for arbiters but also for parties). Practice also covers advice to major estate proprietors, purchase and sale of rural properties and land ventures including Diversification Agreements, opencast mining options and licences.
Prof. Memberships: Society of Writers to H.M. Signet; Law Society of Scotland's Agricultural Law Committee, Agricultural Law Association.
Career: Qualified in 1969. Partner at Anderson Strathern WS since 1972. Accredited by the Law Society of Scotland as a specialist in agricultural law 1993.
Personal: Educated at Lime House School, Carlisle 1954-59, Fettes College, Edinburgh 1959-64 and at the University of Edinburgh 1964-67. Leisure pursuits include sailing, ski-ing, shooting and fishing. Born 1st January 1946. Lives in Edinburgh.

FRASER, Simon
Anderson MacArthur & Co, Stornoway
(01851) 703356
Specialisation: Accredited specialist in Crofting Law. Growing specialism in field of development of legal, constitutional and fiscal aspects of community ownership initiatives. Acted in constitution of Isle of Eigg Heritage Trust and in recent successful acquisition of the Island of Eigg on behalf of the Trust; founder Chairman of Trust.
Prof. Memberships: Member, Crofting Law Group.
Career: School: Nicolson Institute Stornoway; Aberdeen University. Partner of *Anderson MacArthur & Co* since 1986. Chairman North Areas Board of Scottish National Heritage.
Personal: Hillwalking.

GILLIBRAND, R. Martin
Oglethorpe Sturton & Gillibrand, Lancaster
(01524) 67171
Partner in Agriculture Department.
Specialisation: Has over 20 years experience in general agricultural work, including agricultural tax planning and conveyancing, quotas, and law relating to common land. Also handles tax, probate and industrial conveyancing. Clerk to the General Tax Commissioners. Has handled a number of Commons Enquiries and general upland negotiations. Has addressed numerous Moorland seminars.
Prof. Memberships: Agriculture Law Association, Secretary of Moorland Association.
Career: Qualified in 1972. Joined *Oglethorpe Sturton & Gillibrand* in 1972, becoming a

Partner in 1973.

Personal: Born 9th October 1946. Attended Shrewsbury School 1960-65 and Pembroke College, Cambridge 1965-68. Leisure interests include gardening and shooting. Lives in Tatham, near Lancaster.

HALL, Anna

Edmondson Hall, Newmarket
(01638) 560556
Partner in Bloodstock Department.

Specialisation: Acts for all sectors of bloodstock/racing industry. Property, Employment and Licensing. Lectures on Equine Law. Advises major racing charities, leading owners, trainers and studs.

HARGREAVE, R.Hume M.

Dickinson Dees, Newcastle upon Tyne
(0191) 279 9000
Partner and Head of Agriculture Group.

Specialisation: Main area of practice agriculture, encompassing all aspects of land ownership and management, partnerships, agricultural tenancies and European Law. Speaks frequently at RICS/ CAAV conferences and seminars and at AgriLaw seminars; writes regularly for the press.

Prof. Memberships: Agricultural Law Association, AgriLaw (Chairman).

Career: Qualified in 1971. Partner in *Dickinson Dees* since 1974.

Personal: Born 24th September 1940. Shrewsbury School 1954-59, Merton College, Oxford 1959-63.

HARRIS, Edward Kynan

Edward Harris & Son, Swansea
(01792) 652007

Specialisation: Senior Partner specialising in the Law of Commons, the Manorial System and Lordship of Manors and appurtenant rights and interests, also agricultural land tenancies. Other areas of law include rights of way, footpaths and other easements, copyholds, mineral rights, together with countryside law, town and country planning and other areas of agricultural law. Acted in the reported cases of 'Lewis and Others v. Mid Glamorgan County Council' (1995) (House of Lords) 1 ALL ER 760 and 'Re:Merthyr Mawr Common' (1989) 3 ALL ER 451 and 'Hancock v. Brecon Water' etc. plus Commons Commissioners hearings etc. Acts for various Commoners Associations and Lords of the Manors. Appointed by the Countryside Commission to be Welsh Representative on the Common Land Forum. Co-author of Common Land Forum Report 1985. On Department of Environment list of Consultees in respect of Common Land legislation.

Prof. Memberships: Law Society, Agricultural Law Association, Country Land-Owners Association (Legal & Parliamentary Sub-Committee).

Career: Qualified in 1964 (Hons.). Partner at *Edward Harris & Son* since 1965. Senior Partner since 1988.

Personal: Born 2nd April, 1941. Educated at St. Edwards, Oxford 1954-59. Lives in Swansea.

HEAL, Jeremy P W

Howes Percival, Norwich (01603) 762103
Partner, Head of Estates Division

Specialisation: Acts for landowners and others in all areas of agricultural law, tax and land transactions, including agricultural tenancies and contracting agreements,

minerals, farming partnerships, acquisition and disposal of farms and estates, town and country planning, landowners' consortia and joint ventures. Specialises in capital tax planning for landowners, and lectures regularly on inheritance tax and trusts, valuation and other tax-related topics. Work also includes charity law; and is a trustee of a substantial grant-making charity. Author of various articles in *Farmers Weekly, Taxation, Personal Tax Planning Review* and other periodicals.

Prof. Memberships: Agricultural Law Association; Chartered Institute of Arbitrators; Society of Trust & Estate Practitioners; Law Society; Country Landowners Association; Royal Norfolk Agricultural Association.

Personal: Born 1942. Educated Marlborough College and Queen's College, Cambridge. MA, LLM (Cantab), ACIArb, TEP.

HEWITT, Christopher

Ward Hadaway, Newcastle upon Tyne
(0191) 204 4000
Partner in Property Department.

Specialisation: Agricultural holdings, quotas, partnerships business and property law, land use minerals and planning. Wide ranging cases for farmers, landowners and rural institutions. Spoken at CLA, RICS and many other conferences on agricultural law. Regular contributor to local press.

Prof. Memberships: Law Society, Country Landowners Association, Agricultural Law Association.

Career: Qualified in 1971, Partner in 1987 upon joining *Ward Hadaway*.

Personal: Born 16th September 1947. Attended Sedbergh School and the University of Newcastle upon Tyne.

HILL, David

Price & Son, Haverfordwest (01437) 765331

HILL, Stephen

Price & Son, Haverfordwest (01437) 765331

HORNER, Douglas G.

Brachers, Maidstone (01622) 690691
Specialises in Agricultural Law, Environmental Law and Town Planning.

Specialisation: Agricultural Law: agricultural holdings and arbitrations, CAP regimes and legislation, health and safety, UKASTA, NASPM and other contracts and issues. Environmental Law: waste regulation, statutory nuisance, cases involving leachate, methane, water pollution, airbourne pollution and noise. Town planning: advocacy in Public Inquiries, handling High Court appeals and Judicial Review, applications, appeals and cases ranging from industrial development, offices, residential, major and minor farm development to port facilities and aviation. Lectures have included RICS-CPD, Rural Arbrix, CBI, NFU and others.

Prof. Memberships: Law Society's Planning Panel, Legal Associate RTPI, UK Environmental Law Association, Agricultural Law Association, NFU, CLA, Kent Valuers Club, Canterbury Farmers Club.

Career: Qualified 1969, Partner *Brachers* 1972, Head of Agricultural Department and Town Planning and Environmental Law Department 1975: Legal Adviser to Kent County NFU 1975 to date: Legal Adviser to East Sussex NFU: past member Law Society's Civil Litigation Committee and Senate of the Bar Committee on Law Reporting: elected member CBI South East

Region Council: Chairman Kent Economic Forum.

Personal: Born 1945. Sutton Valence School. St John's College Cambridge. Enjoys sailing and lives in Sevenoaks.

HORWOOD-SMART, Adrian

Taylor Vinters, Cambridge (01223) 423444
Partner in Agriculture Department.

Specialisation: Principal area of practice is agriculture. Work includes landlord and tenant, contracting and management agreements, other joint farming operations, partnership arrangements, quota and set-aside transactions and the land law aspects of landed estates and farms. Regularly lectures at seminars and conferences.

Prof. Memberships: Law Society, Agricultural Law Association, Notaries Society.

Career: Qualified in 1977. At *Waltons & Morse* 1977-79 before joining *Taylor Vinters*. Became a Partner in 1983.

KIRKPATRICK, Denbeigh

Turnbull, Simson & Sturrock WS, Jedburgh
(01835) 862391
Partner specialising in agricultural law.

Specialisation: Handles the purchase, sale and leasing of agricultural holdings and associated matters. Also deals with commercial work including purchase of ground for development for housing, arrangement of all necessary servitude rights etc., and subsequent selling as well as the purchase, sale and leasing of shops and other commercial premises. Clients include substantial private landowners and farmers. Convener of the Law Society of Scotland's Agricultural Law Accreditation Panel.

Prof. Memberships: Law Society of Scotland; Society of Writers to Her Majesty's Signet; The Scottish Agricultural Arbiters' Association; The South of Scotland and Border Valuers' Association.

Career: Qualified in 1965. Partner at *Turnbull Simson & Sturrock* since 1967. Member of Council, Law Society of Scotland 1982-88.

Personal: Born 15th December 1940. Educated at Jedburgh Grammar School 1945-51, The Edinburgh Academy 1951-58 and Edinburgh University 1958-64. Leisure pursuits include reading and golf. Lives in Wark, Cornhill-on-Tweed.

KIRKUP, S.

Dickinson Dees, Newcastle upon Tyne
(0191) 279 9000

Specialisation: Handles all aspects of agricultural law. Particular expertise in landlord and tenant issues, quotas and livestock premiums, Agricultural Land Tribunal matters, arbitrations, farming partnerships and farm sales and purchases. Regularly lectures at seminars and conferences.

Prof. Memberships: Agricultural Law Association, AgriLaw.

Career: Attended Sedbergh School 1979-84 and Exeter University 1985-88. Joined *Dickinson Dees* in 1990 and qualified in 1992. Is an Associate in the firm's Agricultural Law Group.

Personal: Born 31 August 1966. Leisure interests including fishing, shooting and sport.

KNIGHT, Matthew

Knights, Tunbridge Wells (01892) 537311
See under Administrative & Public Law, p. 92

KYRKE, Richard Venables
Thomas Eggar Church Adams, Horsham
(01403) 214500
Partner & Head of Agricultural Law Unit.
Specialisation: Handles all aspects of
agricultural law, particularly landlord and tenant
issues, and advises on commercial property
matters, including sales and purchases.
Prof. Memberships: Agricultural Law
Association, CLA, NFU.
Career: Born 1951. Educated Marlborough
College. Qualified 1976. Partner in *Thomas
Eggar Verrall Bowles* since 1979.

LICHTENSTEIN, Jane
Palmer Wheeldon, Cambridge
(01223) 355933
Partner – head of Commercial litigation.
Specialisation: Agricultural Holdings
legislation and farm business matters form main
areas of work. Arbitrations and Agricultural Land
Tribunals, especially succession applications.
Contentious and non-contentious matters
relating to farm partnership, share farming,
licenses. Status of routes across rural land-
public/private rights of way.
Prof. Memberships: Agricultural Law
Association.

MACKAY, Kenneth
Turcan Connell WS, Edinburgh
(0131) 228 8111
Specialisation: Associate partner specialising
in all aspects of rural conveyancing and
agricultural law.
Prof. Memberships:
The Law Society of Scotland.
Career: Attended University of Dundee (LLB
Hons, Dip LP). Articled *Dundas & Wilson CS*
1990-1992; qualified 1992; assistant solicitor
1992-1996; senior solicitor since 1996-1997;
associate 1998.
Personal: Born 1967. Resides Edinburgh.
Leisure interests including sailing.

MACPHEE, Duncan
MacPhee & Partners, Fort William
(01397) 701000
Managing Partner.
Specialisation: Practice includes Commercial
Conveyancing, emphasis on rural and crofting
matters. Accredited Crofting Law Specialist.
Also handles Scottish land law, including rights
of way, agricultural law in the Highlands and
Islands, highland estates, farms, lochs and
rivers and moorings.
Prof. Memberships: Law Society of Scotland,
WS Society, Notary Public, on Committee of the
Crofting Law Group and Scottish Crofters
Union legal advisory panel. Firm won TSB-Law
Society of Scotland Business of Law Awards
1997 for firms up to 6 partners for its work
developing crofting law practice. Finalist
Highlands and Islands Business Awards 1998.
Career: Qualified in 1972. Partner since 1981.
Trustee on several trusts; Clerk to Lochy District
Salmon Fishing Board; Secretary of Local
Moorings Association.
Personal: Born 15th December 1951.
Attended Lochaber High School and Glasgow
University. Past President of Lochaber Rotary
Club, Lochaber Rugby Football Club and Clan
MacPhee Society of Scotland. Leisure interests
include sailing, rugby, skiing and fishing. Lives

in Fort William. Treasurer Fort William and
District Chamber of Commerce. Lochaber Area
Secretary Scottish Crofters Union.

MARGRAVE-JONES, Clive
Margraves, Llandrindod Wells (01597) 825565

MCCLOY, Matthew
Matthew McCloy & Partners, Newbury
(01635) 551515
See under Sports Law, p. 744

MENNIE, William
Grigor & Young, Elgin (01343) 544077

MORRISON, Alastair
Burges Salmon, Bristol (0117) 939 2000

MULCARE, John
Cripps Harries Hall, Tunbridge Wells, Kent
(01435) 860008
Specialisation: Partner dealing with
agriculture; experience includes most aspects
of farming work including ancillary matters e.g.
town and country planning, commercial
litigation, criminal and civil litigation and sitting
as a legal adviser in agricultural arbitration.
Prof. Memberships: Member of the
Agricultural Law Association; an associate
member of the Chartered Institute of Arbitrators
and an accredited mediator with the Centre for
Dispute resolution.
Career: Educated at Hurstpierpont College;
articled at firms in West Sussex and London;
qualified in 1962; partner at *A L Mulcare & Co*
1965; founded *John Mulcare & Co* 1988;
partner, *Cripps Harries Hall* 1996.
Personal: Sailing, hill walking, farming.

NEVILLE, William
Burges Salmon, Bristol (0117) 939 2000

OGG, Robin Stuart
Wright Hassall & Co, Leamington Spa
(01926) 886688
Specialisation: Head of agricultural
department with major agricultural practice.

PLUMMER, Alan J.
Roythorne & Co, Spalding
(01775) 724141
Partner in Litigation Department.
Specialisation: Main areas of practice are
Landlord and Tenant litigation, particularly
relating to Agricultural holdings, contentious
trust matters, employment law, professional
indemnity litigation. Speaker at AgriLaw
seminars and other professional conferences.
Prof. Memberships: ALA
Career: Qualified in 1979. Joined *Roythorne &
Co* in 1976.

QUINN, James Stephen Christopher
Morton Fisher, Worcester (01905) 610410

RENNIE O.B.E., Donald G.
Donald Rennie WS, Edinburgh
(0131) 476 7007

ROBERTSON, Jonathan
Turcan Connell WS, Edinburgh
(0131) 228 8111
Specialisation: Partner. Specialist in Agricultural
Law including all aspects of farm sales and

purchases, agricultural tenancy matters, agricultural
arbitrations and quotas. Other main areas of
work include rural conveyancing, mining and
development work, rural planning and environ-
mental law, forestry, sporting and aquaculture.
Prof. Memberships: Member Agricultural Law
Association. Accredited as a specialist in
agricultural law by the Law Society of Scotland.
Writer to the Signet. Notary Public.
Career: Attended University of Aberdeen (LLB,
DipLP). Articled *Dundas & Wilson CS* 1984-1986;
qualified 1986; assistant solicitor 1986-1990;
associate 1990; Partner 1990-97. Partner *Turcan
Connell* 1997.
Personal: Born 1960. Resides East Lothian.
Leisure interests include walking.

SHARPE, Jeanette L.
Roythorne & Co, Spalding (01775) 724141
Partner in Conveyancing Department.
Specialisation: Main areas of practice are
agricultural and commercial conveyancing,
tenancy and insolvency work and
environmental matters.
Prof. Memberships: UKELA
Career: Qualified in 1975. Practised in the West
Midlands before joining *Roythorne & Co* in 1988.
Personal: Attended Kesteven and Grantham
Girls' School and the University of Birmingham.

SHEARER, Roy G.
Lindsays WS, Edinburgh (0131) 477 8708

SMITH, Graham C.H.
Roythorne & Co, Spalding (01775) 724141
Partner in Private Client/ Agriculture
department.
Specialisation: Partner in Private Client/
Agriculture department. Main area of practice,
agriculture and private client work.
Career: Qualified in 1974 having joined
Roythorne & Co in 1972. Notary Public 1990.
Author of practice text 'Agricultural Law'and
editor of CGT newsletter on Agricultural Law.
Founder member of AgriLaw. Speaker at AgriLaw
seminars, various accountants' and surveyors'
conferences and for Central Law Training on
Agricultural Law.
Personal: Born 19th May 1949.

STEEL, John R.
White & Bowker, Winchester (01962) 844440

STEPHENS, Jonathan
Jonathan Stephens & Co, Usk
(01291) 673344

STONE, James F.
Addleshaw Booth & Co, Leeds
(0113) 209 2000
Partner in Commercial Property Group.
Specialisation: Main areas of practice are
agriculture, commercial property and property
tax. Work includes property investment,
tenancy issues (including termination,
compensation and succession rights), quotas,
property finance, capital taxation and VAT.
Prof. Memberships: Law Society,
Agricultural Law Association.
Career: Qualified in 1981. Joined the firm in
1981, becoming a Partner in 1988.
Personal: Born 9th July 1957. Attended
Bristol Grammar School 1964-75 and Exeter
University 1975-78. Leisure interests include
mountaineering, photography and travel.
Lives in Harrogate.

STRANG STEEL, Malcolm
Turcan Connell WS, Edinburgh
(0131) 228 8111
Specialisation: Handles mainly rural property matters, including landlord and tenant, acting for proprietors of a number of landed estates with let farms. Also taxation in relation to the above. Has acted as clerk in agricultural arbitrations and in the purchase and sale of landed estates, including Grantully, Glenmoriston and Dalgleish Forest. Also in timeshare sales of fishings at Grantully, Taymount and Carron. Has lectured on numerous occasions to Law Society of Scotland and other seminars on agricultural law and sporting law. Convener of Law Society's Agricultural Law Committee and Secretary of Scottish Agricultural Arbitrators Association.

STURROCK, David P.
Turnbull, Simson & Sturrock WS, Jedburgh
(01835) 862391
Managing Partner.
Specialisation: Main area of practice is agricultural law. Handles all aspects of land ownership, Agricultural Holdings (Scotland) Acts, quotas and arbitrations. Also handles wills, succession and inheritance tax planning. Has addressed a variety of Conferences and Seminars.
Prof. Memberships: Law Society of Scotland; Accredited by Law Society of Scotland as a Specialist in Agricultural Law; Writer to the Signet; Notary Public.
Career: Qualified in 1966. Joined *Turnbull, Simson & Sturrock* in 1966, becoming a Partner in 1968 and Managing Partner in 1990.
Personal: Born 16th March 1943. Attended Rugby School 1956-61 and Edinburgh University 1961-65. Lives in Jedburgh.

SWIFT, Robert D.
Wilsons Solicitors, Salisbury (01722) 412412
Specialisation: Advises farmers and landowners on Agricultural Law, business restructuring, farm tenancies (including successions) and in connection with the sale and purchase of farms and estates.
Prof. Memberships: Agricultural Law Association and CLA.
Career: Qualified in 1989. Partner since 1994 in Farms and Estates Department. A member of the Agrilaw Committee and a regular

speaker at agricultural conferences.
Personal: Born 1959. Lives in Broadchalke near Salisbury. Interests include walking and cricket.

SYDENHAM, Angela
Birketts, Ipswich (01473) 232300
Specialisation: Property law, agricultural, business and residential tenancies, milkquota, commons, public and private rights of way, public access, navigation, trusts treasure, experience in judicial and statutory review, public enquiries, arbitration, ALT applications.
Prof. Memberships: Author of numerous books and articles, lectures nationally; Agricultural Law Society; CLA; NFU; TFA; Suffolk Agricultural Association Council Member.
Career: Former Chief Legal Adviser CLA.

TEBBS, Owen E.
Rustons & Lloyd, Newmarket
(01638) 661221

THOMSON, Michael
Arnold Thomson, Towcester (01327) 350266
Partner specialising in agriculture.
Specialisation: Main area of work covers agricultural property, development work, tenancies, quotas and livestock premia. Regularly addresses farming and professional audiences.
Prof. Memberships: Agricultural Law Association, Country Landowners Association, National Farmers Union.
Career: Qualified 1981. Co-founder of *Arnold Thomson* in 1990.
Personal: Born July 1954. Attended Wrekin College 1967-71, then University College, London 1972-76. Leisure pursuits include shooting, golf and cricket. Lives in Blakesley, Northants.

TURCAN, Robert
Turcan Connell WS, Edinburgh
(0131) 228 8111
Specialisation: Joint Senior Partner specialising in land law, trusts and tax planning, adviser to a substantial number of Landowners and farmers.
Prof. Memberships: The Law Society of Scotland, Society of Writers to HM Signet.
Career: Trinity College, Oxford (MA) and University of Edinburgh (LLB). Articled *Shepherd & Wedderburn WS*; qualified 1972;

Partner at *Dundas & Wilson CS* 1973-1997. Chairman of Law and Parliamentary Committee, Scottish Landowners Federation; director of the Abercairny Estates Limited and others.
Personal: Born 1947. Resides Fife. Married with four children. Leisure interests include fox hunting, gardening, shooting and fishing.

WHITTAKER, Geoff
Barker Gotelee, Ipswich (01473) 611211
Specialisation: Joined *Barker Gotelee* autumn 1996. Specialises in agricultural holdings, farm business tenancies, IACS, milk and livestock quotas, land-related transactions and joint ventures.
Prof. Memberships: Law Society, Agricultural Law Association (Committee Member 1997-), Associate Member British Association of Communicators in Business.
Career: Qualified in 1980. Trained in native Liverpool before moving to Midlands, practising for 15 years in a variety of commercial and property-based fields.
Personal: Born 1956. Leisure interests include music (choral and small-group *a capella* singing) and computers. Confirmed cricket nut!

WILLIAMS, Peter Rhys
Burges Salmon, Bristol (0117) 939 2000

WYBAR, David K.
Bankes Ashton, Bury St. Edmunds
(01284) 762331
Specialisation: Acts for farmers, landowners and farming businesses and related throughout East Anglia.
Prof. Memberships: Agricultural Law Association, Country Landowners Association. Council Member of Suffolk Agricultural Association. Suffolk Farming and Wildlife Advisory Group.
Career: Winchester College and St. Andrews University. Trained with *Macfarlanes* in London and worked for *Mills & Reeve* in Norwich immediately before joining *Bankes Ashton* in 1991. Joint Managing Partner since 1995. Chairman of Earl Sohan Parish Council.
Personal: Married with three children. Holiday house in Elie, Fyfe. Member of Bury St. Edmonds Farmers' Club, Royal and Ancient Golf Club of St. Andrews, Aldeburgh Golf Club, Golf House Club, Elie, Gentlemen of Suffolk Cricket Club and Newmarket Real Tennis Club.

ALTERNATIVE DISPUTE RESOLUTION

See also Arbitration

RESEARCH: Our team interviewed specialist solicitors and barristers nationally, organisations offering mediation services and large city institutions currently embracing ADR.

In compiling the tables, we considered all the information available to us, paying particular regard to the market research carried out by our team of ten qualified lawyers. (The researchers' details are set out on page three.)

The rankings, therefore, reflect the opinion of the marketplace as revealed by systematic and objective research: see page four. (Our research is audited every year by the British Market Research Bureau.)

OVERVIEW: The effects of the June 1996 Commercial Court Practice Note are now being felt. Court ordered mediation is increasing and many firms are instituting training programs. The judiciary has also been trained. The use of mediation in the high profile, high value 'DeLorean case' between the government and Arthur Andersen is seen as a crucial development.

There are also various pilot schemes currently underway involving the Central London County Court, Bristol County Court, the Court of Appeal, the family courts' ancillary relief scheme and the NHS. Indications are that the take-up (despite the availability of legal aid in certain cases) is low. Where used, a high proportion of cases have been settled satisfactorily.

Not included in our lists are individuals who work for mediation organisations or retired judges who act as mediators. The following however received many mentions: Eileen Carroll, Bill Marsh and Karl Mackie of CEDR; Andrew Frayley and Brian Beckett of ADRNET; Nick Prior and Lord Griffiths.

LEADING INDIVIDUALS · LONDON

WILLIS Tony Clifford Chance

BROWN Henry Penningtons
MARRIOTT Arthur Debevoise & Plimpton
MILES David Glovers
SHAPIRO David S J Berwin & Co
SIBLEY Edward Berwin Leighton
YORK Stephen Hammond Suddards

KENDALL John Allen & Overy
NEWMARK Chris Baker & McKenzie
ROE Mark Masons

ANDREWARTHA Jane Clyde & Co
CORNES David Winward Fearon
FINCHAM Anthony Cameron McKenna
HANDLER Thomas Baker & McKenzie
HOLLOWAY Julian Greenwoods
LUX Jonathan Ince & Co
MITCHARD Paul Simmons & Simmons
TESTER Stephen Cameron McKenna
THOMAS Andrew Lewis Silkin

SEE PROFILES AT END OF THIS SECTION

LONDON

Tony Willis, Clifford Chance Universally regarded as "first and foremost" in the field, other solicitors have no hesitation using him. With an excellent track record, he often spends up to 25% of his time on ADR matters. Also involved in training lawyers and the judiciary. **Clients/Work:** Has mediated in construction, engineering, insurance, professional negligence, contractual and insolvency related disputes.

Henry Brown, Penningtons An all-round "first class" mediator, with a reputation for settling unsettlable cases. He is the ideal mediator – "cool, calm and a good listener," with a particular interest in relationship disputes, both personal and business. An acknowledged pioneer in the field, he is also involved in writing, training and establishing standards for ADR **Clients/Work:** Family and business disputes.

Arthur Marriott QC, Debevoise & Plimpton A "founding father" and author of the leading text, he has a high profile as an active promoter of mediation. Everyone we spoke to knew of, and respected, the newly appointed silk and his "excellent" book.

David Miles, Glovers Part of the CEDR faculty and an active promoter of ADR. He was one of the first mediators and is seen as a "major player" and a "good chap." Writes and lectures at universities on ADR and is currently lobbying the Official Referees Court to adopt ADR. **Clients/Work:** 5 mediations, including one in the Far East.

David Shapiro, SJ Berwin & Co A professional mediator who acquired much of his expertise in his native US. He is the most experienced mediator in the UK and "a breed of his own." Seen by some as one of "the best mediators this side of the water," others found him "a very tough negotiator." Actively involved in training lawyers and judges and also lectures at LSE **Clients/Work:** Mediated in 5 cases (insolvency, insurance/ reinsurance, environmental and contractual).

Edward Sibley, Berwin Leighton With a high profile, he is frequently requested as a mediator and recently succeeded in a top calibre beauty parade. Admired as a "first class advocate and mediator," he is "quite a canny man, able to pick up hidden agendas." Has acted, either as mediator or advocate, in a total of 51 mediations. **Clients/Work:** This year's selection included 5 professional negligence cases, an international franchise dispute, a banker/client dispute, 2 mediations under the Central London County Court scheme and 1 under the Independent Housing Ombudsman scheme.

Stephen York, Hammond Suddards Admired for his advocacy skills in mediations, he is "experienced and knowledgeable." Currently spends between 50 and 60% of his time on ADR related work. Recently acted as a mediator in the Central London County Court scheme. **Clients/Work:** Represented North West Water in mediation against Oracle; Merlin against Heinz and Kinetica against Keadby Power.

John Kendall, Allen & Overy Best known for his work in expert determinations (an informal but binding form of adjudications), and increasingly more involved in mediations. Considered "nice and able" and a "great sponsor of ADR and arbitration." **Clients/Work:** Having previously acted mainly as an advocate, he mediated in a number of cases this year involving Landlord & Tenant, construction, environmental and health care.

Chris Newmark, Baker & McKenzie Noted for his passionate promotion of ADR, he has spent time training with a mediator in the US. He mainly advises clients but has also acted as a mediator in 9 cases. **Clients/Work:** General commercial disputes. Recently advised in a US$43m telecoms dispute.

Mark Roe, Masons Is a director of CEDR and is involved in drafting adjudication rules for both CEDR and the Official Referee's Solicitors Association. He has done 10 mediations, as mediator and adviser; 4 of these in the last year. **Clients/Work:** Construction and IT.

Jane Andrewartha, Clyde & Co Since qualifying with CEDR in summer 1996, she has done 7 mediations as pupil or co-mediator and another 3 as lead mediator. **Clients/Work:** Commercial litigation, including insurance/re-insurance, marine, banking and construction.

David Cornes, Winward Fearon CEDR accredited, he is making a name as a mediator. Has carried out 18 to date (16 of which have settled on the day). **Clients/Work:** 7 mediations this year (mainly construction), including three four party disputes.

Anthony Fincham, Cameron McKenna An accredited mediator with ADRNET and CEDR, he has mediated in 6 cases and acted as advocate in others. **Clients/Work:** Solicitors' negligence; company/shareholders dispute; building dispute and employment.

Thomas Handler, Baker & McKenzie Has conducted 4 commercial mediations, including one in the Central London County court. Also involved in the Camden neighbourhood disputes scheme (3 mediations). **Clients/Work:** Environmental, neighbourhood and commercial disputes.

Julian Holloway, Greenwoods Involved in CEDR and conducts ad hoc mediations, although he is less active this year.

Jonathan Lux, Ince & Co Has trained as a mediator with CEDR, ADRNET and the British Academy of Experts. Conducted 6 mediations in the last 6 months, mainly as mediator. **Clients/Work:** Maritime, insurance and international trade.

Paul Mitchard, Simmons & Simmons CEDR accredited, this year he successfully resolved a court ordered mediation of a shipping insurance dispute and a 3 party international dispute. He is regarded as "professional and sensible."

Stephen Tester, Cameron McKenna Is a "good and experienced mediator." Mediated 2 cases this year (commercial and contractual dispute and a marine construction project claim). His team have also represented clients in 3 mediations. **Clients/Work:** Commercial, marine, construction, licensing and insurance.

Andrew Thomas, Lewis Silkin Has mediated in 2 cases in the last 6 months and is ADR accredited.

THE REGIONS

Andrew Paton, Pinsent Curtis (Birmingham) Universally respected and still generally regarded as the "crème de la crème," he mediated 11 disputes last year and took another 30 to mediation. **Clients/Work:** He mediated a three party £2.4m multi-jurisdictional insurance dispute, a shipping insurance claim and a £1m professional negligence claim arising from a sewerage scheme collapse.

Phillip Howell-Richardson, Morgan Bruce (Cardiff) A popular choice, he is Chairman of ADRNET and generally seen as outstanding, with some naming him as the best outside London. He is said to possess all the attributes of a great mediator "innovation," "good communication," "an open personality," "commanding manner and presence" and a "long suffering nature." "He appears to physically listen." **Clients/Work:** Successfully ran an ADR pilot scheme for a clearing bank and mediated in numerous disputes, including an emotional dispute between the purchaser of a new house and the building company.

Jonathan Lloyd-Jones, Linnells (Oxford) "First class" and one interviewee called him "the best mediator in the UK." Others found him "gentle," "creative," "calm," "effective" and "good with people." **Clients/Work:** Acted as mediator or advocate in 12 cases this year, including a £3m multi party occupiers liability case, a 4 party professional negligence case represented by a total of 17 people and a family trust dispute.

Tim Wallis, Crutes (Carlisle) "Absolutely tireless" in his promotion of ADR, he writes and lectures on ADR, organises roadshows to disseminate information and spent three months in the US researching ADR. Widely admired for his commitment.

Anthony Glaister, Denison Till (York) Is an active promoter of ADR and "an excellent mediator." Also acts as an advocate and lectures to students and professional bodies. Set up the Association of Northern Mediators. **Clients/Work:** 7 mediations, including housing, construction and partnership disputes and a five year old £450,000 personal injury case.

Bill Goyder, Jacksons (Teeside) Currently less active in ADR due to administrative tasks as managing partner, but still considered "good and personable." "A great pragmatist who cuts through the legal jargon and set clients at ease." **Clients/Work:** Mediated 6 disputes this year.

Euan Temple, Linnells (Oxford) A non contentious lawyer, "he looks for the commercial solution" and has conducted 17 mediations in total, 4 this year. **Clients/Work:** A three party banking/securities dispute; a contractual/agency case and a partnership dispute.

John Winkworth-Smith, Dibb Lupton Alsop (Leeds) Very active in running a firm-wide mediation initiative and training all his firm's litigators. He is also on the Board of CEDR. **Clients/Work:** 4 housing association and general commercial mediations.

Robin Bloom, Jacksons (Teeside) Another Jacksons person, he finds that suggesting ADR often leads to the case settling and that litigation is becoming the last resort. He has recently conducted two mediations and has another two upcoming.

Ronald Bradbeer, Eversheds (Newcastle) A member of the Association of Northern Mediators, he "works hard to get cases settled and has the necessary gravitas

and grey hair." Popular with Scottish litigants. **Clients/Work:** 3 mediations as mediator and 3 as advocate. Mainly construction.

Michael Davies, Veale Wasborough (Bristol) "Experienced" mediator who has conducted 10 mediations, both as mediator and advocate. Seen as "a first class presenter." **Clients/Work:** Includes a three party contractual dispute and two professional negligence claims, one relating to a will and the other to conveyancing/planning.

John Gatenby, Addleshaw Booth & Co (Manchester) Is a director of CEDR and an enthusiastic exponent of ADR who acts primarily as an advocate and trainer. He finds that suggesting ADR often leads to cases then settling.

Robert Langley, Watson Burton (Newcastle) An extremely tough negotiator who is keen on mediation. **Clients/Work:** A construction lawyer, he has mediated in 3 solicitors negligence cases this year, one of which involved an emotional litigant in person.

ANDREWARTHA, Jane
Clyde & Co, London (0171) 623 1244
See under Aviation: Aviation Insurance
Litigation, p. 131

BLOOM, J. Robin
Jacksons, Stockton-on-Tees (01642) 643643
Specialisation: Employment law and
commercial litigation (including use of
alternative dispute resolution).
Prof. Memberships: Law Society. Founder
Member Newcastle Industrial Tribunal User
Group.
Career: Educated: Rugby School, Durham
University and Chester College of Law. Career:
Articled *Cohen Jackson* and *Addleshaw Sons
and Latham*. Admitted: October 1982, worked
for and subsequently partner in *Cohen Jackson*,
now *Jacksons*. Trained as Mediator by ADR Net
Ltd.
Personal: Married with two children. Main
leisure interests are sport (mainly watching but
still play the occasional game of cricket); foreign
travel; gardening.

BRADBEER, Ronald
Eversheds, Newcastle upon Tyne
(0191) 261 1661
See under Health Care, p. 412

BROWN, Henry
Penningtons, London (0171) 457 3000
Consultant in Commercial and Family
Departments.
Specialisation: Principal areas of practice are
ADR (mediation) intellectual property, especially
publishing, partnerships and family
business/matrimonial work. Member of pilot
scheme 'Solicitors in Mediation' (1985-88).
Author of Law Society's Report on ADR (1991),
co-author of Brown & Marriott 'ADR Principles
and Practice' (1993). Has conducted training for
the Family Mediators Association, Centre for
Dispute Resolution and College of Law and
established mediation training programme for
Solicitors Family Law Association and Family
Lawyers of Denmark. Charge-out rate is £220
per hour.
Prof. Memberships: Law Society, Solicitors
Family Law Association, Family Mediators
Association (Founder Member, 1988), UK
College of Family Mediators, Centre For Dispute
Resolution, Mediation UK, Academy of Family
Mediators (US), Society of Professionals in
Dispute Resolution (US), Immigration Law
Practitioners' Association, Clarity.
Career: Qualified in South Africa, 1962 and in
England & Wales 1975. Established *Simanowitz
& Brown* in 1975. Partner at *Birkbeck Montagu's*
1980-91, then *Penningtons* 1991-94. Consultant
from 1994.
Personal: Born 29th May 1939. Educated at
the University of Cape Town (Diploma in Law,
1959) and the University of South Africa (part-
time) (BA, 1967). Certificate in the
Fundamentals of Psychotherapy and
Counselling (Regents College, 1994).
Accredited Mediator (CEDR). Family Mediator
(FMA and SFLA).

CORNES, David L.
Winward Fearon, London (0171) 420 2800
See under Construction & Civil Engineering,
p. 197

DAVIES, Michael
Veale Wasbrough, Bristol (0117) 925 2020
Specialisation: Background in commercial
litigation, financial services litigation and
professional negligence claims. Currently
specialising in employment related litigation.
Career: M.A., Ph.D. Partner *Veale Benson*,
subsequently *Veale Wasbrough*, since 1981.
Personal: Married, two children.

FINCHAM, A.L.R.
Cameron McKenna, London
(0171) 367 3000
Specialisation: Employment and Commercial
Litigation.
Career: Degree in Modern History (Oriel
College, Oxford). Qualified 1980. Partner
Cameron Markby from 1984.
Personal: Married with two children.

GATENBY, John K.
Addleshaw Booth & Co, Manchester
(0161) 934 6000
Email: jkg@addleshaw-booth.co.uk
Partner
Specialisation: Advises English and overseas
private and public companies on international
litigation and arbitration matters, including the
enforcement of foreign judgements. Also advises
on commercial contract disputes including
partnership law. Cases handled include BP
Exploration Co (Libya) Ltd v. Hunt, The Halcyon
the Great, The Halcyon Skies and Noirhomme v.
Walklate. General editor of 'Recovery of Money',
and has also written on discovery and inspection
of documents. Has also contributed articles to
'Modern Law Review', 'Arbitration', and 'Litigation
Letter'. Lectures regularly on civil procedure
matters including international litigation,
discovery, arbitration and ADR.
Prof. Memberships: Law Society, Chartered
Institute of Arbitrators (Fellow), Institute of Credit
Management, IBA, SEG, LSLA, Commonwealth
Lawyers Association, Commercial Law League
of America, Association of Partnership
Practitioners, Director of CEDR.
Career: Qualified in 1975. With *Linklaters &
Paines* 1973-82. Head of Litigation at *Withers*
1983-84. Joined the firm in 1984, becoming a
Partner in 1985.
Personal: Born 26th April 1950. Educated at
West Hartlepool Grammar School 1962-68 and
Trinity Hall, Cambridge 1968-72. Elder, Poynton
Baptist Church.

GLAISTER, Anthony
Denison Till, Leeds (0113) 246 7161
Specialisation: Using the widest spectrum of
alternatives to resolve commercial disputes to
match all means. Experience includes
mediation by executive tribunal and combined
with arbitration. Visiting lecturer on mediation
studies at Leeds Metropolitan University.
Charges £125 per hour or agreed fee.
Prof. Memberships: ORSA Adjudicator, CEDR
Mediator, Administrator Association of Northern
Mediators, and Chartered Institute of
Arbitrators.
Career: Qualified in 1980. Partner in *Fox &
Gibbons*, London from 1985 to 1989 and
Denison Till since.
Personal: Born April 1953. Very active leisure
pursuits where family and farming activities
allow. Regional Deputy Chairman PYBT

GOYDER, William A.
Jacksons, Stockton-on-Tees (01642) 643643
Managing Partner, Member of Commercial
Litigation Department.
Specialisation: Civil and mechanical
engineering Contract disputes, professional
negligence claims, partnership disputes,
insolvency related claims, Mental Health Review
Tribunal representation. Involved in numerous
mediations during 1995-97 including five party
construction claim for £2.5 million.
Prof. Memberships: Director ADR Net Limited,
Member of Law Society Mental Health Panel.
Career: 1963-1964 International Paper Co.,
E42nd Street, New York City. Qualified 1968.
Assistant Solicitor Berkshire County Council.
Assistant Contracts Manager Head Wrightson &
Co., 1970-1973, Partner H*ewitt Brown-Humes &
Hare* 1973-1983, Partner *Jowett & Goyder* 1983-
1990, Partner *Jacksons* 1990-Present.
Personal: Born 12.5.42. Mill Hill School, Trinity
College, Cambridge. Chairman of Governors,
Polam Hall School. Part time jazz musician.

HANDLER, Thomas J.
Baker & McKenzie, London (0171) 919 1000
Consultant in Commercial Litigation Department
and Environmental Law Group.
Specialisation: Practice covers a broad range
of domestic and international commercial
disputes work involving litigation, arbitration and
alternative dispute resolution techniques, as
well as a broad range of environmental law
issues. Major clients include government
instrumentalities and English and multi-national
companies manufacturing and supplying
products and providing services. Has acted as
mediator. Trained and accredited by Centre for
Dispute Resolution and trained by Mediation
UK's Camden Mediation Service. With Chris
Newmark of *Baker & McKenzie* helped
Mediation UK to formulate submissions to Lord
Woolf's enquiry and commented by invitation of
the Lord Chancellor's Department on its draft
consumer booklet on ADR.
Prof. Memberships: Law Society, UK
Environmental Law Association, British-
Hungarian Society.
Career: Qualified in England & Wales 1966 and
in New South Wales, Australia, 1962. Partner at
Baker & McKenzie 1973-1994. Chairman,
Environmental Resolve (The Environment
Council). Member, Board of Directors of The
Environment Council. Member, Board of
Trustees, Foundation for International
Environmental Law and Development. Member,
Executive Committee of the Environmental Law
Foundation.
Personal: Born 25th May 1938, Budapest,
Hungary. Educated Fort Street Boys' High
School, Sydney and University of Sydney, New
South Wales (BA, LLB). Fluent Hungarian and
some German and French. Charity Trustee.

HOLLOWAY, Julian
Greenwoods, London (0171) 323 4632

HOWELL-RICHARDSON, Phillip
Morgan Bruce, Cardiff
(01222) 385385
See under Litigation (Commercial): 200+
Solicitors, p. 525

KENDALL, G. John
Allen & Overy, London (0171) 330 3000
Specialisation: Specialises in arbitration, expert determination and ADR; has appeared as an advocate in international arbitrations, and conducted some major domestic construction disputes. Has written only textbook on Expert Determination. (FT Law & Tax, second edition, 1996). Co-author, with David Sutton and Judith Gill of Russell on Arbitration (Sweet & Maxwell, 21st edition, 1997). An accredited mediator with CEDR. An accredited adjudicator with ORSA. Fellow, Chartered Institute of Arbitrations.
Prof. Memberships: Member The Law Society, The City of London Law Society, Society of Construction Law, The Official Referees Solicitors Association, International Bar Association; Chairman Alternative Dispute Resolution Sub-committee 1994 to 1996.
Career: Articled *Stephenson Harwood*, qualified 1976, Partner *Allen & Overy* 1985.
Personal: Oxford University (1972 BA, 1976 MA). Born 1950.

LANGLEY, Robert Lennox
Watson Burton, Newcastle upon Tyne (0191) 244 4444
See under Construction & Civil Engineering, p. 212

LLOYD-JONES, Jonathan
Linnells, Oxford (01865) 248607
Managing Partner – Head of Commercial Dispute Resolution.
Specialisation: Construction and professional negligence litigation. Company, especially publishing, and general commercial disputes. Mediation.
Prof. Memberships: Law Society. Director of ADR Group Ltd.
Career: Qualified 1979. *Stephenson Harwood* 1977-1980. *Claude Hornby & Cox* 1980-1988 (Partner 1982-1988). *Linnells* 1988 to date (partner 1990). Trained Mediator 1991.
Personal: Born 23rd November 1954. Educated at Sevenoaks School and Southampton University. Interests: Fly fishing, British water colours, family life. Lives in Oxford.

LUX, Jonathan
Ince & Co, London (0171) 623 2011
Partner from 1983 onwards.
Specialisation: Work includes shipping, international trade and insurance advice and litigation. Has acted in many cases and transactions in these fields. Co- author of `The Law of Tug, Tow and Pilotage' and `The Law and Practice of Marine Insurance and Average' and 'Bunkers'. Editor of `Classification Societies'. Author of various other publications in the fields of maritime law and international trade. Regular speaker at conferences and seminars on shipping, international trade and insurance subjects.
Prof. Memberships: Law Society, London Maritime Arbitrators Association, Chartered Institute of Arbitrators, CEDR, ADR Net, British Academy of Experts, International Bunker Industry Association, International Bar Association.
Career: Qualified and joined *Ince & Co.* in 1975. Became a Partner in 1983.
Personal: Born 30th October 1951. Holds LLB (Hons) (Exhib), 1973, and DES from the University of Aix-Marseilles, 1974. Freeman of the City of London, Liveryman of the Worshipful Company of Solicitors, Chairman of the

International Bar Association's Committee on Maritime and Transport Law; Chairman of the Committee 2 (Trial Observations and Interventions) of the International Bar Association's Human Rights Institute, Fellow of the Chartered Institute of Arbitrators and Council Member of the International Bunker Industry Association Ltd. Leisure interests include opera, theatre, golf, sailing and single-seater motor racing (holder of a national licence). Participated in the Peking to Paris Car Rally (1997) finishing First in Class and awarded gold medal. Lives in London.

MARRIOTT Q.C., Arthur
Debevoise & Plimpton, London (0171) 786 9000

MILES, David
Glovers, London (0171) 629 5121
See under Construction & Civil Engineering, p. 200

MITCHARD, Paul
Simmons & Simmons, London (0171) 628 2020
See under Litigation (Commercial): 200+ Solicitors, p. 520

NEWMARK, Chris
Baker & McKenzie, London (0171) 919 1000
Partner
Specialisation: Practice covers a wide range of domestic and international commercial disputes work involving litigation and arbitration as well as alternative dispute resolution techniques. Has advised clients in mediation in both England and the United States. Also practices as mediator for commercial disputes.
Prof. Memberships: The Law Society.
Career: Qualified 1990. At *Baker & McKenzie* since 1988. Elected Partner in 1997. Spent 1993-94 working in the firm's Chicago office. Studied Dispute Resolution at University of DePaul, Chicago in 1993-4. Trained as mediator with CPR, New York in 1994. Accredited CEDR mediator in 1995. Trained community mediator with LAMP (Lewisham Action for Mediation Project). Helped Mediation UK to formulate submissions to Lord Woolf's enquiry and commented by invitation of the Lord Chancellor's Department on its draft consumer booklet on ADR. Member of City Disputes Panel working party on ADR clauses.
Personal: Born 16 January 1964. Educated at Abingdon School, Birmingham University and the University of Limoges, France. Interests include golf and photography. Lives in Blackheath.

PATON, Andrew J.
Pinsent Curtis, Birmingham (0121) 200 1050
Partner and Head of Insurance Litigation in Birmingham office.
Specialisation: Defending claims against professionals on instructions of their insurers. Uses mediation extensively to resolve claims. Acts as mediator in wide range of cases.
Prof. Memberships: Training faculty of CEDR. Director of ADR Net Limited. Member of Council of Birmingham Law Society.
Career: Articled *Cripps Harries Hall & Co*, Tunbridge Wells. Qualified 1981. Joined *Pinsent & Co.* (now *Pinsent Curtis*) September 1981. Partner 1985.
Personal: Born 1957. Educated at Bishop Vesey's Grammar School, Sutton Coldfield and

Exeter University (LLB). Interests include yacht and dinghy racing, cycling and tennis.

ROE, Mark
Masons, London (0171) 490 4000
See under Construction & Civil Engineering, p. 201

SHAPIRO, David
S J Berwin & Co, London
+44 (0)171 533 2222
Specialisation: Alternative Dispute Resolution: He is accredited as a mediator by CEDR (Britain's Centre for Dispute Resolution), is on numerous mediation panels, was Director and Chief Mediator of JAMS Endispute Europe, and is currently Visiting Fellow, Department of Law, London School of Economics and Political Science, where he teaches mediation and mediation advocacy. He was organiser of and lead-off speaker on "Introduction to ADR", part of the Judicial Studies Board's Stage 1 seminars for UK judges, and is a lecturer and writer on mediation issues. Since arriving in the UK in 1996, he has successfully mediated a number of major disputes in this country and Europe. He is a Consultant to *S J Berwin & Co* where he serves as Director of that firm's ADR Services Unit.
Prof. Memberships: Centre for Dispute Resolution; British Assn. of Lawyers Mediators; City Disputes Panel; Int. Bar Assn.; American Bar Assn.; The Chartered Inst. of Arbitrators; Soc. of Professionals in Dispute Resolution (SPIDR).
Career: Formerly senior founding partner and Head of Litigation, *Dickstein, Shapiro & Morin*, New York and Washington DC. In 1995 he was principal engineer of the new national class-action settlement of claims arising out of silicone breast implants, affecting more than 800,000 potential plaintiffs world-wide. In 1990, he was the court-appointed Settlement Master in New York for hundreds of claims for injuries from asbestos. In 1988 he was the court-appointed Examiner (Special Master) in the bankruptcy proceedings for Eastern Airlines. In 1986 he served as Chairman of the American Bar Association's National Institute on "New Techniques for Resolving Complex Litigation." In 1985 he was the court-appointed Settlement Master in the "Agent Orange" litigation brought by Vietnam veterans for their exposure to dioxin. In 1981, after having litigated antitrust cases against American Telephone & Telegraph, leading to the Modified Final Judgement that broke the U.S. telephone monopoly, He was retained by AT&T to resolve a myriad of antitrust actions spawned in part by his earlier representation of plaintiffs. For the next eleven years he served as settlement counsel for AT&T and its offspring, the Regional Bell Operating Companies, as well as numerous other major corporations. Lead trial counsel in landmark U.S. cases from 1950 to the early 1980s.
Personal: Born Brooklyn, New York, 17 June 1928; Military Service: United States Naval Reserve 1944-46; Undergraduate education: University of Wisconsin and Brooklyn College, 1946-47; Legal education: Brooklyn Law School, LL.B 1949.

SIBLEY LI.B, Edward.
Berwin Leighton, London +44 171 760 1000
Senior Partner in Litigation Department.
Specialisation: Principal area of practice is international and domestic civil litigation and

mediation, including insurance and re-insurance disputes, professional negligence, and civil fraud. Has acted as a mediator and advocate in a number of commercial mediations. Publications include `The European Community 1992 and Beyond.' He has addressed conferences worldwide on issues relating to the conflict of laws and comparative law.

Prof. Memberships: Member of Litigation Sub-Committee City of London Law Society; Union Internationale des Avocats; American Bar Association; International Bar Association; The Law Society and the New York State Bar.

Career: Qualified in 1965. Articled with *Clifford Turner* 1961-64 and joined *Berwin & Co.* upon qualification. Became a Partner in 1968. Thereafter became a founder Partner *Berwin Leighton* in 1970 and Managing Partner 1984-86. Also admitted New York State Bar 1985 and Founder Member and Director of the Centre for European Dispute Resolution (CEDR) 1989; CEDR appointed Mediator 1992; Associate Member of the Chartered Institute of Arbitrators 1992; Solicitor Advocate Higher Courts (Civil) 1995.

Personal: Born 21st July 1935. Educated at Rhymney Grammar School and University of Wales 1958-61 (First Class Honours and Sir Samuel Evans Prize for the best student of the year). College of Law, Lancaster Gate 1964. Is a member of the Appeals Committee Youth Clubs UK and a Governor of Daiglen School. Member of Reform Club and MCC.

TEMPLE, Euan M.
Linnells, Oxford (01865) 248607
Specialisation: Partner, Head of European Law. M&A work, competition law, MBOs, joint ventures, partnerships, intellectual property licensing, R&D contracts, mediation.

Prof. Memberships: Director – ADR Group Ltd. Chairman – Law Society's International Awareness Working Party. Chairman – 'Eurolegal' – a pan European network of business lawyers (1974-1994).

Career: Graduated Cambridge. Qualified 1970. Partner in private practice since 1974. More recently 1987-1994 Hunt Dickins and 1994-Linnells Oxford. Trained mediator since 1990.

Personal: Western and central European history. Hockey (player and umpire).

TESTER, Stephen
Cameron McKenna, London
(0171) 367 3000
Specialisation: Practises in construction and surveyors' PI, D & O and Contractor All Risk Insurance (both litigation and policy interpretation and drafting). Clients include insurance companies, Lloyds syndicates, insurance brokers and construction companies. Has extensive experience in alternative forms of dispute resolution both as a mediator and as an adviser to individual parties.

Prof. Memberships: Society of Construction Law. CEDR Accredited Mediator.

Career: KCS Wimbledon and St. John's College Cambridge. Qualified 1981. Partner since 1988.

Personal: Interests include family and friends, golf and squash.

THOMAS, Andrew
Lewis Silkin, London (0171) 227 8000
See under Housing Associations, p. 419

WALLIS, Tim
Crutes, Carlisle (01228) 25446

WILLIS, Tony
Clifford Chance, London (0171) 600 1000
See under Litigation (Commercial): 200+ Solicitors, p. 521

WINKWORTH-SMITH, John
Dibb Lupton Alsop, Leeds (0345) 262728
Partner in Commercial Litigation Department.
Specialisation: Principal area of practice is engineering litigation. Specialises in mechanical engineering. Other main area of practice is ADR. Accredited Mediator (CEDR and the British Academy of Experts). Regular lecturer on ADR.

Career: Qualified in 1970. Partner at *Dibb Lupton Broomhead* since 1972.

YORK, Stephen
Hammond Suddards, London
(0171) 655 1000
Specialisation: Commercial Dispute Resolution and International Arbitration (both as Counsel and as Arbitrator), principally in the Civil Engineering and Construction Industry, Software Engineering and Gas Contracts Industries.

Prof. Memberships: Fellow, Chartered Institute of Arbitrators. Admitted in Hong Kong and ACT, Australia. Member of ORSA and British Computer Society.

Career: Articled at *Slaughter and May* and *Ledbury, Merry, Bristol*; Assistant at *Masons* (1982-84). *Baker & McKenzie*, Hong Kong (1984-86); *Masons*, Hong Kong (1986-1991), Partner in 1988. Partner at *Hammond Suddards*, London in 1993. Author: 'Practical ADR' published by Sweet & Maxwell, December 1996.

Personal: Married with four children. Interests include fast motor cars, gastronomic enterprises and travelling abroad.

ARBITRATION (INTERNATIONAL)

RESEARCH: Our team interviewed specialist practitioners, barristers and LCIA and ICC officials, both here and in Paris. In compiling the tables, we considered all the information available to us, paying particular regard to the market research carried out by our team of ten qualified lawyers. (The researchers' details are set out on page three.)

The rankings, therefore, reflect the opinion of the marketplace as revealed by systematic and objective research: see page four. (Our research is audited every year by the British Market Research Bureau.)

OVERVIEW: Domestically, the most important event of the last year has been the implementation of the new Arbitration Act. Intended to simplify the arbitration procedure but still in its infancy, there is currently much uncertainty and speculation as to the Act's actual operation. Internationally, the recently revised institutional rules of the ICC, LCIA and AAA are seen as significant developments. As with last year, we maintain the distinction between firms participating in many areas of arbitration, and those which concentrate primarily on high volume shipping/commodities and construction areas. It still remains the case that a firm's ranking is largely determined by the high profile of its individuals, as evidenced by *Arthur Marriott QC's* departure from Wilmer, Cutler & Pickering.

Due to the highly confidential and sensitive nature of arbitration, many firms have been unable to provide client/ work details.

LEADING FIRMS ACROSS THE BOARD

- FRESHFIELDS
- CLIFFORD CHANCE
- ALLEN & OVERY
- HERBERT SMITH

HIGHLY REGARDED FIRMS

- Coudert Brothers
- Norton Rose
- White & Case
- Linklaters
- Simmons & Simmons
- Wilmer, Cutler & Pickering
- Denton Hall
- Eversheds
- Lovell White Durrant
- Taylor Joynson Garrett

LONDON

'ACROSS THE BOARD'

Freshfields (9ptnrs/18assts). Still regarded by most as the leaders in "high quality, high level complicated international arbitration," despite serious challenge from Clifford Chance. In 1997, they were involved in more than 50 disputes. The "formidable" *Jan Paulsson* remains the most respected advocate/arbitrator around, recently acting as one of three arbitrators at the Winter Olympics. Regarded by some clients as "the best arbitrator in the world." The "well regarded" *Nigel Rawding* and *Philip Croall* lead the London team. *Nigel Blackaby* is up and coming. **Clients/ Work:** Acted for ENEL SpA in a US$13bn gas supply dispute. Acted in technology dispute contract involving Quebec law, and for a pan-Arabic treaty organisation in construction dispute arising from imposition of sanctions on Iran.

Clifford Chance (3ptnrs/17assts) Universally respected and serious challengers for the top slot. Head of London team is "competent, all-rounder" *John Beechey*, assisted by *Audley Sheppard* and *Robert Lambert*. Also

have arbitration practitioners in Paris, Frankfurt, Amsterdam and Rome and are currently conducting a dozen ICC arbitrations. **Clients/ Work:** Acted for Nigeria LNG Ltd against ENEL SpA in the US$13bn gas supply dispute. Bangladesh Oil, Gas and Mineral Corporation and Balfour Beatty.

Allen & Overy Admired by many but have yet to achieve universal recognition. *David Sutton* (now in London) and *Judith Gill* recently wrote the 21st edition of "Russell on Arbitration." *Andrew Clark* is another leader. **Clients/Work:** Energy, construction, media.

Herbert Smith (18ptnrs – p/t). A "first class" team with prominent and often "academic" individuals. *Lawrence Collins QC* is an "exceptional individual" although he does not practise full-time in this area. With the highly respected *Dr Julian Lew*, he has significantly raised the profile of the firm. *Campbell Mclachlan* is up and coming. **Clients/Work:** Taiwan construction arbitration between Italian joint venture and Taiwan government agency. ICC arbitration between US and Italian parties regarding IP. UNCITRAL ad hoc arbitration between Latin American and Caribbean contractors and Russian oil refinery.

Coudert Brothers Operating mainly from Paris, the firm is "well known and well regarded" for its extensive international practice and its leading light *Laurie Craig*, author, advocate and "good" arbitrator. **Clients/Work:** Recent high value work in Singapore and Hong Kong.

Norton Rose Received many recommendations and move up this year as a result of increasing activity in shipping, construction, insurance and international arbitrations. *Michael Lee* directs the Paris operation. **Clients/Work:** ICC arbitrations conducted in English and French. Substantial international work representing American, Asian and European companies.

White & Case An international firm with offices in all the major world arbitration seats. Heading the Paris office (from which many London arbitrations are handled) is *Christopher Seppala*, legal adviser to FIDIC task group and the "well known" *Stephen Bond* who moves up the rankings this year. **Clients/Work:** ICC arbitration work.

Linklaters (16ptnrs) Led by *Christopher Style*, they acted in 27 arbitrations last year. **Clients/Work:** Acted in the Dabhol Power Project arbitration against the Maharashtra government.

Simmons & Simmons (18ptnrs/16assts world-wide) "Coming up fast," they are involved in increasing areas of arbitration and are seen as "active and competent" with some high quality work. Partners *Paul Mitchard* and "up and coming" *Karyl Nairn* lead the initiative. Clients/Work: Cathiship SA v Allanasons Limited ("Catherine Helen") (key decision on extensions of time under the Arbitration Act 1996).

Wilmer, Cutler & Pickering Lost Arthur Marriott but still has *Gary Born*, a "knowledgeable scholar" with good negotiating /drafting skills. Clients/Work: Acting for sovereign state in territories title dispute; for Latin American utility in trade dispute; and for Russian distributor against Western supplier. Conduct arbitrations under ICC, LCIA, UNCITRAL and ad hoc rules.

Denton Hall (7ptnrs/9assts – not full-time) Clients/Work: Representing Allseas Group in dispute with Sembawang in Singapore arising from vessel conversion contract. Acting for rail operating company against Railtrack plc in performance regime dispute. Also act for Total SA.

Eversheds (5ptnrs/9assts – not f/t) Strengthened by the arrival of *Nicholas Valner* from Frere Cholmeley. Described as "active" in the field. Clients/Work: Acting

LEADING INDIVIDUALS · ACROSS THE BOARD	
LEW Julian Herbert Smith	**PAULSSON Jan** Freshfields
MARRIOTT QC Arthur Debevoise & Plimpton	
BEECHEY John Clifford Chance	**CRAIG William Laurence** Coudert Brothers
BOND Stephen White & Case	**RAWDING Nigel** Freshfields
COLLINS QC Lawrence Herbert Smith	**SUTTON David St. John** Allen & Overy
BORN Gary Wilmer, Cutler & Pickering	**MITCHARD Paul** Simmons & Simmons
CLARK Andrew Allen & Overy	**SEPPALA Christopher** White & Case
CROALL Philip Freshfields	**SHEPPARD Audley** Clifford Chance
GILL Judith Allen & Overy	**STYLE Christopher** Linklaters
LAMBERT Robert Clifford Chance	**VALNER Nicholas** Eversheds
LEE Michael Norton Rose	

UP AND COMING	
BLACKABY Nigel Freshfields	**NAIRN Karyl** Simmons & Simmons
MCLACHLAN Campbell Herbert Smith	

SEE PROFILES AT END OF THIS SECTION

for NATO defence contractor in £m claim against a European government involving missile systems; advising US hotel chain in LCIA dispute with Italian franchisee. Representing Internet service provider in ICC case against European Fund.

Lovell White Durrant (16ptnrs world-wide involved in arbitration, of which 6 are fellows of the CIA. All do other forms of litigation as well). Clients/Work: Act for international insurance companies and Lloyd's syndicates. Known for construction work.

Taylor Joynson Garrett (7ptnrs/10assts – not f/t) Arbitrations in the insurance, construction and shipping/ commodities arenas. Clients/Work: Act for Ericsson Telecommunications, Bounty International and the Cooper Cameron group of companies.

Arthur Marriott QC remains highly regarded at Debevoise & Plimpton.

MAINLY CONSTRUCTION

HIGHLY REGARDED FIRMS CONSTRUCTION
Masons
Cameron McKenna
Lane & Partners
Rowe & Maw

Masons A specialist construction firm in a "category of their own." The arbitration offensive is led by "well known" *Philip Capper* and *Robert Knutson*.

Cameron McKenna Recommended for construction, but also active in many other areas, they handle domestic and international arbitrations under ICC, LCIA, UNCITRAL, ICE, ad hoc and statutory rules. Clients/Work: Acting for Unex in £40m multi-party dispute and Great Ormond St Hospital in £10m action under the new act. Clients include Balfour Beatty and UK Highways.

Lane & Partners Specialist construction firm led by *Terry Lane*, they also handle rent reviews and travel industry disputes in London, Europe, India and the Middle East.

Clients/Work: Acting in a multi-million pound aviation claim.

Rowe & Maw (5ptnrs/8assts – also do litigation) Clients/Work: Commercial disputes in Russia and Germany. Acting for major process plant developers.

LEADING INDIVIDUALS CONSTRUCTION
CAPPER Philip Masons
KNUTSON Robert Masons
LANE Terence Lane & Partners

SEE PROFILES AT END OF THIS SECTION

MAINLY SHIPPING/ COMMODITIES

HIGHLY REGARDED FIRMS SHIPPING/COMMODITIES
Clyde & Co
Holman, Fenwick & Willan
Ince & Co
Middleton Potts
Richards Butler
Sinclair Roche & Temperley

Clyde & Co Highly regarded firm specialising in cargo claims. Also work in other areas and are involved in a number of LCIA cases. Clients/Work: International commercial contracts including commodities.

Holman, Fenwick & Willan Well-known shipping firm which acts for owners/salvors and commodities producers. Clients/Work: A major UNCITRAL arbitration in India and 'across the board' international arbitrations.

Ince & Co (40ptnrs/50assts – also litigation) First firm to obtain Mareva injunctions under the new Act by way of security and in support of a foreign arbitration. Mainly do shipping/commodities arbitrations but also undertake other work, including a number of LCIA arbitrations. Clients/Work: Acting for Sumitomo Heavy Industries Ltd re arbitra-

tion with Oil and Natural Gas Corporation of India arising from construction contract for work in off-shore oil field.

Middleton Potts Niche commodities firm. Clients/Work: Shipping and international trade matters.

Richards Butler An international firm with a specialist commodities practice. Clients/ Work: ICC and UNCITRAL.

Sinclair Roche & Temperley (21ptnrs/ 28assts – not full-time) Clients/Work: Sub-sea engineering dispute for major offshore operator; international dispute relating to North Sea floating production unit; dispute between German container liner operator and Brazilian shipowner.

BEECHEY, John

Clifford Chance, London (0171) 600 1000
Partner. Head of International Commercial
Arbitration Group.
Specialisation: International construction and
infrastructure projects; off-shore structures.
Advising on the adoption and implementation
of dispute resolution procedures generally – in
particular in relation to major international
construction and infrastructure projects;
advising and appearing on behalf of clients in
international arbitrations; advising and
speaking about the practice and procedures of
international commercial arbitration; sitting as
an arbitrator/mediator.
Career: Qualified 1977. Partner 1983.

BLACKABY, Nigel A.

Freshfields, London (0171) 936 4000
Specialisation: International Arbitration
Group. International commercial arbitration,
including acting as counsel in ad hoc
arbitrations and arbitrations under the rules of
the AAA, LCIA, ICC and UNCITRAL. Also
advises on the drafting of arbitration clauses in
international contracts.
Prof. Memberships: Law Society, LCIA.
Career: Articled *Freshfields* 1991 to 1993.
Qualified March 1993. Editor Arbitration
International (1995-), co-chair LCIA Young
Arbitration Practitioners Symposium (1996-).
Personal: Born 20 April 1967. Attended University
of Exeter, Universite d'Aix en Provence and College
of Law, Chester. Speaks French and Spanish.

BOND, Stephen

White & Case, London (44-171) 726 6361
Partner in Arbitration/Litigation Department Also
at *White & Case*, Paris (00 33 1) 55 04 15 15
Specialisation: International commercial law
practice specialising in international
arbitration. Has acted as counsel or arbitrator
in a number of international arbitrations
around the world (under ICC, LCIA,
Stockholm, UNCITRAL and other arbitration
rules) involving disputes in such fields as oil
and gas, construction,computer and
international sales, joint ventures and
distribution. Currently US member of ICC
International Court of Arbitration and was Vice-
President of ICC Working Group to Revise the
ICC Rules of Arbitration.
Prof. Memberships: ABA, IBA, Chartered
Institute of Arbitrators (Fellow), Association
Suisse de l'Arbitrage, Comité Français de
l'Arbitrage. Panel of Arbitrators of: AAA
(International Panel), Arbitral Centre of the
Federal Economic Chamber (Vienna, Austria),
Australian Centre for International Commercial
Arbitrators, Center for Public Resources
International Panel of Distinguished Neutrals,
Court of Arbitration at the Polish Chamber of
Commerce, Hong Kong International Arbitraton
Centre, Korea Commercial Arbitration Board,
London Court of International Arbitration,
Singapore International Arbitrators Centre, US
Council for International Business (ICC Committee
in US), World Industrial Property Organization.
Career: Member New York (since 1969) and
Paris (since 1992) Bars. Law Clerk, Federal
District Court (EDNY) 1968-69; *Stroock & Stroock
& Lavan*, New York, 1969-71; *Law Offices of
Samuel Pisar*, Paris, 1971-73; Office of the Legal
Adviser, US Department of State, Washington &

Geneva, 1974-85; Secretary General ICC
International Court of Arbitration, Paris, 1985-91;
White & Case, Paris, 1991-Present.
Personal: Born 5th July 1943. Educated at
Brown University (BA 1965), Columbia
University Law School (J.D. 1968).

BORN, Gary B.

Wilmer, Cutler & Pickering, London
(0171) 872 1000
Managing Partner in International
Arbitration/Litigation Department.
Specialisation: Principal area of practice is
international arbitration. Represents US,
European, Asian and other corporate clients in
international commercial arbitration under all
major institutional rules (ICC, LCIA, AAA,
Stockholm, IACAC) and ad hoc (UNCITRAL) in
all leading fora. Other main area of practice is
international litigation (US) including advice on
issues of foreign sovereign immunity,
international judicial assistance, conflict of
laws, etc. Important cases handled include
Laker Airways v Lufthansa et al, BCCI
(representing major creditor), Republic of China
v. Liu, Comsat Corporation v Zaire, Citibank v.
Wells Fargo, Aerospatiale v District Court and
Trinidad and Tobago v Tesoro. Author of
'International Commercial Arbitration:
Commentary and Materials' (Kluwer, 1994) and
author of 'International Civil Litigation in United
States Courts' (3rd edition, Kluwer 1996). Has
undertaken numerous speaking engagements.
Editor, *International Litigation Newsletter*.
Prof. Memberships: International Bar
Association, American Bar Association, British
Institute of International and Comparative Law,
Amercan Society of International Law.
Career: Joined *Wilmer, Cutler & Pickering* in
1984. Became a Partner in 1988 and Managing
Partner in London office in 1991.
Personal: Educated at Haverford College,
Haverford, Pennsylvania 1973-78 (BA, summa
cum laude) and University of Pennsylvania Law
School 1978-81 (J.D., summa cum laude).
Proficient in German.

CAPPER, Phillip

Masons, London (0171) 490 4000
Partner, specialising in International Arbitration,
Engineering and Construction.
Specialisation: Recognised authority on legal
aspects of design and construction risks. Great
deal of his practice relates to rail and
infrastructure projects, and advice to projects in
UK, Europe and world-wide (highway, defence,
transportation, high technology, and many
aspects of construction procurement). Since
1989 has represented TML, the consortium
designing and building the Channel Tunnel.
Other major clients include eg GEC-ALSTHOM.
Also advised extensively on the application to
projects of ISO 9000 Quality Assurance.
Worked with brokers and lead underwriters in
drafting a new insurance policy for Design &
Construct. Selected by CIRIA for the legal risk
management aspects of a new report 'A
Client's Guide to Risk in Construction'. For the
ICE, drafted the new Adjudication and Disputes
clauses for the 2nd edition of the New
Engineering Contract.
Prof. Memberships: UK member of the ICC
Commission on International Arbitration,
corresponding member of the ICC Institute of

International Business Law and Practice, and
member of the UK ICC Arbitration national
committee. His national and international lectures
include: in 1992 to a colloquium at the French
Senate on 'L'Europe et les Marchés Publics' for
L'Association Promouvoir la France; in 1993 the
inaugural Lloyds Register Lecture for the Royal
Academy of Engineering of 'Practical
Management of Legal Risks', in 1994 at the USA
DART (Dispute Avoidance and Resolution Task
Force) Multi Disciplinary Conference in
Kentucky, as special invited speaker on key
provisions in the Channel Tunnel Contract; and,
in 1995 at the XVIIth Annual Meeting of the ICC
Institute in Brussels on dispute resolution within
the performance of contracts.
Career: He is also a visiting Professor of
Construction Law at King's College, London
and before joining Masons in 1987 he was
Chairman of the Faculty of Law at the University
of Oxford. He remains a Fellow by special
election of Keble College, Oxford.
Personal: Born 1952.

CLARK, Andrew J.C.

Allen & Overy, London (0171) 330 3000
Specialisation: Partner specialising in
international commercial and corporate litigation
and arbitration. Clients include major corporates
and merchant, commercial and investment banks.
Prof. Memberships: Fellow of the Chartered
Institute of Arbitrators 1993, Member The City
of London Solicitors' Company.
Career: Articled *Allen & Overy*, qualified 1980,
Assistant Solicitor, London 1980-81, Assistant
Solicitor, Dubai 1981-84, Assistant Solicitor,
London 1984-85, Partner, London 1985-89,
Resident Partner, Dubai 1989-94, Partner,
London 1994.
Personal: Trinity College, Cambridge (MA).
Born 29/4/55.

COLLINS, Q.C., Lawrence A.

Herbert Smith, London (0171) 374 8000
See under Litigation (Commercial), p. 519

CRAIG, William Laurence

Coudert Brothers, London (0171) 203 2248
(Also at Coudert Freres, Paris, (331) 43 59 0160.)
Partner in Arbitration and Litigation Department.
Specialisation: Head of *Coudert Brothers*
International arbitration practise in Europe. Has
acted as counsel in more than 150 International
Chamber of Commerce arbitrations, including
numerous disputes involving states and state
agencies (also arbitration involving states
before the International Centre for the
Settlement of Investment Disputes). Acted as
arbitrator (party-appointed, sole arbitrator or
chairman) in 20 ICC arbirations and in numerous
AAA and ad hoc arbitrations. Has represented
parties in oil concession, production sharing, and
operating and exploration agreements. Also
agreements for the joint development of natural
resources, and long term commodity purchase
agreements. Has undertaken contract
negotiations and dispute resolution in Brazil,
Egypt, Kuwait, Qatar, Lebanon, Algeria, Iraq, Iran,
Phillipines, Saudi Arabia and Libya. Co-author,
'Annotated guide to the 1998 ICC Arbitration
Rules' and 'International Chamber of Commerce
Arbitration' (2nd Ed., 1990). Author of articles in
numerous professional publications including
Harvard Law Review, Arbitration International and

the *Yearbook of Commercial Arbitration*.
Career: Admitted to Bars of New York 1958, District of Columbia 1960, US Supreme Court 1963. Admitted in Paris as Conseil Juridique 1972 and as Avocat 1992. Partner at *Coudert Freres*, Paris since 1964. Member, NATO Appeal Board 1972-76. Member, ICC Court of Arbitration 1976-84.
Personal: Born 17th September 1933. Educated at Williams College, Williamstown, Mass., Harvard Law School (Juris Doctor cum laude, 1957) and the University of Paris (Docteur en droit de l'Universite). Lives in Paris, France.

CROALL, Philip. M.
Freshfields, London (0171) 936 4000
Partner specialising in Arbitration, ADR and Commercial Litigation.
Specialisation: Handles all aspects of international commercial arbitration work. Has conducted arbitrations under rules of the key arbitration institutions such as the ICC, the LCIA and ad hoc arbitration under the UNCITRAL Rules. Speaks at seminars and writes articles on arbitration. Also involved in all kinds of commercial litigation including banking and financial services.
Prof. Memberships: Associate of the Chartered Institute of Arbitrators.
Career: Qualified at *Freshfields* in 1985. Partner at *Freshfields* 1992.
Personal: Born 22 August 1959.

GILL, Judith A.E.
Allen & Overy, London (0171) 330 3000
Partner in Litigation Department.
Specialisation: Principal areas of practice are arbitration and commercial litigation. Extensive experience in all forms of arbitration proceedings, both domestic and international, particularly arbitrations under LCIA and ICC rules. Also handles general commercial litigation – acts for a number of large quoted public limited companies on a range of matters including warranty claims, pensions litigation and insurance disputes.
Prof. Memberships: Law Society, City of London Solicitors' Company, Associate Member of the Chartered Institute of Arbitrators.
Career: Qualified in 1985. Joined *Allen & Overy* in 1983 and became a Partner in 1992.
Personal: Born 30th September 1959. Educated at Worcester College, Oxford University 1979-1982. Awarded an MA (Jurisprudence) from Oxford University 1988. Diploma in International Commercial Arbitration from University of London 1990. Lives in Surrey.

KNUTSON, Robert
Masons, London (0171) 490 4000
email: robert.knutson@masons.com
Specialisation: International Commercial Arbitration and Sale of Goods; International Construction Contracts and disputes; Comparative law and conflicts of law; practising arbitrator; advisor on projects valued at greater than £1 billion last year.
Prof. Memberships: Canadian member, ICC Commission on International Arbitration; member, Canadian ICC Arbitration Committee (member qualifications sub-committee); Fellow, Chartered Institute of Arbitrators (England); CIA registered Construction Industry Adjudicator; member, IBA Committees on International Sale

of Goods and sub-committee Chairman International Construction Projects (Newsletter Editor for both committees); ABA Associate member, member, Society of Construction Law; co-founder, and Treasurer, International Arbitration Club.
Career: LLB University of British Columbia, 1982; Barrister and Solicitor, Canada, 1983; LLM, LSE, 1984; Solicitor, England and Wales, 1988; MSc Construction Law and Arbitration, 1991; partner, *Masons* 1996; MPhil University of London 1997; practised in Canadian, American and English law firms, numerous publications; visiting lecturer on arbitration, Kings College, London; regular speaker on international construction and arbitration.
Personal: Born 22/10/56; lives in Dulwich, married, 2 children.

LAMBERT, Robert
Clifford Chance, London (0171) 600 1000
Specialisation: Partner specialising in the law and practice of international arbitration, conflict of laws and jurisdiction. Particular experience in disputes involving: international engineering, constructions and infrastructure projects. Represents clients as Counsel (advocate) before domestic and international arbitral tribunals. Regularly advises on the drafting of dispute resolution provisions for projects and other commercial contracts.
Career: Oxford University (St. Edmund Hall) BA Hons Law (First Class). Trained *Clifford Chance*; Qualified 1989, Partner *Clifford Chance* 1997.
Personal: Born 1965. Resides London.

LANE, Terence M.
Lane & Partners, London (0171) 242 2626
Founding Partner and Senior Partner in Charge of Arbitration and Construction.
Specialisation: Main area of practice is arbitration, with emphasis on construction disputes. Since 1954 has advised on major construction contracts in Saudi Arabia, Kuwait, Abu Dhabi, Libya, Iraq, Iran, Oman, Algeria, Egypt, Tanzania, Botswana, Malawi, Zambia, Mauritius, Indonesia, the Bahamas, Pakistan, Malaysia, South Korea, Singapore, Lebanon and N. Yemen. Has acted as Chairman of an ICC Arbitration Tribunal appointed to determine disputes involving major oil refinery in Saudi Arabia. Through *Lane & Partners*, founder member of the London International Court of Arbitration Users Council. Also handles intellectual property work, particularly licensing. Has acted in numerous international arbitrations, mainly as Counsel for the Contractor, involving claims against Government agencies and ministries and private (non-governmental) employers. Currently representing the Republic of Korea in claims against Iraq through the United Nations Compensation Commission in Geneva. Author of 'English Law of International Licensing Agreements', 'English Law of Trade Secrets and Confidence Agreements', 'Businessman's Guide to the Antitrust Provisions of the Rome Treaty', 'Legal Implications of British Entry to the Common Market' and 'Licensing in Eastern Europe'.
Prof. Memberships: Fellow of the Chartered Institute of Arbitrators, Member of the International Bar Association, Member of the International Fiscal Association, Member of

the Institute of Trade Mark Agents.
Career: Qualified in 1953. Founding Partner of *Lane & Partners* in 1974. Served in the Royal Artillery 1940-46, seconded to the Indian Army as Major; and HM Colonial Administrative Service, District Commissioner and Judge, Chunya District, Tanganyika Territory (Tanzania) 1946-49.
Personal: Born 5th October 1918. Attended London University BA (Hons) (Modern History); Indiana University, USA (Constitutional Law) and College of Law, London. Freeman of the City of London, Liveryman of the Worshipful Company of Arbitrators. Lives in Rake, Liss, Hants.

LEE, Michael J. A.
Norton Rose, France Paris
+33 (0) 1 53 89 56 00
Managing Partner of Paris office and head of International Arbitration Group.
Specialisation: Main areas of practice are international arbitration, particularly ICC and LCIA arbitrations and general commercial and banking litigation, particularly financial services litigation and disciplinary proceedings. Has acted as arbitrator and as counsel in commercial international arbitrations. Author of various articles on arbitration and other related issues. Co-Editor of IBA publication, 'Obtaining Evidence in other Jurisdictions in Business Disputes'.
Prof. Memberships: Fellow, Chartered Institute of Arbitrators; alternate UK Member ICC Court of International Arbitration; Member of ICC Commission on International Arbitration; Member Commercial Court Committee; Member IBA Task Force on Economic Consequences of Litigation; CEDR accredited mediator.

LEW, Julian
Herbert Smith, London (0171) 374 8000
Partner in Litigation and Arbitration Department. 1970 (Bar) 1981 (Solicitor) 1985 (Attorney-at-Law, New York).
Specialisation: Main area of practice is international commercial arbitration, acting as an adviser and representing clients in different forms of arbitrations: concerning all kinds of international contracts, particularly investments, distribution, intellectual property licenses and joint ventures. Has also been appointed as an arbitrator in ICC, LCIA, AAA, Ad hoc and other arbitrations. Author, 'Applicable Law in International Commercial Arbitration' (1978), Editor, 'International Trade: Law and Practice' (1985), 'Contemporary Problems in International Commercial Arbitration' (1985), 'The Immunity of Arbitrators' (1990) and 'Enforcement of Foreign Judgements' (1994). Head of the School of International Arbitration at the Centre for Commercial Law Studies at Queen Mary & Westfield College, University of London; Chairman of the Chartered Institute of Arbitrators' Committee on Arbitral Practice, and Chairman of the ICC Working Party on Intellectual Property Disputes in Arbitration.
Prof. Memberships: British Institute of International and Comparative Law, London Court of International Arbitration, Chartered Institute of Arbitrators, American Society of International Law, American Bar Association, Swiss Arbitration Association, French Arbitration Committee, Hong Kong International Arbitration Centre, International Bar Association, Arbitral Centre of the Federal Economic Chamber, Vienna.

Personal: Born 3rd February 1948. Took an LLB (Hons) London, 1969; Academy of International Law, the Hague, 1970-71; and Doctorat special en droit international, Université Catholique de Louvain, Belgium, 1977. Lives in Hampstead Garden Suburb, London.

MARRIOTT, Arthur
Debevoise & Plimpton, London
(0171) 786 9000

MCLACHLAN, Campbell A.
Herbert Smith, London (0171) 374 8000
See under Litigation (Commercial), p. 520

MITCHARD, Paul
Simmons & Simmons, London
(0171) 628 2020
See under Litigation (Commercial), p. 520

NAIRN, Karyl
Simmons & Simmons, London
(0171) 628 2020
Specialisation: Practises in general international commercial arbitration and litigation specialising in conflict of laws issues. Major cases in 1997/98 include arbitrations for a multi-national oil company, European software company, US property partnership, advising a European pharmaceutical company on US class actions and leading a worldwide investigation on behalf of a major media company. Member of a working group advising the European Telecommunications Platform on dispute resolution issues.
Prof. Memberships: The Law Society of England and Wales, The Law Council of Australia, The Law Society of Western Australia, The City of London Solicitors' Company, American Bar Association, International Bar Association, The Arbitration Club, London Court of International Arbitration.
Career: Qualified as a barrister and solicitor of the Supreme Court of Western Australia and the Federal and High Courts of Australia in 1988, admitted as a solicitor in England and Wales in 1991. 1985-1990 worked at *Michell Sillar McPhee Meyer*, Australia; 1990 Tutor at Law School of University of Western Australia; joined *Simmons & Simmons* in 1991, became a Partner in 1996. Head of *Simmons & Simmons'* International Arbitration Group.
Personal: Educated at University of Western Australia (B.Juris(Hons), L.L.B.(Hons)) and London School of Economics, University of London (L.L.M.).

PAULSSON, Jan
Freshfields, London 0171 936 4000
(Paris Office) Int+ 33 1 44564456
Partner in Litigation/Arbitration Department.
Specialisation: Has acted as counsel or arbitrator in some 300 International arbitral proceedings conducted in English or French in the major venues of Europe and the United States, mostly under the rules of the ICC, but also notably under those of the LCIA, UNCITRAL, ICSID, and the Stockholm Institute; as well as in ad hoc arbitrations. Co-author of the standard text, 'International Chamber of Commerce Arbitration'.
Prof. Memberships: Vice-President London Court of International Arbitration, WIPO Consultative Commission, International Olympic Committee's Tribunal Arbitral du Sport.
Career: Qualified in 1977. Joined *Freshfields*,

in Paris, as a Partner in 1989.
Personal: Born 1949. Attended Harvard University, Yale Law School and University of Paris. Editor of Arbitration International. Lives in Paris.

RAWDING, Nigel K.
Freshfields, London (0171) 936 4000
Partner in Litigation Department and London head of Freshfields' London/Paris International Arbitration Group.
Specialisation: International dispute resolution specialist representing clients in major commercial disputes involving litigation, international arbitration and ADR procedures. International arbitration experience includes ICC, LCIA and UNCITRAL cases. Litigation experience comprises a wide variety of High Court commercial cases. Co-author of The *Freshfields* Guide to Arbitration and ADR (Kluwer, 1992). Regular contributor to arbitration journals and conference speaker on subjects relating to the resolution of international disputes.

SEPPALA, Christopher
White & Case, London 0171 726 6361
Paris Office + (33) 1 55 04 15 15. Partner in Arbitration/Litigation Department.
Specialisation: International commercial law practice in Paris since 1972 specialising in international arbitration. Has acted as counsel or arbitrator in many international arbitrations (ICC, UNCITRAL and other) involving a wide variety of disputes; currently Legal Adviser and member of the FIDIC Task Group for updating FIDIC's forms of international construction contract.
Prof. Memberships: ABA, FIDIC, IBA, ICC organisations, Editorial Boards of I.C.L.R. (London) and R.D.A.I. (Paris).
Career: Member of New York (since 1970) and Paris (since 1974) Bars. At *Sullivan & Cromwell* New York, 1967-72, Law Offices of *S.G. Archibald*, Paris, 1972-1988 (Partner from 1976). Joined *White & Case* as a Partner in 1988.
Personal: Born October 18, 1941. Educated at Harrow School, Harvard University, Columbia University and University of Paris.

SHEPPARD, Audley W.
Clifford Chance, London (0171) 600 1000
Partner in the International Commercial Arbitration Group.
Specialisation: Specialises in the resolution of disputes arising out of infrastructure and energy projects; also advises on public international law issues. Co-rapporteur of the International Commercial Arbitration Committee of the International Law Association. Author of annotations to the Arbitration Act 1996 (Sweet & Maxwell, Current Law Statutes).
Prof. Memberships: Associate of the Chartered Institute of Arbitrators; London Court of International Arbitration; British Institute of International and Comparative Law; International Law Association; International Bar Association.
Career: Barrister and Solicitor New Zealand 1985; Solicitor England 1990; Partner *Clifford Chance* 1995.
Personal: Born 19th August 1960. Attended Victoria University of Wellington, New Zealand (LLB Hons: BCA) and Sidney Sussex College, Cambridge (LLM). Lives in London.

STYLE, Christopher J.D.
Linklaters, London (0171) 456 4286
Specialisation: Specialises in commercial litigation. Has practised in proceedings before the High Court of Justice and Commercial Court. Has conducted numerous arbitrations, both ad hoc and institutional (International Chamber of Commerce, London Maritime Arbitrators' Association, London Court of International Arbitration, etc). Also advised on questions of public international law before international tribunals. Extensive experience of all forms of urgent injunctive relief and a specialist in jurisdictional issues and questions of conflict of laws. Member of London Solicitors Litigation Association and International Bar Association and the City of London Solicitors' Company.

SUTTON, David St. John
Allen & Overy, London (0171) 330 3000
London +44 171 330 3000
Specialisation: Head of the firm's arbitration practice. He specialises in dispute resolution, particularly international arbitration and contentious construction.
Prof. Memberships: Member of the London Court of Arbitration; the International Chamber of Commerce (Mem., Court of Arbitration); Member of the Hong Kong International Arbitration Centre and Fellow of the Chartered Institute of Arbitrators; former member of the Advisory Committee, International School of Arbitration, Queen Mary College and the University of London; visiting lecturer to the Faculty of Law, University of Hong Kong; former joint chairman of committee 'D'; International Bar Association (Settlement of Disputes).
Career: Articled *Robins, Hay, Long & Gardiner*, qualified 1967; Assistant Solicitor 1967-1968; Assistant Solicitor *Allen & Overy* 1968-1970; Partner 1970. Admitted as English and Hong Kong Solicitor; Advocate of Paris bar.
Personal: Born 1941. Educated at Highgate School, Open University (BA).

VALNER, Nicholas E.
Eversheds, London (0171) 919 4500
Head of Commercial Department.
Specialisation: Work includes civil engineering and construction arbitrations, banking disputes, fraud recovery through civil action, royalty and copyright disputes in the music business, insurance policy disputes, Gaming Act proceedings and property investment disputes. Has acted in many arbitrations and Court cases, including Apple Corps v. Apple Computers, Apple Corps v. EMI Records, Polygram v. Royal Reinsurance, Greencap v. Bride Hall, Steerpike (Overseas) Ltd v. Coutts Bank; and leading US/Libya bank cases.
Prof. Memberships: International Bar Association, Chartered Institute of Arbitrators.
Career: Qualified 1979, having joined *Frere Cholmeley Bischoff* in 1977. Became a Partner in 1985. Head of Litigation 1994. Head of Media, Entertainment Group from 1997 to merger with *Eversheds*, London in August 1998.
Personal: Born 14th September 1953. Attended Stonyhurst College 1967-73, then Oxford University 1973-76.

ASSET FINANCE & LEASING

For Consumer Finance (see p 126)

RESEARCH: Our team interviewed specialist practitioners, financiers, operators, deal packagers and others. In compiling the tables, we considered all the information available to us, paying particular regard to the market research carried out by our team of ten qualified lawyers. (The researchers' details are set out on page three.)

The rankings, therefore, reflect the opinion of the marketplace as revealed by systematic and objective research: see page four. (Our research is audited every year by the British Market Research Bureau.)

OVERVIEW: Included are all areas of asset financing and leasing (including aviation finance) with the exception of shipping finance which is dealt with in the Shipping section. Projects/PFI are also dealt with elsewhere although there is overlap on the project finance side.

The 'big ticket' work still remains the preserve of a few City firms. Further divisions may occur as the truly international and global practices break away – particularly on aviation finance. 'Small to middle ticket' work is undertaken by a wider group of firms in London and outside.

In London last year's top five firms remain unchanged with the exception of Wilde Sapte dropping a band. It is difficult to predict the effect of the now aborted Andersens merger on its asset finance practice. Some felt the merger might have caused some problems (including increased conflict situations). Three asset finance/leasing partners (David Smith, Mario Jacovides and Graham Smith) have, in any event, decided to join rival firm Allen & Overy.

The major change in the London market reflects Allen & Overy's up and coming practice. They now rank with Wilde Sapte below the top four firms. The other notable rise up the rankings is Watson, Farley & Williams who move into the leader's table following an overwhelming number of recommendations. Harbottle & Lewis are a new addition to our list and have been recommended for their aviation finance.

Outside London there have been few major changes. Lester Aldridge join Edge & Ellison at the top of the South and Midlands table. Burges Salmon enters our list on recommendation particularly for their rail work.

LEADING FIRMS · LONDON

CLIFFORD CHANCE
FRESHFIELDS
NORTON ROSE
SLAUGHTER AND MAY

ALLEN & OVERY
WILDE SAPTE

CAMERON MCKENNA
HERBERT SMITH
LINKLATERS
LOVELL WHITE DURRANT
THEODORE GODDARD
WATSON, FARLEY & WILLIAMS

HIGHLY REGARDED FIRMS

Berwin Leighton
Field Fisher Waterhouse

Harbottle & Lewis

ASSET FINANCE

LONDON

Clifford Chance (London: 9ptnrs/30assts Overseas: 8ptnrs) Have a strong team which is greatly respected by both practitioners and clients. Active in big and medium ticket deals with a substantial aviation finance practice. Described by clients as providing a "fully fledged international" service with depth which can provide "immediate advice" and "follows business needs." Managed on a global basis with teams in major centres around the world. Following numerous recommendations *Tom Budgett* and *Geoffrey White* join fellow partners *Clive Carpenter* (in Hong Kong) and *Bob Charlton* in the top band of leading individuals. Tom Budgett drew praise for his all round skills and "ability to make things happen." **Clients/Work:** Acting for lenders in connection with the re-fleeting programme of Philippine Airlines. Acting for Airbus in connection with the Iberbus GLL financing of A-340 Aircraft for Iberia. Acting for ECGC and lenders in the financing of Airbus Aircraft for China Southern and China Northern.

Freshfields (16 ptnrs worldwide 4 f/t; 20assts including 1 senior manager) Highly respected international practice handling big and medium ticket work. Substantial general asset and aviation finance work. Seen as having global coverage. Leading individuals based in London include the "excellent" *Tim Lintott, Andrew Littlejohns* (aviation finance) and *Simon Hall* (general asset and aviation). **Clients/Work:** Advising Philippine Airlines on its comprehensive re-fleeting programme, involving the acquisition of 31 new aircraft. Acted for TAP Air Portugal on its financing of 18 Airbus A319 and A320 aircraft. Represented Unitas Finance Limited with the establishment and financing of a global transport equipment leasing company.

Norton Rose (10ptnrs London plus 9 outside London/36assts) Strong team involved in a range of medium to big ticket work. Recognised as one of the pre-eminent firms, operating in the global marketplace. A significant development over the last year has been the growth of the rail asset finance practice. Notable individuals include *Peter Thorne* and *Paul Giles* (aviation/transport finance) who is presently in the firm's Singapore office. *Jeremy Edwards*, who was formerly in Paris, enters our list of 'up and coming' lawyers. Seen doing a lot of aircraft finance work and is viewed as "an all rounder with good technical skills." **Clients/Work:** Advising operating lessor on sale and lease-back of 4 aircraft. Advising lessor on structured lease financing of telecommunications equipment.

Slaughter and May (4ptnrs/12assts) Do not have a specific asset finance department but have well respected partners in company/commercial department with particular expertise in this area. Known for undertaking big ticket work advising a range of international banks, lessors and lessees. The practice covers both general asset and aviation finance and leasing. *Tom Kinnersley* ("one of the best in the business") and *Peter Jolliffe* enjoy excellent reputations. Jolliffe has risen to the top band of leading individuals following recommendations for his technical and all round skills. **Clients/Work:** Advise a range of international banks, UK lessors and lessees.

Allen & Overy (3ptnrs/6f/t and 12p/t assts) A growing reputation in the marketplace particularly for aircraft finance. The imminent arrivals of Mario Jacovides, David Smith and Graham Smith from Wilde Sapte and the continued growth of the practice, both in terms of personnel and reputation, under the respected *Julia Salt* make the firm "one to watch." The international capabilities of the firm mean they have the potential to become one of the market leaders globally. *Andrew Joyce* has gone up from up and coming to leading individuals – "a good all rounder" who has "proved himself." **Clients/Work:** Advising EIB on the European export credit financing of 18 Airbus A320 aircraft for TAP. Acting for Bayerische Landesbank arranging the credit enhancement into a complex French/UK lease structure for ATR (both the French and English side). Acting for Thomson Corporation on the aircraft finance aspects of the flotation of Thomson Travel Group plc.

Wilde Sapte (London: 10ptnrs – includes *Adrian Miles* and *Colin Thaine*, 25assts. Overseas: 3ptnrs) Traditionally strong in the field with a particularly strong UK client base. Practice is primarily medium to big ticket work for financiers. However they also undertake smaller work for leasing companies. Not viewed as having as international a practice as the market leaders. The imminent departures of three partners (Mario Jacovides, David Smith and Graham Smith)

and aborted merger with Andersens mean the firm will be keen to take steps to regain its position as a market leader. **Clients/Work:** Acted for the banks on the US leveraged lease/European ECA-supported financing for Air Canada of approx. 40 Airbus aircraft. Other significant deals in 1997 included acting for UK lessors on the lease financing of a leading international telecommunications company's mobile telephone network and a number of US LILO/UK lease financings of Boeing 767 aircraft for a major UK airline.

Cameron McKenna (6ptnrs/6assts) One year after the merger, the team handling asset finance and leasing is still seen as the product of the old Camerons team. The firm's market presence appears to be at the same level as pre-merger with a mix of aviation and general finance and leasing (including film finance). **Clients/Work:** Have acted for GATX Capital Corporation with the leasing of an Airbus A-320 Aircraft to Luftbrucke, a German travel group, and its sub-lease to San Air. Acted for Cobham Plc on a $57m multiple aircraft lease financing and continues to act for Lloyds Leasing in sale and leaseback of films (eg: 'Tomorrow Never Dies.')

Herbert Smith (London: 5ptnrs/5assts. Overseas: 5ptnrs/4assts) Does not have a team doing asset finance 100 % of the time. Believes in a broad approach. Team undertake a mix of asset finance, securitisation and project finance – "getting a fusion of skills." Not premier league but have a good reputation. Some bankers use them as a second choice and "feel comfortable" with them. Active on rail leasing. Aircraft finance work appears to be growing in the Far East. Aircraft industry insiders have just started to come across the firm in work based on its Hong Kong connections. *Nick Tott* is a recommended individual. **Clients/Work:** Act on number of rolling stock leasing matters for Forward Trust Rail Group. Two aviation financings for Emirates, one using a German tax lease. London office has been working with Hong Kong on number of Chinese aircraft financings.

Linklaters (4ptnrs/9assts in London, 12assts overseas) The four partners in London spend 60% plus of their time on this work. London assistants do a mix of asset finance, banking and projects work. *Ronald Gibbs* is a well regarded name in the field. **Clients/Work:** Middle East executive jet fractional ownership joint venture, operating and management arrangements with Gulfstream involving the aquisition of 12 GIV aircraft. Japanese aircraft operating lease of B767-300 to Skymark Airlines. Aquisition of B767-300ER from Gulf Air and financing with credit Agricole Indosuez.

Lovell White Durrant (3ptnrs/8assts) The team is led by *Robin Hallam* and is part of the banking group. Main area of practice is aircraft finance. Act for a mixture of

financiers, lessors and operators. **Clients/Work:** Key matters included acting for Chase Manhattan on a US $150 million facility for Braathens SAFE (tied closely with export credit and loan facilities for new Boeing deliveries). Acting for Texaco on delivery and full legal defeasance of a £380 million UK tax lease of a North Sea floating production platform and related equipment.

Theodore Goddard (3ptnrs/5assts) About 80% of the firm's asset finance work is aviation but they also do rail and general work. One partner is now doing more PFI work but still does railway and aircraft finance. The other two partners in the group concentrate on aviation finance and contracts. Recently recruited three aviation specialists including the former head of British Midland's legal department. Act for airlines, leasing companies and banks. **Clients/Work:** Aviation work included acting for Lan Chile in the purchase of 3 new Boeing 767-300 Aircraft and acting for TACA International Airlines S.A. in the financing of 3 new Airbus A320-200 Aircraft by a syndicate of banks. Acted for GB Railways Group plc on the acquisition and leasing of new rolling stock.

LEADING INDIVIDUALS · LONDON

BUDGETT Tom Clifford Chance
CARPENTER Clive Clifford Chance
CHARLTON Bob Clifford Chance
GILES Paul Norton Rose
HALL Simon Freshfields
JOLLIFFE Peter Slaughter and May
KINNERSLEY Thomas Slaughter and May
LINTOTT Tim Freshfields
MILES Adrian Wilde Sapte
THAINE Colin Wilde Sapte
THORNE Peter Norton Rose
WHITE Geoffrey Clifford Chance

COLLINS Andrew Wilde Sapte
CRANE David Norton Rose
CROOKES Alan Norton Rose
FALCONER Neil Freshfields
GIBBS Ronald Linklaters
HALL Gordon Norton Rose
HALLAM Robin Lovell White Durrant
HOMAN Hugh Berwin Leighton
JOYCE Andrew Allen & Overy
KAHN Gregory Wilde Sapte
LITTLEJOHNS Andrew Freshfields
SALT Julia Allen & Overy
SMITH David Wilde Sapte
TOTT Nick Herbert Smith
WATTERS James Watson, Farley & Williams
WILLIAMS Geoffrey Watson, Farley & Williams
WILLIAMSON Anne Clifford Chance

UP AND COMING

EDWARDS Jeremy Norton Rose
JACOVIDES Mario Wilde Sapte
VALLANCE Philip Norton Rose

SEE PROFILES AT THE END OF THIS SECTION

Watson, Farley & Williams (London: 6ptnrs/11assts. Overseas: 6ptnrs/6assts) The general consensus is that the firm has been doing a lot of leasing work and has a good reputation for quality people. Are now considered to have a leading asset finance practice. Practitioners have noticed the firm doing more deals as the market picked up and they are now considered "back on track." Leading individuals are *Geoffrey Williams* and *James Watters*. Clients/Work: Acting for lessee on US$525m floating storage and off-take unit in North Sea UK tax lease combined with project finance. Acting for lessee on £104m tax lease of containers. Representing a Canadian bank as defeasance bank in the UK tax lease of a Boeing 767 aircraft on lease to a UK airline.

Berwin Leighton (2ptnrs) Still a recognised name but less active on new lease deals. *Hugh Homan* now concentrates more on advising on the transfer of existing leased assets. Clients/Work: Included acting for Disney Corporation on leases of films, representing CIBC on the restructuring of aircraft lease portfolio and acting for TransAmerica Leasing.

Field Fisher Waterhouse (3ptnrs/ 3assts) Known for its travel and tourism practice but also has an asset finance and leasing practice dealing mainly with aviation finance. Becoming involved in leasing matters in the rail industry. Acts mainly for operators but also do some lessor work. Clients/Work: Advice on operating leases (including wet leases) of numerous Airbus

A320's aircraft. On the rail finance side, advised on the £120m acquisition and leasing of a new fleet of 16 Class 333 trains.

Harbottle & Lewis (1ptnr/1cons/2assts) A new addition to the rankings. Has an aircraft finance specialisation based on acting mainly for airlines and aircraft operators. Clients commended their "speed of response, toughness in negotiations when necessary and general good manner." Have a reasonable practice and are becoming a player. Clients/Work: Acted for UK airlines on the financing of two ATR72 aircraft; the refinancing of one A340. Have also acted for an aircraft operator in relation to operating leases of Boeing 727 and A300 aircraft.

LEADERS' PROFILES · ASSET FINANCE · LONDON

BUDGETT, Tom
Clifford Chance, London (0171) 600 1000
Specialisation: Partner engaged in asset finance and leasing with particular emphasis on tax-based financing for aircraft, ships and other assets. Acts for banks, leasing companies, export credit agencies, manufacturers, operators and defeasance entities. Editor of "Cross-border Aircraft Leasing" LLP 2nd Edition.
Prof. Memberships: Law Society.
Career: Joined *Clifford Chance* in 1972. Partner since 1981. Has worked in London, Hong Kong, Tokyo, Paris and Dubai.
Personal: Born 6th February, 1948. Educated at Culford School and Pembroke College Cambridge (1966-69). Lives in Cambridge.

CARPENTER, Clive
Clifford Chance, Hong Kong
Partner. Asset Finance and Banking Group.
Specialisation: Principal areas of work involve acting for financiers on all aspects of asset finance, leasing and banking in relation to heavy transportation assets (aircraft, ships, rolling stock), satellites and plant and machinery, the securitisation of transportation assets and tax driven structures employed in such financings.
Career: Qualified 1983, Partner 1994.
Personal: B.C.L., M.A. (Oxon) in Jurisprudence.

CHARLTON, Bob
Clifford Chance, London (0171) 600 1000
Partner.
Specialisation: Aircraft finance and leasing, rolling stock procurement, finance and leasing, tax structures, export credit finance, defeasance, cross-border financings, project finance and general asset based finance.
Career: Qualified England (1981), Hong Kong (1986), Brunei (1987). Partner 1987.

COLLINS, Andrew
Wilde Sapte, London (0171) 246 7000
Partner and Head of Corporate Tax Department.
Specialisation: U.K. and cross-border asset financings, principally through leasing of real estate, infrastructure and fixed plant projects, with particular emphasis on taxation and financial analysis and structuring. Advised in connection with the lease financing of Bluewater

Shopping Centre, Kent, and US Lease Structure for UK Power Station.
Prof. Memberships: The Law Society.
Career: Educated at Colchester Royal Grammar School and Lincoln College, Oxford, joined *Wilde Sapte*1976, made partner 1979.

CRANE, David
Norton Rose, London (0171) 283 6000
Specialisation: Partner in the Projects Group, specialising in Project Finance and Asset Finance. He also handles general commercial work. He has advised on numerous major plant leasing transactions, on sales of leasing companies as well as other company acquisitions and joint ventures. He also has considerable experience of public sector financing, particularly relating to local authorities.
Prof. Memberships: Law Society.
Career: Articled at *Norton Rose*. Qualified 1975. Partner since 1985.

CROOKES, Alan
Norton Rose, London (0171) 283 6000
Specialisation: Partner whose principal area of practice is asset finance, particularly equipment leasing. He has acted on two major acquistions of rail rolling stock companies: Angel Train Contracts (for Royal Bank of Scotland); and Eversholt Leasing (for Forward Trust). Major clients include Hambros Leasing, Royal Bank Leasing and Forward Trust.
Prof. Memberships: City of London Solicitors' Company.
Career: Qualified in 1981 while at *Norton Rose*. Became a Partner in 1988.
Personal: Born 27th May 1957. Educated at Durham University 1975-78. Enjoys music (particularly opera). Lives in Shenfield.

EDWARDS, Jeremy
Norton Rose, London (0171) 283 6000
Partner in Banking Department.
Specialisation: Specialises in structured and asset finance, particularly of aircraft and rolling stock. Expertise includes all aspects of operating and finance leases, sales and purchases of aircraft and rolling stock, cross-border leases and export credit financing. Major transactions in 1997/98 included advising on an airline on its award winning export credit financed backed German leveraged lease of an Airbus A340 aircraft, advising the funding bank

in connection with the sale and lease back of six A320 aircraft operated by Gulf Air and advising one of the UK's three rolling stock companies on its purchase and leasing of new and used rolling stock.
Career: Joined *Norton Rose* as a trainee in 1987. Qualified 1989. Spent three years in the firm's Paris office. Elected to partnership May 1997. Speaks fluent French.

FALCONER, Neil
Freshfields, Rome 39 06 844 681
Specialisation: Main practice areas are asset financing and project financing. Recent transactions include acting for TAP-Air Portugal on its fleet financing and on the financing of the Silversea Cruise Ship fleet.
Prof. Memberships: Law Society.
Career: Qualified 1987. Partner 1993.
Personal: Born 1962. Leisure interests include golf and other sports.

GIBBS, Ronald
Linklaters, London (0171) 456 5984
Partner. Project and Asset Finance Department.
Specialisation: Principal area of practice has been in the field of asset finance with emphasis on aviation, including finance, commercial and regulatory aspects of airlines, airports and air traffic control systems. Articled at *Linklaters & Paines*, Partner 1989

GILES, Paul A.
Norton Rose, Singapore 068808 (+65) 223 7311
Managing Partner, Singapore Office.
Specialisation: Specialises in aviation, transportation and asset finance. Work includes cross border tax transactions (including US, German, Japanese, French and UK tax leases), finance and operating leasing and export credit agency financing (utilising various structures and in combination with tax leases). Major clients include Nederlandse Spoorwegen, KLM, Malaysian Airline System, Martinair, SAS and Cathay Pacific.
Prof. Memberships: Law Society.
Career: Qualified in 1973. Partner at *Johnson, Stokes & Master*, 1978-88 (in Hong Kong and Tokyo). Joined *Norton Rose* as a Partner in 1988.
Personal: Born 9th April 1948. Educated at London University.

HALL, Gordon
Norton Rose, London (0171) 283 6000
Specialisation: Partner specialising in Asset Finance: ships; aircraft; rolling stock. Representing lessors and lessees in tax and operating lease transactions, including acting in most of the new lease financing transactions for UK rolling stock throughout 1997.
Prof. Memberships: City of London Solicitor's Company; International Bar Association; Baltic Exchange.
Career: Admitted 1980. Partner at *Norton Rose* 1988. 1985-1988 resident in Singapore office. 1988-1989 resident in Bahrain office.

HALL, Simon A.D.
Freshfields, London (0171) 936 4000
Head of Finance Department.
Specialisation: Main areas of practice are asset and aircraft finance, and banking and project finance. Co-author of 'Aircraft Financing' (Euromoney 3rd edition, 1998); co-author of 'Leasing Finance' (Euromoney 3rd edition, 1997).
Prof. Memberships: Law Society, City of London Solicitors Company, American Bar Association.
Career: Qualified 1979 after joining *Freshfields* in 1977. Became a Partner in 1985.
Personal: Born 6th February 1955. Leisure interests include shooting and fishing.

HALLAM, Robin
Lovell White Durrant, London
(0171) 236 0066
Specialisation: Aviation and asset finance; secured lending, leveraged and operating leasing, tax based and defeased leases, securitisation, export credit and vendor sales finance, engine and equipment leasing principally in aviation but also in ships, containers, rolling stock and other forms of large assets. Substantial experience in aircraft securitisations and other aircraft finance transactions involving capital markets.
Prof. Memberships: City of London Law Society, Aviation Club – Associate Member, American Bar Association.
Career: Qualified 1980. Hong Kong 1981-82; Singapore 1982-83; Partner *Lovell White Durrant* 1995; various articles on aircraft finance.

HOMAN, Hugh
Berwin Leighton, London +44 171 760 1000
Partner in Corporate Department.
Specialisation: Principal area of practice is asset finance, equipment leasing and securitisation. Also handles general corporate finance work.
Prof. Memberships: Law Society, City of London Solicitors Company.
Career: Qualified in 1970. Partner at *Berwin Leighton* since 1975.
Personal: Born 26th June 1945. Educated at Worcester College, Oxford 1964-67. Lives in London.

JACOVIDES, Mario
Wilde Sapte, London (0171) 246 7000

JOLLIFFE, Peter
Slaughter and May, London
(0171) 600 1200
Specialisation: Aircraft and Asset Financing.
Prof. Memberships: The Law Society.
Career: Qualified in 1981 after joining *Slaughter and May* in 1979. Became a Partner in 1989.

Personal: Born 6 June 1957. Educated Downing College, Cambridge. Lives in London.

JOYCE, Andrew L.
Allen & Overy, London (0171) 330 3000
Specialisation: Asset financing and leasing. Acted for UBS in relation to the securitisation of lease receivables for Porterbrook leasing in relation to £380 million's worth of new rolling stock on lease to six train operating companies. Acted for EIB in relation to the financing of 18 Airbus aircraft as a part of the TAP refleeting exercise.
Prof. Memberships: City of London Solicitors.
Career: Oxford University, Keble College. Graduated in 1985 with BA in Jurisprudence. Admitted as solicitor in England and Wales, 1988. Admitted as solicitor, Hong Kong 1991.
Personal: Rugby, skiing. Married with two sons.

KAHN, Gregory
Wilde Sapte, London (0171) 246 7000
Partner, Asset Finance Group, Banking Department.
Specialisation: Asset finance and leasing. Wide experience of UK and cross-border asset-based and tax-based finance structures catering for a variety of credit, security, tax, balance sheet, capital adequacy and asset/project exposure requirements, including leveraged leasing and defeased lease structures in numerous jurisdictions. Has represented banks, leasing companies, airlines and debt providers in financing diverse range of equipment including rolling stock, tram systems, aircraft, ships, power stations, cable television networks.
Prof. Memberships: International Bar Association, Law Society.
Career: Qualified 1986 after joining *Wilde Sapte* in 1984. Became a partner in 1990. Worked in *Wilde Sapte's* Paris office 1993-1995.
Personal: Born 29th December 1956. Educated at Haberdashers' Aske's School, Elstree and The University of Warwick.

KINNERSLEY, Tom
Slaughter and May, London
(0171) 600 1200
Specialisation: General banking, in particular structured finance and asset finance.
Career: Qualified 1972. Partner 1980.
Prof. Memberships: The Law Society.
Personal: Born 28 May 1947. Educated Hertford College, Oxford. Lives in London.

LINTOTT, Tim
Freshfields, London (0171) 936 4000
Specialisation: Asset and project finance, including power stations and transmission, aviation, airports.
Prof. Memberships: Admitted in U.K., Hong Kong.
Career: 1976-94 *Freshfields*, London and New York; 1984-92 *Baker & McKenzie*, Hong Kong; 1992 to date *Freshfields*, London.
Personal: Married, 3 daughters.

LITTLEJOHNS, Andrew
Freshfields, London (0171) 936 4000
Specialisation: Specialises in international banking, international finance, aviation finance, aircraft leasing and equipment leasing. Involvement in aircraft financing includes a wide experience of cross-border tax leases, syndicated multi-option facilities, securitisations, asset value underwriting, joint

ventures, operating leases and regulatory comparison involving a number of jurisdictions.
Career: Education: Lincoln College, Oxford. Became partner in 1987.

MILES, Adrian
Wilde Sapte, London (0171) 246 7000
Partner in Banking Department.
Specialisation: Head of Banking Department. Main area of practice is UK and cross-border asset finance, acting for UK and foreign banks in international financing transactions and cross-border structured finance transactions, frequently with complicated tax aspects. Also handles aviation, leasing and project finance, acting for financing parties in sophisticated and large value transactions in the UK and internationally.
Career: Qualified in 1972. Joined *Wilde Sapte* and became a Partner in 1976.
Personal: Born 16th November 1947. Educated at Rutlish School, Merton 1959-66 and Queen Mary College, London University 1966-69. Recreations include classical music, opera, golf, rugby and chess. Lives in Chislehurst, Kent.

SALT, Julia
Allen & Overy, London (0171) 330 3000
Specialisation: Partner specialising in asset based finance, including aircraft and project financing, telecommunications financing and securitisation.
Career: Articled *Allen & Overy*, qualified 1980, partner 1985.
Personal: Oxford University (1977 BA French and German). Born 1955.

SMITH, David
Wilde Sapte, London (0171) 246 7000

THAINE, Colin
Wilde Sapte, London (0171) 246 7000
Partner and Head of Aviation Group
Specialisation: Specialises in all aspects of aircraft financing with particular emphasis on cross-border leveraged lease and export credit supported debt finance transactions, operating leases, manufacturer's support and aviation insurance.
Career: Has a 24 year record of working in aviation industry having spent earlier part of his career as in-house counsel of BCAL and Qantas and an 18 month secondment to Aribus Industrie.
Prof. Memberships: Royal Aeronautical Society; International Bar Association (former chairman of the aeronautical committee).
Personal: Born 3rd July 1949. Lives in Richmond. He is a contributor to Euromoney Aircraft Financing Third Edition.

THORNE, Peter
Norton Rose, London (0171) 283 6000
Partner in Banking Department.
Specialisation: Asset finance. Clients include airlines, manufacturers, banks, leasing companies and arrangers. Major transactions in 97/98 included advising banks on $2,500,000,000 umbrella facility for major airline and numerous Japanese leveraged leases of aircraft under facility, UK lessor in structured lease financing of telecommunications equipment for Orange and Rosco on purchase leasing of trains and spares for ScotRail financing. Author of 'Aircraft Mortgages' chapter in 'Interests in Goods' (Lloyds of London Press 1993).

Prof. Memberships: International Bar Association, Royal Aeronautical Society.
Career: Qualified 1971. Joined *Norton Rose* that year. Partner since 1977.
Personal: Born 2nd June 1948. Attended Clifton College 1962-65.

TOTT, Nicholas P.
Herbert Smith, London (0171) 374 8000
Specialisation: Principal areas of work include all forms of financing and banking work with particular emphasis on asset finance, leasing, project financing and Private Finance Initiative (PFI) Projects. Seconded to the Private Finance Panel Executive for fifteen months with responsibility for PFI Projects in Scotland, Northern Ireland and the Ministry of Defence. Publications include a chapter "Public Finance in the U.K." in Leasing Finance (Euromoney 1997, 3rd Edition.) Editor (jointly with Jason Fox) of The Private Finance Inititative Handbook (Jordans, due for publication Autumn 1998).
Prof. Memberships: Law Society; City of London Solicitors' Company.
Career: Qualified Scotland (1985), England and Wales (1991). Partner 1992.
Personal: Born 8th May 1960. Educated at Edinburgh University. Leisure pursuits include Golf and Skiing.

VALLANCE, Philip
Norton Rose, London (0171) 283 6000
Specialisation: Principal area of work is structured asset finance transactions. Assets involved have been predominantly aircraft, but include offshore oil production vessels, locomotives, telecommunications and printing presses. Extensive experience in Japanese leveraged leases, UK tax leases, export credit finance, operating leases, debt finance and residual value insurance.
Prof. Memberships: Law Society, City of London Solicitors Company.
Career: Qualified in N.S.W, Australia in 1982, after completing degrees in law and financial studies. Joined *Norton Rose* 1986. Spent two years with Japanese firm in Tokyo 1989-1991. Partner at *Norton Rose* 1993.

WATTERS, James
Watson, Farley & Williams, London
(0171) 814 8000
jwatters@wfw.com
Partner in Finance Group.
Specialisation: Principal areas of practice are banking, asset and trade finance. Work includes the provision of asset finance in the UK and elsewhere by leasing, loan, receivable discounting and other facilities, and the sale and purchase of leasing companies and lease portfolios together with conventional and structured trade finance facilities. Frequent lecturer and co-ordinator of semi-annual conference on 'Law and Leasing'.
Career: Qualified in September 1972. Partner at *Watson Farley & Williams* since May 1992.
Personal: Born 16th March 1948. Educated at KCS Wimbledon and Pembroke College, Oxford. Lives in London.

WHITE, Geoffrey
Clifford Chance, London (0171) 600 1000
Partner. Principal area of practice is asset/project financing and leasing.

WILLIAMS, Geoffrey
Watson, Farley & Williams, London
(0171) 814 8000
gwilliams@wfw.com
Partner in Finance Group.
Specialisation: Main area of work is loan and lease finance for ships, aircraft and other assets (such as satellites and rolling stock). Also advises on aviation, shipping and banking matters generally. Clients include banks and finance lessors, operating lessors, owners and operators, brokers and packagers, manufacturers.
Prof. Memberships: Law Society
Career: Partner *Norton Rose Botterell & Roche* 1974-1982. Partner *Watson Farley & Williams* 1982 to date.
Personal: Lives London W1. BA; LLB.

WILLIAMSON, Anne
Clifford Chance, Frankfurt
(+49) 69 971 55 358
Partner Asset Finance Group.
Specialisation: Aircraft financing, including all kinds of tax leasing, operating leasing, secured financing and enforcement and rescheduling, acting for major international banks, airlines and leasing companies.
Career: Articled *Osborne Clarke*, Bristol; qualified 1978 and joined *Clifford Chance*; Partner since 1986.
Personal: Newham College, Cambridge.

The SOUTH and MIDLANDS

Edge & Ellison (Birmingham) (1f/t and 1p/t ptnr/2assts) *Angela Davis* heads the department. Deal with small to medium ticket leasing work, including advising clients in the equipment leasing sector. **Clients/Work:** Acting for asset finance house and its receivers to "rebank" its entire lease portfolio. Acting for a UK brewery company in relation to letting of equipment. Advising car fleet leasing company on documents.

Lester Aldridge (Bournemouth) (3 lead plus 2 supporting ptnrs/ 3assts) Have a good reputation in the market. Practice is headed by the highly respected *Pip Giddins*. Handle small to medium ticket work including equipment leasing and hire purchase. Also undertake litigious matters. **Clients/Work:** Acted for Johnson & Johnson in negotiation of outsourcing by Birmingham Childrens' Hospital NHS Trust of its requirements for supply and administration of theatre equipment and instruments; acted for Genie Financial Services Europe Ltd; advised On-Line Finance Ltd on successful £58m warehouse line with Merrill Lynch to fund motor finance receivables, structured for a securitisation.

Burges Salmon (Bristol) (1ptnr/3assts) A new entry to our list. Have been seen in the market as active in this area with particular reference to rail work. Also advise on equipment leases. **Clients/Work:** Advising a train company client on setting up a rolling stock company to purchase and lease new trains to operating companies (total facility in excess of £100m). Advised FirstGroup plc on asset finance proposals including reviewing proposed cross-border structures.

Coole & Haddock (Worthing) (2ptnrs/ 2assts) Seen mainly on contentious matters. Also handle small to medium ticket work, mainly involving industrial plant and equipment leasing.

Pinsent Curtis (Birmingham) Team with financing and leasing experience. **Clients/Work:** Major Property Group £30 million tax-driven lease structure.

Pitmans (Reading) Have a general company commercial team doing some asset finance work.

Shakespeares (Birmingham) The firm's practice is built on the reputation of Michael Cronin who is now a part time consultant.

The NORTH

Addleshaw Booth & Co (Leeds, Manchester) (2ptnrs) Part of Banking and Financial Services Dept. Asset finance team has a good reputation with fellow practitioners. The two partners in the team spend 10%-25% of their time on asset finance and the remainder on general banking work. Best known for medium ticket work for banks and leasing companies. **Clients/Work:** Leeds:

Includes the £10m sale and leaseback of plant and equipment; and the disposal of client's business jet fleet and purchase sale and HP back of new executive jet aircraft (£3.6m). Manchester: Leasing of heat and power plants for The Co-operative Bank plc.

Eversheds (Leeds) (2ptnrs/2assts, less than 10% of time) Known among fellow practitioners. Provide ancillary service on asset finance in connection with larger transactions.

Pinsent Curtis (Leeds) (2ptnrs spend 10-30% of time)Experienced in medium and large ticket asset finance transactions but do little aviation finance work. Do a significant amount of transport work including rail and refuse trucks. Also active on factory equipment leasing. **Clients/Work:** Advised a major multinational Plc in relation to equipment leasing to the healthcare industry backed by assignment of rental flows to a financial institution. Also advised on fleet leasing of plant hire and leasing of rail industry fixtures.

Chaffe Street (Manchester) (1ptnr) A growing practice with the partner (who was formerly with Freshfields) spending 35-40% of his time on asset finance. **Clients/Work:** Include acting for Jersey European Airways UK in the acquisition and financing of a total of 4 BAe 146 aircraft for a consideration of US$34m.

Cobbetts (Manchester) (1ptnr 33-50%/1asst) Reputation for small to medium ticket work acting for a number of banks and finance houses. **Clients/Work:** Acted for a Scottish based finance company on a series of 20 asset finance secured loans totalling c. £2m. Clients include Asset Capital Investment Limited and British Linen Asset Finance Limited.

Walker Morris (Leeds) (2p/t ptnrs/1p/t asst) Part of the Banking Group, the work is mainly equipment leasing. **Clients/Work:** Toyota Industrial Equipment, UK Bowling Services and Cattles plc.

SCOTLAND

The Morton Fraser Partnership (9ptnrs/3 assts) Seen as "the leading lights" in Scotland for asset finance work. Led by *Bruce Wood*, the leading Scottish asset finance lawyer, the

practice has some good clients providing high quality work. **Clients/Work:** British Linen Asset Finance Group, Royal Bank Leasing and TSB Asset Finance.

Dundas & Wilson CS (3ptnrs/4assts) Seen as a broad banking practice which picks up asset finance work as a result of its size and general banking experience. **Clients/Work:** Large and medium ticket work for leasing companies. Clients include W&G Lease Finance and Royal Bank Leasing.

McClure Naismith (1ptnr/3assts) Have "genuine expertise" in asset finance. Represent a number of finance houses and have a specialist expert in asset finance and leasing. Well respected amongst leading Scots practitioners. **Clients/Work:** Barclays

Mercantile, RoyScot Trust plc and Close Asset Finance.

Bird Semple (2ptnrs/3assts) Small practice which has a particular involvement in applying Scottish rules to standard English products. **Clients/Work:** transactions financing helicopter fleets and machinery.

Tods Murray WS (2ptnrs) A banking practice which does some asset finance work, mainly for finance houses and involving the motor trade. **Clients/Work:** Aircraft and vehicle related work.

NORTHERN IRELAND

Arthur Cox (1ptnr/2assts) The practice mainly focuses on property and project work but is also involved with plant and machinery leasing.

LEADERS' PROFILES • ASSET FINANCE • REGIONS

DAVIS, Angela C.
Edge & Ellison, Birmingham
(0121) 200 2001
Head of Asset Finance Group.
Specialisation: Principal area of practice, all legal aspects of Asset Finance, Leasing and Consumer Credit with particular expertise on the contentious side and with experience of mediation in the finance sector. Responsible for two leading Court of Appeal decisions; 'RoyScot Trust plc v. Rogerson' and 'RoyScot Trust plc v. Ismail' on damages and indemnities respectively.

Prof. Memberships: Law Society, Birmingham Law Society and Associate of the Chartered Institute of Arbitrators.
Career: Qualified in 1982. Joined *Edge & Ellison*, becoming a Partner in 1990.
Personal: Born 4 March 1958. Attended West Kirby Grammar School for Girls, Wirral 1969-1976. Durham University 1976-79. Leisure interests include antique maps, reading, hockey and Everton FC.

GIDDINS, Pip
Lester Aldridge, Bournemouth
(01202) 786161
Specialisation: Small and middle ticket asset finance. Advises finance houses and captive leasing companies throughout UK on product development, trading relationships, deal making, documentation and funding (including stocking finance and securitisations). Writes articles for legal and trade periodicals.
Prof. Memberships: Member of Finance & Leasing Association Examination Board and

Consumer Credit Trade Association.
Career: Qualified 1976. Lecturer at College of Law Guildford; In-house solicitor with *Lloyds Bowmaker*; Head of Legal Services with *British Credit Trust*; joined *Lester Aldridge* as a partner in 1988. Currently Head of Banking & Finance Department having developed a team of specialist non-contentious and litigation solicitors which is one of the largest in the UK for its market.

WOOD, R. Bruce
The Morton Fraser Partnership, Edinburgh
(0131) 550 1000
Partner and Head of Corporate Division.
Specialisation: Main areas of practice are asset and project finance and leasing, banking

and debt factoring. Acts for Scottish finance companies throughout the UK and for English-based (and foreign-based) finance companies in Scotland: large, medium and small ticket work. Also handles general corporate work. Author of 'Location: Leasing and Hire of Moveables' in the Laws of Scotland, Scottish section of Salinger; 'Factoring Law and Practice', section on Moveables in 'Green's Practice Styles', 'Die Floating Charge Als Kreditsichereit Im Schottischen Recht'. Has lectured widely at legal seminars on, inter alia, leasing of moveables, joint ventures, Consumer Credit Act, banking practices in Scotland, corporate law in Scotland, the globalisation of law firms and of the practice of law.
Prof. Memberships: Law Society of Scotland,

WS Society, Association of Pension Lawyers, Finance and Leasing Association.
Career: Qualified 1976. Joined *Morton Fraser Milligan WS* in 1974, becoming a Partner in 1977 and Head of Corporate Division in 1991. Lecturer in Conveyancing at Edinburgh University 1979-89; Convenor of Conveyancing Teachers of the Scottish Universities in the Diploma in Legal Practice 1986-89. World Chairman of Interlaw 1988-91. Member of the Law Society working party on security over moveables and of the International Relations Committee of the Law Society. Member of the CBI Companies Committee.
Personal: Born 2nd October 1951. Holds an LLB (1st class Hons, Edinburgh 1973) and an LLM (UC Berkeley, 1974). Leisure interests include medieval history and golf. Lives near Penicuik.

CONSUMER FINANCE

OVERVIEW: Consumer Finance is a field in which few firms claim real expertise. There is inevitably an overlap with other areas including asset finance, general consumer law and general commercial law particularly in the way many firms choose to structure their practices. Our list contains the firms with a reputation in consumer finance.

LONDON and the REGIONS

LEADING FIRMS
CONSUMER FINANCE

BERG & CO Manchester
EDGE & ELLISON Birmingham / Leicester
EVERSHEDS Leeds, Cardiff
LESTER ALDRIDGE Bournemouth
MCCLURE NAISMITH Glasgow
MCGRIGOR DONALD Glasgow
PAISNER & CO London

Berg & Co (Manchester) (2ptnrs/3assts) Practice in consumer credit is based on the reputation of *Peter Woolf* who has a "nice practice." Described as "focused."

Eversheds (Leeds, Cardiff) A well respected and "highly" regarded practice lead by the "important player" *Jonathan*

Guest (Leeds), a leading individual in consumer credit law. Cardiff office appears for the first time. The office acts for finance companies, banks and others on consumer credit matters. **Clients/Work:** Leeds: Advised Time Retail Finance Ltd on providing retail credit products to B&Q, Comet Group plc and others. Work for banks includes advising Co-operative Bank plc on its Visa products. Retailer work has included advising Austin Reed Group plc on its in-house operated credit card facilities. Cardiff: Clients include Chartered Trust plc, First Plus Financial Group plc and Investec Asset Finance.

Edge & Ellison (Birmingham, Leicester) (1f\t and 1p/t ptnr, 4f/t and 2p/t assts) A firm "coming in" to the area. A new addition to our table. Do a mix of contentious and non-contentious. Work includes preparing tailor made documentation for credit agreements, loans and HP. **Clients/Work:** Include: GE Capital Equipment Finance Ltd, Ford Credit and RoyScot Trust plc.

Lester Aldridge (Bournemouth) (2 lead and 1 support ptnr/3assts) *Pip Giddins* is an established individual in the area of consumer finance. The firm is a "major player" in the field. **Clients/Work:** Acted for Dixons Stores Group advising on application of Consumer Credit Act 1974 to a complicated credit scheme. Developed new motor finance products involving a Bill of Sale as

security: eg: for On-Line Finance Limited. Acted for Close Consumer Finance on its motor finance documentation.

McClure Naismith (Glasgow) (1ptnr/ 2assts) The "brilliant" and "very nice" *Frank Johnstone* heads the team which does a mix of contentious and non-contentious advisory work. **Clients/Work:** United Dominion Trust, Capital Bank plc and Wagon Finance Ltd.

McGrigor Donald (Glasgow) Have a team who advise on consumer credit related issues. The two partners spend between 10-20% of their time on this area of work. Advise mostly on mortgage and personal loan documentation.

Paisner & Co (London) Part of the Commercial Contracts Group of 4 partners (including the leading individual *Jonathan Kropman*) and 3 assistants. The "able" and respected *Dennis Rosenthal* has recently joined the firm. Act for a mix of lenders and suppliers who utilise financing in the marketing of their business.

LEADING INDIVIDUALS
CONSUMER FINANCE

GIDDINS Pip Lester Aldridge
GUEST Jonathan Eversheds
JOHNSTONE Frank McClure Naismith
KROPMAN Jonathan Paisner & Co
ROSENTHAL Dennis Paisner & Co
WOOLF Peter Berg & Co

GIDDINS, Pip
Lester Aldridge, Bournemouth
(01202) 786161
Specialisation: Small and middle ticket asset finance and consumer credit. Advises finance houses, banks and building societies throughout UK particularly for motor finance, personal loans and credit cards, and application of the Consumer Credit 1974.

Advises on product development, documentation, procedures and advertising/marketing. Writes articles for legal and trade periodicals. Leads the FLA's consumer credit course and in-house training for clients.
Prof. Memberships: Member of Finance & Leasing Association Examination Board and Consumer Credit Trade Association.

Career: Qualified 1976. Lecturer at College of Law Guildford; In-house solicitor with *Lloyds Bowmaker*; Head of Legal Services with *British Credit Trust*; joined *Lester Aldridge* as a partner in 1988. Currently Head of Banking & Finance Department having developed a team of specialist non-contentious and litigation solicitors, which is one of the largest in the UK for its market.

GUEST, Jonathan
Eversheds, Leeds (0113) 243 0391
Specialisation: Consumer credit – acting for banks, building societies, finance houses and retailers and credit card and loan documentation, compliance and advertising issues. Includes data protection compliance, data warehousing arrangements, debt transfer and joint ventures in the retail credit sector.
Prof. Memberships: Consumer Credit Trade Association, Data Protection Forum.
Career: Qualified 1982, Partner 1986.

JOHNSTONE, Frank R.
McClure Naismith, Glasgow
(0141) 204 2700
Partner specialising in Consumer Credit Law, Asset Recovery and Data Protection.
Specialisation: Consumer Credit Law. Represents a number of Finance Houses, Leasing Companies, Banks and Creditcard Companies, with particular emphasis on litigation/debt recovery, sale and supply of goods and data protection. Convener of the Consumer Law Committee of the Law Society of Scotland, Member of the Privacy (Data Protection) Law Committee, Chairman of Money Advice Liaison Group (Scotland) and is a frequent lecturer on Consumer/Credit Law and Data Protection.
Career: Qualified 1982, joined present firm in 1985. Became a partner in 1988.
Personal: Born 12th October, 1957. Graduated M.A., LL.B., Glasgow University, British Universities Lightweight Boxing Champion 1979 – Runner up 1980.

KROPMAN, Jonathan R.
Paisner & Co, London (0171) 353 0299
Partner in Company Department.
Specialisation: Principal area of practice is corporate and commercial law. Work includes commercial law for start-ups and growing businesses with a bias towards suppliers to consumers, leisure, health, communications and technology. Clients include hotel and leisure businesses, mail order catalogue companies, financiers, retailers, pharmacology and biotech industry clients and food suppliers. Contributor to Butterworth's 'Encyclopedia of Forms & Precedents'. Has addressed a Bio-Industry Forum on novel food regulations.
Prof. Memberships: Law Society, Bio-Industry Association Regulatory Affairs Core Group.
Career: Qualified in 1981. Became a Partner at *Paisner & Co* in 1986. Group Head, Company Department since 1991.
Personal: Born 8th September 1957. Educated at the City of London School 1969-75 and Manchester University 1975-78 (LL.B). Trustee of a private charitable trust. Member of Lingfield Sports Club, the Worshipful Company of Basketmakers and the Farringdon Ward Club. Lives in London.

ROSENTHAL, Dennis
Paisner & Co, London (0171) 353 0299
Partner in Company and Commercial Department
Specialisation: Advises banks, finance and leasing companies, building societies and trade associations on all aspects of their commercial activities including standard form documentation, equipment and vehicle financing, retail credit schemes, sales and purchases of receivables and joint ventures. Has devised innovative products relating to credit cards, savings and loans, mortgages and other security. Advises on commercial law, banking law, consumer credit law, advertising and marketing law, financial services law, insurance, fraud prevention, money laundering and data protection. Assistant Editor of Goode: Consumer Credit Legislation, author of "Guide to Consumer Credit Law & Practice" (Butterworths), " Financial Advertising and Marketing Law" (Sweet & Maxwell), contributor to "Consumer Credit" in Halsbury's Laws of England and to various legal journals.

WOOLF, Peter Graham
Berg & Co, Manchester (0161) 833 9211
Partner in Litigation and Matrimonial Department.
Specialisation: Specialises in the litigation of consumer/corporate leasing, matrimonial finance and professional negligence. Has dealt with many matrimonial finance cases involving pensions, trusts, businesses, etc and a large volume of consumer/ corporate leasing cases (the litigation aspect). Also handles contract and debt collection litigation. Clients include Guardian Royal Exchange Group, GE Capital and Thorn Financial Services Limited.
Career: Qualified in 1976. Partner in *Berg & Co* from 1984.
Personal: Born 9th May 1953. Educated at Altrincham Grammar School and Coventry University (BA Hons). Leisure pursuits include tennis, football, table tennis, Chinese philately and music. Lives in Hale Barns, Cheshire.

AVIATION

See also Asset Finance and Leasing

RESEARCH: Our team interviewed specialist practitioners, barristers and in-house lawyers at major airlines, regulatory bodies, insurers, underwriters and other clients at Lloyds. Aviation is a relatively small sector so we were able to conduct a detailed and comprehensive analysis of the legal market.

In compiling the tables, we consider all the information available to us, paying particular regard to the market research carried out by our team of ten qualified lawyers. (The researchers' details are set out on page three.)

The rankings, therefore, reflect the opinion of the marketplace as revealed by systematic and objective research: see page four. (Our research is audited every year by the British Market Research Bureau.)

OVERVIEW: Aviation has evolved into a niche practice area almost exclusively dominated by a small group of expert lawyers in London. We have divided London firms into Regulatory and Insurance/Litigation specialists. A small number of regional firms have some general experience in the field. Leading firms in aviation finance are identified in our Asset Finance section.

Regulatory: Lane & Partners and Wilde Sapte remain at the top of the league and are joined this year by Norton Rose who move up one rank. John Balfour has joined Beaumont and Son and the firm (already top in Insurance/Regulation) enters the Regulatory table. Barlow Lyde & Gilbert also joins the Regulatory table as its work in this field was commended. Niche practice Clark Ricketts is another new entry following recommendation from practitioners. The industry reports a busy period, particularly on commercial and EU matters.

Insurance and Litigation: Beaumont and Son remain at the top of the league notwithstanding the loss of Tony Kilbride and Tim Unmack this year. It remains to be seen whether this will have any long term effect.

LONDON

REGULATORY

LEADING FIRMS · LONDON REGULATORY

LANE & PARTNERS
NORTON ROSE
WILDE SAPTE

HARBOTTLE & LEWIS
LINKLATERS

BEAUMONT AND SON

BARLOW LYDE & GILBERT

HIGHLY REGARDED FIRMS

Clark Ricketts
Lawford & Co

Lane and Partners (3ptnrs/1asst) Unanimously recognised as a leader in this field. The firm's ranking hinges on the established reputation of *Richard Venables* who is "the top guy" – a specialist who does his work "extremely well". **Clients/Work:** Act for Continental on BA/AA alliance. Advising airlines on competition issues in connection with slot allocations. Advice on EC rules on majority ownership and control issues.

Norton Rose (2ptnrs/5assts f/t; 5ptnrs/5assts p/t). No specific aviation department but move up a rank following praise for two key lawyers, *Trevor Soames*, ("brilliant regulator") and *Patrick Farrell* ("practical, commercial and good with clients") who is also in insurance/litigation. **Clients/Work:** Represented Thomson Travel Group in MMC inquiry. Represented Lunn Poly in application for judicial review against customs & excise over insurance premium tax. Acted for Greek government in article 90 ground handling matter.

Wilde Sapte Have an "outstanding" reputation and "belong on top" . The key player is the "able" *Hugh O' Donovan* who has a first class reputation. He is the only partner who specialises in this field, however the firm offers clients a breadth of expertise by drawing on its Asset Finance, Banking, Commercial Property and Employment expertise. **Clients/Work:** Advising Easyjet on regulatory, EC and competition issues including its Article 86 Complaint to the European Commission against KLM for predatory pricing. Advised United Airlines on its submissions to the Office of Fair Trading and the Secretary of State in relation to the proposed BA and AA alliance. Advising United Airlines on the EC's investigations of the alliance with Lufthansa.

Harbottle & Lewis (4ptnrs, including *Colin Howes, Frances Butler-Sloss* and *Dermot Scully*, 1cons, 9assts out of which 5 are 100%). The large team has been praised by contemporaries and clients and is best known for its work for Virgin. Aim to provide airline clients with an all round service. **Clients/ Work:** Advising on regulatory aspects of restructuring part of TNT's operations including re-registration of part of the TNT fleet from Ireland to Denmark. Operator licences.

Linklaters No specific aviation department, but the firm is able to draw on resources as required. Respected for its work for BA. *Bill Allan* is "a good competition lawyer". **Clients/Work:** Act generally for British Airways, including regulatory advice, and anti-trust and competition law.

Beaumont and Son (12ptnrs/28assts undertake regulatory and insurance/litiga-

tion). Already the unrivalled leaders in insurance/litigation, the firm enters the regulatory tables following the acquisition of *John Balfour* ("top notch", "knowledgeable") from Frere Cholmeley Bischoff. **Clients/Work:** John Balfour has undertaken a major study for the EC Commission on airlines' contractual terms. Clients include British Airways, British Midland, Britania Airways, Japan Airlines and KLM.

Barlow Lyde & Gilbert Already in the insurance/litigation tables, the firm now enters the regulatory table due to the spin-off work of 2 ptnrs. *Richard Gimblett* leads the team.

Clark Ricketts (2ptnrs). Much praised niche practice which enters the tables this year. **Clients/Work:** All round aviation service provided to clients including Caledonian Airways, Air and General Finance Limited, General Aviation

Manufacturers and Traders Association.

Lawford & Co (1ptnr/1asst) **Clients/ Work:** Claims arising from Knight air crash, Leeds. Claims arising from helicopter crash in Northern Ireland. Manslaughter case involving crash of gyroglider.

INSURANCE AND LITIGATION

Beaumont and Son (12ptnrs/28assts handle insurance/litigation and regulatory work). Clear leaders in the field. *Sean Gates* has "enormous experience of the Warsaw convention" and is a "hard litigator". *David Clark* is a "conscientious and thorough" lawyer and *David Willcox* is "competent", "cautious" and "gets results". Last year's leaders, Tony Kilbride and Tim Unmack have left the firm, but this does not appear to have damaged their reputation. **Clients/Work:** Crash of Korean Airlines B747 in Guam. Crash of Garuda A300 in Sumatra. Advising the London aviation insurance market on the millennium (Y2K) problem.

Barlow Lyde & Gilbert (3ptnrs/7assts) Highly respected for the quality of their work and particularly commended by counsel for their instructions. Have had a "successful year" and considered by some to be as good as Beaumont and Son. *Ian Awford* stands out as "the big hitter with an immense presence

in the London market". *Richard Gimblett* ("careful solid litigator") and *Nicholas Hughes* move from the regulatory tables as they do more of this type of work. **Clients/Work:** Acted for Saudi Arabian Airlines in the handling of claims and the Conduct of the Court of Inquiry relating to mid air disaster. Representation of Air India in international arbitration. Advice on a proposed transatlantic start-up operation concerning its licence applications to the CAA.

Cameron McKenna (4ptnrs/6assts) Supported by its network of overseas offices, the firm have a strong reputation and a high profile in the insurance market. *Tim Brymer* ("big player with a big presence") is an ex-commercial pilot which "puts him ahead of others on the technical side". **Clients/Work:** Act for airlines and their insurers, engine and component manufacturers and international airports. Successfully defended major international airport in a landmark decision regarding contractual exclusions. Successfully obtained injunction to restrain forum shopping in the USA.

Clyde & Co (2ptnrs/1asst) Primarily involved in the defence of liability claims. *Jane Andrewartha* ("a powerful figure", "well able to hold her corner") is respected by clients for her ability. **Clients/Work:** Act for cargo interests and their insurers.

Dibb Lupton Alsop (4ptnrs/2assts) New department formed last year, including *Tim Scorer* and *Mark Franklin*. **Clients/ Work:** Acting on behalf of Cubana de Aviacion re

AN-24 air crash in Cuba resulting in death of all 39 persons on board. Advising insurers of Fine Airlines re DC-8 crash in Miami Airport resulting in death of 5 people and damage to shopping mall. Representing Schipol Airport (Amsterdam) re crash landing of a Transavia Boeing .

Herbert Smith The firm's excellent reputation for litigation brings it into this league. Not major players in terms of the volume of work handled. *John Reynolds* is regarded as "knowledgeable and competent."

Patrick Farrell at Norton Rose has a strong personal reputation.

THE REGIONS

Bell Lax Litigation (Birmingham) (2ptnrs p/t) A niche firm with expertise in litigation. Act for private individuals and underwriters and have light aircraft and insurance expertise. **Clients/Work:** An assessment of the damages for an air cargo company arising out of an accident to an aircraft parked on the apron of a regional airport. Professional negligence claim against certain aviation insurance brokers concerning a dispute over terms relating to the hull insurance. Advice leading to settlement of potential dispute with insurers as to whether the cover for certain aircraft was vitiated by the aircraft being flown in an alleged unairworthy state.

Cartwrights (Bristol) (3ptnrs/3assts p/t) **Clients/Work:** Act for Bristol, Exeter and Devon Airports. Advise on commercial and property matters, by-laws and on detention of aircraft for non-payment of accounts.

Eversheds (Birmingham) (1ptnr, 3assts p/t) **Clients/Work:** Advice to Birmingham International Airport on Aircraft Wake Vortex incidents with reference to the CAA 1982. EC Ground Handling Directive and redevelopment of the Airport.

Hansell Stevenson (Norwich) (1ptnr f/t, 1ptnr, 1asst p/t) **Clients/Work:** Regulatory, licensing and general commercial advice.

SCOTLAND

Shepherd & Wedderburn WS (1ptnr 25%, 2assts 25%) Move up the tables this year as they have been actively involved in three Court of Appeal cases. Practitioners in London were highly impressed with their work. *Hugh Donald* is recommended. **Clients/Work:** House of Lords litigation involving landmark interpretation of Warsaw Convention. Resolved claims arising out of the Bristol Helicopter disaster.

Maclay Murray & Spens (1ptnr 10%, 1asst 10%) Recommended as a good quality firm. *Richard Clark* is the partner involved. **Clients/Work:** Advising individuals re Silk Air crash in Indonesia. Handling claims for Jetstream Ltd (aircraft manufacturer – subsidiary of British Aerospace).

Simpson & Marwick WS Recommended by London principals for providing good quality agency work. *Peter Anderson* does the work.

LEADERS' PROFILES

REGULATORY

ALLAN, Bill
Linklaters, London (0171) 456 3574
See under European Union/Competition, p. 358

BALFOUR, John
Beaumont and Son, London
(0171) 481 3100
Partner in Aviation Department.
Specialisation: Practice includes regulation, EC, and CAA work; accidents, liability and insurance; sale, purchase and leasing and other commercial arrangements; and international issues. Author of 'European Community Air Law' and of many articles on aviation in the professional press. Lectures extremely widely; recent engagements include conferences and courses organised by IATA, the Institute of Economic Affairs, the European Institute of Public Administration, McGill University, the American Bar Association, Lloyd of London Press and the Royal Aeronautical Society.
Prof. Memberships: Royal Aeronautical Society (Chairman, Air Law Group), European Air Law Association (Treasurer) and Solicitors European Group.
Career: Qualified 1979, having joined *Frere Cholmeley Bischoff* in 1977. Became a Partner in 1986 and Head of the Aviation Group in 1993. Joined *Beaumont and Son* in 1997.

BUTLER-SLOSS, Frances
Harbottle & Lewis, London (0171) 667 5000
Consultant in Aviation Group, Fellow of Royal Aeronautical Society
Specialisation: Handles exclusively aviation work, advising airlines and other aviation companies on licensing, regulatory and competition law, commercial arrangements, airline business and aircraft/ engine leasing.
Personal: Born 13th October 1959.

FARRELL, Patrick
Norton Rose, London (0171) 283 6000
Specialisation: Advises airlines, tour operators and travel agents on the domestic and European regulatory regime. In conjunction with *Norton Rose's* Brussels office, advises start up airlines and their financiers on their relationship with regulators, competitors, airport authorities and contracting parties.
Prof. Memberships: MRAeS, Vice Chairman of the Royal Aeronautical Society Air Law Group, Chairman of the UK ICC Commission on Air Transport, Member of Institute of Travel and Tourism, IBA, LSLA, CLLS (Chairman of the CLLS Aeronautical Law Sub-Committee).

GIMBLETT, Richard
Barlow Lyde & Gilbert, London
(0171) 247 2277
See under Aviation: Aviation Insurance Litigation, p. 132

HOWES, Colin M.
Harbottle & Lewis, London (0171) 667 5000
See under Corporate Finance: 1-125 Fee Earners, p. 229

O'DONOVAN, Hugh
Wilde Sapte, London (0171) 246 7000
Partner in Company Commercial Department and Aviation Industry Group.
Specialisation: Main area of practice is aviation, covering international aviation regulation, commercial agreements in aviation, EC and competition law, airline and airport operations, aircraft leasing and airport financing. Also covers travel agents and tour operators. Regular speaker at various conferences and seminars on aviation-related topics.
Prof. Memberships: Law Society, International Bar Association, Royal Aeronautical Society, Aviation Committee of the UK International Chambers of Commerce, member of Council of the Airport Operators' Association.
Career: Called to the Bar in 1975. Practised as a barrister before joining *Knapp Fishers* in 1985. Left for *Richards Butler* in 1987 (Partner 1989). Presently with *Wilde Sapte* after joining as a partner in 1991.
Personal: Born 19th August 1952. Attended Royal Grammar School, Guildford 1963-69 then Balliol College, Oxford 1970-73. Leisure pursuits include golf, skiing, flying and rugby refereeing. Lives in Witley, Surrey.

SCULLY, Dermot
Harbottle & Lewis, London (0171) 667 5170
Specialisation: Partner and Head of the Aviation Group specialising in regulatory, finance and general aviation commercial work. Practice includes advising airlines, banks, maintenance contractors and other aviation businesses on leasing, regulatory work, competition, debt financing and general commercial matters.

SOAMES, Trevor

Norton Rose, Belgium +32 2 237 6111
Partner in Competition and EC Department.
Specialisation: Main area of practice is all aspects of EC and UK competition, trade and regulatory law in many economic sectors. He is well-known for his air transport expertise. Clients include a wide range of Governments, regulatory agencies and multinational corporations from around the world. In the field of air transport he has represented airlines, airports, Governments and national regulatory bodies. Most recent cases include representing: British Midland (on a variety of major cases including the Aer Lingus Air 86 interlining case, the Brussels Airport Article 90 case, the Aer Lingus and Air France state aid cases); Iberia in the Commission's investigation of the Spanish ground handling monopoly under articles 86 and 90; Olympic Airways and the Greek Government in the Greek ground handling case, successfully closed by a Commission Decision in 1997 dismissing the complainants, as well as in the current Olympic Airways and Spata Airport state aid cases; Ryanair in the AER Lingus Article 86 predatory pricing and state of cases including the recent Ryanair v Commission case before the European Court. He advises airlines and financial institutions on other key aviation regulatory issues including ownership and licensing requirements and represents clients before the UK CAA and EC Commission. He also has specific expertise in the field of UK aviation licensing and scarce capacity procedures, appearing as an advocate before the CAA and other authorities. He has advised various Eastern European Governments on air transport liberalisation related matters including the Czech Republic, Slovenia, Poland and Russia.
Career: Qualified in 1984 as a barrister, now a solicitor. Worked at UK Department of Trade and Industry before entering private practice. Author of many articles on competition and regulatory law as well as being editor of, or contributor to a number of books including: "Corporate Mergers and Acquisitions", "Airline Mergers and Corporation" and "State Aid and Air Transport". Trevor is also an Associate Editor of Butterworths Competition Law Encyclopedia. Recent aviation-related articles include: "Predatory Pricing and Air Transport; "State Aid and Air Transport; "All bark and no bite", Airline Business; "Ground Handling Liberalisation", Journal of Air Transport Management; "European Commission: Great Expectations", Airline Business September; "Ground Handling Liberalistion", Royal Aeronautical Society.
Personal: Born 17 September 1959. Leisure interests are many but unfortunately with insufficient time to pursue them.

VENABLES, Richard

Lane & Partners, London (0171) 242 2626
Head of Aviation and Travel Department.
Specialisation: Principal area of work is aviation law advising British and foreign airlines on regulatory matters including UK and European licensing regulations, competition law and all other matters affecting airlines' commercial operations. Other main area of work is advising UK-based tour operators, particularly on Air Travel Organisers' Licensing, UK and European legal developments and

contractual matters. Acted for a UK scheduled airline in Article 86 (abuse of dominance) litigation in the High Court: also represents a group of British charter airlines on regulatory issues as they arise. Contributor of articles to trade publications.
Prof. Memberships: Chartered Institute of Transport, Royal Aeronautical Society, European Air Law Association.
Career: Qualified in 1971 while with *Gregory, Rowcliffe & Co.*, then joined *Norton Rose* in 1973. Moved to *Booth & Co.* in Leeds 1975-76, then returned to *Norton Rose* 1976-82. Joined *Lane & Partners* in 1982 and became a Partner in 1983.
Personal: Born 6th December 1946. Attended Uppingham School 1960-65, then Keble College, Oxford 1965-68. Leisure pursuits include golf, walking, tennis and family activities. Lives in Hampton, Middlesex.

INSURANCE AND LITIGATION

ANDREWARTHA, Jane

Clyde & Co, London (0171) 623 1244
Partner in Insurance and Reinsurance Department.
Specialisation: Practice is rooted in major insurance and reinsurance litigation, claims and liability work. Acted in the Swazi Airline hijack, involved in personal injury aspect of Piper Alpha claims settlement and reinsurance aspects of the Eastern European Newbuildings. Aviation practice consists of representing insurers and aviation interests in defence and policy matters and most recently case involving TAM crash 1996. Also involved in general aviation – light aircraft and helicopters. Clients include most major London market insurance and reinsurance companies and many Lloyd's syndicates. Is a regular conference speaker and contributor to insurance industry publications.
Prof. Memberships: Law Society, CEDR Accredited Mediator, Update Author of the international publication Journal of Maritime Law & Commerce, Association of Average Adjusters (Associate Member), Lloyds (Associate Member).
Career: Qualified in 1976, having joined *Clyde & Co* in 1974. Became a Partner in 1980. London Head of the firm's Latin American offices from 1989-1997 and Finance Partner from 1993.
Personal: Born 20th December 1952. Attended Exeter University 1970-73 (LLB Hons). Leisure activities include skiing, powerboat racing and swimming. Lives in London.

AWFORD, Ian

Barlow Lyde & Gilbert, London (0171) 247 2277
Senior Partner in Aviation Division.
Specialisation: Main area of practice is aviation law and the law relating to commercial uses of outer space. Also handles insurance law, litigation, arbitration and mediation. Has acted in many major air disaster cases. Author of various publications on legal issues concerning carriage by air, product liability and the law relating to outer space.
Prof. Memberships: International Institute of Space Law of the International Astronautics Federation; International Society of Air Safety Investigators; European Society of Air Safety Investigators; Federation of Insurance and

Corporate Counsel; International Associate of the American Bar Association; Air Law Group of the Royal Aeronautical Society; European Centre for Space Law; Air Law Working Party of the International Chamber of Commerce; Product Liability Advisory Council; International Association of Defense Counsel. European Air Law Association; Aviation Insurance Association; The Guild of Air Traffic Control Officers; International Court of Aviation and Space Arbitration.
Career: Qualified in 1967, and in Hong Kong in 1988. Joined *Barlow Lyde & Gilbert* in 1969, becoming a Partner in 1973. Chairman of the Outer Space Committee of the International Bar Association: Section of Business Law 1987-90; Aerospace Law Committee, Inter Pacific Bar Association 1990-1993; Elected fellow of the Royal Aeronautical Society 1988.
Personal: Born 15th April 1941. Attended Wellingborough School, Northants, then Sheffield University. Leisure interests include skiing, theatre, opera, ballet and painting. Lives in London.

BRYMER, Tim

Cameron McKenna, London
(0171) 367 3000
Specialisation: Partner – Aviation Group specialising in aviation and aerospace law and claims. Represents aviation insurers, airlines and manufacturers worldwide. Responsible for pioneering use of common law injunction in restraining forum shopping following aviation disasters.
Prof. Memberships: Founder member of Lawyers' Flying Association. Member of Guild of Pilots and Air Navigators. Holder of current pilot's licence.
Career: Dulwich College, College of Air Training, Hamble. College of Law, Lancaster Gate. Qualified 1977.
Personal: Art, music, tennis, cycling and flying.

CLARK, David

Beaumont and Son, London
(0171) 481 3100
Partner in Aviation Department.
Specialisation: Main areas of practice are aerospace and litigation insurance; also handles personal injury work for defendants. Deals extensively with matters relating to countries where French or Spanish are spoken.
Prof. Memberships: Law Society.
Career: Qualified 1980.
Personal: Born 8th March 1952. Attended Southampton University of Southampton, and College of Law.

FARRELL, Patrick

Norton Rose, London (0171) 283 6000
Aviation Insurance Litigation Partner in Commercial Litigation Department.
Specialisation: Advises airlines, brokers, banks, financiers and underwriters on aviation insurance matters including liability claims world-wide, coverage disputes, advice on wordings and insurance claims generally. Acts for underwriters in political risk matters arising out of aircraft finance transactions.
Prof. Memberships: MRAeS, Vice Chairman of the Royal Aeronautical Society Air Law Group, Chairman of the UK ICC Commission on Air Transport, Member of Institute of Travel and Tourism, IBA, LSLA, CLLS (Chairman of the CLLS Aeronautical Law Sub-Committee).

FRANKLIN, Mark
Dibb Lupton Alsop, London (0345) 262728
Specialisation: Aviation: predominantly the handling of post accident legal liabilities, but also undertakes commercial and regulatory work. Recent notable projects include acting as Outside Counsel to IATA on the Inter-Carrier Agreement; representing EL AL re claims arising from B747 disaster in Amsterdam.
Prof. Memberships: MRACS
Career: LL.B (Hons) Southampton University: qualified 1984; Partner at *Frere Cholmeley Bischoff* 1993-97; Honorary Solicitor to Aircraft Owners and Pilots Association (AOPA); Contributor to volumes 6 and 7 of 'Encyclopaedia of Forms and Precedents' (Butterworths – 5th ed. & reissue) on 'Carriage by Air' and 'Civil Aviation'; lecturer on international air law issues on courses organised by the College of Aeronautics at Cranfield University.
Personal: Sailing: member of Junior Offshore Group and Royal Yachting Association.

GATES, Sean
Beaumont and Son, London
(0171) 481 3100
Senior Partner and Head of Aviation Claims Department.
Specialisation: Main area of practice is aviation insurance and liability. Represents insurers and airlines in respect of claims made against them, and insurers in respect of policy decisions with airlines and reinsurers. Also handles libel and slander work, representing both plaintiffs and defendants in defamation actions. Acted in Fothergill and Monarch Airlines, Holmes and Bangladesh Biman Airlines, Collins and British Airways, the shooting down of a Korean Airlines plane in 1993 and British Airways Manchester Airport disaster in 1983. Has addressed conferences for American Bar Association and International Bar Association.
Prof. Memberships: Member Royal Aeronautical Society, Chairman Air Law Committee, the RA Society, and the International Association of Defence Counsel.
Career: Qualified in 1972. Joined *Beaumont and Son* in 1973, becoming a Partner in 1978 and Head of Aviation Claims Department in 1991. Senior Partner 1st November 1997. Holds a Diploma in international and German private law 1973. Arbitrator with Cour Internationale d'Arbitrage Aerien et Special.
Personal: Born 4th February 1949. Leisure pursuits include collecting 19th Century illustrated books. Lives in London.

GIMBLETT, Richard
Barlow Lyde & Gilbert, London
(0171) 247 2277
Specialisation: Aviation and Travel Law;

Commercial Litigation.
Career: B.A. Hons (Oxon) (1981) Called to Bar 1982. Legal Adviser, UK Civil Aviation Authority 1985-1988. Admitted as a Solicitor in 1990
Personal: Director of F.T.O Trust Fund Ltd, Private Pilot.

HUGHES, Nicholas M.L.
Barlow Lyde & Gilbert, London
(0171) 247 2277
Partner in Aerospace Department.
Specialisation: Main area of practice is aviation law, covering aviation insurance and reinsurance, liability law, carriage of goods and aviation regulatory law. Also handles environmental law covering liability and insurance. General Editor of 'Contracts for the Carriage of Goods by Land, Sea and Air' (LLP); Editorial Consultant of 'Transport Law and Policy'.
Prof. Memberships: Royal Aeronautical Society, United Kingdom Environmental Law Association, Law Society, International Bar Association, American Bar Association. Member: IATA Faculty of Law Speakers.
Career: Qualified in 1981. Joined *Barlow, Lyde & Gilbert* in 1979, becoming a Partner in 1984. Director of Association of Insurance and Risk Managers (AIRMIC).
Personal: Born 10th October 1955. Attended Sheffield University, BA Law (Hons). Lives in London.

REYNOLDS, John S.
Herbert Smith, London (0171) 374 8000
Specialisation: Domestic and international commercial disputes, including fraud/asset recovery, injunctions, aviation and commodities.
Career: Joined *Herbert Smith* on qualification in 1987; New York office 1989 to 1990; partner 1994.
Personal: Educated at Reading University and University College London.

SCORER, Tim
Dibb Lupton Alsop, London (0345) 262728
Partner in Aviation Department.
Specialisation: Practice deals principally with aviation claims and aviation insurance disputes, litigation and arbitration. Handles a wide range of aviation interests including airlines, aircraft operators, airports and aerodromes, helicopters, gliders and parachuting and contractual documents relative to those interests. Author and lecturer on a wide range of legal issues affecting the aviation industry such as airworthiness, airport operations, carriage by air and aviation legal liabilities generally.
Prof. Memberships: Member of the Royal Aeronautical Society, General Aviation Safety Council (Chairman), Lawyers Flying Association (Chairman), Lawyer Pilots Bar Association

(International Vice-President), City of London Law Society, Guild of Air Pilots and Air Navigators.
Career: Qualified in 1966. 10 years with provincial firm as litigation partner followed by 2 years in the Public Relations Department of the Law Society. Partner in *Barlow Lyde & Gilbert* 1980-1992. Aviation Partner in *Jarvis & Barrister* 1992-97.
Personal: Born 25 June 1941. Attended Repton School, Derbyshire, followed by College of Law. Leisure interests include flying as a Private Pilot, photography and wine growing. Lives in Essex.

WILLCOX, David J.
Beaumont and Son, London
(0171) 481 3100
Partner in Aviation Department.
Specialisation: Main areas of practice are aerospace, commercial litigation and litigation insurance. His practice in aviation law covers handling of passenger and hull claims in respect of major accidents involving fixed and rotary wing operations including a large number of accidents in Africa, passenger cargo and baggage liability claims, advising on rights and liabilities of aviation engineering and maintenance organisations, and commercial litigation.
Prof. Memberships: Law Society.
Career: Qualified in 1981. Became a Partner in 1987.
Personal: Born 25th March 1957. Attended Sheffield University.

SCOTLAND

ANDERSON, Peter
Simpson & Marwick WS, Edinburgh
(0131) 557 1545

CLARK, Richard
Maclay Murray & Spens, Glasgow
(0141) 248 5011
rafc@maclaymurrayspens.co.uk
Specialisation: Senior litigation partner specialising in aviation, environmental law, shipping litigation and fraud and financial services. Recently acted and won for underwriter's/defenders in 'Herd v. Clyde Helicopters Ltd' in the House of Lords. Also acting for Shetland Islands Council in connection with the Braer disaster. Co-author of the Scottish section of Butterworths Aircraft Finance.
Career: Edinburgh University (LL.B 1973).
Personal: Born 1949.

DONALD, Hugh R.
Shepherd & Wedderburn WS, Edinburgh
(0131) 228 9900
See under Medical Negligence: Mainly Defendant, p. 591

BANKING

See also: Asset Finance, Shipping (Ship Finance), Capital Markets and Derivatives – Corporate Finance, Buy-Outs, Projects/PFI. Banking Litigation is covered in the Commercial Litigation Section.

RESEARCH: We interviewed practitioners, bankers and in-house lawyers at major investment banks. In compiling the tables, we considered all the information available to us, paying particular regard to the market research carried out by our team of ten qualified lawyers. (The researchers' details are set out on page three.)

The rankings, therefore, reflect the opinion of the marketplace as revealed by systematic and objective research: see page four. (Our research is audited every year by the British Market Research Bureau.)

OVERVIEW: Banking in this section is taken to include advising lenders and borrowers on all aspects of debt financing. It covers acquisition finance, syndicated loans, and related matters. Banking regulation is also included.

Allen & Overy and Clifford Chance remain the two leading and outstanding banking firms. The general view was that Allen & Overy have an edge over Clifford Chance. However Clifford Chance was recognised as a truly international practice with a global presence and reach.

The biggest upheaval in the banking market amongst the leading firms was the announcement that Stephen Mostyn-Williams and three of his team (including Clifford Atkins) were leaving Ashursts to join US firm Shearman & Sterling. The team have worked together for six years and have a strong reputation in the market particularly with US banks. Shearman & Sterling now have the potential to join the other two US firms in the London table both of which have performed strongly this year. Weil, Gotshal & Manges move up a band (although their great strength was felt to be more on the capital markets side). Baker & McKenzie enter the lists this year.

Norton Rose move up our tables and it remains to be seen what will happen to the banking practice of Wilde Sapte after the failed Andersens merger.

In the South, Osborne Clarke still lead the pack and Lester Aldridge move up to join the leaders this year. In Wales, Eversheds are pre-eminent, while Pinsent Curtis and Wragge & Co dominate the Midlands. In East Anglia, Eversheds and Mills & Reeve continue to handle the lion's share of banking work.

There has been change in the North West this year. Addleshaw Booth & Co no longer dominate as Dibb Lupton Alsop and Eversheds join them at the top of the tables creating a leading triumvirate of firms. Hammond Suddards also move up to join the leading firms. In the North East though, Addleshaws remain ahead of the pack.

There was no change amongst the leaders in Scotland, with Dundas & Wilson CS still ahead, benefitting from their presence in both Edinburgh and Glasgow following their merger with Dorman Jeffrey & Co and their link up with Andersens. In Northern Ireland, both L'Estrange & Brett and Arthur Cox are highly regarded for their banking work.

LEADING FIRMS • LONDON

ALLEN & OVERY
CLIFFORD CHANCE

FRESHFIELDS
LINKLATERS

LOVELL WHITE DURRANT
NORTON ROSE

ASHURST MORRIS CRISP
SLAUGHTER AND MAY
WILDE SAPTE

HIGHLY REGARDED FIRMS

Cameron McKenna
Herbert Smith

Denton Hall
Dibb Lupton Alsop
Dundas & Wilson CS/Garretts
Gouldens
Macfarlanes
Simmons & Simmons
Stephenson Harwood
Taylor Joynson Garrett
Theodore Goddard
Travers Smith Braithwaite
Weil, Gotshal & Manges

Baker & McKenzie
Berwin Leighton
Field Fisher Waterhouse
Nabarro Nathanson
Watson, Farley & Williams
Withers

LONDON

Allen & Overy (43ptnrs/ 200assts worldwide). The most widely respected banking practice in London. The overall consensus is that they have the edge on Clifford Chance ("slightly ahead … more big name partners", "good variety of deals"). *Philip Wood* is regarded more as an "academic" than an active transactional lawyer. Other leading individuals include the "terrific" and "fantastic" *David Morley* and *Anthony Humphrey* ("very good"). *Jonathan Horsfall Turner* was praised as having an "incredible practice … very active," "technically able … practical" and "a good all rounder." *Tony Keal* was described as "a really able lawyer – who can be difficult" doing "complex international deals" who "knows everything there is to know... will screw the other side into the ground." *Stephen Gillespie* ("banks love him and competent with it") moves up into our list of leading individuals. **Clients/Work:** Acted for Goldman Sachs and the other arrangers of the US $10.2bn debt financing for ICI to finance the acquisition of the speciality chemical business of Unilever. Acted for HSBC, Barclays and Goldman Sachs as arrangers of the US $8bn debt financing for the BAT de-merger. Acted for The General Electric Company plc on a Euro 6bn credit facility; the first euro denominated syndicated loan in the market.

Clifford Chance (34ptnrs/150assts London/60+ptnrs/250assts worldwide). A truly international practice with a global presence and reach. The "excellent" and "charming" *Michael Bray* heads the team – "done everything, acted for everybody, remains active doing best transactions despite being a bit long in the tooth … great." *Stuart Popham* ("seen it all … knows it backwards, good all rounder") moves back up our tables. *Mark Campbell* ("does a lot and is good at what he does – puts deals together") was praised by clients as "good all round." The team also includes "able operators" *Mark Stewart* and *Malcolm Sweeting*. **Clients/ Work:** Acting for banks on first ever loan denominated in Euros. GEC Euro 6bn loan. Acted for Banks Advisory Committee on Russian debt rescheduling of approximately US$33bn of debt. Acted on CSFB funding Siebe to acquire Allied Colloids (£1.6bn).

Freshfields (9ptnrs/30assts) Have a strong reputation particularly for their borrower work. Seen as "professional." Undertake a mix of lender and borrower work, the department is headed by Simon Hall who is best known for his asset finance work. Leading individuals include the "top class" *David Ereira* and *Edward Evans*. **Clients/Work:** Acted for ICI on $8.5bn facility in connection with the acquisition of certain Unilever businesses. Acted for Gazprom on $2.5bn facility. Represented Omnitel Pronto Italia on refinancing to increase facilities to Lit 2,800bn.

Linklaters (14ptnrs/33assts in London) A strong reputation for lender and borrower work ("still good, pretty impressive… attractive banking outfit"). "The technical product is good...quality is high." The practice is headed by *Haydn Puleston Jones* described by some as "probably the City's most brilliant draftsman." *Robert Elliott* ("an important part of L&P's banking practice") is a new addition to our tables. **Clients/Work:** Acting for Banque Paribas with £500m syndicated credit facility for General Cable Holdings. Acting for PacifiCorp on 4 syndicated loans worth £2.850bn, US$1.625bn, US$1.575 and US$1.285bn in connection with its June '97 takeover bid for The Energy Group plc. Acting for UBS as arranger and underwriter of US$400m syndicated oil contract prepayment facility and a separate, but related, US$560m syndicated letter of credit facility for the Angolan national oil company.

Lovell White Durrant (12ptnrs/ 32assts) "Good and quite wide banking practice on back of Barclays." The group is headed by the "charismatic" *John Penson* (domestic banking). Clients liked Penson very much and commended the firm for producing "consistently high standard work." *Matthew Cottis* is still up and coming. **Clients/Work:** Acting for Bank of Scotland and Société Générale as co-arrangers of a US$125m syndicated facility to International Mezzanine Investment. Acting for CSFB in making available a total of £82,750,000 by way of senior and mezzanine finance to fund the purchase by CVC of the Britton packaging business. Acting on behalf of Chase Manhattan Bank and others in providing a £3.625b financing to Texas Utilities' UK-based acquisition vehicle to part finance the public offer for the Energy Group Plc.

Norton Rose (24ptnrs/75assts London plus 14 ptnrs in overseas offices) Were recommended to go up the tables to join Lovells due to the relatively broad based nature of their practice and their complex work for financial institutions. Increased profile in the market. However, Douglas Colliver has recently left to join a US firm. Opinions are divided as to the effect of his departure. Appear to be focusing more resources internationally following the decision to dismantle the M5 Group. **Clients/Work:** Advised arranging banks in relation to 3 separate credit facilities aggregating US$340m following the demerger of Cordiant PLC. Advised the national state oil company and the central bank of Angola in a series of structured trade debt financings aggregating US$1.09bn. Represented Rosestbank as the borrower of a US$30m syndicated facility arranged by Bankgesellschaft Berlin.

Ashurst Morris Crisp (9ptnrs/26assts) Marked by the departure of Stephen Mostyn-Williams to Shearman and Sterling and subsequent announcement that he would be joined by some of his team (including *Clifford Atkins*). They were credited with building and successfully marketing the practice. *Justin Spendlove* is the new head of department. Before the announcement, our research had thrown up differing views about the practice. Most had thought that they were "impressive and growing with particular strength in acquisition finance." Some felt that the practice fed off a good corporate client list but that it did not really have the spread. However, with the loss of the core team, there is an inevitable question as to whether they will be able to recover their former position. **Clients/Work:** Acting for Goldman Sachs as debt underwriter and financial adviser on Elis LBO. Advising Bankers Trust and Société

LEADING INDIVIDUALS · LONDON

WOOD Philip Allen & Overy

ALLEN Maurice Weil, Gotshal & Manges
BRAY Michael Clifford Chance
DUNCAN Michael Allen & Overy
EREIRA David Freshfields
EVANS Edward Freshfields
HORSFALL TURNER Jonathan Allen & Overy
HUMPHREY Anthony Allen & Overy
MORLEY David Allen & Overy
POPHAM Stuart Clifford Chance
PULESTON JONES Haydn Linklaters
STEWART Mark Clifford Chance
SWEETING Malcolm Clifford Chance
TUCKER John Linklaters
VINTER Graham Allen & Overy

ATKINS Clifford Ashurst Morris Crisp
BALFOUR Andrew Slaughter and May
CAMPBELL Mark Clifford Chance
CATES Armel Clifford Chance
ELLIOTT Robert Linklaters
FOX Ruth Slaughter and May
FURMAN Mark Macfarlanes
GILLESPIE Stephen Allen & Overy
GLASTONBURY Virginia Denton Hall
HARRIS Julian Allen & Overy
INGLIS Alan Clifford Chance
JOHNSON James Wilde Sapte
KEAL Anthony Allen & Overy
MATHEWS Michael Clifford Chance
MORRISON Neil Rowe & Maw
PENSON John Lovell White Durrant
PETTIT Richard Clifford Chance
RUTHERFORD Brian Dundas & Wilson CS/Garretts
SCHULZ Peter Allen & Overy
SELIGMAN George Slaughter and May
SLATER Richard Slaughter and May
SPENDLOVE Justin Ashurst Morris Crisp
VICKERS Mark Dibb Lupton Alsop
WATSON Martin Watson, Farley & Williams
WYNNE Geoffrey Denton Hall

UP AND COMING

COTTIS Matthew Lovell White Durrant
CULLINANE Lee Clifford Chance
PIERCE Sean Weil, Gotshal & Manges

Générale on parallel debt facilities in England and France in connection with the sale by Générale des Eaux of its private healthcare interests at £1.1bn. Acting as co-ordinating counsel and adviser to the senior banks on the debt financing (underwritten by Bankers Trust) of the purchase of William Hill by Nomura.

Slaughter and May (31 ptnrs) Drew varied responses. The market perception appears to be that the firm acts mainly for corporates. This is partly due to the fact that there is no specific banking department; the relevant partners ("all top quality") are generalists in the company/commercial department. However the firm's clients in bank lending work are both banks and corporates (for whom they do banking work as part of their wider relationship). Most of the banking work is, however, done on behalf of lenders. Leading individuals are *Ruth Fox* ("combines good commercial perspective and legal ability"), *Richard Slater* and *George Seligman* "both excellent and underrated." Still act notably for JP Morgan. **Clients/Work:** Advised Dresdner Kleinwort Benson who arranged a £350m loan facility for Energis PLC. Advised Banque Nationale de Paris and Crédit Commercial de France as co-arrangers for the FRF10bn loan facility for Lafarge, which was made available to fund its bid for Redland plc. Preparing documentation on behalf of JP Morgan Securities Ltd in connection with US$1.75bn multi-currency revolving loan facility involving the re-entry of South African Reserve Bank into the international debt markets.

Wilde Sapte (17ptnrs/60+assts) Even before the failure of the Andersens merger, the firm was perceived to have declined in this area. A recognised banking practice but the perception amongst some is that the reputation is built on acting for NatWest bank. Many saw them as still too heavily dependent on this relationship. However, some interviewees thought that the merger might possibly put off lenders, and this is obviously no longer an issue. The problem now is how the firm will fare post failed-merger. Some bankers used them nationally on medium to high value deals and they were felt to be a "commercially orientated practice." *James Johnson* is rated for "acquisition finance," he "runs a good team to get the job done," and "makes an impression." **Clients/Work:** Acting for Deutsche Morgan Grenfell as arranger of the debt facilities of over £1bn to support Richemont's offer for the part of luxury goods company Vendime it did not already own. Acting for BZW on £100m hybrid debenture stock for Grantchester Finance plc. Acting for the European Investment Bank as arranger of a loan of over £500m for the purposes of financing the £1bn Athens Ring Road.

Cameron McKenna (14ptnrs/ 25assts) Differing opinions as to progress following

the merger. The merger created a wave of energy but despite Cameron's clearing bank strength they are "not conspicuous by high value or niche deals." However many would refer to them on conflict and they appear to have enjoyed a steady stream of work. **Clients/Work:** Acting for Royal Bank of Scotland plc on the financing of the acquisition of Dwyer Group plc. Acting for Rigel Energy Corporation in connection with a syndicated loan and letter of credit facilities totalling Cdn $345m provided by Royal Bank of Canada and others. Concluding the London Club rescheduling of loans to various Russian companies.

Herbert Smith (10ptnrs/30assts) Act for a mix of lenders and borrowers. Seen in the market. "Would refer on conflict." Good at taking advantage of their project finance work **Clients/Work:** Have continued to work on the restructuring of Eurotunnel's £9bn bank debt. Undertaken work (including property finance) for Barclays Bank. Several syndicate facilities for Chase Manhattan Bank including a $220m facility for Intrepid Energy.

Denton Hall (9ptnrs/14assts) Do not have a high profile but those who have come into contact with the group rated them. Notable individuals include the well regarded *Geoffrey Wynne* and *Virginia Glastonbury* ("very good on syndicated deals"). Act for a mix of banks and borrowers. Mix is approximately 70% lender and 30% borrower. **Clients/Work:** Acting for Citibank International Bank plc and Standard Chartered Bank as facility agent and security agent respectively on a syndicated trade receivables financing loan for US$275m to the Ghana Cocoa Board. Acting for Leopold Joseph & Sons Ltd on secured loans to Lloyds' Members' Agents.

Dibb Lupton Alsop (8ptnrs/14assts) A well marketed practice with a good reputation. "Largely driven by acquisition finance." Typical client comment was: "very very good service both in terms of price (and sticking to it), good quality first draft documentation… trusted to get on with the negotiations, they front it. Good after sales service. Practical and commercial." *Mark Vickers* was described as a "good transactional buy-out lawyer and marketeer." Bankers remarked: "he goes to every meeting … hands on … personable with us and other parties involved." **Clients/Work:** Advised Trans-America Corporation on the European aspects of its worldwide acquisition of the trade finance business of Whirlpool Corporation for $1.3bn. Advised Chase Manhattan on syndicated facilities of more than £1.75bn.

Dundas & Wilson CS/Garretts (2ptnrs/ 3assts) *Brian Rutherford* ("commercial, strong negotiator. Knows his law inside out and produces good documents") has joined the Garretts practice as a result of its association with D&W. Some clients remarked "OK in Scotland but the London end has just

been absorbed into Garretts." Rutherford is excellent but queries were raised about the strength and depth of his team. **Clients/ Work:** Clients include AIB Bank, Clydesdale Bank and Bank of Scotland.

Gouldens (4ptnrs/4assts) Have "put together some extremely complex debt structures, sophisticated, all property based." Work is approx. 50/50 bank/borrower in terms of number of deals over last year. **Clients/Work:** Advised ABN Amro in restructuring the group's fixed income business in UK; Pillar Property PLC and Caisse de Dépôt et Placement du Québec in the refinancing of the UK shopping portfolio with a £175m syndicated credit facility.

Macfarlanes (4ptnrs/4assts) Team has "good people" and is headed by *Mark Furman*. A broad practice covering general lending and property finance. Continue to do a lot of acquisition finance. Seen as acting mainly for borrowers. **Clients/Work:** Advised Cordiant advertising group on the financing of its demerger. Acted for JD Wetherspoon on £100m of additional acquisition facilities.

Simmons & Simmons (8ptnrs: 5f/t/30assts) Felt to be stronger in capital markets than mainstream banking. The departure of Moni Mannings was seen as weakening the practice. However their property finance work was rated: "doing more quality work … see a lot on property finance side … mix of borrower and lender." **Clients/Work:** Acting for B.A.T Industries plc on a US$8bn facility taken out in connection with the de-merger of the group's financial services division. The £1.2bn refinancing by Gallaher Group plc on its de-merger from American Brands.

Stephenson Harwood (5ptnrs/9assts) Practice has an international flavour. "Peculiar niche acting for the London branches of smaller overseas banks." Act for banks and borrowers. **Clients/Work:** Acting for Den Norske Bank in the restructuring of a debt of over US$80m incurred to finance the "Spirit of Columbus" oil rig. Acting for The Royal Bank of Scotland plc in its joint venture with Virgin Direct to establish the Virgin One Account.

Taylor Joynson Garrett (6ptnrs/ 7assts) Act for a wide range of financial institutions. Were generally perceived to be "coming along well." **Clients/Work:** Acting for MeesPierson on infrastructure telecom facility to a Russian subsidiary of Deutsche Telecom. Acting for international holding company on a US$60m facility from JP Morgan. Acting for Bank Austria on trade finance facility to Albert Fisher Group plc.

Theodore Goddard (6ptnrs/9assts) Principally act for banks rather than borrowers. **Clients/Work:** Acted for National Westminster Bank Plc on structured finance for various universities. Closed over US$200m structured financings for Nedcor Bank and Hambros Bank Ltd who were brought in to take up half of the funding.

Travers Smith Braithwaite (5ptnrs/ 6assts) Primarily act for banks but also have a significant amount of borrower work. **Clients/Work:** Acted for Westdeutsche Landesbank Girozentrale as arranger on a number of transactions including the $135m multicurrency revolving credit facility for London Forfaiting Company plc. Advised NTL on £875m secured facilities fully underwritten by Chase Manhattan Bank.

Weil, Gotshal & Manges (4ptnrs/14 assocs)"Ignore at peril!". Have moved up a band in our tables. Seen as making immense progress over the last year. Mainly seen in capital markets but making progress in general banking acting for banks rather than borrowers. "Have some excellent practitioners." The practice is headed by the widely admired and praised *Maurice Allen* (who moves up a band in our tables). Amongst other things he was praised for building up the practice from scratch. "Experienced heavyhitter." "Brilliant with clients and good technically ... touch of Philip Wood when he started." *Sean Pierce* remains in our list of up and coming individuals. "Good deals and has a following of US investment banks." **Clients/ Work:** Acting for Czech National Bank on US$2bn syndicated facility to the bank. Acting for Bank of Tokyo-Mitsubishi on 100bn Greek Drachma to Hellenic Railways (first non government guaranteed facility).

Baker & McKenzie (3ptnrs (general lending), 11assts) A new entry to our tables this year. Mainly known for projects orientated work but

have a respectable banking practice doing a mix of lender and borrower work . "Do come across and have some good people." Reputation for international trade/project loans. **Clients/Work:** Represented UBS, as agent and arranger of the $100m structured warehouse refinancing of Sappi Ltd's equity investment in SD Warren Company. Represented Société Générale, as arranger and agent of the $150m syndicated credit facility for the Polish copper product KGHM Polska Miedz SA.

Berwin Leighton (7ptnrs/6assts) As to be expected, strong on the property finance side, four of the partners are concentrated here. Do a mix of lender and borrower work. Clients who used them recently were satisfied with the service. **Clients/Work:** Acting for Bank of Nova Scotia as arranger of a US$1bn letter of credit facility for Cable and Wireless. Preparing standard bilateral agreements for Tesco PLC and advising in relation to numerous facilities.

Field Fisher Waterhouse (3ptnrs/ 1 asst) Act for more than 50 banks. Of these, more than 40 are either foreign or UK subsidiaries of foreign banks. **Clients/Work:** Advising Citibank, NA on various loans, including a £35m syndicated loan to acquire investment property in the City of London, and a £49m loan to BVI corporation to acquire the headquarters of a major pharmaceutical company for investment. Advising a major US bank as lender and security trustee in respect of a credit agreement granted to a US corporation, including a revolving credit facility of

US$25m, a term loan commitment of US $15m and a letter of credit facility of US$5m.

Nabarro Nathanson (2ptnrs/7assts) Also have property finance department with 1prtnr and 2assts. Recognised practice. **Clients/Work:** Acting for Chase Manhattan on the sale of Woolgate House and on a £75m loan note issued by MEPC plc. Acting for BAA-McArthur/Glen Ltd on a series of acquisitions in the UK and Austria for around £91m.

Watson, Farley & Williams (4ptnrs/ 4assts) The general banking (as opposed to ship and asset finance) practice was felt by many to be weakened. Departure of personnel was mentioned although some of these did occur over a year ago. Stronger on the ship and asset finance side. *Martin Watson* is well regarded. **Clients/Work:** Acting for global telecommunications company in the $650m funding of its ground equipment in 12 jurisdictions. Advising the senior and mezzanine lenders in US$90m syndicated facilities to US and European borrowers involved in the manufacture and distribution of water purification systems.

Withers (3ptnrs/1 consultant, 3assts) Banking clients include a number of Italian banks. **Clients/Work:** Acted for a syndicate of Italian banks in a major project financing in Romania to build a wood resin factory with a loan from European Investment Bank being guaranteed by the syndicate.

Neil Morrison at Rowe & Maw was also recommended.

LEADERS' PROFILES · LONDON

ALLEN, Maurice
Weil, Gotshal & Manges, London
(0171) 903 1000
Specialisation: Maurice Allen is Head of the London Office. Maurice has an established reputation in the City as an experienced international finance lawyer who regularly represents the major financial institutions. Maurice has a broad practice covering all forms of syndicated lending and international structured finance, spanning the traditional divide between banking and capital markets work.

ATKINS, Clifford
Ashurst Morris Crisp, London
(0171) 638 1111
Partner in Banking and International Finance Department.
Specialisation: He has a wide experience of both domestic and international banking and has practised both in the United Kingdom and Hong Kong. In recent years he has concentrated on structured and project finance and debt trading and restructuring.
Career: Joined *Ashursts* as a partner in 1991.

BALFOUR, Andrew G.
Slaughter and May, London
(0171) 600 1200
Specialisation: Works mainly on banking and capital markets transactions. Particular experience in syndicated loans, structured finance, project finance, acquisition finance,

international equity issues, Euro-bonds, Euro-commercial paper and medium term notes. Also advises banks and corporate clients on general banking and treasury matters.
Prof. Memberships: The Law Society and International Bar Association.
Career: Qualified 1981 and became a Partner of *Slaughter and May* in 1988. Resident partner in New York office 1991-1993.
Personal: Educated at Nailsea School (1968-75) and Manchester University (1975-78).

BRAY, Michael
Clifford Chance, London (0171) 600 1000, Milan (0039)2 7600 8040
Partner in the Finance Practice since 1976 and Head of Finance Practice since September 1995.
Specialisation: Principal areas of work include all aspects of commercial bank lending, including project finance, structured finance, asset finance, acquisition finance, restructurings for borrowers of all types.

CAMPBELL, Mark
Clifford Chance, London (0171) 600 1000
Specialisation: Partner dealing with banking work including leveraged transactions; insolvency; derivatives; structured finance and corporate reconstruction. Also involved in the development of the Secondary Loan Market as advisor to the Loan Market Association.
Career: Articles *Coward Chance*; qualified 1984; Partner *Clifford Chance* since 1991.

Personal: Oriel College, Oxford (1981 BA).

CATES, Armel C.
Clifford Chance, London (0171) 600 1000
Senior Partner, Finance Area.
Specialisation: Principal area of work involves all aspects of debt securities and banking including trusteeships of bond and debenture issues, secured transactions, securitisation and structured finance, project finance and building society regulation.
Career: Qualified 1969. Partner 1975.
Personal: LL.B (Hons) Southampton University.

COTTIS, Matthew
Lovell White Durrant, London
(0171) 236 0066
See under Corporate Finance: Debt, p. 227

CULLINANE, Lee
Clifford Chance, London (0171) 600 1000
Partner, Finance Area.
Specialisation: General banking with emphasis on project, telecoms and infrastructure finance.
Career: Partner 1995.
Personal: LLB 1985, SFC 1986.

DUNCAN, Michael G.
Allen & Overy, London (0171) 330 3000
Specialisation: Partner dealing in areas of practice comprising all types of banking and corporate finance, including in particular syndicated loans (acting for a variety of banks

and borrowers), acquisition finance, asset financing, property finance, housing association finance and work-outs/reschedulings.
Career: Articled *Allen & Overy*. Qualified 1981, Partner 1987.
Personal: Cambridge University (1978 BA). Born 1957.

ELLIOTT, Robert
Linklaters, London (0171) 456 4478
Specialisation: Banking, structured finance, derivatives and debt markets generally including creditor refinancings and restructurings.
Prof. Memberships: Law Society. American Arbitration Association.
Career: Leeds Grammar School; London University; *Wilde Sapte* 1976-1990; *Linklaters* 1990-date.
Personal: Married with three children. Leisure: sailing, cricket, rugby, reading, music.

EREIRA, David P.
Freshfields, London (0171) 936 4000
Partner in Finance Department.
Specialisation: Responsible for co-ordination of banking practice, acting for banks, international institutions and borrowers in all aspects of banking and finance related work. Responsible for the co-ordination for *Freshfields* property finance practice, acting for bankers, property developers and investors in all aspects of the financing of the acquisition and development of property on property related investments.
Prof. Memberships: Law Society, City of London Solicitors Company sub-committee on Banking Law; International Bar Association, sub-committees B and E; Justice Working Group of the Financial Law Panel.
Career: Qualified in 1981. Worked at *Wilde Sapte* 1981-90, from 1984 as a Partner. Joined *Freshfields* in 1990, becoming a Partner in 1991. Postgraduate student with the Open University studying for an MSc in mathematics. Lives in London.

EVANS, Edward T.H.
Freshfields, London (0171) 936 4000
Partner in Finance Department.
Specialisation: Main areas of practice are banking and project and asset finance. Also handles energy law work. Has addressed numerous conferences and seminars on these subjects.
Prof. Memberships: International Bar Association.
Career: Qualified 1980, having joined *Freshfields* in 1978. Became a Partner in 1986.
Personal: Born 12th December 1954. Attended RGS High Wycombe 1964-72, then Trinity College Cambridge 1973-77. Leisure interests include rugby, fishing and racing. Lives in London.

FOX, Ruth M.
Slaughter and May, London (0171) 600 1200
Specialisation: Practice covers a wide range of commercial work, with an emphasis on banking and capital markets, now focusing on financial regulations. Has acted extensively for banks and also for building societies, including in relation to conversions, and for corporate trustees.
Prof. Memberships: The Law Society.
Career: Qualified in 1979 with *Slaughter and May*. Became a Partner in 1986.
Personal: Born 3 October 1954. Educated at St Helena School Chesterfield and University College, London. Married with three sons. Lives in London and Hertfordshire.

FURMAN, Mark
Macfarlanes, London (0171) 831 9222
Specialisation: Specialises in acquisition finance and property finance and generally acting for lenders and borrowers in all aspects of debt finance.
Career: Dulwich College; St. John's College, Oxford (MA, 1980). Qualified as solicitor 1983.
Personal: Married with two children. Interests: music.

GILLESPIE, Stephen
Allen & Overy, London (0171) 330 3000
Specialisation: Partner in the banking department with experience of all aspects of mainstream international finance, specialising in structured finance, with a particular emphasis on structured acquisition finance, project finance, tele-media finance, infrastructure and transportation finance, equipment and asset finance, and complex restructurings, reconstructions and workouts. Recent/current deals include Bouygues Telecom financing, IPC Magazines LBO, Virgin Rail Group rolling stock financing and Brunner Mond plc bid financing.
Prof. Memberships: Law Society. City of London Solicitors Company.
Career: Articled *Stephenson Harwood* 1985-87, Solicitor *Freshfields* 1987-91, Solicitor *Allen & Overy* 1991-95, Partner 1995.
Personal: Born November, 1962. Educated at Foyle and Londonderry College and Trinity College, Oxford (MA (Hons) Jurisprudence 1984). Interests include family, reading, outdoor pursuits and music. Lives in St. Albans.

GLASTONBURY, Virginia
Denton Hall, London (0171) 320 6226
vg@dentonhall.com
Specialisation: Partner, Banking and Financial Markets Group; Experience in general banking; Private Finance Initiative transactions; secured lending and funding (including project finance, real estate finance, reconstructions, workouts and re-financing) by banks and institutions. Acted for the Royal Bank of Scotland plc, National Westminster Bank plc, Clydesdale and Novia Scotia on £100 million loan facility to J.D. Wetherspoon plc. Also acted for Rentokil Initial plc on refinancing of its £600 million facilities through 10 selected banks. Project leader on two PFI transactions relating to services to prisons and on PFI Pathfinder project for Magistrates Courts at Hereford and Worcester.
Career: Articles at *Denton Hall* 1980-1982; qualified 1982; partner 1988; member of *Denton Hall's* International Partnership board; partner at *Denton Hall* responsible for recruitment of trainee solicitors.
Personal: Born 1957, married with one stepson. Interests include cars, reading, travel, cinema, most sports.

HARRIS, Julian
Allen & Overy, Milan (3902) 290 491
Specialisation: Partner in the finance practice in Milan specialising in structured finance, project finance and securitisation.
Prof. Memberships: Law Society. City of London Solicitors Company.
Career: Articled *Allen & Overy*, partner 1995.
Personal: Born 5/10/60. Educated at Cranleigh School and Peterhouse, Cambridge. Interests include cycling and farming.

HORSFALL TURNER, Jonathan
Allen & Overy, London (0171) 330 3000
See under Project Finance, p. 686

HUMPHREY, Anthony R.
Allen & Overy, London (0171) 330 3000
Specialisation: Partner specialising in financing transactions and with broad experience in company and corporate finance matters; has extensive experience in all aspects of financing, particularly tiered or structured debt/equity financings including international project financings, acquisition financings and other complex multi-sourced financings; has advised on transactions worldwide including the North Sea, North America, the Gulf, the Far East and Australia.
Prof. Memberships: Member, Section on Energy and Natural Resources Law of the International Bar Association.
Career: Articled *Allen & Overy*, qualified 1975, Partner 1981.
Personal: Durham University (1972 BA). Born 1951.

INGLIS, Alan
Clifford Chance, London (0171) 600 1000
Specialisation: Structural and acquisition finance, syndications and corporate reconstructions.
Career: Qualified 1985 (LLB), became Partner in 1992.

JOHNSON, James
Wilde Sapte, London (0171) 246 7000
Partner, General Banking Group, Banking Department.
Specialisation: Advises on all forms of corporate banking but in particular is a leading specialist in acquisition finance, workouts, structured finance and housing assocation finance.
Career: Articled at *Wilde Sapte* and qualified in 1987. Partner at *Wilde Sapte* in 1991.
Personal: Born 1963. Educated: Roundhill College, Thurmaston, Leicester 1974-77, Wreake Valley College, Syston, Leicester 1977-81, Collingwood College, Durham University.

KEAL, Anthony C.
Allen & Overy, London (0171) 330 3000
Specialisation: Partner specialising in structured acquisition finance (LBOs and the like), public bid finance, export credit arrangements and syndicated loans generally.
Prof. Memberships: Law Society and City of London Solicitors Company.
Career: Articled *Allen & Overy*, qualified 1976; legal adviser/CoSec, Libra Bank plc 1976-78; Assistant Solicitor *Allen & Overy* 1979-81; Partner 1981.
Personal: Born 1951. Educated Stowe School and New College, Oxford (1973).

MATHEWS, Michael
Clifford Chance, London (0171) 600 1000
Specialisation: Banking, Project finance and tax-based finance.
Career: Qualified as Solicitor in 1966, became Partner in 1971. Currently joint Senior Partner of financial practice.

MORLEY, David H.
Allen & Overy, London (0171) 330 3000
Specialisation: Partner acting for banks and financial institutions, as well as borrowers, on all types of debt and structured finance

transactions with particular emphasis on syndicated loans, acquisition finance and telecoms, asset finance, project finance, property and housing association finance.
Career: Articled *Allen & Overy*, qualified 1982, trainee solicitor Brussels 1981, assistant solicitor 1982-88. One year on secondment at Chase Investment Bank Ltd 1985, partner 1988. Managing Partner, Banking Department 1998.
Personal: St John's College, Cambridge (1979 MA). Born 1956.

MORRISON, Neil C.
Rowe & Maw, London (0171) 248 4282
Specialisation: Banking, structured finance and project finance. Advising Virgin Rail Group on its fleet renewal for the Cross-country and West Coast Lines. Advising Morgan Stanley International on the proposed financing of a DCMF prison project.
Personal: Fast cars, travel, art and music. Lives in Wiltshire.

PENSON, John
Lovell White Durrant, London
(0171) 236 0066
Specialisation: Wholesale banking generally, and particularly structured finance. Active in: acquisition finance, including senior debt, mezzanine debt and subordinated bonds, vendor loan notes, and all consequential intercreditor issues arising from acquisitions; financing bids and bridging rights issues; project finance (including both senior and mezzanine debt), often in the context of the UK Private Finance Initiative; rescue/restructuring; syndicated loans – for both banks and borrowers, in the context of both structured finance and 'blue chip' facilities; trade finance. Acts mostly for banks (but also for substantial equity and mezzanine houses). Recent major international transactions include the Geberit, Elis, Impress Metal Packaging, Hately Trench, Roventa-Henex, and KNP transactions; substantial UK transactions include acting for financiers of New Look, Pubmaster, Thomson Directories, the Tramway systems in Croydon and Manchester and the Norfolk and Norwich PFI Hospital scheme; the take-private of C.E. Heath, Betterware, and Wellman Industries; the bid by Texas Utilities Company for the Energy Group PLC; Fairey Hydraulics, Britton Packaging, and Pipeline Inspection Services.
Career: Qualified 1980. Partner 1985.
Personal: Born 1955. Lit. Hum., Worcester College, Oxford (1977 BA 1st Class Hons).

PETTIT, Richard
Clifford Chance, London (0171) 600 1000
Partner Finance Area.
Specialisation: Acts for banks or borrowers on a variety of financings, including asset-based and structured transactions.
Career: Qualified 1971; Partner 1976. Property specialist until 1981; Singapore Office 1981-88; finance area in London 1988-present.
Personal: LL.B Bristol.

PIERCE, Sean
Weil, Gotshal & Manges, London
(0171) 903 1000
Specialisation: He is a UK-qualified partner of the London office specialising in finance work. Most recently, in addition to general finance work, he has focused on structured finance work

including cross-border acquisition finance and international project finance. He has a wide range of experience from leveraged buyouts and management buyouts in the late eighties to international project finance and securitisation while in the Far East to restructurings and most recently structured finance work out of London.

POPHAM, Stuart
Clifford Chance, London (0171) 600 1000
Partner Banking and Finance.
Specialisation: Principal area of work relates to finance for corporates including acquisition financing, work-outs, syndicated and capital market financing, structured and tax driven financing with particular reference to media and telecommunications, acting for lenders and borrowers.
Career: Qualified 1978. Partner 1984.
Personal: LLB. 1975.

PULESTON JONES, Haydn
Linklaters, London (0171) 456 4454
Partner in International Finance Department, Banking Group.
Specialisation: Principal area of practice has been in the field of banking. Areas of specialisation include syndicated, secured and structured financings and corporate rescues and recoveries. Has had extensive experience of advising banks, syndicates, steering committees and distressed companies on UK and international defaults and reschedulings.
Prof. Memberships: Member of The Law Society and Chairman of Banking Law Sub-Committee of the City of London Law Society.
Career: Qualified 1973 becoming a Partner with *Linklaters & Paines* in 1979.

RUTHERFORD, Brian
Dundas & Wilson CS, London
(0171) 546 9158
Specialisation: Partner in charge of *Dundas & Wilson's* London office, member of Banking Group dealing with all aspects of banking and corporate finance.
Career: Attended University of Dundee (LLB). Joined *Bonar Mackenzie* 1977; assistant *Bonar Mackenzie* 1979-1980; Partner *Bonar Mackenzie* 1980-1984; Assistant Vice President of Continental Bank (Chicago and London) 1984-1987; Vice President of Continental Bank (Chicago and London) 1987-1989; Director of Charterhouse Bank 1989-1993; Partner in charge of *Dundas & Wilson* London office since 1993. Also Partner *Garretts* since 1997, member of Corporate Department.
Personal: Born 1956. Resides in London.

SCHULZ, Peter F.
Allen & Overy, London (0171) 330 3000
Specialisation: Partner, banking department, specialising in banking and international finance, including domestic and international syndicated and structured lending, export credits and multi-sourced project financings, especially in the emerging markets (having completed numerous transactions throughout Central and Eastern Europe, the Middle East, Africa and India), and also debt restructurings work-outs and par and distressed asset sales, acting for borrowers and export credit agencies as well as arrangers and lenders.
Career: Articled *Allen & Overy*, qualified 1983, partner 1989.

Personal: Educated at Haberdashers' Aske's School, Elstree; Downing College, Cambridge (MA Law) and Sherburn Flying Club, Yorkshire.

SELIGMAN, George E.S.
Slaughter and May, London
(0171) 600 1200
Specialisation: Secured and unsecured loan financings, securitisations, structured financings, banking advisory matters and insolvency law.
Career: Partner in *Slaughter and May* since 1984.

SLATER, Richard
Slaughter and May, London
(0171) 600 1200
Partner in Financial/Commercial Department. Head of Banking Stream.
Specialisation: Principal area of practice is debt financing of all types, including syndicated loan facilities, structured financings, project financings and bond and note issues. Has also acted on international equity offerings, flotations, privatisations and corporate and commercial work of a general nature.
Prof. Memberships: The Law Society.
Career: With *Slaughter and May* throughout. Articles 1970, qualified 1972, Partner 1979. Hong Kong office 1981-1986.
Personal: Born 18 August 1948. Educated at University College School, Hampstead (1956-1965), Lycée Michelet, Paris (1965-1966) and Pembroke College, Cambridge 1966-1969. Lives in London.

SPENDLOVE, Justin
Ashurst Morris Crisp, London
(0171) 638 1111
See under Corporate Finance: Debt, p. 233

STEWART, Mark
Clifford Chance, London (0171) 600 1000
Partner Banking Group.
Specialisation: Principal area of work is general corporate banking acting for banks, corporate borrowers and venture capitalists with an emphasis on highly leveraged transactions, structured debt and acquisition finance.
Career: Qualified 1983, Partner 1990.
Personal: LLB (1st Class Hons) Bristol University, 1980.

SWEETING, Malcolm
Clifford Chance, London (0171) 600 1000
Partner. Main area of practice is banking.

TUCKER, John T.
Linklaters, London (0171) 456 4496
Partner, International Finance Department, Banking Group.
Specialisation: Areas of specialisation include syndicated lending, secured and structured financings, acquisition finance and reorganisation work. Represents banks, bank syndicates and other creditors as well as borrowers in both UK and international financing transactions.
Career: Qualifications LL B (Hons), BA Accountancy. Admitted as a Barrister and Solicitor in South Australia 1980. Qualified, England & Wales, 1988. Became a Partner in 1990.

VICKERS, Mark H.
Dibb Lupton Alsop, London (0345) 262728
Head of Banking Group.
Specialisation: Corporate banking and international finance: specialising in UK and cross-border acquisition finance and leveraged

acquisitions, particularly management buy-outs/buy-ins and institutional purchases; structured finance; global syndicated lending. Expert retained by the leading senior mezzanine lenders and strategic adviser to the banks on trends in the senior debt market. **Career:** Head of Banking at *Alsop Wilkinson* from 1990; National Head of Banking at *Dibb Lupton Alsop* following the firm's merger in 1996. **Personal:** Helicopter pilot.

VINTER, Graham D.
Allen & Overy, London (0171) 330 3000
See under Project Finance, p. 688

WATSON, Martin A.
Watson, Farley & Williams, London
(0171) 814 8000
See under Shipping: Finance, p. 733

WOOD, Philip
Allen & Overy, London (0171) 330 3000
Specialisation: Partner and head of banking department, specialising in all aspects of international banking, including syndicated loans, project finance, title finance, trade

finance, foreign exchange agreements, secured finance, payment and clearing systems, shipping and aircraft, insolvency and business reconstructions, bank regulation, and legal systems, expert in comparative financial law. Head of know-how and training.
Prof. Memberships: Member City of London Law Society Banking Law Sub-Committee; Board of the Institute of Advanced Legal Studies; Visiting Professor, Faculty of Law, Queen Mary and Westfield College. Editorial Board of Butterworth's Journal of International Banking and Financial Law, International Financial Law Review, International Banking and Financial Law Bulletin, Practical Law for Companies, European Financial Services Law. Advisory Board of Asia Business, Law Review, Unidroit correspondent.
Career: Articled *Allen & Overy*, qualified 1970, Partner 1974. Author of eight books on aspects of the law of international finance.
Personal: Born 1942 Livingstone, Zambia. University of Cape Town (BA), Oxford University (MA). Married with 4 children. Interests include landscaping, piano playing, walking, history, literature and astronomy. Lives in Surrey.

WYNNE, Geoffrey L.
Denton Hall, London (0171) 242 1212
Partner, Banking and Financial Markets Department.
Specialisation: Handles all aspects of banking, structured trade and commodity finance, asset and project finance, corporate and international finance, syndicated lending, equipment leasing, financial restructuring, insolvency and bankruptcy, leveraged and management buy-outs. Regularly acts for major financial institutions in the international financial markets. Contributor Sweet & Maxwell's Practical Lending and Security Precedents; editor International Banking & Financial Law (monthly); co-editor Sweet & Maxwell's Company Finance Manual (in preparation); editorial board member Butterworths Journal of International Banking Law. Member of Law Society Committee on Banking.
Career: Qualified 1975; assistant solicitor at *Slaughter and May* 1975-1979; assistant general counsel international Royal Bank of Canada 1979-1985; Partner, *Watson, Farley & Williams* 1985-1996; Partner *Denton Hall* 1997.
Personal: Born 1950. Attended Christ Church, Oxford (1972 BA).

The SOUTH

LEADING FIRMS · THE SOUTH
OSBORNE CLARKE Bristol
BURGES SALMON Bristol
BOND PEARCE Plymouth
LESTER ALDRIDGE Bournemouth

HIGHLY REGARDED FIRMS
Bevan Ashford Exeter
Cameron McKenna Bristol
Lyons Davidson Bristol
Stephens & Scown Exeter

Osborne Clarke (1ptnr/3assts) "Stands out in the region." "They've such a good client base because of NatWest" but "being chased hard by Burges Salmon." Partner *Margaret Childs* "is well respected, technically good and a strong negotiator." All spend 100% of their time on non-contentious banking matters (60% lender/40% borrower). **Clients/Work:** Appointed to 3i panel May 1997. Also act for NatWest, Bank Boston, Bank of Scotland and New Court Credit of Canada.

Burges Salmon (3ptnrs/7assts) *Sandra Forbes* ("knows her stuff") heads the department, and spends 100% of her time on non-contentious banking work. Have a broad spread of work, with a good amount of high value work, and a lot of asset finance – and the team seems to be growing. **Clients/Work:** The review and amendment of Bristol & West plc treasury documentation in light of its acquisition by Bank of Ireland and subsequently redrafting all Bristol & West's commercial loan and security documenta-

tion. Advising Chelsea Building Society on the provision of facilities of £250m in aggregate. Advising Naafi on the £104m sale of its financial services business (including a securitisation of its loan book).

Bond Pearce (3ptnrs/3assts) including the "effective" *Julian Kinsey* who spends 100% of his time in this area. All do non-contentious work, 70% of which is banking, acting for a number of clearing banks and building societies. Practice seen by some as quite insolvency based. **Clients/Work:** £26m advance secured on portfolio of bank branches (acted for lender). Re-structuring £5m facility made by an invoice discounting company (acted for invoice discounter). Act for Chemring plc.

Lester Aldridge (2ptnrs/1asst – 3 other ptnrs in the group handle insolvency and banking litigation). Move up to join the leading firms this year. Many recommended Head of Department *Graham Jeffries* (a "good operator, sensible and always commercial"). **Clients/Work:** Handled over 80 separate matters for Lloyds Bank, including a £30k acquisition financing and lending to five Further and Higher Education Collegess. Preparation of standard facility documentation for lending to the Care sector (London based client). Advised On-Line Finance Ltd when raising £50m and £10m from the city using a structure designed for future securitisation.

Bevan Ashford (3ptnrs/5assts) Handle a mixture of banking and insolvency work. Only firm in the South West which officially sits on the MidWest's panel. **Clients/Work:** For East Kent Medical Services Ltd: Financing of PFI Development by United Bank of Kuwait plc of Private Patient Unit for Thanet Health Authority £2.4m. For Lloyds Bank plc:

Security Audit and Corporate Recovery work. For UCB Bank plc: funding for development in Huddersfield £3.4m.

Cameron McKenna Best known for its litigious banking work, but members of the banking team handle a certain amount of non-contentious work for clients. **Clients/Work:** Lloyds TSB Group. Allied Irish Bank. Alliance & Leicester.

Lyons Davidson (3ptnrs/5assts) Spend a reasonable amount of time on non-contentious banking work. Frequently give transactional advice to senior lenders. **Clients/Work:** Regularly act for Lloyds Bank plc including Acquisition Finance and Commercial Service Offices and in the last year have been involved in senior lending work involving transactions in excess of £27m.

Stephens & Scown (3ptnrs/1 fee-earner) handle non-contentious banking work in the Exeter office ("considered quite good"). Part of a broader finance team doing acquisition finance, restructurings, debt-re-financings and corporate rescue works supported by litigation practitioners. **Clients/Work:** Negotiation of £100.3m variable rate Loan Note isssue and its guarantee by ING Baring, Lloyds and Midland. More generally, secured property lending acting mainly for borrowers but also for the main high street banks and Arbuthnot Latham. Specialise in chattel security.

LEADING INDIVIDUALS THE SOUTH
CHILDS Margaret Osborne Clarke
JEFFRIES Graham Lester Aldridge
KINSEY Julian Bond Pearce
FORBES Sandra Burges Salmon

SEE PROFILES AT END OF THIS SECTION

WALES

Eversheds (2ptnrs/3assts – substantial amounts of time). "In a different league" – have a larger overall practice (national banking and finance practice totals 10ptnrs/25assts) than other Welsh firms, and are leaders both in terms of client base, resources and work. *Kevin Doolan* has a well deserved reputation for excellence and *Philip Vaughan* is also rated. **Clients/Work:** Acted for Barclays on £20m facility for development of a hotel/leisure complex, also on a £14m facility for development of retail complex in Spain (plus retender for client's work nationally). Acted for Firstplus Financial Group in the establishment of a UK funding operation. Acted for Investec Bank on various property and acquisition finance transactions.

Morgan Bruce Spend a substantial amount of their time on non-contentious banking work in areas such as share acquisitions and restructuring of security. Overall, the banking group has increased this year (7ptnrs/7assts overall), following the merger with Newport firm Guthrie Francis. **Clients/Work:** Advised Mitel Corporation on syndicated secured mult-currency facilities of $310m. Acted for a substantial listed property investment company in securing £83m facility.

Edwards Geldard 1 partner specialises in this area (spends all his time on non-contentious work covering banking, insolvency or corporate areas).

MIDLANDS

Pinsent Curtis (6ptnrs (3 f/t)/3assts) Newly restructured banking and finance unit handles the workload. *David Cooke* ("quite an institution" "versatile, good for banking and insolvency work" "considerable expertise") and "good negotiator" *Patrick Twist* maintain the firm's reputation. **Clients/Work:** National Exhibition Centre Ltd £73m bond issue. Major Property Group £30m tax-driven lease structure. NatWest Group £20m facilities for MBO from Krupp. Also act for Midland Bank and Barclays Bank.

Wragge & Co (2ptnrs/2assocs/2assts cover non-contentious banking) *Julian Pallett* ("firm but co-operative") is "good to work with when you're on the other side." Can call on another partner and 2assts for property-related matters. Turnover up by 50% in the last year. **Clients/Work:** For Barclays – acquisition finance for the MBO of ROM Ltd, also acquisition finance for the MBO of Dataform Security. For RBS and RBS Mezzanine Finance – term loan, revolving credit and Capex facilities for Terry Warner Sports Ltd. Handle work for corporate clients, including facilities in excess of £100m in connection with public offers.

Edge & Ellison (3ptnrs/5assts) *Roger Birchall*'s reputation is mainly on the corporate side but he does handle some banking work. The banking team is now part of the acquisition finance unit, within the corporate department. Some felt firm had slipped since departure of Andrew Madden. **Clients/Work:** Barclays Bank plc – MBO of Carrs Paper for which Barclays provided debt facilities aggregating £14.5m. T&S Stornes plc – £90m loan and revolving credit facility in connection with its bid syndicated for M&W plc. Act for all the major clearing banks and a number of US banks on the Eastern Seaboard.

Eversheds (1 ptnr/4assts) *Pat Johnstone* is "well regarded". The firm acts as regional solicitors for National Westminster Bank plc. May well be slightly ahead of Edge & Ellison at present. **Clients/Work:** Acting for Barclays Bank plc in its provision of £10m facilities for the MBO of Maygap Machines Ltd. Negotiating the provision of bank facilities totalling 17 facilities to Headlam Gorup plc in connection with the acquisition by Headlam of MCD (UK) Ltd.

Gateley Wareing (1ptnr + 2corp ptnrs on larger transactional matters/2assts) *Andrew Madden* ("calm under pressure, willing to give commercial advice and gives informed guidance") is individually rated. The firm was involved in acquisiton finance deals for all six of the major UK clearing banks in 1997. **Clients/Work:** Advising on the provision of £10m acquisition finance facilities by Bank of Scotland to Accura Holdings Ltd, including a series of 3 acquisitions. Advising Barclays Bank plc on the provision of facilities to support the £4m MBO/MBI of Birmingham Stopper Ltd.

Martineau Johnson (4ptnrs/6assts – all spend 50% of their time on non-contentious banking work) Combined banking and insolvency team. *Ian Baker* ("a good lawyer, gets results without being overly aggressive," "a serious approach") is new to the tables. **Clients/Work:** Key clients are Lloyds, Bank of Scotland and NatWest. Acted for a clearing bank on a £15m facility on £70m development project which included the assignment of an existing security shareholders' agreement and option. Advised Lloyds Bank Acquisition Finance on £25m MBO.

Dibb Lupton Alsop (1ptnr/1asst/1 consultant) work full time on non-contentious banking matters in newly started up department. **Clients/Work:** Acted for several of the leading Scottish banks on MBO/finance deals.

Shoosmiths & Harrison (2ptnrs/1asst) *John Temple* ("Well respected but better known for insolvency") is in charge of the firmwide Banking Group, which incorporates banking, property finance and banking litigation. **Clients/ Work:** On behalf of Barclays Bank plc and Robert Fleming & Co Ltd in providing £12.5m funding to Bostrom plc for the purposes of a US share acquisition. On behalf of Nationwide Building Society in relation to £17.6m funding for Pemberstone Housing Ltd. On behalf of NatWest Specialist Finance in relation to the funding of an MBO of Coltran Products Ltd.

EAST ANGLIA

Eversheds (4ptnrs p/t in cross-departmental team). "Strong – their national connections help them to maintain their position." *Andrew Croome*, noted individually, spends 40% of his time on banking matters. **Clients/Work:** Major refinancing operation for a Norwich clearing bank. Acting for a borrower regarding syndicated bank loan facilities in aggregate of £60m. Provision of secured finance to care homes operators (over £200m) with control over operators' bank accounts.

Mills & Reeve (1ptnr part time, 3ptnrs when needed)/5/6assts with experience). 50% of banking work handled by firm is non-contentious. Firm handles large amount of banking litigation work for Barclays and get non-contentious instructions on the back of this. *John Lapraik* is the partner best known for non-contentious banking. Firm has seen growth of work in Cambridge office, following relocation of some clearing banks. **Clients/Work:** Act for a number of clearing banks in addition to corporate clients of the firm. Provide advice in connection with debt financing of acquisitions, term loans (both secured rents and unsecured lending) also acting in relation to recoveries work. Act for a large number of higher education institutions on revisions to the terms of their banking arrangements and term and other loans on both tax and non-tax based finances.

Leathes Prior (3ptnrs (30%)/6assts) Handle non-contentious work. Majority of firm's banking work is litigious. **Clients/Work:** Main client is Midland.

NORTH WEST

Addleshaw Booth & Co (3ptnrs/4assts + 2 others who do re-financing) "Strong on the equity side" but are no longer out on their own in their field. *Stephen Clark* ("very able, unafraid to take an aggressive stance on occasion") and *Shaun Rearden* ("seemingly relaxed approach, but underneath it very on the ball") are recognised as players in the Manchester market place. **Clients/Work:** Syndicated development/acquisition finance for Old English Pub Co £36m debt provided by a syndicate of 3 banks (Client: Erstebank as syndicate agent). £30m MBO of Focus DIY, £16m senior debt (Client: The Co-operative Bank plc). Refinancing of Nightfreight plc, £16m secured multi-option facility (Client: Midland Bank plc).

Dibb Lupton Alsop (1ptnr (100% non-contentious banking)/3 assts in Manchester, 2 assts in Liverpool.) "Impressive, doing broad structured deals" – have recovered from the loss of Nigel Dale thanks to the "outstanding" efforts of *Simon Woolley* ("excellent, with a strong local following close to the market, commercially minded and well established"). Deemed to be top dogs along with Addleshaws and Eversheds – loss of Nicholas Fisher not considered to significantly affect firm's standing. **Clients/Work:** Advised Royal Bank of Scotland plc Acquisition Finance in relation to £13m institutional buy-out of Kennedy Civil Engineering; advised Bank of Scotland Structured Finance in relation to the £10.4m instutional offer and de-listing of Instem plc; also act for Barclays and NatWest.

Eversheds (1ptnr/2assts (full time) 2assts part time). "Now part of a leading triumvirate in the North West." *Nigel Dale* ("gets up to speed in seconds, incredibly experienced and quick to take a position") was particularly well thought of by the clients surveyed. **Clients/Work:** Kennedy Construction £60m buy-out acting for Royal Bank of Scotland plc and a syndicate of banks; FKI plc – negotiating a $35m private placement in the US which was then swapped so that interest rates and currency risks are expressed in dollars but the borrowings are provided in Lire; advising Quicks Group plc on the raising of £42m finance on the acquisition of Caverdale Group plc.

Garretts (1ptnr/3assts – all 100%). "Strong at the moment." *Susan Molloy* is individually rated. An extremely competent banking lawyer" "excellent – good on MBO's". Provide a range of services: acquisition and structure finance, property finance and general banking work. **Clients/Work:** Acting for NatWest Bank on acquisition by Scotia Haven Food Group Ltd of Whitworths Ltd and associated companies in May 1997. Client provided Senior Debt, Mezzanine Debt and Revolving Credit Facilities totalling £46m. Acting for Bank of Scotland – made available £12.3m multi-option facility to Quiligotti plc and its subsidiary companies in July 1997 to fund the acquisition of Pilkington's Tiles Ltd

Halliwell Landau (1ptnr/1asst both full time). *Clare Shepherd* ("good technical lawyer") heads up the department and joins the list of individually recommended lawyers this year (the firm has lost Ray McDaid who has gone to Prague). Supported by the corporate department. **Clients/Work:** Act for Royal Bank of Scotland and the Co-Operative Bank on the general lending side. Acted in the MBI of paint manufacturers Cementone Beaver Ltd and sister companies from Cementone Plc for £9.5m and the MBO of John Kennedy (Civil Engineering) Ltd for £25m.

Chaffe Street (2ptnrs/2assts – 80-90% time on non-contentious work). *Christopher Lumsden* is seen as one of the "major players". **Clients/Work:** Acted for Jersey European Airways UK Ltd in the acquisition of 4 BAe 146 aircraft for consideration of approximately US$34m and in the financing of these acquisitions. Acted for British Linen Bank in providing finance for the Stoke City FC Stadium. Acted for Royal Bank of Scotland in financing the reconstruction of the Ferrostatics Group.

Hammond Suddards (3assts) Seen as "doing well," but will miss the input of senior solicitor Sarah Day ("has done an excellent job") who has left to take a partnership at Dibb Lupton Alsop in Leeds. Team work closely with the firm's Leeds office. **Clients/Work:** Acting for Bank of Scotland

Edinburgh on MBO of Brimar Ltd and Cintel International Ltd for £40m, of which BoS provided £25m of senior debt. Acting for Royal Bank of Scotland Manchester in the provision of facilities for the acquisition of Sports & Leisure Foods Ltd and Concept Restaurants, total deal size £9m.

Slater Heelis (2ptnrs/2assts). Act as one of the regional solicitors for NatWest, so handle regular flow of non-contentious work. **Clients/ Work:** Commercial financing documentation work for NatWest and Rothschilds.

Cobbetts (2 ptnr/2assts with 1 ptnr/ 2assts handling contentious/recovery work). *Robin Higham* is "experienced in this area". **Clients/Work:** Acting for The Co-operative Bank plc in connection with multi-million pound facilities to European PGA Tour Courses Plc, secured on properties throughout the UK. Acting for over a dozen financial institutions on 200+ secured commercial loan and development finance transactions in 1997 varying from approximately £100k to over £3m.

Davies Wallis Foyster (4ptnrs/2assts – handle mix of banking and insolvency) A number of other partners involved in various banking finance deals acting for banks. **Clients/Work:** Multi-million pound secured loan by Capital Bank plc for Sunderland's new football ground. £3.25m secured loan for property investment. £11m facility for acquisition of development site.

NORTH EAST

Addleshaw Booth & Co (6ptnrs/12assts – all work closely with the firm's Manchester office). "Definitely the market leader in Leeds." They continue to maintain the position they have historically held – but the competition is growing. *Mark Chidley* is their key player "good on the lender side – thorough, and technically able," and *Richard Papworth* is new to our list of individuals. **Clients /Work:** MBO of SIG Architectural Products from SIG plc (£82m transaction, £35m syndicated senior debt facilities, £10m syndicated debt facilities) for clients National Westminster Bank plc and Midland Bank plc. LSVT facilities for South Oxfordshire Housing Association Ltd, £106m structured facilities – client Bradford & Bingley Building Society.

Eversheds (Leeds) (3ptnrs/3assts full time). "Provide serious competition for Addleshaws." *Stephen Hopkins* "moves swiftly, good at identifying key issues and getting things done" (known for debt funding work) and *John Finnigan* (expertise in the funding needs of the education sector) are both individually rated. **Clients/Work:** Premier Farnell: dissolution of a 20 bank syndicate and leading the construction of 6 bilateral sterling and dollar facilities with 3 US and 3 UK banks of US£150m in aggregate. Acting for Barclays Bank, Bank of Scotland

and NatWest in arranging Term Loan and Revolving Credit Facilities for Group Refinancing and Acquisition Finance, client ISA plc.

Hammond Suddards (2ptnrs/2assts*)*. Rated are *Patrick Mitchell* "extremely effective, and good on acquisition finance" and the "able" *Karen Jarvis*. **Clients/Work:** Acted for Allied Colloids Group plc – 2 US private placements of notes issued by Low Moor Securities Ltd and guaranteed by client and other in the amounts of $125m and $50m. Advised English Partnerships on the financing of the joint venture between English Partnerships and The Royal Bank of Scotland plc creating Priority Sites Ltd. Acted for BZW and Barclays Bank plc on the buy-out of Wallace Arnold.

Pinsent Curtis (6ptnrs/1assoc/4 fee earners). *Andrew Gosnay* is "well known in the Leeds market" and heads the banking department. Of the other partners, two specialise in banking and capital markets, two in secured lending and one in asset finance/capital markets. **Clients/Work:** HSBC Private Equity – £145m AM Paper Group deal financing – largest private equity deal in the North in 1997. US$250m syndication for Bank Boston, N.A. on acquisition of Sylvania Lighting. Banking and financing work globally for Lurpak dairy giant MD Foods plc.

Dibb Lupton Alsop (2ptnrs/3assts). Newly recruited partner *Sarah Day* was regarded as "one to watch" and "definitely able to give partners in competitor firms a run for their money" whilst she was a senior assistant at Hammond Suddards in Manchester. *Mark Smith* is well known – "his clients love him!". **Clients/Work:** Currently acting for a northern-based lender in a £125m term loan facility to refinance investment properties owned by a plc. Acting for Skipton Mortgages Ltd in acquisition of a £42m residential loan portfolio from The Co-Operative Bank plc. Completed the negotiation of the banking and financing aspects of the Berlin Embassy PFI Project acting on behalf of the Foreign Commonwealth Office.

Walker Morris (1ptnr/3assts). *Michael Taylor* is considered knowledgeable. **Clients/ Work:** Acts for Bank of Scotland (approximately 4 deals in 1997, Lloyds and Royal

Bank of Scotland, and have been busy on acquisition finance side in last 12 months.

Dickinson Dees (2 ptns (plus 2 part time)/1 asst). *Chris Harker* is recognised for his expertise. Leading banking practice in Newcastle both in terms of personnel, resources and clients and also complexity and volume of work handled. **Clients/Work:** Acting for Newcastle Building Society, a number of syndicated loan facilities aggregating in excess of £65m to Housing Associations. For Bank of Scotland, £32 m facilities for University of Northumbria at Newcastle. £16m term loan facility for Barclays. Bond issues of £30m and £25m.

Garretts (1ptnr/4 corporate assts with banking experience). Strong relationship with NatWest ensures their ongoing activity in this area. **Clients/Work:** Advising NatWest Equity Ptnrs Ltd in connection with the acquisition of the entire issued share capital of Artform International Ltd. Acting for Cirqual plc in raising a £5.250m bridging facility from Barclays Bank plc in connection with the acquisition of RFI Shielding Ltd and Thos C Wild (Forgings Ltd).

Eversheds (Newcastle-upon-Tyne) (2ptnrs/2assts p/t plus 3 ptnrs on property related secured lending work). Following the merger with Wilkinson Maughan in 1997, the firm has established a dedicated banking unit across Newcastle/Middlesbrough offices. "Now one of the players in Newcastle," they will provide competition for local firms. **Clients/Work:** Clearing banks and financial institutions, involved in acquisition and structured finance plus mainstream secured lending. Also act on behalf of corporate borrowers.

Robert Muckle (2ptnrs/2assts). Team works closely with the firm's corporate and commercial team. **Clients/Work:** £7.5m sterling and foreign currency multi-option

facility. Group re-organisation of £20m facilities and provision of £2.4m new facilities. £3.9m facility to support local high profile MBO.

Ward Hadaway (1 ptnr/1 asst both full time plus 1 property ptnr/1 asst spend 60% of their time in this area). **Clients/Work:**

Instructed by all but one of the English clearers, including Bank of Scotland, Clydesdale Bank and British Linen Bank. Recently acted for 3 banks on a complex inter-creditor arrangement. Also acted for borrowers (£100m deal) on a syndicated revolving credit facility.

SCOTLAND

Dundas & Wilson CS (5ptnrs/18assts). Still perceived as "the major player." "Head and shoulders above" and strengthened by new Glasgow office following merger with Dorman Jeffrey. *Michael Stoneham* is regarded as the leading banking lawyer in Scotland – "excellent on banking matters, despite spending more time on management since the Andersen link-up," "high profile – a real mover and shaker." Firm benefits from its close association with Andersens. **Clients /Work:** Acting for the senior lenders in £45m syndicated bank financing of the institutional buyout of Texstyle World led by Bank of Scotland and The Royal Bank of Scotland, one of the largest in Scotland in 1997. Acting for lenders providing syndicated /junior debt facilities for Dundee City Council's £44m waste to energy PFI project, 1st local authority PFI project completed in the UK.

Maclay Murray & Spens (3ptnrs/ 1assoc). Praised for being "good technically, and up to speed." *Robert Laing* ("good, knowledgeable on both banking and corporate issues") heads the Banking and Finance Unit. Able to offer English and Scottish security work for cross border transactions via Anthony Murray & Laing, firm's associated English practice. **Clients/Work:** Acting for Bank of Scotland on syndicated senior and mezzanine facilities totalling approx. £39m for the MBO of the Bison Group. Acting for Eagle Taverns Ltd providing loan funds by Bank of Scotland and Scottish & Newcastle totalling approx. £33m.

McGrigor Donald (5ptnrs/7assts) Definitely one of the leading Scottish firms for banking although loss of Neil Morrison to London was still commented on, despite the time lapse. *Ian Lyall* is "excellent, known also as a property lawyer but is definitely respected for his banking work." *Iain Macaulay* is "good on pure corporate banking deals." **Clients/Work:** Acting for Scottish Homes in disposal of Scottish loan book. Number of propety funding groups for Royal Bank of Scotland Property Finance Group. Acted for HSBC on purchase funding deal.

Shepherd & Wedderburn WS (1 ptnr/4 fee earners). *Iain Meiklejohn* is "a good general corporate lawyer rather than a banking specialist, but good at whatever he turns his hand to." **Clients/Work:** Acted on behalf of borrowers on secured loans/loan domentation – among them Stagecoach Holdings plc, syndicated loan facilities totalling £170m and Grantchester Group plc, secured funding in respect of Scottish property interests.

Burness (4ptnrs/8assts f/t plus 1 ptnr part time). *Andrew Sleigh* is a "strong personality" and "good guy with many strings to his bow". In the last 12 months, the firm has handled banking deals to the value of £750m. **Clients/Work:** Acting for the Royal Bank of Scotland in revolving credit facility for Donside Paper Mill MBI – one of the major MBI's in Scotland. Acting for Seet plc in setting up bank facilities for acquisition of the Banner Group. Scottish advice for Rabobank International on provision of facilities for Aggreko plc following demerger of Christian Salveson.

Dickson Minto WS (1ptnr/3assts) "Strong this year, with some good clients." *Colin McHale* is "technically good – deals with matters logically, and gets the deal done," "focuses on buy-outs – does quality work." During 1997, completed 35 transactions representing banks, providing acquisition finance, structured finance or working capital facilities. Also has a London team. **Clients/Work:** Lenders: advised on MBO/ IBO of Progenitive Services Ltd by NatWest Equity Partners with senior/ mezzanine debt facilities provided by The Royal Bank of Scotland plc (firm acted for "RBS") and RBS Mezzanine Ltd (value approx.£40m). Borrower: MBI by FPT Gp Ltd of power transmission distribution division of Fenner plc.

Tods Murray WS (2ptnrs/4assts f/t plus 3ptnrs/1asst when needed). Team includes *Graham Burnside* - deemed a "clever guy – good on securitisations" and *Hamish Patrick*. **Clients/Work:** Advised Warburgs re Bank of Scotland securitisation of share depreciation mortgages. Act for Bank of Scotland, TSB, NatWest. Growth in securitisation work.

Biggart Baillie (2 ptnrs plus 3 ptnrs from property/3assoc/3assts). *Colin McKay* is individually rated. Increasingly involved as sole lawyers in cross border work originating in Scotland utilising firm's dual qualified lawyers. **Clients/Work:** Acting for NatWest Bank in provision of facilities to the Sports Connection group in its restructuring. Clydesdale Bank, acted in partial refinancing of a £6m loan facility for Shawland shopping centre in Glasgow.

McClure Naismith (7ptnrs with banking expertise – none f/t). **Clients/ Work:** Lloyds, Barclays Bank, TSB. Involved in S Bucks Hospital Scheme, £60m financing (Had specific role covering banking aspects). For Royal Bank of Scotland, involved in purchase of Scottish Price (£22m).

Brodies WS (10 fee-earners) Banking Group is cross-departmental. Includes 3ptnrs: 2 from corporate and commercial banking, one from private client. **Clients/Work:** Acting for Royal Bank of Scotland plc in preparation and negotiation of standard form documentation for financing of franchisees of the Alldays Group. Provision of all Scots law advice on loan facility provided to House of Fraser Group by Hong Kong and Shanghai Investment Bank plc (£220m). Rescheduling of debt owed to Guiness Mahon & Co Ltd by Western Isles Council.

NORTHERN IRELAND

Arthur Cox (1 ptnr plus 1 property ptnr/2assts f/t) *Angus Creed* heads up the team, which works closely with the Dublin office (5 Ptnrs/ 15 Assts) for cross-border work. **Clients/Work:** First Trust Bank – acted in an MBO deal worth £3.9m. £24m syndicated loan facility (in conjunction with an English firm). £11m property-related transaction for the Bank of Ireland.

L'Estrange & Brett (2ptnrs/2assts substantially plus 1 ptnr/2assts when required) *Brian Henderson* is well thought of. Firm has set up a banking group. **Clients/Work:** Handle a number of transactions for local banks over a wide range of areas, including the voluntary education sector. Acted for UK banks both as primary advisor and as part of a team, giving advice on securitisation especially in the nursing home sector. Have advised on regulatory issues, general banking matters and the modernisation of lending and security documents.

LEADERS' PROFILES · REGIONS

BAKER, Ian P.
Martineau Johnson, Birmingham
(0121) 200 3300
Specialisation: Banking and Insolvency. Advises on banking and debt finance of all kinds including acquisition and project finance, restructurings and security issues and all aspects of non-contentious insolvency. Recent work includes advice on £70m development project, £35m multi-option facility, £20m funding for premiership football club and a number of receiverships and administrations.
Prof. Memberships: SPI.
Career: Bablake School Coventry. Oriel College Oxford (1st Class Hons). Joined *Rylad Martineau* in 1981 becoming partner 1987.
Personal: Arts, cricket, rugby, soccer. Church – missionary and development work in Europe and Africa. Married, 2 children (13 and 11).

BIRCHALL, Roger
Edge & Ellison, Birmingham
(0121) 200 2001
Partner with *Edge & Ellison* and a member of the Company/Commercial Department.
Specialisation: From a background of general acquisition and disposal work, he has developed a particular expertise in management buy-out/buy-in transactions and the venture/development capital sector generally. Whilst he is well known for acting for management teams, he has substantial experience in acting for vendors and a number of the major providors of equity finance. His experience ranges from small local to large cross-border transactions.
Career: Hull University LLB (Hons). College of Law, Chester.

BURNSIDE, Graham M.
Tods Murray WS, Edinburgh
(0131) 226 4771
graham.burnside@todsmurray.co.uk Partner in Corporate and Commercial Department.
Specialisation: Asset and corporate finance, including securitisation, banking and refinancing. Developed, with partner Hamish Patrick, structures used in securitisation of Scottish assets. Has presented papers on securitisation of Scottish assets.
Prof. Memberships: Writer to the Signet.
Career: Qualified in 1978 *Dundas & Wilson CS*. Coal Industry Pension Fund 1979. Joined *Tods Murray WS* in 1983. Partner in 1984.
Personal: Born 1954. Educated at George Heriot's School, Edinburgh University (LLB Hons 1976). Governor of St. Columba's Hospice. Leisure: music, hill-walking.

CHIDLEY, Mark A.
Addleshaw Booth & Co, Leeds
(0113) 209 2000
Partner in Banking and Financial Services Group. Head of Corporate Banking.
Specialisation: Work covers acquisitions, buy-out/buy-in finance, general banking law and venture capital. Also handles general company/commercial work.
Prof. Memberships: IBA.
Career: Qualified in 1979. Articled at *Slaughter and May* 1977-79. Joined the firm in 1982, becoming a Partner in 1984.
Personal: Born 24th March 1955. Attended Ardingly College, Haywards Heath, Sussex 1968-73; then Southampton University 1973-76. Leisure interests include fishing, gardening and 60s/ 70s sports cars. Lives near York.

CHILDS, Margaret E.
Osborne Clarke, Bristol (0117) 984 5442
Head of Corporate Banking
Specialisation: All non-contentious aspects of banking, including acquisition, buy-out/buy-in finance, project finance, syndicated lending, derivative documentation and financial restructuring. (Client base includes English and overseas banks, building societies, venture capitalists and corporate borrowers.)
Career: Qualified 1985. Joined *Osborne Clarke* 1994 after 9 years in the City, including time with *Wilde Sapte*, *McKenna & Co* and Bank of America.

CLARK, Stephen
Addleshaw Booth & Co, Manchester
(0161) 934 6000
Partner in Banking and Financial Services Group.
Specialisation: Corporate Finance; Property Finance; Project Finance; Asset Securitisation; all types of secured and unsecured lending; Refinancings and Work-Outs.
Prof. Memberships: Law Society. Trustee of Patrons of Manchester Art Galleries.
Career: Articled at *Clifford Chance* 1985-1987. Qualified into *Clifford Chance* Banking Department 1987. Joined *Addleshaw Sons & Latham* as a Partner 1993.
Personal: Married to Sally. Plays hockey and cricket for local teams. Enjoys all other types of sports; art; theatre; music; reading.

COOKE, David J.
Pinsent Curtis, Birmingham (0121) 200 1050
Head of Banking and Insolvency Department, Birmingham. Licensed Insolvency Practitioner.
Specialisation: Main area of practice is non contentious banking and corporate insolvency. Work includes lending, security, restructurings, work outs, receiverships and administration. Also handles corporate finance, including mergers and acquisitions.
Prof. Memberships: Law Society, Birmingham Law Society, Insolvency Lawyers Association.
Career: Qualified 1981. Joined *Pinsent & Co.* in 1979, becoming a Partner in 1983.
Personal: Born 1956. Educated at Cambridge University 1975-78. Leisure interests include golf and sailing.

CREED, Angus
Arthur Cox, Belfast (01232) 230007
Partner and Head of Banking Group
Specialisation: Banking security and advisory work.
Prof. Memberships: Law Society of Northern Ireland.
Career: Qualified 1976. In-house lawyer with Bank of Ireland from 1976 to 1987. Joined Norman Wilson & Co. 1987. Became partner in *Arthur Cox – Northern Ireland* in May 1996.
Personal: Born: 10th June 1951. Educated at Campbell College, Belfast and Pembroke College, Cambridge.

CROOME, Andrew
Eversheds, Norwich (01603) 272727
See under General Corporate Finance, p. 246

DALE, Nigel A.
Eversheds, Manchester (0161) 832 6666
Partner and Head of Banking Department, Eversheds, Manchester.
Specialisation: Advises on all aspects of banking related matters, acting for banks and other financial institutions as well as borrowers. Main areas of practice include acquisition finance transactions, the full range of bilateral and syndicated facilities of all types and advising on security. Regularly acts for a large number of banks and other financial institutions including Bank of Scotland, The Royal Bank of Scotland plc, Barclays Bank PLC, Midland Bank PLC, The Co-operative Bank PLC, NM Rothschild & Sons Ltd and Intermediate Capital Group PLC. Significant practice in advising corporate clients of the firm on major banking transactions including advising Quicks Group plc on £54m syndicated facility and Stanley Leisure PLC on £100m syndicated facility as well as other significant funding for other corporates.
Career: Qualified in 1986 whilst at *Eversheds Hepworth & Chadwick*. Joined *Hammond Suddards* 1990 and became Partner at *Hammond Suddards* in 1993. Became Partner at *Eversheds* in 1996.

Personal: Born 1962. Leisure pursuits include motor sports and cars generally, gardening and walking.

DAY, Sarah
Dibb Lupton Alsop, Leeds (0345) 262728
Specialisation: Specialises in corporate and acquisition finance work, including management and institutional buyout transactions, bilateral and syndicated facilities. Also experienced in public/private partnership financing work and corporate restructuring and refinancing previous transactions. Previous transactions include: acting for senior lender on MBO transactions totalling hundreds of £m; acting for project manager and developer on PFI healthcare project in the North East, acting for building societies in a debt for equity swap in the rescue of a building group and acting for institutional investors in obtaining turnaround funding and support for a retail group.
Career: May 1998 *Dibb Lupton Alsop*. Partner, Banking Group. June 1996 *Hammond Suddards*. Banking unit, Manchester. Qualified September 1992. Feb 1992 *Hammond Suddards* Banking unit, Leeds. Sept 1990 *Hammond Suddards* trainee solicitor.
Personal: Good food eaten in or out as long as I am not the cook. Walking, reading from Trollope to trash.

DOOLAN, Kevin J.
Eversheds, Cardiff (01222) 471147
Partner in Banking Department.
Specialisation: National Head of Financial Institutions Group responsible for over three hundred staff, who provide a wide range of advice to banks, building societies, centralised lenders, insurance companies and finance houses including 15 of the largest 20 mortgage lenders in the UK. The Group handles a high volume of cases involving remortgaging, packaged conveyancing, recoveries, claims against professional advisers and property lending, for clients based throughout the UK. Author of articles published in *Mortgage Finance Gazette* on commercial and residential lending. Regular conference speaker on bank lending.
Prof. Memberships: Member of the Institute of Credit Management, Chartered Institute of Bankers, Strategic Planning Society.
Career: Qualified in 1979. Joined *Eversheds* in 1977, becoming a Partner in 1981. Appointed to Urban Investment Grants Panel 1989 by Secretary of State for Wales. Member of Board of Management of *Eversheds* Cardiff and Bristol. MBA Henley 1996. Appointed chairman of the Institute of Credit Management Secured Lenders Group in 1997.
Personal: Born 14th November 1953. Attended University of Wales. Leisure interests include travel, skiing and computer programming. Lives in Cardiff and Thornbury.

FINNIGAN, John H.
Eversheds, Leeds (0113) 243 0391
Corporate Banking Partner. Heads Leeds/Manchester Financial Business Unit
Specialisation: Lead partner for National Westminster Bank plc – Northern Region Corporate Banking. Leader of Housing Association and Educational Lending Teams and PFI funding for *Eversheds* Leeds & Manchester. A number of substantial facilities to Universities and Colleges 1997/98. Major PFI work for a London Borough 1998. Advises corporate borrowers including Austin Reed plc

on Country Casuals takeover.
Prof. Memberships: Law Society: Leeds Law Society.
Career: Gonville & Caius College, Cambridge. BA 1968 MA 1972: Admitted Solicitor 1971. Partner *Hepworth & Chadwick* 1974. Head of Corporate 1991-93. Licensed Insolvency Practitioner 1991-95.
Personal: Married (Hilary) 1974, two sons. Tries to grow grapes on the Pennines. Prefers to drink the products of sunnier climes!

FORBES, Sandra
Burges Salmon, Bristol (0117) 939 2000

GOSNAY, Andrew W.
Pinsent Curtis, Leeds (0113) 244 5000
Partner and Head of Banking, Leeds.
Specialisation: Mainstream banking, asset finance, leasing, property project finance and debt issues. Acted for FKI Plc in US$205m, US$120m US private placings by US subsidiary. Acted in £42m PFI project financing for the Royal Armouries Museum. Handled £123m banking facilities for Lurpak and dairy giant, MD Foods' International Division.
Career: Qualified 1985. *Cameron Markby Hewitt* 1983-86. Joined *Simpson Curtis* in 1986, becoming a Partner in 1990.
Personal: Born 1961. Uppingham School 1974-79; Newcastle University 1979-82 and College of Law 1982-83. Interests include walking, skiing, travel and theatre.

HARKER, Chris
Dickinson Dees, Newcastle upon Tyne (0191) 279 9000
Partner in Company and Commercial Department.
Specialisation: Main areas of practice are banking and commercial lending and venture capital. Works for banks and building societies as well as quoted and unquoted companies as borrowers. Has acted in the last year for Bank of Scotland in various facilities including the syndicated loan of £31m for the University of Northumbria for Newcastle Building society in facilities aggregating over £60m and in the funding for an 8 outlet chain of hotels and pubs.

HENDERSON, Brian L.
L'Estrange & Brett, Belfast (01232) 230426
Partner and head of Banking Unit.
Specialisation: All types of banking and finance work.
Prof. Memberships: The Law Society of Northern Ireland. Member of Non-Contentious Business Committee; Solicitors European Group (NI)
Career: Qualified 1976. Administrative Trainee European Commission; Partner in *L'Estrange & Brett* since 1979.
Personal: Born 1951. Education: Trinity College Dublin, BA (Mod) L.L.B.

HIGHAM, Robin
Cobbetts, Manchester (0161) 833 3333
Specialisation: Leader of *Cobbetts'* Banking team. Particular expertise in the drafting and formation of Banking and Commercial Financing agreements. Previously employed in both private practice and industry enabling him to bring a wide perspective to all financial matters.
Career: Educated Manchester Grammar School and Birmingham University and Chester College of Law. Qualified in 1980. Prior to joining *Cobbetts* in 1994, was senior corporate

solicitor at The Co-operative Bank plc.
Personal: Born 1956. Leisure interests include sailing, golf, football. Married with three children, lives in Stockport.

HOPKINS, Stephen Martyn
Eversheds, Leeds (0113) 243 0391
See under General Corporate Finance, p. 249

JARVIS, Karen
Hammond Suddards, Leeds
(0113) 284 7000
Specialisation: Acquisition finance, financing of MBOs/MBIs, property development and investment finance, project finance, asset finance and syndicated lending.
Prof. Memberships: Law Society.
Career: Qualified 1986. *Clifford Chance* 1986-1991, *Simpson Curtis* 1991-1994 (Partner 1993), *Garrett & Co.* 1994-1996. Joined *Hammond Suddards* as a partner June 1996.
Personal: Born 5 July 1962. Attended Manchester University 1980-1983. Leisure activities include circuit training, cycling and skiing. Lives in Leeds.

JEFFRIES, Graham
Lester Aldridge, Bournemouth
(01202) 786161
Specialisation: Head of Banking Unit acting for clearing, merchant and secondary banks and other financial institutions on lending, property finance, restructuring, workouts, recovery and insolvency matters.
Career: Articled with *McKenna & Co*; qualified 1989. Joined *Lester Aldridge* 1992. Partner Banking and Finance Department 1994.
Personal: Born 1964; resides Christchurch. Educated Wanstead High School; Lady Margaret Hall, Oxford (1985 BA Hons. PPE).

JOHNSTONE, Pat
Eversheds, Birmingham (0121) 233 2001
Specialisation: Investment banking, venture capital, security matters.
Career: Qualified 1986. Joined *Evershed & Tomkinson* in 1984.
Personal: Born 17th March 1955. Educated Dumfries Academy, Glasgow University (MA), Grenoble University. Interests include ballet and horse riding. Lives near Stratford upon Avon.

KINSEY, Julian
Bond Pearce, Plymouth (01752) 266 633
Specialisation: Partner specialising in banking and asset finance work for banks, building societies and other financial institutions. Deals with all aspects of lending, refinancing and security issues for clients based in London and the South. Particular experience of issues relating to the financing of the motor sector.
Career: Qualified in 1984, joined *Bond Pearce* in 1988 having worked for City firm *Linklaters and Paines*, becoming partner in 1993.

LAING, Robert J.
Maclay Murray & Spens, Edinburgh
(0131) 226 5196
rjl@maclaymurrayspens.co.uk
Partner and Head of banking unit.
Specialisation: Acts for major clearing banks and other financial institutions as well as for borrowers in the provision of debt finance, including term loans, secured and unsecured lending and MBO/MBI finance. Also general corporate law.
Career: Qualified in 1977 (England) and 1985

(Scotland). University of Cambridge (MA 1974). At *Slaughter and May* 1975-83.
Personal: Born 1953.

LAPRAIK, John D.
Mills & Reeve, Cambridge
+44 (0)1223 364422
Specialisation: Head of Banking which provides a wide range of advice to Banks. Principally involved in contentious side of Banking with a particular interest in the application of information technology to working practices.
Career: Qualified in 1983. Joined *Mills & Reeve* in 1986 and became a Partner in 1988.
Personal: Born 1958. Interests include travel, sailing, motor sport and hill walking.

LUMSDEN, Christopher
Chaffe Street, Manchester (0161) 236 5800
Partner in Banking Department.
Specialisation: Main area of practice is banking, including debt/equity swaps, documentary credits, management buy-ins and buy-outs, invoice discounting, reconstructions, refinancings and ship and aircraft financing. Also experienced in corporate acquisitions and disposals. Contributed 'Financial Assistance Problems in Management Buy-Outs' to Journal of Business Law.
Prof. Memberships: Law Society.
Career: Qualified 1977. With *Freshfields* in London 1975-82, then *Freshfields* Singapore 1982-84. Moved to *Alsop Wilkinson*, Manchester 1984-90. Practised in Hong Kong 1988. Joined *Chaffe Street* as Partner 1990.
Personal: Born 4th April 1953. Attended Rossall School 1966-70, then University of Newcastle-upon-Tyne 1971-74. Leisure pursuits include tennis, skiing and reading.

LYALL, Ian J.G.
McGrigor Donald, Edinburgh (0131) 226 7777
Head of Commercial Property Department and Secured Lending Unit.
Specialisation: Secured lending and property finance with particular emphasis on Development Funding, Property Investment and cross border finance and lending.
Prof. Memberships: Law Society of Scotland.
Career: Apprenticed to *McGrigor Donald*. Qualified 1980. Assistant in *Baker & McKenzie* 1985-86. Became Partner in *McGrigor Donald* in 1987.
Personal: Born 25th April 1955. Educated Greenock Academy 1960-72 then Aberdeen University (LL.B. 1977; M.A. (Economics),1978); Director and Honorary Legal Advisor to Edinburgh Medical Missionary Society (owns and operates Nazareth Hospital, Israel). Married to Pamela L. Lyall (*Dundas & Wilson*) with three children. Interests include Church, motorcycles, books, sailing and children.

MACAULAY, Iain
McGrigor Donald, Glasgow (0141) 248 6677
Partner in Corporate Banking Unit.
Specialisation: All aspects of debt, funding. Also involved in PFI, insolvency, Consumer Credit and Oil and Gas Exploration work.
Prof. Memberships: Law Society of Scotland.
Career: Qualified in 1984. Worked in-house with BP Petroleum Development Ltd before joining *McGrigor Donald* in 1987. Following a

period with *Cameron Markby Hewitt*, returned to *McGrigor Donald* as principal Banking Partner in Scotland in 1992.
Career: Educated Glyn Grammar School, Epsom and then Aberdeen University. Born 23 April 1960. Married with one daughter. Leisure interests include fresh and sea water fishing.

MADDEN, Andrew
Gateley Wareing, Birmingham
(0121) 236 8585
Specialisation: Partner, Corporate Services Department, specialising in management buy-outs, venture capital and acquisition finance.
Prof. Memberships: The Law Society.
Career: 1981-84, University of Birmingham (LLB); 1984-85, College of Law, Chester; 1985-87 articles *Duggan Lea & Co* 1987-1996 *Edge & Ellison*; 1996 Partner *Gateley Wareing*.
Personal: Birmingham City; Scott (aged 4); Good beer and food.

MCHALE, Colin J.
Dickson Minto WS, Edinburgh
(0131) 225 4455
Partner 1997.
Specialisation: Banking

MCKAY, Colin
Biggart Baillie, Edinburgh (0131) 226 5541
Specialisation: Banking and debt finance generally; more particularly acquistion and MBO/MBI finance, company and group refinancing and PFI transaction finance.
Prof. Memberships: Law Society of Scotland. The Law Society (England and Wales)
Career: *Biggart Baillie & Gifford*: 1986–1988, *Freshfields* (London-Tokyo): 1988-1993, *Biggart Baillie & Gifford*(Glasgow): 1993 to date

MEIKLEJOHN, Iain M.C.
Shepherd & Wedderburn WS, Edinburgh
(0131) 228 9900
Partner in Corporate Department.
Specialisation: Main areas of practice are corporate finance, mergers and acquisitions, banking, company law and insolvency law. Scottish Editor of 'International Bank Secrecy'.
Prof. Memberships: Law Society of Scotland, International Bar Association, Society of Practitioners of Insolvency.
Career: Apprenticed to *Allan Dawson Simpson & Hampton* 1976-78. Qualified in 1976 and joined *Shepherd & Wedderburn WS*. Became a Partner in 1982.
Personal: Born 3rd November 1954. Educated at Edinburgh Academy 1961-72 and Edinburgh University 1972-76. Director of the Scottish Trust for Underwater Archaeology; Director of Stagecoach ESOP Trust Ltd.

MITCHELL, J. Patrick
Hammond Suddards, Leeds
(0113) 284 7000
Partner responsible for acquisition finance in the Corporate Finance and Banking Department.
Specialisation: Acquisition Finance, primarily for structured finance departments of Banks, and related funding issues in the context of buy out/institutional purchase transactions. Also handles bank lending, venture capital and corporate finance generally.
Career: Qualified 1981 with *Cameron Markby*.

Worked for Robert Holmes a Court's company Bell Group before joining *Hammond Suddards* in 1987. Became a Partner in 1989.
Personal: Born 24th February 1957. Attended Ardingly College, Haywards Heath, and Magdalen College, Oxford. Leisure interests include running, riding, football and sport generally. Lives in Harrogate.

MOLLOY, Susan
Garretts, Manchester (0161) 228 0707
Specialisation: Practice covers loan and other credit/facilities letters/agreements, single bank, sydicated, single/multi-borrower, multi-option facilities, tender panel agreements and working capital facilities, acting for senior mezzanine lenders and borrowers. Dealing with property development and investment finance, leasing and hire purchase facilities, guarantees, loan notes, standstills, intercreditors, Providing a full range of banking services. Acts for clearing banks, specialised finance banks, merchant and foreign banks as well as borrowers.
Career: Qualifed in 1981 at *Addleshaw Sons & Latham*. Partner at *Alsop Wilkinson* 1989-95. Joined *Garretts* as a Partner in June 1995.
Personal: Interests include theatre, walking, reading, cinema and wine.

PALLETT, Julian C.
Wragge & Co, Birmingham (0121) 233 1000
Specialisation: Banking: Lending and security arrangements, intercreditor arrangements, project and acquisition finance, transaction funding. Insolvency: Receivership, liquidations, administration, troubled companies, refinancing, restructuring.
Career: Articled *Wragge & Co*. Qualified 1983. Partner at *Wragge & Co* from 1990.
Personal: Born 1958.

PAPWORTH, Richard
Addleshaw Booth & Co, Leeds
(0113) 209 2030
Partner in Banking and Financial Services Group.
Specialisation: Corporate banking, acquisition finance, property finance, housing association finance, project finance, capital markets, asset securitisation, derivatives, reconstructions and receivables finance.
Career: Qualified 1989 at *Travers Smith Braithwaite*. Joined the firm 1991. Appointed Partner 1995.
Personal: Born 25th December 1964. Educated at King Edward VI School, Louth and Christ Church, Oxford. Interests include golf and football. Lives in Harrogate. Married with one son.

PATRICK, Hamish A.
Tods Murray WS, Edinburgh
(0131) 226 4771
hamish.patrick@todsmurray.co.uk
Partner in Banking Department.
Specialisation: Debt finance and recovery, including conventional banking, asset finance, PFI/project finance, innovative funding structures and funding reorganisation. Developed, with partner Graham Burnside, structures for securitisation of Scottish assets. Author, speaker and university examiner in field. Member of Scottish Law Commission Contract Advisory Group.
Career: Qualified 1989. Partner 1992.
Personal: Born 1962. Attended Dollar Academy, Edinburgh University (LLB 1st Class

Hons 1984; DipLP 1985; PhD 1994: Cross-border securities and insolvency). Leisure: family, music sports.

REARDEN, Shaun
Addleshaw Booth & Co, Manchester
(0161) 934 6000
Partner in Banking & Financial Services Group.
Specialisation: Banking with emphasis on facility (including syndicated facilities) and security documentation, acquisition finance, restructuring, project finance and asset finance. Other area of work is regulatory, covering consumer credit, financial services and data protection. Regular presenter at seminars.
Career: Qualified in 1979, while at *Rutherfords* in Liverpool. Was in-house solicitor at Littlewoods 1980-82, then Manager of Legal Department at North West Securities plc to 1986. In-house legal advisor at The Co-operative Bank plc in Manchester 1986-89 before joining *Davies Wallis Foyster* as a Partner. Joined the firm in 1990.
Personal: Born 10th April 1954. Attended West Park Grammar School 1965-72, then King's College, London 1972-75. Leisure pursuits include rugby and sunshine. Lives in Wilmslow.

SHEPHERD, Claire
Halliwell Landau, Manchester
(0161) 835 3003
Specialisation: Acquisition finance and Development finance acting for both banks and borrowers. Acted for the lender on the development of the Reebok Stadium in Bolton and for the lenders on the redevelopment of stadiums of certain other Premiership football clubs.
Career: Cuthbert Hayne School, Torquay – 1977-82. South Devon College of Arts and Technology 1982-84. London School of Economics – 1984-87 (LLB Hons). Articled – *Wilde Sapte* 1988-90. Solicitor *Wilde Sapte* 1990-94. Solicitor – *Clifford Chance* 1994-95. *Halliwell Landau* 1995-now (Partner 1998).
Personal: Cycling, squash and cinema. Lives Hale, Cheshire.

SLEIGH, Andrew F.
Burness, Glasgow (0141) 248 4933
Specialisation: Has acted for most leading joint stocks banks in the legal aspects of major facilities for MBO and MBIs, most recently for The Royal Bank of Scotland plc in relation to Donside Paper.

SMITH, Mark
Dibb Lupton Alsop, Leeds (0345) 262728
Specialisation: The whole range of banking and finance matters, both domestic and cross-border. Since arriving in Leeds in 1991 has built up a thriving practice acting for northern-based clearing banks and building societies and London-based merchant banks and overseas financial institutions. Specialisations include:

acquisition finance, structured property finance, housing association finance, syndicated loans, mortgage-book acquisitions, PFI and restructuring and work-outs.
Career: Matthew Humberstone Foundation School, Cleethorpes 1969-75. St. Edmund Hall, Oxford University 1975-78. Qualified 1984. Partner *Dibb Lupton Broomhead* 1991.
Personal: Rugby, cricket, walking and theatre. Married and lives in Leeds.

STONEHAM, Michael P.
Dundas & Wilson CS, Edinburgh
(0171) 200 7310
Specialisation: Project finance, including oil & gas financing, power plant financing and PFI projects; public sector finance; and shipping finance. Recent major cases include the £45m Baldovic Waste to Energy PFI Project, the £90m Fibrothetford renewable energy refinancing and the £85m Falkirk Schools PFI Project, acting for the senior lenders in each case. Head of Banking and Finance Group which involves managing teams involved in acquisition finance, property finance and financial markets, in addition to leading the project finance team.
Prof. Memberships: Law Society of Scotland, Law Society of England and Wales, W.S. Society, Edinburgh & Leith Petroleum Club, and a member of the Banking Law Sub-Committee of the Law Society of Scotland.
Career: Chatham House School, Ramsgate; Downing College, Cambridge; College of Law, Guildford; Articled with *Allen & Overy* 1978-1980; International Banking with *Allen & Overy* 1980-1984 especially project finance and shipping finance; *Dundas & Wilson* since 1984; qualified Scotland 1985; partner 1987; PFI co-ordinator 1993-1997; non-executive board member 1992 to 1997.
Personal: Born 1955. Married with 3 children and lives in Edinburgh and the Scottish Borders. Leisure interests include tennis, shooting, fishing, skiing, art, opera and children's homework.

TAYLOR, Michael F.
Walker Morris, Leeds (0113) 283 2500
Specialisation: Work includes acquisition finance, MBO/MBI finance and general banking, lending and security advice, restructuring and work outs.
Career: Qualified 1986; Partner *Walker Morris* 1991.
Personal: Attended King Edward VI School, Lichfield and University of Bristol 1980-83. Leisure interests include hockey and fly-fishing. Lives in Leeds.

TEMPLE, John
Shoosmiths & Harrison, Northampton
(01604) 29977
Head of Banking Group and Property Finance Unit.

Specialisation: Property Finance, Housing Association Funding, Syndicated Loans, Commercial Lending, General Banking, Building Society Law, Mortgage Book Acquisition.

TWIST, G. Patrick A.S.
Pinsent Curtis, Birmingham (0121) 200 1050
Partner and Head of Project Finance.
Specialisation: Specialises in all aspects of banking and finance, including acquisition and project finance. Also involved in the development and financing of major projects. Work includes railway infrastructure, energy from waste plants, oil and gas facilities and hospitals.
Prof. Memberships: Chairman, Law Society Banking Law Committee.
Career: Finance and Leasing Association. Ford Credit Europe, Bank of Scotland. Joined *Pinsent & Co.* (now *Pinsent Curtis*) 1987. Partner in 1988.
Personal: Born 1952. Educated Downside School and Keele University.

VAUGHAN, Philip D.
Eversheds, Cardiff (01222) 471147
Partner.
Specialisation: Practice covers a wide-range of non-contentious banking and finance work and includes transactional work (particularly acquisition finance), regulatory advice and drafting of standard documentation for banks, building societies, centralised mortgage lenders and finance companies. Has a particular expertise in sales and purchases of loan portfolios. Also involved in a wide range of non-contentious insolvency work acting for receivers, administrators and liquidators and advising lenders on enforcement of security and restructuring/refinancings.
Career: Qualified 1984. Formerly with *Clifford Chance* and National Westminster Bank Legal Department. Joined current firm in 1987 and became Partner in 1988.
Personal: Born 14th December 1958. Educated at Haverfordwest Grammar School, St. Edmund Hall, Oxford (M.A.) and Emmanuel College, Cambridge (LL.M.).

WOOLLEY, Simon
Dibb Lupton Alsop, Manchester
(0345) 262728
Specialisation: £29m development funding for Leapfrog Day nurseries; £13m public to private buyout of Instern Plc; £20m management buyout of Kennedy Civil Engineering.
Prof. Memberships: Law Society.
Career: Trained at *Travers Smith Braithwaite*. UK Legal Advisor to Istituto Bancario San Paolo di Torino SPA (largest Italian Bank). Joined *Alsop Wilkinson* in September 1993.
Personal: Golf, skiing, motorsport, family. Married with one daughter.

CAPITAL MARKETS AND DERIVATIVES

RESEARCH: Our team interviewed specialist practitioners, in-house lawyers and bankers at the merchant banks who were familiar with the products. In compiling the tables, we consider all the information available to us, paying particular regard to the market research carried out by our team of ten qualified lawyers. (The researchers' details are set out on page three.) The rankings, therefore, reflect the opinion of the marketplace as revealed by systematic and objective research: see page four. (Our research is audited every year by the British Market Research Bureau.)

OVERVIEW: Four City firms dominate the range of capital markets work: Allen & Overy, Linklaters, Clifford Chance and Freshfields. Simmons & Simmons and Slaughter and May also have strong practices although it was generally felt that there was some distance between them and the practices of the leaders. The American firms are building up their UK resources and two of them join the tables this year: Weil Gotshal & Manges join the international debt and equity table and Sidley & Austin join the securitisation and derivatives tables.

As the boundaries between capital markets work and corporate finance, banking and project finance work blur, there are a number of City firms keen to develop their capital markets practices. It was not felt that any outside the established firms, with the exception of Sidley & Austin, currently merit a mention in the tables. Similarly, the focus of the tables remains on London, as there are no significant practices outside the City.

As with last year, we divide the field of capital markets up into three broad categories. The *issuing of debt or equity in the international capital markets*, including acting for issuers and managers in relation to eurobonds, commercial paper and MTN programmes and other debt securities and international offerings of shares. There was some argument for dividing this table up to look at debt and equity separately, but many felt this would not be productive. The second category is *securitisation and repackaging of financial instruments*, which more broadly covers structured finance and the creation of novel financial structures. The final category is *derivatives*, which includes futures, options and swaps. The emphasis here is on OTC derivative products sold by banks rather than those traded on futures and options exchanges. Inevitably, there is some overlap between the tables.

LONDON

Allen & Overy (Cap Mkts: 17ptnrs UK, 9ptnrs globally/93assts UK & globally. Sec/Repack: 5ptnrs/11assts, Derivs: 5ptnrs/21assts plus 16ptnrs globally. There are overlaps). A truly impressive and global capital markets derivatives practice ("have made a real science of it"), due, in no small measure, to the input of expert *Jeffrey Golden* ("Mr Derivatives"). Also recognised as leaders are "senior figure" *Richard Sykes*, *Boyan Wells* ("clear thinking, and fun to deal with") and *Mark Welling* ("outstanding" "technically good, all rounder"). A further six partners are individually rated. *David Benton* is new to the tables this year. Based in Hong Kong is key player *Paul Monk*. *Simon Haddock* has returned from Hong Kong to London). **Clients/Work:** *CapMkts*: Advised on 250

LEADING FIRMS • LONDON INTERNATIONAL DEBT/EQUITY ISSUES

ALLEN & OVERY
LINKLATERS

CLIFFORD CHANCE

FRESHFIELDS

SIMMONS & SIMMONS
SLAUGHTER AND MAY

LOVELL WHITE DURRANT

ASHURST MORRIS CRISP
HERBERT SMITH
NORTON ROSE
WEIL, GOTSHAL & MANGES

LEADING FIRMS • LONDON SECURITISATION & REPACKAGINGS

CLIFFORD CHANCE
FRESHFIELDS

ALLEN & OVERY

LINKLATERS
LOVELL WHITE DURRANT
SIMMONS & SIMMONS

SLAUGHTER AND MAY
WEIL, GOTSHAL & MANGES

NORTON ROSE
SIDLEY & AUSTIN

BERWIN LEIGHTON

LEADING FIRMS • LONDON DERIVATIVES

ALLEN & OVERY

CLIFFORD CHANCE

FRESHFIELDS
LINKLATERS

SIMMONS & SIMMONS
SLAUGHTER AND MAY

BAKER & MCKENZIE
LOVELL WHITE DURRANT

ASHURST MORRIS CRISP
NORTON ROSE
SIDLEY & AUSTIN
WEIL, GOTSHAL & MANGES

FIRMS ARE RANKED ALPHABETICALLY WITHIN THE BANDS

stand-alone debt issues plus numerous individual issues etc including advising the lead managers on Eurobond offering by BT and the Gillette Co. *Sec/Repack:* Acting for Sumitomo on £1.4bn floating rate note issue for Aurora Funding plc – innovative securitisation transaction; *Derivs:* Acting as counsel to ISDA's five Task Forces on EMU: Legal & Regulatory, Documentation, Tax & Accounting, Market Practice and Operations. Completion of the 1997 ISDA Government Bond Option Definitions and the 1997 interest rate and currency derivatives.

Clifford Chance (Cap Mkts: 17ptnrs UK, 13ptnrs overseas (11 full time)/ 95 UK qualified and 24 US qualified assts. Securit: 7ptnrs full time/30assts. Derivs: 8ptnrs/33assts; total of 85 lawyers globally.) Improved their position on the equity side and have strength in depth on the derivatives side. Most notable individual is *Robert Palache* "one of the greats," and well known for securitisation. Also individually rated are *Habib Motani* ("good for ITC's") *David Dunnigan* ("very responsive"), *Stephen Roith* ("good brain") *Chris Oakley* and *Colin Potter* (now back in London). **Clients/Work:** *Cap Mkts:* $33b Russian debt rescheduling agreement reached with banks October 1997, firm had advised the creditor banks' steering committee 1992 onwards on establishing heads of terms and developing financial proposals. *Sec/Repack:* Acted for SBC Warburg Dillon Read as arranger and underwriter in US$650m asset-backed floating rate notes transaction: structured and documented the first securitisation of debt owed by emerging market sovereign debtors. *Derivs*: Increase in work, especially repackaging of instruments such as bonds with a derivative.

Freshfields (Cap Mkts: UK 13ptnrs/ 31assts. Global: 36ptnrs/46assts) Awarded Best Law Firm in Europe by International Securitisation Review and continue to head up our securitisations/repackaging table. *Ian Falconer* is one of the top securitisations lawyers in the country – ("good at creative drafting and has the stamina to keep a clear head in a 24 hour meeting") and joins the top tier of leading individuals this year, as does *Stephen Revell* ("effective operator"). Five other partners are noted for their expertise, including *Jeremy Pitkin* who is rated on debt capital markets and is "sensible on the other side" and *David Trott* ("good all rounder"). Alan Newton has now gone to the Milan office. New to our lists this year is senior US qualified securities lawyer *Tom Joyce*. **Clients/Work:** *Cap Mkts: Debt*: Acting for Barclays Capital Group and UBS as joint lead managers of the $500m subordinated Eurobond offering by Banco Ambrosiano Veneto as part of its L5,300bn capital raising exercise to finance its merger with Cariplo (Cassa di Risparmio delle Provincie Lombarde). *Equity*: Advising UBS on Erste Bank der Oesterreichischen Sparkassen,

Austria's second largest bank, recently completed Sch7bn ($560m) domestic and international share offering. *Sec/Repack:* Acting for the lead manager HSBC Markets and the trustee on the issue of $300m guaranteed mortgaged backed floated rate notes due 2022 by Hong Kong SAR Residential Mortgages, which were secured on mortgages originated by Dah Sing Bank.

Linklaters (Structured Finance Team handles the work: 18ptnrs/66assts – plus similar number overseas) Another strong firm, recognised as leaders across the board especially in capital markets. They have the volume of work and network of offices to top the tables in debt and equity work. This year firm also topped IFLR tables on International Bonds, MTNs and International Equities. Three specialists are ranked at the top of the individuals list for the UK – *Lachlan Burn* "great legal skills – respected in the marketplace," "a really clever guy," *Michael Canby* ("an absolute fount of knowledge") and *Nicholas Eastwell* ("a star in the international equity capital markets"). The further three recommended partners are the "extraordinarily good" *Charles Clark, Simon Firth* and new to the tables *Michael Voisin*. New York based *Caird Forbes-Cockell* ("phenomenal in his work ethic") and *David Barnard* ("an extremely able man," "involved on the management side") are key figures. In Hong Kong, *Andrew Carmichael* ("real expertise" "the guru") has been joined by *Pauline Ashall* "strong on derivatives related matters" and "technically able." **Clients/Work:** *Cap Mkts:* Acting for the Italian Treasury in connection with the privatisation of Telecom Italia, giving both English and US legal advice, also acting for the syndicate of Managers on the 3 bond offerings by The Russian Federation in March, June and October. *Sec/Repack*: Advising UBS on Acres 3, a securitisation of commercial loans originated by the United Bank of Kuwait. *Derivs:* Acted for Credit Suisse Financial Products, IFLR's derivatives house of 1998, on over 30 listed credit-linked note issues in 1997.

Simmons & Simmons (Cap Mkts/ Sec/Repack: 12ptnrs/34assts which includes 4ptnrs/4assts/several US associates from the International Securities Unit. Derivs: 2ptnrs/ plus 3 corporateptnrs/pool of assts). Focus of capital markets practice is on their structured finance and repackaging work, for which the firm is best known and regarded as a leader. No practitioners make the top tier of the individual tables, but five feature in the lists: *James Bresslaw, John Davies, David Dickinson, Alan Karter* and *John Russell*. In 1997 the firm set up an International Securities Unit (ISU), a joint venture with New York firm Fried, Frank, Harris, Shriver & Jacobsen to make an integrated team of English and US lawyers to advise on international equity and debt transactions. **Clients/Work:** *Cap Mkts*: Advising ANZ as lead manager of a $300m sovereign

bond issue for the Islamic Republic of Pakistan. *Sec/Repack*: Development of innovative structures for repackaging Russian treasury bills (MinFin Bonds and GKO's). The transactions raise complex tax and security issues. *Derivs:* Gave high level strategic advice on a variety of regulatory and structural issues to major derivatives brokers/dealers, including a significant secction of the LME community.

Slaughter and May (Cap mkts (debt/equity): 23ptnrs/50assts. *Derivs:* 11ptnrs/15assts. *Securit:* 15 ptnrs). "Terrific corporate firm, but haven't positioned themselves as one of the major players in capital markets." However, *David Frank* ("economical, effective style," "knowledgeable all round,") is rated amongst the leading experts. Five others are individually listed including *Rupert Beaumont* ("meticulous attention to detail," " technically formidable," "in there at the beginning with derivatives"), and *Richard Slater* ("excellent, technically good and can handle the most complex of transactions"). These individuals are also well known for corporate finance work. **Clients/Work:** *Cap Mkts:* Advising the joint global co-ordinators (Dresdner Kleinwort Benson, Jardine Fleming and Salomon Brothers) on the GDR offering for VSNL (India) (the largest GDR offering in India and first GDR offering involving the Government of India). *Derivs:* Synthetic securitisation (through derivatives) of energy contracts.

Ashurst Morris Crisp (International markets/derivatives: 3ptnrs/8assts/1 US qualified asst. *Securit:* 3ptnrs/6assts – overlap between teams). Have raised profile for high yield bond issues this year. *Richard Kendall* ("good to deal with") is the firm's best known practitioner. The firm's derivatives and capital markets work comes from leading investment banks and securities houses and within the firm. Recently received a number of instructions from Latin American clients. **Clients/Work:** *Cap Mkts:* Acting for Cinven and the issuer on the £180m high yield bonds to refinance the acquisition of IPC Magazines. *Securit/Repack:* Acting for Sumitomo Finance International plc as arranger of the L'ARC $2bn asset backed EMTN programme for the securitisation of Japanese corporate loans of Sumitomo Bank.

Baker & McKenzie (Derivs, 2ptnrs full time/2ptnrs part time/6assts). Remain respected for derivatives work, with their team including *Schuyler Henderson* who has "made his mark in derivatives." Can offer both English and US law advice and US tax and securities advice. On the capital markets side, the London team focuses on the UK, Central and Eastern Europe, the CIS, Continental Europe and the Middle East.

Clients/Work: *Derivs:* Acted for a Cayman Islands company which notionally acquired $1bn worth of shares in a Spanish company, funded through a SPV which entered into a series of equity swaps, puts and call.

Berwin Leighton (Sec: 4ptnrs/2assts). Act for housing associations and corporate clients of the firm from time-to-time on one-off securitisations. **Clients/Work:** *Sec/Repack:* Multi-originator Housing Association Funding plc securitisation and first tap issue to it, with further tap issues anticipated in early 1998.

Herbert Smith (Cap Mkts Debt/Equity: 14ptnrs/41assts). There has been an increase this year in US capability to meet client demand. Ranked for their capital markets (debt and equity) work. **Clients/Work:** *Debt:* Acting for Eurotunnel on its implementation of its major restructuring, which will include the issue of complex capital markets instruments. Acting for Bayerische Hypotheken-und-Weschel Bank AG on the issue of several MTN's. *Equity:* Acting for Zhejiang South East Electric Power Company Ltd on its international offering of B shares and GDRs to raise US$239m. Zhejiang was the first company from the People's Republic of China to list GDRs on the London Stock Exchange.

Lovell White Durrant (7ptnrs/10assts London (plus 1 ptnr, 1 asst Hong Kong, 2ptnrs, 2assts in Paris) Partners outside the group also have expertise. Strong performance in the securitisation arena this year, which is the firm's greatest strength. Acted in the securitisation of the Student Loan portfolio. *Peter Voisey*, a securitisation specialist, joins the list of rated practitioners. **Clients/Work:** *Cap Mkts:* Four issues of structured notes for a total principal amount of US$758m equiv, client Credit Agricole Indosuez. *Securit:* Acting for Globaldrive D.V. as issuer and Ford Motor Credit Company as originator: US$5bn Asset Backed Note Programme and DEM1b Series A Asset Backed Floating Rate Notes due 2000. (Deal awarded a "deal of the year" award by three separate publications. *Derivs:* DEM 100m issue repackaging Vnesheconombank loans, by Russian Invest-

ments, a Cayman Islands special purpose vehicle, involving the use of a credit derivative instrument issued by Banque Paribas.

Norton Rose (Debt, securities and derivatives: 3ptnrs/9assts. Equity: 9ptnrs/19assts). *Gilles Thieffrey* is experienced on securities side, and "has a good understanding of different jurisdictions," he heads up the capital markets team handling debt, securities and derivatives. **Clients/Work:** *Cap Mkts:* on debt side, handled AXA-UAP FRF 6m (dual currency) subordinated Perpetual Set-Up notes. On equity side, acted on the international public offer of shares and GDSs in Randgold Resources Ltd, a Jersey incorporated company and its listing on the London Stock Exchange, raising US$2.5m. *Derivs:* Advised Abbey National plc in respect of underlying assets for two guaranteed return index-rated vehicles, each offered to the retail market.

Sidley & Austin (6ptnrs/15assts in International Finance Group, all experienced) Firm is new to two tables this year, Securitisations & Repackagings and Derivs following numerous recommendations – good solid team on the securitisation side. **Clients/Work:** *Sec/Repack:* Advising Bear Stearns on the $132m Anfield Road 1 Ltd collaterised bond obligation. *Derivs* Advising major Italian bank on an innovative US$1bn multi-user, derivative-based financing with a major US investment bank.

Weil Gotshal & Manges (Cap mkts/derivatives: 4ptnrs/15assts in UK, 150 lawyers globally. *Securit:* 1 ptnr/5assts UK). Now appears in all three capital markets tables, and was warmly praised – "making waves – it can now sustain itself for capital markets deals," "don't underestimate this firm," "good for international debt." *Jacky Kelly*, who heads up the securitisation practice, is newly recommended. **Clients/Work:** *Cap Mkts:* Bank Przemyslowo-Handlowy S.A. (Poland) US$100m Exchangeable Bonds. For CSFB as Issuers on Prokom (Poland) International Offering of GDRs (both Reg S and Rule 144A). *Securit/Repack:* Acted for NatWest as lead manager in relation to UK's largest ever residential mortgage-backed deal worth some £1.025bn. The deal through SPV substantially refinanced Bradford & Bingley's acquisition of the £1.5bn mortgage portfolio of Mortgage Express. *Derivs:* Advise on swaps, options, repos and other derivatives as they relate to both rated and unrated asset repackaging and securitisations.

ASHALL, Pauline
Linklaters, Hong Kong ++ 852 2842 4819
Partner. Financial Markets Group.
Specialisation: : Partner in the firm's Financial Markets Group. Specialises in advising banks, securities houses and other financial intermediaries on regulation of their businesses in the UK and European Union and in Hong Kong and the Asia Pacific region. Areas of work include derivatives, stocklending and repos, global custody and handling of investigations and disciplinary action by regulators. Contributed chapters to several publications such as 'EC Financial Markets Regulation and Company Law' eds. Andenas and Kenyon-Slade (Sweet & Maxwell, 1993). 'Mergers and Acquisitions in Europe' (Gee Publishing 1995), 'Business Law in the European Economic Area' (OUP 1994), 'Derivative Instruments' ed. Swan (Graham &Trotman 1994), 'Equity Derivatives' (Asia Law & Practice 1997), 'Custodial Services to 2005' (ISI 1997).
Career: Articled at *Linklaters & Paines,* becoming a Partner in 1992.

BALLHEIMER, Andrew
Allen & Overy, London (0171) 330 3000
Specialisation: International capital markets (including global debt and equity offerings, securitisations, repackagings, structured finance and cross-border MCA. Most high profile transaction was the Bear Bear Steans Global Bond issue where we acted (a first for a non-US firm) on the US SEC registered aspects as well as the London and Hong Kong listings (he led the team).
Prof. Memberships: Law Society, American Bar Association.
Career: *Allen & Overy* – partner 1994 (London), 1994-1996 (Tokyo), 1996 -to date (New York). Cambridge University 1980-1983 (B.A, M.A).
Personal: Married; tennis, squash, theatre, travel.

BARNARD, David
Linklaters, New York 00 1 212 751 1000
Partner in New York office.

BEAUMONT, Rupert R.S.
Slaughter and May, London
(0171) 600 1200
Specialisation: Structured finance and securitisation; project finance.
Prof. Memberships: Association of Corporate Treasurers (Honorary Fellow).

BEDFORD, Paul
Allen & Overy, London (0171) 330 3000
Specialisation: Member of securitisation group.
Career: Qualified 1982. At *Allen & Overy* since 1980. Partner from 1988.
Personal: Born 26th October 1956. Educated at Brighton College and Warwick University. Lives in Islington.

BENTON, David
Allen & Overy, London (0171) 330 3000
Specialisation: Derivatives.

BRESSLAW, James
Simmons & Simmons, London
(0171) 628 2020
Specialisation: Securitisation and structured finance.

Prof. Memberships: Law Society.
Career: *Simmons & Simmons* 1984 to date.

BURN, Lachlan
Linklaters, London (0171) 456 4614
Partner. International Finance Department.
Specialisation: Specialises in banking and capital markets issues, with over 21 years' experience in the field. Typical matters handled include GDRs for Indian issuers, Korean convertible bonds and derivatives of all types. Is Adviser to the International Primary Market Association. Articled at *Linklaters & Paines* and qualified in 1976, becoming a Partner in 1982. Seconded to the Paris office from 1982-86.

CANBY, Michael
Linklaters, London (0171) 456 4624
Partner. International Finance Department.
Specialisation: Specialist in capital markets work. Typical matters include advising on international capital markets work, as regards both debt and equity financing; advising on derivative products and documentation, having been involved for over 9 years in the drafting of the various stages of industry standard documentation; advising on structured financings. Most recently, he has been involved in transactions relating to the introduction of the Euro. Qualified 1980, Partner from 1986. Managing Partner, *Linklaters & Paines*, Paris Office 1992-1995. Partner in charge of the Securities Group, 1995 to present.

CARMICHAEL, Andrew J.
Linklaters, Hong Kong ++ 852 2842 4874
Specialisation: International finance: capital markets and UK corporate fund raising. Work includes international debt, equity related debt and equity issues, derivatives and warrants, synthetic and repackaged securities, and medium term note and debt issuance programmes.
Career: Joined *Linklaters & Paines* 1979. Partner in International Finance Section 1987.

CLARK, Charles
Linklaters, London (0171) 456 4630
Partner. International Finance Department.
Specialisation: Head of Derivatives Group. Specialises in international securities issues. Articled at *Linklaters & Paines*, made Partner 1989.

DAVIES, John
Simmons & Simmons, London
(0171) 628 2020
Partner in Banking and Capital Markets Department.
Specialisation: Work covers a broad range of banking and capital markets work. Acts for banks, securities houses, borrowers, issuers and corporate trustees. Areas of particular emphasis include innovative funding structures, securitisations and project finance.
Prof. Memberships: Law Society, City of London Solicitors Company.
Career: Became a Partner at *Simmons & Simmons* in 1989.

DICKINSON, David
Simmons & Simmons, London
(0171) 628 2020
Managing Partner, Banking and Capital Markets Department.

Specialisation: Main area of practice is capital markets. Has gained a wide range of experience since 1978, including Eurobonds, international equities, repackagings, securitisation and derivatives. Other area is international lending: experienced in syndicated and other bank lending, both secured and unsecured.
Prof. Memberships: Securities Institute, Inter Pacific Bar Association, Law Society.
Career: Qualified 1974. Admitted Hong Kong 1998. Joined *Simmons & Simmons* as a Partner in 1988.
Personal: Born 13th December 1950. Lives in Woldingham.

DUNNIGAN, David
Clifford Chance, London (0171) 600 1000
Partner, Securities Group.
Specialisation: Eurobonds, Medium Term Notes, Commercial Paper, Certificates of Deposit, Warrants and all other terms of debt/derivative instruments.
Career: Qualified December 1986. Partner May 1992.

EASTWELL, Nicholas W.
Linklaters, London (0171) 456 4660
Specialisation: Specialises in capital markets transactions, including issues of debt, equity related debt, equity and depository receipts in international markets, with a particular emphasis on emerging markets (in 1996/7 in particular in Russia, South Africa, Lebanon, Poland and Egypt). Areas of practice include repackagings of bonds, funds and other financial assets, debt issuance programmes and derivatives. Also practises in banking area principally in syndicated lending, both secured and unsecured, revolving underwriting facilities and multiple option facilities.

EDLMANN, Stephen R.R.
Linklaters, London (0171) 456 4512
Partner. International Finance Department.
Specialisation: Has over 15 years' experience in debt and equity capital markets, banking and related matters. Main areas of practice include debt and equity-related issues, banking (syndicated and bilateral), swaps and other derivatives products. Member of International Bar Association. Has contributed to legal text books on capital markets products, including 'The Law & Practice of International Banking', Sweet & Maxwell, 1987. Joined *Linklaters & Paines* in their New York Office in 1981, became Partner in 1985.

FALCONER, Ian
Freshfields, London (0171) 936 4000
Partner in Finance Department.
Specialisation: Main area of practice is complex structured capital markets transactions, in particular securitisations and repackagings. Has been involved in the securitisation market since its inception. Among recent significant transactions he advised the Annington consortium on the £1.66 billion acquisition of the Ministry of Defence Married Quarters Estate, the financing for which included a £904 million securitisation of lease rentals and on subsequent refinancing involving a £3.14 bn property securitisation.
Career: *Freshfields* Assistant 1984. Partner 1990.

FIRTH, Simon
Linklaters, London (0171) 456 3764
Partner. Financial Markets Group, Corporate
Department.
Specialisation: Specialises in product
structuring and development and general
advice regarding all aspects of business
involving the financial markets. Past
responsibilities also include the design and
documentation of the restructured passenger
rail industry of Great Britain.
Career: Articled at *Linklaters & Paines* in 1987,
made Partner in 1996.

FORBES-COCKELL, Caird
Linklaters, New York 00 1 212 751 1000
Partner and Head of the New York office.
International Finance Department.
Specialisation: Has over 15 years' experience
in international finance matters, including
extensive knowledge and experience of
international capital markets, banking,
structured finance and project finance
transactions, in many cases involving
structuring, bankruptcy, securities and
corporate law advice. Articled with *Linklaters &
Paines*, Solicitor from 1981-83 in the London
office, Solicitor 1983-88 in the New York office,
Partner 1988.

FRANK, David
Slaughter and May, London
(0171) 600 1200
Specialisation: Extensive eurobond and
international equity experience with issuers in
the UK and around the world. Also handles
corporate and banking work with a number of
listed plc clients and is active in the venture
capital and project financing areas.
Prof. Memberships: The Law Society.
International Bar Association.
Career: Qualified 1979. Assistant Solicitor,
Slaughter and May, 1979-1986. Partner
Slaughter and May, 1986. Head of Capital
Markets, 1993.
Personal: Born 29 April 1954. Educated
Shrewsbury School 1967-1972. University of
Bristol 1973-1976. Interests include cars and
lawn tennis. Lives in Surrey.

GOLDEN, Jeffrey
Allen & Overy, London (0171) 330 3000
Specialisation: Partner responsible for US law
practice; areas of practice include a wide range
of international capital markets matters,
including swaps and derivatives, international
equity and debt offerings and US private
placements and listings; advises the
International Swaps and Derivatives Association
and a broad range of commercial and
investment banks, borrowers, arrangers,
underwriters and issuers.
Prof. Memberships: American Bar Association
(Chairman US Lawyers Practising Abroad
Committee (1990-96); Council, Section of
International Law and Practice (1996-)). New
Jersey State Bar Association, New York State
Bar Association, American Society of
International Law, International Bar Association,
The Law Society.
Career: Admitted New York Bar 1979, New
Jersey 1978, and the Supreme Court of the
United States 1983.*Cravath, Swaine & Moore*,
New York 1978-83; *Cravath, Swaine & Moore*,

London 1983-94; Partner *Allen & Overy* since
1994.
Personal: Education Duke University, USA; The
London School of Economics and Political
Science; Columbia University School of Law,
USA. Born 1950.

HADDOCK, Simon A.
Allen & Overy, London (Hong Kong)
(00) 852 2840 1282
Specialisation: Partner specialising in all areas
of structured finance, derivatives and
international capital markets.
Prof. Memberships: Law Society.
Career: Articled *Allen & Overy*, qualified
England and Wales 1986, Hong Kong 1992,
assistant solicitor 1986-1992, Partner 1992,
Hong Kong office 1993. London Office 1997.
Personal: Leeds University (1982 LL.B). Born
1960. Resides in the U.K

HENDERSON, Schuyler K.
Baker & McKenzie, London (0171) 919 1000
Specialisation: Practice covers the full range
of lending, credit enhancement and securities
transactions. Since moving to London in 1977,
he has worked closely with many international
financial institutions in creating, developing and
documenting swaps and related derivatives and
structured finance products and advising with
respect to enforcement, regulatory, tax and
capacity issues.
Personal: Obtained his undergraduate degree
(B.A.) from Princeton University in 1967 and his
law degree (J.D.) and business degree (M.B.A.)
from the University of Chicago in 1971 and is a
member of the New York and Illinois bars.

HOOD, Stephen
Clifford Chance, New York
(+1) 212 709 4200
Specialisation: Senior Partner in New York
specialising in Project Finance and Capital
Markets.
Career: LLM (Lond.) 1973, admitted
Queensland 1969, admitted England and Wales
1974, admitted Hong Kong 1980. Partner in
1978.

HUDD, David
Lovell White Durrant, London
(0171) 236 0066
Specialisation: Partner specialising in capital
markets and securitisation. Extensive
experience of bond issues, debt issuance
programmes, international equity and equity-
linked offerings, derivatives, warrants,
securitisations and repackagings.
Prof. Memberships: The City of London
Solicitors' Company, The Law Society.
Career: Christ Church, Oxford University 1977-
1980 (MA Jurisprudence). Qualified 1983.
Linklaters & Paines 1981-1985; Paribas 1985-
1990; Sanwa International 1990-1993; Indosuez
1993-1994; joined *Lovell White Durrant* as a
partner in 1994.

JOHNSON, Nigel
Allen & Overy, London (0171) 330 3000
Specialisation: Partner specialising in capital
markets transactions, acting both for lead
managers as well as issuers; transactions cover
the full range of debt securities from short-dated
instruments (euro-commercial paper and CDs)

through Eurobonds and MTN programmes to
long-dated issues; in addition he has wide
experience of international equity and equity-
related offerings in a number of jurisdictions.
Career: Articled *Allen & Overy*. Qualified 1978.
Assistant Solicitor *Allen & Overy* 1978-80,
Bayerische Landesbank Girozentrale, Munich;
Syndications 1980-1982. Assistant Solicitor
1982-1985, Partner 1985.
Personal: Born 1952. Jesus College, Oxford
(1974 MA Modern Languages). Resides London.

JOYCE, Tom
Freshfields, London +44 171 936 4000
Specialisation: Head of US securities group.
Primarily adviser on US legal aspects of equity
and debt offerings. Active in UK and Italian
privatisations.
Prof. Memberships: IBA, Association of the
Bar of the City of New York and President of the
Society of English and American Lawyers.
Career: BA St John's University, 1960. JD Notre
Dame Law School, 1963. *Shearman & Sterling*,
1963-1996. *Freshfields* 1996-present.
Personal: Leisure interests include reading,
walking and the arts.

KALDERON, Mark
Freshfields, London (0171) 936 4000
Partner Corporate Department.
Specialisation: Main area of practice is capital
markets,particularly involving securitisation and
structured finance. Also handles banking and
financial services regulation.
Career: Qualified in 1983, having joined
Freshfields in 1981. Became a Partner in 1990.
Worked in Tokyo office 1989 – 1992.
Personal: Born 1st March 1957. Attended
Balliol College, Oxford, 1976-79, University of
Chicago Law School 1979-1980. Lives in London.

KARTER, Alan
Simmons & Simmons, London
(0171) 628 2020
Partner in Corporate Department.
Specialisation: Principal area of practice is
corporate and structured finance including
securitisation and venture capital. Other main
area of work involves advising financial
institutions including banks, building societies
and insurance companies. Addresses
conferences on securitisation and investment
advertisements.
Prof. Memberships: Law Society, Law Society
of Scotland.
Career: Qualified 1979 (Scotland). Joined
Simmons & Simmons in 1987 and became a
Partner in 1988.
Personal: Born 12th January 1955. Attended
University of Edinburgh 1974-77. Lives in
London.

KELLEY, Kevin
Clifford Chance, New York
(+1) 212 709 4200
Specialisation: Partner, Resident in New York
Office. US securities partner handling
international financing transactions for issuers
and underwriters involving principally European
and Latin American issuers. Involved in debt,
equity, privatisation and project-related
financings either on an SEC-registered or US
private placement basis.
Prof. Membership: Member American Bar
Association; New York Bar.
Career: *Sullivan & Cromwell* 1986-92 and
Clifford Chance, Partner, since 1992. Head of

firm's US Securities Practice worldwide and Member of the New York Office's Management Committee. JD University of Pennsylvania Law School (1982) and MB/MA, in History, University of Pennsylvania (1979).
Personal: Born 1957. Resides Manhattan, married.

KELLY, Jacky
Weil, Gotshal & Manges, London
(0171) 903 1000
Partner
Specialisation: Heads up the firm's securitisation practice in London. Involved in the UK securitisation market since its inception in the mid-eighties. Practice also covers a broad range of structured finance and derivatives work. Well known securitisation lawyer. Involved in some of the most innovative and high profile transactions with many of the most prominent players in the securitisation market.

KENDALL, Richard
Ashurst Morris Crisp, London
(0171) 638 1111
Partner in Banking and International Finance Department, heads Capital Markets Group.
Specialisation: Eurobonds, GDRs, derivative products and repackagings.
Career: *Linklaters & Paines*, qualifying in 1985. Spent two years in Hong Kong between 1986 and 1988. Joined *Ashurst Morris Crisp* in 1993 becoming a Partner in 1994.
Personal: MA, Queens' College, Cambridge University 1979-82.

KOSNIK, Richard
Clifford Chance, New York +1 212 709 4324
Email: richard.kosnik@cliffordchance.com
Specialisation: Cross-border capital markets transactions, particularly US registered and exempt offerings of equity and debt securities.
Career: US Securities and Exchange Commission, Washington, DC (September 1990 to April 1994). Associate Director, International Corporate Finance and Small Business Policy. Division of Corporation Finance. Responsible for directing the activities of the Office of International Corporate Finance, which is the office within the Division of Corporation Finance responsible for the development and implementation of rulemaking initiatives and interprative policies of the Division pertaining to offerings by foreign issuers in the United States and multinational offerings by foreign and domestic issuers. This position also involved liaison activities with foreign securities regulators and providing technical assistance to developing securities markets abroad. *Simpson Thacher & Bartlett* New York, New York and London, England (September 1982 to September 1990) Associate. Involved with numerous types of transactions in the corporate, securities and banking areas. Georgetown University Law Center JD, 1982. Harvard University AB, cum laude, 1977.

KRISCHER, David S.
Allen & Overy, London (0171) 330 3000
Partner and head of the Securitisation Group.
Specialisation: All forms of securitisation and asset backed transactions in the UK and a variety of European jurisdictions.
Career: Qualified in the US 1982, practised Chicago, U.S.A. 1982-1985. Joined *Allen & Overy* 1986, qualified in UK 1992, Partner 1992.
Personal: Born 1956. BA Oberlin College 1978;

JD Northwestern University, 1982; BCL Oxford University, 1986.

KRUGER, Paul
Clifford Chance, Hong Kong
+852 2810 0229
Email: paul.kruger@cliffordchance.com [SPE]
Head of Securitisation in Asia – Thai, Hong Kong, Malaysian Securitisations; structured finance generally.
Career: University of Auckland (LLB). Started with New Zealand law firm; worked for Citibank, then to Hong Kong with *Clifford Chance*.

LINES, Patrick
Freshfields, Hong Kong
+852 2846 3400
Specialisation: Specialises in capital markets and derivatives work and has advised in connection with securitisations, a wide range of eurobond issues, including convertible and exchangeable bonds, MTN programmes, warrant issues, swaps, stock lending and repo agreements and regulatory matters connected therewith. Recently he has acted for the Hong Kong Monetary Authority (the central bank of Hong Kong) in the establishment of the Hong Kong Mortgage Corporation and subsequently on its day to day operations; the first London listed convertible bond by a PRC company, Zhenhai Refining and Chemical Company; and the International Securities Market Association in connection with the PSA/ISMA Global Master Repurchase Agreement.
Career: Joined *Freshfields* 1987; partner 1998.

MALCOLM, Andrew
Linklaters, Hong Kong
++ 852 2842 4803
Specialisation: Specialist with over ten years' qualified experience in the international capital markets. Typical maters include advising on equtiy and equity-linked securities issues in the Asian and Euro capital markets; advising on debt securities issues in Dragon and Euro Bond Markets; and advsing on derivatives transactions, both listed and OTC, in Hong Kong.
Career: Articled *Linklaters* 1984; qualified 1986; became partner 1993.

MONK, Paul
Allen & Overy, London (0171) 330 3000

MOTANI, Habib
Clifford Chance, London (0171) 600 1000
Specialisation: Banking, capital markets and financial services.
Career: Partner Clifford Chance 1986.

MURRAY, Edward H.
Allen & Overy, London (0171) 330 3000
Specialisation: Partner specialising in international financial transactions, over-the-counter and exchange-traded derivative transactions (including interest rate, foreign exchange, equity, commodity, credit and insurance derivatives), warrants, international securities offerings, stock lending, securities repurchase (repo), agreements, collateral arrangements, netting schemes and structured financing; clients include leading commercial and investment banks, ISDA, fund managers and large corporate end-users.
Career: Qualified New York 1986, England 1992; associate *Sidley & Austin* 1985-90; assistant solicitor *Allen & Overy* 1990-93, partner 1993.

Personal: Trinity College, Dublin (1980 BA Hons). Harvard Law School, USA (1985 JD cum laude). Born 1958, resides Roehampton.

NEWTON, Alan
Freshfields, London (0171) 936 4000
Partner 1989. Milan Office
Specialisation: Practice involves a wide range of capital markets and securities work, including public and private debt and equity issues, securitisations, derivative products and related regulatory work. Advised the Bank of England on UK Government ECU Treasury Bill and Treasury Note Programmes and various UK non-sterling debt issues. Involved in a number of innovative securitisation transactions since inception of the market in 1987. Advises wide range of European financial institutions on capital raising issues.
Prof. Memberships: City of London Solicitors' Company.
Career: Qualified in 1982 with *Freshfields*. Seconded to New York office 1986-88. Moved to Milan Office 1998
Personal: Born 4th January 1957. Attended Exeter College, Oxford 1975-79.

OAKLEY, Chris
Clifford Chance, London (0171) 600 1000
Specialisation: Debt securitisation, structured repackagings, Eurobonds, secured lending and all types of structured finance transactions.
Career: Articled *Coward Chance*, qualified 1983; Partner *Clifford Chance* since 1990.
Personal: Born 1956. Educated at Redborne School, Ampthill, Beds. and Worcester College, Oxford (BA Hons Jurisprudence). Interests include theatre, opera, travel and scuba-diving. Resides in London.

OLDFIELD, Anthony
Clifford Chance, New York
(+1) 212 709 4200
Specialisation: Partner New York Office. Handles international financing transactions, particularly capital markets (including MTN Programmes, Eurobonds, CP and CDs) in Latin America. Also handles corporate matters, particularly cross-border M&A and joint ventures. Member Media, Computer and Telecommunications Group.
Career: Joined *Clifford Chance* in 1987. Became a Partner in 1997.
Personal: Born 1965. LLB (Hons) University of Essex. Resides Manhattan, married with a child.

PALACHE, Robert
Clifford Chance, London (0171) 600 1000
Partner.
Specialisation: Securitisation.
Career: Admitted as a Solicitor 1982. Partner 1988.

PITKIN, Jeremy
Freshfields, London (0171) 936 4000
Partner specialising in Debt and Equity Capital Markets.

POTTER, Colin
Clifford Chance, New York
(+1) 212 750 1440
Partner London Office.
Specialisation: Banking, capital markets and project finance in Latin America and other emerging markets; clients include numerous investment and commercial banks.
Career: Articled *Coward Chance* qualified

1981; Partner *Clifford Chance* 1987; Solicitor of the Supreme Court.
Personal: Cowley Comprehensive, St Helens, Merseyside; Nottingham University (1978 1st Class). Leisure: golf, football, skiing, tennis. Born 1956. Resides London.

QUILLEN, Cecil
Linklaters, New York 00 1 212 751 1000
Specialisation: US in partner in *Linklaters'* international capital markets practice with significant experience in securities, banking and the regulation of financial insitutions.
Career: 1988-89 Law Clerk to US Court of Appeals Judge; 1989-95 Associate, *Sullivan & Cromwell*; 1995 – date *Linklaters*, becoming partner in December 1996.

RAINES, Marke
Allen & Overy, London (0171) 330 3000
Partner in international capital markets department.
Specialisation: Securitisation and structured finance. Acts for investment banks and corporates in developing a wide range of UK and international tax and accounting based structures.
Prof. Memberships: ABA; IBA; City of London Solicitors' Company.
Career: Called to the Bar in Ontario (1982) and New York (1990). Admitted as a solicitor in England and Wales (1990). Practised with Stikeman, Elliott (1982-1989) and *Clifford Chance* (1991-1994). Joined *Allen & Overy* in 1994 (Partner from 1996).
Personal: Born 17th June, 1953. Educated at Simon Fraser University (BA), University of British Columbia (LL.B) and Trinity Hall, University of Cambridge (LL.M). Interests include flying and skiing.

REVELL, Stephen
Freshfields, London (0171) 936 4000
Fax: (0171) 832 7001
E-mail: smr@freshfields.com
Specialisation: Head of the *Freshfields* International Securities Group and has extensive experience of international securities offerings, privatisations and all aspects of capital markets work, derivatives and related regulatory issues. His recent transactions include the international offering and privatisation of PLIVA, the Croatian pharmaceutical company; an international offering of shares in Thistle Hotels; an international share offering of Bank of Scotland shares by Standard Life, an IPO of Erste Bank, Austria and various other equity and debt transactions including the debut eurobonds by the Republic of Croatia.
Career: Joined *Freshfields* in 1979. Qualified in 1981. Partner 1987.
Personal: Born 20 December 1956. Christ's College, Cambridge.

RICE, James
Linklaters, Hong Kong ++ 852 2842 4191
Partner in the International Finance Department, Securities Group.
Specialisation: Specialises in all aspects of capital markets work including equity and equity-related, straight debt and MTNs, structured finance and securitisations.
Career: Qualified 1982 at *Linklaters & Paines*, becoming a Partner in 1989.

ROITH, Stephen
Clifford Chance, London (0171) 600 1000
Partner, Finance Group and Head of Latin America Practice Group.
Specialisation: Principal area of practice is capital markets, banking and structured finance.
Career: Articled *Coward Chance/Clifford Chance*; qualified 1982; admitted Hong Kong 1983; admitted New York Attorney and Counsellor at Law 1987; Hong Kong office *Coward Chance/Clifford Chance* 1983-1986; *White & Case* New York 1986-87; Assistant Solicitor *Clifford Chance* 1987-1989; Partner 1989.
Personal: Cambridge University (Philosophy/Law)

ROUGH, Clive
Freshfields, Hong Kong (852) 2846 3400
Specialisation: Capital markets, securitisation, international finance and banking.

RUDIN, Simon
Freshfields, London (0171) 936 4000
Specialisation: Partner in the Corporate Department advising on all aspects of capital markets work, including private and public debt and equity and commodity linked debt issues, tax structured financings, securitisations, repackagings and all aspects of derivatives transactions. Advises extensively on product development. Head of *Freshfields* Derivatives Unit.
Prof. Memberships: Law Society; City of London Solicitors Company.
Career: Joined *Freshfields* in 1983, qualifying in the Tax Department in 1985; joined the Finance Department in 1993; became a Partner in 1995.
Personal: Born 1961. Attended St. Catherines College, Cambridge.

RUSSELL, John
Simmons & Simmons, London
(0171) 628 2020
Partner in Banking and Capital Markets Department.
Specialisation: Capital markets work with particular emphasis on international equity offerings, derivative issues and structured finance. Emerging markets experience particularly of India. Transactions include US$1.75 billion privatisation of Railtrack plc and a large number of GDR issues, and structured securities programmes and transactions.
Career: Qualified in 1977 and in Hong Kong in 1981. Worked with *Merrill Lynch* 1985-1988. Joined *Simmons & Simmons* in 1988 as a Partner.
Personal: Born 1.6.1953. Attended Southampton University. Lives in Berkhamsted.

SAUL, Christopher
Slaughter and May, London
(0171) 600 1200
Partner Corporate and Financial Department.
Specialisation: Capital markets and financing transactions and general corporate work.
Career: Qualified in 1979. Partner in 1986.

SELIGMAN, George E.S.
Slaughter and May, London (0171) 600 1200
See under Banking, p. 138

SLATER, Richard
Slaughter and May, London
(0171) 600 1200
See under Banking, p. 138

SMITH, Christopher
Slaughter and May, London
(0171) 600 1200
Specialisation: Main areas of practice include securitisations, structured financings and the full range of capital markets and banking transactions.
Career: Qualified 1980; Partner 1987.

SYKES, Richard H.
Allen & Overy, London (0171) 330 3000
Specialisation: Partner specialising in international debt and equity matters since the early 1970s. Has worked with all major international investment banks and has extensive experience of all types of issues of securities, both in the public markets and private placements.
Career: Articled at *Allen & Overy*, qualified 1969, partner 1974. Head of capital markets department 1989.
Personal: Educated at Winchester College and Oxford University. Born 1943.

TAYLOR, Martin
Freshfields, London (0171) 936 4000
Partner in Freshfields. Currently in Freshfields Hong Kong, due to return to London later this year.
Specialisation: Commercial/ corporate/ international capital markets/ joint ventures/ mergers & acquisitions/ securities offerings/ securitisation. Major transactions include advising on the first securitisations in the UK, Hong Kong and Indonesia. In Hong Kong, acted on a number of other capital markets and many corporate finance transactions, including: ICI's acquisition of Unilever's speciality chemicals division, including interests in Hong Kong, the PRC, Korea, Thailand, Japan, Singapore, Malaysia, Indonesia, the Philippines, Taiwan, New Zealand and Australia; Pearson's acquisition of a stake in TVB; the merger of Gestetner's Asian businesses with those of Inchcape. Deals: Advising PT Astra Sedaya Finance on its securitisation of Indonesian auto-loan receivables, the first securitisation in Indonesia.; Acting for Pearson plc in its joint venture to launch a general entertainment Hindi language TV channel for India, the other parties involved were Carlton Communications, Television Broadcasts, Schroders and Hindustan Times; Advising the Hong Kong Monetary Authority on its establishment of the Hong Kong Mortgage Corporation, Hong Kong's equivalent of Fannie Mae.
Career: University of Bristol. Qualified 1986. Articled with *Freshfields* from 1984 to 1986, joined the firm's Company Department in 1986, moved to *Freshfields* Hong Kong 1994, due to return to *Freshfields* London 1998, joined Partnership in May 1994.
Personal: Golf, travel.

THIEFFRY, Gilles
Norton Rose, London (0171) 283 6000
Specialisation: International securities transactions. Leading expert on the implications of EMU on financial markets and on cross border capital raising.
Prof. Memberships: Member of the Paris Bar (Avocat). Member of the New York Bar. Solicitor

of the Supreme Court of England and Wales.
Career: Head of Legal Department at BNP Capital Markets Ltd. (1992-1994). Director of Legal Services UBS Phillips & Drew (1988 – 1992).

TREFNY, Robert
Clifford Chance, Hong Kong
+852 281 00 229
Email: robert.trefney@cliffordchance.com
Specialisation: Head of US Securities (Asia). Involved in all manner of securities offerings (Registered and 144A) for underwriters and issuers. Completes Yankee Bank offerings for US$600 million for a subsidiary of Hopewell Holdings and for US$350 million for Cathay International. Also completed 144A - H Share offerings fror Jingso expressway and Changing Iron & Steel. Also involved in securitisations, (including first 144A lease receivables securitisation transaction for a Japanese issuer), merger and acquisition work and Trustee Counsel work.
Prof. Memberships: NY Bar.
Career: 1992-1994 *Davis Polk & Wardwell*, Corporate Associate (involved in all types of securities offerings, along with merger and acquisition work and some banking). JD-MBA, University of Chicago, Law Review. AB Duke University (Economics), summa cum laude.
Personal: Married, 2 children. Hobbies: golf, travel, history.

TROTT, David
Freshfields, London (0171) 936 4000
Partner in Finance Department.
Specialisation: Deals with banking and finance with a particular emphasis on asset securitisation, structured financing, building societies and banking law. Has lectured at a number of conferences on asset securitisation

and building societies. Author of various articles for Butterworths Journal of International Banking and Finance Law and Journal of International Banking Law and other UK and international publications.
Career: Qualified in 1988. Partner 1997.
Personal: Born in 1963. Attended Durham University.

VOISEY, Peter
Lovell White Durrant, London
(0171) 236 0066
Specialisation: Partner specialising in capital markets, securitisation and structured finance. Extensive experience of securitisations and repackagings, international securities issues (bonds and equities) and derivatives.
Prof. Memberships: City of London Solicitors' Company. Law Society.
Career: Joined *Lovell White Durrant* in 1985. Qualified in 1987. Made partner in 1994.
Personal: Sir Anthony Browne's School, Brentwood. Trinity Hall, Cambridge University 1978 — 1982 (MA Hons Modern and Medieval Languages).

VOISIN, Michael
Linklaters, London (0171) 456 4606
Specialisation: Partner and capital markets specialist with particular expertise in medium term note and commercial paper programmes, eurobands (plain vanilla, structured and subordinated), derivative warrants, swaps and other treasury products, repackagings and structured finance (including property finance).

WELLING, Mark R.
Allen & Overy, London (0171) 330 3000
Specialisation: Partner who advises investment banks, securities firms and issuers in connection with new issues of all types of

debt and equity securities in the international capital markets; particular emphasis on issues for issuers from emerging markets (Asia and Central and Eastern Europe); also advises on capital markets transactions for UK local authorities.
Career: Articled *Allen & Overy*, qualified 1981, partner 1987.
Personal: Educated Emmanuel College, Cambridge University (1978 MA Law). Born 1956. Resides Dorking, Surrey. Vice President Kingston Borough Citizens Advice Bureaux Management Committee.

WELLS, Boyan S.
Allen & Overy, London (0171) 330 3000
Specialisation: Partner, areas of practice include advising managers and issuers on all aspects of international capital markets work, high yield issues and derivative transactions; particular specialisations include medium term note programmes, listed and unlisted warrant issues and programmes and building societies. Spoken at conferences on derivatives and on the Euromarkets.
Prof. Memberships: Law Society.
Career: Articled *Allen & Overy*, qualified 1981, partner 1987.
Personal: Educated Colston's School and Wadham College, Oxford (1978 MA). Born 1956. Resides Dulwich.

WOODHALL, John
Clifford Chance, Hong Kong
+ 852 2810 0229
Regional Managing Partner specialising in securitisation.
Career: 1980 – date *Clifford Chance*. Partner 1988. Educated at Leicester University – LL.B.

CHARITIES

See also Church Law, Education, Trusts and Personal Tax

RESEARCH: Our team interviewed most of the specialist practitioners active in this area and leading charities and independent organisations. In compiling the tables, we considered all the information available to us, paying particular regard to the market research carried out by our team of ten qualified lawyers. (The researchers' details are set out on page three.)

The rankings, therefore, reflect the opinion of the marketplace as revealed by systematic and objective research: see page four. (Our research is audited every year by the British Market Research Bureau.)

OVERVIEW: Bates, Wells & Braithwaite is still regarded as the leading national charities practice, with Allen & Overy, Farrer & Co and Paisner & Co following closely behind. Claricoat Phillips and Winckworth & Pemberton are perceived to have lost ground since last year. SJ Berwin & Co are a new addition to the list. In the regions, Stone King in Bath and Malcolm Lynch in Leeds are the only firms which are regarded as competing directly with the London practices.

Recent developments include a review of the taxation of charities and the Charity Commission's review of the Charities Register. There remains a great deal of activity in charities registration, and there is an increasing volume of work generally, due to more reconstitution and trading work.

LEADING FIRMS · LONDON

BATES, WELLS & BRAITHWAITE

ALLEN & OVERY
FARRER & CO
PAISNER & CO

BIRCHAM & CO
CHARLES RUSSELL
WITHERS

HIGHLY REGARDED FIRMS

Claricoat Phillips
Denton Hall
Goodman Derrick
Nabarro Nathanson
Sinclair Taylor & Martin
Speechly Bircham
Trowers & Hamlins
Winckworth & Pemberton

Ellis Wood
Field Fisher Waterhouse
Harbottle & Lewis
Lee Bolton & Lee
Lee & Pembertons
Payne Hicks Beach
Radcliffes
Witham Weld

S J Berwin & Co
Bristows
Gregory, Rowcliffe & Milners
Hunters
Lawrence Graham
Macfarlanes
Vizards

LONDON

Bates, Wells & Braithwaite (3ptnrs/7assts) Remain the pre-eminent charity practice, and have a superb reputation. Unique in treating charity work as a core business. The "extremely knowledgeable and hard working" *Stephen Lloyd* now appears in the top category of leading practitioners. He has an "excellent feel" for the commercial and trading side. The "sensible and practical" *Fiona Middleton* focuses on charitable status, and senior partner *Andrew Phillips* is also well known. **Clients/Work:** Unification of the British Red Cross Society; re-organisation of the Royal Society of Arts; advice to the Royal Opera House Trust.

Allen & Overy (3ptnrs/6assts) Unusually for a City firm they possess a strong charities practice which draws strength from their impressive private client base. The "astute" and "well-connected" *Peter Mimpriss* has been an eminent name in the field for some time. **Clients/Work:** Prince's Youth Business Trust; University of London; Leverhulme Trust.

Farrer & Co (1ptnr/4assts) Known in education and health fields and for their Crown work. The "intellectually able and practical" *Judith Hill* has been promoted to the top band. She is "particularly well thought of on tax and trading" and known to "run a tight ship." Michael Stewart has left the firm, although they still have a lot of good assistants left. **Clients/Work:** A specialism on the administrative law side. Also dealing with charity constitutions and trading companies.

Paisner & Co (2ptnrs/4 assts) A "commercially minded" firm. They are known for their work for Jewish charities, but have a wide ranging practice. The "dynamic and hard working" *Anne-Marie Piper* has an excellent reputation in the field, and senior partner *Martin Paisner* is a "respected rainmaker." **Clients/Work:** National Lottery Charities Board; Architectural Heritage Fund; Jewish Care.

Bircham & Co Have a relatively low profile in the charities field, although *Simon Weil* is regarded as a competent practitioner. Seen to act for a more traditional market and for landed charities. **Clients/Work:** Blue Cross; Brake; British Horse Society.

Charles Russell (3ptnrs/1asst/1cons) Have maintained their good reputation for this work, which is undertaken by a cross-departmental team drawn from corporate, property, tax and private client groups. *Michael MacFadyen* and *Catriona Syed* have leading reputations in the private client and charity fields. **Clients/Work:** Royal College of Nursing; English Heritage; London Philharmonic Orchestra.

Withers (5ptnrs/2assts) This high profile team also draws upon expertise from lawyers in five other departments and is particularly praised for its work on hospital trusts. Although Michael Carpenter has left the firm, the "extremely able" *Alison Paines* has been recommended this year. **Clients/ Work:** Advising a bio-tech research charity on its IP rights and future re-structuring; discussion with Charity Commission and NHS over NHS legislation; advising educational charity on joint venture with US organisation.

Claricoat Phillips (2ptnrs) A niche firm with a focus on charity registration. Admired for their dealings with the Charity Commission although because of their size it is felt that they cannot service larger clients' needs. *John Claricoat* has a "good mind" and is admired for his negotiating ability. *Hilary Phillips* is recommended for providing "creative solutions" but is seen to be underrated because "she doesn't sell herself." **Clients/ Work:** Balliol College Oxford; Fleet Air-Arm Appeal; International Federation of Guide Dog Schools for the Blind.

Denton Hall/Portrait Solicitors (2ptnrs/4assts) Portrait Solicitors, run by *Judith Portrait*, is the private client arm of Denton Hall. Maintains "a good practice," of which charity work comprises a significant proportion, main clients being Henry Smith Charities and Sainsbury Family Charities. **Clients/Work:** Advice on special projects in plant science, neuroscience, business management and the arts and medical research.

Goodman Derrick (1ptnr/1asst) Possess an impressive client list, and are known for their charity work on the arts side. Also specialise in advice to educational and medical charities. **Clients/Work:** UNICEF; Liver Research Trust; Anna Freud centre.

Nabarro Nathanson (4ptnrs/4assts) A large team services the firm's impressive client list with input from PFI, healthcare, education and local government specialists. Increasing work on constitution of charities and handling Charity Commission enquiries. **Clients/Work:** Save the Children Fund; The British Diabetic Association; Royal National Lifeboat Institution.

Sinclair Taylor & Martin (3ptnrs/3assts) Considered an excellent firm, but possibly limited from competing with the leading firms because of their size. *James Sinclair-Taylor* is known for his work on the corporate side, *Lindsay Driscoll* for her work on charitable status. **Clients/Work:** British School of Osteopathy; Child Poverty Action Group; Age Concern Groups.

Speechly Bircham (3ptnrs) A recommended practice, with a dedicated charity unit which handles a wide range of charity work. **Clients/Work:** RSPB; Bhopal Hospital Trust; Negotiations on behalf of three school fees charities with Charity Commissioners and Inland Revenue successful in averting loss of charitable status.

Trowers & Hamlins (8ptnrs/3assts) Cross-departmental Charities Group which has a good reputation for Housing Associations and property related work. Head of Group, *Jean Dollimore* is recommended for her "practical approach to charity law."

Clients/Work: Advising clients on constitutional issues; National Childbirth Trust; Leonard Cheshire Foundation.

Winckworth & Pemberton (4ptnrs/6assts) Strong on ecclesiastical law, both for the Church of England and Roman Catholic Church. They also have a reputation for Housing Association work and a strong background on the education side. **Clients/Work:** Formation, land transactions, and problems arising from operation of charities, trustee liability, plus all other aspects of charity law.

Ellis Wood (2ptnrs/1asst) Have some well known Roman Catholic clients. **Clients/Work:** Principally property and trust work of all kinds primarily relating to Roman Catholic charities. Also educational, employment and similar work for the same.

Field Fisher Waterhouse (1ptnr/1asst) Have a relatively low profile in charities work, but a long and impressive client list which includes a number of Royal Charter charities. **Clients/ Work:** Aga Khan Foundation; Great Ormond Street Hospital For Sick Children; advising a number of US charities about registration of charities in UK.

Harbottle & Lewis (1ptnr/1asst) Mainly do charities work in the media and entertainment field for which they have an excellent reputation. **Clients/Work:** All legal work for Red Nose Day which raised £26m; advice to Hampstead Theatre Company on a major new twin theatre project; Pilotlight.

Lee Bolton & Lee (4ptnrs) A "very good practice" with a reputation for Church of England and educational charity work. **Clients/Work:** Octavia Hill & Rowe Housing Trust; The Church Housing Trust; Archbishop of Canterbury's Charitable Trust.

Lee & Pembertons (3ptnrs/1asst) Have a respected charities practice which works out of the private client department. **Clients/ Work:** Advice on all aspects of charity law, including the practical aspects of charity administration, accounting and fund-raising.

Payne Hicks Beach (3ptnrs/1asst) The team, headed by Senior Partner *Graham Brown,* services both national and international charities from the strong tax, trust and probate department. **Clients/Work:** Much work relating to tax and accounting issues.

Radcliffes (6ptnrs) Have a respected charities practice, especially in the ecclesiastical field. **Clients/Work:** Charity formation and liaison with the Charity Commission; tax planning; mergers and re-organisations.

Witham Weld (6ptnrs/3assts) An extensive charities practice, with a strong reputation for educational work; also well-known in the ecclesiastical field acting for Catholic clients. **Clients/Work:** Charity formation, conveyancing, educational law, taxation and general charity administration.

SJ Berwin & Co (1ptnr/2assts) A new addition to the list this year, one of the few City firms to have a dedicated charities unit.

Not yet regarded as major players, but have a "sound practice." **Clients/Work:** Friends of Hebrew University of Jerusalem; Royal Academy of Music; The Earth Centre.

Bristows (6ptnrs/3 assts) Have an impressive client list of professional institutions, for which they undertake charities work. **Clients/Work:** Geological Society of London; Institution of Civil Engineers; The Royal Society.

Gregory, Rowcliffe & Milners The firm has a niche expertise in German law and acting for German clients. **Clients/Work:** Advice on the formation and registration of charities; dealings with the Charity Commission and compliance matters; private charitable settlements.

Hunters (2ptnrs/1asst) A traditional firm with a strong reputation in the private client field. Work for charity clients covers registrations, schemes, trading arrangements and housing associations. **Clients/Work:** National Council for YMCAs; Invalid Children's Aid Nationwide; St George's Hospital Medical School.

Lawrence Graham (4ptnrs/3assts) Known to do a "fair amount of charities work" from within the Company and Commercial Department. **Clients/Work:** Assisting major national charity with investigation by the National Audit Office; advising educational charity on appointment of receiver; establishing numerous charitable housing companies and recreational charities taking transfers of local authority assets.

MacFarlanes (7ptnrs pt/11assts pt) Work undertaken from within Tax and Financial Planning Department. Have a recognised charity law capability which is derived from their impressive client list. **Clients/Work:** Establishment of the Trusthouse Charitable Foundation following the take-over of Forte by Granada; advice to a charity exploiting IP rights in a joint venture with a commercial enterprise; advice to a charity on its investment arrangements and arranging wide delegation powers.

Vizards (3ptnrs/4assts) The charity group operates as part of the Business Law Group, and work for charities is carried out in the commercial property and litigation context. **Clients/Work:** Institution of

Environmental Health Officers; Royal British Legion; Dunhill Medical Trust.

Robert Meakin at Simmons & Simmons is a well known figure in the charities field.

LEADERS' PROFILES · LONDON

BROWN, Graham S.
Payne Hicks Beach, London
(0171) 465 4300
Senior Partner, and Head of Tax and Trust Department.
Specialisation: Areas of practice include legal and fiscal advice to shareholders and boards of family and other private companies; landed estates and heritage property; international trusts, probates and family property; charities and educational institutions; French property and succession. Delivered papers on charities and non-profit organisations, trusts and estates at international conferences in London, Paris, Amsterdam, Munich and Taipei.
Prof. Memberships: Associate of Institute of Taxation in Ireland; sometime member of Law Society's Revenue Law Committee Capital Taxes Sub-Committee and of Law Society's Working Party on the Financial Services Act, Committee of Holborn Law Society; member: International Fiscal Association, Franco-British Lawyers' Association.
Personal: Born 1944. Educated at Bristol University (LL.B, 1966), Catholic University of Louvain (Diploma, 1970), and King's College, London (LL.M, 1975). Leisure interests include arts, heritage and music. Fellow of the Royal Society of Arts; Liveryman Clockmakers' Company. Lives in Bath.

CLARICOAT, John
Claricoat Phillips, London (0171) 226 7000

DOLLIMORE, Jean
Trowers & Hamlins, London (0171) 423 8000
Partner, Private Client. Head of Charities Services.
Specialisation: All aspects of charity law with an emphasis on constitutional structures, the establishment of subsidiaries and trading companies, and the powers and duties of trustees. Also experienced in wills and trusts, estate planning, and the administration of estates. Experienced speaker and contributor to charity publications.
Prof. Memberships: Law Society; Member of the Executive Committee of the Charity Law Association; Committee Member of Holborn Law Society; Charities correspondent for Private Client Business.

DRISCOLL, Lindsay
Sinclair Taylor & Martin, London
(0181) 969 3667
Specialisation: All aspects of charity law advising on a wide range of matters including constitutional reviews, establishment of charities, legal aspects of fund raising, trading companies, Charity Commission schemes, trustee issues. Experienced speaker and author of many articles in charity press and co-author of NCVOs Guide to Charities Acts.
Prof. Memberships: Law Society. Charity Law Association. Executive Committee member.
Career: Qualified 1971. At *Biddle & Co.* 1969-73. Assistant Public Trustee Kenya 1974-78,

Lecturer Kenya School of Law 1973-78, Charity Law Consultant 1981-87. Assistant Legal Adviser then Legal Adviser of NCVO 1987-95.
Personal: Born 17th April 1947. Educated St Hugh's College Oxford (MA). Trustee of several charities. As director of International Centre for Not for Profit Law participates in conferences on law and regulation of NGOs all over the world.

HILL, Judith L.
Farrer & Co, London (0171) 242 2022
Partner in charge of the Charity Team and member of the management board.
Specialisation: Main area of practice is charity law, including the establishment of charities, constitutional issues and trading companies. Also experienced in art and heritage law, general private client work, covering trusts, wills, capital taxation. Contributor to Trust Law International, The Charity Law and Practice Review, NGO Finance and Assistant Editor of Art, Antiquity & Law, on Advisory Editorial Board of The Charity Law & Practice Review and the Editorial Board of Trust Law International. Regularly addresses conferences on charity law topics.
Prof. Memberships: Law Society, Holborn Law Society, International Bar Association (Co-Chairman Committee 20), Charity Law Association (Deputy Chairman.)
Career: Joined *Farrer & Co* in 1973, qualifying in 1975. Moved to *Shoosmiths & Harrison* in Northampton in 1979, until 1981. Re-joined *Farrer & Co* in 1985. Partner 1986.
Personal: Born 8th October 1949. Attended Brighton & Hove High School 1956-69, Newnham College, Cambridge 1969-72. Appointed Lieutenant of the Victorian Order in 1995. Leisure pursuits include gardening and reading. Lives in London.

LLOYD, Stephen T.
Bates, Wells & Braithwaite, London
(0171) 551 7777
Partner in Charity and Company Commercial Department.
Specialisation: Acts for a large number of leading charitable organisations on a wide range of matters, including constitutional, contract, intellectual property and charity law. Also provides advice to small and medium sized businesses. Author of 'Barclays Guide to the Law for the Small Business' and 'Charities, Trading and the Law' and of numerous articles. Co-Author with Fiona Middleton of 'The Charities Acts Handbook'. Gave at least 20 lectures in 1997.
Prof. Memberships: Charity Law Association, UK Environmental Law Association, Law Society.
Career: With *Freshfields* 1975-78. Qualified in 1977. Joined *Bates, Wells & Braithwaite* in 1980 and became a Partner in 1984.
Personal: Educated at Bristol University 1969-72 (History) and Cambridge University 1973 (Law). Trustee of three charities. Recreations include reading, cycling, theatre and music.

MACFADYEN, Michael R.
Charles Russell, London (0171) 203 5000
Partner in the Charities Group.
Specialisation: Main areas of practice are charities, private client (national and international), tax planning, trusts, probate and Court of Protection.
Prof. Memberships: Law Society, City of London Solicitors Company, Charity Lawyers Association, Society of Trusts and Estates Practitioners.
Career: Qualified in 1966. Joined *Norton Rose* in 1961, becoming a Partner in 1970. Joined *Charles Russell* 1997.
Personal: Born 1943. Attended Marlborough College 1956-61. Leisure interests include golf, cricket and walking. Lives in Henley-on-Thames.

MEAKIN, Robert
Simmons & Simmons, London
(0171) 353 3290
Specialisation: Practice covers the full range of Charity Law advice including Charitable Status and applications for registration as a charity, applications for Schemes and Orders from the Charity Commissioners and representing charity trustees subject to investigation by the Charity Commissioners. In addition specialises in Charity tax, VAT, trading and fundraising, Commercial Sponsorship, lottery, PFI and partnership funding. Regularly writes articles on charity law and gives seminars to charity officers and trustees. Regularly sits on Charity Law Association Working Party Committees dealing with specialist areas of Charity Law. To coincide with the 50th anniversary of the Foundation of the NHS, is bringing a book out this year entitled 'Charity in the NHS: Policy and Practice' (Jordans).
Prof. Memberships: Charity Law Association
Career: Legal Adviser to the Charity Commissioners 1988-1993. Lovell White Durrant Charity Group 1993-1995. *Speechly Bircham* 1995-1997.
Personal: Born 29/11/63. Married with two children.

MIDDLETON, Fiona
Bates, Wells & Braithwaite, London
(0171) 551 7777
Charity Commision 1979 to 1988. Partner in Charity Department 1990.
Specialisation: Deals with all aspects of law relating to charities and other voluntary organisations. Author (with Andrew Phillips) of 'Charity Investment, Law & Practice' and 'The Charities Acts Handbook' (with Stephen Lloyd). Member of the NCVO/ Charity Commission working party on trustee training which produced the report 'On Trust: Increasing the Effectiveness of Charity Trustees and Management Committees'.
Prof. Memberships: Charity Law Association. Law Society.
Career: Lecturer in Law, Kings College, London University 1972-79. Legal Adviser to the Charity Commission 1979-87. Joined *Bates, Wells &*

Braithwaite in 1988 and became a Partner in 1990.
Personal: Born 18th January 1948. Trustee of Barnardos. Recreations include gardening, bee keeping and opera.

MIMPRISS, Peter
Allen & Overy, London (0171) 330 3000
Partner in Private Client Department.
Specialisation: Main areas of practice are private client and major national charities including universities, professional institutions, national museums and art centres.
Prof. Memberships: Law Society. Charity Law Association.
Career: Qualified 1967. Joined *Allen & Overy* in 1968, and became a Partner in 1972. Chairman of the Charity Law Association in 1992-97. Chairman of the Chariguard Group of Common Investment Funds in 1994.
Personal: Born 22nd August 1943. Trustee or director of The Prince's Trust, Leeds Castle Foundation, Chatham Historic Dockyard, The Edward Heath Charitable Trust, Michael Bishop Foundation, the Edwina Mountbatten Trust and SolCare. Appointed University Solicitor, University of London in 1994. Interests include the development of charity law, maritime history, book collecting, twentieth century paintings and collecting and driving vintage sports cars.

PAINES, Alison J.S.
Withers, London (0171) 936 1000
Partner in Private Client Department, Head of Charities Practice.
Specialisation: Charity law and related tax and trust advice for not-for-profit organisations and their donors. Advises on structure, status, operations (including trading issues) and funding. Particular expertise in charitable issues relating to the NHS. On editorial board and contributor to Kluwer's *'International Charitable Giving: Law and Taxation'* and contributor to Tolley's *'Charities Manual'* and FT Law and Tax's *'Practical Trust Precedents'*.
Prof. Memberships: Charity Law Association (Executive Committee member); Society of Trusts and Estates Practitioners.
Career: Qualified 1981. Solicitor with *Crossman, Block & Keith* 1981-1987; joined *Withers* 1988 and became a partner in 1991.
Personal: Educated Notting Hill and Ealing High School GPDST 1966-1973; Girton College Cambridge 1974-1978 (classics and law); trustee of grant-making foundation.

PAISNER, Martin D.
Paisner & Co, London (0171) 353 0299
Specialisation: Practice embraces tax and estate planning advice with particular emphasis on the high net worth entrepreneur, including trust structures both for a UK based (whether domiciled or not) and an international clientele. In addition, he advises widely on all aspects of charity law involving both grant-making and functional charities and serves as trustee of an honorary solicitor to numerous charitable bodies.
Prof. Memberships: Law Society, Society of Trust and Estate Practitioners, Charity Law Association.
Career: Born 1 September 1943. Attended St Paul's School, London 1956 – 1961, Sorbonnne University , Paris 1961 – 1962, Worcester College, Oxford 1962 – 1965 and Ann Arbor, Michigan 1966- 1967. Honorary Fellow of Queen Mary and Westfield College, University

of London. Qualified 1970. Partner at *Paisner & Co* in 1972.
Personal: Leisure pursuits include antiquarian book-collecting (18th and 19th Century English and American literature), inter-war travel posters, music, reading, communal interests and learning from his children all the things he never knew! Currently Chairman of The Jerusalem Foundation (UK).

PHILLIPS, Andrew Wyndham
Bates, Wells & Braithwaite, London (0171) 551 7777
Founding Partner.
Specialisation: Main areas of practice are charities, business law and defamation. Author of 'Charitable Status: A practical handbook', now in its fourth edition; 'Charity Investment: Law and Practice'; and 'The Living Law', a guide to the law for young people. Also an occasional freelance journalist, and a regular broadcaster, particularly as Legal Eagle on BBC 2's Jimmy Young Show.
Prof. Memberships: Law Society.
Career: Qualified 1964. Founded *Bates Well & Braithwaite, London* in 1970. Still Senior Partner. Co-founder in 1971 and first Chairman of the Legal·Action Group. Founder and first Chairman of the Citizenship Foundation in 1989 (continuing). Initiated the Lawyers in the Community scheme and Solicitors Pro Bono Group. Founder in 1971 of PARLEX Group of European Lawyers.
Personal: Born 15th March 1939. Attended Culford and Uppingham schools, then Trinity Hall, Cambridge. Trustee of Guardian newspapers and various charities. Non-Executive Director of four companies. Leisure pursuits include politics, golf, cricket, history and the arts. Lives in Sudbury, Suffolk.

PHILLIPS, Hilary
Claricoat Phillips, London (0171) 226 7000

PIPER, Anne-Marie
Paisner & Co, London (0171) 353 0299
Head of Firm's Charities Group.
Specialisation: Practice encompasses charity law ranging from the formation and registration of new charities; advice to 'charity trustees' on various matters including permissible activities, trading and commercial activities and tax-efficient fundraising through to the restructuring, variation and dissolution of charities. Acts for sponsors of new charities; directors, trustees and organisers of existing charities; and companies making charitable gifts or having dealings with charities. Frequent contributor of articles to professional publications on charity law subjects.
Prof. Memberships: Charity Law Association (Secretary since 1992).
Career: Called to the Bar in 1980. Noble Lowndes Personal Financial Services 1980-83. Joined Private Client Department at *Richards Butler* in 1983. Admitted as a solicitor in 1988 and became a Partner in 1989. Joined *Paisner & Co.* as a Partner in 1994.
Personal: Born 27th January 1958. Attended North Walsham Secondary School 1969-74, then Norfolk College of Arts & Technology 1974-76. Went on to University College, London, 1976-79 and the Council of Legal Education 1979-80. Charity trustee. Leisure pursuits include family life and reading. Lives in London.

PORTRAIT, Judith
Portrait Solicitors in Association with Denton Hall, London (0171) 320 3888
Specialisation: All aspects of charity law, advising both grant-making and service-providing charities. Also advising on private trusts, estate and tax planning for individuals and trustees.
Personal: Educated St Paul's Girls' School and St Hughs' College Oxford.

SINCLAIR TAYLOR, James
Sinclair Taylor & Martin, London (0181) 969 3667
Partner specialising in charity law.
Specialisation: Main area of practice is charity law. Work includes charity formation, company law, property transactions, internal structure and employment law, trading VAT and contracts with funders. Also deals with not for profit organisations, housing associations, schools and local authorities, advising on property, employment, corporate and charity law. Has substantial involvement in the urban regeneration development trust movement, learned societies, pressure groups, third world charities and housing and residential care. Author of numerous articles and of the Voluntary Sector Legal Handbook. Involved in training for charities and Housing Associations with the A.C.E.N.V.O. Directory for Social Change, Charity Finance Directors Group and other organisations.
Prof. Memberships: Charity Law Association.
Career: Qualified in 1975. Founded *Sinclair Taylor & Martin* in 1981.
Personal: Charity trustee of a wide variety of organisations.

SYED, M. Catriona
Charles Russell, London (0171) 203 5000
See under Trusts & Personal Tax, p. 787

WEIL, Simon P.
Bircham & Co. (incorporating Dyson Bell Martin), London (0171) 222 8044
Specialisation: Specialist areas comprise charities, tax planning, commercial property for institutional investment clients (frequently with charitable status) and the resolution of potentially contentious issues arising out of wills, trusts and co-ownership of property. Important cases have included advising a substantial corporate charity with a turnover running into ten figures on governance and trustee duties; converting an educational trust from an unincorporated charity to a company ltd by guarantee; arranging the reorganisation of a livery company's charitable trust with a view to protecting individual members of the company who had previously been personally liable to third parties; the disposal by legally binding tender to companies invited to bid, of a major commercial site in High Holborn; the establishment of a comprehensive divestment programme for a group of charities with a common trustee, involving the setting up of real property and personalty investment pooling schemes.
Prof. Memberships: CLA. ACTAPS. Law Society.
Career: Served on the Firm's Premises and General Purposes Committee and Staff Committee, becoming the Partner responsible for the firm's practice development in 1988. Continued in the latter role until 1992 and was head of the Tax and Trust/Private Client/Charities Department between 1991 and 1995. Financial

Services Act Compliance Officer between 1991 and 1997 and took a leading role in establishing Bircham Investment Management.

Personal: Opera, singing and music generally; drawing; wine; reading history and novels (normally pre-1900); member of Chatham

House (RIIA) with a particular focus on central Europe; tennis; swimming; riding; member of Oxford and Cambridge Club. Also active within St. Mary's Church Islington.

SOUTH EAST

HIGHLY REGARDED FIRMS
SOUTH EAST

Elizabeth Cairns Maidstone
Manches & Co Oxford
Nabarro Nathanson Reading
Thomson Snell & Passmore Tunbridge Wells
Winckworth & Pemberton

BrookStreet Des Roches Witney
Griffith Smith Brighton
Thomas Eggar Church Adams Chichester

Barlows Guildford
Blake Lapthorn Fareham
Charles Lucas & Marshall Newbury
Cripps Harries Hall Tunbridge Wells, Kent
Furley Page Fielding & Barton Canterbury
Iliffes Booth Bennett Uxbridge
Linnells Oxford

Elizabeth Cairns (Sole Practitioner) The "excellent" *Elizabeth Cairns* has experience at the Charity Commission, and is "good in the field of charity registrations." **Clients/Work:** Charity re-structuring, formation, registration and governance.

Manches (2ptnrs/2assts) Have recently acquired Morrell Peel & Gamlen, and with it an established charity practice. Have close links to Oxford University, and a reputation in work for museums, libraries and other educational charities. The "measured" *Alan Poulter* is recognised as a local specialist in the educational charities field. **Clients/Work:** Islamic Trust; act for over half of the Oxford Colleges.

Nabarro Nathanson (2ptnrs/4assts) The national charity law team is based in Reading. Specialise in commercial side of charity work and is particularly recommended for its work in medical field. The "exceedingly good" *Jonathan Burchfield* "clearly enjoys the law" and is recognised nationally as a leader in charity matters. **Clients/Work:** Defending National Trust against proceedings brought following its decision to end deer hunting on its land; advising RSPCA on structure and systems in legacy department; advising major university on an application to Sport's Council for lottery funding.

Thomson Snell & Passmore (2ptnrs/2assts) A traditional firm with an excellent

reputation undertaking charity work from the private client department. **Clients/Work:** Specialise in the accounting aspects of charities work.

Winckworth & Pemberton (1ptnr/2assts) Have a pre-eminent reputation for Church of England work. *John Rees* advises the Archbishop of Canterbury. **Clients/Work:** Formation, land transactions, problems which arise from the operation of charities, trustee liability, plus all other aspects of charity law.

BrookStreet Des Roches (1ptnr/1asst) A mainly commercial property firm which nevertheless handles a range of charity work for some major Oxford-based clients. *Kenneth Brooks*, co-founder of the firm, is a property lawyer who has a strong reputation in this field although he appears to be less active recently. **Clients/Work:** Oxfam; Merton College; Oxford Literary and Debating Union Charitable Trust.

Griffith Smith (1ptnr/6assts p/t) *Tim Smith* is the only full time charities specialist in Brighton, and focuses on administration of charities and dealings with the Charity Commissioner. He provides an initial free audit service to charities as a method of identifying potential problems. **Clients/Work:** General charity law advice, including incorporation, Charity Commission schemes and charity law compliance.

Thomas Eggar Church Adams (4ptnrs) The well established trust and private client practice of Thomas Eggar Verrall Bowles, recently merged with Church Adams Tatham, has a broad charities practice known for its ecclesiastical perspective. *Richard Thornely* leads the charities unit from the tax and trusts department. **Clients/ Work:** Continue to deal in significant number of charity matters covering broad range of elements within charity law. Over past year firm has dealt with increasing number of Charity Applications for the Charity Commission.

Barlows (2ptnrs/1asst) Predominantly private client firm boasting an impressive client list of national and local charities, and specialising in commercial sponsorship agreements and fund-raising contracts. **Clients/Work:** World Wide Fund for Nature; Great Ormond St; CARE.

Blake Lapthorn (2ptnrs p/t/3assts 1f/t) Widely respected for their work in relation

to medical charities. The "sensible" *Elizabeth Davis* is a recognised specialist in this field who acts as charities adviser to the Charity Business Unit. **Clients/Work:** Advising Portsmouth Area Hospice on commercial participation schemes and a society lottery; advising RNBT in relation to redevelopment of a retirement home, including VAT planning, project management and facilities management; advising on the incorporation of Portsmouth Grammar School.

Charles Lucas & Marshall (3ptnrs/1asst) Will advise on the whole range of charity law matters, including trading and commercial advice. **Clients/Work:** The Mary Hare Grammar School for the Deaf; The Town and Manor of Hungerford; Berkshire Community Trust.

Cripps Harries Hall (5ptnrs) A reputable private client department provides the firm with a "significant" charities practice. **Clients/Work:** Portfolio of work for new clients Great Britain Sasakawa Foundation and Japan Festival Fund.

Furley Page Fielding & Barton A traditional litigation based firm which services charity clients from the private client department.

Iliffes Booth Bennett (1ptnr/1asst) General advice to charity clients including property, litigation and employment advice. **Clients/Work:** Institute of Our Lady of Mercy; Musicians Benevolent Fund.

Linnells (2ptnrs/1asst-60% plus 2 other ptnrs 20%) A reputable local firm with a broad client base amongst which are a range of charities. The partner in charge of the Charities Unit also works part-time as in-house solicitor for Oxfam. **Clients/Work:** Act for a number of Oxford colleges and other charities including Oxfam.

LEADING INDIVIDUALS
SOUTH EAST

BROOKS Kenneth BrookStreet Des Roches
BURCHFIELD Jonathan Nabarro Nathanson
CAIRNS Elizabeth Elizabeth Cairns
POULTER Alan Manches & Co
REES John Winckworth & Pemberton
SMITH Tim Griffith Smith

DAVIS Elizabeth Blake Lapthorn
THORNELY Richard Thomas Eggar Church Adams

SEE PROFILES AT END OF THIS SECTION

SOUTH WEST and WALES

Stone King (1ptnr/2assts) "Undoubtedly leading," the practice is "extremely strong with a good team." Have a national client base, and are distinguished by their work for Roman Catholic and educational charities. *Michael King* is widely respected, and accepted as the main charities player in the south west of England. Also call upon ten other solicitors from other departments. **Clients/Work:** Included reconstructions, mergers and hiving off activities into separate charities; assisting trustees in handling s8 inquiries by Charity Commissioners. Clients include Westminster Diocese.

Burges Salmon (2ptnrs/3assts) The firm has a pre-eminent reputation in the agricultural field, and derives work from land-owning charities. Head of Department *Charles Wyld* is recommended. **Clients/Work:** Advice on Millennium funding for various charities; creation of new private charities.

Osborne Clarke (1ptnr/1asst) A large corporate firm with an excellent reputation for charity work, particularly from the religious angle. Litigator *Robert Johnson* is "highly competent" and "certainly a player" particularly in contentious charity work. **Clients/Work:** Sue Ryder Foundation; Society of Merchant Venturers.

Tozers (2ptnrs/2assts) Have a national reputation for their work for Catholic and educational clients. *Richard King* is widely known for his work in the charities and education field. **Clients/Work:** Plymouth Diocese; National Institute of Social Work; Buckfast Abbey.

Wansbroughs Willey Hargrave (2ptnrs/2assts) Have a reputation in the housing association and NHS field. The "very good" *Mark Woodward* is "an accomplished lawyer who knows the business." **Clients/Work:** McMillan Cancer Relief; Shaw Trust; Home Farm Trust.

Wilsons Known for its "excellent" private client department, *John Emmerson*, (trusts and personal tax expert) is recommended for his charitable trust work, particularly acting for disabled, sporting and educational charities. **Clients/Work:** Royal Commonwealth Society; Salisbury Diocese Fund.

Clarke Willmott & Clarke (1ptnr) Have a "good broadly based practice," but do not have a dedicated charities practice. **Clients/Work:** Working with the Countryside Commission on the Millennium Green Structure work.

Eversheds (2ptnrs) Have an impressive client list, with many clients in the arts and medical fields. Do both charitable funding and private charity work. **Clients/Work:** Wales Millennium Centre; National Museum of Wales; Jane Hodge Foundation.

Michelmores Perform charity work from the private client department. Act for the Anglican Diocese. **Clients/Work:** Act for the Church of England in Devon.

Morgan Bruce (4ptnrs/3assts) Advise on the impact of charity law on education, housing and health sectors. **Clients/Work:**

Millennium Coastal Park; University of Wales, Cardiff.

Parker Bullen (3ptnrs/1asst 15–20% f/t) The private client department deals with charity matters. **Clients/Work:** Setting up a multi-million pound international charity for scholarships in engineering.

Thrings & Long (4ptnrs/1asst) Particular strength in advice to almshouses, educational and medical charities. Other areas of expertise include the arts and museums, church and ecclesiastical bodies and grant making charities. **Clients/Work:** Multi-million pound acquisition and leaseback of an operational and investment property; redrafting of governing instruments and obtaining charity commission schemes; assisting and representing clients with lottery grant applications.

Lester Aldridge (3ptnrs/1asst–10%) Charity work is done by the private client department in which the investment services section manages investments for charities and gives investment advice.

Rickerby Watterson (4ptnrs pt) Recently involved in work on the formation and trading side. **Clients/Work:** The National Star Centre; Barnwood House Trust; YMCA.

Veale Wasbrough (2ptnrs/2assts) A new addition to the list, they are deemed to be good on educational charity work. **Clients/Work:** Acting for South West Arts in relation to its establishment and constitution; acting for St Georges Music Trust in relation to structure, funding, and application for lottery funding; Greater Bristol Foundation.

MIDLANDS

Anthony Collins (1ptnr/1asst) A small firm who are "very active in charities." Have an exclusively active-charity client base, with a principal focus on Christian charity work. *Romaine Thompson* is "practical and knows what she is talking about." **Clients/Work:** Formation and registration; Charity Commission dealings; re-organisations and mergers and acquisitions.

Gateley Wareing (1ptnr) Work carried out within Private Client and Trusts department. *Stephen Gateley* has immense experience in the charities field, especially for Roman Catholic clients. **Clients/Work:** Birmingham Arch-Diocese; Father Hudson's

Society; various Roman Catholic charities.

Harvey Ingram Owsten (1ptnr/1asst) Not treated as a core area of practice, but are recognised as competent practitioners. Seen to act for ecclesiastical clients. **Clients/Work:** Setting up and establishment of charities; advice to charity trustees and directors of charitable companies; charitable trust administration.

Martineau Johnson (1ptnr/2assts) A "highly professional firm" with a broad spread of charity work for "good established clients." Emphasis on church clients. The "very able" *Michael Fea* is a recognised charity lawyer. **Clients/Work:** All aspects of charity law, setting up and compliance; corporate charity work; education.

Shakespeares (2ptnrs/7assts) Have been elevated a place in the tables this year on the recommendation of local competitors. A wide range of general charity work, especially on the employment and educational side. There is a strong commitment to multiculturalism, and the firm has growing international contacts. *Gary De'Ath* is recommended for his commitment to his clients. **Clients/Work:** Community Foundations; multi-cultural education and arts centres.

Wragge & Co (1ptnr/3assts) A large firm with a reputation for acting for private family charities. *Louise Woodhead* is seen as a "good and practical lawyer." **Clients/Work:** Wide range of services including creation and registration, compliance, reconstruction and winding up for clients including Edward Cadbury Charitable Trust Incorporated and Severn Trent Water Charitable Trust.

Hewitson Becke + Shaw (2ptnrs/3assts) Have a "substantial practice," with particular expertise in relation to independent schools and hospitals. **Clients/Work:** RSPB; Northampton Association for the Blind; St Andrews Hospital.

Mander Hadley & Co (3ptnrs/1asst) Known for ecclesiastical charity work including for Anglican clientele. The team does a large amount of pro bono work.

Tallents Godfrey & Co (3ptnrs pt) The main firm for charities work in Newark-on-Trent. Do the full range of work.

EAST ANGLIA

Cozens-Hardy & Jewson (2ptnr/1con) Have a "respectable and wide practice for a small number of clients." The very experienced *Matthew Martin* is a well known figure in the charity field. **Clients/Work:** Endowed charities, in particular Almshouses and educational charities.

Mills & Reeve (5ptnrs/3assts) Have respected private client and education departments, and "impressive clients." *John Herring* is "clearly a leading individual in East Anglia for charities work." **Clients/Work:** Major land owning charities; acquisition and disposal of land; powers and duties of trustees.

Taylor Vinters (3ptnrs/2assts) The firm is known for work for the Cambridge colleges. *Jennifer Warren* does the property based work, and *Michael Womack* the tax and charitable constitution side. **Clients/Work:** Acting for Fitzwilliam College in connection with the development and acquisition of commercial property in Cambridge; acting for University of Cambridge in connection with joint ventures relating to Addenbrookes Hospital; 23 Cambridge colleges.

Eversheds (3ptnrs/1asst) The Norwich office heads the national charities practice which has an established client base of religious charities. *Philip Norton* heads the national group, and specialises in health trusts, education and private foundations. *John Perowne* does work on the trust and tax side. **Clients/Work:** Establishment of charity building hospital in India; Norfolk County Council in relation to Millennium projects; advising local authority in relation to multi-million pound land and property redevelopment where charitable status is required.

Greenwoods (3ptnrs/1asst) Known as a significant local firm; charity work is carried out by the company and commercial department. **Clients/Work:** Charities such as East of England Agricultural Society; colleges such as Wyggeston & Queen Elizabeth I College in Leicester; number of schools.

Leathes Prior (1asst) Anthony Hansell has retired from the firm, but it retains a charities capability. Work undertaken from the private client department. **Clients/Work:** The Great Hospital; RSPCA.

NORTH WEST

Birch Cullimore (2ptnrs/1asst) A "high quality practice" which commands a great deal of local respect. **Clients/Work:** Recent work includes incorporation of existing charities as companies ltd by guarantee; advice in relation to new schemes; advice in relation to Albemarle schemes.

Brabner Holden Banks Wilson (2ptnrs/4assts) A cross-departmental group which draws on the strength of the corporate, private client, property and litigation departments. The "bright and reliable" *Lawrence Holden*, who is a housing association specialist, does much work in the operational charities field. **Clients/Work:** Advice to charitable and public benefit organisations on a range of issues, particularly constitutional and governance matters; Housing Association work.

Oswold Goodier & Co (1ptnr) *Mark Belderbos* is a well known charities practitioner who has 30 years experience in the field. Acts for clients in the ecclesiastical and educational field. Provides commercial property advice to charities. **Clients/Work:** Focus on Catholic diocese and religious order; secular charity work.

Cobbetts (2ptnrs) A general spread of charity work is performed by the private client department. **Clients/Work:** The firm undertakes a full range of work for charities, including foundations and property work.

Cuff Roberts A well respected Liverpool practice which has a reputation for doing competent charities work.

Halliwell Landau (1ptnr/4assts in tax & trusts) A large Manchester firm with a broad client base, advising on administration and on charitable trusts. **Clients/Work:** A range of university and medical charities.

Pannone & Partners (2ptnrs/1asst) Well known for its white collar crime work and commercial practice, the firm also has a respectable charities capability within the private client group which specialises in formation of charities. **Clients/Work:** Setting up two new charities for Manchester Airport plc; advising on creation of a new charity in connection with Millennium Fund bid of National Lottery; advising charity trustees on a claim for lost monies following an inheritance and successfully recovering significant funds.

NORTH EAST

Malcolm Lynch (1ptnr/1asst) A small and very specialised firm with an excellent reputation for charities work. The "well organised and focused" *Malcolm Lynch* is known for his ethical approach to a variety of practice areas. **Clients/Work:** Chaigeley Educational Foundation; Ripon C of E Council for Social Concern; Moulton College Landfill Trust.

Grays (1ptnr) Have a reputation for religious charity work. The firm acts for an increasing number of building preservation trusts, heritage trusts and grant making charities. The "astute and thorough" *Tony Lawton* is rated highly and has a great deal of experience. **Clients/Work:** All aspects of charity law including formation and incorporation of charities, negotiations with the Charity Commission, and acquisition, disposal and leasing of charity land.

Wrigleys (2ptnrs/3assts) Private client firm acting for 30 public charities and a number of private trusts. Advice on formation and administration of a wide range of national and international charities. *Matthew Wrigley* has a traditional client base, especially in the heritage field. **Clients/Work:** Work includes constitutional reorganisations, umbrella funds and preparation of cy-pres application.

Addleshaw Booth & Co (1ptnr/4assts p/t) Work is undertaken by a cross-departmental group including private client, tax and property specialists. Specialise in advice on creation of new charitable bodies, development of trading subsidiaries and day to day running of charities. **Clients/Work:** Act on behalf of charities during investigations by the Charity Commission. Undertaking more trading work.

Pinsent Curtis (1ptnr/2assts) Have a well regarded private client department which can handle charity work well. Good on the tax planning side. **Clients/Work:** Advising a museum on tax efficient sponsorship arrangements; establishing an environmental body on landfill tax purposes which was also a registered charity; advising a hospital trust on restructuring into a company.

Dickinson Dees (3ptnrs/1asst) Have "a sure capability in charities law." **Clients/ Work:** The Freemen of the City of Newcastle; St Mary Magdalene and Holy Jesus Trust; Northern Arts.

Eversheds (1ptnr/1asst) Have taken over the Newcastle office of Wilkinson Maughan which had a longstanding charities practice. The office draws strength from the national charities team. **Clients/Work:** Tyne & Wear Development Corporation; Banks Group; Teeside TEC.

Ford & Warren (3ptnrs/3assts in education and charities group) A long established firm, but with a low profile for this work. Charities work is combined with a notable education practice. Long standing relationship with educational and ecclesiastical charities. **Clients/Work:** The Society of Friends, education and church charities.

Irwin Mitchell (1ptnr/1asst) Advise on charity formation, particularly in personal injury sphere and service sector, and lottery bids. **Clients/Work:** Sheffcare; Sheffield City Trust.

Rollit Farrell & Bladon (1ptnr/3assts + 3 ptnrs when necessary) Possess a strong private client department and some "enviable clients." **Clients/Work:** Joseph Rowntree Housing Trust; The Deep (Hull's £38m Millennium Project); Ampleforth Abbey and College.

SCOTLAND

Balfour & Manson (4ptnrs/1asst) Has an impressive client list. The "active" and "practical" *Brenda Rennie* has a reputation for her work with social charities. **Clients/Work:** Age Concern Scotland; Edinburgh City Mission.

Bell & Scott WS (2ptnrs/1asst) A reputation for work for charities in the media field and medical and special needs charities. *Andrew Kerr* is respected for his work with arts charities. **Clients/Work:** The Edinburgh Festival Fringe Society.

Tods Murray WS (4ptnrs–10%) Have an extensive charities practice, with a reputation for acting for land-owning charities. Offer a broad range of advice on property, employment, tax, constitution and management, and corporate re-organisation. **Clients/Work:** RSPB (Scotland); Royal Highland & Agricultural Society of Scotland; Filmhouse Ltd.

Turcan Connell (3ptnrs/1asst) The new firm is the amalgamated private client department of Dundas & Wilson and Burness and is expected to become a considerable force in the private client market in Scotland. *Douglas Connell* is highly thought of in the charities field as is the "very capable" *Simon Mackintosh*. **Clients/Work:** Lloyds/TSB Foundation for Scotland; Shetland Charitable Trust; Scottish Hospitals Trust.

Gillespie Macandrew WS Have a respected charity capability. **Clients/Work:** Earl Haig Fund; SSPCA; Scottish Spina Bifida Association.

Lindsays WS (1ptnr/1asst) Managing Partner *David Reith* has a broadly based practice, but is known in particular for historic house and other conservation charities. **Clients/Work:** Lothian Homes Trust; Scottish YHA; Edinburgh Children's Holiday Fund.

MacRoberts (2ptnrs/2assts) Based in the Trusts Department. Have a long connection with charities and administer large number of charitable foundations. **Clients/Work:** KIND; SENSE.

Shepherd & Wedderburn WS (2ptnrs) Have a strong client base, and do charity work from the private client department specialising in formation and administration. **Clients/ Work:** Barnados; Dunblane Trust; Edinburgh Voluntary Organisations Council.

T.C. Young & Son (3ptnrs) Are known for their work with medical charities. Gain work from their strong housing association work. **Clients/Work:** Princess Royal Trust for carers; Share Housing Association; Loretto Housing Association.

Alexander Stone & Co (1ptnr/1asst – 50%) Are known to act on behalf of a number of prominent Scottish charities. **Clients/ Work:** Epilepsy Association of Scotland; Enterprise Development Co Ltd; Energy Action Scotland.

LEADERS' PROFILES • REGIONS

BELDERBOS, Mark J.
Oswald Goodier & Co, Preston
(01772) 253841
Specialisation: All aspects of Charity Law, acting for many charitable organisations, both religious and secular. Ecclesiastical and Education. Commercial Property, particularly on behalf of charitable organisations. Substantial amounts of General Trust work.
Career: Qualified 1967. Partner 1968.
Personal: Born 09.11.1942. Educated at Stonyhurst College and University of Liverpool (Ll.B.).

BROOKS, Kenneth Williams
BrookStreet Des Roches, Witney
(01993) 771616
Company and Commercial Partner
Specialisation: All types of commercial property transaction including, in particular, work for national retail chains, site acquisitions and disposals, development work, joint ventures, general estate work, statutory agreements, retail parks, building schemes, security work, funding, planning, taxation and environmental matters. Also specialises in charity work including the establishment and administration of charities and their property work. Clients include a number of publicly quoted companies and banks, charities such as Oxfam and Merton College, Oxford; Co-operative Societies like Oxford, Swindon and Gloucester Co-operative Society Ltd and substantial UK and international retailers like Blockbuster Entertainment Ltd, Electronics Boutique plc and Historical Collections Group plc.
Prof. Memberships: Law Society, Association of Charity Lawyers, European Law Group, Thames Valley Commercial Lawyers Association, Berks Bucks and Oxon Law Society, Oxford & District Solicitors Association.
Career: Qualified in 1982. With *Linnells* from 1980 to 1994; as a partner from 1985. Co-founder of *BrookStreet des Roches* in April 1994.
Personal: Born 23 January 1956. Educated at King Edward VI Guildford. Leisure interests include things historical and archaeological; reading music and walking; dining out and good company. Lives in South Leigh outside Witney.

BURCHFIELD, Jonathan R.
Nabarro Nathanson, Reading
(0118) 925 4606
Partner and Head of Charity Group.
Specialisation: Work includes constitutions of charities, the impact of charity law on all areas of charities' activities; and private client work, including trust and tax planning for individuals. Contributed to 'Charity Appeals: the Complete Guide to Success'.

Prof. Memberships: Charity Law Association committee member, Chartered Institute of Taxation, Society of Trust and Estate Practitioners.
Career: Qualified in 1978, having joined *Turner Kenneth Brown* in 1976. Became a Partner in 1983.
Personal: Born 22nd February 1954. Trustee of Foreign and Colonial Charitable Common Investment Funds. Leisure interests include family and cricket. Lives in Guildford.

CAIRNS, Elizabeth
Elizabeth Cairns, Maidstone (01622) 858191
Specialisation: Specialist Charity law practice established since 1990.
Career: Charity Commission 1972-9; Jaques & Lewis 1979-90 (Partner 1984). Publications: Charities: Law & Practice (Sweet & Maxwell) 3rd edn 1996; Fundraising for Charity (Tolley) 1996

CONNELL, Douglas A.
Turcan Connell WS, Edinburgh
(0131) 228 8111
Specialisation: Joint Senior Partner. Specialist in trusts, tax planning, asset protection, charities and heritage property; acts as principal adviser to many chairmen and chief executives regarding their personal business.
Prof. Memberships: President Scottish Young Lawyers Association 1975-1976; member of Revenue Committee the Law Society of Scotland 1979-1992; chairman Edinburgh Book Festival 1991-1995; member Scottish Arts Council and chairman Lottery Committee, Scottish Arts Council 1994-1997.
Career: Attended University of Edinburgh (LLB). Articled *Dundas & Wilson CS*; qualified 1976; Partner 1979-1997.
Personal: Born 1954. Resides Edinburgh. Leisure interests include books, travel and good food.

DAVIS, Elizabeth
Blake Lapthorn, Portsmouth (01705) 221122
Specialisation: Charities law and Company Commercial law.
Prof. Memberships: Member of the Executive Committee of the Charity Law Association.
Career: Qualified in 1982. Has practised in UK and Hong Kong. First joined *Blake Lapthorn* in 1986, and now practises as the charities adviser to the firm's Charity Business Unit. The Unit provides specialist charity law advice coupled with general, commercial, property, employment and tax issues to charities and voluntary organisations.
Personal: Born 11th January 1956. Non Executive Director of the Royal West Sussex NHS Trust. Lives near Chichester.

DE'ATH, Gary R.
Shakespeares, Birmingham (0121) 632 4199
Partner in Business Services Department
Specialisation: Main areas of practice are charities formation and constitutional issues, operational matters including interpretation and recovery of legacies, fund raising agreements and advice, conflicts of interest, employment matters, property law and general commercial contractual issues.
Prof. Memberships: West Midlands Charitable Trusts Group, West Midlands Charity Trustees Forum, The Institute of Charity Fund-Raising Managers, West Midlands Advisory Panel of WCVO. The Charity Law Association, The Society of Trust and Estate Practitioners.
Career: Qualified in 1976. Joined *Shakespeares* in 1986 and became a Partner in 1989.
Personal: Born 21st December 1951. Educated at Gilberd School, Colchester 1963-70 and Kings College, University of London 1970-73.

EMMERSON, John C.
Wilsons Solicitors, Salisbury (01722) 412412
See under Trusts & Personal Tax, p. 793

FEA, Michael
Martineau Johnson, Birmingham
(0121) 200 3300
Specialisation: 30 years specialisation in Estate Planning, all aspects of charity law, wills, trusts, succession and probate. Trustee/Clerk to a number of charities.
Prof. Memberships: Society of Trust and Estate Practitioners; Charity Law Association; Law Society.
Career: Partner 1971. Notary Public. Deputy Chairman West Midlands Mental Health Tribunal. Deputy Registrar Birmingham Diocese.
Personal: Born 1939. Attended Winchester College (1954-1958). Recreations include: tennis, shooting, concerts, opera and gardening. Lives in Worcestershire.

GATELEY, Stephen
Gateley Wareing, Birmingham
(0121) 236 8585
Partner in Charity Trust and Private Client Department.
Specialisation: Acts for Roman Catholic Diocese and religious orders and schools on charity trust matters. Also handles conveyancing, probate, wills and IHT tax planning. Is the Partner in charge of the Private Client Department. Writes newsletter for CSRCDRO.
Prof. Memberships: S.T.E.P. (Member) Conference of Solicitors acting for Roman Catholic Diocese and Religious Orders (CSRCDRO Secretary).

Career: Joined *Gateley Wareing* in 1956. Qualified in 1966 and became a Partner in 1967.
Personal: Born 5th July 1940. Attended Erdington Abbey 1952-56, Birmingham College of Commerce 1956-58 and the University of Birmingham (1960). Governor of Newman College, Governor of St. Nicholas J & I School, Member of Council of Maryvale Institute. Lives in Sutton Coldfield.

HERRING, John
Mills & Reeve, Norwich +44 (0)1603 660155
Specialisation: All aspects of charity law with particular emphasis on ecclesiastical charities and charity property. Also Registrar of Diocese of Norwich and legal secretary to the Bishop of Norwich.
Prof. Memberships: Law Society, Ecclesiastical Law Association (Executive Committee Member), Ecclesiastical Law Society.

HOLDEN, Lawrence
Brabner Holden Banks Wilson, Liverpool (0151) 236 5821
See under Housing Associations, p. 424

JOHNSON, Robert I.
Osborne Clarke, Bristol (0117) 923 0220
See under Litigation (Commercial), p. 524

KERR, Andrew M.
Bell & Scott WS, Edinburgh (0131) 226 6703

KING, Michael
Stone King, Bath (01225) 337599
Partner in Charity and Education unit.
Specialisation: Charity and Education Law, originally amongst religious and educational charities but growing involvement with service-providing charities in other parts of the sector.
Prof. Memberships: Law Society, Charity Law Association, Education Law Association.
Career: Articled: *Stone King & Wardle*, and *Charles Russell & Co.* 1969-74 Qualified 1974; Partner *Stone King* 1975 (Chairman: 1996); Opened London Office 1990. Chairman, Catholic Charity Conference since 1991. Chairman, Charity Law Association since 1997
Personal: Born 9th February 1949. Trustee of several charities. Leisure interests include tennis, sailing, shooting and watching rugby. Married with 3 children; lives in Bath.

KING, Richard
Tozers, Exeter (01392) 207020

LAWTON, F. A. (Tony)
Grays, York (01904) 634771
Partner in 1967.
Specialisation: Main area of practice is charity law, especially conveyancing in relation to charity property, formation of charities and negotiating with Charity Commissioners. Also experienced in work relating to education (especially statutory interpretation of the Education Acts and representations to the Education Assets Board), unincorporated associations, non-Companies Act companies and housing associations.
Prof. Memberships: Law Society, Yorkshire Law Society, Education Law Association.
Career: Qualified 1966. Joined *Grays* in 1967. Partner 1967. Home Office Correspondent of Approved School 1967-73. Board Member Trustee Savings Bank of Yorkshire & Lincoln 1976-89. Committee Member Conference of

Solicitors acting for Catholic Dioceses and Religious Orders 1967-present. (Chairman 1998-)
Personal: Born 9th July 1940. Attended Bordeaux University 1958-59, then Corpus Christi College, Cambridge 1959-62. Leisure pursuits include history, gardening and foreign travel. Lives in York.

LYNCH, Malcolm
Malcolm Lynch, Leeds (0113) 242 9600

MACKINTOSH, Simon A.
Turcan Connell WS, Edinburgh (0131) 228 8111
Specialisation: Main areas of practice are tax, trusts and charities. Work includes tax planning, heritage property, charity law and practice and trust establishment, variation and practice. Co-author of 'Revenue Law in Scotland', 1987. Member of Law Society of Scotland Tax Law Committee, and Convener of Capital Taxes Sub-committee.
Prof. Memberships: Society of Trust and Estate Practitioners, International Academy of Estate and Trust Law.
Career: Non-executive Director of Macphie of Glenbervie Ltd and director of the Edinburgh Book Festival.

MARTIN, Matthew T.
Cozens-Hardy & Jewson, Norwich (01603) 625231
Consultant in Private Client Department.
Specialisation: Main areas of practice are charity law and administration. Solicitor and Clerk to trustees of a number of charities, including Norwich Consolidated Charities, Norwich Town Close Estate Charity, Anguish's Educational Foundation, The Memorial Trust of the 2nd Air Division USAAF and Laura Elizabeth Stuart Memorial Trust.
Prof. Memberships: Law Society, Charity Law Association.
Career: Joined *Cozens-Hardy & Jewson* in 1962. Qualified in 1967. Became Partner in 1969. Consultant in 1996.
Personal: Born 28th June 1943. Attended Bradfield College, Berkshire 1957-61. Under Sheriff of City of Norwich 1987-94. Leisure pursuits include golf and gardening.

NORTON, Philip
Eversheds, Norwich (01603) 272727
Specialisation: The administration of estates and the creation and administration of charities. Honorary Solicitor for Age Concern Norwich, Norwich Crossroads, the Ted Ellis Trust, Norfolk and Norwich Medical Benevolent Society, Friends of Kelling Hospital and the Norfolk & Norwich Healthcare NHS Trust Hospital Arts and Heritage Project. Also acts as solicitor for and trustee of a number of hospital based charities e.g. Norfolk Renal Fund and NANIME Charitable Trust and large private foundations. Lectures to charities, hospital management and retirement groups on charity law and personal affairs.
Prof. Memberships: Law Society, Charity Law Association, Norfolk & Norwich Medico-Legal Society, Society of Trust and Estate Practitioners.
Career: Qualified 1984 while with *Hill & Perks*, now *Eversheds*, and became a Partner in 1990.
Personal: Born 17th September 1959. Attended Queen Elizabeth's School, Barnet 1972-78, then Sheffield University 1978-81. Member of Norwich Castle Round Table.

Leisure includes mountain walking, travel, food and wine. Lives in Wymondham, Norfolk.

PEROWNE, John
Eversheds, Norwich (01603) 272727
Specialisation: Probate, Trust, Charity, Personal Tax and Wills.
Prof. Memberships: STEP
Career: Partner *Eversheds* (previously *Daynes Hill & Perks* previously *Daynes Chittock*) since 1978.

POULTER, Alan
Manches & Co, Oxford (01865) 722106
Email: alan.poulter@manches.co.uk.
Specialisation: Principal areas of practice include work for charitable and educational institutions, including universities and the colleges of Oxford University, private trusts, tax-planning and related work for private clients.
Prof. Memberships: Charity Law Association; Society of Trust and Estate Practitioners.
Career: Qualified 1971 while at *Biddle & Co*. Joined *Morrell Peel & Gamlen* 1974 and became a Partner in 1975. Became partner in *Manches & Co* on the merger of Morrell Peel and Gamlen in 1997.
Personal: Born 4th November 1945. Attended Berkhamsted School 1953-64, then New College, Oxford 1964-68. School Governor and Trustee of various charities. Lives in Oxford.

REES, John
Winckworth & Pemberton (incorporating Sherwood & Co), Oxford (01865) 241974
See under Ecclesiastical (Church of England), p. 171

REITH, David S.
Lindsays WS, Edinburgh (0131) 477 8708
Partner in Commercial Department.
Specialisation: Main area of practice is commercial property, but specialises in charities, including building preservation and other conservation work. Acted for Lothian Building Preservation Trust in successful campaign to save Mavisbank House, near Edinburgh, from demolition. Has spoken at various seminars on charities.
Prof. Memberships: Law Society of Scotland, WS Society.
Career: Qualified in 1974, having joined *Lindsays WS* in 1972. Became a Partner in 1976. Director of Scottish Historic Buildings Trust, Cockburn Conservation Trust, Scottish Sculpture Trust, Boilerhouse Theatre Company and other charitable companies. Secretary of Scottish Seabird Centre and Queensberry House Trust. Treasurer of the Cockburn Association and Fet-Lor Youth Centre.
Personal: Born 15th April 1951. Educated at Fettes College 1965-69 and Aberdeen University 1969-72. Leisure interests include winemaking, gardening and architectural heritage. Lives in East Lothian.

RENNIE, Brenda L.
Balfour & Manson, Edinburgh (0131) 200 1200
Head of Private Client Department.
Specialisation: As part of a general private client practice, has developed a particular interest in charities. Has considerable experience in setting up charities and giving ongoing advice. The administration of private charitable trusts is a specialty. Is the Solicitor to Age Concern Scotland.

Prof. Memberships: W.S.; Member of the W.S. Society Legal Education Committee; Member of Society of Trust and Estate Practitioners; Member of Board of EDINVAR Housing Association; Trustee – High Blood Pressure Foundation.
Career: Qualified in 1971, having joined *Balfour & Manson* in 1969. Became a Partner in 1976.
Personal: Born 21st December 1947. Educated in Aberdeen and graduated University of Aberdeen LLB Hons 1969. Enjoys reading, walking and looking at buildings when time permits. Lives in Edinburgh.

SMITH, Tim
Griffith Smith, Brighton (01273) 324041
Specialisation: Specialises in all aspects of Charity Law (registration, constitutional issues, charity property, fundraising etc.) and provides an initial free 'legal audit' service as a way of identifying potential problems. He also draws on his experience of working full-time in charity management throughout the 1980s which gives him particular understanding of the practical issues facing charity managers and trustees.
Prof. Memberships: Charity Law Association.
Career: Qualified as Solicitor in 1979. Worked full time in charity management 1981-1990. With Griffith Smith since 1990 (Partner 1991).
Personal: Married with two children. Interested in wide range of social and community issues – and jazz and hill-walking when time allows.

THOMPSON, Romaine
Anthony Collins Solicitors, Birmingham (0121) 200 3242
Partner and Head of the Charities Department.
Specialisation: Provides specialist legal services to numerous charities and churches throughout the UK. The department advises charities on all legal aspects of their activities such as formation and registration, compliance with the Charity Commission requirements, restructuring, fund-raising, employment law, copyright, property management and trustee training. The department publishes a free news-letter to clients updating them on legal issues

and also offers a fixed fee legal audit service.
Prof. Memberships: She is a member of the Charity Law Association, the Ecclesiastical Law Society and the Society of Trust and Estate Practitioners.
Career: Educated at Trinity Hall, Cambridge. Qualified 1988. She joined *Anthony Collins Solicitors* in 1989 and became a Partner in 1993. She has written articles for professional journals and lectures on charity law issues.

THORNELY, Richard
Thomas Eggar Church Adams, Horsham (01403) 214500
See under Trusts & Personal Tax, p. 795

WARREN, Jennifer
Taylor Vinters, Cambridge (01223) 423444
Specialisation: Partner dealing with all property aspects of Charity Law. Acting for a wide range of charities and educational institutions, advising on the purchase, development, management and disposal of property holdings and investments, and the making and documentation of charitable grants. Recent transactions include acting for a disability charity on two joint ventures and for Cambridge University on several developments.
Career: Qualified 1981. With *Bischoff & Co* 1979-1991. Associate partner from 1986. Joined *Bates Wells & Braithwaite* 1991 as head of property department. Partner 1992. Joined *Taylor Vinters* as Partner 1996.
Personal: Exeter University 1967-1970. Arts adminstrator and Member of Tate Gallery Educational Committee 1971-1977. Governor of Anglia Polytechnic University. Visual arts, reading, riding.

WOMACK, Michael
Taylor Vinters, Cambridge (01223) 423444
Specialisation: Mainly educational and fundraising charities, universities, colleges, schools and grant awarding bodies. Major technical achievements this year include consolidation of public examination bodies and the merger of two charities operating hospices.

Prof. Memberships: Law Society; Anglo-German Lawyers; Law Society European Group; Licensing Executive's Society; Educational Law Association.
Career: Trinity Hall, Cambridge; LLM University College, London. Articled in City firm and joined *Taylors* as it then was in 1975.
Personal: Ornithology, hill-walking, photography, foreign languages and travel.

WOODHEAD, Louise S.
Wragge & Co, Birmingham (0121) 233 1000
See under Trusts & Personal Tax, p. 796

WOODWARD, Mark
Wansbroughs Willey Hargrave, Bristol (0117) 926 8981
Head of Charity Unit.
Specialisation: Acts for several national as well as local charities, advising on all aspects of charity law. Advises an increasing number of NHS trusts on charitable funds, in particular on fundraising agreements, trading and legacy disputes. Is particularly interested in establishing new charities and acting for charities in legacy disputes. Also handles charity commission investigations.
Career: Qualified in 1985. Legal Officer for the Charity Commission, London, 1987-88, before joining *Wansbroughs Willey Hargrave* in 1988.

WRIGLEY, Matthew
Wrigleys, Leeds (0113) 244 6100
Partner.
Specialisation: Private client and charities, particularly agricultural, heritage property, educational, religious and conservation charities.
Career: Qualified 1972. Partner *Biddle & Co* 1975. Partner *Dibb Lupton Broomhead* 1978. Partner *Wrigleys* 1996.
Personal: Born 1947. Educated Westminster School (Queen's Scholar), King's College, Cambridge (Scholar). Partner *Biddle & Co* 1975. Partner *Dibb Lupton Broomhead* 1978. Partner *Wrigleys* 1996.

WYLD, Charles
Burges Salmon, Bristol (0117) 939 2000

CHURCH LAW

RESEARCH: In compiling the tables, we considered all the information available to us, paying particular regard to the market research carried out by our team of ten qualified lawyers. (The researchers' details are set out on page three.)

The rankings, therefore, reflect the opinion of the marketplace as revealed by systematic and objective research: see page four. (Our research is audited every year by the British Market Research Bureau.)

OVERVIEW: This section is divided into two sections. Only firms which act for the Church of England can be said to practise 'Ecclesiastical Law' in the strict sense. Those included in the 'Other Denominations' section practise property, trusts, charity and other law insofar as it relates to a specific type of client. These will usually be clients in the Roman Catholic community, but also include Free Church or Orthodox bodies, and other institutions.

Most firms act for clients of one denomination, although there are exceptions. For example, Winckworth & Pemberton act for the Church of England and Roman Catholic bodies.

LONDON

CHURCH OF ENGLAND

Lee Bolton & Lee The firm is one of the two clear leaders in London. *Peter Beesley* is the senior partner specialising in ecclesiastical law. Partner *Nick Richens* also has a strong reputation for this type of work and is active on the education side of church law. **Winckworth & Pemberton** The other leading firm in London. One of the few firms advising Roman Catholic bodies as well as Church of England clients. The Ecclesiastical and Education Law Department is headed by *Paul Morris*, who has acted in many controversial cases. *Michael Thatcher's* particular expertise lies in Church school law and education.

LEADING FIRMS CHURCH OF ENGLAND
LEE BOLTON & LEE
WINCKWORTH & PEMBERTON

LEADING INDIVIDUALS CHURCH OF ENGLAND
BEESLEY Peter Lee Bolton & Lee
MORRIS Paul Winckworth & Pemberton
RICHENS Nicholas Lee Bolton & Lee
THATCHER Michael Winckworth & Pemberton

SEE PROFILES AT END OF THIS SECTION

OTHER DENOMINATIONS

Ellis Wood *Simon Howell* is known for his work for Roman Catholic clients. **Witham Weld** A broad practice in which leaders *Charles* and *Nicolas Bellord* serve clients from a range of denominations including Roman Catholic, Anglican and Orthodox. **Camerons** do work for Baptist clients. **Pothecary & Barrett** have a longstanding reputation for acting on behalf of Methodists. **Wansbroughs Willey Hargrave** do some work for Catholic clients.

HIGHLY REGARDED FIRMS OTHER DENOMINATIONS
Ellis Wood
Witham Weld
Camerons
Pothecary & Barratt
Wansbroughs Willey Hargrave

LEADING INDIVIDUALS OTHER DENOMINATIONS
BELLORD Charles Witham Weld
BELLORD Nicolas Witham Weld
HOWELL Simon Ellis Wood

SEE PROFILES AT END OF THIS SECTION

The SOUTH and WALES

CHURCH OF ENGLAND

Winckworth & Pemberton's Oxford and Cheltenham offices, operating as a team with the London office, dominate this specialist area outside London. The team is headed by *Dr Frank Robson* (Chair of Ecclesiastical Law Society) and includes *Brian Hood* and *John Rees* (Solicitor to the Anglican Consultative Council). **Follett Stock** Team is led by *Martin Follett*. **Harris & Harris** *Timothy Berry* does the work. **Michelmores** *Richard Wheeler* enjoys a strong reputation.

    Thomas Eggar Church Adams (the merged firm of Thomas Eggar Verrall Bowles and Church Adams Tatham) is considered a strong practice. Senior partner *Clifford Hodgetts* heads a team which includes *Guy Scoular*, who does work on the property side. The firm's ecclesiastical practice includes the Diocese of Chichester and the Dean and Chapter of Westminster. **Brutton & Co** acts for the Portsmouth Diocese, and *Hilary Tyler* maintains a good reputation in the sector.

    Claytons has a good reputation in the field as does **Osborne Clarke**.

    White & Bowker's team is headed by *Peter White* who also has experience in the field of Methodist property.

LEADING FIRMS • THE SOUTH AND WALES • CHURCH OF ENGLAND	
WINCKWORTH & PEMBERTON Chelmsford/Oxford	

HIGHLY REGARDED FIRMS	
Follett Stock Truro	Michelmores Exeter
Harris & Harris Wells	Thomas Eggar Church Adams Chichester
Brutton & Co Fareham	Osborne Clarke Bristol
Claytons St Albans	White & Bowker Winchester

LEADING INDIVIDUALS • THE SOUTH AND WALES • CHURCH OF ENGLAND	
ROBSON Frank Winckworth & Pemberton	
BERRY Timothy Harris & Harris	HOOD Brian Winckworth & Pemberton
CHEETHAM David Claytons	REES John Winckworth & Pemberton
FOLLETT Martin Follett Stock	WHEELER Richard Michelmores
HODGETTS Clifford Thomas Eggar Church Adams	WHITE Peter White & Bowker
SCOULAR Guy Thomas Eggar Church Adams	TYLER Hilary Brutton & Co

SEE PROFILES AT END OF THIS SECTION

OTHER DENOMINATIONS

Both **Stone King & Wardle** and **Tozers** have strong reputations for their work for Roman Catholic institutions. Tozers acts for the Roman Catholic Diocese of Plymouth. *Michael King* at Stone King, and *Richard King* at Tozers are highly recommended for their advice for Catholic clients.

    Hugh James advises the Presbyterian Church of Wales as well as Baptist and Methodist clients. **Allington Hughes** and **L G Williams & Prichard** retain their reputations for their work in Roman Catholic matters.

    Donne Mileham & Haddock has long experience of acting for religious institutions, and currently acts for two Roman Catholic dioceses, as well as various free churches and religious orders and bodies. They often also advise individual members of the clergy.

    Rodgers Horsley Whiteman acts for clients from the Russian Orthodox church.

HIGHLY REGARDED FIRMS • THE SOUTH AND WALES • OTHER DENOMINATIONS	
Stone King & Wardle Bath	Tozers Exeter
Allington Hughes Wrexham	Hugh James Cardiff
Camerons Harrow	LG Williams & Prichard Cardiff
Donne Mileham & Haddock Brighton	Rodgers Horsley Whitemans Guildford

LEADING INDIVIDUALS THE SOUTH AND WALES OTHER DENOMINATIONS
KING Michael Stone King
KING Richard Tozers

SEE PROFILES AT END OF THIS SECTION

MIDLANDS and EAST ANGLIA

CHURCH OF ENGLAND

All the named individuals enjoy strong reputations and maintain their positions on the leaders' tables. The ecclesiastical work of both **Leeds Day** and **Mills & Reeve** has a particular emphasis on property work.

HIGHLY REGARDED FIRMS • MIDLANDS AND EAST ANGLIA CHURCH OF ENGLAND	
Edwards Geldard Derby	Martineau Johnson Birmingham
Manby & Steward Wolverhampton	Wellman & Co Lincoln
Harvey Ingram Owston Leicester	Rotheras Nottingham
Leeds Day Sandy	Mills & Reeve Norwich

LEADING INDIVIDUALS • CHURCH OF ENGLAND	
BATTIE James Edwards Geldard	THORNEYCROFT John Manby & Steward
CARSLAKE Hugh Martineau Johnson	WELLMAN Derek Wellman & Co
BLOOR Richard Harvey Ingram Owston	HODSON Christopher Rotheras

SEE PROFILES AT END OF THIS SECTION

OTHER DENOMINATIONS

Gateley Wareing acts for the Roman Catholic Archdiocese of Birmingham. *Stephen Gateley* is Secretary of and writes the newsletter for the Conference of Solicitors acting for Roman Catholic Dioceses and Religious Orders.

HIGHLY REGARDED FIRMS • MIDLANDS AND EAST ANGLIA OTHER DENOMINATIONS	
Gateley Wareing Birmingham	
Anthony Collins Solicitors Birmingham	

LEADING INDIVIDUALS • MIDLANDS • OTHER DENOMINATIONS
GATELEY Stephen Gateley Wareing

SEE PROFILES AT END OF THIS SECTION

Anthony Collins Solicitors acts for a number of individual community and independent churches throughout the country, typically advising on structures, organisation, charity regulations, and property matters. The firm also advises a number of individual Anglican churches, mainly in the Midlands but sometimes further afield.

The NORTH

CHURCH OF ENGLAND

Denison Till is pre-eminent in the North East as is *Lionel Lennox* amongst the individuals.

Birch Cullimore *Alan McAllester* heads the practice.

Dixon, Coles & Gill advise some Methodist clients in addition to their Church of England work; *Linda Box* is recommended.

Gamon Arden & Co *Roger Arden* retains his position at the top of the table.

M C Darlington *Michael Darlington* (who is a sole practitioner although he is also a partner in H.L.F Berry & Co) is also recommended, and is solicitor to the Manchester Diocesan Board of Finance and Board of Education; other clients include parish church councils and Church of England schools. *Tom Hoyle* of Roebucks is also a respected practitioner.

Gordons Wright & Wright act for Methodist clients as well as Church of England. *Jeremy Mackrell* has retired as a partner, but continues to act as Registrar for the Bradford Diocese from the firm's offices.

LEADING FIRMS • THE NORTH • CHURCH OF ENGLAND	
DENISON TILL Leeds	

HIGHLY REGARDED FIRMS	
Birch Cullimore Chester	**Gamon Arden & Co** Liverpool
Dixon, Coles & Gill Wakefield	**Gordons Wright & Wright** Keighley
M C Darlington Manchester	**Roebucks** Blackburn

LEADING INDIVIDUALS • THE NORTH • CHURCH OF ENGLAND	
ARDEN Roger Hollins Gamon Arden & Co	**LENNOX Lionel** Denison Till
BOX Linda Dixon, Coles & Gill	**McALLESTER Alan** Birch Cullimore
DARLINGTON Michael M C Darlington	
HOYLE Thomas Roebucks	**MACKRELL Jeremy** Gordons Wright & Wright

SEE PROFILES AT END OF THIS SECTION

OTHER DENOMINATIONS

Lancashire is an area where Roman Catholicism is particularly strong, so it is not surprising to find that the three main firms in the north west act for Catholic clients.

Grays Still at the top of the heap in the North. *Anthony Lawton* is strongly recommended. Although Grays is primarily associated with Roman Catholic clients, the firm has also acted for the Dean and Chapter of York for 300 years and advises in relation to Church of England schools. **Hill Dickinson** advises the Archdiocese of Liverpool. **Oswald Goodier & Co** acts for the Diocese of Lancaster. **Fieldings Porter** also acts for Roman Catholic clients. *Mark Belderbos* and *Edward Nally* remain in the tables this year on recommendation.

HIGHLY REGARDED FIRMS THE NORTH OTHER DENOMINATIONS	
Grays York	
Hill Dickinson Liverpool	
Oswald Goodier & Co Preston	
Fieldings Porter Bolton	

LEADING INDIVIDUALS THE NORTH OTHER DENOMINATIONS
LAWTON Tony Grays
BELDERBOS Mark Oswald Goodier & Co
NALLY Edward Fieldings Porter

SEE PROFILES AT END OF THIS SECTION

LEADERS' PROFILES • LONDON AND REGIONS

ARDEN, Roger Hollins
Gamon Arden & Co, Liverpool
(0151) 709 2222

BATTIE, James S.
Edwards Geldard, Deeside (01332) 31631
Specialisation: Solicitor to Derby Diocesan Board of Finance since 1972. Diocesan Registrar and Legal Secretary to the Bishop of Derby since 1986.
Prof. Memberships: Law Society. Ecclesiastical Law Association. Ecclesiastical Law Society.
Career: Ashby Boys Grammar School and Keble College Oxford. Partner *Hollisbriggs & Co* and *Edwards Geldard* 1966-96 (now consultant).
Personal: Gardening. Hill walking. Follows most sports (especially cricket). Trips overseas to sites of historic interest. Church of England lay reader.

BEESLEY, Peter
Lee Bolton & Lee, London (0171) 222 5381
See under Education (mainly institutions), p. 286

BELDERBOS, Mark J.
Oswald Goodier & Co, Preston
(01772) 253841
See under Charities, p. 164

BELLORD, Charles E.T.
Witham Weld, London (0171) 821 8211

BELLORD, Nicolas J.
Witham Weld, London (0171) 821 8211
Partner in Tax and Trusts Department.
Specialisation: Main area of practice is charities, advising on all aspects of the law with particular emphasis on religious charities including Roman Catholic, Anglican, Orthodox and Eastern European. Other area of practice is computer law: founder member and secretary of Society for Computers and the Law, 1975-84. Author of 'Computer Science and Law' (CUP 1980) and 'Computers for Lawyers' (Sinclair Browne 1983).
Prof. Memberships: Law Society, Society for Computers and the Law. British Cybernetics Society.
Career: Qualified 1963. Became a Partner in 1967. UK representative on the Committee of Experts on Legal Data Processing, Council of Europe, 1980-84.
Personal: Born 24th April 1938. Attended Downside School 1952-54, Fribourg University in Switzerland 1954-56, then Oxford 1957-60. Leisure interests include running a vineyard in Portugal. Lives near Haywards Heath.

BERRY, Timothy F.
Harris & Harris, Wells (01749) 674747

BLOOR, R.H.
Harvey Ingram Owston, Leicester
(0116) 254 5454
Specialisation: General Ecclesiastical including litigation. Numerous cases within diocese of Leicester. Lectures on ecclesiastical law and contributions to Ecclesiastical Law Journal.
Prof. Memberships: Solicitor Law Society Planning Panel, Ecclesiastical Law Association, Ecclesiastical Law Society.
Career: LL.B Hons (University College London) Solicitor of Supreme Court (1960).
Personal: Leisure interests – Church of England.

BOX, Linda
Dixon, Coles & Gill, Wakefield
(01924) 373467
Specialisation: Ecclesastical Law, Charity Law.
Prof. Memberships: Law Society.
Ecclesiastical Law Association; Ecclesiastical
Law Society.
Career: LLB 1970; Qualified solicitor December
1973; Deputy Diocesan Registrar 1979 – 1993;
Diocesan Registrar 1994 to date.
Personal: Married with two sons. Interests
include walking in the Lake District, theatre and
the opera.

CARSLAKE, Hugh
Martineau Johnson, Birmingham
(0121) 200 3300
Partner in Private Client Department.
Specialisation: Main area of practice covers
tax planning, trusts and estate planning and
ecclesiastical law. Acts for the owners of landed
estates and private individuals in their personal
and trustee capacities. Registrar for and legal
adviser to the Diocese of Birmingham.
Prof. Memberships: Law Society, STEP.
Ecclesiastical Law Association (ELA).
Career: Qualified in 1973, having joined
Martineau Johnson in 1972. Became a Partner in
1974, Notary Public in 1981, Head of Private
Client Department in 1991 and Diocesan
Registrar in 1992.
Personal: Born 15th November 1946. Attended
Rugby School, 1960-65, then Trinity College,
Dublin, 1966-70. Chairman of the Barber
Institute of Fine Arts (University of Birmingham);
Council Member of the Birmingham and
Midland Institute; Member of the Council of the
University of Birmingham; Trustee of the
Worcester Cathedral Appeal Trust. Council
Member of the Notaries Society. Leisure
interests include family, music and gardening.
Lives in Warwickshire.

CHEETHAM, David N.
Claytons, St. Albans (01727) 865765
Partner in Ecclesiastical, Charity and General
Property Department
Specialisation: Principal areas of practice are
ecclesiastical and charity law. Acts as legal
adviser to the Church of England in the Diocese
of St. Albans and Registrar of the St. Albans
Consistory Court. Has some experience of
advocacy in other Consistory Courts. Has been
involved in the establishment of two hospices.
Deals with general work in relation to charity
owned property and over 130 church schools.
Has handled cases involving access through
churchyards and sale of church treasures.
Panel member at various Ecclesiastical Law
conferences. Has appeared on local radio.
Prof. Memberships: Law Society,
Ecclesiastical Law Society, Ecclesiastical Law
Association (Chairman 1996-98), SBA.
Career: Joined *Claytons* as a clerk in 1962.
Qualified in 1971. Became a Partner in 1972.
Senior Partner from 1985. Registrar of St.
Albans Diocese from 1978.
Personal: Born 3rd August 1941. Educated at
Merchant Taylors School, Crosby, and
Dunstable Grammar School. School governor,
local charity trustee, Red Cross trustee. Leisure
pursuits include exploring old churches and
some sporting interests. Lives in St. Albans.

DARLINGTON, Michael C.
M C Darlington, Manchester (0161) 834 7545

FOLLETT, Martin
Follett Stock, Truro (01872) 241700

GATELEY, Stephen
Gateley Wareing, Birmingham
(0121) 236 8585
See under Charities, p. 164

HODGETTS, Clifford L.
Thomas Eggar Church Adams, Chichester
(01243) 786111
Also at Worthing and Horsham. Senior Partner.
Specialisation: Principal area of practice
covers ecclesiastical and charities work.
Registrar of the Diocese of Chichester and
Legal Secretary to the Bishop of Chichester.
Clerk to the Dean and Chapter of Chichester
and its associated charities. Also acts as legal
adviser to the Dean and Chapter of
Westminster. Other main area of work is private
client and commercial conveyancing. Recent
article in Law Society Gazette relating to
Practise Rule 5- Hived Off Businesses.
Prof. Memberships: Ecclesiastical Law
Association, Law Society, Ecclesiastical Law
Society.
Career: Qualified 1958. Joined *Thomas Eggar
Verrall Bowles* in 1960, became a Partner in
1961, and Senior Partner in 1986.
Personal: Born 12 May 1934. Attended Bristol
University 1953-56. Deputy Lieutenant of West
Sussex. Director of Chichester Festival Theatre
Ltd (1989). Governor of Westbourne House
School Educational Trust. Leisure pursuits
include fishing, tennis, golf, shooting, travel.
Member of MCC. Lives in Graffham.

HODSON, Christopher
Rotheras, Nottingham (0115) 910 0600
Specialisation: As Diocesan Registrar for the
Diocese of Southwell involved in all aspects of
Ecclesiastical law including advice to Bishops,
Archdeacons, Clergy, Parochial Church
Councils and any persons requiring
Ecclesiastical legal advice. The extent of the
work includes property matters, Clergy
discipline matters, advice as to qualifications
and rights of marriage, Ecclesiastical Planning
law, i.e. Faculty jurisdiction and even extends to
having advised other Dioceses in connection
with Ecclesiastical matters. In addition works for
the Southwell Diocesan Board of Finance which
is the Administrative Authority for the Church of
England in the Diocese of Southwell and in this
context is required to give advice in all areas of
work affecting Church of England including
commercial matters, property matters and
employment matters.
Prof. Memberships: Member of the
Ecclesiastical Lawyers Association, the
Ecclesiastical Law Society and the Notaries
Society.
Career: Qualified 1969 with *Perry, Parr & Ford*,
Solicitors of Nottingham which amalgamated
into the firm of *Rotheras* in 1970 (Partner from
1973 and became Senior Partner in 1993).
Deputy Diocesan Registrar for the Diocese of
Southwell 1970-1990. Became Registrar of the
Diocese of Southwell in 1990 which position is
still held. Became Notary Public in 1981.
Personal: Born 27th May 1945. Education at

Mundella Grammar School, Nottingham and
Southampton University (First Class Honours
Degree LLB). Interests include singing, theatre,
sport and walking. Lives in Southwell,
Nottingham.

HOOD, Brian J.
Winckworth & Pemberton (incorporating
Sherwood & Co), Chelmsford
(01245) 262212
Partner in Ecclesiastical Department
(Chelmsford).
Specialisation: Specialises in ecclesiastical
law. Deputy Registrar to Bishop of Chelmsford
1976-89. Registrar and Bishop's Legal Secretary
since 1989. Also handles property and charities
law, private and commercial matters.
Prof. Memberships: Ecclesiastical Law
Association, Ecclesiastical Law Society.
Career: Qualified as a solicitor in New Zealand
in 1966. Qualified in the UK in 1976. Joined
Winckworth & Pemberton as a Partner in 1977.
Personal: Born 8th February 1943. Educated at
Marlborough College, New Zealand 1956-62
and the University of Canterbury, New Zealand
1963-67 (LLM Hons). Leisure interests include
golf, tennis, music and theatre. Lives in Terling,
Essex.

HOWELL, Simon P.J.
Ellis Wood, London (0171) 242 1194
Specialisation: Partner specialising in charity
law. Practice covers both charitable trusts and
property related work. Acts for major national
Catholic charities, religious orders and
dioceses. Also advises schools and colleges,
mainly in the voluntary (Roman Catholic) sector.
Prof. Memberships: The Charity Law
Association; Conference of Solicitors Acting for
Catholic Dioceses and Religious Orders
(Committee Member).
Career: Qualified 1971. Partner, *Ellis Wood*
since 1976.

HOYLE, Thomas
Roebucks, Blackburn (01254) 668855
Specialisation: Ecclesiastical and Charity Law.
Recent reported cases include Re: Holy Trinity,
Freckleton (vernacular names on grave-stones);
Re: St Peter's Shipley (telecommunication
antennae on church tower).
Prof. Memberships: Ecclesiastical Law
Association; Ecclesiastical Law Society; Past
President, Association of North Western Law
Societies. Notaries Society (Council Member).
Career: Diocesan Registrar and Legal
Secretary to the Bishop of Blackburn; Solicitor
to various Boards and Committees including
the Diocesan Board of Finance and Diocesan
Board of Education.
Personal: Qualified as Solicitor 1976;
Ecclesiastical Notary 1985; Notary Public 1989.

KING, Michael
Stone King, Bath (01225) 337599
See under Charities, p. 165

KING, Richard
Tozers, Exeter (01392) 207020

LAWTON, F. A. (Tony)
Grays, York (01904) 634771
See under Charities, p. 165

LENNOX, Lionel
Denison Till, York York (01904) 611411
Partner. Main area of practice is ecclesiastical law. Registrar of the Province and Diocese of York; Registrar of the Convocation of York; Legal Secretary to the Archbishop of York; Member of the Legal Advisory Commission of the General Synod. Also handles town and country planning and charity law. Advanced Professional Diploma in Planning and Environmental Law from Leeds Metropolitan University 1994. Legal advisor to various charities. Spoke at a conference re planning law and ecclesiastical listed buildings; has particular interest in listed buildings. Notary Public 1992.
Prof. Memberships: Yorkshire Law Society, Ecclesiastical Law Society.
Career: Qualified in 1973. Worked at *Denison Suddards* as a Partner 1976-80; Assistant Legal Advisor to the General Synod of the Church of England 1981-7. Joined *Denison Till* as a Partner in 1987.
Personal: Attended St John's School Leatherhead 1962-67 and University of Birmingham 1967-70. Notary Public 1992. Lives in York.

MACKRELL, Jeremy G.H.
Gordons Wright & Wright, Keighley (01535) 667731
Specialisation: Ecclesiastical Law. Commercial Property.
Prof. Memberships: Ecclesiastical Law Association. Law Society.
Career: Joined *Wright & Wright* on qualifying in 1963. Partner in 1964. Senior Partner 1990, and since merger in 1993 Joint Senior Partner of Gordons *Wright & Wright*. Bradford Diocesan Registrar and Bishop's Legal Secretary since 1977. Notary Public.
Personal: Born 24th April 1937. Trinity College Glenalmond. Leiutenant RNR 1955-57. Leeds University 1957-60. Honorary Lay Canon Bradford Cathedral. Interests include all field sports.

MCALLESTER, Alan K.
Birch Cullimore, Chester (01244) 321066

MORRIS, Paul C.E.
Winckworth & Pemberton (incorporating Sherwood & Co), London (0171) 593 5000
Partner and Head of Ecclesiastical and Education Law Department.
Specialisation: Head of Department since 1987; previously Joint Head of Institutional Property Department 1984-87, with expertise in commercial property law. Has acted in controversial cases involving clergy discipline, re-ordering of church buildings and re-development of redundant churches and church land.
Prof. Memberships: Law Society, City of Westminster Law Society, Ecclesiastical Law Society, Ecclesiastical Law Association.
Career: Qualified in 1978. Joined *Winckworth &*

Pemberton in 1978, becoming a Partner in 1981. Registrar and Bishop's Legal Secretary, Diocese of London. Registrar and Bishop's Legal Secretary, Diocese of Southwark. Joint Registrar, Diocese of Leicester. Solicitor to Southwark Diocesan Board of Finance. Solicitor to the London Diocesan Fund. Chapter Clerk of Southwark Cathedral.
Personal: Born 21st September 1950. Attended Westminster Abbey Choir School 1960-64, Westminster School 1964-68 and UCNW Bangor 1968-72. Leisure interests include music and the family. Lives in West London and Charlbury, Oxfordshire.

NALLY, Edward
Fieldings Porter, Bolton (01204) 387742
Specialisation: Acts as Diocesan Solicitor for Salford Roman Catholic Diocese and has also represented various religious and educational charities.
Prof. Memberships: Council member of the Law Society for Central Lancashire and Northern Greater Manchester.
Career: De La Salle College, Salford and Nottingham University.
Personal: Married with two children

REES, John
Winckworth & Pemberton (incorporating Sherwood & Co), Oxford (01865) 241974
Partner in ecclesiastical, education and charities department.
Specialisation: Main area of practice is ecclesiastical law. Joint Registrar, Diocese of Oxford: Deputy Registrar, Province of Canterbury: Legal Adviser to the Anglican Consultative Council (the international liaison body for the Anglican Communion worldwide). Extensive experience in contested faculty cases, including Court of Arches Judgment in Re St. Luke, Maidstone: wide acquaintance with education law issues, both for voluntary and grant-maintained school sectors.
Prof. Memberships: Ecclesiastical Law Association, Ecclesiastical Law Society (Treasurer).
Career: Qualified 1975. Joined *Winckworth & Pemberton* 1986. Partner 1988.
Personal: Born 21 April 1951. Holds LLB (Southampton 1972), MA (Oxon 1984) and MPhil (Leeds 1984). Leisure interests include photography and cycling. Lives in Oxford.

RICHENS, Nicholas J.
Lee Bolton & Lee, London (0171) 222 5381
Specialisation: Education Law and Charity Law, particularly with reference to church schools and school sites. Advised the General Synod Board of Education on the School Standards and Framework Bill. Joint contributor to Volume 13(2) Encyclopaedia of Forms and Precedents – Ecclesiastical Law. Joint author of "Charity Land and Premises" (Jordans 1996). Deputy Registrar, Diocese of Guilford.
Prof. Memberships: Ecclesiastical Law

Society (Deputy Secretary); Ecclesiastical Law Association (Assistant Secretary); Charity Law Association.
Career: Admitted 1985. Joined *Lee Bolton & Lee* in 1991.
Personal: Born 1960; Educated Marple Hill High School, Stockport and Downing College Cambridge. Lives in East London.

ROBSON, Frank E.
Winckworth & Pemberton (incorporating Sherwood & Co), Oxford (01865) 241974
Consultant in Ecclesiastical Department.
Specialisation: Main area of practice is ecclesiastical law. Registrar to Diocese of Oxford since 1970; Registrar to Province of Canterbury and legal adviser to the Archbishop since 1982; Vice-Chairman of Legal Advisory Commission of the General Synod. Also handles education law: legal adviser to Oxford Diocesan Board of Education.
Prof. Memberships: Ecclesiastical Law Association (Chairman 1984-86), Ecclesiastical Law Society (Chairman 1996-).
Career: Qualified 1954. Joined *Winckworth & Pemberton* in 1958, becoming a Partner in 1960 and Senior Partner in 1990.
Personal: Born 14th December 1931. Attended Selwyn College, Cambridge 1954-57. Leisure interests include supporting Oxford United, walking and travel. Lives in Stanton St. John, Oxford.

SCOULAR, Guy
Thomas Eggar Church Adams, Horsham (01403) 214500
Specialisation: Ecclesiastical property and charities work, also private clients and general conveyancing.
Career: Qualified 1965. Joined *Thomas Eggar & Son* in 1966. Partner 1969.
Personal: Born 16.1.1940. Attended Loretto School. Officer in Territorial Army (Royal Sussex Regiment) 1958-1966.

THATCHER, Michael C.
Winckworth & Pemberton (incorporating Sherwood & Co), London (0171) 593 5000
See under Education (mainly institutions), p. 287

THORNEYCROFT, J.P.
Manby & Steward, Bridgnorth (01746) 761436

TYLER, Hilary A.G.
Brutton & Co, Fareham (01329) 236171

WELLMAN, Derek
Wellman & Co, Lincoln (01522) 536161

WHEELER, Richard K.
Michelmores, Exeter (01392) 436244

WHITE, Peter M.
White & Bowker, Winchester (01962) 844440

CIVIL LIBERTIES

See also Admin and Public Law; Crime (General); Immigration and Nationality

RESEARCH: We interviewed specialist practitioners, barristers and advice centres. Most interviewees knew the legal market intimately in this small practice area. In compiling the tables, we considered all the information available to us, paying particular regard to the market research carried out by our team of ten qualified lawyers. (The researchers' details are set out on page three.)

The rankings, therefore, reflect the opinion of the marketplace as revealed by systematic and objective research: see page four. (Our research is audited every year by the British Market Research Bureau.)

OVERVIEW: Most of the specialist civil liberties firms are based in London and there has been little change to the tables this year. Bindman & Partners and BM Birnberg & Co remain at the top, with Geoffrey Bindman and Gareth Pierce retaining their high profiles. Raju Bhatt of Birnbergs and Jane Deighton of Deighton Guedella are new entries to the tables following consistent recommendations from their peers. In the regions, Tyndallwoods in Birmingham and A S Law in Liverpool stand out.

There was a certain amount of diversity in the definition of civil liberties when practitioners in the field were questioned. This stems from the fact that civil liberties law can and often does arise from other areas of law such as employment, crime and immigration, and there is inevitably some overlap with these sections of the directory. In order to give a full picture, we give civil liberties a wide definition and include prisoners' rights, actions against the police, public order, discrimination, free speech and miscarriage of justice.

LEADING FIRMS · LONDON

BINDMAN & PARTNERS
B.M. BIRNBERG & CO

HIGHLY REGARDED FIRMS

Christian Fisher
Deighton Guedalla
Taylor Nichol
Winstanley-Burgess

Fisher Meredith
Simons Muirhead & Burton
Stephens Innocent

LONDON

Bindman & Partners (13ptnrs, 10assts – the whole firm handles civil liberties work in conjunction with other areas). *Geoffrey Bindman* is hailed nationwide as the star of the civil liberties legal world. His high profile and experience mean that the firm maintains its status at the top. More of the day to day work is perhaps being handled by his team, which includes *Stephen Grosz*, who is particularly well known in the administrative and public law domain. Particularly good on discrimination. **Clients/Work:** Ongoing work includes the Hanratty and Silcott miscarriage of justice cases and R v Secretary of State for the Armed Forces ex p. Smith and others (involving homosexuals in the armed forces). Also acting for anti-roads protesters.

B.M. Birnberg & Co (2ptnrs, 14assts – all handling civil liberties work as required). "Up there at the top with Bindmans" was how this firm was consistently described. Some practitioners even rated them above

Bindmans, particularly for miscarriages of justice where *Gareth Pierce* has made her name. The team was also praised, particularly *Rajv Bhatt* who was variously described as "outstanding", "very pleasant to deal with" and "trustworthy". He heads the firm's police action team and is known for his death in custody cases and work with the DPP. He joins the table. **Clients/Work:** Particularly well known for miscarriages of justice in Northern Ireland, inquest work and also immigration.

Christian Fisher (3ptnrs, 5assts). Known especially for inquest work. The "extremely able" *Louise Christian* remains well respected and *Sadiq Khan*, also experienced, was made a partner in February this year. **Clients/Work:** Recent successful judicial reviews and damages against the police. Recently obtained £20,000 damages for Jamaican refused entry to UK.

Deighton Guedalla (2ptnrs, 2assts) Especially well regarded for work in race and sex discrimination. *Jane Deighton* ("tough plaintiff lawyer") was consistently singled

out for praise and is a new entry to the tables. **Clients/Work:** Representing Dwayne Brooks in the Stephen Lawrence inquiry. Acting for Danny Goswell.

Taylor Nichol (2ptnrs, 1asst) *Jim Nichol* was praised and moves up a band and the assistant solicitor has written a book on youth justice. **Clients/Work:** High proportion of miscarriage of justice and public order cases and judicial review. Known for previous work for Myra Hindley and Bridgewater Four.

Winstanley-Burgess (5ptnrs, 6assts) Known for immigration and refugee work. Main client base is the non-English speaking community (eg. Kurdish, Turkish, Chinese and Filipino) **Clients/Work:** Handles domestic slavery cases especially for members of the Filipino community. Represents transsexuals. Handles claims against the police and national security work.

Fisher Meredith (6assts handle actions against the police and immigration) Clients/Work: A reputable high street practice known mainly for crime and large amount of legal aid work. Currently have 450 live cases against the police.

Simons Muirhead & Burton Specialise in appeals to the Privy Council on behalf of individuals sentenced to the death penalty in countries like Jamaica and Trinidad. Praised particularly for their commitment to pro bono work. **Clients/Work:** Cases before the UN Human Rights Committee and the Inter-American Commission of Human Rights. Also domestic miscarriage of justice cases.

Stephens Innocent (3 fee-earners) Maintain a good reputation in this field despite the feeling among some that they are more commercial and media-orientated. **Clients/Work:** Most notable case of 1998 was the "stolen body parts" case involving artist Anthony Noel Kelly. Anti-roads protesters and free speech cases. Lethal force cases from foreign jurisdictions. European Court of Human Rights cases.

LEADING INDIVIDUALS · LONDON
BINDMAN Geoffrey Bindman & Partners
PIERCE Gareth B.M. Birnberg & Co
BHATT Rajv B.M. Birnberg & Co
CHRISTIAN Louise Christian Fisher
DEIGHTON Jane Deighton Guedalla
KHAN Sadiq Christian Fisher
NICHOL James Taylor Nichol
GROSZ Stephen Bindman & Partners

MIDLANDS

LEADING FIRMS · MIDLANDS
TYNDALLWOODS Birmingham

HIGHLY REGARDED FIRMS
George Jonas & Co Birmingham
Glaisyers Birmingham

Tyndallwoods (2ptnrs spend between 30-60% of time on civ libs). Predominantly a legal aid practice. Recognised by regional and London firms as the leading player in the Midlands. *Mark Phillips* received praise from practitioners throughout the country. **Clients/Work:** Significant cases this year concerned transsexuals in the police; DSS liability for damages or breach of statutory duty in their failure to pay benefits on time; immigration and domestic slavery. Expertise in poll tax cases.

George Jonas & Co (2ptnrs, including *Steven Jonas* and 4assts spend 15 – 20% of time on civ libs). Known principally for its busy criminal practice, but also experienced in this field. **Clients/Work:** No high profile cases this year, but sustaining a high volume of work particularly actions against the police and miscarriage of justices cases.

Glaisyers (1ptnr 1asst). Entered the table last year and have maintained their good reputation for crime-related civil liberties issues. **Clients/Work:** Worked with television companies producing public interest programmes such as "Rough Justice" and "Trial and Error". Acting for Jeremy Bamber, challenging his "natural life tariff" prison sentence.

LEADING INDIVIDUALS · MIDLANDS
PHILLIPS Mark Tyndallwoods
JONAS Steven George Jonas & Co

The NORTH

LEADING FIRMS · THE NORTH
A S LAW Liverpool

HIGHLY REGARDED FIRMS
Harrison Bundey & Co. Leeds
Howells Sheffield
Irwin Mitchell Sheffield
David Gray & Company Newcastle upon Tyne
Robert Lizar Manchester

A S Law (2ptnrs 2assts) Previously Edwards Frais Abrahamson, the firm's reputation stems from the "very able" *Elkan Abrahamson* himself, whose top ranking was upheld by practitioners nationwide. **Clients/Work:** Known for prisoners rights cases, acting particularly for those serving life sentences. Various rights of access issues (including access to computers, condoms and sex changes).

Harrison Bundey & Co (2ptnrs including *Ruth Bundey*, 6assts part-time) High Street practice, with majority of income from legal aid. **Clients/Work:** Death in custody and inquest work. Represented David Greene (aged 15) who hanged himself. Judicial review (Re W: established that a single sex couple could adopt children). Actions against the police and immigration.

Howells (3ptnrs, 2assts 10 %) A popular Sheffield practice which has seen some staff changes, but is still highly recommended, mainly because of *Danny Simpson*. **Clients/Work:** Judicial review. Right of silence cases – some going to the ECHR or ECJ. Appeals for life sentence prisoners and remand in custody cases.

Irwin Mitchell (1ptnr, 4assts devote 40% of their time to civ libs) Particularly well-known for bringing actions against the police. Commended by several firms in the midlands and north. A separate department deals with unlawful arrest and false imprisonment. **Clients/Work:** High profile clients include demonstrators at Swalesmoor Mink Farm, Hillgrove Farm and Whatley Quarry. Many actions against the police. Approximately 7-800 live civ lib cases.

David Gray & Company (6ptnrs, 12assts – all undertake the work when required) Recommended by some of the top London firms as a solid practice. **Clients/Work:** Local lobby groups, hunt saboteurs, anti-vivisectionists and anti-roads protesters.

Robert Lizar (3ptnrs, 2assts handle work as necessary) **Clients/Work:** Famed for representing Manchester Airport protesters. Have also advised terrorist suspects and gay rights activists.

LEADING INDIVIDUALS · THE NORTH
ABRAHAMSON Elkan A S Law
BUNDEY Ruth Harrison Bundey & Co.
SIMPSON Danny Howells

ABRAHAMSON, Elkan
A S Law, Liverpool (0151) 707 1212
Partner in Litigation Department.
Specialisation: Main area of practice is prisoners' rights. Enforces and extends the rights of prisoners by way of judicial review, parole tribunals and litigation. Other area of practice is child care, representing children and parents in care proceedings. Also has special expertise in representing the mentally ill.
Prof. Memberships: Child Care Panel, Lawyers for Children.
Career: Qualified 1983. Solicitor of the Supreme Court of Hong Kong 1984. Partner since 1991.
Personal: Born 31st July 1953. Holds an LLB from Jerusalem 1978, and an LLM London 1979. Lives in Liverpool.

BHATT, Rajv
B.M. Birnberg & Co, London
(0171) 403 3166

BINDMAN, Geoffrey
Bindman & Partners, London
(0171) 833 4433
See under Defamation, p. 278

BUNDEY, Ruth
Harrison Bundey & Co., Leeds
(0113) 237 4047
See under Immigration & Nationality, p. 433

CHRISTIAN, Louise
Christian Fisher, London (0171) 831 1750
Partner in Civil Litigation Department.
Specialisation: Main area of practice is administrative law/judicial review, inquests, trades union and employment work, personal injury and disaster law, actions against the police and government departments and immigration work.
Prof. Memberships: Civil Liberties Trust, Law Society Human Rights Working Party, Association of Personal Injury Lawyers, Immigration Law Practitioners Association, Inquest Lawyers Group, British Panel of the International Federation of Human Rights, Advisory Boards of Kurdistan Human Rights Project and the Redress Trust. Law Society Personal Injury Panel member.
Career: Qualified in 1978 while at *Lovell White & King*. Solicitor, Plumstead Community Law Centre 1979-81, then Advisor to the GLC Police Committee 1981-84. Co-founded *Christian Fisher* with Michael Fisher in November 1985.

DEIGHTON, Jane
Deighton Guedalla, London
(0171) 359 5700

GROSZ, Stephen
Bindman & Partners, London
(0171) 833 4433
See under Administrative & Public Law, p. 87

JONAS, Steven
George, Jonas & Co, Birmingham
(0121) 212 4111
See under Crime (General – see also Commercial Fraud), p. 404

KHAN, Sadiq
Christian Fisher, London (0171) 831 1750
Partner in Civil Litigation Department.
Specialisation: Main area of practice is actions against the police, employment law, personal injury work, judicial reviews, Inquests. Involved in all areas of civil liberties work. In 1997 gave oral evidence to the Home Affairs Select Committee which looked at police complaints and discipline. He is also one of the authors of the written submission of the Police Action Lawyers Group to the Lord Chancellors Department on the changes to Legal Aid. Sadiq lectures and writes extensively on civil liberties issues.
Prof. Memberships: Police Action Lawyers Group, Executive Committee of Legal Action Group, Inquest Lawyers Group, Society of Labour Lawyers. Executive Committee of Liberty, APIL.
Career: Trainee Solicitor with *Christian Fisher & Co.* where he is now a Partner. He is a visiting lecturer in Employment Law at the University of North London.
Personal: Awarded Sweet & Maxwell Law Prize, Governors Award, Windsor Fellowship, Esso Law Bursary and Awarded Society of Black Lawyers bursary. Labour Councillor in Wandsworth since 1994 . Deputy leader of the Labour Group since 1996. Representative on Police Consultative Committee and Racial Incidents Panel. Involved in human rights visits to Kurdish areas of Turkey.

NICHOL, James
Taylor Nichol, London (0171) 272 8336

PHILLIPS, Mark
Tyndallwoods, Birmingham (0121) 624 1111
See under Immigration & Nationality, p. 434

PIERCE, Gareth
B.M. Birnberg & Co, London (0171) 403 3166

SIMPSON, Danny
Howells, Sheffield (0114) 249 6666
Partner and Head of Criminal Law Department.
Specialisation: All aspects of criminal law, including miscarriage of justice cases and a range of civil liberties issues. Last year in particular was involved in two notable cases – a successful private prosecution for rape which the CPS had rejected and the action which overturned the Home Secretary's interpretation of prisoners release dates.
Prof. Memberships: Haldane Society, Law Society.
Career: BA (Hons) Degree, Exeter College, Oxford, Politics, Philosophy and Economics, qualified as a solicitor in 1984 and employed at *Bindman & Partners* solicitors becoming a partner in 1989, before moving to Sheffield in 1990 as a partner, Head of Department and later Development partner at Howells solicitors.
Personal: Lives in Sheffield, married to GP practising locally, with 3 children. Member of Labour Party and Local Authority Community Safety panel.

COMMODITIES

RESEARCH: In compiling the tables, we consider all the information available to us, paying particular regard to the market research carried out by our team of ten qualified lawyers. (The researchers' details are set out on page three.)

The rankings, therefore, reflect the opinion of the marketplace as revealed by systematic and objective research: see page four. (Our research is audited every year by the British Market Research Bureau.)

OVERVIEW: *Physicals*: Due to changes in GAFTA and FOSFA rules, solicitors are less likely to appear in arbitrations, but are still heavily involved behind the scenes preparing submissions and coaching their clients. Furthermore, as a result of the Arbitration Act 1996, leave to appeal from arbitrations is becoming rarer.

Practitioners report that the grain trade is relatively static, with more work arising from the oil, gas and metal markets. Non-contentious work is seen as a growth area, particularly in the disciplinary, regulatory, financing and transactional field. Richards Butler edge ahead this year due to their vitality and efforts in this field. In terms of leading individuals, Christopher Potts and David Pullen clearly stand out from the rest and move up accordingly.

Futures: Comprises finance (derivatives) and physical commodities. There is little change in the hierarchy of leading players, Clifford Chance still dominate.

LONDON

PHYSICALS

LEADING FIRMS • LONDON PHYSICALS

RICHARDS BUTLER

MIDDLETON POTTS

CLIFFORD CHANCE
CLYDE & CO
HILL TAYLOR DICKINSON
HOLMAN, FENWICK & WILLAN
INCE & CO
SINCLAIR ROCHE & TEMPERLEY
TURNER & CO

HIGHLY REGARDED FIRMS

Herbert Smith
Holmes Hardingham
Lovell White Durrant
More Fisher Brown
R.D.Black & Co.
Shaw and Croft
The Simkins Partnership
Simmons & Simmons
Thomas Cooper & Stibbard

Richards Butler (4ptnrs/4assts) Seen as just having the edge over Middleton Potts, due to their "very bright team." Clients like their "youth" and feel they have re-energised. All four partners rate as leading individuals. *David Pullen* is "incredibly active and the leading figure in this field", although much of the firm's high profile is attributed to "the outstanding technical ability" of the "energetic" *Richard Swinburn* and the "hard hitting" *Diane Galloway*. *John Emmott* is also a leader. **Clients/Work:** Cocoa Association; Louis Dreyfus; Glencore.

Middleton Potts (5ptnrs/5assts – also do international trade) This niche firm has 3 leading individuals, including acknowledged guru, the "commercial and incredibly experienced" *Christopher Potts*. "Solid" *David Lucas* and *Robert Parson* are also well liked by clients. **Clients/Work:** Acted in Toepfer v Cargill and the 'Taria'. Represented a major grain trading house in the leading case on penalties in GAFTA contracts. Also acted in an arbitral dispute between two grain trading houses over force majeure and prohibition.

Clifford Chance (1ptnr/7assts f/t, plus others from shipping and futures on ad-hoc basis) John Bassindale's retirement is seen as a blow to the practice, although most felt they were strong enough to cope. *Ed Patton* is "one of the elder statesmen." **Clients/Work:** Refined Sugar Association and the Sugar Association of London. Involved in barter dispute between Russia and Cuba concerning their "oil for sugar" deal.

Clyde & Co (8 ptnrs (6 f/t)/12 assts (some f/t)) Led by *David Best* and *Andrew Wells,* the practice is regarded as "strong" and "on the up." **Clients/Work:** Acting in Glencore v Metro and in "Operation Patricia" (JH Rayner/ Mincing Lane Ltd v Federative Republic of Brazil). Also act for Citoma Trading Ltd, Banque Nationale de Paris and Inter-Continental De Cafe.

Hill Taylor Dickinson Described as "sound and pleasant to work with." *Jeff Isaacs* and "excellent" *Peter MacDonald-Eggers* are well regarded by clients. **Clients/Work:** Cargill International SA; Andre & Cie; Eximco-op/Grainco-op.

Holman, Fenwick & Willan (9ptnrs/18assts) Seen as an active practice and admired by clients. *Patricia Francies* is a respected individual. **Clients/Work:** Grains et Fourrages SA v Huyton; Navigas Ltd of Gibraltar v Enron Liquid Fuels Inc. Also act for Vitol SA; Cargill SA and Continental Grain Company.

Ince & Co (9 ptnrs/8assts – p/t) The team includes *Denys Hickey* ("a sensible, level-headed, commercial problem-solver"), the "excellent" *Jonathan Lux*, *Andrew Iyer* and *Stuart Shepherd*. Clients/Work: Vitol; Euromin; Tate & Lyle; Sonatrach.

Sinclair Roche & Temperley (4ptnrs/4assts) *Ben Leach* "is easy to deal with" yet "a formidable lawyer", and the firm generally "understands the market." Clients/Work: Cargill SA; Enron; Marc Rich; Société Générale Energie.

Turner & Co (2ptnrs/2assts – p/t) Headed by *Paul Turner*, this niche firm is a respected force in the commodities arena. Clients/Work: Glencore UK Ltd; Gill & Duffus SA; Phillip Brothers

Herbert Smith (3ptnrs – 50%) Involved in some large cases, but otherwise not a major presence in this market. Clients/Work: Act for Codelco in copper litigation and Borealis in a Court of Appeal gas case against Bergesen.

Holmes Hardingham (3ptnrs/4assts – also do other work) The "solid" *Nicholas Walser* is the main commodities player at this firm, which has less of a presence this year than previously. Clients/Work: Legal adviser to FOSFA.

Lovell White Durrant (6ptnrs/7assts – 70%). Also do futures). This large firm certainly has the expertise required for this field, but is not seen as a major player. Their activities are directed by *Philip Quenby*. Clients/ Work: Act for ED & F Mann. Represented Petroleum Authority of Thailand in proceedings by North Sea Energy Holdings N.V.

More Fisher Brown Known primarily for shipping, they also have a small, well-regarded commodities practice headed by *Adrian Moylan*.

R.D. Black & Co *Richard Black* is "an experienced and hard litigator." Clients/Work: Has been heavily involved representing English brokers in the Sumitomo copper affair.

Shaw and Croft (3ptnrs/3assts) Seen as small, but active. Clients/Work: Acting in the Metro Bunker Trading collapse.

The Simkins Partnership (2ptnrs/1asst) *Dominic Free* leads this team, which is perceived as having a small presence in the market. Clients/Work: Peter Cremer Group; Toepfer Group; Grosvenor Grain & Feed

Simmons & Simmons (4ptnrs/4assts p/t) Known more for their futures work, but also do some physicals.

Thomas Cooper & Stibbard (4ptnrs/2 assts) Regarded as a good, sound practice. Clients/Work: Acted in Bem Dis A Turk Ticaret SA v International Agri Trade Co Ltd ('The Selda'). Act for Chilean National Oil Company.

LONDON

FUTURES

Clifford Chance (3ptnrs/11assts – p/t) Still viewed as the leading firm for financial futures, largely due to their clearing house client base. *Tim Plews, David Mayhew* and *Lynn Johansen* are particularly admired. The firm is also rated for commodities futures. Clients/Work: LIFFE; IPE; OMLX; Hong Kong Futures Exchange.

Arnheim & Co (2ptnrs/6assts – p/t) *Martin Cornish* and his team are well regarded, and continue to be active players. Clients/Work: IPE arbitration re non-delivery of gas. OTE documentation for natural gas trading. Swap documentation for LME brokers.

Denton Hall (5ptnrs/8assts – p/t) Led by *Robert Finney*, the firm is seen as a strong financial and commodities futures practice. Clients/Work: Acted for Citibank International Bank plc and Standard Chartered Bank in US$275m syndicated commodity financing for Ghana Cocoa Board; and for Standard Chartered Bank in syndicated cotton financing for the Zimbabwe Cotton Company. Also act for Total and IPE.

Simmons & Simmons (8ptnrs – p/t) Strong in financial futures with two leading individuals, *Iain Cullen* and *Jonathan Melrose*. Clients/Work: Act for Sogemin Metals in continued copper futures litigation with Codelco.

Linklaters (2ptnrs/7assts – p/t) *Simon Firth* leads the derivatives team and does mainly commodities futures. Clients/ Work: London Metal Exchange.

Lovell White Durrant (6ptnrs/7assts – 70%). Also do physicals) *David Moss* spearheads this part of the firm's practice. Clients/Work: Continental Grain; Amerada Hess; Banque Paribas. Represented Paribas Futures Ltd and AIC Ltd in disciplinary proceedings by the International Petroleum Exchange.

Mayer Brown & Platt *Eric Bettelheim* directs the London team of lawyers handling contentious and non-contentious futures work for this U.S. firm.

Norton Rose Despite the lack of high profile individuals, the firm is known to do some work in this market. Clients/Work: Advised on two long-term coal contracts for Indian and Indonesian power projects.

Richards Butler (4ptnrs/4assts – also do futures) The undoubted star in the physicals sphere, the firm has less of a high profile for futures, although this is expected to change given its general resurgence. Clients/Work: Continue to be involved in the Sumitomo copper affair.

PHYSICALS

BEST, David
Clyde & Co, London (0171) 623 1244
Specialisation: Disputes concerning oil and gas, metal, sugar and other international commodity contracts, both in arbitration and court, and related charterparty and bill of lading disputes.

BLACK, Richard
R.D.Black & Co., London (0171) 600 8282
Partner specialising in Shipping and Commodities Litigation.
Specialisation: Wide experience since 1978 of maritime and commodity arbitrations (both physical and futures), and Commercial Court hearings relating to shipping, trading, insurance and commercial litigation disputes and regulatory work with a particular emphasis on charterparty and cargo claims and commodity disputes including GAFTA, FOSFA, the crude oil and petroleum product trade and LME arbitrations. Clients include international trading houses, commodity and derivatives traders, oil majors and traders, P&I and charterers' liability clubs, ship owners, charterers and marine insurers. Also handles commercial litigation and white collar crime. Major cases included Deutsche Schachtbau und Tiefborgesellschaft v. Raknoc & Shell International; Kloeckner v. Gatoil; the M.V. 'P', The 'Taria', Comdel v Siporex. Currently heavily involved in representing English brokers in the Sumitomo Affair.
Prof. Memberships: Law Society.
Career: Qualified in 1077. Joined *Middlcton Potts* from *Coward Chance* in 1984, becoming a Partner in 1985. In December 1996, resigned from Middleton Potts to set up R.D. Black & Co.
Personal: Born 22nd March 1951. Holds an LLB from Manchester, 1969-72. Leisure interests include golf, tennis, chess and reading. Lives in Oxshott.

EMMOTT, John
Richards Butler, London (0171) 247 6555
Partner in Shipping Unit.
Specialisation: Specialises in international trade and commodities.
Career: Qualified in 1978 (Australia), 1985 (UK). Partner at *Richards Butler* since 1986.
Personal: Born 1953. Educated at the University of Sydney (BA, LL.B).

FRANCIES, Patricia
Holman, Fenwick & Willan, London
(0171) 488 2300
Partner in Commercial Litigation Department.
Specialisation: Litigation, soft and hard commodities, oil and gas trading disputes, international sale of goods including acting for Fiat's railway division in the Channel Tunnel disputes, the Santa Clara House of Lords Case for Vitol SA, acts for Cargill SA, Continental Grain, Minermet SA and many others.
Prof. Memberships: Supporting member of LMAA, GAFTA, member of Law Society.
Career: LL.B Auckland 1978, LL.M London 1979, called to New Zealand Bar 1980, admitted as solicitor in England/Wales 1988. P&I Club 1979-1987. Claims Manager *Tindall Riley & Co.* (Director of the Management Co. 1983-1987). *Middleton Potts* 1988-1990. *Holman Fenwick and Willan* 1990-present. Partner 1993.

FREE, Dominic
The Simkins Partnership, London
(0171) 631 1050
Partner in Litigation Department.
Specialisation: Litigation and arbitration of commercial disputes particularly in relation to international business transactions and intellectual property matters.
Career: Qualified in 1985. Partner *Richards Butler* 1989-92. Partner *The Simkins Partnership* 1993.
Personal: Born 16th November 1956. Educated in New Zealand (LLB, Auckland 1979) and the USA (LLM, Cornell University 1982).

GALLOWAY, Diane
Richards Butler, London (0171) 247 6555
Specialisation: Principal areas of practice are commodities arbitrations and litigation, including in Grain and Feed Trade Association, Liverpool Cotton Association, Refined Sugar Association and FOSFA. Recent experience also includes Chinese Trade Arbitration (CIETAC). Has recently lectured for GAFTA and Sugar Association of London. Also specialises in sanctions related litigation.
Career: LL.B Trinity College, Cambridge, then Masters in International Law, Harvard Law School, USA. Joined *Richards Butler* in 1984 after internship with New York firm.

HICKEY, Denys
Ince & Co, London (0171) 623 2011
Partner
Specialisation: A major part of his practice involves oil and gas trading disputes. Has acted in disputes involving many of the Majors and independant oil traders in connection with contracts for the sale of crude, products and gas. Also involved in metals trading including LME disputes, tolling contracts, offtake agreements and other aspects of metals trading with particular reference to the FSU. Involved in disputes relating to time and voyage charters, long term contracts of affreightment, storage contracts, and shortage and contamination claims. Has advised on short and long term contracts and problems arising out of letters of credit and trade finance and the application of EU and UK competition law. He has spoken at numerous conferences on the legal aspects of transport, trading, letters of credit and EC competition law, and is a regular speaker at the Centre for Petroleum and Mineral Law at the University of Dundee, and the College of Petroleum Studies in Oxford.
Career: Post-graduate studies in Public International and EC Law, then qualified as a barrister. Joined *Ince & Co.*, requalified as a solicitor and became a Partner in 1986.
Personal: Born 1952. Lives Saffron Walden. Leisure interests include golf and skiing.

ISAACS, Jeffrey
Hill Taylor Dickinson, London
(0171) 283 9033
Partner.
Specialisation: Practice covers the full range of maritime and Sale of Goods law, but with a specialisation in 'dry' shipping and Commodities disputes including both High Court litigation and arbitration at the various Trade Associations, including GAFTA, FOSFA, The Refined Sugar Association, The Sugar

Association of London and LME. Regularly sits as legal assessor to arbitration panels at the Sugar Associations and GAFTA. Author of articles on Shipping and Commodities matters. Speaks at seminars and on the GAFTA Trade Education Course. Shipping Editor of 'Law and Transport Policy'. An Editor of International Trade Law Quarterly.
Prof. Memberships: Law Society, and through *Hill Taylor Dickinson* GAFTA, FOSFA and Refined Sugar Association.
Career: Qualified in 1983 having joined *Hill Taylor Dickinson* in 1981. Associate in 1987. Partner in 1989.
Personal: Born 11th April 1959. Attended Dulwich College then Christ's College, Cambridge (BA 1980). Leisure interests include tennis, badminton, horse riding, wine making and tasting and skiing. Lives in Putney.

IYER, Andrew
Ince & Co, London (0171) 623 2011
Partner specialising in Commodities Law and Shipping Law.
Specialisation: Principal areas of practice are shipping and commodities work, covering dry and wet shipping disputes involving both litigation and arbitration, and the full range of contentious and non-contentious physicals and futures work, including disputes on GAFTA, FOSFA, Coffee Trade Federation, Refined Sugar Association and London Metal Exchange contracts. Also deals with all areas of oil trading and energy. Does a lot of work for clients dealing with emerging markets in the FSU and Black Sea region. Other main areas of work are letter of credit disputes, trade finance, insurance, construction and engineering disputes in all forums. Articles written are: 'Legal Effects of War on International Trade Contracts', 'Letters of Credit and the Doctrine of Strict Compliance', and co-author 'Nomination of Vessels Under FOB and CiF Contracts'.
Prof. Memberships: GAFTA, FOSFA, (via *Ince & Co*). LLMA.
Career: Trained with *Middleton Potts*. Joined *Ince & Co* in 1991.
Personal: Leisure pursuits include diving and skiing. Lives in London.

LEACH, Ben
Sinclair Roche & Temperley, London
(0171) 452 4000
Partner; Head of Litigation.
Specialisation: Main area of specialisation is commodity trades, from litigation and arbitration to drafting and advising on commodity sales, contracts and associated documentation. Instructed in several of the milestone commodity trade cases in the last 15 years, e.g. Bunge v. Tradax (H.L. 1981), Italgrani v. Sosimage (C.A. 1986), State Trading Corporation v. Golodetz (C.A. 1989), Cargill v. Kadinopoulos (H.L. 1992). Conducted over 100 arbitrations before GAFTA, FOSFA, Refined Sugar Association, London Metal Exchange, London Rice Brokers' Association and various other hard and soft commodity trade associations in London and abroad. Contributed to the Law Commission Working Group on title to goods forming part of a bulk. Also a specialist in shipping and oil litigation (see separate listing under Shipping & Maritime Law).

Prof. Memberships: Law Society
Career: Articled to *Richards Butler* in 1969, qualified as a solicitor in 1971, joined *Sinclair Roche & Temperley* in 1975 and became a partner in 1978.
Personal: Born 24th October 1945. Attended Leeds University 1965-68. Accredited CEDR mediator.

LUCAS, Charles David
Middleton Potts, London (0171) 600 2333
Partner in Commercial Litigation Department.
Specialisation: Main area of practice is commodities and shipping. Extensive experience of arbitration and litigation, acting for commodity trading houses (including the majors), oil companies and traders, shipowners, insurers and P&I Clubs. Major cases handled include 'Bremer v Vanden-Avenne', 'The Montone', 'The Caspian Sea', 'The Pegase', 'The Afovos', 'The Golden Bear' and 'The Future Express'.
Prof. Memberships: Law Society
Career: Qualified in 1972. Associate, *Crawley & de Reya* 1974-76. Founding Partner at *Middleton Potts* in 1976.
Personal: Born 15th December 1947. Attended St Paul's School 1960-65, then Bristol University 1966-69.

LUX, Jonathan
Ince & Co, London (0171) 623 2011
See under Alternative Dispute Resolution, p. 113

MACDONALD EGGERS, Peter
Hill Taylor Dickinson, London
(0171) 283 9033
Specialisation: All aspects of commodities disputes and transactions, including Commercial Court litigation and arbitration. Also specialises in shipping, insurance and international projects.
Prof. Memberships: Law Society, and through Hill Taylor Dickinson, GAFTA, FOSFA and Refined Sugar Association. Contributing Editor, Chitty on Contracts; General Editor, International Trade Law Quarterly.
Career: Qualified in New South Wales in 1987 and in England and Wales in 1991. Joined *Hill Taylor Dickinson* in 1988, Associate in 1993, Partner in 1995.
Personal: Born 1964. Attended Sydney Grammar School, University of Sydney and Magdalene College, Cambridge.

MOYLAN, Adrian
More Fisher Brown, London
(0171) 247 0438

PARSON, Robert Michael
Middleton Potts, London (0171) 600 2333
Partner in international trade and commodities department.
Specialisation: Wide experience since 1987 in all aspects of law and practice relating to the international sale of goods and commodity trading including advice on related maritime and trade finance. Regularly involved in GAFTA, FOSFA, IGPA, LME and other trade arbitrations as well as LMAA arbitration. Clients include major international trading houses, shippers, receivers, insurers, banks and carriers.
Prof. Memberships: Law Society.
Career: Qualified 1986. Joined *Middleton Potts*

from *Richards Butler* in 1992. Partner in 1995.
Personal: Born 7th February 1961. Sheffield University LLB 1979-1982.

PATTON, Edwin
Clifford Chance, London (0171) 600 1000
Partner Shipping and International Group.
Specialisation: Principal areas of work include the international trading of commodities and its financing, marine oil pollution and the litigation and arbitration of all kinds of commercial shipping disputes.
Career: Lecturer in Law, University of Bristol 1964-1967. Qualified 1970. Partner 1974.
Personal: LL.B (Queen's, Belfast) 1963.

POTTS, Christopher Reginald
Middleton Potts, London (0171) 600 2333
Senior Partner at *Middleton Potts*.
Specialisation: Over 30 years experience of law and practice relating to commodities, carriage of goods, insurance (marine and non-marine) and international trade. Many major cases handled are leading authorities. Clientele includes major trading houses, carriers, insurers and banks. Regularly lectures to trade audiences.
Prof. Memberships: Law Society
Career: Qualified in 1965. Partner at *Crawley & de Reya* 1967-76. Founding Partner of *Middleton Potts* in 1976, and is currently Senior Partner.
Personal: Born 1st July 1939. Attended University of London 1958-61. Lives in London.

PULLEN, David
Richards Butler, London (0171) 247 6555
Partner in International Trade and Commodities.
Specialisation: Main area of practice is commodity trading disputes, including arbitration and advice work in grain (GAFTA), vegetable oil (FOSFA), sugar (RSA and SAOL) and oil trading (ICC). Also handles documentary credits advice work, and advises on litigation disputes in customs and EC matters. Cases have included the 1973 US Prohibition cases, Naxos, Panchaud Freres and Toepfer v Continental Grain. Instructor at the University of Pennsylvania Law School 1963-64. Regular speaker at trade related conferences.
Prof. Memberships: Supporting Member of London Maritime Arbitration Association
Career: Qualified 1967, and has been at *Richards Butler* since 1964.
Personal: Born 1941. Attended Taunton School 1954-59, then University College Oxford 1960-63. President of Chesterfords Cricket Club. Leisure interests include sports. Lives in Great St Chesterford, Essex.

QUENBY, Philip
Lovell White Durrant, London
(0171) 236 0066
Specialisation: Commodity trading and financing (physicals and futures), covering crude and refined petroleum products, LNG, LPG, agriproducts, metals and other bulk commodities. Includes IPE and LME transactions and all aspects of transactional shipping work.
Prof. Memberships: Law Society, London Maritime Arbitrators' Association.
Career: Articled *Lovell White & King* (now *Lovell White Durrant*); qualified 1986; Solicitor 1986-1992; Partner *Lovell White Durrant* 1992.

SHEPHERD, Stuart
Ince & Co, London (0171) 623 2011
Specialisation: Main areas of practice are shipping and commodities. Handles all aspects of dry shipping work, with particular emphasis on carriage of goods by sea and charterparty disputes and is involved in advising those trading in various commodities, in particular oil, oil products and commodities traded on GAFTA terms, with particular emphasis on litigation. Leading reported cases have included ' 'Mathraki' (1989), 'Lefthero' (1992), 'Boucraa' (1993) and 'Kriti Rex' (1996). Chairman of International Bar Association Committee on Commodities and author of articles on a number of shipping matters. Speaks at Lloyds of London shipping seminars and on the GAFTA Training and Education course.
Prof. Memberships: Member of IBA, LMAA, and through *Ince & Co.*, GAFTA, FOSFA and Refined Sugar Association.
Career: Qualified in 1984, having joined *Ince & Co.* in 1982. Became a Partner in 1990.
Personal: Born 17th October 1959. Attended Bexhill Grammar 1971-78, then University College, Cardiff 1978-81. Leisure interests include golf and skiing. Lives in Mayfield, East Sussex.

SWINBURN, Richard
Richards Butler, London (0171) 247 6555
Specialisation: Advises trading companies, trade associations, banks and governments on all aspects of the buying, selling, financing and transporting of commodities.
Career: Qualified in 1988. Partner at *Richards Butler* 1994.
Personal: Born 1963. Educated at Sedbergh School, Cumbria and Robinson College, Cambridge.

TURNER, Paul
Turner & Co, London (0171) 480 7991
Founder Partner handling Commodities.
Specialisation: Work includes trade arbitrations before the Sugar Associations, GAFTA, FOSFA, Cocoa Association, Coffee Trade Federation and Rice Association. Also handles oil disputes, bills of lading and charter party disputes, largely before commercial courts or the London Maritime Arbitrators Association.
Prof. Memberships: Law Society, Associate Member of the Sugar Association of London.
Career: Qualified 1973. Partner with *Thomas Cooper & Stibbard* from 1977-85. Founder Partner of *Turner & Co.* in 1985.
Personal: Born 16th September 1948. Attended Skegness Grammar School 1960-67, then University College, London, 1967-70. Leisure interests include walking, travelling and eating. Lives in Esher, Surrey.

WALSER, Nicholas
Holmes Hardingham, London
(0171) 283 0222
Partner specialising in 'dry' shipping law.
Specialisation: 'Dry' shipping law, including commodity trade disputes. Work covers charterparty disputes, cargo loss/ damage claims, and international sale contracts including agricultural commodities (GAFTA and FOSFA contracts) and oil trading. Major cases include the 'TFL Prosperity' (1984) and Soules v.Intertradex (1991). Fluent French. Working knowledge of German.

Prof. Memberships: Law Society, AIJA.
Career: Qualified in 1977. Partner in *Ingledew Brown Bennison & Garrett* 1979-89. A Founding Partner of *Holmes Hardingham* in 1989.
Personal: Born 31st December 1952. Attended Cambridge University (MA 1975). Lives in London.

WELLS, Andrew
Clyde & Co, London
(0171) 623 1244
Partner.
Specialisation: Drafting and advising on commodity contracts, international trade agreements, international joint ventures and associated finance documents. Clients include commodity traders, oil majors, banks, shipowners, charterers and trading houses. Experienced in structuring and negotiating contracts in a wide variety of jurisdictions and in the production of clear, practical commercial documentation.
Personal: Born 1953. MA Cambridge University. Partner at *Clyde & Co* since 1984.

FUTURES

BETTELHEIM, Eric
Mayer Brown & Platt, London
(0171) 246 6200

CORNISH, Martin
Arnheim & Co, London (0171) 939 1660
See under Investment Funds, p. 497

CULLEN, Iain
Simmons & Simmons, London
(0171) 628 2020
See under Investment Funds, p. 497

FINNEY, Robert
Denton Hall, London (0171) 242 1212
Partner in Banking and Financial Markets Group. Main areas of practice are: Securities and derivatives dealing, investment management and related regulatory matters; Capital markets, especially derivative products and structured finance; Funds; and Commodities (covering non-contentious work in respect of physicals and futures, including OTC derivatives). Author of various articles, especially in 'Futures and Options World' and Butterworths' 'Journal of International Banking and Finance Law'. Has addressed seminars and conferences on regulatory and derivatives issues.
Prof. Memberships: Law Society, ICSA (FCIS), Futures & Options Association, US Managed Futures Association.
Career: Qualified in Scotland 1979, (England and Wales 1991). In-house counsel with Pearson Group, then with Credit Suisse First Boston and Morgan Stanley International before joining *Denton Hall* in 1990. Became a Partner in 1992.
Personal: Born 1955. LLB Edinburgh University 1977. Leisure interests include theatre and cycling.

FIRTH, Simon
Linklaters, London (0171) 456 3764
See under Capital Markets: International Capital Mkts & Derivatives, p. 152

JOHANSEN, Lynn
Clifford Chance, London (0171) 600 1000
Partner Finance Group.
Specialisation: Principal area of work is advising on derivatives and financial regulation with a particular focus on exchange traded derivatives issues for exchanges and clearing houses, banks, securities houses and other investment firms and commodity derivatives.
Career: Qualified 1985. Partner 1995.
Personal: MA (CANTAB) in History 1981.

MAYHEW, David
Clifford Chance, London (0171) 600 1000
See under Fraud: Regulation and Investigation, p. 401

MELROSE, Jonathan
Simmons & Simmons, London
(0171) 628 2020
Partner in Corporate Department.
Specialisation: Handles all types of work relating to commodities, derivatives/ securities, collective investment vehicles and asset management. Regular speaker at conferences and seminars.

Prof. Memberships: Union Internationale des Avocats, Law Society, The Securities Institute, Member of Commodities Committee of the Futures and Options Association, Joint Editor of the Financial Services Newsletter of the Union Internationale des Avocats.
Career: Qualified 1985, having joined *Simmons & Simmons* in 1983. Became a Partner in 1991.
Personal: Born 21st April 1959. Holds an MA (Hons) Oxon, 1981. Lives in Suffolk.

MOSS, David
Lovell White Durrant, London
(0171) 236 0066
Specialisation: Principal area of practice is non-contentious commodities, trade finance and shipping work. Expertise in commodity trading (particularly futures and commodity derivatives) commodity financing, structured trade financing, Islamic financing and transactional shipping work. Advises banks, oil companies and trading companies.
Prof. Memberships: Law Society; London Maritime Arbitrators' Association; American Arbitration Association Panel of neutrals.
Career: Articled *Lovell, White & King* (now *Lovell White Durrant*); qualified 1981; solicitor London office 1981-83, Hong Kong office 1983-85 and London office 1985-87; seconded to law firm in Tokyo 1987-90; partner *Lovell White Durrant* 1988; partner resident in Tokyo office of *Lovell White Durrant* 1990-93.

PLEWS, Tim
Clifford Chance, London (0171) 600 1000
Specialisation: Chairs the Firm's International Financial Markets Group; expertise in law and regulation of stock and derivatives exchanges and other financial markets, clearing and settlemnt systems; financial sector mergers and acquisitions; acts for governments, exchanges, banks, brokers and dealers.
Prof. Memberships: Law Society; Futures Industry Association.
Career: Durham School; Trinity College, Cambridge. Articled *Coward Chance*; qualified 1988; Partner *Clifford Chance* 1994.
Personal: Born 1962; Resides Godalming, Surrey.

COMPUTER & IT

RESEARCH: In compiling the tables, we consider all the information available to us, paying particular regard to the market research carried out by our team of ten qualified lawyers. (The researchers' details are set out on page three.)

The rankings, therefore, reflect the opinion of the marketplace as revealed by systematic and objective research: see page four. (Our research is audited every year by the British Market Research Bureau.)

An index to all profiles is on page 67.

OVERVIEW: This is a highly competitive and rapidly developing area of practice, so there are considerable changes in the tables of leading firms. However, the level of expertise and experience necessary to establish a reputation in the field means that there are few alterations to the list of leading individuals.

Bird & Bird joins Clifford Chance and Baker & McKenzie in the leading band on the basis of almost unanimous recommendation. Masons remains in the second category due to its outstanding litigation practice.

New niche firms which enter the list for the first time are Kemp & Co and Robertson & Co. Tarlo Lyons goes up one place, as does Theodore Goddard since its incorporation of Arnold Segal.

In the South, The Law Offices of Marcus J. O'Leary goes from strength to strength. In the Midlands, Wragge & Co have pulled away from local competitors, with Pinsent Curtis also doing well this year. In the North, Masons is out on its own at the top and in Scotland Bird Semple is a new addition to our tables.

LEADING FIRMS · LONDON

BAKER & MCKENZIE
BIRD & BIRD
CLIFFORD CHANCE

MASONS

ALLEN & OVERY
DENTON HALL
DIBB LUPTON ALSOP
HERBERT SMITH
LOVELL WHITE DURRANT
OLSWANG
OSBORNE CLARKE

HIGHLY REGARDED FIRMS

Bristows
Field Fisher Waterhouse
Hammond Suddards
Harbottle & Lewis
Kemp & Co
Linklaters
Simmons & Simmons
Slaughter and May
Taylor Joynson Garrett

Ashurst Morris Crisp
Garretts
Nabarro Nathanson
Robertson & Co, Technology Law Practice
Rowe & Maw
Singletons
Tarlo Lyons
Theodore Goddard

LONDON

Baker & McKenzie (5ptnrs/14assts) Described as "one of the leading computer litigation firms in London." Their strengths are seen to derive from their solid commercial base, their IP practice, and the quality of their leading individuals. *Donald Jerrard* and *Harry Small* appear in the highest band of leading individuals, and *Michael Hart* also features in the list. *Graham Allen* enters the up & coming category. Active in emerging areas such as electronic commerce, Euro issues and Year 2000 compliance. **Clients/Work:** Acted for Oracle in leading litigation against North West Water re interpretation of software warranties and the enforceability of IT industry exclusion clauses. Acting for Psion Software plc structuring and negotiating two operating software licenses. Acted for Kelloggs in the out-sourcing of their European IT systems.

Bird & Bird (15 ptnrs/25assts) Elevated to the highest band. Considered "strong in non-contentious work," and in litigation, "difficult" for their opponents. Widespread admiration for their team, which is led by the "excellent"

Hamish Sandison. Simon Chalton now focuses on the advisory and academic side, and is fondly described as the "elder statesman of computer law." *Roger Bickerstaff* performs "impressive government transactional work," and on the corporate side, *Christopher Rees* has "a great deal of common sense." *Hilary Pearson* is respected as a litigator, as is *Graham Smith*, who is "measured in what he says and transparently nice, which is unusual for a litigator." **Clients/Work:** Advised Yorkshire Electricity on deregulation. Advised the Environment Agency in its dispute with Logica re WAMS software project. Renegotiated the RAF LITS contract for the implementation of a new logistics system for all RAF operations (£290m).

Clifford Chance (34ptnrs – 17f/t) Have a "strong practice," which is seen to undertake the biggest deals. Team includes the "friendly and personable" *Christopher Millard*, *David Griffiths* "respected for his work on big commercial IT contracts", and the "dynamic" *Vanessa Marsland* who practises in the IP dept, but is also seen as an accomplished IT lawyer. **Clients/Work:** Act mainly for service providers, plus financial services and

corporate clients. Specialise in international transactions and internet and e-commerce. Also have a strong telecoms practice.

Masons (6 ptnrs/13 assts) Have a unique IT practice in that they undertake little transactional work, but are highly respected litigators. *Robert McCallough* is "a positive and bullish litigator," and *Rachel Burnett* is "a well respected player." The firm has lost Liam McNieve, who has left to establish a sole practice, and Peter Bullock has moved to the Hong Kong office. *Iain Monaghan* and *Clive Seddon* are also recommended. **Clients/Work:** Market data licensing work for LIFFE;

contentious work for WH Smith and The ICL Group; non-contentious work for ICI, the London Stock Exchange and United Utilities.

Allen & Overy (5ptnrs/18assts) A firm which is "good at everything they turn their hands to" have developed a respected practice, and *Laurence Jacobs* enters the list as a leading individual for the first time. **Clients/Work:** EDS; Mondex project; Chase Manhatten E-banking project.

Denton Hall (6 ptnrs/12 assts) Are particularly known for their large scale contract work. *Nicholas Higham* is described as a "good thinker who can cut to the quick on a commercial deal." The "quiet and intelligent" *John Worthy* is "a good operator," and "the kind of person you can do business with." **Clients/Work:** Advised Bank of Scotland re business process re-engineering systems. Advised BG plc on 3 major transactions. Advising Western Digital Corp on its dispute with Amstrad relating to disk drives.

Dibb Lupton Alsop (4ptnrs/11assts) Have a national presence in the IT field, and are seen to be "good on outsourcing." *David Barrett* is "a good technical lawyer and commercially aware." *Alistair Maughan* has been acclaimed as "one of the best commercial IT lawyers in the City." *George Godar* is also recommended. **Clients/ Work:** TranSys consortium; ACCORD Project for the DSS; outsourcing for Save & Prosper.

Herbert Smith (3ptnrs/3assts) Have "some good people, especially on the litigation side." Their IT service to blue chip companies is seen to take strength from the IP practice, and the department has been bolstered by the arrival of *Mark Turner* from Garretts. **Clients/Work:** Acted for CAA on new IT facilities; outsourcing for Department of National Savings; acted for Amstrad against Seagate.

Lovell White Durrant (4ptnrs/8assts) Are "commercially excellent" and "do more IT work than they let on." *Quentin Archer* is an "impressive" computer lawyer, and the "bright" *Conor Ward* has been elevated from up and coming as he is "making a good name for himself." **Clients/Work:** BZW; Pearson; Barclays Bank.

Olswang (4 ptnrs/7assts) Have a formidable reputation as a media law firm, and from this have developed a respected IT practice. *Kim Nicholson* has a "good reputation," but reservations have been expressed about the ability of the firm to compete with other leaders if the practice relies upon media related work. **Clients/Work:** BBC Worldwide; UUNET; Daiwa Bank.

Osborne Clark (7ptnrs/8assts) Have a "useful practice which is doing extremely well." The team includes the "dynamic" *Simon Rendell* who is a "sound lawyer." *Nigel Wildish* is a "thoughtful lawyer who you can trust with commercial matters." *Paula Staunton* is joined in the up & coming section by the frequently recommended

Paul Gardner. **Clients/Work:** Negotiated Encryption Certification Authority Agreement with BT for VeriSign Inc; advised NatWest IT fund on their investment in STB Ltd; acquired Sequelogic Ltd for Diagonal.

Bristows (9ptnrs/8assts) A respectable IT practice, which "they don't make a song and dance about," stems from their pre-eminent IP reputation. The department is headed by the "self-effacing" *Philip Westmacott* who is "hard working and thorough." **Clients/Work:** Opticom; Motorola; IBM.

Field Fisher Waterhouse (3ptnrs/10assts) Have suffered from a lack of exposure in the IT field, as most competitors are unaware of their client base. The merger with Allison & Humphreys may help their profile, and the "nice and straightforward" *Michael Chissick* is respected as a "good technical lawyer." **Clients/Work:** ComputerLand; Thomas Cook; Software Europe.

Hammond Suddards (2ptnrs/4assts) Have a strong litigation department and "some good computer people," including the "rigorous and methodical" *Michael Mahony*. **Clients/Work:** One2One; Dixons; Sharp.

Harbottle & Lewis (2ptnrs/5assts) Known as an entertainment firm and enter IT from the internet and multi-media side. **Clients/Work:** ICL; Virgin Atlantic; TNT.

Kemp & Co (2 ptnrs/1asst) The new firm set up by the "energetic and innovative" *Richard Kemp*, formerly of Garretts. The firm are expected to make a significant impact on the IT scene over the coming years. **Clients/Work:** Microsoft; FTSE International; Deloitte & Touche.

Linklaters (3ptnrs/12 assts) Have an IT practice as a spin-off from their commercial and banking practices, and are "good, especially on litigation." **Clients/Work:** Advising BP on development and exploitation of their integrated business operations system; advising British Airways and KPMG on outsourcing.

Simmons & Simmons (2ptnrs/8assts) Have a highly regarded IT practice linked to their outstanding IP practice. **Clients/Work:** Advising UK clearing banks on their role as settlement banks for CREST. Advising Railtrack on a number on high value strategic IT development contracts; Network Technology plc on LSE listings, including full IT due diligence.

Slaughter and May (2ptnrs/11assts) Excellent on the corporate side. However, it is felt that the firm's policy of each individual being a generalist prevents them from being real IT experts. **Clients/Work:** Advising ICL on Year 2000 issues; advising Kwik-Fit and JP Morgan in relation to outsourcing and procurement.

Taylor Joynson Garrett (3ptnrs/7assts) Lost Ranald Robertson this year but are building up a reasonable IT practice,

although it is still currently seen as based upon their expertise in IP. **Clients/Work:** Acting for major banks in outsourcing agreement and branch equipment contracts; acted for Thomson Holidays in the outsourcing of their computer operations to IBM; acting for Sony Computer Entertainment Europe in its anti-piracy programme.

Ashurst Morris Crisp (4ptnrs/10assts) Have a strong telecommunications practice, but their IT work is perceived more as corporate work for IT companies rather than IT work for companies. However, "whatever they do, they do well." **Clients/Work:** MIH Holdings; Cyberlife Technology; Legal & General.

Garretts (1ptnr/5assts) Suffered a major setback with the loss of Richard Kemp and

Mark Turner, but retain some IT capability. **Clients/Work:** Include Waterford Wedgwood; PPL; Arthur Andersen.

Nabarro Nathanson (4ptnrs/9assts) Operate an IT practice from their London and Reading offices, although they have not made a great impact on the London IT market this year. **Clients/Work:** Granada Computer Services; CSL (subsidiary of Deloitte & Touche); Sema Group Plc.

Robertson & Co, Technology Law Practice A new firm set up by *Ranald Robertson,* formerly of Taylor Joynson Garrett.

Rowe & Maw (5ptnrs/11assts) Received praise for their non-contentious practice, and the work of the "competent and sensible"

Michael Webster. **Clients/Work:** Advised NEC Corporation re supply of software systems to enable ICO Global Mobile Communications Network to operate. Procurement contracts for M&G Group plc. Advising Prime Response Ltd re standard form documentation and a series of transactions.

Singletons (1 principal) *Susan Singleton* has "an awful lot of energy," and is well known for her writing and lecturing activities. She advises on competition law as well as "doing an incredible job running her own IT practice." **Clients/Work:** Advising in a computer contract dispute concerning assignment of copyright in computer game. Advising leading plc on year 2000 issues.

Tarlo Lyons (5ptnrs/6assts full-time) Have "a fair amount of good IT work" which is "impressive." Undertake general outsourcing, IT sales and M&As in the IT sector. **Clients/Work:** Prudential Group; Schroders; Energis.

Theodore Goddard (5ptnrs/5assts) Have recruited the "practical" *Arnold Segal;* a non-contentious specialist who is "particularly good at contract drafting." **Clients/Work:** AMX Digital Ltd; Western Provident Association; Vic Tokai.

Jeremy Newton has recently joined Cameron McKenna from Pitmans. He was well regarded in Reading, and combines IT with IP work.

LEADERS' PROFILES · LONDON

ALLAN, Graham
Baker & McKenzie, London (0171) 919 1000
Specialisation: Practises exclusively in commercial and contentious information and communication technology law. Particular areas of expertise include software development and system integration contracts, outsourcing, electronic commerce and internet law, major systems disputes, and millennium compliance advice. Acts for a broad range of technology suppliers (from start-ups to the largest of Silicon Valley multinationals) and customers in a number of different industry sectors, including the banking, pharmaceutical and retail.
Prof. Memberships: Member of Society for Computers & The Law and Legal Advisor to the Business Accountancy Software Developers' Association (BASDA).
Career: Joined *Baker McKenzie* in 1989, after graduating from Manchester University. Obtained a Diploma in IP law from Bristol University in 1992. Worked in *Baker & McKenzie's* Palo Alto and San Francisco Offices (1994-96), advising leading Silicon Valley multinationals and a broad range of start-up software houses. Now a Senior Associate in the London Office.
Personal: Interests: Fell walking and Leeds United Football Club.

ARCHER, Quentin
Lovell White Durrant, London
(0171) 236 0066
Specialisation: Partner specialising in all aspects of IT law, both contentious and non-contentious, particularly computer contracts (including projects under the Private Finance Initiative), electronic commerce and the introduction of new technology. One of the first lawyers to move (in 1985) from the IT industry back into private practice. Most clients outside the IT sector are in the financial services, defence, and media fields.
Prof. Memberships: Law Society; US Computer Law Association; British-Russian Law Association; Treasurer, British Czech and Slovak Law Association.
Career: Qualified 1981. In-house solicitor at Acorn Computer Group PLC, 1984-85. Rejoined *Lovell White Durrant* in 1985, partner 1987.

BARRETT, David
Dibb Lupton Alsop, London (0345) 262728
Partner and Head of IT and Telecommunications Group.

Specialisation: Partner and Head of Communications, Technology and Intellectual Property. Responsible for *Dibb Lupton Alsop's* practice in information technology, communications, broadcasting, media and EU and computer technology transfer; Information systems and business systems outsourcing; telecommunications IT & Telecommunications procurement and supply; multimedia and international projects.

BICKERSTAFF, Roger
Bird & Bird, London (0171) 415 6000
Partner in Company Department.
Specialisation: Principal area of practice is information technology. Work encompasses all aspects of IT law, including contract negotiation, dispute resolution, protection of rights, Year 2000, impact of EC legislation and impact of new technology (e.g. Internet). Also advises on all aspects of EC/GATT procurement law. Clients include the Government's Central Computer and Telecommunications Agency (CCTA), where he is Head of CCTA's Legal Services, government departments and major private sector IT purchasers.
Prof. Memberships: Society for Computers and Law. Company Secretary of Taskforce 2000 and Action 2000.
Career: Qualified in 1990. At *Linklaters & Paines* 1990-92. Joined *Bird & Bird* in 1992 and became a Partner in 1995.
Personal: Born 1961. Attended King's College, Cambridge 1980-84. Lives in London.

BURNETT, Rachel
Masons, London (0171) 490 4000
Partner in Information & Technology Group.
Specialisation: Practice covers the full range of IT and multimedia industry transactions and related commercial matters, including IT and outsourcing contract negotiation. Acts for vendors, system integrators, software publishers, resellers, major corporate and public sector users. Co-author of "Drafting and Negotiating Computer Contracts" (Butterworths, 1994), author of "Outsourcing IT- The Legal Aspects" (Gowes, 1998), and contributor of legal column in "The VAR". Writes and lectures widely on IT-related matters.
Prof. Memberships: Institute for Information Systems Management (IMIS) (Council Member); Worshipful Company of Information Technologists (Livery Member); British Computer Society; Law Society.

Career: Qualified 1980. Former IT professional. Joined *Masons* in 1990. Partner in 1994.
Personal: Exeter University (BA Soc. Studies). Associate, Institute of Linguists (French). Chair, Association of Women Solicitors, 1990-91.

CHALTON, Simon
Bird & Bird, London (0171) 415 6000
Consultant to Information Technology Group.
Specialisation: Computer law including intellectual property rights in computer programs and databases; computer system procurement; computer-related contracts; computer-related liabilities, disputes and ADR (CEDR trained WIPO listed mediator); data protection; competition law and European and international law relating to computers and telecommunications. Co-editor Sweet & Maxwell's 'Encyclopedia of Data Protection'; co-author 'Data Protection Law'; consultant contributor 'Encyclopedia of Information Technology Law'. Editorial Board member Computer Law and Security Report, Computer Law and Practice; and frequent contributor to many other legal and professional journals. Conference speaker at an international level.
Prof. Memberships: Law Society, International Bar Association (former Chairman of Computer and Database Committee), British Computer Society (former Chairman of Intellectual Property Commitee and Deputy Chairman of Professional Issues Board), National Computing Centre (former Chairman of Legal Group), Chartered Institute of Arbitrators (Fellow), Society for Information Management (USA) (Member of Procurement working group), College of Law Practice Management (USA) (Fellow), American Bar Foundation (USA) (Fellow).
Career: Qualified 1958. Solicitor, subsequently Partner and Senior Partner with *Dibb Lupton & Co* in Leeds until 1989. Consultant to *Dibb Lupton Broomhead 1989-93.* Consultant to *Masons* 1993-94. Joined *Bird & Bird,* 1995.
Personal: Born 1932. Lives in High Kilburn near York.

CHISSICK, Michael
Field Fisher Waterhouse, London
(0171) 481 4841
Videophone: (0171) 488 0796 email: michael.chissick@ffw.sprint.com
Specialisation: Head of IT, and Internet Group which comprises a team of 8 specialist lawyers. Main areas of practice include: outsourcing projects, advising both service providers and

companies seeking to outsource; data protection; digital mixed media; and a rapidly growing Internet practice. He is the author of 'Internet Law' published in October 1997 by FT Publications. In the past year has advised on several major outsourcing projects, including advising Thomas Cook on various outsourcing to Cap Gemini.
Prof. Memberships: Law Society; Solicitors European Group; FAST Legal Advisory Group; Computer Law Association.
Career: 1st Class Degree in Law (LLB); Law Society Finals 1st Class; Masters Degree in IT and Telecommunications.

GARDNER, Paul
Osborne Clarke, London (0171) 634 1606
Specialisation: Handles all apsects of intellectual property and commercial law relating to the digital media industries, with particular emphasis on the entertainment software and educational software industries. Advised: mail order company in connection with the establishment of an on-line shop; educational software publisher in connection with the exploitation of its products as part of an on-line database; leading computer game publishers and developers in connection with a variety of joint ventures, publishing agreements and intellectual property issues.
Prof. Memberships: Executive Committee of the British Interactive Multimedia Association (BIMA) and works closely with the European Leisure Software Publishers Association (ELSPA).
Career: Joined *Titmuss Sainer Dechert* as trainee in 1985 and made partner in 1992. Joined *Osborne Clarke* as partner IT, Telecoms and Media department February 1998.

GODAR, George
Dibb Lupton Alsop, London (0345) 262728
National Head of Intellectual Property. Partner in Communications, Technology and Intellectual Property Group.
Specialisation: Principal area of practice is intellectual property, commercial, computers and competition. Handles both litigation and advisory work in relation to patents, trade marks, copyright, design rights, technology, franchising, software and hardware. Also deals with EC law, including competition and public procurement. Has been involved in engineering, technology and pharmaceutical litigation, including claims arising out of the collapse of the Milford Haven box girder bridge, subsidence at Oldbury nuclear power station, the collapse of the Emley Moor television mast and the Ronan Point tower block. Has spoken at conferences on trade marks, intellectual property licensing, technology transfer, competition law and computer contracts.
Prof. Memberships: Law Society, Solicitors European Group, Society for Computers and Law, London Solicitors Litigation Association, International Trademark Association, Intellectual Property Lawyers Association, Federation Against Software Theft Legal Advisory Group and Competition Law Association.
Career: Qualified in 1974. Partner with *Wilkinson Kimbers* from 1975 and Head of Intellectual Property and Computer Law Department from 1985. Partner with *Alsop Wilkinson* from 1988. National Head of Intellectual Property with *Dibb Lupton Alsop* from 1996. Admitted as a solicitor in Hong Kong in 1988.
Personal: Born 11th November 1948.

Educated at Nottingham High School 1959-67 and King's College, Cambridge 1968-71 (MA, Engineering Science and Law). Interests include theatre, running, classic cars and travel. Lives in Berkhamsted, Herts

GRIFFITHS, David
Clifford Chance, London (0171) 600 1000
Partner in Media, Computer and Communications Group.
Specialisation: Specialises in computer law, communications and multimedia. Author of 'Restraint of Trade and Business Secrets' (Longmans, 1991), co-ordinating editor 'Law and Regulation in European Multimedia' (Longmans, 1994).
Career: Partner since 1990.
Personal: Born 13th February 1958. Educated at Cambridge University 1976-79. Leisure activities include golf, skiing and tennis. Lives in London.

HART, Michael
Baker & McKenzie, London (0171) 919 1000
Specialisation: Contentious and non-contentious information technology lawyer. Has conducted software and hardware infringement actions, computer fraud cases and numerous computer contract disputes and has drafted and negotiated a wide variety of computer and IT related agreements ranging from distribution and licensing agreements to networking and interactive communications contracts. Clients he has represented include Sony, Platinum Technology, Apple Computer, the Electronic Industry Association of Japan and Informix. He is a contributor to the Sweet & Maxwell Encyclopedia of Information Technology Law and has recently written and spoken at seminars and on Radio 4's 'In Business' programme on legal aspects of the Internet, on-line services and email/Internet policy and on IT and ADR.
Career: Qualified in 1983. With *Linklaters & Paines* 1983-87. Joined *Baker & McKenzie* in 1987 and became a Partner in 1990.
Personal: Born 12th August 1959. Educated at City of London School 1970-77 and Exeter College, Oxford 1977-80. Leisure activities include theatre, cinema, horse racing, tennis and hockey. Lives in London.

HIGHAM, Nicholas
Denton Hall, London (0171) 242 1212
email: nach@dentonhall.com
Specialisation: Partner in Media and Technology Group. Main areas of practice are telecommunications, information technology, digital media and copyright. Work includes regulation (14 countries), privatisation (4 countries), outsourcing and system development agreements. Acted on the establishment of the first Trans-European network for telecoms and for satellite operators, and for The British Library on its Digital Library Project for a digital terrestial broadcaster, and for Internet Service Providers. Author of many articles on regulation, communications and I.T. Regular lecturer on telecommunications, multimedia and I.T.
Prof. Memberships: Associate of Chartered Institute of Patent Agents, International Institute of Communications, Trade Marks Agent, IBA.
Career: Qualified in 1971. Joined *Denton Hall* as a Partner in 1992. Previously at *Linklaters & Paines* 1975-1981, solicitor and Partner at *SJ Berwin* 1981-1992.

Personal: Born 1947. Leisure interests include bridge. Lives in London.

JACOBS, Laurence
Allen & Overy, London (0171) 330 3000
Specialisation: Contentious and non-contentious information technology law and related intellectual property matters. Advising suppliers and customers on outsourcing and electronic commerce projects, advising on development of new digital products and services. Also advised on major contract and copyright disputes in the IT sector.
Prof. Memberships: News editor Computer and Telecommunications Law Review. Chair of the International Communications Round Table (ICRT) Copyright Working Party.
Career: Qualified *Clifford Chance* 1990. Partner *Allen & Overy* 1997.
Personal: Born 1960. Educated Queens College and Kings College, Cambridge University.

JERRARD, Donald
Baker & McKenzie, London (0171) 919 1000
Senior Partner of Intellectual Property and Information Technology Law Department.
Specialisation: Main areas of practice are intellectual property, information technology and competition law, including patent, trade mark and copyright litigation, technology transfer, computer contracts, computer disputes, and competition law (domestic and EC). Has acted for many leading companies in the Computer and Consumer Electronic industries (including Sony, Lotus, 3Com, Mitsubishi Electric) in corporate acquisitions and major infringement actions. Has written numerous articles on IP and IT law. Member of the editorial board of 'Computer Law and Security Report'. Editor "Protecting Computer Technology" (Longmans, 1985) and contributor to "Guide to Intellectual Property in the IT Industry" (Sweet & Maxwell, 1988). Speaker and Chairman at many conferences, especially on IT law, in the UK and abroad.
Prof. Memberships: Law Society, London Computer Law Group.
Career: Qualified in 1976 and joined *Baker & McKenzie* in 1977. Became Head of Department in 1983 and a Partner in 1985. Board Member, Federation against Software Theft (1988-91). Chairman, Fast Legal Advisory Group (1988-91).
Personal: Born 21st March 1950. Educated at Winchester College (1963-68) and Emmanuel College, Cambridge (1969-73). Leisure pursuits include swimming, tennis, watching most sports and landscape gardening. Lives in Greatham, near Liss, Hampshire.

KEMP, Richard
Kemp & Co, London (0171) 600 8080
Specialisation: Practice covers intellectual property, competition/EU regulatory and general business law for the full range of computer, internet, software, content and telecoms sectors, acting for both suppliers and acquirers.
Prof. Memberships: Law Society; Chartered Institute of Patent Agents; International Co. Editor of Computer Law Association Bulletin; Computer Law and Security Reports – Editorial Board Member. Profiled in '40 under 40' (Legal Business 1996); Guide to the World's Leading Patent Lawyers (1997).
Career: *Clifford-Turner* (1978-1984); *Hopkins & Wood* 1984-1991 (Partner 1985); (*Hammond*

Suddards (1991-1995 (head of IT Group; Founder Partner London Office)); *Garrett & Co.* (Partner 1995, IP/IT London Office Group Head 1996; IP/IT European Service Line Head, 1997). Set up *Kemp & Co* in November 1997 to specialise in computer, information and communications work – firm now has 6 lawyers and 10 staff.
Personal: Born 8th July 1956. Educated Oakham School, St. Catharine's College Cambridge, Universite Libre de Bruxelles.

MAHONY, Michael
Hammond Suddards, London
(0171) 655 1000
Specialisation: All aspects of legal work for users and suppliers of information technology products and services including intellectual property, licensing and distribution, development, systems integration, outsourcing, use of the Internet and services, telecommunications, broadcasting and dispute resolution.
Career: Articled Clerk at *Ashurst Morris Crisp* 1986 and Assistant Solicitor in 1988. Counsel *IBM United Kingdom Ltd* 1990 to 1993. Assistant Solicitor 1993 and then Partner 1996 at *Hammond Suddards*.
Personal: Born 1964. Resides in London.

MARSLAND, Vanessa
Clifford Chance, London (0171) 600 1000
See under Intellectual Property, p. 482

MAUGHAN, Alistair
Dibb Lupton Alsop, London (0171) 796 6004
Partner in IT and Telecommunications Group.
Specialisation: Acts for government departments (e.g. the DSS in Lytham St. Anne's, Inland Revenue), educational bodies and manufacturing entities nationwide. Involved in major IT PFI projects (BA – POCL, Home Office – Police mobile radio replacement project) Specialises in IT, multimedia and technology acquisition/ supply contracts. Work is mainly non-contentious and divided equally between major government contracts and contracts for private sector clients. Handled the Inland Revenue Information Technology Office outsourcing and the DVOIT privatisation (first privatisation of a UK government executive agency). Author of several articles on computer law and export controls. Has lectured on outsourcing of IT, multimedia, export controls and acquiring computer systems.
Prof. Memberships: Law Society, New York State Bar, NY State Bar Association, Society for Computers and Law, Computer Law Association.
Career: Qualified in 1987. With *Boodle Hatfield* 1985-89, then *Crowell & Moring* in Washington D.C, 1989-92. Qualified in New York in 1990. At *Theodore Goddard* 1992-93, before joining *Dibb Lupton Broomhead* in 1993. Became a Partner in 1994.

MCCALLOUGH, Robert
Masons, London (0171) 490 4000
Partner and Head of Information & Technology.
Specialisation: Specialises in computer and telecommunications disputes. Leads a team of contentious and non-contentious lawyers. Involved in project management disputes relating to software engineering, hardware and software procurement disputes, integration of mainframes and PC networks, etc. Has lectured

extensively for professional bodies, Government Departments, commercial organisations (eg IBC).
Prof. Memberships: Hong Kong Law Society; English Law Society; the N.C.C.; European workshop for resolution of telecommunications disputes and the Worshipful Company of Information Technologists.
Career: Qualified in 1975. At *Hill & Perks*, Norwich 1975-78. Member of Attorney General's Chambers in Hong Kong 1978-83. Joined *Masons* (Hong Kong) in 1983. Became a Partner in 1984.
Personal: Born 30th May 1950.

MILLARD, Christopher
Clifford Chance, London (0171) 600 1000
Specialisation: Partner in the Media, Computer and Communications Group; specialises in online services and the Internet, telecommunications regulation and contracts, data protection, outsourcing, computer procurement and distribution arrangements, software development and licensing, intellectual property rights in software and data.
Career: Articled *Clifford Turner*, qualified 1986; Partner *Clifford Chance* since 1992; senior visiting fellow University of London teaching LLM courses in IT Law and Telecommunications Law; president International Federation of Computer Law Associations; general editor OUP 'International Journal of Law and Information Technology;' board member Computer Security Research Centre LSE; board member of 'Cyberspace Lawyer,' 'Telecommunications Policy' and many other IT and telecoms journals.
Personal: Born 1959. Educated at Manchester Grammar school, University of Sheffield (1980 LLB Hons); University of Toronto (1982 MA, 1983 LLM). Married with two children, resides in London. Interested in music.

MONAGHAN, Iain
Masons, London (0171) 490 4000
Partner Information & Technology Group
Specialisation: Outsourcing (particularly of IT and telecommunications); systems integration contracts; electronic commerce. Involved over the last year in major outsourcings in the financial and industrial sectors; in research on the development of electronic tendering in public procurement; and in initiatives to bring enhanced electronic communications/information networks to the financial community.
Prof. Memberships: Law Society
Career: MA (Cantab)

NEWTON, Jeremy
Cameron McKenna, London
(0171) 367 3000
Specialisation: Principal areas of expertise are computer and telecommunications law. Workload is primarily non-contentious, relating to IT procurement and telecommunications regulation: includes advising on major software development projects, turnkey agreements, facilities management and outsourcing, together with electronic publishing, multimedia and the Internet. Lectured widely on IT and telecommunications and general IP in 1997-98, including: Internet update (*British Computer Society law and specialist group*), legal environment for directory and operator services (*SMI Conferences*), copyright aspects of

software contracts (*Central Law Training*), Year 2000 projects in the oil and gas industries (*EuroForum*), annual review of intellectual property law (*Central Law Training*).
Prof. Memberships: Law Society, British Computer Society (and Law Specialist Group), FAST, Society for Computers and Law, Computer and Law, Computer Law Association and National Computer Centre's Legal Affairs Committee.
Career: Articled *Slaughter and May*, qualified 1991; assistant solicitor *Slaughter and May*, 1991-94; assistant and partner *Pitmans*, 1994-97; partner *Cameron McKenna*, 1997 to date.
Personal: Married with 2 daughters. Lives near Hook, Hampshire. Leisure interests including literature, occasional marathons and spending time with his children.

NICHOLSON, Kim
Olswang, London (0171) 208 8731
See under Media & Entertainment: Digital Media, p. 568

PEARSON, Hilary
Bird & Bird, London (0171) 415 6000
Partner in Information Technology and Intellectual Property Groups.
Specialisation: Main areas of practice are intellectual property and computer law. Barrister in patent chambers then worked in Silicon Valley 1980-83, becoming involved in the start of the personal computer industry. Since then has represented a wide range of hardware, software and component suppliers. Work includes intellectual property and computer contract litigation and non-contentious issues. Author of 'Computer Contracts' (1983) and 'Commercial Exploitation of Intellectual Property' (1990). Contributor to 'Internet Law and Regulation' (1996).
Prof. Memberships: American Bar Association, Computer Law Association, Licensing Executives Society, American I.P. Law Association.
Career: Qualified 1976. New Court, Temple 1977-80; *Rosenblum, Parrish & Bacigalupi*, San Francisco 1980-83; *Arnold White & Durkee*, Houston 1983-90. *Simmons & Simmons*, London 1990-95. Joined *Bird & Bird* in 1995. Member of the Californian Bar 1981 and Texas Bar 1985; US Patent Attorney.
Personal: Born 1943. Holds BA/ MA (Oxon) Hons Physics 1965-69, and LLB (London) 1975.

REES, Christopher W.
Bird & Bird, London (0171) 415 6000
Partner in Company Department and Co-Chair of IT Group.
Specialisation: Principal area of practice is computer law covering all aspects in that field acting for both users and suppliers; including rights acquisition, licensing, distribution policies, data protection, database licensing, use of the Internet, joint ventures and M + A work. Experienced in multinational dispute resolution with Japanese and US suppliers. Author of 'Patents for Software: The Holy Grail for the Computer Industry' (Copyright World) and 'The Quest for Quality' (Law Society Gazette). Co-editor of "The New Law of Databases (Jordan, 1998). Presents two-day seminar: 'Negotiating Software Contracts'. Chairman of National Computing Centre's Legal Affairs Committee, Chairman of IBA Computer and Database Committee.
Career: Qualified in 1979. Managing Partner of *Bird & Bird* 1993-1996

Personal: Born 1955. Attended Christ's College, Cambridge 1973-76. Lives in London.

RENDELL, Simon
Osborne Clarke, London (0171) 600 0155
Partner and Head of IT and Telecommunications.
Specialisation: In addition to IT and telecommunications, advises on EC Competition law, UK Restrictive Trade Practices, Intellectual Property and all aspects of commercial law. Advises manufacturers, importers, distributors and OEM's. Advises on the Internet, multimedia software development, intellectual property protection, tendering for contracts, contractual negotiations, trade practices, unfair competition law and outsourcing and systems integration. For telecommunications, advises carriers, service providers and re-sellers, users of telecom services, radio-communication operators, satellite services operators, importers and manufacturers of such equipment and various businesses engaged in providing communication services. Advises on legal and regulatory issues and developments. Obtained the first UK international simple resale licence used by DTI. Consultant editor for IT Law Today and International Computer Law Adviser. Lectures on all aspects of IT law.
Prof. Memberships: FAST Legal Advisory Group, Public Network Operators Interest Group, Competition Law Association.
Career: Qualified in 1991 at *Hopkins & Wood*. Appointed Partner and Head of Department in 1991. Previously qualified as a Barrister in 1986. Joined *Osborne Clarke* as Head of IT and Telecommunications in April 1996.

ROBERTSON, Ranald
Robertson & Co, Technology Law Practice, London (0171) 731 4626
Specialisation: Focus of practice is IT/computer work, with over 17 years experience in this field. Advises a mix of UK and overseas user and supplier clients on computing, software, database and internet matters. Includes major IT procurement projects (outsourcing, software development, systems integration), distribution agreements, software acquisition and licensing, on line/Internet issues, database contracts, IP protection, Year 2000, data protection, hi-tech start ups and business ventures. Author of 'Legal Protection of Computer Software' and Computer Contracts section of Butterworths Forms and Precedents. Co-author of 'European Computer Law'. Editorial Panel of IT Law Today.
Prof. Memberships: Law Society, British Computer Society, Worshipful Company of Information Technologists, London Computer Law Group, Founder Chairman of 14 country pan-European IT Law Group/Europe network of which *Roberston & Co* is UK member.
Career: Legal Services Manager with CAP/SEMA systems integration group (1980-1987); Partner and head of IT groups at *Stephenson Harwood*, *Field Fisher Waterhouse* and *Taylor Johnson Garrett* (1987-1997) before establishing own firm in September 1997. Qualified 1980.
Personal: Born 23rd April 1948. Attended University of Auckland, New Zealand 1969-72. Lives in London.

SANDISON, Hamish
Bird & Bird, London (0171) 415 6000
Partner in Company Department and Head of Information Technology Group.

Specialisation: Main area of practice is IT law. Acts for both public bodies and private sector companies on IT procurement. Heads team representing CCTA (the Government's Central Computer and Telecommunications Agency). Intellectual property and multimedia work is also covered, especially advising on copyright law. Clients include Motion Picture Export Association of America and numerous scientific and technical publishers. European Counsel to Software Publishers Association. Co-author of 'Computer and Software Protection Law', 1989. Contributing Editor 'International Copyright and Neighbouring Rights', 1990. Lectures frequently in both UK and US. Appears on Legal Network TV
Prof. Memberships: Council of Intellectual Property Institute, FAST Legal Advisory Group, Intellectual Property Committee of the British Computer Society.
Career: Admitted to Washington DC Bar 1980. Qualified in UK 1989. Joined *Bird & Bird* 1992 as a Partner.
Personal: Born 1952. Attended University College School, London 1960-70, Jesus College, Cambridge 1971-74, then University of California, Berkeley 1974-75. Lives in Usk, Monmouthshire

SEDDON, Clive
Masons, London (0171) 490 4000
email: clive.seddon@masons.com
Specialisation: Specialises in computer and telecommunications disputes acting for a variety of users, suppliers and service providers. Increasing involvement in supporting I.T. project and contract management teams to avoid disputes. Leads *Masons'* team advising upon all aspects of the Year 2000 problem.
Prof. Memberships: Law Society; Society for Computers and the Law; Management Board, Construct I.T. Centre of Excellence; European workshop for resolution of telecommunications disputes.
Career: Articled *Mason & Moore Dutton*. Joined *Masons* upon qualification in 1987. Partner since May 1993.
Personal: Born 1962. Educated Wrekin College; Exeter University (1983 LLB Hons). Married. Resides in North Bedfordshire. Interests include country sports.

SEGAL, Arnold
Theodore Goddard, London
(0171) 606 8855
Head of IT Law Group
Specialisation: Computer and IT law including software licensing, distribution, copyright, hardware, maintenance, turnkey, facilities management, Internet and computer games. Has lectured frequently to professional audiences, user groups and law courses.
Prof. Memberships: Law Society, FAST Legal Advisory Group, Society for Computers and Law, BCS, FRSA.
Career: Assistant Legal Adviser/Company Secretary Alcan Aluminium. Legal Adviser Morgan Crucible. Partner *Spark & Co.* Established *Arnold Segal* in 1986. Joined *Theodore Goddard* in 1997.
Personal: Born 17th July 1943. Attended King's College, London. Leisure pursuits include travel, theatre, cinema and reading. Lives in London.

SINGLETON, E. Susan
Singletons, Pinner (0181) 866 1934
Senior Partner of firm since 1994.
Specialisation: Main area of practice is EC Competition law, intellectual property and computer law. Handles compliance,

competition law notifications, abuse of market power, licensing and EU law generally. Advises on ownership of rights, licences, EU intellectual property directives, general commercial law, agency (particularly Commercial Agents (Council Directive) Regulations), distribution and contract law. Acted in ready mixed concrete investigations and in various EC notifications. Author of 'Year 2000: Law and Liability' (Sweet & Maxwell 1998), 'IT 2000' (Monitor Press 1997), Financial Times Management Reports 'EC Competition Law' (2nd ed. 1996) and EU Intellectual Property (1996), Introduction to Competition Law', 'Getting Value from Professional Advisers' and contributor to 20 other books including Croner's:-'I.T. Guide', 'Europe' and 'Model Business Contracts'. Editor of 'Comparative Law of Monopolies' looseleaf and journals – I.T. Law Today and Trading Law. Writes and speaks widely on legal issues at home and abroad.
Prof. Memberships: Competition Law Association, Licensing Executives Society, Law Society, Society of Computers and Law, Computer Law Association and Institute of Export.
Career: Qualified 1985, having joined *Nabarro Nathanson* in 1983. Joined *Slaughter and May* in 1985, then *Bristows* in 1988. Established *Singletons* in 1994.
Personal: Born 14th December 1961. Attended Westfield School, Newcastle-upon-Tyne 1972-79, then Manchester University 1979-82 and Chester Law College 1982-3. Leisure interests include singing, piano, reading, writing and children. Lives in Pinner.

SMALL, Harry
Baker & McKenzie, London (0171) 919 1000
Partner in Intellectual Property and Information Technology Law Department.
Specialisation: Principal area of practice is IT Law, including computer litigation, software protection and IT contracts (especially outsourcing). Other main area of work is IP law, covering enforcement of IP rights, copyright and designs law and multimedia contracts. Acted in many significant computer systems and high technology disputes including amongst others Exel -v- Dun & Bradstreet Software and Vodafone -v- Orange. Contributor to Sweet & Maxwell 'IT Encyclopaedia' and author of numerous articles on IP and IT law for various legal periodicals. Regularly addresses conferences and is lecturer on designs on Bristol University Intellectual Property Diploma course. Expert to EU Economic and Social Committee on various IT and IP related draft legislation.
Prof. Memberships: Law Society, Computer Law Group, Patent Solicitors Association.
Career: Articled with *Linklaters & Paines* 1979-81 and then Assistant Solicitor 1981-86. Joined *Baker & McKenzie* in 1986 and became a Partner in 1989.
Personal: Born 20th April 1957. Attended St. Alban's Grammar School 1968-75, then Oriel College, Oxford 1975-78. Leisure pursuits include travel, railways, computers, books and sleeping. Lives in London.

SMITH, Graham
Bird & Bird, London (0171) 415 6000
Partner Digital Media Group.
Specialisation: Computer project disputes, commercial litigation in computer and telecommunications industries. Evidence, document imaging and computer records.

Internet law including domain name disputes, website advice, internet/e-mail use policies and regulatory issues. Intellectual property disputes. Gave evidence to the House of Lords Science and Technology Select Committee on Digital Images as Evidence. Contributes a section on Non-Contractual Liability to the loose-leaf "Encyclopedia of Information Technology Law"(Sweet & Maxwell). Editor and a co-author of the book "Internet Law and Regulation" (Sweet & Maxwell, 2nd edition December 1997). Speaks and writes regularly in the UK and abroad mainly on IT and Internet legal issues.
Prof. Memberships: American Intellectual Property Law Association. Council Member, Society for Computers and Law. Computer Law Association. Electoral Commerce Association Legal Advising Group.
Career: Qualified 1978. Joined *Bird & Bird* 1983. Partner 1985.
Personal: Born 27 September 1953. Educated Uppingham School, Rutland; Bristol University. Lives London.

STAUNTON, Paula
Osborne Clarke, London (0171) 634 1616
Specialisation: Information technology law/telecoms. Advising suppliers/users on all forms of IT contracts. IT support, software development, licensing, distribution. Recently reviewing and re-drafted IT supplier's standard agreements. Assisted telecoms supplier with university tenders/contractual negotiations for supply of telecoms services to UK universities.
Prof. Memberships: French Chamber of Commerce
Career: Bishop Fox's Girls Grammar School – Taunton. Richard Huish Sixth Form College – Taunton. Surrey University. Hopkins & Wood 1989-1996. Osborne Clarke 1st April 1996 -.
Personal: Married. Interests: Swimming, hill walking, cinema, eating!

TURNER, Mark
Herbert Smith, London (0171) 374 8000
Partner in Intellectual Property and Technology Group
Specialisation: Practice covers a wide range of commercial and intellectual property issues in the IT and new media industries. Specialist experience in information technology, Internet and online services, CD-Rom and electronic publishing. Clients include many internationally known businesses and organisations. Publications: Co-author of Butterworths 'Encyclopedia of Competition Law', chapter on licensing of intellectual property rights. Co-author of a chapter on complex licensing issues in 'International Technology Transfer' (Kluwer). Correspondent for 'Computer Law and Security Report'. Many articles in national, legal and trade press.
Prof. Memberships: International Chamber of Commerce, Committee on Telecoms and IT. Intellectual Property Institute, Multimedia Committee. International Bar Association. Computer Law Association.
Career: Qualified 1983. *Macfarlanes* 1981-1985. *Denton Hall* 1985-1995 (Partner from 1989). *Garrett & Co.* 1995 – 1997. Joined *Herbert Smith* as a partner in 1998.
Personal: Born on 3rd September 1956. Educated Latymer Upper School and University College, Oxford (Exhibitioner).

WARD, Conor
Lovell White Durrant, London
(0171) 236 0066
Specialisation: Partner in the firm's computers, communications and media unit. Work includes advising on the contentious and non-contentious aspects of systems acquisition and development; facilities management and outsourcing (including telecommunications services); electronic commerce and electronic data interchange; encryption technologies, anti-piracy and computer crime. Practises exclusively in the information technology field often where the technological issues are most complex. Cases in which he has acted include 'J Mc Conville & Ors v. Barclays Bank PLC & Ors', 'Stephenson Blake (Holdings) Ltd v. Streets Heaver Ltd', 'Novell Inc. v. Persona PLC', 'Computer Associates Ltd v. DVOIT' and 'R v. Richard Pryce'.
Prof. Memberships: The British Computer Society (where he sits on its Year 2000 Working Group), The Computer Law Association, member of editorial board of the Computer and Telecommunications Law Review published by Sweet and Maxwell.
Career: 1980-84 The Queen's University, Belfast (Law LL.B (Hons)); 1984-88 IBM United Kingdom Laboratories Ltd – development programmer; 1987 called to the Bar of England & Wales; 1988-1990 *Heald Nickinson* – assistant; 1990 to date *Lovell White Durrant*, assistant solicitor; 1994 admitted as a solicitor; Partner 1998.

WEBSTER, Michael
Rowe & Maw, London (0171) 248 4282
Specialisation: Computer & telecoms, software & service supply contracts, ranging from software development & distribution contracts, VAR & franchising, turnkey supply and system integration agreements, joint ventures, technology transfer, outsourcing & long term supply of services agreements.
Prof. Memberships: Law Society, Society for Computers & the Law, Computer Law Group, IBA Committee on International Computer & Technology Law, Worshipful Company of Information Technologists.
Career: Articled *Herbert Smith*, qualified in 1967, partner *Rowe & Maw* 1973. Long term involvement with specialisations has led to many invitations to speak and write articles on a number of topics such as liability arising from computer contracts, the 'Millennium Timebomb', outsourcing and joint ventures.
Personal: Born 1942. Educated at Berkhamsted School and Bristol University (LLB hons). Interests include tennis, long distance walking and tree felling. Member of The Honourable Artillery Company and Liveryman of the Worshipful Company of Upholders.

WESTMACOTT, Philip G.
Bristows, London (0171) 400 8000
Partner in Intellectual Property Department.
Specialisation: The full range of intellectual property work, contentious and non-contentious, with an emphasis on disputes involving, and advice to, the IT and computer industries. Has given evidence as an expert on UK IP law in US proceedings. Cases include, for the plaintiff, IBM v. Phoenix, Monsanto v. Maxwell M Hart and Monsanto v. Stauffer and, for the defendant, Smith Myers

Communications Ltd v. Motorola and Norton Christensen v. Foseco. Lecturer and marker on the Bristol University Diploma in Intellectual Property Law and Practice.
Prof. Memberships: Law Society, Associate of Chartered Institute of Patent Agents, London Computer Law Group, AIPPI, Society for Computers and Law.
Career: Undergraduate trainee at Tube Investments Ltd 1971-74. Joined *Bristows Cooke & Carpmael* on qualification in 1978 and became a partner in 1985.
Personal: Born 15th April 1954. Educated at Cambridge University 1972-75 (Engineering and Law). Enjoys sailing, walking, skiing and cycling. Lives in London.

WILDISH, Nigel D.
Osborne Clarke, London (0171) 600 0155
e-mail: nigel.wildish@osborne-clarke.co.uk
Specialisation: IT Commercial Law: acting for suppliers and customers in relation to a wide range of IT contracts, including systems and software development and procurement, networking, marketing and distribution agreements, outsourcing contracts and service level agreements. Electronic Publishing, Electronic Commerce and Internet Law: drafting and negotiating data provider and database publishing agreements, web development and exploitation agreements; advising on all legal aspects of the Internet, including contracts over the Internet, cross-jurisdictional liability and name/brand protection. Mergers and Acquisitions in IT, Telecoms and Electronic Publishing: due diligence, joint ventures, acquisitions and sales.
Prof. Memberships: IBA (Technology and Intellectual Property Committees) National Computing Centre (Member, Law Group) Computer Law Association
Career: Clare College, Cambridge. Partner: *Turner Kenneth Brown* (1974-1995); *Nabarro Nathanson* (1995-1997); *Osborne Clarke* (1997-).
Personal: Married with 2 teenage children. Active in squash, golf, cricket. Active member of Church of England. Member: MCC.

WORTHY, John
Denton Hall, London (0171) 242 1212
email: jnw@dentonhall.com Partner in Media and Technology Group.
Specialisation: Electronic banking, electronic commerce, Internet, IT system integration, software development, facilities management, encryption, export control; data transfer, data protection, multimedia; telecoms transactions and privatisations, joint ventures, regulatory issues, network services, satellite transponder leases, satellite construction and launch, satellite financing. Major clients include: S.W.I.F.T., Credit Suisse First Boston, Bank of Scotland and group companies, Springboard Internet Services, Daiwa Institute of Research Europe, Advanced Radio Telecom, Europay International.
Prof. Memberships: Law Society. Telecommunications Managers Association. Editorial Board, Computer Law and Security Report.
Career: MA, Law, Cambridge University. *McKenna & Co* 1983-92. *Allen & Overy* 1992-96, *Denton Hall*, Partner, 1996. In-house counsel at British Aerospace (1992) and News Digital Systems (1994).
Personal: Born 1961. Leisure: travel, skiing, walking.

The SOUTH

Clark Holt (Swindon) (1ptnr/1asst) Small commercial law firm with niche IT capability headed by the "enthusiastic" *Jeremy Holt*. Clients/Work: AIT Plc; a Government Agency.

The Law Offices of Marcus J. O'Leary (Bracknell) (3ptnrs/1asst) Have "amazing IT clients," and *Marcus O'Leary* is "focused on the industry and experienced." Move up the tables. Clients/Work: Hardware and software transactional and dispute work for internationally recognised companies.

Nabarro Nathanson (Reading) (2ptnrs/6assts) Described by some as "the best IT department in the south." *Tony Bailes* "knows his IT and is active in this area." Clients/Work: EDS; Siemens Nixdorf; Sun Microsystems Ltd.

Garretts (Reading) (1ptnr/3assts) The Reading office has performed relatively well. *Alison Harrington* was praised. Clients/Work: Research Machines Plc; Formida Software; Axxia Systems Ltd.

Paul Klinger & Co (Reading) *Paul Klinger* "definitely knows what he's talking about." Acts for Silicon Graphics where he is European General Counsel and maintains his consultancy association with Shoosmiths & Harrison. Clients/Work: Principally contract negotiating and drafting.

Manches & Co (Oxford) (1ptnr/1asst) *David Tighe* is considered "mild mannered and easy to get on with," and the firm's position has been strengthened by the acquisition of Morrell Peel & Gamlen. Clients/Work: Datasure; Research Machines plc; Staffware plc.

Osborne Clarke (Bristol) (2ptnrs/5assts) Operate a respected IT practice from their London and Bristol offices. Clients/Work: Advising the University of Bath on contracts for its BIDs on-line academic publications catalogue on the Internet. Advising the Wildscreen Trust on contracts for creation of Internet archive of endangered animal species.

Willoughby & Partners (Oxford) (4ptnrs/5assts) Increased in size since the acquisition of most of the staff of Dallas Brett. Better known for IP than IT. *Ben Goodger* handles the IT work. Clients/Work: Pitman domain name case; Prince domain name case; UK aspects of sale of major part of Wang to Kodak.

Anstey Sargent & Probert (Exeter) The only Exeter firm to be recognised as having an IT capability, they undertake software licensing, source code advice, internet advice, code ownership disputes and other general computer work. *Edmund Probert* is recommended. Clients/Work: Mainly act for software companies, particularly writers rather than distributors.

Boyes Turner & Burrows (Reading) (1 ptnr/1asst) IT work is done by the intellectual property unit. Clients/Work: Advising leading food distributor on major computer implementation project.

Burges Salmon (Bristol) (4 ptnrs/6 assts) Act for suppliers and manufacturers, with emphasis on non-contentious work.

Clients/Work: Science Systems Plc; Naafi; Ministry of Defence.

Clyde & Co (Guildford) (2ptnrs/3 assts and other fee-earners as needed). A strong international reputation based upon shipping and finance provides computer work for the Guildford office. Clients/Work: Act for suppliers, users, telecoms companies. Joint venture between domestic telecoms company and Scandinavian company for managed network services. Distribution work for suppliers.

Donne Mileham & Haddock (Brighton) (2ptnrs/1asst) Building an independent IT group to complement their IP practice. Clients/Work: Academic institutions; software infringement disputes.

Laytons (Bristol) (3ptnrs/7assts in IP/IT) Offer an IT service within a wide ranging practice. Clients/Work: Zuken-Redac Group; Somerfield; Smoby UK.

Lester Aldridge (Bournemouth) (3ptnrs/1asst in IP/IT) Deal with contentious and non-contentious matters for suppliers and users. Clients/Work: Cadre Ltd; Ibcos Ltd; ESSP Ltd.

Wansbroughs Willey Hargrave (Bristol) (1 ptnr/2assts) A "respectable and traditional" practice. *Alan Wood* is regarded as "good on the technical side of IP and IT." Clients/Work: IT advice to health service clients. Procurement of command and control system for an Ambulance Trust.

WALES, MIDLANDS and EAST ANGLIA

Wragge & Co (Birmingham) (1ptnr/6assts) Have "without doubt the best IT department in the Midlands," and *Bill Jones* is singled out as the leading IT practitioner in the region. *Sarah Sasse* enters the up and coming list for the first time. Clients/Work: AT&T; Albert E Sharp; Windsor Life.

Hewitson Becke + Shaw (Cambridge/Northampton) (6ptnrs/8assts in IT and IP) Have respected IP and IT practices which operate from the Cambridge and Northampton offices. Clients/Work: Microsoft Research Ltd; Pegasus; Novell.

Pinsent Curtis (Birmingham) (1ptnr/2assts) Have a good local reputation, and an excellent client base. Clients/Work: ICL; Lanner Group; Misys.

Dibb Lupton Alsop (Birmingham) *Neil Maybury* mixes IT work with his IP practice. Not yet regarded as major players in the Midlands IT market. Clients/Work: Acting for Cybermedia Inc on copyright infringement action of computer software; CDS.

Edwards Geldard (Cardiff) (1ptnr/3assts) Do respectable IT work from the IP department. Clients/Work: Fly Fishing Technology Ltd; Ensigma Ltd; general Year 2000 and EMU issues.

Eversheds (Nottingham) (1 ptnr/8assts: 4 p/t) Known for their outsourcing work. *Nigel Sternberg* spends 80% of his time on IT and telecoms work. **Clients/Work:** Driving Standards Agency; Nottingham Building Society; NatWest UK Purchasing.

Eversheds (Cardiff) (2ptnrs/2assts) Handle general IP related work, outsourcing and Year 2000 work. The office benefits from its national client base. **Clients/Work:** Pearl Insurance; Chartered Trust; Carlyle.

Morgan Bruce (Cardiff) (5ptnrs/4assts) A commercial practice with clients which require IT advice. **Clients/Work:** Admiral plc; BP; Target Computer Group.

The NORTH

Masons (Leeds, Manchester) (Leeds – 1ptnr, 6assts; Manchester – 1ptnr, 2assts) Have a "team of strong players," including the experienced *Shelagh Gaskill*, and the "efficient and tenacious" *Zoe Ollerenshaw*, who is recommended for her knowledge of outsourcing. **Clients/Work:** Leeds: outsourcing deals for ICI and Rolls Royce; advising major utilities organisations on IT procurement. Manchester: acting for The Co-operative Bank plc in its plan to outsource IT systems to IBM.

Addleshaw Booth & Co (Leeds, Manchester) (5ptnrs/9assts) *Ian Sampson*

"has good client relationships," and *Paul Bentham* is an up and coming name in IT. **Clients/ Work:** BBA Group; Newcastle Building Society; Tenhill Computers.

Oxley & Coward (Rotherham) (2ptnrs/ 2assts) Known for their NHS work and are "exceptionally good." The "friendly and efficient" *John Yates* is liked by competitors for his "constructive attitude." **Clients/Work:** £400m outsourcing contract between Cap Gemini and British Steel; £7m outsourcing contract for payroll service between consortium of NHS trust and NSA; representing NHS trust at mediation of £1m dispute with supplier.

Pinsent Curtis (Leeds) (4ptnrs/6assts) Have a credible IT practice and *Michael Peeters* has a "very good understanding of a broad range of IT" **Clients/Work:** Hackney Borough Council; DTI; Gremlin Group Plc.

Eversheds (Leeds) (2ptnrs: 1pt/t; 5assts: 3pt/t) Still a leading player but may miss the presence and "technical knowledge" of Dai Davis who was Chairman of the firm's National Computer Law Group. But do have an excellent client base of computer suppliers and acquirers. **Clients/Work:** Intentia; Pindar; Exel Logistics; Asda.

Dibb Lupton Alsop (Sheffield) Have a nationally respected IT and IP practice, acting for both users and suppliers. **Clients/Work:** ICI; Gremlin Inter-active; On Demand Information.

Halliwell Landau (Manchester) (2ptnrs/ 3assts in IP/IT) *Jonathan Moakes* is seen as "highly competent." Act for companies wanting to acquire systems, and suppliers and distributors. **Clients/Work:** Dedicated Microcomputers Ltd; AromaScan Plc; UMIST Ventures Ltd.

Garretts (Leeds) (2ptnrs/8assts) Undertake IT work from the IP department, including general IT and computer game work. **Clients/Work:** Consortium of Yorkshire Universities – Yhman Project; Confounding Factor; Mindseye Productions.

SCOTLAND

Maclay Murray & Spens (Glasgow) (3ptnrs/10assts in IP/IT) *Fiona Nicolson* is a respected IP lawyer who also undertakes IT work. *Gillian Cameron* enters the up and coming list for the first time. **Clients/Work:** Adobe Systems; Microsoft; Nominet UK.

McGrigor Donald (Glasgow) (2ptnrs/ 5assts) Combined IT/IP department, headed by *Shonaig MacPherson*. **Clients/Work:** Student Loans Company Ltd; Land Registry in Northern Ireland; acting for two major financial institutions in a unique mutual disaster recovery shared resource centre.

Dundas & Wilson CS (Edinburgh) (3ptnrs/6assts) *Lorne Byatt* is known for large scale work. **Clients/Work:** Bank of Scotland; Britannia Life Ltd; Memory Corporation Plc.

MacRoberts (Glasgow) (2ptnrs/5assts in IP/IT) The internet work of *David Flint* was singled out for praise. **Clients/Work:** Giltech Ltd; Challenger UK Ltd; Inner Workings.

Bird Semple (Glasgow) (2 ptnrs/8assts in technology and media) The firm and team

leader, *John Salmon*, are new entries to the list this year. **Clients/Work:** Red Lemon Studios Ltd; Grampian Pharmaceuticals disposal; re-organisation of Spektra Systems plc.

BAILES, Tony
Nabarro Nathanson, Reading
(0118) 925 4602
Partner and Head of IT Communications and
New Media Group.
Specialisation: Sole area of practice is in IT
disputes of all types, acting for a wide range of
major US and European owned multi-national
computer and communication companies,
including EDS and Siemens. Jointly led the
team acting for the major complainant in the
landmark Digital case before the EC
Commission. Acted with a fast growing
specialist team in relation to over 30 substantial
high-value disputes arising from systems
integration and software development
contracts, outsourcing contracts and PFI based
projects.
Personal: 15.05.51

BENTHAM, Paul
Addleshaw Booth & Co, Manchester
(0161) 934 6000
Partner in Intellectual Property Department,
Commercial Group
Specialisation: Intellectual property and
technology including patents, trade marks,
passing off, copyright and designs, trade
secrets and confidential information and related
areas of competition law. Particular expertise in
information technology contracts including the
acquisition of computer systems, the licensing
of computer software and outsourcing
agreements. Also has considerable experience
in technology licensing and advising on
intellectual property matters in respect of
corporate acquisitions and joint ventures.
Prof. Memberships: Licensing Executives
Society, Solicitors European Group and The
Society for Computers and Law.
Career: Articled with the firm and qualified in
1989 and became a partner in 1995.
Personal: Born 30th June 1964, educated at
the University of Leicester (1984-87), (LL.B
Hons, Law with French) Universite de
Strasbourg (Diplome d'Etudes juridiques
francaises). Leisure interests include foreign
travel and supporting Manchester United.

BYATT, Lorne
Dundas & Wilson CS, Edinburgh
(0131) 228 8000
email: lorne.byatt@dundas-wilson.com
Specialisation: Partner in Technology Law
Group. Main area of practice is intellectual
property with particular reference to information
technology and legal issues raised by the
increasing commercial use of the Internet. Has
advised on web-site design and operation,
internet set-up and operation, e-commerce, and
many other software development and licensing
transactions. Acts for a number of high-tech
start-up companies.
Prof. Memberships: Law Society of Scotland,
Society for Computers and Law, Licensing
Executives Society, Federation Against Software
Theft. City Disputes Panel "Year 2000" Working
Party.
Career: Attended Winchester College 1969-
1973; Pembroke College, Cambridge 1974-
1977 and University of Edinburgh 1977-1979.
Qualified *Shepherd & Wedderburn WS* in 1981;
Stagiaire, European Commission (DG-8) 1981;
Atlantic Drilling Co Ltd 1982-1986; and Acorn

Computer Group plc 1986-1990. Joined
Dundas & Wilson CS in 1990 as an Associate.
Partner 1997.
Personal: Born in 1955. Lives in Edinburgh.
Leisure interests include sailing, hillwalking,
archery, languages and travel. Has also been
recommended as a Leader in the Field of
Intellectual Property.

CAMERON, Gillian J.
Maclay Murray & Spens, Glasgow
(0141) 248 5011
gjc@maclaymurrayspens.co.uk;
Associate in Intellectual Property Department.
Specialisation: Specialises in IP generally and
IT in particular for a wide range of clients and
with a growing practice of internet related and
year 2000 work.
Prof. Memberships: Member of Licensing
Executives Society.
Career: LLB (Hons) Edinburgh University
(1987); Dip LP (1988); Joined *Maclay Murray &
Spens* in1996; previously Head of Technology
Law Unit at *Bird Semple*.

FLINT, David
MacRoberts, Glasgow (0141) 332 9988
Partner in Corporate and Commercial
Department.
Specialisation: Corporate and commercial
matters including commercial contracts,
patents, trade marks, copyright and other
intellectual property licensing, computer and
technology contracts, agency and distribution
agreements, restrictive practices and
competition law in terms of both EU and UK law.
Author of 'Liquidation in Scotland' (Jordan &
Sons Ltd, 2nd edition 1990); EU Competition
Law Section of Stair Memorial Encyclopaedia of
the Laws of Scotland. Extensive lecturing
experience on a variety of legal and IT subjects.
Member of Joint Working Party of Scottish,
English and Northern Irish Law Societies and
Bars on Competition Law (since 1981). Member
of CBI Competition Panel; Member of Law
Society of Scotland Intellectual Property Law
and International Relations Committees.
Licensed Insolvency Practitioner.
Prof. Memberships: Licensing Executives
Society, Insolvency Practitioners Association,
Society of Practitioners of Insolvency, Institute of
Credit Management, The Computer Law
Association Inc., Union Internationale des
Avocats, UK Association for European Law.
American Bar Association (Associate).
Career: Qualified in 1979. Assistant in
MacRoberts Company and Commercial
Department 1979-84 and Partner from May
1984. Admitted Notary Public 1980. Chairman
of Scottish Lawyers European Group 1985 – 1995.
Personal: Educated at the High School of
Glasgow 1964-73, the University of Glasgow
(LLB 1976 and LLM 1982), and the Europa
Instituut, Universiteit van Amsterdam (Diploma
in European Integration 1978). Director of
Giltech Ltd, The Shareholding & Investment
Trust Ltd, and Advoc Ltd.

GASKILL, Shelagh
Masons, Leeds (0113) 233 8905
Partner and Head of Information & Technology
Group in Leeds.
Specialisation: Industrial and commercial IT
outsourcing deals, information law, data

protection law, database design, international
data flows, electronic and new media and major
infrastructure projects.
Prof. Memberships: Associate Member of
BCS.
Career: Lecturer – Faculty of Law, University of
Leeds 1979-84. Qualified 1986. At *Dibb Lupton
Broomhead* 1984-1994 (Partner from 1993).
Joined *Masons* as a Partner in 1994.
Personal: Interests: opera and bridge.

GOODGER, Ben
Willoughby & Partners, Oxford
(01865) 791 990
Partner in Intellectual Property Department.
Specialisation: All aspects of I.T. multimedia
and Internet law; trade marks and brand
management; technology transfer and
biotechnology; other general I.P and
commercial law, including advertising and
trading standards.
Prof. Memberships: President of Licensing
Executives Society; Secretary: Society for
Computers & Law (Thames Valley Group); IPI;
SEG; TVCLA, INTA.
Career: Exhibition to Keble College, Oxford;
Frere Cholmeley 1986-90; *Denton Hall* 1990-93;
*Dallas Brett*1993-97. *Willoughby & Partners* 1997
to date.
Personal: Married with three children; plays the
bassoon; architecture; drama; drawing.

HARRINGTON, Alison
Garretts, Reading (01189) 490000
Specialisation: Practice covers all aspects of
computer and technology law including media
and communications. Areas of practice include
computer software development, systems
integration, network maintenance, information
provision, IT distribution, internet and new
media related work. Work also includes the
protection and exploitation of copyright, trade
marks, designs, patents and confidential
information.
Prof. Memberships: Law Society, Committee
Member Thames Valley Branch of the Society
for Computers and Law, Federation Against
Software Theft, the Intellectual Property Lawyer
Organisation.
Career: Qualified in 1989 – *Denton Hall* (1987-
1994). *Garretts* 1994 to date (Head of IT/IP
Group – *Garretts* Reading), Partner from
September 1997.
Personal: Born 13 July 1963. Educated at
Harrogate College/Harrogate Grammar School
and St Edmund Hall, Oxford University. Lives in
Henley-on-Thames. Leisure interests include
sailing, mountain biking and hill walking.

HOLT, Jeremy
Clark Holt, Swindon (01793) 617444
Partner specialising in computer law.
Specialisation: Advises on all aspects of non-
contentious work including software rights,
system purchase agreements and maintenance
contracts.
Prof. Memberships: Society for Computers
and Law, British Computer Society.
Career: Qualified in 1980, co-founded Clark
Holt, Commercial Solicitors in 1995.
Personal: Born 1956. Leisure interests include
military history, 5 a side football and reading
computer magazines.

JONES, Bill
Wragge & Co, Birmingham (0121) 233 1000
Partner and Head of Computer and
Communications Group (CCG), and of the
larger Intellectual Property Group of which CCG
forms part.
Specialisation: Principal area of practice is
information technology, including contract
negotiation, outsourcing and facilities
management, data protection, dispute
resolution, Year 2000, Internet, and intellectual
property issues. Also communications,
telecommunications, multimedia and
broadcasting. Acted for one of defendants in
'IBCOS' in Court of Appeal. Acts for a wide
range of well known supply side and user clients,
both nationally and internationally. Frequent
speaker at conferences and seminars. Author of
numerous articles. Co-author: 'The TRIPS
Agreement', ch in 'International Protection of
Intellectual Property', Sweet & Maxwell, 1997.
Prof. Memberships: British Computer Society;
The Society for Computers and Law; FAST
Legal Advisory Group; Institute of Trade Mark
Agents; Chartered Institute of Patent Agents.
Career: Qualified in 1984 at *Wragge & Co.*
Partner 1990.

KLINGER, Paul
Paul Klinger & Co, Reading (01734) 498765

MACPHERSON, Shonaig
McGrigor Donald, Edinburgh
(0131) 226 7777
Partner in Corporate Department, Head
Intellectual Property Unit.
Specialisation: Handles all aspects of
intellectual property and information technology
work. Advise on protection strategies, funding
for technology projects, licensing, research
contracts, litigation and dispute resolution,
expertise on software licensing, systems
developments and procurement, outsourcing
and facilities management contracts. Speaker
at Glasgow IT summits in 1993 and 1994, and at
the International Science Festival in Edinburgh
in 1992,1993 and 1994, Chicago 1996.
Prof. Memberships: Law Society (England &
Wales), Law Society (Scotland), Licensing
Executives Society, Royal Society, Scottish
Biomedical Association, Scottish Biomedical
Research Trust. Visiting Professor at Heriot-Watt
University, Society for Computers and the Law.
Career: Qualified in 1984 in England & Wales
with *Norton Rose.* Assistant Company Secretary
(Legal) Storehouse plc, then Legal Director of
Harrods 1987-89. Partner at *Calow Easton* in
London 1989-91. Qualified in Scotland 1991.
Joined *McGrigor Donald* in 1991 and became a
Partner in 1992.
Personal: Born 29th September 1958. Director
of Edinburgh Chamber of Commerce and
Enterprise. Recreations include theatre, opera
and reading. Lives in Edinburgh.

MAYBURY, Neil
Dibb Lupton Alsop, Birmingham
(0345) 262728
Partner I.T. and Intellectual Property Group.
Specialisation: Advises on all aspects of
computer and IT law both contentious and non-
contentious. Acts for many software publishers
both national and international. Regular speaker
at computer law seminars.

Prof. Memberships: Federation Against
Software Theft-legal Advisory Group, Society for
Computers and Law.
Career: Qualified 1969 with *Clifford-Turner* (now
Clifford Chance), partner *Pinsent & Co* (now
Pinsent Curtis) 1975-1995, joined *Dibb Lupton
Broomhead* as a partner 1995.

MOAKES, Jonathan
Halliwell Landau, Manchester
(0161) 835 3003
See under Intellectual Property, p. 492

NICOLSON, Fiona
Maclay Murray & Spens, Glasgow
(0141) 248 5011
See under Intellectual Property, p. 493

O'LEARY, Marcus
The Law Offices of Marcus J. O'Leary,
Bracknell (01344) 303044
Specialisation: Main area of practice is IT,
including the drafting and negotiation of
computer and software distribution,
development, tpm, outsourcing, evaluation and
licensing arrangements. All areas covered
especially multi-media, disaster recovery,
software piracy and hardware/software
disputes. Very active in providing advice,
documentation and support to companies
providing access to and utilising the Internet.
Other principal area of practice is intellectual
property where experience encompasses
copyright, design, patent, biotechnology, trade
mark, passing off, confidential information,
advertising, sales promotion, trade libel, music,
media and entertainment, franchising and
character merchandising issues as well as
intellectual property health checks and IP
litigation. Experienced in providing legal
services in connection with contractual and
licencing issues in the Asia Pacific area. Acts for
many well known international technology
companies. Author of a number of articles in the
IP/IT press and has been interviewed by the
BBC on software piracy issues.
Prof. Memberships: Law Society, Society for
Computers and the Law, British Japanese Law
Association and member of the legal advisory
group to FAST.
Career: Previously an accountant, called to the
Bar in 1984 and later requalified as a solicitor.
Manager of Legal Affairs at Hewlett Packard,
and an Intellectual Property Lawyer for the
United Biscuits Group. Formerly Head of IP/IT at
Garrett & Co. Set up own practice in 1995.
Personal: Born 31st October 1952. Educated
at London University and the Inns of Court
School of Law. Enjoys sailing, writing, and
learning Japanese. Occasional rock climber.
Lives in Eversley, Hampshire.

OLLERENSHAW, Zoe
Masons, Leeds (0113) 233 8905
Specialisation: All types of computer,
intellectual property and telecommunications
agreements for both end users and suppliers;
from advising on the terms of outsourcing and
facilities management contracts, software
licence, procurement and distribution
agreements, to advising on the acquisition of
intellectual property, multimedia titles and
technology transfer licences.
Career: Qualified in 1987. Helped to establish

the Intellectual Property Department of *Dibb
Lupton Broomhead*'s Sheffield office in 1991.
Joined *Masons* on the opening of its Leeds
office in August 1994.
Personal: LLB University of Sheffield. Interests
include travelling, hiking, mountain biking and
antiques. Lives in Sheffield.

PEETERS, Michael
Pinsent Curtis, Leeds (0113) 244 5000
Partner in Commercial Department, Leeds
Specialisation: Principal area of practice is
information technology law including major I.T.
procurement contracts, data protection,
telecommunications, electronic trading, software
licensing and distribution, and dispute
resolution. Other main area of work is intellectual
property law, particularly international software
copyright. Frequently addresses seminars and
conferences. Registered Trade Mark Agent.
Career: *Clifford Chance* 1986 until 1992, then
became Head of I.T. Law Unit at *Simpson Curtis*
in Leeds.

PROBERT, Edmund A.W.
Anstey Sargent & Probert, Exeter
(01392) 411221
Partner in charge of Commercial Department.
Specialisation: Intellectual property with
particular emphasis on computer software
licensing. Employment law, especially
negotiating and drafting employment contracts,
staff handbooks and advising on disciplinary
and redundancy procedures.
Prof. Memberships: Society for Computers &
Law; Employment Lawyers Association.
Career: Qualified in 1978 with *Anstey Sargent &
Probert* after articles with *Gouldens.* Became a
Partner in 1982.
Personal: Born 13 March 1953. Attended
Clifton College and Christ's College,
Cambridge. Leisure interests include
windsurfing, running, badminton, 'Tractions
Avant' and computers.

SALMON, John Alexander
Bird Semple, Edinburgh (0131) 459 2345
Specialisation: Non-contentious intellectual
property/IT, in particular software developers,
computer games, multimedia, biotech. Major
transactions include Red Lemon Studios –
publishing agreements for games; Spektra
Systems (software solutions provider) – various
contracts; Keith McMahon (inventor of medical
products) – deal with New Medical Technology;
KAC – deal with NCR; Rackwick – deal with
Bank of Scotland.
Prof. Memberships: Member of Law Society
of Scotland, Electronic Services Working Party,
Scottish Committee of Society of Computers &
Law, Scottish Software Federation, Interactive
Media Alliance Scotland.
Career: Joined *Bird Semple* 1995. 1987-1991
Edinburgh University, LLB (Hons). 1991-1992
Strathclyde University, Dip. L.P. Formerly IT
programmer/consultant.
Personal: Hockey for the firm and the Grange
Hockey Club in Edinburgh.

SAMPSON, Ian
Addleshaw Booth & Co, Leeds
(0113) 209 2000
Partner in Intellectual Property Department,
Commercial Group.
Specialisation: Acts for a wide range of
software suppliers (eg Oxford Molecular, Lynx
Financial Systems) and users (including major

PLC's and national financial institutions) on information technology contracts millennium and Euro compliance issues and Internet trading. Has lectured at Leeds Business School/Institute of Directors seminars, conferences in the UK and continental Europe and at Capitol University, Columbus, Ohio.
Prof. Memberships: LES, IBA, Society for Computers and Law.
Career: Qualified at *Baker & McKenzie* in 1987. Joined the firm in 1988, Partner in 1992.
Personal: Born 1960. University of Kent. Enjoys competitive distance running. Lives in Sicklinghall, North Yorkshire.

SASSE, Sarah
Wragge & Co, Birmingham (0121) 233 1000
Specialisation: Specialist in non contentious computer and IT related matters within the Computer and Communications Group. Wide experience of system supply agreements, software development, maintenance and support arrangements and facilities management. Other interests include Internet trading, domain name disputes, Year 2000 compliance and data protection.
Prof. Memberships: Member of Licensing Executives Society.
Career: Articled at *Macfarlanes*. Qualified 1992. Associate *Wragge & Co* 1996.
Personal: Born 1967.

STERNBERG, Nigel P.
Eversheds, Nottingham (0115) 950 7000
See under Education (mainly institutions), p. 292

TIGHE, David P.
Manches & Co, Oxford (01865) 722106
Specialisation: Main area of practice is IT, dealing with all types of non-contentious IT related agreements. These include software licensing, distribution and marketing agreements, software development contracts, facilities management and computer bureau agreements, system supply agreements, supply agreements for hardware and other equipment and support and maintenance contracts. An increasing amount of Internet related work. Corporate finance work, ranging from start-ups and venture capital deals to acquisitions/disposals and flotations, concentrating in the IT field. Also writes articles on IT issues.
Prof. Memberships: Society for Computers and Law.
Career: Attended Marist College, Hull and Trinity College, Cambridge. Qualified as a solicitor in 1982. At *Boodle Hatfield* from 1980-1985. Head of Legal Services at Logica plc from 1986-1988. *Manches & Co* since 1989. Partner since 1990.
Personal: Born 1 March 1958. Leisure interests include squash, cricket and skiing.

WOOD, Alan
Wansbroughs Willey Hargrave, Bristol (0117) 926 8981
Partner in Commercial Department.
Specialisation: Main areas of practice are computer and IT, competition and public procurement, and intellectual property. Acts for both public bodies and private sector companies. IT projects range from complex, high-value IT system procurements, with advice on tendering procedures, review and incorporation of technical specifications, contract drafting and award and ongoing contract support, to advice on standard supply, licence and maintenance terms. Also includes advice on public procurement rules, the Private Finance Initiative, out-sourcing and facilities management. Intellectual property advice includes IP protection, trade mark licensing and character merchandising, publishing contracts, multimedia projects, franchising and technology transfer.
Career: Qualified at *Linklaters & Paines* in 1975. With *Linklaters & Paines* 1975-1987. *Osborne Clarke* 1987-1997. Joined *Wansbroughs Willey Hargrave* May 1997.

YATES, John
Oxley & Coward, Rotherham (01709) 510999
Partner in Commercial Department.
Specialisation: Main area of practice is computer law, including computer contracts and disputes. Clients include national and international computer companies, health authorities, NHS trusts and other public bodies. Author of numerous articles on all aspects of computer law. Regular speaker on outsourcing and computer disputes.
Prof. Memberships: Council member of Society of Computers and Law.
Career: Qualified in 1984. IBM In-house lawyer 1984-87. Partner at *Theodore Goddard* in Computer Group, 1987-93. Joined *Oxley & Coward* as a Partner in 1993.
Personal: Born 8th May 1959. Attended Leeds University (LLB) and Oxford University (BCL). Leisure interests include mountaineering and rock climbing. Lives near Sheffield.

CONSTRUCTION & CIVIL ENGINEERING

RESEARCH: In compiling the tables, we consider all the information available to us, paying particular regard to the market research carried out by our team of ten qualified lawyers. (The researchers' details are set out on page three.)

The rankings, therefore, reflect the opinion of the marketplace as revealed by systematic and objective research: see page four. (Our research is audited every year by the British Market Research Bureau.)

OVERVIEW: The firms listed in this section range from niche construction boutiques to the largest City practices undertaking 'construction' for their corporate clients as part of a complete package of services. Unsurprisingly they do not have the same client profile or undertake the same work. Historically many firms acted for one sector of the market, either main contractors, sub contractors, employers, funders, insurers, etc. Whilst this is not as true as it was, many firms retain a bias towards a particular type of client. For these reasons several interviewees suggested having a number of separate tables. The majority, however, preferred that we retain a single composite table for both contentious and non-contentious work.

Masons have enhanced their position as the leading construction practice in the UK, with London, Bristol, Leeds and Manchester being joined by new offices in Dublin and Glasgow.

The big changes in London this year are the disappearance of Bristows (formerly Bristows Cooke & Carpmael) from the lists following the exodus of James Hudson and his team to Nicholson Graham & Jones. Tony Blackler's departure from Rowe & Maw was expected but his move to a non-leading construction practice – Macfarlanes – came as a surprise to many.

Whilst we have ranked the Birmingham, Leeds, Manchester, Newcastle and Bristol firms within their regions, many are doing work that London firms would be proud of. More often than not regional firms come up against London firms rather than their neighbours. As a general rule 'Leading' regional firms would be 'Highly Regarded' in London. Some firms could give the London firms stiff competition (such as Wragges in Birmingham, Mills & Reeve in Cambridge or MacRoberts in Scotland) and they have the added advantage of significantly lower overheads. In Scotland the *'Big Three'* (MacRoberts, McGrigor Donald and Dundas & Wilson CS) have consolidated their position at the top. However, as a surprise gambit, Masons has opened a Glasgow office and filched two of the top lawyers from D&W and McGrigors. They enter our tables at a high three and are expected to achieve significant inroads into the Scottish market.

Researching the Northern Ireland section posed some unusual problems. One interviewee commented that he was going to be less than candid because "in the Province you never know who's listening." The other difficulties are that it is a small, isolated and rather introverted legal market place, that has procedures peculiar to the Province. In consequence no mainland law firm would comment on the practices in Northern Ireland. At present there is little building work so the law firms rely on disputes for their bread and butter. No firm was thought to dominate the market. Indeed several leaders said it was unfair to rank the firms. Few do enough work to be called true construction purists and the material distinction between the firms was said to be cost. We have therefore listed the firms which were considered to have a good reputation in construction but have not compared them against each other.

LEADING FIRMS · LONDON

MASONS

CAMERON MCKENNA

ROWE & MAW

HIGHLY REGARDED FIRMS

Ashurst Morris Crisp
Berwin Leighton
S J Berwin & Co
Clifford Chance
Davies Arnold Cooper
Fenwick Elliott
Hammond Suddards
Herbert Smith
Linklaters
Lovell White Durrant
Nicholson Graham & Jones
Shadbolt & Co
Taylor Joynson Garrett
Winward Fearon

Berrymans Lace Mawer
Denton Hall
Edge & Ellison
Freshfields
Glovers
Norton Rose
Trowers & Hamlins
Warner Cranston
Wedlake Bell

Allen & Overy
Baker & McKenzie
Barlow Lyde & Gilbert
Beale and Company
Corbett & Co
Dibb Lupton Alsop
Manches & Co
Nabarro Nathanson
Simmons & Simmons
Speechly Bircham

Chambers & Partners

LONDON

Masons (22ptnrs/30assts) "Whatever you do in construction, and wherever you do it, you run up against Masons." Although they do have some serious competition, no single firm approaches them in terms of being able to deploy massed ranks of specialists across the full range of construction activities. At the moment it is hard to imagine who else could be No.1. Masons' reputation was built on its contentious work for contractors but over the last five years much of the UK contentious work has been moved to their regional offices. The London office now concentrates on matters which require big teams, deal with highly specialised areas (transport, process & energy, water, etc.), international work (where the majority of work is for employers) or disputes located in the South East. Head of department is the "cerebral" *Martin Harman*, although for many Masons is still epitomised by *John Bishop*, a man with "great vision and a mind like a man-trap." *Martin Roberts* "doesn't take dumb points" and *Mark Lane* "solves problems – if you can get him," the latter a fairly common complaint about the top lawyers at Masons. The "flamboyant street fighter" *Mark Roe* has "a good grasp of the crucial issues." *Phillip Capper* ("horribly good") is a new but obvious entrant to the lists. On the down side many interviewees suggested that, although the senior lawyers are superb, many of the foot soldiers are "average." **Clients/Work:** Advising the successful consortium for Nottingham Light Rail urban transportation project (+£150m); Campenon/Maeda Corporation joint venture in a dispute with the government of Hong Kong concerning the Strategic Sewerage Disposal Scheme.

Cameron McKenna (7ptnrs/18assts) The theory behind the merger was to combine the construction strengths of McKenna with Cameron's banking practice and stun the business world with a potent projects group. In non-contentious CMcK are "top quality," doing so much work that some practitioners claim to have built careers almost exclusively litigating documents bearing *Ann Minogue's* initials. On the contentious side there is a feeling that the merged firm might be on the way back up. Ann Minogue, "a million miles away from being a pushover," is "streets ahead of the rest" in contract drafting – "she's SO fast." *Peter Long* ("capable and clever"), *Trevor Butcher* ("the unsung hero") and *Henry Sherman* ("goes to the heart of the problem") are a little overshadowed but well thought of. **Clients/Work:** Acting for Prudential Assurance Company Ltd on all construction work, including shopping centre at Cribbs Causeway, Bristol and new business park at Reading. Advising on the extension to the Royal Opera House, Covent Garden.

Advising the trustees of the British Museum on all of the construction documentation for the Great Court Project at the Museum.

Rowe & Maw (5ptnrs/10assts) Describes itself as "a commercially minded practice that does not waste time and money running silly arguments." Everyone else agreed. If "you will have to work with your opponent again" R&M may be the firm for you. Described variously as "extremely good to deal with" and "always professional," other practitioners look forward to a sensible dispute with them. *John Rushton* heads the team which also includes *Michael Regan* ("exceptionally good...a real heavy hitter") and *Gillian Birkby*, "dedicated to her clients' cause." The sole criticism was that the firm "never quite put the boot in." It remains to be seen how the loss of Tony Blackler (previously perceived as key to the firm's success) to Macfarlanes will affect the firm's position. **Clients/Work:** Advising Guy's and St. Thomas' NHS Trust in dispute over the redevelopment of Guy's Hospital. Acting for Hayden Young in the dispute over airconditioning system in Lloyds Building, London. Advising on the construction aspects of the Laing/Serco joint venture for the refurbishment of the National Physical Laboratory.

Ashurst Morris Crisp (3ptnrs/10assts) A heavyweight City firm, best known for project and PFI work with blue chip employers and funders. But as they are also handling more than £100m of claims at the moment it would be wrong to write off their contentious practice. Not surprisingly there is a bias towards employers and funders but other clients include AMEY, Balfour Beatty and Robert McAlpine. *Chris Vigrass* ("sensible and thorough") joins the leaders list for the first time. **Clients/Work:** Several PFI projects that went to financial close, including Croydon Tramlink, DLR, Lewisham Extension, the A19 and M6 DBFO projects. Visag Power Project.

SJ Berwin (5ptnrs/10assts) A good set up and tipped as a firm to watch. Known particularly for their work with developers they have a good mix of contentious and non-contentious work. The team includes the "thorough" *Julian Critchlow* who joins our leaders list for the first time. **Clients/Work:** Triton Square development for British Land. King's College PFI project for Bouyges S.A. Acting for the Earth Centre.

Berwin Leighton (5ptnrs/8assts) *Terry Fleet* is a "social animal with a nice way about him" and "very client orientated." So are the people he has surrounded himself with. Noted for a "refreshing absence of over arching egos," at BL "everyone pulls together." This approach is paying off and the firm was described as "solid," particularly on the non-contentious side. *Michael Gibson* is also rated and *John Hughes-D'Aeth* is "definitely" up and coming. **Clients/Work:**

£300m New Parliamentary Building, Westminster. £80m new headquarters for the Department of Environment, Transport and Regions. £200m development of Greenwich Peninsula for English partnerships as part of the Millenium project.

Clifford Chance (4ptnrs/15assts) Just what you would expect: "solid...able...not likely to make mistakes...deliver the goods," but partners thought to be overstretched. *Tim Steadman*, who leads the department, is seen to be growing the practice and generating some "home spun" clients. To date they are mainly known for non-contentious work for employers and funders and for overseas projects. **Clients/Work:** Advising on $240m power project in Vemagiri, India. Advising Wates on the development of CityPoint, the largest office development in the City of London. Conducting an adjudication for Bangladesh Oil, Gas and Mineral Corporation in connection with delay to the completion of a gas treatment facility.

Davies Arnold Cooper (6ptnrs/12assts) To lawyers in private practice 'DAC' spells insurance. But if you ask some of the UK's largest contractors DAC is a "top firm" in pure contentious construction (60% of their construction work is not insurance related). Clients have a lot of time for *Danny Gowan*, "a straight forward fellow" who "knows what he's doing" and "isn't taken in by irrelevancies." *John Bolton*, an engineer and former VP of Foster Wheeler, also makes a great contribution. Practice is geared up to high value work rather than high volume. **Clients/Work:** Advising the Petroleum Company of Trinidad & Tobago in mediation and arbitration proceedings with a large Canadian contractor; Unites Utilities plc in relation to Bangkok Waste Water Project; The Professional Indemnity Insurers with respect to the Channel Tunnel and Heathrow Tunnel Collapse.

Fenwick Elliott (9 ptnrs/5 assts) A small niche practice best known for contentious work. *Robert Fenwick Elliott* (a noted individualist, "author of that useful book" and "one of the cleverest people around") is the firm's greatest strength and, perversely, its greatest weakness. Perhaps somewhat unfairly, the market perception is a one dimensional firm that lacks depth. In fact the firm does handle major disputes (a recent claim which ran for seven years was for £200m) and even the firm's detractors agree that "if Robert is handling the work his clients can sleep safely at night." **Clients/Work:** Advising the Oderbrecht Group on the conversion of an oil tanker in to floating stage in the North Sea (£110m in dispute). Advising Asia Petroleum Ltd on disputes on the pipeline in Pakistan from Pipri to the Hub Power complex ($18m). Advising an American/Japanese consortium in contract with the Malaysian Government to implement a Total Airport Management System (£100m).

Hammond Suddards (3ptnrs/9assts) Are there two firms called 'Hammond Suddards' in London? One is described as a "growing force," "doing really good stuff," "as good as anyone" and noted for a "sensi-ble, strategic, commercial approach." The other follows "an antagonistic style of litigation that went out in the 80s." Fortunately most people come into contact with the "nice" Hammond Suddards. *David Jones* is a "super guy," "switched on" and "always a tough opponent." The most successful of the regional practices, particularly in contentious work (75% of their total workload.) **Clients/Work:** Advising Kier in connection with challenges to an Arbitration Clause in respect of a civil works contract; London Underground Ltd v Kenchington Ford; Stachan & Henshaw v Stein Industrie UK relating to the construction of HRSG Boilers.

Herbert Smith (4ptnrs/10assts) Moving up a band from last year, the firm is seen working for the big players and making a good job of it. A typical comment was that "you don't want to get into a fight with Herbert Smith unless you're well organised." The higher profile is due in part to the firm's success in PFI and projects – and due to its already strong reputation for arbitration and litigation, particularly overseas. *Michael Davis* is a well known face on the construction 'cocktail circuit'. **Clients/Work:** Representing a major US multi-national in connection with an ICC arbitration against the supply of equipment in a plant in India. Litigation for Blue Circle defending claim over construction of the biggest waste-to-energy project in the UK. Advising Hammerson UK Properties plc in relation to developments including the Bull Ring Birmingham and The Oracle.

Linklaters (4ptnrs/18assts) Have had a great year, recruiting nine new assistants to keep pace with all the work, most of which has been non-contentious/major projects/PFI. Acting for major corporate clients, the firm was praised for its "efficient and fast service" and "for doing a bloody good job." *Marshall Levine* ("a lovely chap...typical Linklaters") and *Simon Burch* ("a great guy for a massive engineering deal") oversee a team which produces quality work. But with only four partners, they are spread thinly. Not so strong on the contentious side. **Clients/Work:** Instructions from Swiss Re, Merrill Lynch, ABN Amro and Goldman Sachs relating to the relocation or major expansion of their headquarters. Advising SmithKline Beecham on a major bottling plant development. Litigation disputes in relation to five power stations (UK and overseas).

Lovell White Durrant (6ptnrs/13assts) Once a serious contender, LWD lost a lot of people in the early 90s but are now firmly on the way back up. Strong internationally, the construction team (which forms part of a broader PFI & energy department) were praised for their "excellent" approach to litigation. *Nicholas Gould* heads the diverse team which includes *Iain Smith*, "the old campaigner," and "a very clever chap." **Clients/Work:** Engaged in five separate power station disputes including TBV Power Ltd and Tarmac plc v Elm Energy and Recycling (UK) Ltd.

Nicholson Graham & Jones (5ptnrs/6assts) *James Hudson* ("an excellent litigator") and his team might just be what NGJ need. It certainly looks like a good match. Bristows had a strong litigation practice, particularly for M&E sub-contractors, whilst NGJ under *David Race* were known for non-contentious. The merged practice should be a good all rounder but it is too early to say. **Clients/Work:** Project risk assessment for Blue Circle's £180m cement works in the Medway Valley, Kent; acting for Pirelli on disputes on major transportation project. Other clients inclue Eurotunnel Plc, Yanbu Cement Co.

Shadbolt & Co (7ptnrs/8assts/1consultant) Based in Reigate but with a City reputation. *Dick Shadbolt* "keeps a firm hand on the tiller." *Dominic Helps* is helping to increase the firm's profile which was not as high as the firm deserves given the amount and quality of work they handle. **Clients/Work:** Two ICC arbitrations over major hotel project in Egypt (claims over £10m); advice on $multi-million disputes in China. Team have advised on amendments to the FIDIC Form of International Construction Contract.

Taylor Joynson Garrett (5ptnrs/3assts) "Real contractors' litigators." *Christopher Bourgeois* is "a raw steak for breakfast kinda guy" but he gets results, as does *Peter Shaw*, although some thought they lacked the special quality of Freedmans, their former home. **Clients/Work:** Representing Welsh Water over £3m claims relating to defective design of water treatment plants; South Bank University over £3.5m claim relating to delays in construction of student accommodation.

Winward Fearon (7ptnrs/5assts) One of the problems with construction lawyers is they cover their opinions in caveats. "Winward Fearon tell it the way they see it." The "highly impressive" *David Cornes* ("a qualified engineer") understands the technical issues and *Richard Winward* "knows his stuff" too. A popular choice for small to middling matters but doubts were raised whether they had "enough bodies" for the big disputes. **Clients/Work:** Major power generation projects in Indonesia and India. BOT waste-to-energy scheme for a UK public authority.

Berrymans Lace Mawer (10ptnrs/6assts) Thought of as a good insurance firm although there are signs that they might be trying to move into pure construction. *Victoria Russell* was described as "extremely knowledgeable" and "meticulous." **Clients/Work:** Acted for defendents in action relating to the British Library brought by Dept. of National Heritage; involved in mediation relating to high profile public building in Berlin; successful litigation in Riyadh on a housing development.

Denton Hall (3ptnrs/8assts) *Julian Pope,* "a quietly assured lateral thinker" and "a genuinely decent guy," leads a highly able and much praised team that gets a lot of quality work. Particularly strong on the PFI side. **Clients/Work:** Acted for the Tarmac-led consortium on the first major PFI hospital contract to reach financial close. Acting for Skanska in the negotiation of agreements for the construction of a new headquarters for Reuters in Moscow. Acted for Cleanaway against ABB in arbitration proceedings arising out of construction of a hazardous waste incineration plant at Ellesmere Port.

Edge & Ellison (1ptnr/4assts) *Jonathan Hosie* is "a guy you can trust" who "doesn't waste time huffing and puffing." He has certainly put E&E on the map in the last two years but will need to do great things to live up to the marketing. Both Jonathan and E&E move up one band. **Clients/Work:** Acting for US Corporation in relation to claim under contract for supply of telecommunications equipment for oil rig.

Freshfields (8ptnrs/16assts – not all full time) "A big City player with a small construction department" *Sally Roe* ("fearsome!") fields some good people but not enough. Viewed as a practice whose work falls off the back of the firm's corporate clients, they are not seen as doing "hard-core construction," but what they do they do well. **Clients/Work:** Acting for consortium of European and Asian contractors in High Court proceedings arising out of the construction of the Iraq-Trans-Saudi Arabia pipeline. Acting for CSFB in connection with proposed acquisition of extension to existing premises by Canary Wharf Ltd.

Glovers (3ptnrs/3assts) The "gentlemanly" *David Miles* leads a small specialised team that "knows its onions." Although "experienced in quality work," the firm may be too small to handle a large case load. **Clients/Work:** For Fondelile Foundations in a dispute concerning a shopping centre in Sutton; for the appellant before the Privy Council in a dispute concerning a hotel in Grenada.

Norton Rose (4ptnrs/11assts) "A top ten firm but not a name that immediately springs to mind in the context of construction." *Peter Rees* (a first rate operator) and the "marvellous" *Martin Bridgewater* will be hoping to change that perception. Strong on the international side and recommended for doing a "thorough and competent job." **Clients/Work:** The Millenium Dome; advising CERN on a £1bn underground particle accelerator on the Franco/Swiss border.

Trowers & Hamlins (7ptnrs/5assts) *David Mosey* is pushing hard to establish a broad based construction practice. The perception at the moment is that "the reality is lagging somewhat behind the marketing" (except in the niche area of Housing Associations where Trowers is the market leader).

However, there is no doubt that David has built up a good team, including an ex-Tarmac man and the firm could quickly become more heavyweight in this area. **Clients/Work:** Acting for Tower Hamlets over largest UK urban regeneration project for refurbishment of up to 13,000 properties for the Poplar and Cityside Housing and Regeneration Community Associations (up to £510m); Metropolitan Housing Trust over Urban regeneration redevelopment of Chalkhill Estate, Brent.

Warner Cranston (2ptnrs/4assts) *John Wright* and his team are "effective," "have a good take on things," "give you a run for your money." John "always seems to have the right answer." Also described as "focused," the partners were praised for coming clean when they are too busy – "If a partner says he'll do the work he does. You don't find yourself shuffled off to someone else."

Wedlake Bell (2ptnrs/1asst) *Suzanne Reeves* is a well respected litigator. The firm beat some bigger names to win the Drake & Skull beauty parade. **Clients/Work:** Drafting documentation for a major US bank for out fit of offices and dealing room, plus installation of IT equipment. Acting for clients in relation to an action concerning damage to an historic building.

Allen & Overy (9 fee-earners dedicated to non-contentious, 3 to contentious.) Excellent firm but without a vast amount of construction expertise. Added four of their non-contentious associates this year. Although mainly known for non-contentious, A&O was recommended for its approach to litigation – "polite, dignified and sensible." **Clients/Work:** Acting for the Banks on the Istrian Motorway Project, Croatia. $465m Sutton Bridge Power Project which involved a novel construction structure using a 'turnkey wrap'. Acting for Oman LNG LLC on its multi-billion dollar two train LNG projects at Al. Ghalilah, Oman.

Baker & McKenzie (2ptnrs/6assts) *Jeremy Winter* is that "rare combination of a rocket scientist with a hard commercial edge," but the firm has lost a lot of senior people. **Clients/Work:** A2 Toll Motorway in Poland reported by the World Bank to be the largest infrastructure project currently being undertaken in the world; Cross Israel Highway – electronic toll road project. Representing Attiko Metro, owner/operator of the Athens Metro in responding to claims by the consortium of contractors building two new underground lines in Athens.

Barlow Lyde & Gilbert (4ptnrs/5assts) Handles a broad range of construction work. The team is described as "legally astute," "highly able" but "less commercial than some." **Clients/Work:** Acting for TML in ICC arbitration proceedings arising out of installation work in the Channel Tunnel. Acting for insurers in relation to allegations of defective deisgn and delay claims arising out

of a civil engineering project in Asia.

Beale & Co: (6ptnrs/5assts) A long established and respected construction practice. Particularly well known as advisers to engineers (the firm are solicitors to the ACE). **Clients/Work:** Acting for a group of consulting engineers against the Highways Agency, arising from the termination of road building contracts. Acting for a government agency and a local authority in an arbitration concerning coastal defences on the South Coast. Drafting the new Standard Conditions of the Accounts of Consulting Engineers for the ACE.

Corbett & Co (1ptnr/3assts) "If you can get Sooty he'll do a good job for you." Everyone who knows *Edward Corbett* (ex-Masons) speaks highly of him. He has "lots of energy," is "fun to deal with" and "knows FIDIC inside out." With a heavy bias towards international work, the firm suffers from low visibility in the UK and a perception that the '& Co' is decorative rather than descriptive. **Clients/Work:** Acting for The African Development Bank to prepare standard bidding documents for use by the World Bank. Advising SIETCO, the Chinese contractor, on the recovery of $4m form the Tanzanian Electricity supply company by means of negotiation or ICC arbitration.

Dibb Lupton Alsop Nationally, a large construction practice with 8 partners and 17 assistants (excluding those fee earners who do insurance based work). 3ptnrs/6assts are based in London. Other firms do not come across Dibbs often although those that did found them "unflappable and realistic." Overall the work is split evenly between employers and contractors/sub-contractors but in London there is a bias towards contractors. **Clients/Work:** Bromley Hospital PFI preferred bidder; ABB Power – advice concerning power distribution contracts.

Manches (3ptnrs/6assts) Have been hiding under a bushel. They have built up a portfolio of quality contentious and non-contentious work together with a formidable reputation in M&E (mainly in the Far East), water treatment and sewage. **Clients/Work:** Acting for Bouyues through its subsidiary Saur, for a significant number of the privatised water companies in England. Acting for the Jardine Schindler Group in SE Asia.

Nabarro Nathanson (8ptnrs/10assts) Have lost a lot of constuction lawyers over the last few years. It is too early to write them off but it is a long way back to their previous standing. **Clients/Work:** Continuation of major arbitration proceedings and numerous related court actions on behalf of Zanen Dredging against Costain and Tarmac arising out of the construction of the Conwy Tunnel in North Wales. Contract documentation for US$100m condensate refinery in the Gulf.

Simmons & Simmons (3ptnrs/5assts) *Robert Bryan* leads a small team best known for its work in the rail sector. The firm's reputation may be lagging behind their volume of work. **Clients/Work:** Advising Railtrack on £1.9 billion West Coast Main Line remodernisation project, part of £4 billion infrastructure maintenance and redevelopment of Paddington Station; advising the MoD on pathfinder PFI projects.

Speechly Bircham (2ptnrs/3assts) One of the chasing pack. **Clients/Work:** Acting for Kian Gwan – Greater London House on refurbishment/modernisation of 1920's building.

Helen Garthwaite, head of construction at Lewis Silkin, was also recommended.

BIRKBY, Gillian
Rowe & Maw, London (0171) 248 4282
Specialisation: Construction and Engineering Law, both contentious and non-contentious. Recently worked on probably the largest piece of construction litigation in the country. Expert in the application of the CDM Regulations (Health and Safety).
Prof. Memberships: ACIArb. Honorary Member of the Association of Planning Supervisors. Chairman of the Construction Industry Council's Task Force on Health and Safety.
Career: Joined the construction and engineering group of *Rowe & Maw* in 1982. Became a partner in 1988.
Personal: Walking, archaeology.

BISHOP, John
Masons, London (0171) 490 4000
Senior Partner. Chairman of the Board, and Partner in Construction and Engineering Department.
Specialisation: Worked on projects in over 20 countries in Europe, Africa, Middle East and Far East and has substantial UK practice. Major matters include LRTS and Second Harbour Crossing in Hong Kong, Cairo Plaza, Tiffany oil platform and the Channel Tunnel. Particular interests include international arbitration, ADR, cost effective litigation and use of technology. Non-contentious work includes joint ventures, all types of project documentation, BOT schemes, negotiating and drafting of contracts, insurances, guarantees, performance bonds, quality assurance, procurement, project management and project execution contracts. Contentious work involves litigation, arbitration, and ADR in the UK and internationally.
Prof. Memberships: Past Chairman (now President) of Official Referees Solicitors Association; Member of Official Referees Users Committee, OR's Rules Committee, OR's IT Committee, ADR Committee, Past Member Law Society Civil Litigation Committee, ICE Sub Committee on Expert Evidence, Founder Member of CEDR, previously served on (inter alia) Chartered Institute of Arbitrators' Committees on new forms of arbitration and ADR, British Academy of Experts Sub Committee, Blundel Memorial lecturer; Annual Address to NCG; Editorial Board of Construction Law Journal.
Career: Qualified 1971, Partner 1972. Admitted in Hong Kong 1983. Managing Partner 1986-1990 and Senior Partner from 1990.
Personal: Attended Sherborne School. LLB Hons Queen Mary College, University of London. Leisure interests include golf, fishing, riding, tennis and bonfires.

BLACKLER, Anthony
Macfarlanes, London (0171) 831 9222
Partner, Property Department.
Specialisation: Tony Blackler graduated from Downing College, Cambridge, as a Harris Scholar in law, and qualified as a solicitor in 1967. He has since specialised in construction law, initially on the contentious side, where he has been involved over the years in major disputes before the courts and in arbitration. More recently he has become involved in front-end work, negotiating contract documentation and advising on procurement generally. Until recently he chaired a sub-committee of the International Bar Association's Committee T (International Construction Projects). He is a lecturer, and currently writes a column for Building magazine. He was the principal author of a book published by Sweet & Maxwell on the JCT Management Contract. He is a trained and accredited mediator, and undertakes mediations when he is available to do so. He has advised a number of industry bodies in recent years about the legislation affecting construction contracts which is now embodied in the Housing Grants, Construction & Regeneration Act 1996.

BOLTON, John
Davies Arnold Cooper, London (0171) 936 2222
Partner in Construction Department.
Specialisation: Principal area of practice is construction and energy litigation and arbitration within the UK and overseas, representing contractors, engineers, architects and owners in construction and process plant disputes. Has 25 years' practical experience in the construction industry. Construction management expert with expertise in project control systems and contractual and construction management formulations for large industrial turnkey projects. Has prepared detailed claims for disruption and delay and acted as an expert witness. Involved in projects in the USA, UK, Turkey, Tunisia and South Africa. Major cases handled include Royal Bank of Scotland v. Allianz Etal; Circle Ltd Partnership v. Bovis International Inc. and Trafalgar House Construction Ltd; and Makers Industrial v. London Borough of Lambeth. Author of articles on delay and disruption, fast track project management and negotiating techniques in the construction industry. Lectures frequently for the Chartered Institute of Arbitrators on award writing and managing arbitrations. Currently an assessor of Lord Woolf's Committee on Access to Justice and review of civil litigation procedure.
Prof. Memberships: Chartered Institute of Arbitrators, Law Society.
Career: Construction industry experience includes Andco Incorporated (Group Financial Director); Andreco Incorporated (Managing Director); and Andreco Anderson Incorporated (Executive Vice President). Qualified as a solicitor in 1987 and joined *Davies Arnold Cooper*, becoming a Partner in 1991.
Personal: Born 29th September 1943. Attended Canisus College, Buffalo, New York. Leisure pursuits include golf. Lives in Bristol.

BOURGEOIS, Christopher
Taylor Joynson Garrett, London (0171) 353 1234
Partner in Construction and Engineering Department.
Specialisation: Principal area of practice is construction and engineering, and on and off-shore contract law. Advises employers, main contractors, specialist subcontractors, professionals and insurers on all forms of contract, standard form and 'bespoke', and all points of practice and procedure. ADR and mediaion. Clients include national and international construction and engineering companies (including process engineering), UK and foreign companies engaged in the manufacture of electrical and other technical components, UK and foreign government agencies, water companies, professional indemnity insurers, health trusts and developers. Lectures to local authorities, architects, engineers, quantity surveyors and management on building and engineering contracts, contentious and non-contentious matters, company reorganisations.
Prof. Memberships: Society of Construction Law, Worshipful Company of Arbitrators. Fellow of the Chartered Institute of Arbitrators.
Career: Qualified in 1975. Joined *Freedmans* in 1977 and became a Partner in 1979.
Personal: Born 17th May 1946. Leisure interests include shooting, vintage car and property restoration. Lives in Bookham, Surrey.

BRIDGEWATER, Martin
Norton Rose, London (0171) 283 6000
Partner in Construction and Engineering Group.
Specialisation: Main area of practice covers non-contentious construction work and engineering contract work, both UK and International, and associated project finance and export credit arrangements. Generally advises developers or contractors on major UK building projects and banks or sponsors on infrastructure, process plant and independent power projects.
Prof. Memberships: International Bar Association, Society of Construction Lawyers.
Career: Qualified in England and Wales in 1976, and in Hong Kong in 1978. Joined *Nabarro Nathanson* in 1980, became a Partner in 1984 and headed their Construction Department from 1986-1997. Joined *Norton Rose* in 1997.

BRYAN, Robert
Simmons & Simmons, London (0171) 628 2020
Partner and Head of Construction Group.
Specialisation: Main field of activity concerns contentious and non- contentious construction law. Non-contentious work includes the preparation of and advice on construction contracts, consultant's appointments, collateral warranties, bonds, guarantees and other related documentation on a wide variety of projects for developers, funders, contractors and consultants both in the UK and overseas. Contentious work has been of an equally varied nature, with the resolution of disputes either by High Court litigation, domestic and international arbitration

or ADR. Approved ORSA Adjudicator. Author of articles for the Pipeline Industries Guild and *British Property Review* and the publication of the firm's quarterly Construction Law Newsletter.
Prof. Memberships: Society of Construction Law, Official Referees' Solicitor's Association.
Career: Qualified in 1981. Joined *Simmons & Simmons* in 1985, becoming a Partner in 1987.
Personal: Born 6th March 1955. Holds a BA (Hons) in Law.

BUNCH, Anthony
Masons, London (0171) 490 4000
Partner in Construction and Engineering Department.
Specialisation: Has experience in all aspects of contentious and non-contentious matters relating to construction law. Has drafted a full range of contracts for major projects (including BOT schemes) in the UK and the Far East on behalf of employers, major contractors and international consultants. Has conducted proceedings to all levels, including the House of Lords, and in other countries including Hong Kong, Singapore and China. Also handles arbitration and ADR work. Acted in the Channel Tunnel House of Lords case. Author of numerous articles on dispute resolution and in particular ADR. Joint author on the chapter on Hong Kong in the International Handbook on Commercial Arbitration and the specialist chapter on construction issues. Speaks widely on construction issues. Member of the Departmental Advisory Committee on the new Arbitration Act 1996.
Prof. Memberships: Chartered Institute of Arbitrators.
Career: Qualified in 1978, having joined *Masons* in 1976. Became a Salaried Partner in 1980 and Equity Partner in 1982. Admitted as a Solicitor in Hong Kong in 1985; Senior resident Partner in Hong Kong office 1985-90. Became Managing Partner in 1991.
Personal: Born 8th February 1953. Holds a BA (Hons) from Nottingham. Leisure interests include cycling, music and theatre. Lives in Radlett, Herts.

BURCH, Simon
Linklaters, London (0171) 456 3582
Partner in Construction & Engineering Unit, Commercial Property Department.
Specialisation: Has been involved in a wide range of major construction projects in the UK and abroad. Highly experienced in drafting and advising on concession agreements, construction contracts and other project-related contracts such as operations and maintenance agreements, fuel supply and facilities management agreements. Also advises on resolution of disputes over a wide variety of projects including substantial commercial office redevelopments, civil engineering projects, power station projects, industrial petrochemical projects and offshore projects. Qualified 1974 (New Zealand), 1991 (UK).

BUTCHER, Trevor
Cameron McKenna, London
(0171) 367 3000
Partner in Projects Group.
Specialisation: Main areas of practice are construction and major projects, particularly private finance work in the UK and internationally including central and eastern Europe. Particular specialisation in infrastructure projects especially roads, rail, water and power. During 1994 based

in Hong Kong advising the Hong Kong Government on projects related to the new airport. Worked on numerous DBFO Roads Projects in the UK and overseas. Author of various articles and speaker at a number of conferences on subjects including project management, construction in the former Soviet Union, partnering and DBFO Roads.
Career: Qualified in 1986, having joined *McKenna & Co.* in 1984. Became a Partner in 1992.
Personal: Born 10th February 1960. Graduated from Leicester University in 1983.

CAPPER, Phillip
Masons, London (0171) 490 4000
See under Arbitration, p. 117

CORBETT, Edward
Corbett & Co, Teddington (0181) 943 9885
Specialisation: Active in the UK and all over the world advising contractors, clients, consultants and others on building and civil engineering procurement, contract preparation and negotiation, on dispute avoidance, management and resolution including mediation, adjudication and, if unavoidable, arbitration. Author of 'FIDIC 4th – A Practical Legal Guide'. Regular seminar speaker.
Prof. Memberships: FCIArb, SCL, IBA Committee T – Chair, FIDIC Sub-committee, ORSA, Affiliate Member of FIDIC, FIDIC Mediator and Adjudicator, AAA Panellist. Former partner at Masons.
Personal: Born 10th September 1957. MSc in Construction Law and Arbitration, King's College. MA Jurisprudence, Oxford; Accredited Adjudicator and Mediator. Keen sailor and windsurfer.

CORNES, David L.
Winward Fearon, London (0171) 420 2800
Founding Partner.
Specialisation: Gives advice to those involved in building, civil engineering and the construction professions (architects, engineers and quantity surveyors) and their insurers. Handles High Court and arbitration work, including abroad. Involved in major non-contentious projects including private finance. Author of 'Design Liability in the Construction Industry', contributor to 'Construction Contract Policy'. Joint author of 'Collateral Warranties'. CEDR Mediator. Arbitrator. Regular speaker at conferences in the UK and occasionally abroad.
Prof. Memberships: Fellow of the Institution of Civil Engineers, Fellow of the Chartered Institute of Arbitrators, Law Society, Society of Construction Law, Official Referees Solicitors Association, International Bar Association.
Career: Qualified in 1979. Worked with contractors and consulting engineers before joining *Masons* in 1976. Partner *Fenwick Elliott & Co.*, 1982-85, before founding *Winward Fearon* in 1986.
Personal: Born 31st August 1944. Attended King's College, University of London. Member of Electoral Reform Society and Charter 88. Leisure interests include walking, travelling, opera. Lives Berkhamsted, Herts.

CRITCHLOW, Julian
S J Berwin & Co, London
+44 (0)171 533 2222
Specialisation: Partner specialising in both non-contentious and contentious construction matters with particular emphasis on the

construction aspects of infrastructure projects and on arbitration. Author of Making Partnering Work in the Construction Industry (Chandos 1998), Co-editor of Construction Law Newsletter (LLP), Arbitration Editor of Amicus Curiae.
Prof. Memberships: Fellow of the Chartered Institute of Arbitrators; CEDR accredited mediator; ORSA registered adjudicator; Associate Fellow of the Society for Advanced Legal Studies; member of ORSA; member of the Arbitration Club, member of the American Judicature Society; member of King's College Construction Law Association; adviser on civil litigation on LPC course, London Guildhall University.
Career: Qualified 1984. University College London (LL.B. 1981). King's College London (M.Sc. 1993). King's College London (Ph.D. commenced 1994). Articled *Field Fisher and Martineau*.
Personal: Born 1958. Married, two children. Leisure interests include riding, shooting, English poetry.

DAVIS, Michael E.
Herbert Smith, London (0171) 374 8000
Specialisation: Has specialised in major national and international construction and civil engineering projects since qualification, advising and conducting construction and civil engineering disputes both within the English jurisdiction and in international arbitrations worldwide. He is also responsible for the preparation and negotiation of contracts for all aspects of construction and civil engineering projects acting on behalf of all sectors of the industry, project companies and banks and has advised in numerous projects both nationally and internationally including a number of major infrastructure projects.
Prof. Memberships: Law Society, City Solicitors Company, International Bar Association, Society of Construction Law, United Kingdom Energy Lawyers Group, British Academy of Experts, Founder Member of the Centre for Dispute Resolution (Alternative Dispute Resolution), Founder Member of the City Disputes Panel.
Career: Qualified in 1977, became a partner in 1986, head of construction and civil engineering law 1986. Lectured widely in respect of construction, civil engineering and arbitration, including the International Bar Association and the Law Society Commerce and Industry Group and most recently published a paper in the Sweet Lectures "Comparative Studies in Construction Law" entitled "Choice of Law Rules in International Construction Contracts". Born 14th August 1951, educated BA (London).

EDWARDS, Anthony A.
D J Freeman, London (0171) 583 4055
Partner and Senior Construction Lawyer.
Specialisation: Construction Law. Principally dispute resolution and claims work but also extensive contract advice and drafting experience. Principal client base – employers, developers, investors, and public authorities, but also advises contractors, consultants and their insurers. Covers domestic and international claims. Led the Eagle Star building law team in the Carlton Gate Action by John Mowlem. More recently advising on dispute resolution of town centre redevelopment claims and ADR for high profile London 'south bank' projects. Promotes successful use of computerised Litigation Support techniques in

construction disputes.
Career: Qualified at Masons 1976, partner
1978. Joined *D J Freeman* as partner in 1986.
Prof. Memberships: Law Society.
Personal: Born October 1949. Educated at
Llandovery College and St Johns College
Cambridge (MA). Interests embrace the
classical choral tradition, the garden and family.
Lives in the Kent High Weald.

FENWICK ELLIOTT, Robert J.
Fenwick Elliott, London (0171) 956 9354
Senior Partner in Construction Department.
Specialisation: Senior Partner of firm, which
specialises in construction law. Emphasis on
resolution of disputes in the area of building and
civil engineering contracts. Also advises on the
drafting of building contracts. Has handled
many large cases, including Norwich Union v.
Schal. Editor of the 'Construction Industry Law
Letter'. Author of 'Building Contract Litigation'
and 'Building Contract Disputes: Practice and
Precedents'. Accredited ORSA, CIC, CIOB
Adjudicator. Qualified CEDR mediator.
Prof. Memberships: ORSA (Official Referees
Solicitors Association) Committee Member.
Society of Construction Law Member.
Career: Qualified 1977. Worked at *Masons*
from 1976 to 1980 before founding *Fenwick
Elliott* in 1980.
Personal: Born 17th March 1952. Attended
Eastbourne College 1965-69, then the University
of Kent 1969-72. Leisure interests include music
and motorbikes. Lives in London.

FLEET, Terry
Berwin Leighton, London +44 171 760 1000
Partner in Construction Department.
Specialisation: Principal area of practice is
construction law advising on building and civil
engineering projects in the UK and
internationally, including procurement strategy,
contract drafting and negotiation, bonds,
warranties, insurance, contract advice and
dispute resolution. Has advised in connection
with major projects in the UK, the Carribean,
Europe (including Eastern Europe), Africa, the
Middle East and the Far East. Currently involved
in the New Parliamentary Building, major office
and retail developments in the UK, and projects
in Hungary, Poland, and Russia. Clients include
institutions, government departments, funders,
developers, major construction and engineering
companies and professional architectural and
civil engineering consultants. Has written
articles in *Construction Law*, *Building*, *Property
Week*, *Estates Gazette* and *Chartered Surveyor
Weekly*. Speaks at conferences on construction
law matters.
Prof. Memberships: The Law Society,
International Bar Association and Society of
Construction Law.
Career: Qualified in 1980. Articled at *Heald &
Nickinson* 1977-79 and moved to *Speechly
Bircham* 1979-80. Legal Advisor to Costain
Group 1980-82, Babcock International 1982-84
and Cementation International, (Trafalgar
House) 1984-87. Joined *Berwin Leighton* in
1987 before becoming a Partner in 1988.
Personal: Born 1954. Attended Southampton
University (graduated 1976 LLB Hons.). Leisure
interests include flying, travel and family. Lives in
Twickenham.

GARTHWAITE, Helen
Lewis Silkin, London (0171) 227 8000
Specialisation: All aspects of construction
contract drafting, negotiation and advice,
drafting and advising in connection with project
finance and security taking; advising on day to
day contract administration issues and on their
solution including arbitration and dispute
resolution. Has acted for a wide range of
corporations and institutions owning, occupying
and investing in commercial property and
involved in development projects in the office,
retail, industrial and leisure sectors and
engaged in civil engineering projects. Writes
and lectures regularly. Joint Editor of
Construction, Law and the Environment.
Prof. Memberships: Council Member, Society
of Construction Law; Associate, Chartered
Institute of Arbitrators.
Career: Qualified 1990. Solicitor, *Nabarro
Nathason* 1990-1996. Partner and Head of
Construction and Engineering Unit, *Lewis Silkin*
1996.
Personal: M.Sc. Construction Law and
Arbitration (1992). Interests include yachting.
Resides in Westminster.

GIBSON, Michael R.
Berwin Leighton, London +44 171 760 1000
Partner.
Specialisation: All aspects of law and practice
relating to construction procurement and
process engineering in the UK and
internationally, advising authorities, developers,
funds, Government agencies, Health Trusts,
contractors and designers on contracts for
design, construction, financing and facilities
management of major building and engineering
projects and resolution of disputes arising from
them. Significant involvement with projects
assembled under the Government's Private
Finance Initiative.
Prof. Memberships: Society of Construction
Law.
Career: Admitted in 1977. Legal department of
Costain Group 1975-78. Head of Legal
Department, Construction Division, Trafalgar
House plc, 1981-87. Joined *Berwin Leighton* in
1987.
Personal: Born 19th February 1952. Educated
at St. Edward's School, Oxford 1965-70 and
Southampton University 1970-74. Lives in
Oxshott, Surrey.

GOULD, R. Nicholas H.
Lovell White Durrant, London
(0171) 236 0066
Specialisation: Principal area of practice is
construction, with particular emphasis on
engineering and international projects and
energy. Has drafted, advised on, and helped
resolve disputes on a wide range of
construction, project, engineering and energy
contracts over 30 years in the UK and many
overseas countries. Has experience of project
finance and of all forms of dispute resolution.
Co-authored the book "International
Commercial Arbitration" (LLP 1996).
Prof. Memberships: Law Society, International
Bar Association, (Member of the Council of the
Section on Business Law and immediate past
Co-Chairman of the International Contruction
Projects Committee), Fellow of the Chartered
Institute of Arbitrators and Associate of the

Chartered Institute of Patent Agents.
Career: Qualified in 1967 with *Lovell White &
King* (now *Lovell White Durrant*) became a
partner in 1971. Established construction and
engineering practice in the late 1960s.

GOWAN, Daniel
Davies Arnold Cooper, London
(0171) 936 2222
Partner in Construction Department.
Specialisation: Handles all aspects of
contentious and non-contentious construction
work, contract drafting and reviewing, joint
ventures, arbitration and litigation. Experienced
in mechanical and civil engineering and
building. Also handles construction insurance,
including professional indemnity, contractors all
risks and public liability claims. Acted for Laing
Management Ltd in Chelsea & Westminster
Hospital dispute; Petrotrin (Trinidad) in dispute
with SNC Lavalin; PI insurers in Heathrow Tunnel
collapse and Eurotunnel disputes; Project Insurer
on Hong Kong Airport. Has spoken on many
publicly-paid-for seminars for Hawkesmere, and
for a number of in-house seminars and
presentations to the construction industry.
Prof. Memberships: Fellow, Chartered
Institute of Arbitrators; Current Secretary of
London Branch.
Career: Qualified in New Zealand in 1976, and
in England in 1983. Worked at *Meredith Connell
& Co.*, New Zealand, 1975-78, then *Freedman &
Co.*, London, 1980-83. Joined *Davies Arnold
Cooper* in 1983, becoming a Partner in 1987.
Personal: Born 2nd October 1951. Leisure
interests include cricket, tennis, golf, theatre,
opera, music and reading. Lives in Rotherwick,
Hampshire.

HARMAN, Martin
Masons, London (0171) 490 4000
Partner and Head of Construction and
Engineering Practise Area.
Specialisation: Main area of practice is
engineering and construction, covering
contentious (litigation, arbitration and
mediation) and non-contentious (drafting
construction and related contracts) work.
Particular focus upon international major
infrastructure projects. Advising various
international entities, both governmental and
private, upon the privitisation of major
infrastructure projects and in that capacity,
advising upon contract procurement strategy
and drafting of project documentation. Has
undertaken international arbitrations in Hong
Kong, Singapore, Egypt, Kuwait, Yemen,
Pakistan and India, with particular emphasis
upon ICC arbitrations. Author of various articles
on International arbitration. Lectures widely for
various international conference organisers.
Prof. Memberships: Faculty of Building,
International Bar Association, Law Society of
Hong Kong. Member of editorial team of the
International Arbitration Law Review; member of
Chartered Institute of Transport; Chairman
British Consultants Bureau's East Asia and
Pacific Group, committee member of DTI's Asia
Pacific Advisory Group.
Career: Qualified in 1971. Joined *Masons* in
1975, becoming a Partner in 1976. Admitted in
Hong Kong 1983; first resident Partner at
Masons in Hong Kong 1983. Head of
Construction Department of *Masons*.
Personal: Born 24th December 1946. Attended
Brighton College, Brighton 1960-65, then Bristol
University 1966-69. Leisure interests include

tennis, walking, golf, reading and music. Lives in London.

HELPS, Dominic
Shadbolt & Co, Reigate (01737) 226277
Specialisation: Specialises in all sorts of contentious and non-contentious construction work, both domestic and international. Has handled major cases including London Borough of Merton -v- Stanley Hugh Leach and Crest Homes -v- Marks (HL). Major projects include the Heathrow Express, the Tsing Ma Bridge in Hong Kong and the Elm Energy tyre-to-electricity plant. Experienced in drafting building contract amendments, consultants appointments and warranty documentation associated with development and property transactions and health and safety matters. Regular contributor to the construction press and speaker at conferences and seminars. Also lectures in construction law at Kingston University. Accredited adjudicator (ORSA).
Prof. Memberships: Official Referees Solicitors Association (Committee Member); Society of Construction Law; Law Society; Arbitration Club.
Career: Articled and qualified with *Linklaters & Paines* 1983. Joined *Lovell White & King* (later *Lovell White Durrant*) in Hong Kong in 1985, returning to London office in 1986. Became a Partner with *Shadbolt & Co* in 1996.
Personal: Born 8th July 1956. Attended Radley College, Oxon, then Cambridge University 1975-1978 and 1979-1980. In between was staff writer for Management Today. Leisure interests include playing cricket, Arsenal FC, scuba-diving, reading novels/history and cinema. Lives in Reigate.

HOSIE, Jonathan
Edge & Ellison, London (0171) 404 4701
Specialisation: Partner in charge of the Construction and Engineering Law practice of *Edge & Ellison* in London. Handling drafting of documentation for construction and major projects particularly under the PFI. Also deals with resolution of construction and professional negligence disputes. Recent assignments include representing Allied Colloids on the negotiation of contracts for the engineering, procurement and construction of a large chemical plant in the USA, acting for Drake & Scull Engineering in a 3 party arbitration involving a multi-million pound dispute. Also represents and advises developers, main contractors and sub-contractors in claims for payment in respect of variations, delay and disruption, acceleration, extensions of time, quantum meruit and claims for damages for breach of construction and process engineering contracts generally. Has published a number of articles and regularly addresses conferences and seminars on the legal aspects of construction and arbitration.
Prof. Memberships: Society of Construction Law (Council member); Official Referees' Solicitors Association (ORSA accredited adjudicator); Chartered Institute of Arbitrators; Arbitration Club, King's College Branch (Vice Chairman), Member of Working Group 3 of the Design Build Foundation.
Career: Qualified 1984. Associate with *Baker & McKenzie's* Construction and Engineering Law Department 1989-95 before joining *Edge & Ellison*.
Personal: Educated at the University of Wales (LL.B Hons) and at King's College, London (MSc Construction Law and Arbitration) 1989-

91. Winner of the Alfred Hudson Prize awarded by Society of Construction Law 1993. Interests include family and Manchester United FC. Born 5th December 1958. Lives in London.

HUDSON, James J.S.
Nicholson Graham & Jones, London (0171) 648 9000
Partner in Construction and Engineering Department.
Specialisation: Principal area of practice is construction and civil engineering law. Has extensive experience of litigation and arbitration in this field. Acts for employers, contractors, specialist subcontractors and professionals. Important cases have included 'Minter v. WHTSO' and 'ICI v. Bovis' and others. Speaker at construction seminars.
Prof. Memberships: Official Referees Solicitors Association (Chairman), Society of Construction Law, International Bar Association, Member of the Official Referees Working Group to the Woolf Enquiry.
Career: Called to the Bar in 1972. Qualified as a Solicitor in 1977. Joined *Bristows Cooke & Carpmael* in 1979 and became a Partner in 1984. Joined *Nicholson Graham & Jones* as a Partner in 1998.
Personal: Born 13th May 1949. Educated at Winchester College 1962-66 and King's College, London (LL.B Hons, 1971). Leisure activities include golf, tennis and cricket. Lives in London.

HUGHES-D'AETH, John
Berwin Leighton, London +44 171 760 1000
Specialisation: All aspects of the law and practice relating to construction procurement, both in the UK and internationally, including contract drafting, negotiation and post-contract advice. Acts for developers, institutions, public bodies, contractors and consultants on major building and civil engineering projects, including PFI projects. Recently advised AMEC in connnection with the redevelopment of the DSS Newcastle Estate under the PFS. Editor of the firm's Construction Review and a regular contributor to Building magazine.
Prof. Memberships: Society of Construction Law.
Career: Gonville & Caius College, Cambridge – B.A. (Law) 1983, M.A. 1987. Called to Bar (Middle Temple) 1984. Requalified as a solicitor in 1992. Legal Advisor to Building Employers' Confederation, 1985-1988. Joined *Berwin Leighton* in 1988, became a partner in 1997.
Personal: Born 1962; lives in St Albans. Leisure interests include bellringing (member of Westminster Abbey Company), family, sport and classical music.

JONES, David
Hammond Suddards, London (0171) 655 1000
Specialisation: Large scale construction and civil engineering disputes both in the UK and abroad. Experienced in ADR and has successfully concluded a number of Mediation/Conciliations for clients as well as more traditional forms of Dispute Resolution, Arbitration, Litigation (including a year long trial in the Caribbean). He is also an expert in Environmental Law, Construction Insurance and Health & Safety. He has been involved in non-contentious work from Hotels to Hospitals and more recently Tunnelling contracts and some PFI work.

Prof. Memberships: Official Referees Solicitors Association; Court Member of the Company of Water Conservators.
Career History: Qualified 1976; Articles at *Lovell White Durrant*; *Masons* (Equity Partner 1982-94) 1980-94; *Hammond Suddards* (Equity Partner) 1995.
Personal: Married with two teenage daughters. Interests: football and golf.

LANE, Mark
Masons, London (0171) 490 6214 (Direct Line)
email: mark.lane@masons.com
Partner in Construction, Engineering Department.
Specialisation: Principally contract drafting and dispute resolution. Includes ICC arbitrations, domestic litigation and contract drafting for international and UK construction projects. Also handles EU public procurement advising contracting authorities (including government departments, agencies and utilities) on tendering procedures and structuring tendering procedures under PFI schemes. Acted for Eric Cumine Associates on Harbour City litigation in Hong Kong. Member of the firm's team on Channel Tunnel and Canary Wharf projects and on a number of PFI projects including hospitals (procurement issues) and waste water treatment works (construction issues). Contract drafting on other water related projects in the recent past includes projects in India, the Philippines, Australasia, and Scotland. Has extensive African experience (much of it FIDIC related) including matters in Nigeria, Gambia, Ghana, Mozambique, Kenya and Mali. Has recently worked on projects in Maldives (airport) and Belgium. In the spring of 1998, led Masons' team acting for the Government of Ukraine in negotiations to establish the Project Management Unit to manage the project to render the Chernobyl Nuclear Reactor No4 safe.
Prof. Memberships: Society of Construction Law; IBA (Committee T) Chairman of sub-committee on International Procurement in Construction Projects; European Construction Institute (Member of Executive Committee) (Chairman of European Legislation Task Force).
Career: Qualified in 1975. Partner at *Masons* since 1988.
Personal: Born 18th March 1950. Educated at Cranleigh School 1962-67 and Trinity College, Cambridge 1968-72. Lives in London.

LEVINE, Marshall F.
Linklaters, London (0171) 456 3580
Specialisation: Partner and Head of the Construction and Engineering Unit. Involved in a wide range of property and construction matters, including advice in relation to many major property joint ventures, property developments and finance agreements. Highly experienced in drafting construction contracts, and in advising on dispute resolution over a wide variety of projects including substantial office redevelopment, relocations and refurbishment as well as PFI transactions in the health, property and transportation sectors. Was involved in the *BR* privatisaton. Publications include 'Construction Insurance' (Lloyds); 'Commercial Development Property Precedents' (Longman).

LONG, Peter
Cameron McKenna, London (0171) 367 3000
Partner in Construction Group.
Specialisation: Specialist in construction law

with over 20 years experience advising contractors, consultants and employers in the construction industry. Includes advice on construction aspects of major projects and PFI schemes, procurement advice, drafting and negotiation of construction contracts, consultancy agreements, collateral warranties, concession agreements and operating and maintenance agreements. Also advising on contractual claims against and by contractors and consultants, dispute resolution procedures and conduct of litigation, arbitration and ADR procedures. Experienced in all kinds of construction projects including large-scale commercial buildings, civil engineering projects and process plant and heavy engineering. Contributor of articles to the construction press. Speaker at construction law seminars. Accredited mediator with CEDR (Centre for Dispute Resolution).
Prof. Memberships: Law Society, Society of Construction Law, Official Referees Solicitors Association, Associate of the Chartered Institute of Arbitrators, CEDR Board Member.
Career: Qualified in 1978, having joined *McKenna & Co.* in 1975. Became a Partner in 1984. Worked in Hong Kong office 1981-1985, having qualified as a solicitor in Hong Kong in 1981. Partner in *Cameron McKenna* 1997
Personal: Born 18th October 1950. Attended Balliol College, Oxford 1969-1973 (1st Class Honours in Classics). Leisure interests include music and family. Lives in Hampton Hill, Middlesex.

MILES, David
Glovers, London (0171) 629 5121
Partner in Construction Department.
Specialisation: Has specialised in construction since 1978. Deals with contract negotiations, joint venture agreements, claims involving both arbitration and litigation acting both for employers and contractors in the UK and overseas. Acted in the cases Rees Hough, Viking Grain and St Martins. Contributing Author 'Construction Conflict Management and Resolution.' Co-Author 'Commercial Dispute Resolution – an ADR Practice Guide'. Member of CEDR and ORSA training faculty and lecturer on ADR. Mediator (CEDR/BAE). Adjudicator (ORSA).
Prof. Memberships: F.C.I.Arb, Committee Member Official Referees Solicitors Association, Society of Construction Law.
Career: Commission Regular Army (1966-1971). Joined *Alan Wilson & Co.* in 1978, Partner 1979. Merged with *Glovers* in 1986.
Personal: Born 22nd June 1946. Haileybury 1960-64. Chairman of Moreton Cricket Club. Leisure interests: tennis, cricket, shooting, opera.
Lives in North Moreton, Oxon.

MINOGUE, Ann
Cameron McKenna, London
(0171) 367 3000
Partner in Construction Group.
Specialisation: Principal area of work is procurement advice and drafting building and construction-related contracts for major developments and projects. Other main area of work is construction disputes. Drafted standard forms for ACA and BPF. Handled construction work on Broadgate, Canary Wharf, and Minster

Court. Contributes two monthly column to 'Building' magazine.
Prof. Memberships: University of Reading, Construction Management Forum, and Design-Build Foundation, BPF Construction Committee, 'Justice' Committee (legal remedies for home-owners), Latham Working Group 10, JCT Drafting Sub-Committee.
Career: Joined *McKenna & Co.* in 1978 as an articled clerk. Qualified in 1980 and became a Partner in 1985.
Personal: Born 17th October 1955. Attended Aylesbury Girls' High School 1966-73, then Clare College, Cambridge 1974-77. Speaks Russian. Leisure pursuits include films and tennis. Lives in Buckinghamshire.

MOSEY, David
Trowers & Hamlins, London (0171) 423 8000
Partner, Commercial. Head of Projects and Construction Group.
Has advised for more than 18 years on UK and international construction law, including major projects in the commercial, industrial, housing, urban regeneration, health and education sectors. Increasing involvement in PFI, with six projects reaching financial close in 1997. Particular expertise in procurement strategies, risk analysis, standard and bespoke contracts and professional appointments. Joint author of Butterworths Building & Engineering Contracts: A Construction Practitioners Guide, Tutor in Msc Construction Law course at Kings College London and highly experienced conference/seminar speaker.

POPE, Julian
Denton Hall, London (0171) 242 1212
email: jlp@dentonhall.com
Specialisation: Principal area of practice for over 20 years has been construction projects, including contract drafting, negotiating, advisory work and disputes resolution in the UK and overseas. Particular emphasis in recent years on privately financed infrastructure and power projects under concessions, BOT and PFI contracts. Acted for UK Department of Transport for 2 DBFO roads projects; for Ministry of Defence on PFI projects; and for private sector clients on a number of independent power projects in various countries and other projects in the transport, health and ports sectors.
Prof. Memberships: Law Society; International Bar Association.
Career: Born 1952. Qualified in 1977 with *Lovell White and King* (1975-1980); Joined *Denton Hall* 1980, becoming a partner 1982. Worked in Hong Kong office 1980-1988.

RACE, David W.
Nicholson Graham & Jones, London
(0171) 648 9000
Head of Construction and Engineering Department.
Specialisation: Main areas of practice are construction and engineering law. Handles major infrastructure projects, particularly in transport and international project work in process engineering and related fields. Also undertakes general commercial work including project finance, joint ventures, procurement, tendering and contracting in the private and public sectors. Major clients include Blue Circle

Industries PLC, London Underground Ltd and Eurostar (UK) Ltd. Author of various articles for professional journals. Visiting lecturer to Crown Agents on international procurement and engineering law.
Prof. Memberships: Institute of Arbitrators, Society of Construction Law. Official Referees Solicitors Association.
Career: Qualified in 1974. Joined *Nicholson Graham & Jones* as Partner in 1987. Before qualifying worked in overseas banking 1969-71. Subsequently legal adviser to Mass Transit Railway Corp., Hong Kong 1978-82 and Chief Solicitor to Blue Circle Industries PLC 1985-87.

REES, Peter
Norton Rose, London (0171) 283 6000
Head of *Norton Rose* Litigation Department and Senior Partner in the Construction and Engineering Law Group.
Specialisation: All aspects of contentious and non-contentious construction and engineering law. Particular expertise in international arbitration (especially ICC) and in BOT and PFI projects. Has advised government departments, multilateral agencies, international organisations and international contractors.
Prof. Memberships: Vice-Chairman International Construction Projects Committee of IBA; past Secretary Official Referees Solicitors Assocation; Fellow Chartered Institute of Arbitrators; accredited ORSA adjudicator; Board of Advisers, Centre for International Legal Studies.
Career: Qualified 1981 with *Norton Rose*. Partner 1987.
Personal: Born 21st April 1957. MA from Downing College, Cambridge University. Leisure interests include football (still crazy enough to be playing), golf and scuba diving.

REEVES, Suzanne
Wedlake Bell, London (0171) 395 3000
Partner and head of the construction team.
Specialisation: Construction and Engineering. Acts for all sectors of the industry, particularly specialist subcontractors, consulting engineers and insurers. Non-contentious work focuses on consultants, developers and financial institutions. Contributor at industry publications. Frequent speaker at industry seminars and conferences. Has close association with major subcontractor organisations and places emphasis on finding cost-effective solutions in both contentious and non-contentious matters.
Prof. Memberships: Accredited adjudicator, Law Society, Official Referees Solicitors Association.
Career: Qualified in 1979. Joined *Wedlake Bell* the same year, becoming a Partner in 1986. Currently Head of Construction Team.
Personal: Born 13th August 1955. LLB (Exon) 1976. Lives in London.

REGAN, Michael
Rowe & Maw, London (0171) 248 4282
Partner in and Head of Construction and Engineering Department.
Specialisation: Advises contractors, employers and professionals, and also insurers, particularly in relation to professional indemnity matters.
Prof. Memberships: Law Society, Chartered Institute of Arbitrators, Society of Construction Law.
Career: Qualified in 1980, having joined *Rowe & Maw* in 1978. Became a Partner in 1985.
Personal: Born 4th October 1955. Attended Westcliff High School 1969-74, then Pembroke

College, Oxford 1974-77. Leisure interests include watching cricket, talking about football and playing tennis. Lives in London and Gloucestershire.

ROBERTS, Martin
Masons, London (0171) 490 4000
Partner Construction & Engineering department, Head of Power Industry Sector.
Specialisation: Specialises in dispute resolution and non-contentious advice on construction and engineering matters. Leads team of lawyers advising contractors, employers, professionals and insurers on wide range of issues and projects. Recently involved in advising on Jubilee Line Extension, Croydon Tramlink, Peterborough and Corby CCGT Power Stations, Navotas Power Station where advised successful Plaintiff in Hopewell Project Management Ltd v. Ewbank Preece Ltd 1998 1 LLR. Currently advising on issues relating to HGCR Act and Arbitration Act. Accredited CEDR Mediator and Adjudicator.
Prof. Memberships: Law Society, elected committee member of City of London Law Society, member of Litigation Sub-Committee of City of London Law Society, Society of Construction Law, ORSA, CEDR.
Career: Qualified 1979, partner with Masons 1983, member of Mason's Partnership Strategy Board 1992 to 1997.
Personal: Born 11th April 1955. Attended City of London Freeman's School, Kingston University (BA Hons) Law. Leisure interests include theatre, cinema, pop music, tennis, swimming and two children. Lives in Sussex.

ROE, Mark
Masons, London (0171) 490 4000
mark.roe@masons.com. Partner specialising in dispute resolution in the Construction Industry.
Specialisation: Expert in resolution of disputes in construction and related industries both in the UK and abroad. Also project management with particular experience in construction and Information Technology. Has advised and acted extensively in the resolution of disputes by mediation and mini-trial/ structured settlement procedures, arbitration and expert determination and has acted successfully as a mediator. Also advises on PFI matters. Author of articles of ADR. Speaks regularly on ADR, project management and construction law matters.
Prof. Memberships: ORSA Committee Member, Director of CEDR, Accredited Mediator.
Career: Qualified 1981. Joined Masons in 1981. Partner of Masons since 1985.
Personal: Born 30th May 1955. Attended the John Fisher School 1965-73, Balliol College, Oxford 1974-77. Leisure interests include rugby, tennis, cycling, skiing, theatre and furniture, jewellery and textiles of the arts and crafts movement. Lives in Central London.

ROE, Sally
Freshfields, London (0171) 936 4000
Partner in Litigation Department. Authorised to exercise rights of audience in the Higher Courts (Civil Proceedings), July '95.
Specialisation: Head of Construction and Engineering Group. Extensive experience of litigation and arbitration in these fields, acting for employers and contractors. Also handles non-contentious projects including property developments and infrastructure projects. Other areas of practice include advising on the application of the EC Procurement Regime.

Prof. Memberships: City of London Solicitors Company.
Career: Qualified in 1981. Joined *Freshfields* in 1988, becoming a Partner in 1990.
Personal: Born 4th September 1956. Attended Wakefield Girls' High School 1965-74 and St Hilda's College, Oxford 1974-77.

RUSHTON, John Michael
Rowe & Maw, London (0171) 248 4282
Partner in Construction Department.
Specialisation: Acts or has acted for all sides of the construction industry: developers, building owners, consultants, main contractors, sub-contractors, insurers, trade associations and arbitrators regarding building and civil engineering projects. Handles litigation and arbitration. Cases have involved dredging, ground conditions, mechanical and electrical disputes, decontamination contracts and defects claims, fee claims and claims of loss and expense and extensions of time. Drafts and advises on terms of construction contracts. Accredited adjudicator of the Official Referees Solicitors Association. Lectures both for private and for public organisations. Accredited mediator with the Centre for Dispute Resolution. Has some advocacy experience in the High Court and before arbitrators.
Prof. Memberships: Chartered Institute of Arbitrators (Fellow), Institution of Civil Engineering Surveyors (Fellow), Society of Construction Law. Regular contributor to Construction press. Firm has corporate or associate membership of British Academy of Experts and Confederation of Construction Specialists.
Career: Qualified 1975. Joined *Rowe & Maw* in 1980, becoming a Partner in 1981.
Personal: Born 22nd March 1950. Attended Uppingham 1963-68, then Sidney Sussex College, Cambridge, 1969-72. Liveryman of the Worshipful Company of Arbitrators. Leisure interests include MCC and family life: he has two children. Lives in Loughton.

RUSSELL, Victoria E.
Berrymans Lace Mawer, London (0171) 638 2811
Partner in Construction Department.
Specialisation: Handles contentious and non contentious construction and engineering matters with a special emphasis on litigation and arbitration. Advises employers, main contractors, specialist subcontractors and members of the professional team on a variety of points of law, practice and procedure. Has dealt with a number of complex construction matters, some arising from the various JCT and ICE standard forms of contract and others from "tailor made" contractual arrangements. Fluent German speaker. Practising arbitrator, CEDR accredited mediator and ORSA adjudicator. Charge-out rate is £185 per hour.
Prof. Memberships: ORSA, IBA (Business Section), LCIA, Society of Construction Law (Council Member since 1990, Secretary 1996-98, Vice-Chairman 1998-), Chartered Institute of Arbitrators (Fellow (1991). Member of the Diploma in Arbitration Advisory Board of the College of Estate Management in Reading (1991-97). Member of the Court of Assistants of the Worshipful Company of Arbitrators and Chairman of its Charitable Trust.
Career: Qualified and joined *Freedmans* in 1981. Became a Partner in 1985. Joined *Berrymans* in 1996.
Personal: Born 12th October 1956. Educated

at Benenden School, Kent 1968-73 and Exeter University 1974-77 (LL.B Hons). Member of Benenden School Trust and Alumni Board of Exeter University. Leisure time spent responding to the challenges of two small sons. Lives in West London.

SHADBOLT, Richard A.
Shadbolt & Co, Reigate (01737) 226277
Senior Partner.
Specialisation: Main area of practice is construction law, including work on engineering and major projects, with experience in UK and internationally since 1967. Particular experience of structuring and drafting of contracts for major projects and construction. Litigation and arbitration work covered as well as environmental, trade and other commercial matters. Involved with the drafting of the widely praised Association of Consultant Architects standard contract form. Author of articles in professional and other periodicals and occasional lecturer on International Construction Contracts. Regular speaker at professional conventions and international conferences on construction contract and other legal topics.
Prof. Memberships: Law Society, Law Society of Hong Kong, American Bar Association (Associate Member), International Bar Association, Inter-Pacific Bar Association, British Consultants Bureau.
Career: Joined *E T Ray & Co.* in Bletchley in 1965. Qualified 1968. Joined *McKenna & Co.* in London in 1967. Partner, *McKenna & Co.* in London, Brussels, Bahrain, Hong Kong, Singapore, Tokyo and Jakarta, from 1971 until 1991. Established *Shadbolt & Co.* as Senior Partner in 1991.
Personal: Born 18th December 1942. Attended Okehampton Grammar School 1954-60; King's College, London 1961-64 then College of Law, Guildford 1967. Leisure pursuits include family life.

SHAW, Peter R.
Taylor Joynson Garrett, London (0171) 353 1234
Partner specialising in construction and engineering law.
Specialisation: Handles both contentious and non-contentious matters. Non-contentious work includes contract procurement, commercial drafting, collateral warranties, bonds, funding agreements, professional service agreements, project insurance, legal audits, contract adminstration procedures and BOT and PFI projects. Also provides representation in all forms of arbitration tribunal and ADR, pleading and affidavit drafting, opinions and advices. Examples of contentious work include advising clients in an arbitration dispute with a main contractor regarding design and construction work during the building of a railway in Jordan for the transport of phosphates (FIDIC contract); acting for clients as plaintiffs in litigation concerning the construction of a hospital in Suva, Fiji (JCT contract); representing plaintiffs in disputes with quarry owners concerning the construction of a £25 million mineral processing and crushing plant in the UK (I Chem E contract), and joint action in court by services engineering companies against oil rig jacket constructors in one of the English North Sea fields involving the joining of the Oil Companies Consortium as third parties (amended ICE contract). Clients include national and

international construction companies, government agencies, health trusts and professional indemnity insurers in construction design disciplines. Contributor to legal section in trade/ professional publications that circulate in the construction industry. Also presents seminars and lectures to various bodies and institutions involved in the construction industry. Member of the British Academy of Experts Committee on "The Language of ADR". Charge-out rate is £185 per hour.
Prof. Memberships: Official Referees Solicitors Association (Committee Member), Reading Construction Forum, IBA Business Section.
Career: Qualified in 1980. With *Freedmans/ Freedman Church* since 1973. Became a Partner in 1980 and Senior Partner in 1991.
Personal: Born 10th January 1946. Educated at Huddersfield Grammar School and the University of Lancaster (BA Hons in History). Interests include golf, sailing, skiing, gardening, walking and good food and wine. Lives in London and Dartmouth.

SHERMAN, Henry C.
Cameron McKenna, London (0171) 367 3000
Partner in Construction Group.
Specialisation: Main practice area is domestic and international construction advice. Acts for all sectors of the construction industry in relation to major construction projects and disputes in the United Kingdom, Central and Eastern Europe and the Middle and Far East. Specialises in international arbitration and litigation as well as disputes resolution by mediation, adjudication and other informal routes. Regularly addresses seminars and workshops and writes on legal subjects in the construction and legal press.
Prof. Memberships: Society of Construction Law, Official Referees Solicitors' Association.
Career: Qualified in 1977. Worked at *Frere Cholmeley* 1975-83. Joined *McKenna & Co* in 1983, becoming a Partner in 1986. 1985-7 Hong Kong with *McKenna & Co* and 1997/8 with *Cameron McKenna*.
Personal: Born 16th February 1952. University of Oxford 1970-73 (BA) and University of Aix-Marseilles 1973-4. Leisure interests include idling whenever possible with his family on the Isle of Wight. Lives in Teddington, Middlesex.

SMITH, I.D.
Lovell White Durrant, London (0171) 236 0066
Specialisation: Principal work area is the drafting and negotiation of contracts for national and international construction and energy projects. Recent work includes the construction contracts for the new Hong Kong airport,

construction and operation contracts for cogeneration facilities, a range of EPC, alliance, target price, leasing and operating contracts for North Sea oil and gas developments, DBFO road and rail contracts and hospital projects as part of the Private Finance Initiative and build/operate contracts for distribution centres. Works closely with the firm's property team on the construction documentation for all types of development.
Prof. Memberships: Law Society, Society of Construction Law.
Career: Articled to *Lovell White & King*. Qualified 1976 and became a Partner in 1981. Resident Partner in Hong Kong 1984 to 1989.

STEADMAN, Tim
Clifford Chance, London (0171) 600 1000
tim.steadman@cliffordchance.com
Partner. Head of Construction.
Specialisation: Construction aspects of private/ project finance transactions in the UK and internationally. Was involved in the pioneering of privately financed infrastructure projects in Asia in the 1980s. Has since been active in the wider use of such structures in the UK and western and eastern Europe. Recent extensive involvement in PPP/ PFI projects in the UK and in IPP/ EPC contracts in the UK and is a member of advisory bodies on construction/ project finance established by UNCITRAL, the CBI and the UN/ ECE.
Career: BA Oxon 1975. Qualified in 1978; partner in *Baker & McKenzie* (in Hong Kong and London offices) 1984 to 1987; partner in *Clifford Chance* from 1997.
Personal: Born 13 January 1955. Lives in London.

VIGRASS, Christopher
Ashurst Morris Crisp, London (0171) 638 1111
Specialisation: Contentious Construction and Engineering. Major cases include acting for (i) 'Docklands Light Railway' against 'Balfour Beatty'; Court of Appeal – "Crouch" point (ii) 'Smith New Court' against 'Citibank'; House of Lords – quantum of damages for fraud (iii) 'British Shipbuilders' against 'VSEL'; expert determination and relationship with court.
Prof. Memberships: Fellow of Chartered Institute of Arbitrators. Accredited Mediator (CEDR). Accredited Adjudicator (ORSA).
Career: Bradford Grammar School; MA (Law) Gonville & Caius College, Cambridge. Articled and Assistant *Linklaters & Paines* 1978-1986. Assistant and Partner since 1988 with *Ashurst Morris Crisp*.
Personal: Fellwalking, squash, badminton and family.

WINTER, Jeremy
Baker & McKenzie, London (0171) 919 1000
Partner and Head of Construction Department.
Specialisation: Resolution of construction disputes by litigation, arbitration and ADR. Particular expertise in civil engineering matters. 15 years' experience of construction law in a total of 25 countries around the world (particularly Europe, Africa and the Middle East). Conducts own advocacy in arbitration and (where permitted) in High Court. Frequent speaker and writer on construction topics. Outspoken advocate of reforms of arbitration law and civil procedure to make them quicker and cheaper.
Prof. Memberships: Hon Fellow of Institution of Civil Engineering Surveyors, Society of Construction Law, Official Referees Solicitors Association. Member of Association for Project Management, Member of the Geological Society.
Career: Qualified 1979. Joined *Baker & McKenzie* London 1980. Worked in B&M Sydney Office 1982-4. Partner 1987.
Personal: Born 26 December 1953. Educated at Bradfield College and Warwick University (LLB Hons 1975). Lives in Toys Hill, Kent.

WINWARD, Richard
Winward Fearon, London (0171) 420 2800

WRIGHT, John
Warner Cranston, London (0171) 403 2900
Specialisation: John Wright handles a wide variety of contentious matters acting for contractors, sub-contractors, professional indemnity insurers and employers. He has dealt with many High Court disputes and both domestic and international arbitrations. Recent reported cases include 'Vascroft Contractors Ltd-v-Seeboard plc' (interpretation of aspects DOM/1 Form of Contract) and 'John Barker Construction Ltd-v-London Portman Hotel Ltd (landmark case on assessing a contractor's claim for delay). He has particular experience in arbitration and mediation.
Prof. Memberships: Fellow of the Chartered Institute of Arbitrators and is currently Chairman of the London Branch. He is an accredited mediator with CEDR (Centre for Dispute Resolution) and accredited adjudicator with ORSA (Official Referees' Solicitors' Association) and a member of the ORSA Committee. He is also a member of the International Bar Association. He frequently writes and lectures on construction topics.
Career: Qualified in 1976. With *Coward Chance* 1976-79 and *McKenna & Co* 1979-83. Joined *Warner Cranston* as a Partner in 1984.
Personal: Born 2nd May 1952. Educated Hereford Cathedral School 1963-69 and St John's College, Cambridge 1970-73 (BA 1973, MA 1977). Leisure interests include golf, cricket, wine tasting and theatre. Lives in Richmond, Surrey.

SOUTH EAST

Blake Lapthorn (6ptners/ 6assts) "A good regional firm," 3 partners and 1 assistant deal with construction matters almost exclusively. Non-contentious is handled within the commercial department whilst contentious work is in the civil litigation group. Client base stretches from Sussex to Dorset and as far north as Berkshire **Clients/Work:** Advising Isle of Wight College on a PFI £12m project for the development of a new college campus; advising the London Borough of Brent on tendering and documentation; acting for Pirelli Construction Ltd in multi-million sub-contract claim against its main contractor arising out of work for London Underground.

Cole & Cole (1 f/t, 2p/t ptnrs and 1f/t and 4 p/t assts). One of the assistants is ex-Nabarros and Mowlem and the firm's non-contentious specialist ("good on the details"). Most of the work is linked to property development. **Clients/Work:** Acted for contractors on Queen's Square development in Liverpool for Amey; acted for employers on residential scheme for Oxford Brookes University; acted for consultants for RPS in relation to site remediation.

Cripps Harries Hall (2ptnrs/2assts) Contentious work is handled within the commercial litigation department by *Peter Ashford.* The firm acts for main contractors and subbies as well as employers. **Clients/Work:** Include Wates Construction Ltd; HJ Gleeson Gp plc.

Clarks 1ptnr and 2assts make up the specialist construction department that is new to our tables this year. **Clients/Work:** Relocation of a bus depot for Reading Transport Ltd. Drafting of and advising on contractual documentation for a consolidation project at Royal Berkshire Hospital.

Linnells (1ptnr/1asst – not exclusively) A heavy bias towards contentious, the firm acts for small to medium sized contractors and a few employers, particularly a local institution of some repute. Also new to the lists this year. **Clients/Work:** Advising the owner and developer on a Design & Build Contract for student accommodation. Prosecution of a claim in relation to a large new faculty building with structural defects.

SOUTH WEST

Masons (4ptnrs/7assts) "Vastly bigger than anyone else," they have been in Bristol for ten years but do not dominate the local market as much as Masons, Manchester. Recommended for "not being afraid to put their necks out," all four partners appear in this years tables. *Mark Collingwood* is "sensible," "an effective operator" and "well liked by clients." *Adam Harris* is "the guy for the definitive commercial answer." *Richard Foley* has "the right attitude" and a rare and much valued (by clients) attribute – "if he doesn't know the answer he says so." *Lawrence Davies* has up and come into the third band. Handle big ticket litigation on a national basis and act for local contractors **Clients/Work:** Acting for the Main Contractor with disputes arising out of the new £50m Sun Life HQ, Bristol; acting for contractor of Hereford Hospital PFI over procurement and delivery.

Laytons (2ptnrs/5assts) Competent construction practice. *John Redmond's* personality and ability makes up for a perceived lack of back room support. Team also includes *Nicholas Guppy* – "charming and competent." Majority of work is contentious for which Redmond has a national reputation. **Clients/Work:** LG Construction Ltd semiconductor plant in S.Wales; Cardiff Millenium Stadium – acting for Drake & Scull contract preparation; acting for Matthew Hall in multi-party litigation for major government facility in Southampton.

Bevan Ashford (2ptnrs/4assts/1consultant) Well thought of by the Construction Federation, they move up to 'Leading' this year. Handle both non-contentious and contentious, mainly for employers, particularly health trusts. Recommended for their approach – "they know all the risks and the procedures." Some thought them "too adversarial." **Clients/Work:** Claims for: Gloucester Health Authority; major property company in respect of construction contract with significant overrun company (£6m+).

Burges Salmon (2ptnrs/2assts) Team includes *Marcus Harling* ("straight as a die.") Strong reputation for non-contentious, acting mainly for employers, developers and local authorities. **Clients/Work:** £65m Harbourside development – the largest arts project outside London. 'Bristol 2000' – a £95m Millennium project. Advising the MOD on the £800m Defence Fixed Telecommunications System.

Veale Wasbrough (2ptnrs/3assts) Historically most of their work was acting for engineers' insurers. Over the last few years have become more mainstream, with the PI now constituting between 30-50% of the total. Work is split evenly between contentious and non-contentious. *Roger Hoyle,* "the doyen of the local PI scene" and a "humorous man" who "does a good job for his clients." His name on a document is a "guarantee of quality." *Martin Howe* is "knowledgeable." **Clients/Work:** Drafting new suite of standard form contracts for the MOD. £m arbitration for Magnox Electric Plc; acting for consulting engineers (and their insurers) in Lidle UK Properties GmbH v Clarke Bond Partnership.

Wansbrough Willey Hargrave (1ptnr/3assts) *John Vasey* (ex McKenna) heads a small team mainly known for its PI practice although approx. two thirds of the work is non-contentious. **Clients/Work:** Reviewing contracts for appointment of principal engineers on Millennium Dome; acting for architects defending a £10m claim on planning problem a major road/rail distribution site.

Bond Pearce (1assoc/3assts) Handle contentious and non-contentious. **Clients/ Work:** Advising and drafting for development of prime City Centre site for retail use; advice on construction matters for the new National Marine Aquarium in Plymouth.

Stones Cann & Hallett: (2ptnrs (one f/t, one p/t) 1asst) *Peter Buechel* enters the tables for the first time as an 'up & coming'. A small Exeter based practice, the firm was recom-

mended for sub-contractor disputes. Handle non-contentious as well as advice to arbitrators.

Townsends (2ptnrs/3assts) Some big firms felt confident to give Townsends conflict work and they have not had any complaints. Handle a mix of work. **Clients/Work:** Include

Impreglio Spa and Impresa Castelli Spa – two major italian contractors; Johnson Control Systems Ltd; acted for major engineering company in dispute concerning Heathrow to Paddington Rail Link.

WALES

Eversheds (2ptnrs/7assts) Noted for its "pragmatic approach" clients seem to be well satisfied with the strategic and tactical advice given by *Peter Jones* and his team – "bags of common sense." Handle both contentious and non-contentious. **Clients/Work:** Acting on behalf of public body and advising as to propriety and adequacy of tendering procedure; acting on behalf of a public body in advising on liability of designers who undertook site investigation of contaminated land. Advising public authority on claim for negligent design and supervision.

Hugh James (3ptnrs) Described as "a rather traditional firm," they are noted for their litigation expertise. *Michael Jefferies* is experienced and is "a good man for the technical side." *Michael Jones* was seen as a good and enthusisatic negotiator. *Mark Robinson* joins the tables following his work on the Millennium Stadium project. **Clients/Work:** Instructed by Vale of Glamorgan Council on renovation of Dryyryn House; continuing representation before local and London Official Referees on harbour redevelopment scheme and for industrial/retail park at Portishead.

Morgan Bruce (2ptnrs/3assts) "Rock solid." *Philip Howell-Richardson* is a specialist litigator who contributes to the job in hand and is "pragmatic." *Jeremy Williams* was recommended for his negotiation skills. Handle a broad mix of work. **Clients/Work:** Advising: R.F. Brooks on procurement of a £30m food factory; Cardiff Bay Development Corporation on scheme linking harbour to City centre. Retained by General Accident to handle claims against engineers in Wales under the ACE scheme.

Edwards Geldard (2assts) Joining the tables for the first time, handle a mix of construction work. *Paul Newman*, a barrister, was recommended as a technical litigator with an academic style. **Clients/Work:** Contractual advice on the Cardiff Bay Barrage. Advice on drafting the contract arrangements for appointment of consultants and construction manager at National Botanic Garden of Wales (£20m).

MIDLANDS

Neil F. Jones & Co (5ptnrs/6assts) A niche litigation practice with a national reputation, "do an amazing amount of work considering their resources." The firm is synonymous with contractor and sub-contractor disputes. The firm's focus on disputes means that for large areas of practice it would not be an

appropriate choice. *Kevin Barrett* ("absolutely spot on") and *Simon Baylis* are joined by *Ian Yule* ("an excellent fellow!") in this year's tables.

Wragge & Co (1ptnr/8assts – plus 2 additional ptnrs part time) Recommended for doing quality work with the critical mass as a firm to handle the big cases. Do a mix of work. *Ashley Pigott*, "a thoroughly decent chap who knows his stuff." **Clients/Work:** Acted successfully for Mellowes vs Bell Projects, establishing as legal principle that delay on a construction project is not ground for abatement of the contract price. Acting for Harmon CFEM Facades (UK) Ltd in connection with a £14m claim arising out of alleged breaches of Procurement Regulations.

Dibb Lupton Alsop (4ptnrs/1consultant) *Graham Bradley* ("proactive," ex-Masons) is raising the profile in Birmingham. Act for both contractors and employers. *Francis Kirkham* retains her place in the table although she now sits as a Recorder. **Clients/Work:** Acting for Bryant, Ibstock; major arbitration for Therman Engineering.

Edge & Ellison (2ptnrs/9assts) *David Lloyd Jones* heads a dedicated team of construction lawyers who are "serious about what they do." Contentious work predomi-

nates (the split is 70:30) but the firm also acts on some massive building projects including two Millennium projects (total value £150m). Reputation for being "good technical litigators." **Clients/Work:** Advising Birmingham"s Millenium Trust on £120m development. Acting for mechanical and electrical contractor in High Court and ICC Arbitration proceedings relating to works at a Russian factory.

Gateley Wareing (2ptnrs/3assts) *Peter Davies* has a "jolly good reputation." Handle a mix of work but are particularly known for building defects disputes. **Clients/Work:** Include George Wimpey plc, Christiani &

Nielsen Ltd, Wrekin Group plc. Resisting application for injunction in High Court in London to prevent multi-million pound development; advising on contracts for project in Far East for engineering client.

Pinsent Curtis (3ptnrs/5assts) Moves up one band on recommendation. **Clients/ Work:** Factory Advisors to the Government Agency Property Advisors to the Civil Estate (PACE) on new editions of government construction contracts. Acting for GEC ALSTHOM Ltd in the successful conclusion of three multi-million pound arbitrations, involving two power stations.

Eversheds (Birmingham) (2ptnrs/5assts) Have good PR and were noted for their non-contentious work. However there was some question about the strength in depth of the specialist construction team. **Clients/Work:** Expansion joints on M1 motorway network for HSC (UK) Ltd. Advising Birmingham International Airport in relation to its redevelopment scheme; Star Site Plc leisure centre development at Heartlands Star Park.

Hacking Ashton (6ptnrs/9assts) *Malcolm Hacking* is a well known local figure dealing mainly with contentious work (85% of the caseload) and is a qualified arbitrator and adjudicator. The firm is currently handling 14 arbitrations with an average value of £100k and a maximum value of £2m. On the building side, they advise some local authorities and developers. **Clients/Work:** Advice to Ciba Specialty Chemicals over new office redevelopment; appointed by Derbyshire County Council to draft contracts for civil engineering and building works and to advise the Council on its appointment of a developer.

Ashton Bond Gigg (4ptnrs/3assts) Handle mainly contentious work with an increasing amount of building work. None of the fee earners are full time construction specialists. **Clients/Work:** Include Wilson Bowden plc; extensive mineral work for Lefarge; major restructuring of the property portfolio for the Wheatley Group of companies.

Eversheds (Nottingham/Derby) (1ptnr/ 3assts) Exclusively non-contentious. Disputes are referred to the Newcastle office. **Clients/ Work:** Advising Simon Estates Ltd on redevelopment of Swansea City Centre's retail core; advising Astra on construction, engineering and process plant contracts in excess of £60m.

Freeth Cartwright Hunt Dickins (4 ptnrs/3assts) Described as "competent but not specialists," the firm does an equal mix of contentious and non-contentious. **Clients/ Work:** Documentation for Castle Wharf Development at Canal Street, Nottingham. Acted for Stanifer Hotels Ltd in the acquisition and construction documentation for nine hotels throughout the country

Garretts (1ptnrs/3asst) Have a qualified team with the head of department being the author of two textbooks on construction. However, their profile is not high in this area. **Clients/Work:** Advisors to Dresser Ltd regarding new manufacturing facility in Newcastle; Sandvik AB over Italian Subsidiary Project advice for Major M&E contracts.

Knight & Sons (2ptnrs – neither f/t) **Clients/Work:** Advising Josiah Wedgwood on the procurement of a £m global processing centre; Morrison Construction Ltd; Alton Towers.

Merricks (2ptnrs/4assts) Recommended for their expertise and experience in contentious disputes. **Clients/Work:** Acted for Inserco in Inserco v Honeywell Control Systems; acted for Ellison in Ellison v MoD; advice to State of Jersey in relation to major civil engineering project.

EAST ANGLIA

Mills & Reeve (3ptnrs/3assts) "The Premier division firm in East Anglia." *Ronald Plascow* (ex-LWD and Trafalgar) was described as "erudite and knowledgeable." He heads a specialist construction team that operates on a national and international basis with a client base that stretches from Scotland to a secret (but wet) location in Africa. *Raith Pickup* concentrates his "excellent brain" exclusively on non-contentious matters but overall the firm handles equal amounts of contentious. **Clients/Work:** Two major multi-million pound disputes on behalf of higher education clients; advising in relation to a dispute over a HEP station in Africa; advising a contractor in a multi-party dispute relating to sheltered housing accommodation.

Greenwoods (3ptnrs/2assts – one an ex-Ove Arup engineer of 18 years standing) A true regional firm, 75% of the construction group's work is based in or related to the region. *John Hardwick* pursues matters vigorously and was described as a "doughty litigator" but "not averse to reaching sensible settlements." *Martin Wood* is also recommended. **Clients/Work:** Advising Geest plc on a £10m+ new food production factory in Bourne, Lincolnshire. Panel solicitors for Architects & Professional Indemnity Association; Dragomar SpA (italian).

Hewitson Becke + Shaw (1ptnr 3assts) *Tim Richards* joined two years ago (from Linklaters) to head up the firm's construction team which now handles equal amounts of contentious (generally for contractors) and non-contentious (for developers). The majority of the firm's work is located within East Anglia, the East Midlands and North London. **Clients/Work:** London Borough of Brent advising street lighting project contract; advising Cambridge City Council over refurbishment of local swimming pool; advising Canadian Car Components Manufacturer on European HQ and Production Plant in the UK.

Birketts (2ptnrs/3assts) Joining the list for the first time, *Simon Oats* and his team were recommended as "very helpful." The firm acts for a number of national and regional contractors, civil engineers and specialist sub-contractors, with a slight bias towards contentious.

Eversheds (2ptnrs/1asst) Not known outside Norwich, but reputed to have a reasonable practice. **Clients/Work:** Successfully representing Eternit (UK) Ltd (designers, developers and suppliers of roofing materials) in relation to the alleged failure of key products. Acting for the plaintiff in a dispute concerning whether a surveyor was liable for incorrect "off the cuff" advice – successful in the Court of Appeal. Multi-party dispute concerning a major food production agency.

Merricks (1ptnr) The contact partner is exclusively a litigator, mainly for contractors and specialist sub-contractors. 70% of the work is insurance related.

Prettys (5ptnrs/2assts – not exclusively) Work mainly for medium sized local contractors and specialist sub-contractors, with a slight bias towards disputes. **Clients/Work:** PFI based instructions and contentious work in the healthcare sector. Instructions from a national contractor in connection with claim arising from the method of construction of a building (£0.5m).

SEE PROFILES AT END OF SECTION

NORTH WEST

Masons (4ptnrs/19assts) The Manchester office has been a success, with some preferring it to London, saying it was "less aggressive." Working mainly in the North West (although there is an international aspect), the split is 70:30 between contentious and non-contentious. The team of "extremely good people" which "stands out from the crowd" includes *Edward Davies*, a "true specialist." (Ian Radford has relocated to Hong Kong and Peter Wood to London). **Clients/Work:** PFI Prison acting for a main contractor. Acting on $100m water project in China. Multi million dispute relating to a gas process facility in Bangladesh.

Addleshaw Booth & Co (3ptnrs/8assts) Perceived as being "employer oriented", and described as "solid." *Huw Baker* gets conflict work from Masons. Work is split 50/50 between contentious and non-contentious. **Clients/Work:** South Manchester University Hospitals NHS Trust – major PFI project involving the redevelopment of Wythenshawe Hospital; contracts for JD Williams & Co Ltd for construction of automated warehouse/distribution facility; acting for Barlows plc on development of leisure park.

Hammond Suddards (2ptnrs/7assts) Very active in contentious work, *David Moss* and *Chris Wilcock* (ex-Masons) put up a good fight for their clients but were considered less strong on non-contentious. **Clients/ Work:** New instructions received from North West Water, Biwater Europe, Bowmer & Kirkland. Also involved in advising P&O on construction related aspects of the sale of the Arndale Centre in Manchester.

Kirk Jackson (3ptnrs/1asst) A small general practice that has a specialised construction group. A number of firms would happily poach *Kenneth Salmon* who was well regarded for medium to largish disputes, particularly when acting for sub-contractors. Other members of the team were recommended for their willingness to sit down and talk about the issues.

Davies Arnold Cooper (2ptnrs/2assts) Less focused on contentious work than the London office, 80% is insurance related; the rest is split evenly between disputes and non-contentious. Lost *Andrew Willcock* to Trowers & Hamlins. *Nigel Proctor* is up and coming. **Clients/Work:** Advising British Aerospace Ltd over large construction disputes; large national distribution centre development for Littlewoods Home Shopping; Thurnall Plc – large mechanical plant dispute.

Dibb Lupton Alsop (2ptnrs/3assts) One partner in Manchester and one in Liverpool. Handle a mix of work with an employer bias. **Clients/Work:** Advising Environment Agency on construction department re£84m Maidenhead, Windsor & Eton Flood Alleviation scheme; advising on construction documentation on developments/ acqusitions such as for Ropemaker Properties Ltd on Heywood Distribution Park worth £75m.

Halliwell Landau (3ptnrs/3assts) Traditionally construction has been closely linked with the property group, although the firm is now well known for litigating performance bonds. **Clients/Work:** General Surety & Guarentee Co Ltd; John Sisk; Taylor Woodrow Developments Ltd.

Elliott & Company (2ptnrs/6assts) A "decent man," people have a great deal of respect for *Mike Woolley* who enters the tables for the first time as does his firm. A litigation specialist, the firm acts predominantly for contractors, engineers, architects and their insurers (50% of the caseload is insurance based).

Hill Dickinson (5ptnrs/5assts f/t, with 5ptnrs/5assts p/t) David Chinn although not in our construction lists has a good name as a litigator. The firm recently merged with a Chester firm which specialised in development. **Clients/Work:** Successfully defeated a £4m plus claim against an employers agent in relation to its duties under a Design and Build contract. Acting for developers such as Wainhomes, McAlpine and Bellway.

Pannone & Partners (2ptnrs/2assts) Having snaffled the team from Glaisyers, the firm's stated aim is to vie for second place behind Masons. They have some way to go. **Clients/Work:** Claims totalling £6.5m for Capper Engineering Services (Norwest Host Group); GMPTE, University of Manchester.

Andrew Willcock ("logical negotiator") has left Davies Arnold Cooper to set up a construction and PFI practice at Trowers & Hamlins.

NORTH EAST

Addleshaw Booth & Co (3ptnrs/3assts/1 legal exec – 6 other fee earners do some construction litigation) "Some lawyers know how to draft – for them precedents are nothing more than the answers to other people's problems. Others don't have a clue. *Richard Cockram* is definitely in the first category." In the murky waters of the Leeds "shark pond," Addleshaws "make things better" for their clients – blue chip employers and funders. **Clients/Work:** Include GMI Construction Group plc, Marshall Construction and Jarvis Facilities.

Eversheds (Newcastle) (5ptnrs/ 4assts) "THE construction firm in Newcastle." *Nigel Robson* must have discovered how to get more than 24 hours out of a day to maintain his reputation as a "first rate litiagator" and handle all his management responsibilities. *Mary Herbert* is "excellent," a "pleasure to deal with" and so on top of the details that ill prepared opponents have a hard time keeping up. **Clients/Work:** £42m Coach Lane Campus at University of Northumbria. £53m at International Cntre for Life. Acting for Newcastle Building Society in defects claim in the Europoean Headquarters.

Masons (2ptnrs/6assts) "An unbelievably good reputation" said contractors "but they haven't made as much of a splash in Leeds as you'd expect." Nevertheless Masons move into the top band, and into a new office. There are 19 of them at the moment but, worryingly for the competition, the office is designed to hold fifty lawyers. "I'm always pleased to have *Mark Richards* on my side" commented interviewees, "he delivers the goodies." *Keith Hartley* was described as a "Dirty Harry" type – a no-nonsense character who ploughs his own furrow. He thinks up innovative ideas – "and executes them." **Clients/Work:** Acting for a Sir Robert McAlpine led consortium in their bid for £30m for the Norfolk Police Constabulary new Headquarters. Acting for Amec Process and Energy Ltd over Floating Production Unit dispute woth £15m.

Dibb Lupton Alsop (Sheffield, Leeds) (2ptnrs) Not as heavyweight in construction compared to other parts of the firm's practice. Nevertheless *Bruce Bentley* was described as "a first class lawyer" who "doesn't mess about or waste time with unpleasantness." *Paul Dally* is "a delight to deal with" and joins the lists as an up and coming. **Clients/Work:** East Midlands Airport; Hepworth Plc; acting for Sheffield City Council in a £120m redevelopment of Sheffield City Centre.

Dickinson Dees (1ptnr/5assts) A "solid firm with a serious profile" undertaking a mix of work. The department is headed by *Simon Lewis*. **Clients/Work:** Advising six gas fired power stations in the South of England for major utility client; advice in relation to the construction of Luton Airport's railway station for Thameslink; advice provided to the receivers of the £3m + claim relating to the development of the Docklands.

Eversheds (Leeds) (3ptnrs/6assts) "If Leeds Eversheds are on the other side you know you're dealing with someone competent who'll go the extra mile to settle." The team is headed by the "no nonsense" *Alison Staniforth* and includes the "down to earth" *Simon Palmer*. They are solid on litigation but less so on non-contentious. **Clients/Work:** Advising a London Borough on a £24m claim arising from outsourcing of construction services. Acting for a cable

telecommunications company in a £10m arbitration against a North Midlands contractor, involving a civil engineering and construction contract.

Hammond Suddards (2ptnrs/7assts) *Mark Hilton* has a "big personality" that goes down well with clients and an "individual litigation style." Whilst other law firms sometimes find them "bullish," clients found them "useful" and "sound on strategy." **Clients/Work:** Successful appeal against an arbitrator's award and application for remittance for misconduct. Acting for engineering contractor on £55m claim. Advisors to Caddick Construction and Allied Colloids Group Plc.

Robert Muckle (1ptnr/2assts) *Roddy Gordon* was described as an "effective" lawyer and a "great litigator." 90% of the work is contentious, mainly for medium sized NE based contractors. **Clients/Work:** Advising the developer in litigation involving the purchaser and contractor of the European headquarters of Newcastle Building Society. Advising a major sub-contractor on a dispute concerning the Second Severn crossing.

Walker Morris (1ptnr/3assocs/2assts) The largest Leeds firm that does not have national aspirations, they "know the boundary between undue aggression and being tough." The team includes *Martin Scott* and act mainly for developers, corporate clients and funders. **Clients/Work:** Negotiation of a contract for Northern Foods for a blow moulding bottle plant at value of £10m with two bakeries valued at £6m each. Review of Halifax Plc contract packages.

Watson Burton Some contractors described the team as tenacious whilst other lawyers found them "professional."

Denison Till (3ptnrs/2assts) "You could almost trip over *Tony Glaister* he's so active." The firm has a slight bias towards contentious and contractors but with an increasing amount of developer work. **Clients/Work:** Leisure Development on

behalf of P S Turner (Contructions) Ltd.

Nabarro Nathanson (1ptnr/ 3 other fee-earners) **Clients/Work:** Contract documentation for University of Westminster's refurbishment; contracts for subsidiaries of Baltic Property Finance Plc for the redevelopment of the Grand Hotel, Manchester.

Hay & Kilner (2ptnrs) Some good people but thought to suffer from a lack of resources. **Clients/Work:** Acting in relation to a civil engineering scheme arising out of a road improvement scheme (£850,000). Settlement negotiation in Norwegian Commercial Court arising out of a contract in the offshore industry where claims were in excess of £500,000.

Ward Hadaway (2ptnrs/1asst) A new entrant to the tables, the firm was described as "proactive" and "hungry to do more." **Clients/Work:** Advising DSS major dispute with contractor over DSS Quarry House HQ in Leeds.

LEADING INDIVIDUALS NORTH EAST	
BENTLEY Bruce Dibb Lupton Alsop	
COCKRAM Richard Addleshaw Booth & Co	
ROBSON Nigel Eversheds	
GLAISTER Anthony Denison Till	
GORDON Roderick Robert Muckle	
HARTLEY Keith Masons	
HERBERT Mary Eversheds	
HILTON Mark Hammond Suddards	
LANGLEY Robert Lennox Watson Burton	
LEWIS Simon Dickinson Dees	
PALMER Simon Eversheds	
RICHARDS Mark Masons	
SCOTT Martin Walker Morris	
STANIFORTH Alison Eversheds	

UP AND COMING
DALLY Paul Dibb Lupton Alsop

SCOTLAND

LEADING FIRMS · SCOTLAND
MACROBERTS Glasgow Edinburgh
DUNDAS & WILSON CS Glasgow
MCGRIGOR DONALD Glasgow
MASONS Glasgow

HIGHLY REGARDED FIRMS
Bird Semple Edinburgh
Burness Edinburgh
Maclay Murray & Spens Glasgow
Biggart Baillie Glasgow
Bishop and Robertson Chalmers Glasgow
Simpson & Marwick WS Edinburgh
Lindsays WS Edinburgh
Steedman Ramage WS Edinburgh

MacRoberts (13ptnrs/6assts) *Jim Arnott* would be the first to agree that there is life in the old dog yet. The acknowledged guru of the Scottish construction scene has overseen a good year at MacRoberts. The firm is now widely perceived as having achieved the elusive "clear blue water" between it and its nearest rivals. Has strength in depth and, more importantly, quality in depth, in both contentious and non-contentious work. The team includes *Neil Kelly* ("a great technician... a clever chap... extremely bright") and the much talked about solicitor-advocate *Lindy Patterson,* a "commercially aggressive" litigator and the clients' choice if they want someone to "knock heads". She recently joined from Bird Semple. The respected David Henderson leaves the construction list as he is now devoted full time to PFI.

Clients/Work: Acted for three Scottish Universities in separate arbitrations; acted in major litigation relating to Forth Road Bridge; acted for West Lothian Council in relation to heat leasing contract.

Dundas & Wilson CS (5ptnrs/6 assts) The CS stands for *'Clerks to the Signet,'* a historical tag that belongs to D&W's roots in eighteenth century Edinburgh. There is nothing outdated about D&W's construction practice. Although D&W are not seen as being on the same level as MacRoberts this is a reflection of the relative size of the departments rather than the quality of the work. *Alistair McLean* is well thought of and is developing as a "competent, commercially minded" practitioner. The relatively youthful team, with its "imaginative approach" and willingness to get down to the crucial issues was described as "one to watch" – and then Alastair Morrison left to join Masons. Now the future is less clear. **Clients/Work:** Contentious and non-conentious work is split 50:50. Advised Hyundai Semiconductor Europe Ltd on documentation regarding their semiconductor manufacturing facility in Fife worth 200m. Advised Buchanan Galleries on Scotland's largest city centre shopping development.

McGrigor Donald (7ptnrs /10assts) Have a reputation for driving deals forward and are a "solid firm with no tricks about them". This pragmatic approach is epitomised by the "terrific" and "approachable" *Brandon Nolan*, a " safe pair of hands" who joins Jim Arnott (MacRoberts) in the star category for the first time. *Edward MacKechnie* is also "coming on." McGrigor's have a UK wide construction presence and have recruited a senior associate from MacRoberts to spearhead their non-contentious business. However this year they lost partners to Clifford Chance, MacRoberts and Masons. **Clients/Work:** Defending Floods of Queensferry Ltd which has raised novel issues such as the right of assignment under the standard form of sub-contract used and the ability of a ltd company to be granted legal aid. Development of new HQ building at Broomielaw, Glasgow for BT by Pillar Property Investments.

Masons (2ptnrs/2assocs) Established in the early summer of '98, they have managed to lure two key construction lawyers from D&W and McGrigor's. *Alastair Morrison* was D&W's "star." A "good guy," Morrison has been less visible in the market place recently due to his work on several massive inward investments. His peers describe him as "a strategist who sees the big picture... clients value his judgement". *Vincent Connor* (ex-McGrigor's) was widely praised for his advocacy skills and persistence. In the first two months of its existence the office was instructed by five of the UK's top ten contractors.

Bird Semple (3ptnrs/6 assts). A big name in Scottish construction, they are considered to be damaged by last year's defections. No one is writing them off – they are still heavily involved in construction. But, for the moment, they are not the force they were. Seen as relying heavily on a few

talented individuals, the firm's weakness is that there are not enough of them. On the positive side *Fenella Mason* is "coming of age" and is joined by Sandra Cassels from Shepherd & Wedderburn. The consensus amongst the lawyers was "it is too early to say" – a view not shared by Mowlem. The firm won a beauty parade to do all Mowlem's Scottish legal work, contentious and non-contentious, *after* Ms Patterson's departure. **Clients/Work:** Arbitration for East of Scotland Water against Norwest Host over engineering contract for installation of Central Scotland Water Mains Advising M J Gleeson on building contract for PFR project at Inverness Airport. Advising Chunghwa Picture Tubes (UK) Ltd on substantial construction management contract.

Burness (5ptnrs/5assts – not all full time construction lawyers) Pushing hard to establish a presence in the market, particularly on the non-contentious side, the firm has a decent construction department. *Martin Sales* and his team are all good at what they do and overall move up our tables. However, getting accepted as a serious player by the Big Three will be a hard struggle. **Clients/Work:** Ballast Wiltshier's first Scottish schools project (£60m). Project for the Department of Social Security PRIME (£4.6bn). Strathclyde Police New Force Training and Recruitment Centre (£12m)

Maclay Murray & Spens (2ptnrs/ 3assts full time, 3 more assts 50% of time) Known for its work with universities, the firm are seeking a higher profile having recently established a dedicated construction department. **Clients/Work:** Advice to the St Enoch Centre. Erskine Hospital Extension; Scottish Enterprise (College Yard, Pacific Quay).

Biggart Baillie (2ptnrs) The team are regarded as technically good. They were joined by a lawyer from Miller Hendry recently. Perceived as general practitioners doing some construction work with some big clients eg: Kvaener. **Clients/Work:** Acting for a major international contractor in a number of significant arbitrations. Drafting construction and O & M contracts for variety of PFI/PPP and CHP projects including the Basingstke District General Hospital.

Bishop and Robertson Chalmers (2ptnrs/3assts) To make it into the major league the firm will need to poach a 'name'.

For the time being they are known essentially for their PI practice, particularly engineering disputes, and for *John Welsh's* regular appearances as an arbiter's clerk. **Clients/Work:** Contract advice to Glasgow Caledonian University on various construction projects in the city campus.

Simpson & Marwick WS (3ptnrs: 1 part-time/2assts: 1 full-time) *Andrew Renton* is an astute engineer who is confidently building his practice – currently largely insurance based claims. Described as "unflappable" and "an able negotiator" some of the larger firms are happy to refer conflict work to him. **Clients/Work:** ERDC Ltd v HM Love & Others; Norwest Holst Construction Ltd V Strathclyde Regional Council (representing the respondents).

Lindsays WS (13ptnrs/9assts) A healthy commercial property practice – construction is seen as a spin off. *Alan McKay* is well known as an arbiter's clerk.

Steedman Ramage (2ptnrs/2assts) To date, known solely for its non-contentious work for retail and developer clients. Thought to be looking for a construction specialist. **Clients/Work:** Advising Helical Retail Ltd in connection with retail development in Glasgow. Advising J Sainsbury Ltd on building contracts relating to retail warehouse park development in Dumfries. Advising Haden Young (subcontractor) on several arbitrations.

LEADING INDIVIDUALS **SCOTLAND**	
ARNOTT James MacRoberts	
NOLAN Brandon McGrigor Donald	
MCLEAN Alistair Dundas & Wilson CS	
MORRISON Alastair Masons	
PATTERSON Lindy MacRoberts	
CONNOR Vincent Masons	
KELLY Neil MacRoberts	
MACKAY Alan Lindsays WS	
MACKECHNIE Edward McGrigor Donald	
MASON Fenella Bird Semple	
RENTON Andrew Simpson & Marwick WS	
SALES Martin Burness	
SHAW Murray Biggart Baillie	
WELSH John Bishop and Robertson Chalmers	

NORTHERN IRELAND

Carson McDowell (1ptnr/2assts) "Well capable of serving the needs of its clients." *Peter Davison* is "a solid and extroverted performer." **Clients/Work:** Largest Civil Engineering contract: Duncree St Sewage. Total worth £30/40m.

Cleaver Fulton & Rankin (2ptnrs/2assts – not all exclusively construction) A large firm for NI with a number of good people.

Elliott Duffy Garrett (3ptnrs/1assts – 10% to 30% of their time) Construction litigation is dealt with as part of a wider practice. The firm has an association with A & L Goodbody in Dublin.

Johns Elliot (3ptnrs/no assts) The practice revolves around *Maurice Butler*,

("excellent") with a long involvement in construction. Maurice is noted for doing his own advocacy rather than using counsel. The firm acts for the Northern Ireland Housing Executive (NIHE), the largest builder in the Province.

Kennedys (1 resident ptnr, 4ptnrs spend some time in the Province/2assts 65% of their time) "The new kid on the block." "Hard working" and "tenacious," *Sean Craig* "is adapting

Carson & McDowell Belfast

Cleaver Fulton & Rankin Belfast

Elliott Duffy Garrett Belfast

Johns Elliot Belfast

Kennedys Belfast

L'Estrange & Brett Belfast

McKinty & Wright Belfast

Mills Selig Belfast

Tughan & Co Belfast

to the local way." Also qualified in the Republic, Sean is setting up to operate on an all-Ireland basis. **Clients/Work:** Advising consortium partner on possible disputes involving $3.5bn desalination unit in the Middle East. Acting for erection company on $20m ICC arbitration dispute involving sulphur storage

facility. Assistance to the parties involved in the Heathrow Airport Tunnel Collapse.

L'Estrange & Brett (1ptnr 25% of time/2assts 10% of time) Known as a contractors law firm; *Sam Beckett* is "courteous" and "looks after his clients' interests." **Clients/Work:** Acted in the case of Gilbert-Ash Ltd vs Beaufort Developments Ltd currently before the House of Lords in an issue relating to arbitration.

McKinty & Wright (4 ptnrs do some) With a deliberately low profile *Owen Catchpole* is considered to be "knowledgeable" but is not a construction specialist. He is well known for PI work and is also a leading defamation lawyer in the Province.

Mills Selig (3ptnrs) Well known for its work in relation to commercial property, *Brian Ham* was recommended for his "gentlemanly representation".

Tughan & Co (1ptnr/ 3assts) The other of the two firms that act for NIHE. *Keith Cowan* is well known.

Masons The recently established Dublin office is doing some PFI projects in the Province, at present it is unable to do pure construction work there.

BECKETT Samuel L'Estrange & Brett

BUTLER Maurice Johns Elliot

COWAN Keith Tughan & Co

DAVISON Peter Carson & McDowell

HAM Brian Mills Selig

CATCHPOLE Owen McKinty & Wright

CRAIG Sean Kennedys

LEADERS' PROFILES · REGIONS

ARNOTT, James M.
MacRoberts, Glasgow (0141) 332 9988
Senior Partner and member of Litigation Department.
Specialisation: Main area of practice is construction, both contentious and non-contentious, including High Court and arbitration proceedings, insurance claims arising in the construction sphere and drafting and negotiation of contracts. Also handles commercial litigation: contractual and delictual business issues. Has handled many leading construction cases in Scotland and also English arbitrations. Contributor to 'Building Contracts' in the Stair Memorial Encyclopedia. Author of papers for IBA, ICLR, IBL, Law Society and commercial bodies. Frequent speaker on construction matters.
Prof. Memberships: Law Society of Scotland, Writer to the Signet, Solicitor to the Supreme Court, International Bar Association.
Career: Qualified in 1956. Joined *MacRoberts* in 1962, becoming Partner in 1963. Former Convenor of Law Reform Committee of Law Society of Scotland and Convenor of Law Society Working Party on Arbitration. Chairman of Committee of Law Society on Construction Specialism. Secretary and Legal Adviser to Scottish Building Contracts Committee. Director and Secretary of Scottish Council for International Arbitration.
Personal: Born 22nd March 1935. Attended Merchiston Castle School 1948-53, then University of Edinburgh 1953-56. Leisure interests include cricket. Lives in Edinburgh.

ASHFORD, Peter
Cripps Harries Hall, Tunbridge Wells, Kent (01892) 506113
Partner in Commercial Litigation Department.
Specialisation: Principal area of practice is construction litigation. Has eleven years experience of handling disputes and is familiar with all the standard forms of building contracts. Particular experience in disputes involving JCT81 with contractors design, DOM/2 'Blueform' and various in-house forms of contracts. Has handled several claims in excess of £1 million for sub-contractors and main contractors. Clients include suspended ceiling/ partition sub-contractors and

national construction and civil engingeering main contractors, including work for Wates Building Group Ltd and M J Gleeson Group Plc. Also handles insolvency and is regularly instructed by "big six" accountancy firms on insolvency matters. Additional interest in professional negligence work and is a member of the team which is a panel member for Solicitors Indemnity Fund Ltd.
Prof. Memberships: Law Society.
Career: Qualified in 1986. Joined *Cripps Harries Hall* in 1987. Became an Associate in 1989 and a Partner in 1991.
Personal: Born in 1961. Educated at Oxted County School and Keele University (BSoc Sci, 1983). Interests include sailing, tennis and cycling. Lives in Tunbridge Wells.

BAKER, Huw J.
Addleshaw Booth & Co, Manchester (0161) 934 6000
Partner in charge of construction in the Manchester office.
Specialisation: Work covers all aspects of contentious and non-contentious construction and engineering work.
Prof. Memberships: Society of Construction Lawyers. Member of ORSA. ORSA accredited Adjudicator.
Career: Qualified in 1987 while with *McKenna & Co*, then joined *Booth & Co* in Leeds in 1990. Joined *Addleshaw Sons & Latham* (now *Addleshaw Booth & Co*) in 1993 as Partner in the Construction Team in Manchester.
Personal: Born 22nd September 1962. Graduated from Cambridge University in 1984 with First Class Honours in Law. Leisure pursuits include gardening, walking and reading. Lives in Hebden Bridge, West Yorkshire.

BARRETT, Kevin John
Neil F. Jones & Co, Birmingham (0121) 643 1010
Qualified 1985; Partner 1989.
Specialisation: Construction litigation, arbitration and alternative dispute resolution as well as non-contentious work relating to the drafting of contracts, bonds, warranties and guaranties and general advisory work in relation

to construction. Lectures on the law relating to construction.
Prof. Memberships: Law Society, Fellow of the Chartered Institute of Arbitrators and Committee Member of the West Midlands Branch. Member of the Birmingham Official Referees Users Committee. *Career:* Joined Neil F. Jones & Co. 1987. Partner 1989.
Personal: Born 1957. Attended Sheffield University, graduating in Law.

BAYLIS, Simon E.
Neil F. Jones & Co, Birmingham (0121) 643 1010
E-mail: seb@neilfjones.co.uk
Specialisation: Building and civil engineering work, both contentious and non-contentious. Particular interest in adjudication and arbitration, and has acted as arbitrator. Non-contentious work includes drafting sub-contracts for use with major Government contract. Lectures extensively on construction contracts and related issues; co-author of third edition of 'The JCT Intermediate Form of Contract'.
Prof. Memberships: Fellow of the Chartered Institute of Arbitrators; Associate of the Royal Institution of Chartered Surveyors; Law Society; ORSA.
Career: Formerly practised in construction industry as Chartered Quantity Surveyor; called to Bar 1985; joined *Neil F. Jones & Co.* in 1989.
Personal: Born 1st September 1954. Educated Bristol Grammar School and University of Sheffield.

BECKETT, Samuel R.
L'Estrange & Brett, Belfast (01232) 230426
See under Litigation (Commercial): 200+ Solicitors, p. 536

BENTLEY, Bruce
Dibb Lupton Alsop, Sheffield (0345) 262 728
Partner in Property Group and Construction Law Unit.
Specialisation: Engineering project work. Involves contracts for the implementation of building and engineering development projects and the negotiation and drafting of development agreements, construction and engineering

contractors and related documents relating to office and industrial developments,disputes and arbitrations between public and private employers and contractors. Delivered a paper at first International Construction Management Conference, UMIST, 1992. Lectured on building contract terms, collateral warranties, JCT insurance clauses and JCT insolvency provisions. Contributor to Construction Management and Resolution.
Prof. Memberships: Society of Construction Law.
Career: Qualified with *Oxley & Coward*, Rotherham, 1971. Partner 1972. Left to join *Dibb Lupton Broomhead* as Partner in 1986.

BRADLEY, Graeme
Dibb Lupton Alsop, Birmingham
(0345) 262728
Specialisation: Contentious and Non-Contentious Construction matters. International Arbitration (Construction). ADR.
Prof. Memberships: Law Society/Arbitration Club/Society Construction Law.
Career: *Masons* 1985-1989 (London). *Masons* 1989-1993 (Hong Kong) Hong Kong Solicitor. *Archibald Andersen* 1993-1995 (Paris) (French Avocat). *Eversheds* 1995- 1997, Head of Construction group. 1997 to date Partner Construction Group DLA.
Personal: Main interests: family, fun and information technology for lawyers.

BUECHEL, P.M.M.
Stones Cann & Hallett, Exeter
(01392) 666 777
Specialisation: Construction, drawn from a wide ranging experience representing the interests of funds, developers, employers, contractors, sub-contractors and professionals both in the context of contentious issues and project documentation at all levels.
Prof. Memberships: Fellow of the Chartered Institute of Arbitrators and Committee Member and Public Relations Officer of the Western Counties Branch of the Chartered Institute of Arbitrators, Member of the Society of Construction Law, Member of the Arbitration Club (King's College Branch), Member of Devon and Exeter Incorporated Law Society.
Career: Qualified 1986, *Herbert Oppenheimer, Nathan & Vandyk* 1986-1988, *Speechly Bircham* 1988-1993, *Stones* 1993 until merger of *Stones* with *Cann & Hallett* on 1 May 1998. Partner of *Stones* 1996, Partner of *Stones Cann & Hallett* 1 May 1998.
Personal: Born 8 April 1962. Educated at Poole Grammar School and Oxford University (Honours School of Jurisprudence) BA 1983, MA 1989. King's College London MSc in Construction Law and Arbitration 1992. When not in the office enjoys sailing, rugby and the pleasures of being a father to Cathryn and Marcus and husband to Karen.

BUTLER, Maurice R.
Johns Elliot, Belfast (01232) 326881
See under General Corporate Finance, p. 259

CATCHPOLE, Owen
McKinty & Wright, Belfast (01232) 246751
See under Defamation, p. 283

COCKRAM, Richard
Addleshaw Booth & Co, Leeds
(0113) 209 2000
Partner, Head of Construction Unit, Leeds.
Specialisation: Construction litigation, arbitration and drafting. Visiting lecturer in Construction Law at Leeds Metropolitan University.
Prof. Memberships: Fellow, Chartered Institute of Arbitrators. Member, Society of Construction Lawyers.
Career: Qualified 1973. Partner, *McKenna & Co.*, 1986-89. Joined the firm in 1989. Publications: "Manual of Construction Agreements" (Jordans, 1998).
Personal: Born 4th November 1947. Cambridge University 1967-70: MA in law. Interests include books and walking. Lives in Leeds.

COLLINGWOOD, Mark
Masons, Bristol (0117) 924 5678
Partner in Construction and Engineering Department.
Specialisation: Heads *Masons'* twenty-five lawyer Bristol office and the firm's Construction Department in Bristol. Specialist construction lawyer since qualification. Particular specialisms include litigation, arbitration and dispute resolution generally, contract and project documentation negotiation and drafting. Has acted in many 'heavyweight' construction cases — civil engineering and building in the UK and abroad. Drafted project documentation for £350m Devonport dockyard redevelopment scheme. Recent reported cases have included Wessex v. HLM. Lectures frequently on the law relating to the construction industry.
Prof. Memberships: Law Society, Faculty of Building.
Career: Qualified in 1980. Articled at *Crossman Block and Keith* 1978-80, before joining *Masons*. Became a Partner in 1985.
Personal: Born 19th December 1954. Attended Durham University, taking a BA in law and politics. Leisure interests include tennis. Has four young children.

CONNOR, Vincent
Masons, Glasgow (0141) 314 3968
Partner in Litigation Department.
Specialisation: Specialist in contentious law, including tactical and strategic advice and the pursuit and defence of claims in litigation, arbitration and ADR.
Prof. Memberships: Law Society of Scotland.
Career: Qualified in 1989. Also qualified as a Notary Public in 1989. Joined *McGrigor Donald* in 1990, became an Associate in 1993 and assumed as a Partner in 1995. Accredited by the Law Society of Scotland as a Solicitor Mediator in 1994. Joined Masons' Glasgow office (associated) when it was opened on 1st May 1998.
Personal: Born 17th April 1964. Educated at Glasgow University 1982-1987 (LLB 1st Class Hons. 1986, DipLP 1987). Leisure interests include running, swimming, skiing, cinema and literature. Lives in Glasgow.

COWAN, Keith C.E.
Tughan & Co, Belfast (01232) 553300
Partner in Commercial Litigation and Insolvency Department.
Specialisation: Main area of practice is construction law and general commercial

litigation. Has over 15 years experience in acting for major construction companies and government departments advising on all areas of JCT/ICC, FIDIC and other similar contracts. Has considerable arbitration experience particularly in construction and has conducted arbitrations in Finland, England and Ireland.
Prof. Memberships: Law Society, Society of Practitioners of Insolvency.
Career: Educated Pembroke College, Cambridge. Partner Tughan & Co, 1989.

CRAIG, Sean T.
Kennedys, Belfast (01232) 240067
Specialisation: Construction related litigation. Disputes against professionals: Architects, Engineers, Surveyors, Geophysicists etc. Also claims against brokers and financial advisers. Acted for Lewis and Tucker on the BBL case. Acting for the Engineer on DED v Kennedys & Co, Loughrey Agnew etc.
Prof. Memberships: Qualified: English Bar, 1985; Law Society (England), 1988; Law Society (Northern Ireland), 1994; Law Society (Republic of Ireland), 1998.
Career: Joined *Kennedys'* City office in June 1987, becoming a Partner in January 1993. Helped establish *Kennedys'* Belfast office which opened in March 1996.

DALLY, Paul
Dibb Lupton Alsop, Leeds (0345) 262728
Specialisation: Professional Indemnity litigation/dispute resolution, acting for a wide variety of construction professionals including architects, surveyors and engineers. Resolution of commercial claims related to all aspects of the construction industry. A particular interest in mediation as a form of dispute resolution.
Career: 1982-1985 University of Sheffield LLB (Hons). 1985-1986 Law Society Finals, Trent Polytechnic. 1986-1991 *Schilling and Lom* Solicitors, London. 1991 to date *Dibb Lupton Alsop Solicitors*, Leeds.
Personal: All sport but particularly football, circuit training and running.

DAVIES, Edward
Masons, Manchester (0161) 877 3777
Partner in Construction Department, *Masons*.
Specialisation: Construction and engineering work, together with technology expertise. Projects throughout UK and abroad involving building, civil engineering, process, transportation, water and energy matters. Advises on all forms of dispute resolution, drafting of contracts, warranties, insurance and bonds. Particular experience in contract drafting for major projects – especially transport and infrastructure – and construction aspects of the PFI. Particular interest in infrastructure projects in People's Republic of China. Training in the field of ADR as a mediator by American Arbitration Association in San Francisco. Lectures extensively on all aspects of construction and engineering law to individual companies and on continuing education courses. Visiting Research Fellow, University of Manchester Institute of Science and Technology (UMIST).
Prof. Memberships: Law Society, Manchester Law Society, Society of Construction Law, American Arbitration Association, Chairman steering group of joint venture between UMIST and *Masons* researching into construction industry disputes. Joint co-ordinator of the CIB (Conseil International du Batiment pour la Recherche, L'Etude et la Documentation)

international task group working on conflict management and dispute resolution in the construction industry.
Career: Qualified in 1982. Joined *Masons* in 1986 in London. Became Partner and moved to the Manchester office on its establishment in 1989.
Personal: Born 25th May 1958. Attended Leeds Grammar School until 1975; Manchester University 1976-79 (LLB); College of Law, Guildford 1980-81 then Kings College, London 1988-90 (part-time MSc). Lives in Manchester.

DAVIES, Lawrence
Masons, Bristol (0117) 924 5678
Partner in Construction and Engineering Department.
Specialisation: Specialises in contentious and non-contentious work related to the construction and engineering industries for contractors, sub-contractors, employers and consultants. Represented Tarmac in the case of Tarmac v Esso (1996).
Prof. Memberships: Law Society. Member of Society of Computers & Law. Secretary of Bristol Construction Law Forum. ORSA adjudicator.
Career: Articled at *Lovell White & King*. Qualified in 1984. Assistant solicitor *Lovell White & King* (then *Lovell White Durrant*) 1984-1990. Joined *Masons* in 1990. Became a Partner 1992.
Personal: Born 1959. Lives in North Somerset. Leisure interests include squash, golf, gardening and DIY.

DAVIES, Peter G.
Gateley Wareing, Birmingham (0121) 236 8585
Specialisation: Construction – mainly contentious but some non-contentious.
Career: Trained at *Needham & James*, Birmingham (now *Dibb Lupton Alsop*) and spent many years there, becoming an equity partner. Moved to *Gateley Wareing* in 1992.
Prof. Memberships: Law Society, Chartered Institute of Arbitrators, The Arbitration Club, Official Referees' Solicitors' Association.

DAVISON, Peter William
Carson & McDowell, Belfast (01232) 244951
Specialisation: Over 20 years of practical experience in general Commercial Litigation, with particular reference to construction matters, working for both Private and Public Sector under ICE/JCT/GC and other forms of contract. Established links with leading Construction Counsel in Belfast and London and experienced expert witnesses if required.
Prof. Memberships: Law Society of Northern Ireland.
Career: 1974 MA Trinity College, Dublin (Legal Science), joined *Carson & McDowell* and admitted solicitor 1977. Partner 1979.

FOLEY, Richard
Masons, Bristol (0117) 924 5678
Specialisation: A specialist construction lawyer undertaking contentious and non-contentious work principally for contractors and employers. Recently advised on suite of contracts for multimillion pound processing facility and acted in major arbitration regarding defects and cost overruns.
Career: Qualified in 1987. Joined *Masons* in 1990. Partner 1997.
Personal: Born 6th November 1962. Educated at Colston's School and Liverpool University (LLB). Interests include golf, cricket, rugby and squash.

GLAISTER, Anthony
Denison Till, Leeds (0113) 246 7161
Specialisation: All areas of construction law to include Arbitration and Alternative Dispute Resolution. Solicitor for NFB and FMB regional members. Charges £125 per hour.
Prof. Memberships: ORSA Adjudicator, CEDR Mediator, Administrator Association of Northern Mediators, and Chartered Institute of Arbitrators. Visiting Lecturer on adjudication and mediation at Leeds Metropolitan University.
Career: Qualified in 1980. Partner in *Fox & Gibbons*, London from 1985 to 1989 and *Denison Till* since.
Personal: Born April 1953. Very active leisure pursuits where family and farming activities allow. Regional Deputy Chairman PYBT.

GORDON, Roderick C.P.R.
Robert Muckle, Newcastle-upon-Tyne (0191) 232 4402
Partner in Construction Unit. Head of Litigation Department. Main area of practice covers construction and engineering disputes, including High Court, arbitration and Alternative Dispute Resolution work as well as non-contentious work.
Career: Qualified 1988. Moved from *Masons* to *Robert Muckle* as a Partner in 1993.
Personal: Born 17.3.1959.

GUPPY, W. Nicholas
Laytons, Bristol 0117 929 1626

HACKING, Malcolm R.
Hacking Ashton, Newcastle-under-Lyme (01782) 715555

HAM, Brian E.
Mills Selig, Belfast (01232) 243878
See under Litigation (Commercial), p. 536

HARDWICK, John
Greenwoods, Peterborough (01733) 555244

HARLING, Marcus
Burges Salmon, Bristol (0117) 939 2000

HARRIS, Adam
Masons, Bristol (0117) 924 5678
Email: adam.harris@masons.com
Partner in Construction and Engineering Department.
Specialisation: Contentious and non-contentious work with a particular interest in PFI. A specialist in the building, civil engineering, process plant and electricity industries. Acts for both contractors and employers.
Career: Qualified 1981. *Lovell White Durrant* 1982-1988 (Hong Kong 1983-1987). Admitted Hong Kong 1984. Partner at *Masons* 1990.
Personal: Born 3rd January 1956. Educated Wellington School and Birmingham University (LLB). Interests include cricket and gardening.

HARTLEY, Keith
Masons, Leeds (0113) 233 8905
Partner in Construction & Engineering Department
Specialisation: Leads 10-lawyer Construction Dept in Leeds. Dispute resolution including High Court, arbitration and ADR and major project work, including many PFI and BOT schemes. Particular interests are transport systems and infrastructure and off shore process installations. Worked in UK and several Asian countries.

Prof. Memberships: Law Society, Chartered Institute of Arbitrators, Pacific Lawyers Association.
Career: Joined *Masons* in1980. Admitted as solicitor in England (1982) and in Hong Kong (1984) and became a partner in 1986. Resident in Hong Kong for 10 years before becoming Managing Partner of Leeds office in 1995.
Personal: Born 11 October 1957. Educated at King's College, London. Lives at Adel near Leeds.

HERBERT, Mary
Eversheds, Newcastle upon Tyne (0191) 261 1661
Specialisation: Defects claims, particularly claims against professionals, loss and expense claims. Considerable experience of health sector, power, offshore and micro-electronics, as well as general building and engineering. Also very experienced in contract drafting, amending and professional appointments and warranties.
Prof. Memberships: Law society.
Career: Qualified in 1988 and joined Eversheds, becoming a Partner in 1993.
Personal: Theatre, art and gardening. Lives in Durham.

HILTON, Mark W.
Hammond Suddards, Leeds (0113) 284 7000
Partner and National Head of the Construction and Engineering Unit.
Specialisation: Main area of practice is construction law. Acts on behalf of contractors, sub-contractors and employers in relation to non-contentious and contentious matters and contractual and other disputes in all areas of construction, in arbitration and litigation. Also handles commercial litigation work. Acted in Duquemin v. Slater, Preston v. Torfaen, Yorkshire RHA v. Fairclough and Percy Thomas, Strachan and Henshaw v. Stein Industrie.
Prof. Memberships: Law Society, ORSA, Fellow of the Chartered Institute of Arbitrators.
Career: Qualified in 1982. Worked at *Last Suddards* in Bradford 1980-82, *Barlow Lyde & Gilbert* 1982-84 and rejoined *Last Suddards* (later *Hammond Suddards*) in 1984, becoming a Partner in 1985.
Personal: Born 15th July 1958. Attended Wrekin College 1972-76 and University of Leeds 1976-79. Leisure interests include swimming, scuba diving, skiing and tennis. Lives in Harrogate.

HOWE, Martin
Veale Wasbrough, Bristol (0117) 925 2020
Partner.
Specialisation: Construction law, both contentious and non-contentious.
Career: Qualified 1983. With *Lawrance Messer* 1980-85. With *Veale Wasbrough* (formerly *Stanley Wasbrough*) since 1985. Partner since 1989.
Personal: Born 10/11/58. Educated at Bristol Cathedral School and King's College, London. Interests include: running, mountain-biking, swimming, music and family. Lives in North Nibley, Gloucestershire.

HOWELL-RICHARDSON, Phillip
Morgan Bruce, Cardiff (01222) 385385
See under Litigation (Commercial): 200+ Solicitors, p. 525

HOYLE, Roger V.
Veale Wasbrough, Bristol (0117) 925 2020
Partner in Commercial Litigation Department.
Specialisation: Construction law. Has
extensive experience of dispute resolution in the
construction industry, involving claims
concerning defective design and construction,
the liability of professionals and their insurers,
and the interpretation and enforcement of
contracts, including claims for loss and expense.
Prof. Memberships: Committee Member of
the Official Referees Solicitors Association, Law
Society (London and Bristol).
Career: Qualified in 1971. Joined *Stanley
Wasbrough*, now *Veale Wasbrough*, in 1972.
Became a Partner in 1973.
Personal: Born 6th March 1947. Educated at
Sedbergh School. Leisure interests include
trekking and walking, photography, archery,
family, food and wine. Lives in Bristol.

JEFFERIES, Michael
Hugh James, Cardiff (01222) 224871
Partner in Construction and Civil Engineering
Department.
Specialisation: Has specialised in
construction law for over 20 years, engaged in
major litigation and arbitration for all sectors of
the industry, as well as advising on non-
contentious matters. Particular emphasis on
professional indemnity matters, acting on behalf
of a variety of professionals including architects,
engineers, surveyors and their insurers
(including contractor's design liability insurers).
Important cases handled include Mid
Glamorgan C.C. v. Devonald Williams; H.H.C v.
W.H.T.S.O and Mid Glamorgan C.C. v. Land
Authority for Wales. Member of Salford
University Working Party on Intelligent Authoring
of Building Contracts. Lead Partner for the
Welsh Rugby Union redevelopment of the
National Stadium.
Prof. Memberships: Institute of Arbitrators.
Career: Joined *Hugh James* in 1970. Qualified
and became a Partner in 1972.
Personal: Born 21st November 1947. Educated
at University College, London. Lives in Cardiff.

JONES, Michael L.N.
Hugh James, Cardiff (01222) 224871
See under Litigation (Commercial): 200+
Solicitors, p. 525

JONES, Peter
Eversheds, Cardiff (01222) 471147
Specialisation: Commercial litigation,
particularly construction and engineering and
property related litigation. Has considerable
experience in major construction disputes and
professional negligence in relation to earthworks
design and claims for loss and expense. Has
practised as a mediator and is an accredited
mediator with CEDR and the ADR Group.
Prof. Memberships: Fellow Chartered Institute
of Arbitrators; member of the Law Society.
Career: Articled with Phillips & Buck, now
Eversheds. Partner 1986.
Personal: Educated University of Wales;
University of Aix-en-Provence; has a university
doctorate in Comparative Law. Fluent French
and Welsh speaker. Is a semi-professional
musician.

KELLY, Neil J.
MacRoberts, Edinburgh (0131) 226 2552
Specialisation: Practice covers full range of
advice to commercial clients in connection with
dispute avoidance and resolution (Arbitration,
Court, ADR) with particular reference to the
construction and civil engineering industries
acting for related professions, contractors, sub-
contractors and suppliers.
Prof. Memberships: Notary Public, Associate
of the Chartered Institute of Arbitrators,
Commissioner of the Scottish Council for
International Arbitration.
Career: Born 28th June 1961. Aberdeen
University (LLB with Distinction and Dip. L.P.).
Interests include opera and classical music.
Lives in Edinburgh.

KIRKHAM, Frances
Dibb Lupton Alsop, Birmingham
(0345) 262728
Specialisation: Construction, engineering,
power engineering, major capital projects,
litigation, arbitration, ADR, practising arbitrator,
assistant recorder, higher rights (civil).
Prof. Memberships: The Law Society, ORSA,
Association of Women Solicitors, Birmingham
Law Society, Fellow of the Chartered Institute of
Arbitrators.
Career: Head of construction at *Edge & Ellison*
until 1985. Now head of construction at *Dibb
Lupton Alsop*, Birmingham.
Personal: Linguist.

LANGLEY, Robert Lennox
Watson Burton, Newcastle upon Tyne
(0191) 244 4444
Partner in Commercial Litigation Department.
Member of construction unit. Accredited
Mediator.
Specialisation: Specialises in construction law
and professional indemnity. Head of
Commercial Litigation. Handles contractual
disputes in construction, engineering and
fabrication. Also undertakes professional
indemnity and professional negligence work,
both tortious and contractual. Has acted in a
wide range of disputes including those in the
construction process, injunctive work
particularly in the context of off-shore fabrication
and engineering, minority oppression and a
number of major arbitrations. Clients include
fundholders, developers, further education
institutions, design consultants, estate
surveyors and valuers, foreign lawyers and
Underwriters. Regular speaker at conferences
and seminars including the RICS National
Briefing Conference for Building Surveyors.
Prof. Memberships: Law Society, Official
Referees Solicitors Association, Chartered
Institute of Arbitrators. ADR Net.
Career: Qualified in 1979. Articled at *Watson
Burton*, Newcastle upon Tyne. Partner in 1981.
Personal: Educated at Oxford University (BA
Jurisprudence 1974). Leisure interests include
yachting, skiing, the hills and history. Lives in
Newcastle upon Tyne.

LEWIS, Simon
Dickinson Dees, Newcastle upon Tyne
0191 279 9000
Specialisation: Covers full range of
Construction Law, including offshore and
minerals industries. In particular deals with

dispute resolution, including litigation,
arbitration, ADR and Adjudication. Also
extensively involved in PFI work. Acts for all
sectors of the Construction industry. Writes and
lectures extensively on construction law and PFI
issues. Has a regular column in Building
magazine.
Prof. Memberships: Associate of the
Chartered Institute of Arbitrators, member of
ORSA (accredited adjudicator) and ARCOM.
Career: Qualified 1986. Joined Lovell White
Durrant 1988. Joined Dickinson Dees 1992
(Partner from 1995).
Personal: Born 20 November 1960. Bristol
University 1979 – 1983: LL.B, LL.M. Interests
include: cinema, hillwalking and American
Football. Lives in Newcastle upon Tyne

LLOYD JONES, David
Edge & Ellison, Birmingham
(0121) 200 2001
Specialisation: Extensive experience in
contentious and non-contentious construction.
Principal areas of work involve drafting and
negotiation of construction and engineering
contracts and development agreements
covering all aspects of property development,
rail, road and engineering projects whether
acting for developers, owners, funders,
contractors or consultants.
Prof. Memberships: Fellow, Chartered
Institute of Arbitrators, Official Referees
Solicitors Association (Committee Member),
Society of Construction Law.
Career: Joined Edge & Ellison in 1989 (Partner
from 1991).

MACKAY, Alan D.
Lindsays WS, Edinburgh (0131) 477 8708
Partner in Litigation Department.
Specialisation: Main areas of practice are
building and construction arbitration and
litigation. Acts for contractors, sub-contractors
and employers in building and civil engineering
work both contentious and non-contentious.
Acts as legal clerk and adviser to arbiters in
construction arbitrations in Scotland. Has
lectured for the Law Society of Scotland and the
Chartered Institute of Arbiters. Accredited by the
Law Society of Scotland as a Specialist in
Construction Law.
Prof. Memberships: Law Society of Scotland,
Society of Writers to the Signet, Chartered
Institute of Arbiters (Fellow), on list of
adjudicators kept by the Law Society of
Scotland acting as a nominating body in terms
of the Scheme for Construction Contracts
(Scotland).
Career: Qualified in 1968. Joined *Lindsays WS*
as a Partner in 1987.
Personal: Born 19th January 1944. Attended
George Watson's College 1952-62 and
Edinburgh University 1962-65. Leisure interests
include golf, reading, theatre and family. Lives in
Edinburgh.

MACKECHNIE, Edward M.
McGrigor Donald, Glasgow (0141) 248 6677
Specialisation: Provision of advocacy services
in relation to construction related Arbitrations –
four Major Construction/Engineering Arbitrations
over the last year. Advising generally in relation
to a wide range of construction related issues.
Prof. Memberships: Law Society of Scotland.
Career: Glasgow Academy, Glasgow
University, Partner *Bishop & Company* 1975 to
1986; Partner *McGrigor Donald* 1986 to date.

Dual qualified England and Scotland.
Personal: Leisure interests include golf and skiing. Married with two daughters.

MASON, Fenella Mary
Bird Semple, Edinburgh (0131) 459 2345
Specialisation: Partner in *Bird Semple's* Construction and Engineering Unit. Fenella's practice encompasses all aspects of the law in relation to construction and engineering, from advising on contractual arrangements, drafting bespoke contracts, warranties etc., through to resolution of substantial disputes through negotiation, litigation and arbitration. Acts for contractors, sub-contractors and employers in wide range of major public and private sector projects and disputes.
Prof. Memberships: Scottish Regional Co-ordinator for The Society of Construction Law.
Career: Qualified 1989. Partner in *Bird Semple* 1995.

MCLEAN, Alistair
Dundas & Wilson CS, Edinburgh
(0131) 228 8000
Specialisation: Partner and Head of Construction and Engineering Group and member of Information Technology Group. Work undertaken includes all types of construction related disputes (both litigation and arbitration), advising on procurement methods and drafting contract documents. Acts for a broad base of institutional and commercial developers, main contractors and large sub/trade contractors, including Scottish Widows, Hyundai, Tarmac and The Miller Group. Has advised on a number of software related disputes for a mixture of users and software houses. Lectures at Strathclyde University on LLM course on Construction Law.
Prof. Memberships: The Law Society of Scotland and admitted as a solicitor in England and Hong Kong. Society of Construction Law.
Career: Attended University of Glasgow (LLB, DipLP). Articled *McClure Naismith*; qualified 1985; *McGrigor Donald* 1986-88; *McKenna & Co*, Hong Kong 1988-90; *Masons*, London 1990-94; *Dundas & Wilson CS* Partner since 1996.
Personal: Born 1962. Resides Edinburgh. Leisure interests include rugby, golf and tennis. Alistair McLean has also been recommended as a Leader in the Field of Litigation (Commercial).

MORRISON, Alastair
Masons, Glasgow (0141) 221 8586
Specialisation: Partner providing legal and strategic advice on all aspects of construction projects, drafting of bespoke contracts and construction arbitration and litigation.
Prof. Memberships: International Bar Association Construction Division.
Career: Attended University of Cape Town, University of Glasgow (LLB Hons, Dip LP). Assistant solicitor *Digby Brown* 1986 – 1989; assistant solicitor *McGrigor Donald* 1989 – 1993; associate partner *Dundas & Wilson CS* 1993 – 1994; Partner and Head of Construction and Engineering Group 1994-1998; Partner, *Masons*, July 1998.
Personal: Born 1962. Resides Glasgow. Leisure interests include running and rugby.

MOSS, David J.
Hammond Suddards, Manchester
(0161) 830 5000
Partner in Construction and Engineering Unit.
Specialisation: Principal area of practice is contentious construction and engineering industry claims. Wide experience of the standard form of building and engineering contract (including JCT, ICE, RMR '80, MF/I, IMechEE). Has advised main mechanical subcontractors on numerous power stations, waste incinerators and chemical process plants and both contractors and employers on various 'build' schemes. Part-time lecturer at the University of the City of Leeds. Addresses conferences and seminars both internal and external.
Prof. Memberships: O.R.S.A., ACIAArb, Society of Construction Law, O.R.S.A. Accredited Adjudicator.
Career: Qualified in 1986. Joined *Hammond Suddards* in 1990.
Personal: Born November 1961. Educated at Edge End High School, Nelson. University of Sheffield 1980-83. The College of Law Guilford. Leisure activities include family, cricket, football and golf. Lives in Addingham.

NEWMAN, Paul
Edwards Geldard, Cardiff (01222) 238239
Senior Associate – Construction
Specialisation: Principally contentious, but also some non-contentious construction law. Regularly appears as advocate in Arbitration hearings. Most recently relating to a gas works remediation site. Currently has conduct of an arbitration on a major roadworks scheme. In addition to arbitration, regularly appears for clients in matters conducted as Official referee's Business and has an interest in ADR/conciliation of claims. Non-contentious work includes advising the funder on the Millennium Syadium, Cardiff and acting for Wales Millennium Centre on procurement issues. Has provided seminar on construction law to many organisations, including the College of Law and professional bodies. Author and/or co-author of various books and papers on construction law, including tactics in construction litigation 1996, ADR 1998 and securing payment and other obligations under construction contracts 1998.
Prof. Memberships: Called to the Bar by Gray's Inn November 1982, Associate of the Chartered Institute of Arbitrators, accredited Adjudicator for the Royal Institute of British Architects and the Construction Industry Council.
Career: Called to the Bar in November 1982 and joined *Edwards Geldard* as a non-practising barrister in 1990.
Personal: Born 5 March 1958. Educated at Clare College, Cambridge (1976-1980), City University, London (1980-1981) and the Inns of Court School of Law (1981-1982).

NOLAN, Brandon
McGrigor Donald, Glasgow (0141) 248 6677
Specialisation: All aspects of contentious and non-contentious matters relating to construction law. Currently involved in substantial projects in England and Northern Ireland as well as in Scotland. Has conducted the advocacy in a number of substantial arbitrations. A frequent speaker at commercially organised seminars.
Prof. Memberships: Associate of the Chartered Institute of Arbitrators; Society of Construction Law; International Bar Association; Official Referees Solicitors Association.
Career: Qualified 1980 with *McGrigor Donald & Co* (as it was then). Became a partner in 1987. Head of the Construction and Engineering Unit at *McGrigor Donald*.

Personal: Born 4th November 1955. Educated at Glasgow University 1974-1978. Leisure interests include visiting a gym and films.

OATS, Simon D.
Birketts, Ipswich (01473) 232300
Specialisation: Construction and engineering related law encompassing contractual advice and disputes resolution. Acts for a number of substantial construction clients including employers, developers, contractors and professionals. Particular experience in engineering contracts, official referees business and arbitration.
Prof. Memberships: Law society, Society of Construction Law, Interact.

PALMER, S.D.
Eversheds, Leeds (0113) 243 0391
Specialisation: Construction engineering disputes: Official Referees High Court litigation; arbitration; forms of Alternative Dispute Resolution. Advising on construction contracts, consultants' appointments and collateral warranties. Head of the Eversheds ADR Initiative. Visiting lecturer on various construction matters at Leeds Metropolitan University, Leeds University and Leeds College of Building. Speaker on a wide range of construction issues to other forums.
Prof. Memberships: Associate of the Chartered Institute of Arbitrators; Honorary Secretary of the North East Branch of the CIArb; member of the Society of Construction Law and regional co-ordinator of the Society's Leeds focus; member of the Yorkshire Construction Association, Visiting lecturer.
Career: Qualified in 1987. Trained with *Eversheds*, Leeds office (then Hepworth & Chadwick) and has been with them ever since. Partner in 1994.
Personal: Born 21.5.63. BA in law at Durham University. Interests include: music, rugby, walking, skiing, socialising. Lives in York.

PATTERSON, Lindy A.
MacRoberts, Edinburgh (0141) 332 9988
Specialisation: Specialises in contentious building and civil engineering matters. Lindy is widely regarded as one of Scotland's leading construction and civil engineering law experts. She acts for a number of the UK's leading construction and engineering companies, including Taylor Woodrow regularly handling disputes in arbitration and litigation covering all aspects of building and civil engineering disputes. She represents clients in the Commercial Court and the Court of Session, as one of Scotland's first Solicitor-Advocates and the first female Solicitor Advocate. She speaks regularly at industry seminars and contributes to building and civil engineering publications.
Prof. Memberships: Member of Law Society Accreditation Panel for Construction Law; Judicial Procedure and Insurance Committees; Member of Commercial Court Working Party set up to establish the need for and rules of such a Court; Member of the Consultative Committee on the Commercial Court to monitor its progress; Member of Working Party set up by Scottish Office to advise on Scheme for Constuction Contracts required by Housing Grants Construction and Regeneration Act 1996. Liaison Committee of the Department of Building & Surveying, Napier University.
Career: Trainee Solicitor *W & J Burness* 1980-1982. Solicitor *Biggart Billie & Gifford* and *Menzies Dougal* 1982-1985. Joined *Bird Semple* 1985,

became partner 1988; solicitor-Advocate 1993.
Personal: Graduated LLB (Hons) Edinburgh
University 1980. Skiing, hillwalking and
watersports.

PICKUP, Raith
Mills & Reeve, Cambridge
+44 (0)1223 364422
Specialisation: Has extremely wide experience
of drafting and negotiating the documentation
for many substantial projects. These include
business parks, retail developments, university
campuses, hospitals and large infrastructure
projects such as power stations. Also conducts
construction arbitrations and litigation. He
heads the *Mills & Reeve* Private Finance
Initiative (PFI) team and has advised on more
than 20 PFI projects in the health, education
and local authority sectors.
Prof. Memberships: Lectures regularly on the
legal aspects of the building and engineering
industries as well as PFI and is a member of the
Society of Construction Law.

PIGOTT, Ashley R.
Wragge & Co, Birmingham (0121) 233 1000
Specialisation: Advises major public utilities
on power station projects. Acts for a number of
national and international contractors and
developers. All aspects of construction and
engineering law.
Prof. Memberships: Committee member
Chartered Institute of Arbitrators, West Midlands
Region, member Official Referees Solicitors
Association and Society of Construction Law.
Career: Articled *Macfarlanes*. Qualified 1986.
Partner at *Wragge & Co* from 1995.
Personal: Born 1962.

PLASCOW, Ronald H.
Mills & Reeve, Cambridge Int
+44 (01223) 364422
Partner in Construction and Civil Engineering
Department.
Specialisation: Has practised exclusively in
construction and civil engineering since 1982
beginning in industry at Trafalgar House Plc.
Regularly advises on the JCT, ICE and most
other forms of standard contracts used in the
UK and on the FIDIC Contract used abroad.
Represents employers and contractors involved
in litigation in the Courts, or in arbitration. A
trained mediator familiar with the use of other
ADR techniques to resolve disputes and has
represented clients in mediations. Prepares and
drafts construction contracts, consultants'
appointments and bonds and warranties. Editor
of Arbitration Practice and Procedure,
Interlocutory and Hearing Problems (Lloyd's of
London Press Ltd) first edition, regular speaker
at conferences arranged by the RICS, RIBA, ICE
and CIArb. Past Secretary to the East Anglia
Branch of the CIArb.

PROCTOR, Nigel
Davies Arnold Cooper, Manchester
(0161) 839 8396
Partner in Construction Group.
Specialisation: Chartered Civil Engineer and
Solicitor handles all aspects of contentious and
non-contentious construction and engineering
work. Contentious work includes major
domestic and international disputes. Non-
contentious work includes advising on property

development schemes, various forms of
management contract and PFI. Currently acting
for Petrotrin (Trinidad) in dispute with SNC Lavalin
and disputes for North West Water Ltd. Acting for
the Consortium in major hospital PFI advising
on construction and service provider elements.
Prof. Memberships: Member Institution of Civil
Engineers. Chartered Engineer. Society of
Construction Law. Official Referees Solicitors
Association.
Career: Civil Engineer 1977 – 1984. Joined
McKenna & Co 1984. Qualified 1990. Joined
Davies Arnold Cooper 1995. Partner 1997.
Personal: Born 20 May 1956. Leisure interests:
include golf, football and family. Lives in
Wilmslow, Cheshire.

REDMOND, John V.
Laytons, Bristol (0117) 929 1626

RENTON, Andrew L.
Simpson & Marwick WS, Edinburgh
(0131) 557 1545

RICHARDS, Mark
Masons, Leeds (0113) 233 8905
Specialisation: Specialises in construction
and engineering both contentious and non-
contentious work. Has recently been involved in
the drafting and negotiation of the construction
management contracts for the making safe of
the Chernobyl Nuclear Power Plant in Ukraine.
Leads a team advising both public and private
sector organisations in relation to PFI projects.
Is involved in running a number of multi-million
pound engineering and construction disputes
for contractors.
Prof. Memberships: Law Society. Society of
Construction Law. International Bar Association.
Lighthouse Club.
Career: Qualified 1987. Joined *Masons* 1988.
Became a partner in1993. LLB(Hons)
Birmingham University 1982. Msc in
Construction Law and Arbitration – King's
College London.
Personal: Born May 1961 – 2 children. Leisure
interests: cricket, golf, squash.

RICHARDS, Tim
Hewitson Becke + Shaw, Cambridge
(01223) 461155
Specialisation: Head of construction dealing
with all aspects of construction law including
drafting and advising on all forms of project
documentation and the litigation and arbitration
of disputes. Currently advising the preferred
bidder on a local authority Pathfinder PFI project.
Prof. Memberships: Society of Construction
Law
Career: Caterham School, Surrey; University
College Cardiff (1982 LLB Hons); Articled
Evershed & Tomkinson, Birmingham; Qualified
1985 *Linklaters & Paines* (1985-96); Partner,
Head of Construction, *Hewitson Becke & Shaw*
1996 to date.
Personal: Born 1959; Resides Abbotsley,
Cambs; Leisure – rugby, skiing and golf.

ROBINSON, Mark G.C.
Hugh James, Cardiff (01222) 224871
Specialisation: Construction and civil
engineering, in particular, non-contentious
aspects of large scale retail, commercial, leisure
and housing projects. Also contentious matters

by way of Arbitration and Official Referees
Litigation. Major projects in the last twelve
months include the Millennium Stadium, retail
park at Portishead, shopping centre
development in Ebbw Vale, renovation of
Dyffryn House for Vale of Glamorgan and advice
to the Welsh Office on the Secretary of State for
Wales' involvement in the Bute Avenue PFI
Project.
Prof. Memberships: The Law Society. The
Concrete Society (Welsh Region-Committee
Member). Panel Solicitor-Federation of Master
Builders (Welsh Region).
Career: Born 18th May 1959. Graduate of
University College of Wales, Aberystwyth (Law).
Calcoff Pryce essay prize winner of UCW Law
Department, 1980. Joined *Hugh James* in
October 1980. Became an Equity Partner in May
1996.
Personal: Has two children. Leisure interests
include cricket and allotment gardening.

ROBSON, Nigel R.
Eversheds, Newcastle upon Tyne
(0191) 261 1661
Partner in Construction and Engineering Unit.
Specialisation: Principal area of practice
involves handling contractual disputes arising
from construction or engineering projects on
JCT, ICE, GC Works forms of contract or
individual off-the-shelf contracts with particular
emphasis on loss and expense claims and
defects claims. Has considerable experience in
relation to hospitals, process engineering,
power stations, off-shore, waste incinerators
and major civil engineering projects. Other main
area of work involves drafting and amending
commercial agreements for construction and
engineering projects.
Prof. Memberships: Law Society; Fellow,
Chartered Institute of Arbitrators.
Career: Qualified in 1977 and went on to join
Eversheds, becoming a Partner in 1980.
Chairman of *Eversheds'* Construction Group
since 1989. Board Member and Managing
Partner of *Eversheds* North East since 1992.
Personal: Born 23rd May 1951.

SALES, Martin
Burness, Edinburgh (0131) 473 6000
See under Planning, p. 657

SALMON, Kenneth T.
Kirk Jackson, Manchester (0161) 707 3000
Partner Construction Law Department.
Specialisation: Main area of work is building
and civil engineering disputes, both in court and
at arbitration, and advising on contract
documentation. Conducts in-house seminars
for clients.
Prof. Memberships: Law Society, Official
Referee's Solicitors Association, Northern
Arbitration Association, Manchester Law
Society, A.C.I. Arb.
Career: Qualified 1973 while at *Kirk Jackson*
and became a Partner in 1975.
Personal: Born 16th April 1946. Leisure
pursuits include cycling, five-a-side soccer, hill-
walking, music and reading. Lives in
Warrington.

SCOTT, Martin L.
Walker Morris, Leeds (0113) 283 2500
Partner and Head of Construction Group.
Specialisation: Practice covers the full rage of
construction and engineering law, both
contentious and non-contentious. Particularly

active in the field of disputes where defects whether by design or in construction are the central issue. Acts mainly for Employers/Developers and specialist sub-contractors but also undertakes work for main contractors within the region.
Career: Qualified 1985. At *Scott Turnbull & Kendall*, now *Walker Morris*, since 1984. Became a Partner in 1992.
Personal: Born 13th August 1959. Educated at Ashville College, Harrogate and Leicester Polytechnic BA Law. Interests include flying, farming and family. Lives in Harrogate.

SHAW, Murray W.A.
Biggart Baillie, Glasgow (0141) 228 8000
Specialisation: Partner in the litigation department specialising in construction law (contentious and non-contentious) and insolvency law. Law Society accredited in both areas as well as Licensed Insolvency Practitioner. Work includes commercial litigation including contract disputes, building contract diputes and arbitration, and planning (with particular reference to the energy industry). Author of chapter on liquidation in 'Scottish Insolvency Casebook', and has written several articles on insolvency for the IBA Journal. Regular speaker on courses on insolvency and building contracts.
Prof. Memberships: International Bar Association; Law Society of Scotland.
Career: Qualified 1982. Assistant solicitor, *Biggart, Baillie & Gifford* 1982-85 and 1986/1987 Assistant *Speechly Bircham*, London, 1985-86. Partner, *Biggart, Baillie & Gifford* since 1987.
Personal: Educated at Dundee University (LL.B Hons 1980).Leisure pursuits include golf, reading and rugby. Born 25th September 1957. Lives in Glasgow.

STANIFORTH, Alison J.
Eversheds, Leeds (0113) 243 0391
Partner in Litigation Department (Head of Construction and Engineering).
Specialisation: Principal area of practice is construction and engineering disputes including litigation, arbitration and ADR on the JCT and ICE families of contracts, bespoke contracts (including joint ventures, both domestic and international) and FIDIC forms. Also handles non-contentious construction and engineering work, including drafting and negotiating amendments to standard and bespoke forms of contracts, warranties, performance bonds, parent company guarantees and professional appointments. Important matters handled include developments for student accomodation; teaching facilities and science laboratories; facilities management agreements; power generation projects; PFI for waste recycling. Other clients include N G Bailey, Yorkshire Electricity, British Waterways Board, Weir Pumps Ltd, Cameron Taylor Bedford, Morrison Construction and Hays Specialist Distribution Ltd. Visiting Lecturer at Leeds Metropolitan University (MSc in Arbitration and Construction Law). Regular conference speaker for e.g. APM, RICS, CIOB and the Institute of Structural Engineers.
Prof. Memberships: CIARB, ORSA, Common Purpose Graduate, OPP 2K, Network.
Career: Qualified in 1985. With *Herbert Smith* 1983-86. Joined *Hepworth & Chadwick* in 1986 and became a Partner at *Eversheds Hepworth & Chadwick* in 1991.
Personal: Born 13th December 1957. Leeds

University 1976-79 (LL.B) and Trinity Hall, Cambridge 1980-83 (MLitt). Interests include golf, malt whiskey and gardening.

VASEY, John R.
Wansbroughs Willey Hargrave, Bristol (0117) 926 8981
Head of Construction Group.
Specialisation: Acts for developers, contractors (both private and public sector) and insurers in often high value and high profile litigation. Experienced in all types of construction contracts, disputes, insured construction risks and professional indemnity claims. Recent experience includes complex multi-party arbitration proceedings, disputes on major civil engineering and building contracts, and advising on construction implications of fire and flood related claims. He is a keen exponent of all types of ADR, including expert determination and adjudication.
Career: Qualified in 1980. *Oppenheimer Nathan & Vandhyke* 1981-83; *McKenna & Co* 1984-87. Joined *Wansbroughs Willey Hargrave* in 1988.

WELSH, John
Bishop and Robertson Chalmers, Glasgow (0141) 248 4672
Partner in the Litigation Division.
Specialisation: Main area of practice is construction law, including professional negligence claims against engineers, architects and surveyors, arbitrations, drafting and advising on construction law contracts, appointments and warranties. He is a regular contributor of articles for Construction Industry Publications. Speaker at conferences on collateral warranties and methods of procurement under building contracts.
Prof. Memberships: Law Society of Scotland, Royal Faculty of Procurators in Glasgow.
Career: Qualified in 1968. Assistant Solicitor and Partner at *Robertson Chalmers & Auld* 1969-86. Partner with *Bishop and Robertson Chalmers* from 1986. Accredited by the Law Society of Scotland as a Specialist in Construction Law in 1993 and as a Solicitor-Mediator in 1994.
Personal: Born 12th September 1945. Educated at Glasgow University 1963-66. Enjoys golf and fishing. Lives in Bearsden.

WILCOCK, Christopher
Hammond Suddards, Manchester (0161) 830 5000
Specialisation: Main practice areas are construction and engineering. Contentious and non-contentious work. Lectured on adjudication/arbitration. Acted for P&O on sale of Arndale Centre, Manchester. Acting for local authority on major road project.
Prof. Memberships: Associate: Chartered Institute of Arbitrators. Member: Pipeline Industries Guild.
Career: Qualified 1987. Specialised in construction/engineering since then.
Personal: Leisure interests – Manchester United FC. Two young children. Not much time for anything else!!

WILLCOCK, Andrew
Trowers & Hamlins, Manchester (0161) 833 9293
Partner in Construction Department.
Specialisation: Main areas of practice are construction and civil engineering. Includes both

contentious and non-contentious matters involving building, civil engineering and mechanical engineering work. Also specialises in PFI.
Prof. Memberships: Official Referees Solicitors Association, Society for Computers and Law.
Career: Qualified in 1972. Joined *Davies Arnold Cooper* in 1991. Became Partner in 1993. Joined *Trowers & Hamlins* as Partner in 1998.
Personal: Born 13th September 1945. Leisure pursuits include hill walking. Lives in Manchester.

WILLIAMS, Jeremy
Morgan Bruce, Cardiff (01222) 385385
Specialisation: Construction and Engineering Law. Heads the five lawyer Construction Team. Specialises in contentious and non-contentious work relating to construction, engineering, process plant, facilities management and large scale PFI projects.
Prof. Memberships: Societyof Construction Law.
Career: Qualified in 1988; joined *Morgan Bruce* from *Linklaters* in 1992.
Personal: Born 10/11/61; Educated at Neath Grammar School and University of Wales, Aberystwyth.

WOOD, Martin
Greenwoods, Peterborough (01733) 555244

WOOLLEY, Michael D.
Elliott & Company, Manchester (0161) 834 9933
Specialisation: All construction related litigation and arbitration cases including those with a foreign element, for Employers, Contractors and their Insurers. Construction related Professional Indemnity work. Recent cases include claims for time and money for power stations, water treatment works and office buildings. In addition claims for defective work on several projects including a Theme Park ride.
Career: Admitted 1987. Joined *Elliott & Company* 1988 – Heads Construction Team. Northern Arbitration Association. North West Official Referees User Group.
Personal: Married with two children.

YULE, Ian R.
Neil F. Jones & Co, Birmingham (0121) 643 1010
Specialisation: Handles contentious and non-contentious construction and engineering matters. Emphasis is on arbitration, litigation and mediation. Also advises on forms of contract, bonds, warranties. Lectures on I.Chem.E and MF/1 Forms. Recent work includes partnering agreement for the Dudley Southern Bypass. Acts for insurers of construction professionals and has contributed book chapters on architect's liability to "Professional Liability: Law and Insurance" (ed. Hodgin) and "Professional Negligence in the Construction Industry" (Neil F Jones & Co) both published by Lloyds of London Press. Has also written and lectured widely on construction and professional indemnity matters.
Prof. Memberships: F.C.I. Arb, O.R.S.A, Society of Construction Law.
Career: Qualified in 1984, joined *Neil F Jones & Co* in 1990 becoming a partner in 1992.
Personal: Born 1958. Educated Worcester College, Oxford. Leisure interests include squash, tennis and West Ham FC.

CORPORATE FINANCE/COMPANY

RESEARCH: Our team carried out extensive interviews with solicitors, accountants, venture capitalists, bankers and listed companies. This was supplemented with a written survey amongst clients (extracts of which are published below). In compiling the tables, we consider all the information available to us, paying particular regard to the market research carried out by our team of ten qualified lawyers. (The researchers' details are set out on page three.) The rankings, therefore, reflect the opinion of the marketplace as revealed by systematic and objective research: see page four. (Our research is audited every year by the British Market Research Bureau.)

OVERVIEW: All aspects of company/corporate finance work, including flotations, privatisations, company mergers and acquisitions (public and private), business sales and purchases and (providing the issues raised are essentially corporate) joint ventures are dealt with in one general section within the regions. In London, there are separate tables covering both the debt and equity sides of buy-outs to reflect the fact that in the City there are an identifiable number of firms and individuals with particular and specialist practices in this area.

The leading triumvirate of large London firms remains the same: Freshfields, Linklaters and Slaughter and May, with almost unanimous agreement that there is clear water between these firms and their nearest rivals. Of the Highly Regarded firms, Cameron McKenna topped the list. As with last year, we have given lower rankings to many top corporate finance lawyers who hold positions as managing or senior partner, to reflect the fact they are not fee-earning full time.

The **South East** has seen significant changes since last year with two Thames Valley firms, Clarks and Cole & Cole, joining south coast firm Blake Lapthorn at the top of the table. There are four new firms, the most significant being Bond Pearce (Southampton) following its merger with Hepherd Winstanley & Pugh. Osborne Clarke's new Reading office has got off to a running start. Brachers and Shadbolt & Co are the other two new entries.

The main changes to the **South West** region reflect the diminishing reputation of Bevan Ashford's Bristol Office and the increasing reputation of the firm's Exeter office which enters our table. Burges Salmon and Osborne Clarke remain the top two firms. There are also three new entrants: Foot & Bowden, Michelmores and Trumps.

There have been major changes in **Wales**. Eversheds drop following the departure of partners Laurence James and Alan Whiteley. Edwards Geldard and Morgan Bruce (who have merged with Newport firm Guthrie Francis) are the new leaders. Berry Smith enter as highly regarded.

In the **Midlands**, Wragge & Co have pulled ahead of Pinsent Curtis. Dibb Lupton Alsop are improving their practice following the arrival of Chris Rawstron from Edge & Ellison. Garretts Birmingham office enters our list following numerous recommendations.

THE TOP CORPORATE FINANCE FIRMS

This table differs from the other tables in *Chambers*. It is based solely on the opinions of clients – of in-house heads of legal, company secretaries and other buyers of legal services in the top 1,000 companies in the UK. They were sent a list of the top corporate finance firms (as indicated by research we had already done) and were asked to rank them in order from 1 to 10, indicating at the same time which they had actually used. (Each questionnaire listed the firms in a different order, at random.)

TOP TWELVE:
Ranked by users and non-users

Firms	Overall scores '98 ('97)	No. of first scores '98 ('97)
1) SLAUGHTER AND MAY 2	631 (595)	20 (21)
2) LINKLATERS 3	618 (540)	19 (15)
3) FRESHFIELDS 1	611 (598)	16 (19)
4) CLIFFORD CHANCE 4	517 (532)	11 (14)
5) ALLEN & OVERY 5	494 (466)	5 (8)
6) HERBERT SMITH 6	355 (394)	8 (7)
7) ASHURST MORRIS CRISP 7	329 (353)	7 (6)
8) NORTON ROSE –	257 (–)	1 (–)
9) SIMMONS & SIMMONS –	244 (–)	2 (–)
10) LOVELL WHITE DURRANT 8	239 (306)	0 (0)
11) MACFARLANES 9	132 (209)	0 (1)
12) TRAVERS SMITH B'WAITE 10	127 (147)	4 (2)

TOP TWELVE: Ranked by users only

Firms	Overall scores '98 ('97)	No. of first scores '98 ('97)
1) SLAUGHTER AND MAY 2	370 (270)	17 (12)
2) LINKLATERS 5	328 (216)	17 (11)
3) FRESHFIELDS 3	268 (265)	12 (12)
4) CLIFFORD CHANCE 1	232 (276)	8 (11)
5) ALLEN & OVERY 4	218 (230)	8 (7)
6) HERBERT SMITH 6	194 (188)	7 (6)
7) ASHURST MORRIS CRISP 8	166 (101)	7 (4)
8) SIMMONS & SIMMONS –	132 (–)	2 (–)
9) NORTON ROSE –	123 (–)	1 (–)
10) LOVELL WHITE DURRANT 7	80 (142)	0 (0)
11) TRAVERS SMITH B'WAITE 10	59 (35)	3 (1)
12) MACFARLANES 9	80 (51)	0 (1)

The figure in brackets denotes the position and the scores of the firm in 1997

In **East Anglia** also Garretts improve their position along with Bankes Ashton and Greene & Greene.

In the **North West** and the **North East** there is little movement from last year, the same four firms tend to dominate with varying degrees of strength in different commercial centres. Addleshaw Booth & Co continue to retain their pre-eminence overall, but Eversheds Leeds has had a notable year and the merger with Wilkinson Maughan has definitely strengthened their Newcastle presence.

In **Scotland**, Dundas & Wilson dominate the table, benefitting from Brian Dorman's firm, and, in terms of profile, from Andersens.

Overall Garretts have had an interesting year, and generally are beginning to be seen in the corporate market place a little more, but without creating the impact long expected.

LONDON

250+FEE-EARNERS

LEADING FIRMS · LONDON 250+ FEE-EARNERS
FRESHFIELDS
LINKLATERS
SLAUGHTER AND MAY
ALLEN & OVERY
ASHURST MORRIS CRISP
CLIFFORD CHANCE
HERBERT SMITH
LOVELL WHITE DURRANT
NORTON ROSE
SIMMONS & SIMMONS

HIGHLY REGARDED FIRMS
Cameron McKenna
Denton Hall
Nabarro Nathanson
Wilde Sapte

Freshfields (London: 40ptnrs/96assts, Overseas:53ptnrs/150assts) As per other firms, they are "doing extremely well." They also have some good younger lawyers in the ascendant. On the M&A side, have a strong cross-border element to the deals. *Gavin Darlington* heads up the corporate department and *Barry O'Brien* ("getting quite grand now" "extraordinarily able" "instinctive approach – sometimes impulsive rather than considered" "willing to take a firm stand") heads corporate finance. Ranked individuals include *Charles ap Simon* ("gives a considered view"), *Mark Rawlinson* ("pretty clever, combining practicality with great people skills"), senior partner *Anthony Salz* ("undoubtedly one of the market leaders" "still brilliant"), *Philip Richards* ("always takes a sensible view"), *Edward Braham* ("effective, pragmatic and a good project manager. Thinks creatively and construc-

tively." "Good negotiator, intellectually rigorous but still commercial"), *James Davis* ("dangerously wonderful"). *William Lawes* "has definitely made a name for himself" and new to the lists *David Graham* "thrives on challenge." *Laurie McFadden* has transferred to the firm's Milan office. **Clients/Work:** M&A private: acting for Reed Elsevier on its disposal of IPC to an MBO group financed by Cinven and financed as to debt by Goldman Sachs for a consideration of £860m. On public side, acting for Zurich Group on its proposed £23bn merger with the financial services arm of BAT Industries plc, (includes Farmers in US, Eagle Star and Allied Dunbar in UK).

Linklaters (London:60 ptnrs/199 assts. Overseas: 25ptnrs/65 assts.) "An excellent, very together firm – understated and good to deal with." Strong for UK corporate work. Head of department *Anthony Cann* ("enviable reputation" "sensible – can always see the main picture"), *David Cheyne* ("charming, long established" "diplomatic, gets results") and *Richard Godden* ("so good at what he does") receive top ranking. Senior Partner *Charles Allen-Jones* is highly thought of, but less active on deals as a result of his management role. Also rated are *Tim Clarke* ("good technically, he's self assured and has a straightforward approach"), *John Ellard, Peter King* ("good to work with, gets the deal done" "quietly effective, and thorough" "technically superb" "good on privatisations") and *Michael Sullivan.* **Clients/ Work:** M&A: UK legal advisers to Billiton on its demerger from Gencor Ltd, a $.5bn new issue and its subsequent listing on the London and Johannesburg stock exchange (value £3.5bn + US£1bn new issue). Acted on conversion and subsequent flotations of Halifax BS (£18bn) Woolwich BS (£5.3bn) and Alliance & Leicester BX (£5.6bn). Acted for Worms & Cie on hostile bid by Evran S.A (largest ever hostile bid in France).

Slaughter and May Known for their flexible approach: many lawyers handle a broad range of corporate, banking and com-

mercial work (accordingly, it is difficult to assess team sizes). The firm's name is synonymous with real quality and expertise for corporate finance. They "continue to concentrate on quality in a London market obsessed with globalisation at the expense of quality control." *Nigel Boardman* is viewed as outstanding by both lawyers and clients ("a real air of authority," "sometimes high-handed, but he can afford to be, he's so effective" and "ebullient.") *Michael Pescod* "quite simply, he's just a brilliant lawyer" excels in an understated way, *William Underhill* "clearly among the best, you want him to be on your side." Other rated lawyers include *Tim Clark* "a serious operator," *Stephen Cooke* "a good all rounder," *Anthony Newhouse* "intelligent, not afraid to take a strong view," and *Robert Stern* "sound, hardworking." New to our list is *Frances Murphy* – "ferocious, tenacious and gets results." **Clients/Work:** Acting for Grand Metropolitan plc on its merger with Guinness plc to create Diageo, a company with a market capitalisation of £20.6bn. Acting for Unilever on the sale of its international speciality chemical businesses (National Starch aand Chemical Company, Quest International, Unichem International and Crosfield) to ICI for a cash consideration of US$8bn. Acting for the Energy Group when subject to competing offers, in excess of £4bn, from PacifiCorp and Texas Utilities.

Allen & Overy (39ptnrs/123assocs) "Coming up," was the general consensus and emerging out of the shadow of their banking practice. "Good all rounders" and doing

LEADING US FIRMS WITH AN INTERNATIONAL CORPORATE FINANCE REPUTATION
CRAVATH, SWAINE & MOORE
DAVIS POLK & WARDWELL
SHEARMAN & STERLING
SKADDEN, ARPS, SLATE, MEAGHER & FLOM LLP
SULLIVAN & CROMWELL

better quality deals. Noted practitioners are *Richard Cranfield* "good for M&A," *Alan Paul* "good on public side" "amazingly shrewd guy," *Keith Godfrey*, *Peter Holland* and *David Wootton* "charming lawyer who has the capacity to save deals from collapsing." **Clients/Work:** 1997, M&A practice involved in 36 transactions, each with a value of over £100m (including 5 public takeovers each with value over £1bn). Public deals include bids by Merrill Lynch for Mercury Asset Management, T&N by Federal-Mogul and by Yorkshire Holdings for Yorkshire Electricity. Private deals: ICI's disposal programme, including its UK fertiliser business to Terra Industries and its polyesters and films business.

Ashurst Morris Crisp (London: 40 ptnrs/100assts. Overseas: 8ptnrs/25assts). "Smaller than some, but perfectly formed." Some considered them one of the best firms in the City, "commercial, uniformly excellent." They are thought to be able to handle a large volume of work and the quality of their lawyers is high "totally focused," and "on excellent form at the moment." Leading reputation for MBO's (see separate section) and also have a "strong venture capital team" although there was some feeling that they had "slipped a bit in the global march." Ranked individuals include *Adrian Knight* ("really shrewd," "rolls his sleeves up and gets on with it") is "going places." *David Macfarlane* is "commercial and easy to do business with." **Clients/Work:** Flotations: Acted for Baring Brothers re formation of Cable & Wireless Communications plc and on its listing on the London Stock Exchange, valuing company at £4.5bn. M&A: Acted for Morgan Stanley and UBS on a recommended takeover bid by Energy for London Electricity plc (£1.26bn bid). Advised the syndicate of investors in relation to £726m sale of Eversholt Holding Ltd.

Clifford Chance (London: 30ptnrs/97 assts. Overseas: 23ptnrs/90assts.) Naturally, the firm's work has strong international emphasis. Although some felt that recent defections (inc Peter Brooks) had damaged the practice, opinion was mixed and others felt the practice was still "impressive and definitely one of the heavyweights." Head of department *David Childs* is "commercial in his approach," "the firm's real heavy hitter" and "razor sharp." *Jeremy Brownlow* ("down to earth – good to deal with") is a star player. Also recommended is newcomer to the tables *Adam Signy* ("down to earth, with a good corporate finance practice"). **Clients/Work:** In 1997, 150 M&A (total value approx. £40bn – advised CSFB on its acquisition of the UK and continental European equities, equity capital markets and M&A advisory businesses of BZW from Barclays Bank plc. Advised GE Capital on recommended cash offer for Woodchester Investments plc (consideration £547m).

Advised Burton Group plc on plans to demerge Debenhams department stores into a separately quoted public company.

Herbert Smith (London: 32ptnrs/78 assts. Overseas: 14ptnrs/40 assts). "Strong public deal group, and a good flow of work." Seven individuals make the Leaders list which is more than their immediate competitors although none make the top rank. Head of department is *Richard Bond*. Other leaders include: *Anthony Macaulay* ("superb on takeovers"), *Margaret Mountford* ("an amazingly clever lawyer and good all rounder, although she doesn't suffer fools," "good news to have on a deal"), *Stephen Barnard*, the "able" *Edward Walker-Arnott*, *James Palmer* ("really excellent – he's definitely made his mark") and *Chris Parsons* "knowledgeable." **Clients/Work:** M&A's: Acting for BAT Industries plc on proposed £30bn reconstruction, involving demerger of its financial services businesses (Allied Dunbar, Eagle Star (UK) and Farmers (US) and subsequent merger with Zurich Insurance Group. Acting for Argos on the £1.68bn hostile bid by GUS. Flotations: Advising BZW, the sponsor and underwriter on the highly successful £136.4m flotation of conservatory roof manufacturer Ultraframe Group plc.

Lovell White Durrant (London: 22ptnrs/48assts. Overseas: 13ptnrs/20assts) A busy year, with turnover up 21% across the corporate area. Can call on resources in international offices, notably Paris, Prague, New York and Hong Kong. A key figure is *Dan Mace* who "has done really well for the firm, considering he has a relatively small number of individuals to back him compared to the largest firms." New to this year's tables is *Nigel Read* – "outstanding, he's bright, creative and a practical thinker who is good at problem solving." **Clients/Work:** M&A. Acted on 11 public bids, including Granada Group PlC offer for Yorkshire Tyne-Tees Television plc (£711m) and Interim Services Inc re their offer for Michael Page plc (£346m). Flotations: Acted for JP Morgan (financial adviser and sponsor) in flotation of Alliance & Leicester (£3.3bn) and Northern Rock (£2.05bn).

Norton Rose (29 ptnrs/70+ assts. Overseas: 13 ptnrs) This year they have been busy with some excellent deals, seen to be "flexing their muscles" and "especially good on the public deals side." Senior partner *David Lewis* "has made his name" and is "good to work with." *Simon Sackman* also received particular mention. **Clients/Work:** Acted as lead corporate lawyer for Guinness plc in £23b merger with Grand Metropolitan (merged company Diageo is world's largest food and drinks company). Acted for Forward Trust, leasing arm of Midland Bank, on its acquisition of Eversholt Holdings (total consideration £765m). Flotations included Bovis Homes Plc (£225m) and Galen Holdings plc (£182m).

Simmons & Simmons (London: 31ptnrs/54assts. Overseas: 10ptnrs) Have had an interesting year although many questioned their position post Railtrack and after the Andersens discussions. *William Knight* "forceful, confident personality" – heads the team and specialises in public and private mergers, acquisitions, disposals, joint ventures, MBO's and initial public offerings. *William Charnley* is also ranked. **Clients/ Work:** M&A: Acted for Gallaher Group plc on US$3bn demerger from Fortune Brands Inc and its subsequent listing on both the London and New York Stock Exchanges. Privatisions: included US$700m+ offerings of Global Depositary Receipts representing shares in the Gas Authority of India Ltd and the Container Corporation of India (acting for Indian government).

Cameron McKenna (London: 25ptnrs/ 35assts. Overseas: 12ptnrs/33assts) Team handle mixture of corporate and corporate finance work. Of the highly regarded firms, this firm leads the pack – "have been getting noticed since the merger." *Arfon Jones*, joint head of the practice area, merits an individual mention. Have been active in flotation work. **Clients/**

Work: M&A: in past year undertook 50 private company transactions, combined value of over £2b; six public company takeovers, combined value £550m – successful representation of Nomura in auction of William Hill (£750m). Generally: Global offering of ordinary shares and American Depository Shares valuing Energis at £846m. Acting for string of biotechnology clients: Stock Exchange flotations of CaT and PowderJect.

Denton Hall (London:12 ptnrs/ 22assts. Overseas: 8ptnrs/14assts) Corporate deals have a focus on the energy, media and techonology sectors. Andrew Daws has now left the group to pursue a career outside the law. **Clients/Work:** Advised Apax Ptnrs on the £85m purchase of Virgin Radio by Chris Evans; advised on the establishment of Sainsbury's bank; advised GE Capital Fleet Services on the acquisition of BRS Car Lease for £120m.

Nabarro Nathanson (26 ptnrs/59assts) Not one of the obvious corporate players, but able when they turn their hands to it.

Clients/Work: Acted for vendors of Books Etc. Ltd in its sale for an undisclosed sum to Borders Group Inc. Acted for Granada Group plc on the sale of its Granada Computer Services International Division, which operates throughout Europe, to an MBO team for £89m in cash.

Wilde Sapte (London company/commercial group: 8 ptnrs/19 assts specialise in M&A) "A disruptive year" with the talks with Andersens and their consequent termination perceived as a distraction by the marketplace. Have a respectable buy-outs practice on the debt side. **Clients/Work:** Acted on the offer by Greenwich Insurance Holdings plc comprising part of the 2nd generation scheme for conversion from unLtd to Ltd liability underwriting at Lloyd's. Public bids: Tibbett & Britten Group bid for Applied Distribution. Completion of the 19 jurisdiction acquisition by Elekta AB of the Philips Medical Systems radiotherapy business.

LONDON

125–250 FEE-EARNERS

LEADING FIRMS · LONDON
125–250 FEE-EARNERS

| MACFARLANES |
| TRAVERS SMITH BRAITHWAITE |

| S J BERWIN & CO |
| GOULDENS |

| BAKER & MCKENZIE |
| BERWIN LEIGHTON |
| RICHARDS BUTLER |
| ROWE & MAW |
| THEODORE GODDARD |

| EVERSHEDS |
| TITMUSS SAINER DECHERT |

| STEPHENSON HARWOOD |

HIGHLY REGARDED FIRMS

| Dibb Lupton Alsop |
| Field Fisher Waterhouse |
| Lawrence Graham |
| Taylor Joynson Garrett |
| Watson, Farley & Williams |

| Clyde & Co |
| Davies Arnold Cooper |
| D J Freeman |
| Nicholson Graham & Jones |
| Radcliffes |
| Sinclair Roche & Temperley |

| Beachcroft Stanleys |
| Speechly Bircham |

Macfarlanes (13ptnrs/20assts) Seen as "truly outstanding for their size, can easily hold their own against the larger firms." Regarded as "sensible and commercial." They tended to evoke strong reactions. *Robert Sutton* is seen as "the best lawyer outside the large firms," he will be taking over as senior partner next year. *Jonathan Macfarlane* and *Mary Leth* are also rated. **Clients/Work:** Acting for Compagnie Générale des Eaux in the £1.1bn disposal of its healthcare business. Handling the £112.5m flotation of SGB Group plc. Acting on the £297m agreed bid for Midland Independant Newspapers by Mirror Group.

Travers Smith Braithwaite (16ptnrs/30 assts) Thought to have "put recent traumas aside." They still have the breadth and quality of work although they have a little ground to make up. "Revving up their private equity side" recently. Generally they are "pithy" with "good juniors" although "lacking in international pretensions." Experienced senior partner *Alan Keat* is perceived as "absolutely excellent" but more of a figurehead these days although he is full time fee-earning. The "grand" *Christopher Bell* is known for his long experience and is "good to deal with." **Clients/Work:** Acting in the £112.5m flotation of SGB Group. Acting for NTL in the $600m acquisition of Comcast UK. Advising in the EASDAQ flotation of Esprit Telecom.

SJ Berwin & Co (23ptnrs/37assts) An "impressive, extremely well run firm" giving "first class service," known for their assertive style. Strong on setting up VC funds and a reasonable deal flow from the institutions, seen as having some good individuals but can be "a bit patchy" at times. *Robert Burrow* specialises in M&A and is regarded as

"delightful and capable," a top notch player. **Clients/Work:** Acting for Ladbroke Group plc on its acquisition of the Coral Group of Companies from Bass plc. Acting as joint advisor to Guinness plc on its merger with Grand Metropolitan. Acting for British Land Company plc on the establishment of a 50/50 joint venture to acquire certain leisure properties from The Rank Group with a value in excess of £100m.

Gouldens (16ptnrs: 2 p/t/16assts) "Their star is rising." Known for a cohesive approach. "Bright" but "slightly aggressive." *Adam Greaves* "deserves his slot in the rankings" and is rated highly by clients. Team also includes "idiosyncratic" and well thought of *Patrick Burgess*. **Clients/Work:** Domestic flotations: Ashtenne plc and Ted Baker plc. M&A: Acting for Hanson plc in the demerger of the Energy Group plc at market capitalisation of £2,800m.

Baker & McKenzie (14 ptnrs p/t; 19 assts p/t) Managing partner *Nigel Carrington* is part of the team and *Tim Gee* leads the European M&A Group. Have lost Christopher Bown to Freshfields. **Clients/Work:** Acting for Swissair on its purchase of British Airways' £1.5bn contract catering business. Acting for Tyrrell on disposal of racing team to British American Racing. Acting for Oriflame International on its reverse takeover and relisting of the enlarged group on the London Stock Exchange with market capitalisation of £500m.

Berwin Leighton (11 ptnrs 100% 4 ptnrs up to 50%/23 assts.) "Nice firm to deal with," liked by clients for an assertive style. *John Bennett* heads the Corporate Department. **Clients/Work:** Acting for Tesco plc in £630m acquisition of Associated British Foods.

Acting for Southern Water in £90m divestment programme following the acquisition by Southern Water of Scottish Power in a contested bid. Acting for fashion retailer Monsoon plc in its London Stock Exchange listing capitalising at £352m.

Richards Butler (8 ptnrs/13assts) Have a strong international emphasis and are working to increase their UK profile. **Clients/Work:** Include The Rank Group plc, MTV and Sea Containers doing a range of general corporate-M&A, disposals, Blue Book work.

Rowe & Maw (20 ptnrs/33 assts) "Doing well at the moment," with "clients singing their praises," for a "good quality" "trustworthy" corporate practice. Other practitioners do not see them as frequently, but they do act for 10 of the FTSE250 (Commercial Lawyer Survey: Issue 19) although not necessarily all corporate work. Team includes "respectable" *Paul Maher*. **Clients/Work:** Acting for Unilever in its £80m disposal of the distribution and dealership rights for Caterpillar in the UK and parts of Africa. Acting for ICI plc on its sale of its 62.4% shareholding in ICI Australia Ltd, raising AUS$2.2bn by way of a global offering. Acting for Cable and Wireless Communications in their £60m acquisition of the Anite Networks business.

Theodore Goddard (13ptnrs/17assts) Have a strongly reputed US connection. Respected for involvement in "a small number of high value transactions." *Martin Chester* is an "extremely impressive" member of the department. **Clients/Work:** Acting as lead legal adviser for Guinness plc in the £23bn merger with Grand Metropolitan. Advising Johnson Fry Utilities Trust plc on its £150m merger with Johnson Fry Second Utilities Trust under a s425 Companies Act 1985 scheme of arrangement. Acting for Signet Group on its £500m capital reorganisation involving the conversion of 5 classes of share capital into one class.

Eversheds (10 ptnrs/16 assts) "Sensible and pleasant firm" which should benefit from the Frere Cholmeley merger which is thought to "give more depth to their practice." Team includes *Martin Issitt*. Corporate practice nationally has gained serious credibility after acting for DuPont. **Clients/Work:** Acting for DuPont on its $3bn acquisition of ICI's industrial chemicals business. £165m joint venture between Hotel Properties Ltd (the client, a Singapore based company), Canary Wharf Ltd and Pidemco for a development at Canary Wharf. Four AIM floats including Charlton Athletic plc and Nottingham Forest plc.

Titmuss Sainer Dechert (9ptnrs,1 ptnr 75%/ 10 assts) Have an increasingly recognised presence in the French market. *Michael Steinfeld* has a positive reputation as a "strong senior lawyer" seen as "extremely good" by clients. **Clients/Work:** Acting for Etam Development on its £90m take-over of Stock Exchange listed Etam plc. Acting for the

shareholders of Badenoch and Clark Ltd on the sale of the company to AccuStaff Incorporated. Acting for a consortium of banks comprising Credit Agricole Indosuez, Banque Nationale de Paris and J Henry Schroder & Co Ltd on the flotation of Etam Developpement.

Stephenson Harwood (9ptnrs 100%/ 24assts) Reasonable corporate practice but have lost the head of corporate finance Richard Ufland to Lovell White Durrant so doubts cast as to their market position. **Clients/Work:** Acting for Capital Corporation plc in hostile bid by London Clubs referred to the Monopolies and Mergers Commission. The bid failed as a result of the MMC decision. Acting in a series of significant disposals on behalf of Harrisons & Crosfield plc.

Dibb Lupton Alsop (5 ptnrs 100% 3 ptnrs 60%/ 37 assts up to 100%) "Firm has some good people, even if they're not all household names," seen as "aggressive." *Peter Wayte* is associated more with a management role now but when doing deals he has a reputation for being "commercial." **Clients/Work:** Acting for CIA Group Plc in £30m acquisition of a Scandinavian group with £17m placing. Acting in the £27.69 m-disposal by Sutcliffe Speakman plc of the Carbons and Environmental Engineering Businesses to Waterlink.

Field Fisher Waterhouse (5ptnrs/ 11assts) Merger with Allison & Humphreys has given firm added expertise in communications and media sector, placing firm in a good position to advise on the corporate and commercial matters arising from digital convergence. **Clients/Work:** Advised on the disposal of 51% of the share capital of BBL Marketing Communications Ltd to the subsidiary of a French advertising company. Advised ComputerLand (UK) Plc on its admission to AIM and on fundraising activities. Advised the Minister of Agriculture Fisheries and Food on the sale of ADAS, and agricultural service, to an MBO team.

Lawrence Graham (11 ptnrs: 4 100%; 19assts) Well regarded by clients. *Michael Storar* manages the department. Perceived as having targeted smaller AIM flotations and are known for M&A. Company/Commercial work accounts for 20% of the firm's turnover. **Clients/Work:** M&A's handled for Legal & General Group plc, Land & Urban plc and Moss Bross Group plc amongst others.

Taylor Joynson Garrett (17ptnrs/ 20assts) Considered a "reasonable" practice but not seen as much in the market despite handling some good sized deals. This may be due to the fact that approx 35% of the deals they handled last year were actually for US clients. Strong on M&A side. *Martin Dillon* is a recognised player in the department. **Clients/Work:** Acting for Rutland Trust plc in the sale of Thamesport for £112m. Acting for Macmillan Publishers in the sale of health service journals publication division for

£103m to Emap and separately acquisition of Heinemann ELT division from Reed Elsevier for a sum of £38m. Acting for TBWA International BV in acquisitions in UK, Finland, Holland, Austria, Brazil, India and Israel.

Watson Farley Williams (13ptnrs/23 assts) Strong on their AIM work and traditionally considered a finance firm. Highly regarded for strong central and eastern european work. **Clients/Work:** ICO Global Communications (Holdings) Ltd – advising in connection with a rights issue and other equity issues to raise US$500m from existing shareholders and new investors.

Clyde & Co (8 ptnrs/11assts) Known for a shipping bias in corporate finance and increasing profile in venture capital work. **Clients/Work:** Acting in the recommended takeover of The Brockbank Group plc. Advising on the AIM flotation of the Longmead Group plc. Acting for Peel, Hunt & Company Ltd in the open offer and subscription for Sunleigh plc.

Davies Arnold Cooper (16ptnrs up to 100%/15assts up to 100%). Often act for insurance and reinsurance clients but also focus on technology and automotive work. **Clients/Work:** Acting for Norwich Union plc in the £56m sale of its maritime insurance arm, Maritime Insurance Company to CNA, Chicago. Acting for Raynard in the establishment of the Formula 1 racing team. Acting in a £25m debenture for Fuller Smith & Turner plc.

D J Freeman (3ptnrs/10assts) "A strong focused firm," known for corporate insurance which represents 25% of the department's work. **Clients/Work:** Acting for Lloyd's subsidiaries Lioncover Insurance Company and its managers Syndicate Underwriting

Management in preparation of the reinsurance contract between Lioncover and Equitas Reinsurance. Acting for Sedgwick Oakwood Capital in pooled conversion with total underwriting capacity of £55m.

Nicholson Graham & Jones (19ptnrs upto 100%/13assts up to 100%) *Michael Johns* is managing partner. **Clients/Work:** Acting for the ITE Group Ltd in reverse takeover and open offer for Cemenstone plc. Advising Eurodis Electron plc in strategic alliance with Pioneer – Standard Electronics Inc and share issue. Acting for 4Front Group plc and 4Front International Software Inc in acquisition of French companies Eurosystems GA, France SA and Netrix SA.

Radcliffes (5ptnrs /2assts) One of the smaller firms in this size category, they have a reasonable corporate practice. **Clients/**

Work: Recently completed the initial public offering of Avalon Oil plc on AIM with net proceeds of £31.7m and market capitalisation of £76.3m.

Sinclair Roche & Temperley (3ptnrs/ 10assts) Handling corporate finance/company and commercial work feeding off their shipping work. Have a reputation for privatisation work from Eastern Europe – Bucharest and Far East. **Clients/Work:** Acting for UK Active Value Fund in takeover of their first UK listed company, John Mansfield plc. Acting for Concerto Capital Corporation representing the interests of Brian Myerson and working with the Stewart-Liberty family in the replacement of the entire Board of Directors of Liberty plc. Acting for Carnival Cruise Lines Inc in US$500m acquisition of Cunard.

Beachcroft Stanleys (7ptnrs/7assts) Known for water company work but generally low profile in the London market. **Clients/Work:** Acting for Cambridge Water plc in £4m market buy back of 10% of the issued share capital. Acting for CMP Media Inc in £2.36m acquisition of outstanding 50% of shares in Information Week Ltd and the businesses of the Network group. Acting for UCB SA in £33.7m acquisition from ICI and Orica Australia Pty Ltd of their polypropelene film businesses in UK, Belgium and Australia.

Speechly Bircham (8ptnrs/10 assts) Considered low profile in the market. **Clients/Work:** Acting for Ashstead plc on the £39m takeover of Sheriff Holdings plc. Acting for PA Consulting in the £200m reconstruction of the group.

LONDON

1–125 FEE-EARNERS

LEADING FIRMS · LONDON
1-125 FEE-EARNERS

FOX WILLIAMS
HAMMOND SUDDARDS
OLSWANG

PAISNER & CO
PINSENT CURTIS

WARNER CRANSTON

HIGHLY REGARDED FIRMS

Lewis Silkin
Memery Crystal
Osborne Clarke

Biddle
Bird & Bird
Harbottle & Lewis
Hobson Audley Hopkins & Wood
Howard Kennedy
Marriott Harrison

Charles Russell
Coudert Brothers
Forsyte Saunders Kerman
Laytons
Manches & Co
Rakisons

Barnett Alexander Chart
Middleton Potts
Wedlake Bell

Fox Williams (4 ptnrs: 1 ptnr 80%, 3 ptnrs 20%/ 6 assts) "An excellent firm." The "brilliant"*Christine Williams* "projects a good image" and is generally seen as effective. **Clients/Work:** Acting for Cinram Ltd in its acquisition of Polygram Manufacturing and Distribution Centres BV. Acting for Elsevier

Science BV in its acquisition of UK and US companies in the Current Science Group. Handling a number of capital raising projects in film financing for Trimax Films plc and King Lear plc.

Hammond Suddards (6ptnrs/17assts) The London office of this national firm has benefitted from the arrival from Manchester of *Richard Burns* who is now National Head of Corporate Finance. **Clients/Work:** Acting for Fine Art Developments plc on the £140m demerger of Creative Publishing plc. Acting for the management on the £140m MBO of Hansen Electrical. Acting for Viad Corporation in the £150m disposal of Crystal Holidays Ltd and Jetsave Ltd.

Olswang (9 ptnrs 75%/ 16 assts 75%) "A firm where they make things happen." "Getting bigger all the time, they've come up dramatically" doing "decent private equity work" which feeds off their media practice. They are also prominent in AIM listing. The team is seen as "dynamic" with clear and strong leadership. "Solid"*Adrian Bott* has a good name and a positive reputation as a deal doer who "sees deals from the clients' perspective." *Graeme Levy* is a "technically brilliant lawyer" who is "conscientious and puts in incredible effort to solve difficult and demanding issues." *Simon Morgan* has joined from Frere Cholmeley following the merger with Eversheds. **Clients/Work:** Acting for Chris Evans and Ginger Group of Companies in the £81m Virgin Radio deal. Acting for Anite Group plc in the disposal of Case Technology Ltd and Case Technolgy A/s. Acting for BBC Worldwide Ltd in the £400m twin joint venture structure with Flextech plc.

Paisner & Co (10ptnrs/11assts) "Well rated firm." *Keith Stella* is head of Corporate Finance and *Stephen Rosefield* is well regarded. **Clients/Work:** Acting for the Great Universal Stores plc in £900m joint venture with The British Land Company plc. Acting for Allied London Properties plc in joint

venture with Clerical Medical Investment Group Ltd. Acting for Medisys plc in reverse takeover of Needle Incinerator Company Ltd and its AIM admission with market capitalisation of £40m approx.

Pinsent Curtis (12ptnrs/14assts) Regarded as "doing more and better work" and benefiting from having two ex-Clifford Chance partners. The firm is strong on takeovers and flotations and are known for the number of smaller investment banks they act for. **Clients/Work:** Advising Triplex Lloyd plc on the £184m recommended offer by Doncasters plc. Advising the vendors of Pharmavene Inc on its acquisition for $170m by Shire Pharmaceuticals plc. Advising N M Rothschild & Sons Ltd on the London Stock Exchange flotation of Core Group plc raising £25m.

Warner Cranston (8ptnrs/11assts) Sporting a reputation for international deals this firm was not seen as high enough profile in the London market to merit a higher ranking – "don't question the quality just the size." "Talks a good talk" head of department *Ian Fagelson* is a "professional." **Clients/Work:** Acting on the acquisitions by Thermo Electron Corporation of Peek for £98m; acting for GEO Interactive Media Group in £300m capitalised admission to the full list; acting for Courtaulds plc and Vickers plc.

Lewis Silkin (4 ptnrs 100% 2 ptnrs 50% 2ptnrs 25%/ 7 assts) Have lost one partner and an assistant to Pinsent Curtis this year but have recruited to make up numbers. The "charming" but "formidable"*Clare Grayston* is known for her AIM work acting for sponsors and she " knows her way round that market well." **Clients/Work:** Acting for Abbott Mead Vickers plc on a series of six acquisitions on an earn out basis totalling a maximum £26m. Acting for the sponsor on the subscription, placing and open offer and move from AIM to the Official List by Dean Corporation plc.

Memery Crystal (2 ptnrs75% 2 ptnrs 50% /4 assts 50-75%) Have a good reputation for sports clients and AIM work, the senior partner with his "entrepreneurial style" *Peter Crystal* is well regarded. **Clients/Work:** Acting for BGRplc on its AIM admission raising £3m. Acting for Boustead plc and sponsor Ellis & Partners on its readmission to the Official List following its acquisition of Hong Kong company Sunlink Group raising £13.8m. Acting for Micro Focus Group plc in itsUS$18m acquisition of XDB Systems Inc and listing on London Stock Exchange.

Osborne Clarke (6ptnrs 100%/1 ptnr 40% 1 ptnr 20% /12 assts 100%) Known for relationship with one of the clearing banks and new issue work. Thought to "have some good people doing a steady flow of interesting and decently sized work. This London office is good." *Timothy Birt* ("intellectual and commercial") has an excellent reputation as "a man you can do a deal with." **Clients/Work:** Acting for Diagonal plc on its £11.8m placing and admission to the official list. Advising Activision Inc on the £26m acquisition of Combined Distribution Holdings Ltd. Acting for Torex plc on the £10m disposal of its tool hire division and accompanying Super Class 1 circular.

Biddle (10 ptnrs/10 assts) "Good 'City' style firm." *Martin Winter* is the senior partner and *Martin Webster* continues to be rated. **Clients/Work:** Acting on venture capital investments and acquisitions/disposals totalling over £40m.

Bird & Bird (13ptnrs 75-100% 5ptnrs 50-75% 16 assts 50-100%) Known for their telecoms practice. **Clients/Work:** Acting for the Q Group plc in its AIM flotation raising £4m capitalising to some £20m. Advised on the formation of joint venture between four international businesses to open up digital interactive TV services. Advised CSFB on the sale of Citymax Integrated Information Systems Ltd to EDS International UK Ltd with related provision of services to CSFB.

Harbottle & Lewis (4ptnrs/14assts) Reputed for their Branson connections, *Colin Howes* is well known. **Clients/Work:** Acting for the principals of advertising agency Howell Henry Chaldecott Lury on its merger with Chime Communications plc. Acting for shareholders of Computer Film Company on its £7m acquisition of Megalomania plc. Advising on UK law aspects of Virgin Express Holdings plc's simultaneous $200m dual flotation on NASDAQ and in Brussels.

Hobson Audley Hopkins & Wood (5ptnrs/8assts) "A solid practice" with "good quality corporate work" regarded as "good all-rounders" with strength in IT and Telecoms. Old hand *Max Audley* "has a good track record" and is seen as the driving force behind the firm. **Clients/Work:** Acting for management team in £1bn MBO of General Healthcare Group from Companie

Générale des Eaux and subsequent merger with Amicus Healthcare. Acting for Energy Capital Investment Company plc on its £21.5m placing and open offer of unsecured loan stock. Acting for vendors of MOCOM Group on sale to Misys plc.

Howard Kennedy (4ptnrs,1ptnr 50%/3assts) Did extremely well at high volume/lower value BES deals for one or two corporate finance providers. This work has now largely dried up, and the firm has moved more into venture capital deals. **Clients/Work:** Acting as solicitors and stock exchange sponsors to Elderstreet Downing VCT plc raising £14m. Acting for Ex-Lands Properties in £21.1m merger with Marylebone Warwick Balfour Group plc. Advising in private placing by Next Generation Clubs Ltd raising £20m approx.

Marriott Harrison (3ptnrs/4assts) Known for entertainment clients and involvement in film finance. *Jon Sweet* has a solid reputation. **Clients/Work:** Advising Shepperton Holdings Ltd in relation to acquisition of controlling stake in The Mill (Facility) Ltd. Advising Essex Radio plc in recommended offer by Daily Mail Group Trust plc. Acting for management on MBO of Guiness Mahon Development Capital Ltd.

Charles Russell (9ptnrs /9assts) Good firm "coming into clearer waters"and recognised for corporate telecoms work. **Clients/Work:** Advising Reichhold Chemicals Inc in acquisition of Jotun Polymer. Acting for Freepages plc in £40m international and US public offerings and NASDAQ listing.

Coudert Brothers (5ptnrs/5assts) "Good" internationally connected firm. Known name *Steven Beharrell* has a reputation in oil and gas work. **Clients/Work:** Acting for Minerals Technologies Inc in £20m purchase of precipitated calcium carbonate business from Rhodia Ltd. Acting for ICN Pharmaceuticals Inc on $45m acquisition from SmithKline Beecham plc.

Forsyte Saunders Kerman (5ptnrs/1asst) Small team including *Paul Di Biase* who is rated as "a competent operator." This work accounts for 13% of turnover. **Clients/Work:** Acting for Lombard Tricity Finance, SJA Brand Holdings and HFC Bank.

Laytons (5ptnrs/3assts) Handle medium sized general corporate work. **Clients/Work:** Acting for Oxford Instruments plc in purshase of part of Vickers plc Medical Division. Acting for AMEC plc in purchase of Babcock Process and Energy Division.

Manches & Co (3ptnrs/4assts) "Keeping a low profile," focusing on acquisitions and disposals and AIM and full listings. **Clients/Work:** Advising Saur Water Services plc on £100m joint bid for Mid Kent Holdings plc. Acting for Eidos on $48m takeover of CentreGold plc and on UK aspects of its ADR offering and NASDAQ listing.

Rakisons (3 ptnrs/4assts) Predominantly known for litigation, their corporate work is thought of as "esoteric." **Clients/Work:** £40m acquisition of a world wide film services group for Panavision Inc. Acting for the vendors in £50m MBI of Nichol Beauty Products Ltd.

Barnett Alexander Chart (3ptnrs/5assts) Known in the market for PFI work, nonetheless have a reasonable corporate practice. **Clients/Work:** Acting for Maher Booksellers Ltd in development capital deal. Acting in the MBO of Momart plc and £20m MBO of Container Recovery Ltd.

Middleton Potts (3ptnrs /10assts) Seen as a niche shipping/commodities firm whose corporate department is "moderate." Their clients are 85% foreign or foreign controlled corporations. **Clients/Work:** Acting for Assicuazioni Generali on its sale of Harris & Dixon Lloyds brokers to BMS Group. Acting for Jenoptik in acquisition of English and Irish Group supplying equipment automation products.

Wedlake Bell (3ptnrs/3assts) Seen as "reasonable." *Andrew Baker*, chairman of CISCO, heads up the corporate finance team. **Clients/Work:** Acting for The African Lakes Corporation plc in £13.4m share issue by way of open offer and placing. Acting for the management of Libra Health Group plc in its aggregate£24m sale to Westminister Health Care Group plc.

Michael Hatchard of **Skadden, Arps, Slate, Meagher & Florn LLP** is rated by investment bankers for high quality international equities offerings where he is said to "compete with Allen & Overy well."

LEADING INDIVIDUALS · LONDON 1-125 FEE-EARNERS
AUDLEY Max Hobson Audley Hopkins & Wood
BEHARRELL Steven Coudert Brothers
BOTT Adrian Olswang
HATCHARD Michael Skadden, Arps, Slate, Meagher & Flom LLP
WILLIAMS Christine Fox Williams
BAKER Andrew Wedlake Bell
BIRT Timothy Osborne Clarke
BURNS Richard Hammond Suddards
CRYSTAL Peter Memery Crystal
DI BIASE Paul Edward Lewis
FAGELSON Ian Warner Cranston
GRAYSTON Clare Lewis Silkin
HOWES Colin Harbottle & Lewis
LEVY Graeme Olswang
MORGAN Simon Olswang
ROSEFIELD Stephen Paisner & Co
STELLA Keith Paisner & Co
SWEET Jon Marriott Harrison
WEBSTER Martin Biddle
WINTER Martin Biddle

LONDON

BUY-OUTS
EQUITY AND DEBT

OVERVIEW: We include two tables for equity and debt buy-out work. Equity buy-out work includes acting for equity provider and management team.

On the equity side Ashurst Morris Crisp remain the leading firm. Travers Smith Braithwaite had an exceptional year and move up. Alistair Dickson of Dickson Minto received much praise for his equity buy-out work and joins Charles Geffen of Ashurst Morris Crisp in the top band of leading individuals. Berwin Leighton and Nabarro Nathanson are building reputations and enter our tables this year.

On the debt side, a smaller number of firms maintain reputations as specialists. Lovell White Durrant has had a good year and moves into our top band. Ashurst Morris Crisp drop a band on the debt side and will be closely watched following the departure of banking head Stephen Mostyn-Williams.

LEADING FIRMS • LONDON EQUITY
ASHURST MORRIS CRISP
CLIFFORD CHANCE
LOVELL WHITE DURRANT
ALLEN & OVERY
DICKSON MINTO WS
MACFARLANES
TRAVERS SMITH BRAITHWAITE

HIGHLY REGARDED FIRMS • EQUITY
S J Berwin & Co
Cameron McKenna
Dibb Lupton Alsop
Berwin Leighton
Hammond Suddards
Herbert Smith
Nabarro Nathanson
Simmons & Simmons

LEADING FIRMS • LONDON DEBT
ALLEN & OVERY
CLIFFORD CHANCE
LOVELL WHITE DURRANT
ASHURST MORRIS CRISP
WILDE SAPTE
DIBB LUPTON ALSOP
DICKSON MINTO WS
NORTON ROSE

Ashurst Morris Crisp (Equity: 9 ptnrs; Debt: 4 ptnrs) The leading equity buy-out practice in London who have "a great franchise in this area." The firm still has "the best contacts at equity houses" and have concentrated on this market. Known for both large UK deals and European cross-border work. A "premier" buy-out practice. The "great" *Charles Geffen* received all round praise including being "a pleasure to have on the other side, a worthy opponent." Highly praised by venture capitalists. Whilst *Geoffrey Green* is less active on deals, he still has an enviable reputation in the market and is "hugely respected." The experienced and "practical" *Bruce Hanton* joins our Leading Individuals. *Simon Beddow* ("extremely able and personable lawyer with sense of humour") enters our tables as up and coming.

On the debt side the firm also has a strong practice but its future will be closely watched following the departure earlier this year of former Banking head Stephen Mostyn-Williams who had been doing "great work" for his clients. *Justin Spendlove* is seen as a "quality performer" whilst the "excellent" and "extremely organised" *Nigel Ward* is newly recommended. **Clients/Work:** Equity: Advised Cinven on the £860m buy-out of IPC magazines. Acted for Unipoly SA and Legal & General Ventures on the £620m buy-out of BTR's Polymer Products Group. Debt: Advising Bankers Trust and Société Générale on parallel debt facilities in England and France in connection with the sale by Générale des Eaux of its private healthcare interests at £1.1bn.

Clifford Chance (Equity: 6 ptnrs – 3f/t; 20 assts; Debt: 12 ptnrs – 5 f/t, 30 assts) An all round practice that has performed well on both the equity and debt sides. Had a particularly good year on the equity side including a "good start to [1998]..done some quite significant deals." Because of overseas network attracting more instructions due to internationalisation of equity buy-outs. Seen in some quarters as making up ground on Ashursts. Recommended partners include *James Baird*, the "commercial" and "able" *Matthew Layton* and the "highly spoken of" *Julia Clarke*.

On the debt side the firm has been seen "doing "big cross border" work and "a lot of larger deals." Partners include "good guy" *Mark Stewart*. **Clients/Work:** Advising PPM Ventures on the acquisition of Gala Bingo for £300m. Advising Merrill Lynch and SBC Warburg Dillon Read in relation to the senior debt and high yield issue securities for the acquisition of HMV Media Group (value £850m). Acting for BCI and Citibank on SEAT buy-out (£1.4bn).

Lovell White Durrant (Equity: 6ptnrs, 12assts; Debt: 4ptnrs – 3 f/t, 12assts – 6 f/t) Have "strong players with good following and pick up work on conflicts – recognised reputation in market place." *Marco Compagnoni* continues "to raise profile successfully in buy-out market" and is seen doing a lot of big deals. Other leading individuals are "senior guy" *John Kitching* and *Allan Murray-Jones* ("proactive lawyer, commercial and practical in approach, ... clients do love him.")

The debt side of the practice has had a good year with a particularly strong team. On the up "on basis of number of deals and quality of people." Seen by one interviewee as a having a "cracking practice." Lawyers are "nimble on feet." *John Penson* moves up a band. He is "highly regarded by clients and others – has technical ability and practical," a "wonderful performer" and "extremely commercial." *Matthew Cottis* also rises up,

he is "doing the deals and is competent at it." **Clients/Work:** Deals on the equity side included acting for Doughty Hanson on the £770m buy-out of the Geberit Group and the £510m buy-out of Impress, both multi-jurisdictional transactions. The debt team acted for the senior debt providers, Credit Suisse First Boston, on the £205 m buy-out of Trench Group.

Allen & Overy (Equity: 6 ptnrs, 20 assts; Debt: 6 ptnrs of which 3 dedicated (ie 75-80% of time), 15 dedicated assts) The equity practice is known more for "quality rather than quantity of deals." Have a "good reputation at top end...technical ability." *Alan Paul* is a "broad corporate finance lawyer...very clever" but is seen by some as less active on buy-out work than in the past.

The debt practice includes "big cross-border" work. *Anthony Keal* is reportedly doing more borrower work than in the past and maintains his reputation for assertiveness on deals. The "terrific" *David Morley* is a "talented performer" and has a reputation for buy-out and general banking work. The "excellent" *Stephen Gillespie* is "making a big push..doing well." *Euan Gorrie* is viewed by many as up and coming. He is "good technically," "cool ... knows his stuff." **Clients/Work:** Advised Investcorp in connection with the MBI of Watmoughs/British Printing company which had a combined purchase price of £400m ignoring debt repayment. Advising the management and the purchaser on the buy-out of Dalgety Agriculture from Dalgety plc. Acted for Goldman Sachs International as sole arranger and lead underwriter of senior and mezzanine debt facilities to Cinven Ltd in connection with the £860m acquisition of IPC Magazines.

Dickson Minto WS (Equity: 2ptnrs/5assts; Debt: 2ptnrs/5assts) Both the equity and debt practices have performed well. The equity practice is seen as "steady" and has a "strong relationship with clients." Have reputation for "quality roles involved on management side." The "very able" *Alastair Dickson* stands out as one of the top equity buy-out lawyers. Compliments included "wonderful..great artist … clever – is star" and "does a lot of work … commands enormous respect … one of three wise men of equity."

The debt practice acts for debt providers and management teams. One banker praised the firm's "extremely good corporate banking lawyers." *Michael Barron* has "commercial ability and manner."

Macfarlanes (Equity: 5 ptnrs, 8 assts plus 3 spending some of time) The equity practice reputation is mainly for smaller UK deals but has done some substantial transactions. "Have some good people." The "constructive" *Charles Martin* is "clearly able," "personable" and "works hard" – a "quick witted all rounder." *Kevin Tuffnell* and *Peter Turnbull* are the other leading individuals **Clients/Work:** Acting for Legal & General Ventures on the MBI of Henley's Motor Division valued at £110m. Acting for Candover Investments on the £360m MBO of UPN from United News and Media. Acting for management on the £860m MBO of IPC from Reed Elsiver.

Travers Smith Braithwaite (Equity: 6 ptnrs (3 of which is main area of practice), 12 assts (of which 3-4 nearly full time MBO/MBI). Had an exceptional year on equity buy-out work and rise up our tables. "Been doing quite a lot… more high profile deals… got good people." "Have made quite a lot of progress… acting for management and equity." "Done wonderful job this year getting act together." *Chris Hale* heads the Private Equity Group. *Mark Soundy* enters our table as up and coming. He is a "good all round guy" who is "business like, robust, energetic" and has had a really good year. *Charles Barter* also received recommendations, seen on beauty parades and has been busy. **Clients/Work:** Acting for management in six countries in the international buy-out of the metal packaging operations of Schmalbachubeca AG and Pechiney SA to form Impress Metal Packaging Group (deal size £469m). Acting for NatWest Equity Ptnrs Ltd and the offeror on the public bid for Betterware PLC funded using a private equity structure (deal size £127m). Acting

for the management on the HMV/Waterstones buy-out (total deal value £800m).

S J Berwin & Co (Equity: 7 ptnrs (50% of time), 20 assts) Best known for fund-raising for equity players but also have an established buy-out practice doing "smaller deals." "Terrific funds practice." *Jonathan Blake's* reputation is primarily as a funds lawyer rather than a transactional buy-out lawyer but does "both funds and buy-out." **Clients/Work:** Acting for Phildrew Ventures on MBO of transport division of Hogg Robinson PLC. Acting for Whitecross Group PLC on public to private MBO. Acting for Apax Partners on management and employee buy-out of Future Publishing Ltd and Edicorp Publications S.A from Pearson plc for £142m.

Cameron McKenna (Equity: 10 ptnrs of which 7 do a substantial amount, 15 assts of which 7 do a substantial amount) The equity practice is headed by *Anthony Lewis*. The firm has had a "reasonably good year… some interesting deals." **Clients/Work:** Equity: Acting for Nomura on £700m institutional purchase of William Hill Betting Shops chain. Acting for NatWest Equity Partners on the £49m MBO of Riva Clubs. Acting for the management team on the £77m MBO of Harwich International Ports.

Dibb Lupton Alsop (Equity: 5 ptnrs – 3 f/t, 6 assts. Debt: 6ptnrs, 11assts) A firm with "depth of experience, committed to the buy-out market" which is "doing a lot of management team" work as well as acting for equity providers. *Peter Wayte* is a member of the firm's management board and conse-

quently less transactionally active than in the past. He has a good reputation – "Clearly a leading individual."

On the debt side have a reputation for UK work. Bankers use "primarily on UK side. Have … good commercial style." The "extremely good" *Mark Vickers* has "got quite a name in terms of volume of transactions" and is a "big name in general UK deals." **Clients/Work:** Equity: Acting for HSBC Private Equity Europe and its clients on the institutional buy out of Harwich International Port for £77m. Acting for Natwest Equity Partners in the MBO of Marchpole Group Ltd for £130m. Debt: Acting for Bank of Scotland in relation to the public to private takeover/buy-out of JLI.

Berwin Leighton (Equity: 3 ptnrs(1p/t), 8 assts) A new addition to our tables for equity buy-out work. Doing a reasonable amount and making an effort to develop speciality in field. Act for a mix of private equity houses and management teams. **Clients/Work:** Advised Gresham Trust plc and the Newco on its £28m re-engineered MBO of Beck & Pollitzer Engineering Ltd. Advised Lloyds Development Capital Ltd and the Newco on the £15m buy-out of The Hymatic Group Ltd from Cobham plc. Acted for Foreign & Colonial Ventures Ltd and the Newco on the MBO of SodaStream from Cadbury Schweppes.

Hammonds Suddards (2ptnrs/12 assts on private equity of which 8 spend majority of time) An equity practice whose best known partner, Simon Inman, has recently retired from the law. "Enthusiastic" partner *Daljit Singh* is "up and coming" has a "good reputation and doing deals." **Clients/Work:** Acted for Murray Johnstone on £94 m MBO of INEOS from Inspec Group. Advised the management in the £145m MBO of Electrium. Advised Primary Capital on the MBO of Lowthers Cakes.

Herbert Smith (Equity: 4ptnrs/10assts) A low profile equity practice with "good quality product." Advise equity providers and management. **Clients/Work:** Acted for Electra Investment Trust and the other funds managed by Electra Fleming Ltd on a number of new investments, including £35m MBO of Aspen Healthcare. Advised management on the abortive MBO of Dalgety Foods.

Nabarro Nathanson (Equity: 4ptnrs/8assts) Enter our table on equity side as highly regarded. Have some ex-Turner Kenneth Brown partners who are "now back on scene" and "have good and strong contacts at equity houses." Act for equity providers and management teams. **Clients/Work:** Acted for the management on the £6m buy-out of Woolf Ollins. Acted for Alchemy Partners in respect of the acquisition of AG Stanley Holdings Plc (FADS). Acted for the management team and newco on the MBI of the CAMAS highway construction, maintenance and surfacing business (approx £14m).

Simmons & Simmons (Equity: 3 ptnrs/6assts) A rounded equity practice acting for equity providers and management

teams. Also involved acting for vendors. Potential in some bankers' opinions to "move up into big league." **Clients/Work:** Advising the management team on the MBO of Crystal Holidays Ltd and Jetsave Ltd (total funding £150m). Advising Charterhouse Development Capital on its £17m investment in Sheffield Wednesday Football Club PLC. Advising Booker PLC on its £57m sale of its prepared foods group to an MBI team backed by 3i plc.

Wilde Sapte (Debt: Core banking team consists of 3 ptnrs plus 1 ptnr approx 33%, 10 assts) A debt buy-out practice with a reputation for a good year "doing volume deals." Have good quality people including the "seriously good" *James Johnson* who does a lot of buy-out work and "banks would give a ring due to reputation."*Nick Syson* is still up and coming. **Clients/Work:** Acting for National Westminster Bank plc in relation to the acquisition of Dutton-Forshaw Ltd (deal size £113m). Acting for the Bank of Scotland in relation to the acquisition of Greenhall Cellars Ltd (deal size £100m). Acting for Citibank N.A. and UEGC in relation to the

acquisition of Demoservice (deal size £650m).

Norton Rose (Debt: 3 ptnrs 50%/7assts) A debt buy-out practice on the way up after a good year. Have had some success and luck at picking up instructions where other firms are conflicted. Good on big debt transactions and appear in large transactions. Client comments included – "Get good commercial viewpoint;" "Use more than anybody else. Doesn't that say it all?" *Tim Polglase* "has reputation for complex transactions." *Philip Whale* is seen as up and coming and "commercial" and "consistent… sensible." **Clients/Work:** Advising Chase Manhattan in relation to the £395m senior financing of the £700m acquisitions of Watmoughs (Holdings) and The British Printing Company. Acting for Royal Bank of Scotland and RBS Mezzanine on the £65m Public to Private MBO of Healthcall Group. Advising the equity consortium on the £244m acquisition of Castle Transmission from the BBC, including the £162.5m credit facilities and subsequent £125m high yield bond issue.

LEADERS' PROFILES · LONDON

ALLEN-JONES, Charles M.
Linklaters, London (0171) 456 3720
Senior Partner.
Specialisation: Specialist in corporate matters, particularly equity issues, public and private acquisitions, reorganisations and projects. Responsible for managing the firm's relationships with several key clients.
Career: Partner in charge of *Linklaters' International Finance Department 1981 – 83;* Partner in charge of Corporate Department 1985 – 91. Qualified 1963.
Personal: Born 1939. Lives in London. Leisure activities include travel, reading, gardening and tennis.

AP SIMON, Charles
Freshfields, London (0171) 936 4000
London (0171) 832 7125 direct line. Email: capsimon@freshfields.com
Partner in Corporate Department.
Specialisation: Main area of practice is corporate and corporate finance. Advises corporate and merchant banking clients on corporate, stock exchange and take-over related issues, including securities issues, joint ventures and private acquisitions and disposals.
Prof. Memberships: Law Society and City Solicitors' Company. London Stock Exchange Listing Rules Committee member.
Career: Qualified in 1977. Joined *Freshfields* in 1977, becoming a Partner in 1982.
Personal: Born 28th June 1947. Attended Epsom College 1960-65 and Christ's College Cambridge 1966-69 (MA, LLB).

ASHWORTH, Chris John
Ashurst Morris Crisp, London
(0171) 638 1111

AUDLEY, Max
Hobson Audley Hopkins & Wood, London
(0171) 450 4500
Specialisation: Head of Company Department. Specialises in Corporate Finance, IPOs, MBOs, take-overs mergers and acquisitions.
Prof. Memberships: International Bar Association – Company Law Committee. Associate of American Bar Association – Business Law Section. Association of German-speaking lawyers.
Career: Qualified 1980. Co-founded *Hobson Audley* 1983. Has built up a team of experienced corporate lawyers.

BAIRD, James
Clifford Chance, London (0171) 600 1000
Partner.
Specialisation: Partner specialising in management buy-outs and buy-ins with broad experience of general company and commercial work; corporate finance; M&A and takeovers.
Career: Qualified 1978. Partner Clifford Chance 1985.
Personal: University College, Oxford, BA Jurisprudence 1975.

BAKER, Andrew P.
Wedlake Bell, London (0171) 395 3000
Partner. Head of Corporate Finance.
Specialisation: Commercial and Corporate. Acts for a wide range of listed companies, brokers and venture capitalists with regard to mergers and acquisitions, equity issues and flotations. Speaker at seminars and conferences with regard to corporate governance and buying and selling companies.
Career: Articled with *Slaughter and May* in 1970. Qualified 1972 joining the commercial department of *Slaughter and May*. Joined *Wedlake Bell* 1979 becoming a partner in 1982.

Head of Corporate Finance 1985 to date. Also President of the international association of independent commercial law firms, TELFA (Trans European Law Firms Alliance) and chairman of CISCO. Member of legal and tax and corporate governance committees of European Association of Securities Dealers.
Personal: Born 12th October 1946. LLB(Hons) Birmingham 1969. Lives in Surrey. Also a Director of The Global Group plc, The Egyptian-British Chamber of Commerce and Lambeth Building Society.

BARNARD, Stephen G.
Herbert Smith, London (0171) 374 8000
Partner in Corporate Department.
Specialisation: Heads one of the firm's corporate groups and deals with a broad range of company and commercial work including corporate finance, mergers and acquisitions, venture capital and leveraged transactions, privatisations and major projects. His work involves acting for a number of listed clients as well as financial intermediaries, institutions and government.
Career: Qualified in 1974. Partner at *Herbert Smith* since 1983.
Personal: Educated at Southampton University.

BARRON, Michael J.
Dickson Minto WS, London (0171) 628 4455
Specialisation: Management buy-outs and buy-ins, especially structured debt finance and other credit facilities. Acts for major financial institutions and banks active in the venture capital and development capital market.
Career: Qualified as a solicitor in Scotland 1977 and in England 1986. Educated University of Edinburgh. Solicitor with 3i plc 1984 to 1987 then with *Dickson Minto WS*, as a partner since 1989.

BARTER, Charles S. J.
Travers Smith Braithwaite, London
(0171) 248 9133
Partner in Corporate Finance Department
Specialisation: Corporate Finance in particular venture capital, buyouts, buyins, disposals and reconstructions. Clients include leading venture capital houses, quoted and private companies.
Prof. Memberships: Law Society, City of London Solicitors Company.
Career: Articled Clerk 1985; Partner 1995.
Personal: Motorcycling, gardening, natural history, Church.

BEDDOW, Simon
Ashurst Morris Crisp, London
(0171) 638 1111
Specialisation: Management Buyouts but also advises a number of listed companies. Significant deals include £370 buyout of Williams Holdings' European building products division; £150m buyout of Crystal Holidays; £103 million 'White Knight' bid for William Cook plc; £50million public to private takeover of B. Elliott plc.
Career: University of Bristol (LLB 1986); Qualified 1989: Partner *Ashurst Morris Crisp* 1998.
Personal: Married with one daughter and one son.

BEHARRELL, Steven
Coudert Brothers, London (0171) 203 2222
E-mail: beharrell@london.coudert.com
Specialisation: Senior Partner and head of all English law activities for Coudert Brothers internationally. Specialises in energy and natural resources, infrastructure investment, project finance, transportation and privatisation. Has 25 years experience advising on oil and gas law in the Middle East, Asia, North Sea and Russia. Also involved in electricity and other privatisations since the late 1980s. Regularly addresses conferences and seminars on the subject of energy and privatisation law. Editor of Butterworths 'International Commercial Forms and Precedents' (1998).
Prof. Memberships: International Bar Association; member of the Oil Committee of the Section on Energy and Natural Resources Law.
Career: Assistant solicitor, Denton Hall 1966-72 and partner 1972-90. Founder and head of the Energy and Privatisation Groups. Partner, Coudert Brothers since 1990.
Personal: Educated at Sorbonne University, Paris 1961-62 and the College of Law, London 1964-66. Lives in London. Born 22nd December 1944.

BELL, Christopher C.
Travers Smith Braithwaite, London
(0171) 248 9133
Specialisation: Corporate and Corporate Finance – Mergers and Acquisitions, Equity Financings, MBOs and MBI's. Corporate governance issues.
Prof. Memberships: Member of the Company Law sub-committee of the City of London Solicitors Company.
Career: Qualified April 1971. Partner at *Travers Smith Braithwaite* since 1975, having joined the firm in 1971 after Articles at *Crossman Block & Keith*.

BENNETT, John E.
Berwin Leighton, London +44 171 760 1000
Specialisation: Corporate finance, private acquisitions and disposals, takeovers, flotations, joint ventures and general company and securities law advice.
Prof. Memberships: City of London Law Society Company Laws Sub-Committee.
Career: Qualified in 1983 with *Berwin Leighton*. Became a partner in 1987.

BIRT, Timothy D.
Osborne Clarke, London (0171) 634 1622
See under Advertising & Marketing, p. 95

BLAKE, Jonathan E.
S J Berwin & Co, London
+44 (0)171 533 2222
Specialisation: Partner in the Corporate Finance Department advising generally on mergers and acquisitions of private and public companies and specialising in the establishment of private equity and other funds, the structuring of companies, venture capital investment, MBOs as well as reorganisations, flotations and associated taxation matters.
Prof. Memberships: Associate of the Chartered Institute of Taxation (ATII); British Venture Capital Association; International Bar Association; European Venture Capital Association.
Personal: Educated at Haberdashers' Aske's School, Elstree and Queens' College, Cambridge (MA LL.M). Qualified 1979. Born 7th July 1954.

BOARDMAN, Nigel P.G.
Slaughter and May, London
(0171) 600 1200
Specialisation: M&A, Corporate Finance, Corporate and Commercial. Advises UK and overseas companies and investment banks on the full range of corporate transactions, including acquisitions, disposals, takeovers, joint ventures, financings, flotations, MBOs and general corporate advice.
Career: Qualified in 1975 while with *Slaughter and May*. Joined the Corporate Finance Department of Kleinwort Benson Ltd before returning to *Slaughter and May*, becoming Partner in 1982 and Head of Corporate in 1996.

BOND, Richard
Herbert Smith, London (0171) 374 8000
See under Energy – Oil and Gas, p. 330

BOTT, Adrian J.A.
Olswang, London (0171) 208 8888
Partner and Head of Corporate Group.
Specialisation: Main areas of practice are corporate and finance. Since 1980, has been consistently involved in activities ranging from M&A, MBOs and MBIs, through flotations (including many on AIM), rights issues, placings and other means of financing, to Venture Capital (acting for both providers and consumers), both in domestic and international transactions. Clients are predominantly quoted or subsidiaries of multinationals. Many have an electronics or media bias. Also active in significant corporate joint ventures (such as BBC Worldwide/Flextech) and banking work (involving all types of facilities and financial instruments) and a broad spectrum of commercial contracts and employee share schemes. Has handled numerous consortium

arrangements, leading a variety of consortia in bids for various TV and radio broadcasting licences (ITV Channel 3 and Channel 5, and INRI (Classic FM)).
Prof. Memberships: Law Society, British Venture Capital Association.
Career: Qualified in 1980. *Rooks Rider* 1978-87, from 1984 as a Partner. Partner at Olswang from 1988.
Personal: Born 9th June 1956. Charterhouse School 1969-73, Manchester University 1974-77 and Guildford Law School 1977.

BRAHAM, Edward
Freshfields, London (0171) 936 4000
Specialisation: Partner in corporate department specialising in mergers and acquisitions and corporate finance matters.
Prof. Memberships: Law Society.
Career: Qualified 1987, Partner 1995.
Personal: Born 1961. Educated at Worcester College, Oxford 1980-1984 (BA, BCL).

BROWNLOW, Jeremy
Clifford Chance, London (0171) 600 1000
Partner.
Specialisation: Main area of work is company and commercial including corporate finance and mergers and acquisitions. Principally advising public listed companies and merchant banks on recommended and hostile public takeovers and domestic and international corporate transactions.
Career: Qualified 1970. Partner 1973.
Personal: MA (camb).

BURGESS, Patrick
Gouldens, London (0171) 583 7777
Senior Partner.
Specialisation: Corporate finance and international specialist. Recent activities include advising on drafting of the new Stock Exchange Yellow Book, membership of the Stock Exchange Working Party on smaller companies and the Alternative Investment Market Panel of the London Stock Exchange, and tax and legislation advice to the Unquoted Companies Group. Speaker at numerous conferences and seminars.
Career: Qualified in 1972. Joined *Gouldens* in 1968 and became a Partner in 1974.
Personal: Born 31st October 1944. Recreations include sailing, shooting, rowing, reading and opera. Lives in London and Chichester.

BURNS, Richard
Hammond Suddards, London
(0171) 655 1000
Partner.
Specialisation: Specialises in corporate finance work and, in particular, mergers and acquisitions for public companies and rights issues.
Prof. Memberships: Law Society.
Career: Articled *Last Suddards*; qualified 1983; Partner *Hammond Suddards* 1986.
Personal: Born 1958; resides Knightsbridge and Burley-in-Wharfedale. Enjoys sailing. Prior to retirement played rugby, football and cricket for a number of clubs, now relegated to the role of spectator; member of Sandmoor Golf Club.

BURROW, Robert P.
S J Berwin & Co, London
+44 (0)171 533 2222
Partner in Corporate Finance Department.
Specialisation: Main area of practice is international merger and acquisition work and

investment funds.
Prof. Memberships: Law Society.
Career: Qualified in 1975. Joined *S J Berwin & Co* as a Partner in 1985. Managing Director of J Rothschild & Co Ltd 1982-85.
Personal: Born 24th March 1951. Educated at Fitzwilliam College, Cambridge 1969-72. Leisure interests include cars, tennis, and skiing. Lives in London.

CANN, J.W.Anthony
Linklaters, London (0171) 456 3592
Head of Corporate Department.
Specialisation: Specialises in company law and corporate finance, including mergers and acquisitions, takeovers and issues, with responsibility for relationships with several major public companies. Transactions have included advising British Gas plc on its proposed demerger, advising Scottish and Newcastle on the acquisition of Courage Brewing and Chef & Brewer, advising British Airways on several transactions, advising Allied Domecq on the acquisition of Pedro Domecq and related 'trombone' rights issue, advising on the defence of Racal Electronics to the bid from Williams Holdings, Elf Aquitaine in relation to its joint venture with Enterprise Oil, Zeneca Group on its demerger from ICI, Bell Cablemedia plc on its simultaneous acquisitions and listing and then its takeover of Videotron Holdings and merger into Cable & Wireless Communications, advising Chubb Security on its takeover by Williams Holdings.

CARRINGTON, Nigel M.
Baker & McKenzie, London (0171) 919 1000
Managing Partner. Member of the Corporate Department.
Specialisation: Principal area of practice involves international corporate transactions including mergers, acquisitions, joint ventures and privatisations. Editor of 'Acquiring Companies and Businesses in Europe' (Wiley Chancery Law 1994).
Prof. Memberships: Law Society, City of London Law Society.
Career: Joined *Baker & McKenzie* as an Articled Clerk in 1979, qualified in 1981. Assigned to Chicago Office (Foreign Trade Department) 1983-84 and became a Partner in 1987. Appointed Managing Partner of the firm's London office in 1994.
Personal: Born 1st May 1956. MA Jurisprudence, St John's College, Oxford.

CHARNLEY, William F.
Simmons & Simmons, London
(0171) 628 2020
Head of Corporate Finance
Specialisation: Principal area of practice is corporate finance covering flotations, mergers and acquisitions and capital raising for companies acting for underwriters and issuers of securities, private equity transactions and general corporate advice.
Prof. Memberships: Law Society, Institute of Chartered Secretaries and Administrators, The Drapers Company.
Career: Articled at *Slater Heelis* in Manchester 1985-87, then joined *Booth & Co.* and became a Partner in 1990; joined *Simmons & Simmons* as a Partner in 1994.
Personal: Born 21st August 1960. Attended Rivington and Blackrod Grammar School 1971-78, Bolton Institute 1978-80, Sheffield Hallam University 1980-81, Lancaster University 1981-

83 and Manchester Metropolitan University 1984-85. Trustee of Children's Heart Surgery Fund, Killingbeck Hospital. Leisure pursuits include country sports, art, opera and wine. Lives in London.

CHESTER, Martin G.
Theodore Goddard, London
(0171) 606 8855
Specialisation: Corporate finance, including mergers and acquisitions, public offerings, flotations, share capital and debt restructuring, investment trusts, corporate governance and general corporate advice. Recent major transactions include the Lloyds TSB merger, reorganisation of the 5 classes of share capital of the Signet Group plc into a single class, and the disposal by Blagden Industries plc of their packaging division.
Career: Qualified 1967. Partner in *Theodore Goddard* since 1972. Chairman of the Company Law Sub-Committee of the City of London Law Society 1990-93 and of the Law Society's Company Law Committee 1993-96. Educated at St. Albans School and Exeter University.
Personal: Leisure interests include swimming, scuba diving and enjoying good food and wine.

CHEYNE, David W.
Linklaters, London (0171) 456 3174
Partner in Corporate Department.
Specialisation: Involved in a wide range of corporate transactions including M&A work, flotations, general corporate finance work and Stock Exchange related matters.
Career: Qualified 1974. Became a Partner in 1980. Partner, *Linklaters & Paines*, Hong Kong office, 1981-1986.

CHILDS, David
Clifford Chance, London (0171) 600 1000
Specialisation: Head of the corporate practice area, specialising in mergers and acquisitions, primary and secondary securities issues and privatisations. For example, led the Clifford Chance team advising British Gas on its £1.5bn privatisation by international offering.
Career: Sheffield University; University College, London (LLB, LLM). Articled Clifford Chance; qualified 1976; Partner Clifford Chance since 1981.
Personal: Born 1951; resides Sevenoaks.

CLARK, Adrian S.
Ashurst Morris Crisp, London
(0171) 638 1111
Specialisation: Company Department.
Career: Qualified 1983. *Slaughter and May* 1981-1986; *Ashurst Morris Crisp* 1986 onwards. Partner 1990. Seconded to Take-over Panel 1988-1990.

CLARK, Tim N.
Slaughter and May, London
(0171) 600 1200
Specialisation: Principal area of practice is UK and international corporate work, corporate finance and mergers and acquisitions (including public takeovers, flotations, international equity offerings), advising corporate and investment bank clients. Practice also involves demutualisatons (building societies and insurance companies).
Prof. Memberships: The Law Society.
Career: Qualified 1976 with *Slaughter and May*. Became Partner in 1983.
Personal: Born 9 January 1951. Educated at

Sherbourne School and Pembroke College, Cambridge. Interests include theatre, sport, Italy and flying. Lives in London.

CLARKE, Julia
Clifford Chance, London (0171) 600 1000
Partner.
Specialisation: Partner specialising in venture capital and management buy-outs and buy-ins including cross-border European deals with broad experience of corporate finance and mergers and acquisitions.
Career: Guildford County School; St. Hugh's College, Oxford (1984, MA). Articled *Clifford Chance*; qualified 1989; Partner 1994.
Personal: Born 1962; resides London.

CLARKE, Tim
Linklaters, London (0171) 456 3304
Specialisation: Partner with significant experience of corporate finance, M&A and takeovers; significant experience of UK and international privatisations, both primary and secondary, including British Aerospace, Rolls Royce, National Power, British Telecom, Cable & Wireless, Railtrack and Associated British Ports.

COMPAGNONI, Marco
Lovell White Durrant, London
(0171) 236 0066
Specialisation: Specialises in a range of mergers and acquisitions work and corporate law. A particular specialisation is private equity transactions (MBOs and MBIs) acting primarily for institutional investors. Equity institutions for whom he has acted regularly include Mercury Asset Management and 3i. He also has extensive experience of joint ventures, purchase and sales of companies and businesses (both domestic and cross border). Significant recent transactions include acting for ING in its purchase of Barings and advising Doughty Hanson on its purchase of the Ilford Photo Business.
Prof. Memberships: Member of the British Venture Capital Association, the British Italian Law Association and the City of London Solicitors Company.
Career: Articled at *Lovell White & King*; qualified in 1987 and became a partner in 1993.

COOKE, Stephen J.
Slaughter and May, London
(0171) 600 1200
Partner in Company/Commercial Department.
Specialisation: Principal area of practice is company and commercial work with a particular emphasis on M&A.
Prof. Memberships: The Law Society.
Career: Qualified in 1984 while with *Slaughter and May*. Worked in the New York office 1989-90, and became a Partner in 1991. Publications include "Takeovers" (1997).
Personal: Born 7 March 1959. Educated Lincoln College, Oxford (1978-81). Lives in London.

COTTIS, Matthew
Lovell White Durrant, London
(0171) 236 0066
Specialisation: Expertise in management buy-outs/buy-ins, bids and takeovers and other types of acquisition finance, property development finance and general syndicated loans.
Career: Articled Lovell White Durrant 1985-87, Partner 1993.

CRANFIELD, Richard
Allen & Overy, London
(0171) 330 3000
Specialisation: Has a wide range of corporate finance experience including domestic mergers and acquisitions, privatisations and buy-outs and capital markets work (both international and domestic) for equity and debt financings. Recent corporate finance experience includes advising Cable and Wireless on formation of Cable & Wireless Communications. Privatisation experience includes advising the DTI on the privatisation of British Energy. Currently advising DFID on the public/private partnership for Commonwealth Development Corporation.
Career: Articled 1978, qualified 1980, Partner 1985 at *Allen & Overy*.
Personal: Born 19/01/56. Educated at Winchester College and Fitzwilliam College, Cambridge. Married with four children.

CRYSTAL, Peter
Memery Crystal, London
(0171) 242 5905
Senior Partner in Corporate/ Commercial Department.
Specialisation: Corporate finance and sports law. Advises management and companies on take-overs, AIM and OFEX and company flotations, capital raising, MBO, MBI, and commercial sports law, including transaction structures, sponsorship and corporate aspects. Acts, inter alia, for Wembley plc and Lennox Lewis. Examiner with the Law Society in Company Law and Partnership 1974-78. Lib Dem Parliamentary candidate on three Elections. Conference spokesman on Guinness Case.
Prof. Memberships: Law Society, Sports Lawyers Association.
Career: Qualified in 1972. Articled at *Simpson Curtis*: with *Clifford Turner* 1973-78; Founded *Memery Crystal* in 1978.
Personal: Born 1948. Attended Leeds Grammar School; St Edmund Hall Oxford (MA Hons PPE); College of Law; McGill University, Montreal (LLM). Played rugby and boxed for Oxford, captained Otley RUFC. Leisure interests include all sports, reading and travel. Lives in London.

DARLINGTON, Gavin L.B.
Freshfields, London (0171) 936 4000
Specialisation: Head of corporate department and has particular expertise in cross-border transactions and specialises in mergers and acquisitions and joint ventures. He has recently acted for the Zurich group, on its proposed merger with BAT Industries' Financial Services arm and GEC on its proposed global offering of shares in GEC Alsthom.

DAVIS, James P.L.
Freshfields, London (0171) 936 4000
Specialisation: Corporate Finance, acting for companies and investment bank on M&A and equity issues. Clients include Schroders, Cinven, Wolseley, Hays, Compass.
Career: Balliol College, Oxford. Partner since 1976.
Personal: Wife (Sally) and four children. Interests include golf and fishing.

DI BIASE, Paul
Edward Lewis, London
(0171) 404 5566
Partner in Company and Commercial Department.
Specialisation: Principal areas of practice are mergers and acquisitions and corporate finance, including sales and acquisitions of companies and businesses, MBOs and MBI's mainly for the management team.
Prof. Memberships: Law Society.
Career: Qualified in 1961. Partner with *Forsyte Saunders Kerman* since 1965. Chairman of the firm's Partnership Board.
Personal: Born 21st July 1934. Educated at Rutlish School, Merton 1946-53 and University College, Oxford 1954-57. Lessee of The Richmond Golf Club. Leisure interests include golf, cinema, theatre, travel, food and wine. Lives in Weston Green, Esher, Surrey.

DICKSON, Alastair R.
Dickson Minto WS, London
(0171) 628 4455
Specialisation: Mergers and acquisitions; leveraged buy-outs; acting for major financial institutions and banks; involved in over £8 billion of financial buy-outs.
Prof. Memberships: Member of Law Society of Scotland; Writer to Her Majesty's Signet.
Career: Educated Edinburgh University 1971. *Dundas & Wilson* 1971-73. *Maclay Murray & Spens* 1973-76. *Dundas & Wilson* 1976-85 (partner from 1978). Founding partner of *Dickson Minto WS* 1985.
Personal: Golf, squash, hill walking.

DILLON, Martin L.G.
Taylor Joynson Garrett, London
(0171) 353 1234
Qualified 1965. Partner 1970. Corporate Commercial Department. Main areas of practice are corporate acquisitions, sales and reorganisations, international tax, international note issues and reinsurance disputes. Educated at The Queen's College, Oxford (1st Class Hons. Law).

ELLARD, John
Linklaters, London (0171) 456 3324
Specialisation: Partner in the corporate department with extensive experience of tax and corporate finance, particularly in the field of privatisations.

FAGELSON, Ian B.
Warner Cranston, London (0171) 403 2900
Partner in Company/ Commercial Department.
Specialisation: Handles corporate and financial transactions, including corporate finance, mergers and acquisitions and banking. Wide experience of both public and private corporate and financial transactions, including complex international mergers and acquisitions, disposals, financings, restructurings, debt and equity issues (public and private) and joint ventures. Also deals with insurance and reinsurance, including the establishment of innovative structured reinsurance programmes. University lecturer 1977-79. Subsequently regular conference and seminar lecturer on corporate and banking topics.
Prof. Memberships: Law Society, American Bar Association.

Career: Qualified in 1980, having joined *Warner Cranston* in 1979. Became a Partner in 1981 and Senior Partner in 1997.
Personal: Born 22nd April 1952. Educated at the University of Southampton 1970-73 (LLB) and Oxford University 1973-75 (BCL). Enjoys theatre, reading and loafing. Lives in London.

GEE, Tim
Baker & McKenzie, London (0171) 919 1000
Specialisation: Public and private company M&A, privatisation and equity capital markets transactions, acting for underwriters and issuers. Extensive cross-border and emerging markets experience and identified as one of the UK's leading privatisation lawyers in Euromoney's Guide to the World's Leading Privatisation Lawyers. Head of *Baker & McKenzie's* European M&A Practice Group.
Prof. Memberships: The Law Society; City of London Solicitors Company.
Career: Educated at Worcester College, Oxford. Qualified in 1986 with *Baker & McKenzie*. 1989-1990 *Baker & McKenzie*, Hong Kong. 1991 *Baker & McKenzie*, Budapest. Partner in 1992.
Personal: Married with one son. Interests include Rugby and fly fishing.

GEFFEN, Charles S.H.
Ashurst Morris Crisp, London
(0171) 638 1111
Specialisation: General corporate and corporate finance.
Career: Head of Buy Outs.
Personal: Married, three children.

GILLESPIE, Stephen
Allen & Overy, London (0171) 330 3000
See under Banking, p. 137

GODDEN, Richard W.
Linklaters, London (0171) 456 3610
Partner. Corporate Department.
Specialisation: Has wide experience both in general corporate advisory work and corporate transactions in the UK and the Far East. Advises a wide range of corporate clients and merchant and investment banks in connection with public takeovers, the establishment of joint ventures, private merger and acquisition transactions, flotations, other corporate equity fund raising, and advising corporations of various sizes in relation to their on-going affairs (e.g. issues connected with general meetings, scrip dividend schemes, removal of directors, etc.)

GODFREY, Keith G.
Allen & Overy, London (0171) 330 3000
Specialisation: Partner in the corporate department, specialising in corporate finance, mergers and acquisitions, joint ventures and securities offerings.
Prof. Memberships: Member of Law Society's Standing Committee on Company Law since 1988.
Career: Articled Allen & Overy, qualified 1976, Partner 1981.
Personal: London University 1972. Born 1951.

GORRIE, Euan
Allen & Overy, London (0171) 330 3000
Specialisation: Structured finance and leveraged buy-outs lending to partnerships, secured loans, work outs.
Career: Glenalmond; New College Oxford; Articled *Allen & Overy*, Partner 1996.
Personal: Married; two children.

GRAHAM, David
Freshfields, London (0171) 936 4000
Specialisation: Partner in the Corporate Department specialising in mergers and acquisitions, demergers and equity offerings. Acted for Morgan Stanley on demerger of Gallaher from American Brands, flotation of ARM Holdings and offer by Federal Mogul for T&N. Clients include Morgan Stanley, Takeover Panel, Dresdner Kleinwort Benson and ScottishPower.
Prof. Memberships: Law Society, City of London Solicitors Company.
Career: Qualified in 1984, becoming a partner in 1991. *Freshfields* New York office (1987-1990). Seconded to Takeover Panel (1990-1992). Seconded to Morgan Stanley (1993-1994).
Personal: Born in 1958. Attended Lincoln College Oxford. Married with two daughters. Leisure pursuits include tennis, golf and skiing.

GRAYSTON, Clare
Lewis Silkin, London (0171) 227 8004
Specialisation: Partner in Corporate Department, covering mergers and acquisitions and corporate finance. Wrote for Butterworths Encyclopaedia of Forms and Precedents (Fifth Edition) on 'Public Issues of Shares.' General editor of Kluwer Law International titles 'Sale of Private and Public Companies by Auction' (1996), Protection of Minority Shareholders (1997). National President of the International Association of Young Lawyers (1995-97).
Prof. Memberships: International Association of Young Lawyers, International Bar Association, Law Society, Westminster Law Society, Association of Women Solicitors.
Career: Qualified in 1985. Other interests: Director (Chair of Finance Committee) of Women in Film and Television (UK) Ltd (1992-1998), Director of Living Earth Foundation (1995-1996).
Personal: Born 18th December 1960. BA (Hons) Law and French. Lives in central London.

GREAVES, Adam
Gouldens, London (0171) 583 7777
Partner in Company/ Commercial Department.
Specialisation: Very diversified practice covers venture capital, management buy-outs and buy-ins, mergers and acquisitions (private and public), flotations, corporate finance, corporate reconstructions and commercial agreements and joint ventures. Major clients include Nash Sells & Partners, BancBoston Capital, Gresham Trust, Collins Stewart, Credit Lyonnais Securities and several listed companies.
Career: Qualified in 1982. Joined *Nabarro Nathanson* in 1980, joining and becoming a Partner of *Gouldens* in 1986.
Personal: Born 9th July 1958. Attended Bradfield College 1972-76, Selwyn College, Cambridge 1976-79 and Guildford College of Law 1979-80. Leisure interests include fly fishing (member of the Red Sea Casters), bridge, hockey, walking and cooking. Lives in London.

GREEN, Geoffrey.S.
Ashurst Morris Crisp, London (0171) 638 1111
Partner, Head of Company Department.
Specialisation: Principal area of work is mergers and acquisitions, including cross-border mergers and acquisitions and corporate finance generally, including new issues. Other main area of work is buy-outs acting primarily for equity institutions.
Prof. Memberships: Law Society.
Career: Qualified in 1975 while with *Ashurst*

Morris Crisp and became a Partner in 1979.
Personal: Forest School; St. Catharine's College, Cambridge. Leisure pursuits include tennis, golf and riding. Lives in London and Wiltshire.

HALE, Chris
Travers Smith Braithwaite, London (0171) 248 9133
Specialisation: Main area of practice: Buy-outs (head of Travers Smith Private Equity Group); also advises on new issues and a number of listed companies and financial advisers on equity raising and mergers and acquisitions. Significant recent deals: £120m public to private buyout of Betterware Plc; £104m buyout of Blagden Packaging; £58m buyout of Fairey Hydraulics; flotation of Quester VCT 2 Plc.
Prof. Memberships: Hon. Treasurer and Executive Committee member of Society of Advanced Legal Studies; author of articles appearing in legal journals.
Career: King's College School, Wimbledon. Emmanuel College, Cambridge MA. Wolfson College, Cambridge LLM. *Kingsley Napley*, articled clerk then assistant solicitor 1979-82. *Travers Smith Braithwaite*, assistant solicitor 1983-87. Partner 1987.
Personal: Football, reading, gardening, walking, legal history.

HANTON, Bruce
Ashurst Morris Crisp, London (0171) 638 1111
Specialisation: Principal area of work is corporate finance particularly private equity transactions. Recent transactions include the Unipoly buy-out (Legal & General Ventures) and the acquisition of RoadChef Plc (Nikko Europe).
Prof. Memberships: Law Society.
Career: Qualified in 1988 with *Ashurst Morris Crisp*. Became Partner in 1996.
Personal: Born 7 February 1962. Educated Alleyn's School and Bristol University (LL.B and LL.M). Married with two children.

HATCHARD, Michael E.
Skadden, Arps, Slate, Meagher & Flom LLP, London (0171) 519 7000
Partner specialising in corporate finance and M&A.
Specialisation: Principally mergers, acquisitions and joint ventures and the full range of securities distribution transactions, particularly where significant UK/US implications arise.
Career: Qualified 1980 with *Theodore Goddard*, partner 1985. Joined *Skadden, Arps* as a partner in 1994 with responsibility for the English legal and regulatory aspects of global securities offerings and cross-border transactions.
Personal: Born 21st November 1955.

HENDERSON CBE, Giles I.
Slaughter and May, London (0171) 600 1200
Senior Partner and Partner in Corporate Department.
Specialisation: Corporate, corporate finance and commercial law, with particular experience in privatisations.
Prof. Memberships: The Law Society. Member, Hampel Committee on Corporate Governance.
Career: Qualified 1970. Partner since 1975. Senior Partner since 1993.
Personal: Born 1942. Educated at Michaelhouse School, South Africa and at

Witwatersrand University, South Africa (BA) and Magdalen College, Oxford (MA, BCL).

HOLLAND, Peter Rodney James
Allen & Overy, London (0171) 330 3000
Specialisation: Partner in Corporate Department. Main area of work is corporate law, principally mergers, acquisitions, privatisations and new issues in the UK, as well as building societies affairs. Has handled acquisitions of companies and undertakings of varying sorts by UK and overseas clients. Acted on the merger of the Leeds Permanent and Halifax Building Societies and on aspects of the latter's conversion; acted for Banque Indosuez on its disposal of Gartmore Plc and for ABN AMRO on the acquisition of Hoare Govett and other entities; acted for South West Water plc on its privatisation and, subsequently, on the proposed bids for it by other water companies. Acts for a number of major building societies on matters ranging from conversion proposals to general constitutional matters. Heads the firm's Building Societies Group. Contributor to 'Mergers & Acquisitions' and 'A Practitioner's Guide to Take-overs and Mergers;' Joint Editor of 'Contemporary Issues on Corporate Governance.' Has spoken at various conferences.
Prof. Memberships: Law Society, City of London Law Society.
Career: Qualified in 1968. Joined *Allen & Overy* in 1966, becoming a Partner in 1972. Member of the Law Society's Company Law Committee 1978-88 and Chairman 1983-87; Member of the City EEC Committee 1983-87; Member of the City of London Law Society's Company Law Sub-Committee 1983-87; Member of Institute of Directors Council and Policy and Executive Committee.
Personal: Born 31st July 1944. Attended Oxford University 1962-65 (MA Jurisprudence). Governor St Edmund's School Canterbury. Leisure interests include outdoor activities. Lives in Long Sutton, Hants.

HOWES, Colin M.
Harbottle & Lewis, London (0171) 667 5000
Partner in Company/ Commercial Department.
Specialisation: Handles regulatory and company/commercial work for a variety of clients, most of whom are in the entertainment, leisure and travel industries. Author of 'Slot Allocation at Heathrow Airport: The Legal Framework.' Addressed the 1993 EALA conference and the 1988 Theatre Managers Association Annual Conference (on the impact of the Financial Services Act 1986 on theatre producers).
Prof. Memberships: Law Society, European Air Law Association.
Career: Qualified in 1981. Joined *Harbottle & Lewis* in 1979, became a Partner in 1984.
Personal: Born 3rd March 1956. Attended Ipswich School 1967-74, then Oriel College, Oxford 1975-78. Lives in London.

ISSITT, Martin
Eversheds, London (0171) 919 4500
Specialisation: Range of mergers and acquisitions and corporate work for public and private companies, including MBOs/ MBIs and joint ventures. Frequently cross-border elements.
Career: Qualified 1984. Partner at *Eversheds* since 1994, having joined firm from *McKenna & Co.*
Personal: Born 1958. Married, 2 children. Lives London.

JAMES, Glen W.
Slaughter and May, London
(0171) 600 1200
Specialisation: Practice covers all work in the fields of Company/Corporate Finance, including mergers and acquisitions, issues and flotations and corporate restructurings. Additional interest in non-contentious insurance and reinsurance work.
Prof. Memberships: The Law Society; Securities Institute.
Career: Qualified 1976. Articled at *Slaughter and May* 1974-76. Assistant Solicitor 1976-1983. Partner since 1983.
Personal: Born 22 August 1952. Educated at King's College School, Wimbledon and New College, Oxford.

JOHNS, Michael S.M.
Nicholson Graham & Jones, London
(0171) 648 9000
 Managing Partner and Partner in the Company and Commercial Department.
Specialisation: Main area of practice is corporate finance. Work includes acquisitions, mergers, venture capital, buy-outs, equity issues, yellow book work and general corporate work for public listed companies. Member of sports group; acts for organisations and individuals in the sports field including sponsors and sports organisers. Has spoken at seminars both in the UK and USA on subjects such as buy-outs, international strategic activities, law firm management and sports sponsorship. Non-Executive Director of Merchant Retail Group Plc since 1979.
Prof. Memberships: Institute of Directors, Law Society. Chairman of Globalex.

JOHNSON, James
Wilde Sapte, London (0171) 246 7000
See under Banking, p. 137

JONES, Arfon
Cameron McKenna, London
(0171) 367 3000
Specialisation: Corporate finance, including M & A, flotations and equity and debt capital issues. Major transactions include the recent £75 million Rolfe & Nolan/Sungard Data Systems offer, the £9 billion Glaxo/Wellcome take over and the US$1billion Exchangeable Capital units issue by National Australia Bank.
Prof. Memberships: Law Society; Company Law Sub-Committee; City of London Solicitors Company.
Career: Bristol Grammar School, Clare College, Cambridge. Joined *Markbys* 1968. Partner 1970 to date in *Markbys*, *Cameron Markby*, *Cameron Markby Hewitt*, *Cameron McKenna*.
Personal: Married, 2 sons, 1 daughter. Interests: skiing, golf.

KEAL, Anthony C.
Allen & Overy, London (0171) 330 3000
Specialisation: Partner specialising in structured acquisition finance (LBOs and the like), public bid finance, export credit arrangements and syndicated loans generally.
Prof. Memberships: Law Society and City of London Solicitors Company.
Career: Articled Allen & Overy, qualified 1976; legal adviser/CoSec, Libra Bank plc 1976-78;

Assistant Solicitor Allen & Overy 1979-81; Partner 1981.
Personal: Born 1951. Educated Stowe School and New College, Oxford (1973).

KEAT, Alan M.
Travers Smith Braithwaite, London
(0171) 248 9133
Specialisation: Company Department. Company law specialist.
Career: Qualified 1966. Partner 1970.
Personal: Born 12.5.1942

KING, Peter D.S.
Linklaters, London (0171) 456 3448
Partner. Corporate Department.
Specialisation: Experienced in all aspects of corporate finance, including, in particular, international equity offers, privatisations, mergers and acquisitions and advice to financial institutions on regulatory matters.
Career: Articled at *Linklaters & Paines*, Solicitor 1983-90, becoming Partner in 1990.
Personal: Educated in Modern Languages at St John's College, Cambridge. Born 1960.

KITCHING, John
Lovell White Durrant, London
(0171) 236 0066
Specialisation: Principal area of practice is venture capital which he started in 1983, having previously been in the corporate tax department. Expertise in MBOs, equity investments and cross border transactions. Mainly acts for UK investing institutions although quite prepared to act for management teams if there is not a conflict. Now actively involved in fund raising advice.
Prof. Memberships: City Law Club, Law Society.
Career: Qualified in 1971 with *Lovell White & King* (now *Lovell White Durrant*.) Partner 1976. During his career he has been a Partner in corporate tax, construction, corporate finance and financial services departments (where he currently resides).

KNIGHT, Adrian G.
Ashurst Morris Crisp, London
(0171) 638 1111
Partner in Company Department.
Specialisation: Specialises in corporate finance, mergers and acquisitions and corporate transactions.
Career: Qualified in March 1984. Became a Partner at *Ashurst Morris Crisp* in 1992.
Personal: Graduated from Cambridge University in 1980.

KNIGHT, William
Simmons & Simmons, London
(0171) 628 2020
Senior Partner.
Specialisation: Main area of practice involves corporate finance and company work. Author of Acquisition of Private Companies (7th ed.) and member of Editorial Board of PLC magazine.
Prof. Memberships: Chairman Law Society Company Law Committee 1990-93, Institute of Advanced Legal Studies Research Committee, CCBE (Conseil Barreaux de la Communaute Europeenne) Company Law Committee.
Career: Qualified in 1969. Partner at *Simmons & Simmons* 1973. Admitted as Hong Kong

Solicitor 1979, and Head of Hong Kong office 1979-82. Leader of one of the corporate finance groups 1984-94. Appointed head of corporate department 1994. Appointed Senior Partner in September 1996.

LAWES, William P.L.
Freshfields, London (0171) 936 4000
Specialisation: Main practice areas are mergers and acquisitions, demergers, joint ventures, international offerings and UK domestic issues of all types. Acts for a range of corporate clients (with a media bias) and investment banks. Recent significant M&A transactions include acting for the financial advisers/ underwriters on Rentokil's bid for BET, Pearson on the UK aspects of its acquisition of Simon & Schuster, Capital Radio on its acquisition of two radio stations, Scottish Media on its bid for Grampian TV and its stake in Ulster TV and Amersham on the mergers with Nycomed and the life science business of Pharmacia & UpJohn. Recent introductions include acting for the sponsors on the Halifax flotation and the demerger of the Energy Group from Hanson. Recent restructurings include acting on the demerger and sale of C&J Clark's factory outlets centres and in relation to the demerger of Lonrho Africa.
Prof. Memberships: Law Society, City of London Solicitors Company.
Career: Qualified as Barrister and Solicitor in New Zealand in 1986. Judges' Clerk at New Zealand Court of Appeal 1985. Joined *Freshfields* in 1986. Partner in Corporate Department 1994.
Personal: Born 2 January 1964. Educated in England and New Zealand. Victoria University, Wellington N.Z. 1981 – 1985. Gonville and Caius College, Cambridge 1985/86. Leisure pursuits include golf and family.

LAYTON, Matthew
Clifford Chance, London (0171) 600 1000
Partner in the Corporate Group.
Specialisation: Partner specialising in venture capital and management buy-outs/buy-ins and realisations from such investments; and with broad experience of mergers and acquisitions and corporate finance.
Career: Qualified 1986. Partner Clifford Chance 1991.
Personal: LL.B (Hons) Leeds 1982.

LETH, Mary H.
Macfarlanes, London (0171) 831 9222
Specialisation: Partner Company Commercial and Banking Department. Deals with corporate finance including acquisitions, mergers, demergers and corporate reconstructions.
Career: Educated in United States: University of Colorado. Articled at *Macfarlanes*; qualified 1988; Partner 1995. Admitted States of Colorado 1977; New York 1984.
Personal: Born 1952. Resides London. Interests include music, opera, walking, cycling.

LEVY, Graeme
Olswang, London (0171) 208 8888
Partner and Head of Insolvency Unit.
Specialisation: Specialises in corporate and insolvency matters, acting for corporates, institutions, insolvency practitioners and banks. Work includes mergers and acquisitions, joint ventures and public issues, as well as all aspects of insolvency. Author of "Practical Insolvency Precedents" *Sweet and Maxwell* and

consulting editor to Butterworths Encyclopedia of Forms and Precedents.
Career: Qualified 1985. Previously at *Herbert Oppenheimer, Nathan & Vandyk, Richards Butler* and *S J Berwin & Co*, (partner there from 1990). Joined *Olswang* as a partner in 1995.
Personal: Born April 1959. Educated at Trinity Hall, Cambridge. Interests include tennis, theatre (musicals) and playing the guitar.

LEWIS, Anthony
Cameron McKenna, London
(0171) 367 3000
Specialisation: Partner in the Corporate department with 25+ years experience in all aspects of corporate finance work. Has particular experience in buy-outs and other venture capital transactions, company acquisitions and disposals and flotations. Has recently gained experience of corporate transactions concerning Lloyds.
Career: Joined *Cameron Markby Hewitt* in 1969, qualified as a solicitor in 1972 and was made a Partner in 1973.

LEWIS, David T.R.
Norton Rose, London (0171) 283 6000
Partner in Corporate Finance Department; Senior Partner.
Specialisation: Main area of practice is corporate finance, including take-overs (public and private), flotations, stock exchange work of all types, MBOs, schemes of arrangement, international global offerings, all types of commercial agreements, and debt restructurings. Has handled over 100 listings and numerous take-overs including HSBC Holdings/ Midland, GEC Siemens/ Plessey, Imperial Group/ Hanson/ UB, BA/ B-Cal, BMW/ Rover, Redland/ Steetley, Ladbroke/ Hilton, Dixons/ Currys, Guinness/Grandmet, Ciba/Allied Colloids, BMW/Rolls Royce. Author of articles in Gazette and PLC; also the Norton Rose Guide to Take-overs. Has chaired and spoken at numerous conferences. Member of the Law Society of London Company Law Committee 1982-97.

MACAULAY, Anthony D.
Herbert Smith, London (0171) 374 8000
Partner in Corporate Finance Department.
Specialisation: Experienced in company and commercial matters, especially corporate finance work, including takeovers and flotations. Has particular expertise in relation to the Takeover Code (having spent two years as Secretary of the Takeover Panel) and insider dealing.
Career: Qualified in 1974. Became a Partner at *Herbert Smith* in 1983.
Personal: Educated Keble College, Oxford.

MACE, Dan
Lovell White Durrant, London
(0171) 236 0066
Specialisation: Corporate finance transactions including takeovers and securities issues; company and securities law advice (including corporate governance issues); merger and acquisitions; collective investment schemes. Advised bidders, targets and financial advisers in agreed, contested and competitive situations. Sometime contributor to Acquisitions Monthly, In-House Lawyer and PLC. Speaker on In-House lawyers and corporate governance (June 1996 EuroForum In-House Lawyers Conference); speaker on takeovers and mergers (April 1997 IBC Conference).
Prof. Memberships: Law Society Company

Law Committee (leader of Working Party on 13th Directive on company law (takeovers)); City of London Law Society Company Law Sub-Committee (Chairman 1993-1998); Justice; member of Primary Markets Committee of the London Stock Exchange.
Career: 1968-1970 Articles with *Lovell White & King* (now *Lovell White Durrant*); Partner from 1976-date.

MACFARLANE, David J.
Ashurst Morris Crisp, London
(0171) 638 1111
Specialisation: General Corporate. Corporate Finance.
Career: Head of Corporate Finance.

MACFARLANE, Jonathan
Macfarlanes, London (0171) 831 9222
Partner in Company, Commercial & Banking Department.
Specialisation: Corporate finance and mergers and acquisitions. Work includes company and business acquisitions and disposals, flotations and secondary equity issues for company/ sponsor public take-overs. Also deals with environmental law matters. Acted for Community Hospitals Group plc on disposal of Nursing Homes Division and aquisitions of further private hospitals.
Prof. Memberships: Law Society, City of London Solicitors Company.
Career: Qualified in 1980 while with *Macfarlanes*. Became a Partner in 1985.

MAHER, Paul J.
Rowe & Maw, London (0171) 248 4282
Specialisation: Corporate finance including specifically M & A, Joint Ventures, MBOs and MBIs. Main focus in recent years has been transactional work in both the telecoms and chemicals sectors.
Prof. Memberships: Law Society.
Career: Articled to *Boodle Hatfield* 1982-1984, Solicitor ICI group legal department,1984-1990. *Rowe & Maw* 1990 to date.
Personal: Born 30th July 1959. London Law Degree, LLB Bristol. Interested mainly in books, politics and travel. Other leisure pursuits include running, football and squash. Lives in Wandsworth Common.

MARTIN, Charles D.Z.
Macfarlanes, London (0171) 831 9222
Specialisation: MBOs/Venture capital. M&A (especially cross-border) and Corporate finance/securities.
Career: Bristol University 1982. Qualified 1985. Partner 1990. Worked in the US 1988-9.
Personal: Married with three children. Lives in London.

MCFADDEN, Laurie
Freshfields, London (0171) 936 4000
Specialisation: Main area of practice is corporate and corporate finance. Advises corporate and merchant banking clients on corporate, stock exchange and take-over related issues, including securities issues, joint ventures and private acquisitions and disposals.
Prof. Memberships: Law Society.
Career: Qualifed first in Canada. Joined Freshfields in 1987, becoming a partner in 1991.
Personal: Born 10 July 1957. Educated University of Alberta, Canada (LL.B.) and Magdalene College, Cambridge (LL.M.). Leisure interests include tennis and skiing.

MORGAN, Simon
Olswang, London (0171) 208 8888
Partner, Corporate.
Specialisation: Corporate Finance. Advises businesses and professional advisers on business start-ups, joint ventures, equity issues, acquisitions, disposals and take-overs. Recent transactions have included representing the shareholders of SBC Cable Comms on its merger with Telewest, acting for Cox Communications on its acquisition of an interest in Flextech, acting on the bid for Central Motor Auctions and advising Two Way TV, an interactive television operator, in connection with a number of equity issues.
Career: Qualified in 1987. Joined *Frere Cholmeley Bischoff* in 1985, becoming a Partner in 1994. Joined *Olswang* in August 1998.
Personal: Born 25th June 1963. Attended Oakwood Comprehensive School 1974-79, Thomas Rotherham College 1979-81 and Pembroke College, Cambridge 1981-84.

MORLEY, David H.
Allen & Overy, London (0171) 330 3000
See under Banking, p. 137

MOUNTFORD, Margaret
Herbert Smith, London (0171) 374 8000
Partner in Company Department.
Specialisation: Principal area of practice is corporate, corporate finance and commercial matters. Advises corporate clients and intermediaries (investment banks, brokers, etc) on a wide range of transactions including mergers, flotations, takeovers, private company and assets acquisitions/ disposals, joint ventures and venture capital.
Prof. Memberships: Law Society, British German Jurists Association.
Career: Qualified in 1976. Became a partner at *Herbert Smith* in 1983.
Personal: Born 24th November 1951. Educated at Strathearn School, Belfast 1963-70 and Girton College, Cambridge 1970-73 (MA). Leisure interests include opera and travel. Lives in London.

MURPHY, Frances
Slaughter and May, London
(0171) 600 1200
Specialisation: General practice consists principally of acting for corporate clients on corporate finance and M&A transactions, both in England and overseas, and generally on corporate matters. Wide experience of acquisitions and disposals (both public and private), joint ventures and of equity and debt financing structures. Also has a significant practice in relation to demutualisation of building societies.
Prof. Memberships: The Law Society.
Career: Qualified in 1983 after articles with *Slaughter and May*. Became a Partner in 1990, after a year in the Hong Kong office.
Personal: Born 24 September 1957.

MURRAY-JONES, Allan
Lovell White Durrant, London
(0171) 236 0066
Specialisation: Corporate finance law including cross border mergers and acquisitions, and private equity generally.
Prof. Memberships: The Law Society.
Career: Qualified in Australia and moved to England in 1980. Partner 1986.

NEWHOUSE, Anthony
Slaughter and May, London
(0171) 600 1200

NORMAN, Guy T.D.
Clifford Chance, London (0171) 600 1000
Specialisation: Principal area of practice is
corporate and corporate finance. Advises
corporate and investment banking clients on
takeovers and mergers, capital raising, stock
exchange issues, joint ventures, private
acquisitions and disposals. Has particular
expertise in relation to the Takeover Code and
related matters.
Prof. Memberships: Law Society.
Career: Articled with *Clifford Chance* 1989-91,
qualified in September 1991 and became a
Partner in 1998. *Schroders* corporate finance
(on secondment) 1994. Secretary of Takeover
Panel (on secondment) 1997-99.
Personal: Born 1966. Educated Sevenoaks
School and Downing College Cambridge.
Interests include cars, tennis and golf. Lives in
London.

O'BRIEN, Barry
Freshfields, London (0171) 936 4000
Partner in Corporate Department: head of
Corporate Finance Group.
Specialisation: Corporate finance including
mergers and acquisitions, new issues: advising
Lloyd's on its reconstruction.
Prof. Memberships: Law Society.
Career: Qualified in 1978. Joined *Freshfields* in
1983 and became a Partner in 1986.
Personal: Born 27th October 1952. Educated
at University College, London. Enjoys sport.
Lives in London.

PALMER, James E.
Herbert Smith, London (0171) 374 8000
Specialisation: Principal areas of work are
mergers and acquisitions, corporate finance
and general corporate, including takeovers, UK
and international equity offerings, demergers,
schemes of arrangement and joint ventures.
Also formation/restructuring of international
banking and financial services businesses.
Prof. Memberships: City of London Solicitors
Company, Company Law Sub-Committee.
Career: Joined 1986, qualified 1988, Partner
1994.
Personal: Born 10.9.1963. Educated at
Winchester College and Queens' College
Cambridge 1982-85.

PARSONS, Chris
Herbert Smith, London (0171) 374 8000
Specialisation: Extensive corporate finance
experience acting for leading investment banks
and major corporate clients. One of the key
relationship partners for CSFB. Practice
includes cross border M&A and international
equities work. Also head of *Herbert Smith*'s
Italian Practice Group; new clients last year
included Olivetti and Pirelli.

PAUL, Alan D.
Allen & Overy, London (0171) 330 3000
Partner in the Corporate Department.
Specialisation: Principal area of work is
corporate finance, particularly corporate
acquisitions with a specialisation in public
takeovers and management buy-outs. Other

main area of work is equity-linked financings,
including flotations. Author of 'Corporate
Governance in the Context of Takeovers of UK
Public Companies' in 'Contemporary Issues in
Corporate Governance' (1993) and has written
numerous articles for various legal journals.
Prof. Memberships: Law Society.
Career: Articled with *Allen & Overy* 1978-80,
qualified in March 1980 and became a Partner
in 1985. Secretary of Takeover Panel (on
secondment) 1985-88.
Personal: Born 19th July 1954. Attended St.
Paul's School 1966-72, then University College,
Oxford 1973-77. Lives in London.

PENSON, John
Lovell White Durrant, London
(0171) 236 0066
See under Banking, p. 138

PESCOD, Michael
Slaughter and May, London
(0171) 600 1200
Partner 1977.
Specialisation: Corporate Department. Main
areas of practice are corporate finance,
commercial and corporate law.

POLGLASE, Timothy
Norton Rose, London (0171) 283 6000
Specialisation: Advises on management buy-
outs, buy-ins and other leveraged acquisitions;
export and project finance-related transactions;
bond and other capital markets issues and on
derivative products; regulatory issues (with
particular emphasis on banking regulation).
Career: Articled *Norton Rose*; qualified 1986;
seconded to *Milbank, Tweed, Hadley & McCloy*
(New York) 1988-1989; seconded to Banking
Supervision Division, Bank of England 1990-
1991; partner *Norton Rose* 1994.
Personal: Born 1962. Educated at St. John's
College, Oxford.

RAWLINSON, Mark S.
Freshfields, London (0171) 936 4000
Specialisation: Partner in the Corporate
Department specialising in cross border and
domestic mergers, acquisitions, disposals and
joint ventures. Work also covers corporate
finance and IPOs including flotations, rights
issues and other issues. Publications include 'A
Practitioners Guide to Corporate Finance and
the Financial Services Act 1986' (contributor)
and 'Rights Issues Practice Manual' (contributor
and editor).
Career: Qualified 1984. Assistant solicitor,
Freshfields 1984-90. Partner since 1990.
Personal: Educated at Haberdashers' Aske's
School, Elstree and Sidney Sussex College,
Cambridge 1976-80. Interests include family
and sport. Born 3rd May 1957. Lives in London.

READ, Nigel
Lovell White Durrant, London
(0171) 236 0066
Specialisation: Mergers & acquisitions,
corporate finance, securities and general
corporate law. Particular expertise in public
takeovers, both recommended and hostile, and
Stock Exchange flotations and secondary
issues. Advises corporate clients across a wide
range of industry sectors, particularly media,
leisure and property. Also acts for a number of

invesment banks in their capacity as sponsors,
financial advisers and underwriters.
Prof. Memberships: Law Society, City of
London Solicitors Company.
Career: Qualified at *Freshfields* in 1984.
Investment banker at Lazard Brothers & Co., Ltd
1990-93. Joined *Lovell White Durrant* in 1993
and became a partner in 1996.
Personal: Educated at Marlborough College
and St Catharines College, Cambridge. Leisure
interests include golf, tennis, skiing and watersports.

RICHARDS, Philip
Freshfields, London (0171) 936 4000
See under Insurance & Reinsurance: Non-
contentious Insurance, p. 469

ROSEFIELD, Stephen M.
Paisner & Co, London (0171) 353 0299
Partner in Company Commercial Department.
Specialisation: Main area of practice is
mergers and acquisitions and corporate finance
including takeovers (both public and private),
purchase and sale of businesses, MBOs, joint
ventures and reconstructions. Acts for a wide
range of listed property, trading and investment
companies. Writes and speaks widely on the
purchase and sale of companies and
businesses, and joint ventures including having
contributed to Butterworths Encyclopaedia of
Forms & Precedents Vol. 11.
Prof. Memberships: Law Society.
Career: Qualified in 1977, having joined *Paisner
& Co* in 1975. Became a Partner in 1980.
Personal: Born 19th December 1952. Educated
at St. Paul's School 1965-70 and St. Edmund
Hall, Oxford 1971-74. Recreations include theatre,
music, tennis and soccer. Lives in London

SACKMAN, Simon
Norton Rose, London (0171) 283 6000
Partner and Head of Corporate Finance.
Specialisation: Main area of practice is mergers
and acquisitions (both public and private),
flotations and other equity issues, demergers and
other restructurings and investment trusts. Also
experienced in regulatory investigations and the
hotel sector. Important transactions handled
include the sale of Hambros Bank to Société
Générale and the subsequent restructuring of
Hambros plc, the restructuring of GPA Group, the
flotation of Harvey Nichols, the enquiry into
Lanica's bid for CWS and numerous hotel
acquisitions, including the Caledonian in
Edinburgh and the Landmark of London. Clients
include merchant banks (Samuel Montagu,
Hambros, Morgan Grenfell and Charterhouse),
hotel groups and investment trusts.
Prof. Memberships: Law Society, City of
London Solicitors Company, International Bar
Association.

SALZ, Anthony M.V.
Freshfields, London (0171) 936 4000
Senior Partner and Partner in Corporate
Department.
Specialisation: Main area of practice is
mergers and acquisitions and all aspects of
corporate finance work, both in the UK and
internationally.
Prof. Memberships: Law Society.
Career: Qualified 1974. Joined *Freshfields* in
1975. 1977/8 *Davis Polk & Wardwell*, New York.
Partner in Corporate Department 1980. Senior
Partner 1996.
Personal: Born 30th June 1950. Attended
Summerfields 1958-63, Radley College 1964-67.

Exeter University 1968-71. Leisure pursuits include golf, family and fishing and supporting Southampton FC.

SIGNY, Adam

Clifford Chance, London (0171) 600 1000
Specialisation: Corporate partner specialising in corporate finance; mergers and acquisitions; private equity.
Career: Qualified 1982; Partner *Clifford Chance* 1987.
Personal: Born 1955; married with three children; lives in London and Suffolk.

SINGH, Daljit

Hammond Suddards, London
(0171) 655 1000
Fax: (0171) 655 1001 E-Mail:
daljit.singh@hammondsuddards.co.uk
Specialisation: All aspects of corporate finance including Blue & Yellow Book, M & A (UK and cross border); private equity transactions (whether for the equity house, management or other funders) and securities work.
Prof. Memberships: Law Society, IOD
Career: London University, Law College (Chancery Lane), *Baker McKenzie*, *Alsop Wilkinson*, *Hammond Suddards*.
Personal: Football (especially Chelsea football club), entertaining, music, Business and the family (married, 2 girls and 1 boy).

SOUNDY, Mark

Travers Smith Braithwaite, London
(0171) 248 9133
Specialisation: Private equity, particularly buy-outs/buy-ins and realisations. Also experienced in corporate finance and general corporate work. Major clients include institutional investors and a number of private and smaller quoted companies. Significant recent deals: Heal's float, BIMBO of Motorcycle City, £27m MBO of Webb Fasteners, £30m MBO of Jigsaw Day Nurseries and £800m MBO of HMV Media Group.
Prof. Memberships: Law Society, American Bar Association, Society of Advanced Legal Studies.
Career: Education: Radley College, Oxford; Trinity College, Cambridge (MA1990). Admitted to New York State Bar (1992). *Travers Smith Braithwaite*: articles (1987-1989), assistant solicitor (1989-1997), partner (1997-to date).

SPENDLOVE, Justin

Ashurst Morris Crisp, London
(0171) 638 1111
Banking Department.
Specialisation: Partner in the banking department specialising in structured acquisition finance involving secured and unsecured financings.
Career: Articled at *Wilde Sapte* where he became a partner in 1989. Joined *Ashurst Morris Crisp* as a partner in 1996.

STEINFELD, Michael

Titmuss Sainer Dechert, London
(0171) 583 5353
Partner in Corporate Finance Group, Business Law Department.
Specialisation: Corporate finance, mergers and acquisitions, and general company and commercial work, involving mainly Stock Exchange listed and overseas companies.
Career: Qualified in 1970, having joined *Titmuss Sainer & Webb* (now *Titmuss Sainer Dechert*) in 1968. Became a Partner in 1972.

Personal: Born in 1943. Educated at Pembroke College, Oxford. Interests include skiing, football, good food and France. Lives in London.

STELLA, Keith G.

Paisner & Co, London (0171) 353 0299
Partner and head of Corporate Finance.
Specialisation: Practice covers the full range of corporate finance activities, including flotations, secondary offerings, bids and takeovers (both public and private). Acts for wide range of listed and private companies, as well as for banks, brokers and other intermediaries. Also undertakes work for a range of leasing clients in asset finance and related activities.
Career: Qualified 1978. Partner from 1980. Educated at City of London School and University College, London (LL.B 1st Class Hons). First Class Hons in Law Society Finals.
Personal: Born 1954. Living in Hertfordshire. Interests include classical music, antiques and wine.

STERN, Robert C.

Slaughter and May, London
(0171) 600 1200
Specialisation: General practice consists principally of acting for corporate and investment bank clients on corporate finance and M&A transactions, both in England and overseas and generally on corporate matters. Wide experience of acquisitions and disposals (both public and private), joint ventures and of equity and debt financing structures.
Career: BA in French and German at The Queen's College, Oxford. Qualified as a solicitor in 1986. Became a Partner in 1993.

STEWART, Mark

Clifford Chance, London (0171) 600 1000
See under Banking, p. 138

STORAR, Michael J.

Lawrence Graham, London (0171) 379 0000
Partner in Company/Commercial Department.
Specialisation: Main area of practice is corporate finance, covering mergers and acquisitions, flotations, listings and venture capital. Also handles advertising and marketing. Advised the Government and the Director General of the National Lottery on its structure and start up.
Career: Qualified in 1981. Worked at *Ashurst Morris Crisp* 1978-83. Joined *Blyth Dutton* in 1983, which merged to become *Lawrence Graham*.
Personal: Born 25th October 1955. Attended Cranleigh School 1963-73, Camberwell 1973-4 and Birmingham 1974-7. Lives in Suffolk.

SULLIVAN, Michael

Linklaters, London (0171) 456 3166
Partner, Corporate Department.
Specialisation: Specialist in corporate law including mergers and acquisitions, initial and secondary public offerings, corporate reorganisations and demergers and privatisations.
Career: Qualified 1988. Became a Partner 1994.
Personal: Attended King's College, University of London, LL B (Hons).

SUTTON, Robert H.

Macfarlanes, London (0171) 831 9222
Partner in Company, Commercial and Banking Department.
Specialisation: Work covers mergers and

acquisitions, corporate finance, securities law, take-overs (private and public, friendly and hostile), flotations and corporate reconstructions, representing corporate and investment banking clients. Led team involved in acting for controlling shareholder in Forte Plc in connection with bid by Granada, and represented BET in defence of bid from Rentokil. Acts for worldwide advertising groups Omnicom and Cordiant; represented Deutsche Morgan Grenfell in Gulf Canada bid for Clyde Petroleum and works closely with several investment banks.
Prof. Memberships: Law Society.
Career: Qualified in 1979 while with *Macfarlanes*. Became a Partner in 1983. Spent a year on secondment to *White & Case*, New York 1980-81.

SWEET, Jon

Marriott Harrison, London (0171) 209 2000
Partner in Corporate Department.
Specialisation: Main area of practice is corporate and commercial, principally venture capital, mergers and acquisitions and general corporate finance. Handles a mix of private and public company work, but primarily private company. Has a broad range of experience in company/ business sales and purchases, complex company and group restructurings, financings (debt and equity) and joint ventures as well as more general commercial advice such as agency and distribution. Past experience has included the full range of stock exchange and take over code work. Also handles banking and insolvency.
Prof. Memberships: Law Society, Associate Member of BVCA.
Career: Qualified in 1982. Worked at *Slaughter and May* 1980-90 (including 1986-88 in the Hong Kong office). Partner at *Iliffes* 1990-93, and at *Marriott Harrison* since 1993.
Personal: Born 7th March 1956. Attended Trinity College Glenalmond 1969-74, Brunel University 1975-79 and Guildford Law College 1979-80. Leisure interests include target rifle shooting, motor sport and classic cars. Lives in Hertfordshire.

SYSON, Nicholas

Wilde Sapte, London (0171) 246 7000
Specialisation: Partner specialising in acquisition finance and reconstructions. He acts for banks providing funding in relation to management buy-outs, management buy-ins, corporate acquisitions (both domestic and cross border) and public company bids. He also acts for the Co-ordinating bank in cross border 'London Approach' workouts and for the administrative receivers on any subsequent insolvency.
Career: Articled *Flint Bishop & Barnett* (Derby) 1985-1987; joined *Wilde Sapte* 1990; Partner 1994. Appointed to management board 1997.

TUFFNELL, Kevin

Macfarlanes, London (0171) 831 9222
Partner in Corporate Commercial & Banking Department.
Specialisation: Venture capital, corporate finance, mergers and acquisitions and flotations. Handled the Allders and Lombard flotations and many substantial buy outs and financial purchases. Author of articles, e.g. in 'Company Law' in 1993.
Career: Qualified in 1984 while with *Macfarlanes*. Became a Partner in 1989.

TURNBULL, Peter

Macfarlanes, London (0171) 831 9222
Partner and Head of Company, Commercial
and Banking Department.
Specialisation: Principal area of practice is
institutional equity financings encompassing
venture and development capital, MBOs/ MBIs
and MEBOs. Also handles general corporate
work such as sales, acquisitions and 'ordinary
course' commercial matters.
Prof. Memberships: Law Society.
Career: Qualified in 1968 while with
Macfarlanes. Became a Partner in 1974. Head of
Company, Commercial and Banking
Department since 1986.

UNDERHILL, C.William Y.

Slaughter and May, London
(0171) 600 1200
Specialisation: Specialises in corporate
finance, including acting for underwriters and
issuers of securities, M&A, London Stock
Exchange rules and regulations and FSA
compliance. Also experienced in mortgage and
other asset securitisation, and other mortgage-
backed financing. Editor of Weinberg and Blank
on Takeovers and Mergers.
Career: Qualified 1983 with *Slaughter and May*.
Partner 1990.

VICKERS, Mark H.

Dibb Lupton Alsop, London (0345) 262728
Head of Banking Group.
Specialisation: Corporate banking and
international finance: specialising in UK and
cross-border acquisition finance and leveraged
acquisitions, particularly management buy-
outs/buy-ins and institutional purchases;
structured finance; global syndicated lending.
Expert retained by the leading senior mezzanine
lenders and strategic adviser to the banks on
trends in the senior debt market.
Career: Head of Banking at *Alsop Wilkinson*
from 1990; National Head of Banking at *Dibb
Lupton Alsop* following the firm's merger in 1996.
Personal: Helicopter pilot.

WALKER-ARNOTT, Edward I.

Herbert Smith, London (0171) 374 8000
Senior Partner.
Specialisation: Has extensive experience as a
company lawyer and as a commercial lawyer
involved in insolvency, banking, insurance,
securities, employment, tax, venture capital,
management buy-outs, intellectual property
rights, media and broadcasting, accountancy,
sport, monopolies, competition, EC law and
takeovers and mergers. Led the firm's
privatisation teams for Britoil, British Gas and
British Coal and participated in the team on
electricity. Sat on the Cork Enquiry into
insolvency law between 1977 and 1982, the
report of which resulted in the enactment of the
Insolvency Act 1986. Was one of the first
nominated members of the Council of Lloyd's
(sitting on the Council from 1983 to 1989) and
chaired the Investigations Committee at Lloyd's
in the late 1970s and early 1980s.
Career: Qualified in 1963 and became a
Partner at *Herbert Smith* in 1968.
Personal: Educated at London University (LL.M).

WARD, Anthony

Ashurst Morris Crisp, London
(0171) 638 1111
Specialisation: Specialist in structured finance
including acquisition finance, restructurings,
property finance and trade finance.
Career: BA in Russian Language and Literature,
London University. Articles – *Barlow Lyde and
Gilbert*. 1996 – Partner at *Ashurst Morris Crisp*.

WARD, Nigel T.

Ashurst Morris Crisp, London
(0171) 638 1111
Specialisation: General banking law including
acquisition finance, structured finance, property
finance and restructuring.
Prof. Memberships: Member of Banking Law
Sub-committee of the City of London Law Society.
Career: Educated St. Catherine's College,
Oxford. Qualified in 1985. Partner in 1992.
Personal: Born 1961. Married with three
children. Plays golf and tennis.

WATSON, Sean M.

Cameron McKenna, London
(0171) 367 3000
Partner in Corporate Department.
Specialisation: Advises corporate, merchant
banking and venture capital clients on all areas
of corporate finance including reconstructions,
take-overs, mergers and acquisitions, flotations
and venture capital transactions, with primary
specialisation in stock exchange transactions.
Prof. Memberships: Law Society, City of
London Solicitors Company.
Career: Qualified in 1972. Joined *McKenna &
Co* in 1979, becoming a Partner in the same year.
Personal: Born 5th April 1948. Attended The
Leys School, Cambridge, 1961-66 and
Manchester University 1966-69. Leisure
interests include tennis, golf, skiing, gardening
and family. Lives in Weybridge, Surrey.

WAYTE, Peter B.

Dibb Lupton Alsop, London (0345) 262728
Corporate Finance, Equity:
Specialisation: Mergers & Acquisitions,
Corporate Finance, MBOs/ MBI's. Acted for
management on two Swedish buyouts funded
by Morgan Grenfell Development Capital and
Charterhouse Development Capital, for
Charterhouse Development Capital and
management on the disposal of Metric Group
and NatWest Ventures and management on the
disposal of ACT, and for Kleinwort Benson
Development Capital in several investments
including Tractiv Holdings.
Corporate Finance, 125-250 Fee Earners:
Specialisation: Mergers & Acquisitions,
Corporate Finance, MBOs/MBIs. Acted for
Sutcliffe Speakman Plc on the disposal of its
Carbons Division, for Keller Group Plc on its
acquisition of Franki Asia, for Bellwinch Plc in
connection with the recommended bid for that
company and for the shareholders of Melrose
Group Ltd on their demerger from Melrose Plc
and subsequent acquisition of various limited
partnerships.
Prof. Memberships: Law Society.
Career: LL.B Sheffield. Articled *Wilkinson
Kimbers & Staddon*; Partner *Dibb Lupton Alsop*
(and Predecessor firms) 1976 to date.
Personal: Married; three children. Outside
interests: squash, skiing, walking and gardening.

WEBSTER, Martin

Biddle, London (0171) 606 9301
Partner in Company Commercial Department.
Specialisation: Main areas of practice are
corporate finance and commercial advice to
company clients. In recent years, has
particularly specialised in MBOs/MBIs etc.
Acted in the establishment of Parliamentary
Broadcasting Unit Ltd, the vehicle for the
dissemination of Parliamentary broadcasting,
which is owned by the major broadcasters but
ultimately controlled by Parliament. Is secretary
of that company.
Prof. Memberships: Institute of Taxation, Law
Society, City of London Law Society
Commercial Law Sub-committee.
Career: Qualified in 1983. ATII 1986. Joined
Biddle in 1981, becoming a Partner in 1987.
Personal: Born 1st July 1958. Attended Christ's
College, Cambridge, 1976-79. Leisure interests
include music, theatre and golf. Lives in London
SE11.

WHALE, Philip

Norton Rose, London (0171) 283 6000
Specialisation: Advises on: a broad range of
structured finance transactions including, in
particular, on the financing of leveraged
acquisitions (MBOs, MBIs, institutional buy-
outs, public takeovers, increasingly involving
complex cross-border transactions and
innovative debt structures), infrastructure
projects and the travel industry; syndicated and
bilateral credit facilities and restructurings.
Prof. Memberships: Member of the Law
Society Banking Law Sub-Committee.
Career: Qualified in New Zealand; worked in
commercial law in Auckland for five years;
joined *Norton Rose* in 1986; partner in *Norton
Rose* in 1992.

WILLIAMS, Christine J.

Fox Williams, London (0171) 628 2000
Partner in Corporate Department.
Specialisation: Principal area of practice is
corporate finance. Work includes mergers and
acquisitions, capital raising, joint ventures,
restructurings and partnership law. Has acted
on many purchases and sales of companies,
both quoted and unquoted, including
management buy-outs and buy-ins. Member of
Company Law Sub-Committee of City of
London Law Society.
Prof. Memberships: Law Society, City of
London Law Society, International Bar
Association, Association of Partnership
Practitioners.
Career: Qualified in 1977. Partner at
Oppenheimers 1981-88. Formed and joined *Fox
Williams* as a Partner in 1989.
Personal: Born 15th February 1953. Educated
at St Anne's College, Oxford 1971-74. Leisure
interests include theatre and cinema. Lives in
Buckinghamshire.

WINTER, Martin A.S.

Biddle, London (0171) 606 9301
Senior Partner. Head of Company Commercial
Department.
Specialisation: Main areas of practice are
venture capital, joint ventures, acquisitions and
disposals.
Prof. Memberships: British Venture Capital
Association (by firm).
Career: Qualified in 1978. Assistant Solicitor at
Norton Rose, 1979-84. Joined *Biddle* in 1984.
Partner in 1985.

Personal: Born 13th April 1954. Graduated in English from St Edmund Hall, Oxford, 1975. Nationally ranked waterskier, twice a Conservative Parliamentary Candidate.

WOOTTON, David
Allen & Overy, London (0171) 330 3000
Specialisation: Corporate finance specialist, in particular mergers & acquisitions, flotations,

public and private takeovers, joint ventures, corporate restructurings. Led the team advising the sponsors and underwriters on the flotations in 1997 of Billiton Plc and advising MISYS Plc on its acquisition of Medic Computer Systems Inc, funded by an innovative rights issue, both transactions being amongst the largest of their type in recent years. He also led the team acting for the issuer and the selling shareholder on the

flotation in 1998 of Thomson Travel Group Plc.
Career: BA Cambridge University 1972. MA Cambridge University. Admitted as solicitor 1975. Associate *Allen & Overy* 1975-79; Partner *Allen & Overy* since 1976.

SOUTH EAST

LEADING FIRMS · SOUTH EAST

BLAKE LAPTHORN Fareham
CLARKS Reading
COLE & COLE Oxford, Reading

BOND PEARCE Southampton
DONNE MILEHAM & HADDOCK Brighton, Crawley

CRIPPS HARRIES HALL Tunbridge Wells
GARRETTS Reading
MANCHES & CO Oxford
MUNDAYS Esher
PARIS SMITH & RANDALL Southampton
PITMANS Reading
RAWLISON & BUTLER Crawley
THOMSON SNELL & PASSMORE Tunbridge Wells

HIGHLY REGARDED FIRMS

Burstows Crawley
B.P. Collins & Co Gerrards Cross
Kimbell & Co Milton Keynes
Nabarro Nathanson Reading
Osborne Clarke Reading
Stevens & Bolton Guildford
Thomas Eggar Church Adams Chichester

Brachers Maidstone
Shadbolt & Co Reigate

Blake Lapthorn (8 f/t, 2 p/t ptnrs, 11 f/t and 2 p/t assts) Highly rated south coast practice with strength and depth. "Have good plc pedigree. Regarded as premier blue chip firm." "Was impressed by professionalism." *Caroline Williams* has an "excellent reputation…," but is seen less often on deals – due to her management responsibilities. **Clients/Work:** Acting for Kerry Group PLC in relation to the acquisition by Kerry Foods of the Milling and Ingredients business of Dalgety PLC for £330m. Sale of Walker Hammill Ltd to Marlborough International PLC for £17.6m. Acting for management in MBO of Webbs Country Foods Ltd for £60m.

Clarks (4 ptnrs/5 assts: 1 p/t) Thames Valley firm with a big reputation. "Firm with greatest commitment to area, well dug in, well respected, professional." Have had a good year and a high profile. *Richard Lee* drew widespread praise for being a "good

bloke" who was also "thorough and professional." "Excellent!" **Clients/Work:** Acted for Newco and management in the £40m acquisition of Nicol Beauty Products Ltd. Handled sale (for vendors) of Action International Marketing Services to Quintiles Transnational Corporation Inc. for £22m settled in quoted shares. Flotation of Optoplast Plc on the AIM.

Cole & Cole (4 ptnrs: 1p/t; 4assts) Another leading and "professional" Thames Valley firm with a well-established office in Oxford and a commitment to their Reading office. Active and well liked. "Can't speak highly enough of them. Would go to before anybody else… " Leading individuals at the firm are the "just excellent" and "responsive" *Joe Pillman* and *Jonathan Loake* who has joined from the now defunct Dallas Brett. **Clients/Work:** Acted for Xerox on acquisition of City Paper. Raising $21m for Bookham Technology by private placement. Flotation of Screen on AIM.

Bond Pearce inc. Hepherd Winstanley & Pugh (6ptnrs: 3f/t; 10assts) Recently merged practice with Bond Pearce entering Southampton. A new entry to our tables, they both have "strong practices, put together they will be premier." "Good reputation, kick off well." "Strong on corporate finance… will be number one firm in Southampton." *Moray Macpherson* and *Simon Hewes* enter as leading individuals."Both have high profiles and get around… good technically." **Clients/Work:** Acting for the shareholders of Rapid Deployment Ltd in the disposal of their shares for £15m. Acting for the management of Warings Construction Group in their MBO. Various transactions for Chemring Group Plc.

Donne Mileham & Haddock (4ptnrs/3assts) "Good strong provincial firm" which does not appear to have been significantly affected by Andrew Trotters departure a year on. Leading individual *Derek Sparrow* is a "pretty able bloke" and is "rated highly." **Clients/Work:** Acted for shareholders on the sale of The Woodgate Farms Dairy Ltd. £15m acquisition for Cory Waste Management Ltd of waste disposal company. Acted for vendors on sale of motor dealership for £6.5m.

Cripps Harries Hall (5ptnrs/5assts) Have a stronger reputation for corporate finance and company work amongst accountants and clients than fellow practitioners.

They "do a good job," and are "switched on." **Clients/Work:** Acted for North Downs Dairy Co Ltd on sale of shares to Adam Foods Ltd. Acted for FM Contract Services on sale of all issued share capital to Kier Group plc for £4.5m.

Garretts (2ptnrs/9assts). A firm on the up but seen as reliant on the Andersen connection which has both positive and negative aspects. Some thought that the recent flow of "big deals" would continue because of the AA link whilst accountants commented that they would not choose to instruct them. Whatever, they are "making big efforts locally and doing bloody well." Thought to be "highly professional" with "some good ex-City support lawyers." **Clients/Work:** Advised AdProTech on spin out and venture capital financing of a biotech unit from SmithKline Beecham. Acting for management team on MBO of Peacock's Stores for £78m. Acting for Hypertec on its MBO for £7.6m from Hypetec's Australian parent.

Manches & Co (4ptnrs/3assts) Have a strong reputation with both accountants and practitioners who would refer work to them. A firm on the up. Are "well-liked" and have some good people including *Peter Angel* who is "one of the best guys around." "Technically good," he is "well known," and obviously "able." **Clients/Work:** Acted on behalf of the MBO team on the MBO of Hogg Robinson Transport (total consideration about £23m). Advised Navigators Group, Inc with its acquisition of Lloyd's managing agent, Mander, Thomas & Cooper (Underwriting Agencies) Ltd. Acted for the shareholders of M&J Seafoods on the sale of a proportion of their shareholding (£20m+).

Mundays (3ptnrs/1asst) Active firm with a growing reputation and market presence. "Well geared up… .recruited in and built up strong team. Leading firm in their area for this type of work." They appear to be getting the deals and are thought "underrated." *Peter Munday* enters the lists, "a good dealmaker;" "Commercial… does good job for clients… experienced." **Clients/Work:** Advised Granger Telecom (Holdings) Plc on its flotation on EASDAQ – shares sold at US$25m. Advising Octagon Developments Ltd on their joint venture with Xaloc (Property Developments) Ltd to create Octagon (Bryanston Square) Ltd. Advising UniChem

PLC on the acquisition of the Triocare group of companies for just under £6 m.

Paris Smith & Randall (3ptnrs/2assts) An expanding practice that goes up our tables following many favourable comments. Interviewees found them "pro-active, courteous, good lawyers." Despite the lack of a "brand name" people feel comfortable with them. They have been doing some "good work over the last 12 months" and were perceived to be "highly competent." *Andrew Heathcock* is "commercial and technical." **Clients/Work:** Acted for vendor shareholders in MBO of Webbs Country Foods Ltd. Sale of Citybus to FirstBus for an offer value of £7.2m. Acted for Hawker Pacific Aerospace Ltd with acquisition, for £13m, of the business carried on by British Airways Plc repairing and overhauling aircraft landing gear.

Pitmans (3ptnrs/7assts) A good firm who are "well known" and decent. *John Hutchinson* is good with clients. "Personable guy...good manner," and "effective." **Clients/Work:** Include: Porsche GB, De Beers and Q Drive Bus Group.

Rawlinson & Butler (2ptnrs/2assts) "Good... well respected by institutions" who rated their quality. *James Chatfield* was described as a "practical sort of bloke, a good lawyer... commercial." **Clients/Work:** Acted for Ringway Group Ltd in acquisition of the Highway Maintenance Division of Lincolnshire County Council. Acting for the Vendors in their disposal by way of BIMBO of Warth International Ltd. Acting for Sidcup Plant Hire plc and C L Faulks in the disposal of the plant hire business to Hewden Stewart plc.

Thomson Snell & Passmore (4ptnrs/1asst) "Quite strong." Team includes the well regarded *James Partridge* ("Does good job," "Good chap. Would use again no hesitation. Diligent and commercial"). **Clients/Work:** Acting for a company raising £5m new equity for a high technology business by a private placing. Acting for vendors in the food sector over sale of shares of a company for £6m. Acting for MBO/MBI team on acquisition of manufacturing company for £3.9m.

Burstows (2ptnrs/5assts doing a mix of company/commercial) Well respected small "sensible" firm who practitioners would be "happy to introduce a management team to." **Clients/Work:** Private company mergers, acquisitions and disposals and MBO's.

B. P. Collins & Co (4ptnrs/2assts doing a mix of corporate and commercial) "Well respected" with some "effective and experienced practitioners." Cover a range of work including M&A, joint ventures and MBOs. **Clients/Work:** Act for owner managed business clients and a number of plc's and multinationals.

Kimbell & Co (2ptnrs/3assts) Small but well regarded practice with good people. Known by interviewees and thought competent. "More or less mopped up good work in the Milton Keynes area. For smallish firm, do substantial deals." **Clients/Work:** Work has included MBO of an insolvent company and the reorganisation of European subsidiaries of a public company to integrate with the target group following an acquisition.

Nabarro Nathanson (2ptnrs/2assts) Do a mix of work and inspire mixed views. "Will leap into action... are sleeping giants capable of doing more." The IT practice has a much stronger profile in Reading whilst the corporate finance practice is perceived as "managed by London – one day a week." **Clients/Work:** Acted for Birchin International plc (formerly Rushmere Wynne Group) on 2 reverse takeovers , totalling approximately £10m. Acted for Silver Shield Group plc on its acquisition of Swansea City Football Club.

Osborne Clarke (1ptnr/5assts) Opened their office in Reading in January this year but off to a flying start. "Treat as serious player in market for future competition. Have put heavyweight partner in." They present a serious face in the Thames Valley and are expected to succeed in the long term. **Clients/Work:** 3i; Smith & Jones Communications.

Stevens & Bolton (4ptnrs: 1 p/t; 5 assts: 2 p/t) A Guildford practice with a "pretty solid" reputation for corporate work. Thought to be focused on commercial and corporate finance matters. **Clients/Work:** Acting for the selling shareholders on the £10m sale of Aston Electronic Designs Ltd to a venture capital backed MBI team. Acting for Energy Systems Ltd on £multi-m parallel transactions with several Regional Electricity Companies.

Thomas Eggar Church Adams (2ptnrs/1asst) Possibly the only "corporate finance firm in Chichester ... highly regarded." **Clients/Work:** Acted for Argo

Interactive Group plc on second round offering of shares via the internet. Acted for Hendy Lennox Group on acquisition of car dealership.

Brachers (2ptnrs/3assts) A new name to our tables. "Seen a niche and got someone in to do it. Moving away from sleepy firm to more go-getting." *Stuart Butler-Gallie* is up and coming. Only just partner, but interviewees had no hesitation in recommending him. He "seems to be making quite an impression and is one to watch." **Clients/Work:** Acted for The Weeks Group Plc on the acquisition of The Lawrence Hewitt Partnership Ltd. Acted for Charlton Athletic plc on placing of 4m new ordinary shares raising £2m. Acted for Environet Ltd on the sale of its computer network business to Bull Information Systems Ltd.

Shadbolt & Co (1ptnr/2assts) Practice led by ex-Donne Mileham partner *Andrew Trotter* ("thorough, hard working, dilligent and commercial"). Although the corporate practice is still small, there is interest in how the practice develops and it is thought as "one to watch." **Clients/Work:** MBO from a US quoted company of a cash drawer manufacturing company. Sale of the issued share capital of an international software company. Acting for Arcadian International PLC in a proposed joint venture.

SEE PROFILES AT END OF THIS SECTION

LEADERS' PROFILE · SOUTH EAST

ANGEL, Peter G.
Manches & Co, Oxford (01865) 722106
Email: peter.angel@manches.co.uk
Partner in the Company & Commercial Department.
Specialisation: General corporate finance and venture capital work, with particular interest in corporate and regulatory aspects of the Lloyd's insurance market. Regular speaker at seminars on corporate finance topics.
Career: Qualified 1970.
Personal: Born 27th July, 1946. Attended Maidstone Grammar School 1959-64 and then University College London. Board member of The College of Estate Management. Lives in Oxford.

BUTLER-GALLIE, Stuart
Brachers, Maidstone (01622) 690691
Specialisation: Concentrates on M&A work, debt and equity funding, listed company work, (acted on AIM flotation of Charlton Athletic plc March 1997 and 2 subsequent placings) joint ventures (UK and international), corporate reorganisations and reconstructions, MBOs/MBIs, all aspects of general company

law and full range of commercial advice.
Career: Articled: *Denton Hall* 1988-90.
Qualified: *Denton Hall* 1990. Worked in Banking
and Financial Services, moving to Corporate
Finance in 1991. Joined *Brachers* Jan 96,
Partner May 97.
Personal: Born 1.3.1964. St. Dunstan's College
Catford. Sheffield University (LLB). Law School
Chester. SSVC in Regular Army 1PWO (Prince
of Wales Own Regiment of Yorkshire). Married 3
children. Cross country running, military history.

CHATFIELD, James H.T.
Rawlison & Butler, Crawley (01293) 527744
Partner and Head of Corporate Department.
Specialisation: Over 20 years experience of
UK and international corporate and commercial
work. This has included cross-border work,
investment in the UK and Europe, joint ventures,
commercial agreements and financing. Has
advised UK and non-UK companies on mergers
and acquisitions and on setting up in Europe.
Has acted for Plcs making strategic acquisitions
in the UK, Europe and worldwide, and in
reorganisations of companies. Has carried out
speaking engagements for the CBI, DTI, Union
Internationale des Avocats and at the firm's
seminars.
Prof. Memberships: Law Society (Member of
Solicitors European Group), Union
Internationale des Avocats (Member of
Commission on the Future of the Lawyer).
Career: Worked for *Linklaters & Paines* 1974-
1984, with a year at Swiss Bank Corporation
International in London (1980-81). Qualified in
1977. Joined *Rawlison & Butler* as a Partner and
Head of Corporate Department in 1984.
Currently Chairman of the firm's Management
Committee.
Personal: Born in 1952. Educated at Ardingly
College, Sussex and Trinity College Oxford
(M.A. in History). Leisure interests include
cricket, theatre, literature, history and
gardening. Member of the MCC.

HEATHCOCK, Andrew E.
Paris Smith & Randall, Southampton
(01703) 482482

HEWES, Simon P.
Bond Pearce, Southampton (01703) 632211
Partner in the Corporate Group.
Specialisation: Specialises in Company and
Commercial, including Insolvency, Company
and Business Sales and Acquisitions,
Reorganisations, Management Buy-outs and
Venture Capital Transactions, Insolvency,
Banking and Lending Work and general
corporate work.
Prof. Memberships: Society of Practitioners of
Insolvency (Committee Member for Southern
Region).
Career: Qualified in 1987 with *Pinsent & Co.*,
Birmingham (now *Pinsent Curtis*). Joined
Hepherd Winstanley & Pugh in 1992, becoming
a Partner in 1994 and joining *Bond Pearce* in
1998 on merger.

HUTCHINSON, John C.
Pitmans, Reading (0118) 9580224
Specialisation: Company/Commercial
specialist whose main areas of work include
MBO/MBIs, acquisitions, disposals and joint
ventures.
Career: Qualified 1990. Partner 1994.
Personal: Born 7th December 1961. Lives in
Oxford. Interests include golf, football and opera.

LEE, Richard
Clarks, Reading (0118) 958 5321
Partner in Company Department.
Specialisation: Work covers company law,
corporate finance and venture capital, public
issues, company acquisitions, banking and
employee share schemes. Advises large
corporates, financiers and buy out teams in
management buy out and buy in transactions.
Prof. Memberships: Thames Valley
Commercial Lawyers Association (Co-Founder
1987, Committee Member 1987-1994,
Chairman 1991-93).
Career: Qualified in 1976. Held various
marketing positions with Shell International
1969-72; trained with *Norton Rose* specialising
in corporate finance until 1980. A Partner at
Simpson Curtis 1981-1986. Head of Company
Department at *Clarks* since 1986.
Personal: Born 16th June 1947. BSc
(Economics and Politics) from Bristol University
1969. Leisure interests include golf, music and
theatre. Lives in Reading.

LOAKE, Jonathan
Cole & Cole, Oxford (01865) 262600
Specialisation: Company acquisitions and
mergers, group reorganisations, MBOs, venture
capital subscriptions, corporate transactions in
the music industry. Clients include a wide range
of companies in different industrial sectors,
including publishers, record companies,
software houses and food companies.
Prof. Memberships: IBA; Thames Valley
Commercial Lawyers' Association (former
Chairman).
Career: Editor with Hodder & Stoughton.
Qualified with *Denton Hall* in 1979; left after four
years to co-found *Dallas Brett*. Joined *Cole &
Cole* in 1997.
Personal: Born 21 March 1951. Educated at
Rugby School and Trinity College, Oxford.
Married with three children. Leisure pursuits
include sport, reading and music.

MACPHERSON, Moray
Bond Pearce, Southampton
(01703) 332 001
Partner in the Corporate Group.
Specialisation: Specialises in corporate
finance: M&A, MBOs etc for management,
equity investors and banks. Several
transactions for Chemring Group plc; MBO for
Scott Closures International; Industrial Rubber
plc reconstruction and sale to management;
MBO of Penny & Giles Instrumentation.
Prof. Memberships: Member of the British
Venture Capital Association.
Career: Qualified 1985, becoming partner with
Boodle Hatfield 1990. Joined *Bond Pearce* 1995
on the firms acquisition of the Southhampton
Office of *Boodle Hatfield*.

MUNDAY, Peter J.
Mundays, Esher (01372) 809000
Head of Corporate Department and Senior
Partner.
Specialisation: Mergers, acquisitions and
disposals. Clients include: Alliance UniChem
Plc, Corporate Express Inc, Air Express
International (UK) Ltd, E. Moss Ltd, Fine
Frangrances & Cosmetics Ltd, Morgan Elliott
Group Ltd, Granger Telecom (Holdings) Plc.
Has undertaken lecture tours of USA under the
title "Building a Bridge To The United States of
Europe."
Career: Qualified in 1968 – Notary Public 1975.

Personal: Born 31.10.1938. Educated: College
of Law Guildford. Leisure interests include
playing hockey, squash and cricket – member
of the MCC. Lives in Oxshott, Surrey.

PARTRIDGE, W.M. James
Thomson Snell & Passmore, Tunbridge Wells
(01892) 510000
Partner in Commercial Department.
Specialisation: Deals with all company and
commercial matters but specialises in the sale
and purchase of companies and businesses,
management buy-outs, the establishment of
joint ventures, corporate finance and intellectual
property licensing.
Career: Qualified in 1983. Trained and practised
in London before joining *Thomson Snell &
Passmore* in 1986. Became a Partner in 1987.
Personal: Born 14 March 1958. Educated at
Lancing College and Trinity College, Cambridge
BA(CANTAB) 1977-80. Other interests: member
of the Territorial Army. Lives in Tunbridge Wells.

PILLMAN, Joe
Cole & Cole, Oxford (01865) 262600
Partner in Company Commercial Department.
Specialisation: Handles general company law
including flotations, mergers and acquisitions,
MBOs, MBIs and reconstructions. Important
matters handled include the management buy-
outs of Early's of Witney plc and Cambridge
Industries Ltd, acquisitions by Xerox and Amey,
the sales of Carfax Publishing to Routledge and
Supergas to Centrica, and the flotation of
Screen on AIM.
Career: Qualified in 1977. Partner with *Cole &
Cole* since 1983.
Personal: Born 7th July 1952. Educated at
Rugby School 1965-69 and Cambridge
University 1970-74. Lives in Northumberland.

SPARROW, Derek T.
Donne Mileham & Haddock, Crawley
(01293) 605000
Specialisation: Company and Commercial
work generally, with particular experience in
handling mergers and acquisitions,
management buy-outs/buy-ins and computer
contracts.
Prof. Memberships: Law Society; Institute of
Directors.
Career: Qualified 1961. Partner of *Coole &
Haddock 1963* (merged *Donne Mileham &
Haddock* 1970). Senior Partner Company
Commercial Department. Appointed chairman
of *Donne Mileham & Haddock* 1996.
Personal: Born 1935. Educated Denstone
College and Keble College Oxford, MA (Oxon)
1958. Assistant examiner – Law Society
accounts 1966-1988. President Sussex Law
Society 1984/85. Directorships – Brighton
Festival Trust, Old Ship Hotel (Brighton) Ltd;
secretary – Sussex Chamber of Commerce
Training and Enterprise, Business Link Sussex
and Wired Sussex. Interests include golf and
after dinner speaking.

TROTTER, Andrew
Shadbolt & Co, Reigate (01737) 226277
Partner and head of Corporate Department.
Specialisation: Main area of practice is
company sales and purchases and corporate
finance, including MBOs, MBIs, venture capital,
joint ventures and cross-border transactions.
Leads a team which also handles general
company commercial work, including
franchising, IT contracts and intellectual

property. Regular lectures on his subject, including a series of seminars 'Buying and Selling Unquoted Companies.'
Career: Qualified in 1981. At *Withers* 1977–1983, *Norton Rose* 1983-85, *Donne Mileham & Haddock* 1985-1997 and *Shadbolt & Co* from May 1997.
Personal: Born 5th August 1954. Educated at Lancing College and Oxford. Lives in Cuckfield in Sussex. Interests include football and golf.

WILLIAMS, Caroline
Blake Lapthorn, Fareham (01489) 579990
Specialisation: Commercial specialist with particular interest in corporate structures and taxation; advises many boards of directors and acts as a non-executive director; leads a team of corporate finance specialists dealing with mergers, acquisition, MBOs, Stock Exchange work and privatisation arrangements.
Prof. Memberships: Chairman Portsmouth

Area Committee, Hampshire Incorporated Law Society (1993-1995).
Career: Joined *Blake Lapthorn* as an articled clerk in 1976. Qualified in 1978 and became a partner in 1981. Head of Commercial Department and Exchequer Partner.
Personal: Married with two children. Chairman of Board of Governors of University of Portsmouth (1995-) Governor Portsmouth High School. Member of CBI Southern Regional Council (1997-). Recreations: Sailing and water sports.

SOUTH WEST

LEADING FIRMS • SOUTH WEST

BURGES SALMON Bristol
OSBORNE CLARKE Bristol

BOND PEARCE Plymouth, Exeter

BEVAN ASHFORD Exeter

HIGHLY REGARDED FIRMS

Anstey Sargent & Probert Exeter
Cartwrights Bristol
Lawrence Tucketts Bristol
Laytons Bristol
Lester Aldridge Bournemouth
Stephens & Scown Exeter, St Austell
Veale Wasbrough Bristol

Bevan Ashford Bristol
Charles Russell Cheltenham
Clarke Willmott & Clarke Bristol
Foot & Bowden Exeter, Plymouth
Lyons Davidson Bristol
Michelmores Exeter
Trumps Bristol

Burges Salmon (6ptnrs) Still felt to be one of the top two practices in the region. Leading individuals include the "significant" and "technically very very good" *Alan Barr*, *Christopher Godfrey* who has a "positive attitude to getting deals done" and *Roger Hawes* who has been seen doing some big deals this year. *David Marsh* is seen as less active on deals now he is joint senior partner. **Clients/Work:** Acting for Naafi in the disposal of its financial services division to an institutionally backed MBI to which Naafi re-invested in the newco (deal value of around £104m). Acting for FirstBus plc in the acquisition of a controlling stake in Bristol International Airport (£40m+). Acting for the company on the flotation of Science Systems plc.
Osborne Clarke (7ptnrs/13assts) Some thought they had a slight edge over Burges Salmon this year. *Simon Beswick* is department head and is "sensible, easy to deal with" and in some accountants opinions "head and shoulders above rest – tops the lot." *Paul Cooper* has a "good commercial instinct"

but can be "aggressive." Senior partner *Chris Curling* appears to be less active as a dealmaker. *Clive Watts* is well regarded by clients: "practical, effective and commercial." *Bruce Roxburgh* was said to be "good to deal with." *Patrick Graves* is seen as "up and coming." **Clients/Work:** Acting for Newcourt Credit Group Inc. of Canada on acquisition of the Business Technology Finance division of Lloyds Bowmaker for £235m. Acting for 3i Group on IBO of Webbs Country Foods Ltd. Acting for Bolton Wanderers F.C. on reverse take-over of Mosaic Investments plc.
Bond Pearce (4 ptnrs: 2p/t, 6assts) Position reflects firm's strength in Exeter/Plymouth but are opening office in Bristol which will be watched with interest. *Roger Acock* has impressed: "Nice chap – technically pretty good." "Sensible; gets deals done." **Clients/Work:** Acted for the Company in connection with the admission of AB Airlines PLC to the Official List of the London Stock Exchange. Sale of Midas Homes to Galliford Plc for £4.9m. Acting for Epwin Group Plc in purchase of Dekura.
Bevan Ashford (Exeter) (2ptnrs/3assts) A strong office distinct from the firm's Bristol office. They are key players in Exeter and have "competent people behind lead individual." *Simon Rous* "is a prominent operator" and is without doubt "a leading light." He "has a national perspective. Is committed and prepared to go where the work is." **Clients/Work:** Transit International Group Ltd: sale of UK businesses and reinvestment in Australian transport lines in excess of £36m. The Robinia Group Plc: acquisition of Advantage Enterprises. Sale of The Workshop to Argosy Recruitment Ltd for £6.3m.
Anstey Sargent & Probert (3ptnrs/2 assts – not all f/t) A well regarded, solid Exeter practice with a good client base. The team is rated and includes *Richard Coombs* who was described as "helpful, responsive and commercial." **Clients/Work:** Acting for The Beer Seller on £8.5m acquisition of free-trade wholesaling of Gibbs Mew plc. Acting for major UK foods importer on £5m joint venture agreement with Italian pasta manufacturer. Advising local company on new partnership between family management and employees, including implementing a

£1m plus unapproved company buy in of shareholdings.
Cartwrights (2ptnrs/2assts) Reputation as an active practice with a niche in brewery sector. Also active in leisure, transport and hi-tech sectors. They have impressed those who have dealt with them and their profile is expanding. *Christopher Mitchell* ("professional") was described as a "sensible fellow" who "works hard." **Clients/Work:** Acted for the management of Ritz Bingo Clubs on buy-out of Vardon Plc (value £30m). Acted for the vendors on the sale of Stanley Gibbons Holdings to Flying Flowers plc (sale price £13.5m). Acting on the acquisition and for management in relation to an MBO of Discovery Inns to create Lionheart Inns.
Lawrence Tucketts (3ptnrs/8assts) Most interviewees thought this firm was "coming more into the picture" and although not the biggest was making a "better name" for themselves in corporate work. An "interesting firm with good individuals." **Clients/Work:** Appian Traffic Technologies – OFFEX float. Sale of R & B to Hazelwood Foods for £11m. Acting for Powell Duffryn PLC on sale of interest in Coral Montany (£8.1m).
Laytons (2ptnrs/2 assts – all spend 50% of time) An "established" practice with a rep-

LEADING INDIVIDUALS
SOUTH WEST

BARR Alan Burges Salmon
BESWICK Simon Osborne Clarke
COOPER Paul Osborne Clarke
GODFREY Christopher Burges Salmon

ACOCK Roger Bond Pearce
BELLEW Derek Veale Wasbrough
COOMBS Richard Anstey Sargent & Probert
CURLING Chris Osborne Clarke
HAWES Roger Burges Salmon
MARSH David Burges Salmon
MITCHELL Christopher Cartwrights
ROUS Simon Bevan Ashford
ROXBURGH Bruce Osborne Clarke
WATTS Clive Osborne Clarke

UP AND COMING

GRAVES Patrick Osborne Clarke
HUNT Robert Clarke Willmott & Clarke
WHITFIELD Stuart Veale Wasbrough

utation for doing mid-sized deals. "Trying hard and are highly regarded." One client said "rate very highly, absolutely excellent." **Clients/Work:** Acted for the MBO team on the MBO of Lister Shearing. Acted for Bank of Scotland on the Bohlin Instruments MBO.

Lester Aldridge (3ptnrs/2assts) South coast firm handling a range of corporate matters. **Clients/Work:** Acting for R E Bath Travel Service Ltd in its acquisition of Tappers Travel Service Ltd. Acting for ITW Ltd on the disposal of businesses.

Stephens & Scown (3ptnrs/2assts) A good year on the back of the Terry Adams transaction where the firm was seen to have done a good job and "impressed." **Clients/Work:** Acted for Terry Adams Group Ltd in the tender and sale of the group to South West Water for £105m. Acting for Howden Group on acquisition of TSL Group of Companies.

Veale Wasbrough (5ptnrs/3assts) Accountants found them "professional and solid." Technically good and "improving." Department head *Stuart Whitfield* has a higher profile and enters our tables. He is "commercial, practical… ..takes time to understand deal." *Derek Bellew* has a "good client book – always busy." Accountants remarked "rate very very highly...really good bloke...technically good and handles clients well." **Clients/Work:** Advised West Midland Farmers on its transition from an Industrial and Provident Society to Ltd Company status. MBO of subsidiary of the Wimpey

Group. Advised management team on buyout of Ray Plastics from the Lilleshall Group.

Bevan Ashford (Bristol) (3 ptnrs: 1p/t; 3assts) The loss of Paul Cooper and Patrick Graves has hit the firm's Bristol profile hard. They are perceived as a health practice concentrating on areas other than corporate finance. Seen less in the market. **Clients/Work:** Acted for vendors on disposal of Aeron Valley Cheese Group of companies to Milkmarque Ltd. Acted for the purchaser on acquisition of powered access division of Brandon Hire Plc.

Charles Russell (2ptnrs/1asst) Do a mix of company and commercial. "Feature more and more...are impressive." Received some good client approbation: "fantastic, professional – looking to add value." **Clients/Work:** Acted for Britannia Group plc on their takeover bid for British Building & Engineering Appliances plc. Acted for management team on Healthcare Services Group plc MBI. Acquisitions for Trifast plc.

Clarke Willmott & Clarke (3ptnrs/ 6assts) The consolidation of their Bristol office has made a qualitative difference to the firm's profile. They are "coming on to the scene and trying hard." People that had dealt with them found them to be "strong players with a good client base" and "pragmatic in their approach – do provide solutions." This is partly due to new leading individual *Robert Hunt* who is beginning to make an impact and

is a "practical, commercial guy." **Clients/Work:** Several pre-float acquisitions for Autologic plc. Share sale and joint venture agreement to value of £2m for Portcullis Publications Ltd. Acted for Bridport Gundry Plc in relation to the sale of three divisions to respective MBO teams totalling £2.7m.

Lyons Davidson (3ptnrs/3assts) Understated team that does not "publicise themselves." They too have been seen around more recently and are "rated highly. Have some good clients and good people." **Clients/Work:** Includes company reorganisations and purchases.

Michelmores (2ptnrs/1asst) Increased profile and getting around. Have recruited specialist. "Concentrated on quality for size ... quite a unique animal… rate very very highly." Also thought to have some significant clients. **Clients/Work:** Sale of St Mellion International Ltd. Sale/purchase of two franchise motor dealerships for group in the motor trade. Advising the MBO team on the acquisition of glass and glazing business from Pilkington.

Trumps (1ptnr/2assts) "Starting to do work." "A good solid commercial firm for the smaller client. Medium level deals (£1-5 m)." Targeting a niche in the computer industry. **Clients/Work:** Creation of a group for an international software house. Advised BYO Restaurants PLC on a company restructure and a £1m venture capitalist investment with 3i.

LEADERS' PROFILES · SOUTH WEST

ACOCK, Roger
Bond Pearce, Exeter (01392) 221185
Specialisation: Partner in the Corporate Group specialising in corporate finance and general company law. Regularly leads *Bond Pearce* teams on many high profile MBO, MBI, IBI and other corporate finance transactions across the southern region. Special interest and experience in waste management and aviation law.
Prof. Memberships: Member of the International Bar Association and Solicitors European Group. Secretary of the Devon and Cornwall Branch of the Institute of Directors. Director of Environmental Trust and PLC Employee Share Trust.
Career: Qualified 1980. Partner 1985. Previous firm *Durrant Piesse* (now *Lovell White Durrant*).

BARR, R. Alan
Burges Salmon, Bristol (0117) 939 2000

BELLEW, Derek J.
Veale Wasbrough, Bristol (0117) 925 2020
Partner in Company Commercial Department.
Specialisation: Work covers company sales and purchases, MBOs, corporate finance and professional partnerships. Detailed experience and knowledge of Track Access in the Rail Industry. Specialist practice in medical partnerships.
Career: Qualified in 1967. A Partner at *Veale Wasbrough* since 1971 and Managing Partner since 1993.
Personal: Born 5th April 1942. Attended St

John's College, Oxford 1961-64. Chairman of St George's Music Trust. Leisure interests include golf and music.

BESWICK, Simon A.
Osborne Clarke, Bristol (0117) 984 5280
Head of Company Department.
Specialisation: Practice covers all company and corporate finance work with a particular emphasis on MBOs/MBIs and venture capital. Recent deals include the £60m IBO of Webbs Country Foods, £35m sale of Bailey Newspaper Group, £55m MBO of Fairey Hydraulics Ltd, £21m IBO of Westcote Semiconductors Ltd. £22m MBO of an agri-chemical business, the £11m MBI of Tile City, the MBO of the Thomas Hardy Brewery, the £35m MBO of Integrated Process Technologies and the £88m MBO of Lister Petier. Editor of 'Wine & Beswick: Buying and Selling Private Companies and Businesses.'
Prof. Memberships: Law Society.
Career: Qualified in 1986, having joined *Osborne Clarke* in 1985. Became a Partner in 1989. Articled at *Lee Crowder*; previously sponsored by TI plc.
Personal: Born 2nd March 1961. Attended Bishop Vesey G.S., and Newcastle-upon-Tyne University. Leisure interests include football, golf, cricket, squash, skiing and reggae music. Lives in Bristol.

COOMBS, Richard
Anstey Sargent & Probert, Exeter
(01392) 411221
Partner, Commercial Department.
Specialisation: Corporate finance, mergers, acquisitions, MBOs, MBIs, share schemes, FSA compliance, friendly societies.
Prof. Memberships: IOD, SWEL, Chamber of Commerce. External Examiner in Corporate Finance for Exeter University.
Career: Qualified 1979. *Clifford Chance* 1977-80, *Turner Kenneth Brown* 1980-81, *British Coal* 1981-85, *Bond Pearce* 1985-94 (Partner from 1988). Joined *Anstey Sargent & Probert* as Partner in 1994.
Personal: Born 16th March 1954. Attended Kings School Chester, Cardiff High School, Downing College, Cambridge (First in Law). Interests: walking and music. Lives in Ivybridge.

COOPER, Paul
Osborne Clarke, Bristol (0117) 984 3586
Partner in the Company and Commercial Department in Bristol.
Specialisation: Main area of practice covers corporate finance and company and business disposals and acquisitions. Responsible for numerous transactions involving clients receiving venture capital, as well as acting for venture capitalists, such as Charterhouse and NatWest Equity Partners. Also deals with Stock Exchange and Company Offer documents, handling Yellow Book work for listed clients.

Experienced in requirements for prospectuses, circulars and listing particulars. Acted for Old English Pub Company PLC on the purchase of Country Style Inns and its admission to the Official List (£60million) and on the agreed bid for Colleagues Group PLC by Moore Group (£25 million) in 1997 and on the establishment by acquisition of a plant hire division for MITIE Group PLC in 1998.
Prof. Memberships: Law Society.
Career: Qualified in 1977, having joined *Boodle Hatfield* in 1975. Moved to *Norton Rose Botterel & Roche* in 1978. Left to join *Bevan Ashford* in 1980, becoming a Partner in 1981. Partner *Osborne Clark* 1997.
Personal: Born 6th February 1953. Attended Oxford School 1964-70, then Selwyn College, Cambridge 1971-74. Director of Westward Commercial Vehicles Ltd.

CURLING, Chris J.
Osborne Clarke, Bristol (0117) 984 5246
Partner in Company/ Commercial Department and Senior Partner of *Osborne Clarke*.
Specialisation: Main area of practice is corporate. Principal clients are dynamic private companies and listed groups. Main activity areas are acquisitions, disposals, new issue work and shareholder/ boardroom/ partnership break-ups. He has responsibility for a number of the firm's listed medium and large clients throughout the South of England. Brings a 'strong commercial flavour' to his legal work. Former contributor to Butterworths Company Law Service. Has spoken at numerous conferences and other events on law-firm management.
Prof. Memberships: Law Society.
Career: Qualified 1976. Assistant Solicitor at *Slaughter and May* 1976-78. Joined *Osborne Clarke* in 1978, becoming a Partner in 1980. Was the firm's Managing Partner from 1988 until 1994.
Personal: Born 21st April 1950. Attended Brentwood School 1961-68, then Queens' College, Cambridge, 1968-71. Trustee of Greater Bristol Foundation and of the Underfall Restoration Project in Bristol. Leisure interests include tennis, cycling and fishing. Lives in Bristol.

GODFREY, Christopher
Burges Salmon, Bristol (0117) 939 2000

GRAVES, Patrick
Osborne Clarke, Bristol (0117) 984 5294
Specialisation: Practice covers all company and corporate finance work with a particular emphasis on listed work.
Career: Qualified 1989 , *Linklaters & Paines*; 1992-95 *Ashurst Morris Crisp*; 1996-97 Partner

Bevan Ashford; 1997 Partner *Osborne Clarke*.
Personal: Fishing, writing, hillwalking, cycling, bird-watching, and all forms of organised sport.

HAWES, Roger
Burges Salmon, Bristol (0117) 939 2000

HUNT, Robert
Clarke Willmott & Clarke, Bristol
(0117) 941 6600
Specialisation: Corporate finance, M&A, pensions. Acting on the acquisition of Deptich Designs for Relyon Group plc for £7m. Represented Brunel Holdings plc in the disposal of Titman Tip Tools Ltd for approximately £3.5m.
Prof. Memberships: Pensions Management Institute.
Career: Westwoods Grammar School, Northleach, Glos 1968-75, Pembroke College, Oxford 1975-78, trained *Rowe & Maw* 1979-81, Assistant Solicitor *Herbert Smith* 1981-83, Assistant Solicitor/Associate *CW&C* 1983-88, Partner *CW&C* 1988 to date.
Personal: Tennis, squash, golf, opera, music – married with two children.

MARSH, David J.
Burges Salmon, Bristol (0117) 939 2000

MITCHELL, Christopher J.
Cartwrights, Bristol (0117) 929 3601
Partner and Head of Commercial Client Department.
Specialisation: Main area of practice is corporate finance work, handling mergers and acquisitions, venture capital, joint ventures; also deals with the 'tie' and beer supply agreements. Was involved in the sale of Discovery Inns Plc (1997), management buy out of Ritz Bingo Clubs (1997), sale of Stanley Gibbons Holdings Plc (1998) and the organisation by Wolverhampton & Dudley Breweries Plc's lager portfolio (1997/98).
Prof. Memberships: Law Society, SBO.
Career: Qualified in 1981. Joined *Cartwrights* in 1986 and became a Partner in 1987.
Personal: Born 3rd October 1957. Educated at Portsmouth Grammar School 1969-73. Brockenhurst College, Hampshire 1973-75 and St. Catherine's College, Oxford 1975-78. Recreations include sport, hill walking and all things French. Lives in Bristol.

ROUS, Simon
Bevan Ashford, Exeter
Direct Line: (01392) 663333
Specialisation: Multi-million pound corporate financings for clients including: BPC Books and Journals Ltd, Centrax Ltd, Environ Products

Inc., Flambards Theme Park, Gemini Radio Ltd, Group SMB Linited, Healthex Ltd, Home Hardware South West Ltd, Lowman Manufacturing Ltd, Lloyds Bank Plc, Midland Bank Plc., Orchard Media Ltd, Parkins Group, Schlumberger Technologies, Stenner Ltd, The Eurotech Group Plc, Teignbridge Propellors Ltd, Transit International Group Ltd, Wrafton Laboritories Ltd.
Career: Spent 11 years with *Clifford Turner* (now *Clifford Chance*) in London, France, Belgium, Saudi Arabia and the USA. Now Managing Partner of *Bevan Ashford* Exeter office and member of this firm's Management Board.

ROXBURGH, Bruce O.
Osborne Clarke, Bristol (0117) 984 5210
Specialisation: Partner dealing with a wide variety of corporate finance and other corporate transactional work including MBOs; MBIs; share and asset sales and purchases; private and public company takeover offers; rights issues, placings and other share offers.
Career: Blundells School; Sidney Sussex College, Cambridge; College of Law, Guildford. Articled *Freshfields* 86-88; joined *Osborne Clarke* 1988; Partner 1991. Director Bristol and Avon Enterprise Agency.
Personal: Resides in Bath

WATTS, Clive
Osborne Clarke, Bristol (0117) 923 0220
Specialisation: Partner dealing with company law, M&A, MBOs. Acts for Prism Rail plc and its subsidiaries.
Career: Monmouth School. Articled *Imperial Group plc*; qualified 1977; legal department 1963-1986; deputy solicitor *Imperial Tobacco Ltd* 1986-1987; *Osborne Clarke* 1987; partner 1988.
Personal: Resides Bristol.

WHITFIELD, Stuart
Veale Wasbrough, Bristol (0117) 925 2020
Partner in the Company Commercial section of the Business Services Department.
Specialisation: Main area of practice covers corporate finance and business and company acquisitions and disposals. Recent work has included large public/ private sector PFI/ partnering transactions and acquisitions and mergers in the IT and semiconductor sector.
Prof. Memberships: Law Society; Princes Youth Business Trust. Institute of Directors.
Career: Exeter University; Articled at *Bond Pearce*; Qualified 1990; Partner at *Veale Wasbrough* 1997.
Personal: Lives in Bristol; Leisure interests include basketball, photography, walking, music and cars.

WALES

Edwards Geldard (5ptnrs/5assts) Have handled a "nice volume of work" recently and are enhanced by *Jeff Pearson* and *Andrew Morris* – who are both new to our table of leading individuals. Morris "likes what he does," – "good corporate work for big clients." Pearson is seen as an "all rounder" who is known for his work for Welsh Water.

Has established himself over last 4/5 years and "knows the community – handles buy in/buy out work as well." **Clients/Work:** The simultaneous handling of the £55m Pendragon Rights Issue and acquisition of Lex Dealerships. The £94m disposal of Cortworth plc. The sale of Kears Group Ltd to Greencore.

Morgan Bruce (5ptnrs/6assts) Merged with Guthrie Francis, Newport which will

strengthen the practice. Both leading individuals are "technically able, know community well... constructive deal doing lawyers [and] commercial." *Graeme Guthrie* is a superb corporate lawyer who now has the right support. *Duncan Macintosh* "knows his stuff... personable and gets work in." **Clients/Work:** Advised management team on buy-out of Parker Plant Ltd. Acted for BP Chemicals in the sale of its subsidiary,

LEADING FIRMS · WALES

EDWARDS GELDARD Cardiff
MORGAN BRUCE Cardiff
EVERSHEDS Cardiff

HIGHLY REGARDED FIRMS

Hugh James Cardiff

Berry Smith Cardiff
Bevan Ashford Cardiff

Cellobond to Blagden Chemicals for £13m. Advised Mitel Corporation in their purchase of the Plessey Semi-Conductor business from GEC for $225m.

Eversheds (1ptnr/5assts) Have recently lost two main corporate partners Alan White-

ley and Laurence James. The practice has taken a "significant knock" and will need to rebuild. Seen to be in a "process of change...need to promote replacements in market." Still have a big client base: the question is who will look after it? **Clients/Work:** Align-Rite International Inc – £5m purchase of photomask business in Germany. Swansea Rugby Club Ltd – incorporation and capital raising. Caverdale Plc – five acquisitions in the £1-5m range.

Hugh James (3 ptnrs – do commercial as well) Handle smaller corporate cases: "do a sensible job."

Berry Smith (1ptnr) A new entry. A small practice based on one partner who is "competent" and "a safe pair of hands." Are picking up conflict work. "Done a few deals...active."

Bevan Ashford (1ptnr/1asst) In a state of change with a new partner brought in earlier this year. Seen as struggling on the corporate side although they have "done a couple of quite decent deals in Cardiff this year." **Clients/Work:** Celtic House Investment Partners Ltd, Gilesport Plc and Culver Holdings plc.

LEADING INDIVIDUALS · WALES

GUTHRIE Graeme Morgan Bruce
MACINTOSH Duncan Morgan Bruce
PEARSON Jeffrey Edwards Geldard

UP AND COMING

MORRIS Andrew Edwards Geldard

SEE PROFILES AT END OF THIS SECTION

LEADERS' PROFILES · WALES

GUTHRIE, Graeme
Morgan Bruce, Cardiff (01222) 385385
Specialisation: Corporate Finance. Mergers & Acquisitions. General Company/ Commercial legal team in the acquisition of Plessey Semi Conductor Group by Mitel Telecom Ltd from GEC Plc in February 1998 for US $235m.
Prof. Memberships: Law Society.
Career: Liverpool University Partner in *Francis* 1978-1996. Partner in *Guthrie Francis & Co.* 1996-1997. Merged with *Morgan Bruce* 1997.

MACINTOSH, Duncan J.G.
Morgan Bruce, Cardiff (01222) 385385
Specialisation: Main area of practice is corporate finance. Work includes mergers and acquisitions and venture capital based transactions, including management buy-outs, management buy-ins and institutional investments. Acted for management in the MBIs of Regent and Postern to form The Assembly Group of Companies Ltd, and of Parker Plant International Ltd. Also, the MBO of Glamalco Ltd

and other venture capital financings.
Prof. Memberships: Member of the Law Society of England and Wales, the Law Society of Scotland, Society of Writers to H M Signet. Qualified in Scotland in 1984, becoming a Partner in an Edinburgh legal practice before joining 3i plc; and then in England and Wales in 1992. Joined Morgan Bruce in 1990.
Personal: Born 11 October 1957. Attended Glenalmond College in Perthshire and Glasgow University. Leisure interests include cricket and golf. Lives in Llanblethian, Vale of Glamorgan.

MORRIS, Andrew
Edwards Geldard, Cardiff (01222) 238239
Specialisation: Corporate finance, company and business acquisitions and disposals, management buy-outs and buy-ins, joint ventures and reorganisations, acts for clients receiving venture capital and bank funding and for banks and venture capital organisations on the provision of such funding.
Prof. Memberships: Law Society.

Career: Assistant Solicitor at *Edwards Geldard* between 1989 and 1995. Partner in *Edwards Geldard* since 1995.
Personal: Born 1965. Educated at Lady Mary High School, Cardiff and University of Glamorgan. Lives in Cardiff.

PEARSON, Jeffrey
Edwards Geldard, Cardiff (01222) 238239
Specialisation: Corporate finance, public takeovers, mergers and acquisitions and multi-jurisdictional joint ventures. Recent work includes a number of transactions for Hyder plc, Hicking Pentecost plc and the recommended offer for Cortworth plc.
Prof. Memberships: Law Society.
Career: *Slaughter and May*, London between 1984 and 1991. Partner in *Edwards Geldard* since 1991.
Personal: Born 1961. Educated at Bishop Gore SC, Swansea and University College of Wales, Aberystwyth. Married with two children. Lives in Cardiff.

MIDLANDS

LEADING FIRMS · MIDLANDS

WRAGGE & CO Birmingham

EVERSHEDS Birmingham
PINSENT CURTIS Birmingham

DIBB LUPTON ALSOP Birmingham
EDGE & ELLISON Birmingham, Leicester

Wragge & Co (13ptnrs/24assts) "In a league of their own." The general opinion was that the firm is now *the* market leader in Birmingham having clearly pulled ahead of Pinsent Curtis in size and terms of volume of business. They have "good continuity and direction." The "excellent" *Ian Metcalfe* was seen as "a star, all round individual – well connected, affable... is business getter." *Maurice Dwyer* ("excellent – good reputa-

tion") had a good year. He moves up to our top band of Leaders. *Richard Haywood* was described as a "good head and good lawyer." *Jeremy Millington* has "arrived," and is "young, energetic and excellent at what does... involved in good quality deals." **Clients/Work:** Advised directors of Care First Group in relation to BUPA's hostile takeover bid which was eventually increased and recommended by the directors. Acted for Doncasters on its £194m recommended takeover of Triplex Lloyd. Acted for Aer Rianta International and NatWest Equity Partners with their co-investment in Birmingham International Airport Ltd.

Eversheds (Birmingham) (7ptnrs/ 20assts) A well respected "high quality" practice with a "good plc client base and some good practitioners" who had quite a good year. The "jolly good" *Milton Psyllides* was described as "one of the top two in town."

Susan Lewis has a good reputation as does *Peter McHugh. Chris Garnett* ("good technical lawyer," "gets deals done," "dependable public company practitioner") enters our lists this year. **Clients/Work:** Acting for Partco Group in its £103m acquisition of Dana Distribution Europe. Acting for Headlam Group plc in the acquisition of MCD (UK) Ltd. Acting for Lucas Varity plc in the sale of its assembly and test systems to DT Industries Inc for £30m.

Pinsent Curtis (10ptnrs/14assts) A practice with a reputation that extends beyond the Midlands. "Excellent, high quality firm." Mixed views as-to progress over the last year with some interviewees feeling that the firm had not moved forward. The team is headed by *Andrew Eastgate* who appears to be less active on deal doing. Leading individuals include *David Hughes, Amanda Allen* (who was seen leading some good deals) and *Simon Gronow* ("absolutely first rate… excellent lawyer… technical and commercial… good all rounder"). *James Lavery* is still "up and coming." **Clients/Work:** Working with MBO team on £84m management MBO of Bristol Street group of companies from Britax International. Advising Avonmore Foods plc on the £50m purchase of Beni Foods Ltd and on the UK aspects of the £350m merger of Avonmore Foods with Waterford Foods plc. Acting for Triplex Lloyd plc on £194m recommended bid by Doncasters.

Dibb Lupton Alsop (7ptnrs/24assts) The arrival of *Chris Rawstron* ("excellent") and others has strenghtened their position. On balance have now achieved 'Leading Firm' status but eyes are on future development. "Have grown in way needed to – recruited Chris Rawstron. Now starting to get critical mass in Midlands." **Clients/Work:** Manchester & London Investment Trust plc – admission to the Official List of the London Stock Exchange. £52m MBO of Arnolds, National Veterinary Supplies and Dales Pharmaceuticals – legal advisors to the management team and acquisition. Legal advisors to Wellman plc on £73m recommended offer by Alchemy Partners.

Edge & Ellison (B'ham: 8ptnrs/18assts. Leicester: 1ptnr/4assts) The Birmingham office has seriously suffered due to the loss of personnel including Digby Jones (to KPMG) and Chris Rawstron (to Dibbs). Still a leading firm but mixed views as to the long term position. They do have leading individuals *David Hull* and *Paul Cliff* who is making a reputation for himself and is up and coming. He is known for his public company work, flotations/fund raising. "Measured, good attention to detail. Calm, thoughtful, capable style appeals to clients." Leicester practice is highly regarded. Some think of it as one with the firm's Birmingham practice whilst others feel

it operates in discrete marketplace. **Clients/Work:** Advising Forward Group plc on recommended offer by PCB Investments for entire share capital for £129m. Acting for Leicester City on recommended offers by Soccer Investments plc (renamed Leicester City plc) for the entire share capital of Leicester City Football Club plc, value £36m. Advising Ocwen Financial Corporation on the acquisition of of UK operations of Cityscape Financial Corporation (£275m).

Browne Jacobson (6ptnrs/12assts) A highly regarded Nottingham practice. "Good operation, good quality team." *Robin Metcalfe* ("no nonsense, gets on with it") has a good reputation locally and " a good following." **Clients/Work:** £40m fund-raising and reorganisation for Derby County Football Club. Acting for Saint-Gobain on £37m acquisition of Glynwed Foundry Products businesses. Advising vendors on £28m sale of Technolog to Utillitec plc.

Eversheds (Nottingham: 5ptnrs/6 assts. Derby: 2ptnrs/5 assts) The team advises a range of clients including plc's. "Good client base in Nottingham." *Victor Semmens* is "the face of Eversheds Nottingham." *David Wild* at the Derby office is not widely known outside the area but is highly rated in it, he is "active and successful in developing office. Good quality operator." **Clients/Work:** Advised Nottingham Group Holdings Plc on its £31m merger with Philip Harris Plc. Acted for Rolls Royce Power Engineering on the sale of Power Combustion to ABB. Acted for principal shareholders and company on sale of Sheriff to Ashtead Group plc.

Gateley Wareing (3ptnrs/4assts) Have carved a successful niche in the MBO/venture capital market. Thought to have "placed themselves in right market – profitable niche at the lower MBO range." The young team are effective networkers and includes *Paul Hayward* who is busy. **Clients/Work:** Solicitors to the acquisition and management on MBOs of Trident Alloys Ltd and Page & Moy Marketing Ltd. For the purchaser on acquisition of Courtaulds Aerospace division by Reinhold Industries Inc.

Martineau Johnson (9ptnrs/13assts: 11f/t) A broad practice which has been seen "doing a lot of sale work." The "super" *Andrew Stilton* is liked and highly regarded. **Clients/Work:** Acting for the management on the buy-out/buy-in of Prism Group for over £10m. Acting for the nominated advisers on the AIM flotation of IS Solutions PLC. Acting as sponsors and legal advisers on the flotation of the Foresight Technology Venture Capital Trust.

Shoosmiths & Harrison (6ptnrs:3f/t; 9assts) The well regarded Robert Cooper is now a consultant. **Clients/Work:** Acting for Tomkins plc on disposal of Axis Resources to a MBO team for £13m. Acting for combined management team on double BIMBO

of Murmar Fabrics Ltd and Phipps-Faire Ltd for a combined acquisition price of £13m. Acting for Radstone Technology plc on rights issue and placing.

Garretts (3ptnrs/7assts: 5f/t) A new entry to our tables on the back of recommendations from other practitioners. A growing practice with increased market presence handling quality work on the back of Andersens association. One to watch. "Could become major players." **Clients/Work:** Acting for management and Newco on MBO of National Railway Supplies Ltd worth £48m. Acting for Finning (UK) Ltd on its acquisition of the entire issued share capital of H. Leverton Ltd from Unilever UK Holdings Ltd – £50,751,000.

George Green & Co (3ptnrs/1asst – 90% of time) A respected niche buyout practice in Black Country. **Clients/Work:** Acting for ECI Ventures in further investment in Westley Group Plc. Advising joint venture company on £18 m demerger.

Hewitson Becke + Shaw (3ptnrs:3 f/t; 2 p/t assts) Active Northampton firm . "Have reasonable quality people but static." **Clients/Work:** Acting for Pegasus Group PLC in a £6.7m Super Class 1 acquisition from Microvitec. Acting for the MBO team in its buy-out from Texas Instruments of power semi-conductors business.

Howes Percival (4ptnrs/2assts) Have opened new office in Leicester which is gaining a good reputation. "Have more of a commercial practice" although the perception is they are doing more quality corporate deals." Strength across the two offices (Milton Keynes and Leics.) **Clients/Work:** Clients include Silverstone Racing Circuit, Shanks & McEwan and Groupe Norbert Dentressangle.

Kent Jones and Done (5ptnrs/4assts) A good year . "Increasing quality of work." Teams seen to be "on the ball." **Clients/Work:** Lead advisers in Metsin's management backed cash offer for Instem plc. Advising Alchemy Partners in the £9m re-financing and buyout of Ashbury Confectionery Ltd.

Knight & Sons (5 ptnrs: 4 almost f/t; 1 asst) A growing reputation and seen in the market place. **Clients/Work:** Acted for the management of International Freight Brokers Ltd in the MBO of the company. Acted for James Crean plc in the sale of its florist sundries subsidiary Douthwaites for £7.3m.

Lee Crowder (4 ptnrs: 3 almost f/t; 5

assts) A good firm mainly known for their 3i work but also have some decent commercial clients. The full impact of their move into the city centre is still to be felt. **Clients/Work:** Advised Airflow Streamlines plc in relation to the disposal of its vehicle contract hire business to Paragan Vehicle Contracts Ltd and its Ford dealership business to Ryland. Advised 3i Group plc in relation to £20m funding of an MBI of Pizza Piatza.

Eking Manning (1ptnrs/2assts) A fairly small operation concerntrating on MBO/ MBIs, mainly acting for management teams at the bottom end MBO/MBI. Carved a good niche. **Clients/Work:** Advising management on the MBI of Jeenay from Grove Industries. Acting for management team in MBO of Star Beauty from Star Nail Products Inc for £4.1m.

Freeth Cartwright Hunt Dickens (3ptnrs/5assts) A reasonable sized practice , handling a volume of deals. **Clients/Work:** Advised management on the £7.5m MBI of Library Services UK, Moreley Book

Company and Greenhead Books. Advised management team on management/employee buy-out of Translinc for £7.2m.

Harvey Ingram Owston (5ptnrs: 4f/t; 1 asst) Well regarded practice known for their corporate work. **Clients/Work:** Acquisition by Stead & Simpson of the business of Shoe Express. Ford & Slater double acquisition of the issued share capital of Peterborough Engineering Ltd and Carrow Commercial.

Higgs & Sons (5ptnrs/1asst p/t) Black Country practice at Brierley Hill with an established reputation there.

Shakespeares (2ptnrs: 2 f/t; 2 p/t assts) Much of the corporate work is advising owner managed businesses on acquisitions, disposals and joint ventures. Tend to act for management on MBOs. **Clients/Work:** Advised Allied Leisure plc on the sale to Sanctuary Leisure plc of six bowling based family entertainment centres. Advising Morris & Company Ltd on the acquisition of Ernest Newton Group Ltd.

LEADERS' PROFILES · MIDLANDS

ALLEN, Amanda
Pinsent Curtis, Birmingham (0121) 200 1050
Partner in Corporate Finance Department.
Specialisation: Handles all types of company and commercial work including mergers and acquisitions, MBOs/ MBIs, joint ventures, flotations, etc. Recent deals include advising Bristol Street group of companies on a series of acquisitions and disposals and Ecko Group Ltd on a £12 million acquisition from Rexam Plastic Packaging Ltd.
Career: Qualified in 1986. Partner at *Pinsent Curtis* since 1992.
Personal: Born 1960. Leisure interests include golf, skiing and travel.

BRAITHWAITE, Stephen
Wragge & Co, Birmingham (0121) 233 1000
Partner in Corporate Group.
Specialisation: Handles corporate finance work and mergers and acquisitions for Public Companies, acquisition and disposals, flotations and new share issues, joint ventures and general corporate matters.
Prof. Memberships: Law Society.
Career: Qualified in 1973. Articled with *Turner Kenneth Brown* 1971-73, worked with *Freshfields* 1973-76, joined *Wragge & Co* in 1976, and became a Partner in 1980.
Personal: Born 3rd May 1947. Interests include sailing, shooting, fishing and walking.

CLIFF, Paul
Edge & Ellison, Birmingham
(0121) 200 2001
Partner and member of the Corporate Department
Specialisation: Corporate Finance, Acquisitions & Disposals, Public share issues including flotations. Specialises in acquisitions, disposals, takeovers and mergers (UK and overseas) primarily for public companies. Clients include some of the firm's listed plcs in a variety of industry sectors. Also regularly acts for either sponsors or issuers in new and secondary issue work and has considerable

experience in these areas. Also a member of the firm's Healthcare Group.
Prof. Memberships: Law Society, Birmingham Law Society and Solicitors European Group.
Personal: Educated at Spondon School, Derby, Lancaster University LL.B (Hons), College of Law, Chester. Interests include football, travel, cricket and golf.

CRABTREE, John
Wragge & Co, Birmingham (0121) 233 1000
Partner in Corporate Group.
Specialisation: Specialising in M&A and Stock Exchange work.
Career: Qualified in 1973. Joined *Wragge & Co* in 1971, becoming a Partner in 1976. Head of Corporate Department 1986-1990; Managing Partner 1990-1993; Senior Partner 1993-present day.
Personal: Born 5th August 1949.

DWYER, Maurice J.
Wragge & Co, Birmingham (0121) 233 1000
Specialisation: Head of Private Equity. Corporate finance, mergers and acquisitions. Structuring of equity and debt finance.
Career: Articled *Freshfields*. Qualified 1983. *Wragge & Co* 1983-86 and 1987 to date. *3i plc* 1987. Partner at *Wragge & Co* from 1990.
Personal: D.O.B. 19.7.57. Author of 'Management Buyouts' (Sweet & Maxwell 1997).

EASTGATE, Andrew
Pinsent Curtis, Birmingham (0121) 200 1050
Partner in Corporate Finance Department.
Specialisation: Mergers and acquisitions for private and public companies. Recent work includes advising Avonmore Foods on UK aspects of £350million merger with Waterford Foods plc; Avonmore Waterford Group on £14 million sale by subsidiary of juice business to subsidiary of Mitsubishi Corporation; acquisitions by Epwin Group plc and Belgian company Tessenderlo Chemie NV on acquisition by UK subsidiary.
Prof. Memberships: Law Society.

Career: Qualified in 1980. Assistant Solicitor with *Stephenson Harwood* 1980-83. *Pinsent & Co.* from 1983. Partner in 1985 and Head of Corporate, Birmingham in 1997.
Personal: Born 1953. Attended Uppingham School and Mansfield College, Oxford.

GARNETT, Chris J.
Eversheds, Birmingham (0121) 233 2001
Specialisation: Mergers and Acquisitions for private and public company clients, flotations and other public company capital issues, corporate restructuring and reorganisations.
Prof. Memberships: Law Society.
Career: Birmingham University. Articled to *Eversheds* (formerly *Evershed & Tomkinson*) 1983-85, Associate 1989, Partner 1992.
Personal: Married to Kathryn; with 2 children, Daniel (aged 5) and Anna (aged 3). A keen interest in natural history, particularly ornithology, and enjoys playing tennis and watching football and cricket.

GREEN, Guy
George Green & Co, Warley (01384) 410410
Specialisation: Corporate finance, M&A for both private and public companies, MBOs/MBIs and venture capital. 1997 deals include £18 million de-merger of metal recycling joint venture company, £18 million sale of foundry and acting for ECI Ventures in investment in Westley Engineering PLC.
Career: Qualified at *Bird & Bird* in 1982. Became partner at *George Green & Co* in 1989.
Personal: Leisure interests include sailing, hockey, skiing and golf.

GRONOW, Simon D.V.
Pinsent Curtis, Birmingham (0121) 200 1050
Partner in Corporate Finance Department.
Specialisation: Principally engaged in corporate matters undertaking "Yellow Book" work for public companies and merchant banks/brokers, including flotations, rights issues, takeover offers, acquisitions and disposals.
Prof. Memberships: Law Society.

Career: Qualified 1986. Joined *Pinsent Curtis* in 1984, Partner in 1991.
Personal: Born 1961. Educated at King's College Cambridge 1979-83.

HAYWARD, Paul A.
Gateley Wareing, Birmingham
(0121) 236 8585
Specialisation: Corporate Finance, General Corporate, Mergers and Acquisitions and Corporate Reconstruction.
Prof. Memberships: Law Society, Society of Practitioners of Insolvency.
Career: Alleyne's School; Nottingham Trent University; Chester Law College; Articles *Edge & Ellison* – Assistant Solicitor 1982-1985; *Needham & James* – Assistant/Associate 1985-1988; Partner *Gateley Wareing* 1988 to date.
Personal: Member of Edgbaston Golf Club and Moor Hall Golf Club. Interests: All sport, music.

HAYWOOD, Richard
Wragge & Co, Birmingham (0121) 233 1000
Specialisation: Head of Corporate Finance; wide range of M&A experience; acts for AT&T, EMAP, Powell Duffryn, PowerGen, Severn Trent, The London Stock Exchange, TRW Wagon Plc and Muller UK.
Career: Qualified 1980; Partner *Wragge +Co* 1986.
Personal: Born 1955. Chairman of the NSPCC Birmingham Business Group.

HUGHES, David J.
Pinsent Curtis, Birmingham (0121) 200 1050
Head of Corporate Finance, Birmingham.
Specialisation: Corporate finance, including mergers and aquisitions, takeovers and primary and secondary equity issues. Recent work includes a series of transactions for Evans Halshaw Holdings plc; UK and international transactions for IMI plc and the recommended bid for Triplex Lloyd plc by Doncasters.
Career: Qualified in 1980. Partner in 1987. Worked at *Nabarro Nathanson* 1978-82, then *Slaughter and May* 1982-85, before joining *Pinsent & Co.* in 1985.
Personal: Born 1955. Attended Wolverhampton Grammar School 1966-73, then Jesus College, Oxford 1973-77.

HULL, David Julian
Edge & Ellison, Birmingham
(0121) 200 2001
National Head of Corporate Finance, *Edge & Ellison*.
Specialisation: Specialises in corporate finance and company commercial work. Primary expertise is mergers and acquisitions, Stock Exchange work, international cross-border transactions and entertainment and leisure contracts.
Prof. Memberships: LL.B (Hons) (Sheff'd). Member of the Firms Partnership Council and is responsible for many of the firms large corporate clients. Regular writer of legal articles and visiting lecturer at the University of Wolverhampton.
Career: Qualified 1986. *Dibb Lupton Broomhead* 1984-86, *Hammond Suddards* 1986-87, *Edge & Ellison* 1987 to date (Partner from 1990).
Personal: Born 18th October 1961. Educated at Banbury School and Sheffield University. Interests include theatre and West Bromwich Albion FC. Lives in Knowle Solihull.

LAVERY, James
Pinsent Curtis, Birmingham (0121) 200 1050
Specialisation: Partner in corporate finance department. Main practice areas are MBOs MBIs, financial purchases and venture capital and M&A work for private and public companies. Recent deals include the MBOs of Ravenstock Tam from Goode Durrant and Safeguard UK from its US parent, and the disposal of the Doncaster/ Triplex automotive division to management backed by Phildrew Ventures.
Prof. Memberships: Law Society.
Career: Educated at King Edward's School, Birmingham and Exeter University. Qualified 1990. Joined *Pinsent Curtis* in 1994. Partner 1996.
Personal: Born 1964. Leisure interests include golf and music.

LEWIS, Susan
Eversheds, Birmingham (0121) 233 2001
Specialisation: Mergers and acquisitions, principally (but not exclusively) for listed companies. During 1997 was involved in a number of transactions with an international dimension.
Career: Oxford University 1976-79. Articled at *Evershed & Tomkinson*, became a partner in 1988. Has been with *Eversheds* throughout career.
Personal: Married with 2 small children. The time for non-work related external interests is almost non-existent, and limited to children and Aston Villa!

MCHUGH, Peter J.
Eversheds, Birmingham (0121) 233 2001
Head of Corporate Services, Birmingham. Chairman of National Corporate Practice Group.
Specialisation: Handles mainly public company work, share acquisitions and disposals, management buy-outs and general corporate advice.
Prof. Memberships: Birmingham Law Society.
Career: Qualified in 1982. Became a Partner in *Eversheds Wells & Hind* in 1989.
Personal: Born 23rd July 1958. Lives in Hartlebury, Worcestershire.

METCALFE, Ian
Wragge & Co, Birmingham (0121) 233 1000
Specialisation: Corporate Finance: Flotations, public takeovers, company mergers and acquisitions. Important Cases: Acting for BI Group Plc on recommended offer for Cortworth Plc; acting for Independent Parts Group Plc on recommended offer by Finelist Group Plc; acting for Specialist Computer Holdings on sale of Byte; acting for Innovative Technologies Group plc on acquisition of Polymedica Inc and associated fundraising; acting for company on flotation of ITNET plc; acting for British Airways Plc on formation of GO.
Career: King Edward's School; St Catharine's College, Cambridge (MA Hons Law). Articled O'Dowd & Co; qualified 1983; Partner *Wragge & Co* 1992.
Personal: Born 1958; married to Judy; Two children – James 10, Annie 7. Leisure: Rugby, Cricket, Golf. Vice president Moseley FC(RU); Warwickshire CCC General Committee; General Purposes and Finance Sub-Committee; Chairman Catering Board; Lord's Taverner's General Committee (West Midlands); Member Edgbaston Golf Club.

METCALFE, Robin H.
Browne Jacobson, Nottingham
(0115) 950 0055
Specialisation: Corporate and corporate finance, insolvency, banking. Wide experience of transaction oriented work heading unit which advises buyers, sellers and funders (equity and debt).
Prof. Memberships: Law Society, Licensed Insolvency Practitioner.
Career: Articled *Eking Manning*. Qualified 1980. Partner *Browne Jacobson* 1985.
Personal: Born 1956; Educated Barnard Castle School, Co. Durham and Nottingham University (LLB Hons). Resides Nottingham. Interests: football, cricket, squash, watersports, hill walking, travel and music.

MILLINGTON, Jeremy S.
Wragge & Co, Birmingham (0121) 233 1000
Specialisation: Partner in corporate group specialising in flotations, takeover offers, securities offerings, acquisitions and disposals.
Prof. Memberships: Member of The Law Society and The Birmingham Law Society; Member of the Birmingham Law Society Company and Commercial Law Sub-Committee.
Career: Qualified 1988. Joined *Wragge & Co* in 1986; Partner in 1995.
Personal: Born 1964. Lives in Edgbaston, Birmingham.

PSYLLIDES, Milton N.
Eversheds, Birmingham (0121) 233 2001
Partner.
Specialisation: Public company transactions, including flotations, mergers and acquisitions, new issues and funding transactions.
Prof. Memberships: Member of the Law Society and the Birmingham Law Society. Council member of the Birmingham Law Society. Secretary of the Birmingham Law Society Company and Commercial Law sub-committee.
Career: Qualified March 1978 with *Evershed & Tomkinson*. Partner May 1984 with *Evershed & Tomkinson*. *Eversheds* national firm created May 1989.
Personal: Born 30th October 1953. Brockley County Grammar School and Liverpool University. Married with one daughter and one son.

RAWSTRON, Chris
Dibb Lupton Alsop, Birmingham
(0345) 262728
Head of Corporate Department (Birmingham).
Specialisation: Main area of practice is corporate finance. Work includes mergers and acquisitions, flotations, rights issues, MBOs, MBIs, disposals and general corporate advice. Sector experience covers automotive, retail and engineering. Has handled numerous acquisitions for quoted and unquoted companies; disposals; bids; flotations and reverse takeovers. Frequent author of articles for press and specialist publications.
Prof. Memberships: Law Society.
Career: Qualified in 1986. Joined *Edge & Ellison* in 1984, becoming a Partner in 1990. Joined *Dibb Lupton Alsop* as a Partner in November 1997.
Personal: Born 29th July 1962. Attended Clitheroe Royal Grammar School 1978-80, Birmingham University 1980-83 and College of Law 1983-84. Holds various trusteeships and directorships. Leisure interests include golf,

Burnley FC and cricket. Lives in Hagley, near Stourbridge.

SEABROOK, Michael R.
Eversheds, Birmingham (0121) 233 2001
Deputy Senior Partner (Birmingham) in Corporate Services Department.
Specialisation: Corporate finance specialist. Work includes MBOs/ MBIs, mergers and acquisitions, public companies and venture capital. Recent transactions handled include the buy-outs of Axis Resources, GWK Group, Carrs Paper, Fab'n Fix and Policy Master and Policy Master's subsequent AIM flotation.
Prof. Memberships: Law Society, Securities Institute.
Career: Qualified in 1976. Assistant solicitor at *Clifford Turner* 1977-79. With *Needham & James* 1980-86 (Partner from 1981). Joined *Evershed & Tomkinson* as a Partner in 1986. Now Deputy Senior Partner (Birmingham).
Personal: Born 24th March 1952. Educated at King Edward's School, Birmingham 1963-70

and Exeter University (LL.B) 1970-73. Recreations include cricket, golf, soccer, rugby, and horse racing. Lives in Dorridge, Solihull.

SEMMENS, Victor W.
Eversheds, Nottingham (0115) 950 7000
Specialisation: Partner, specialises in corporate finance, M & A, takeovers and tax.
Career: Articled Stollard & Limbrey, qualified 1964, partner Eversheds 1968.
Personal: Born 1941. Education Blundells. Resides Nottingham.

STILTON, Andrew J.
Martineau Johnson, Birmingham (0121) 200 3300
Specialisation: Corporate finance: buy-outs, buy-ins and general and acquisition work as well as venture capital and flotation work. Also some banking work.
Prof. Memberships: Law Society, Securities Institute, member of the Law Society's Company Law Committee.

Career: Qualified in 1981. Partner in *Ryland Martineau* in 1985. Partner in *Martineau Johnson* on merger in 1987.
Personal: Born 31st October 1957. Educated at Trinity Hall, Cambridge. Leisure interests include cricket, football, music and travel until parenthood intervened.

WARD, Michael J.
Gateley Wareing, Birmingham (0121) 236 8585

WILD, David W.
Eversheds, Derby 01332 360992
Senior Partner (Derby).
Specialisation: Corporate Finance, MBOs, Insolvency.
Prof. Memberships: Council Member, Derby Law Society.
Career: Articled Wells & Hind, Nottingham. Qualified 1981. Partner Eversheds, 1985.
Personal: Born 1956. Educated Nottingham High School and Jesus College, Cambridge.

EAST ANGLIA

Eversheds (7ptnrs/6assts) A well respected practice with a good reputation in the area. *Terry Gould* is well known as is the "bright" *Andrew Croome.* **Clients/Work:** Acting for Ransomes plc in connection with its takeover by Textron (US) for £137m. Acting for the management team of William Clowes in the MBO from Rexam plc. Acting for Tamaris plc in reltion to the £46m acquisition of Quality Care Homes.

Mills & Reeve (8ptnrs: 7f/t; 7assts: 6 f/t) A quality practice which "can offer an excellent regional service." Team includes *Nick Fischl* and *Glynne Stanfield* whose name was mentioned a lot this year. **Clients/Work:** Advising management teams on MBOs including Mills Manufacturing Technology Ltd and the contracting division of Eastern Group. Acting for Barnham Broom PLC in connection with its acquisition by Daveney PLC pursuant to a scheme of arrangement.

Hewitson Becke + Shaw (4ptnrs/ 5assts) Have a good market position in Cam-

bridge and regional spread. *Bridget Kerle* is "sound." **Clients/Work:** Group reorganisation and sale of business in the food industry. Sale of software company to a US NASDAQ company for $40m.

Taylor Vinters (3ptnrs: 2 almost f/t; 3 assts: 2f/t) Maintain their reputation as a leading corporate practice in the region. The experienced *John Short* has a "well known track record." *Steve Sharratt* was reported as being "active." **Clients/Work:** Acting for the shareholders in Symbionics Group Ltd in its sale to Cadence Design Systems Inc. Preliminary advice to the Bulgarian Minister of State Administration on corporate structures and a companies registry.

Birketts (2ptnrs/1asst) The "leading and longest established practice in Ipswich." Deal with a mix of corporate work including mergers, acquisitions and disposals. **Clients/Work:** Acted for the purchaser and dealt with the UK aspects of the global acquisition of the safety restraint business of Allied Signal. Acted for the management of Inspectorate plc on its sale to BSI.

Garretts (1ptnr/2assts) A "very small" but "up and coming practice" in Cambridge. Undoubtedly benefitting from the Andersens connection and doing work of "reasonable quality." *Gerard Fitzsimons* is an "extremely capable corporate lawyer." **Clients/Work:** Dexion Group Ltd – advising the management on the £70m buy-out of an international racking and material company. Advised a global packaging company on the reorganisation of its European group structure with a value of US$200m.

Greenwoods (3ptnrs/1asst in company and commercial department) A well respected corporate practice in Peterborough which continues to act on acquisitions and disposals of businesses and companies. The company/commercial department is headed by the respected *Michael Evans.*

Prettys (1ptnr: the up and coming *Ian Waine.*) The firm has a highly regarded but small corporate practice handling transactions for public and owner-managed companies.

Bankes Ashton (2 ptnrs:approx 40%) Established firm with a "sound practice." Do a mix of company work including acquisitions, disposals and joint ventures. Some substantial clients.

Gotelee & Goldsmith (2ptnrs/1asst) Ipswich firm with a company/commercial practice providing a range of corporate services.

Greene & Greene (4ptnrs) A good firm which is "long established" in the area. Handles a mix of corporate work including take-overs and MBOs. *Christopher Thomson* is kept busy. **Clients/Work:** Acted for Weston Medical Ltd on their raising £4m of venture capital from 3i Group plc and Phildrew Ventures. Acted for management team on MBO of Pelcombe Training Ltd . Acted for management team in MBO of Foulger Transport Ltd.

SEE PROFILES AT END OF THIS SECTION

ALEXANDER-SINCLAIR, Ian
Mills & Reeve, Norwich +44 (01603) 660155
Partner in Company Department.
Specialisation: Main area of practice is
company law, covering mergers and
acquisitions and corporate finance. Other area
is commercial, including joint ventures and
distribution and agency agreements.
Prof. Memberships: Law Society, Norfolk and
Norwich Law Society.
Career: John Mackrell Prize and City of London
Solicitors Company Prize 1971. At *Slaughter
and May* from 1969 to 1977. Joined *Mills and
Reeve* in 1977, becoming a partner in 1979.

CROOME, Andrew
Eversheds, Norwich (01603) 272727
Specialisation: Non Contentious company
and banking work handling a wide variety of
matters for lenders and borrowers.
Career: Qualified in 1978 with *Allen & Overy*.
Joined *Eversheds* in 1979 becoming a Partner in
1982.
Personal: Born in Essex in 1954. Educated in
Essex, Suffolk and at Trinity Hall, Cambridge.
Lives in North Norfolk.

DIX, John T.
Hewitson Becke + Shaw, Cambridge
(01223) 461155
Specialisation: Main area of practice is
corporate finance work: acquisitions, disposals,
MBOs/MBIs and venture capital funding. Acts
for two venture capital providers and many high
technology and biotech companies.
Prof. Memberships: Law Society.
Career: University of Sydney BA(Hons) and
LLB. Solicitor New South Wales 1986. Qualified
in UK 1991. *Hewitson Becke + Shaw* since
1988. Partner 1996.
Personal: Born 1961. Resides Cambridge.

EVANS, Michael
Greenwoods, Peterborough (01733) 555244

FISCHL, Nicolas J.
Mills & Reeve, Norwich +44 (0)1603 660155
Partner in Corporate Servies Group.
Specialisation: Work includes corporate
finance, MBOs, MBIs, venture capital, joint
ventures/ facilities management and other
computer/ IT agreements.
Prof. Memberships: Law Society, Norfolk and
Norwich Law Society.
Career: Qualified 1979. Joined *Mills & Reeve* in
1984, becoming a Partner in 1986.

FITZSIMONS, Gerard
Garretts, Cambridge (01223) 355977
Managing Partner, Cambridge Office.
Specialisation: Practice focuses on
acquisitions and disposals, venture capital,
corporate finance for private and public
companies, MBOs, MBIs, joint ventures,
banking and insolvency (including taking and
enforcing security), corporate reorganisation.
Prof. Memberships: Law Society.

Career: Qualified in 1984 after articles with
Coward Chance. With *Shearman & Sterling,* New
York 1984-85 and Coward Chance *1986-87*. Joined
Taylor Vinters in 1987. Joined *Garretts* in 1996.
Personal: Born 28th August 1959. Educated in
University College, Oxford 1978-81. Lives in
Cambridge.

GOULD, Terry
Eversheds, Norwich (01603) 272727
Specialisation: Head of Corporate
Department in East Anglia. Practice covers
mergers and acquisitions and corporate
finance. Extensive experience in the media
sector with newspaper publishing and
commercial radio. Recent work includes
acquisition of a listed plc., MBO and joint
ventures. Addresses seminars.
Prof. Memberships: Law Society.
Career: Qualified 1977 with *Freshfields*. Joined
present firm in 1978 and became a Partner in
1981.
Personal: Born 7th March 1952. Attended
Downing College, Cambridge 1971-74.
Governor Norwich School. Leisure pursuits golf
and football. Lives in Norwich.

KERLE, Bridget A.
Hewitson Becke + Shaw, Cambridge
(01223) 461155
Head of Company Commercial Department.
Specialisation: Advises corporate clients,
including quoted and other public companies
on funding, acquisitions and disposals,
flotations and MBOs. Also handles employee
share schemes for growing and quoted
companies. There is a large international
element to her work.
Prof. Memberships: Law Society.
Career: Qualified in 1977. Joined *Hewitson Becke
+ Shaw* in 1977, becoming a Partner in 1980.
Personal: Born 1953. Attended St Hilda's
College, Oxford 1971-74. Main leisure pursuit is
her family. Lives in Wilburton, Cambridgeshire.

SHARRATT, Steve
Taylor Vinters, Cambridge (01223) 423444
Specialisation: Corporate Finance
Transactions, including MBOs MBIs, Mergers
and Acquisitions, Venture Capital for Private Ltd
Companies. Also handles international matters
with a Central European bias.
Prof. Memberships: Law Society.
Career: Qualified 1989. Trainee and Solicitor at
Edge & Ellison Legal Advisor at BP Plc,
Managing Director Neville Industrial Securities
Ltd, Director Neville Group Ltd, Solicitor *Gepp &
Sons*, Partner *Connolly Sharratt*, Partner *Taylor
Vinters*. Currently acts as Non-Executive
Chairman of six private Companies.

SHORT, John
Taylor Vinters, Cambridge (01223) 423444
Partner in Company/ Commercial Department.
Specialisation: Work covers acquisitions and
sales, reconstructions, venture capital,
investment, and MBO/MBIs. Also handles

insolvency and banking, advising receivers and
liquidators. Advises on taking and enforcing
security. Occasional lecturer in legal topics at
Madingley Hall, Cambridge.
Prof. Memberships: Law Society, Associate
Member of Society of Practitioners of
Insolvency.
Career: Qualified 1974. Trainee and solicitor at
Prettys, Ipswich, 1972-75; Assistant Solicitor at
Coward Chance, London, 1976-78. Joined
Taylor Vinters in 1979. Became a Partner in 1982.
Secretary of Cambridgeshire and District Law
Society, 1983-87.
Personal: Born 28th December 1949. Attended
Sheffield University 1968-71. Leisure interests
include walking, music and photography.

STANFIELD, Glynne
Mills & Reeve, Cambridge
+44 (01223) 364422
Specialisation: Advises on wide range of
corporate and commercial matters with an
emphasis on management buy-outs and buy-
ins where he usually advises the incoming
management team. Recently he has also been
involved in a US NASDAQ listing and a London
Stock Exchange flotation. Acts for several
acquisitive clients. Particular interest in the
funding of higher education by conventional
and unconventional/ innovative financing
methods including tax based schemes.

THOMSON, C.J.
Greene & Greene, Bury St. Edmunds
(01284) 762211
Specialisation: Acts regularly for growing
businesses seeking equity finance and also for
providers of such finance to private companies.
Has acted on numerous MBOs, takeovers,
public offers of securities and equity
involvement in private companies. Handles
Stock Exchange compliance work and has
written material on company law for the
Association of Certified Accountants.
Career: Articled with *Daynes Hill & Perks*,
Norwich, joined *Greene & Greene* in 1989,
became a Partner in 1991 and a Notary Public in
1995.
Personal: Educated in East Anglia, having first
studied Business Studies and then gained a first
class honours degree in Law at UEA in 1985.
Aged 34.

WAINE, Ian
Prettys, Ipswich (01473) 232121
Specialisation: Main areas of work include
company law, mergers and acquisitions,
corporate finance, insolvency and advice on
directors liabilities. Work has also included
advice on Private Finance Initiative projects and
privatisations.
Career: Qualified 1986. Partner at *Prettys* since
1989.
Personal: Born 1961. Educated at Walton
School, Stafford and Southampton University.
Interests include golf and cricket. Lives in Great
Finborough, Suffolk.

NORTH EAST

Addleshaw Booth & Co (16ptnrs/30assts) Known as "steady" for their 3i work and still pre-eminent in the region. "Figurehead" *Maurice Cowen* is well known but thought to be less active than in the past. Lower profile – *Ian McIntosh* receives praise whilst partner *Timothy Wheldon* is considered "good, bright and able." **Clients/Work:** Advising Fastline Group Ltd on £50m sale to Jarvis plc. Acting for Yorkshire Group plc on the £37m sale of its leather and speciality chemicals division. Acting for sponsor Singer & Friedlander Ltd Ltd in £33m flotation of ScS Upholstory plc.

Dibb Lupton Alsop (Leeds: 6ptnrs/ 10assts. Sheffield: 4 ptnrs/9assts) *Alastair Da Costa* is head of the department in Leeds. *Andrew Darwin* continues to be rated but is seen as lower profile in the North East since his duties as Group Head of Corporate involve a greater commitment in London. The "steady"*Julia Wood* is "hard working." **Clients/Work:** Acting for US corp. Interface Inc in acquisition of Readicut International plc(£30m). Acting for Charles Sidney plc in takeover by Sanderson Bramall Motor Group plc (£37.5m). Acting for Sytner Group plc in £55m flotation.

Eversheds (Leeds) (8 ptnrs/16assts) Rated as the strongest office in the national firm, "they have the perceived market edge in Leeds after Du Pont." Department Head *David Gray* is good and regarded as "the best technical lawyer" whilst *Ian Richardson* has taken on more of an international development focus this year. *Stephen Hopkins* is said

to "work hard for his clients" **Clients/Work:** Acting in the purchase by International Maritine Group Ltd of Stephenson Clarke Shipping. Sale of Hartlepool Water plc to Anglian Water plc. IBO of Joyce Loebl Ltd by 3i.

Hammond Suddards (7ptnrs/12assts) A well regarded office of this national firm. "Figurehead" *Noel Hutton* is a recognised personality with the "truly exceptional." *David Armitage* and *Richard James* rated for wide ranging corporate finance work. **Clients/Work:** Acting for FKI plc in £131m acquisition of Bridon plc. Acting for Bradford & Bingley Building Society in £64m acquisition of Mortgage Express Group from Lloyds TSB Group. Acting for Great Lakes Chemical Corporation on UK aspects of demerger of the petroleum additives business.

Dickinson Dees (11ptnrs: 2p/t/18assts: 50-100%) "A big fish" in Newcastle. "Strong" with a good client base. Many competitors said they would refer conflicted clients. Head of Department *Nigel Bellis* is seen as "quiet and competent,"and the assertive *John Flynn* is "commercial." Other known name *Graham Wright* is now senior partner. New entry to the rankings *Chris Harker* is considered "excellent," "doesn't mess around and always has an eye on finishing the deal." Team includes *Jamie Pass.* **Clients/Work:** Acting for Ropner plc in £34m agreed takeover by Jacobs plc. Acting for Quality Care Homes plc in £55m agreed takeover by Principal Healthcare plc. Acting for Northern Recruitment Group plc in £17.6m flotation.

Pinsent Curtis, (8ptnrs/15assts) Perceived by clients and competitors alike as "still reeling" from last year's defections.The firm is however making a come back, having brought in *Alan Greenough* from Birmingham. He is seen as being the mainstay of the practice and a "real deal doer." The team is rated for the quality of work, and clients are satisfied with their service. **Clients/Work:** Acting for HSBC/Newco in £145m private equity deal with AM Paper Group Ltd. Acting for SIG plc in the £65m sale of Architectural Products. Acting for SCS Upholstery plc in £33m full listing.

Eversheds (Newcastle) (9ptnrs: 5 p/t; /7 assts. Middlesborough: 1 ptnr) Accountants from the big six' thought the merger last year with the well rated Wilkinson Maughan beneficial for the office, "given them an edge and also given Dickinson Dees something to think about." They are "coming through" enthused some clients. Their peer firms perceive them to have "the wherewithal to challenge"for the top of the tables. *Michael Spriggs* is rated and is doing the deals. The " quiet and easy going" *Andrew Davison* is "competent." **Clients/Work:** Acting in the purchase by International Maritine Group Ltd of Stephenson Clarke Shipping. Sale of Hartlepool Water plc to Anglian Water plc. IBO of Joyce Loebl Ltd by 3i.

Garretts (5ptnrs: 1p/t; 9assts) "Supremely sensible and practical" with "a broad spread of skills" the team includes the "stunningly good" *Sean Lippell* and "good operator" *Nick Painter.* Andersens have recently acquired the Natwest Markets team, and it will be interesting to see whether this has impact on the Leeds corporate practice. **Clients/Work:** Acting for Natwest Equity Partners/Newco in IBO of Artform International. Acting for the management of Wellman Plc in IBO by way of delisting with a significant transactional value. Acting for ISA International plc on their Super Class 1 acquisition of Atapco (UK) Ltd and the John Heath group of companies from Atapco International Inc. for initial £29m.

Walker Morris (3ptnrs/8assts) A good firm but not seen as much in the market in the last 12 months. "Highly rated" *Ian Gilbert* is thought to be "a real deal doer." *Peter Smart* is managing partner but "is still doing the work." Team also includes the rated *Paul Emmett.* **Clients/Work:** Acting for Golsborough Healthcare plc in £80m recommended offer by BUPA. Advising NatWest

Markets in the Newcastle United plc flotation. Advising Hambros Bank in the IMS Group plc £44m flotation, now acting for IMS.

Andrew M Jackson (2 100%, 1 p/t ptnrs/4 f/t, 1 p/t assts) Have a " quality commercial team who get on with the job." **Clients/Work:** Northern Foods plc acquisition of Woodgate Farms Dairy for £17m (acting for Purchaser). Victoria Dock School, Hull PFI Project (acting for Sewell Construction plc as developer/service provider). EYMS Group/National Holidays demerger (acting for 50 % shareholder).

Gosschalks (5ptnrs 100%/3assts 100%) Decent firm with a local reputation for "a good commercial team." **Clients/Work:** Acting for Dixon Motors plc in the acquisition of Carnell Motor Group plc. Acting for Mill House Inns plc in a syndicated loan facility of £50m. Acting in the acquisition of the Rugby Club of London Ltd from Jeff Butterfield.

Irwin Mitchell (Sheffield:4ptnrs 1p/t/ 4assts 1p/t. Leeds 1ptnr/2assts) Although rated by some clients as "extremely good" they are perceived as constrained by size although the individual players are well regarded. *Kevin Cunningham* heads the Leeds office. "Quality operator" *Andrew Harrison* jointly heads up the larger Sheffield office with newcomer to the rankings *Michael Jelly* of whom one client said "stunning, one of the brightest most capable negotiators...he's superb. He's worked miracles for me...especially good at calming down emotional clients when a deal is getting critical." **Clients/Work:** Advised on sale of Swiss and Luxembourg based group of companies (with operations in 44 jurisdictions) for substantial sum to Dutch purchaser financed by Union Bank of Switzerland's London office. Acting for United Dominion Industries Inc on acquisition of the Radiodetection multinational group. Acted on acquisition by ANI Aurora plc of specialist steel fabrications company Cromdane.

Robert Muckle (3 ptnrs: 1p/t/8 assts) "A lively lot" including *Ian Gilthorpe* who accountants think "does a good job," he is also managing partner, *Hugh Welch* is thought to "work hard and is more than competent." **Clients/Work:** Hathaway Roofing Ltd management buy-out (£10m). Seaward Electronic Ltd acquisition of Clare Instruments Ltd. Thomas Armstrong Holdings Ltd acquisition of Coulthards Concrete Products Ltd (£2.5m)

Rollit Farrell & Bladon (6ptnrs/3assts) Seen as "a reasonable firm in this area" the partners are highly regarded by accountants. **Clients/Work:** Acting in £20m acquisition for Persimmon Homes (East Yorkshire) Ltd. Advising in the £37m millenium project for City of Hull known as 'The Deep.' Acting in the £85m re-financing for Kingston Communications (Hull) plc.

Ward Hadaway (4ptnrs/7assts) A favourite with accountants – "known for smaller MBOs." Figurehead *Peter Allan* has been on sabbatical for 3 months and is coming up for retirement. **Clients/Work:** Acting for Kennametal Inc in £15m acquisition of Presto Engineers Cutting Tools Ltd. Acting in the £7.2m MBO of Dataform Print Management from Sage Group plc. Acting for Northumbrian Water plc.

Watson Burton (6ptnrs: 3p/t; 2assts 75-90%) Also popular with accountants, the team includes new to the list *Gillian Hall* who is particularly rated by clients. **Clients/Work:** Acting for MBO teams in acquisitions of Premier Books (UK) Ltd and Heating Components & Equipment Ltd. Advising the vendors in the disposal of Morley Electronic Fire Systems Ltd to a US group.

Gordons Wright & Wright (3ptnrs/ 1asst) Quiet in the market but generally rated by those who knew them. **Clients/Work:** Sale of entire issued share capital FC Heaton Ltd to Amberley Group plc; sale of Gisburn Park Hospital to Abbey Hospitals; VC subscription £1.25m in TIB plc acquisition of PC Wise Ltd.

Jacksons (3ptnrs/1asst) Not thought of as a high profile player nonetheless well regarded when seen. Mainly act locally. **Clients/Work:** Sale of three companies, largest valued at £1.5-2m. Corporate acquisition worth £5m.

Keeble Hawson Moorhouse (3ptnrs/ 3assts) A respectable Sheffield firm in this field. **Clients/Work:** Acting in the completion of the MBO of Hallamshire Hardmetal Products Ltd. Dealing with the sale of Noble Macaulay Ltd. Advising 9 of Yorkshire's Top 100 companies.

Lupton Fawcett (2ptnrs/4assts) Seen as having "a good name" for smaller ticket general corporate work. **Clients/Work:** Acting in the flotation of ICM Computer Group plc. Acting on behalf of Shorco Group Holdings plc on £9.2m acquisition of Peterhouse Group and Lowfields Technology. Advising Concept Foods Ltd on a fund raising from 3i.

LEADERS' PROFILES · NORTH EAST

ALLAN, Peter R.
Ward Hadaway, Newcastle upon Tyne
(0191) 204 4000
Partner in Commercial Department.
Specialisation: Corporate Finance.
Prof. Memberships: Law Society and Institute of Directors
Career: Qualified in 1960. Lecturer in Law prior to joining *Ward Hadaway* in 1962. Became Partner in 1964, Senior Partner 1990 and Joint Senior Partner 1997.
Personal: Born 5th July 1936. Attended Queen Elizabeth Grammar School, Hexham 1947-54, then St Catharine's College, Cambridge 1954-57 (MA, 1st Class Honours in Law). Council Member of Northern Region CBI. Board Member of Prince's Youth Business Trust.

ARMITAGE, David W.K.
Hammond Suddards, Leeds
(0113) 284 7000
Specialisation: Corporate partner specialising in national and international merger and acquisition work, MBOs and MBIs, joint ventures, competition issues, commercial contracts, sponsorship and endorsement work; corporate restructuring; capital issues and Yellow Book and Blue Book work for plc clients.

Recent highlights include: acting for FKI plc on its £196m acquisition of the Hawker Siddeley Electric Power Group from BTR plc; acting for FKI plc on its £185 million hostile bid for Newman Tonks Group plc; acting for Allied Colloids Group plc in its $390million Super-Class 1 acquisition of CPS Chemical Company Inc. and associated £173 million rights issue; acting for Bradford & Bingley Building Society in its £1.5 billion acquisition of Mortgage Express Holdings; acting for FKI plc on its £131 million recommended bid for Bridon plc.
Prof. Memberships: Law Society.
Career: Rydal School; Queens' College, Cambridge (1980 BA, 1983 MA). Articled *Alexander Tatham*, Manchester; qualified 1983; Ferranti plc 1985-1986; joined *Hammond Suddards* 1986; partner since 1988.
Personal: Born 1958; resides Harrogate; married with two children. Leisure interests include golf, rugby, motor sports; Abersoch Golf Club.

BELLIS, Nigel D.
Dickinson Dees, Newcastle upon Tyne
(0191) 279 9000
Partner in Company and Commercial Department.
Specialisation: Handles flotations, share issues, mergers and acquisitions, IT contracts and complex commercial agreements. Clients include public companies, utilities and substantial private companies, as well as public sector organisations.
Prof. Memberships: Law Society.
Career: Qualified in 1977. Joined *Dickinson Dees* in 1980 and became a Partner in 1982.
Personal: Born 1953. Educated at Cambridge University 1971-74. Lives in Newcastle upon Tyne.

COWEN, Maurice C.
Addleshaw Booth & Co, Leeds
(0113) 209 2010
Partner in Corporate Finance Group.
Specialisation: Main areas of practice are corporate, corporate finance and inward investment work principally for US companies.
Prof. Memberships: Law Society.
Career: Qualified in 1970. Worked at *Slaughter and May* 1968-73. Joined the firm in 1973, becoming a Partner in 1975.
Personal: Born 29th January 1946. Attended Sheffield University 1964-67 (LLB). Board Member of Leeds Financial Services Initiative and British American Business Group North East. Leisure interests include opera, music, literature and walking. Lives in Harrogate.

CUNNINGHAM, Kevin G.
Irwin Mitchell, Leeds (0113) 234 3333
Specialisation: Corporate finance, mergers and acquisitions and venture capital. Acting in particular for MBO teams and funds. Buy-outs include Viscount, Gloystarne, Baldwin & Francis, Three Star, RFS, Cowen Barrett and Marc Wheatley. Trade deals include the acquisition of the Multi-Compact Group for John Mowlem & Co plc and the Clarkson Osborn group for Hydra Tools International.
Prof. Memberships: The Law Society.
Career: Qualified 1979. Joined *Irwin Mitchell* 1983. Partner 1985 and appointed to Management Board in 1989.
Personal: Born 1956. Interests include tennis and skiing.

DA COSTA, Alastair
Dibb Lupton Alsop, Leeds (0345) 262728
Specialisation: Corporate finance lawyer specialising in mergers and acquisition and public company work, including Stock Exchange and takeover code work. Recent transactions include: Recommended bid for Charles Sidney plc (£38m); acting for Interface Europe Ltd in acquisitions of Readiat plc carpet businesses (£30m); acting for Filtronic plc in two acquisitions (£16m); actng for Natwest Markets in recommended bid for Healthcall Group plc (£50m).
Prof. Memberships: Law Society. Company Secretary of Leeds Financial Services Initiative.
Career: Ripon Grammar School; Leeds University (LLB Hons); Leeds Metropolitan University (Management Certificate); Articled with *Slaughter and May*; qualified 1990; joined *Dibb Lupton Alsop* in 1992; Partner in 1995, Head of Leeds Corporate Group from 1997.
Personal: All sports, particularly football, tennis, rugby union and golf.

DARWIN, Andrew
Dibb Lupton Alsop, Leeds (0345) 262728
Also London and Sheffield.
Specialisation: Corporate finance (flotations, secondary issues, takeovers and mergers) venture capital (UBOS/ UBIS; acting for institutions and management) and mergers and acquisitions.
Career: 1981 to date *Dibb Lupton Broomhead*.
Personal: Education – Queens' College, Cambridge.

DAVISON, Andrew J.
Eversheds, Newcastle upon Tyne
(0191) 261 1661
Partner in Corporate Department.
Specialisation: General Company Law with particular reference to public company, corporate finance, and mergers and acquisitions work.
Prof. Memberships: Law Society, Newcastle upon Tyne Incorporated Law Society. Member of Law Society Standing Committee on Company Law.
Career: Qualified in 1985. Joined *Wilkinson Maughan* in 1983, becoming a Partner in 1986.

EMMETT, Paul D.
Walker Morris, Leeds (0113) 283 2500
Partner in Corporate Department.
Specialisation: Principal area of practice is corporate finance, mergers and acquisitions. Work includes flotations, rights issues, other forms of equity financing, acquisitions and disposals. Other main area of practice is

general corporate advice. Important transactions have included the £190million flotation of Newcastle United PLC, £50million flotation of IMS Group PLC, £30million merger of Rosebys PLC and Rexmore PLC, £75 million flotation of City Technology Holdings PLC, £35million acquisition of Sheffield Forgemasters Group Ltd, £20million acquisition of the Scottish division of Laing Homes Ltd. Author of several articles in the Yorkshire Post and legal journals. Has spoken at seminars on Stock Exchange listing rules and director's duties.
Prof. Memberships: Law Society.
Career: Qualified in 1987. With *Slaughter and May* 1985-91. Joined *Walker Morris* in 1991 and became a Partner in 1993.
Personal: Born 7th November 1961. Educated at Cheadle Hulme School, Cheshire 1974-80 and King's College, London University 1981-84. Lives in Leeds.

FLYNN, John
Dickinson Dees, Newcastle upon Tyne
(0191) 279 9000
Partner in Corporate Department.
Specialisation: Work includes mergers and acquisitions, flotations, rights issues and similar related Stock Exchange work, as well as joint ventures. Acted in the flotation of Go-ahead Group plc, the investment by Northern Electric in Ionica and the £300million acquisition by Cowie of British Bus. Led the team voted U.K. Regional Corporate Team of the Year by Legal Business Magazine.
Prof. Memberships: Law Society.
Career: Qualified in 1979. Joined *Dickinson Dees* in 1981, becoming a Partner in 1986.

GILBERT, Ian M.
Walker Morris, Leeds (0113) 283 2500
Partner in Corporate Department.
Specialisation: Main area of practice is corporate finance, management buy-outs and venture capital. Has been involved in venture capital and development capital for 17 years, acting on both sides. Involved in numerous MBOs of varying size and complexity as well as public and private company acquisitions and disposals, flotations, joint ventures, and share issues.
Career: Qualified in 1981. With 3i Group Plc 1979-85, latterly as Senior Legal Advisor. Joined *Walker Morris* in 1985 and became a Partner in 1986.
Personal: Born 22nd July 1957. Educated at Sheffield University 1975-78. Recreations include tennis, walking, squash and rebuilding a house. Lives in Follifoot.

GILTHORPE, Ian M.
Robert Muckle, Newcastle-upon-Tyne
(0191) 232 4402
Partner in Commercial Department. Managing Partner.
Specialisation: Main area of practice is corporate finance, including MBOs, acquisitions, disposals, sources of finance, debt re-structuring and flotation. Also a Licensed Insolvency Practitioner.
Career: Qualified in 1978. Partner 1979.
Personal: Born 9.5.1953.

GRAY, David
Eversheds, Leeds (0113) 243 0391
Head of the Corporate Department in Leeds and Manchester
Specialisation: David, head of corporate in Leeds and Manchester, handles all aspects of

corporate finance work with a particular emphasis on international work. His clients include Premier Farnell, McCains, Peter Black, Heywood Williams and Waddington. Independent comments include: "a good business adviser hightly rated by his competitors,""considered an outstanding player in the Leeds market . . . widely regarded as a class act."
Career: Qualified in 1979. Became a Partner in 1982.
Personal: Born 9th January 1955. Member of Yorkshire and Humberside CBI Council. Leisure interests include golf and horse racing.

GREENOUGH, Alan Edward
Pinsent Curtis, Leeds (0113) 244 5000
National Head of Corporate Department.
Specialisation: MBOs, MBIs, BIMBOs, VIMBOs, MEBOs, Financial purchases, Venture capital, private company disposals and acquisitions, international offerings, international placings and underwritings. Handles M&A for both private and public companies, including cross-frontier deals. 1997 deals include ROM MBO (£21m); Carrs Paper disposal (£30m), and AM Paper (£145m). 1998 deals include Carcraft (£50m) and Newmond sale of Swish.

HALL, Gillian Mary
Watson Burton, Newcastle upon Tyne
(0191) 244 4444
Specialisation: Corporate Finance work – acquisitions and disposals, MBOs, MBIs, joint ventures both in UK and overseas. Also technology transfer and intellectual property licensing generally accredited mediator.
Prof. Memberships: Law Society, Institute of Directors, ADR NET.
Career: Qualified in 1985. Articled at *Lovell White & King*. Partner 1988. Educated at Cambridge University (BA Law 1982)

HARKER, Chris
Dickinson Dees, Newcastle upon Tyne
(0191) 279 9000
See under Banking, p. 145

HARRISON, Andrew M.
Irwin Mitchell, Sheffield (0114) 276 7777
Specialisation: Corporate transactions, international and domestic, highlights include: purchase of Salisbury chain from Receiver of Facia Ltd for Mr Minit Plc; sale of Bredel Holdings Brand subsidiaries to Watson Marlow Ltd (part of Spirax); management buyout of William Cook plc by Steel Castings Investments plc for the management.
Career: Doncaster Grammar School. Christ Church, Oxford MA. BCL (Oxon).

HOPKINS, Stephen Martyn
Eversheds, Leeds (0113) 243 0391
Specialisation: Leads the firm's commercial lending team and undertakes significant banking and funding work principally for debt and working capital providers. He specialises in acquisition finance having undertaken some of the most significant deals in the area such as the £65m institutional purchase from Sheffield Insulation Group and the £60m MBO of Kennedy Construction. Deals with major syndicated and club facilities having completed a $150m six bank bilateral arrangement and a £36m three bank deal. He is part of the firm's hugely successful MBO team and leads this with John

Shinwell. Has dealt with a number of major corporate deals in the last twelve months includig the dsiposal of Leyland Trucks, Fotoprocessing and the acquisition of Carpets International. His work load is increasingly biased towards merger, acquisition and venture capital.
Prof. Memberships: Law Society
Career: Qualified in 1984. Joined *Eversheds* in 1988. Became a Partner in 1991.
Personal: Born 17th March 1960. Attended Sheffield University 1978-1981. Leisure interests include golf, cricket and rugby. Lives near Wetherby.

HUTTON, C. Noel
Hammond Suddards, Leeds
(0113) 284 7000
Partner in Corporate Finance Department.
Specialisation: Specialises in mergers and acquisitions (principally by and on behalf of listed companies) and new issue work.
Career: Qualified in 1973. Partner at *Hammond Suddards* since 1977.
Personal: Born 4th November 1949. Interests include sailing, motor sports and sport generally. Lives in Ilkley.

JAMES, Richard
Hammond Suddards, Leeds
(0113) 284 7000
Specialisation: Partner in Corporate Finance Unit specialising in MBO/MBI, development capital, acquisition and disposals. Highlights of 1997/8 included formation and flotation of Quantica plc.
Prof. Memberships: Law Society.
Career: Rawlins, Quorn, Leicestershire; Trent Polytechnic. 2:1 BA Legal Studies; Trent Law Journal Prizewinner 1983. Articled *Allen & Overy*; qualified 1986. Assistant solicitor *Simpson Curtis* 1987-1989; Associate 1989-1991; Partner 1991-1994. Partner *Garrett & Co* (Leeds) May 1994 – January 1996. May 1996, Partner *Hammond Suddards*.
Personal: Born 1960. Resides Leeds. Leisure interests include golf (member of Alwoodley Golf Club).

JELLY, Michael
Irwin Mitchell, Sheffield
(0114) 276 7777
Specialisation: Partner and Head of Corporate Services, specialising in transactional work and competition law. Recent work includes various transactions concerning league football clubs including the £17m public issue by Sheffield Wednesday. Advising on the impact of European law and regulation on the Australia National Industries Ltd employee share plan for five jurisdictions. Advising on the merger regulation implications of various transactions including the sale of MINIT SA and Radio Detection Ltd.
Career: Articled *Kingsford Dorman*; qualified 1968. Assistant Solicitor *Lawrence Messer* 1968-71. Solicitor *Kershaw Tudor* 1971, Partner 1972, Senior Partner 1986. Partner *Irwin Mitchell* 1994, Director Hallamshire Investments Plc, Peak Park Trust Ltd. Chairman Thorntons Plc pension funds.
Personal: Born 1943, resides Hathersage. Interests include skiing, music, walking.

LIPPELL, C. Sean
Garretts, Leeds (0113) 207 9000
Northern Managing Partner and Partner in Corporate Department.
Specialisation: Principal area of practice is corporate finance. Work includes public issues, MBO'/MBIs and development capital, mergers and acquisitions (including cross-border/international transactions), demergers and corporate reconstructions and corporate joint ventures.
Prof. Memberships: Law Society.
Career: Qualified in 1979 at *Simmons & Simmons*. *Freshfields* 1979-83. *Pinsent & Co.* 1983-1987 (Partner 1984). *Simpson Curtis* in 1987 as a Partner, became Head of Corporate Department in 1993, and Joint Chief Executive in 1994. Appointed National Head of Corporate Department, May 1995. Joined *Garretts* May 1997 as Northern Managing Partner.
Personal: Born 21 September 1950. Educated at Kelly College, Tavistock and Durham University. Leisure interests include running, walking, reading and films. Lives in North Yorkshire.

MCINTOSH, Ian W.
Addleshaw Booth & Co, Leeds
(0113) 209 2000
Partner in Corporate Finance Group.
Specialisation: Corporate finance and company law including mergers and acquisitions, joint ventures, MBOs and private and public capital raisings. Acts for a range of public and private companies, banks and venture capitalists.
Prof. Memberships: Law Society
Career: Qualified 1983. At *Turner Kenneth Brown* 1981-1984 and *Travers Smith Braithwaite* 1984-1988. Joined the firm in 1988, becoming a partner in 1989.

PAINTER, Nick
Garretts, Leeds (0113) 207 9000
Partner in Corporate/Commercial Department.
Specialisation: Principal area of practice is corporate finance. Work includes flotations, UK and cross-border mergers and acquisitions, demergers and corporate reconstructions, management buy-outs, transport infrastructure projects and corporate joint ventures. Other areas of practice are competition law, employee share schemes and local authority law. Represents clients in monopolies and mergers enquiries and Competition Act investigations, advises on employee share ownership plans, especially in relation to employee buy-outs, and advises on local authority statutory powers. Important assignments include the sale of West Midlands Travel Ltd by West Midlands PTA (1991), the flotation of Holliday Chemical Holdings PLC (1993), the management/ employee buy-out of London United Busways Ltd from London Regional Transport (1994), and representing Stagecoach Busways in the North East of England buses-monopoly enquiry (1995/6). Major clients include quoted and unquoted companies, particularly in the transport and chemical sectors, and Passenger Transport Authorities and Executives. Regular seminar speaker. Fixed fees by prior arrangement.
Prof. Memberships: Law Society, Leeds Law Society.
Career: Qualified in 1983. With *Howes Percival*, Northampton 1983-85, then *Simpson Curtis*

1985-94 (Partner from 1988). Joined *Garretts* as a Partner in May 1994.
Personal: Born 3rd February 1959. Educated at Gowerton Comprehensive School 1970-74, Haverfordwest Grammar School 1974-77 and Keble College, Oxford 1977-80. Leisure interests include cricket, squash, badminton, films, outward bound activities and hill walking. Lives in Ilkley, West Yorkshire.

PASS, Jamie
Dickinson Dees, Newcastle upon Tyne
(0191) 279 9000
Specialisation: Mainstream corporate finance, mergers & acquisitions and new issues work.
Prof. Memberships: Law Society.
Career: Educated Doncaster Grammar School & Jesus College, Cambridge. *Clifford Chance* 1986-1992. Joined *Dickinson Dees* in 1992. Partner 1995.
Personal: Born Doncaster, resides Newcastle upon Tyne.

PHILLIPS, R.J.
Robert Muckle, Newcastle-upon-Tyne
(0191) 232 4402
Specialisation: General Corporate Finance. Partner – quality commercial work for both public and private companies. Specialisation in corporate sales and acquisitions and investment venture capital.
Career: Educated, Ponteland Comprehensive School; Leeds University (1987 LLB Hons); Chester Law College. Articled *Denton Hall*; work in corporate finance sector; 2 years with *Memery Crystal*. Qualified 1990. Partner 1997.

RICHARDSON, Ian A.
Eversheds, Leeds (0113) 243 0391
Specialisation: Handles all aspects of corporate finance work, venture capital, MBOs and MBIs, concentrating in particular on acting for management teams. Acquisitions and Disposals. Acting for several listed companies in respect of their M&A work. Director of Firth Holdings plc and Peterhouse Group plc both fully listed companies. He is joint author of "Running a Partnership," published by Jordons.
Prof. Memberships: Law Society.
Career: Qualified in 1983 and became a Partner in 1989.
Personal: Born on 23rd April 1959. Lives near Boroughbridge, North Yorkshire. Leisure interests: running, sport and history.

SMART, Peter C.
Walker Morris, Leeds (0113) 283 2500
Head of Corporate Department.
Specialisation: Main areas of practice are corporate finance, M & A work, venture capital and shareholder disputes.
Prof. Memberships: Law Society.
Career: Qualified in 1979, having joined *Walker Morris* in 1977. Became a Partner in 1981, Managing Partner in 1993 and Head of Corporate in 1998.

SPRIGGS, Michael I.
Eversheds, Newcastle upon Tyne
(0191) 261 1661
Partner in Corporate Group
Specialisation: Corporate finance, covering MBOs, MBIs, mergers and acquisitions, joint ventures, shareholder disputes and listed company work. Also public sector work, with particular experience of privatisation and development work. Legal Practice Course

external examiner. Member of advisory board of Durham University Careers Advisory Service.
Prof. Memberships: Law Society, CBI, BURA.
Career: Banker with Standard Chartered Bank, Hong Kong 1979-81. Trained at *Frere Cholmeley*, London. Qualified as a solicitor in 1985. Joined *Wilkinson Maughan*, becoming Partner in 1987.

WELCH, Hugh B.
Robert Muckle, Newcastle-upon-Tyne
(0191) 232 4402
Specialisation: General Corporate Finance. Partner, head of commercial department and joint head of corporate finance unit: scope of work includes a wide range of high quality commercial work for both public and private companies with sector specialisation in tax-driven corporate structures and reorganisations and in the corporate needs of substantial manufacturing companies.
Career: Articled *Dickinson Dees*: qualified 1981: assistant solicitor 1979-1985: partner *Robert Muckle* 1985: current directorships:

Cedardell Ltd: Cederdell Inc; Mobex North East Ltd.
Personal: Educated at St Bees School, Cumbria; Cambridge University (1979 BA Hons, 1983 MA Hons Evan Lewis Thomas Law Scholar).

WHELDON, Timothy
Addleshaw Booth & Co, Leeds
(0113) 209 2000
Partner in Corporate Finance Group.
Specialisation: Corporate/commercial; PFI; project finance; venture capital.
Prof. Memberships: Law Society.
Career: Articled *Gosschalks*, Hull; qualified 1983; partner 1985 to 1990. Joined the firm as partner in 1990.
Personal: Hymers College, Hull; Manchester Polytechnic BA(Hons) Law and French. Born 1959; lives in Leeds.

WOOD, Julia
Dibb Lupton Alsop, Sheffield (0345) 262728
Specialisation: Corporate finance, mergers and acquisitions, MBOs, stock exchange.
Career: Reading University. Articled with *Broomheads*. Qualified 1987; 1993 partner *Dibb Lupton Broomhead*.
Personal: Hiking, gardening.

WRIGHT, Graham
Dickinson Dees, Newcastle upon Tyne
(0191) 279 9000
Specialisation: Main practice areas are mergers and acquisitions, yellow and blue book work; corporate finance.
Career: Qualified 1972. Joined *Dickinson Dees* in 1975. Partner Company and Commercial Department 1977. Managing Partner 1990. Senior Partner 1997. Council Member of Northern Region CBI.
Personal: Educated at Queen Elizabeth Grammar School, Darlington and Jesus College, Cambridge.

NORTH WEST

LEADING FIRMS · NORTH WEST
ADDLESHAW BOOTH & CO Manchester
DIBB LUPTON ALSOP Liverpool, Manchester
EVERSHEDS Manchester
HALLIWELL LANDAU Manchester

HIGHLY REGARDED FIRMS
Brabner Holden Banks Wilson Liverpool
Chaffe Street Manchester
Cobbetts Manchester
Davies Wallis Foyster Liverpool, Manchester
Garretts Manchester
Hammond Suddards Manchester
Slater Heelis Manchester
Wacks Caller Manchester
Aaron & Partners Chester
Berrymans Lace Mawer Liverpool
Cartmell Shepherd Carlisle
Kuit Steinart Levy Manchester
Pannone & Partners Manchester

Addleshaw Booth & Co (16ptnrs/30assts) Rated as "clear number one in Manchester"and "the IBM of the Manchester market" with an "enviable client base." "They have enough good quality bodies to throw at a deal," commented competitors. However, have recently lost department head Andrew Needham who is co-founding an IT services business. Senior partner *Paul Lee* is well reputed for closing deals. Team includes *Darryl Cooke* seen as "extremely good, practical and down to earth" who has "done well – a smart operator and the VC's like him." *Keith Johnston* "inspires confidence in clients" together with *Richard Lee* ("a star") and *Paul Devitt*.
Clients/Work: Acting for Design to Distribu-

tion Ltd and Celestia International Inc.in acquisition of part of ICL's UK business involving assets in excess of £100m. Advising Barlows plc in £46.3m recommended takeover of Rowlinson Securities plc. Acting in £43m acquisition by Dan-Loc Corporation of the Flexitallic business of T&N plc.
Dibb Lupton Alsop (Liverpool: 5ptnrs/7assts. Manchester:10ptnrs/6assts) Seen as high profile in the venture capital market and busy. *Andrew Holt* has a reputation as a buy-outs specialist with "a lot of work from 3i." *Michael Prince* has a good reputation and *William Holt* is "loved by clients." *David Cadwallader* is well regarded in the Liverpool market. *Jonathan Brown* is also part of the team. **Clients/Work:** Acting for MTL Rail Ltd in acquisition and funding of Regional Railways North East. Acting for T&N plc on £20m disposal in MBO of its Tenmat Division. Acting for management team in £18m MBO of the Engineering Division of Graystone plc.
Eversheds (9ptnrs/13assts) Does not have the reputation of the Leeds office but is nonetheless popular with accountants. Star player *Edward Pysden* is "a great lawyer – he rolls up his sleeves and does the details," known for having "the monopoly on work for Bodycote International." "Self-reliant." *Geoffrey Blower* and "hard working" *Daniel Hall* are well regarded. **Clients/Work:** Acting for Quicks Group plc on its £45.5m superclass 1 acquisition of Group's motor retailing division and the associated £15m rights issue and £2.3m placing. Acting for Bodycote International plc on a £99.3m rights issue and £60.7m acquisition of HIT SA. Acting for the Car Group plc on its acquisition of Empress.
Halliwell Landau (12ptnrs/14assts) Department is "busy" with "good technical lawyers" they have been visible in the market recently. Known name *Rebecca Grisewood*

is "pretty good." **Clients/Work:** Acting for Farringford plc in £10m acquisition of Lingfield Park 1991 Ltd. £16m MBO of Curtina Ltd. Acting for NM Rothschild & Sons Ltd in the introduction of Lorien plc to the official list.
Brabner Holden Banks Wilson (4ptnrs 40-75% /3 assts 50%) "An excellent firm" that have gone up in the rankings. Their reputation is for acting for owner managed businesses, for which *Tony Harper* is rated. Competitors would have no hesitation in

LEADING INDIVIDUALS
NORTH WEST
PYSDEN Edward Eversheds
HOLT Andrew Dibb Lupton Alsop
LEE Paul Addleshaw Booth & Co
PRINCE Michael Dibb Lupton Alsop
COOKE Darryl Addleshaw Booth & Co
CRAIG Alexander Halliwell Landau
HALL Daniel Eversheds
LEE Richard Addleshaw Booth & Co
BLOWER Geoffrey Eversheds
CADWALLADER David Dibb Lupton Alsop
DOWNS William Hammond Suddards
GRISEWOOD Rebecca Halliwell Landau
HARPER Tony Brabner Holden Banks Wilson
HOLT William Dibb Lupton Alsop
JOHNSTON Keith Addleshaw Booth & Co
LUMSDEN Christopher Chaffe Street
MCMAHON Greg Garretts
O'CONNOR Mark Davies Wallis Foyster
STREET Robert Chaffe Street
WARBURTON Mark Slater Heelis

UP AND COMING · NORTH WEST
BROWN Jonathan Dibb Lupton Alsop
DEVITT Paul Addleshaw Booth & Co
FITZGERALD Sean Chaffe Street
SEE PROFILES AT END OF THIS SECTION

referring work. **Clients/Work:** Advising management team in £2.85m MBO of EPMoulding. Acting for management team in: £4m MBO of Hydraroll Ltd; MBI of A Warren & Sons.

Chaffe Street (6ptnrs/10assts) "Reasonable firm with a number of highly rated, good technical lawyers" including *Sean Fitzgerald, Christopher Lumsden* and *Robert Street.* **Clients/Work:** Acted for AM Paper in £145m HSBC investment in AM Paper Group. Acted for management in £6m+ MBO of Signs and Labels Ltd. Acted for shareholders in sale of Thompson Carmichael Holdings Ltd to Delaware Capital Holdings Inc.

Cobbetts (5ptnrs/4assts) Known for a strong emphasis on owner-managed businesses. Still seen as a "self confident" general practice "moving from strength to strength." **Clients/Work:** Acting for Lancashire County Council in a £50m disposal of an 80% interest in Lancashire Waste Services Ltd. Advising Alfred McAlpine plc in £6m disposal of the Ffestiniog Welsh Quarry Group. Acting for Cookson Group plc on £12m sale of its horticultural plastics business to Synbra (UK)Ltd.

Davies Wallis Foyster (6ptnrs/10assts) Have kept a low profile recently, *Mark O'Connor* is well regarded in the Liverpool office. **Clients/Work:** £60m acquisition on behalf of Caterpillar Inc. $1.3bn acquisition of UK automotive manufacturer Perkins on behalf of Caterpillar Inc. Princes acquisition of F.E. Barber drinks business from Hillsdown Holding plc.

Garretts (4ptnrs/6assts)The Andersens' connection has raised market doubts as to future deal flow. Generally seen as "patchy." However do have *Greg McMahon* who is highly regarded as an individual. **Clients/Work:** For Hampton Trust plc advising on a capital reduction and distribution of Australian listed securities together with £15m acquisition of property portfolio. £62m MBO of Kennedy Construction in association with Grant Thornton. £48m 3i funded MBO by Image Precision International of Brimar and Cintel.

Hammond Suddards (4ptnrs/10assts) Generally perceived as having fallen behind recently. The departure of Richard Burns to London to be Head of National Corporate Finance has not been viewed as positive for this office. However, newcomer to the rankings *William Downs* appears to be filling Burns' place "very well" **Clients/Work:** Acted for Fine Art Developments plc on demerger of Creative Publishing plc for £140m. Acted for Ultraframe plc on its £135m flotation. Advising Graystone plc on £18m MBI sale of engineering department.

Slater Heelis "A solid firm with good people with a strong set of traditional values" Partner *Mark Warburton* is seen as "good."

Wacks Caller (5ptnrs/5assts) Reputed for having "decent clients"and for "doing a lot of venture capital work" **Clients/Work:** Acting for Premier Group plc in full list flotation and subsequent takeover. Handling the AIM flotation of Independent British Healthcare plc and takeover by Community Health Group plc. Acting for Carabiner International Inc in acquisition of WCT Live Communications Ltd.

Aaron & Partners (5ptnrs p/t, 6assts p/t) Regarded as "a small niche outfit." **Clients/Work:** Acting in telecommunications business acquisition approx. £8.5m. Acting in MBO of regional manufacturing business from Scottish parent company.

Berrymans Lace Mawer (6ptnrs/4assts) Small practice worthy of note. **Clients/Work:** Acting for T J Hughes plc in placing and open offer of new shares fully underwritten by Charterhouse Tilney Securities Ltd for £6.6m. Acting for API Ltd in sale of shares in excess of £7m to US corporation Harbinger.

Cartmell Shepherd Felt to "have got the Carlisle market sown up."

Kuit Steinart Levy (4ptnrs/4assts) Seen as doing good work for their well known client Seaton Health Care plc. **Clients/Work:** AIM float of Hartford Group plc. Sale of Stationary Box Ltd to MBI funded by PRECOOA.

Pannone & Partners (8ptnrs p/t/4assts p/t) Known for having work from Swedish banks, a reasonable practice with some international connections. **Clients/Work:** Advising Prestolite Electric Inc and subsidiary in purchase of Lucas' heavy duty products division in UK, South Africa and Argentina, initial consideration £25m. Advising Newell Co. in recent corporate reorganisation of its UK subsidiaries.

LEADERS' PROFILES · NORTH WEST

BLOWER, Geoffrey
Eversheds, Manchester (0161) 832 6666
Head of Corporate Department, Eversheds, Manchester.
Specialisation: Main area of practice is Corporate Finance including mergers and acquisitions, flotations, management buy-outs, disposals, stock exchange and "Blue Book" work and non-contentious corporate work. Sector experience includes dairy industry, pharmaceuticals, leisure, automotive and engineering. Principal transactions include the Co-operative Wholesale Society's £111m disposal of its Food Manufacturing Group; again for the Co-operative Wholesale Society he spearheaded the team which dealt with the complex exchange of assets and businesses with Dale Farm Dairy Group where the total assets involved were £30m; Quicks Group Plc acquisition of the Motor Retail Division of Coverdale Group plc for £45.5m; Stanley Leisure plc in its £15m recommended take-over of Gus Carter plc. Also acts for Waterford Foods, McLeod Russel Holdings plc and Eurocamp plc.
Prof. Memberships: Law Society, Securities Institute.
Career: Qualified in 1972 and became a Partner in 1974.
Personal: Born 14th March 1948. Leisure pursuits include walking, cricket and theatre.

BROWN, Jonathan A.
Dibb Lupton Alsop, Liverpool (0345) 262728
Partner
Specialisation: Main area of practice is corporate finance work. Work includes acquisitions, disposals, flotations, joint ventures and venture capital. Major transactions include (acquisition) MTL London Northern Ltd; (flotations) Cammell Laird Holdings Plc and Dawn Til Dusk Holdings Plc; (acquisition) Stalbridge Linen Services for Johnson Group Cleaners Plc; (joint venture) Benfield Sports International Ltd; (acquisition) The Gibraltar Dockyard from the Government of Gibraltar.
Prof. Memberships: Law Society.
Career: Sheffield University 1984-1987, SOL (Hons). Chester College of Law 1988. Admitted October 1990 *Addleshaw Sons & Latham* (1990-1993), *Dibb Lupton Alsop* (*Alsop Wilkinson*) 1993 – to date. Partner 1996.
Personal: Born 18 September 1966. Golf (Caldy G.C. & Formby Hall Golf Club Plc). Cricket (Neston C.C.), Hockey (Neston C.C.). The Liverpool Racquet Club.

CADWALLADER, David H.
Dibb Lupton Alsop, Liverpool (0345) 262728
Head of Liverpool Corporate Department.
Specialisation: Main area of practice: Corporate Finance. Work includes mergers and acquisitions, MBO/MBIs (advising institutional investors and management teams), venture and development capital, flotations, joint ventures. In addition to transactional work has advised upon and negotiated 'key' commercial contracts and project agreements.
Prof. Memberships: Law Society.
Career: Qualified in 1987. Joined *Alsop Stevens* in 1985. Became partner in 1990.
Personal: Attended Liverpool University and Chester College of Law. Leisure interests include, family activities, golf and football. Lives in Parbold, West Lancashire.

COOKE, Darryl J.
Addleshaw Booth & Co, Manchester (0161) 934 6000
Partner in Corporate Finance Group.
Specialisation: Principal areas of practice are venture capital, management buy-outs and corporate finance. Author of 'Management Buy-outs' (FT: Law and Tax); 'Venture Capital: Law and Practice' (FT: Law and Tax) and 'Due Diligence: A Practical Guide' (Sweet & Maxwell).
Career: Became a Partner at the firm in 1995.
Personal: Born 1st January 1959. Educated at Hulme Grammar School, Oldham, and Leeds University (LLB, LLM). Plays golf and squash in his spare time as well as fell running. Lives in Kerridge, Cheshire.

CRAIG, I. Alexander
Halliwell Landau, Manchester
(0161) 835 3003
Partner, Head of Corporate Department.
Specialisation: Work includes MBOs and MBIs, many in excess of £25m; and flotations, mergers, sales and acquisitions. Specialist in institutional fundraising in the hitec/biotec area. Has spoken at numerous seminars and conferences.
Prof. Memberships: Law Society, Institute of Management, Securities Institute.
Career: Qualified in 1985, joining *Halliwell Landau* in the same year. Became a Partner in 1989.
Personal: Born 28th September 1957. Attended Sheffield University 1979-82 then College of Law 1983. Public Company non executive director. Leisure interests include soccer, squash and fell walking. Lives in Alderley Edge.

DEVITT, Paul
Addleshaw Booth & Co, Manchester
(0161) 934 6000
Partner in Corporate Finance Group.
Specialisation: Company and Corporate Finance, with particular specialisation in public company and public issue work: flotations; public issues; other public company/stock exchange-related advice; acquisitions and disposals of companies and businesses.
Prof. Memberships: Law Society.
Career: Qualified 1988. At *Turner Kenneth Brown* 1988-1991 and *Freshfields* 1991-1993. Joined the firm in 1993 (Partner from 1995).
Personal: Born 19th August 1964. Educated at Barrow-in-Furness Grammar School for Boys and University of Bristol (LL.B). Lives in Wilmslow.

DOWNS, William
Hammond Suddards, Manchester
(0161) 830 5000
Specialisation: Merger and acquisition work, flotations and Yellow Book work generally. Recent transactions include acting for Ultraframe PLC on its flotation and acting for Babcock International on the privatisation of the Rosyth Royal Dockyard.
Prof. Memberships: Law Society, RSA.
Career: Bradford Grammar School; Downing College, Cambridge.
Personal: Golf, tennis, gardening. Married with three children.

FITZGERALD, Sean
Chaffe Street, Manchester (0161) 236 5800
Specialisation: Corporate finance including mergers and acquisitons, venture and development capital and management buy-outs and buy-ins.
Prof. Memberships: Law Society.
Career: Articled at *James Chapman & Co.* Qualified in 1984. Joined *Chaffe Street* in 1988. Became a partner in 1991.
Personal: Born 22nd January 1960. Attended St Bede's College, Manchester and Hull University. Leisure interests include golf, cricket and football. Lives in Greenmount, Lancashire.

GRISEWOOD, Rebecca
Halliwell Landau, Manchester
(0161) 835 3003
Specialisation: Handles a range of corporate finance work principally mergers, acquisitions, venture and development capital transactions, MBOs and MBIs.
Career: Articled *Halliwell Landau*. Qualified 1987. Partner 1995, Corporate Development.

Personal: Born 3 January 1963. Liverpool University 1981-84 (LLB). Lives in Saddleworth.

HALL, Daniel C.J.
Eversheds, Manchester (0161) 832 6666
Specialisation: Mergers and acquisitions and corporate finance for public and private companies with a specialism in primary and secondary issues by public companies. Acted on the flotation in 1998 of James R. Knowles (Holdings) Ltd. Heads the Eversheds flotation and PLC know-how unit in Manchester. Expertise in Takeover Code Offers. Acted in May 1998 on the substantial acquisition by The Lubrizol Corporation of the fuel and lubricant additive business of British Petroleum in 9 jurisdictions. Visiting lecturer in law at Manchester University. Regular speaker at seminars and conferences.
Prof. Memberships: Law Society. British American Business Group. Institute of Directors.
Career: Trainee Solicitor, *Eversheds* (Manchester) 1985-1987, Solicitor (Company Dept.) *Clifford Chance* 1987-1992. Partner *Eversheds* (Manchester) 1992.
Personal: Born 29th August 1962. Educated Repton Preparatory School, Repton School, Bristol University and London College of Law. Leisure pursuits include golf and shooting. Lives in Wilmslow, Cheshire. Married.

HARPER, Tony
Brabner Holden Banks Wilson, Liverpool
(0151) 236 5821
Specialisation: Head of Corporate Department. Work includes corporate finance, MBOs, MBIs, venture and development capital, mergers, acquisitions and disposals, housing association funding.
Prof. Memberships: Law Society, Liverpool Law Society.
Career: Educated at St. Ambrose College, Altrincham; University of Liverpool. Articled at Brabner Holden 1981-1983 becoming Partner in 1986.
Personal: Born 1959. Interests include golf, fell walking, Round Table. Married with three children. Lives in Stockton Heath.

HOLT, Andrew D.
Dibb Lupton Alsop, Manchester
(0345) 262728
Specialisation: Company acquisitions and disposals, corporate finance, MBOs, MBIs and venture capital investments.

HOLT, William E.
Dibb Lupton Alsop, Manchester
(0345) 262728
Specialisation: Corporate Finance, mergers and acquisitions and takeovers.

JOHNSTON, Keith T.
Addleshaw Booth & Co, Manchester
(0161) 934 6000
Partner in Corporate Finance Group.
Specialisation: Principal area of practice is corporate finance mainly for listed companies. Other main areas of work include partnerships and joint ventures between public and private sector parties relating to economic development, regeneration and infrastructure initiatives, advice to public sector bodies on transactional and constitutional matters, PFI work and advice to private sector and public sector parties on grant assistance. (see separate entry)

Prof. Memberships: Law Society. Chairman: North West Company Secretaries' Forum. Head of Projects Group at the firm.
Career: Qualified in 1976. Became a Partner in 1981. 1991-94 Member of board of *Norton Rose* M5 Group. Board member of *Addleshaw Booth & Co*.
Personal: Born 3rd July 1952. Attended Bootle Grammar School 1963-70, then London University 1970-73 (External). Governor of The Grange School, Hartford, Cheshire. Leisure pursuits include badminton (Manchester League), chess and tennis. Lives in Hale, Cheshire.

LEE, Paul
Addleshaw Booth & Co, Manchester
(0161) 934 6000
Senior Partner and Chairman of the Board of *Addleshaw Booth & Co*, Partner in the Corporate Finance Group.
Specialisation: Work covers acquisitions and disposals for both listed and non-listed companies. MBOs and venture capital specialising in strategic advice and business planning. Has acted on numerous large transactions including acquisition of Thomson Newspapers by Trinity International for £327.5m in 1995, the agreed Barlows plc offer for Rowlinson Securities plc valued at £46.5m in 1997 and the sale of Mottram Group for £62m in 1998. Addresses conferences and seminars.
Career: Qualified 1970. Joined the firm in 1970, becoming a Partner in 1973, Managing Partner in 1991 and Senior Partner in 1997.
Personal: Born 26th January 1946. Attended Manchester Central Grammar School, then Clare College, Cambridge. Director of several companies, both public and private, including textiles, banking, and property. Deputy Chairman of the CBI -North West. Keenly interested in art and education. Chairman of the Royal Exchange Theatre. Chairman for the Governors of Chethams School of Music and a Board member of the Royal Northern College of Music. Director of Opera North and Northern Theatre Ballet. Leisure interests include the arts, sport and wine. Lives in Manchester.

LEE, Richard N.F.
Addleshaw Booth & Co, Manchester
(0161) 934 6000
Partner in Corporate Finance Group.
Specialisation: Main area of practice is corporate finance. Work covers mergers and acquisitions, including City Code take-overs, flotations and secondary issues. Also deals with general corporate work including Stock Exchange compliance. Flotations have included Airtours plc, BWI plc, Manchester United plc, Gradus Group plc and Nord Anglia Education plc (acting for company) and Lilliput Group plc and JJB Sports plc (acting for sponsor). Equity issues have included BWI plc, Airtours plc and European Colour plc Rights Issues and Airtours plc and BWI plc Open Offers (acting for company) and Rexmore plc Open Offer (acting for sponsor). Acted in Airtours plc's acquisitions of Pickfords Travel Service Ltd and Hogg Robinson Leisure Travel, in Trinity International Holdings plc's acquisition of Scottish & Universal Newspapers Ltd, in Whitecroft plc's sale of its Housebuilding Division and in the sale of Mottram Group plc's UK businesses to Heywood Williams Group plc. Advised Airtours plc in relation to the £100million subscription, and associated partial offers, by Carnival Corporation, Rexmore plc in relation to its

recommended takeover by Roseby's plc, Gradus Group plc in its recommended takeover by Headlam Group plc and Barlows plc in its recommended takeover of Rowlinson Securities plc.

Prof. Memberships: Law Society, Manchester Law Society.

Career: Qualified in 1983 with *Rowe & Maw* before joining the firm in 1986. Became a Partner in 1988.

Personal: Born 27th March 1959. Educated at Sexey's Grammar School, Blackford, Somerset 1970-77 and Trinity College, Cambridge 1977-80. Leisure interests include sport and raising children. Lives in Wilmslow, Cheshire.

LUMSDEN, Christopher
Chaffe Street, Manchester (0161) 236 5800
See under Banking, p. 146

MCMAHON, Greg
Garretts, Manchester 0161 228 0707
Specialisation: Venture and development capital, MBOs, MBIs, acquisitions and disposals and reorganisations of public and private companies and businesses. Public and private infrastructure projects.

Prof. Memberships: Law Society.

Career: Qualified 1985. Articled at *Addleshaw Sons & Latham* 1983 – 1985. Partner 1991 – 1995. Joined *Garrett & Co.* as a Partner in 1995.

Personal: Born 21 September 1960. Educated at Xaverian College, Manchester and Manchester University (LLB (Hons) 1982) and College of Law, Chester. Interests include hill walking, cooking and Oldham Athletic. Lives in Oldham.

O'CONNOR, Mark I.
Davies Wallis Foyster, Liverpool
(0151) 236 6226

PRINCE, Michael J.
Dibb Lupton Alsop, Liverpool (0345) 262728
Regional Managing Partner.

Specialisation: Main area of practice is corporate finance. Work includes MBOs, venture and development capital, mergers and acquisitions and flotations. Also handles corporate joint ventures. Author of various articles in local and national newspapers and in Investors Chronicle. Has addressed numerous conferences and seminars.

Prof. Memberships: Law Society.

Career: Qualified 1979. Worked with *Addleshaw Sons & Latham* 1977-81, then for 3i plc 1981-86 as Legal Adviser. Joined *Alsop Wilkinson* as a Partner in the Corporate Department in 1986.

Personal: Born 20th December 1954. Attended Birmingham University. Committee Member of Fairbridge Trust (charity), Liverpool Chamber of Commerce (council member). Leisure interests include golf, tennis, squash and skiing. Lives in Aughton, Lancashire.

PYSDEN, Edward
Eversheds, Manchester (0161) 832 6666
Senior Partner specialising in Corporate and Commercial work.

Specialisation: Corporation finance covering flotations, acquisitions, MBOs and Yellow Book work, recently with a great deal of international flavour. In the last 18 months he has led Bodycobe's £60million acquisition of HIT s.a., a French company listed on the Lyon Stocks Exchange and other acquisitions in Europe and the US. For five years he has been voted top North West Corporate Lawyer by readers of Insider Magazine. Lectures on Company Law at the Manchester Business School and the Henley and Ashridge Schools of Management.

Director of Brukens Thermotreat AB and Marketing Manchester.

Prof. Memberships: Securities Institute, Law Society, Institute for Fiscal Studies.

Career: Articled at *Alexander Tatham* 1970-72 and became a Partner in 1974. Appointed Senior Partner of the firm (now *Eversheds, Manchester*) in 1993.

Personal: Born 6th May 1948. Attended Dulwich College 1959-60, King's School, Macclesfield 1960-66, and Manchester University 1966-69. Leisure pursuits include golf, real tennis, classical music, food and wine. Lives in Macclesfield.

STREET, Robert H.
Chaffe Street, Manchester (0161) 236 5800
Partner in Company/ Commercial Department.

Specialisation: Handles all areas of company commercial work including corporate finance, company and business acquisitions and disposals, intellectual property and commercial contracts.

Prof. Memberships: Law Society.

Career: Qualified in 1975. Articles at *Coward Chance*. Became a Partner at *Harold Chaffe & Co.* in 1978. Partner at *Chaffe Street* since 1983.

Personal: Born 25th May 1951. Involved with North West Kidney Research. Leisure interests include golf, cricket, fell walking and skiing. Lives in Pott Shrigley, Cheshire.

WARBURTON, Mark
Slater Heelis, Manchester (0161) 228 3781
Specialisation: Company and Commercial and Commercial Property.

Career: Articled: Slater Heelis. Qualified: 1975. Partner Slater Heelis 1986.

Personal: Born 1950. Education: Kings School Chester and Selwyn College Cambridge. Resides Wilmslow. Leisure: Golf.

SCOTLAND

Dundas & Wilson CS (13ptnrs/28assts) The reputation of the Glasgow office has been augmented by the merger this year with Dorman Jeffrey and they are thought to benefit from Andersens. Strong in general corporate finance although not as high profile in the venture capital market, despite recruiting a new partner with VC experience. Once exclusively Shetland Islands Counsel *David Hardie* is a "leading light," *Christopher Campbell* is regional managing partner for Andersens northern legal network, *Maureen Coutts* is "efficient and practical," *Kenneth Rose* is "reasonable." *Brian Dorman,* thought to be one of the bonuses of the merger, is seen as "extremely competent." **Clients/Work:** Acting for Dunedin Enterprise Investment Trust plc in its £20m hostile offers for Baronsmead Investment Trust plc. Acting for Scottish Hydro-Electric's £100m acquisition of Norweb's interest in the Keadby joint venture power project. Acting in the MBO of Johnston Press plc's bookbinding division.

Dickson Minto WS (11ptnrs up to 95%;

41assts) "Doing a lot of VC and banking," they are highly rated for their "solid approach, quality and commercial attitude" Strong on quoted work. "Legend" and "highly motivated"*Bruce Minto* has led some substantial M&A's coordinated with the London Office. *Roddy Bruce* is seen as "first class professional operator," *Kevan McDonald* is also part of the team. **Clients/Work:** Acting for Somerfield in the £1.6bn merger with Quicksave. Acting for Streamline Holdings plc in £200m recommended bid by Jarvis plc. Advising Newco and the management team in £70m IBI from Fenner plc of its automotive parts business worldwide.

Maclay Murray & Spens (16 ptnrs (2 in London office); 20 assts) Highly rated by venture capitalists and holding on to their big Scottish plc's. They are "snapping at Dickson Minto's heels." *Ian Lumsden* "knows his law and is a good man to have around." *Bruce Patrick* has some reputational ground to make up but is seen as "intelligent and able." Department head, known for private equity MBOs, *Magnus Swanson* is considered "brilliant" and "pragmatic" – favoured

lawyer for some VC's, he is also "easy going and pleasant." New name to the list managing partner *Michael Walker* is rated by peers and VC's alike. **Clients/Work:** Acting in the £1.9bn demutualisation of Scottish Amicable. Acting on the refinancing of Sports Division. Acting in the institutional purchase by 3i of Eagle Taverns.

McGrigor Donald (9ptnrs/12assts) Doing some good work but thought by some to be "off the boil" recently. The "dogged" *Morag McNeill,* seen as "incisive and good," was voted , Top Corporate Lawyer' by peers in an informal cocktail party pole conducted by 3i. "Extremely competent and bright"*Colin Gray* moves up the rankings this year. **Clients/Work:** Acting for 3i in £70m investor lead buy-out of Grampian Pharmaceuticals Ltd from Grampian Holdings plc. Flotation of BCO Technologies plc with market capitalisation of £25m. Flotation of Core Group plc with market capitalisation of £125m.

Shepherd & Wedderburn WS (11ptnrs/20assts) Have opened a Glasgow office this year and are known for their stock exchange work and Bank of Scotland connection. The retirement of former leading name Ian Inglis is not seen as causing difficulties. *Iain Meiklejohn* is well known, *Paul Hally* leads the department's PFI unit. As department head *James Will* is seen as wearing his marketing hat to the detriment of his deal making profile but there is little doubt about his capabilities when he does have his sleeves rolled up. **Clients/Work:** Acting for Bank of Scotland in its £90-100m recommended offer for EFT Group plc. Acting for Ivory and Sime plc in its £132m merger with Friends Provident. Acting for Scottish Settlements, the joint venture between Scottish Power and Scottish Hydro Electric to oversea the Scottish Electricity market trading valued at £1bn per annum.

Burness (8ptnrs/7assts) Known for quality banking work. "Respected and active,"*Andrew Sleigh* thought to have "suffered a bit from too much of an insolvency bias" is now seen as having "a finger in every corporate pie." *John Rafferty* gets the job done. **Clients/Work:** Acting for The Royal Bank of Scotland in a revolving credit facility for the Donside Paper Mill MBI. Advising and providing all Phase I finance documentation for £36m debt and equity financing of Fife Power. Acting for SEET plc in setting up bank facilities for its acquisition of the Banner Group.

MacRoberts (Glasgow: 4ptnrs:1 p/t; 7 assts. Edinburgh: 1ptnr/1asst) "An excellent practice" favoured for smaller to medium sized deals by the VC's. Top name *Ian Dickson* is "a fine man to deal with" who does a "good solid job" and *Neil Cunningham* is seen as strong on unquoted work. Up and coming and "understated"*James McGinn* is seen as having a "strong practice and a pleasant style." **Clients/Work:** Acting for Johnston

Press plc in its agreed £54m offer for Home Counties Newspapers Holdings plc. Acting for Inner workings Group plc in its AIM placing of Ordinary Shares. Acting for Semple Cochrane plc in its flotation on the London Stock Exchange.

Paull & Williamsons (6ptnrs/9assts) Seen as dominating the Aberdeen market. "A tight ship" with some impressive rainmakers including: "first class" *Sidney Barrie* who "handles his clients superbly, a high flying, practical lawyer;" "good all rounder"*Gordan Buchan*, considered "excellent and able." **Clients/Work:** Acting for Asco Group plc in substantial share consideration acquisitions of two John Wood Group plc logistics companies. Acting in the MBO of Ensign Geophysics Ltd. Acting for CHC Helicopter Corporation of St John's, newfoundland, Canada of Hunting Airmotive Ltd.

Biggart Bailie (1ptnr 100%, 4ptnrs 30%/ 1asst 100%/8assts 30%) Emphasis on equity investments and AIM listings. Ranked partner *Campbell Smith* is "super." **Clients/Work:** Acting for Southern Water plc in the Scottish part of the £90m divestment programme of 16 English businesses. Advising the buy-out team in MBO of neo-natal testing unit from Shield Diagnostics Group plc. Acting in first joint list on AIM and DCM for UK nominated advisor Bell Lawrie White and Irish sponsors Goodbody Corporate Finance in £10m flotation of BCO Technologies.

Brodies WS (3ptnrs/7assts) Well regarded for some decent work. **Clients/Work:** Franchising of ScotRail on behalf of OPRAF (£1.6bn). Sykes Enterprises, Inc on the acquisition of the entire issued share capital of McQueen International Ltd for $70m. Advising on the raising, by way of prospectus, of £8m for Highland Timber plc and admission to AIM.

Tods Murray WS (5 ptnrs/8 assts) Known for good quality general corporate work. **Clients/Work:** Acting in the stock exchange placing of preference stock for the Bank of Scotland (£100m). Acting in the sale of part of the Global Group of companies (£18m). Admission to AIM of Dobbie's Garden Centre plc.

Fyfe Ireland WS Edinburgh "A small but quality corporate team" has impressed this year moving the firm up the ranks.

Henderson Boyd Jackson WS (6ptnrs/ 6assts) "High profile in a lot of the smaller deals" the Edinburgh office is "trying hard" and has raised the profile. **Clients/Work:** Acting in the listing of Heart of Midlothian plc. Acting in the raising of £28m for Greenshields Shipping Ltd. Advising in the Joe Bloggs acquisition of Elizabeth Emmanuel International.

Ledingham Chalmers (7ptnrs/6assts) Recently appointed to 3i's panel. Managing partner *David Laing* is "an excellent operator, liked by his clients." **Clients/Work:** Acting for the MBO/MBI team in £8m

acquisition of Ross & Bonnyman Ltd. Acting for ESL Group Ltd in £5m disposal to Wyko plc. Acting for shareholders including 3i and Abtrust Scotland Investment Company plc in £2.5m disposal of Abtex Computer Systems Ltd

McClure Naismith (6ptnrs /8assts) One partner down on last year the team is known for VC, M&A and banking work. **Clients/ Work:** Acting for the vendor shareholders in MBI of Lamar Industries Ltd. Acting for the management team in £13m MBI/IBO of Howden Packaging Equipment Ltd's English and Dutch interests.Acted for APC Ltd in further equity investment by 3i plc and Royal Bank of Scotland of £3.38m.

Bird Semple (1ptnr 95% 1ptnr 60%/ 2 assts 95% 4 assts 60%).Moving down the rankings this year as their market profile for pure corporate /corporate finance work is at a low ebb. Such work as is done is handled within the Techmedia and Corporate Property Departments. **Clients/Work:** Advising Integration Environmental Solutions in fund raising for product development project.

Iain Smith & Company (4ptnrs/3assts) "Pragmatic, practical and commercial." Corporate reputation hangs on the work of one large client. **Clients/Work:** Acting for

SEE PROFILES AT END OF THIS SECTION

Grampian Country Food Group Ltd in purchase of New market Foods Ltd and Halls of Broxburn. Acting in the IBI of Progenitive Services Ltd.

Steedman Ramage WS (2ptnrs/2assts) Have acquired an ex-Dickson Minto partner this year. Known to be working hard in the

market. **Clients/Work:** Acting for Stannifer Group Holdings in joint venture with J Sainsbury plc to acquire and develop a retail/leisure centre at Romford, Essex. Acting for Macdonald & Muir Ltd in £7m acquisition of Ardbeg business and distillery from Allied Domecq plc

Thorntons WS (2ptnrs /2assts) A well regarded Dundee firm. **Clients/Work:** Acting for Bank of Scotland in £7.5m MBO of Ross and Bonnyman. Advising Hillcrest Housing Association and Abertay Housing Association in £5m and £13m stock transfers, respectively.

LEADERS' PROFILES · SCOTLAND

BARRIE, Sidney
Paull & Williamsons, Aberdeen
(01224) 621621
Specialisation: Partner in the Corporate Department specialising in MBOs and acquisitions and disposals. Also advises on general corporate law, including reconstructions, investment documentation and contractual work.
Prof. Memberships: Law Society of Scotland; Society of Advocates in Aberdeen.
Career: Apprentice, James & George Collie 1971-73. Joined Paull & Williamsons 1973, partner 1978.
Personal: Educated at Robert Gordon's College, Aberdeen 1962-68 and at Aberdeen University 1968-71. Leisure pursuits include golf and watching football. Lives in Aberdeen. Born 14th June 1950.

BRUCE, Roderick L.
Dickson Minto WS, Edinburgh
(0131) 225 4455
Specialisation: General Corporate, Mergers and Acquisitions, Venture Capital, Re-organisation.
Prof. Memberships: Law Society of Scotland; Writer to the Signet.
Career: Boroughmuir Secondary School; Edinburgh University (LLB (Hons 2.1)).
Personal: Wife: Jane; Four children: 3 girls, 1 boy. Squash, skiing, golf, rugby (spectating), theatre.

BUCHAN, Gordon A.
Paull & Williamsons, Aberdeen
(01224) 621621
Specialisation: General corporate law, particularly acquisitions and disposals. Also oil and gas law.
Career: Qualified 1976; Partner at *Paull and Williamsons* since 1981. Non-executive director of Aberdeen Football Club.
Personal: Born 1952.

CAMPBELL, Christopher R.J.
Dundas & Wilson CS, Edinburgh
(0131) 228 8000
Managing Partner of *Dundas & Wilson* and Regional Managing Partner of *Garretts*.
Specialisation: Mergers and acquisitions, MBOs/MBIs and joint ventures. Advised Murray International Holdings Ltd on major re-organisation 1992; as part of a consortium funded by UK Know How Fund, provided advice on establishment of a commercial property market in St Petersburg 1992; advised Babtie Group Ltd on externalisation of Highways and Planning Department of Berkshire County Council (the largest local authority externalisation effected in the UK) 1993; acted for liquidators of Clydesdale Electrical Stores (largest liquidation in Scotland for ten years) 1994; advised Sidlaw Group on disposal of its Textiles Division to three MBO teams 1994-95; advised Murray International Holdings on sale of interests in Mimtec Ltd 1996;

acted for Sidlaw Group in disposal of its oil services division 1996.
Prof. Memberships: Writer to the Signet; Notary Public; Honorary Professor in Faculty of Law at University of Glasgow.
Career: Attended University of Edinburgh (LLB (Hons)). Articled *Dundas & Wilson CS*; qualified 1982; assistant solicitor 1982; Partner since 1987; Partner in Charge (Glasgow) since 1991; Managing Partner since 1996; Regional Managing Partner since 1996.
Personal: Born 1958. Resides Edinburgh, married with two children. Leisure interests include golf (Murrayfield Golf Club), football, music, photography.

COUTTS, Maureen S.
Dundas & Wilson CS, Edinburgh
(0131) 228 8000
Specialisation: Partner in Technology Group, Banking Group and PFI Group, specialising in outsourcing deals, technology biased commercial contracts, mergers, acquisitions and investments.
Prof. Memberships: The Law Society of Scotland; The Law Society of England and Wales; Writer to the Signet.
Career: Attended University of St Andrews (MA (Hons)). Articled *Birketts* 1975-1977; assistant *Middleton Potts & Co*, London 1977-1981; assistant *Dundas & Wilson CS* 1981-1984; Partner since 1984; Head of Corporate Department (administrative) 1986-1991; Head of mergers and acquisitions 1991-1996.
Personal: Born 1952. Resides East Lothian. Leisure interests include swimming.

CUNNINGHAM, Neil
MacRoberts, Glasgow (0141) 332 9988
Specialisation: Corporate Finance, Mergers and Acquisitions, Reconstructions and Partnership Law. Recent deals include acting for: Ford Motor Company Ltd in its sale of a regional distribution business; Cookson Group plc in the sale of its tool and mould manufacturing division; Kirker Enterprises Inc in establishing a new European group and its acquisition of ATC Cosmetics Ltd; R Frazier Group Ltd in relation to various matters; Morning Foods Ltd in its acquisition of Grampian Oat Products; Adams Hotels Ltd in its group reorganisation.
Prof. Memberships: Law Society of Scotland, Institute of Chartered Accountants in England & Wales, Institute of Chartered Accountants of Scotland.
Career: Price Waterhouse, Chartered Accountants, London and Glasgow 1984-1988; *Ledingham Chalmers*, Solicitors, Aberdeen 1989-1991; *MacRoberts*, Solicitors, Glasgow 1991 – to date (became a Partner in 1995).
Personal: Born August 6, 1964. Married with two daughters. Leisure interests include golf, football and squash.

DICKSON, Ian
MacRoberts, Glasgow (0141) 332 9988
Partner in Corporate Department.
Specialisation: Although Principal area of practice is corporate law and corporate finance, he also practices in electricity (and in particular) nuclear energy law. He acts for British Energy.
Prof. Memberships: Law Society of Scotland, International Bar Association, American Bar Association, Institute of Directors.
Career: Qualified 1971. Joined *MacRoberts* in 1973. Partner in 1977, now its Senior Corporate Partner. Non-executive Director of Johnston Press plc.
Personal: Born 10th April 1950. Attended Hillhead High School, Glasgow 1962-68; then Strathclyde University 1968-71. Chairman of Friends of the Beatson Oncology Centre. Leisure interests include music, golf and football. Lives in Glasgow.

DORMAN, A. Brian
Dundas & Wilson CS, Glasgow
(0141) 221 8586
Partner in Corporate Department.
Specialisation: Corporate and Commercial; mergers and acquisitions, management buyouts, sales and purchase of companies, refinancings and contract.
Prof. Memberships: Law Society of Scotland; Fellow of the Institute of Management.
Career: Qualified in 1969. Founded *Dorman Jeffrey & Co.* in 1979.
Personal: Born in 1945. Attended University of Glasgow 1963-67. Leisure interests include current affairs, music and occasional golf. Lives in Hurlford, Ayrshire.

GRAY, Colin F.
McGrigor Donald, Glasgow (0141) 248 6677
Specialisation: Acquisition and Sales of businesses/ companies (both listed and non-listed). Acting on Institutional Investments (on both debt and equity sides). General Corporate (including inward investment franchise, supply, licence etc. agreements). Last Quarter Deals: advised Bowie-Castlebank Group on the acquisition of Foto Processing (March 1998); Foxteq on inward nvestment into Scotland (April/May 1998); advised J.Trevor & Webster Group on merger with Gooch & Wagstaff (April/ May) 1998); advised Murray Johnstone on investment into Aberdeen F.C (May 1998); advised on the buy-out of the Merchandising Division of Hewden Stuart plc (June 1998).
Prof. Memberships: Law Society of Scotland; Law Society of England and Wales; Society of Scottish Lawyers in London.
Career: 1980-1984 Glasgow University (LLB, DipLP), 1987 to date *McGrigor Donald* (Partner – November 1991).

Personal: Married June 1993 to Lee (nee Robertson). Two children, Hannah and Oliver. Leisure interests include golf and trying to keep fit by cycling to and from work.

HALLY, Paul W.
Shepherd & Wedderburn WS, Edinburgh
(0131) 228 9900
Partner in Corporate Department.
Specialisation: Main area of practice is corporate finance. Work includes PFI mergers and acquisitions, MBOs, development and venture capital, banking and insolvency.
Prof. Memberships: Law Society of Scotland, Society of Writers to the Signet, Institute of Directors.
Career: Qualified in 1983. Worked at *Fyfe Ireland WS* 1982-4 and joined *Shepherd & Wedderburn WS* in 1984, becoming a Partner in 1987.
Personal: Born 23rd June 1959. Holds an LLB (Hons) Dip LP Edinburgh (1977-84).

HARDIE, David
Dundas & Wilson CS, Edinburgh
(0131) 228 8000
Specialsation: Partner, Head of Corporate Finance Group, specialising in corporate finance including flotations, rights issues, placings and takeovers, M & A and Blue Book and Yellow Book work. Acts for several of Scotland's leading companies including Scottish Media Group, Dawson International and Clydeport.
Prof. Memberships: Law Society of Scotland; International Bar Association.
Career: Attended University of Dundee (LLB (Hons)). Articled *Dundas & Wilson CS*; qualified 1978; solicitor 1978-1983, Partner 1983. Notary Public; Writer to the Signet.
Personal: Born 1954. Resides Edinburgh, married with three children. Leisure interests include swimming, golf and motor cycling.

LAING, David K.
Ledingham Chalmers, Aberdeen
(01224) 408510
Managing Partner.
Specialisation: Corporate finance; oil and gas. Clients include several oil and gas and oil service companies. Actively involved in firm's activities in Turkey, Azerbaijan and Falkland Islands.
Career: Qualified 1976. With *C & P H Chalmers* 1976-1990 (Partner from 1978) and with merged firm *Ledingham Chalmers* since 1991.
Personal: Born 17th June 1953. Educated at Robert Gordons College, Aberdeen and Edinburgh University. Interests include family, music and outdoors.

LUMSDEN, Ian G.
Maclay Murray & Spens, Edinburgh
(0131) 226 5196
igl@maclaymurrayspens.co.uk Partner in Corporate Finance Department.
Specialisation: Partner specialising in corporate finance and mergers and acquisitions. Work includes flotations, rights issues and other fund raising activity for plc's as well as acquisitions and disposals for listed and unlisted companies.
Career: Qualified in 1976. University of Cambridge (BA 1972), University of Edinburgh (LLB 1974). Spent two years working with *Slaughter and May* in London 1978-80.
Personal: Born 1951.

MCDONALD, Kevan
Dickson Minto WS, Edinburgh
(0131) 225 4455
Specialisation: Partner in Corporate Department. Main areas of practice are corporate and commercial: mergers and acquisitions, management buy-ins and outs, sales and purchases of companies and businesses, refinancings and corporate finance. Some recent deals include sale of the Cashmere Store of Scotland, Inveresk plc's Tissue Division, the MBI (£33m) of Donside Paper's businesses in the UK and USA from Fletcher Challenge (all 1997) and the £64m MBI of Fenner's Worldwide PT Distribution business for FPT Group Ltd and purchase of Klaper for Oil States Industries of the USA (1998).
Prof. Memberships: Law Society of Scotland, IBA.
Career: Qualified in 1982. Joined *Dickson Minto WS* as Senior Assistant in 1985 and assumed as a Partner in 1987.
Personal: Born 7th July 1958. Attended Aberdeen University 1976-79 (LLB) and Dundee University 1979-80 (Diploma in Petroleum Law). Leisure interests include fishing, swimming and squash. Lives in Edinburgh.

MCGINN, James
MacRoberts, Glasgow (0141) 332 9988
Specialisation: Corporate finance including mergers and acquisitions, management / institutional buy-outs / buy-ins and yellow book. Recent deals include the £45.5 million institutional buy-out of PSL on behalf of Nat West Equity Partners.
Prof. Memberships: Law Society of Scotland. Law Society (England and Wales)
Career: Qualified 1986 with *Levy & McRae* Glasgow. Joined *Taylor Vinters* Cambridge,1988, *Dickson Minto* London 1990 and *MacRoberts* Glasgow 1997. Partner 1998. University of Glasgow 1980 – 85.

MCNEILL, Morag
McGrigor Donald, Glasgow (0141) 248 6677
Specialisation: Corporate finance including mergers, acquisitions, MBOs, MBIs, IBOs and Flotations. Deals – acted. for 3i plc in the £74 million leveraged investor buy-out of Grampian Pharmaceuticals Ltd; for the shareholders of Mimtec Electronics in the sale of the Laird group plc; for the board of Ewart plc in the £25 million hostile bid by Dunloe House plc; for BCD Technologies plc in its flotation on Aim and the Dublin DCM; for Royal Bank of Scotland plc in the funding of the MBO of Broderick Structures Ltd from Riberoid plc.
Prof. Memberships: Member of the RSA.
Career: 1977-1983 Edinburgh University (LLB, DipL, LLM). 1983-1986 Trainee and Assistant, *Pairman Miller & Murray WS*, Edinburgh. 1986-1988 Assistant *Herbert Oppenheimer Nathan & Vandyke*, London. Joined *McGrigor Donald* July 1988, Associate November 1989, Partner May 1991, Head of Corporate Finance 1994. Member of McGrigor Donald Management Committee.
Personal: Married to David P. Sellar, advocate. No children. Leisure interests include Cinema, swimming and the arts.

MEIKLEJOHN, Iain M.C.
Shepherd & Wedderburn WS, Edinburgh
(0131) 228 9900
See under Banking, p. 146

MINTO, Bruce
Dickson Minto WS, Edinburgh
(0131) 225 4455
Founding Partner in Corporate Department.
Specialisation: Work includes Stock Exchange listings, Yellow Book work generally, mergers and acquisitions and institutional finance.
Prof. Memberships: Law Society of Scotland.
Career: Qualified in 1981. Formed *Dickson Minto WS* in 1985.
Personal: Born 30th October 1957. Attended Edinburgh University 1975-79. Leisure interests include golf, shooting and music. Lives in Edinburgh.

PATRICK, Bruce R.
Maclay Murray & Spens, Edinburgh
(0131) 226 5196
brp@maclaymurrayspens.co.uk
Specialisation: Partner experienced in all areas of corporate law but most notably in venture capital, MBOs/ MBIs, receiverships and ship finance. Vice-Convenor of the Company Law Committee of the Law Society of Scotland. Has been a panel solicitor for 3i plc for over 20 years.
Career: Qualified 1973. University of Oxford (BA 1967) and University of Edinburgh (LLB 1971). Former Managing Partner of *Maclay Murray & Spens* (1991-1994).
Personal: Born 1945.

RAFFERTY, John C.
Burness, Edinburgh (0131) 473 6000
Chairman and Partner in Corporate Department.
Specialisation: Main areas of practice are company law and corporate finance. Particular experience in AIM work, flotations of football clubs and venture capital investments (including EIS and reinvestment relief schemes). Has also worked on numerous capital reconstruction schemes and refinancings, especially debt roll-over and receivership acquisitions. Has developed various executive incentive schemes, including ESOPs. Member of the Securities Institute.

ROSE, Kenneth
Dundas & Wilson CS, Edinburgh
(0131) 228 8000
Specialisation: Partner in Corporate Finance Group involved in a large number of flotations and other share issues on the Official List and on AIM as well as public company takeovers and mergers. Considerable experience in recent years in the Lloyd's of London insurance market. Has also been involved in numerous MBO/MBIs, company acquisitions and disposals.
Prof. Memberships: The Law Society of Scotland.
Career: Attended University of Edinburgh (LLB Hons, DipLP). Trained *Dundas & Wilson CS*; qualified 1988; assistant 1988-1993; associate 1993-1995; Partner since 1995.
Personal: Born 1963. Resides Edinburgh. Leisure interests include golf (member of Royal Dornoch Golf Club) and music.

SIMMONS, William G.
Tods Murray WS, Edinburgh
(0131) 226 4771
See under Projects/PFI (Both), p. 693

SLEIGH, Andrew F.
Burness, Glasgow (0141) 248 4933
Specialisation: Has significant experience in all aspects of private company corporate

finance, including acting for management, venture capital houses and vendors involved in MBO and MBI transactions. Notable recent deals include acting for Royal Bank Development Capital in investment in Holiday Inn Express and acting for Big Beat International in acquisition of Simpson Trading Company which involved innovative corporate finance aspects.

SMITH, W.W. Campbell
Biggart Baillie, Glasgow (0141) 228 8000
Managing Partner and Partner in Corporate Department.
Specialisation: Main area of practice is corporate transactions. Work includes acquisitions and disposals of private companies and assets. Also insurance companies and friendly societies. Former Director of the Joint Insolvency Examination Board; member of several Law Society Committees.
Prof. Memberships: Law Society of Scotland, International Bar Association.
Career: Qualified in 1972. Assistant at *Herbert Smith & Co.* 1972-73 and *Biggart Baillie & Gifford* (now *Biggart Baillie*)1973-74. Became Partner there in 1974.
Personal: Born 17th May 1946. Attended Glasgow Academy 1951-65, St Catharine's College, Cambridge 1965-68 and the University of Glasgow 1968-70. Member of Convocation, University of Strathclyde; ex-Deacon Incorporation of Barbers, Glasgow. Leisure interests include golf, croquet, barbershop and choral singing. Lives in Glasgow.

SWANSON, Magnus P.
Maclay Murray & Spens, Glasgow
(0141) 248 5011
email: mps@maclaymurrayspens.co.uk
Partner in Corporate Department.
Specialisation: Partner and Head of Corporate Department. Principle areas of work are MBOs/MBIs, mergers and acquisitions and joint ventures. Recent transactions include the £30m MBI of Phillips International Auctioneers and the acquisition of Prestwick Airport by Stagecoach.
Career: Qualified in 1982. University of Edinburgh (LLB 1980). Spent 18 months working in New York with *Paul Weiss Rifkind Wharton & Garrison.* (1986-87).
Personal: Born 1958.

WALKER, Michael J.
Maclay Murray & Spens, Glasgow
(0141) 248 5011
Partner in Company Department and Managing Partner of firm since 1994.
Specialisation: Main area of practice is mergers and acquisitions, acting for Hewden

Stuart plc, Grampian Holdings plc, and many other listed company clients, including investment trusts.
Prof. Memberships: Law Society of Scotland, IBA.
Career: Qualified in 1976 and joined *Maclay Murray & Spens* in the same year. Became a Partner in 1981.
Personal: Born 23rd October 1952. Educated at Glenalmond College 1966-70 and Dundee University 1971-74. Non executive director of John Menzies plc, Scottish Screen Ltd, and other companies. Enjoys playing golf. Lives in Glasgow and London.

WILL, James R.
Shepherd & Wedderburn WS, Edinburgh
(0131) 228 9900
Partner in Corporate Department.
Specialisation: Main areas of practice are Stock Exchange work, company law, mergers and acquisitions, major start-ups and development capital, with emphasis on the technology sector.
Prof. Memberships: Law Society of Scotland, Society of Writers to Her Majesty's Signet.
Career: Qualified in 1978. With *Tods Murray WS* 1978-79 and *Clifford Chance* 1980-81. Joined *Shepherd & Wedderburn* in 1981 and became a Partner in 1982.
Personal: Born 30th April 1955. Educated at Merchiston Castle and Aberdeen University.

NORTHERN IRELAND

HIGHLY REGARDED FIRMS
NORTHERN IRELAND

Carson & McDowell Belfast
Elliott Duffy Garrett Belfast
L'Estrange & Brett Belfast

Arthur Cox Belfast
Mills Selig Belfast
Tughan & Co Belfast

Cleaver Fulton & Rankin Belfast
Johns Elliot Belfast
Johnsons Belfast
McKinty & Wright Belfast

Carson & McDowell (1 ptnr 75-100% 1 ptnr 100%/2 assts 100%) *Michael Johnston* is the lead name in this well respected practice known to be "pragmatic and easy to deal with." *David Jamison* has been made a partner this year. **Clients/Work:** Acting for Belleek Group in the purchase of the Aynsley China Group. Acting for NIE plc in the sale of its retail division and associated internal reorganisation. Acting for Electronic Manufacturing Systems Inc in the acquisition of Bemac Engineering Ltd.
Elliott Duffy Garrett (3ptnrs/3assts) "Experienced" firm. Heavyweight senior

partner *Brian Garrett* is rated for venture capital work. *Jacqueline Kerr* is also part of the team. **Clients/Work:** Acting in the MBI of the Northern Ireland Electricity plc "Shop Electric" business and chain. Acting for First Trust Bank in the joint venture and funding of the creation of Orchard Brae Developments with Morrison Homes of Scotland. Acting for Abbey Retail Park Ltd in the acquisition and development of retail park at Newtownabbey, County Antrim.
L'Estrange & Brett (3ptnrs/4assts) Highly rated by peers, the corporate finance work is led by the "excellent" *John Irvine.* *Richard Gray* has moved up the rankings this year due to further recognition of his expertise. **Clients/Work:** Advising W&R Barnett Ltd and IAWS Group plc on acquisition of animal feed business of Dalgety plc. Acting for Bemac Engineering Ltd on sale to EMS of Denver Colorado. Advising J P Cory Group on acquisition of Coen Group.
Arthur Cox (1ptnr/1asst) Although a small team seen as strong in corporate finance and banking the firm has a presence both sides of the border. **Clients/Work:** Acting for Supervalue & Central Distribution (Northern Ireland) Ltd part of the Musgrave Group of Companies in acquisition of 21 supermarket businesses from F A Wellworth & Co Ltd a subsidiary of Fitzwilton plc. Handled various deals totalling approx. £65m.
Mills Selig (2ptnrs/2 assts) Known as an all round corporate practice with "good expe-

rience." Ivan Selig is retired now. New name *Richard Fulton* is rated by VC's for his "commercial approach." **Clients/Work:** Acting in the sale of Masstock Arable (UK) Ltd to MBO team. Acting in four major investments on behalf of Hambros Northern Ireland Ventures Ltd and Enterprise Equity (NI)Ltd. Acting for shareholders of Connors Chemists Ltd in the £18m sale to Boots the Chemist Ltd.
Tughan & Co (1ptnr/2assts) Seen as having a "strong approach"*John-George Willis* leads the team. **Clients/Work:** Acting for Boots the Chemist Ltd in £18m acquisition of Connors Chemist Ltd. Acting for Glen Farm Holdings Ltd in £7.2m acquisition of the business of Lisburn Proteins from IAWS.

LEADING INDIVIDUALS
NORTHERN IRELAND

GARRETT Brian Elliott Duffy Garrett
IRVINE John L'Estrange & Brett

BOYD Frederick McKinty & Wright
BUTLER Maurice Johns Elliot
FULTON Richard Mills Selig
GRAY Richard L'Estrange & Brett
JOHNSTON Michael Carson & McDowell
MARSHALL John Johnsons
WILLIS John-George Tughan & Co

UP AND COMING

JAMISON David Carson & McDowell
KERR Jacqueline Elliott Duffy Garrett

SEE PROFILES AT END OF THIS SECTION

Cleaver Fulton & Rankin (3ptnrs/ 2assts) The firm has increased its corporate department this year. **Clients/Work:** Acting for Principal Healthcare Finance Ltd in £50m acquisition of 30 nursing homes owned by The Sandown Group. Acting for Fitzwilton plc in disposal of its interests in part of the Wellworth chain of supermarkets to the Musgrave Group.

Johns Elliot (3 ptnrs 40% /1 asst 30%) "Traditional" firm with increasing amount of joint venture work. *Maurice Butler,* seen as a good lawyer, continues to be well regarded. **Clients/Work:** Acting in sale of Northern Ireland Carpets Ltd, buy-out of Pilot Engineering Co. Ltd and sale of Maxwell Engineering Supplies.

Johnsons (1ptnr 50% /2assts 50%) Although a small department the "pragmatic and commercial" *John Marshall* is known for his deal closing abilities.

McKinty & Wright (2ptnrs/2assts) Small niche practice with venture capital at the forefront. *Frederick Boyd* is highly regarded. **Clients/Work:** Acting for 3i.

LEADERS' PROFILES • NORTHERN IRELAND

BOYD, Frederick W.J.
McKinty & Wright, Belfast (01232) 246751
Specialisation: Corporate and commercial law and practice (including corporate acquisitions and disposals, venture capital, lending, commercial property).
Prof. Memberships: Law Society of Northern Ireland.
Career: Graduated from Queen's University Belfast, in Law (LLB) in 1976 and in Business Studies (MBA) in 1977. Admitted to the role of Solicitors in Northern Ireland in 1978. Became partner in *McKinty & Wright* in 1983.

BUTLER, Maurice R.
Johns Elliot, Belfast (01232) 326881
Specialisation: Construction Claims/Arbitrations. Involved in two recent landmark appeals by way of Cases Stated to High Court from an arbritrator.
Prof. Memberships: Law Society of Northern Ireland.
Career: Graduated QUB 1965. Qualified 1968. Partner 1972, Senior/Managing Partner 1997. Appointed to Solicitor's Disciplinary Tribunal in 1986. Appointed Deputy County Court Judge in 1990.
Personal: Sailing (National Judge) and Bridge. Abbeyfield Society – Member of Regional Council and Chairman of Abbeyfield NI Development Society Ltd. Married with two daughters.

FULTON, Richard
Mills Selig, Belfast (01232) 243878
Specialisation: Main areas of practice are mergers, acquisitions, joint ventures and corporate finance generally. Represents two major venture capital houses. Has extensive experience in mergers and acquisitions and joint ventures both locally and internationally.
Prof. Memberships: Law Society of Northern Ireland.
Career: Queens University, Belfast LLB 1976. Qualified England and Wales 1980. Qualified Northern Ireland 1990. Formerly Senior Company/Commercial Partner with Blaser Mills. Joined *Mills Selig* January 1991.
Personal: Waterskiing, windsurfing, countryside, literature. Lives outside Belfast.

GARRETT, Brian
Elliott Duffy Garrett, Belfast (01232) 245034
Specialisation: Company and Commercial Law (including Banking).
Prof. Memberships: Fellow of Chartered Institute of Arbitrators. Member of Northern Ireland Law Society.
Career: Admitted as Solicitor in 1962. First place and Medal Solicitors' Finals. Senior Partner. Deputy County Court Judge. Author of various articles on Northern Ireland Law.
Personal: Former Visiting Fellow (Centre for International Affairs), Harvard University.

GRAY, Richard
L'Estrange & Brett, Belfast (01232) 230426
Partner, Corporate Department.
Specialisation: Main areas of practice are corporate, corporate finance and banking work. Also active in project finance and PFI work.
Prof. Memberships: Law Society of Northern Ireland; Law Society of England and Wales.
Career: Called to the Northern Ireland Bar in 1989. Admitted as a solicitor in England and Wales in 1992 and in Northern Ireland in 1992. Assistant solicitor with *Cameron Markby Hewitt* (now *Cameron McKenna*) 1989-1992. Partner in *L'Estrange & Brett* since 1996.
Personal: Born 1966. Education: Queen's University of Belfast (LLB). Course Adviser (Company Law): Institute of Professional Legal Studies, Belfast.

IRVINE, John W.
L'Estrange & Brett, Belfast (01232) 230426
Partner and Head of Corporate Department.
Specialisation: Main area of work: Corporate and commercial law.
Prof. Memberships: Law Society of Northern Ireland.
Career: Lecturer in law: Queen's University, Kingston, Ontario; University of Central Lancashire. Tutor in law, University of Exeter; Course tutor, Institute of Professional Legal Studies, Belfast. Qualified 1986. Partner in *L'Estrange & Brett* since 1988.
Personal: Born 1957: Education: Queen's University, Belfast (L.L.B.), Queen's University, Kingston, Ontario (L.L.M.)

JAMISON, David
Carson & McDowell, Belfast (01232) 244951
Specialisation: Emphasis on mergers acquisitions disposals and PFI transactions.
Prof. Memberships: Law Society of Northern Ireland and Law Society of England and Wales.
Career: Born 1964. Qualified 1989. University of Manchester. Articled and practised in London and latterly in North of England prior to returning to Northern Ireland in 1995. Partner 1998.

JOHNSTON, Michael C.
Carson & McDowell, Belfast (01232) 244951
Partner Company/ Commercial Department
Specialisation: Work includes mergers and acquisitions, PFI, management buy-outs and management buy-ins, venture capital, joint ventures and general corporate/ commercial advice.

KERR, Jacqueline A.
Elliott Duffy Garrett, Belfast (01232) 245034
Specialisation: All aspects of Corporate and Commercial law, secured lending and related banking law, including company and business acquisitions and disposals joint venture and management buy-ins and buy-outs, venture capital investments, company start ups etc.
Prof. Memberships: Law Society of England and Wales; Law Society of Northern Ireland.
Career: Qualified 1989. *Allen and Overy*, London 1989 – 1991. *Wilkinson Maughan*, Newcastle Upon Tyne 1991 – 1995. *Elliott Duffy Garrett* 1995 – date (admitted Partner July 1996).

MARSHALL, John
Johnsons, Belfast (01232) 240183

WILLIS, John-George
Tughan & Co, Belfast (01232) 553300
Specialisation: Handles all types of company and commercial work including mergers and acquisitions. MBOs/MBAs, joint ventures and public and private share issues.
Career: Qualified 1984. Assistant Solicitor at *Tughan & Co* 1987-92. Partner since 1992.
Personal: Educated at The Royal School, Dungannon and Queen's University Belfast. Interests include family and sport.

CRIME (GENERAL)

See also Commercial Fraud

RESEARCH: In compiling the tables, we consider all the information available to us, paying particular regard to the market research carried out by our team of ten qualified lawyers. (The researchers' details are set out on page three.) The rankings, therefore, reflect the opinion of the marketplace as revealed by systematic and objective research: see page four. (Our research is audited every year by the British Market Research Bureau.)

We do not consider size, volume of work or public exposure to be determinative. The tables are not exhaustive. We intend merely to provide the reader with a selection of firms considered by other practitioners to provide a high quality of service. The work of a number of the firms is detailed below, with any particular areas of expertise highlighted.

OVERVIEW: In London, Christian Fisher & Co, Magrath & Co, Offenbach & Co, Thanki Novy Taube and Whitelock & Storr move up to the top band following particular recommendation for these firms and their teams. In the South East, Gepp & Sons of Chelmsford move up to the top band and Woodfine Batcheldor replaces Gareth Woodfine & Partners. There are no movements in the South West, while in Wales, Graham Evans & Partners, Huttons and Robertsons move up to the top band. In the Midlands, Banners, Barrie Ward & Julian Griffiths and Brethertons move up to the top band and Fletchers of Nottingham and Kieran & Co of Chesterfield enter the table. In East Anglia, Overbury Steward & Eaton move up and Cole & Co enter the tables. In the North West, Garstangs and Miller Gardner move up and The Berkson Globe Partnership in Liverpool is a new entry, while in the north east there is no change. Scotland and Northern Ireland also remain substantially the same, with the addition of one new firm – McClenahan Crossey & Co in Coleraine.

LONDON

Bindman & Partners Although it covers every area of criminal defence work, the firm specialises in cases with civil liberties implications, including miscarriage of justice cases, defence of minority rights and public order charges, especially in connection with environmental and other public demonstrations. They also have a wealth of experience in defending against charges of terrorism and in representation at public inquiries. *Adrian Clarke* and *Neil O'May* are the firm's best known criminal practitioners.

B. M. Birnberg & Co Headed by *Gareth Pierce*, this firm maintains its excellent reputation in criminal defence work and linked matters including extradition, immigration, prison law and judicial review as it relates to prisoners' cases. The firm has particular strength in appellate work and has also represented convicts on two referrals to the Criminal Cases Review Commission.

Recently involved in the 'Whitemoore escape' trial which was stayed through the firm's efforts on the grounds of the effect on the prisoners of being incarcerated in secure units. Over the last year the firm has secured acquittals in three separate trials of difficult cases involving allegations of terrorism.

Christian Fisher & Co Regarded as a firm "par excellence", Christian Fisher & Co. deal with the general range of criminal work but are particularly well known for their involvement in allegations of terrorism. They are recommended for their efficient handling of serious cases. Move up to the top band following consistent praise. *Michael Fisher* has been recommended again.

Fisher Meredith (3ptnrs/7assts) Considered by some to be "by far the best criminal firm covering the south of London," this firm defends clients against the whole spectrum of criminal charges, including allegations involving drugs, sex and violence. They maintain a strong reputation

LEADING FIRMS · LONDON

BINDMAN & PARTNERS
B.M. BIRNBERG & CO
CHRISTIAN FISHER
FISHER MEREDITH
MAGRATH & CO
OFFENBACH & CO
POWELL SPENCER & PARTNERS
SAUNDERS & CO
TAYLOR NICHOL
THANKI NOVY TAUBE
WHITELOCK & STORR

ANDREW KEENAN & CO
DUNDONS
EDWARD FAIL BRADSHAW & WATERSON
HALLINAN, BLACKBURN, GITTINGS & NOTT
HENRY MILNER & CO
HICKMAN & ROSE
HODGE JONES & ALLEN
J.R. JONES
REYNOLDS DAWSON
RUSSELL-COOKE, POTTER & CHAPMAN
SIMONS MUIRHEAD & BURTON
T.V. EDWARDS
VENTERS & CO
VICTOR LISSACK & ROSCOE
WINSTANLEY-BURGESS

ALISTAIR MELDRUM & CO
CLAUDE HORNBY & COX
DARLINGTON & PARKINSON
DOWSE & CO
DUTHIE HART & DUTHIE
KINGSLEY NAPLEY
JOY MERRIAM & CO
MATTILA
McCORMACKS
TUCKERS
VENTERS
J.B. WHEATLEY & CO

for defence of psychiatrically disturbed clients and have successfully fought an appeal to have life sentences commuted to hospital orders. Through their involvement in R. v. Milton Browne, reported in The Times earlier this year, the firm played an instrumental role in the alteration of the courts' approach to cross-examination of witnesses by alleged rapists. *Stephen Hewitt* has an excellent reputation amongst practitioners.

Offenbach & Co *Bernard Carnell*'s team undertake a wide range of cases, including specialist work in connection with large scale drug supply, importation, VAT offences and confiscation. They have carved a niche in obscenity work and have conducted two cases in the past year involving allegations of obscenity on the internet. Move up to the top band.

Powell Spencer & Partners In north west London, *Greg Powell*, *Richard Spencer* and four other partners have built up a community-based practice with a strong presence in the magistrates' courts and on Duty Solicitor schemes. Heavyweight cases are regularly handled in all areas of criminal practice including importation and drug offences and homicide. One solicitor specialises in Youth Court work. Move to the top band following praise from peers.

Saunders & Co *James Saunders*' practice has recently been strengthened by the addition of two partners and the creation of a Prison Rights Team. The firm handles day to day crime including juvenile, sexual and motoring offences, homicide and armed robbery and has also been involved in high profile actions against the police. Recently acted in a large cocaine importation case involving complex issues of disclosure and Public Interest Immunity.

Taylor Nichol *James Nichol*, a highly regarded criminal and civil liberties practitioner, regularly handles cases attracting media attention. Also deals with rank and file cases of all descriptions. Team includes *Carolyn Taylor* and *Mark Ashford*, a specialist in Youth Court work.

Thanki Novy Taube Both *Girish Thanki* and his firm are highly respected nationwide. They handle large cases, often with an international element. Move up in the tables following praise from contemporaries.

Whitelock & Storr *John Zani* is consid-

ered by many to be outstanding in his field. He heads a team of five solicitors dedicated to criminal defence. The team boasts over twenty years experience in criminal work of all types but with notable specialisations in drugs, fraud and extradition. Recently the firm successfully represented two Italians in the Divisional Court, saving them from extradition. In one case, the Italian government has been refused leave to appeal to the House of Lords. Both the firm and Zani move up to the top bands.

Andrew Keenan & Co *Andrew Keenan* has been a sole practitioner since 1985 and continues to handle all areas of general crime from his south east London office.

Hallinan Blackburn Gittings & Nott *Colin Nott* specialises in criminal defence, extradition and judicial review work from this Victoria-based firm.

Henry Milner & Co *Henry Milner* has many years experience in defending serious criminal cases of all types.

Hickman & Rose *Jane Hickman* founded Hickman & Rose in 1991 and specialises in complex criminal cases and cases involving negligence by the legal profession.

Hodge Jones & Allen The department acts for clients from the local community via police and magistrates' court duty schemes. The team includes *Mark Studdert*.

Reynolds Dawson Established in 1982, this firm specialises exclusively in criminal law with *Colin Reynolds* heading the team.

Russell-Cooke Potter & Chapman The firm handles a full range of criminal work and *Ian Ryan* specialises in complex cases, often with medical and forensic aspects.

Simons Muirhead & Burton An increasing reputation for general crime over the last year. The firm handles the entire spectrum of criminal matters, concentrating on defence. The expanding Wandsworth office presently holds five fee earners. *Anthony Burton* enters the table following strong recommendation.

Venters & Co Well respected for the excellent quality of their work. *June Venters* is highly regarded and has been described as an extremely thorough, hard working lawyer. She enters the table as a result.

Claude Hornby & Cox *Michael Butler, Christopher Green* and *Richard Hallam* continue to handle crime in London and the south east. Particular emphasis on serious crime,

LEADING INDIVIDUALS · LONDON
BURTON Anthony Simons Muirhead & Burton
BUTLER Michael Claude Hornby & Cox
CARNELL Bernard Offenbach & Co
CLARKE Adrian Bindman & Partners
EDWARDS Anthony T.V. Edwards
FISHER Michael Christian Fisher
GRANT Kenneth Darlington & Parkinson
GREEN Christopher Claude Hornby & Cox
HALLAM Richard Claude Hornby & Cox
HASLAM Mark Magrath & Co
HEWITT Stephen Fisher Meredith
HICKMAN Jane Hickman & Rose
KEENAN Andrew Andrew Keenan & Co
MILNER Henry Henry Milner & Co
MURPHY Shaun Duthie Hart & Duthie
NICHOL James Taylor Nichol
NOTT Colin Hallinan, Blackburn, Gittings & Nott
O'MAY Neil Bindman & Partners
PIERCE Gareth B.M. Birnberg & Co
POWELL Greg Powell Spencer & Partners
PRESTON Edward Edward Fail Bradshaw & Waterson
ROSCOE Robert Victor Lissack & Roscoe
SAUNDERS James Saunders & Co
THANKI Girish Thanki Novy Taube
VENTERS June Venters & Co
ZANI John Whitelock & Storr
ASHFORD Mark Taylor Nichol
BROWN Robert Darlington & Parkinson
CADMAN Peter Russell-Cooke, Potter & Chapman
HUBER Bernard Duthie Hart & Duthie
MATTILA Terry Mattila Solicitors
MERRIAM Joy Joy Merriam & Co
REYNOLDS Colin Reynolds Dawson
RYAN Ian Russell-Cooke, Potter & Chapman
SPENCER Richard Powell Spencer & Partners
STUDDERT Mark Hodge Jones & Allen
TAYLOR Carolyn Taylor Nichol

SEE PROFILES AT END OF THIS SECTION

with experience in the criminal, civil and military courts.

Darlington & Parkinson *Kenneth Grant, Robert Brown* and their team handle white collar and general crime. Experience ranges from serious fraud to sexual offences – Grant once defended Cynthia Payne.

Duthie Hart & Duthie *Shaun Murphy* and *Bernard Huber* head a large team of lawyers with a range of experience in this field. Murphy is a Higher Courts Advocate.

ASHFORD, Mark
Taylor Nichol, London (0171) 272 8336

BROWN, Robert T.J.
Darlington & Parkinson, London
(0181) 601 9910
Specialisation: Practice encompasses all areas of criminal defence work, mainly in London but also in the Provinces.
Prof. Memberships: Law Society, Central and South Middlesex Law Society, London Criminal Courts Solicitors Association (Committee Member).
Career: Qualified 1983, Partner *Darlington and Parkinson* 1985. Has lectured on Criminal Justice in England and overseas.
Personal: Educated at Cambridge University. Resides West London. Interests include literature, painting and sport.

BURTON, Anthony
Simons Muirhead & Burton, London
(0171) 734 4499
See under Crime: Fraud, p. 396

BUTLER, Michael
Claude Hornby & Cox, London
(0171) 437 8873
Specialisation: All aspects of criminal defence work in London and throughout the South East. Has an extensive and varied practise, with particular emphasis on serious crime, including terrorism, murder, sexual offences and large-scale fraud. Also considerable experience representing defendants in courts martial and in professional disciplinary proceedings.
Prof. Memberships: Law Society.
Career: Qualified 1992. Partner 1997.
Personal: Born in 1965. Lives in London.

CADMAN, Peter
Russell-Cooke, Potter & Chapman, London
(0171) 405 6566

CARNELL, Bernard
Offenbach & Co, London (0171) 434 9891
See under Crime: Fraud, p. 397

CLARKE, Adrian
Bindman & Partners, London
(0171) 833 4433
Specialisation: Experience in wide range of criminal defence work. Areas of practice include miscarriage of justice work, homicide cases, contempt and other cases involving press freedom, extradition, serious fraud, public inquiries, prisoners rights, judicial review and civil actions against the police.

EDWARDS, Anthony
T.V. Edwards, London (0171) 791 1050
Senior Partner. Criminal and Licensing Department.
Specialisation: Criminal law. Author of 'Advising the suspect in the police station' and 'Standard Fees in the Magistrates Court: A Survival Guide.' Contributor to Criminal Law Society Practice Guides. Regular contributor to Law Society Gazette and other periodicals . Lecturer on all aspects of criminal practice, and specialist in criminal costs and professional conduct.
Prof. Memberships: Law Society, London Criminal Courts Solicitors Association.

Career: Qualified in 1974, having joined *T.V. Edwards* in 1972. Became Senior Partner in 1993. Solicitor Member of the Criminal Justice Consultative Council.
Personal: Born 6th December 1949. Attended Bristol University, taking a first class LLB in 1972. Leisure interests include walking, reading, and theatre.

FISHER, Michael
Christian Fisher, London (0171) 831 1750
Specialisation: Criminal defence work including many serious criminal trials (political cases, fraud cases, murder, miscarriages of justice). Acted in IRA trials and for defendants accused of riot and major fraud. Specialises in civil liberties cases.
Prof. Memberships: Law Society; Member of Central London Duty Solicitor Scheme.
Career: *Vizards* 1970-1973; *DJ Freeman* 1973-1976; founded *Michael Fisher & Co* (later *Fisher Meredith*) 1976-1985. Co-founded *Christian Fisher* with Louise Christian in 1985.

GRANT, Kenneth I
Darlington & Parkinson, London
(0181) 601 9910
Senior Partner in Criminal Department.
Specialisation: Handles white collar crime and general crime. Has been involved in a range of cases, from defending Cynthia Payne, to acting on behalf of two defendants in the Harrovian fraud, the largest alleged mortgage fraud to date, and the source of the largest single claim against the Solicitors Indemnity Fund (trial anticipated in 1998/9).
Prof. Memberships: Law Society, Central and South Middlesex Law Society, London Criminal Courts Solicitors Association.
Career: Qualified in 1977. Joined *Darlington & Parkinson* in 1977 and became a Partner in 1979. Chairman Ealing Duty Solicitor Committee, Member London Legal Aid Area Committee, Deputy Metropolitan Stipendiary Magistrate, Solicitor-Advocate (Higher Courts Criminal).
Personal: Born 14th November 1951. Educated at the University of Sussex. Leisure interests include opera and ballet. Lives in London.

GREEN, Christopher
Claude Hornby & Cox, London
(0171) 437 8873
Consultant in Criminal Department.
Specialisation: Wide experience of criminal litigation both in the civil and military courts. Whilst instructed, for the most part, for the defence, he has prosecuted as agent for the CPS; and, has prosecuted copyright pirates for the film industry. His career has encompassed successful defences in homicide, assault, fraud and dishonesty, major and minor, and road traffic allegations; both for corporate and private clients. Degrees in psychology and law have enhanced his recognition of the importance not only of the law but also of the stress particular to the accused. He teaches on aspects of criminal law and advocacy, and professional ethics. He sits as legal assessor to the disciplinary committees of a number of professional bodies and defends regularly in professional disciplinary proceedings.
Prof. Memberships: British Academy of Forensic Sciences, City of Westminster Law

Society (Criminal Law Committee), London Criminal Courts Solicitors Association.
Career: Qualified 1970 while with *Claude Hornby & Cox* became a Partner in 1972, and a consultant in 1997.
Personal: Born 9th August 1944.

HALLAM, Richard S.
Claude Hornby & Cox, London
(0171) 437 8873
Partner in Criminal Litigation Department since 1989.
Specialisation: Crime. Has substantial experience of conducting cases in the Magistrates Courts, Higher Criminal Courts and before Courts Martial in UK and Germany. Normally instructed as a defence advocate, but has experience of prosecuting for the CPS and will prosecute privately for individuals or organisations. Nationwide experience of prosecuting video piracy cases. Defends in professional disciplinary proceedings. Has successfully represented defendants facing allegations of murder, terrorism, large-scale drugs importation and fraud, but equally interested in defending clients charged with less serious offences.
Prof. Memberships: City of Westminster Law Society, London Criminal Courts Solicitors Association, Legal Aid Practitioners Group.
Personal: Born 24th April 1948. Educated at the King's School, Canterbury and Oxford University. Lives in London.

HASLAM, Mark
Magrath & Co, London (0171) 495 3003

HEWITT, Stephen
Fisher Meredith, London (0171) 622 4468
Specialisation: Head of department of one of the largest and most successful criminal defence teams in London. Wide range of criminal defence and civil liberties work including advocacy with lengthy experience of major homicide cases, drug trafficking cases and white collar crime. Specialist in acting for mentally disturbed defendants and undertaking difficult appeals to the Court of Appeal. Lecturer on aspects of criminal practice, legal aid franchising and practice management. Co-author of "Legal Aid Practice Manual" and on committee of London firms negotiating with Legal Aid Board on crime block contracting.
Prof. Memberships: Law Society, London Criminal Courts Solicitors Association.
Career: Qualified 1980. Joined *Fisher Meredith* as partner in 1986.
Personal: Born 14th November 1953. Lives in London.

HICKMAN, Jane
Hickman & Rose, London (0171) 700 2211

HUBER, Bernard
Duthie Hart & Duthie, London
(0181) 472 0138
Partner in Criminal Litigation Department.
Specialisation: Has a large and varied criminal law case load with daily advocacy. Involved in conducting prosecutions on behalf of the North East London Probation Service and the Port of London Authority.
Prof. Memberships: London Criminal Courts Solicitors Association, West Essex Law Society,

Child Care Panel, Duty Solicitor Schemes (Newham and Thames).
Career: Qualified in 1980 after articles at *Duthie Hart & Duthie*. Partner since 1982.
Personal: Born 30th October 1955. Educated at Leeds University (LL.B Hons, 1977). Leisure interests, most sports; playing and spectator. Lives in Wanstead, London.

KEENAN, Andrew
Andrew Keenan & Co, London
(0181) 659 0332

MATTILA, Terry
Mattila Solicitors, London (0171) 274 7821

MERRIAM, Joy
Joy Merriam & Co, London (0181) 980 7171
Specialisation: Senior Partner of an East London Criminal Practice established in 1987. Substantial expertise in all areas of criminal law and attributes her firm's success and large client following to giving equal attention to all cases whether involving major crime or not.
Prof. Memberships: Member of the Law Society, Committee member of the LCCSA and Thames Duty Solicitor Committee.

MILNER, Henry
Henry Milner & Co, London (0171) 831 9944
Principal of firm.
Specialisation: Main area of practice is criminal defence work. Has twenty-two years specialist experience defending in serious criminal cases of all types. Defence solicitor in all Brinks Mat robbery trials and many other important trials of the 1980s and 1990s. Author of 'Time Wasting at Magistrates Courts' in the Law Society Gazette.
Prof. Memberships: Law Society.
Career: Qualified in 1975. Established *Henry Milner & Co.* in 1978.
Personal: Born 23rd April 1947. Holds a law degree from London School of Economics. Leisure interests include bridge, football and traditional American music. Lives in London.

MURPHY, Shaun
Duthie Hart & Duthie, London
(0181) 472 0138
Partner in Criminal Litigation Department. Assistant Crown Court Recorder.
Specialisation: Criminal law specialist. Advocate in criminal proceedings on a regular basis in courts throughout the London area. Qualified as a Higher Courts Advocate. Also a Privy Council Agent. Other areas of practice are care proceedings and civil litigation. Involved in prosecution work on behalf of North East London Probation Service and the Port of London Authority. Member of Duty Solicitor Schemes (Newham and Thames) and Child Care Panel. Member of Legal Aid Board Area Committee.
Prof. Memberships: London Criminal Courts Solicitors Association, Criminal Law Solicitors Association, West Essex Law Society.
Career: Qualified in 1979 after articles at *Duthie Hart & Duthie*. Became a Partner in 1986.
Personal: Born 10th June 1956. Educated at Warwick University 1974-77 (LL.B Hons). School Governor. Enjoys most sports. Lives in Wanstead, London.

NICHOL, James
Taylor Nichol, London (0171) 272 8336

NOTT, Colin
Hallinan, Blackburn, Gittings & Nott, London
(0171) 834 3135
Specialisation: Specialist in criminal Defence Work, Extradition and Judicial review.
Prof. Memberships: LLB (Hons)
Career: Qualified 1978. Sole practitioner 1979-1982. Joined *Hallinan Blackburn Gittings & Nott* as a Partner – 1982.
Personal: Born 27.6.52. Educated Weymouth Grammar School, London University. Interests: sport, rugby and football in particular, theatre and travel.

O'MAY, Neil
Bindman & Partners, London
(0171) 833 4433
Specialisation: Wide range of criminal defence work from murder and terrorist cases to more general crime. All types of serious fraud (including SFO cases), particularly those involving professionals (solicitors and accountants) as defendants. Particular expertise in large-scale public order arrests and multi-defendant trials. Specialist in cases involving complex scientific and expert evidence. Extensive experience in defending journalists on civil liberties issues and other "professionals in trouble" (including professional body disciplinary proceedings). Defending against top prosecution teams, including the Anti-Terrorist Squad (most recently in the Israeli Embassy bombing case and the IRA mortar attack on Heathrow airport). Experience in the defence of complex drugs cases. Fresh evidence appeals in the Court of Appeal and investigations of miscarriages of justice. Inquests including deaths in police custody. Two ground-breaking cases in the House of Lords ('R. v. Doody & Others' and 'R. v. Aziz & Others'). Writer, lecturer, and broadcaster on legal issues.
Prof. Memberships: Law Society, London Criminal Courts Solicitors Association.
Career: Qualified 1985. Joined *Bindman & Partners* as Head of Criminal Department in 1990.
Personal: Degree in Biochemistry, BSc (Hons). Londoner.

PIERCE, Gareth
B.M. Birnberg & Co, London
(0171) 403 3166

POWELL, Greg
Powell Spencer & Partners, London
(0171) 624 8888
Specialisation: Criminal defence; especially murder, conspiracies to import and supply drugs, armed robbery. Magistrates Court advocacy. Acting for an increasing number of professional clients; accountants, doctors, estate agents, solicitors etc.
Prof. Memberships: Law Society, Haldane Society, Liberty.
Career: Qualified 1973. Degrees in Law (LSE) and Psychology (Birkbeck) and co-author of a Practical Guide to the Police and Criminal Evidence Act.

PRESTON, Edward
Edward Fail Bradshaw & Waterson, London
(0171) 790 4032

REYNOLDS, Colin
Reynolds Dawson, London (0171) 839 2373
Specialisation: Qualified in 1978. Since establishment of this Practice in 1982 it has been concerned exclusively with the field of

criminal law. This rigorous specialisation allows a highly motivated and conscientious specialist staff to handle the whole range of criminal offences. The Senior Partner in particular has specialised in white collar crime and extradition cases, including three recent Appeals before the House of Lords. The Practice has defended and advised a number of cases with international implications, as well as in serious and complex domestic fraud where the accused are professionals. The Practice has established a close-working relationship with Counsel experienced in these fields and related experts.
Prof. Memberships: The Law Society, London Criminal Courts Solicitors Association; International Bar Association; City of Westminster Law Society.
Career: Graduated in 1975. Qualified as Solicitor in 1978. In Partnership with *Victor J Lissack* to 1982. In Partnership with Mr S Dawson 1982 to 1994, until his appointment as a Metropolitan Stipendiary Magistrate.

ROSCOE, Robert
Victor Lissack & Roscoe, London
(0171) 240 2010
Partner in Crime Department.
Specialisation: Main areas of practice are white collar fraud, serious criminal offences, and general criminal practice.
Prof. Memberships: Law Society, City of Westminster Law Society, London Criminal Courts Solicitors' Association, Criminal Law Solicitors' Association.
Career: Qualified in 1976. Higher Courts (Criminal Proceedings) Qualification 1994. Joined *Victor Lissack & Roscoe* in 1969, becoming a Partner in 1978. Law Society Council Member since 1992; Chairman of Criminal Law Committee since 1995; LCCSA: President 1996-1997, Committee Member and Advocacy Training Officer 1983-93; Chairman of no. 14 Regional Duty Solicitor Committee (1991-1997), Legal Aid Board Costs Appeals Committee (1993-4).

RYAN, Ian
Russell-Cooke, Potter & Chapman, London
(0181) 788 0005
Specialisation: Deals with the full range of criminal defence work with particular expertise in complex and weighty cases including murder, sexual offences, importation of drugs, extradition, sanction evasions and fraud. Magistrates' Court and Crown Court advocacy and experience of professional disciplinary Tribunals.
Prof. Memberships: Solicitor Advocate in the Crown Court. Member LCCSA.
Career: Qualified 1987. Partner from 1995.

SAUNDERS, James
Saunders & Co, London (0171) 404 2828
Senior Partner.
Specialisation: Criminal Law; Legal Aid Franchise and Private Client. Covers all aspects of Criminal Law, particularly complex and heavy trials including fraud, serial murder, drugs, sexual offences, robbery, official secrets and civil liberties. Also deals with scientific, medical and other expert issues; DNA, computers, firearms, confiscation of assets, motoring and London Agent matters.
Career: Articled at the North Kensington Neighbourhood Law Centre. Qualified 1972. Established *Saunders & Co* in 1974.

Personal: Born 1948. Attended King Edward VII School, Sheffield and University of Leicester (LLB).

SPENCER, Richard
Powell Spencer & Partners, London
(0171) 624 8888
Specialisation: A Criminal Law Specialist for over 20 years covering the whole range of defence work, but particularly drug importation and VAT 'boot legging' offences. Excellent Magistrates Courts defence advocate practising throughout the London area.

STUDDERT, Mark
Hodge Jones & Allen, London
(0171) 482 1974
Specialisation: Partner in large franchised criminal department dealing with wide range of offences. Own specialisation – homicide, drug importation, fraud.
Prof. Memberships: Member Liberty, Haldane

Society, London Criminal Courts Association, Prisoners Advice Service. Organiser and administrator of Highbury and Old Street Duty Solicitor scheme.
Career: Qualified 1979. Joined *Hodge Jones & Allen* 1985, partner 1987.
Personal: Lives in Stoke Newington with partner and new baby. Interests: film, popular culture, food.

TAYLOR, Carolyn S.
Taylor Nichol, London (0171) 272 8336

THANKI, Girish
Thanki Novy Taube, London
(0171) 833 5800
Specialisation: Wide range of criminal defence and civil liberties work including murder, armed robberies and white collar crime with considerable experience of handling complex and weighty cases. Specialist knowledge of forensics and scientific issues.

Active extradition practice with particular emphasis on the USA. Recent case involved arguing fairness of trial for black defendants in the State of Missouri. Judicial reviews and appellate work including the House of Lords.
Prof. Memberships: LCCSA, BAFS, Medico-Legal Society, IBA, Liberty, Justice (Criminal Justice Panel Member), Prisoners' Advisory Service, Inquest, Law Society, Holborn Law Society.
Career: Co-founded the practice with Rod Novy and Martin Taube in 1992. Educated Dame Alice Owen's School and University of East Anglia.
Personal: Lives in London with barrister wife and two children. Leisure interests confined to food, wine, travelling and armchair politics and cricket.

VENTERS, June
Venters & Co, London (0171) 277 0110

ZANI, John
Whitelock & Storr, London (0171) 242 8612

SOUTH EAST

DUKES ARNOLD DU FEU High Wycombe, Oxford
GEPP & SONS Chelmsford, Colchester
PICTONS Watford, St. Albans, Hemel Hempstead, Luton, Stevenage
TWITCHEN MUSTERS & KELLY Southend-on-Sea
WOODFINE BATCHELDOR Bedford

BERNARD CHILL & AXTELL Southampton
BRADLEYS Dover
DAVID CHARNLEY & CO Romford
ERIC ROBINSON & CO Southampton
MARSH, FERRIMAN & CHEALE Worthing
MAX BARFORD & CO Tunbridge Wells
PARK WOODFINE Bedford
STEPHEN RIMMER & CO Eastbourne
WHITE & BOWKER Winchester

Dukes Arnold du Feu The firm has offices in High Wycombe and Oxford. It is a highly regarded criminal defence practice, taking on "anything that comes through the door." The firm also prosecutes on behalf of the Post Office.

Gepp & Sons Based in Chelmsford and Colchester, the firm covers a wide geographical area in Essex and beyond. It is praised for both national and international litigation. Particularly well known for representing clients charged with importation of drugs and pornography.

Pictons With eight partners and twenty four fee earners, Pictons remains at the forefront of criminal practice in the South East. The firm covers a wide area, with offices in St. Albans, Watford, Hemel Hempsted, Luton and Stevenage.

Twitchen Musters & Kelly Particularly well regarded for their advice on appeals

referred. Involved in heavyweight, serious crime, in particular in connection with drugs offences, importation and homicide. They were strongly recommended by a prisoner from H.M.P. Downview who commended their well placed advice, dedicated and efficient manner, and their ability to get down to the "nitty gritty." *Philip Kelly* and *Patrick Musters* were particularly recommended.

Woodfine Batcheldor The product of the merger in April 1998 of Gareth Woodfine & Partners and Batcheldor & Co. The new firm is recommended for all areas of criminal practice.

SOUTH WEST

BOBBETTS MACKAN Bristol
DOUGLAS & PARTNERS Bristol
JOHN BOYLE AND CO Redruth

CROSSE & CROSSE Exeter
FOOT & BOWDEN Plymouth
STEPHENS & SCOWN Exeter
WOLFERSTANS Plymouth
WOOLLCOMBE BEER WATTS Newton Abbot

Bobbetts Mackan Well known for the quality of their representation in courts martial.

Also respected for the full range of criminal work which they undertake. *Anthony Miles* was recommended again.

Douglas & Partners Enjoy a strong reputation in racially sensitive criminal matters and work for Support Against Racist Incidents ("SARI"). Unusually, they boast a Youth Court department. *Roy Douglas* and *David Fanson* remain highly regarded.

John Boyle and Co *John Boyle* is well-known throughout the south east as a solicitor-advocate and has particular experience of large drugs smuggling cases. He and two other partners handle a range of work.

Crosse & Crosse Undertake all types of criminal work with particular specialisms in Youth Court work and Mental Health.

They are regarded within the profession as a "very good" general criminal practice.

Stephens & Scown Have developed an excellent reputation for miscarriage of justice cases and have successfully represented clients at the Criminal Cases Review Commission.

Wolferstans The firm maintains its reputation for representing police officers at disciplinary hearings. Also involved in the defence of military personnel in courts martial. *David Gabbitass* regularly appears for prosecution and defence in Magistrates' and Crown courts.

Woollcombe Beer Watts With six partners and one assistant specialising in crime, this firm is recommended for the quantity and quality of its work. A substantial amount of serious crime work is undertaken. Based in Newton Abbot, it enjoys a good reputation in South Devon and beyond.

WALES

LEADING FIRMS · WALES
GAMLINS Rhyll
GRAHAM EVANS & PARTNERS Swansea
HUTTONS Cardiff
MARTYN PROWEL, EDWARDS & DAVIES Cardiff
ROBERTSONS Cardiff
SPICKETTS Pontypridd
SPIRO GRECH & CO Cardiff
HORNBY, BAKER JONES & WOOD Newport
LEO ABSE & COHEN Cardiff

Gamlins This newly merged firm continues to handle Crown Court advocacy. *Gwyn Jones* has recently been involved in a large fraud conspiracy case and covers all aspects of crime for individual and corporate clients.

Graham Evans & Partners Well known in the Swansea area for their solid general crime practice.

Huttons Particularly well known for their involvement in the 'Cardiff news agent Three' case, this firm deals with a broad range of serious criminal matters including drugs, fraud and homicide. *Stuart Hutton* leads the team and the firm moves up the tables.

Martyn Prowel, Edwards & Davies Deal with every aspect of criminal work from shoplifting to homicide. Many high profile cases. *Martyn Prowel* has handled complex fraud cases as well as prosecutions for the RSPCA and general Crown Court defence.

Robertsons The three offices of this firm continue to undertake general crime and fraud work. *Ian Williams* was recommended again.

LEADING INDIVIDUALS · WALES
BIRD Jeremy Hugh James
HUTTON Stuart Huttons
JONES Gwyn Gamlins
PROWEL Martyn Martin Prowel, Edwards & Davies
WILLIAMS Ian Robertsons

SEE PROFILES AT END OF THIS SECTION

MIDLANDS

LEADING FIRMS · MIDLANDS
BANNERS Chesterfield
BARRIE WARD & JULIAN GRIFFITHS Nottingham
BERRYMAN & CO Nottingham
BRETHERTONS Rugby
FLETCHERS Nottingham
GEORGE, JONAS & CO Birmingham
GLAISYERS Birmingham
THE JOHNSON PARTNERSHIP Nottingham
KIERAN & CO Worcester
NELSONS Nottingham
THE SMITH PARTNERSHIP Derby
TYNDALLWOODS Birmingham
WOODFORD-ROBINSON Northampton
EDDOWES WALDRON & CASH Derby
ELLIOT MATHER SMITH Chesterfield
FREETH CARTWRIGHT HUNT DICKINS Nottingham
HAWLEY & RODGERS Loughborough
MARRON DODDS Leicester
REES PAGE Wolverhampton
SILKS Warley

Banners General defence work. Two full time advocates specialising in crime. Recently they have been particularly noted for their involvement in date rape cases.

Barrie Ward & Julian Griffiths The eponymous partners deal with a wide range of criminal work, including civil liberties. Both *Barrie Ward* and *Julian Griffiths* enter the table of leaders.

Brethertons Involved in a broad range of criminal work. Specialising in defence work, they run two local Duty Solicitor Schemes.

Fletchers Regarded as a good, solid firm. *Caroline Goldbourne* is generally well respected as an accomplished advocate.

George Jonas & Co Maintain a solid reputation for general crime and fraud and *Steven Jonas* is "very experienced."

Glaisyers Strong team including *Charles Royle* who has experience of a range of criminal matters including youth work and motoring offences.

Kieran & Co This Chesterfield firm is a new entry to the table following recommendation from other practitioners in the area. *Kevin Tomlinson* was particularly highly regarded.

Nelsons The general crime department has grown considerably in strength following the addition of Cash from Eddoes, Waldron & Cash. There are now five partners and six assistants handling much of the larger criminal work in the area, from murders and rapes to large drugs conspiracies. There are also two higher court advocates allowing the firm to retain a large proportion of advocacy in-house, ensuring consistency of representation up to Crown Court level. *Richard Nelson* has a leading reputation.

Freeth Cartwright Hunt Dickins A criminal defence practice, regarded by some as the best in Nottingham. It provides a high quality service, covering the full range of criminal defence work, including youth work. Perhaps even better known for their fraud work. *Jane Winfield* was recommended.

LEADING INDIVIDUALS MIDLANDS
GOLDBOURNE Caroline Fletchers
GRIFFITHS Julian Barrie Ward & Julian Griffiths
HOLMES Murray Dennis Faulkner & Alsop
JONAS Steven George, Jonas & Co
MATHER Bertie Elliot Mather Smith
NELSON Richard Nelsons
ROYLE Charles Glaisyers
TOMLINSON Kevin Kieran & Co
WARD Barrie Barrie Ward & Julian Griffiths
WINFIELD Jane Freeth Cartwright Hunt Dickins

SEE PROFILES AT END OF THIS SECTION

EAST ANGLIA

Copleys *Kevin Warboys* and his firm maintain their leading repuation for all aspects of criminal law.

Hunt & Coombs Undertake criminal work from their offices in Peterborough and Oundle. Remain well respected by other firms in the area and *John Henson* maintains his leading individual status.

Overbury Stewart & Eaton Describe themselves as a general high street practice, yet they are well known and respected for their involvement in high profile drugs cases and other matters which have attracted public attention.

Cole & Co This Norwich firm has been strongly recommended by other leading East Anglian practices.

NORTH WEST

Burton Copeland Generally regarded as the leading criminal firm in the North West. It is regularly employed in high profile cases, for example representing sporting celebrities. *Michael Mackey* is one of the most experienced criminal lawyers in the country and *Nicholas Freeman* is considered by many to be the best criminal defence lawyer for drink-driving cases. They are well supported by the largest criminal defence team in the UK with more than sixty fee earners including *Shahid Ali*. The team covers all areas of criminal defence work, from minor offences to major drugs importations, violent crime, homicide and commercial fraud. Private defence work makes up a large part of their caseload but they also have a strong legal aid practice. They are leading the way in the use of DNA testing in criminal trials.

The Berkson Globe Partnership A new entry to the list following praise from contemporaries. *Valerie Lamont* and *Peter Charles* received particular commendation.

Jones Maidment Wilson *Peter Grogan* heads the team at this firm which maintain their reputation for high quality general crime work.

Maidments Set up in 1993 by *Allan Maidment* (formerly of Jones Maidment Wilson) this firm continues to feature in serious crime and commercial fraud matters.

Shaun Draycott has been with the firm almost from inception and has particular experience in robbery and drug importation as well as murder and manslaughter.

Miller Gardner Undertake a broad spectrum of criminal defence work, including large drug trafficking cases, assault, homicide and fraud. Many of their cases gain public attention.

Tuckers A strong criminal defence practice handling private client and legal aid work. *Franklin Sinclair* was recommended again and has particular experience in large scale drugs importation and armed robbery cases.

NORTH EAST

LEADING FIRMS · NORTH EAST

LUMB & MACGILL Bradford
SUGARÉ & CO Leeds

DAVID GREY & CO Newcastle
GRAHAME STOWE, BATESON Leeds
HOWELLS Sheffield
IRWIN MITCHELL Sheffield
LEVI & CO Leeds
MAX GOLD & CO Hull

GOSSCHALKS Hull
HENRY HYAMS & CO Leeds
MYER WOLFF & MANLEY Hull

Lumb & Macgill Highly respected for the quality of their criminal defence work. *Kerry Macgill* is a renowned advocate, with rights of audience in the higher courts. Peter Sutcliffe ws a former clients.

Sugaré & Co Maintain a strong reputation for criminal defence. *Anthony Sugaré* is an experienced advocate and handles road traffic work together with general crime.

LEADING INDIVIDUALS
NORTH EAST

MACGILL Kerry Lumb & Macgill
SUGARÉ Anthony Sugaré & Co

SCOTLAND

LEADING FIRMS · SCOTLAND

BELTRAMI & CO Glasgow

GILFEDDER & MCINNES Edinburgh
GORDON & SMYTH Glasgow
McCOURTS Edinburgh
MORE & CO Edinburgh

ADAMS Edinburgh
BLAIR & BRYDEN Greenock
CONDIES Perth
GALLEN & CO Glasgow
GEORGE MATHERS & CO Aberdeen
HALL & HAUGHEY Glasgow
HAMILTON BURNS & MOORE Glasgow
LIVINGSTONE BROWNE Glasgow
McKAY & NORWELL WS Edinburgh
NESS GALLAGHER Motherwell

Beltrami & Co. Based in Glasgow, the six practitioners at this "excellent" firm concentrate mainly on criminal defence work and are often involved in high profile cases. *Joseph Beltrami* maintains his position as the premier Scottish criminal lawyer and *Murray Macara* also enjoys an envied reputation.

Gilfedder & McInnes *Brian Gilfedder* and *John McInnes* continue to feature highly as major criminal specialists in Edinburgh. They have a strong team of ten fee-earners concentrating on general crime.

Gordon & Smyth *Maurice Smyth* was recommended again as a high profile solicitor advocate who is regularly seen on the circuit.

McCourts This specialist criminal firm has experience of both every day matters and high profile crime. It has a strong team including three leaders: *Alistair Duff, Douglas Main* and *Alexander Prentice*.

LEADING INDIVIDUALS
SCOTLAND

BELTRAMI Joseph Beltrami & Co

DUFF Alistair McCourts
GILFEDDER Brian Gilfedder & McInnes
MACARA Murray Beltrami & Co
MAIN Douglas McCourts
McINNES John Gilfedder & McInnes
MORE George More & Co
PRENTICE Alexander McCourts
SMYTH Maurice Gordon & Smyth

More & Co This Edinburgh practice again features highly in our tables and *George More* continues to handle a range of criminal matters.

NORTHERN IRELAND

The table of recommended firms remains the same as last year, with the addition of McClenahan Crossey & Co. of Coleraine, following recommendation from other practitioners in and outside Belfast.

LEADING FIRMS · NORTHERN IRELAND

BABINGTON & CROASDAILE Londonderry	**MADDEN & FINUCANE** Belfast
BOGUE AND McNULTY	**McCLENAHAN CROSSEY & CO** Coleraine
BRENDAN KEARNEY KELLY & CO Derry	**MILLAR SHEARER & BLACK** Cookstown
DONNELLY & WALL Belfast	**RICHARD MONTEITH** Portadown
FLYNN & McGETTRICK Belfast	**TREVOR SMYTH & CO** Belfast

LEADERS' PROFILES · REGIONS

ALI, Shahid
Burton Copeland, Manchester
(0161) 834 7374
Specialisation: Had considerable input in and personal dealings in high calibre criminal work which has also attracted media attention. Built up and established a strong base in the areas of Bolton and Bury. Fluent in the languages of Urdu, Punjabi, Hindi and Gujerati.

BECKFORD, Trevor
Leathes Prior, Norwich (01603) 610911

BELTRAMI, Joseph
Beltrami & Co, Glasgow (0141) 221 0981
Specialisation: Consultant and Solicitor advocate specialising in criminal law. Instructed in more than 300 murder and manslaughter cases. Acted in the only two Scottish Royal Pardons this century on matters of substantive crime — Maurice Swanson in 1975 and Pat Meehan in 1976. In each case compensation was awarded to the client. Also acted in the cases of W.S.Ellis, A.Thompson, D. Boyle, Howard Wilson, Thos Docherty, Johnny

Ramensky and Alan Hasson. First solicitor advocate to appear before the Criminal Appeal Court (1993) and the first to lead in a successful murder acquittal (June 1994). Author of 'The Defender' (1980), 'Beltrami's Tales of the Suspected' (1988), and 'A Deadly Innocence' (1989). Has written numerous articles for 'New Law Journal,' 'Scottish Law Journal,' the Police Federation.
Prof. Memberships: Solicitor Advocate, Solicitor to the Supreme Court.
Career: Qualified in 1953. Detachment

Commander in the Intelligence Corps 1954-56. Founding Partner of *Beltrami & Co*, established in 1958.
Personal: Born 15th May 1932. Educated at St. Aloysius's College, Glasgow and Glasgow University. Recreations include bowls, soccer, snooker, writing and boxing. Lives in Bothwell.

BILES, Peter
Fosters, Norwich (01603) 620 508

BIRD, Jeremy S.
Hugh James, Blackwood (01495) 223 328

BOYLE, John
John Boyle and Co, Redruth
(01209) 213507
Founder Partner specialising in criminal law.
Specialisation: Has practised as a solicitor advocate before Crown Courts in Cornwall for 18 years, both prosecuting, defending and conducting jury trials. Probably the most regular Crown Court solicitor advocate. Appears regularly before Court of Appeal. Also handles general common law. Has dealt with numerous large drugs importation cases involving millions of pounds of drugs smuggled by sea and landed around the Cornish coast. Author of articles for The Times, Solicitors Journal, and Law Society Gazette.
Prof. Memberships: Cornwall and National Law Societies.
Career: Qualified in 1980. Articled with *Herbert Smith* 1978-80. Assistant solicitor and Partner at *Stewart & Knight* until established *John Boyle and Co* in 1986. Higher Courts (Criminal Proceedings) Qualification.
Personal: Born 22nd June 1954. Attended St Catherine's College, Oxford (Hons Degree, PPE 1976). Owner of Shark Bay Films, producers of underwater documentary films sold to world-wide television. Author of articles on scuba diving around the world. Leisure interests include scuba diving, film making, snowboarding, watersports, squash and walking.

BROUDIE, Robert
R.M. Broudie & Co, Liverpool
(0151) 227 1429
Specialisation: Criminal Law. Judicial Review.
Prof. Memberships: Criminal Law Practitioners Association. Association of Higher Court Advocates.
Career: LL.B 2(i). Cert. Eur. Integ.

CHARLES, Peter
Louis Berkson & Globe, Liverpool
(0151) 236 1234

CUTTLE, M.B.
M.B. Cuttle & Co, Manchester
(0161) 835 2050
Specialisation: Criminal Law. Appointed as solicitor in the Strangeways prison riots to negotiate between prisoners and officers towards ending of individual personal disputes in 1990.
Prof. Memberships: Law Society.
Career: Qualified in January 1963. Worked with the Crown Prosecution Service in Manchester. Promoted to new CPS Department in charge of Bolton Borough, thereafter in Lanchashire County Prosecutions. Formed *MB Cuttle & Co*.

1972. Thereafter dealing with much crime of all levels, much fraud conspiracy murders. Now senior partner of *MB Cuttle & Co*.
Personal: Educated at Worksop College in Nottinghamshire. Married with 3 children and upon leaving school at Worksop, became heavily involved in swimming, particularly long distance and raising many thousands for good causes; all sports; became an officer in the Cheshire RGT. Shena (wife) teacher and current president of Soroptimist International Manchester Club; Louise (daughter) bar clerk; Fiona (daughter) nurse; Fraser (son) studying law and is an officer with the Cheshire RGT.

DOUGLAS, Roy
Douglas & Partners, Bristol (0117) 955 2663
Specialisation: Criminal Defence, particularly heavy crime, public order policing and civil rights cases. Occasional lecturing on issues of criminal justice.
Prof. Memberships: Law Society. Bristol Law Society. Criminal Law Solicitors Association. Legal Aid Practitioners Group. Solicitor representative in Avon and Somerset Area Criminal Justice Liason Committee. Member of Bristol Court Users Group.
Career: Leighton Park School 1966-70; Cambridge University 1971-74; Partner *Douglas & Partners* 1980-98; Consultant.
Personal: Married with three children. Interests include music, literature, politics and gardening.

DRAYCOTT, Shaun
Maidments, Manchester (0161) 834 0008

DUFF, Alistair
McCourts, Edinburgh (0131) 225 6555

FANSON, David
Douglas & Partners, Bristol (0117) 955 2663
Specialisation: General Crime, heavy crime and serious fraud.
Prof. Memberships: Member of Bristol Law Society Council. Chairman of Bristol Criminal Law Committee. Police and Magistrates Court Duty Solicitor.
Career: Educated at Bristol Polytechnic. Senior Partner at *Douglas & Partners*.
Personal: Rugby, scuba diving, skiing, gardening and computers. Married with two children.

FREEMAN, Nicholas
Burton Copeland, Manchester
(0161) 834 7374
Specialisation: Road traffic matters, particularly drink driving on a national basis including defence of several high profile sports and acting celebrities. Private crime court martials and hearings before Board of Visitors.
Career: Uppingham School, BA Law Honours, Articles: *Johnstone Sharp & Walker*. Qualified in 1981, prosecutor for Greater Manchester Police 1981-1983. Partner at *Burton Copeland* 1983 onwards.
Personal: Born 1956, reside at Mere in Cheshire, Leisure: golf, squash, tennis, family, swimming and travel. Modern and classic cars.

GABBITASS, David
Wolferstans, Plymouth (01752) 663295
Partner specialising in criminal advocacy.
Specialisation: Regular advocate for prosecution and defence in the Crown Court

and Magistrates' Courts and for the defence at Courts Martial for all branches of the services. Represents police officers at disciplinary hearings, solicitors at Solicitors' Disciplinary Tribunals and also appears at inquests. Former agent for the DPP, Treasury Solicitor and Bank of England. Currently agent solicitor for the DTI. Member of Justice Committee on Fraud Trials. Appears on television and radio, as well as regularly having articles published in the local press. Chairman S.S.A.T., Adjudicator Criminal Injuries Compensation Panel. Member Criminal Injuries Compensation Board.
Prof. Memberships: Law Society, Fellow of the Chartered Institute of Arbitrators, Higher Courts Advocates Association.
Career: Plymouth City Police 1956-59. Joined practice in 1959, became Partner in 1965, Senior Partner in 1980 and Managing Partner in 1986. President of Plymouth Law Society, 1987. Obtained Higher Court advocacy rights in 1994.
Personal: Born 19th July 1935. Attended Huish's Grammar School, Taunton 1945-51. President of Plymouth Albion RFC, 1985-90. Past President of Rotary Club of Drake, Plymouth. Member of Management Committee of Somerset County Cricket Club and ECB Discipline Committee. Lords Taverner. Leisure interests include cricket and rugby.

GILFEDDER, Brian
Gilfedder & McInnes, Edinburgh
(0131) 553 4333

GOLDBOURNE, Caroline
Fletchers, Nottingham (0115) 959 9550

GRIFFITHS, Julian
Barrie Ward & Julian Griffiths, Nottingham
(0115) 9412622

GROGAN, Peter
Jones Maidment Wilson, Manchester
(0161) 832 8087

HENSON, John S.
Hunt & Coombs, Peterborough
(01733) 565312

HOLMES, Murray A.L.
Dennis Faulkner & Alsop, Northampton
(01604) 620161
Specialisation: All areas of Criminal Law including "white Collar" crime. Within last year, successfully defended local youth charged with Murder; local farmer and wife charged with Manslaughter; and Territorial Army soldier charged with Causing Death by Dangerous Driving – all high profile locally and received significant national coverage.
Prof. Memberships: Law Society. Northamptonshire Law Society.
Career: Educated Mill Hill School, London and University of Wales. Articled *Rance & Co* of Islington; thence Assistant Solicitor *Lucien Fior*, Regent Street, London. Joined *DF&A* approx. 30 years ago. Currently Senior Partner.
Personal: Married. Three children. President of Northampton Rugby Football Club.

HUTTON, Stuart
Huttons, Cardiff (01222) 378621
Senior Partner. Criminal Department.
Specialisation: Has been primarily involved in criminal work for over 20 years. Also deals with child care, adoption and fostering. Has been

on the Child Care Panel for over 10 years. Has handled some notable murder cases, including the high profile Tooze double Farmhouse murder and the acquittal of Jonathan Jones, another the subject of the 'Bloody Valentine' book, and 'vigilante' killing Penrhys, Rhondda, Mid Glamorgan. Has had continuing success in taking miscarriages of justice to the Court of Appeal. Former part time Chairman of Social Security Appeals tribunals. Has special interest in entertainment and media law.
Career: Qualified in 1975. With *Edwards Geldard* 1973-86 (as a Partner from 1976). Established own practice, *Hutton's*, in August 1986. The practice has a reputation for specialist litigation.
Personal: Born 21st October 1946. Lives in Cardiff.

JACKSON, Brian
The Paul Rooney Partnership, Liverpool (0151) 227 2851

JONAS, Steven
George, Jonas & Co, Birmingham (0121) 212 4111
Partner specialising in crime and personal injury work.
Specialisation: Deals with all areas of crime, from the most serious (e.g. murder) to minor traffic offences, with particular development recently in white collar and commercial crime. Acts for both legal aid and private clients. Also handles personal injury work, including road traffic accidents and factory accidents, with particular emphasis on medical negligence. Acts for both legal aid and private clients in this area also. Has been involved with several high profile criminal cases (e.g. 'Home Alone' Heidi Colwell) and personal injury cases (e.g. 'failed vasectomy,' Mr & Mrs Stobie). Author of publications in the 'New Law Journal' on costs in criminal cases. Has a large amount of media experience involving newspapers, radio and television, both local and national.
Prof. Memberships: Law Society, Birmingham Law Society, Personal Injury Panel, AVMA, APIL, Liberty.
Career: Qualified in 1981. Joined *George Jonas & Co.* as a Partner in 1982. Became Senior Partner in 1993. Chairman of Birmingham Young Solicitors Group 1989-90. Member of Birmingham Law Society's Council since 1990 (Library Committee since 1990, Civil Litigation Committee 1991-1995 and Criminal Litigation Committee since 1995). Member of Legal Aid Board No.6 Area Committee and of the Law Society Personal Injury Panel from 1994.
Personal: Born 30th December 1956. Educated at Moseley School, Birmingham until 1975, then Manchester University 1975-78. School Governor in 1974. Enjoys mountaineering, listening to music and good food and wine. Lives in Birmingham.

JONES, Gwyn
Gamlins, Rhyl 01745 343 500
Consultant and Head of Crime and Licencing Unit.
Specialisation: Personally covers and supervises all aspects of serious cases from the outset to their conclusion for both individuals and corporate clients. Conducts large scale and multi defendant public disorder matters, often through the medium of Welsh. He has extensive experience in representing those charged with sexual abuse and drug

trafficking offences. Regularly appears in the Crown Court and disciplinary proceedings, mostly defending but occasionally prosecuting. Appears frequently on TV and Radio as legal expert.
Prof. Memberships: Law Society.
Career: Qualified 1984. *Leo Abse & Cohen* 1982-96 (Partner from 1986). Became Higher Court Advocate in 1995. Joined *Gamlins* in 1996.
Personal: Born 22.07.1960. Chair Llamau Housing Society Ltd 1988-91. Duty Solicitor Committee Member. Interests: Travelling, eating out and mountain biking.

KELLY, Philip L.
Twitchen Musters & Kelly, Southend-on-Sea (01702) 339222
Specialisation: Specialist in all areas of Criminal Litigation with particular emphasis on murder, international drug importation, armed robbery, white collar fraud and supergrass cases. Has represented defendants attracting national and international notoriety.
Prof. Memberships: Law Society, Criminal Law Solicitors Association, Association of Higher Court Advocates, London Criminal Courts Solicitors Association.
Career: Admitted January 1980. Higher Court Advocate April 1994.
Personal: Born 22 February 1951. Avid supporter of Welsh Rugby. Family lives in Stebbing, Essex.

LAMONT, Valerie
Louis Berkson & Globe, Liverpool (0151) 236 1234

LINSKILL, Julian
Linskills Solicitors, Liverpool (0151) 236 2224

MACARA, J.D. Murray
Beltrami & Co, Glasgow (0141) 221 0981
Specialisation: Solicitor Advocate specialising in criminal law. Has appeared in all courts throughout Scotland. Has appeared in numerous cases in the High Court.
Prof. Memberships: Society of Solicitors in the Supreme Court.
Career: Qualified in 1973. Partner in *Beltrami & Co* since 1975.
Personal: Born 22.7.49. Educated at Loretto School Musselburgh & Glasgow University. Interests: most sports, travel, dining out. Lives in Glasgow.

MACGILL, Kerry M.P.
Lumb & Macgill, Bradford (01274) 730666
Partner in Criminal Department.
Specialisation: Extensive experience of criminal matters. Has handled in excess of 50 Homicide cases including "Yorkshire Ripper," Peter Sutcliffe; Ian Wood, a Sheffield solicitor; and Arthur Hutchinson, a triple murder case. Specialises in representing solicitors on fraud charges, Prosecutes for the Department of Social Security in the Crown Court. Member of Child Care Panel and Mental Health Tribunal Panel. Elected Chairman of the Solicitor's Association of Higher Court Advocates, June 1997. Appointed to the Law Society Council October 97 as Criminal Law and Legal Aid Practice member chairing working party of Law Society to produce a national Criminal Law Accreditation Scheme. Tutor on courses assessing solicitors for Higher Rights. Involved

as advocate in Crown Court trials and has appeared three times in the Court of Appeal.
Prof. Memberships: Criminal Law Solicitors Association, Solicitors' Association of Higher Court Advocates.
Career: Qualified 1975. Joined *Lumb & Macgill* in 1978. Senior Partner. Acting Stipendiary Magistrate 1989-95. Appointed Recorder 1995.
Personal: Born 30th April 1950. Governor of Bradford Grammar School. Leisure pursuits include sailing, fell running and golf. Lives in Huddersfield.

MACKEY, Michael
Burton Copeland, Manchester (0161) 834 7374

MAIDMENT, Allan
Maidments, Manchester (0161) 834 0008
Specialisation: Senior Partner of *Maidments* Solicitors. Worked exclusively in Crime and Commercial Fraud. Founded *Maidments* in 1993 as a specialist criminal law practice with particular emphasis on Serious Crime and Commercial Fraud. Developed the firm into one of the country's leading criminal law practices with three offices in Manchester and offices in Birmingham, Liverpool, London and Bolton.
Prof. Memberships: A member of the Law Society and Local Societies in Manchester and Birmingham. Former member of the Manchester Duty Solicitor Committee. Member of the Criminal Law Solicitors Association.
Career: Educated in Scotland, LLB Leeds University. Qualified in 1976.

MAIN, Douglas
McCourts, Edinburgh (0131) 225 6555

MASTERS, Peter
Peter Masters & Co, Cambridge (01223) 462700

MATHER, B.J.M.
Elliot Mather Smith, Matlock (01629) 584885

MCINNES, John
Gilfedder & McInnes, Edinburgh (0131) 553 4333

MILES, Anthony
Bobbetts Mackan, Bristol (0117) 929 9001
Partner responsible for Criminal Defence Department. 24-hour Criminal Defence helpline (0117) 929 8987
Specialisation: Main area of practice is criminal defence and advocacy. Engaged in the conduct of all cases before the Criminal Courts and at Courts Martial. Has developed an expertise in the defence of cases before Courts Martial, District and General. Has handled serious fraud cases; offences involving serious dishonesty and violence and complex murder and drugs cases. Conducts advocacy training courses for Bristol Law Society.
Prof. Memberships: Law Society, Bristol Law Society (Former President), CLSA, LAPG.
Career: Qualified in 1972. Joined *Bobbetts Mackan* in 1972, becoming a Partner in 1974.
Personal: Born 12th February 1947. Leisure interests include sailing, walking, skiing and reading.

MORE, George M.
More & Co, Edinburgh (0131) 557 1110

MUSTERS, Patrick H.A.
Twitchen Musters & Kelly, Southend-on-Sea
(01702) 339222
Specialisation: Specialist in all areas of
Criminal Litigation especially serious crime,
drug importation and serious fraud.
Prof. Memberships: Law Society, Criminal
Law Solicitors Association, Association of
Higher Court Advocates, London Criminal
Courts Solicitors Association, British Academy
of Forensic Scientists. Member of Legal Aid
Board Area Committee and formerly Regional
Duty Solicitor Committee.
Career: Admitted June 1978. Higher Court
Advocate April 1994.
Personal: Born 20 July 1952. Educated
Allhallows School, Lyme Regis. Interests
include Law Society Golf Club (especially when
beating the Welsh Solicitors Golf Club), running
and skiing. Acted as a consultant to both BBC
Radio Essex and Essex Radio on matters
relating to criminal law.

NELSON, Richard
Nelsons, Derby (01332) 206111
See under Crime: Fraud, p. 405

NUNN, Stephen
Stephens & Scown, Exeter (01392) 210700
Specialisation: Criminal law specialist in all
aspects of defence work, with substantial
experience of trial advocacy and Youth Court.
Partner in charge of firm's criminal litigation
departments. Caseload ranging from murder to
summary cases. Acted in large MOD land fraud
conspiracy and other white collar cases.
Granted Higher Court rights in June 1994,
experience of jury trials.
Prof. Memberships: Area Criminal Justice
Liaison Committee, Magistrates & Crown Court
user groups, council member Devon & Exeter
Law Society (past chairman litigation committee).
Administrator of Exeter & Devon duty solicitor
schemes. 24 hour and court duty solicitor.
Career: Qualified 1981. 1979-1985 *Trump &
Partners*, Bristol. 1985 to date, *Stephens &
Scown*. Partner, 1990. Joint Winner of Law
Society centenary 'My favourite Solicitor'
competition for pro bono work in high profile
miscarriage of justice case. Regular television
appearances on this and other legal issues.
Personal: Born 24.12.55. Married with

children. Lives in Exeter. Leisure interests
include cinema and computer technology,
including programming, Internet and games.

PRENTICE, Alexander
McCourts, Edinburgh (0131) 225 6555

PROWEL, Martyn
Martin Prowel, Edwards & Davies, Cardiff
(01222) 496316

ROYLE, Charles
Glaisyers, Birmingham (0121) 233 2971
Specialisation: Crime, all areas including
Youth & Motoring, Licensing – liquor & gaming.
Prof. Memberships: Law Society, Birmingham
Law Society, Duty Solicitor.
Career: Palmers School Grays, George Dixon
Grammer School Birmingham, Sheffield
University. Articled *George Jonas*, Partner with
Jonas Grove & Co, Partner with *Glaisyers* since
1979, now Senior Partner.
Personal: Keen Sportsman & Fan; Cricket,
Tennis, Golf, Soccer, Rugby. Married with 3
children; President of Edgbaston Nursery
School.

SINCLAIR, Franklin
Tuckers, Manchester (0161) 835 1414
Senior Partner.
Specialisation: In overall control of large
criminal practice dealing in all aspects of
criminal defence work. Particular specialisation
as an advocate defending the rights of clients
in a robust manner and dealing with many
serious cases, including extensive involvement
in preparation from the outset of a case to its
conclusion. Has dealt with numerous murder
cases and specialises, particularly, in large
scale drugs' importation and armed robbery
cases. Has previously dealt with the first case
involving challenge to D.N.A. evidence which
initially was successful at the Court of Appeal.
Prof. Memberships: Manchester Law Society.
Solicitor Member of Criminal Justice Liaison
Committee for the North-West. Vice Chairman
of Criminal Law Solicitors' Association
(C.L.S.A.).
Career: Qualified 1982. Partner with Barry
Tucker in *Tuckers Solicitors* since 1984.
Personal: Manchester Grammer School;
Manchester University; College of Law, Chester.

Married with three children. Interests include
Golf, Environmental Issues, Gardening. Born
28th June 1958. Lives in Cheshire.

SMYTH, Maurice T.
Gordon & Smyth, Glasgow (0141) 332 5705

SUGARÉ, Anthony
Sugaré & Co, Leeds (0113) 244 6978
Senior Partner and founder of firm 1974.
Specialisation: Experienced advocate
specialising in criminal and road traffic matters.
Recommended by leading motoring
organisation. Provides representation for
defendants in all areas of criminal law, both
legal aid and private. Wide expertise in
representing sportsmen and sporting
associations.
Career: Qualified in 1970. Founded and
became Senior Partner of *Sugaré & Co.* in
1974. Member of the Leeds Duty Solicitor
Committee. Criminal Law Officer of Leeds Law
Society and Chairman of Solicitors
Representatives on the Leeds Court Users
Group.
Personal: Born 16th July 1943. Attended
Leeds Grammar School and Manchester
University. Leisure pursuits include rugby
league, golf and horse racing. Lives in Leeds.

TOMLINSON, Kevin
Kieran & Co, Worcester (01905) 28635

WARBOYS, Kevin
Copleys, St. Ives. Huntingdon
(01480) 456191

WARD, B.A.
Barrie Ward & Julian Griffiths, Nottingham
(0115) 9412622

WILLIAMS, I.M.
Robertsons, Cardiff (01222) 237777

WINFIELD, Jane
Freeth Cartwright Hunt Dickins, Nottingham
(0115) 936 9369
Specialisation: General crime including Youth
Court.
Career: Articled *Hunt Dickins*; qualified 1989;
assistant/ associate solicitor *Hunt Dickins*
1989-1994; partner *Freeth Cartwright Hunt
Dickins* 1994.
Personal: Horse riding.

CUSTOMS & EXCISE

See also Tax (Corporate) & VAT

LONDON

Baker & McKenzie (1ptnr, 1 sen asst, 1jun asst) *Andrew Hart* ("head of the bunch", "senior chap with a wealth of experience") heads the team which handles mainly advisory work, some dispute resolution but little litigation. **Clients/Work:** Main client base tends to be multi-national "high-tech" companies and other industry sectors including alcoholic beverages and chemicals. Recent work includes transfer pricing inquiry advice and challenging the classification of imported CD Roms.

Titmuss Sainer Dechert (2ptnrs, 5assts) Gavin Macfarlane (last year's leader) is now a consultant and still advises on non-contentious customs matters, but the first point of contact for clients is *Malachy Cornwell-Kelly.* **Clients/Work:** Act for top five accountancy firms, large commercial organisations and private individuals. Customs duty cases in VAT & Duties Tribunal and the High Court on origin, valuation and tariff classification. Judicial reviews of excise duty drawback for alcohol sales to Calais, and of Ministry of Agriculture on import restrictions for pesticides.

LEADING FIRMS · LONDON
BAKER & MCKENZIE
TITMUSS SAINER DECHERT

LEADING INDIVIDUALS
HART Andrew Baker & McKenzie
CORNWELL-KELLY Malachy Titmuss Sainer Dechert

AN INDEX TO ALL PROFILES IS ON PAGE 67.

The NORTH

Dibb Lupton Alsop (Manchester) *David Hanman* specialises in the criminal aspects of Customs & Excise and Inland Revenue investigations.

LEADING FIRMS · THE NORTH
DIBB LUPTON ALSOP Manchester

LEADING INDIVIDUALS
HANMAN David Dibb Lupton Alsop

AN INDEX TO ALL PROFILES IS ON PAGE 67.

LEADERS' PROFILES · LONDON AND THE NORTH

CORNWELL-KELLY, Malachy
Titmuss Sainer Dechert, London
(0171) 583 5353
International Trade and Customs Division.
Specialisation: Negotiates and handles disputes with Customs and Excise and IBEA on all VAT, customs and excise duty matters. Work covers investigation cases, tariff classification, valuation and transfer pricing issues, origin, duty preference, export rebates, CAP questions, import and export licensing, anti-dumping duties, and appeals to and appearances before the VAT and Duties Tribunal and the European Court. Cases have included agricultural levy disputes and CAP export refunds, tariff classification, origin disputes, customs duty panel, VAT liability, Single Market excise liabilities, collateral insurance rights, judicial review of Customs & Excise and United Nations trade sanctions. Author of 'European Community Law,' 2nd edition, a regular column in The In-House Lawyer and The Practical Tax Lawyer, and articles in Taxation, The Law Society's Gazette and Exporting Today. Frequent conference speaker.
Prof. Memberships: Law Society VAT and Duties Committee, VAT Practitioners Group, Customs Practitioners Group, Institute of Indirect Taxation, Law Society representative on Joint Customs Consultative Committee.
Career: Qualified in 1971. Worked at Customs and Excise Solicitor's Office 1972–77, then *Richards Butler* 1977–83. Joined the Law Society as Revenue Law Committee Secretary in 1983 before becoming Director of Tax Investigations for the Parliamentary Ombudsman in 1988. Joined *Titmuss Sainer & Webb* (now *Titmuss Sainer Dechert*) in 1993.

Personal: Born 11th May 1947. Attended King's College, London, 1965–68 (LLB), then College of Law, London, 1968–69, Ecole Nationale d'Administration, Paris, 1975. Secretary of the Tax Law Review Committee at the Institute for Fiscal Studies 1993–95, chairman of the VAT and Duties Tribunal and deputy special commissioner. Leisure interests include cider and beer making and collecting Customs memorabilia. Lives in Sevenoaks, Kent.

HANMAN, David
Dibb Lupton Alsop, Manchester
(0345) 262728
Specialisation: Criminal – representing clients involved in Tax Investigations conducted by the National Investigation Service (NIS) of HM Customs & Excise and the Special Compliance Office (SLO) of HM Inland Revenue. Civil – advice to clients of Value Added Tax and Customs & Excise matters.
Prof. Memberships: Law Society; Chartered Institute of Taxation (CIOT); Institue of Indirect Tax (AIIT); VAT Practice Group (VPG); Customs Practitioner Group (CPG).
Career: Qualified 1992: *Vaudreys* 1992-94. *Wacks Caller* called 1994-1996. Joined Commercial Regulatory Group a *Dibb Lupton Alsop* Jan 1997.
Personal: Tae Kwon-do.

HART, Andrew
Baker & McKenzie, London (0171) 919 1000
Partner in EU, Competition and Trade Law Department.
Specialisation: Principal area of practice is commercial and trade law, notably customs and VAT law. Advises multinational and domestic companies on practice and procedures relating to their business, especially the impact of customs duties and other taxes, and maximizing the benefit to be derived from various customs regimes and reliefs. Assists clients in responding to enquiries and investigations into compliance with customs and VAT obligations, including negotiation and settlement of investigations by the Customs National Investigation Service and other parts of H.M. Customs & Excise. Clients include Digital, Seagate, Octel, IBM, and Informix. Writes Customs Update for Butterworth's monthly *De Voil's Indirect Tax Intelligence.* Author of Customs and VAT sections of Sweet & Maxwell's 'Encyclopedia of Information Technology Law'. Has undertaken speaking engagements in the US, UK and India on various aspects of UK and EU trade, customs, VAT and tax law and practice. Charge-out rate is £350–£400 per hour.
Prof. Memberships: Law Society (Member of VAT and Duties Sub-Committee of Revenue Law Committee), Customs Practitioners Group (Hon. Secretary).
Career: Qualified in 1972. Partner at *Baker & McKenzie* since 1980. [PER] Born 2nd August 1947. Educated at Nottingham University 1966–69 (LL.B Hons). Leisure interests include football and squash. Lives in London.

DEBT RECOVERY AND FACTORING

RESEARCH: In compiling the tables, we consider all the information available to us, paying particular regard to the market research carried out by our team of ten qualified lawyers. (The researchers' details are set out on page three.) The rankings, therefore, reflect the opinion of the marketplace as revealed by systematic and objective research: see page four. (Our research is audited every year by the British Market Research Bureau.)

Overview: Firms listed in this section fall into one of two categories. Some practices provide a bespoke service to other debt collectors, factors and corporate clients. Such firms tend to be in London or the large regional centres, and draw on the expertise and experience of their associated litigation departments. Other firms provide high volume and low cost debt recovery services to various companies.

In London, Braby & Waller (in particular) and Wilde & Partners still stand out for the volume and quality of their work. Leading units outside London include Eversheds, Greenwoods and Hewitson Becke + Shaw in East Anglia; Bermans in Liverpool; and Addleshaw Booth & Co, Dibb Lupton Alsop, and Hammond Suddards in the Leeds area. In Scotland, McClure Naismith and The Morton Fraser Partnership are most prominent. Babington & Croasdaile and Comerton & Hill in Northern Ireland are at the top. Because much of the work is of a similar nature we only mention the top firms in each area, and we have considerably diminished the size of the lists this year.

LEADING FIRMS · LONDON

BRABY & WALLER (DEBT RECOVERY DIVISION OF IRWIN MITCHELL SOLICITORS)

WILDE & PARTNERS

HIGHLY REGARDED FIRMS

Wilde Sapte

Davies Arnold Cooper
Jeffrey Green Russell

Edge & Ellison
Nabarro Nathanson
Sprecher Grier
Tucker Turner Kingsley Wood & Co

LONDON

Braby & Waller Experienced and long-standing in debt recovery, and benefit from large clients. No-one had a bad word to say about them. The firm has merged with Irwin Mitchell, and is now effectively the debt recovery section of the firm.

Wilde & Partners A small commercial firm with a high profile in the field, and particularly well thought of in factoring. The unit has a high turnover, with a focus on trade and consumer debt recovery in the High Court and County Court.

Wilde Sapte (4ptnrs/6assts) Seen to do a high volume of medium-sized retail bank work.

Davies Arnold Cooper Insolvency based practice, with much debt recovery for the banking sector. Have "good people" working in this area.

Jeffrey Green Russell (5ptnrs/11assts) Focus on High Court and Companies Court matters. Well thought of by other firms for their "aggressive approach" and "good quality work." Act for many commercial clients, especially in the electrical and building industries. Also undertake local authority collection, particularly non-domestic rates.

SOUTH EAST

Blake Lapthorn (1ptnr/1asst, plus 6 other fee-earners) A well regarded debt recovery practice which is based in the litigation department. Have a dedicated debt collection department. **Clients/Work:** Act for First Direct Ltd; Zurich Life Assurance Company; Coopers & Lybrand (now Price Waterhouse Coopers).

Boyes Turner & Burrows (1ptnr) Assisted by three other fee earners. The firm has an "excellent" insolvency department, and their debt recovery practice benefits from this reputation. **Clients/Work:** Act for Kelly Services (UK) Ltd; Merloni Domestic Appliances Ltd; Bax Global Ltd.

Brachers (1ptnr, plus 16 other fee-earners) Recognised as regional leaders, with a large and dedicated team. Act for clients in the construction, transport and credit card industries. **Clients/Work:** Act for many well known national and international clients. The firm has reciprocal arrangements with firms in Scotland and other European countries.

Donne Mileham & Haddock (1ptnr/3assts) Have a "small but very good unit." Considered "well organised" and have a "good dedicated practice." **Clients/Work:** Act for clients such as the Bank of Scotland, Ann Summers Ltd and the Civil Service Motoring Association.

Shoosmiths & Harrison Considered a big name in debt collection and have a national network of offices. Strong in repossession work. **Clients/Work:** Act for institutional lenders, including clearing banks and building societies.

Tarlo Lyons The Southend office deals with the bulk of the firm's debt recovery work, although the litigation department in London handles more complex matters. **Clients/Work:** Act for high street banks, mail order firms, finance companies and building societies.

HIGHLY REGARDED FIRMS • SOUTH EAST	
Blake Lapthorn Fareham	**Donne Mileham & Haddock** Brighton
Boyes Turner & Burrows Reading	**Shoosmiths & Harrison** Reading
Brachers Maidstone	**Tarlo Lyons** Southend-on-Sea
Clarks Reading	**Stevens & Bolton** Guildford
Clyde & Co Guildford	**Thomson Snell & Passmore** Tunbridge Wells
Cole & Cole Oxford	**Trethowan Woodford** Southampton
Cripps Harries Hall Tunbridge Wells, Kent	**White & Bowker** Winchester
Glenisters Ruislip	
Clarkson Wright & Jakes Orpington	**Rawlison & Butler** Crawley
Linnells Oxford	**Turbervilles with Nelson Cuff** Uxbridge
Matthew Arnold & Baldwin Watford	**Underwoods** St. Albans
Moore & Blatch Southampton	**Wynne Baxter Godfree and**
Mundays Esher	**Selwood Leathes Hooper** Brighton

SOUTH WEST and WALES

Bevan Ashford (Bristol) A "good firm which fully deserves its reputation." Considered "very strong" in the region and has "reliable people" in charge. **Clients/Work:** Small to medium-sized businesses and trade debtors.

Burges Salmon (Bristol) Have been elevated in the bands this year, and are considered "highly professional." **Clients/Work:** Act for Halifax, Nationwide and Cheltenham & Gloucester.

Clarke Willmott & Clarke (Taunton, Yeovil) (1ptnr/2assts) A solid commercial practice with "lots of West Country clients." Recent re-organisation has resulted in the formation of a dedicated Debt Recovery and Factoring Unit in Yeovil. Have a growing profile in the food and parcel carrying sector. **Clients/ Work:** Advice on credit control procedures and risk analysis assessment. Clients include Northern Foods Ltd; Amtrak; Ginsters.

HIGHLY REGARDED FIRMS • SOUTH WEST AND WALES	
Bevan Ashford Bristol	**Osborne Clarke** Bristol
Burges Salmon Bristol	**Stephens & Scown** Exeter / Truro
Clarke Willmott & Clarke Taunton, Yeovil	
Anstey Sargent & Probert Exeter	**Eversheds** Cardiff
Bond Pearce Plymouth	**Lawrence Tucketts** Bristol
Cartwrights Bristol	**Townsends** Swindon
Douglas-Jones Mercer Swansea	**Wansbroughs Willey Hargrave** Bristol
Edwards Geldard Cardiff	
Davies and Partners Gloucester	**Pardoes** Bridgwater
Dickinson Manser Poole	**Porter Dodson** Yeovil
Guthrie Francis Newport	**Steele Raymond** Bournemouth
Lester Aldridge Bournemouth	**Veale Wasbrough** Bristol
Michelmores Exeter	**Withy King** Bath

Osborne Clarke (Bristol) A team of four fee earners deals with debt recovery. The firm is also known for its insolvency practice. **Clients/Work:** Clients include Chesterton plc, Danish Bacon plc and Bristol & West.

Stephens & Scown (Exeter/Truro) (2ptnrs spend 10% of their time on this area). Four other fee earners also deal with debt matters. **Clients/Work:** Connect South West; KPMG.

MIDLANDS

Edge & Ellison 3 fee-earners deal with debt recovery. Also have an insolvency section. Strong on mortgage repossession and finance work. **Clients/Work:** Act for a number of breweries including Carlsberg Tetley, and the leading supplier of white goods in the UK; also act for Thomas Cook.

Freeth Cartright Hunt Dickins Have a "very good reputation in this area." Act for smaller clients than other firms in the band, but deal with a high volume of work. Offer a one-stop-shop service which includes mediation and ADR. **Clients/Work:** Act for a wide range of clients including those in the consumer, retail and commercial sectors.

HIGHLY REGARDED FIRMS • MIDLANDS	
Edge & Ellison Birmingham	**Hewitson Becke + Shaw** Northampton
Freeth Cartwright Hunt Dickins Nottingham	
Browne Jacobson Nottingham	**Toller Hales & Collcutt** Northampton
Eversheds Birmingham / Nottingham	**Warner Cranston** Coventry
Howes Percival Northampton	
Blunts Walsall	**Shakespeares** Birmingham
Gateley Wareing Birmingham	**Willcox Lane Clutterbuck** Birmingham
Lanyon Bowdler Shrewsbury	**Wragge & Co** Birmingham
Pinsent Curtis Birmingham	

Hewitson Becke + Shaw Known for their high turnover of work and international client base. Based in the Northampton office. **Clients/Work:** Work for banks and companies in many jurisdictions, including Australia, Croatia, Colombia, Pakistan and Saudi Arabia. Offer an internet service to clients.

Eversheds (1ptnr/2assts) Assisted by 15 other fee earners, the core team handles mortgage repossessions, shortfall recovery, unsecured debt collection, professional negligence, contested recoveries and general banking litigation. Client base mainly comprises financial institutions. **Clients/Work:** Repossessions for Natwest Home Loans; banking litigation for Natwest; general litigation for Midland Bank.

EAST ANGLIA

Eversheds (1ptnr/2assts) Assisted by a team of 4 further fee earners. **Clients/Work:** Undertake bulk insolvency proceedings for HM Customs & Excise.

Greenwoods 3 fee-earners handle debt recovery work with the assistance of five others. Act only for commercial clients. **Clients/ Work:** Railtrack plc; Norwich & Peterborough plc; Thomas Cook plc.

LEADING FIRMS • EAST ANGLIA	
EVERSHEDS Norwich	**HEWITSON BECKE + SHAW** Cambridge
GREENWOODS Peterborough	

HIGHLY REGARDED FIRMS	
Bankes Ashton Bury St. Edmunds	**Greenland Houchen** Norwich
Birketts Ipswich	**Leathes Prior** Norwich
Gotelee & Goldsmith Ipswich	**Leeds Day** Sandy

NORTH WEST

Bermans (2ptnrs/6assts) Plus 14 other fee earners. Act for several leasing companies. Have a good reputation in the field. **Clients/Work:** London Borough of Camden; Environment Agency; Carlsberg.

Cuff Roberts (1ptnr plus 4 other fee-earners) Carry out a wide range of debt recovery work for a variety of commercial organisations, with the benefit of the back-up from a good litigation department.

HIGHLY REGARDED FIRMS • NORTH WEST	
Bermans Liverpool	
Addleshaw Booth & Co Manchester	**Lees Lloyd Whitley** Liverpool
Aaron & Partners Chester	**Davies Wallis Foyster** Liverpool
Cobbetts Manchester	**Halliwell Landau** Manchester
Cuff Roberts Liverpool	**Thomas Higgins** Wirral

Clients/Work: Act for three major consumer credit banks/institutions, for accountants and for major agricultural companies.

NORTH EAST

Addleshaw Booth & Co (1ptnr/5assts) Very strong on institutional debt recovery, especially banks and building societies. Also act for clients in the public sector. 90 other fee earners are involved to a lesser extent. **Clients/Work:** Mortgage arrears, general debt recovery for commercial clients. Act for 21 institutions. Offer online facilities to clients.

Dibb Lupton Alsop Debt recovery work is undertaken by the Business Services Group. **Clients/Work:** Debt collection, repossessions and recoveries. Offer one-stop-shop for debt recovery and debt management. Possess an advanced computerised recovery system.

Hammond Suddards The Bradford office is dedicated to providing lender services, and they advise on recovery, repossessions and volume conveyancing

LEADING FIRMS • NORTH EAST	
ADDLESHAW BOOTH & CO Leeds	**HAMMOND SUDDARDS** Bradford
DIBB LUPTON ALSOP Bradford	
EVERSHEDS Leeds	

HIGHLY REGARDED FIRMS	
Carrick Carr & Wright Kingston upon Hull	**Walker Morris** Leeds
R.C. Moorhouse & Co Leeds	
Ford & Warren Leeds	**Read Hind Stewart** Leeds
Irwin Mitchell Sheffield	**Robert Muckle** Newcastle-upon-Tyne
Lupton Fawcett Leeds	**Wilkin Chapman** Grimsby
Pinsent Curtis Leeds	

services. Possess an impressive client base. **Clients/Work:** Deal with 30,000 live transactions at any one time for clients across the country. Act for Halifax plc, Bradford & Bingley Building Society and Prudential Banking plc.

Eversheds Seen to handle more bulk debt recovery work than local competitors.

SCOTLAND

McClure Naismith (1ptnr f/t and 5 p/t; 10 assts also involved) Offer a "cost effective" and "aggressive" debt recovery service. Considered "excellent." **Clients/Work:** Birmingham Midshires Mortgage Services Ltd; Barclays Bank plc; Dalziel Ltd.

The Morton Fraser Partnership Have a large and respectable debt recovery service. **Clients/Work:** Act for large banks and commercial institutions.

Bonar MacKenzie WS (3ptnrs/1asst) The firm has a strong commercial reputation, and is considered "excellent" on debt matters.

Brodies WS The debt recovery service benefits from the commercial excellence of the firm in general and has "outstanding leadership."

LEADING FIRMS · SCOTLAND	
MCCLURE NAISMITH Glasgow	**THE MORTON FRASER PARTNERSHIP** Edinburgh
BONAR MACKENZIE WS Edinburgh	**BRODIES WS** Edinburgh

HIGHLY REGARDED FIRMS	
Dundas & Wilson CS Glasgow	**Miller Samuel & Co** Glasgow
Kidstons & Co Glasgow	
Anderson Fyfe Glasgow	**Fyfe Ireland WS** Edinburgh
Balfour & Manson Edinburgh	**Macdonalds** Glasgow
Bennett & Robertson Edinburgh	**McGrigor Donald** Glasgow
Bishop and Robertson Chalmers Glasgow	
Aitken Nairn WS Edinburgh	**Brechin Tindal Oatts** Glasgow
Bird Semple Glasgow	**Henderson Boyd Jackson WS** Glasgow
Blackadder Reid Johnston Dundee	**Wright, Johnston & Mackenzie** Glasgow

NORTHERN IRELAND

Babington & Croasdaile 2 ptnrs deal with factoring. **Clients/Work:** General debt recovery, and also act directly for creditors.

Comerton & Hill 4 assts deal with debt recovery. **Clients/Work:** Act for finance houses with some work in the building industry.

HIGHLY REGARDED FIRMS · NORTHERN IRELAND	
Babington & Croasdaile Londonderry	**Comerton & Hill** Belfast
Carson & McDowell Belfast	**S.J. Diamond & Son** Belfast
Cleaver Fulton & Rankin Belfast	**John McKee & Son** Belfast
Hewitt & Gilpin Belfast	**J.W. Russell & Co** Newtonards
O'Reilly Stewart Belfast	**Wilson Nesbitt** Belfast

DEFAMATION

See also Media & Entertainment

RESEARCH: In compiling the tables, we consider all the information available to us, paying particular regard to the market research carried out by our team of ten qualified lawyers. (The researchers' details are set out on page three.) The rankings, therefore, reflect the opinion of the marketplace as revealed by systematic and objective research: see page four. (Our research is audited every year by the British Market Research Bureau.)

OVERVIEW: The major change in London is the elevation of Schilling & Lom and Partners to the top band of firms, following a very successful year and praise from competitors and clients. Farrer & Co, Olswang and Peter Carter-Ruck and Partners remain at the top of the table, reflecting the majority rather than a unanimous opinion.

Crockers Oswald Hickson move up a band as the merger is felt to be working well. Theodore Goddard also move up following recommendation from competitors and clients. Roderick Dadak has left The Simkins Partnership and joined Lewis Silkin, bringing the latter firm into the list. Liz Hartley has left DJ Freeman and joined Reynolds Porter Chamberlain and they too enter the table. Harbottle & Lewis joins the list following various recommendations from Counsel, and Stephens Innocent is another new entry, mainly because of its work for US newspapers.

We have amalgamated the other regions and only two firms in the south west, Foot & Bowden and Wiggin & Co, stand out as having a major strength in defamation. In Scotland Bird Semple and Levy and McRae appear to have the majority of the work. In Northern Ireland Paul Spring has left Cleaver Fulton & Rankin and joined Mills Selig bringing them into the tables.

LEADING FIRMS • LONDON

FARRER & CO
OLSWANG
PETER CARTER-RUCK AND PARTNERS
SCHILLING & LOM AND PARTNERS

CROCKERS OSWALD HICKSON
DAVENPORT LYONS
THEODORE GODDARD

BIDDLE
BINDMAN & PARTNERS
CLIFFORD CHANCE
DAVID PRICE & CO
D J FREEMAN
GOODMAN DERRICK
HARBOTTLE & LEWIS
HENRY HEPWORTH
RUSSELL JONES & WALKER
STEPHENS INNOCENT
SWEPSTONE WALSH

HIGHLY REGARDED FIRMS

Lewis Silkin
Lovell White Durrant
Manches & Co
Mishcon de Reya
Simons Muirhead & Burton

Davies Arnold Cooper
Reynolds Porter Chamberlain

LONDON

Farrer & Co (2ptnrs 100%/2assts 100%) *Robert Clinton* ("one of the top men in the field," "a star," "the big hitter") leads the team and it is felt that the firm's reputation in this field is built on "his connections and ability." Highly recommended by clients. **Clients/ Work:** Acting for Newsgroup re the drugs allegations concerning Jack Straw's son. Acting for Guy Snowden in his appeal re the Richard Branson/GTec libel action. Representing the Telegraph re Saif Gaddafi's action. Involved in police litigation.

Olswang (2ptnrs/4assts) *Geraldine Proudler* has had "a fantastic run" and is generally acknowledged as one of the toughest opponents in the field. Her recent high profile victories have consolidated her pre-eminent position as the "star of the London defamation scene." *Julia Palca* remains highly respected. **Clients/Work:** Successfully defended the Guardian in Jonathan Aitken's libel action. Acted for Marks & Spencer in recovering £700,000 from Granada TV in action arising from a World In Action programme. Settled libel action for Jupiter Asset

Management Ltd against London Financial News obtaining front page apology.

Peter Carter-Ruck and Partners (8ptnrs 100%, 1ptnr 50%/5assts) The firm and *Peter Carter-Ruck* himself remain "very highly regarded – despite the passage of time." Praised by clients for their ability to "see the issues immediately and deal with them quickly and effectively." *Alasdair Pepper* has a no-nonsense style, gets things done and clients like him. *Andrew Stephenson* is knowledgeable and for some clients "the first port of call." *Nigel Tait* was praised for his unassuming style and his negotiating skills. It remains to be seen how the firm will cope with the recent internal problems. **Clients/Work:** Acting for the Barclay Brothers against the Sunday Times, for The Express against Edwina Currie and for Cornell University against Dr Laurence Godfrey. Also act for Hello magazine, Michael Winner and Viscount Rothermere.

Schilling & Lom and Partners (4ptnrs/ 7assts) Move up to the top band following a successful year and praise from clients. Respected for their use of the law of confidence to protect the reputations of their

celebrity clients. *Keith Schilling* has a "fearsome reputation" and the "tough/bordering on aggressive approach" gets results and was commended. **Clients/Work:** Major success in obtaining six figure sum of damages and front page apology for Brooke Shields within one week of publication. Successful libel actions for Elizabeth Hurley against the Daily Mirror; for Eamon Holmes against the Express and Daily Star and for Warner Bros against the Daily Mail regarding the New Avengers film.

Crockers Oswald Hickson (4ptnrs 75%-100%/3assts) Described as "a safe pair of hands for defendants – cautious and sensible." *Richard Shillito* is seen as "effective and competent" and *Rupert Grey* and *Paul Davies* are solid members of the team. **Clients/Work:** Defending the Independent against Kojo Tsikata. Acting for Neil

Hamilton against Mohammed Al Fayed. Acted for former Irish Prime Minister Albert Reynolds against the Sunday Times.

Davenport Lyons (3ptnrs/5assts) *Kevin Bays* ("tough," "terrific negotiator") and *Philip Conway* (*"good if you want a settlement"*) are the main players at the firm. Have mostly defendant clients. **Clients/Work:** Representing Marketing Week in case concerning the disclosure of journalists' powers. Acting for Penguin Books in libel claim brought by David Irving over books about the Holocaust. Recovered £30,000 for Bodker against the Mail on Sunday.

Theodore Goddard *Martin Kramer* ("shrewd operator," "good negotiator") received praise from contemporaries for his effective handling of both plaintiff and defendant matters. *Katherine Rimmel* was also singled out as a name to watch and she enters our up and coming list. **Clients/Work:** Acting for the Sunday Times in the Albert Reynolds appeals. Acting for MORI in their dispute with the BBC. Obtained apology and damages for Western Provident in cyber-libel case against Norwich Union.

Biddle Team led by the "very intelligent" *David Hooper* who is "an extremely tough opponent." **Clients/Work:** Defending Conde Nast against Mohammed Al Fayed's libel action. Acted for Chris Patten against the Mail on Sunday. Acted for defendants in Berezovsky and Glouchkov v Forbes magazine involving decision on appropriate forum for libel actions.

Bindman & Partners (2ptnrs 25% – 50%/2assts 50% – 100%) *Geoffrey Bindman* has a "loyal following" and the firm's strength appears to rest on his personal reputation. **Clients/Work:** Acting for plaintiffs in Tsikata v The Independent and McPhilemy v Sunday Times. Acted for Tessa Sanderson v Sunday Mirror. Other clients include New Statesman, Gay Times, The Big Issue.

Clifford Chance (1ptnr 50%/6assts 50%) International and corporate bias to the work. *Michael Smyth* "knows his stuff" – he's a fighter and useful for heavy duty City libel." **Clients/Work:** Defending the "Dagens Naeringsliv" (a Scandinavian business publication) in three libel actions brought by Fiba Nordic Securities arising out of the Morgan Grenfell affair. Acting for City Mortgage Corporation in its libel action against Times Newspapers. Also act for Mirror Group, Reuters and GMTV.

David Price & Co (1ptnr/2assts 70%) *David Price* (a solicitor-advocate) is "capable and thorough," while *Paul Fox* is "self effacing and competent." **Clients/ Work:** Established that political party cannot sue for defamation in Sir James Goldsmith and the Referendum Party v Bhoyrul action. Involved in the landmark ruling on disclosure of sources by journalists in Ernest Saunders v Punch.

D J Freeman (3ptnrs including the "experienced" *Susan Aslan*). Have lost Elizabeth Hartley to Reynolds Porter Chamberlain but retain most of their work. **Clients/ Work:** Defended Channel 4 in libel actions against Dr Nixon and Terry Venables. Pre-publication advice to Reed Business Information.

Goodman Derrick (4ptnrs/3assts) *Patrick Swaffer* and *Jeffery Maunsell* are "extremely good." The team have a reputation for being "effective and pleasant," "not self publicists – just get on and do an excellent technical job for their clients." **Clients/ Work:** Defended Granada TV against Marks & Spencer. Defended Yorkshire TV against Urbanovitz.

Harbottle & Lewis (2ptnrs/5assts undertake media litigation) A new entry to the table following recommendation from practitioners and clients. Have an impressive celebrity client list. Much work involves preventing the publication of damaging material. **Clients/Work:** Represented Richard Branson in his high profile action against GTECH and Guy Snowden. Acting for publishers, Little Brown, in action which has now gone to the Court of Appeal.

Henry Hepworth (2ptnrs/1 asst) The new firm seems to have settled down well and *Brian Hepworth* remains respected for his wealth of experience. *Jason McCue* is "capable" and developing a "good reputation." **Clients/Work:** Representing Express Newspapers against Tom Cruise and Nicole Kidman. Acting for Times Newspapers against Sean McPhilemy and against Thomas and Patrick Murphy.

Russell Jones & Walker (3ptnrs/4assts) Known for their main client, The Police Federation. *Barton Taylor* "gets good results." **Clients/Work:** Acted for Kirby (solicitor) against Daily Telegraph. Acted for Sergeant Evans and Ors in 5 actions against News of the World, Today, Sunday Express, Daily Express and Guardian. Acted for Constables Bennett and Ors against Time Out Magazine Ltd.

Stephens Innocent (2ptnrs/1assoc/6assts) **Clients/Work:** Act for 9 US newspapers including Wall Street Journal, International Herald Tribune and Washington Post. Also represent satellite channels like MedTV. Involved in internet libel.

Swepstone Walsh *Rhory Robertson* and *Patrick Stewart* are the most prominent figures at this small but experienced practice. **Clients/Work:** Acting for Newspaper Publishing plc against Robert Kilroy Silk; for Mirror Group Newspapers Ltd against Neil Ruddock and for Sharon Feinstein against Punch Ltd.

Lewis Silkin *Roderick Dadak* has left The Simkins Partnership to join Lewis Silkin. He is an experienced practitioner with a good reputation. It remains to be seen whether he can establish a stable practice. **Clients/Work:** Acting for James Hewitt

against Direct Line and News Group Newspapers. Defending Express Newspapers against an action brought by Stephen Scott re the serialisation of a book in the Express. Acting for EUROMED against GEM Medical in a slander/malicious faleshood case re drug testing device.

Lovell White Durrant Sill rated for doing some good work. **Clients/Work:** Acting for the Barclay Brothers against the BBC. Settled action for The Independent against the main Versace company.

Manches & Co (2ptnrs including *John Rubinstein*/2assts – p/t) **Clients/Work:** Defending the European Journal of Clinical Hypnosis against claim by Paul McKenna. Defending RAC Motoring Services Ltd against claim by Cardata Ltd.

Mishcon De Reya (1ptnr 100%/1 consultant 100%/2 othr consts/5assts – p/t) Not as prominent as in previous years and Simon Gallant and Anthony Julius are now consultants. *Julie Scott-Bayfield* is seen to be "keeping the show on the road." **Clients/Work:** Defending Channel 4 against a claim by a doctor. Defending the International Herald Tribune against a claim by a Russian businessman. Acting for the late Diana, Princess of Wales against Express Newspapers re a report that she was keeping and not donating the proceeds of the auction of her dresses.

Simons Muirhead & Burton (2ptnrs 100%/1 asst 50%) *Razi Mireskandari* has been building up a solid reputation over the past few years. **Clients/Work:** Acting for Paula Yates against the Mirror and the Mail. Acting for Time Out against Givenchy and for a barrister against Business Age Magazine.

Davies Arnold Cooper (4ptnrs including *Keith Mathieson*/5assts in the IP/Media/Defamation team). **Clients/Work:** Successfully defended a professional food consultant at trial. Acted for printers of a satirical magazine sued by Linford Christie. Acted for daily newspaper in CA: plaintiff's case struck out.

Reynolds Porter Chamberlain (1ptnr/3assts) After many years with DJ Freeman, *Elizabeth Hartley* has joined Reynolds Porter Chamberlain, where she will continue to do some defamation work. **Clients/Work:** Representing the Evening Standard in the Belmarsh Prison contempt proceedings. Acting for the Daily Mail against various celebrities including Anna Pasternak and Michael York.

Frank Presland, ex Frere Cholmeley is now at Eversheds, and was also recommended.

LEADERS' PROFILES · LONDON

ASLAN, Susan
D J Freeman, London (0171) 583 4055
Partner in Media & Communications Department.
Specialisation: Principal area of practice is advising terrestrial and satellite broadcasting companies in relation to libel, contempt of court, breach of copyright and other programme content issues. Also undertakes a smaller amount of plaintiff work and covers breach of confidence and contractual disputes including claims in relation to programme format rights. Important cases handled include Thames Television v. Dixons (libel trial); Channel 4 v. Jani Allan (libel trial); Press Alliance v. Sherill (libel jurisdiction case before the European Court of Justice); Channel 4 v. Dr Nixon (libel trial) and others. Clients include Channel 4, BSkyB, Thames and Carlton. Co-author of 'A Short Guide to Small Screen Law.' Has appeared on ITV, radio, etc on libel matters. Charge-out rate is £275 per hour.
Prof. Memberships: Media Society.
Career: Qualified in 1985. Partner at *D J Freeman* since 1991.
Personal: Educated at The Latymer Grammar School and the University of York. Leisure interests include hill walking, theatre, books and horse riding. Lives in London.

BAYS, Kevin
Davenport Lyons, London (0171) 468 2600
Fax: (0171) 437 8216 E-mail: kbays@davenport-lyons.co.uk Partner in 1982.
Specialisation: Defamation, publishing and media law. Principal solicitor for 'Private Eye' for over 12 years. Other publisher clients include Mirror Group Newspapers, Express Newspapers and major book and magazine publishers. Also acts for plaintiffs in defamation cases. Handles general commercial litigation with an entertainment bias. Currently acting for Penguin Books in a major libel action brought by revisionist historian David Irving arising out of a book entitled 'Denying the Holocaust.'
Prof. Memberships: Law Society.
Career: Qualified 1979, having joined *Wright Webb Syrett* in 1977. Became a Partner in 1982.
Personal: Born 24th April 1955. Leisure interests include skiing, golf, cricket, football and travelling. Member of The Media Society and The Groucho Club.

BINDMAN, Geoffrey
Bindman & Partners, London
(0171) 833 4433
Senior Partner.
Specialisation: Specialises in civil liberties and human rights, media law, defamation, anti-

discrimination and general litigation. Author of numerous articles in the professional and national press on these subjects, and has broadcast frequently. Has represented the ICJ, IBA, Amnesty International, and other bodies in human rights missions in many countries.
Prof. Memberships: Law Society (Member of the Equal Opportunities Committee). Chairman, Discrimination Law Association.
Career: Established *Bindman & Partners* in 1974. From 1966 to 1976 was Legal Adviser to the Race Relations Board and thereafter until 1983 to the Commission for Racial Equality. Visiting professor, U.C.L.A (1982). Visiting Professor of Law at University College London and Honorary Fellow in Civil Legal Process at the University of Kent.
Personal: Born 3rd January 1933. Attended Newcastle RGS and Oriel College, Oxford.

CARTER-RUCK, Peter Frederick
Peter Carter-Ruck and Partners, London
(0171) 353 5005
Senior Consultant to Media, Intellectual Property and Trusts Departments.
Specialisation: Principal areas of practice are libel and copyright litigation for plaintiffs and defendants and checking written matter for libel, contempt of court and copyright for newspapers, magazines and T.V. companies. Also advises on literary and financial trusts, probate and matrimonial matters. Has acted in many leading cases including the copyright action and subsequent negotiations leading to the production and vesting of the copyright in Kevin McClory, the producer of the James Bond Film "Thunderball," the Hamilton and Howarth libel actions against the BBC and others, the case of Sir Ranulph Fiennes against Macleans Magazine and the King of Malaysia against the "Daily Mirror". Clients have included many Members of Parliament, Cabinet Ministers, Ambassadors and High Court Judges, Express Newspapers, Associated Newspapers, provincial newspapers, National Magazines and book publishers, Time Warner, the late Lord Olivier and the late Sir Terence Rattigan. Has written 'Libel and Slander' (Butterworths), 'Copyright: Modern Law and Practice' and 'The Cyclist and The Law' and has contributed numerous articles on media and newspaper law for the *Newspaper Society*. Has spoken extensively on media law and has more recently taken part in debates at Cambridge, Oxford and Durham Universities.
Prof. Memberships: Member, The International Bar Association, Justice, International Commission of Jurists (English Section), the Solicitors Benevolent Association

and the Institute of Journalists. Formerly specialist member of the Council of the Law Society and President of the City of Westminster Law Society.
Career: Qualified in 1937. Joined *Oswald Hickson, Collier & Co.* where he became Senior Partner 1945-81. Founded *Peter Carter-Ruck and Partners* in 1982 as Senior Partner.
Personal: Born 26th February 1914. Educated at Thorpe House Preparatory School, St. Edward's School, Oxford, 1928-31. Past Governor of St. Edward's School, Oxford, 1950-78, former Chairman and Governor of Shiplake College, Henley, past President of the Media Society, Member of Council of Justice since 1968, past Commodore of the Law Society Yacht Club and past Commodore of the Ocean Cruising Club. Leisure interests include sailing, walking, field work, carpentry, wood-turning and photography. Lives in Great Hallingbury, Herts.

CLINTON, Robert G.
Farrer & Co, London (0171) 242 2022
Partner. Head of Litigation, Managing Partner.
Specialisation: Main areas of practice are defamation and publishing related litigation. Involves extensive range of plaintiff and defendant work for prominent individuals and institutions, including newspaper and publishing companies. Pre- and post-publication advice including breach of confidence, contempt etc. Intellectual property work, covering general trademark and passing off work for commercial clients.
Prof. Memberships: Media Society. International Bar Association.
Career: Joined *Farrer & Co.* in 1972. Became Partner in 1979.
Personal: Born 19th August 1948. Attended Brasenose College, Oxford 1967-71. Lives in London.

CONWAY, Philip
Davenport Lyons, London (0171) 468 2600
Fax: (0171) 437 8216 E-mail: pconway@davenport-lyons.co.uk
Partner in Litigation Department.
Specialisation: Main area of practice is defamation, especially with regard to the newspaper and entertainment industries. Acted for Gorden Kaye (against the Sunday Sport), The Daily Star (against Gillian Taylforth) and Carmen Proetta (against The Sunday Times). Sunday Mirror (against Barry Jones). John Prescott (against Daily Telegraph). Chris Bodker (against The Mail on Sunday). The Sunday Express (against Ian Brady).
Prof. Memberships: Law Society (Member of

Privacy and Defamation Working Committees). **Career:** Qualified in 1984. Joined *Wright Webb Syrett* in February 1986. Became Partner in August 1988. Joined *Davenport Lyons* as a Partner on Merger with *Wright Webb Syrett* in March 1995.
Personal: Born 15th April 1959. Attended Aldenham School 1972-77. Former Director Southend United Football Club. Member of The Media Society, Groucho Club and a Barker of The Variety Club of Great Britain.

DADAK, Roderick
Lewis Silkin, London (0171) 227 8000
Head of Defamation.
Specialisation: Main areas of practice are defamation - libel, slander and malicious falsehood and handling complaints to the Press Complaints Commission and the Broadcasting Standards Commission. Wide experience acting for the media and, in particular, newspapers and publishers. Undertakes both plaintiff and defendant work, and pre-publication libel reading. Has represented newspapers in major libel trials (e.g. Kiffin, Sethia, and Lucas Box); judicial reviews (e.g. AN v Pickering); confidence actions (e.g. Stephens v Avery); copyright actions (e.g. Associated Newspapers v News Group Newspapers Ltd); contempt actions (e.g. acted for the Daily Star in successfully defending contempt proceedings brought by the Attorney General concerning Geoff Knights, and prior to that A.G. v ITV and Express Newspapers PLC) and passing off actions (e.g. Associated Newspapers v Insert Media, Associated Newspapers v News UK Ltd) also in important wardship cases (e.g. Re: W). Acted for many celebrities and high profile individuals in libel actions (e.g. Clare Latimer in Scallywag/New Statesman cases, John Cleese, Jenny Pitman, James Hewitt and numerous MPs). Acts for Express Newspapers PLC and other newspaper, book and magazine publishers. Lectures regularly on defamation matters.
Prof. Memberships: Law Society.
Career: Qualified in 1972. Articled *Theodore Goddard*, Partner *Swepstone Walsh* in 1983, becoming Senior Partner in 1991. At *The Simkins Partnership* 1996-1998. Joined *Lewis Silkin* 1998.
Personal: Attended Lancing College and King's College, London. LLB (Hons). Leisure pursuits include tennis, cinema, theatre and holidaying in Provence. Lives in Farnham. Married with three sons.

DAVIES, Paul
Crockers Oswald Hickson, London
(0171) 353 0311 / 583 5333
Consultant in Media Department.
Specialisation: Principal area of practice is libel (defamation). Important cases handled include Morgan v. Odhams Press, Cassell and Broome and Spycatcher as well as cases relating to protection of journalist's sources, notably in re an Inquiry under the Company Securities (insider dealing) Act 1985, X v. Morgan-Grampian and others and in re Saunders. Also regarding the extent of common law privilege in Tsikata v. Newspaper Publishing [1994]. In addition to libel, practice covers all other aspects of media law - contempt of court, reporting restrictions, copyright, injunctions, advertising, computer misuse, competition law, betting, gaming and

lotteries and newspaper competitions. Clients include national and international broadsheet newspapers, major regional newspaper groups, major trade business and specialist interest magazine publishers, Lloyd's syndicates and other insurers in the UK and abroad.
Prof. Memberships: Law Society.
Career: Qualified in 1964. Partner at *Oswald Hickson Collier* between 1965 and 1997.
Personal: Born 13th May 1939. Educated at Beaumont College 1952-57. Leisure interests include reading, music and gardening. Lives in Cobham, Surrey.

FOX, Paul
David Price & Co, London (0171) 916 9911
Specialisation: Main area of practice is defamation, and intellectual property, including pre-publication advice and High Court advocacy.
Career: Qualified, 1986. *Peter Carter-Ruck & Partners* 1984-1988, moving to *Turner Kenneth Brown*, England 1988, and Hong Kong in 1994 and joined *David Price & Co* in 1995.

GREY, Rupert C.
Crockers Oswald Hickson, London
(0171) 353 0311
Joint Senior Partner; Head of Media Department.
Specialisation: Principal area of practice is defamation and copyright. Retained by leading book, magazine and newspaper publishers and their insurers to advise on libel and allied matters prior to publication and post publication complaints. Also by leading photographic/syndication agencies to handle matters connected with literary and artistic copyright. Lectures, writes and gives seminars. Also retained by high profile individuals in advisory, preemptive and plaintiff work. Clients include: The Financial Times, Telegraph Group, Emap, Hello! Limited, Centaur Communications Limited, The Liverpool Institute for Performing Arts and Members of Parliament.
Prof. Memberships: Fellow of Royal Geographical Society.
Career: Qualified in 1975, served articles with *Farrer & Co*. Joined *Crockers* in 1981, Partner in 1983, Head of Department in 1989, Senior Partner in 1997. Previous lives include prospecting for copper in the Fiji Islands, for nickel in Australia, as a roughneck in the Yukon and freelance photo-journalism.
Personal: Born 8th September 1946. Educated Wellington College and UCL. Principal leisure activities are expeditions to wild places and building barns. Married to Jan Sinclair, three daughters; lives in the South Downs.

HARTLEY, Elizabeth B.A.
Reynolds Porter Chamberlain, London
(0171) 242 2877
email: ebh@rpc.co.uk Partner and Head of Media, Communications and Technology Group
Specialisation: A very experienced litigator whose principal areas of practice are defamation work for defendants and publishers, both pre-publication advice and defending libel, contempt of court, breach of confidence, copyright actions and complaints to the Press Complaints Commission. High profile cases include Homan v. Associated Newspapers, the Geoff Knights, Magee and Belmarsh prison contempt actions and

Pasternak v. Associated Newspapers. Also experienced in information technology disputes and has represented both users and suppliers of IT products and services. Has advised on IT disputes in banking, manufacturing, publishing, health, aviation and privatisations.
Prof. Memberships: Association Internationale des Jeunes Advocats; Honorary Fellow of the American Bar Association; the Media Society; The Society for Computers and the Law; International Bar Association; and London Solicitors Litigation Association.
Career: Qualified 1982. Chairman of London Young Solicitor's Group 1987-88; Partner, *D J Freeman* 1987, Head of Commercial Litigation from 1996. Joined *Reynolds Porter Chamberlain* as a partner 1997.
Personal: Born 1957; Royal Masonic School for Girls; University of Sheffield. Resides London. Leisure: horse riding, gardening, theatre, opera, her children.

HEPWORTH, Brian
Henry Hepworth, London (0171) 242 7999
Partner in Litigation Department.
Specialisation: Main areas of practice are defamation and media, including contempt and contentious copyright. Acts mainly for television, newspapers and publishers. Handles pre-publication clearance, injunctive work and post-publication litigation. Acted for broadcasters in successfully defending the injuctions concerning the broadcast of recorded interviews with mass murderers Denis Nilsen and Beverley Allitt. Major clients include Central Television, Carlton Television, IPC Magazines, Express Newspapers and Mirror Group Newspapers. Highly experienced in US and UK insurance claims.
Prof. Memberships: Law Society, Media Society.
Career: Qualified in 1981. Partner *Peter Carter-Ruck & Partners* 1982-88. Joined *Mishcon de Reya* as a Partner in 1988 and *Goodman Derrick* as Partner in 1995. One of Founding Partners of *Henry Hepworth* 1 May 1997.
Personal: Born 14 November 1950. Attended Salford Grammar Shcool 1962-69 and King's College London 1969-72. Leisure interests include Rugby and contemporary literature. Lives in St Albans.

HOOPER, David
Biddle, London (0171) 606 9301
Partner in Media Department.
Specialisation: Main area of practice is media and defamation. Also handles entertainment, copyright matters, publishing and broadcasting and issues involving multimedia. Acted for Peter Wright and the publishers in the Spycatcher case. Successfully involved in defending libel actions brought by Robert Maxwell. Acted for John Major in his libel action and prevented attempt by the Government to injunct Andy McNab's book. Acted for Chris Patten against HarperCollins. Publications include 'Public Scandal Odium and Contempt' and 'Official Secrets: The Use and Abuse of the Act.' Has contributed many articles on defamation and media matters in periodicals and the national press and regularly addresses conferences.
Prof. Memberships: Law Society, International Bar Association.
Career: Qualified in 1971 as a Barrister and in 1977 as a Solicitor. Joined *Biddle* as a Partner in 1986.
Personal: Born 5th January 1949. Attended

Eton College 1961-66, then Balliol College 1967-70. Leisure pursuits include cricket, theatre and country activities. Lives in London.

KRAMER, Martin
Theodore Goddard, London
(0171) 606 8855
Specialisation: Media-related litigation for corporate and individual clients, both plaintiffs and defendants. Main newspaper clients are The Sunday Times and The Times. Areas of expertise include libel and slander; malicious falsehood; contempt of court; human rights cases relating to freedom of expression; confidentiality and official secrets; copyright and passing off. Recent and current cases include acting for the Sunday Times in the appeals arising out of the libel action brought by the former Prime Minister of Ireland, Albert Reynolds; for Western Provident Association, the medical insurance company, which successfully sued Norwich Union for defamation on its email; and for MORI and Robert Worcester in their libel action against the BBC.
Prof. Memberships: Law Society.
Career: Main areas of practice are media-related litigation and administrative and public law. Qualified 1969. Partner 1978.

MATHIESON, Keith
Davies Arnold Cooper, London
(0171) 936 2222
Partner in IP and Media Department.
Specialisation: Main area of practice is media law, particularly defamation, but including contempt of court, reporting restrictions, copyright and passing off. Has acted for and against numerous national and regional newspaper and magazine groups and their insurers. As well as litigation, advises a wide range of publishers on copy clearance. Has written various articles for legal and other publications.
Career: Qualified 1983 with *Lovell White & King*. Joined *Oswald Hickson Collier* 1990. Partner 1992. Joined *Davies Arnold Cooper* in 1997.
Personal: Born 1959. Caius College, Cambridge 1977-80. Postgraduate diploma in UK and European law of copyright, King's College, London 1997.

MAUNSELL, Jeffery
Goodman Derrick, London (0171) 404 0606
Partner and Head of Media Litigation Department
Specialisation: Intellectual property, defamation, copyright and all aspects of media law. Is one of the most experienced practitioners in libel and general litigaton. Specialises in representing television companies and undertaking work requiring pre- and post-transmission expertise. Has acted in many celebrated and successful cases involving films (Oscar Wilde; Oliver!; The Charge of the Light Brigade) and politicians including Harold Wilson (-v- The Move pop group); Reginald Maudling (-v- Granada Television); Jonathan Aitken (both for him in 1970 in his Official Secrets case and against him in the libel trial of Aitken -v- Granada Television which collapsed so bizarrely in June 1997). Enjoys the cut and thrust of litigation and getting to the nub of the intractable problems

facing the client.
Career: Joined *Goodman Derrick* in 1956 and has been a Partner since 1972.
Personal: Born 1936. Lives in London.

MCCUE, Jason
Henry Hepworth, London (0171) 242 7999
Partner in Media Litigation department.
Specialisation: Media Law: Defamation, Copyright (including music), Publishing, Trade Mark, Advertising, Confidentiality, Privacy, Contempt. Acted and advised on all aspects of media law (pre-publication/broadcast clearance, injunctions and litigation) for national broadcasters (e.g Carlton Television), national newspapers (e.g. Express Newspapers, News Group Newspapers, The Sunday Times, The Mirror Group), publishers (e.g. IPC, Granta Books), journalists, authors, public figures (e.g. businessmen, celebrities, clergy and musicians) and corporations. Defamation Speciality: Complex case investigation (particularly in relation to politics, matters of investigative journalism, security forces and international terrorism), advising and managing Irish and Northern Irish litigation, internet and cross-border libel. Acted in many leading cases for the above clients including the recent victory for The Sunday Times against Thomas "Slab" Murphy, who was proven to be a prominent member of the Provisional IRA. Presently defending several actions on behalf of national newspapers and television companies against alleged terrorists, and overseeing litigation in Ireland on behalf of major media corporations and insurance companies.
Prof. Memberships: The usual! And the National Farmers Union.
Career: Queen Mary College, London University. Joined *Mishcon de Reya* in 1991. Moved to *Goodman Derrick* in 1995 and then left to become a partner and set up the media firm *Henry Hepworth* in May 1997. Previously spent time at an advertising agency in Tokyo and in South America.
Personal: Born in 1969. Living in a renovated Islington Pub. Spends time writing, expressing creative frustrations on canvas, cross county skiing, hiking, farming and enjoying folk music, Ireland and travel adventures.

MIRESKANDARI, Razi
Simons Muirhead & Burton, London
(0171) 734 4499
Partner 1989. Head, Civil Litigation Department.
Specialisation: Main areas of practice are media-related. Particularly noted for defamation. Acts for publishers, authors' agents, writers, journalists and a wide variety of clients in the media and entertainment world, ranging from rock bands to restaurants.
Career: Qualified in 1986.

PALCA, Julia
Olswang, London (0171) 208 8888
Partner and Head of Litigation Department 1987.
Specialisation: Main area of practice is media litigation. Represents both print and broadcast defendants, and some plaintiffs, in defamation, breaches of copyright and other media and entertainment-related disputes including judicial review of decisions of media regulatory and quasi-regulatory bodies. Also advises mainly employers on all aspects of employment

law, including unfair and wrongful dismissal, discrimination and the application of restrictive covenants. Author of 'Employment Law Checklists' and numerous articles on media and employment issues. Acted as an in-house libel litigator to a major newspaper group 1985-86. Speaks on both media and employment law issues.
Career: Qualified in 1980. Joined *Olswang* in 1986, becoming Partner and Head of Litigation Group in 1987.

PEPPER, Alasdair G.T.
Peter Carter-Ruck and Partners, London
(0171) 353 5005
Partner in Media Litigation Department.
Specialisation: Main area of practice is media law, with emphasis on defamation and related areas, contempt and copyright. He acts for both plaintiffs and defendants and also undertakes election law (acted for the Referendum Party), advertising law and more general areas of litigation. He has experience in preparing submissions to regulators such as the Medicines Control Agency, Advertising Standards Authority and Broadcast Advertising Clearance Centre and appearing before the Broadcasting Standards Commission.
Prof. Memberships: Law Society, IBA.
Career: Qualified in 1984. Has remained with *Peter Carter-Ruck and Partners* since qualification. Became a Partner in 1986.
Personal: Born 13th May 1960. Attended Radley College, then Guildford College of Law. Leisure interests include tennis, squash, riding and walking. Lives in Farnham, Surrey.

PRESLAND, Frank
Eversheds, London (0171) 919 4500
Joint Senior Partner of *Eversheds*.
Specialisation: Specialising in Defamation, Commercial Litigation and Arbitration.
Prof. Memberships: Member of London Court of Arbitration.
Career: Qualified 1973. Joined *Frere Cholmeley* in 1973; became partner 1976; Chairman 1992-1998 and the firm's merger with *Eversheds*, London.
Personal: Born 1944. Education: London University and Fairbridge Commonwealth Undergraduate Scholar, University College of Rhodesia and Nyasaland.

PRICE, David
David Price & Co, London (0171) 916 9911
Specialisation: Principal area of practice is defamation and media litigation acting for both plaintiffs and a wide range of publishers. A solicitor - advocate who offers a "one-stop" service, including representation at trial. In the past 12 months has acted in the following notable cases; Referendum Party v Bhoyrul (establishing that a political party cannot sue for defamation), Oliver v Sammut (First solicitor to act as an advocate in a High Court defamation trial, for the successful defendant), Ernest Saunders v Punch (disclosure of sources by journalists), Liam Gallagher v Here! (defence of public interest to breach of confidence), R v Brown (liability of a director for articles published by a newspaper managed by him), Linford Christie v John McVicar. Cases handled include 'Michael Foot v. Rupert Murdoch,' ' Godfrey v. Hallam Baker' (first libel action on the internet), 'Watts v. City of London Police' (first (unled) solicitor in the Court of Appeal civil division), 'British Data Management

v. Boxer' (leading authority on pre-publication injunctions) and John Major v Scallywag. Author of 'Defamation: Law, Procedure and Practice' published by Sweet & Maxwell 1997.
Prof. Memberships: Media Society, British Association for Sport and Law.
Career: Qualified as a solicitor (1990). Barrister (1991), Principal of *David Price & Co* since 1993.
Personal: Born 16th October 1963. Educated at Haberdashers' Aske School (1970-82) and Harvard High School, Los Angeles (1982-83). Manchester University (1983-86). Enjoys spending time with his family and playing cricket and football. Lives in Highgate.

PROUDLER, Geraldine
Olswang, London (0171) 208 8888
Head of Defamation
Specialisation: Main area of practice is media law including defamation, contempt of court, breach of confidence, broadcasting complaints and associated matters. Acts for both plaintiffs and defendants including national and regional newspapers and magazines. Acted for the Guardian in its successful defences against Jonathan Aitken and Neil Hamilton, and acted for Marks and Spencer Plc in its successful action against Granada Television.
Prof. Memberships: Law Society, Media Society.
Career: Qualified 1980. Became a partner with *Lovell White & King* (now *Lovell White Durrant*) in 1987. Joined *Olswang* as a partner 1995.
Personal: Born 2 July 1956. BA Law at Nottingham University 1974-1977. Lives in London.

RIMELL, Katherine
Theodore Goddard, London
(0171) 606 8855
Specialisation: Main areas of practice are media related litigation, particularly defamation, malicious falsehood, confidence, human rights and also public law. Acts for a variety of corporate and individual clients, both plaintiffs and defendants. Recent cases include defending The Sunday Times in a libel action brought by the Barclay brothers and defending The Mirror in the retrial of the action brought by Rupert Allason for malicious falsehood.
Prof. Memberships: Law Society
Career: Qualified in 1985. Partner of *Theodore Goddard* in 1997.

ROBERTSON, Rhory
Swepstone Walsh, London (0171) 304 2100
Specialisation: Practice covers full range of media and commercial litigation; in particular defamation and intellectual property. Acts for substantial Newspapers and Publishing Groups; independent production companies, authors and broadcasters.
Prof. Memberships: Law Society
Career: Qualified 1977. BBC Solicitor 1978-1984. Mirror Group Legal Adviser 1987. Joined *Swepstone Walsh* 1988.
Personal: Born 31st July 1952. Educated Ardingly College and Southampton University (LLB).

RUBINSTEIN, John
Manches & Co, London (0171) 404 4433
Specialisation: All aspects of media law and electronic publishing; defamation, malicious falsehood, copyright, obscenity, trade mark infringement, passing off, rights of privacy and personality. Also practices in publishing,

multimedia and computer law. Has contributed articles to The Times and to professional publications and has appeared on BBC and Sky TV. Cases include 'Stern v Piper' (CA) 1996, 'The Conde Nast Publications Ltd v MGN Ltd,' 'The Conde Nast Publications Ltd v News Group Newspapers Ltd' (both settled) (additional statutory damages for photographic copyright infringement) and 'Cilla Black Ltd v. Granada TV and C4.' Also led a 22 person team Anton Piller search for Business Software Alliance against The Mirror Group.
Prof. Memberships: International Bar Assocations (Co-Chairman of Art and Cultural Property Law Committee), Media Society, TIPLO, Association of the Bar of the City of New York.
Career: Admitted in 1977; admitted to New York Bar and Federal Courts ED and SD New York 1979; with *Manches & Co* since 1994 on merger with *Rubinstein Callingham Polden & Gale*.
Personal: Educated at Marlborough and Magdalen College, Oxford. Interests: reading, theatre, bridge, croquet, visiting art galleries and collecting prints.

SCHILLING, Keith
Schilling & Lom and Partners, London
(0171) 453 2500
Senior Partner
Specialisation: Main area of practice is media and internet litigation especially libel. Represents insurers, broadcasters, newspapers, other publishers, film producers, film distributors, sportsmen, internet users and many leading celebrities. Other areas of practice in media litigation include copyright, breach of confidence, passing off and divorce. Contributor on libel, breach of confidence and copyright in the Entertainment Law Review.
Prof. Memberships: Law Society, City of Westminster Law Society.
Career: Qualified in 1981. Articled at *Wright Webb Syrett* before forming *Schilling & Lom* in 1984.
Personal: Born 25 July 1956. Attended Bromley Technical High School Boys 1967-72, Master of Arts (European Business Law), City of London Polytechnic 1980-82. Member of 'Groucho's' and Chelsea Arts Club and Institute of Directors. Leisure interests include reading, music, mountaineering. Lives in Hampstead.

SCOTT-BAYFIELD, Julie
Mishcon de Reya, London (0171) 440 7000
Specialisation: Main areas of practice are defamation, media and copyright law. Main Clients: publishers, newspapers, authors and scriptwriters. Involved in all aspects of defamation work for both Defendant and Plaintiff. Advises on pre-publication work as well as handling litigation including injunctions. Writes, broadcasts on television and radio and lectures on defamation. Recent cases: successful defence on behalf of Penguin Books Ltd of first major infringement of copyright case involving a world map; acted for the Poetry Society in one of the first libel actions in the UK involving defamation on the internet; successful defence of journalist Neil Hyde and INS News Group Limited against action for disclosure of source by Broadmoor Hospital; advised on publication of 'In the Public Interest' by Gerald James concerning arms to Iraq; advised on publication of Fiasco concerning derivative trading; acted for Thistle Hotels plc in libel action. Author: 'Defamation: Law and Practice' 1996.
Prof. Memberships: Law Society, City of London Solicitors Company, Media Society,

Holborn Law Society (Committee Member).
Career: Qualified 1965 Samuel Herbert Easterbrook Prize. 1966-1981 Partner, *Oswald Hickson Collier & Co*. 1982-1988 Partner, *Peter Carter-Ruck and Partners*. Joined *Mishcon de Reya* as Partner in 1988.
Personal: Member of Reform, Groucho, Royal Ocean Racing Club, Forum (UK) Ltd. Interests include sailing and walking.

SHILLITO, Richard A.
Crockers Oswald Hickson, London
(0171) 353 0311
Partner in Media Department.
Specialisation: Main area of practice is defamation. Acts for a large number of national, regional and trade press clients and their insurers. Other areas of expertise are contempt, reporting restrictions and copyright. Contributor to the Yearbook of Media and Entertainment Law (OUP, 1997/8).
Career: Qualified in 1976, having joined *Oswald Hickson, Collier & Co.* in 1973. Became a Partner in 1984. Previously a trainee journalist at Yorkshire Weekly Newspaper Group Limited, 1970-72.
Personal: Born 13th March 1948. Attended Westminster School, then Magdalen College, Oxford (1970, PPE (Hons)). Leisure interests include music and sailing. Lives in London. Married, with three daughters.

SMYTH, Michael T.
Clifford Chance, London (0171) 600 1000
See under Administrative & Public Law, p. 89

STEPHENSON, Andrew James
Peter Carter-Ruck and Partners, London
(0171) 353 5005
Partner in Litigation Department.
Specialisation: Main area of practice is defamation. Includes 15 years' experience acting both for plaintiffs, including government ministers, members of Parliament and sports and music personalities, and for defendants including book, magazine and newspaper publishers and television companies. Also experienced in media law generally, including the law of contempt, copyright and passing off work. Advised and assisted on chapter on defamation law in McNae's Essential Law for Journalists.
Prof. Memberships: Law Society, Media Society.
Career: Joined *Peter Carter-Ruck & Partners* in 1982. Qualified 1983. Became Partner in 1986.
Personal: Born 11th September 1956. Attended University College, London 1975-78. Council of Stock Exchange 1979-81. Leisure pursuits include literature and theatre. Lives in Wokingham, Berkshire.

STEWART, Patrick
Swepstone Walsh, London (0171) 404 1499
Specialisation: Media law including defamation, Contempt of Court, copyright, breach of confidence, passing off and pre-publication clearance. Acts for national newspapers, book and magazine publishers, video production companies and plaintiffs. Also does some general commercial litigation.
Prof. Memberships: Law Society and Media Society
Career: Qualified 1973. Legal Adviser Mirror Group Newspapers 1985-1990. Joined *Swepstone Walsh* 1990.
Personal: Born 6th July 1948. Educated Stoneyhurst College and Durham University.

SWAFFER, Patrick
Goodman Derrick, London (0171) 404 0606
Partner in Media Department.
Specialisation: Main areas of practice are broadcasting and publishing. Includes pre- and post-publication advice on defamation, contempt, confidence and copyright, rights exploitation, contractual issues and regulatory advice for the broadcasting industry.
Career: Joined *Goodman Derrick* in 1974. Qualified 1976. Became Partner in 1979 in Media Department.
Personal: Born 12th February 1951. Lives in London.

TAIT, Nigel G.T.M.
Peter Carter-Ruck and Partners, London (0171) 353 5005
Partner in Media Department.
Specialisation: Main area of practice is media law, acting for plaintiffs and defendants and giving pre-publication advice. Cases of interest include Beta Construction v. Channel 4 (award of

£568,000: highest ever libel award paid to a company); Vladimir Telnikoff v. Vladimir Matusevitch (first libel case to go to House of Lords for over a decade. Award of £240,000); Jack Slipper v BBC (£50,000 damages: a leading case on liability for republication); Jonathan Hunt (aged 6) v. The Sun (settlement of £35,000 plus costs to mother and son; youngest ever libel plaintiff); Victor Kiam v. Sunday Times (£45,000 damages - the first and only libel award to be upheld by the Court of Appeal since the Courts and Legal Services Act 1990). Shah v. Standard Chartered Bank. The leading case on reasonable grounds to suspect. Also undertakes personal injury work, acting for plaintiffs (highest award £755,000). Contributor to 'Carter-Ruck on Libel and Slander,' 5th edition. Regular lecturer on media law and defamation. Has spoken at the Oxford Union Debating Society in each of the last 3 years on law reform. Member of Law Society Privacy and Defamation working committees.
Prof. Memberships: Law Society. International Bar Association.

Career: Qualified in 1988, having joined *Peter Carter-Ruck and Partners* in 1986. Became a Partner in 1990. Managing Partner 1997.
Personal: Born 5th April 1963. Attended Nottingham University 1981-84. Leisure interests include family and football. Lives in Clapham, London.

TAYLOR, Barton
Russell Jones & Walker, London
(0171) 837 2808
Partner and Head of Commercial Litigation Department.
Specialisation: Defamation, acting only for Plaintiffs. Has acted successfully against all national daily, most Sunday newspapers, against magazines, book publishers, and TV companies. Other area of practice is commercial litigation including, in particular, professional negligence.
Prof. Memberships: Law Society.
Career: Qualified 1971, joined *Russell Jones & Walker* as a Partner in 1977.
Personal: Born 3rd August 1944. Attended Hereford Cathedral School. Leisure interests include golf, tennis, family and friends.

THE REGIONS

Foot & Bowden Exeter
Wiggin and Co Cheltenham

Bevan Ashford Bristol
Brabner Holden Banks Wilson Liverpool
Cobbetts Manchester
Knights Tunbridge Wells

Eversheds Cardiff
Pannone & Partners Manchester
Wragge & Co Birmingham

Foot & Bowden (Exeter) (2ptnrs) *Anthony Jaffa* (now based in the Exeter office) has a national reputation acting for defendants. **Clients/Work:** Newspaper groups and publishers including the Northcliffe Newspaper Group.
Wiggin and Co (Cheltenham) (1ptnr/ 4assts) Have a "powerful" practice. Their strong reputation is largely due to *Caroline Kean* who is ex-Olswang and retains London clients. **Clients/Work:** Acted for Northern &

Shell Publishing in action against News Group Newspapers. Represented John Alford (actor and popstar) against News of the World.
Bevan Ashford (Bristol) (4ptnrs 10%) **Clients/Work:** Mainly NHS Trusts and consultants.
Brabner Holden Banks Wilson (Liverpool) (1ptnr *Mark Manley* 75%/1 asst 15%) **Clients/Work:** Panel Solicitor for Radio City and Radio Piccadilly. Also act for individual celebrities.
Cobbetts (Manchester) (1ptnr/1 asst 35%) *Peter Stone* described as "excellent." **Clients/Work:** Successfully defending editor in contempt proceedings having given pre-publication advice. Libel action in Republic of Ireland. Advise Manchester Evening News and the Chester Chronicle Group.
Knights (Tunbridge Wells) (2ptnrs/2assts 25-30%) Known for their work for countryside organisations, including the Field Sports Society. **Clients/Work:** Acting for plaintiff in action against Sporting Life. Obtained damages and costs for Southampton University against the Express on Sunday.

Eversheds (Cardiff) (1ptnr 100%/2ptnrs and 4assts help when required) **Clients/Work:** Pre publication advice to HTV on news and current affairs programmes.
Pannone & Partners (Manchester) (2ptnrs 40-50%/1 asst 25%) **Clients/Work:** Manchester City Council; local politicians; sports personalities and other individual plaintiffs.
Wragge & Co (Birmingham) (1ptnr/2assts 15%) The only firm in the Midlands known to have a defamation capacity. *Gordon Harris* is an IP litigator who mainly advises corporate clients on media issues. **Clients/Work:** Obtained apology and retraction for Carefirst plc over misleading statement by Channel 4. Pre-broadcast advice for Birmingham Live TV.

JAFFA Anthony Foot & Bowden
KEAN Caroline Wiggin and Co

HARRIS Gordon Wragge & Co
MANLEY Mark Brabner Holden Banks Wilson
STONE Peter Cobbetts

SCOTLAND

Bird Semple Glasgow
Levy & McRae Glasgow

Bannatyne, Kirkwood, France & Co Glasgow
Dundas & Wilson CS Edinburgh
McGrigor Donald Glasgow

Bird Semple (2ptnrs including *Derek Currie*/2assts 35%) **Clients/Work:** Defending News of the World in action by Mohammed Sarwar (Labour MP) for £750,000 damages. Represent the Press Association for all Scottish work.
Levy & McRae (2ptnrs including *Peter Watson*/2assts 20%) **Clients/Work:** Clients include Scottish Television, Grampian Television, Daily Record, Channel 4, ITN, Reuters and Sky.

CURRIE Derek Bird Semple
MACLEOD Euan Dundas & Wilson CS
SCOTT Niall McGrigor Donald
SMITH Martin Bannatyne, Kirkwood, France & Co
WATSON Peter Levy & McRae

Bannatyne, Kirkwood, France & Co (3ptnrs/2assts) *Martin Smith* has many years defamation experience. **Clients/Work:** Act for The Scotsman Publications Ltd; Scottish & Universal Newspapers Ltd and Associated Newspapers Ltd.

Dundas & Wilson CS (3ptnrs 100%, including *Euan Macleod*/2assts 10%) **Clients/Work:** Radio Forth; Radio Tay.

McGrigor Donald (4ptnrs/ 4assts in the litigation dept handle media and entertainment work including defamation) *Niall Scott*

heads the team. **Clients/Work:** Defending Sunday Mail against former world boxing champion Jim Watt and his wife Margaret. Defending BBC against claim by nursing home in Lanark.

NORTHERN IRELAND

Elliott Duffy Garrett (2ptnrs including *Brian Deeny* 30%) **Clients/Work:** Ongoing work for the the Mirror Group. Continuing involvement in the Private Lee Clegg case.

Johnsons (1ptnr 15%) *Paul Tweed* has a strong reputation particularly for plaintiff work. Opponents "hate to hear he is on the other side." **Clients/Work:** Successfully represented Robert McCarthy QC/MP against the Irish Times.

McKinty & Wright (2ptnrs 60% – 25%/1 asst 20%) *Owen Catchpole* ("top rate solid operator") leads the team. **Clients/Work:** Involved in the appeals in the Private Lee Clegg case. Defending Sunday Life in two actions brought by Magistrates.

Mills Selig (1ptnr 80%/1asst 100%) The firm enters the table for the first time following the acquisition of *Paul Spring* ("knowledgeable," "first class operator") from Cleaver Fulton & Rankin. **Clients/**

Work: Mainly defendant work for newspaper clients, including Sunday Newspapers Ltd, Independent Newspapers Ltd, The Sun and The News of the World. Also acts for book publishers such as Simon & Schuster and Little Brown and magazine publishers such as IPC.

LEADERS' PROFILES · REGIONS

CATCHPOLE, Owen
McKinty & Wright, Belfast (01232) 246751
Partner.
Specialisation: Principal area of practice is what in Northern Ireland is described as Commercial List work. This includes not only 'straight' commercial litigation but also non-medical professional negligence and what in England would be classed as Official Referees business. Also extensive defamation work both advisory and litigation, for print and broadcast media.
Prof. Memberships: Law Society of Northern Ireland, Northern Ireland Supreme Court Rules Committee.
Career: Qualified 1973, Partner in *McKinty & Wright* since 1975.
Personal: Graduated in Legal Science from Trinity College Dublin. Recreations include yoga and target shooting.

CURRIE, Derek Gordon
Bird Semple, Glasgow (0141) 221 7090
Specialisation: Defamation: Acts for Times Newspapers Limited, publishers of The Times, The Sunday Times and The Sunday Times Scotland; News Group Newspapers Limited, publishers of The Sun and The News of the World, and D C Thomson & Co Limited, publishers of The Sunday Post, for all pre-publication advice and any subsequent litigation; The Press Association as well as for a number of publishers. Employment Law: Advises employers on all aspects of labour law, including European legislation, involving unfair dismissals, redundancy, TUPE legislation. Represents clients at Industrial Tribunals and, where necessary, Employment Appeal Tribunals.
Prof. Memberships: Member of The Law Society of Scotland Industrial Law Group. British Member of the Labour & Employment Law Committee of Lex Mundi a worldwide

organisation of lawyers. Member of Employment Law Committee of UIA (Union Internationale des Avocats).
Career: Graduated LLB (I Ions) Glasgow University 1977. Assumed as a Partner in the Litigation Department in 1983.
Personal: Married with 2 children. Golf, hillwalking, sport in general.

DEENY, Brian
Elliott Duffy Garrett, Belfast (01232) 245034
Specialisation: Defamation, Commercial litigation and professional negligence. Acts for 6 national newspapers in defence of claims in N. Ireland. Also extensive experience acting for Plaintiffs in libel actions.
Prof. Memberships: Law Society of N. Ireland.
Career: Graduated University College, Dublin 1982. Admitted solicitor 1985. Admitted partner 1990.

HARRIS, Gordon D.
Wragge & Co, Birmingham (0121) 233 1000
Partner in Commercial and Intellectual Property Group.
Specialisation: Main areas of practice are intellectual property, franchising and defamation. Work includes preparing franchise agreements (advising both franchisors and franchisees), intellectual property litigation (especially patents), and defamation litigation for plaintiffs and defendants. Assisted in establishment of Rosemary Conley Diet & Finess Clubs franchises and Drinkmaster franchises. Author of 'Franchising: A Commercial and Legal Guide' (1993), numerous articles in trade journals on franchising, merchandising and intellectual property. Has addressed national seminars on franchising and international seminars on intellectual property and character merchandising.
Prof. Memberships: Intellectual Property

Lawyers Association, *Wragge & Co.* Nominee for the British Franchise Association (Affiliate), Chartered Institute of Patent Agents (Associate), Institute of Trade Mark Agents, Patent Litigators Association, International Trade Marks Association, Licensing Industry Merchandisers' Association. Anti Counterfeiting Group.
Career: Qualified in 1984, joined *Wragge & Co.* in 1982. Partner in 1990.
Personal: Born 13th October 1959.

JAFFA, Anthony
Foot & Bowden, Exeter (01392) 203980
Fax: (01392) 203 981
Email: 106636.3565@compuserve.com
Partner.
Specialisation: Handles libel, contempt of court, court secrecy orders and related law for media clients. Author of articles and reviews on all aspects of media law. Speaker at conferences for the Newspaper Industry.
Prof. Memberships: Law Society, Society of Notaries.
Career: Qualified in 1980. Articled at *Boyce Hatton & Co.* 1978-80. Worked at *Wilde Sapte* 1980-83, before joining *Foot & Bowden* in 1983. Became a Partner in 1987. Chairman of the Devon Young Solicitors Group 1989-90; Member of National Committee of Young Solicitors Group 1988-89. Notary Public 1989.
Personal: Born 6th August 1956. Attended St Boniface's College, Plymouth 1967-74 and Oxford University 1974-77. Leisure interests include windsurfing, sailing and cycling. Married with two children. Lives in Torquay.

KEAN, Caroline Mary
Wiggin and Co, Cheltenham (01242) 224114
Partner, Head of Litigation Department.
Specialisation: Main areas of practice are defamation and media related litigation.

Includes contentious work for plaintiffs, defendants and insurers, advising on copy pre-publication and broadcast, confidence, copyright and passing off. Commercial/Property litigation work also covered. Speaks frequently on BBC Radio and specialises in private seminars to companies and organisations on issues which include media handling/damage limitation and systems. Author of "Considerations for the Libel Defendant," "International Media Law:"Ideas in the Need of Protection,"Television; 'Obscenity: Have the New Kids Come of Age?', International Media Law; 'Protection Rackets,' 'Director' magazine, 'Libel Damages: literally the cost of an arm and a leg?', International Media Law.
Prof. Memberships: Law Society, The Media Society (Council Member). Legal Adviser to Women in Journalism.
Career: Articled *Rubinstein Callingham*. Qualified 1985. Partner 1987. Partner *Olswang* 1989-1995. Joined *Wiggin and Co* 1995 as a partner and Head of Litigation 1995.
Personal: Born 1960. Burford School 1971-78, Newnham College, Cambridge 1978-81. College of Law, Lancaster Gate 1981-82.

MACLEOD, Euan
Dundas & Wilson CS, Edinburgh
(0131) 228 8000
See under Employment Law, p. 322

MANLEY, Mark J.
Brabner Holden Banks Wilson, Liverpool
(0151) 236 5821
Partner in Commercial Litigation Department.
Specialisation: Main area of practice is defamation, acting for newspapers, radio stations, broadcasters and publishers. Also acts for plaintiffs in libel cases. Panel member on Lloyd's Syndicate 702 Libel Panel. Approved EMAP Radio advisor. Also handles general commercial litigation. Has acted in libel actions against several MPs, the ex-Lord Mayor of Liverpool, and in several commercial libel cases both for and against newspapers. Author of numerous articles on financial services. Spent two years as Partner in Lawyers Planning Services lecturing on financial services, practice management and defamation.
Prof. Memberships: Law Society, British Association for Sport and the Law.
Career: Qualified in 1987, becoming an Assistant Solicitor at *Loosemores*. Partner in Lawyers Planning Services since 1989. Joined *Brabner Holden* in 1991, and appointed Partner in 1992.
Personal: Born 17th August 1962. Attended St Nicholas and De La Salle Schools, then Liverpool University and Christleton College of Law. Leisure interests include his daughter Zoe, sports (squash and snooker) and writing music. Lives in Chester.

SCOTT, J.Niall
McGrigor Donald, Glasgow (0141) 248 6677
Specialisation: Pre and post publication editorial advice in relation to Contempt of court

and Defamation. Advised the BBC in relation to the Zircon Affair and the raid by Special Branch on the headquarters of BBC Scotland. Advised Robert Maxwell in relation to actions of Defamation raised in Scotland.
Prof. Memberships: Law Society of Scotland. Royal Faculty of Procurators, Glasgow.
Career: Jordanhill College School, Glasgow. LLB University of Aberdeen. Qualified as a solicitor in 1975. 1991-1993 External examiner for diploma in legal practice, University of Glasgow. Managing Partner, *McGrigor Donald* from April 1994 to August 1997.
Personal: Married to Judith with four children Edward, Antonia, Virginia and Nicholas. Hill walking, golf, tennis, skiing and swimming.

SMITH, Martin B.
Bannatyne, Kirkwood, France & Co, Glasgow (0141) 221 6020
Specialisation: The practice which was established in Glasgow in 1785 covers the full range of intellectual property work and includes all aspects of defamation and media law with particular reference to Scotland. The practice numbers amongst its clients major newspaper and publishing companies and also acts for British Actors Equity Association in Scotland.
Prof. Memberships: Martin Smith is a former journalist who graduated in Law at Edinburgh University and is admitted as a Notary Public in Scotland.
Career: He qualified in 1971 and joined *Bannatyne, Kirkwood, France, & Co* in 1973 attaining the position of Senior Partner in 1995. He is also a partner of Messrs. *Peter Carter-Ruck & Partners* in London, being a Registered Foreign Lawyer.
Personal: He was educated at the High School of Glasgow and University of Edinburgh. Interests include writing on media matters and lecturing on the subject. In addition, he is a former Chairman of the Queen's Park Football Club Limited and has represented the Club at Scottish Football League and Scottish Football Association levels. He is currently a Director of the Club and has an involvement with the major reconstruction work that is taking place at the Club's Stadium, Hampden Park.

SPRING, Paul
Mills Selig, Belfast (01232) 243878
Litigation partner.
Specialisation: Main area of practice is libel. Represents several national newspapers, broadcasting organisations and book and magazine publishers. Extensive experience of libel litigation for both defendants and plaintiffs. Areas of practice include breach of confidence, contempt of Court, press complaints, copyright and pre-publication work. Other major areas of practice are commercial litigation and product liability litigation.
Prof. Memberships: Law Society of Northern Ireland.
Career: Qualified 1983. Formerly Litigation Partner since 1988 at *Cleaver Fulton & Rankin*, Belfast. Joined *Mills Selig* March 1998.

Personal: Educated at Belfast Royal Academy and London School of Economics (graduating in Law in 1981). Lives near Belfast.

STONE, Peter J.W.
Cobbetts, Manchester (0161) 833 3333
Specialisation: Over 20 years experience in litigation for national and regional blue-chip clients. Particular expertise in commercial property litigation (forfeiture, dilapidations, covenants, contested lease renewals, Brewery/Licensed Retailer work) and in defamation (Plaintiff and Defendant) for individual and media clients.
Prof. Memberships: Law Society. Notaries Society.
Career: Educated at Rossall School and Liverpool University (LLB Hons 1st class). Articled at *Cobbetts*, 1974. Qualified 1976, Partner 1979.
Personal: Born 1951. Leisure interests include fellwalking, climbing and scuba diving.

TWEED, Paul
Johnsons, Belfast (01232) 240183
Specialisation: Defamation (the most well known case being for B J Eastwood against the boxer Barry McGuigan - £450,000 award, and more recently acted for Mr Robert McCartney QC, the MP for North Down, who was awarded £80,000 in a high profile case against the Irish Times on the eve of the General Election). Acts for a number of political, public, business and legal personalities and also on the Defence side for several newspapers and publications. Other areas of practice include copyright and related media work.
Prof. Memberships: Incorporated Law Society of Northern Ireland (1978). Law Society of England and Wales (1993).

WATSON, Peter B.
Levy & McRae, Glasgow (0141) 307 2311
Specialisation: Media; Defamation; Libel; Aviation; International Claims and Litigation; Personal Injury Litigation; Public & Fatal Accident Inquiries; civil and criminal litigation; Inland Revenue and Customs & Excise Investigation; employment law; partnership law; Secretary of the Lockerbie Air Disaster Group; Secretary of Braer Disaster Group; Member of the Steering Committee of the Piper Alpha Disaster Group; 'Gecas v. Scottish Television plc;' 'Cavendish v. The Scotsman Publications & Others;' representing the Dunblane Families at the Dunblane Public Inquiry; involved in litigation in more than 12 countries other than the UK.
Prof. Memberships: Law Society of Scotland; SSC Society; APIL; ATLA; President of the Society of Solicitor Advocates; Chairman of the Scottish Mediation Bureau; Member of the IBA.
Career: BA in Economics, University of Strathclyde; Bachelor of Law, University of Edinburgh; research at Scandinavian Maritime Institute and thereafter at Dundee University, Centre for Petroleum and Mineral Law Studies; Visiting Scholar in International Law, Nova University, Florida, USA; on the Board of Anglia Sports Law Research Centre.
Personal: Horseracing; travel; married with two daughters, Anna and Sophie.

EDUCATION

RESEARCH: In compiling the tables, we consider all the information available to us, paying particular regard to the market research carried out by our team of ten qualified lawyers. (The researchers' details are set out on page three.) The rankings, therefore, reflect the opinion of the marketplace as revealed by systematic and objective research: see page four. (Our research is audited every year by the British Market Research Bureau.)

OVERVIEW: Within education law there are two quite different types of practice, and our tables are organised accordingly. Some firms have an institutional client base, acting for universities, colleges of further and higher education, schools and funding organisations. Other firms act for pupils, parents or students who wish to take action against institutions or local authorities. Some firms act for both types of client.

In London the Eversheds team maintains its pre-eminence amongst firms acting for institutional clients. Smaller, more specialist firms tend to act for individuals and are joined this year by new firm John Ford.

Several national firms have excellent education practices. Veale Wasbrough in Bristol and Martineau Johnson in Birmingham compete with Eversheds for institutional work, and Peter Liell has a national reputation for his work on behalf of individuals. New additions to the list this year are John Hall Solicitors and Bevan Ashford. In the North the well-regarded Elaine Maxwell has left Marsden Huck to form her own practice. In Newcastle, Eversheds has strengthened its practice by acquiring Wilkinson Maughan.

LONDON

FIRMS ACTING FOR INSTITUTIONS

LEADING FIRMS
LONDON • INSTITUTIONS

EVERSHEDS

BEACHCROFT STANLEYS
LAWFORD & CO
REYNOLDS PORTER CHAMBERLAIN
WINCKWORTH & PEMBERTON

LEE BOLTON & LEE
WITHAM WELD

Eversheds (2ptnrs/10assts) Head of the national educational practice is *John Hall* who has a high profile and is active in the educational field. He mainly undertakes governance work and provides commercial advice to institutions. *David Hetherington* works on the employment aspects of educa-tion. The London office focuses on higher and further education. **Clients/Work:** Advising UCAS on issues such as tuition fees, gap years and arbitration; Thames Valley University; Hackney Community College.

Beachcroft Stanleys (1ptnr/1asst) The firm now offers a one-stop-shop service to universities in alliance with Price Waterhouse Coopers. *Julian Gizzi* is regarded as pre-eminent on the funding side, and has "an almost aggressive profile for developing the law in relation to special needs." **Clients/Work:** The Further Education Funding Council; University of London; National Foundation for Educational Research.

Lawford & Co (3ptnrs/5assts) *Richard Gold* joined the firm from Bennett Taylor Tyrrell after BTT merged with Finers. He has an excellent reputation for his schools work, which compliments Lawford's traditional specialism in further education and for teaching unions. **Clients/Work:** Advises on grant maintained and independent schools; further education; PFI advice.

Reynolds Porter Chamberlain (3ptnrs/4assts) Have a notable presence in educa-tional work, in particular for unions. **Clients/Work:** NASUWT; ATL; recent cases include Wilson v St Helens Borough Council;

Winckworth & Pemberton (1ptnr/1asst) A "very impressive firm" with a substantial schools practice. The experienced *Michael Thatcher* has an "extremely good reputation" in this area and acts for a wide range of clients. **Clients/Work:** Act for a large number of schools; Diocesan Boards of Education for London and Southwark.

Lee Bolton & Lee (2ptnrs/1asst) Have developed a respected schools specialism from their work for religious communities.

LEADING INDIVIDUALS
LONDON • INSTITUTIONS

HALL John Eversheds

GIZZI Julian Beachcroft Stanleys
GOLD Richard Lawford & Co
THATCHER Michael Winckworth & Pemberton

BEESLEY Peter Lee Bolton & Lee
HAWTHORNE Peter Witham Weld
HETHERINGTON David Eversheds

Peter Beesley is "very sound" on educational matters. **Clients/Work:** Work for colleges and maintained and independent schools; National Society of the Church of England; General Synod Board of Education.

Witham Weld (3ptnrs/1asst – 20% of time) Have a respected practice mainly derived from their Roman Catholic client base. *Peter Hawthorne* has a broad practice within education which includes employ-

ment advice and issues of child abuse. **Clients/Work:** Involved in work for independent and state sector, with a focus on secondary school level.

FIRMS ACTING FOR INDIVIDUALS

LEADING FIRMS
LONDON • INDIVIDUALS
TEACHER STERN SELBY
BINDMAN & PARTNERS
DAVID LEVENE & CO
GILLS
JOHN FORD

Teacher Stern Selby (1ptnr/3asst) Mainly undertake judicial review and negligence work, and also have a reputation for tribunals and grant issues. *Jack Rabinowicz* "knows education law backwards" and is known for his work on cutting-edge cases, particularly in relation to special needs. **Clients/Work:** Recent cases include Phelps v LB Hillingdon, Anderton v Clwyd County Council, Burridge v LB Harrow.

Bindman & Partners (2ptnrs/1asst 20%) Have a good reputation for their work in the educational field. *Stephen Grosz* has earned a good reputation for several high profile cases. **Clients/Work:** Act for pupils who have been excluded from school, for parents in cases of schools selection and against HE and FE institutions in relation to discipline and academic failure.

David Levene & Co (1ptnr/3assts – 1f/t) *David Ruebain* does a lot of work on disability and special needs. The firm has a reputation for work in the public law field. Clients are referred by a wide range of specialist education and disability organisations who assist families and children. **Clients/Work:** Recent cases include R v IAC ex parte Mayor & Burgess of the LB of Enfield – re the reinstatement of a permanently excluded child; R v The Governing Body of Dame Alice Owen School concerning the refusal to give a child a place at the establishment.

Gills (1ptnr/1asst) *Jaswinder Gill* is known nationally for his work on behalf of students with grievances against local/ university authorities. **Clients/Work:** Act for adult students in grants' disputes amongst other issues.

John Ford (1ptnr/1asst p/t) New name in the lists this year, he has a reputation for good work on behalf of individuals, especially in the context of special needs. **Clients/Work:** All aspects of education law affecting pupils, parents and students.

LEADING INDIVIDUALS	
LONDON • INDIVIDUALS	
RABINOWICZ Jack	Teacher Stern Selby
FORD John	John Ford Solicitors
GILL Jaswinder	Gills
GROSZ Stephen	Bindman & Partners
RUEBAIN David	David Levene & Co

LEADERS' PROFILES • LONDON

BEESLEY, Peter
Lee Bolton & Lee, London (0171) 222 5381
Senior Partner in Ecclesiastical Education and Charity Department.
Specialisation: Particular expertise in Church of England work. Chapter Clerk of St Alban's Cathedral; Joint Registrar of the Diocese of Ely; Registrar of the Diocese of Guildford; Joint Registrar of the Diocese of Hereford; Registrar of the Faculty Office of the Archbishop of Canterbury; a member of the Legal Advisory Commission of the General Synod of the Church of England. Also handles education and charity work. Solicitor to the National Society; and to the Board of Education of the General Synod; Registrar of the Woodard Corporation. Joint Contributor to Volume 13 (2) 'Encyclopaedia of Forms and Precedents- Ecclesiastical Law.' Speaker at and promoter of several conferences and seminars on ecclesiastical charity and education matters.
Prof. Memberships: Law Society, City of Westminster Law Society (ex-President), Ecclesiastical Law Association (Secretary), Ecclesiastical Law Society (Secretary), Charity Law Association (member of Executive Committee).
Career: Qualified 1967. Joined *Lee Bolton & Lee* in 1968, becoming a Partner in 1969.
Personal: Born 30th April 1943. Attended Kings School Worcester, then Exeter University 1961-64 and College of Law 1964-65. Lives in London.

FORD, John
John Ford Solicitors, London
(0171) 288 1066
Specialisation: Education, personal injury (including medical negligence), general civil litigation.

Prof. Memberships: ELAS, APIC, Liberty, Inquest Lawyers Group, MIND, NACRO, Legal Action Group.
Career: Admitted 1975. Strong civil rights background. Author of Education Law and Practice book due to be published by Legal Action Group, September1998. Duty Solicitor and member of Clerkenwell & Hampstead Duty Solicitor Committee.
Personal: School governor.

GILL, Jaswinder
Gills, Southall (0181) 893 6869
Specialisation: Offers expert legal advice in protecting and promoting students' legal rights in the law of Higher Education. Has gained a nation-wide reputation as the leading lawyer in the country in this area in challenging local authorities and Universities, previously being unfamiliar territory. Set up his own firm to offer specialist guidance and advice for students aggrieved by decisions made by the above bodies. Also involved in bringing about a greater sense of awareness of legal remedies available to students within a complex framework of education law. Many cases involve novel issues and will have a strong element of wider public importance issues for all students. Specialises in challenging (a) local authorities' decisions refusing discretionary and mandatory awards in the area of student funding and (b) decisions made by Universities/Colleges regarding examination results, by way of judicial review proceedings. In respect of the latter, also handling cases involving damages for breach of contract and/or negligence. Also focusing on judicial review proceedings within the education field embracing Statements of Special

Educational Needs and Appeals, exclusion appeals and admissions.

GIZZI, Julian
Beachcroft Stanleys, London
(0171) 242 1011
Partner, Head of Education Department.
Specialisation: All aspects of education law including funding matters, incorporations, mergers, learning difficulties, enquiries, judicial reviews and the private finance initiative.
Prof. Memberships: Law Society, Education Law Association.
Career: Qualified in 1981, having joined *Beachcroft Stanleys* in 1979. Became a partner in 1986. Member of the Structure and Governance Working Group of the National Committee of Inquiry into Higher Education. Fellow of the Royal Society of Arts. Member of the Admissions and Exclusions Appeals Panel of the Schools' Commission.
Personal: Born 13 February 1957. Educated at Downside School and Cambridge University. Lives in Little Chart, Kent.

GOLD, Richard
Lawford & Co, London (0171) 353 5099
Partner specialising in education work.
Specialisation: Education Law. Acts for schools and parents in all aspects of education law including governor training and PFI projects. Also covers property and private client work, including commercial and residential property matters, wills and trusts. Addresses conferences and seminars organised by IBC and Education Law Association and others. Co-author of "Running a School 1998 – Legal Duties and Responsibilities."

Prof. Memberships: Education Law Association (ELAS) (Member of Executive Committee and Treasurer).
Career: Qualified 1968. Joined *Lawford & Co* in 1998 as a Partner.
Personal: Born 21st October 1941. Attended William Ellis School 1953-61, then Trinity College, Cambridge 1961-65. Chair of Governors, William Ellis School 1978-87. Chair of Trustees, William Ellis School 1978-present. Governor, Ravenscroft School 1992-1996. Governor, Jews Free School 1994-present. Member, London Borough of Barnet Admissions and Exclusions Appeal Committee. Leisure pursuits include music, theatre, reading and sport.

GROSZ, Stephen
Bindman & Partners, London
(0171) 833 4433
See under Administrative & Public Law, p. 87

HALL, John T.
Eversheds, London (0171) 919 4500
Partner and Chairman of *Eversheds* Education Group.
Specialisation: Work includes governance, the Education Acts, employment law, industrial relations, judicial review, the student relationships, commercial law, funding and asset management. Clients include in excess of two hundred education institutions, mainly universities and colleges of higher and further education. Also handles company/commercial and employment and constitutional advice for professional and other bodies. Contributor to 'Education and the Law,' the 'Times Education Supplement' and education press. Author of further and higher education module in University of Buckingham Postgraduate Diploma in Education Law and contributor on 'Higher Education and the Law' (Open University Press).
Prof. Memberships: Law Society, Education Law Association, Fellow of the Royal Society of Arts. Fellow of the Institute of Continuing Professional Development.
Career: Qualified in 1975. Partner at *Wedlake Saint* 1978-93. Chair, London Young Solicitors' Group, 1985; Company Secretary, Polytechnics and Colleges Employers' Forum, 1988; Governor, Barnet College of Further Education, 1992; Company Secretary, Colleges' Employers' Forum, 1992. Joined *Eversheds* in 1994 as a Partner.
Personal: Born 23rd December 1948. College Governor. Leisure interests include walking, history, art and Spain. Lives in Hadley Wood, Barnet, Herts.

HAWTHORNE, Peter J.M.
Witham Weld, London (0171) 821 8211
Partner in Litigation Department.
Specialisation: Main areas of practice are education and employment law. Advises

colleges, schools and a Local Authority. Also advises religious institutions on procedures for safeguarding their clients' welfare and furthering their work in a secular world. Has acted in judicial reviews of pupil exclusions, governor removal, admission policies of RC state-maintained schools and religious special educational needs. Lectured on child protection and employment issues to conferences of religious orders.
Prof. Memberships: Law Society, Education Law Association, Catholic Union.
Career: Qualified 1976, having joined *Witham Weld* in 1974. Became a Partner in 1978. Governor of Wimbledon College Preparatory School since 1990, St Christina's Independent Catholic Girls' School, London since 1993.
Personal: Born 14th May 1949. Attended Beaumont College 1962-67, then LL.B (Hons), London. Leisure interests include HCPT and family.

HETHERINGTON, David
Eversheds, London (0171) 919 4500
Member of the firm's Education and Employment Groups.
Specialisation: Main areas of practice are employment and education law. In particular, acts for universities and colleges of higher and further education in relation to contentious and non-contentious matters concerning employment and industrial relations law.
Career: Qualified in 1975. With *Slaughter & May* 1979-90 as Assistant Solicitor in its Litigation Department. Associate with *Wedlake Saint*, where specialised in employment law, 1990-93. Joined *Eversheds* in 1994.

RABINOWICZ, Jack
Teacher Stern Selby, London
(0171) 242 3191
Partner in Litigation Department.
Specialisation: Main areas of practice include education, medical negligence, and personal injury work.
Prof. Memberships: Director of Disability Law Service, Chair of Education Law Association (ELAS), Steering Committee of Whooping Cough Claims, Action for Victims of Medical Accidents (AVMA), American Trial Lawyers Association (ATLA), Medico-Legal Society, Association of Personal Injury Lawyers (APIL), Law Society's Group for the Welfare of People with a Mental Handicap, Council of Registration of Schools teaching Dyslexia (CresTeD).
Career: Qualified in 1977. Currently a partner with *Teacher Stern Selby*.

RUEBAIN, David
David Levene & Co, London (0181) 881 7777
Head of Education and Disability Law Department.
Specialisation: The Department specialises in all aspects of education law, health law, community care law and disability

discrimination. He has published and taught extensively on education and disability law and is author of the Code of Practice on Admission, Exclusion and Reinstatement Appeals for Maintained Schools in England and Wales; co-author of the 1995 Disabled Persons' (Civil Rights) Bill; consultant editor to Disability Discrimination: Advising on the Law and Practice; author of Notes on the Disability Discrimination Act; co-author of Taking Action, a guide for parents of children with Special Educational Needs; an editorial board member of Disability and Society; and co-author of the Legal Action Group's Education and the Law.
Prof. Memberships: Trustee of the Disability Discrimination Act Represention and Advice Project, a trustee of the Disability Law Service, Vice Chair of the Rights Now Campaign, a member of the Law Society's Mental Health and Disability Sub-Committee, Vice Chair of Disability Equality in Education and a member of the Advisory Board of the Disablement Policy and Law Research Unit.

THATCHER, Michael C.
Winckworth & Pemberton (incorporating Sherwood & Co), London (0171) 593 5000
Partner in Education, Ecclesiastical and Charities Department.
Specialisation: Acts for voluntary aided schools, grant maintained schools, voluntary controlled schools, Church of England and Roman Catholic boards of education and finance, further education colleges and local education authorities. Also acts for charities, airlines, and in general commercial and property law. Has acted in Judicial Review of Appeal Committee decisions, all types of disciplinary and appeal hearings, and Commission for Racial Equality proceedings against Governors. Author of various editorials in the specialist press. Has spoken at a wide range of conferences and seminars on various aspects of education and employment law.
Prof. Memberships: Law Society; Ecclesiastical Law Association; Ecclesiastical Law Society; Education Law Association.
Career: Qualified in 1968. From 1969 to 1989 was clerk to the Governors of St Clement Danes School, to St Clement Danes Parochial Charities and to Isaac Ducketts Trustees. Registrar to the Diocese of Rochester and Joint Registrar to the Diocese of London.
Personal: Born 19th May 1943. Attended Ardingly College 1956-60, then King's College, London 1961-64, and College of Law 1964-65. Clerk to the Worshipful Company of Cooks, Secretary to the Reunion des Gastronomes, Parish Councillor. Leisure interests include running, shooting, fishing and gardening. Lives in Guildford.

SOUTH EAST

FIRMS ACTING FOR INSTITUTIONS

| HIGHLY REGARDED FIRMS |
SOUTH EAST • INSTITUTIONS
Birkett Long Colchester
Cole & Cole Oxford
Donne Mileham & Haddock Brighton
Manches & Co Oxford
Thomas Eggar Church Adams Chichester
Wollastons Chelmsford
Winckworth & Pemberton Oxford

Birkett Long (1ptnr/8assts) Have a broad range of clients, and partner *Philip George* is considered "highly professional." Clients/ Work: Essex University; Colchester Institute; Colchester Sixth Form College.

Cole & Cole (3ptnrs/5assts) A respected local practice which benefits from its proximity to a large number of educational institutions. Clients/Work: Oxford Brookes University; Westminster College; The Dragon School.

Donne Mileham & Haddock (3ptnrs/ 1con) A leading southern commercial practice in which a cross-departmental team handles a range of work for educational institutions. Clients/Work: Advice to the University of Sussex on library extension; leading ultra vires case of Baldry v Feintuck; Roman Catholic Diocese of Arundel and Brighton.

Manches & Co Have recently acquired Morrell Peel & Gamlen, and with it a client base which includes many Oxford colleges.

Thomas Eggar Church Adams (2ptnrs/ 2assts) Education work is done by individuals from various departments, although the firm has a reputation in the ecclesiastical field.

Wollastons (1ptnr p/t) Cross-departmental team. *Nicholas Cook* is in the commercial property department, but possesses "genuine specialist expertise" in education field. Clients/Work: University of East Anglia; general education law advice; employment and property advice for institutional clients.

Winckworth & Pemberton (1ptnr) Most of the education work comes from firm's Church of England connections, but also have some Catholic clients. Clients/ Work: Oxford Diocesan Board of Education.

| LEADING INDIVIDUALS |
SOUTH EAST • INSTITUTIONS
COOK Nicholas Wollastons
GEORGE Philip Birkett Long

FIRMS ACTING FOR INDIVIDUALS

| LEADING FIRMS |
SOUTH EAST • INDIVIDUALS
PETER LIELL Potters Bar

Peter Liell (1 principal) Niche firm specialising in education work. *Peter Liell* has "tremendous academic knowledge"and 20 years of experience. Acts for children and students, and also parents or groups of parents. Clients/Work: For students and parents who wish to challenge the decisions, acts or omissions of school governors, LEAs or government departments. Has handled about 30 judicial review cases relating to education.

| LEADING INDIVIDUALS |
SOUTH EAST • INDIVIDUALS
LIELL Peter Peter Liell

SOUTH WEST

FIRMS ACTING FOR INSTITUTIONS

| LEADING FIRMS |
SOUTH WEST • INSTITUTIONS
VEALE WASBROUGH Bristol
MICHELMORES Exeter
RICKERBY WATTERSON Cheltenham
STONE KING Bath
TOZERS Exeter

HIGHLY REGARDED FIRMS
Osborne Clarke Bristol
Bevan Ashford Bristol
Bond Pearce Plymouth
Steele Raymond Bournemouth

Veale Wasbrough (6ptnrs/8assts) Act for independent schools and have a "good and quite aggressive unit." *Robert Boyd* heads the firm's schools practice, and he is known for his work on governance and parent contracts. Have the largest national practice for independent schools. Clients/Work: Legal advice to Sedburgh school when it became wrongly involved in Operation Clarence; acting for the school governors in Grenar v The Royal School Hindhead; advising on the rescue of Sherborne Preparatory School.

Michelmores (2ptnrs/5assts) The firm mainly does finance and re-structuring work for institutional clients. Act for most of the Church schools in Devon. *Malcolm Dickinson* does this work from the company and commercial department. Clients/ Work: University of Exeter; act for a wide range of institutions, universities, schools and colleges, particularly in relation to property and finance. Have an established reputation for raising sums of money for educational institutions.

Rickerby Watterson (7ptnrs) Act for a number of local private schools and grant maintained schools. Recently involved in high profile employment cases, and a growing number of pupil rights and discipline cases. Clients/ Work: Cheltenham Ladies College; Cheltenham and Gloucester College of Higher Education; Dean Close School.

Stone King (1ptnr/2assts) Traditional presence amongst voluntary aided, grant maintained and independent Catholic schools. *Michael King* has an excellent reputation in the charities and educational field. Clients/Work: Reorganisation of constitutions and property of independent schools; property management arrangements between trustees and governors of voluntary aided and grant maintained schools; general advice to schools on expulsions/ exclusions, child abuse, confidentiality, employment and charities matters.

Tozers A "very sound firm" which is known as a leading Catholic practice. Clients/Work: Advises educational charities and schools in the state and private sector.

Osborne Clarke (1ptnr/2asst) Have several regional higher education institutions as clients. *Joachim Steinbach* is considered "able and knowledgeable." Clients/Work: Advice on the creation of a network of university colleges for University of Plymouth; advice on two major healthcare education contracts for local NHS excutive; University of Bath.

| LEADING INDIVIDUALS |
SOUTH WEST • INSTITUTIONS
BOYD Robert Veale Wasbrough
DICKINSON Malcolm Michelmores
KING Michael Stone King
STEINBACH Joachim Osborne Clarke

Bevan Ashford (3ptnrs/3assts) A new addition to the list this year, they act for several HE institutions, and have a reputation on the property and planning side. Clients/Work: Bristol University; Newbury College; University of Glamorgan.

Bond Pearce (10ptnrs spend half their time acting for educational institutions) A leading southern commercial practice with a respectable education law capability. Clients/Work: College of St Mark and St John; Cornwall College; other colleges of higher education and schools.

Steele Raymond (4ptnrs) Large Bournemouth firm with a respected education practice. Clients/Work: All contractual work on newly-built 500 bed student accommodation block; education franchise agreements between a university and a chartered institution; contentious education law matters.

FIRMS ACTING FOR INDIVIDUALS

A.E. Smith & Son (1ptnr/1asst) *Robert Love* is a "superb lawyer" and well respected by colleagues and competitors for work on behalf of clients with special educational needs. Clients/Work: Particularly in the area of special needs including acting for parents in Special Educational Needs Tribunal Appeals, also judicial review and Order 55 Appeals on points of law against decisions of SEN Tribunals; some work in relation to admission and exclusion appeals; many educational negligence cases.

WALES

FIRMS ACTING FOR INSTITUTIONS

Eversheds (5ptnrs/8assts) Clearly leaders in the further education legal market in Wales. Clients/Work: Tax advice to colleges; acting in litigation over university buildings; IP advice.

Morgan Bruce (8ptnrs/7assts) Another leading firm acting for universities and schools, with an emphasis on HE. Clients/Work: University of Wales; acting for Bridgend College in contract to provide education services to HM Prison Parc.

FIRMS ACTING FOR INDIVIDUALS

Hugh James *Michael Jones* has a broad and impressive practice, which includes acting for children, parents and students. Work for Welsh language schools and for pupils with mental disabilities. Clients/Work: Handles constitutional issues and claims against LEAs.

MIDLANDS

FIRMS ACTING FOR INSTITUTIONS

Martineau Johnson (3ptnrs/3assts) A well-respected education unit with a reputation extending beyond the Midlands. The "sensible" *Simon Arrowsmith* is highly experienced in HE work and has "good all-round education law knowledge." *Paul Pharaoh* "really knows his education law." Clients/Work: Universities of Birmingham, Coventry and Warwick.

Eversheds (3ptnrs/8assts) Run a dedicated team from within public sector department. The Nottingham and Derby offices focus on PFI projects for schools, with *Nigel Sternberg* enjoying a good reputation for this type of work. Clients/Work: Clarendon College on the first education sector PFI project to be signed off; act for over 35 further education colleges and five universities.

Wragge & Co (6ptnrs/9assts) A leading commercial practice which has a large team servicing an extensive institutional client list. Clients/Work: Walsall College – European Design Centre building project and financing; confidentially advising a college on a claim brought by the Commission for Racial Equality; North Birmingham College.

Shakespeares (1ptnr) Practice is limited to one partner only but is noted for work in the multi-cultural educational area, and is regarded as a "flexible and practical" firm. Clients/Work: Al Furqan School – first grant maintained school in the UK for Islamic Studies.

FIRMS ACTING FOR INDIVIDUALS

Young & Lee Possess a specialist children's law and education department with a focus on special needs.

EAST ANGLIA

FIRMS ACTING FOR INSTITUTIONS

Eversheds (4ptnrs/6assts) Are the leading regional practice in further education, and also do some schools work. **Clients/Work:** Whole range of advice in the further education sector, including tax, employment and mergers.

Mills & Reeve (4ptnrs/9assts) Described as "an excellent firm with focused people" offering a "good service to clients." *Glynne Stanfield* is known for his work for higher education clients, and is considered an "effective operator." **Clients/Work:** Setting up Quality Assurance Agency for Higher Education; advising consortium of four universities on their acquisition of shares in Natural Resources International Ltd; advising a university on funding and constitutional aspects of new campus and its subsequent tax-based financing.

FIRMS ACTING FOR INDIVIDUALS

Hunt & Coombs (2ptnrs) Peterborough based practice with a reputation for representing individual children or parents. **Clients/Work:** Act for individuals on special needs cases and also exclusion matters. Also Special Educational Needs Tribunals, judicial review and negligence claims.

The NORTH and SCOTLAND

FIRMS ACTING FOR INSTITUTIONS

Eversheds (Leeds/Manchester) (4ptnrs/30assts) Have an excellent local reputation and an enviable national client base. The "pragmatic" *John Boardman* is regarded as the leading northern education solicitor. **Clients/Work:** UMIST; Manchester and Leeds Universities; 55 FE colleges.

Addleshaw Booth & Co (Manchester) Cross-disciplinary team which draws on 24 specialists from property, tax, employment and construction. **Clients/Work:** Acted for the Royal Northern College of Music on its pathfinder £5m PFI students' accommodation project; acted for Barclay's Bank on its £4m loan to Salford University; Leeds University.

Eversheds (Middlesborough/Newcastle) (5ptnrs/5assts) A cross-departmental team drawing on the strength of the national practice. *Chris Hugill* specialises in educational property work, and in particular PFI. Have recently acquired the team from merged Newcastle firm Wilkinson Maughan. **Clients/Work:** Education law in mergers, employment, construction, property, general commercial, PFI, all litigation and IP.

Dibb Lupton Alsop (Liverpool) Education is not treated by the firm as a specialist area, but they possess some valuable clients and perform a large amount of PFI work for schools and colleges. **Clients/Work:** PFI work for Northern Ireland Department of Education; £15m redevelopment of city centre campus for Liverpool Hope University College; VAT planning for a number of institutions such as Liverpool University.

Ford & Warren (Leeds) (3ptnrs/3assts) *Edward Brown* heads the education department, which advises further education colleges and schools. Undertake commercial property and employment advice and other work for the education sector including service provider contracts. **Clients/Work:** Society of Friends; ISIS; advice on the closure of Ayton School.

Pinsent Curtis (Leeds) A cross-departmental unit drawing on all departments of firm. Mainly work for higher and vocational education sectors. **Clients/Work:** Harassment and discrimination advice; student relations; Cardinal Heenan High School.

Dundas & Wilson CS (Edinburgh) (9ptnrs) Various members of the Industry Group do work for this client sector. An excellent client base gives the firm a steady stream of educational work. **Clients/Work:** University of Edinburgh on relocation of Medical School; principal legal advisors to University of Glasgow; The Institute of Chartered Accountants in Scotland.

Burnetts (Carlisle) Known for their contentious work. **Clients/Work:** Act for most FE and HE colleges in Cumbria and north Lancashire; acting for grant maintained schools; representing individuals in relation to special needs or admissions.

Grays (York) (3ptnrs p/t) Have a cross-departmental unit which advises institutions on property, employment and other matters. Known mainly for their non-contentious work. **Clients/Work:** Act for two FE colleges, the Roman Catholic Diocese of Leeds and of Middlesborough (which has about 100 schools). Also act for a number of independent schools.

FIRMS ACTING FOR INDIVIDUALS

Elaine Maxwell & Co (Lancaster) (1principal/1asst) *Elaine Maxwell* has recently left Marsden Huck taking her assistant with her. She regularly advises children and parents, particularly in relation to special needs. Also involved in a growing number of student cases. **Clients/Work:** Judicial reviews on failure to educate, discrimination, schools admission; appeals to special needs tribunals, admission appeals and actions for negligence.

Campbell Smith WS (Edinburgh) (1ptnr/1asst – 30%) The Edinburgh firm has a niche expertise in relation to advice on children with special needs. **Clients/Work:** Advises solely in relation to children with special education needs.

LEADERS' PROFILES · REGIONS

ARROWSMITH, Simon
Martineau Johnson, Birmingham
(0121) 200 3300
Partner in the Education Department.
Specialisation: The department provides and/or co-ordinates a full in-house service to all institutional educational clients, principally universities, colleges and schools. Particular interests or expertise include: constitutional, public and administrative law, specialist contracts (including joint ventures with private sector partners), statutory interpretation and compliance, project management, audit and other process consultancy, disciplinary and other management advice.
Career: Qualified in 1984, having joined *Martineau Johnson* in 1982. Became a partner in 1987. Head of Education 1992-1997.

BOARDMAN, John
Eversheds, Manchester (0161) 832 6666
Leeds (0113) 243 0391. Partner in Education Law Department.
Specialisation: Principal area of work is education law advising higher education, further education grant-maintained schools and TECs. Also advises other non-profit making bodies. Contributes articles to various specialist education law journals and gives numerous lectures and seminars on these areas.
Prof. Memberships: ELAS, Charity Law Association.
Career: Qualified 1979 while at *Alexander Tatham*, now *Eversheds* and became a Partner in 1986.
Personal: Born 26th July 1955. Attended Manchester Grammar School 1966-73 and Downing College, Cambridge 1973-76. Former Governor of a further education college. Leisure pursuits include pottery, plants, films, books, music and guinea pigs. Lives in Mellor, Derbyshire.

BOYD, Robert P.
Veale Wasbrough, Bristol (0117) 925 2020
Partner and Head of Schools Unit.
Specialisation: Partner in charge of the Education Department which has advised more than 500 independent schools and some special and grant maintained schools in the last decade. Also handles professional indemnity and personal injury litigation for insurers and plaintiffs. Author of VWSU Legal Summaries for Independent Schools and a textbook 'Independent Schools: Law, Custom and Practice' being published in autumn 1998 and of the Parent Contract and numerous other education templates and articles on education issues. Advises schools in the areas of governance, management, structural change, incorporation, charity and trust issues, the parent contract and many other concerns. Since 1996 has advised in high profile cases concerning playing fields, threats to kill, bogus qualifications and other crisis management. Advised ISJC on compilation of its Compliance Checklist for Inspectors. An invited speaker at seminars all over the country for HMC, GBA, IAPS, GSA, ISBA and SHMIS.
Prof. Memberships: Law Society; Academy of Experts; Bristol Law Society (Council Member 1986/88); Bristol Medico-Legal Society; ELAS.
Career: Qualified in 1972. Joined *Veale Wasbrough* as a Partner in 1988. Council of Bristol Law Society 1986-88; practising expert and Council Member of Academy of Experts 1989; Co-opted to Judicial Committee 1992.
Personal: Born 21st December 1946. Attended Stonyhurst College 1960/65 and Birmingham University 1966/69. Leisure interests include family, sailing and woodwork; charity pianist. Lives in Bristol.

BROWN, Edward V.
Ford & Warren, Leeds (0113) 243 6601
Partner in Property and Trusts Department.
Specialisation: Area of practice includes acting for a wide variety of educational establishments, principally for private and non-maintained special schools sector. Acts for a major further education college in Leeds. Extensive experience acting for education and ecclesiastical charities. Acts for the Society of Friends (the Quakers), former chair of the Society of Friends Joint Bursary Scheme and currently vice-chairman of Governors of Frobelian School and a director of Ackworth School Estates Limited. Regularly chairs seminars under the auspices of ISIS and *Ford & Warren* to headmasters of independent schools on a wide range of legal matters affecting education.
Prof. Memberships: Law Society, Leeds Law Society.
Career: Qualified in 1969, having joined *Ford & Warren* in 1967. Became a Partner in 1970.
Personal: Born 3 February 1945. Attended Bootham School, York 1958-63, then Leeds University, 1963. Leisure interests include hockey and tennis. Lives in Poole-in-Wharfedale.

COOK, Nicholas D.
Wollastons, Chelmsford (01245) 211211
Partner in Commercial Property Department.
Specialisation: Head of commercial property department, specialises in commercial leasehold advice. Supervises the firm's provision of legal services to education corporations. Acts for a university and a number of other further education colleges and schools.
Prof. Memberships: Law Society, Mid Essex Law Society (Hon Sec 85-96, President 97). Chairman South East Essex Centre Institute of Directors.
Career: Qualified 1983, Partner at *Wollastons* in 1986. Notary Public since 1993.

DICKINSON, Malcolm K.
Michelmores, Exeter (01392) 436244

GEORGE, Philip W.
Birkett Long, Colchester (01206) 217300
Partner in Company Commercial Department.
Specialisation: Advises a university, further education and sixth form colleges and a wide range of grant maintained and independent schools on contractual and constitutional issues, and upon the interpretation of statutes.
Prof. Memberships: Education Law Association.
Career: Qualified April 1975. Partner since 1976. Heads the firm's Education Unit.

HUGILL, Chris J.
Eversheds, Newcastle upon Tyne
(0191) 261 1661
Partner and head of education in the North East.
Specialisation: Property aspects of education

work including PFI. General education work.
Career: LL.B Sheffield 1974. Author of
'Business Tenancies' (Cavendish) – 3 editions.

JONES, Michael L.N.
Hugh James, Cardiff (01222) 224871
See under Litigation (Commercial), p. 525

KING, Michael
Stone King, Bath (01225) 337599
See under Charities, p. 165

LIELL, Peter Mark
Peter Liell, Potters Bar (01707) 665540

LOVE, Robert J.
A.E. Smith & Son, Stroud (01453) 757444
Partner. Special Educational Needs.
Prof. Memberships: Law Society, Convenor of
Special Needs Interest Group of Education Law
Association, Member of Advisory Board –
Education & Public Law Journal.
Career: Qualfied 1975. Partner in *A.E. Smith &
Son* since 1988.
Personal: Has been practising in this area for
the last eleven years.

MAXWELL, Elaine
Elaine Maxwell & Co, Lancaster
(01524) 840810
Specialisation: Now running own specialist firm
handling solely education law and community
care. Area of practice covers admissions,
exclusions, employment in education, transport
cases etc with particular expertise in special
educational needs and claims by students.
Provides seminars and advice to parent groups
on statementing system. Recent cases include
group actions for judicial review by parents
against statementing policies of local education
authorities, group actions by students following
withdrawal of funds by University, and actions

for negligence against universities and local
education authorities.
Prof. Memberships: Education Law
Association (Regional Co-ordinator),
Employment Lawyers Association.
Career: Called to Bar 1974, has advised on
education law since 1990, admitted as solicitor
1991, Partner *Marsden Huck* 1995 - 1998, set up
Elaine Maxwell & Co 1998.
Personal: Born 1951, attended Nottingham
High School for Girls, then Manchester
University.

PHARAOH, Paul
Martineau Johnson, Birmingham
(0121) 200 3300
Partner in Education Department.
Specialisation: Handles contractual, property-
related and constitutional issues for higher and
further education institutions and schools.
Author of articles in various legal journals,
chapters on judicial review in "Higher Education
and the Law" and on due diligence in
forthcoming publication "Managing Mergers,"
and module on law affecting pupils in school
for University of Buckingham Diploma in
Education Law. Speaker on education law and
judicial review at various conferences and
seminars.
Prof. Memberships: Law Society, ELAS.
Career: Qualified in 1971. Joined *Bettinsons* in
1969, becoming partner in 1973. Partner in
Shakespeares on merger 1990. Partner in
Martineau Johnson 1996. Law Society Council
Member since 1990, currently Chairman of
Compliance and Supervision Committee.
Midlands convenor for Education Law
Association.
Personal: Born 1947. Attended Manchester
University 1965-68 and Liverpool College of
Commerce 1968-69.

STANFIELD, Glynne
Mills & Reeve, Cambridge
+44·(01223) 364422
See under General Corporate Finance, p. 246

STEINBACH, Joachim
Osborne Clarke, Bristol (0117) 984 5374
Specialisation: Advises universities, health
service bodies and other publicly funded
institutions on public law and contractual
issues, including constitutional compliance,
public procurement, healthcare education
agreements, investment of treasury funds and
participation in public service pension schemes.
Prof. Memberships: Association of Pension
Lawyers.
Career: Qualified 1987. *Stephenson Harwood*
1984-87; *Bond Pearce*1987 -94; joined *Osborne
Clarke* as a partner in 1994.

STERNBERG, Nigel P.
Eversheds, Nottingham (0115) 950 7000
E-mail: nigelsternberg@eversheds.com
Partner in Commercial Department.
Specialisation: Practice covers intellectual
property work, with specalisation in IT, data and
distance learning. He has extensive experience
of outsourcing and large system developments,
both in the public and private sectors. He has
specialist knowledge of the Higher Education
and Banking sectors.
Prof. Memberships: Licensing Executive
Society and ELAS.
Career: Lecturer at the University of Durham
(1977 to 1980); qualifed 1982 *Branson Bramley*,
Sheffield (partner from 1984); joined *Eversheds*
(then *Wells and Hind*) as a partner 1987;
sometime Chairman of the Evershed Computer
IT BDU. Part-time lecturer University of Durham
(1977 to date).
Personal: Born November 1954; educated at
Staveley-Netherthorpe Grammar School,
Staveley and Oriel Oxford. MA in Jurisprudence.
Interests include mountain biking, food and
wine. Lives Chesterfield.

EMPLOYEE SHARE SCHEMES

RESEARCH: In compiling the tables, we consider all the information available to us, paying particular regard to the market research carried out by our team of ten qualified lawyers. (The researchers' details are set out on page three.) The rankings, therefore, reflect the opinion of the marketplace as revealed by systematic and objective research: see page four. (Our research is audited every year by the British Market Research Bureau.)

OVERVIEW: The market in employee share schemes is still busy and complex following changes in tax legislation and the Cadbury, Greenbury and Hampel reports, which have increased the demand for corporate governance advice. Cadbury has stimulated a new trend for payment of non-executive directors in shares.

Only the big corporate firms have the resources to provide employee share schemes expertise. It is a difficult area to dabble in and there are limited numbers of specialists, particularly outside London.

The threat of the accountants in this area does not seem to have materialised and even the Andersens/Garretts/Dundas & Wilson link-up has not yet had an impact. One positive effect of the competition is that practitioners are looking beyond narrow legal advice to provide more of a consultancy service.

In London the large Linklaters' team has maintained its strong hold on the market under the leadership of the dynamic Janet Cooper. There have, however, been some significant moves with the loss of Patrick Moon from private practice and the movement of David Cohen to Norton Rose leaving Paisners and Nabarro Nathanson with no practices to speak of and catapulting Norton Rose into the lists for the first time.

The regional and Scottish practices tend not to have national reputations, with the notable exception of star David Pett's Birmingham practice at Pinsent Curtis, which has pretensions to be a truly national practice.

LEADING FIRMS · LONDON
LINKLATERS
CLIFFORD CHANCE
FRESHFIELDS
ALLEN & OVERY
ASHURST MORRIS CRISP
HERBERT SMITH
LOVELL WHITE DURRANT
SLAUGHTER AND MAY

HIGHLY REGARDED FIRMS
Norton Rose
Travers Smith Braithwaite
Field Fisher Waterhouse
Nicholson Graham & Jones
Baker & McKenzie

LONDON

Linklaters (1ptnr/13assts) "Are known to have the advantage in numbers and in doing very big deals." The practice is "in a class of its own" and competitors also commented on the team's good database of background information. *Janet Cooper* "leads with panache and is a good team leader." She is "very much a corporate/employment person dealing in strategies, concepts etc" as opposed to consultant *Ann Croft* who is a "good technician, a detailed tax lawyer." *Graham Rowlands-Hempel* is a new partner who is "competent and one to watch for the future." **Clients/Work:** Major launch of share plans for British Airways in 80 countries. Designing and project managing launch of international share schemes for US, European, Australian and Japanese multi-nationals. Innovative executive and employee incentive arrange- ments (working with Halifax on ProShare Award winning arrangements).

Clifford Chance (2ptnrs/1cons/13assts) The team (including *Robin Tremaine*) is part of the tax department. Has its own consultancy firm, Newbridge Street Consultants, who are known nationally by practitioners, and gets some of its clients through them. **Clients/Work:** Advising British Energy on their ESOP funded purchase of shares and setting up of new Inland Revenue approved all employee share scheme; advising Unilever on establishing new Executive Share Option Scheme with shareholder approval; advising Burtons on compensating participants in share schemes for effects of demerger including facility for optionholders to roll over options into new employing entity.

Freshfields (2ptnrs) Now doing more share scheme work with US implications. Work divides almost 50:50 into M&A or flotation work and advisory. *Simon Evans* heads the team. The "excellent" *Jocelyn Mitchell* is "always up to date." **Clients/Work:** Northern Rock – share scheme aspects of demutualisation, including arrangements for distributing free shares to employees; advising Remuneration Committee on an executive share scheme and a wide variety of remuneration issues. Bovis Homes – share scheme aspects of flotation. Merrill Lynch – share scheme aspects of acquisition of Mercury Asset Management.

Allen & Overy (2ptnrs including *Stephen Chater* /9assts all of whom spend 50% of their time on it). Seen to be "trying to build up a good practice" and known for work arising from their "good M&A practice." Go up our tables this year. *Mervyn Parry* is "seen a lot on corporate transactions." **Clients/Work:** Establishment of Cable & Wireless Communications by merger of Mercury/Nynex/

Bell Cablemedia and Videotron. Bid by Lafarge S.A. for Redland plc. Bid by Merrill Lynch for Mercury Asset Management.

Ashurst Morris Crisp (1ptnr/4assts) A good practice which is known for having several solid people with experience in transactions and international executive share work. *Paul Randall* "has a lot of experience and is a capable pair of hands" but he keeps a low profile so is not a well-recognised name. Go up our tables this year. **Clients/Work:** Acting for Debenhams on demerger from the Burton Group; acting for J Bibby on its acquisition by Barlow of South Africa; acting for Forbes of South Africa on its acquisition of Nelson Hurst plc.

Herbert Smith (1ptnr/4assts) Handle work across the board. *Colin Chamberlain*, partner in the employment and trust group, is "absolutely first class and regarded as something of a guru." **Clients/Work:** Impact on share schemes of share buy-backs eg BG. Impact on share schemes of various demergers including British American Tobacco/ Allied Zurich. Share scheme aspects of various takeovers including GUS/Argos.

Lovell White Durrant (1ptnr/4assts) Located within the corporate finance group. Do a full mix of flotation and M&A type work as well as advisory work for listed and private companies. Have a prominent practitioner in *Louise Whitewright* who is "very enthusiastic" and has a growing reputation. **Clients/Work:** Advising Granada Group plc on the employee benefits implications of the recommended bid for Yorkshire Tyne Tees; advising the Mirror Group plc on their acquisition of Midland Independent Newspapers; acting for a number of US corporations extending their employee share schemes worldwide.

Slaughter and May (4ptnrs p/t;16assts p/t) The firm's generalist approach means that all members of the Pensions and Employment Department will spend some time on employee share scheme work. Known as an excellent corporate practice, *Edward Codrington* gets a lot of work on the strength of it and is a "big player but without a high public profile." *Jonathan Fenn* is building up a reputation. **Clients/Work:**

Include advising existing corporate clients on share option schemes, profit-sharing, restricted share schemes, LTIPs etc.

Norton Rose (2ptnrs/3assts) *David Cohen* formerly of Paisners and currently Chair of Share Schemes Lawyers Group, joined the firm as Head of Employee Benefits on 1 May 1998 taking some of his practice with him. The Norton Rose practice was previously dependent on M&A spin-off advice but Cohen will be seeking to build up stand-alone share scheme work for his new firm's large corporate clients. **Clients/Work:** Advice on share scheme implications of: sale of Hambros Bank by Hambros PLC and related transactions, sale of Eversholt Leasing to Forward Trust and £4.4billion acquisition of The Energy Group PLC by Texas Utilities Company.

Travers Smith Braithwaite (2ptnrs/ 2assts f/t, 3assts p/t) The practice operates from within the tax department. Particular niche is in MBO and flotation work. Also now busy on international trusts. *Victoria Nicholl* enjoys a growing reputation. **Clients/Work:** Principal advisers to Guinness (now Diageo) on Share Scheme aspects of the merger with GrandMet and now appointed to advise on Diageo's employee share schemes on an ongoing basis. share schemes and employee tax issues on 8 flotations and £1bn of MBO deals in 1997. International share schemes in over 50 countries this year.

Field Fisher Waterhouse (1ptnr/1asst and others from time to time) This small practice is relatively low profile but does have an international dimension which involves seminars on employee ownership all over the world and in conjunction with the UK Know-How Fund. **Clients/Work:** Growth in work for new NASDAQ listed technology companies. Continuing to help genuine employee ownership in private companies through use of Employee Benefit Trusts operating phantom share plans for benefit of workforce. Developing new incentive schemes such as dividend based incentive scheme.

Nicholson Graham & Jones (1ptnr/ 2assts) The "very very knowledgeable" and "personable" *Michael Jacobs* comes from a

tax background; he "loves the detailed tax in the area." The only criticism is that he "spreads himself too thin." He also appears as a leader in the trusts section. **Clients/Work:** Advising target of reverse takeover company resulting in ITE Group Plc. Advising Merrydown Plc on their reorganisation. Advising fund managers and stockbrokers on share schemes tailored to their special needs.

Baker & McKenzie (2ptnrs/1barrister) Work for a number of non-UK based multinationals so have experience of setting up and maintaining UK sub-plans of foreign share plans. Team is headed by *Michael Ingle* who is known as a specialist although he is also seen as an employment lawyer. **Clients/ Work:** Advising Avis Europe plc re extension of profit-sharing plan to nine other European countries. Establishing tax approved share option plans as sub-plans of US stock plans for number of major US multinationals including AT&T. Advising UK and foreign companies on maintenance and operation of UK share plans eg:Inspec Group PLC.

LEADERS' PROFILES · LONDON

CHAMBERLAIN, Colin
Herbert Smith, London (0171) 374 8000
Partner in Employment Department.
Specialisation: Specialises in employee share schemes and benefit arrangements in the UK and overseas including employee cash incentives, ESOP's, corporate personal equity plans and profit-related pay. He is author of 'Tolley's Practical Guide to Employees' Share Schemes.'
Career: Qualified in 1977. Between 1985 and 1989 he worked as a director of the former CC&P, now part of Bacon & Woodrow. Became

a Partner at *Herbert Smith* in 1989.
Personal: Educated at Sussex University. ATII.

CHATER, Stephen
Allen & Overy, London (0171) 330 3000
Specialisation: Specialises in employee tax and share incentives in an international context. Deals with flotations, privatisations, mergers and acquisitions and management buy-outs and advises on the establishment, operation, variation and termination of employees' share schemes.
Prof. Memberships: Law Society; Share

Scheme Lawyers Group; Society of Share Scheme Practitioners.
Career: Joined *Allen & Overy* 1979. Qualified 1981. Partner 1989.
Personal: Educated at Hartlepool Grammar School and Christ Church, Oxford. Lives in Surrey.

CODRINGTON, Edward A.
Slaughter and May, London (0171) 600 1200
Specialisation: Main areas of practice are employee benefits, pensions and employment. Deals with the establishment of all types of employee benefit plans, both cash and share

based, ESOPs and profit related pay. Also handles pensions work including setting up, merger and termination of pension schemes.
Prof. Memberships: The Law Society, Association of Pension Lawyers, Share Scheme Lawyer Group.
Career: Joined 1974, qualified 1976, Partner 1985.
Personal: Born 12 April 1951. St Benedict's School, Ealing 1957–1970. Birmingham University 1970–73. Interests include family and sport (watching).

COHEN MA FTII, David Henry
Norton Rose, London (0171) 283 6000
Partner in Human Resources Department. Head of Employee Benefits Group. Visiting Fellow in Employee Share Ownership Law at the Centre for Commercial Law Studies at University of London.
Specialisation: Handles mainly employee share schemes and employee benefits work. Author of 'Employee Participation in Flotations 1987–1997.' Contributor to the 'Encyclopaedia of Forms and Precedents.' Regular contributor to the Financial Times.
Prof. Memberships: Fellow of the Chartered Institute of Taxation, Chairman of the Share Scheme Lawyers Group. Member of editorial board of Palmer's Company Law.
Career: Qualified in 1980. With *Titmuss Sainer & Webb* 1978–82. Assistant Solicitor and Partner at *Nicholson Graham & Jones* 1982–86. Partner at *Paisner & Co.* 1986–1998. Joined *Norton Rose* as a Partner in May 1998.
Personal: Born Cardiff 15th December 1955. Educated at Jesus College, Oxford 1974–77. Governor of Independent Jewish Day School. Enjoys sport. Married with 4 sons. Lives in London.

COOPER, Janet
Linklaters, London (0171) 456 3662
Partner 1991. Employment and Employee Benefits Group, Head of the Employee Share Schemes team.
Specialisation: Specialises in employee share schemes, executive incentives, international employee share arrangements and related matters. On qualification was a general corporate lawyer before specialising in employee share schemes and executive incentives and therefore familiar with how corporate transactions affect employee share schemes. Main areas of practice include advising on, designing and drafting documentation in connection with a variety of employee share schemes, and executive incentives, including revenue approved schemes, restricted share plans, bonus conversion plans, employee share ownership plans (ESOPs) and international employee and executive share schemes.

CROFT, Anne
Linklaters, London (0171) 456 3706
Specialisation: Specialises in tax, in particular employee-related tax and national insurance contributions. Practice areas include employee share schemes, ESOPs (including ESOP financing techniques), unapproved pension arrangements, employment contracts and flexible remuneration packages, termination of employment and international employment contracts. Transactional work has included privatisations (electricity, water, rail), mergers and acquisitions (GUS/ Argos, Somerfield/ Kwiksave, several electricity companies),

schemes of arrangement (Royal Sun Alliance, Lloyds TSB) and B Share issues (Bass, WH Smith).
Prof. Memberships: Fellow of the Chartered Institute of Taxation, Share Scheme Lawyers Group.
Career: Called to the Bar 1975; LLM, tax and company law (University of London) 1976. Requalified as a solicitor 1990; Consultant 1998.

EVANS, Simon
Freshfields, London (0171) 936 4000
Partner in Employment Pensions and Benefits Department.
Specialisation: Specialises in share option, restricted share plan and ESOP arrangements, relating both to establishment of schemes and advice on the impact of corporate transactions on schemes. Also handles employment law, notably executive appointments and dismissals. Devised numerous long term incentive plans and other tailor-made incentive schemes. Regularly lectures on share scheme topics.
Prof. Memberships: Share Scheme Lawyers Group.
Career: Qualified in 1983. Joined *Freshfields* in 1981, becoming a Partner in 1991.
Personal: Born 16th June 1957. Attended Rugby School 1970–75; MA from Sidney Sussex College, Cambridge, 1976–79. Lives in Staplehurst, Kent.

FENN, Jonathan
Slaughter and May, London (0171) 600 1200
Specialisation: Principal area of practice is employees' share schemes, both Inland Revenue approved and unapproved, including deferred bonus and long-term incentive schemes and ESOPs. Also advises on pensions, including in particular the pensions aspects of M&A and corporate transactions, as well as general pensions advice.
Prof. Memberships: The Law Society, Association of Pension Lawyers (member of Legislative and Parliamentary Sub-Committee), Share Scheme Lawyers Group (member of Committee), Society of Share Scheme Practitioners.
Career: Qualified 1986. At *Slaughter and May* 1984 to date. Became a Partner in 1995.
Personal: Born 30 May 1961. Educated at Maidstone Grammar School and King's College, London. Lives in Kent.

INGLE, Michael
Baker & McKenzie, London (0171) 919 1000
Specialisation: Practice covers the full range of employee benefits and employment taxation. Co-ordinates the firm's practice in the area of share schemes and incentive plans. Clients include banks and numerous multinational companies. Is a contributing editor of the FT Law & Tax publication Practical Tax Planning.
Prof. Memberships: Share Schemes Lawyers Group; Society of Share Schemes Practitioners.
Career: Qualified 1981. At *Dunham Brindley & Linn* 1979–1984, Engineering Employers Federation 1984 to 1985 and *Baker & McKenzie* from 1985 (Partner from 1990).
Personal: Born 27 April 1951. Educated in Canada and obtained LLB degree from the University of Western Ontario in 1974. Lives in London.

JACOBS, Michael
Nicholson Graham & Jones, London (0171) 648 9000
Head of Private Client Department.
Specialisation: Tax on M & A transactions; employee share schemes; international tax, trusts, charities, and public sector bodies. Author of 'Tax on Take-overs' (7 editions) and 'Rewarding Leadership' (published by CISCO, February 1998); contributor to 'Tolley's Tax Planning' and 'Tolley's VAT Planning.' Consultant editor of Tolley's Trust Law International.
Prof. Memberships: Trust Law Committee (Founder Member and (1994–97) Secretary); Share Scheme Lawyers Group (Founder Member and Vice-Chairman); Employee Share Scheme Committee (Chairman) CISCO; STEP; IFA; IFS; Charity Law Association.
Career: Articled at *Nicholson Graham & Jones* 1970; Partner 1976. Head of Tax Department 1981.

MITCHELL, Jocelyn
Freshfields, London (0171) 936 4000
Specialisation: Main areas of practice are share schemes and employee benefits. Deals with the establishment and ongoing advisory work relating to share option schemes, long term incentive plans, ESOPs, QUESTs and international share schemes. Has extensive experience of share schemes and employment issues on mergers and acquisitions and flotations. Also advises on senior executive terminations, employment tax and the law relating to directors and corporate governance.
Prof. Memberships: Share Scheme Lawyers Group.
Career: Qualified in 1985. *Freshfields* 1995 (partner 1997).

NICHOLL, Victoria
Travers Smith Braithwaite, London (0171) 248 9133
Specialisation: UK corporate tax and UK and international employee incentives and employee taxation. Handles share schemes, ESOPs and benefits both generally and in relation to MBOs, flotations and corporate transactions.
Career: Qualified 1987. Joined *Travers Smith Braithwaite* 1989. Partner 1995.

PARRY, Mervyn
Allen & Overy, London (0171) 330 3000
Specialisation: Specialises in employee share schemes and employee tax and benefits, as well as pensions. Advises employers on all forms of share option and other incentive schemes, employee share ownership trusts, QUESTS, phantom plans, international aspects (e.g. the Americas, Europe and Australia). Also advises on corporate governance and national insurance issues. Handles setting up, merging and winding-up all forms of pension scheme and all transactional aspects.
Prof. Memberships: Share Schemes Lawyers Group; Association of Pension Lawyers.
Career: Educated at Kings College School, Wimbledon and Downing College Cambridge (1969–1972). Joined *Allen & Overy* and articled clerk 1973. Became partner 1985.
Personal: Born 1951. Married, two daughters. Lives in Wandsworth.

RANDALL, Paul

Ashurst Morris Crisp, London
(0171) 638 1111
Partner and head of the Employment and
Benefits Group.
Specialisation: Designs and implements
domestic and international employee share
schemes and incentives, including ESOPs,
QUESTs, profit sharing schemes, executive and
savings related share options, restricted share
schemes, bonus arrangements and Long Term
Incentive Plans, both generally and in the con-
text of MBOs, flotations, mergers and privatisa-
tions. Major clients include Albert Fisher, Allied
Domecq, National Grid, NFC and Sun Alliance.
Prof. Memberships: Law Society and Share
Scheme Lawyers Group.
Career: Qualified in 1984. Joined *Ashurst
Morris Crisp* 1987, partner 1995.

ROWLANDS-HEMPEL, Graham

Linklaters, London (0171) 456 3680
Specialisation: Specialist in employee share
plans, executive incentives and related matters.
On qualification was a corporate tax lawyer
before specialising in employee share plans
and executive incentives. Main areas of practice
include advising on, designing and drafting
documentation in connection with a variety of
employee share plans and executive incentives,
including UK Revenue approved plans, restricted
stock plans, employee share ownership plans
(ESOPs) and other executive incentive arrangements. Typical matters include: dealing with
employee share plans in various major

corporate reorganisations and transactions.
Examples include the British Gas demerger and
the flotations of Denby Pottery, Orange, AEA
Technology and Biocompatibles International
plc; advising and helping with the design of
several restricted share plans including British
Airways and BP; and advising on and helping
with the design of many international share
plans including supervising and co-ordinating
the overseas legal advice. Examples include
working with BP, British Airways and Waterford
Wedgwood. Articles in professional journals.
Frequent speaker at lectures and seminars,
most recently at the annual conference of The
National Centre for Employee Share Ownership
in Chicago and ProShare Conference on
Extending Share Ownership beyond the UK.
Prof. Memberships: Member of Society of
Share Scheme Practitioners and the Share
Scheme Lawyers' Group.
Career: 1998 to date – Partner, Employment &
Benefits Group, *Linklaters*. 1994–1998 –
Senior Assistant, Employment & Benefits Group,
Linklaters. 1987–1994 – Assistant Solicitor, Tax
Group, *Simmons & Simmons*. Education –
University of South Bank – LLB.

TREMAINE, Robin

Clifford Chance, London (0171) 600 1000
Partner. Head of the Employee Share Schemes
Unit.
Specialisation: Specialises in advising on the
design, establishment and operation of all
types of employee share schemes (including
long term incentive plans, performance share

plans, restricted share schemes and equity
partnership plans). Advises on all aspects of
ESOP financing, acting both for companies
and banks. Specialist expertise in international
share schemes. Also handles corporate and
international tax.
Prof. Memberships: Share Scheme Lawyers'
Group; Society of Share Scheme Practitioners.
Career: Qualified as a barrister in 1979.
Requalified as a solicitor in 1986. Partner in
Clifford Chance in 1989.
Personal: Plymouth College; Trinity Hall,
Cambridge MA 1978.

WHITEWRIGHT, Louise

Lovell White Durrant, London
(0171) 236 0066
Specialisation: Principal area of practice
is employee share schemes and employee
benefits advising on all aspects of the design,
structure, establishment and operation of
approved and unapproved employee share
schemes (including ESOPS, restricted share
schemes and international share schemes) for
private and public companies. Deals with all
aspects of these schemes on flotations,
takeovers, privatisations etc. Contributor of
section in CCH Editions Employment Manual
and to other publications.
Prof. Memberships: Law Society; Share
Scheme Lawyers Group (Secretary and member
of Executive Committee). ESOP Centre.
Career: Articled *Rakisons* 1984–1986; qualified
1986 with *Lovell White Durrant* as an assistant
solicitor in the tax group. Specialised in employee
share schemes from 1987 and became a Partner
in 1996.

THE REGIONS

PINSENT CURTIS Birmingham, Leeds

ADDLESHAW BOOTH & CO Manchester, Leeds

WRAGGE & CO Birmingham

EVERSHEDS Birmingham

HIGHLY REGARDED FIRMS

Malcolm Lynch Leeds

Burges Salmon Bristol
Dundas & Wilson CS Edinburgh
Garretts Leeds
Hammond Suddards Leeds
McGrigor Donald Glasgow
Osborne Clarke Bristol

Pinsent Curtis (Birmingham, Leeds)
(4ptnrs/6assts) Kept ahead by their extremely high profile leader. *David Pett* in
Birmingham made a good move when he
wrote "the Book" on Employee Share
Schemes and turned himself into the "household name" in this area of practice. *Judith
Greaves* operates from the Leeds office. She
tends to be known in the market-place more
for corporate tax than employee share
schemes. *John Christian* is a corporate tax

lawyer who is "increasingly getting into the
area" and commands wide respect from
other practitioners throughout the UK.
Clients/Work: Advising employees and
trustees on sale of country's largest employee-owned company to a large listed company.
Developing QUEST idea for a continuing
range of listed and private companies.
Developing innovative linking of SAYE
share option schemes and discretionary
share option schemes and significantly
enhancing value of tax reliefs available to
employee-owned company (XTRAC Ltd).

Addleshaw Booth & Co (Manchester,
Leeds) (2ptnrs/1cons/4assts) The practice is
located within the commercial tax department. *Richard Hayes* is "on the ball." Have
recruited a consultant from Buck Consultants in Leeds to provide remuneration
consultancy to industry and commerce.
Clients/Work: Trinity International Holdings
plc – establishment of replacement share
option schemes and of a QUEST. Calderburn
plc – establishment of replacement share
option schemes. Oxford Molecular Group
plc – amendment of unapproved share option
scheme to allow increased incentives to key
executives.

Wragge & Co (Birmingham) (1ptnr/
1asst do up to 30%) The team functions out
of the corporate department led by *Peter*

Smith. He "knows what he's about" and "does
a lot of things … commands respect." Some
question the team's strength in depth.
Clients/Work: BI Group plc: offers in
relation to the share option schemes of
Cortworth plc. Doncasters plc: offers in relation to the share option schemes of Triplex
Lloyd plc. Independent Parts Group plc: new
executive and savings related share schemes.

Eversheds (Birmingham) (1ptnr/1asst)
The team has two dedicated share incentive
lawyers and works closely with the Leeds/
Manchester offices. *Lawrence Green* is a
senior associate spending most of his time in
this area. **Clients/Work:** Advising Vision
Express Group Ltd on its Employee Share
Ownership Plan for arrangements relating to
its share option schemes in connection with
the £500m merger with Grand Photo-Service
SA to form a company listed on the French
Stock Exchange. For Britax International plc
to put in place new LTIP.

Malcolm Lynch (Leeds) (1ptnr/1asst)
An interesting niche firm with a national
client base which was set up by *Malcolm
Lynch* who came from a trade union background and works for unions, charities and
progressive commercial clients who desire
real hands-on employee share ownership.
Clients/Work: Advising a winner of the
Queen's Award for Export for Industry (Aber

Instruments Limited) on a profit sharing scheme. Developing with others a national telephone advisory service for SME owners seeking advice on ESOPs as a succession strategy.

Burges Salmon (Bristol) (1ptnr/3assts) Pensions and tax specialists have share schemes expertise. Practice is increasingly slanted towards putting in place LTIPs for plcs. **Clients/Work:** Application to High Court regarding use of pension fund surplus on a winding-up. Longterm incentive plans for Bridport Gundry plc, FirstGroup plc and Brandon Hire plc.

Dundas & Wilson CS (Edinburgh) (2assts, 90%/20%) Team works out of the Human Capital Services Group; it is headed by an associate from Dorman Jeffrey, since the takeover in September 1997. Provide tax and national insurance planning advice for equity and non-equity incentives. Provide multi-disciplinary approach through link-up with Andersens. **Clients/Work:** Advising on setting up of international cross-border share schemes and use of employee share trusts. Dealing with all compliance aspects including advising on ABI guidelines, the Greenbury and Hampel committee reports.

Garretts (Leeds) (3assts) The Share Scheme Team operates as part of Human Capital Services Group and are said to "do a lot on the back of Andersens" so provide a multi-disciplinary approach for clients.

Hammond Suddards (Leeds) (1ptnr/ 2assts-Leeds; 3assts Manchester) Team is located in the corporate tax department and covers a broad cross-section of work including flotations, demergers and general administration advice. Their reputation is local rather than national. **Clients/Work:** Acting for Fine Art Developments plc and Creative Publishing plc on establishment of new employee share schemes at time of demerger. Advising FKI plc on arrangements for participants in employee share schemes operated by Bridon following takeover of Bridon by FKI.

McGrigor Donald (Glasgow) (1ptnr/ 2assts) Do mainly advisory work from within the corporate tax department. **Clients/ Work:** Stakis plc – introduction of new "super option" arrangements for key directors and senior management. Core Group plc – establishment of share option, profit sharing and ESOP arrangements upon flotation. Edinburgh Petroleum Services Ltd –

renegotiation of option arrangements.

Osborne Clarke (Bristol) (1ptnr f/t; 1ptnr p/t; 1asst) Have a dedicated Pensions and Benefits Group out of which the share schemes team operates. The partner heading the team comes from a corporate tax background but now specialises. **Clients/ Work:** Advising on setting up of a long-term incentive plan for Chesterton International plc. Advising on setting up an ESOP trust and international share scheme for HP Bulmer Holdings PLC. Advising on setting up a profit-sharing scheme for Prism Rail plc.

LEADING INDIVIDUALS
THE REGIONS

PETT David Pinsent Curtis

GREAVES Judith Pinsent Curtis

GREEN Lawrence Eversheds

HAYES Richard Addleshaw Booth & Co

LYNCH Malcolm Malcolm Lynch

SMITH Peter Wragge & Co

UP AND COMING

CHRISTIAN John Pinsent Curtis

SEE PROFILES AT END OF THIS SECTION

LEADERS' PROFILES · REGIONS

CHRISTIAN, John M.S.
Pinsent Curtis, Leeds (0113) 244 5000
See under Tax (Corporate), p. 757

GREAVES, Judith
Pinsent Curtis, Leeds (0113) 244 5000
Partner in Corporate Tax Department.
Specialisation: Main areas of practice are employee share schemes: approved and unapproved schemes, long term incentive plans, ESOPs, employee buy outs and international schemes; and corporate tax, covering acquisitions and disposals, group reorganisations, financing and property transactions and MBOs.
Prof. Memberships: Share Schemes Lawyers Group.
Career: Qualified 1986 with *Linklaters & Paines*. Joined *Simpson Curtis* in 1988, becoming Partner in 1991.

GREEN, Lawrence
Eversheds, Birmingham (0121) 233 2001
Senior Associate in Tax Department.
Specialisation: Advises on planning and implementation of all types of employee share incentive arrangements. Acts for a range of quoted and private companies on UK and overseas implications. Charge-out rate is £190 per hour.
Career: Trained with *Evershed & Tomkinson* and qualified in 1988. Senior Associate at *Eversheds* since 1996.
Personal: Born 8th March 1964. Educated at

Queen Elizabeth Grammar School, Trinity Hall, Cambridge and Chester Law School. Leisure interests include cycling and mountain walking. Lives in Sutton Coldfield.

HAYES, Richard
Addleshaw Booth & Co, Manchester (0161) 934 6000
Partner in Commercial Tax Department, Commercial Group.
Specialisation: Head of Commercial Tax Department providing specialist tax services to the firm. Specialises in employee share schemes including ESOPs, option schemes and long term incentive schemes for both public and private companies.
Prof. Memberships: Law Society, Manchester Law Society; Society of Share Scheme Practitioners.
Career: Qualified in 1972. Joined the firm in 1973, becoming a Partner in 1975. Treasurer of the Manchester Incorporated Law Library Society.
Personal: Born 31st October 1947. Attended Trinity Hall, Cambridge (MA 1969, LLB 1970). Chairman of the Manchester Midday Concerts Society. Leisure interests include railways, opera, classical music and sheep.
Lives in Chapel-en-le-Frith.

LYNCH, Malcolm
Malcolm Lynch, Leeds (0113) 242 9600

PETT, David
Pinsent Curtis, Birmingham (0121) 200 1050
National Practice Head of Tax and Pensions.
Specialisation: Leader of a team of acknowledged specialists in the fields of corporate tax and employee share schemes. David is responsible for devising many of the more innovative share schemes for public and private companies including long-term incentive plans; the use of QUEST, with SAYE option schemes; the tax efficient buyout of companies using employee trusts; and international schemes. Author of 'Employee Share Schemes' (Sweet and Maxwells 2 volume updated looseleaf).
Prof. Memberships: Active member of The Share Scheme Lawyers Group and the Society of Share Scheme Practitioners.
Career: Qualified 1980, became a partner in 1985.
Personal: Educated at Lincoln College, Oxford.

SMITH, Peter
Wragge & Co, Birmingham (0121) 233 1000
Specialisation: Employees' and Executives' share (or equity linked) incentive and share ownership schemes and arrangements of all kinds.
Prof. Memberships: International Fiscal Association.
Career: Educated at West Bromwich Grammar School and Jesus College, Oxford. Qualified 1978. Partner at *Wragge & Co* from 1983.
Personal: Born 1952.

EMPLOYMENT LAW

See also Employee Share Schemes; Health & Safety; Pensions

RESEARCH: In compiling the tables, we consider all the information available to us, paying particular regard to the market research carried out by our team of ten qualified lawyers. (The researchers' details are set out on page three.) The rankings, therefore, reflect the opinion of the marketplace as revealed by systematic and objective research: see page four. (Our research is audited every year by the British Market Research Bureau.)

OVERVIEW: With Tony Blair and Cherie Booth both being employment lawyers, it is no surprise that the new Labour government has brought major change. The UK accession to the Social Chapter means a raft of legislation awaits enactment. Employment lawyers are going to be busy. The Disability Discrimination Act 1996 and high compensation awards for sexual harrassment cases have increased the number of discrimination claims as an automatic add-on to unfair dismissal claims.

Personalities are of primary importance in this area. 'Client-friendliness' is paramount. The personality cult is particularly significant in London, where clients may refuse to settle for anyone other than the figurehead partner. Some firms whose leaders do not promote themselves as part of the "magic circle"of the Employment Lawyers Association or similar organisations may suffer in terms of profile.

The employment market remains relatively unchanged throughout the country. The most significant move in our tables is the top ranking of Simmons & Simmons ahead of Baker & McKenzie in London. Nationwide, Eversheds' branches continue to consolidate their position as a cost-effective alternative by diversifying into HR consultancy work. They lead in both Wales and the Midlands.

Cole & Cole, led by Sue Ashtiany, retains pole position as the only firm in the South East with a truly national reputation.

In the North East there is some difficulty in comparing the Leeds market with firms in Newcastle. That said, Pinsent Curtis headed by the indomitable John McMullen continues to play top dog, helped by the team in London.

Mackay Simon, the one niche employment firm in Scotland, continues to provide an impressive service and stay ahead of the big commercial firms. In Northern Ireland there is an increase in firms specialising in employment law, although it remains a far smaller market than on the mainland. Niche firm Jones & Cassidy emerges for the first time as a leader.

In terms of the legal marketplace, employment is developing as a 'sexy' area of practice for new qualifiers. This has led to an increase in quality in the specialist firms. Firms trying to get into the field have floundered. In the provinces, accountancy firms and independent consultancies are beginning to provide real competition.

David Warner (of Warner Cranston) is planning to open up a boutique employment practice in London with ex-barrister Michael Johns in September '98.

LEADING FIRMS · LONDON
MAINLY RESPONDENT

SIMMONS & SIMMONS

BAKER & MCKENZIE

EVERSHEDS
FOX WILLIAMS
LOVELL WHITE DURRANT
ROWE & MAW

HIGHLY REGARDED FIRMS

Cameron McKenna
Herbert Smith
Lewis Silkin
Paisner & Co
Salans Hertzfeld & Heilbronn HRK
Slaughter and May
Warner Cranston

Allen & Overy
Beachcroft Stanleys
Charles Russell
Clifford Chance
Richards Butler
Stephenson Harwood
Theodore Goddard

S J Berwin & Co
Boodle Hatfield
Denton Hall
D J Freeman
Freshfields
Langley & Co
Linklaters
Macfarlanes
Norton Rose
Osborne Clarke
Speechly Bircham
Taylor Joynson Garrett
Titmuss Sainer Dechert

LONDON

MAINLY RESPONDENT

Simmons & Simmons (5ptnrs/17assts) The firm's large and growing team maintains its strong reputation for technical competence and strength in depth, and has forged ahead in terms of breadth of work. Opposing solicitors praise them as "fair and balanced to deal with." *Janet Gaymer's* high profile as the "doyenne of employment law" leaves her capable team to carry the bulk of client work. *William Dawson* commands widespread respect. *Simon Watson* received several recommendations. **Clients/Work:** Advised on the global integration of Dresdner RCM, global investors bringing together the investment arm of Kleinwort Benson and Thornton Management. Advised the Royal Shakespeare Company on the employment aspects of its move to the Barbican. Setting up European Employment Forum.

Baker & McKenzie (4ptnrs/1cons/ 17assts) "International in character, technically good." During 1997, acquired a dedicated know-how officer. Run the European Labour Lawyers Practice Group which advises on the establishment of European works councils. *Fraser Younson* is "excellent," *Caroline Cheshire* has "good technical expertise and appreciates a commercial problem," and *Christine O'Brien* is "highly competent." **Clients/Work:** Advising a leading global brand on claims of alleged breaches of its European works council agreement. Acting for a prominent Formula 1 racing car team over the recruitment of the world's leading racing car designer, before the expiry of his employment contract with another prominent Formula 1 racing car team. Acting in one of the biggest wrongful dismissal claims in recent years, with potential damages of £10m.

Eversheds (2ptnrs/13assts) Benefits from the support of its nationwide regional offices, allowing it to provide an efficient and low cost Industrial Tribunal service although not the kind of high profile strategic work attracted by the other leaders. The "knowledgeable and hard-working" *Elaine Aarons* is perceived as "good news" for the firm, being "a safe pair of hands." Following the election she set up a Forum on Social Policy. **Clients/Work:** The team won a beauty parade to act for new Financial Services Authority, advising them on the transfer of employees from eight regulatory bodies into one. Advised on a $3bn share purchase from ICI by Dupont. Acting on the termination of contracts of a number of Laura Ashley directors.

Fox Williams (3ptnrs/8assts) A "small but premier firm." The employment team, led by "class act" *Ronnie Fox*, is enormously strengthened by the "brilliant and extremely

busy" *Jane Mann*. The team is perceived to be at a crucial point in its development – between being a small firm and having the critical mass to field the teams expected by large clients. **Clients/Work:** Have acted for Deutsche Morgan Grenfell, Charter plc and Republic National Bank of New York.

Lovell White Durrant (4ptnrs/9assts). Well-established "quality outfit." Continues to act for a high-profile client base although it suffers from the relatively low profile of its partners. The "straight-talking, commercial" *Andrew Williamson* heads the team, his "aggressive" style a contrast to *David Harper*, who "quietly gets on with the job" and is praised as being both "practical" and "quick to respond." New partner *Naomi Feinstein* is "impressive." **Clients/Work:** Advising on the employment aspects of the BZW takeover of Credit Suisse. Defending the BCCI "stigma claims" in the High Court. Acting for several high-profile senior executive terminations.

Rowe & Maw (2ptnrs/6assts). Small but expanding practice. Reputation still rests largely upon the "very, very knowledgeable" *Julian Roskill*, "a solid pair of hands" who has increased his profile over the last year. *Nick Robertson* is newly recommended for being "calm under pressure." **Clients/Work:** Acting for Argos in an early TUPE case following Suzen, Johnson v Network SI Group and others, in which the client got a cost order for being wrongly joined into the case. Acting in AEEU v Thorn in the EAT, a claim for a protective award for failure to consult about the closure of a business, involving technical arguments on the meaning of 'establishment.' Acting for a Formula One chief designer leaving to join McLaren, involving issues of garden leave, restrictive covenants etc.

Cameron McKenna (2ptnrs/8assts) The merger, which combines the litigation strength of CMH with the more non-contentious bent and corporate clients of McKennas, "seems to have jelled well." The firm had numerous recommendations to go up. The "excellent" *Simon Jeffreys* is "a bright cookie." **Clients/Work:** Successful on behalf of IGE in the Employment Appeal Tribunal v Halfpenny, dealing with the rights of women to return from maternity leave to work. Acting for Mr Bill Harrison on departure from Barclays and joining Deutsche Bank. Advising Nomura in acquisition of William Hill.

Herbert Smith (2ptnrs/7assts) Team consists of *John Farr* ("first class"and "the ultimate gentleman") and *Peter Frost* (" a real employment lawyer"). The firm is considered more impressive than other City practices and goes up the rankings this year. **Clients/Work:** Acting for Jardine Lloyd Thompson for ex parte injunction application. Acting for First Choice plc in wrongful dismissal claim. Defending race discrimination case for major hotel chain involving £800k claim by former Managing Director.

Lewis Silkin (4ptnrs/8assts) The team is seen as conscientious. *Michael Burd* is known as a general litigator rather than an employment specialist. The "enthusiastic" *James Davies* is "bright and loved by clients." **Clients/Work:** Successfully represented 73 bus drivers in the House of Lords who were dismissed for taking industrial action in 1990; Crosville Wales Ltd v Tracey and others (no2). Reached agreements for 6 ex-directors of Shandwick plc who broke away and formed new public relations agency Hogarth Partnership. Acting in a heavily contested Mareva injunction case against former bank general manager accused of wrong-doing; recent reported decision in the case has important implications.

Paisner & Co (1ptnr/5assts) The "highly effective" *Stephen Levinson* has "achieved an historically high profile." **Clients/Work:** Collective bargaining and TUPE issues, consultation by Agricultural Wages Board. Industrial tribunal cases involving race, sex and disability discrimination for institutional clients. High level executive terminations.

Salans Hertzfeld & Heilbronn HRK, formerly Harris Rosenblatt and Kramer (1ptnr/2assts) The effects of the merger on 1st January 1998 have yet to make their mark on the wider world. In employment the firm seems to be generally perceived as a one-man band. The "one man" is department head *Barry Mordsley*, "one of the grey-haired doyens of employment law." **Clients/Work:** Lloyds UDT – industrial tribunals. Remploy-general advice. Infoproducts – general advice.

Slaughter and May (4ptnrs/18assts) Practitioners do not specialise solely in employment but also do pensions and employee share schemes. The department's work is slanted towards high-profile terminations. *Howard Jacobs* is a "shrewd operator" who "never takes a silly point, an extremely good practitioner."

Warner Cranston (2ptnrs/8assocs) Still recovering from David Warner's departure. *David Dalgarno* was thought useful and competent. All fee-earners do their own advocacy. **Clients/Work:** Act for United Airlines, NatWest Markets and Courtaulds plc among others.

Allen & Overy (2ptnrs/10assts) *Mark Mansell* heads the unit and is "sensible and competent." **Clients/Work:** Disposal ICI bulk chemicals businesses. Merger of UBS and SBC. Merger of cable businesses of Mercury, Nynex, Bell Cablemedia and Videotron.

Beachcroft Stanleys (2ptnrs/7assts) A "solid public-sector practice." The practice is led by the "articulate" *Elizabeth Adams* who has a reputation as "a real people person." *Rachel Dineley*, recently made a partner, is newly recommended this year. **Clients/Work:** Advising the project company on the TUPE aspects of the South Bucks PFI. VNU Business Publications Ltd-v-Adam Yates in the High Courts.

Charles Russell (3ptnrs/7assts) *David Green* ("the big man") is "first class." **Clients/Work:** Acted for KLM in authority case on the Transfer of Undertaking Regulations; Acting for 90 pilots against British Airways; Taken over conduct of Goodwin v CableTel (health and safety issues to the Industrial Tribunal).

Clifford Chance (3ptnrs/13assts) The feeling is that the department "needs more resourcing," but it does include the "well-respected" *Chris Osman*. **Clients/Work:** Advising Receivers and Administrators in relation to wrongful dismissal claims; successfully challenging the scope of Abrahams v Performing Rights Society in the Court of Appeal in Gregory v Mountleigh Services (in administration).

Richards Butler (4ptnrs/4assts) Members of the team also advise on pay, benefits, bonuses and pensions rights. The department is not seen to have grown and has yet to prove that arrival of "effortlessly bright" *Georgina Keane* will make it a success. **Clients/Work:** Includes drafting and advising on contracts, TUPE, EU employment law and industrial relations.

Stephenson Harwood (3ptnrs – 1 pt/t/6assts – 2 pt/t) "Very city, formal traditional firm." Some comment was made that the department was "short on leading individuals at the moment." However others still thought it high calibre with *Kate Brearley* in our lists of leaders and the arrival of Tom Flanagan, formerly at Addleshaw Booth & Co in Leeds, should strengthen the team. **Clients/Work:** Acting in a Court of Appeal case involving waivers in fixed term contracts; Dr Baht v Charing Cross and Westminster Hospital. Litigation involving stress and permanent health insurance schemes with relation to ME.

Theodore Goddard (3ptnrs/5assts) "Quite aggressive and do it well." *Peter Cooke* is "determined on behalf of his clients." **Clients/Work:** Acting for Guinness plc in relation to its merger with Grand Metropolitan plc. Acting for Dialog plc on acquisition of Knight Ridder Information. Advising GB Railways Group plc in winning the Anglia Railways Passenger Rail Franchise.

S J Berwin & Co (2ptnrs – 1 pt/t; 6assts) Seen as being active in the market. *Nicola Walker* is up and coming. **Clients/Work:** Advising on TUPE issues arising from a major retailer's acquisition of a large property portfolio. Acting for a senior executive in a negotiation of severance arrangements in the light of impending departure from Fidelity Brokerage Services.

Boodle Hatfield (4ptnrs/6assts) *Russell Brimelow* has "brilliant intellect and ability" for which he has been newly recommended but consensus is that he "needs to build the practice." **Clients/Work:** Conducted successfully the first ever equal pay claim for a major UK-based international insurance company. Currently acting for an individual against a major plc in what may be a test case under the Disability Dicrimination Act.

Denton Hall (3ptnrs/1const/5assts) The group acts for stand-alone clients and services employment and immigration requirements of clients elsewhere in the firm.

Stephanie Dale is department head. **Clients/Work:** Advising British Airways plc over cabin crew dispute 1997; acting for BET Ltd Clark v BET; Acting in the Industrial Tribunal and Employment Appeal Tribunal on behalf of over 150 Swedish Seamen in Addison & Others v Denholm Ship Management Ltd.

D J Freeman (2ptnrs/4assts) A "credible" department led by the highly-rated *Jane Moorman*. **Clients/Work:** Involved in complex joint venture arrangements between Tarmac & Bovis' plant hire businesses involving TUPE. Advised on high profile redundancy negotiations and agreements for the Royal Opera House. Advised on employment issues arising from the Shell Acquisition of Gulf Oil.

Freshfields (5ptnrs/25assts) The department covers employment, pensions and benefits work as an integrated practice. A particular specialism is advice on corporate governance. **Clients/Work:** Employment aspects of the acquisition of Unilever's speciality chemicals business. Advising Barclays Bank/BZW on the sale of the company's equity and corporate advisory business to Credit Suisse First Boston. Advising the PPM Consortium on the employment implications of the acquisition and leaseback of the DSS estate.

Langley & Co (3ptnrs/6assts) Niche practice dealing with all aspects of employment law for corporate clients and offering a range of fixed price services. The "excellent" *Dale Langley* effects a manner of "studied lugubriousness" that belies a "solid" workload. **Clients/Work:** Discrimination cases potentially involving large sums of money. High profile sexual harrassment cases. Particularly interesting TUPE case.

Linklaters (1ptnr/13assts) Described as "thorough and competent" although the team is seen as "part of the corporate machine." *Raymond Jeffers* is a "black-letter lawyer" described as "intellectually challenging." **Clients/Work:** Advising on the demerger of British Gas and Centrica. The first successful hospital PFI contract (Carlisle). An employee investigation into losses arising from derivatives trading (NatWest Markets).

Macfarlanes (3ptnrs/6assts) Principal areas of work include garden leave and restrictive covenants, service agreements, severance negotiations, corporate acquisitions and TUPE. Seen by some as "a victim of the wider success of the firm." *Tony Thompson* is seen more in the context of litigation but is described as "a pleasure to deal with" and "one of the best employment lawyers around, both sensible and effective." **Clients/Work:** For Zenith Media Ltd re garden leave and restrictive covenants. Acted for the employer AOC in Brompton v AOC International Ltd and UNUM Ltd, the latest case relating to permanent health insurance benefits. Employment issues arising from the demerger of Saatchi & Saatchi from the Cordiant Plc Group.

Norton Rose (2ptnrs/5assts) Team works out of Human Resources Department. Said to suffer from "corporate firm domination." Clients/Work: Advice to Safe Service on litigation in EAT in Edinburgh on a transfer of undertakings issue. Advice on the acquisition terms and employment arrangements following the privatisation of the BBC Home Transmission Service.

Osborne Clark (2ptnrs/9assts) Undertake full-range of employment law advice for employers and high-level employees. Clients/Work: Acting for P&O European Ferries in two high-profile sex discrimination claims. Support to team acting for Lloyds Bowmaker on £250m acquisition of Newcourt credit of Canada. Acting for employees in Rock-it Cargo v Green.

Speechly Bircham (2ptnrs/3assts f/t 1asst p/t) Mainly work for senior executives. *Alan Julyan* is "a blackletter lawyer,"an "unassuming, good drafter and negotiator." Clients/Work: Acting for J Ecclestone, former Deputy General Secretary of the NUJ and CRTUM to secure an order challenging the refusal by the union to list him as a candidate in 'the election' for the vacant office of Deputy General Secretary.

Taylor Joynson Garrett (3ptnrs/5assts) "Professional and solid," and "good team work," were some of the comments we received about the employment practice. The firm enters our lists for the first time this year. Clients/Work: Have a lot of transactional work: employment advice on the acquisition of Meespierson by Fortis plc; also act for Southbank University.

Titmuss Sainer Dechert (1ptnr/ 2assts) Act for employers and senior executives. *Charles Wynn-Evans*,("impressive, mature for level of qualification") heads this small team. Clients/Work: Recovering £135,000 compensation on behalf of Colchester Football Club in relation to a dispute with Ipswich Football Club over the poaching of their manager. Acting for well-known listed retailer on some important executive departures and allegations of fraud.

Ian Hunter of Bird & Bird and *Pamela Davies* of Monier-Williams & Boxalls are also known for their employment work.

MAINLY APPLICANT

Pattinson & Brewer (5ptnrs/4assts) "Competent and consistent practice over many years"which is praised for its "strength in depth." This year received more recommendations than any other applicant firm. *David Cockburn* ("solid and thorough, works ridiculously hard") and *Simon Auerbach* ("has a growing reputation") lead the team. Clients/Work: Securing Government concession in Francovitch litigation over TUPE. Successfully defending applications for injunctions sought to prevent RMT (Rail) Union taking industrial action. Advising on merger of CPSA with PTC to form the country's largest civil service union.

Rowley Ashworth (4ptnrs/3assts) Particularly known for its expertise in employment and personal injury claims on behalf of trade unions and their members. *Michael Short* leads the team. Clients/Work: Acting for TNG in connection with cabin crew dispute with BA. Advising AEWU on changes in rules from having a full-time executive to a lay executive. Settling over 1,000 Paramount claims re Leyland DAF and Ferranti and many others still outstanding.

Russell Jones & Walker (4ptnrs/6assts also doing pensions and public sector work) The team has a specific discrimination capability. *Edward Cooper* leads. Clients/Work: Inspector Dana Fleming v Chief Constable of Lincolnshire, discrimination case.Acting for steelworker Joe Davey in a high profile dismissal for trade union activities case. Alan England v PTC, a complaint about procedure for balloting on amalgamation between PTC and CPSA.

Thompsons (3ptnrs/3assts) Well-known TU firm based at Congress House, with a specialist employment rights unit covering all aspects of industrial and employment law. *Stephen Cavalier* is "one of the few Trade Union lawyers who think about the law and give clients sensible advice.'" Clients/Work: Achieved highest settlement in a disability discrimination claim. Taking a part-time pensions case to the European Court. Pursuing a Francovich claim regarding the Government's failure to implement the Acquired Rights Directive.

Bindman & Partners (4ptnrs/1asst) The firm's aim is to provide legal services to promote human rights and civil liberties. Most of their employment work centres around

discrimination on the grounds of sexual orientation. Clients/Work: Advised a large scale employer on the investigation of serious allegations of sexual harrassment against a senior executive, leading to disciplinary action. Have conducted one major case of sexual harrassment relating to the armed forces. Test cases on aspects of discrimination law affecting part time workers, including rights to return after maternity, dicrimination in flexible working hours and pay and pension provisions.

Hodge Jones & Allen (1ptnr/2assts) The non-contentious and employment unit deals with all claims for racial discrimination and employment issues in the High Court, County Court and industrial tribunal. Act for local businesses. Clients/Work: Representing appellant in Tuckett v Lansdowne Tutors; successful appeal against dismissal of unfair dismissal complaint. Representing applicant in Dando v Hackney Independent Living Trust; applicant successful in claim for racial discrimination. Defending City and Islington College in two week unfair dismissal case, conducting solicitor did own advocacy.

Lawford & Co (2ptnrs/3assts f/t, 3assts p/t) Represents predominantly trade union members and private clients. Clients/Work: Advising Labour Party/Government and TUC on Employment White Paper. Barry v Midlands Bank in House of Lords. Halloram v Corporation of London, much publicised equal pay case.

LEADERS' PROFILES • LONDON

AARONS, Elaine
Eversheds, London (0171) 919 4500
Partner in Employment and Pensions Group.
Specialisation: Main area of practice is employment law, advising private companies, public sector employers and senior management on all aspects of the employment relationship, including contracts, staff

handbooks, service agreements, changing terms & conditions of employment, collective consultation, board room disputes, restrictive covenants, and employment related litigation. Has particular experience in flexible benefits and disability discrimination. Has lectured for Industrial Relations Services, IPD, Euroforum, IBC, Croners and CCH. Regularly invited to

speak to private business audiences. Co-author of book entitled 'Flexible Working Practices' published by Croners. Currently co-writing book on Stress.
Prof. Memberships: Employment Lawyers Association (Association's Training Co-ordinator 1992-1997, Association's Secretary 1997- and member of its Management Committee),

International Bar Association (Labour Law Committee), Industrial Law Society, Employment Law Sub-Committee of City of London Law Society.
Career: Qualified in 1982 and has specialised in employment law since that date. Practised for 9 years with *Norton Rose*. Joined *Jaques & Lewis* (now *Eversheds* London) as Employment Partner in 1989. Now heads a department of 13 lawyers specialising exclusively in employment law. Her clients include: HSBC Investment Bank plc (including HSBC James Capel & Samuel Montagu), NatWest Markets, National Gallery, Scope, Alliance & Leicester Building Society and Toronto Dominion Bank.

ADAMS, Elizabeth
Beachcroft Stanleys, London
(0171) 242 1011
Specialisation: Practice covers contentious and non-contentious employment work undertaken for both public and private sector clients including discrimination claims on the grounds of sex, race, disability and trade union activities including harassment claims. Has also developed a particular expertise in industrial relations disputes and interlocutory relief. Has in depth knowledge of the Transfer of Undertakings (Protection of Employment) Regulations 1982 (TUPE). Particular interest in EU social policy aspects. Lectures extensively on all aspects of expertise. Regular contributor to the firm's Employment Working Brief and contributor to "Strategic Procurement for the NHS" (The NHS Confederation). Member of the City of London Employment Law Sub-Committee, CBI Competing for Quality Advisory Group, Member of the Employer Lawyers Association Management Committee, Employment Lawyers Working Party on Working Time Directive, Employment Lawyers Association and Industrial Law Society.
Prof. Memberships: LLB (Hons) Law 1977.
Career: Admitted 1980 at *Beachcroft Hyman Isaacs* (now *Beachcroft Stanleys*) from 1981. Partner 1986 to date.
Personal: Born 15th April 1955. Interests include reading and travel. Lives in Horsley.

AUERBACH, Simon
Pattinson & Brewer, London (0171) 400 5100
Partner in Employment Department.
Specialisation: Practises in all areas of labour, employment and discrimination law. Particular interest in transfers of undertakings, industrial conflict and trade union law. Co-author of 'A Guide to The Employment Act 1988' and author of 'Legislating for Conflict' (OUP, 1990) and 'Derecognition and Personal Contracts' (IER, 1993). Has had articles published in *Industrial Law Journal* and *Political Quarterly*. Regular writer in specialist publications and conference speaker. Has addressed meetings of the Industrial Law Society, Employment Lawyers' Association and the Institute of Employment Rights. Occasional media commentator.
Prof. Memberships: Industrial Law Society, Institute of Employment Rights, Employment Lawyers' Association.
Career: Qualified in 1985. Partner with *Pattinson & Brewer*.
Personal: Born in 1961. Educated at Oxford University (BA in Jurisprudence, 1st Class Hons, 1982 and D.Phil, 1988). Lives in London.

BREARLEY, Kate
Stephenson Harwood, London
(0171) 329 4422
Specialisation: Handles all aspects of contentious and non contentious employment law acting on behalf of clients in both the public and private sectors and for some individual Senior Executives/Directors and for teams of employees. Work includes preparation of Service Agreements, handling Industrial Tribunal, County and High Court claims, boardroom disputes, stress and discrimination claims, employment aspects of business mergers/takeovers/mbo's (in particular the application of the Transfer of Undertaking Regulations), and establishment of European Works Councils. Leading expert on competition in the employment field and co-author of Brearley & Bloch, 'Employment Covenants and Confidential Information; Law Practice and Technique' (Butterworths). Has Lectured for IBC, EuroForum and CLT on employment related topics.
Prof. Memberships: City of London Solicitors Company (Member of the Employment Law Sub-Committee), Employment Lawyers Association, Industrial Law Society and United Kingdom Environmental Law Association.
Career: Called to the Bar 1979 and has specialised predominantly in employment law since qualification. Joined *Stephenson Harwood* in 1986 and qualified as a solicitor in 1989. Became a Partner in 1989.
Personal: Born 1957. Educated Harrogate Ladies College and Exeter University 1975-1978, LL.B Hons.

BRIMELOW, Russell
Boodle Hatfield, London (0171) 629 7411
Partner and Head of Employment Group.
Specialisation: Practice covers all aspects of employment law for companies, individuals, staff bodies and other associations, including educational establishments. Particular areas of expertise include work on business transfers, working time, executive terminations, discrimination law and equal pay actions. Regularly appears as an advocate in the Industrial Tribunal. A regular contributor to Personnel Today and other journals. Active member of a number of Employment Lawyers Association's working parties. On editorial board of Croner's Questions and Answers, Bulletin and European Newsletters. Regular lecturer for many of the commercial conference organisers.
Prof. Memberships: Employment Lawyers Association, Industrial Law Society, Law Society.
Career: Qualified 1991. With *Denton Hall* 1988-1994. Joined *Boodle Hatfield* in 1994, becoming an Associate in 1996 and a Partner in 1997.
Personal: Born 1963. Attended Oxford University 1983-1986 BA. Father of two. Keen traveller, cyclist, piano and guitar player.

BURD, Michael
Lewis Silkin, London (0171) 227 8000
Partner.
Specialisation: All aspects of employment law, with emphasis on contentious work. Particular areas of interest include dismissal and redundancy, Industrial Tribunal claims and advice aimed at preventing employment disputes.

Prof. Memberships: Employment Lawyers Association. Committee Member, London Solicitors Litigation Association. Consultant Editor: Croner's "Managing Termination of Employment." Section Editor: Employment Section, FT Practical Tax Planning and Precedents. President of City of Westminster Law Society (1995/96).
Career: Qualified 1986. Partner at *Lewis Silkin* 1988. Head of Employment at *Lewis Silkin*.
Personal: Born 07/02/58. BA Columbia University 1980. MPhil Cambridge University 1982.

CAVALIER, Stephen
Thompsons, London (0171) 637 9761
Specialisation: Head of Employment Rights Unit. Partner specialising in employment and trade union law. Practice covers a range of employment and trade union work including transfer of undertakings, European law, dismissals, trade union law, rule books, industrial disputes and all aspects of collective and individual labour law. Involved in a number of significant cases on the application of the TUPE Regulations to competitive tendering, including the leading Court of Appeal case, conducting Francovich claims against UK government under Acquired Rights Directive and Judicial Review challenging the Consultation Regulations. Expert witness to the European Parliament on Acquired Rights Directive. Frequent speaker at union conferences, fringe meetings and seminars. Author of "Transfer of Undertakings: Employment Rights" and several articles and publications.
Prof. Memberships: Industrial Law Society (Executive Committee), Institute of Employment Rights, ETUC Legal Experts Network.
Career: Qualified in 1986. Joined *Thompsons* in 1987 and became a Partner in 1989.
Personal: Born 26th February 1962. Educated at St Edmund Hall, Oxford 1980-83. Member of Labour Party.

CHESHIRE, Caroline
Baker & McKenzie, London (0171) 919 1000
Specialisation: Senior Associate in Employment Department of *Baker & McKenzie*, specialising in all aspects of employment law – sex, race and disability discrimination, equal pay, maternity, senior executive dismissals; calculating severance packages, employment tax; transfer of undertakings; restrictive covenants; unfair dismissal and redundancy, Industrial Tribunal claims, worker representatives and European works councils, European labour law, drafting contracts handbooks and policies. Contributor of articles on employment law issues to PLC, In-house Lawyer and Tolleys. Regular speaker at employment law conferences, both internally for *Baker & McKenzie* and externally (e.g. for IBC and IRS)
Prof. Memberships: Employment Lawyers Association; The Law Society; Former Member of ELA Legislative and Policy Sub-Committee. Sat on the ELA Committee which reviewed the draft disability legislation.
Career: Attended Cambridge University. Qualified as a solicitor in January 1989 with *Macfarlanes*. Moved to *Baker & McKenzie* in 1990.
Personal: Born 5 May 1962. Lives in London.

COCKBURN, David
Pattinson & Brewer, London (0171) 400 5100 Partner in Employment & Trade Union Law Department.
Specialisation: All areas of trade union, employment and discrimination law.
Prof. Memberships: Chair of Employment Law Committee of the Law Society. Immediate past chair of the Employment Lawyers Association. Vice President of the Industrial Law Society. Vice-chair of EAT Users Group. Treasurer of the Institute of Employment Rights. Co-author of Know-How for Employment Lawyers.
Career: Joined *Pattinson & Brewer* in 1972. Qualified 1975, Partner 1978.
Personal: Born 30.11.48. Educated at Kings School, Pontefract, and at LSE for LLB and MSc (Econ) -Industrial Relations (distinction).

COOKE, Peter
Theodore Goddard, London (0171) 606 8855
Specialisation: Employment – main areas of practice include corporate transactions, executive contracts, outsourcing particularly in information technology and cleaning and catering and employment litigation. Recent cases and matters include 'Credit Suisse v Armstrong and Others,' the Guinness and GrandMet Merger, and advising the Business Services Association on the Acquired Rights Directive.
Prof. Memberships: City of London Solicitors Company – Vice Chairman of the Employment Law Sub-Committee.
Career: B.Sc – Electrical Engineering, Southampton Unversity; Legal Adviser – Engineering Employers Federation 1978-83; Partner – *Theodore Goddard* 1986.
Personal: Interests: Sailing, Music. Married, four children.

COOPER, Edward J.O.
Russell Jones & Walker, London (0171) 837 2808
Partner and Head of Employment Department.
Specialisation: Principal area of practice is trade union and employment law. Advises on a wide range of industrial employment and constitutional issues. Also covers administrative and public law. Advises on police terms and conditions of service, acts on union mergers, major privatisations, terms and conditions reviews, new legislation, health and safety, pensions, discrimination and other employment cases. Clients include the TUC, Police Federation and trade unions in the public and private sectors. The department (now of eleven executives and with a national presence) has growing employee private client writ. Author of the trade union section of Butterworths 'Encyclopedia of Forms and Precedents.' Charge-out rate is £130-£175 per hour.
Prof. Memberships: Industrial Law Society.
Career: Qualified in 1984. With *Simmons & Simmons* 1982-85. Joined *Russell Jones & Walker* in 1985 and became a Partner in 1988.
Personal: Born 12th June 1959. Educated at Bristol University 1977-80. Leisure interests include family, jazz, cricket, theatre and tennis. Lives in London SW15.

DALE, Stephanie
Denton Hall, London (0171) 242 1212 email: sjd@dentonhall.com Partner in Employment and Immigration Group.
Specialisation: Covers the whole range of contentious and non-contentious employment law. Work includes director + senior management packages, industrial relations, discrimination issues, redundancies, review and rationalisation of employment practices for employers, transactional work including Transfer of Undertakings Regulations, employment documentation and termination. Seconded to British Airways 1990-91 to advise on a wide range of employment issues. Speaker at professional conferences and writer of articles.
Prof. Memberships: International Bar Association, Industrial Law Society, Institute of Personnel and Development, Devonshire House Management Club, ILPA, Employment Lawyers Association
Career: Qualified 1985. Legal Adviser, A.T.L. (Teachers' Trade Union) 1986-87. Joined *Denton Hall* in 1987 and became a Partner in 1993.
Personal: Educated at the University of Newcastle 1979-82 (LLB).

DALGARNO, David
Warner Cranston, London (0171) 403 2900 Partner and Head of Employment group of nine specialist lawyers.
Specialisation: Undertakes all types of advisory and employment work, contractual and statutory, contentious and non-contentious; primarily for employers, but also acts for senior executives: principal interests include management of integration and organisational change programmes, collective and trade union issues, discrimination, trial advocacy. He frequently speaks on employment law issues; the author of the CCH Employment Contracts manual and founder member of the European Labour Lawyers Group. Clients include UK and global financial institutions, major industrial concerns, airlines, foreign law firms, 'Fortune 500' companies and senior executives.
Prof. Memberships: Employment Lawyers Association, City of London Law Society, Employment Law Sub Committee, Industrial Law Society.
Career: Called to the Bar at Inner Temple 1978; in-house lawyer specialising in employment and labour law at *Courtaulds plc* 1979-1987; assistant solicitor *Warner Cranston* 1987-1989, then Partner 1989.
Personal: Born in 1955. Educated at Hatfield School 1969-74 and Warwick University 1974-77. Leisure interests include tennis, wine, and loafing.

DAVIES, James
Lewis Silkin, London (0171) 227 8000 Partner.
Specialisation: All areas of employment law and business immigration. Particular interests include EC employment law, discrimination law and TUPE.
Prof. Memberships: ELA (Treasurer, Management Committee and Chair of Working Group on Age Discrimination), ILS, IPD, ILPA, and BASL. Management Committee of the AIRE Centre. Active participant in the Employers Forum on Age.
Career: Qualified in 1988. At *Denton Hall* 1986-90. Joined *Lewis Silkin* in 1992.
Personal: Born 26th February 1962. Educated at Ysgol Gyfun, David Hughes, Menai Bridge; Leicester University (L.L.B. and L.L.M.); and Strasbourg University (Dip. Ed. Jr. Fr.). Interests: long-suffering supporter of Glamorgan Cricket and Welsh rugby; most sports and travel.

DAVIES, Pamela Benady
Monier-Williams & Boxalls, London (0171) 405 6195 Partner.
Specialisation: Has specialised in all aspects of employment law since 1971. Acted for Mr Shove in the leading case on compensation for dismissal, 'Shove v. Downs Surgical plc.' Clients include major public companies and banks, advising personnel directors and in-house lawyers.
Career: Called to the Bar in 1955. Practised in partnership *Benady & Benady*, Gibraltar, as a barrister and solicitor. First woman barrister to appear in a Court Martial. Co-editor of 'Phipson on Evidence.' Qualified as a Solicitor in 1971 and joined *Rowe & Maw*, becoming a Partner in 1974. Left in 1985. Now a Partner in *Monier-Williams & Boxalls*.

DAWSON, William S.
Simmons & Simmons, London (0171) 628 2020
Specialisation: William has advised on numerous acquisitions, disposals and mergers and transfers of undertakings, both UK and internationally, for major corporations and institutions and has a strong City-based practice acting for insurance, banking and financial services institutions covering a wide range of complex issues associated with "high flyers." He acted in the Allied Dunbar v Frank Weisinger case, a leading case on post termination restrictive covenants and has handled many interlocutory matters. William was voted an 'Expert's Expert' in the Legal Business 1997 review.
Prof. Memberships: Law Society and American Bar Association.
Career: William joined the Employment Law Department at *Simmons & Simmons* in 1981 and became a partner in 1986. William is an employment law practitioner and the Department's Managing Partner. He gained his MA (Hons) Law degree from Cambridge University in 1977 and admitted as a solicitor in England and Wales in 1980.

DINELEY, Rachel
Beachcroft Stanleys, London (0171) 242 1011
Specialisation: Practice in both contentious and non-contentious employment work on behalf of employers and individuals in the public and private sectors. Regularly deals with commercial transactions and preparation/negotiation of executive service agreements as well as board room disputes, dismissals and executive termination packages. Has developed a particular expertise in the field of protection of confidential information and enforcement of restrictive covenants. Has an in depth knowledge of discrimination law and is a member of the Editorial Board of Croner's "Discrimination Law Briefing" in addition to writing the chapter on race discrimination and contributing to two other chapters of Croner's book "Discrimination Law." Regularly lectures on these and other topics.
Prof. Memberships: Member of the Employment Law Association, Industrial Law Society, Institute of Personnel and Development and chairs the Employment Committee of City Women's Network.
Career: University of Exeter Scholar LLB (Hons) 1979. Admitted in 1981. Solicitor and then

Partner at *Denton Hall* before joining *Beachcroft Stanleys* in December 1994.
Personal: Married and lives in the Chiltern Hills. Interests include theatre (and occasional amateur dramatics), extensive travel, photography, skiing and walking.

FARR, John

Herbert Smith, London (0171) 374 8000
Partner and Head of Employment Section.
Specialisation: Deals with a wide range of employment issues. Well known for his representation of companies and senior individuals in contentious matters including injunction applications in connection with restrictive covenants: competing businesses and group defections; boardroom disputes and dismissals; redundancies; pension disputes and Ombudsman referrals; discrimination claims and equal pay investigations. He also deals with partnership disputes, directors' disqualification and has defamation experience. Non-contentious work covers, inter alia, business transfers and reorganisations, and the devising and implementation of new terms of employment.
Career: Qualified in 1974. Became a Partner at *Herbert Smith* in 1982. Member of the City of London Solicitors' Company Employment Law Committee.
Personal: LL.B. (London).

FEINSTEIN, Naomi

Lovell White Durrant, London
(0171) 236 0066
Specialisation: Deals with all aspects of employment law, both contentious and non contentious, including advice on employment contracts, restrictive covenants, termination packages, wrongful and unfair dismissal, redundancies and reorganisations, discrimination and the employment aspects of corporate transactions.
Career: Articled *Osborne Clarke* and *Lovell White and King*. Qualified 1987. Partner 1997.

FOX, Ronnie

Fox Williams, London (0171) 628 2000
Email:rdfox@foxwilliams.co.uk
Specialisation: Main areas of practice are employment law and partnership law. Specialises in advising on the calculation and taxation of payments on termination of employment. Frequently negotiates on behalf of the boards of listed companies on the departure of senior executives. Author of "Payments on Termination of Employment" (now in its third edition). Master of the City of London Solicitors' Company, Chairman of the Practice Management Sub-Committee of the IBA; Member of the Law Society Law Management Section Advisory Group. Frequently Broadcasts and is the author of numerous articles in the professional and national press on employment, partnership and management topics.
Prof. Memberships: IBA, Law Society, City of London Law Society, Employment Lawyers' Association.
Career: Qualified 1972. Senior Partner at *Fox Williams*.
Personal: Born 27th September 1946.

FROST, Peter

Herbert Smith, London (0171) 374 8000
Partner in Employment Section
Specialisation: Deals with both contentious and non-contentious employment matters with particular expertise in transactional work, executive severances, team defections, the drafting and enforcement of special arrangements for executives (including restrictive covenants), proceedings in the industrial tribunal and the High Courts (including injunctive relief), collective matters (including works councils and industrial action) and discrimination issues.
Career: Emmanuel College, Cambridge. Qualified in 1985. Became a Partner at *Herbert Smith* in 1994.

GAYMER, Janet

Simmons & Simmons, London
(0171) 628 2020
Head of Employment Law Department.
Specialisation: Employment and Immigration Law. Work covers collective and individual, contentious and non-contentious matters and occupational health and safety. Acted for the Ministry of Defence on the contractorisation of the Royal Dockyards and for Railtrack on the British Rail privatisation. Written numerous articles on employment law and is a frequent lecturer on employment law topics. Founder Chairman of the Employment Lawyers Association and (in 1988) of the European Employment Lawyers Association. Voted "The Times" Woman of Achievement in the Law in 1997.
Prof. Memberships: UIA, IBA, Institute of Advanced Legal Studies (Honorary Fellow). Visiting Law Fellow, St Hida's College, Oxford (1998).
Career: Articled with *Simmons & Simmons* in 1971, qualified in 1973 and became a Partner in 1977. Currently Head of Employment and Immigration Law Department.
Personal: Born 11th July 1947. Attended Nuneaton High School for Girls 1958-65, then St Hilda's College, Oxford 1966-70. Read LLM at London School of Economics 1976-78. Leisure pursuits include theatre, music and learning to play the flute. Lives in Effingham.

GREEN, David

Charles Russell, London (0171) 203 5000
Partner in Employment, Pensions and Employee Benefits Unit.
Specialisation: Handles all aspects of employment law, including individual employment rights, employee benefits, contractual and policy documentation, discrimination, health and safety, equal opportunities, wrongful dismissal, redundancy, protection of confidentiality and goodwill, collective labour law, immigration and employment issues resulting from mergers and acquisitions. Member of editorial board of Croners Employer, Industrial Relations and Discrimination Briefing Notes. Author of various articles in a range of publications, including Management Consultancy and Tolleys Employment Law. Author of 'Business Basics Staff.' Has spoken at and chaired a number of seminars.
Prof. Memberships: Association of Employment Lawyers.
Career: Qualified in 1978. Worked at *Taylors Newmarket* 1976-83 (from 1981 as a Partner); then *McKenna & Co.* 1983-85 and *Clifford*

Chance 1985-91. Joined *Charles Russell* in 1991 as a Partner.
Personal: Born 1953. Attended John Lyon School, Forest School and University of London. Committee Member of Downham Town FC. Follows all forms of sports. Leisure interests include gardening. Lives in Downham Market, Norfolk.

HARPER, David

Lovell White Durrant, London
(0171) 236 0066
Specialisation: Deals with all aspects of employment law both collective and individual, including executive contracts and severance packages (plus tax, pension and employee benefits aspects), all tribunal litigation, redundancies, discrimination, restrictive covenants and employment policies and practices such as working time and pay issues. Handles all employment aspects of transactional work, particularly TUPE. Regularly appears as an advocate in industrial tribunals. Substantial experience of collective labour law issues and injunction proceedings. Principal editor of CCH Employment Manual and regular writer on employment matters.
Prof. Memberships: Employment Lawyers' Association, City of London Solicitors Company Employment Sub-committee.
Career: Articled with *Lovell White & King* (now *Lovell White Durrant*); qualified 1978; partner 1986.
Personal: Born 1954. Educated Stowe School and Keble College Oxford. Lives in Richmond.

HUNTER, Ian

Bird & Bird, London (0171) 415 6000
Partner in the Employment and Immigration section of the Company Commercial Department.
Specialisation: Main area of practice is employment law. Specialises in negotiation of payments on termination of employment, the Transfer of Undertakings Regulations, employment aspects of acquisitions and disputes, immigration and sex and race discrimination. Has handled departures from the boards of listed companies and advised on major outsourcing projects. Co-author of 'Britain's Invisible Earnings.' Regular contributor to The Independent and author of forthcoming WHICH? Guide to employment law. Employment Law specialist appeared regularly on Channel 5's 'Serious Money.' Author of numerous articles in the national and professional press.
Prof. Memberships: Law Society, Employment Lawyers' Association.
Career: Qualified in 1989. Joined *Bird & Bird* in 1996.
Personal: Born 20th July 1961. Attended Campbell College, Belfast, then Bristol University. Interests include writing and current affairs. Lives in London.

JACOBS, Howard

Slaughter and May, London (0171) 600 1200
Specialisation: Executive engagements and dismissals. TUPE.
Prof. Memberships: City of London Solicitors Company Employment Law Sub-committee.
Career: Winchester College. Pembroke College, Cambridge. *Slaughter and May* since 1975.
Personal: Married, three children. Interests: family and gardening.

JEFFERS, Raymond

Linklaters, London (0171) 456 2000
Partner. Employment and Employee Benefits
Group.
Specialisation: Head of Employment and
Benefits Group, specialising in employment and
employee benefits law. Covers all aspects of
this area, principally advising public sector and
private sector clients of the firm (national, multi-
national and foreign) on all aspects of
employment law.
Prof. Memberships: Founder member of City
of London Solicitors' Company Employment
Sub-Committee, member of Employment
Lawyers Association, and member of the
International Bar Association.
Career: Editor of the International Handbook of
Contracts of Employment. Articled at *Linklaters
& Paines*, becoming Partner in 1986.
Personal: Born 1954.

JEFFREYS, Simon

Cameron McKenna, London
(0171) 367 3000
Partner Employment Group.
Specialisation: Has specialised in
employment and labour relations law since
qualifying, advising predominantly employer
clients in the public and private sectors on all
aspects of their legal relationship with
employees and trade unions. Work includes
contractual documentation, corporate policies
towards employees, workforce reductions,
negotiations with trade unions, anti-
discrimination law, employee and trade union
aspects of mergers, acquisitions and disposals,
together with general advice on all aspects of
the day to day employment relationship and the
resolution of disputes with employees and trade
unions. Has appeared as an advocate in the
Industrial Tribunal and has conducted litigation
for clients in the Employment Appeal Tribunal,
County Court, High Court and Court of Appeal.
Frequently advises clients on interpretation of
legislation and the impact of proposed
legislation. Has spoken at numerous
conferences and seminars. Contributor of
employment precedents to Sweet & Maxwell's
'Practical Commercial Precedents' and
'Commercial Checklists,' joint editor of their
'Employment Prededents and Company Policy
Documents' and 'Transfer of Undertakings' and
author of 'Hiring and Firing Senior Executives'
1995.
Prof. Memberships: Employment Lawyers
Association, Industrial Law Society, City of
London Law Society (Member of Employment
Law Sub-Committee), Member Law Society
Employment Law Committee.
Career: Joined *McKenna & Co* in 1980 and
qualified in 1982. Became a Partner in 1988.

JULYAN, Alan

Speechly Bircham, London (0171) 353 3290
Specialisation: Practice covers full range of
employment and labour law specialising in the
employment and corporate governance issues
arising on the recruitment and termination of
senior executives, TUPE and the management
of organisational change. Author "Key
Employees-Drafting Service Agreements" and
Editor of "Checklists for Solicitors." Joint Editor
of "Employment Precedents and Employment
Policies" all published by Sweet & Maxwell.
Prof. Memberships: Law Society. Committee
member of the Employment Law Subcommittee
of the City of London Law Society, the Industrial

Law Society, and the Employment Lawyers
Association.
Career: Qualified 1974. Joined *Speechly
Bircham* and became partner in 1977.
Personal: Born 14th October 1949. Educated
at Bristol Grammar School and Lanchester
Polytechnic. Interests include tennis, painting
and jazz. Lives in New Malden.

KEANE, Georgina

Richards Butler, London (0171) 247 6555
Partner and Head of Employment Unit. Handles
all aspects of employment law, discrimination
and trade unions, as well as employee benefits
including share option schemes and ESOPS.
Has conducted numerous speaking
engagements at conferences and training for a
wide variety of organisations and for clients.
Prof. Memberships: Employment Lawyers
Association, Industrial Law Society, American
Bar Association.
Career: Qualified in 1988. Called to the Bar in
1975, practised at the common law Bar until
1984. Then became Employment Law Adviser
to the Confederation of British Industry. Joined
Titmuss Sainer Dechert in 1986 as Head of
Employment Unit; requalified as a solicitor and
became a Partner in 1988. Joined *Richards
Butler* in 1996 as Head of Employment.
Personal: Born 3rd February 1954. Married
with two sons. Leisure interests include theatre
and music.

LANGLEY, Dale

Langley & Co, London (0171) 397 9650
Specialisation: All aspects of Employment
Law, for both individual and corporate clients,
with particular knowledge of Company Law, tax
and stock exchange requirements. Often acts
for senior city brokers, analysts and traders, and
for top executives, including the main board of
FTSE 100 companies. Has completed a
number of seven-figure settlements over the
past year. Counts two top-twenty city law firms
amongst his corporate clients.
Prof. Memberships: Employment Lawyers
Association, Law Society.
Career: Downer Grammar School.
Southampton University LLB 2(1) in 1978
(Maxwell Prizewinner 1977). Articled at
Stephenson Harwood, qualifying in 1981; in
1986 joined *Ashurst Morris Crisp*, establishing
their Employment Law Group in 1988. Left in
1993 to set up *Langley & Co*, on his own. The
firm now has 14 people, specialising only in
Employment Law.
Personal: Cycling and Tennis. Four children.

LEVINSON, Stephen

Paisner & Co, London (0171) 353 0299
Partner in Employment Department
Specialisation: Advises on all aspects of
employment law from the acquisition and sale
of businesses to individual claims. Has dealt
with cases at all levels from the Industrial
Tribunals to the House of Lords. Has extensive
experience as an advocate. Also advises on
European Law and Discrimination.
Prof. Memberships: Chairman of the Industrial
Law Society. Founder member of the Law
Society's Employment Law Committee.
(Chairman of Law Society's Discrimination Law
Review Working Party Committee). Fellow of the
Chartered Institute of Arbitrators.
Career: Joined *Paisner & Co* in 1974. Qualified
as a solicitor in 1976. Partner since 1978.
Formed the Employment Department in 1988

and became Head of Employment Law in 1988.
Personal: Born 12th February 1949. Educated
at Claysmore School, Dorset and Leicester
University. Lives in St Johns Wood. Interests
include tennis, reading and theatre.

MANN, Jane

Fox Williams, London (0171) 628 2000
Email jemann@foxwilliams.co.uk
Partner in Employment and Immigration
Department.
Specialisation: Advises a number of large
employers in relation to employment law issues
and business immigration. Works closely with in-
house legal and personnel departments to
provide an integrated service to line
management. Has handled a number of difficult
and high profile cases. Also acts for senior
executives in relation to the termination of
employment. Discrimination law is a particular
interest. Contributor to books on employment law
published by Tolleys and FT Law and Tax. Legal
contributor to ExeComp, software to calculate
executive compensation. Frequent lecturer at
conferences. Member of several editorial boards.
Writes regularly for various journals. Chairman of
the Employment Lawyers Association Working
Party or the Working Time Directive.
Prof. Memberships: Co-founder of
Employment Lawyers Association and currently
its Deputy Chairman. Former Treasurer of the
Immigration Law Practitioners Association.
Member of the International Bar Association and
a member of the committee of the IBA's
Womens Interest Group. Member of the
Industrial Law Society; the Employment Law
Sub-Committee of the City of London Law
Society; and The American Immigration
Lawyers Association. Associate Member of the
Institute of Personnel and Development.
Career: Qualified 1981. Worked at *McKenna &
Co.* 1979-86, then at *Denton Hall* until 1994,
where became a Partner. Joined *Fox Williams* in
1994 as a Partner.
Personal: Born 1957. Attended Cambridge
University 1975-78.

MANSELL, Mark

Allen & Overy, London (0171) 330 3000
Partner
Specialisation: Partner in the employment and
pensions department, specialising in
employment law and dealing with the full range
of contentious and non-contentious matters.
His experience includes advising on major
redundancy and restructuring exercises,
including changing terms and conditions of
employment and working practices, designing
and implementing redundancy procedures and
negotiating and consulting with recognised
trade unions. He has experience in advising on
and drafting services agreements, terms and
conditions of employment and other
employment practices. He has experience of
European law and its implementation in the UK
including advising on employee rights on the
transfers of businesses or the contracting out of
services. He has advised on outsourcing
employment issues for many clients including
contractors, government agencies and
companies outsourcing out services and
changing contractors.
Prof. Memberships: Member of the
Employment Law Sub-Committee of the City of
London Solicitors Company.
Career: LLB (Hons) London University.
Admitted as Solicitor 1985. Legal Advisor, CBI

Employment Affairs. Directorate 1985-87, Assistant Solicitor *Allen & Overy* 1987-91, Partner *Allen & Overy* since 1992.

MOORMAN, Jane
D J Freeman, London (0171) 583 4055
Partner and Head of the Employment Law Group.
Specialisation: Practice covers the full range of employment law work and in particular transfer of undertakings issues arising on transactions, policy advice, particularly in the context of equal opportunities, advising on changing contracts of employment in the context of industrial relations and flexible working. Restrictive covenant enforcement, injunctions and executive level dismissals. Wide experience of media related employment work. Speaks regularly at conferences and writes on the subject of employment law.
Prof. Memberships: Member of the Law Society, the Employment Lawyers Association and a member of its Training Sub-Committee, and the CBI Employee Relations Panel.
Career: Qualified 1984. At *D J Freeman* 1982 to date. Partner 1992.
Personal: Born 12 May 1958. Educated at the London School of Economics and Political Science. Interests include theatre, gardening and swimming. Lives in Wimbledon.

MORDSLEY, Barry
Salans Hertzfeld & Heilbronn HRK, London (0171) 509 6000
Partner and Head of Employment Department.
Specialisation: Deals with all employment law issues, contentious and non-contentious, including contracts and handbooks, restrictive covenants, discrimination, transfer of undertakings and executive terminations. Advocate in the Industrial Tribunal and Employment Appeals Tribunal. Co-author of Butterworths Emploment Law Guide and Butterworths Older Clients Service and Croners Discrimination law. Regularly contributes to Croners Bulletins and is on the Editorial Board of Croners Discrimination Law Briefing. Lectures widely to conferences, professional organisations, educational institutions and clients.
Prof. Memberships: Membership of Employment Lawyers' Association Management Committee, former member of the Law Society's Employment Law Committee, a Member of the Employers' Forum on Age Members' Advisory Group, and a Fellow of the Institute of Personnel and Development.
Career: Qualified 1972. Academic career: Principal Lecturer London Guildhall University; Visiting Professor, Cornell University, USA; Visiting Lecturer Queen Mary & Westfield College. Ran own practice specialising in labour law before joining *Harris, Rosenblatt & Kramer* as a Partner in 1989. A Chairman of Industrial Tribunals (England and Wales) since 1984.
Personal: Born:19.01.47. Interests include theatre and music. Avid cricket and football fan (supporter of Middlesex and Chelsea respectively). Plays squash frequently.

O'BRIEN, Christine
Baker & McKenzie, London (0171) 919 1000
Specialisation: Contentious and non-contentious employment law. Has acted in high profile discrimination cases and the enforcement of covenants and other contractual terms in the High Court. Frequent speaker at external conferences. Has developed a large practice acting for Investment Banks and other financial institutions.
Prof. Memberships: Law Society, Employment Lawyers Association, Industrial Law Society.
Career: Qualified 1987 with *Simmons & Simmons*. Joined *Baker & McKenzie* in 1989 and became a partner in 1995.
Personal: Born 6 September 1959.

OSMAN, Christopher
Clifford Chance, London (0171) 600 1000
Partner. Head of the Employment Unit.
Specialisation: All aspects of individual and collective employment law.
Career: Articled *Coward Chance*; qualified 1976; Partner *Clifford Chance* 1981. Editor of 'Harvey on Industrial Relations and Employment Law;' advisory editor 'Butterworths Employment Law Guide;' frequent conference speaker.
Personal: Educated at Ramsden School; Southampton University (LLB) 1973. Born 1951. Resides Keston. Interests include hot air ballooning.

ROBERTSON, Nicholas
Rowe & Maw, London (0171) 248 4282
Specialisation: Recent work has included advice on the Transfer Regulations, agreeing termination packages for senior executives, (acting for employers or senior executives) and dealing with a wide range of issues arising on termination of employment. He has also represented employers before the Industrial Tribunal and Employment Appeals Tribunal. He has also assisted with collective redundancy exercises and with fair procedures, consultation issues and the best way to avoid claims for unfair dismissal in redundancy situations. He is also advising on the potential impact on employers of the forthcoming changes in employment law, in particular the draft Working Time Regulations and the White Paper on Fairness at Work.
Career: Edinburgh Academy, Leicester University.

ROSKILL, Julian
Rowe & Maw, London (0171) 248 4282
Specialisation: Has been specialising in employment law since he qualified in 1974. He deals with the full range of employment and industrial relations law and practice for business and senior individuals. His special interests are restrictive covenants, discrimination, contracting-out and business transfers and collective issues. Acted in 'Dupont Steels v Sirs' (1980); the 1984 Fleet Street Dispute; 'John Michael Design v Cooke' (1987); 'Rolls Royce Motor Cars v Price' (1993); 'Rolls Royce Motor Cars v Mair' (1993); 'New Victoria Hospital v Ryan' (1993); 'Credit Suisse v Armstrong' (1996); 'AEEU v Thorn' (1997). Regular speaker and writer on a variety of employment topics.
Prof. Memberships: Law Society, City of London Solicitors Company, Employment Lawyers Association, Industrial Law Society.
Career: Qualified in 1974. Joined *Rowe & Maw* in 1986, became a partner in 1988. Member of Editorial Advisory Board of Croners Industrial Relations Briefings. Chairman of Employment Sub-Committee of City of London Solicitors Company.
Personal: Born 22nd July 1950. Attended Horris Hill 1958-63, then Winchester College 1963-69. Leisure interests include tennis, photography and music, theatre and opera (listening!). Lives in London.

SHORT, Michael
Rowley Ashworth, London (0181) 543 2277
Partner and Head of Trade Union & Employment Law Department.
Specialisation: Handles trade union and employment law for employees and unions. Work includes trade union constitution, rules, amalgamations etc., collective employment law (including industrial action) and individual employment law (including discrimination). Also deals with defamation and pensions litigation.
Prof. Memberships: Law Society, Industrial Law Society.
Career: With *Lovell White & King* 1977-80. Qualified in 1979. With *Lawford & Co* 1980-87 (Partner from 1983). Joined *Rowley Ashworth* as a Partner in 1988.
Personal: Born 2nd May 1951. Educated at St. Philips Grammar School, Birmingham 1962-69 and Sussex University 1970-73 (BA in Philosophy).

THOMPSON, Tony
Macfarlanes, London (0171) 831 9222
Specialisation: Contentious and non-contentious employment law. Drafting and advising on employment contracts, service agreements, secondments and consultancies. Employment policies and procedures. Transfers of undertakings. Drafting and enforcement of restrictive covenants.
Prof. Memberships: Law Society. Employment Lawyers Association. City of London Solicitors Company Employment Law Sub-Committee. Currently secretary of the Committee.
Career: Oundle School. MA Cantab (St Catharine's College). Articled at *Markbys* (now part of *Cameron McKenna*). Admitted as a Solicitor June 1976. Joined *Macfarlanes* 1980, Partner 1986, Head of Litigation 1989. Head of Employment Group.

WALKER, Nicola S.
S J Berwin & Co, London
+44 (0)171 533 2222
Specialisation: Partner and Head of Employment Group. Undertakes all aspects of employment law including directors' duties, boardroom disputes, severance arrangements for senior directors, large scale redundancies, transfer of undertakings advice, team moves, restrictive covenant advice and injunctions. Writes and speaks regularly on employment law topics.
Prof. Memberships: Holborn Law Society Law Reform Committee (Employment Law Representative). Employment Lawyers Association and Industrial Law Society member.
Career: Admitted 1980. With *Macfarlanes* 1982-1984. Joined *S J Berwin* in 1984, becoming a partner in 1987.
Personal: Leisure Interests: reading, cinema and astrology.

WATSON, Simon
Simmons & Simmons, London
(0171) 628 2020
Specialisation: Employment Law. Simon has a strong City-based Employment Law practice acting for insurance and major corporations and regularly advises on the employment aspects of acquisitions, disposals and mergers including the Transfer of Undertakings Regulations and recently advised on the

employment aspects of a £383 million public offering. In addition, Simon has extensive experience of handling litigation both in the industrial tribunal and the High Court, including applying for interlocutory relief, injunctions and Anton Piller orders and has acted in the Court of Appeal case Abrahams vs PRS, which is now the leading authority on termination payments/payments in lieu of notice.
Prof. Memberships: Law Society
Career: St. Catherines's College, Oxford, College of Law, *Simmons & Simmons*
Personal: Bridge, Opera

WILLIAMSON, Andrew P F
Lovell White Durrant, London
(0171) 236 0066
Specialisation: Employment and labour law.
Prof. Memberships: Prof. Membership: Past chairman and current member of City of London Law Society Employment Law Sub-Committee.
Career: Career: Partner *Bowman Gilfillan & Blacklock* Johannesburg 1971-1978 practising in insurance and general commercial litigation and political criminal cases; articled *Lovell White & King* (now *Lovell White Durrant*) 1978; qualified England 1980, Partner 1982.

WYNN-EVANS, Charles
Titmuss Sainer Dechert, London
(0171) 583 5353
Specialisation: Deals with all aspects of contentious and non contentious employment law, including discrimination, transfers of undertakings, share option and incentive schemes, senior executive appointments and departures and restrictive covenant matters. Regularly writes on employment law for a variety of journals.
Prof. Memberships: Industrial Law Society, Employment Lawyers' Association, Law Society.
Career: Joined *Titmuss Sainer & Webb* (now *Titmuss Sainer Dechert*) in 1990. Qualified 1992. Appointed partner 1997.
Personal: Born 1967. Educated at King Henry VIII School Coventry; Bristol University (LL.B 1988) and Merton College Oxford (BCL 1990). Interests include cricket, rugby and current affairs. Lives in Kennington, London.

YOUNSON, Fraser
Baker & McKenzie, London (0171) 919 1000 (Bar 1975) Partner and Head of Employment Department. Chairman of European Labour Law Practice Group.
Specialisation: Main area of practice is

employment law, covering executive termination, employment aspects of mergers and acquisitions, sex, race and disability discrimination, restrictive covenants, unfair dismissal and redundancy, wrongful dismissal, collective labour law, industrial disputes, worker representation and European Work Councils, EC labour law, Industrial Tribunal advocacy and compensation claims, transnational reorganisation and collective redundancies. Author of Employment Law Handbook, Employment Law and Business Transfers – A Practical Guide, Croner's Industrial Relations Law, and contributor to PLC and the Law Society Gazette on employment law issues. Lectures extensively on labour law; Transfers of Undertakings (Sweet & Maxwell).
Prof. Memberships: Law Society, Industrial Law Society, Former Chairman and joint founder of Employment Lawyers Association.
Career: Qualified for the Bar in 1975, and for the Law Society in 1987. Previously Employment Law Adviser to British Aerospace Group HQ, and previously Editor of IDS Brief. Joined *Baker & McKenzie* in 1983, becoming a Partner in 1990.
Personal: Born 11th November 1952. Attended Oxford University. Lives in Houghton, Cambs.

SOUTH EAST

LEADING FIRMS • SOUTH EAST

COLE & COLE Oxford

HIGHLY REGARDED FIRMS

Donne Mileham & Haddock Brighton
Henmans Oxford

Brachers Maidstone
Clarks Reading
Clarkson Wright & Jakes Orpington
Cripps Harries Hall Tunbridge Wells, Kent
Pattinson & Brewer Chatham
Pickworths Hemel Hempstead
Stevens & Bolton Guildford
Thompsons Ilford
Underwoods St. Albans

Cole & Cole (2ptnrs/4assts) Act mainly for employers, their client base covers a large geographical area. Extremely well thought-of dedicated team which has a national reputation, based upon the reputation of leader *Sue Ashtiany*, who is known particularly for her discrimination work. **Clients/Work:** Major clients include Equal Opportunities Commission, The Police Federation and Oxford University.

Donne Mileham & Haddock (2ptnrs/1const/1asst) All practitioners conduct their own cases in the tribunals and Employment Appeal Tribunal. *Quintin Barry* is now acting as a consultant. He is also part-time Industrial Tribunal Chair. **Clients/Work:** Instructed by Retained Firefighters Union in respect of high profile sexual harrassment

claim within fire service listed for 12 day hearing. Acted in multi-party IT case relating to TUPE Regulations. Acting in reported Employment Appeal Tribunal case of Bromley Hospitals NHS Trust v Portman.

Henmans (1ptnr/2assts) Small dedicated team undertaking employer and employee work. *Colin Henney* does his own advocacy in industrial tribunal and before EAT. **Clients/Work:** Advising on one of first Disability Discrimination Act cases to be heard by Industrial Tribunal and then on appeal to Employment Appeal Tribunal (O'Neill v Symm & Co Ltd) Providing training to ACAS.

Brachers (2ptnrs/3assts) "An all-round firm" which represents a wide range of employers from major international companies to local farmers. **Clients/Work:** Advice on employment policy and service contracts at senior levels involving share options.

Clarks (4ptnrs/4assts) The firm has combined Employment Services Unit. Lead partner is a member of the CBI's Employee Relations Panel. **Clients/Work:** Reported EAT case for SmithKline Beecham on variation of terms of employment. Continuing to provide employment-related support for Blue Circle Industries Plc. Reported EAT case on Disability Discrimination Act for Novacold.

Clarkson Wright & Jakes (2ptnrs/2assts) Act for respondents and employees/directors/shareholders of small and medium-sized companies. **Clients/Work:** Advising on and preparing settlement agreement for Finance Director of large service provider. Representing building maintenance company in IT on a race discrimination claim. Providing ongoing telephone advice to managers of

a care provider (nursing homes, care in the community).

Cripps Harries Hall (2ptnrs/2assts) Involved with range of employment issues including collective redundancies, TUPE transfers and discrimination claims. **Clients/Work:** Involved with employment issues arising from transfer of employees abroad. Discrimination claim in the EAT.

Pattinson & Brewer (1ptnr/1asst) Act for Unions. Chairman of the Partnership was a part-time Chairman of the Industrial Tribunals. His practice accounts for about 10% of firm's work. **Clients/Work:** Bradley v Department of Employment, a "Francovich" case for the TGWU, currently in High Court on quantum issues. Ongoing advice to National Union of Marine Aviation and Shipping Transport Officers and Commercial Workers Union and members.

Pickworths (2ptnrs/1asst) Advise employers (80%) and employees (20%) on resignation, dismissal and redundancy and representation at Industrial Tribunals. Partners conduct their own advocacy. **Clients/Work:** Include Employee Advisory Resource Ltd, Greene King Plc and Schroff UK Ltd. Recent cases involved constructive dismissal, sexual harrassment and TUPE.

Stevens & Bolton (1ptnr/2assts) A dedicated team acting primarily for employers although also doing some senior employee

LEADING INDIVIDUALS
SOUTH EAST

ASHTIANY Sue Cole & Cole
BARRY Quintin Donne Mileham & Haddock
HENNEY Colin Henmans

termination packages as well as discrimination applications.

Thompsons (1barrister/2assts) This branch of the trade union firm is extremely well set up for employment matters. **Clients/Work:** Successfully establishing that a transfer can occur between a group of companies. Claiming under Disability Discrimination

Act on behalf of a colour-blind train-driver, and succeeding in finding alternative employment for him. Settling a sexual harrassment claim involving a leading City firm, citing the European Guidelines on Sexual Harrassment.

Underwoods (2ptnrs/2assts) Run by a Chairman of the Industrial Tribunals who is

also on the Employment Law Advisory Scheme, the team does a 50:50 mix of applicant and respondent work. **Clients/Work:** Acting for Appellant in EAT to overturn management of Health & Safety at Work Regulations for breach of Pregnant Workers Directive.

LEADERS' PROFILES · SOUTH EAST

ASHTIANY, Sue
Cole & Cole, Oxford (01865) 262600
Partner in Employment and Discrimination Law Department.
Specialisation: Heads a specialist department in employment and discrimination law. Acts for several major clients in the public and private sector and has taken a number of cases for the Equal Opportunities Commission, especially complex ones or new points such as 'Robinson v Oddbins.' Major clients have included Midland Bank Plc, Oxford and Anglia NHS Executive, University of Oxford, Oxford Radcliffe NHS Trust, Apollo Leisure, Amey plc and Unipart Ltd. Writes and lectures extensively on employment law and discrimination matters including training for Civil Service College and the Cabinet Office. Regular contributor to the Equality Network, Contributing Editor to the Tolley loose-leaf encyclopaedia on Employment Law: author of chapter on Racial Discrimination. Also Contributing Editor to FT Law & Tax Employment Precedents and Company Policy Documents.Individual charge-out rate is approximately £175 per hour.
Prof. Memberships: Law Society, Solicitors' European Group, Industrial Law Society.
Career: Qualified in 1986, having joined *Cole and Cole* in 1984. Became a Partner in 1989. Previously, worked extensively in immigration, including for the UN High Commissioner for Refugees.

Personal: Educated in Iran and the UK. Non-Executive Director of Oxfordshire Ambulance NHS Trust and Advisory Board of Oxford Common Purpose. Leisure interests include music and walking. Lives in Oxford.

BARRY, Quintin
Donne Mileham & Haddock, Brighton (01273) 744268
Partner 1961. Commercial department – Employment Group.
Specialisation: Main area of practice is employment law. Advises on all aspects and conducts employment related litigation, including advocacy before industrial tribunals and EAT. Also advises on general commercial law. Major clients include Forbuoys Ltd., Vosper Thornycroft (UK) Ltd, East Sussex Health Authority, various NHS trusts, University of Sussex. Regularly addresses conferences and seminars.
Prof. Memberships: ELA, Law Society, Sussex Law Society, Legal Aid Practitioners Group.
Career: Qualified 1958. Assistant solicitor, *Cronin & Son* 1959-60. Assistant solicitor, *Mileham Scatliff & Allen* 1960-62. Partner, *Mileham Scatliff & Allen* 1962-70. Managing Partner, *Donne Mileham Haddock* 1970-91, Chairman 1991 to January 1st 1997. Part-time Chairman Industrial Tribunal 1994 to date.
Personal: Born on 7th March 1936. Educated at Eastbourne College and Open University.

Principal hobby is the study and writing of history. Chairman Southern FM, Deputy Chairman South Downs Health NHS Trust. Lives in Shoreham-by-Sea.

HENNEY, Colin C.
Henmans, Oxford (01865) 722181
Partner and Head of Employment Department.
Specialisation: Sole area of practice is employment. Handles the full range of employee and employer work, both contentious and non-contentious. Has appeared before EAT as well as undertaking almost all advocacy in cases before ITs. Involved in ACAS training, giving seminars at individual conciliation officer workshops since 1990. Also provides training to major employer clients and insurers.
Prof. Memberships: Employment Lawyers' Association, Industrial Law Society.
Career: Qualified in 1982. Articled with *Rickerby Watterson* 1980-82; joined *Henmans* in 1983, becoming a Partner in 1987; Managing Partner 1991-3.
Personal: Born 25.11.1957. Attended Daniel Stewart's and Melville College, Edinburgh 1962-75, and Oxford University 1976-79 (Law, BA). Leisure interests include music, golf and languages. Lives in Eynsham, Oxfordshire.

SOUTH WEST

LEADING FIRMS · SOUTH WEST

BOND PEARCE Plymouth
BURGES SALMON Bristol
OSBORNE CLARKE Bristol

VEALE WASBROUGH Bristol

HIGHLY REGARDED FIRMS

Bevan Ashford Bristol
Eversheds Bristol
Pattinson & Brewer Bristol
Thompsons Bristol

Cartwrights Bristol
Lester Aldridge Bournemouth
Stephens & Scown Exeter
Stone King Bath
Thrings & Long Bath
Wansbroughs Willey Hargrave Bristol

Bond Pearce (1ptnr/2assts) "Efficient, user-friendly firm." *Nikki Duncan* is "mature and sensible in approach." **Clients/Work:** Dealt with number of test issues on TUPE.

Some of first cases under DDA including first where costs order made against applicant. Test case before EAT on health and safety related dismissal.

Burges Salmon (1ptnr/2assocs/3assts.) The team derives its traditional style from *George Dyson,* who sits as Deputy Chair of Tribunals. He "brings a gravitas to the work." **Clients/Work:** Acting for two listed plcs in removal of their chief executive/managing director. Advising association of contractors in construction industry on managing transition of their members working from contractor to employee status. Advising leading financial institution on redundancy programme and negotiation with recognised trades union.

Osborne Clarke (2ptnrs/2assocs/3assts) The firm "has lacked a big-hitter"in the past and David Ticehurst has recently been made a High Court Judge, leaving the department without a high-profile leader. A new partner joined this year from Nicholson Graham & Jones in London. The partner from the London office is now Head of the Employment Unit and spends 50% of his time in Bristol.

Clients/Work: Advising on employment and industrial relations issues arising out of United News and Media's agreed bid for HTV. Advice on large-scale redundancy programme for Parragon Books; subsequently defending multiple claims for protective awards brought at Industrial Tribunals throughout the country. Successful defence of one of the first claims brought under Disability Discrimination Act for C & J Clark.

Veale Wasbrough (2ptnrs/4assts) The big news is that Chris Southam, head of

LEADING INDIVIDUALS
SOUTH WEST

DUNCAN Nikki Bond Pearce
DYSON George Burges Salmon

BROWN Anthony Wansbroughs Willey Hargrave
MOORE Nigel Stephens & Scown
WIDDOWSON David Bevan Ashford

UP AND COMING

LAMONT Sarah Veale Wasbrough
RANKIN Claire Eversheds

SEE PROFILES AT END OF THIS SECTION

employment, moved at the end of February to Hammond Suddards in London and "will be a big loss"since "he built up the department." *Sarah Lamont*, new partner, now heads the team. The verdict at the moment is that she is unlikely to achieve the same reputation. However she is "one to watch, a safe pair of hands" and "so good she could keep the practice together." **Clients/Work:** Acting for Barry Town AFC in defence of a wrongful dismissal claim brought by a former manager. Successfully defended Dartford Securities Ltd in both unfair dismissal claim and race discrimination claim. Has also dealt with a substantial equal pay claim on behalf of an employee.

Bevan Ashford (3ptnrs/2assocs/2assts) The department acts for a number of NHS Trusts but lacks a high profile for its employment work. *David Widdowson* specialises in health sector respondent work. **Clients/Work:** Advised on employment aspects of public sector PFI schemes. Advised on transfer of staff, implications of care in community schemes on reprovisioning of mental healthcare in several NHS trusts. Have advised on at least four sensitive dismissals of chief executives.

Eversheds (3assts) Not as successful as the Cardiff office. The "capable" *Claire Rankin* "tries hard." The team is seen to"bask in the reputation" of Martin Warren from the Cardiff office who spends 50% of his time in Bristol. **Clients/Work:** Advising Walkers Snack Foods Ltd, nationally on major contractual changes and handling Industrial Tribunal and High Court Litigation. Advising

Bluebird Toys (UK) Ltd in connection with TUPE and collective issues.

Pattinson & Brewer (1ptnr/2assts) Firm traditionally acts for Trade Unions so employment work is primarily for applicants. Advice is given across the spectrum. **Clients/Work:** Disability discrimination claim in the EAT on a preliminary point. Successful sex discrimination claim in the industrial tribunal. Application for interim relief.

Thompsons (1ptnr/1asst) Trade Union firm acting for applicants. **Clients/Work:** Contractual disputes re TUPE Regs. Cases arising from Disability Discrimination Act 1995. Equal Pay claims.

Cartwrights (1ptnr/3assts) The legal team works with two consultants with senior human resources backgrounds. Over past year have received instructions for approx 153 Industrial Tribunal applications. **Clients/Work:** Acting for Safeway plc in the leading case of Safeway v Burrell which has become the latest authority on the redundancy rules. Launching a practical employment training company with external consultants for large corporates.

Lester Aldridge (4ptnrs/1asst) Act mainly for employers but also some senior executives. "Strong in their own area." **Clients/Work:** Provided an advice line to all the members of the Registered Nursing Homes Association. Advised employers on redundancy and relocation programmes, and the effect of TUPE to listed company clients involved in the defence industry .

Stephens & Scown (3ptnr/2assts in Exeter and Truro) Employment work is a sig-

nificant part of the litigation workload. *Nigel Moore*,who has High Court rights of audience, is a "good advocate who knows his stuff." Reputation as "an aggressive litigator." **Clients/Work:** For Cornwall Care, substantial local authority privatisation involving highly complex issues under Transfer Regulations appealed to Employment Appeal Tribunal, may go to the European Court.

Stone King (8ptnrs/14assts: 3p/t) Employment work comes out of their education and charities base.

Thrings & Long (5ptnrs/4assts) Act principally for employers and senior employees. Members of the department have a particular expertise in dealing with educational institutions, sports institutions and agricultural employment matters. **Clients/Work:** Act for Bath Rugby Club. Tribunal work involving unfair dismissal, sexual discrimination,equal pay, enforcement of post employment restrictions, redundancy and contract variations. Matters involving European Law implications.

Wansbroughs Willey Hargrave (1ptnr/2assts) Acts principally for employers, particularly in the insurance, health and charities sectors. *Anthony Brown* handles IT contracts work in particular on behalf of major companies and NHS Trusts. **Clients/Work:** Currently acting for a local NHS Trust in proceedings by its part-time employees for parity with full time colleagues about provisions relating to pensions. Recently completed a review of restrictive covenants in the employment contracts of the underwriting staff of a major insurance client.

LEADERS' PROFILES • SOUTH WEST

BROWN, Anthony
Wansbroughs Willey Hargrave, Bristol
(0117) 926 8981
Partner in National Employment Unit.
Specialisation: Broad experience of all contentious and non-contentious aspects of employment law, including drafting employment contracts and disciplinary procedures, employee remuneration, discrimination and TUPE. In particular, he handles Industrial Tribunal work acting on behalf of major companies, as well as NHS Trusts.
Prof. Memberships: He is an active member of the Industrial Law Society, Employment Lawyers' Association and the Industrial Tribunal Users Consultative Committee.
Career: Qualified 1983. *Laytons* 1981-83, *Osborne Clarke* 1983-84; joined *Wansbroughs Willey Hargrave* in 1984. Partner in 1988.

DUNCAN, Nikki S.
Bond Pearce, Plymouth (01752) 266633
Partner and Head of Employment Law Group.
Specialisation: All aspects of employment law. Has considerable experience in employment law litigation, advocacy and the employment aspects of corporate transactions and discrimination law issues. Regulary speaks at, or chairs, both regional and national

employment law seminars and conferences. Has had published numerous articles and given radio and television interviews on topical employment law issues.
Prof. Memberships: Elected member of the Management Committee of the Employment Lawyers Association and their UK Training Coordinator – first time anyone outside London has been appointed to this key role. Also member of the European Employment Lawyers Association and the Regional IT Users Consultative Committee.
Career: Qualifed in 1979. Joined *Bond Pearce* in 1982, becoming partner 1985. Previous firm *McKenna & Co*.

DYSON, George
Burges Salmon, Bristol (0117) 939 2000

LAMONT, Sarah
Veale Wasbrough, Bristol (0117) 925 2020
pecialisation: Head of Employment Law Department dealing with all aspects of contentious and non contentious employment law. Including: employment aspects of corporate transactions; TUPE; service agreements; sex, race, disability discrimination; equal pay; restrictive covenants; trade unions/industrial action; and employment

litigation including tribunals and advocacy. Co-author of Jordan's Secretarial Administration, Jordan's/IPD Employment Service and Sweet & Maxwell's Public and Private Partnerships. Regularly publishes articles and speaks at employment seminars/courses, including tailored training for clients, and lectures on the Legal Practice Course.
Prof. Memberships: Law Society, Institute of Personnel and Development, Employment Lawyers Association, Industrial Law Society, Bristol Law Society Training & Equal Opportunities Committee, Regional Industrial Tribunal Users Consultative Committee.
Career: MA Cambridge University, trained *Macfarlanes*, London. Qualified 1992. Partner at *Veale Wasbrough* 1998.
Personal: Astronomy, mythology, painting and sketching, squash.

MOORE, Nigel
Stephens & Scown, Exeter (01392) 210700
Specialisation: All aspects of contentious employment law, acting mainly for employers as regular advocate in Industrial Tribunals and the Employment Appeal Tribunal, advising on corporate aspects of employment law including TUPE and Service Agreements, executive terminations and restrictive covenants.

Prof. Memberships: Law Society.
Career: Called to the Bar in 1978, Harmsworth Scholar, Middle Temple. 1982-1986 Assistant Editor IDS Brief; 1986-1990 Assistant, *Simmons & Simmons*, December 1989, admitted as solicitor. Joined *Stephens & Scown* in 1990 becoming a partner in 1994.
Personal: Educated Plymouth College and Southampton University 1974-1977.

RANKIN, Claire
Eversheds, Bristol (0117) 929 9555
Specialisation: Handles all aspects of

employment law and is an experienced Industrial Tribunal advocate. Has particular expertise in dealing with large scale redundancy, contract change and TUPE issues. Regular speaker at regional and national conferences for organisations including the IPD and Croners. Writes frequently for employment law publications and updates the Unfair Dismissal section of the Croner Case Law Index.
Prof. Memberships: IPD; Institute of Directors.
Career: Birmingham University. Qualified and joined *Eversheds* in 1993.

WIDDOWSON, David G.
Bevan Ashford, London
(0171) 421 4400
Specialisation: Employment and Industrial Relations Law, principally for employers. Specialism in Health Sector.
Prof. Memberships: Member Management Committee Employment Lawyers Association; Member CBI Employment Relations Panel; Fellow of Chartered Institute of Arbitrators; Institute of Personnel and Development.
Career: Penarth County Grammar School. Birmingham University.
Personal: Rugby, cricket, Whitwell Players, Neath RFC.

WALES

EVERSHEDS Cardiff
MORGAN BRUCE Cardiff

Leo Abse & Cohen Cardiff
Edwards Geldard Cardiff
Thompsons Cardiff

Eversheds (3ptnrs/14assts) A "decent well-established firm." They have a reputation for their "aggressive" style and for "taking tribunal cases all the way." *Viv Du-Feu* "an experienced and well-respected practitioner" was the first in Wales to specialise in employment law 20 years ago. *Martin Warren* now focuses almost exclusively on employment matters, but retains an interest in environmental law as well. He is "practical, sound technically, and wants to understand the business" and is even "threatening to eclipse the reputation of Viv Du-Feu. *Audrey Williams* has a strong reputation as a discrimination expert; she is "more academic in approach." **Clients/Work:** Advising First Plus Bank in

the US in establishing its UK subsidiary. Acting for the Directors and Senior Managers of HTV in relation to the takeover by United News and Media in July 1997. Acting for the Welsh Development Agency.
Morgan Bruce (2ptnrs/8assts) Known for health and public sector work, but "more service oriented; not nationally known as employment lawyers." Headed by the "aggressive" *Michael Clarke* who "knows his stuff." The team has grown in the last four years at a rate of two fee-earners per year. **Clients/Work:** Advising companies on the implications of the Disability Discrimination Act upon performance appraisal, salary increases, redundancy selection criteria. Involved in the termination of a Managing Director's contract worth in excess of £1m.
Leo Abse & Cohen (1ptnr/1assoc/1asst) Act mainly for applicants in the firm's tradition. *Alison Love* is "practical, prepared to be flexible and capable." Promoted in the tables this year. **Clients/Work:** Acted in relation to a sex disrimination claim funded by the Equal Opportunities Commission regarding a failure to allow an employee to return to part time following maternity leave. Acted on behalf of an employer in a claim against an ex-employee for breach of contract. Acting on behalf of approx. 250 plaintiffs in a

claim against adminstrative receivers for contractual redundancy payments – worth over £200,000.
Edwards Geldard (2ptnrs/2assts do employment and pensions) Act primarily for respondents who consist of public sector and corporate clients. Seen to lack a leader. **Clients/Work:** Advising on the dismissal of approximately thirty employees for taking part in industrial action. Advising in respect of relocation of a group of employees.
Thompsons (2ptnrs/1asst) Handles full range of personal and collective employment cases for individuals and trade unions. **Clients/Work:** Acting in major race discrimination claim for probation officer, resulting in award of £73k. 250 union members in High Court breach of contract claim against multi-national resulting in payment of £1m.

DU-FEU Vivian Eversheds
WARREN Martin Eversheds
WILLIAMS Audrey Eversheds
CLARKE Michael Morgan Bruce

LOVE Alison Leo Abse & Cohen

SEE PROFILES AT END OF THIS SECTION

CLARKE, Michael H.
Morgan Bruce, Cardiff (01222) 385385
Specialisation: Partner and Head of Employment Group in Cardiff. Has extensive experience in handling all types of contentious and non-contentious employment law for leading public and private sector clients. An experienced advocate who represents many of the region's major employers in the Industrial Tribunal. Speaker at Employment Law conferences arranged by the CBI, Institute of Personnel and Development, NHS Staff College and Institute of International Affairs. Author of numerous articles on employment law. Recognised by Legal Business 1998 as one of the leading employment law specialists practising in the Regions. In the past year has provided advice and guidance to Wales' largest

employer on a wide variety of complex employment law matters including the transfer of undertakings and industrial action.
Prof. Memberships: Member of Employment Lawyers Association. The Law Society.
Career: Qualified as a Solicitor in England and Wales in January 1985. Admitted as Solicitor of Supreme Court of Hong Kong in April 1985 and June 1990. Joined *Morgan Bruce* in July 1991 and became Partner 1993.
Personal: Married and lives in Cardiff.

DU-FEU, Vivian
Eversheds, Cardiff 01222 471 147
A Partner and Head of the Employment Law Department at Cardiff.
Specialisation: Head of the *Eversheds* national Employment Law Group of over 100 lawyers.

Has wide experience in providing advice on all aspects of contentious and non-contentious employment law. Lectures and writes regularly on various employment issues and is a member of the Editorial Advisory Board for Croners.
Prof. Memberships: A Fellow of the Institute of Personnel and Development (IPD); Director of Principle Training Limited.
Career: Graduate of University of Wales College of Cardiff. Qualified in 1979. Became a Partner in 1984.
Personal: Married and resides in Cardiff.

LOVE, Alison
Leo Abse & Cohen, Cardiff (01222) 383252
Specialisation: An experienced employment lawyer who advises on all aspects of employment law, both contentious and non-

contentious, on behalf of employers and employees. Particular experience of all types of discrimination claims, including having represented Applicants and Respondents in some of the first claims to be brought under the Disability Discrimination Act 1995. Acts on behalf of approximately 200 Plaintiffs on one of the largest Paramount claims in the High Court. Author of articles on employment law and a regular speaker at seminars.

Prof. Memberships: Employment Lawyers Association, member of the Institute of Personnel & Development, committee member of the South East Wales branch of the Institute of Personnel & Development.

Career: Personnel management background, followed by a law degree at University College of Wales, Cardiff and Law Society finals at University of The West of England. Qualified 1993, joined *Leo Abse & Cohen* June 1995, became an Associate Partner in 1996.

Personal: Born 11th November 1960. Resides with partner and two young sons in the Vale of

Glamorgan. Previously a competitive swimmer, now only to keep fit.

WARREN, Martin
Eversheds, Cardiff (01222) 471147
Partner and Head of the Industrial Relations Unit at *Eversheds* Cardiff.

Specialisation: An experienced employment lawyer with particular expertise in dealing with large scale redundancy, contract change, industrial action and the management of multi-applicant Industrial Tribunal litigation. Acted successfully for employer clients in reported cases including 'O'Dea -v- ISC Chemicals' (Court of Appeal 1995) and 'Alcan Extrusions -v-Yates' (EAT 1996).

Prof. Memberships: Member of the Employment Lawyers Association; member of Cardiff Industrial Tribunal User Group; Fellow of the Royal Society of Arts; member of the Reform Club.

Career: Qualified in 1985. Joined *Phillips & Buck* in 1986 (now *Eversheds*). Became a

Partner in 1989.

Personal: Director of Principle Training Limited. Resides in Magor, Gwent.

WILLIAMS, Audrey M.
Eversheds, Cardiff (01222) 471147
Specialisation: A Partner in the Employment Law Department at *Eversheds* Cardiff. Specialises in all aspects of employment law. Particular experience of sex discrimination, race discrimination and disability discrimination. Advises on equal opportunities, maternity and harassment and bullying policies; providing advice and training for establishing such policies; grievance procedures and counselling. Author of a number of publications.

Prof. Memberships: Graduate of the Institute of Personnel and Development.

Career: Graduate of Southampton University; qualified in 1989, joined *Eversheds Phillips and Buck* in 1989 (now *Eversheds* Cardiff); became a partner in 1993.

Personal: Married and resides in Cardiff.

MIDLANDS

Eversheds (2ptnrs/14assts) Largest dedicated team in the region. Department benefits from the national branding of the Eversheds product. Taken on senior HR professional offering consultancy services. The "extremely capable all-rounder" *Martin Hopkins* is known for his litigation expertise. *David Beswick* is "excellent." **Clients/Work:** Advising Grand Metropolitan Plc on the employment implications of their merger with Guinness Plc. Advising the registrar's department of the Bank of England on a major restructuring and redundancy programme at their Gloucester premises. Advising Carlsberg Tetley on their reorganisation following the rejection by DTI of their proposed merger with Bass.

Dibb Lupton Alsop (2ptnrs/3assoc/2assts) Benefit from their national marketing and have recruited an HR specialist to sell in-house training services. Team includes *Peter Thompson* and *Alan Jones*, a "tough litigator" with an "aggressive style." **Clients/Work:** Defended a test case for Humberside

Independent Care Association in excess of 100 claims alleging unfair dismissal and breach of contract. Act for Tesco, Makro and Habitat.

Edge & Ellison (2ptnrs/3assocs/6assts) The "talented" *James Retallack* has now become Senior Partner and the general view is that this "will inevitably have an impact" on the practice. Although he "has a good team behind him" he was the "dominant individual." New National Head of Employment is *Veronica Dean*; although "bright and able" with a "pragmatic, robust, commonsense view" of employment matters she does not have the same profile as yet. Team also includes *Julia Edwards*. **Clients/Work:** Acting in the EAT for the appellant in Senior Heat Treatment v Bell, Hand & Hipwood; acting for the Chief Executive and Finance Director of Leigh Interests plc with the negotiation of their severance terms following the General Utilities acquisition. Representing a national IT services supplier against a number of ex-employees following the loss of a contract. The case raised significant issues under the 1981 Transfer Regulations and the Suzen decision.

Pinsent Curtis (2ptnr/5assts) A "traditional, polite firm." Head of employment is *Colin Goodier* ("as an intellectual presence he takes some beating"). *Jane Ellis* is "client-friendly." **Clients/Work:** Negotiating departure and severance package for Chief Executive of Triplex Lloyd plc. Advising Luton Airport on bidding for Airport Concession contract. For Britannic Assurance plc dealing with test cases for hearing in January 1998, representing some 300 claims arising out of a major restructuring exercise in 1997.

Wragge & Co (2ptnrs/3assocs/4assts) The firm has recently taken on a new "high-flier" *Martin Chitty* , a "sound chap." **Clients/Work:** Exit arrangement for Chief Executive of recently merged public company seeking to

gain board control and subsequent executive packages on further takeover. Injunction proceedings to stop defecting football manager. Advice on new airline employee contracts.

Higgs & Sons (2ptnrs/1asst) Small niche firm; employment is a strong feature. The team consists of "two extremely good individuals." *Roger Field* is "well-liked and technically competent."

Browne Jacobson (1ptnr/1asstf/t 1asst p/t) Small team does most of its own advocacy and claims to have lost only one tribunal over a 12-month period. *Edward Benson* is the specialist partner. **Clients/Work:** Successfully acting for Nottinghamshire Police in a complex sex and race discrimination claim. Abbey National sex discrimination claim, going to appeal in the EAT. Acting for an NHS Trust in a claim by a doctor dismissed for his refusal to accept changed working patterns.

Martineau Johnson (1ptnrs/5assts) Represent individuals as well as corporate clients in ongoing advice work and transactional work. Team is headed by *Ian Marshall*. **Clients/Work:** Acting for football league club in action by former member of coaching staff for breach of contract. Advising major Midland builder on takeover of construction and maintenance work from local authority.

Tyndallwoods (1ptnr/1asst) The firm acts for applicants. Madeleine Rees was the "high-profile" practitioner but she has left the firm and is spending some months in Bosnia in her capacity as Deputy Ombudsman. It remains to be seen what happens to the practice, but they retain their ranking on the basis of the work they have done over the past year. **Clients/Work:** PvS: ECJ established that transexuals have rights under EC law. AvB: IT found that the Sex Discrimination Act must be interpreted to provide protection for transsexuals; now in Court of Appeal. Armed forces pregnancy dismissal cases.

The Lewington Partnership (2ptnrs/1assoc/4assts) Have little profile outside their NHS work; they are however expert in NHS employment regulations. Known in this context as "a dominant supplier of legal services to the West Midlands." **Clients/Work:** North Staffordshire NHS Trust v Payne – advising on a staff breach of confidentiality; Stirzaker v Birmingham Health NHS Trust, employment aspect of large PFI project for North B'ham Community NHS Trust.

Shakespeares (3ptnrs/3assts) The team have "proved to be capable lawyers" in opposition. **Clients/Work:** Dealt with more tribunal cases than in any previous year. New clients include subsidiary of major plc. Many disability discrimination cases.

LEADERS' PROFILES • MIDLANDS

BENSON, Edward
Browne Jacobson, Nottingham
(0115) 950 0055
Specialisation: Practice covers full range of employment law services including drafting contracts of employment, general employment advice, County and High Court Litigation and representation at industrial tribunals in complaints relating to unfair dismissal, redundancy pay, discrimination, equal pay, wages act, etc. Contributor and General Editor of Employment Law Service for IPD, published by Jordans.
Career: Admitted 1980. *Slaughter and May* 1978-1982. Assistant Editor of Handbooks and supplements at IDS (1982-1984). Editor of Industrial Relations Legal Information Bulletin (1985-89). Joined *Browne Jacobson* 1989, Partner since 1993.

BESWICK, David
Eversheds, Birmingham (0121) 233 2001
Specialisation: Contentious and non-contentious employment law, advising mainly employers, including education institutions, with strengths in Executive Severance packages, TUPE issues, restructuring and restrictive covenants.
Prof. Memberships: Law Society. Employment Lawyers' Association. Education Lawyers' Association.
Career: Joined *Eversheds* in 1985, Partner 1996.
Personal: Born: 18.2.63. Attended Newcastle University 1981-84. Leisure interests include badminton, walking and theatre.

CHITTY, Martin
Wragge & Co, Birmingham (0121) 233 1000
Head of employment team.
Specialisation: Interests include TUPE in public and private sector, collective disputes, senior executive contracts, severance and use and abuse of restrictive covenants.
Career: Articled *Pinsent & Co.* Qualified 1986. Partner *Pinsent & Co* 1993-1995. Partner *Wragge & Co* from 1995.
Personal: Born 1961.

DEAN, Veronica
Edge & Ellison, Birmingham (0121) 200 2001
Head of Employment
Specialisation: All areas of contentious and non-contentious employment law with a particular interest in TUPE and discrimination issues. A regular tribunal advocate.

Prof. Memberships: Law Society, Employment Lawyers Association, Birmingham Industrial Tribunal Users Group.
Career: Qualified 1984, Joined *Edge & Ellison* 1986, partner 1993.
Personal: Born 1959, Graduate of University of Wales, Cardiff. Interests include art, gardening and entertaining. Lives in Worcestershire.

EDWARDS, Julia C.
Edge & Ellison, Birmingham (0121) 200 2001
Specialisation: All aspects of employment law including unfair, wrongful and constructive dismissal, sex, race and disability discrimination, executive severance and injunctive proceedings.
Prof. Memberships: Employment Lawyers Association. Association of Women Solicitors.
Career: Articled *Edge & Ellison*. Admitted 1992 becoming an Associate 1996 and a Partner in 1998.
Personal: Born 1968. Alice Ottley School, Worcester, 1973-1986 and Bournemouth University 1986-1989. Lives in Worcestershire.

ELLIS, Jane
Pinsent Curtis, Birmingham (0121) 200 1050
Specialisation: Partner specialising in all types of employment law. Particular experience in TUPE, employment aspects of PFI Projects, Discrimination Law (particularly Disability Discrimination), Working Time Directive and Regulations (Chair of Birmingham Chamber of Commerce and Industry Working Party on Working Time Regulations), Employment Issues in Rail and Automotive Industries (number of clients in these areas including GT Railway Maintenance)
Prof. Memberships: Employment Lawyers Association, Birmingham Law Society.
Career: St Albans Girls' School. Oxford University, Hertford College. College of Law, Chester. 2:1 Law Degree from Oxford – 1988; Law Society Finals (2nd Class Hons.) – 1989 Trained with *Eversheds*. Moved to *Pinsent Curtis* after qualification. Made up to partner in May 1998.
Personal: Active gym and tennis club member, scuba diving, pianist.

FIELD, Roger
Higgs & Sons, Dudley (01384) 342000
Specialisation: All aspects of employment law, 80% employer – 20% employee. Emphasis on national retailer clients. Contentious and non-contentious. Part-time Chairman of Industrial Tribunals.

Prof. Memberships: Law Society, Birmingham Law Society, Employment Lawyers Association.
Career: Qualified in 1970. Joined *Higgs & Sons* in 1968, becoming a Partner in 1974.
Personal: Born 13th January 1946. Educated at Dudley Grammar School and The London School of Economics. Interests include crosswords, railways and cricket. Lives in Stourbridge.

GOODIER, Colin
Pinsent Curtis, Birmingham (0121) 200 1050
Head of Employment Department, Birmingham.
Specialisation: Employment law including contentious and non-contentious work, advice on individual and collective rights and heavy involvement in TUPE, employee consultation and employment aspects of M&A.
Prof. Memberships: Chairman of Industrial Tribunals (England & Wales). Founder member of managing committee of Employment Lawyers' Assoc. Member of Birmingham Industrial Tribunal Users' Group.
Career: Admitted 1972. Specialist in Employment Law throughout career. Partner *Bettinsons* Birmingham 1976. Partner *Pinsent & Co.* (now *Pinsent Curtis*) 1987. Head of Litigation (Birmingham) 1995. Head of Employment (Birmingham) 1996.
Personal: Born 1947. Educated Hertford College, Oxford. Interests include renovation of timber-framed cottage; walking; old prints. Elected FRSA 1996.

HOPKINS, Martin W.
Eversheds, Birmingham (0121) 233 2001
Partner and Head of Employment.
Specialisation: Main area of practice is Employment and Industrial Relations Law. Has wide experience of handling all types of contentious and non-contentious employment work in both the public and private sector. Particular strength in executive severance, change management and industrial relations law. Leads team of 19 specialist employment lawyers, trainers and HR professionals. Co-author of 'Health and Safety: Are You at Risk?' (1993) and of 'The Maternity Manual' (1994). Speaks frequently on employment issues and regularly delivers in-house tailored training courses for clients.
Prof. Memberships: Member of Institute of Personnel and Development and Employment Lawyers Association.
Career: Joined *Eversheds* 1980, qualified in 1982, and made Partner and Head of

Employment in 1989.
Personal: Born 28th October 1957. Attended Warwick School 1971-76 and Coventry University 1976-79. Leisure interests include family and travel. Lives in Lighthorne, near Warwick.

JONES, Alan
Dibb Lupton Alsop, Birmingham
(0345) 262728
Employment Law Partner and Head of Employment in Birmingham office.
Specialisation: Principal area of practice is the whole spectrum of employment law including unfair dismissal, discrimination, executive severance and restrictive covenant work. Both contentious and non-contentious but with an emphasis on the former. A regular and experienced advocate primarily on behalf of such clients as Makro, Tesco, Employment Service, and AMEC Group Plc amongst others. Also acts for senior executives in dispute with their employer. Occasional speaker at conferences, and does a lot of in-house training on related subjects.
Prof. Memberships: Law Society, Employment Lawyers Association.
Career: Qualified with *Needham & James* in 1978 becoming a Partner in 1983. Originally a criminal lawyer, moving to employment from 1985. Partner with *Dubb Lupton Broomhead* upon merger in November 1993, and *Dibb Lupton Alsop* since October 1996.
Personal: Born 17 May 1953. Interests include most sports, particularly rugby, skiing and wind

surfing. Married with three children. Lives near Stratford upon Avon.

MARSHALL, Ian
Martineau Johnson, Birmingham
(0121) 200 3300
Specialisation: 'All aspects of Employment law, contentious and non-contentious, largely for employers. Trial experience includes actions against a trade union, injunctions, contempt of court, and wrongful dismissal. Advice on TUPE, severance agreements, restrictive covenants and equality issues in the private and educational sectors.
Prof. Memberships: Employment Lawyers Association, Birmingham Law Society, Birmingham Law Society representative on Birmingham Industrial Tribunal Users Group.
Career: Rugby School and Magdalene College, Cambridge. Articled *Ryland Martineau & Co.*; Partner in *Ryland Martineau & Co.* 1976; *Martineau Johnson* 1987; Head of Employment Department 1994.
Personal: Born 1947. Lives in Edgbaston, Birmingham. Council Member, Edgbaston High School, Birmingham and Edgbaston Debating Society. St Paul's Club, Birmingham. Fell Walking.

RETALLACK, James
Edge & Ellison, Birmingham (0121) 200 2001
DDI: (0121) 214 2531
Senior Partner of *Edge & Ellison*
Specialisation: All aspects of employment, human resource and Industrial Relations law

and employment and personnel training.
Prof. Memberships: Law Society, Employment Lawyers Association, Birmingham Industrial Tribunal Users Committee.
Career: Qualified in 1981. Joined *Edge & Ellison* in 1981, becoming a Partner in 1988 and Senior Partner in 1998.
Personal: Born 8th July 1957. Attended Malvern College 1970-74 and Manchester University 1975-78. Leisure interests include reading, skiing, gardening and American Football. Lives in Worcester.

THOMPSON, Peter
Dibb Lupton Alsop, Birmingham
(0345) 262728
Employment Law Partner, Head of DLA Consulting.
Specialisation: Main area of practice is employment and has specialised since 1978. An experienced advocate and leader of corporate in-house and external training. Has instigated the merger of legal and personnel expertise and heads DLA's/National Consulting Division.
Career: Qualified 1970. Group Solicitor The Littlewoods Organisation 1975-78. Personnel Director Littlewoods Mail Order Companies 1978-82. Part-time Chairman of Industrial Tribunals 1983-96, previously Head of Employment and Managing Partner *Howes Percival*.
Personal: Born 18.1.46. Interests include Golf (member Northamptonshire and Royal Birkdale Golf Clubs and Rugby (member Northampton)). Lives – Northamptonshire.

EAST ANGLIA

LEADING FIRMS · EAST ANGLIA
EVERSHEDS Norwich, Ipswich
HEWITSON BECKE + SHAW Cambridge
MILLS & REEVE Norwich, Cambridge
STEELE & CO Norwich

HIGHLY REGARDED FIRMS
Greenwoods Peterborough
Taylor Vinters Cambridge
Leathes Prior Norwich
Prettys Ipswich

Eversheds (4ptnrs/3assts) The team is "strong"in the region. *Owen Warnock* is highly prominent; he has an "excellent reputation"and a "great deal of experience on public sector and TUPE." *Tracy Yates* is "a competent lawyer."

Hewitson Becke + Shaw (1ptnr/5assts Cambridge1ptnr/1asst Northampton) Also handle share schemes work. *Nick Sayer* has a good reputation as does his team.
Clients/Work: Advised clients on the impact of recently issued EU directives. Handled more than 200 armed forces pregnancy and discrimination cases as agent for the Treasury Solicitor. Dealing with the first cases arising from the Disability Discrimination Act 1995.

Mills & Reeve (5ptnrs/5assts – 1p/t) A "well-regarded quality firm" have just recruited a qualified barrister for tribunal advocacy work. There is however some criticism that they "need to work to maintain their position." Colin Tweedie, their well-regarded department head, has recently left the Norwich office to head the Addleshaw Booth & Co employment law department. *Nicola Brown* and *Sally Boyle,* who was newly recommended this year, hold the fort in Cambridge. **Clients/Work:** Two major multi-day tribunal cases for a major financial institution. TUPE advice on complex farming acquisition and multiple disposal. Acting for a university on TUPE effect on changing terms and conditions.

Steele & Co (1ptnr/3assts) *Norman Lamb* has a "wealth of experience" on sex discrimination and equal pay matters. His reputation is enhanced by his work on armed forces pregnancy litigation. **Clients/Work:** Settlement of a substantial number of equal pay claims brought against the MoD relating to female Army Recruiting Sergeants. Defended a claim brought in the County Court under the Commercial Agents Regulations. Advised Sixth Form Colleges on restructuring proposals involving redundancies as a result of funding shortfalls.

Greenwoods (1ptnr/2assts) 90% practice for corporate entities. Sex, race and disability discrimination work. *Robert Dillar-*

stone is a strong contentious lawyer. **Clients/Work:** Won a number of clients from a training programme they provided. Secured the employment work of a major packaging company. The restructuring involved advice on redundancies.

Taylor Vinters (1ptnrs/2assts) Service commercial clients including substantial institutions and high technology industries. Head of department *Mandy Lyne* is newly recommended this year. **Clients/Work:** Dealing with cases of judicial review, discrimination and breach of contract brought by university lecturer for Cambridge University. Defending industrial tribunal case and review on discrimination allegation on non-appointment for school headship.

LEADING INDIVIDUALS EAST ANGLIA	
LAMB Norman Steele & Co	
SAYER Nicholas Hewitson Becke + Shaw	
WARNOCK Owen Eversheds	
BROWN Nicola Mills & Reeve	
DILLARSTONE Robert Greenwoods	
YATES Tracy Eversheds	

UP AND COMING	
BOYLE Sally Mills & Reeve	
LYNE Amanda Taylor Vinters	

SEE PROFILES AT END OF THIS SECTION

Leathes Prior (2ptnrs/5assts) Have an innovative fixed price package centred on an Employment Management System and advice line. **Clients/Work:** Over 40 new clients won over last year. Regular seminars for Business Link.

Prettys (1ptnr/1asst) Act for clients in agriculture, shipping and transport, construction, health and retail sectors. **Clients/Work:** Re-organisation of workforce in a large East Anglian agricultural estate. Acting in a large number of transport related tribunal claims. Growth in restrictive covenant claims.

LEADERS' PROFILES · EAST ANGLIA

BOYLE, Sally
Mills & Reeve, Cambridge
+44 (0)1223 364422
Specialisation: Employment Law – advising private and public sector clients on drafting service agreements, contracts of employment and policies, representing clients in unfair/ wrongful/ discrimination and injunction proceedings, advising on TUPE (particularly in PFI projects), running in-house training for clients, regularly speaking at seminars on topical employment issues.
Prof. Memberships: Employment Lawyers Association.
Career: Cheltenham Ladies' College; Queens' College, Cambridge; *Simmons & Simmons*; *Mills & Reeve*; Diploma in Employment Law and Industrial Relations, Leicester University.
Personal: Tennis, Jazz and D.I.Y.

BROWN, Nicola
Mills & Reeve, Cambridge
+44 (0)1223 364422
Specialisation: Specialises in all aspects of employment law acting mainly for employers both in the public and private sector. Deals with contract drafting, advice on dismissals and industrial tribunal claims. Increasing emphasis on discrimination claims and advice on the Transfer of Undertaking Regulations.
Career: 1983 – LLB University of Southampton; 1987 – Qualified as a solicitor; 1987-1990 – Assistant solicitor *Kennedys*, Chiswell Street, London; 1990-1995 – Senior solicitor *Mills & Reeve*, Cambridge; 1995 to date – Partner *Mills & Reeve*, Cambridge.

DILLARSTONE, Robert
Greenwoods, Peterborough (01733) 555244

LAMB, Norman
Steele & Co, Norwich (01603) 627107
Specialisation: Main areas of practice: Employment and discrimination plus entertainment licensing, advocacy. Tribunal advocacy, drafting and advising on terms and conditions, and reorganisations of companies, trade unions recognition issues, collective redundancy consultation, works councils and advice on Commercial Agents Regulations. Regularly lectures and presents training sessions on Employment Law.
Prof. Memberships: Employment Lawyers Association, Discrimination Law Association.
Career: Qualified in 1984.
Personal: Born 16.9.1957.

LYNE, Amanda
Taylor Vinters, Cambridge (01223) 423444
Partner and Head of Employment Department
Specialisation: All aspects of employment law, national and European, contentious and non-contentious for companies, institutions and individuals. Contracts and benefits. Reorganistaions and redundancies. Dismissals. Transfers of undertakings. Discrimination. Restrictive Covenants. In-house training. Tribunal advocacy. Clients include major high tech, biotech, telecoms, education (including Cambridge University and many colleges, and major schools).
Prof. Memberships: Law Society, Employment Lawyers Association, Industrial Law Society.
Career: Called to the bar in 1969. Qualified as a solicitor in 1981. Joined *Vinters* in 1986 (becoming *Taylor Vinters* after merger in 1988). Became partner in 1989.
Personal: Educated at Adelaide, Australia and Cambridge (MA, LLB). Keen sailor, tennis player, theatre, film and concert goer.

SAYER, Nicholas
Hewitson Becke + Shaw, Cambridge (01223) 461155
Partner and Head of Employment Law Department.
Specialisation: Principal area of practice is contentious employment matters, particularly injunctive relief, trade secret and confidential information matters, non-competition, non-solicitation and non-dealing covenants, Anton Piller orders, orders for delivery up,etc. Also deals with other contentious and non-contentious employment matters, wrongful dismissal, unfair dismissal, redundancy, discrimination, trade disputes and other Trades Union matters, transfers of undertakings, drafting contracts of employment. Has presented seminars to other professionals and clients.
Prof. Memberships: The Employment Lawyers Association, The Industrial Law Society, The Institute of Employment Rights.
Career: Joined *Hewitson Becke & Shaw* in 1985. Qualified in 1987. Became a Partner and Head of Employment Law in 1993.
Personal: Born 26th September 1961. Educated at the Cambridgeshire High School for Boys 1973-80 and Leicester University 1981-84. Awarded an LLM in Law and Industrial Relations from Leicester University in 1993. Leisure pursuits include cricket, photography and gardening. Lives in Cambridge.

WARNOCK, Owen
Eversheds, Norwich (01603) 272727
Specialisation: Has specialised in employment law for 16 years and heads the *Eversheds* East Anglian employment department, consisting of 9 lawyers. He has considerable Industrial Tribunal advocacy experience and has particular strength in discrimination law and Health Service employment law. He is Consultant Legal Editor to the CCH Disability Manual (1996) and co-author of Employment Law in the NHS (Cavendish 1995). A regular speaker on employment law issues at events ranging from local IPD groups to CBI and similar national conferences. Employment law is main area of practice, but also advises on food and drink law.
Prof. Memberships: Employment Lawyers Association, Industrial Law Society, The Food Law Group.
Career: Qualified 1982 with *Daynes Hill & Perks* (Partner 1985).
Personal: Born 5 April 1957. Graduated in Law from Cambridge University in 1979. Lives in Norwich.

YATES, Tracy
Eversheds, Norwich (01603) 272727
Specialisation: Employment, handling unfair and wrongful dismissal claims, including advocacy in the industrial tribunal and courts. Advising employers and senior employees in respect of compromise agreement/severage packages; Advising on all aspects of employment law – commercial clients and senior employees (TUPE, redundancy, dismissals etc); Drafting, and advising on Service Agreements and Statements of Main Terms and Conditions of Employment. Immigration: – Advising on applications for entry clearance (and appeals against refusal), work permits and naturalisation.
Prof. Memberships: Law Society and Employment Lawyers Association.
Career: Qualified October 1986. 1984-86 – Trainee Solicitor, *Daynes, Chittock & Back*; 1986-89 – Assistant Solicitor, *Daynes, Chittock & Back/Daynes, Hill & Perks*; 1989-92 – Associate, *Daynes, Hill & Perks*; 1992 to date Partner, *Eversheds*.
Personal: Two daughters – Helena and Sophia.

NORTH WEST

Addleshaw Booth & Co (2ptnrs/11assts in Leeds and Manchester offices) The firm is known for its traditional, academic approach. "They lay down the law." Both partners describe themselves as generalists and do their own advocacy. *Malcolm Pike* is head of the employment department. He is "decent to deal with." *Andrew Chamberlain* "can be aggressive" and is "good but has no national reputation yet." **Clients/Work:** S. Manchester Universtiy Hospitals Trust (employment aspects of PFI). Aliance Paper Group v Prestwich (C of A). AAH plc - relocation of head office and drawing up new contracts, staff handbook, etc. following acquisition of Lloyds Chemists plc.

Hammond Suddards (1ptnr/10assts) *Sue Nickson* "has a tremendous reputation and national profile." "Intelligent and personable, she drives the team forward on a day-to-day basis." She also has departmental back-up and "has built a client-friendly team." **Clients/Work:** Acting in the Ashworth Special Hospital Public Enquiry into the running of its PD Unit. Success survey of IPD line. Involved in substantial corporate support work (e.g Guilbert-Ofrex WHS, Lorien Acquisitions etc).

Dibb Lupton Alsop (2ptnrs/5assts) Their "profile has diminished" in recent years. *Paul Nicholls* is now Regional Managing Partner, so has little time to spend on employment law. *Mary Clarke* "does the main work" and is "good, quite self-effacing

and reasonable but does not have the national reputation." **Clients/Work:** Successfully resisting a sex/race discrimination claim against Merseyside Racial Equality Council. For GPT, test cases to settle approximately 450 industrial tribunal claims(decision pending). Acting for Liverpool John Moores University on a successful sex/equal pay/unfair dismissal claim by law lecturer against the Law Department.

Whittles (1ptnr/1asst) A medium-sized firm specialising mainly in plaintiffs' personal injury work but also universally praised for its applicants' employment work for which the style is "no waffle, they just get on with it." *Charles Hantom* who is Senior Partner is a "flamboyant character," a lawyer "in the old style." He is assisted by the hardworking *Helen Parkinson* who is "lower key in approach but also sound and competent."

Eversheds (1ptnr/5assts) "Not such a specialist unit"although they give "good competent advice." *Peter Norbury* has a reputation for his "aggressive style" but "seems to have mellowed recently." However he "keeps his clients happy" and "fells it as it is." **Clients/Work:** Acting for DuPont on £1.8bn acquisition of part of ICI. Acting for Wigan Rugby League Club in a major management personnel change. Advised on a couple of major executive terminations for Plc clients.

Mace & Jones (Liverpool: 3ptnrs/ 5assts. Manchester 2ptnrs – 1p/t; 1asst) Leaders in Liverpool, but their name means little in Manchester. Clients praise them as "absolutely first-class" and for giving "a good service." *Michael Malone* is "sensible and pragmatic." *Martin Edwards* is also recommended. **Clients/Work:** Retainer to conduct over 100 separate cases nationwide for insurance company. Major TUPE-related litigation for onc of thc UK's major care service employers. Successful joint tender to undertake employment work for the Countryside Commission.

Cobbetts (1ptnr/1assoc/2assts) Do a substantial amount of applicant work as well as respondent work. *Judith Watson* is team leader ("a good solid doer"). **Clients/Work:** Advising independent schools on loss of assisted places scheme with consequent reduction in numbers of staff and general associated employment/staffing issues.

Advising employee representatives on redundancy/TUPE issues.

Halliwell Landau (2ptnrs/2assts) Head of department *Stephen Hills* "does a lot of Industrial Tribunal work and is more litigation based." He particularly specialises in post employment protection issues and restrictive covenants and has a "workmanlike approach." **Clients/Work:** Employment advice on transactions eg Sun Alliance sale of National Vulcan, Scotia Haven and acquisition of Whitworth Group of Companies. Prevalence of claims involving sex and race discrimination, particularly harrassment.

Davies Wallis Foyster (3ptnrs/2assts) The firm's work is "extremely competent, they cannot be faulted on preparation." *Andrea McWatt* is a part-time Industrial Tribunal Chair; there is a feeling abroad that they need a full-time partner. **Clients/Work:** Employment support role in contesting EOC-supported discrimination action against Liverpool John Moores University. TUPE action involving implications of Suzen. Employment advice on Caterpillar's $1.3bn purchase of Perkins.

Pannone & Partners (3ptnrs/2assts) Have not replaced Sue Nickson, and there was some question as to who would maintain the practice. **Clients/Work:** Appointed as employment law adviser to Co-operative Bank PLC. Successful defence of a claim made against a chiropodist of infamous conduct. Sex discrimination case defended for Texaco. Successfully assisted Motorola in changing its terms of employment.

LEADERS' PROFILES · NORTH WEST

CHAMBERLAIN, Andrew
Addleshaw Booth & Co, Manchester
(0161) 934 6000
Partner in Employment Department, Commercial Group.
Specialisation: All aspects of employment law including the drafting of service agreements, Transfer of Undertakings Regulations, restrictive covenant injunctions and all contentious employment matters (including advocacy at the

Industrial Tribunals), employment aspects of M & A work, and immigration matters.
Prof. Memberships: Employment Lawyers Association, Manchester Industrial Relations Society.
Career: *Freshfields* 1986-1992. *Dibb Lupton Broomhead (Manchester)* 1993-1995 (Partner from May 1994). Joined the firm in September 1995.
Personal: Educated at King Edward VII School,

Lytham and the University of Nottingham. Interests: golf, rugby, cricket and squash. Lives in Knutsford.

CLARKE, Mary
Dibb Lupton Alsop, Manchester
(0345) 262728
Specialisation: Main areas of practice – employment law contentions including High Court actions on restrictive covenants and

share option schemes, group tribunal claims and non-contentious including business transfer issues, drafting. Lectures widely on employment law issues.
Prof. Memberships: Employment Lawyer Association.
Career: Qualified 1985 at *Pannone & Partners*. Joined *Alsop Wilkinson* 1988. MSc Employment Studies 1995.

EDWARDS, K.Martin
Mace & Jones, Liverpool (0151) 236 8989
Head of Employment Law Department.
Specialisation: Employment law specialist with extensive advocacy experience. Advises on all aspects of industrial relations law and acts for major clients in the public and private sectors throughout the UK. Also expert in relation to computer contracts. Major cases include 'Lavery v. Plessey Telecommunications' (maternity leave). Advised on film 'Letter to Brezhnev.' Author of 'Dismissal Law,' 'Managing Redundancies,' 'Careers in the Law,' 'How to get the Best Deal from your Employer,' 'Understanding Computer Contracts' and numerous articles. Founder member of Law Society's Employment Law Committee.
Prof. Memberships: Law Society, Liverpool Law Society, Employment Lawyers Association, Society for Computers and Law, Society of Authors, Crime Writers Association.
Career: Qualified in 1980 while at *Mace & Jones*. Became a Partner in 1984.
Personal: Born 7th July 1955. Attended Balliol College, Oxford 1974-77. First Class Honours Degree in Law. Leisure pursuits include writing crime novels about Liverpool Solicitor Harry Devlin, the first of which was nominated for the award for best first crime novel of 1991. Lives in Lymm, Cheshire.

HANTOM, Charles C.
Whittles, Manchester (0161) 228 2061
Senior Partner.
Specialisation: Main areas of practice are employment, trade union and industrial. Handles Industrial Tribunal and EAT work. Undertakes advocacy for industrial tribunals. Also handles High Court Injunctive proceedings. Predominantly Trade Union practice. Gives occasional seminars for Trade Union clients.
Prof. Memberships: Employment Lawyers Association.
Career: Qualified 1967. Joined *Whittles* in 1969, becoming a Partner in 1972.
Personal: Born 24th January 1942. Attended Windermere Grammar School 1954-60, Nottingham University 1960-63, and College of Law 1966. Leisure interests include walking, classic cars and outdoor pursuits. Lives in Bowdon.

HILLS, Stephen
Halliwell Landau, Manchester
(0161) 835 3003
Partner in Employment in Department.
Specialisation: Handles all aspects of contentious and non-contentious employment matters. An experienced advocate who regularly appears in the Industrial Tribunal in England and Scotland. Particular experience in transfer of undertakings and discrimination. Regularly presents seminars.

Prof. Memberships: Law Society, Employment Lawyers Association, Industrial Law Society.
Career: Qualified in 1986. Joined *Halliwell Landau* in 1990, becoming a Partner in 1992. Previously with *Mills & Reeve*, Norwich.
Personal: Born 20th September 1959. Attended University of East Anglia 1980-83. Leisure interests include walking and gardening. Lives in Appleton, Cheshire.

MALONE, M. D.
Mace & Jones, Manchester (0161) 236 2244
Partner in Employment Department.
Specialisation: Extensive advocacy experience notably in complex sex discrimination and equal pay cases. Deals with the whole range of employment work acting mainly for employers. Recent publications include "Your Employment Rights," "Discrimination Law – A Practical Guide" and the Employment Law Section of "Butterworths Guide on Law for Accountants." Has also spoken regularly at conferences and seminars.
Prof. Memberships: Law Society; International Bar Association; Associate Member of Institute of Personnel & Development.
Career: Admitted in 1968; partner at *Henry Fallows & Co* in Bolton from 1968-1991; Partner in *Mace & Jones* since 1991.
Personal: Born Bury 1943, educated at Brasenose College, Oxford. Leisure pursuits include tennis, bridge, walking, theatre. Lives in Bolton.

MCWATT, H. Andrea
Davies Wallis Foyster, Liverpool
(0151) 236 6226

NICHOLLS, Paul
Dibb Lupton Alsop, Manchester
(0345) 262 728
Employment Law Partner and North West Regional Managing Partner.
Specialisation: Main areas of practice are employment and discrimination. Has practised in these fields since 1982. DLA's employment law team is the largest in the country. Experienced advocate, reported cases include 'CRE v. Lambeth LB' & 'Sharma v. British Gas.' Author of Tolley's Discrimination Law Handbook (now in 2nd ed). Set up DLA Business and Law Training, a substantial and well respected training subsidiary of the firm, for which he lectures extensively.
Career: Qualified in 1980 at the Bar and 1990 as a Solicitor. Commission for Racial Equality 1982-88, *Paisner & Co* 1988-92. *Dibb Lupton Alsop* 1992 (London), promoted to Regional Managing Partner in North West from 1994 based in Manchester.
Personal: Born July 2nd 1953. Interests include classic cars (Armstrong Siddely Owners Club) and politics (Lib PPC 1987 General election).

NICKSON, Sue
Hammond Suddards, Manchester
(0161) 830 5000
Partner in charge of Manchester Employment Unit of eleven specialist employment lawyers and joint head of the National Employment Unit.
Specialisation: Handles the full ambit of contentious and non-contentious employment law issues ranging from public to the private sector, including acting for retail, manufacturing

and construction companies. Also handles NHS Trust work. Particular speciality is advice in relation to the Transfer of Undertakings regulations. Has contributed to various journals, and lectures frequently.
Prof. Memberships: Law Society, Employment Lawyers Association, Member of Salford University Council.
Career: Qualified in 1988. Worked at *Pannone & Partners* 1986-94, as a Partner from 1991 and as Head of Employment Department from 1992. Joined *Hammond Suddards* as a Partner in 1994.
Personal: Born 1st January 1964. Holds a First Class Honours Degree from Caius College, Cambridge 1982-85, with a TAPP postgraduate scholarship. Associate Member of Institute of Linguists. Leisure interests include motor bike riding, ballroom dancing, theatre and Manchester United.

NORBURY, Peter
Eversheds, Manchester (0161) 832 6666
Head of Employment for Leeds and Manchester.
Specialisation: Experienced advocate before Industrial Tribunals throughout the UK and Employment Appeal Tribunal, together with representation at Joint Industries Board hearings. Particular expertise in executive terminations, TUPE and discrimination. Key work on collective issues including de-recognition. Regular speaker at seminars and conferences and contributor to publications. Reported cases include 'Stoker v. Lancashire County Council,' 'Monsanto v. TGWU,' 'Roevin, BP v. Gillick,' 'Akzo Coatings v. Thompson and others' and 'Rock Refrigeration -v- Seward.'
Prof. Memberships: Employment Lawyers Association, Industrial Law Society, RSA, EFSP Working Party.
Career: Qualified in 1978 and stayed with the firm before being made partner in 1984.
Personal: Born 12.1.53. Educated at Manchester Grammar School and Sheffield University. Interests include football, cricket and golf. Lives in Saddleworth.

PARKINSON, Helen L
Whittles, Manchester (0161) 228 2061
Specialisation: Specialises in all aspects of contentious employment law including advocacy at industrial tribunals and the Employment Appeal Tribunal, acting mainly for trade unions and employees.
Career: Qualified 1989. Joined *Whittles* in 1990 and became a partner in 1996.

PIKE, Malcolm J.
Addleshaw Booth & Co, Manchester
(0161) 934 6000
Partner & Head of Commercial Group.
Specialisation: Main areas of practice are employment and industrial relations. Includes drafting and advising on terms and conditions of employment, personnel policies and collective agreements, industrial relations and other trade union matters, discrimination and equal pay, defending and prosecuting High Court and industrial tribunal proceedings and advising on employment aspects of the sale and reorganisation of companies and businesses. Various publications include 'The Lawyers Factbook,' 'Essential Facts Employment' and 'Butterworths Encyclopaedia of Forms and Precedents' and 'Workplace Discrimination.' Regular speaker at seminars and conferences. Acted in 'Doughty v. Rolls

Royce Plc' (1992), 'Micklefield v. SAC Technology Ltd' (1990) , 'Alliance Paper Group plc v. Prestwich' (1995), and Qureshi v. Victoria University of Manchester (1997).
Prof. Memberships: Law Society, Employment Lawyers Association, Industrial Law Society, Manchester Industrial Relations Society, IBA, ABA.
Career: Qualified in 1984 with *Hepworth & Chadwick* in Leeds. Moved to *Freshfields*, London in 1984. Left to join the firm in Manchester as a Partner in 1992.

Personal: Born 22nd August 1959. Attended Leicester University 1978-81. Leisure pursuits include golf. Lives in Wilmslow, Cheshire.

WATSON, Judith
Cobbetts, Manchester (0161) 833 3333
Specialisation: Partner and head of Employment Law Team. Specialist interest in discrimination issues and acts as a regular media spokesperson for the firm on all issues concerning human resources and employment.
Prof. Memberships: Committee Member and

firm's representative of the European Law network, Eurolegal. Member of the Employment Lawyers Association.
Career: Educated at Sheffield High School for Girls and Sheffield University (1981-4). Articled with *Leak Almond & Parkinson* which subsequently became *Cobbett Leak Almond* and then *Cobbetts*. Qualified in 1987. Became a Partner in January 1997.
Personal: Born 31 January 1963. Leisure interests include swimming and travel. Lives in Timperley, Cheshire.

NORTH EAST

LEADING FIRMS • NORTH EAST

PINSENT CURTIS Leeds

ADDLESHAW BOOTH & CO Leeds
DIBB LUPTON ALSOP Leeds / Sheffield
HAMMOND SUDDARDS Leeds
SHORT RICHARDSON & FORTH Newcastle-upon-Tyne

DICKINSON DEES Newcastle-upon-Tyne
EVERSHEDS Newcastle upon Tyne
ROLLIT FARRELL & BLADON Hull
THOMPSONS Newcastle-upon-Tyne

HIGHLY REGARDED FIRMS

Ford & Warren Leeds
Jacksons Stockton-on-Tees
Nabarro Nathanson Sheffield
Read Hind Stewart Leeds
Walker Morris Leeds
Wansbroughs Willey Hargrave Sheffield

Bridge McFarland Grimsby
Gordons Wright & Wright Bradford
Irwin Mitchell Sheffield
Ward Hadaway Newcastle upon Tyne

Hay & Kilner Newcastle-upon-Tyne

Pinsent Curtis (3ptnrs/2assocs/6assts/ 1 technical support lawyer) "Definitely head of the queue" with a somewhat "academic" approach. Their "absolute star" is *John McMullen*, a bit of a "elusive figure" around Leeds since he spends much of his time in London. He is a national player in terms of TUPE and an "exceptional lawyer" who "raises the firm above the rest." *Chris Booth* is "a good mix." **Clients/Work:** Dealing with one of largest divestments from a utility involving a TUPE transfer for 2000 employees. Successfully defending TUPE related litigation involving 103 applicants in a multi-party industrial tribunal case. Number of high-profile discrimination law cases for police constabularies including successful defence of Williamson v North Yorkshire Police.
    Addleshaw Booth & Co (2ptnrs/11assts in Leeds and Manchester) The merger has made the combined practice more high-pro-

file. Some thought they "had a slight edge over the others in their band in the table." However Tom Flanagan, former leader, moved to Stephenson Harwood in July and has been replaced by *Colin Tweedie,* formerly of Mills & Reeve. **Clients/Work:** Preston v Wolverhampton BC/Fletcher v Midland Bank. Acted for Midland, representing the whole of the UK banking sector in this part-timers case. Advising Banque Indosuez on their merger with Credit Agricole. Advising Leeds Community and Mental Health Care NHS Trust on the TUPE and other employment aspects of outsourcing its IT function – the first outsourcing of an IT function under PFI.
    Dibb Lupton Alsop (2ptnrs/4assts in Leeds;1ptnrs/4assts in Sheffield) "Competent large commercial practice"with an aggressive approach. Thought to be stronger in Sheffield where *David Bradley* is particularly recommended ("good at talking his way out of a paper bag.") The "first class" *David Hill* heads the Leeds team. **Clients/Work:** Defending over 300 IT claims arising from national bargaining arrangement in woodworking sector of construction industry. EAT/ IT cases relating to correct conduct of employer with national implications for supported placement scheme facilitating employment opportunities for disabled persons.
    Hammond Suddards (2ptnrs/5assts) "Competent team" with a "tough" style. Good for clients who prefer "a bombastic approach." *Tim Russell* ("assertive") and "confident and clever"*Mark Shrives* lead the team. **Clients/Work:** European business of Crown inc, after instructed by Carnaud Metalbox. Advised employment contract changes following company reorganisations for several companies involving over 15,000 staff, including a brand name clothing manufacturer and a major public school. Instructed in a major TUPE high court case for IDI involving 400 employees.
    Short Richardson & Forth (2ptnrs/ 2assts – 1 pt/t) Have a "long-standing reputation." The well-respected *Michael Short* is a "frequent advocate." He makes a good team with the "capable" new partner *Sharon Langridge* who is "building up a good reputation in the North East." **Clients/Work:**

LEADING INDIVIDUALS
NORTH EAST

MCMULLEN John Pinsent Curtis

BOOTH Christopher Pinsent Curtis
CROSS Stefan Thompsons
GORAJ Ann Wansbroughs Willey Hargrave
MOLYNEUX Pauline Rollit Farrell & Bladon
RUSSELL Timothy Hammond Suddards
SHORT Michael Short Richardson & Forth
TWEEDIE Colin Addleshaw Booth & Co

BRADLEY David Dibb Lupton Alsop
BRIDGE John Bridge McFarland
DRAKE Ronald Read Hind Stewart
FLETCHER Kevin Jacksons
HEARN Keith Ford & Warren
HILL David Dibb Lupton Alsop
PUGH Keith Nabarro Nathanson
SHRIVES Mark Hammond Suddards

UP AND COMING

LANGRIDGE Sharon Short Richardson & Forth
PREST Catherine Eversheds

SEE PROFILES AT END OF THIS SECTION

Employment advice to Greggs plc, Nissan Motor Manufacturing (UK) Limited and North Tyneside College.
    Dickinson Dees (2ptnrs/1assoc/2assts) Have an "enviable client base"and do "quality employment work." **Clients/Work:** TUPE advice in relation to PFI project at Carlisle Hospital; advising an NHS Trust on defending over 200 equal pay claim applications; advising an Arriva subsidiary on its appeal to House of Lords on compensation for dismissal following industrial action.
    Eversheds (1ptnr/9assts/1const selling training services) Strong in Newcastle and seen as aggressive litigators although they have "lost ground historically and will take time to develop." *Catherine Prest* is able. **Clients/Work:** Dealing with substantial multi-site redundancies for Readicut Plc involving in excess of 300 redundancies. Acting for Trust Motor Group Plc in relation to departing executives and sale of Wallace Arnold Travel Company. EAT Appeal on variation of terms and conditions post outsourcing of nursing homes.
    Rollitt Farrell & Bladon (3ptnrs/ 2assocs) A small practice which is "*the* firm on Humberside." The "assertive"*Pauline*

Molyneux is "impressive"and particularly knowledgeable on TUPE. **Clients/Work:** Emphasis on race, sex and disability discrimination.

Thompsons (2ptnrs/ assts) *Stefan Cross* is "a doughty fighter, highly competent on the collective side"who "does lots of innovative litigation."

Ford & Warren (2ptnrs/3assts) The well thought of *Keith Hearn*, who is Managing Partner, heads the team, which handles all its own advocacy work as well as providing management training to clients including NHS Trusts and bus operators. **Clients/ Work:** Hundreds of Equal Pay claims for United Leeds Teaching Hospitals NHS Trust. Also act for Travel West Midlands and National Blood Authority.

Jacksons (2ptnrs/1assoc/1asst) Biggest firm on Teesside. *Kevin Fletcher* is "good and held in high regard." **Clients/Work:** Acted for British Bakeries Ltd in multi-applicant cases involving changes to terms and conditions. First application under the Disability Discrimination Act received by British Steel plc. Won eight day case under the Sex Discrimination Act for the Environment Agency.

Nabarro Nathanson (2ptnrs/4assts) Members of the team also do pensions work. Advise on TUPE, industrial disputes, outsourcing and insourcing as well as all contentious matters. *Keith Pugh* heads the team. **Clients/Work:** Acting for British Fuels Limited in Meade and Another v British

Fuels Limited, decision appealed to House of Lords. Acting for The Football Association in sex discrimination claim brought by female football coach, appealed to EAT.

Read Hind Stewart (2ptnrs/2assts) *Ron Drake* is a part-time IT Chair. **Clients/Work:** Janciuk v Winerite Limited [1998]. Appearance on Channel 4 documentary "Cutting Edge"on sexual harrassment.

Walker Morris (1ptnr/3assts) **Clients/ Work:** G M Goodwill v Mountleigh Group plc(in administrative receivership and liquidation) – "Paramount" claim. Hartgrove and others v Meridian Business Support and Proctor & Gamble – TUPE and agency issues.

Wansbroughs Willey Hargrave (1ptnr/2assocs/1asst) The main reputation of the practice is founded on its health sector respondents work. *Ann Goraj* is head of the firm's national employment unit and a part-time IT Chair; she has a "powerful intellect" and is "well to the fore" in this region. **Clients/Work:** Representing applicant in high profile sexual orientation discrimination claim against MoD currently pending application to European Court of Human Rights. Successfully guiding NHS Trust through major restructuring of terms and conditions, avoiding any IT claims.

Bridge McFarland (1ptnr; 2assts pt/t) *John Bridge* specialises in the Grimsby office and another solicitor spends 15% of his time on employment matters in the Lincoln office. Practice has developed as an off-shoot to its

historical practice of acting for plaintiffs involved in accidents at sea. **Clients/Work:** 70% of work is for applicants; act for local trade unions.

Gordons Wright & Wright (1ptnr/1asst pt/t) Head of employment is a part-time IT Chair; the team is "very good." **Clients/ Work:** Include Wm Morrison Supermarkets Plc, JCT 600 Limited, Pace Micro Technology Plc. Mass changes to terms and conditions of employment for an acute hospital NHS Trust. Successfully seen off industrial action for an educational institution.

Irwin Mitchell (3ptnrs/1cons/3assts) Act for both applicants and respondents. **Clients/Work:** Investigating fraudulent employee activities involving dealings between client and customer. Dealing with suspension of Regi Blinker by UEFA for Sheffield Wednesday plc.

Ward Hadaway (1ptnr/1assoc/1asst) New associate recruited this year. Act predominantly for respondents. **Clients/Work:** Multi-party claim defending respondent involving 120 tribunal applications. Acting on behalf of respondent in defending equal pay claims.

Hay & Kilner (2ptnrs/1cons/1ass) Acting for applicants and respondents across the full range of employment issues. **Clients/ Work:** Negotiating terms of executive termination and acting for independent school in race discrimination case taken up by Commission for Racial Equality.

LEADERS' PROFILES · NORTH EAST

BOOTH, Christopher
Pinsent Curtis, Leeds (0113) 244 5000
Specialisation: Specialises in employment law dealing with high-profile executive terminations, restrictive covenants and discrimination cases.
Prof. Memberships: Management Committee of Employment Lawyers Association (ELA) as North East representative (including membership of European Working Party). Leeds Law Society.
Career: Educated at Hull University (LLB 1984). Joined former *Simpson Curtis* in 1987 on qualification. Partner 1993.
Personal: Born 1963. Leisure interests: golf, skiing, cooking, family and personal computer.

BRADLEY, David John
Dibb Lupton Alsop, Sheffield (0345) 262728
Specialisation: All areas of Employment Law, primarily on behalf of employers with particular experience in Senior Executive disputes. Transfers of Undertakings, managing change through contract variation, redundancy programmes and discrimination matters. A regular advocate in Industrial Tribunals and co-author of the annual Industrial Relations Survey. David has been involved in a number of high profile matters involving variations to working terms and conditions and strategic redundancy programmes including negotiating with Trade Unions alongside the senior management teams.
Prof. Memberships: Law Society; CBI; Employment Lawyers Association.

Career: National Head of the Human Resources Group at *Dibb Lupton Alsop*. Articled with *Broomheads* (predecessor firm of *Dibb Lupton Alsop*). Former President of T.S.G. (Sheffield). Nottingham University. South East Essex Sixth Form College, Greensward School Essex.
Personal: Mainly sport – Rugby Union and golf. Married with two sons.

BRIDGE, John
Bridge McFarland Solicitors, Grimsby (01472) 311711

CROSS, Stefan
Thompsons, Newcastle-upon-Tyne (0191) 261 5341
Regional Co-ordinator for Thompsons Employment Rights Unit.
Specialisation: Covers all aspects of employment law for Trade Unions and their members, in particular TUPE, Collective Consultation Rights, Discrimination, Equal Pay and Industrial Action. Regular speaker at conferences, seminars and TUC courses.
Prof. Memberships: Regional Industrial Tribunal Users Group. Society of Labour Lawyers.
Career: Qualified 1985. *Brian Thompson & Partners* 1986. Partner 1989. *Thompsons* 1996 Partner.
Personal: Born 5th October 1960; LL.B

Southampton University 1982; LL.M (Law and Employment Relations) Leicester University 1990; Newcastle City Councillor 1990 to 1998; Newcastle United Platinum Club Member.

DRAKE, Ronald S.
Read Hind Stewart, Leeds (0113) 246 8123
Specialisation: Unfair/Wrongful dismissal, redundancy, equal pay, discrimination and harrasment industrial action., TUPE transfer and contracting out. Involved as lead Solicitor in 'Tanks & Drums v T & GWU,' 'Kelman v Care,' 'Jancuik v Winerite,' and the Staffordshire Legionnaires' Disease Public Inquiry.
Prof. Memberships: Associate of the Chartered Institute of Arbitrators, Affiliate of the Institute of Personnel & Development, Member of the Employment Lawyers Association, Industrial Law Society, Competition Law Association and The British-Nordic Lawyers Association.
Career: Bradford GS, Manchester University and Chester College of Law. Articles to J Aucott at *Edge & Ellison*; Birmingham. Partner *Last Suddards* (later *Hammond Suddards*) 1981-1990. Partner *Read Hind Stewart* 1990 to date. Part-time Chairman of Industrial Tribunals (Newcastle Region) 1997.
Personal: Married to ex-Solicitor Teacher, two children. Interests in Choral singing and classical music. Scandinavian Culture and Music. Director of Yorkshire & Humberside Business in The Arts.

FLETCHER, Kevin J.
Jacksons, Stockton-on-Tees (01642) 643643
Senior Partner and head of Company /
Commercial Department.
Specialisation: Principal area of practice is
employment law advising and representing
mainly employers in all aspects, both
contentious and non-contentious. Advocates in
tribunals throughout the country. Also handles
company/commercial work and commercial
litigation. Major clients include British Steel Plc,
British Bakeries Ltd, Black and Decker and the
National Farmers Union. Part-time chairman of
Industrial Tribunals in 1991. Regularly gives
seminars to clients, local professional bodies
and employers' associations.
Prof. Memberships: Law Society and
Employment Lawyers' Association.
Career: Qualified in 1971. Appointed a Partner
at *Jacksons* in 1972. Became Senior Partner in
1995.
Personal: Born 6th March 1947. Educated at
Hull Grammar School 1958-65; St Catharine's
College, Cambridge 1965-68 and The College
of Law, Guildford 1968-69. Leisure interests
include music, sport, art, reading and travel.
Lives in Middlesbrough.

GORAJ, Ann
Wansbroughs Willey Hargrave, Sheffield
(0114) 272 7485
Head of Employment.
Specialisation: Acts for both public and private
sector clients, particularly health trusts and
authorities. Has specialist experience of
employment law affecting the health service
including Whitley Council provisions, medical
disciplinary issues, and local terms and
conditions. Work includes complex race and
sex discrimination cases, drafting contracts,
restructuring working arrangements and
advising on TUPE. She is a regular contributor
to NHS Personnel and a part time Industrial
Tribunal Chairman.
Career: 1982 Qualified; 1990 joined *Oxley &
Coward*, Sheffield; 1995 transferred to
Wansbroughs Willey Hargrave, Sheffield.

HEARN, Keith
Ford & Warren, Leeds (0113) 243 6601
Managing Partner and Head of Employment
Law.
Specialisation: Experienced since 1973 in all
aspects of employment law. Acted as labour
relations adviser on construction of Sullom Voe
Oil Terminal and other major projects. Deals
with competition issues arising out of human
resources matters. Extensive experience in full
range of applications before Industrial Tribunals
including sex and race discrimination. Regularly
appears before the Employment Appeal
Tribunal. Extensive experience involving
management training. Received degree of
Master of Laws in European Management and
Labour Law in 1995, the subject matter of the
dissertation being Fair Competition in the Road
Haulage industry. Works closely with his fellow
specialists in transport and now leads the multi
national group claiming damages in respect of
the 1996 French Lorry Drivers Blockade. Has
handled high profile cases including of late
whistle blowing in the public health service.
Principal clients including PSV and HGV
operators and hospital trusts and other public
health bodies. Editor of Commercial Motor
Employment Bulletin sponsored by DAF.
Speaker at 1997 Malta Conference of Road

Haulage Association on Competition in Europe
in the Road Transport Industry.
Prof. Memberships: Industrial Law Society.
Career: Joined *Ford & Warren* in 1974. Became
Partner in 1976. Became Managing Partner in
1989. Leeds University LL.B 1966-70. Leicester
University LL.M 1995.
Personal: Leisure interests include scuba
diving instructor and racing cars.

HILL, David G.
Dibb Lupton Alsop, Leeds (0345) 262728
Partner and Head of Employment Department,
Leeds.
Specialisation: Deals with all aspects of
employment law for private and public sector
clients. Specialises in business transfers,
employment contracts, policies and
procedures, contract variation, restrictive
covenants and handling redundancies.
Experienced advocate in the Industrial Tribunals.
Prof. Memberships: Member of the
Employment Lawyers Association. Part-time
lecturer on Employment Law, Bradford
University.
Career: Qualified 1978. Partner since 1982.
Personal: Born 1954. Educated at Worcester
College, Oxford.

LANGRIDGE, Sharon E.
Short Richardson & Forth, Newcastle upon
Tyne (0191) 232 0283
Specialisation: Has a number of years'
experience in employment law, acting for both
Respondents and Applicants. Deals with all
areas including contracts, reorganisations,
TUPE, and a full range of Tribunal claims.
Conducts own advocacy in Tribunals locally and
nationally, including complex multi-day
hearings. Particular interest in sex
descrimination and maternity cases, and dealt
with 30 pregnancy dismissal claims against the
Armed Forces in 1994. Presents seminars to
clients and also TV/radio/press involvement.
Prof. Memberships: Employment Lawyers
Association, Industrial Law Society, active in the
Association of Women Solicitors (including
advice for the maternity helpline), Industrial
Tribunal Users' Committee.
Career: BA (Hons) German and French,
London University (1984). Joined *Baker and
McKenzie*, London after graduating. Diploma in
Industrial Relations, PCL (University of
Westminster) (1988). Admitted 1994 after
completing legal qualifications while at *Latimer
Hinks*, Darlington. Joined *Short Richardson &
Forth* in October 1995, becoming a partner in
March 1997.
Personal: Married and lives in Newcastle upon
Tyne. Interests include books, music, hill-
walking and cycling.

MCMULLEN, John
Pinsent Curtis, Leeds (0113) 244 5000
Partner and National Head of Employment
Department, based in Leeds
Specialisation: Acts for a wide range of
household name plcs, national and
multinational, universities and public sector
organisations. Leading authority on transfer of
undertakings. Expert on European Works
Councils. Part-time Professor of Labour Law at
University of Leeds. Author "Business Transfers
and Employee Rights," "Butterworths
Employment Law Guide," "Aspects of
Employment Law," "Acquired Rights of
Employees," "Tolley's Employment Law" (Joint),

"Redundancy: The Law and Practice,"
"Jordans/IP2 Employment Law Service."
Contributes widely to legal journals such as
Modern Law Review, Industrial Law Journal,
Company Lawyer, Civil Justice Quarterly, New
Law Journal and Cambridge Law Journal. Also
contributes to human resources and business
journals such as PLC, People Management and
Personnel Today.
Prof. Memberships: FIPD. FRSA. Founder
member Law Society's Employment Law
Committee. Industrial Law Society Executive
Committee, International Bar Association,
Associate Fellow, Society for Advanced Legal
Studies.
Career: Qualified in 1978. With *Rotheras* 1978-
80. Fellow in Law at Girton College, Cambridge
1980-86. Bye Fellow since 1986. Partner,
Rotheras 1986-91. Partner and Head of
Employment, *Simpson Curtis* 1991. National
Head of Employment, *Pinsent Curtis* 1995.
Personal: Born 1954. Educated Emmanuel
College, Cambridge (BA 1975, double 1st Class
(Hons), MA 1979, PhD 1993).

MOLYNEUX, Pauline
Rollit Farrell & Bladon, Hull (01482) 323239
Partner in Commercial Department.
Specialisation: Head of Employment Law Unit.
Covers all aspects, contentious and non-
contentious, including boardroom disputes and
negotiation of severerance arrangements,
review and drafting of documentation,
advocacy before Tribunals, the conduct of High
Court cases and advising on employment
consequences of commercial sales,
specialising in matters involving TUPE. Has
been involved in a variety of Tribunal cases
including sex, race and disability discrimination
claims and equal pay claims; cases involving
the application of the Transfer of Undertakings
Regulations and cases involving injunctions to
enforce post-termination employment
restrictions. Author of articles in various law
journals.
Prof. Memberships: Employment Lawyers
Association, Industrial Law Society, Law Society.
Career: Qualified in 1977. *Clifford Turner* 1977-
79, *Field Fisher and Martineau* 1979-84. Senior
lecturer at the College of Law, Lancaster Gate,
1984-86; *Clifford Chance* 1986-89. Joined *Rollit
Farrell & Bladon* as a Partner in 1989. Part-time
Chairman of Industrial Tribunals (appointed 1995).

PREST, Catherine
Eversheds, Leeds (0113) 243 0391
Specialisation: Advises on all areas of
contentious and non-contentious employment
work. Particular experience in discrimination
law, strategic employment advice and transfer
of undertakings.
Prof. Memberships: Employment Law
Association, Governor Leeds College of Building.
West Riding Oxford and Cambridge Club.
Career: Qualified as Barrister in 1988. Former
In-House Lawyer with Alliance and Leicester
Building Society. Joined *Eversheds* in 1993,
became a Partner in May 1997.
Personal: Born 22nd May 1966. Educated
Notre Dame High School Leeds, St Hilda's
College Oxford University.

PUGH, Keith
Nabarro Nathanson, Sheffield
(0114) 279 4000
Specialisation: Employment law specialist for
15 years dealing with both contentious and non-

contentious issues ranging from drafting employment contracts policies and procedures; Tribunal claims; restrictive covenants and garden leave; trade union recognition and collective issues; industrial action and transfer of undertaking. Instructed by BFL in BFL v. Meade (House of Lords).

Prof. Memberships: Law Society. Employment Lawyers Association. Industrial Law Society. **Career:** Admitted 1980. British Coal Legal Department 1980-1990. Joined *Nabarro Nathanson* as a partner in 1990. Head of Employment Department. **Personal:** Music, food, wine and gardening.

RUSSELL, Timothy
Hammond Suddards, Leeds
(0113) 284 7000
Partner in Employment Unit.
Specialisation: Specialises in employment law. Head of Employment Law Unit. Has handled many major transfer of undertakings and sex discrimination cases. An advocate for over 200 industrial tribunal cases. Contributor to many publications and journals, including 'Personnel Today,' 'Modern Management,' 'Lloyd's List,' 'The Estates Gazette' and the Law Society's 'Gazette.' Speaker for the Industrial Society and lecturer for Commerce and Industry Group. Regularly speaks at seminars and has made radio and television appearances. Practical approach based on in-house commercial experience.
Prof. Memberships: Law Society, Employment Lawyers Association, CBI Employee Relations Panel, Industrial Law Society, Local Chamber of Commerce.
Career: Worked with *Wilde Sapte* 1982-86. Qualified in 1985 and was Ciba Geigy's legal

adviser 1986-87. Senior legal adviser at Lloyds Bank 1987-91. Joined *Hammond Suddards* in 1991 and became a Partner in 1992.
Personal: Born 17th June 1960. Educated at Pocklington School and Cambridge University. Enjoys all sports. Lives in Leeds.

SHORT, Michael C.
Short Richardson & Forth, Newcastle upon Tyne (0191) 232 0283
Founder Partner in Employment Law Department.
Specialisation: Has twenty-five years' experience in employment law, acting on both sides of industry and dealing with the full range of employment law matters including appearing before Industrial Tribunals regularly throughout the country and lecturing regularly on employment law matters to Companies.
Prof. Memberships: Member of the Law Society's Employment Law Committee, Employment Lawyers Association, and Industrial Law Society.
Career: Qualified in 1967. Senior Partner and founding Partner of *Short Richardson & Forth* since 1978.
Personal: Born 20th April 1943. Attended Durham University LLB (Hons) 1964. Leisure interests include theatre. Lives in Newcastle-upon-Tyne.

SHRIVES, Mark
Hammond Suddards, Leeds
(0113) 284 7000
Specialisation: Partner – employment unit. Specialising in all aspects of contentious and non-contentious employment and discrimination law acting predominately for multi-national and large corporate clients and

senior executives. Conducts all own advocacy before industrial relations and employment appeal tribunal. Also handles work permit and other employment-related immigration issues. Speaks regularly on a wide-range of employment issues.
Prof. Memberships: Law Society. Local Chamber of Commerce. Employment Lawyers Association.
Career: Articled at *McKenna & Co.* Qualified 1990. *Eversheds* (Manchester) 1990-1992. *Hammond Suddards* 1992 onwards. Partner 1995.
Personal: Born 13 April 1964. Educated Downing College, Cambridge, BA (Hons) 1986. LLM (1st Class honours) 1987. Law Society Finals (1st Class honours) 1988. Resides in Calderdale. Interests include gardening, DIY, music & cinema.

TWEEDIE, Colin
Addleshaw Booth & Co, Leeds
(0113) 209 2000
Partner in Employment Law Department.
Specialisation: Has specialised exclusively in employment law since qualification. Deals with all aspects, mainly for employers, including appearing before industrial tribunals throughout the country. Conducts in-house seminars for clients, lectures and has appeared on local radio. Author of occasional articles.
Prof. Memberships: Employment Lawyers Association.
Career: Qualified in 1978. With *McKenna & Co* 1976-83. Moved to *Mills & Reeve* in 1983 and became a Partner in 1985.
Personal: Born 29th June 1953. Educated at Grangemouth High School 1965-68, Doncaster Grammar School 1968-71 and Fitzwilliam College, Cambridge 1972-75. Leisure interests include sports, railways and Scottish history. Lives in Norwich.

SCOTLAND

Mackay Simon (2ptnrs/5assts/1const/1 policy and practice advisor) The firm have carved a niche and fill it well." A young practice headed by the "dynamic" *Malcolm Mackay* who is widely recognised as a "leading light on TUPE issues," "God of employment law in Scotland, he makes no song and dance about it, but his feel for a case is extremely good." There is felt to be a good balance between him and his partner *Shona Simon* who "is strong on discrimination." Generally they are "reasonable, easy to deal with and don't take silly points."

MacRoberts (2ptnrs/3assts) The firm has a "considerable reputation" as a "big tough well-resourced traditional firm" which is recognised as having a "top notch" employment department. However there is some perception that the firm's "star has fallen" and that *Raymond Williamson* does not have an heir apparent. He is "particularly strong on TUPE and a leading light in the Industrial Law Society." He is seen to fit in well with the more traditional client. **Clients/Work:** Acting for Tate & Lyle in an unfair dismissal case; British Aerospace in an important redundancy exercise; involved in the re-

organisation and rationalisation of Local Authorities and FE Colleges.

Burnside Kemp Fraser (3ptnrs/3assts) A small Aberdeen practice specialising in employment aspects of the oil industry. *David Burnside* is recommended as is *Sandy Kemp* ("good solid pair of hands.") **Clients/Work:** Involved in complicated employment matters principally in oil industry and educational field.

Dundas & Wilson CS (2ptnrs/3assts) Good for clients who want employment as part of a package. "Nice people, easy to deal with." *Euan MacLeod* is recommended as an employment lawyer on the commercial side. They are growing their employment department; a lawyer has been brought in to set up the Human Capital Services Group, a "one-stop shop" incorporating employee benefits and pensions. **Clients/Work:** Advised Pringle of Scotland Ltd on Court of Sessions proceedings about redundancy selection procedures. Advised on a $75m disposal of shares from McQueen International to Sykes Entertainment Incorporated. Advised on the acquisition of Grampian TV by the Scottish Media Group.

Harper MacLeod (2ptnrs ;1assoc p/t; 2assts) "On the map in Glasgow." "Particularly recognised for applicants work." Well-established, quite aggressive. *Rod McKenzie* is "flamboyant and robust." **Clients/Work:** Advising GA Construction in the harmonisation of terms and conditions of employment throughout the UK with Kyle Stewart and Higgs & Hill. Advising and representing clients in the longest running Industrial Tribunal case in Scotland.

McGrigor Donald (3ptnrs/2assocs/ 3assts do 55%) Big firm, they "do everything." Known for "bright people." Team includes *James Young, Craig Connal* and the newly recommended *David Walker.* **Clients/Work:** Acting on employment status of casual workers in newspaper industry. Acting for McDonalds Restaurants Limited in complaint by transsexual of discrimination on grounds of sex. Dealing with first tribunal to take evidence by way of video conferencing from witness in Australia (for Clydesdale Bank).

Paull & Williamsons (3ptnrs – 2p/t; 3assts p/t) Perceived by many to have been very tied up in the Piper Alpha litigation to the detriment of their employment work but they are now seriously building it up again. *James Tierney* is not primarily employment. The "clever" *Sean Saluja* is newly recommended.

Brodies WS (3ptnrs/1cons/2assts) A traditional "classy practice with many landed clients." The team is known for its sensible approach. *David Williamson* is a Part-time Chair, so his role is diminished and he now does mainly advice work. *Joyce Cullen* has been highly recommended for "taking a realistic practical approach," and has improved the firm's ranking in the tables. **Clients/Work:** Acting in Union-backed case involving 73 applicants arising from plant closure. US company Sykes purchased McQueens of Scotland, advised on employment aspects. Negotiated Senior Executive contracts.

Kidstons & Co (2ptnrs/1asst) *Iain Atack* has a good reputation.

Maclay Murray & Spens (1ptnr/ 3assocs) Have offices in Glasgow and Edinburgh. The practice in the east is slanted towards severance negotiations for employers and employees: that in the west towards advising industrial companies. **Clients/Work:** Advising Robert Wiseman Dairies plc in their acquisition of parts of fresh milk business of Scottish Pride.Advising on TUPE implications of dissolution of Scottish Film Council and setting up of Scottish Screen. Advising Scottish Amicable on employment issues arising from deal with Prudential.

McClure Naismith (2ptnrs/5assts) In this large commercial firm the employment practice in Glasgow and Edinburgh principally advises employers. **Clients/Work:** Acting in a series of cases before Industrial Tribunal for National Semiconductor (UK) Ltd relating to variation of terms and conditions. Acting for a group of directors handling claims in receivership of Scottish Pride Ltd. Advising the Post Office on industrial action.

Raeburn Christie & Co (2ptnrs/2assts) The "experienced"*Reginald Christie* heads the team in this Aberdeen firm.

Shepherd & Wedderburn WS (4ptnrs/ 9assts) Large commercial firm doing employment law as part of its full service to corporate clients. *Ian Macleod*, their Court partner, heads the team. **Clients/Work:** Advising SLC Turnbury Limited in the purchase of Nitto World Co Ltd owners of Turnbury Hotel, golf courses and spa. Advising Scottish Rugby Union on the contractual arrangements for the National Team and management. Advising BMA.

Simpson & Marwick WS (1ptnr/1asst) Known mainly for its reparation work. Advise on a range of employment law issues with particular interest in NHS-related and Public Authority work, acting primarily for respondents. *John Griffiths* does mainly commercial work. **Clients/Work:** Acting for large local authority in complex dispute with largest teacher's TU in Scotland, resulting in 94 IT applications, of which two test cases have so far been successful. Instructed by large passenger transport authority in TUPE problem, now settled. Acting for university in defending sex discrimination claim.

Thompsons (2ptnrs/2assts) One partner and one assistant in each of Edinburgh and Glasgow offices. Received many recommendations to go to the top of 'Highly Regarded' on their own.

Bishop & Robertson Chalmers (1ptnrs) Team is led by *David Whyte.*

Blackadder Reid Johnston (2ptnrs/ 1assts) A respondents' practice headed by *Sandy Meiklejohn.* **Clients/Work:** Act for employers in contentious and non-contentious matters.

Brechin Tindal Oatts (3ptnrs/2assts) Team includes *William Speirs*

Maxwell MacLaurin (1ptnr/1asst) Team includes *Alistair Cockburn.*

The Morton Fraser Partnership (4ptnrs/1asst) Does mainly respondent work, is "nice to deal with." *David Stewart* is Part-time Chairman. **Clients/Work:** Continuing employment advice for UKAEA, BP Chemicals Ltd and United Distillers.

ATACK, Iain F
Kidstons & Co, Glasgow (0141) 221 6551
Senior Partner.
Specialisation: Main area of practice is employment law: accredited as a specialist by the Law Society of Scotland. Advises mainly employers on all aspects of Employment law. Represents at Tribunals in Scotland and England. Also handles general civil litigation and factoring law. Advises on contractual disputes and claims for damages for personal injuries. Advises invoice factors on all commercial matters. Major clients include

several large Plc's operating both in England and Scotland, banks, financial institutions and many medium sized companies. Lectures at conferences. Formerly Tutor in Advocacy & Pleading at Glasgow University.
Prof. Memberships: Law Society of Scotland, Royal Faculty of Procurators in Glasgow, Industrial Law Group. Member Law Society of Scotland Employment Law Committee.
Career: Qualified in 1971. Joined *Kidstons & Company* in 1972, becoming a Partner in 1975 and Senior Partner in 1993. Council Member of Royal Faculty of Procurators 1989-92. Committee

Member of Industrial Law Group since 1984. Chairman of NHBC Appeal Tribunal since 1990.
Personal: Born 22nd November 1947. Attended Kelvinside Academy, Glasgow 1954-66, then St Andrew's University 1966-69. Leisure interests include walking and skiing. Lives in Killearn.

BURNSIDE, David
Burnside Kemp Fraser, Aberdeen
(01224) 624602
Senior Partner in Court Department.
Specialisation: Main area of practice is employment. Has handled industrial tribunal

cases since 1967 in the fields of redundancy, unfair dismissal, sexual and racial discrimination and Transfer of Undertakings. Acts for a number of major clients in these matters. Accredited by the Law Society of Scotland as an Employment Law Specialist. Also handles personal injury work. (Member of Personal Injury Panel.) Since 1970 has worked predominantly for claimants. Has substantial experience of offshore cases, although also deals with many cases involving injury at work or in road traffic accidents and medical negligence. Joint lead negotiator in Piper Alpha for claimants. Group spokesman for steering committees involving major helicopter crashes. Gives occasional lectures for Aberdeen University, the Law Society, IPM and other outside bodies. Has considerable media experience arising from matters of local and national interest.
Prof. Memberships: Law Society of Scotland, Society of Advocates in Aberdeen, Association of Personal Injury Lawyers, Aberdeen Bar Association, Employment Law Group, A.T.L.A.
Career: Qualified in 1966. Established *Messrs Burnside Advocates* as Senior Partner in 1989; firm became *Burnside Kemp Fraser* in 1994. President of Junior Chamber of Commerce, Aberdeen, 1978-79; President of Aberdeen Bar Association 1987-89; Board Member of Legal Defence Union since 1990; Scottish convenor and member of National Executive Committee of APIL 1990-1996. Treasurer of Employment Law Group.
Personal: Born 5th March 1943.

CHRISTIE, Reginald
Raeburn Christie & Co, Aberdeen
(01224) 640101
Partner specialising in employment law.
Specialisation: Full range of issues relating to all aspects of employment law.
Prof. Memberships: Law Society of Scotland, Industrial Law Group of Scotland.
Career: Qualified in 1971. Partner in *Raeburn Christie & Co.* 1975.

COCKBURN, Alistair
Maxwell MacLaurin, Glasgow
(0141) 332 5666
Partner in Litigation Department.
Specialisation: Main area of practice is employment law, primarily the representation of employers in relation to proceedings before industrial tribunals throughout the whole of the UK including representation before the Employment Appeal Tribunal. Also represents individual employees before tribunals in Scotland and to both in relation to the formation of service agreements and the implications at termination, particularly with regard to covenants. Also handles litigation generally.
Prof. Memberships: Law Society of Scotland, Royal Faculty of Procurators in Glasgow, Glasgow Bar Association.
Career: Qualified in 1972. Joined *Tilston MacLaurin* in 1970, becoming a Partner in 1974. Accredited as a Specialist in Employment Law by the Law Society of Scotland in 1992.
Personal: Born 8th March 1950. Attended High School of Glasgow 1961-67, then University of Glasgow 1967-70 (LLB). Member of Committee of Management of local Victim Support Group. Leisure interests include golf. Lives in Brookfield, Renfrewshire.

CONNAL, R. Craig
McGrigor Donald, Glasgow (0141) 248 6677
See under Planning, p. 653

CULLEN, Joyce
Brodies WS, Edinburgh (0131) 228 3777
Specialisation: Partner within Litigation Department's Employment Law Group providing a full range of advice to companies, institutions, partnerships and individuals, including a major Scottish Bank, national retailers, colleges, professional firms and clients in the industrial and manufacturing sectors. Specialises in employment contracts, change management policies, business transfers and redundancies. Extensive experience as an advocate in Industrial Tribunals, EAT and the Court of Session.
Prof. Memberships: Member of the Management Committee of the Employment Lawyers Association, Industrial Law Group, Institute of Directors.
Career: Qualified 1981. With *Brodies*, initially as an Assistant Solicitor and as a Partner since 1986. Management Board Member. Accredited Specialist in Employment Law and Solicitor Advocate with extended rights of audience in the Civil Courts.
Personal: Born 1958. Educated Leith Academy, Edinburgh and Dundee University. Married with three children. Interests include travel and politics.

GRIFFITHS, John
Simpson & Marwick WS, Edinburgh
(0131) 557 1545

KEMP, Sandy
Burnside Kemp Fraser, Aberdeen
(01224) 624602
Specialisation: Has specialised in employment law and personal injury claims throughout career. Accredited as an Employment Law Specialist by the Law Society of Scotland and member of Assessment Committee for Personal Injury Panel. Advises employers and individuals on all aspects of employment law, particularly in relation to offshore oil industry. Has lectured for Law Society and others on employment law, negotiation and on personal injury claims, both generally and arising from offshore industry.
Prof. Memberships: Law Society of Scotland, Employment Law Group, Association of Personal Injury Lawyers, Association of Trial Lawyers of America.
Career: Qualified 1983. Partner at *Philip and Kemp* 1986. Joined *Burnside* 1994 and established *Burnside Kemp Fraser*.
Personal: Born 8 February 1959.

LEFEVRE, Frank Hartley
Lefevre Litigation, Aberdeen (01224) 208208
See under Personal Injury; Mainly Plaintiff, p. 637

MACKAY, Malcolm
Mackay Simon, Edinburgh (0131) 240 1400
Partner.
Specialisation: Practises only in the field of employment law. Co-author of 'Employment Law Update' in the Journal of the Law Society of Scotland; Co-editor of Greens Employment Law Bulletin. Lectures in employment law at various universities. Particular interests – Industrial Relations, Transfer of Undertakings and Discrimination.
Prof. Memberships: Society to Writers of HM Signet; Member of Institute of Personnel and Development. Law Society of Scotland Employment Law Committee.
Career: Qualified in 1975. Founded *Mackay WS* now *Mackay Simon* in 1988.
Personal: Born 24th January 1953. Attended Edinburgh University. Lives in Edinburgh.

MACLEOD, D. Ian K.
Shepherd & Wedderburn WS, Edinburgh
(0131) 228 9900
See under Litigation (Commercial): 200+ Solicitors, p. 534

MACLEOD, Euan
Dundas & Wilson CS, Edinburgh
(0131) 228 8000
Specialisation: Partner in Human Capital Services. Active in employment aspects of business sales and acquisitions, outsourcing, re-organisation of all types of business including variation of terms and conditions of employment and senior executive service contracts and severance terms. Regularly appears before Industrial Tribunals and the Employment Appeal Tribunal. Employment clients include City Centre Restaurants plc, Dawson International plc, Drake & Scull Engineering Limited, GEC-Marconi Avionics Limited, Hewlett-Packard Limited, Rank Hovis McDougall plc, Scottish Media Group plc, Scottish Widows Fund & Life Assurance Society and Zeneca Limited. Advisor on issues of possible defamation and contempt of court. Has lectured at seminars on defamation.
Prof. Memberships: Law Society of Scotland, Society of Writers to H.M. Signet, Scottish Law Agents Society, Scottish Media Lawyers Society; accredited by the Law Society of Scotland as an Employment Law Specialist; member of Employment Lawyers Association.
Career: Attended University of Edinburgh (LLB). Qualified at *Davidson & Syme WS* 1967; Partner *Dundas & Wilson CS* since 1972; responsible for *Dundas & Wilson CS* Information Notes on Employment Issues; Conference Speaker at IBC Conferences on Transfer of Undertakings, 1994 and 1996; Keynote Conferences on Employment Law for G.Ps 1998.
Personal: Leisure interests include theatre, sport, reading and walking. Has also been recommended as a Leader in the Field of Defamation.

MCKENZIE, Rod
Harper Macleod, Glasgow (0141) 221 8888
Specialisation: Lead partner in the Litigation Department specialising in employment law. Undertakes work for major public companies, local authorities, Trades Unions, and the Equal Opportunities Commission. Law Society of Scotland accredited specialist in employment law. Regularly lectures and writes on the subject. Also specialises in planning and environmental law, construction law and mining and mineral law.
Prof. Memberships: Law Society of Scotland; Industrial Law Group.
Career: Qualified 1982. Assistant solicitor, *Harper Macleod* 1982-84. Partner since 1984.
Personal: Educated at High School of Stirling 1970-76, Strathclyde University 1976-79, and Stirling University 1979-80. Leisure pursuits include golf and gardening. Born 1st July 1958. Lives in Uddington, Lanarkshire.

MEIKLEJOHN, Sandy
Blackadder Reid Johnston, Dundee
(01382) 229222
Partner in Commercial Department.
Specialisation: Main area of practice is
employment law. Appeared regularly before
industrial tribunals from 1975 until appointed as
part-time Chairman in 1993; Advises a wide
range of employers and individual employees
on employment law matters. Accredited as an
employment law specialist by the Law Society of
Scotland.
Prof. Memberships: Law Society of Scotland.
Career: Qualified in 1973. Joined *Blackadder
Reid Johnston* in 1973, becoming a Partner in
1978. Appointed as part-time Chairman of
Industrial Tribunals in 1993. Tutor in Department
of Legal Practice at Dundee University since
1984.
Personal: Born 9th February 1951. Attended
High School of Dundee 1956-69, then
Edinburgh University 1969-73. Leisure interests
include skiing and golf. Lives in Dundee.

SALUJA, Sean A.
Paull & Williamsons, Aberdeen
(01224) 621621

SIMON, Shona M.W.
Mackay Simon, Edinburgh (0131) 240 1400
Specialisation: Practises only in the field of
employment law. Co-author of 'Employment
Law Update' in the Journal of the Law Society of
Scotland; Co-editor of Greens Employment Law
Bulletin. Lectures in employment law at various
Universities. Particular interests – Discrimination
and Maternity. Currently acting for the appellant
in 'Brown v Rentokill' which has been referred
by the House of Lords to the European Court of
Justice.
Prof. Memberships: Member of Institute of
Careers Guidance.
Career: MA (Hons) English Literature and
English Language – 1983. Diploma in Careers
Guidance – 1984. LLB (Dist) – 1990. Diploma in
Legal Practice – 1991; Qualified 1993; worked
for a number of years as careers adviser with
special responsibility for advising on equal
opportunities issues; traineeship with *Mackay
WE* (now *Mackay Simon*).
Personal: Born 1960, resides Edinburgh.

SPEIRS, William Stewart Colin
Brechin Tindal Oatts, Glasgow
(0141) 221 8012
Specialisation: Accredited as Employment
Specialist by Law Society of Scotland since
1990. Specialist areas: Transfer of
Undertakings, Redundancy Schemes, Sex
Discrimination, Director's Service Contracts.
Prof. Memberships: Law Society of Scotland,
The Society of Solicitors to the Supreme Court,
The Royal Faculty of Procurators in Glasgow.
Career: Graduated in 1972, LLB (Hons) Public
Law, Glasgow University, Notary Public. Practised
Employment Law since 1978. Partner 1984.
Personal: Golf and Travel.

STEWART, David
The Morton Fraser Partnership, Edinburgh
(0131) 550 1000
Partner in Litigation Department; Head of
Commercial Litigation.

Specialisation: Main area of practice is
commercial and maritime litigation and
employment law. Certified as an Employment
Law specialist by the Law Society of Scotland.
Gives lectures to courses organised by the Law
Society and other bodies.
Prof. Memberships: Law Society of Scotland,
WS Society.
Personal: Born 18th March 1942. Attended
Trinity Hall, Cambridge University 1961-64 and
Edinburgh University 1964-67. Leisure interests
include skiing and sailing. Lives in Edinburgh.

TIERNEY, James
Paull & Williamsons, Aberdeen
(01224) 621621
Specialisation: Principal areas of practice are
employment law and commercial litigation,
advising principal employers on all aspects of
employment law. Lectures occasionally.
Prof. Memberships: Law Society of Scotland,
Society of Advocates in Aberdeen Employment
Law Group.
Career: Graduated from Edinburgh University
1969; enrolled as solicitor 1971; partner
Littlejohns Stirling, 1975, *Paull & Williamsons*
Aberdeen 1982.
Personal: Born 1947; Married, 3 adult children.

WALKER, David James
McGrigor Donald, Glasgow (0141) 248 6677
Specialisation: Accredited by the Law Society
of Scotland as an Employment Law Specialist.
Advises mainly employers on all employment
and industrial relations issues. Regularly
appears in Tribunals throughout Scotland and
England. Recent experience includes advising
on managing business transfers, down sizing,
sexual harassment, executive terminations and
disability discrimination. Seminar speaker and
presenter of training programmes to clients.
Prof. Memberships: Law Society of Scotland.
Career: Glasgow University LLB (Hons).
Diploma in Legal Practice. Qualified 1984.
Personal: Born: 11th May 1959. Interests
include travel and sport.

WHYTE, David
Bishop and Robertson Chalmers, Glasgow
(0141) 248 4672
Partner in Litigation Department.
Specialisation: Main area of practice is
employment law. Has 15 years practical
experience. Accredited by Law Society of
Scotland as a specialist in employment law.
Also handles debt recovery, divorce and general
civil litigation. Lectures on employment law and
debt recovery.
Prof. Memberships: Industrial Law Group
(Scotland). Institute of Credit Management.
Career: Qualified in 1976. Joined *Bishop and
Robertson Chalmers* in 1976. Became a Partner
in 1981.
Personal: Born 1st July 1954. Attended
Kelvinside Academy 1959-72 and Glasgow
University 1972-76. Enjoys sailing and hill-
walking. Lives in Glasgow.

WILLIAMSON, David
Brodies WS, Edinburgh (0131) 228 3777
See under Litigation (Commercial): 200+
Solicitors, p. 535

WILLIAMSON, Raymond
MacRoberts, Glasgow (0141) 332 9988
Partner in Employment Unit.
Specialisation: Specialist in employment law
since the early 1970's. Advises on the drafting
of contracts of employment, on management of
staff, on redundancies and disciplinary matters.
Also experienced in representing clients'
interests before industrial and other tribunals.
Holder of Specialist Authorisation from the Law
Society of Scotland in Employment Law.
Convener of the Law Society's Employment Law
Committee and Chairman of the Employment
Law Specialisation Committee. Lectures
extensively on employment matters for various
course giving bodies and has been an external
examiner on employment law at Glasgow
University. Author of the chapter on employment
law in Greene & Fletcher's 'The Law and
Practice of Receivership in Scotland.'
Prof. Memberships: Law Society of Scotland,
Royal Faculty of Procurators in Glasgow.
Career: Joined *MacRoberts* Solicitors in 1966
and qualified in 1968. Became a Partner in
1972.
Personal: Born 24th December 1942.
Educated at the High School of Glasgow 1949-
60 and the University of Glasgow 1960-66.
Governor of the Royal Scottish Academy of
Music and Drama, Governor of The High School
of Glasgow, Chairman of the John Currie
Singers Ltd. Chairman Scottish Childrens Music
Foundation in Scotland, Chairman National
Youth Choir of Scotland, Deputy Chairman
Scottish International Piano Competition.
Leisure interests include music and gardening.
Lives in Glasgow.

YOUNG, James
McGrigor Donald, Edinburgh
(0131) 226 7777
Specialisation: Has been involved in
Employment Law since the initiating UK
legislation in the 1970's. Head of *McGrigor
Donald*'s Employment Law Unit and provides
advice on a full range of Employment Law
issues. Particular concerns of clients in the past
year have included the impact of Suzen on
transfers; trade union issues; the increase in
discrimination claims; post-termination
restrictions and the impact of new legislation.
Has represented and continues to represent a
large number of clients at Industrial Tribunals.
Member of the Law Society Committee of
Employment Law; member of Institute of
Personnel and Management; speaker at
conferences on various aspects of employment
law; Scottish contributor to Employment
Precedents and Company Policy documents.
Prof. Memberships: Law Society of Scotland;
Institute of Personnel and Management.
Career: Qualified in 1975 at *McGrigor Donald &
Co.* After two years as Legal Officer West
Lothian District Council and two years as
Assistant Solicitor at *Moncrieff Warren Patterson
& Co.*, became Partner in 1979 and joined
McGrigor Donald as Partner in 1985.
Personal: Born 26 February 1950. Educated at
Hutchesons' Boys Grammar School and the
University of Glasgow. Leisure interests include
watching and participating in sport (now mainly
golf), Contemporary Scottish Art and Theatre.
Lives in Edinburgh.

NORTHERN IRELAND

LEADING FIRMS
NORTHERN IRELAND

JONES & CASSIDY Belfast

HIGHLY REGARDED FIRMS

Cleaver Fulton & Rankin Belfast
Elliott Duffy Garrett Belfast
L'Estrange & Brett Belfast

Carson & McDowell Belfast
Culbert and Martin Belfast
C & H Jefferson Belfast
Johns Elliot Belfast
Tughan & Co Belfast

Jones & Cassidy (2ptnrs/2assts) Niche firm specialising in discrimination law. Stand out this year as the leading firm in the region. *Beverley Jones* is "sharp on Equal Pay and sex discrimination" but her style might not suit some of the more "macho" manufacturing clients. *Fiona Cassidy* is "quietly competent," particularly at advising on religious discrimination.

Cleaver Fulton & Rankin (2ptnrs/2assts) A large commercial firm which is "hot on marketing." *Patrick Cross* is a part-time Industrial Tribunal Chair and cannot represent clients in IT. Most contentious work is therefore taken on by *Rosalie Prytherch*. Clients/Work: Acting for respondent in sex discrimination case where leave is now being sought to appeal to House of Lords on issue of whether outworker is employee. Continued involvement in TUPE cases in Northern Ireland. Involvement in number of High Court injunction cases where instructed to restrain employees from breaching contracts.

Elliott Duffy Garrett (2ptnrs) *Henry Coll* has a "sensible practical approach" and "takes a commercial view. His position as an Industrial Tribunal Chair "doesn't detract from his position at the top. He goes out of his way to do work for his clients." He is "ably" assisted by partner *Adrienne Brock.*

L'Estrange & Brett (1ptnr 90%/2assts substantial amounts) Act mainly for respondents. *Adam Brett* is experienced in Equal Pay cases. Clients/Work: Successfully defended series of discrimination claims in the Industrial Tribunal for Queens University Belfast. Reviewing employment procedures for major manufacturing clients.

Carson & McDowell (2ptnrs p/t; 2assts) The "practical, straightforward" *Brian Turtle* does a lot of railway work and "brings a lot of sense to the area." Clients/Work: Significant corporate and commercial client emphasis which provides a substantial employment caseload.

Culbert & Martin (2ptnrs/1const/2assts do emp work to some degree). A small firm which handles mainly applicants' work. *David Gray* is "good in a discrete way;" he specialises in discrimination cases, spending 50% of his time working for the Equal Opportunities Commission and Fair Employment Commission, and he is a member of the Northern Ireland Disability Council. Clients/Work: Represented applicant in Baird v Cookstown District Council. Also represented applicant in Allan & Ors v Stockham Valve Ltd, multiple applicant equal pay claim for clerical staff comparing themselves with shopfloor workers.

C & H Jefferson (1ptnr p/t; 2assts p/t) Act for respondents, they have a reputation for religious discrimination work. Known for "taking a determined view." *Alana Jones* is newly recommended, she "knows her stuff." Clients/Work: Representing Shorts Missile Systems Limited in test religious discrimination case challenging redundancy selection omitting length of service as a criterion. Advising VF Northern Europe Ltd on sale of undertakings in Northern Ireland. Advise on union recognition issues.

Johns Elliott (2ptnrs/1asst) Act entirely for respondents, concentrating on handholding advice work, drafting severance agreements as well as representing at ITs. Clients/Work: Public/private companies. Northern Ireland Tourist Board.

Tughan & Co (8ptnrs/6assts) *Grahame Loughlin* is known particularly for his litigation work in the employment context.

LEADING INDIVIDUALS
NORTHERN IRELAND

BRETT Adam L'Estrange & Brett
CASSIDY Fiona Jones & Cassidy
COLL Henry Elliott Duffy Garrett
JONES Beverley Jones & Cassidy

CROSS Patrick Cleaver Fulton & Rankin
GRAY David Culbert and Martin
LOUGHLIN Grahame Tughan & Co
PRYTHERCH Rosalie Cleaver Fulton & Rankin
TURTLE Brian Carson & McDowell

UP AND COMING

BROCK Adrienne Elliott Duffy Garrett
JONES Alana C & H Jefferson

SEE PROFILES AT END OF THIS SECTION

LEADERS' PROFILES • NORTHERN IRELAND

BRETT, Adam
L'Estrange & Brett, Belfast (01232) 230426
Partner. Main area of work: Employment law and discrimination law.
Prof. Memberships: Law Society of Northern Ireland.
Career: Qualified 1981. Partner in *L'Estrange & Brett* since 1985.
Personal: Born 1957. Education: Oxford University (M.A.). Committee Member Employment Lawyers Group in Northern Ireland and Member Employment Lawyers Association.

BROCK, Adrienne M.
Elliott Duffy Garrett, Belfast (01232) 245034

CASSIDY, Fiona
Jones & Cassidy, Belfast (01232) 642290

COLL, Henry A.
Elliott Duffy Garrett, Belfast (01232) 245034
Partner and Head of Employment and Education Law Unit.
Specialisation: Practice covers all aspects of employment and discrimination Law including advising on contractual arrangements for senior employees, dispute resolution and representation at Tribunals and elsewhere. Clients include Public Authorities, Third Level Educational Institutes and Commercial Sectors.
Prof. Memberships: Employment Lawyers Association, American Bar Association.
Career: Qualified 1973. Partner in *Elliott Duffy Garrett* since 1975.
Personal: Born 1946. Educated at Queen's University, Belfast. Awarded O.B.E. in 1994 for services to employment.

CROSS, Patrick
Cleaver Fulton & Rankin, Belfast (01232) 243141
Specialisation: Employment Law aspects of Company Commercial Law including drafting Employment Contracts and handling employment disputes. Part-time Chairman of Industrial Tribunals.
Career: Qualified at *Metson Cross & Co* London in 1966, qualified in Northern Ireland 1968 and joined *Cleaver Fulton & Rankin*, (Partner in 1970).
Personal: Born 3rd April 1943.

GRAY, David
Culbert and Martin, Belfast (01232) 325508

JONES, Alana
C & H Jefferson, Belfast (01232) 329545
Specialisation: Practice covers all aspects of employment, discrimination and industrial relations law. Acting almost exclusively for employers, clients include public and private sector companies, employment agencies, charities, insurers and educational establishments. Often instructed as agents for practices in Great Britain and Republic of Ireland.
Prof. Memberships: Committee Member of Employment Lawyers' Group (NI); Solicitors' European Group; Law Society of Northern Ireland.
Career: Graduated LL.B 1989. Graduated LL.M in Discrimination Law 1990. Employed as a Lecturer at The Queen's University of Belfast. Qualified at *C & H Jefferson* 1993. Speaker at numerous conference and training events.

JONES, Beverley
Jones & Cassidy, Belfast (01232) 642290

LOUGHLIN, Grahame
Tughan & Co, Belfast (01232) 553300
Specialisation: Advising clients, mainly
employers, regarding unfair and wrongful
dismissal claims; claims of discrimination under
Fair Employment and Equal Opportunities
legislation; drafting and varying Contracts of
Employment; drafting Termination/Severance
Agreements; Transfer of Undertakings
Regulations on sale and purchase of
businesses. The firm has acted in the leading
cases in this jurisdiction on Sunday working and
discovery of documents in discrimination
claims.

Prof. Memberships: Law Society of Northern
Ireland. Northern Ireland Employment Lawyers
Group.
Career: Graduated in 1973 – Queens
University, Belfast. Partner from 1981 to date.

PRYTHERCH, Rosalie
Cleaver Fulton & Rankin, Belfast
(01232) 243141
Specialisation: Acting almost exclusively for
employers, practice includes all aspects of
employment law including general advice,
drafting, claims handling, advising in area of
restraint of trade clauses and advice to

companies with regard to dismissal of senior
executives. Interactive approach with
commercial dept, regarding TUPE implications
arising in sales and acquisitions.
Prof. Memberships: Employment Lawyers'
Group (NI). Law Society of Northern Ireland.
Career: Qualified 1987. Partner in *Cleaver
Fulton & Rankin* 1996.

TURTLE, W.Brian W.
Carson & McDowell, Belfast (01232) 244951
See under Litigation (Commercial): 200+
Solicitors, p. 536

ENERGY & NATURAL RESOURCES

RESEARCH: Our sample this year consisted of interviews with solicitors, barristers and in-house lawyers at the leading O&G (both up and down stream), water, renewables and mining companies as well as PESs and regulators. In compiling the tables, we consider all the information available to us, paying particular regard to the market research carried out by our team of ten qualified lawyers. (The researchers' details are set out on page three.) The rankings, therefore, reflect the opinion of the marketplace as revealed by systematic and objective research: see page four. (Our research is audited every year by the British Market Research Bureau.)

OVERVIEW: The major players took hold of the energy market in the 70s and 80s and have not let go since. Most energy work is shared out, unevenly, amongst the twelve leading firms. The rest operate in a single sector or isolated projects.

The usual suspects do not have a monopoly on the necessary skills: Simmons & Simmons acted for the industry on the Green Peace judicial review, NGC uses Martineau Johnson in Birmingham for regulatory work and the Falkland Islands Government went to Michelle Dunne and Martin Byatt (formerly of Penningtons, now with Clyde & Co) to develop their O&G regulations. Nabarros in Sheffield is a leading coal practice and Bond Pearce in Plymouth is well known in the ethereal world of wind farms. However no 'Highly Regarded Firm' had done enough this year to join the 'Leading Firms.' If anything, the gap between the true holistic energy practices and the rest has widened.

Denton Hall and Herbert Smith are still the leading firms having focused resources on energy as a discrete practice area. However within the various sectors, other firms were at least as strong if not stronger, particularly in project finance. Whether they retain their position over the coming years will depend on their success overseas. The UK is seen as a mature market and those firm's which fail to become truly international will invariably shrink.

A number of US firm's have sizeable energy practices based in London and are included in the main table. This year we have a separate US firm's table which is an un-ranked list of firms recommended for their practice outside the UK.

In Scotland the leading firms are all within the Central Belt and advise the Scottish electricity generation and supply companies. The next two firms are based in Aberdeen and service the oil and gas industry, although most of the 'serious' work is still done from London.

Many commented that energy companies are becoming more litigious. Whether it is due to the market price of gas moving away from contract prices or the influence of aggressive new entrants, energy companies have become more open minded about taking an early advantage. Every interviewee named either Herbert Smith or Denton Hall as their usual opponent in energy disputes and those two firms named the other as their most regular combatant by far.

If there is an industry star, it is undoubtedly Charles Wood at Denton Hall for his work on the Network Code.

Energy companies use a wide selection of firms and are ideally placed to evaluate their lawyers. The in-house departments are so strong that private practice lawyers are as likely to be up against an in-house team as not. Indeed, many interviewees commented that if in-house teams were included in the following tables, many would do rather well, with BP's team appearing close to the top.

LEADING FIRMS · LONDON

DENTON HALL
HERBERT SMITH

ALLEN & OVERY
ASHURST MORRIS CRISP
CAMERON MCKENNA
CLIFFORD CHANCE
FRESHFIELDS
LINKLATERS

LOVELL WHITE DURRANT
NABARRO NATHANSON
NORTON ROSE
SLAUGHTER AND MAY

HIGHLY REGARDED FIRMS

Clyde & Co
Coudert Brothers
Lawrence Graham
Le Boeuf Lamb Greene & Macrae
Simmons & Simmons

Baker & McKenzie
Eversheds
Field Fisher Waterhouse
Holman, Fenwick & Willan
Ince & Co
Masons

Beachcroft Stanleys
Edge & Ellison
Richards Butler
Trowers & Hamlins
Watson, Farley & Williams

NOTABLE US FIRMS

Milbank, Tweed, Hadley & McCloy
Shearman & Sterling
Skadden, Arps, Slate, Meagher & Flom LLP
Vinson & Elkins
White & Case

LONDON

Denton Hall (8ptnrs/2consultants/1barrister/11assts*).* "Still the one to beat." Playing to its strengths and focusing on energy as a practice area in itself rather than being merely one part of a project finance capability. Remain the leading gas practice and, for many, "in a class of its own" in energy overall. *Malcolm Groom* ("one of the good people, with the confidence to make a deal") heads a lengthy list of leading individuals, with every partner and many assistants having experience of working in-house. The best known are *James Dallas* (the firm's chairman and "a gifted showman who always says the right thing, at the right time, in the right way"), *Charles Wood* ("genius"), *Myles Cave-Browne-Cave* ("an outstanding character with an intimate knowledge of the industry and powerfully destructive of weak arguments"), *Blanche Sas* ("a useful addition to any energy department"), *David Moroney* ("combines detailed knowledge with finely tuned legal skills") and *Michael Brothwood,* now a consultant and recently the specialist adviser to a House of Lords sub committee considering the Gas Directive. The firm has a specialist energy litigation team of 3 partners and 5 assistants. **Clients/Work:** Advising Premier Oil on gas sales and transportation in Indonesia and Singapore, on JOAs and licences in Albania, an upstream project in Myanmar and gas field development in Pakistan. International legal advisors to National Power Corporation of the Philippines on a tender for a US $11bn power tolling agreement and the building of a new IPP. Advising the Government of Abu Dhabi on the restructuring and regulation of its electricity and water supply industries.

Herbert Smith (19ptnrs/30assts) "Too bloody good." Nobody knows the UK electricity industry better than Herbert Smith – they acted for the RECs on privatisation and currently act for all 14 public electricity suppliers (PESs) on the introduction of full supply competition. Although their profile in O&G is less than it was, as they are one of the leading energy litigation practices and the leading water practice, few questioned their right to be at the head of the UK table. Internationally the firm did not rate so highly. *Richard Bond is* a "charming, astute and heavyweight player." So is the "wholly realistic" *Alan Jowett.* Other well known names are the "hands on" *Mark Newbery* a noted electricity specialist and *Trevor Turtle,* the "best water lawyer in private practice." *Adrian Clough* has played a key role advising the PESs. *Henry Davey* is another new, "personable and pragmatic" entrant whilst Ted Greeno is the best known litigator in the industry with a team of 4 partners and up to 9 assistants. **Clients/Work:** Advising Northern Ireland Electric plc on its corporate restructuring and its challenge to the

regulation refusal to implement the MMC's decisions. Advising CalEnergy Gas on the acquisition of producing and exploration assets and interests in off-shore pipelines on the UKCS. Advising on the 2x350MW Hefei No.2 power project in Anhui Province, PRC.

Allen & Overy (14ptnrs/40 assts) "Has the ability to field excellent people at every level" Described as "first rate," and "a respected adversary," the firm is "top in project finance" but not seen in day-to-day matters. With a truly global practice and a "dynamic marketing strategy" the firm is "going somewhere on a bullet." During 1997, they advised on 35 power projects with a total project cost of $21.5bn and a combined capacity of 23,183MW; *Roger Davies* is "dogged but flexible" and "can handle anything if he's minded to." *Doran Doeh,* based in Moscow, and *Ian Elder* ("excellent in electricity") were also recommended, as was Graham Vinter (see project finance) -

LEADING INDIVIDUALS
OIL and GAS

BOND Richard Herbert Smith
CARVER Jeremy Clifford Chance
DALLAS James Denton Hall
DAVIES Roger Allen & Overy
GRIFFIN Paul Ashurst Morris Crisp
GROOM Malcolm Denton Hall
ROBERTS Martin Slaughter and May
SALT Stuart Linklaters
SAUNDERS Mark Nabarro Nathanson
STANGER Michael Lovell White Durrant
TAYLOR Michael Norton Rose
WOOD Charles Denton Hall

BANKES Charles Simmons & Simmons
BROTHWOOD Michael Denton Hall
BROWN Douglas Eversheds
BYATT Martin Clyde & Co
CAVE-BROWNE-CAVE Myles Denton Hall
COFFELL Howard Field Fisher Waterhouse
DAVEY Henry Herbert Smith
DOEH Doran Allen & Overy
DUNNE Michelle Clyde & Co
FELTER Peter Clyde & Co
HIGGINSON Tony Lovell White Durrant
JONES Alan LeBoeuf, Lamb, Greene & MacRae
JONES Gareth Nabarro Nathanson
JONES Richard Linklaters
JOWETT Alan Herbert Smith
KHAN Rafique Cameron McKenna
PEGG Garry LeBoeuf, Lamb, Greene & MacRae
PICTON-TURBERVILL Geoffrey Ashurst Morris Crisp
REES Jonathan Freshfields
SAS Blanche Denton Hall
SAYER Stephen Richards Butler
TYNE Sally Cameron McKenna
VERRILL John Lawrence Graham

UP AND COMING
OTWAY Linda Lawrence Graham
SEE PROFILES AT END OF THIS SECTION

LEADING INDIVIDUALS
ELECTRICITY

DALLAS James Denton Hall
LANE Robert Cameron McKenna
ROBERTS Martin Slaughter and May
SALT Stuart Linklaters
TAYLOR Michael Norton Rose
WOOLF Fiona Cameron McKenna

BLAKE Peter Clifford Chance
BOND Richard Herbert Smith
CLOUGH Adrian Herbert Smith
DAVEY Henry Herbert Smith
ELDER Ian Allen & Overy
MORONEY David Denton Hall
NEWBERY Mark Herbert Smith
PICTON-TURBERVILL Geoffrey Ashurst Morris Crisp
ROWEY Kent Freshfields
SAS Blanche Denton Hall
SAYER Stephen Richards Butler
SIMPSON Paul Clifford Chance
STACEY Paul Slaughter and May
TUDWAY Robert Nabarro Nathanson
WALLACE Patrick Freshfields

LEADING INDIVIDUALS · MINING

BYRNE John Dorsey & Whitney
HURST Philip Ashurst Morris Crisp
MORONEY David Denton Hall

BOND Richard Herbert Smith
BYATT Martin Clyde & Co
REES Jonathan Freshfields
TAYLOR Michael Norton Rose

LEADING INDIVIDUALS · WATER

TURTLE Trevor Herbert Smith
SEE PROFILES AT END OF THIS SECTION

Clients/Work: Advising the Sutton Bridge Project Company on all aspects of its greenfield gas fired power station, including the £337m financing by way of a dual listed euro bond and 144a offering. Appointed as international legal adviser to the Petroleum Authority of Thailand (PTT), the Thai state-owned O&G corporation, on its proposed privatisation. Advising the Armenian government on the development of their mining industry.

Ashurst Morris Crisp (9ptnrs in London, 6ptnrs overseas/19assts) Although still a leader, they have lost their image as the hot firm. *Paul Griffin* is "exceptionally good, one of the best in the industry and commands respect" but heads a group perceived to be losing people. Paul's name was built on gas purchase agreements but he increasingly works on power projects, LNG and oil. *Geoffrey Picton-Turbervill* is strong in electricity and oil. *Philip Hurst* was recommended for hard rock mining. Energy work is also handled in the firm's Tokyo and Delhi offices. **Clients/Work:** Acting for Azerbaijan International Operating Company (a consortium of 12 companies including BP,

Statoil, Exxon and Amoco) on the export of petroleum from the Caspian; acting for BG on the renegotiation of long term take-or-pay contracts with gas suppliers; acting for Energy Group Plc on power tolling arrangements with Rolls Royce at the Heartlands Power Project in the Midlands.

Cameron McKenna (9ptnrs/10assts) "Making a lot of noise." Over the last year they have built up an impressive team with "plenty of skill and experience" but which has yet to match its PR and potential, except in electricity where they even gained work in North America – "an outstanding achievement" given the local competition. The firm's most public face is the "globe trotting" *Fiona Woolf*, a "brilliant woman" who commands confidence. *Sally Tyne* has a "personality that suits the O&G industry," whilst *Robert Lane* is "astute and easy to deal with." Other team members include *Rafique Khan* and a new recruit from Deminex. Unique amongst City firms in having an Aberdeen office. **Clients/Work:** Advising California Independent System Operator Corporation and California Power Exchange Corporation on the establishment of electricity trading arrangements in California; advising BP on all gas supply and Network Code aspects of its Saltend Co-generation Project; advising Dresdner Kleinwort Benson on a Scottish PFI waste water project.

Clifford Chance The Energy & Natural Resources Group is part of a larger projects group of 15 partners and 45 lawyers active in the UK, Russia, South America, the Middle East, China, Vietnam and a few countries in between. Good on the finance side and now making serious efforts to move into mainstream energy work. The firm generally acts for industry in electricity matters (clients include National Power, Intergen, Southern and MEB) and for banks on O&G projects. The team includes *Peter Blake* ("a terrific lawyer – he only makes good points and knows when to shut up "), the sage *Jeremy Carver* (head of the Public International Law group) and *Paul Simpson*. **Clients/Work:** Lead arrangers of the US$2.2bn financing for the expansion of an ethylene cracker and polyethylene plant, Yanpet, owned and operated by Saudi Yanbu Petrochemical Company. Acting for the arrangers, JP Morgan, Chase, BCI and UBS on the Omnitel GSM Telecoms project. Advising the sponsors of the 1200MW CCGT merchant power station at Saltend, Humberside.

Freshfields (24ptnrs/42assts) One of the big international players, they are highly rated in electricity, nuclear, mining, energy litigation and "anything involving complex funding issues." Thought not to be as expert on gas issues. *Jon Rees* is "as good as they get and doesn't let a difficult negotiation spoil his sense of fun." "Bright and imaginative," he "makes good points reasonably." The London Energy Group "work their

hearts out" and are "extremely professional and helpful." It includes *Kent Rowey* (a US qualified lawyer and head of the firm's International Project Finance Group) and *Patrick Wallace*. Chris Pugh has made a name for himself acting for J-Block against Enron as a "skilful operator who gets things done." He leads a specialist energy litigation team. The firm's overseas offices have impressive CVs in their own right. **Clients/Work:** Advising Gazprom on its strategic alliance with Royal Dutch/Shell advising the project sponsors, Electricité de France and GEC Alsthom on the Laibin B power project, 2 x 360MW coal fired power plant in the PRC. Advising Tractabel and Sembawang Corporation, the project sponsors, on a BOO project for a utilities centre to provide the Singapore grid and steam, water and waste treatment to the industrial customers on the island of Pulau Sakra, Singapore.

Linklaters A great approach, an international presence, in depth industry knowledge and superb resources make them a force to be reckoned with, particularly on corporate and finance led deals. *Stuart Salt* combines all the virtues that make an outstanding lawyer: technical knowledge, speed of thought, pragmatism, stamina (although he is rumoured to flag at 3am), and a sense of humour. Opponents enjoy being around him and several oil majors commented that they would use him more but he is always working for BP. **Clients/Work:** Acting on the £5billion plus demerger of the base metal mining business of Gencor; an LNG extraction, processing, liquefaction and regasification project in Qatar; the Laibin B, Changsha, Hanfeng and Hefei No.2 power projects in China.

Lovell White Durrant (15 ptnrs/12 assts) A bit adrift in the energy market. Have a niche in claims validation and trying to make headway in electricity and power projects but it is slow going. The core team of 4 lawyers includes two well known individuals. *Michael Stanger* ("a sharp witted fellow… wouldn't hesitate to use him for anything") represented the shippers on the development of the Network Code and is "as good a gas expert as you'll find." *Tony Higginson* (ex-Sun and Philips) knows the business and, in negotiations, can be "aggressive but effective." **Clients/Work:** Acquisition of UNOCAL Britain Ltd, the operator of the Heather field. Acting on the conversion of a tanker into an FPSO. Acquisition of SWEB Gas for Amerada Hess.

Nabarro Nathanson (12 ptnrs/12assts) Up and coming, and already well established in up stream O&G and CHP. The "nice bunch to work with" includes *Mark Saunders* ("a fine fellow and as sharp a lawyer as you could hope to find") and *Gareth Jones* ("a master of O&G and project finance"). *Robert Tudway* (a "good guy" and "the one who wrote Halsbury's on Energy Law") heads the electricity group. John Byrne has now left the

firm. **Clients/Work:** Acting for Elf on the Elgin Franklin project; advising Oil Spill Response, an industry environmental disaster response organisation comprising 22 major oil companies, on all aspects of their business; advising on a high profile/value oil trading dispute.

Norton Rose (16ptnrs/31assts) *Michael Taylor* is highly rated but is the only well known name. However he is now joined by a partner from Denton Hall. Intimately associated with the development of the UKCS and the firm retains a lot of goodwill. But nowadays they are hardly visible outside domestic IPP (where they have been extremely successful). O&G litigation forms a core specialist area within the shipping litigation team which acted for Enron on J-Block and CATs. **Clients/Work:** Acting on three out of the five UK IPP to reach financial close in 1997. Advising TOTAL, Statoil, Norsk Hydro and Maraven on a JV to produce and refine heavy oil reserves in the Orinoco basin, Venezuela. Four water projects in Scotland for Scotia Water Consortium with a combined value of £220m.

Slaughter and May (10ptnrs – no specific dept) "If they set their mind to it they could be one of the major players in almost any area." However the firm is not as heavily involved in O&G as one would expect. Their profile in electricity is higher – they acted for the Electricity Pool on the introduction of competition ("there must be some tortured minds at Slaughters after that project.") *Martin Roberts* ("there is integrity behind all his comments") attracts most of the energy work. *Paul Stacey* was also recomended as a sound technician. **Clients/Work:** Acting on the acquisition and power purchase arrangements for the Hwange power station in Zimbabwe; Monument's swap with Mobil of interests in Columbia for the Hudson field; Nippon's acquisitions of the Alba, Hutton and Hudson fields.

Clyde & Co (5ptnrs/1assoc/5assts in London, 2ptnrs/2assts in Guildford, 2ptnrs/ 3assocs overseas) "An oily practice with a wealth of experience in FPSO's." Visibly building up the energy practice. Took on ex-Britoil lawyer, *Michelle Dunne* ("makes good points ") and *Martin Byatt* from Penningtons to strengthen the team headed by *Peter Felter*. Other energy specialists are based in Venezuela, St Petersburg, Dubai and Guildford. Through Michelle Dunne they are now advising BG on the Interconnector. Also well known for energy litigation. **Clients/Work:** Glencore International Ab. Falklands Islands Government. Issues in turbulent and developing jurisdictions.

Coudert Brothers (4ptnrs/2assts) Good in the CIS and central and eastern Europe for O&G, the firm has been effective in attracting quality work and clients. Thought to be too small (in energy terms) to bat in the big league. Steven Beharrell (ex Denton Hall) heads the group in London with a further 12 partners overseas. **Clients/Work:** Representing Total on its production-sharing agreement in Russia; advising Wärtsilä NSD Power Development on a long term sale agreement to the Kenyan Power and Light Corporation to underpin a 74MW diesel power generation project; advising ESB, the Irish state electricity utility, on long term gas supply contracts for Power Station in Dublin.

Lawrence Graham (4ptnrs/2assts) *John Verrill* "understands the O&G industry" and has raised the firm's profile to the point where they might soon be knocking on the door of the next division. Well known for their work for LASMO, the firm was praised for "not treating clients like idiots." *Linda Otway* ("a pleasure to deal with") was tipped as a rising star and joins the up and coming list. **Clients/Work:** Clients include LASMO, Halliburton/Brown & Root and Enterprise Oil.

Le Boeuf Lamb Greene & Macrae Big overseas, especially in the FSU, but not a major force in the UK – 85% of the practice is overseas. The energy team is headed by *Alan Jones* and *Garry Pegg*, the latter particularly recommended for his work on claims validation.

Simmons & Simmons (10ptnrs/10assts) Not the obvious choice to represent the industry in the 17th Licensing round, nevertheless the firm made a positive impression and is now a name that the majors (other than Shell who knew them anyway) know. Strong in areas that overlap into energy (particularly environmental law) they are moving forward, focusing on the FSU and the Middle East. *Charles Bankes* is the sole external adviser to OFGAS. Energy work is also handled in the Abu Dhabi, Lisbon, Paris, Hong Kong and Shanghai offices. **Clients/ Work:** Advising Tidewater Inc on the US$328m acquisition of the marine divsion of Ocean Group plc. Advising Law Debenture Trust Corporation plc as security trustee in the US£3bn Qatar gas financing. Advising the Electricity Generating Authority of Thailand on the Nam Therm II project, a 681MW hydroelectric power plant in Laos PDR.

Baker & McKenzie (6ptnrs/10assts) No one ever gets sacked for using Baker & McKenzie. A huge global reach and undoubted energy capability. The London office has a substantial practice in North Sea upstream with an increasing involvment in overseas transactions. **Clients/Work:** Acquisition and disposal of various interests in oil and gas licences in Kazakstan, Russia and Africa. IPP deals in Eastern Europe, the FSU, the Middle East and North Africa.

Eversheds (3ptnrs/2assts) A national Energy Group based in London, Birmingham, Cardiff, Leeds and East Anglia. *Douglas Brown* (ex BG) is the best known individual. Known for their work in the regulatory sector. **Clients/Work:** Sale of interest in Brazilian Gas distribution company involving review of drilling contracts in Brazil, Tunisia and elsewhere.

Field Fisher Waterhouse Drafting the interconnector agreement has given the firm a foundation to build on. *Howard Coffell* heads a cross departmental group that works on oil, gas and electricity but is best known for pipelines. **Clients/Work:** Advising Avocet Mining on a US$5.5m convertible loan facility. Advising Enfield Energy Centre Ltd on a 12.5 km pipeline connecting a CCGT power station in Enfield to the BG National Transmission Pipeline System. Advising Interconnector (UK) Ltd on the Bacton to Zeebrugge gas pipeline.

Ince & Co (9ptnrs/15assts) A shipping firm with a longstanding presence in upstream O&G. "An ideal choice for an insurance or shipping or offshore installation related dispute." **Clients/Work:** The purchase and upgrading of a drilling unit for an independent oil company. Representing a Far Eastern yard on a dispute arising from the construction of a FPSO for operation in the North Sea.

Masons (25ptnrs/30assts – none exclusively) "Potential." Building on their construction expertise, Masons have been gaining work that other lawyers expected would go to a more established firm, particularly power and water projects. **Clients/Work:** Acting for Independent Energy Holdings Plc on the acquisition of UK gas reserves and general corporate transactions; acting for Renewable Energy Systems Ltd and B9 Energy on the project financing of a 15MW

wind farm in Ireland.

Beachcroft Stanleys (8ptnrs/8assts) A new entrant on the basis of the firm's reputation in the water industry. The cross departmental group has been involved in water for 60 years and "knows the industry inside out." **Clients/Work:** Acting for Dee Valley water on its acquisition of of Chester Water. Advising WOCs, including Bournemouth & West Hampshire Water and Mid Kent Water, in relation to a High Court case which held budget payment meters to be unlawful.

Edge & Ellison (4ptnrs/1asst) Active in waste to energy schemes and gas sales. **Clients/Work:** Two CHP projects in south east England for Van Heyningen Brothers Ltd. Preparation of standard form data collection and aggregation agreements for the electricity supply market for 1998.

Richards Butler (10ptnrs) Seldom come across by other practitioners nowadays. Nevertheless *Stephen Sayer* retains a reputation as someone who does O&G and electricity "better than most." **Clients/Work:** Government of Kyrgystan. Saudi Aramco. Rosneftegazstroy International.

Trowers & Hamlins (3ptnrs in London) A strong Middle East reputation for O&G, power and water. The firm has offices in Dubai/Abu Dhabi, (3ptnrs) Bahrain (1ptnr) and Oman (2ptnrs). **Clients/Work:** Advising Charus, the lead promoter of a consortium forming the Sohar Aluminium Smelter Company in Oman, project value in excess of US$3bn. Advising the Ministry of Planning in Jordan on the implementation policy for BOOT/BOO.

Watson, Farley & Williams (9ptnrs) Originally a shipping firm with an involvement in upstream O&G, mainly through FPSOs, they are now developing a name in power and CHP projects in Eastern and Central Europe. **Clients/Work:** Advising on the first project financed power project in the Czech Republic; representing a FPSO operating company in the $450million refinancing of three FPSOs; brought in by the EBRD to prepare a Lithuanian CHP company from privatisation.

John Byrne has now left Nabarro Nathanson to join American firm, Dorsey & Whitney.

LEADERS' PROFILES · LONDON

BANKES, Charles
Simmons & Simmons, London
(0171) 628 2020
Partner – EC, Competition and Regulatory Law Group.
Specialisation: Specialises in EC, competition and regulatory law with particular emphasis on gas regulation. External adviser to Ofgas on a wide range of issues and members of its team for the 1996-97 MMC inquiry into BG Transco price controls; also advises Ofreg on gas

related matters in Northern Ireland. Has extensive experience of the application of EC and UK competition law to both upstream and downstream oil and gas issues; advised oil company licensees on EC issues in relation to Greenpeace's judicial review of the 17th offshore round. Has also advised widely on gas and electricity regulation in Asia. Has written and lectured on the application of EC competition law in the energy sector, EC liberalisation initiatives and on regulation.

Career: Qualified 1991, joined *Simmons & Simmons* 1994, Partner *Simmons & Simmons* 1998.
Personal: Born 1960, married with two sons.

BLAKE, Peter M.W.
Clifford Chance, London (0171) 600 1000
See under Project Finance, p. 684

BOND, Richard
Herbert Smith, London (0171) 374 8000
Partner and Head of Corporate Department.
Specialisation: Wide ranging experience of corporate transactions, particularly in the fields of energy and natural resources, utilities and privatisations. Is a Council Member of the Energy and Natural Resources Section of the International Bar Association and Chairman of its Oil Committee.
Career: Qualified in 1969. Partner with *Herbert Smith* since 1977.

BROTHWOOD, Michael
Denton Hall, London (0171) 242 1212
email: mb@dentonhall.com
Consultant to Energy and Natural Resources Group – former partner and head of the Energy and Infrastructure Group.
Specialisation: Main area of practice is energy law. As senior legal adviser to British Gas Corporation, was responsible for drafting and negotiating numerous major contracts for the purchase of natural gas from both UK and Norwegian Shelf. Also covered EEC and UK Competition law, asset disposal programs and legal aspects of relations with the government. As senior legal adviser to the British Steel Corporation, was responsible for international joint ventures and construction projects and for legal aspects of integration of British Steel into the European Community. Cases have included drafting and negotiating LNG purchase contracts; giving advice as a Consultant to Danish National Oil and Gas Company in connection with EC law issues; advising on numerous regulatory and competition matters and EC law relating particularly to third party access; and advising and drafting UK gas transportation agreements. Legal Expert to the European Parliament, in connection with its proposals for third party access to gas and electricity networks (1992); Specialist Adviser to the House of Lords' Committee reviewing the EU Gas Liberalisation Directive (1997); project leader for Phare Legislation/Regulation project on the European Energy Charter (1994), and legal expert in supplementary Energy Charter Treaty project (1996). Other EEC projects include Advising the European Commission (Synergy Progamme) in connection with a project in the 'Consequences of the future accession of countries of Central and Eastern Europe: Energy Strategies & Legislation' and Advising the European Commission under a PHARE programme project on a regulatory regime for gas in Slovenia. Member of the editorial boards of the European Law Review and the Oil and Gas Law and Taxation Review. Has written and lectured widely on European and Energy Law.
Prof. Memberships: Law Society, Solicitors' European Group, International Bar Association.
Career: Qualified in 1959. Worked at *Slaughter and May* 1956-65; Counsel to *Casey Lane & Mittendorf*, New York, 1965-67; Senior Legal Adviser for British Steel Corporation 1967-74. Resident Partner at *Freshfields*, Paris, 1974-81; Senior Legal Adviser for British Steel Corporation 1981-85; Partner with *Denton Hall* 1985-1994. Consultant to Energy and Natural Resources Group since 1994.
Personal: Born 22nd September 1932. Holds an MA in law from Cambridge 1953-56. Leisure interests include cycling, walking, gardening and French culture. Lives in London.

BROWN, Douglas
Eversheds, London (0171) 919 4725
Specialisation: Extensive experience of UK and international on shore and off shore gas projects, oil and gas refining projects, pipelines and gas purchasing contracts with particular expertise in formulating contracting strategies (including Alliancing) for major projects. Currently involved in UK power generation projects, overseas transporter electricity transmission/telecoms projects. Has experience in drilling and in the mining sector. Specialises in power generation, gas purchasing and long term supply agreements, EPP and construction related aspects of oil and gas projects and mining sectors. In addition to UK, current international experience includes large gas – to – electricity CCGT trans-border project in Africa and mining project in the West Indies. Contributor to "Energy Day."
Prof. Memberships: IBA Section on energy and natural resources law; UK Energy Lawyers; Institute of Petroleum; Member of the Pipelines Industries Guild; Companion of the Institution of Chemical Engineers.
Career: Senior legal adviser British Gas plc 1981-1988; partner 1990.

BYATT, Martin P.
Clyde & Co, London (0171) 623 1244
A member of *Clyde & Co* Energy Trade and Finance Group.
Specialisation: Main area of practice is energy law. Handles the commercial, regulatory, environmental and financing aspects of the exploration for and extraction, production, processing, storage, distribution and sale of oil, gas and minerals generally. Also handles corporate finance work, covering all aspects of Yellow and Blue Book work including flotations, rights issues, prospectuses and takeovers. Has handled numerous international natural resource joint ventures and financing of cross border natural resource projects.
Prof. Memberships: Law Society, International Bar Association (Energy Sector).
Career: Qualified in 1968. Partner in own practice 1970-93. Now Partner at *Clyde & Co*.
Personal: Born 7th March 1946. Attended College of Law. Leisure interests include horse riding, gardening and wine appreciation. Lives in Cambridgeshire.

BYRNE, John
Dorsey & Whitney, London (0171) 588 0800
Partner in Commercial Department.
Specialisation: Main area of practice is contractual negotiation. Adviser to various Energy Companies (including coal buyers, sellers and traders) on a range of projects, (including privatisations). Has presented and published various papers on a range of Energy related subjects.
Career: Qualified in 1985. Articled clerk at British Rail 1983-85. Solicitor at British Coal 1985-90. Partner at *Nabarro Nathanson* 1990 to 1998. Joined *Dorsey & Whitney* February, 1998.
Personal: Born 28th December 1958. Holds LLB (London) 1981 and LLM (London) 1983.

CARVER, Jeremy
Clifford Chance, London (0171) 600 1000
Partner. Head of Public International Law Group.
Specialisation: Represents States, government agencies and international organisations in relation to proceedings in England and elsewhere; representing Kuwait's Oil Sector companies in claims to the United Nations Compensation Commission. Areas of expertise include state and diplomatic immunity; upstream oil and gas operations; international economic sanctions; maritime and territorial boundary issues; world trade law; jurisdiction, conflicts of laws, extraterritoriality. Contributions to numerous books and professional journals.
Career: University: Trinity College, Cambridge (1961-1964). Degree: MA (Engineering). Qualified 1969. *Coward Chance* 1969-1987. Partner 1974. Resident Manager, Brussels 1973-1974. Resident Partner, Singapore 1982-1983. *Clifford Chance* 1987-date.
Prof. Memberships: Hon. Treasurer, International Law Association, British Branch 1981-1998; Vice President, International Law Association, British Branch 1998-present. Member, Executive Council, International Law Association 1991- present. Member, ILA International Trade Law Committee 1996-present. Member, Executive Committee, British Institute of International and Comparative Law 1996-present; Council of Management, British Institute of International and Comparative Law, 1998 – present. Chairman, British Invisibles CIS Panel 1993-1995. Member Kazakh-British Trade and Industry Council 1994-present. Member, Uzbek-British Trade and Industry Council 1994-present. Member, Export Promotion Forum 1996-present. Member, City Promotion Panel 1995-present.
Personal: Born 1943; resides London.

CAVE-BROWNE-CAVE, Myles
Denton Hall, London (0171) 242 1212
email: mcbc@dentonhall.com
Specialisation: Partner; extensive experience both in industry and private practice in all aspects of the exploration for, production, transportation, processing, marketing and sale of oil and gas in the UK and continental Europe. Also experience in the Middle East and Japan.
Career: Qualified: 1974. Joined *Denton Hall* 1975. Partner of *Denton Hall* 1980.
Personal: Born: 1949.

CLOUGH, Adrian
Herbert Smith, London (0171) 374 8000
Specialisation: Partner in *Herbert Smith's* Projects Group, specialising in privatisation, major restructurings and infrastructure projects, particularly in the electricity sector. Involvement with the electricity sector began when part of the team advising the Area Boards of England and Wales on the 1990 restructuring and their subsequent privatisation. Has continued to advise various members of the industry on contractual and regulatory issues. For the last two years has had day to day responsibility for the *Herbert Smith* team advising the 14 Public Electricity Suppliers in Great Britain on the major revisions to the industry's contractual and regulatory structure which are necessary to enable full supply competition. Has also advised British Gas in relation to the Northern Ireland electricity privatisation and the Magnox division of Nuclear Electric on the restructuring that preceded the privatisation of British Energy. Regular speaker at electricity related conferences.

Career: Educated at Christ Church, Oxford (MA); qualified as a solicitor 1988; partner of *Herbert Smith* 1995. Seconded for two years as an Assistant Director of the Office of Passenger Rail Franchising, leading the development of the new contractual and regulatory structure of the railway industry as it developed.

COFFELL, Howard
Field Fisher Waterhouse, London
(0171) 481 4841
Partner Commercial Property Department. Head of Pipeline Services Unit.
Specialisation: Practice covers acquisition, disposal and development of commercial property including industrial sites, oil and gas terminals and facilities and the construction of cross-country pipelines. Acts for a number of major UK oil and gas companies and pipeline operators.
Prof. Memberships: Law Society.
Career: Qualified 1974, having joined *Field Fisher Waterhouse* in 1972. Became a Partner in 1978.
Personal: Born 23rd November 1948. Attended King Henry VIII School, Coventry and Magdalen College, Oxford.

DALLAS, James
Denton Hall, London (0171) 242 1212
jad@dentonhall.com
Chairman of *Denton Hall* Partner in Energy and Infrastructure Group.
Specialisation: Experienced in oil and gas work, including project finance; gas, electricity and rail privatisation and regulation in the UK and internationally; private finance initiative projects in the UK. Regular speaker at conferences on privatisation and regulation issues. Editor of the *Utilities Law Review*.
Prof. Memberships: Law Society; UK Oil Lawyers Group; Centre for the Study of Regulated Industries (committee member).
Career: Qualified 1979 while articled with a City firm. Joined *Denton Hall* in 1985, became a Partner in 1986 and Chairman 1996.
Personal: Born 1955. Attended Eton College and St Edmund Hall, Oxford 1973-76 (MA Jurisprudence).

DAVEY, Henry
Herbert Smith, London (0171) 374 8000
Specialisation: Electricity: Involved in the privatisation and restructuring of the UK electricity industry in 1990, acting on behalf of the 12 Regional Electricity Companies and in the restructuring of the electricity industry in Northern Ireland. Continues to advise on the UK electricity industry, including UK power projects (Humber Power, Sutton Bridge, Kingsnorth, Porth yr Ogof, Salt End, South Denes), and advises on innovative electricity and gas trading contracts. Advises on international power projects and on electricity transmission projects (gas, coal and hydro-electric) including in Europe, India and the Middle East.
Specialisation: Oil and Gas: Advises on UK and international oil and gas projects, including UK oil and gas field developments and asset acquisitions and disposals (including the Alba, Beryl, Boulton, Brae, Britannia, Everest, Gallahad, Hudson, Hutton, Audrey & Johnston, Markham and Victor fields) and on all aspects of oil and gas contracts, including joint ventures and joint operating agreements; advises on gas sales and transportation agreements, including sales of gas to power stations and gas to gas

trading and the Network Code. Advises on international oil and gas transactions, including acquisitions and disposals, production sharing agreements, licensing and concession agreements and development contracts in various jurisdictions (including Russia, Kazakstan, Falkland Islands, South America and India).
Prof. Memberships: Member of IBA. Member of the United Kingdom Energy Lawyers Group.
Career: Partner in *Herbert Smith*. Joined *Herbert Smith* as a trainee in September 1986; qualified in 1988. MA Cantab (Queens' College), Law; Nottingham High School.

DAVIES, Roger
Allen & Overy, London (0171) 330 3000
Specialisation: Partner in charge of oil and gas group; other areas of practice include international joint ventures and commercial contracts; also specialises in hotel sale and purchase and management contracts.
Career: Articled *Allen & Overy*, qualified 1972, Partner 1976, Partner in charge of Dubai office 1980-83.
Personal: Fitzwilliam College, Cambridge 1969. Born 1946.

DOEH, Doran
Allen & Overy, London Moscow:
(00 7) 501 258 3111
Specialisation: Based in Moscow office. Covers all aspects of oil and gas and minerals transactions in Russia, including licensing, production sharing agreements, joint ventures, acquisitions and disposals, financing and securities.
Prof. Memberships: Law Society; Honorary Associate, Institute of Petroleum and Minerals Law and Policy, University of Dundee.
Career: Qualified as barrister 1973; solicitor 1987. Joined *Allen & Overy* 1986, Partner *Allen & Overy* 1995. 1975-86 Legal Adviser, Burmah Oil North Sea Limited/The British National Oil Corporation/Britoil Plc.
Personal: Born 14.5.48 in New York. Educated Dartmouth College (USA), Oxford University (England), London University (England). Leisure: cooking, wine, opera, tennis.

DUNNE, Michelle
Clyde & Co, London (0171) 623 1244
Partner in Energy, Trade and Asset Finance Group.
Specialisation: Main area of practice is energy. Specialises in oil and gas work, including joint operating agreements, unit operating agreements, transportation and distribution, licensing, FPSOs, safety case requirements and operational issues generally, gas sales and asset sales and purchases and swaps. Work in domestic and international, particularly Continental Europe, Scandinavia, South America, Falklands Islands and FSU.
Prof. Memberships: Law Society, International Bar Association.
Career: Qualified in 1979 (Scotland) and 1985 (England). Since 1981 main practice area has been natural resources (in-house and private practice).

ELDER, Ian
Allen & Overy, London (0171) 330 3000
Specialisation: Partner specialising in major projects and joint ventures with particular emphasis upon infrastructure and electricity projects.
Prof. Memberships: Law Society (England

and Scotland), IBA, City of London Solicitors Company.
Career: Apprenticed *Dundas & Wilson*; qualified Scotland 1977, England 1984; Solicitor ICI legal department 1977-87; Assistant Solicitor, *Allen & Overy* 1987-89; Partner 1989.
Personal: St Andrew's University (1972 MA); Edinburgh University (1974 LLB). Born 1951.

FELTER, Peter
Clyde & Co, London (0171) 623 1244
Partner and Head of Energy.
Specialisation: Chairman, *Clyde & Co.* Energy, Trade & Asset Finance Group. Extensive international experience of oil and gas; upstream and downstream; onshore/offshore, FPSO's, pipelines, platforms, refineries etc. Also extensive experience in power projects, intern. gas, metals and minerals. Crossborder and government transactions, finance arrangements, wind power.
Prof. Memberships: Danish Law Society and UKOGLG.
Career: Danish Advocate 1985; Editorial Board Member OGTLR; former manager within Maersk Oil and Gas, North Sea operator of DUC.
Personal: LLM (CPH); PhD (Cantab).

GRIFFIN, Paul
Ashurst Morris Crisp, London
(0171) 638 1111
Partner in Energy Group.
Specialisation: Wide experience in energy law, in particular the oil, gas and electricity sectors, both in the UK and overseas. Recently, has been involved in the re-negotiation of long term take-or-pay contracts in liberalised gas and electricity markets and has also been much involved in energy related disputes in court and before experts and arbitrators. Currently working on LNG sales, power generation and projects for the export of petroleum from the Copious Ice area to international markets.
Prof. Memberships: Writes and lectures widely.

GROOM, Malcolm
Denton Hall, London (0171) 242 1212
email: mdjg@dentonhall.com
Partner in Company and Commercial Department (Head of Energy and Infrastructure Group).
Specialisation: Areas of expertise include oil and gas regulatory work and production sharing agreements, joint ventures and project financing, long-term gas purchase contracts, gas marketing, pipeline finance, construction and carriage arrangements. Has substantial international experience, including former Soviet Union countries, Europe, Australia and Africa.
Prof. Memberships: International Bar Association. UK Oil and Gas Lawyers Association. Law Society.
Career: Qualified in 1974 after articles at *Linklaters & Paines*. Legal Adviser, Union Oil Co., California 1974-83. Joined *Warrens* as a Partner in 1983.
Personal: Born 16th June 1950. Educated at Kingston Grammar School, Manchester Grammar School and Trinity Hall, Cambridge (1st Class Hons in Law). Leisure pursuits include marathon running and chess.

HIGGINSON, Tony
Lovell White Durrant, London
(0171) 236 0066
Specialisation: Energy & Natural Resources: advising both in the UK and internationally on

energy projects, including: concession and production sharing contracts; corporate and asset transactions; gas supply and marketing contracts; LNG; transportation and tariffing; downstream refining and product sales and power generation.
Prof. Memberships: International Bar Association; Institute of Petroleum; Association of International Petroleum Negotiators.
Career: MA, Emmanuel College, Cambridge (1971); Graduate PMD Harvard Business School 1987; Articled *Herbert Smith*; legal adviser Vickers Plc, 1974-6; attorney Phillips Petroleum Company Europe – Africa and Phillips Petroleum Company, Oklahoma 1976-84; General Counsel Sun Oil International; Managing Director Sun Oil Britain Limited, Far East Regional Manager, Sun Oil, 1984-1992; partner *Lovell White Durrant* 1996.

HURST, Philip
Ashurst Morris Crisp, London
(0171) 638 1111
Partner in Projects Group.
Specialisation: Heads mining team and electricity team. Leading practitioner in natural resources law, especially in Africa, Middle East and South Asia. Extensive experience in advising sponsors of independent power projects, particularly in India and Pakistan, eg Hub River, Tractebel Khaleej, Triveni Zond, Indus Grid (NGC). Currently advising on privatisation and refinancing of Zambia Consolidated Copper Mines.
Career: BA, LLB(ANU), MA, LLM (Virginia). 1981-1985 associate *White & Case*, New York; 1985-1987, Counsel, The World Bank, Washington DC; 1988-1992, Solicitor *Linklaters & Paines*, London.

JONES, Alan
LeBoeuf, Lamb, Greene & MacRae, London
(0171) 459 5000
Specialisation: Main areas of practice are corporate and project finance, international privatisations and cross-border acquisitions, utilities, water and energy. Numerous articles published in legal and energy publications and has been a frequent speaker at conferences and seminars.
Prof. Memberships: Law Society, International Bar Association (SERL), Association of International Petroleum Negotiators and the UK Energy Lawyers Group.
Career: Qualified as a Solicitor in 1983. He joined *Clifford Chance* in 1981, was partner between 1990 and 1995 and was the partner in charge of the energy group. He joined *LeBoeuf, Lamb, Greene & McRae* as a partner in July 1995.
Personal: Born 1958. LLB (Hons) University College, London 1980. Lives in Richmond, Surrey.

JONES, Gareth
Nabarro Nathanson, London
(0171) 493 9933
Energy law. Power station and infrastructure projects. Power and gas supply/distribution/transportation contracts. Related Regulatory Advice. Oil and gas projects.
Prof. Memberships: Law Society, Institute of Petroleum.
Career: Qualified in 1980. Worked at *Thomas Cooper & Co.*, 1980-83. Joined *Nabarro*

Nathanson in 1983 onwards (Partner in 1986).
Personal: *Nabarro Nathanson.* London
(0171) 518 3209

JONES, Richard
Linklaters, London (0171) 456 2000

JOWETT, Alan
Herbert Smith, London (0171) 374 8000
Partner in Corporate Department.
Specialisation: Main area of practice is energy law, projects and related project finance work. Heads the firm's Central and East European Group.
Career: Qualified in 1977. Joined *Herbert Smith* in 1974 and became a Partner in 1986.

KHAN, Rafique
Cameron McKenna, London
(0171) 367 3000
Specialisation: Specialises in oil and gas particularly in the areas of natural gas production, transportation and supply with an additional emphasis on project-financed CCGT Power Projects. Has extensive experience of the European natural gas industries both in the commercial and regulatory field. Speaker on legislative, regulatory and commercial issues facing the gas industries in the UK, elsewhere in the European Union and Central and Eastern Europe.
Prof. Memberships: Law Society of England and Wales; The Institute of Petroleum.
Career: Graduated in 1982 from the University of Leeds; articled clerk and senior legal adviser at *British Gas* 1984-1992. In 1992 joined *McKenna & Co* as Assistant Solicitor and since 1994 a partner in the Energy, Projects and Construction Group.
Personal: Cinema, Opera, Eating, Walking and Climbing.

LANE, Robert
Cameron McKenna, London
(0171) 367 3000
Partner specialising in utilities law and regulation.
Specialisation: Extensive experience of electricity projects and restructurings in the UK and overseas. Adviser to The National Grid Company plc. From 1988 to 1990 advised on the restructuring of the England and Wales electricity industry, including drafting the Grid Code for the England and Wales system, with extensive involvement in the design of the regulatory regime and pooling arrangements and in drafting and advising on many of the other documents (e.g. those dealing with connection to and use of the system). Continues to advise on these topics. Also adviser to Northern Ireland Electricity plc on its re-structuring and privatisation and adviser to the ESI Reform Unit of the State Government of Victoria (which involved consideration of and scoping of the regulatory, contractual and code structures and critiquing the licences, codes and contracts). He has also worked on power purchase agreements relating to Electricidade de Portugal and the Public Power Corporation of Greece and advised on all aspects of the restructuring of the electricity supply industry in Orissa, India. Adviser to Electricity Supply Board in Eire and to Ontario Hydro in Canada.

Advising in a number of jurisdictions on the implementation of the Internal Electricity Market Directive, including drafting legislation and transitional regimes. Regular speaker at conferences throughout the world.
Prof. Memberships: International Bar Association (Member of Section on Energy and Natural Resources Law and vice-chairman of Utilities Law Committee).
Career: Qualified in 1982. Joined *McKenna & Co* eight years ago.
Personal: Educated at University College, London.

MORONEY, David
Denton Hall, Singapore (65) 5381551
email: dfm@dentonhall.com.sg
Head of Projects, Asia.
Specialisation: Specialises in energy and natural resources law. Work includes international projects, financing and transactions, privatisation, and drafting of legislation for developing markets. Particular expertise in oil and gas, electricity and mining sectors. In addition to UK, international experience includes former Soviet countries, Asia, Australia, Africa and Europe. Considerable experience in-house. Experienced conference lecturer.
Prof. Memberships: International Bar Association (Section on Energy & Natural Resources Law – Chairman).
Career: Qualified as a Solicitor in New South Wales 1969. Legal and Lands Manager, Burmah Oil, London & Australia 1969-77. UK Legal Adviser, Deminex Oil and Gas, London 1977-80. Uranium Contracts Manager and Corporate Solicitor, Western Mining Corporation Ltd, Melbourne 1980-81. General Counsel, International Energy Development Corporation, Switzerland and UK 1981-86. Solicitor *Allen Allen & Hemsley*, Sydney 1987-88. Qualified in England & Wales and joined *Denton Hall* in 1988. Became a Partner in 1989.
Personal: Born 20th October 1945. Educated at the University of Sydney (LL.B).

NEWBERY, Mark
Herbert Smith, Singapore (65) 536 7990
Managing Partner of the Singapore Office.
Specialisation: Has experience in a wide range of corporate matters including major project finance transactions; has considerable experience of the electricity industry having acted for the 12 regional electricity companies in the restructuring of the supply industry prior to privatisation in 1990 and having led the team acting for all 14 public electricity suppliers in the development of the regulatory and contractual matrix required for the introduction of full competition in the supply of electricity in 1998; has also acted on numerous independent power generation projects in the UK and restructurings and projects overseas.
Career: Educated at Nottingham University; qualified 1982; partner *Herbert Smith* 1989.

OTWAY, L.
Lawrence Graham, London (0171) 379 0000
Specialisation: Main area of practice is energy law, mainly upstream oil and gas and in particular asset sales and purchases, swaps, farm-ins, and reorganisations. Recently completed a placement at a major oil company during which advised on a range of oil industry contracts and issues.
Prof. Memberships: The Law Society

Career: Reading University (BA Psychology). Qualified as a solicitor in 1991.
Personal: Lives in North London and Hertfordshire. Enjoys the gym, reading, wine, dancing and newly – acquired family.

PEGG, Garry
LeBoeuf, Lamb, Greene & MacRae, London (0171) 459 5000
Specialisation: Main areas of specialisation are corporate and commercial work focussing on projects, particularly in the Energy and Natural Resources Sector, and Private International Law generally.
Prof. Memberships: Law Society, International Bar Association (SERL), Association of International Petroleum Negotiators and the UK Energy Lawyers Sub Group. Numerous articles published in Legal and energy publications and has been a frequent speaker at conferences and seminars.
Career: Qualified as a Barrister in 1981 and requalified as a solicitor in 1994. Began his career with the West of England P & I Club, was staff legal adviser at Chevron UK Limited between March 1986-1990, and Senior International Counsel at BHP Petroleum Limited between 1990 – 1992. Was with *Clifford Chance* between 1992-1995 and joined *LeBoeuf, Lamb, Greene & MacRae* as a partner in June 1996. Currently acts as a Director of a number of energy companies including Claims Validation Services Limited.
Personal: Born 1958. BA (Hons) Law Class 2.1 University of Kent 1981. Lives in London.

PICTON-TURBERVILL, Geoffrey
Ashurst Morris Crisp, London (0171) 638 1111
Partner in Energy Group.
Specialisation: Commercial lawyer specialising in energy and natural resources law, in particular upstream and downstream oil and gas and power both in the UK and overseas. His work covers all aspects of oil and gas and electricity industries, and he has particular expertise in mergers and acquisitions and project work.
Prof. Memberships: India Editor of 'Oil & Gas Law & Taxation Review,' and the author of the chapter on 'Oil and Gas Acquisition Agreements' for Sweet & Maxwell.

REES, Jonathan
Freshfields, London (0171) 936 4000
Specialisation: Head of the Freshfields Energy Group; specialises in international M&A, oil and gas and natural resource work. Clients include oil companies, mining companies and investment banks.
Prof. Memberships: International Bar Association (Section on Energy and Natural Resources Law).
Career: *Freshfields* 1982, qualified in 1984 and became a partner in 1992.
Personal: Educated at Wadham College, Oxford (MA).

ROBERTS, Martin J.D.
Slaughter and May, London (0171) 600 1200
See under Project Finance, p. 687

ROWEY, Kent
Freshfields, London (0171) 936 4000
Specialisation: Head of *Freshfields'* international project finance group, with over ten years experience representing lenders, sponsors and suppliers in independent power projects

throughout Europe, Asia and the United States. Currently involved in power projects in Peru and the UK. Recently closed power projects include representing the largest lender to the Uch Power Project in Pakistan and the Saba Power Project in Pakistan, and acting as project counsel to the Khimti Power Project in Nepal.
Prof. Memberships: State Bar of California, American Bar Association, International Bar Association.
Career: B.A. Philosphy, University of California, Los Angeles, (Magna cum laude) J.D. New York University. Partner, *Perkins Coie*, London. Associate *Milbank, Tweed, Hadley & McCloy*, Los Angeles, London.
Personal: Lives in Oxfordshire with wife Rosalie and two children, Allison and Austin. Avid (but average) golfer, and infrequent (but fairly useful) sailor.

SALT, Stuart
Linklaters, London (0171) 456 5912
See under Project Finance, p. 687

SAS, Blanche
Denton Hall, London (0171) 242 1212
Brussels 00 32 2 223 0621
email: 100675.3157@compuserve.com
Fax 00 7 502 213 9214.
Head of Brussels Office. Responsible for Central and Eastern Energy Practice.
Specialisation: Specialist in energy legislation and commercial contracts in Eastern Europe and former Soviet Union; international and comparative law in relation to petroleum regimes; upstream oil and gas contracts in particular Production Sharing Agreements (PSA); downstream energy law in particular, pipeline regulation and contracts; privatisation and regulation of electricity and gas industries; energy sales contracts (electricity, gas, oil, coal and uranium) and oil trading. Editor of *Oil and Gas Law and Taxation Review* and author of numerous publications on energy law.
Prof. Memberships: International Bar Association.
Career: Lecturer in petroleum law at Dundee University 1985-91. Joined *Denton Hall* in 1991.
Personal: Born 28th March, 1948. Fluent French, English and Italian – working Russian.

SAUNDERS, Mark
Nabarro Nathanson, London (0171) 518 3204
Partner specialising in all aspects of energy law and corporate law.
Specialisation: Head of the firm's Energy Group specialising in all aspects of energy law particularly oil and gas. Seconded to a major oil and gas company in the mid 1980s. Outside counsel to a number of the integrated majors as well as service companies within the sector. Also solicitor to oil industry environmental response collective. An editor of OGLTR, frequent speaker at energy conferences worldwide, contributed to Sweet & Maxwell's "Upstream Oil and Gas Agreements." Listed in Chambers Survey of Leading UK Commercial Lawyers as one of the eight leading commercial lawyers in the United Kingdom 1997-1998.

SAYER, Stephen T.
Richards Butler, London (0171) 247 6555
Specialisation: Specialises in energy law, competition law and international commercial law. Is head of the firm's Energy Group and has extensive practical experience in this area. In the

energy field he has represented governments and oil companies in a wide range of oil, gas and electricity related matters. Has experience of drafting legislation and regulations relating to electricity and oil, joint production arrangements, supply agreements, concession agreements and special tax arrangements between oil companies and governments. He has similar experience in relation to gas agreements. Has negotiated energy import/export agreements for several Central European and Middle Eastern countries and advised on refinery projects in Panama and Russia. Has also represented the European Commission in relation to the Energy Charter Treaty. In the field of Energy regulation, he has advised on regulation of state owned monopolies in newly emerging economies, including Kyrgyzstan and Lithuania. Is a contributor to Longman's 'Practical Commercial Precedents' and other publications. Has written numerous papers and lectured extensively around the world. In particular, he has lectured on all aspects of EU energy policy, including speeches on the creation of an internal electricity market and on the EU energy policy White Paper. Through the British "Know-How" Fund, he has been a speaker at international seminars on energy subjects in Poland and Hungary.
Prof. Memberships: Institute of Petroleum, United Kingdom Oil Lawyers Group, the City of London Solicitors Company.
Career: Qualified in 1968 and joined *Richards Butler* in the same year. Became a Partner in 1974.
Personal: Born 8th July 1945. Interests include racquets, real tennis, golf and theatre. Lives in London.

SIMPSON, Paul
Clifford Chance, London (0171) 600 1000
See under Project Finance, p. 688

STACEY, Paul
Slaughter and May, London (0171) 600 1200
See under Project Finance, p. 688

STANGER, Michael
Lovell White Durrant, London (0171) 236 0066
Specialisation: Practice covers a wide range of work related to the gas industry; heavily involved in the recent structural changes in the UK, acting on behalf of gas shippers in relation to the drafting of the Network Code and the 'Claims Validation' agreements; and acting for the Bacton Agent's Group in relation to gas flows through the Interconnector to Continental Europe. Practice also covers gas trading agreements, gas supply agreements, gas storage and work related to the development of independent gas pipeline systems.
Prof. Memberships: Law Society, City of London Solicitors Company, Institute of Petroleum, UK Energy Lawyers Group.
Career: Field Engineer in the oil industry for SPE Schlumberger, mainly in Africa, 1975 to 1978; articled *Lovell White & King* (now *Lovell White Durrant*); qualified 1981; Partner 1986.

TAYLOR, Michael
Norton Rose, London (0171) 283 6000
email: taylormpg@nortonrose.com
Partner, Project Group, *Norton Rose*.
Specialisation: Project finance and energy and natural resources. Has specialised in the development and financing of projects in the energy and natural resources fields since joining *Norton Rose* in 1974; became a partner

1979. A member of the editorial board of Oil and Gas Law and Taxation Review and contributing editor to Butterworth's Financial Services Law and Practice. Co-author of a book on oil and gas joint ventures.

TUDWAY, Robert
Nabarro Nathanson, London
(0171) 493 9933
Specialisation: Energy Law.
Prof. Memberships: International Bar Association. Statute Law Society.

TURTLE, Trevor W.
Herbert Smith, London (0171) 374 8000
Partner since 1987 in Company Department, with general corporate and commercial practice.
Specialisation: Specialisations include non-contentious insurance, particularly insurance insolvency and demutualisation, regulatory, project and corporate work in water sector.

TYNE, Sally M.
Cameron McKenna, London
(0171) 367 3000
Specialisation: Specialises in oil and gas, with particular emphasis on acquisitions and disposals of UKCS and international petroleum interests via share or asset deals. Extensive experience of oil industry contracts and joint venture issues. Speaker on licensing, unitisation, JOAs and oil & gas acquisition agreements. Co-author of second edition of Taylor & Winsor on Joint Operating Agreements (standard industry textbook).
Prof. Memberships: United Kingdom Energy Lawyers Group (IBA); Law Society.
Career: Educated Trinity College, Oxford.

Joined *Cameron Markby Hewitt* (prior to merger with *McKenna & Co*) as an oil & gas partner in London, reinforcing *CMH*'s strong existing energy practices in London and Aberdeen. Previously specialised in oil & gas for ten years at *Norton Rose*.
Personal: Married with three children.

VERRILL, John
Lawrence Graham, London (0171) 379 0000
See under Insolvency, p. 444

WALLACE, Patrick
Freshfields, London (0171) 936 4000
Specialisation: Advised on establishing the UK electricity market structure at privatisation. Acted on a wide range of electricity projects in the UK and internationally. Advises on energy and natural resources, project financing, regulatory issues, privatisation, commercial contracts and corporate transactions. Speaks English, German and French.
Career: Holds degrees from London, Paris and Harvard Universities. Qualified in 1986. Partner since 1992. Now in Frankfurt with *Deringer Tessin Herrmann & Sedemund* in association with *Freshfields*.

WOOD, Charles
Denton Hall, London (0171) 242 1212
email: cwcw@dentonhall.com
Specialisation: Partner, experience includes commercial contracts and regulation in gas and electricity sectors and LNG projects. Adviser to BG Transco on UK network code.
Career: Articled at *Denton Hall*. Qualified 1980. Partner 1984.
Personal: Born 1955.

WOOLF, Fiona
Cameron McKenna, London
(0171) 367 3000
Energy Projects and Construction Group.
Specialisation: Main areas of practice are electricity restructurings and privatisations, regulation and the introduction of wholesale and retail competitive markets in the power sector, projects and financings. Worked exclusively on banking and project finance transactions in Bahrain, 1982-85. Acted in the Channel Tunnel project as one of the lead negotiators on the Concession Agreement and the Treaty with British and French Governments. Led a team of 40 people acting for The National Grid Company plc on the privatisation of the Electricity Supply Industry in England and Wales and advised on the Northern Ireland Electricity restructuring and privatisation. Advised Electricidade de Portugal on the Tapada do Outeiro and Pego power projects and the project to bring natural gas to Portugal. Worked on independent transmission projects in Pakistan and Malaysia and the privatisation of the transmission system of Argentina. Has worked on power sector restructurings, utility regulation and privatisations in Australia, Canada, India, California and the Republic of Ireland. Contributor to 'Utilities Law Review' and the Electricity Journal; regular speaker at conferences.
Prof. Memberships: Council Member of the Law Society.
Career: Qualified in 1973. Worked at *Coward Chance* 1973-78 before joining *McKenna & Co*. in 1978. Became a Partner in 1981.
Personal: Born 11th May 1948. Attended Keele University 1966-70. Leisure interests include wine and opera. Lives in Esher, Surrey.

The SOUTH and WALES

HIGHLY REGARDED FIRMS
THE SOUTH AND WALES

Bond Pearce Plymouth
Deborah Mills Associates Marlow
Veale Wasbrough Bristol
Foot & Bowden Plymouth
Stephens & Scown Exeter

Bond Pearce (Plymouth) (3ptnrs/2assocs/2assts) *Marcus Trinick* and his team "do some things brilliantly." Those "things" include wind farm developments and waste to energy schemes. **Clients/Work:** Advising on renewable energy projects throughout the UK and Ireland, including site acquisition, planning and corporate finance for projects exceeding 700MW.

Deborah Mills & Associates (Marlow) (2ptnrs/1assoc/2assts) "A private practice that can act like an in-house oil & gas team." **Clients/Work:** Acted for Risel in its acquisition from Conoco of a 20% interest in the MacCullock field. Acted for Mitsubishi, Esso and Ranger on a regular basis, including Andrew Field, Elgin/Franklin and CTAP.

Veale Wasbrough (Bristol) (1ptnr/1asst) *Tim Smithers* (a member of the Pipeline Industry's Guild) has successfully established a niche practice advising the oil and gas industry on pipeline issues. **Clients/Work:** Advisors to Esso Petroleum Company Ltd on its national oil pipeline network. Advisors to Fina PLC on pipeline management. Advising on Seabank Power's 27km gas pipeline constructed to serve a new power station on Sevenside.

Foot & Bowden (Plymouth) (3ptnrs/1 planning-landuse barrister) Reputation for mines and minerals work. **Clients/Work:** The senior partner edits the Mines & Minerals section of the Encyclopedia of Forms & Precedents.

Stephens & Scown (Exeter) (8ptnrs/1 consultant) Newly recommended this year for their minerals practice and renewables practice. **Clients/Work:** Advising on renewables WFFO order and generation of electricity from methane gas. NFFO3 application for a hydroelectric scheme. Handling of mineral waste tipping application for ECC International.

LEADING INDIVIDUALS
THE SOUTH AND WALES

MILLS Deborah	Deborah Mills Associates
SMITHERS Tim	Veale Wasbrough
TRINICK Marcus	Bond Pearce

MIDLANDS

Martineau Johnson (Birmingham) (3ptnrs/4assts) One of the few regional firms involved in main stream energy work in both gas and electricity. *Andrew Whitehead* heads an "impressive" utilities department. *Paul Brennan* (ex senior legal adviser at BG Transco) was recommended for his knowledge of the Network Code, gas sales, transport and allocations issues. Clients/Work: Sole legal adviser on the creation of the world's first market in Reactive Power, involving advice to the National Grid Company Plc and the Electricity Pool. Advice on the provision of a black start capability at a gas fired power station. Launch of "CODE UPDATE," a monthly journal which analyses developments in the UK gas industry.

Wragge & Co (Birmingham) (4ptnrs/7assts) The core team act as project leaders, pulling in lawyers from a pool of 70. Recommended more for project work in the energy sector than for pure energy issues, although

one plc went so far as to describe them as "better than Freshfields on gas." *David Hamlett* is highly regarded. *Neil Upton* is an "able lawyer." Clients/Work: Acting on 6 CHP projects, including the construction and sale of a 140MW CHP project in mid Cheshire for PowerGen. Acting on a major private sewerage upgrade. Acting for 11 RECs and 2 generators in a £7m MBO of EATL.

Edge & Ellison (Birmingham) (2ptnrs/3assts) *Gwyn Williams* (ex Tarmac and "a practical lawyer with great experience") is a well known character in minerals. One interviewee went so far as to say "he can do no wrong." Clients/Work: Acting for Eastern Group on the development of Eastern Gas. Acquiring a site for RMC Group as a waste disposal facility. Advising Aggregate Industries on a joint venture for the development of a road surfacing material.

Edwards Geldard (Derby) (1ptnr/2assts) Most of the firm's energy work is centred in Derby where the commercial contract and utilities team act for a number of RECs on electricty and gas issues. Clients/Work: Advising East Midlands and SWALEC on the Pool, power purchase agreements, other supply agreements, gas sales and gas trading.

Eversheds (Birmingham) (1ptnr/2assts) Within the firm's overall Energy, Utilities & Natural Resources unit, the Birmingham office concentrates on gas issues. Newly joined by the charismatic ex-senior partner of mining specialist, Kent Jones & Done, who is expected to develop a minerals practice. Clients/Work: Advising a regional power company and its subsidiaries on gas and electricity issues, including the Network Code, trading documentation and supply

agreements. Windfarms and other renewables.

Pinsent Curtis (Birmingham) (4ptnrs/2assts) Clients/Work: Hampshire Waste Management Contract including three waste to energy plants. NFFO IV Contracts for Offer. Energy contracts for Centrica.

Crane & Walton (Leicester) One of a dying breed of Midlands coal experts.

Kent Jones & Done (Stoke-on-Trent) (1ptnr/1assoc/1asst) A mining and minerals practice. Despite losing some key players in recent years, the practice was thought to be in reasonable shape. Clients/Work: Purchase of the minerals interests at a quarry in the Staffordshire Moorlands. Ongoing title audit for a major plc. Negotiating and preparing mineral leases for a major plc.

Knight & Sons (Newcastle Under Lyme) (2ptnrs/2assts) Another minerals practice acting for some of the largest companies in the sector. *Tony Bell* has been in the business for a long time and "knows how to get things done." Act for both extractors and landed estates. Clients/Work: ARC, Hepworth Minerals and Chemicals Ltd, the Crown Estate.

SEE PROFILES AT END OF THIS SECTION

The NORTH

Eversheds (Leeds) (1ptnr/2assts) *Neil Brown* is the epicentre of the firm's national energy practice. The Leeds office is best known for electricity. Clients/Work: Power project for Yorkshire Cogen Ltd including 2 on-site 50MW CGT/CHP schemes and one stand-alone embedded CCGT scheme. Five on-site power generation schemes ranging form 50MW to more than 100MW for a variety of industrial users. Agreements between

Yorkshire Electricity and NGC to provide a probalistic frequency response service.

Nabarro Nathanson (Sheffield) (5ptnrs/5assts) Having taken on most of the old NCB/British Coal legal team it is no surprise that the firm "knows a lot about coal." The group are also involved in O&G matters and there is a specialist minerals and mining litigation group. *Mike Renger* has a national reputation. Clients/Work: Disposal of an oil refinery. Acquisition of CRC Evans Pipeline Inc group of companies by Natural Gas Partners. Acting for Coal Products in the successful defence of a group action by local residents who claimed a coking plant was causing damage.

Dickinson Dees (Newcastle-Upon-Tyne) (4 fee earners) The leading north-east minerals practice and advisers to Northern Electric and Northumbrian Water on regulatory and commercial issues, and on small power projects. Clients/Work: Advising Northern Electric on gas purchase and transportation agreements, take or pay contracts, connection agreements and terms and con-

ditions of industrial and domestic supply.

Pinsent Curtis (Leeds) (4ptnrs/1assoc/1asst) A cross departmental group known for its work in minerals and waste. Clients/Work: Over 10 million cubic metres of mineral deposits and airspace. Landfill gas exploitation arragements. CHP project valued at £60m over the life of the project.

Aaron & Partners (Chester) (4ptnrs/1asst) A well known minerals and waste practice. Clients/Work: Planning and environmental agreements for a sand and gravel extraction and waste disposal site in Hertfordshire. Planning inquiry/appeals re calcite and limestone extraction and processing in Derbyshire. Acting for a water authority in planning/compulsory purchase inquiries.

SEE PROFILES AT END OF THIS SECTION

Malcolm Lynch (Leeds) (2ptnrs) A niche renewables practice. **Clients/Work:** Advising The Wind Company UK Ltd on the financing and construction of a five turbine wind cluster in Cumbria. Advising the Bay- wind Energy Co-operative Ltd on a share issue to raise finance for a wind cluster at Harlock Hill in Cumbria. A feasibility study on Biomass development for Dulas Ltd.

Wake Dyne Lawton (Chester) (2ptnrs/ 1asst) The firm set up by *Brian Wake* when he left Aaron & Partners. A dedicated min- erals, waste, environment and transport firm.

SCOTLAND

HIGHLY REGARDED FIRMS SCOTLAND
Biggart Baillie Glasgow
Dundas & Wilson CS Edinburgh
MacRoberts Glasgow
Shepherd & Wedderburn WS Edinburgh
Cameron McKenna Aberdeen
Ledingham Chalmers Aberdeen
Burness Edinburgh
Deborah Mills Associates Aberdeen
McGrigor Donald Glasgow
Paull & Williamsons Aberdeen

Biggart Baillie (4ptnrs/3assts) The firm with the lions' share of ScottishPower's work. *David Ross* is the "main man" and "one of the best energy lawyers in private practice" according to some clients. "He spots the right issues and doesn't mess about." Increasing involvement in gas issues. **Clients/Work:** Advising the 14 PESs on the Scottish aspects of the introduction of competition in the elec- tricity market. Advising ScottishPower on a CHP plant in the London Borough of Barnet and on a proposed gas storage project in North Yorkshire, one of the few such projects in the UK not operated by BG Transco.

Dundas & Wilson CS (4ptnrs/10assts) The jewel in the practice's crown is Scottish Hydro-Electric, Scotland's second largest vertically integrated electricity company. Merged with Dorman Jeffrey & Co, a firm which had a reputable energy practice. Also experienced in coal and minerals. The "quiet and reserved" *Donald Cumming* has a repu- tation in electricity. **Clients/Work:** Acting for Scottish Hydro-Electric in the buy-out of Norweb's interest in the Keadby Power Sta- tion joint venture and on long term gas sup- ply and storage contracts. Acting for the lenders on Dundee City Council's £44m waste to energy plant.

MacRoberts (3ptnrs/2assts) *Ian Dick- son,* "a great technician, draftsman and nego- tiator," and his small team are well known, mainly in nuclear. **Clients/Work:** British Energy plc, Scottish Nuclear Ltd and Nuclear Energy plc.

Shepherd & Wedderburn (5ptnrs/ 10assts) The lead firm in establishing Scot- tish Settlement System, the Scottish equiva- lent of the Electricity Pool, a joint venture between ScottishPower and Scottish Hydro- Electric. *James Saunders* "got in at the ground floor and knows his stuff." **Clients/Work:** Advising ScottishPower on the Northern Ireland interconnector. Cairn Energy/Shell joint venture in Bangladesh. Advising ScottishPower on the revision of its composite licence in relation to the imple- mentation of supply competition.

Cameron McKenna (2ptnrs/10assts) "Generally good, they're on the spot which counts for a lot." Have plenty of practical, day to day experience of up stream, operational work. *Penelope Warne* is "reliable, knows what she's doing and has tremendous drive." A steadily expanding office which this year takes on a second partner. Most lawyers are dual qualified. **Clients/Work:** Advising on gas issues for BP's Saltens Co-Gen project at Hull. Combining with the Petroleum Centre at Dundee University for its 3rd joint conference in Houston.

Ledingham Chalmers (3ptnrs/9assts) *Robert Ruddiman,* a "can do guy," has his foot firmly in the door. Despite less back up than Camerons, Bob's team was recom- mended for its "high average level of com- petence and experience," particularly at the operational, off-shore supply end of the busi- ness. The firm has offices in Baku, Istanbul and the Falklands, the latter staffed by a senior assistant and a trainee. **Clients/Work:** Ramco Energy plc on their issue of ADR's and admission to the American stock exchange. Acting for Elf Exploration UK plc on aspects of the Elgin/Franklin field. Talis- man Energy (UK) Ltd.

Burness (4ptnrs/4assts) A new entrant on the back of strong recommendations. **Clients/Work:** Re-appointed as Scottish solicitors for Magnox Electric plc following privatisation of the nuclear industry. Gas and electricity sale and supply contracts for Fife Power, the UK's first Advanced Fuel Tech- nology-Intergrated Gasification Combined Cycle power station on behalf of Global Energy Inc.

Deborah Mills & Associates (1assoc/ 1asst) The newly opened office of the niche oil practice. Described as a "body shop" pro- viding consultants who know the industry. **Clients/Work:** Acted for Elf in corporate assignment of Elgin/Franklin interest between subsidiaries. Targeting sub-contractor indus- try in Aberdeen. Close connections with the O&G department at Aberdeen University.

McGrigor Donald (2ptnrs/3assts) By acting for the Government on the privatisa- tion of the utilities in Scotland, McGrigor's gained "all the expertise but none of the clients" amongst the companies that now dominate the Scottish scene. **Clients/Work:** Acting for Northern Ireland Electricity on the interconnector between Scotland and the Province. Advising BP on the enhancement of the electricity supplies to the Grange- mouth petrochemical complex. Acting for BP Energy Ltd on small CHP projects in northern England and Northern Ireland.

Paull & Williamson A competent practice in up stream oil and gas. Many in-house teams in Aberdeen have a few ex P&W lawyers.

LEADING INDIVIDUALS SCOTLAND
ANDREWS Patrick Shepherd & Wedderburn WS
CUMMING Donald Dundas & Wilson CS
DICKSON Ian MacRoberts
ROSS David Biggart Baillie
RUDDIMAN Robert Ledingham Chalmers
SAUNDERS James Shepherd & Wedderburn WS
WARNE Penelope Cameron McKenna

LEADERS' PROFILES · REGIONS

ANDREWS, Patrick
Shepherd & Wedderburn WS, Edinburgh
Glasgow (0141) 566 9900
Partner in Commercial Property Department.
Specialisation: Main areas of practice are commercial property and contracts. Work has included the privatisation of Scottish Electricity Companies; the proposed interconnection between Scotland and Northern Ireland and various renewable energy projects and the property aspects of telecommunications infrastructure. Has particular knowledge of infrastructure and wayleaving.
Prof. Memberships: Law Society, WS Society.
Career: Qualified in 1984. Articled *Dundas & Wilson CS* 1984-86. Joined *Shepherd & Wedderburn WS* in 1987, becoming a Partner in 1989.

Personal: Born 10th April 1962. Holds an LLB/ DipLP from Aberdeen University. Leisure interests include sailing, hill walking, cycling and gardening. Lives West Coast.

BELL, Tony
Knight & Sons, Newcastle-under-Lyme
(01782) 619225

BRENNAN, Paul

Martineau Johnson, Birmingham
(0121) 200 3300
Specialisation: Advises a number of energy companies on gas transportation and gas storage, also advises major users on energy purchase and generation projects. Editor: Code Update. Career highlights include international litigation involving production assets in Kazakhstan, de-merger of British Gas plc and associated gas purchase and transportation arrangements, drafted Network Code for Phoenix Natural Gas.
Prof. Memberships: Law Society, UK Energy Lawyers Association, Society for Computers & Law.
Career: Stonyhurst College, Durham University, Leeds University, College of Law, Articled *TV Edwards & Co*. Various positions BG plc, Partner, *Martineau Johnson Solicitors* 1997.
Personal: Born 1961, resides Warwick with daughter and wife. Interest/Pastimes – cricket, football and the other arts.

BROWN, Neil

Eversheds, Leeds (0113) 2430391
Partner. Head of *Eversheds* Telecoms and Energy Utility Groups.
Specialisation: Leads a combined team of 8 specialist lawyers. Main area of practice is work of a commercial/regulatory nature for clients in Telecoms and Energy industries. Telecoms work includes regulatory advice, industry specific commercial agreements, network and infrastructure development, and some international projects. Telecom clients include Martin Dawes, Torch, PSI Net, Orange, Eskom Telecommunications (South Africa) and St Olav (Poland). In the Energy sector he has recently handled 4 major independent power projects, 2 for Yorkshire Electricity and 2 for major industrial buyers of power. Well-known also as an adviser on canals and inland waterways.
Prof. Memberships: International Bar Association (Communications and Utilities Committees).
Career: Joined *Breeze & Wyles*, Hertford 1981. Qualified 1983 and left to join *Watson Burton*, Newcastle. Moved to *Eversheds* in 1986. Partner 1988.
Personal: Born 17th January 1957. Attended Richard Hale, Hertford 1969-77, then Warwick University 1977-80. Leisure pursuits include supporting Newcastle United F.C., performing magic, the theatre and languages (Spanish and French). Lives near Ilkley.

CUMMING, Donald

Dundas & Wilson CS, Edinburgh
(0131) 228 8000
Specialisation: Partner in Infrastructure Group; specialist in electricity law, power projects and PFI schemes. From 1989 to 1991, worked on the restructuring and privatisation of the Scottish electricity industry. In 1996 adviser to Scottish Office on transfer of assets to implement the reorganisation of the Scottish water and sewerage industry. Heavily involved with Scottish Hydro-Electric plc in power projects, CHP schemes and other gas and electricity-related matters. Recent projects include Seabank Power joint venture and the Rocksavage independent power project.
Prof. Memberships: Law Society of Scotland, Society of Writers to Her Majesty's Signet.
Career: Attended University of Edinburgh (LLB (Hons)). Articled *Dundas & Wilson CS*; qualified 1976; assistant solicitor 1976-1981; Partner since 1981.
Personal: Born 1952. Resides Edinburgh.

DICKSON, Ian

MacRoberts, Glasgow (0141) 332 9988
See under General Corporate Finance, p. 256

HAMLETT, David

Wragge & Co, Birmingham (0121) 233 1000
Specialisation: Head of Energy/Utilities group and has a very wide experience of general corporate and commercial matters including several large scale joint ventures on which he has a proven track record. Has considerable experience in the energy field in relation to contractual and regulatory matters.
Career: Articled *Linklaters & Paines*. Qualified 1980. Joined *Wragge & Co* 1983. Became a Partner 1988.

MILLS, Deborah

Deborah Mills Associates, Marlow
(01628) 487 711

RENGER, Michael

Nabarro Nathanson, Sheffield
(01302) 344455
See under Environmental Law, p. 351

ROSS, David

Biggart Baillie, Glasgow (0141) 228 8000
Partner in Corporate Department.
Specialisation: Leads team of several lawyers working extensively in this field. Main areas of Practice are electricity and gas law. Widely involved in the drafting and negotiation of a wide variety of contracts relating to the Electricity Industry, including connection, Use of System, Supply and Sales Agreement for Electricity Companies. Work covered both the vertically integrated industry in Scotland and the industry in England and Wales. Advised on the review of the Agreement for the Nuclear Industry to supply fifty per cent of Scotland's electricity. Adviser on Scottish aspects of the contracts required for all the Public Electricity Suppliers in Great Britain post 1988. Advised on first Energy PFI contract in Health sector in England, and currently advising on Glasgow Energy Initiative £500m. PFI project to provide heating to 80,000 Council houses in Glasgow. Involved in advising on a range of CHP projects. Also extensively involved in gas law matters. Particularly drafting and negotiating contracts for the purchase and sale of gas throughout the supply stream from the field to the domestic customer, including contracts for use throughout Great Britain in the domestic gas market. Separately advises those holding Transporters, Shippers and Suppliers licences and the legal aspects of the development of gas storage in the UK. Author of text for internal circulation in the firm on energy matters; lectures to seminars for firms and clients.
Prof. Memberships: Law Society of Scotland, International Bar Association Section Energy and Natural Resources Law, Insolvency Lawyers Association.
Career: Qualified in 1972. Worked at *Maclay Murray & Spens* 1970-75. Joined *Biggart Baillie & Gifford* in 1975, becoming a Partner in 1977.
Personal: Born 14th January 1948. Attended Trinity College, Glenalmond 1961-65, then Glasgow University: Engineering 1965-66 and Law 1966-70. Business Committee, University of Glasgow 1990-96, Law Society

representative, Scottish Council Development and Industry 1995 to date. Director, Glasgow Chamber of Commerce 1996 to date. Chairman Euro-American Lawyers Group 1997 to date. Leisure interests include gardening and windsurfing. Lives in Glasgow.

RUDDIMAN, Robert J.A.

Ledingham Chalmers, Aberdeen
(01224) 408408
Specialisation: Oil and gas exploration and production. bidding agreements, licence applications, joint operating agreements, production sharing agreements, unitisation, pipeline and transportation agreements, trading in field and licence interests, onshore/offshore construction agreements, drilling contracts, logistics agreements and all aspects of contracting and operational philosophy.
Prof. Memberships: Law Society of Scotland, The Law Society.
Career: Qualified in Scots Law 1989, English Law 1994. Articled and assistant with *Shepherd & Wedderburn W.S.* 1987-1991. Legal counsel Elf Exploration 1991-1993. *Cameron Markby Hewitt* 1993-1997. Partner *Ledingham Chalmers* 1997.

SAUNDERS, James

Shepherd & Wedderburn WS, Edinburgh
(0131) 228 9900
Partner in Corporate Department.
Specialisation: Main areas of practice are energy law and I.P. (including computer law). Advises on electricity agreements and on I.P. agreements including licensing and turnkey. Also advises on telecommunications law, giving advice on supplier and infrastructure agreements.
Prof. Memberships: Intellectual Property Committee of Law Society of Scotland.
Career: Qualified in 1984. Trainee with *McClure Naismith*, Glasgow 1983-85. Worked for ICI plc 1986-87 and *Freshfields* 1987-93. Joined *Shepherd & Wedderburn WS* in 1993.

SMITHERS, Tim M.D.

Veale Wasbrough, Bristol (0117) 925 2020
Partner in Property Services Department.
Specialisation: Main areas of practice are development, energy and environmental law with specialisms in waste management, contaminated land and Pipelines Act work. An editor of Butterworths' Property Law Service. Regular contributor to professional publications and speaker at seminars.
Prof. Memberships: Law Society, Pipeline Industries Guild, Institute of Wastes Management, Environmental Services Association.
Career: Qualified in 1982. Joined *Veale Wasbrough* in 1986, becoming a Partner in 1988.
Personal: Born 1958. Attended University of Wales LLB(Hons) 1979 (Cardiff). Lives in Bristol.

TRINICK, G. Marcus

Bond Pearce, Plymouth (01752) 266 633
See under Planning, p. 657

UPTON, Neil

Wragge & Co, Birmingham (0121) 233 1000
Specialisation: Interests include power projects and project financing; utilities regulation. Has advised on the setting up of a major UK gas trading business including risk management structure, IPE trading and

contracts. He has advised on CHP and Renewables Projects with a value in excess of £600 million and is experienced in both UK and Overseas BUT Projects. He is a regular contributor at conferences on utilities matters.
Career: Dove Grammar School 1970-1997; Ran a leasing company before college. 1984-1985 North East London Polytechnic 1st Class Degree LL.B (Hons). Winner of Sweet & Maxwell Law Prize. Articled *Slaughter & May* 1989. Qualified 1991. Partner at *Wragge & Co* May 1996.
Personal: Ex Youth International Golfer; Cricket; Squash; Operetta and Cookery.

WAKE, Brian
Wake Dyne Lawton, Chester (01829) 773100
See under Environmental Law, p. 352

WARNE, Penelope
Cameron McKenna, Aberdeen
(01224) 622002 ex 4412/4437
Specialisation: Practice covers commercial agreements and advice of all types associated with oil & gas exploration and production; dealings in oil and gas interests, farm-ins and farm-outs; unitisation and joint operating agreements; partnering, alliances and joint ventures; and service contracts including pipleline, construction and drilling contracts.
Career: Qualified in English Law in 1981. Articled and assistant solicitor with *Slaughter and May* 1976-83. Thereafter in-house legal adviser to Marks & Spencer plc before establishing own practice in Aberdeen. 1993 joined *Cameron Markby Hewitt* to establish the Aberdeen office. Became a partner in 1994. Also qualified in Scots law.

WHITEHEAD, Andrew R.
Martineau Johnson, Birmingham
(0121) 200 3300
Specialisation: Head of Utilities Department whose clients include several major utilities in the energy sector. Leads a team advising The National Grid Company plc on contractual, regulatory and pool issues affecting its Transmission Services business, in particular the procurement of ancillary services. Advises South Staffordshire Water PLC on statutory and regulatory issues.
Prof. Memberships: Law Society.
Career: South Hunsley School, Birmingham University (1985 LLB). College of Law, Chester (1986). Articled *Ryland Martineau* (now *Martineau Johnson*). Qualified 1988; Partner 1994.
Personal: Born 1963, resides Warwick with wife and daughter. Music (plays piano and oboe). Member UK Energy Lawyers Association. Associate London College of Music, piano, curries.

WILLIAMS, Gwyn
Edge & Ellison, Birmingham (0121) 200 2001
See under Environmental Law, p. 349

ENVIRONMENTAL LAW

See also Planning; Energy & Natural Resources

RESEARCH: In compiling the tables, we consider all the information available to us, paying particular regard to the market research carried out by our team of ten qualified lawyers. (The researchers' details are set out on page three.) The rankings, therefore, reflect the opinion of the marketplace as revealed by systematic and objective research: see page four. (Our research is audited every year by the British Market Research Bureau.)

OVERVIEW: Environmental law is still a relatively new area of practice, with many firms yet to develop units dedicated to this field. A complete environmental practice will include litigation, judicial review, criminal work, corporate and property transactional work and regulatory advice. Each firm will come to environmental law from one or more of these perspectives.

The top firms are still Freshfields and Simmons & Simmons. Leigh Day & Co remains the pre-eminent plaintiff litigation firm, and as such is different to the other firms in the list. Clifford Chance and Denton Hall but are not perceived to have stand-alone environmental units on a par with the leading firms. Of the highly regarded firms, the ones most capable of competing with them are Berwin Leighton and Bristows. Barlow Lyde & Gilbert enters the list on the basis of its insurance related work. The list is smaller this year to reflect the development of the larger and more specialist practices.

In the South, Blake Lapthorn and Lyons Davidson have made progress and been promoted in the bands. In the Midlands, Tyndallwoods continues to impress with its work for plaintiffs.

In the North East, Eversheds remains the most accomplished practice, but Nabarro Nathanson also has an excellent reputation. In the North West, the work is mainly non-contentious and practitioners rarely come across each other. However, three firms still stand out for their work – Dibb Lupton Alsop, Eversheds and Masons. New to the list is the Manchester office of Leigh Day & Co which was highly regarded by London practitioners. Aaron & Partners has now been replaced by the off-shoot practice Wake Dyne Lawton.

LEADING FIRMS · LONDON

FRESHFIELDS
SIMMONS & SIMMONS

ALLEN & OVERY
CAMERON MCKENNA

LEIGH, DAY & CO

HIGHLY REGARDED FIRMS

Berwin Leighton
Bristows
Clifford Chance
Denton Hall

Ashurst Morris Crisp
S J Berwin & Co
Herbert Smith
Lawrence Graham
Nicholson Graham & Jones
Norton Rose

Baker & McKenzie
Barlow Lyde & Gilbert
Berrymans Lace Mawer
Gouldens
Linklaters
Lovell White Durrant
Nabarro Nathanson
Rowe & Maw
Slaughter and May
Stephenson Harwood
Trowers & Hamlins
Wiseman Solicitors

LONDON

Freshfields (2 ptnrs/12 assts) Made their reputation in nuclear work, and are now regarded as "the leaders in environmental litigation defence." The department possesses a "high level of professionalism and knowledge," and is strengthened by its "sophisticated corporate practice." *Paul Bowden* has a "good intellect," and is "without question the leader" in corporate environmental litigation. *Malcolm Forster* "brought environmental law to where it is today" and has "very wide expertise," especially on the international side. Like many other specialists in this field, *Paul Watchman* has an academic background. *Jonathan Isted* is an up and coming name at the firm and is known for his work on electromagnetic field

cases. **Clients/ Work:** Advising ICI on its acquisition of speciality chemicals business of Unilever; advising Export-Import Bank in connection with the environmental aspects of financing a gold and copper mine in Indonesia; advising various power generating companies on the environmental aspects of constructing new power stations in the UK.

Simmons & Simmons (2 ptnrs/5 assts) Still considered the premier environmental firm "which everyone would use as a benchmark," but has a "slightly lower profile than it used to." Seen as particularly strong on advisory and regulatory work, and has an eminent and established team. *Stephen Tromans* spends much of his time speaking and writing. He is regarded as a pathfinder in environmental law and "an absolute star

on academic grounds." *Kathy Mylrea* is considered an "excellent environmental lawyer," and also recommended is *Mike Nash* "who is acquiring quite a name for himself." **Clients/Work:** Three Valleys Water during the outbreak of cryptosporidiosis in London; acted for General Utilities on its £116m acquisition of Leigh Interests plc, the largest waste industry transaction of 1997; advised the government on a project for the disposal of radioactive waste.

Allen & Overy (2 ptnrs/5 assts) Has "a good client base" and a free standing environmental practice. It does "a lot of major transactional work," and is seen as particularly strong on packaging and waste. The team is perceived to have slightly weakened in past years, but still includes *Owen Lomas*, who is "one of the original environmental lawyers," and "knows the issues inside out." *Ross Fairley* is promoted to the leading individuals' table. He is "knowledgeable and bright" and "contributes significantly to the department's strength." **Clients/Work:** Acting for ICI in relation to the environmental issues arising from a series of disposals of industrial assets; advising the sponsors on the flotation of Billiton plc; advising Glasmo Ltd on the PWRR.

Cameron McKenna (2 ptnrs/5 assts) Has a large regulatory practice, and is also considered "top for advice." The "dynamic" *Pamela Castle* has a high profile, and is a "considered lawyer." **Clients/Work:** Environmental information for Cable & Wireless; judicial review of Northumbria Water's reluctance to fluoridate drinking water; World Wide Fund for Nature.

Leigh Day & Co (4 ptnrs/8 assts) A "cutting edge" firm which undertakes important work on behalf of plaintiffs, especially in PI cases. As such they are significantly different to the other firms in the table. The "tenacious" *Martyn Day* is a "good team leader" and "understands the broad picture in environmental matters." **Clients/Work:** Ongoing tobacco and electromagnetic field litigation; traffic pollution litigation.

Berwin Leighton (3 ptnrs/4 assts) Possess a "big development practice" and are "good on strategic advice." *Andrew Waite* is one of the "founders" of environmental law, and a client described him as "a careful lawyer, which is what you need for this area." **Clients/Work:** Strategic advice to BG Properties; advising Tesco on contaminated land problems; advising WH Smith on noise problems.

Bristows (1 ptnr/3assts) A "tremendously professional" firm which is strong on the IP side. The "vastly experienced" *Richard Burnett-Hall* is a "doyen of environmental law" and admired by colleagues as a "practical and sensible chap." Some reservations were expressed about the extent to which the team relies upon his reputation. **Clients/Work:** Barratt Southern Counties; Bristol Myers Squib.

Clifford Chance (2 ptnrs/6 assts) Has an enviable client base, and much work is derived from corporate referrals. The department is "very strong on power stations," and has a team of "excellent individuals." They include *Christopher Napier*, who "knows his way around the business," and the "quiet and detailed" *Michael Redman*, who has a "good legal mind," and is recognised for his work on nuclear privatisation. **Clients/Work:** Mediation of substantial claim on an envi-

ronmental indemnity given in an acquisition for GE Lighting; defended case against Anglo United over alleged dioxin contamination of land; Burmah Castrol plc.

Denton Hall (3 assts) "Strong in oil and gas," but also does a wide range of general environmental law. The "very able" *Jacqui O'Keeffe* has a high profile in the environmental field, and the reputation of the department is enhanced by the presence of John Salter, who is still a consultant. **Clients/Work:** Due diligence for the Bulgarian government on privatisation of Bulgarian ship yards and steel works; registering Valpak with the EA; advising Dockgrange Ltd on judicial review.

Ashurst Morris Crisp (1 ptnr/2 assts) Derives much of its work from its "effective corporate practice." **Clients/Work:** Acted for Unipoly SA and Legal & General Ventures on the £620m buyout of BTR's Polymer Products Group; acting for Cinven Ltd and Argent Group on the £74m buyout of seven businesses from Hillsdown Holdings.

S J Berwin & Co (1 ptnr/3 assts) Seen to come at environmental law from the planning perspective. *Mark Brumwell* is recommended as an up and coming name in the field. **Clients/Work:** Acted for The British Land Company plc on joint venture with Rank Properties concerning contaminated sites; acted for Phildrew Ventures on the purchase of Hogg Robinson Transport; London City Airport Ltd.

Herbert Smith (2 ptnrs) Offers environmental services from its property and litigation departments. *David Brock* is recognised for his work in planning and minerals. **Clients/Work:** Defended South West Water in high profile prosecution; acted for EMI in litigation relating to environmental indemnity deed following the sale of its light source business to General Electric; acting for Anglian Water and their insurers.

Lawrence Graham (2 ptnrs/2 assts) *Caroline May* is "active in the environmental field" and is a "good litigator," but the firm as a whole has a lower profile than her presence would suggest. **Clients/Work:** Acting for Legal & General on the development of Reading Football Club on ex-landfill waste site; acting for BT on acquisition of commercial office space on ex-industrial site; development of industrial site at Lakeside, Thurrock.

Nicholson Graham & Jones (3 ptnrs/2 assts) Emphasis on contentious work, especially against local government. *John Garbutt* is "one of the original environmental lawyers" and "an expert on waste matters." **Clients/Work:** Blue Circle; general advice relating to the extraction of peat for Levingtons; judicial review of planning decision on landfill site for Essex County Council.

Norton Rose (2 ptnrs/4 assts) A respected environmental practice has grown from its planning department. The "high profile" and "outgoing" *Brian Greenwood*

has a "good understanding of the area." **Clients/ Work:** Due diligence for the Millennium Dome; Carter Cement Ltd on alternative fuels; due diligence for BMW on the purchase of Rolls Royce.

Baker & McKenzie (3 ptnrs/5 assts) Have the advantage of a major international practice, but are not seen as treating environmental law as a service in its own right. *Thomas Handler* has retired as a partner and is now a consultant. **Clients/Work:** Advising major speciality chemicals company on clean up liabilities following the acquisition of a contaminated land site; advising a prospective bidder for the Royal Ordnance factory; advising German chemical company on its disposal of its foundry chemical business.

Barlow Lyde & Gilbert (4 ptnrs/2 assts) Possesses a "strong insurance practice" and is now "beginning to take environmental law seriously." *Valerie Fogleman* is new to the list this year, and has forged a high profile on the back of much speaking and writing. **Clients/Work:** Policy drafting and advice to insurers on specialist environmental policies for the UK market; representing excess insurers in a major toxic tort coverage claim; drafted and advised on pollution cover and

---

LEADING INDIVIDUALS · LONDON

BOWDEN Paul Freshfields
BURNETT-HALL Richard Bristows
CASTLE Pamela Cameron McKenna
DAY Martyn Leigh, Day & Co
FORSTER Malcolm Freshfields
LOMAS Owen Allen & Overy
MYLREA Kathy Simmons & Simmons
TROMANS Stephen Simmons & Simmons
WAITE Andrew Berwin Leighton
WATCHMAN Paul Freshfields

CUCKSON David Stephenson Harwood
GARBUTT John Nicholson Graham & Jones
GREENWOOD Brian Norton Rose
KEEBLE Ed Slaughter and May
MAY Caroline Lawrence Graham
NAPIER Christopher Clifford Chance
O'KEEFFE Jacqui Denton Hall

BROCK David Herbert Smith
DEANESLY Clare Gouldens
DEVAS Hugh Rowe & Maw
DOOLITTLE Ian Trowers & Hamlins
FAIRLEY Ross Allen & Overy
FOGLEMAN Valerie Barlow Lyde & Gilbert
HANDLER Thomas Baker & McKenzie
REDMAN Michael Clifford Chance
WISEMAN Andrew Wiseman Solicitors

UP AND COMING

BRUMWELL Mark S J Berwin & Co
HAVARD - WILLIAMS Vanessa Linklaters
ISTED Jonathan Freshfields
NASH Mike Simmons & Simmons
PHILIPS Vicky Nabarro Nathanson

SEE PROFILES AT END OF SECTION

---

exclusions in public liability and other insurance policies for a Lloyd's syndicate.

Berrymans Lace Mawer (1 ptnr/3assts) Derives its environmental work from a healthy personal injury and insurance practice. The firm has also acted for water companies involved in personal injury actions. **Clients/Work:** Insurers, Lloyds syndicates.

Gouldens (2ptnrs/2 assts) *Clare Deanesly* is recognised as a "capable environmental lawyer," who mainly undertakes landfill and waste management cases. **Clients/Work:** Greenways; Hanson Bank; Erinstone.

Linklaters Does "good solid work" in the environmental field for a variety of large clients. *Vanessa Havard-Williams* is listed as an up and coming name. **Clients/Work:** Consideration of the environmental issues on the demerger between BG plc and Centrica; advising the Turks and Caicos Islands government on the proposal to take over an un inhabited island; Enfield Power Project.

Lovell White Durrant Has a well regarded environmental practice, and also undertakes litigation. **Clients/Work:** Cliftons and Prudential v PowerGen plc; representing a major chemical company in an investigation and prosecution following a major explosion and release of gas; acting for Taylor Woodrow in its appeal against Customs &

Excise's decision to withdraw a landfill tax exemption certificate.

Nabarro Nathanson Has a reputation nationally, in particular in the mining field. Most of the practice is based in Sheffield, but the "on the ball" *Vicky Philips* is a new addition to the up and coming names in London. **Clients/Work:** Include British Coal.

Rowe & Maw (1ptnr/2assts) Environmental work is done from the corporate department. The team includes the "understated but effective" *Hugh Devas*. **Clients/Work:** Due diligence and risk asssment, espcially for US clients making acquisitions in the manufacturing sector; Thorn EMI demerger; National Physical Lab PFI project.

Slaughter and May (3ptnrs/3 assts) Generally low-key in environment, but has an "extremely high quality practice." It is strong on transactional matters, particularly when there is an environmental question with M&As. *Ed Keeble* "thinks broadly" when dealing with environmental matters and "has a feel for the commercial side too." **Clients/Work:** Acted for Unilever on the sale of speciality chemicals division to ICI; advice to Blue Circle Industries on a range of matters.

Stephenson Harwood (1 ptnr plus 14 others as required) Regarded as "good on transactional work," and are headed by the

"steady and knowledgeable" *David Cuckson*; a well known environmental specialist who is "unflappable." **Clients/Work:** Advised Harrisons & Crosfield (now Elementis) on environmental issues in relation to the offer of the sale of five business divisions; report on environmental constraints on the expansion of Heathrow Airport; advising Federal Mogul on potential exposure to environmental liability in relation to its take-over bid for T&N.

Trowers & Hamlins (1 ptnr/1 asst, plus 4 others) Acts for local authorities on transactional matters, and recommended for the experienced *Ian Doolittle*. **Clients/Work:** Advised a hazardous waste company which specialises in the production of waste derived fuels; advised a local authority on the environmental and landfill tax issues arising from a major landfill development; working with SERM on the rating model to assess environmental and work safety.

Wiseman Solicitors Enters the London lists having moved its offices, sole practitioner *Andrew Wiseman* has a "solid reputation," and City firms admit to a "sneaking admiration for him." **Clients/Work:** Acting on behalf of an Italian national in the European Court on the definition of waste; planning work for the Environmental Law Foundation; act for Greenpeace.

LEADERS' PROFILES · LONDON

BOWDEN, Paul
Freshfields, London (0171) 936 4000
See under Litigation (Commercial), p. 518

BROCK, David M. J.
Herbert Smith, London (0171) 374 8000
Partner in Planning and Environmental Group.
Specialisation: Has a wide ranging planning, environmental and minerals law practice, advising on new settlements, urban regeneration, minerals and waste planning, integrated pollution control, judicial review and parliamentary matters, together with planning and environmental aspects of corporate transactions. Experienced advocate. Contributor to 'Commercial Environmental Law and Liability' (FT Law and Tax).
Career: Qualified in 1980. Partner at *Herbert Smith* since 1989.
Personal: Born in 1954. Educated at Dame Allan's Boys School, Newcastle, Marylebone Grammar School and University College, London (LL.B). Practising Christian. Enjoys opera, skiing and modern art. Resides near Saffron Walden.

BRUMWELL, Mark
S J Berwin & Co, London
+44 (0)171 533 2222
Specialisation: All areas of environmental law with particular emphasis on environmental aspects of corporate transactions, due diligence, contaminated land and land use planning. Recently dealt with the acquisition of a portfolio of over 40 properties with various industrial uses and has advised on the environmental aspects of pharmaceutical production, food processing and paper making.

Prof. Memberships: Member of the Law Society's Planning Panel. Legal Associate of the Royal Town Planning Institute. Member of the United Kingdom Environmental Law Association. Associate of the Institute of Environmental Science.
Career: University of Bristol – LLB (Hons). Law Society's Finals. Articled with *Simmons & Simmons*. With *Ashurst Morris Crisp* for 7 years including a period of secondment to the London Docklands Development Corporation. Environment Group at *S J Berwin & Co* since March 1996.
Personal: Married and lives in Harrow. Leisure interests include motorsport, photography, hill walking and badminton.

BURNETT-HALL, Richard H.
Bristows, London (0171) 400 8000
Head of Environmental Law Group.
Specialisation: Environmental law. Handles all aspects of UK and EC environmental law and regulation, and their impacts on business transactions and activities; also technology protection and exploitation, particularly enviromental techniques. Author of "Environmental Law," a legal practitioners' textbook, published by Sweet & Maxwell. Has written and given numerous articles and papers on environmental issues.
Prof. Memberships: Law Society, UK Environmental Law Association, Environmental Industries Commission (Member, Advisory Council), Chartered Institute of Patent Agents (Fellow).
Career: Qualified as Chartered Patent Agent 1966. Qualified as solicitor and partner

McKenna & Co in 1974. Joined *Bristows Cooke & Carpmael* 1995.
Personal: Born 5th August 1935: Trinity Hall, Cambridge 1956-59 (BA Natural Sciences 1959; MA 1963).

CASTLE, Pamela
Cameron McKenna, London
(0171) 367 3000
Partner, Head of Environmental Law Group.
Specialisation: Handles a range of environmental law matters. Provides compliance advice on all areas of UK and EC environmental law, in particular the regulatory control of emissions to air and water, the transport, labelling and disposal of waste, the handling and storage of hazardous substances and health and safety at work. Advised the water and electricity industries on environmental issues before and during privatisation and acted for the Department of the Environment in Northern Ireland on the restructuring of the water industry there. Has advised local authorities on the transfer of their waste disposal functions into arms-length companies in relation to contaminated land issues. Conducts environmental audits and advises on the results, especially in the context of mergers and acquisitions and property transactions, with particular focus on contaminated land issues. Also advises on the terms of waste disposal contracts and on the liabilities of owners and occupiers of waste disposal sites and the generators of waste, as well as defending criminal prosecutions in the magistrates court by regulatory authorities, particularly the Environment Agency. Council Member of the

Environmental Auditors Registration Association. Member of the CBI Environmental Protection Water and Effluent Panel and the Environment Agency Flood Defence Committee. On the Environmental Committee of the Association of British Healthcare Industries. Frequently speaks at public conferences and has had a number of articles published in journals such as *Oil and Gas Law and Taxation Review* and *European Construction Lawyer*.
Prof. Memberships: Law Society, Vice Chairman UK Environmental Law Association, City of London Solicitors Company, Institute of Wastes Management, Institute of Environmental Assessment (accredited environmental auditor), Royal Society of Chemistry, Fellow of the Royal Society of Arts.
Career: With Shell Chemical Company, New York 1965-67. Head of European Operations of Paul de Haen, Inc., New York (research company associated with the pharmaceutical industry) 1967-84. Joined *McKenna & Co* in 1986 and became a Partner in 1994.
Personal: Born 7th September 1941. Educated at the University of London (Queen Mary College) 1960-63 (BSc, 1st Class Hons in Chemistry) and the College of Law 1984-86. Interests include music, reading, theatre and walking. Lives in London.

CUCKSON, David M.
Stephenson Harwood, London (0171) 329 4422
Partner in Property Department.
Specialisation: Head of Environmental Law Group. Specific work includes issues relating to contaminated land, environmental warranties and waste management. Also handles property law work relating to education, local government and other public bodies, including PFI. Writes on environmental law topics and speaks at conferences and seminars. Treasurer of UKELA, member of Contaminated Land and Waste Working Parties.
Prof. Memberships: UK Environmental Law Association.
Career: Qualified in 1978. Held various posts in local government, most recently as Borough Secretary and Solicitor to Test Valley Borough Council. Joined *Stephenson Harwood* in 1989, becoming a Partner in 1992.
Personal: Born 1942. Fitzwilliam College, Cambridge 1961-65. United Reformed Church Minister 1966-74.

DAY, Martyn
Leigh, Day & Co, London (0171) 650 1200
Partner in Environment and Product Liability Department.
Specialisation: Main area of practice is environmental and product liability law. Heads team of 14 lawyers specialising in representing groups of injured people in complex actions. Acts for smokers in litigation against tobacco companies, prisoners of war against the Japanese government, and childhood cancer victims against the electricity industry. Co-Author of 'Toxic Torts,' 'Personal Injury Handbook,' 'Multi-Party Actions' and 'Environmental Action: A Citizens Guide.' Regularly addresses lectures, seminars and media on environmental issues.
Prof. Memberships: APIL, Executive Committee Member of Society of Labour Lawyers, Director of Greenpeace.

Career: Qualified in 1981 with *Colombotti & Partners*. Moved to *Clifford Chance* and then *Bindman & Partners* in 1981. Left to join *Leigh Day & Co.* as a Partner in 1987.
Personal: Born in 1957.

DEANESLY, Clare
Gouldens, London (0171) 583 7777
Partner and Head of Environmental Law Group.
Specialisation: Member of UKELA Waste Working Party. Member of ICC Committee on Environment and ESA Commercial Contracts Sub-committee. Principal area of practice is environmental law, dealing with minerals, waste management, landfill and contaminated land cases. Also handles general commercial property work including landlord and tenant matters and retail and development work. Acted for the Landfill Division of ARC (Greenways) in their acquisition of Econowaste from Tarmac plc 1993; 1993 and 1996 acted for London Brick Property Limited on sale of substantial landfill void to Shanks & McEwan; 1996 acted for minerals division of ARC in Midlands joint venture with Tarmac plc. Other major clients include Hanson Plc and BFI Limited. 1997: acted on landfill and minerals sites in connection with sale of Hanson Properties. Advised on landfill tax and environmental bodies. Author of 'Badlands: Essential Environmental Law for Property Professionals' (1993) and author of various articles on waste management property issues for professional publications. Environmental contributor to T.E.N. Video Network (the lawyers' educational channel). Contributor to ESA training seminar on Duty of Care. Speaker on waste management issues at conferences and seminars. Individual charge-out rate varies depending on type of job, degree of complexity and other relevant factors.
Prof. Memberships: Law Society, UKELA, ESA.
Career: Qualified in 1977 while at *Field Fisher Martineau*. Joined *Gouldens* in 1978 and became a Partner in 1980.
Personal: Born 30th May 1953. Attended Edgbaston C of E College for Girls, Birmingham 1957-71, then Southampton University 1971-74 (LLB Hons). Leisure pursuits include family, skiing, walking, tennis, travel and theatre. Lives in London.

DEVAS, H.E.
Rowe & Maw, London (0171) 248 4282
Partner, Head of Environment Group.
Specialisation: Environmental assignments of all types, including transactional and project finance support work. Specialises in waste management, contaminated land and regulatory compliance for industry, with a particular focus on clean technology and the pulp and paper sector. Advises on sustainable development issues for capital market clients and the preparation of corporate environmental policy documents. Recent assignments have included specialist support for the acquisition by Lear Corporation of the Chapman Group, the National Physical Laboratory PFI Project, the acquisitions of Darrington Quarries Ltd for Waste Recycling Group plc and Kenal Services group (chemical waste treatment and oil recovery) for Hillbridge Investments Ltd and the disposal by ICI of its Propafilm business. Lectures and writes widely on environmental

issues. Author of industry guide 'The Impact of Environmental Legislation on the European Paper Industry' (1994).
Prof. Memberships: United Kingdom Environmental Law Association (Member of the Waste Working Party). Paper Industry Technical Association Environmental Working Group. Editorial Board of 'The Green Paper' (Newsletter on sustainability issues for the Pulp and Paper Industry).
Career: Spent two years as a transaction lawyer before taking up a partnership outside London. Joined *Rowe & Maw* as a partner in 1988 specialising increasingly in the environmental aspects of property transactions, transferring to the Corporate Department as Head of the Environment Group in 1994.
Personal: Married with four children, living in Hampshire. Leisure interests: tennis, skiing, sailing and the performing arts.

DOOLITTLE, Ian
Trowers & Hamlins, London (0171) 423 8000
Partner, Public Sector. Head of Environmental Law.
Specialisation: Specialist in environmental law, especially transactional and regulatory work (including contaminated land and waste management). Editor of 'Garners Environmental Law.' Author of 'Butterworths Environmental Regulation.' Vice Chairman of the International Bar Association's sub-committee on European Environmental Law. Also specialist in public sector law.

FAIRLEY, Ross
Allen & Overy, London (0171) 330 3000
Environmental Law
Specialisation: Involved in all aspects of UK and EU environmental law particularly environmental policy, management and audit, contaminated land and lender liability. Works closely with environmental consultants advising on the findings of detailed site and management audits, writes and speaks regularly on environmental matters and is a contributor to Croner's 'Environmental Management – Caselaw' and FT Law and Tax's 'Commercial Environmental Law and Liability' and Legal Editor of Gee's "Environmental Risk Manager."
Prof. Memberships: Law Society, Council Member of the United Kingdom Environmental Law Association, Environmental Auditors Registration Association (registered as associate auditor), Associate Member of the Institute of Environmental Management.
Career: Born 11.10.68, educated at Leicester University LLB Law; qualified with *Allen & Overy* in 1993.
Personal: Interests include all sports, particularly hockey, cricket and driving an old Austin Healey 'Frogeye' Sprite.

FOGLEMAN, Valerie
Barlow Lyde & Gilbert, London (0171) 247 2277
Specialisation: All aspects of environmental law including specialist environmental insurance policies, environmental insurance coverage claims, environmental liability matters, particularly contaminated land, environmental aspects of commercial transactions, due diligence, criminal and civil environmental litigation, lender liability, environmental management and audits. Author of Hazardous Waste Cleanup, Liability and Litigation: A Comprehensive Guide to Superfund Law

(Quorum); Guide to National Environmental Policy Act (Quorum); Pollution Liabilities and Insurance in the United States and Great Britain (forthcoming). Contributing author: Commercial Environmental Law & Liability (Sweet & Maxwell); Environmental Law Practice Guide (Matthew Bender); Sustainable Development and the Energy Industries (Royal Institute of International Affairs/ Earthscan Publications). Numerous articles on environmental liabilities and environmental insurance in UK and US publications including monthly article in Insurance Day; frequent speaker in UK and overseas; joint editor, Insurance and Reinsurance Law Newsletter (LLP); assitant editor, International Journal of Insurance Law (LLP).
Prof. Memberships: Convenor, United Kingdom Environmental Law Association (UKELA) Insurance Working Party. Member: Association of Insurance and Risk Managers (AIRMIC) Environmental Task Group; UKELA Contaminated Land Working Party; Law Society; City of London Solicitors' Company Planning and Environmental Law Subcommittee; Amercian Bar Association (ABA) Section on Natural Resources, Environment and Energy Law, ABA Tort and Insurance Practice Section; State Bar of Texas; Environmental Law Section.
Career: Admitted to Texas State Bar 1986; Natural Resource: Law Fellow, Northwestern School of Law, Lewis and Clark College, Portland, Oregon 1986-1987; Teaching Fellow, University of Illinois College of Law, Champaign, Illinois 1987-1988; private practice, Corpus Christi, Texas 1988-1992; joined *Barlow Lyde & Gilbert* 1992; qualified in England 1995. University of Illinois (1992 LLM); Texas Tech University (1989 Master of Science, 1989 Juris Doctor, 1983 Bachelor of Landscape Architecture).
Personal: Interests include reading, gardening and listening to country and western music. Lives in Surrey.

FORSTER, Malcolm
Freshfields, London (0171) 936 4000
Litigation Department (Environment Group).
Specialisation: Advises and represents on regulatory challenges and liability disputes in the environmental field. Manages preparation of environmental statements for major projects and ensures statutory compliance. Handles corporate indemnity and warranty disputes over environmental issues. Gives environmental support for international investment, including project financing. Has special interest in matters with transitional and transnational elements; supervising partner Pan-European environmental practice; advises international organisations. Editor of Environmental Law & Management, Editor, author or contributor to numerous books and articles in legal journals. Professor of International Environmental Law at the Durrell Institute for Conservation and Ecology, at the University of Kent. Sometime Deputy Chairman, United Kingdom Environmental Law Association.
Prof. Memberships: International Bar Association, Selden Society.
Career: Qualified in 1992, having joined *Freshfields* in 1991. Partner 1995. Director of the Centre for Environmental Law at the University of Southampton 1973-84 and 1987-91. General Counsel for the Commission on Environmental Law at the International Union for Conservation

of Nature and Natural Resources, Bonn, Germany, 1984-87.
Personal: Born 22nd October 1948. Attended University of Southampton 1967-70. Interests include ecclesiastical law, naval history, legal history and equestrianism. Lives in,Crow Hill, Hants.

GARBUTT, John
Nicholson Graham & Jones, London (0171) 648 9000
Head of Planning and Environment Unit.
Specialisation: Planning and environmental law, including appeals, development plans, environment disputes, audits and policy, compulsory purchase, rating, Lands Tribunal, major planning inquiries concerning minerals, waste management, leisure developments, and judicial reviews. Author 'Environmental Law- A Practical Handbook,' 'Waste Management Law: A Manager's Handbook.' Contributor 'Commercial Environmental Law and Liability' (Longman). The firm is a member of the Land Pollution Consortium.
Prof. Memberships: UKELA, CBI Minerals Committee and Environment Protection Panel, Mining & Mineral Law Group.
Career: Qualified in 1963. Local government 1965-69. Blue Circle Industries (1978-85) and Chief Executive, Blue Circle Industrial Minerals 1986-88 and Blue Circle Waste Management 1989. *Nicholson Graham & Jones*, Partner 1991.

GREENWOOD, Brian J.
Norton Rose, London (0171) 283 6000
Head of Environmental Services Unit.
Specialisation: Corporate acquisitions, disposals and funding; environmental due diligence (acting on the Greenwich Millennium Dome), project finance, waste, water and IPC including appeals and advocacy (acted for Castle Cement in judicial review of Environment Agency re alternative fuels); international practice with considerable experience in Eastern Europe. Author "Butterworths Planning Law Service," Co-author "Environment Regulation and Economic Growth," Editor Butterworths Planning Law Handbook.
Career: Qualified in local government, with posts at Westminster, South Yorkshire and Kent before being appointed Chief Solicitor at Bedfordshire County Council. Joined *Norton Rose* in 1985, partner in 1988.
Prof. Memberships: Chairman Law Society's Environmental Law Committee, CBI Environmental Protection Panel; UKELA.

HANDLER, Thomas J.
Baker & McKenzie, London (0171) 919 1000
Consultant in Environmental Law Group and Commercial Litigation Department.
Specialisation: Practice covers a broad range of environmental law, corporate, regulatory, liability and litigation issues, UK and international; and commercial litigation and arbitration UK and international, as well as alternative dispute resolution. Major clients include government instrumentalities and English and multinational companies manufacturing and supplying products and providing services. Contributor to and editor of *Baker & McKenzie's* 'Regulating the European Environment' (2nd edition published by John Wiley & Sons). Legal consultant to the Environmental Law Foundation publication *ELFline*. Mediator trained and accredited by the Centre for Dispute Resolution and Mediation UK.

Prof. Memberships: Law Society, UK Environmental Law Association, British-Hungarian Society.
Career: Qualified in England & Wales 1966 and in New South Wales, Australia, 1962. Partner in *Baker & McKenzie* 1973-1997. Member, Board of Trustees, Foundation for International Environmental Law and Development. Member, Executive Committee of the Environmental Law Foundation. Chairman, Environmental Resolve (The Environment Council). Member, Board of Directors of The Environment Council.
Personal: Born 25th May 1938, Budapest, Hungary. Educated Fort Street Boys' High School, Sydney and University of Sydney, New South Wales (BA, LLB). Fluent Hungarian and some German and French. Charity Trustee.

HAVARD – WILLIAMS, Vanessa
Linklaters, London (0171) 456 4280
Specialisation: Specialist in environmental law (contentious and non-contentious) and EC commercial and litigation. Founding member of L&P's Environmental Unit. Typical environmental instructions include drafting of environmental indemnities in sale and purchase agreements, advising on the assessment and allocation of environmental risks in the context of privatisations, flotations and share issues. EC litigation – advising on the conduct and defence of claims under Articles 85 and 86 of the EC Treaty, and under the EC procurement rules. General commercial litigation.

ISTED, Jonathan
Freshfields, London (0171) 936 4000
Specialisation: Defence of multi-party toxic tort claims, including Sellafield childhood leukaemia cases, electromagnetic field and mobile phone litigation, disaster litigation, product liability and contaminated land liability claims. Also general commercial litigation. Member of Lord Woolf's Advisory Group on Multi-Party actions.
Prof. Memberships: Law Society, UKELA.
Career: Articled with *Freshfields* 1987-89. Qualified as an assistant solicitor in *Freshfields'* Litigation Department in 1989. LLM (with Distinction) in Advanced Litigation from Nottingham Trent University in 1996. Partner in *Freshfields* 1998.
Personal: Born 5 May 1964. Educated at Newport Free Grammar School and Durham University, College of Law (Chester) 1987. Leisure activities include golf, squash, running and travel. Reform Club.

KEEBLE, Ed F.
Slaughter and May, London (0171) 600 1200
Specialisation: Wide range of environmental matters, including major transactions, due diligence, contaminated site litigation and general environmental law advice.
Prof. Memberships: United Kingdom Environmental Law Association.
Career: Ipswich School, Cambridge University. Qualified in 1988 and became a Partner at *Slaughter and May* in 1995.

LOMAS, Owen
Allen & Overy, London (0171) 330 3000
Partner and Head of Environmental Law Group.
Specialisation: All aspects of UK and EU Environmental and Health & Safety law notably contaminated land, air and water pollution, waste management (including packaging recycling obligations) and corporate

environmental policy, management and audit. Acted for VALPAK, the industry organisation set up to negotiate the packaging industry's recycling obligations with HMG, the DTI on environmental aspects of the privatisation of the nuclear power industry and for a wide range of major industrial companies and banks on environmental aspects of their businesses and on acquisitions and disposals. Joint editor of Commercial Environmental Law and Liability (1994), editor of Environmental Law, journal of the UK Environmental Law Association and author of numerous articles on environmental law 1989-1997.
Prof. Memberships: Past Chairman of the UK Environmental Law Association standing committee on air pollution and member of the standing committees on integrated pollution control and environmental liability. Law Society. The Council of Management of the UK Environmental Law Association 1987-1996.
Career: Articled *Simons, Muirhead & Allen*, London; qualified 1980; lecturer in Law, University of Birmingham 1979-88; Lecturer in Law University of Warwick 1988-91; Professor in law, University of Trier, Germany 1991-92. Joined *Allen & Overy* 1992; Partner 1995.
Personal: London University (1976 LL.B); University of Birmingham (1987 LL.M). Born 1955. Lives near Saffron Walden.

MAY, Caroline
Lawrence Graham, London (0171) 379 0000
Specialisation: Partner specialising in all aspects of environmental law, with particular specialisation in contentious issues but increasingly involved in transactional work including acquisitions and disposals, planning and property development issues. Her work has an international flavour with multi-national and transatlantic corporations with varied environmental concerns. Particular specialisms include dioxin and methane emission problems, chemical waste managment issues and contaminated land. One the development side, she has become increasingly involved in the liability issues arising from brownfield site remediation on behalf of commercial property developers, institutional investors and banks. Regular speaker at public seminars and trade assocation events. Also undertakes in-house training tailored to client needs and contributes articles to various legal and environmental publications.
Prof. Memberships: Member of the National Council of the United Kingdom Environmental Association and member of its Noise and Finance Working Parties. Freeman of the City of London and winner of the Institute of Energy Roscoe Prize 1995.
Career: Articled *Beachcroft Stanleys* 1985-1987; qualified October 1987. *Clifford Chance* solicitor 1988-1994. Joined *Lawrence Graham* 1994, made partner November 1995.
Personal: Durham University BA Hons, CPE and Law Society Final Examination, Chester College of Law.

MYLREA, Kathy
Simmons & Simmons, London
(0171) 628 2020
Partner in Environmental Law Department.
Specialisation: Advises on all aspects of UK and EU environmental law including regulatory matters, transaction work involving allocation of environmental liabilities, criminal and civil litigation, environmental assessment and environmental audits. Examples of matters handled include appeals against Integrated Pollution Control Authorisation conditions, co-ordination of legal input to environmental audits at European facilities of major manufacturing companies, acting for the applicant in a major planning inquiry against refusal of planning permission for a hazardous waste incinerator, and defending numerous prosecutions under environmental legislation. Organises and conducts training seminars on the application of environmental law to individual businesses and business sectors. Major clients include Tate & Lyle, Royal Ordnance, Lloyds TSB Group, Owens Corning, Rhone Poulenc Rorer, Smithkline Beecham, General Utilities, BASF and Railtrack.
Prof. Memberships: Law Society, International Bar Association, UK Environmental Law Association (Member of Working Parties on Waste, Integrated Pollution Control and Air).
Career: Qualified in Ontario, Canada in 1986 and in England & Wales in 1992. With *McKenna & Co* 1988-1992. Joined *Simmons & Simmons* in May 1992.
Personal: Born 6th November 1958. Educated at Brown University, Providence, Rhode Island, USA (BA 1980) and the University of Toronto (LL.B, 1984). Fellow of the Royal Society of Arts. Outside interests include skiing, scuba diving and ballet. Lives in London.

NAPIER, Christopher
Clifford Chance, London (0171) 600 1000
Specialisation: Partner in charge of environmental and health and safety dispute resolution. Experienced in litigation, arbitration and mediation. A founder partner of the *Clifford Chance* European Environment Group in which he has worked since 1989. Defends clients facing environmental and health and safety prosecutions, regulatory proceedings and civil claims; and deals with all insurance recovery aspects of these sometimes complex and technical cases. Advises in environmental and health and safety liabilities, regulation, and legal risk control; on legal aspects of environmental auditing and management systems; and on insurance cover for environmental liabilities. Has managed a number of high profile and complex environmental court cases in the higher Courts in England, and the resolution of environmental disputes using mediation. He is qualified as a facilitator for the resolution of environmental conflict by process of consensus building and stakeholder dialogue. Editor of, and a contributing author to "Environmental Conflict Resolution" published by Cameron May 1998.
Career: Articled *Clifford Turner/ Clifford Chance*; qualified 1979; 14 years as a Seaman Officer in the Royal Navy, mainly submarines; Partner *Clifford Chance* since 1983.

NASH, Mike
Simmons & Simmons, London
(0171) 628 2020
Specialisation: Practises in all areas of UK and EU with particular emphasis on waste, contaminated land, chemicals and water law and its application to commercial transactions and in litigation. Assistant Editor of the Encyclopaedia of Environmental Law and co-author of The Environment Acts 1990-95 (annotated). Major cases over the year include judicial review on IPC issues, defence contractorisation, a defended 152-charge prosecution, disposals of heavy engineering businesses and a project for the Department of the Environment assessing the efficacy of the draft statutory guidance on contaminated land. Major clients over the last year include Procter & Gamble, Railtrack, PowerGen, BTR, Celtic Energy, VSEL, Caird Group, RPR, Country Landowners' Association, London Electricity, Lloyds TSB Group.
Prof. Memberships: Law Society of England and Wales.
Career: BA (First Class Honours) New College, Oxford University. Joined *Booth & Co*, Leeds in 1991. Joined *Simmons & Simmons* in 1994.
Personal: Married with two children. Interests – football, reading, travel.

O'KEEFFE, Jacqui
Denton Hall, London (0171) 242 1212
Head of Environmental Group.
Specialisation: Principal areas of work covers environmental, health and safety and related planning law. Main areas of practice include waste management issues including transfrontier shipments of waste, corporate and property due diligence, environmental auditing, contaminated land, regulatory compliance, and advice on applications for transfer or appeals of environmental permits, environmental and health and safety litigation (in particular judicial reviews) and the preparation and co-ordination of environmental statements for major projects. Advice covers both UK, EC and international legislation and conventions. An increasing amount of work also includes advising on health and safety issues both contentious and non contentious. Recent projects include advising the Government of Bulgaria as part of the European consortia on the environmental liabilities arising from the privatisation of its shipbuilding and steel works industries. Has advised a number of environmental trade associations and associated bodies such as the British Metals Federation, Entrust, Environmental Services Association and Valpak Ltd. Primary author and co-ordinating editor of Croner's Environmental Case Law (1995) and is a contributing author to a number of environmental publications e.g a book on Nuisances edited by Gordon Wignall to be published by Sweet & Maxwell. Has published numerous articles and has spoken at many conferences both in the UK and abroad.
Prof. Memberships: Elected member of the Council of UKELA in 1997. Law Society, International Bar Association.
Career: Qualified in 1982. Local government solicitor until 1987, *Field Fisher Martineau* 1987-1989, *S J Berwin* 1989-1995, *Denton Hall* 1996.
Personal: Born in Canada in 1955, attended University of South Bank 1974-1977 (LLB Hons). Enjoys white water rafting, wilderness camping and motorcycling.

PHILLIPS, Vicky
Nabarro Nathanson, London
(0171) 493 3318
Specialisation: All aspects of UK and EC environmental law, especially contaminated land, waste management and nature conservation legislation. Also Health and Safety and EC law. Recent work includes representing a dredging company in connection with the first revocation of a planning consent under the habitat directive and due diligence/negotiations on major poperty portfolio acquisitions.
Prof. Memberships: UKELA
Career: BA University of Sussex (1984), Qualified 1988, joined *Nabarro Nathanson* 1991, LLM Environmental Law, University of London (1992).
Personal: Growing organic vegetables, walking, travel.

REDMAN, Michael
Clifford Chance, London (0171) 600 1000
Environmental Law Solicitor advocate (qualified in criminal and civil jurisdiction).
Specialisation: He has experience in dealing with the environmental aspects of corporate, banking and property transactions and infrastructure projects. A considerable depth of expertise in electricity sector going back to his time at the bar, he has been involved in British Coal and Nuclear Electric privatisations as well as a number of independent power projects. Advised Eurorail in relation to the environmental aspects of its bid to build and operate the Channel Tunnel Rail Link.
Prof. Memberships: UKELA.
Career: Barrister (1975); Solicitor (1986).
Personal: Rugby referee.

TROMANS, Stephen R.
Simmons & Simmons, London
(0171) 628 2020
Partner and Head of Environmental Law Department.
Specialisation: Work covers waste management, due diligence, environmental litigation, contaminated land, pollution control, water resources and environmental audit and compliance. Has acted recently in the environmental aspects of the contractorisation and sale of major defence establishments, for Railtrack plc on rail privatisation and for a wide range of major industrial companies, banks and governments public authorities. Author of 'Planning Law, Practice and Precedents'(1990), 'The Environment Acts,' 1990-95 (1996) and 'Contaminated Land' (1994), 'The Law of Nuclear Installations and Radioactive Substances' (1997). Associate Lecturer at University of Cambridge. Very frequent speaker in the UK and abroad.
Prof. Memberships: UKELA (Chairman 1992-95), specialist advisor to House of Lords Environment Committee; former Chairman of Environmental Law Sub-Committee of the Law Society. Member of the Council of English Nature, Member of Environmental Advisory Panel, National Grid Company.
Career: Qualified 1981. Lecturer at Cambridge University 1981-87, then a Partner at *Hewitson Becke + Shaw* from 1987-90. Joined *Simmons & Simmons* as a Partner in 1990.
Personal: Born 2nd February 1957. Attended Selwyn College, Cambridge 1975-78. Lives in Cambridge.

WAITE, Andrew
Berwin Leighton, London +44 171 760 1000
Partner and Co-ordinator of the Environmental Group.
Specialisation: Specialist in environmental liability and pollution controls, dealing principally with contaminated land, waste management, noise, and water resources issues. Also handles integrated pollution controls and air pollution. Advises on environmental liabilities in corporate and property transactions, lender liability issues, environmental litigation and legal issues involved in establishing and operating environmental management systems. Clients advised include English Partnerships, Blue Circle, BG Plc, Tesco, Royal Bank of Scotland, Girobank, Prudential Property Management, W.H.Smith, Hainischfegen Industries and Transamerica. Advises Waste Facilities Audit Association on waste management issues and the Brownlands Group on law and policy developments relating to contaminated land. Has advised the Bulgarian and Ukrainian governments with regard to their proposed environmental legislation and has drafted forestry legislation for Sierra Leone as well as contributing to the Environmental Protection Act 1990 and the Environment Act 1995. Member of the International Court of Environmental Arbitration and Conciliation. Member of CBI ad hoc working party on environmental liability and former Chairman of the UKELA working party on contaminated land. Co-author of Environmental Law in Property Transactions (Butterworths 1997); Editor of Butterworths' Environmental Handbook (2nd edition 1997) and author of numerous articles on environmental law. Frequent speaker at national and international conferences on environmental law, with TV and radio experience.
Prof. Memberships: Vice-President of the European Environmental Law Association, Co-founder and former Secretary of the UK Environmental Law Association.
Career: Qualified 1975, Lecturer in law at Southampton University from 1980-88; acting director of the Centre for Environmental Law at Southampton University 1984-87; visiting Professor in Environmental Law at the University of Georgia 1987. Head of Environmental Law Group at *Masons* 1988-90 and Co-ordinator of the Environment Group at *Linklaters & Paines* 1990-93. Joined *Berwin Leighton* in 1993.
Personal: Born 25th February 1950. Attended Lincoln College, Oxford, 1969-72. Leisure interests include history, archaeology, wildlife, theatre, cinema and walking in the countryside. Lives in Chandlers Ford, Hampshire.

WATCHMAN, Paul Q.
Freshfields, London (0171) 936 4000
Property Department: Environment Group.
Specialisation: Principal area of work is environmental law, including contaminated land, water pollution, waste management, energy and minerals. Other main area of work is planning law, covering mineral developments (including coal mining and coastal superquarries), planning inquiries and retail office and business developments. Author or co-author of books and articles on environmental planning and public law. Lectures regularly on planning and environmental law.
Prof. Memberships: Law Society, Law Society of Scotland.
Career: Qualified as a Scottish Solicitor in 1977 and as an English Solicitor in 1994, Partner *Freshfields*, 1995.
Personal: Born 17th November 1952. Lives in Surrey.

WISEMAN, Andrew
Wiseman Solicitors, London
(0181) 244 5463
Specialisation: Practice covers the full range including noise, waste, contaminated land, pollution and planning. Former member of London Waste Regulation Authority. Visiting lecturer at Brunel University. Has addressed numerous conferences and been interviewed on TV and radio.
Prof. Memberships: Treasurer UK Environmental Law Association, City of London Law Society (Planning and Environmental Law Sub-Committee), Environmental Law Foundation, International Bar Association. European Environmental Law Sub Committee.
Career: Qualified in 1989. Former Partner at *Shindler & Co* and *Finers*.
Personal: Fellow of the Royal Society of Arts.

SOUTH EAST

Andrew Bryce & Co (1 principal) *Andrew Bryce* is a sole practitioner who "took a decent practice from Camerons and it continues to grow." He is "a person the industry looks to." Acts mainly for waste management companies and in oil, plus some criminal work. **Clients/Work:** Review of standard contracts for large waste contractor; successful defence of waste company on three day trial relating to explosion; advising range of industrials on packaging waste issues.

Blake Lapthorn (2 ptnrs/3assts) A large local firm with a respected environmental practice, especially in pollution. *Colin Barlow* is a recognised planning and environmental specialist and the firm moves up our tables. **Clients/Work:** River/water pollution cases; management licensing; litigation involving alleged pollution of farming land.

Brachers (2 ptnrs) Environmental law is tackled from a public law perspective, especially for companies and individuals against Local Authorities and the EA. Known also for their farm work and waste management. *Henry Abraham* is known on the planning side, and *Douglas Horner* is "solid" on environmental matters. **Clients/Work:** Instructed by seven waste management companies on corporate, planning and waste regulation issues; successful defence of an enforcement notice attempting to discontinue a major truck repair/fabrication business.

Bond Pearce Hepherd Winstanley & Pugh have been incorporated into Bond Pearce, and *Robert Davies* undertakes the environmental work from the commercial property department. **Clients/Work:** Environmental aspects of property transactions for developers.

Donne Mileham & Haddock (2 ptnrs/1 asst) Considered an "important player" on the south coast for environmental matters, and *Anthony Allen* is recommended. **Clients/Work:** Advised Sussex based industrial client on purchase of extensive north England industrial site with history of uses liable to cause contamination; represented property arm of major insurer on prosecution for incorrect handling of waste; other cases relating to noise, statutory nuisance and contaminated land.

Griffith Smith (2 ptnrs/1 asst p/t) Deal with the environmental aspects of property transactions, and the recommended partner is *Robert Simpson*. **Clients/Work:** Water pollution, contaminated land, water supply, drainage and related matters.

White & Bowker *John Steel* has "clear expertise" in the field, and he spends about 20% of his time on environmental matters, which are dealt with by the Agriculture department. **Clients/Work:** Act for companies, landowners and parish councils.

LEADERS' PROFILES • SOUTH EAST

ABRAHAM, Henry
Brachers, Maidstone (01622) 690691
See under Planning, p. 652

ALLEN, Anthony
Donne Mileham & Haddock, Brighton
(01273) 744451
See under Planning, p. 652

BARLOW, Colin
Blake Lapthorn, Fareham (01489) 579990
Partner 1968. Head of Environmental and Planning Unit.
Specialisation: Main area of practice is planning and environmental law. Also a senior member of the employment department. Involved in appeals re: mineral extraction, landfill and "wind farm" development, hazardous substances and statutory nuisance. Lectures frequently to architects, surveyors and planning consultants on environmental law matters.
Prof. Memberships: Royal Town Planning Institute (Legal Associate), Law Society (Member of Planning Panel), Law South Group of Solicitors.
Career: Qualified in 1959. Joined *Blake Lapthorn* in 1967 and became a Partner in 1968.
Personal: Born 18th August 1935. Attended Nottingham University 1953-56. Member of MCC. Leisure pursuits include cricket and walking. Lives in Havant.

BRYCE, Andrew John
Andrew Bryce & Co, Colchester
(01376) 563123
Specialisation: A specialist in environmental law, including waste management, contaminated land, water law, criminal defence, corporate, banking and property due diligence and environmental training programmes. The practice also includes planning and environmental assessment on major projects. Author of numerous magazine articles and papers. Has spoken at many conferences in the UK and abroad.
Prof. Memberships: Law Society, UK Environmental Law Association (Chairman 1988-91),
Career: Qualified in 1971, having joined *Cameron Markby Hewitt* in 1969. Became a Partner in 1973. Vice-Chair of UKELA 1987-8, and Chairman of UKELA 1988-91. Vice Chair of City of London Law Society, Planning and Environmental Sub-Committee, 1990-1996. Convenor tof UKELA Waste Working Party.
Personal: Born 31st August 1947. Attended Thorpe Grammar School, Norwich to 1965, then Newcastle University 1965-68. Leisure interests include birdwatching, tennis, walking, decorative arts and music. Lives in Coggeshall, Essex.

DAVIES, Robert
Bond Pearce, Southampton
(01703) 632 211
Partner in the Commercial Property Department.
Specialisation: Principal area of practice covers environmental aspects of major

commercial property transactions. Other main area of work is general corporate, including commercial property and business sales and purchases and commercial agreements. Defended Marwell Zoological Park against charge of polluting controlled waters.
Prof. Memberships: UKELA.
Career: Qualified in 1973 while with *Hepherd Winstanley & Pugh* and became a Partner in 1975, joining *Bond Pearce* in 1998 on merger.

HORNER, Douglas G.
Brachers, Maidstone (01622) 690691
See under Agriculture & Bloodstock, p. 107

SIMPSON, R.J.
Griffith Smith, Brighton (01273) 324041
Specialisation: Practice covers Pollution, Nuisance, Contaminated Land and Waste Disposal.
Prof. Memberships: UKELA (Contact for South East Region). Environmental Law Federation.
Career: Qualified 1970. Worked in Private Practice and in Law Centre. In 1976 joined Yorkshire Water Authority, Legal Department, until 1988. Joined *Griffith Smith* (Partner since 1990).
Personal: Born 23rd July, 1945. Strong interest in and supporter of Environmental Protection Groups.

STEEL, John R.
White & Bowker, Winchester (01962) 844440

SOUTH WEST

Bond Pearce (5ptnrs/3assts) Possesses a "good strong practice" in the development and transactional fields. Specialised focus in renewable energy, and in particular *Marcus Trinick* is deemed the "number one in the country for wind farms." The "bright" *Sarah Holmes* also works in the energy field.

Clients/Work: Currently advising on legal framework for offshore wind energy development; advising ABP on environmental issues in connection with its proposals to construct a new port in Dibden Bay; major transactions in the waste and minerals sector.

Burges Salmon (4ptnrs/4assts) The firm is generally known for its agriculture

and property work, and also has a "strong local profile" in environmental matters. Is seen to be "making a big effort in environmental regulation." **Clients/Work:** Residential groups and companies in the chemical and mineral sectors.

Osborne Clarke (1 ptnr/5 assts) A commercial firm which offers environmental advice as a service. Described as "good on the technical side." *Alan John* undertakes a wide range of non-contentious environmental work. **Clients/Work:** Obtaining environmental body status for national charity despite its owning an active landfill; advising leading manufacturer on civil and criminal liability for long term diesel tank leak above aquifer; negotiating complex environmental indemnities in acquisition of substantial electronics business located on contaminated land.

Clarke Willmott & Clarke (1ptnr/6 assts) Criminal prosecutions and defence for individuals and companies, and also regarded as strong on planning. *Tim Hayden* is well known on the prosecution side. **Clients/Work:**

Appointed to the Road Haulage Association Panel for solicitors specialising in transport law; substantial work for the National Farmers Union.

Lyons Davidson (1ptnr/2assts) The "enthusiastic and committed" *Kevin Gibbs* is "active," bringing experience from his planning background. The firm has been elevated from the highly regarded band into the list of leading practices. **Clients/Work:** Advice on combined heat/power plants CHP using landfill gas nationally; EPA advice and threatened pros; due diligence for High St Bank on transactions involving potentially contaminated land.

Bevan Ashford (2ptnrs/2 assts) A "very good firm" with a reputation for planning, and considered "sound" on environmental matters. **Clients/Work:** Merck Ltd; Churngold Waste Management Ltd; Energy Power Resources.

Lawrence Tucketts A "good environmental practice" essentially based on the firm's property practice, is spearheaded by *Stephen Pasterfield*. **Clients/Work:** Noise, nuisance and waste disposal cases.

Veale Wasbrough (1ptnr/1asst) Has a reputation for easements and power lines in the general property field, and is also recommended for its work on contaminated land. **Clients/Work:** Waste management planning and licensing issues; land/lease acquisition for landfill purposes; redevelopment of contaminated land sites.

Fynn & Partners (2ptnrs/1 asst) The firm is the demerged environmental and planning office of Penningtons, and is known for its work in the leisure business. **Clients/Work:** Noise abatement notices; defending prosecutions for breaches of waste disposal and pollution regulations.

Lester Aldridge (1 ptnr) Environmental work is handled from its litigation department. **Clients/Work:** Acted for UK Waste – defending prosecutions brought by regulators such as the Environment Agency; acted for United Biscuits in an important public enquiry following environmental objections to its goods vehicle operators (work won in opposition to two city firms).

Stephens & Scown (5 ptnrs spend 5-10% of their time in this area) A local firm with a respected waste practice. **Clients/Work:** Advice on various statutory nuisances in connection with mineral, landfill and tourist and shipping services industries; mining and quarrying waste management.

SEE PROFILES AT END OF THIS SECTION

LEADERS' PROFILES • SOUTH WEST

GIBBS, Kevin
Lyons Davidson, Bristol (0117) 904 6000
See under Planning, p. 654

HAYDEN, Tim
Clarke Willmott & Clarke, Taunton
(01823) 442266
Partner in Advocacy Department.
Specialisation: Main area of practice is environmental. Work includes prosecution and defence of industrial pollution cases, agricultural pollution and noise abatement. Also handles commercial criminal work, including health and safety, trade descriptions, food and drugs, road haulage and licensing. Gives lectures to Environmental Health Officers and to RICS on legal aspects of pollution.
Prof. Memberships: UKELA.
Career: Qualified in 1981. Joined *Clarke Willmott & Clarke* in 1979, becoming a Partner in 1985. Qualified as a Higher Courts Advocate in 1995.
Personal: Born 10th December 1956. Attended Bristol Grammar School 1968-74, University College Cardiff 1974-78 and College of Law Guildford 1978-79. Leisure interests include golf and cricket. Lives in Taunton.

HOLMES, Sarah C.
Bond Pearce, Plymouth (01752) 266 633
Associate in the Commercial Property Group.
Specialisation: Specialises in planning and environmental law, with a Master of Arts Degree in Environmental Law (1997). Advises on planning and environmental legal and policy isssues for a client base spanning institutional, commercial, and individuals, and in the public and private sectors. Has been actively involved in major transactions in the waste and minerals sector. Special interest in contaminated redevelopment, waste management issues and nature conservation. Lectures widely in this country on environmental and planning law policy and practice. In 1995 was runner up Assistant Solicitor of the Year in the National Hifal Awards sponsored by The Lawyer and was awarded a Wind Energy Pioneer Award by the BWEA in recognition of her contribution to national, regional and local planing policy on renewable energy developments.
Prof. Memberships: Member of the UK Environmental Law Association (Treasurer of UKELA South West).
Career: Qualified in 1991. Joined *Bond Pearce* in 1989, becoming Associate in 1997.

JOHN, Alan
Osborne Clarke, Bristol (0171) 984 5260
Specialisation: Advising upon renewable energy projects (wind, water, waste, methane, biomass), landfill and contaminated land, waste disposal, due diligence and warranty/indemnity protection in corporate transactions, obtaining, appealing and varying authorisations, water pollution and statutory nuisance claims and director and receiver environmental liability.
Prof. Memberships: UKELA, ELF, ESA.
Career: Qualified 1984 at *Osborne Clarke*. *McKenna & Co* 1984-87. Rejoined *Osborne Clarke* in 1987 and became partner and head of environmental unit in 1990.

PASTERFIELD, Stephen
Lawrence Tucketts, Bristol (0117) 929 5252
See under Planning, p. 656

TRINICK, G. Marcus
Bond Pearce, Plymouth (01752) 266 633
See under Planning, p. 657

WALES

Eversheds *Martin Warren* has an "excellent local reputation," and presently spends about 10% of his time on environmental issues. Clients/Work: British Aluminium; British Gas Properties; Welsh Development Agency.

Morgan Bruce (2ptnrs/1asst) Deal with a broad range of environmental matters, especially waste and minerals. *Luke Bennett* is "methodical, detail conscious and easy to get on with." Clients/Work: Contaminated land advice for a Lead Acid Battery factory; compliance advice in relation to the new Packaging Waste Regulations; pollution cases.

Edwards Geldard Has had a "steady year," with the "bright" *Richard Lloyd* dealing with environmental work. He devotes about 30% of his time to this area, mainly dealing with issues from a property perspective. Clients/Work: Advice on waste and polluted water; M&A work; contaminated land advice for a range of clients.

LEADERS' PROFILES · WALES

BENNETT, Luke
Morgan Bruce, Cardiff (01222) 385385
Specialisation: Associate, co-ordinates *Morgan Bruce's* Environmental Law practice. Advises a diverse range of public and private sector clients upon environmental and safety law compliance and liabilities, including transaction related and stand-alone work. Practice includes contaminated land, industrial regulation, mining and transportation law. Frequent speaker art seminars.
Prof. Memberships: UK Environmental Law Association; Chairman of The Association of European Lawyers UK Environmental Law Special Interest Group; Mining & Mineral Law Group.
Career: LLB (Hons), University of Wales Cardiff;; qualified 1992 with *Morgan Bruce*.
Personal: Born 14/7/67. Lives Cardiff.

LLOYD, Richard
Edwards Geldard, Cardiff (01222) 238239
Associate – Public Law
Specialisation: Principal areas of practice encompass environmental and planning law. Has conducted defence cases in environmental prosecutions and enforcement proceedings, including the first water pollution prosecution of the designer of engineering works; also statutory nuisance cases for railway companies, as well as construction noise and breach of waste "duty of care" prosecutions. Environmental issues and matters involved in company share and asset sales and acquisitions. Currently retained in connection with the sale of a major oil refinery. Also undertakes advice on planning and compulsory purchase, including statutory challenges and judicial reviews.

Prof. Memberships: Law Society. Committee Member, South and Mid-Wales branch of the National Association for Clean Air and Environmental Protection. Member of the United Kingdom Environmental Law Association.
Career: Attended Aberdare Boys Comprehensive School, then University College Wales, Aberystwyth 1988-1991 (LLB Hons). *Edwards Geldard* 1992 to date. Qualified 1994, Associate, Public Law Department 1997.
Personal: Leisure pursuits include music, football and travel.

WARREN, Martin
Eversheds, Cardiff (01222) 471147
See under Employment Law, p. 311

MIDLANDS

Wragge & Co (1ptnr/ 4 p/t assts) Has a good client base in the manufacturing sector, and one competitor "wouldn't consider referring anywhere else." *John Turner* is recognised as a leading environmental practitioner in the Midlands. He dedicates most of his time to environmental law and also does some health and safety work. Clients/Work: Equal split between contentious and non-contentious. Clancy major air pollution control appeal against Dudley MBC; major appeal against statutory noise nuisance notice for Alumasc plc; various matters for Moxley plc.

Edge & Ellison (2ptnrs/4assts) Possesses a respected environmental practice which focuses on waste, contaminated land, taxes and water. The "self effacing" *Gwyn Williams* undertakes non-contentious work, and is considered "extremely competent" in quarrying and land fill. He spends about half of his time on environmental matters. Clients/Work: Acting for the Irish government on issues relating to the proposal by NIREX for a nuclear waste repository at Sellafield; acting for Teesside Development Corporation in relation to the funding of a major international wildlife reserve utilising monies from the landfill tax credit scheme; advising National Grid on its appeal in relation to its rights regarding the grant of water discharge contents by the EA.

Pinsent Curtis (2ptnrs/3assts) Recognised as an effective non-contentious environmental practice which has made a "strong comeback" after a "difficult re-structuring period." Deemed to be "knowledgeable," but there is no recognised leader at the firm. Clients/Work: Acting for major industrial operator in connection with criminal prosecution relating to cyanide pollution; acting in defence of criminal proceedings for a radioactive waste disposal company in relation to a contamination incident; completion of a major long term contract for Hampshire Waste Services Ltd with regard to disposal of waste.

Eversheds (5 p/t fee-earners) Has a relatively low profile in the Midland environmental market, but "generally underestimated." *Rod Bull* is a new addition to the list, who concentrates on non-contentious matters. Clients/Work: Advising Ford/Jaguar and Coventry City Council on major industrial park proposal; conducting Shropshire Local Minerals Plan Inquiry on behalf of the County Council.

Browne Jacobson (2 ptnrs/3 assts – all p/t) No dedicated environmental team but has a "competent environmental capability." Clients/Work: Retained to carry out nature conservation enforcement on behalf of English Nature; won a month long multi-party nuisance action defended on behalf of Nottingham County Council; Knitting Industries Federation appeals.

Tyndallwoods Undertakes quite different work to the other firms, concentrating on high profile public law matters. The "outstanding" *Phil Shiner* has a national reputation for his work on behalf of plaintiffs and third parties and the firm goes up the tables this year. **Clients/Work:** Recent CAP case on Bolton incinerators; test case on combustion of solvent waste in cement and lime kiln; 6 other reported cases in 1997/8.

Kent Jones & Done Has specialist expertise in the field of coal mining and waste management. **Clients/Work:** Norcros plc; FG Chambers Co Ltd.

Knight & Sons Known for its capability in aggregates, mining and quarrying. **Clients/Work:** ARC; H & R Johnson; Hepworth Minerals & Chemicals.

LEADERS' PROFILES · MIDLANDS

BULL, Rod
Eversheds, Birmingham (0121) 233 2001
See under Planning, p. 652

SHINER, Phil
Tyndallwoods, Birmingham (0121) 243 3105
Partner and Head of Planning and Environmental Department.
Specialisation: Specialises in enviromental protection work especially judicial review for individuals and communities. Particular emphasis on air quality/ incineration cases and mineral planning. Instructed in a number of reported cases including the judicial reviews concerning the incineration of hazardous waste by the cement and lime industry: *R v Rochdale MBC ex parte Brown; R v Derbyshire CC ex parte Woods; R v North Somerset DC ex parte Garnett; R v SomersetCC ex parte Dixon; R v Bolton MBC ex parte Kirkman; Lubrizol Limited v Tyndallwoods; R v Environment Agency ex parte Learn; R v Environmental Agency ex parte Gibson; R v Environmental Agency ex parte Sellers and Petty.* Has written and spoken extensively on environmental and planning law, housing, urban policy/urban funding and community regeneration.

Prof. Memberships: Law Society's Planning Panel, Member of UKELA, ELF, CATS, Friends of the Earth and Labour Party.
Career: Solicitor, *Robin Thompsons* 1981-2; Small Heath Law Centre 1982-4; Birmingham Council Estates Project 1985-8; Birkenhead Resource Unit 1992-5; *Tyndallwoods* 1995. Also worked in community development for Barnardos.
Personal: Born 25 December 1956. Educated, Bishop Ullathorne RC School, Coventry 1968-75; Birmingham University 1975-8; Warwick University 1984-6 (LLM by research). Married with three children. Leisure interests include contemporary music especially indie, cycle racing, running, fell walking and real ale.

TURNER, John R.
Wragge & Co, Birmingham (0121) 233 1000
Specialisation: Head of the Environmental Law Group with very wide experience in all aspects of air pollution, water, contaminated land and waste law for commercial clients. Specialises in litigation and regulatory law as well as advising on corporate acquisition and due diligence matters.
Prof. Memberships: Director, Midlands Environmental Business Club Limited; Director,

Birmingham Groundwork; Member, Chartered Institution of Water and Environmental Management (C.I.W.E.M.); Member, UKELA.
Career: Articled *Mills and Reeve.* Qualified 1980. Joined *Wragge & Co* 1982. Partner at *Wragge & Co* from 1989.
Personal: Born 3.7.55.

WILLIAMS, Gwyn
Edge & Ellison, Birmingham
(0121) 200 2001
Partner.
Specialisation: Main areas of practice are in energy and natural resources law including the environmental and financing aspects of the mineral exploration and development, power generation, waste to energy and liabilities regulation. Also has experience of rail privatisation and the development of large rail terminals and railway infrastructure projects.
Prof. Memberships: Law Society.
Career: Qualified in 1970, Tarmac Group Legal Department 1972. Company Secretary and Solicitor Tarmac Quarry Products 1981-1989. Partner with *Edge & Ellison* since 1990.
Personal: Educated at Liverpool University. Leisure interests include industrial archaelogy.

EAST ANGLIA

LEADING FIRMS · EAST ANGLIA

RICHARD BUXTON Cambridge

EVERSHEDS Norwich
HEWITSON BECKE + SHAW Cambridge
MILLS & REEVE Norwich

Richard Buxton The "solid and respectable" *Richard Buxton* undertakes "high quality work" for plaintiff individuals and environmental organisations. Has an enviable reputation in public law and is associated with some ground breaking cases. **Clients/Work:** Several judicial reviews testing the EA directive, including quarrying (exp Brown and Cartwright), forestry (Swan), and development (re Berkeley); cases and inquiries covering town and country planning; application of the Birds and Habitats Directives, and aircraft and other nuisance including work in the ECHR.

Eversheds (1 ptnr) Nicholas Jones has relocated to the Leeds office, but the Norwich office continues to undertake environmental work. **Clients/Work:** Due diligence for DuPont on acquisition of parts of ICI; due diligence for company involved in genetically engineered wheat; dispute over SSSI in Wales.

Hewitson Becke + Shaw The "extremely bright" *Peter Brady* is primarily a planner, but also has a local reputation for his work on waste. **Clients/Work:** Advice on all aspects of contaminated land issues in property and corporate transactions, commissioning and assessing environmental

audits, as well as representing clients in criminal and civil proceedings.

Mills & Reeve (2ptnrs/3 assts) Partner *Beverley Firth* is well respected as a planner and environmental practitioner, and new to the list is *Rebecca Carriage.* **Clients/Work:** Acting for a local university in the acquisition of a brown field site to be restored and developed for student accommodation; acting for a local food company in defence of a criminal prosecution.

LEADING INDIVIDUALS
EAST ANGLIA

BUXTON Richard Richard Buxton

BRADY Peter Hewitson Becke + Shaw
CARRIAGE Rebecca Mills & Reeve
FIRTH Beverley Mills & Reeve

LEADERS' PROFILES · EAST ANGLIA

BRADY, Peter J.
Hewitson Becke + Shaw, Cambridge
(01223) 461155
See under Planning, p. 652

BUXTON, Richard
Richard Buxton, Cambridge (01223) 328933
Sole Practitioner, environmental lawyer.
Specialisation: Water (esp. abstraction licensing), nature conservation, environmental assessment, noise (esp. aircraft noise) and

other nuisance work. Context: judicial review, human rights, other litigation, planning inquiries and appeals, general advice, lectures. Advises statutory agencies, local authorities, charities, groups, private clients, other solicitors. Cases include Heathrow night flights *Lappel Bank* for

RSPB, several current cases and appeals on environmental assessment, and *Cambridge trishaws*.
Prof. Memberships: UK Environmental Law Association. Institute of Environmental Assessment.
Career: Qualified 1978 with *Farrer & Co. Sinclair Roche & Temperley* 1978, shipping disputes work. Legal adviser, Japan Line, Tokyo 1981-84. Environmental consultancy, Nova Scotia 1986-89, marine and fisheries issues. *Mills & Reeve*, Cambridge 1989. Independent since 1990.
Personal: Born1953. Lives and works in Cambridge.

CARRIAGE, Rebecca
Mills & Reeve, Norwich +44 (0)1603 660155
Specialisation: Town and Country Planning, Environmental and compulsory Purchase/Compensation. Highlights last 12 months: defended number of locally significant statutory nuisance prosecutions; two major referrals to the Lands Tribunal (questions of valuation and law); enrolling local business environment club as Environmental Body (Landfill Tax Regulations 1996); instructed in respect of major mineral planning appeal in highly protected area; involved in emerging local waste plan for Norfolk.

Prof. Memberships: United Kingdom Environmental Law Association. Steering Group member of East Anglian Business Environment Club. Committee member of Norfolk & Norwich Incorporated Law Society Associate member of Quarry Products Association.
Career: Articled *Hill & Perks* (now *Eversheds*). Moved to *Mills & Reeve* 1998.
Personal: Married. Hobbies: History of Imperial Rome; 1940's Cinema; Birdwatching.

FIRTH, Beverley
Mills & Reeve, Cambridge
+44 (0)1223 364422
See under Planning, p. 654

NORTH EAST

LEADING FIRMS · NORTH EAST

EVERSHEDS Leeds

NABARRO NATHANSON Sheffield

ADDLESHAW BOOTH & CO Leeds

HIGHLY REGARDED FIRMS

Dibb Lupton Alsop Sheffield

Dickinson Dees Newcastle upon Tyne

Hammond Suddards Leeds

Pinsent Curtis Leeds

Wilbraham & Co Leeds

Rollit Farrell & Bladon Hull

Eversheds (2ptnrs/5assts) A "strong reputation" in the litigation field. *Paul Smith* is an eminent litigator who forms "marvellous relationships with his clients." He has a reputation as an all-rounder, with experience of corporate deals and appeal work. *Professor Stuart Bell* is a part time consultant with a specialism in contaminated land and packaging waste. *Nicholas Jones* has moved to Leeds from the Norwich office. **Clients/Work:** Due diligence for DuPont in relation to its £3 billion purchase of ICI's industrial chemicals business; defending Hickson International plc and Yorkshire Water in relation to a number of civil claims from employees following a chemical spill; defending over 500 toxic tort claims brought against Monsanto and Flexsys following a leak of hydrogen sulphide.
Nabarro Nathanson (2ptnrs/5 other fee earners) Has an outstanding reputation in

coal, minerals and mining, especially on the contentious side. *Michael Renger* is a coal specialist with a reputation on the waste field, and *Ray Clarke* is also considered "sound." **Clients/Work:** Advising the coal authority; noise advice to a major construction company; acting on behalf of a national concern regarding the disposal of a radio-active source.
Addleshaw Booth & Co (2ptnrs/5assts) Contentious and non-contentious work in the property and commercial field. *Victoria Joy* is a consultant who has a reputation for general work and due diligence, and group leader *John Pike* is also recommended as a leading player. **Clients/Work:** Increasing amount of due diligence, contaminated land, and defence in EA prosecutions.
Dibb Lupton Alsop (1ptnr/2assts) A well regarded national environmental practice. The "knowledgeable" *Teresa Hitchcock* has a "good understanding of the technical side." **Clients/Work:** British Steel; Hepworth Building Products; ANI Aurora.
Dickinson Dees Considered the major Newcastle environmental practice, with a dedicated specialism in this field. *Denise Dowen* is recommended as a leader. **Clients/Work:** Large scale coastal reclamation scheme; due diligence on company acquisitions; water pollution prosecutions.
Hammond Suddards (1ptnr/2assts) Most of the environmental profile is generated from their Leeds office, but the Manchester office also has a highly regarded non-contentious practice. **Clients/Work:** Defence of National Starch on prosecution following a catastrophic explosion at a fac-

tory in Hull; acted for ICI Chemicals & Polymers against the EA on two spillage cases.
Pinsent Curtis (2ptnrs) A "high profile" local practice featuring *Peter Atkinson*, who undertakes prosecutions for the EA. **Clients/Work:** Advising on environmental issues for Smith & Nephew; corporate transaction in refinancing AM Paper for £145m for HSBC.
Wilbraham & Co Has a distinguished planning practice, and also has a reputation for environmental impact assessment. *Richard Wade-Smith* is a known planner and environmental specialist.
Rollit Farrell & Bladon (3ptnrs in environment and planning) Act for a wide range of clients on litigation, impact assessment, authorisations and permits. **Clients/Work:** Civil and criminal litigation; advice to industry, commerce, land owners, developers, public authorities, individuals and pressure groups.

LEADING INDIVIDUALS
NORTH EAST

RENGER Michael Nabarro Nathanson
SMITH Paul Eversheds

BELL Stuart Eversheds
HITCHCOCK Teresa Dibb Lupton Alsop
JONES Nicholas Eversheds
JOY Victoria Addleshaw Booth & Co
PIKE John Addleshaw Booth & Co
WADE-SMITH Richard Wilbraham & Co

ATKINSON Peter Pinsent Curtis
CLARKE Ray Nabarro Nathanson
DOWEN Denise Dickinson Dees

LEADERS' PROFILES · NORTH EAST

ATKINSON, Peter
Pinsent Curtis, Leeds (0113) 244 5000
Specialisation: Provides comprehensive environmental advice including applications for authorisations, consents and licences. Advises on enforcement and prosecution for breaches of environmental legislation; contaminated land;

pollution; waste management and disposal; statutory and common law nuisance; health and safety. Acted on a number of high profile prosecutions including 'HMIP v. Coalite Products Limited.' Clients include Case; Smith & Nephew; Ellis & Everard; Synthetic Chemicals and Serviceteam.

Prof. Memberships: United Kingdom Environmental Law Association. Institute of Wastes Management.
Career: Sir William Turners School, Redcar. Nottingham Trent University. Leeds Metropolitan University.

BELL, Stuart
Eversheds, Leeds (0113) 243 0391
Consultant.
Specialisation: Main area of practice is environmental law. Also advises on planning and administrative matters. Advised national and regional utilities on a range of issues from the construction of overhead power lines to the development of water treatment works. International work has involved advising National Governments on the drafting of new environmental legislation. Clients have included the World Health Organisation and the Australian Commonwealth Environmental Protection Agency. Editor of the Environmental Law Reports and Water Law. *Eversheds* Professor of Environmental Law at Nottingham Law School.

CLARKE, Ray
Nabarro Nathanson, Sheffield
(0114) 279 4000
Specialisation: Environmental litigation including advocacy. Advised on resolution of minewater pollution litigation, emissions from power stations, environmental prosecutions and appeals. Due Diligence – acquisition and disposals with contaminated and IPC sites. Privatisation – mines and chemicals. Urban regeneration – chemical site for international nature reserve and landfill; oil contamination polluting aquifer, sub-regional shopping centre (Dumplington). Construction – environmental procedures manual and contract issues.
Prof. Memberships: Fellow of the Institute of Quarrying, Member of UKELA Council. Visiting Tutor, International Development Institute, Rome.

DOWEN, Denise
Dickinson Dees, Newcastle upon Tyne
(0191) 279 9000
Specialisation: Practice covers all aspects of environmental law in relation to company and property transactions including EIAs, waste management, water pollution, process authorisations and contaminated land. Acts for developers, lending institutions and waste management companies.
Prof. Memberships: Law Society. Chair of the Environment Committee of the Royal Town Planning Institute (Northern Branch).
Career: Qualified in 1990. Trained with Avon County Council before moving to private practice. Joined *Dickinson Dees* in 1994.
Personal: Born July 1965. Read Law at the University of Leeds. Interests include dancing, jazz music and team sports.

HITCHCOCK, Teresa
Dibb Lupton Alsop, Sheffield (0345) 262728
Specialisation: Environmental Law: a) Advice to industrial organisations on compliance issues; b) Environmental input into corporate finance transactions; c) Regulatory Investigations and d) Involvement in environmental litigation. Also advice on Health & Safety at Work, Crisis Management, Product Safety and Food Safety. A significant proportion of this work comprises transactions and projects for high profile, blue chip companies and major plcs.

Prof. Memberships: Institute of Environmental Health. Law Society. UKELA.
Career: Environmental Health Degree 1981. 12 years in local government as a principal environmental health officer dealing with enforcement of environmental pollution, health & safety and food safety issues. Honours Law Degree 1988.
Personal: Equestrian activities. Netball. Walking.

JONES, Nicholas W.
Eversheds, Leeds (0113) 243 0391
Specialisation: All aspects of environmental law including pollution regulation, environmental liability (toxic torts etc), waste disposal and management, contaminated land, due diligence and compliance audits, corporate environmental management, environmental planning, nature conservation. Writes on environmental issues e.g. contributor "Concise Lexicon of Environmental Terms" (1993), "Know Your Rights" (Reader's Digest 1996) and is a regular speaker at seminars. Has been involved in major corporate environmental due diligence, notably for Eastern Group and DuPont.
Prof. Memberships: Royal Geographical Society (Fellow), Chartered Institution of Water and Environmental Management, Institute of Legal Executives (Fellow), UKELA (Member and sits on Nature Conservation Working Group).
Career: Local Government: 1970-1982; Trade Unions: 1982-1989; Private Practice: 1989 to date. Previously with *Hewitson Becke & Shaw* and *Overbury Steward & Eaton*. Joined *Eversheds* 1995.
Personal: Born 18th January 1950, MA (Environmental Law) 1994.

JOY, Victoria
Addleshaw Booth & Co, Leeds
(0113) 209 2334
Environmental Consultant
Specialisation: Advises principally on environmental issues arising from corporate transactions, lender/investor liability and enforcement actions. Also conducts environmental audits and advises on regulatory compliance, pollution control and land remediation. Project Manager of the National Brownfield Land Study for Urban Mines.
Prof. Memberships: Graduate Member of IMechE, UKELA, Leeds Environmental Business Forum.
Career: DoE, 1982-85. FCRA 1985-88, then Environmental Services Manager at British Textile Technology Group, Leeds. Joined the firm in 1993.
Personal: Born 26th February 1960. BA St. Hilda's College, Oxford, MSc Glasgow University.

PIKE, John D.
Addleshaw Booth & Co, Leeds
(0113) 209 2000
Head of Commercial Property Group (includes Commercial Property, Environmental, Construction, Planning and Property Litigation).
Specialisation: Main area of practice is commercial property work, covering development, banking, environmental,

investment and joint venture matters. Environmental law experience includes contaminated land remediation, waste and lender risk. Numerous articles in property and environmental journals.
Career: Joined the firm in 1969. Qualified 1972. Partner 1976.
Personal: Born 4th October 1947. Jesus College Cambridge (MA: Hons). De Montfort University (MA: Environmental Law). Governor Moorlands School, Leeds. Director: Leeds Environmental Business Forum. Interests include sports and family. Lives in Wetherby.

RENGER, Michael
Nabarro Nathanson, Sheffield
(01302) 344455
Partner and Head of Environment Department.
Specialisation: Extensive industrial, energy and property client base. Projects include construction and modification of power stations, waste to energy plants, regional waste facilities, major mineral developments and environmental litigation. Chaired Environment Agency/CIRIA project for construction industry "Building a Cleaner Future." Legal Member of Environment Steering Group of Institute of Chartered Accountants.
Prof. Memberships: Legal Associate of RTPI; Law Society's Planning Panel; UKELA.

SMITH, Paul A.
Eversheds, Leeds (0113) 243 0391
Partner in Commercial Litigation Department.
Specialisation: Main area of practice is environmental law. Heads *Eversheds'* National Environmental Law Group, having established the unit in 1988. Acts principally for major industrial companies in the UK, US and Europe. Also covers employment law. Successfully took the River Derwent test case to the House of Lords. In the crisis management field he acted in the Hickson & Welch Castleford incident, the Hickson International Cork incident and the Associated Octel fire at Ellesmere Port. Co-Author of College of Law Environment Law and Environmental Manual published by CCH Publications. Has lectured for IBC, Industrial Society, College of Law, CBI, European Business Seminars, US Mining Congress in Florida on the Environment. Regular contributor to BBC radio programmes. *Eversheds* client partner for Dupont in the UK.
Prof. Memberships: UKELA, Law Society, ABA, IBA.
Career: Qualified in 1982, having joined *Freshfields* in 1980. Joined *Eversheds Hepworth & Chadwick* in 1984 and became a Partner in 1987.
Personal: Born 14th November 1956. Attended Warwick University 1975-79. Governor of Richmond House School. Member of Hickson International Plc Supervisory Board. Professional Puppeteer. Lives in Menston, West Yorks.

WADE-SMITH, Richard
Wilbraham & Co, Leeds (0113) 243 2200
See under Planning, p. 658

NORTH WEST

LEADING FIRMS · NORTH WEST

DIBB LUPTON ALSOP Manchester
EVERSHEDS Manchester
MASONS Manchester

HIGHLY REGARDED FIRMS

Addleshaw Booth & Co Manchester
Hammond Suddards Manchester
Leigh, Day & Co Manchester
Wake Dyne Lawton Chester

Dibb Lupton Alsop *Andrew Dawson* undertakes general environmental work on waste and contaminated land and is known as a litigator. **Clients/Work.** British Steel; Hepworth Building Products; ANI Aurora.

Eversheds (1ptnr/2assts) *Elizabeth Shepherd* does non-contentious corporate environmental work, and is described as "a hard-nosed but amicable negotiator." **Clients/Work:** Advised DuPont on its £1.8b

purchase of ICI's industrial chemical business; Hickson International plc on its sale of Pharmachem to Warner Lambert; the Royal Bank of Scotland.

Masons (1ptnr/4assts) The well respected *John Moritz* has a name for general environmental work, and the firm is known for their work in the construction field. **Clients/Work:** Urban Regeneration Partnership Scheme in Bradford; Rochdale Canal Restoration Project; large scale landfill gas migration case.

Addleshaw Booth & Co (2ptnrs/5assts) Perform environmental work from the commercial property department. **Clients/Work:** Purchase by Dutch company of a manufacturing company with significant environmental processes and properties with historic contamination; appeal against the imposition of landfill tax on engineering materials; prosecution for noise nuisance joint construction works.

Hammond Suddards (1ptnr/2assts) Part of the national team, the "very competent" *Michael Shepherd* acts for defendants, and also undertakes Health and Safety work.

Clients/Work: Defence for ICI; Scottish & Newcastle; One2One.

Leigh Day & Co (2ptnrs/6assts) The preeminent northern plaintiff litigation firm, concentrating on PI work. **Clients/Work:** Ongoing tobacco and electromagnetic field litigation; traffic pollution litigation.

Wake Dyne Lawton (2ptnrs/1asst) *Brian Wake* is a new entry to the list this year, having set up the practice after leaving Aaron & Partners. The firm has undergone a recent expansion, merging with Jonathon Lawton **Clients/Work:** Offer specialist advice on minerals and waste law.

LEADING INDIVIDUALS
NORTH WEST

DAWSON Andrew Dibb Lupton Alsop
MORITZ John Masons
SHEPHERD Elizabeth Eversheds
SHEPHERD Michael Hammond Suddards
WAKE Brian Wake Dyne Lawton

SEE PROFILES AT END OF THIS SECTION

LEADERS' PROFILES · NORTH WEST

DAWSON, Andrew
Dibb Lupton Alsop, Manchester
(0161) 830 4321
Partner within Commercial Regulatory Group.
Specialisation: Practice covers the full ambit of environment and health and safety law and includes advice and representation before criminal Courts as well as inquiries. Advice is also given in relation to corporate transactions. Pollution matters and waste are particular specialisms.
Prof. Memberships: UKELA.
Career: Qualified in 1988 in Local Government before joining *Alsop Wilkinson* in 1991 (Partner 1996).
Personal: Born 10th November 1963. Educated St Margaret's High School and Liverpool University (LLB).

MORITZ, John
Masons, Manchester (0161) 234 8234

SHEPHERD, Elizabeth
Eversheds, Manchester (0161) 832 6666
Specialisation: Environmental and Corporate. Head of Manchester Environmental Team advising on transaction related environmental issues and general environmental compliance,

carrying out legal environmental audits and formulating on behalf of clients corporate environmental policies and management systems.
Prof. Memberships: UKELA (United Kingdom Environmental Law Association). CBI North West Environment Business Forum, GMEA (Greater Manchester Environmental Association) and Law Society Environmental Law Sub-Committee.
Career: Cambridge University, Churchill College M.A. First Class Honours. Admitted as a Solicitor in October 1984. Articled with *Eversheds Alexander Tatham* in Manchester and appointed partner of Eversheds in 1988.
Personal: Elizabeth lives near Knutsford, Cheshire, and her interests include classical music, opera, skiing & gardening.

SHEPHERD, Michael L.
Hammond Suddards, Manchester
(0161) 830 5000
Partner in Litigation Department. Head of Safety Health and Environment Group.
Specialisation: Main areas of practice are Environmental, Health and Safety, Food Safety and Trading Standards.
Prof. Memberships: Law Society.

Career: Qualified in 1969. Worked in Town Clerk's office, Manchester 1966-72. Joined *Hammond Suddards* in 1972, becoming a Partner in 1974.
Personal: Born 26th September 1944. Attended Bradford Grammar School 1954-1963, then The Queen's College, Oxford 1963-66. Leisure interests include cricket, football, golf and foreign languages (Portuguese, French and Spanish). Lives in East Bierley.

WAKE, Brian
Wake Dyne Lawton, Tattenhall, Chester
(01829) 773100
Specialisation: Mineral extraction, waste management, land reclamation and environmental law. Acts for major mineral companies and landowners, and advises regularly on contaminated land and pollution control matters.
Prof. Memberships: Fellow of the Institute of Quarrying. Founder, United Kingdom Environmental Law Association North West Section.
Career: Qualified 1978 with *Linklaters & Paines*. Tarmac Quarry Products 1981-86.
Personal: Born 19.9.53 Hong Kong. Speaks Cantonese. LLB Liverpool 1975.

SCOTLAND

Brodies WS (2ptnrs) A "solid environmental firm" which offers "sound advice." Has a one-stop shop service in conjunction with surveyors to advise on contaminated land. *Charles Smith* has a company and commercial background, and "continues the excellent tradition of the firm." **Clients/Work:** Contaminated land advice for housebuilders;

advice on waste management licensing; landfill tax advice.

The Morton Fraser Partnership (2ptnrs/2 others) "An old and honourable firm" known for its litigation practice. *Donald Reid* has "superb knowledge and ability" and now also does consultancy work. The firm has a reputation for a wide range of environmental matters, including nuclear waste (has worked for the Atomic Energy

Authority). **Clients/Work:** BP Chemicals; UKAEA, BNFL.

Bishop and Robertson Chalmers (2ptnrs) Known for its practice in contaminated land, prosecutions and insolvency related work. *Kenneth C. Ross* spends between a third and a half of his time on environmental matters. He "knows and understands licensing and permits very well." **Clients/Work:** Advisory work on property or company trans-

LEADING FIRMS · SCOTLAND

BRODIES WS Edinburgh

THE MORTON FRASER PARTNERSHIP
Edinburgh

BISHOP AND ROBERTSON CHALMERS
Glasgow

MCGRIGOR DONALD Glasgow

HIGHLY REGARDED FIRMS

Burness Edinburgh

Maclay Murray & Spens Glasgow

Dundas & Wilson CS Edinburgh

MacRoberts Glasgow

Tods Murray WS Edinburgh

Steedman Ramage WS Edinburgh

actions in relation to contaminated land; also on contracts, legal liability, discharge consents and prosecutions; prosecutions relating to water pollution.

McGrigor Donald (1ptnr/3assts) Has a commercial client base with an industrial focus. The "trusted and respected" *Patricia Hawthorn* "strongly represents her clients" and "definitely knows her stuff," although the profile of the practice is lower than the quality of the work would suggest. **Clients/Work:** Tilcon (Scotland) Ltd; acting

for the M6 joint venture; Environmental Trust for Scotland.

Burness (5ptnrs/3assts) The environmental aspects of corporate, property or planning deals are dealt with by the two recommended leaders, *Kenneth A. Ross* and *Martin Sales*, who are both known for their planning work. **Clients/Work:** Contaminated land advice; banking sector advice on environmental issues; advice on large scale developments in sensitive areas.

Maclay Murray & Spens Undertakes much due diligence and waste advice. *Andrew Primrose* is a "safe pair of hands" and "has good knowledge of water law." **Clients/Work:** Pilkington Optronics Barr & Stroud Ltd; British Waterways Board.

Dundas & Wilson CS Has a strong industrial property practice, and are known for its major infrastructure projects and landfill work. The firm recently acquired Dorman Jeffrey & Co, which brings an established environmental client base and capable environmental practitioners to add to the Dundas & Wilson team. *John Watchman* is recommended. **Clients/Work:** Greenpeace; several PFI projects.

MacRoberts *James Grant* pays "good attention to detail" and is known on the property and planning side. **Clients/Work:**

Scottish Nuclear Energy; Crouch Mining and Catchment Ltd.

Tods Murray WS Does land based environmental work. *Ian McPake* comes from the corporate and PFI angle, and is regarded as a competent environmental lawyer. **Clients/Work:** Tends to act for agricultural, estate and forestry clients.

Steedman Ramage (2ptnrs) Does "good back up work for the commercial property department," and *Kenneth Cumming* is regarded as good on litigation. **Clients/Work:** UK Waste; Marine Harvest McDonnell; judicial review regarding diseased fish.

LEADING INDIVIDUALS
SCOTLAND

REID Donald The Morton Fraser Partnership

SMITH Charles Brodies WS

HAWTHORN Patricia McGrigor Donald

PRIMROSE Andrew Maclay Murray & Spens

ROSS Kenneth C. Bishop and Robertson Chalmers

CUMMING Kenneth M. Steedman Ramage WS

GRANT James MacRoberts

MCPAKE Ian Tods Murray WS

ROSS Kenneth A. Burness

SALES Martin Burness

WATCHMAN John Dundas & Wilson CS

NORTHERN IRELAND

HIGHLY REGARDED FIRMS
NORTHERN IRELAND

Cleaver Fulton & Rankin Belfast

Cleaver Fulton & Rankin *Neil Faris* is listed as the leading Northern Ireland environmental practitioner, with particular emphasis on waste enquiries. **Clients/Work:** Contaminated land issues in property transactions.

LEADING INDIVIDUALS
NORTHERN IRELAND

FARIS Neil Cleaver Fulton & Rankin

LEADERS' PROFILES · SCOTLAND AND NORTHERN IRELAND

CUMMING, Kenneth M.
Steedman Ramage WS, Edinburgh
(0131) 260 6600
See under Litigation (Property), p. 548

FARIS, Neil C.
Cleaver Fulton & Rankin, Belfast
(01232) 243 141
See under Property (Commercial), p. 724 and Administrative & Public Law, p. 91

GRANT, James R.
MacRoberts, Glasgow (0141) 332 9988
Specialisation: Main area of practice in planning and environmental law, although he also does some commercial property work (especially licensed trade).
Prof. Memberships: Law Society of Scotland.
Career: Edinburgh University 1979-84. Mitchells Roberton 1984-88 (trainee/assistant). *Maclay Murray & Spens* 1988-91

(assistant/associate). *MacRoberts* 1991 – present (assistant/associate/partner (1993)).
Personal: Born 29 June 1961. Lives Glasgow. Leisure interests include sailing, music and gardening.

HAWTHORN, Patricia
McGrigor Donald, Glasgow (0141) 248 6677
Specialisation: Environmental Law with a particular focus on mineral extraction and waste management, also renewable energy and regulatory issues in water and sewerage PFI projects. Highlights: 4 major minerals acquisitions, advising funders on first PFI Sewerage Scheme, currently involved in 2 further PFI Sewerage Schemes, 3 renewable energy projects and 1 roads scheme.
Prof. Memberships: CBI, UKELA (United Kingdom Environmental Law Association) and IEM (Institute of Environmental Managers).
Career: Hutchesons' Grammer School,

Glasgow University LLB (Hons 1st Class). Assumed a Partner in *McGrigor Donald* 1995.
Personal: Married with two children. Leisure interests: Skiing, golf and swimming.

MCPAKE, Ian A.H.
Tods Murray WS, Edinburgh
(0131) 226 4771 ian.mcpake
Specialisation: Work includes PFI, commercial property and environmental law.
Prof. Memberships: Member of United Kingdom Environmental Law Association.
Career: Qualified in 1971. Articled *J & W Buchan, Peebles* 1969-72. *Ranken & Reid SSC* 1972-90, Partner 1973. Joined *Tods Murray WS* as a Partner in 1990.
Personal: Born 1948. Attended George Watson's College, Edinburgh and St Andrew's University (LLB 1969). Leisure: cricket, swimming, skiing, reading. Lives in Edinburgh.

PRIMROSE, Andrew H.
Maclay Murray & Spens, Glasgow
(0141) 248 5011
Email: ahp@maclaymurrayspens.co.uk
Specialisation: Senior commercial property
partner and head of environment unit. Qualified
to practise in both Scotland and England.
Established the firm's London office and was
previously Managing Partner. In-depth
experience of all property and environmental
issues, including those relating to acquisitions,
disposals and risk assessment. Author of
numerous publications. Vice Chairman, IBA's
Section on Legal Practice.
Prof. Memberships: UK Environmental Law
Association, Scotland Europa Environmental
Group, Scottish Environmental Industries
Association.
Career: Oxford University (BA 1961) and
Glasgow University (LL.B 1964).
Personal: Born 1939.

REID, Donald A.
The Morton Fraser Partnership, Edinburgh
(0131) 550 1000
Partner and Head of Environmental Law Group.
Specialisation: Advises on all aspects of
environmental law and liability including
legislative compliance, property transactions,
civil litigation and corporate environmental
strategy, with a particular emphasis on
European and international environmental law.
Frequent contributor to environmental law
journals and conferences. Lecturer to
universities and industrial groups throughout
the UK and abroad.
Prof. Memberships: UK Environmental Law
Association (Chairman), CBI Environment
Committee, Law Society of Scotland
Environment Committee (Convenor). Director
ENTRUST.
Career: Qualified in 1968. Joined *Morton Fraser
Milligan WS* as a Partner in 1975.
Personal: Born 14th February 1945. Educated
at George Watson's College 1949-62 and
Edinburgh University 1962-66. Leisure interests
include sailing, hill walking and music. Lives in
Aberdour, Fife.

ROSS, Kenneth A.
Burness, Edinburgh (0131) 473 6000
Managing Partner and Partner in Commercial
Property Department.
Specialisation: Deals primarily with developers
and retailers and major overseas investors.
Contributes to conferences on planning law,
environmental law, VAT and commercial leases.
Member of the Environmental Law Committee
of the Law Society of Scotland. Accredited by
the Law Society as a specialist in commercial
leasing.

ROSS, Kenneth C.
Bishop and Robertson Chalmers, Glasgow
(0141) 248 4672
Partner in Business Law Division. Head of
Environmental Law Group.
Specialisation: All aspects of environmental
law, with particular reference to contaminated
land and waste. Frequent lecturer to
conferences, and author of articles regarding a
variety of environmental law topics, particularly
contaminated land and its connection with
commercial property transactions, waste
management licences and other waste issues.
Author of chapter on Contaminated Land in
Second Edition of Greens Guide to
Environmental Law in Scotland.
Prof. Memberships: UK Environmental Law
Association (Member of its National Council and
Chairman of its Scottish Committee),Secretary
General of the Environmental Commission of
Union des Avocats Européens. Member of Law
Society of Scotland Environmental Law
Committee.
Career: Qualified in 1982. Joined *Robertson
Chalmers & Auld* in 1984 and became a Partner
the same year. Became a Partner in *Bishop and
Robertson Chalmers* in 1986.
Personal: Born 30th September 1958.
Graduate of Glasgow University (LLB 1st Class
Hons 1980). Spare time interests include
archaeology. Lives in Glasgow.

SALES, Martin
Burness, Edinburgh (0131) 473 6000
See under Planning, p. 657

SMITH, Charles
Brodies WS, Edinburgh (0131) 228 3777
Partner in Corporate Department.
Specialisation: Advises on environmental law
and liability generally and in respect of land,
water and air pollution, sales and purchases of
land, assets and shares, leases and
security/banking transactions. Also handles
major commercial contracts (including PFI and
privatisations) and banking transactions.
Advises various housebuilders on
environmental liability, contractors on waste
management licensing and the landfill tax, and
numerous clients on contaminated land.
Continues to advise on Ravenscraig Steelworks
Site. Co-author of "Pollution Control: The Law in
Scotland," published in November 1997.
Prof. Memberships: Law Society of Scotland,
United Kingdom Environmental Law
Assocation, Royal Society of Arts, Commerce
and Manufactures, Scottish Environmental
Industries Association.
Career: Qualified in 1987 having joined *Brodies
WS* in 1985. Became a Partner in 1990.
Personal: Born 21st October 1960. Attended
Perth Academy 1972-78, Exeter College, Oxford
1978-82, then University of Edinburgh 1982-85.
Lives in Edinburgh.

WATCHMAN, John
Dundas & Wilson CS, Edinburgh
(0131) 228 8000
Associate in Commercial Property Group,
Member of Planning and Environment Group.
Specialisation: All aspects of both
environmental and planning law. Wide
experience gained in both the public and private
sectors. Frequent contributor to "Scottish
Planning and Environmental Law."
Prof. Memberships: Law Society of Scotland,
Legal Associate of Royal Town Planning
Institute, Associate of Chartered Institute of
Arbitrators, United Kingdom Environmental Law
Association.
Career: Attended University of Glasgow
(LLB).Qualified as a Scottish solicitor in 1982;
Solicitor/Principal Solicitor in Local Government
in Scotland 1983-1989; Crown Counsel/Senior
Crown Counsel Attorney General's Chambers,
Hong Kong 1989-1994; qualified as a Hong
Kong solicitor in 1990; joined *Dundas & Wilson
CS* in 1995; qualified as an English solicitor in
1996, Associate since 1998.
Personal: Born 1958. Resides Edinburgh.
Leisure interests include sport, reading and
music.

EUROPEAN UNION/COMPETITION

RESEARCH: In compiling the tables, we consider all the information available to us, paying particular regard to the market research carried out by our team of ten qualified lawyers. (The researchers' details are set out on page three.) The rankings, therefore, reflect the opinion of the marketplace as revealed by systematic and objective research: see page four. (Our research is audited every year by the British Market Research Bureau.)

OVERVIEW: Researching the leading London firms proved fairly straightforward. Many of the leading practitioners are involved in M&A work, and know each other well. However, the highly regarded firms proved more difficult. Their work tends to be advisory rather than mainstream corporate, and clients are unwilling to allow them to give publicity to their activities. The strengths of the highly regarded firms tend to lie in specific industry sectors.

At time of going to press, Linklaters announced that The Alliance was definitely going ahead, which means that their European presence overall will be greatly strengthened. In Brussels, they will have merged with Belgian firm De Bandt, van Hecke & Lagae which will reinforce their EU practice. There was a widespread recognition of the strength of Lovell's Brussels practice, and of the quality of its pure competition rather than just M&A-based work.

This year, Freshfields are promoted to the top band, as are two of the firm's practitioners – Rachel Brandenburger and Deidre Trapp. The firm also formed an alliance with German competition firm Deringer Tessin Herrmann and Sedemund.

Among the highly regarded firms, Stephen Kon at SJ Berwin & Co and Richard Whish at Watson, Farley & Williams continue to stand out as leading individuals, enabling their firms to punch above their weight.

Outside London, there are few specialist competition departments, with most competition work coming from the firms' company/commercial departments. However, there are several leading individuals of note. Geraldine Tickle at Martineau Johnson and Guy Lougher at Wragge & Co are both high profile practitioners. They are joined this year by Kate Rees at Pinsent Curtis.

The section covers UK competition matters, article 85 and 86 and the free movement of goods/services provisions of the Treaty of Rome, state aid, public procurement and anti-dumping work. Regulatory matters are a natural spin-off from this work and are normally dealt with by EU/competition lawyers, and therefore covered by this section.

This year sees two major developments in competition law. The Competition Bill is due to come into force later this year but is yet to mean new work for law firms, as clients await the Bill's final wording. However, there is concern among some practitioners that those law firms that have traditionally advised on domestic merger work may miss out in the future, as the new law mirrors EU rather than existing domestic legislation.

LEADING FIRMS · LONDON

FRESHFIELDS
LINKLATERS
LOVELL WHITE DURRANT
SLAUGHTER AND MAY

HERBERT SMITH

ALLEN & OVERY
ASHURST MORRIS CRISP
SIMMONS & SIMMONS

S J BERWIN & CO
CLIFFORD CHANCE
NORTON ROSE

HIGHLY REGARDED FIRMS

Baker & McKenzie
Denton Hall

Theodore Goddard
Watson, Farley & Williams

Bristows
Cameron McKenna
Eversheds
Holman, Fenwick & Willan
Richards Butler
Rowe & Maw

SOLE PRACTITIONERS

MICHAEL HUTCHINGS

LONDON

Freshfields (London:5 ptnrs. Brussels: 3 ptnrs. Also 30 assts) Recent link-up with German competition firm Deringer Tessin Herrmann and Sedemund was one of this year's most significant developments in the EU/competition law market. Brussels-based partner and communications and media specialist *Rachel Brandenburger* moves up to the top band of leading individuals. She is described as "technically excellent, but cautious" for her regulatory work. Her London-based colleague, the utilities specialist *Deirdre Trapp,* is also promoted this year, having returned from maternity leave in November 1997. "Commercial, with an eye for detail," she has a substantial client list. **Clients/Work:** Acted for MCI in the EC merger notification of its aborted merger with BT. Acted for ICI in notification of its purchase of Unilever's specialty chemicals business. Article 85 notifications include acting for American Airlines on its proposed merger with British Airways. Restrictive practices work includes acting for Rolls Royce plc in defence of its trademark licence following a complaint to the European Commission from Vickers.

Linklaters (London 7ptnrs/17assts. Brussels: 1ptnr/5assts) A large London team boasts significant corporate-based leading individuals, including *Bill Allan*, *Christopher Bright* and *David Hall* – "the pre-eminent practitioner in London," "very experienced." *Alec Burnside* leads in Brussels. Also have two non fee-earning researchers including Dan Goyder, ex-deputy chairman of the MMC – an external consultant. **Clients/Work:** Significant transactions for the London office include acting for Pacificorp on its £4.35 billion acquisition of the Energy Group and for British Airways on its proposed merger with American Airlines. In Brussels, transactions include advising BT on its joint venture with Cegetel.

Lovell White Durrant (London: 2.5 ptnrs, Brussels: 4.5 ptnrs, 20 assts/other fee earners) Widely regarded as having one of the best stand-alone EU/competition law practices not dependent purely on the firm's corporate work. Also has a strong Brussels practice. *Simon Polito* (London) *Philip Collins* (Brussels) *John Pheasant* (Brussels/London) are acknowledged leaders, while *Lesley Ainsworth* also has a good reputation. Variant of "Polito proposals" were used as a basis of new EC merger regulations. **Clients/Work:** Merger work includes acting for Barclays Bank on the EC clearance of disposal of the BZW businesses. Also acted for Granada on its bid for Yorkshire Tyne Tees. Non-merger work includes representing Mars in its dispute with Unilever over ice cream distribution practices and for Nintendo on its defence of alleged competition law infringements relating to licensing of IP rights for the development of video games.

Slaughter and May (London: 3ptnrs. Brussels: 2ptnrs. Also 21 other fee earners) Excellent reputation in merger control work, although perceived to be stronger in London than Brussels and on non-contentious rather than contentious work. Leading practitioners include utilities specialist *Malcolm Nicholson* (London) "excellent" and contentious specialist *Laura Carstensen* (London) (goes up to top band this year), described as "good at dealing with clients, practical and intelligent" and "really tough." *William Sibree* (Brussels, former barrister at Monckton Chambers) also rises to the second band this year, and is

described as "terribly clever, incisive, grasps facts quickly." **Clients/Work:** Merger work included acting for Grand Metropolitan on its merger with Guinness to form Diageo, for The Energy Group on the MMC enquiry regarding its proposed merger with PacifiCorp, and for Williams Holdings on its acquisition of Chubb. Contentious work includes advising Unilever in the EC Commission proceedings relating to ice cream cabinet exclusivity. Monopoly references included acting for Airtours relating to foreign package holidays.

Herbert Smith (London: 5ptnrs/10assts. Brussels:2ptnrs/4assts) Moves up to second ranking this year thanks to the growing quality of its practitioners and Brussels-based trade law practice. *Jonathan Scott* and public procurement specialist *Dorothy Livingston* are the firm's leading individuals. *Stephen Kinsella* is tipped as a major future player. *Elizabeth McKnight* moves up a rank on the strength of her growing reputation in the IP and regulated industries field. **Clients/Work:** Acting for both Price Waterhouse and Coopers & Lybrand on their merger. Other major clients include advising British American Tobacco on its merger with Zurich Reinsurance and British Sky Broadcasting in cases under Articles 85 and 86. Trade law work includes defending 10 major Indian steel producers in anti-dumping investigation.

Allen & Overy (London: 2ptnrs/16assts. Brussels: 2ptnrs/7assts) Separate UK and Brussels practices, also building up Italian presence following merger with Bricio Casati. Leading partner *Michael Reynolds* (Brussels) heads the world-wide practice, and is described as a "big name." *Mark Friend* is described as "clear" and "an exacting opponent." **Clients/Work:** Represented Lafarge on its acquisition of Redland plc, the first time that the European Commission handed back jurisdiction to two member states (UK and France). Other clients include GEC/Alsthom, Seagrams and T&N.

Ashurst Morris Crisp (London:3ptnrs. Brussels:3ptnrs. Also 12 assistants) Team operates as part of firm's corporate department, although the firm does offer a 'stand-alone practice' for competition enquiries, investigations, litigation and advocacy. The firm also employs two full-time economists, both former employees of the OFT. Leaders include *Roger Finbow* "good at merger work" and *Nigel Parr*, the head of the firm's London group, who also has a growing reputation. Former barrister *Mark Clough*, who is strong in transport and telecoms, is promoted this year from up and coming. He has "a leading reputation in Brussels." **Clients/Work:** Acted for Stena on the EC, OFT and MMC merger clearance on its merger with P&O short sea ferry service and for Allied Domecq on representations to the merger task regarding the Guinness-Grand Metropolitan merger.

Simmons & Simmons (5ptnrs/10assts, 3 know-how officers) Wide ranging practice covering corporate finance and cartel to free movement of goods work. However, group suffers from lack of star individuals. Group head *Peter Freeman* – joint general editor of Butterworths Competition Law – has for some an "outstanding reputation." *Martin Smith* remains highly regarded. **Clients/Work:** Acted for Bass on Bass/Carlsberg-Tetley merger proposals and on competition aspects of the disposal of its 1,400 leased pubs. Also acted for OFGAS on the final stages of MMC Transco price control inquiry.

Clifford Chance (London: 4ptnrs/12assts. Brussels: 2ptnrs) Has 40 lawyers across Europe working on competition law, mainly in media, energy, banking, retail and transport. *Jim Wheaton* is described as a "top class player," although the team has suffered from the loss of Ulick Bourke, who left in April. **Clients/Work:** Acted for JVC and Sharp in the MMC enquiry into the supply of domestic electrical goods in the UK. Also acted for Whitbread in the MMC enquiry in the proposed acquisition of Carlsberg-Tetley by Bass.

SJ Berwin & Co (5ptnrs/8assts) Team divided between London and Brussels, with strong litigation practice. *Stephen Kon* has universal appeal among his competitors, although perceived to be a somewhat "one man band." Comments include "an amazing operator with a good range of clients" and "strong academically and good on detail." *Ralph Cohen*, head of the Brussels office, is highly rated, and is included on this year's up and coming list for the first time. However, the firm lost competition consultant Lord Clinton-Davis, who left to become minister for trade at the DTI. **Clients/Work:** Acted for Guinness plc on the $24 billion merger with Grand Metropolitan. Other clients include the European Commission, Ladbroke Group, PolyGram and Procter & Gable.

Norton Rose (London:1ptnr/11 fee-earners. Brussels: 2ptnrs/10 fee-earners) The departure of competition department head John Cook to Macfarlanes was one of this year's best-known moves. The firm is still rated but the competition department is perceived to be on probation. The department is now headed by *Martin Coleman* who, while less high-profile, is described as a "good operator" with "a pretty good reputation," particularly in energy, transport, telecommunications, banking and financial services sectors. **Clients/Work:** Acted for Carlsberg on joint venture agreement with Coca-Cola on production, sale and distribution agreements in the Nordic region. Also advised Stena Line in the Stena-P&O joint venture and Sea-Land Services on its world-wide co-operation agreement with Maersk.

Baker & McKenzie (2ptnrs/8assts) *Lynda Martin Alegi* has a good reputation and "terrific client loyalty." Strong in merger control, customs and trade law work. **Clients/ Work:** Clients include high-tech, consumer goods and computer companies.

Denton Hall (3ptnrs/6assts) Offer a mixture of stand-alone competition and existing company/commercial clients work. *David Aitman* ("excellent with good client loyalty,") is the firm's public competition face and recently advised the DTI on the new competition bill. The practice's main strengths include utilities and media related competition advice. **Clients/Work:** Advised the Premier League on OFT litigation over collective licensing of football rights and for the Ofreg in relation to two monopolies and mergers inquiries into electricity generation, transmission, distribution and supply agreements in N. Ireland. Also acted on merger clearance work for the aborted Ernst & Young/KPMG link-up.

Theodore Goddard (2ptnrs/8assts) The competition law team is in the media and entertainment group, and works between London and Brussels. It specialises in competition and regulatory matters affecting the audio-visual and IT sectors. Also work in the transport sector, particularly road and rail. *Guy Leigh* is well-regarded. **Clients/Work:** Advised the Russian Aluminium Producers Association on trade implications of Russia joining the WTO and Video Performance Ltd in dispute with MTV over the use of VPL members' music videos.

Watson, Farley & Williams (2ptnrs/ 5assts, spend 100% of time on competition work in the international corporate group.) *Richard Whish*, who heads the group, combines his role as a partner at the firm with his role as professor of law at King's College London. Formerly a consultant to Oftel. He is described as "a walking encyclopaedia of competition law," "good at explaining simple competition issues to people that should know them – but don't" and "good at detail." However, he is thought to overshadow the rest of the firm's competition lawyers. **Clients/Work:** Clients include corporations in chemicals, pharmaceuticals, motor vehicle, food and drink, retailing and power, telecoms and satellite communications sectors.

Bristows (2ptnrs/4assts) The competition group mainly works on IP/IT related matters, particularly in the pharmaceutical, biotech, engineering and medical sciences sectors, although the firm lacks recognised leaders. **Clients/Work:** Acted for Panasonic UK Ltd on UK and EC competition aspects of the formation of British Interactive Broadcasting joint venture. Other clients include Monsanto, Rizla and Nestle.

Cameron McKenna (London: 3ptnrs. Brussels: 1ptnr/7assts) The 1997 merger of Cameron Markby Hewitt and McKenna & Co led to the expansion of the competition group, but it is still felt to be lacking in star individuals. **Clients/Work:** Main clients include BP and other major construction, brewing, rail, telecoms, utilities and healthcare companies.

Eversheds (10ptnrs/3assts) The firm recently lost its Brussels practice to Dibb Lupton Alsop, although its competition practice is still headed by *Rosalind Kellaway*, who splits her time between London and Brussels. The firm is perceived to offer "text book" legal competition advice. *Stephen Rose* remains in up and coming this year. **Clients/Work:** Acted for the Electricity Association in lobbying government over Competition Bill. Also acted for Bang & Olufsen in relation to MMC inquiry into domestic electrical goods.

Richards Butler (4ptnrs/4assts) Mainly work in the food & drink, broadcasting, leisure and computer sectors, but lack star players. **Clients/Work:** Acted for the Foster Brewing Group on the Commission notification of the Inntrepreneur pub group leases. Also acted for the BBC in the RTPA Premier League case over broadcasting rights.

Rowe & Maw 5 fee earners in Brussels with some other fee earners in London work occasionally on competition law. **Clients/ Work:** Merger clearance work includes acting for NBC in joint venture with Dow Jones and GE Silicones on joint venture with Bayer. Also act for Zeneca, EMI and Air Miles.

Michael Hutchings *Michael Hutchings*, previously a partner at Lovell White Durrant, is a highly respected and experienced practitioner in this field. He started to practise on his own account in early 1996. Good reputation as a lobbyist.

LEADING INDIVIDUALS · LONDON

AITMAN David Denton Hall
ALLAN Bill Linklaters
BRANDENBURGER Rachel Freshfields
BRIGHT Christopher Linklaters
CARSTENSEN Laura Slaughter and May
COLLINS Philip Lovell White Durrant
FREEMAN Peter Simmons & Simmons
HALL David Linklaters
KON Stephen S J Berwin & Co
MARTIN ALEGI Lynda Baker & McKenzie
NICHOLSON Malcolm Slaughter and May
PHEASANT John Lovell White Durrant
POLITO Simon Lovell White Durrant
REYNOLDS Michael Allen & Overy
SMITH Martin Simmons & Simmons
WHISH Richard Watson, Farley & Williams

AINSWORTH Lesley Lovell White Durrant
CHAPPATTE Philippe Slaughter and May
COOK John Macfarlanes
DAVIES John Freshfields
FINBOW Roger Ashurst Morris Crisp
HUTCHINGS Michael Sole Practitioner
LIVINGSTON Dorothy Herbert Smith
McKNIGHT Elizabeth Herbert Smith
PARR Nigel Ashurst Morris Crisp
SCOTT Jonathan Herbert Smith
SIBREE William Slaughter and May
SOAMES Trevor Norton Rose
SPEARING Nicholas Freshfields
WHEATON James Clifford Chance

BOYCE John Slaughter and May
BURNSIDE Alec Linklaters
CLOUGH Mark Ashurst Morris Crisp
COLEMAN Martin Norton Rose
FLECK Richard Herbert Smith
FRIEND Mark Allen & Overy
KELLAWAY Rosalind Eversheds
KINSELLA Stephen Herbert Smith
LEIGH Guy Theodore Goddard
MORRIS Anthony Linklaters
OSBORNE John Clifford Chance
TRAPP Deirdre Freshfields
WOTTON John Allen & Overy

UP AND COMING

COHEN Ralph S J Berwin & Co
ROSE Stephen Eversheds
ROWE Michael Slaughter and May

SEE PROFILES AT END OF THIS SECTION

LEADERS' PROFILES · LONDON

AINSWORTH, Lesley M.
Lovell White Durrant, London
(0171) 236 0066
Specialisation: Specialist work includes UK and EC competition law (advisory work, investigations by the Office of Fair Trading, the Monopolies and Mergers Commission and the EC Commission and proceedings before the European Court of Justice and national courts – advice on the proposed UK Competition legislation); state aids; free movement of goods and services; public procurement; EC customs legislation: EC agricultural regimes; advice on proposed EC legislation and the implementation of EC legislation in Member States.
Prof. Memberships: Examiner, Qualified Lawyers Transfer Test Board; Member, Solicitors' European Group.
Career: Articled Lovell White & King (now Lovell White Durrant); qualified 1981; *Lovell White & King*, London 1979-1983; Brussels office 1983-1985; secondment to *LeBoeuf, Lamb, Leiby & McRae* 1985-1986; London since 1986; partner *Lovell White Durrant* 1988.

AITMAN, David
Denton Hall, London (0171) 242 1212
Partner, Head of Competition and EC Group,
Company and Commercial Department.
Specialisation: Advising on all areas of EC
and domestic competition law, particularly in
the energy, transport, manufacturing, retail,
communications and media sectors; and on
regulation, in connection with privatised utilities,
practice covers, notifications and complaints to
the European Commission, the Office of Fair
Trading, the Monopolies and Mergers
Commission, Oftel, the Restrictive Practices
Court and the DTI. Editor of section on
intellectual property licensing in Butterworth's
'Encyclopedia of Competition Law' of the
sections on competition law in Practical
Intellectual Property and in the Yearbook of
Media Law. Lectures on EC and UK
competition law and is a regular contributor of
articles to the legal and trade press.
Prof. Memberships: Competition Law
Association, International Bar Association.
Career: Qualified in 1982 after articles at
Denton Hall. Became a Partner of the firm
in 1988.
Personal: Born 1956. Educated at Clifton
College, Bristol, then Sheffield University
1975-78 (English Literature) and the Royal
Academy of Music (1978). Leisure interests
include music, theatre, reading, wind-surfing
and skiing.

ALLAN, Bill
Linklaters, London (0171) 456 3574
Partner 1982. Corporate Department.
Specialisation: Specialises in EC and UK anti-
trust law, mergers and acquisitions, and other
competition and trade-related areas of the law.
In conjunction with this work, he has
maintained a broader commercial law practice.
He has extensive experience in the UK and EC
context, representing clients from diverse
industries including utilities, food, transport,
brewing, leisure, chemicals, construction
materials and computers. Publications include
'Competition Laws of the United Kingdom and
Republic of Ireland,' which he co-authored.
Qualified 1976.

BOYCE, John D.
Slaughter and May, London
(0171) 600 1200
Specialisation: Qualified 1987. Partner 1994 in
EU/Competition Group. Based in Brussels
office (00-32-2) 737 9411. Specialises in EU
and UK Competition law for a broad range of
clients. Includes merger control notifications, as
well as European Commission, Monopolies
and Merger Commission and Office of Fair
Trading monopoly and competition
investigations, state aid rules and European
Court proceedings.

BRANDENBURGER, Rachel
Freshfields, London (0171) 936 4000
Brussels (00) 322 230 0820
Main areas of practice are EU and UK
competition and regulatory law. Has led many
cases in front of the European Commission
and the UK regulators (including the Office of
Fair Trading, the Monopolies and Mergers
Commission and the industry specific
regulators for telecommunications,

broadcasing, electricity and water). Has a wide
range of clients from the UK, continental
Europe and North and South America. Major
cases have included EC Merger Regulation
(first and second stage) reviews; Articles 85
and 86 inquiries into joint ventures and cartels;
state aid and free movement of goods cases;
and Office of Fair Trading and Monopolies and
Mergers Commission mergers and monopolies
reviews. Has written and spoken widely on a
range of competition and regulatory matters in
different jurisdictions. Co-author of the section
on Mergers in Butterworths Competition Law
Encyclopedia.
Prof. Memberships: Treasurer of the
Solicitors' European Group, committee
member of the Competition Law Sub-Group of
the City of London Law Society.
Career: Articled with *Freshfields*; qualified in
1979; became a partner in 1988.
Personal: Born 2 April 1954. Educated at
North London Collegiate School (1961-72) and
St Hilda's College, Oxford (1973-76) (MA
Jurisprudence).

BRIGHT, Christopher R.
Linklaters, London (0171) 456 3408
Partner in EC Competition and Regulatory
Group.
Specialisation: Practises in the field of EC and
UK competition and regulatory law and policy.
Extensive experience before the European
Commission, Office of Fair Trading, Monopolies
and Mergers Commission, Office of Electricity
Regulation and Office of Water Regulation.
Advises particularly on strategic issues arising
from corporate deals, commmercial policy and
regulatory alternatives. Lecturer in Law.
Prof. Memberships: Committee Member,
Competition Law Association; Member, CBI EC
Public Procurement Panel; Advisory Board,
Regulatory Policy Institute, Oxford University;
Editor, International Trade Law and Regulation
Review; Advisory Board, Oxford Centre for the
Advanced Study of European and Comparative
Law OECD; Member, Business and Industry
Advisory Committee (Competition).

BURNSIDE, Alec
Linklaters, Brussels
+32 2 513 7800
Partner and Head of the Brussels Office.
Specialisation: Specialises in EC and
competition law. Substantial experience in
commercial matters involving anti-trust law and
merger control, including notifications to EC,
UK, and other national authorities; policy
representation on behalf of clients to EC
institutions; development of EC policy and
single market legislation; dumping and trade
law. Major deals include BP/ Mobil joint
venture, Commercial Union/ General Accident
and Groupe Victoire, Allied Lyons/ Pedro
Domecq.
Career: Qualified 1986, becoming a Partner
in 1993.
Personal: Associate of Institute of the
Linguists. Fluent in French and German to legal
translator standard.

CARSTENSEN, Laura
Slaughter and May, London
(0171) 600 1200
Partner, EU/Competition Department.
Specialisation: Practice in UK and EU
Competition law, predominantly in relation to
strategic corporate events (M&A; key changes
in business policy and practice) and
contentious situations (cartel/abuse of
dominance inquiries). Extensive experience
before the European Commission, Office of
Fair Trading and Monopolies and Mergers
Commission.
Prof. Memberships: The Law Society.
Career: Qualified 1987 with *Slaughter and May*
and became a Partner in 1994.
Personal: Born 11 November 1960. Educated
Withington Girls School, Manchester then
St.Hilda's College, Oxford (English Lang. &
Lit.). Lives in Hampstead, London.

CHAPPATTE, Philippe P.
Slaughter and May, London
(0171) 600 1200
Specialisation: Competition law specialist.
Provides a wide range of UK and EU
Competition law advice (including on state aid)
in connection with transactions, litigation and
regulatory investigations and has been
responsible for a number of notifications to the
EC Commission under the EC Merger
Regulation and Article 85. Major cases have
included the Alcazar project (the proposed
merger of SAS/KLM/Austrian Airlines/Swissair
in 1993), the Montedison/Shell JV in
polypropylene and polyethylene, the
SAS/Lufthansa Alliance and the Richemont-
Telepió pay-TV joint ventures. Recent deals
include Canal +/ Nethold (pay-TV),
Williams/Chubb (security and fire protection)
and Shell/BASF polyethylene JV (Elenac). He
has also been involved in a number of
European Court cases. Experience of UK
Competition law has included Monopolies and
Mergers Commission investigations both in
monopoly and in merger cases and contempt
proceedings under the UK Restrictive Trade
Practices Act.
Prof. Memberships: Co-founder of European
Competition Lawyers Forum. Contributor to
Bellamy & Child 'Common Market Law of
Competition.'
Career: Bryanston School. Oxford University
(BA Law, First Class). Université Libre de
Bruxelles (Lic.Sp.Dr.Eur., Highest Distinction).
Qualified *Slaughter and May* 1982. Partner
1989. Responsible for running and
development of Brussels office between April
1991 and August 1996.
Personal: Three children.

CLOUGH, Mark
Ashurst Morris Crisp, London
(0171) 638 1111
Specialisation: Solicitor Advocate (Partner
1995) specialising in European Union law
(competition, mergers, state aid, anti-
dumping), WTO, UK competition law and
related sectoral regulation including:
telecommunications, broadcasting, energy,
transport and insurance. Advocacy practice
before European and National Courts.
Established author (including books on EU
competition, mergers and international trade).
Member Editorial Board International Trade Law
and Regulation (Sweet & Maxwell). Expert,
ECOSOC, Brussels (telecommunications

policy: convergence, numbering, UMTS); Vice President AMCHAM EU Committee Industrial Affairs Subcommittee Brussels.
Prof. Memberships: IBA.
Career: Bar, 1978 (Grays Inn). Solicitor Advocate (All Higher Courts), 1996.
Personal: Born 1953.

COHEN, Ralph J.
S J Berwin & Co, London
+44 (0)171 533 2222
Specialisation: Partner specialising in EC and UK Competition Law and EC Trade and Customs Law. Has extensive experience representing clients before the OFT, MMC and European Commission. Recent matters include EC merger clearance for the Guinness and GrandMet merger, MMC inquiry into distribution of ice cream and EC anti-dumping investigation into car audio products.
Prof. Memberships: Solicitors European Group.
Career: Qualified 1983. Partner at *S J Berwin & Co* 1991.
Personal: Born 10th May 1959. Attended Clifton College, and University of Southampton. Married with three sons.

COLEMAN, Martin A.
Norton Rose, London (0171) 283 6000
Specialisation: Partner specialising in EC and UK competition and general EC law. Advises businesses, governments and government agencies on matters relating to merger control; restrictive agreements; abuse of market power; state aids; free movement of goods, services and capital; freedom of establishment. Also advises on the application of UK and EC regulations in areas such as energy, transport, telecommunications, banking and financial services. Regular speaker at conferences on EC and competition law topics, and has written a number of articles for both specialist and more general publications.
Personal: Born 19th November 1952. Lives in Essex.

COLLINS, Philip G.H.
Lovell White Durrant, Brussels
+32 2 647 0660
Specialisation: EC and UK competition law; advises mainly multinational corporations on business practices, pricing and discount issues, commercial agreements and corporate alliances, joint ventures and transactions; handles complaints, investigations and administrative and judicial proceedings on competition issues. Also advises on other areas of EU law and legal developments affecting businesses including the four freedoms, public procurement and the development of European legislation and its implementation in the Member States.
Prof. Memberships: Competition Law Sub-Committee, City of London Solicitors Company; Anti-trust Section, American Bar Association; Competition Law Committee, International Bar Association.
Career: Qualified *Lovell White & King* (now *Lovell White Durrant*) in 1973; partner 1978. Following secondment to industry, established the firm's specialist competition group. Based in Brussels since 1993.

COOK, C. John
Macfarlanes, London (0171) 831 9222
Partner, Competition and EC Unit.
Specialisation: Competition law, EC law, (including international trade, public procurement and state aids) and transport and utilities regulation. A regular conference speaker and writer, he is the author, with C.S. Kerse, of "EC Merger Control," the leading text book on EC merger control – published by Sweet & Maxwell – second ed. 1996.
Career: Called to the Bar of Grays Inn in 1975. Lectureship, Magdalen College, Oxford 1976-81. UK government legal service 1976-88. *Norton Rose* 1988-1997 (established and headed its competition and EC Department). Joined *Macfarlanes* 1997.

DAVIES, John G.
Freshfields, London (0171) 936 4000
Brussels (00) 32 2 230 0820
Specialisation: Main areas of practice are competition and regulatory law at both EC and national levels (including the co-ordination of cases before several European competition authorities). Has broad experience across a wide range of industries – acting for notifying parties, defendants and complainants. Has also a number of clients in regulated industries, notably in the telecommunications and gas sectors. Has written and spoken widely on a range of competition issues in different jurisdictions.
Prof. Memberships: Visiting senior lecturer and member of the Executive Council of the Centre for European Law at London University (King's College); Committee Vice Chairman of the International Anti-trust Committee of the American Bar Association.
Career: Prior to joining *Freshfields* he worked as a case officer in the Competition Directorate-General of the European Commission (1981-1983); became a partner in 1988. Head of the Brussels office since 1989.
Personal: Born 1956. Educated at Bristol University (LLB Hons, 1977). Resides Brussels.

FINBOW, Roger J.
Ashurst Morris Crisp, London
(0171) 638 1111
Specialisation: Partner in Company Department. Member of Competition Group. Head of Sports Law Group. Handles all aspects of corporate and commercial law for principally public company clients; and competition law, especially dealing with UK regulatory bodies. Recent matters include: MMC inquiries into the acquisition by National Express of Scotrail and Central Trains; the proposed mergers of Lloyds Chemists Plc with Unichem and GEHE; the acquisition by Nutricia of Valio International and Milupa A.G., and other inquiries; the regulatory aspects of Imperial Tobacco Group's acquisition of Douwe Egberts Van Nelle; joint author of 'UK Merger Control: Law and Practice.'
Career: Qualified in 1977. Joined *Ashurst Morris Crisp* in 1975, becoming a Partner in 1984.
Personal: Born 13th May 1952. Attended Woodbridge School 1963-70 and Mansfield College Oxford 1971-74 (MA 1977). Leisure interests include classic cars, collecting model cars, badminton, ballet and gardening. Director of Ipswich Town Football Club Co. Limited; trustee of Adfam (Suffolk). Lives in the Suffolk/Essex borders.

FLECK, Richard J.H.
Herbert Smith, London (0171) 374 8000
Partner in EC and Competition Law Section.
Specialisation: Handles EC and competition law, commercial disputes and accounting law. Has extensive experience of references of proposed merger and monopoly situations to the Monopolies and Mergers Commission and on other competitive and regulatory matters such as investigations under the Competition Act. Also of European competition authorities, the Department of Trade and the Bank of England. Other areas of expertise include major commercial disputes and advising major accounting firms and the Institute of Chartered Accountants on technical and accounting matters. He is the only lawyer on the Auditing Practices Board.
Career: Qualified in 1973. Partner at *Herbert Smith* since 1979.
Personal: Educated at Southampton University.

FREEMAN, Peter J.
Simmons & Simmons, London
(0171) 628 2020
Head of EC and Competition Law and Managing Partner of Commercial and Trade Law Department.
Specialisation: Main area of practice is the law of the European Community, particularly its competition law and UK competition and regulatory law including mergers, RTPA and monopolies. Industrial sector specialisations include beer, railways, gas and broadcasting. Joint General Editor (with Richard Whish) of 'Butterworths Competition Law.' Vice Chairman of the Regulatory Policy Institute, Oxford.
Prof. Memberships: IBA, UIA, Law Society, Competition Law Association.
Career: Qualified 1977, and as a Barrister (Middle Temple) 1972. Joined *Simmons & Simmons* in 1973 and became a Partner in 1978.
Personal: Born 2nd October 1948. Attended Kingswood School, Bath, 1961-66, Goethe Institut, Berlin, 1967, Trinity College, Cambridge 1967-71, and Université Libre de Bruxelles 1972-73. Vice President of British Maritime Charitable Foundation. Leisure interests include naval history and music.

FRIEND, Mark
Allen & Overy, London (0171) 330 3000
Specialisation: Partner specialising in UK and EC competition law and utilities regulation. Has wide experience of dealing with the OFT, MMC, sectoral regulators and the EC Commission. Author of numerous articles in leading academic and professional journals.
Prof. Memberships: Member of City of London Law Society Competition Law Sub-Committee, Solicitors European Group, IBA.
Career: Qualified 1982, Partner 1990.
Personal: Cambridge University (1979 BA Law) Université Libre de Bruxelles (Lic Spec en Droit Eur 1983). Born 1957.

HALL, David F.
Linklaters, London (0171) 456 3412
Partner. Head of EU/Corporate Department.
Specialisation: Is also Chairman of the Competition Working Party of the UK Bars and Law Societies, UK Delegate to the Competition Committee of the Council of the Bars and Law Societies of the European Community. Has written and contributed to several publications.

Is the Co-author of EEC Anti-trust; 'Principles & Practice' (Butterworths), 1975; and 'Procedure and Enforcement in EC and US Competition Law' (Sweet & Maxwell), 1993.
Career: Articled at *T Haynes Duffell & Son*, Birmingham, then joined *Linklaters & Paines* as a Solicitor in 1969, made Partner in 1976. Born 1945.

HUTCHINGS, Michael B.
Michael Hutchings, Warminster
(0468) 105777
Fax: (01373) 832785
Sole Practitioner
Specialisation: Advice on all aspects of EU law, especially internal market, competition and regulation;UK implementation of EU law; UK competition law.
Prof. Memberships: British Institute of International and Comparative Law (Chairman of Executive Committee). Solicitors European Group (Former Chairman). European Competition Law Review (Editorial Board).
Career: Qualified 1973; articled with *McKenna & Co;* partner *Lovell White Durrant* 1981-1996; established independent sole practice 1996.
Personal: Born 8 November 1948.

KELLAWAY, Rosalind
Eversheds, London (0171) 919 4500
Specialisation: Rosalind Kellaway chairs the Eversheds national EU and Competition Group. Her practice covers all aspects of EU and competition law practice with particular expertise in utilities work. She handles all types of related commercial work including distributive and licensing systems and complex contractual work generally. She is a member of the CBI Competition Law Committee and of the OFFER legal advisory working group advising on the opening of the UK electricity market to full competition in 1998.
Prof. Memberships: Solicitors European Group, Competition Law Association, CBI Competition Law Committee.
Career: Qualified in 1984. Joined *Jaques & Lewis* (now Eversheds) in 1981, becoming a Partner in 1989.
Personal: Born 10th June 1957. Attended Lewes Priory School and the University of Sussex 1979 (BA Law with French). Leisure interests include riding. Lives in Lewes.

KINSELLA, Stephen
Herbert Smith, London BRUSSELS
(32) 2 511 7450
Specialisation: Stephen Kinsella is managing partner of the Brussels office, where he has resided since 1989. He specialises in European and UK competition law with particular emphasis on mergers and acquisitions, intellectual property, licensing and media. Current cases include notifications to the Commision of agreements relating to motor sport and instructions from the European Commission to assist in defending one of its merger decisions before the European Court.
Prof. Memberships: Vice President, British Chamber of Commerce in Belgium. Editor, Merger Control Reporter (Kluwer). Editor, IBA Committee C (antitrust and trade law) Newsletter. Member of International Chamber of Commerce (Paris); Air Law Association; European Competition Lawyers Forum.

Career: Graduate in Law (MA Hons) Trinity Hall, Cambridge, 1982. Qualified 1985. Partner 1991.
Personal: 5 a side football, cinema, theatre, the bars and restaurants of Brussels.

KON, Stephen D.
S J Berwin & Co, London
+44 (0)171 533 2222
Specialisation: Partner specialising in EU and competition law. Stephen heads the department which has been named 'Competition Team of the Year' at the recent Legal Business Awards. He acts in a wide variety of EC Law and competition matters, including UK and EC merger clearances. He regularly appears before the European Commission, the Monopolies and Merger Commission, the Office of Fair Trading and The Court of First Instance and European Court. Significant recent mergers clearance work has included acting for Guinness on the second phase EU clearance of the merger with Grand Metropolitan (reportedly Europe's largest merger) and for Ladbroke, in successfully opposing the bid for Capital Corporation before the OFT and MMC. He has acted in a large number of competition cases before the European Courts and has been instructed to act for the European Commission in a number of competition cases before the CFI and ECJ. Other successful cases before the CFI and Court of Justice include Allen & Hanburys v Generics concerning the compatibility of provision of UK patent legislation with community law and the Commerzbank case on the compatibility of certain provisions of UK taxation legislation with community law. Publications include: 'Competition and Business Regulation in the Single Market' as well as articles in 'The European Competition Law review,' 'The European Law Review,' amongst others.
Prof. Memberships: International Bar Association; National Committee of the English Section of the Union International Des Avocats. Law Society's Solicitors' European Group.
Career: Law lecturer at Reading University and Sussex University. Qualified in 1980. Partner at *S J Berwin & Co* 1982.
Personal: Educated at Sussex University (BA Hons). Born 26th September 1949. Lives in London.

LEIGH, Guy I.F.
Theodore Goddard, London
(0171) 606 8855
Head of Competition and Regulation Department.
Specialisation: Extensive experience of a wide range of EU and UK competition law issues and transactions, including acting before EU and national courts and administrative bodies. Experienced in various sectors such as IT, media, transport and brewing. Particular expertise in the relationship between I.P/ I.T. and competition law and in issue management/lobbying and compliance.Cases have included Magill TV listings before ECJ; state aids issues relating to the privatisation of Rail Freight Distribution; EC & UK competition law concerns relevant to the Brent Walker reconstruction; MMC National Newspaper Distribution Inquiry; MMC Credit Card Inquiry;

MMC Inquiry into acquisition by British Airways of British Caledonian; and numerous newspaper merger references. Co-author of 'The EEC and Intellectual Property.' Author of numerous articles on EU and UK competition law. Frequent speaker at conferences and seminars. In keeping with the international spirit of his work he speaks German, French, Italian and Spanish.
Prof. Memberships: Past General Rapporteur and International Rapporteur, and current Council member, of the International League for Competition Law, Committee of the English Competition Law Association, Law Society Bar Joint Working Party on Competition Law. Member of British Board European Competition Lawyers Forum.
Career: Qualified 1974. Joined *Theodore Goddard* in 1974, Partner 1978.
Personal: Born Kent 1944. University of Pennsylvania and Trinity Hall, Cambridge. Leisure include travel, languages, boating, photography, swimming and theatre. Lives in London.

LIVINGSTON, Dorothy K.
Herbert Smith, London (0171) 374 8000
Partner, Deputy Head of European and Competition Law Group and Head of Public Sector and Utilities Procurement Unit.
Specialisation: Her areas of expertise cover the full range of EU and UK competition law, including restrictive agreements, monopolies, anti-competitive practices, abuse of dominant position, mergers, public procurement, state aids and utility regulation. Also contributes to the work of the firm's international finance and banking department with particular reference to European Monetary Union. She is the joint author of 'Competition Law Sources' and author of 'Competition Law and Practice' (both FT Law and Tax) and has contributed three chapters on competition and EC law to 'Finance Leasing' (Euromoney, 3rd ed.), as well as being author of 'The Competition Act' [1998] (Sweet & Maxwell, in preparation). Sits on the advisory board of the Centre for European Law at King's College, London.
Prof. Memberships: City of London Law Society (Chairman of Banking Law and Member of EC and Competition Law Sub-Committees), Financial Law Panel Working Party on State Aids.
Career: Qualified in 1972. With *Herbert Smith* since articles. Became a Partner in 1980.
Personal: Educated at St Hugh's College, Oxford.

MARTIN ALEGI, Lynda
Baker & McKenzie, London (0171) 919 1000
Partner in EC, Competition and Trade Department.
Specialisation: Main area of practice is competition law. Also distribution, franchising, computers and I.T. Author of competition chapter in Sweet & Maxwell's 'Encyclopaedia of Information Technology Law.'
Prof. Memberships: Law Society, Competition Law Society. International Bar Association.
Career: Qualified in 1977, having joined *Baker & McKenzie* in 1975. Became a Partner in 1981. Member of the CBI Competition Panel. Member of the International Chamber of Commerce UK Competition Law Committee.
Personal: Born 7th March 1952. Educated at Cambridge University (MA in Law, 1973) and the Institute of European Studies, Brussels (1975). Lives in London.

MCKNIGHT, Elizabeth S.

Herbert Smith, London (0171) 374 8000
Specialisation: Principal area of work covers UK and EC Competition law, including cases relating to the exploitation of intellectual property rights and cases relating to regulated industries (electricity, water, gas, telecommunications, media).
Prof. Memberships: Law Society, International Bar Association.
Career: Qualified in 1988 and became a partner in 1994.
Personal: Born 3rd May 1961. Attended Jesus College, Oxford 1979-1983, then took an LLM at London School of Economics, 1989.

MORRIS, Anthony L.

Linklaters, London (0171) 456 3416
Partner in the Corporate Department.
Specialisation: Has specialised in all aspects of competition law since 1976. Main areas of practice include privatisation/regulatory work, restrictive trade practices cases, competition cases before the Commission in Brussels and when necessary before the European Court in Luxembourg. Also monopolies and mergers work before the Office of Fair Trading and Monopolies and Mergers Commission references.
Prof. Memberships: Chairman, City of London Law Society Competition Law Sub-Committee.
Career: Assistant Author 'Common Market Law of Competition' (2nd Edition Bellamy & Child). Articles at *Herbert Smith*. Qualified 1976. Became a Partner 1985.

NICHOLSON, Malcolm G.C.

Slaughter and May, London
(0171) 600 1200
Specialisation: EC, competition and regulatory law. Head of *Slaughter and May*'s EU Competition Group. His practice covers the full range of UK and EU antitrust work for a number of blue chip clients (including RECs and other utilities), governments and regulatory authorities. On the UK competition front, he has extensive experience before the MMC, including both merger and monopoly enquiries and deals regularly with the OFT. On the European front he has been engaged in a number of competition cases before the Commission and Court of Justice and in obtaining regulatory clearances from the Merger Task Force. He was heavily involved in the regulatory and competition aspects of the major UK privatisations and currently advises a number of electricity and water utilities with regard to price controls and other regulatory matters.
Career: Qualified in 1974 with *Slaughter and May*, and became a Partner in 1982.
Personal: Born March 1949. Educated Haileybury, Cambridge University, Brussels University. Married with six children.

OSBORNE, John

Clifford Chance, London (0171) 600 1000
Partner in Competition and EC Law Group.
Specialisation: Full range of EC and UK competition law from merger control, strategic alliances, joint ventures and commercial agreements to monopoly and cartel investigations. Extensive experience in conducting cases and investigations before the EC Commission, the OFT, the MMC and the CFI for parties and complaints, and co-

ordinating clearances in cross-border transactions. Acts for clients across a wide-range of business sectors including banking, financial services and broadcasting. Also advises on the EC law generally and utility regulation. Contributing editor and author of "Butterworths Competition Law" division on permitted horizontal agreements.
Prof. Memberships: IBA, Solicitors European Group, Competition Association.
Career: Qualified 1973. Partner 1980.
Personal: Born 23 October 1947. LLB Bristol (1968); LLM London School of Economics (1969). Leisure interests include military history, cricket and horseracing. Lives in Richmond.

PARR, Nigel

Ashurst Morris Crisp, London
(0171) 638 1111
Specialisation: Advises in relation to all aspects of UK and EC competition law and utilities regulation, particularly merger control. Has acted in relation to 17 MMC inquiries including monopoly investigations, mergers and anti-competitive practices for clients including Alcatel, Allied Domecq, Smith & Nephew, United News and Media, Pioneer, Express Dairies and Northern Foods. He has acted in relation to a number of bids in the utility sector, and regularly acts for clients in relation to notifications and investigations by the EC Commission.
Career: LLB, LLM, PhD, partner in the Company Department and Head of the Competition Group, co-author (with Roger Finbow) of 'UK Merger Control Law & Practice' (Sweet & Maxwell, 1995), and author of the competition section of PLC's Asset Purchases Manual, as well as numerous articles on EC law and competition-related matters. Committee member of the Solicitors European Group; tutor in EC law and intellectual property law at Exeter University 1984-86.

PHEASANT, John E.

Lovell White Durrant,
London (0171) 236 0066
Brussels (00) 32 2 647 0660
Specialisation: EC competition law in all its aspects, but particularly contentious proceedings and competition policy/regulation. Significant experience as an advocate before the Commission in administrative proceedings, and before the Court of First Instance and European Court of Justice on appeals (including interim measures). Co-author 'Competition Law' (Butterworths) and Editor of division on prohibited horizontal agreements.
Prof. Memberships: Member of the Advisory Board of the Regulatory Policy Institute, Oxford. Member of the European Association of Lawyers EC Commission Liaison Sub-Committee.
Career: Articled *Lovell, White & King* (now *Lovell White Durrant*). Qualified 1979; partner since 1985. *Lovell White Durrant* Brussels office: 1980-1983 and 1986 – present.

POLITO, Simon W.

Lovell White Durrant, London (0171) 236 0066
Specialisation: Principally EC and UK competition law. Expertise acquired since late 1970s in numerous Commission cases under Articles 85 and 86 and the Merger Regulation as well as UK merger and monopoly inquiries. Advises mainly UK, European and US multinationals on competition issues affecting

manufacturing and service industries. Also advises on regulatory aspects of privatised industries, utilities and broadcasting.
Prof. Memberships: Member Joint Working Party on Competition Law of UK and Irish Bars and Law Societies; also of UK Committee of ICC on Competition Law.
Career: Called to Bar (Middle Temple) 1972. Qualified as Solicitor with *Lovell White & King* in 1976, Partner 1982. Worked in Brussels 1977-1981 (including 1990 "stage" with the Commission) and as a resident Brussels partner from 1988. Now based primarily in London.

REYNOLDS, Michael J.

Allen & Overy, London Brussels
(00) 32 2 234 5000
Partner and Head of EC Law Group.
Specialisation: Main areas of practice are EC law and UK anti-trust law. Has acted in numerous major transactions by the European Commission. Recent cases include: Anglo/ Lonrho; Global One/ Atlas; business/ travel Met/CMB/ Crown Cork; British Airways/ American Airlines; Coca-Cola/ Cadbury Schweppes; Santa Cruz/ Microsoft; World loan/Met. Author of over twenty articles in the professional legal and business press. Speaks at conferences on EC law in Europe, the US and Japan. Was invited to address the newly constituted EC Merger Task force by the EC Commission in Ostend in 1990. Has spoken at the Fordham Law Institute's Annual Seminar and at the Mitsubishi Research Institute of Tokyo. Presented evidence at the House of Lords Select Committee on the European Communities in relation to competition practice in 1993.
Prof. Memberships: Represents the Solicitors' profession on the European Committee of British Invisibles. Member of the Advisory Board of European Business Law and of the Advisory Board of the Centre for International Studies, University of Toronto. Former Chairman of the International Bar Association's Anti-Trust and Trade Law Committee. IBA EU Co-ordinator. Visiting Professor in European Competition Law at the University of Durham. Project Director and Advisory Board Member of Global Forum on Competition and Trade Policy.
Career: Qualified Supreme Court of Judicature in 1977, having joined *Allen & Overy* in 1974. Became a Partner in 1981. In 1978 spent six months in the EC Commission's Legal Service, establishing the firm's Brussels office in 1979.
Personal: Born 8th October 1950. Attended Keele University 1969-73. Leisure interests include boats, gardening, swimming, travel and learning languages (French, Spanish, Dutch, Italian, Portuguese and German).

ROSE, Stephen

Eversheds, London (0171) 919 4500
Specialisation: All aspects of EU and UK competition law with a focus on mergers, acquisitions and joint ventures.
Prof. Memberships: Solicitors European Group (National Committee Member). Competition Law Association.
Personal: Born 27.5.65. Lives in Great Chesterford Essex.

ROWE, Michael
Slaughter and May, London
(0171) 600 1200
Specialisation: Practises all aspects of EU and UK competition law with particular expertise in M&A related competition issues. Recent matters include on-going proceedings before the European Commission, the Irish Courts and the European Courts in relation to impulse ice cream freezer cabinet exclusivity; notifications to the EU Commission and other authorities of British Aerospace's acquisition of a controlling stake in Saab, the merger of Alliance Santé and UniChem and Dalgety's disposal of its pet foods business to Nestlé.
Prof. Memberships: The Law Society, Solicitors' European Group.
Career: Qualified with *Slaughter and May* in 1994. Has practised in the firm's EU/Competition group since that date.
Personal: Born 1968. Educated at Wesley College, Dublin, Trinity College, Dublin (LLB) and Christ Church, Oxford (BCL).

SCOTT, Jonathan W.
Herbert Smith, London (0171) 374 8000
Head of EC/Competition Department.
Specialisation: Work includes mergers, joint ventures, anti-trust investigations and European Court of Justice work. Acted in major investigations involving the television industry, electricity industry, the food and drink industry, and most recently the travel, dairy and domestic appliance industries and EC merger investigations in the glass, spirits, titanium and petro-chemical industries. Editor of EC Merger Reporter. Editor merger chapters of Longman's 'Competition Law and Practice.'
Prof. Memberships: IBA.
Career: Qualified in 1981. Worked at the Council of Europe Human Rights Directorate 1979. Joined *Herbert Smith* in 1979, becoming a Partner in 1988.
Personal: Born 4th May 1956. Attended Shrewsbury School 1969-74, then St Catharine's College, Cambridge 1975-78. Lives in Cambridge.

SIBREE, William
Slaughter and May, London
(00) 32 2 230 5631
Specialisation: All areas of EU and UK competition law both contentious and non-contentious, including mergers, monopoly and Competition Act references, cartel investigations, Article 86 proceedings, state aid and litigation before the Court of Justice and Court of First Instance.
Career: Admitted to the Bar (Inner Temple) 1984. Pupillage at Monckton Chambers (1984-1985). Joined *Slaughter and May* 1986. Partner 1993.
Personal: Born 19 March 1961. Educated at Eton College and Queens' College, Cambridge (MA). Fluent in French and German. Interests include bridge, opera and skiing.

SMITH, Martin
Simmons & Simmons, London
(0171) 628 2020
Partner.
Specialisation: Main area of practice is European Community Law with particular emphasis on competition and regulatory work

(both EC and UK). Has experience of dealing with all the main EC and UK competition law authorities. His experience extends to a number of regulated industries, notably water and radio. Also undertakes more general commercial work, usually with a significant competition law or regulatory element. Author of two major divisions of the three-volume 'Butterworths Competition Law.' Has also written a number of articles. Frequently speaks at conferences and seminars.
Prof. Memberships: Law Society, City of London Solicitors' Company Competition Law Sub-Committee, CBI Competition Panel, Solicitors European Group, International Bar Association, American Bar Association.
Career: Qualified in 1981. Joined *Simmons & Simmons* in 1977, becoming a Partner in 1986, having worked at *Dechert Price & Rhoads* (Philadelphia) 1978 and *Linklaters & Paines* 1983-5.
Personal: Born 27th August 1955. Attended St Catharine's College, Cambridge 1974-77 (MA) and University of Pennsylvania (LLM) 1978-9. Leisure interests include sport, music and walking. Lives in London.

SOAMES, Trevor
Norton Rose, Belgium +32 2 237 6111
Partner in Competition and EC Department.
Specialisation: Main area of practice is all aspects of EC and UK competition, trade and regulatory law with a wide variety of experience ranging from major merger and joint venture cases (most recently Stena/ P&O involving the simultaneous and at times potentially contradictory application of EC and domestic competition law) to important multi-national cartel cases (such as Cement, Cartonboard, PVCII, Cross-Channel Ferries, Greek Ferries). His many cases include major recent decisions of the European Commission under Articles 85, 86 and 90. In addition, Trevor has handled a number of state aid cases before the European Commission and the European Court on behalf of complainants as well as for donor Governments and recipients. Trevor is an experienced litigator and proficient advocate, representing clients before the European Commission and European Court, as well as before the UK competition authorities.
Career: Qualified in 1984 as a barrister, now a solicitor. Worked at UK Department of Trade and Industry before entering private practice. Author of many articles on competition and regulatory law as well as being editor of, or contributor to a number of books. Associate editor of Butterworths Competition Law Encyclopedia.
Personal: Born 17 September 1959. Leisure interests are many but unfortunately with insufficient time to pursue them.

SPEARING, D.Nicholas
Freshfields, London (0171) 936 4000
Head of Competition Group.
Specialisation: Main area of practice is EC/Competition law. Extensive experience in monopolies, mergers and restrictive practices cases at both UK and EC levels. Acted for leading companies in MMC inquiries into car prices, perfumes, ice-cream, electrical goods and underwriting fees. Merger control work for a range of clients including ICI, Nestlé, PepsiCo, Kingfisher, Maiden and PowerGen.

Co-Author of 'Mergers' section of Butterworth's Competition law. Numerous contributions to legal journals.
Prof. Memberships: Law Society, City of London Solicitors Company, Former Chairman Solicitors' European Group.
Career: Joined *Gordon, Dadds & Co.* in 1976, qualifying in 1978. Left to join *Freshfields* in 1978. Partner 1984. Head of Competition Group.
Personal: Born 4th May 1954. Attended Caterham School 1965-72, then Hertford College, Oxford 1972-75. Leisure pursuits include family, travel and golf. Lives in Haslemere, Surrey.

TRAPP, Deirdre
Freshfields, London (0171) 936 4000
Specialisation: Main area of practice is competition and regulatory law. Has conducted monopolies, mergers and restrictive practices cases under both EU and UK jurisdictions. Extensive experience in utility, transport and media regulation.
Prof. Memberships: Law Society, City of London Solicitor's Company, Solicitor's European Group.
Career: Joined *Freshfields* in 1987. Partner 1995.
Personal: Born 21 September 1961. Attended Gunley House Convent School 1973-1980 then St. Hilda's College Oxford 1980-1983 reading Philosophy, Politics and Economics. Married with three daughters. Enjoys contemporary architecture and art, travel and food.

WHEATON, James
Clifford Chance, London (0171) 600 1000
Specialisation: Principal area of practice is EC and competition law: UK and EC competition and regulatory law including mergers, monopolies and cartels, and control of regulated utilities. Also handles public procurement and government contracts, with particular emphasis on the defence sector.
Prof. Memberships: A member of the CBI Competition Law Panel and the CBI Defence Contracts Panel.
Career: Attained LLB (1st Class Hons) Birmingham University (1970), Qualified 1973, Partner 1978.
Personal: Leisure pursuits include tennis, swimming and music. Born 13.11.1948.

WHISH, Richard P.
Watson, Farley & Williams, London
(0171) 814 8000
Email: rwhish@wfw.com
Partner in Corporate Group/ Professor of Law, King's College London, University of London.
Specialisation: Main areas of practice are UK and EC competition law including mergers, joint ventures, distribution agreements, licences of intellectual property rights and the control of market power. Author of several books including 'Competition Law' 3rd edition (Butterworths, 1993); Co-editor of Butterworths 'Competition Law,' 1991; Editor of Volume 47 of 'Halsbury's Laws of England' (Trade and Industry); contributor to 'Chitty on Contracts on Competition Law.'
Prof. Memberships: Member of the Executive Council of the Centre of European Law at King's College, London; Member of the Advisory Board of the Centre for the Study of Regulated Industries; Member of the Editorial Board of the European Business Law Review.
Career: Qualified 1977. Lecturer in Law at

Bristol University 1978-88, then Reader in Commercial Law at Bristol University 1988-90. Joined *Watson Farley & Williams* in 1989. **Personal:** Born 23rd March 1953. Holds a BA, BCL Oxon. Leisure interests include opera, travelling, gardening and India. Lives in London and Marshfield.

WOTTON, John P.
Allen & Overy, London (0171) 330 3000
Specialisation: Partner specialising in EC competition law and broadcasting law; monopoly and merger investigations; EC investigations, complaints and clearance applications; international anti-trust matters; state aids and public procurement; acted for clients from a wide range of industrial and service sectors in these matters, including newspapers and publishing, chemicals,

pharmaceuticals, sports, media, telecommunications and the motor industry; acted for many years for television and radio regulators in the UK; competition and regulatory issues in the utilities sector, particularly in water and the railways.
Career: Articled *Allen & Overy*; qualified 1978; partner 1984.
Personal: Born 7th May 1954. Graduate of Jesus College, Cambridge 1972-75.

The SOUTH and WALES

HIGHLY REGARDED FIRMS
THE SOUTH AND WALES

Burges Salmon Bristol
Maitland Walker Minehead
Edwards Geldard Cardiff
Eversheds Cardiff
Morgan Bruce Cardiff
Mundays Esher
Veale Wasbrough Bristol

Burges Salmon (Bristol) (4ptnrs/4assts) *Simon Coppen* is one the region's leading competition lawyers and *Laura Claydon* heads the department. **Clients/Work:** Includes domestic and EU competition advice, acting for FirstBus on FirstGroup/SB Holdings MMC enquiry and for Slovenia regarding the country's entry into the EU. Clients include NFU, Honda, oil and gas and utilities clients, plus EU agricultural work.

Maitland Walker (Minehead) (1ptnr/2assts) *Julian Maitland Walker* is a well-known EC and competition law specialist, working for commercial clients, individual traders, companies and trade associations. Also editor of European Company Law Review. Also works as a consultant in competition law for Veale Wasbrough. **Clients/Work:** Include Inntrepreneur tenants group action litigation in dispute over beer ties in pub tenancy agreements. Acted for Esso Licensed Retailers Association in complaint against Esso.

Edwards Geldard (Cardiff) (1ptnr/3assts in the company/commercial department). Spend a small proportion of their time working on competition law, including public procurement work.

Eversheds (Cardiff) (2 ptnrs, 1 asst, part-time in the firm's company and commercial department) Mainly on non-contentious work. The firm works for local authorities, government bodies and health trusts. **Clients/Work:** Include the Welsh Development Agency, the University of Glamorgan and the DVLA.

Morgan Bruce (Cardiff) (2ptnrs/1asst in the firm's commercial law team) Spend a fair amount of time on competition issues, supported by a consultant at the University of Glamorgan.

Mundays (Esher) Former EC Commission official *Bryan Harris* continues to advise the firm, although he is now based in the US and Brussels.

Veale Wasbrough (Bristol) (3 ptnrs/1asst in the company/commercial department) Work on non-contentious IP and public procurement matters. Also has two consultants, Julian Maitland Walker and Brenda Sufrin, lecturer in competition law at Bristol University.

LEADING INDIVIDUALS
THE SOUTH AND WALES

CLAYDON Laura Burges Salmon
COPPEN Simon Burges Salmon
HARRIS Bryan Mundays
MAITLAND WALKER Julian Maitland Walker

SEE PROFILES AT END OF THIS SECTION

MIDLANDS and EAST ANGLIA

HIGHLY REGARDED FIRMS
MIDLANDS AND EAST ANGLIA

Pinsent Curtis Birmingham
Wragge & Co Birmingham
Martineau Johnson Birmingham
Eversheds Birmingham, Norwich

Pinsent Curtis (Birmingham) (3ptnrs/5assts) Work in Birmingham, Leeds and Brussels on a wide range of competition matters, especially utilities work. *Kate Rees* is ranked for the first time. "She's worked bloody hard, even if she isn't on the circuit." "She knows her stuff, can find a competition problem in anything." **Clients/Work:** Advising London Luton Airport on competition and public procurement issues arising out of proposed grant of long-term concession for operation of airport and Avonmore Foods on competition aspects of merger with Waterford. Other clients include IMI plc and NHS Supplies Authority.

Wragge & Co (Birmingham) (1ptnr/4assts) Work within the commercial department on a mixture of contentious and non-contentious work. *Guy Lougher* ("competent,") is the merger control, trading and IP licensing agreements specialist. **Clients/Work:** Defending client in RPTA over price fixing cartel, several merger notifications in the motor industry. Also work for ABB Adtraz.

Martineau Johnson (Birmingham) (4ptnrs/2assts) Work in the trade and utilities department, which covers general commercial, competition and utilities work. *Geraldine Tickle* is highly regarded for her competition work, particularly for motor industry IP-related work. Active speaker.

Eversheds (Birmingham/Norwich) (2ptnrs/3assts in Birmingham within the firm's commercial department and 3ptnrs/4assts in Norwich) However, work is perceived to be London rather than locally led. **Clients/Work:** Advising Birmingham International Airport on EU merger clearance and Headlam Group plc's OFT clearance following its acquisition of MCD (UK) Ltd.

LEADING INDIVIDUALS
MIDLANDS AND EAST ANGLIA

LOUGHER Guy Wragge & Co
REES Kate Pinsent Curtis
TICKLE Geraldine Martineau Johnson

SEE PROFILES AT END OF THIS SECTION

The NORTH

Addleshaw Booth & Co (Manchester/Leeds) (4ptnrs/6assts within the trade and regulatory department) *Garth Lindrup* "has a national reputation, but is somewhat academic." *Jonathan Davey* and *Gillian Holding* write extensively on competition law matters. **Clients/Work:** Include Adidas, Airtours, Ministry of Defence, Unipoly, Yorkshire Water

Dibb Lupton Alsop (Sheffield, London, Brussels) (1 ptnr/1 asst work full-time with assistance from other members of the communications and technology group) Unit practices from London, Sheffield and Brussels. *Stephen Hornsby* is good, but there is a question over the firm's strength and depth. **Clients/Work:** Include First Division

Rugby Clubs, Daewoo, East Midlands and Manchester Airports and Connex.

Eversheds (Leeds/Manchester) (Leeds: 2 ptnrs/1asst. Manchester: 2 ptnrs/1 assts) Automotive, brewing and pharmaceutical sector specialist *Adam Collinson* was made partner in February 1998 and is committed to making a reputation. **Clients/Work:** Advised Asda in defence of Italian Parma Ham Consortium dispute over EC designation of origin regulation, and over resale price maintenance dispute for over the counter pharmaceuticals.

Eversheds (Newcastle-upon-Tyne, Middlesbrough) (1ptnr/2assts across Newcastle-upon-Tyne and Middlesbrough) *Geoff Harrison* is experienced. **Clients/Work:** Main work includes merger control advice, competition law and public sector procurement rules compliance. Clients include BTR, Nissan, AEA Technology and Century Inns. Public sector clients include the Universities of Durham and Northumbria.

Pinsent Curtis (Leeds) (2ptnrs/1asst) Part of national team with 2 partners in Birmingham. **Clients/Work:** Involved in a price-fixing cartel investigation and merger clearance. Clients include Smith & Nephew, DfEE and Pace Micro Technology plc.

Berrymans Lace Mawer (Liverpool) (4ptnrs/2 assts) **Clients/Work:** Include

Commission notification of BPB plc and St Gobain's glass fibre insulation joint venture and SITA SA on EC and UK merger rules for its US$1.5 billion acquisition of Brown Ferring Industries. Other clients include British Gypsum and Pilkington UK Ltd.

Dickinson Dees (Newcastle-upon-Tyne) (3ptnrs/2 assts) Work between Newcastle and Leeds in the commercial department, mainly in merger and acquisitions (particularly in transport), MMC enquiries, inward investment and anti-dumping. **Clients/Work:** Act on 10 per cent of all Commission merger applications. Also acted on Arriva plc's (formerly Cowie plc's) acquisition of the British Bus Group.

SCOTLAND

Burness WS (Edinburgh) (3ptnrs/3assts) Work in the corporate department, mainly on the back of the firm's company and corporate work. *James McLean* is the most active. More public procurement work expected following the firm's expanding PFI practice. **Clients/Work:** Include Fife Power, Magnox Electric plc, BSkyB, Pepsico.

Dundas & Wilson CS (Edinburgh) (2ptnrs/1assts form a specialist unit in the firm's corporate and commercial group) **Clients/Work:** Advised electronics firm on the referral of a state aid package to the European Commission. Also acted for the University of Edinburgh on public procurement issues and The Royal Bank of Scotland on competition law compliance.

Maclay Murray & Spens (Glasgow/Edinburgh) Six fee earners work in this area, headed by *Michael Dean*, formerly of McGrigor Donald. **Clients/Work:** Work includes assisting Robert Wiseman Dairies plc in the MMC enquiry into acquisition of Scottish Pride and defending a client from European Commission 'dawn raid.' Other work comes from local authorities and other public bodies on public procurement compliance.

MacRoberts (Glasgow) Small number of partners and assistants spend a 'modest' amount of time on competition issues. *David Flint* sits on CBI competition panel. **Clients/Work:** Various PFI projects. Also acted on Scottish Nuclear/BNFL contracts and amendments.

McGrigor Donald (Glasgow) (1ptnr/3assts in sub-group of the firm's corporate department) Frank Doran replaces Michael Dean, who went to Maclay Murray & Spens. **Clients/Work:** Mainly public procurement work, although some domestic M&A support and distribution and agency agreements.

NORTHERN IRELAND

Cleaver Fulton & Rankin (Belfast) Three lawyers spend a small proportion of their time on this work. **Clients/Work:** Handle

competition work relating to commercial agreements and environmental-related EU issues.

CLAYDON, Laura
Burges Salmon, Bristol (0117) 939 2000

COLLINSON, Adam G.
Eversheds, Leeds (0113) 243 0391
Partner in Commercial Department and Head
of EC/competition practice for
Leeds/Manchester.
Specialisation: EC and UK competition and
related commercial law. Significant exposure to
automotive, brewing and pharmaceutical
sectors. Particular experience in UK merger
control and in preparing appropriate structures
for UK, European and US clients to get their
products to market. Advised Asda in its
campaigns to end resale price maintenance for
books and OTC medicines.
Prof. Memberships: Solicitors European Group
(Committee member – Yorkshire Branch).
Career: Joined *Eversheds* in 1994 after 6 years
at *McKenna & Co* (including Articles). Became
a Partner in 1998. Educated at Oundle School
and Durham University (Hatfield College).
Personal: Married with two daughters. Lives in
Wetherby. Trustee of Constance Green
Foundation.

COPPEN, Simon A.
Burges Salmon, Bristol (0117) 939 2000

DAVEY, Jonathan
Addleshaw Booth & Co, Manchester
(0161) 934 6000
Partner in Trade & Regulatory Department,
Commercial Group.
Specialisation: Main areas of work in this field
are UK and EC competition law (including the
law relating to restrictive practices, mergers
and anti-competitive behaviour), public
procurement law and state aids. Has been
involved in the recent past in a number of
significant notifications and complaints to the
EC Commission and has considerable
experience of UK Merger Control and of
advising on UK competition law generally.
Prof. Memberships: Association
Internationale des Jeunes Avocats, President of
Distribution Law Commission, CBI National
Consumer Law Advisory Panel, North West
Solicitors European Group.
Career: Joined the firm in 1986 and qualified in
1988. Became an Associate in 1992 and a
Partner in 1994.
Personal: Educated at Manchester University
1982-85 (LL.B Hons) and the College of Law,
Chester 1985-86 (1st Class Hons in Law
Society Final Examination). Treasurer,
Manchester University Law Graduates
Association (MULGA). Enjoys hill walking, travel
and good food. Lives near Knutsford.

DEAN, Michael
Maclay Murray & Spens, Glasgow
(0141) 248 5011
Specialisation: Partner in the Corporate
Department specialising in EU and UK
competition law. Practice covers agency,
distribution, EC and UK, merger clearances,
MMC inquiries, advice on pricing and discount
structures, private finance initiative and
outsourcing projects. Also advises both the
public and private sector on procurement
issues, procedures and notices. Recent cases
have involved the successful mediation of a

$15m claim against a US client by a European
agent; advising on competition issues in the
financial services sector; provision of
Eurodefence in Scottish courts in licensing
litigation; advising public sector bodies on state
aid obligations; retained by several
multinationals for competition investigations;
advised on a range of Bosman issues; has
advised Law Society of Scotland. Frequently
gives presentations to the business sector on
export and European issues.
Prof. Memberships: Law Society of Scotland;
Scottish Lawyers European Group. Chairman
German-British Chamber of Commerce in
Scotland, Chair, Glasgow Export Club.
Career: Qualified 1986. Assistant solicitor,
McKenna & Co., London 1986-1988. Assistant
solicitor, *Lovell White Durrant*, London 1988-
1990. Assistant solicitor and partner *McGrigor
Donald* 1990-1995. Recruited by *Maclay Murray
& Spens* as partner. Former external examiner,
Europa Institute, Edinburgh.
Personal: Educated at St. Aloysius College,
Glasgow 1968-1978, University of Glasgow
(LL.B Hons and Diploma in Legal Practice)
1978-1983, and at the College of Europe,
Bruges 1983-1984. Interests include local
politics. Leisure pursuits include badminton.
Born 15th January 1960. Lives in Glasgow.

FLINT, David
MacRoberts, Glasgow (0141) 332 9988
See under Computer Law & I.T., p. 189

HARRIS, Bryan
Mundays, Brussels 00 322 502 2752
Specialisation: A special consultant to
Mundays advising on European Community
policy and law. Advises generally on the
administrative, legislative and policy-making
procedures of the EC institutions; and
particularly on questions involving the
competition rules and intellectual property
rights (patents, trade marks, copyright etc).
Career: He was a senior official of the
Commission of the European Community from
1973 to 1983 and served as Head of the
Intellectual Property Division. He is now
Director of Legal Research and Adjunct (Part-
Time) Professor of European Union Law at the
Franklin Pierce Law Centre, New Hampshire,
USA, and gives Post-Graduate courses on EU
Constitutional Law and on Intellectual Property
and Anti-Trust Law in the EU. During the last 20
years he has written and lectured extensively
on legal and economic matters. He has written
several full-length books 'The Law of the
European Communities,' [Butterworths, 1973];
'Franchising in the European Community,'
[Longmans, 1991]; has contributed numerous
articles to learned or specialised journals,
including The European Law Review, [London,
England], The Journal of Law and Technology,
[Concord, NH, USA], The Common Market Law
Review [Leyden, The Netherlands], The
International Contract Law Review [Lausanne,
Switzerland], and the European Intellectual
Property Review [Oxford, England]; he also
wrote the section on the Common Agricultural
Policy [Title 'Agriculture'] for the Fourth Edition
of Halsbury's Laws. He is Editor of the monthly
publication, 'Competition Law in the European
Communities,' published by the Fairford Press
in England, with an international readership.

HARRISON, Geoffrey
Eversheds, Middlesbrough (01642) 247456
Specialisation: Practises in EU and UK
competition law. Experience of other national
systems. Advises major UK, European and US
clients on merger control, pricing, supply policy
and regulatory investigations.
Prof. Memberships: Law society.
Career: University of Leicester 1971.
Admitted 1974.

HOLDING, Gillian E.
Addleshaw Booth & Co, Leeds
(0113) 209 2000
Partner in Trade and Regulatory Department,
Commercial Group.
Specialisation: Principal area of practice is
European, competition/regulatory and public
procurement law. Work includes UK and EU
merger control advice; OFT, MMC and
European Commission enquiries and
investigations; restrictive trade practices.
Prof. Memberships: Solicitors European
Group (current Chairman of Yorkshire branch).
Career: Qualified in 1984 with *Linklaters &
Paines* until August 1990 (1986 – 1988 in Paris
office). Joined the firm September 1990.
Personal: Born 4th March 1959. Educated at
the University of Birmingham 1977-81 (LL.B
Hons, Law with French), Université de Limoges,
France 1979-80 (Diplome d'etudes juridiques
Francais) and City University 1983-85 (MA in
Business Law). Leisure interests include
walking, painting, gardening, food, travel,
French cinema and literature. Lives in Leeds.

HORNSBY, Stephen
Dibb Lupton Alsop, Sheffield (0345) 262728
Specialisation: EU/U.K. competition and
regulatory. Media/Telecoms and sport.
Prof. Memberships: Law Society, Solicitors
European Group, I.B.A.
Career: 1983-86 Official in Competition
Directorate EC Commission. 1986-90 *Allen &
Overy*, London Office. 1991-92 British Telecom
Legal Services – Regulatory Division. 1993 to
date Partner at *Dibb Lupton Alsop*.

LINDRUP, Garth
Addleshaw Booth & Co, Manchester
(0161) 934 6000
Partner in Trade & Regulatory Department,
Commercial Group.
Specialisation: Work includes mergers and
joint ventures, distribution, agency and
franchising, public procurement, state aid,
restrictive and anti-competitive practices,
dominant positions and complex monopolies.
Particular sectors include motor vehicles,
books, beer, milk, air transport, buses, steel
and pharmaceuticals. Editor, 'Butterworths
Competition Law Handbook' and 'Butterworths
Public Procurement and CCT Handbook;'
Chairman, Law Society's Solicitors European
Group 1994/95.
Prof. Memberships: IBA, LIDC, Competition
Law Association, Law Society.
Career: Qualified in 1975. Joined the firm in
1979 and became a Partner in 1984. Member
of Law Society's 1992 (subsequently
International) Awareness Working Party,
1989-93.
Personal: Born 1948. Holds BA, LLM
(Cantab).

LOUGHER, Guy
Wragge & Co, Birmingham (0121) 233 1000
Head of EC/Competition Group.
Specialisation: EU and competition law,
particularly its application to merger control,
trading and IP Licensing Agreements.
Prof. Memberships: Member of Solicitors
European Group, Competition Law Association,
Competition Law Committee of the ICC United
Kingdom (International Chamber Of
Commerce).
Career: Qualified 1989. Joined *Wragge & Co*
1994, made Partner 1996.
Personal: Born 1964.

MAITLAND-WALKER, Julian
Maitland Walker, Minehead (01643) 707777
Specialisation: Main area of Practice is
European trade and competition law including
UK restrictive trade parctices, monopolies and
merger control, state aids, public procurements
and anti-dumping issues. Has acted in several
references to the MMC, including Beer Supply,
Motor Vehicle Distribution and the
Pharmaceutical Industry. Other areas of
practice include intellectual property,
registration and licensing, agency distribution,
franchising, joint ventures and R & D
agreements. Editor of the *European
Competition Law Review* and author of several
texts including 'Competition Laws of Europe'
(Butterworths), 'A Guide to European Company
Laws' (Sweet & Maxwell), 'EC Insurance
Directives' and 'EC Banking Directives' (Lloyds
of London Press).

MCLEAN, James
Burness, Edinburgh (0131) 473 6000
Specialisation: Jim McLean graduated in
English and Scots Law at Cambridge and
Edinburgh Universities. He is Convenor of the
Law Society of Scotland's Intellectual Property
Committee. He also represents the Law Society
of Scotland on the joint UK Law Societies' and
Bars' working party on Competition (anti-trust)
Law. His practice covers assignation, disposal
and licensing of intellectual property including
property and insolvency aspects.

REES, Kate
Pinsent Curtis, Birmingham (0121) 200 1050
Specialisation: EU and Competition Law
including UK and EU merger clearances and
OFT, MMC and European Commission
enquiries. Very extensive public procurement
practice.
Career: LLB Hons 1st class. Qualified in 1988.
Partner in *Pinsent Curtis*.
Personal: Resides in Oxfordshire.

TICKLE, Geraldine
Martineau Johnson, Birmingham
(0121) 200 3300
Specialisation: Competition and EU Law. Also
advises on public procurement and non-
contentious IP.
Prof. Memberships: Competition Law
Association – UK Rapporteur General; Ligue
International De Droit de la Concurrence –
Rapporteur General Adjoint; Solicitors
European Group; IBA – Anti Trust Committee.
Heads the firm's Automotive Group which
specialises in providing competition law, IP and
commercial advice to clients engaged in
manufacturing and distribution in that sector.
Contributor to a number of books on
competition law and non-contentious IP.
Member of government advisory group on
automotive distribution.
Career: LLB Hons. Called 1973 Grays Inn.
Admitted 1983. Joined *Martineau Johnson*
1995. Head of Trade Department.

FAMILY/MATRIMONIAL LAW

RESEARCH: In compiling the tables, we consider all the information available to us, paying particular regard to the market research carried out by our team of ten qualified lawyers. (The researchers' details are set out on page three.) The rankings, therefore, reflect the opinion of the marketplace as revealed by systematic and objective research: see page four. (Our research is audited every year by the British Market Research Bureau.)

OVERVIEW: In London, Manches & Co and Withers remain at the top of the tree, while Bates Wells & Braithwaite and Sears Tooth move up the tables. Although not all agree with the approach of the latter firm, most interviewees were impressed with its results. New firm Levison Meltzer Pigott (made up of three ex Collyer-Bristow partners) should be one to watch. In the south west, the Ian Downing Family Law Practice and Woollcombe Beer Watts move up on recommendation and in the north east, Zermansky & Partners and Jones Myers Gordon were felt to be doing well. There was little significant movement in the other regions. The increasing popularity of mediation, which is now enshrined in The Family Law Act 1996, is evident in both London and the regions, as most firms are taking a keen interest in this rapidly expanding field.

LEADING FIRMS · LONDON

MANCHES & CO
WITHERS

BATES, WELLS & BRAITHWAITE
CHARLES RUSSELL
SEARS TOOTH

COLLYER-BRISTOW
DAWSON CORNWELL & CO
FARRER & CO
GORDON DADDS
KINGSLEY NAPLEY
LEVISON MELTZER PIGOTT
MILES PRESTON & CO
MISHCON DE REYA

HIGHLY REGARDED FIRMS

Anthony Gold, Lerman & Muirhead
Barnett Sampson
The Family Law Consortium
Fisher Meredith
Goodman Ray
Payne Hicks Beach
Reynolds Porter Chamberlain

Bindman & Partners
David du Pré & Co
David Truex and Company
Dawson & Co
Druces & Attlee
Hodge Jones & Allen
Margaret Bennett
Osbornes
Penningtons
Russell Jones & Walker
Stephenson Harwood

Edward Fail Bradshaw & Waterson
Forsters
Hunters
Russell-Cooke, Potter & Chapman
The Simkins Partnership
Wright Son & Pepper

LONDON

Manches & Co (5ptnrs/8assts) Together with Withers this is the leading family department in London and the team is easily one of the largest and most prestigious in the country. Boasting such figures as *Helen Ward* ("a good, tough lawyer") and the "talented" *Richard Sax* the team is headed by the "excellent" *Jane Simpson*. The newly recommended *William Massey* also enters the table. **Clients/Work:** The department specialises in high net worth clients, complex children and residence cases and international forum shopping.

Withers (6 ptnrs/7assts) With numerous high profile cases throughout the past twelve months, Withers easily justifies its top ranking in the table. It boasts several leaders including the "excellent and well rounded" *Gill Doran*, *Charles Doughty*, *Andrew Gerry*, *James Harcus* and *Diana Parker*. **Clients/Work:** Work covers divorce, surrogacy and child abduction, much of which has an international dimension.

Bates Wells & Braithwaite (2ptnrs/4assts ft/1asst pt) The expanding department continues to be headed by the "very able" *Frances Hughes* and *Pauline Fowler*. Often quoted in the press due to the number of high profile cases undertaken in the last year. Move up the tables as a result. **Clients/Work:** Undertaking an increasing amount of media and entertainment work alongside the usual big money ancillary relief and general family work.

Charles Russell (5ptrs/6assts) Retaining its position as one of the leading family law firms in London, this highly respected team is headed by *Peter George*, a founder member of the International Academy of Matrimonial Lawyers, and is backed by four other "notable" partners (*David Davidson*, *Grant Howell*, *Maryly La Follette* and *William Longrigg*). **Clients/Work:** Specialising in medium and high net worth divorce work, private client children work and numerous child abduction cases. Particular expertise in pensions, cross-jurisdictional and international family work.

Sears Tooth (4ptnrs/2assts) Though some may object to his direct and confrontational style, most agree that the "exceptional" *Ray Tooth* "doggedly pursues the interests of his clients." Especially noted for tackling the "messiest of divorce cases." **Clients/Work:** Specialises in divorce and general matrimonial work, much of which has an international flavour.

Collyer-Bristow (3 prtrs/4 assts) With the departure of Jeremy Levison, Claire Meltzer and Simon Pigott, many practitioners predicted the demise of Collyer Bristow. However the arrival of the widely respected *Geoffrey Rutter*, formerly of Rutter & Co, is felt to have "saved the day." The firm also retains the "truly exceptional" new head of

LEADING INDIVIDUALS · LONDON

LEVISON Jeremy Levison Meltzer Pigott	**TOOTH Ray** Sears Tooth	**WARD Helen** Manches & Co

ALEXIOU Douglas Gordon Dadds	**GERRY Andrew** Withers	**SAX Richard** Manches & Co
CORNWELL John Dawson Cornwell & Co	**HARCUS James** Withers	**SHACKLETON Fiona** Farrer & Co
DAVIS Sandra Mishcon de Reya	**HUGHES Frances** Bates, Wells & Braithwaite	**SIMPSON Jane** Manches & Co
DORAN Gill Withers	**PARKER Diana** Withers	
DOUGHTY Charles Withers	**PRESTON Miles** Miles Preston & Co	
DRAKE Michael Collyer-Bristow	**RAE Maggie** Mishcon de Reya	

ALEXANDER Peter Dawson & Co	**HARPER Mark** Anthony Gold, Lerman & Muirhead	**PEARSON Philippa** The Family Law Consortium
BEATSON Kim Anthony Gold, Lerman & Muirhead	**HODSON David** The Family Law Consortium	**PEAT Kathryn** Druces & Attlee
BISHOP Gillian The Family Law Consortium	**HOWELL Grant** Charles Russell	**PEMBRIDGE Eileen** Fisher Meredith
CHAPMAN Elspeth Barnett Sampson	**HUTCHINSON Anne-Marie** Dawson Cornwell & Co	**PHILIPPS Susan** Penningtons
COLLIS Pamela Kingsley Napley	**KEIR Jane** Kingsley Napley	**PIGOTT Simon** Levison Meltzer Pigott
CROWTHER Felicity Bindman & Partners	**LA FOLLETTE Maryly** Charles Russell	**PIRRIE James** The Family Law Consortium
DAVIDSON David Charles Russell	**LEVERTON David** Payne Hicks Beach	**RAY Peggy** Goodman Ray
FISHER Jeremy Gordon Dadds	**LONGRIGG William** Charles Russell	**ROBINSON Sara** The Family Law Consortium
FOWLER Pauline Bates, Wells & Braithwaite	**MARCO Alan** Collyer-Bristow	**RODGERS Hilary** Forsters
GEORGE Peter Charles Russell	**MELTZER Claire** Levison Meltzer Pigott	**RUTTER Geoffrey** Collyer-Bristow
GOODMAN Judith Goodman Ray	**PARRY Richard** Farrer & Co	**WALSH Jonathan** Stephenson Harwood

UP AND COMING

BAKER Miranda Kingsley Napley	**MASSEY William** Manches & Co

SEE PROFILES AT END OF THIS SECTION

department *Michael Drake* and the "noteworthy" *Alan Marco*. **Clients/Work:** Since the merger with Rutter & Co the firm has become increasingly involved in international work, such as forum shopping, child abduction and the recognition of foreign decrees. The firm is also on the Lord Chancellor's Child Abduction Panel. Also now has expertise in cohabitation law and pre-nuptial agreements.

Dawson Cornwell & Co (6 ptnrs/3 assts) Team headed by the "widely respected" *John Cornwell*. Move up the table as a result of a successful year. **Clients/Work:** Clients range from those whose net worth is in excess of £30 million to those who are legally aided. Notable cases include Re P, P v P, and Re S.

Farrer & Co (4 ptnrs/4assts ft, 2assts pt) This high profile department led by the "direct" and "more than efficient" *Fiona Shackleton* has had another busy year. Team includes *Richard Parry*. **Clients/Work:** Cover a wide range of family and matrimonial work, most notably for several members of the Royal family and other "elite" clients.

Gordon Dadds (3 ptnrs/2 assts) Headed by the "excellent" *Douglas Alexiou*, this department has gone from strength to strength over the past twelve months. Also highly rated by his peers in London is "effective operator" *Jeremy Fisher*. **Clients/Work:** Divorce, financial disputes, children and some international work.

Kingsley Napley (4ptnrs/3assts)Led by *Pamela Collis*, this established department continues to be respected by other leading firms and still attracts mainly big money clients. Team includes *Jane Keir* and the newly recommended *Miranda Baker*. **Clients/Work:** In the past twelve months they have been particularly successful in children cases, including child abduction and contested international custody disputes. Also disputed residence applications.

Levison Meltzer Pigott (3ptnrs/2assts) The combined talents of the "truly exceptional" *Jeremy Levison*, "the very able" *Simon Pigott* and the "highly experienced" *Claire Meltzer* have joined forces to form this new firm, which promises to "rival the best." **Clients/Work:** High net worth individuals and complex children's cases dominate the workload. Increasing emphasis on international work such as forum shopping and the recognition of foreign decrees. Clients range from actors and singers to professionals and business people.

Miles Preston & Co (3ptnrs/2assts) Described by some as a "first class specialist practice." The team is headed by the "elegant, solution driven" *Miles Preston*. Following a policy of deliberately slow but steady expansion. **Clients/Work:** The firm only deals with matrimonial and family law. Recently handled some high profile cases.

Mishcon de Reya (2ptnrs/5assts) Heading a department with a £1.3m turnover last year, *Sandra Davis* and *Maggie Rae* have maintained their team's standing as one of the leading firms in London. Claim to be expanding at the moment and becoming increasingly international in outlook. **Clients/Work:** Building on their media foundations, they have a particular expertise in family work with a media aspect. Services range from divorce and separation advice for high profile individuals to controversial international matters such as international adoption and abduction. The two partners are trained mediators.

LEADERS' PROFILES · LONDON

ALEXANDER, Peter J.
Dawson & Co, London (0171) 421 4800
Partner in Matrimonial Department.
Specialisation: Twenty-five years experience as a matrimonial specialist. Acted in the famous case of B v. B, decided by Mr Justice Ward. Has commented on legal developments on The 6 O'Clock News.
Prof. Memberships: Law Society, Solicitors Family Law Association.
Career: Qualified in 1970. Partner in *Gamlens* 1970-89. Partner in *Penningtons* 1989-93.

Joined *Dawson & Co.* as a Partner in July 1993.
Personal: Born 16th November 1943. Educated at Haileybury and I.S.C. 1957-62, then University of Manchester 1963-66. Lists his leisure interests as 'looking after my family, going to the pub, and following my sons' careers with interest.' Lives in Alton, Hants.

ALEXIOU, Douglas
Gordon Dadds, London (0171) 493 6151
Senior Partner and Head of Family Law Department.

Specialisation: Covers all areas including divorce, judicial separation, financial disputes, co-habitation, children (including Children Act applications, Child Support Act) and international aspects (including recognition and enforcement). Lectures, gives TV, radio, magazine and newspaper interviews; workshop leader at the 'Big Money' conference.
Prof. Memberships: Law Society, Solicitors Family Law Association (Chairman of London Regional Group 1992-1996), Vice-President International Academy of Matrimonial Lawyers

(also President, European Chapter), City of Westminster Law Society, Member of the Family Mediators Association.
Career: Qualified in 1970. Joined *Gordon Dadds* in February 1971, and was made a Partner later that year. Became Senior Partner in 1986. Director of Tottenham Hotspur Football Club since 1980. Chairman 1982-84. Director of Tottenham Hotspur Plc 1983-91 and 1993 to date. Member of 1996 British Olympic Appeal Council.
Personal: Born 24th May 1942. Attended St Paul's School 1955-59, Kings College London (LLB Hons) 1965 and College of Law. Leisure interests include golf, tennis and association football. Lives in Kingston-upon-Thames.

BAKER, Miranda
Kingsley Napley, London (0171) 814 1200
Specialisation: All aspects of family law, including complex children and ancillary relief applications. Advice in relation to the legal implications of surrogacy arrangements. Occasional writer and lecturer on family law. SFLA trained mediator.
Career: Qualified 1981. With *Collyer-Bristow* 1983-86, *Rubinstein Callingham* 1986-94 (partner from 1989) and *Manches & Co* (following the merger with *Rubinstein Callingham*) 1994-95. Joined *Kingsley Napley* as a partner in 1995.
Prof. Memberships: SFLA (member of Children Committee since 1989), National Council for Family Proceedings.
Personal: Born 16/05/56. Attended Wimbledon High School, then New Hall, Cambridge (1974-77). Leisure interests include travel, opera, football and swimming. Lives in London.

BEATSON, Kim
Anthony Gold, Lerman & Muirhead, London (0171) 940 4000
Partner in Matrimonial Department.
Specialisation: Exclusively Family Law particularly financial disputes. Occasional lecturer and accredited Family Mediator.
Prof. Memberships: SFLA, SFLA Mediation Training Board, Family Mediators Association and UK College of Family Mediators.
Career: Qualified in 1984. Became a Partner and Head of Family Law Department, *Russell-Cooke, Potter & Chapman* 1986. Joined *Anthony Gold, Lerman & Muirhead* as a Partner in 1996.

BISHOP, Gillian
The Family Law Consortium, London (0171) 420 5000
email: flc@tflc.co.uk
Partner.
Specialisation: Expertise in all types of ancillary relief and children issues including permanent removal from the jurisdiction applications and international child abduction. Mediation.
Prof. Memberships: Solicitors Family Law Association (Member Education Committee and National Committee) Family Mediators Association, UK College of Family Mediation. Trustee of The Oxford Institute of Legal Practice. Trustee of London Marriage Guidance Council. Co-author 'Divorce Reform: A Guide for Lawyers and Mediators.'
Career: Qualified 1982. Partner at *Brecher & Co.* 1988-1995; Co-Founder of *The Family Law Consortium* in 1995.
Personal: Born 25th September 1958. Educated at The Old Palace School 1972-1976.

Queen Mary College, London (LLB Hons. 1979). Leisure pursuits include walking, cooking, reading and Liverpool Football Club. Lives in Sevenoaks.

CHAPMAN, Elspeth
Barnett Sampson, London (0171) 831 7181
Specialisation: Partner in the Family Department. Specialises in substantial ancillary relief applications, often with an international, trust or offshore aspect. Also undertakes private children's applications. Has written a number of articles and book reviews.
Prof. Memberships: Founder member and current Treasurer of the Solicitors Family Law Association; accredited member of the Family Mediators Association.
Career: Qualified in 1972. Partner at *Finers* 1973-84. Partner at *Barnett Sampson* since 1984.
Personal: Educated at Howells School, Denbigh 1957-63 and University College, London (LL.B 1968). Leisure pursuits include travel, horse riding, cooking, reading and gardening.

COLLIS, Pamela
Kingsley Napley, London (0171) 814 1200
Head of Family Department.
Specialisation: International and domestic family law work; particularly financial aspects of marriage and cohabitation breakdown, and Children Act work. Contributor to legal journals and speaker on matters relating to family law.
Prof. Memberships: International Academy of Matrimonial lawyers, SFLA (Committee Member London Regional Group), City of London Law Society, Member Principal Registry Family Division Users Group, Justice.
Career: Qualified 1981. Joined *Kingsley Napley* in 1982 and became a Partner in 1984.
Personal: Born 9th March 1957. Attended Rosemead School for Girls, then Bristol University (LLB 1978). Leisure pursuits include sailing, books and family life. Lives in London.

CORNWELL, John
Dawson Cornwell & Co, London (0171) 242 2556
Partner handling family and matrimonial and private client matters.
Specialisation: Main areas of practice are family and matrimonial work (private law only). Practises on own account as a mediator. Deputy District Judge in Principal Registry since 1987. Also handles private client matters, including administration of estates, trusts and wills. Writes articles in SFLA newsletters and for 'Family Law.' Has frequently addressed conferences.
Prof. Memberships: SFLA, FMA.
Career: Qualified in 1969. Founding Partner of *Dawson Cornwell* in 1972. Founder of the SFLA, Chairman 1982-87 and returned to the Committee in 1994. Co-founder of FMA, Vice Chairman 1992-93 and Board Member from inception until 1994. Deputy District Judge since 1987.
Personal: Born 21st September 1943. Educated at St. Paul's School 1957-62 and Bristol University 1962-65. Leisure interests include theatre and cricket. Lives in London.

CROWTHER, Felicity
Bindman & Partners, London (0171) 833 4433
Partner in Family Department.
Specialisation: Work includes ancillary relief, residence and contact, cohabitation disputes and international child abduction.

Prof. Memberships: Solicitors Family Law Association, Family Mediators Association. Deputy District Judge of the Principal Registry of the Family Division.
Career: Qualified in 1974. Joined *Bindman & Partners* in 1974, becoming a Partner in 1976.
Personal: Born 14th January 1947. Lives in London. Married with three children.

DAVIDSON, David
Charles Russell, London (0171) 203 5114
Partner in Family Law Department.
Specialisation: Handles all areas of family law with emphasis on substantial financial applications, frequently with an international aspect. Author of "A Charles Russell Guide to Pensions and Marriage Breakdown." Writes, lectures and broadcasts on Taxation and Pension issues relating to separation and divorce. Joint author latest edition of Solicitors Family Law Association Precedents for Consent Orders.
Prof. Memberships: Solicitors Family Law Association, International Academy of Matrimonial Lawyers.
Personal: Born 30th January 1947. Educated Winchester College and Edinburgh University. Leisure pursuits include hill walking in the Highlands.

DAVIS, Sandra S.
Mishcon de Reya, London (0171) 440 7000
Head of Family Department.
Specialisation: Work includes international and domestic 'big money' cases, international child abduction, divorce and separation, cohabitation disputes and contact and residency disputes. Author of 'International Child Abduction' (1993) and numerous articles. Lectured to the 1st World Family Congress in Sydney, 1993 and the IBA Conferences, 1993, 1994, 1995. Chaired, and lectured at the *Mishcon de Reya* and IBC conferences on 'Big Money,' 'International Child Abduction,' 'Middle Money' and 'International Money.' Lord Chancellor's Department panel solicitor; Radio 4 'You & Yours' panel member.
Prof. Memberships: Solicitors Family Law Association, Holborn Law Society, Law Society. Fellow of the International Academy of Matrimonial Lawyers; Fellow of the RSA.
Career: Qualified with *Mishcon de Reya* in 1981, becoming a Partner in 1984.
Personal: Born 3rd July 1956. Attended University of Sussex 1974-78 and Université Aix-en-Provence, France, and studied European Studies/ Law. Languages: French and German. Leisure interests include travel, painting and photography. Lives in London. Married with two children.

DORAN, Gill
Withers, London (0171) 936 1000
Partner in Family Law Department.
Specialisation: Has specialised in family and matrimonial work for 20 years. Has written articles about family matters, addressed conferences and done committee work for the Solicitors Family Law Association (SFLA).
Prof. Memberships: International Academy of Matrimonial Lawyers (IAML), Family Mediators Association (FMA).
Career: Qualified in 1974. Joined *Gordon Dadds* (1979-1996). Joined the Family Law Department at *Withers* in 1996.
Personal: Born 28th September 1949. Educated at The Abbey School 1960-68 and Manchester University 1968-71. Leisure

interests include music, opera and horses. Lives in London.

DOUGHTY, Charles
Withers, London (0171) 936 1000
Consultant in Family Law Department.
Specialisation: Family law specialist.
Prof. Memberships: International Academy of Matrimonial Lawyers (IAML), Solicitors Family Law Association (SFLA).
Career: Qualified in 1961, having joined *Withers* in 1958. Became a Partner in 1963.
Personal: Born 21st December 1935. Educated at Eton 1948-53 and Magdalen College, Oxford 1955-58. Leisure interests include fishing and hunting.

DRAKE, Michael J.
Collyer-Bristow, London (0171) 242 7363
Head of Matrimonial Department.
Specialisation: Handles all areas of matrimonial and family law, particularly where there is a commercial, financial or international element. Also advises on litigation and business law, including contract and commercial advice and employment issues. Author of various textbooks, SFLA publications, articles. Co-author of 'Divorce and the Family Business,' published in 1997 by Jordans. On the editorial board of 'The Family Practitioner.' Has lectured and broadcast on radio and television.
Prof. Memberships: SFLA (National Committee 1987 to 1994).
Career: Qualified in 1971. Joined *Collyer-Bristow* as a partner in 1984.
Personal: Born 14 August 1947. Educated at Haberdasher's Askes's Elstree (to 1965) and Selwyn College, Cambridge (to 1968). Recreations include travel, arts reading and tennis. Lives in London.

FISHER, Jeremy
Gordon Dadds, London (0171) 493 6151

FOWLER, Pauline J.
Bates, Wells & Braithwaite, London (0171) 551 7777
Specialisation: Partner, family law department. Work includes complex financial settlements, regularly with an overseas element; all aspects of children's law including international adoption; mediation; cohabitation and Inheritance Act cases.
Prof. Memberships: SFLA (serves on London regional committee); FMA (sits on FMA Board); BAAF legal group.
Career: Liverpool University (1972-75); College of Law (1979-81); articled to Henry Hodge, *Hodge Jones & Allen* (1981-83) and then stayed on after qualification; *Bates Wells & Braithwaite* from 1985 where became a partner in 1990. Trained as mediator with FMA 1992 and now practises as FMA accredited sole and co-mediator. Lectures and writes on family law.
Personal: Born 1955; lives in London; leisure interests include Chamber music.

GEORGE, Peter
Charles Russell, London (0171) 203 5098
Partner in Family Department.
Specialisation: Handles all areas of family law.
Prof. Memberships: Chair Council for Family Proceedings, International Society of Family Law, International Academy of Matrimonial

Lawyers, Family Mediators Association. Solicitors Family Law Association.
Personal: Born 12th January 1935. Attended Ampleforth. Leisure interests include people, music, reading, bridge and chess.

GERRY, Andrew
Withers, London (0171) 936 1000
Partner in Family Law Department.
Specialisation: Full-time family law practice.
Prof. Memberships: International Academy of Matrimonial Lawyers (IAML), American Bar Association (ABA) (Family Law Section), Solicitors Family Law Association (SFLA) (Secretary for 6 yrs).
Career: Factory Manager from 1964 to 1969. Management Consultant from 1969 to 1974. Qualified in June 1977, having joined *Withers* in 1974.
Personal: Born 27th March 1938. Educated at Cambridge University 1959-62. Enjoys golf, fishing and walking. Lives in London.

GOODMAN, Judith
Goodman Ray, London (0171) 254 8855
Partner specialising in family law.
Specialisation: Main areas of practice are divorce, ancillary relief and Children Act work including care work. Deputy District Judge. Member of Law Society Children Panel since 1985. Member of Legal Aid Area Appeals Committee.
Prof. Memberships: SFLA, LAPG, Association of Lawyers for Children, Law Society.
Career: Qualified in 1980. Partner at *Goodman Ray* since 1985.
Personal: Born 23rd March 1955. Educated at Liverpool University 1974-77 (LL.B Hons). Lives in London. Married with three children.

HARCUS, James
Withers, London (0171) 936 1000
Partner in Family Law Department.
Specialisation: Specialises in matrimonial finance and taxation, children, cohabitation and pre-marital contracts. Acted in 'Robinson v. Robinson' 1982 (case involving setting aside for material non-disclosure) and 'Cornick v. Cornick' 1994 (Barder principles). Co-Author of articles in Family Law. Has lectured for the Solicitors Family Law Association and the Institute of Financial Planning.
Prof. Memberships: Fellow of the International Academy of Matrimonial Lawyers (IAML). Treasurer of the Solicitors Family Law Association (SFLA) 1982-87.
Career: Qualified in 1974. Partner of *Gordon Dadds* (1981-1996). Joined Family Law Department at *Withers* in 1996.
Personal: Born 15th April 1949. Educated at Exeter University 1968-71. Leisure interests include riding, skiing, sailing and gardening. Lives in London.

HARPER, Mark
Anthony Gold, Lerman & Muirhead, London (0171) 940 4000
Head of 9 strong specialist Family Law Department.
Specialisation: Exclusively Family Law and, in particular, in substantial financial cases including those with an international element and child abduction. Author of articles in Family Law and SFLA Newsletter. Author of Model

Letters for Family Lawyers (Jordans). Lectures on family law with CLT. Has broadcast on TV and radio.
Prof. Memberships: SFLA National Committee 1992 – 1998, SFLA Family Law Bill team, SFLA Cohabitation Working Group Chairperson 1995 to date, SFLA Press Officer 1997 – 1998, Law Society.
Career: Qualified in 1988. Became a Partner in 1990 at *Anthony Gold* after articles with the firm. Head of Family Law Department since 1991.
Personal: Born 2 February 1962. Educated at Malvern College and Pembroke College, Oxford. Enjoys travel, architecture and classic cars. Lives in Balham, South London

HODSON, David
The Family Law Consortium, London (0171) 420 5000
email: flc@tflc.co.uk
Partner.
Specialisation: Principal area of practice is financial aspects of family breakdown, with emphasis on cases involving complex or substantial assets or an international element.
Prof. Memberships: Solicitors Family Law Association National Committee, Ancillary Relief Reform Committee (chairman) and Good Practice Committee and International Committee; Fellow, International Academy of Matrimonial Lawyers; Lawyers Christian Fellowship; Society of Computers and the Law; Trustee, Marriage Resource counselling organisation. Regular lecturer and writer on family law. Co-Author of 'Divorce Reform: A Guide for Lawyers and Mediators' (Sweet & Maxwell) and 'The Business of Family Law' (Jordans), and Consulting Editor of 'Family Law in Europe' (Butterworths). Deputy District Judge, Principal Registry of the Family Division. Family Proceedings Rules Committee.
Career: Qualified 1978. Previously with *Theodore Goddard* and *Frere Cholmeley Bischoff*. Co-Founder in 1995 of new solicitors' and mediation practice, *The Family Law Consortium*. Qualified 1997 as family mediator with Family Mediators Association. Member, UK College of family mediators.
Personal: Born October 1953. Educated at Southampton and Leicester University. Married. Lives in Guildford.

HOWELL, Grant
Charles Russell, London (0171) 203 5000
Specialisation: Handles all areas of family law. Lectures and writes on the subject. Author "Family Breakdown and Insolvency" (Butterworths).
Prof. Memberships: Member National Committee Solicitors Family Law Association (SFLA) (1993-98). Member Training Committee SFLA. (1991 to date: Chairman 1993-98). Member Family Justice Studies Committee.
Career: Qualified 1980. At *Batchelor Street Longstaffe* till 1985; then *Bennett Taylor Tyrrell* till 1990 when joined *Charles Russell* as a Partner.
Personal: Born 4th February 1956. LLB from Birmingham University. Leisure interests include Chelsea Football Club and music.

HUGHES, Frances
Bates, Wells & Braithwaite, London (0171) 551 7777
Partner and Head of Family Law Department.
Specialisation: Practice covers the full range of family law, especially international cases, and cases involving trust law or complex offshore

corporate entities, also complex children's work. Clients include City professionals, entertainment clients and other lawyers. Writes, lectures and broadcasts on family law, nationally and internationally, contributing editor Butterworth Family Law Service.
Prof. Memberships: International Academy of Matrimonial Lawyers; SFLA (serves on SFLA Mediation Training Management Board); Co-ordinator of SFLA Mediation Training. Accreditied SFLA and FMA Mediator.
Career: Qualified in 1981. Assistant at *Theodore Goddard*. Joined *Bates Wells & Braithwaite* to establish the Family Department in 1983 and became a Partner in 1984.
Personal: Born 15th June 1954. Oxford 1973-76. School Governor. Enjoys opera and gardening. Lives in London and Wiltshire.

HUTCHINSON, Anne-Marie
Dawson Cornwell & Co, London
(0171) 242 2556
Specialisation: Practises exclusively in family law, specialising in international custody disputes and child abduction. Chair of Re-unite, Council for Abducted Children and member of the All Party Parliamentary Working Group on Child Abduction. Consultant Editor Hershman and McFarlane's "Children Law and Practice" and co-author "International Parental Child Abduction" both published by Jordan. Regular speaker and lecturer on the subject of child abduction, frequently appearing on the media and in the press. Her expertise in child abduction law is widely acknowledged by practitioners and the family bar.
Prof. Memberships: Law Society, Solicitors Family Law Association, International Bar Association, International Society of Family Law, Association of Lawyers for Children.
Career: Admitted 1985. Partner and Head of Family Department at *Beckman & Beckman* from 1987, Partner and Head of Children's Department at *Dawson Cornwell & Co* from 1998.

KEIR, Jane
Kingsley Napley, London (0171) 814 1200
Partner.
Specialisation: Specialises in family law and handles particularly children and financial cases. Has a particular specialisation in international abduction cases and domestic and international custody and financial disputes. Writes and lectures on developments in private children law and child abduction.
Prof. Memberships: Chairs the international committee of the SFLA and sits on its children committee. Member of the Institute of Advanced Legal Studies Working Group on the cross border movement of children (Sharila law sub group). Member of Reunite; the National Council for Family Proceedings and the International Bar Association.
Career: Qualified December 1987. Joined *Kingsley Napley* in September 1989 and became a partner in the family law department in November 1992.
Personal: Born 4th March 1962. Lives in London. Leisure interests include horses and National Hunt racing, tennis and travel.

LA FOLLETTE, Maryly
Charles Russell, London (0171) 203 5000
Partner in the Family Department.
Specialisation: International Divorce, ancillary relief and child related work (private law).
Prof. Memberships: Solicitors Family Law

Association; Family Mediators Association.
Personal: Born 18 October 1942; Attended San Francisco University, University of California at Berkeley, Columbia University (New York). Interests include tennis, skiing, reading, music and charitable work.

LEVERTON, David. J.
Payne Hicks Beach, London
(0171) 465 4300
Head of Family Law Department.
Specialisation: Founder member of International Academy of Matrimonial Lawyers. Very experienced specialist in all aspects of matrimonial law with particular expertise in complex financial matters and in negotiating financial settlements.
Career: Qualified 1958 at *Ridsdale & Son* of Westminster: joined *Payne Hicks Beach* in 1959. Became Partner in 1963. Managing Partner of firm. Member of Solicitors Disciplinary Tribunal.
Personal: Born 8th September 1935. Educated at The Haberdashers' Askes' School, Hampstead. Enjoys fine art, music and rugby. Lives in London.

LEVISON, Jeremy I.
Levison Meltzer Pigott, London
(0171) 556 2400
Specialisation: Along with leading practitioners Claire Meltzer and Simon Pigott has opened the specialist divorce and family law firm, *Levison Meltzer Pigott*. Handles all aspects of matrimonial work, with particular interest in high worth clients, cohabitation, cases with a foreign element and children.
Prof. Memberships: International Academy of Matrimonial Lawyers. Solicitors' Family Law Association. American Bar Association (Family Section).
Career: Qualified in 1974 and worked for *Theodore Goddard* until 1980. *Collyer-Bristow* 1980-1998. *Levison Meltzer Pigott* from 1st June 1998.
Personal: Born 3rd February 1952. Educated at Charterhouse School 1965-1969 and the University of Kent 1970-73. Enjoys fine art, music, cricket, classic cars and France. Lives in London.

LONGRIGG, William
Charles Russell, London (0171) 203 5000
Partner in Family Department.
Specialisation: Main areas of practice are divorce, ancillary relief and child-related work (private law).
Prof. Memberships: Solicitors Family Law Association (Member SFLA Mediation Committee; Chairman SFLA London Regional Group).
Career: Qualified in 1987. Joined *Charles Russell* in 1985, becoming a Partner in 1992.
Personal: Born 6th July 1960. Attended Dragon School, Oxford 1968-73, Shrewsbury School 1973-78 and Warwick University 1979-82. Leisure interests include drawing, writing and junk shops. Lives in London.

MARCO, Alan
Collyer-Bristow, London (0171) 242 7363
Partner, Matrimonial Department.
Specialisation: Handles all areas of family and matrimonial law with emphasis on financial provision applications. Deputy District Judge at Principal Registry of the Family Division
Prof. Memberships: Solicitors Family Law Association.

Career: Qualified in 1965. Partner at *Baileys Shaw & Gillett* 1972-1996. Partner *Collyer-Bristow* 1996.
Personal: Born in Devon. Married with three children.

MASSEY, William
Manches & Co, London (0171) 404 4433
email: william.massey@manches.co.uk
Specialisation: Practises exclusively in family and matrimonial law.
Prof. Memberships: Solicitor's Family Law Association, member of London Guildhall University LPC Advisory Panel.
Career: Qualified in 1990 at *Freshfields*. *Penningtons* 1991-1994. Joined *Manches & Co* in 1994.
Personal: Born 3rd May 1964. Educated at Oundle School and Exeter University. Married with two children. Enjoys music, walking and most sports.

MELTZER, Claire
Levison Meltzer Pigott, London
(0171) 556 2400
Specialisation: Along with leading family practitioners Jeremy Levison and Simon Pigott opened specialist family and divorce law firm, *Levison Meltzer Pigott*. Handles all aspect of family work. Special knowledge of high profile financial and children's cases and pensions on divorce. Regular broadcaster and lecturer.
Prof. Memberships: Solicitors Family Law Association. American Bar Association (Family Sector). Family Mediators Association.
Career: Qualified 1979. Partner in *Theodore Goddard* 1983-1985. Partner in *Collyer-Bristow* 1985-1998. Partner in *Levison Meltzer Pigott* 1998.
Personal: B.A. Hons (Eng. Lang. & Lit:). Lives in London.

PARKER, Diana C.
Withers, London (0171) 936 1000
Partner in Family Law Department.
Specialisation: Exclusively family law. Co-author of Longman's Practical Matrimonial Precedents' and 'Know How for Family Lawyers.' Author of articles in professional journals and elsewhere. Occasional lecturer, speaker at conferences and contributor to the media.
Prof. Memberships: Solicitors Family Law Association (SFLA); Family Mediators Association (FMA); International Academy of Matrimonial Lawyers (IAML).
Personal: MA (Cantab) MPhil (Cantab). Lives in London and Oxford.

PARRY, Richard
Farrer & Co, London (0171) 242 2022
Specialisation: Partner in Family team. Main area of practice is family law.
Prof. Memberships: Solicitors Family Law Association.
Career: Qualified in 1976. Joined *Farrer & Co.* in 1974, becoming a partner in 1983.
Personal: Born 6 December 1951. Educated at Eton College (1964-1969) and Balliol College, Oxford (1970-1973). Governor of Downe House. Leisure interests include golf, bridge and music. Lives in London.

PEARSON, Philippa
The Family Law Consortium, London
(0171) 420 5000
email: flc@tflc.co.uk
Partner

Specialisation: Solicitor and SFLA mediator. Experienced in all areas of family law including ancillary relief, Children Act (both public and private law) and Inheritance Act applications. Legal Aid work undertaken. Author of articles in professional journals and contributor to the Law Society's family law handbook and Butterworths Family Law Service. Regularly lectures and appears on TV and radio.
Prof. Memberships: Chair of Solicitors Family Law Association Legal Aid Committee and Member of Solicitors Family Law Association National Committee.
Career: Qualified 1988. *Penningtons* 1988-90. *Charles Russell* 1990-92. Former partner and head of matrimonial department at *Osbornes* 1994-1998; joined *The Family Law Consortium* 1998.
Personal: B.A. (Oxon) 1982-1985. Date of birth 25th November 1963.

PEAT, Kathryn
Druces & Attlee, London (0171) 638 9271
Specialisation: All areas of family law, with particular specialisation in 'big money' cases and those involving disputes over children.
Prof. Memberships: Law Society. Solicitors Family Law Association.
Career: Reading University. Sits on S.E. Circuit as Assistant Recorder.
Personal: All spare time spent with husband and 2 children. Would like to garden, read, cook, walk, play tennis and cycle!

PEMBRIDGE, Eileen
Fisher Meredith, London (0171) 924 9124 (Family Dept.)
Senior Partner and Head of Family Department.
Specialisation: Deals with all aspects of family law, but especially complex ancillary relief on divorce and other financial matters. Has always taken on legal aid work. Will also handle defamation where there are important public issues to address. Has written various opinion pieces in 'Family Law' and the legal profession. Has lectured on the Childrens Act and addressed sessions on Family Law at the Law Society's National Conference.
Prof. Memberships: Law Society (Council Member for London South since 1990, Chair of Family Law Committee 1992-95, on Courts and Legal Services Committee since 1987, International Human Rights working party Committee since 1993 and Equal Opportunities Committee since 1994), SFLA, LAPG (Committee Member since 1982 and Chair 1987-88). International Family Law Association.
Career: Worked as a freelance interpreter for the UN 1967-73 and casually thereafter until 1983. Qualified in 1975. Co-founder of *Fisher Meredith* in 1975, now 80 strong. Challenged Law Society convention by standing for election of President, July 1995.
Personal: Born 15th March 1944. Educated at Worcester Girls' Grammar School; Newnham College, Cambridge (Natural Sciences degree and postgraduate Russian), and Bath University (postgraduate language studies). FRSA. Interests include Amnesty, animal welfare, childrens activities, sailing, horse-riding, hill-walking, vegetable-growing and reading novels in French, Russian and Spanish. Lives in Dulwich Village, London.

PHILIPPS, Susan
Penningtons, London (0171) 457 3000
Partner and Head of Family Law Department.
Specialisation: Covers all areas of family and matrimonial law. SFLA Trained Mediator.
Prof. Memberships: Solicitors Family Law Association. Serves on Education and Mediation Committees of the SFLA.
Career: Qualified in 1984. Joined *Ward Bowie* in 1982 and became a partner in 1986 on merger with *Penningtons*. Head of Family Law Department since 1994.
Personal: Born 9th April 1957. Lives in London.

PIGOTT, Simon
Levison Meltzer Pigott, London (0171) 556 2400
Specialisation: Along with leading practitioners Jeremy Levison and Claire Meltzer opened *Levison Meltzer Pigott*. Handles all aspects of matrimonial work including cases involving complex financial issues and children. Practising family mediator. Lecturer and broadcaster.
Prof. Memberships: Solicitors Family Law Association. American Bar Association (Family Section). Family Mediators Association. United Kingdom College of Family Mediators.
Career: Qualified 1982. *Wright Webb Syrett* 1978-1983; *Theodore Goddard* 1983-1985; *Collyer-Bristow* 1985-1998 (partner from 1987); *Levison Meltzer Pigott* 1998.
Personal: Born October 1956. Mill Hill School 1970-1974. University of Southampton 1974-1977. Lives in Wolverton, Hants. Married with three daughters.

PIRRIE, James M.
The Family Law Consortium, London (0171) 420 5000
email: flc@tflc.co.uk Partner
Specialisation: Focusing on the entire range of practical effects of relationship breakdown, whether inside or outside marriage, bringing to the process mediation, conveyancing, wills etc skills as well as a keen interest in CSA legislation and procedure.
Prof. Memberships: Solicitors Family Law Association National Committee, Good Practice, Legal Aid, CSA and Chair Procedure Committee; member of mediation unit of Institute of Family Therapy; member of Society Trusts and Estates Practitioners; member advisory group to Social Policy Research Unit investigation on child maintenance; writes/lectures on legal aid, child support, pensions, financial matters, cohabitation and mediation; secretary Child Support Practitioner's Group.
Career: Qualified 1985; previously with *Crossman Block and Keith*, *Russell Jones and Walker*; joined *The Family Law Consortium* 1998; qualified as NFM mediator 1994.
Personal: Born 1960; educated Orwell Park School, Felsted, Leicester University; lives Saint Albans, married with 2yo son.

PRESTON, Miles
Miles Preston & Co, London (0171) 583 0583
Founding Partner 1994.
Specialisation: Practises exclusively in matrimonial and family law.
Prof. Memberships: Solicitors Family Law Association, International Academy of Matrimonial Lawyers.
Career: Qualified in 1974. Partner with *Radcliffes & Co.* 1979-94. Served on Sir Gervaise Sheldon's Family Law Liaison Committee 1982; Founder Member SFLA 1982; served on Main Committee of SFLA 1982-88; Chaired working party on procedure 1982-88; Founder Member of IAML 1986; Governor IAML 1986-89; Parliamentarian to Main Committee 1989; President of English Chapter 1989; President of European Chapter 1989-92; President Elect of Main Academy 1992-94. President of Main Academy 1994-96. Member of the President's International Family Law Committee (chaired by Lord Justice Thorpe) since 1994.
Personal: Born 1950. Educated Shrewsbury School 1963-68. Leisure interests include food, travel and classic cars. Lives in Greenwich, London.

RAE, Maggie
Mishcon de Reya, London (0171) 440 7000
Partner. Family Department.
Specialisation: Work includes divorce, children, adoption, employment and education. Also all aspects of family and children work. Author of 'Women and the Law,' 'Children and the Law,' 'First Rights' and 'Child Care Law.' Lectured at Warwick University. Undertakes frequent teaching, lecturing and writing assignments.
Prof. Memberships: Solicitors Family Law Association, Education Law Association, British Association for Adoption and Fostering, Inter Country Adoption Lawyers Association, International Academy of Matrimonial Lawyers, member of the Government's consultation panel on Pensions and Divorce, the President of the Family Division's International Committee and special advisor to the Social Security Select Committee in relation to Pensions and Divorce, Fellow of the RSA.
Career: Qualified in 1973. Barrister 1973-77. Partner at *Hodge Jones & Allen* 1978-92. Joined *Mishcon de Reya* in 1992, becoming a Partner in 1993.
Personal: Born 20th September 1949. Attended Great Yarmouth High School 1961-68 and University of Warwick 1968-71. Leisure interests include walking, cooking and gardening. Lives in London.

RAY, Peggy
Goodman Ray, London (0171) 254 8855
Specialisation: Practice covers all areas of child care work including both public and private law cases, adoption and associated areas such as judicial review, education law, and administrative law. Speaker and trainer in child care. Former Member of the Law Society Family Law Committee, current member of Solicitors Family Law Association children committee, member of the Expert Witness Group, and member of the Inner London Children Act Business Committee. Member of the Law Society Children Panel since 1985. Member of Legal Aid area Committee.
Prof. Memberships: Solicitors Family Law Association, Association of Lawyers for Children, NaGALRO, National Council for Family Proceedings, BAAF.
Career: Qualified 1980. Established own practice with Judith Goodman in Hackney in 1985.

ROBINSON, Sara

The Family Law Consortium, London
(0171) 420 5000
email: flc@tflc.co.uk
Partner.

Specialisation: Expertise in negotiation of family law financial settlements; investigation, location of matrimonial assets worldwide and enforcement of matrimonial orders. Residence and contact issues. Accredited co- & sole solicitor mediator with The Family Mediators Association and Solicitors Family Law Association, including comprehensive mediation. Acts for a number of high profile pop star and media clients and those in public life.

Prof. Memberships: Solicitors Family Law Association, Family Mediators Association, UK College of Family Mediators Committee Member, SFLA International Committee and of Central and South London Group of the Family Mediators Association. Former SFLA National Press Officer for the Solicitors Family Law Association and member of its Media team. Co-author of Scandinavian chapters of the Solicitors Family Law Association 'Guide to Family Law in Europe' and also 'Divorce Reform: A Guide for Lawyers and Mediators.'

Career: Qualified in 1981. Partner and Head of Family Department at *The Simkins Partnership* 1990-95. Co-Founder of *The Family Law Consortium* 1995.

Personal: Born 1955. Educated at Leeds University. Secretary of Spare Tyre Theatre Company. Enjoys eating, drinking good wines, listening to music, photography, gardening, interior decorating, the company of friends and coastal walking. Lives in Chiswick.

RODGERS, Hilary

Forsters, London (0171) 863 8333

Specialisation: Head of Family Law practice, specialising in complex financial divorce settlements. Also experienced in issues of jurisdiction, taxation, trusts and pensions in relation to matrimonial matters.

Prof. Memberships: Solicitors Family Law Association Member, also SFLA Procedure Committee and Chair of the Cohabitation Working Group, International Bar Association, and International Academy of Matrimonial Lawyers.

Career: Admitted 1987. Assistant at Theodore Goddard. Joined Frere Cholmeley Bischoff 1991. Partner 1994. Founder Partner of Forsters, August 1998.

Personal: Born 1962. Married, lives in North London.

RUTTER, Geoffrey M.

Collyer-Bristow, London (0171) 242 7363

Specialisation: Many years experience in family law, principally involving substantial financial issues resulting from marriage breakdown. Considerable knowledge of and experience in the investigative elements of domestic and international work including offshore trusts and structures. Regularly advises on the commercial and tax considerations involved in financial negotiations and settlements.

Prof. Memberships: Solicitors Family Law Association, International Academy of Matrimonial Lawyers.

SAX, Richard

Manches & Co, London (0171) 404 4433
email: richard.sax@manches.co.uk
Partner in Family Department.

Specialisation: Advises on all areas of family law, particularly complex financial and children issues arising from matrimonial and relationship breakdown including International, Trust and Tax aspects.

Prof. Memberships: Solicitors Family Law Association. International Academy of Matrimonial Lawyers, Law Society.

Career: Qualified in 1967. 1968 Partner and subsequently Managing Partner at *Rubinstein Callingham* (which merged with *Manches* in 1994). Sits as a Deputy District Judge at the Principal Registry. Past Chairman of the Solicitors Family Law Association. Member of Law Society Family Law Committee. Governor and secretary/Treasurer International Academy of Matrimonial Lawyers European Chapter. Member of the DSS Consultation Panel on Pension Sharing and The President's International Committee. Co-Author 'Know how for Family Lawyers,' published by Longmans. Joint General Editor Butterworth Family Law Service.

Personal: Born 26th December 1938. Attended Tonbridge School, Scholar St John's College, Oxford. National service. Member MCC. Liveryman Skinners Company. Married with three daughters. Leisure: Family. Gardening. Archaeology. Visiting churches and art galleries. Watching cricket. Current affairs. Theatre.

SHACKLETON, Fiona

Farrer & Co, London (0171) 242 2022
Partner in Family Team.

Specialisation: Principal area of practice is family law. Author of 'The Divorce Handbook.'

Prof. Memberships: SFLA, IAML.

Career: Qualified in 1980. Became a Partner with *Brecher & Co* in 1982. Joined *Farrer & Co* in 1984 and became a Partner in 1987.

Personal: Born 26th May 1956. Attended Benenden School and Exeter University Governor of Benenden School since 1985. Leisure pursuits include opera and bridge. Lives in London.

SIMPSON, Jane

Manches & Co, London (0171) 404 4433
email: jane.simpson@manches.co.uk
Partner and Head of Family Law Department.

Specialisation: Deals in particular with divorce and complex financial issues, children, tax, and the commercial implications of divorce and separation; international aspects of divorce and separation and forum shopping. Has addressed and chaired many family law conferences and seminars, and appeared on radio and television. Member of Lord Chancellors Advisory Committe on Ancillary Relief and Lord Chancellor's Family Law Advisory Board.

Prof. Memberships: Solicitors Family Law Association, International Academy of Matrimonial Lawyers, Law Society.

Career: Qualified in 1967. Marriage Guidance Counsellor 1972-77. Joined *Manches & Co* as a Partner and Head of Family Law Department in 1977. Member of Management Board from 1990. Founder member of Solicitors Family Law Association (1982), Chairman of its Education Committee 1982-90, Chairman 1993-95.

Personal: Born 15th July 1942. Educated at Channing School, Highgate, and London University 1961-64. Non-executive director of

Tavistock and Portman NHS Trust from 1994. Leisure interests include reading, walking, music and food. Lives in London. Two adult daughters and son.

TOOTH, Ray

Sears Tooth, London (0171) 499 5599

Specialisation: All aspects of matrimonial matters with particular emphasis on financial cases, often of an international nature. We have habitually been involved on difficult cases.

Prof. Memberships: The Law Society.

Career: Dragon School. Oxford. Kings School, Canterbury. Univeristy College Oxford.

Personal: Extensive horse racing interests, including breeding.

WALSH, Jonathan

Stephenson Harwood, London
(0171) 329 4422
Head of Matrimonial and Family Department.

Specialisation: Many years' experience of family, matrimonial and private client work. Has addressed conferences on various aspects of family law.

Prof. Memberships: SFLA.

Career: Qualified in 1968. Previously Head of Litigation Department and Matrimonial and Family Department at *Joynson-Hicks* and later at *Taylor Joynson Garrett*, where he was also Head of the Private Client Department. Joined *Stephenson Harwood* as a Partner in 1991.

Personal: Born 1944. Educated at Eton College 1957-62 and Sorbonne University. Enjoys tennis, real tennis and shooting.

WARD, Helen

Manches & Co, London (0171) 404 4433
email: helen.ward@manches.co.uk
Partner in Family Law Department.

Specialisation: Handles all areas of family law, particularly complex financial aspects of matrimonial and relationship breakdown involving an international element.

Prof. Memberships: Solicitors Family Law Association, International Academy of Matrimonial Lawyers, Law Society.

Career: Qualified in 1978. Partner at *Ward Bowie* from 1978, which subsequently became *Penningtons*. Joined *Manches & Co* as a partner in July 1994. Deputy District Judge in the Principal Registry and Assistant Recorder.

Personal: Born 28th May 1951. Attended King Alfred School, London 1955-69 and Birmingham University 1970-73. Her family come first but her leisure interests include music, theatre, tennis and her garden.

WALSH, Jonathan

Stephenson Harwood, London
(0171) 329 4422
Head of Matrimonial and Family Department.

Specialisation: Many years' experience of family, matrimonial and private client work. Has addressed conferences on various aspects of family law.

Prof. Memberships: SFLA.

Career: Qualified in 1968. Previously Head of Litigation Department and Matrimonial and Family Department at *Joynson-Hicks* and later at *Taylor Joynson Garrett*, where he was also Head of the Private Client Department. Joined *Stephenson Harwood* as a Partner in 1991.

Personal: Born 1944. Educated at Eton College 1957-62 and Sorbonne University. Enjoys tennis, real tennis and shooting.

SOUTH EAST

Blandy & Blandy (4ptnrs, including *Andrew Don*, 3 other fee earners) Continues to lead the field in the south east. **Clients/Work:** All areas covered. Recently launched 'Stepahead' – a one stop counselling, mediation and legal advice service.

Darbys (2ptnrs/2assts) This Oxford based firm has gone from strength to strength this year. The use of mediation has become increasingly popular within this firm. **Clients/Work:** Recently involved in Court of Appeal adoption case. Particularly strong in ancillary relief.

Leonard Gray (2ptnrs/1asst/2other fee earners) The "well respected" *Richard Randall* heads this large and experienced department. **Clients/Work:** Most areas covered, though over the last twelve months there has been a significant increase in guardian and ancillary relief work.

Linnells (3ptnrs/1assoc/1other fee earner) Recent high profile cases coupled with an increasingly popular mediation service has led to a substantial increase in this firm's workload. A mix of both private and public

law offered. **Clients/Work:** Recent Court of Appeal case, 'Re M,' concerning dispensing of consent of the natural mother which resulted in guidelines being produced for this area. Court of Appeal case , 'Re M'(unrelated), concerning possible breach of the Hague Convention. Also increase in local authority work.

Thomson Snell & Passmore (2ptnrs/1asst/1assoc) Known as one of the "leading lights" of the south east, *Barbara Wright* heads an "efficient" and "well organised" team. Most areas of family law are covered and they have a particular reputation for dealing with heavyweight ancillary relief matters.

SOUTH WEST

Lester Aldridge (1ptnr/8fee-earners) *Stephen Foster* heads the team, whose quality caseload is more similar to a leading London firm than its regional counterparts. **Clients/Work:** Reputation for cases with offshore and foreign element alongside top drawer divorce cases. Many big money clients and currently dealing with three cases with assets in excess of £10,000,000. Also known for commercial approach and expertise in related commercial disputes.

Bond Pearce (1ptnr/3assts) Noted for her writing as well as her professional skills, *Wendy Boyce* has been described as a "safe pair of hands." Noted for the high quality of their work. **Clients/Work:** Tackle the most complex of cases. Chiefly dealing with high net worth ancillary relief cases, with particular interest in pensions.

Burges Salmon (1ptnr/2assts) "Very reliable." Known both for the volume and quality of its work. **Clients/Work:** All aspects of private client divorce and matrimonial matters, including complex ancillary relief disputes for wealthy individuals.

Clarke Willmott & Clarke (2 ptnrs/9 other fee earners) Described as "an extremely good family lawyer" *Felicity Shakespear* heads the team. Have a "firm but fair" reputation. **Clients/Work:** Broad client base. Private client side deals mainly with financial matters and custody/child disputes, while public law sector deals with Children's Act cases.

Hartnell & Co (1ptnr/4assts) Over the past year this specialist firm has expanded in the areas of mediation and public law. *Norman Hartnell* leads the team. **Clients/Work:** Recently expanded their public work caseload by acquiring a Legal Aid franchise for mediation.

Ian Downing Family Law Practice (1ptnr) Sole practitioner in this fledgling firm has had a busy year. Since striking out on his own *Ian Downing*'s reputation as "a first rate family law practitioner" has attracted so much work that expansion appears inevitable. He is the chair of the regional SFLA. **Clients/Work:** Mainly high net worth clients, dealing with ancillary relief matters with a speciality in pensions. Some child work undertaken but no public law.

Hooper & Wollen (2ptnrs/2assts) This noted matrimonial practice has had a busy year with leading partner *Ian Scofield* piloting a mediation scheme in the West Country, as well as becoming a trainer for mediators in the south west region. **Clients/ Work:** Substantial and increasing public work load. Other areas of speciality include divorce, ancillary relief and mediation.

Tozers Described as a "competent" firm, this practice has numerous branch offices around Southern England. Noted in the Exeter branch are *Philip Kidd* and "highly rated" *Julie Shrimpton* who are known regionally as "quality practitioners." **Clients/Work:** Almost exclusively child care work, although a small amount of general family law is undertaken.

Trumps This "solid" department led by *David Woodward* has expanded to a total of 5 fee earners. The team has been joined recently by *Ian Walker* who raises the number of mediators to three. **Clients/Work:** Legal aid work and big money private clients.

Wolferstans This widely known practice is headed by the "well regarded" *Philip Thorneycroft*. On the child care side, *Jeremy Bennet* is also "widely respected." Team also includes *Susan Jury* who was newly recommended this year. **Clients/Work:** Wide scope of family law, ranging from big money divorces to mental health to child abuse.

WALES

Larby Williams (2ptnrs/1asst) The noted *Frances Williams* has joined forces with Adrian Larby to form this new firm out of the ashes of Anthony & Jarvie. Frances Williams' reputation for being a "safe pair of hands" still holds as she remains one of the leading lights of the Welsh circuit. **Clients/Work:** Frances Williams undertakes some child work but is better known for her high value ancillary relief work. Adrian Larby deals with general family matters in conjunction with other practice areas.

Martyn Prowel Edwards Davies (1ptnr/2other fee earners) *Robert Edwards* heads this widely respected team and the firm is felt to be going from strength to strength. **Clients/Work:** All areas of family work are handled, including child care and High Court advocacy. Particular emphasis on divorce and high value settlements.

Morgan Bruce (1ptnr/1asst) This small team is noted for being "efficient" and "client friendly." Although Rosemary Gregory-Jones has left the firm, it appears to retain its strength through *Jane Williams*. Strong in the field of mediation. **Clients/Work:** Most areas of family law covered, including divorce, child care and adoption work.

Nicol, Denvir & Purnell (2ptnrs/1ptnr 40%/1asst) *Frazer Nicol* heads the team. Mixed legal aid family practice. Growing interest in mediation. **Clients/Work:** The department mixes matrimonial and child care to offer a full range of family law services.

MIDLANDS

Barbara Carter *Barbara Carter* has been described as "the very model of a family lawyer." Carter's high reputation among Midland legal circles justifies her position in the table. **Clients/Work:** Well known for the quality of her public and private child care work.

Blair Allison & Co (3ptnrs/3assts) The firm has been chosen to be on the Lord Chancellor's Mediation pilot scheme. **Clients/Work:** Legally-aided matters and child care ranging to substantial financial settlements on divorce.

Freeth Cartwright Hunt Dickins (5ptnrs, including *Hugh Young*, 2assts) Though reduced in size to 7 fee earners, they have maintained the quality of their work. **Clients/Work:** Specialists in high value ancillary relief work coupled with a reputable child care practice.

Nelsons (1ptnr/8 other fee earners) This large and "extremely well regarded" department consists of 9 fee earners who exclusively practice family law. Headed by *John Nash* who has plans to further develop the department and enhance its reputation as a strong SFLA firm. **Clients/Work:** Solid practice handling divorce and ancillary relief matters as well as public law child care.

Rupert Bear Murray Davies (3ptnrs/5 assts) This Nottingham-based niche firm boasts a large team of 8 fee earners and has been described by opponents as "extremely good at what they do." Noted member of the department is *Rupert Bear* himself. **Clients/Work:** Full range of family law offered. Legal aid franchise.

Tyndallwoods (1ptnr/3assts ft, 2assts pt) This small but "efficient" team of family lawyers enjoys a high standing among Midland law firms for the quality of its work. **Clients/Work:** The three main areas of speciality are child care and public law, divorce and matrimonial and cases relating to the Children's Act.

Wace Morgan (4 fee earners) This "well respected" team are generally perceived as "good all-rounders." The firm runs a 24-hour 'TraumaLine' for victims of domestic violence. **Clients/Work:** General matrimonial work including divorce, ancillary relief and both public and private child care work.

EAST ANGLIA

HIGHLY REGARDED FIRMS
EAST ANGLIA

Buckle Mellows Peterborough
Eversheds Norwich
Fosters Norwich
Greenwoods Peterborough
Hunt & Coombs Peterborough
Miller & Company Cambridge
Silver Savory Smith Cambridge
Ward Gethin King's Lynn

Cozens-Hardy & Jewson Norwich
Hatch Brenner Norwich
Mills & Reeve Norwich
Palmer Wheeldon Cambridge
Rudlings & Wakelam Thetford

Graeme Carmichael Ipswich

Buckle Mellows (2ptnrs/4assts) Large general family department based in Peterborough. The team has a good reputation in the area as being sympathetic to the needs of the clients. **Clients/Work:** Particular strength dealing with high net worth individuals. Specialists in divorce and matrimonial matters. Also Legal aid franchise

Eversheds (1ptnr/1asst) Over the past year the firm has scaled down the family department leaving the "respected" *David Sisson* as the only partner aided by one assistant. Claim to be concentrating on the more exclusive end of the market , "reducing and refining" their workload while focusing on the needs of their high net worth clients.

Clients/Work: Exclusively private client. Work is referred from London, and often has an international element. Emphasis on serving the needs of high net worth individuals who have previous dealings with the firm.

Fosters (3prtnrs/2assts) Accepted on the legal mediation pilot scheme. *Catherine Iliff* is an experienced mediator and will steer the department through this transitional phase. Expanding services to include counselling and mediation. **Clients/Work:** Divorce, separation, financial consequences and dealing with children. Domestic violence, including 24 hour helpline. General child care work. Private and legal aid work.

Greenwoods (1ptnr/3other fee earners) Led by *Jane Proctor*. Increase in the handling of high value matrimonial cases, especially in the area of ancillary relief. Though previously noted equally for both child care and matrimonial work the focus of the department has shifted more to the latter. **Clients/Work:** High value matrimonial work, some child care.

Hunt & Coombs (3ptnrs/3assts) *John Henson* ("well-liked," "sensible" and a "straight operator") is the best known individual. The department at times overlaps with other disciplines in the firm and can call upon their expertise to help – this is particularly evident in the field of education law. **Clients/Work:** Deal equally with public and private law matters.

Miller & Company (1ptnr/3assts) Good reputation among other East Anglian firms who described them as "sound operators." Headed by partner *Rosemary Sands*. Specialising in ancillary relief. **Clients/Work:**

Broad range of family work, but particularly known for child care on behalf of guardians and the local authority. Strong in mediation.

Silver Savory Smith (3ptnrs/3assts) *Raphael Silver* received widespread praise as an "excellent, much respected" child care lawyer. The team was also praised. They are known for handling their own advocacy. **Clients/Work:** Child care and general matrimonial work.

Ward Gethin (2ptnrs/3other fee earners) This established and experienced team continues to be well regarded in Norfolk and surrounding areas. Described as a "reliable outfit." **Clients/Work:** The department balances private and public with financial and child work. Special adoption expertise. Legal aid franchise.

LEADING INDIVIDUALS
EAST ANGLIA

BAMBER Roger Mills & Reeve
CARMICHAEL Graeme Graeme Carmichael
FIFE Peter Ward Gethin
HENSON John Hunt & Coombs
ILIFF Catherine Fosters
O'DONNELL Caroline Miller & Company
O'REGAN Timothy Rudlings & Wakelam
PROCTOR Jane Greenwoods
SANDS Rosemary Miller & Company
SILVER Raphael Silver Savory Smith
SISSON David Eversheds
WHITE Iain Cozens-Hardy & Jewson
WILSON Bruce Mills & Reeve

NORTH WEST

HIGHLY REGARDED FIRMS
NORTH WEST

Berrymans Lace Mawer Manchester/Liverpool
Farleys Blackburn
Green & Co Manchester
Jones Maidment Wilson Manchester
Pannone & Partners Manchester

Burnetts Carlisle
Cuff Roberts Liverpool
Forbes & Partners Blackburn
Jackson & Canter Liverpool
Morecroft Urquhart Liverpool
Nightingales Manchester
Rowlands Manchester
Roy Pybus Liverpool
Stephenson Flint & Holmes Salford

Berrymans Lace Mawer (1ptnr/3other fee earners) The past twelve months have seen major changes within the department. The number of fee-earners has reduced from six to four, "major player" Helen Meadows has

gone to the bench, and the "pleasant" and "charming" *Nigel Shepherd* is now head of the department. **Clients/Work:** Cases for high net worth individuals are a speciality.

Farleys (2ptnrs/8assts) This Blackburn firm is well known locally for its family work. *Kathryn Hughes* has a good reputation as a "tough operator." **Clients/Work:** Child care, public law and increasingly "big money" cases.

Green & Co (1ptnr/5other fee earners) Led by *Michael Green*, described as "an absolutely superb public child care lawyer." **Clients/Work:** Whole range of family litigation is covered. Particularly strong in public child care matters.

Jones Maidment Wilson Headed by *Iain Hamilton*. Particularly strong on child care matters. Also expertise in higher-value matrimonial finance work, which enables it to compete against the larger Manchester firms practising in this area. Team includes *Paula Milburn.*

Pannone & Partners (5ptnrs/6other fee earners) Proved to be one of the leading firms in the north west. *Catherine Jones* has been described by peers as "an excellent and able operator." *Beth Wilkins*, chair of the 1998

national SFLA conference, is also held in "very high esteem." Growing interest in mediation with two partners practising it to date. **Clients/Work:** Increase in high net worth clients and big money ancillary relief work over the last twelve months. Involved in high profile child cases, many with an international element. No public law.

LEADING INDIVIDUALS
NORTH WEST

JONES Catherine Pannone & Partners
MCGOLDRICK John Jones Maidment Wilson
SHEPHERD Nigel Berrymans Lace Mawer

BALDWIN Lorraine Rowlands
COTTRELL Patricia Cuff Roberts
DEVLIN Michael Stephenson Flint & Holmes
GREEN Michael Green & Co
HAMILTON Iain Jones Maidment Wilson
HARDMAN Peter Nightingales
HUGHES Kathryn Farleys
MILBURN Paula Jones Maidment Wilson
PYBUS Roy Roy Pybus
WILKINS Beth Pannone & Partners

NORTH EAST

Addleshaw Booth & Co Maintained its position as the leading family law department in the north east. Headed by the "truly exceptional" *David Salter*, the practice has expanded into Manchester. Though David Salter is the leading light in the region, holding the prestigious accolade of being one of only two Fellows of the International Academy of Matrimonial Lawyers outside London, Addleshaws is by no means a one man band. The "efficient " and "talented" team boasts leader *Philip Way*. **Clients/Work:** Mainly high net worth clients, including leading business and professional people and landed gentry from the rural areas surrounding Leeds. Private client divorce and ancillary relief work over the past year including some high profile cases.

Dickinson Dees (2ptnrs/2other fee earners) Highly rated by his competitors, *Lyn Rutherford* heads this prestigious department. Over the past twelve months there has been a substantial increase in high value cases with the firm reporting 30 cases with assets in excess of £1,000,000. Top drawer private client base which includes leading figures of the business world and the landed gentry of the North. **Clients/Work:** All aspects of divorce, matrimonial finance and child care work, especially at the high net worth end of the market, though some legal aid work is accepted. Complicated cases, especially with tax and pension implications are a speciality as they have the support and resources of other departments.

Irwin Mitchell (6fee-earners) New partner, Alison Straw is a child care expert. Offer full range of services to all sections of the community. High net worth ancillary relief to legal aid matters.

Jones Myers Gordon (3ptnrs including *Peter Jones*/2assts) Client base includes titled land owners in north of England. Mainly divorce and ancillary relief work.

Zermansky & Partners (1ptnr/4other fee earners) The ever-increasing reputation of this Leeds-based firm has justified their promotion into the leading firms band. Headed by *Norman Taylor* who has been described as a "safe pair of hands." **Clients/Work:** Particular speciality in child care work. Both public and private work undertaken.

Andrew M Jackson (1ptnr/4other fee earners) Increase in higher value private client work. The team have all been trained as mediators and have recently launched "SOLUTIONS," a 'one-stop shop' incorporating legal advice, a counselling service and a qualified social worker.

Gordons Wright & Wright (2ptnrs/5assts) Headed by the "highly respected" *Peter Foskett*. Team includes a child care and abduction specialist.

SEE PROFILES AT END OF THIS SECTION

SCOTLAND

Anne Hall Dick & Co Devoted exclusively to family law, with a specific focus on mediation. Senior partner *Anne Dick* is described as an "honest and highly respected" practitioner. The team is also well regarded. **Clients/Work:** Handle divorce, financial disputes, child care disputes and aim to resolve these through mediation, as well as court action.

Balfour & Manson Even with the departure of the pre-eminent Ian Balfour, Balfour & Manson has maintained its position as one of the leading Scottish family law firms. The department is headed by the "talented" *Andrew Gibb* who acted for Dr Margaret Cook, wife of the Foreign Secretary in her divorce action. Rising star *Wendy Sheehan* (involved in Paterson v Marke) was also praised. **Clients/Work:** Expertise in child abduction illustrated by the high profile cases of Singh v Singh and Pirrie v Sawacki. Private client divorce, ancillary relief, child care work and international work.

Loudons WS (1ptnr/7other fee earners) This growing niche practice, operating exclusively in the field of family law, is headed by the "respected" *Alasdair Loudon*. Litigation and negotiation take precedence over mediation. **Clients/Work:** International child abduction cases (Cameron v Cameron). Divorce proceedings involving financial provision (Maclachlan v Machlachlan).

Drummond Miller WS (2ptnrs f/t, 3ptnrs ft, 3assts ft, 6assts pt) This Edinburgh based practice has a good reputation among other firms in the area. Headed by the "admired" *Fiona Tait*. **Clients/Work:** Divorce, financial provision, child abduction, adoption and parental rights.

Erkine MacAskill *Sarah Erskine* is well thought of at this predominantly Legal Aid practice. She has been praised for her com-

SEE PROFILES AT END OF THIS SECTION

mitment to the victims of abuse, domestic violence and child abduction.

Iain Smith & Co (1ptnr, 3other fee earners) *Iain Patience* is an accredited family law specialist and qualified in mediation. The team is described as "both capable and efficient." **Clients/Work:** Growing expertise in mediation.

Morton Fraser Partnership (1ptnr/ 3other fee earners) Department head, *Leonard Mair*, was one of the first solicitor

mediators to be accredited by the law society in Scotland. Supported by the residential property, commercial enterprise, taxation, agricultural and trusts departments when required. **Clients/Work:** All family and child care law including mediation. Acted on behalf of the mother in the McDonald case where the son sued for alimony to support his studies – settled out of court.

Burnett & Reid (1ptnr/2assts) *Joan Catto* is an accredited specialist in both

family and child care law. Handle private and legal aid cases.

Mowat Dean & Co WS (1ptnr/3other fee earners) The "dedicated" *Tom Ballantine* has "a good knowledge of his cases" and a commitment to his work. The firm encourages mediation. **Clients/Work:** Separation, divorce, children, financial issues and protection.

NORTHERN IRELAND

Most Northern Ireland firms have a family law capacity. The firms in our table are the specialists, usually with dedicated departments. Like last year, special mention goes to the "resourceful and professional" *Patrica Hyland*, and to *George Palmer* of Peden & Reid, who is felt to have cornered the market in big money ancillary relief cases (recently dealt with several divorce settlements in excess of £500,000).

LEADERS' PROFILES · REGIONS

ANDERSON, Heather
Blacks, Leeds (0113) 243 3311

ASHLEY, Jacqueline S.
Gill Akaster, Plymouth (01752) 500111
Partner and Head of Family Department.
Specialisation: Main areas of practice are public law, child-care and ancillary relief. Member of Law Society's Children Panel since March 1986. Experienced practitioner for children, guardians and parents. Handles all aspects of marriage and cohabitation breakdown, both private and legal aid. Lecturer from 1983-88 on Legal Executive Course. Committed member of Children Act Business and Services Committees for Plymouth. Currently Chair of SFLA Children Committee.
Prof. Memberships: Law Society, Children Panel, Committee Member of Local SFLA.
Career: Qualified in 1984. Previous training as Legal Executive. Joined *Gill Akaster* in 1975, becoming a Partner in 1985.
Personal: Born 28th April 1950. Attended College of Law, Guildford 1982-83. Leisure interests include walking, theatre and amateur theatre. Lives in Plymouth.

BALDWIN, Lorraine
Rowlands, Manchester (0161) 835 2020
Specialisation: Child Care
Prof. Memberships: Member of Law Society Child Care Panel, Child Concern and a Legal aid Franchisee.
Career: Educated at Maricourt High School Liverpool and Liverpool Polytechnic. Qualified in 1988.
Personal: Single parent living in Charlton with one child and two dogs.

BALLANTINE, Tom
Mowat Dean & Co WS, Edinburgh (0131) 555 0616
Specialisation: Main area of practice is family law covering separation, divorce, children, financial issues and protection. Accredited by Law Society of Scotland as Family Mediator. On Management Councils of Lothian Marriage Counselling Service and Scottish Adoption Association.
Prof. Memberships: Law Society of Scotland, Family Law Association, CALM.
Career: Qualified 1986, set up *Mowat Dean & Co.* Family Law Department in 1994.
Personal: Born 3rd May, 1959, obtained MA at Cambridge University 1978-1981, LL.B at Edinburgh University 1982—1985. Current Editor of Family Law Association Bulletin. Leisure interests include walking, football and reading. Lives on outskirts of Edinburgh.

BAMBER, Roger
Mills & Reeve, Cambridge (01223) 64422
Partner in Family Department.
Specialisation: With partner Bruce Wilson, leads the largest and most specialist team in the region. He has lectured extensively within the profession as well as appearing on radio and television. He is the chairman of the National Family Law Group. Work includes financial provision, children law, divorce and Inheritance Act claims. Co-author of Pensions and Insurance on Matrimonial Breakdown. Editor of "The Family Through Divorce," which is a comprehensive guide to the personal, financial and legal aspects of family breakdown, with marital therapist Dr Janet

Reibstein, and colleagues, Jackie Wells, Sarah Attle, and Dr Jeannette Josse.
Prof. Memberships: Law Society, SFLA.
Career: Qualified in 1981. Joined *Mills & Reeve* as a Partner in 1988. Member of the Training Committee of SFLA 1988-90; Chairman of the Cams and West Suffolk SFLA 1989-94.
Personal: Born 5th February 1955. MA Cantab. Leisure interests include family and the Arts. Lives in Cambridge.

BEAR, C. Rupert
Rupert Bear Murray Davies, Nottingham (0115) 924 3333
Specialisation: All aspects of relationship breakdown with a concentration on resolving high profile financial claims.
Prof. Memberships: Solicitors Family Law Association, Nottinghamshire Chamber of Commerce.
Career: Qualified 1964. At *Wells & Hind* 1964-1989; *Evershed Wells & Hind* 1989-1992; founded *Rupert Bear & Co* 1992.
Personal: Born 29 November 1938. Married with 6 children. Educated Ipswich School and King's College, London. Member Trent Wine & Food Society. Lives in Bingham, Nottinghamshire and Middleton-by-Youlgreave, Derbyshire.

BENNETT, Jeremy
Wolferstans, Plymouth (01752) 663295
Partner 1980. Head of Childrens Department.
Specialisation: Specialist Child Care Lawyer also dealing with proceedings relating to children generally, mental health and welfare rights. Legal aid specialist. SFLA Trained All Issues Mediator.
Prof. Memberships: SFLA, Association of

Lawyers for Children, BAAF, NAGALRO, LAG, CPAG and LAPG.
Career: Qualified 1975. Joined *Wolferstans* 1978. Partner 1980. President Plymouth Law Society 1994/95. Part-time Chairman Child Support and Social Security Appeal Tribunals.
Personal: Born Penzance 8th August 1949. School Winchester and Croydon. University in Leeds. Early career London and Shrewsbury before returning to West Country. Senator British Junior Chamber. Leisure pursuits include running, walking, vegetable gardening and Crystal Palace.

BONNER, Margaret
Foot & Bowden, Plymouth
(01752) 675000
Partner. Head of Child Care Law Department.
Specialisation: Acts in cases involving children, in both public and private law. Work includes adoption, child abduction, divorce and ancillary relief matters. Lectures for College of Law and SFLA. Conference Chairman at the SFLA fifth conference in 1993.
Prof. Memberships: Solicitors Family Law Association. Member of Children Panel. Association of Lawyers for Children. Association of Women Solicitors, Plymouth Child Care Support Group, Family Mediators Association. SFLA Lawyer Mediator.
Career: Qualified in 1985. Joined *Foot & Bowden* in 1985, becoming a Partner in 1986. Previously Nursing Auxiliary in Geriatric Hospital, Trainee Assistant Editor of Cookery magazine and personal assistant to Clinical Psychologist.
Personal: Born 31st August 1946. Attended University of Sussex 1965-68. Leisure interests include yoga, walking, food and wine.

BOYCE, Wendy A.
Bond Pearce, Plymouth
(01752) 266 633
Partner and Head of the Family Law Group.
Specialisation: Has specialised in family law since qualifying. Specialising in particular in matters involving loss of pension benefits on divorce, business issues and insolvency related problems. Her skilled approach in dealing with the often complicated commercial aspects of a dispute has established her reputation in this field. Handles all aspects which arise on marriage or relationship breakdown relating to finance and children, within both divorce and separation proceedings. Lectures extensively to the legal profession and other professionals on various family law topics and is a key figure in Jordans Publishing Annual National Lectures speaking on a range of topics including the Child Support Act and Pensions and Insolvency on family breakdown, amongst other publications. General editor of the Jordans books entitled 'Debt and Insolvency on Family Breakdown' and contributor to 'Pensions and Insurance on Family Breakdown,' amongst other publications.
Prof. Memberships: Member of the Devon & Cornwall Solicitors Family Law Association.
Career: Qualified in 1980. Joined *Bond Pearce* in 1978, becoming partner in 1987.

CALDWELL, Anne I.M.
Flynn & McGettrick, Belfast
(01232) 244212

CARMICHAEL, Graeme
Graeme Carmichael, Ipswich
(01473) 252159
Specialisation: Principally work concerning children in public and private law, including advocacy. Balance of caseload divorce and related issues.
Prof. Memberships: Law Society Children Panel; SFLA (Regional Chairman); Association of Lawyers for Children.
Career: Qualified 1976. Previously family Law Partner at *Eversheds* (Norwich) and *Prettys* (Ipswich).
Personal: Born 1950. Educated Fettes College and Newcastle University.

CARTER, Barbara
Barbara Carter, Birmingham
(0121) 441 3238
Specialisation: Children's Law.
Career: Qualified 1983. Own firm since 1988.
Prof. Memberships: S.F.L.A., Birmingham Children's Panel, BAAF Midland Legal Executive.

CATTO, Joan
Burnett & Reid, Aberdeen (01224) 644333
Partner in Court Department.
Specialisation: Main area of practice is family law. Deals with numerous divorce cases including ancillary issues such as financial arrangements and residence and contact orders. Also handles child law: acts as curator ad litem and reporter in adoptions, residence and contact disputes. Was for 10 years Safeguarder to the Children's Panel and to the Sheriff Court. Acted as safeguarder in W. which went to the Inner House of the Court of Session. Acted on behalf of the petitioners in K Petitioners and for child in Cameron v Cameron. Has participated in and organised numerous Family Law Seminars in Aberdeen and elsewhere.
Prof. Memberships: Member of Family Law Association, Member of Family Mediation (Grampian). Board member Scottish Children's Reporter Administration.
Career: Qualified in 1968. Joined *Burnett & Reid* in 1988, becoming a Partner in 1991. As well as working full-time as a solicitor in private practice, has been part-time Social Security Appeal Tribunal Chairman since 1983, and part time Child Support Appeal Tribunal Chairman since 1993.
Personal: Born 30th April 1946. Attended Aberdeen High School for Girls and Aberdeen University. Non-executive Director with Grampian Healthcare NHS Trust. Member of Business Committee, General Council, Aberdeen University; Committee Member, Aberdeen Civic Society. Leisure interests include needlework, walking and foreign travel. Lives in Aberdeen, and Glenbuchat.

COTTRELL, Patricia A.
Cuff Roberts, Liverpool (0151) 227 4181
Partner in Family Department
Specialisation: Specialises in high-profile, high-value matrimonial cases. Practice deals with all aspects of Family Law, particularly divorce, separation, ancillary relief, co-habitation and Private Law Children cases.
Prof. Memberships: Law Society, Liverpool Law Society, Solicitors Family Law Association (SFLA)
Career: Qualified 1983. Joined *Cuff Roberts* in 1981, now franchise Partner and Head of

Family Department. Former Chairman Merseyside SFLA; Currently member of Liverpool Law Society General Committee; Chairman of Liverpool Law Society Family Business Committee; Solicitor to Liverpool Branch of Relate; Member of Merseyside Legal Aid Board Appeals Committee, Deputy District Judge.
Personal: Leisure interests include walking, theatre, gardening, reading and travel. Lives on the Wirral Peninusla.

CRAIG, Clare
Anne Hall Dick & Co, Glasgow
(0141) 636 0003

DARBYSHIRE, Chris
Rowberry Morris & Co, Reading
(0118) 958 5611
Specialisation: Child care, Adoption, Family Law. Has represented Local Authorities, parents, children, guardians ad litem, adoptive applicants and others in full range of child care and family matters in Magistrates, County and Higher Courts. Has acted as guardian ad litem for children in County and High Court proceedings.
Prof. Memberships: SFLA, Association of Lawyers for Children, Solicitors Association of Higher Court Advocates.
Career: Admitted 1973. In Local Government until 1979 when went into Private Practice. With *Rowberry Morris* since 1982. Child Care panel 1985. Higher Courts (Civil Proceedings), Qualification for Advocacy (1994).

DAVIES, Murray
Rupert Bear Murray Davies, Nottingham
(0115) 924 3333

DEVLIN, Michael
Stephensons,incorporating Flint & Holmes, Salford (0161) 832 8844
Specialisation: Care proceedings; adoption; complex residence and contact cases. Provides training on this area of the law for lawyers, GALs and social workers.
Prof. Memberships: The Law Society, The Children Panel.

DICK, Anne
Anne Hall Dick & Co, Glasgow
(0141) 636 0003

DON, Andrew M.W.
Blandy & Blandy, Reading
(0118) 958 7111
Specialisation: Divorce or separation and issues arising namely financial settlement and arrangements for children. Accredited mediator with the Family Mediators Association since 1992. Trains other solicitors to be mediators.
Career: Qualified 1981. Partner 1984.
Prof. Memberships: Solicitors Family Law Association. Family Mediators Association
Personal: Born 1.12.52. Educated at Malvern College and Liverpool University. Lives in Hampshire. Enjoys cricket, Rackets and gardening.

DOWNING, Ian
Ian Downing, Plymouth (01752) 226224
Specialisation: Family law generally and particularly: high asset ancillary relief claims involving company/business matters and pensions; Inheritance Act claims; cohabitee disputes.

Prof. Memberships: Chairman, Devon & Cornwall SFLA.
Career: Qualified 1984. Family law partner, *Bond Pearce*, 1990. Left to set up specialist family practice 1997. Contributing writer to Pensions and Insurance on Family Breakdown, Debt and Insolvency on Family Breakdown, and Humphreys Family Proceedings.
Personal: Born 20.09.59. Newcastle upon Tyne University LLB (Hons). Married. Interests include windsurfing, skiing, scuba diving, theatre, travel.

EDWARDS, Robert Nigel
Martin Prowel, Edwards & Davies, Cardiff (01222) 496316

ERSKINE, Sarah R.
Erskine MacAskill & Co, Edinburgh (0131) 557 1520
Partner.
Specialisation: Main area of practice is family law, covering matrimonial, separations, agreements, violence, financial arrangements, child law, custody, children in care and children's hearings. Also handles other civil court work, damages and criminal work. Acts for Shakti Women's Aid and has become involved in cases concerning marital disputes amongst ethnic minorities, child sexual abuse, non-accidental injury cases and abduction cases. Gave a family mediation child abduction seminar; on advisory group of Scottish Child Law Centre; on Management Group managing housing for homeless women.
Prof. Memberships: SSC (Solicitor to the Supreme Court), Notary Public,
Career: Qualified in 1980. Joined *Erskine Macaskill & Co* in 1984 as a Partner.
Personal: Educated at St. Brides' School, Helensburgh, then Edinburgh University LL.B. Leisure interests include politics, hill walking, bird watching and reading. Lives in Edinburgh.

FIFE, Peter R.G.
Ward Gethin, King's Lynn (01553) 773456

FLINT, Peter
Lanyon Bowdler, Shrewsbury (01743) 236400
Specialisation: Head of Family Law Department, *Lanyon Bowdler* – based in firm's Shrewsbury office, specialising in all aspects of Family Law. Articled to *J.C.H. Bowdler & Sons*, Shrewsbury, in 1967. Qualified in 1971. Admitted into parternship with *J.C.H Bowdler & Sons* in 1972.
Prof. Memberships: Member of Legal Aid Area (No 12) Committee. Member of S.F.L.A. and of Family Mediators Association.
Career: Educated at St Martin's Prepatory School, Northwood, Haileybury and I.S.C, Hertford and College of Law. Passed Law Society Pt II exams with 2nd class honours.
Personal: Married, with 3 daughters. Lives in Bayston Hill, near Shrewsbury. Interests include golf and tennis.

FOSKETT, Peter W.
Gordons Wright & Wright, Bradford (01274) 202202
Partner in the Family Department.
Specialisation: All aspects of family law, but especially complex ancillary relief on divorce and other financial matters and child-related work.
Prof. Memberships: SFLA, WYFMC (West Yorkshire Family Mediation Council – Vice Chairman), FMA.
Career: Qualified 1981. At *Addleshaw Sons & Latham* 1979-1982. Joined *Gordons* in 1983. (Partner from 1985).
Personal: Born 27 May 1957. Educated at Leeds University (LLB). Lives in Bingley.

FOSTER, Stephen
Lester Aldridge, Bournemouth (01202) 786161
Specialisation: Head of Family Law Unit, leading a team of six specialist lawyers dealing with all areas of family law work, financial and children. Specialises in dealing with substantial financial and property matters within divorce and cohabitee proceedings, including related shareholding and other company disputes. Cases often involve an international element. Also specialises in solicitors' negligence covering all areas of family law.
Prof. Memberships: Solicitors Family Law Association.
Career: Qualified 1986. *Bircham & Co Westminster* 1986-1992 as lead family lawyer and member of the commercial litigation team. Joined *Lester Aldridge* in 1993 as a partner to head up large Family Law unit.
Personal: Born 1959. Educated at Newport High School and University of Wales, University College Swansea (1980 BA History). Lives near Dorchester, Dorset. Interests include English and American literature, swimming and squash.

FOTHERINGHAM, John M.
Ross & Connel, Dunfermline (01383) 721156

GIBB, Andrew T.F.
Balfour & Manson, Edinburgh (0131) 200 1200
Partner in Litigation Department.
Specialisation: Has a substantial practice in family law in both the Court of Session and Sheriff Court, also involving drafting of separation agreements with particular regard to financial provision. Other main areas are education and employment law. Is involved in all aspects of education law including contract disputes, disciplinary matters, criminal prosecutions and accident cases. Provides employment law advice to both employers and employees. Solicitor to The Educational Institute of Scotland, the main teaching union in Scotland. Joint editor of 'The Family Law Bulletin' and regular contributor to 'Update' (Education Department of Law Society of Scotland) on family law matters.
Prof. Memberships: Law Society of Scotland, Family Law Association.
Career: Qualified in 1971. Became a partner in *Balfour & Manson* in 1975. Member of Council of Law Society of Scotland 1981-93 and President of Law Society of Scotland 1990-91.
Personal: Born 17th August 1947. Educated at Perth Academy 1959-65 and Edinburgh University 1965-69. Chairman, Management Committee Lothian Allelon (Probation hostel); Leisure interests include golf and music. Lives in Edinburgh.

GREEN, Michael
Green & Co, Manchester (0161) 834 8980

GREGORY-JONES, Rosemary
Leo Abse & Cohen, Cardiff (01222) 383252
Specialisation: Family Law, particularly practising in the area of complex ancillary relief cases, also Children Act applications and claims under the Inheritance (Provision for Family and Dependant) Act. I also practice as a family mediator.
Prof. Memberships: Degree in Economic History from Leicester University. Thereafter I qualifed as a solicitor. At *Morgan Bruce*, Cardiff, for 15 years, 9 of which as a partner.

HALLAM, Catherine
Burges Salmon, Bristol (0117) 939 2000

HAMILTON, Iain M.
Jones Maidment Wilson, Manchester (0161) 832 8087

HARDMAN, Peter
Nightingales, Manchester (0161) 832 6722
Partner in Matrimonial/Family Law Department.
Specialisation: Specialises in all aspects of family law, advising mainly strongly contested high value cases of privately funded clients, with limited representation otherwise. Experienced advocate. Main areas: Ancillary relief; settlements; children issues. Clients include high achievers both socially and professionally. Introduction is usually by recommendation.
Prof. Memberships: Law Society. Manchester Law Society.
Career: Experienced Deputy District Judge. Legal Aid appeals adjudication.

HARTNELL, Norman A.
Hartnell & Co, Exeter (01392) 421777
Principal. Family Law specialist.
Specialisation: Main areas of practice are family law, child care law and family mediation. Member of Law Society Children Panel; accredited mediator and sole mediator with FMA; joint organiser of Devon Family Forum (interdisciplinary group); former member of Plymouth Family Courts Business and Services Committees; FMA trainer and supervisor. Has acted for children in a number of private law cases, and handled substantial ancillary relief and children cases.
Prof. Memberships: Family Mediators Association; Devon and Cornwall SFLA (past Secretary); Devon & Exeter Law Society. Member of Relate Quality Partnership.
Career: Qualified in 1979. Established own specialist family law firm in 1991, now has staff of 13. Previously Partner with *Dunn & Baker* from 1988. Assistant Solicitor with *Stones* in Exeter 1985-87. Previous positions with *Rimmers*, Aylesbury; *Reynolds Parry-Jones*, High Wycombe; *Landons*, Brentwood and *Whiskers*, Harlow and Epping.
Personal: Born 1st October 1953. Attended Aylesbury Grammar School, then Selwyn College, Cambridge (1974-76, MA) and Chester College of Law 1978. Lives in Exeter.

HENSON, John S.
Hunt & Coombs, Peterborough (01733) 565312

HOPKINS, Wendy
Wendy Hopkins & Co, Cardiff
(01222) 342233

HUGHES, Kathryn Lesley
Farleys, Blackburn (01254) 606060
Partner in Family Law Department. Main areas of practice are child care and ancillary relief in divorce, together with the law relating to cohabitants. Handles all aspects, both privately paid, legal aid, both public and private law cases. Children Panel Member. Has acted in instances from the most straightforward ancillary relief case to the case where the wife obtained, inter alia, a lump sum of £1 million; from uncomplicated children matters to the most difficult; and adoptions with a foreign element. Contributing author to Butterworths Family Law Service since 1992.
Prof. Memberships: Law Society Family Law Committee Member; SFLA, Child Concern.
Career: Qualified in 1985. Past member of the Bar (called 1977). Joined *Farleys* in 1983, becoming a Partner in 1985. Assistant Recorder since 1994, sitting on Crime, Civil, and most recently, private family law matters.
Personal: Born 5th June 1954. Leisure interests include walking, sailing, swimming and reading. Lives in Hale, Altrincham.

HYLAND, Patricia
Patricia U. Hyland, Belfast (01232) 324035

ILIFF, Catherine
Fosters, Norwich (01603) 620508
Bungay (01986) 895251
Specialisation: Partner in *Fosters'* substantial family law department. Solid experience in all aspects of family work for private clients. Significant mediation experience, having been accredited as a mediator since 1991.

JONES, Catherine E.
Pannone & Partners, Manchester
(0161) 909 3000
Partner in Family Department.
Specialisation: Work includes divorce, separation, financial provision, children including contested adoption and cohabitation.
Prof. Memberships: Law Society, Manchester Law Society, SFLA.
Career: Qualified 1977. Joined *Pannone & Partners* in 1982, now Client Care Partner and Joint Head of Family Department. Currently member of Manchester Family Court Forum, North West SFLA secretary and regional representative, Management Committee of the Manchester and Salford FSU.
Personal: Leisure interests include walking, sailing, theatre and travel. Lives in Altrincham.

JONES, Peter
Jones Myers Gordon, Leeds
(0113) 246 0055
Specialisation: Main areas of practice Divorce and Ancillary Relief together with Cohabitation Disputes and Mediation.
Career: Qualified 1980. Founded 6 years ago a Specialist Family Law Practice.
Prof. Memberships: Former National Chairman of the Solicitors Family Law Association, Committee Member of the Council for Family Proceedings, Lecturer and Member of the UK College of Family Mediators.
Personal: Born 4th June 1948. Married with 2 daughters. Lives in Harrogate.

JURY, S.N.
Wolferstans, Plymouth (01752) 663295
Family/Matrimonial
Specialisation: Family Law including all areas of divorce work, child law, including both public and private law, cohabitee matters. Member of SFLA and Law Society's Children Panel Committee member of National Association of Women Solicitors. Member of the Law Society.
Prof. Memberships: Articled *Wolferstans* 1987, qualified 1990, became a partner 1995.
Career: Tavistock School; Huddersfield University; Chester College of Law; LL.B.
Personal: Year of birth: 1964; town of residence: Plymouth; main leisure activities, clubs: rowing; skiing; sailing; Plymouth Amateur Rowing Club.

KIDD, Philip E.
Tozers, Torquay (01803) 291898

LAMBERT, Tracy
Tozers, Torquay (01803) 291898

LOUDON, Alasdair
Loudons WS, Edinburgh (0131) 662 4193
Founding Partner.
Specialisation: Sole area of practice is family law, including divorce cases, particularly those involving claims for capital payments or property transfer orders. Also handles substantial number of cases involving the negotiation of separation agreements. Acts in Court of Session and Sheriff Court. Former tutor in criminal advocacy at Edinburgh University. Accredited by the Law Society of Scotland as a specialist in Family Law and Child Law.
Prof. Memberships: WS Society, Edinburgh Bar Association (Past President), Family Law Association.
Career: Qualified in 1978. Apprentice at *Tods, Murray & Jamieson WS* 1978-80. Qualified Assistant at *Warner & Co.* 1980-82 and Partner 1982-92. Founded *Loudons WS* in 1992.
Personal: Born 7th April 1956. Attended Dundee University 1974-78. Leisure interests include golf (member of Bruntsfield Links and Luffness New) and football (Hearts Season Ticket holder). Lives in Edinburgh.

MAIR, Leonard
The Morton Fraser Partnership, Edinburgh
(0131) 550 1000
Partner in Civil Litigation Department.
Specialisation: Main areas of practice are family law, negotiating financial divorce settlements, ADR and mediation. Has covered a wide range of work over a 21 year period and has developed ADR and mediation skills since 1993. Has also handled reparation and contract work in general practice over 21 years. Mediator with Family Mediation Service; Accredited Mediator with CEDR; Accredited 'solicitor-mediator' with Law Society of Scotland.
Prof. Memberships: Law Society of Scotland, Writers to the Signet, College of Family Mediators.
Career: Qualified in 1975. Joined *The Morton Fraser Partnership* in 1972, becoming a Partner in 1977.
Personal: Born 5th September 1949. Attended Stirling University 1967-71 and Edinburgh University 1971-73. Former Vice Chairman of Lothian Marriage Counselling Service. Former part-time Chairman CSAT. Leisure interests

include fly fishing, sailing and the arts. Lives in East Lothian.

MCGOLDRICK, John
Jones Maidment Wilson, Manchester
(0161) 832 8087

MCGOWAN, Maureen
The Morton Fraser Partnership, Edinburgh
(0131) 550 1000

MILBURN, Paula
Jones Maidment Wilson, Manchester
(0161) 832 8087

NASH, John
Nelsons, Nottingham (0115) 958 6262
Partner and Head of Family Law Department.
Specialisation: Main area of practice is dealing with substantial ancillary relief cases and private law children cases.
Prof. Memberships: Chairman of Notts branch of SFLA for several years.
Career: Admitted in 1980, Head of *Nelsons* Family Law Department since 1987.
Personal: Aged 42. Married with one child. Attended Andover Grammar School (Lord Denning's old school) and Nottingham University.

NICOL, Frazer
Nicol, Denvir & Purnell, Cardiff
(01222) 796311

O'DONNELL, Caroline
Miller & Company, Cambridge
(01223) 366741

O'REGAN, T.G.
Rudlings & Wakelam,
Thetford (01842) 754151
Bury St. Edmunds (01284) 755771
Specialisation: Specialises in child law, particularly child care and adoption. Original member of the Children Panel. Head of Child Law Department at *Rudlings & Wakelam*.
Prof. Memberships: Secretary to Children Committee of the Solicitors Family Law Association, member of the Association of Lawyers for Children, member of British Agencies for Adoption and Fostering, associate member of National Association of Guardians ad Litem and Reporting Officers, solicitor representative on the Suffolk Family Court Business Committee, member Law Society Child Law sub-committee.
Career: Admitted as solicitor in 1975, Partner since 1978. Writes and lectures regularly on child law and adoption.

PALMER, George
Peden & Reid, Belfast (01232) 325617

PATIENCE, Iain
Iain Smith & Company, Aberdeen
(01224) 878417
email: iainp@iainsmith.com
Partner.
Specialisation: Law Society accredited specialist in Family Law and Family Mediation.
Career: Admitted December 1979, joining *Iain Smith & Company* the same year. At *Iain Smith & Company* ever since. Partner since 1983.

PAYNE, Peter
Stephens & Scown, Exeter
(01392) 210700
Specialisation: Family and child care work.
Prof. Memberships: Member of SFLA and on Child Care Panel.

PROCTOR, E. Jane
Greenwoods, Peterborough
(01733) 555244

PYBUS, Roy
Roy Pybus, Liverpool (0151) 475 4400

RANDALL, Richard M.
Leonard Gray, Chelmsford
(01245) 251411
Specialisation: All aspects of family law including complex cases involving substantial financial assets or children. Particular specialisation in contact cases involving hostile parents and the representation of teenage children in legal proceedings. Broadcasts, lectures and writes on family law and related issues.
Prof. Memberships: Solicitors Family Law Association. Founder member British Association of Lawyer Mediators.
Career: Qualified 1972. Partner *Leonard Gray* 1975. Head of Family Law Department 1984. Senior Partner 1991. Sole Family Mediator 1996.
Personal: Born 17th May 1948. Educated at Brentwood School, LLB London. Lives and works in Chelmsford. Enjoys performing choral music and opera, cricket, cycling. Married with two teenage children.

RUTHERFORD, Lyn
Dickinson Dees, Newcastle upon Tyne
(0191) 279 9000
Partner and Head of Family Law Department.
Specialisation: The practice covers a full range of family law matters. In particular specialisation in high net worth private clients and major ancillary matters.
Career: Qualified 1972. Thereafter 1 year at Clayton Mott in Nottingham. Joined *Dickinson Dees* in January 1974. Became a Partner in 1976.
Personal: Born 20 January 1948. Educated at Hookergate Grammar School and Liverpool University – LLB Degree. Interests include sports, particularly horse racing, football and reading. Lives in Newcastle upon Tyne.

SALTER, David A.
Addleshaw Booth & Co, Leeds
(0113) 209 2000
Partner and Head of Family Law Department.
Specialisation: Handles all aspects of family law, but principally financial relief with an emphasis on pensions. Author or joint author of 'Humphreys Family Proceedings,' 'Matrimonial Consent Orders and Agreements,' 'Family Finance and Tax' and 'Family Courts: Emergency Remedies and Procedures.' Editor of 'Pensions and Insurance on Family Breakdown' and 'Longman Litigation Practice.' Contributor to 'Insolvency on Family Breakdown' and 'Butterworths Family Law Service.' Frequent lecturer on family law topics.
Prof. Memberships: SFLA (Chairman). International Academy of Matrimonial Lawyers (Fellow).

Career: Qualified in 1972. Joined the firm in 1975, becoming a Partner in 1978. Recorder (North Eastern Circuit); Member of Supreme Court Procedure Committee Family Division Sub-committee; Member of the Family Committee of the Judicial Studies Board.
Personal: Born 27th August 1948. Educated Pembroke College, Cambridge.

SANDS, Rosemary
Miller & Company, Cambridge
(01223) 366741

SCANLAN, Margaret
Russells Gibson McCaffrey, Glasgow
(0141) 332 4176
Specialisation: Family law and child law, including negotiating settlements and court work. Law Society Accredited specialist in Family Law.
Prof. Memberships: Family Law Association, Sheriff Court Rules Council, Scottish Legal Aid Board.
Career: Qualified 1972 after apprenticeship with *Flowers & Co*. Thereafter wide general practice, specialising in Family Law for last 10 years. Founder member and past chair of Family Law Association.
Personal: Bad golf, good food.

SCOFIELD, Ian D.
Hooper & Wollen, Torquay
(01803) 213251
Specialisation: Head of department advising on all aspects of family law and child care. Specialises in financial and property issues and has a substantial case load of high value divorces involving complex negotiation. Accredited mediator with the Family Mediators Association and one of the few mediators in the South West with a regular case load. National committee member of the Solicitors Family Law Association and a member of the Law Society's Child Care Panel.

SHAKESPEAR, Felicity
Clarke Willmott & Clarke, Bristol
(0117) 941 6600
Specialisation: Partner, Head of Family Department. Has specialised in Family Law since qualification and is now Leader of 8 specialist lawyers. All areas of family law are covered, in particular, high asset ancillary relief claims involving companies and farmers, and also Public Law child care.
Prof. Memberships: Member of Children Panel. SFLA Regional Committee Member.
Career: Qualiified in 1973. Partner with *Darlington & Parkinson* (Ealing, London) 1976-1986. President of Central and South Middlesex Law Society 198. Joined *Clarke Willmott & Clarke* in 1986, becoming a Partner in 1989.
Personal: Born 1948. LLB Southampton. Leisure interests include gardening, bridge and running a large apple orchard.

SHEEHAN, Wendy
Balfour & Manson, Edinburgh
(0131) 200 1200
Specialisation: Practises solely in Family Law both in the Sheriff Court and Court of Session dealing with inter alia provision on divorce, parental rights, residence and contact cases,

spousal maintenance/CSA and separation agreements. Appointed as an independent court reporter in child residence and contact cases. Also accredited by the Law Society of Scotland as a Family Law Mediator with a substantial mediation practice.
Prof. Memberships: Family Law Association, Notary Public, C.A.L.M.
Career: Born 26th December 1968. Educated at St. George's School for Girls and University of Aberdeen. Admitted as a solicitor in 1991.
Personal: Lives in Edinburgh. Author for Butterworths Family Law Service, Vice Chair of Lothian Marriage Counselling Service. Leisure interests include music and water sports.

SHEPHERD, Nigel G.
Berrymans Lace Mawer, Liverpool
(0151) 236 2002
Specialisation: Main areas of practice are financial issues and private Children Act work; lectures on family law topics; has written articles for Family Law Journal and Family Matters.
Prof. Memberships: SFLA (National Chairman 1995-97; North West Chairman 1987-91); Law Society.
Career: Born 9.11.1956; BA (Hons) Manchester Polytechnic 1978; Married: two daughters; Lives in Stockport; Leisure interests include sport, music and wine.

SHRIMPTON, Julie E.
Tozers, Plymouth (01752) 206460

SILVER, Raphael
Silver Savory Smith, Cambridge
(01223) 562001
Senior Litigation Partner.
Specialisation: Childcare, crime.
Career: Admitted 1984. Litigator/advocate. Dealt with all types of serious crime before turning to Childcare work in 1991. Now deals mainly with Public Law Children work acting for Local Authority, children and parents.
Prof. Memberships: Law Society Children Panel. SFLA. Associate Member NAGALRO and BAAF.
Personal: Born 1960, Liverpool. Graduated Durham University. Married. Lives in Saffron Walden. Interests include cricket, gardening and wine.

SIMPSON, Barbara
Cole & Cole, Oxford (01865) 262600
Specialisation: All types of private children law and ancillary relief issues. In particular dealing with substantial financial cases including those with an international element or complex commercial issues. Child abduction is a further speciality.
Prof. Memberships: First chair of Solicitors Family Law Association Oxford.
Career: Qualified 1974. Head of family law teams in *Cole & Cole* since1984. Deputy District Judge in Principal Registry of Family Law Association.
Personal: Born 31 March 1948. Educated at Durham University. Leisure pursuits including Latin American dancing, skiing, books and family life.

SISSON, David
Eversheds, Norwich 01603 272727
Specialisation: Exclusively Family Law, with emphasis on Finance.
Prof. Memberships: SFLA; SFLA International Committee.

Career: Qualified 1977. Partner *Eversheds* 1985. Head of *Eversheds* Family Law Department since 1991.
Personal: Born 5th May 1951. Leisure interests include Bridge and Golf.

SMITH, Caroline
Loudons WS, Edinburgh
(0131) 662 4193
Partner dealing with family law .
Specialisation: Twelve years experience dealing exclusively with family law. Accredited by Law Society of Scotland as specialist in Family Law and as a Family Mediator. Member of local panel of Reporting Officers/ Curators ad litem for adoption proceedings. Prepares child welfare reports for Sheriff Court.
Prof. Memberships: Family Law Association, Edinburgh Bar Association. W.S. Society, Scottish Association of Children's Curators, UK College of Family Mediators.
Career: Qualified MB.Ch.B 1979 and worked as hospital doctor 1979-82. Assistant *Warner & Co.* 1985-88. Qualified LLB 1986. Assistant (Litigation) *Morton Fraser Milligan WS* 1988-93. Joined *Loudons WS* as an Associate in October 1993. Partner July 1994.
Personal: Born 23rd June 1955. Educated St. Denis School, Edinburgh 1960-73 and Edinburgh University 1973-79 and 1982-85. Lives in Edinburgh.

SMITH, Cathryn
Foot & Bowden, Plymouth (01752) 675000
Partner: Head of Family Law Department.
Specialisation: All aspects of ancillary relief within divorce. Work includes high finance, pensions, section 8 applications. Lectures for SFLA. Member of SFLA National Training Committee and Chairman of Devon and Cornwall SFLA.
Prof. Memberships: Solicitors Family Law Association, Association of Women Solicitors.
Career: Qualified in 1986. Joined *Foot & Bowden* in 1990, becoming a Partner in 1993.
Personal: Born 10th July 1961. Attended Birmingham University 1980 to 1983. Leisure interests include sailing, walking and good food.

SPEKER, Barry N.
Samuel Phillips & Co, Newcastle upon Tyne
(0191) 232 8451
Senior Partner and Head of Litigation Department.
Specialisation: Principal area of work is medical negligence, personal injury, family and matrimonial including child care and adoption and employment law cases. Legal adviser for Newcastle Health Authority and various NHS trusts, NSPCC Newcastle upon Tyne and Barnardo's North East. Regular lecturer on child care law, mental health law, medical negligence and employment law. Affiliate of Institute of Risk Management.
Prof. Memberships: Law Society (Medical Negligence and Children Panels), Law Society, Lawyers for Business Users Committee.
Career: Qualified 1971 while with *Leigh Gold & Co.*, then joined *Samuel Phillips & Co*. Became a Partner in 1973 and Senior Partner in 1987. Deputy District Judge. Part time Industrial Tribunal Chairman.
Personal: Born 28th June 1947. Attended Heaton Grammar School and London University. Member of Mensa. Leisure pursuits include golf (Arcot Hall Golf Club), debating

and the Times Crossword. Lives in Newcastle upon Tyne.

STAKES, John Anthony
Cranswick Watson, Leeds (0113) 245 2450
Specialisation: Family Law: Divorce, Finance, Cohabitation and Abduction.
Career: Qualified 1971. Partner 1975
Prof. Memberships: Former National SFLA Regional Press Officer and currently Chairman of West and North Yorkshire SFLA.
Personal: Married with two children and three step-children. Leisure interests include walking, amateur dramatics and cricket.

STEVENSON, Lorraine
Wilson Nesbitt, Bangor (01247) 271035
Specialisation: All aspects of family law, including separation, divorce, ancillary relief and the law as it relates to children.
Prof. Memberships: Member of the Children Panel, Northern Ireland Solicitors Family Law Association.
Career: Qualified in 1993 joining *Wilson Nesbitt* on qualification. Associate and Head of Matrimonial Department.
Personal: Born 2 May 1969. Leisure interests include travel, running and reading.

TAIT, Fiona
Drummond Miller WS, Edinburgh
(0131) 226 5151
Partner in Sheriff Court Department.
Specialisation: Main area of practice is family law. Work includes divorce, child law and children's hearings. Tutor at the University of Edinburgh LLB Course in commercial law (1990 – 1997).
Prof. Memberships: Law Society of Scotland, Edinburgh Bar Association Council Member (1993 – 1996).
Career: Qualified in 1991. Joined *Drummond Miller WS* in 1989, becoming a Partner in 1996.
Personal: Born 9th January 1966. Attended University of Edinburgh: LLB (Hons) 1988, DipLP 1989. Lives in Edinburgh.

TAYLOR, Norman S.
Zermansky & Partners, Leeds
(0113) 245 9766
Specialisation: Ancillary relief in divorce and cohabitation disputes.
Prof. Memberships: West and North Yorkshire S.F.L.A. Committee.
Career: Qualified July 1975. With *Zermansky & Partners* since February 1974. Educated at University of Newcastle upon Tyne (LL.B)
Personal: Born 14 January 1951. Married with three children. 1st Dan Black Belt Japan Karate Association (retired). School Governor. Lead Guitarist in Charity Rock Band.

THORNEYCROFT, Philip M.
Wolferstans, Plymouth (01752) 663295
Partner 1990. Head of Matrimonial Department.
Specialisation: Main areas of practice are child-care and family law. Acts on behalf of parents and children in Care proceedings and related matters. Acts for private and legally aided clients in divorce, ancillary relief, injunctions, and domestic violence matters. Lectured on child-care update to a conference run jointly by Plymouth University and Plymouth Law Society. Has made a number of appearances on local radio dealing with such issues as sexual abuse, cohabitation contracts and the effect of pensions on divorce.

Prof. Memberships: Solicitors Family Law Association, Member of Children Panel, a founder member of the Plymouth Child-care Support Group. Associate Member of the National Association of Guardians ad Litem and Reporting Officers.
Career: Qualified in 1982. Joined *Wolferstans* in 1982, becoming a Partner in 1990. Member of the Plymouth Hockey Club.
Personal: Born 2nd December 1957. Attended Chesterfield Grammar School 1970-76, Hull University 1976-79 and Chester Law College 1979-80. Leisure interests include hockey, skiing, music and Sheffield Wednesday. Lives in Plymouth.

WALKER, Ian
Trumps, Bristol (0117) 946 8200
Specialisation: Family Law including ancillary relief and children both private and public law. SFLA Mediator.
Prof. Memberships: Law Society Children Panel; SFLA and Association of Lawyers for Children.
Career: University of Essex, qualified 1992. *Christopher Green & Partners* 1990-92, *Berry & Berry* 1992-94, *Brethertons* 1995-98, joined *Trumps* 1998.
Personal: Born 8th June 1968. Married with growing family which does not leave much time for leisure.

WAY, Philip
Addleshaw Booth & Co, Leeds
(0113) 209 2000
Specialisation: Deputy Head of Family Law Department. Deals with all aspects of privately funded family Law, in particular, high value applications for ancillary relief. SFLA trained mediator. Contributor to 'Humphreys Family Proceedings,' 'Insolvency on Family Breakdown' and 'Family Finance and Tax.' Regular Author of Articles for legal journals.
Prof. Memberships: SFLA. Associate of H/C College of Family Mediators.
Career: Educated at Durham University.
Personal: Born 9th August 1967. Married. Lives in Wakefield.

WHITE, Iain
Cozens-Hardy & Jewson, Norwich
(01603) 625231
Family Department.
Specialisation: Specialises in child-related work, divorce and matrimonial finance.
Prof. Memberships: Member of the Children Panel.
Career: Qualified 1977. Partner 1986.

WILKINS, Beth D.
Pannone & Partners, Manchester
(0161) 909 3000
Partner in Family Department.
Specialisation: Work includes children, divorce, matrimonial finance and cohabitation. Regularly appears on local Radio and television, author of local and national press features and regularly lectures and chairs seminars on family law.
Prof. Memberships: Manchester Law Society, SFLA.
Career: Qualified in 1981. Joint Head of Family Department. Currently a member of the Manchester Law Society Council, PR Officer of North West SFLA, SFLA Good Practice Committee Member.
Personal: Leisure interests include gluttony,

theatre, cinema, the arts and travel. Lives in Manchester.

WILLIAMS, Frances
Larby Williams, Cardiff (01222) 472100
Specialisation: All aspects of Family Law, including substantial ancillary claims in divorce, child care representing parents and guardians, and advocacy from Family Proceedings Court to High Court.
Prof. Memberships: Member of Children Panel, Association of Lawyers for Children, BAAF Legal Group; Regional Chairman – SFLA, and AWS; Junior Vice President – Cardiff and District Law Society.
Career: Educated – Caerphilly Girls' Grammar School and Manchester University (BA in Politics and Modern History). Qualified 1976. 23 years' experience as matrimonial specialist. 1997 to date partner with *Larby Williams*, Cardiff and Cowbridge.
Personal: Married. Leisure interests include golf, skiing, theatre and books.

WILLIAMS, Jane R.
Morgan Bruce, Cardiff (01222) 385385

WILSON, Bruce
Mills & Reeve, Norwich +44 (0)1603 660155
Specialisation: High value and complex applications for ancillary relief with emphasis on landed estates.
Prof. Memberships: Solicitors' Family Law Association.

WOODS, Paul L.
Wolferstans, Plymouth (01752) 663295
Family/Matrimonial
Specialisation: Specialising in divorce for private and legally aided clients, including ancillary relief and advocacy.
Prof. Memberships: Qualified in 1975; Became partner with *Rundle McDonald & Rendle* 1979; Became partner with *Wolferstans*

following merger in 1992; Part time Chairman Social Security Appeal Tribunal 1988 to date; President Plymouth Law Society 1996-97; Founder member & past committee member Devon & Cornwall SFLA.
Career: Wellford Grammer School, Durham; Liverpool University; LL.B. 1972.
Personal: Year of birth: 1949; town of residence: Plymouth; main leisure activities, clubs: Chairman, Plymouth Albion Rugby Football Club 1996 to date; member St Mellion and Yelverton Golf Clubs; golf, rugby, theatre.

WOODWARD, David W.
Trumps, Bristol (0117) 946 8200
Partner in Family Law Department.
Specialisation: Main areas of practice are divorce, ancillary relief and children. Acted in Richardson 1994 1FLR 188, B v. B 1995 IFLR 9 and Richardson (No2) 1996 2 FLR 617. Contributor to Western Daily Press. Experience includes cable television work.
Prof. Memberships: SFLA, Law Society, Chairman Bristol SFLA.
Career: Qualified in 1975. Joined *Trumps* in 1979, becoming a Partner in 1981.
Personal: Born 10th January 1950. Holds an LLB from Bristol. Leisure interests include cycling, badminton and cricket. Lives in Bristol.

WRIGHT, Barbara J.
Thomson Snell & Passmore, Tunbridge Wells (01892) 510000
Partner and Head of Family Department.
Specialisation: Deals with all areas of family breakdown. Particular interest in financial aspects.
Prof. Memberships: Member of the College of Family Mediators and Solicitors Family Law Association. Founding Chair of Kent Solicitors Family Law Association and member of National Committee of SFLA from March 1997.
Career: Qualified 1979. Joined *Thomson Snell & Passmore* in 1987. Equity partner from 1995.

Honorary Legal Adviser to West Kent Relate. Accredited mediator trained by the Family Mediators Association.
Personal: Born 16th March 1955. Honours Law degree Sheffield University. Second Class Honours in Part II Law Society's examinations. Interests include English and French history, current affairs, cuisine. Lives in the Tunbridge Wells area. A Soroptimist.

WYATT, Alexandra
Gill Akaster, Plymouth (01752) 500111
Specialisation: Partner. Deals with all aspects of family law, both private and legal aid. Main areas of practice are divorce, ancillary relief, children (private and public law), domestic violence matters and cohabitation. Also mental health work.
Prof. Memberships: Law Society, Committee Member of Local SFLA, Member of Children Panel.
Career: Joined *Gill Akaster* in May 1993, qualified in September that year. Became a partner in July 1997.
Personal: Born 9-7-66. Attended Kent University 1984-1987, University of East Anglia 1988-1989, Chester Law College 1989-1991. Lives in Plymouth.

YOUNG, Hugh
Freeth Cartwright Hunt Dickins, Nottingham (0115) 936 9369
Specialisation: Partner in the Family Law Department and Head of Private Client Services specialising in matrimonial work.
Career: Articled *Simmons & Simmons*. Qualified 1970. Partner in *Freeth Cartwright* (now *Freeth Cartwright Hunt Dickins*) since 1973.
Personal: Born 1943. Educated at Ampleforth and Pembroke College, Cambridge. Resides in Nottingham. Married with 4 children. Interests include all sports principally now as spectator.

YOUNG, Ian
Young & Lee; Birmingham (0121) 633 3233

FINANCIAL SERVICES

RESEARCH: In compiling the tables, we consider all the information available to us, paying particular regard to the market research carried out by our team of ten qualified lawyers. (The researchers' details are set out on page three.) The rankings, therefore, reflect the opinion of the marketplace as revealed by systematic and objective research: see page four. (Our research is audited every year by the British Market Research Bureau.)

OVERVIEW: This is an area which will see great change over the coming years with the creation of the Financial Services Authority and the proposed new Financial Services Reform Act. The structure of firms' financial services practice will in many cases modify to reflect changes to the regulatory framework.

Traditionally financial services relates to the Financial Services Act 1986 and the regulatory framework created by it. Financial services advice covers:

1. Transactional compliance advice – this is required in relation to transactional activity, such as advising on a merger, take-over or acquisition.
2. Pure compliance advice – advice as to procedures required to comply with new or existing regulations.
3. Advice relating to enforcement and disciplinary actions taken by the regulators.

Financial services advice also extends to the regulation of other financial areas such as the insurance market and the specialist rules relating to Lloyds and The Stock Exchange. Whilst banking regulation is included under our Banking section there is inevitably overlap with this section. This section does not cover everyday investment advice to clients.

The London table is unchanged with Clifford Chance and Linklaters retaining top slot. The only addition to the tables is the Leeds firm, James Kendall. The re-organisation of the regulatory framework may well produce dramatic changes to the relative position of the firms in the future. Those firms with strong banking practices have much to gain as banking, securities and insurance regulation move closer together.

LEADING FIRMS · LONDON
CLIFFORD CHANCE
LINKLATERS
CAMERON MCKENNA
FRESHFIELDS
ALLEN & OVERY
S J BERWIN & CO
LOVELL WHITE DURRANT
NORTON ROSE
SIMMONS & SIMMONS
SLAUGHTER AND MAY
TRAVERS SMITH BRAITHWAITE
WILDE SAPTE

LONDON

Clifford Chance (7ptnrs/30assts) Cover all areas of financial services regulation, non-contentious and contentious. The team is led by the "brilliant," "extremely able" and "well known" *Tim Herrington* who "continues to give sensible, statesman-like advice. Have a "lot of in-depth knowledge." Also includes *James Barlow*. **Clients/Work:** Acting for PIA/IMRO on the establishment of the Financial Services Authority and the transfer of their staff to the authority. Advised CSFB on acquisition of BZW's UK and European Equities Business, structuring financial services aspects of the transaction and advising on regulatory issues. Advised Deutsche Morgan Grenfell in relation to the acquisition of the equity derivative business of NatWest Markets.

Linklaters (2ptnrs/3cnslts/12assts) The Financial Markets Group is led by *Paul Nelson* who is "strong on business development." Cover a full range of financial services. The group has extended its Blue Flag© advisory service by launching Blue Flag© UK providing English legal advice (through the Internet) to firms and banks conducting investment business in, into or from the UK. **Clients/Work:** Large number of leading investment firms and banks.

Cameron McKenna (4ptnrs/12assts) The "active" and "solid" *Simon Morris* is "well known" for his work on financial services, both non-contentious and enforcement work. The firm has a "respectable practice" which has "been active" and seen on a "lot of PIA type work." **Clients/ Work:** Advising 20 major product providers on fulfilling the requirements of the SIB/PIA pensions review, including representing three firms before IMRO/PIA Disciplinary Tribunals. Successfully handling five regulatory investigations for a major merchant bank and a life office. Acting for bidders for Albany Life.

Freshfields (16ptnrs – 10f/t 20assts p/t) A well respected practice. One regulator commented that the practice is "strong on banking side in terms of the relationship with the regulator" and that "relative strength in banking regulation gives an edge" in relation to the new regulatory framework changes being introduced. The "strong" *Guy Morton* heads the Financial Services Group. *Annabel Sykes* and *Anthony McWhirter* are the group's other leading individuals. **Clients/Work:** Acted for Merrill Lynch on its takeover of Mercury Asset Management. Advised the Bank of England on the implementation of the real time gross settlement system and other matters. Advised ISMA on its UK status.

Allen & Overy (6ptnrs/13assts) An established practice with experience in the regulatory field. The firm's strong banking and finance practice puts them in a good position to benefit from the regulatory changes as the Financial Services Authority becomes fully operational. *Paul Phillips* specialises. **Clients/ Work:** Advise regulators and regulated including banks, building societies, securities houses and insurance companies. Advising UBS on the merger between UBS and SBC Warburg. Advising Canadian Imperial Bank of Commerce on the regulatory aspects of the re-organisation of their UK business as a result of their merger with Royal Bank of Canada.

S J Berwin & Co (4ptnrs/4assts) Have a good reputation in the market including regulators "in both amount and quality." They "understand business." The widely known and respected *Charles Abrams* has an individual reputation and is "well regarded." He specialises in securities law and regulatory issues. The practice "stands out" and is a popular choice for conflict work. *Tamasin Little* also understands clients' business and is "commercially aware." **Clients/Work:** The UK end of the demerger of the proprietary derivatives trading group of First Marathon to form Maple Partners Financial Group Inc. Structuring digital deposit facilities for Banque Nationale de Paris p.l.c. Advising Gartmore Investment Limited (in conjunction with its in-house legal department) on the tendering arrangements and contract negotiations for the outsourcing of £32bn of global custody assets to Bank of New York.

Lovell White Durrant (8ptnrs/14assts) The securities and investments group advises on a range of regulatory and securities law issues. The non-contentious part of the practice covers transactional and pure compliance advice. Have a focus on funds work. "One of the broader and more impressive teams." The City litigation group has broad experience of regulatory matters and the conduct of disciplinary matters by regulators. *Richard Stones* "knows his stuff and is extremely nice to deal with." *Rachel Kent* ("good grasp of detail" with "sensible commercial judgement") has recently been appointed partner and enters our list of up and coming this year.

Norton Rose (6ptnrs/18assts) The team is co-ordinated on a cross departmental basis and covers non-contentious and contentious matters. Thought to be "making a great push" in the area. Leading individuals are *Tim Marsden* (non-contentious) and *James Bagge* (contentious) "who is trying to build practice" and is "flexible and practical in approach." **Clients/Work:** Appointed by Hambros Bank to report on the Bank's role in the abortive take over for the Co-operative Wholesale Society. Acted for Market Investigations Division of LIFFE on disciplinary matters. Advising major German bank on the implementation of the Second Banking Directive and Investment Services Directive in the UK and Germany and its effect on cross-border custody business and notification arrangements.

Simmons & Simmons (4ptnrs/10assts on non-contentious plus core litigation unit on contentious side of 4ptnrs/3assts) The practice has 2 dedicated teams, one on non-contentious and the other on contentious. *Richard Slater* has a good reputation particularly on funds related work. *Iain Cullen* was mentioned by both regulators and practitioners for his derivatives and funds related work and enters our lists of leading individuals. The contentious team advise the regulated on investigations. **Clients/Work:** Advised the Association of Payment Clearing Services in relation to the upgrading of the Central Gilts Office settlement system maintained by the Bank of England. Advised Cowen & Co on the establishment of investment banking and market making activities in the UK. Gerald Limited – advice and advocacy in connection with an appeal against certain penalties imposed by LIFFE.

Slaughter and May (8ptnrs/6assts) The firm has restructured its practice into a new Financial Regulation group to mirror the areas which are to be covered by the new Financial Services Authority. Janine Edge retired earlier this year and *Ruth Fox* heads the new group and "will step into the role well." Perceived to offer a "full service" but not seen as "specialists." However the new

structure of the group is a timely response to the regulatory changes taking place. **Clients/Work:** Advising Deutsche Morgan Grenfell on regulatory matters which arose in respect of investment funds managed by Peter Young.

Travers Smith Braithwaite (5ptnrs/5assts) *Margaret Chamberlain* maintains an excellent reputation for financial services work. Clients rated her highly..."advice is good...very available... practical and helpful." Leading practitioners said she was "good in private equity.....on wish list!" Seen to have done a good job on work generated by CRESTCo Limited's settlement system. *Rachel Ford*, a senior assistant, was recommended as an up and coming lawyer. **Clients/Work:** Advised CRESTCo Limited on a wide range of issues. Advised Woolwich plc on the establishment of the share dealing service put in place in connection with its flotation to enable shareholders to deal in Woolwich shares.

Wilde Sapte (4ptnrs/1asst) Suffered a setback with the departure of Richard Caird in-house to Commerz Bank. Continue to handle a mix of non-contentious compliance and disciplinary work mainly for financial institutions. **Clients/Work:** Advice to a number of SFA and IMRO members.

LEADERS' PROFILES · LONDON

ABRAMS, Charles
S J Berwin & Co, London
+44 (0)171 533 2222
Specialisation: Advises almost exclusively on securites law and regulatory issues including EC Directives, the marketing of investment funds, insider dealing and the disclosure of interests in shares, primarily to investment and private banks, venture capital fund managers, stockbrokers, and corporate finance houses. Has developed a niche specialisation in advising clients on how to reorganise group structures or activities to minimise regulation and financial resources requirements, often as a result of persuading regulators to agree with helpful interpretations of EC and UK rules. Co-author of a leading introductory text book on the Financial Services Act, "Guide to Financial Services Regulation" (CCH, 3rd Edition 1997) and contributor to "Bond Market Compliance" (IFR) for which he wrote an analysis of the FSA's money market exemption, "Futures Trading Law and Regulation" (Longmans) for which he wrote an analysis of customer categorisation rules

and "International Survey of Investment Advisor Regulation" (Kluwer 2nd Edition 1998) for which he wrote an analysis of UK regulatory law relevant to investment and fund managers. Member of the editorial advisory board of European Financial Services Law (Kluwer Law International). Writes and lectures frequently on regulatory issues. Is and was formerly a member of the CBI's City Regulatory Panel, and was formerly an arbitrator for SFA's Consumer Arbitration Scheme and a special adviser to IMRO on Venture Capital.
Prof. Memberships: Chartered Institute of Arbitrators.
Career: Qualified in 1976 with *Linklaters & Paines* and moved to *S J Berwin* in 1985. Became a partner in *S J Berwin* in 1988.

BAGGE, James
Norton Rose, London (0171) 283 6000
See under Fraud: Regulation and Investigation, p. 401

BARLOW, James
Clifford Chance, London (0171) 600 1000
Partner.
Specialisation: Principal area of practice encompasses collective investment schemes and financial services.

CHAMBERLAIN, Margaret
Travers Smith Braithwaite, London
(0171) 248 9133
Specialisation: Specialist in trading, clearance, settlement, investment management and custody issues. Part of team at *Travers Smith Braithwaite* which advised The Bank of England and CREST Co. Limited on the legal arrangements for the introduction of CREST and continues to advise CREST CO. Advises venture capital firms on the legal and regulatory requirements relevant to the establishment and management of funds.
Prof. Memberships: Chairman Regulatory Committee of the British Venture Capital Association and member of BVCA Council. Member of City of London Law Society Regulatory Working Party. Contributor to Tolley's Company Law and Palmer's Company Law. Chairman of sub-Committee Q6 (Settlement and Clearance), International Bar Association.
Career: Qualified September 1985. Partner *Travers Smith Braithwaite* 1991.
Personal: Educated at University College, Oxford. Married.

CULLEN, Iain
Simmons & Simmons, London
(0171) 628 2020
See under Investment Funds, p. 497

FORD, Rachel H.
Travers Smith Braithwaite, London
(0171) 248 9133
Specialisation: Specialises in advising financial institutions and pension fund trustees on regulatory, investment management, custody and securities trading issues.
Career: Trained at *Travers Smith Braithwaite*, qualifying there in 1992.
Personal: Born 1967. Educated at Sidney Sussex College, Cambridge.

FOX, Ruth M.
Slaughter and May, London (0171) 600 1200
Specialisation: Practice covers a wide range of commercial work, with an emphasis on banking

and capital markets, now focusing on financial regulations. Has acted extensively for banks and also for building societies, including in relation to conversions, and for corporate trustees.
Prof. Memberships: The Law Society.
Career: Qualified in 1979 with *Slaughter and May*. Became a Partner in 1986.
Personal: Born 3 October 1954. Educated at St Helena School Chesterfield and University College, London. Married with three sons. Lives in London and Hertfordshire.

HERRINGTON, Timothy
Clifford Chance, London (0171) 600 1000
Specialisation: Partner specialising in financial services, particularly investment management issues and the structuring, creating and marketing of investment funds of all kinds; securities trading and regulatory issues (including global custody stocklending and repos); mergers and acquisitions and other corporate work for the financial services industry.
Prof. Memberships: Chairman Law Society's Committee on Company Law; Vice Chairman Investment Fund's Committee of the International Bar Association.
Career: Articled *Clifford Chance*; qualified 1978; Partner *Clifford Chance* since 1985.
Personal: Born 1954; Queen Mary's Grammar School, Basingstoke; Bristol University (LLB, first class honours). Leisure: cricket, travel, walking, rare breeds, winc. Resides Sevenoaks.

KENT, Rachel
Lovell White Durrant, London
(0171) 236 0066
Specialisation: Corporate tax partner specialising in all aspects of busines tax including taxation implications of mergers, acquisitions and joint ventures (particularly cross-border), UK equipment leasing and property transactions and North Sea oil tax.
Prof. Memberships: Law Society, City of London Solicitors' Company.
Career: Articled *Lovell White & King* (now *Lovell White Durrant*; qualified 1980; partner 1986; specialised in UK corporate tax since qualification.

LITTLE, Tamasin
S J Berwin & Co, London
+44 (0)171 533 2222
Specialisation: Specialises in financial markets and regulatory matters including structuring derivatives, funds and other investment products and advising investment managers, banks, brokers, accountants and insurance companies on regulatory and related matters.
Prof. Memberships: City of London Law Society, International Bar Association, EASD Legal and Tax Committee.
Career: First class BA Jurisprudence, Oxford, LLM London School of Economics. Legal Associate seconded to the Bank of England's Legal Risk Review Committee 1991/2. Partner *Stephenson Harwood* 1992-1996. Partner *S J Berwin & Co* Securities Group 1996 to date.

MARSDEN, Tim
Norton Rose, London (0171) 283 6000
See under Investment Funds, p. 498

MCWHIRTER, Anthony
Freshfields, London (0171) 936 4000
See under Investment Funds, p. 498

MORRIS, Simon
Cameron McKenna, London
(0171) 367 3000
Partner in Financial Services Group.
Specialisation: Advises financial institutions on acquisitions, joint ventures, new funds and products, distribution and regulatory issues; and advises and represents institutions in their dealings with FSA regulators, including over 50 investigations and disciplinary cases. Author of 'Financial Services: Regulating Investment Business' (Second Edition, 1995). Chairman of eight annual conferences for IMRO and PIA members on compliance organised by IBC.
Prof. Memberships: Compliance Institute.
Career: Qualified in 1982, having joined *Cameron Markby* in 1980. Became a Partner in 1988.
Personal: Born 24th January 1958. Attended Cambridge University. Member of Council, London Topographical Society. Leisure interests include travel and cartography. Lives in Islington.

MORTON, Guy
Freshfields, London (0171) 936 4000
Specialisation: Specialises in banking and securities regulation, payment systems and trading law, repos and securities lending. He is particularly experienced within the banking, securities dealing, investment trading and insurance sectors.
Career: Became Partner in *Freshfields* in 1986. Corpus Christi College, Oxford.

NELSON, Paul M.
Linklaters, London (0171) 456 3766
Partner, Head of Financial Markets Group
Specialisation: Specialises in the regulations, applying to derivatives and other wholesale transactions of financial services institutions including investment banks, securities houses and insurance companies in the UK, Europe and internationally.
Prof. Memberships: Member of the Company Law Committee of The Law Society. Senior visiting fellow of Queen Mary College, London lecturing on securities regulation, (1993-95).

PHILLIPS, Paul
Allen & Overy, London (0171) 330 3000
Specialisation: His experience is in financial services and the regulatory field, including the Financial Services Act, Banking Act, SRO Rules – restrictions on marketing investments, prospectuses, advertisements, collective investment schemes, regulatory aspects of acquisitions, reorganisations, drafting and negotiating terms of business for investment activities, investment management, custody arrangements, advice on capital adequacy and conduct of business rules.
Career: MA Cambridge University (first class honours) 1982; Barrister 1983-87; admitted as a Solicitor 1988; Assistant Solicitor, *Allen & Overy* 1987-1994; Partner 1994.

SLATER, Richard E.H.
Simmons & Simmons, London
(0171) 628 2020
Partner in Corporate Department.
Specialisation: Corporate and regulatory work with a particular emphasis on the financial services industry. Work covers regulatory advice on the formation and promotion of investment vehicles of all types, the acquisition and disposal of financial services businesses and the reconstruction and merger of investment trust companies, unit trusts and other

investment entities. Transactional advice includes public and private company take-overs and acquisitions, joint ventures, initial share offerings and flotations.
Career: Qualified in 1977, after joining *Simmons & Simmons* as an articled clerk in 1975. Became a Partner in the Corporate Department in 1981.
Personal: Born 9th November 1950. Attended City University 1979-82, then Cambridge University 1982-84. Lives in London.

STONES, Richard
Lovell White Durrant, London
(0171) 236 0066

Specialisation: Advises financial services business, mostly on regulatory matters, the establishment and marketing of unit trusts and other investment funds and other legal issues affecting the industry. Has a general corporate and commercial training, and deals with corporate transactions involving businesses in his sector. Also advises a number of major pension funds on investment management issues. Has contributed to the CCH *Financial Services Reporter* and Securities Transactions in Europe. He speaks regularly at seminars on regulatory and investment fund topics.
Prof. Memberships: He is a member of the Securities Institute, and of the City of London

Law Society Regulatory Working Party.
Career: Joined *Lovell White & King* (now *Lovell White Durrant*) 1977; qualified 1980; Partner 1987.

SYKES, Annabel
Freshfields, London (0171) 936 4000
Specialisation: Partner dealing with regulatory and other issues for broker-dealers, asset managers and other institutions in the financial services and insurance sectors. Has advised Lloyd's on various regulatory matters including the admission of corporate capital and the recently completed reconstruction and renewal proposals.
Prof. Memberships: Law Society.
Career: Trinity College, Cambridge; University of Auckland.
Personal: Born 1961.

The SOUTH and WALES

Burges Salmon (Bristol) (3ptnrs/4assts) The practice focuses on compliance for IMRO members including general compliance for networks and product advice. Also do some enforcement work. **Clients/Work:** Product and compliance advice for Nationwide Building Society, J Rothchild Assurance and Hargreaves Lansdown plc.

Wansboroughs Willey Hargrave (Bristol) (2ptnrs) Do a mix of transactional and pure compliance work. **Clients/Work:** Advise ethical and other banks on regulatory and compliance work.

Davies and Partners (Gloucester) (2ptnrs/2assts) Act for networks and independent advisers. Provide pure compliance advice and transactional compliance advice on acquisitions and disposals.

Eversheds (Cardiff) Part of overall banking practice undertaking some FSA work. Involved in advice on FSA compliance and related issues. **Clients/Work:** Recent work has included advising NPI on specific product and Investec Bank on compliance issues.

MIDLANDS

Pinsent Curtis (Birmingham) (3ptnrs/4assts) Practice covers both non-contentious and contentious areas. Continue to have an

emphasis on pensions mis-selling litigation. **Clients/Work:** Represent the UK interests of New York Life International Inc. Ongoing advice in relation to corporate finance transactions. Advice to corporates on regulatory structure and FSA authorisation requirements.

Edge & Ellison (Birmingham) (3ptnrs/2assts) A practice "active in field" covering all the core areas of transactional advice, pure compliance advice and disciplinary work. **Clients/Work:** Advice to KPMG Corporate Finance, Williams de Bröc plc, Craig Middleton & Co Limited, Neilson Cobbalds Smith and Williamson plc.

Wragge & Co (Birmingham) (1ptnr/5assts) A "strong firm" with a Financial Services Unit providing advice on a mix of regulatory, compliance and product matters. **Clients/Work:** Advising on ISA Products and companies in relation to compliance, regulation and audit processes involving IMRO and PIA.

Blythe Liggins (Leamington Spa) (2ptnrs/1asst) The practice provides a range of general non-contentious compliance advice and does little contentious.

The NORTH

Addleshaw Booth & Co (Leeds) (2ptnrs p/t) Richard Garmon-Jones has left the firm

but market perception is that they are still active on financial services work particularly bearing in mind their client list. "Always will be strong in area … have good mix of financial and institutional clients." Principally provide general compliance advice and also transactional compliance advice. **Clients/Work:** Advising international insurance company on need to register under the Financial Services Act for UK activities. Advising UK brokers re pensions review. Advising UK institution re internet advertising.

Dickinson Dees (Newcastle-upon-Tyne) (3ptnrs/2assts) Offer transactional and pure compliance advice to clients. Also do some contentious financial services work advising

on regulatory matters. **Clients/Work:** Stockbrokers and investment managers.

Eversheds (Leeds/Manchester) (4ptnrs/1asst) An expanding team following the arrival of an ex-Wilde Sapte partner dealing with a mix of contentious and non-contentious matters. *Antony Gold* has a reputation for dealing with contentious financial services matters. **Clients/Work:** A mix of disciplinary and mainstream compliance work. Negotiated settlement for investors in the Second Greig Middleton Enterprise Zone Trust. Representing Trustee of the Concept Regional Portfolio.

Chaffe Street (Manchester) (1ptnr, assts as required from a pool of 5) A specialist commercial firm mainly involved with advising clients on pure compliance and transactional compliance. Do not do disciplinary work. *Chris Lumsden* is recommended. **Clients/Work:** Advising on terms of business for financial intermediaries; general compliance and regulation advice to clients.

Halliwell Landau (Manchester) Do not have a dedicated financial services team but provide advice within banking and corporate finance. **Clients/Work:** Stockbrokers and other financial intermediaries.

James Kendall (Leeds) (1ptnr) A new firm formed in 1997 by 2 in-house lawyers previously working with a venture capitalist. Provide pure compliance and transactional compliance advice. Advice in areas such as seeking authorisation under FSA in terms of law and process. *James ("Jim") Gervasio* is an IMRO compliance officer and is building a reputation for financial services work.

Malcolm Lynch (Leeds) (1ptnr) *Malcolm Lynch* has a non-contentious practice with a particular emphasis on unlisted securities issues and enterprise investment

scheme work where compliance advice is given in context. Also provides advice around growing new companies.

LEADING INDIVIDUALS
THE NORTH

GERVASIO James James Kendall	
GOLD Antony Eversheds	
LUMSDEN Christopher Chaffe Street	
LYNCH Malcolm Malcolm Lynch	

SCOTLAND

LEADING FIRMS · SCOTLAND

DUNDAS & WILSON CS Edinburgh
SHEPHERD & WEDDERBURN WS Edinburgh
TODS MURRAY WS Edinburgh
DICKSON MINTO WS Edinburgh
MACLAY MURRAY & SPENS Glasgow
MCGRIGOR DONALD Glasgow

Dundas & Wilson CS (Edinburgh) (3ptnrs/6assts) A leading financial services practice which is "strong in unit trusts and bank related" work. Deal with a spectrum of non-contentious and disciplinary work. Are striving to service the whole financial industry. Leading individuals are *Philip MacKay*, *Michael Polson* and *James Watt* who is quite significantly involved in this area. **Clients/Work:** Advising GA Unit Trust Managers on rationalisation of its unit trusts.

Shepherd & Wedderburn WS (Edinburgh) (2ptnrs/3assts) *Sue Inglis* has an excellent reputation with a range of clients. Provide pure and transactional compliance advice for fund management groups and life companies. Do not handle contentious side.

Clients/Work: Advising Ivory & Sime on its reverse takeover of FP Asset Management to create Friends Ivory & Sime (value £232 million). Advising Kleinwort Benson Private Bank and Scottish Life International on the launch of The Kleinwort Benson Private Investment Bond. Advising McInroy &Wood on the launch of various investment products, including its managed PEP.

Tods Murray WS (Edinburgh) (3ptnrs/2assts) Following the arrival of *Chris Athanas* have an increasing presence in the area of financial services. *Martin Thurston Smith* continues to have a good reputation in the market. **Clients/Work:** Acted for Bank of Scotland on the sale of its Corporate Trustee business to State Street Bank & Trust Co of Boston. Acted for Edinburgh Unit Trust Managers Ltd and for The Royal Bank of Scotland plc in connection with the disposal to Premier Fund Managers of Edinburgh Enterprise Fund. Acting for Clydesdale Bank PLC in connection with FSA regulatory issues affecting Waverley Unit Trust Management Limited.

Dickson Minto WS (Edinburgh) (3ptnrs/4f/t, 1p/t asst) The practice principally feeds off fund management side but is breaking into other areas. Provide transactional and pure compliance advice. *Bruce*

Minto is the best known individual in the firm handling financial services work. *Andrew Todd* is also well respected.

Maclay Murray & Spens (Glasgow) *Michael Livingston* leads the financial services practice.

McGrigor Donald (Glasgow) (1ptnr/2assts) A Glasgow firm with a financial services practice providing transactional and pure compliance advice including advice on marketing material. Limited involvement on disciplinary side. *Frank Doran* heads the practice. **Clients/Work:** Funds managers, life companies and banks.

LEADING INDIVIDUALS
SCOTLAND

ATHANAS Christopher Tods Murray WS	
INGLIS Sue Shepherd & Wedderburn WS	
MACKAY Philip Dundas & Wilson CS	
THURSTON SMITH Martin Tods Murray WS	
DORAN Frank McGrigor Donald	
LIVINGSTON Michael Maclay Murray & Spens	
MINTO Bruce Dickson Minto WS	
POLSON Michael Dundas & Wilson CS	
TODD Andrew Dickson Minto WS	
WATT James Dundas & Wilson CS	

LEADERS' PROFILES · REGIONS

ATHANAS, Christopher
Tods Murray WS, Edinburgh
(0131) 226 4771
See under Investment Funds, p. 497

DORAN, Frank
McGrigor Donald, Glasgow (0141) 248 6677
Specialisation: Advises on securities law and regulatory issues generally including compliance with SIB and SRO Rule books, insider dealing legislation, global custody and insurance regulations. Also involved in the development and marketing of retail financial products and establishment and management of investment funds.
Prof. Memberships: Member of the Law Society of Scotland Investor Protection Committee.
Career: Qualified in 1985 with *Maclay Murray & Spens* and then moved to *McGrigor Donald*. Became a partner in *McGrigor Donald* in 1991.

GERVASIO, James
James Kendall, Leeds (0113) 294 5059
Specialisation: Regulatory compliance, with particular reference to IMRO.
Prof. Memberships:
Member of the Securities Institute.
Career: BSc Econ. (Hons); LLB; IMRO Compliance Officer.
Personal: Married – two adult daughters. Walking, theatre.

GOLD, Antony
Eversheds, Manchester (0161) 832 6666
See under Litigation (Commercial), p. 530

INGLIS, Sue
Shepherd & Wedderburn WS, Edinburgh
(0131) 228 9900
Partner in Corporate Department.
Specialisation: Main areas of practice are

financial services, collective investment funds, investment products, listed securities (acting for both sponsors and investment funds) and corporate finance transactions for fund management and life insurance companies.
Career: Qualified and joined *Shepherd & Wedderburn* 1988. Partner 1993.
Personal: Born 13.08.1964.

LIVINGSTON, Michael B
Maclay Murray & Spens, Glasgow
(0141) 248 5011
mbl@maclaymurrayspens.co.uk
Specialisation: Partner specialising in corporate finance and financial services. Particular experience working with public companies and in the insurance sector. Has advised a number of public companies in connection with listings, rights issues and takeovers.

LEADERS' PROFILES • REGIONS continued

Career: Strathclyde University (LL.B First Class Hons 1979). After qualifying, spent 7 years working in corporate finance and asset finance with *Noble Grossart* and with Edinburgh Financial Trust. Corporate Director of Lilley plc (1990-1992). Joined *Maclay Murray & Spens* in 1992.
Personal: Born 1958.

LUMSDEN, Christopher
Chaffe Street, Manchester (0161) 236 5800
See under Banking, p. 146

LYNCH, Malcolm
Malcolm Lynch, Leeds (0113) 242 9600

MACKAY, Philip
Dundas & Wilson CS, Edinburgh
(0131) 228 8000
Specialisation: Partner in Banking and Finance Group specialising in retail financial services, banking, building society and insurance law. Also involved in company and information technology law. Main areas of practice are retail financial services, banking and insurance law acting mainly for insurance, banking and building society groups advising on joint ventures, new products, collective investment schemes and investment funds (particularly unit trusts, OEICs etc.) and compliance.
Prof. Memberships: Member of the Society of Writers to the Signet.
Career: Attended University of Edinburgh (LLB (Hons)). Articled *Dundas & Wilson CS*; qualified 1982; Partner since 1986.
Personal: Born 1957. Resides Edinburgh. Leisure interests include swimming, cycling and personal computing. Has also been recommended as a Leader in the field of Insurance and Reinsurance, Investment Funds and Building Societies.

MINTO, Bruce
Dickson Minto WS, Edinburgh
(0131) 225 4455
See under General Corporate Finance, p. 257

POLSON, Michael
Dundas & Wilson CS, Edinburgh
(0131) 228 8000
See under Investment Funds, p. 499

THURSTON SMITH, Martin
Tods Murray WS, Edinburgh (0131) 226 4771
See under Investment Funds, p. 499

TODD, Andrew G.
Dickson Minto WS, Edinburgh
(0131) 225 4455
See under Investment Funds, p. 499

WATT, James P.
Dundas & Wilson CS, Edinburgh
(0131) 228 8000
See under Investment Funds, p. 499

FRANCHISING

See also Intellectual Property

RESEARCH: In compiling the tables, we consider all the information available to us, paying particular regard to the market research carried out by our team of ten qualified lawyers. (The researchers' details are set out on page three.) The rankings, therefore, reflect the opinion of the marketplace as revealed by systematic and objective research: see page four. (Our research is audited every year by the British Market Research Bureau.)

OVERVIEW: The number of firms with a genuine franchising specialism has diminished. Firms which are listed act for franchisors or franchisee associations, and not simply for individual franchisees. True dedicated franchising departments are restricted to the leading London firms, and a select number of leading regional firms. The only addition to our lists is the new niche firm Chambers & Co in Norwich.

LEADING FIRMS · LONDON

EVERSHEDS

FIELD FISHER WATERHOUSE

DAVID BIGMORE & CO

HIGHLY REGARDED FIRMS

Peters & Peters

Taylor Joynson Garrett

LONDON

Eversheds Have led the field in franchising for some years. Particularly recommended for the quality of their advice and the strength in depth of their team, which is "the most well rounded in the sector." With Field Fisher Waterhouse they dominate the London franchising market, and also have broad international experience. The department is led by the "immensely experienced" *Martin Mendelsohn,* who has "phenomenal international contacts" and maintains a high professional and academic profile. **Clients/ Work:** Mainly franchisor clients. Structuring domestic and international franchise arrangements.

Field Fisher Waterhouse (3 ptnrs/13 assts) Newer to franchising than Eversheds, but are established as a "dedicated and growing" team which is respected for its national and international practice. *Mark Abell* is "knowledgeable and has genuine international experience." **Clients/Work:** Threshers; Sears Plc; Pizza Hut.

David Bigmore & Co (1 principal/2 assts) A niche franchising firm which offers a good service and has made "real strides in the last year." Their size limits their potential to undertake a wide range of work. *David Bigmore* ("knowledgeable and bright.") is a respected franchising specialist. **Clients/Work:** Setting up franchises in the UK for foreign clients (especially from the Far East and the US); advising on regulatory matters (eg Trading Schemes Act 1996); advising on global master licensing.

Peters & Peters (Can call on 11 ptnrs/7assts) Used to be major players in this area but now their profile is not so high. **Clients/Work:** Kinko's/Virgin Group joint venture; Cevdant Corp/Days Inn & Howard Johnson Hotels.

Taylor Joynson Garrett (3 ptnrs, 3 assts part-time) Have some respectable clients, but are not considered major players in the field. **Clients/Work:** Kentucky Fried Chicken; Toyota; Haagen-Dazs.

LEADING INDIVIDUALS · LONDON

ABELL Mark Field Fisher Waterhouse

MENDELSOHN Martin Eversheds

BIGMORE David David Bigmore & Co

SEE PROFILES AT END OF THIS SECTION

THE REGIONS

LEADING FIRMS · THE REGIONS

MUNDAYS Esher

OWEN WHITE Slough

PINSENT CURTIS Birmingham

BRODIES WS Edinburgh

COLEMANS Manchester

EVERSHEDS Newcastle upon Tyne

LEATHES PRIOR Norwich

WRAGGE & CO Birmingham

Mundays (Esher) (1 ptnr/3 assts) "Undoubtedly a leading firm in the regions," the franchising team includes *Manzoor Ishani,* who "knows franchising and has been doing it for years," and *Ray Walley.* **Clients/Work:** ELC; TDK; Clarks International.

Owen White (Slough) (5ptnrs/10assts) Renowned for their international experience. *Anton Bates* is widely known and respected; "does a lot of work but doesn't shout about it," and *Jane Masih* is also known. **Clients/Work:** Dyno-Rod case; Saks Hair and Beauty Salons; Humana.

Pinsent Curtis (Birmingham) (2 ptnrs/ 5assts) The national practice may be weakened by the departure of John Chambers from the Leeds office. *John Pratt* is now managing partner and may do less hands-on work, but he still has a high profile and a good reputation. **Clients/Work:** Carlton Cards; Bass Plc; Dollond & Aitchison.

Brodies WS (Edinburgh) (3 ptnrs/4 assts – all part time) Described as the "lead-ing Scottish firm." *Julian Voge* acts mainly for franchisees and associations. **Clients/Work:** ORRAF for the ScotRail Franchise (Apr 1997).

Colemans (Manchester) (2 ptnrs (one f/t one p/t, 1 asst p/t) Generally respected for high quality work. *Pauline Cowie* is highly rated for her "constructive and common sense approach." **Clients/Work:** Felicity Hat Hire; The Handwash; Russells Piano Cafes.

Eversheds (Newcastle Upon Tyne) (1 ptnr, 5 assts) Have experience of the international side of franchising and litigation, and are "very good at what they do." *Paul Heatherington* was in-house, "which gives him an edge and a wide perspective." **Clients/Work:** Prontaprint; Bang & Olufsen; Seattle Coffee Company.

Chambers & Co Norwich
Dundas & Wilson CS Edinburgh
Halliwell Landau Manchester
Lawrence Tucketts Bristol
Levy & McRae Glasgow
Wright, Johnston & Mackenzie Glasgow

Leathes Prior (Norwich) (2 ptnrs, 2assts) Have "a high profile in franchising," and are led by the "sensible and reasonable" *Jonathan Chadd*, who "handles his clients well," and is considered "good at franchising contracts." **Clients/Work:** Metal Supermarkets; Belvoir Property Mangement; Grinders Gourmet Coffee Ltd.

Wragge & Co (Birmingham) Team includes *Gordon Harris*. Have an outstanding IP practice, and are consistently good on franchising. Have an increasing amount of international work. **Clients/Work:** Rosemary Conley; Drinkwater; Finelist (Autela, Nationwide and Roaduser).

Chambers & Co (Norwich) (1 principal) Since leaving Pinsent Curtis, the "ambitious" *John Chambers* has established himself as a sole practitioner. He has "loyal clients," a "no-nonsense approach" and "gets things done." **Clients/Work:** Birthday Card Shops; Mailboxes; French Connection.

Dundas & Wilson CS (Edinburgh) Full services to franchisors and masterfranchisees. **Clients/Work:** Pierre Victoire; Toni & Guy; Scotwork International.

Halliwell Landau (Manchester) (1 ptnr/2 assts) The IP team perform franchising work when necessary. **Clients/Work:** Swinton Insurance; Pronuptia Young.

Lawrence Tucketts (Bristol) (1ptnr *Robin Staunton* spends 40% of his time and 1asst spending 60-70% of his time). Have set up 28 franchises. **Clients/ Work:** Local free newspaper and advertising magazine; company specialising in the sale and maintenance of agricultural parts and spares across England.

Levy & McRae (Glasgow) (1 ptnr, 1 cons) Have an established reputation for franchising work, and *Anthony Caplan* is admired for his "good practical advice."

BATES Anton Owen White
ISHANI Manzoor Mundays
PRATT John Pinsent Curtis

CHADD Jonathan Leathes Prior
CHAMBERS John Chambers & Co
COWIE Pauline Colemans Solicitors
HARRIS Gordon Wragge & Co
HEATHERINGTON Paul Eversheds
VOGE Julian Brodies WS

CAPLAN Anthony Levy & McRae
MASIH Jane Owen White
MCCRACKEN Kenneth Wright, Johnston & Mackenzie
STAUNTON Robin Lawrence Tucketts
WALLEY Ray Mundays

Wright, Johnston & Mackenzie (Glasgow) *Kenneth McCracken* is the contact although he is better known for his litigation expertise.

ABELL, P. Mark
Field Fisher Waterhouse, London
(0171) 481 4841
Partner heading the Intellectual Property Department.
Specialisation: Main areas of practice are franchising and licensing. Work covers negotiating, drafting and advising generally on international and domestic master, area and unit franchises, development agreements, concessions, subordinated equity arrangements, technology transfers, merchandising, endorsement and sponsorship. Advises the United Nations WIPO on the appropriate legal regime for franchising and trademark licensing and evaluation of I.P in developing countries. Other area of practice is the negotiating, drafting and advising generally on the distribution of branded products internationally and domestically. Acted in the Moosehead decision of the EC Commission, an important trademarks and anti-trust case. Author of 'The Franchise Option,' 'The International Franchise Option,' 'European Franchising- Law and Practice in the European Community Vol. I & II,' 'International Technology Transfer for Profit,' 'Franchising in India,' chapters in ten textbooks and over 300 articles on franchising, licensing and I.P. Expert adviser to WIPO. Visiting lecturer and external examiner at University of London. Lectures regularly in the USA, Japan, PRC and Europe. Editorial Board Member of Trade Mark World and Franchise Law and Business Review, I.P World and I.P Business.
Prof. Memberships: IFA, IBA, INTA, UIA, LES, Society of Franchising, British Franchise Association (BFA).
Career: Worked for Japanese company in Japan 1980-81. Qualified in 1984. Joined *Field Fisher Waterhouse* in 1985 and became a Partner in 1987.
Personal: Born 19th February 1957. Attended Southampton University 1975-78. Vice President of UIA's Franchise Commission. BFA Legal Committee Member. Leisure interests include Japanese and Chinese culture (Japanese speaker), scuba diving, keeping fit, opera, travelling and his family.

BATES, Anton B.
Owen White, Slough
(01753) 536846 Fax: (01753) 691360
Partner leading the Commercial Department.
Specialisation: Main area of practice is franchising. Legal Advisor to British Franchise Association since advising founder members and drafting constitution in 1977. Chairman of BFA legal committee and BFA representative on European Franchise Federation legal committee. Has advised scores of franchisors and franchisees including companies engaged in international franchising. Acts for many household names in the franchising industry. Author of many articles in various specialist magazines and newspapers. Organiser and speaker at numerous seminars in the UK (for the BFA) and abroad.
Prof. Memberships: Law Society, Chartered Institute of Arbitrators.
Career: Qualified in 1967. After 5 years as a Partner in a large city firm, joined *Owen White* as a Partner in 1973.

BIGMORE, David
David Bigmore & Co, London
(0171) 600 3191
Franchising Department.
Specialisation: Has specialised in franchising since 1986. Has acted for numerous international franchisors, domestic franchisors and large franchisee associations. Special Adviser to British Franchise Association on Trading Schemes Act 1996. DTI amended the Exclusions Regulations to cure two mistakes which David pointed out. Also handles mergers and acquisitions, joint ventures and corporate law, with twenty years experience of such work. Author of numerous articles. Other experience includes lecturing and conducting seminars.
Prof. Memberships: Law Society, BFA, Member of BFA's Legal Committee.
Career: Qualified in 1972. Set up *David Bigmore & Co.* in 1992.
Personal: Born 27th March 1948. Attended Merchant Taylor's School, Crosby, 1957-64, Bedford Modern School 1964-66, and Worcester College, Oxford, 1966-69. Leisure interests include squash and tennis. Lives in Wimbledon Village.

CAPLAN, Anthony M.
Levy & McRae, Glasgow (0141) 307 2311

CHADD, R. Jonathan
Leathes Prior, Norwich (01603) 610911

CHAMBERS, John
Chambers & Co, Norwich (01603) 616 155

COWIE, Pauline
Colemans Solicitors, Manchester
(0161) 236 5623
Specialisation: Head of Commercial Department. Provides wide ranging strategic corporate advice principally to entrepreneurs and owner-managed businesses. Franchising is increasingly predominant with advice given to both franchisors and franchisees on a national and more recently international basis. Has advised clients on over 150 franchise systems and developed a substantial computerised franchising database. A frequent contributor of articles on franchising and speaker at seminars on franchising.
Prof. Memberships: Law Society, Manchester Law Society, Affiliate member of the British Franchise Association, Solicitors European Group, Association of Women Solicitors, Secretary of Network North.

Career: Qualified in 1985 joining *Janet Scowcroft & Co* on qualification. Became a partner in 1988 and remained a partner on merging the practice with *Coleman & Co* to form *Colemans Solicitors* in 1991.
Personal: Born 1961, resides Wilmslow, married, two children.

HARRIS, Gordon D.
Wragge & Co, Birmingham (0121) 233 1000
See under Defamation, p. 283

HEATHERINGTON, Paul
Eversheds, Newcastle upon Tyne
(0191) 261 1661
Partner in Commercial Department since 1994.
Specialisation: Franchising. 18 years experience of work for franchisors. Involved in early expansion of Prontaprint, gaining experience in the myriad of issues relevant to rapid franchise expansion. Handles numerous transactions and contractual disputes in UK and internationally. Lectures in UK and abroad. Regularly contributes articles to press and periodicals.
Prof. Memberships: Law Society, BFA, IFA, IBA.
Career: Qualified 1980 (also admitted in Ireland and Northern Ireland). Director of Prontaprint Limited 1989-93.
Personal: Born 11th May 1948. Lives County Durham.

ISHANI, Manzoor G.K.
Mundays, Esher (01372) 809000
Partner and Head of Franchising Unit.
Specialisation: Principal area of practice (for over 20 years) in UK and international franchising, including franchise dispute resolution and joint ventures with overseas companies. Over past three years has helped UK companies franchise into more than 23 countries. Other main area of work is EC Competition Law. Has advised Clarks International, TDK, London International Group Plc, Prêt à Manger, Redland Roofing Systems, Ribbon Revival, Stagecoach Theatre Arts, Securicor Pony Express, Early Learning Centres, John Menzies [UK] Ltd, The Meteorological Office, Jigsaw and E. Moss Chemists (Alliance UniChem Plc). Regular columnist on legal and commercial aspects of franchising for Business Franchise Magazine, Franchise World and Business Money Magazine. Author of 'The European Community' (Fourmat Publishing [Tolley] 1992) and co-author of 'Franchising in the UK;' (Second Edition, Franchise World Publications 1989); 'Franchising in Europe' (Second Edition, Cassey Publications 1993); 'Franchising in Canada' (MacMillan Canada 1992); and 'The Business Franchise Guide-Franchise Handbook' (Seventh Edition, CGB Publishing 1994). European Contributing Editor. Advisory Editor: Journal of International Franchising and Distribution Law (1986-1991). Lectures frequently on legal and commercial aspects of franchising to businessmen, academics and lawyers worldwide and Legal Advisor to the Franchise Consultants Association.
Prof. Memberships: British Franchise Association (Legal Committee), International Bar Association (Franchise Committee – Section of Business Law), American Bar Association (Forum Committee on Franchising), International Association of Lawyers (Franchising Committee), International Association of Young Jurists (Working Commission on Franchising), Association of Swiss Arbitrators.
Career: Qualified 1976. Previously a Partner with City practice. Joined *Mundays* as a partner in 1992.
Personal: Born 6th October 1949. Attended St. Edmund's School Canterbury 1963-68, then the University of St. Andrews 1969-72. Leisure pursuits include classic cars, reading and jazz. Lives in Oxshott, Surrey.

MASIH, Jane
Owen White, Slough (01753) 536846
Partner in Company & Commercial Department.
Specialisation: Over ten years experience in drafting franchise agreements and advising franchisors in all aspects of franchising. In addition involved in commercial work related to the IT industry, advising on a broad range of commercial issues, including negotiating and drafting documentation. Has lecturing experience, addressing local interest groups, including the Chamber of Commerce.
Prof. Memberships: Law Society, Thames Valley Commercial Lawyers Association.
Career: Qualified in 1987, having joined *Owen White* in 1986. Became a Partner in 1989.

MCCRACKEN, Kenneth
Wright, Johnston & Mackenzie, Glasgow
(0141) 248 3434
Partner in Corporate Department.
Specialisation: Advising franchisors and franchisees on all aspects of franchising including developing the Scottish Market (in part through master franchiser and area development agreements). Also advises on agency, distribution and licensing agreements (including intellectual property).
Prof. Memberships: Law Society of Scotland, and member of British Franchise Association.
Career: Qualified in 1987. Joined *Wright, Johnston & Mackenzie* in 1990 and became a partner in 1995.
Personal: Born 1962. Lives in Glasgow.

MENDELSOHN, Martin
Eversheds, London (0171) 919 4500
Specialisation: Has 38 years experience of handling a wide range of commercial, corporate and international transactions. Has particular expertise in franchising, distribution, agency and licensing transactions, both domestic and international, as well as UK and EC competition law. Has been active in many parts of the world in providing support and assistance to Franchise Associations. Has twice visited Indonesia to advise its Government at the request of the ILO and UNDP as well as visiting Eastern Europe and countries at the request of the OECD to explain franchising to Government Departments. Led the *Eversheds* teams in advising the Russian Government in franchising under the Know How Fund. Visiting Professor of Franchising and Director of the Centre for Franchise Research at City University Business School. Visiting Professor of Franchising Middlesex University Business School where he has helped develop a post graduate diploma in franchise management. Member of the International Institution for the Unification of Private Law (UNIDROIT) study group on franchising. Member of the American Bar Association's Forum Committee on Franchising. Current publications include 'The Guide to Franchising' (5th edition), and 'How to Evaluate a Franchise' (6th edition) and 'The Ethics of Franchising' (2nd edition), 'How to Franchise Internationally' (2nd edition). He is also co-author of several publications, including 'How to Franchise your Business' (4th edition) 'Franchising and the Block Exemption Regulation' and 'Franchising.' Editor of the 'Journal of International Franchising and Distribution Law' and editor of and contributor to 'Franchising in Europe.' Legal consultant to the British Franchise Association. Assisted in the introduction of a franchising law course by Queen Mary & Westfield College, London University as a subject for the University's Master of Law Degree and lectures regularly there. Frequent lecturer at conferences and seminars world-wide. Regular contributor to journals and publications. Was first chairman of the International Franchising Committee of the International Bar Association.
Prof. Memberships: Fellow of the Chartered Institute of Arbitrators, Law Society, International Bar Association, American Bar Association.
Career: Qualified in 1959. Joined *Jaques & Lewis* (now *Eversheds*) as a partner in 1992.
Personal: Born 6th November 1935. Lives in Stanmore, Middlesex.

PRATT, John
Pinsent Curtis, Birmingham (0121) 200 1050
Managing Partner, Birmingham office.
Specialisation: Main area of practice is franchising. Drafts franchise agreements, advises on international franchising and prepares documentation. Expertise also in competition law including anti-trust compliance programmes, notifications and general advice. Has prepared franchise agreements for 100 UK franchisors including FT 100 companies. Author of 'Franchising Law & Practice,' and 'Franchising.' Contributor to "New Frontiers in Competition Law" and "Il Franchising Internazionale." Lectures in the UK and overseas.
Prof. Memberships: Law Society; Birmingham Law Society.
Career: Qualified in 1976. Worked at *Lovell White Durrant* from 1974-83, then *Needham & James* 1983-93. Joined *Pinsent & Co.* as a Partner in 1993. Previously Chairman of Young Solicitors of England and Wales.
Personal: Born 1951. Attended Dulwich College 1960-69; Oxford University 1969-72 and Université D'Aix-Marseille 1972-73. Interests include theatre, wine, food and sport.

STAUNTON, R.M.
Lawrence Tucketts, Bristol (0117) 929 5252
Specialisation: From a background in corporate work, especially business structures, Robin Staunton has now been involved in establishing or reorganising 28 franchised businesses, ranging from new retail concepts, to mobiles and service franchises, as well as manufacturing and 'wholesale' systems. A particular strength is practical advice to integrate the commercial objectives with the legal arrangements. Franchisee disputes are a growing area of work. Other areas: corporate finance, funerals and crematoria, high-tech and computers. Born 1957.

VOGE, Julian C.A.
Brodies WS, Edinburgh (0131) 228 3777
Partner 1987. Corporate Department.
Specialisation: Main areas of practice are corporate and contract law, including franchising and licensing. Author of chapters on

Scots law for 'Franchising Law and Practice'
and 'International Franchising Law.'
Prof. Memberships: Law Society of Scotland,
Writer to the Signet. Also admitted as a solicitor
in England and Wales.
Career: Qualified 1982. Articled at *Tods Murray*.
Then worked at *Brodies* and *Berwin Leighton*,
before re-joining *Brodies* as a Partner in 1987.
Personal: Born 3rd February 1958. Attended
Daniel Stewarts & Melville College 1964-76,
then University of Edinburgh 1976-80. Lives in
Edinburgh.

WALLEY, Ray D.
Mundays, Esher (01372) 809000
Partner and head of Intellectual Property
Department and Managing Partner.
Specialisation: Principal area of practice is
intellectual property, especially trade marks,
copyright, and software issues, including the
licensing and disposal of rights. Also
specialises in franchising, licensing and
distribution. Clients include E.Moss
Pharmacists, Unichem plc, ICS Identcode
Systems, Granger Telecom Plc, Photo-Me
International Plc, Renaissance Cosmetics Inc.,
Bluepoint Plc. and Yonex. Has conducted two
lecture tours of the U.S. under the title of
'Building a Bridge To The United States Of
Europe' and has spoken extensively at
conferences in the U.K. and in Europe.
Prof. Memberships: Member of Institute of
Directors, Chartered Institute of Bankers and
Licensing Executives Society.
Career: Qualified in 1976. Became a Partner in
Mundays in 1976 and Managing Partner in 1992.
Personal: Born 29th July 1944. Educated at
King Edward VII G.S., Sheffield 1956-62, and at
Durham University. Law Society Qualification
1972-76. At Lloyds Bank 1963-72. Leisure
interests include computing and walking. Lives
in Cobham, Surrey.

FRAUD

See also: Insolvency (e.g. wrongful trading and director's disqualification), Financial Services and Commercial Litigation (e.g. mareva injunctions and Anton Pillar orders).

RESEARCH: In compiling the tables, we consider all the information available to us, paying particular regard to the market research carried out by our team of ten qualified lawyers. (The researchers' details are set out on page three.) The rankings, therefore, reflect the opinion of the marketplace as revealed by systematic and objective research: see page four. (Our research is audited every year by the British Market Research Bureau.)

OVERVIEW: There are relatively few firms which have an established reputation for white collar fraud work. This will involve defending individuals and corporations facing prosecutions brought by the CPS, SFO, Customs & Excise or other bodies. Burton Copeland, Kingsley Napley and Peters & Peters remain the pre-eminent names in the field, and new firms in the table are Ralph Hume Garry and Oury & Colhoun. Outside London, Nelsons and Irwin Mitchell have had a good year and have risen in our rankings.

We have a separate London table for the regulation and investigation of fraud. This area of practice can be separate from the criminal justice system, for example when disciplinary proceedings are initiated by the DTI, the SFA or other regulatory bodies. This work is sometimes undertaken by the specialist fraud firms, but the strongest practices are the city firms which draw on their expertise in commercial matters.

LEADING FIRMS · LONDON GENERAL FRAUD

BURTON COPELAND
KINGSLEY NAPLEY
PETERS & PETERS

RUSSELL JONES & WALKER
SIMONS MUIRHEAD & BURTON

HIGHLY REGARDED FIRMS GENERAL FRAUD

Garstangs

Claude Hornby & Cox
Offenbach & Co
Oury Colhoun & Co
Ralph Hume Garry
Titmuss Sainer Dechert
Victor Lissack & Roscoe

LONDON

GENERAL FRAUD

Burton Copeland (8ptnrs/5assts) Have been successful since establishing a practice in London, and undertake both commercial fraud and regulatory work. "Quick thinking and straight to the point," *Ian Burton* is one of the most eminent large scale fraud practitioners, as is the "exceptional" *Jeffrey Bayes*. Other well known names at the firm include *Catherine Mather*, who has "great potential," *Karen Peacock* and *Harry Travers*. **Clients/Work:** Involved in the defence of Eagle Trust; Darius Guppy; Maxwell and BCCI.

Kingsley Napley (7ptnrs/7assts/6 fulltime) An established white collar fraud practice led by the experienced *John Clitheroe*. *Michael Caplan* is considered a "good operator" and *Christopher Murray* "good on strategy." The "tactically astute" *John Harding* is thought "very hard working and client orientated." *Stephen Pollard* is also recommended as a leading practitioner.

Clients/Work: Hill Samuel case; Sipra case; Investco money laundering case.

Peters & Peters (7ptnrs/5assts) Considered "tough in defence of their clients," they have been leaders in fraud for many years. "Canny" *Monty Raphael* is "the most phenomenal rainmaker," and "have no fear that he will get the right result." The "dedicated and tenacious" *Keith Oliver* is "aggressive but charming at the same time," and *Julia Balfour-Lynn* also takes the "direct approach." *David Corker* is considered "very bright," and *Louise Delahunty* "knows exactly what she's doing." *Michele O'Neill* and *Joanne Rickards* provide support for this established and impressive team. **Clients/ Work:** Defending Judge Gee; Hinchcliffe; Fininvest.

Russell Jones & Walker Known predominantly for their police work, but have been successful in penetrating the fraud market. *Rod Fletcher* brings valuable experience of the civil law to the department, and also recommended is *Scott Ingram*. **Clients/Work:** Maxwell 1 and 2 (for Trachtenberg), Barings and Butte Mining.

Simons Muirhead & Burton (4ptnrs/4assts) Have a well established and dedicated fraud team which includes the "responsive and constructive" *Anthony Burton*, *Brian Spiro*, and the "experienced and completely unflappable" *David Kirk*. The firm are recommended highly for fraud defence work, and are close to breaking into the top tier. **Clients/Work:** Defending Jamshid Hashemi; defending in British Bus/First National Bank of Boston corruption case; defending company director in first case under new insider dealing legislation.

Garstangs (2ptnrs/2assts) Have made in-roads into fraud in the capital having originally been based in the north. Seen as a "tough" law firm, and in particular *Richard Cornthwaite* is described as an "excellent fraud lawyer." **Clients/Work:** Defences of Neil Kelly; Robert Pollock and Colin Keyes.

Claude Hornby & Cox (2ptnrs/ 4assts) Good general crime firm which also performs significant and respected fraud work. Undertake both defendant work and assist on private prosecutions. **Clients/Work:** Largest ever mortgage fraud which involves 20 defendants; assisting individual in the Wickes investigation; investigation in relation to Etam.

Offenbach & Co Undertake general criminal defence work, and the "conscientious and hard working" *Bernard Carnell* is regarded as a leading fraud practitioner. Clients/Work: Large scale corruption and multi-million pound fraud cases. Act for company directors and financial institutions.

Oury Colhoun & Co (2ptnrs) *Aileen Colhoun* has established this new firm after leaving Magrath & Co, and is well known for her experience in big fraud cases. Clients/Work: White collar fraud; general criminal litigation; pro bono work on behalf of defendants facing the death penalty in the USA.

Ralph Hume & Garry (6ptnrs/3assts) *John Hume* left Titmuss Sainer Dechert to join the Ralph Garry Partnership. His "good sound judgement" makes him ideal for delicate City fraud matters. Clients/Work: Co-operative Wholesale Society v Regan & Lyons; Inland Revenue Inquiry following raids on Coopers & Lybrand; R v Philips & Schofield.

Titmuss Sainer Dechert (2ptnrs/8assts) Despite the loss of John Hume they maintain a general fraud practice. The "extremely highly regarded" *Matthew Frankland* focuses on criminal prosecutions,

and enters the list for the first time. Clients/Work: Revenue and Customs prosecutions; Jyske bank case; Launder case.

Victor Lissack & Roscoe A mixed practice. Also good on white collar crime.

Clients/Work: Specialise in both fraud and general crime, including mortgage fraud and Customs & Excise matters.

LEADING INDIVIDUALS • LONDON GENERAL FRAUD	
BURTON Ian Burton Copeland	**RAPHAEL Monty** Peters & Peters
CLITHEROE John Kingsley Napley	
BAYES Jeffrey Burton Copeland	**KIRK David** Simons Muirhead & Burton
BURTON Anthony Simons Muirhead & Burton	**MURRAY Christopher** Kingsley Napley
CAPLAN Michael Kingsley Napley	**OLIVER Keith** Peters & Peters
COLHOUN Aileen Oury Colhoun & Co	**POLLARD Stephen** Kingsley Napley
CORNTHWAITE Richard Garstangs	**SPIRO Brian** Simons Muirhead & Burton
BALFOUR-LYNN Julia Peters & Peters	**INGRAM Scott** Russell Jones & Walker
CARNELL Bernard Offenbach & Co	**MATHER Catherine** Burton Copeland
CORKER David Peters & Peters	**O'NEILL Michele** Peters & Peters
DELAHUNTY Louise Peters & Peters	**PEACOCK Karen** Burton Copeland
FLETCHER Rod Russell Jones & Walker	**RICKARDS Joanne** Peters & Peters
HARDING John Kingsley Napley	**TRAVERS Harry** Burton Copeland
HUME John Ralph Hume Garry	

UP AND COMING	
FRANKLAND Matthew Titmuss Sainer Dechert	

SEE PROFILES AT END OF THIS SECTION

LEADERS' PROFILES • LONDON (GENERAL FRAUD)

BALFOUR-LYNN, Julia M.
Peters & Peters, London (0171) 629 7991
Partner in Litigation Department.
Specialisation: Principal area of practice is business crime, encompassing major cases instituted by the SFO, Inland Revenue, Customs and Excise and other regulatory authorities involving fraud, tax and securities offences, Customs infractions and general financial regulatory problems. French Speaker.
Prof. Memberships: Law Society, The City of Westminster Law Society, Association Internationale des jeunes advocats (AIJA), International Bar Association
Career: Qualified 1984. Joined *Peters & Peters* in 1986 and became a Partner in 1988.
Personal: Graduated University College, London. Lives in London.

BAYES, Jeffrey
Burton Copeland, London (0171) 430 2277
Partner in Commercial Fraud Department.
Specialisation: Has over 35 years experience of general crime. For the last 20 years has specialised in the defence of fraud cases including SFO, DTI, Inland Revenue and VAT and extradition cases. Has handled cases with foreign elements, and advised local lawyers concerning criminal law and extradition in USA, Scotland, France, Cyprus, Israel, Egypt, Sweden, Malta etc. Author of various articles and book reviews in Law Society Gazette, New Law Journal and Solicitors Journal. Author of Criminal Law section of Law Society Directory of Expert Witnesses. Has made numerous radio and television appearances and lectured on criminal law – especially fraud.
Prof. Memberships: Law Society, London Criminal Courts Solicitors' Association (President 1989-90), Criminal Law Solicitors'

Association (Chairman 1990-91). British Academy of Forensic Sciences (Executive Council Member 1995-1998).
Career: Qualified 1963. Joined *Burton Copeland* as a Partner in 1991. Member of Law Society Criminal Law Committee since 1989-1997. Former Member of Number 13 (London East) Legal Aid Area Committee.
Personal: Attended St Paul's School and London University (LLB). Freeman of the City of London. Former Chairman of Holloway Prison Board of Visitors. Leisure interests include family, cricket and rugby, travel, book-shop browsing and book collecting. Lives in London.

BURTON, Anthony
Simons Muirhead & Burton, London (0171) 734 4499
Senior Partner.
Specialisation: Main area of practice is white collar crime and enquiries by investigatory or regulatory bodies: DTI, SFO, Customs and Excise and Inland Revenue. Also handles other criminal defence work and libel. Has written for law journals and national newspapers, and lectured on criminal law. He is also a regular broadcaster.
Prof. Memberships: Law Society, London Criminal Courts Solicitors Association and International Bar Association. Member of the Council of Justice.
Career: Qualified 1972, joining *Simons Muirhead & Burton* as Partner in 1976. Assistant Recorder.
Personal: Born 1947. Vice Chairman of the board of the Royal Court Theatre. Groucho Club.

BURTON, Ian
Burton Copeland, London
(0171) 430 2277 & (0161) 834 7374
Commercial Fraud Department.
Specialisation: All aspects of national and international white collar crime. Advising and representing both prior to and during investigation by bodies such as the DTI, SFO, Customs & Excise, and following charge. Extensive experience in major cases involving fraud, tax and Customs investigations including general financial regulatory problems, advising professionals facing disciplinary proceedings and cross jurisdictional cases.
Career: Qualified in 1972; Partner *Nigel Copeland Glickman & Co* (1971-1975); Partner *Gardner Burton* (1975-1982); founder and Senior Partner *Burton Copeland*.
Prof. Memberships: Law Society, London Criminal Courts Solicitors' Association.
Personal: Born 1947. Resides Cheshire and London.

CAPLAN, Michael
Kingsley Napley, London (0171) 814 1200
Partner in Criminal Litigation Department.
Specialisation: Work includes criminal law, advocacy, extradition, casino applications, gaming and licensing, and prosecuting for and advising professional and regulatory bodies. Sits as an Assistant Recorder. Rights of audience in the Crown Court. Advises TEN on Criminal Law. Secretary of the Solicitors Association of Higher Court Advocates
Career: Qualified in 1977. Joined *Kingsley Napley* in 1978 and became a Partner in 1982.
Personal: Born 3rd May 1953. Attended Kings College, London: LLB (Hons), AKC. Leisure interests include family, sport and reading. Lives in London.

CARNELL, Bernard
Offenbach & Co, London (0171) 434 9891
Senior Partner in Criminal Department.
Specialisation: Work includes commercial fraud, insider dealing, drug related crime, obscene publications and all areas of general crime. Particular experience of legal aid regulations and international and financial investigations. Acted in R v. Kellard and Others (Britannia Park Fraud trial, the longest in English history); BCCI Investigation; R v. Fisher (the first insider dealing trial); R v. Adelaja and Others (the first trial using computers); R v. Howard Marks and others (one of the largest and well-publicised drug cases); the inquest of Cynthia Jarrett (Tottenham riots); and R v Gay News Ltd and Lemon (Blasphemy trial) and numerous Divisional Court, Court of Appeal and House of Lords proceedings. Individual charge-out rate is usually £150-£180 per hour, depending on nature and seriousness of case.
Prof. Memberships: Law Society.
Career: Qualified in 1972. Joined *Offenbach & Co* in 1976, becoming a Partner in 1982.
Personal: Born 13th December 1947. Attended LSE (1966-69) and Law College. Lives in London. Former Board Director of Release.

CLITHEROE, John
Kingsley Napley, London (0171) 814 1200
Senior Partner.
Specialisation: Work covers white collar crime, international crime, tax and customs investigations and professional litigation. Also handles licensing and gaming. Author of 'Conducting a Criminal Defence', 'Criminal Risks in International Trade' and 'Data Protection in UK'. Recent major cases include Blue Arrow, Barlow Clowes, BCCI, Barings and Maxwell. Contributor to TV and radio on legal matters.
Prof. Memberships: Law Society, London Criminal Courts Solicitors Association (President 1992-1993), British Academy of Forensic Sciences, Chairman of the Criminal Law Committee of the International Bar Association, Chairman of the Editorial Board of the Journal of Criminal Law.
Career: Qualified in 1958. Joined *Kingsley Napley* in 1962, becoming a Partner in 1965 and Senior Partner in 1994. Past member of Law Society Standing Committee on Criminal Law; member of the International Bar Association Committee on Business Crime; member of Solicitors Disciplinary Tribunal.
Personal: Born 3rd June 1935. Attended Royal Grammar School, Guildford. Leisure interests include reading, opera, theatre, sport and travel; member of Athenaeum Club, RAC. Lives in Kingston-upon-Thames.

COLHOUN, Aileen
Oury Colhoun & Co, London
(0171) 629 8844
Partner specialising in criminal litigation.
Specialisation: Practice covers all areas of criminal work, particularly large scale white collar criminal defence work. Advises in investigations conducted by other regulatory bodies.
Prof. Memberships: Law Society, London Criminal Courts Solicitors Association, International Bar Association, British Academy of Forensic Scientists, Committee Member of City of Westmister Law Society and Chairman of its Criminal Law Sub-Committee, Justice.
Career: Qualified in 1983. Worked at *Kingsley*

Napley 1981-87, then *Powell Magrath & Spencer* 1987-90. Partner at *Magrath & Co.* 1990-97. Founding partner of *Oury Colhoun and Co* 1997.
Personal: Born 14th September 1957. Attended University of Bristol 1976-79 (LLB), then University of Cambridge (MPhil in Criminology 1979-80). Leisure interests include reading, cinema and live music. Lives in London.

CORKER, David
Peters & Peters, London (0171) 629 7991
Partner in white collar crime/general crime.
Specialisation: Dealing with all aspects of white collar crime and general crime. Acts for clients in a wide variety of criminal cases largely concerned with all aspects of national and international white collar crime. Experience includes arms to Iraq, public sector corruption, insolvency fraud, fraudulent trading, mortgage and investment frauds. Commended by Crown Court judges for trial preparation.
Prof. Memberships: Member of the British Academy of Forensic Sciences, the Law Society and the London Criminal Courts Solicitors Association.
Career: BA in Law from Oriel College Oxford MA in Socio-Legal studies from the University of Sheffield. Metropolitan Police Officer 1984 - 1987. Returned to law in 1987. Joined *Peters & Peters* in 1990, partner in 1996. Author 'Disclosure in Criminal Proceedings' (Sweet & Maxwell, 1997). Lectures widely on money laundering, disclosure and related issues.
Personal: Lives in London.

CORNTHWAITE, Richard
Garstangs, London (0171) 242 4324
Specialisation: Specialises in the defence of fraud cases, including SFO, Inland Revenue, Customs and Excise and D.T.I prosecutions. Also handles ancillary commercial litigation, particularly in relation to fraud and asset recovery in the Chancery Division. Acted in the Guinness, Eagle Trust, Thermastor and Brent Walker cases. Also secured the acquittal of Kevin Taylor in the 'Stalker Affair'. Recently represented a principal defendant in Chancery proceedings brought by Jyske Bank (Gibraltar) Limited. During last twelve months represented defendants acquitted in two cases prosecuted by Customs and Excise. Currently acting in Alpine Double Glazing and Richmond Oil & Gas PLC (SFO prosecutions) and three major Customs and Excise investigations.
Prof. Memberships: Law Society.
Career: Qualified in 1977. Joined *Garstangs* as a Partner in 1990.
Personal: Born 12th November, 1951. Keele University 1970-74. Lives in London and Manchester.

DELAHUNTY, Louise
Peters & Peters, London (0171) 629 7991
Partner in Litigation Department.
Specialisation: Has extensive experience in business crime including defence of major prosecutions instituted by the SFO, Customs and Excise, and the Department of Trade & Industry. International work includes extradition law and advice on proceedings in the European Union, the USA and the Far East. Has wide experience in civil and commercial litigation including jurisdictional disputes, contempt, employment and civil and commercial fraud.
Prof. Memberships: Law Society, The City of Westminister Law Society, Hong Kong Law

Society. London Criminal Courts Solicitors Association, International Bar Association and AIJA.
Career: Joined *Peters & Peters* in 1982 and qualified in 1984. Spent 4 years in Hong Kong between 1986 and 1990, practising in both criminal and commercial litigation. Returned to *Peters & Peters* in 1990 and became a Partner in 1991.

FLETCHER, Rod
Russell Jones & Walker, London
(0171) 837 2808
Partner and Head of Criminal and Business Investigations Department.
Specialisation: Main area of practice is criminal defence. Has particular involvement with white collar/ business crime and major miscarriage of justice cases. Also regularly instructed in disciplinary cases. Represents individuals attending a number of government and other public inquiries: examples include the Scott Inquiry and the Stephen Lawrence Inquiry. Acted in many miscarriage of justice cases, including the representation of the police officers prosecuted following the Birmingham Six, Guildford Four and Broadwater Farm investigations. Acted in the Maxwell, Barings and Bute Mining cases.
Prof. Memberships: Law Society, LCCSA, IBA
Career: Qualified in 1981. Worked with *Kingsley Napley*, 1979-83. Left to join *Russell Jones & Walker* in 1983, becoming a Partner in 1985.
Personal: Born 21st April 1957. Attended Berkhamstead School, then Birmingham University 1975-8. Leisure interests include sailing, golf, cricket and music. Lives in London.

FRANKLAND, Matthew
Titmuss Sainer Dechert, London
(0171) 583 5353
Partner in the Investigations Department.
Specialisation: Specialises in defence of national and international fraud/white collar crime cases, including those brought by the SFO, DTI, CPS, Inland Revenue and Customs & Excise. Particular experience of High Court confiscation and restraint proceedings. Also handles regulatory investigations by the FSA including those of IMRO, SFA and PIA. He has handled litigation arising from Criminal Law in the House of Lords and European Court of Human Rights. Also advises on investigations by professional institutes and insurers.
Prof. Memberships: Law Society, Criminal Law Solicitors' Association, Society of Practitioners of Insolvency.
Career: Qualified in September 1991. Joined *Titmuss Sainer Dechert* in 1995.
Personal: Born 1964, attended University of Wales, resides London and Lincoln. Leisure interests include sport, travel and art.

HARDING, John
Kingsley Napley, London (0171) 814 1200
Specialisation: Partner in Criminal Litigation Department dealing with white collar and general crime. Recent cases include SFO and Inland Revenue Investigations, European Leisure and International case work involving sanctions legislation and fraud.
Prof. Memberships: Law Society; LCCSA; CLSA; BAFS.
Career: Qualified in October 1988. Joined *Kingsley Napley* in 1990 and became a partner in 1994.
Personal: Born 9th April 1993. Educated at Derby School and Brunel University.

HUME, John
Ralph Hume Garry, London (0171) 831 3737
Specialisation: Partner specialising in corporate litigation civil and criminal with an emphasis on fraud related shareholder and partnership disputes. Experience encompasses international fraud actions, large white collar crime trials, takeover battles, post company acquisition claims, directors disqualification applications and commonwealth capital appeals. Represents professionals in all disciplinary regulatory inquiries, tribunals and criminal matters.
Prof. Memberships: Liveryman and member of the Court of the City of London Solicitors' Company, past Committee member of the London Litigation Solicitors' Association and member of London Criminal Courts Solicitors Association.. Solicitor Advocate Higher Courts (Civil).
Career: Qualified in 1970. Articled at *Titmuss Sainer & Webb*. Partner in 1973. Partner *Ralph Hume Garry* August 1997.
Personal: Born 1945. Educated at Cranleigh School and College of Law, Lancaster Gate. Interests include shooting, scuba diving, watching cricket, rugby, motor racing and collecting classic cars.

INGRAM, Scott
Russell Jones & Walker, London
(0171) 837 2808
Specialisation: White collar crime. Practice covers wide range including mortgage fraud, pensions, City insurance and full range of financial fraud. Represented client in Butte Mining S.F.O. prosecution. Involved in many 'High Profile' cases.
Prof. Memberships: International Bar Association, London Criminal Courts Solicitors Association.
Career: Qualified 1983. Trainee and post-qualification experience with *Wontner & Sons*, including prosecution work. Joined *Russell Jones & Walker* in 1986. Partner from 1990.
Personal: Born 8th August 1958. Educated at Warriston School, Dumfriesshire and Brunel University (LLB). Interests include golf, motor cycle racing and soccer. Married, lives in Wandsworth.

KIRK, David
Simons Muirhead & Burton, London
(0171) 734 4499
Partner in Criminal Department.
Specialisation: Commercial Fraud (including SFO, DTI, Inland Revenue and Customs & Excise investigations), Regulation, Investigations. Co-author of 'Serious Fraud – Investigation and Trial' (2nd Edition, Butterworths 1997).
Prof. Memberships: IBA.
Career: Qualified in 1989. Called to the Bar 1974. Worked at the office of the DPP 1976-85, and the Law Officers Department 1985-88. Partner at *Stephenson Harwood* 1989-94; joined *Simons Muirhead & Burton* as a Partner in 1994.
Personal: Born 1949. English Language & Literature MA (Hons) degree (Oxford, 1971). Lives in London.

MATHER, Catherine
Burton Copeland, London (0171) 430 2277
Specialisation: White collar and general crime.

Regulatory proceedings; involvement in following trials: Guinness, Blue Arrow, Nissan UK, Levitt, Maxwell.
Career: Assistant Solicitor at Metropolitan Police Solicitors Department; Senior Crown Prosecutor Inner London; Associate – Fraud and Regulation Unit, *Stephenson Harwood*. Joined *Burton Copeland* in 1994 and made Partner December 1995.

MURRAY, Christopher
Kingsley Napley, London (0171) 814 1200
Specialisation: Partner and head of the Criminal Litigation Department. Specialises in both white collar and general crime with a strong emphasis on the international aspects and pre-inquiry stages of this area. Particular expertise in money laundering, blackmail, corruption and fraud cases. Involved in many highly publicised cases including Maxwell, Polly Peck, Guinness, Banco Ambrosiano, Jeremy Thorpe, the Helen Smith Inquest, Ian Ball (Kidnap of H.R.H. Princess Anne) and the Simon Hayward case. Presented paper to American Bar Association, Orlando 1996 "Undercover Sting Operations: How to Protect Professionals – The UK Experience". Presented papers to International Bar Association, Berlin 1996 "Money Laundering – The Hidden Problems for UK Lawyers; /Delhi 1997 "The Role of the Civil Practitioner in a Civil Investigation"; Vienna 1998 "Mutual Assistance – Obtaining Evidence in the Absence of a Treaty". Speaks regularly at national and international conferences and writes on money laundering, lawyer confidentiality and international co-operation in white collar crime. Regular contributor to TV and radio on criminal law matters. Vice Patron Missing Persons Helpline. PUBLICATIONS New Law Journal September 1996 "Fair is Foul and Foul is Fair" – the implications of the Criminal Procedure & Investigations Act 1996. International Enforcement Law Reporter October 1996 "Undercover Sting Operations – How to Protect Professionals – The UK Experience". The Gazette January 1997 "Beware the Bill" – the threat to lawyer client confidentiality in the Police Act (1997). Currently co-writing a book on mutual assistance in criminal matters.
Prof. Memberships: London Criminal Courts Solicitors Association (LCCSA) (President 1997/8); LCCSA Committee on Payments to Witnesses; LCCSA Committee on Corruption; LCCSA Committee on Disclosure (Chairman); Law Society Criminal Law Committee, Author of Law Society Guidance on Conflicts of Interest; Law Society Criminal Law Sub Committee on Juries in Serious Fraud Trials. City of London Solicitor's Society (sub-committee on Judicial Appointments for City Solicitors) CLSA, IBA, British Academy of Forensic Sciences; Justice (Sub Committee on Serious Fraud).
Career: Qualified 1972. Partner at *Kingsley Napley* since 1974. Assistant Recorder of the Crown Court.
Personal: Educated at Kings College, Taunton 1961-65, and University College, London (LLB) 1966-69. Member of the Athenaeum and 2 Brydges Place. Leisure pursuits include music, theatre, modern art and design, 20th Century English literature. Born 6 November 1947.

O'NEILL, Michele
Peters & Peters, London (0171) 629 7991
Partner in white collar crime/general crime.
Specialisation: Dealing with all aspects of white collar crime and general crime. Involved in a number of high profile fraud cases brought about by the Serious Fraud Office, the Fraud Investigation Group, HM Customs and Excise, the Inland Revenue, the Department of Trade and Industry and as a result of investigations by the London Stock Exchange and other City regulatory authorities.
Prof. Memberships: Law Society, Westminster Law Society; London Criminal Courts Solicitors Association; International Association of Irish Lawyers; member of the London Legal Aid Board Area Committee.
Career: Qualified 1990; joined *Peters & Peters* 1990; Associate in 1993; Partner 1996.
Personal: Attended Sussex University. Lives in London.

OLIVER, Keith
Peters & Peters, London (0171) 629 7991
Partner in Business Crime and Commercial Litigation.
Specialisation: Main areas of expertise are business crime and civil and commercial litigation, from both a domestic and international perspective. Has extensive experience in business crime including defence of major prosecutions instituted by the Serious Fraud Office and other agencies. Among the best known are Anthony Parnes (one of the Guinness Four) and Kevin Maxwell. Has done considerable work involving the powers of the SFO and the privilege against self-incrimination both at Common Law and under insolvency legislation. Wide experience of DTI Companies Act and various regulatory enquiries. President of AIJA Business Crime Sub- committee. Lectures, and has delivered papers on insider trading, money laundering and abuse of process.
Prof. Memberships: Association Internationale de Jeunes Avocats (AIJA), IBA, Law Society, British Italian Law Association, London Criminal Courts Solicitors Association
Career: Qualified in 1980, having joined *Peters & Peters* in 1978. Became a Partner in 1983.
Personal: Lives in London.

PEACOCK, Karen
Burton Copeland, London (0171) 430 2277
Partner in Commercial Fraud Department.
Specialisation: All types of commercial fraud. Background in commercial litigation particularly banking. Defended in substantial SFO prosecutions including BCCI and the successful defence of George Walker.
Prof. Memberships: Law Society, LCCSA.
Career: Qualified 1990. At *Slaughter & May* 1988-1992; *McKennas* 1992-1993; *Harkavys* 1993-1994; *Burton Copeland* 1995.
Personal: Educated at Longsands College and London University.

POLLARD, Stephen
Kingsley Napley, London (0171) 814 1200
See under Fraud: Regulation and Investigation, p. 401

RAPHAEL, Monty
Peters & Peters, London (0171) 629 7991
Senior Partner.
Specialisation: Main area of practice is business crime and associated litigation.

Handles major cases involving fraud, tax and securities offences, customs infractions and general financial regulatory problems. Has specialised in commercial fraud for 30 years. Author of numerous articles and publications on the subject. Has spoken widely at conferences held by, among many others, the American Bar Association, American Bankers Association, American Society of Criminology, The Crown Agents, Commonwealth Secretariat, Jesus College, Cambridge, British-German Jurists Association, the Anglo-French Law Society and the Bank of England.
Prof. Memberships: Law Society, The City of Westminster Law Society, London Criminal Courts Solicitors' Association, British Academy of Forensic Science, International Bar Association, International Fiscal Association, International Association of Penal Law.
Career: Qualified 1962; has been a Senior Partner of *Peters & Peters* since 1983. In 1979 became the first Advocacy Training Officer appointed by the London Criminal Courts Solicitors' Association, (President 1982-84). Provided detailed written and oral evidence on the prosecution and trial of commercial fraud to the Roskill Committee and to the Royal Commission on Criminal Justice. Founder and past Chairman of the Business Crime Committee of the Section on Business Law of the International Bar Association. Served as a member of the Home Office Working Party advising on the proposed alterations to 'right to silence' in 1988-89. Chairman of the White Collar Crime Unit at the Liverpool Business School. Assisted the Council of Europe in its programme to help the emergent economies of Eastern Europe in their transition to a market economy. Has advised a number of offshore jurisdictions on money laundering measures. This year has been appointed Honorary Solicitor to the Howard League for Penal Reform.

Member ICAEW and Fraud Advisory Panel.
Personal: Lives in London.

RICKARDS, Joanne
Peters & Peters, London (0171) 629 7991
Partner in Business Crime Department.
Specialisation: Principal area of practice is white collar crime encompassing SFO, DTI, Customs and Excise and Inland Revenue cases. Has extensive experience in all types of investment fraud, also disciplinary and regulatory work with SRO's, the Joint Disciplinary Scheme of the Institute of Chartered Accountants and Solicitors' Complaints. She prepared the first case to make a successful application for dismissal under the Criminal Justice Act 1987 and has represented both suspects and witnesses in numerous s.2 inquiries. Also has experience of the banking tribunal of the Bank of England and a large part of her practice involves defending high profile clients in proceedings brought under the Company Directors Disqualification Act. She was mentioned in the '40 under 40' profile published by Legal Business in 1995.
Prof. Memberships: Law Society, International Bar Association, Westminster Law Society, Association Internationale des Jeunes Avocats (AIJA).
Career: Qualified in 1989 while at *Peters & Peters* and became a Partner in 1992.
Personal: Attended University College, London 1982-85 (LL.B Hons).
Lives in London.

SPIRO, Brian
Simons Muirhead & Burton, London (0171) 734 4499
Partner in Criminal Litigation Department.
Specialisation: Criminal defence litigation, specialising in business crime, drugs law and serious offences against the person. Also fraud investigation and international consultancy

work. Regular contributor to legal journals and broadcaster.
Prof. Memberships: Law Society, LCCSA, I.B.A, A.I..J.A.
Career: Qualified in 1984, having joined *Simons Muirhead & Burton* in 1982. Became Partner in 1986. Author of "Police Station Adviser's Index" (FT Law & Tax).
Personal: Born 1959. Educated at Manchester Grammar School 1969-76 and Nottingham University 1976-79.

TRAVERS, Harry
Burton Copeland, London (0171) 430 2277
Commercial Fraud Department
Specialisation: Partner specialising in all aspects of white-collar crime, often with an international element, including tax fraud, corruption, insolvency/banking/insurance fraud and money laundering. Also specialises in Lloyd's-related work, acting for professionals facing disciplinary proceedings, and directors' disqualifications. Acted for Darius Guppy, Dieter Abt, George Hendry (the European Leisure case), and Hisham Alwan (R v Allcock & Others). Disciplinary work has included acting for Derek Walker (Lloyd's Disciplinary Proceedings relating to Gooda Walker), and for barrister acquitted of professional charges arising from Cook Report. Currently acting in Bijan jewellery fraud case, and advising Victoria Aitken.
Career: Qualified as a barrister in 1986, a Solicitor in 1990. 1987-1991: *Berwin Leighton* Tax & Trusts Dept specialising in tax investigations/litigation/trusts. 1991 joined *Burton Copeland* Commercial Fraud Dept. Partner February 1995. Educated at Manchester Grammar School and St Edmund Hall, Oxford (BCL MA).
Prof. Memberships: LCCSA, BISLA.
Personal: Leisure interests include football, golf, languages and music.

REGULATION AND INVESTIGATION
··

Allen & Overy (3ptnrs in litigation) "Extremely impressive and professional" when dealing with fraud matters. Act for both prosecutors and defendants. **Clients/Work:** Acting in connection with criminal proceedings arising out of fraud perpetrated in Jersey and Sweden by a well known family of Swedish industrialists; acting for the News Corporation in the widely reported Clinger fraud case; acting for a member of a prominent Royal family.

Clifford Chance (4ptnrs/5assts) Possess a strong fraud team which includes *John Potts* and *Jeremy Sandelson*. The "hugely capable" *David Mayhew* is known for his own advocacy, and the department is strengthened by the return of the high profile *George Staple QC* from the SFO. **Clients/ Work:** Include governments, companies, banks and other financial and regulatory institutions.

Herbert Smith (3ptnrs) Considered "real crunchers for litigation," and also undertake regulatory work, *Philip Carrington*

"really fights for his clients." **Clients/ Work:** Acting for Codelco in the prosecutions arising from huge losses on the London and New York stock exchanges; Jyske Bank case; Acting for the American Endeavour Fund in complex litigation arising from fraud by pension fund managers.

Linklaters (2ptnrs/1asst) Elevated a place in the rankings on the basis of their impressive work for banks. A new entry to the list is *Alan Walls,* who is considered "good on the investigations side." **Clients/ Work:** Ernst & Young: BCCI litigation; Natwest Group

Norton Rose (1ptnr/4assts) A "high profile" City fraud practice which maintains its position in the top rank of firms. The "able and energetic" *James Bagge* is thought "sensible and easy to deal with." Mainly known for their work in financial services and banking, both prosecuting and defending. **Clients/Work:** Advice on the administration of MCC; acting in relation to a trust claim being litigated in Bermuda worth about $1.5 billion; involved in claims against an insurance company by the administration of Atlantic Computers.

Stephenson Harwood (11ptnrs/10assts) Maintain an excellent reputation in City fraud matters. The "impressive" *Anthony Woodcock* is "methodical and thorough," and a new entrant to the list of leading individuals is the "hugely experienced" *John Fordham*. Clients/Work: Defending large firm of accountants in a disciplinary matter; representing members of Hambros Bank in relation to an SFA inquiry; acting for the directors of a company threatened with censure by the London Stock Exchange.

Cameron McKenna (4ptnrs/8assts) Considered "good all-rounders" for regulatory matters and investigation of fraud. New to the list is the "solid" *Tony Marks* who is admired for his "quiet and constructive approach." Clients/Work: Investigation of banking fraud; asset tracing; defending individuals on disciplinary tribunals.

Kingsley Napley (1 specialist partner plus the general fraud team) Well known for their defence work in high profile cases, they also maintain a reputation for regulation and investigative work. *Stephen Pollard* is respected by colleagues because he "plays straight." Clients/Work: Henry Sweetbaum (Wickes investigation); Erik Langaker (Morgan Grenfell case); Michael Palmer (Hashemi case).

Lovell White Durrant The civil fraud team acts for companies and liquidators. Have been elevated a place in the rankings on the recommendations of several competitors. Clients/Work: Multi-jurisdictional criminal proceedings; debt recovery and asset tracing; BCCI litigation.

MacFarlanes *Paul Phippen* "looks after his clients well" and is thought of as a "safe pair of hands with lots of experience." Look after both individuals and institutions on civil fraud matters. Clients/Work: Tracing, freezing and recovery of assets; advising prosecution witnesses in relation to SFO prosecutions.

Peters & Peters (5ptnrs/4assts) Well respected for their work on tax investigations as well as representing individuals facing investigations on regulatory matters. *Monty Raphael* in particular is recognised as a leader in this field. Clients/Work: Atlantic Computers Plc case; Young case; large IR Special Compliance Office investigations.

Simmons & Simmons The banking and financial services litigation group acts for defendant organisations, and are considered very good. *Paul Li* is recommended. Clients/Work: Focus is on regulatory investigations by regulatory bodies such as the SIB, as well as commercial fraud litigation.

Slaughter and May Regulatory and investigation work is performed by the Litigation and Arbitration team. The "tough and impressive" *Elizabeth Barrett* is experienced in disciplinary investigations. Clients/Work: Deutsche Morgan Grenfell; Hambros; major roles in Guinness and Blue Arrow inquiries.

Titmuss Sainer Dechert (2ptnrs/8assts) Although the firm has lost John Hume, they have expanded their fraud investigations team. *David Byrne* is recommended. Clients/Work: Advised on aspects of SFO prosecutions, including Brent Walker, Guinness, Barlow Clowes and Blue Arrow.

SJ Berwin (3ptnrs/5assts) A firm with a strong reputation in banking and finance. Offers regulatory advice to a range of corporate clients. Clients/Work: New leading case on the privilege against self-incrimination in the Court of Appeal which may necessitate changes to Anton Pillar Orders; Trustor v Lord Moyne & Others; Prince Mohammed Bin Fahd v Sayed Ayas & Others.

Denton Hall (3ptnrs/2assts) Clients/Work: Acting for the pension funds of Chrysler (Canada) Ltd; acting for a UK bank in relation to transactions concerning the Bank of England; acting for the Official Receiver in relation to illegal snowball schemes including Titan and One Life.

DJ Freeman (4ptnrs/4assts) A well respected practice offering regulatory advice on the back of their insolvency work. Clients/Work: Acted for the receivers of De Lorean Motor Cars; litigation arising from the BCCI liquidation; currently acting in relation to international money laundering investigation by a foreign government.

Eversheds Defend individuals and organisations on investigative matters. Clients/Work: Acting for Lloyds Underwriters.

Jeffrey Russell Green (3ptnrs/1asst) The firm draws on the experience of the property and commercial departments. Clients/Work: White collar fraud, regulatory, income tax and VAT investigations, in both the courts and in the tribunals. Actions against the SFO and IR.

Memery Crystal A niche corporate and property firm which performs fraud work from the commercial litigation department. Clients/Work: Criminal prosecutions and regulatory proceedings.

Richards Butler (5ptnrs/2assts) Do regulatory work as part of as general commercial and finance practice. Clients/Work: Dealing with UK prosecuting authorities and regulators concerning Sumitomo copper trading; involved in SFO investigation and litigation arising from the acts of Maxwell fund management companies; involved in proceedings arising from the collapse in Canada of the Castot group.

Theodore Goddard (2ptnrs/4assts) Undertake regulatory fraud work and asset recovery, with a focus on the banking and securities sector. Clients/Work: Recoveries on behalf of the 1986 Noteholders in the fraud on Barings by Nick Leeson; defending a client in fraud allegations made against it by a local authority and dealing with the police inquiry; acting for one of the defendants in the Normaco metal trading claims.

Wilde Sapte (3ptnrs/4assts) The recent departure of Richard Caird (in-house) will affect the profile and status of the commercial litigation practice, but the firm maintains a reputation in general civil fraud. Clients/Work: Deals with investigations and contested cases of fraud in all its manifestations.

Graeme Brister of Pinsent Curtis was also recommended.

BAGGE, James

Norton Rose, London (0171) 283 6000
Partner in Commercial Litigation Department.
Specialisation: Practice focuses on fraud and
the regulation of investment and banking
business, in particular advising on all forms of
investigations, statutory or private, and
associated legal proceedings involving the SFO,
DTI, SRO and Revenue authorities. Advised the
Board of Banking Supervision on the Barings
inquiry. Has acted for LIFFE in relation to market
investigations and enforcement actions.
Conducted the Banking Act inquiry into
Hambros involvement with the aborted bid for
the Co-operative Wholesale Society.
Prof. Memberships: International Bar
Association.
Career: Qualified 1979. Spent eight years at the
Criminal Bar and two years on secondment to
the Serious Fraud Office. Joined *Norton Rose* in
1990 and became a Partner in 1993.

BARRETT, Elizabeth A.

Slaughter and May, London (0171) 600 1200
Partner in Litigation Department.
Specialisation: Principal area of practice is
commercial litigation (including defamation) with
particular emphasis on civil and commercial
fraud and corporate crime, and extensive
experience of a broad range of statutory regulatory
and disciplinary investigations and enquiries.
Prof. Memberships: The Law Society.
Career: Qualified 1981. Partner *Peter Carter-
Ruck and Partners* 1982-1986. Joined *Slaughter
and May* 1986; Partner 1989.
Personal: Born 23 November 1956. Attended
University College, London (LLB Hons 1978).

BRISTER, Graeme

Pinsent Curtis, London (0171) 418 7000
Partner in Litigation Department.
Specialisation: Specialises in banking and
financial services. Advises leading investment
banks, commercial banks, securities houses
and insurance companies on litigation,
regulatory investigations and other contentious
problems. He has acted on many of the leading
financial services regulatory matters over the
last five years. Fourteen years working in the
Middle East acting for Middle East institutions
and US/European banks. Eighteen years'
experience working in US litigation including
negotiating the settlement of anti-trust litigation
and class actions for a major airline.
Career: Qualified 1979 at *Linklaters & Paines*,
becoming a Partner in 1985. Became Managing
Partner, *Pinsent Curtis*, London in 1997.

BYRNE, David

Titmuss Sainer Dechert, London
(0171) 583 5353
Partner and head of the Investigations Department.
Specialisation: Responsible for all aspects of
investigation work ranging from disciplinary
hearings and insurance disputes to serious fraud.
He specialises in civil and criminal commercial
fraud for both plaintiff and defendant. In particular,
he has specialised in cases brought by the SFO,
City regulators, Inland Revenue and Customs &
Excise. He has acted for clients involved directly
and indirectly in Barlow Clowes, BCCI, Resort
Hotels, Polly Peck, Guinness, Blue Arrow, Leyland
Daf and Hare Wines. He has acted for the only
successful defendant in the recent Jyske Bank

case in the Chancery Division. He also deals with
investigations arising from Insolvency matters.
Prof. Memberships: Law Society, Society
Practitioners of Insolvency.
Career: Qualified in 1978. Articled at *Norton
Rose*. Solicitor *Norton Rose* 1978-1983. *Clifford
Turner* (now *Clifford Chance*) 1983-1985. Partner
Titmuss Sainer & Webb (now *Titmuss Sainer
Dechert*) since 1987.
Personal: Born 1951. Attended Kings College
London, Masters degree in insurance law,
Sweet & Maxwell prize for company law.
Interests include golf and fell walking.

CARRINGTON, Philip

Herbert Smith, London (0171) 374 8000
Partner in Litigation and Arbitration Department.
Specialisation: Specialises in commercial
litigation including corporate and securities
related fraud and insolvency. Also handles
regulatory work and investigations and
professional negligence.
Career: Qualified 1982. Partner at *Herbert
Smith* since 1989.

FORDHAM, John

Stephenson Harwood, London
(0171) 329 4422
Specialisation: Principal areas of litigation and
arbitration experience; banking, insolvency,
corporate and commercial – fraud investigations
and asset-tracing – cross-border disputes.
Career: Qualified 1974. Partner 1979. Head of
Litigation 1995.
Personal: Born 1948. Education: Dulwich
College and Gonville & Caius College,
Cambridge (First Class degree, Law). Good
French. Cricket.

LI, Paul

Simmons & Simmons, London
(0171) 628 2020
Specialisation: Banking and financial services
litigation, Companies Act investigations and
financial services regulatory enforcement and
disciplinary proceedings.

MARKS, A.L.

Cameron McKenna, London
(0171) 367 3000
Partner in Litigation and Dispute Management
Group.
Specialisation: Litigation involving financial
services, banking, pensions and accountants;
representation of parties before disciplinary
tribunals, including Exchanges, financial
services regulators, ICAEW; conduct of
investigations into fraud and regulatory matters;
Companies Act investigations. Recent cases
include investigation of British Biotech share
dealings, Belling pension fund litigation, private
prosecution by Camelot Group plc of William
Hill, Ladbroke and Coral.
Prof. Memberships: The City of London Law
Society Litigation Sub-Committee; Committee
member of The London Solicitors Litigation
Association.
Career: Qualified 1975; *Clifford-Turner* from
1973 to 1979; Joined *McKenna & Co* in 1979;
Partner 1983.
Personal: Born 1949. Bristol University LLB.
Interests include cricket, golf, sailing and opera.
Lives in London.

MAYHEW, David

Clifford Chance, London (0171) 600 1000
Specialisation: Complex disputes and
investigations in the financial services sector. A
solicitor advocate entitled to appear in all forums
in civil proceedings. Appears as advocate
before regulatory tribunals, both for and against
regulators, and as adviser to various disciplinary
panels in the financial futures markets.
Career: Qualified in 1976 (New Zealand) and
1983 (England); Partner in 1987. Responsible
for managing the firm's Advocacy Unit and its
complete service initiative.

PHIPPEN, Paul

Macfarlanes, London (0171) 831 9222
Specialisation: Partner with a broad
commercial litigation practice and a particular
specialty in City regulatory fraud and DTI inquiries.
Prof. Memberships: City of London Law
Society Litigation Sub-committee.
Career: Exeter University LLB 1979. Qualified
1982. Partner *Macfarlanes* 1989.
Personal: Born 1957.

POLLARD, Stephen

Kingsley Napley, London (0171) 814 1200
Partner in Criminal and Regulatory Department.
Specialisation: Practice covers all criminal
work, but particularly white collar fraud and 'city
crime'. Also handles regulatory work including
disciplinary proceedings before the Self-
Regulating Organisations. Acted for Lou Macari
in the revenue prosecution of Swindon Town FC,
and in the SFO prosecution of the directors of
DPR Futures. Currently represents Nick Leeson,
the ex-Barings trader and parties in the
Deutsche Morgan Grenfell and Hambros
enquiries. Appears regularly on TV and radio on
criminal law matters.
Prof. Memberships: AIJA, London Criminal
Courts Solicitors' Association, City of London
Solicitors.
Career: Qualified 1985. Worked at *Payne Hicks
Beach* 1982-87, including 1984-5 as a Member
of Secretariat of the European Commission of
Human Rights, Strasbourg. One year with the
Crown Prosecution Service 1987-88. Joined
Kingsley Napley in 1989, becoming a Partner in
1990.
Personal: Born 5th September 1958. Attended
Manchester Grammar School 1972-77, and
Pembroke College, Oxford 1977-80. Leisure
interests include reading, sport, theatre and
family. Lives in Putney, London. Married with
three children.

POTTS, John

Clifford Chance, London (0171) 600 1000
Lead Partner. Corporate/Commercial Litigation
Group.
Specialisation: All aspects of
corporate/contract litigation. Specialises in SFA
Regulatory Investigations and Tribunals, Fraud
and White Collar Crime.
Career: Qualified 1982. Partner 1987.
Personal: BSc (Hons) Man. 1968.

RAPHAEL, Monty

Peters & Peters, London (0171) 629 7991
Senior Partner.
Specialisation: Main area of practice is
business crime and associated litigation. Handles
major cases involving fraud, tax and securities

offences, customs infractions and general financial regulatory problems. Has specialised in commercial fraud for 30 years. Author of numerous articles and publications on the subject. Has spoken widely at conferences held by, among many others, the American Bar Association, American Bankers Association, American Society of Criminology, The Crown Agents, Commonwealth Secretariat, Jesus College, Cambridge, British-German Jurists Association, the Anglo-French Law Society and the Bank of England.
Prof. Memberships: Law Society, The City of Westminster Law Society, London Criminal Courts Solicitors' Association, British Academy of Forensic Science, International Bar Association, International Fiscal Association, International Association of Penal Law.
Career: Qualified 1962; has been a Senior Partner of *Peters & Peters* since 1983. In 1979 became the first Advocacy Training Officer appointed by the London Criminal Courts Solicitors' Association, (President 1982-84). Provided detailed written and oral evidence on the prosecution and trial of commercial fraud to the Roskill Committee and to the Royal Commission on Criminal Justice. Founder and past Chairman of the Business Crime Committee of the Section on Business Law of the International Bar Association. Served as a member of the Home Office Working Party advising on the proposed alterations to 'right to silence' in 1988-89. Chairman of the White Collar Crime Unit at the Liverpool Business School. Assisted the Council of Europe in its programme to help the

emergent economies of Eastern Europe in their transition to a market economy. Has advised a number of offshore jurisdictions on money laundering measures. This year has been appointed Honorary Solicitor to the Howard League for Penal Reform. Member ICAEW and Fraud Advisory Panel.
Personal: Lives in London.

SANDELSON, Jeremy
Clifford Chance, London (0171) 600 1000
Partner.
Specialisation: Principal area of practice is Commercial litigation, concentrating on fraud and international commercial litigation. In addition, long experience of corporate litigation with particular emphasis on disputes following public and private company acquisitions. Recently involved in a number of Regulatory disputes.
Career: MA (Cantab) 1978. Qualified 1981. Partner Clifford Chance 1987. 1990/2 Secretary: Takeovers and Mergers Panel.

STAPLE, George
Clifford Chance, London (0171) 600 1000
Specialisation: Investigation of regulatory breach and criminal conduct in the field of financial services. Proceedings before regulatory Tribunals.
Career: Qualified 1964. Q.C. (Hon) 1997. DTI Inspector Consolidated Gold Fields plc 1986, Aldermanbury Trust plc 1988, Director of Serious Fraud Office 1992-1997, Partner *Clifford Chance* 1967 to 1992 and from 1997.

WALLS, W.Alan
Linklaters, London (0171) 456 4258
Specialisation: Partner dealing with commercial litigation, principally banking and insolvency, but encompassing regulatory work, investigations, industrial relations, employment issues and other types of commercial dispute.

WOODCOCK, Anthony
Stephenson Harwood, London
(0171) 329 4422
Partner and Head of Fraud and Regulation Unit.
Specialisation: Main area of practice is white collar crime and business and professional regulation, including fraud, insider dealing, and prosecuting and defending before professional disciplinary tribunals. Also deals with financial and professional investigations, conducting investigations for regulatory bodies in financial services, accounting and insolvency. Co-author of 'Serious Fraud: Investigation and Trial' (Butterworths). Speaker at conferences. Regular television appearances in relation to fraud and regulatory issues.
Career: Called to the Bar 1976. At the Office of the DPP 1979-85 and the Office of the Treasury Solicitor 1985-87. With *Slaughter and May* 1987-90. Requalified 1989. Joined *Stephenson Harwood* 1990.
Personal: Born 1954. Educated at University College, London 1972-75. School Governor; Chairman of Education Act Appeal Committee. Interests include reading, cycling, running, swimming and music.

The SOUTH and WALES

HIGHLY REGARDED FIRMS
SOUTH AND WALES

Blake Lapthorn Fareham

Bobbetts Mackan Bristol
Donne Mileham & Haddock Brighton
Martin Prowel, Edwards & Davies Cardiff

Cartwrights Bristol
Gamlins Rhyl
Huttons Cardiff
Leo Abse & Cohen Cardiff
Wolferstans Plymouth
Woollcombe Beer Watts Newton Abbot

Blake Lapthorn (Fareham) (2ptnrs/1asst) Are considered "excellent on tax fraud," and *John Mitchell* is recommended from the firm. **Clients/Work:** Defence of individuals and companies; also have expertise in relation to tachograph fraud, mortgage fraud and health and safety prosecutions.

Bobbetts Mackan (Bristol) (1ptnr/ 5assts) Possess a "substantial practice," and "know what they are doing" with regulatory and fraud matters.

Donne Mileham & Haddock (Brighton) (3ptnrs) *Roger Hartwell* does the commercial fraud work for the firm. **Clients/Work:** White collar crime, specialising in regulatory defences relating to the environment, building, health and safety.

Martyn Prowel, Edwards & Davies (Cardiff) (5ptnrs/4assts) Highly regarded for fraud in South Wales, and have been promoted a place in the tables this year. *Martyn Prowel* is a "well respected advocate and lawyer who does hard fraud cases." **Clients/Work:** Defence in 14 defendant VAT cases; number of high profile trials.

Cartwrights (Bristol) (1ptnr/2assts) Not considered a major player in this field, but do have a reputation for doing some disciplinary work. **Clients/Work:** White collar and corporate fraud.

Gamlins (Rhyl) *Gwyn Jones* is recommended for his general fraud practice. The firm does commercial fraud work and blue collar fraud. **Clients/Work:** Full range of criminal fraud, including VAT, credit card and mortgage fraud.

Huttons (Cardiff) A small local practice with emphasis on crime and civil litigation.

Leo Abse & Cohen (Cardiff) (1ptnr/ 3assts) Have a specialism in corporate crime

and VAT investigations, and offer in-house advocacy expertise. **Clients/Work:** International insurance fraud involving top six City institutions; inter-company fraud involving £1.3m; solicitor fraud of over £1m.

Wolferstans (Plymouth) (1ptnr/2assts) A respected local practice. *David Gabbitass* has a high profile and undertakes his own advocacy. **Clients/Work:** Commercial crime, including forgery and false accounting. Undertake DTI prosecutions in relation to bankruptcy and insolvency.

Woollcombe Beer Watts (Newton Abbot) (5ptnrs/ 5assts) Act mainly for company directors and professionals. **Clients/Work:** Fata Morgan and Jazz cases (undercover Customs operations involving millions of pounds worth of drugs).

LEADING INDIVIDUALS
SOUTH AND WALES

GABBITASS David Wolferstans
HARTWELL Roger Donne Mileham & Haddock
JONES Gwyn Gamlins
MITCHELL John Blake Lapthorn
PROWEL Martyn Martin Prowel, Edwards & Davies

SEE PROFILES AT END OF THIS SECTION

MIDLANDS

Edge & Ellison (1ptnr/3assts) *Steven Edmonds* looks after the commercial clients of the firm who require fraud advice. Recognised as specialists on the investigative side. **Clients/Work:** Director charged with two counts of fraudulent trading acquitted after three month trial; defended company and manager on charge of illegal exports; defend-ed manager charged with conspiracy to corrupt and conspiracy to defraud a public official.

Freeth Cartwright Hunt Dickens (3ptnrs) Moving their fraud department from Nottingham to Leicester. Led by the well regarded *Mark Wilson*. Involved in large scale commercial fraud, and regulatory work. **Clients/Work:** £1m VAT fraud; £470k tax fraud; £2m conspiracy to defraud.

Nelsons (1ptnr/8assts) A medium sized mixed practice who "do the majority of Nottingham fraud." *Richard Nelson* is the senior partner with a good reputation. Specialise in business crime. **Clients/Work:** Defence in cases of tax investigations, and charges of fraudulent trading and false accounting.

George Jonas & Co (1ptnr/3assts) *Steven Jonas* "runs a good ship," and the firm is considered a "major player" on the Midlands fraud scene. **Clients/Work:** Emphasis on the defence of individuals facing prosecution or disciplinary proceedings.

Glaisyers (11ptnrs/13assts) A "good Birmingham firm," and the "lively" *Charles Royle* is well regarded as a fraud practitioner.

Berryman & Co (3ptnrs/3assts in general crime) Undertake general and DSS fraud as part of a mixed crime practice. **Clients/Work:** Customs & Excise fraud; DSS fraud; Building Society and credit card fraud.

Howell & Co (2ptnrs/4assts) A "shrewd" firm which is "small but does good work" in the general fraud area. **Clients/Work:** R v KDC; R v Mr and Mrs N; R v R (a solicitor).

The NORTH

Burton Copeland (Manchester) Have the largest general fraud practice in the North, and have "lots of quality fraud work." *Michael Kenyon* is "clearly a specialist and knows what he's talking about," and *Lesley Burrows* is also recommended. Although *Ian Cooper* "can be abrasive" he "knows the game" and is "good on tactics." **Clients/Work:** Butte Mining case; Barlow Clowes.

Irwin Mitchell (Sheffield) (1ptnr/2assts) Have a "good general fraud practice," and have been promoted into the leading firms category. *Kevin Robinson* is a "good operator and does big cases." **Clients/Work:** Doncaster MBC corruption inquiry; DTI inquiries; defence of individuals and companies.

Betesh Fox & Co (Manchester) (3ptnrs/2assts) The leading individuals in the firm were highly recommended. *Stephen Fox* is considered "low key and discreet," and the experienced *Andrew Kenyon* is described as "thoughtful and reliable." **Clients/Work:** R v Grosberg; Colin Youell; R v Peter Tuegal.

Dibb Lupton Alsop (Manchester) (2ptnrs/4assts full-time plus 2 others in Commercial Regulatory Group) Act for individuals and companies. *Richard Smyth* is recommended as "methodical and careful," and *Neil Gerrard* has "excellent understanding and directional skills" and handles work from London office. The national team has been joined by *Roy Tozer* from Edge & Ellison. **Clients/Work:** Defence in SFO prosecutions and advises in Customs & Excise and Inland Revenue investigations. Also act for individuals on DTI prosecution, and the DTI itself.

Eversheds (Leeds) (4ptnrs) Handle civil fraud and investigative work for national clients. **Clients/Work:** Advising a London Borough in relation to the recovery of sums paid to former executive officers; advising a major meat supplier in a fraud investigation; acting for a leading Plc in relation to an IR raid.

Garstangs (Bolton) As Richard Cornthwaite mainly practices now from London, the Bolton office has a diminished profile. However, they retain a capability and reputation for fraud work. **Clients/Work:** Defences of Neil Kelly; Robert Pollock and Colin Keyes.

Jones Maidment Wilson (Manchester) Recognised as competent local fraud practitioners.

McCormicks (Leeds) (4ptnrs: 20-30% of their time/2assts) The "larger than life" *Peter McCormick* does fraud work within a broad practice. **Clients/Work:** Acting in a fraud where it is alleged that over 4000 investors have been defrauded; represented a former director of Manchester United in a substantial fraud trial; recently dealt with time-share fraud.

Pannone & Partners (Manchester) (2ptnrs/2assts) Regional prosecutors for the DTI, and undertake defence work too. Forged a reputation in the field on the back of Asil Nadir and Ernest Saunders, but have lacked exposure in the field since the departure of two partners. **Clients/Work:** Papermill fraud in excess of £1m; factoring fraud case; defending former MD of financial services company.

BURROWS, Lesley
Burton Copeland, Manchester
(0161) 834 7374
Specialisation: Commercial fraud defence
work including liquidation, banking, stock
market, loan and leasing and mortgage and
property fraud. Considerable experience of SFO
investigations and prosecutions having acted
for the first defendants in the Arrows and Butte
Mining prosecutions.
Prof. Memberships: Law Society and Criminal
Law Solicitors Association.
Career: Qualified 1980. Partner at *Burton
Coplend* from 1990.
Personal: Attended Arnold School in Blackpool
and the University of Sheffield.

COOPER, Ian
Burton Copeland, Manchester
(0161) 834 7374
Specialisation: Partner specialising in
business and corporate fraud, investment,
offshore and tax fraud, mortgage and property
fraud, professional misconduct matters, share
and securities fraud.
Prof. Memberships: Criminal Law Solicitors'
Association.
Career: Articled *Copeland Glickman*; qualified
1987; Assistant Solicitor *Hugh Pond & Co* 1987-
1989; Assistant Solicitor *Burton Copeland* 1989-
1991, Partner 1991. King Edward VII School.
Liverpool University (1973 BA Hons).

EDMONDS, Steven James
Edge & Ellison, Birmingham (0121) 200 2001
See under Health & Safety, p. 408

FOX, Stephen
Betesh Fox & Co, Manchester
(0161) 832 6131
Senior Partner.
Specialisation: International and UK Fraud,
Commercial Crime and Defendant injunctive
work including defence of DTI, Excise and
Revenue prosecutions, Solicitors Tribunal and
professional proceedings. Defence of
Extradition proceedings.
Prof. Memberships: The Law Society, The
Manchester Law Society
Career: Instructed by Defendants in Eagle
Trust, BCCI, Arrows, IRL Group Australia
(Malcolm Johnson), Kevin Taylor (the Stalker
Affair), Jyske Bank, Alliance Resources,
Harrovian Property, G Grosberg and other
Solicitor Defendants.
Personal: Born 8 October 1948. Educated
Manchester G.S. College of Law. Interests:
Rugby League and writing.

GABBITASS, David
Wolferstans, Plymouth (01752) 663295
See under Crime (General – see also
Commercial Fraud), p. 268

GERRARD, D.Neil
Dibb Lupton Alsop, London (0345) 262728
Specialisation: Neil Gerrard's career in law has
been spent in the defence of companies under
investigation from various regulators (eg Health
and Safety, Environmental Protection, Finance
Services, Inland Revenue and Customs &
Excise). His expertise also includes representing
individuals/companies in respect of Serious
Fraud Office and DTI investigations. His main

activities at present include advising a multi-
national company in respect of a £100+ million
Customs & Excise investigation. He is also
advising/assisting a number of Accountants as
to Customs & Excise/Inland Revenue inquiries,
and advising a petro-chemical company in
respect of regulatory matters.
Prof. Memberships: Law Society.
Career: Born in 1955, Neil Gerrard was a
Policeman in the Metropolitan Police for ten
years whereafter he took his law degree in
Manchester (LLB (Hons)). He is now a Partner
and Head of the Commercial Regulatory Group
in the firm of *Dibb Lupton Alsop*. He is now
based in London but acts for clients nationwide.
Personal: Neil Gerrard is married with two
daughters aged 9 and 12. His interests include
golf, sailing and spectating at equestrian
activities where his wife and daughters
compete.

HARTWELL, Roger
Donne Mileham & Haddock, Worthing
Worthing (01903) 235026
Specialisation: Licensing, crime (business
defence)
Career: Qualified 1966. Prosecuting solicitor,
Brighton Borough Council 1966-1969, Partner
Donne Mileham & Haddock 1973, Managing
Partner 1994.
Personal: Year of birth 1943. Education
Maudlin College School Brackley and Bristol
University 1960-1963. Interests: endurance
sports. Lives in Worthing.

JONAS, Steven
George, Jonas & Co, Birmingham
(0121) 212 4111
See under Crime (General – see also
Commercial Fraud), p. 269

JONES, Gwyn
Gamlins, Rhyl 01745 343 500
See under Crime (General – see also
Commercial Fraud), p. 269

KENYON, Andrew
Betesh Fox & Co, Manchester
(0161) 832 6131
Specialisation: Partner in Serious and
Commercial Crime Department. Commercial
Fraud and Business Crime including defence of
cases instituted by SFO, DTI, Inland Revenue
and Customs and Excise: and other areas of
white collar crime.
Prof. Memberships: The Law Society.
Career: Qualified 1970. Practised in both
Private Practice and Crown Prosecution
Service. Joined *Betesh Fox & Co* as Partner in
1993. Instructed by Defendant's in Arrows,
Financial Services Group plc, Ahmed (British
Telecom Fraud), Herr Peter Tuegel, Allgemeine
Handels and Effectenbank AG, BancEurope.
Personal: Born 13th March 1946. Educated
Oundle School and Leeds University. Interests
include sport, walking, theatre and cinema.

KENYON, Michael J.
Burton Copeland, Manchester
(0161) 834 7374
Specialisation: Commercial Fraud
Investigation and Defence including Prospectus
Fraud, loan and leasing fraud, insider dealing,
fraudulent trading, frauds on investors, property

and mortgage fraud, corruption and tax
investigations. Considerable recent experience
of advising and defending in Customs Duty and
VAT cases. Defended numerous solicitors
charged with mortgage and other frauds.
Prof. Memberships: Law Society, Criminal
Law Solicitors Association.
Career: Qualified in 1980. Partner at *Chafes*,
Stockport 1985-1986 Senior Crown Prosecutor
in Manchester 1987-1989. Partner at *Burton
Copeland* from 1990.
Personal: Born 1956. Attended Manchester
Grammar School and University of Kent. Leisure
interests include salmon fishing, game
shooting, military and political history and
opera. Lives in Cheshire and Scotland.

MCCORMICK, Peter D.G.
McCormicks, Leeds (0113) 246 0622
Senior and Managing Partner.
Specialisation: Over 20 years experience of
complex fraud cases of all types – defending
white collar fraud; DTI investigations,
prosecutions and applications to disqualify
Directors; Inland Revenue, VAT, back duty and
other Customs and Excise prosecutions and
inquiries on an international basis including
appearing in the High Court on Mareva and
other restraining order hearings; conducts
cases before the VAT Tribunals and
Commissioners of Inland Revenue. Holds the
Higher Courts (Criminal Proceedings)
Qualification, conducting cases in the
Magistrates and Crown Courts and the Court of
Appeal. Has conducted a number of substantial
and high profile cases internationally including
the first case of extradition from Uruguay (the
bullion dealer Harvey Michael Ross – alleged
£20m fraud), the first G.P. to be prosecuted for
conspiracy to defraud the Health Service, the
largest fraud case ever prosecuted by the West
Yorkshire Fraud Squad and taxation cases
where the tax involved has exceeded £25m.
Other areas of practice include: Sports Law and
Media and Entertainment Law (Leader in the
Field in both – see elsewhere) and
commercial/commercial litigation. Lectures
widely. Resident legal expert on Radio Leeds,
Yorkshire Television and the Yorkshire Post. Also
writes for the Gazette, the Lawyer and other
legal and business journals.
Prof. Memberships: Member of the Economic
Law and Tax Committee of the Leeds, Bradford
and North Yorkshire Chambers of Commerce.
Director of Leeds United Holdings Plc.
Chairman of the Yorkshire Young Achievers
Awards. President of Harrogate Town F.C.;
Member of the Editorial Board, I.P. Business
Magazine; Member of the Advisory Board,
Sports Law Centre, Anglia University; Head of
Sports Law Unit, EuroLink for Lawyers; Vice-
President of The Outward Bound Trust; Solicitor
to The Duke of Edinburgh's Award; Member of
the Legal Working Party of the F.A. Premier
League.

MITCHELL, John
Blake Lapthorn, Fareham (01489) 579990
Partner in charge of Criminal Courts
Department.
Specialisation: Main areas of practice are
white collar and corporate fraud. Has
specialised in criminal law since qualification
and now concentrates on defending all types of

commercial fraud prosecutions, especially tax fraud. Also defends businesses against regulatory investigation, sanction and prosecution by local and national Government Departments and by Tax authorities.
Prof. Memberships: Law Society.
Career: Qualified in 1979. Joined *Blake Lapthorn* in 1977, becoming a Partner in 1984.
Personal: Born 2nd March 1954. Attended Portsmouth Grammar School 1962-72, Pembroke College, Cambridge, 1973-76, and Guildford College of Law 1977. Lives in Hampshire.

NELSON, Richard
Nelsons, Derby (01332) 206111
Specialisation: Leads substantial Business Crime Department comprising in-house Solicitors and Barristers covering full range of business related investigation and prosecution acting for companies and individuals. Practice involves cases over wide geographical area. Recent case work of Fraud (including computer fraud) Revenue and Customs & Excise including tax and importation, Trading Standards, HSE, Companies Act, Dti and Insolvency offences, also corporate and other individual crime and SFO prosecutions. Often involves pursuit and consideration of large volumes of evidence (2,000,000 documents in one case) and liaison with technical and forensic experts. The firm also has a separate department dealing with general and other serious crime.
Prof. Memberships: Area Criminal Justice Liaison Committee. Chairman of Notts Law Society Criminal Business Committee. Council Member Notts Law Society.
Career: Qualified 1975. 1972-1977 *J A Bright Richards & Flewitt.* 1977-1983 *Freeth Cartwright & Sketchley* (Partner from 1983). 1983 Formed *Nelson, Johnson & Hastings* (now *Nelsons*) with two partners and no staff in 1983. *Nelsons* is now one of the largest firms in the region.
Personal: Born 14.06.50. Educated Nottingham High School and Bristol University. Interests include sport and comedy.

PROWEL, Martyn
Martin Prowel, Edwards & Davies, Cardiff (01222) 496316

ROBINSON, Kevin
Irwin Mitchell, Sheffield (0114) 276 7777 Partner heading Business Crime Unit.
Specialisation: Acted in the major Iraqi arms export cases and also Astra/BMARC disqualification proceedings. Involved in arms export prosecutions in the US. Represents Company directors, managers and professionals charged with fraud, fraudulent trading and ancillary offences. Also represents Corporations including multi-nationals and Plc's in criminal proceedings arising out of their commercial activities.
Career: Qualified in 1973. Joined *Irwin Mitchell* in 1974 became a partner in 1975. Former Treasurer of Criminal Law Solicitors Association. Higher Courts Rights of Audience 1995.

ROYLE, Charles
Glaisyers, Birmingham (0121) 233 2971
Specialisation: Crime, all areas including Youth & Motoring, Licensing – liquor & gaming.
Prof. Memberships: Law Society, Birmingham Law Society, Duty Solicitor.
Career: Palmers School Grays, George Dixon Grammer School Birmingham, Sheffield University. Articled *George Jonas*, Partner with *Jonas Grove & Co*, Partner with *Glaisyers* since 1979, now Senior Partner.
Personal: Keen Sportsman & Fan; Cricket, Tennis, Golf, Soccer, Rugby. Married with 3 children; President of Edgbaston Nursery School.

SMYTH, Richard
Dibb Lupton Alsop, London (0345) 262728
Specialisation: Representation of companies and individuals defending enquiries and prosecutions commenced by Customs and Excise, Inland Revenue, DTI and Serious Fraud Office. Played a major part in Barlow Clowes and Seil Trade Finance litigation. Currently involved in Butte Mining litigation and discreet representation of several national/international companies. Also represents solicitors and accountants in professional Disciplinary Tribunal proceedings.
Prof. Memberships: The Law Society.
Career: Qualified 1977. *Millers Solicitors* 1977-1987. *Burton Copeland* 1987-1996 (Founder member of Commercial Fraud Department). 1996 joined Commercial Regulatory Group of *Dibb Lupton Alsop*.
Personal: Born 4/1/53. Lives in Todmorden. Interests: wooden boats/sailing.

TOZER, Royston C.L.
Dibb Lupton Alsop, London (0345) 262728
Specialisation: An Associate with *Dipp Lupton Alsop* and a member of the Commercial Regulatory Group. Joined the firm in 1998 and specialises in criminal litigation. He was previously employed by Birmingham City Council as a prosecuting solicitor. He has invaluable experience, therefore, of both sides of a criminal prosecution. Has wide experience in dealing with corporate crime and regulatory prosecutions. He undertakes fraud and Customs & Excise enquiries and acted in the longest Inland Revenue fraud prosecution. He acts for a large number of retail, manufacturing, transport and leisure service clients.

WILSON, Mark
Freeth Cartwright Hunt Dickins, Nottingham (0115) 936 9369
Offices at Derby and Leicester
Specialisation: Partner in Forensic Law Department specialising in high quality defence of all types of fraud, corporate and regulatory crime. Recent experience in Revenue, C&E, DTI, PIA, OFT, Environment Agency, trading standards, HSE investigations and prosecutions.
Career: Birmingham University (LLB Hons). Articled *Kidd Rapinet*. Qualified 1985. Partner since 1990.
Personal: Born 1961; married with 3 children. Leisure: family, motor racing, mountain biking, skiing.

HEALTH AND SAFETY

RESEARCH: In compiling the tables, we consider all the information available to us, paying particular regard to the market research carried out by our team of ten qualified lawyers. (The researchers' details are set out on page three.) The rankings, therefore, reflect the opinion of the marketplace as revealed by systematic and objective research: see page four. (Our research is audited every year by the British Market Research Bureau.)

OVERVIEW: This section concerns those practices which deal with the commercial and regulatory side of health and safety work, and not simply those who act on personal injury matters for insurers. The firms mentioned in the tables treat health and safety as a self-contained area of law. They tend not to deal with each other, but deal with the Health and Safety Executive (HSE) and local authorities in relation to enforcement.

Firms will advise on HSE investigations, write policies for companies, undertake risk assessment and represent individuals and companies. There has been no change in the tables this year as there are few dedicated health and safety specialists and the market is stable.

LONDON

LEADING FIRMS · LONDON
CAMERON MCKENNA
MASONS
NABARRO NATHANSON
SIMMONS & SIMMONS

Cameron McKenna (2ptnrs/9assts in Pharmaceuticals, Regulatory and Health & Safety) Contentious and non-contentious work with a focus on the bio-tech industry, and also known for their work in the construction field. The "wonderful" *Mark Tyler* is one of the few dedicated health and safety practitioners, and has a very high profile. One client considered him "excellent on strategic advice." *Alison Brown* acts for corporations on enforcement issues, especially in relation to crisis management. **Clients/Work:** Recent advice on gas explosions, hazardous substances, railway accidents and faulty electrical equipment; defence of individuals; advice on policies.

Masons Known as construction specialists, they also have an "excellent practice" in health and safety, and despite the fact that Christopher Dering no longer does this work, the firm retain a good reputation.

Nabarro Nathanson (2ptnrs/4assts) Health and safety work is dealt with by a well respected national team. Much property related work, for both owners and occupiers, especially in the construction industry. Also undertake advice on health and safety policy. *Thomas Symes* has a property background. **Clients/Work:** Due diligence and general policy advice; advice on HSE prosecutions; allocation of risk on PFI projects.

Simmons & Simmons (7ptnrs/7assts) Have a reputation for health and safety work from an employment angle. The health and safety group draws on the expertise of departments such as environment, insurance, transport and EC law. **Clients/Work:** Defence of Sensormatic Ltd on regulatory prosecution; tendering exercises for Halfords and Boots Properties.

LEADING INDIVIDUALS · LONDON
TYLER Mark Cameron McKenna
BROWN Alison Cameron McKenna
SYMES Thomas Nabarro Nathanson

The SOUTH and WALES

Osborne Clarke (Bristol) (1ptnr/2assts) *Richard Bretton* "does a good job" for this "switched on firm," which is active in promoting health and safety law. They have a substantial and broadly-based commercial practice, and also do a lot of insurance related work. **Clients/Work:** Advised on several criminal prosecutions; problems of implementing the Health & Safety (Consultation with Employees) Regulations 1996; training for government agencies, Bristol & West plc and others; homeworking advice.

Bevan Ashford (Bristol) (2ptnrs) Substantial amount of prosecutions, and also defence work. Have been involved in high profile cases recently. *Richard Annandale* is also known for his work in the healthcare field. **Clients/Work:** Risk assessment; advice

LEADING FIRMS THE SOUTH AND WALES
OSBORNE CLARKE Bristol
BEVAN ASHFORD Bristol
EVERSHEDS Cardiff
LESTER ALDRIDGE Bournemouth
HUGH JAMES Cardiff
LYONS DAVIDSON Bristol
VEALE WASBROUGH Bristol

on breaches of health and safety regulations; prosecuting and defending cases in the Magistrates and Crown Court.

Eversheds (Cardiff) (1ptnr/2assts) The experienced *Martin Warren* has a respected mixed practice which involves employment, environment and health and safety. He is known for defending prosecutions relating to injuries in the workplace. **Clients/Work:** Luxfer Group Holdings; Celtic Energy.

Lester Aldridge (Bournemouth) (2ptnrs/ 1asst) *Richard Byrne* handles prosecution and defence work in conjunction with his employment work. **Clients/Work:** Preparing comprehensive health and safety

policies; act for HSE in relation to agricultural, construction and factory related offences; act for Proctor & Gamble plc.

Hugh James (Cardiff) A large firm with a reputation in the commercial field, they are also recommended for their work on health and safety issues. **Clients/Work:** Defence on behalf of clients in the construction, electronics manufacturing, railway and car industries. Prosecutions are also undertaken on behalf of the HSE.

Lyons Davidson (Bristol) Good on the PI side. Some health and safety work but not high profile. **Clients/Work:** Mainly advise the construction and licensing industries.

Veale Wasbrough (Bristol) Very much on the litigation side, with a health and safety capacity, but not dedicated specialists. **Clients/Work:** Risk management and accident avoidance. Clients include Great Mills group of companies.

LEADING INDIVIDUALS
THE SOUTH AND WALES
BRETTON Richard Osborne Clarke
ANNANDALE Richard Bevan Ashford
BYRNE Richard Lester Aldridge
WARREN Martin Eversheds

SEE PROFILES AT END OF THIS SECTION

MIDLANDS and The NORTH

LEADING FIRMS
MIDLANDS AND THE NORTH
NABARRO NATHANSON Sheffield
EDGE & ELLISON Birmingham
EVERSHEDS Leeds
HALLIWELL LANDAU Manchester
HAMMOND SUDDARDS Manchester

Nabarro Nathanson (Sheffield) (2ptnrs/4 assts) The "impressive" and "level headed" *Gareth Watkins* is head of the national team. He undertakes the litigious aspects of health and safety, and is known for his work on the consequences of accidents. **Clients/Work:** Due diligence for several company acquisitions and disposals; drafting health and safety policies; advising clients on liabilities arising from multiple fatality accidents.

Edge & Ellison (Birmingham) *Steven Edmonds* is known primarily for his advocacy. He undertakes a wide range of regulatory work. **Clients/Work:** Defences in Magistrates and Crown Courts, and also prosecutions for the HSE. Lectures on health and safety to corporate clients.

Eversheds (Leeds) (2ptnrs/2assts) Have experience of crisis management, and the "outgoing" *Paul Burnley* is known for large scale disaster cases. Particular experience of the chemical industry. **Clients/Work:** Defence of Northern Supplies Ltd following a major fire and explosion at its liquid peroleum gas plant. Defended Hickson International PLC. Defence of The Associated Octel Company Ltd following a fire at its Ellesmere Port plant.

Halliwell Landau (Manchester) *Christopher Phillips* has a national reputation, and is known in particular for his work for insurers. He specialises in industrial disease. **Clients/Work:** Representing ICI in an appeal to the House of Lords in a WRULD claim;

Zeneca Specialities; English, Welsh and Scottish Railways.

Hammond Suddards (Manchester) Good on litigation, and do substantial amounts of insurance work. *Michael Shepherd* heads the national team, and undertakes his own advocacy. He is recommended for his "robust common sense." **Clients/Work:** Defence of National Starch and Chemical Ltd. Acted for ICI in defending proceedings following the loss of 50 tonnes of oil into the River Tees. Acting for ICI following the loss of 150 tonnes of Chloroform at Runcorn.

LEADING INDIVIDUALS
MIDLANDS AND THE NORTH
WATKINS Gareth Nabarro Nathanson
BURNLEY Paul Eversheds
EDMONDS Steven Edge & Ellison
PHILLIPS Christopher Halliwell Landau
SHEPHERD Michael Hammond Suddards

SEE PROFILES AT END OF THIS SECTION

SCOTLAND

LEADING FIRMS
SCOTLAND
DUNDAS & WILSON CS Edinburgh
McCLURE NAISMITH Glasgow

Dundas & Wilson CS (Edinburgh) (1ptnr/ 5assts) Act mainly for insurance companies in litigation. **Clients/Work:** Advise companies on health and safety policy; advice on industrial diseases and repetitive strain injury; increase in work related stress claims.

McClure Naismith (Glasgow) (4ptnrs/ 6assts) Health and safety work is dealt with

in the litigation department. **Clients/Work:** Acting on behalf of a manufacturing company facing health and safety prosecution following fatalities in an industrial accident. Acting in defence of a criminal prosecution arising out of fatality at the Oasis concert at Loch Lomond.

LEADERS' PROFILES · LONDON AND REGIONS

ANNANDALE, Richard
Bevan Ashford, Bristol (0117) 923 0111
See under Medical Negligence: Mainly Defendant, p. 582

BRETTON, Richard
Osborne Clarke, Bristol (0117) 984 5298
Specialisation: Advises a wide range of institutions and businesses on health & safety management, documentation, systems and training and related employment issues. Also

handles claims and prosecutions for insurers, businesses and claimants. *Osborne Clarke's* Health & Safety Club was launched in October 1994. Its benefits include a 24 hour advice line, regular workshops, briefings on significant developments in the law, and access to a comprehensive library. The Club has more than 100 members from all over the country. Health & safety work can be done from both the Bristol and London office.
Career: Qualified in 1978; partner *Veale*

Wasborough 1987-1993; partner and head of health & safety unit *Osborne Clarke* 1993.
Prof. Memberships: Law Society Personal Injury Panel; Law Society Accident Line Scheme; Association of Personal Injury Lawyers; Action for Victims for Medical Accidents; Institution of Occupational Safety & Health.
Personal: Born in 1954. Educated Tonbridge School, and University of Bristol.

BROWN, Alison
Cameron McKenna, London
(0171) 367 3000
Assistant Solicitor in Healthcare Department.
Specialisation: Advises on civil and criminal aspects of a wide range of health and safety matters and acts for companies faced with criminal prosecutions, inquests and claims for damages. Also handles related litigation, including product liability litigation. Has written several articles for legal journals and spoken at conferences and seminars. Editor of the Enforcement Law chapter of Tolley's Health and Safety at Work handbook. Holds the NEBOSH National General Certificate in Occupational Safety and Health.
Career: Joined *McKenna & Co* in 1988 and qualified in 1990.
Personal: Born 12th June 1966. Educated at Latymer Grammar School, Edmonton 1977-84 and Bristol University 1984-87.

BURNLEY, Paul
Eversheds, Leeds (0113) 243 0391
Specialisation: Principal area of practice is acting for corporate/commercial clients in complex environmental and health and safety litigation. Wide experience of crisis management, having represented clients in major incidents, disasters and product recall. Experienced in all aspects of environmental issues. Attends various venues as a guest speaker.
Prof. Memberships: UKELA
Career: Qualified April 1980. 9 years as a Prosecuting Solicitor, he joined *Eversheds* in 1989 becoming a Partner in May 1996. A Gamekeeper turned poacher!
Personal: Born 31 August 1955.

BYRNE, Richard
Lester Aldridge, Bournemouth
(01202) 786161
Specialisation: Advises on all aspects of health and safety legislation, company health and safety policies and their management. Provides representation in connection with Health and Safety at Work Act prosecutions. Advises and represents the Health and Safety Executive in prosecutions. Part time industrial tribunal chairman. Visiting lecturer at Bournemouth University in Health and Safety Law.
Prof. Memberships: Employment Lawyers Association.
Career: Qualified in 1978. Joined *Lester*

Aldridge 1983 becoming a partner in 1984.
Personal: Born 1955. Honorary Secretary of The Royal Geographical Society. Lives near Romsey, Hampshire.

EDMONDS, Steven James
Edge & Ellison, Birmingham
(0121) 200 2001
Specialisation: Practice covers all aspects of regulatory work in consumer protection, food safety, health and safety, retailing, trading standards and contentious environmental law. Acts for large national companies particularly in food industry and retailing.
Prof. Memberships: Law Society and Food Law Group.
Career: Qualified 1978. Principal of own firm in Coventry until 1988 when joined *Edge & Ellison*.
Personal: Born 1954. Educated at Bromsgrove and Warwick University (Upper Second). Higher Court Advocate (Criminal) since 1994.

PHILLIPS, Christopher
Halliwell Landau, Manchester
(0161) 835 3003
Specialisation: Head of Insurance Litigation Department. Has considerable experience of Defendant personal injury issues, both within the Industry and private practice. Is currently regarded as one of the leading UK specialists in Industrial Disease and Environmental Litigation. He writes articles and gives seminars on many specialist disease issues. He has a reputation for success in a number of leading disease cases.
Career: Articled Greater London Council; Qualified 1986; Partner *Hammond Suddards* 1992 – 1994; Partner *Halliwell Landau* 1994.
Personal: Born 1953, resides Halifax.

SHEPHERD, Michael L.
Hammond Suddards, Manchester
(0161) 830 5000
See under Environmental Law, p. 352

SYMES, Thomas
Nabarro Nathanson, London
(0171) 493 9933
Specialisation: Partner, commercial property department. In addition, advises on health and safety policy and legislation, particularly on structuring contractual arrangements to allocate responsibility for health and safety risks.
Prof. Memberships: Law Society. Anglo American Real Property Institute.

Career: LLB, Reading University. Joined *Nabarro Nathanson* 1982, partner 1986.
Personal: Resides London. Hobbies: Skiing, running, family.

TYLER, Mark
Cameron McKenna, London
(0171) 367 3000
Partner in Product Liability and Health & Safety.
Specialisation: Main areas of practice are product liability and health and safety. Co-author of 'Product Safety' and 'Safer by Design'; Consultant Editor of Health and Safety Liability and Litigation; legal reviewer for Croner's Management of Construction Safety. Contributor to 'Buildings and Health: The Rosehaugh Guide to the Design Construction and Management of Buildings', 'A New Balance: A Guide for Property Owners and Developers', 'Environmental Issues in Construction' – CIRIA Special Report, and CIOB Handbook Facilities Management.
Prof. Memberships: Law Society, CBI Health and Safety Panel, CBI Consumer Affairs Panel, Forum of Insurance Lawyers, International Association of Defense Counsel.
Career: Joined *McKenna & Co* in 1984 and qualified in 1986. Became a Partner in 1992.
Personal: Born 10th October 1960. Educated at Sir William Borlase's Grammar School, Marlow, Worcester College, Oxford and Kings College, London.

WARREN, Martin
Eversheds, Cardiff (01222) 471147
See under Employment Law, p. 311

WATKINS, Gareth
Nabarro Nathanson, Sheffield
(0114) 279 4000
Partner in Litigation Department.
Specialisation: Main area of practice is health and safety. Gives advice to clients on health and safety policies, organisation, inquests, public inquiries and Health and Safety at Work Act prosecutions. Also handles occupational health and industrial diseases. Has published numerous papers and articles in professional journals, magazines and newspapers. Has given several radio broadcasts on subjects connected with health and safety. Regular conference speaker. Edits the 'Encyclopedia of Health & Safety at Work' and published the 'Health and Safety Handbook' in 1997.

HEALTH CARE (INCORPORATING MENTAL HEALTH)

See also Medical Negligence; Product Liability; PFI

RESEARCH: In compiling the tables, we consider all the information available to us, paying particular regard to the market research carried out by our team of ten qualified lawyers. (The researchers' details are set out on page three.) The rankings, therefore, reflect the opinion of the marketplace as revealed by systematic and objective research: see page four. (Our research is audited every year by the British Market Research Bureau.)

OVERVIEW: This section includes a range of practices offering differing services to the health industry. This year we have divided London firms into two tables: general healthcare and pharmaceuticals. The first table includes those firms which offer an all-round service to healthcare bodies, such as NHS Trusts or individual medical practitioners. Advice may include commercial litigation, property, employment and medical negligence.

Those firms listed in the pharmaceuticals section tend to have a more corporate background and advise clients on regulatory and contentious issues. (This sometimes overlaps with product liability).

Firms *only* advising NHS Trusts on PFI projects are dealt with elsewhere although many of the firms listed here do handle a substantial amount of PFI work for NHS trusts. This section should be cross-referenced with the medical negligence and product liability sections of this book.

LONDON

GENERAL HEALTHCARE

LEADING FIRMS · LONDON GENERAL HEALTHCARE

BEACHCROFT STANLEYS
CAPSTICKS

HEMPSONS
LE BRASSEUR J TICKLE

BEVAN ASHFORD
BIRD & BIRD
DAVIES ARNOLD COOPER

Beachcroft Stanleys (17ptnrs/43assts divided into Health Litigation, Projects, Property and Employment teams) Unanimously praised as one of the major players in the healthcare field. The team includes several leading individuals: *Barry Francis* ("at the top of his field") *Marisa Broadhurst* and *Trevor Blythe*. Clients/Work: Principal client base is in London and the South East. Act for 118 NHS bodies, GP practices, private health care providers and companies providing healthcare to NHS. Leading the RAGE class litigation on behalf of the NHS (100+ claims in relation to post-operative radiology treatment). Successfully representing Camden & Islington Health Authority re claim brought against them by Christopher Clunis in connection with his killing of Mr Zito.

Capsticks (11ptnrs/14assts) "Longstanding depth of experience." *Brian Capstick*, an "effective senior partner,"and *Hilary Blackwell* are both leading individuals. Clients/Work: Act for approximately 100 NHS Trusts and Health Authorities. Representation of three London health authorities in a major fraud case, including obtaining a Mareva injunction. Advising in connection with threatened judicial reviews of decisions to close Edgware Hospital and Harperbury Hospital. One of the two "pathfinder" non acute PFI schemes recognised by the Department of Health for community hospital reprovision.

Hempsons (11ptnrs/10assts divided into three teams) "Lots of GP work." *Bertie Leigh* remains a leading figure in the health world. Clients/Work: Act for 81 NHS bodies (19 Health Authorities and 62 NHS Trusts) across the country. Also act for a number of regional NHS Executive offices, The MDU, the BMA and BDA. Re MB(1997) 8 Med Law 217 Court of Appeal Guidelines on Involuntary Caesarean Section. Recombinant Factor 8 – decision on Judicial Review of resources.

Le Brasseur J Tickle (14ptnrs/13fee-earners) Known for their "all-round involvement with the NHS." Clients/Work: Review of new health related legislation to ensure clients' compliance with both new and existing UK law and EU directives. Advised on a number of PFI projects including the construction of a private patients wing and additional theatres with the acquisition of an ultrafast CT scanner. Also advised on EC Procurement Rules.

Bevan Ashford (2ptnrs/3assts) A new office which opened on 1st May 1998 with the aim of servicing London clients. For the moment, the firm's strength is felt to be at its Bristol office.

Bird & Bird (10ptnrs/6assts) The team received praise for its regulatory work. Clients/Work: Acted for a London NHS Trust on two separate outsourcing transac-

LEADING INDIVIDUALS · LONDON GENERAL HEALTHCARE

CAPSTICK Brian Capsticks
FRANCIS Barry Beachcroft Stanleys

BLACKWELL Hilary Capsticks
BLYTHE Trevor Beachcroft Stanleys
BROADHURST Marisa Beachcroft Stanleys
LEIGH Bertie Hempsons

tions. Acted for an NHS Trust in a PFI project to procure a new community hospital. Advised a major professional regulatory body on conduct procedures and precedent system.

PHARMACEUTICALS

Cameron McKenna (6ptnrs/9assts) Leading pharmaceuticals and product liablility firm particularly on regulatory work. The well-known *Ian Dodds-Smith* heads the team. Clients/Work: Act for over 100 pharmaceutical and healthcare companies in the UK and EC, ranging from multi-nationals to smaller niche biotech companies. Biotech and medical device regulatory law. Cosmetics,

Davies Arnold Cooper (4ptnrs/7assts) within the Healthcare, Pharmaceutical, Product Liability and Mass Tort Department)The firm has been appointed to the NHSLA panel and as a result, will probably try to develop its

pesticides and biocides regulatory law; both contentious and non-contentious.

Davies Arnold Cooper (4 ptnrs/7assts) Essentially regarded as an insurance firm, they also have a pharmaceuticals and product liability practice. Clients/Work: Acting on Halcyon litigation.

Herbert Smith (10ptnrs) Perceived as a corporate firm which has a profile in pharmaceuticals, mainly in relation to intellectual property issues. Clients/Work: Advising Hoffmann-La Roche AG on patent matters relating to its PCR DNA amplification technology. Represented Akzo Nobel NV in its major patent battle with Chiron concerning Hepatitis C testing kits. Boehringer Mannheim GmbH (international patent war concerning the rights to the recombinant human hormone erythropoietin).

all-round service to its health authority clients. At present it is better known for its corporate and insurance background. Clients/Work: Co-ordinating Hepatitis C litigation for the NHSLA. Co-ordinating HIV litigation.

Simmons & Simmons (7ptnrs/14assts form the Pharmaceutical and Medical Group) A new entry to the tables following several recommendations. Particularly rated for its regulatory work. Clients/Work: Represented SmithKline Beecham in major claim for patent infringement and breach of confidential information. Advising EFPIA on its intervention before the Court of First Instance in Bayer's action against the European Commission. Advising Rhône-Poulenc Rorer on application for judicial review of decision by the Medicines Control Agency.

The SOUTH, WALES and EAST ANGLIA

Bevan Ashford (Bristol: 22ptnrs/over 60 other fee earners divided into the following teams: NHS Litigation, Construction, Property. Environment & Planning, Energy, Employment and Commercial Litigation, Public Sector Commercial, Public & Administrative Law; Cardiff: 1ptnr/3assts) The firm has experienced some upheaval in the past year with the resignation of Ian Fairbairn and several of his colleagues from the Commercial team. Nevertheless it is perceived as strong enough to weather the storm and retain its large market share. A firm with "all-round expertise" and a good track record.

Mills & Reeve (Cambridge, Norwich) (6ptnrs/15assts) "A good bunch." *Raith*

Pickup heads the team. Clients/Work: Sale and leaseback of staff residential accommodation on behalf of a major hospital. Approximately 25 PFI projects for 13 trusts including Ipswich, Harrow & Hillingdon, Mid-Essex NHS Trusts and the NHS Executive.

Wansbroughs Willey Hargrave (Winchester: A dedicated 'Health' Department 3ptnrs/ 14 fee-earners plus 1ptnr and 4 further fee-earners who handle insurance work. Bristol: 6ptnrs/18 fee-earners across a number of departments – commercial, property, employment, IT/IP and construction) A "first division firm" with acknowledged expertise in the field. *Tim Wright* of the Winchester office received particular recognition. Clients/Work: The Winchester office acts for over 30 NHS Trusts and health organisations.

Brachers (Maidstone) (10ptnrs/12 assts across the medical negligence, employment, property and commercial departments) A "sensible firm" with a "respectable reputation" in the health care field. Clients/Work: Act for 10 National Health Trusts, a Health Authority and the Secretary of State for Health. Three current conveyancing transactions in excess of £1m. Instructed by Medway Trust for a £37.1m hospital redevelopment.

Clarks (Reading) (4ptnrs/7assts) Not as high profile as some firms, but still well regarded. Clients/Work: Acted for NHS Executive on disposal of three major hospital sites. Appointed solicitors to the Oxfordshire

Community Health NHS Trust to advise on estate matters. Advised major acute unit (The Royal Berkshire & Battle Hospitals NHS Trust) on a PFI project (abortive).

Cole & Cole (Oxford) (6ptnrs/13assts) Although the practice is not currently on the NHSLA panel for medical negligence work, it can continue to advise on other healthcare issues and is well-regarded. Clients/Work: Clients come from London and the whole of the south east. NHS employment clients are located from Cornwall to the north of England. NHS pilot project mediations.

Morgan Bruce (Cardiff) (16ptnrs/ 19assts) Generally well-regarded. Clients/Work: Advised the HFEA re legal implications of human cloning, including appearing before a Select Committe of the House of Commons on behalf of the Authority. Dealt with 10 sales of surplus hospital sites. Employment advice to one of the largest trusts in the UK on restructuring of middle management contracts.

Donne Mileham & Haddock (Brighton) (8ptnrs/3assts) *Michael Long* is recommended Clients/Work: Eastbourne & County Healthcare PFI Project. Wheelchair and child safety equipment provision schemes for East Sussex Brighton & Hove Health Authority. Constitutional and other work for Association of British Paediatric Nurses.

Osborne Clarke (Bristol: 2ptnrs/ 2assts) **Clients/Work:** Acting for United Bristol Healthcare NHS Trust in the paediatric cardiac surgery group of claims. Also medico-

legal advice on matters such as mental health and persistent vegetative state.

MIDLANDS and the NORTH

LEADING FIRMS
MIDLANDS AND THE NORTH

HEMPSONS Harrogate, Manchester
WANSBROUGHS WILLEY HARGRAVE
Birmingham, Leeds, Sheffield

DICKINSON DEES Newcastle upon Tyne
EVERSHEDS Newcastle upon Tyne, Nottingham
THE LEWINGTON PARTNERSHIP Birmingham

Hempsons (Harrogate: 3ptnrs/22assts divided into four teams; Manchester: 7ptnrs/ 22assts divided into seven teams). *Tim Young* is a leader based in Harrogate. **Clients/Work:** The Harrogate office is the firm's national base for PFI/Projects work. The Manchester office handles 'white coat' crime as well as general healthcare and medical negligence work.

Wansbroughs Willey Hargrave (Birmingham: 1ptnr/3assts; Leeds: 3ptnrs/ 12 fee-earners about 33% of the time; Sheffield: 8ptnrs/20 fee-earners) The "effective" *Diane Hallatt* at the Sheffield office was widely praised. Team also includes *John Evans* and *Peter Lee*. **Clients/Work:** The

Birmingham team includes a medical negligence litigator and a property lawyer and provides advice on commercial issues including corporate governance, PFI, commercial property, employment, construction and commercial contracts. Leeds focuses on commercial property, construction and PFI. The Sheffield office's strength is in medical negligence litigation and health advice.

Dickinson Dees (Newcastle) (20-30 fee-earners across all depts including *Andrew Jackson*) A "pleasant firm" where the team "know what they're talking about," particularly for PFI work. **Clients/Work:** Cumberland Infirmary PFI (£86m).

Eversheds (Newcastle, Nottingham) (3ptnrs – f/t/15 – p/t/4assts – f/t/13p/t) Seen as high profile in health authority work. *Ronald Bradbeer* heads the team. **Clients/Work:** Act for eight acute trusts, nine non-acute trusts, health authorities and other health service providers. Dealing with over 100 claims on behalf of Hartlepool and East Durham NHS Trust. Appointed by Tees Health Authority and Hartlepool and East Durham NHS Trust to act in the claim of Beverley Palmer arising from the murder of Rosie Palmer.

The Lewington Partnership (Birmingham) (8ptnrs/28assts) The firm has had a difficult year with its absence from the

NHSLA panel restricting its ability to do medical negligence work. Nevertheless it is still a player and this may be a temporary setback. Both *Stuart Knowles* and *Sheila Waddington* are rated as leading individuals with the latter perceived to be "taking the reins" at the firm. **Clients/Work:** Totally dedicated to healthcare work with the practice divided into Employment, Commercial Property, Litigation, Public Sector and Healthcare departments. Work includes advising public bodies and NHS clients on merger, establishment, corporate governance, community care, joint commissioning, fund holding arrangements, primary care and audit committees.

LEADING INDIVIDUALS
MIDLANDS AND THE NORTH

BRADBEER Ronald Eversheds
EVANS John Wansbroughs Willoy Hargrave
HALLATT Diane Wansbroughs Willey Hargrave
LEE Peter Wansbroughs Willey Hargrave
YOUNG Tim Hempsons

KNOWLES Stuart The Lewington Partnership
WADDINGTON Sheila The Lewington Partnership

JACKSON Andrew Dickinson Dees

MENTAL HEALTH

Practitioners in the field of mental health fall into two broad categories: those advising health authorities, hospitals and trusts; and those representing patients before the Mental Health Review Tribunal. Some are also increasingly involved in community care work. The majority of leading individuals are either sole practitioners or in niche practices. The main development in the last year has been the House of Lords case of L v Bournewood which will mean many more patients being sectioned under the Mental Health Act and thus a substantially increased workload for mental health lawyers.

The "brilliant, feisty" *Lucy Scott-Moncrieff* remains pre-eminent in the field. Several practitioners spoke of her outstanding contribution on behalf of patients. She "has the keys to Broadmoor" according to a fellow solicitor. *Anselm Eldergill*, formerly of T.V. Edwards but now a sole practitioner has recently written a book on Mental Health and is considered "authoritative." *Nicola Mackintosh* of T.V. Edwards is "very

energetic and "very good at what she does." She is heavily involved in community care work and during 1997 brought the first carers case under the Carers (Recognition & Services) Act 1995. *David Mylan* is "an excellent tribunal lawyer." *Colin McCloskey* is recognised as doing a variety of mental health work including housing, community care, tribunals and complaints. *Andrew Parsons* is head of the Health Group at Radcliffes and specialises in mental health law. His work is advisory on behalf of hospitals and health professionals.

Outside London *Peter Edwards* was highly recommended by several interviewees. He runs the Institute of Mental Health Law, is heavily involved in teaching work and "knows his stuff." *Neil Confrey* is recommended for tribunal work. *Christopher Topping* specialises in both personal injury and mental health law at Jackson & Canter. *Tim Wright's* work at Wansbroughs Willey Hargrave is entirely advisory on behalf of a number of NHS Trusts.

LEADING INDIVIDUALS
LONDON • MENTAL HEALTH

SCOTT-MONCRIEFF Lucy Scott-Moncrieff, Harbour & Sinclair

ELDERGILL Anselm Sole Practitioner
MACKINTOSH Nicola T.V. Edwards
MCCLOSKEY Colin Jacqueline Everett & Co
MYLAN David Sole Practitioner

PARSONS Andrew Radcliffes

LEADING INDIVIDUALS
THE REGIONS • MENTAL HEALTH

EDWARDS Peter Peter Edwards & Co, Merseyside

CONFREY Neil Confreys, Cardiff
DURKIN Timothy Myer Wolff & Manley, Hull
TOPPING Christopher Jackson & Canter, Liverpool
WRIGHT Tim Wansbroughs Willey Hargrave, Winchester

BLACKWELL, Hilary
Capsticks, London (0181) 780 2211
Specialisation: Head of Property &
Commercial Department comprising 6 partners
and 5 solicitors specialising in NHS property
and contracts issues, including the Private
Finance Initiative Special interest in care in the
community and pioneered the Lewisham
Partnership approach to Joint Commissioning.
Contributor to "The Provision of Staff
Accommodation in the NHS - Problems Issues
& Opportunities." Research Report prepared for
the Regional Estates Management Group.
Prof. Memberships: Law Society.
Career: LL.B (Hons) University of Bristol,
College of Law, Guildford. Articles *Veale Benson*
(now *Veale Wansborough*). 1992 joined
Capsticks to head Property and Commercial
Department, 1993 Partner. Member of firm's
management committee.
Personal: Family and bridge.

BLYTHE, Trevor
Beachcroft Stanleys, London
(0171) 242 1011
Specialisation: His principal areas of practice
are general Health Service Law and
Administrative Law, including Judicial Review.
Has advised widely on NHS commercial,
primary care and estates issues and on the
powers and duties of NHS bodies, with
particular reference to hospital closures, the
dissolution and establishments of NHS Trusts
and related issues. Currently working on a
number of PFI projects. He is joint Chairman of
the Health Law Group and speaks both at
internal seminars and external conferences.
Prof. Memberships: The Law Society.
Career: Admitted 1974 at *Beachcroft Hyman
Isaacs* (now *Beachcroft Stanleys*). Partner 1980
to date.
Personal: Born 4th October 1947. Educated at
Read Grammer School, Yorkshire. Graduate of
London University.

BRADBEER, Ronald
Eversheds, Newcastle upon Tyne
(0191) 261 1661
Senior Partner and Senior Litigation Partner.
Specialisation: Principal area of practice is
medical negligence. Principal legal advisor to
area health authorities and trusts for many
years. Specialised in medical negligence for
over 25 years. Also handles commercial
disputes specialising in commercial contracts,
industrial tribunal cases and construction
matters
Prof. Memberships: Accredited Mediator with
Centre for Dispute Resolution, Law Society.
Career: Joined *Wilkinson Maughan* in 1960.
Qualified in 1963. Partner in 1967, Managing
Partner in 1993 and Senior Partner in 1997.

BROADHURST, Marisa
Beachcroft Stanleys, London
(0171) 242 1011
Specialisation: Practice covers a full range of
services on all types of estates and commercial
property transactions, projects, public law and
constitutional law issues connected with
property deals. Currently Lead Partner for the
Guy's Hospital, Lambeth Hospital and St
Thomas' Hospital projects for the
redevelopment of these hospitals. Also, the

property partner on a number of other hospital
redevelopments under the private finance
initiative. Regular contributor to the firm's Health
Law Bulletin and speaker at both internal
seminars held for clients and external public
conferences.
Prof. Memberships: Law Society.
Career: Admitted 1970, articles at *Max Bitel
Greene & Co*, a Partner from 1970-71, the
Greater London Council from 1971-76, the
London Residuary Body from 1988-89 and
Beachcroft Stanleys from 1989 to present, a
Partner from 1991.
Personal: Born 8th June 1947. Educated at
The Convent of Our Lady of Sion and at the
University of Lille (France) and the University of
Valladolid (Spain). Interests include cinema and
theatre. Lives in Wimbledon, London.

CAPSTICK, Brian
Capsticks, London (0181) 780 2211
Specialisation: Practices in the areas of
administrative and employment law. Has
successfully defended many of the most
sensitive judicial cases to have been brought
against the NHS since 1980, relating to such
matters as consultation over changes in the
provision of services and the powers of
management. His published work on obstetric
risk management is well known and he lectures
frequently on the conference circuit. He also
devised a software-assisted claims
management system in the early 1980s, which
is now the Datix system licensed to hospitals
and legal practices up and down the country
and abroad.
Career: Trained at *Philip Harner & Co*. Qualified
1977. Founded *Capsticks* 1979. Designed Datix
software for managing claims 1982 (winner
Society for Computers & Law award 1990).
Winner TSB (Business of Law Award) 1993,
Lawyer/HIFAL Firm of the Year 1997 (Best
Medium-Sized Firm).
Personal: Born 1948. Educated Bishops
Wordsworth's, Salisbury and University of
Lancaster. BA 1968, MA 1969. Leisure interests
include skiing, mountain walking and music.

CONFREY, Neil
Confreys, Cardiff (01222) 458080

DODDS-SMITH, Ian C.
Cameron McKenna, London
(0171) 367 3000
Fax: (0171) 367 2000 Partner and Head of
Healthcare Group.
Specialisation: Main area of practice is
healthcare related. Deals with the law relating to
pharmaceuticals, medical products and
devices and products in the cosmetics and food
sectors. Specialist in licensing and related
regulatory affairs, and on product liability
issues. Also covers product liability generally,
and personal injury litigation. Has handled many
product liability cases, many multi-claimant and
with international elements including hormone
pregnancy tests, oral contraceptives, blood
products, benzodiazepines, IUCDs, pesticides
and heart valves. Has dealt with several
regulatory cases to the E.C.J. including R v.
Licensing Authority ex parte Scotia and R v.
Licensing Authority ex parte Generics UK and
ER Squibb. Author of 'Product Liability for
Medical Products' in 'Medical Negligence'

(Butterworths) and 'Legal Liabilities in Clinical
Trials' in 'Early Phase Human Drug Evaluation.'
Joint Editor with Sir Abraham Goldberg of
'Pharmaceutical Medicine and the Law' (The
Royal College of Physicians). Author of various
articles on regulatory and liability issues.
Frequent lecturer in the UK and abroad.
Consultant Editor to the Personal and Medical
Injuries Law Letter, and to the Regulatory Affairs
Journal.
Prof. Memberships: Law Society, American
Bar Association, Drug Information Association,
Fellow of the Royal Society of Medicine.
Career: Joined *McKenna & Co* in 1974 and
qualified in 1976. Became a Partner in 1984.
Member of the Royal College of Physicians
Working Party on Research at Phase 1 in
Healthy Volunteers 1985-86. Member of the
Medical Research Council Working Party on
legal and ethical issues raised by Research in
the Mentally Incapacitated (1988). Temporary
Adviser (1987) to W.H.O. on the law relating to
clinical trials. Legal adviser to the Clinical
Sciences Ethics Committee of the University of
London and University College Hospital.
Personal: Born 31st July 1951. Educated at
Solihull School and Downing College,
Cambridge 1969-72. Recreations include
gardening and National Hunt racing. Lives in
London.

DURKIN, Timothy
Myer Wolff & Manley, Hull (01482) 223693
Specialisation: Mental Health Review
Tribunals, private Children Act, Divorce and
Ancillary Relief.
Prof. Memberships: Solicitors Family Law
Association, The Law Society. UK College of
Mediators.
Career: LL.B. Admitted 1973. Senior Partner
1994. London Borough Councillor early 1970s.
Co-opted member Humberside Social Services
Committee 1980 to 1990, developing mental
health and learning disability policies. Has been
undertaking Mental Health Tribunals for over 20
years and member of the Law Society Panel
since 1985.
Personal: National Chairman of MIND 1988 to
1994 and continuing membership of
Management Council of MIND. Chairman
MIND/Millennium Commission Awards from
1997.

EDWARDS, Peter Charles
Peter Edwards & Co, Hoylake
(0151) 632 6699
Founding Partner in Mental Health Department.
Specialisation: For 22 years has represented
patients detained under the Mental Health Act
1983 who wish to appeal against their
detention. Advises in other aspects of mental
health law, including consent to treatment,
capacity, and vulnerable adults in police
stations. Acted for Michael Fagan who entered
Buckingham Palace. Director of NW Law
Conferences.
Prof. Memberships: Member of NACRO
Mental Health Advisory Committee. Chair of
Merseyside Community Mental Health Services
and Dove Enterprises. Founder member of the
Law Society Mental Health and Disability
Committee; Member of the Law Society Mental
Health Review Tribunal panel.
Career: Qualified in 1975. Worked at *Yaffe*

Jackson & Ostrin 1971-76, *Rollo Mills Roberts* 1976-80 and *Aneurin Rees & Davies* 1980-89. Founded *Edwards Frais Abrahamson* in 1989. Member of the Mental Health Act Commission 1983-89, also being a member of the Central Policy Committee. Director of the Institute of Mental Health Law. Former member of national MIND and until recently was the Chair of Liverpool MIND.
Personal: Born 10th January 1952. Attended Leighton Park, Reading 1965-70.

ELDERGILL, Anselm
Anselm Eldergill, London (0171) 284 1006
Specialisation: Specialist in mental health law, in particular the detention, tribunal and criminal law provisions. Inquiries, conferences, lecturing, policy drafting and training for NHS trusts and local authorities. Discussant, *XXIIIrd International Congress on Law and Mental Health*, Sorbonne (July 1998). Chairman, IBC Conference, Mental Health Law, Regents Park (May 1998). Keynote speaker, 1st National Conference on *Risk Management in Mental Health*, Royal College of Physicians (June 1998). [PUB] Mental Health Review Tribunals - Law and Practice (*Sweet & Maxwell*, 1997, *lxxvii*, 1333pp); "The law and individual rights" in *The Treatment of the personality disordered offender* (ed. R Blackburn, *et al.*, Butterworth-Heinemann, 1998)
Prof. Memberships: Mental Health Act Commissioner (Chairman of the Legal & Ethics Committee); Alexander Maxwell Law Trust Scholar; member of, and interviewer for, the Mental Health Review Tribunal panel; David Hallett Prize for Government.

EVANS, John
Wansbroughs Willey Hargrave, Sheffield (0114) 272 7485
Partner in Health Department.
Specialisation: Healthcare law, NHS administrative law, corporate governance, untoward incidents, medical disciplinary cases, commercial issues, clinical governance and risk management. Untoward incident experience includes dealing with the aftermath of the Hillsborough, Kegworth and Allitt incidents and the Abbie Humphreys abduction and other high profile NHS cases.
Prof. Memberships: Secretary to the Queens Medical Centre, Nottingham, University Hospital NHS Trust.
Career: 1968 qualified; 1974 Solicitor; Cotswold District Council; 1977 Regional Solicitor, Trent Regional Health Authority; 1994 Secretary to the Trust, Queens Medical Centre; 1996 joined *Wansbroughs Willey Hargrave*.

FRANCIS, Barry
Beachcroft Stanleys, London (0171) 242 1011
Specialisation: PFI projects and other commercial transactions in the health and other public sectors including public sector/private sector joint ventures, facilities management contracts and procurement and administrative law advice. Current projects include major hospital building and services projects (PFI). Head of *Beachcroft Stanleys'* Projects Department and Joint Chairman of the Health Law Group. Regular speaker at conferences and seminars. Contributor to a range of specialist publications. A member of the Editorial Board of 'The PFI Report.'
Prof. Memberships: Law Society
Career: Admitted 1977, at *Beachcroft Hyman*

Isaacs (now *Beachcroft Stanleys*) Associate 1979-80, Partner 1980 to date.
Personal: Born 14th March 1953. Educated at Enfield Grammar School and University of Bristol. Interests include travel, history and food. Lives in North London.

HALLATT, Diane
Wansbroughs Willey Hargrave, Sheffield (0114) 272 7485
Partner and National Head of Health.
Specialisation: Specialises in defendant medical negligence and health service related law. Has detailed knowledge of medical negligence, risk management, inquests, the Children Act, the Mental Health Act, complaints handling, ethical issues, class actions and major untoward incidents. Has experience of a wide range of health service and public administrative law issues and has defended several Judicial Reviews. Advised in the Beverley Allit case and was involved in overseeing the HIV haemophilia litigation and in the Myodil and Benzodiazepine class actions.
Career: Qualified 1980. Trent Regional Health Authority 1986-89. Partner at *Oxley & Coward* 1989-95 and at *Wansbroughs Willey Hargrave* from February 1995.

JACKSON, Andrew
Dickinson Dees, Newcastle upon Tyne (0191) 279 9000
Specialisation: Partner and Head of the Health Sector Group at *Dickinson Dees*, specialising in defendant medical negligence claims and medico-legal advice for NHS Trusts and Health Authorities, with particular interest in cases involving obstetrics, anaesthesia, paediatrics, orthopaedics, and neurosurgery. Lectures regularly to claims managers, doctors and nurses.
Prof. Memberships: Law Society. Medico-Legal Society.
Career: Qualified in 1984. Joined *Dickinson Dees* in 1995 to develop the Health Sector Group.
Personal: Born 29 November 1955. Educated at Reeds School, Cobham 1970-1975, and University of Reading 1975-1978. Lives in Stocksfield, Northumberland. Leisure interests include running and motor racing.

KNOWLES, Stuart
The Lewington Partnership, Birmingham (0121) 454 4000
Specialisation: Medical Negligence, especially claims of utmost severity and brain damaged children. Successfully defended 'Sherlock v. Birmingham HA,' which went to the Court of Appeal, and 'Birmingham HA Brain Tumour Cases.' Works as leading member of the Birmingham County Court Medical Negligence Pilot Scheme. Also expert on Patient Confidentiality and Consent to Treatment, Medical Ethics, Inquests and Personal Injury.
Prof. Memberships: The Law Society. Birmingham Medico - Legal Society.
Career: Oxford graduate who qualified in 1986. Joined West Midlands RHA in 1988 to specialise in medical negligence. Partner in *The Lewington Partnership* 1995. Regular contributor to medical journals.
Personal: Hobbies: Travel, motorcycling, radio and diving.

LEE, Peter
Wansbroughs Willey Hargrave, Sheffield (0114) 272 7485
Specialisation: A commercial, corporate and public sector lawyer, acting for public sector organisations, particularly in the health service. Extensive experience of health service law, European Law and contracting in the public sector including PFI.
Career: Qualified 1980; Managing Partner *Oxley & Coward*, Sheffield; Qualified Public Notary 1991; joined *Wansbroughs Willey Hargrave* in 1995.

LEIGH, Bertie
Hempsons, London (0171) 836 0011
Senior Partner.
Specialisation: Principal area of practice is medical law, with particular interest in cases involving obstetrics, anaesthesia, paediatrics, orthopaedics, neurosurgery and general practice. Other main area of expertise is National Health Service Acts and associated Regulations. Has dealt with a number of Court of Appeal cases including Gregory v. Pembrokeshire (1989), Hughes v. Waltham Forest (1991), and Bull & Wakeham v. Devon Health Authority (1989), DeFreitas v. O'Brien (1994), Thomas v Brighton HA (1998), R v Nottingham HA (1996), Re MB (1997) . Major clients include the Association of Anaesthetists and the Royal College of Paediatrics and Child Health of which he is an Hon. Fellow. Author of chapters in 'Ethics & Obstetrics & Gynaecology' (RCOG 1994) and 'Safe Practice in Obstetrics & Gynaecology' (1994) 'Neonatology' (Ed Roberton & Rennie) 1997. Lectures regularly to lawyers and doctors.
Prof. Memberships: Medico-Legal Society.
Career: Qualified in 1976, having joined *Hempsons* in 1973. Became a Partner in 1977.
Personal: Born 30th August 1946. Educated at St. Christopher School, Letchworth 1960-65 and the University of East Anglia 1966-69. Lives in Clapham.

LONG, Michael
Donne Mileham & Haddock, Brighton (01273) 744240
Specialisation: Commercial/Public Authority and Health Care Unit. Head of commercial group and public authority and health care unit, specialising in NHS and local authority corporate, contractual and general matters; clients include many authorities and trusts in the south east. Other specialist areas include company transactions, commercial and marketing contracts, computer contracts, charities, IPR, insolvency, pensions and employment contracts.
Career: St. John's College Cambridge (1968 MA); articled *Stephenson Harwood*; qualified 1971; joined *Donne Mileham & Haddock* 1973; partner 1976; Law Society Council member, inner Sussex 1982 to date.
Personal: Born 1947; resides Hove, East Sussex; enjoys Scotland, opera, theatre; member United Oxford & Cambridge Club.

MACKINTOSH, Nicola
T.V. Edwards, London (0171) 791 1050
See under Administrative & Public Law, p. 88

MCCLOSKEY, Colin
Jacqueline Everett & Co, London (0181) 664 6042

MYLAN, David
David Mylan, London (0181) 347 7270
Specialisation: Mental Health Review Tribunals in particular restricted cases.
Prof. Memberships: Law Society Mental Health Panel. Convenor Mental Health Review Tribunals Advocates Group. Legal Member of Mental Health Review Tribunals North Thames Region.
Career: B.Sc. in Behavioural Science. Qualified as Solicitor 1981.

PARSONS, Andrew E.
Radcliffes, London (0171) 222 7040
Partner in Litigation Department (Head of Health Group).
Specialisation: Principal area of practice is Healthcare Law. Specialises in substantial claims and has acted in cases relating to most medical specialities, particularly psychiatric, obstetric and paediatric cases. Also advises on the administration and powers of the NHS. Extensive experience of psychiatric related issues and the Mental Health Act. Also advocacy at inquests. Advised on innovative commercial contract with local authority for provision of accommodation by NHS Trust. Has acted in several drug related fatal cases and advised on drug testing protocols. Acts for Health Authorities and NHS Trusts, Teaching Hospitals, private clinics and health insurers. Also acts for institutional, property investment fund and NHS clients in connection with property and general commercial litigation matters. Author of 'Tenant Default Under Commercial Leases' (1993, 2nd edition published 1996). Lectures widely to doctors, nurses and other NHS staff.
Prof. Memberships: Law Society, City of Westminster Law Society (Senior Vice President), Royal Society of Medicine, Secretary of Queen Elizabeth Hospital Research Fund.
Career: Qualified in 1987 having been at *Radcliffes* since 1985. Became a Partner in

1992.
Personal: Born 5th February 1963. Educated at Norwich School 1971-1980 and the University of Reading 1981-84. Leisure pursuits include music, sports and handicrafts. Member of Mensa and RAC. Lives in London.

PICKUP, Raith
Mills & Reeve, Cambridge
+44 (0)1223 364422
Specialisation: Head of PFI at *Mills & Reeve*. Considerable experience of advising on capital projects in the NHS. Currently (June 1998) advising on approximately 20 PFI schemes in the health sector. His work includes joint ventures between NHS trusts and other public sector bodies or the private sector; EC procurement and tendering; CIM and Concode compliance, income generation schemes. He is a regular speaker at NHS seminars.

SCOTT-MONCRIEFF, Lucy
Scott-Moncrieff, Harbour & Sinclair, London (0171) 242 4114

TOPPING, Christopher Paul
Jackson & Canter, Liverpool (0151) 298 1166
Specialisation: Specialist in Mental Health - representation at tribunals for clients detained under the Mental Health Act 1983. In the last year represented two clients with immigration and nationality difficulties who faced deportation under Section 86 Mental Health Act. Specialist in other civil liberty matters such as civil actions against Police.
Prof. Memberships: Member of Mental Health Review Tribunal Panel. Member of Law Society Personal Injury Panel. Member of Association of Personal Injury Lawyers.
Career: LLB (Hons) Sheffield University 1985. Law Society Finals (Chester) 1986. Partner in firm of *Jackson and Canter* since 1992.

WADDINGTON, Sheila
The Lewington Partnership, Birmingham (0121) 454 4000
Specialisation: Corporate Governance; powers and responsibilities of NHS bodies; corporate advice and interpreting the law on the NHS; joint commissioning and funding schemes; intellectual property; income generation; public procurements; competitive tendering and market testing. National expert on mergers and acquisitions of NHS trusts; community care; primary care and GP fundholding arrangements. Public Private Partnerships.
Prof. Memberships: The Law Society.
Career: Born and educated in USA. Mature entrant to profession. Worked in local government before joining West Midlands RHA as Secretary to the Authority and Deputy Regional Legal Adviser. Founded *The Lewington Partnership* in 1993.
Personal: Large family. Gardening. Reading and walking. Classical music.

WRIGHT, Tim L.
Wansbroughs Willey Hargrave, Winchester (01962) 841444
See under Medical Negligence: Mainly Defendant, p. 580

YOUNG, Tim
Hempsons, Harrogate (01423) 522331
Health Care.
Specialisation: Partner heading the Commercial and PFI team. Specialises in advising Health Authorities and NHS Trusts on commercial, constitutional and organisational issues including PFI, market testing and corporate governance. Has advised on various mergers of NHS Trusts. Joined *Hempsons* in 1996 and has been dealing with various PFI Schemes for the provision of health care facilities. During 1997/98 has brought four PFI schemes through to completion including two community hospitals and a mobile communications system for an Ambulance NHS Trust.

HOUSING ASSOCIATIONS

RESEARCH: In compiling the tables, we consider all the information available to us, paying particular regard to the market research carried out by our team of ten qualified lawyers. (The researchers' details are set out on page three.) The rankings, therefore, reflect the opinion of the marketplace as revealed by systematic and objective research: see page four. (Our research is audited every year by the British Market Research Bureau.)

OVERVIEW: With the list of leading individuals starting to look suspiciously like Trowers & Hamlins' notepaper, they have such a dominance of the social housing market that their position, for the present, looks unassailable. Not only are they significantly larger than other firms but they have a geographical presence in the regions which makes them unique. Of the competition, Devonshires is chasing the hardest.

Catherine Hand and Keith Jenkins' firm continues to go from strength to strength and despite a tiny work force (just the two of them) many interviewees reckoned they had the profile of all but the largest firms.

In the regions we have separated Wales from the South West. Not only is Wales a separate market but it is regulated under a different regime, by Housing for Wales (soon to become part of the Welsh Office in the run up to devolution). In the Midlands the major change is the recognition of a number of firms in the East Midlands. In the North, Trowers has a slight lead based in part on its ability to call on the resources of the London office.

This year we have a separate table dealing with the English firms that advise funders lending to associations. Whilst most of the firms ranked in the main tables will act on funding matters for associations, few firms undertake significant amounts of work for lenders. In addition the major players in the field, Allen & Overy and Clifford Chance, have no involvement in social housing except as advisers to funders. Whilst Fladgate Fielder received a number of recommendations for inclusion in this table, the firm's clients are no longer actively lending in the market.

LEADING FIRMS · LONDON

TROWERS & HAMLINS

DEVONSHIRES
PRINCE EVANS

JENKINS & HAND
LAWRENCE GRAHAM
LEWIS SILKIN
WINCKWORTH & PEMBERTON

HIGHLY REGARDED FIRMS

Maclays
Manches & Co

Evans Butler Wade
G.L. Hockfield & Co
Marsons Solicitors

Andersen Solicitors
Dawson & Co
Edwin Coe
Hodge Jones & Allen

LONDON

Trowers & Hamlins (22ptnrs/25assts). "A good mob that you can't really knock." Benefitting from the IBM Syndrome and destined to stay at the top of the tree until "a whole gang of their competitors merge." Not seen to be grafting for work as hard as some of the others but they don't need to. Whilst many associations use other firms for day to day matters they almost instinctively go to Trowers for the complex issues. The team include the "fun to work with" *Jonathan* 'The Governor' *Adlington,* the "shrewd" *Sarah Hayes,* the "impressive and focused" *Jennifer Gubbins, Ian Doolittle, Ian Graham, Rosemary Hart* and *James Hawkins,* "defi-

nitely up & coming." The firm also has a dedicated housing finance team of six partners and five assistants. **Clients/Work:** Acting for Western Challenge HA and Poole NHS Trust on a £4m PFI staff accommodation project. Acting for English Churches Housing Group on the transfer of dual registered care home from charity to charitable HA to provide accommodation and care through its charitable subsidiary, Heritage Care, to residents. Housing Corporation sale of a loan book portfolio of more than £1bn. Rushmoor HA, the first HA to be financed by capital market bond issue.

Devonshires (25 fee-earners) "First rate." With 165 HA clients in England & Wales, the firm may no longer be lean but it remains as hungry as ever, particularly out-

side the South East. In one year the percentage of work coming from north of Watford has increased from between 5-15% to 48%. The "personable bunch" includes *Andy Cowan* ("puts himself about and works enormously hard") and *Allan Hudson.* **Clients/Work:** Acting on all the major Eurobond issues in the housing sector, raising over £100bn for clients. Contractual advice relating to replacement computer systems for housing associations. Advising on corporate structures for HAs, involving mergers/demergers and conversions to charitable status.

Prince Evans The firm's success in HA work is envied by other small practices. Acting for over 80 associations, the firm is described as "great on ideas." The west

London location and the consequent difficulty of attracting the right people is seen to be the main limiting factor on future growth. Three heavyweight partners stand out: *Louis Roberts, Trevor Morley* and *Robert Jennings*. **Clients/Work:** Transfer of £50m public sector loan portfolio for a foreign bank. Acting on the LSVT for the London Borough of Brent to Fortunegate Ltd. Acting for a newly formed housing company in the provision of £28m of finance as part of the first wave of ERCF funding.

Jenkins & Hand (2ptnrs) *Catherine Hand* and *Keith Jenkins* are as niche as you can be, limited capacity but enormously successful, acting for 70 HAs in their first year. Perceived as consultants structuring transactions at the early stages rather than sweating away at the paper mill, although they actually do more than just analyse and advise. No assistants or legal executives or plans to recruit any. **Clients/Work:** Advising 10 associations on the implementation of group structures. Acting for 3 HAs on the acquisition of substantial portfolios of National Health staff accommodation. Keith Jenkins drafted the new Model Rules for the National Housing Federation published in 1997.

Lawrence Graham (2ptnrs/2assts in the Local & Public Authority Unit, 8 other fee earners throughout the firm.) Already "the other solicitors instructed on LSVTs" and fairly aggressive in their efforts to build up a presence in more general housing work. During 1997 the firm acted for 25 HAs. *Simon Randall* has a long history of personal involvement in the area. *Nick Turner*, a new entrant to the lists, is the firm's principal financing guy, leading a specialist HA finance team of 5 ptnrs and 2 assts. **Clients/Work:** Completion of large scale voluntary transfers of housing stock to top £1bn and over 65,000 houses. Signature of heads of terms for the £200m regeneration of Edmonton Town Centre for LB of Enfield. Advising South Oxon HA on a £106m facility from Bradford & Bingley Building Society. Advising Elgar HA on the restructuring of its £90m facility.

Lewis Silkin (5ptnrs/8assts) Have 60 social housing clients in London and the South East. "Fantastic" remains the most popular description of *Gillian Bastow*. *Andrew Thomas* was also recommended. **Clients/Work:** Major regeneration project for an LSVT association involving the buy-back of properties sold under Right to Buy, demolition and the creation of a mixed tenure scheme. Advising on a Model Form of Conditions of Contract for high value term maintenance contracts for social landlords. A sensitive possession case consistent with the new provisions in the '96 Housing Act to deal with "bad neighbours."

Winckworth & Pemberton (3ptnrs/11assts) According to one school of thought, last year's departures have made a positive

contribution to the firm's future even if their profile in the short term has suffered. Still a strong practice, with their turnover up 30% since the departures even if they are not as visible. 10% of housing work is finance related, acting for lenders and borrowers. Have taken on a tax adviser specialising in social housing. *Andrew Murray* is "always a pleasure to deal with," as is *Roger Fitton*. **Clients/Work:** Completing a PFI transaction acting for an association in partnership with the London Borough of Islington. Completing and implementing a tax efficient group structure strategy for a Home Counties association. Documenting the regeneration of a 700 unit scheme in the London Docklands in a partnership between housebuilders, housing associations and local authorities for a complete new build scheme.

Maclays The English arm of Maclay Murray and Spens is a new entrant having recruited the well regarded *Chris Smith* from Stones Porter. Handle work for 25 HAs. **Clients/Work:** Instructed by two large HAs to advise on their employment matters. Acting on a 250 unit re-provision exercise on the South Coast. Representing a Royal Charter charity on a rule change involving the Privy Council.

Manches & Co (2ptnrs/2assts) *Richard Frost* has been active in social housing for 30 years and the firm acts for 25/30 associations ranging from the huge to the minute. **Clients/Work:** Anchor Trust on its PFI acquisition of 17 residential care homes from Surrey County Council. Christian Action (Enfield) HA Ltd's acquisition and financing of a foyer for young people in Edmonton. National Housing Federation resolving issues of registration under the Registered Homes Act.

Evans Butler Wade (4ptnrs/3assts) "Effective." Two thirds of the firm's work is for social landlords, split evenly between property and housing management. The work is consistent with the firm's size (eg loans under £10m). Can claim 40 HA clients. *Chris Evans* – "has a personal style and clients love him for it." **Clients/Work:** Acting for three HAs on the acquisition of the £7m Danesbury schools site. Acquiring a site in California Road for Threshold HA.

G.L. Hockfield & Co (2ptnrs/2assts) Predominantly involved in litigation and advising on housing management. Do not get involved on the development side or in acquisitions. A number of big name clients. **Clients/Work:** Acting for a local authority obtaining injunctions in respect of anti-social behaviour. Drafting a management agreement for a tenants' co-operative. Acting for an association in possession proceedings when the Court of Appeal found that the County Court judge had wrongly exercised his discretion to set aside a possession order.

Marsons Solicitors (1ptnr/2assocs) "The nuisance specialists, who deliver what

clients want." Housing management, litigation and urban regeneration for 12 HAs and a large number of housing cooperatives but do not do development or funding work. *Kevin Lee* has a fearsome reputation and enters the lists as a consequence. **Clients/Work:** Major nuisance trial for Hyde HA reported in a four page article in the Sunday Times magazine. Extended grounds for possession cases for LB of Lambeth under the '96 Act. Regeneration projects in Greenwich/Deptford.

Andersens Solicitors (3ptnrs/2assocs/2assts) Based in Croydon, a new entrant following a number of strong recommendations. Act for over 20 HAs ranging up to 10,000 units.

Dawson & Co (1ptnr/1asst) Perfectly competent but not a big player. Handle acquisition and sales, development schemes, transfers and contentious issues.

Edwin Coe (2ptnrs/1asst) Not a major operator in the field but act for half a dozen HAs, mostly on constitutional and financial issues. Also handle litigation for associations.

Hodge Jones & Allen (1ptnr/1asst) Act for half a dozen small to medium HAs and housing cooperatives. Four other lawyers act for tenants. **Clients/Work:** Represented appellant in Payne v Barnet London Borough on the liability for structural defects in relation to the right to buy leases. Advised Bridge HA on a group re-organisation.

LEADING INDIVIDUALS · LONDON

ADLINGTON Jonathan Trowers & Hamlins
BASTOW Gillian Lewis Silkin
COWAN Andrew Devonshires
DOOLITTLE Ian Trowers & Hamlins
GRAHAM Ian Trowers & Hamlins
GUBBINS Jennifer Trowers & Hamlins
HAYES Sarah Trowers & Hamlins
JENKINS Keith Jenkins & Hand
MURRAY Andrew Winckworth & Pemberton
ROBERT Louis Prince Evans

BURGESS Despina Clifford Chance
EVANS Chris Evans Butler Wade
FITTON Roger Winckworth & Pemberton
FROST Richard Manches & Co
HAND Catherine Jenkins & Hand
HART Rosemary Trowers & Hamlins
HUDSON Allan James Devonshires
MORLEY Trevor Prince Evans
RANDALL Simon Lawrence Graham
SMITH Chris Maclays
THOMAS Andrew Lewis Silkin

UP AND COMING

HAWKINS James Trowers & Hamlins
JENNINGS Robert Prince Evans
LEE Kevin Marsons Solicitors
TURNER Nicholas Lawrence Graham

SEE PROFILES AT END OF THIS SECTION

FIRMS ADVISING LENDERS UK WIDE

Allen & Overy (5ptnrs/20assts) The top lending firm. Operating only in the financial context, advising on capital markets and financing issues rather than constitutional matters. Adam Kleil's team are "incredibly professional." **Clients/Work:** Halifax plc on

£88.5m facility for Lichfield District HA to finance the LSVT from Lichfield DC. Hambros Bank, the lead manager, and the Prudential Trustee Company Ltd on a £46.3m bond issue by Haven Funding, the proceeds of which were on-lent to Hyde HA, Devon and Cornwall HA and Portsmouth HA.

Clifford Chance (6ptnrs/20assts) A leading firm acting for funders. *Despina Burgess* is "straight-talking." Considered to be the most innovative in this field. **Clients/Work:** For Banque Paribas and Abbey National on the first ERCF transfer to a stand-alone housing company (Poplar HARCA). For Banque Paribas arranging the first bond issue for a LSVT for London & Quadrant. For Nationwide on the first ERCF housing loan to a local housing company, part of the group structure arranged for Anglia Housing Group.

Addleshaw Booth & Co (Leeds/ Manchester) (4ptnrs/9assts) The "two

Richards" lead a well respected and high profile, detail conscious team, advising funders lending to HAs. Involved in 30 LSVTs, eight acting for the lead funders, with a total aggregate value of approx. £8bn. **Clients/Work:** Advising Bradford & Bingley on £106m loan facilities to South Oxfordshire HA to fund the LSVT of South Oxfordshire DC's housing stock. Acting for Britannia Building Society in connection with loans facilities to fund the transfer of housing stock of Scottish Homes to various associations. Acting for Northern Rock on the £25m refinancing of Waverley Housing Trust.

Wilde Sapte (4ptnrs/10assts) Act for funders lending to associations. **Clients/Work:** For Dresdner Kleinwort Benson as arranger of the North British HA's £100m secured bond issue and Northern Counties HA's £30m guaranteed secured stock issue. Bayerische Vereinsbank's purchase of the entire housing loan portfolio of Yamaichi.

LEADERS' PROFILES · LONDON

ADLINGTON, Jonathan
Trowers & Hamlins, London (0171) 423 8000
Partner. Head of Property Department.
Specialisation: Vast experience of housing law and the housing association movement having built a specialist practice over more than 20 years. Deals with all aspects of commercial and residential property, from purchases, sales and mortgages to development agreements, structures and funding. Instrumental in the development of private finance for social housing. Acts for Housing Associations, Local Authorities and lenders. Regular speaker at housing events and for funding bodies.

BASTOW, Gillian
Lewis Silkin, London (0171) 227 8000
Partner and Head of Social Housing Group.
Specialisation: All aspects of housing association activity including land acquisition and development, partnerships involving housing associations, local authorities/health authorities, private and public finance, care in the community schemes, landlord and tenant issues, constitutional matters and specialist work with housing co-operatives.
Prof. Memberships: Law Society, Solicitors European Group, NHF Lawyers Sub-Group, Housing Association Committee Member.
Career: Qualified 1981 with *Lewis Silkin*. Partner 1984.
Personal: Born October 1953. Attended Somerville College Oxford (MA) and Leicester University (LLM). Lives in London.

BURGESS, Despina
Clifford Chance, London (0171) 600 1000
Specialisation: Housing association finance.
Career: Admitted 1987, *Clifford Chance* 1987-1995, *Allen & Overy* 1996-1997, *Clifford Chance* 1997 - Head of Housing Finance.

COWAN, Andrew
Devonshires, London (0171) 628 7576
Specialisation: Partner and head of finance leading the housing association finance unit which has negotiated about £1.6 billion of

housing association funding since 1988 from the capital markets, banks and building societies; acts for ten banks, building societies and over 165 RSL based all over England and Wales and a group association borrowing vehicle. More recently involved with group structures, PFI's for NHS Trusts and RSLs. Lectures widely on finance, ERCF/SRB bids and RSL strategies
Career: Articled *Hobson Audley*; qualified 1989; *Trowers & Hamlins* 1990-1991; *Devonshires* 1991; Partner 1993; regular speaker on housing finance; committee member of a London based housing association.
Personal: Educated University of East Anglia (1986 LL.B Hons. 2(2)). Born 1964: resides London. Leisure: backpacking, football, swimming, Latin America.

DOOLITTLE, Ian
Trowers & Hamlins, London (0171) 423 8000
Partner, Public Sector, Head of Public Sector.
Specialisation: Team leader on many housing stock transfers, first LSVT and more recently urban estate-based transfers. Is an authority on public/private sector partnerships. Also specialist in environmental law.

EVANS, Chris
Evans Butler Wade, London
(0181) 858 8926
Specialisation: Advises social landlords on a wide range of matters including acquisition and development, loans and finance, partnerships and constitutional, student accommodation. Also handles employment contracts, claims and discrimination cases.
Prof. Memberships: Employment Lawyers Association. Education Law Association. Member of London Committee of N.B.H.A.
Career: Admitted 1980. Partner in *Stitt & Co.* 1980. Founded own firm in 1985 with Gill Butler.
Personal: Born March 1952. Queens College Cambridge. Lives in London. The renaissance of Welsh Rugby.

FITTON, Roger
Winckworth & Pemberton (incorporating Sherwood & Co), London (0171) 593 5000
Specialisation: Housing law with emphasis on urban regeneration projects, NHS transfers and constitutional work. Highlights of last year include: acquisition of 700 unit inner London scheme in partnership between associations, housebuilders and local authorities; completion of 5 NHS stock transfers; re-structuring the use by associations of their "corporate trusteeship" of legally independent registered charities.
Prof. Memberships: Law Society.
Career: Oulder Hill Community School, Rochdale 1974-1979; Exeter College, Oxford, Law 1980-1983; Trained, *Boodle Hatfield* 1984-1986; Assistant Solicitor, *Denton Hall* 1986-1989; Assistant, then partner, *Winckworth & Pemberton* 1989-1998.
Personal: Horticulture, architecture and landscapes. Lives Clapham, London.

FROST, Richard
Manches & Co, London (0171) 404 4433
Email: richard.frost@manches.co.uk
Specialisation: Main areas of practice are housing associations and other social landlords and retirement housing.
Career: Qualified in 1970. Joined *Manches & Co* and became a Partner in 1971 then merged with *Manches & Co* in 1993.
Personal: Born in 1944. Educated at Haileybury and Worcester College, Oxford. Recreations include tennis and music. Lives near Dorking, Surrey.

GRAHAM, Ian
Trowers & Hamlins, London (0171) 423 8000
Partner, Housing.
Specialisation: Work for Associations includes advising on group structures, powers, consortium development, assured and secure tenancies, management contracts with local authorities, stock transfer, local housing companies, CCT/VCT, joint ventures to provide student/nurse accommodation, shared ownership, care in the community schemes and

partnerships with local authorities. Also deals with the PFI and Health Sector work, including joint ventures with Associations. A prolific author and public speaker.

GUBBINS, Jennifer
Trowers & Hamlins, London (0171) 423 8000
Partner, Company & Commercial. Head of Housing Finance.
Specialisation: A corporate finance specialist and leading practitioner in funding for the housing movement. Experience includes innovative work on securitisation as well as stock/bond issues, loans and the acquisitions/transfers of public sector companies and undertakings. Experience covers the PFI, Charity law, Local Housing Companies and Health. Member of The National Blood Authority and on editorial board of Charity Law & Practice Review.

HAND, Catherine
Jenkins & Hand, London (0171) 222 5002
See under Local Government, p. 553

HART, Rosemary
Trowers & Hamlins, London (0171) 423 8000
Partner, Housing.
Specialisation: Works primarily for housing associations, voluntary and public sector bodies. Experience includes: property acquisition and development including projects in the Private Finance Initiative relating to staff and student accommodation, nursing and care homes, joint ventures and security work; nomination agreements, leases, tenancies, constitutional advice, care in the community and management schemes. Regular author and speaker.

HAWKINS, James
Trowers & Hamlins, London (0171) 423 8000
Specialisation: Partner Public Sector Department. Specialist in public/ private sector partnerships. Is an authority on housing stock transfers and, in particular, urban transfers, local housing companies and the Estates Renewal Challenge Fund. Also specialises in group structure and residential care home transfers.
Career: University of Birmingham; Qualified 1989. *Trowers & Hamlins* 1991 to date. Partner 1996.

HAYES, Sarah
Trowers & Hamlins, London (0171) 423 8000
Partner, Housing/Corporate Finance.
Specialisation: General expertise in property finance, secured and unsecured. Particular specialism in housing finance, acting for borrowers and lenders. Experience covers hedging arrangements, stock issue, syndicated lending, bonds and securities, group structures, general commercial and charitable issues. Writes regularly for housing and charitable press. Experienced speaker at housing, charitable and funding events.

HUDSON, Allan James
Devonshires, London (0171) 628 7576
Partner in Housing Association Development and Finance Department.
Specialisation: Principal area is complex consortium developments of sites and provision of private finance. Also patient hotels. Practice

also covers commercial property work, including acquisition, disposal and management of investment property. Has done pioneering work on patient hotels in Glasgow, Liverpool and Nottingham.
Career: Qualified in 1978. At *Penningtons* 1978-81, *Nabarro Nathanson* 1981-82 and *Knapp Fishers* 1982-84. Joined *Devonshires* in 1984 and became a Partner in 1985.
Personal: Born 7th July 1954. Educated at Poole Grammar School and Durham University (BA 1st Class Hons). Leisure interests include theatre, cinema and gardening. Lives in Godalming.

JENKINS, Keith
Jenkins & Hand, London (0171) 222 5002
Specialisation: Closely involved with the Housing Association movement for about twenty years, he specialises in Housing, Co-ops and local authorities. He has made a significant contribution to the growth and development of social housing. He is regarded as one of the most imaginative achievers in this sector.
Career: Qualified in 1974. Joined *Winckworth & Pemberton* in 1972, becoming a partner in 1977. Set up *Jenkins & Hand* 1996.
Personal: Born 10th May 1949. Read law at Lincoln College, Oxford. Leisure interests include reading & rock music. Lives in London.

JENNINGS, Robert
Prince Evans, London (0181) 567 3477
Specialisation: Litigation Partner; experienced in all aspects of corporate, commercial and public sector litigation; particular emphasis on construction (including non-contentious drafting of build contract documentation) property litigation and employment; advising/ drafting the build contract documentation in respect of the redevelopment of the Blackbird Leys Estate, Southwark Five Estates together with Church End and Roundwood Estate (Fortunegate Community Housing). Has written articles and lectured on a variety of construction and housing management issues.
Prof. Memberships: Member of London Solicitor's Litigation Society.
Career: Qualified 1987; became a partner at *Prince Evans* in 1988; Born 21 June 1961; Lives in Ealing.

LEE, Kevin Aidan
Marsons Solicitors, Bromley
(0181) 313 1300
Specialisation: Specialises in housing management issues for R.S.L.'s and local authorities including high level estate management litigation and nuisance litigation. Urban regeneration and full range of housing and landlord and tenant litigation. Also lectures on environmental and landlord and tenant issues.
Prof. Memberships: Law Society, Chartered Institute of Housing, Property Litigation Association.
Career: Qualified 1990. Partner *Marsons* 1992. Head of property litigation.
Personal: Born London 1964. Lives Croydon. Leisure includes Crystal Palace Football Club and soul music.

MORLEY, Trevor
Prince Evans, London (0181) 567 3477
Partner in Housing and Public Sector Department.
Specialisation: Experienced in all aspects of housing association finance, including banking facilities and capital markets issues, with particular emphasis on shared ownership finance. Also undertakes property work, including acquisitions, development, consortium arrangements, long and short term funding, disposals and vires issues. He is a committee member of Network Housing Association, and has lectured extensively on housing related topics.
Personal: Born 28th December, 1953. Lives in Cobham.

MURRAY, Andrew J.
Winckworth & Pemberton (incorporating Sherwood & Co), London (0171) 593 5000
Partner in Housing and Local Government.
Specialisation: Main area of practice is housing law, with particular expertise in finance and development projects. Addresses various seminars organised by professional bodies and clients.
Prof. Memberships: Law Society.
Career: Qualified in 1987. Joined *Winckworth & Pemberton* in 1988, becoming a Partner in 1989.
Personal: Attended Manchester University 1978-81 (English Language and Literature). Lives in Richmond, Surrey.

RANDALL, Simon
Lawrence Graham, London (0171) 379 0000
See under Local Government, p. 553

ROBERT, Louis
Prince Evans, London (0181) 567 3477
Senior Partner in Housing Regeneration and Public Sector Department.
Specialisation: Principal area of practice is new initiatives and joint ventures in housing, health and community care. Also handles housing association corporate matters and funding. Acted in the redevelopment of the Blackbird Leys Estate, Oxford, Hackney NOW, Southwark Five Estates and Lewisham major SRB projects and currently on Local Housing Companies in Brent and Tower Hamlets HAT and Care Home Transfers in several boroughs, legal author of the report by the Audit Commission on the financial/ legal framework for Community Care. Has written articles and lectured on a variety of housing and healthcare issues and lectured extensively on a range of housing related topics. Member of the NHF Legal Working Party.
Career: Qualified in 1969. Became a Partner at *Prince Evans* in 1972. Now Senior Partner.
Personal: Born 23rd July 1943. Lives in Kew, Surrey.

SMITH, Chris
Maclay Murray & Spens, London
(0171) 606 6130
Partner in Housing Association Department.
Specialisation: Principal area of practice covers all aspects of social housing work with particular expertise in employment law, constitutional work and Care in the Community. Other main area of practice is development work including consortium arrangements. Currently engaged in a major south coast reprovision project involving two hundred and fifty properties and associated amenities.

Career: Qualified in 1978. Became a Partner with *Asshetons* in 1980 and in the merged firm of *Manches & Co.*, then joined *Stones Porter* as a Partner in 1993, and *Maclays* (associated with *Maclay Murray & Spens*) in 1998.
Personal: Born 22 October 1953. Attended University College, Cardiff 1972-75. Leisure pursuits include golf and squash. Lives in Godalming.

THOMAS, Andrew
Lewis Silkin, London (0171) 227 8000
Partner in Property Department.
Specialisation: Advises housing associations in all aspects of the activities including property, purchasing developing and financing, landlord and tenant law and organisation and stuctures.

Qualified mediator since 1993.
Prof. Memberships: Law Society Practice and Remuneration Development Committee 1988-1993, Member of Legal Aid Board 1993-1996, Deputy District Judge since 1996.
Career: Qualified at *Lewis Silkin* in 1974, having joined them in 1972. Partner since 1976.
Personal: Married with two daughters. Lives in Dulwich SE21. Hobbies include choral singing, opera and triathlon.

TURNER, Nicholas
Lawrence Graham, London (0171) 379 0000
Specialisation: Partner in *Lawrence Graham's* banking team and specialises in advising housing associations and local housing companies on all aspects of financing. Particular

specialisation in the funding aspects of large scale voluntary transfers, syndicated and bilateral lending arrangements, restructuring and refinancing of facilities, funding issues relating to group structures, security documentation and issues relevant to all of the above. Experience also includes development facilities, derivatives, PFI and ERCF. General experience in most aspects of banking and finance (and in particular property finance) and capital markets.
Career: Prior to joining *Lawrence Graham* spent one year as a money/derivatives broker with *EXCO Plc*. Qualified at *Lawrence Graham* in 1989 and became a partner in 1997.
Personal: Educated at University of East Anglia (LLB (Hons)). Lives in North London. Married with two children.

SOUTH EAST

LEADING FIRMS • SOUTH EAST
COFFIN MEW & CLOVER Portsmouth
OWEN WHITE Slough
PENNINGTONS Newbury
CRIPPS HARRIES HALL Tunbridge Wells
FITZHUGH GATES Brighton
SHERRARDS St. Albans
WHISKERS Harlow

Coffin Mew & Clover (7ptnrs/6assts) By far the best known firm in the South East. Social Housing is headed by *Jennifer Bennett,* "someone who asks intelligent questions, always a sign of quality." **Clients/Work:** Advising on corporate, commercial and partnering aspects of Hyde HA and partners in the Southampton Single Regeneration Budget Programme. Eastleigh HA's acquisition of two blocks of market rental flats under an innovative leasing scheme from an institutional investor. Transfer of properties following group structure re-organisation.

Owen White (3ptnrs/4assts – do varying amounts) Acting for 21 HAs on the development and management side of things. **Clients/Work:** 100% success rate in nuisance injunctions for Airways, Hart and Sanctuary. Leasehold development arrangements turning office accommodation above shops into rented units for Beacon.

Penningtons (1ptnr/1asst) Team is part of the commercial property department, based in Newbury. Have a reputation in social housing. Act for four HA's

Cripps Harries Hall (2ptnrs/2assts) One dedicated partner acting for five HAs. A lead-ing firm in Kent and Sussex, with a reputation for litigation.

Fitzhugh Gates Tony Foot is building a following on the South Coast.

Sherrards (3ptnrs/3assts) Active in HA litigation, acting for associations in "tenant from hell" situations and related matter*s*. Non-contentious work is not a major part of the practice. **Clients/Work:** Serious nuisance cases on behalf of HAs where tenants are involved with violence, prostitution and drug dealing. Rent arrears, mutual exchanges, new powers under the Housing Act 1996, breach of covenant and all forms of possession claims.

LEADING INDIVIDUALS SOUTH EAST
BENNETT Jennifer Coffin Mew & Clover

SOUTH WEST

LEADING FIRMS • SOUTH WEST
BURGES SALMON Bristol
TROWERS & HAMLINS Exeter
STONES CANN & HALLETT Exeter
BEVAN ASHFORD Bristol

Burges Salmon (3ptnrs/3assts) *Stephen McNulty* is well known for social housing in the Bristol area and is joined by an assistant – the former head of legal resources at Kingfisher HA, now specialising in constitutional and regulatory matters. **Clients/Work:** Major refunding exercise for an association. Completing an inner city regeneration scheme. Stock transfer of former MoD accommodation.

Trowers & Hamlins (2ptnrs) *Joseph Acton* ("highly competent and gets the job done") and *Peter Keuls* ("an absolutely superb operator") do more or less everything from Exeter except negotiating loan documents. **Clients/Work:** Acting for Kerrier Homes Trust Ltd on the transfer to the trust of Kerrier DC's housing stock. Acting for Sanctuary HA on the provision of student accommodation for Falmouth College of Arts. Representing Midas Homes Ltd, The Guinness Trust, Devon & Cornwall HA and Sovereign HA on a consortium agreement to redevelop a site at Chaddleworth, Plymouth for both speculative and social housing.

Stones Cann & Hallett (2ptnrs) "Given their size, the quality of their work is excellent." Do "everything" but concentrate on non-contentious work, including funding and site acquisition. *Nick Dyer* is newly recommended. **Clients/Work:** Acting for Western Challenge HA on the purchase of 10.5 acres of development land where the association will construct 88 houses to be leased to the MoD, and in connection with a management agreement with Somerset CC to provide care in the community accommodation for 200 people with learning disabilities. Acting for two of the main clearing banks completing charges over a number of HA residential developments.

Bevan Ashford Core team of five based in Bristol, however some work may be carried out from offices local to an association if appropriate. *Ken Mortimer*, an associate and the lead solicitor, is "co-operative and turns things around quickly." Act for 12 HAs, and starting to do more funding work. **Clients/Work:** Advising on the £2m Bristol Foyer project, funded by the Housing Corporation, EC Urban Funding and managed by Knightstone HA to provide accommodation and training facilities for 16 to 25 year olds. Site acquisition of 76 affordable houses for rent at Weston-Super-Mare.

LEADING INDIVIDUALS SOUTH WEST
KEULS Peter Trowers & Hamlins
MCNULTY Stephen Burges Salmon
ACTON Joseph Trowers & Hamlins
DYER Nick Stones Cann & Hallett

UP AND COMING
MORTIMER Ken Bevan Ashford

WALES

Hugh James (4ptnrs – varying amounts) Traditionally known for handling large amount of housing work in Wales. Clients/Work: Wales & West HA, Aelwyd HA, Housing for Wales, national banks and building societies

Morgan Bruce (8ptnrs/6assts) Acting for 21of the 30 HAs in Wales and seeking to expand into the South West. Clients/Work: Refinancing of Hafod HA's porfolio. £15m refinancing facility and work on two Foyer Schemes for Clwyd Alyn HA.

Eversheds (Cardiff) All Eversheds offices deal with HA work to some degree but the Cardiff office is the centre of the National HA Unit, headed by Anne Hayward. The Cardiff office does all Barclays lending work in Wales. The firm has also opened a HA unit in Bristol. Clients/Work: Winning Swansea HA and Bro Myrddin HA as new clients. Acquiring development sites for Eastern Valley HA including a variety of related finance drawdowns. Acting for Bourneville Village Trust on potential judicial review advice on tenant incentive scheme grant and group re-structuring of merger of subsidiaries.

MIDLANDS

Anthony Collins (7ptnrs/15assts) One of the few in the Midlands who do a significant amount of housing law as opposed to just property work. *Martin* "the Man" *Knox* might be a bit intense for some people but has a "well earned reputation for constitutional work." The practice covers the South and the North West as well as the Midlands. Clients/Work: Work for LSVT associations on the transfer of housing stock, housing management, conveyancing and development. Conversions to charitable status. PFI and ERCF.

Irwin Mitchell (3ptnrs/6assts) Regional heavyweights. *Hugo Stephens* is "an excellent magician," with a wealth of experience (he came from Prince Evans) "well above anyone else locally" according to some. Clients/Work: Advising South Oxfordshire DC and Oldham Metropolitan BC on their housing stock transfers. Advising Toynbee Housing Group on £20m new facilities. Advising Harden HA on its conversion to charitable status and its new group structure.

Browne Jacobson A new leader in the East Midlands concentrating on property acquisition and development work. *David Huddleston* is "a nice chap, always keen to help out and extremely professional." Clients/Work: Acquisition and funding of two sites for student accommodation in Leicester. Acting on the redevelopment of 170 local authorities to produce in excess of 260 units. Acting for an association in moving a Derbyshire village followed by the subsequent charging of the properties for £5m.

Freeth Cartwright Hunt Dickins (1ptnr/4assts between 25 to 75% of their time) One of the leading practices in the East Midlands, acting for some of the largest and best known HAs. Clients/Work: Concluding the Trivett Square project for Nottingham Community HA with funding from English Partnerships. Acquiring the former Baker & Plumb department store in Nottingham for Derwent HA for mixed development. Acting for the Salvation Army HA on the redevelopment of a site at Charter Row, Sheffield.

Harvey Ingram Owston (2ptnrs/1assoc/1asst) A big name in Leicester. Most work is property related, including mortgage work and property litigation. Clients/Work: Bede Island North, Leicester. Epperstone Court, West Bridgeford. Various transfers of housing between registered social landlords.

Lee Crowder (2ptnrs/2assts – varying amounts) A known name but not as visible this year as last.

Needham & James (4ptnrs/1asst) A firm on the up and "clearly a player." *Andrew Dudley* is liked, well known and acts for 12 HAs across the country. Clients/Work: Acting for Orbit Bexley HA on a 4,000 property, £87m LSVT from the London Borough of Bexley. Acting on the PFI refurbishment and management of residential and office accommodation for a Birmingham hospital.

Shakespeares (2ptnr/3assts) "Doing housing rather than specialising in it." Regularly act for 10 HAs doing the full range of work except LSVTs. Clients/Work: Involved in £1m transfer of assets between local associations. Restructuring of a loan term agreement between an association, a health authority and a district council for the financing of residential care provision for people with learning disabilities. Acting for an association on a £10m loan facility from CLF Municipal Bank.

Wright Hassall & Co (7ptnrs/1asst) *Carol Matthews* (ex Winckworth & Pemberton) has been successful in raising the firm's profile. The core team of two fee earners concentrate on transfers, LSVTs, group structures, housing management and conversions to charitable status. Others handle development work, litigation and employment matters. Clients/Work: Acting for one of the top five association groups on the conversion of the parent to charitable status and a revised group structure. Acting on LSVT and undertaking an estate based transfer. Trickle transfer agreement with subsequent purchase of 499 properties.

The NORTH

Trowers & Hamlins (Manchester) (5ptnrs/3assts) *Graham Turner* heads this northerly outpost of the Trowers housing empire, the first port of call for many associations, but not as good a reputation as the London office. All 30 members of staff do some housing work. **Clients/Work:** Acting for Waterloo HA on a £27m refinancing package from NatWest; advising on the estate regeneration of the Perry Common district of Birmingham; advising on a major redevelopment for Longhurst HA.

Brabner Holden Banks Wilson (Liverpool) (3ptnrs/3assts) Can call on a further 20 fee earners. *Lawrence Holden* has had a foot in the social housing door for as long as anyone and is the best known name in the region. "He has a clear idea of what needs doing and why." However, despite a "wonderful" core team, there is no heir apparent. Predominantly a Merseyside practice actively working for 5 HAs, and 20 others to a lesser extent. **Clients/Work:** 3 stock transfers of housing stock from Liverpool CC to HA clients. Acquisition of numerous substantial sites for residential development.

Dickinson Dees (Newcastle) (3ptnrs/5assts) 30% of the practice is acting for lenders to HAs. 15 active HA clients, with development work being the single largest practice area. **Clients/Work:** Acting for North British HA in a pathfinder PFI with Berwick council for 250 units over five years.

Acting for three HAs establishing group structures in order to minimise corporation tax liability. Advising the Royal Bank of Scotland on a £2m facility to Brunel & Family HA.

Howarth Goodman (Manchester) (6ptnrs/5assts) Treading water rather than moving forward but still highly respected. Act for 70 associations nationally, providing a complete service. **Clients/Work:** Acting for three associations on LSVTs.

Rollit Farrell & Bladon (Hull/York) (Hull: 2ptnrs/ 1asst p/t. York: 3 ptnrs) The premier Hull lawyers known for their work for the Joseph Rowntree Foundation. **Clients/Work:** Developing the concept of a continuing care community at Hartrigg Oakes, near York. Housing stock refinancing for a major association. Advising North Hull Housing Action Trust on the regeneration of residential estates in North Hull.

Slater Heelis (Manchester) (1ptnr/ 4assts) *Michael Gaskell,* someone "interested in social housing beyond his immediate instructions," has years of experience in the sector and has consolidated the firm's practice in the last few years. They are expected to continue taking significant strides. **Clients/Work:** 10 HAs including West Pennine HA and North British HA. Banks and building societies.

Walker Charlesworth & Foster (Leeds) (2ptnrs/3assts) "For a small firm they are big players in housing." The "pragmatic" *Colin Birtwistle* and his team act for 21 associations, from the largest to the very small. **Clients/Work:** Acting on an agreement between Leeds City Council and Leeds Partnership Homes where the council transferred £33m of land for enhanced nominations by five associations who then provided social housing on the majority of the land transferred.

Walker Morris (Leeds) (2ptnrs/1assoc/ 2assts) A small but well respected team undertaking a full range of work for five HAs. However they recently lost their specialist Andrew Hurst. **Clients/Work:** Acting on an estate regeneration partnership. Development and funding of Foyer project.

A.Halsall & Co (Birkenhead) (1ptnr/ 1asst) A small firm that works for associations as far south as Bromley. **Clients/Work:** Harewood HA. Wirral Methodist HA. Co-ownership Housing Society Scheme.

Croftons (Manchester) (3ptnrs/1asst) A niche housing practice since the 70s. With two partners and an assistant working almost exclusively in housing for 10 associations. Social housing is a considerable part of the

firm's total practice. **Clients/Work:** Advising a major association charging over 6,500 units to secure private finance via a bond issue. Representing Northern Counties and Irwell Valley on the Manchester Renewal project, acquiring substantial numbers of properties for refurbishment. Advising two associations in establishing streamlined systems for debt recovery and possession actions.

Eversheds (Manchester) (3ptnrs/2assts) At the moment, "more marketing than reality" even if the reality is catching up. Nevertheless *Michael Rhatigan* has a good reputation in Manchester especially and the North generally. **Clients/Work:** Advising Manchester and District HA in negotiations with Stockport council in relation to their sites at Offerton and Belmont. Acting for the developer for part of the Hulme Regeneration Order.

Ward Hadaway (Newcastle) (1ptnr/ 2assts) Part of the commercial property department. **Clients/Work:** Acting for the association on the first LSVT in the North East. Advising associations on charitable status of HAs, special needs schemes and the acquisition of development land. Acting for an association on the securitisation of a loan facility.

Gorna & Co (Manchester) One partner has a reputation as an efficient social housing practitioner.

Savage Crangle (Skipton) (3ptnrs) The surprise new home of former Walker Morris partner, *Andrew Hurst.* **Clients/Work:** Advising a large association which is the preferred bidder on a £60m PFI project to develop and manage new and existing facilities for an NHS trust.

Bell Lamb & Joynson (Liverpool) A good capability but largely unrecognised. A new entrant into our lists this year.

SCOTLAND

Brechin Tindal Oatts (5ptnrs/2assocs /2assts – ranging from 100% to as and when) One of the recognised names in Scottish housing with a specialised Social Housing Unit. "A wealth of people experienced in the area."

Henderson Boyd Jackson WS (3ptnrs/ 7assts) *Fraser Jackson* and *Kate Dewar* were recommended for LSVTs and funding work. **Clients/Work:** Acting on behalf of Northern Rock in its £23m refinancing of Waverley Housing Trust Ltd. Acting for Linstone HA in the acquisition of 2000 homes in Paisley. Acting for Paragon HA in their acquisition of 1000 properties in Falkirk.

Shepherd & Wedderburn WS (1ptnr/ 1assoc/ 2assts) 20 active HA clients. *Alison Campbell* "makes it her business to know what's going on in Scottish housing" and is the working head of the firm's dedicated housing unit with three fee earners working full time in the area. Also have a specialist litigation team. **Clients/Work:** Acting for the Royal Bank of Scotland in completing a number of facilities to associations. Advising the Scottish Federation of HAs on a number of projects including the production of the new model rules and a new model tenancy agreement. Advising on and researching projects for housing consultants and Scottish Homes on the granting of s.9 consents, group structures and gro-grant securities.

Burness (3ptnrs/6assts) Act for 12 Scottish associations and the Scottish Federation of Housing Associations. Involved in the sector since the 70s. Their best known name is *Paul Pia*. **Clients/Work:** Appointed by Edinburgh Council to advise on the development of a model for a local regeneration company at Craigmillar, Edinburgh. A major loan redemption on behalf of Link HA with Scottish Homes. Acting for Clydesdale Bank on the financing of Patrick HA in Glasgow.

Harper MacLeod (3ptnrs/3assts) "The best in the West" according to one enthusiastic interviewee. Another described them as "the most impressive firm acting for lenders" and praised *Leonard Freedman's* businesslike approach. Out there aggressively looking for housing work all the time. **Clients/Work:** Acting for Scottish Homes advising on the disposal of housing stock in Ayrshire and Dumfriesshire to Home HA and Shire HA. Acting on behalf of Irvine HA in the acquisition of the Irvine Development Corporation housing stock. Advisers to Nationwide Building Society for all their social housing funding in Scotland.

T.C. Young & Son (3ptnrs/2assts) Real specialists with a fine, long standing reputation. The principal solicitors for 30 associations (size range between 24 and 3,000 units). *Andrew Robertson* is a "significant figure in the West of Scotland" whilst *Andrew Cowan* is "developing an expertise." **Clients/Work:** Advising the HA Ombudsman in Scotland. Establishment of Scottish HA subsidiary of Home Group Ltd. Co-ordination of the provision of housing stock for Thenew and other associations assisting in the discharge programme for residents from Lennox Castle Hospital.

Alan J. Baillie (2ptnrs/1assoc) The -leading housing practice in Dundee, headed by *Kenneth Swinton*. **Clients/Work:** 8 associations, 2 clearing banks and 1 building society.

Anderson Fyfe (2ptnrs/3assts) Act for 7 associations, mainly within Glasgow. **Clients/Work:** Acting for Springburn & Possilpark HA refinancing Scottish Homes loan with a private funder. Acting on behalf of Glasgow West HA in a multiple stock transfer from Scottish Homes. Acting for Horizon HA on the acquisition and sale of a shared ownership development at South Gyle, Edinburgh.

Anderson Strathern WS (3ptnrs/ 2assts) A new entrant to the list on the back of some strong recommendations. **Clients/Work:** Acting for East Lothian HA and Wester Hailes HA in all matters, including security work, acquisition and disposals. Acting for Dunfermline Building Society negotiating funding and loan agreements with a variety of HAs.

Baird & Co (3ptnrs/1asst) Act for 6 associations, ranging from the small to large general needs associations within the Fife and Dundee area. *Charles Milne* devotes 40% of his time to the area. **Clients/Work:** Second phase of an LSVT. Increasing client portfolio for court related matters including anti-social tenants. Major refinancing transactions.

Ledingham Chalmers (2ptnrs) Leaders in the North East, with a finger in most Grampian pies and a nice approach to things. Historically acted for funders (Dunfermline Building Society) but now also act for two local authorities developing schemes for local housing companies.

MacLeod & MacCallum (1ptnr/1asst) A small firm but the largest in the Highlands. Specialising in work for associations, trusts and charities in all points north and west of Inverness. **Clients/Work:** Pentland HAs purchase of housing stock in Thurso. LSVT of 313 houses in Easter Ross and Nairn from Scottish Homes for Albyn Housing Society. Development of a shared equity pilot scheme for Albyn.

Dundas & Wilson CS (2ptnrs/5assts) An active adviser to funders lending to associations. **Clients/Work:** LSVT of 3,000 units to Fife Special HA from Scottish Homes financed by the Bank of Scotland. Development funding for Fountainbridge HA financed by TSB Scotland plc. Development funding for Hanover (Scotland) HA financed by NatWest.

Golds (1ptnr/1assoc/1asst) A well known name acting for lenders to associations. In a particularly price sensitive sector, the firm relies on standardised documentation to keep costs down. Other firms reluctantly agreed their proforma documents were "excellent." **Clients/Work:** Bank of Scotland, Clydesdale Bank and the Bradford & Bingley and Britannia building societies.

NORTHERN IRELAND

Wilson Nesbitt (2ptnrs/1assoc). The preeminent social housing practice in the Province, acting for clients active throughout Northern Ireland. **Clients/ Work:** Act for Fold Housing Association and the Northern Ireland Housing Executive.

LEADERS' PROFILES · REGIONS

ACTON, Joseph
Trowers & Hamlins, Exeter (01392) 217466
Specialisation: Advises upon all areas of Housing Association law and practice including acquisition and development, building contracts, PFI matters, homelessness initiatives, funding and major consortium agreements and joint ventures. Speaks regularly at client seminars on matters of current interest.
Prof. Memberships: Member of the Law Society.
Career: Torquay Grammar School (1977-84); Magdalen College Oxford (1984-87); *Trowers & Hamlins* (1989-date). Partner from 1995.
Personal: Chairman of Governors of Priory School Torquay.

BENNETT, Jennifer
Coffin Mew & Clover, Fareham, Hants (01705) 812511
Partner. Head of Social Housing Department.
Specialisation: Over 20 years experience in Housing Association Law, with particular interest in new housing initiatives and low cost home ownership schemes, but with a very broad expertise in this sector. Heads a team of dedicated professionals who provide comprehensive services to a large number of local and regional RSLs.
Personal: Born 1955. Educated University College, London. Admitted 1979. Non-executive Director of Portsmouth Hospitals NHS Trust and a Trustee of an independent girls school.

BIRTWISTLE, Colin
Walker Charlesworth & Foster, Leeds (0113) 245 3594
Specialisation: Housing Association Law and Practice particularly in the field of constitutional matters for Housing Associations e.g. dealing with several rule changes and mergers. Also heavily involved from 1990 to date with Leeds Partnership Homes which dealt with the transfer of £33m of City Council land largely for Housing Association development but also for outright sale. Now involved with the Single Regeneration Budget Agreement for Leeds. Also with a stock transfer to a local housing company.
Prof. Memberships: The Law Society, Leeds Law Society and Solicitor Benevolent Fund Member.
Career: LLB Birmingham Class 2(i). Senior Partner in the Leeds office of *Walker Charlesworth & Foster* which has three other branches.
Personal: Family: married with three children aged 19, 17 and 13. Outside interests – sport, fell walking and Charity work.

BODE, Adrian F.
Trowers & Hamlins, Manchester (0161) 833 9293
Specialisation: A partner since 1983 and has acquired wide ranging experience. Particular specialisations are large scale acquisitions and disposals, joint venture work and private finance.
Career: University of Nottingham. Qualified 1978. *Trowers & Hamlins* (1978-to date) – Partner 1983.

BROWN, Mitch
Dickinson Dees, Newcastle upon Tyne (0191) 279 9000
Specialisation: Partner in the Commercial Property Department and Head of the Social Housing Group. Handles all aspects of housing association work in the fields of development, governance and finance. Has in the past year dealt with housing association/housebuilder partnerships, creating over 1,000 new dwellings, and 2 local authorities' stock transfer projects. Currently dealing with 3 foyer schemes and a Pathfinder PFI project for social housing.
Prof. Memberships: Law Society.
Career: Born 1962. Educated Royal Grammar School, Newcastle upon Tyne. University of Newcastle upon Tyne 1984 (LLB). Qualified 1987, became a partner in 1995.
Personal: Leisure interests include sport, music, art and reading. Married with 3 daughters.

CAMPBELL, Alison
Shepherd & Wedderburn WS, Edinburgh (0131) 228 9900
Specialisation: Handles all aspects of housing association law including stock transfers, public/private housing partnerships, commercial contracts funding, policy, corporate structures, tenancies, tenures, shared ownership developments, site acquisition and development.
Prof. Memberships: Law Society (Scotland), Notary Public.
Career: Qualified 1988; Associate *Shepherd & Wedderburn WS* 1995.

COWAN, Andrew
T.C. Young & Son, Glasgow (0141) 221 5562
Specialisation: Housing Association tenancies and housing management issues. Representation in all areas of litigation and employment related disputes. He has an extensive knowledge of the regulatory regime for secured and assured tenancies and regularly contributes to training conferences and seminars.
Prof. Memberships: Law Society of Scotland and Chartered Institute of Arbitrators.
Career: Dundee University LL.B 1984 *T.C. Young & Son* Trainee 1985 -87 *McArthur Stanton* partner 1986 -95 *T.C. Young & Son* partner 1995-

DEWAR, Kate M.
Henderson Boyd Jackson WS, Edinburgh (0131) 226 6881
Specialisation: With a background in Commercial Law has worked extensively in the last 5 years on multi variety transactions for and involving Housing Associations, Housing Management Companies and similar bodies. Has been involved in all aspects of Large Scale Voluntary Transfers from Scottish Homes and the New Town Corporations. Involved in the legal formation of Housing Associations, local Housing Companies and Housing Partnerships. Has been involved in new build and housing development projects with both the public and private sector. Advises on tenancy and compliance issue for Housing Associations. Has also acted extensively for a variety of funders on housing projects.
Prof. Memberships: Law Society of Scotland. Writer to the Signet, Notary Public.
Career: Qualified as a Solicitor in 1982 and after initially working in the field of litigation joined Henderson Boyd Jackson and has worked in the areas of domestic followed by commercial conveyancing for the past 12 years. Since working full time has been partner in the firm's Commercial Department specialising in Housing and Public Sector work.
Personal: Obtained Law Degree (Honours) from Edinburgh University; married to an Advocate at the Scottish Bar and has 3 children. Lives in Edinburgh. Interests include swimming and travelling.

DUDLEY, Andrew P.
Needham & James, Stratford upon Avon (01789) 414 444
Specialisation: Acted for Housing Associations since 1982. Specialises in site acquisition and disposal, nomination rights, planning and planning agreements, infrastructure agreements and environmental issues. Lead solicitor advising Orbit Bexley Housing Association Limited in the acquisition of the housing stock of the London Borough of Bexley (LSVT).
Prof. Memberships: Law Society.
Career: Kings Norton Grammar School Birmingham. LLB (Hons) Wales (Cardiff). Qualified 1981.
Personal: Married. Enjoys cricket, soccer, motor racing, theatre and travel. Vice-President Old Nortonians Assocation. Member of Housing Today Readers Panel.

DYER, Nick J
Stones Cann & Hallett, Exeter (01392) 666 777
Specialisation: Specialised in Housing Association work for nearly 20 years. Experience of site acquisition and development

funding, Management Agreements with Health Trusts and Local Authorities, Shared Ownership and LSE schemes and other issues involving Housing Associations.
Career: Law graduate (Trinity Hall, Cambridge). Partner (latterly Managing Partner) in *Cann & Hallett* for over 20 years, and now partner in *Stones Cann & Hallett* in charge of Housing Association work.
Personal: Married with young daughter. Interests include foreign travel, skiing, trying (and largely failing) to keep fit.

FREEDMAN, Leonard
Harper Macleod, Glasgow (0141) 221 8888
Head of firm's Corporate Department.
Specialisation: Has led the firm's Social Housing Unit in LSVT deals of just over £40 million in the last 12 months and in excess of £70 million since 1995. Also Scottish Adviser in relation to Bond Issues in excess of £100 million for the Social Housing Market. Particular interest in Public/Private Partnerships and group structures generally and is presently advising various Local Authorities, Funders and Developers. Devised structuring arrangements for Thistle Marches Shopping Centre, one of Scotland's most successful Joint Ventures between Public and Private Sector.
Prof. Memberships: Regular and well known speaker on public/private partnerships, funding and group structure issues relative to profit and not-for-profit organisations. For some years tutor in Company Law and Formation at University of Glasgow.

GASKELL, Michael
Slater Heelis, Manchester (0161) 228 3781
Specialisation: Advising Housing Associations – group structures, joint ventures, stock transfer, acquisition and development, landlord and tenant. Currently advising on four group structures and five stock transfers.
Prof. Memberships: Law Society.
Career: LLB Liverpool. Advising Housing Associations for fifteen years.
Personal: Married. Three children.

HOLDEN, Lawrence
Brabner Holden Banks Wilson, Liverpool (0151) 236 5821
Senior Partner.
Specialisation: Principal area of practice involves advising a number of major housing associations and charities. Also deals with general property and private client work. Advised in relation to many charitable incorporations and group structures. Author of a number of articles on computers and the law and law practice management and legal education. Was a Panel Member of NFHA Independent Inquiry into Governance of Housing Associations 1994-5. Article on "Charities and Governance" in Charity Law and Practice Review Vol. 4 Issue 4.
Prof. Memberships: Law Society, Charity Law Society, National Federation of Housing Association Solicitors' Group, Society for Computers and Law.
Career: Qualified in 1965 while with *Brabner Holden*, became a Partner in 1966 and now Senior Partner. Past President Liverpool Law Society, President of Council Liverpool University. Deputy Lieutenant of Merseyside.

Personal: Born 19th September 1940. Attended Liverpool College 1951-59, then Liverpool University 1959-62. Leisure pursuits include fell walking, gardening and wood sculpture. Lives in Birkenhead.

HUDDLESTON, David
Browne Jacobson, Nottingham (0115) 950 0055
Partner in Property Department
Specialisation: Advising both local and national Housing Associations on acquisitions of sites for residential developments including a consortium of a number of Associations. Advising Housing Associations on private financing and security agreements. David has been involved in securing lending for Associations in excess of £30 million and has also acted for the Royal Bank of Scotland on lending for Housing Association projects. These projects total £11 million. Advising on acquisition of development sites for residential, office and industrial developments. Advising on development agreements associated with acquisition of sites and subsequent sales and leases. Acting for developers on the development of sites including financing and subsequent sales either by grant of leases (including industrial, retail and offices) or to investors of whole development. Advising major retailers on leases on retail parks. Clients include North British Housing Association Limited (the largest in the Country); Metropolitan Housing Trust Limited; East Midlands Housing Association Limited, Leicester Housing Association Limited.

HURST, Andrew L.T.
Savage Crangle, Skipton (01756) 794611
Partner, specialising in Housing Association and property work.
Specialisation: Work includes acquisition, development funding and general advice on governance Housing Association Law. Have advised a number of Housing Associations on refunding Housing Corporation debt and use of long tern SWAP agreements. Instructed on four substantial PFI Projects in Health Sector.
Career: Articled – *Walker Morris & Coles*. Qualified 1978. Appointed Partner 1981. *Walker Morris* 1981-98. 1998 joined *Savage Crangle*
Personal: Loughborough and Selby Grammar Schools. Manchester Polytechnic. Married – 3 children, lives in Bingley. Leisure interests – tennis, motorcycling, history.

JACKSON, Fraser S.
Henderson Boyd Jackson WS, Edinburgh (0131) 226 6881
Specialisation: Worked extensively in last four years in large scale voluntary transfers from Scottish Homes and new town corporations to housing associations and similar bodies. Instrumental in developing what is now the standard format of contract for such transactions. Currently extensively involved in advising on public/ private housing partnerships.
Prof. Memberships: Law Society of Scotland, Writer to the Signet, Notary Public.
Career: Qualified solicitor since 1977. Worked in local government and with Shell Expro before joining *Henderson Boyd Jackson* in 1982. Partner in firm's Capital Projects Group.
Personal: Educated at George Watsons

College and Edinburgh University. Married with four children. Lives in Edinburgh. Interests include soccer, ski-ing, canoeing and golf.

KEULS, Peter
Trowers & Hamlins, Exeter (01392) 217466
Specialisation: Housing associations, local housing companies, large scale voluntary transfers of housing stock: East Dorset, West Dorset, Penwith, North Dorset, Basingstoke & Deane, Kennet, Kerrier, West Somerset, West Devon.
Career: North School, Sussex; College of Law, Guildford; Qualified 1977, *Trowers & Hamlins* (1972-date) – Partner 1982.

KNOX, Martin
Anthony Collins Solicitors, Birmingham (0121) 200 3242
Specialisation: Provides specialist legal services on Housing and Local Government Law to over 40 Housing Associations, over 20 Local Authorities and numerous Charities and Businesses. Pioneered significant initiatives for increased investment in the provision and management of social housing. Particular experience of major urban regeneration including SRB funding and of joint venture companies, particularly local housing companies.
Career: Qualified 1980. Martin worked as legal adviser to Sheffield, and the Birmingham City Councils' Housing Committees. Since joining *Anthony Collins Solicitors* in 1989, Martin has been closely involved in creating innovative solutions to housing and regeneration in urban local authorities. He has developed the community association model in a number of locations throughout the Country both for provision of new stock and improvement of existing Council housing.

MATTHEWS, Carol A.
Wright Hassall & Co, Leamington Spa (01926) 886688
Specialisation: Constitutional Issues and Structures for Registered Social Landlords and Housing Groups. Lead Solicitor in a number of LSVTs in acting for both a Housing Association and the Council and in dealing with Property work. Acting on the purchase of Development Sites and advising on Housing Management Issues. Giving seminars and lectures on all aspects of Housing Law.
Career: Qualified in 1980, joined what is now *Rodgers & Burton* becoming Partner, subsequently with *Winckworth & Pemberton* in Westminster before joining *Wright Hassall & Co.* in June 1995 heading the Housing & Local Government Department.
Personal: Born 7th December 1954. Educated at Grammar school in Hertfordshire and Warwick University. Married with two daughters. Interests include literature and theatre. Lives in Stratford-upon-Avon.

MCNULTY, S.J.
Burges Salmon, Bristol (0117) 939 2000

MILNE, Charles M.
Baird & Company, Cupar (01334) 656644
Partner in Cupar office.
Specialisation: Principal area of practice is housing law, housing association work, conveyancing and commercial leasing. Acted in cases relating to damages for injury caused by dampness in dwellings. Also handles

employment law and some criminal and matrimonial work. Has co-ordinated major housing association refinancing projects. Born 23.7.1954.

MORTIMER, Ken
Bevan Ashford, Bristol (0117) 923 0111
Career: Qualified with *Bevan Hancock & Co.* in 1975 and returned to *Bevan Ashford* in 1984 having worked in the meantime with *Lawrence Tucketts*.
Personal: Three children. Main hobbies include the Territorial Army (a member since 1971 and now a Senior Officer) and canal narrow boating.

PIA, Paul D.
Burness, Edinburgh (0131) 473 6000
Specialisation: A corporate lawyer specialising in business formations in their operation and in amalgamation, including industrial and provident societies, housing associations, local housing companies, co-operatives, corporate trusts, group structures and joint ventures for housing associations, both with local authorities and the private sector. Has extensive knowledge of the regulatory regime affecting housing associations: Scottish Homes, registrations, charities law and the register of friendly societies, property matters and all commercial contracts and arrangements affecting housing associations. Advises Scottish Federation of Housing Associations and Institute of Housing in Scotland; Co-author of 'Care, Diligence and Skill,' a hand book for directors. Fellow of the Institute of Directors.

RHATIGAN, Michael
Eversheds, Manchester (0161) 832 6666
Partner in Commercial Property department.
Specialisation: All property aspects for Housing Association law including acquisition development and letting of properties and funding.
Career: Partner *Maurice Rubin Clare* 1979-1990; Partner *Davies Arnold Cooper* 1990-1995; Partner *Eversheds* 1995.
Personal: Born 1952. Leisure interests include Bolton Wanderers and opera.

ROBERTSON O.B.E., Andrew O.
T.C. Young & Son, Glasgow (0141) 221 5562
Senior Partner.
Specialisation: Has acted for Housing Associations in Glasgow from the early 1970s being particularly closely involved in the development of the Community Based Model. He has worked for Charitable and Generalist Housing Associations as well as Fully Mutual and Non Fully Mutual Co-ops. More recently the firm has completed a number of LSVTs from Local Authorities, Scottish Homes and the MoD. Shared Ownership and Shared Equity have been pioneered by T.C. Young & Son and he has recently contributed to an analysis of Shared Equity for Scottish Homes. He acts on behalf of Housing Associations across the whole field of their activity. He was instrumental in the forming of the first Employers Federation for Housing Association Committees (now EVH) and provided a full secreterial and legal service from 1978 until 1993 when full time staff were appointed.
Prof. Memberships: Law Society of Scotland.
Career: LLB Edinburgh 1964. Trainee *Maclay Murray & Spens* 1964 1967. Partner, *T.C. Young & Son* 1968.
Personal: Chairman of the Scottish Housing Associations Charitable Trust from 1992 to date. Trustee of HACT from 1991 to 1997.

STEPHENS, Hugo
Irwin Mitchell, Birmingham (0121) 200 3343
Specialisation: Corporate, constitutional and finance for registered social landlords. Experience includes stock transfers, local housing companies, group structures, transfers of engagements and conversions to charitable status; particular expertise in housing finance acting for borrowers and lenders; wrote the National Housing Federation's guide to Understanding Loan Documentation.
Prof. Memberships: Law Society.
Career: Qualified in 1989 with *Trowers & Hamlins*; 1989-94, Assistant Solicitor *Trowers & Hamlins*; 1994-97, Senior Assistant Solicitor *Prince Evans*; 1997, Partner *Irwin Mitchell*; head of RSL Corporate, Constitutional and Funding team.
Personal: Born 20th March 1956. Member of the Magic Circle.

SWINTON, Kenneth W.
Alan J. Baillie, Dundee (01382) 202444

TURNER, Graham F.
Trowers & Hamlins, Manchester
(0161) 833 9293
Partner, Head of Manchester Office.
Specialisation: Has specialised in housing association law for almost 25 years, heading a team of seven Manchester lawyers (five Partners) who provide a comprehensive housing law service on a regional and national basis. Experience ranges from stock transfer major development and partnership projects, urban renewal and regeneration to private finance and group structures. Constitutional and Vires issues. All legal issues relating to the housing movement are covered by the Manchester office, including litigation, construction and environmental matters.

IMMIGRATION AND NATIONALITY

See also: Administrative and Public law, Civil liberties, Parliamentary and Public Affairs

RESEARCH: In compiling the tables, we consider all the information available to us, paying particular regard to the market research carried out by our team of ten qualified lawyers. (The researchers' details are set out on page three.) The rankings, therefore, reflect the opinion of the marketplace as revealed by systematic and objective research: see page four. (Our research is audited every year by the British Market Research Bureau.)

OVERVIEW: We maintain the distinction between business and personal immigration. Business immigration is undertaken by both city firms and specialist firms, and includes work permits and investor applications. Overall there has been little movement in the tables. Warner Cranston did well this year in the business immigration table and Wesley Gryk stood out in the personal.

Personal immigration work relates to political asylum, students, nationality, marriage applications and family reunion cases. It is usually legally aided and is undertaken by niche firms, criminal law and civil liberties firms, and high street firms. It has been a good year for Wesley Gryk, which enters the highest band of firms, and Glazer Delmar are recommended for the first time. Darbys in Oxford and A S Law in Manchester have also been promoted.

LEADING FIRMS • LONDON

- CAMERON MCKENNA
- KINGSLEY NAPLEY
- SIMMONS & SIMMONS
- STURTIVANT & CO

- BATES, WELLS & BRAITHWAITE
- GHERSON & CO
- MAGRATH & CO
- NORTON ROSE
- SIMONS MUIRHEAD & BURTON
- WARNER CRANSTON

- GULBENKIAN HARRIS ANDONIAN

HIGHLY REGARDED FIRMS

- Baker & McKenzie
- Campbell Hooper
- Eversheds
- Fladgate Fielder
- Pullig & Co

- Fox Williams
- Harbottle & Lewis
- Radcliffes

LONDON

BUSINESS

Cameron McKenna (2ptnrs/11assts) Offer an "excellent and comprehensive service" to business clients, who "get confidence from dealing with them." The "impressive" *Julia Onslow-Cole* leads the department, which "she raised by sheer hard work and creativity." Regarded by many as the pre-eminent city immigration practice and act for a large number of multi-national corporations. **Clients/Work:** Established a new US immigration service; a number of high profile applications including same sex applications.

Kingsley Napley (2ptnrs/3assts) Seen to serve a niche market for medium sized corporate clients, with a specialisation in European Association Agreements. The "marvellous" *Elspeth Guild* is "academically streets ahead on EU law," and splits her time between London and Europe. *Lesley Kemp* "thinks laterally and knows her subject," and has been elevated a place in the rankings this year. **Clients/Work:** All areas of immigration and nationality except asylum; act for many clients in the hotel and catering industry, entertainers and sports people; also act for central and eastern Europeans wishing to establish businesses in the UK.

Simmons & Simmons (1ptnr/6assts) A leading city business immigration practice with an emphasis on work permits. *Hilary Belchak* "works hard and has a good reputation." **Clients/Work:** Advised a major multi-national on managing the immigration aspects of a proposed merger and also on switching immigration categories from TWES to full work permits; act for International Cricket Council and Williams Grand Prix, and are developing a sports immigration law capacity.

Sturtivant & Co (1 principal/1asst) Are "very focused" on business immigration, and perform "good quality work." *Karen Sturtivant* herself is described as a "superb practitioner." **Clients/Work:** Include commercial companies, financial institutions, professional firms and leading US and foreign firms.

Bates, Wells & Braithwaite (1ptnr/1asst) Undertake a combination of good personal and business immigration work. *Peter Moss* is recommended as "solid, reliable and consistent." **Clients/Work:** Advise corporations and individuals on work permits, applications for overseas representatives; also personal immigration work, representation at appeals and judicial reviews.

Gherson & Co (1ptnr/1asst) A niche firm with experience of a range of immigration work, led by the "very good" *Roger Gherson*. **Clients/Work:** A full range of business immigration for companies; focus on high net worth individuals.

Magrath & Co (2ptnrs/6assts) Have "a good client base" comprised almost exclusively of corporate clients. The highly rated *Christopher Magrath* has "good technical knowledge." **Clients/Work:** Advise many multi-national/international corporate clients.

Norton Rose (1ptnr/3assts) Struggled to maintain a high profile following the loss of departmental head last year. Their work has been described as "exceptionally thorough," and *Caron Pope* is recommended. Act for a range of City clients, and an increasing number of computer companies. **Clients/Work:** Advising the British Chamber of Shipping on the potential liability of its members to pay detention and removal costs under the Immigration Act 1971, arising from the mass influx of asylum seekers from the Czech and Slovak Republics; advising Texas Utilities on the relocation of senior personnel following its acquisition of the Energy Group.

Simons Muirhead & Burton (1 cons) *Larry Grant* has been seen less recently, although he is an adjudicator and considered "an excellent lawyer." **Clients/Work:** Mainly business immigration work, but also acts for individuals at tribunals and on judicial review.

Warner Cranston (1 ptnr/1asst) Have a "huge client base," and are described as "creative and pro-active on the work permit side." The "low key and experienced" *Peter Alfandary* has been promoted in the rankings. **Clients/Work:** Include: Hitachi; TI Group; Courtaulds Plc.

Gulbenkian Harris Andonian (10ptnrs/ 3assts) Have a long established business immigration practice which includes *Paul Gulbenkian* and *Peter Wyatt.* **Clients/Work:** British American Tobacco; BAA; L'Oreal.

Baker & McKenzie (3assts) Considered good on work permits, but only have relatively junior people. Known in particular for professional Japanese immigration. **Clients/ Work:** Work permit applications and naturalisation matters for clients such as Kelloggs, Honda and Toyota.

Campbell Hooper A medium sized firm which offers immigration advice from the family department. **Clients/Work:** Entertainment clients, some financial institutions and corporate clients.

Eversheds (3ptnrs/1asst) Undertake immigration work for corporate clients and have a "good national practice." **Clients/ Work:** Produced a report of the work permit scheme for HR managers.

Fladgate Fielder (2ptnrs) Undertake respectable business immigration work from their employment department. **Clients/ Work:** Work permit applications.

Pullig & Co (4ptnrs) Have an established reputation as a quality niche immigration practice. Act for corporate clients including media companies and individuals. Strong emphasis on judicial review. **Clients/Work:** Work permits, business applications sole representatives and investors. Also undertake personal immigration.

Fox Williams (1ptnr/2assts) *Jane Mann* spends 20% of her time on immigration, although she is known more for employment work. The firm specialises in immigration in relation to employment and business. **Clients/Work:** Include: Winterthur International Insurance Co Ltd; Carlson Europe; Hasbro Europe.

Harbottle & Lewis (2ptnrs/ 4assts) 1asst spends 100% of her time on Business immigration, predominantly for clients in the media and entertainment world, and others include it in a mixed practice. **Clients/Work:** Include: Sale Rugby Club; Charner Wallis; Ginger TV.

Radcliffes (2ptnrs/2assts) Offer immigration advice from a cross-departmental team, and have close associations with South Africa. **Clients/Work:** Pearson Television; Foster Plan; major relocations for US software enterprises and new set-ups in the UK.

PERSONAL

Bindman & Partners (1 ptnr/ 2 other fee earners) Have a reputation for big human rights cases, and possess a widely respected personal immigration practice. Recommended individuals at the firm include the "dynamic" *Alison Stanley* who is considered an "innovative thinker," and *Graham Smith*, who is known for family reünion cases in Asia. **Clients/Work:** Yiadom; nationality and asylum work; particular emphasis on south Asia and Bangladesh.

B.M. Birnberg & Co *Nigel Leskin* possesses an "agile mind" and is "very committed to his clients." *Fiona Lindsley* is respected for her prison work and habeus corpus applications. **Clients/Work:** Particularly political asylum cases, deportation, illegal entry and habeus corpus cases in the High Court.

Deighton Guedalla (2ptnrs/2assts) A "small but very good" niche firm which concentrates on asylum matters. *Vicky Guedalla* is considered "thorough and focused." **Clients/Work:** Niche expertise in unaccompanied children cases; act for a large number of Sudanese and Turkish clients.

Jane Coker & Partners Are known for high quality work on a "full spread of personal immigration." *Jane Coker* is a "determined and committed immigration lawyer," and she is aided by the well respected *Jawaid Luqmani.* **Clients/Work:** Kerrouche v SS; Kondova; Terho & Others (challenge to education regulations on the basis of discrimination against EU students). **Wesley Gryk** (1principal/3assts) Have had an excellent year, which is reflected in their promotion to the leading band of firms. They are known for gay rights cases and refugee law. *Wesley Gryk* himself has enhanced his profile and reputation considerably and has been elevated in the tables. He is "committed to his clients, has thorough knowledge and an understanding of his client's needs." The team has been augmented by the arrival of the experienced *Lanis Levy* from Bates, Wells & Braithwaite, and *Barbara Coll* enters the list as an up and coming name. **Clients/Work:** Belsham and Berisha cases; acting for the UNHCR in an intervention in the Lords for the Shahana Islam cases; expertise on Association Agreements.

Winstanley-Burgess (3ptnrs/2assts) Have been established in the immigration field for many years, with "extremely high quality individuals" who offer a "good ser-

vice." The "intellectually agile" *David Burgess* is considered by some as "the best immigration lawyer in private practice." Other members of the team include the "knowledgeable" *Christopher Randall*, the "solid and thorough" *Martin Penrose* and *Fiona Ripley.* She is known as a specialist in asylum law, especially relating to Turkey. **Clients/Work:** ECJ case of Radiom (national security and EC nationals); representation of Czech Romany asylum seekers.

Bartram & Co (1 principal/ 3 other fee earners) One of the generalist immigration firms who perform "good quality" work. *Peter Bartram* is recommended. **Clients/ Work:** Asylum cases, especially from Afghanistan and Algeria; unaccompanied children cases; also undertake EAA advice.

Glazer Delmar (2assts) Enter the list for the first time this year. They are considered "extremely good, especially on asylum." Also entering the list of individuals is the "co-operative" *David Rhys Jones.* **Clients/Work:** Predominantly asylum, especially from Latin America, plus all other aspects of immigration.

Powell & Co Have a "good solid reputation" for a "full range of immigration work." *Belayeth Hussain* is a recognised specialist practitioner. **Clients/Work:** Much community based work, including referrals from local agencies.

Stuart Miller Maintain a reputation in the field despite the loss of Sally Thompson to Gherson & Co. *Lisa Smith* is seen as "solid." **Clients/Work:** Mainly political asylum, and to a lesser extent student, marriage and family reunion cases.

Taylor Nichol Predominantly a crime practice, but active in immigration recently. *Carolyn Taylor* devotes the most time to immigration. **Clients/Work:** Emphasis on legal aid work, especially in relation to Kurdish asylum applications and unaccompanied minors. Also work for Algerian, Angolan, Ethiopian, Nigerian and Somalian clients.

Wilson & Co An "immigration factory." Considered "definitely the best for Somali cases." *Michael Hanley* is "a thoughtful lawyer." **Clients/Work:** Full range of personal immigration, including same sex cases, asylum and family reunions.

Gulbenkian Harris Andonian (10ptnrs/3assts) *Bernard Andonian* is a highly experienced and distinguished name in the field of personal immigration, who has "excellent contacts." **Clients/Work:** Case of Islam and Shah (on definition of membership of a

LEADING INDIVIDUALS • PERSONAL • LONDON

BURGESS David Winstanley-Burgess	**LUQMANI Jawaid** Jane Coker & Partners
COKER Jane Jane Coker & Partners	**RANDALL Christopher** Winstanley-Burgess
GRYK Wesley Wesley Gryk	**RIPLEY Fiona** Winstanley-Burgess
GUEDALLA Vicky Deighton Guedalla	**STANLEY Alison** Bindman & Partners
ANDONIAN Bernard Gulbenkian Harris Andonian	**LEVY Lanis** Wesley Gryk
BARTRAM Peter Bartram & Co	**LINDSLEY Fiona** B.M. Birnberg & Co
DAVIES Matthew Wilson & Co	**PENROSE Martin** Winstanley-Burgess
HANLEY Michael Wilson & Co	**SMITH Graham** Bindman & Partners
HUSSAIN Belayeth Powell & Co	**TAYLOR Carolyn** Taylor Nichol
KEMP Lesley Kingsley Napley	**THOMPSON Sally** Gherson & Co
LESKIN Nigel B.M. Birnberg & Co	

UP AND COMING

COLL Barbara Wesley Gryk	**SMITH Lisa** Stuart Miller
JONES David Rhys Glazer Delmar	

SEE PROFILES AT THE END OF THIS SECTION

particular social group); case of Livingstone on same sex couples.

LEADERS' PROFILES • LONDON

BUSINESS

ALFANDARY, Peter
Warner Cranston, London (0171) 403 2900
Partner and Head of Corporate Immigration Department.
Specialisation: Corporate immigration. 15 years of experience advising national and multinational corporations on work permits and related immigration issues with the Home Office and Department of Education and Employment. Advice on nationality law, overseas investor rules and business related immigration for individuals. Author of chapter on immigration in 'CCH Employment Contracts Manual.'
Prof. Memberships: Law Society; Immigration Law Practitioners Association.
Career: Articled *Lovell White & King*; qualified 1983. Spent a year in industry and a year with a leading firm of French advocates. Joined *Warner Cranston* as a partner in 1982. Managing Partner 1991-93.
Personal: Born 10 January 1953, resides in London. Educated at Lycée Francais de Londres, University of Kent and London School of Economics. Interests include Theatre, Music and Anglo-French relations. Deputy-President French Chamber of Commerce; decorated by the French Government as a *Chevalier dans L'Ordre Nationale du Mérite* in 1991.

BELCHAK, Hilary
Simmons & Simmons, London
(0171) 628 2020
Partner in Litigation Department.
Specialisation: Main areas of practice are UK immigration and nationality law. Has fourteen years experience in this field. Presently covering corporate immigration such as work permits, immigration advice to high net worth individuals wishing to settle in the UK and nationality issues. Contributor to 'Central and Eastern European Business Law Review' IBA journal 'International Legal Practitioner' and 'Corporate Counsel's International Adviser.' Has spoken at ILPA and the immigration committees of AILA, IBA and IPBA annual conferences as well as conferences of CBI Employee Relocation Council, IBC UK, Employment Lawyers Association, the Japan

Institute for Overseas Investment and In-house Seminars.
Prof. Memberships: ILPA, IPBA, AILA. Chair IPBA's Immigration Committee. 1997-9 Past Secretary of ILPA (Dec 1995 – Dec 1997).
Career: Qualified in 1984. Senior lecturer at North London Polytechnic 1971-81; worked at *Winstanley Burgess* 1982-84 and *Clinton Davis & Co.* 1984-88. Joined *Simmons & Simmons* in 1988, becoming a Partner in 1994.
Personal: Born 17th March 1949. Holds an LLB (1970) and LLM (1971). Leisure interests include opera and cinema. Lives in London.

GHERSON, Roger M.
Gherson & Co, London (0171) 724 4488
Principal of firm.
Specialisation: Practices exclusively in immigration and nationality. Work includes work permits, business investors, sole representations, writers and artists visas, appeals before the adjudicators and the Tribunal, as well as judicial review matters in the High Court.
Prof. Memberships: Law Society, Immigration Law Practitioners' Association.
Career: Qualified in 1981. Established *Gherson & Co.* in 1988.
Personal: Born 24th August 1954. Attended University College, London 1975-78.

GRANT, Larry
Simons Muirhead & Burton, London
(0171) 734 4499
Consultant in Immigration and Nationality Department.
Specialisation: Handles all areas of law and practice including applications to the Home Office, Department of Employment and overseas posts. Co-editor of 'Civil Liberty: the NCCL Guide;' co-author of 'Immigration Law and Practice,' and 'Immigration and Asylum Emergency Procedures' and Consultant Editor of 'Tolley's Immigration and Nationality Law and Practice.' Gives regular seminars on immigration law.
Prof. Memberships: Law Society, Immigration Law Practitioners Association.
Career: Qualified in 1967. Legal Officer, National Council for Civil Liberties 1970-74, solicitor, Law Clinic at the University of Kent 1974-77. Partner at *Seifert Sedley Williams* 1977-

91. Partner at *Simons Muirhead & Burton* 1991-97. Founder member and former Chair of the ILPA. Member of Immigration Law sub-committee of Law Society. Part time immigration appeals adjudicator.
Personal: Born 1943.

GUILD, Elspeth
Kingsley Napley, London (0171) 814 1200
Partner, Immigration Department.
Specialisation: Primarily specialises in European Community law relating to free movement of persons including the transfer of staff from companies in one Member State to another Member State, the right of self-employment and provision of services. Wide expertise in UK immigration and nationality law generally. Frequent lecturer and has written many articles on UK immigration and nationality issues. Author of two textbooks on Free Movement of Persons in the European Union and the Developing Immigration and Asylum Policy of the European Union. A further book is to be published on the Position of the European Convention on Human Rights in the Community Legal Order.
Prof. Memberships: Chair of the Immigration Law Practitioners' Association European Group; Member of the Council of Justice; UK Expert to the European Commission's Network: Free Movement of Persons; British representative of the European Sections of the International Commission of Jurists; Member of the Executive Committee, Centre of European Law, Kings College London; Legal Expert to Migrant's Forum. Coordinator, Centre of Migration Law, University of Nijmegen.
Career: 1989 to 1997 *Baileys Shaw & Gillett*: Head of Immigration Department; joined *Kingsley Napley* as a Partner in March 1997.

GULBENKIAN, Paul
Gulbenkian Harris Andonian, London
(0171) 937 1542
Immigration Department.
Specialisation: Principal area of practice covers business and private immigration and nationality law including nationality applications, UK immigration and advice and obtaining work permits. Other main area of work covers family, defamation and general litigation. Appointed

Part-time Immigration Adjudicator 1989 and Assistant Recorder in the Crown Court 1992. Joint editor of "European Immigration Law & Business" and "Entry and Residence in Europe." Author of numerous articles in legal and other journals.
Prof. Memberships: Law Society, Institute of Directors, ILPA, European Immigration Lawyers Group, Council of Immigration Judges, SFLA and the British Armenian Lawyers Association. Fellow of the Royal Society of Arts (FRSA).
Career: Qualified 1964 while with *Penningtons, Lewis & Lewis*. Joined *Isadore Goldman & Son* 1966. Administration Partner in charge of Litigation Department 1970. Became Senior Partner of *Gulbenkian Harris Andonian & Isadore Goldman* in 1989. President Holborn Law Society 1984-85, Hon. Auditor Law Society 1988-89.
Personal: Born 23rd March 1940. Attended King's College School, Wimbledon 1953-58, then London School of Economics 1958-61 (LL.B). Leisure pursuits include walking, music, tennis and squash. Lives in Weybridge, Surrey.

KEMP, Lesley
Kingsley Napley, London (0171) 814 1200
Partner. Head of Immigration Department.
Specialisation: Primarily specialises in business/employment related immigration (business investors; EC Association Agreement applications; work permits (including work permits for entertainers, sports people and hotel and catering); TWES; sole representatives; Expertise in all aspects of United Kingdom immigration and nationality is provided including personal immigration applications e.g. investors; retired persons of independent means; spouse applications. Lectures and has published articles on immigration issues.
Prof. Memberships: City of London Law Society. Member of Immigration Law Practitioners' Association (past Treasurer and member of the Executive Committee [1995-1997]).
Career: Qualified February 1989, assistant solicitor 1989 – 1993 *Kingsley Napley*; assistant solicitor and partner and Head of Immigration at *Magrath & Co* 1993-1995; returned to *Kingsley Napley* in November 1995.
Personal: Born 1960. Tiverton Grammar School; University of Kent (BA Hons); College of Law, Chancery Lane.

MAGRATH, Christopher
Magrath & Co, London (0171) 495 3003
Senior Partner and Head of Immigration and Employment Department.
Specialisation: Practice has substantially specialised in immigration and nationality law since 1985, primarily in the corporate field of executive expatriate transfer on a global basis, as well as for numerous individual clients over the last ten years. Also practises employment law in both contentious and non-contentious circumstances. Co-author of 'Practitioners Guide to the Police and Criminal Evidence Act 1984' (Longmans) and 'Working in the United Kingdom- A Guide for Foreign Nationals' (Handbook). Has published numerous articles in both professional and commercial magazines. Has made many conference addresses worldwide over the last twenty years, on immigration and employment related issues arising from expatriate transfer and relocation. Regular broadcaster on legal affairs, in particular with LBC and London News Radio since 1983.
Prof. Memberships: Law Society, ILPA, American Immigration Lawyers Association, International Bar Association, London Criminal

Courts Solicitors' Association.
Career: Qualified in 1975. Admitted to New York Bar in 1986. Set up *Magrath & Co* as Senior Partner in 1990.
Personal: Born 12th May 1948. Attended Campbell College, Belfast, 1961-66 and Trinity College Dublin (BA degree) 1972. Leisure interests include tennis, restaurants, dogs and skiing. Lives in London.

MANN, Jane
Fox Williams, London (0171) 628 2000
Partner in Employment and Immigration Department. email: jemann@foxwilliams.co.uk
Specialisation: Specialises in immigration related to business and employment. Advises multi-national companies relocating employees to the UK, overseas companies establishing an office in the UK for the first time and overseas nationals wishing to establish a UK business. Handles problems with both immigration and employment law aspects.
Prof. Memberships: Founder Member of Employment Lawyers Association and currently its Deputy Chairman. Former Treasurer of the Immigration Law Practitioners Association. Member of The International Bar Association and The American Immigration Lawyers Association. Associate Member of the Institute of Personnel and Development.
Career: Qualified 1981. Worked at *McKenna & Co.* 1979-86, then at *Denton Hall* until 1994, where became a Partner. Joined *Fox Williams* in 1994 as a Partner.
Personal: Born 1957. Attended Cambridge University 1975-78.

MOSS, Peter
Bates, Wells & Braithwaite, London (0171) 551 7777
Immigration and Nationality Advisor.
Specialisation: Advises on immigration and nationality matters and conducts advocacy in appeals. Main area of practice covers commercial immigration: work permits and applications for entry clearance as businessmen, overseas representatives, and under the Europe Agreements with Eastern European countries. Also specialises in applications outside the immigration rules for long term residents and couples who cannot marry. Other main area of work for private clients including persons of independent means, self-employed artists and family settlement cases. Author of articles for 'Immigration Law and Practice' and the 'Hong Kong Law Society Gazette.'
Prof. Memberships: Treasurer of Immigration Law Practitioners' Association, 1992-1996. Many years service on the Executive of I.L.P.A., and its European sub-committee.
Career: HM Immigration Officer, Dover 1973-75. Immigration Counsellor with the United Kingdom Immigrants Advisory Service 1975-76, then Senior Counsellor 1976-89. Immigration and Nationality Advisor with *Thomson Snell & Passmore* 1989-92, then joined *Bates Wells & Braithwaite*.
Personal: Born 11th July 1949.

ONSLOW-COLE, Julia
Cameron McKenna, London (0171) 367 3000
Partner and Head of UK Immigration and Nationality Group.
Specialisation: Partner responsible for Immigration and Nationality Group, which is the largest in the UK and ranked No. 1 by Legal

Directories. In 1998 *Cameron McKenna* became the first City firm to offer a US immigration law service. The Group advises on all aspects of UK and US immigration and nationality law except asylum and refugee. The Group's principal clients are major multi-nationals and financial institutions who are seeking prompt, accurate and cost-effective advice to enable their employees to move rapidly to the UK or to the US. *Cameron McKenna*'s team have a practical and expeditious approach to work permits and during 1998 we made a number of complex applications. We have substantial business experience and make many successful business, sole representative and investor applications. We also make many applications for retired persons of independent means and applications for British citizenship. In addition, we advise individual clients from all parts of the world, including artists and sportsmen. On the US side we specialise in international transfers, professionals and investors. The Group also offers advice on European immigration law and has made several applications at the cutting edge of European and UK immigration law. Julia Onslow-Cole is the Chairman of the International Bar Association's Immigration and Nationality Committee which has a membership of approximately 300 immigration lawyers throughout the world. Through these members and *Cameron McKenna*'s several international offices the Group can also assist clients who require immigration advice outside of the US and UK. Voted Expert's Expert by Legal Business. Contributing co-editor of Butterworths Immigration Law Service. Author of numerous articles. Has lectured and spoken at conferences in South Africa, Japan, Hong Kong, the USA and in Europe.
Prof. Memberships: Chairman of International Bar Association, Immigration & Nationality Committee, Member of Immigration Law Sub-Committee of Law Society, secretary of Immigration Law Practitioners Association, and Joint Chair of Immigration Law Practitioners Business and Employment Sub-Committee, Trustee to the Immigration and Nationality Research and Information charity.
Career: Qualified 1984. Worked for British Coal 1982-86, then *Simmons & Simmons* as I lead of UK Immigration and Nationality Department 1986-90. Joined *Cameron Markby Hewitt* in 1990 as Head of UK Immigration and Nationality Group, Partner from 1991.
Personal: Born 30th September 1959. Took an LLB(Hons) in 1981, Law Society exams in 1982.

POPE, Caron
Norton Rose, London (0171) 283 6000
Specialisation: Broad range of work permit applications with particular expertise in obtaining permits for outside hires which have not been advertised. Training and work experience permits. Sole representative and other permit free employment categories. Business applications. Applications under Home Office concessions, settlement and naturalisation applications. Marriage and student applications; Advising on the application of European law.
Prof. Memberships: Immigration Law Practitioners Association. Associate member – Canada / UK Chamber of Commerce; Member Inner Pacific Bar Association (IPBA).
Career: Croydon High School for Girls 1977 – 1984. University of East Anglia, Norwich 1984-1987 (LLB Hons). Guilford College of Law. *Cameron Markby Hewitt* 1988-1996. Articled Clerk

(1988-1990). Solicitor, Immigration & Nationality Law Group (1990-1996). *Norton Rose* August 1996 to date. Caron has spoken at a number of seminars over the last 12 months. She presented a paper at the IPBA AGM in Auckland, New Zealand in May 1998 and co-presented a seminar for ILPA "Basic Business Immigration Law."

STURTIVANT, Karen L.
Sturtivant & Co, London (0171) 486 9524

TROTT, Philip
Bates, Wells & Braithwaite, London
(0171) 551 7777
Partner in Immigration and Employment Department.
Specialisation: Commercial Immigration law, advising individuals and corporations on how they can be economically active in the UK and advising on Home Office and Department of Employment unpublished practices and concessions. Regular lecturer on professional courses on immigration and employment law issues. Lectures and broadcasts.
Prof. Memberships: Law Society, Immigration Law Practitioners' Association, Chair of Business and Employment sub-committee, Employment Lawyers Association, American Immigration Lawyers' Association.
Career: Qualified in 1979. Assistant Solicitor *Lawford & Co* 1979-1982. Partner *Lawford & Co* in 1982. Joined *Thomson Snell & Passmore* as Head of Immigration and Employment Law Department in 1989, and moved to *Bates, Wells & Braithwaite* in 1992, Head of Immigration Department.
Personal: Born 5th June 1952. University College, London 1973-76. Fluent in French.

WYATT, Peter
Gulbenkian Harris Andonian, London
(0171) 937 1542
Fax (0171) 938 2059. Partner in Immigration Department.
Specialisation: Main areas of practice are immigration and nationality law. Handles all aspects including work permits, businessmen, sole representatives, independent means, investor, writers and artists applications, nationality and citizenship applications, and refugee and asylum cases. Also handles conveyancing and company work. Addresses conferences.
Prof. Memberships: Immigration Law Practitioners Association, Law Society, International Bar Association, West London Law Society.
Career: Qualified in 1980. Previously worked for a Central London Practice in London, Saudi Arabia and USA. Joined *Gulbenkian Harris Andonian* in 1992, becoming a Partner in 1994.
Personal: Born 27th October 1953. Attended Fettes College Edinburgh, Dundee University and College of Law. Leisure interests include skiing and golf. Lives in London.

PERSONAL

ANDONIAN, Bernard
Gulbenkian Harris Andonian, London
(0171) 937 1542
Partner in Immigration Department.
Specialisation: Principal area of practice is UK immigration and nationality law and US business immigration. Deals with UK business immigration including work permit applications and business

and sole representative applications; preparation and submission of business and investor plans; independent means and asylum applications. Also handles appeals against Home Office or Entry Clearance Officer decisions and cases before the Adjudicator, Immigration Appeal Tribunals and judicial review. Acted in the Court of Appeal in the asylum case of 'Islam' on social groups creating new law in this area. Contributor to numerous articles for The Law Society Gazette, Solicitors Journal, International Legal Practitioner, Immigration and Nationality Law and Practice. Lectures on immigration; appointed by Lord Chancellor as part-time Immigration Adjudicator, and Special Adjudicator. Also deals with general commercial litigation, matrimonial finance and property disputes and has a speciality in intellectual property.
Prof. Memberships: Member of Immigration Law Practitioners Association, and former Executive Committee Member; the International Bar Association, Law Society, Holborn Law Society.
Career: Qualified 1985 while at *Gulbenkian Harris Andonian*, and became a Partner in 1986.
Personal: Born 11th September 1949. Attended City of London and Thames Valley Universities. Obtained Distinction in Intellectual Property for the MA Degree. Leisure pursuits include reading, rambling, table tennis, snooker, swimming. Lives in Osterley, Middlesex.

BARTRAM, Peter
Bartram & Co, Hounslow (0181) 814 1414
Specialisation: Head of Practice near Heathrow Airport devoted to all aspects of UK Immigration and Asylum Law (Private and Legal Aid) including appeal representation and judicial review.
Prof. Memberships: Immigration Law Practioners Association.
Career: Qualified 1981. Immigration specialist for 14 years in Law Centres, Advice Centres and private practice.
Personal: Born 21 August 1957. Bristol University (LLB, 1978) and Brunel University (MA, 1988). Spanish and French speaker.

BURGESS, David C.W.
Winstanley-Burgess, London
(0171) 278 7911
Partner in immigration department.
Specialisation: Main area of practice is immigration, including refugee work. Acted in Re M (H.L.), asylum case involving Ministers' liability to contempt; Re Sivakumaran (H.L. and European Court of Human Rights), 'refugee' definition case and Chahal (European Court of Human Rights) national security case establishing the absolute nature of Article 3. Has acted in other national security cases including NSH and Gulf War detainees. Has conducted cases before the European Court of Human Rights and the European Court of Justice. Involved in actions against carriers, police and immigration officers for unlawful removal of asylum seekers. Other areas of practice include transsexual cases before the European Court of Human Rights. Author of articles and book reviews concerning immigration matters. Has appeared on television and radio, as well as teaching at seminars in Europe.
Prof. Memberships: Law Society, Immigration Law Practitioners Association, Refugee Legal Group, European Legal Network on Asylum

(Joint UK Representative).
Career: Qualified in 1972. Partner at *Winstanley-Burgess* from 1975.
Personal: Born 25th September 1947. Attended Cambridge University (MA, 1969). Lives in London.

COKER, Jane
Jane Coker & Partners, London
(0181) 885 1415
Partner specialising in immigration.
Specialisation: Work includes deportation, asylum, appeals representation and judicial review, and contempt of court. Cases have included National Security, Deportation of EC Nationals, Association Agreements and the inter-relation between the Children Act and immigration law. Author of numerous articles for Immigration Nationality Law Journal, LAG and Socialist Lawyer. Lectures on ILPA, LNTV and LAG courses. Addresses WNS, UKCOSA and medical conferences. Numerous TV and radio interviews.
Prof. Memberships: Immigration Law Practitioners Association, Law Society
Career: Qualified 1980. Set up *Jane Coker & Partners* in 1982.
Personal: Born 11th July 1954. Holds a BSc in Biological Sciences. Trustee to Haldane Educational Trust.

COLL, Barbara
Wesley Gryk, London (0171) 240 8485
Specialisation: Handles immigration and nationality cases. Main area of work is political asylum, particularly Kosovan, Iraqi and Iraqi Kurdish, Somali and unaccompanied minor cases. Also handles marriage, EC association agreement, same sex and exceptional cases as well as judicial review including the lead cases on the safety of Greece as a third country, ex parte Elshani and Berisha.
Prof. Memberships: Law Society, Immigration Law Practitioners Association, Refugee Legal Group.
Career: Studied Law at South Bank University. Presently studying LLM – University of London intercollegiate degree (part time). Previously worked at *B.M. Birnberg & Co.* Solicitors and moved to *Wesley Gryk* Solicitors in February 1995. Qualified at *Wesley Gryk* in 1996.
Personal: Born 2.2.1971.

DAVIES, Matthew
Wilson & Co, London (0181) 808 7535

GRYK, Wesley
Wesley Gryk, London (0171) 240 8485
Specialisation: All areas of UK immigration and nationality law.
Prof. Memberships: Law Society, Immigration Law Practitioners Association, Association of the Bar of the City of New York.
Career: Qualified in 1990, admitted to the Bar of New York in 1976. Federal Judicial Clerk, Southern District of New York, 1975-76; Associate, *Shearman & Sterling,* New York and Hong Kong, 1976-80; Deputy Representative and Legal Advisor, UN High Commissioner for Refugees, 1980-81; Deputy Head of Research Department, Amnesty International, 1981-86; *B.M. Birnberg & Co*, London, 1988-1994; established own firm 1995.
Personal: Born 12th May 1949; attended East Catholic High School, 1963-67; Harvard College, 1967-71, BA; Warsaw University, 1971-72, Fulbright Scholar; Harvard Law School 1972-75, JD. Trustee of the Refugee Legal

Centre and the Redress Trust. Active in the work of Stonewall and the Terrence Higgins Trust. Has travelled widely on human rights missions for Amnesty International and Article 19.

GUEDALLA, Vicky
Deighton Guedalla, London (0171) 359 5700

HANLEY, Michael
Wilson & Co, London (0181) 808 7535

HUSSAIN, Belayeth
Powell & Co, London (0181) 854 9131

JONES, David Rhys
Glazer Delmar, London (0171) 639 8801
Specialisation: Refugee Law, detained cases (esp. children), Latin America.
Prof. Memberships: ILPA, Refugee Legal Group.
Career: Refugee Counsellor, UKIAS Refugee Unit 1987-1989, Appeals Counsellor, UNHCR funded project, Hong Kong 1989-1991, Legal Officer, UNHCR, Thailand, 1991-1993, Caseworker/ Casework Manager, RLC 1994-1997, Legal Advisor to Association of Visitors to Immigration Detainees. Conference speaker, Toronto 1997; Comparative use of detention in Europe and legal challenges in the UK.
Personal: Born in 1954. Attended Wolverhampton Polytechnic (LLB).

KEMP, Lesley
Kingsley Napley, London (0171) 814 1200
See under Immigration & Nationality. Business Immigration, p. 429

LESKIN, Nigel
B.M. Birnberg & Co, London (0171) 403 3166

LEVY, Lanis
Wesley Gryk, London (0171) 240 8485
Immigration & Nationality Specialist.
Specialisation: All areas of immigration, nationality and asylum law, with a specific interest in 'family' cases. Further specialisation in artists, designers, writers and composers. Extensive experience of representation before the Immigration Appellate Authority.
Prof. Memberships: ILPA member since 1987 and Executive Committee member 1989-1997. Co-opted member of the Stonewall Immigration Group Management Committee.
Career: At United Kingdom Immigrants' Advisory Service 1987-1993 and the Joint Council for the Welfare of Immigrants (JCWI) 1993-1995. Went into private practice in January 1996 and established the immigration department at *Lloyd & Associates*. At *Bates, Wells & Braithwaite* September 1996 to April 1998. Joined *Wesley Gryk* at the end of April 1998.
Personal: Born in New York City. Educated at Brooklyn Friends School, University of Rhode Island (BA (Hons.) + B.Sc. (Hons.)), London School of Economics (M.Sc.) and University of Westminster (Graduate Diploma in Law). Russian speaker.

LINDSLEY, Fiona
B.M. Birnberg & Co, London
(0171) 403 3166

LUQMANI, Jawaid
Jane Coker & Partners, London
(0181) 885 1415
Partner specialising in immigration.
Specialisation: Work includes judicial review and Habeas Corpus at High Court and Court of Appeal in immigration and related areas of housing, education and crime. Cases include interrelationships between asylum and terrorism, asylum and crime and free movement for non EU nationals. Co-author of 'Recent Development in Immigration' for LAG and author of immigration sections in Defending Suspects at Police Stations.' Lecturer for ILPA, LAG and CAB. Numerous Television and Radio interviews in respect of topical immigration issues.
Prof. Memberships: Executive Committee Member of ILPA since 1992, Law Society.

PENROSE, Martin
Winstanley-Burgess, London
(0171) 278 7911
Specialisation: Senior solicitor in the immigration department specialising in refugee law, Judicial Review and general immigration law. Has experience of teaching for ILPA and community organisations and has appeared on radio and television. Has travelled to Turkey for Amnesty International and the Law Society to monitor Human Rights trials. Specialist interest and experience in Sudanese casework.
Prof. Memberships: Immigration Law Practitioners Association; Refugee Legal Group.
Career: Graduate of Balliol College, Oxford. Qualified at *Winstanley-Burgess* in 1992.
Personal: Born 1965. Amateur string musician.

RANDALL, Christopher W.
Winstanley-Burgess, London
(0171) 278 7911
Partner in Immigration Department.
Specialisation: Handles refugee law, judicial review and general immigration law. Solicitor in the cases of R v. Special Adjudicator ex parte Mehari and R v. SSHD ex parte RADIOM. Author of 'An Asylum Policy for the UK' in 'Strangers and Citizens,' published by IPPR in 1994 and co-author of the trimonthly article 'Recent Developments in Immigration Law' in Legal Action. Has experience of teaching for ECRE, ILPA, the Refugee Council and community organisations, and has appeared on radio and television.
Prof. Memberships: Immigration Law Practitioners Association executive committee member, European Legal Network on Asylum (joint UK representative).
Career: Joined *Winstanley-Burgess* in 1985 and qualified 1987. Partner since 1990.
Personal: Born in 1959. Attended Oxford University 1978-81 and the City of London Polytechnic 1983-85. Lives in South East London.

RIPLEY, Fiona
Winstanley-Burgess, London
(0171) 278 7911
Partner in immigration department.
Specialisation: Specialises in refugee law, judicial review and all aspects of immigration law. Has organised and participated in human rights delegations and seminars relating to Turkey and Kurdistan. Has appeared on

television. Co-founder of the Refugee Legal Group. Provides training for and works closely with refugee community organisations particularly Turkish Kurdish refugee groups.
Prof. Memberships: Immigration Law Practitioners Association, Refugee Legal Group.
Career: Qualified at *Winstanley Burgess* in 1987. Partner since 1990.
Personal: Born in 1961. Attended SOAS (University of London) 1981-84.

SMITH, Graham
Bindman & Partners, London
(0171) 833 4433
Specialisation: All areas of immigration and nationality law, especially family settlement and deportation appeals for South Asian and African clients; advocacy before Adjudicators and the Tribunal; applications outside the rules.
Career: Educated Barry Grammar School and SOAS, graduating in 1973 with a degree in Marathi and Hindi. After 3 years' research in Hindu Law, joined *Bindmans* in 1977 as immigration adviser. Visits South Asia annually (since 1980) conducting enquiries for clients and Law Centres in immigration and family cases. Speakes Sylheti, and translates Bengali literature

SMITH, Lisa
Stuart Miller, London (0181) 881 7440
Specialisation: Work covers all aspects of immigration, particularly asylum and work with unaccompanied minors.
Prof. Memberships: ILPA, Refugee Legal Group.
Career: Qualified at *Bindman & Partners* in 1994. Became Head of Immigration Department at *Stuart Miller & Co* in 1997.
Personal: Born 1963. Graduate of Sussex University.

STANLEY, Alison
Bindman & Partners, London
(0171) 833 4433
Specialisation: Practice covers all aspects of Immigration, Asylum and Nationality law.
Prof. Memberships: Member of the Law Society's Immigration Law Sub-Committee, Immigration Law Practitioner's Association and the Refugee Women's Legal Group.
Career: Articled at *Winstanley-Burgess*. Subsequently worked for 4^1/2 years as the solicitor to the Joint Council for the Welfare of Immigrants. Joined *Bindman & Partners* in July 1994. Became Partner and Head of Immigration Department in May 1995.

TAYLOR, Carolyn S.
Taylor Nichol, London (0171) 272 8336

THOMPSON, Sally
Gherson & Co, London (0171) 724 4488
Specialisation: All aspects of immigration and nationality work with emphasis on asylum. Judicial Review cases have included challenges of visa posts abroad as well as decisions of the Home Office in the UK.
Prof. Memberships: ILPA, Law Society, RLG.
Career: Articled in London and Reading. Qualified in 1991. Head of Immigration Department *Stuart Miller and Co* April 1994 to June 1997. Joined *Gherson and Co* as Associate Solicitor July 1997 to head the Legal Aid Department.

The SOUTH and WALES

Darbys (Oxford) Have been promoted to the top band of regional practitioners, and in particular *Jenny Harvey* is up and coming. **Clients/Work:** Mainly personal immigration work, including political asylum, family reunion, same sex cases and judicial review.

Linnells (Oxford) The "experienced" *Philip Turpin* has a "brilliant reputation," and is widely admired by colleagues as "co-operative and trustworthy." **Clients/Work:** Substantial amount of political asylum. Also business immigration.

Trethowan Woodford (Southampton) *Gordon Denson* has "great experience" in personal immigration law, and has also been more noticed on the business side recently. **Clients/Work:** Personal and business immigration, with particular expertise offered in relation to Indian and South African citizens with British ancestry.

Bobbetts Mackan (Bristol) (2assts) Spend half their time on personal immigration work. **Clients/Work:** Act for individuals, including asylum and family reunion.

Eric Robinson & Co (Southampton) (1asst) Kathy Askew no longer practises immigration law, and the work is now dealt with by an assistant. **Clients/Work:** All areas of personal immigration, including political asylum, detention, marriage applications and family reunion.

Eversheds (Cardiff) The major Welsh business immigration practice, with 1 ptnr and 1asst spending about 10% of their time in this field. **Clients/Work:** Mainly corporate immigration work, such as work permits and applications for sole representatives, but also personal work.

Wollastons (Chelmsford) (2ptnrs) Offer business immigration advice as a service to clients. **Clients/Work:** Business immigration, including work permits and advising on arrangements for dependants of foreign nationals.

MIDLANDS and EAST ANGLIA

McGrath & Co (Birmingham) Head of the team is the "vastly experienced" *Manjit Singh*. The firm mainly does legal aid work. **Clients/Work:** Political asylum, appeals and judicial review; 24 hour emergency call-out; some business work as well.

Tyndallwoods (Birmingham) An "extremely professional" firm with a strong team led by the "genial" *Mark Phillips* who "takes the work very seriously." In up and coming are the "enthusiastic, committed and sensible" *Margaret Finch*, and *Sue Conlan*, who "really knows her stuff, especially on asylum." Most of the firm's work is legally aided. **Clients/Work:** Mainly personal immigration, with clients from all parts of Africa, the Americas and eastern Europe.

Gross & Co (Bury St. Edmunds) *Graeme Kirk* does mainly business immigration and some private client work. **Clients/ Work:** Corporate clients, including financial institutions in London, and some individuals.

Leathes Prior *Tim Cary* spends about 70% of his time on immigration, and is supported by 1asst. **Clients/Work:** Mixture of personal and business work; specialises in Eastern Europe applications for asylum.

Nelsons (1ptnr/1asst) The firm undertakes "good quality work" in the immigration field, and the team includes the experienced *David Smith*, who is aided by a dedicated immigration assistant. **Clients/ Work:** The 'Wok permit case' (obtaining a permit for a dim sum chef); general personal immigration; mainly legal aid.

The NORTH

David Gray & Co (Newcastle) *David Gray* is considered an "excellent immigration lawyer," and the firm has a reputation for a wide range of quality immigration work. **Clients/Work:** Known for political asylum and refugee law, family settlement, student work and nationality law.

Harrison Bundey & Co (Leeds) (9ptnrs/20assts) The "extremely good" *Ruth Bundey* is "very good on public law," and is also known for her civil liberties work. **Clients/Work:** Full range of personal immigration including asylum, students, marriage and same sex cases.

Howells (formerly John Howell & Co) They are considered an "excellent immigration firm." *John Donkersley* is "one of the few full time dedicated immigration lawyers," and has been elevated to the list of leading practitioners. **Clients/Work:** Mainly legal aid; clients from the Yemen and Somalia, Pakistan and the Middle East.

James & Co (Bradford (1 principal) Sole practitioner *Charles James* has a "good success rate," and "serves an established Asian client base in Bradford." He performs "a lot of spouse cases to a high standard." **Clients/Work:** Personal immigration including asylum and welfare, as well as business immigration, and ministers of religion cases.

Asylum work, particularly from Iraq and the former Yugoslavia.

A S Law (Liverpool)(2ptnrs/3assts) The "superb" *Peter Simm* and his firm have been promoted to the top band. He does a lot of his own advocacy, and is "genuinely committed to his clients." **Clients/Work:** R v Sec of State ex parte Obi; public campaign of Bayo Omoyiola; staff visit to refugee camps in Ethiopia.

Jackson & Canter (Liverpool) (1ptnr/ 1asst) Considered a "major immigration firm" in the north of England. *Andrew Holroyd* spends half of his time on a wide range of immigration work. **Clients/Work:** A varied caseload of personal immigration work, such as marriage and student applications, and some business immigration.

Ramsbottom & Co (Great Harwood) Suffered from a lower profile recently as

Mamta Dave has been on maternity leave, but the firm retains a capability in this area. **Clients/Work:** Mainly personal immigration with some business immigration. Specialises in spouse entry clearance and marriage applications.

Davis Blank Furniss (Manchester) (1 ptnr spends 25% of his time in this area) Wide range of immigration, more on the private client side. **Clients/Work:** Mixture of personal and business immigration work, including applications for those setting up businesses in the UK, as well as asylum and associated work.

J. Keith Park & Co (Toxteth) (2assts) Spend 20% of their time on immigration matters **Clients/Work:** Deportation, housing and child cases; mainly for Caribbean, African and Asian communities.

Robin Ince (Manchester) New entry to the list this year, *Robin Ince* is a sole practitioner who does some immigration work. He established his own firm after leaving Dunderdale Wignall. **Clients/Work:** Applications for asylum, leave to enter or remain; acts for student, family or business clients.

Samuel Phillips & Co (Newcastle) (1 ptnr/1asst) **Clients/Work:** Applications for refugee status, nationality, extensions. Emergency attendances also undertaken.

LEADERS' PROFILES • REGIONS

BUNDEY, Ruth
Harrison Bundey & Co., Leeds
(0113) 237 4047
Partner specialising in crime and immigration.
Specialisation: Main areas of practice since 1980: crime, immigration and inquests. Acted in the Helen Smith inquest, the case of the Bradford 12 and of Anwar Ditta, and various Yorkshire drug operations. Contributor to the Liberty Guide 'Know Your Rights' and member of the Liverpool 8 Inquiry which published 'Loosen the Shackles.'
Prof. Memberships: Law Society, Leeds Law Society, Liberty. Chairs Law Society Immigration Sub-Committee.
Career: Qualified in 1980. Formed Ruth Bundey & Co in 1986. Merged in 1993 to form Harrison Bundey & Co.
Personal: Educated at the University of Kent (BA Hons in English & American Literature). Awarded Honorary Master of Arts Degree for services to law in November 1995: University of Kent. Independent Governor, Leeds Metropolitan University. Management member of Chapeltown CAB and of Umoja House (hostel) and a member of West Yorkshire Justice for Women. Lives in Chapeltown, Leeds.

CARY, Tim
Leathes Prior, Norwich (01603) 610911

CONLAN, Sue
Tyndallwoods, Birmingham (0121) 624 1111
Specialisation: All aspects of immigration, including asylum, family reunion, illegal entry, deportation and detention. Experienced and special interest in advocacy before Adjudicators and Immigration Appeal Tribunal. Experienced in Judicial Review (including emergency cases) and in preparing appeals for Court of Appeal.
Prof. Memberships: Immigration Law Practitioners' Association.
Career: Graduated with a B.A. (Hons.) Law degree from Kingston Polytechnic (1980) and with an LLM (Welfare Law) from Leicester University (1990). Specialised in immigration law since July 1987. Joined *Tyndallwoods* in March 1996.
Personal: Born 14 November 1958, Birmingham.

DAVE, Mamta
Ramsbottom & Co, Blackburn
(01254) 672222

DENSON, Gordon F.
Irethowan Woodford, Southampton
(01703) 321000
Partner in Immigration Department.
Specialisation: Work covers all areas of immigration, nationality and asylum law. Conducts own appeals before adjudicators. Other areas of practice are commercial and conveyancing. Has undertaken personal visits to India to organise visas for children on compassionate grounds.
Prof. Memberships: JCWI.
Career: Qualified 1975. Joined *Woodford & Ackroyd* 1976. Partner 1980. Deputy Coroner for Southampton and New Forest District 1993. Appointed part-time Immigration Adjudicator 1995.
Personal: Born 22nd May 1950. Rotary member. Leisure interests include road running, walking, ornithology and foreign travel.

DONKERSLEY, John
Howells, Sheffield (0114) 249 6666
Specialisation: All aspects of immigration. Recently concentrating on representation of appeals, Yemeni and Somali asylum cases and family reunion cases. Contributor to local radio. Teaches immigration courses for local groups and NACAB.
Prof. Memberships: Law Society, ILPA.
Career: Welfare Rights worker and freelance trainer 1985-88. Articled, and qualified 1991 at current firm where cut teeth representing detained Iraqis during Gulf War.
Personal: Born 1st December 1961. Attended London School of Economics (University of London), LLB (Hons) 1985. Leisure interests include amateur radio, computers and internet.

FINCH, Margaret
Tyndallwoods, Birmingham (0121) 624 1111
Specialisation: Has practised immigration exclusively since qualification in 1993. Asylum work forms approximately 80% of current caseload, but other personal immigration work also handled. Conducts own advocacy when possible, including *pro bono* on occasion. Has strong track-record of investigating and substantiating asylum cases which have previously been rejected.
Prof. Memberships: ILPA, Law Society
Career: Graduated 1984. Taught English in Palestinian refugee camps in the Gaza Strip & worked in Switzerland before undertaking law conversion course. Trained at *John Howell & Co* before moving to *Tyndallwoods* in 1993.
Personal: Born 22.2.62. BA English Literature 1984. Fluent French speaker. Leisure interests include music (piano and flute player) & hillwalking.

GRAY, David
David Gray & Company, Newcastle upon Tyne
(0191) 232 9547
Founding Principal.
Specialisation: Main area of practice is immigration. Handles a wide range of casework including family settlement, nationality, illegals, students, political asylum and refugees, including judicial review (deportation) and European Contention cases. Also handles mental health work (Member of Law Society MHRT Panel). Contributor to local radio, TV and press on current legal issues, with particular reference to immigration law.
Prof. Memberships: Law Society, Immigration Law Practitioners Association, Legal Action, LAPG.
Career: Qualified in 1970. Worked at the University of Malawi 1970-73, Newcastle Law Centre 1974-79, and established *David Gray & Company* in 1979.
Personal: Born 16th November 1944. Attended University of Manchester (LLB Hons, 1963-66). Member of Liberty, Amnesty, Greenpeace, the Labour Party. Part time chair SSAT and DAT. Solicitor member Northern Legal Services Committee. Leisure interests include family, walking, cycling and Newcastle United. Lives in Newcastle upon Tyne.

HARVEY, Jenny
Darbys, Oxford (01865) 247294
Specialisation: All aspects of immigration work including family reunion, asylum applications and business/employment matters. Recently involved in an asylum case which was taken to the Court of Appeal – Case of 'Lawrence Kagema v Secretary of State 1997 Imm.Ar.' Have developed close links with Asylum Welcome, a local charity set up to assist asylum seekers and refugees.
Prof. Memberships: Law Society, Immigration Law Practitioners Association, Joint Council for Welfare of Immigrants.
Career: Degree in modern history at Lady Margaret Hall, Oxford (2:1). Worked in Sydney Legal Centre, Australia upon completion of law finals. Completed articles at *Darbys* and qualified in October 1994.
Personal: Involved in Oxford Amnesty International Group, Travel, Sport.

HOLROYD, Andrew
Jackson & Canter, Liverpool (0151) 708 6593
Partner in Immigration and Small Business Department.
Specialisation: Principal area of practice covers all aspects of immigration law including business immigration matters, with an emphasis on dealing with small businesses operated by ethnic minorities. Involved in Positive Action Scheme to encourage black entrants to the legal profession.
Prof. Memberships: Law Society Council Member and member of Law Society Immigration Sub Committee. Past President of Liverpool Law Society. ILPA.
Career: Qualified 1974 while with *Alsop Stevens Batesons* in Liverpool, then joined *Jackson & Canter*. Became a Partner in 1977.
Personal: Born 13th April 1948. Attended Bradford Grammar School and Nottingham University. Methodist Local Preacher. Leisure pursuits include music and walking. Lives in Liverpool.

INCE, Robin
Robin Ince, Manchester (0161) 839 2550

JAMES, Charles
James & Co, Bradford (01274) 729900

KIRK, Graeme
Gross & Co., Bury St. Edmonds (01284) 763333 & (0171) 935 5541.
Senior Partner and Partner in Immigration and Commercial Department.
Specialisation: Principal area of practice is immigration and nationality law. Other main area of work is company/commercial for private companies and businesses, including foreign businesses seeking to establish a UK presence. Handles work permit, self-employment, investor,

business sole representative independent means and all other immigration cases. Addressed IBA conferences regularly since 1991 and has given seminars throughout the world. Acts as Consultant in immigration law to solicitors firms throughout the UK. Lectures on Business Immigration for CLT.
Prof. Memberships: Law Society, IBA, ILPA, Solicitors European Group.
Career: Qualified in 1981. Assistant solicitor with *Radcliffes & Co.* 1981-84, then joined *Gross & Co.* in 1984 and became a Partner in 1986. Appointed Chairman of NIS Group November 1992. Currently Vice-Chairman of the Migration & Nationality Committee of the International Bar Association, and recently co-chaired IBA conference in London.
Personal: Educated at Westminster School and University of East Anglia. A member of Bury St. Edmunds Rotary Club. Leisure pursuits include cricket, badminton, opera and the violin. Lives in Bury St. Edmunds.

PHILLIPS, Mark
Tyndallwoods, Birmingham (0121) 624 1111
Partner and Head of Civil Liberties Department.
Specialisation: Main area of practice is immigration and public law, mainly refugee, marriage and family reunion cases. Undertakes advocacy and judicial review work. Other area is miscarriages of justice and Mental Health Review Tribunals, including judicial review for plaintiffs in education, health, local authority, prison and other cases. Author of 'Tenants Control' (Council Housing Co-operatives). Has lectured for LIBERTY on civil liberties issues (especially policing) and for ILPA and IISA on judicial review and immigration appeals advocacy. Member of Amnesty International and Joint Council for the Welfare of Immigrants. Member of the Law Society Immigration Law Sub-Committee, Chairperson Midland Immigration Practitioners (MIP). Member of Area 6 Legal Aid Committee.
Prof. Memberships: Law Society, Birmingham Law Society, Immigration Law Practitioners Association.
Career: Paralegal advisor at Stepney Green Law Centre 1973-75. Action/ research project on tenant's co-operatives 1975-77. Articled clerk at *T.V. Edwards* 1978-81. Assistant solicitor at *Geffens* 1981-83. Senior solicitor at Handsworth Law Centre, Birmingham, 1983-85. Joined *Tyndallwoods* in 1985, becoming a Partner in 1988.
Personal: Born 10th May 1947. Educated at Lymm Grammar School, Cheshire, 1958-64; Dame Allen's School, Newcastle-on-Tyne, 1964-66; Hull University 1967-70; then London School of Economics 1970-71. Married with two children. Leisure interests include mountain biking and struggling with the guitar. Lives in Walsall.

SIMM, Peter
A S Law, Liverpool (0151) 707 1212
Partner in Immigration Department.
Specialisation: Handles all aspects of immigration law, particularly family reunion, refugee cases and European Court/Commission. Acted in Yousef v. UK, a case taken to the European Commission of Human Rights on the rights of an immigrant father to remain in the UK to exercise access to his child. Local lecturer.
Prof. Memberships: Immigration Law Practitioners Association, Amnesty International.
Career: Qualified 1982. Solicitor at Liverpool 8 Law Centre 1987-1990; then Partner at *Edwards Frais Abrahamson* since 1991.
Personal: Born 17th February 1953. Attended Liverpool Polytechnic (BA(Hons) Law, 1982).

SINGH, Manjit
McGrath & Co, Birmingham (0121) 643 4121
Solicitor and Head of Immigration Department
Specialisation: All areas of personal immigration law.
Career: Worked in Advice Centres and Law Centres in the Midlands between 1983-1990. Senior Immigration Case Worker at the Greater Manchester Immigration Aid Unit from 1990-1992. Then entered into private profession, at all times specialising in Immigration & Nationality work. Joined *McGrath & Co* Solicitors as Head of Immigration Department in September 1996.

SMITH, David
Nelsons, Nottingham (0115) 958 6262
Partner, Head of Immigration Unit.
Specialisation: Developed immigration work from scratch at *Nelsons* since 1989. Works across full range of individual and corporate immigration cases.
Prof. Memberships: Law Society, Immigration Law Practitioners Association. Panel solicitor for Stonewall and Refugee Legal Centre.
Career: After ten years in social work qualified as a solicitor in 1989. Partner at *Nelsons* since 1995.
Personal: Born 5/3/54. BA Philosophy 1976, Master in Social Work 1978.

TURPIN, Philip B.C.
Linnells, Oxford (01865) 248607
Assistant Solicitor and Head of Immigration Department.
Specialisation: Handles exclusively immigration and nationality matters, involving work permits, investors, business people, visitors, students, academics, family settlement and asylum and representing both private and corporate clients. Regular course lecturer for ILPA.
Prof. Memberships: ILPA.
Career: Attended the Inns of Court Law School 1981-82, followed by pupillage at 2 Paper Buildings. Employed by UKIAS 1983-86, Paddington Law Centre 1986-88 and *McGrath & Co* in 1988-95. Joined *Linnells* 1995.

INSOLVENCY

RESEARCH: In compiling the tables, we consider all the information available to us, paying particular regard to the market research carried out by our team of ten qualified lawyers. (The researchers' details are set out on page three.)

The rankings, therefore, reflect the opinion of the marketplace as revealed by systematic and objective research: see page four. (Our research is audited every year by the British Market Research Bureau.)

OVERVIEW: The trend towards solvent schemes of arrangement and corporate reconstruction has continued. The economic crisis in the Far East has led to those firms with offices in Thailand, Singapore and Hong Kong gearing up for a rush of lucrative big ticket work along the lines of the Peregrine collapse in Hong Kong.

In London, the top firms are the ones that have seen the most upheaval. Although Allen & Overy's position is still unassailable, Lovells are down this year after losing some key figures, Wilde Sapte have to recover from the Andersens debacle and Clifford Chance have to weather the senior defections and shady resignations that have virtually removed all their leading insolvency lawyers.

Doing well this year are Herbert Smith who have achieved leading status, in major part due to the arrival of Stephen Gale from Hammond Suddards; Freshfields who acquired Sandy Shandro from Clifford Chance, and Linklaters. For the first time, we include the London offices of two US law firms which have been making serious efforts in terms of recruitment and work. We have incorporated the insurance insolvency table into the main one this year as activity in this specialist area has decreased to a level not meriting a distinction.

Many regional firms have rationalised their insolvency practices, although a few have retained dedicated departments in anticipation of the predicted downturn at the end of 1998. This latter group of firms received stronger recommendations from accountants than the former. However, we have taken care in the research to ensure that the true experts in this field, who may not necessarily be doing insolvency work full time, are still recognised.

In the North, the departure of Shân Spencer and team from Addleshaw Booth & Co has put that firm down and resulted in the appearance of Chaffe Street for the first time. In Scotland, the incorporation of Dorman Jeffrey & Co as the Corporate Recovery Division of Dundas & Wilson means the top firm name has changed but the faces are the same.

LONDON

Allen & Overy (4ptnrs/12assts) Now the pre-eminent insolvency practice due to the upheavals at the other top firms. The high profile team comprises *Gordon Stewart,* and *Peter Totty* ("the grand old men of insolvency"), *Judith Naylor* ("well liked and steady") and *Nicholas Segal* . **Clients/Work:** Acting in the restucturing of oil and gas project Bell Lines on behalf of UK merchant bank.

Advising the trustees of major bond issues in Korea, Thailand and Indonesia. Handling the Administration of Fosters Menswear plc.

Lovell White Durrant (11ptnrs/1consultant/17assts) Have recently lost some of their big hitters. Christopher Hanson has retired to become a consultant. The team is split between contentious and non-contentious players. Well known team members are *Christopher Grierson,* the "first class" *Keith Gaines, Deborah Gregory* and

Joe Bannister, known for corporate reconstruction, also part of the insurance insolvency team with *Robin Spencer.* **Clients/Work:** Acting for Deloitte & Touche the UK liquidators of BCCI in the BCCI employees 'stigma' claims and Re BCCI (No 8) [1997] establishing a bank's right to take a charge over its deposits as security for lending. Acting for the Admin Receivers (Deloitte & Touche) of Yorkshire Foods with an aggregate debt of US$120m. Acting in the receivership of Bell Gas Ltd, the first ever receivership of a UK privatised utility.

Cameron McKenna (6ptnrs: 1 p/t / 15assts) "Good firm, good people" with a reputation for being "a banking driven practice." Department's best known individuals are the "indefatigable" *John White* (head of the banking and international finance department) who "consistently does a good job," *Anthony Loring* and ex-barrister *Stephen Foster*, well rated by accountants. *David Kidd* ("good man") and *Dan Hamilton* have gone to the Hong Kong office this year to strengthen the team there. **Clients/Work:** Acting for the liquidators of a stockbroker in successfully resisting a High Court action to set aside a transaction claimed to be at an undervalue. Instructed by Coopers & Lybrand in the administration of the Anglo Corporation plc group. Advising a banking client on recoveries in a cross border insolvency involving a US Chapter 11 of a Swiss company and its UK parent, parallel Swiss insolvency proceedings and English security.

Herbert Smith (2ptnrs/6assts) The firm has implemented a firm wide corporate recovery network to marshall their expertise. Lead partners are the excellent *Richard Obank* and "exceptional" *Stephen Gale* who has joined from Hammond Suddards, greatly boosting the department's perceived strengths and moving them into leading firm status. *Trevor Turtle* continues to be recognised for insurance insolvency expertise. **Clients/Work:** Acting for the administrators of the Mayking Group and of Knickerbox Ltd. Advising the Thai Government in the implementation of new law to deal with the economic crisis. Handling various subsidiaries of the liquidated Peregrine Group in Hong Kong.

Wilde Sapte (17ptnrs/34assts) "An enjoyable firm to work with." The general market view was that they will be preoccupied with recovery after being jilted by Arthur Andersen. Consistently recognised as players, the department includes *Mark Andrews, Richard Bethell-Jones, Mark Gill* ("impressive"), *Nigel Barnett* and *Richard Scopes*. **Clients/Work:** Administrative Receiverships include Leyland DAF Ltd Group and Resort Hotels plc. Administrations include Paramount Airways Ltd and Nyckeln Finance Ltd. Specialist Insolvency Litigation Unit cases include Re Paramount Airways Ltd/Leyland DAF Ltd [H of L].

Clifford Chance (4ptnrs/11assts) The loss of Andrew Wilkinson and Sandy Shandro has affected the perception of this firm in the market and with Ashley Booker's hasty departure it has been an interesting year. The remaining and well regarded partners are *Mark Hyde,* who is spending a lot of time in Hong Kong, and *David Steinberg*, known for insurance insolvency work, also handles mainstream corporate recoveries. New to the list, *Adrian Cohen* has impressed this year.

Clients/Work: Acting for Price Waterhouse as liquidators for the Peregrine Group in Hong Kong. Advising in the restructuring of Thai companies Alphatec and TPI Polin. Acting in the liquidation of Anglo-American Insurance.

Denton Hall (4ptnrs/6assts)Known for Official Receiver work. *Michael Steiner* and *Neil Griffiths* are both highly rated by accountants. **Clients/Work:** Acting for the 1996 bondholders in numerous Barings related proceedings including the "flip litigation." Acting for the administrators of MTi Group in attempt to challenge the administration order. Acting for the Official Receiver as provisional liquidator of Alchemy Marketing Ltd/One Life Ltd and Vanilla Accumulation Ltd and subsequently for BDO Stoy Hayward, Grant Thornton and Morrison Stoneham in proceedings against de jure and de facto directors of these companies.

Dibb Lupton Alsop (21ptnrs approx/ 30assts) "Lots of good people"and rated by accountants. *Paul Gordon-Saker* has been replaced as national head of insolvency by Leeds partner Peter Cranston. Insolvency work accounts for about 8% of total fee income. **Clients/Work:** Advising National Westminster Bank plc on administration of Millwall F.C. Advising Lloyd's of London on insolvency aspects of reconstruction and renewal. Acting for the Scheme Administrators of Trinity Insurance Company Ltd and Bryanston Insurance Company Ltd.

Freshfields (16ptnrs/12assts) One of the firms considered to be in a position to challenge for the top of the rankings in the next few years "they have really geared themselves up recently." The "very able" *Sandy Shandro* ("well respected") was the key hire this year. **Clients/Work:** Advising SBC Warburg on the financial restructuring of the Azlan Group. Acting for the scheme administrators of the five insolvent insurance companies KWELM in arbitration proceedings to make reinsurance recoveries due from major reinsurer. In Hong Kong acting for a number of creditors following the Peregrine collapse.

Hammond Suddards (3ptnrs/6assts) "Good professional firm" **Clients/Work:** Acting for Coopers&Lybrand/Buchler Phillips joint liquidators of Leyland Daf. Acting for Deloitte & Touche and Ernst & Young dealing with applications for change of office holder due to retirement or resignation of various practitioners.

Lawrence Graham (6ptnrs/3assts) Head of the Insolvency Team, *John Verrill* is the acknowledged "senior" player **Clients/Work:** Acting in the Court of Appeal matter Park Air Services. Clients include Polly Peck International, Deloitte & Touche and Royal Bank of Scotland.

Linklaters (22ptnrs worldwide/24assts) "Doing well" and "higher up the food chain

than many." *Richard Wright* is praised as "profoundly extraordinary" and *Tony Bugg* is well rated by accountants. **Clients/Work:** Advising Banque Nationale de Paris, Crédit Lyonnais, Midland Bank plc and National Westminster Bank plc as agents for the senior and junior lenders to Eurotunnel (£8.4bn debt) for restructuring of Eurotunnel. Acting for Arthur Andersen, the administrators of NSM PLC and its subsidiaries on a series of disposals of mining and other assets as going concerns.

Nabarro Nathanson (Core: 2ptnrs, additional firm wide 6ptnrs/19assts) Can feed off their substantial property and banking practices. *Michael Prior* is Head of Department which includes *Peter Sigler* and

Patricia Godfrey who is rated for contentious insolvency work. **Clients/Work:** Receiving instructions from the liquidators of CTC Travel in Australia, to apply and obtain provisional liquidation orders against CTC Shipping (charter travel company) involving international preservation of assets. Acting for Lombard Tricity Finance leading up to and following the demise of the Maples Group.

Norton Rose (7ptnrs/38assts) Head of Insolvency *Sandy Pratt* is rated by accountants. **Clients/Work:** Acting for the Administrative Receivers (Deloitte & Touche) of Maple Stores. Acting as UK advisor to Alliance Entertainment Corp, a US corporation in Chapter 11, on the UK aspects of the insolvency relating to the solvent UK subsidiaries. Continuing to act for the Administrators of Maxwell Communication plc.

Simmons & Simmons (2ptnrs up to 100% /6assts) *John Houghton* is head of the non-contentious side of the The Corporate Recovery Group. This year has seen two known names, Jonathan Downey and James Roome depart for Weil Gotshal & Manges and Cadwallader respectively. There has been some high level recruiting to counteract this loss though. Team includes *Alison Pascoe*. **Clients/Work:** Acting for the receivers of Telesure Ltd reported in Re Telesure Ltd [1997] BCC 580. Continuing to advise the board of directors of Brent Walker/William Hill including effecting an exit strategy for 127 group companies following the sale of William Hill.

Stephenson Harwood (9ptnrs/13assts) Accountants rated them for "good sound advice," and they are busy. Known names are "fair minded personality" *Geoffry Woolf* and *Peter Fidler* ("technically good"), known for insurance insolvency work. **Clients/Work:** Acting for the Administrators of British & Commonwealth including appearing in the House of Lords on the question of the ranking of B&C's claims against Atlantic. Acting for the Joint Liquidators of Bishopsgate Investment Management Ltd, the Maxwell pension trustee company, against insurers and recovering losses as a result of dishonest misappropriation by officers/employees.

Ashurst Morris Crisp (6ptnrs/7assts) The "thoroughly capable and fair minded" *Nick Angel* is head of the group and appointed specialist reconstruction and insolvency partner, *David Kershaw* is also part of the group. **Clients/Work:** Acting for the directors of the Maples Group Ltd in the receivership and liquidation. Acting for the administrative receivers of Landhurst Leasing plc to recover debts due.

Davies Arnold Cooper (3ptnrs/6assts) Their profile is in insurance insolvency. *Nigel Montgomery* ("calm and measured") is head of the insurance insolvency unit and has close working relationships with accountants. **Clients/Work:** Acting for HIR (UK)

Ltd, a solvent insurance company run-off, on the formulation of proposals for a solvent Scheme of Arrangement. Acting for the provisional liquidators of Marina Mutual Insurance Association Ltd, the first insolvent P&I Club, advising on the best method of maximising realisations for creditors.

DJ Freeman (3ptnrs/5assts) Known for insurance insolvency work. *Vivien Tyrell* is the specialist partner. **Clients/Work:** Acting for the provisional liquidators of United Standard Insurance Company Ltd preparing scheme of arrangement. Advising the liquidators of The Continental Assurance Company of London plc.

Isadore Goldman (3ptnrs: 1p/t / 4assts: 1p/t) "Good on personal insolvency," and also known for one big client National Westminister Bank plc. "Leading light" *Danny Schaffer* ("quick concise and knowledgeable") is extremely well regarded for his bankruptcy expertise.

Nicholson Graham & Jones (7ptnrs: 4 p/t / 10assts: 8p/t) "Aggressive team" and a "good quality practice" The "indefatigable" *Shashi Rajani*, has "good technical expertise" and is seen as an expert on directors disqualification, he is considered an asset for the firm. **Clients/Work:** Continuing involvement in ongoing BCCI matters in London and Luxembourg. Representing respondent directors in disqualification proceedings and subsequently advising monitoring accountants where conditional leave has been granted.

Slaughter and May (4ptnrs/6assts) Seen as lower profile but have good quality work. *Jonathan Rushworth* is one of the principal partners involved. **Clients/Work:** Continuing to advise the administrators and liquidators of companies in the Barings group particularly following the involvement of the City Disputes Panel. Successfully concluding the various financial restructurings of the Costain Group plc.

Barlow Lyde &Gilbert (6ptnrs/6assts) Well regarded for insurance insolvency work. **Clients/Work:** Acting for one of the defendants in the Bermudan court case of The Bermuda Fire & Marine Insurance Company Ltd (in liquidation) v BF&MLtd. On-going role for Liquidators of National Employers Mutual General Insurance Association Ltd.

Berwin Leighton (8ptnrs: 7p/t / 10assts) Acquisition of *Keith Bordell* ("strong") from Allen & Overy has boosted the firm's market profile. **Clients/Work:** Acting for Martin Birrane in his acquisition of Lola motor racing team and associated business from the administrators. Acting for Administrative Receivers – BDO Stoy Hayward, of Cafe des Amis/Michels Brasserie group of restaurants in disposal of the group as a going concern.

Biddle (5ptnrs/4assts) The insolvency practice was seen to be "coming on." *Chris Mallon* "knows his stuff and presents it well,"

and is well known for asset tracing. **Clients/Work:** Acting for Global Opportunity Fund, a Cayman fund in liquidation. Advising English and Cayman liquidators in BCCI. Acting for liquidators of various Virgin Retail Group Companies in members' voluntary liquidation.

Clyde & Co Known as a good quality insurance insolvency practice.

Edge & Ellison (3ptnrs/4assts) Received "solid" reviews. **Clients/Work:** Acting for the administrative receivers of Ozwald Boateng Limited. Acting for the administrator of Lola Cars Ltd in a complex case involving UK, US and French jurisdictions.

Edwin Coe (3ptnrs/2assts) "Established" practice. New name to the rankings *Chris Berry* ("superb") is highly regarded by accountants. **Clients/Work:** Acting in the De Lorean Liquidation litigation and the Grupo Torras litigation.

Eversheds (7ptnrs: 6p/t;3assts) Have a good reputation. **Clients/Work:** Include Price Waterhouse, KPMG and Coopers & Lybrand

Holman Fenwick & Willan Highly rated for insurance insolvency.

Kennedys (3ptnrs/3assts) With "good people" and some "ex-Wilde Sapte" lawyers, the firm has a growing reputation and joins the list new this year. **Clients/Work:** Acting on behalf of the joint liquidators of a marine reinsurance broker regulated by Lloyds of London. Acting on behalf of Grant Thornton, Administrative Receivers of Cabouchon Ltd, appointed by Midland Bank plc in March 1998.

Olswang (3ptnrs/1asst) Seen as a good practice. **Clients/Work:** Advising the receivers of Reducta Sales Ltd (instructed by receivers from Coopers & Lybrand) and the liquidator in relation to the solvent liquidation of the Girovend business (instructed by liquidators from Latham Crossley & Davis).

Osborne Clarke (3ptnrs: 2p/t / 3assts: 1p/t) A smaller practice than the Bristol office but nonetheless well regarded. **Clients/Work:** Acting in the acquisition by Diagonal plc of an Oracle service provider Sequelogic Ltd in Administrative Receivership. Sucessfully acting for Finnforest OY in injunction proceedings brought by the Administrative Receiver.

Richards Butler (4ptnrs/4assts) *Ian Fletcher* continues to be recognised as a player. **Clients/Work:** Acting in major insolvencies including The Ostrich Farming Corporation plc and the administration of Millwall Football Club – acting for the in-going management.

Sprecher Grier (3ptnrs/1asst) Well known partner *Ian Stephen Grier* has a reputation for "swift to the point advice" **Clients/Work:** Proceedings in the Companies Court on behalf of liquidators against former directors for wrongful trading and misfeasance leading to the successful recovery in several cases of substantial sums for the benefit of creditors.

Taylor Joynson Garrett (8ptnrs: 6p/t / 12assts: 10p/t) Acknowledged as players but have a lower profile. **Clients/Work:** Acting for Finn Associates the administrators of Reliant Motors, and assisting in the sale of the company's business and assets. Acting for Kidsons Impey in relation to their appointment as the administrators of Dino Music Ltd and Dino Entertainment Ltd.

Travers Smith Braithwaite (2ptnrs/3assts) Firm rated by accountants. New to the ranks *Stephen Pearson* and *Jeremy Walsh* are both seen as "leading individuals" with complimentary strengths. **Clients/Work:** Acting for Barclays Bank plc in relation to the restructuring of WEW Group plc. Acting for Barclays as co-ordinator of the banking syndicate in the insolvency of Lister & Co plc. including the appointment of Administrators – Ernst & Young.

Withers (4ptnrs – all f/t; 1cons 25%; 3assts p/t) They are popular with accountants and clients for an assertive style and tough litigation stance – "good at asset tracing and other complex cross border matters." **Clients/Work:** Continue to act for liquidator of Bond Corporation Holdings Ltd of Australia including an application in the UK courts by the liquidator of a division of the company for the examination of Sir William

Purves and directors of Hong Kong & Shanghai Banking Corp.

Cadwalader, Wickersham & Tuft (2ptnrs/7assts) Have recruited *Andrew Wilkinson* from Clifford Chance and *James Roome* from Simmons & Simmons this year and are seen as making a big push into the UK. In the Far East, they are known for doing a lot of US debt trader work where they have capitalised on their US distressed debt owner clients buying up Hong Kong and Thai distressed debt. They do not have a great history of association with institutional clients which puts them at a disadvantage in more UK dominated jurisdictions but gives them an edge in Seoul which is a US influenced area. **Clients/Work:** Acting for the 94 noteholders on Barings. Acting for Zurich/Centre Re in connection with Anglo American Insurance company. Acting for the provisional liquidators on the KWELM Scheme of Arrangement.

Weil Gotschal & Manges (3ptnrs/3assts) Have gained *Jonathan Downey* from Simmons & Simmons and are making determined efforts to gain a slice of the UK market. Known as being a key insolvency player in the US, the London office has been focusing on banking and finance and is approaching "critical mass" in this area. **Clients/Work:** Advising SBC Warburg on final stages of restructuring of Isosceles debt; advising committee of junior creditors on restructuring proposals.

LEADERS' PROFILES • LONDON

ANDREWS, Mark B.
Wilde Sapte, London (0171) 246 7000
Senior Partner and Head of Insolvency Group.
Specialisation: Main areas of work are insolvency, advising on administrations, receiverships, liquidations, bankruptcies, voluntary arrangements, work-outs and restructurings, directors' liabilities and banking, advising on insolvency, security and restructuring issues. Has acted in innumerable corporate insolvencies for a wide range of clients. He is a very well-known practitioner. Member of Editorial Board for Insolvency Bulletin and Receivers, Administrators & Liquidations Quarterly. Member CLSC Insolvency Law Sub-Committee. Chairman CBI Insolvency Panel. Regularly chairs and addresses conferences on insolvency issues.
Prof. Memberships: Law Society, City of London Solicitors Company, Society of

Practitioners of Insolvency, Insolvency Lawyers Association, AEPPC, INSOL and IBA.
Career: Articled with *Clark & Son* Reading 1974-76. Joined *Wilde Sapte* in 1976 and became a Partner in 1979. Became Head of Insolvency in 1991 and Senior Partner in 1996.
Personal: Born 12th July 1952. Attended Reading Grammar School 1963-69, then Hertford College, Oxford 1970-73. Trustee of Pimlico Opera. Leisure pursuits include music, playing the French horn, singing, history, ornithology and farming. Lives in London.

ANGEL, Nick
Ashurst Morris Crisp, London
(0171) 638 1111
Specialisation: Corporate turnaround and insolvency law.
Prof. Memberships: Insolvency Lawyers Association. Society of Practitioners of Insolvency.

Career: Southend High School for Boys, Bristol University. Joined *Ashurst Morris Crisp* in 1993. Partner 1997.

BANNISTER, Joe
Lovell White Durrant, London
(0171) 236 0066
Specialisation: Partner specialising in all aspects of business reconstruction and insolvency; particular (but not exclusive) experience in financial services insolvencies, especially exit strategies for troubled insurance or reinsurance companies, Lloyd's members agencies and pools. Main cases in past year: acting for the scheme administrators of The London and Overseas Insurance Company PLC in various matters arising from the implementation of the scheme of arrangement for those companies. Acting for the Joint Liquidators of Bank of Credit and Commerce

International SA in the landmark House of Lords' Ruling (BCCI No. 8[1997] 3 WLR 909) establishing finally that a bank could take charges over its customers' deposits as security for those customers liabilities to it. Acting for the Joint Administrative receivers of Kendell PLC and for Sunday Business Publishing Limited in the acquisition of Sunday Business from its joint administrative receivers.
Prof. Memberships: Subscriber member of the Society of Practitioners of Insolvency; member of Law Society.
Career: School: King William's College, Isle of Man (1974-1980). University: Magdalene College, Cambridge (1981 – 1984). Career: *Lovell White Durrant* (1985 to date). Partner 1997. Published: Co-editor with Peter Horrocks (*Lovell White Durrant*) and Professor Harry Rajak (University of East Sussex) of 'European Corporate Insolvency – A Practical Guide' – published by Wiley Chancery – September 1995. Contributor to Television Education Network, insolvency videos and speaker at external conferences – eg Euroforum seminar on insurance fraud in June 1998.

BARNETT, Nigel
Wilde Sapte, London (0171) 246 7000
Partner in Insolvency Group.
Specialisation: Handles all aspects of insolvency, but with particular emphasis on insolvency litigation. Cases include: The Reject Shop Plc, Lancer Boss Group Plc, Leyland Daf Ltd, Resort Hotels Plc, Nyckeln Finance Co Ltd., Dunn & Co Ltd, Galileo Group Ltd and the restructuring of Cityjet.
Prof. Memberships: International Bar Association, Insolvency Lawyers Association.
Career: Qualified in 1985. Partner at *Wilde Sapte* since 1991. Appointed Deputy Bankruptcy Registrar of the High Court January 1997.
Personal: Educated at Southampton University 1979-82 and Guildford College of Law 1983-84.

BERRY, Christopher R.
Edwin Coe, London (0171) 691 4000
Specialisation: Personal insolvency. The Gruppo Torres litigation. Euro Express Ltd disqualification proceedings. Many conditional fee arrangements successfully agreed.
Prof. Memberships: Law Society. MSPI. FCI Arb. Insolvency Lawyers Association (Technical Committee).
Career: Partner *Edwin Coe*. Crown Court Recorder. Law Society Nominee, Insolvency Court Users-Committee.
Personal: Early morning squash. Chairman, Warman Sports Trust.

BETHELL-JONES, Richard J.S.
Wilde Sapte, London (0171) 246 7000
Partner in Banking and Finance Department.
Specialisation: Specialist in banking. Areas of practice include banking, secured and unsecured lending, including management and leveraged buy-outs and project finance, drafting and take up of security, rescheduling and work-outs and sale of loan assets, administrations and administrative receiverships. Also handles insurance insolvency. Acted for the administrators of Fairbriar Plc, the German trustee and paying agent for ECU and DM bonds issued by Maxwell Communications Corporation and the provisional liquidators of Pine Top Insurance Company Limited in relation to a proposed

scheme of arrangement. Acts for banks, administrative receivers and administrators. Contributor to numerous publications and journals. Has spoken at a number of seminars.
Prof. Memberships: City of London Law Society, International Bar Association, Society of Practitioners of Insolvency, Insolvency Lawyers Association.
Career: Qualified in 1970. Partner in *Wilde Sapte* from 1974.
Personal: Born 16th September 1945. Educated at St Johns School Leatherhead 1957-63 and Churchill College, Cambridge 1964-67. Leisure pursuits include tennis, sailing and cinema. Lives in London.

BORDELL, Keith S.
Berwin Leighton, London +44 171 760 1000
Specialisation: All aspects of business rescue and reconstruction, workout and insolvency law including voluntary arrangements, administrations, receiverships and liquidations.
Prof. Memberships: Law Society; Society of Practitioners on Insolvency; Insolvency Lawyers' Association; AEPPC/ EIPA.
Career: Articled at *Cameron Markby*. Qualified 1988. Joined *Berwin Leighton* as a partner in February 1988.
Personal: Born 1963. Educated at Chigwell School and The London School of Economics. Married with two sons. Interests include music, theatre, cinema and family.

BUGG, Anthony
Linklaters, London (0171) 456 4470
Specialisation: Principal area of practice is corporate insolvency and business reorganisations. Wide experience of all aspects of contentious and non-contentious insolvency work acting for insolvency practitioners, banks and other financial institutions. Recent assignments include acting for the liquidator of Toshoku Finance UK PLC and the administrator of Tulip Computers UK PLC.
Prof. Memberships: Insolvency Lawyers' Association (Council Member), SPI (Member of PR Committee), Law Society, AEPPC, IPA, IBA.
Career: Qualified 1981. Partner *William Prior & Co* 1982. Partner *Dibb Lupton Broomhead* 1990. Joined *Linklaters & Paines* 1997; became partner 1998. Licensed Insolvency Practitioner since 1987.

COHEN, Adrian Leon
Clifford Chance, London (0171) 600 1000
Specialisation: All aspects of domestic and international corporate insolvency and corporate reconstruction, with an emphasis on advice on insolvency aspects of structured finance, securitisation and other banking and capital market transactions, security enforcements and asset realisation.
Prof. Memberships: Law Society, Middle Temple.
Career: Called to the Bar 1988, practising barrister 1988-1990, joined *Clifford Chance* corporate practice 1990 and then the firm's Insolvency Group 1991 to the present date. Partner May 1998.
Personal: Married with one son.

DOWNEY, Jonathan
Weil, Gotshal & Manges, London (0171) 903 1000
Specialisation: Jonathan is Head of Corporate Recovery at the London office of *Weil, Gotshal & Manges*. An expert in his field,

Jonathan has over eight years experience of corporate recovery and insolvency law and practice. Jonathan regularly advises banks, insolvency practitioners, companies and directors on all aspects of insolvency and restructuring work. He has been involved in a wide variety of receiverships, liquidations and administrations. He joined the firm from *Simmons & Simmons*.
Prof. Memberships: Society of Practitioners of Insolvency, Insolvency Lawyers Association and Law Society.
Career: Liverpool John Moores University LLB (Hons) 1985-1988. Guildford College of Law 1988-1989. Joined *Simmons & Simmons* in March 1990, qualified May 1992. Joined *Weil, Gotshal & Manges* in 1998.
Personal: Born 24 November 1965. Interests include wine and Manchester United.

FIDLER, Peter
Stephenson Harwood, London (0171) 329 4422
Partner in Banking Department (Insolvency & Asset Recovery Group).
Specialisation: Specialised in banking since 1967 and in insolvency for over 20 years. Main editor, Sheldon & Fidler's Practice and Law of Banking, 11th Edition, 1982. In the last five years has specialised in schemes of arrangement for insolvent insurance companies. Has been involved in recovery of assets from abroad using compulsory interrogation techniques here and abroad.
Prof. Memberships: City of London Law Society Insolvency Law Sub-Committee. SPI International Committee.
Career: Admitted as solicitor 1967. *Coward Chance* (now part of *Clifford Chance*), May 1967 to March 1972. *D J Freeman & Co* March 1972 to January 1984 (partner from 1973 to 1984). *Stephenson Harwood* partner since 1984.
Personal: Bradford Grammar School. St John's College, Oxford 1959-1963 – Open Scholarship in Classics. Classical Honour Moderations 1961. First Class Honours. First Class Honours Literae Humaniores (Classics) 1963. First Class Honours Law Society Part II Qualifying examination and John Mackrell, Daniel Reardon and Cecil Karuth Prizes.

FLETCHER, Ian
Richards Butler, London (0171) 247 6555
Specialisation: Partner, Company and Commercial Group, Corporate Recovery and insolvency work and MBO/MBI work against a general corporate law background.
Prof. Memberships: Council of the Law Society of Scotland (currently convener Insolvency Solicitors Committee and Insolvency Practitioners Adjudication Panel), Council of the Society of Practitioners of Insolvency (member of the International Committee); Law Society of England & Wales; Council Insolvency Lawyers' Association Ltd; President of the Insolvency Lawyers' Association 1995/96; IBA (Member Committee J (Joint Chairman of Sub-Committee on Remedies under Security Interests: Section on Business Law); the Society of Scottish Lawyers, London (past president); Institute of Directors; British Venture Capital Association; LTCL, LRAM, ARCO, MinstD, MIPA, FSPI, WS. Joint author 'The Law and Practice of Receivership in Scotland' (1987 2nd ed. 1992) and 'The Law and Practice of Corporate Administrations 1994, 1st ed., joint contributor to a chapter on Insolvency and

Finance in the Transportation Industry (1993). Joint author of contribution on UK Corporate Insolvency Law for Norton Annual Bankruptcy Serving – International Section. Joint Editor of 'Guide to International Insolvency' incorporating contributions from 35 jurisdictions to be published by Oceana Publications Inc in late 1998.
Personal: Educated Glasgow University (LLB). Qualified Scotland 1971, England 1978. Interests include music, golf and swimming.

FOSTER, Stephen J.
Cameron McKenna, London
(0171) 367 3000
Partner in Banking & Insolvency Department.
Specialisation: Principal area of practice is insolvency. Work includes advising banks on domestic banking questions and pre-insolvency issues, including options to maximise recovery and advising Insolvency Practitioners in receiverships, administrations and liquidations. Other main area of practice is UK and US distressed debt funds, advising on documentation and insolvency issues. Has lectured to the Institute of Bankers, SPI and for various commercial lecture providers on banking and insolvency topics.
Prof. Memberships: Law Society, Insolvency Lawyers Association, AEPPC.
Career: Qualified in 1989. Became a Partner at *Cameron Markby Hewitt* in 1991.
Personal: Born 4th January 1958. Educated at Pembroke College, Cambridge. Interests include walking, music and film. Lives in London.

GAINES, Keith
Lovell White Durrant, London
(0171) 236 0066
Specialisation: Principal areas of work: contentious insolvency, commercial fraud, asset tracing. Wide experience with emphasis on cross border situations encompassing many jurisdictions from USA through Caribbean to Europe and Far East. Advised on several key legal developments in last 10 years; acted on several high profile cases, including liquidation of BCCI. Advises UK accountants, overseas lawyers, UK and overseas financial institutions. Experienced in dealings with Serious Fraud Office and other regulatory bodies. Contributes to publications on civil fraud.
Prof. Memberships: The Law Society, International Bar Association, Society of Practitioners of Insolvency, AEPPC.
Career: Qualified 1981; seconded to New York 1984-1986; partner 1986, London; admitted Hong Kong solicitor 1986.

GALE, Stephen
Herbert Smith, London (0171) 448 1000
Partner and Head of Corporate Recovery at Herbert Smith.
Specialisation: Principal area of practice is corporate rescue and company reorganisation. Has wide experience of acting for banks and other financial institutions in work-outs and reorganisations. Also has considerable insolvency related experience, particularly in corporate insolvencies. Recent cases include BCCI, Paramount, Leyland Daf, Peregrine, Knickerbox. Chairman of General Technical

Committee of SPI. Lectures widely on insolvency – related issues.
Prof. Memberships: Law Society, Institute of Credit Management, SPI, IPA, AEPPC.
Career: Qualified in 1982. Associate with *Simpson Curtis* 1984, then Partner with *Masons & Marriott* in Hong Kong, 1985. Joined *Hammond Suddards* in 1987 as a Partner. Partner *Herbert Smith* January 1998.
Personal: Born 15th October 1957. Attended Blackpool Grammar School and Sixth Form College, then Sheffield University. Leisure pursuits include fell walking, windsurfing, horseriding, skiing and classical music. Married with two children.

GILL, Mark S.
Wilde Sapte, London (0171) 246 7000
Partner in Commercial Litigation Department.
Specialisation: Acts mainly for banks, frequently on insolvency related issues. Regularly delivers lectures on banking and insolvency topics. Joint Editor of Credit Finance Law.
Prof. Memberships: Subscriber to the Society of Practioners for Insolvency, Associate Member of AEPPC.
Career: Qualified in 1977. Articles with *Alsop Stevens & Batesons* 1975-77. Lecturer for The College of Law 1977-79. Joined *Wilde Sapte* in 1979. Became a partner in 1985.
Personal: Born 15th March 1953. Educated at St Anselm's College, Birkenhead and University College London (LL.B). Lives in London.

GODFREY, Patricia
Nabarro Nathanson, London
(0171) 493 9933
Specialisation: Handles all aspects of insolvency and corporate recovery work. Advises lenders and insolvency practitioners on both formal insolvency proceedings and workouts and reorganisations. Recent cases include acting for a major tenant at *Canary Wharf*, for the liquidators of *Edennote plc* and for the administrative receivers of the *Facia Group of Companies*. Regular speaker at insolvency conferences including SPI. Contributor to the Legal Network TV specialist insolvency programmes. Associate Editor of Tolleys Insolvency Law & Practice. Fluent German speaker and heads the Firm's German Group.
Prof. Memberships: SPI. AEPPC. ILA.
Career: Qualified 1986. LLB London School of Economics. Partner *Nabarro Nathanson* 1991.

GORDON-SAKER, P.D.
Dibb Lupton Alsop, London (0345) 262728
Specialisation: Contentious insolvency, international asset tracing, acts for insolvency practitioners, banks and other creditors. Recent cases include Polly Peck International plc and Brent Walker Group plc.
Prof. Memberships: Law Society, Insolvency Lawyers' Association, Insolvency Practitioners Association, Society of Practitioners of Insolvency, American Bankruptcy Institute, AEPPC.
Career: Partner 1973. Licensed Insolvency Practitioner.

GREGORY, Deborah
Lovell White Durrant, London
(0171) 236 0066
Specialisation: Insolvency and business recovery; dealing with corporate and personal insolvency and insurance insolvency including individual and corporate voluntary arrangements, schemes of arrangements, administrations, receiverships, liquidations, and corporate reconstructions; advising in relation to the Insolvency Act and related provisions. A licensed insolvency practitioner. Recent cases include acting for Proton on the acquisition of Lotus, acting for ING on the Barings acquisition and the proposed Scheme of Arrangement and acting for the Receivers of Yorkshire Food Group Plc and its 27 subsidiaries.
Prof. Memberships: Law Society; Fellow of the Society of Practitioners in Insolvency; AEPPC; Insolvency Lawyers Association; International Women's Insolvency & Restructuring Confederation; British Insurance Law Association; International Association of Insurance Receivers.
Career: Qualified in 1984 with *Lovell White & King* 1989 Partner in *Lovell White Durrant*.

GRIER, Ian Stephen
Sprecher Grier, London (0171) 544 5555
Partner in Litigation and Insolvency Department.
Specialisation: Deals with all aspects of corporate and individual insolvency, principally working for administrative receivers, liquidators and trustees in bankruptcy as well as for banks and creditors. Substantial involvement in rescue schemes for limited companies, partnerships and individuals by way of corporate and individual voluntary arrangements. Also has considerable experience in relation to court appointed receiverships and LPA receiverships. Other main area of practice is corporate litigation including contractual disputes, construction work, intellectual property, banking litigation and debt recovery. Important cases have included Re Brightlife Limited (leading case on fixed and floating charges); Re Cranley Mansions Limited (leading case in relation to individual voluntary arrangement); Scottish Enterprise v. Bank of East Asia Limited. Clients include one of the clearing banks, merchant banks, a substantial number of firms of insolvency practitioners and major firms of chartered and certified accountants, international airlines and international employment agencies. Lectures widely to the SPI, firms of chartered accountants and other professional bodies in relation to the law and practice of insolvency. Co-author of three published works on corporate and individual insolvency and of numerous articles.
Prof. Memberships: Law Society, Fellow of the Society of Practitioners of Insolvency (Member of the Small Practices Issues Committee).
Career: Qualified in 1972. Joined with David Sprecher to form *Sprecher Grier* in 1984.
Personal: Born 23rd February 1945. Educated at London University (LL.B 1967, LL.M 1968). Former local councillor. Leisure interests include theatre, playing poker and bridge. Lives in London.

GRIERSON, Christopher K.
Lovell White Durrant, London
(0171) 236 0066
Specialisation: International litigation with particular emphasis on insolvency, fraud and asset recovery matters, and insurance and reinsurance. Has acted in a number of prominent cases, including BCCI, Barings and EMLICO. Licensed insolvency practitioner. Contributed chapters in 'Current Developments in International and Comparative Corporate Insolvency Law' (Clarendon Press, 1994) and 'Current Issues in Cross-Border Insolvency and Reorganisations' (Graham & Trotman, 1994).
Prof. Memberships: International Bar Association (Chairman of Committee J5: Insolvency of Regulated Financial Institutions and Vice-Chairman of Committee J (Insolvency)), American Bar Association, American Bankruptcy Institute, European Association of Insolvency Practitioners, London Solicitors Litigation Association, The Law Society (England), City of London Solicitors' Company.
Career: 1976-1980 Assistant Solicitor in *Durrant Piesse*; 1980 Partner in *Durrant Piesse*; 1988 Partner in *Lovell White Durrant* (following merger of *Durrant Piesse* with *Lovell White & King*,) including 1991-1994 Partner in its New York office and 1992-1994 managing partner of that office.

GRIFFITHS, Neil
Denton Hall, London (0171) 242 1212
Partner in Insolvency Group Litigation Department. email: nrg@dentonhall.com
Specialisation: All aspects of insolvency, both corporate and personal; in particular fraud, financial services, insurance and reinsurance insolvency; licensing and disciplinary matters for insolvency practitioners; Criminal Justice Act 1988 and Drugs Trafficking Act 1994 receiverships.
Prof. Memberships: IBA, SPI
Career: Qualified 1986. *Durrant Piesse/Lovell White Durrant* 1984-1993; *Denton Hall* 1993 to date (partner 1995).
Personal: Born 1959. Educated at Royal Grammar School, Newcastle upon Tyne and Wadham College, Oxford.

HAMILTON, Dan
Cameron McKenna, London
(0171) 367 3000
Partner in Banking Group.
Specialisation: Principal area of practice is insolvency and reconstruction. Has wide experience of insolvency and rescue work including receiverships, administrations, liquidations, corporate and individual voluntary arrangements and schemes of arrangements. Also has wide experience of advising directors of troubled companies, banks and creditor groups on restructuring and rescues. Advised the administrators in putting together the Polly Peck International PLC scheme of arrangement and advised the administrative receivers of the Union International/ Dewhurst Group. The firm acts for the leading firms of accountants and insolvency practitioners and has numerous banks among its clients. During Summer 1998 he was a member of the team establishing the firm's corporate rescue and recovery practice in Hong Kong and South East Asia. Regular lecturer to clients and occasional conference speaker.
Prof. Memberships: Society of Practitioners

of Insolvency (Associate Member), Insolvency Lawyers Association, European Insolvency Practitioners Association.
Career: Qualified in 1988. Joined *Cameron Markby* in 1986 and became a partner at *Cameron Markby Hewitt* in 1994.
Personal: Educated at Reigate Grammar School 1973-80 and Worcester College, Oxford 1981-84.

HOUGHTON, John
Simmons & Simmons, London
(0171) 628 2020
Partner in Corporate Department.
Specialisation: Principal area of practice is insolvency and reconstructions. Work includes rescues and reconstructions, administrations, receiverships and liquidations and cross-border insolvencies. Recently advised Portsmouth Football Club on its dispute with Terry Venables and Advanced Banking Solutions on its buyout of the Winter Partners business from administration. Also handled the receivership of Colorvision plc, Team Lotus administration, the Travers Morgan administrations and the de Savary companies receiverships. Advised on various reconstructions and workouts including Heron and Brent Walker.
Prof. Memberships: Society of Practitioners of Insolvency, Law Society, Insolvency Lawyers Association, and the European Insolvency Practitioners Association.
Career: Qualified in 1989, became a Partner in 1994.
Personal: Born 20th February 1962. Educated at Brunel University and University College, London 1980-84 (LL.B Hons, First Class) 1984-85 (LL.M). Interests include wine, Manchester United, music and an E-Type. Lives in London.

HYDE, Mark
Clifford Chance, London (0171) 600 1000
Specialisation: Contentious and non-contentious corporate insolvency work often with an international cross-border element.
Prof. Memberships: President of the Insolvency Lawyers Association, member of the Society of Practitioners of Insolvency.
Career: Articled *Philip Conway Thomas*; qualified 1984; partner *Clifford Chance* 1993; licensed insolvency practitioner. Admitted to practice in Hong Kong and Brunei.
Personal: Born 1958. Educated at Bootham School, York and Birmingham University (1980 LLB Hons). Resides in London.

KERSHAW, David R.
Ashurst Morris Crisp, London
(0171) 638 1111
Partner in company department.
Specialisation: He specialises in corporate work for listed companies including debt related and insolvency work, in particular debt restructurings and corporate rescues. Projects have included rescheduling the banking arrangements of two listed UK property companies combined with public offerings, the bid for Barings (in administration) and the Scan Re scheme of arrangement. He specialises in the property sector and the hi-tech/engineering sector. He is the editor of the bi-monthly supplement to Gore-Bowne on Companies and contributor of the Company Law Bulletin to PLC magazine. He is a contributing author to the Practitioners' Guide to Corporate Insolvency and Corporate Rescue.

Prof. Memberships: Member of the Union International des Avocats, UK member of the Corporate Commission of the UIA.
Career: Qualified 1978, became partner in *Ashursts* 1986.
Personal: Educated at Urmston Grammar School, Manchester and Trinity College, Cambridge (MA Hons). Married with four children, interests include the violin, painting, literature and music, windsurfing and sailing.

KIDD, David John
Cameron McKenna, Hong Kong
(852) 2846 9100
Partner in Corporate Recovery and Restructuring Group.
Specialisation: Principal area of practice is acting for banks, creditors, administrators, receivers and liquidators in all areas, from debt restructuring through to formal insolvency procedures, including dispute resolution and cross-border issues. Experienced in general commercial litigation, particularly fraud, obtaining Mareva and Anton Piller relief and asset tracing. Acted in Sugar Properties (Derisley Wood) Ltd (bloodstock receivership), Aveling Barford Group of Companies (manufacturing receivership), Atlantic Computers Group of Companies (computor leasing administration), Polly Peck International Plc (electronics, leisure and fresh produce administration), GVDC Zambia (agricultural receivership) and BCCI (bank liquidation). Acted for Court appointed receiver in Derby v. Weldon litigation. Clients include Arthur Andersen, Coopers & Lybrand, Price Waterhouse, Deloitte & Touche, KPMG, banks and creditors. Has lectured at conferences organised by Euroforum, IBC and the Society of Practitioners of Insolvency.
Prof. Memberships: Law Society, SPI (Assoc.), AEPPC, IBA.
Career: Qualified in New Zealand in 1982. Barrister and Solicitor with *Simpson Grierson* 1982-83. Joined *Cameron Markby Hewitt* in 1984 and became a Partner in 1990. Qualified as a solicitor in England and Wales in 1988. Relocated to *Cameron McKenna* in Hong Kong in 1998.
Personal: Born 8th April 1959. Educated at St Paul's Collegiate School, Hamilton, New Zealand 1972-76 and Auckland University (LL.B/ BCom) 1977-81. Leisure interests include cricket, theatre, golf and sailing. Lives in Hong Kong.

LEWIS, Jonathan
Finers, London (0171) 323 4000
Specialisation: All aspects of corporate recovery and insolvency work, corporate and personal, together with a corporate law practice. Advises lenders, debtors, and insolvency practitioners. Emphasis on cross-border insolvency and on strategic planning. Most recently, has acted for the Trustee in successfully resisting a heavily litigious challenge in the UK to a complex Chapter 11 Plan of Reorganisation in the *Inoco* case, and for the liquidators of English and Cook Island subsidiaries of the *Australian Bond Corporation*. Speaker and author on insolvency topics. Authorised insolvency practitioner.
Prof. Memberships: Law Society Company Law Sub-Committee; Insolvency Lawyers Association; AEPPC; Society of Practitioners of Insolvency; International Bar Association (Creditors' Rights Committee J); Insol International.

Career: Qualified 1971. Partner in Insolvency Group at *Finers*.
Personal: Born 1946. Educated at Harrow County Grammar School and Downing College Cambridge. Interests include walking, theatre and family.

LORING, Anthony
Cameron McKenna, London
(0171) 367 3000
Specialisation: Partner advising insolvency practitioners on receiverships, administrations and liquidations; companies on the alternatives to insolvency and lenders on debt recovery. Also advises on private equity financing, acquisitions and joint ventures.
Career: Born in 1954. Qualified in 1979. Became a partner in the Bahrain office of *McKenna & Co* in 1988 and in the London office in 1990.

MALLON, Christopher
Biddle, London (0171) 606 9301
Partner in Insolvency Group.
Specialisation: All areas of Insolvency law and asset tracing. Particular expertise in cross-border insolvency and complex bank fraud.
Prof. Memberships: Insolvency Lawyers Association, City of London Solicitors Company.
Career: Qualified in Australia in 1982. Practised at *Jackson McDonald*, Perth, 1982-1985, *Allen & Overy* 1985-1986. Joined *Lovell White & King* 1987. Admitted in England 1987. Joined *Biddle* as a partner in July 1995.
Personal: Born 6th May 1956. Attended Aquinas College, Perth, Western Australia and the University of Western Australia. Lives in Stockwell.

MONTGOMERY, Nigel
Davies Arnold Cooper, London
(0171) 936 2222
Partner in charge of Insurance Insolvency and Corporate Rescue/Insolvency Departments.
Specialisation: Principal area is advising on schemes of arrangement for solvent and insolvent insurance and reinsurance companies and pools. Current schemes include RMCA Re; ICS Re; Charter Re; MGI; ICS UK; Pan Atlantic; UIC; Hawk Insurance Company.Also advises receivers, administrators, supervisors of CVAs and banks on corporate insolvency and companies, banks and shareholders on rescue and turnaround strategies. Acted in the receiverships of Clarke Foods/Lyons Maid and for a major bidder for Ferranti receivership assets. Frequently lectures and writes on insurance insolvency in UK and USA. Is a licensed Insolvency Practitioner and has previously acted as receiver liquidator and administrator of a wide variety of companies while a partner in an accounting firm.
Prof. Memberships: Law Society; Society of Practitioners of Insolvency; International Association of Insurance Receivers; AEPPC; Insolvency Lawyers Association.
Career: Qualified 1981.

NAYLOR, Judith P.
Allen & Overy, London (0171) 330 3000
Specialisation: Banking partner specialising in business reconstruction, debt rescheduling, workouts and all aspects of insolvency law,

particularly receiverships, administrations and liquidations; recently acted for the receivers of the Pentos Group (Dillons/Rymans), the Ferranti Group, Healthcare International, the administrators of the Maxwell private companies and of Olympia & York and the liquidators of Meridien International Bank Limited, the old Magnet Group and the Cresvale Group.
Prof. Memberships: Chairman of the Women's Group of the Society of Practitioners of Insolvency and member of the Education, Courses and Conferences Committee of the Society of Practitioners of Insolvency and its Legal sub-committee, the Law Society, City of London Solicitors Company, International Bar Association, Associate member of the AEPPC and Insolvency Lawyers Association.
Career: Articled *Cameron Markby Hewitt*, qualified 1986, Partner 1993.
Personal: Born 1961. St Peters College, Oxford (1983). Leisure: riding, tennis, skiing and music. Contributor to FT Insolvency.

OBANK, Richard
Herbert Smith, London (0171) 374 8000
Specialisation: Partner handling a wide range of corporate matters of both a contentious and non-contentious nature; work includes restructurings/ reorganisation and all forms of formal insolvency procedures, frequently of an international nature.
Prof. Memberships: Law Society (City of London Society), Society of Practitioners of Insolvency; Insolvency Lawyers' Association; INSOL; AEPPC/EIPA; Committee J, International Bar Association.
Career: Trained *A.V Hammond & Co*; assistant solicitor in national corporate recovery department of *Hammond Suddards* (Leeds and London). Joined *Herbert Smith* 1995; partner (corporate recovery) 1997; successful candidate in JIEB examinations (November 1997); licensed insolvency practitioner.
Personal: Born 13 June 1964. Educated at Fulneck School for Boys, Pudsey, West Yorkshire; Manchester University (1986 LLB Class 2 (1)); Guildford College of Law (1987); Honorary Fellow to the Institute of Advanced legal Studies at the University of London; Member of the Advisory Board for the Centre for Law and Business at the University of Manchester. Interests include most sports, family and travel. Lives in London and West Yorkshire.

PASCOE, Alison
Simmons & Simmons, London
(0171) 628 2020
Specialisation: All aspects of non-contentious insolvency, acting both for insolvency practitioners and banks. Major cases include MacMillan v Bishopsgate (1996); Re; BCCI (No. 10) (1997) and Kempe v Mentor (1997) (Privy Council).
Prof. Memberships: Society of Practitioners of Insolvency; Insolvency Lawyers' Association; AEPPC; SPI Womens Group.
Career: Aberdeen University LLB Scottish Law 2(i) 1986; trained *Clifford Chance* 1989-91; Qualified 1991 *Clifford Chance*; Joined *Simmons & Simmons* September 1997.

PEARSON, W Stephen
Travers Smith Braithwaite, London
(0171) 248 9133
Specialisation: Specialises in Insolvency Litigation, acting for Insolvency Practitioners, Banks and Creditors. Has particular expertice in relation to claims for Wrongful and Fraudulent Trading, Preferences and Transactions at an Undervalue.
Prof. Memberships: Law Society, Law Society of Scotland, SPI (Associate), ILA, AEPPC, IBA.
Career: Qualified in Scotland in 1985. Requalified in England in1989. Made Partner in *Travers Smith Braithwaite* in 1994. Seconded to Deloitte & Touche in 1988.
Personal: Born 25 March 1961. University of Glasgow. Leisure interests include music (piano and singing), tennis, family.

PRATT, Sandy
Norton Rose, London (0171) 283 6000
Partner in Banking Department.
Specialisation: Principal area of practice is corporate rescue and insolvency, acting for receivers, administrators and liquidators, as well as for companies in financial difficulty and for banks and other financial institutions in connection with companies in financial difficulty. Also handles banking and corporate lending. Acted for the Administrators of *Maxwell Communication Corporation plc*, the Receivers of *Maples Stores plc,*, the Liquidators of *Riverbus Ltd* and the Receivers of *Reymerston Golf Club*. Author of 'Corporate Insolvency Law & Practice' (a *Norton Rose* booklet) and numerous articles on insolvency.

PRIOR, Michael
Nabarro Nathanson, London 0171 518 3205
Specialisation: Insolvency, Corporate Recovery, National/International. Cases include: Maxwell Personal Bankruptcy, Epic Group, Dallhold (Alan Bond), Olympia & York. 1996/97: Facia Group, Fairview Currency Exchange Group (Sweden/UK/US), YC Group, Administration & CVA Millwall Football Club; Project Rose, Restructuring/Financing Large Solicitors Firm; Melita Group of Shoe Companies and Lister Group of Textile Companies (1998).
Prof. Memberships: COMMJ, IBA; INSOL, SPI, IPA, ILA, Various Technical Committees (ILA, SPI, CBI).
Career: Epsom College, England; Sorbonne University, France.
Personal: Heli-skiing, cricket, opera, Peninsular War History. Large growing family.

RAJANI, Shashi H.
Nicholson Graham & Jones, London
(0171) 648 9000
Specialisation: Insolvency. Partner and head of Corporate Rescue and Insolvency group. Specialising in corporate insolvency and reconstruction. Licensed Insolvency Practitioner since 1986. Actively involved in all aspects of corporate rescue and insolvency matters for accountant, banking and corporate clients. Also advises banking and individual clients on personal insolvency matters. Acts as consultant to the other departments and groups of the firm on insolvency matters. As Head of Corporate Rescue and Insolvency Group, responsible for managing and developing the practice of that Group and providing formal and on-the-job training in corporate insolvency to the members of the firm.

Prof. Memberships: The Law Society; including its alternate representative on the Insolvency Licensing Committee of the Insitute of Chartered Accountants in England and Wales, and Insolvency Assessor on the Society's Post-Qualification Coursework Committee; The City of London Solicitor's Company; The City of London Law Society; and its Insolvency Law Sub-Committee; Society of Practitioners of Insolvency (member of the Membership Committee); Insolvency Lawyer's Association (Council Member until April '97); European Insolvency Practitioners Association (AEPPC); Insolvency Law Committee of JUSTICE. Publications and seminars include: 1. author of: (a) Tolley's Corporate Insolvency Law Handbook (1990); (b) Tolley's Corporate Insolvency (1995); (c) Chapters on Liquidations and Dissolution and Revival in Tolley's Company Law (1st Edition); (d) Chapters on Insolvency: General, Administration Orders, Liquidators, Receivers, voluntary Arrangements and Dissolution and Revival in Tolley's Company Law (2nd Edition); (e) Chapters as in (d) above and, in addition, Chapters on insolvency: Special Provisions for Financial Markets and Director's Disqualification in Tolley's Company Law (3rd – looseleaf – edition); (f) Chapter on 'Equitable Assistance in the Search for Security' in Insolvency Law – Theory and Practice by Harry Rajak (Sweet & Maxwell – 1993); (g) Tolley's Insolvency Fees and Costs (1995-1997). 2. Joint Chief Editor of 'Insolvency Law & Practice' (Tolley); 3. Joint Consulting Editor of Tolley's Insolvency Law – 1996 looseleaf; 4. Contributor of the Insolvency/Corporate Rescue section of Corporate Briefing (until 31 December 1993). 5. Writer of a number of articles on various aspects of Corporate Insolvency Law and Practice in domestic and international journals. 6. Speaker at a number of external insolvency seminars and courses. 7. Visiting Professor, London Guildhall University.
Career: 26 November 1956 to 12 July 1964 – In practice as an advocate in Dar es Salaam, Tanzania and also in Tabora, Tanzania as senior partner. 12 July 1964 – Appointed to the Tanzanian Civil Service as Assistant Administrator-General. 1 July 1967 – Promoted to Senior Assistant Administrator-General. 31 March – Resigned from the Civil Service and moved to England. 1 June 1970 to 31 December 1976 – With *Coopers & Lybrand*, London as Manager in their Insolvency Department. 1 January 1977 to April 1988 – With *Linklaters & Paines*, London as Senior Assistant Solicitor. 25 April 1988 to 31 December 1988 – With *Cameron Markby* (now *Cameron McKenna*) as Senior Assistant Solicitor. 1 January 1989 to 31 December 1993 – Partner in *Cameron Markby Hewitt*. Since 1 January 1994 – Partner in *Nicholson Graham & Jones* and Head of its Corporate Rescue and Insolvency Group.

ROOME, James H.D.
Cadwalader, Wickersham & Taft, London (0171) 456 8500
Partner in Financial Restructuring Group.
Specialisation: Principal area of work is corporate law, including insolvency and reconstructions. Corporate recovery work includes cross-border and multinational insolvency, receivership administration and liquidations. Handles acquisitions and disposals of both troubled and healthy companies, and secondary insolvency litigation.

Prof. Memberships: Society of Practitioners of Insolvency, Law Society, Insolvency Lawyers Association, European Insolvency Practitioners Association.
Career: Qualified in 1984 and in Hong Kong in 1985. Became Partner at *Simmons & Simmons* Hong Kong office in 1987 and at London office in 1988. Licensed Insolvency Practitioner from March 1990. Became Partner at *Cadwalader, Wickersham & Taft* in 1985.
Personal: Born 7th October 1958. Educated at Wellington College 1971-76 and Southampton University 1978-81 (LL.B Hons).

RUSHWORTH, Jonathan E.F.
Slaughter and May, London
(0171) 600 1200
Partner.
Specialisation: Has a wide-ranging company, corporate finance and capital markets practice, acting in particular for listed and other companies and also for corporate trustees in capital markets issues. He has a particular interest and specialisation in insolvency work, advising companies and their directors in refinancing and insolvency issues, banks and other creditors, and also insolvency practitioners. His practice involves domestic and cross-border insolvency matters. He has been involved in many of the recent large insolvencies, in particular acting for the administrators of the Barings Group. He has lectured extensively on the subjects of reconstruction and insolvency, written numerous papers on the subject and has written a book on receivership.
Prof. Memberships: Creditors' Rights Committee of the International Bar Association. The Law Society's Standing Committee on Company Law.

SCHAFFER, Danny
Isadore Goldman, London (0171) 242 3000
Partner.
Specialisation: Specialises in all aspects of insolvency including related litigation and bank recovery. Licensed Insolvency Practitioner.
Prof. Memberships: Society for Practitioners of Insolvency, Insolvency Practitioners Association, Insolvency Lawyers Association.
Career: Qualified in 1975. Partner at *Isadore Goldman* since 1978. Appointed Deputy Registrar in Bankruptcy at High Court in February 1992.
Personal: Born 2nd September 1950. University of Birmingham 1969-71. Spare time activities include being a football referee. Lives in London.

SCOPES, Richard H.
Wilde Sapte, London (0171) 246 7000
Specialisation: Principal practice areas: corporate insolvency and insolvency related banking work, including business reconstruction and work-outs. Acts together with his colleagues for insolvency practitioners from all the main accounting practices as well as for major banks and financial institutions. Recent important matters include acting for the administrative receivers of the Coloroll Group, the Leyland DAF Group, Dunn & Co and the Sweater Shop Group as well as for the liquidator of Galileo Group Ltd.
Prof. Memberships: Law Society, City of London Solicitors Company, Society of Practitioners of Insolvency, Insolvency Practitioners Association, AEPPC, Insolvency

Lawyers Association (Council Member).
Career: Qualified 1969. Joined *Wilde Sapte* in 1976. Partner 1980. Licensed Insolvency Practitioner.
Personal: Born 1944. Educated at University College School and Magdalene College, Cambridge. Interests include wine, opera and playing bad golf better.

SEGAL, Nicholas A.
Allen & Overy, London (0171) 330 3000
Specialisation: Partner in the banking department dealing with a wide range of banking transactions (including secured lending, project finance, securitisation; global custody and distressed debt trading), work-outs and insolvency with an emphasis on international restructurings.
Prof. Memberships: Society of Practitioners of Insolvency; American Bankruptcy Institute; Fellow of the Society Law Advanced Legal Studies.
Career: Articled *Cameron Markby*, qualified 1982, assistant solicitor *Cameron Markby*, Partner *Cameron Markby*; Partner *Allen & Overy*. Senior Visiting Fellow at Queen Mary and Westfield College, University of London 1987 – date. Contributor to Gore-Brown on Companies; Current developments in International and Comparative Corporate Insolvency Law (OUP). Insolvences of Banks (FT Law & Tax) and Restitution and Banking Law (OUP).
Personal: Educated at St Peter's College, Oxford (1979 MA First Class). Born 1956. Married with one son. Interests include opera and golf.

SHANDRO, Philip Alexander (Sandy)
Freshfields, London (0171) 936 4000
Partner in Restructuring and Insolvency Group
Specialisation: All aspects of Insolvency including; advising on insolvency risk – avoidance at the pre-transaction stage; advising creditors, debtors and boards of directors on restructurings; advising officeholders of all types in formal insolvency procedures. Much cross-border experience. Fluent French. Frequent speaker and author. Member of editorial board of Receivers, Administrators & Liquidators Quarterly.
Prof. Memberships: City of London Law Society Insolvency Sub-Committee, Insolvency Lawyer's Association, AEPPC, INSOL, Canadian Bar Association.
Career: Qualified in 1978 (British Columbia) and 1992 (England & Wales). Solicitor Advocate. CEDR Accredited Mediator.
Personal: Born 14th July 1951. Educated in Canada (BA, Alberta, 1972; MA McGill, 1974) and at Oxford University (BA 1976, BCL 1978). Vice-President, Canada-UK Chamber of Commerce. Lives in London.

SIGLER, Peter
Nabarro Nathanson, London
(0171) 518 3169
Partner and Head of Litigation Department.
Specialisation: Main area of practice is commercial litigation (including contentious insolvency). Representing Sheikh Khalid Bin Mahfouz in proceedings brought by the liquidators of BCCI.
Prof. Memberships: Law Society, International Bar Association.
Career: Qualified in 1975. Joined *Nabarro Nathanson* in 1982 as a Partner.
Personal: Born 3rd October 1948. Attended

Hendon County Grammar School and Magdalen College, Oxford. Leisure interests include opera, cricket, golf and travel. Lives in London.

SPENCER, Robin
Lovell White Durrant, London
(0171) 236 0066
Specialisation: Business Reconstruction and Insolvency group specialising in insolvent insurance and reinsurance companies, insurance-related insolvency matters and troubled financial services companies, as well as other more general types of insolvency and reconstruction. Major assignments include the insolvencies of: Mentor Insurance Limited; Drexel Burnham Lambert Group; British & Commonwealth Merchant Bank plc; The London and Overseas Insurance Company PLC; Gooda Walker Limited; Feltrim Underwriting Agencies Limited; Stockholm Re (Bermuda) Ltd; Dawnay, Day Securities Limited; Sovereign Marine & General Insurance Company Limited.
Career: Qualified as Barrister 1981; solicitors' office HM Customs & Excise 1983-1986; joined *Lovell White Durrant* 1987 (including two year secondment to *Appleby, Spurling & Kempe*, attorneys, Bermuda); requalified as solicitor 1991; partner 1994; member of International Association of Insurance Receivers, Society of Practitioners of Insolvency.
Personal: Born 1958. Educated at Birkenhead School (1969-76); Pembroke College, Cambridge (1980 BA Hons (Cantab); 1984 MA (Cantab)). Resides Chesham, Buckinghamshire.

STEINBERG, David Jeremy
Clifford Chance, London (0171) 600 1000
Specialisation: Insolvency and Corporate Restructuring for the insurance and reinsurance industry. Also provides general insolvency and restructuring advice, advising banks and other secured lenders to troubled debtors, advising unsecured creditors of troubled debtors, advising shareholders and directors of troubled debtors on reorganisation and solvency issues, advising insolvency practitioners such as administrators, receivers, and liquidators. Partner 1994.

STEINER, Michael
Denton Hall, London 0171 320 6887
Partner in Litigation Department. email: mxs@dentonhall.com
Specialisation: Main area of practice is insolvency and corporate reconstruction. Specialises in all areas of insolvency law, including official and unofficial corporate reconstruction, administrative receiverships and liquidations, personal insolvency (including voluntary arrangements) and asset recovery, particularly in relation to trans-national insolvencies. Acts for provisional liquidators on public interest petitions and has advised regulatory bodies.
Prof. Memberships: International Bar Association Creditors Rights Section (Former Joint Chairman of Sub-Committee on Model International Bankruptcy Legislation); Bar and Law Society's Joint Working Party on Insolvency Law; Chairman of City of London Solicitors' Insolvency Society Sub-Committee.

Member of SPI International Committee.
Career: Qualified in 1964. Partner with *Booth & Blackwell* 1964-90. Joined *Denton Hall* as a Partner in 1990. Solicitor member of the Lord Chancellor's Insolvency Rules Advisory Committee 1986-92. Consultant to the Czech Government on privatisation with responsibility for insolvency legislation. Adviser to the Russian Federation Ministry on Insolvency. Co-author of 'Insolvent Partnerships' (Jordans, 1996).
Personal: Born in 1938. Educated at St. Paul's School, London and Lincoln College, Oxford (MA 1961). Leisure pursuits include theatre, cinema and walking the dog.

STEWART, Gordon C.
Allen & Overy, London (0171) 330 3000
Partner in Banking Department and Head of Business Reconstruction and Insolvency Group.
Specialisation: Work includes corporate and business rescues and reconstructions, receiverships, administrations, voluntary arrangements and liquidations. Also handles other aspects of banking, including loan and security documentation. Major matters including acting for: numerous administrators including those of the Maxwell private companies and the Coal Investments Group (mining); numerous receivers including those of the Ferranti International (industrial), Athena, Pentos (Dillons/ Ryman) (retail), Astra Training Services Group (services), Broadwell Land (property), Leyland DAF Finance (securitisation) and Blackspur Leasing (leasing); numerous liquidators including those of Meridien International (international conglomerate), Bell Lines (international freight) and the Wallace Smith Trust private bank (banking); banks on the successful restructuring of the Charles Church Group; banks and companies on numerous other confidential restructurings; represented the insolvency profession in connection with the Paramount case in the House of Lords. Author of Administrative Receivers and Administrators (1987). Contributor to Leasing Law in the European Community, Euromoney (1994). Author of numerous articles in this field. Regular lecturer at, and Chairman of, seminars and conferences.
Career: Qualified in 1980. Joined *Allen & Overy* as a Partner in 1989. Member of the Lord Chancellor's Insolvency Rules Committee from 1993; President of the Society of Practitioners of Insolvency (SPI) 1996-97 – first lawyer to hold the post; Chairman of the Law Society insolvency law sub-committee.
Personal: Born 16th May 1956. Attended Hutchesons' Boys Grammar School, Glasgow 1970-74 and University College, Oxford 1974-77. Leisure interests include running, golf and humour. Lives in London.

TOTTY, Peter G.
Allen & Overy, London (0171) 330 3000
Partner in Banking Department and Member of Business Reconstruction and Insolvency Group.
Specialisation: Principal area of practice is banking, debt rescheduling, work-outs and insolvency. Has over 30 years experience in this area. Recent cases include acting for

administrators of Olympia & York (Canary Wharf) and receivers of Ferranti International and advising banks on Peregrine. Co-author of 'Corporate Insolvency' (McGraw Hill) and 'Insolvency' (Sweet & Maxwell 5 vols). Regular contributor of articles to professional journals and lectures on banking and insolvency related topics. Past president of the Insolvency Lawyers Association. Fellow American college of Bankruptcy, member 'Ferris' working party on insolvency fees.
Prof. Memberships: Law Society, INSOL (Council Member), Insolvency Lawyers Association.
Career: Qualified in 1964. MA Oxon.
Personal: Born 10th June 1938. Attended Jesus College, Oxford 1958-6 . Leisure pursuits include sailing. Lives in London and New Forest.

TURTLE, Trevor W.
Herbert Smith, London (0171) 374 8000
See under Energy – Water, p. 334

TYRELL, Vivien M.
D J Freeman, London (0171) 583 4055
Partner in the Insurance Department.
Specialisation: Authorised insolvency practitioner. Acting for officeholders and advising in relation to all aspects of insolvency. The largest proportion of her work is insurance insolvency involving drafting international schemes of arrangement. She has unwound joint venture agreements and vehicles, pursued actions for the repatriation of assets using injunctions and officeholders' interrogation procedures both here and abroad. Wrongful trading, directors' mispeason and other directors' liability issues. Advice in relation to returns to creditors and shareholders whose interests are in insurance companies in run-off.
Prof. Memberships: International Association of Insurance Receivers, AEPPC (European Insolvency Practitioners Association), INSOL, ILA and SPI.
Career: Qualified 1980. Joined *D J Freeman* 1981 (Partner from 1985).
Personal: Educated at South Shields Grammar School for Girls and Somerville College, Oxford (BA Hons Jurisprudence). Interests include opera, skiing, sailing, hot air ballooning.

VERRILL, John
Lawrence Graham, London (0171) 379 0000
Partner in Company Commercial Department.
Specialisation: Significant area of practice is insolvency. Acted in the company voluntary arrangement of London Securities PLC and gave advice to boards of British and Commonwealth and Polly Peck after administration orders made. Author of Butterworths "Insolvency Meetings Manual." Frequent speaker and writer on insolvency topics. Recent work includes restitution and wrongful trading actions arising out of ultra vires local authority contracts. Also has significant area of practice in oil and gas law. Work covers all aspects of upstream asset management, including sales and purchases, farm-ins and earn-ins, transportation and joint ventures. Has worked in the UK and Norwegian sectors of the North Sea and on first major offshore gas development in Bangladesh in the summer of 1996, a project structured around the industry's new "alliancing" concept.
Prof. Memberships: Insolvency Practitioners

Association, Fellow of Society of Practitioners in Insolvency, Insolvency Lawyers Association (Council Member and Vice-President). UK Energy Lawyers Group, International Bar Association Section on Energy and Resources Law.
Career: Qualified in 1981. Licensed Insolvency Practitioner 1990. Joined *Lawrence Graham* in 1983, becoming a Partner in 1986.
Personal: Born 25th March 1954. Attended University College School Hampstead, then University College, London (LLB Hons). Leisure interests include shooting, rowing, child minding, sailing, sea fishing and gardening. Lives in South Oxfordshire.

WALSH, Jeremy M.
Travers Smith Braithwaite, London
(0171) 248 9133
Specialisation: Partner specialising in corporate rescue, reconstruction and insolvency, acting for banks, companies, insolvency practitioners, creditors and investors. Has wide experience including rescues, reconstructions, administrations, receiverships, liquidations, voluntary arrangements and schemes of arrangement. Licensed insolvency practitioner since 1994.
Prof. Memberships: Law Society, Society of Practitioners of Insolvency, Insolvency Lawyers Association, European Insolvency Practitioners Association and International Bar Association.
Career: Qualified in 1985. Partner in *Travers Smith Braithwaite* since 1994. Seconded to Coopers & Lybrand in 1990.
Personal: Born 4 November 1960. University of Manchester. Interests include family, films, theatre, swimming and music.

WHITE, John J.
Cameron McKenna, London
(0171) 367 3000
Partner and Head of Banking and Insolvency Group.
Specialisation: Insolvency work includes multi-bank support operations, administrations and administrative receiverships. Banking work

includes clearing bank lending, property and project finance, trade finance and syndicated facilities. Acted for the administrators of Polly Peck, the examiner of the Maxwell Communication Corporation and the administrators of Air Europe. Addresses around twenty conferences per year.
Prof. Memberships: Law Society, Chartered Institute of Bankers, Society of Practitioners in Insolvency, Insolvency Lawyers Association, International Bar Association, City of London Solicitors Company, Association Europeene des Practiciens des Procedures Collectives.
Career: Qualified in 1963. Having joined *Cameron Markby Hewitt* in 1957, became a Partner in 1964. Fellow of the Chartered Institute of Bankers.
Personal: Born 6th July 1938. Leisure interests include hockey, cricket and port. Lives in London. Clubs: Athenaeum and West Herts.

WILKINSON, Andrew J.D.
Cadwalader, Wickersham & Taft, London
(0171) 456 8500
Partner. Leads the London office's corporate insolvency and insurance restructuring practices. Mr Wilkinson is an experienced corporate insolvency practitioner. He has pioneered the use of schemes of arrangement for the work out of troubled insurance companies and is expert in run-off issues involving recovery from reinsurers, security rights, cut-throughs, communations, policyholder rights, broker accounting and setoff. Mr Wilkinson is also extensively involved in M&A work in the insurance industry.

WOOLF, Geoffrey
Stephenson Harwood, London
(0171) 329 4422
Partner in Banking Department (Insolvency & Asset Recovery Group).
Specialisation: Principal area of practice is corporate insolvency and reconstruction. Also handles banking work including secured and unsecured lending and debt restructuring.

Advises a clearing bank on its standard forms. Has acted as an expert witness in a number of cases. Regularly speaks at conferences and publishes articles.
Career: Qualified in 1970 after articles at *Stephenson Harwood*. Former Head of the Property Department and former Finance Partner.
Personal: Born 1946. Educated at Harrow County Grammar School and King's College, London (LL.B 1967).

WRIGHT, Richard W.
Linklaters, London (0171) 456 3477
Specialisation: Has acted in all areas of insolvency but in recent years has concentrated on contentious and investigatory matters. Acted for the Trustees in Bankruptcy of A Nadir, K Maxwell and M B Murjani, and in the administration of British & Commonwealth. Also practises in the field of fraud and financial services malfeasance.
Prof. Memberships: Member of the Insolvency Practitioners Association, the Society of Practitioners of Insolvency and the Insolvency Lawyers Association. Former President and Council Member of the Insolvency Lawyers Association. Member of the Justice Committee on Bankruptcy in the mid-1970s.
Career: Bryanston School, Dorset; MA (Cantab) – articled and at *Simmons & Simmons* 1964-1967, partner *Williams Prior & Co* 1968-1990, partner *Dibb Lupton Broomhead* 1990-1996, Of Counsel to *Linklaters & Paines* 1996 to date.
Personal: Sports: golf and tennis. Leisure interests: opera and classical music, antiques, history. Married with two daughters.

SOUTH EAST

Boyes Turner Burrows (6ptnrs: 5 p/t / 3assts) The firm is a "significant player with an innovative approach" and thought to be "really switched on." *Christopher Branson* has been consistently rated as a star in the region this year. **Clients/Work:** Acting in the Total Records Ltd liquidation. Dealing with the Onyx Group Ltd rescue package. Acting for the trustee in bankruptcy of Jimmy White.

Burstows (Brighton: 2ptnrs/4assts. Crawley: 1ptnr 50%/1asst 50%) "Dominate in Brighton,"and specialise in bankruptcy. *Andrew Taylor* heads a team which also includes *Andrew Clinton* who is "a good crisp lawyer,"with a reputation for contentious work. **Clients/Work:** Acting for Penny Armstrong, partner and mother of the children of Paolo Gucci in defence of international insolvency proceedings brought by his US Chapter 11 Trustee. Acting for the Secretary of State for Trade and Industry in directors disqualification action against political commentator Vincent Hannah

deceased. Advising the IVA Supervisor of two partners in collapsed unlicensed deposit taker with £5+m debts.

Bunkers (1ptnr 90%/1asst 90%) A"small" but well regarded practice which boasts *Julian Dobson* who is "excellent and amiable." **Clients/Work:** Act for the top 6 accountancy firms and others in small to medium sized insolvencies.

Blake Lapthorn (1ptnr f/t 4ptnrs 25%/1asst f/t 4assts 25%) The firm goes up the tables and was perceived to be "coming on in leaps and bounds." New to the lists are "top player" *Nicholas Keitley* ("commercial, responsive, pragmatic and friendly") and "up and coming" senior assistant *Matthew Barker* who has impressed this year. **Clients/Work:** Acting for Coopers & Lybrand on the administration of BrazierLtd. Acting for Price Waterhouse on the administrative receivership of Bowman Yachts Ltd. Acting for Ernst & Young in administrative receiverships of Park Elder Ltd and Charles Murphy Ltd.

Bond Pearce (1ptnr/2assts) Merged with Hepherd Winstanley & Pugh last year and are considered "a good firm" which is used on a regular basis by accountants. However, the loss of Adrian Owen was seen as a cause for concern amongst the IP's. **Clients/Work:** Acting in the Administration sale of building merchants in Essex involving complex directors' application; advising on administrative receivership and liquidation sales; acting for office holders on the investigation of claims against company directors.

Cole & Cole (2ptnrs: 1-30% / 3assts – 30%) Thought to "know what they are doing." Team includes *Bruce Potter* who has a more general commercial reputation and *Paul Rippon* who is fully committed to insolvency work. **Clients/Work:** General insolvency with a corporate bias, liquidations and CVA's. Acting in smaller receiverships and partnership voluntary arrangements.

Parrott & Coales (1ptnr 75% / 1asst 10%) Small team but seen as "active." *Elizabeth Taylor* is well known and well thought of. "A good all round corporate and personal insolvency lawyer," she joins the lists for the first time this year. Ian Taylor has retired. **Clients/Work:** Acting for liquidators and trustee in bankruptcy involving adjustment of prior adjustment. Acting for Supervisors of IVA's and for directors in defending proceedings under the Directors Disqualification Act 1986.

Sherwin Oliver (2ptnrs 80-90%, 1ptnr 50%/1asst 50%) Handle both contentious and non-contentious matters. *David Oliver* is a good senior insolvency lawyer who has

been "around the block." *Nigel Craig* ("excellent") and *Christopher Brockman* are both recognised players. **Clients/Work:** Acting for the DTI, Nationwide Building Society-Business Finance, KPMG and Smith & Williamson.

Lamport Bassitt (1ptnr 25%, 2ptnrs 10%/ 2assts p/t) "A small practice" which includes *Sean Kelly* who is respected for his insolvency work although it is not his main area of practice. **Clients/Work:** Advising receivers of property company with its equitable charge as security over shares in another company. Acting in preference claim brought by liquidators against former director of insolvent company.

Paris Smith & Randall (4ptnrs 40% / 1asst 40%) Not a firm with a dedicated insolvency department but *Malcolm Le Bas* is good. Known to represent IP's at their own disciplinary tribunals. **Clients/Work:** Acting for the administrator of a substantial plc in Wiltshire involving sale of the business and assets and complex arrangements in the administration. Acting for joint Administrative Receivers of Southampton plc in sale of assets and advice relating to issues of priorities against chargeholders.

Cripps Harries Hall (3ptnrs/5assts) Reputation for corporate recoveries on behalf of secondary banks. **Clients/Work:** Acting for the Administrative receivers of H&K Medway Ltd in application for directions relating to preferential creditor pay-out entitlement. Acting for Coopers & Lybrand and Grant Thornton.

Thomas Eggar Church Adams (4ptnrs p/t / 3assts p/t) Recently merged and com-

mended for their "lateral thinking." **Clients/Work:** Litigating on the question of liability of contributions when winding up a partnership as if it is a company. Advising on the interlinking of failed CVA's and cross guarantees.

Paul Davidson Taylor (1ptnr f/t, 5ptnrs p/t; 1asst p/t) A new firm to our lists recommended as having a "true insolvency practice" which is highly rated by insolvency practitioners. **Clients/Work:** Handling a mix of liquidations, administrative receiverships and IVAs, partnership winding up and bankruptcy.

LEADERS' PROFILES · SOUTH EAST

BARKER, Matthew
Blake Lapthorn, Fareham (01489) 579990
Specialisation: All aspects of corporate and personal insolvency, restructuring and rescue work, acting primarily for Insolvency Practitioners.
Prof. Memberships: Law Society; Society of Practitioners of Insolvency.
Career: Qualified in 1995 following articles with *Blake Lapthorn*. Solicitor in the Insolvency and Business Rescue Group at *Blake Lapthorn* since qualification.
Personal: Born 1969. Married. Hockey, tennis, film, music and walking.

BRANSON, Christopher
Boyes Turner & Burrows, Reading
(0118) 959 7711
Partner in Insolvency Group.
Specialisation: Principal area of practice is corporate and individual insolvency. Acts for receivers, liquidators and administrators in corporate insolvency situations and for trustees in bankruptcy as well as nominees and supervisors in CVAs and IVAs. Acts for office-holders in areas of fraud and asset tracing, often abroad. Advises banks and financial institutions on security and lending issues. Clients include Cork Gully, Coopers & Lybrand,

Ernst & Young, KPMG, Price Waterhouse, Deloitte & Touche, Grant Thornton and Barclays Bank. Has lectured at IBC Conferences, SPI South conferences as well as giving internal lectures and talks to accountancy firms. Charge-out rate of £160 per hour.
Prof. Memberships: Law Society, IPA, SPI. Insolvency Lawyers Association.
Career: Qualified in 1981. At *Hewett Pim & Dixon* 1981-1987 (Partner from 1983). Partner at *Boyes Turner & Burrows* from 1988.
Personal: Born in 1955. Educated at Kingston University 1975-78 (BA Hons in Law). Leisure activities include water sports, mountain biking and squash. Lives in Caversham, Reading.

BROCKMAN, Christopher C.
Sherwin Oliver, Portsmouth (01705) 832200
Specialisation: Deals with all aspects of individual and corporate insolvency, from administration to voluntary arrangements, particularly on the contentious side. Acts for many of the leading and smaller insolvency practitioners on the South Coast. Also prosecutes for the DTI and acts for directors facing disqualification proceedings. Regularly gives talks at professional seminars. Has a particular interest in the effect of the incorporation of the European Convention on

Human Rights into UK law on insolvency proceedings.
Prof. Memberships: Law Society, Society for Practitioners of Insolvency, LawNet Insolvency Unit.
Career: Called to Bar 1985, transferred to solicitors 1988, joining *Sherwin Oliver Solicitors* in 1992 from a leading London firm.
Personal: Born 1962, lives in Broughton, Hampshire. Designing and building own house, sailing.

CLINTON, Andrew
Burstows, Crawley (01293) 603603

CRAIG, Nigel S.
Sherwin Oliver, Portsmouth (01705) 832200
Partner in Corporate/Commercial and Corporate Rescue Department.
Specialisation: Principal area of practice is corporate restructuring, mergers, acquisitions and disposals, with and without insolvency related issues. Approximately half of the department's cases are insolvency-related and involve acting for the Insolvency Practitioner on a restructuring/hive down prior to sale, and subsequently on the sale, or acting for the clients acquiring from receivers, administrators or liquidators. Has dealt with twenty to thirty

group re-structurings for groups of various values, the acquisition and disposal of insurance companies and insurance brokerages and the acquisition, disposal and re-structuring of major cross-channel ferry companies and shipping companies. Also handles management buy-outs and provides management and general corporate advice. Has advised on the setting up of nationwide franchise operations and re-structuring of a franchise group. Author of a number of articles published in legal journals and newspapers. Lectures regularly and has been interviewed and spoken on radio on legal topics. Charge out rate for normal work is in the region of o135 per hour plus VAT.
Prof. Memberships: Law Society, Insolvency Lawyers' Association (Associate Member), LawNet Insolvency Unit.
Career: Qualified 1981. Shortly afterwards set up with David Oliver as *Oliver & Co*. The firm merged with *Sherwins* to produce *Sherwin Oliver* in May 1989.
Personal: Born 16th December 1956. Educated at Southern Grammar School, Portsmouth 1968-75, Kingston-upon-Thames Polytechnic 1975-78 and Guildford Law College 1978-79. Leisure pursuits include sailing (racing two-man catamarans), badminton and gardening. Lives in Emsworth, Hampshire.

DOBSON, Julian C.
Bunkers, Hove (01273) 329797

KEITLEY, Nicholas
Blake Lapthorn, Fareham (01489) 579990
Specialisation: Partner and Head of Insolvency and Business Rescue Group, dealing with all types of corporate and personal insolvency work; also undertakes banking and factoring work. Recent insolvency work includes acting for Coopers & Lybrand on the administration of Brazier Limited, acting for Price Waterhouse on the administrative receivership of Bowman Yachts Limited and acting for Ernst & Young on the administrative receivership of Parkelder Limited and Charles Murphy Limited.
Prof. Memberships: Law Society, member of the Society of Practitioners of Insolvency.
Career: Articled *Stoneham Langton &*

Passmore; qualified 1985; Assistant Solicitor at *Lovell White Durrant* (formerly *Durrant Piesse*) 1985-1993; Assistant Solicitor *Hammond Suddards* 1993-1995; joined *Blake Lapthorn* 1995; Partner *Blake Lapthorn* 1996. Educated at Epsom College and Leeds University; Bachelor of Laws (Hons) 2:1; Insolvency Practitioners Licence obtained in 1990.

KELLY, Sean
Lamport Bassitt, Southampton (01703) 634931
Partner in Company and Commercial Department.
Specialisation: Specialises in company and commercial work and insolvency, acting for accountants, banks and the leisure industry.
Prof. Memberships: Law Society.
Career: Qualified in 1976. Partner at *Lamport Bassitt* since 1978.
Personal: Born 8th January 1951. Lives in Winchester.

LE BAS, Malcolm H.
Paris Smith & Randall, Southampton (01703) 482482

OLIVER, David C.
Sherwin Oliver, Portsmouth (01705) 832200
Senior Partner in Insolvency and Litigation Department.
Specialisation: Practice covers all areas of corporate and individual insolvency, acting for all of the major insolvency practitioners in the Southern region and some outside. Acts for various firms of chartered surveyors in relation to LPA receiverships. Also handles general civil litigation and major fraud prosecutions. Work includes construction arbitration contract disputes, involving claims in excess of £5 million each (obtained an Administration Order in relation to a Lloyds managing agent company with claims against it of approximately £90 million) and major fraudulent trading cases, representing one director of a company with a deficiency in excess of £12 million. Has lectured to Portsmouth University, LawNet, Chambers of Commerce and the Insolvency Practitioners Association. Charge-out rate is £150 per hour.
Prof. Memberships: Law Society, Insolvency

Lawyers Association, AEPPC, Chartered Institute of Arbitrators, Institute of Directors, Society of Practitioners of Insolvency.
Career: Senior Litigation Partner at *Sherwin Oliver* since 1985. Fellow of Chartered Institute of Arbitrators since 1993. Appointed Deputy District Judge in June 1993. Past Chairman Lawnet Insolvency Unit.
Personal: Born 13th March 1944. Leisure interests include golf, tennis, walking, swimming, films and theatre. Trustee of three national charities. Lives in Portsmouth.

POTTER, Bruce J.
Cole & Cole, Reading (0118) 955 3000
Specialisation: Corporate and Individual Insolvency, particularly Administrations, Receiverships and Professional Partnership VA's. Also specialist insolvency advice to lenders, including Factoring/Invoice Discounting Clients and General Corporate/Reconstruction advice.
Prof. Memberships: Chairman Thames Valley Commercial Lawyers Association 1997-1998.
Career: Qualified 1985. Joined *Cole & Cole* 1986. Partner 1989.
Personal: Born June 1958. Oxford University 1977-1980. Married. Rugby and skiing.

RIPPON, P.D.W.
Cole & Cole, Reading (0118) 955 3001
Specialisation: Corporate and Individual Insolvency: particulary Receiverships, Liquidations, Company and Individual Voluntary Arrangements and Bankruptcies. Recent large liquidation, DHV Holding (UK) Limited group of companies and recent large receivership, Regisbrook Group Limited group of companies. Also specialist insolvency advice to lenders.
Career: Qualified in 1972. Joined *Cole & Cole* 1976. Partner 1979.
Personal: Born June 1948. Leicester University 1966-69. Sport, films, theatre and opera.

TAYLOR, Andrew C.
Burstows, Crawley (01293) 603603

TAYLOR, E.E.
Parrott & Coales, Aylesbury (01296) 482244

SOUTH WEST

Bond Pearce (2ptnrs/5assts) Strong in the South West and acquiring a profile in Bristol. **Clients/Work:** Restructuring of a number of leisure attractions in the South West. Acting in administrative receiverships of investment property in Durham, major haulage business and meat processing factory. Handling a series of restructurings and receiverships in the agricultural sector.

Osborne Clarke (2ptnrs: 1p/t / 9assts) A large team which is good on personal insolvency. *Patrick Cook* ("good bloke") was on sabbatical this year but is now back in the saddle. **Clients/Work:** Acting for the joint Administrative Receivers appointed by Lloyds over Bournemouth & Boscombe Athletic Football Club Company Ltd. Acting

for the Disqualification Unit of the Insolvency Service in some 200 disqualifications during the year including reported cases Country Farm Inns Ltd and Admiral Energy Group Ltd. Acting for National Westminister Bank plc.

Burges Salmon (6ptnrs: 5p/t / 5assts: 3p/t) Interviewees recommended the practice as "strong across the board" with particular expertise in agricultural insolvency. Managing partner *Guy Stobart* and *Paul Haggett* are acknowledged players. **Clients/Work:** Acting for all major accountants, Lloyds TSB Group and UCB Bank plc.

Anstey Sargent & Probert (3ptnrs/ 2assts) Known by accountants and lawyers for personal insolvency matters but well regarded for corporate recoveries too. Often seen acting for the Official Receiver. Lead

partner *Stephen Lawson* is considered "excellent." **Clients/Work:** Acting for the prosecution in Re CS Holidays Ltd (1997) BCC172. Acting in major insolvencies of the estates of A S Collard, deceased (in Bankruptcy) and T M Elwick (in Bankruptcy) involving the administration of a Compensation scheme for investors. Acting for the Debtor in Re Eileen Davies (1997) BPIR 619.

Cameron McKenna (1ptnr/3assts) Have a good practice but a lower profile in the South West insolvency market than their London office. **Clients/Work:** LPA Receiverships including one involving portfolio of 20 properties. Restructurings and rescues ranging in value from £250,000 to £2.5m. Insolvency litigation including Receiver's application for directions to determine the ownership of book debts circa £400,000.

LEADING FIRMS · SOUTH WEST

BOND PEARCE Plymouth
OSBORNE CLARKE Bristol

BURGES SALMON Bristol

ANSTEY SARGENT & PROBERT Exeter
LAYTONS Bristol

HIGHLY REGARDED FIRMS

Cameron McKenna Bristol
Lester Aldridge Bournemouth

Meade-King Bristol
Stephens & Scown Exeter
Trumps Bristol

Clarke Willmott & Clarke Taunton
Lawrence Tucketts Bristol
Rickerby Watterson Cheltenham

Laytons (2ptnrs: 1p/t / 3assts 25-100%) Have gone up in the rankings this year after several strong recommendations. Accountants rated them for personal insolvency. Team includes the "slightly maverick" *Anthony Harris* who is appreciated for his "lateral thinking on knotty problems." He does a "respected mix" of corporate and non-contentious work. New in this year is *Gordon Bon*. **Clients/Work:** Acting in the Administration order of Lamberhurst Vineyard Ltd and the CVA of Sweatfield Ltd (formerly J T Design and Build)

Lester Aldridge (1ptnr f/t, 3ptnrs 25%/ 3assts) A relatively sizeable insolvency practice in the region which includes *Malcolm Niekirk* who is well rated. **Clients/ Work:** Acting for AFC Bournemouth Trust Fund in constructing a rescue package for AFC Bournemouth in CVA and receivership including dealing with High Court challenge to the validity of the creditors decision in the CVA.

Meade-King (2ptnrs/3assts) A well regarded mainly contentious practice. *Clare Harris* is "excellent" and is considered "a true insolvency expert." **Clients/Work:** Acting in TSB Bank plc v Platts (1998) (No. 2) BPIR 284 dealing with equitable set off in a bankruptcy petition. Acting in Re: Keenan (1998) BPIR 205 deciding whether culpability on the part of a debtor a prerequisite for IVA failure under s 276(1)(a) IA1986.

Stephens & Scown (1ptnr 75%, 3ptnrs p/t / 2assts 15%) "The team has good advocates" including *Matthew Wald* and go up in the rankings for quality work. **Clients/Work:** Acting in Director's disqualification Court of Appeal case Country Farms Inns Ltd [1997] BCC 801. Instructed by most insolvency practices in South West.

Trumps (3ptnrs 20-40%/3assts 10-40%) A well regarded firm. New to the ranks, *Philip May* is rated by peers as a player. *Robert Bourns* continues to be recognised for individual insolvency work. **Clients/Work:** Acting nationally for the Official Receivers in disposing of interests in bankruptcy estates. Handling reciverships acting for IPs, lenders/appointors and purchasers. Acting in Re South West Car Sales Ltd (in liquidation) [1998] BCC 163 relating to the proper treatment of VAT monies following the appointment of a liquidator.

Clarke Willmott & Clarke (1ptnr) Small department but expanding to Bristol office. **Clients/Work:** Acting for receivers in receivership of South West construction company. Acting in large IVA concerning an abattoir in LPA Receivership. Acting for large London insolvency accountant in "Centrebind"business rescue package.

Lawrence Tucketts (4ptnrs:1 p/t / 4assts: 1 p/t) Were recommended by accountants. **Clients/Work:** Acting for Barclays Bank plc in Huish v Ellis and others, a claim against bank receiver.

Rickerby Watterson (1ptnr 100%; 3ptnrs 40-60%; 2ptnrs 20-40%/ 2assts) A good practice which was quite well-known. **Clients/Work:** Acting in the creation of a company restructuring to avoid a receivership using a debt equity swap. Advising the liquidator in a multi-million pound theft by the directors of a wine company. Acting on directors disqualification and LPA Receiverships.

LEADING INDIVIDUALS SOUTH WEST

COOK Patrick Osborne Clarke
LAWSON Stephen Anstey Sargent & Probert
NIEKIRK Malcolm Lester Aldridge
STOBART Guy Burges Salmon
TETTMAR Victor Bond Pearce

BOURNS Robert Trumps
HARRIS Anthony Laytons
HARRIS Clare Meade-King
MAY Philip Trumps
WALD Matthew Stephens & Scown

UP AND COMING

BON Gordon Laytons
HAGGETT Paul Burges Salmon

LEADERS' PROFILES · SOUTH WEST

BON, Gordon E.
Laytons, Bristol (0117) 929 1626

BOURNS, Robert H.G.
Trumps, Bristol (0117) 946 8200
Specialisation: Principal area of practice is insolvency. Supervises contract to Insolvency Service (37 offices in England & Wales). Other work for insolvency practitioners, in particular addition to individual insolvency. Also employment law, settling terms and conditions of employment, acting for employers and employees on termination of employment. Prosecutes for DTI under the Insolvency Act 1986 and CDDA 1986. Charge-out rate is £140 per hour.
Prof. Memberships: Law Society, Employment Lawyers Association.
Career: Qualified 1980 *Osborne Clarke* 1978-83. *Trumps* 1983 to date. (Partner from 1987).
Personal: Born 11th May 1956. Educated Bristol. Leisure pursuits include dinghy sailing; swimming.

COOK, Patrick D.
Osborne Clarke, Bristol (0117) 984 5225
Partner in Insolvency Department.
Specialisation: Licensed insolvency practitioner. Has acted for office holders in over 450 administrative receiverships, 300 Law of Property Act receiverships and twelve administration orders together with numerous liquidations and bankruptcies, CVA and IVA. Appointed Company Inspector by Secretary of State for Trade and Industry for Insider Dealing investigation in City of London. Solicitor to the Insolvency Service in conducting applications for the disqualification of Directors under the Company Directors Disqualification Act 1986. Also handles litigation in corporate and contractual disputes. Acted in the rescue of Swansea City FC from liquidation through Company's Schemes of Arrangement. Also acted in the administration of Newport County FC. Advised in the administrative receivership and subsequent sale of Bournemouth Football Club. Frequent lecturer at conferences and seminars.
Prof. Memberships: SPI, IPA, ILA, Law Society.
Career: Qualified 1981. Joined *Osborne Clarke* in 1983, becoming a Partner in 1986.

Personal: Born 11th July 1956. Attended Abingdon School 1967-75, then Oxford University 1975-78. Leisure interests include golf, tennis and family. Lives in Stone Allerton.

HAGGETT, Paul S.N.
Burges Salmon, Bristol (0117) 939 2000

HARRIS, Anthony
Laytons, Bristol (0117) 929 1626

HARRIS, Clare
Meade-King, Bristol (0117) 926 4121

LAWSON, Stephen A.
Anstey Sargent & Probert, Exeter (01392) 411221
Partner in Insolvency Department.
Specialisation: Handles all areas of corporate and personal insolvency, including LPA receiverships. Also handles bank litigation and professional negligence, including acting as expert witness in these fields. Author of 'Individual Voluntary Arrangements' and 'LPA Receivers.' Has extensive lecturing experience for *Jordans*, College of Law and others.
Prof. Memberships: Law Society, IPA, SPI,

Institute of Credit Management.
Career: Qualified in 1969. Joined *Anstey Sargent & Probert* in 1964, becoming a Partner in 1973. Former President and Secretary of Devon and Exeter Law Society. Deputy High Court Bankruptcy Registrar.
Personal: Born 27th August 1945. Attended Queens College Taunton 1956-64. Methodist local preacher and School Governor.

MAY, Philip N S
Trumps, Bristol (0117) 946 8200
Specialisation: Principal area of practice is business breakdown and insolvency. Acts for Official Receivers and Insolvency Practitioners nationally, particularly in connection with corporate insolvency and contentious matters. Also acts for respondents in CDDA 1986 cases. Recent reported cases include: Re: South West Car Sales Ltd (in liq) BCC 163. Charge-out rate is £140 per hour.
Prof. Memberships: Law Society, Bristol Law Society, S.P.I.
Career: Educated Southend-on-Sea, Essex and Lincoln College, Oxford Articled *Osborne Clarke* Bristol 1982-84. Assistant Solicitor to Partner *Osborne Clarke* Bristol 1984-1995. Joined *Trumps* as Partner 1995.
Personal: Born 16th March 1959; married with 2 children; lives in Bristol. Leisure pursuits include golf, snooker and skiing.

NIEKIRK, Malcolm
Lester Aldridge, Bournemouth (01202) 786161
Specialisation: Head of the Corporate Recovery Unit. Licensed insolvency practitioner. Deals almost exclusively with non-contentious corporate insolvency, generally administrative receiverships (with a particular interest in structured receiverships), but also including fixed charge receiverships, administrations, liquidations and voluntary arrangements. Usually advises banks and other financial institutions, insolvency practitioners and sometimes businesses buying assets from receivers and companies in financial difficulties. Occasional conference speaker. Supports plain English drafting.
Career: Articled *Moore & Blatch*, Southampton; qualified 1987. Joined *Lester Aldridge* 1990. Partner 1994. Insolvency practitioners licence 1998.
Personal: Born 1963. Educated Royal Grammar School, High Wycombe; Southampton University (1984 LL.B Hons). Lives in Lyndhurst.

STOBART, Guy W.
Burges Salmon, Bristol (0117) 939 2000

TETTMAR, Victor
Bond Pearce, Bristol (0117) 929 9197
Partner and Head of the Banking and Insolvency Group.
Specialisation: Licensed Insolvency Practitioner specialising in all aspects of non contentious insolvency, realisations and rescues. Practice includes banking, property and finance work for banks, other financial institutions and insolvency professionals. Particular interest in security documentation, enforcement and auditing, agricultural and construction insolvency, and rescues and restructuring.
Prof. Memberships: Member of the Society of Practitioners of Insolvency, the Insolvency Lawyers Association and Non-Administrative Receivers Association. Has undertaken a number of book reviews and contributed a chapter on 'Distribution' to Tolley's Insolvency Service 1996.
Career: Manchester University. Remained with *Bond Pearce* on qualifying in 1985, becoming partner 1991.

WALD, Matthew
Stephens & Scown, Exeter (01392) 210700
Qualified 1982. Partner. Is a Higher Court Advocate and specialises in Insolvency and Banking/Financial Litigation. Has acted in a number of reported insolvency cases.

WALES

LEADING FIRMS • WALES

EVERSHEDS Cardiff
MORGAN BRUCE Cardiff
EDWARDS GELDARD Cardiff
HUGH JAMES Cardiff

HIGHLY REGARDED FIRMS

Dolmans Cardiff

Eversheds (3ptnrs/3assts all p/t) *Philip Vaughan* heads the team, and is seen as doing most of the bigger ticket insolvency work in Wales. **Clients/Work:** Acting for the administrative receivers (Deloitte & Touche) of Steelfab Ltd and I G Hale Ltd and the administrators of GTS Fabrications Ltd.

Morgan Bruce (2ptnrs 25%; 4assts 25%) Merged with Guthrie Francis in Newport adding to their personal insolvency client base. Head of the Business Services Group *Bleddyn Rees* is highly rated by accountants and peers although not seen as concentrating on insolvency work. **Clients/Work:** Acting for the joint administrators of GTS Fabrications Ltd. Work received from Ernst & Young, Coopers & Lybrand and KPMG

Edwards Geldard (1ptnr/1asst) A small insolvency practice. **Clients/Work:** Dealing with nursing home insolvencies and other general administrations, LPA receiverships and bankruptcies.

Hugh James Seem to be quite "busy" and are thought "good for bankruptcy," however not seen as high profile. *Catrin Wyn Thomas* ("able") seen as "mainly litigation

and good at it." **Clients/Work:** Advising the Welsh Rugby Union on the insolvency of one of their clubs. Advising directors of insolvent company part owner of the Laura Ashley Group.

Dolmans (1ptnr 40%/1asst 25%) On the Barclays Bank panel. Known for an active bankruptcy practice of smaller value work. *John Wilkins* has a good reputation. **Clients/Work:** Handling bankruptcies, IVA's and acting for a number of IP's.

LEADING INDIVIDUALS
WALES

REES Bleddyn Morgan Bruce
THOMAS Catrin Hugh James
VAUGHAN Philip Eversheds
WILKINS John Dolmans

LEADERS' PROFILES • WALES

REES, Bleddyn
Morgan Bruce, Cardiff (01222) 385385

THOMAS, Catrin Wyn
Hugh James, Cardiff (01222) 224871
Partner and Head of Insolvency and Debt Recovery Unit.
Specialisation: Handles all aspects of personal, partnership and corporate insolvency. Acts on behalf of a variety of clients including insolvency practitioners, banks and other financial institutions, directors, shareholders and many professional individuals (mainly

architects and accountants). Deals with contentious and non-contentious insolvency work and also commercial litigation including banking litigation and litigation between directors and shareholders.
Prof. Memberships: Law Society, Insolvency Lawyers' Association.
Career: Qualified in 1983. Became a Partner at *Hugh James* in 1986. Licensed Insolvency Practitioner since 1989, the only one in Wales amongst the legal profession.
Personal: Born 26th September 1956. Educated at the University of Wales,

Aberystwyth 1975-78 (LL.B) and Emmanuel College, Cambridge 1980-81 (LL.M). Leisure interests include reading, music, theatre, travel and watching rugby and cricket. Lives in Cardiff.

VAUGHAN, Philip D.
Eversheds, Cardiff (01222) 471147
Partner.
Specialisation: Practice covers a wide-range of non-contentious banking and finance work and includes transactional work (particularly acquisition finance), regulatory advice and drafting of standard documentation for banks,

building societies, centralised mortgage lenders and finance companies. Has a particular expertise in sales and purchases of loan portfolios. Also involved in a wide range of non-contentious insolvency work acting for receivers, administrators and liquidators and advising lenders on enforcement of security and restructuring/refinancings.
Career: Qualified 1984. Formerly with *Clifford Chance* and *National Westminster Bank* Legal Department. Joined current firm in 1987 and

became Partner in 1988.
Personal: Born 14th December 1958. Educated at Haverfordwest Grammar School, St. Edmund Hall, Oxford (M.A.) and Emmanuel College, Cambridge (LL.M.).

WILKINS, John R.
Dolmans, Cardiff (01222) 345531
Qualified 1969 Partner in Insolvency and Commercial Litigation Department.
Specialisation: Advises Administrators,

Administrative Receivers, Liquidators, Supervisors and Trustees in Bankruptcy on all aspects of insolvency practice both contentious and non contentious and assists in the realisation of assets and sales of business. Advises Directors on their responsibilities and potential liabilities both before and after Insolvency. Advises Individuals and Partnerships on their business and other financial matters.

MIDLANDS

LEADING FIRMS • MIDLANDS

EVERSHEDS Birmingham

DIBB LUPTON ALSOP Birmingham
MARTINEAU JOHNSON Birmingham

EDGE & ELLISON Birmingham
GATELEY WAREING Birmingham

HIGHLY REGARDED FIRMS

Pinsent Curtis Birmingham
Wragge & Co Birmingham

Irwin Mitchell Birmingham
Shoosmiths & Harrison Northampton

Actons Nottingham
Freeth Cartwright Hunt Dickens Nottingham
Knight & Sons Newcastle-under-Lyme

Eversheds (3ptnrs/4assts) A "top drawer" department who have"virtually cornered the market." Team leaders are the "coveted" *Jeff Drew* and *Louise Pheasant* who has a "brilliant bedside manner" **Clients/Work:** Acting for Price Waterhouse on the receiverships of Beck Food Group and Jacques Marisa. Acting for KPMG on the receivership of WG Allen (Birmingham). Acting For Robson Rhodes on a multiple site LPA receivership.

Dibb Lupton Alsop (3ptnrs: 1p/t / 4assts) Are beginning to present serious competition for Eversheds, "dealing with bigger ticket work." *Jeremy Bowden* is a dedicated insolvency man with a "definite style" and associate *Huw Dolphin* continues to be recognised. **Clients/Work:** Acting on the Administrative Receivership of Archway Valves Ltd for BDO Stoy Hayward. Advising Coopers and Lybrand in Willenhall Automation Ltd. Acting for accountants Ernst & Young, Deloitte & Touche and KPMG.

Martineau Johnson (4ptnrs/6assts) Have strengthened their practice and go up the rankings. *Ian Baker* ("able, reliable, solid performer") is concentrating on his banking practice at present. Have acquired the "super" *Helen Readett* from Edge & Ellison. **Clients/Work:** Acting for the Administration

of CBE (2000)Ltd and Cuspo (2000) Ltd (Coopers & Lybrand) including negotiating complex supply agreements. Acting for Hong Kong International Airport renegotiating letters of credit and supply arrangement and other contracts and disposal. Acting for liquidator of John Hill & Sons (Foundaries) Ltd (Ernst & Young).

Edge & Ellison (2ptnrs p/t/ 5assts) Team includes *John Sullivan* who is seen to be "doing more international litigation work these days." **Clients/Work:** Acting for the joint Administrative Receivers of Towles plc involving the disposal of an equity investment in solvent associated company. Advising the Administrators in the administration of the British Athletic Federation including the appointment of interim managers.

Gateley Wareing (2ptnrs 90%/ 3assts 85%) Are "known for middle value domestic work." Senior partner *Brendan McGeever* "has great connections."

Pinsent Curtis (1ptnr 20%/1asst + 7 litigation assts 5%) Seen as moving away from a dedicated insolvency practice, *David Cooke* ("superb") is known for a good bankruptcy and corporate recoveries practice, although he is concentrating more on banking work at present. **Clients/Work:** Acting in the Administration and subsequent liquidation of an insolvent finance company. Acting in a number of agricultural receiverships.

Wragge & Co (4ptnrs p/t; 8assts p/t / 10assts 100% on DTI work) "Have the ability and the potential" and are generally "a brilliant firm" but lacking the breadth in insolvency work. Do a significant amount of DTI directors disqualification work. *Julian Pallett* "is a technically good insolvency man." **Clients/Work:** Acting in the administrative receiverships of UVG (Bus & Coach) Limited (Arthur Anderson) and Peter Hollingworth Limited (Deloitte & Touche), and the administration of Moseley Football Club Limited (Buchler Phillips).

Irwin Mitchell (1ptnr + 2ptnrs 30% / 2assts + 2assts 30%) Merged with Rigbeys and are seen as stronger as a result. Reputation for having a "high volume, lower value" practice. **Clients/Work:** Advising Coopers & Lybrand in trading Receivership of sports kit manufacturer and eventual sale of the busi-

ness as a going concern for consideration in the region of £750,000. Appointment to panel of two firms (along with Denton Hall) to advise Abbey Legal Protection on insolvency cases.

Shoosmiths & Harrison (7ptnrs/5assts all – p/t) Have some good people. **Clients/Work:** Acting in the widely publicised Receivership of a well known lingerie manufacturer in Nottingham including the sale of two divisions as a going concern. Acting in the bankruptcy case of Judd v Williams [1998] BPIR88.

Actons (5ptnrs/3assts – all p/t) **Clients/Work:** Handle contentious and non-contentious work. Act for national accountants and local IPs. Also Directors' disqualification proceedings. Received recommendations and one interviewee thought them a "super" firm.

Freeth Cartwright Hunt Dickins (3ptnrs/ 5assts) Insolvency unit is part of the commercial litigation department. **Clients/Work:** Acting for a "big five" accountant as administrative receiver in multi-million pound claim against a public utility, settled. Acting on misfeasance and related claims for a "big five" accountant as liquidator resulting in large settlement.

Knight & Sons (2ptnrs p/t / 2assts) Well placed to take advantage of recession in the potteries, concentrating on personal insolvency. **Clients/Work:** Corporate insolvency including Administrative Receiverships and liquidations and bankruptcies, acting for IPs.

LEADING INDIVIDUALS
MIDLANDS

BAKER Ian Martineau Johnson
DREW Jeff Eversheds

BOWDEN Jeremy Dibb Lupton Alsop
COOKE David Pinsent Curtis
MCGEEVER Brendan Gateley Wareing
PALLETT Julian Wragge & Co
PHEASANT Louise Eversheds
READETT Helen Martineau Johnson
SULLIVAN John Edge & Ellison

UP AND COMING

DOLPHIN Huw Dibb Lupton Alsop

BAKER, Ian P.
Martineau Johnson, Birmingham
(0121) 200 3300
See under Banking, p. 144

BOWDEN, Jeremy
Dibb Lupton Alsop, Birmingham
(0121) 2005046
Specialisation: Head of Corporate Recovery
and Insolvency Birmingham. All aspects of
contentious and non-contentious corporate and
individual insolvency. Corporate turnarounds and
work outs. Clearing Bank defence litigation.
Prof. Memberships: Law Society, Society of
Practitioners of Insolvency, Insolvency Lawyers
Association, Institute of Credit Management.
Career: Qualified 1987. Partner 1992. Licensed
Insolvency Practitioner. (Passed JIEB exams.)
Personal: Flying, motorsport, country pursuits.
Married.

COOKE, David J.
Pinsent Curtis, Birmingham (0121) 200 1050
See under Banking, p. 144

DOLPHIN, Huw
Dibb Lupton Alsop, Birmingham
(0345) 262728
Specialisation: Advises on all areas of
insolvency and recovery work both contentious
and non-contentious but with particular
emphasis on liquidation and receiverships.
Acts for insolvency practitioners, banks and
other lenders and commercial clients needing
solutions in this area.
Prof. Memberships: Society of Practitioners
of Insolvency. Insolvency Lawyers Association.
Career: Manchester University 1985-1988.
Qualified 1991. *Dibb Lupton Broomhead –
London* office 1992-1993. *Dibb Lupton
Broomhead*, then *Dibb Lupton Alsop –
Birmingham* office 1993 to date. Licensed
insolvency practitioner since 1995.
Personal: Married with two children. Lives near
Shrewsbury. Interested in sport particularly
football and motor racing.

DREW, Jeff
Eversheds, Birmingham (0121) 233 2001
Partner in Insolvency and Banking Group.
Chairman of *Eversheds'* Insolvency Group.
Specialisation: Advises insolvency
practitioners in connection with all aspects of
insolvency law and banks in connection with
the taking and realising of charges. Speaks
widely at conferences and seminars.
Prof. Memberships: Society of Practitioners
of Insolvency.
Career: Qualified in 1980. Worked at *Wragge &
Co.* 1978-82, then *Edge & Ellison* 1982-92 (from
1984 as a Partner). Joined *Eversheds* (then
Eversheds Wells & Hind) as a Partner in 1992.
Personal: Born 12th October 1954. Attended
Solihull School and St Edmund Hall, Oxford
1974-77. Leisure interests include tennis,
squash and badminton. Lives in Birmingham.

MCGEEVER, Brendan G.
Gateley Wareing, Birmingham
(0121) 236 8585
Senior Partner and Partner in Banking and
Insolvency Department.
Specialisation: Main areas of practice are
insolvency, banking and commercial litigation.
Acts for administrative receivers, liquidators,
administrators and trustees in bankruptcy on all
aspects of insolvency law. Also advises banks
and other financial institutions in relation to
securities and realisations.
Prof. Memberships: Law Society.
Career: Qualified in 1983. Joined *Gateley
Wareing* in 1984, becoming a Partner in 1986
and Senior Partner in 1993.
Personal: Born 11th February 1958. Attended
St Mary's College, Middlesbrough 1971-76 and
Birmingham University 1976-79. Leisure
interests include golf, soccer and rugby. Lives
in Birmingham.

PALLETT, Julian C.
Wragge & Co, Birmingham (0121) 233 1000
See under Banking, p. 146

PHEASANT, Louise A.
Eversheds, Birmingham (0121) 233 2001
Specialisation: Banking and insolvency. Acts
for lenders and insolvency practitioners on all
aspects of insolvency law, security and asset
realisations.
Prof. Memberships: SPI – Society of
Practitioners of Insolvency, Law Society.
Career: Birmingham University (1st Class
Hons) Midland Bank plc 1979-1983, BBC 1983-
1984, *Eversheds* 1988 becoming partner 1997.
Personal: Cinema, contemporary art, West
Bromwich Albion. Married.

READETT, Helen A.
Martineau Johnson, Birmingham
(0121) 200 3300
Specialisation: Advises Insolvency
practitioners on all types of Insolvency work
and Banks and lending institutions on putting
security in place and enforcing it.
Prof. Memberships: Licensed Insolvency
Practitioner and member SPI. Law Society
member.
Career: Qualified 1982. *Edge & Ellison* partner
until 1998. Now partner with *Martineau
Johnson*.
Personal: Married with young son. Used to
enjoy travel, keeping fit and theatre.

SULLIVAN, John C.P.
Edge & Ellison, Birmingham
(0121) 200 2001
Head of, and Partner in, Insolvency and
International Litigation Departments.
Specialisation: Handles banking and
insolvency work of all types with international
work as a specialist skill.
Prof. Memberships: Member of Society of
Practitioners in Insolvency.
Career: Qualified in 1980. Joined *Edge &
Ellison* in 1978, becoming a Partner in 1987.
Personal: Born 10th August 1956. Attended
Oxford University 1974-77.

EAST ANGLIA

Eversheds (5ptnrs/7assts) *Anthony*
"young" *McGurk* (based in the company
commercial department) and *Paul Matthews*,
based in commercial litigation, jointly lead
the team. **Clients/Work:** Acting for
Administrative Receivers in disposal as
going concerns of six Burger King franchises. Acting for Administrative Receivers and
LPA Receivers in a number of property disposals. Advising and acting for Insolvency
Practitioners and Creditors on a variety of
contentious issues.

Mills & Reeve (3ptnrs/6assts) A
"strong" firm with a team spanning Norwich
and Cambridge. Work for all the major
accountants and are led by *Bryony Falkus* in
Norwich and *Jamie Wheatley* in Cambridge.
Clients/Work: Anglian Processors Ltd – in
administrative receivership. CVA Royston
Steel Fencing. Conducting four cases on conditional fee agreements.

Leathes Prior (4ptnrs: 3p/t / 6assts: 4p/t)
Have a good reputation in personal insolvency; also do some corporate insolvency
work and directors disqualification work,
acting for directors. *Mark Oakley* is recommended although neither he nor his partners
work full-time on insolvency work. **Clients/
Work:** Successfully acting for liquidator in
dispute re priority of fees. Acting for a debtor
in successful negotiations to reschedule

multi-million £ indebtedness to several creditors. Acting for a director who had been disqualified under CDDA 1986. Appeal against disqualification was allowed.

Prettys (1ptnrs/2assts) *Ian Waine* has a good reputation with local insolvency practitioners on the non-contentious side.

Taylor Vinters (3ptnrs/2assts) Act for office-holders and creditors in pursuing and resisting claims in insolvency. Not seen around town as much as in previous years. *John Short* specialises from the Corporate and Commmercial Group. **Clients/Work:** Advising Grant Thornton, Deloitte & Touche and KPMG on appointments and disposal of insolvent businesses.

Nicholsons (1ptnr/2assts: 1p/t) Have had a lower profile over the last 12 months. However *Mark Nicholson* can "give you a good run for your money."

Birketts (2ptnrs) Said to be fighting Prettys and Eversheds for the Ipswich work. Although a small practice they are rated for "a detailed knowledge of insolvency." **Clients/ Work:** Acting in relation to pubs, nursing homes, receiverships of companies in haulage/shipping and transport industry.

Hewitson Becke + Shaw (3ptnrs) Acting for local and regional insolvency practitioners advising on all aspects of insolvency proceedings. Known for their work with Barclays Bank. **Clients/Work:** Acting

for one of the Big Five accountancy firms, succeeded in obtaining an urgently required administration order within 48 hours.

Palmer Wheeldon (2ptnrs/2assts) During the current work 'low' in East Anglia, the firm have been heard of less than others, although they continue to do receivership work and pursuit of directors for misdealing. *Ian Mather* leads the team. **Clients/Work:** Advising 5 insolvency practitioners in claims against directors following liquidation. Advising administrative receiver in sale of assets in total worth over £500,000.

LEADERS' PROFILES • EAST ANGLIA

FALKUS, Bryony J.
Mills & Reeve, Norwich +44 (0)1603 660155
Partner in Corporate Department.
Specialisation: Work covers corporate insolvency generally and in particular receiverships and administrations, acting for banks, specialised lending institutions and insolvency practitioners. Major clients include Coopers and Lybrand, KPMG and other accountants. Also handles acquisitions and sales, reconstructions, offers of securities and yellow book work.
Prof. Memberships: Law Society, SPI.
Career: Qualifed 1976; Partner *Pickering Kenyon* 1980; Partner *Mills & Reeve* 1992.

MATHER, Ian Philip
Palmer Wheeldon, Cambridge
(01223) 355933
Partner in Litigation Department.
Specialisation: Principal area of practice is insolvency. Advises insolvency practitioners on all aspects of insolvency law. Advised for the liquidators in Re: Corfe Joinery Limited on preference payments to directors. Other main area of practice is employment law. Largest employer client is the Royal British Legion Attendants Co Ltd.
Prof. Memberships: Law Society; Associate Member of the Society of Practitioners of Insolvency.

Career: Partner since 1986. Managing Partner since 1992.
Personal: Born 13th June 1958. Educated at York University (BA Hons Economics, 1979) and Newcastle Polytechnic 1981-82 (CPE and Law Society Finals). Vice President of Cambridge Chamber of Commerce since November 1995.

MATTHEWS, Paul
Eversheds, Norwich (01603) 272727
See under Litigation (Commercial): 200+ Solicitors, p. 528

MCGURK, Anthony J.G.
Eversheds, Norwich (01603) 272727
Specialisation: Handles all aspects of corporate insolvency and reconstruction work, including acting for insolvency practitioners in connection with administrative receiverships, LPA receiverships, administrations, IVA's and liquidations. In addition, specialises in company/ corporate work, including mergers and acquisitions and banking.
Prof. Memberships: SPI
Career: Qualified in September 1989. Became a Partner at *Eversheds* in May 1995.
Personal: Educated at Downside School, Nr. Bath, Graduated in Law from Hull University. Obtained First Class Honours in Law Society finals.

NICHOLSON, M.J.
Nicholsons, Lowestoft (01502) 532300
Specialisation: Bankruptcy and personal insolvency and liquidations. Acts for insolvency practitioners.
Career: Qualified May 1977. Licensed Insolvency Practitioner.
Personal: Born 14.6.52.

OAKLEY, Mark Robert
Leathes Prior, Norwich (01603) 610911

SHORT, John
Taylor Vinters, Cambridge (01223) 423444
See under General Corporate Finance, p. 246

WAINE, Ian
Prettys, Ipswich (01473) 232121
See under General Corporate Finance, p. 246

WHEATLEY, Jamie G.
Mills & Reeve, Cambridge
+44 (0)1223 364422
Specialisation: Practices in all areas of corporate and personal insolvency work.

NORTH WEST

LEADING FIRMS • NORTH WEST

DIBB LUPTON ALSOP Liverpool / Manchester
ADDLESHAW BOOTH & CO Manchester
SLATER HEELIS Manchester
HALLIWELL LANDAU Manchester
HAMMOND SUDDARDS Manchester

HIGHLY REGARDED FIRMS

Chaffe Street Manchester
Davies Arnold Cooper Manchester
Davies Wallis Foyster Liverpool
Eversheds Manchester
Cuff Roberts Liverpool

Dibb Lupton Alsop (4ptnrs/6assts in Manchester and Liverpool) Now *the* leading practice. Act for major banks and their work incorporates big administrations and receiverships. All members of the team work full-time in this practice area. *Peter Manning* is "excellent" and well-respected for both contentious and non-contentious work. Graham Wilkinson has now left practice. **Clients/Work:** Acting in partnership administration order of J&H Kyrris and administrative receivership of Genesis Fast Food Ltd on behalf of office holders, Latham Crossley & Davis; Pannell Kerr Forster and Royal Bank of Scotland Plc involving sale of BurgerKing franchised restaurants. Acting for Arthur Andersen and National Westminster

Bank Plc in relation to Kiely Developments Ltd. Acting for Begbies Traynor as administrators and supervisors of Doncaster Rovers Football Club.

Addleshaw Booth & Co (6ptnrs/7assts) Leader Shân Spencer has left taking a team of one partner and two assistants with her. This has significantly affected confidence in the team's ability to do the work. Traditionally taken a lot of work from its banking clients but is now developing insolvency from its corporate practice. *Nick Goodman* is recommended for his contentious work. **Clients/Work:** SBD Tool Co Ltd (in Administrative Receivership). JDK Ltd (in Administrative Receivership) (part of the Helene Group of Companies). Advising

Pension Trustees of H H Robertson (UK) Ltd (in Administrative Receivership).

Slater Heelis (2ptnrs/3assts) Heavily weighted towards NatWest work but also covers pre-insolvency matters. Have a big practice in directors' disqualification work. *Egan Brooks* is "tremendous; bright, well-respected and personable." *John Joyce* is also recommended. **Clients/Work:** Brotherton Engineering Ltd (Deloitte & Touche). Energy (UK) PLC Group of Companies (Kidsons Impey). PM Group of Companies Ltd (Buchler Phillips).

Halliwell Landau (3ptnrs/4assts) A broad practice, lots of bankruptcy work, liquidations and receiverships. *Andrew Livesey* is well-known and "a good marketeer" **Clients/Work:** Acting for administrator of John Siddall & Son Ltd involving first formal insolvency of Crest registered stockbroker since commencement of Crest paperless settlement system. Acting for administrators of The Statesman and Nation Publishing Company Ltd. Acting for administrators of Business Newspapers Publishing Ltd and other group companies.

Hammond Suddards (1ptnr/4assts) Good reputation overall but insolvency group has not made as much of an impact on the Manchester market as other parts of the practice. *Duncan Haymes* is seen as benefit-ing from his knowledge of the players from his days at Addleshaw Booth & Co. **Clients/Work:** Advising KPMG on liquidation of Maples Stores plc. Advising Neville Russell on administration of E J Bostock & Sons. Acting for Grant Thornton (appointed by Barclays Bank) Receivership of Peakdale Ltd.

Chaffe Street (4ptnrs/2assts) The firm did not have much of an insolvency practice until *Shân Spencer* and her team arrived from Addleshaws. Her reputation alone will ensure that the firm will get reasonable work, although it is said that they must attract work from the banks to really build a practice. **Clients/Work:** Focusing on corporate recovery.

Davies Arnold Cooper (3ptnrs/6assts) Their consultant is retiring. Handle a moderate workload. **Clients/Work:** Continuing to act for Provisional Liquidators of eg.- Municipal General Insurance Ltd on formulation of Schemes of Arrangement. Acting for HIR (UK) Ltd on proposals for a solvent Scheme of Arrangement, approved by the DTI.

Davies Wallis Foyster (5ptnrs:3 p/t / 5assts 3 p/t) Not seen much on the higher value work over the last year. Known to be good on the liquidation and personal side in particular. **Clients/Work:** Acting for Alan Sutton on transfer of insolvency appointments upon retirement from Baker Tilly. Dealing with a number of administrations. Pursuing substantial claim for wrongful trading against directors re company involved in aviation industry.

Eversheds (1ptnr/2assts) Seem to be very quiet, and there were questions of "What are they doing?" Answers may soon be forthcoming from *Simon Waller* who moved there from Halliwell Landau to replace Richard Glithero. **Clients/Work:** Acting for Royal Bank of Scotland in reorganisation of group of companies. Acting for Ernst & Young on liquidation of wine warehouse. Substantial Receivership for Leonard Curtis.

LEADERS' PROFILES • NORTH WEST

BROOKS, Egan R.
Slater Heelis, Manchester (0161) 228 3781
Specialisation: Senior Partner and Head of Banking and Insolvency Department.
Prof. Memberships: The Law Society. Licenced Insolvency Practitioner and Notary Public.
Career: Articled: *Slater Heelis*. Qualified: 1966. Assistant Solicitor *Slater Heelis* 1966-69. Partner 1969.
Personal: Born 1943. Educated at Manchester Grammar School and Manchester University (LLB First Class Honours). Lives in Hale.

GOODMAN, Nick
Addleshaw Booth & Co, Manchester (0161) 934 6000
Partner in Banking and Financial Services Group.
Specialisation: Deals with the full range of insolvency matters with the emphasis on corporate insolvency including administrative receiverships, administrations, liquidations (both compulsory and voluntary) and corporate voluntary arrangements.
Prof. Memberships: Society of Practitioners of Insolvency, Law Society of England and Wales, Insolvency Lawyers Association.
Career: Qualified in 1982. *Wilkinson & Grist*, Hong Kong 1982-1987. *Dibb Lupton Broomhead* 1989-1995. Joined the firm as a Partner in 1995. Member of the North West Regional Committee of the SPI 1994-1996.
Personal: Attended Warwick School 1969-1974 and Southampton University 1974-1977. Leisure interests include theatre, golf and sailing. Lives in Cheshire.

HAYMES, Duncan R.
Hammond Suddards, Manchester (0161) 830 5000
Partner in Insolvency and Corporate Recovery Department.
Specialisation: Banking, Corporate Recovery and Insolvency law. Has addressed conferences and seminars.
Prof. Memberships: Law Society; Society of Practitioners of Insolvency; Insolvency Lawyers Association.
Career: Joined *JW Hollows & Co* in 1975, moving to *Pilkington Brothers* in 1980. From 1983-90, was at *William Prior & Co* and from 1990-92, was at *Addleshaw Sons & Latham*. Joined *Hammond Suddards* as a Partner in 1992.
Personal: Born in 1953. Lives in Manchester.

JOYCE, John
Slater Heelis, Manchester (0161) 228 3781
Specialisation: Banking and Insolvency.
Career: Articled: *Slater Heelis*. Qualified: 1988. Assistant Solicitor *Slater Heelis* 1988-93. Partner 1993.
Personal: Born 1963. Educated at De La Salle College Salford and Manchester University (1985 LLB Hons.). Law Society Finals (1986 Second Class Hons.). Resides Atherton.

LIVESEY, Andrew J.
Halliwell Landau, Manchester (0161) 835 3003
Specialisation: Lead Partner in Insolvency and Corporate Recovery Department. Handles all types of corporate insolvency and personal insolvency, corporate recovery and reconstruction. Banking.
Prof. Memberships: Society of Practitioners of Insolvency, Insolvency Lawyers Association, INSOL.
Career: Qualified in 1985. Joined *Halliwell Landau* as a Partner in 1991.
Personal: Born 23rd August 1960. Educated at Queen Elizabeth's Grammar School, Blackburn and University College, Durham 1979-82. Leisure interests include golf, Blackburn Rovers FC, and Lancashire County Cricket Club. Lives in Chorley, Lancashire.

MANNING, Peter R.
Dibb Lupton Alsop, Manchester (0345) 262728
Partner and head of North West Corporate Recovery and Insolvency Group.
Specialisation: Corporate insolvency, banking and security reviews. Regular lecturer on insolvency matters on behalf of SPI and others.
Prof. Memberships: Law Society, Society of Practitioners in Insolvency, Insolvency Lawyers Association.
Career: Articled with *Memery Crystal & Co*, qualifying in 1986. Assistant solicitor with *Hepworth & Chadwick* 1986-1989. Joined *Alsop Wilkinson* in 1989, becoming a Partner in 1990.
Personal: Born 1959. Attended Hertford College, Oxford 1978-82.

SPENCER, Shân
Chaffe Street, Manchester (0161) 236 5800
Specialisation: Deals with the full range of insolvency matters with the emphasis on

corporate insolvency including administrative receiverships, administrations, liquidations and CVAs. Also acts for banks in recovery matters and risk positions. Has acted in cases including Keith Prowse, ELS, Kumar Brothers, Doctus plc, Habit Group, Paddy Hopkirk Limited, Australia House Limited and Production Steel Group. Addresses SPI conferences.
Prof. Memberships: Society of Practitioners of Insolvency, (Vice Chairman North West

Region), Insolvency Lawyers Association, Insolvency Practitioners Association, Association Europeene des Practiciens des Procedures Collective.

WALLER, Simon
Eversheds, Manchester (0161) 832 6666
Specialisation: Partner; Head of Insolvency and corporate recovery, Manchester; specialises in insolvency and corporate reconstruction. Acts for all of the main

accountancy practices and for a number of banks and secondary lenders; previously acted (whilst at *Wilde Sapte*) for the Receivers of Leyland Daf Limited and the Administrators of Paramount Airways Limited amongst others.
Prof. Memberships: SPI
Career: Articled *Booth & Co*; qualified 1989; *Wilde Sapto* to 1996; partner *Halliwell Landau* 1996-1998; partner *Eversheds* 1998; sits on editorial board of Receivers, Administrators and Liquidators quarterly.
Personal: St Cuthbert's School; Durham University (BA Hons Law); sport, cinema, reading; resides Manchester; one daughter.

NORTH EAST

LEADING FIRMS • NORTH EAST

WALKER MORRIS Leeds

DIBB LUPTON ALSOP Leeds/ Sheffield

ADDLESHAW BOOTH & CO Leeds

HIGHLY REGARDED FIRMS

Carrick Read Insolvency Leeds

Dickinson Dees Newcastle upon Tyne

Eversheds Leeds

Hammond Suddards Leeds

Lupton Fawcett Leeds

Pinsent Curtis Leeds

Robert Muckle Newcastle-upon-Tyne

Brooke North Leeds

Eversheds Newcastle upon Tyne

Irwin Mitchell Sheffield

Keeble Hawson Moorhouse Sheffield

Ward Hadaway Newcastle upon Tyne

Walker Morris (5ptnrs/10assts) A locally based practice in Leeds with seemingly no ambition to become a national firm. In insolvency they lead in the North East. *Philip Mudd* ("class operator, the driver behind Walker Morris practice")became Managing Partner on 1 May 1998 but will continue as head of department, focusing on large, complex cases. *David Hinchcliffe* is "the guy who knocks on doors, shakes hands and does the business." *Michael Taylor* is also part of the team. **Clients/Work:** The £10m administration of Transperience acting for Coopers & Lybrand. Liquidation of Dunn & Co acting for Deloitte & Touche. Administration of Medd Construction Group.

Dibb Lupton Alsop (8ptnrs/8assts) A "sophisticated" practice in size, amount and quality of work, divided into separate sub-units eg. liquidation, personal insolvency and DTI work. The "academically good" *Peter Cranston* is now National Head of Insolvency leaving the reigns in the hands of *Mark Jackson*. **Clients/Work:** Acting for liquidators of Pacific & General Insurance Company Ltd. Acting for joint administrators of English & American Insurance Holdings plc and English & American Group plc. Acting

for Scheme Administrators of Trinity Insurance Company Ltd.

Addleshaw Booth & Co (7ptnrs/11assts) There is some concern in the marketplace that losing Shân Spencer from the Manchester office may weaken this office since they market themselves as a cross-office team. *William Ballmann* comes from a "serious insolvency background" and heads the team. *Jane Evason* is up-and-coming. **Clients/ Work:** Acting for Poppleton & Appleby on administrative receivership of Wade & Hotson Ltd.Acting for Arthur Andersen as administrative receivers of D F Hoult & Partners Ltd. Acting for lender in reconstruction and rescue of Top 20 firm of accountants.

Carrick Read Insolvency (4ptnrs) An interesting practice which amalgamates the insolvency practices of Garwood Devine in Hull and Read Hind Stewart in Leeds. Do a lot of Corporate Voluntary Arrangement work. *Chris Garwood* is Senior Partner. *Andrew Laycock* is an "effective if tough operator" who does not make friends with insolvency practitioners since he acts both for and against them.

Dickinson Dees (3ptnrs/4assts) Have a dedicated directors disqualification team. *John Pennie* ("sound") heads the team. **Clients/Work:** Significant recoveries on pensions side of Brims receivership. Advising Grant Thornton in successful corporate recovery of Robot Simulations Ltd resulting in company being handed back to shareholders. Directors disqualification team has now handled in excess of 100 cases.

Eversheds (1ptnr/1cons/6assts) Doing increasing amounts of reconstruction work. Said to have suffered from the loss of David Hinchcliffe to Walker Morris and their market-share is widely perceived to have dwindled accordingly. *Julian Horrocks* leads the team. **Clients/Work:** Acting for IP in proceedings on whether or not a creditor's claim was correctly rejected; creditor appealing to Court of Appeal. Assignment of substantial litigation rights by Liquidator to major creditor. Advising Administrative Receivers appointed over various professional practices, both partnerships and limited and unlimited liability companies.

Hammond Suddards (3ptnrs/8assts) Said to be struggling since the departure of Stephen Gale to Herbert Smith left them without a leader. Reputation for good relations with small accountants on liquidations and voluntary arrangements. **Clients/Work:** Continuing to advise Luxembourg liquidators of BCCI SA on various issues between them and other group liquidators(£500m). Liquidation of Design Conservatories Ltd(substantial consumer credit issues). Receivership English Village Nurseries. Receivership of Prelude UK Ltd and subsequent asset sale in excess of £1m.

Lupton Fawcett (2ptnrs/3assts) Deal particularly in the field of small and medium-sized receiverships and company voluntary arrangements. 50% of their work comes out of London. *Kevin Royle* ("a big hitter") and *Richard Marshall* ("a tremendously fun and flamboyant lawyer") both joined from Dibb Lupton Alsop. "Great things were expected of them," but they have yet to make that impact. **Clients/Work:** CVA of a major Plc. Acting on behalf of receivers in case

LEADING INDIVIDUALS
NORTH EAST

CRANSTON Peter Dibb Lupton Alsop

MUDD Philip Walker Morris

BALLMANN William Addleshaw Booth & Co

BROWN Robert Keeble Hawson Moorhouse

CORR Patrick Pinsent Curtis

FRIEZE Steven Brooke North

HINCHCLIFFE David Walker Morris

HORROCKS Julian Eversheds

FRITH Stuart Brooke North

GARWOOD Christopher Carrick Read Insolvency

GILTHORPE Ian Robert Muckle

JACKSON Mark Dibb Lupton Alsop

JEFFRIES Jonathan Pinsent Curtis

LAYCOCK Andrew Carrick Read Insolvency

MARSHALL Richard Lupton Fawcett

PENNIE John Dickinson Dees

ROYLE Kevin Lupton Fawcett

TAYLOR Michael Walker Morris

UP AND COMING

EVASON Jane Addleshaw Booth & Co

SEE PROFILES AT END OF THIS SECTION

involving massive VAT fraud. Corporate rescue of a very well-known Yorkshire restaurant.

Pinsent Curtis (5ptnrs/1assoc/4assts) Their practice is slanted towards technical and bank receivership work. *Patrick* "Paddy" *Corr* ("pulls work in") and *Jonathan Jeffries* head the team. **Clients/Work:** Major security review for Gulf Oil(Great Britain)Ltd. Acting on receivership of Greenfield Holdings. Acting for Administrator of Keighley Cougars Rugby Football League Club.

Robert Muckle (4ptnrs: 2 p/t / 1cons / 2assts) Their reputation is for large-scale work although in the recent climate there has been a greater amount of personal insolvency and intensive care work. *Ian Gilthorpe* is a recognised practitioner. **Clients/Work:** Share acquisition of Robot Simulations Ltd from administrator,Grant Thornton. Wares Building Services Ltd – administrative receivership for Ernst & Young. R Curry Ltd – administrative receiverships for Deloitte & Touche.

Brooke North (3ptnrs/2assts) Do a large amount of personal insolvency and voluntary arrangements of all sorts. Also heavily

involved in issues of pensions and insolvency. They have a reputation for doing "their work very very well." The team is led by *Stephen Frieze* who is extremely highly regarded but who is known by other practitioners more for his academic work than for his practice. **Clients/Work:** Wide variety of insolvency work including personal insolvency and court appointments. Secretary of State v Cleland on company directors' disqualification. Double S Printers Ltd on position of fixed as opposed to floating charge.

Eversheds (3ptnrs: 2p/t / 3assts:1p/t) Took over Wilkinson Maughan which is seen to have increased their profile in Newcastle; the Eversheds brand-name is a door opener now. **Clients/Work:** The only Newcastle firm on the Midland Bank panel and one of two firms on Barclays Bank panel. Advised on 4 substantial receiverships, two potential administration orders and large number of liquidations and bankruptcies.

Irwin Mitchell (Leeds: 3ptnrs: 2p/t/ 4assts: 20 – 100%. Sheffield: 5ptnrs: 4p/t/ 5assts 30-100%) Currently known only for their Sheffield office but have made up a full

time partner in Leeds in the last year to increase their profile there. **Clients/Work:** Successfully struck out criminal proceedings with costs against a company, in administration, which faced litigation brought by Customs and Excise. Handling Partnership Voluntary Arrangement and administration for solicitors' practice. Restructuring of a number of companies in engineering sector, saving approx 150 jobs.

Keeble Hawson Moorhouse (7ptnrs: 4p/t / 2assts: 1p/t) This year has seen the merger of R.C.Moorhouse & Co with Sheffield firm Keeble Hawson Rogers & Howe and the perception is that they "have rejuvenated themselves and increased their profile." *Robert Brown* received several strong recommendations this year as a "capable industrious performer doing good work well." **Clients/Work:** Carried out a conditional fee agreement – first in region.

Ward Hadaway (3ptnrs/2assts) Act for all the major accountancy practices in Newcastle. **Clients/Work:** Cross border insolvency for national Building Society. Administrative receivership for national building society.

LEADERS' PROFILES • NORTH EAST

BALLMANN, William
Addleshaw Booth & Co, Leeds
(0113) 209 2000
Partner in Banking and Financial Services Group.
Specialisation: Handles all aspects of contentious and non-contentious corporate and personal insolvency work. Also covers related banking work. Contributor of articles and updates to 'Insolvency Practitioner.' Speaker at SPI conferences and seminars.
Prof. Memberships: Law Society, SPI, ILA (Council Member), AEPPC.
Career: Qualified in 1983. Joined the firm as Partner and Head of Insolvency Department in 1992.
Personal: Attended Esher Grammar School and the University of Leeds (LLB 1978). Leisure interests include golf, skiing and scuba diving.

BROWN, Robert
Keeble Hawson Moorhouse, Sheffield
(0114) 272 2061

CORR, Patrick
Pinsent Curtis, Leeds (0113) 244 5000
Specialisation: Head of Corporate Recovery, Leeds. Advises insolvency practitioners on all aspects of insolvency. Also advises banks and other financial institutions on security issues. Recently acted for the Receivers of Brookbank Nursing Home and advised the Administrator of the Posh Windows and Conservatories Ltd Group of Companies. Has presented seminars to accountants and banks on corporate recovery and banking issues.
Prof. Memberships: Young Solicitors Group. The Insolvency Lawyers Association. Subscriber to the Society of Practitioners of Insolvency.
Career: LLB (Hons), Leeds Metropolitan University. Joined *Pinsent Curtis* in 1988. Qualified in 1990. Partner 1996.

CRANSTON, Peter
Dibb Lupton Alsop, Leeds (0345) 262728
Licensed insolvency practitioner.
Specialisation: Partner dealing with a full range of issues arising from commercial insolvency, with emphasis on taking and enforcement of security, restructuring and asset recovery.
Prof. Memberships: Member Law Society; SPI.

EVASON, Jane
Addleshaw Booth & Co, Leeds
(0113) 209 2000
Solicitor in Banking and Financial Services Group.
Specialisation: A Senior Solicitor in the Corporate Recovery Department of *Addleshaw Booth & Co*, dealing with all aspects of corporate recovery, insolvency and related banking and building society work. Acts for insolvency practitioners in all of the major accounting practices and many of the smaller firms, all of the major building societies and a large number of banks.
Prof. Memberships: Speaker at conferences for and is a member of the Society of Practitioners of Insolvency. Law Society, AWS, SPI member.
Career: Shortly after qualifying as a solicitor in 1988, Jane joined *Addleshaw Sons & Latham* helping to develop the firm's department in Manchester, then in Leeds.
Personal: Outside interests include skiing and walking.

FRIEZE, Steven A.
Brooke North, Leeds (0113) 283 2100
Specialisation: All aspects of contentious insolvency with a bias towards personal insolvency but including cross border issues.
Prof. Memberships: SPI, ILA, Commercial

Law League of America, Licensed Insolvency Practitioner.
Carcer: Leeds Grammar School; Trinity College, Oxford (1965-1968). Admitted 1971. Partner 1976. Deputy District Judge 1982-1994. Author of Handbook of Personal Insolvency, Weavings Notes on Bankruptcy, Compulsory Winding Up Procedure, and Practice Note: Insolvency in their various editions from 1982 to date.
Personal: General editor of Insolvency Intelligence (1988 to date).

FRITH, Stuart J.
Brooke North, Leeds (0113) 283 2100
Specialisation: Contentious insolvency of all types with particular interest in the environmental consequences of insolvency; acting on behalf of Respondents in directors disqualification proceedings. Recent cases involved Secretary of State v Cleland (acceptability of undertaking); Re Double S Printers Limited (fixed charge on book debts).
Prof. Memberships: Law Society; Council Member of Insolvency Lawyers Association; SPI; IPA.
Career: Qualified October 1983; Articled at *Jacksons Monk & Rowe*, Middlesbrough; Joined *Brooke North* in 1984; Partner 1989; Licensed Insolvency Practitioner 1989.
Personal: Born 6 December 1957; Educated Spalding Grammar School; Leeds University.

GARWOOD, Christopher
Carrick Read Insolvency, Hull
(01482) 211160
Senior Partner.
Specialisation: Has specialised in all aspects of personal and corporate insolvency since 1975 and is an authorised insolvency practitioner. Through Senior Partnership with

associated firm *Garwood Devine* also deals with general commercial work.

Prof. Memberships: Law Society, Insolvency Lawyers Association (Founder member and 1993/4 President), SPI, AEPPC.

Career: Qualified 1973 before establishing *Carr & Garwood*, which merged in 1979 to become *Carrick Carr & Garwood*. Was licensed to act as an insolvency practitioner in 1986 after working on the Law Society Committee dealing with the 1985 Insolvency Act. Established *Carrick Read Insolvency* in 1990, and in 1992 established the primarily commercial practice of *Garwood Devine*: currently Senior Partner of both.

Personal: Born 15th June 1949. Attended Pocklington School 1959-67, then Worcester College, Oxford 1967-70. Leisure interests include golf. Lives in Wansford, near Driffield, East Yorkshire.

GILTHORPE, Ian M.
Robert Muckle, Newcastle-upon-Tyne (0191) 232 4402
See under General Corporate Finance, p. 249

HINCHCLIFFE, David
Walker Morris, Leeds (0113) 283 2500
Specialisation: Advises insolvency practitioners on all aspects of insolvency with particular emphasis upon company and individual rescue, often through voluntary arrangements. Also specialises in liquidations, administrations and bankruptcies. Significant instructions have included acting for the liquidators of Medchoice Holidays and Sir James Hill. Recently instructed to act for the liquidators of Dunn & Co. Speaker at Regional SPI Conference.
Prof. Memberships: Society of Practitioners of Insolvency, Insolvency Lawyers Association.
Career: Qualified 1989. Became a partner at *Walker Morris* immediately upon joining the firm from *Eversheds* in 1996.
Personal: Born 1965. Played rugby for Otley RUFC. Leisure pursuits include supporting Bradford Bulls, beer and food (preferably lots) and heavy rock music.

HORROCKS, Julian
Eversheds, Leeds 0113 243 0391
Fax: (0113) 2450 6188
Specialisation: Partner and Head of Insolvency Department in Leeds comprising a team of seven specialists. Acts in relation to formal insolvency procedures, reconstructions, negotiated settlements and informal compromise agreements. Advises banks, creditors, Insolvency Practitioners, debtors (both companies and individuals) and directors.
Career: Age: 41. Qualified 1981. Partner since 1988.

JACKSON, Mark S.
Dibb Lupton Alsop, Leeds (0345) 262728
Specialisation: Banking, insolvency and corporate reconstruction.
Prof. Memberships: Society of Practitioners in Insolvency.

JEFFRIES, Jonathan D.
Pinsent Curtis, Leeds (0113) 244 5000
Partner, Licensed Insolvency Practitioner and Head of Financial Services Group, Leeds.
Specialisation: Advises insolvency practitioners on all aspects of insolvency, and banks and other financial institutions on re-financing and security. Acted for the Receivers of Greenfield Holdings Limited and the administrators of Charnley Davies Limited, James Ferguson Holdings Plc (of which Barlow Clowes was a subsidiary). Advises a number of banks on financial recovery strategies. Lectures to banks and accountants on corporate recovery, debt recovery and banking law.
Prof. Memberships: Member of the Society of Practitioners of Insolvency; Fellow of the Insolvency Practitioners Association; Member of the Education Courses and Conference Committee of the Society of Practitioners of Insolvency.

LAYCOCK, Andrew
Carrick Read Insolvency, Leeds (0113) 243 2911
Partner.
Specialisation: Main area of practice is insolvency. Handles small to medium receiverships, CVAs, administrations, liquidations, bankruptcy and IVAs. Transactions have included numerous heavy engineering cases, the insolvency of Hull Grammar (the first charity administration order), and the administration of Doncaster RLFC. Contributor to Insolvency Intelligence, Solicitors Journal, and Legal Executive Journal. Regularly addresses conferences to bankers, accountants and the SPI. Honorary Solicitor to the Bankruptcy Association.
Prof. Memberships: Insolvency Lawyers Association, SPI, AEPPC.
Career: Qualified in 1983. *Established Carrick Read Insolvency* in 1980 with Chris Garwood.
Personal: Born 5th December 1957. Attended St Michael's College, Leeds 1970- 1976: Emmanuel College Cambridge 1977-1980. Leisure interests include rugby and cricket. Director of Leeds C F & A Ltd and Leeds R.L. Married with two daughters and lives in Thorner, near Wetherby.

MARSHALL, J. Richard
Lupton Fawcett, Leeds (0113) 280 2000
Specialisation: Department deals with all aspects of both corporate and personal insolvency, acting for insolvency practitioners, companies, private individuals and directors.
Prof. Memberships: Associate member of SPI and ILA.
Career: Qualified 1987. At *Dibb Lupton Broomhead* 1985 to 1992. Joined Lupton Fawcett as a Partner in 1992.
Personal: Born 1960. Educated at Scarborough College and Leeds Metropolitan University (LLB (Hons)). Interests include family, shooting, fishing, racing, eating and drinking. Lives near Huddersfield.

MUDD, Philip J.
Walker Morris, Leeds (0113) 283 2500
Partner and Head of Banking and Insolvency Department.
Specialisation: Deals with insolvency and banking issues for lenders, insolvency practitioners and corporate clients with an emphasis on debt restructuring and corporate rescue in addition to mainstream insolvency, lending and realisation work. Acted for lender in reconstruction of UK Land plc. Recent work includes administration of Transperience Limited, the receivership of On Demand Information plc and the liquidation of Dunn & Co. Contributor to 'Insolvency Law and Practice.' Speaker at local and regional SPI conferences.
Prof. Memberships: Fellow of Society of Practitioners of Insolvency, Insolvency Lawyers Association.
Career: Qualified 1983, and joined *Walker Morris* the same year. Became a Partner in 1985. Licensed insolvency practitioner.
Personal: Born 19th January 1959. Attended Bristol University 1977-80. Leisure interests include music, skiing and sailing. Lives in Huddersfield.

PENNIE, John A.
Dickinson Dees, Newcastle upon Tyne 0191 279 9000
Specialisation: A specialist in both personal and corporate insolvency, leading a team of nine lawyers. JIEB Moderator in Personal Insolvency. Member of the Law Society Insolvency Authorisation Casework Committee. Treasury Solicitor's Northern Agent for Disqualification cases. Licensed Insolvency Practitioner.
Prof. Memberships: Law Society.
Career: MA (Cantab) Partner with *Dickinson Dees* since 1985.

ROYLE, Kevin A
Lupton Fawcett, Leeds (0113) 280 2000
Specialisation: Partner specialising in corporate insolvency.
Prof. Memberships: Fellow Society of Practitioners of member of Insolvency Practitioners Association and Insolvency and Insolvency Lawyers Association.
Career: Articled *Addleshaw Sons & Latham*; qualified 1979; assistant solicitor 1979-1981; partner *William F Prior & Co* 1981-82; assistant solicitor *Deacons*, Hong Kong 1982-84; partner *Dibb Lupton Broomhead* 1985; partner *Lupton Fawcett* 1995.
Personal: Born 1953; resides Ripponden. Shooting, travel, food and wine, antiques.

TAYLOR, Michael F.
Walker Morris, Leeds (0113) 283 2500
Specialisation: Work includes all aspects of non-contentious corporate insolvency, restructuring and work outs.
Career: Qualified 1986; Partner *Walker Morris* 1991.
Personal: Attended King Edward VI School, Lichfield and University of Bristol 1980-83. Leisure interests include hockey and fly-fishing. Lives in Leeds.

SCOTLAND

Dundas & Wilson CS (4ptnrs/8assts) Merged with last year's lead firm Dorman Jeffrey and now operate out of their Corporate Recovery Services Group. There were initially doubts amongst rival practitioners as to whether the "Andersen connection" may in fact weaken the practice; this does not appear to have happened. *Ian Cuthbertson* is said to stand out as someone who exclusively works in insolvency, "gets more work than anybody" and is now involved in more pre-insolvency work. *Yvonne Brady* is also highly regarded. **Clients/Work:** Receiverships for Scottish Pride Group. Receiverships for Rowco Group. Administrations for Virtuality Group.

Burness (5ptnrs/5assts) Act for institutions, receivers and companies in financial difficulties in particular in the field of potential insolvency of professional partnerships. *Andrew Sleigh* is seen as an omission from previous years – "does more buying/selling on receiverships than anybody else." **Clients/Work:** Acting for Ernst & Young in receivership of William Grant Mining Ltd. Peter Craig receivership for Price Waterhouse involving serious allegations of fraud. Increasing evidence of confidential advice in relation to receiverships being sought from firm.

Shepherd & Wedderburn (6ptnrs/ 10assts) The practice has a strong reputation for its Customs & Excise work on VAT liq-

uidations. *Paul Hally* is actually a corporate finance specialist with an insolvency reputation. Former leader Jim Birrell is more on the training side these days. **Clients/Work:** Liquidation of John Gardiner Environmental Services Ltd. Liquidation of Alval Process Engineering Ltd. Reveivership of Langley Group Ltd.

Maclay Murray & Spens (5ptnrs/1asst) Seen more on receiverships than liquidations and sequestrations. *Magnus Swanson* in Glasgow and *Bruce Patrick* in Edinburgh are known for receivership work. **Clients/Work:** Acting for Waste Systems International Inc who successfully petitioned to liquidate Scotsafe Ltd. Recently appointed to act for receivers of Lockerbie Meatpackers Ltd and receivers of Oregon Development Company Ltd. Continuing to act in relation to Brewing Products Receivership.

MacRoberts (4ptnrs/3assts) Admit to having done less and less insolvency work in the past two years and are concentrating more on advisory work and avoidance. *David Flint* is perceived as spending more time on his IP practice. **Clients/Work:** Acting for Campsie Ltd. Advising Elmeg Communications GmbH in relation to international retention of title problem. Acting for provisional liquidator of Falkirk Football Club in relation to liquidation and ultimate rescue.

Biggart Baillie (2ptnrs) *Murray Shaw* is an accredited insolvency specialist and an authorised insolvency practitioner. **Clients/ Work:** Pursuing a number of applications under the Company Directors Disqualification Act 1986 on behalf of DTI. Acting in several smaller liquidations for a number of insolvency practitioners. Securing appointment to advise receivers of Jolly Giant.

Bird Semple (3ptnrs/5assts) Known for their large-scale receivership work although have been busy on property-related insolvencies in the last year. *Gordon Hollerin* is a well regarded partner. **Clients/Work:** Conclusion of sale of T.C.Farries & Co, a major bookbinding business in Dumfries. Sale as a going concern of Silver Choice Leisure. Continuing liquidation of car and parts dealership, Prossers Ltd, including ongoing wrongful trading actions against directors.

Bishop and Robertson Chalmers (4ptnrs) Work for the big six accountancy firms. *Russell Lang* is an insolvency specialist with a lot of experience in personal and corporate insolvency and on corporate res-

cue work. **Clients/Work:** Currently acting for receivers in landmark insolvency case of Lindop v Stuart Noble & Sons Ltd (In Receivership).

Iain Smith & Company (4ptnrs/3assts) Led by *Roy Roxburgh* who is seen to be active in the market. **Clients/Work:** Acting in the receiverships of Fridge Freight (Fyrie) Ltd and Uppa Crust (South) Ltd

McGrigor Donald (2ptnrs/4assts) Described as "genuinely having good expertise both on corporate and court side" *John Macfarlane* has "always had a good reputation on the corporate side." **Clients/Work:** Advising particularly in the field of strategic advice on corporate recovery for financial institutions and trade investors. Acting as legal advisor for liquidator of Monktonhall Mineworkers Ltd.

Pagan Macbeth (4ptnrs: 2p/t / 2assts) Team includes *John Clarke*.

Paull & Williamsons A strong contender in the Aberdeen market.

Stronachs (2ptnrs/1asst) The team has been involved mainly in liquidation and personal and partnership bankruptcies. *James Merson* is a litigator who is also a licensed insolvency practitioner. **Clients/Work:** Acting for joint liquidators of property company owning leased properties and development sites in Scotland.

Brodies WS (2ptnrs/1asst) Appear on behalf of the Accountant in Bankruptcy. Advise receivers re environmental issues and heavily involved in liquidation and receivership.

BRADY, Yvonne T.
Dundas & Wilson CS, Glasgow
(0141) 221 8586
Partner in *Dorman Jeffrey*, Insolvency Division of *Dundas & Wilson*.
Specialisation: Main area of practice is corporate reconstruction and insolvency. Also deals with licensing, mainly in insolvency situations. Contributed two chapters to 'A Scottish Insolvency Casebook,' published autumn 1994. Regularly convenes and lectures at Institute of Chartered Accountants seminars. Has presented seminars for Law Society courses and is a member of the examining team for the Joint Insolvency Examination Board, member of the SPI Technical Committee.
Prof. Memberships: Law Society.
Career: Qualified in 1984, having joined *Dorman Jeffrey & Co.* in 1982. Became a Partner in 1990.
Personal: Born 3rd July 1961. Educated at Strathclyde University 1978-82. Leisure pursuits include cooking, entertaining and reading (mainly thrillers and biographies). Lives in Glasgow.

CLARKE, John B.
Pagan Macbeth, Edinburgh Cupar
(0131) 220 3334
Also at Dunfermline (01383) 626666 and Cupar (01334) 657000 Partner in Commercial and Insolvency Department.
Specialisation: Licensed Insolvency Practitioner. Accredited Insolvency Specialist with the Law Society of Scotland. Handles all areas of corporate law. Also involved in intellectual property and computer law.
Prof. Memberships: Law Society of Scotland. SPI.
Career: Qualified in 1977. Worked with *Dundas & Wilson* 1977-81, joining *Pagan Osborne* in 1981. Founded *Pagan Macbeth* as a Partner in 1994 (remaining a Partner in *Pagan Osborne*).
Personal: Born 8th April 1955. Attended University of Edinburgh 1973-77. Leisure interests include shooting and skiing. Lives in Cupar.

CUTHBERTSON, Ian
Dundas & Wilson CS, Glasgow
(0141) 221 8586
Specialisation: Receiverships, reconstructions, portfolio control, securities enforcement, administrations, waitouts, risk management, bank advisory, liquidations, turnaround, asset quality management.
Prof. Memberships: Law Society of Scotland; Society of Practitioners in Insolvency; Insolvency Practitioners Association; Insolvency Lawyers Association.
Career: Jordanhill College School; University of Glasgow; 1972-1979 *Boyds* 1979-1997 *Dorman Jeffrey & Co* 1997-date *Dundas & Wilson, Garretts* and *Dorman Jeffrey.*
Personal: Rugby, football, movies, reading.

FLINT, David
MacRoberts, Glasgow (0141) 332 9988
See under Computer Law & I.T., p. 189

HALLY, Paul W.
Shepherd & Wedderburn WS, Edinburgh
(0131) 228 9900
See under General Corporate Finance, p. 257

HOLLERIN, Gordon Craig
Bird Semple, Glasgow (0141) 221 7090
Partner in Litigation Department.
Specialisation: Main areas of practice are corporate recovery and insolvency, including administrations, receiverships, liquidations and company voluntary arrangements. Also specialises in property litigation. Accredited as ADR Mediator by Centre for Dispute Resolution and the Law Society of Scotland. Head Partner on receivership of Lilley plc and Group Companies and on Scottish aspects of receivership of Rush & Tompkins Group. Contributor to 'ADR in Scotland' published in 1995. Has widespread experience as seminar speaker on ADR and Insolvency.
Prof. Memberships: Member of Law Society of Scotland's ADR Committee and Solicitor-Mediator Accreditation Panel, CEDR Scotland Board member, AIJA, Property Litigation Association.
Career: Qualified in 1980. Joined *Bird Semple* in 1978, becoming a Partner 1985.
Personal: Born 23rd January 1957. Attended University of Glasgow 1974-78 (LLB with Honours in Private Law). Leisure interests include mini-rugby coaching. Lives in Glasgow.

LANG, J. Russell
Bishop and Robertson Chalmers, Glasgow
(0141) 248 4672
Partner in Corporate Unit of Business Law Division. Has specialised in all aspects of personal and corporate insolvency and corporate rescue work since 1976. Has been involved in all aspects of corporate and commercial law since 1990. Licensed Insolvency Practitioner since 1987. Accredited as a specialist in insolvency law by the Law Society of Scotland. Member of Joint Discussion Group for insolvency specialists set up by the Law Society of Scotland and the Institute of Chartered Accountants of Scotland. Lecturer on courses run by the Law Society of Scotland, Institute of Chartered Accountants of Scotland and Strathclyde University. Appointed Moderator by Joint Insolvency Examination Board in September 1993. Appointed member of the Scottish Technical Committee of the Society of Practitioners of Insolvency.
Prof. Memberships: Law Society of Scotland, Insolvency Lawyers Association.
Career: With *McGrigor Donald, Solicitors* in Glasgow 1974-80. Qualified in 1976. Joined *Bishop & Co, Solicitors*, Glasgow in 1980 and became a Partner in 1982. Firm became *Bishop and Robertson Chalmers, Solicitors* in 1986. Partner in the Litigation department 1986-90. Partner in the Corporate and Commercial Unit of the firm's Business Law Division from 1990.
Personal: Educated at Edinburgh University 1970-74.

MACFARLANE, John
McGrigor Donald, Edinburgh
(0131) 226 7777
Partner in Company Department.
Specialisation: Principal area of practice is corporate insolvency. Also handles general corporate work. Acted in the receiverships of Pierre Victoire Ltd, Lees Group (Scotland) Ltd, Allan Timber Products Group, Charles Gray (Builders) Ltd. Major clients include KPMG,

Ernst & Young, Coopers & Lybrand and Grant Thorton. Contributor to legal journals on insolvency and related topics (e.g.'Impecunias'). Formerly tutor in Diploma of Legal Practice, Strathclyde and Edinburgh Universities. Speaker at various conferences e.g. 'Insolvency and the Construction Industry.'
Prof. Memberships: Law Society of Scotland; Joint Insolvency Specialists Group.
Career: Qualified 1971. Partner at *Bird Semple Ireland* 1976-90. Joint Convenor, Joint Insolvency Specialists Group (Law Society of Scotland/ Institute of C.A. Scotland) from 1995.
Personal: Born 18th September 1949. Educated at Glasgow University 1967-71 (LL.B Hons). Interests include horse riding and point to point (not riding). Lives in East Lothian.

MERSON, James T.
Stronachs, Aberdeen (01224) 845845
Partner in Commercial Litigation Department. Head of Department.
Specialisation: Specialist area of practice is insolvency. Licensed insolvency practitioner and certified by Law Society of Scotland as a specialist in insolvency law. Also handles civil litigation, spanning all types of commercial disputes and litigation.
Prof. Memberships: Law Society of Scotland. Aberdeen Bar Association.
Career: Qualified in 1974. Joined *Stronachs* in 1974, becoming a Partner in 1978.
Personal: Born 24th April 1951. Attended Aberdeen University 1969-72. Leisure interests include bridge and golf. Lives in Aberdeen.

PATRICK, Bruce R.
Maclay Murray & Spens, Edinburgh
(0131) 226 5196
See under General Corporate Finance, p. 257

ROXBURGH, Roy
Iain Smith & Company, Aberdeen
(01224) 645454
Email: roy@iainsmith.com
Partner in Company & Commercial Department.
Specialisation: Main areas of practice are mergers and take-overs, MBO's, MBI's and corporate insolvency, acting for both purchasers and vendors of businesses, investors both private and institutional, and receiverships. Involvement in insolvency is generally on a specialist basis. Author of a chapter on diligence for the ICAS 'Insolvency Case Book.' Convener 1993 to 1995 of the Law Society/ ICAS's Insolvency Specialist Group.
Prof. Memberships: Law Society of Scotland (Member of Insolvency Solicitors Committee since 1992, and Insolvency Specialist Accreditation Panel since 1994), S.P.I. (Member of Scottish Technical Committee).
Career: Qualified in 1974. Joined *Iain Smith & Co* as a Partner in 1977. External Examiner JIEB since 1993 and External Examiner at Robert Gordon University since 1992. Notary Public.
Personal: Born 29th September 1950. Educated at Dunfermline High School 1961-68 and Edinburgh University 1968-72. Recreations include ski-ing, golf and football. Lives in Aberdeen.

SHAW, Murray W.A.
Biggart Baillie, Glasgow (0141) 228 8000
See under Construction & Civil Engineering,
p. 215

SLEIGH, Andrew.
Burness, Glasgow (0141) 248 4933
See under Banking, p. 147 and General
Corporate Finance, p. 257 and Sports Law, p. 745

SWANSON, Magnus P.
Maclay Murray & Spens, Glasgow
(0141) 248 5011
See under General Corporate Finance, p. 258

NORTHERN IRELAND

LEADING FIRMS
NORTHERN IRELAND
NAPIER & SONS Belfast
CARSON & MCDOWELL Belfast
JOHN MCKEE & SON Belfast
KING & GOWDY Belfast
L'ESTRANGE & BRETT Belfast
MCMANUS & KEARNEY Belfast
TUGHAN & CO Belfast
CLEAVER FULTON & RANKIN Belfast
COMERTON & HILL Belfast
ELLIOTT DUFFY GARRETT Belfast

Napier & Sons (3ptnrs/2assts) Still head and shoulders above the other insolvency practices in Northern Ireland, *John Gordon* is described as "particularly good;" his expertise covers both corporate and personal insolvency.

Carson & McDowell (1ptnr p/t/1asst f/t)
John McKee & Son (2ptnrs/2assts) Act particularly in administrative receiverships, and on the personal insolvency side. Well-known and respected as specialists. *Lex Ross* has "excellent judgment"and is widely respected by other insolvency lawyers. **Clients/Work:** O'Hara's Bakeries Ltd – administrative receivership. James Anderson Ltd – administrative receivership. G Kinnaird Ltd – administrative receivership.

King & Gowdy Act for one of the banks. "Very good, very sound, do a lot."

L'Estrange & Brett (1ptnr/3assts) Work purely on the corporate side. *Brian Henderson* does this work.

McManus & Kearney (2ptnrs/3assts) A general corporate firm known for its bankruptcy work. One partner is a licensed insolvency practitioner. **Clients/Work:** Enquiries from creditors/clients on how to make individual voluntary arrangements more effective and increasing requirement to attend and advise at creditors meetings. Significant increase in requirements for legal advice by other insolvency practitioners.

Tughan & Co (2ptnrs/2assts) Known particularly for their directors disqualification proceedings work.

Cleaver Fulton & Rankin (1ptnr/1assoc/1asst) **Clients/Work:** General insolvency work on the corporate side both for creditors and debtors.

Comerton & Hill Said to be "genuine specialists."

Elliott Duffy Garrett (2ptnrs/2assts) One of the partners is a licenced insolvency practitioner.

LEADING INDIVIDUALS
NORTHERN IRELAND
GORDON John Gerard Napier & Sons
HENDERSON Brian L'Estrange & Brett
ROSS Alexander John McKee & Son

LEADERS' PROFILES · NORTHERN IRELAND

GORDON, John Gerard
Napier & Sons, Belfast (01232) 244602
Managing Partner.
Specialisation: Licensed Insolvency Practitioner. Presents seminars for Law Society and lectures at Institute of Professional Legal Studies. Contributor of Northern Ireland chapter to Grier & Floyd Personal Insolvency. Main area of practice is Individual Voluntary arrangements and C.V.A.'s.
Prof. Memberships: Law Society N.I. Treasurer and council member S.P.I.
Career: LL.B. Queen's University Belfast.
Certificate Professional Legal Studies, Queen's University Belfast. Qualified 1981. Managing Partner *Napier & Sons* 1985. Member of the Lord Chancellor's Advisory Rules Committee on Insolvency.

HENDERSON, Brian L.
L'Estrange & Brett, Belfast (01232) 230426
See under Banking, p. 145

ROSS, Alexander T.
John McKee & Son, Belfast (01232) 232303
Specialisation: Advises office holders particularly Administrative Receivers on all legal matters arising from corporate recovery and insolvency including sales of businesses and assets and claims by creditors. Also advises banks on lending and security.
Prof. Memberships: Law Society of Northern Ireland.
Career: Qualified 1967; Partner in *John McKee & Son* from 1972.
Personal: Born 23.12.1942. Educated at Strathallen School, Perthshire and Queens University, Belfast.

INSURANCE AND REINSURANCE

See also Personal Injury and Professional Negligence

RESEARCH: In compiling the tables, we consider all the information available to us, paying particular regard to the market research carried out by our team of ten qualified lawyers. (The researchers' details are set out on page three.) The rankings, therefore, reflect the opinion of the marketplace as revealed by systematic and objective research: see page four. (Our research is audited every year by the British Market Research Bureau.)

OVERVIEW: This year, the section is divided into three areas: General Claims, Reinsurance and Non-Contentious. We have included a General Claims section this year as an overall guide to the 'insurance' reader, although inevitably this table overlaps with our Defendant Personal Injury and Professional Negligence sections.

The recent mergers of several key insurance, reinsurance and life companies as well as brokers have had a knock on effect on the firms. The sources of legal work are fewer, and increasingly there is a demand for "one-stop shops" with the specialisation to handle all of their clients insurance needs. There is likely to be a spate of client-driven mergers amongst the insurance firms, which need to avoid becoming victims of the "panel slashing" taking place at major insurance companies. The gap between major and minor players is predicted to widen.

The General Claims table is dominated by the same firms as the Reinsurance tables. Accordingly insurance specialists Barlows, Camerons, Clyde's, DAC and Ince's receive top billing. This is unsurprising as there is a large amount of cross-over between reinsurance and general claims. The leading band of highly regarded firms contains two types of firm: large litigation heavyweights known for high value work and smaller firms known for their work for composites. The nationwide firms have been recruiting heavily and appear at the bottom end of the tables.

In the reinsurance market, Barlow Lyde & Gilbert stay ahead – just. There were numerous recommendations for Ince & Co who join Clyde & Co in the number two slot and seem serious contenders for the reinsurance crown. Of the highly recommended firms, DJ Freeman received many compliments. Those interviewed commented on the settling down of the London market, following the advent of Equitas. Due to the current "soft market," most observed a general reluctance on their clients' part to litigate, with a greater emphasis on pre-emptory advisory work and mediation.

The non-contentious category includes demutualisations, mergers, take-overs and flotations of insurance companies and can be divided into three areas: life assurance, Lloyds work and non-life/provincial insurance work. 1997 was another busy year for the small group of specialised non-contentious insurance practitioners competing for this lucrative work. Niche firms appear to be suffering as non-contentious insurance work gravitates towards larger firms with a corporate base. It is becoming more common for headline deals to be handled by corporate finance firms rather than insurance experts. Also, although all firms are keen to stress their "strength in depth," in this complex area of law, individual profiles are extremely important. When a team leader changes firm, it has an immediate and detrimental impact on the firm's original position.

LONDON

GENERAL CLAIMS

Barlow Lyde & Gilbert (10ptnrs/25assts). "Undeniably one of *the* names in the world of insurance." Individually rated are head of department *Graham Dickinson,* deputy head of department *Roger Doulton, Tim Hardy* and newly arrived "resourceful" *Sheila Simison.* **Clients/Work:** Digital vs Hampshire County Council 1997. White vs QCE 1997. Berryman vs London Borough of Hounslow [CA] 1997.

Cameron McKenna (13ptnrs/22assts) "Can handle all the really complex cases." "Have built up a good practice from strong professional negligence roots." The team includes the "forceful" *Mark Elborne, John Hall* ("a truly excellent litigator") and *Belinda Schofield* ("hard worker, really thorough in her approach"). **Clients/Work:** Act for Capital Counties plc in a £17m fire claim. Negotiated a settlement of the Contractors All Risks insurance claim following the Heathrow Expressway collapse in October 1994. Successfully acted for promotional insurance underwriters in a claim regarding promotions which offered free flights to retail customers upon proof of purchase of certain goods (DSG Retail Ltd v QBE International Insurance Ltd & Others)

Clyde & Co (12ptnrs/17assts) An excellent practice. "Serious players for both marine and non-marine work." Team includes *Michael Payton* ("extremely experienced," "a senior figure"), and *Rod Smith* ("calm, pragmatic and gives well balanced advice"). The group (handling commercial litigation, insurance and reinsurance) has a diverse practice, with strength in credit and political risk work for insurers and their insureds. **Clients/Work:** Acted for the plaintiffs in TGA Chapman Ltd and Anor v Christopher and Sun Alliance." Acted for successful Defendants in a large war risk insurance dispute (Boskalis v Mountain). Also acted for the Underwriters in the "Nukila" a latent defect case.

Davies Arnold Cooper (25ptnrs/133 fee-earners) "Good all-rounders" – insurance litigation accounts for 75-80% of the firm's billings. Individually ranked are *David McIntosh* (Senior Partner – "seems less directly involved now, but knows his stuff"), *Nicholas Sinfield* and *Kenneth McKenzie* ("knows the market"). **Clients/Work:** Ranges from high volume, low value claims in EL/PL, motor and professional indemnity to highly complex and substantial matters, accountancy, construction and energy, product liability, mass tort). Important cases include the BZW Jurisdictional litigation (HL).

Ince & Co (17ptnrs/17assts). "Strong on marine side, but also respected for non-marine." *Peter* ("Mr Insurance") *Rogan* who is "excellent for any insurance problem," jointly heads the team. *Christopher Jefferis* and *Alan Weir* both have recognised expertise. **Clients/Work:** Acting for hull underwriters in the litigation between the Dutch Government and underwriters over the building of submarines for the Royal Dutch Navy (The State of Netherlands v Youell). Birmingham Midshires v David Parry & Co, key appeal decision restricting the liability of solicitors to mortgage lenders (HL refused leave to the plaintiff). Ford v GRE, acted for insurance company in successfully bringing civil case, following an acquittal in a criminal case involving conspiracy to commit arson (insurance company not obliged to pay out monies).

Berrymans Lace Mawer (2ptnrs/2assts in London – work closely with regional teams). The merger seems to have been successful and the firm is thought to be excellent on the composite side. "Going places." **Clients/Work:** Royal and Sun Alliance, General Accident, Commercial Union. Acted in Pride Valley v Independent Client: Independent Insurance Co (own client).

Freshfields (9ptnrs:4f/t/20assts). "Good for the high value cases." The firm has the resources to handle large, complex cases but, as with the other corporate litigation firms, does not handle volume work. **Clients/Work:** Acting for Lloyds in test cases against non-accepting Names to recover unpaid debts including resisting defences based on Article 85 and fraud (achieved commercially successful victory in CA ensuring settlement remained in place). Acting for Equitas in the appeal to HL in Baker (Syndicate 947) v Black Sea/Baltic, the leading authority regarding the sharing of investigation, settlement and defence costs under proportional reinsurance treaties.

Herbert Smith (8ptnrs/20assts). "Very professional" and "capable of cutting edge stuff." *Martin Bakes* ("always finds creative solutions") is part of the team who handle insurance litigation and concentrate on complex high value claim work (often international). *David Higgins* and *Michael Munden* were also recommended. **Clients/Work:** Southall Rail Crash – instructed by insurers of one of the parties potentially involved in claims arising out of the crash. Akai Pty Ltd v Peoples Insurance Company Ltd – claim under a credit insurance policy which raised complex issues of private international law (acted for successful insurer). Also act for Royal & Sun Alliance, Sedgwick and Lloyds syndicates.

Holman Fenwick & Willan (4ptnrs/ 1manager/10assts spend 1/3 of their time). Have the capacity to handle complex, international disputes. "Real expertise," but with a smaller team than the leaders. *Paul Wordley* ("flexible, knowledgeable") is individually recognised. **Clients/Work:** Acting for the insured/captive insurer of a major mining company in proceedings arising out of major EAR/Property Damage/ Business Interruption losses in the United States. Acting for underwriters in a number of major property damage disputes in diverse jurisdictions including Italy, Saudi Arabia, Peru and Brazil (both involved multi-million dollar losses).

Kennedys (34ptnrs/54assts/24 legal execs). Admired for their "excellent house style" and noted for their ability to handle an extremely varied caseload. *Nicholas Williams* is "one of the best around" and is "capable across the whole spectrum." The "formidable" *Nicholas Thomas* is also ranked. Firm took on the London office of Elliot & Co this year. **Clients/Work:** Acted for Commercial Union Assurance Co plc in case concerning duty of utmost good faith in a Consumer Policy context. Involved in valuers tortious claims – no duty to an undisclosed principal of whom valuer not aware at time of valuation (Secured Residential Funding v Nationwide Building Society. Acted in Orssank S.A. v Spencer Associates (use of interlocutory procedure to minimise clients' costs exposure and achieve early end to potentially expensive claim).

Lovell White Durrant (London: 6ptnrs. Worldwide: 13ptnrs). Good on the international side. **Clients/Work:** Several continuing aspects for Assurances Generales de France arising out of the liquidation of NEMGIA and the ensuing litigation.

Continuation of the Mirror Group litigation concerning the death of Robert Maxwell, following the 1996 preliminary ruling (MGN v New Hampshire).

Reynolds Porter Chamberlain (12ptnrs/ 24assts. Also 7ptnrs/18assts (construction specialists)) "A good, solid insurance firm." *Simon Greenley,* is "a popular figure" who is "enthusiastic and gives excellent advice." **Clients/Work:** Outsourced insurance work (non-marine claims of all types – 6 dedicated claims handlers, 3 of them solicitors). Appointed this year to the panel of two major Lloyds Syndicates specialising in general liability work.

Beachcroft Stanleys (8ptnrs/17assts). Currently act for three of the top ten general insurers and cover the full range of insurance claims including major disaster litigation and fire/fraud. **Clients/Work:** Acting for Allianz and 11 reinsurers in connection with a $175m insurance dispute arising out of two incidents at a USA copper smelting plant. Acting for Allianz in an insurance dispute arising out of the collapse of the Heathrow Expressway Tunnel. Also act for Norwich Union, Guardian and Cornhill Insurance plc.

Clifford Chance (6ptnrs (2 in Lloyds) /18assts). "Have the capability to handle complex, high value cases," although not traditionally seen as an insurance firm. *David Cohen* ("bright") is individually recommended. **Clients/Work:** Specialise in advising on political risk and major construction project financial risk insurance coverage. Assist with insurance problems arising out of innovative asset and project financings, including securitisations, and M&A. Advise Lloyds underwriters on international directors' and officers' coverage. Represented Kleinwort Benson successfully in the Den Dansk and Others v Skipton Building Society litigation.

D J Freeman (5ptnrs/10assts). Insurance coverage work accounts for 35% of team's workload. "Doing well for themselves." Turnover grew by 40% this year. Cover both marine and non-marine insurance claims. **Clients/Work:** Act for insurers of three largest cigarette manufacturers in the American tobacco litigation and have commenced arbitrations in London to resolve coverage disputes. Acted for owners of Turkish charter jet which crashed in Puerto Rico in 1996 killing 131 passengers in the owners' dispute with their insurers and brokers over coverage – successfully obtained full indemnity for client at trial.

Elborne Mitchell (6ptnrs/6assts – substantial amount of time) Well established niche firm – recent departures following the settling of the Lloyds litigation were "no surprise" to the marketplace but they remain well thought of. **Clients/Work:** Acting for American reinsurers on London market (Personal Accident LMX spiral). Advising continental reinsurers concerning commutation of claims.

Hill Taylor Dickinson (17ptnrs/ 5assocs/10assts). *Robin Williams* ("high profile") is a key member of the team, all of whom spend approx. 65% of their time on general insurance work. **Clients/Work:** Acted in the "Star Sea," leading case on the extent of the duty of good faith owed by an insured in the presentation of insurance claims. Represented the underwriters in Fraser Shipping Ltd v NJ Colton & Others. Acted in significant claim arising out of the Gulf War – Royal Boskalis Westminster NV v TR Mountain & Others.

Richards Butler (10ptnrs/11assts in insurance/reinsurance dept) Cover both marine and non-marine work. *Mark Connoley* was recommended. **Clients/Work:** Represent US and other overseas carriers with several coverage disputes in the London market. Represented a Swiss finance house in 17 commercial mortgage disputes and related negligence actions against valuers. Represent several brokers in the Lloyds internal disputes in their strike out application against the Gooda Walker Names.

Rowe & Maw (7ptnrs f/t /15-20assts). The nature of the work is non-marine. Firm has a dedicated Lloyds office. **Clients/Work:** Advise leading Lloyds liability syndicates and their representatives. Large proportion of insurance related work is in professional negligence field for high profile insureds.

Dibb Lupton Alsop (Marine 3ptnrs/ 4assts, non-marine 3ptnrs/4assts). Actively looking to increase their market share in London. A speciality is energy and technical claims. **Clients/Work:** Include Royal & Sun Alliance, Cigna and Gan Insurance Co.

Edward Lewis (9ptnrs/23assts) In addition to UK work, firm acts in European and international insurance claims. **Clients/Work:** Represent major UK and European insurance companies on contentious matters involving third party disputes and policy interpretation matters.

Fishburn Boxer (13ptnrs/19assts/ 5 insurance market professionals run claims handling unit) *Stephen Leonard* is their best known partner. **Clients/Work:** Handle claims on behalf of Lloyds underwriters and insurance companies. Active in new professional indemnity markets such as IT and media and development of products such as litigation protection insurance.

Hammond Suddards (4ptnrs/14assts with 3 further assts if required) Have "ambition." Dedicated Lloyds office handles insurance litigation (largest legal presence within Lloyds). **Clients/Work:** Major Lloyds underwriters, also non-Lloyds insurers.

Hextall Erskine (14ptnrs/7assts/ 7 legal execs) Over 80% of the firm's workload is insurance related. **Clients/Work:** Act for UK composites, Lloyds syndicates.

Wansbroughs Willey Hargrave (10ptnrs/35assts handling defendant insurance work). Seen to be "beefing up their insurance team" in London. 50% of workload relates to general and property-related insurance litigation. **Clients/Work:** Acted for the insurers of the defendant in the case of TGA Chapman Ltd v Christopher.

LEADING INDIVIDUALS · LONDON GENERAL CLAIMS

ROGAN Peter Ince & Co	
BAKES Martin Herbert Smith	
COHEN David Clifford Chance	
CONNOLEY Mark Richards Butler	
DICKINSON Graham Barlow Lyde & Gilbert	
DOULTON Roger Barlow Lyde & Gilbert	
ELBORNE Mark Cameron McKenna	
FARTHING Peter Clyde & Co	
GREENLEY Simon Reynolds Porter Chamberlain	
HALL John Cameron McKenna	
HARDY Tim Barlow Lyde & Gilbert	
HIGGINS David Herbert Smith	
JEFFERIS Chris Ince & Co	
LEONARD Stephen Fishburn Boxer	
McINTOSH David Davies Arnold Cooper	
McKENZIE Kenneth Davies Arnold Cooper	
MUNDEN Michael Herbert Smith	
PAYTON Michael Clyde & Co	
SCHOFIELD Belinda Cameron McKenna	
SIMISON Sheila Barlow Lyde & Gilbert	
SINFIELD Nicholas Davies Arnold Cooper	
SMITH Roderick Clyde & Co	
THOMAS Nicholas Kennedys	
WEIR Alan Ince & Co	
WILLIAMS Nicholas Kennedys	
WILLIAMS Robin Hill Taylor Dickinson	
WORDLEY Paul Holman, Fenwick & Willan	

SEE PROFILES AT THE END OF THIS SECTION

REINSURANCE

Barlow Lyde & Gilbert (13ptnrs/14assts/1 consult). Have "an enviable reputation" and are "committed to providing advice to the market." In 1997, they won Professional Service Provider of the Year in The Review's Worldwide Reinsurance Awards. *Colin Croly* is "knowledgeable" and "really specialised." He is undoubtedly a key figure. Individually recognised are *Tim Hardy* ("gets very involved") *John Hanson* and *Michael Mendelowitz* who is "unsurpassed for advisory work." **Clients/Work:** GIO v Brown and in major (confidential) arbitrations. Advised on implications of "Y2K" and have taken a lead in drafting wordings and providing intelligence and analysis to the market. Involved in new risk transfer products, alternative risk financing, cut throughs, contract wordings.

Clyde & Co (10ptnrs(f/t), 8ptnrs (experienced). 13assts.) Have an "excellent client base," and are always there for reinsurance. Senior partner *Michael Payton* "wears lots of different insurance hats," including reinsurance. His role is as an "umbrella figure" – but he's still a leading expert. *Peter Harvey* is good on the marine side and *Nigel Brook* "knows his stuff." **Clients/Work:** Acted in Brown v GIO where the CA decided that a clause making the reinsured sole judge as to what constitutes an "event" is valid and effective. Also acted in Commercial Union v Victory (CA found that a judgement against the reinsured on the original claim is conclusive at the reinsurance level, although the same is not true of a settlement) and Eastern European Newbuildings (reinsurance disputes).

Ince & Co (6ptnrs/8assts) "Go from strength to strength,"and are "seriously good." Much of this is due to the activities of joint team head *Peter Rogan* ("very hands on," "terribly able guy," "always commercial") who received a phenomenal number of individual recommendations. Members of the team include *Steven Fox*, *Alan Hepworth* and newly recommended *Alan Weir* who is "worth watching." **Clients/Work:** Denby v English & Scottish, represented various reinsurers in important market dispute over the proper interpretation of the aggregate extension clause and its applicability to professional indemnity practices. Represented Liverpool v London, major P&I Club, who placed reinsurance with GIO (GIO purported to avoid those reinsurances and have commenced an action in the Commercial Court).

Cameron McKenna (4ptnrs specialise, 16ptnrs with expertise/15-18assts). "Have consolidated their practice post-merger." *Mark Elborne* ("great brain – and confident") and *Vere Wheatley* ("clever, understands the market and gives good advice") are the recommended reinsurance experts. Work closely with the six strong insurance team in Hong Kong. **Clients/Work:** Acted for a US reinsurer of London market PA LMX spiral (value of dispute in excess of $100m) and in a dispute between a major Lloyds Syndicate, Australian reinsurers and retrocessionaires based in London on a whole account reinsurance originally intended to run for three years (value of approx. $100m). In Aneco Re v Johnson & Higgins successfully acted for Aneco Re (judgement given that J&H were negligent in placing excess of loss protections as brokers on behalf of client).

Davies Arnold Cooper (14ptnrs/ 13assts) Have a solid reputation for insurance work and are "commercial and pragmatic." There was a perception that the firm had "more strength in their team work, than individually." *Michael Dobias* "a familiar face," heads up the team, assisted by *Gerald O'Mahoney.* **Clients/Work:** Include twelve insurance schemes of arrangement for insurers and reinsurers.

Clifford Chance (6ptnrs, up to 80%/18assts, 50%) Firm gained exposure through recent involvement in the Aneco matter. Concentrate on major complex cases with international elements.Key partners are *Stephen Lewis* and the "brilliant" *Terry O'Neill.* **Clients/Work:** Represented Johnson & Higgins in major Commercial Court litigation concerning placing of reinsurance, due to go to CA (Johnson & Higgins/Aneco). Represented NRG Victory (reinsurance company in run-off) in major reinsurance litigation arising out of the Exxon Valdez oil spill (won in Court of Appeal).

D J Freeman (5ptnrs specialise/up to 16 assists can support – 25% of insurance team's workload is reinsurance). "Doing well" was the general consensus – the firm moves up

the tables this year. *David Kendall* is a well established figure who "gives extremely realistic advice"and is "intellectually sound." *David Tiplady* is also individually ranked. **Clients/Work:** Acted for English & American in its dispute with the Outhwaite syndicates at Lloyds over the recovery of reinsurance claims and the right of the syndicates to inspect English & American's books and records. Advised Alexander Howden (now Aon) on the formation of KeyAction Ltd and the assignment to KeyAction of reinsurance claims due to 50 of Howden's clients.

Freshfields (5ptnrs/pool of 20assts) Have established themselves in the marketplace. Practice is focused on high value, international work which often combines reinsurance, insurance and insolvency issues. *Raj Parker* is seen as "technically and tactically good" but perceived as spending less time on pure reinsurance work than some of the other experts. **Clients/Work:** Acting for Alexander & Alexander (now Aon) and the provisional liquidators of Orion Insurance in a dispute with Baloise (eight week trial going to CA March and December 1998). Acting for scheme administrators of KWELM which participated in the Weavers underwriting pool· in arbitration proceedings to recover substantial reinsurance recoveries.

Holman Fenwick & Willan (2/3ptnrs plus 1 ptnr/1 manager/10assts) "Increasingly active." *John Duff* is well known in the market and is described as "a powerhouse." *Andrew Bandurka* is his right hand man. **Clients/Work:** Successfully acted for a reinsurer of Sovereign Marine and General in proceedings which led to the well publicised liquidation of Sovereign by its parent company Willis Corroon in July 1997. Acted for reinsurer of an insurance pool, which denied liabilities flowing from the provisional liquidation of North Atlantic Insurance Company, case decided in Commercial Court.

Lovell White Durrant (6ptnrs/12assts). Have been active in matters relating to EMLICO. "Possess some excellent individual practitioners: *John Powell* ("a very good intellect"), *Peter Taylor* (highly recommended) and *Christian Wells*. The team work closely with the firm's Chicago office. **Clients/Work:** Acting for INSCO against ACIC in an action relating to the type of cover provided in the retrocessional market for Savings and Loans collapse. Acting for Yasuda against Lloyds Syndicates (Equitas) on the meaning of the opening sentence of the Aggregate Extension Clause and its application to the Minets Line Slip.

Elborne Mitchell (5ptnrs/6assts) Despite several recent departures, (including leader Ed Stanley to Hammond Suddards) the firm continues to have many supporters – "historically, a player," "will have something up their sleeve" "still know their stuff." *Tim Akeroyd* is "technically good, smart and hardworking." Clients/Work: Acted successfully for Prudential & Pearl in dispute about reinsurance of a book of marine liability business produced by a niche Lloyds broker (C J Mander & Others v Prudential & Pearl). Advised Centre Re in provision of contingent capital in the form of a special reinsurance contract when Sedgwick Oakwood created a conversion vehicle for its unlimited liability Names.

Herbert Smith (8ptnrs/20assts). Always strong on the litigation side. *Michael Munden* – "able, though perhaps less active in this area than in former years" is long established. As with general insurance litigation, concentrate on high value, complex matters. Handle many international matters, and team work closely with specialist insurance groups in Hong Kong and Paris. Clients/Work: Involved in highly technical reinsurance dispute with the Pacific and General Insurance Company, case going to appeal this year. Acted in a dispute under facultative reinsurance contract relating to machinery breakdown policy from a problem in Saudi Arabia.

Norton Rose (2ptnrs/6assts) *Francis Mackie*, who is well known in the industry heads up the reinsurance team. Clients/Work: The Eastern European Ship Building reinsurance arbitration dispute. Syndicate 947 v Black Sea & Baltic – recovery of costs from reinsurers. Denby v Marchant – aggregate extension clauses.

Eversheds (4ptnrs/8assts substantially involved – plus recently recruited 2ptnrs/1asst) Have been team building over the last year but at present stay static in the rankings. Many in the market expected more impact when the Waltons & Morse team joined. Clients/Work: Acted for one of the members of the Personal Accident LMX Spiral Working Party – advice has formed part of the working party's programme.

Fishburn Boxer (3ptnrs/assts as required) Clients/Work: E&O underwriters of reinsurance brokers and for both cedants and reinsurers in disputes before the courts and arbitrators. Advise both Lloyds syndicates and reinsurers in their dealings with Equitas.

Hill Taylor Dickinson (17ptnrs/5 assoc/10assts – all 35% of time) Are "keen to maintain a presence"and expanded last year after taking on McKenna's Lloyds' team. Clients/Work: Acted for London Market Reassureds with the proper meaning of the extent of "follow settlement" clauses in an XL/reinsurance contract – $24m.

Paisner & Co (5ptnrs/8assts focus primarily on reinsurance). Smaller scale than many, but have a reputation. Have picked up work recently from Equitas. *Jonathan Sacher* ("amiable character who has developed a following") has achieved a "good deal on much more limited resources than many competitors." Clients/Work: Appointed by Equitas Ltd on significant projects. Conducted two major arbitrations for European reinsurers with London Market reinsureds involving over $20m in dispute.

LEADING INDIVIDUALS · LONDON REINSURANCE

ROGAN Peter Ince & Co	
CROLY Colin Barlow Lyde & Gilbert	
BROOK Nigel Clyde & Co	
DOBIAS Michael Davies Arnold Cooper	
DUFF John Holman, Fenwick & Willan	
ELBORNE Mark Cameron McKenna	
FARTHING Peter Clyde & Co	
KENDALL David D J Freeman	
MENDELOWITZ Michael Barlow Lyde & Gilbert	
PAYTON Michael Clyde & Co	
POWELL John Lovell White Durrant	
TAYLOR Peter Lovell White Durrant	
WHEATLEY Vere Cameron McKenna	
AKEROYD Tim Elborne Mitchell	
BANDURKA Andrew Holman, Fenwick & Willan	
FOX Steven Ince & Co	
HANSON John Barlow Lyde & Gilbert	
HARDY Tim Barlow Lyde & Gilbert	
HEPWORTH Allan Ince & Co	
LEWIS Stephen Clifford Chance	
MACKIE Francis Norton Rose	
O'MAHONEY Gerald Davies Arnold Cooper	
O'NEILL Terry Clifford Chance	
PARKER Raj Freshfields	
SACHER Jonathan Paisner & Co	
STANLEY Ed Hammond Suddards	
TIPLADY David D J Freeman	
WEIR Alan Ince & Co	
WELLS Christian Lovell White Durrant	

SEE PROFILES AT THE END OF THIS SECTION

NON-CONTENTIOUS

LEADING FIRMS · LONDON NON-CONTENTIOUS

CLIFFORD CHANCE
FRESHFIELDS
HERBERT SMITH
LOVELL WHITE DURRANT

CLYDE & CO
LINKLATERS
SLAUGHTER AND MAY

HIGHLY REGARDED FIRMS

Ashurst Morris Crisp
Barlow Lyde & Gilbert
D J Freeman
Eversheds
Norton Rose
Titmuss Sainer Dechert

Clifford Chance (4ptnrs/15assts) The "bright" *Katherine Coates* leads a team providing specialist expertise on large transactions. Their substantial resources and capacity for high volume, particularly in Lloyds work has kept the firm in our top band. As "good journeymen," they were felt to be on a par with other leading firms.

Clients/Work: Advised sellers on the disposal of a majority interest in Bankside to LIMIT; advised Murray Lawrence Holdings Ltd in relation to a strategic investment by three US investors, and the creation of a new Bermudan holding company; advised US mutual insurer on auction sale of Albany Life Group to Canada Life.

Freshfields (9ptnrs/12assts) The team is headed by *Philip Richards* who enjoys a reputation for providing a "top class" service to his clients. Geared less towards high volume work, it has been involved in several major deals in the past year. Clients/Work: Scottish Amicable on its proposed demutualisation and acquisition by Prudential; Zurich Insurance on its proposed merger with BAT Industries' financial services business; participated in the successful worldwide demutualisation of Australia's largest mutual insurer, AMP Society.

Herbert Smith (11ptnrs plus "a significant number of assts") Felt to be preeminent in Life Assurance work by many practitioners. The "highly impressive" *Marian Pell* heads a large team which advised on a number of notable deals in 1997. Clients/Work: BAT Industries on the proposed demerger of its financial services division; AXA-UAP on the sale of AXA divisions; Securitas Capital and Swiss Re on the demutualisation and flotation of Scottish Amicable.

Lovell White Durrant (3ptnrs/10assts) The widely respected *John Young* leads a "genuinely dedicated" team and the firm is regarded as a "major player" with a level of resource and expertise which sets them apart from lower placed firms. Clients/Work: Acted for Prudential Corporation plc in successful £2.9bn bid in the demutualisation of Scottish Amicable; Acted for Unionamerica in US$215m takeover by MMI Companies Inc.; Acted for Liverpool Victoria's (reportedly) £60m acquisition of the motor and household insurance business of Landmark Insurance Company Ltd.

Clyde & Co (5ptnrs/2assts) The firm's slight drop in placing this year is a reflection of the fact that *Verner Southey* is now practising as a consultant and a general perception that as a niche practice it can no longer compete with the larger firms for "headline-grabbing deals." Despite this, Mr Southey is well-regarded in the field and his team is "near dedicated" to non-contentious work. Clients/Work: Munich Re on its investment in the Lloyds marine market through the acquisition of Apollo Underwriting Ltd and Syndicate 457 Capital Ltd; Generali

Worldwide Insurance Company Ltd on acquisition from Royal & Sun Alliance group of its Guernsey-based offshore life and pensions subsidiary.

Linklaters (3ptnrs/8assts plus a further pool of solicitors and fee-earners) Recent involvement in several major deals has raised their profile and indicates that they may be closing in on the leading firms. Their corporate strength enables the team, led by *Alan Barker*, to provide substantial specialist transactional advice. **Clients/Work:** Kleinwort Benson on the £1.75bn Norwich Union flotation: Sun Life and Provincial Holdings in the £900m acquisition of AXA Equity & Law Life Assurance, AXA Insurance and AXA Equity & Law Investment Managers from AXA-UAP.

Slaughter and May (9ptnrs/c.30assts) As with Linklaters, the firm's increasing presence in the field and ability to call on a strong corporate team indicates that they are catching up with the top firms. The department is headed by *Glen James*. **Clients/Work:** Norwich Union on its demutualisation and flotation; Guardian Royal Exchange in relation to the acquisition of PPP Healthcare Group plc; Abbey National plc in relation to its bid for Scottish Amicable.

Ashurst Morris Crisp (9ptnrs and a large number of assts form the insurance and reinsurance team) Described as "upwardly mobile" in the quality of transactions it has been dealing with in the last year. *Jeremy Hill* leads a "solid" department. **Clients/Work:** Acted for St Paul Companies on the sale of Minet Group to Aon; acted on takeover of Matheson Lloyds Investment Trust plc by Goshawk Insurance Holdings plc.

Barlow Lyde & Gilbert (5ptnrs/11assts) While most acknowledged the firm's strength in contentious insurance work, many expressed doubts that it had a sufficient market share or the resources to be considered a leading firm in non-contentious insurance. The team is led by *Michael Jones* and is considered to be biased towards litigation. **Clients/Work:** Advised on four catastrophe bond issues involving the securitisation of insurance portfolios; advised Liberty International (Holdings) Inc, Liberty Risk Services Ltd, Christchurch Holdings Plc and Churchill Insurance Company Ltd on their respective acquisition programmes.

DJ Freeman (3ptnrs/10assts) The presence of the well respected *Richard Spiller* ensures the firm's ranking. **Clients/Work:** Euclidian, Centre Re, Raphael Zorn Hemsley, SUM (Lloyds), Sedgwick, Chartwell.

Eversheds (3ptnrs/4assts) Have had a lower presence in non-contentious work in 1997 although the department head, *Hugh Bohling* remains a well-known name in the field. Recently recruited Jonathan Evans and Michael Wainwright for this department and it remains to be seen whether they will succeed in attracting higher profile work. **Clients/Work:** Advised Wren Underwriting Agencies Limited on its promotion of an Interavailablity Conversion Vehicle (Cathedral Capital Plc); acted for EW Blanch on the acquisition of Lloyds Brokers, Swire Fraser Insurance Holdings.

Norton Rose (2ptnrs/6assts plus 2 other ptnrs) Enter the list for the first time this year following several recommendations of the team. **Clients/Work:** The sale by Landmark (a subsidiary of AIG) of its household & motor insurance business to Liverpool Victoria Insurance Company; the demutualisation of Ansvar Mutual by the transfer of its insurance portfolio to Ansvar Limited.

Titmuss Sainer Dechert (4ptnrs/6assts) A number of changes took place during 1997, including department head Andrew Holderness moving to Clyde & Co. Questions were therefore asked about the department's capacity to succeed without him. However, Michael Smith is stepping down as senior partner to head the department full time. **Clients/Work:** Advised The Benfield & Rea Investment Trust plc on the acquisition of a portfolio of shares in Lloyds investment trusts from Fidelity.

LEADING INDIVIDUALS · LONDON NON-CONTENTIOUS

COATES Katherine Clifford Chance	
PELL Marian Herbert Smith	
RICHARDS Philip Freshfields	
YOUNG John Lovell White Durrant	
BARKER Alan Linklaters	
BOHLING Hugh Eversheds	
HILL Jeremy Ashurst Morris Crisp	
JAMES Glen Slaughter and May	
JONES Michael Barlow Lyde & Gilbert	
SOUTHEY Verner Clyde & Co	
SPILLER Richard D J Freeman	

SEE PROFILES AT THE END OF THIS SECTION

LEADERS' PROFILES · LONDON

AKEROYD, Tim
Elborne Mitchell, London (0171) 320 9000
Qualified 1971. Partner 1974. Specialist areas of practice are insurance and reinsurance litigation, including Lloyds litigation and professional indemnity defence. Born 1947.

BAKES, Martin
Herbert Smith, London (0171) 374 8000
Partner in Litigation Department (Insurance Section).
Specialisation: Has expertise in a wide range of insurance work, including policy disputes between insureds and insurers, subrogated actions against all types of professionals, local authorities, banks and many others, acting for major UK brokers and their errors and omissions insurers.
Career: Qualified in 1980. Became a Partner at *Herbert Smith* in 1987.
Personal: Educated at Downing College, Cambridge.

BANDURKA, Andrew A.
Holman, Fenwick & Willan, London
(0171) 488 2300
Partner in Insurance/Reinsurance Department.
Specialisation: Principal area of practice is insurance and reinsurance related. Work covers insurance and reinsurance and professional negligence (insurance/ reinsurance brokers and managing agents). Author of numerous articles in *Lloyds List* and other publications. Regular speaker at seminars world wide.
Prof. Memberships: British Insurance Law Association.
Career: Degrees in Mathematics and Statistics. Masters degree in Operational Research. Called to the Bar in 1989. Qualified as a solicitor in 1989. Became a Partner at *Holman Fenwick & Willan* in 1993.
Personal: Born 31st December 1956.

BARKER, Alan V.
Linklaters, London (0171) 456 3388
Partner 1986. Corporate Department.
Specialisation: Responsible for insurance companies practice, dealing with a wide range of corporate work including acquisitions, disposals, joint ventures, reconstructions, regulatory problems, etc., particularly in relation to insurance companies. Advises a number of leading UK insurance companies, both life and non-life and both listed and mutual. In addition, advises many non-UK insurance companies on UK and European legal matters.

BOHLING, Hugh Hovey
Eversheds, London (0171) 919 4500
Specialisation: Specialises in the introduction and structuring of corporate capital to Lloyds of London: corporate finance and mergers and acquisitions in the insurance industry; group reorganisations; corporate and regulatory advice for Lloyds agents and brokers; directors' responsibilities; run off agreements. Is a member of BILA and of the Lloyds Advisers Group.
Prof. Memberships: Was a founder Committee member of Lloyds Corporate Capital Association where he remains Secretary. As a member of Lloyds Agents' Lawyers Group, reviewed contracts with Equitas and Lloyds Settlement and Contribution Agreements. Sponsor of applications for corporate Membership of Lloyds. Is Director of Malayan Insurance Company (UK) Limited and adviser to many companies both public and private. Speaks and writes regularly.
Career: Articled at *Allen & Overy*, qualified in 1983 and admitted Partner in 1987 at *Waltons & Morse*. Joined Eversheds in May 1996 when the *Waltons & Morse* corporate and insurance teams joined *Eversheds*.

BROOK, Nigel
Clyde & Co, London (0171) 623 1244
Specialisation: Reinsurance disputes, mainly London market; on the direct side, credit insurance, professional indemnity and regulatory. Drafts and advises on wordings. Author of various articles and editor of Clydes' "Reinsurance Update."
Career: Qualified 1981, partner 1985.

COATES, Katherine
Clifford Chance, London (0171) 600 1000
Partner in Securities Group.
Specialisation: Specialises in non-contentious insurance matters including UK and European regulation, start-ups, mergers and acquisitions, demutualisations, capital raising, distribution arrangements, product development, Lloyds; investment funds including venture capital, futures, UCITS, investment trusts, derivatives, exchange regulation and other financial services matters.
Career: Articled Coward Chance/Clifford Chance; qualified 1983; Partner Clifford Chance since 1990.
Personal: Educated at King Edward VI High School for Girls, Edgbaston, Birmingham; Somerville College, Oxford (MA Jurisprudence); Law Society Finals. Born 1959; resides Godalming.

COHEN, David
Clifford Chance, London (0171) 600 1000

CONNOLEY, Mark F.
Richards Butler, London (0171) 247 6555
Partner and Head of the Insurance and Reinsurance Group.
Specialisation: Practice extends across a broad range of insurance (both marine and non-marine) and reinsurance matters usually, although not exclusively, from the contentious standpoint. Has recently had considerable involvement in the 'Lloyds' Litigation. Has acted for policyholders, overseas reinsurers, brokers, E&O underwriters and London Market companies.
Career: Qualified 1980. Partner at Richards Butler since 1987.
Personal: Born 1955. Attended St Edmund Hall, Oxford (Jurisprudence).

CROLY, Colin V.
Barlow Lyde & Gilbert, London
(0171) 247 2277
Partner and Head of Reinsurance and International Risks.
Specialisation: Advises on all areas of reinsurance and international risks, including contract wording and dispute resolution. Joint Editor 'Reinsurance Practice and the Law,' published by LLP. Speaks regularly on a number of aspects relating to reinsurance/insurance at various conferences, including such matters as drafting and construction of reinsurance contracts and coverage issues in respect of asbestos, environmental, tobacco and Y2K issues.
Prof. Memberships: Secretary General of AIDA (Association Internationale de Droits des Assurances), and Chairman of the Reinsurance Working Party. Government Appointed member Insurance Brokers Registration Counsel (IBRC).
Career: Qualified in 1971 in the Republic of

South Africa. Practising attorney in Transvaal 1974-75. Qualified in England and Wales 1980. Joined Barlow Lyde & Gilbert 1976, Partner 1980.
Personal: Born 9th October 1949. Read economics and law at Cape Town University, followed by a Masters Degree in International Law at London University. Recreations include gardening, reading, theatre, gym. Lives in Central London.

DICKINSON, Graham
Barlow Lyde & Gilbert, London
(0171) 247 2277
Specialisation: All aspects of insurance liability work but primarily Employers Liability, Industrial Disease, Motor and Public Liability claims. Extensive experience in major injury and loss claims and defence of group action.
Prof. Memberships: Member of the Chartered Insurance Institute
Career: Qualified 1978. Partner Robin Thompson & Partners 1980. Founding Partner Dickinson Simpson (Birmingham) 1983. Senior Partner Rowley Dickinson (Birmingham) 1989. Appointed Head of General Insurance Division, Barlow Lyde & Gilbert 1994.

DOBIAS, Michael
Davies Arnold Cooper, London
(0171) 936 2222
Partner and Head of Reinsurance Interest Group.
Specialisation: Main areas of practice in insurance and reinsurance matters, both domestic and international, covering arbitration and litigation. Includes facultative and treaty contracts. Primarily represents defendants. Author of 'The Trials of Treaty Disputes' jointly with David McIntosh and 'The Scales of Justice: the Need for a Defence Bar Representation Body.' Lectured extensively at conferences and seminars on insurance and reinsurance issues.
Prof. Memberships: Law Society, International Association of Defence Counsel, London Solicitors Litigation Association.
Career: Joined Davies Arnold Cooper in 1973. Qualified in 1975. Partner 1980. Head of Reinsurance Interest Group.
Personal: Born 28th September 1950. Attended Birmingham University 1969-72. Leisure pursuits include sport, cinema and wine tasting. Lives in Chigwell, Essex.

DOULTON, Roger
Barlow Lyde & Gilbert, London
(0171) 247 2277
Specialisation: Insurance and reinsurance policy coverage and wording disputes, policy drafting, professional indemnity (especially brokers and surveyors), property claims (subrogation actions, fraudulent arson, wording), fidelity claims.
Prof. Memberships: Member of the Chartered Institute of Insurers, Fellow of the Royal Society of Arts, Member of the Academy of Experts and, Accredited Mediator for the centre of Dispute Resolution (CEDR). Past Chairman City Forum and Editor of British Insurance Law Journal.
Career: Assistant Solicitor at Herbert Smith & Co. and Davies Arnold Cooper. Founder partner of Winward Fearon & Co. Since 1995 partner at Barlow Lyde & Gilbert.

Personal: French horn playing, sailing, incompetent cricket, the arts generally (especially opera), sport (especially rugby football and cricket), politics, food, his wife and children. Education: M.A.(Oxon), Rugby School.

DUFF, John
Holman, Fenwick & Willan, London
(0171) 488 2300
Partner in Insurance/Reinsurance Department.
Specialisation: Main areas of practice are reinsurance and professional indemnity. Author of various articles and a frequent speaker worldwide.
Career: Qualified in 1982. Joined Holman Fenwick & Willan in 1983, becoming a Partner in 1987.

ELBORNE, Mark E.M.
Cameron McKenna, London
(0171) 367 3000
Partner in Insurance and Reinsurance Department.
Specialisation: Principal areas of practice involve acting in claims and disputes for insurers and reinsurers of banks and financial institutions, directors and officers, accountants, financial advisers and stockbrokers, Lloyds agents and Lloyds brokers; advising insurers and reinsurers on policy wordings and construction in insurance and reinsurance contracts; acting in major reinsurance arbitration and litigation disputes and advising Reinsurers generally with clients in the London market, Europe, Middle and Far East, USA and Bermuda. Lectured in Bermuda at International Reinsurance Congress and in Hong Kong and London at various conferences on financial institutions insurance, Directors' and Officers' liability cover and on reinsurance.
Prof. Memberships: Law Society, Chartered Institute of Insurers, Society of Insurance Receivers.
Career: Qualified 1983 while at Cameron Markby Hewitt and became a Partner in 1988.
Personal: Born 22nd January 1958. School Trustee. Leisure pursuits include golf, swimming, tennis, shooting and opera. Lives near Uppingham, Rutland. Married with 5 children.

FARTHING, Peter
Clyde & Co, London (0171) 623 1244
Specialisation: Has covered almost every aspect of insurance and reinsurance: marine: hull, cargo, war and liability, contract frustration; non-marine: property, jewellers' block, fine art, goods in transit, kidnap and ransom, E & O, D & O, pollution, personal accident, personal stop loss, employers' liability, product liability, performance guarantee, contractors' all risks; reinsurance: excess of loss, quota share, run-off covers, LMX, pools, commutations; brokers' liabilities; issues involving Lloyds Names, Managing and Members' Agents; recently involved in 'Napier v. Kershaw' (1993), a case of fundamental importance in subrogation law.
Career: Clyde & Co. 1973 to date. Became a Partner in 1977.

FOX, Steven C.
Ince & Co, London (0171) 623 2011
Specialisation: Specialises in commercial litigation (both court and arbitration) principally involving insurance/ reinsurance disputes (both marine and non-marine) and shipping matters. Has taken matters as far as the House of Lords on three occasions.

Career: Articled *Ince & Co*; qualified 1983; Partner 1989.

Personal: Educated Trent College, Nottingham; St John's College, Oxford (1980 BA Jurisprudence).

GREENLEY, Simon K.P.T.

Reynolds Porter Chamberlain, London
(0171) 242 2877
Partner in Insurance, Reinsurance and Professional Indemnity Department.

Specialisation: Main area of practice is insurance, reinsurance and professional liability litigation. Work covers litigation for professional indemnity underwriters, including banks and other financial institutions, financial advisors, brokers, accountants, surveyors, Directors and Officers, acts in a wide range of non-marine insurance and reinsurance disputes for Lloyds syndicates and Company underwriters, including commercial property risks, property, fine arts and jewellers' block policies. Also handles policy disputes and liability litigation (US, European and domestic).

Prof. Memberships: Law Society. British Insurance Law Association.

Career: Qualified in 1980. Became a Partner in 1983.

Personal: Born 29 January 1957. Leisure interests include golf, tennis, rackets, squash, art, antique furniture. Hurlingham Club and Walton Heath Golf Club. Married and lives in London.

HALL, J.E.

Cameron McKenna, London
(0171) 367 3000

Specialisation: Reinsurance, Professional Indemnity, Contingency Insurance and General Insurance Advice. Major cases in recent years include Pan Atlantic -v- Pine Top (for the brokers, BRS), First State -v- St Katherine's, Yasuda (and others) (for the brokers, PWS) and Schal -v- Norwich Union (for the quantity surveyors Gardiner and Theobald). Highlights of the past year include: Successes in DSG Retail -v-QBE International (for the Defendants Insurers) and Alfred McAlpine -v- BAI (Run-off) Limited (for the Plaintiffs). In addition, currently acting for Lincoln National Reinsurance Companies in relation to the personal accident LMX spiral.

Career: Ardingly College (1958-1967); Sidney Sussex College, Cambridge University (1968-1971); *Parlett Kent & Co* (1980-2); *Berrymans* (1982-6); *Hewitt Woollatt & Chown*; Subsequently *Cameron Markby Hewitt*; Subsequently *Cameron McKenna* (1986-date); Became a partner 1989.

HANSON, John

Barlow Lyde & Gilbert, London
(0171) 247 2277
Partner

Specialisation: Main areas of practice are insurance brokers, property insurance, reinsurance and international risk transfer. Author of various articles; joint author of Lloyds of London Press 'Reinsurance Practice and the Law.' Co-author of 'All Risks Property Insurance' textbook published by Lloyds of London Press 1995 and winner of the 1996 B.I.L.A. book prize. Contributing author to 'Insurance Coverage Disputes' shortly to be published by LLP . Has made regular conference appearances, particularly with DYP and EuroForum.

Career: Admitted in England 1977. Admitted as a Barrister and Solicitor in Western and Northern Australia in 1978. Partner Commercial Litigation in Australia 1981-5. Joined *Barlow Lyde & Gilbert* in 1986, becoming a Partner in 1987.

Personal: Born 19th January 1952. Attended Oxford University. Jurisprudence 1973; Law Society Part II 1974. Lives in Whitstable, Kent. Interest include tennis, swimming, cycling, reading, cinema, art (visual).

HARDY, Tim

Barlow Lyde & Gilbert, London
(0171) 247 2277

Specialisation: For over 16 years has advised and represented participants in the insurance and reinsurance markets in London and around the world upon policy coverage issues and resolution of disputes in multi-national litigation, arbitration or other forms of dispute resolution in most leading jurisdictions. Extensive experience of London Market pooling and underwriting agency problems and coverage issues associated with North America and other long-tail liabilities, insolvencies and commutations. Additional wide experience of insurance cases with an international element in respect of liability/ property programmes, bond and credit and political risk insurance, mortgage indemnity, contingency/ cancellation coverage and overseas motor and other schemes. Presently serving on London Market committees advising upon policy drafting in wake of leading insurance and reinsurance cases. In addition to conference presentations and published articles, contributing author of 'Reinsurance Practice and the Law' (LLP 1993, looseleaf). In 1998 became CEDR accredited mediator.

Prof. Memberships: Chairman of the British Insurance Law Association since 1996; Chartered Insurance Institute; Law Society.

Career: *Barlow Lyde & Gilbert* since qualification in 1982, partner since 1987.

Personal: Educated at RGS High Wycombe and Balliol College, Oxford graduating in Jurisprudence. Lives in London.

HEPWORTH, Allan

Ince & Co, London (0171) 623 2011

Specialisation: Specialises in non-marine and marine reinsurance litigation. In recent years his practice has had particular emphasis on London market reinsurance problems arising out of the various LMX spirals. He has also handled major reinsurance disputes such as the 'Pan Atlantic v. Pine Top' litigation and the dispute arising out of the death of Robert Maxwell. His practice also extends to dealing with numerous direct insurance problems involving in recent years major disputes arising out of loss of hire open covers, cargo insurances and political risk contracts.

Career: Allan was educated at Rugby School and obtained a Law with French degree from Birmingham University. He joined *Ince & Co* as an articled clerk in 1986, qualified in 1988 and became a partner in 1995. In the early 1990s, Allan spent 15 months on secondment to the Legal Department of the reinsurance division of a major US insurance and reinsurance company.

HIGGINS, David E.A.

Herbert Smith, London (0171) 374 8000
Partner and Head of Insurance Litigation Section.

Specialisation: Specialises in insurance and reinsurance law. Many of his cases have an international element requiring advice on jurisdiction and choice of law.

Prof. Memberships: Assistant Recorder of the Crown Court and Chairman of the Insurance Law Sub-Committee of the City of London Law Society.

Career: Qualified in 1970 and joined *Herbert Smith* in 1971. Became a Partner of the firm in 1977.

Personal: Educated at St. Peter's School, York and Newcastle University.

HILL, Jeremy G.

Ashurst Morris Crisp, London
(0171) 638 1111
Partner in Company/ Commercial Department. Head of Insurance.

Specialisation: Lloyds of London and London Market: handles all non-contentious matters, particularly policy wordings; acquisition, disposal, flotation of agencies, brokers and insurance and reinsurance companies; regulatory issues; captive insurance vehicles; insurance reconstructions and insolvencies; and creation and registration of Lloyds Corporate Members. Acted in the flotation of Delian Lloyds Investment Trust PLC, HCG Lloyds Investment Trust PLC and Archer Dedicated PLC; advised on the agreed merger of Angerstein Underwriting Trust PLC with Delian Lloyds Investment Trust PLC and the establishment of London Processing Centre; acted for the St Paul Companies on the sale of Minet to Aon and for Goshawk Insurance Holdings plc on its takeover of Matheson Lloyds Investment Trust plc. Author of 'Willis Corroon Guide to Directors' and Officers' Liability,' and of articles in publications on Lloyds and the London Insurance market.

Prof. Memberships: Chartered Insurance Institute, Law Society.

Career: Qualified in 1984. Joined *Ashurst Morris Crisp* in 1982, spending a year seconded to Lloyds of London in 1985, and becoming a Partner in 1992.

Personal: Born 4th November 1958. Attended Bootham School, York 1972-77 and Pembroke College, Oxford 1977-80. Leisure interests include sailing, fishing and antiques. Lives in London.

JAMES, Glen W.

Slaughter and May, London
(0171) 600 1200

Specialisation: Practice covers all work in the fields of Company/Corporate Finance, including mergers and acquisitions, issues and flotations and corporate restructurings. Additional interest in non-contentious insurance and reinsurance work.

Prof. Memberships: The Law Society; Securities Institute.

Career: Qualified 1976. Articled at *Slaughter and May* 1974-76. Assistant Solicitor 1976-1983. Partner since 1983.

Personal: Born 22 August 1952. Educated at King's College School, Wimbledon and New College, Oxford.

JEFFERIS, Chris J.Q.

Ince & Co, London (0171) 623 2011

Specialisation: Chris has a diverse practice within the main core area of insurance and reinsurance, ranging from drafting and advising on specialist wordings for underwriters and brokers through to advising reinsurers on making or defending claims to dealing with all

types of dispute resolution often involving a multi-jurisdictional element. In recent years he has been involved in the major litigation arising out of the mortage indemnity guarantee class as well as other credit, political risk and contigency insurance problems. He also regularly advises in relation to problems concerning brokers both in a professional indemnity context as well as more general advice often involving insolvency matters. Has recently been involved in the GIO v Liverpool & London case ultimately resolved through ADR and settlement at the doors of the Court. Chris also specialises in insurance and contractual problems which arise in the offshore sphere and is currently involved in matters concerning FPSOs and complex offshore production platforms. More recently, the hanging regulatory climate at Lloyds has led to involvement in advising in relation to Lloyds investigatory powers and in disciplinary proceedings.
Career: Educated Churston Ferrers Grammar School and Magdalene College, Cambridge (BA 1981). Articled at *Ince & Co*, qualified 1984, seconded to Lloyds Regulatory Department for a spell, partner of *Ince & Co* 1990.

JONES, Michael E.
Barlow Lyde & Gilbert, London
(0171) 247 2277
Specialisation: Specialises in the formation, authorisation, regulation, sale and purchase and restructuring of insurance businesses both in the Lloyds and company markets. Advises on applications for corporate membership of Lloyds. Has structured and advised on products emerging as alternative ways of financing risk such as catastrophe bonds as well as on forms of traditional risk financing, including advice on the formation and operations of direct and reinsurance captives, mutual companies and all related issues. Advised H M Government in connection with Pool Re and Equitas Limited. Author of various articles on insurance and a contributor to 'Reinsurance and the Law' published by Lloyds of London Press. Speaker at seminars and conferences.
Prof. Memberships: Law Society. Solicitors' European Group. British-German Jurists Association. The City of London Solicitors' Company (Insurance Law Sub-Committee) and The Chartered Insurance Institute.
Career: BA (Hons) in Law and German. Qualified in 1981, *Clifford Chance* 1982-1988. Partner with *Barlow, Lyde & Gilbert* from 1988.
Personal: Lives in London. Speaks German. Leisure interests include tennis, rugby, golf and music. Tenor with London Symphony Chorus and London Welsh Chorale.

KENDALL, David R.
D J Freeman, London (0171) 583 4055
Partner and Head of Insurance Department.
Specialisation: Main area of practice is insurance and reinsurance. Acts for Lloyds syndicates, for major UK and overseas insurers and reinsurers, for liquidators and for Lloyds brokers in litigation and arbitration. Has particular experience of advising on pool and syndicate group reinsurance programmes and on insurance coverage. Advises on regulatory, structural and management issues affecting

Lloyds, particularly in relation to run-off and corporate capital. Lloyds panel arbitrator. Cases have included 'PCW Syndicates v PCW Reinsurers' (reinsurance), 'Suncorp v Milano' (pools/reinsurance), 'DR Insurance v Central National' (jurisdiction), 'Munich Re v Weavers' (reinsurance), 'Milano v Walbrook' (reinsurance) and Re: A Company 1991 (insurance insolvency). Regularly contributes articles to ReActions, Lloyds List and other insurance publications. Speaks regularly at conferences and *D J Freeman* seminars.
Prof. Memberships: Law Society, Federation of Insurance and Corporate Counsel, BILA, ARIAS, LMAA, British-German Jurists and SEG.
Career: Qualified in 1981. Worked at *Hedleys* 1979-87, from 1985 as a Partner. Joined *D J Freeman* in 1988 as a Partner, becoming Head of Department in 1993.
Personal: Born 17th September 1955. Holds an LLB (Hons) 1976, and MA (Business Law) 1982.

LEONARD, Stephen M.
Fishburn Boxer, London (0171) 925 2884
Partner since 1992 in Insurance and Reinsurance Litigation Department.
Specialisation: Principal area of practice is insurance and reinsurance litigation and arbitration. Advises insurers and reinsurers in a wide array of actual and potential disputes. Other main area of practice is product development including drafting insurance and reinsurance documentation. Acts for Lloyds syndicates, insurance and reinsurance companies and insurance brokers.
Personal: Born 16th June 1959. Educated at St Edmund Hall, Oxford and LL.M in Commercial Law from the University of London.

LEWIS, Stephen
Clifford Chance, London (0171) 600 1000
Specialisation: Commercial: Insurance and reinsurance law - advisory, litigation and arbitration.
Career: Qualified as Solicitor in 1974, LLB (Lond) 1979. Became Partner in 1985.

MACKIE, Francis
Norton Rose, London (0171) 283 6000
Specialisation: Partner practising in the international commercial insurance and reinsurance market, with clients being London market insurers (Lloyds and the company market) and the international insurance market, with clients from Europe, USA, Middle East and the Far East. The practice involves both contentious matters and policy advisory work as well as regulatory matters and advising on the creation of the insurance companies. Current high profile cases are - acting for the Plaintiffs in the continuing 'SAIL v Farex' litigation in London, acting for the successful Lloyds Syndicate Plaintiffs in the Aggregate Extension Clause/MIPI Lineslip litigation, acting for a section of reinsurers (and successfully) in a London Arbitration concerning the major property loss/damage claim arising out of Iraq's invasion of Kuwait, acting for reinsurers in the ongoing large and complex Eastern European ship building disputes/arbitrations, also continuing to act on behalf of the Plaintiffs in the ongoing 'Syndicate 947 v Black Sea & Baltic' litigation which may go to the House of

Lords on the question of recovery of legal costs from reinsurers.
Career: Admitted 1976. After qualification practised for two years in Newcastle and then moved to London, becoming a partner at *Clyde & Co.* in 1984. In November 1993 he moved over to *Norton Rose* to become a partner in the Insurance Group.

McINTOSH, David
Davies Arnold Cooper, London
(0171) 936 2222
See under Personal Injury: Mainly Defendant, p. 619

McKENZIE, Kenneth
Davies Arnold Cooper, London
(0171) 936 2222
Partner in Litigation Department.
Specialisation: Main areas of practice are insurance and reinsurance litigation, with emphasis on financial risks and institutions, professional indemnity, directors and officers, and Lloyds related matters. Acted in 'Iron Trades v. Imperio Banerto' and 'Stockwell v. Outhwaite.' Author of various articles on insurance, reinsurance and particularly directors' and officers' liability. Has given numerous lectures and seminars.
Prof. Memberships: Law Society.
Career: Qualified in 1978. Assistant Solicitor at *Clyde & Co* 1978-83. Joined *Davies Arnold Cooper* in 1984, becoming a Partner in 1986.
Personal: Born 18th June 1953. Attended Trinity School, Croydon, 1964-71 and the University of Exeter 1971-4. Leisure interests include music and golf. Lives in Chiswick, London.

MENDELOWITZ, Michael
Barlow Lyde & Gilbert, London
(0171) 247 2277
Partner in Reinsurance Division.
Specialisation: All aspects of insurance and reinsurance, with emphasis on complex reinsurance claims, environmental and other long-tail problems, insurance insolvency and disputes concerning intepretation of contracts.
Prof. Memberships: Association Internationale de Droit des Assurances (Assistant Secretary-General), British Insurance Law Association, UK Enviromental Law Association, Law Society and Chartered Insurance Institute.
Career: Practised as a barrister in South Africa before joining *Barlow Lyde & Gilbert* in 1987. Re-qualified as a solicitor in 1989 and became a partner in 1990. Frequent speaker at conferences in UK and overseas on topics ranging from arbitration and alternative dispute resolution in reinsurance to liability for pollution and toxic torts. Numerous articles published in legal and market journals. Co-author and co-ordinating editor of 'Reinsurance Practice and the Law' (Lloyds of London Press, 1993)
Personal: Born 1952. Educated at University of the Witwatersrand (B.A., LI.B.) and Oxford University (B.C.L.) as a Rhodes Scholar. Lives in North London. Interests include his family, music and skiing holidays.

MUNDEN, Michael R.
Herbert Smith, London (0171) 374 8000
Partner in Insurance and Reinsurance Group.
Specialisation: Michael Munden is a senior partner in the firm who is responsible for the firm's insurance practice internationally. He has regularly advised many of the world's leading insurance and reinsurance organisations in

most aspects of insurance and reinsurance law as well as many aspects of the general law. He has particular experience in dealing with disputes involving insurance brokers. He has advised on and conducted litigation and arbitration in London and in many foreign jurisdictions. Michael has considerable experience in alternative dispute resolutions procedures. He is Chairman of the Litigation sub-committee of the City of London Law Society.

O'MAHONEY, Gerald
Davies Arnold Cooper, London
(0171) 936 2222
Partner in Commercial Litigation Department.
Specialisation: Handles commercial litigation and arbitration, insurance, reinsurance, professional indemnity and liability. Has written several articles on law reform and Lloyds disciplinary procedures. Charge-out rate is £195 - £240 per hour.
Prof. Memberships: Law Society.
Career: Started as a Legal Executive. Previously with *Robert Gore & Co* 1977-82 and *Colombotti & Partners* 1983-85. Qualified in 1984. Joined *Davies Arnold Cooper* in 1985 and became a Partner in 1987.
Personal: Born 1st November 1953. Educated at Gunnersbury Grammar School 1965-70 and the College of Law 1982-83. Interests include golf, rugby, good food and wine, reading and current affairs. Lives in London.

O'NEILL, Terry
Clifford Chance, London (0171) 600 1000
Partner.
Specialisation: Contentious and non-contentious insurance, reinsurance, Lloyds and professional indemnity.
Career: Called to Bar Lincoln's Inn 1973; joined *Clifford Turner* 1977; qualified as Solicitor 1978; Partner *Clifford Chance* since 1980; Solicitor Advocate (Civil) 1994.
Personal: Educated at Ratcliffe College, Leicester; University College, London (1965 LLB, 1973 PhD). Born 1944. Resides London.

PARKER, Raj D.
Freshfields, London (0171) 936 4000
Partner in Litigation Department, Solicitor Advocate.
Specialisation: Main area of practice is insurance and reinsurance work. Regular speaker at insurance industry seminars. Substantial general commercial dispute resolution practice. Also deals with sports law, acting for the Football Association in all advisory and contentious work.
Prof. Memberships: Law Society; Society of Solicitor Advocates. Nominated Court of Arbitration for Sport ('CAS') Arbitrator. Member of British Insurance Law Association, British Association for Sport and the Law.
Career: Attended Bar School (1983) and practised as a barrister until 1985. At the Corporation of Lloyds for a year 1985-86 on an Inquiry. Joined *Freshfields* in 1986 and became a Partner in 1993.
Personal: Born 19th September 1960. Educated at Christ's College 1972-79 and Southampton University 1979-82. Recreations include sport, music, theatre and ornithology. Lives in London.

PAYTON, Michael
Clyde & Co, London (0171) 623 1244
See under Professional Negligence, p. 670

PELL, Marian
Herbert Smith, London (0171) 374 8000
Partner and Head of Insurance Section of Company Department.
Specialisation: Has expertise in corporate insurance and reinsurance work involving mutual and proprietary life and general insurance companies, including mergers and acquisitions, demutualisation, restructuring of insurance businesses and the establishment, authorisation and regulation of insurance businesses and insurance intermediaries.
Career: Qualified in 1976 and became a Partner at *Herbert Smith* in 1984.
Personal: Educated at Southampton University.

POWELL, John F.
Lovell White Durrant, London
(0171) 236 0066
Specialisation: International Insurance and Reinsurance dispute resolution, particularly arbitration. Regular conference speaker and contributor on Insurance, Reinsurance and Arbitration to various publications.
Prof. Memberships: ARIAS - Vice Chairman, Committee member and co-founder. Fellow of the Chartered Institute of Arbitrators. CEDR accredited mediator.
Career: Qualified 1970. Joined *Lovell White Durrant* in 1993. Involved in insurance dispute resolution for whole of professional career. Initially maritime insurance. Since 1980 predominantly reinsurance, advisory and dispute resolution worldwide: US, Bermuda, Japan and Far East as well as UK and Europe.

RICHARDS, Philip
Freshfields, London (0171) 936 4000
Partner in Corporate Department. Head of Insurance Group.
Specialisation: Deals with corporate law including mergers and acquisitions, joint ventures and specialises in transactions involving utilities and mutual and proprietary life and general insurance companies, and regulatory matters.
Prof. Memberships: Law Society.
Career: Qualified in 1980, becoming a Partner in 1987.
Personal: Born in 1956. Attended Lincoln College, Oxford.

ROGAN, Peter J.H.
Ince & Co, London (0171) 623 2011
Peter Rogan is the current Chairman of the International Bar Association Insurance Committee. He specialises in advising in the insurance and reinsurance fields and is joint Chairman of the *Ince & Co* Insurance Business Group. His reinsurance practice is litigation oriented and diverse, acting for clients both in London and abroad on high profile non-marine, aviation and marine reinsurance disputes, including, in 1998, GIO v Liverpool & London (for the Club), for HIH in the Charman Whole account dispute and representing US interests in a major long tail arbitration. Past cases included a number setting important precedent in areas of legal difficulty, such as Pine Top, on non disclosure, and PCW on moral hazard. In direct insurance work, his practice is almost as broad, again encompassing a variety of classes, most significanty professional indemnity insurance mátters for brokers, accountants and solicitors and others in a range of high value cases arising from major

market losses and disputes since the late 1970s.
Prof. Memberships: Aside from the IBA, he is a Committee member of ARIAS (UK).
Career: Educated at Stellenbosch University and Kings College, London, he spent two years at London brokers *Willis Faber* before joining *Ince & Co* in 1977, to become a partner in 1982.
Personal: Born 1950, resides London, leisure interests include family, theatre, tennis, golf and skiing. Lives in London.

SACHER, Jonathan
Paisner & Co, London (0171) 353 0299
Specialisation: Head of *Paisner & Co's* Insurance/Reinsurance Group. Work focuses on reinsurance/ insurance litigation and arbitration and commutation for a wide variety of UK and international insurers and reinsurers. Writes for numerous publications including *ReActions, Review, Reinsurance* and *Insurance Day* and has spoken at a number of International Insurance/Reinsurance conferences. Has acted in the following reported Reinsurance/Insurance cases: In 'Re a Company ex parte Pritchard;' In 'Re a Company 1991;' 'Pan Atlantic v Hassneh;' 'Sun Alliance v RJL and Webster;' 'R v Insurance Ombudsman ex parte Aegon Life Assurance Limited.'
Prof. Memberships: Vice Chairman of the British Insurance Law Association, member of ARIAS (UK); International Association of Insurance Receivers; former member of the Law Society International Committee and China Working Party; past chairman of the London Young Solicitors Group.
Career: Arts and Law degree from Cape Town University, South Africa; solicitor of the Supreme Court of England and Wales (1981); Advocate of the Supreme Court of South Africa (1978).

SCHOFIELD, Belinda
Cameron McKenna, London
(0171) 367 3000
Partner in Insurance and Reinsurance Group.
Specialisation: Principal areas of practice are handling professional indemnity claims against accountants, actuaries, Lloyds agents, financial institutions and insurance brokers and Directors' & Officers' liability acting for insurers and insured. In addition advising on general insurance and reinsurance matters including advising on policy wording construction. Experienced in handling commercial disputes. Speaks at numerous market seminars.
Prof. Memberships: Law Society.
Career: Qualified in 1980 became a partner in *Hewitt Woollacott & Chown* in 1986 which merged with *Cameron Markby* 1989, which merged with *McKenna and Co* in 1997.
Personal: Born 11th June 1956.

SIMISON, Sheila
Barlow Lyde & Gilbert, London
(0171) 247 2277
Specialisation: Partner specialising in all aspects of non-marine /general/ direct insurance claims, coverage disputes, drafting policy wording, litigation, subrogation and third party claims; property insurance, bloodstock, contigency, non-appearance, brokers E&O, jewellers' block are specialities. Has considerable experience in conducting commercial court litigation. With partner,

Yvonne Jefferies, acted for insurers in Gerling-Konzern General Insurance Company -v- Polygram Holdings Inc.
Prof. Memberships: Member of the Commercial Court Users Committee for 10 years.
Career: Trained *Hewitt Woollacott & Chown*; qualified 1979; assistant *Clyde & Co* 1981 - 1984, partner 1984 -1997, partner *Barlow Lyde & Gilbert* 1997 onwards.
Personal: Born 1954; Educated at Faringdon County Grammar School for Girls and at Birmingham University (1976 LLB Hons); Interests include music and horse racing. Lives in London.

SINFIELD, Nicholas
Davies Arnold Cooper, London
(0171) 936 2222
Head of Insurance Services Sector and National Head of Litigation.
Specialisation: Partner specialising in professional indemnity, coverage and reinsurance litigation. Practice also covers fire and property insurance coverage disputes. Interesting cases include the JD Wood consequential insurance litigation; Asbestos London Market Coverage disputes; defence of RMH Outhwaite (Underwriting) Agency in Names litigation; Judicial Review process of PIA Pensions; Daichi and Kobe reinsurance litigation and Spanish D&O cases relating to the Banesto scandal. Regularly addresses conferences and has lectured as a guest of Stamford Law School on catastrophe excess of loss insurance. Has written various articles on insurance and fraud, and insurance/reinsurance coverage issues.
Prof. Memberships: Law Society; British Insurance Law Association, Arson Prevention Bureau.
Career: Qualified 1984. *Reynolds Porter Chamberlain* 1984-1987. *Davies Arnold Cooper* since 1987, partner since 1989.
Personal: Educated at Bedford School 1965-1977, University College, London 1977-1980 and at the College of Law 1981. Leisure pursuits include ergometer and gym training. Born 22nd March 1959. Lives in Chiswick. Married with four children

SMITH, Roderick
Clyde & Co, London (0171) 623 1244
Specialisation: Insurance and Reinsurance Disputes. Serves London Market and overseas insurers. Has wide experience of marine and non-marine insurance disputes often of an international nature. Marine cargo, goods in transit, contingency, delayed start-up and business interruption, credit, political and financial risks, fine art, jewellers' block, cash in transit, professional indemnity, personal accident including Key Man insurance. Reinsurance: excess of loss, quota share, run-off reinsurance and commutations. Has also represented parties in relation to Lloyd's disciplinary investigations and proceedings. Experienced in the use of Mediation. Extensive involvement in drafting and review of insurance and reinsurance wordings including new product development.
Career: Qualified as an attorney in South Africa in 1976. Joined *Clyde & Co* in 1977. Qualified in England and Wales in 1980. Partner in *Clyde & Co* in 1982.

SOUTHEY, Verner
Clyde & Co, London (0171) 623 1244
Consultant with Clyde & Co.
Specialisation: Corporate insurance work in all its aspects for public and private corporations and partnerships engaged in insurance activities at Lloyds and in the London, European and international insurance markets.
Career: Formerly practised as attorney in Rhodesia (now Zimbabwe). Practised in the City and admitted as a solicitor in England in 1977 and joined *Clyde & Co.* as Head of Corporate in 1986. Since September 1996 acts as Consultant to *Clyde & Co* and to entities in the insurance industry.
Personal: Born 1st October 1942. Educated Grahamstown and University of Cape Town, South Africa. Lives in London and the Dordogne and devotes leisure to wife, wine, sport, music and international commuting.

SPILLER, Richard J.
D J Freeman, London (0171) 583 4055
Partner
Specialisation: Company commercial lawyer specialising in insurance. Practice covers corporate finance, M & A, insolvency and run-off, agency agreements and policy wordings. Recent transactions include the £800m reinsurance of Lioncover Insurance Company to Equitas Reinsurance.
Prof. Memberships: Member of City of London Law Society Commercial and Insurance sub-committees.
Career: Qualified 1980. At *Norton Rose* 1981-1983. Joined *D J Freeman* 1983, Partner 1985.

STANLEY, Ed
Hammond Suddards, London
(0171) 655 1089
Fax: (0171) 655 1001 Email: ed.stanley
Specialisation: Reinsurance and all areas of commercial insurance litigation, notably professional indemnity disputes involving brokers and underwriting agencies.
Career: Articled *Elborne Mitchell*, Qualified 1984. Assistant Solicitor *Elborne Mitchell* 1984-1997. Partner *Elborne Mitchell* 1989-1997. Partner *Hammond Suddards* 1997 to date.
Personal: Born 1959. Educated at St Brendan's College, Bristol and Exeter College, Oxford. Leisure: football and playing keyboards. Resides: London.

TAYLOR, Peter L.
Lovell White Durrant, London
(0171) 236 0066
Specialisation: Worked in marine insurance and dry shipping litigation before specialising in reinsurance dispute resolution. Experienced in toxic tort, latent disease and liability insurance and reinsurance, chiefly from viewpoint of the London, continental and Far East markets' absorption of the longtail liability risk emanating from the USA. Concentrates on the companies market, in London and abroad. Regular contributor to industry seminars, conferences and publications; on editorial board of International Insurance Law Review.
Prof. Memberships: The Law Society.
Career: Called to the Bar 1979; in-house Counsel to Marine Liability Insurer 1981-1983; private practice with an English law firm in Paris

1983-1987; admitted as solicitor 1988; joined *Lovell White Durrant* as partner 1993.

THOMAS, Nicholas
Kennedys, London (0171) 638 3688
See under Professional Negligence, p. 670

TIPLADY, David
D J Freeman, London (0171) 583 4055
Partner in Insurance Litigation Department.
Specialisation: Insurance and re-insurance litigation and arbitration. Acts for and advises Lloyds Agencies; insurance companies; liquidators, scheme administrators, run-off companies, and Lloyds Names. Recent cases include 'Aiken v. Stewart Wrightson Ltd' and 'Brown v. KMR Services Ltd' (Court of Appeal). Author of books and articles on commercial law subjects. Editor of D J Freeman Insurance Review. Examiner in commercial law and the law of international trade, London University.
Prof. Memberships: Law Society, B.I.L.A.
Career: Former professor of commercial law. Barrister (Gray's Inn) 1975. Solicitor 1991.
Personal: Educated in Newcastle Royal Grammar School and Lincoln College, Oxford.

WEIR, Alan H.M.
Ince & Co, London (0171) 623 2011
Specialisation: Alan Weir has specialised since 1985 in advising insurance and reinsurance market participants, and other professionals especialy those in London and the USA. Cases reported in 1998 are Mander v Commercial Union, representing CU and AXA in a P&I reinsurance dispute, the successful appeal in Denby, acting for XL reinsurers on the Aggregate Extension Clause and the dismissal for subrogated energy/ property insurers of shipowners' appeal in The Sivand. Current editor of Ince Insurance Law Update. Direct insurance dispute practice is predominantly professional indemnity, both for and against professionals, (and their insurers) especially brokers on placing/ claims issues and market problems (e.g. assisted Julian Hill advising Lloyds brokers on Reconstruction and Renewal). Also handling large accountants,' lawyers' and other professionals' E&O matters, particularly those involving substantial investigations. Reinsurance has included close involvement in London disputes triggered by APH deteriorations, issues arising for US markets in the Excess of Loss context and several open cover cases. Worked on the PCW XL reinsurance and the Pine Top appeals. Recently engaged in resolving disputes arising in the energy and P&I reinsurance fields.
Prof. Memberships: British Maritime Law Association.
Career: Educated at Fettes College, Edinburgh, University of Virginia and Trinity College, Cambridge. Partner in 1991.

WELLS, Christian
Lovell White Durrant, London
(0171) 236 0066
Specialisation: Insurance partner specialising in the operation of insurance businesses and markets; work undertaken in addition to claims includes the drafting of wordings including asset finance and finite risk insurances; the management of syndicates at Lloyds; underwriting agencies; mutual insurance associations including P&I clubs; insurance market administration; risk management; run-offs and insolvency related problems.

Prof. Memberships: City of London Law Society: Insurance Sub-Committee.
Career: Article *Waltons & Morse*; qualified 1980; Partner *Lovell White & King* (now *Lovell White Durrant*) 1986.

WHEATLEY, Vere A.
Cameron McKenna, London
(0171) 367 3000
Partner in Insurance and Reinsurance Group.
Specialisation: Main area of practice is reinsurance and professional indemnity insurance.
Career: Qualified in 1982. Practised in New York 1985-89. Admitted as a lawyer in New York state 1987. Joined *Cameron Markby Hewitt* in 1989, becoming a partner in 1992.

WILLIAMS, Nicholas D.
Kennedys, London (0171) 638 3688
Specialisation: Handles a wide range of insurance and reinsurance disputes, often of an international nature. Has extensive experience of Directors' and Officers' claims and also property insurance/reinsurance disputes. Represented defendant insurers in the Policyholders Protection Act test case which went to the House of Lords. Involved in a number of other reported cases including 'Arkwright Mutual Insurance Co v Bryanston Insurance Co,' a Court of Appeal decision on jurisdiction issues in reinsurance and 'Middleton v Hargreaves Clearwaste,' representing Commercial Union in the Court of Appeal. Lectures extensively at insurance and reinsurance conferences and seminars.
Career: Qualified 1980 with *Kennedys*. Partner since 1983.
Personal: Born 28 December 1955. Attended Guisborough Grammar School and Nottingham

University. Leisure interests include theatre, cricket, golf, and squash.

WILLIAMS, Robin
Hill Taylor Dickinson, London
(0171) 283 9033
Specialisation: Has over 20 years' experience in the fields of reinsurance and brokers' errors and omissions claims, not only in the UK but also in the USA and Australia; and has represented parties in many of the major disputes which have troubled the London Market during this period, most recently acting for Lloyds Auditors in the Names' Litigation. Also specialises in Contractors' All Risks and environmental insurances, subjects on which he has written numerous articles and spoken widely at seminars and conferences.
Prof. Memberships: Law Society.
Career: Qualified in 1973. Joined *McKenna & Co* in 1971. Partner in *McKenna & Co* from 1979 to 1996. Partner in *Hill Taylor Dickinson* from 1996.
Personal: Born 6th February 1949. Attended Hampton School 1960-67 and University College Oxford MA (Oxon). Leisure interests include football, golf, gardening and family. Lives in Woking, Surrey.

WORDLEY, Paul
Holman, Fenwick & Willan, London
(0171) 488 2300
Partner in Insurance/Reinsurance Department.
Specialisation: Principal areas of practice encompass insurance/ reinsurance industry disputes, Lloyds professional indemnity litigation, captive insurance/ reinsurance disputes, insurance/ reinsurance coverage disputes and reinsurance run-off/pool disputes. Also acts in professional negligence and

environmental litigation, including U.S. litigation support, environmental insurance claims and discovery proceedings. Chairman/ speaker at seminars in the U.S. and U.K.
Prof. Memberships: Member of CII, Institute of RISK Managers, Society of English and American Lawyers, British Insurance Law Association and Law Society.
Career: Qualified in 1994. Called to the Bar in 1982. Practised at the Bar 1982-86 and worked in the insurance industry 1986-91. Joined *Holman, Fenwick & Willan* in 1991 where he became a Partner in 1994.
Personal: Born 12th July 1959. Educated at Highgate School 1972-77 and Bristol University 1978-81. Lives in Hertfordshire.

YOUNG, John
Lovell White Durrant, London
(0171) 236 0066
Specialisation: Advises on the formation, regulation, sale and purchase of insurance companies and businesses in the UK and Europe. Co-ordinates the activities of *Lovell White Durrant*'s lawyers who advise the insurance industry on non-contentious matters. Has acted on numerous transactions within the industry, including recent life assurance demutualisations. Author of various articles on insurance; author of the insurance chapter in the revised CCH Common Market Reporter (1996). Speaks regularly on topics relating to the regulation of insurance and mergers and acquisitions in the industry.
Prof. Memberships: Law Society.
Career: Articled *Lovell White & King* (now *Lovell White Durrant*) 1979-1981: qualified 1981; partner 1987.

REGIONS

....

This table includes a mixed group of firms doing 'insurance work.' Many firms have developed large and specialised teams for professional negligence and personal injury claims and these may be found in other sections of the book.

This table is for remaining contentious work – fire/flood claims, coverage disputes, insurance fraud etc. There is inevitably some overlap as the majority of firms will have an "insurance department" dealing with a spread of claims for their insurer clients. Therefore the table is a summary of firms with insurance litigation skills 'across the board.'

We have tried to give some idea of the resources of each firm in the text. On the non-contentious side, there are a few niche firms doing Lloyds work and general regulatory work, as well as reinsurance.

Cartwrights (Bristol) (5ptnrs/8assts working in all insurance areas.) Their reputation as a good liability practice providing a consistently high standard of service has lifted them into the top rank this year. *David*

HIGHLY REGARDED FIRMS • REGIONS	
Cartwrights Bristol	**Hill Dickinson** Liverpool
Clyde & Co Guildford	**Manches & Co** Oxford
Dibb Lupton Alsop Liverpool	**Wansbroughs Willey Hargrave** Bristol, Leeds
Eversheds Newcastle upon Tyne	**Wragge & Co** Birmingham
Berrymans Lace Mawer Birmingham, Liverpool, Manchester, Southampton	**Eversheds** Cardiff
	Hammond Suddards Leeds
Bond Pearce Exeter, Plymouth, Southampton	**James Chapman & Co** Manchester
Browne Jacobson Nottingham	**Keogh Ritson** Bolton
Buller Jeffries Birmingham	**Wansbroughs Willey Hargrave** Birmingham
Cameron McKenna Bristol	**Weightmans** Liverpool
Berryman & Co Nottingham	**Kennedys** Brentwood
Davies Arnold Cooper Manchester	**Lyons Davidson** Bristol, Plymouth
Dibb Lupton Alsop Leeds	**Merricks** Chelmsford, Ipswich
Dutton Gregory Winchester	**Mills & Reeve** Cambridge, Norwich
Elliott & Company Manchester	**Peter Rickson and Partners** Preston
Humphreys & Co. Bristol	**Prettys** Ipswich
Jacksons Middlesbrough, Newcastle Upon Tyne, Stockton-on-Tees	**Vaudreys** Manchester
	Weightmans Birmingham

Vernalls leads the insurance department which incorporates several specialist units.
Clients/Work: Panel solicitors for several major composite insurers

Clyde & Co, (Guildford) (25ptnrs/plus a number of assts working in reinsurance, non-

contentious and general claims.) Known primarily as a City firm, the Guildford branch is one of the few outside London to offer a specialised service in reinsurance and non-contentious insurance work. Much of the work is in fact generated in London.

Clients/Work: Brown v GIO (Court of Appeal); Agnew v Lansforsakringsbolagens (Court of appeal) – on jurisdiction in reinsurance; FAI v Ocean Marine – reinsurance dispute for P&I club.

Dibb Lupton Alsop (Liverpool) (2ptnrs/11fee-earners) While some practitioners felt them "aggressive," most felt that the Liverpool branch has earned a solid reputation, particularly in shipping insurance. **Clients/Work:** Acted in Municipal Mutual v Sea Insurance Co and others (CA) – consideration of aggregation and proof of loss under a reinsurance contract and Seismik Securitac AG v Sphere Drake Insurance plc – involved non-disclosure and coverage defences.

Eversheds (Newcastle) (3ptnrs/5fee-earners) *Lex Dowie* heads the insurance department which specialises in marine insurance and international trade. **Clients/Work:** Highlights of the last year include drafting new leasing documents for a factory and redrafting a policy for an aquaculture (fish farming) company, which is the largest aquaculture insurance policy in the world.

Hill Dickinson (Liverpool) (1ptnr/2assts forming part of a much larger insurance department) "Big market players," was the consensus opinion about the firm who are better known for their personal injury work. The firm opened a new office in Manchester April 1998. **Clients/Work:** The Insurance Policy Group also acts for a number of major composite insurers in drafting and amending insurance policies.

Manches & Co (Oxford) (3ptnrs/1asst) Niche practice which claims to be the only firm outside London specialising in corporate and regulatory work for the Lloyds market. **Clients/Work:** Almost exclusively Lloyds corporate and regulatory work for underwriting agents and Lloyds agents.

Wansbroughs Willey Hargrave (Bristol: 4ptnrs/20fee-earners, Leeds: 5ptnrs/17fee-earners working on "volume" and "big ticket" work, including professional negligence and personal injury) Differing quality is reported between Wansbroughs' various offices. The Leeds office is considered "professional" and the Bristol office is well respected. **Clients/Work:** Include Royal & Sun Alliance, GAN, Ecclesiastical Insurance Group, General Accident.

Wragge & Co (Birmingham) (6ptnrs/17assts) *Susan Dearden*, a "doughty lady" according to practitioners, leads a substantial insurance department which prides itself on its personal injury work but also deals with general claims and reinsurance. **Clients/Work:** Advising insurers on claims, outsourcing and agreements; drafting policy wordings, binding authorities and agreements for conducting insurance via EDI links with brokers; advising insurers in multi-million pound subrogated recovery claims.

Berrymans Lace Mawer (Birmingham, Liverpool, Manchester, Southampton) (31ptnrs/65assts across the four offices doing personal injury, professional indemnity and general insurance) Lawyers throughout the country praised this "powerful practice" which appears to be going from strength to strength since the merger of two already highly regarded firms. It has risen in our ranking and may well reach our top band next year if it continues on current form. **Clients/Work:** Include Royal & Sun Alliance, Iron Trades, Commercial Union, Guardian, NFU Mutual, Independent, ITT London & Edinburgh, GA. Handle coverage disputes, fraud, fire/subsistence, environmental, construction.

Bond Pearce (Plymouth/Exeter: 8ptnrs/1assoc/14assts/1paralegal; Southampton: 2ptnrs/1assoc/2assts/1claims handler) Have risen in our tables. The insurance caseload is spread between the three branches, doing "all insurance work" including personal injury, professional indemnity, medical negligence and health and safety matters. This "highly reliable" firm, which merged with Hepherd Winstanley & Pugh on 1 May 1998, is one of the the largest insurance practices in the South. **Clients/Work:** Include composite insurers, Lloyds Syndicates, life assurance companies and permanent health insurers. Specialise in advice on policy issues.

Browne Jacobson (Nottingham) (12ptnrs/48assts) Unanimously good reports of the firm's work have lifted it up a band. The department is separated into three groups: Professional Indemnity, General Insurance and Public Authority (including personal injury). **Clients/Work:** Act for a number of major national insurers.

Buller Jeffries (Birmingham) (3ptnrs/6assts alternate between general liability and personal injury work) "Not Johnny-come-latelys" says Geoff Lewis of his team, a comment borne out by the favourable views of the market which have raised it to a higher band this year. **Clients/Work:** Successful defence of a products claim for multiple insurers where damages claimed were in excess of £100m; resolution of a major asbestos class action securing a contribution from asbestos suppliers towards settlement of E.L. claims.

Cameron McKenna (Bristol) (3ptnrs/12assts doing a variety of insurance work) Maintains its good reputation although known more for its work in professional indemnity. **Clients/Work:** ITT London & Edinburgh, Syndicates at Lloyds, Independent Insurance, General Accident.

Eversheds (Cardiff) (2ptnrs/6 fee-earners) The Cardiff office is felt to have some good practitioners. **Clients/Work:** Act for over 30 insurer clients.

Hammond Suddards (Leeds) (4ptnrs/21assts) A "high quality" firm currently investing heavily in new IT systems and moving up our ranking at the same time.

Clients/Work: Cross v Kirklees MBC (CA) – acted for defendant and its insurers in case dealing with the duties of Highway Authorities in relation to the clearing of snow and ice on highways.

James Chapman & Co (Manchester) (4ptnrs/3assts combine general liability and professional indemnity work) *John McKenna* leads a team known better for its knowledge of professional indemnity but highly regarded by fellow practitioners and clients alike for its insurance presence. **Clients/Work:** Act for a number of major composite insurers on a combination of coverage disputes and professional indemnity work.

Keogh Ritson, (Bolton) (2ptnrs/2assts) Praise for its "close relationship with insurance clients" and the quality of its work, earned them promotion in our tables. **Clients/Work:** Policy interpretation advice and representation in range of insurance disputes from measure of indemnity to policy repudiation and fraud/arson by the insured. Have "household name" clients including major composites, direct insurers and Lloyds syndicates.

Wansbroughs Willey Hargrave (Birmingham) (3ptnrs/14assts) One of Wansbroughs' smaller offices although generally well regarded. **Clients/Work:** Royal and Sun Alliance, Guardian Insurance, Ecclesiastical Insurance.

Weightmans (Liverpool, Birmingham) (17ptnrs/27assts form the Insurance and Personal Injury Department) The Liverpool office received particular praise but the bulk of the firm's insurance work is personal injury related. **Clients/Work:** Act for more than fifty insurance companies, amongst them eight of the top ten market leaders.

Berryman & Co (Nottingham) (3ptnrs/5 other fee earners doing a variety of insurance work) Team are well located geographically to serve their insurance clients. Perceived to be doing well.

Davies Arnold Cooper (Manchester) (3ptnrs/7fee earners doing general liability and professional indemnity work.) "Hasn't set the world on fire" was the universal feeling about the Manchester office of this well respected London firm. Undaunted, last year the firm opened a new office in Newcastle dedicated to insurance litigation. **Clients/Work:** Acting for an Excess of Loss insurance market in a coverage dispute with their insured and an Irish Government department concerning a £22m fire claim; policy interpretation concerning serious fire damage claim, value potentially £3–4m.

Dutton Gregory (Winchester) (2ptnrs/4 fee earners make up a general insurance department, including personal injury work) The team deals with both contentious and contentious insurance work. **Clients/Work:** Number of Lloyds syndicates.

Elliott & Co. (Manchester) (2ptnrs/3assocs) Not felt to be a major player by some, particularly now that the London office has been taken over by Kennedys. The insurance team deals with professional indemnity and coverage claims.

Humphreys, (Bristol) (2ptnrs/1asst) A small firm known for its reinsurance work.

Jacksons, (Middlesbrough, Stockton-on-Tees, Newcastle) (7ptnrs/7assts work in insurance litigation, including personal injury) The only new entry to our list this year following several recommendations although better known for their personal injury work.

Lyons Davidson (Bristol, Plymouth) (1ptnr) *John Gore* acts for insurer clients on policy disputes and insurance fraud as part of a much larger insurance department.

Merricks (Ipswich, Chelmsford) Generally well-respected. Deals more with personal injury and professional indemnity as part of its insurance department.

Mills & Reeve (Cambridge, Norwich) (2ptnrs/3assts form the team for general liability work, including personal injury.) A firm with a "pre-eminent reputation" although better known in other fields. **Clients/Work:** Act for approximately 30 different insurers, Underwriters, Lloyds Syndicates and Loss Adjusters.

Peter Rickson & Partners (Preston) Felt to be "slipping" by some interviewees although there was praise for the "impressive" *Mark Field* who leads the team.

Prettys (Ipswich) (4ptnrs, each leading a team of 4 lawyers, form the insurance department) A relatively small but well regarded firm which provides a "consistently high standard."

Vaudreys (Manchester) (4ptnrs/16assts doing a wide range of work, specialising in commercial transport claims and disease

work) Persistent rumours of merger have not helped the firm's profile, but they do act for some good clients. **Clients/Work:** British Aerospace plc, Iron Trades Insurance Group, General Accident, NFC plc, Archer Underwriting.

LEADING INDIVIDUALS · REGIONS	
ANGEL Peter Manches & Co	
BELL Raymond Clyde & Co	
DOWIE Lex Eversheds	
DEARDEN Susan Wragge & Co	
FIELD Mark Peter Rickson and Partners	
GORE John Lyons Davidson	
MCKENNA John James Chapman & Co	
MILLER Glenn Wansbroughs Willey Hargrave	
VERNALLS David Cartwrights	

SCOTLAND

HIGHLY REGARDED FIRMS SCOTLAND
Dundas & Wilson CS Edinburgh
McGrigor Donald Edinburgh
Maclay Murray Spens Glasgow
Shepherd & Wedderburn WS Edinburgh
Simpson & Marwick WS Edinburgh
Biggart Baillie Glasgow
Bishop and Robertson Chalmers

Dundas & Wilson CS (Contentious: 3ptnrs/8fee-earners; Non-contentious: 2ptnrs/6assts plus a further team of up to 30 fee-earners for major transactions) Pamela Lyall leads the contentious insurance team which acts for insurers in employer liability, motor and public liability claims and in policy wording and coverage disputes. With a strong corporate background and "in a class of their own" for non-contentious insurance work, the second team is led by *Philip Mackay*. Some predict that becoming part of Andersens and losing the private client department may deter their insurer clients. This remains to be seen. **Clients/Work:**

Advising Swiss Re and its affiliate Securities Capital on the Scottish aspects of the proposals for demutualisation of Scottish Amicable; the joint venture arrangements between The Royal Bank of Scotland plc, Royal Scottish insurance, Direct Line Assurance and Scottish Widows relating to collaboration and the provision of certain services for The Royal Bank Group; advising Hiscox Select Insurance Fund plc on its "reverse interavail deity" conversion scheme for Roberts & Hiscox Names at Lloyds.

McGrigor Donald (1ptnr/1asst forming part of the construction department) A new entry to our list following several recommendations, its main strength is in construction related work.

Maclay Murray Spens Another new firm which is felt to be a presence in this area of insurance litigation.

Shepherd & Wedderburn WS (4ptnrs/ 4assts form the insurance department, which includes personal injury and professional indemnity work) The firm has recently set up a Devolution Unit to look at the effect of the new Scottish Parliament on legal transactions, including insurance work.

Simpson & Marwick WS Praise from fellow practitioners and clients has raised this

firm in our ranking this year.

Biggart Baillie (6ptnrs/8assts form the corporate department including non-contentious insurance work) One of the few Scottish firms to do both non-contentious and insurance litigation. Other practitioners see them as more lively in this field. Clients perceive them to be developing more expertise. *Campbell Smith* leads the non-contentious team while James Roxburgh heads litigation. **Clients/Work:** Deal with acquisitions and restructurings in the life insurance and friendly society sector as well as providing advice on insurance regulatory matters. Contentious work includes disputes arising out of substantial fire claims.

Bishop and Robertson Chalmers (4ptnrs/5assts in personal injury/reparations) "Pushy and efficient" was the comment about this firm which is known more for its work in other fields.

LEADING INDIVIDUALS SCOTLAND
COCHRAN Neil Dundas & Wilson
MACKAY Philip Dundas & Wilson
SMITH Campbell Biggart Baillie

ANGEL, Peter G.
Manches & Co, Oxford (01865) 722106
See under General Corporate Finance, p. 236

BELL, Raymond
Clyde & Co, Guildford (0171) 623 1244
Specialisation: Specialises in insurance and reinsurance law often with an international dimension. Disputes on which he acts include policy construction, placing issues and brokers' responsibilities and subrogation claims in diverse fields of commercial activity. Litigation can be in Court proceedings or Arbitration and involve jurisdiction and law issues under various international conventions. Has acted at different times for many of the different interests for example assureds, insurers, brokers and reinsurers. Major matters include involvement in the Lloyd's Litigation acting for the Lloyd's Agents E&O Insurers in cases such as Cox v Bankside and Cox v Deeny. In the reinsurance field Axa v Field and Brown v GIO on important market issues of 'event' and Equitas v Trygg Hansa on the new Arbitration Act. In the energy insurance context successfully acted in the landmark case of National Oilwell v Davy on subrogation rights against co-assureds. The collapse of the Swedish credit insurance industry in the early 1990's spawned major international litigation icluding the case of Trade Indemnity v Njord on jurisdiction under the Lugano Convention. Handled the further recent decision on the Convention in Agnew v LFAB for reinsurers which is currently on its way to the House of Lords. Major litigation has also arisen recently in the field of P&I Club reinsurance and Ray acts for FAI against the Ocean Marine Club which is due to go to Trial in the year 2000. Lectures regularly in the UK and abroad on topical legal issues and contributes articles to various periodicals. Practises from both Guildford and City Offices.
Career: Qualified in 1984. First Class Law Degree and First Class Honours in law society finals.
Personal: Married with 4 children, lives in Guildford.

COCHRAN, Neil
Dundas & Wilson CS, Edinburgh
(0131) 228 8000
See under Professional Negligence p. 675

DEARDEN, Susan J.
Wragge & Co, Birmingham (0121) 233 1000
Specialisation: Specialises in Defence of general liability claims and and is head of the Insurance Practice at *Wragge & Co*. Particular expertise in serious injury and fatal accident claims as well as industrial disease and work related upper limb disorders.
Prof. Memberships: BIIBA (West Midlands Region). BII. Birmingham Medico Legal Society.
Career: Birmingham University LLB 2:1. Articled with *Wragge & Co*. Partner from May 1995.
Personal: Husband is head of employment at *Wragge & Co*. Hobbies: Golf, Travel, Food & Drink, Skiing.

DOWIE, Lex
Eversheds, Newcastle upon Tyne
(0191) 261 1661
See under Shipping & Maritime Law, p. 735

FIELD, Mark A.
Peter Rickson and Partners, Preston
(01772) 556677
Specialisation: Specialises in litigation for insurers involving contractual disputes and property damage. Also deals with insurance policy coverage and interpretation and is experienced in all aspects of personal injury litigation.
Prof. Memberships: FOIL and NFU Professional.
Career: Qualified in 1981. *Greenwoods* 1981-1986, *Davies Arnold Cooper* 1987-1990, *Peter Rickson and Partners* since 1990.
Personal: Born 1995. Leisure interests include Italian opera and football. Lives in Preston.

GORE, J. I.
Lyons Davidson, Bristol (0117) 904 6000

MACKAY, Philip
Dundas & Wilson CS, Edinburgh
(0131) 228 8000
See under Financial Services (FSA, Compliance etc), p. 390

McKENNA, John
James Chapman & Co, Manchester
(0161) 828 8000
See under Professional Negligence, p. 677

MILLER, Glenn
Wansbroughs Willey Hargrave, Leeds
(0113) 244 1151
See under Professional Negligence, p. 677

SMITH, W.W. Campbell
Biggart Baillie, Glasgow (0141) 228 8000
See under General Corporate Finance, p. 258

VERNALLS, David Francis
Cartwrights, Bristol (0117) 929 3601
See under Personal Injury: Mainly Defendant, p. 632

INTELLECTUAL PROPERTY

See also Computer IT; Franchising; Media & Entertainment

RESEARCH: In compiling the tables, we consider all the information available to us, paying particular regard to the market research carried out by our team of ten qualified lawyers. (The researchers' details are set out on page three.) The rankings, therefore, reflect the opinion of the marketplace as revealed by systematic and objective research: see page four. (Our research is audited every year by the British Market Research Bureau.)

OVERVIEW: There are few changes to the rankings of firms: last year's listings were considered an accurate reflection of the market. Cross border litigation has been developing, in particular pan-European injunctions. The EU Green Paper on patents will affect the future of UK patent litigation, and the pharmaceutical, bio-technology and communications sides of IP continue to grow.

Patent work is generally deemed to be such a distinct area of law that it justifies a separate list to non-patent work. Bird & Bird, Bristows and Simmons & Simmons are almost universally accepted as the leading patent practitioners.

The list of leading non-patent firms is largely unchanged. Some firms are focusing more on IT work at the expense of their soft IP practices. Only minor alterations have been made to the list of highly regarded non-patent practices. Llewellyn Zietman have strengthened their team, and Olswang have made substantial progress in developing their soft IP practice.

In the South East there has been some change, with Willoughby & Partners' acquisition of some of the lawyers from Dallas Brett, and Garretts in Reading entering the list on the basis of recommendations from local competitors.

In the Midlands there has been slight movement. Martineau Johnson has performed well but Eversheds was affected by the retirement of Lionel Howard. In East Anglia, the move of Isabel Napper from Taylor Vinters to Mills & Reeve has affected the relative standings of both firms.

In the North West, Halliwell Landau have been raised to the top band of leading firms.

LEADING FIRMS
LONDON • NON-PATENT

BIRD & BIRD
CLIFFORD CHANCE
EVERSHEDS
LOVELL WHITE DURRANT
SIMMONS & SIMMONS
TAYLOR JOYNSON GARRETT

ALLEN & OVERY
BAKER & MCKENZIE
BRISTOWS
LINKLATERS
NEEDHAM & GRANT
WILLOUGHBY & PARTNERS

HIGHLY REGARDED FIRMS

Ashurst Morris Crisp
Cameron McKenna
Denton Hall
Dibb Lupton Alsop
Freshfields
Hammond Suddards
Herbert Smith
Llewelyn Zietman
Rowe & Maw
Slaughter and May

Briffa & Co
Macfarlanes
Maycock's
Nabarro Nathanson
Norton Rose
Olswang
Reynolds Porter Chamberlain
Roiter Zucker
Stephenson Harwood
Titmuss Sainer Dechert

Charles Russell
Collyer-Bristow
Field Fisher Waterhouse
Gouldens
Henry Hepworth
Hobson Audley Hopkins & Wood
Wilde Sapte

LONDON

Bird & Bird (9ptnrs/24assts) "Absolutely top-notch" for patent work. *Trevor Cook* is a renowned hard IP specialist. *David Harriss* is also rated. They are still ranked as a leader in non-patent, but reservations have been expressed about the extent to which this relies upon IT related work rather than pure IP such as trade marks. *Morag MacDonald* is a "walking encyclopaedia of IP caselaw" and is "pleasant and focused, but a terrier when she needs to be." She is particularly known for her internet work. *Miles Gaythwaite* is also recommended. **Clients/Work:** Acted for International Rectifier against SGS Thomson on semi-conductor patent infringment case; acting for Chocosuisse against Cadburys; acted for Labsystems in substantial design copyright infringement case against Biohit.

Clifford Chance (5ptnrs/20 assts) Offer a "comprehensive IP service," and are led by the highly respected *David Perkins. Vanessa Marsland* specialises in the IT aspects of IP, and has a "to the point" style. Their patent work is gaining a higher profile, and they have been involved in a respectable number of big cases. *Peter Taylor* is also recommended. **Clients/Work:** Acting for Bodum against Household Articles; acting for Kimberley-Clark against Fort-Sterling; for ICO against TRW.

Eversheds (3ptnrs/7assts) Have several provincial IP departments in addition to the London office. *Isabel Davies* is accepted as one of the national experts on trade marks. She leads a "young and well regarded team" which includes the "practical and commercial" *Paul Harris*. Clients/Work: Acted for Boston Scientific against Johnson & Johnson; acting for Nabisco in relation to Nestlé's claim to unbranded ring-shaped confectionary; drafting copyright laws of Lithuania.

Lovell White Durrant (7ptnrs/31assts) Are well respected for a wide range of IP work, and boast an impressive client list. Their patent practice is seen to be weighted towards the non-contentious side. *Robert Anderson* is the most experienced member of a "solid team," which includes the "balanced and sensible" *Nicholas Macfarlane*. It remains to be seen how the loss of James Marshall to Taylor Joynson Garrett affects them. Clients/Work: Act for Discovision Associates in patent litigation against Disctronics; advising Nintendo on the EC Commission investigation into Nintendo's policy of patent and know-how licensing in relation to video games; advised Vickers on its selling off of Rolls Royce.

Simmons & Simmons (7ptnrs/17assts) Are deemed to be "superb" on patents, and also rank in the highest category for non-patent work. *Gerry Kamstra* is recommended for his bio-tech patent work, but it remains to be seen how the departure of Mark Hodgson affects their patent practice. *Kevin Mooney* is described as "a smooth operator who surrounds himself with good lawyers." *Rowan Freeland* is "an excellent IP lawyer," and *Helen Newman* is known for her trade mark practice. *Michelle Paver* is also recommended. Clients/Work: Bristol-Myers Squib v Napro Biotherapeutics and BNP; Union Carbide; TRW.

Taylor Joynson Garrett (13ptnrs/23assts) *Richard Price* heads an "excellent department" which includes the highly experienced (and now part-time) David Petterson. *Gary Moss* is considered a "driving force" in the firm." The profile of their IP practice will be enhanced by the arrivals of *James Marshall* from Lovells, and *Mark Hodgson* from Simmons & Simmons. The latter is described as "top class" in pharmaceutical patents, and a "pleasant person to work with who gets things done." *Glyn Morgan* is also recommended. Clients/Work: Hoechst Celanese Corp v BP; Visa's transactional work and TM litigation; advising Mechanical-Copyright Protection Society Ltd.

Allen & Overy (6ptnrs/19assts) As a major commercial law firm, most of their IP practice stems from corporate spin-offs. Although "she hides her light under a bushel," *Catriona Smith* is respected for both her IT and IP work. *Stephen Jones* has been added to the leaders list for the first time. Clients/Work: Acted for MGM/United Artists in a TM dispute; acted for ICI on its disposal programme in relation to its industrial chemicals businesses; acted for NDM in a dispute over a medical device success-

fully appealed to the Court of Appeal.

Baker & McKenzie (5ptnrs/14 assts in IP and IT) Are regarded as stronger for soft than hard IP. They service many high profile clients, and have an excellent international base. *Harry Small* is best known as a litigator in the IP and IT field, and *Michael Hart* also features as a leader. Clients/Work: Represented Orange successfully against Vodafone in High Court trade marks action; represented Ralph Lauren in leading parallel import trade marks law test case; represented European Association of Consumer Electronic Equipment Manufacturers in relation to the EU proposed Directive on Copyright in the Information Society.

Bristows (13ptnrs/30assts) Have been known for many decades as a leader in patent work, although the perception that they undertake more contentious IP than Bird & Bird may be changing. They also have a substantial non-patent practice which includes a TM filing service. The team is led by the "experienced and knowledgeable" *Ian Judge*, and includes *Sally Field* who is admired for her "strength of mind." *David Brown* is "experienced in patent work." *Edward Nodder* and *Paul Walsh* also received recommendations. Clients/Work: Acted for Electrolux-Dyson on a matter concerning infringement of trade mark and falsehood in relation to comparative advertising; act for many large clients in the sector including GEC and Glaxo Wellcome.

Linklaters (6ptnrs/25 assts) A strong team includes the experienced *Robert Swift* and *Jeremy Brown*. *Robin Whaite* is regarded as "clever" and "pragmatic," and has done "good work on pharmaceuticals." The "energetic" *Ian Karet* has been elevated two places from the up and coming band due to several recommendations. *Nigel Jones* enters the list for the first time. Known in particular for their non-contentious practice. Clients/Work: Patent litigation matters include Fort Dodge v Akzo, and also acted for Cordis Corporation against Boston Scientific. Also undertake Microsoft's anti-counterfeiting work.

Needham & Grant (3ptnrs/1asst) A small but "delightful" firm who are highly respected for both their patent and non-patent work. They are "cost effective and do a good job." *Gregor Grant* is a specialist patent litigator, and is "easy to get on with, personable, and knowledgeable." *Adam Cooke* is also a "tenacious patent litigator." *David Gibbins* undertakes a wider range of work, including trade marks. Clients/Work: Unilever; British Telecom; Thames Water.

Willoughby & Partners (5ptnrs/9assts in IT/IP) Maintain their status as one of the leading non-patent specialists. *Anthony Willoughby* is accepted as the pre-eminent name in trade marks (along with Isabel Davies at Eversheds), and has been elevated this year to the highest band of leading individuals. Also have a strong international

anti-counterfeiting practice. Clients/Work: Acting for Prince Plc against Prince Sports in a domain name dispute; acting for Pitman Publishing in a domain name dispute; acted for Economist Newspaper Ltd in TM dispute over the use of the name "European Voice."

Ashurst Morris Crisp (5ptnrs/15assts) Led by the "first class" *Ian Starr*, who has been raised a band due to his increasing profile, and favourable accounts of the quality of his work. He is considered "clear and concise." Clients/Work: Substantial litigations and transactions for Motorola, Smith & Nephew, and Allied Domecq.

Cameron McKenna (5ptnrs/13assts) The work of the department is split evenly between contentious and non-contentious. Have recently been pushing the IT practice. Clients/Work: Advised Warner-Lambert Company in relation to the European aspects of their joint venture with Glaxo-Wellcome; acting in the Elvis Presley TM litigation; acting for CBS Inc in relation to litigation with the Trustees of the estate of George Bernard Shaw relating to the rights in My Fair Lady.

Denton Hall (5ptnrs/13assts) *Clive Thorne* and *Hilary Newiss* are rated as leading individuals, and in general the firm are seen to be strong on the entertainment side of IP. Despite the loss of James Irvine to Llewellyn Zietman, they maintain their position in the tables. Clients/Work: Alan Clark v Associated Newspapers; advise Hasbro on trade marks, domain name and general IP; advised Sainsburys on licensing deal with Microban for antibacterial products.

Dibb Lupton Alsop (5ptnrs/9assts) Have a highly regarded non-patent practice, in particular in the branding and anti-counterfeiting field. Seen to be considerably stronger on the computer side. Clients/Work: Lek Pharmaceutical & Chemical Company; Pitman Training; IPC Magazines.

Freshfields (3ptnrs/13assts) The department includes *Avril Martindale*, who has

LEADING FIRMS
LONDON • PATENT

BIRD & BIRD
BRISTOWS
SIMMONS & SIMMONS

LINKLATERS
LOVELL WHITE DURRANT
NEEDHAM & GRANT
TAYLOR JOYNSON GARRETT

CLIFFORD CHANCE
HERBERT SMITH

HIGHLY REGARDED FIRMS

Allen & Overy

Baker & McKenzie
Eversheds
Hammond Suddards

Rowe & Maw

been described as one of "the best non-contentious IP lawyers in the City." She has entered the leaders' table from up and coming. *Hugh Stubbs* also appears in the list, and is known as a litigator. **Clients/Work:** Advised Capital Radio on its proposed acquisition of Virgin Radio; strategic advice to the FA Premier League in relation to international TM portfolio; advised ICI on its acquisition of Unilever's speciality chemicals division.

Hammond Suddards (5ptnrs/19assts) Highly regarded for both their patent and non-patent practice, but it is the formidable reputation of the "dynamic" *Larry Cohen* which gives the department its prestige. He is a "nightmare for opponents" with an "unorthodox style," and "gets results quickly." **Clients/Work:** Acted for Lotus against Chaplin; acted for Zeneca against Chemiculture in application for Supplementary Protection Certificate; acted for Murex against Chiron in world-wide HCV litigation.

Herbert Smith (6ptnrs/12assts) Have a "good patent department," and also undertake highly regarded non-patent work. Christopher Tootal has a reduced workload as he prepares for retirement, but the experienced *Bill Moodie* is developing a higher profile. *Nick Gardner* is appearing more frequently in the courts as a solicitor-advocate, and has been elevated one place in the rankings. *Andrew Rich* and *Mark Shillito* have been recommended as up and coming names this year. **Clients/Work:** Acting for the Automobile Association in proceedings commenced by the Ordnance Survey in a copyright matter; acting for Akzo in the important new pan-European patent action against Fort Dodge; act for Virgin.

Llewellyn Zietman (7ptnrs/4assts) The "bright" *David Llewellyn* is expanding his soft IP practice, and has recruited *James Irvine* from Denton Hall, who is recognised as "an experienced and wide ranging practitioner." The highly experienced and well respected *Hugh Brett* has also joined the team following the dissolution of Dallas Brett. **Clients/Work:** Iomega Corporation; acted for L'Oreal SA in TM and passing off dispute; acted for DC Congress Gesellschaft GmbH against Mecklermedia Ltd in a passing off case.

Rowe & Maw (4ptnrs plus 10 other fee-earners dedicated to IP) Their patent work is relatively low profile, but the department is boosted by the "energetic" presence of *Ian Wood* who is "extremely good with clients." **Clients/Work:** Patent related matters for Samsonite; TM work for Hodder & Stoughton; non-contentious work for ICI and Unilever.

Slaughter and May (2ptnrs/11assts in IP and IT) Known mainly for the quality of their commercial work, they also have a respected soft IP practice. *Chris Hickson* appears in the list, as does *Nigel Swycher*. He

is considered "imaginative" and "commercially sensible." **Clients/Work:** Acted for EMAP against SPL; advised on GEC's disposal of Marconi instruments; acting for Nomura on flotation of Quadrant.

Briffa & Co (1principal/4assts) A small niche firm under the guidance of *Margaret Briffa*. **Clients/Work:** Gorag v Xylum; Farmers Build v Carrier; advised on the copyright infringement of a documentary programme.

Macfarlanes (4ptnrs/3assts) Offer a competent IP service within a wide ranging practice. Undertake both patent and non-patent matters. **Clients/Work:** Patent work for Walk Off Mats Ltd; advise DC Thomson & Co Ltd on trade marks; acting for Tag PC Ltd against Microsoft on copyright and TM infringement case.

Maycock's (1principal/2assts) A small niche firm that operates solely in the IP field. **Clients/Work:** Act for AOL in defence of TM infringement/passing off/copyright infringement claim; acting for Besalon Ltd in the Designs Appeal Tribunal in a successful appeal resulting in the cancellation of a registered design relating to roof tiles; acting for McNicholas Construction in patent infringement proceedings concerning plastic moulding supports.

Nabarro Nathanson (2ptnrs/8assts) Have kept a relatively low profile since the departure of Andrew Inglis to Olswang. **Clients/ Work:** Successful challenge to the English court's jurisdiction to hear foreign patent infringement claims for Coin Controls/Suzo; also act for the FT and Planet Hollywood.

Norton Rose (2ptnrs/6assts in commercial/corporate, 4assts on contentious matters) Have had a quiet year for IP work, with many practitioners unaware of their practice. **Clients/ Work:** New Millennium Experience Company; Dawnay Day v Cantor Fitzgerald; particular expertise in relation to advertising, merchandising and passing off.

Olswang (2ptnrs/4assts) Developed a broad soft IP practice since the arrival of *Andrew Inglis.* They have been elevated a band due to a consensus that they are making a significant impact on the IP market. **Clients/Work:** Mecklermedia; Budejovicky Budvar Norodni Podnik (Budweiser TM); Massmould (Tiny Metal Box Co).

Reynolds Porter Chamberlain (3ptnrs/4assts) Have a strong commercial base, of which the IP service is an integral part. **Clients/ Work:** Successfully defended Scandecor Ltd in a major passing off action; undertake copyright, design, patent, and trade mark work for Mag Instrument.

Roiter Zucker (2ptnrs/1asst) Are perceived to have a restricted client base, but do some "solid" patent work. **Clients/Work:** Wide variety of work for Norton Healthcare Ltd; Bioglan Pharma plc; Antigen Pharmaceuticals Ltd.

Stephenson Harwood (2ptnrs/6assts) Undertake a wide range of work on IP matters. Also offer a patent and TM filing service. **Clients/Work:** Ansell Group; Arrows Grand Prix International; British Aerospace Plc.

Titmuss Sainer Dechert (3 ptnrs/ 1asst) Have a well regarded IP "one stop shop" practice which includes a comprehensive TM filing service. **Clients/Work:** Acted for the Evening Standard against Alan Clark; Pannini Spice Girls case; ELSPA.

Charles Russell (3ptnrs/3assts) Traditional media firm that offers IP work as part of a general service. **Clients/Work:** Acted for Royal College of Nursing against Macmillan Magazines Ltd in comparative advertising dispute; acted for AVS in a patent dispute against Antec International Ltd; Reichold Chemicals Inc.

Collyer-Bristow (1ptnr/3assts) Offer a mixture of commercial and entertainment based advice. **Clients/Work:** Act for various multi-national corporations, particularly in the food/drink and energy sectors.

Field Fisher Waterhouse A new entry to the tables this year. Have an extensive patent and TM filing practice, and a high profile in international IP matters. The focus is on non-contentious work, and they are described as "practical and sensible." The firm has an impressive client list, and treat IP as a core area of practice. Although most of their practice is based on soft IP, they are seen to be making a push in patents too. **Clients/Work:** Acting for the Music Gallery against Direct Line Insurance and TBWA regarding copyright ownership and trade mark rights in the jingle used in Direct Line adverts. Enforcing Crown Copyright on behalf of Ordnance Survey.

Gouldens (3ptnrs/7assts) Considered "diligent, down to earth and not aggressive" by a client." *Charters MacDonald-Brown* is now managing partner, and has been described as "thorough and careful, but prepared to tough it out if necessary." **Clients/Work:** Acted for Warner Music against Pioneer; Bhs plc; advised Marks & Spencer in design right infringement claim.

Henry Hepworth Is a small specialist practice which includes media work and soft IP. *Michael Henry* appears in the leaders list. **Clients/Work:** Substantial client base in the media and entertainment field including the BBC; excellent client list of publishing clients, such as Express Newspapers and IPC magazines.

Hobson Audley Hopkins & Wood (2ptnrs/3assts) Have struggled to make an impression on the IP market since the departure of Ian Wood. *Robert Bond* maintains a reputation for IP work, although he heads the IT department. **Clients/Work:** Successfully defended Isoact in domain name dispute; acted for Dawnay Day & Co Ltd in TM case; act for the Institute of Physics.

Wilde Sapte (1ptnrs/3assts/1consultant) The "quiet and intellectual" *John Hull* leads the IP services. **Clients/Work:** Acted on the acquisition of the Philips Radio-Therapy Business by Elekta AB; the sale by University College London of UCL press; the setting up by UCL of UCL-Istar.

LEADERS' PROFILES · LONDON

ANDERSON, Robert
Lovell White Durrant, London
(0171) 236 0066
Specialisation: Intellectual property and technology. Both the litigious and commercial aspects of intellectual property including patents, designs, copyright, trade secrets and trade marks. Particular experience of R & D agreements and acquisitions and joint ventures involving technology based businesses. Also deals with other matters involving computers, pharmaceuticals or otherwise having a high technology content.
Prof. Memberships: AIPPI, Associate Member Chartered Institute of Patent Agents, Solicitors European Group, Law Society.
Career: BSc Edinburgh (Natural Sciences), 1968. Articled *Bristows Cooke and Carpmael*, admitted 1972; joined *Lovell White and King* (now *Lovell White Durrant*) 1974; partner 1978.

BOND, Robert
Hobson Audley Hopkins & Wood, London
(0171) 450 4500
Head of IT and Media Law Group.
Specialisation: Practice covers software, hardware, telecoms, database, multimedia and electronic commerce transactions; patents, copyright, registered designs, trademarks, trade secrets and international technology transfer. Also undertakes international trade, agency, distribution and franchising agreements. Author of "Understanding Software Contracts" and "Negotiating Tactics and Techniques for Software and other Hi-tech Agreements", both published by Thorogood. Regularly writes and publishes on internet law, electronic commerce law, data protection law and information technology legal issues. Chairman ICC (UK) Electronic Commerce Working Group and Legal Counsel to the Electronic Commerce Project of the International Chamber of Commerce world headquarters in Paris.

Prof. Memberships: Law Society of England and Wales; Notaries Society; City of London Solicitors Company; IBA; ABA; British Computer Society; Licensing Executives Society; Inter Pacific Bar Association; Computer Law Association; CyberNotaries (UK) Association.
Career: Qualified as a solicitor in 1979 and as a notary public in 1989 with *Goodger Auden*. Joined *Hobson Audley* as a partner in 1995.
Personal: Born 29th September, 1954. Educated at Repton School, 1968-73 and then at University of Wolverhampton 1973-76. Research Fellow, Leicester University 1995. Leisure pursuits include travel, swimming, keep fit, riding, ski-ing, gardening and antiques. Lives in Derbyshire.

BRETT, Hugh
Llewelyn Zietman, London (0171) 842 5400
Consultant
Specialisation: Intellectual property specialist dealing with patents, trade marks, designs and copyrights, confidentiality arrrangements, publishing and multi-media agreements, software protection and exploitation of intellectual property rights. Experience of handling major intellectual property transactions including licensing and sale of intellectual property rights in the fields of entertainment, publishing and brand management. Is a member of the intellectual property section of the British Computer Society. Also sits on the intellectual property committee of the Law Society and sat on The Copyright Tribunal. Has lectured in the UK and abroad on intellectual property matters and has acted as an expert for the European Commission on technology transfer and copyright issues raised by multi-media. Author of articles on anti-trust law, copyright, patent licensing and technology transfer and has written books on *The Patents Act 1977* and The Protection of Computer Software. Founder and co-editor of *European Intellectual Property Review* and founder and

member of *The Institute of Intellectual Property*. He is a Committee Member of The Intellectual Property Lawyers' Organisation and a Professorial Fellow in the Centre for Commercial Law Studies at QMW, University of London.
Prof. Memberships: Law Society, British Literary and Copyright Association.
Career: Qualified with *Linklaters & Paines*. Co-founder of *Dallas Brett* in 1981. Joined *Llewelyn Zietman*, April 1998.
Personal: Born 14th June 1941. Educated at Keble College, Oxford. Leisure pursuits include fishing. Lives in Oxford.

BRIFFA, Margaret
Briffa & Co, London (0171) 288 6003
Principal of niche intellectual property practice Briffa & Co.
Specialisation: Main area of practice dispute resolution in copyright, design, patent and trade mark matters. Co-author of 'Contracts for your Multimedia Business' (1997). Regular speaker at intellectual property seminars.
Career: Qualified in 1987. *Boodle Hatfield* 1987-1991, *Clifford Chance* 1991-92, *Rouse & Co.*1992-95. Established Briffa & Co. in 1995.
Personal: Born 18 September 1961. Educated Ursuline High School, East London and London School of Economics. Enjoys dancing, boats, travel, gardening and family pursuits. Lives Crouch End, North London.

BROWN, David
Bristows, London (0171) 400 8000
Partner in Intellectual Property Department.
Specialisation: Practice covers the full range of intellectual property and includes disputes in relation to patents, copyright, design rights, trade secrets and antitrust issues. Co-ordinates multi-forum disputes. Acts for international companies in the manufacturing, pharmaceutical, electronic and engineering industries. Had conduct of major cases such as 'Pilkington v. PPG' and 'Glaxo v. Generics'.

Recent and current cases include 'Beloit v. Valmet', 'Ocular Sciences v. Aspect', 'Pifco v. Philips', 'Electrolux v. Dyson', 'Tetra Pak v. APV', 'Texas Instruments v. Hyundai' and 'Napp Pharmaceuticals v. Asta-Medica'.
Career: Member Royal Corps of Naval Constructors 1960-1966. Joined *Bristows Cooke & Carpmael* 1966. Qualified as Solicitor in 1973; Partner from 1974; Executive Partner from 1992-1997. Member of Editorial Board of Patent World and Intellectual Property World.
Personal: Born 8 May 1942. Educated at Royal High School Edinburgh, Royal Naval Engineering College Plymouth and Royal Naval College Greenwich (Honours Degree in Naval Architecture). Interests include the Turf. Lives in Ecclestone Square, London and Oxfordshire.

BROWN, Jeremy
Linklaters, London (0171) 456 5748
Specialisation: Head of Intellectual Property and Information Technology Department, *Linklaters & Paines*. Jeremy has degrees in chemical engineering and law and is an English solicitor and a South African patent attorney. He has over 25 years experience in intellectual property practice, with particular reference to issues affecting the pharmaceuticals, chemical, electronics and luxury goods industries. His experience includes UK and multi-jurisdictional patent and trademark litigation, combating unlawful parallel imports, advising on exhaustion of intellectual property rights in Europe and internationally, and advising on EC competition law implications of trademark, patent and technology licences and other intellectual property related collaborations.

COHEN, Laurence
Hammond Suddards, London
(0171) 655 1000
Specialisation: Contentious and non-contentious intellectual property matters including patents, trademarks, copyright, design right and trade secrets. Also deals with regulatory law, particularly in the area of agrochemicals and medicines. Acted in Chiron v. Murex (client), Harrods Limited (client) v. Harrods (Buenos Aires) Limited, GEC v. FKI (client), Coin Controls (client) v. Suzo and Philips Electronics v. Ingman (client). Author of 'World Litigation Law and Practice: Unit B1 England and Wales' (1986) and CIPA/ ITMA Trademarks Handbook section on Civil Litigation (1992). Contributor of numerous articles to a variety of specialist publications on intellectual property topics and regular conference speaker.
Prof. Memberships: CIPA, ITMA, INTA, IBA, Law Society.
Career: Qualified 1976. Assistant Solicitor with *Bristows Cooke & Carpmael* from 1976, and became a Partner in 1981. Joined *Hammond Suddards* in 1992 and is currently Head of Intellectual Property Unit.
Personal: Born 12th September 1951. Attended Emmanuel College, Cambridge 1970-73. Leisure pursuits include tennis, squash and skiing. Lives in Radlett, Hertfordshire.

COOK, Trevor
Bird & Bird, London (0171) 415 6000
Partner in Intellectual Property Department.
Specialisation: Main areas of practice are litigation, transactional and advisory work in relation to patents, copyright, trademarks and

other intellectual property rights and associated regulatory law issues, particularly in the information technology and pharmaceutical/biotechnology sectors. Contributor to 'Information Technology and the Law', 'CIPA Guide to Patents Act' and European Patents Handbook; co-author of 'Pharmaceuticals Biotechnology and the Law' and 'Practical Intellectual Property Precedents'; author of "The Protection of Regulatory Data". Frequent writer and speaker on various intellectual property and regulatory topics.
Prof. Memberships: Treasurer of the International Association for the Protection of Industrial Property (AIPPI) (British Group), member of Licensing Executives Society, associate member of Chartered Institute of Patent Agents, Secretary of the British Computer Society Intellectual Property Committee, Secretary of British Copyright Council Working Group on Copyright & Technology.
Career: Qualified in 1977. Joined *Bird & Bird* in 1974, became a Partner in 1981.
Personal: Born 1951. Attended Southampton University (BSc Chemistry, 1973).

COOKE, Adam
Needham & Grant, London (0171) 242 5866

DAVIES, Isabel
Eversheds, London (0171) 919 4500
Partner and Head of Intellectual Property at Eversheds, London. Head of Eversheds National Intellectual Property Group.
Specialisation: Work includes patents, trademarks, copyright, designs, competition and EC law. Cases have included Jif, Coloplast v. Mentor 1994, Boston Scientific v Palmez 1998. Editor of Sweet and Maxwell's European Trade Mark Litigation Handbook. Co-editor of Eversheds IPEye. Legal Editor of Journal of Brand Management, Editorial Board of Trademark World and Country Correspondent for EIPR. Has spoken widely at conferences on I.P. issues, often taking the Chair.
Prof. Memberships: ITMS, CIPA, INTA, ACG. Member of Intellectual Property Sub-committee of the Law Society.
Career: Qualified in 1976. Partner at *Wragge & Co.*, 1979-85. Joined *Woodham Smith Taylor Joynson Garrett* as partner in 1986, then *Jaques & Lewis* (now *Eversheds*) in 1994.
Personal: Born 30th May 1952. Attended St Albans Girls' Grammar School, Leicester University and Guildford College of Law. Leisure interests include travel, theatre, squash, skiing, food and wine. Lives in Twickenham.

FIELD, Sally
Bristows, London (0171) 400 8000
Partner in Intellectual Property Department.
Specialisation: Intellectual Property litigation. Work covers advising on full range of intellectual property including patents, trade marks, copyright, designs and confidential information. Cases include Allen & Hanbury's (Glaxo) v. Generics, IBM v. Phoenix, and Peaudouce v Kimberly-Clark. Writes articles for specialist periodicals. Regular speaker at intellectual property conferences and seminars.
Prof. Memberships: Law Society, Associate Member Chartered Institute of Patent Agents, Associate Member Institute of Trade Mark Agents.
Career: Articled with *Clifford Turner* 1979-81, then moved to *Bristows Cooke & Carpmael* in 1983. Became a Partner in 1987.

Personal: Born 16th May 1957. Attended Durham University 1975-78. Leisure pursuits include golf, tennis and skiing. Lives in London.

FREELAND, Rowan
Simmons & Simmons, London
(0171) 628 2020
Specialisation: Intellectual Property litigation particularly patents and designs. Major cases include Allied Colloids v American Cynamid, General Instrument v Intel, Southco v Dzus and Hallen v Brabantia. Also IT law. Commissioning Editor, then Editorial Board Member, 'Patent World'.
Prof. Memberships: AIPPI, AIPLA, LES, CLA.
Personal: Born 1956. Education Wellington, St Catherines College Oxford (BA 1978). Joined *Simmons & Simmons* 1980, qualified 1982, partner 1988. Married with three daughters. Interests reading, gardening, opera.

GARDNER, Nick
Herbert Smith, London (0171) 374 8000
Partner in Intellectual Property and Technology Group.
Specialisation: Deals with intellectual property and technology, specialising in matters involving technical issues in the computing and electronics field. Contentious and non-contentious work. Admitted as a Solicitor Advocate with rights of audience in all civil proceedings.
Career: A number of years experience in the electronic and computing industries before becoming a solicitor. Qualified in 1988 and became a Partner at *Herbert Smith* in 1994. Handled the first Internet domain name case in front of the English courts, acting for Harrods. Acted for Amstrad in its record breaking £50 million plus judgment against Seagate Technology.
Personal: Educated at the University of Nottingham.

GAYTHWAITE, Miles
Bird & Bird, London (0171) 415 6000
Partner in Intellectual Property Department.
Specialisation: Principal area of practice is patents, patent and know-how licensing, trade marks and copyright. Also pharmaceuticals and software. Important cases handled include 'L.B. Plastics v. Swish'; 'Holtite v. Jost'; 'Unilever v. Gillette'; 'Societe Francaise Hoechst v. Allied Colloids Ltd'; 'Kakkar v. Ferring'; 'BICC plc v. Burndy Corporation', ' Amersham v. Corning', 'Hässle v. SmithKline Beecham, Cynamid and Knoll' and Connaught Laboratories v. SmithKline Beecham.
Prof. Memberships: Chartered Institute of Patent Agents, Licensing Executives Society, APRAM.
Career: With *Elkington & Fife*, Chartered Patent Agents 1967-74. Qualified as a Chartered Patent Agent in 1972. Joined *Bird & Bird* in 1974 and became a Partner in 1978.
Personal: Born 1943. Educated at Glasgow University 1960-64 (BSc, Chemistry) and Cambridge University 1964-67 (PhD, Organic Chemistry). Lives in London.

GIBBINS, David
Needham & Grant, London (0171) 242 5866

GRANT, Gregor
Needham & Grant, London (0171) 242 5866

HARRIS, Paul
Eversheds, London (0171) 919 4500
Partner *Eversheds* London Intellectual Property
Group.
Specialisation: Patents, trademarks,
copyright, designs. Notable cases include
Coloplast [1993]; Wagamama v. City Centre
Restaurants [1995]; Electrolux v. Black &
Decker [1996]. Author of various IP articles;
regular lecturer including Bristol University: IP
Diploma course.
Prof. Memberships: ITMA; CIPA; INTA
(member of Aisa Pacific sub-committee); AIPPI;
UNION; Royal Society of Chemistry.
Career: Qualified in 1987. *Bristows Cooke &
Carpmael*; *McKenna & Co [1988-1992]*; Taylor
Joynson Garrett *[1992-94]*; *Eversheds* formerly
Jaques & Lewis[[1994-], became partner in
1995.
Personal: Born 17th May 1961; Keele
University; Leisure interests include squash;
badminton; running; theatre; wine. Lives in
Westminster.

HARRISS, David
Bird & Bird, London (0171) 415 6000
Specialisation: Partner in Intellectual Property
Department. Senior Partner. Main area of
practice is intellectual property litigation.
Includes UK and international patent
infringement litigation, trademark infringement,
passing off, copyright infringement, design
infringement and breach of confidence. Acted in
Akzo/ Du Pont, PLG/Ardon, BP/Hoechst
Celanese, BP/Union Carbide and Exxon/
Lubrizol. Member of Editorial Boards of World
Intellectual Property Review and Patent World.
Prof. Memberships: Law Society, Chartered
Institute of Patent Agents (Fellow).
Career: Qualified as Patent Agent 1969.
Worked for AA Thornton & Co. 1965-70, then
Langner Parry from 1970-73 (Chartered Patent
Agents). Joined *Bird & Bird* in 1973. Qualified as a
Solicitor 1977. Partner 1977. Senior Partner 1993.
Personal: Born 1943. Attended Epsom College
1956-61, then Christ's College, Cambridge
1961-64. Lives in Chobham, Surrey.

HART, Michael
Baker & McKenzie, London (0171) 919 1000
Partner in Intellectual Property and Information
Technology Law Department.
Specialisation: Principal area of practice is
contentious and non-contentious IP Law. Work
includes copyright, trade marks and passing
off, patents and trade secrets, computer
copyright disputes, broadcasting and media
law. Also deals with government regulations and
trade libel. Has represented various trade
bodies in lobbying activities relating to UK and
EU legislative proposals, including the copyright
in the Information Society Directive. Has acted
in numerous IP court actions representing
companies such as Versace, Fila, Hasbro,
Labatts, Apple Inc. and Sony. Contributor to
Sweet & Maxwell's "Guide to Intellectual
Property in the IT Industry." Has written
numerous articles on IP issues. One of Radio 4
"Today" programme experts on Copyright law
issues. Frequently speaks at seminars.
Prof. Memberships: Anti-counterfeiting
Group, AIPPI, Intellectual Property Lawyers
Association.
Career: Qualified in 1983. With *Linklaters &*

Paines 1983-87. Joined *Baker & McKenzie* in
1987 and became a Partner in 1990.
Personal: Born 12th August 1959. Educated at
City of London School 1970-77 and Exeter
College, Oxford 1977-80. Leisure activities
include theatre, cinema, horse racing, tennis
and hockey. Lives in London.

HENRY, Michael
Henry Hepworth, London (0171) 242 7999
See under Media & Entertainment: Film, p. 567

HICKSON, Chris
Slaughter and May, London (0171) 600 1200
Specialisation: Head of group specialising in
contentious and non-contentious intellectual
property and information technology matters.
Practice comprises principally litigation and
advice on patents, trade marks, passing off,
copyright and designs, the protection of trade
secrets, and advertising. Has a wide experience
of IP in the context of corporate transactions,
intellectual property licensing and general
litigation.
Prof. Memberships: ITMA, ACG, INTA, AIPPI.
Career: Admitted 1977. With *Slaughter and May*
since 1975. Became a Partner in 1984.
Personal: Born 10 December 1951. Educated
at St. Joseph's College, Beulah Hill and
Birmingham University (LLB). Interests include
stamps, books and mountaineering. Lives in
Surrey.

HODGSON, Mark
Taylor Joynson Garrett, London
(0171) 353 1234
Partner in Intellectual Property Department.
Head of Pharmaceutical and Medical Group.
Specialisation: Specialises in patent litigation
in the U.K. courts and in the European Patent
Office. Also handles pharmaceutical, medical
device and biotechnology matters, including
regulatory issues, product liability, advertising,
parallel importation and clinical trial contracts.
Acted in respect of Smith Kline and French
Laboratories Ltd.(Cimetidine) Patents, Bonzel v.
Intervention, R v. Licensing Authority ex parte
Smith Kline and French Laboratories Ltd,
Merck/SB v. Primecrown, Smithkline Beecham
v. Norton/LEK and Biogen v. Medeva. Clients
include Eli Lilly and Smith Kline Beecham. Has
written articles for legal and pharmaceutical
journals and lectures extensively on matters
such as E.C. medical device regulations, patent
term restoration and parallel importation.
Prof. Memberships: Member Law Society,
AIPPI, IBA and Secretary of Intellectual Property
Lawyers Association.
Career: Qualified in 1983 whilst at *Woodham
Smith* 1981-85. Joined *Simmons & Simmons* in
1985 where he became a Partner in 1989.
Joined *Taylor Joynson Garrett* in 1998.
Personal: Educated at Barnard Castle School
1969-77 and at Emmanuel College Cambridge
1977-80. Chester Law School 1981. Leisure
interests include Newcastle United F.C. and
chauffeuring his children to parties. Lives near
Gamlingay, Cambs.

HULL, John
Wilde Sapte, London (0171) 246 7000
Partner in Commercial Litigation.
Specialisation: Principal area of practice is
intellectual property. Handles a range of

intellectual property litigation, with an emphasis
on copyright, trade mark and passing off
issues. Special interest in breach of confidence,
trade secrets, privacy and data protection. Also
computer law, including hardware and software
supply disputes, and non-contentious IP work
including advice and drafting, especially related
to banking and finance and industry/university
collaboration. Other main area of practice is
judicial review, particularly in relation to
commercial matters and the educational
sphere. Important cases handled include G.D.
Searle v. Celltech [1982] (employees/breach of
confidence/biotechnology), Swedac Ltd v.
Magnet and Southerns PLC [1989] (Anton Piller/
striking out/copyright infringement/ interference
with trade), PA. v. Manchester City [1986]
(photocopying/copyright infringement), CIS v.
Forward Trust [1987] (computer
programs/copyright infringement/"look and
feel"), Dalgety Spillers Foods Ltd v. Food
Brokers [1994] (passing off/get up/ survey
evidence), R v. Joint Committee on Higher
Surgical Training ex p. Milner [1994] (judicial
review/consultant's training) and R v. Cardiff City
Council ex p. Gooding [1995] (judicial review/
EPA 1990/local authority tendering). Clients
include multinational food companies, UK and
international banks, insurance companies,
universities and research institutes. Author of
"Commercial Secrecy: Law and Practice"
(Sweet & Maxwell 1998) and over fifty articles,
case notes and reviews on intellectual property,
commercial litigation and company law.
Member of the Editorial Advisory Board of
Commercial Judicial Review. Frequent
conference speaker on intellectual property and
commercial legal subjects.
Prof. Memberships: Society for Computers
and the Law, Chartered Institute of Patent
Agents (Associate Member), Intellectual
Property Lawyers Organisation, Licensing
Executives Society.
Career: Qualified in 1979. Lecturer in Law at
Exeter University 1978-81. At *Coward Chance*
1981-89. Joined *Wilde Sapte* in 1989 and
became a Partner in 1990.
Personal: Born 22nd June 1951. Educated at
Southmoor School, Sunderland 1962-69,
Monkwearmouth College, Sunderland 1969-70,
Warwick University 1970-73 (LL.B Hons) and
the London School of Economics 1973-74
(LL.M). Leisure interests include writing, squash
and wine. Lives in London.

INGLIS, Andrew
Olswang, London (0171) 208 8888
Specialisation: Patents, trademarks,
copyright, confidential information, advertising
and marketing. Deals with a mixture of litigation
and commercial work. Cases have included
'Glaverbell S.A v. National Smokeless Fuels and
Anor' and 'Airtec SRL v. Bance', 'Mecklermedia
v. DC Congress' and acting for the Czech
Brewery against Anheuser Busch in the recent
trademark appeal to the High Court. Writes
widely on intellectual property issues including
contributing the UK section of "Intellectual
Property Laws of Europe" published by Wiley.
Prof. Memberships: CIPA, ITMA, INTA, AIPPI.
Career: First qualified in Australia in 1981.
Qualified in England in 1990 and became a
partner at *Nabarro Nathanson* in 1991.
Subsequently became head of *Nabarro
Nathanson's* I.P. department. Joined *Olswang*
February 1997 as a partner and head of the I.P.
Group.

Personal: Born 1957 in Surrey, England. Lived in Australia & U.K. Educated at University of Queensland. Lives in South West London. Leisure interests include collecting antique silhouette profiles and antique prints.

IRVINE, James
Llewelyn Zietman, London (0171) 842 5400
Partner.
Specialisation: Specialises in IP litigation, particularly major patent and trademark litigation and anti-counterfeiting work for international companies. Clients in industries ranging from computer software to fashion accessories. Co-author of chapter on Hong Kong in book about IP rights in Hong Kong and other countries. Lectures on IP issues. Regular contributor of articles to IP magazines.
Prof. Memberships: Institute of Trade Mark Agents (Associate Member), Chartered Institute of Patent Agents, Marques, Law Society of Scotland, AIPPI, INTA.
Career: Admitted in Scotland in 1983, Hong Kong in 1984 and England and Wales 1995. With *Johnson Stokes & Master* in Hong Kong 1984-88. Joined *Denton Hall* in 1988 and became a Partner in 1990. In their Hong Kong office 1988-92. Joined *Llewelyn Zietman* in November 1997.
Personal: Born 24th August 1959. Educated at Aberdeen University 1977-82 (LL.B Hons, DLP). Interests outside the law include golf and bridge.

JONES, Nigel
Linklaters, London (0171) 456 5804
Specialisation: Specialist in intellectual property and technology related matters, particularly in the pharmaceuticals field. Main areas of practice include IP aspects of major acquisitions and disposals, corporate fund raising, and licensing (including drafting and reviewing patent, know-how, trade mark and software licences, both from the commercial and EC anti-trust viewpoints); drafting and negotiating IP licences, manufacturing agreements and distribution agreements and general advisory work. IP litigation, including patent litigation (in the biotech and general healthcare fields), breach of confidence actions and trade mark and copyright disputes.
Prof. Memberships: Licensing Executives Society, International: Vice-Chair, European Committee. Licensing Executives Society, Britain & Ireland: Member of Council and Chairman of EEC Laws Committee. Associate Member of the Chartered Institute of Patent Agents and American Intellectual Property Lawyers Association. Member of Editorial Board of BioScience Law Review.

JONES, Stephen
Allen & Overy, London (0171) 330 3000
Specialisation: Intellectual property litigation and advice work including patents, trade marks, designs and copyright; passing off; technology related litigation and dispute resolution, including information technology; IP aspects of corporate transactions and commercial agreements.
Prof. Memberships: CIPA (Fellow); EPI; ITMA; ECTA; LES; AIPPI (British Group); PTMG; Royal Society of Chemistry (Associate).
Career: BSc (Chemistry) Imperial College; ARCS; LLB (London); Chartered Patent Agent; European Patent Attorney; Registered Trade Mark Agent; solicitor; partner *Allen & Overy*.
Personal: Born 22 January 1956; married with three children.

JUDGE, Ian
Bristows, London (0171) 400 8000
Partner in Intellectual Property Department.
Specialisation: Work covers litigation and licensing of the full range of intellectual property, including patents, trade marks, copyright, designs and confidential information. Has had conduct of major patent cases such as Beecham v. Bristol Myers and Du Pont v. Akzo (both H.L.) and Chiron v Organon Teknika. Speaker at seminars on specialist intellectual property topics.
Prof. Memberships: Law Society, Chartered Institute of Patent Agents (Associate Member), Chairman – Intellectual Property Lawyers Association, AIPPI.
Career: Joined *Bristows Cooke & Carpmael* 1964, became a Partner in 1969.
Personal: Born 4th December 1941. Attended Cambridge University (BA 1963, MA 1967).

KAMSTRA, Gerry
Simmons & Simmons, London (0171) 628 2020
Partner in Intellectual Property Department.
Specialisation: Principal area of practice is intellectual property law, including financings, commercial transactions and litigation within the pharmaceutical and biotechnology industries. Acted in SmithKline & French v. Evans Medical, Bonzel & Schneider (Europe) v. Intervention & Advanced Cardiovascular Systems and Chiron Corporation & Ortho Diagnostics v. Organon/Akzo & United Biomedical. Clients include The Liposome Company Inc, Alizyme plc, Inhale Therapeutic Systems and Bristol-Myers Squibb. Has written numerous articles for legal journals and sub-editor of Journal of Biotechnology in Healthcare and Blackstones IP Business. Is a regular speaker at conferences.
Prof. Memberships: Member Intellectual Property Advisory Committee of BioIndustry Association and Associate Member of Chartered Institute of Patent Agents and Member of The Society for Advanced Legal Studies.
Career: Qualified in 1986. Joined *Simmons & Simmons* 1986 where he became a Partner in 1992.
Personal: Born 13th May 1954. Educated at Hymers College, Hull 1963-71, Keble College, Oxford 1972-75 (Psychology & Physiology), Leicester University 1975-80 (Ph.D in Neuroendocrinology) and Trent Polytechnic 1982-84. Leisure interests include running, swimming and travel. Lives in London and Essex.

KARET, Ian
Linklaters, London (0171) 456 5800
Specialisation: Specialist in intellectual property and technology related matters, particularly in patents. Main areas of practice include IP aspects of major acquisitions and disposals, corporate fund raising and licensing (including drafting and reviewing patent, know-how, trade mark and software licences, both from the commercial and EC anti-trust viewpoints); drafting and negotiating IP licences, manufacturing agreements and distribution agreements and general advisory work. IP litigation, including patent litigation (in the biotech and general healthcare fields), trade mark and copyright disputes and software exploitation.
Prof. Memberships: Associate Member of the Chartered Institute of Patent Agents. Member of the Royal Society of Chemistry and Chartered Chemist.

LLEWELYN, David
Llewelyn Zietman, London (0171) 824 5400
Founding Partner specialising in intellectual property law.
Specialisation: Main area of practice is intellectual property. Deals with all aspects, both contentious and non-contentious. Also covers information technology and pharmaceutical law. Has been involved in a number of major IP related transactions and cases, many cross-border. Clients come principally from the cosmetics, food and drink, pharmaceuticals and retail sectors. Also computer companies (especially software) and multimedia. Author of numerous articles published in legal journals, Editor, IIC. Has also delivered many conference papers in the UK and abroad. Senior Visiting Fellow in Intellectual Property, Centre for Commercial Law Studies, Queen Mary and Westfield College, London.
Prof. Memberships: Law Society, Pharmaceutical Trade Marks Group, International Trademark Association.
Career: Research Fellow at Max Planck Institute for Patent, Copyright and Competition Law, Munich 1980-81. Qualified in 1985. With *Linklaters & Paines* 1982-87, then Partner at *McKenna & Co* 1987-94. Founded *Llewelyn Zietman* in July 1994.
Personal: Born 15th July 1956. Educated at Wallingford Grammar School 1967-74, Southampton University 1974-77 (LL.B) and Worcester College, Oxford 1978-79 (BCL, 1st Class Hons). German speaker. Lives in London SW7.

MACDONALD, Morag
Bird & Bird, London (0171) 415 6000
Partner in Intellectual Property Department.
Specialisation: Work includes litigation, transactional and advisory work in relation to patents, trade marks, copyright and other intellectual property rights. Also handles electronics and computer law. Acted in 'Mentor/Hollister', 'Compaq/Dell', 'Richardson Vicks/Reckitt & Coleman'; Chocosuisse/Cadbury.
Prof. Memberships: CIPA, ITMA, INTA, ECTA.
Career: Called to the Bar in 1984. Qualified as a Solicitor in 1988, having joined *Bird & Bird* in 1985. Became a Partner in 1989. Contributor on IP issues to "Internet Law and Regulation" (FT Law and Tax, 2nd edition, 1998). Co-author of "Designs & Copyright Protection of Products: World Law & Practice". (FT Law and Tax).
Personal: MA in Mathematics, Physics and Law from Cambridge.

MACDONALD-BROWN, Charters
Gouldens, London (0171) 583 7777
Specialisation: Head of Intellectual Property Group. Advised in numerous patent, copyright, trade mark and other IP cases. Executive Council of AIPPI (UK). Editorial Board – Trademark World. Honorary adviser to the Legal and Parliamentary Committee of the Royal Society of Chemistry. Regular conference speaker. Lectures on IP courses at Bristol University and QMW (part of London University).
Prof. Memberships: Law Society, IBA, CIPA, ITMA, AIPPI, ABA, AIPLA, INTA, ECTA, LES.
Career: Qualified 1974. Partner from 1977.

MACFARLANE, Nicholas
Lovell White Durrant, London
(0171) 236 0066
Specialisation: Patents; trade marks; passing-off; copyright; misuse of confidential

information; trade libel and other allied areas of competition law; largely involved in litigation. Involved in many leading intellectual property cases concerning inter alia; patentability of software; the movement of patented pharmaceuticals within the EU; extent of relief in Anton Piller Orders; comparative advertising and counterfeiting.
Prof. Memberships: Member of and former Secretary of Intellectual Property Lawyers Association; member Council British Group of AIPPI; associate member Chartered Institute of Patent Agents and Institute of Trade Mark Agents; member European Trade Mark Association (Anti-Counterfeiting Committee).
Career: Lancaster University 1974 BA (Hons). Articled *Richards Butler*; qualified as solicitor 1977. Joined *Faithfull Owen & Fraser* 1978 partner 1980. In 1985 the firm amalgamated with *Durrant Piesse* which in turn merged with *Lovell White & King* in 1988.

MARSHALL, James
Taylor Joynson Garrett, London
(0171) 353 1234
Specialisation: All areas of intellectual property, both contentious and non-contentious. In particular, patent, trade mark, copyright and breach of confidence litigation; licences and other agreements concerning exploitation of intellectual property including in competition law context.
Prof. Memberships: Solicitor's Association of Higher Courts Advocates; Associate of Chartered Institute of Patent Agents; AIPPI; IP Advisory Committee of BioIndustry Association.
Career: BSc (Mathematics and Physics), University of Bristol. Called to the Bar in 1986 with pupillage in Chambers of (then) Stephen Gratwick QC. 1987 joined *Lovell White Durrant*, subsequently requalifying as a solicitor. 1995 obtained Solicitor-Advocate (Higher Courts Civil) qualification. 1997 joined partnership of *Taylor Joynson Garrett*.

MARSLAND, Vanessa
Clifford Chance, London (0171) 600 1000
Intellectual Property: Partner.
Specialisation: Intellectual property, computer and media law.
Prof. Memberships: Director of the Federation Against Software Theft and of the Computer Law Association, Inc.; member of the Publishers Association publishing law group.
Career: Law (Cambridge) 1978. Admitted as solicitor in 1981. Became Partner in 1987.Currently practising in intellectual property and media, computer and communications groups.

MARTINDALE, Avril
Freshfields, London (0171) 936 4000
Partner specialising in intellectual property.
Specialisation: Main area of practice covers intellectual property. Deals with commercial, advisory and transactional aspects of intellectual property, including relevant EC and competition law. Author of various articles on intellectual property and EC law, and a regular speaker at intellectual property conferences.
Prof. Memberships: Law Society of England & Wales, Law Society of Scotland, Licensing Executives Society, Competition Law Society, INTA.

Career: Qualified in Scotland in 1985. With Scottish firm *Dickson Minto WS* 1985-88, then *McKenna & Co.* 1988-93. Qualified in England & Wales in 1992. Joined *Bristows Cooke & Carpmael* as a Partner in 1993. Joined *Freshfields* August 1997.
Personal: Born 1st June 1961. Educated at Glasgow University 1978-83.

MOODIE, Bill
Herbert Smith, London (0171) 374 8000
Head of the Intellectual Property and Technology Group.
Specialisation: Specialises in intellectual property law, particularly patents, copyright and trade marks involving the electronics, communications and computer industries. Extensive litigation experience but also substantial non-contentious practice. Clients include Logica, Quantel, IBM, Guinness, Formula One, BSkyB, Bridgestone/Firestone, Price Waterhouse, Warner, Vodafone, Procter & Gamble and many others.
Career: South African patent agent and attorney – 1975; Solicitor in England and Wales – 1979; Partner at *Herbert Smith* – 1984; Head of IP Group – 1996.
Personal: Education – University of Cape Town (B.Sc Elec. Eng.) First Class Honours – 1969; University of South Africa (LL.B) – 1975.

MOONEY, Kevin
Simmons & Simmons, London
(0171) 628 2020
Senior Partner in Intellectual Property Department.
Specialisation: Principal area of practice is patent litigation, especially in the pharmaceutical industry. Important cases handled included Beecham Group Ltd v. Bristol-Myers Co [1978] (infringement and revocation action concerning Hetacillin, in High Court, Court of Appeal and House of Lords – a leading case on non-literal infringement); Anheuser-Busch Inc. v. Budejovicky Budvar Narodny Podnik [1984] (passing-off case concerning the "Budweiser" trade mark); Generics (UK) Ltd v. Smith Kline & French Laboratories Ltd [1992] (European Court decision relating to the application of the Treaty of Rome to a licence of right under pharmaceutical patents in the UK), and Biogen v. Medeva Plc (patent infringement/validity action in Patents Court and EPO. Patent relates to Hepatitis B virus antigen). Also handles product liability work. Acts for Gallaher in the smoking and health litigation. Clients include Smith Kline Beecham, Eli Lilly, Bristol Myers Squibb, Pharmacia & Upjohn, Courtaulds, Union Carbide, Procter & Gamble, Intel Inc, Gallaher and Norsk Hydro. Member of Nuffield Bioethics Council Working Party on Human Tissue (report published April 1995). Experienced speaker at seminars and conferences. Charge-out rate is around £300 per hour.
Prof. Memberships: ABA, AIPLA, AIPPI, City of London Solicitors Company (Member of Intellectual Property Sub-Committee).
Career: Qualified in 1971. Partner at *Simmons & Simmons* since 1973.
Personal: Born 14th November 1945. Educated at Bristol University (LL.B 1968). Leisure activities include gardening and supporting Q.P.R. Lives in Ealing, West London.

MORGAN, Glyn
Taylor Joynson Garrett, London
(0171) 353 1234
Specialisation: All aspects of intellectual property and information technology law, including litigation and transactional work. Substantial expertise in copyright infringement actions relating to computer software, disputes relating to the supply of computer systems and in major IT – related transactions including outsourcing and IT systems supply and procurement.
Prof. Memberships: The Society for Computers and The Law, Computer Law Association.
Career: Qualified 1988. At *Woodham Smith* 1986 to 1990. Joined Taylor Joynson Garrett 1990 (Partner from 1994).
Personal: Born 23 January 1963. Educated Royal Hospital School, Holbrook and University College, Cardiff, University of Wales (LL.B). Interests include skiing, film, literature, food and wine.

MOSS, Gary
Taylor Joynson Garrett, London
(0171) 353 1234
Currently the Head of *Taylor Joynson Garrett's* Intellectual Property Department.
Specialisation: Practice covers all areas of intellectual property, but with particular emphasis on patents, biotechnology, information technology and technology transfers. Also handles both contentious and non-contentious matters within the field of information technology including licence disputes, fitness for purpose disputes and copying/ plagiarism disputes. Examples of important cases handled are 'Pall Corporation v. Commercial Hydraulics', 'SKM v. Wagner Spraytech', 'Single Buoy Moorings v. Brown Brothers and Vickers plc', 'Brugger v. Medic-Aid Limited' and Amgen v. Boehringer Mannheim & Genetics Institute (major litigation relating to biotechnology patents). Clients include Amgen Inc, Visa, Pall Corporation, Norcros plc, Vickers plc and NCR Limited. Member of the Editorial Boards of *The Biotechnology Law Report* and the Journal of Brand Management. Has spoken at seminars on information technology and acquisitions/ protection of computer hardware and software.
Prof. Memberships: Law Society (Member of Intellectual Property Sub-Committee).
Career: Qualified in 1977. With *Clifford Turner* 1977-79, then *Woodham Smith* 1979-90 (Partner from 1981). Joined *Taylor Joynson Garrett* as a Partner in 1990.
Personal: Born 7th April 1953. Educated at the University of Leicester 1971-74 (1st Class Hons) and the College of Law (1st Class Hons). Recreations include theatre, opera and golf. Lives in London.

NEWISS, Hilary
Denton Hall, London (0171) 242 1212
hjn@dentonhall.com
Partner in Intellectual Property Group.
Specialisation: Practice covers all aspects of intellectual property advice and litigation, including patent, copyrights, trade marks, confidential information and designs. Acts for a range of Technology and Media clients.
Prof. Memberships: CIPA, AIPLA, AIPPI, Union, City of London Law Society (Intellectual Property Committee Member), BioIndustry Association Committee on Intellectual

Property,Computer Law Association.
Career: Qualified 1981. Partner – *Denton Hall* 1990.
Personal: Born 1956. Educated Harrogate College and Somerville College, Oxford.

NEWMAN, Helen
Simmons & Simmons, London
(0171) 628 2020
Partner and Managing Partner of Intellectual Property Department.
Specialisation: Principal area of practice is advising on a wide range of contentious and non-contentious intellectual property matters. Conducts litigation involving patents, know-how, copyright, designs and trade marks in the UK, and co-ordinates or instructs corresponding litigation overseas. Other main area of work is advising on the acquisition, disposal, re-structuring and exploitation of intellectual property rights portfolios. Has spoken at a number of conferences on intellectual property matters.
Prof. Memberships: International Trademark Association, Institute of Trade Mark Agents, MARQUES, Anti-Counterfeiting Group, European Communities Trade Mark Association.
Career: Articled with *Simmons & Simmons*. Qualified 1980 and became a Partner in 1985.

NODDER, Edward
Bristows, London (0171) 400 8000
Partner in Intellectual Property Department.
Specialisation: Advises on the full range of contentious and non-contentious intellectual property, including patents, trade marks, copyright, designs and confidential information, computers and IT and biotechnology. This includes advice on European competition and harmonisation laws as they impact on intellectual property, including the European Patent Office and the Community Trade Mark Office. Amongst numerous cases, acted for the plaintiff in 3M v. Rennicks and Gillette v. Edenwest and for the defendant in Murray v. NEC and Kastner v Rizla. Has been involved in opposition proceedings at European Patent Office for British Gas and other clients and developed the trade marks aspects of the X/Open Branding Programme for Open IT Systems. Author of articles for specialist periodicals such as 'Patent World'. Regular speaker at intellectual property conferences and seminars.
Prof. Memberships: Law Society, Associate Member of Chartered Institute of Patent Agents, AIPPI.
Career: Joined *Bristows Cooke & Carpmael* in 1978. Became a Partner in 1986.
Personal: Born 29th June 1956. Educated at Cambridge University 1974-77 (MA in Natural Sciences and Law). Enjoys opera, chamber music, tennis, gardening and the Languedoc. Lives in Lewes, Sussex.

PAVER, Michelle
Simmons & Simmons, London
(0171) 628 2020
Specialisation: Patent litigation – cases: Courtaulds v. Lenzig, Fidia v. Seikagaku
Career: MA, Biochemistry (First Class), University of Oxford 1979-83; Admitted 1987; made a Partner of *Simmons & Simmons* 1993.
Personal: Writing and travelling.

PERKINS, David
Clifford Chance, London (0171) 600 1000
Partner.
Specialisation: Principal area of practice is intellectual property encompassing patents, designs, trademarks copyright and trade secrets, competition and antitrust law, pharmaceuticals and biotechnology.

PRICE, Richard
Taylor Joynson Garrett, London
(0171) 353 1234
Partner in Intellectual Property Department.
Specialisation: Intellectual property specialist dealing with patents, trade marks, copyright, confidential information and trade libel litigation, IP intensive acquisitions and disposals and licensing. Important cases handled include successful appeal to House of Lords concerning Asahi Chemical's Patent Application in 1991 (priority of competing patent applications and the need for an enabling disclosure; brought UK back into line with Europe; first IP case ever taken to House of Lords by a Japanese company), Reckitt & Colman Plc v Borden Inc [1990] (successful prevention of JIF lemon lookalike. House of Lords), Unilever v Johnson Wax [1989] (successful defence of a trade mark infringement action re LIFEBUOY/LIFEGUARD and rectification of Unilever's marks) and Lancer Boss v Henley Forklift [1975] (one of the few patent cases to go as far as an enquiry into damages). Also acted for Canon in one of the last appeals to the Privy Council from Hong Kong (patent issues successful; copyright issues re spare part for PC printer also successful.) Current heavy cases include two for Hoechst Celanese Corporation against BP Chemicals (patents for more efficient production and decontamination of acetic acid). The first was successful at trial in February 1997 and, although the infringement issue is under appeal, is proceeding to an account of profits in September 1998.
Prof. Memberships: Chairman, 1994-1997 The Intellectual Property Lawyer's Association (formerly Patent Solicitors Association , City of London Solicitors' Company, Law Society's Intellectual Property Committee, Solicitors European Group, AIPPI (UK). Lecturer Bristol University IP Diploma.
Career: Qualified in 1970. With *Joynson-Hicks & Co* 1968-75 (partner 1973-75), then Partner at *Courts & Co* 1975-77 and at *Woodham Smith* 1977-90. Joined *Taylor Joynson Garrett* as a Partner in 1990.
Personal: Born 7th January 1946. Educated at Kingston Grammar School 1957-64 and Bristol University (LLB) 1964-67. Leisure interests include wildlife, tennis and sailing. Trustee, British Ornithologist's Club. Lives in Berkshire. Married with 3 sons.

RICH, Andrew
Herbert Smith, London (0171) 374 8000
Specialisation: All areas of intellectual property law, contentious and non-contentious. Has been involved in a number of the leading cases in this area including the Boehringer-Mannheim-Amgen patent litigation (recombinant erythropoietin), the Sandvik -v-Iscar and Sandvik -v- Emporia patent actions, an action for Hoffmann-La Roche concerning the PCR patents, actions brought by the owners of the UK Quiksilver trade marks to prevent parallel imports, the patent action between

Carter-Wallace and Unilever relating to pregnancy test kits, a contested application by BASF for a supplementary protection certificate and a number of oppositions in the European Patent Office.
Prof. Memberships: Member of the Intellectual Property Advisory Committee of the UK BioIndustry Association. Member of AIPPI, IPLA and associate member of CIPA and ITMA.
Career: Degree in Biology from Liverpool University (First Class Honours) – 1984. Articled at *Lovell White Durrant* – 1987-1989. Joined *Hammond Suddards* in Yorkshire in 1992. Joined *Herbert Smith* in 1994. Partner 1996.

SHILLITO, Mark
Herbert Smith, London (0171) 374 8000
Specialisation: All aspects of intellectual property work, contentious and non-contentious; extensive trial experience; has acted in a number of the leading cases in the fields of patents (Chiron v. Organon Teknika; Strix v. Otter); trade marks (Vodafone v. Orange); plant variety rights (Germinal v. Fell & Rowsell); copyright (BSkyB v. PRS); and breach of confidence (Berkeley Administration v. McClelland).
Prof. Memberships: AIPPI; AIPLA; CIPA; ITMA; INTA; IPLA; TIPLO.
Career: Articled at *Herbert Smith*; qualified 1989; partner 1996. Queen Mary & Westfield College, London (Dip.IP). University College London (LLB Hons).

SMALL, Harry
Baker & McKenzie, London (0171) 919 1000
See under Computer Law & I.T., p. 185

SMITH, Catriona Macdonald
Allen & Overy, London (0171) 330 3000
Specialisation: Partner dealing with patent, trade mark, copyright, designs and trade secrets litigation, with emphasis on pharmaceuticals, computers and hi-tech products; banking and insolvency related IP, in particular post-insolvency asset disposal; dispute resolution and malicious falsehood.
Prof. Memberships: Honorary Secretary Union of European Practitioners in Industrial Property; Sub-Committee Chair, International Trade Mark Association; Council Member Intellectual Property Lawyers Association, Member of the Intellectual Property Lawyers Organisation, American Intellectual Property Lawyers Association, Association of Intellectual Property Practitioners in Industry.
Career: Articled *Clifford-Turner* (now *Clifford Chance*); qualified 1982; *Clifford Turner* (Clifford Chance) 1980-89; *Allen & Overy* 1989 to present; partner 1992.
Personal: St Andrew's University (MA). Interests include mountain climbing, music and languages.

STARR, Ian
Ashurst Morris Crisp, London
(0171) 638 1111
Specialisation: Patent, trade mark, confidential information and copyright, particularly litigation in the UK and across Europe. Clients range from a number of multi-national telecommunications, computer and healthcare companies to both large and small UK and foreign companies in the general engineering and fmcg industries.
Prof. Memberships: Active member of, and speaker at, a wide range of specialist intellectual property and competition law organisations.

STUBBS, Hugh
Freshfields, London (0171) 936 4000
Specialisation: Head of Intellectual Property Department, handling a wide range of matters relating to copyright, patents, trade marks and designs. Author and co-author of various articles in International Legal Practitioner.
Prof. Memberships: International Bar Association (Chairman of Section on General Practice; Chairman of Civil Litigation Committee 1988-92). Partner 1977. Hong Kong Office 1986-1990.
Personal: Born 6th August 1946. Attended Exeter University. Lives at Hampton Court, London.

SWIFT, Robert
Linklaters, London (0171 456 5806
Partner, Intellectual Property and Information Technology Department.
Specialisation: Specialist with over 30 years experience in all aspects of the intellectual property field. Typical matters include: resolving disputes about trade marks, copyright; designs and unfair trading through negotiations and litigation where necessary; interlocutory injunctions and damages assessments against 'pirates' and 'counterfeiters'; protection of computer software; drafting and negotiating licence agreements of various IP rights; EC and UK competition law issues arising out of complex licensing structures; IP aspects of major corporate deals.

SWYCHER, Nigel
Slaughter and May, London (0171) 600 1200
Specialisation: Intellectual property and information technology law. Primarily involved in non-contentious matters, including the IP and IT aspects of acquisitions, disposals, flotations and privatisations; involved in technology, licensing and transfer, franchising and sponsorship and IT procurement and development.
Prof. Memberships: ITMA, BioIndustry Association.
Career: Admitted 1987 with *Slaughter and May*. Partner 1994.
Personal: Born 6 June 1962. Educated at Denstone College, Staffordshire and Durham University. Magician.

TAYLOR, Peter D
Clifford Chance, London (0171) 600 1000
Partner.
Specialisation: Principal area of practice is intellectual property matters generally and advertising and marketing work.

THORNE, Clive
Denton Hall, London (0171) 320 6802
email: cdt@dentonhall.com Partner in Intellectual Property Group, Litigation Department.
Specialisation: Specialises in contentious intellectual property work, including copyright law, patents, trade marks, passing off, marketing law, computer law and trade secrets. Also commercial litigation, arbitration and employment law. Fellow of the Chartered Institute of Arbitrators. Co-author of 'Intellectual Property – the New Law', joint author of 'Sony Guide to Home Taping and Users Guide to Copyright. Lectures on and has written numerous articles about intellectual property. Leading cases have included: Alan Clark v. Associated Newspapers; Halifax B.S. v. Urquhart DyRes; Interlego A.G. v. Tyco Industries; Sony Corporation v. Saray Electronics; Robin Ray v. Classic FM; Dormeuil v. Nicolian; Dormeuil v. Ferlaglow; Karoon v. Bank of Tokyo.
Prof. Memberships: A founding member of The Intellectual Property Lawyers Organisation. Member of Patent Solicitors Association, International Trade Mark Association, Institute of Trade Mark Agents (Associate Member), Anti-counterfeiting Group, Computer Law Group, Chartered Institute of Patent Agents (Associate Member), panel of arbitrators WIPO and Patents County Court.
Career: Qualified in 1977. Articled *Clifford Turner*. Admitted in Hong Kong in 1984 and Victoria, Australia in 1985. Joined *Denton Hall* as a Partner in 1987.
Personal: Born 1952. Educated at Trinity Hall, Cambridge 1971-74 (BA Hons in Law). Interests outside the law include politics, playing the flute, opera and English music.

WALSH, Paul
Bristows, London (0171) 400 8000
Partner in Intellectual Property Department.
Specialisation: Practice spans both contentious and non-contentious intellectual property matters including computer contracts and related disputes. Legal adviser to the British Brands Group, an alliance of leading manufacturers in the FMCG industry concerned with lookalike products. Also interested in emergency interlocutory applications, Anton Piller Orders and Mareva injunctions, and has been appointed by the High Court to supervise in the conduct of such orders. Cases include Pilkington v. PPG (confidential information arbitration), PPG v. Pilkington (anti-trust arbitration), Assidoman Multipack v. Mead Corporation and Altertext Inc. v. Advanced Data Communications Ltd. Lecturer on technology transfer litigation, trade mark law, biotechnology law and Anton Piller Orders. Author of various articles for *Trade Mark World* and *Corporate Briefing*.
Prof. Memberships: Licensing Executives Society, Associate Member of the Institute of Trade Mark Agents, European Community Trade Mark Association, Law Society.
Career: Qualified and joined *Bristows Cooke and Carpmael* in 1983. Became a Partner in 1988.
Personal: Born 21st December 1956. Educated at Salvatorian College 1968-75 and Oxford University 1976-79. Leisure interests include tennis, squash, literature and wine. Lives in London.

WHAITE, Robin
Linklaters, London (0171) 456 5828
Partner, Intellectual Property and Information Technology Department.
Specialisation: Considerable experience in commercial and litigious matters involving IP rights and technology. Particular knowledge of issues arising in the healthcare, chemical and computer industries. Main areas of practice include patent, copyright, trade marks and trade secrets litigation; technology joint ventures and IP aspects of corporate finance and restructurings; technology transfer generally, including EC and UK anti-trust and competition law considerations; pharmaceutical law, including regulatory affairs. Member of IP panel of the London Chamber of Commerce and Industry and the Government's Standing Advisory Committee on Intellectual Property.

WILLOUGHBY, Anthony
Willoughby & Partners, London (0171) 345 8888
Partner.
Specialisation: All areas of Intellectual Property, but particularly litigation relating to trade marks, passing off, copyright, designs and confidential information.
Prof. Memberships: ITMA, INTA, LSLA.
Career: Qualified 1970. At the Distillers Co Ltd 1970-73, *Herbert Smith* 1973-1994. Partner from 1977. Joined present firm as a partner in 1994.
Personal: Born 29th February 1944. Educated at Westminster School. Interests include music, sport and wine. Member of the Governing Body of Westminster School.

WOOD, Ian
Rowe & Maw, London (0171) 248 4282
Partner and Head of Intellectual Property Department.
Specialisation: All aspects of intellectual property law, including patents, trade marks and copyright and allied rights, although primarily involved in the area of dispute resolution. Acts for a broad range of clients from large multinational corporations to smaller more locally based businesses, covering a broad spectrum of industries and services extending from those involved in newly emergent technologies to those in more established areas of business. Responsible for the conduct of several notable actions in the High Court, including the following leading reported patent infringement actions: Mölnlycke v. Procter & Gamble; Unilever v. Akzo and Chefaro; Honeywell v. ACL. Author of several articles and regularly invited to speak at conferences and seminars (including those attended by fellow professionals).
Prof. Memberships: CIPA; ITMA; INTA; AIPPI; IPLA.
Personal: Born 1950. Attended Durham University (BSc Physics and MSc Nuclear Physics). Qualified as a solicitor in 1977.

SOUTH EAST

The Law Offices of Marcus J O'Leary
(2ptnrs/1asst) Focus on soft IP and IT work. *Marcus O'Leary* and *Celia Nortcliff* feature in the list of leading local IP specialists. **Clients/Work:** Can draw on an excellent client list. General soft IP and IT related work.

Willoughby & Partners (formerly Dallas Brett's office) (2ptnrs/3assts) Willoughby & Partners have taken over parts of Dallas Brett, although Hugh Brett has left. *Anna Booy* enters the IP list as her work is becoming more IP than IT based. **Clients/Work:** All brand and product clearance for a major retailing group; work for various record companies and composers; website agreements and advice on liability, on trading, database agreements and licensing and facilities management.

Garretts (1ptnr/3assts) Breaking into the listing for the first time after recommendations from local competitors. The Reading office continues to impress. **Clients/ Work:** Optical Express; RP Scherer Ltd; Rolls Royce.

Nabarro Nathanson (2ptnrs/5assts) The driving force of the firm is commercial, and their IP work is spearheaded by litigator *Tony Bailes*. **Clients/Work:** Morray Engineering; Sun Microsystems Ltd; Save the Children Fund.

Donne Mileham & Haddock (5ptnrs/ 3assts) Have a good commercial reputation, and undertake mostly IP litigation. *Tim Aspinall* is a commercial litigator, but is also known for his IP work. **Clients/Work:** Successfully represented the defendant in Link Miles v Hughes Rediffusion (a multi-million pound claim relating to visual displays in flight simulators); act for commercial clients in Hi-tech sector.

Lochners Technology Solicitors (2ptnrs/2assts) A niche IP firm in Godalming who are well regarded for their patent work. **Clients/Work:** Defended Remington in an action brought by Philipps NV of the Netherlands for alleged trade mark and registered design infringement relating to Philips' three-headed rotary shaver; represented British Airways before the Copyright Tribunal; also act for Sauflon Pharmaceuticals.

LEADERS' PROFILES · SOUTH EAST

ASPINALL, Tim
Donne Mileham & Haddock, Brighton
(01273) 744319
Managing Partner.
Specialisation: Practice focuses on intellectual property and computer related litigation and other heavyweight commercial litigation cases concerning high technology products and services. Work covers the full range of intellectual property litigation including copyright, design rights, trademarks, patents, passing off and breaches of confidential information. Also handles information technology disputes. Acted for the successful defendant in the reported patent dispute Hughes Rediffusion v. Link-Miles (a multi-million pound patent infringement claim concerning visual displays on flight simulators). Clients include several major flight simulator companies, a major US conglomerate quoted on New York Stock Exchange with subsidiaries throughout Europe, NHS Trusts and academic institutions. Lectures to other lawyers around the country and regularly speaks at conferences.
Prof. Memberships: Society for Computers and the Law, Law Society.
Career: Qualified in 1982. Spent a year at West Sussex County Council before joining *Donne Mileham & Haddock* in 1983. Appointed Partner in 1987 and Head of Litigation Department in 1994. Appointed Managing Partner 1997.
Personal: Born 30th June 1956. Educated at Huddersfield New College 1967-74, York University 1975-78 (BA Hons, History) and Leeds Law School 1979-80 (CPE and LSF). Plays golf and enjoys cricket and theatre. Trustee of local charity. Lives in Brighton.

BAILES, Tony
Nabarro Nathanson, Reading
(0118) 925 4602
See under Computer Law & I.T., p. 189

BOOY, Anna
Willoughby & Partners, Oxford
(01865) 791 990
Consultant in Intellectual Property Department.
Specialisation: All transactional intellectual property work especially in the industry areas of computer software, the internet, multimedia, publishing, music and entertainment, the fine arts, food and drink, advertising and brand management.
Prof. Memberships: SCL, TIPLO, IPI, SEG, TVLO, and honorary member of Society of Professional Composers (legal advisor).
Career: Qualified both UK and Australia.
Personal: Born 19th June 1962. Educated at the University of Queensland (BA LLB Hons.) and University College, London. (LLM in Intellectual Property).

NORTCLIFF, Celia
The Law Offices of Marcus J. O'Leary, Bracknell (01344) 303044
Specialisation: Full range of Intellectual Property work with emphasis on Computer Industry; advice includes Software Licensing and Distribution; Hardware Sales and Distribution; Competition; Advertising and Marketing; Facility Management; CCTA Contracts; Public Procurement; Disaster Recovery; Acts for several multinational companies.
Prof. Memberships: Law Society
Career: Qualified 1971. Ten years in City finally as Partner at *Rowe & Maw*; 1982 onwards in Reading becoming Partner and Head of Intellectual Property at *Brain & Brain* in 1991; joined *The Law Offices of Marcus J O'Leary* as a partner in 1996.
Personal: Born on 31 January 1947; educated Lowestoft Grammar School then Manchester University. Leisure interests – plays flute and piano; enjoys travel and reading.

O'LEARY, Marcus
The Law Offices of Marcus J. O'Leary, Bracknell (01344) 303044
See under Computer Law & I.T., p. 190

SOUTH WEST

Osborne Clarke (2ptnrs/4assts) The largest dedicated IP practice in the south west includes *Andrew Braithwaite* who "gets the job done." **Clients/Work:** Advised Hallmark Cards on infringement action in respect of 'Forever Friends' design; advised on the creation of a video library on the internet for HTV Group; telephone shopping service via radio for GWR Group.

Laytons (3ptnrs/7assts in IP/IT) A highly regarded IP practice includes the "experienced" *Richard Brown*. **Clients/Work:** Several software related transactions for Zuken-Redac Group; several TM infringement actions for Somerfield.

Lester Aldridge (3ptnrs/1asst) Deal in both contentious and non-contentious matters in relation to hard and soft IP. **Clients/Work:** Bishopsgate Insurance; Sunseeker (International) Boats Ltd; Deverill Plc.

Wansbroughs Willey Hargrave (1ptnr) They include the well respected *Alan Wood* who is considered "good on the technical side of patents and trade marks." Known in particular for their litigation expertise. **Clients/Work:** Growth in outsourcing and procurement; much work from the health sector, especially advising on hospital and clinical information.

Bevan Ashford (2ptnrs/3assts) *Gareth Jones* includes IP work in his general company and commercial practice. **Clients/Work:** Pittards Plc; Biotrace International Plc; Glastonbury Festivals.

Burges Salmon (4ptnrs/6assts) Undertake a broad spread of IP work, with strong commercial support. **Clients/Work:** IP aspects of flotation of Science Systems Plc and Gooch & Housego Plc; Naafi.

Clarke Wilmott & Clarke (1ptnr/1asst) A general IP practice which also undertakes IT work. **Clients/Work:** Somerset TEC year 2000 advice; BSI; patent work for Samson Technology Plc.

Humphreys & Co The well known *Robert Humphreys* is particularly respected for his internet work.

LEADERS' PROFILES • SOUTH WEST

BRAITHWAITE, Andrew
Osborne Clarke, Bristol (0117) 984 5237
Partner in IT, Telecoms and Media.
Specialisation: Main areas of practice are commercial and intellectual property work, focusing on IT, telecoms and media. Advises retail, software suppliers on computer program development, licensing and distribution as well as systems integration and facilities management. In the media field, advises multimedia content providers, independent TV producers on productions and sports bodies on sponsorship and merchandising.
Career: Qualified in 1985. Worked with *Ingledew Brown Bennison & Garrett* 1983-85, then *Finers* 1985-88. Joined *Wansbroughs Willey Hargrave* in 1989.

BROWN, Richard
Laytons, Bristol (0117) 929 1626

HUMPHREYS, Robert
Humphreys & Co., Bristol (0117) 929 2662
Senior partner in commercial department.
Specialisation: Intellectual property and reinsurance.
Prof. Memberships: Law Society.
Career: Qualified 1981. With *Simmons & Simmons* 1979-85. Partner *Cartwrights* 1985-86. Co-founded *Humphreys & Co.* 1986.
Personal: Born 1953. Educated Dr Morgan's School, Bridgwater and New College, Oxford. Leisure interests include cricket. Lives near Bristol.

JONES, Gareth
Bevan Ashford, Bristol (0117) 923 0111
Specialisation: Technology transfer agreements, all aspects of IT procurement in public and private sectors including framework agreements, software licencing agreements

and advice on national guidance issued by public sector bodies.
Prof. Memberships: Licensing Executives Society; Society for Computers and Law (Committee member – South West Region); The Intellectual Property Organisation.
Career: University College Wales, Aberystwyth – LLB Hons. Qualified 1980. 1985-1991 Partner *Eversheds* Cardiff (formerly *Phillips & Buck*). 1991 to date Partner – *Bevan Ashford*.
Personal: Golf, rugby.

WOOD, Alan
Wansbroughs Willey Hargrave, Bristol
(0117) 926 8981
See under Computer Law & I.T., p. 191

WALES

Edwards Geldard (1ptnr/3assts) With Eversheds, they dominate the Welsh IP market. *Ceri Delamore* is the head of the team, and is considered "perceptive and quick to grasp the point." **Clients/Work:** Reviewing and advising on TAC's new commissioning agreement relating to digital television; produced a handbook on IP for BTR plc; acting for Fly Fishing Technology Ltd in a patent infringement matter.

Eversheds (2ptnrs/2assts) *Heather McNabb* leads their IP practice. They act for manufacturers, local authorities, government bodies, educational institutions, financial organisations and retailers. **Clients/Work:** Act for Norgine Ltd on contentious and non-contentious matters relating to pharmaceuticals; advising Osprey Metals on licensing of its patents throughout the world; advising a University on the protection and exploitation of IP rights.

Morgan Bruce (5ptnrs/4assts) Are recognised for their work on the IP elements of the media. **Clients/Work:** Acting for a university, companies and the NHS on patent licensing matters.

LEADERS' PROFILES • WALES

DELEMORE, Ceri
Edwards Geldard, Cardiff (01222) 238239
Partner, Head of Intellectual
Property/Information Technology
Specialisation: All aspects of intellectual property and information technology law including transactional work, collaboration agreements, licensing, IT procurement, FM contracts, bespoke software developments and litigation. Also handles media work.
Prof. Memberships: The Intellectual Property Lawyers Organisation. The Law Society's Solicitors' European Group. Society for Computers & the Law. Affiliate of Chartered Institute of Arbitrators.

Personal: B.A. (Hons.) English and French Law Class 1, University of Kent at Canterbury: Diplome de droit francais de l'universitÇ, de Paris-Sud. Articled *Slaughter & May*; qualified 1986; *Slaughter & May* 1984-88; joined *Edwards Geldard* 1988: partner 1991. Author of "Copyright Explained" published by RIBA.

McNABB, Heather
Eversheds, Cardiff (01222) 471147
Specialisation: Partner and Head of Intellectual Property Unit. Specialises in all aspects of Intellectual Property and IT work. Extensive experience of drafting and negotiating on a wide range of licenses and agreements and advises generally on the protection, maintenance and exploitation of intellectual property rights. Practice covers the full range of contentious and non-contentious IP. Particular interest in trade mark issues, technology-based businesses, the Internet and Year 2000 issues.
Prof. Memberships: Member of the Licensing Executives Society; member of the Society for Computers and Law; Member of the Intellectual Property Lawyers Association.
Career: Attended University of Wales, Cardiff (LLB Hons. 1986) Qualified in 1989. Joined *Eversheds* in 1994, becoming a partner in 1995.
Personal: Married and resides in South Wales.

MIDLANDS

Wragge & Co (4ptnrs/7assts) Although *Bill Jones* is more known for his IT than his IP work, they have a strong practice. **Clients/Work:** Acting for a BI Group subsidiary in connection with 13 patent actions in the Cinpres v Melea Ltd case; acting for Brita in relation to Patent and Design Right Licences with Boots plc in the context of manufacturing agreements; acting in the Parlock v Jonesco patent infringement action.

Edge & Ellison (5ptnrs/6assts) *Michael Luckman* is respected for the general spread of IP work he undertakes, although reservations were expressed about the strength in depth of the team. **Clients/Work:** European Trading Corporation against Customs & Excise; franchise agreements for Dunkin Donuts; Premier Brands.

Martineau Johnson (3ptnrs/6assts) Praised for the quality of their work. The "friendly and approachable" *William Barker* is known mainly for his contentious work. **Clients/Work:** Carflow Products v Linwood Securities; Orwin v AG; Griggs Group.

Pinsent Curtis (1ptnr/8assts) A well respected IP practice which includes *Cerys Wyn Davies*, and on the litigation side *Marie McMorrow*. **Clients/Work:** Joint venture agreement between Xenova Plc and Finnish company; advising TI Group plc on copyright dispute; advising LucasVarity on a wide range of IP matters including licensing, development and joint venture programmes all relating to their core technologies.

Dibb Lupton Alsop (1ptnr/3assts) Developing a "one stop shop" policy under the guidance of *Neil Maybury*. **Clients/Work:** Anton Piller TM infringement action for Puma; acting for Cybermedia Inc in relation to copyright infringement of computer software; JBA Plc.

Browne Jacobson (3ptnrs/2assts) Have *Peter Ellis* in the list of leading solicitors, and undertake both patent and soft IP matters. **Clients/Work:** Appointed by the University of Nottingham to assist in creating a joint venture with industry to allow the University to maximise the value of IP generated by its bio-chemistry research; ongoing patent licensing work world-wide.

Freeth Cartwright Hunt Dickens (2ptnrs/2assts) John Lewis has left to set up his own practice, although the arrival of Helen Driscoll from Eversheds may sustain the quality. **Clients/Work:** General advice to Experian Ltd; Coldseal Ltd; Paul Smith Ltd; acted for the National Airline Commission for Papua New Guinea in a passing off dispute.

Hewitson Becke + Shaw (6ptnrs/ 8assts in IT/IP) Regarded as strong in anti-counterfeiting, with IP lawyers floating between the Northampton and Cambridge offices. **Clients/Work:** Pegasus plc; Novell; RPC Group plc design right work.

Shoosmiths & Harrison Have an "aggressive but good" IP practice.

Eversheds (4ptnrs/6assts in commercial the department) Lionel Howard is now a consultant. They have a specialism in advertising and sales promotion work. **Clients/Work:** Currently acting for Metsec Plc and its subsidiary companies in relation to a patent infringement case; advised Lucas Varity on IP aspects of the disposal of two large divisions spread across several jurisdictions; also act for the Bourne Leisure Group.

Wansbroughs Willey Hargrave The experienced *Jeremy Roper* has a "strong IP base" in addition to his commercial work. **Clients/Work:** Much of the work comes from the health sector, such as advising on clinical and hospital information.

John Lewis, now a sole practitioner, remains a leading individual.

LEADERS' PROFILES · MIDLANDS

BARKER, William
Martineau Johnson, Birmingham
(0121) 200 3300
Partner, Head of Intellectual Property Department.
Specialisation: Areas of practice include contentious and non-contentious intellectual property and computer law. Experienced in anti-counterfeiting and has particular experience of trade marks, copyright and patents. Has written various articles on the protection and enforcement of intellectual property rights and has addressed seminars in Birmingham and Singapore. Experienced in the application and execution of Anton Piller Orders and is on the Birmingham Law Society list of supervising solicitors.
Prof. Memberships: Anti-counterfeiting Group and Licensing Executives Society.
Career: Articled: *Laces & Co*, Liverpool; Qualified 1986; Assistant Solicitor, *Pinsent & Co* 1986-1990; Associate, 1990-1991; Partner, *Martineau Johnson* 1992.
Personal: Born 4th January 1962. Educated at Merchant Taylors School, Crosby, Liverpool. BSc in Law and Mathematics. Leisure interests include tennis, member Edgbaston Priory LTC and golf, member Moor Hall Golf Club.

ELLIS, Peter
Browne Jacobson, Nottingham
(0115) 950 0055
Specialisation: Practises in all aspects of Intellectual Property litigation and dispute resolution including patents, copyright and design rights (registered and unregistered), confidential information, passing off trade secrets; acting for computer software and hardware companies, telecommunications, engineering and clothing companies. In 1998 involved in the trademark for major fashion house, assisting/representation with clients in US patent litigation.
Prof. Memberships: TIPLO, LES, AIPPI.
Career: Qualified 1976. At *Wells & Hind* 1976-1980. *Browne Jacobson* 1981 to present (Partner from 1984).
Personal: Born 3.6.52. Interests include family, golf, cricket and sports generally. Lives in Nottingham.

JONES, Bill
Wragge & Co, Birmingham (0121) 233 1000
See under Computer Law & I.T., p. 190

LEWIS, John
John Lewis Solicitor Advocate, Southwell
(01949) 851 513
Solicitor Advocate and Registered Trade Mark Attorney.
Specialisation: Trade Marks, Patents, Copyright and Designs, Passing off, confidential information, Media Law. As one of the first Solicitor Advocates to qualify in this country, John has the right to appear in open court in all Civil Courts in the country up to the House Lords, and he also appears on a regular basis in the Trade Mark Registry in invalidity/revocation and opposition proceedings. Reported decisions include GRANIT TM and GRANITE Revocation (Trade Mark Registry) and LEEC v Morquip (Laddie J). John also handles non-contentious IP work including licensing. He is competent in French, German and Italian.
Prof. Memberships: Corporate Member of the INstitute of Trade Mark Agents; Chairman, Software, IT and Multimedia group, Licensing executivess' Society; AIPPI; TIPLO; SEG; SAHCA.
Career: Registered Trade Mark Attorney; Supreme Court Advocate (Civil Courts); MITMA.
Personal: Educated at Loughborough; Oxford University (MA Hons).

LUCKMAN, Michael
Edge & Ellison, Birmingham (0121) 200 2001
Specialisation: Complete range of commercial and contentious intellectual property and information technology work. Specialist areas of advice include biotechnology and technology, the Internet and the retail sector – brands and counterfeit issues.
Prof. Memberships: Licensing Executives Society. The Intellectual Property Lawyers Organisation. British In Vitro Diagnostics Association.
Career: St Brendan's College, Bristol. Exeter University (LLB Hons). *Simmons & Simmons* (1983-1988). *Slaughter and May* (1989-1994). Qualified 1985. Partner *Edge & Ellison* 1995.
Personal: 2 beautiful daughters. Interests include fly fishing, watching rugby, reading, skiing.

MAYBURY, Neil
Dibb Lupton Alsop, Birmingham
(0345) 262728
Partner I.T. and Intellectual Property Group.
Specialisation: Advises on all aspects of computer and IT law both contentious and non-contentious. Acts for many software publishers both national and international. Regular speaker at computer law seminars.
Prof. Memberships: Federation Against Software Theft-legal Advisory Group, Society for Computers and Law.
Career: Qualified 1969 with *Clifford-Turner* (now *Clifford Chance*), partner *Pinsent & Co* (now *Pinsent Curtis*) 1975-1995, joined *Dibb Lupton Broomhead* as a partner 1995.

MCMORROW, Marie
Pinsent Curtis, Birmingham (0121) 200 1050
Associate in Intellectual Property Department.
Specialisation: Deals with contentious and non-contentious intellectual property matters, chiefly IP litigation. Areas of expertise include patent and trade mark disputes, passing off, copyright, know-how and design infringement and breach of confidence. Such litigation is also co-ordinated on an international, multi-forum basis for clients. Work includes competition and EC law litigation.
Prof. Memberships: Licensing Executives Society, Institute of Trade Mark Agents, Anti-Counterfeiting Group and TIPLO
Career: Articled: *Wragge & Co* in 1987; qualified 1989. Associateship: *Wragge & Co*, May 1993. Joined *Pinsent Curtis*, June1996.

ROPER, Jeremy James
Wansbroughs Willey Hargrave, Birmingham
(0121) 631 4099
Specialisation: Advises on both contentious and non-contentious intellectual property, including patents, copyright, designs, trade marks and confidential information; also technology transfers, and IP licensing, EC law, IT procurement and outsourcing.
Career: 1977 *Wragge & Co*; 1980 *Dibb Lupton Broomhead*; 1983 became partner; 1995 Joined *WWH*.

WYN DAVIES, Cerys
Pinsent Curtis, Birmingham (0121) 200 1050
Commercial Partner
Specialisation: Full range of intellectual property and information technology work, emphasis on non-contentious matters including IP/IT due diligence in connection with transactions; technology and biotechnology licensing; multimedia licensing; research and development and collaboration agreements; confidentiality arrangements; trade marks licensing and advice including matters relating to the Internet and the impact of the millennium.
Prof. Memberships: Licensing Executives Society. TIPLO. FAST.
Career: Qualified 1985. *Coward Chance* 1983-87 and *Clifford Chance* 1987-95. Joined *Pinsent Curtis* in 1995 as Partner.
Personal: Born 1961. Graduated from Exeter University 1982 (LLB) First Class Honours and Sweet and Maxwell prize winner. Diploma in Intellectual Property Law, University of London 1991 – Distinction in all four heads. Interests include theatre, walking and skiing.

EAST ANGLIA

HEWITSON BECKE + SHAW Cambridge
MILLS & REEVE Norwich

EVERSHEDS Norwich
TAYLOR VINTERS Cambridge

Greenwoods Peterborough

Hewitson Becke + Shaw (6ptnrs/8assts in IT/IP) The team of *Ian Craig* and *Niel Ackermann* work from both the Northampton and Cambridge offices. **Clients/Work:** Microsoft Research Ltd; Nike; Chiroscience.

Mills & Reeve (6ptnrs/6assts) Elevated a place after the arrival of *Isabel Napper* from Taylor Vinters, who is considered particularly strong on non-contentious bio-tech work. *Alasdair Poore* is experienced in the general science and electronics field. **Clients/Work:** Imperial College London; increasing work in the health sector, such as NHS Trusts and major clients in the pharmaceutical and bio-tech fields such as Celsis International and Ethical Pharmaceuticals.

Eversheds (4ptnrs/4assts in Norwich and Ipswich) A strong national IP practice which can draw on the resources of several offices. **Clients/Work:** Advising Ransomes plc on technology licence-in for all new wheel drive technology; act for Sinclair International Ltd on technology licences-out in countries such as Chile and New Zealand; advice on sub-licensing agreements relating to new gardening equipment technology in the USA for Atco-Qualcast Ltd.

Taylor Vinters (2ptnrs/2assts) Profile dented by the departure of Isabel Napper, but still undertake IP work. **Clients/Work:** Symbionics Ltd; MDSI; Olivetti.

Greenwoods Known for their IP work as well as publishing, and are led by *Philip Sloan*. The firm undertakes patent and non-patent work. **Clients/Work:** Acted on behalf of an American company against a Japanese company in an ICC Arbitration in Paris on claim for unpaid royalties in respect of IP licensing agreement; successfully acted for plaintiff in Gerber v Lectra; EMAP plc.

CRAIG Ian Hewitson Becke + Shaw

ACKERMANN Niel Hewitson Becke + Shaw
NAPPER Isabel Mills & Reeve
POORE Alasdair Mills & Reeve
SLOAN Philip Greenwoods

ACKERMANN, Niel
Hewitson Becke + Shaw, Cambridge
(01223) 461155
Specialisation: Qualified 1981. Intellectual Property Group, undertaking only Intellectual property work. Has specialised in IP since qualifying, including two years as Assistant Solicitor at Bird & Bird and 6 years as a Partner at Pettman Smith. Work covers the full range of intellectual property litigation, including copyright, design rights, trade marks, patents, passing off and breaches of confidential information. Has acted in a number of reported cases.
Career: Admitted to the Bar in South Africa and was a journalist for three years during which he was sent as a foreign correspondent to London, commenced playing rugby for the Law Society RFC and qualified as a solicitor. Educated at Groote Schuur High School, Cape Town; University of Cape Town (BA LLD); Open University (BSc).
Prof. Memberships: Member of Anti-Counterfeiting Group, Society for Computers and the Law.
Personal: Lives in Cambridge has four young children. Interests include computing and rugby.

CRAIG, Ian
Hewitson Becke + Shaw, Cambridge
(01223) 461155
Partner in the Intellectual Property Group.
Specialisation: Technical background comes from 11 years service in the Submarine branch of the Royal Navy, in both conventional and nuclear powered submarines. Now undertakes all forms of contentious and non-contentious Intellectual Property work. Advising extensively on all copyright issues, including copyright in computer programs, also upon patents and unregistered design rights, trademarks and passing off. Undertakes consultancy from major public companies in relation to Intellectual Property and sits on two Intellectual Property Committees for substantial public companies as the external adviser. Lectures widely on the subject of Intellectual Property to companies and University students. Has overseen a number of teams of lawyers executing Anton Piller orders.
Career: Qualified in 1982. Previously served as a Commissioned Officer in the Royal Navy 1967-78. Joined *Wild, Hewitson + Shaw* in 1980, becoming a Partner in 1985 and Head of Intellectual Property Department in 1993. Now runs Intellectual Property Group. Associate member of the American Bar Association, and Society for Computers and The Law.
Personal: Born 21st January 1949. Attended Kelvinside Academy, Glasgow, 1959-67; then College of Law, Chancery Lane, 1978-80. Leisure interests include reading, travel and water colour painting, sports, skiing and rugby. Lives in Cambridge.

NAPPER, Isabel
Mills & Reeve, Cambridge
+44 (0)1223 364422
Specialisation: Strong London City background dealing in all aspects of intellectual property law. Her move to Cambridge, where she has already acquired a substantial reputation, enables her to use that experience to advantage of clients. Enjoys handling a wide variety of IP issues relating to patents, designs, trade marks and confidential information. Often called in to advise companies of all sizes on how to deal with their intellectual property in order to protect and exploit it efficiently. Frequently lectures and gives seminars to clients and professional bodies. Extensive practical experience of litigation and dispute resolution. Has a particular interest in technology transfer and biotechnology.
Prof. Memberships: Chartered Institute of Patent Agents, Society for the Application of Research, Licensing Executives Society.
Career: Masters Degree (London). Qualified 1984. Specialist IP lawyer with *Lovell White Durrant*. 1991 IP partner *Hopkins & Wood*. 1998 Partner in IP team *Mills & Reeve*.
Personal: Born 1958. Keen on good food, wine and enjoying life.

POORE, Alasdair
Mills & Reeve, Cambridge
+44 (0)1223 364422
Specialisation: Wide range of intellectual property work including commercial (licensing and other agreements, computer contracts, competition law and M&A) and litigation and dispute resolution. Experience and particular interest in high-tech areas including electronics, computers and software, and also chemicals and biotechnology. Recent work has included a substantial patent action involving plastic interlocking floors, a multi-million pound refunding of recognition software, a renewable energy venture and licensing and advice on a significant web browsing technology.
Prof. Memberships: Chartered Patent Agent, Registered Trade Mark Agent, Council Member of CIPA and Chairman General Laws Committee, Patent Litigators Association, Licensing Executives Society, INTA.
Career: MA (Cantab) Law and Natural Sciences; Shell International Petroleum Co; *Lovell White Durrant*; *Clyde & Co.*; *Mills & Reeve*.
Personal: Squash, real tennis, mountaineering, music

SLOAN, Philip
Greenwoods, Peterborough (01733) 555244

NORTH EAST

Addleshaw Booth & Co (4ptnrs/13assts) *Richard Kempner* made a big impact with the Asda case, and is well known for his soft IP work. Have an impressive client list. **Clients/Work:** All IP work for Asda; acting for Ferrari in litigation against Sony for TM infringement; acting for Sir Roger Penrose in much publicised copyright infringement case against Kimberley Clark for their double velvet toilet paper.

Dibb Lupton Alsop (4ptnrs/6assts) Used to dominate the regional IP field, and are still well respected for their practice, which includes a patent filing operation. The "methodical" *Christopher Tulley* is a described as a "feisty fighter." **Clients/Work:** Acting for Microstill Ltd in two major patent revocation actions by Ladbrokes and Coral Racing; acting for the Early Learning Centre in TM/passing off to prevent 18 million 'Mr Men Early Learning' Cards; acting for Yorkshire Electricity Group plc in TM/passing off case against Yorkshire Electricity and Gas Ltd.

Lupton Fawcett (2ptnrs – 1p/t; 2assts) Have a well established IP practice, which is led by *John Sykes*. **Clients/Work:** Client base focused on the manufacturing, chemical IT, textiles and bio-technology.

Pinsent Curtis (2ptnrs/ 10assts) The "solid" *Stephen Chandler* is head of the commercial group, and is known for his non-contentious practice. **Clients/ Work:** Pace Microtechnology patent claims; acting for Allied Colloids Group plc in a major joint venture to settle US patent litigation; acting for Smith & Nephew plc in a major patent revocation action involving complex multi-jurisdictional and foreign law issues.

Walker Morris (1ptnr/2assts) *Patrick Cantrill* is known as a trade mark specialist, and the firm also has a reasonably strong TM filing practice. **Clients/Work:** Re-vamping Leeds University's IP contracts; advising Kalon on an infringement case against PJ Paints; acting on behalf of Surfachem Ltd in a patent infringment in the Dutch courts.

Eversheds (2ptnrs/6assts) The strength of the department lies chiefly in IT work, although they are still highly regarded for their IP practice. **Clients/Work:** General advice for Asda; litigation work for Philips; TM administration and licensing arrangements across the world for Austin Reed.

Hammond Suddards (1ptnr/3assts) The reputation of the Leeds office is enhanced by the name of Larry Cohen, but he practises mainly from London. *Andrew Clay* enters the list for the first time. **Clients/Work:** Netlon v Tensar; R v MAFF ex parte ISK; ISA v Stannell.

Dickinson Dees (1ptnr/2assts) Offer a "competent IP service" on the back of a commercial and insolvency practice. **Clients/Work:** Trade mark registration; soft drinks manufacturer; patent work for marine equipment manufacturer.

LEADERS' PROFILES · NORTH EAST

CANTRILL, Patrick
Walker Morris, Leeds (0113) 283 2500
Specialisation: Practice covers the full range of contentious and non contentious intellectual property work including advice on the securitisation and management of IP. Case load relates to a broad client base. Has acted in a number of patent infringement 'look-a-like' disputes and high profile technology licensing deals. Has lectured extensively in the UK and abroad and has been a speaker for the Patent Office Roadshow.
Prof. Memberships: Chairman of the North East chapter of Licensing Executives Society; Anti-Counterfeiting Group; INTA; ECTA.
Career: Qualified 1984. Also admitted in Hong Kong in 1986. Joined *Walker Morris* as a partner and head of the Intellectual Property Group in 1992.
Personal: Educated at Wycliffe College and University College, London. Lives in York.

CHANDLER, Stephen
Pinsent Curtis, Leeds (0113) 224 5000
National Head of Commercial and Partner in Commercial Department, Leeds.
Specialisation: Intellectual property,including protection, exploitation and enforcement of patents, trade marks, copyrights, design rights and trade secrets, as well as consultancy in the management of IP. Acted in 'Provident v. Halifax', acts for Holliday Chemical Holdings Plc in chemical and pharmaceutical patent matters, Pace Microtechnology in telecoms matters; worked for the NHS in developing a framework for the management of its intellectual property,

acts for Smith & Nephew plc, Case Corporation and a number of NHS Hospital Trusts.
Career: Qualified in 1980. Partner in 1985.
Personal: Born 1955. Educated St. John's College, Cambridge 1974-77.

CLAY, Andrew
Hammond Suddards, Leeds
(0113) 284 7000
Specialisation: Intellectual Property Litigation and the commercial exploitation of intellectual property. Particular specialisation in heavyweight patent, copyright and breach of confidence litigation. Cases include Re GEC's Patent, Halifax Building Society v. Urquhart-Dykes & Lord, R v MAFF (Ex Parte ISK Biosciences) – a case on data protection in relation to pesticide regulatory data and Tensar Inc v. Netlon Limited – a major intellectual property arbitration.
Prof. Memberships: CIPA. Solicitor's European Group.
Career: Harrogate Grammar School, St. Andrews University (first class honours BSc. degree. Law school in Leeds, *Herbert Smith* 1989-1992. 1992 – to date *Hammond Suddards*, Partner 1997.
Personal: Resides in Harrogate. Hobbies include cinema, theatre, cycling.

KEMPNER, Richard
Addleshaw Booth & Co, Leeds
(0113) 209 2000
Partner and Head of Intellectual Property (Leeds), Commercial Group.
Specialisation: Handles both disputes and

transactions involving patents, copyright, trade marks, designs, confidential information and IT. Clients include Asda, Becton Dickinson, Sir Roger Penrose, Yorkshire Water, Reckitt & Colman. Speaks and writes extensively internationally on protection, licensing and enforcement.
Prof. Memberships: LES, Honorary Representative Canada (UK) Chamber of Commerce, INTA
Career: *Linklaters & Paines* 1985-1990. Joined the firm in 1990. Partner 1992.
Personal: Born 30th July 1962. Educated at Durham University 1981-84.

SYKES, John
Lupton Fawcett, Leeds (0113) 280 2000
Specialisation: John Sykes has substantial experience in handling all aspects of intellectual property work since 1982 when he began specialising in this field. His knowledge and experience is based on both National and International work in this field, whether as part of a dispute or as part of a commercial deal, and covers patents, trade marks, copyright including media and entertainment industry work, confidential information and all types of design rights. John Sykes has particular expertise and interest in patents and trade marks, and intellectual property rights relating to the information technology industry.
Prof. Memberships: Associate Member of the Chartered Institute of Patent Agents; Member of the Licensing Executives Society.

Career: 1982-1986, Trainee and Qualified Solicitor with *Philip Conn & Co* Manchester. Niche Intellectual Property Practice. 1986-1989, Solicitor with *Dibb Lupton Broomhead*, specialising in Intellectual Property Law, Leeds. 1989-1992, Partner with *Dibb Lupton Broomhead*, Leeds. 1992-Date, Partner *Lupton Fawcett*, Leeds.
Personal: Born 8 May 1957. Particular interests include sailing and golf when family and work allow.

TULLEY, Christopher
Dibb Lupton Alsop, Leeds (0345) 262728
Specialisation: Full range of intellectual property litigation including patents, trade marks, copyright and design right, passing off and breach of confidence.
Prof. Memberships: Chartered Institute of Patent Agents (Associate), Intellectual Property Lawyers Association, Patent Litigators Association, Law Society.

Career: Qualified 1985. Joined *Dibb Lupton* in 1987. Partner in 1992. Head of the Yorkshire IP Group 1995.
Personal: Born 1961. Attended Leeds University. Lives in Harrogate.

NORTH WEST

LEADING FIRMS · NORTH WEST
ADDLESHAW BOOTH & CO Manchester
HALLIWELL LANDAU Manchester
HILL DICKINSON Manchester

HIGHLY REGARDED FIRMS
Davies Wallis Foyster Liverpool
Dibb Lupton Alsop Liverpool
Hammond Suddards Manchester
Kuit Steinart Levy Manchester
Lawson Coppock & Hart Manchester
Taylors Blackburn

Addleshaw Booth & Co (4ptnrs/13assts) A large and well regarded IP department, and considered especially good on the non-contentious side. *Robert Stoker* is described as "amiable" and has "good drafting and commercial skills." *Paul Bentham* also features in the up & coming list. **Clients/Work:** Successfully defended Satake UK Ltd against Buhler AG in a multi-million pound patent dispute relating to grain milling machinery; advised Flexitallic Group on the IP aspects of the acquisition of Dan-Loc Corporation in relation to the industrial gasket sealing business purchased from T&N plc for £70m; act for AAH Pharmaceuticals Ltd.

Halliwell Landau (2ptnrs/3assts) *Jonathan Moakes* undertakes mainly non-contentious IP work, and the department has been strengthened by the addition of *Richard Boardman*, who is known for his work on the media and music side. **Clients/Work:** Trinity Pharmaceuticals; Swinton Group Plc; Tepnel Life Sciences.

Hill Dickinson (formerly Philip Woods & Co) (2ptnrs/1asst) Philip Woods & Co have been taken over by Hill Dickinson, and Stephen Aldred has left the firm. *Philip Woods* himself remains, and continues to operate "primarily as an IP litigator." **Clients/Work:** Large clients in utilities, TV, manufacturing, software and universities. Predominantly litigation, including Patent Court work.

Davies Wallis Foyster (4ptnrs/1asst) Offer IP advice as part of a general commercial practice. **Clients/Work:** Acquisition of "Prestige" Intellectual Property for Meyer International Holdings; legal advisors to Mirror Group TV; Liverpool John Moores University.

Dibb Lupton Alsop The Manchester office is seen to be making progress in IP over the last year, and offers advice on a range of IP issues. **Clients/Work:** Acting for Charlesworth/Extradakerb in a patent matter; acting for D Jacobson on its acquisition of 'GOLA' brand; acting for Stagecoach Plc in passing off and TM action.

Hammond Suddards (5assts) A strong national litigation practice underpins the reputation of the firm's IP work. **Clients/Work:** See Leeds office details.

Kuit Steinart Levy (3ptnrs/2 assts – none f/t) A small commercial firm which maintains a reputation in IP for their work for a pharmeceutical client. **Clients/Work:** Emphasis of work is in the sports merchandising and character licensing, and healthcare sectors.

Lawson Coppock & Hart (4ptnrs do some IP) A small firm which undertakes well regarded soft IP work, especially trade marks and copyright. **Clients/Work:** General soft IP work, with a particular focus on trade marks and copyright.

Taylors (2ptnrs/4assts) Undertake the IP spin-offs from their textile industry work, mainly design and copyright. **Clients/Work:** Large client base among textile manufacturers (75% in home furnishing).

LEADING INDIVIDUALS NORTH WEST
BOARDMAN Richard Halliwell Landau
MOAKES Jonathan Halliwell Landau
STOKER Robert Addleshaw Booth & Co
WOODS Philip Hill Dickinson

UP AND COMING
BENTHAM Paul Addleshaw Booth & Co
SEE PROFILES AT END OF THIS SECTION

LEADERS' PROFILES · NORTH WEST

BENTHAM, Paul
Addleshaw Booth & Co, Manchester
(0161) 934 6000
Partner in Intellectual Property Deaprtment, Commercial Group
Specialisation: Intellectual property and technology including patents, trade marks, passing off, copyright and designs, trade secrets and confidential information and related areas of competition law. Particular expertise in information technology contracts including the acquisition of computer systems, the licensing of computer software and outsourcing agreements. Also has considerable experience in technology licensing.
Prof. Memberships: Licensing Executives Society, Solicitors European Group and The Society for Computers and Law and advising on intellectual property matters in respect of corporate acquisitions and joint ventures.
Career: Articled with the firm and qualified in

1989 and became a partner in 1995.
Personal: Born 30th June 1964, educated at the University of Leicester (1984-87), (LL.B Hons, Law with French) Universite de Strasbourg (Diplome d'Etudes juridiques francaises). Leisure interests include foreign travel and supporting Manchester United.

BOARDMAN, Richard
Halliwell Landau, Manchester
(01132) 416107
Partner in the Intellectual Property and Information Technology Department.
Specialisation: Handles all aspects of commercial and dispute related intellectual property and information technology work together with associated anti-trust matters. This work covers patents, trade marks (including registrations, copyright, design right, confidential information and passing-off). Also deals with character and personality

merchandising, media and entertainment law and multimedia. Represents a wide range of clients from international corporations to smaller private companies in the United Kingdom and abroad (particulary in the United States). Recent work has been in areas as diverse as chemicals, biotechnology, engineering, retailing, manufacturing, publishing, media and entertainment, advertising and information technology.
Prof. Memberships: The Chartered Institute of Patents Agents (Associate), The Royal Television Society, The Computer Law Association, The Licensing Executives Society, The Federation Against Software Theft, The FAST Legal Advisory Group, The British Interactive Multimedia Association, The Law Society and The International Association of Entertainment Lawyers.
Career: Qualified in 1989. Employed as trainee solicitor, assistant and associate at *Simpson Curtis* 1987-1994. Joined *Garrett & Co* in 1994.

Appointed Partner in 1995. *Halliwell Landau* 1998 as Partner.

MOAKES, Jonathan
Halliwell Landau, Manchester
(0161) 835 3003
Partner and head of Intellectual Property Department.
Specialisation: Work includes patents, copyright, designs, trade secrets, technology transfer and exploitation agreements, trade marks and disputes. Particular experience in acting for high tech businesses – member of the firm's high tech/biotech unit. Other area of practice is computer law, including software licensing, supply contracts and disputes. Author of International Information Technology Law – England and Wales and the Encyclopaedia of Information Technology Law – Export Licensing Control. Has addressed numerous conferences on intellectual property and computer law issues.
Prof. Memberships: Chairman of North West Branch of the Licensing Executives Society, Society for Computers and Law, Solicitors European Group.
Career: Qualified 1984. Worked at *Baker & McKenzie* 1982-88, then *Halliwell Landau*, becoming a Partner in 1989.
Personal: Born 1960. Attended Queens' College, Cambridge 1978-81. Leisure interests include sailing, skiing, fell walking, tennis and playing the violin. Lives in Wilmslow.

STOKER, Robert
Addleshaw Booth & Co, Manchester
(0161) 934 6000
Partner in Intellectual Property Department, Commercial Group.
Specialisation: Work includes the acquisition, exploitation and enforcement of patents, trade marks, copyright and designs, confidential information and related areas of competition law. Other areas of practice are sport, media and entertainment and information technology including all types of computer contracts involving the acquisition, disposal or licensing of software, hardware purchase and maintenance, facilities management and computer bureau agreements. Has been appointed to advise the organising committee of the 2002 Commonwealth Games in respect of IP matters. Has dealt with the IP aspects of pharmaceutical and healthcare joint ventures and the acquisition of portfolios of international agrochemical products, the merchandising of various internationally known brands and various total solution computer hardware and software installation transactions. Former lecturer at University College of Wales, Aberystwyth. Has spoken on various intellectual property and information technology related topics in the UK and USA.
Prof. Memberships: Licensing Executives Society, INTA, LIDC, Solicitors European Group, Law Society, British Association for Sport and Law.

Career: Qualified in 1981. Assistant Secretary at ICI Paints 1987-89. Joined the firm in 1989 and became a Partner in 1991.
Personal: Born 5th June 1953. Educated at Sir William Borlase's School, Marlow 1964-71 and St Catharine's College, Cambridge 1972-75 and 1976-77. Leisure interests include angling, music, journalism, photography and Sunderland A.F.C. Lives in Whitegate.

WOODS, Philip
Hill Dickinson, Manchester (0161) 278 8800
Specialisation: Partner in Technology and Intellectual Property Group of *Hill Dickinson* specialising in all aspects of intellectual property and computer law, both contentious and non-contentious.
Prof. Memberships: Chartered Institute of Patent Agents (Associate); Institute of Trade Mark Agents (Associate); UNION; FICPI; AIPPI; Society for Computers and Law; Committee Member of LES (North West Group); TIPLO (founder member).
Career: Qualified 1974. Admitted Hong Kong 1975. *Deacons* (Hong Kong) 1975-81. Partner, *Wilkinson & Grist* (Hong Kong) 1981-89. Partner, *Eversheds Alexander Tatham* (head of IP Department) 1989-94. Chairman of Eversheds National IP Group until 1994. Partner, *Philip Woods & Co* 1994-1997. Presently Partner *Hill Dickinson*.
Personal: Leisure pursuits include classic cars, wines, walking, reading and gardening. Lives in Prestbury, Cheshire. Born 23rd December 1950

SCOTLAND

LEADING FIRMS • SCOTLAND

MACLAY MURRAY & SPENS Glasgow
MCGRIGOR DONALD Edinburgh

DUNDAS & WILSON CS Glasgow
MACROBERTS Glasgow

HIGHLY REGARDED FIRMS

Burness Edinburgh
Shepherd & Wedderburn WS Edinburgh

Steedman Ramage WS Edinburgh

Maclay Murray & Spens (3ptnrs/10assts in IP/IT) Split between non-contentious (1ptnr/4assts) and contentious (1ptnr/2assts). *Fiona Nicolson* offers "experience and expertise," and is aided by the up and coming *Gill Grassie*. An impressive reputation in the software licensing field. **Clients/Work:** Scottish Widows; British Aerospace; Rover Group.

McGrigor Donald (2ptnrs/5assts in IP/IT) *Shonaig MacPherson* is a well respected figure on the Scottish IP scene. **Clients/Work:** Acting for Cadence Design Systems Inc in Project Alba; acting for William Grant & Son Ltd in their litigation with Glen Catrine in respect of the IP rights to the Grant name for Gin and Vodka; acting

for Scottish Biomedical Research Trust and member universities in relation to the establishment of the Yoshitomi Institute of Neurological Sciences in Glasgow.

Dundas & Wilson CS (3ptnrs/6assts in the Technology Group) An established and respected non-registered IP practice. *Lorne Byatt* ("technically able") undertakes a range of general IP, predominantly from an IT perspective. **Clients/Work:** Principal legal advisors to the University of Glasgow; advised Buck Chemicals Ltd on the acquisition from Stafford Miller of TM and related patent technology; advised the Memory Corporation on Technology Licensing transactions including VCM licences with Taiwanese and Korean clients.

MacRoberts (2ptnrs/5assts in IP/IT) *David Flint* comes from an insolvency background, and his internet work has been commended in particular. **Clients/Work:** Giltech Ltd – international licensing of Arglaes SRP in relation to wound management; Challenger UK Ltd – passing off actions in the UK and Ireland; Inner Workings – various international multimedia deals including Lemon Dog in Soundlands.

Burness (3ptnrs/3assts – none f/t) A large commercial firm. *James McLean* is a leader in this field and is known for his "academic ability." **Clients/Work:** Act for the Patent Agents Kennedy & Co; advise on origin destinations for several companies such as Harris Tweed

Authority; various matters in the food industry.

Shepherd & Wedderburn WS (3ptnrs/7assts in IP/IT) The "methodical" *James Saunders* leads the IP team. He and three assistants work full time in IP. Have recently opened a Glasgow office. **Clients/Work:** Scottish Electricity Settlements Ltd on framework agreement required for the introduction of competition in domestic supplies and on the procurement of hardware and software; New Medical Technology with regard to its flotation; Turnberry Hotel.

Steedman Ramage WS (2ptnrs/1asst) *Scott Kerr* has recently joined from Dickson Minto. **Clients/Work:** Aspects Software Ltd; Glemorangie; Scottish Publishers Association.

LEADING INDIVIDUALS
SCOTLAND

NICOLSON Fiona Maclay Murray & Spens

BYATT Lorne Dundas & Wilson CS
FLINT David MacRoberts
MACPHERSON Shonaig McGrigor Donald

KERR Scott Steedman Ramage WS
MCLEAN James Burness
SAUNDERS James Shepherd & Wedderburn WS

UP AND COMING

GRASSIE Gill Maclay Murray & Spens

SEE PROFILES AT END OF THIS SECTION

BYATT, Lorne
Dundas & Wilson CS, Edinburgh
(0131) 228 8000
See under Computer Law & I.T., p. 189

FLINT, David
MacRoberts, Glasgow (0141) 332 9988
See under Computer Law & I.T., p. 189

GRASSIE, Gill
Maclay Murray & Spens, Edinburgh
(0131) 226 5196
gg@maclaymurrayspens.co.uk
Specialisation: Litigation partner specialising
in major Court of Session IPR infringement
litigation including trademark, patent, copyright
infringement and passing off and trade secrets
violation.
Career: Edinburgh University (LL.B Hons
1984). Writer to the Signet. Law Society IP
Committee member; Associate member of
CIPA; member of TIPLO; Scottish
correspondent for CIPA guide. Member of
Editorial Committee for Sweet & Maxwell
European Trade Mark Reports; author of
Scottish chapters of Sweet & Maxwell European
Trade Mark Litigation Handbook and of Monitor
Press IT 2000 Handbook. Worked for *Bristows*
IP litigation department, London (1991-92) and
Drostes, Munich (1992-93).
Personal: Born 1963.

KERR, Scott
Steedman Ramage WS, Edinburgh
(0131) 260 6600
E-mail: strk@srws.co.uk Partner. Qualified 1985
Specialisation: Main areas of practice include:
acquisition and licensing of trademarks,
patents, copyright and designs; advising both
licensors and licensees on all aspects of
computer contracts (hardware and software);
publishing and media contracts; advising on UK
and EU competition law.

MACPHERSON, Shonaig
McGrigor Donald, Edinburgh
(0131) 226 7777
Partner in Corporate Department, Head
Intellectual Property Unit.
Specialisation: Handles all aspects of
intellectual property and information technology
work. Advise on protection strategies, funding
for technology projects, licensing, research
contracts, litigation and dispute resolution,
expertise on software licensing, systems
developments and procurement, outsourcing
and facilities management contracts. Speaker
at Glasgow IT summits in 1993 and 1994, and at
the International Science Festival in Edinburgh
in 1992,1993 and 1994, Chicago 1996.
Prof. Memberships: Law Society (England &
Wales), Law Society (Scotland), Licensing
Executives Society, Royal Society, Scottish
Biomedical Association, Scottish Biomedical
Research Trust. Visiting Professor at Heriot-Watt
University, Society for Computers and the Law.
Career: Qualified in 1984 in England & Wales
with *Norton Rose*. Assistant Company Secretary
(Legal) Storehouse plc, then Legal Director of
Harrods 1987-89. Partner at *Calow Easton* in

London 1989-91. Qualified in Scotland 1991.
Joined *McGrigor Donald* in 1991 and became a
Partner in 1992.
Personal: Born 29th September 1958. Director
of Edinburgh Chamber of Commerce and
Enterprise. Recreations include theatre, opera
and reading. Lives in Edinburgh.

MCLEAN, James
Burness, Edinburgh (0131) 473 6000
See under European Union/Competition, p. 366

NICOLSON, Fiona
Maclay Murray & Spens, Glasgow
(0141) 248 5011
fmmn@maclaymurrayspens.co.uk
Partner and Head of Intellectual Property
Department.
Specialisation: Specialises in Intellectual
Property and Information Technology work for
clients both national and international, including
start-ups, listed companies, venture capitalists
and educational institutions.
Prof. Memberships: President – Licensing
Executives Society, (Britain and Ireland) Council
Member. Chairman of the Law Society of
Scotland panel for accreditation of intellectual
property.
Career: Joined *Maclay Murray & Spens* in 1993.
Previously partner and Head of IP at *Bird
Scmple*, Fyfe Ireland.
Personal: Glasgow University MA (1974) LLB
(1983). Born 1954.

SAUNDERS, James
Shepherd & Wedderburn WS, Edinburgh
(0131) 228 9900
See under Energy & Utilities, p. 337

INVESTMENT FUNDS

RESEARCH: In compiling the tables, we consider all the information available to us, paying particular regard to the market research carried out by our team of ten qualified lawyers. (The researchers' details are set out on page three.) The rankings, therefore, reflect the opinion of the marketplace as revealed by systematic and objective research: see page four. (Our research is audited every year by the British Market Research Bureau.)

OVERVIEW: All areas of investment funds work are covered in this section – UK Unit Trusts, UK Investment Trusts, open ended investment companies (OEICs) and Offshore Funds. The overall leading firm this year is Linklaters out on their own. The merger of Frere Cholmeley Bischoff and Eversheds means that the new merged firm retains Frere Cholmeley Bischoff's reputation as the leading unit trust and OEIC practice.

Our London table contains two new firms which have based their practices around the former partners of M W Cornish – Arnheim & Co (Martin Cornish) and Titmuss Sainer Dechert (Peter Astleford).

The only English firm outside London is Burges Salmon in Bristol. Scotland has a thriving funds market. The two leading firms remain Dundas & Wilson CS and Shepherd & Wedderburn WS. However they are being caught up by Dickson Minto WS and Tods Murray WS.

OEICs are starting to become more popular particularly in the conversion of unit trusts but there has not been any mad rush. They do not appear to have attracted much offshore funds money back to the UK.

LEADING FIRMS · LONDON

LINKLATERS

CLIFFORD CHANCE
HERBERT SMITH
NORTON ROSE
SLAUGHTER AND MAY

ASHURST MORRIS CRISP
EVERSHEDS
MACFARLANES
SIMMONS & SIMMONS

HIGHLY REGARDED FIRMS

Allen & Overy
S J Berwin & Co
Freshfields
Lawrence Graham
Lovell White Durrant
Stephenson Harwood
Travers Smith Braithwaite

Arnheim & Co
Rowe & Maw
Speechly Bircham
Titmuss Sainer Dechert

LONDON

Linklaters (10ptnrs: 4 f/t, 30assts) Have established themselves as the "leading funds lawyers" with a "full spread" of work. Are involved with many new types of fund and seen as one of the most active firms on emerging markets. Particularly strong on offshore funds and closed ended funds. Provide a full service of "high quality." The "excellent" *Paul Harris* heads the practice. *Timothy Shipton* does a lot of offshore and was praised for being "good at finding solutions" particularly "in tricky markets like India." *Matthew Middleditch* is a "quality" performer with a reputation as a corporate finance lawyer who also handles investment funds work. He is "commercially and technically extremely good." Senior assistant *Jonathan Perkins* ("concientious," "efficient") enters as up and coming and has already done a lot of deals. Clients/Work: Advised on the launch and structuring of Regent Russian Real Estate

Fund. Advised on the Ecu 1.1bn equity capital raising for BC European Capital VI, BC Partners' new European private equity fund. Advised Midland Bank plc (the Issuer) and HSBC Investment Bank plc (the Issue Agent) in relation to the issue of FTSE 100 TRAINS (Traded Index Securities).

Clifford Chance (5ptnrs of whom 4 spend most of time, 22assts) A substantial and "strong" investment fund practice covering a broad spectrum of work. Are "heavyweight in unit trusts" and significant players in emerging markets. Have been seen doing "innovative" deals. The team includes the "great" and "well respected" *Timothy Herrington* and *James Barlow*. Clients/Work: Advising Geared Income Investment Trust PLC on its offers for General Consolidated Investment Trust PLC. Advised Charterhouse Development Capital on the establishment of CCP VI which raised total commitments of £800m. Advising Chase Manhattan Bank and E D & F Man

Investment Products in relation to the issue of guaranteed leveraged bonds by Man-IP 220 Limited (a Bermudan investment company).

Herbert Smith (7ptnrs (3 of whom spend bulk of time), 10assts) An "outstanding" firm with a growing reputation. *Nigel Farr* is "making a mark for himself" on investment trusts. He is seen as "technically good and commercial." One interviewee thought him the "best investment trust lawyer in the country... been involved in a lot of big deals." Clients/Work: Acted on the reconstructions of The Scottish National Trust and of Kleinwort Overseas Investment Trust. Acted in the flotation of Abtrust New Preferred Income Investment Trust.

Norton Rose (8ptnrs: 4 p/t, 12 core groupassts plus 6 as necessary) An "extremely good" practice with a growing market presence and "good quantity and quality." Particularly strong on investment trusts and "do a lot of offshore." Were active on Egyptian funds in 1997. Leading individuals are *Simon Cox* and the "successful" and "energetic" *Tim Marsden* who does offshore and is "driving the practice forward." **Clients/Work:** Friends' Provident Life Office (reverse takeover of Ivory & Sime PLC). Abbey National Dublin Investment Fund PLC (closed-ended Irish protected-capital investment company; approximate value £100 million). Abtrust High Income Trust PLC (reduction of share premium account to finance proposed share buy-back scheme of issued ordinary share capital).

Slaughter and May (5ptnrs 2 of which virtually full time, 10assts) A "first class practice" which is stronger on offshore and closed-ended than on unit trusts. Have been involved with many new types of funds. Clients rated them for their work on "investment trusts and strategic advice." *Colin Hall* has an "excellent reputation" and "commercial approach." *James Cripps* was commended for doing "a lot of quite difficult and innovative work." **Clients/Work:** Advised the £350m Baring Tribune Investment Trust plc on reconstruction proposals. Advised The Saudi Arabian Investment Fund Limited and Baring Brothers on the establishment of investment vehicle permitting foreign access to the Saudi Arabian securities market. Advised 3i in connection with the establishment of 3i EuroFund II.

Ashurst Morris Crisp (6ptnrs/7assts) Have a reputation based on the "back of investment trust work....great UK investment trust expertise." Seen on venture capital funds and fundraising work. Also involved with unit trusts. The "excellent" *Roger Walsom* is particularly well known for investment trusts. **Clients/Work:** Acted for the Carlyle Group of the US on its European limited partnership fund of approximately 1 billion ECU. Acted for Dresdner RCM Endowment Policy Trust 2010 plc on its placing and offer for subscription of 25 million ordinary shares at £1 each, sponsored by Merrill Lynch International. Acted for INVESCO Blue Chip Trust plc on its winding up and reconstruction.

Eversheds (4ptnrs, 1cons, 6assts plus 1 tax assistant) At the time of the merger announcement the old Frere Cholmeley Bischoff practice continued to dominate the unit trust market and OEICs. The practice is still seen to be based around this niche. *Richard Millar* is now a consultant. *Pamela Thompson* is still a high-flier. **Clients/Work:** Threadneedle Asset Management Limited (establishment of OEIC and conversion of 38 authorised unit trust schemes into sub-funds of the OEIC). Save & Prosper (establishment of an OEIC). Fidelity (establishment of institutional investment company).

Macfarlanes (4 f/t and 2 p/tptnrs, 4assts including 1 p/t) Particularly strong on unit trusts and have recently made a "big push on OEICs." Cover offshore and onshore. *Timothy Cornick* is a leading unit trust lawyer

and "OIEC man." *Bridget Barker* also has a strong reputation. **Clients/Work:** Legal & General Industrial Property Fund (UK limited partnership for property investment). Legal & General Ventures 1998 Private Equity Limited Partnership (2 parallel UK limited partnerships for venture capital investment which raised £190.5m). Gartmore Controlled Risk UK Equity Fund, a guaranteed unit trust.

Simmons & Simmons (3ptnrs (most of time) plus 2ptnrs doing 5-10%, 11assts) A "capable firm" which does offshore and onshore. Particularly visible on unit trusts work with "good clients." *Richard Slater* is good with clients. *Iain Cullen* has a good workload. **Clients/Work:** Advised UK investment manager on the NeuAlpha Hedge Fund, an OEIC incorporated in the Cayman Islands. Advised Cazenove Unit Trust Management Ltd in connection with the launch of 2 new Common Investment Funds for charities. Advised Barclays Funds Limited in relation to the reorganisation of the Barclays Unicorn range of unit trusts.

Allen & Overy (8ptnrs: to varying degrees) Have created an investment structures group to build on international capabilities. Have "some good clients." **Clients/Work:** Advising on proposed establishment of a US$200m fund investing in Russia and Ukraine. Advised in connection with conversion of a large number of unit trusts into a UK OEIC. Advised a Luxembourg based open-ended company on its registration for the marketing and sale of its shares in Korea.

SJ Berwin & Co (4ptnrs/11assts) Have a particularly strong reputation for venture capital fund practice/limited partnerships. "Fantastic venture capital." *Jonathan Blake* enters our tables as a "leading funds lawyer" who "does a lot of limited partnerships." **Clients/Work:** Funds include: Mercury Asset Management (£250 million private equity fund), NatWest Equity Partners (over £500 million European investment fund) and Prelude Trust plc (£20.84 million fund).

Freshfields (6ptnrs, 2 of whom f/t/ 10assts) Investment funds practice with leading individual *Anthony McWhirter* who is known for his tax knowledge. Have been involved in a variety of new launches, reconstructions and venture capital/private equity funds matters. **Clients/Work:** Advance UK Trust plc (launch of London listed investment trust to invest in other UK oriented investment trusts and closed-ended funds whose shares are trading at large discounts to net asset value). Guinness Flight (advising on the merger of Guinness Flight and Hambros offshore funds following the merger of Guinness Flight and Hambros.)

Lawrence Graham (2ptnrs/2assts) The funds team is known for unit trusts and investment trusts work. **Clients/Work:** Acting for the sponsor on introduction to the

Official List of Manchester & London Investment Trust Plc. Acting for the sponsor on introduction and placing of Tea Plantation Investment Trust to Official List.

Lovell White Durrant (4ptnrs/4assts) Practice covers unit trusts, investment trusts and offshore funds. The group is headed by the "active" and "excellent" *Richard Stones.* **Clients/Work:** Acting for INVESCO on the reconstruction of Continental Assets Trust plc, by liquidation and distribution of assets into a new investment trust (INVESCO Continental Smaller Companies Trust plc) and 2 Invesco unit trusts.

Stephenson Harwood (1ptnr/4assts) "Good reputation for offshore work." The practice is focused and led by the "creative"*Andrew Sutch* who is "bright and able" and "gets on well with clients." **Clients/Work:** Johnson Fry Second Utilities Trust plc (Scheme of Arrangement). Manek Growth Fund (launch of new unit trust for Jayesh Manek). Launch of various offshore funds.

Travers Smith Braithwaite (3ptnrs/4assts) Following Nigel Campion-Smith's departure the practice still has "good players" in investment funds. **Clients/Work:** Advised on the launch of an Islamic Fund and a Russian debt fund for ANZ. Also acted for Guinness Flight.

Arnheim & Co (2ptnrs/4assts) The practice is primarily based on part of the old M W Cornish practice. "Specialist" *Martin Cornish* has "done a good job" and is "knowledgeable... been in industry and private practice." **Clients/Work:** Espirito Santo Activos Financeiros (advising on the reorganisation of an umbrella fund). Partners Group of Zug, Switzerland (advising on the establishment and structuring of an offshore master umbrella fund and US feeder fund).

Rowe & Maw (2ptnrs(50% and 30%), 1 asst (30%)) *David Ive* heads the practice with an emphasis on unit trusts and OEICs. **Clients/Work:** Tax Committee of Unit Trust

Association. Particular focus on stamp duty and mergers.

Speechly Bircham (1ptnr/1asst) Specialise in unit trusts and OEICs. **Clients/Work:** Clients include ABN Amro Pembroke Carrington, Scottish Life and Tilney.

Titmuss Sainer Dechert (4ptnrs: 2 f/t, 5assts) The team is led by ex M W Cornish partner *Peter Astleford* who is a "good prob-

lem solver" and has been in-house as well as private practice. Particularly involved in offshore with a transatlantic capability due to the firm's association with US firm Dechert Price Rhoads. **Clients/Work:** Launch of the Société Générale Landenburg Thalmann Ukraine Fund (an Irish listed Guernsey company). Open ending and UK registration of Atlantis Korean Smaller Companies Fund sponsored by Barings.

SOUTH WEST

Burges Salmon (1ptnr/2assts) The firm has a specialist investment funds practice focusing on unit trusts and OEICs. Led by *Chris Godfrey*. **Clients/Work:** Issue of 5,800,000 zero dividend preference shares for Asset Management Investment Company PLC. Acting for Premier Portfolio Managers Limited in the acquisition of a mandate from

Edinburgh Unit Trusts Managers Limited. Scheme of amalgamation for Premier Portfolio Managers Limited.

SCOTLAND

Dundas & Wilson CS (3ptnrs: 2 f/t/4assts plus 3 as and when necessary) A leading investment funds practice. *Philip Mackay* "does a wide spread of work." *James Watt* has a continuing involvement with collective investments. The "very good" *Michael Polson* is seen more on the investment trust side of the practice. **Clients/Work:** Advising Templeton on a scheme for the conversion of 3 existing authorised unit trust schemes into a new OEIC. Advising GA Unit Trust Managers on its rationalisation of its unit trusts and those formerly managed by Provident Mutual Unit Trust Managers Limited. Advising Martin Currie on the acquisition of 3 private investment companies and the associated launch of Martin Currie Income & Growth Trust.

Shepherd & Wedderburn WS (2ptnrs/3assts) Reputation for being "large on the investment trust side." Have "big market credibility in closed ended side." *Sue Inglis*, rated highly, is "investment trust

focused and commercial." **Clients/Work:** Advising Undervalued Assets Trust on its successful hostile bid for Pilot Investment Trust. Advising Ivory & Sime Optimum Income Trust on the recommended proposals for the reconstruction of Ivory & Sime Optimum Income Trust II. Advising Dunedin Worldwide Investment Trust, Edinburgh Worldwide Investment Trust and Edinburgh Investment Company on the recommended proposals for the reconstruction of DWIT into EWIT and EIT.

Dickson Minto WS (3ptnrs/4assts) A practice with a growing reputation particularly on investment trusts side. *Bruce Minto* is "commercial...gets the job done." *Andrew Todd* – has a "crisp City" style and is "quality." **Clients/Work:** Unitisation of the British Investment Trust. Reconstruction of Voyageur European Smaller Companies Trust and launch of Capital Opportunities as a successor investment vehicle. Reconstruction of BZW Convertible Investment Trust.

Tods Murray WS (3ptnrs/2assts) The practice is seen as "focused on the unit trust side particularly acting for managers and trustees." *Christopher Athanas* has "expertise" on this side" and was described by some as the "leading unit trusts lawyer in Scotland." Other leading individuals are *David Dunsire* and *Martin Thurston-Smith*. **Clients/Work:** Acting for Edinburgh Unit Trust Managers Limited and for The Royal Bank of Scotland plc in the restructuring of The British Investment Trust PLC. Acting for The Royal Bank of Scotland plc as Authorised Depositary in the setting up of

the Fleming/Save & Prosper OEIC. Acting for Baillie Gifford and The Royal Bank of Scotland plc in the rebranding and updating of BG's range of 11 authorised unit trusts.

McGrigor Donald (2ptnrs/1asst) Practice covers investment and unit trusts and other funds. *Frank Doran* enters our table of Leading Individuals and is praised for being "good technically." **Clients/Work:** Reconstruction of Saracen Value Trust plc. Reconstruction of Scottish National Trust plc (acted for Scottish National Trust plc in connection with the takeover offer which it received from Second Scottish National Trust plc). The Murray Open Ended Investment Company ICVC (acted in respect of the incorporation of Murray Open Ended Investment Company and the subsequent amalgamation of two authorised unit trusts with two sub funds of this new OIEC).

Maclay Murray & Spens Glasgow firm with a financial services and funds practice.

ASTLEFORD, Peter

Titmuss Sainer Dechert and Dechert Price & Rhoads, London (0171) 583 5353

Partner and Head of the Joint Financial Services and Investment Management Group, London.

Specialisation: Peter specialises in all aspects of onshore and offshore mutual funds and attendant legal and regulatory issues applicable to the funds and their promoters/ investment managers/ other service providers. His unit also provides a one-stop-shop dealing with UK and US regulatory issues including dual purpose compliance manuals. Peter is a frequent contributor to the financial press and speaker at related conferences.

Career: Qualified in 1986. Peter specialised in financial services/ investment funds with a leading City of London law firm and subsequently became Group Legal Advisor and then Head of Corporate Services at the London listed holding company to a major international financial services group. Appointed a dual partner of the integrated practices of *Dechert Price & Rhoads* and *Titmuss Sainer Dechert* in 1997.

Personal: Born 1962.

ATHANAS, Christopher

Tods Murray WS, Edinburgh (0131) 226 4771
email: chris.athanas@todsmurray.co.uk

Specialisation: Specialises in Corporate Financial Services and Investment Funds; all aspects of collective investment schemes including unit trusts, open-ended investment companies (OIEC's), investment trust companies, investment products (including PEPs and ISAs), related regulatory and compliance law.

Prof. Memberships: Law Society of Scotland.

Career: Qualified 1966 *Paull & Williamsons*; *Dundas & Wilson*1968; Partner 1969-1996; Partner *Tods Murray* 1996.

Personal: Born 1941. Attended Fettes College, Edinburgh; Aberdeen University (1962 MA) 1964 (LLB); WS. Leisure: Angling, walking, golf, the arts.

BARKER, Bridget

Macfarlanes, London (0171) 831 9222

Partner in Company, Commercial and Banking Department.

Specialisation: Specialises in investment funds and financial services, acting for a number of on-shore and off-shore investment funds, covering a range of investment areas. Also experienced in corporate finance work, acting for a number of listed companies. Recent matters include advising venture capital fund work for HSBC Private Equity (and property fund work for Legal & General as well as drafting two notebooks for Lloyds). Author of articles on investment funds, financial services and money laundering.

Prof. Memberships: Law Society, International Bar Association. Vice Chairman of Committee on Specialised Investment Funds. Association of Women Solicitors.

Career: Qualified with *Macfarlanes* in 1983. Became a Partner in 1988.

BARLOW, James

Clifford Chance, London (0171) 600 1000

See under Financial Services (FSA, Compliance etc), p. 387

BLAKE, Jonathan E.

S J Berwin & Co, London
+44 (0)171 533 2222

See under Corporate Finance: Equity, p. 226

CLARKE, Dominic

Herbert Smith, London (0171) 374 8000

Partner in Company Department.

Specialisation: Specialises in investment funds within the UK and overseas and in the regulation of the financial services and insurance industries. His work in connection with investment funds includes the formation and restructuring of unit trusts, open-ended investment companies, investment trusts, limited partnerships, common investment funds for charities, off-shore funds and other investment vehicles. His regulatory practice covers the application of regulations governing the financial services and insurance industries. Other areas of expertise include acting for trustees of debenture and loan stock issues and the raising of private sector finance by housing associations.

Career: Qualified in 1975. Became a Partner at *Herbert Smith* in 1987.

Personal: Educated at Leeds University.

CORNICK, Timothy

Macfarlanes, London (0171) 831 9222

Partner in Company/ Commercial Department.

Specialisation: Work covers Financial Services Act regulatory and securities work. Main area of practice is collective investment schemes. Substantial involvement in matters on behalf of investment managers and trustees. Particular experience of the unit trusts industry. Contributor to Butterworths Financial Services Law and Practice and Encyclopaedia of Forms and Precedents. Lead editor, 'Collective Investment Schemes Law and Practice.' Author of articles in International Business Lawyer, Journal of International Banking and Financial Law and Compliance Monitor. Speaker at conferences and seminars for IBC, Cadogan and Investment Education.

Prof. Memberships: Law Society.

Career: Qualified in 1982, having joined *Kenneth Brown Baker* in 1980. Became a Partner of *Turner Kenneth Brown* in 1988. Joined *Macfarlanes* as a Partner in 1995.

Personal: Born 1st November 1957. Attended Weymouth Grammar School 1969-76, then Worcester College, Oxford 1976-79 and College of Law Guildford 1979-80. Society of Dorset Men; Primary Club. Leisure interests include cricket, wine, jogging, reading and history. Lives in Kent.

CORNISH, Martin

Arnheim & Co, London (0171) 939 1660

Senior Partner 1991.

Specialisation: Main area of practice is full range of commodities and related derivatives and funds transactions including structuring exchange and OTC and on-shore and off-shore products. Other main area of work is financial services and securities documentation and regulation, particularly leveraged transactions and related security/netting issues. Author of numerous articles in the professional press. Regular speaker at conferences and seminars.

Prof. Memberships: Law Society.

Career: Qualified in 1980. Partner with

Simmons & Simmons 1980-88, then European Legal Director at *Lehman Brothers* 1988-92. Established *M.W. Cornish & Co.* in 1992. As of July 1997, the firm's financial services practice joined *Arnheim & Co*, the UK correspondent law firm of *Price Waterhouse*.

Personal: Born 28th February 1955. Attended Millfield School 1970-74, then Downing College, Cambridge 1974-76. Leisure pursuits include tennis and golf. Lives in Billericay, Essex.

COX, Simon

Norton Rose, London (0171) 283 6000

Partner in Corporate Finance Department.

Specialisation: Main areas of practice are collective investment schemes, corporate finance and financial services work. Has a wide-ranging securities and corporate practice with an emphasis on collective investment and international and domestic corporate finance, particularly in relation to emerging markets. Contributor to 'A Practitioner's Guide to the Stock Exchange Yellow Book' and author of various articles. Has spoken at a number of UK and overseas conferences on funds and Financial Services Act issues and on investment in the former Soviet Union.

Prof. Memberships: Securities Institute, IBA, Law Society, City of London Solicitors Company.

Career: Qualified in 1980, having joined *Norton Rose* in 1978. Became a Partner in 1988.

Personal: Born 17th January 1956. Attended Eton College 1967-73 and Trinity College, Oxford 1974-77. Trustee of two Charitable Trusts. Lives in London.

CRIPPS, James

Slaughter and May, London (0171) 600 1200

Partner in Commercial Department.

Specialisation: General and international corporate and corporate finance practice with emphasis on listed and unlisted collective investment schemes (in particular hedge funds and emerging markets) and advice to providers of financial services and financial products.

Prof. Memberships: The Law Society, Securities Institute, Company of Fuellers.

Career: Joined *Slaughter and May* 1978, qualified 1980, Partner 1989.

Personal: Born 15 March 1956. Educated Eton and St. Catharine's College, Cambridge. Married, three sons two daughters. Lives in London and Buckinghamshire. Leisure interests include farming, forestry, opera and golf.

CULLEN, Iain

Simmons & Simmons, London
(0171) 628 2020

Partner in Corporate Department.

Specialisation: Handles all types of work relating to commodities, futures and options, unit trusts, offshore funds and investment management. Author of numerous articles in the professional press. Regular speaker at conferences and seminars.

Prof. Memberships: Law Society, International Bar Association, American Bar Association, Alternative Investment Management Association, Board of Editors of Futures and Derivatives Law Report, International Law Letter, Advisory Board of The Futures and Derivatives Law Review, Advisory Board of World Securities Law Report.

Career: Qualified in 1980, having joined

Simmons & Simmons in 1977. Became a Partner in 1986.
Personal: Born 13th May 1953. Took a BA in Law in 1975. Lives in London.

DORAN, Frank
McGrigor Donald, Glasgow (0141) 248 6677
See under Financial Services (FSA, Compliance etc), p. 389

DUNSIRE, David
Tods Murray WS, Edinburgh (0131) 226 4771
email: david.dunsire@todsmurray.co.uk
Partner in Corporate Department.
Specialisation: Specialises in financial services particularly unit trusts, acting principally for trustee. Also handles corporate finance and general corporate work, with an emphasis on acquisitions and disposals, MBO's and start-ups.
Prof. Memberships: Law Society of Scotland.
Career: Qualified 1982, having joined *Tods Murray WS* in 1980. Partner *Tods Murray WS* 1986. Departmental Managing Partner 1998.
Personal: Born 1958. Attended Buckhaven High School, Fife 1970-76, then Edinburgh University 1976-80 (LLB). Leisure: family, gardening and music.

FARR, Nigel J
Herbert Smith, London (0171) 374 8000
Specialisation: Transactional and advisory work in the funds sector, mainly in relation to investment trusts but with increasing involvement with offshore funds. Acts for funds, management groups and financial advisers. Particular emphasis on the design, launch, merger and restructuring of funds. Also broad corporate finance experience.
Career: Joined Herbert Smith in 1985; Partner in 1994.
Personal: Educated at Wimbledon College and Gonville & Caius College, Cambridge. Interests include food and wine, horse racing, cinema and travel.

GODFREY, Christopher
Burges Salmon, Bristol (0117) 939 2000

HALL, Colin
Slaughter and May, London (0171) 600 1200
Partner in Company/Commercial Department.
Specialisation: Main areas of practice are investment funds and corporate finance. Has extensive experience in advising on the structuring, establishment and marketing of all types of investment funds (corporate and non-corporate) in the UK and major offshore financial centres. Also handles general corporate work for UK companies, including UK investment groups.
Career: Worked for HM Diplomatic Service 1967-69. Member of The Law Society Collective Investment Scheme Sub-Committee and the Association of Investment Trust Companies Legal and Regulatory Committee. Joined *Slaughter and May* in 1969, becoming a Partner in 1978.

HARRIS, Paul
Linklaters, London (0171) 456 3104
Partner, Corporate Department and Investment Funds Group.
Specialisation: Specialises in investment

funds matters. Has over 25 years experience in structuring, creating and organising funds for investment in property of all types (securities, derivatives, financial instruments, real estate, etc) onshore and offshore, domestic and international, public and private, retail and institutional.
Prof. Memberships: Member of the Law Society sub-committee on Unit Trusts. Former Editor of "Unit Trusts – The Law and Practice."
Career: Articled at *Linklaters & Paines*, and made Partner in 1976.
Personal: Born 1943.

HERRINGTON, Timothy
Clifford Chance, London (0171) 600 1000
See under Financial Services (FSA, Compliance etc), p. 387

INGLIS, Sue
Shepherd & Wedderburn WS, Edinburgh (0131) 228 9900
Partner in Corporate Department.
Specialisation: Main areas of practice are financial services, collective investment funds, investment products, listed securities (acting for both sponsors and investment funds) and corporate finance transactions for fund management and life insurance companies.
Career: Qualified and joined *Shepherd & Wedderburn* 1988. Partner 1993.
Personal: Born 13.08.1964.

IVE, David
Rowe & Maw, London (0171) 248 4282
Partner in Corporate Taxation Department.
Specialisation: Experienced in all aspects of taxation, especially in relation to financial services, collective investment schemes, unit trusts, offshore funds and life assurance taxation. Drafted the current trust deed of M&G Group plc Charifund Unit Trust. Author of articles in various tax journals, including 'British Tax Review' and 'Tax Journal.' Lecturer on tax topics, especially collective investment schemes and unit trusts. Member of the Taxation Committee of the Associators of Unit Trusts and Investment Funds.
Prof. Memberships: Law Society.
Career: Qualified in 1972. Worked with *Allen & Overy* 1976-84. Spent 1 year at the Tax Bar (1984-85), then joined *Rowe & Maw* in June 1985. Became a Partner in 1986.
Personal: Born 2nd January 1950. Attended Highgate School 1963-68, then Birmingham University 1968-71. Chairman of the Association of Liberal Democrat Lawyers. Joint author of a number of Liberal Democrat publications on constitutional reform. Leisure pursuits include opera and swimming. Lives in London.

MACKAY, Philip
Dundas & Wilson CS, Edinburgh (0131) 228 8000
See under Financial Services (FSA, Compliance etc), p. 390

MARSDEN, Tim
Norton Rose, London (0171) 283 6000
Partner in Corporate Finance Department.
Specialisation: Corporate finance with particular emphasis on financial services operations and collective investment schemes, both on-shore and off-shore. Advises on

acquisitions and disposals in the financial services sector and advises both public and private sector entities on financial services regulation generally. Commonly advises on corporate and collective investment transactions involving emerging markets. Lectures on financial services, investment trusts and unit trusts.
Career: Qualified 1984; Barrister 1984-85. Joined *Norton Rose* 1986. Partner in 1993
Personal: Born 9th September 1961. Honorary solicitor to DEBRA. Leisure interests include sport and social activities.

MCWHIRTER, Anthony
Freshfields, London (0171) 936 4000
Partner in Tax Department.
Specialisation: Main practice area is investment funds. Advises on all aspects of the structuring, operation and winding up of investment funds and other collective investment arrangements including tax planning and regulation. Author of various articles; has spoken widely at conferences.
Prof. Memberships: Law Society of City of London, AUTIF.
Career: Qualified in 1979, having joined *Freshfields* in 1977. Became a Partner in 1985.
Personal: Born 5th October 1954. Attended Downing College, Cambridge 1973-76.

MIDDLEDITCH, Matthew
Linklaters, London (0171) 456 3144
Partner. Corporate Department.
Specialisation: Specialises in UK corporate finance and company law. Main areas of practice include advising companies and merchant banks on: mergers and acquisitions, including public takeovers and private acquisitions of shares and businesses; flotations; secondary issues, including acting on rights issues, vendor placings and open offers; reorganisations; joint ventures and general corporate work.
Career: Articled with *Linklaters & Paines* and qualified in 1982. Born 1958.

MILLAR, Richard
Eversheds, London (0171) 919 4500
Specialisation: Main area of practice is collective investment schemes: has acted for managers of authorised unit trusts since 1965 and for promoters of offshore funds and managers of unauthorised trusts subsequently. Also advises generally on financial services law as well as broader company law. Regular speaker at conferences.
Prof. Memberships: Law Society, IBA. Member of Law Society's Company Law Committee and Chairman of its Sub-committee on Collective Investment Schemes.
Career: Qualified in 1963. Joined *Bischoff & Co.* in 1965, becoming a Partner in 1967 and Senior Partner and Managing Partner in 1990. Firm merged with *Frere Cholmeley* in 1993 and with *Eversheds*, London in 1998.

MINTO, Bruce
Dickson Minto WS, Edinburgh (0131) 225 4455
Founding Partner in Corporate Department.
Specialisation: Work includes Stock Exchange listings, Yellow Book work generally, mergers and acquisitions and institutional finance.
Prof. Memberships: Law Society of Scotland.
Career: Qualified in 1981. Formed *Dickson Minto WS* in 1985.

Personal: Born 30th October 1957. Attended Edinburgh University 1975-79. Leisure interests include golf, shooting and music. Lives in Edinburgh.

PERKINS, Jonathan M. J.
Linklaters, London (0171) 456 3092
Specialisation: Principal areas of practice are all aspects of investment fund work for managers and promoters, including the structuring, establishment and reorganisation of different forms of collective investment vehicles (open and closed companies, unit trusts and limited partnerships), both domestic and offshore, institutional and retail.
Prof. Memberships: Member of the AUTIF International Advisory Group, Law Society.
Career: Trainee solicitor at *Linklaters*; qualified 1992.

POLSON, Michael
Dundas & Wilson CS, Edinburgh
(0131) 228 8000
Specialisation: Partner in Corporate Finance Group specialising in work for listed public companies and fund management companies including mergers, acquisitions and divestments. Recent major transactions include the acquisition by Martin Currie of three private investment companies and the associated launch of Martin Currie Income and Growth Trust, the unitisation of General Consolidated Investment Trust and offers by Dunedin Enterprise Investment Trust for Baronsmead Investment Trust.
Prof. Memberships: The Law Society of Scotland.
Career: Attended University of Edinburgh and Edinburgh University Management School (LLB (Hons), DipLP, MBA). Articled *Dundas & Wilson CS*; qualified 1989; seconded to *Ashurst Morris Crisp* 1991; senior solicitor *Dundas & Wilson CS* 1992-93; associate 1993-95; Partner since 1995.
Personal: Born 1964. Resides Edinburgh. Leisure interests include golf, cricket, football, rugby and cycling. Has also been recommended as a Leader in the Field of Financial Services.

SHIPTON, Timothy
Linklaters, London (0171) 456 3100
Partner in Corporate Department.
Specialisation: Specialist in offshore fund work advising domestic and foreign clients on the corporate, regulatory and tax aspects of structuring, creating, organising and marketing funds for investment in property of all types (securities, derivatives, financial instruments, debt, real estate, onshore and offshore, domestic and international, public and private, retail and institutional). He has been involved in international capital market issues of debt and equity securities joint ventures and project financing work.

SLATER, Richard E.H.
Simmons & Simmons, London
(0171) 628 2020
Partner in Corporate Department.
Specialisation: Corporate and regulatory work with a particular emphasis on the financial services industry. Work covers regulatory advice on the formation and promotion of investment vehicles of all types, the acquisition and disposal of financial services businesses and the reconstruction and merger of investment trust companies, unit trusts and other investment entities. Transactional advice includes public and private company take-overs and acquisitions, joint ventures, initial share offerings and flotations.
Career: Qualified in 1977, after joining *Simmons & Simmons* as an articled clerk in 1975. Became a Partner in the Corporate Department in 1981.
Personal: Born 9th November 1950. Attended City University 1979-82, then Cambridge University 1982-84. Lives in London.

STONES, Richard
Lovell White Durrant, London
(0171) 236 0066
See under Financial Services (FSA, Compliance etc), p. 388

SUTCH, Andrew
Stephenson Harwood, London
(0171) 329 4422
Specialisation: Specialises in investment funds, both UK and offshore, and financial services regulation. Transactional work has involved a number of fund takeovers or restructurings and advice on launches of a number of emerging markets funds. Lectures on open-ended investment companies and other aspects of financial services law.
Prof. Memberships: Law Society, IBA.
Career: Educated at Haileybury and Oxford. Qualified in 1979. Seconded to Stephenson Harwood and Lo in Hong Kong, 1982-86. Partner in 1984 and Head of Corporate Department in 1997.

THOMPSON, Pamela
Eversheds, London (0171) 919 4500
Partner and Head of Financial Services Group.
Specialisation: Main areas of practice are collective investment schemes, pooled investments and financial services regulatory work. Handles onshore schemes including authorised and unauthorised unit trusts and limited partnerships and offshore schemes such as trusts, open ended companies and closed ended funds. Also handles general financial services work, including regulatory advice, structuring, taxation and marketing investment schemes.
Prof. Memberships: Association of Women Solicitors.
Career: Qualified in 1982, having joined *Bischoff & Co.* in 1980. Became a Partner in 1986.
Personal: Born in 1956. Attended St Hilda's College, Oxford 1974-78.

THURSTON SMITH, Martin
Tods Murray WS, Edinburgh (0131) 226 4771
email: martin.thurston.smith@todsmurray.co.uk
Partner in Corporate Department.
Specialisation: Specialises in collective investment schemes, financial services and pension schemes. Also handles corporate and commercial work including other commercial applications of trusts.
Prof. Memberships: Law Society of Scotland.
Career: Joined *Tods Murray* 1974. Qualified 1977. Partner 1978.
Personal: Born 1951. Attended The Edinburgh Academy 1957-69 and Christ's College Cambridge 1970-1974. Leisure: hillwalking. Fluent German and French.

TODD, Andrew G.
Dickson Minto WS, Edinburgh
(0131) 225 4455
Specialisation: Main areas of practice are Stock Exchange work, financial services and venture capital work.
Prof. Memberships: Law Society of Scotland, Writer to the Signet.
Career: Joined *Dickson Minto* in 1987; Partner 1995.
Personal: Born 1964. Edinburgh University 1982-1987.

WALSOM, Roger
Ashurst Morris Crisp, London
(0171) 638 1111
Specialisation: A partner in the company department involved in a wide range of corporate work including corporate finance and investment funds. Deals with most areas of investment fund work, particularly investment trusts and limited partnerships. Also has broader corporate finance experience.
Prof. Memberships: Law Society.
Career: Qualified in 1980. Joined *Ashursts* in 1983. Became a Partner in 1988.

WATT, James P.
Dundas & Wilson CS, Edinburgh
(0131) 228 8000
Specialisation: Partner in Corporate Finance Group; specialist areas include corporate financial services law, stock exchange and pensions law; acts for fund management companies and carries out a full range of work in investment trusts, unit trusts, other collective investment schemes (including open-ended investment companies), overseas funds and sales and acquisitions of financial services businesses; compliance and regulatory matters, PEPs and other savings schemes, investment agreements and marketing documents, joint ventures and EC aspects of the financial services area; pension schemes (including surpluses, deficits, documentation, unapproved schemes, winding-ups, mergers and acquisitions).
Prof. Memberships: Writer to the Signet, Notary Public.
Career: Attended University of Edinburgh (LLB Hons, BComm), Harvard Law School (LLM). Legal Assistant *Slaughter & May*, London 1972-74; articled *Dundas & Wilson CS*; qualified 1976; assistant 1976-77; Partner since 1977.
Personal: Born 1943. Resides Edinburgh, married, four children. Leisure interests include golf (the Royal Burgess Golfing Society of Edinburgh; the Golf House Club, Elie, Luffness New Golf Club), swimming and reading. Has also been recommended as a Leader in the Field of Financial Services.

LICENSING

RESEARCH: In compiling the tables, we consider all the information available to us, paying particular regard to the market research carried out by our team of ten qualified lawyers. (The researchers' details are set out on page three.) The rankings, therefore, reflect the opinion of the marketplace as revealed by systematic and objective research: see page four. (Our research is audited every year by the British Market Research Bureau.)

OVERVIEW: Licensing work divides broadly into three main areas: liquor, betting and gaming. Most firms undertake general liquor licensing. A smaller number of firms also handle betting and gaming.

In England most of the betting work is undertaken by Richards Butler, Trethowan Woodford in Southampton and Gosschalks in Hull. This is because they act for the three major national bookmakers. There are firms which take on work for independent bookmakers but these are few and far between. Firms which handle liquor licensing generally also deal with public entertainment work.

The Shipley case went to the Court of Appeal at the end of 1997 and has created complications and therefore extra work, in relation to special hours certificates for nightclubs.

The three firms mentioned above, together with the other top band London firms, Cartwrights in Bristol, Poppleston Allen in Nottingham and Cobbetts in Manchester are known nationally for their liquor and public entertainment work. The two individuals who featured most prominently in our research were Les Green of Gosschalks and Jeremy Allen of Poppleston Allen.

LEADING FIRMS · LONDON

ALLEN & FRASER
FIELD FISHER WATERHOUSE
JEFFREY GREEN RUSSELL
KINGSFORD STACEY BLACKWELL
PAISNER & CO
RICHARDS BUTLER

HIGHLY REGARDED FIRMS

Joelson Wilson & Co
Kingsley Napley
Pullig & Co
Swepstone Walsh

Biddle
Howard Kennedy
Loxleys

LONDON

Allen & Fraser (2ptnrs/1asst) The firm has a strong reputation with *David Lavender* ("excellent", "cool, calm and collected") regarded as the doyen of the London licensing scene. He is said to be able to read magistrates extremely well. *Robin Walter* is also well-known. The firm is known for its capacity to handle volumes of work. **Clients/Work:** Full range of services for Scottish & Newcastle Retail Ltd, Pizza Express Ltd, Forte/Granada plc and other blue chip clients.

Field Fisher Waterhouse (1ptnr/1asst) *Peter Glazebrook* and the firm have a solid reputation. He is described as a good advocate ("a fighter") and good on presentation. **Clients/Work:** Act for clients such as London Clubs, Pizza Hut and Whitbread Plc across England and Wales. Handle all types of liquor and entertainment licensing as well as gaming and betting (act for The Lotteries Council of Great Britain).

Jeffrey Green Russell (4ptnrs – 2f/t, 2p/t/2assts) Perceived to be active in this field. *Julian Skeens* is high profile and well regarded in and out of London. **Clients/Work:** Deal mainly with liquor licensing (large brewery client) but also deal with gaming (bingo). Involved in the Shipley case going to the Court of Appeal and are still working to change the result. Accredited to train and certify bouncers.

Kingsford Stacey Blackwell (2 ptnrs – 1f/t, 1p/t/3assts – 1f/t, 2 p/t) Kingsford Stacey have merged with Booth & Blackwell to form this new firm. *Robert Edney* is known as an extremely good, straightforward licensing lawyer. This solid reputation also applies to the rest of the team. **Clients/Work:** Public entertainment and liquor licensing for clients such as Pitcher & Piano and Allied Domecq Retailing.

Paisner & Co (1ptnr/2assts) *Craig Baylis* is "doing good work" and developing the practice. **Clients/Work:** The concentration is on liquor licensing but the firm has seen an increase in public entertainment work. Handle all the licensing work for clients such as Prêt-à-Manger, Spaghetti House and Corney & Barrow.

Richards Butler (1ptnr/3assts) Described as a good, solid practice by other leading practitioners. The "highly experienced" *Elizabeth Southorn* has been recommended again. **Clients/Work:** Handle a range of licensing issues nationwide. Deal with leisure sites e.g. all the new major multi-leisure sites for Rank Group, all the Odeon Cinema licences and work for THT plc. Specialise in unusual/one-off licences. Also act for Coral.

Joelson Wilson & Co (2ptnrs/3assts) A good team, headed by *David Clifton* who is praised for his gaming experience. The popular *Suzanne Davies* has joined the firm from Edge & Ellison. **Clients/Work:** Undertake gaming, liquor and entertainment work throughout the country. Clients include Grosvenor Casinos (recent new licences in London and Newcastle), Regent Inns Plc and Restaurants GB Ltd. Advise trade organisations and involved in the drafting of new legislation.

Kingsley Napley (2ptnrs/2assts) Particularly respected for their gaming work. **Clients/Work:** Include casinos and large breweries.

Pullig & Co (1ptnr – f/t) *Christopher Hepher* is widely praised and the firm, though small, is well thought of. **Clients/Work:** All liquor and entertainment work for a range of clients from independent shop owners to major breweries.

Swepstone Walsh (1ptnr/2assts – 1f/t, 1p/t) Attempting to recruit and rebuild the practice following the loss of two senior licensing lawyers. **Clients/Work:** Have recently doubled the capacity of a prestigious

casino and obtained favourable licence conditions for a football club.

Biddle (Gaming and Leisure Group – 12 lawyers) Good reputation for gaming. *Julian Harris* heads the team. **Clients/Work:** Casino work and lottery advice as well as other types of gaming work and some liquor licensing.

Howard Kennedy The Commercial Property Department deals with licensing in relation to developments. The firm are known but not seen as much as other leaders on the licensing scene. **Clients/Work:** Act for a hotel group, a department store chain and for Ask Central plc.

Loxleys Best known for *Graeme Harris* who has a "down to earth style". **Clients/Work:** Advising brewing industry clients on new licence applications.

LEADERS' PROFILES • LONDON

BAYLIS, Craig
Paisner & Co, London (0171) 353 0299
Partner in Litigation Department and Head of the Business Regulation Unit.
Specialisation: Main area of practice is licensing and leisure. Handles all aspects for the leisure, retailing and brewing industries including advocacy at all levels throughout the UK. Other area of expertise is business protection and environmental law. Advises and represents on all regulatory matters, health and safety, food safety, trading standards and environmental health. Author of 'Food Safety: Law and Practice' and 'Environmental Regulation – Its Impact on Foreign Investment'.
Prof. Memberships: Food Law Group.
Career: Qualified 1981. Solicitor for the Metropolitan Police 1981-84; Partner at *Field Fisher Waterhouse* 1984-92. Joined *Paisner & Co.* in 1992 and became a Partner in 1993.
Personal: Born 9th February 1957. Attended Exeter University 1975-78. Lives in London.

CLIFTON, David R.G.
Joelson Wilson & Co, London
(0171) 580 5721
Partner in Charge of Licensing Department.
Specialisation: Liquor, betting, gaming and late-night entertainment licensing. Acts for a range of leading public companies, appearing as advocate in magistrates courts and crown courts and before local authorities throughout England and Wales. Advises two of the leading trade organisations in the leisure field which has resulted in involvement in the drafting of national licensing legislation and membership of working parties on licensing law reform. Appointed "Legal Expert" for The Publican Newspaper in April 1998. Regularly speaks at seminars and conferences. Clients include Grosvenor Casinos and Regent Inns Plc.
Prof. Memberships: Law Society. International Association of Gaming Attorneys, Society of Entertainment Licensing Practitioners, Association of Licensed Multiple Retailers.
Career: Attended Wellingborough School (1963-74) and University of Reading (1974-78). Articled at *Joelson Wilson & Co* in 1979 and has remained there ever since. Appointed Partner in 1983, Head of Litigation Department 1988 and Head of Licensing Department in 1993.

Personal: Born 14th March 1955. Lives in West Sussex. Leisure interests include family, theatre and cricket.

DAVIES, Suzanne
Joelson Wilson & Co, London
(0171) 580 5721
Licensing Lawyer
Specialisation: Acts for, amongst others, Regent Inns plc, Restaurants GB Limited, Grosvenor Casinos Limited, Association of Licensed Multiple Retailers. One of the firm's legal experts who write for "The Publican".
Prof. Memberships: Hotel Property Network.
Career: Manchester University, American Studies BA (Hons) 1982-1986, Pennsylvania State University, USA 1986-1987, College of Law, Chester – CPE and LSF 1987-1989.
Personal: Interests include theatre, cinema and travelling.

EDNEY, Robert
Kingsford Stacey Blackwell, London
(0171) 447 1200
Partner in Licensing Department.
Specialisation: Acts for major brewery clients and others in the leisure industry at all levels in relation to liquor and entertainment licensing and related work.
Career: Qualified in 1970, having joined *Kingsford Stacey* in 1968. Became a Partner in 1972.
Personal: Born 8th September 1946. Educated at Cambridge University (MA 1968). Chairman of local tennis club. Enjoys tennis, food and wine. Lives in Aston, near Stevenage with his wife and family of five.

GLAZEBROOK, Peter G.
Field Fisher Waterhouse, London
(0171) 481 4841

HARRIS, Graeme
Loxleys, London (0171) 377 1066
Partner in Licensing Department.
Specialisation: Acts for major companies and individuals on liquor licensing and Gaming Act matters. Also advises on entertainment licensing. Other area of practice is commercial property, acting for companies and individuals with particular reference to licensing and attendant matters.

Has acted in a wide range of licensing cases related to liquor and entertainment licensing.
Prof. Memberships: Law Society, London Brewery and Licensing Solicitors Association (Chairman).
Career: Qualified in 1960. Joined *Loxleys* in 1960, becoming a Partner in 1965.
Personal: Born 27th September 1936. Attended Westminster School 1950-54, then College of Law. Leisure interests include theatre, bowls and watching other sports. Lives in Eltham, London.

HARRIS, Julian A.
Biddle, London (0171) 606 9301
Partner in Litigation Department.
Specialisation: Main area of practice is gaming licenses. Spent six years with solicitors for Gaming Board. Now acts for several major casino and leisure groups. Also handles food law: acts for national and international food manufacturing and catering companies.
Prof. Memberships: International Association of Gaming Attorneys, Food Law Group.
Career: Qualified in 1980. Articled at *Beechcroft Hyman Isaacs* 1978-80, on qualification, *Gregory Rowcliffe & Co.* 1980-86, becoming a Partner in 1983; *Nicholson Graham & Jones* 1986-88 and *Shoosmiths & Harrison* 1988-93, as Partner and Head of Litigation in the London office. Joined *Biddle* as a Partner in 1993.
Personal: Born 15th May 1955. Attended Wellingborough School 1963-73 and Magdalene College, Cambridge 1974-77. Lives in Richmond, Surrey.

HEPHER, Christopher
Pullig & Co, London (0171) 353 0505

LAVENDER, F.D.
Allen & Fraser, London (0171) 437 4001
Specialisation: Liquor and entertainment licensing for public houses, restaurants, clubs, discotheques, off licences, hotels and casinos. Acts for several national companies as well as for individual applicants.
Career: Qualified 1966. Partner since 1968. Clerk to Board of Green Cloth Verge of the Palaces since 1984. Clerk to General Commissioners of Taxes.

Personal: Born 23 August 1942. Educated at St Peter's School York and Worcester College Oxford.

SKEENS, Julian M.
Jeffrey Green Russell, London
(0171) 339 7000

Partner in charge of Licensing and Gaming Law Department with another partner, two assistant solicitors, three paralegals and other support staff. Works closely with other departments which have specialist knowledge of the leisure industry.
Specialisation: Specialist in liquor licensing, betting, gaming, public entertainment and lotteries: undertakes cases nationwide. Known for his creative approach to licensing. Cases successfully handled include the UK's first multi-activity centre, the UK's first 24-hour public entertainment licence and the UK's largest licensed premises (600 acres). Last year he

represented the industry in the leading case of Shipley and obtained a new licence for a 3,000 capacity nightclub in Leicester Square, London.
Prof. Memberships: Law Society, Business in Sport and Leisure (Director), Society for the Study of Gambling, International Association of Gaming Attorneys, European Society for the Study of Gambling, Society of Entertainment and Licensing Practitioners (Fellow).
Career: Qualified 1980. Joined *Jeffrey Green Russell* in 1987 as a Partner to establish the now thriving specialist Licensing and Gaming Department.
Personal: Born 26th December 1951. LLB (Hons) (1974).

SOUTHORN, Elizabeth
Richards Butler, London (0171) 247 6555
Specialisation: Licensing of liquor, betting, gaming, late night entertainment and large new multi-leisure sites. Acts for major players in the

leisure industry such as the Rank Group, national bookmakers Coral, Sir Terence Conran and many of the most active developers including THI plc. Lectures in all aspects of licensing.
Prof. Memberships: Business in Sport and Leisure; Association of London Brewery Solicitors; the Law Society.
Career: Articled *Oswald Hickson Collier & Co.*; Qualified in 1974; *Clyde & Co* 1980-82; *Crossman Block & Keith* 1982-88; Partner and Head of Licensing at *Penningtons (London)* 1988-93. Joined *Richards Butler* in 1993. Currently Partner and Head of Licensing Unit.
Personal: St Anne's College, Oxford (MA Jurisprudence) 1968-71. Leisure interests include family, sailing, opera and reading.

WALTER, Robin
Allen & Fraser, London (0171) 437 4001

SOUTH EAST

Trethowan Woodford (2ptnrs – 1f/t, 1p/t/3assts) Definite leaders in the south east especially for betting work, for which they have a national reputation. *Michael Messent* is notable. The firm was described by local competitors as "very helpful". **Clients/Work:** Handling an increasing amount of casino work but the mainstay of the department is the exclusive work for Ladbrokes nationwide. Also act for Pizza Hut and Tower Casino Group.

Blake Lapthorn (2ptnrs/2assts) The firm is held in high esteem and was described as "a big player in liquor licensing". *Walter Cha* is considered "highly competent." **Clients/Work:** Liquor licensing for major breweries, supermarkets and stores locally

and nationally.

Allan Janes (1ptnr – p/t/1asst – p/t) *David Hay* is a "very good lawyer" but the loss of a major betting client in the last few years is still being felt. **Clients/Work:** Liquor licensing – acting for Surrey Free Inns, independent licencees and the leisure and hotel industry.

Argles & Court (3ptnrs – 1f/t, 2p/t. 2assts – 1f/t, 1p/t) **Clients/Work:** Handle liquor licensing for historic houses (Leeds Castle), nightclubs (The Gallery, Maidstone), pubs, etc. Clients include Whitbreads.

Blandy & Blandy (2ptnrs/1asst) **Clients/Work:** Much work relates to exhibition or conference halls, sports stadia both in London and around the country. In 1997 obtained an on-licence for Wembley Stadium and handled work for Oval cricket ground.

Cole & Cole (2ptnrs – 1p/t. 1asst – p/t) **Clients/Work:** Mainly liquor work and public entertainment but handle gaming and betting as well. Much of the work is in Oxford but the firm also handles nationwide matters. Clients include Morland Plc and Hobgoblin brewery.

Donne Mileham & Haddock (4ptnrs – p/t) A "big established practice which is good to deal with." **Clients/Work:** Working from all the firm's offices, handle liquor work, club work and public entertainment for clients such as regional hotel chains, pubs and national breweries.

Field Seymour Parkes (1ptnr – p/t. 2assts – p/t) This firm has incorporated Brain & Brain – a leading licensing firm last year. The licensing practitioners continue to handle a reasonable amount of work.

Lamport Bassitt (2ptnrs – p/t. 1asst – p/t) Known for being heavily involved in licensing in the Southampton area. **Clients/Work:** Mainly liquor and entertainment licensing, with a lot of nightclub work.

Act for the Alehouse Co Ltd and handle agency work for leading national firms.

Turbervilles (1ptnr p/t. 1asst) Renowned for handling a high volume of work and for having good clients. **Clients/Work:** Locally and nationally cover all types of work relating to liquor. Nuance Global Traders Ltd, British Airways Plc and Booker Plc are among the clients as well as local pubs, clubs and hotels.

Brachers (1ptnr) Handle a small amount of work competently. **Clients/Work:** Work for a first division football club and for educational institutions, pubs and shops.

Girlings (3ptnrs – p/t) **Clients/Work:** Work on all aspects of licensing from liquor to betting from three offices in the south east.

McLellans (2ptnrs – 1f/t, 1p/t/3assts – p/t) The firm's main specialism is licensing but they were not widely known by other practitioners in the region. **Clients/Work:** Clients include JD Wetherspoon and McMullen & Sons Ltd. Recently obtained the licensing for the Prince of Wales Theatre Development in Cardiff.

Penningtons (2ptnrs – p/t) **Clients/Work:** Handle much work locally as agents for the major national firms. Have recently arranged licences for vineyards to sell their product.

Mullis & Peake Small firm acting as agents.

CHA, Walter
Blake Lapthorn, Fareham (01489) 579990
Partner in Commercial Department.
Specialisation: Main area of practice is
licensing: has specialised since 1985, acting for
national and regional brewers undertakes own
advocacy. Also handles commercial
conveyancing for licensed premises. Acts on
behalf of brewers in landlord and tenant matters
and acquisitions and disposals of premises.
Individual charge-out rate of £120 per hour.
Career: Qualified in 1983, having joined *Blake*

Lapthorn in 1981. Became a Partner in 1987.
Personal: Born 9th August 1959. Married with
two children. Leisure interests include rugby,
golf, tennis, theatre and family. Lives in
Southsea.

HAY, David Leslie
Allan Janes, High Wycombe
(01494) 521 301

MESSENT, Michael J.
Trethowan Woodford, Southampton
(01703) 321000
Partner in Licensing Department.
Specialisation: Head of Department with
extensive experience as advisor and advocate
in betting, gaming and liquor licensing law.
Career: Qualified 1971. Joined *Woodford &
Ackroyd* 1973. Partner 1976.
Personal: Born 15th August 1947. Court
Member of the Cooks Company. Leisure
interests include golf, walking and world travel.

SOUTH WEST

CARTWRIGHTS Bristol

EVERSHEDS Bristol

FYNN & PARTNERS Bournemouth

Andrew Gregg & Co Bristol
Clarke Willmott & Clarke Taunton
Crosse & Crosse Exeter
Foot & Bowden Plymouth
Lester Aldridge Bournemouth
Rickerby Watterson Cheltenham

Bevan Ashford Bristol
Ford Simey Daw Roberts Exeter
Frank & Caffin Truro
Nalder & Son Truro
Stephens & Scown Exeter
Thompson & Jackson Plymouth

Beviss & Beckingsale Chard
Stones Cann & Hallett Exeter
Woollcombe Beer Watts Newton Abbot

Cartwrights (3ptnrs/2assts) Maintain their
extremely high profile and strong reputation
in licensing nationwide. Handle a large
volume of work and boast an impressive team
of specialists. *Timothy Davies* ("weight of
knowledge", "very effective") heads the
team. Other members include *Kathryn
Eardley* ("very good") and *Michael Parrott*
("highly competent"). *David Hamilton* now
works part time as a consultant.
Clients/Work: Deal with all licensing matters
for a range of clients including Safeway, Top
Rank, Greenalls and Victoria Wine. In the
last year made the first successful application for alcohol consumption for cinema
movie watchers.

Eversheds (1ptnr/5assts) The firm has
a burgeoning reputation nationally for its
licensing work, with the Bristol office leading the way. *Jeremy Phillips* ("shrewd") is
well known and highly regarded. He is the
author of Phillips' Licensing Law Guide and
will jointly edit the liquor section of
Halsbury's Laws. **Clients/Work:** All types of
licensing matters handled for a large client

base including clients such as Esso, Scottish
& Newcastle, and exclusively, Somerfield
and 7-Eleven.

Fynn & Partners (3ptnrs: 1p/t. 1asst, 1
consultant p/t) Described as "a household
name" in licensing. *Lionel Fynn* ("flamboyant") is well regarded. Other members of the
team include *Julia Palmer* ("sound", "able"
and "thorough") and *Graham Gover* ("well
prepared"). **Clients/Work:** Deal with the
whole range of licensing work in the South.
Clients include Surrey Free Inns (Litten Tree
superpub), Sheridan Group (Imax Leisure
Centre) and Wessex Bowlplex.

Andrew Gregg & Co (1ptnr/1asst – p/t)
Very well known in Bristol. *Andrew Gregg*
is experienced and has "good court presence." **Clients/Work:** Work mainly in Bristol
for many small pubs and the Falcons Inn
Group. Handle many oppositions and work
linked with food safety. Recently obtained
licences for Babington House and a six a.m.
licence for the Powerhouse Nightclub.

Clarke Willmott & Clarke (1ptnr/6assts)
Maintain a good reputation in this sphere.
Clients/Work: Liquor work for breweries,
pubs and caterers throughout the south west.
Clients include Co-operative Retail Ser-
vices Ltd, Ushers Brewery and Sutcliffe
Catering.

Crosse & Crosse (1ptnr/1asst) Said to
be "at the forefront in Exeter". **Clients/Work:**
Much work as agents for leading firms.
Handle entertainment licences for nightclubs
and festivals, and conduct oppositions in the
local area.

Foot & Bowden (1ptnr/1asst) **Clients/
Work:** Applications and oppositions for
brewery and individual clients. Also
involved in gaming and public entertainment.

Lester Aldridge (2ptnrs) A strong local
practice. *Colin Patrick* is "very experienced"
and a good advocate. **Clients/Work:** Still
handling a lot of nightclub related work in
Bournemouth. Have seen a fall in the amount
of gaming work recently. Act for Greenalls;
the Dorset Police in many objections.

Rickerby Watterson (2ptnrs/2assts)
Clients/Work: Handle work for clients such
as Greenalls Plc, Whitbread Plc and Roadchef Plc. In 1997 were involved in the restruc-

turing of Gloucester Rugby Club's licensing
requirements.

Bevan Ashford (1ptnr/1asst – p/t in
Bristol office. Other offices also handle
licensing) **Clients/Work:** Act for Lidl UK
Properties GmbH; Allied Domecq; arrange
the licensing for the Glastonbury Festival.

Ford Simey Daw Roberts (1ptnr 20%,
1asst 20%) **Clients/Work:** Act for individual
licencees in transfers, occasional licences
and new applications.

Frank & Caffin (4ptnrs: 3p/t. 1asst)
Clients/Work: Handle all the work in
Cornwall for a major brewer. Also deal with
all types of liquor work for pubs, clubs, stores.

Nalder & Son (1ptnr/2assts – all p/t)
Clients/Work: Handle all types of liquor
licensing. Retained by Appleby Westward
Plc. Handling of licence applications for new
Spar stores in Cornwall and Devon.

Stephens & Scown (2ptnrs; 2assts – all
p/t) **Clients/Work:** Operate across Devon and
Cornwall for breweries, shops, hotels and
leisure parks. Clients include St. Austell
Brewery, Haven Holidays and Primex UK
Ltd.

Thompson & Jackson (1ptnr p/t) Have
many years experience in licensing and are
perceived to handle a reasonable amount of
work.

Beviss & Beckinsale (1ptnr p/t)
Clients/Work: All types of liquor licensing
in Devon, Somerset and Dorset. Handle
agency work for city firms.

Stones Cann & Hallett Stones has
recently merged with Cann & Hallett to form

DAVIES Timothy Cartwrights
FYNN Lionel Fynn & Partners
PHILLIPS Jeremy Eversheds

EARDLEY Kathryn Cartwrights
PALMER Julia Fynn & Partners
PARROTT Michael Cartwrights
PATRICK Colin Lester Aldridge

GOVER Graham Fynn & Partners
GREGG Andrew Andrew Gregg & Co
HAMILTON David Cartwrights

this new firm. Continue to handle licensing work for local publicans, hoteliers, restaurateurs and off-licence owners.

Woollcombe Beer Watts (5ptnrs; p/t/2assts: 1p/t) **Clients/Work:** Deal with a high volume of liquor licensing throughout the south west. Specialities include golf clubs and holiday facilities.

LEADERS' PROFILES · SOUTH WEST

DAVIES, Timothy L.
Cartwrights, Bristol (0117) 929 3601
Specialisation: Adviser and advocate for all liquor, entertainment and gaming licence cases. As Head of Licensing Department, provides licensing input to commercial partners on licensed property acquisitions and disposals. By way of example acts for Marks & Spencer, Tesco, Stakis, Mecca, Virgin Cinemas and many other leading companies in the retail and leisure sectors. Has run licensing workshops and training for the trade and witness training exercises for clients. Legal consultant to the British Retail Consortium.
Personal: Born 2nd April 1953. Attended Clifton College and University College London. Married with 3 children and lives in Bristol.

EARDLEY, Kathryn A.
Cartwrights, Bristol (0117) 929 3601
Partner in Licensing Department.
Specialisation: Specialises in the administration of licensed estates for national retailers and breweries.
Career: Qualified in 1978, while articled with *George Brown & Co* and then moved to *Blatch & Co*. Spent six years with Hampshire Magistrates' Court Committee. Joined *Cartwrights* in 1988 and became a Partner in 1990.
Personal: Educated at University of Sheffield, 1971. Lives in Bristol.

FYNN, Lionel C.
Fynn & Partners, Bournemouth (01202) 551991
Partner, and Head of Environmental Licensing and Planning Department.
Specialisation: Regular advocate in a wide range of planning environmental and licensing matters. One of the first solicitors in the country to conduct a Crown Court Licensing Appeal and has since acted in numerous such cases involving liquor licensing, betting and gaming subjects. Has personally conducted noise related proceedings and civil actions and numerous Town Planning enquiries and specialises in High Court challenges/Judicial Review.
Prof. Memberships: Member of Business in Sport and Leisure.
Career: Lecturer at major seminars on Licensing and Planning Subjects. Produced 'cassette law' audio series in collaboration with Oyez IBC and the Law Society and subsequently produced two Licensing videos. A third on the new Children's Certificates legislation was released late 1994 and has been widely acclaimed. Now involved in the production of a new Town Planning video on urban design.

GOVER, Graham
Fynn & Partners, Bournemouth (01202) 551991
Associate in Environmental Licensing Department and Planning Department.
Specialisation: Every aspect of liquor and entertainment licensing, particularly for the outdoor events industry and sports and leisure operators. Also acts for a major convenience

store represented nationally, in particular for obtaining off-licences at petrol stations. With a background as a prosecutor and Local Authority Solicitor, also conducts appeals and defends criminal proceedings in these areas and advises on all Local Authority and environmental issues. He is a regular speaker at training events and seminars.
Prof. Memberships: Law Society, UKELA, Food Law Group, Fellow of the Society of Entertainment Licensing Practitioners.
Career: LLB Brunel University. Qualified 1983. Magistrates Clerk 1980-1995. Prosecutor 1985-1988. Local Government Solicitor 1988-1993. Joined the Bournemouth office of *Penningtons* (now *Fynn & Partners*) 1993, becoming Associate in 1994.

GREGG, Andrew
Andrew Gregg & Co, Bristol (0117) 925 8123
Specialisation: All aspects of law concerning food, licensing and health and safety. Acts for wide variety of food and drink manufacturers, processors and retailers. See 'R v. Gateway Foodmarkets Ltd' C.A. TLR 2.1.97.
Prof. Memberships: Secretary Food Law Group, Vice President Bristol Law Society, Council Member Notaries Society.
Career: The Dragon School Oxford, The Kings School Canterbury. Solicitor D.o.A. 1970, Notary Public D.o.A. 1984. For 20 years partner with a leading Bristol firm before setting up own niche practice in 1992.
Personal: Born 12.9.43. Interests include rugby, sailing, motor racing and restoration of vintage cars. Owns and campaigns a 1933 Lagonda. Chairman Bristol and Avon Federation of Clubs for Young People.

HAMILTON, David J.
Cartwrights, Bristol (0117) 929 3601
Consultant in Licensing Department.
Specialisation: Main area of practice is specialist licensing advice in connection with applications for gaming, liquor, public entertainment, betting and similar licences. Also provides advice in connection with prosecutions of clients arising under consumer protection and in particular Food Safety Legislation. Joint author with Kerry Barker of 'Betting, Gaming and Lotteries'. (Fourmat Publishing 1993).
Career: Served in the Royal Navy for 3 years after leaving university, then pursued a career in industry. Studied for the Solicitors qualifying exam part-time 1973-76. Qualified and joined *Cartwrights* in 1976. Became a Partner in 1980; and Consultant in 1996.
Personal: Born 1934. Educated at Fitzwilliam House, Cambridge 1953-56 (MA Natural Sciences).

PALMER, Julia C.
Fynn & Partners, Bournemouth (01202) 551991
Partner in Environmental Licensing and Planning Department.
Specialisation: All aspects of liquor, entertainment and betting and gaming licensing, and Local Authority matters affecting

the leisure industry. Clients include major leisure Plcs, breweries, and a major stadium operator. Good record of obtaining "superpub" licences on previously unlicensed sites. Appears before Courts and Committees throughout England and Wales. Has regularly both organised and given talks at seminars in this field; author of articles in various publications.
Career: Qualified in 1980. Court Clerk, Bournemouth Magistrates Court 1982-88. Joined the Bournemouth office of *Penningtons* in 1988 (now *Fynn & Partners*), becoming a Partner in 1991.
Personal: Born 11th April 1952. Leisure interests include gliding, archery, walking, photography, classical music and crosswords.

PARROTT, Michael Kindersley
Cartwrights, Bristol (0117) 929 3601
Specialisation: Partner specialising in all aspects of licensing law including liquor, entertainment and gaming licences on behalf of major Plcs. Practice has involved applications for judicial review of interpretation and implementation of licensing justices' policy. Also acts for national food retailers on food law matters.
Career: Articles in Magistrates Courts Service, *Cartwrights* in 1985, appointed Partner in 1987.
Personal: Educated at Exeter School 1965-71 and Leicester University 1972-1975. Leisure pursuits include squash, tennis, skiing and photography. Born 1953. Lives in Bristol.

PATRICK, Colin
Lester Aldridge, Bournemouth (01202) 786161
Specialisation: Chairman of the firm, Partner and specialist in licensing law. Practice covers liquor, public entertainment (especially night-clubs), betting and gaming. Has written a number of articles on licensing matters for Hotel and Restaurant Association publications.
Prof. Memberships: The Law Society.
Career: Qualified 1957. Partner, *Lester Aldridge* 1962. Chairman, *Lester Aldridge* since 1990.
Personal: Educated at Canford School, Wimborne 1948-1952. Law Society Finals 1957 (2nd Class honours). Hampshire Law Society Prize 1957. Bournemouth Law Society Prize 1957. Trustee of the Bournemouth Orchestras Foundation. Governor of Canford School, Wimborne. President, Summer Music Society of Dorset. Leisure pursuits include music, theatre, food and wine, antiques, art, gardening, architecture, travel and the countryside. Born 28th August 1934. Lives in Poole, Dorset.

PHILLIPS, Jeremy
Eversheds, Bristol 0117 929 9555
Eversheds, Cardiff, (01222) 471147. Partner in Employment, Pensions and Licensing.
Specialisation: Main area of practice is licensing and leisure, acting on behalf of breweries, licensed property companies, independent operators, multiple specialist off licences and convenience stores throughout England and Wales. Also retail work, defending and advising companies concerning food safety, trades descriptions, weights and

measures and environmental legislation. Advisor to industry groups concerning legislative reform. Regular contributor to legal journals concerning licensing matters. Conducts seminars on licensing law for national

multiple operators, financial institutions and professional practices. Joint editor of Paterson's Licensing Acts. Author of Phillips: Licensing Law Guide published by Butterworths; joint editor Halsbury's 'Licensing Statutes' . Chairman of

Eversheds' National Licensing Group.
Prof. Memberships: A.B.I.I.
Career: Partner in 1982, Co-founder of *Holt Phillips* in 1984.
Personal: Lives outside Bristol.

WALES

Morgan Bruce (3ptnrs – p/t/2assts – p/t) The firm maintains its position in Wales. The quality of the team and their work were highly praised. *Robin Havard* works out of the Cardiff office and *Rosemary Morgan* works

in Swansea. *Claire Rawle* enters our up and coming list. **Clients/Work:** Work in the whole of Wales and a large part of England. Cover liquor licensing, betting and gaming. Clients include Whitbread Plc and Allied Domecq.

Edwards Geldard (1ptnr – p/t/1asst – p/t) **Clients/Work:** Handle a large volume of licensing work in south Wales for a major brewer. Also act for private clients in liquor and gaming.

Cartwrights Adams & Black (1ptnr – p/t/1asst – p/t) Well known and enjoy a good reputation in licensing. **Clients/Work:** Mainly liquor work but deal with betting and gaming as well. Work for a local Cardiff brewery.

Eversheds (2ptnrs – p/t. 1asst p/t) Looking to increase its presence in the Welsh

market. The firm is respected amongst competitors. Jeremy Phillips, who is a leading individual in the south west, also heads the team in Wales. **Clients/Work:** Undertake a range of licensing work in Wales and England. Clients include Surrey Free Inns, Inntrepeneur and Wales National Ice Rink.

LEADERS' PROFILES • WALES

HAVARD, Robin
Morgan Bruce, Cardiff (01222) 385385
Partner in General Insurance Department.
Specialisation: Principal area of practice is general insurance work including advocacy. Also handles licensing, health and safety and environmental prosecutions. Has dealt with a number of acquisitions of new development sites for one of the big six national breweries

and all licensing work necessary. Other clients include a national convenience store chain, local hotels, restaurants, publicans and a large independent bookmaker.
Prof. Memberships: Law Society, FOIL. Higher Courts (all proceedings) Qualification.
Career: Qualified in 1981. Partner at *Morgan Bruce* since May 1987.
Personal: Born 7th May 1957. Educated at the

Cathedral School, Cardiff, Epsom College and University College, Cardiff. Lives in Cardiff.

MORGAN, Rosemary
Morgan Bruce, Newport (01633) 244988

RAWLE, Claire
Morgan Bruce, Cardiff (01222) 385385

MIDLANDS

Poppleston Allen (2ptnrs/4assts) One of the best known practices in the country, this niche licensing firm is highly rated. Their work with nightclubs is especially lauded. *Jeremy Allen* ("detailed", "effective") is one of the top licensing lawyers in the country, while *Susanna Poppleston* is considered to

be "very, very good" and an "excellent advocate." *Lisa Sharkey* features and *Kirsty Pearson* has arrived from Eversheds to add further strength to this excellent team. **Clients/Work:** Handle liquor and entertainment licensing for clients up and down the country and have an increasing workload. Act exclusively for European Leisure Plc, Luminar Leisure Plc, Bass Leisure and Pizza Express Plc as well as doing the major part of Scottish and Newcastle's work.

Anthony Collins (1ptnr/1asst) Small but highly rated team. *Anthony Collins* ("good and thorough") received many commendations as did *Deborah Shaw* ("good fighter in court"). **Clients/Work:** Work mainly in the West Midlands dealing with all aspects of liquor licensing e.g. new applications, late night licences. Wolverhampton & Dudley Breweries Plc and Whitbread Seven Inns are two of the major clients.

Edge & Ellison (2ptnrs/3assts) Said to do more work than any other firm in the Birmingham area. *Andrew Potts* ("tenacious") gets the results. *Stephanie Perraton* is good with clients. **Clients/Work:** Deal with liquor and gaming work in Birmingham and the rest of the country. Have seen an increase in turnover in the last year. Clients include

Apollo Leisure Plc, Marston Thompson Evershed Plc and Aston Villa Football Club.

Eversheds (1ptnr/3assts) This office of the national firm has a good reputation with

David Young described as "a safe pair of hands." **Clients/Work:** Working with clients such as Esso and Greenalls Inns, handle a range of liquor licensing matters. In the last year have obtained outline grants for a proposed re-development near Spaghetti Junction.

Shacklocks (2ptnrs/1asst) A good team, with *Robin Wilson* featuring prominently. They act for Mansfield Breweries and this keeps their profile high. **Clients/Work:** Liquor licensing work for a range of businesses. Other clients include the Nottinghamshire Police and Vaux Brewery.

Young & Pearce (3ptnrs – 1f/t, 1p/t/1asst) *John Pearce* comes highly recommended and the firm's reputation in licensing is largely due to him. **Clients/Work:** Nationwide, for large companies, dealing with pubs, nightclubs, casinos and off-licences.

Challinors Lyon Clark (7ptnrs/1asst) A substantial practice which is well known locally. *Trevor Lee* gets high praise and moves up a band. **Clients/Work:** Liquor and gaming work for breweries, clubs, off-licences and supermarkets.

Freeth Cartwright Hunt Dickins (2ptnrs – 1f/t, 1asst – p/t) *Malcolm Radcliffe* has joined the firm from Ironsides, bringing his good reputation with him. The firm moves up a band. **Clients/Work:** Opening a new office in Leicester to deal with liquor licensing. Act for Aldi stores, the Leicestershire Police and cafes and hotels.

Kenneth Curtis & Co (1ptnr – p/t) *Tony Curtis* is thought of as a "good, aggressive advocate."

Ellis Moxon (2ptnrs – p/t) Leader *Ian Moxon* is known as the "licensing king of the Potteries."

Knight & Sons (1ptnr 20%/1asst 5%) Have a "solid" reputation. **Clients/Work:** Recently obtained a special hours certificate in Stoke-on-Trent for Allied Domecq.

Lanyon Bowdler (5ptnrs – 1f/t, 4p/t) *Robin Onions* was highly recommended for his work for off-licences and is a new entry to the table this year. **Clients/Work:** Handle all licensing for AF Blakemore & Son Ltd (Spar), and work for Spar Independent retailers. Also undertake work re pubs, garage forecourts and nightclubs.

Nelsons (1consultant – pt/2assts – 1f/t, 1p/t)) **Clients/Work:** Deal with all liquor licensing matters and also handle gaming work. Clients include Scottish & Newcastle, Greenalls and a leading amusement arcade company.

LEADERS' PROFILES • MIDLANDS

ALLEN, Jeremy
Poppleston Allen, Nottingham
(0115) 953 8500
Partner and Co-Founder.
Specialisation: Specialises in licensing and leisure work, including liquor, public entertainment, betting and gaming. Also handles associated crime work, including trades descriptions and breach of conditions. Legal Director of B.E.D.A. (British Entertainment and Discotheque Association). Major clients include Bass Leisure Entertainment, European Leisure Plc, Kingfisher Leisure Plc, Luminar Leisure, Pizza Express, Rank Leisure Plc, Scottish and Newcastle, Wolverhampton & Dudley Breweries and many university student unions.
Prof. Memberships: Law Society. Secretary Nottinghamshire Law Society 1977-84; President East Midlands Association of Local Law Societies (Secretary 1981-86). Founder Chairman Law Society's Child Care Working Party; member Law Society Council 1986-92; member Magistrates' Courts Rule Committee since 1982; Chairman Law Society's Criminal Law Committee 1987-1991; member Lord Chancellor's Efficiency Commission 1987-89; member of Home Office Review of Procedure Committee. First Higher Courts (crime) Advocacy course leader, current Chairman of Advocacy Training Sub-Committee.
Career: Qualified in 1970. Articled at *Johnstone Sharp & Walker* 1962-68. *Raleigh Industries* 1968-72. Joined *Hunt Dickins* in 1972, becoming a Partner in 1973 and Managing Partner in 1987. Co-founded *Poppleston Allen Licensing Solicitors* in 1994.
Personal: Born 5th July 1944. Attended Bedales and College of Law. Leisure interests include theatre, hockey and running. Lives in Nottingham.

COLLINS, Anthony Ralph
Anthony Collins Solicitors, Birmingham
(0121) 200 3242
Specialisation: Specialises in licensing applications of all types, particularly for national brewers and entrepreneurs. A majority of the applications are concentrated within the West Midlands conurbation and clients are also

advised throughout England & Wales. Other areas of specialisation within the firm include liquor licensing, secured lending for breweries, local government and housing, charity, employment, professional & medical negligence and child care.
Prof. Memberships: Referral Panel Solicitor for Action for Victims of Medical Accidents.
Career: Articled *Wragge & Co* and qualified in 1970, joined *Tilley Carson & Finlay* in Toronto 1970 and admitted as a Barrister and Solicitor to the Law Society of Upper Canada in 1972. Founded *Anthony Collins Solicitors* in 1973.
Personal: Married. Three children. Bradfield College. Chairman Education & Training Committee Birmingham Law Society. Family history and fly fishing.

CURTIS, Anthony G.
Kenneth Curtis & Co, Birmingham
(0121) 356 1161

LEE, Trevor A.
Challinors Lyon Clark, Edgbaston
(0121) 455 6333
Specialisation: Licensing (gaming, betting and liquors). Leisure. Heads an enlarged licensing team with wide client base throughout West Midlands in all forms of licensed premises. Undertakes work for Bass Taverns Enterprise Inns and instructed by Richardson Brothers for licensing work at prestigious development of Merry Hill Waterfront.
Prof. Memberships: Vice President of Birmingham Law Society.
Career: Admitted 1969. Worked in licensing since then with present firm where he is Senior Partner.
Personal: Married, sons 16 and 18. Golf, cricket, skiing, good wines.

MOXON, Ian
Ellis Moxon, Stoke-on-Trent (01782) 577700
Specialisation: Partner in charge of Licensing. Fourth generation of family specialising in licensing for private clients, breweries and bookmakers. Full range of licensing work undertaken.
Prof. Memberships: Past President North Staffordshire Law Society. Past Chariman

Solicitors Benevolent Association.
Career: Qualified in 1962. Partner in present firm since 1963.

ONIONS, Robin W.
Lanyon Bowdler, Shrewsbury
(01743) 236400
Specialisation: Liqour licensing. Crime. Representing major company in off licence applications throughout UK. Licensing major night club in Telford. Solicitor advocate – appearing to prosecute and defend in crown courts.
Prof. Memberships: Law Society, Child Care Panel, Solicitor Advocate (1994), Crown Court Recorder (1995).
Career: Priory School, Shrewsbury. LSE LL.B (1970). Solicitor (1993). Senior Partner *Lanyon Bowdler* (1993 –).
Personal: Sport – football, skiing, cricket, travel, gardening! reading, driving. Married – Catherine (educational psychologist), 2 children.

PEARCE, John
Young & Pearce, Nottingham
(0115) 959 8888

PEARSON, Kirsty
Poppleston Allen, Nottingham
(0115) 953 8500
Specialisation: Specialises in licensing and leisure work, including liqour and public entertainment. Major clients include Bass Leisure Entertainment, European Leisure plc, Kingfisher Leisure plc, Luminar Leisure plc, Pizza Express, Rank Leisure plc, Scottish and Newcastle and works for an increasing number of student unions.
Prof. Memberships: Law Society; Nottingham Law Society.
Career: Joined *Poppleston Allen* in March 1998 having worked for *Eversheds*, Birmingham for six years. Educated at Manchester University (law degree) and Chester College of Law.
Personal: Holidays spent exploring and trekking. Leisure time devoted to outdoor pursuits, food and sport. Reads and cross-stiches when it is raining. Lives in Sollhull.

PERRATON, Stephanie

Edge & Ellison, Birmingham (0121) 200 2001
Partner with Edge & Ellison since May 1996.
Specialisation: Key member of a Specialist Team of Lawyers operating exclusively on behalf of the Licensed Trade. Acts on a day to day basis for a wide range of operators from listed companies to individual entrepreneurs, advising and making applications on behalf of theatres, cinemas, concert halls, entertainment venues, breweries, stores, hoteliers, sports facilities, pub and club owners, off-licences, post offices and newsagents. She has considerable experience in acting on behalf of receivers of licensed premises.
Prof. Memberships: Member of the Law Society (local and international), BEDA (British Entertainment and Disco Association) and a co-opted governor of Fairfax Grant Maintained School.

POPPLESTON, Susanna

Poppleston Allen, Nottingham
(0115) 953 8500
Partner and Co-founder.
Specialisation: Main area of practice is licensing and leisure. Work includes liquor, betting and gaming, public entertainment and pay parties. Legal correspondent and columnist for Licensee and Morning Advertiser, a trade paper for the licensed trade. Former Notts advocacy training officer; now advocacy trainer with the National Law Society. Major clients include Bass Leisure Entertainment, European Leisure plc, Kingfisher Leisure plc, Luminar Leisure, Pizza Express, Rank Leisure plc, Scottish and Newcastle and Wolverhampton & Dudley Breweries.
Prof. Memberships: Nottinghamshire Law Society (Former President), Law Society.
Career: LLB. Bristol 1969. Qualified in 1972. Articled at *Shacklocks* (subsequently merged with *Ashton Hill & Co.*) 1969-72, setting up own criminal department in 1972 and becoming a Partner in 1974. Set up and ran the first branch office in Nottingham. Co-founded *Temple Wallis* in 1979, which merged to create *Hunt Dickins* in 1987. First woman Vice-President of the Nottingham Law Students' Society. Co-founded *Poppleston Allen* in 1994.
Personal: Born 24th June 1948. Educated Nottingham and Bristol University. Leisure interests include reading, cooking, fell walking and eating. Lives in Nottingham.

POTTS, Andrew J.

Edge & Ellison, Birmingham (0121) 200 2001
Partner in Litigation Department.
Specialisation: Main area of practice is licensing: Head of a department of two partners and four fee earners. Also handles employment law. Author of numerous articles in the professional press and has wide experience of addressing conferences and seminars.
Prof. Memberships: Law Society, Birmingham Law Society.
Career: Qualified in 1971. Joined *Edge & Ellison* in 1970, becoming a Partner in 1976. Part time Industrial Tribunal Chairman from 1983-95.
Personal: Born 7th September 1944. Attended Aldenham School 1958-63 and Bristol University 1963-66. Leisure interests include tennis, hockey and cricket. Lives in Leamington Spa.

RADCLIFFE, Malcolm

Freeth Cartwright Hunt Dickins, Leicester (0115) 936 9369
Partner in Licensing and Commercial Department.
Specialisation: Principal area of practice is licensing. Also handles commercial conveyancing. Major clients include Leicestershire Police; Aldi Stores; and has written a guide to the 1988 Licensing Act which was distributed to all major brewers and organisations in the leisure industry. Individual charge-out rate is normally £130 per hour.
Prof. Memberships: Law Society, Solicitors Benevolent Association.
Career: Qualified in 1972. With *Ironsides* from qualification and became a Partner in 1974. Partner in *Freeth Cartwright Hunt Dickins* 1998.
Personal: Born 22nd November 1948. Educated at Oakham School 1959-66. Parish Councillor and Vice Chairman of local primary school governors.

SHARKEY, Lisa

Poppleston Allen, Nottingham
(0115) 953 8500
Specialisation: Specialises in licensing and leisure work, including liquor, public entertainment and pay parties. Writes legal column for 'Agenda', a magazine for the Professional Association of Student Union Managers. Major clients include Bass Leisure Entertainment, European Leisure plc, Kingfisher Leisure plc, Luminar Leisure plc, Pizza Express, Rank Leisure plc, Scottish and Newcastle and works for an increasing number of student unions. Involved with B.E.D.A. in Drugs issues and the campaign to Legalise Sunday dancing.
Prof. Memberships: Law Society; Nottingham. Law Society; Society of Entertainment Licensing Practitioners.
Career: LLB: (Hons) Leeds 1989. Lectured Law at the University of Derby 1991. Articled at *Hunt Dickins* 1992. Left *Hunt Dickins* in 1994 with Jeremy Allen and Susanna Poppleston when they formed *Poppleston Allen* Licensing Solicitors.
Personal: Leisure interests include drinking and dancing, eating, netball and Tae Kwon Do.

SHAW, Deborah

Anthony Collins Solicitors, Birmingham
(0121) 200 3242
Specialisation: Deborah Shaw is a solicitor in the firm's licensing and leisure department specialising in licensing applications of all types, particularly for national breweries and entrepreneurs. Applications are made throughout England and Wales but with a special concentration in the West Midlands. Deborah has wide experience of handling betting and gaming licensing. The firm's licensing expertise incorporates a licensing property department with a substantial secured lending emphasis. Other areas of specialisation within the firm include local government and housing law, charity, employment, professional & medical negligence and child care.
Prof. Memberships: Birmingham Law Society.
Career: Qualified in 1984. Deborah has 11 years experience with two leading licensing practices.
Personal: Educated at Birmingham University; interests include mountaineering, fell walking, films and theatre, reading, travel when time and family permit.

WILSON, Robin K.

Shacklocks, Nottingham (0115) 941 0789
Senior Partner, Managing Partner; Head of Licencing Department.
Specialisation: Department deals exclusively with licencing, and includes highly experienced partner David Lucas and an assistant solicitor. Acts for major regional brewer throughout its entire estate, together with other brewers, an international night club proprietor, and other independent operators of all sizes across central and north eastern England, in all types of licensed premises, clubs and betting offices. Also acts or licencing justices and police.
Career: Qualified 1970. Partner, *Shacklocks* since 1972.
Personal: Born 1945. Educated Jesus College Cambridge (MA).

YOUNG, David A.

Eversheds, Birmingham (0121) 233 2001
Partner in Litigation Department.
Specialisation: Main area of practice is liquor licensing. Acts principally for leisure and retail clients. Work covers new licences, both on and off, structural alteration programmes, special hour certificates, supper hour certificates, childrens' certificates, public entertainment licensing etc. Also handles general regulatory work including health and safety matters, trading standards, food law and environmental prosecutions. Examples of matters dealt with in the past are the re-licensing of two terminals at an international airport, the management of the licensing programme for conversions of well over 100 public houses to three branded operations and petrol station forecourt shop off-licences. Together with other *Eversheds'* licensing lawyers is coordinating a Licensing Guide for publication in 1997. Writes regularly for In-House Lawyer as well as speaking at seminars. Runs a team of 5 licensing lawyers as well as working closely with other *Eversheds'* licensing lawyers, in particular the team run by Jeremy Phillips from the Bristol/Cardiff offices.
Prof. Memberships: Law Society, Food Law Group.
Career: Qualified in 1984. Became a Partner at *Eversheds* in 1993.
Personal: Born 11th October 1959. Educated at Solihull School 1971-78, University College, London 1978-81 and The College of Law, Chancery Lane 1981-82. Leisure time devoted to squash, family life and travel. Lives in Solihull.

EAST ANGLIA

Howes Percival (1ptnr 70%) Still leading the way in East Anglia. *Alan Kefford* handles the work. **Clients/Work:** Liquor and entertainment licensing for a range of individuals and organisations, including work for Ryan Elizabeth Holdings Plc and most of the Scottish and Newcastle work in the area. The firm is now an accredited examiner for the National Licencees Certificate.

Eversheds (2 ptnrs – p/t) Sound licensing practice with *Malcolm Partridge* ("very competent") respected for his work. **Clients/Work:** Deal with a range of licensing matters for leisure industry clients.

Greenwoods (1ptnr – p/t/1asst – p/t) Recognised for their work in the Peterborough area. **Clients/Work:** Liquor and entertainment work for pubs, clubs etc. Act for a national pub chain.

Kenneth Bush (1ptnr – p/t/1asst – p/t) Known locally for their work for leisure groups. **Clients/Work:** Have applied for many new licences for holiday site providers throughout the country in the last year.

Mills & Reeve (1ptnr – p/t/1asst – p/t) The death of Anthony Jordan is a blow to the firm and he will be sorely missed.

Clients/Work: Mainly work related to the tourist industry in Norwich and East Anglia.

Nicholls & Co (1ptnr 15%) *Simon Nicholls* handles licensing work in conjunction with his criminal practice. **Clients/Work:** Liquor and gaming work for big hotels and individual licencees. Act for Stakis Plc and Dunstan Hall.

Ward Gethin (1ptnr – p/t) Work mainly in the King's Lynn area and considered a good, local practice. **Clients/Work:** Liquor licensing for pubs, off licences and restaurants. Agency work.

LEADERS' PROFILES · EAST ANGLIA

KEFFORD, Alan
Howes Percival, Norwich (01603) 762103
Managing Partner for East Anglian office and Head of firm's Liquor and Leisure Division.
Specialisation: Main area of practice covers all aspects of liquor and entertainment licensing. Also includes gaming matters. Addressed a number of seminars for representatives of the leisure industry.
Prof. Memberships: Director of Anglian Archives plc and The Leisure Stop Ltd.
Personal: Born 1st May 1944. Attended Malvern College 1958-62, then University College, London 1963-66. Leisure pursuits include walking, cricket and Norwich City F.C. Lives in Norwich.

NICHOLLS, Simon J.
Nicholls & Co, Norwich (01603) 499999

PARTRIDGE, Malcolm
Eversheds, Norwich (01603) 272727
Specialisation: Specialisations include all aspects of liquor and entertainment licensing for both independent operators and national concerns. Contributor to monthly licensing section of 'In-House Lawyer'.
Prof. Memberships: Norfolk and Norwich Law Society (Vice-President), Employment Lawyers Association.
Career: Qualified 1970. Partner in Norwich since 1976. Considerable advocacy experience. Specialist in licensing law for twenty years.
Personal: Born 16th January 1945. University of Sheffield 1964-67.

NORTH WEST

Cobbetts (2ptnrs/1asst) Maintaining their position at the top of the tables, this firm is felt to have the best brewing clients. Head of the team, *Hamish Lawson*, is "straight", "industrious" and "a pleasure to work with." *Simon Jones* is "level headed", and very much in the mould of Lawson. **Clients/Work:** Handle a range of liquor licensing matters, with particular expertise in new developments. The firm advises the North West Brewers and Retailers Association and a host of brewing clients including Greenalls, Whitbreads and Allied Domecq. In the past year they have seen an increase in the volume of work with more national deals.

Davies Wallis Foyster (2ptnrs/3assts) *Nick Dickinson* is well regarded at this leading firm. **Clients/Work:** Act for many stores and supermarkets in England and are one of the few English firms to work in Scotland. In the past year have acted increasingly in objections.

Weightmans (3ptnrs: 2p/t; 6assts – p/t) The other leading firm in Liverpool. *Mark Owen* ("very clued up", "solid", "straight bat") has many admirers. **Clients/Work:** Deal with all types of licensing. Betting work for five independent bookmakers. Clients include Whitbreads, Merseyside Police and Liverpool Football Club. Recently acted on the successful licensing of Queen Square, Liverpool which involved 12 provisional grants for new pubs, clubs and restaurants.

Elliott & Company (1ptnr – p/t/1asst – p/t) *Barry Holland* ("ebullient, "great character") is the basis of the firm's reputation. **Clients/Work:** Clients include Threshers, Majestic and First Leisure.

Halliwell Landau (1ptnr/2assts) *Anthony Horne* ("good scrapper", "very able") is highly rated. **Clients/Work:** Liquor, entertainment, betting and gaming work is undertaken. In the last year acted in two successful appeals. Grosvenor Casinos Ltd, Manchester University and Bargain Booze are some of the firm's clients.

Pannone & Partners (2ptnrs/2assts) The popular *Anthony Lyons* has a good reputation as head of licensing and the firm was widely praised. It moves up the tables accordingly. **Clients/Work:** Mainly liquor licensing for clients such as Granada Entertainments Ltd, Jennings Brewery and McAlpines. Advise the Federation of Licensed Victuallers and are accredited to run British Institute of Innkeepers courses for the National Licensees Certificate.

Barker, Booth & Eastwood (1ptnr–p/t) Good firm doing a reasonable amount of work in Blackpool.

Bermans (1ptnr/1asst in Liverpool office and 1ptnr/1asst in Manchester office) Nigel

Copeland is behind the firm's good reputation, however he is due to retire in August.

Bullivant Jones & Co (2ptnrs–p/t/1asst p/t) Known by competitors mainly due to their work for Iceland, although they also

undertake other liquor licensing work for hotels and convenience stores.

A. Halsall & Co (1ptnr – p/t) *Christopher Johnson* handles the licensing work at this small but competent practice.

LEADERS' PROFILES ·NORTH WEST

DICKINSON, Nicholas H.
Davies Wallis Foyster, Liverpool
(0151) 236 6226

HOLLAND, Barry K.
Elliott & Company, Manchester
(0161) 834 9933
Notary Public 1980. Partner in Licensing Department.
Specialisation: Acts for major off licence chains in England and Wales and for a national bookmaker and a pools company. Also handles entertainment and liquor licensing for major brewing clients and night club operators. Other areas of practice are food safety and health and safety at work acting on a nationwide basis for national supermarket chains. Chairman of the Food Law Group. Cases have included successful challenges of the liquor licensing policies of Sheffield and Birmingham, and the successful defence of a national supermarket chain in a substantial MAFF prosecution. Has lectured for the Law Society and given both in-house and client seminars on liquor, betting licensing, food safety and health & safety.

HORNE, Anthony
Halliwell Landau, Manchester
(0161) 835 3003
Specialisation: Sole area of practice is licensing and leisure. Work includes liquor, gaming and public entertainment. Cases successfully handled include licensing the U.K.'s first indoor cycling arena (Manchester Velodrome) and two substantial appeals at Liverpool and Manchester Crown Courts. Major clients include MacDonald Hotels plc, Top Rank Ltd, Grosvenor Casinos Ltd, UMIST and Bargain Booze.
Prof. Memberships: Law Society. Fellow to the Society of Entertainment Licensing Practitioners.
Career: M.A. (Cantab.) 1983. Admitted 1985. Articled at *Nigel Copeland*, which merged with *Burton & Co.* in 1985 to become *Burton Copeland*. Appointed head of licensing *Davies Arnold Cooper* (Manchester) 1993. Joined *Halliwell Landau* as licensing partner 1996.
Personal: Born 29 July 1957. Leisure interests include swimming, reading and dining out.

JOHNSON, Christopher R.
A. Halsall & Co, Birkenhead (0151) 647 6323
Qualified 1971. Partner 1973. Head of Licensing Department. All aspects of Liquor licensing including Off Licence work. Acting for National Companies England and Wales.

JONES, Simon
Cobbetts, Manchester (0161) 833 3333
Partner in Commercial Property Department.
Specialisation: Specialises in licensing and leisure work including all aspects of liquor licensing, public entertainment and Gaming Act matters, representing a wide range of brewing, restaurant and retail interests in the licensed trade. Also provides assistance and representation in related prosecutions – food safety, consumer protection, trading standards, environmental protection (in particular noise nuisance), weights and measures and health and safety legislation. Has extensive experience in appearing before courts and committees throughout the North of England and in negotiating with enforcing authorities. Was involved in Drury v Scunthorpe Licensing Justices (dealing with the purported surrender of a Justices' Licence).
Prof. Memberships: Law Society, Manchester Law Society, Food Law Group.
Career: Articled with *Leak Almond & Parkinson* which subsequently became *Cobbett Leak Almond* and qualified in 1978. Became a Partner in 1982.
Personal: Born 28th March 1953. Educated at Birkenhead School 1965-71 and Oxford University 1972-75.

LAWSON, Hamish K.
Cobbetts, Manchester (0161) 833 3333
Partner in Commercial Property Department.
Specialisation: Main area of practice is licensing. Acts for most of the breweries and major licensed retail operators represented in the north west, especially with regard to new site applications. Also handles food law, acting for two major national food manufacturers. Acted in Drury & Samuel Smith Old Brewery (Tadcaster) v. Scunthorpe Licensing Justices on surrender of licences. Firm advises North West Brewers and Licensed Retailers Association. Has

addressed numerous conferences and seminars including 'The 24 Hour City' in Manchester in 1993.
Prof. Memberships: Law Society of England and Wales, Manchester Law Society.
Career: Qualified in 1978. Joined *Cobbett Leak Almond* in 1976, becoming a Partner in 1981.
Personal: Born 23rd June 1951. Attended Oxford University 1969-72. Leisure interests include theatre (acting and directing) and sport. Lives in Bramhall, Cheshire.

LYONS, Anthony S.
Pannone & Partners, Manchester
(0161) 909 3000
Partner in Licensing Department.
Specialisation: Specialist Liquor Licensing Solicitor handling all aspects of liquor and entertainment licensing law including agency work. Particular strengths in Public House, Nightclub, Theatre, Off licence and Restaurant work. Solicitors to the Federation of Licensed Victuallers Associations. His firm has been accredited by the British Institute of Innkeeeping as a training and examination centre for licensees seeking their National Licensee's certificate. client base includes City Centre Restaurants Plc., Whitbread, Alfred McAlpine, Texaco and many other household names.
Career: Former partner of *Lyons Vilsons*. October 1993 formed *Copeland Lyons* which practice merged with *Pannone & Partners* in 1997.
Personal: Resides in Manchester. Leisure interests include cycling, snow skiing, fell walking and classic cars (Annual Entrant Mille Miglia).

OWEN, Mark D.
Weightmans, Liverpool (0151) 227 2601
Specialisation: All areas of liquor licensing. Represents major brewers on national basis particularly relating to new off licences. Also covers Public Entertainment Licensing and Betting and Gaming.
Prof. Memberships: Law Society.
Career: Qualified 1987 – Partner 1992.

NORTH EAST

Gosschalks (3ptnrs) A major licensing presence in the north and well-known nationwide. *Les Green* ("flamboyant", "robust", "a brilliant character") is perhaps the best known and most respected licensing lawyer in the country. **Clients/Work:** Act for private and corporate clients in the leisure industry countrywide. Act exclusively for William Hill, Yates Wine Lodge and Northern Leisure.

Dibb Lupton Alsop (4ptnrs – 1f/t, 1p/t/

2assts–p/t) A solid team including the "quiet but effective" *Martin Cowell*. **Clients/Work:** Deal with all licensing matters, including those relating to property acquisitions. Act non-exclusively for Thistle Hotels, Vaux Breweries and Bass.

John Gaunt & Partners (2ptnrs/1asst) The firm, and in particular *John Gaunt* ("effective", "gets things done") received a lot of praise. **Clients/Work:** Work for clients such as Whitbread and Queens Moat Houses in the north east and further afield.

McKenzie Bell (1ptnr/1asst – p/t with help when needed from other partners). *William Temperley* is described as a highly academic licensing lawyer. **Clients/Work:** Handle liquor licensing work in the Tyneside and Sunderland areas. Act as agents for in-house department of a large brewery as well as taking on work for Scottish & Newcastle.

Mincoffs (1ptnr/1consultant) Well known in the area. *Austen Science* is seen as "reliable" and "a good advocate". He edits the section on gaming in the Butterworths guide. **Clients/Work:** Involved in liquor and gaming work. Obtained the first liquor licence for a bowling alley in central London.

Richard Hall & Partners (3ptnrs) This firm was created from firms Goodswens and Harvard & Co. *Richard Hall* ("very sound") is "very impressive." **Clients/Work:** Deal with gaming, betting, liquor and entertain-

ment. In the last year have been involved in high profile work in the Newcastle quayside area with Pitcher & Piano and Bannatynes. Also some work in relation to property acquisitions.

Eaton Smith Marshall Mills (3ptnrs p/t, 1asst p/t) In the tables last year as Eaton Smith & Downey. Merged with Marshall Mills & Sykes and this has increased the number of people handling licensing work. **Clients/Work:** All types of licensing but mainly liquor work, acting for two major breweries.

Gordons Wright & Wright (2ptnrs –1f/t, 1p/t/2assts – 1f/t, one p/t) **Clients/Work:** In the last year obtained 11 on-licences for a proposed leisure venue and a number of off licences for WM Morrison Supermarkets Plc.

Brooke North (2ptnrs – p/t) **Clients/Work:** Handle a number off-licence oppositions.

Eversheds (3ptnrs – 2f/t, 1p/t/3assts – p/t) Took over Wilkinson Maughan who were included last year and the combined licensing departments should do well in the future. **Clients/Work:** Much work relates to property acquisitions for clients such as Scottish & Newcastle, Fenwick Ltd and Victoria Wine.

Freemans (2ptnrs) An effective team. **Clients/Work:** Handle all liquor licensing matters. Act for Bass.

Lupton Fawcett (1ptnr – p/t, assistance from other members of the dept) **Clients/Work:** Liquor licensing. Applications and objections re petrol station forecourts, pubs and clubs.

Read Hind Stewart (3ptnrs – p/t/1asst –p/t) **Clients/Work:** Undertake liquor licensing for free houses and general commercial clients.

Walker Morris (1ptnr/3assts) The licensing department is fairly new to the scene and appears to be developing well. **Clients/Work:** Handling betting and liquor work. Clients include Demmy the Bookmaker, Alldays, Carlsberg Tetley.

LEADERS' PROFILES · NORTH EAST

COWELL, M.
Dibb Lupton Alsop, Sheffield (0114) 2833474
Partner in Litigation Department.
Specialisation: Main area of practice is licensing – has specialised since 1979. Established and became head of firm's licensing unit in 1989. Deals with all types of liquor licensing, as well as public entertainment, gaming and bingo licensing and lotteries. Acts for National and Regional brewers, various companies operating public houses, major hotel chains, restaurant operators, leisure groups and supermarket operators together with individual entrepreneurs and licensees. Also handles white collar and corporate crime, covering fraud, health and safety, food safety and trading standards prosecutions. Has given various seminars on Licensing and Food Safety, including IBC conferences on Revocations.
Career: Qualified in 1975, having joined *Dibb Lupton Alsop* in 1973. Became a Partner in 1979.

GAUNT, John R.T.
John Gaunt & Partners, Sheffield
(0114) 266 8664
Specialisation: Main area of practising is licensing and leisure. Retained as regional licensing solicitor by a major brewer for 18 years. Has developed a wide client base including several PLCs and operates nationally, handling a number of important applications throughout the country. Also covers general commercial litigation, particularly in relation to the brewing and leisure industries and landlord and tenant matters. Has handled a number of high profile licensing applications, attracting significant media attention and coverage, particularly in recent years.

Prof. Memberships: Law Society.
Career: Qualified in 1976. Became a Partner in Wake Smith in 1977 and latterly a member of the firm's Management Committee. Co-founded *John Gaunt & Partners* in 1995, a specialist commercial litigation and property practice particularly for the liquor and leisure industries.

GREEN, Richard Leslie
Gosschalks, Hull (01482) 324252
Senior Partner and Head of the Licensing and Leisure Department.
Specialisation: Sole Licensing Advisor to William Hill Organisation Ltd., Yates Wine Lodge, Tom Cobleigh, First Leisure Corporation and Northern Leisure. Undertakes substantial work for Greenalls, Allied Domecq, Scottish and Newcastle, and Waterfall Holdings. During the last year the Department has dealt with all licensing arrangements for the newly constructed "Stadium of Light".
Prof. Memberships: Law Society.
Career: Articled *Pettit & Westlake*; Qualified 1969; Partner *Gosschalks* 1972; Senior Partner 1993; Joint Editor Patersons Licensing 1995. Attended Bedford Modern. Hull University 1965 LLB.
Personal: Born 1944. Resides Beverley. Leisure interests include music, reading and cinema. Member of RAC, Gerry's and the Academy.

HALL, Richard
Richard Hall & Partners, Middlesbrough
(01642) 218444
Partner in Commercial and Civil Litigation Department.
Specialisation: Principal area of practice is licensing and leisure. Deals with all aspects of

liquor and entertainment licensing, gaming, sales and purchases of licensed premises and financing of operations. Clients include hotels, bars, public houses, off licences, social clubs, night-clubs, restaurants, casinos, sports and entertainment centres. Dealt with all Licensing matters at new Middlesbrough Football stadium and several high profile licensing applications on the Quayside, Newcastle upon Tyne. Author of articles in various legal journals.
Prof. Memberships: Lawyers for Licensing North.
Career: Qualified in 1970. In private practice in Middlesbrough until creating own firm in 1997. Appointed Deputy District Judge in 1984.
Personal: Born 13th November 1945. Educated at Bradford Grammar School 1954-64 and Exeter University 1964-67. Leisure pursuits include chess. Lives in Castleton, North Yorkshire.

SCIENCE, Austen
Mincoffs, Newcastle-upon-Tyne
(0191) 281 6151
Leisure Department Head.
Specialisation: Main area of practice is licensing, covering liquor licensing, gaming, amusements, and town and country planning. Acted in R v. Herrod, ex parte Leeds City District Council, a House of Lords decision on amusement premises; R v. Newcastle upon Tyne Gaming Licensing Committee, ex parte Whiteheart Enterprises Ltd on the exhibition of statutory notices; R v. Burt & Adams, a House of Lords decision validating trading up in amusement premises. Major clients include Rank, Mecca, Scottish & Newcastle, Century Inns and Pubmaster. Editor of section on Clubs in Halsbury's Laws of England and Clubs and Betting and Gaming in Encyclopaedia of Forms and Precedents.

Prof. Memberships: Law Society Planning Panel, National Vice President of the British Amusement Caterers Trade Association.
Career: Qualified in 1961.
Personal: Born 11th August 1938. Attended Clifton College. Leisure interests include golf. Lives in Newcastle upon Tyne.

TEMPERLEY, William B.
McKenzie Bell, Sunderland (0191) 567 4857
Partner in Licensing and Leisure Department.

Specialisation: Principal area of work covers liquor and public entertainment licensing including sports grounds, betting and theatre licences and all types of applications and offences under the Licensing Act 1964. Handles applications to Justices and local authorities and Appeals to Crown Court throughout five North Eastern counties. Handles objections and applications for late licences, revocations and opposed renewals on behalf of police and licensees.

Prof. Memberships: Lawyers for Licensing North. Fellow of the Society of Entertainment Licensing Practitioners.
Career: Articled with *McKenzie Bell* and became a Partner in 1966.
Personal: Born 1940. Attended Bristol University 1958-61. Leisure pursuits include theatres and railways. Lives in Sunderland.

SCOTLAND

LEADING FIRMS • SCOTLAND

BRUNTON MILLER Glasgow
R. & J.M. HILL BROWN & CO Glasgow
JOHN BATTERS & CO Glasgow
MACROBERTS Edinburgh

BLACKADDER REID JOHNSTON Dundee
MCARTHUR STANTON Dumbarton
MCGRIGOR DONALD Glasgow
PAULL & WILLIAMSONS Aberdeen

HASTIES Edinburgh
LINDSAYS WS Edinburgh

HIGHLY REGARDED FIRMS

Dundas & Wilson CS Edinburgh
Grigor & Young Elgin
Harper Macleod Glasgow

Adam Cochran Aberdeen
James & George Collie Aberdeen
Johnston & Herron Lochgelly
Ledingham Chalmers Edinburgh
Mackintosh & Wylie Kilmarnock
The Morton Fraser Partnership Edinburgh
Thorntons WS Dundee

Brunton Miller (3ptnrs/1consultant) Probably the "biggest licensing firm in Scotland", the firm is said to handle a large volume of work. *Douglas Dalgleish* ("powerful on his feet", "very good off the cuff") is the "elder statesman" of the team. *Archie MacIver* "known for his expertise." *Robin Morton* is well known and has an "off the wall" style. **Clients/Work:** All types of licensing work for clients such as Bass, Whitbread and Safeway. In the last year the team obtained a regular 4 a.m. extension for a nightclub and obtained the first casino licence to be granted in Glasgow in twelve years.

R & JM Hill Brown & Co (2ptnrs – 1f/t, 1p/t/1asst – p/t) A highly regarded licensing team. *Jack Cummins* ("intellectual", "enthusiast", "specialist") lectures and writes on the subject. *Peter Lawson* is said to be a "smart, straight" lawyer with a "laid back" style. **Clients/Work:** Much work in the leisure industry. The team is instructed for pure

licensing work, i.e. which does not arise from related property transactions. Clients include Bass Leisure, First Leisure and Allied Domecq.

John Batters & Co A sole practitioner with over 20 years experience, *John Batters* has an "easy-going style" and has a high success rate with the licensing board. Said to do a lot of good work in Glasgow and central Scotland **Clients/Work:** Liquor, gaming and betting work for a range of clients, such as G101 Off Sales Ltd, the Noble Organisation, Aldi and King City Leisure Ltd.

MacRoberts (1ptnr/2assts, assistance from other ptnrs when needed) *John Loudon* ("finger on the pulse", "successful") is one of the outstanding Edinburgh players. **Clients/Work:** Licensing work of all types including gaming, entertainment and taxis. Handle work for Scottish Highlands Hotels, Mecca Bingo Ltd and Allied Domecq. In the last year acted in a successful judicial review: Date Lock Ltd v City of Edinburgh District Council.

Blackadder Reid Johnston (1ptnr – p/t/1asst – p/t) **Clients/Work:** Liquor and entertainment licensing for pubs and small businesses in the area.

McArthur Stanton (1ptnr p/t/1consultant) A "good local practice." *John Gilmour* is retiring and will act as a licensing consultant. However, the reputation of the firm has not been adversely affected. **Clients/Work:** The main body of work is as agents for the city firms and for private clients. Specialism in liquor licensing.

McGrigor Donald (2assts – p/t) *Audrey Ferrie* is considered "very able." **Clients/Work:** Liquor, gaming and betting work is undertaken for clients such as Tote Bookmakers Ltd, Stakis Plc and Tom Cobleigh Plc. In the last year the firm has obtained the licences in Scotland for the first Yates Wine Lodge and Hard Rock Cafe.

Paull & Williamsons (1ptnr – p/t) *David McLeod* ("serious and well prepared") was highly recommended again. **Clients/Work:** Mainly liquor licensing but all types of licensing work are undertaken.

Hasties (2ptnrs – 1f/t, 1p/t/1asst – p/t) Still have a recognised licensing capacity.

Lindsays WS (1ptnr – p/t/2assts – p/t) **Clients/Work:** Mainly liquor licensing but also handle the licensing of sports venues including Murrayfield Stadium and events such as the Open Golf Championships. Clients include Century Inns, Whitbread and Granada.

Dundas & Wilson CS (2ptnrs – p/t/4assts – p/t) Recently took over Dorman Jeffrey & Co who also appeared in the licensing lists last year and the two teams are now combined. **Clients/Work:** Work all over Scotland for clients such as Stanley Casinos Ltd, Alldays, City Centre Restaurants and the Gleneagles Hotel.

Grigor & Young (1ptnr – p/t) **Clients/Work:** Handles liquor licensing at all levels as well as late hours catering, taxis and street traders.

Harper McLeod (3ptnrs/3assts) Relatively new to the licensing scene but making a concerted effort and have a growing reputation. **Clients/Work:** Act for owner-operated businesses, as well as clients such as William Hill (in Scotland), the Scottish Licensed Trade Association and Chris Hart & Co. Liquor, betting and gaming work is undertaken.

Adam Cochran (1ptnr – p/t/1asst – p/t) Have recently lost Alexander Carle and it is felt that the firm will not be as strong without him. **Clients/Work:** Liquor licensing for a range of clients from corner shops to big companies.

James & George Collie (1ptnr – p/t/1asst – p/t) Small but well regarded.

LEADING INDIVIDUALS
SCOTLAND

BATTERS John John Batters & Co
CUMMINS Jack R. & J.M. Hill Brown & Co
DALGLEISH Douglas Brunton Miller
LOUDON John MacRoberts

FERRIE Audrey McGrigor Donald
JOHNSTON Tom Johnston & Herron
LAWSON Peter R. & J.M. Hill Brown & Co
MACIVER Archibald Brunton Miller
MCLEOD David Paull & Williamsons
MORTON Robin Brunton Miller
GILMOUR John McArthur Stanton

Johnston & Herron (1ptnr p/t, with help from other ptnrs when required) Well-regarded firm, renowned for its work in the Fife area. *Tom Johnston* is highly rated. **Clients/ Work:** A whole range of licensing work (liquor, gaming, taxis, late hours catering) for mostly private individuals.

Ledingham Chalmers (1ptnr/1asst) Have good clients and a good reputation. Do a lot of work in the north east of Scotland.

Clients/Work: Handle liquor work and some gaming work for corporate and individual clients including Victoria Wine and Eagle Taverns Ltd.

MacKintosh & Wylie (3ptnrs) **Clients/ Work:** Undertake all types of licensing work in the area. Deal mainly with pubs, hotels, stores and off licences.

The Morton Fraser Partnership (2ptnrs – p/t) Known in Edinburgh for their

work. **Clients/Work:** Handle liquor licensing for Scottish & Newcastle and Ibis Hotels (first licence in Scotland). Also work for private individuals.

Thorntons WS (3ptnrs – p/t) **Clients/Work:** Working from their offices in Dundee, Angus and Perth, handle liquor licensing for pubs and hotels.

LEADERS' PROFILES · SCOTLAND

BATTERS, John A.
John Batters & Co, Glasgow
(0141) 427 6884

CUMMINS, Jack
R. & J.M. Hill Brown & Co, Glasgow
(0141) 332 3265
Partner in Licensing Department.
Specialisation: Handles licensing, gaming, leisure and retail matters, representing a wide range of brewing, restaurant, retail and entertainment interests in the licensed trade. Author of 'Licensing Law in Scotland' (Butterworths, 1993); contributor to 'Scots Law Times', 'Journal of the Law Society of Scotland' and 'Scottish Licensed Trade News'. Reporter for 'Scottish Civil Law Reports' and Editor of 'Scottish Licensing Law and Practice'. Scottish Consulting Editor to 'Licensing Review'. Accredited as a specialist in liquor licensing law by The Law Society of Scotland. Keynote speaker, National Conferences for Licensing Boards 1994, 1995 and 1996. Chairman 1997. Contributor to various radio programmes. Law Society of Scotland 'Update' speaker. Convenor of Certificate in Liquor Licensing Course, Central Law Training/ University of Glasgow 1995 and 1998; Convenor and keynote speaker Annual Licensing Conference, Central Law Training 1996, 1997 and 1998. Member of Licensing Law Committee of the Law Society of Scotland.
Prof. Memberships: Law Society of Scotland.
Career: Joined *R & JM Hill & Brown & Co.* in 1976. Qualified in 1978 and became a Partner in 1980.
Personal: Born in 1952. Educated at the University of Glasgow (M.A., 1974, LL.B. 1976) and University of Montpellier (1972-1973). Leisure pursuits include motoring. Lives in Glasgow.

DALGLEISH, Douglas S.
Brunton Miller, Glasgow (0141) 337 1199
Senior Partner.
Specialisation: Has been involved in licensing work for over thirty years. Widely experienced, acting for several major breweries and supermarket chains. Also handles general commercial work. Regular contributor to various licensed trade publications. Has addressed numerous conferences and seminar groups. Scottish Legal Adviser to B.E.D.A. and to Scottish Golf Union, lives in Helensburgh.
Prof. Memberships: Law Society of Scotland.
Career: Qualified in 1956. Became Senior Partner of *Brunton Miller* in 1974. Member of Law Society Working Party on licensing law.
Personal: Born 26th December 1927. Attended Glasgow University 1949-55. Chairman of Dumbarton FC; Past President of Scottish Golf

Union; Chairman of Caledonian Golf Travel Limited. Leisure interests include golf and football. Lives in Helensburgh.

FERRIE, Audrey
McGrigor Donald, Glasgow (0141) 248 6677
Specialisation: Liquor, betting and gaming licensing throughout Scotland, acting for a hotel and casino operator, several English pub chains expanding into Scotland and one major bookmaker. Highlights – new casino in Edinburgh and first Hard Rock Cafe in Scotland.
Prof. Memberships: Accredited as a specialist in liquor licensing by Law Society of Scotland.
Career: Educated Notre Dame High School, Glasgow and Glasgow University, trained with well-known criminal litigation firm in Glasgow (*Hughes Dowdall & Co*) then to *Moncrieff Warren Paterson* who merged with *McGrigor Donald.*
Personal: Married to Glasgow lawyer, 2 children. Leisure interests include travel and attempting to keep fit – when time permits.

GILMOUR, John A.G.
McArthur Stanton, Dumbarton
(01389) 762266

JOHNSTON, Tom
Johnston & Herron, Lochgelly
(01592) 780421
Partner specialising in Liquor Licensing.
Specialisation: Main area of practice is liquor licensing. Accredited Liquor Licensing Specialist. Advises on and attends at Licensing Boards. Deals with purchase, sale and finance of licensed properties. Author of 'How Not to Lose Your Licence', published in April 1994. Has lectured extensively to solicitors and to licensees. Regular contributor to Scottish Licensing Law and Practice.
Prof. Memberships: Law Society of Scotland (Member of Specialist Accreditation Committee on Liquor Licensing).
Career: Apprentice and assistant at *Allan McDougall & Co.* 1976-79. Qualified in 1978. Partner *Johnston & Herron* in 1979. Past Dean of Dunfermline District Society of Solicitors. Member of Law Society Council 1989-92.
Personal: Born 10th July 1954. Educated at Edinburgh University 1972-76. Leisure interests include reading, cooking and wine. Lives in Edinburgh.

LAWSON, Peter J.
R. & J.M. Hill Brown & Co, Glasgow
(0141) 332 3265
Partner in Licensing Department.
Speclalisation: Principal area of practice is licensing. Deals with new licence applications, provides an advice service to multiple operators

and individuals, court representation (including trading standards, consumer protection, etc.) and renewal/ review service for existing clients. Also handles commercial/ employment matters, providing a full commercial service, advice and representation in relation to employment law. Clients include most national brewers, supermarket chains and national entertainment companies. Has written various articles for trade magazines and lectured on Glasgow University Licensing Course. Co-presenter of licensing seminars throughout Scotland.
Prof. Memberships: Law Society of Scotland.
Career: Qualified in 1981. Partner at *McSherry Halliday, Irvine* 1984-90. Joined *Hill Brown* as a Partner in 1990.
Personal: Born 25th March 1958. Educated at Peterhouse, Zimbabwe, Marr College, Troon and Glasgow University. Holds various directorships. Director of Tron Theatre, Glasgow. Leisure interests include theatre and skiing. Lives in Glasgow.

LOUDON, John A.
MacRoberts, Edinburgh (0131) 226 2552
Partner.
Specialisation: Main areas of practice are liquor licensing and gaming. Accredited as a specialist in liquor licensing by the Law Society of Scotland in July 1993. Also advises on related commercial work. Author of a number of articles on licensing matters in various journals. Lectures for Law Society Update Courses, Central Law Training and to other bodies.
Prof. Memberships: SSC Society.
Career: Qualified in 1973. Joined *J.A. Hastie* in 1973, becoming a Partner in 1975 and Senior Partner in 1989. Joined *MacRoberts* in 1996.
Personal: Born 5th December 1949. Attended Edinburgh Academy 1955-68 and University of Dundee 1968-71. High Constable of Edinburgh. Past member of Council of Law Society of Scotland. Leisure interests include skiing and shooting. Lives in Edinburgh.

MACIVER, Archibald D.
Brunton Miller, Glasgow (0141) 337 1199
Partner.
Specialisation: Main area of practice is licensing. Extensive experience in all aspects of liquor licensing work. Also involved heavily in licensing under Civic Government (Scotland) Act such as public entertainment licences, street traders and late hours catering licences. Regular columnist in 'Scottish Licensed Trade News'. Has addressed many seminar groups on licensing matters.
Prof. Memberships: Law Society of Scotland, Scottish Law Agents Society, Glasgow Bar Association.
Career: Qualified in 1982. Worked at *Levy &*

McRae 1981-88, from 1984 as a Partner. Joined *Brunton Miller* in 1988 as a Partner. Accredited by the Law Society of Scotland as a Specialist in Liquor Licensing Law in 1993.
Personal: Born 13th December 1959. Attended Hutchesons' Grammar School 1972-77 and University of Strathclyde 1977-81. Leisure interests include sport (especially football), keeping fit, cinema and reading. Lives in Glasgow.

MCLEOD, David F.
Paull & Williamsons, Aberdeen
(01224) 621621
Partner in Commercial Property Department.
Specialisation: Handles the purchase, sale and leasing of all types of commercial property, particularly licensed premises. Also handles liquor licensing: accredited as a specialist by the Law Society of Scotland. Acted for Jurys Hotel Group on the purchase of the Pond Hotel, Glasgow. Has successfully obtained many new licences of various categories for licensed premises in Aberdeen and the North East. Acted for the developers of Forte Posthouse

Hotel Aberdeen. Recently involved in advising the developers of 'The Academy' retail/leisure development currently under construction and the recently completed leisure development at Queen's Links, Aberdeen on the licensing aspects of those projects.
Prof. Memberships: Law Society of Scotland.
Career: Qualified in 1978. Worked at *Dundas & Wilson CS* 1976-81. Joined *Paull & Williamsons* in 1981, becoming a Partner in 1984.
Personal: Born 8th April 1954. Attended Banff Academy 1959-72; University of Edinburgh 1972-76. Leisure interests include shooting, skiing and football. Lives in Aberdeen.

MORTON, Robin J.M.
Brunton Miller, Glasgow (0141) 337 1199
Mobile Telephone No: 07970 272953.
Consultant in Licensing Department.
Specialisation: Handles liquor licensing, leisure and entertainment law. Acts for major organisations as well as individuals in obtaining and operating liquor licences, appearing at many boards throughout Scotland. Also acts for banks, purchasers and sellers in the property

and commercial aspects relating to licensed premises. Has been involved in a number of reported cases, including one which resulted in a change of law (Mount Charlotte Investments v. City of Glasgow District Licensing Board). Accredited by the Law Society of Scotland as a specialist in liquor licensing. Regular contributor to 'Scottish Licensed Trade News' Legal Clinic. Frequently lectures on liquor licensing law and is on the panel of lecturers for the First Annual Advanced Licensing Seminar.
Prof. Memberships: Law Society of Scotland.
Career: Qualified in 1975. With *Brunton Miller,* Solicitors 1975-1978. Assistant Director of Legal Aid for the Hong Kong Government 1978-81. Partner with *Brunton Miller* 1981-88. Joined *McClure Naismith Anderson & Gardiner* as a Partner in 1988, established *Robin Morton Solicitors* in 1995. Consultant with *Brunton Miller,* 1996-Date.
Personal: Born 1st October 1951. Educated at Glasgow Academy 1961-69, then Glasgow University 1969-72. Leisure pursuits include music and football.
Lives in Glasgow.

NORTHERN IRELAND

LEADING FIRMS
NORTHERN IRELAND

E. & L. KENNEDY Belfast
SHEAN DICKSON MERRICK Belfast
MCCANN & GREYSTOKE Belfast
O'REILLY STEWART Belfast
O'NEILL & CO Belfast

E. & L. Kennedy (3ptnrs (50%, 10%) The firm has a good name amongst competitors. **Clients/Work:** Mainly liquor licensing and pharmaceutical licensing for Tesco and Boots Pharmaceutical Department. Also handle pub and club work.

Shean Dickson Merrick (2ptnrs (80%, 60%)/1asst – p/t) **Clients/Work:** Deal mainly with liquor licensing and club registration (Northern Ireland Federation of Social Clubs). Clients include Guinness and Sheridan Restaurants. In the last year have handled a large multi-party case and obtained an

opposed grant of a new pub licence in Belfast City Centre after a High Court appeal.

McCann & Greystoke (1ptnr – p/t) Well-known and are said to handle a lot of work, especially in relation to off-licences.

O'Reilly Stewart (1ptnr – p/t) **Clients/ Work:** Licensing work (liquor, gaming, entertainment) is undertaken for a range of clients (pubs, nightclubs, sports clubs, off licences, hotels and restaurants).

O'Neill & Co Have a reputation for licensing work for clubs and bookmakers.

LITIGATION (COMMERCIAL)

RESEARCH: In compiling the tables, we consider all the information available to us, paying particular regard to the market research carried out by our team of ten qualified lawyers. (The researchers' details are set out on page three.) The rankings, therefore, reflect the opinion of the marketplace as revealed by systematic and objective research: see page four. (Our research is audited every year by the British Market Research Bureau.)

OVERVIEW: Most firms predict a downturn in litigation as a result of the upturn in the economy. The larger firms expect to replace this work with cases of a more international nature, but as yet there are few substantial cases around. The Woolf reforms remain at the forefront of most litigators' agendas, and conditional fee arrangements are also receiving attention. Many firms are actively embracing new forms of commercial dispute resolution, recognising the need for flexible and commercial solutions.

Our rankings in London are grouped according to size of firm (number of solicitors includes partners and assistants only). In the 200+ size category Herbert Smith retain the top slot, but their dominance is challenged by the next four firms. Certainly, there is no longer clear water between them. Amongst the smaller sized firms, Barlow Lyde & Gilbert stands out in the 100+ category as a quality litigation firm whose work could be considered on a par with the larger firms despite the size differential.

Amongst firms in the South East, Donne Mileham & Haddock and Blake Lapthorn emerged as head and shoulders above the rest. Elsewhere, Bevan Ashford (Bristol) and Edwards Geldard (Cardiff) have risen through the ranks; Pinsent Curtis have ended Wragge & Co's domination of the Midlands in this field.

In the rest of the country, there has been no movement at the top of the tables and only small shifts further down. In general, the large commercial firms in each region dominate the litigation field.

LEADING FIRMS · LONDON
200+ SOLICITORS

HERBERT SMITH

CLIFFORD CHANCE
FRESHFIELDS
LINKLATERS
LOVELL WHITE DURRANT

ALLEN & OVERY

HIGHLY REGARDED
200+ SOLICITORS

Ashurst Morris Crisp
Cameron McKenna
Norton Rose
Simmons & Simmons

Denton Hall
Slaughter and May

LONDON

200+ SOLICITORS

Herbert Smith (50ptnrs/100assts). Their "aggressive, no holds barred approach" attracts some criticism, but they are "still number one in terms of sheer skill" and they "run the university for litigation." Eight partners are regarded as leading individuals, including "brilliant" *Lawrence Collins QC,* "tough" *David Gold,* "first rate*" Charles Plant,* and "good pro" *Harry Anderson. David Natali* is felt to embody "all the virtues of a Herbies partner – fearsomely intelligent, aggressive and focused." **Clients/Work:** Acted for Central Area Transmission System in a send or pay dispute under a gas transportation contract. Amstrad v Seagate (£85m sale of goods case). Represented Jyske Bank in £56m international fraud action

Clifford Chance (42ptnrs/132assts- all areas) Generally seen as "professional, reasonable, firm and tough." Banking is still a key area and the firm is an obvious choice for complex litigation. One enthusiastic client loved them for their "technical, pragmatic, solution oriented approach and their complete understanding of business." *Jeremy Sandelson* is "hot stuff – the most serious performer at CC." Solicitor advocate *David Mayhew* is popular with clients. *Tony Willis* is seen as "great and good" with "a magisterial quality." **Clients/Work:** Acting for Nomura International in regulatory proceedings. Kredietbank, Antwerp v Midland Bank plc

(construction of letters of credit). Acting for liquidators of BAH.

Freshfields (25ptnrs/80assts) Are one of the few firms to attract no criticism at all. Seen as "professional and reasonable to deal with" by opponents, and the "favourite by a long way" with many clients. Leading individuals are *Paul Bowden, Paul Leonard, Raj Parker* and *Ian Taylor.* **Clients/Work:** J Block v Enron ($440m gas sales agreement dispute). Acting for liquidators of EMLICO in multi jurisdictional proceedings. Acting for Lloyd's in relation to non accepting Names.

Linklaters (16ptnrs/50assts). Seen variously as "bloody minded," "hard fighters," "high quality" and "commercial." Many felt that litigation was not one of their mainstream activities, although as with other areas of practice they tend to excel at what they do."

HIGHLY REGARDED FIRMS
100+ SOLICITORS

Barlow Lyde & Gilbert
S J Berwin & Co
D J Freeman
Macfarlanes
Stephenson Harwood

Baker & McKenzie
Berwin Leighton
Clyde & Co
Eversheds
Gouldens
Nabarro Nathanson
Titmuss Sainer Dechert
Wilde Sapte

Davies Arnold Cooper
Dibb Lupton Alsop
Field Fisher Waterhouse
Hammond Suddards
Lawrence Graham
Richards Butler
Rowe & Maw
Taylor Joynson Garrett
Theodore Goddard
Travers Smith Braithwaite

HIGHLY REGARDED FIRMS
40-100 SOLICITORS

Berrymans Lace Mawer
Harbottle & Lewis
Holman, Fenwick & Willan
Reynolds Porter Chamberlain
Sinclair Roche & Temperley
Warner Cranston

Biddle
Lewis Silkin
Nicholson Graham & Jones
Wedlake Bell

Fladgate Fielder
Howard Kennedy
Jeffrey Green Russell
Kennedys
Manches & Co
Memery Crystal
Mishcon de Reya
Pinsent Curtis
Radcliffes
Rosling King

HIGHLY REGARDED FIRM
UNDER 40 SOLICITORS

Glovers
Goodman Derrick
Hamlin Slowe
Kingsford Stacey Blackwell

Bower Cotton
Lane & Partners
LeBoeuf, Lamb, Greene & MacRae
Mackrell Turner Garrett
Seddons
Sheridans

Leading lights include "safe pair of hands" *John Turnbull,* "technical and strategic" *Christopher Style,* "well respected" *Diana Good,* "well known" *Brinsley Nicholson,* and "solid" *Mark Humphries.* Clients/Work: Masterminded Co-op's defence of hostile take-over bid by Andrew Regan. Advised Davy International on recovery of confidential information from ex-employees and a competitor. Acted for Natwest Group in relation to £90.5m interest rate derivatives losses.

Lovell White Durrant (38ptnrs worldwide/115assts – none full-time) Not seen as equally strong across the board, but have acknowledged leaders of high quality. Noted individuals include *Patrick Sherrington,* "straight guy" *John Trotter,* "resolute" *Neil Fagan,* "technical whizz" *Russell Sleigh,* and "innovative" *Michael Seymour.* Clients/Work: Acted for joint liquidators of BCCI in Morris v Agrichemicals (bank may take charge over deposits as security). Acting for Bank of Zambia in multi-jurisdictional enforcement proceedings by Camdex (including Court of Appeal decision on Mareva injunctions). Defending Petroleum Authority of Thailand in oil supply dispute with North Sea Energy.

Allen & Overy (16ptnrs/44assts) Have "wall to wall competence despite a relatively small practice." Recently appointed a silk, (one of only three solicitors to share that distinction) "heavy hitter" *David Mackie* and *Peter Watson* are particularly admired. Banking work a specialty. Also known for derivatives-related disputes. Clients/Work: Acting for Prince Jefri of Brunei against the Manoukian brothers and for News Corporation in multi-jurisdictional Clinger fraud trial. Continue to act for Queens Moat House in action against its former senior management.

Ashurst Morris Crisp (9ptnrs/40assts) "Punch above their weight," thanks to the likes of "the extremely impressive" *Edward Sparrow.* Clients/Work: Represent NM Rothschild & Sons Ltd in Atlantic Computers litigation. Act for the first defendant in the Grupo Torras action. Acted for Daimler Benz AG in injunctive proceedings against Christies to prevent an auction and recover motor racing memorabilia.

Cameron McKenna (44ptnrs/100assts – none full-time) Clients/Work: Represented Camelot's interests in the Branson v Snowden libel action. Advised Cynamid in relation to prospective group action concerning anti acne antibiotics. Represented Procter & Gamble in action against Merck, Sharp and Dohme (breach of industry code of practice).

Norton Rose (26ptnrs/69assts- also do other litigation) Continue to present two distinct faces. Many interviewees felt they had "had a good year, are quite good, and are definitely a player." In short, they "do a sound job." Others perceive them as "not having enough spread or intensity." *Valerie Davies* is "a forceful operator." Clients/Work: Act-

ing for Kuwait Investment Authority in proceedings by Grupo Torras; Chancery PLC in breach of fiduciary duty case, and an individual in $1.5 billion breach of trust claim in the Bahamas.

Simmons & Simmons (18ptnrs/42assts) Liked by clients for their "subtle approach," S&S seem to be "on the up." *Jonathan Kelly* and *Paul Mitchard* are leading individuals. Clients/Work: Represented 17 oil companies opposing Greenpeace's attempt to judicially review the Government's grant of oil exploration licences. Representing SACE in £100m dispute with Deutsche Morgan Grenfell. Co-ordinating defence of first tobacco/health related litigation.

Denton Hall (19ptnrs/35assts) Seem to be "holding their own" with "some quite good work." However they have yet to find a suitable replacement for Bob Goldspink. Litigation was not perceived as a key area for this high profile energy and media practice. Clients/Work: Co-ordinated multi jurisdictional litigation for the Chrysler pension fund arising from a £300m fraud. Acting for Total Gas Marketing on its successful appeal in a gas purchase agreement dispute with ARCO. Acting for FA Premier League in proceedings in the Restrictive Practices Court by Director General of Fair Trading in relation to broadcasting agreements.

Slaughter and May (7ptnrs/35assts – also do other areas) Regarded as "intensely practical and intellectual," but many in the market do not perceive them as a firm with a high commercial litigation profile. However, they have handled some quality work and the "sensible and businesslike" *Richard Grandison* and *Nick Archer* continue to be seen as leading individuals. Clients/Work: Kredietbank NV v Midland Bank plc (letter of credit); Sakura Bank v Nuova Safim (SWAPS dispute); acting for Metallasallschaft in litigation with Codelco.

HIGHLY REGARDED FIRMS: 100+ SOLICITORS

Barlow Lyde & Gilbert (25ptnrs/42assts-not all full time) Although they have a strong reputation as an insurance firm, they are also seen as "first rate, efficient, hard nosed" litigators who "never lose sight of the commercial objective." Move up our tables this year. The firm was also highly rated in a survey carried out by the Journal of International Commercial Litigation ('97) who ranked the firm alongside much larger firms in sixth position. Clients/Work: Acted for McDonalds in the McLibel trial.

Represented PW in Bank Austria v Price Waterhouse. Acted for major management consultancy in multi million pound dispute concerning IT system.

SJ Berwin & Co. (11ptnrs/18assts-none full time) Reputation for being "tough" and "commercial." *Tim Taylor* heads the department. Clients/Work: Acted for American Express against BCCI liquidators, 49's in litigation with Camelot plc and the government of Malawi in proceedings against former President Hastings Banda.

DJ Freeman (8ptnrs/14assts) Consistently praised by practitioners and clients as a "solid" firm with "presence" who have a good all round commercial litigation practice. Clients/Work: Shell UK, Post Office, British Tourist Authority, Itochu Europe Ltd, Rhodes Benson Management Ltd.

Macfarlanes (5ptnrs/20assts) A quality firm that can still impress. Clients/Work: Continue to act for Government of Abu Dhabi in connection with BCCI collapse and Dieter Bock in his long running dispute with Tiny Rowland.

Stephenson Harwood (9ptnrs/28assts) Are regarded as pleasant to deal with and can be "impressive." The "down to earth, commercially sensible" *John Fordham* heads up the department and is often chosen by some of the bigger firms to act in conflict situations. Clients/Work: Act for Capital Corporation plc in claim against former employees for conspiracy to damage, and Wang(UK) Ltd in multi million pound computer dispute. Represented plaintiff in Sierra Leone Telecommunications Co Ltd v Barclays Bank plc.

Baker & McKenzie (7ptnrs/15assts- not full time) Team includes *Nick Pearson,* "a thoughtful, tough but sensible litigator." Clients/Work: Represented plaintiffs in Mitsubishi Heavy Industries v Gulf Bank KSC (interpretation of counter indemnity) and Orange v Vodafone (malicious falsehood and trademark infringement in advertising campaign). Representing Camdex in dispute with Bank of Zambia (including Court of Appeal decision on Mareva injunctions).

Berwin Leighton (7ptnrs/13assts) Have a reputation for being "fairly uncompromising" litigators. Clients/Work: Acted for Alliance & Leicester plc in connection with judicial review of issues concerning Solicitors Compensation Fund. Act for NationsBank NA in civil fraud and asset tracing case. Acting for Nottingham Forest FC in FA inquiry.

Clyde & Co (10ptnrs/15assts- also do insurance) In litigation circles their profile is as "a highly technical insurance firm." But they do have "some first class players" which elevates them. Clients/Work: Acted for plaintiffs in TGA Chapman v Christopher and Sun Alliance (insurer's liability for costs exceeding indemnity). Represented defendant in

Boskalis v Mountain (war risk insurance-dispute). Involved in "Nukila" case (latent defects).

Eversheds (11ptnrs/22assts-also defamation, IP and arbitration) The merger with Frere Cholmeley Bischoff should put Eversheds on the map. Frere's "outstanding" public international work and reputation as strong litigators combined with Eversheds' "volume", should benefit the profiles of both practices. *Alan Jenkins* (ex-Freres) is a "sensible, businesslike performer." Clients/Work: Acting for the German government in connection with the recovery of a painting allegedly stolen during WW2 and on sale through Sotheby's, London. Advising on the Yemen-Eritrea Red Sea Island dispute and Iran/US oil platforms case. Involved in Camdex litigation.

Gouldens (5ptnrs/18assts) Generally perceived as being "sensible to deal with," this "serious commercial litigation practice" earned promotion in our tables this year. Clients/Work: Acted on the cases of: Pioneer Electronics Capital Inc v Warner Music Manufacturing Europe GmbH, Henry Ansbacher & Co Ltd v Binks Stern (a firm), DTI v John Gunn.

Nabarro Nathanson (8ptnrs/17assts) Perceived as "effective and very good." Clients/Work: Acted in United Mizrahi v Doherty and U.S Sec v Warren (major "Mareva" action). Acted for Islington Borough Council in landmark Westdeutsche Landesbank Gironzentrale case. Successfully acted on behalf of Pension Trustees of major plc in a substantial dispute (£7m) with the Inland Revenue.

Titmuss Sainer Dechert (6ptnrs/14fee-earners) Opinions differed about this firm , but most agreed that they were "serious players." Clients/Work: Act for national and multinational manufacturing PLCs, banks (domestic and foreign),UK and foreign liquidators, European and other international law firms, directors, national newspapers.

Wilde Sapte (4ptnrs/4assts) The litigation practice related to civil fraud and banking matters is highly rated. Clients/Work: Allied Irish Bank v Ashford Hotels Ltd; Bank of Scotland v Kustow (undue influence); acting for BCCI in attempt to recover loans to former employees.

Davies Arnold Cooper Primarily an insurance firm, they are "good, relatively hard." *Nicholas Rochez* is "a bright operator, with lots of initiative."

Dibb Lupton Alsop (10ptnrs/25assts) Generally seen as "pushy, aggressive publicity seekers," their profile was affected when they were dis-instructed from the Polly Peck case. Clients/Work: Acting for Regulator in disciplinary action against Deutsche Morgan Grenfell arising from £200m unit trusts irregularities; Henry Ansbacher (Bahamas) Ltd in US$160m claim for breach

of trust and fraudulent misrepresentation against Central Bank of Ecuador: Home Office in dispute over award of £1.5 billion public procurement contract.

Field Fisher Waterhouse (5ptnrs/13fee-earners plus several specialist units) The litigation team was enlarged with the incorporation of Allison & Humphreys on 1st January 1998. It is too early to comment on whether the enlarged practice has yet made its mark. Clients/Work: ICI, Zeneca and Whitbread. Acted in the Atlantic Computers and British & Commonwealth administrations litigation; the Netherlands Reinsurance Group case; the Base Metal Trading Limited/Ross Metals case.

Hammond Suddards (2ptnrs/8assts) Not quite established in London yet but have a reputation for being good on volume. Clients/Work: One 2 One, United Biscuits

UK Ltd, London Regional Transport.

Lawrence Graham (4ptnrs/7assts) Regarded by many as a "fine" firm. Have specialist areas in insurance, shipping, property, construction, environment and planning litigation. **Clients/Work:** Grupo Torras litigation; In re Park Air Services; Barings BV (competing issues of US$150m floating rate notes).

Richards Butler (29ptnrs/45assts-also do other work) Primarily undertake banking, finance and regulatory litigation. Felt by some to have now established a general commercial litigation practice and undergone something of a resurgence. *Lista Cannon* has just returned from secondment to the FSA. **Clients/Work:** Involved in The

Canada Trust Co v Stolzenberg; Direct Line Group v Direct Line Estate Agency; Internationale Nederlanden Aviation Leases BV v Civil Aviation Authority.

Rowe & Maw (5ptnrs/8assts) Received a mixed review but are in the main considered to be a "good, solid, decent" practice. **Clients/Work:** Involved in Grupo Torras and South West Trains Pension Scheme litigation.

Taylor Joynson Garrett (26ptnrs/36assts – also do other litigation). Regarded as " a formidable opponent." **Clients/Work:** Acting for National Bus Company Pension Trustees Ltd in £300m pension fund surplus case against Secretary of State for Transport; Republic of Nigeria in US$ 42.5m promis-

sory notes claim, and National Farmer's Union in connection with BSE crisis.

Theodore Goddard (4ptnrs/10assts) A "very competent team." **Clients/Work:** Advising Standard Chartered Bank in connection with breach of trust claim by George Walker's children, Republic of Cote d'Ivoire in claim by Moutafian Commodities Ltd and LDC trustees in Barings Noteholders litigation.

Travers Smith Braithwaite (5ptnrs/11assts) **Clients/Work:** Involved in Maxwell litigation. Represent VAI in $1 billion commercial espionage proceedings against Kvaerner. Greenalis Management Ltd v Canavan (upheld injunction requiring tenant to comply with his beer tie).

HIGHLY REGARDED
25 – 100 SOLICITORS

Berrymans Lace Mawer (2ptnrs/4assts for recovery work plus specialist teams for professional indemnity and construction) A "straightforward" firm which includes recoveries and insurance related work as part of its commercial litigation department. **Clients/Work:** Acted on: London Borough of Dagenham v Stamford Asphalt; Verity & Spindler v Lloyds; Kruger Tissue (Industrial) Ltd v Frank Galliers Ltd.

Harbottle & Lewis (3ptnrs/3assocs/8assts) Best known for their high quality work in music and entertainment rather than general commercial litigation. *Gerrard Tyrrell* is a leading individual. **Clients/Work:** Virgin Group Companies, Caribjet, British World Airlines, Debonair, TBG Airways, Chrysalis, Ecosse Films, Nissan, Primesight International.

Holman, Fenwick & Willan (8ptnrs/6assts) A "first class practice," particularly in their niche area of shipping litigation. The firm also deals with other litigation including banking and insolvency, insurance, environmental and general contractual disputes. However, have recently lost three litigation lawyers to Coudert Brothers. **Clients/Work:** Act for the Danish Credit Fund and the Danish Government in a claim amounting to US$50m arising out of the collapse of the Wheelock Marsden Shipping Group in Hong Kong; involved in litigation involving the Haji-Ioannou and Frangos families concerning breach of trust allegations; for Powergen in relation to insurance and environmental litigation arising out of orimulsion burning in the UK.

Reynolds Porter Chamberlain (6ptnrs/10assts- also do other work) Have a long standing reputation in this field and most saw them as "professional, decent, sensible." Known primarily as an insurance/professional indemnity firm. **Clients/ Work:** Atlas Copco Manufacturing Ltd; Morgan Crucible Co plc; Frigoscandia Ltd

Sinclair Roche & Temperley (2ptnrs/6assts) Although their general litigation profile is in shipping related matters, they are perceived to be excellent and are thus ranked at the top of their size band. **Clients/Work:** Successful "recovery" of domain name on behalf of an Internet trader; recovery of profit share of a major movie; a number of substantial offshore construction disputes relating to installations mainly intended for new North Sea Development

Warner Cranston (2ptnrs/7fee-earners) Unanimously favourable comments were received from fellow practitioners about this "worthy opponent" which has been expanding in the international market, particularly in the USA, the Middle East and Europe (40% of the firm's turnover comes from overseas clients). **Clients/Work:** Project-led assets recovery operation involving multiple and sophisticated frauds amounting to some $600m; involved in much of the litigation arising out of the Lloyd's disputes – particularly where cross border issues occur.

Biddle (11ptnrs/17assts) Despite having a strong defamation biased profile, the litigation department is also rated as an "all round practice." The work handled also includes banking, insurance and professional indemnity work. **Clients/Work:** During 1997 acted on several major Anton Piller and Mareva injunction cases as well as a variety of pensions litigation, including acting for six Maxwell Pension Schemes seeking recovery of assets.

Lewis Silkin (9ptnrs/16assts including several specialised units) The majority of our interviewees regarded them highly. Work handled is largely media related. **Clients/Work:** Kleinwort Benson v Glasgow (House of Lords) – international jurisdiction element in a SWAPS case; GPR v Ketchum Communications Inc. – successful appeal in the Court of Appeal in relation to construction of a share sale agreement; Wire TV (Mirror Television) v CableTel (UK) Ltd – obtaining judgment for the TV subsidiary of Mirror

Group involving a perpetual injunction against CableTel.

Nicholson Graham & Jones (12ptnrs/18assts divided into specialist teams) A "highly competent" firm involved in a number of high profile cases this year. **Clients/Work:** Acted on: Manoukian v Prince Jefri of Brunei, Eurotunnel, PGA European Tour v KLO.

Wedlake Bell (3ptnrs/7assts) The firm received some extraordinary praise this year and was considered "a serious opponent" by some of our interviewees. **Clients/Work:** Handle range of general commercial litigation.

Fladgate Fielder (6ptnrs/5assts) Felt by some to be "retracting," but praised by clients as running "a professional ship." **Clients/Work:** Focusing more on international litigation. Have acted for corporate clients from the UK and abroad, as well as a number of overseas lawyers.

Howard Kennedy (4ptnrs/4assts) Not a huge presence but generally felt to be "going strong." **Clients/Work:** Commercial litigation work includes IP, professional negligence and debt collection as well as contractual disputes.

Jeffrey Green Russell (6ptnrs/7assts) The "commercial litigation" department actually deals with most areas of litigation and received particular mention for media and debt collection. **Clients/Work:** The department incorporates specialist teams devoted to insolvency and banking; construction and plant hire; employment; media and IP; defamation; white collar crime and boardroom struggles; breach of contract; professional negligence and personal injury.

Kennedys (29ptnrs/46assts) Primarily known as an insurance firm but aim to offer range of commercial services to its insurer clients, including litigation advice. **Clients/Work:** Cases in 1997 included: Secured Residential Funding Plc v Nationwide Building Society – professional indemnity; acting for insurers of a zinc galvanising plant in a £1m product liability dispute; acting on a

$20m ICC arbitration dispute involving a sulphur storage facility.

Manches & Co (5ptnrs/8assts) The department is divided into construction, insurance, banking and insolvency teams **Clients/Work:** Acted for the Plaintiff on: Mannai-v-Eagle Star (HL) – in which the House of Lords overturned by a 3:2 majority a unanimous Court of Appeal finding against Mannai; Malik-v-BCCI(HL)–acted for two former BCCI employees in their claim for compensation for the stigma of being associated with BCCI. The House of Lords ruled that the claim could go ahead in this situation.

Memery Crystal (3ptnrs/10fee-earners) A "small outfit" compared to some in these tables, this "punchy little firm" has been involved in some high profile litigation in the last year. **Clients/Work:** Acted on : GTech v Branson;Park Air Services;BCCI.

Mishcon de Reya (8ptnrs/3consts/ 11assts) More comments were received about Mishcons than any other firm in these tables. Practitioners had widely differing views on the impact, if any, of Anthony Julius' decision to become a 3 day a week consultant. Remain a presence. **Clients/ Work:** Government of Egypt, Burdale Acceptances Ltd, UCB Bank Plc, Ladbroke Group Plc, The Thomson Group of Companies, Tate & Lyle Plc. Acting for various parties in a shareholder dispute, acting for a quoted company on recovering substantial losses suffered in subsidiary – full recovery with one mandatory injunction.

Pinsent Curtis (5ptnrs/1assoc/ 7fee earners) A "very professional" firm. **Clients/Work:** Advised a number of financial institutions in relation to regulatory issues involving the SFA, SIB/FSA, LME and PIA; acted for a major plc on a multi-

million pound negligence firm against a City law firm; advised a number of clients in relation to shareholder disputes in the UK and Europe.

Radcliffes (4ptnrs/2assocs/6assts) The team is closely involved with dispute resolution as part of commercial litigation. **Clients/Work:** International trade and jurisdiction disputes, professional negligence, environmental law claims, insurance, employment and the law relating to charities and universities.

Rosling King (8ptnrs/17assts) Have a niche reputation for handling professional indemnity work for building societies and other financial institutions. Also advise on commercial lending secured on property. **Clients/Work:** Acted on:Agnew v LF Insurance Company – a case on the competent jurisdiction to handle disputes between EU member states

---

UNDER 25 SOLICITORS

Glovers (3ptnrs/3assts) A well respected firm whose commercial litigation department includes disputes arising out of property, banking, white collar fraud and contractual disputes. *Anthony Bourne* leads the team. **Clients/Work:** American Express Group; Robert McAlpine Group; Kleinwort Benson; UCB Bank plc; University College London; Winkworths; Steelcase Strafor plc;

Regis Europe Ltd.

Goodman Derrick (3ptnrs/1assoc/ 4assts) Generally popular with other practitioners, the commercial litigation emphasis is on banking and insolvency work.

Hamlin Slowe (8ptnrs/8assts) A firm which "knows what it's doing" according to fellow practitioners. **Clients/Work:** Commercial litigation includes professional negligence, secured lending, media and entertainment, defamation and general

contractual disputes. Phonographic Performance Ltd-v-Maitra (CA); National Home Loans Corp. plc-v-Bromley Hyde & Robinson.

Kingsford Stacey Blackwell (9ptnrs/ 10assts) Noted for its debt recovery work. **Clients/Work:** Clients include local authorities, insurance companies, national retailers, banks/building societies. Work handled includes debt recovery, factoring insolvency, property litigation , IP, employment.

ANDERSON, Harry R.A.
Herbert Smith, London (0171) 374 8000
Head of Litigation and Arbitration Department.
Specialisation: Heads one of the firm's general commercial litigation sections with substantial experience in litigation arising out of corporate transactions, such as claims for misrepresentation and breach of warranty.
Career: Joined *Herbert Smith* as an articled clerk in 1968. Qualified 1970. Partner since 1976.
Personal: Educated at Jesus College, Cambridge.

ARCHER, Nick J.
Slaughter and May, London
(0171) 600 1200
Principal area of practice is commercial litigation and arbitration.
Specialisation: Handles a wide variety of domestic and international disputes in the commercial context. Has particular experience in banking disputes and has worked extensively on litigation and arbitration both for and against Indian banks and corporates.
Prof. Memberships: The Law Society; International Bar Association; Indian Council of Arbitration.
Career: Qualified in 1981 with *Slaughter and May* and became a Partner in 1988.
Personal: Born 15 May 1956. Attended Oakham School and Durham University. Lives in London.

BOURNE, Anthony
Glovers, London (0171) 629 5121
Specialisation: Banking litigation, commercial disputes, employment disputes (banking related). Ata -v- American Express Bank Ltd - Successfully defended a claim by the plaintiff amounting to approx $350,000,000. Concluded two Compromise Agreements for employees where the negotiated settlement figure was in excess of $1.5 million.
Prof. Memberships: Law Society. Westminster Law Society.
Career: Kings School. LLB London.
Personal: Married to Susan. Travel, politics, antiques.

BOWDEN, Paul
Freshfields, London (0171) 936 4000
Partner in Litigation Department.
Specialisation: Environmental and complex multi-party litigation. An author and editor of 'Environmental Law' (Tolleys) and contributor to 'Transnational Rules in International Commercial Arbitration' (ICC).
Prof. Memberships: Membership: Joint Bar/ Law Society Working Party on Civil Justice (1992-93); Lord Woolf's advisory committee on multi-party actions (1995-96); International Nuclear Lawyers Association Insurance; Non-executive director of Nottingham Law School.
Career: Qualified with *Freshfields* in 1981. Partner in 1987, Qualified in Hong Kong, 1986.

Personal: Born 1955. Educated: Bristol University 1973-78.

CANNON, Lista M.
Richards Butler, London (0171) 247 6555
Specialisation: As a lawyer qualified in New York and England & Wales, her practice covers the full range of commercial litigation work with particular emphasis on transnational (cross-border) commercial disputes and litigation, sovereign immunity issues, risk assessment and dispute resoluton and government advisory work. She has a strong banking, finance and regulatory practice. Her work includes ICC arbitration and energy related contract disputes.
Prof. Memberships: In September 1998 she was seconded for six months to the Financial Services Authority as a Senior Legal Advisor and Acting Head of Enforcement. Law Society, admitted to New York State Bar in 1976, Federal Bar Council, ICC UK Environmental Committee.
Career: Litigation lawyer at *Sullivan & Cromwell*, New York, 1975-1980. Established commercial litigation department, (*Boodle Hatfield*), London 1980-1992; Member of the Partnership Board of *Richards Butler* since May 1998.
Personal: Educated at New York University 1969; University of London LLB (hons) 1971. Trustee British American Educational

Foundation since 1980, member of India House, New York and Reform Club.

COLLINS, Q.C., Lawrence A.
Herbert Smith, London (0171) 374 8000
Partner in Litigation and Arbitration Department.
Specialisation: International commercial litigation and arbitration with particular emphasis on banking questions, competition and securities law, commercial fraud and arbitration. He has advised and represented several foreign governments. He has acted in ICC, LCIA and ad hoc arbitrations, and has acted as Chairman in major international cases. He is general editor of 'Dicey and Morris on the Conflict of Laws' (12th edition, 1993), with special responsibility for the section on international arbitration and the author of other works on international litigation and arbitration.
Career: Qualified 1968. Partner at *Herbert Smith* since 1971. Appointed Queen's Counsel, 1997; Deputy High Court Judge since 1997; elected fellow of British Academy, 1994.
Personal: Educated at Cambridge University (LL.D. 1994) and Columbia University, New York.

DAVIES, Valerie E.M.
Norton Rose, London (0171) 283 6000
Partner in Commercial Litigation Department.
Specialisation: Main areas of practice are banking, corporate and financial litigation, insolvency and commercial fraud with particular emphasis on the recovery of assets. Valerie heads *Norton Rose*'s insolvency litigation team and has wide experience of cross border international insolvency. She is also an Assistant Recorder and a CEDR accredited mediator.
Prof. Memberships: Law Society; City of London Solicitors Company; Treasurer of IBA Committee on International Litigation.
Career: Qualified 1979. Partner at *Norton Rose* since 1986.

FAGAN, N.J.
Lovell White Durrant, London
(0171) 236 0066
Specialisation: Senior partner of 'city litigation group' specialising in financial, 'City' and commercial regulatory issues and commercial dispute resolution. He also heads the firm's public policy practice.
Prof. Memberships: Member of the City of London Solicitors' Company and former Chairman, Employment Law Sub-Committee City of London Solicitors' Company; member International Association of Gaming Attorneys; member International Bar Association Commercial Litigation and Labour Law Committees.
Career: Articled *Durrant Cooper & Hambling* (was *Durrant Piesse* until 1988 now *Lovell White Durrant*); qualified 1971; partner 1975.

FORDHAM, John
Stephenson Harwood, London
(0171) 329 4422
See under Fraud: Regulation and Investigation, p. 401

GOLD, David L.
Herbert Smith, London (0171) 374 8000
Partner in Litigation and Arbitration Department.

Specialisation: Main area of practice is general commercial litigation, often with an international connection. Also handles company/partnership disputes, local authority law, computer law and injunctions. Led the legal team responsible for pursuing the former owner of Rumasa SA, a large private company expropriated in Spain in 1983, involving litigation in England, Jersey, Switzerland, Holland and the United States. Led the teams dealing with the Hammersmith loan swaps dispute and Le Gavroche health prosecution. Represented Tottenham Hotspur plc, Alan Sugar and others against Terry Venables and led the team representing Amstrad in its successful litigation against US disk drive manufacturer, Seagate. Has recently represented a major Israeli company in its successful claim against insurers arising out of the expropriation of a timber concession in Liberia. Has also been representing the institutional shareholders in Secton 459 proceedings relating to Astec (BSR) plc. Is currently instructed in proceedings brought following both the collapse of Bermuda Fire & Marine Insurance Company Limited in Bermuda and the Cambridge Group in Ireland and is also representing one of the Defendants in the Atlantic Computer/B&C litigation. He is also representing John Reid Enterprises in its claim against Michael Hatley.
Prof. Memberships: Law Society.
Career: Qualified in 1975. Joined *Herbert Smith* in 1973, becoming a Partner in 1983.
Personal: Born 1st March 1951. Attended LSE 1969-72. Leisure interests include theatre, bridge and family. Lives in Thorpe Bay, Essex.

GOLDSPINK, Robert
Morgan, Lewis & Bockius, London
(0171) 747 5500 / 839 1677
Partner in Litigation Department.
Specialisation: Main areas of practice are international commercial litigation and arbitration. Has particular experience in advising companies who have been the victims of fraud on how to handle the issues arising and recover their losses. Cases include Alexander Howden, PCW, Lloyds litigation, Lonrho v. Fayed, 'Operation Cheetah' (Liverpool and Derek Hatton), Grupo Torras, and the Canada Trust Company and Others v W.O Stolzenberg and Others. Member of joint working party of the general counsel of the Bar and the Law Society which in 1993 reviewed Britain's civil courts and made wide ranging recommendations for the reform of the English Civil Litigation process. Member of the 'Mariott' committee which produced draft legislation for the reform of British arbitration law, eventually taken up by the DTI. Member of committee assisting Court of Appeal in mediation. Member of the Advisory Board of the Centre of Advanced Litigation of Nottingham Law School. Teaches law regularly at conferences and seminars .
Prof. Memberships: City of London Law Society, London Litigation Solicitors' Association.
Career: Qualified in 1975. Joined *Denton Hall* in 1980, becoming a Partner in 1981.
Personal: Born 8th August 1949. Attended Eltham College 1959-67, then Cambridge

University 1968-72 (receiving an MA & LLM). Leisure interests include gardening and fishing.

GOOD, Diana
Linklaters, London (0171) 456 4328
Partner. Litigation Department.
Specialisation: Specialises in commercial litigation, and has extensive experience of advising clients, settling and fighting a wide range of commercial disputes including banking and insurance, and financial services work. Also has experience in EC law disputes including competition law (both EC and UK); and tax litigation.

GRANDISON, Richard
Slaughter and May, London
(0171) 600 1200
Head of Commercial Litigation and Arbitration department.
Specialisation: Extensive experience in commercial litigation, arbitration and commercial judicial review for a wide range of corporate clients in commercial disputes in England and overseas - including international trade and commodity disputes, sovereign immunity issues, oil and gas and financial services.
Prof. Memberships: The Law Society and City of London Solicitors Society.
Career: Qualified in 1978 with *Slaughter and May* . Partner since 1987. Educated at Fettes College, Edinburgh and Pembroke College, Cambridge.

GREENO, Ted
Herbert Smith, London (0171) 374 8000
Partner in Litigation and Arbitration Department.
Specialisation: Wide range of experience in both litigation and arbitration work spanning a number of commercial, industrial and professional sectors including the oil and gas industry, engineering and construction, media, product liability and accountancy.
Career: Qualified 1983. Partner at *Herbert Smith* since 1989.
Personal: Educated at King's College, London.

HUMPHRIES, Mark
Linklaters, London (0171) 456 4250
Partner. Litigation Department.
Specialisation: Main area of practice is commercial litigation. Is an experienced solicitor-advocate and practises in the High Court and many other courts and tribunals. Has experience of handling a wide range of commercial disputes but with an emphasis on industrial and insurance cases. Seconded to *Morgan Lewis Bockius,* Washington DC in 1988. Educated at Cambridge University.

JENKINS, Alan D.
Eversheds, London (0171) 919 4500
Head of International department in London.
Specialisation: Main area of practice is commercial litigation. Includes professional negligence, fraud, breach of warranty, insurance/reinsurance, unfair prejudice and investigatory work. Environmental law work also undertaken. Acted in: Bromley 475 Names Action Group litigation; also BCCI-related litigation; Mentor-related litigation; Elton John v. Dick James Music; Alexander Howden-related litigation; Harrods (Buenos Aires) Ltd.
Prof. Memberships: Law Society, IBA (Committee on International Litigation), UIA, FRSA.

Career: Articled at *Frere Cholmeley*, qualified 1977. Partner 1983. Previously Head of Litigation Department. Head of Environmental Group 1991. Managing Partner 1996-1998 and the firm's merger with *Eversheds*, London.
Personal: Born 27th May 1952. Attended New College, Oxford.

KELLY, Jonathan P.

Simmons & Simmons, London
(0171) 628 2020
Partner in Commercial Litigation Department and Head of the Banking Litigation Group.
Specialisation: Main areas of practice are banking and financial services litigation, specialising in securities, commodities and derivatives disputes, and regulatory issues arising in these areas. Experienced in corporate disputes and large scale commercial fraud actions. Further area of specialism is defamation with experience of advising both publisher defendants and a wide range of plaintiffs. Has handled securities and commodities disputes and regulatory investigations arising under The Financial Services Act, derivatives litigation and claims of multi-jurisdictional international commercial fraud. Clients include UK, US and European commercial and investment banks, investment institutions, brokers and commodity houses and, in relation to defamation, UK public companies and Lloyd's insurers, foreign multi-nationals and international sports bodies and personalities.
Prof. Memberships: Law Society, Society of English and American Lawyers.
Career: Qualified in 1989 after articles at *Simmons & Simmons*. Became a Partner in 1995.
Personal: Born 11th August 1964. Educated at Stonyhurst College 1972-82, Balliol College, Oxford 1983-86 and The College of Law, Lancaster Gate, 1986-87. Leisure pursuits include salmon fishing, squash and tennis.

LEONARD, Paul M.

Freshfields, London (0171) 936 4000
Partner in Litigation Department.
Specialisation: Main areas of practice are international litigation, arbitration and mediation. Cases include Ocean Island case (Tito v. Waddell), Westinghouse Uranium Contract litigation and the Alexander Howden insurance fraud cases. Acting in numerous ICC arbitrations. Also involved in insurance insolvency litigation, acting in the KWELM and Electric Mutual (EMLICO) cases. A CEDR accredited mediator.
Prof. Memberships: Law Society and IBA.
Career: Articled at *Freshfields*. Qualified in 1966. Partner in 1972. Head of Litigation Department 1988-91.
Personal: Born 14th January 1942. Educated at Finchley Grammar School and Sheffield University (LL.B.). Leisure interests include cricket, fishing and an old Aston Martin.

MACKIE, Q.C., David L.

Allen & Overy, London (0171) 330 3000
Head of Litigation.
Specialisation: Litigation and arbitration.
Prof. Memberships: Law Society.
Career: Qualified 1971, having joined *Allen & Overy* in 1969. Became a Partner in 1975 and

Head of Litigation in 1988. Assistant Recorder 1989-92, and a Recorder of Crown Court since 1992. Higher Court Advocate (all courts), Fellow Chartered Institute of Arbitrators. Queen's Counsel 1998.
Personal: Born 1946. Attended various schools 1951-63, then St Edmund Hall, Oxford 1964-7. Leisure interests include climbing. Lives in London.

MAYHEW, David

Clifford Chance, London (0171) 600 1000
See under Commodities: Futures, Fraud: Regulation and Investigation, p. 179, 401

MCLACHLAN, Campbell A.

Herbert Smith, London (0171) 374 8000
Partner in Litigation and Arbitration Department.
Specialisation: Specialises in international commercial litigation and arbitration including public and private international law, investment disputes, multi-national fraud and cross-border banking . He is Vice-Chairman of the IBA Committee on International Litigation, and Joint Secretary of the British Branch of the ILA. His book, 'Transnational Tort Litigation' is published by OUP.
Career: Qualified New Zealand 1984 and England and Wales 1991. Partner at *Herbert Smith* since 1992.
Personal: Educated at Victoria University of Wellington, New Zealand, the University of London and Hague Academy of International Law (Diploma cum laude).

MITCHARD, Paul

Simmons & Simmons, London
(0171) 628 2020
Head of Litigation.
Specialisation: Main areas of practice are international arbitration and commercial litigation, covering the conduct of ICC, LCIA, RSA, Lloyd's arbitrations, commercial, financial and administrative and public law disputes. Also handles dispute resolution and mediation. Accredited CEDR mediator, member of CPR's panel of distinguished neutrals and a Fellow of the Chartered Institute of Arbitrators. Has represented domestic and international companies and State organisations in a number of major disputes. Has given seminars in London, the USA and the Middle East on international arbitration.
Prof. Memberships: Law Society, American Bar Association, International Bar Association, City of London Solicitors' Company, City of London Law Society Litigation Sub-Committee.
Career: Qualified in 1977. Worked at *Slaughter and May* 1977-84 in London and Hong Kong. Joined *Simmons & Simmons* in 1984, becoming a Partner in 1985 and Head of Litigation in 1994.
Personal: Born 2nd January 1952. Attended Taunton School 1960-70 and Lincoln College, Oxford 1971-4. Leisure interests include travel, reading and walking. Lives in Chalfont St. Giles, Bucks.

NATALI, David P.

Herbert Smith, London (0171) 374 8000
Specialisation: Cross-border fraud; asset tracing in jurisdictions noted for their banking, trust and corporate secrecy laws; commodities disputes; partnership disputes; professional

negligence; defamation and major international disputes of all kinds. Currently acting for Codelco, the Chilean state-owned copper company, in claims arising from $178m losses on the futures markets; and for Price Waterhouse in defending claims which arose following the collapse of BCCI.
Career: Articled *Herbert Smith;* qualified 1963; partner 1968. Head of one of the Commercial Litigation Groups. Former member of the firm's Management Committee. Former member of Joint Bar/Law Society Working Party on the Civil Courts.
Personal: Born 1940.

NICHOLSON, Brinsley

Linklaters, London (0171) 456 4364
Partner, Head of Litigation Department.
Specialisation: Practised in proceedings before the High Court and the Commercial Court; experienced in obtaining urgent injunctions (particularly to freeze assets), dealing with jurisdictional issues, questions of conflict of laws and handling substantial disputes. Also experience of arbitration, insolvency, financial services, investigations, banking and white collar crime. Member of IBA, AEPPC and City of London Solicitors Company. Joined *Linklaters & Paines*, 1972. Became a Partner in 1977. Admitted as a Solicitor of the Supreme Court of Hong Kong, and Litigation Partner in the Hong Kong office 1986-89.

PARKER, Raj D.

Freshfields, London (0171) 936 4000
See under Insurance & Reinsurance: Reinsurance, Sports, p. 469,741

PEARSON, N.P.

Baker & McKenzie, London (0171) 919 1000
Specialisation: Civil Fraud, insolvency, and international disputes. Significant experience in managing large multi jurisdictional claims.
Prof. Memberships: Licensed insolvency practitioner. Member of Society of Practitioners of Insolvency, Insolvency Lawyers Association, Insolvency Practitioners Association, and European Insolvency Practitioners Association.
Career: Qualified 1976. Articled with and remained at *Herbert Smith* 1974-1979. *Baker & McKenzie*, Hong Kong 1979-1988. Partner *Baker & McKenzie* 1982. *Baker & McKenzie*, London 1988-date.
Personal: Educated King Edwards School, Birmingham and Lincoln College, Oxford. Keen sportsman. Married, two children.

PLANT, Charles W.

Herbert Smith, London (0171) 374 8000
Specialisation: Principal area of practice is commercial litigation with particular reference to media, oil and gas and construction industries. Also provides expert advice on international arbitration law.
Prof. Memberships: Law Society, International Bar Association (Secretary of the International Litigation Committee).
Career: Qualified in 1969 while at *Herbert Smith*. Became a partner in 1976. Head of Litigation Department 1988 - 1995. Member of Lord Chancellor's Advisory Committee on Legal Education and Conduct (appointed April 1994).
Personal: Born 1944. Attended Cambridge University 1963-66. Lives in Tunbridge Wells.

ROCHEZ, Nicholas
Davies Arnold Cooper, London
(0171) 936 2222
Senior Litigation Partner.
Specialisation: Specialist in insurance and reinsurance. Also has extensive and wide ranging experience in all fields of commercial litigation, including world wide jurisdictions. Author of many articles and papers on insurance and reinsurance over the past ten years.
Prof. Memberships: Law Society.
Career: Qualified in 1980. Joined *Davies Arnold Cooper* in 1978. Became a Partner in 1984, Managing Partner in 1987 and Senior Litigation Partner in 1992.
Personal: Born 13th November 1954. Attended Ardingly College, West Sussex; then Middlesex Polytechnic (BA Law) and City of London (MA in Business Law). Leisure interests include family, motor sports and horse racing. Lives in Hambledon, Hampshire.

SANDELSON, Jeremy
Clifford Chance, London (0171) 600 1000
See under Fraud: Regulation and Investigation, p. 402

SEYMOUR, Michael J.
Lovell White Durrant, London
(0171) 236 0066
Specialisation: Main area of practice commercial litigation and arbitration often involving an international dimension, particularly in the area of trade and business. Has acted for foreign governments in cases involving state immunity and for banks, insurers and other companies in professional negligence, fraud, and property related cases.
Prof. Memberships: Law Society, Chartered Institute of Arbitrators, Committee member (President: 1994-1996) of London Solicitors Litigation Association, member of the joint working party of the Bar and the Law Society on the Civil Courts.
Career: Articled at *Lovell White & King* (now *Lovell White Durrant*); Qualified 1974; Partner 1982.

SHERRINGTON, Patrick
Lovell White Durrant, London
(0171) 236 0066
Specialisation: Commercial Litigation. Extensive experience of international commercial litigation, arbitration and ADR, especially in the fields of banking and finance, insolvency, energy, product liability and professional negligence. Author of: 'Civil Litigation' published in Hong Kong by Longmans, 2nd edition 1996; writes and regularly speaks on his specialist areas of practice.
Prof. Memberships: Admitted in the UK, Hong Kong and Australia (NSW). Law Society of England & Wales, Solicitors' European Group, City of London Solicitors' Company, Fellow of the Chartered Institute of Arbitrators, Law Society of Hong Kong, Inter-Pacific Bar Association, LawAsia, International Bar Association.
Career: Articled *Lovell White & King* (now *Lovell White Durrant*) 1978-1980; resident in New York 1982-1984; Partner 1985; resident in Hong Kong 1987-1996; registered UK insolvency practitioner; Higher Courts (Civil proceedings) qualification; Law Society of Hong Kong Council Member 1990-1996; Vice President

1993-1996; Council Member Inter-Pacific Bar Association 1990-1996; Governor Advocacy Institute of Hong Kong 1992-1996.

SLEIGH, Russell H.P.
Lovell White Durrant, London
(0171) 236 0066
Specialisation: Experienced in wide range of international commercial litigation, in particular corporate, banking and regulatory disputes and multi-jurisdictional fraud issues. Acted on numerous governmental and quasi-governmental investigations on behalf of the authorities and of other participants. Also experienced in media law issues.
Career: Qualified 1973. Partner 1980. New York office 1977-80. Paris office 1990-93.

SPARROW, Edward C.A.
Ashurst Morris Crisp, London
(0171) 638 1111
Specialisation: General commercial litigation and dispute resolution with experience in: financial sector disputes (mergers and acquisitions, Stock Exchange transactions and management and trading of securities/other financial instruments); energy sector disputes (offshore construction, exploration and extraction contracts); professional negligence, insolvency and insurance; city and professional regulation.
Prof. Memberships: Law Society.
Career: Ampleforth College; Lincoln College, Oxford. Articled *Ashurst Morris Crisp*; qualified 1977; partner 1981; head of litigation department 1993.
Personal: Born 1953; resides London.

STYLE, Christopher J.D.
Linklaters, London (0171) 456 4286
See under Arbitration, p. 119

TAYLOR, Ian
Freshfields, London (0171) 936 4000
Partner in Litigation Department.
Specialisation: Main area of practice is commercial litigation, particularly in relation to banking and financial services, fraud and asset recovery. Also represents financial institutions in regulatory, DTI and SFO inquiries.
Prof. Memberships: Law Society; Member of Commercial Court Committee.
Career: Qualified in 1976, having joined *Freshfields* in 1974. Became a Partner in 1982.
Personal: Born 20th June 1951. Attended Gonville & Caius College, Cambridge 1969-73. Lives in London.

TAYLOR, Tim
S J Berwin & Co, London
+44 (0)171 533 2222
Specialisation: Complex commercial litigation with an emphasis on cross-border disputes. Co-author of Sweet and Maxwell's European Litigation Handbook. Major cases in the last 12 months include: acting for Corals, Ladbrokes and William Hill in proceedings brought by Camelot and for Lloyd Thompson in Commercial Union v Lloyd Thompson Ltd as well as various BCCI related litigation.
Prof. Memberships: International Bar Association; American Bar Association.
Career: MA Oxon.

TROTTER, John
Lovell White Durrant, London
(0171) 236 0066
Specialisation: Main area of practice is litigation and other dispute resolution involving insurance and re-insurance, including professional indemnity and product liability. Has been involved in numerous actions and arbitrations in these areas, including the defence of major claims against lawyers.
Prof. Memberships: Co-Chairman of the Professional Indemnity Insurance Sub-Committee of the International Bar Association. Member of the London Solicitors Litigation Association and the City of London Law Society.
Career: Qualified in 1977 with *Lovell, White & King* (now *Lovell White Durrant*); worked in their New York office 1980-1982; Partner in 1983.

TURNBULL, John W.
Linklaters, London (0171) 456 4310
Specialisation: Partner, Litigation Department specialising in corporate finance litigation and all contentious aspects of mergers and acquisitions work, including acting on Plessey/GEC, Minorco/Consolidated Gold Fields and others, and major litigation for British Airways and British Aerospace. He has extensive experience of professional negligence and banking work, advising Ernst & Whinney in relation to BCCI and NatWest Bank in relation to the Maxwell affair. He has recently represented the CWS in relation to its defence of the failed Regan Galileo bid. He advises the Financial Reporting Review Panel. After qualifying in 1983 he became a Partner in 1989.

TYRRELL, Gerrard
Harbottle & Lewis, London (0171) 667 5000
Partner in Litigation Department.
Specialisation: Main area of practice is commercial litigation with emphasis on the media and entertainment industries. Acted in the Virgin/BA libel dispute, Richard Branson/G-Tech dispute.
Prof. Memberships: IBA.
Career: Qualified in 1981. Joined *Harbottle & Lewis* in 1981, became a Partner in 1984.
Personal: Attended University of Bristol and College of Law. Member of Council Institute of Contemporary Arts. Lives in London.

WATSON, Peter M.
Allen & Overy, London (0171) 330 3000
Specialisation: Deals with the full range of contentious commercial work in particular aviation, professional negligence, banking and finance, commercial fraud, judicial review and trade promotion issues.
Career: Assistant solicitor *Allen & Overy* 1981-86, seconded to *Allen & Overy* Dubai office 1984-86; partner *Allen & Overy* 1987.
Personal: BA Oxford University 1978. Born 1956.

WILLIS, Tony
Clifford Chance, London (0171) 600 1000
Specialisation: All forms of Commercial Dispute Resolution especially Cross-border, Finance, Regulatory and other complex matters. Litigation partner since 1973, led the Litigation Practice from 1989 to 1996 after 2 years (1987-1988) as a full-time Managing Partner of the Firm. Specialises in Mediation and other forms of ADR. CEDR Accredited Mediator, member of CEDR Training Faculty

and Director CEDR. Member European Advisory Committee and Panel of Distinguished Mediators, CPR Institute for Dispute Resolution, New York. Member International Academy of Mediators (US). Regular lecturer and trainer on ADR including 10 sessions for Judicial Studies Board (1997), Society of Practitioners in Insolvency (3 sessions) and many others. Acts as Mediator and Mediator Party Advocate. Advises on Dispute Resolution Process design. Member Commercial Court Working Party on ADR 1995-96 leading to June 1996 Practice Direction. FCIArb. and Member of several Arbitration Panels.

Prof. Memberships: Law Society, Liveryman City of London Solicitors Company, IBA, ABA, LawAsia, New Zealand Law Society.
Personal: Born 29th November 1941, New Zealand, LLB Victoria University of Wellington 1966.

SOUTH EAST

LEADING FIRMS · SOUTH EAST
DONNE MILEHAM & HADDOCK Brighton
BLAKE LAPTHORN Fareham

HIGHLY REGARDED FIRMS
Cole & Cole Oxford
Paris, Smith & Randall Southampton
Thomas Eggar Church Adams Chichester
Thomson Snell & Passmore Tunbridge Wells
Barlows Guildford
Brachers Maidstone
Burstows Brighton
Clarks Reading
Cripps Harries Hall Tunbridge Wells, Kent
Furley Page Fielding & Barton Canterbury
Matthew Arnold & Baldwin Watford
Pitmans Reading
Rawlison & Butler Crawley
Stevens & Bolton Guildford
Burt Brill & Cardens Brighton
Lamport Bassitt Southampton
Shoosmiths & Harrison Banbury, Reading, Southampton
Taylor Walton Luton
Wollastons Chelmsford

Donne Mileham & Haddock (5ptnrs/7assts – virtually full-time) Have a "huge presence" with a "good, strong team." 15% of the firm's turnover derives from pure commercial litigation work. Managing partner *Tim Aspinall* heads up the team; in 1997 he acted as the supervising solicitor on the execution of four Anton Piller orders. He is "a first class litigator, with lots of flair." **Clients/Work:** Act for Mandy Allwood in action for breach of contract and fiduciary duty against former publicist Max Clifford. Also act for Arcadia Group plc and Thomson CSF.

Blake Lapthorn (6ptnrs/6assts full time) "Non aggressive" *David Higham* leads a "heavyweight" and quality litigation department which with Donne Mileham is "streets ahead" of the competition. **Clients/Work:** Pirelli UK plc, Alcatel and University College London. Involved in Credit Lyonnais Bank v Burch.

Cole & Cole (2ptnrs/6assts) Regarded as "approachable" and are "well known" in the South East.

Paris Smith & Randall (2ptnrs/4assts) *Clive Thompson* is a leading litigator."

Thomas Eggar Church Adams (5ptnrs/10assts) It remains to be seen what the effect of the merger between Thomas Eggar Verrall Bowles and Church Adams Tatham will be. The new firm remains highly regarded. **Clients/Work:** Frazer Nash Technology; Kurekess SIA; Alliance Unichem plc.

Thomson Snell & Passmore (9ptnrs/7assts- also professional negligence and property) **Clients/Work:** RICS, SIF, Marley plc

Barlows (3ptnrs/5assts) Have a particular reputation for injunctive work. **Clients/Work:** Include large educational establishments and major plcs. Represent car franchisees suing Fiat and Honda. Obtained injunction to remove sub-contractors from construction site, and Mareva injunction for small family business in contractual dispute. Also acted for employers to obtain breach of covenant injunction.

Brachers (4ptnrs/2assts) **Clients/Work:** Represented an Indian exporter in £5,000,000 bills of exchange claim against English importer.

Burstows (6ptnrs/2assts) Perceived as a "growing, bullish firm" **Clients/Work:** Instructed by exporters of live animals in claim for damages against Dover Harbour Board.

Clarks (5ptnrs/1asst – all do other areas) Considered "solid" with "depth." **Clients/Work:** Blue Circle Industries plc, SmithKline Beecham plc, University of Reading.

Cripps Harries Hall (7ptnrs/16assts- also do other areas) Known primarily for their professional indemnity work, they are regarded as a "strong, efficient team" with "City type polish." **Clients/Work:** SIF, Britannia Life Ltd, NPI

Furley Page Fielding & Barton (4ptnrs (2 full-time)/4assts (2 full-time)) Undertake a broad spread of litigation.

Matthew Arnold & Baldwin (3ptnrs/4assts – also do other areas) **Clients/Work:**

Europcar, The Home Video Channel, Sanyo Information Systems.

Pitmans (5ptnrs/8assts- also do other areas) Perceived as having "considerable depth and a good reputation." **Clients/Work:** Represented plaintiff in Jones v Secretary of State for Wales (taxation of costs- regional solicitors who specialise in commercial work can claim a higher hourly rate than local non-specialist firms).

Rawlison & Butler (1ptnr/4assts) Composed mainly of ex-City solicitors, the practice has a reputation for being "tough."

Stevens & Bolton (3ptnrs/4assts) Continue to be regarded as a "go ahead, up and coming firm." **Clients/Work:** Acted in Ibero Travel v Pallas Leasing. Represent Proctor & Gamble; IAF Group plc; Gerling Namur and Rugby Football Union.

Burt Brill & Cardens (1ptnr/2assts) Main activity is debt recovery for a plc involved in the hire of consumer durables. **Clients/Work:** Acted for a major plc in lift installation and associated building works dispute.

Lamport Bassitt (3ptnrs/2assts) **Clients/Work:** Act for Alehouse Co Ltd and Petrol Express.

Shoosmiths & Harrison Known mainly by virtue of their national presence, the south eastern offices seem not to have established individual profiles.

Taylor Walton (2ptnrs/5assts) **Clients/Work:** Acting for former partners in partnership dissolution; commercial contract involving inquiry into damages on a cross-undertaking given in emergency injunction application; action for steel trader involving injunctions and orders for delivery up of unpaid consignment of steel.

Wollastons (3ptnrs-50%/3assts-30%/1 other-80%) Act for a number of Plcs & pharmaceutical companies.

LEADING INDIVIDUALS SOUTH EAST
ASPINALL Tim Donne Mileham & Haddock
HIGHAM David Blake Lapthorn
THOMSON Clive H. Paris Smith & Randall

ASPINALL, Tim
Donne Mileham & Haddock, Brighton
(01273) 744319
See under Intellectual Property, p. 485

HIGHAM, David
Blake Lapthorn, Fareham (01489) 579990
Specialisation: Head of Civil Litigation at
Blake Lapthorn. Personal specialisation is
professional negligence and commercial

litigaton. Has particular expertise in cases
involving professional fraud. Lectures on
management of litigation.
Career: First career as submarine officer in the
Royal Navy. Joined *Blake Lapthorn* as Articled
Clerk in 1976, qualifying in 1979. Partner in
1980. Appointed head of Civil Litigation in
1991. LLM in Advanced Litigation at
Nottingham Trent University 1996. Advocacy
trainer with NITA (UK)

THOMSON, Clive H.
Paris Smith & Randall, Southampton
(01703) 482482

SOUTH WEST

Bond Pearce (8ptnrs/1assoc/11assts) A
"strong practice" regarded by many as insurance based. Team leader *Simon Richardson*
is "genuinely excellent." Plans for a new
office in Bristol should strengthen their base
in the South West. **Clients/Work:** The
commercial litigation department handles
matters arising from insurance,professional
indemnity, banking, insolvency and IP
sectors. Media related litigation was an
important part of the firm's work in 1997.
Also act on dealer litigation for multinational
vehicle wholesalers.

Burges Salmon (4ptnrs/20assts) "Technically good and commercial" according to
clients although some practitioners view
them as having an agricultural bias. *Adrian
Llewelyn Evans* is "tough and shrewd."
Clients/Work: The department includes
insurance, insolvency, banking, product
liability, construction, employment.

Osborne Clarke (2 teams incorporating
1ptnr/3-6assts in each team) Highly rated by
many for its "strength and depth" and "corporate bias." Also for the presence of *Robert
Johnson*, "a commercial litigator of renown."
Clients/Work: Include Ministry of Defence,
Allied Domecq Spirits and Wines Ltd, Bristol & West plc, National Westminster Bank
plc. Acting for Greek Cypriot interests in
relation to two forthcoming appeals, in the
House of Lords and the Court of Appeal
respectively.

Bevan Ashford (3ptnrs/1assoc/2assts)
Promoted in our tables following many
commendations of the firm's "wide-ranging
portfolio" and "good people." *David Owens*
was recommended for his NHS related work.
Clients/Work: Midland Bank Plc, Allied
Dunbar Assurance Plc, Bristol & West Plc,
Orange PCS Ltd, Intcl, Allied Domecq
Spirits and Wines. Areas of advice include
contractual disputes, economic torts, banking, fraud and equitable remedies, minority
shareholders and Company Court work.

Eversheds (3ptnrs/7assts/6 other fee
earners) Generally regarded as having less of
a profile in Bristol although the team leader
Peter Morris is a new entry in recognition of
his involvement in some important litigation
recently. **Clients/Work:** Act for: Rhone-
Poulenc Chemicals Ltd (now Rhodia Ltd);
Somerfield Stores. The workload of the team
has been dominated by one major case now
involving one partner and five other fee earners.

Laytons (2ptnrs/2assts) A "solid"
practice felt to be heavily biased towards construction work. **Clients/Work:** Act for:
Somerfield Stores; Bowthorpe Plc and subsidiaries. "Commercial litigation" includes
professional indemnity, IP, defamation,
product liability, general breach of contract.

Veale Wasbrough (5ptnrs/5assts)
Simon Pizzey is a leading individual.
Clients/Work: Act for Lloyds Bank on recovery work and professional negligence
actions; West Wiltshire District Council in a
major piece of litigation on the duties of auditors which has been to the Court of Appeal;
Bristol & West Building Society in the conduct of another major piece of litigation.
Judgments obtained included: Penn v Wil-
son(CA); Kramer; May,May & Merrimans
(Mothew) (CA); Nelsons; Fancy & Jackson.

Wansbroughs Willey Hargrave
(2ptnrs/3assts plus a further 5ptnrs/15assts
for professional indemnity) Strongly
weighted towards professional indemnity
work rather than general commercial litigation. **Clients/Work:** Includes professional
indemnity, construction, IT, IP, banking,
insolvency.

Anstey Sargent & Probert (4ptnrs/
5assts) Less of a presence although the team
received praise for its insurance work.
Clients/Work: Deal with property disputes,
banking litigation, professional indemnity
and employment litigation.

Cartwrights (1ptnr/1asst) Generally
well respected by fellow practitioners.
Clients/Work: Act for: Railtrack plc, Dalgety
Agriculture Ltd, Bristol International
Airport, Standard Life Assurance Co. Ltd,
Reading Borough Council, South Wales
Transport, Jefferson Smurfit Group. Claims
include acting for Railtrack following a rail
crash in South Wales.

Clarke Willmott & Clarke (3ptnrs/
11assts) Perceived as a "county firm" rather
than mainstream commercial litigation practice. **Clients/Work:** Work includes sale of
goods, international trade and arbitration.

Davies and Partners (3ptnrs/3assts)
Promoted in our tables following praise from
fellow practitioners. **Clients/Work:** Shareholder disputes, professional indemnity,
judicial review, insolvency and debt collection apart from general contractual disputes.

Foot & Bowden (4ptnrs/8assts divided
into subdivisions) **Clients/Work:** Commercial litigation is divided into specialist areas:
shipping, construction, banking and media.

Lawrence Tucketts (7ptnrs/18other fee
earners) Better known for property litigation,
the department also deals with construction
disputes, banking and financial recoveries.
Clients/Work: During 1997 dealt with two
major engineering contract disputes.

Lester Aldridge (2ptnrs/2assts) **Clients/
Work:** Represented plaintiff where a claim
for damages resulting from breach of contract and duty in the design and project management of nuclear fuel containers and mod-
ular flask grabs; recovered damages of
approximately £3m for 120 Plaintiffs in a
multi-party action for misrepresentation;
acted for Plaintiffs in an action for breach of

dealership agreements and abuse of dominant market position under Article 86 of the Treaty of Rome.

Lyons Davidson (3ptnrs/2assts)The department includes Health & Safety, licensing, professional negligence and property litigation as well as commercial and contractual disputes. **Clients/Work:** Acted for a plaintiff in the petro-chemical industry. The claim involved cross border litigation with a Trade Mark dispute and was in excess of £1m; acted for a plc in respect of a bond guarantee where the claim was in excess of £1.75m.

Rickerby Watterson (3ptnrs) Have a "good client following." **Clients/Work:** Commercial litigation includes insolvency, professional negligence and shareholder disputes

Trumps (3ptnrs/5assts) **Clients/Work:** The Commercial Litigation department is divided into three teams dealing with Personal Injury, General Commercial/-Professional Negligence and Insolvency, Banking and Business Breakdown.

Wolferstans (2ptnrs/1asst) Has risen in our tables this year. **Clients/Work:** Commercial litigation includes professional indemnity and IP.

Stephens & Scown (4ptnrs/4assts who spend 35-100% of their time on commercial litigation) **Clients/Work:** Acted in a number of cases involving applications to disqualify company directors, one of which went to the Court of Appeal and established new law; also undue influence and misrepresentation cases which went to trial with successful outcomes.

Townsends (4ptnrs/2assts) **Clients/Work:** Acting for a major importer and distributor of commercial vehicles in dispute over design of depots in UK; acting for former staff of supplier to motor racing industry, acting as mediator in a banking dispute.

Wilsons Solicitors (2ptnrs/4assts who also do property litigation and personal injury work) **Clients/Work:** Principal specialist area is employment law.

LEADING INDIVIDUALS SOUTH WEST		
JOHNSON Robert Osborne Clarke		
LLEWELYN EVANS Adrian Burges Salmon		
RICHARDSON Simon Bond Pearce		
MORRIS Peter Eversheds		
OWENS David Bevan Ashford		
PIZZEY Simon Veale Wasbrough		

SEE PROFILES AT END OF THIS SECTION

LEADERS' PROFILES · SOUTH WEST

JOHNSON, Robert I.
Osborne Clarke, Bristol (0117) 923 0220
Partner in Litigation Department.
Specialisation: Main areas of practice include banking, charities, medical and educational work. Has acted for Westminster and National Westminster Banks since 1964 in Wales, South of England and South-West England. Has advised the central Bristol Teaching Hospitals on all aspects of hospital, medical and nursing law since 1964. Acts for Universities Chartered Professional bodies. Has also advised on the running down and winding up of charitable schools, especially as relates to the issue of personal liability of charitable trustees. Has lectured and given seminars on medical law, community health law, aspects of charitable law and the responsibilities of a professional person.
Prof. Memberships: Law Society, Notaries Society, Council Member Sue Ryder Foundation. Legal Aid Board Committee (since 1970), Director Avonline Communications Limited.
Career: Qualified in 1963. Joined *Osborne Clarke* in 1964, becoming a Partner in 1967.
Personal: Born 20th September 1940. Attended Bristol Grammar School 1948-57, then Bristol University 1957-60. Leisure interests include the economic history of the UK, the history of communications (received gold medal from Postal History Society of America) and 'growing things'.

LLEWELYN EVANS, Adrian
Burges Salmon, Bristol (0117) 939 2000

MORRIS, Peter
Eversheds, Bristol (0117) 929 9555
Specialisation: Head of banking and commercial litigation in *Eversheds's* Bristol office. All types of commercial litigation particularly for financial institutions. Professional negligence for financial and commercial clients mainly as Plaintiff against solicitor and valuer Defendants. Heavily involved in recent years in managed litigation against multiple defendants. Also property litigation, mainly Landlord and Tenant, for retail and developer clients.
Prof. Memberships: Bristol Law Society; CBI.
Career: Qualified in 1982. *Kenwright & Cox* 1982-86, partner 1985. *Holt Phillips* 1986-1994, partner 1986, becoming *Eversheds* partner in 1994.
Personal: Born 1957. Lives outside Bristol. Interests include hill walking, smallholding and real ale.

OWENS, David
Bevan Ashford, Bristol (0117) 923 0111
Partner in Public Sector Commercial.
Specialisation: After twelve years experience working in the Commercial Litigation Department of *Bevan Ashford*, his focus on public law issues, particularly Judicial Review, has increased to the extent that he is now working with the Public Sector Commercial team. His work has involved commercial litigation on a wide range of topics both for NHS and private sector clients, together with a significant degree of advice on more general matters on the law and practice of the NHS and other public sector bodies.Currently main practice areas are Judicial Review within the NHS and associated public law matters and some employment litigation matters involving the public sector.
Prof. Memberships: Bristol Law Society, Employment Lawyers' Association, Society of Computers and Law.
Career: Joined *Bevan Ashford* in 1982.

Qualified 1984. Partner 1990.
Personal: Born 23rd July 1958. Attended Oxford University 1977-80.

PIZZEY, Simon F.
Veale Wasbrough, Bristol (0117) 925 2020
Partner.
Specialisation: Commercial litigation in the fields of banking, commercial fraud, business breakdown (corporate and partnership) and professional negligence. Clients include building societies, banks, local authorities, central government agencies, professional partnerships and corporates.
Prof. Memberships: Bristol Law Society Panel of Supervising Solicitors for the enforcement of Anton Piller Orders.
Career: Qualified in 1982. *Payne Hicks Beach* 1983-87. Joined *Veale Wasbrough* in 1987. Partner in 1989. Head of *Veale Wasbrough's* Litigation Department.
Personal: Born 1957. Educated at Trowbridge High School and Birmingham University. Lives near Bath. Enjoys family life and most sports.

RICHARDSON, Simon
Bond Pearce, Southampton (01703) 332001
Partner and Head of the Commercial Group.
Specialisation: Specialises in commercial litigation in particular employment, fraud related litigation and business dispute litigation. Handles international business disputes in foreign jurisdictions.
Prof. Memberships: An accredited mediator and member of the Institute of Directors.
Career: Qualified in 1983. Joined *Bond Pearce* in 1989, having worked for City firm *Lovell White Durrant*, becoming a Partner in 1991.

WALES

Hugh James (8ptnrs/8assts) Have "strength in the valleys" and are seen as a cohesive unit across their many offices. Some see them as "aggressive." *Michael Jefferies* "of the older generation" is "technically fine and a tough litigator." *Michael Jones* is an "able litigator who you either love or hate" and a "good hands on man." **Clients/Work:** Acting for Welsh Rugby Union in action by Cardiff RFC; continue to act as lead solicitors for Hoover in defending "free flight" litigation.

Morgan Bruce (23ptnrs (including 7ptnrs in London)/37assts- not all full time) Following an internal reorganisation, the head of litigation is based in the London office, but *Phillip Howell-Richardson* remains in Wales where he is regarded by some as "an aggressive litigator" who "gets down in the arena with his clients." **Clients/Work:** Acting for Cardiff Rugby Club in its dispute with the Welsh Rugby Union. Also act for Associated British Ports, BP and TBI plc.

Eversheds (5ptnrs/9assts) "Have a corporate feel" and are seen as "determined." *Peter Jones* "will roll his sleeves up and get on with the job." **Clients/Work:** Act for British Gas plc in clearance of 150 business tenants; Burger King (grant of overriding lease) and Cardiff Bay Development Corporation

Edwards Geldard (1ptnr/4assts) Are "more distinguished than ever." **Clients/Work:** Rackline Ltd v National Library of Wales (contractual duty to appoint nominated sub-contractors), Coslett (Contractors) Ltd v Mid Glamorgan County

Council (claim by administrator for delivery up). Advising Welsh Development Agency in litigation relating to land in Aberdare

Dolmans (4ptnrs/3assts) Seen as "reliable and reputable."

Palser Grossman (4ptnrs: 2p/t; 5assts: 2p/t) The practice is seen to be "growing quickly" and can be "quite forceful" when necessary. **Clients/Work:** Rhondda Waste Disposal: high profile eviction of pickets from sensitive waste tip; successful defence of Director of local company against proceeding to disqualify brought by DTI who discontinued half way through; successful defence of arbitration claim brought by timeshare owners against Directors of management company.

LEADERS' PROFILES · WALES

HOWELL-RICHARDSON, Phillip
Morgan Bruce, Cardiff (01222) 385385
Partner & Head of Commercial Litigation.
Specialisation: Heavyweight High Court Litigation arbitration and dispute resolution. Has extensive experience in advising institutions, companies, banks, government bodies and individuals on a wide range of corporate, financial and statutory issues. Has conducted or led actions ranging from substantial corporate fraud to money and asset recovery to defamation. Has developed an expertise in construction litigation and a long standing involvement in mediation in the UK. Has developed expertise as an experienced mediator and taken part in pilot mediation programmes as well as conducting mediations in a wide range of disputes around the country. Cases have included arbitration involving a public company and a claim in excess of £10 million which settled successfully after the first phase of the hearing. Addresses conferences on the development of ADR.
Prof. Memberships: Law Society, Chairman of ADR Net, ORSA, Association of European Lawyers, Wales Medico-Legal Society. A

member of the panel of Court of Appeal Mediators.
Career: Qualified in 1975. *Stanley Wasbrough* from 1975-76, then *Osborne Clarke* 1976-81. Joined *Morgan Bruce* in 1981, becoming a Partner in 1982.
Personal: Born 21st June 1950. Clifton College, Bristol 1963-69, University of Kent 1969-72. Leisure interests include sailing, tennis and restoration of classic cars. Lives in Cardiff.

JEFFERIES, Michael
Hugh James, Cardiff (01222) 224871
See under Construction & Civil Engineering, p. 212

JONES, Michael L.N.
Hugh James, Cardiff (01222) 224871
Senior Partner and Head of Civil Litigation Department.
Specialisation: Handles a wide variety of commercial litigation work including intellectual property. Acts for numerous clients including advertising agencies, building companies and manufacturers. Also handles construction

arbitration and litigation matters acting for housing associations and architects amongst others. Cases handled include R v South Glamorgan County Council ex parte Evans concerning parents' choice in education. High Court Advocate. Lecturer on civil advocacy courses at Cardiff Law Society
Prof. Memberships: Chartered Institute of Arbitrators, past President of Cardiff Law Society, Law Society Welsh Spokesman for over 20 years.
Career: Joined *Hugh James* in 1963. Qualified in 1966 and become a Partner the same year. Senior Partner in 1970.
Personal: Born 14th January 1943. Educated at Neath Boys' Grammar School 1953-60 and Jesus College, Oxford 1960-63. School Governor. Past Chairman of Parents for Welsh Education. Leisure pursuits include gardening and music. Lives in Peterston-S-Ely, Cardiff.

JONES, Peter
Eversheds, Cardiff (01222) 471147
See under Construction & Civil Engineering, p. 212

MIDLANDS

Pinsent Curtis (6ptnrs/13assts full-time, another 5ptnrs and 9 assts- 25%) "Stylish" and "sensible," a firm that is "a pleasure to do business with." Quality individuals and work. *Carl Garvie* and *Greg Lowson* feature as leading individuals. **Clients/Work:** Acting for Nottingham County Council in £10m claim for misfeasance in public office and GEC Alsthom Ltd in three multi million

pound arbitrations. Also act for IMI plc, Misys plc and GKN plc.

Wragge & Co (4ptnrs/14assts) The "efficient" team includes *Paul Howard* although they have a reputation for sometimes being overly forceful. **Clients/Work:** Involved in the multi-million pound class action for 125 farmers against the National Farmers Union in respect of compensation for loss of milk quota. Act for BG, Massey-Ferguson, Rover and PowerGen.

Eversheds (8ptnrs/29assts (not all f/t) spread over Birmingham, Nottingham and Derby) Another "efficient" litigation department including husband/wife team *Sarah* and *Martin McKenna*. **Clients/Work:** Involved in claims by Investors Compensation Scheme seeking to recover compensation paid to 700 investors and claims by West Bromwich Building Society against 400 solicitors. Also act for Norwich Union, Thorntons plc and The University of Derby.

Edge & Ellison (8ptnrs/15assts) Head of litigation *Digby Rose* continues to have a high profile. *Jayne Willetts* is "a good operator" who appeared as a solicitor advocate in two Court of Appeal cases this year (Jones v Midland Bank Trust Co and Cott(UK) Ltd v FE Barber Ltd). **Clients/Work:** Represent Leicester City FC in dispute with supporters over travel to Madrid for UEFA match. Acted in Iberotravel Ltd v Pallas Leasing (payments into court).

Browne Jacobson (5ptnrs/25assts-80%) One of the leading litigation practices in the East Midlands - "very able and pleasant to deal with." **Clients/Work:** Acted for Stanton plc in nuisance case and Knitting Industries Federation in water case.

Martineau Johnson (3ptnrs/5 assts) *Andrew Spooner* is the head of the firm's litigation department which is regarded as "professional, straight down the line, not a soft touch." **Clients/Work:** Antonio Merloni SpA v National Homecare Ltd; Reflex

Developments Ltd v Millward; Maple Mechanical Services Ltd (in liquidation) v Maddox.

Freeth Cartwright Hunt Dickins (8ptnrs/14assts) A major player in the East Midlands. Their "thorough understanding of business" makes them popular with clients. *Guy Berwick* remains well regarded. **Clients/Work:** Daylay Foods Ltd, Coldseal Windows Ltd, British Gas Energy Centres Ltd.

Gateley Wareing (1ptnr/7 others) Seen as "sensible, competent and commercial" and particularly noted for banking work. **Clients/Work:** Cradley Group Holdings plc, Clydesdale Bank plc, Wilson Finance plc.

Kent Jones and Done (1ptnr/5assts) "Fairly strong litigators." **Clients/Work:** Handling category A action against the Coal Authority in respect of allegedly negligent replies to mining enquiries; acting for charity being sued for repayment of donations by the Foundation for New Era Philanthropy. Act for JCB plc; Norton plc and The Crown Estate.

Knight & Sons (3ptnrs/9assts) Perceived as a "safe pair of hands" and a "quality practice." **Clients/Work:** Advising steelwork subcontractor in multi million pound dispute relating to Royal Saudi Arabian Navy contract; advising US Fortune 500 corporation in relation to Hong Kong power station; advising local MEP on World Cup ticket allocation.

Dibb Lupton Alsop (4ptnrs/14assts) The Birmingham office is "growing strongly" but has yet to make a "major impression" in litigation. **Clients/Work:** Satnam Investments Ltd v Tesco Stores Ltd (declaration that property development contract had been abandoned); Satnam v Dunlop Heywood (breach of confidence); advising Conoco in judicial review against Customs & Excise.

George Green & Co (2ptnrs/3assts) Based in the Black Country they continue to make a favourable impression in the Midlands. **Clients/Work:** Include three FE colleges, large industrial (metal) manufacturers, and large local builders.

Hewitson Becke + Shaw The Midlands team is less high profile than its Cambridge counterpart. **Clients/Work:** Act for 1,500 Barings preference shareholders in proceedings brought by liquidators and one of the parties in £1 billion claim arising out of collapse of British & Commonwealth Bank.

Shakespeares (4ptnrs/12assts- not all full time) Considered a "highly professional firm."

Shoosmiths & Harrison (6ptnrs/9assts) Are regarded by some as a "bulk work" firm, well-known for their national presence. **Clients/Work:** Acted in The Mead Corporation v Riverwood Multiple Packaging; Cardona and Williams.

Bell Lax Litigation (2ptnrs/4assts) A dedicated litigation firm. **Clients/Work:** Challenged ICC arbitral award in the High Court. Acted for an accountant "partner" in bringing section 459 proceedings. £1m claim for professional negligence against accountants and solicitors relating to tax law and duties in matrimonial proceedings.

Herbert Wilkes (5ptnrs/4assts) Have a good reputation and a pleasant approach. **Clients/Work:** Jewson, Avis, EMI records

Lee Crowder (2ptnrs f/t; 3ptnrs 50%; 5assts-70%) A "niche firm," who are "making progress." **Clients/Work:** Include Wesleyan Assurance Society, IM Properties plc and NFC plc. British Fittings plc v Taylor (breach of warranty). R v Ashworth & Ball – Landhurst Leasing plc (white collar fraud).

LEADERS' PROFILES · MIDLANDS

BERWICK, Guy
Freeth Cartwright Hunt Dickins, Nottingham
(0115) 936 9369
Offices at Derby and Leicester
Specialisation: Solving problems, especially complex disputes, at the right time, in the right way, ensuring the most realistic result at the right price. Wide experience of all commercial disputes especially construction, engineering, artbitration and insolvency recovery. Considerable experience of injunctive work, often acts as supervising solicitor in Anton Piller injunctions. Developed his firm's bespoke innovative "Winning Without Trial®" dispute resolution service.
Prof. Memberships: Fellow of the Chartered Institute of Arbitrators.
Career: 1979: LLB Nottingham University.

1994: FCIArb. 1996: LLM Advanced Litigation (with Distinction) - Nottingham Law School. Qualified 1982. Joined present firm 1983, Partner, Commercial Litigation
Personal: Interests include Football and Blackburn Rovers. Married to Kathy, two daughters, Katrina and Stephanie.

GARVIE, Carl
Pinsent Curtis, Birmingham (0121) 200 1050
Specialisation: Head of litigation in Birmingham. Specialises in corporate and commercial litigation including warranty claims, shareholder disputes, fiduciary duty claims and commercial contractual disputes. Considerable experience in Mareva, Anton Piller and other injunctive relief applications, including acting as the court-appointed supervisor of Anton Piller orders.

Prof. Memberships: Law Society.
Career: MA Trinity Hall, Cambridge. Articled at *Pinsent & Co.* Qualified in 1986. Partner in 1991. Head of litigation (Birmingham) in January 1997.
Personal: Soccer, music, gymnasium.

HOWARD, Paul
Wragge & Co, Birmingham (0121) 233 1000
Specialisation: Commercial litigation; construction
Career: Articled *Wragge & Co.* Qualified 1975. Partner at *Needham & James* 1980-1993, Partner *Dibb Lupton Broomhead* 1993-94, Partner *Wragge & Co* from 1995.
Personal: Born 1948.

LOWSON, Greg
Pinsent Curtis, Birmingham (0121) 200 1050
Specialisation: Commercial litigation; arbitration and construction. Recently completed three multi-million pound construction arbitrations, one of which was successfully determined in the Court of Appeal and which set the first law on the M/F1 form of engineering contract. Also head of banking litigation unit, regularly obtaining Mareva injunction relief without using counsel for a number of financial institutions on a national basis.
Prof. Memberships: Law Society; Insolvency Lawyers Association.
Career: Qualified 1984. Joined *Pinsent & Co* as partner in 1981 from *Ashurst Morris Crisp*.
Personal: Tennis; golf.

MCKENNA, Martin N.
Eversheds, Birmingham (0121) 233 2001
Partner. Head of Litigation.
Specialisation: Main areas of practice are commercial litigation and dispute resolution. Has a wide experience of professional negligence and contract disputes with particular expertise in handling group actions. Other areas of interest include insolvency and financial services litigation.
Prof. Memberships: Law Society. Birmingham Law Society. Society of Practitioners of Insolvency. European Insolvency Practitioners Association. Insolvency Lawyers Association.
Career: Articled at *Evershed & Tomkinson*. Qualified 1980. Partner 1987. Head of Department 1994+.
Personal: Born 1955. Educated at Birmingham University and Lincoln College, Oxford. Interests include rugby and cricket.

MCKENNA, Sarah L.
Eversheds, Birmingham (0121) 233 2001
Partner in Litigation Department.
Specialisation: Work covers contract, negligence, insurance (including personal injury and medical negligence) and all types of commercial litigation; recently, with a particular specialism in Group actions. Also handles intellectual property and defamation work. Marker for Law Society Final Examinations. Tutor at Birmingham University 1982-83.

Prof. Memberships: Law Society, Birmingham Law Society, Birmingham Medico Legal Society.
Career: Qualified in 1984. Articled at *Wragge & Co.* 1982-84. Joined *Eversheds* in 1984, becoming a Partner in 1992.
Personal: Born 26th January 1959. Attended Queenswood School, Hatfield 1969-75; Loughborough Technical College, 1976-78 and Birmingham University 1978-81. Leisure interests include photography, music and swimming.

ROSE, Digby H.
Edge & Ellison, Birmingham
(0121) 200 2001
Head of Litigation.
Specialisation: Commercial dispute resolution and litigation. Has wide experience covering contractual disputes, computer claims and contentious intellectual property work. Other areas of interest include defamation and professional negligence. Also advises on partnership issues. Cases include substantial disputes concerning computer systems, industrial machinery, engineering plant and media contracts as well as claims resulting from the acquisition and sale of businesses. Member of the Editorial Board of Current Law Week and regular contributor - Focus on Civil Litigation.
Prof. Memberships: Law Society, Birmingham Law Society.
Career: Qualified in 1975. Worked in London for four years before joining *Edge & Ellison* in 1979. Became Head of Commercial Litigation in 1990.
Personal: Born 16th September 1950. MA Gonville & Caius College, Cambridge. Honorary Secretary of Birmingham Botanical Gardens. Leisure interests include music. Lives in Birmingham.

SPOONER, Andrew Nicolas
Martineau Johnson, Birmingham
(0121) 200 3300
Partner and Head of Litigation Department.
Specialisation: Main area of practice is commercial litigation (both in the High Court and arbitration). In particular, handles claims arising from product liability and defective

goods and machinery in the engineering industry. Has acted in a variety of large claims involving the engineering industry, including robots, cranes, mining equipment, furnaces, diesel trains, power stations, industrial conveyors, plastic extrusions, computers, boilers, radiators and domestic appliances. Author of articles for 'Court Brief'. Addressed seminars on Trading Conditions, the Millennium Bomb and gave a presentation on High Court litigation in the UK at a conference in Hong Kong. Has supervised the acquisition and installation of a fully computerised Document Management System for *Martineau Johnson*.
Prof. Memberships: Chartered Institute of Arbitrators, Centre for Dispute Resolution.
Career: Qualified in 1978. Partner in 1980 and Head of Litigation in 1989. Fellow of the Chartered Institute of Arbitrators in 1995 and Accredited Mediator (CEDR).
Personal: Holds an LLB (1975). Leisure interests include golf, cricket, walking the dog and the Arts.

WILLETTS, Jayne
Edge & Ellison, Birmingham
(0121) 200 2001
Specialisation: Partner - Commercial Litigation Department. Specialises in most aspects of commercial litigation including professional negligence, pensions litigation and trust and probate litigation. Principal asset is depth and breadth of litigation experience. Qualified as first woman High Court Solicitor Advocate 1994.
Prof. Memberships: First female Chairman Law Society National Young Solicitors' Group 1990 - 1991; member Birmingham Law Society Council and Civil Litigation Committee; also Deputy Vice-President and Public Relations Officer for Birmingham Law Society; member Court Users Committees for both Mercantile Court and the Chancery Division in Birmingham. Member American Bar Association.
Career: Qualified in 1982. Joined *Edge & Ellison* 1988 - Partner from 1991.
Personal: Born 1958. Educated at Stourbridge High School for Girls and University College London. Leisure interests include equestrian sports, tennis and gardening. Lives Stourbridge.

EAST ANGLIA

Eversheds (Ipswich: 1assoc/1asst; Norwich: 4ptnrs/2assts) A firm with a "good profile" that you "can do business with." *Paul*

Matthews is "thorough" and *Max Roessler* is "technical" and a "good litigator." **Clients/Work:** North Norfolk District Council v Tesco – acted for Local Authority in dispute over the implementation of planning permission for a supermarket site; Peak v RW Peak (King's Lynn) & Others – acting in a shareholders dispute involving a claim for rectification of the register of members; QV Foods v Eternit UK Ltd & Others – successfully defended a buildings product liability claim.

Mills & Reeve (5ptnrs/8assts with the larger team based in Cambridge) Highly regarded although most felt the firm's main strength now lies in the Cambridge office. Nevertheless the "well respected" and "smooth" *Edward Callaghan* is based in Norwich, keeping this office in the tables as well. **Clients/Work:** Include: Anglian Group Plc, Oceonics Group Plc, Sentry Farming Group

Plc, Barnham Broom Plc, NHS Trusts. £20m breach of contract claim for a university; successfully struck out professional negligence claim for £350m; pursuing £6.5m claim for damages/consequential loss for the manufacturer of printed circuit boards.

Birketts (5ptnrs/2assts) *Robert Wright* is highly regarded. **Clients/Work:** Work is spread across several departments including shipping and international trade, construction and general commercial litigation.

Greenwoods (3ptnrs/3fee-earners) Particularly rated for construction work. **Clients/Work:** Work is handled by the Commercial Dispute Resolution Group and the department actively promotes mediation. Acting for English subsidiary of German parent company in defence of claim for £4.5m for breach of contract; acting on behalf of a minority shareholder in Isle of

Man company dispute to protect property assets of that company in Spain; acting for a farming co-operative with a Court of Appeal contractual dispute concerning terms of payments due to its members.

Hewitson Becke + Shaw (2ptnrs/6assts) **Clients/Work:** Act for a major energy supplier on a dozen multi-million pound claims, including one involving a syndicate of 12 County Councils and 64 District Councils; represent one of the parties involved in a £1bn claim arising out of the collapse of the British & Commonwealth Bank; represented a client involved in jurisdictional dispute over Formula 1 sponsorship contract.

Prettys (2ptnrs/6 fee-earners) Felt to be predominantly insurance based and now under pressure from larger firms in the area, but *Peter Blake* received several recommendations. **Clients/Work:** Handle debt recovery, shipping and transport, arbitration and general commercial litigation. A multi faceted cross jurisdictional dispute with a supplier involving several sets of proceedings; instructions include construction contracts, professional indemnity, agency and general debt collection from a major Plc.

Howes Percival (1ptnr, 3 fee-earners plus an insolvency team) Best known for insolvency work, the firm was generally recommended. **Clients/Work:** Number of contractual disputes. Clients include the DTI.

Taylor Vinters (2ptnrs/5fee-earners) *Edward Perrott* heads the team. **Clients/**

Work: Majority of work relates to contractual disputes with professional negligence claims also forming a large part of the caseload. Conducted large claims in the telecommunications and technical fields for Philips and other leading companies.

LEADERS' PROFILES · EAST ANGLIA

BLAKE, Peter L.B.
Prettys, Ipswich (01473) 232121
Specialisation: Handles a range of commercial litigation including sale of goods, warranty claims, carriage of goods by road (domestic and CMR), freight forwarding and construction. Clients include insurance, construction, road haulier and freight forwarding companies.
Prof. Memberships: Law Society, Eastern Builders Federation, Felixstowe Port User's Association.
Career: Qualified in 1987. Partner in *Prettys* Commercial Litigation Department since 1991.
Personal: Born 1963. Educated at King Edward VI School, Norwich 1973-81, Exeter University 1981-84 and Guildford College of Law.

CALLAGHAN, Edward J.
Mills & Reeve, Norwich +44 (0)1603 660155
Partner in Commercial Litigation Department.
Specialisation: Main areas of practice include banking, insolvency and building/construction litigation. Also covered is professional indemnity work relating to architects, surveyors, engineers and solicitors. Has addressed seminars to Barclays Bank and Building Employers Confederation.
Prof. Memberships: Law Society, Legal Panel Eastern Builders Federation, Former Council Member Norfolk and Norwich Medico-Legal Society.
Career: Qualified with *Mills & Reeve* in 1974. Became Partner in Commercial Litigation Department in 1979.
Personal: Born 25th February 1950 in

Middlesex. Attended Franciscan College, Buckingham 1961-68, then Exeter University 1968-71. Chairman Norwich Chamber of Commerce. Leisure pursuits include squash, orienteering, reading and the Internet. Lives Norfolk Broads.

MATTHEWS, Paul
Eversheds, Norwich (01603) 272727
Partner in Commercial Litigation Department.
Specialisation: Principal area of practice is contract-based litigation and dispute management including sale of goods and services in various commercial and industrial sectors (chemicals, manufacturing, agriculture and motor retail). Also handles insolvency matters and land compensation. Acts for insolvency practitioners in pursuing and defending a wide variety of claims arising during mainly corporate insolvencies. Has been involved in a wide variety of high value contract disputes. Insolvency work has included R.O.T cases, challenging IVA's, director disqualification, wrongful trading and preferences. Experienced in various forms of alternative dispute resolution. Charge-out rate is £165 per hour.
Career: Qualified in 1982. Became a Partner at *Eversheds Daynes Hill & Perks* in 1985. Has obtained CEDR Mediator accreditation.
Personal: Born 25th September 1953. Educated at Culford School 1966-71, Hatfield Polytechnic 1971-75 (BA Hons in Business Studies) and the College of Law. Leisure activities include golf, shooting, jazz saxophone, wine and food. Lives in Mattishall, Dereham, Norfolk.

PERROTT, Edward
Taylor Vinters, Cambridge (01223) 423444
Partner and Head of Commercial Litigation.
Specialisation: Specialising in leading edge technology, precision engineering and high quality manufacturing clients. Litigation covering infringement of intellectual property rights, contractual disputes and professional negligence.
Prof. Memberships: Law Society.
Career: Jesus College, Cambridge 1965-68; Retail business owner in Beirut 1968-73; Trained and practised in London with *Crossman Block and Keith* 1974-1980; Joined *Taylor Vinters* in 1981.
Personal: Interests include skiing (Member of the Downhill Only Club), sailing and cricket.

ROESSLER, Max
Eversheds, Norwich (01603) 272727
Specialisation: Professional Negligence, Construction, Product Liability.
Prof. Memberships: Law Society
Career: Admitted: 1981. Partner: 1986

WRIGHT, Robert J.
Birketts, Ipswich (01473) 232300
Specialisation: Commercial litigation. Professional Negligence.
Prof. Memberships: Law Society.
Career: Qualified 1975. Joined *Birketts* from *Slaughter and May*. Partner since 1984.
Personal: Educated at Dulwich College and Christ's College Cambridge. Interests in sport, music and cinema. Fluent in French.

NORTH WEST

Dibb Lupton Alsop (Liverpool – 3ptnrs/5assts; Manchester – 6ptnrs/3assocs/8assts) The Liverpool office received particular commendation but both offices are "good to deal with" and "tough, but not stupidly so." People hear good things about *Tony Winterburn*. **Clients/Work:** Stagecoach plc, CRT Group plc, Guardian, British Waterways, Granada Entertainments Ltd. Instructed in a mediation concerning a government supply contract; advising a processing company in a multi-party toxic tort case; a million pounds plus warranty claim arising from a share sale agreement.

Eversheds (5ptnrs/14assts) Perceived as a small but high quality office. *Antony Gold* has a good name and heads the team in Manchester (which also includes *Mark Mattison*) as well as being National Head of Litigation for Eversheds. **Clients/Work:** BTR and British Aerospace plc. Successfully pursued one action valued in the region of £8m on behalf of all 236 individual investors against a stockbroker in relation to the collapse of an investment scheme; Anton Piller orders and Mareva injunctions.

Addleshaw Booth & Co (7ptnrs/10assts who also work at the Leeds office) "Some good commercial litigation work on the back of a fabulous corporate department" was the generally held view about the practice. Team includes *John Gatenby* and *John Gosling*. **Clients/Work:** Arthur Andersen, Asda Stores Plc, Derbyshire Tertiary College, Leeds

DIBB LUPTON ALSOP Liverpool
EVERSHEDS Manchester
ADDLESHAW BOOTH & CO Manchester
COBBETTS Manchester
DAVIES WALLIS FOYSTER Liverpool
HILL DICKINSON Liverpool
HALLIWELL LANDAU Manchester
HAMMOND SUDDARDS Manchester

**HIGHLY REGARDED FIRMS
NORTH WEST**

Berg & Co Manchester
Pannone & Partners Manchester
Berrymans Lace Mawer Liverpool, Manchester
Brabner Holden Banks Wilson Liverpool, Preston
Chaffe Street Manchester
Cuff Roberts Liverpool
Davies Arnold Cooper Manchester
Slater Heelis Manchester
Vaudreys Manchester
Weightmans Liverpool

United plc, Sheffield United plc, Scottish Provident, Trouw UK. Acted for Plaintiff on Lancaster City Council -v- Unique Group Ltd (A Noel Edmonds Company) – Unique claimed damages estimated at £7m, the case was settled for £950k inclusive of interest and costs; advised international manufacturer of electrical sanitary ware, Vortoplast (UK) Ltd in action for malicious falsehood brought by Saniflo Ltd.

Cobbetts (2ptnrs/4assts) Generally well regarded, with a "strong property background." The team has a reputation for being "sensible and constructive." *Robert Roper* is "realistic, efficient and commercial." Clients/Work: CRS, Royal Bank of Scotland Plc, P&O Properties, Royal Sun Alliance, Lookers plc, Cheshire BS, Brittannia BS and other societies.

Davies Wallis Foyster (6ptnrs/10assts) Professional negligence is a major part of the "solid" commercial litigation practice which is highly thought of by most interviewees. *Christopher Sorrell* is "canny and astute." Edward Bootland has left the firm for Willan Bootland White, and remains in our lists. Clients/Work: £30m professional negligence claim; £20m+ injunction/judicial review for a national retailer; breach of confidentiality claim for a major UK clearing bank.

Hill Dickinson (8ptnrs/10-11assts form the mercantile department) A highly praised practice with an insurance bias, and some "cracking insurance clients." Clients/Work: The mercantile department deals both with general commercial disputes and specialised disputes such as shipping, environmental, construction and goods in transit.

Halliwell Landau (7ptnrs/12assts excluding further teams for insurance litigation, insolvency and IP) Received a mixed

review this year although they clearly have a substantial team (including *Paul Rose* and *Paul Thomas*) and client base. Clients/Work: Successful appeal to the House of Lords in the matter of GSG and Trafalgar House; successful appeal to the Court of Appeal on the leading authority on the responsibilities and liabilities of stakeholders in commercial transactions. Presently advising on professional indemnity claims value £100m+.

Hammond Suddards (2ptnrs/4assts) Seen as working from a corporate base and with a smaller presence than some of their other offices. Clients/Work: Include a major pension fund dispute; a multi-million pound warranty claim in the photocopying industry; international mediation for an opthalmic distributor.

Berg & Co (5ptnrs/6assts) "A small operation but well run." *Charles Khan* heads the team. Clients/Work: Barry Dale v The Littlewoods Organisation Plc – successfully negotiating settlement of the Plaintiff's claim for wrongful dismissal; identifying and attacking the perpetrators of multi-million pound property fraud in retail sector; acting for a freight forwarding and warehousing company and securing leave to enforce security under a general lien.

Pannone & Partners (7ptnrs/5assts/6 other fee-earners) Felt to be stronger in other areas but now expanding their commercial litigation team rapidly. Clients/Work: The Granada Group, Manchester Airport Plc, Texaco Ltd. Substantial and complex "realisation of security action" for a major brewery client; defending a client who was sued for patent infringement and successfully counterclaiming to challenge that patent's validity; multi-million pound off-shore loan dispute.

Berrymans Lace Mawer (6ptnrs/9assts) Regarded as an insurance based personal injury practice rather than mainstream commercial litigators. Clients/Work: Alleged commercial fraud involving a high street bank (est. value £2m); acting for a record producer in a claim against a number of parties for studio failure (est. value £5-£10m); acting for an international company in proceedings arising from explosion (est. value £800K).

Brabner Holden Banks Wilson (Liverpool: 2ptnrs/6assts; Preston: 2ptnrs/3assts who also do work in other areas of litigation.) An "old established firm," generally well respected. Clients/Work: Case that tests the extent and effectiveness of an arbitrator's judicial immunity from suit; successfully removing a liquidator in circumstances where there was no allegation of misconduct against him but because he must be seen to be independent; instructions to act for a Franchise Group (30) alleging Directors' misrepresentation.

Chaffe Street (5ptnrs/3other fee-earners) A "small but effective" practice that contains the highly regarded *Ian Tranter*. Clients/Work: National Computing Centre, Endress & Hauser, Hosokawa Micron and CMP Batteries. Successfully defeating a £15m contractual claim arising in South East Asia and acting on a number of complex banking claims each of over £2.5m.

Cuff Roberts (4ptnrs/6assts form the litigation department which includes contractual disputes) A "weighty firm" for its size, the only criticism being that they can sometimes be "too nice!" Clients/Work: Represent a number of large commercial organisations and Plc's.

Davies Arnold Cooper (2ptnrs/6assocs) Considered to have "good people" but yet to make their full impact on the Manchester market. Clients/Work: Focus on dispute prevention, resolution and litigation in the areas of employment, pensions, insolvency, turnaround and intellectual property.

Slater Heelis (4ptnrs/10other fee-earners) A popular, "traditional" firm which received praise from several practitioners. Clients/Work: NatWest, DTI, Housing Associations, United Norwest Cooperatives, ADT/Thorn Security, the Weir Group.

Vaudreys (2ptnrs/6assts) "Well liked" and "strong on employment" but better known for their insurance-related work. Clients/Work: Handle claims arising out of fire, flood, subsidence, product liability and professional indemnity. Handled Court of Appeal case and successfully negotiated a substantial settlement in a six figure insurance policy wording dispute.

Weightmans (1ptnr/3assts) An "efficient" firm with "good tactical sense." Clients/Work: High profile international enforcement of English arbitration award against Tanzanian nationalised cotton industry. Total of awards approx US$25m; other multi-jurisdictional proceedings in USA, Netherlands, Bulgaria, Turkmenistan, Singapore, Hong Kong, Pakistan, Malawi and Zambia, some going to the highest appellate courts.

**LEADING INDIVIDUALS
NORTH WEST**

GOLD Antony Eversheds
KHAN Charles Berg & Co
MATTISON Mark Eversheds
ROPER Robert Cobbetts
BOOTLAND Edward Willan Bootland White
GATENBY John Addleshaw Booth & Co
GOSLING John Addleshaw Booth & Co
ROSE Paul Halliwell Landau
SORRELL Christopher Davies Wallis Foyster
THOMAS Paul Halliwell Landau
TRANTER Ian Chaffe Street
WINTERBURN Tony Dibb Lupton Alsop

BOOTLAND, Edward T.
Willan Bootland White, Manchester
(0161) 839 1922
Partner in Commercial Litigation Department.
Specialisation: Principal area of practice is
general commercial contract disputes, asset
leasing, hire purchase and sale of goods
disputes involving large pieces of plant and
machinery, trucks and cars. These include
disputes as to title and quality as well as non-
payment and recovery of assets. Clients
include various finance houses and other
trading and manufacturing companies.
Experienced conference speaker. Course
Director for Manchester Law Society Advocacy
Training Courses.
Prof. Memberships: Manchester Law Society
(Member of council), Institute of Credit
Management.
Career: Qualified in 1972. Partner at *Pricketts*
1974-79. Partner at *Foysters* from 1980 *Davies
Wallis Foyster* (1989-1998) *Willan Bootland
White* from 1998. Member of Legal Aid Appeals
Committee since 1985. Deputy District Judge
since 1992.
Personal: Born 5th October 1947. Educated at
King's School, Macclesfield 1956-66 and
Manchester University 1966-69. Colonel,
Territorial Army (Royal Engineers). Member of
Council of the Order of St. John, Greater
Manchester. Leisure interests include skiing,
walking, shooting, music, good food and wine.
Lives in Mobberley, Cheshire.

GATENBY, John K.
Addleshaw Booth & Co, Manchester
(0161) 934 6000
Email: jkg@addleshaw-booth.co.uk
Partner
Specialisation: Advises English and overseas
private and public companies on international
litigation and arbitration matters, including the
enforcement of foreign judgements. Also
advises on commercial contract disputes
including partnership law. Cases handled
include BP Exploration Co (Libya) Ltd v. Hunt,
The Halcyon the Great, The Halcyon Skies and
Noirhomme v. Walklate. General editor of
'Recovery of Money', and has also written on
discovery and inspection of documents. Has
also contributed articles to 'Modern Law
Review', 'Arbitration', and 'Litigation Letter'.
Lectures regularly on civil procedure matters
including international litigation, discovery,
arbitration and ADR.
Prof. Memberships: Law Society, Chartered
Institute of Arbitrators (Fellow), Institute of
Credit Management, IBA, SEG, LSLA,
Commonwealth Lawyers Association,
Commercial Law League of America,
Association of Partnership Practitioners,
Director of CEDR.
Career: Qualified in 1975. With *Linklaters &
Paines* 1973-82. Head of Litigation at *Withers*
1983-84. Joined the firm in 1984, becoming a
Partner in 1985.
Personal: Born 26th April 1950. Educated at
West Hartlepool Grammar School 1962-68 and
Trinity Hall, Cambridge 1968-72. Elder, Poynton
Baptist Church.

GOLD, Antony
Eversheds, Manchester (0161) 832 6666
Head of Litigation - *Eversheds* Manchester.
Former Chairman of *Eversheds* National
Litigation Group.
Specialisation: Main area of practice is
Intellectual Property and Contract Litigation.
Has dealt, in particular, with a number of
substantial passing off cases but deals also
with trade mark, patent and copyright litigation.
Other previous experience includes acting in
'Brady v. Brady' (House of Lords, 1988), Barlow
Clowes, BCCI, Lancashire and Yorkshire
Assurance Society. Has acquired extensive
media experience.
Prof. Memberships: Law Society. International
Bar Association, International Arbitration Club.
Career: Qualified in 1983, joined *Eversheds
Alexander Tatham* in 1984 and became a
Partner in 1988. Chairman of *Eversheds'*
National Litigation Group 1993-1998.
Personal: Born 26th August 1958. Attended
Birkenhead School 1969-76, then Manchester
University 1976-9 and Chester College of Law
1979-80. Leisure interests include climbing and
mountaineering. Lives in Adlington, Cheshire.
Married, three children.

GOSLING, John A.
Addleshaw Booth & Co, Manchester
(0161) 934 6000
Head of Litigation and Dispute Resolution
Group.
Specialisation: Professional negligence work,
particularly financial services industry claims,
valuers, surveyors and barristers,
predominantly on behalf of insurers.
Experienced in broader heavyweight
commercial disputes and property based
claims.
Prof. Memberships: Law Society, Manchester
Law Society.
Career: Qualified in 1984. Employed at
Addleshaw Sons & Latham since 1982. Became
partner in 1990. Appointed Head of Group in
May 1998.
Personal: Born 22nd July 1959. Educated at
Shrewsbury School 1973-77 and Durham
University 1978-81. Leisure pursuits include
sport and family. Lives in Wilmslow, Cheshire.

KHAN, Charles
Berg & Co, Manchester (0161) 833 9211
Specialisation: Charles Khan is a Partner in
the Commercial Litigation Department. He
specialises in commercial litigation, including in
particular contract disputes (special expertise
in disputes in the textile and clothing sector),
concerning quality, title, non-payment;
professional negligence; landlord and tenant;
advising office holders, companies and
individuals on insolvency related matters. He was
appointed a Deputy District Judge in June 1994.
Prof. Memberships: Law Society; Manchester
Law Society.
Career: Qualified in 1980. Joined *Berg & Co* in
1982 and became Partner in 1984. Appointed
Deputy District Judge in the Northern Circuit in
1994.
Personal: Born 21 June 1956. Educated Stand
Grammar School and Hull University. Enjoys
cycling, football, cricket, cinema. Lives in
Prestwich, Greater Manchester.

MATTISON, Mark
Eversheds, Manchester (0161) 832 6666
Partner in Commercial Litigation Department.
Specialisation: Main areas of practice are
construction litigation, shareholder disputes
and professional negligence claims.
Prof. Memberships: Law Society. Past
President of Manchester Law Society.
Associate, Chartered Institute of Arbitrators.
Member Society of Construction Law. Council
Member Manchester Chamber of Commerce
and Industry. Chairman Franco British Business
Club. CEDR accredited mediator.
Career: Articled at *Alexander Tatham* (now
Eversheds) 1972-1974 and became a partner in
1978.
Personal: Born 26/4/1951. Attended Liverpool
College and studied Law in Liverpool. Leisure
pursuits include cycling, swimming and
overseas travel. Lives in Hale, Cheshire.

ROPER, R.A.
Cobbetts, Manchester (0161) 833 3333
Partner in Commercial Department.
Specialisation: Principal area of practice is
intellectual property. Work includes litigation on
all types of trade mark, passing off, copyright
and design right matters as well as mechanical
and electrical patent proceedings. Also handles
commercial litigation including large
commercial contract disputes with overseas
elements and/or competition law issues (e.g.
Restrictive Trade Practices Act Article 85/86).
Has considerable experience in injunction work
including Anton Piller Orders both in intellectual
property matters and commercial litigation.
Important cases handled include McMillan
Graham & Others v. R R UK Ltd (contempt of
court for breach of interlocutory undertakings in
passing off/copyright case) and DTI v. D C
Wilson and others (acted for the major
intermediaries sued by the DTI in the Barlow
Clowes collapse).
Prof. Memberships: Law Society, Manchester
Law Society, Licensing Executive Society.
Career: Qualified in 1979 while at *Cobbett
Leak Almond*. Became a Partner in 1983.
Personal: Born 11th August 1953. Educated at
Altrincham Grammar School 1964-71 and the
University of Wales Institute of Science and
Technology 1973-76 (LL.B Hons).

ROSE, Paul M.A.
Halliwell Landau, Manchester
(0161) 835 3003
Partner in Insolvency Department.
Specialisation: Principal area of practice is
receivership and liquidations. Experienced in
handling all types of receivership and
liquidation work for banks and insolvency
practitioners. Regularly presents papers on
insolvency topics at seminars, particularly for
the Society of Insolvency Practitioners. Also
handles non-contentious construction work.
Wide experience in preparing construction
documents, including professional
appointments and collateral warranties.
Recently advised on the construction
documentation for a major office development
in Manchester.
Prof. Memberships: Law Society, Manchester
Law Society, Society of Practitioners in
Insolvency (Associate Member), Fellow of the

Institute of Continuing Professional Development.
Career: Qualified in 1973. Partner at *Halliwell Landau* since 1984. Honorary Lecturer in Law at the University of Manchester.
Personal: Born 30th July 1948. Educated at Manchester Grammar School 1959-67 and St Edmund Hall, Oxford 1967-70. Chairman of First Organisation (formerly Greater Manchester Youth Association). Leisure interests include golf. Lives in Sale, Cheshire.

SORRELL, Christopher R.J.
Davies Wallis Foyster, Manchester
(0161) 228 3702

THOMAS, Paul A.
Halliwell Landau, Manchester
(0161) 835 3003
Partner, 1981. Head of Litigation Department.
Specialisation: All types of commercial litigation, professional indemnity work, Mareva

injunctions and Anton Pillar Orders, landlord and tenant, other property-related disputes.
Prof. Memberships: Law Society of England and Wales.
Career: Qualified 1979, partner at *Halliwell Landau* since 1981.
Personal: Born 1954; squash, rugby, foreign languages.

TRANTER, Ian Victor Keith
Chaffe Street, Manchester (0161) 236 5800
Partner in Litigation Department.
Specialisation: Handles commercial civil litigation including employment law, shareholder disputes and injunctions. Acted in 'Bird Precision Bellows' (minority shareholdings) and 'Hungarian International Bank v. First Energy' (ostensible authority) 'Parkinson v March Consulting Limited' (establishment of reason for dismissal). Clients include financial institutions, public and private companies, and private clients.

Prof. Memberships: Law Society.
Career: Qualified 1982. Partner at *Chaffe Street* since 1989.
Personal: Born 1955. Educated at Chetham's Hospital School, Manchester and St Catharine's College, Cambridge. Interests include skiing, cricket, golf, wine, art history and antiques. Lives in Henbury, Cheshire.

WINTERBURN, Tony
Dibb Lupton Alsop, London (0345) 262728
Specialisation: Associate in Commercial Litigation Department. Main area of practices are commercial contract and warranty disputes, bank recovery and insolvency and corporate litigation, including shareholder disputes.
Career: Qualified 1988 and rejoined *Alsop Wilkinson* (now *Dibb Lupton Alsop*) in 1989.
Personal: Born 17th November 1962. Attended Hull University 1981-84. Leisure pursuits – sport. Lives in Didsbury, Manchester.

NORTH EAST

LEADING FIRMS · NORTH EAST

ADDLESHAW BOOTH & CO Leeds
DIBB LUPTON ALSOP Leeds
EVERSHEDS Leeds
HAMMOND SUDDARDS Leeds

PINSENT CURTIS Leeds
WALKER MORRIS Leeds

HIGHLY REGARDED FIRMS

Andrew M Jackson & Co. Hull
Dickinson Dees Newcastle upon Tyne
Eversheds Newcastle upon Tyne
Hay & Kilner Newcastle-upon-Tyne
Irwin Mitchell Sheffield
Lupton Fawcett Leeds
Ward Hadaway Newcastle upon Tyne

Brooke North Leeds
Ford & Warren Leeds
McCormicks Leeds
Robert Muckle Newcastle-upon-Tyne
Rollit Farrell & Bladon Hull
Wansbroughs Willey Hargrave Leeds
Watson Burton Newcastle upon Tyne

Gordons Wright & Wright Bradford
Gosschalks Hull
Linsley & Mortimer Newcastle-upon-Tyne
Shulmans Leeds

Addleshaw Booth & Co (7ptnrs/10assts who also work at the Manchester office) A "major player" felt to be a leader in terms of volume of work, with a "traditional" style. The "dry" *Peter Cherry* who leads the team received praise, as did *John Priestley.* **Clients/Work:** Arthur Andersen, Asda Stores Plc, Derbyshire Tertiary College, Leeds Utd Plc, Scottish Provident, Sheffield Utd Plc. Writ and injunction against Everton F.C. and Manager Howard Kendall on behalf of Sheffield Utd F.C. – substantial cash settle-

ment obtained; judgement handed down October 1997 in £20m "retrospective taxation" case in European Court of Human Rights on behalf of Yorkshire B.S.; acted for Stockton Borough Council in defeating court action to quash CPOs for £40m City Centre redevelopment scheme.

Dibb Lupton Alsop (2ptnrs/3assocs/ 4assts) A "weighty litigation practice" whose "top people are very good." **Clients/Work:** Stylo Plc – involved on dispute/negotiation with Hush Puppy UK Ltd/Wolverine Inc., Kuwaiti Investment Bank – acting on contract/professional negligence action against UK firm of solicitors, Rugby Joinery, Early Learning Centre, Nestle (UK) Ltd, Halifax Plc, Yorkshire County Cricket Club.

Eversheds (4ptnrs/11assts/5other fee earners) Widely praised by many as having "real strength" and "pre-eminent in commercial litigation." The "highly able" *John Heaps* was also strongly recommended and unanimously praised. **Clients/Work:** Partnership dispute following dissolution of a legal firm; disputes for minority shareholders claiming unfair prejudice; successful defence of claims brought against puppet directors of company under guarantees.

Hammond Suddards (5ptnrs/11assts) Obviously a "major player." In general, the firm was felt to be "highly competent" with "lots of young, hungry people." *Michael Henley* was described as commercial. John Heller was seen to be more involved with managing the firm now. **Clients/Work:** Babcock International Group plc, BBA Group plc, David Brown plc, Fine Art Developments plc, FKI plc, ICI plc

Pinsent Curtis (8ptnrs/4assocs/14other fee earners) Interviewees could not agree about Pinsents in Leeds. Some saw the office as more of a "corporate" practice whilst others saw it as having excellent litigation. Generally, they remain as one of the leading practices. *John Browne* was praised as an

"experienced senior litigator" and a "safe pair of hands," and the team has been strengthened with the arrival of Nigel Kissack, formerly a leading individual at Dibbs in Manchester. **Clients/Work:** Case Inc, Eurocopy plc, Groupe Schneider, MD Foods plc, MDIS, Polypipe plc, Premier Farnell plc, SIG plc, Smith & Nephew plc

Walker Morris (6ptnrs/12assts/25fee earners) Have a "good local reputation," and particularly recommended for its insolvency work. The firm is seen to be good at marketing, dynamic, and successful in building relationships. **Clients/Work:** Croda plc, Empire Stores Group plc, Carlsberg Tetley; Work in 1997 included: advising on a £1.5m claim against insurers for refusal to indemnify; advising on a £2m claim on behalf of an American Corporation; £1.5m defended claim on behalf of a textile machinery manufacturer.

Andrew M. Jackson & Co (3ptnrs/ 5assts) "Well regarded in Hull" as capable litigators. **Clients/Work:** Successful Court of Appeal hearing in resisting an application to stay proceedings in relation to a repair contract for road haulage tankers; successful application for specific performance on a contract for £3.75m followed by successfully resisting an appeal made to the Judge; successfully settled through mediation six figure dispute relating to PVC windows between an international company and a UK window company thereby avoiding proceedings.

Dickinson Dees (4ptnrs/2assoc/5assts) A "well respected" and "excellent" firm which many felt was underrated in the table last year and has accordingly been promoted. Considered by some to have "a monopoly in their region." **Clients/Work:** Several multimillion pound contract claims, several warranty claims in excess of £1m, various instructions on private company shareholder disputes.

Eversheds (4ptnrs/16fee-earners) With the acquisition of Wilkinson Maughan, the firm is now regarded as a major player in the North East. **Clients/Work:** Partnership dispute following dissolution of a legal firm; disputes for minority shareholders claiming unfair prejudice; successful defence of claims brought against puppet directors of a company under guarantees.

Hay & Kilner (6ptnrs/2assts/1fee-earner some of whom do predominantly insurance work) "Not high profile but solidly doing good work," "a super firm but on a small level." Their profile is higher in insurance related work rather than general commercial litigation. *Martin Soloman* is often mentioned. **Clients/Work:** Application to the Court of Appeal to overturn a refusal to grant a Gaming Permit; acting for the ousted Director/shareholder in a shareholder dispute where settlement was negotiated after litigation in the High Court and Industrial Tribunal; a number of cases of breaches of warranty arising out of acquisitions/disposals of companies.

Irwin Mitchell (7ptnrs/2consts/10assts) Better known for insurance and personal injury work. **Clients/Work:** Successfully pursued joint claims for Avesta Sheffield Ltd and British Steel plc; acted on behalf of 8,000 purchasers under the Right to Buy scheme in an action against a local authority relating to service charges; successfully concluded a complex shareholder/breach of warranty dispute relating to an emerging IT business – over £1.5m was recovered for client shareholders.

Lupton Fawcett (4ptnrs/4assts/2 legal execs) Not felt to be a "big player" and with a higher profile in other areas the firm is nevertheless well regarded. **Clients/Work:** Contractual/corporate disputes, professional negligence claims, construction work, partnership issues, landlord and tenant and general litigation.

Ward Hadaway (4ptnrs/7assts) A solid litigation practice with two leading individuals in *Ian Collinson* and *Robert Elliott*. **Clients/Work:** Several multi million pound insurance related disputes; two related multi million pound international product liability disputes; multi million pound contractual

claim against a major television company.

Brooke North (7ptnrs/3assts) Many commented on the predominance of the firm's insolvency practice although to others the team are "good commercial litigators" with a "solid reputation." **Clients/Work:** Rights of way work; Yorkshire Water and claims against the 'Dirty Thirty' based on effluent treatment changes; act for 'deposed' senior company executives; IVA's and bankruptcy; construction and property litigaton.

Ford & Warren (3ptnrs/5assts) A "respectable" firm better known in other fields. **Clients/Work:** Specialise in litigation arising out of Road Transport. Act for Road Haulage Association, Freight Transport Association and Irish Road Haulage Association. Dealing with new claims against the French Government arising out of strike action in 1997; also work in all areas of contract dispute including CMR, Goods in Transit and Carriage of Goods,

McCormicks (5ptnrs/4assts) A well regarded up and coming firm. **Clients/Work:** Major piece of litigation relating to the shareholding and management of a group of sixteen companies operating throughout the country; acting for the Australian Rugby League against The Rugby Football League in connection with its involvement in World Cup 1995; acting in successful litigation claiming malicious presentation of a winding up petition.

Robert Muckle (2ptnrs/1const/9other fee-earners) Received praise for their quality although many felt that size was a limitation. **Clients/Work:** Commercial contract disputes, insolvency, construction and employment.

Rollit Farrell & Bladon (3ptnrs/2assoc) Perceived to act for "some excellent clients," they have a good throughput of work. **Clients/Work:** The commercial and general litigation groups deal with contract disputes, intellectual property, construction, landlord and tenant and property disputes.

Wansbroughs Willey Hargrave (3ptnrs/7fee-earners) A firm which received high praise for its insurance profile rather than general commercial litigation. **Clients/Work:** Act on behalf of insurers and corporate clients. A significant part of the

work is health related, eg.supplier disputes, defending Trusts against allegations of officers' misfeasance and against an allegation of contaminating a local water supply.

Watson Burton (6ptnrs/7fee-earners) Good firm, promoted in the table following favourable comments. **Clients/Work:** The principal activities of the Commercial Litigation Group are employment, construction, professional indemnity, trade and corporate disputes.

Gordons Wright & Wright (5ptnrs/7assts) A "small player" but "solid" with a "constructive commercial approach." **Clients/Work:** Judicial Review of Planning Consents, IP and breach of contract claims as well as general commercial litigation. Clients include Lidl UK GmbH, Wm Morrison Supermarkets Plc, JCT600 Limited and Halewood International Ltd.

Gosschalks (5ptnrs/3assts) The firm's reputation lies in licensing work rather than general commercial litigation but it is felt to have good clients. **Clients/Work:** Primarily deals with litigation for the firm's property and licensing clients but also handles mix of general commercial, IP, construction and insolvency.

Linsley & Mortimer "Small, but very good at what they do," the firm is regarded as mainly insurance based.

Shulmans (2ptnrs/2assts) Not a high profile firm but generally well regarded as "small and competent." **Clients/Work:** Securing and obtaining Mareva type injunctions through the Leeds Mercantile Court, acting for a client who purchases printing machines for onward sale – injunctions are frequently required to preserve the asset while the contract is complied with.

LEADERS' PROFILES · NORTH EAST

BROWNE, John
Pinsent Curtis, Leeds (0113) 244 5000
Partner in litigation department.
Specialisation: Practice covers full range of commercial disputes including construction litigation and arbitration and professional negligence in fields of accountancy, engineering and agriculture.
Career: Qualified 1970. Partner *Simpson Curtis* (now *Pinsent Curtis*) 1977. Former Head of Litigation, Leeds
Personal: Born 1943. Educated at Clee

Humberstone Foundation School and Manchester University (LLB). Interests include wine, Georgian architecture, music and theatre.

CHERRY, Peter J.
Addleshaw Booth & Co, Leeds
(0113) 209 2000
Specialisation: Partner in Litigation and Dispute Resolution Group, dealing with contract disputes and arbitrations.
Prof. Memberships: Qualified 1978, Partner at the firm 1983.
Career: BA Durham 1975.

Personal: Leisure interests include prehistory, wine and coping with small children.

COLLINSON, Ian H.
Ward Hadaway, Newcastle upon Tyne
(0191) 204 4000
Specialisation: Head of Commercial Litigation with particular expertise in professional negligence, insurance and defamation.
Career: Birkenhead School and Kings College, London. Qualified in 1982. Articled and subsequently partner with *Dawson & Co*, London. Head of litigation 1989. Moved to

Newcastle and *Ward Hadaway* 1991. Partner 1992. Head of litigation 1993.
Personal: Golf, sailing and fishing.

ELLIOTT, Robert G.
Ward Hadaway, Newcastle upon Tyne
(0191) 204 4000
Specialisation: Partner dealing with wide range of commercial litigation, primarily heavy/light engineering, IT/high tech, and other manufacturing businesses. Particular interests in intellectual property, company/business sales disputes, shareholders disputes, faulty machinery/manufacturing processes, EU/international.
Career: Attended RGS Newcastle, then Manchester University. Qualified 1983. Practised in London 1981-93; *Herbert Smith, Clifford Chance, Richards Butler* (Partner), Returned to Newcastle 1994 joining *Ward Hadaway* as Partner in 1996.
Personal: Lives in Wall (nr Kexham); married, one daughter;
Interests: hill walking, gardening and cooking.

HEAPS, John
Eversheds, Leeds (0113) 243 0391
Partner. National Head of Litigation. Head of Litigation Department, Leeds and Manchester.
Specialisation: Main area of practice is the management and negotiation of business disputes. Particular expertise in the fields of information technology and company disputes including warranty claims.
Prof. Memberships: Vice-Chairman to Committee 12 (Civil Litigation SGP)

International Bar Association. Fellow of The Chartered Institute of Arbitrators.
Career: Qualified 1978 *Hepworth & Chadwick*, Leeds. *Freshfields* 1978-1984. Joined *Eversheds*, Leeds 1984, partner 1985.
Personal: Born 8th July 1953. Ratcliffe College then Liverpool University 1972-75. Lives near Harrogate, North Yorkshire.

HENLEY, Michael
Hammond Suddards, Leeds
(0113) 284 7000
Specialisation: National Head of Commercial Dispute Resolution Unit and Partner in charge of the Yorkshire office. Specialises in litigation corporate clients, and litigation for various institutional clients such as banks and building societies. Highlights of 1996 included leading the team which successfully salvaged the £28.5 million acquisition of Leeds United Football Club by Caspian, the media group.
Prof. Memberships: Law Society, Leeds Law Society.
Career: Whitley Bay High School, Leicester University and Chester College of Law (1982 LLB). Articled *Broomheads*; qualified 1985. Assistant solicitor *AV Hammond & Co* 1985; specialised insolvency and commercial litigation work 1985-1989. Partner 1989. Head of Commercial Litigation, Leeds, 1994-96. National Head of Commercial Dispute Resolution 1997. Partner in charge of the Yorkshire Offices of *Hammond Suddards*.
Personal: Born 1960. Resides Ilkley. Leisure interests include Football, tennis, guitar,

golf and Nintendo. Member of Ilkley Lawn Tennis and Squash Club and Bradford Golf Club.

PRIESTLEY, John C.
Addleshaw Booth & Co, Leeds
(0113) 209 2000
Specialisation: Litigation with emphasis on banking, building society and insolvency law.
Prof. Memberships: Law Society; Licensed insolvency practitioner.
Career: Articled with the firm 1969-1971; qualified 1971; Partner 1976; Head of Litigation 1990; Head of Banking Group 1993; joint Senior Partner 1993; Head of Banking and Financial Services February 1997.
Personal: Born 1947; King's College, London (LLB AKC MSPI); leisure includes family, sport, reading, theatre and travel.

SOLOMAN, Martin
Hay & Kilner, Newcastle-upon-Tyne
(0191) 232 8345
Specialisation: Full range of commercial disputes including contract, warranty claims, professional negligence and insurance litigation, construction, intellectual property litigation and defamation.
Prof. Memberships: Law Society, Chairman of a Health Authority Disciplinary Committee.
Career: Educated at University of Kent 1971-1974. Joined *Hay & Kilner* in 1984 becoming a Partner that year.
Personal: Born 1953. Lives in Newcastle upon Tyne; leisure pursuits include family, skiing, music and cycling.

SCOTLAND

LEADING FIRMS · SCOTLAND
DUNDAS & WILSON CS Edinburgh
MCGRIGOR DONALD Glasgow
MACLAY MURRAY & SPENS Edinburgh
BRODIES WS Edinburgh
SHEPHERD & WEDDERBURN WS Edinburgh

HIGHLY REGARDED FIRMS
Paull & Williamsons Aberdeen
Simpson & Marwick WS Edinburgh
Anderson Strathern WS Edinburgh
Bird Semple Glasgow
Bishop and Robertson Chalmers Glasgow
Burness Edinburgh
The Morton Fraser Partnership Edinburgh
Anderson Fyfe Glasgow
Balfour & Manson Edinburgh
Biggart Baillie Glasgow
Fyfe Ireland WS Edinburgh
Henderson Boyd Jackson WS Edinburgh
Tods Murray WS Edinburgh
Wright, Johnston & Mackenzie Glasgow

Dundas & Wilson CS (5ptnrs/11assts) Since the merger with Dorman Jeffrey & Co, have a wide litigation practice although they are best known for professional negligence.

Colin Macleod is "sound, commercial and a first class fighter" whilst *John Innes* "has a brain second to none." **Clients/Work:** Acted for Greenpeace in £1.25 damages claim; ten Premier Division football clubs in proposed departure from Scottish Football League; National Union Of Journalists and Shetland News in internet case.

McGrigor Donald (9ptnrs/26assts-50%) Have a spread of work, "some good people" and an extensive client base. Some find them "aggressive" but they are generally considered "very professional." *James Taylor* is a "well regarded, intrepid and able" solicitor advocate." *James Young* and *Eddie MacKechnie* are also highly regarded. **Clients/Work:** Advising BP in proceedings against Greenpeace relating to their protest; FIFA in defence of action relating to Estonia/Scotland match; Imperial Tobacco Ltd in numerous tobacco litigation cases.

Maclay Murray & Spens (6ptnrs-85%; 1asst-90%) An "extremely professional firm" who have "consolidated their position." *Alayne Swanson* has a good reputation, and a "strong personality." Colleague *Ewan Easton* is also recognised as a leading individual. **Clients/Work:** Hiram Walker v Drambuie and Herd v Clyde Helicopters Ltd (aviation). Advising Lazio FC in relation to Paul Gascoigne's transfer to Glasgow Rangers

Brodies (6ptnrs/23 others- all do other

work) *David Williamson* is a "first rate, top man" with a "good brain," currently acting as temporary sheriff. He leads the litigation practice at this "gentleman's firm." **Clients/Work:** Secretary of State for Scotland and Revival Properties Ltd v City of Edinburgh Council; Girvan v Inverness Dairies Ltd; Shetland Times case

Shepherd & Wedderburn (4ptnrs/7 fee earners) A large Scottish firm. The litigation operation is directed by "sensible chap" *Ian Macleod*; he is "very knowledgeable" and is "one of the best." **Clients/Work:** Acting for BA in Abnett v British Airways (claim by passengers held as part of Saddam Hussein's human shield). Represented Scottish Life Assurance Co in landlord and tenant claim involving Agfa Gevaert Ltd. Acted in Aubrey Investments Ltd v E S Crawford Ltd (in receivership) (effect of receivership on lease).

Paull & Williamsons Are an "excellent firm," who are "strong and active." They are the only firm in Aberdeen to feature in this list.

Simpson & Marwick WS (4ptnrs- not full time) Their main strength is in insurance related work, rather than pure commercial litigation. *Peter Anderson* is a "clever chap." **Clients/Work:** Acted for various sub contractors in the Piper Alpha litigation. Also involved in the fatal accident inquiry into the deaths in Lanarkshire from the E.Coli outbreak

Anderson Strathern WS (7ptnrs/10assts-not full-time) *Robert Fife* is recognised as a leading individual. **Clients/Work:** Smith v Bank of Scotland (cautionary obligations)and Universal Import Export GMBH v Bank of Scotland (multiple poinding). Advising Scotmid in connection with E-coli outbreak.

Bird Semple (8ptnrs-70%/7assts) Perceived as a "small, but quality" firm. **Clients/Work:** Hamiltonhill Estates Ltd v Stirling Council; Defending News Group Newspapers Ltd in action by Mohammed Sarwar MP. Act for East of Scotland Water

Bishop and Robertson Chalmers (5ptnrs/4assts-none full-time) Recognised players in the field **Clients/Work:** Involved in Commercial Procedure action for a freight forwarding company; acting for a textile company in connection with a mill purchase dispute; acted for an Italian manufacturer/ lessor of leases to prevent forward sale/lease.

Burness (4ptnrs/7assts-also other work) Continue to have a good reputation. **Clients/Work:** Tarmac Construction Ltd; FairBriar plc. Multi million pound arbitration for oil sector client.

The Morton Fraser Partnership (3ptnrs/3assts) An able firm but they have a relatively low profile in this area. **Clients/Work:** Scottish & Newcastle v Bondway (planning judicial review). Act for numerous parties in claims arising from Braer Oil spill.

Anderson Fyfe (3ptnrs (2 full-time)/ 3 assts) Are seen more as a personal injury firm, but do some commercial litigation. **Clients/Work:** Royal Bank of Scotland, Scottish Enterprise, Conoco (UK) Ltd.

Balfour & Manson (7ptnrs/6assts- 30%) This is an active team with a reputation for "quality," however their profile is much stronger as a leading personal injury firm.

Biggart Baillie (5ptnrs/7assts) Regarded as having "good people and good clients" but without their previous profile. **Clients/Work:** Scottish Power v Britoil (Exploration) Ltd (construction of contracts); Millar & Bryce v Keeper of the Land Register (alleged abuse of position under European law; Norwich Union v /Young (challenging repossession of Name's property arising from Lloyd's membership)

Fyfe Ireland WS (2ptnrs/5assts) Perceived to be "going places," the firm is a worthy inclusion in our lists.

Henderson Boyd Jackson WS (5ptnrs-70%; 4assts) Handle commercial litigation but do not have a high profile. **Clients/Work:** Action concerning recovery and use of documents obtained under "Dawn Raid." Acting for major developers in dispute with local authority over the development of a new town centre for approximately £5m.

Tods Murray WS (3ptnrs/3assts-50%) Players in this field, although to a lesser extent than others. **Clients/Work:** CIS, AA, Slough Estates, Bank of Scotland

Wright Johnston & Mackenzie (1ptnr/2assts) Well-regarded litigation firm. **Clients/Work:** Acting for a local authority in a dispute with developers relating to the letting of an office block; representing a liquidator in a bid to retrieve a director's loan of £230,000, and acting in a partnership dispute.

LEADERS' PROFILES · SCOTLAND

ANDERSON, Peter
Simpson & Marwick WS, Edinburgh
(0131) 557 1545

EASTON, Ewan R.
Maclay Murray & Spens, Edinburgh
(0131) 226 5196
ere@maclaymurrayspens.co.uk
Specialisation: Partner and Head of Litigation Department. Specialises in property litigation, planning issues and employment law. Initiated the series of "stay open" clause litigations in Scotland which have resulted in orders requiring banks, a supermarket and numerous other traders to keep trading operations alive.
Career: University of Glasgow (LL.B 1980). Member of the Council of the WS Society. Worked for *Herbert Smith*, London (1984-85).
Personal: Born 1958.

FIFE, Robert D.M.
Anderson Strathern WS, Edinburgh
(0131) 220 2345
Specialisation: General commercial litigation, advising local authorities, liability insurance litigation and Health Service law.
Career: Qualified 1978. Partner in Litigation Department. Solicitor Advocate. Temporary Sheriff (part-time appointment).
Personal: School Governor.

INNES, John A.D.
Dundas & Wilson CS, Edinburgh
(0131) 228 8000
Specialisation: Partner in Commercial Litigation Group specialising in intellectual property, building and construction law and medical negligence. Acted for Morgan Trust in leading SWAPS case in Scotland (major review by five-judge court of Scottish law of restitution); and in Shetland Times v. Shetland News case on copyright on the Internet; currently acting on leading building design copyright case and in other copyright, trademark and patent litigation.
Prof. Memberships: The Law Society of Scotland.
Career: Attended University of Edinburgh (LLB). Apprentice *Dundas & Wilson CS* 1963-65; qualified 1965; assistant solicitor 1965-66; Partner specialising in litigation since 1966.
Personal: Born 1940. Resides Edinburgh. Leisure interests include music, hill walking and skiing.

MACKECHNIE, Edward M.
McGrigor Donald, Glasgow (0141) 248 6677
Specialisation: Provision of advocacy services in relation to construction related Arbitrations - four Major Construction/Engineering Arbitrations over the last year. Passing off and trademark infringement proceedings in Court of Session and various foreign jurisdictions on behalf of a major Scottish Whisky Company.
Prof. Memberships: Law Society of Scotland.
Career: Glasgow Academy, Glasgow University, Partner *Bishop & Company* 1975 to 1986; Partner *McGrigor Donald* 1986 to date. Dual qualified England and Scotland.
Personal: Leisure interests include golf and skiing. Married with two daughters.

MACLEOD, Colin
Dundas & Wilson CS, Edinburgh
(0131) 228 8000
See under Professional Negligence, p. 676

MACLEOD, D. Ian K.
Shepherd & Wedderburn WS, Edinburgh
(0131) 228 9900
Partner in Litigation Department.
Specialisation: Main areas of practice are general commercial litigation and employment law. Accredited as Employment Law Specialist by Law Society of Scotland. Solicitor in Scotland to Department for Education and Employment. Also solicitor in Scotland to HM Customs & Excise and to Health and Safety Executive. Occasional lecturer in post qualification legal education; Member of Court of Session Rules Council.
Prof. Memberships: Law Society of Scotland, WS Society, Scottish Law Agents Society, Edinburgh Bar Association.
Career: Qualified in 1960. Joined *Shepherd & Wedderburn WS* in 1957, becoming a Partner in 1964.
Personal: Born 19th April 1937. Attended Aberdeen and Edinburgh Universities 1954-59 (MA, LLB). Governor of Rannoch School; Lt. Cdr. RNR (Rtd.)

SWANSON, Alayne
Maclay Murray & Spens, Glasgow
(0141) 221 8586
Specialisation: Partner in Litigation Department; 14 years of experience as a commercial litigator; specialist areas include

contractual disputes, arbitration, employment law, media law, debt collection, and insolvency.Major Cases include: Intellectual Property dispute between Universities of Glasgow and Liverpool concerning the ownership of an academic journal, an Arbitration for Sheraton Hotels, and one of the first cases under the new Commercial Agents Regulations. Appears regularly in Sheriff Court and Court of Session.
Career: Attended University of Edinburgh (LLB Hons, Dip LP). Articled at *Shepherd & Wedderburn* 1982-1984; assistant solicitor Glasgow 1984-1985; foreign associate at *Hughes Hubbard & Reed*,New York 1986-1987; assistant solicitor *Bird Semple Fyfe Ireland* 1987-1990; partner 1990-1993; Partner *Dundas & Wilson* 1994-1997; Solicitor Advocate 1996.
Personal: Born 1959. Resides Glasgow. Leisure interests include music, playing cello and piano, walking.

TAYLOR, James A.
McGrigor Donald, Edinburgh
(0131) 226 7777
Specialisation: Qualified as a solicitor advocate in 1993 and now acts as firm's in-house advocate in the Court of Session. Specialises in commercial litigation.

Represented Central Scotland Police in Lord Cullen's Inquiry into the Dunblane killings.
Prof. Memberships: Convenor of the Rights of Audience Training Course for solicitor advocates.
Career: Attended Aberdeen University, graduating BSc in 1972 and LLB in 1975. Partner in *A. C. Morrison & Richards*, Aberdeen from 1980 to 1986. Partner in *McGrigor Donald* in 1987. Currently the head of litigation department.
Personal: Married to Lesley Macleod and has two children. Interests include golf, good food, fine wine and jazz

WILLIAMSON, David
Brodies WS, Edinburgh (0131) 228 3777
Partner in Litigation Department.
Specialisation: Solicitor-Advocate handling general commercial litigation and specialising in intellectual property, employment law and partnership disputes. Experienced speaker at conferences and seminars. Lectured for over 5 years at University of Edinburgh in Civil Procedure.
Career: Qualified in 1971. With *Simpson & Marwick* 1969-75, latterly as Partner. Joined *Brodies WS* as a Partner in 1976. Part time Industrial Tribunals Chairman and Temporary

Sheriff. Criminal Injuries Compensation Board member.
Personal: Born in 1949. Educated at Royal High School, Edinburgh and University of Edinburgh. Leisure interests include cricket and hill walking. Lives in Edinburgh.

YOUNG, James
McGrigor Donald, Edinburgh
(0131) 226 7777
Specialisation: Has acted in a wide range of commercial claims. Has continual involvement in contractual disputes; in defamation actions; contentious intellectual property disputes and professional negligence.
Prof. Memberships: Law Society of Scotland; Institute of Personnel and Management.
Career: Qualified in 1975 at *McGrigor Donald & Co.* After two years as Legal Officer West Lothian District Council and two years as Assistant Solicitor at *Moncrieff Warren Patterson & Co.*, became Partner in 1979 and joined *McGrigor Donald* as Partner in 1985.
Personal: Born 26 February 1950. Educated at Hutchesons' Boys Grammar School and the University of Glasgow. Leisure interests include watching and participating in sport (now mainly golf); Contemporary Scottish Art and Theatre. Lives in Edinburgh.

NORTHERN IRELAND

HIGHLY REGARDED FIRMS
NORTHERN IRELAND

Carson & McDowell Belfast
Elliott Duffy Garrett Belfast
L'Estrange & Brett Belfast
McKinty & Wright Belfast
Cleaver Fulton & Rankin Belfast
Johnsons Belfast
Tughan & Co Belfast
C & H Jefferson Belfast
Johns Elliot Belfast
Mills Selig Belfast

Carson & McDowell (3ptnrs/5assts, some of whom also work in other areas of litigation) An "excellent" firm where the team includes the respected *Brian Turtle*. Clients/Work: Many cases in the High Court 'commercial list.'

Elliott Duffy Garrett (4ptnrs/3assts) "A well-known firm in commercial litigation." *Michael Lynch* was recommended and *Michael Wilson* is a new entry this year following strong praise. Clients/Work: Professional negligence, defamation, insolvency, construction, planning, arbitration and general contractual disputes. Also product liability – act for tobacco manu-

facturer in major litigation.
L'Estrange & Brett (2ptnrs/2assts) Perceived as "a growing firm" with "more younger partners." *Samuel Beckett* is a well known figure in the field. Clients/Work: Construction and employment law. Work in 1997 included Gilbert Ash Ltd v Beaufort Developments Ltd (House of Lords) which dealt with an issue in relation to arbitration.

McKinty & Wright (3ptners/2assts) A well-regarded firm, not least because of the strong reputation of *Owen Catchpole*. Clients/Work: Includes professional negligence and general commercial disputes.

Cleaver Fulton & Rankin (2ptnrs/2assts) A firm which is perceived as a real specialist in commercial litigation but which lost partner Paul Spring earlier in the year and may therefore have lost some momentum. *Patrick O'Driscoll* heads the team. Clients/Work: Deal with IP, product liability, debt recovery, construction, employment, EEC matters and breaches of contract.

Johnsons (2ptnrs/6assts) A "considerable presence" and a busy year which earned the firm promotion in our tables. Clients/Work: Act for over 20 insurance groups and companies doing "all litigation work."

Tughan & Co (1ptnr/3assts) Have "a significant litigation arm," and handle construction, and insolvency.

C & H Jefferson (3ptnrs/3assts) Recognised primarily for a "huge volume of insurance work." Clients/Work: Contractual disputes, including those involving professional negligence.

Johns Elliot (4ptnrs/1asst) Better known in other areas but also good in commercial litigation. Clients/Work: Contentious construction work. Acting for NIHE the firm had two successful appeals to the High Court by way of Case Stated from an arbitrator.

Mills Selig (2ptnrs) A small firm which has been strengthened by the arrival of Paul Spring (who is a recommended leader in defamation) and his caseload. *Brian Ham* is a leading individual although he may now have a lower profile for this area of work. Clients/Work: Defamation, product liability and company disputes.

LEADING INDIVIDUALS
NORTHERN IRELAND

BECKETT Samuel L'Estrange & Brett
CATCHPOLE Owen McKinty & Wright
HAM Brian Mills Selig
LYNCH Michael Elliott Duffy Garrett
O'DRISCOLL W Patrick Cleaver Fulton & Rankin
TURTLE W.Brian Carson & McDowell
WILSON Michael Elliott Duffy Garrett

BECKETT, Samuel R.
L'Estrange & Brett, Belfast (01232) 230426
Partner.
Specialisation: Main area of work: Civil litigation, including construction and planning law.
Career: Qualified 1980. Partner in *L'Estrange & Brett* since 1986.
Prof. Memberships: Law Society of Northern Ireland.
Personal: Born 1957. Education: Queen's University, Belfast (L.L.B.)

CATCHPOLE, Owen
McKinty & Wright, Belfast (01232) 246751
Partner.
Specialisation: Principal area of practice is what in Northern Ireland is described as Commercial List work. This includes not only 'straight' commercial litigation but also non-medical professional negligence and what in England would be classed as Official Referees business. Also extensive defamation work both advisory and litigation, for print and broadcast media.
Prof. Memberships: Law Society of Northern Ireland, Northern Ireland Supreme Court Rules Committee.

Career: Qualified 1973, Partner in *McKinty & Wright* since 1975.
Personal: Graduated in Legal Science from Trinity College Dublin. Recreations include yoga and target shooting.

HAM, Brian E.
Mills Selig, Belfast (01232) 243878
Specialisation: Property based litigation.
Prof. Memberships: Law Society of Northern Ireland. The Environmental & Planning Law Association for Northern Ireland.
Career: Qualified 1969. Joined *Mills Selig* 1971. Became Partner 1984.
Personal: Sailing, Gardening and Architecture.

LYNCH, Michael P.
Elliott Duffy Garrett, Belfast (01232) 245034

O'DRISCOLL, W Patrick M.
Cleaver Fulton & Rankin, Belfast (01232) 243141
Specialisation: Commercial litigation, serious fraud, multi-document litigation, intellectual property, product liability and judicial review.
Prof. Memberships: The Law Society of Northern Ireland.
Career: Educated at Glenstal Abbey School,

Republic of Ireland and Queen's University of Belfast (BSc Econ). Qualified 1972. Became a Partner in *Cleaver Fulton & Rankin* 1975.
Personal: Born 7 December 1947. Running. Happily married with four children.

TURTLE, W.Brian W.
Carson & McDowell, Belfast (01232) 244951
Specialisation: Commercial litigation (25 years of practice in all major areas). Professional Negligence. Employment law/Industrial relations to include unfair dismissal and religious and sex discrimination claims.
Prof. Memberships: Law Society of Northern Ireland
Career:
1968: LLB – QUB; joined *Carson & McDowell*
1971: Admitted as solicitor
1973: partner in *Carson & McDowell*.

WILSON, Michael W.C.
Elliott Duffy Garrett, Belfast (01232) 245034
Specialisation: Product Liability, including defence of "Tobacco Claims". Insolvency Litigation.
Prof. Memberships: Society of Practitioners of Insolvency.

LITIGATION (PROPERTY)

RESEARCH: In compiling the tables, we consider all the information available to us, paying particular regard to the market research carried out by our team of ten qualified lawyers. (The researchers' details are set out on page three.) The rankings, therefore, reflect the opinion of the marketplace as revealed by systematic and objective research: see page four. (Our research is audited every year by the British Market Research Bureau.)

OVERVIEW: There is some debate amongst practitioners as to whether property litigation is really litigation at all. This is because parties are seeking changes or solutions to problems in the context of continuing long-term relationships rather than dividing the spoils of an irrevocable split. A property litigator does not wish to go to court. Some teams therefore operate out of the property department rather than out of litigation.

It follows that arbitration is commonly used in this field, and last year the Royal Institution of Chartered Surveyors and the Law Society set up training sessions for 30 chartered surveyors and 30 lawyers to sit on a combined panel as arbitrators and independent experts known as PACT ("Professional Arbitration on Court Terms") arbitrators. We have tried to indicate where our leaders are PACT qualified.

In London, while Nabarros remains pre-eminent, Linklaters is storming up into close second place.

In the South East, firms have little experience of each other's work. There were no significant changes in the South West. We have separated Bobbetts Mackan from the other firms as it is distinct in acting for residential tenants. The Welsh market place is limited and dominated by the usual big names. Hugh James are however making particular inroads. Work is becoming more polarised in the Midlands towards Edges, Wragges and Eversheds. Pinsent Curtis move into our North East lists for the first time behind Addleshaws who are still ahead of the Leeds game. In the North West Cobbetts, Dibbs and Eversheds were widely thought to be the lead firms, with dedicated property litigation teams. The picture in Scotland also remains fairly constant.

LEADING FIRMS · LONDON

NABARRO NATHANSON

LINKLATERS

BERWIN LEIGHTON
S J BERWIN & CO
CLIFFORD CHANCE
DENTON HALL
HERBERT SMITH
LAWRENCE GRAHAM
LOVELL WHITE DURRANT

CAMERON MCKENNA
MASONS
ROWE & MAW
SIMMONS & SIMMONS
TITMUSS SAINER DECHERT

HIGHLY REGARDED FIRMS

Ashurst Morris Crisp
Dibb Lupton Alsop
D J Freeman
Macfarlanes
Olswang
Speechly Bircham
Stephenson Harwood

Boodle Hatfield
Dewar Hogan
Maxwell Batley
Radcliffes
Thomas Eggar Church Adams

Druces & Attlee
Field Fisher Waterhouse
Forsyte Saunders Kerman
Maples Teesdale

LONDON

Nabarro Nathanson (3ptnrs/10assts) The largest department and, for many people, the best. Three partners give the firm an edge over the rest. *Iain Travers* runs the show whilst *Nicholas Cheffings* "never fires off something he's not thought about" and "is the sort of guy you can have a spat with and still get on with afterwards." The "formidable" *Jennifer Rickard* is "stunning in every possible way." Recruiting a new assistant in the late summer. Clients/Work: Acting for Eagle Star Life Assurance Co. Ltd against Mannai Investment Co. Ltd in House of Lords in case on validity of break clauses. Acting for Lewisham Investment Partnership against Peter Morgan in case on surveyors negligence and valuation principles in a rent review. Acting for Straudley Investments Ltd against Mount Eden Land Ltd concerning a landlord's unreasonable withholding of consent to an assignment.

Linklaters (2ptnrs/4assts) "You can nearly always cut a deal with Linklaters." Consistently praised for their litigation style. "Settle if you can, and if you can't, litigate on a sensible basis." *Katie Bradford* epitomises this approach and is "thoroughly professional" but "stands her ground when she has to." Clients/Work: Acting for Lehman Brothers on its review of premises at 1/2 Broadgate. Somerfield v Dukeminster in which the Court of Appeal affirmed that a rent review clause must be applied commercially. Conducting Prudential v Messila, the longest trial of a party wall dispute concerning ownership of a strip of land adjacent to a highway. The case is a leading authority on estoppel and adverse possession.

S J Berwin (2ptnrs/2assts) *Vivien King* ("born to win") has focused the group on what matters. **Clients/Work:** Acting for Marks & Spencer plc re Telford shopping centre service charge dispute. Acting for British Land re major rent review of office premises in Broadgate. Acting for Hill Samuel Property Unit Trust re rent review of a whole shopping centre in South Wales.

Berwin Leighton (1ptnr/9assts, banking recovery 3ptnrs/5assts) The "extremely able" *Roger Cohen* "always has original contributions to make to any discussion" and is "pleasant to deal with". **Clients/Work:** Acting for Tesco on a £1.5 million claim against consultants for alleged negligent environmental advice. The dispute was referred to mediation. Acting for Prudential on a claim for rent arrears from an insolvent tenant who counterclaimed for disrepair. A global settlement was acheived with the tenants' receivers.

Clifford Chance (2ptnrs/4assts) "Pleasant to deal with and oozing self confidence." *Wendy Miller* is "just great" and always "aims to get the job done in the most sensible and cost effective way." *John Pickston* is "client friendly and never misses a thing, even when he's working at speed." Focusing on high quality work rather than day to day stuff. **Clients/Work:** Giving strategic litigation advice to Burford Group plc re its £100m acquisition of Stratton St/Berkeley St property portfolio. Acting for Arcadian International plc on its £45m redevelopment of the Great Eastern Hotel, Liverpool St. Acting for Bankers Trust in High Court proceedings concerning professional negligence against a valuer: settled before trial for £2m representing full recovery to the client.

Denton Hall (2ptnr/8assts in London and Milton Keynes) "Tough and effective." You only hear positive things about the "straightforward and no frills" *Carole Peet.* **Clients/Work:** Acting for South Australia Asset Management Corporation in their successful £8m claim against Finers re advice given and not given in connection with the financing of various properties. Appointed to act for Sears Group Properties on a significant proportion of their portfolio. Advising Dockgrange Ltd on a landmark judicial review concerning trans- frontier shipments of waste.

Herbert Smith (2ptnrs/7assts) Their reputation is measured and reasonable. People "like and respect" the "easy to deal with" *Lucy Hutchinson.* **Clients/Work:** The landlord and tenant aspects of the CTRL at Kings Cross/St. Pancras for London & Continental Railways Ltd. Redevelopment of the Bullring, Birmingham for Hammerson. Acting for Standard Life in Court of Appeal case against Unipath.

Lawrence Graham (3ptnrs/7assts) The "no nonsense" *Penny Francis* is "no soft touch." She is now heading the commercial property group. The team will be strengthened by the arrival of a partner from the now disbanded Forsyte Saunders Kerman. (The whole property team of FSK joined in July 1998). **Clients/Work:** Removing tenants from a large site in Oxford St required by Legal & General for a new retail development. National Farmers Union Mutual Insurance Society Ltd v Next plc in a case concerning consent for an assignment given in correspondence before document completed following the Prudential v Mount Eden case. Universities Superannuation Scheme Ltd v M&S plc – a service charge dispute.

Lovell White Durrant (1ptnr/11assts) *Anne Waltham* has impressed. A well-resourced and effective team. **Clients/Work:** Acting for Barclays against Harries in a Court of Appeal case which upheld the bank's entitlement to part of the sale proceeds of a farm, attributable to the milk quota attached to the farm and to the proceeds from leasing the quota out. Acting for the Estates Trustees of the Dulwich Estate seeking approval to vary a Scheme of Management affecting 5000 properties. Acting for BAA in a claim for a substantial turnover rent from a tenant where the tenant unilaterally reduced its rent, claiming BAA had abused its dominant position under Article 86 of the Treaty of Rome.

Cameron McKenna (2ptnrs/7assts) Strong firm seen as "worthy competitors" and very active in this area. *Andrew Walker* heads the department and comes up with good ideas." *Michael Langdon* is "sound." **Clients/Work:** Commencing and dealing with High Court proceedings for Moorfield Estates Plc against tenant to recover arrears of rent and obtain a declaration that the tenant was not entitled to exercise a break-clause. Commencing and dealing with High Court proceedings on behalf of a major US insurance company against a City of London law firm in respect of negligent advice and failure to exercise a break-clause. High Court proceedings in Northern Ireland for an Irish retailer against the landlord of a shopping centre for breach of landlord's covenants following extension works to shopping centre.

Masons (2ptnrs/9assts) *Anne Molyneux* "has the knack of translating complex legal issues into points that even the least sophisticated client can understand." *Siobhan Cross* is "terrific to work with." Taken on two more assistants this year. **Clients/Work:** Acting for Inntepreneur Estates (GL) Ltd in the Court of Appeal against Moore. The CA overturned a finding of fact by a County Court judge and laid down guidelines for dealing with allegations of misrepresentation. Acting for Inntrepreneur against Star Rider Ltd in a test case concerning set off against rent and Article 85 of the Treaty of Rome. Acting for a landlord in connection with the recovery of a series of multi million pound debts in a concerted group of actions involving injunctions and property

insolvency. Achieved 100% recovery.

Rowe & Maw (3ptnrs/1assts) *Michele Freyne* is a "well respected tough cookie" who also does matrimonial work. **Clients/Work:** Acting for the successful tenant in Thameside Properties v Brixton Estates, the leading authority on interpretation of a lease where the mechanisms for ascertaining managing agents' fees has failed. Acting for the successful landlord in Dunn & Bradstreet v Provident Mutual in the Court of Appeal, an authority on agency, estoppel, and conditions precedent to a break clause. Acting for Provident Mutual against Greater London Employers' Association concerning service of notices.

Simmons & Simmons (2ptnrs/6assts) *Carol Hewson* has "presence and a total grasp of the facts." **Clients/Work:** Acting for Bass Lease Company Ltd in a series of actions by tenants of tied houses for damages for alleged breaches of Article 85 the Treaty of Rome. Advising DTZ Debenham Thorpe, the LPA Receivers of the landlord of South Quay Plaza, Docklands in relation to issues arising from the IRA bombing of the building in 1996. Acting for Gallaher Ltd in High Court proceedings for damages for dilapidations.

Titmuss Sainer Dechert (2ptnrs/9assts – also do construction) The firm has a specialist Property Litigation Unit and is traditionally very strong in the retail sector and known for acting for developer clients. The partners can be tough opponents but are considered "effective." **Clients/Work:** Co-operative Insurance Society Limited v Argyll Stores (Holdings) Limited: acting for Argyll Stores in House of Lords re enforcement of keep open covenants by specific performance. Advising landlords and tenants affected by terrorist activities in Canary Wharf and Manchester. Acting for PACE (Property Advisers to the Civil Estate) in substantial proceedings re landlord's dilapidations claim in excess of £18m.

Ashurst Morris Crisp (1ptnr/7assts) Traditionally known for their strong property practice. *Michael Madden* has a reputation for being "hard nosed" and getting the job done. **Clients/Work:** Armgrade Ltd v Parkside Clubs; favourable result in rent review arbitration. R v London Borough of Brent ex parte O'Malley; successfully defending judicial review proceedings arising out of borough's decision to redevelop large housing estate. Thamesworld v Docklands Light Railway.

Dibb Lupton Alsop (1assoc/1asst) Leslie Webber has left and the practice is now small. Reputation based on the firm's client base rather than on the profile of any individual. **Clients/Work:** Landlord & Tenant 1954 matters. Involved in one rent review which will be one of the biggest in the City. Enfranchisement applications under the Leasehold Reform, Housing and Urban

Development Act 1993 and Leasehold Reform Act 1967.

D J Freeman (1ptnr/4assts) Going through a time of change. Property litigation is handled by a small group within the property services department. Two senior assistants were replaced by newly qualifieds in the reorganisation. **Clients/Work:** Department continues to act for range of institutional and entrepreneurial clients.

Macfarlanes (1ptnr/4assts) Leading individual *Willie Manners* divides his time between this and employment work. **Clients/Work:** Acting for administrators of Fosters Menswear re Fosters retail premises. R v Wiltshire CC, ex parte Nettlecombe Ltd and Pelham – injuncted the council from making an order modifying the Definitive Map and Statement, side-stepping the cumbersome statutory inquiry procedure.

Olswang (1ptnr/3assts) "Have a growing reputation" in this field, which is not one automatically associated with them. *Marcus Barclay* is "doing a great job"and is " enthusiastic." **Clients/Work:** Acting for a leisure industry developer in multi-party, multi-million pound construction litigation which resulted in a settlement. Acting for a retail client in an action for negligence against its former solicitors which broke new law on tenant's right of compensation under Landlord & Tenant Act 1954 Part II. Acting for Landlord in contested actions for forfeiture by physical re-entry, the re-entry was upheld by the Court of Appeal.

Speechly Bircham (4ptnrs/2assts) Have had a specialised property litigation department for 25 years. *David Masters* heads the team. **Clients/Work:** Acting for successful appellant in case of Cheverell Estates v Haddon & Harris. Acting for P&O in dilapidations claim of approximately £18m. Acting for Howard de Walden Estates, comprising approximately 1,200 properties, in successfully opposing a 1954 Act lease renewal in the Court of Appeal in an action crucial to the new Conran development in Marylebone.

Stephenson Harwood (2ptnrs/6assts) Described as "low-profile" but a "good, primarily Landlord & Tenant practice." **Clients/Work:** Hammerson UK Properties plc v Commercial Union Assurance Company plc, involving issues of privilege and whether trivial breaches of repairing

covenants nullify tenant's break notice. St.Martins Property Investments Ltd v Citibank plc and CIP Properties Limited, a rent review case going to the Court of Appeal.

Boodle Hatfield (3ptnrs/3assts) Known primarily for their Grosvenor Estate work and for doing insurance and professional indemnity property work. **Clients/Work:** Reported case in Court of Appeal regarding exclusion from security of tenure under Landlord and Tenant Act 1954.

Dewar Hogan (2ptnrs/2assts/1consultant) Unique in being a niche property litigation firm. Set up by ex-Nabarros partner *Ronald Hogan* who also founded the Property Litigation Association. He is praised as "sensible and commercial, a real property lawyer who can litigate – rather than a litigator who turns his hand to property work." **Clients/Work:** Enfranchisement case in the Court of Appeal re statutory interpretation of Restrictive Covenants. Dispute with Building Society re treatment of part redemptions. Proper approach to valuation of improvements in assessing price to be paid by residential leaseholders for an extended lease.

Maxwell Batley (2ptnrs/4assts) Their "good client base means they get good high profile work" and property litigation is an adjunct to their property practice. **Clients/Work:** Drafting lease for Possfund (North-West) Ltd – involving unsuccessful challenge of £1m sinking fund by tenant. Acting for Britel Fund Trustees Limited, plaintiffs in pending action re defective shopping mall in Guildford. Acting for Regent Holdings defending pending action by Sir David Alliance re disputed £10m property sale.

Radcliffes (4ptnrs/6assts) They "keep their clients happy". Head of Department *Rob Highmore* is Vice Chair and Membership Secretary of the Association of Property Litigators. **Clients/Work:** Church Commissioners for England v Baines [1998], a Court of Appeal decision concerning sub-tenants of mixed residential and business premises and their protection under Rent Act 1977. Advising on seven Estate Management schemes (currently part-heard).

Thomas Eggar Church Adams (6ptnrs/3assocs/5assts) The department is "impressive." **Clients/Work:** Railtrack, Perfect Pizza

Druces & Attlee (2ptnrs/2assts) Their

work is mainly forfeiture and possession actions and contested assignments. "A small practice relying on establishment clients and breweries."

Field Fisher Waterhouse (1ptnr/1asst p/t) Act mainly for an institutional client-base. **Clients/Work:** Trial on liability to repair issue – Shell v Macbeth Scott. ICI v Frogmore Investments; extent of parties' obligations where no contract for sale exists. Yamato Transport v Washington Lands; litigation over effect of a break clause after two fires.

Maples Teesdale (2ptnrs –1p/t; 2assts – 1p/t) **Clients/Work:** Now acting for new clients: Wates, Virgin Interactive and PPM Limited.

Richard Butler of Norton Rose was also highly recommended, as was *Lesley Webber* of Beachcroft Stanleys. *Guy Willetts* at Theodore Goddard is an up and coming name.

LEADING INDIVIDUALS · LONDON
BRADFORD Katie Linklaters
CHEFFINGS Nicholas Nabarro Nathanson
COHEN Roger Berwin Leighton
FRANCIS Penelope Lawrence Graham
FREYNE Michele Rowe & Maw
HEWSON Carol Simmons & Simmons
HUTCHINSON Lucy Herbert Smith
KING Vivien S J Berwin & Co
MADDEN Michael Ashurst Morris Crisp
MASTERS David Speechly Bircham
MILLER Wendy Clifford Chance
MOLYNEUX Anne Masons
PEET Carole Denton Hall
PICKSTON John Clifford Chance
RICKARD Jennifer Nabarro Nathanson
TRAVERS Iain Nabarro Nathanson
WALTHAM Anne Lovell White Durrant
WEBBER Lesley Beachcroft Stanleys
BARCLAY Marcus Olswang
BUTLER Richard Norton Rose
CROSS Siobhan Masons
HIGHMORE Robert Radcliffes
HOGAN Ronald Dewar Hogan
LANGDON Michael Cameron McKenna
MANNERS John (Willie) Macfarlanes
WALKER Andrew Cameron McKenna

UP AND COMING
WILLETTS Guy Theodore Goddard

LEADERS' PROFILES · LONDON

BARCLAY, Marcus Robert
Olswang, London (0171) 208 8888
Partner in Litigation Department.
Specialisation: Principal area of practice is property litigation. Handles all aspects of commercial property litigation, including contentious lease renewals, forfeiture actions, rent review arbitrations, service charge disputes and privity actions. Also deals with insolvency including

security enforcement for banks, and acting for liquidators and administrative receivers on all matters arising out of liquidations or receiverships. Important cases include 'Ropemaker Properties v. Noonhaven Ltd' [1989] (considerations which will influence the Court to grant relief from forfeiture) and 'Commercial Union Life Assurance Co Ltd and another v. Woolworths PLC' [1994] (binding variations to rights and obligations of landlord and

tenant to be taken into account on rent review). Clients include leading commercial property companies, major high street retailers, banks and insolvency practitioners.
Prof. Memberships: Law Society.
Career: Qualified in September 1988. At *Rubinstein Callingham Polden & Gale* 1986-90. Joined *Simon Olswang* in August 1990. Became a Partner at *Olswang* in May 1994.

Personal: Born 12th December 1961. Educated at Holland Park School 1971-76, Abingdon School 1976-78 and Warwick University 1981-84. Leisure pursuits include music, sports, cooking, theatre and cinema. Lives in London.

BRADFORD, Katie

Linklaters, London (0171) 456 4234
Partner and Head of Property Litigation Unit.
Specialisation: Specialises in all aspects of property litigation and arbitration, including landlord and tenant; rent reviews; solicitors/surveyor's negligence; insolvency related disputes. Acted for Parisbas in recent rent review case (to the House of Lords: 2 interlocutory points in CA and a record breaking arbitration); acted for BBL in Pointwest litigation; acted for CWS in headline rent cases in CA.

BUTLER, Richard

Norton Rose, London (0171) 283 6000
Partner in Commercial Litigation Department
Specialisation: Specialises in property litigation and arbitration, including landlord and tenant disputes (especially rent review), disputes arising from land transactions, insolvency issues relating to land and secured lending problems. Has conducted cases in all courts up to and including the House of Lords.
Prof. Memberships: Fellow of the Chartered Institute of Arbitrators. Member of the RICS and Law Society PACT Panels. Member of ARBRIX. Member of the Law Society.
Career: Lectures and writes regularly on property and dispute resolution issues.

CHEFFINGS, Nicholas

Nabarro Nathanson, London
(0171) 493 9933
Partner in Property Litigation Department.
Specialisation: All aspects of contentious property work such as landlord and tenant (including major rent reviews), planning/judicial review, rights of light, Lands Tribunal work, professional negligence, environmental litigation, vendor/purchaser and development disputes. Acts as a legal assessor to rent review arbitrators. Instructed in several reported cases. Sits as Mediator. Author of numerous articles and regular speaker at conferences.
Prof. Memberships: Fellow of Chartered Institute of Arbitrators.
Career: Qualified 1983. Partner 1990.

COHEN, Roger D.

Berwin Leighton, London +44 171 760 1000
Partner in Litigation Department.
Specialisation: Main area of practice is property litigation including landlord and tenant, planning-related litigation, environmental claims, rating, ADR, and professional indemnity. Acts as a mediator. Other areas are general commercial litigation and arbitration. Acted for Tesco Stores Ltd in planning gain litigation, Prudential and Central Government. Major clients also include PDFM and Legal & General. Conducts client seminars and regularly contributes articles to the property press.
Prof. Memberships: Fellow Chartered Institute Of Arbitrators, CEDR Accredited Mediator, Administrative Law Bar Association, City of London Solicitors Company, Law Society, Law Reform Sub-Committee, Property Litigation Association.

Career: Articled with *Donnelly & Elliott* in Gosport, then joined *Matthew Arnold & Baldwin* in Watford. Joined *Berwin Leighton* in 1984 and became a Partner in 1989. Head of Contentious Property Group.
Personal: Born 2nd June 1959. Attended Portsmouth Grammar School 1970-77. Leisure pursuits include soccer, music and reading. Lives in London.

CROSS, Siobhan

Masons, London (0171) 490 4000
Partner in Property Litigation Department.
Specialisation: Practice covers all areas of property litigation including Landlord and Tenant litigation such as rent reviews, dilapidations, possession proceedings, and lease renewals and other property related litigation including disputes over joint venture developments, relevant professional negligence claims and rights of light and air.
Prof. Memberships: Property Litigation Association and Landlord and Tenant Committee of CEDR.
Career: Qualified in 1987. Joined *Masons* in 1988 and became a partner in 1993.
Personal: Born 21 July 1962 and lives in North London.

FRANCIS, Penelope J.L.

Lawrence Graham, London (0171) 379 0000
From 1 May 1998, Head of Property Department Partner in Litigation Department.
Specialisation: Main area of practice is property litigation, covering rent reviews, insolvency, shopping centre and portfolio management, lease renewals and dilapidations. Lectures for RICS, ARBRIX and other conferences.
Prof. Memberships: Law Society, Women in Property, Property Litigation Club, Reform Club.
Career: Qualified in 1984. Worked at *Beachcroft Stanleys* 1982-88. Joined *Lawrence Graham* in 1989, becoming a Partner in 1991.
Personal: Born 9th November 1959. Attended University of Bristol 1978-81, then College of Law 1981-2. Leisure interests include ballet, eating and travel. Lives in London.

FREYNE, Michele

Rowe & Maw, London (0171) 248 4282
Specialisation: Main area of practice is property litigation. Started first specialist team in 1980 which has grown into team of 3 partners, 2 assistants, 1 legal executive and 2 trainees. Also specialises in matrimonial law (about 15% of total workload).
Prof. Memberships: Solicitors Family Law Association
Career: Qualified in 1978. Joined *Rowe & Maw* in 1979, became partner in 1984. Group Managing Partner, Commercial Litigation 1993-94.

HEWSON, Carol

Simmons & Simmons, London
(0171) 628 2020
Partner in Litigation Department.
Specialisation: Main area of practice is commercial litigation, with particular experience in all aspects of commercial property and landlord and tenant litigation. Acts for institutional landlords, property developers and banks, as well as for commercial and retail tenants. Also has extensive experience in rent

review disputes, including arbitration, service charge disputes, forfeiture claims and litigation under the Landlord and Tenant Act 1954. Experienced in insolvency litigation, acting primarily for banks and insolvency practitioners. Acted for Bass Lease Company Limited in a series of actions brought by tenants of tied houses for damages for alleged breaches of Article 85, Treaty of Rome. Addressed seminars for Euroform on "Watertight Commercial Leases" and for Central Law Training at their annual Commercial Landlord and Tenant Conference.
Prof. Memberships: Law Society; City of London Solicitors Company; Member of Property Litigation Association.
Career: Qualified in April 1980, after joining *Stephenson Harwood* as an articled clerk in 1978. Left for *Simmons & Simmons* in 1983, Partner in 1986.
Personal: Born 8th October 1955. Attended Kings College, London 1974-1977. Deputy Chairman of Management of Broomleigh Housing Association and Chairman of its Audit Committee. Leisure pursuits include fell walking, skiing and horse racing. Lives in London.

HIGHMORE, Robert P.

Radcliffes, London (0171) 222 7040
Litigation Partner and Head of Property Litigation Team.
Specialisation: Principal area of practice covers full range of property and landlord and tenant litigation and dispute resolution including commercial and residential property and professional negligence actions. Acts for both landlords and tenants including major institutions, pension funds, the NHS, Banks and Life Assurance companies. Also handles general commercial litigation.
Prof. Memberships: Vice-Chairman and founder committee member of Property Litigation Association; British Property Federation; Law Society; City of Westminster Law Society.
Career: Qualified 1982, at *Radcliffes & Co* since 1980. Became a partner in 1987.
Personal: Born 9th February 1957. Educated at Cambridge and County High School (1968-71), Beverley Grammar School, East Yorkshire (1971-75), Trinity Hall, Cambridge (1976-79). Leisure pursuits include squash, Ceroc, Rotary (Chislehurst). Lives in Bromley, Kent.

HOGAN, Ronald D.

Dewar Hogan, London (0171) 246 2929
Specialisation: All types of contentious property matters and related litigation in connection with commercial and residential property. Instructed in relation to property management disputes (including dilapidations, arrears, forfeiture, and rent reviews); professional negligence cases involving solicitors and valuers; enforcement of securities and other insolvency related work; leasehold enfranchisement and estate management schemes. Instructed in a number of reported cases, author of articles in the property press and speaker at conferences on property issues. Chairman of the Property Litigation Association 1995-96.
Career: Formed the niche property litigation practice of *Dewar Hogan* in 1991. Formerly at *Nabarro Nathanson*.

HUTCHINSON, Lucy
Herbert Smith, London (0171) 374 8000
Head of Property Litigation: Partner in Litigation and Arbitration Department.
Specialisation: Deals with specialised property litigation involving major property and landlord and tenant disputes relating to commercial, retail, industrial and residential property. Does rent review work, including acting as legal assessor to Arbitrators. Acts for a number of institutional investors including Hermes and Standard Life. Also does regulatory work and general commercial litigation.
Career: Qualified in 1982. Became a Partner at *Herbert Smith* in 1989.
Personal: Educated at Southampton University.

KING, Vivien M.
S J Berwin & Co, London
+44 (0)171 533 2222
Specialisation: Caseload includes all aspects of contentions property matters including real property, mortgage and leasehold concerns. Venues for dispute include both the courts and arbitration. Particular legal interests include trespass, dilapidations and rent reviews. PACT arbitrator and member of Arbrix. Founder member of Institute of Continuing Professional Development.
Prof. Memberships: Lectures extensively at the Law Society, the RICS and at *S J Berwin & Co.*
Career: BA in Law. Qualified 1987. Partner at *Turner Kenneth & Brown* 1989 – 1993; partner *Bower Cotton & Bower* 1993-1994; became partner at *SJ Berwin & Co* 1995.
Personal: Old houses, antique glass, cooking and France. Born 1950.

LANGDON, M.C.
Cameron McKenna, London
(0171) 367 3000
Property Litigation and Arbitration and associated advice.Cases Include: 'Brewers Company v. Viewplan plc' (1989); 'Pembroke St. Georges Ltd v. Cromwell Developments Ltd' (1991), 'British Airways Plc v. Heathrow Airport Ltd' (1992); (all rent review); 'Briargate Developments Ltd v. Newprop Co. Ltd' (1990) (specific performance); 'Special Trustees of St. Bartholomews and Another v. BRB and Another' (1992) (repeal of statutory pre-emption rights); 'Crown Estate Commissioners v. TTT Money Corp Limited' (1996) (refusal of consent to assignment).
Prof. Memberships: British Italian Law Association; Property Litigation Association.
Career: *McKenna & Co.*, admitted 1981, Partner 1987.
Personal: Born – 27th February 1956.

MADDEN, Michael
Ashurst Morris Crisp, London
(0171) 638 1111
Specialisation: Partner in charge of the property litigation group at *Ashursts*. He advises on matters such as development agreement disputes, mortgage and property financing actions, adjoining owner/party wall/adverse possession claims in addition to landlord and tenant, estate management, and other general property disputes. Acts for both landlords and tenants in contested rent review arbitrations and expert determinations. The group advises on both liquor and game licensing matters.
Prof. Memberships: Accredited mediator with CEDR. ACIArb. Member of Property Litigation Group Law Reform Committee.

MANNERS, John (Willie) H.R.
Macfarlanes, London (0171) 831 9222
Partner in Litigation Department.
Specialisation: Practice is focused on contentious property and employment cases as well as covering a broad mix of general commercial work. Important reported cases include Johnston & others v. Duke of Westminster (leasehold enfranchisement), Edelman v. Lonhro plc (dispute about notices under section 212 of the Companies Act 1985) and Dun & Bradstreet Software Services (England) Ltd & others v Provident Mutual Life Assurance Association (break notice under a lease and estoppel). Charge-out rate is £300 per hour.
Prof. Memberships: London Solicitors Litigation Association, Country Landowners Association.
Career: Qualified in 1980, having joined *Macfarlanes* as a trainee in 1976. Became a Partner in 1987. Spent a year on secondment to major US litigation firm *Fulbright & Jaworski* in Houston, Texas.
Personal: Born 5th May 1956. Educated at Eton College 1969-74 and The College of Law, Guildford 1976-79. Interests include farming, gardening and shooting. Trustee of Avon Tyrrell House Charitable Trust. Lives in London.

MASTERS, David C.
Speechly Bircham, London (0171) 353 3290
Specialisation: Practice covers full range of property litigation including rent reviews, dilapidations claims, applications under the Landlord and Tenant Act 1954 and recovery of possession of land. Acts for large and small property companies, life assurance companies, shopping centre landlords, local authorities, landed estates, and private individuals.
Prof. Memberships: Property Litigation Association.
Career: Qualified 1981. At *Joynson-Hicks* 1984-1986. *Nabarro Nathanson* 1986-88, *Speechly Bircham* since 1988 (Partner from 1990).
Personal: Born 7.11.56. Educated at Felsted School and Reading University. Married. Interests include Theatre, Skiing and Tennis. Lives in Coggeshall Essex.

MILLER, Wendy
Clifford Chance, London (0171) 600 1000
Partner and Head of Property Litigation Unit.
Specialisation: Specialising in all aspects of contentious property work including rent reviews; development disputes; nuisance and trespass; landlord and tenant; professional negligence; lease renewals; secured lending disputes; insolvency issues.
Prof. Memberships: Property Litigation Association.
Career: Articled Clifford-Turner; qualified 1984; partner Clifford Chance 1991; Blundell Memorial Lecturer 1993; CEDR qualified mediator 1996. Has published and lectured widely on property issues, including articles in Rent Review and Lease Renewal, lectures to the RICS and the Arbrix Club.

MOLYNEUX, Anne
Masons, London (0171) 490 4000
Partner and Head of Property Litigation Department.
Specialisation: Handles all areas of High Court litigation. Cases have included Inntrepreneur Estates v. Boyes (covering European law, application of Article 85 and

severance), Inntrepreneur v. Mason (covering the status of comfort letters), Little v. Courage (covering status of option) and Star Rider v. Inntrapreneur (equitable right of set off). Addressed Law Society National Conference on litigation; has addressed conferences on dilapidations, insolvency, litigation and rent review. Worked on a TEN video. Presented programmes for BBC World Service.
Prof. Memberships: Law Society.
Career: Qualified in 1983. Associate at *Lawrence Messer & Co.*, before joining *Masons* in 1987. Became a Partner in 1989.
Personal: Born 12th January 1959. Member of Ealing and Fulham Book Club. Lives in Ealing. Has two children.

PEET, Carole
Denton Hall, London
(0171) 320 3905 / 01908 690 260
email: cep@dentonhall.com Partner: Head of Litigation Group in Milton Keynes.
Specialisation: Practice covers all aspects of contentious property law. Emphasis on landlord and tenant disputes, including rent reviews, business lease renewals, possession actions, dilapidations claims and litigation involving the refusal or withholding of licences. Has contributed articles to Estates Gazette, Property Review, Lawyer, Lease Renewal and Rent Review, Property Week and Solicitors Journal. Lectures frequently to invited audiences.
Career: Qualified 1985. Assistant Solicitor with *Boodle Hatfield* 1985-88. Joined *Denton Hall* 1988 and became a Partner in 1993.
Personal: Born 1958. Lives in Buckinghamshire and London.

PICKSTON, John
Clifford Chance, London (0171) 600 1000
Partner. Property Litigation Unit.
Specialisation: Property related litigation and advice on contentious aspects of property transactions including development disputes, rent reviews, landlord and tenant disputes, professional negligence and property aspects of insolvency disputes. Acts for a diverse range of clients including developers, banks, property institutions, hoteliers, retailers and manufacturing clients.
Career: Qualified 1986. Partner 1996.

RICKARD, Jennifer
Nabarro Nathanson, London
(0171) 518 3330
Partner Property Litigation Department.
Specialisation: All aspects of Property litigation. Acted in 'Mannai Investment Company Ltd v. Eagle Star Life Assurance Ltd', 'Lewisham Investment Partnership v. Morgan', 'Straudley Investment v. Mount Eden Land', 'Grundy v. Summit Group Holdings' and 'Pontsarn v. Kansallis Osake Panke'. Speaker at Blundell Memorial Lectures, Henry Stewart conferences, RICS, IBC conferences, Central Law Training. Speaker on Owlion cassettes on Dilapidations 1996, Lease Renewals 1998, Rent Reviews 1998 and Property law updates 1997-98.
Career: Qualified 1983. Partner 1989.

TRAVERS, Iain
Nabarro Nathanson, London
(0171) 493 9933
Head of Property Litigation.
Specialisation: Property litigation and arbitration generally. Acted in St. Bartholomew's Hospital Trustees v. British Railways Board' and

'Techno Ltd v. Allied Dunbar Assurance Ltd. Member of ARBRIX.
Prof. Memberships: Fellow of Chartered Institute of Arbitrators. Member of Law Society working party and on panel for arbitration in business tenancy renewals. Chairman of Law Reform sub-committee of Property Litigation Association.
Career: Qualified 1977. Partner 1980.

WALKER, Andrew
Cameron McKenna, London
(0171) 367 3000
Partner in Property Litigation Group.
Specialisation: Main area of practice covers all types of property disputes including landlord and tenant (breaches of covenants, rent reviews, statutory renewals of commercial leases, breaches of statutory obligatons, insolvency and applications to the Leasehold Valuation Tribunal for Estate Management Schemes), claims arising out of contracts for the sale and purchase of land/buildings, breach of statutory obligations, disputes on boundaries, trespass, rights of way, professional negligence by surveyors or solicitors in relation to property matters.
Prof. Memberships: Law Society, Property Litigation Association.
Career: Qualified 1986 while with Masons. Joined *Cameron Markby Hewitt* in 1987 and became a Partner and Head of Property Litigation Group in 1993.
Personal: Born 8th December 1959. Leisure pursuits include walking, gardening, cars and family life. Lives in London and Ross-on-Wye.

WALTHAM, Anne
Lovell White Durrant, London
(0171) 236 0066
Specialisation: Manages the property litigation group having became a partner in May 1998.

Specialises in property litigation, dealing with a wide variety of landlord and tenant and real property disputes, including advising the firm's property department on potentially litigious matters. Particular expertise in rent review disputes acting for leading institutional landlords. Familiar with running substantial landlord and tenant cases and has dealt also with a number of property related professional negligence cases. Acted for the Prudential in The Prudential Assurance Company Ltd. v. Mault Eden Land Ltd. Contributes to a number of publications including the Estates Gazette, Property Week and Commerical Lawyer and to seminars on aspects of property litigation. Recently delivered a paper on the Arbitration Act 1996 to the Arbrix Club.
Prof. Memberships: Law Society; Property Litigation Association.
Career: Qualified in 1982 and joined *Lovell White Durrant* in 1989: (partner: 1998).

WEBBER, Lesley
Beachcroft Stanleys, London
(0171) 242 1011
Partner, Head of Property Litigation and Planning Department.
Specialisation: Principal area of practice is property litigation including rent reviews, lease renewals, dilapidations and service charge disputes, possession and forfeiture, rating and professional negligence actions. Also acts as arbitrator and as legal assessor to arbitrators. Other main area of work is town and country planning covering planning applications, agreements and appeals, local planning advice and representation, compulsory purchase orders and environmental assessments. Acted in 'PHIT v. Holding & Management', 'Shield Properties v. Anglo Overseas Transport Ltd', 'Zubaida v. Hargreaves', 'Sterling Estates v. Pickard', 'Morgan Sindall v. Sawston Farms' and

in the original arbitration of 'National Westminster Bank v. Arthur Young'. Member of Law Society RICS Working Party on Landlord and Tenant Act 1954 and draftsman of PACT scheme for lease renewals. Member of Property Advisory Group to the Department of the Environment, Transport and the Regions.
Prof. Memberships: Fellow of the Chartered Institute of Arbitrators, Honorary Member of ARBRIX.
Career: Qualified 1980 while with *Freshfields*. Joined *Masons* in 1984 and became a Partner and Head of the Property Litigation and Planning Department in 1985. Partner London office of *Dibb Lupton Broomhead* from 1993. Joined *Beachcroft Stanleys* in 1997.
Personal: Born 10th April 1956. Attended Birmingham University 1974-77. Winner of SLSS Prize for Planning Law.

WILLETTS, Guy
Theodore Goddard, London
(0171) 606 8855
Specialisation: All aspects of property litigation including landlord and tenant disputes, land disputes, nuisance claims and environmental prosecutions. Major cases include 'Esselte A.B and another -v- Pearl Assurance'.
Prof. Memberships: Member of Property Litigation Association.
Career: LLB with French Law at LSE followed by Articles with *Robert Gore and Company*, Grosvenor Street, to 1988; *McKenna & Co* to 1994. Currently associate at *Theodore Goddard* and Head of Property and Environmental Litigation.
Personal: Still two daughters and a bass guitar.

SOUTH EAST

DONNE MILEHAM & HADDOCK Brighton	
COFFIN MEW & CLOVER Portsmouth	
DENTON HALL Milton Keynes	
THOMSON SNELL & PASSMORE Tonbridge	
BRACHERS Maidstone	
CRIPPS HARRIES HALL Tunbridge Wells, Kent	

Harold Benjamin & Collins Harrow	
Rawlison & Butler Crawley	
Burstows Crawley	

Donne Mileham & Haddock (2ptnrs/1 assoc/3assts in Brighton and Crawley) The property litigation team is part of the firm's combined Commercial Property Services group. They are "the big boys; still a force to be reckoned with." One client recommended

them for giving "an instant response, always on top of the case and dealing successfully with complex issues." *Martin Allen* is well thought of but is rarely seen in court these days." **Clients/Work:** Acting for Lloyds TSB re a series of restrictive covenant cases impending disposal of surplus bank premises. Acting for a farm consortium re arbitration of complex multi-million pound sale agreement and option. Acting for Arun District Council re injunction proceedings to enforce planning decisions precluding gypsies from using their freehold land as caravan site, involving complex and important issues of law and policy.

Coffin Mew & Clover (2ptnrs/1asst do varying amounts) The partners now have an assistant working for them, so have expanded since last year. Come across less frequently by other practitioners in the last year. **Clients/Work:** Acting for the plaintiff in Southampton Community Healthcare Trust v Crown Estates Commissioners, a 6-day High Court trial reported in the Estates Gazettes. Continuing to act for existing clients.

Denton Hall (1ptnr/5assts) **Clients/ Work:** See under London leading firms.

Thomson Snell & Passmore (1ptnr (1assoc)/1asst) The firm is part of the Law South network. The property litigation team acts for the Solicitors Indemnity Fund among others. Opponents describe them as "good and capable." **Clients/Work:** Leasehold enfranchisement – several cases, for both landlords and tenants. Trespass claims by land owners against hunting associations. Environmental pollution and statutory nuisance – advising and acting on several matters, both enforcement and civil liability. Also involved in contested mortgage possession work.

Brachers (10ptnrs/6assts – p/t) There is no dedicated team, but various members of the firm deal with property litigation matters, largely serving the firm's extensive agricultural practice. **Clients/ Work:** Work in the Lands Tribunal, Agricultural Lands Tribunal and agricultural arbitration in addition to courts.

Cripps Harries Hall (2ptnrs/2assts) The team is described by opponents as "always fair to deal with." **Clients/Work:** Major rent review work, some under Arbitration Act 1996, as well as site redevelopment work and property-related insolvency work.

Harold Benjamin & Collins (3ptnrs/1assoc) Act for a variety of clients ranging from major commercial and industrial groups, property developers and major housing association to individuals and small businesses. **Clients/Work:** Appeals re proposed superstore development. Negligence claim against other solicitors re acquisition of commercial property. Acting for tenant in lease renewal re premises within a building damaged by an IRA bomb.

Rawlinson & Butler (2ptnrs/4assts) The firm has a "good commercial practice." The property litigation team function out of the commercial property department. **Clients/Work:** Advising a housing association re negligence/nuisance action against neighbouring land owners/contracted engineers/architects re major landslip, resulting in seven figure settlement for HA. Advising/representing division of leading UK commercial development group of companies re action against local authority for breach of covenant to provide adequate drainage facilities to major residential development. Representing foreign based international commercial development group re professional negligence claim re access problems experienced with UK-based development.

Burstows (3ptnrs/4assts) Work out of the commercial property department and deal with land disputes and litigation arising out of town planning. However other practitioners in the region "do not deal with them regularly."

SOUTH WEST

Burges Salmon (4ptnrs/15assts) The biggest and the best property litigation practice in the South West. Tough and extremely professional. *Richard Bedford* ("a good technician") concentrates on real property disputes, insolvency and professional negligence. *Neil Ham,* a new entrant, specialises in landlord & tenant and "doesn't mess about." Peter Williams, the partner responsible for establishing and building up the practice, now devotes most of his time to agricultural matters. **Clients/ Work:** High Court interlocutory injunction for leading telecommunications operator to allow the erection of a telecommunications mast. High value option dispute over development land.

Osborne Clarke (1ptnr/2associates/2assts) A good practice, particularly known for its work for NatWest – "they have a firm grasp of what is important." *James Orme* ("effective") moves up to the top band. *Leona Briggs* ("bright and will go far") is part of the team. **Clients/Work:** Dealing with one of the first references under the PACT scheme. Acting on defended mortgage possession actions for National Westminster bank. Property-related negligence actions against solicitors and surveyors.

Veale Wasbrough (1ptnr/1asst) A team within the property services department which "makes sensible points, at the right time and in the right way." Headed by the "no nonsense and delightful" *Julie Exton.* **Clients/Work:** Acting for landlord of a commercial site where occupier claiming lease, not licence. A substantial service charge dispute for a number of tenants of an out of town retail park. Dilapidations claims, especially for PACE (South West & Midlands regions) and Barclays Bank Group Property Services.

Bond Pearce (1ptnr/3assts) All work in other fields as well although one assistant is almost full time in this area. **Clients/Work:** Refurbishment of historic listed building involving Prosecution and Defence of various actions brought by residential tenants of the building, and litigation with local authority over levels of improvement grants. Defending proceedings for adverse possession through the invocation of local by-laws for a major land owner. Defending proceedings in Lands Tribunal for discharge of restrictive covenants.

Cartwrights (1ptnr/3assts) The "solid and tenacious" *Nigel Puddicombe* and his small but growing team "see the client's objective and work towards that rather than getting bogged down in legal argument." **Clients/Work:** Acting for Reading BC on substantial development compensation claim. Acting for Tesco defending claim for loss of use and opportunity relating to business premises and defeating a claim for a new business lease.

Eversheds (2ptnrs/4assts) A team that operates across Eversheds' Bristol and Cardiff offices. *Peter Morris* ("focused") is a new entrant. James Rees is a recent arrival from Denton Hall. Their strength is seen to be recovery work for financial institutions. **Clients/Work:** Acting for Burger King in the first case within the region involving the grant of an overriding lease.

Lyons Davidson (1ptnr/1asst) *Martin Bastow* doesn't waste time scoring unnecessary points and is always helpful. **Clients/Work:** HB Property Developments Ltd v SofS for Environment; a Court of Appeal decision where the tenant successfully appealed re a disputed break clause. Acting for AEM (Avon) Ltd against Bristol City Council; the council's action to recover rates previously refunded in error by means of a liability order in a magistrates court was ultra vires. Hughes v MacPherson and UCB Bank; acting for the plaintiff to set aside the deed of gift of his home procured by the first defendant's undue influence.

Bevan Ashford (1ptnr/3assts) It is "early days" for the team but the signs are good. **Clients/Work:** One of the first cases involving the application of Section 17 of the 1995 Act. Removing 50 squatters from property in the West Country. Assisting a client in enforcing his right to allow customers free car parking.

Foot & Bowden (1ptnr/2assts) A dedicated unit with individuals specialising in landlord & tenant, land use disputes etc. The team now includes a barrister. **Clients/Work:**

Acting for plaintiff against West Devon BC in High Court case concerning negligent misstatements made by local government offer which were relied upon by a developer. Acting for Looe Harbour Commissioners re termination of business tenancy under the '54 Act. Acting for the defendants in Roberts and Roberts v Heritage Parklands and others, involving application for rectification of original option agreement concerning golf course and residential development which plaintiffs sought to prevent.

Lawrence Tucketts (2assts) Associate *Julia Lucas* (ex Masons and in-house at Inntrepreneur) joined the firm in June '97 to develop a contentious property practice. Recommended for her expertise in this field.Known to act for some large commercial landlords and tenants, particularly in the retail sector, and local authorities. **Clients/Work:** C & J Clark International Ltd: Acting for a major national retailer re application for declaration that their landlord was not acting reasonably in withholding consent to sub let. South Gloucestershire Council: Defending claim for damages for trespass (alternatively the value of an alleged ransom strip) over part of land covered by Compulsory Purchase Order. G E Capital Information Technology Solutions (UK) plc: re action for possession of land comprising warehouse premises and surrounding areas.

Wansbroughs Willey Hargrave (1ptnr/3assts) Not this firm's major area of practice but they are seen to be doing well regarded work in this field. **Clients/Work:** Defending golf club against nuisance dispute arising from change in land use which impacted on the water table and affected a nearby river. Resisting renewal of lease of substantial investment property in multiple occupation. Acting for development company over rescission of lease for fraudulent misrepresentation.

Bobbetts Mackan (1ptnr/2assts) A focused residential tenants' firm. They know how to work the system, and have agreed protocols with large landlords to cut out needless argument. *Brian Cox* heads the team.

WALES

Eversheds (2ptnrs – 1p/t; 4assts) In the course of the last year the firm has developed a dedicated property litigation department across the board and set up a Property Litigation Roadshow to tour the country and "brand" the unit. Their main clients are developers and funders. They "have the best coverage in Wales in terms of size and national presence." **Clients/Work:** Acting for BG plc in the clearance of 150 business tenants from 30 acres of commercial premises in Chelsea. Acting for major plc to obtain injunction against adjoining land-owner restraining him from excavating beside client's office building, where the excavation was causing water to enter into a main frame computer room. Acting for public sector client in obtaining vacant possession of a site where unlawful occupation was holding up a multi-million pound construction contract.

Hugh James (2ptnrs – 1pt; 1asst) Known primarily for their Housing Association work and for doing more tenant work than the other leaders, the firm is "very strong in South Wales" and "proactive" in property litigation. **Clients/Work:** Acting for Housing Associations in a range of cases, particularly nuisance cases some of which have led to significant trials. Major dilapidations claims; acting for tenants, the largest of whom is Companies House. Acting for tenants in lease renewals under the Landlord & Tenant Act 1954, some of which have led to Court proceedings..

Morgan Bruce (1ptnr/3assts in Cardiff, 1ptnr/2assts in Swansea, support from other fee-earners as required) Seen as "big players" in South Wales. Property litigation is run as a cross-office group with London. The teams in Cardiff and Swansea continue their work with Housing Associations but the majority of work is for commercial landlords.

Edwards Geldard (1ptnr/1asst) A small dedicated property litigation team working out of the commercial litigation department which is "seeking to develop more." **Clients/Work:** Continuing to act for major development company in dispute in Official Referees' Court with its former tenant re damages for dilapidations worth around £2m. Defending claim worth approx £200,000 against major land owner re damages for alleged illegal distraint. Pursuing claim for local company against local authority for damages arising from nuisance and/or negligence in failing to adequately maintain a bridge running over the client's property.

MIDLANDS

Edge & Ellison (1ptnr/4assts) A "solid" reputation. One assistant is a specialist in agricultural property litigation. The majority of their clients are in the brewery and retail sectors, although they have increasing work for institutional landlords. One client had "nothing but positive feedback on them, they are brilliant, very very good." *Gordon Scott* heads the Unit and is a "positive feature" of the team. **Clients/Work:** Judicial review against Law Society on decision on property matter. Dealt with a number of Commons Registration Act applications. Advising on professional negligence cases against surveyors and solicitors.

Wragge & Co (2ptnrs/3assts) The firm "is top." Acting for institutional-type clients, the team has a "very good reputation." *Suzanne Lloyd-Holt* "is a first rate technician and knows her area extremely well, which gives her an edge." She is also "a practical lawyer who seeks to obtain a benefit for her commercial client." She is a trained arbitrator on the combined RICS and Law Society PACT panel. **Clients/Work:** Comprehensive redevelopment of retail site with complex Landlord & Tenant Act 1954 aspects (Hampshire Centre, Bournemouth for Castlemore Securities). Casino contested 54 Act renewal for Stakis. Alienation dispute re hangar for British Airways.

Eversheds (1ptnr/2assocs/2assts) Now have a partner in charge of this department, seen as having "got its act together." One client praises them as "impressive, give a very quick response." *Gary O'Brien* came from Pinsent Curtis, Leeds and "has shaken things up a bit." *Hilary Harrison* "ran things before Gary came along, has been around for a while and certainly knows her stuff." *Jason Pinkney* is an associate based in the Derby office. **Clients/Work:** Acting for businesses with substantial estates re break notices providing important strategic advice and detailed legal support, including proceedings. Substantial dilapidations claim for government agency handled without recourse to court. Acting in quasi opposed lease renewal re new prestige development at Martineau Square in Birmingham on behalf of the tenant.

Anthony Collins Solicitors (2ptnrs/2assocs/3assts of whom 1 assoc and 1 asst are full-time) The team "gets involved in a different sort of work;" primarily within the social housing sector as well as the leisure industry. **Clients/Work:** Successfully defending dilapidations claim for national charity – reducing their potential liability from £0.5million to £32,000. Becoming exclusive providers of property litigation services to one of the largest Housing Associations in the region. Acting for LPA receivers and advising on duties.

Freeth Cartwright Hunt Dickins (1ptnr) Niche work for many licensed premises. Known by their reputation as "fairly aggressive."

Martineau Johnson (2assocs/1asst) Professional and capable in this area. Not a

dedicated unit. **Clients/Work:** Staffordshire University v Winton Properties Limited; major piece of property litigation for a university client, involving complex dilapidations and planning aspects.

Pinsent Curtis (1ptnr) "A good firm with good clients; they always maintain a high standard." **Clients/Work:** Large dilapidation dispute involving petrochemical contamination. Declaratory proceedings on rent review interpretation. Action for specific performance of agreement to vary contract.

Browne Jacobson (1ptnr/1asst) **Clients/Work:** Acting for major plc clients including Fii Group plc, Abbey National plc and Wilkinson Hardware Stores Ltd.

Lanyon Bowdler "Good on rural type property work," the team is rated for its agricultural work and practice.

McGrath & Co (4ptnrs/8assts) A different practice from the other firms on our lists; primarily acting for legally-aided clients; travellers, gypsies, and others in housing

need. They are described as "extremely good" and "hot on housing association work." **Clients/Work:** Working with squatters in Luton who were facing eviction from a farm they had squatted and renovated; they are now buying the farm. Establishing ownership of land from adverse posssession for two gypsies parked under a fly-over. Achieving record settlement for disrepair, including damages relating to asthma in children.

Shoosmiths & Harrison (1ptnr/3assocs/2assts) Litigation covering all aspects of landlord and tenant and property disputes, mainly of a commercial nature.

LEADING INDIVIDUALS
MIDLANDS

LLOYD-HOLT Suzanne Wragge & Co	
O'BRIEN Gary Eversheds	
SCOTT Gordon Edge & Ellison	
HARRISON Hilary Eversheds	
PINKNEY Jason Eversheds	

EAST ANGLIA

LEADING FIRMS · EAST ANGLIA

EVERSHEDS Ipswich/Norwich
MILLS & REEVE Norwich

HIGHLY REGARDED FIRMS

Hewitson Becke + Shaw Cambridge
Lawrence Wood Norwich

Eversheds (3assts/1barrister) Led by "Knowledgeable" associate *John Scannell*. **Clients/Work:** Recent high profile case

involving removal of protesters against genetically modified crops from agricultural land outside Norwich. Complex property-related matters for RMC Group plc. Other clients include Scottish and Newcastle Retail Limited.

Mills & Reeve (1ptnr/3assts) A sizeable, specialist team and a respected adversary. The "excellent" *James Falkner* has been a property litigator since 1982 undertaking landlord & tenant, residential and agricultural matters.

Hewitson Becke + Shaw (1ptnr/2assts) Concentrate mainly on contentious property and have a "sensible approach." **Clients/**

Work: Successful in attracting property-based instructions, including work from Environment Agency, Minster General Housing Association and London Brick Property Co Ltd.

Lawrence Wood (1ptnr) Tim Quince spends 30% of his time on contentious matters, split evenly between residential and commercial.

LEADING INDIVIDUALS
EAST ANGLIA

FALKNER James Mills & Reeve	
SCANNELL John Eversheds	

NORTH WEST

LEADING FIRMS · NORTH WEST

COBBETTS Manchester
DIBB LUPTON ALSOP Manchester
EVERSHEDS Manchester

ADDLESHAW BOOTH & CO Manchester
HALLIWELL LANDAU Manchester
PANNONE & PARTNERS Manchester

GORNA & CO Manchester

HIGHLY REGARDED FIRMS

Weightmans Liverpool

Cobbetts (1ptnr/1asst) An established firm with a solid reputation. *Peter Stone* is thorough and "does a good job for clients." **Clients/Work:** Instructed by 3 brewers/pub companies re claims by their tenants that the

"tied" provisions in their leases were contrary to Article 85 of the Treaty of Rome. Acting for landlord after a tenant sought reduction of payable rent from £86k pa to £47k pa. – new lease ultimately agreed at £86k. Refusal of adjoining owner to comply with terms of an award made by an agreed surveyor in a party wall act/easement dispute.

Dibb Lupton Alsop (1ptnr/2assts) *Steven Jennings* "knows his stuff and gets down to the real issues quickly." **Clients/Work:** Acting for British Gas in dilapidations claim made against it for £600k re large office block owned by PDFM – claim settled at nil. Acting for tenants in Manchester office block facing service charge claim from their landlords arising out of £5m scheme to renovate steel-work. Acting for consortium of tenants in Arndale Centre Manchester fighting post-IRA bomb service charge and rent claims.

Eversheds (4assts) *Lee Ranson* "gets

hold of issues and takes sensible decisions." Other members of the team are based in Leeds. **Clients/Work:** 3C Waste Ltd v Waste Management Ltd, a lease dispute involving a waste disposal site which has now settled in arbitration. Acting for Barlows Investment Properties Ltd against Laidlaw Thompson and others in contested service charge proceedings re office development in Manchester. Acting for Stanley Casinos Ltd in dispute with Bilton plc involving contested right of way allowing access to large casino in the south of England.

Addleshaw Booth & Co (2assts) A dedicated department headed by a partner based in Leeds. *Alan Walker* is "thorough, competent and a true specialist." The firm mainly acts for landlords and blue chip tenants. **Clients/Work:** Carried out large quantity of work for AAH plc and Barlows plc, as well as handling £500,000 dilapidations claim on behalf of Deloitte & Touche.

Halliwell Landau (2ptnrs/3assts 50%) *Paul Thomas* and his team "know the rules and how to use them to get results." *Karen Spencer* joins the up and coming table. Clients/Work: Acting on behalf of Swinton Group Limited, subsidiary of Royal Sun Alliance re proposal to withdraw from franchising and reorganise franchise branches. Acting for large development company re potentially large dispute arising out of construction of office space in Barbirolli Square, Central Manchester. Pursuing claim against firm of consulting engineers in negligence re construction of blocks of flats for Blackburn Borough Council where damage could run into millions of pounds.

Pannone & Partners (4ptnrs/5assts) Good generalists rather than specialists. *Vincent O'Farrell* heads the commercial litigation department which does a significant amount of contentious property. Clients/Work: Million plus property dispute recovering property estate from "buyer at undervalue" now heading towards High Court trial. Acting for brewery against licensee/borrower, recovering substantial secured debt by way of LPA receivership of commercial premises. Court of Appeal success in £1m + claim against local authority arising out of compulsory purchase by local authority of client's premises.

Gorna & Co (1ptnr) *Helen Hoath* is a competent full time property litigator. Clients/Work: Successfully arguing that a blue chip covenant tenant's attempt to break a 25 year lease was unsuccessful (the tenant had only applied 2 coats of paint not the required 3, an error that cost the tenant £610,000). Settling Allied London Industrial Properties Ltd v Castleguard Properties Inc.

– pending appeal to the House of Lords.

Weightmans (3ptnrs/1assoc/4assts) A respected firm with some genuine specialists." Clients/Work: Brewers, hoteliers, developers and bankers.

NORTH EAST

Addleshaw Booth & Co (1ptnr/4assts) View themselves as commercial property experts with a litigation bent. *Philip O'Loughlin* is "the name people know for property litigation in Leeds." Clients/Work: A 5-day arbitration in Manchester handled by Leeds and Manchester fee earners over disputed service charges for Jeyes (UK) Ltd. Acting for former trustees of Yorkshire County Cricket Club in dispute over proposals by the club to vacate the Headingley ground and relocate to Wakefield. Acting for defendants in BRS Northern Limited v Templeheights Ltd and Sainsbury's Supermarkets Ltd.

Dibb Lupton Alsop (Leeds: 1ptnr/2assocs, Sheffield: 1ptnr/2assts) Describe themselves as "dominating retail property." Their client list backs this up. Many instructions come from London from clients who traditionally used City firms. Clients/Work: The Burton Group Plc; Debenhams Plc; Boots Properties Plc.

Eversheds (Leeds: 2ptnrs/4assts; Newcastle: 4ptnrs/7assts, some p/t) The Newcastle team merged with Wilkinson Maughan last year which has augmented their numbers. Chris Hugill, who was previously a leader in this section, is now concentrating on education. *Penny Belcher*, who heads the Leeds team, is gaining a reputation as "very competent, a safe pair of hands and sensible to deal with." Clients/Work: Representing North Herts College in complex application to the Lands Tribunal for the removal of covenants which have a severe impact on the marketability of land (Leeds). For Warmfield seeking judicial review of a planning decision which will impact on major development of a land fill site (Leeds).

Hammond Suddards (2ptnrs/5assts) The team works out of its Commercial Dispute Resolution Department. Generally well-regarded, although they have "never made a splash." Clients/Work: Acting for William Morrison Supermarkets Plc in judicial review proceedings against Teesside Development Corporation, successfully challenging grant of planning permission in respect of rival supermarket to be operated by Asda. Acting for Bradford Property Trust Plc in leasehold enfranchisement dispute before the Lands Tribunal. Acting for local authority through its insurers in defending a £2m claim brought by property developer.

Pinsent Curtis (1ptnr/1assoc/1asst) Enter the tables new this year. Clients/Work: Act for DTI on range of issues for properties in Leeds, Manchester, Nottingham and London. Court of Appeal case of Sledmore v Dalby which dealt with proprietary estoppel to obtain possession order. Involved in BRS v Templeheights Ltd dealing with application for consent to assignment of lease.

Dickinson Dees (1ptnr/1assoc/1asst) Not generally known by other practitioners but have a strong Newcastle practice. Clients/Work: Advising clients with a long leasehold interest in part of a commercial property in London where the head lease was forfeited after clients had contracted to assign their interest to a third party. Acting for landlords to obtain declaration that a lease continued to subsist on grounds that the tenants had not successfully exercised a conditional break clause option contained in their lease.

Nabarro Nathanson (2assts) Have not established an independent profile separate from their London office. Clients/Work: Successfully resisting compensation claim exceeding £1m under the Railway Clauses Consolidation Act 1845 by a mineral operator against the Secretary of State for Defence acting by its agent, the Oil & Pipeline Agency. Dealing with property litigation arising from Fads and Homestyle Stores throughout the UK.

Walker Morris (1ptnr/1assoc/1asst) Act mainly for household name retail clients. Clients/Work: Acting for receivers of Periquito Hotels Ltd in dispute arising from sale of Periquito Queensgate Hotel, London. Acting in dispute under Trusts of Land and Appointment of Trustees Act 1996 involving development land worth £4.6m. Advising LPA Receivers on dilapidations claim exceeding £900,000 on office premises in Bradford.

SCOTLAND

Dundas & Wilson CS (1ptnr/1assoc/1asst, and recruiting two more) Well-resourced, dedicated team with "the right people to deal with all the issues." The partner heading the team is regarded as "solid and dependable". Two other partners and several assistants get involved as required **Clients/Work:** Acting for Chartwell Land in appeal against Axis West Developments Ltd re former Goodyear Factory site in Glasgow – on appeal to House of Lords. Acting for landlords, Legal & General, in conducting two 'test' rent review arbitrations re Paisley Town Centre leading to favourable awards for Landlord. Pursuing Court of Session claim for damages in excess of £1m re refurbishment of major Scottish baronial property resulting in favourable settlement.

Maclay Murray & Spens (1ptnr/1assoc/ 3assts) The "able" *Ewan Easton* leads a specialist team noted for their pragmatic approach whilst "always rooting for their client." **Clients/Work:** Acting for Sears in first big inherent defects insurance claim in the UK against SCOR and Allianz. Acting for Asda in dispute against Glasgow City Council re ransom strips. Acting for United Friendly in dispute re land anchors.

Steedman Ramage (2ptnrs/1asst) A smaller but well respected firm. Acting for retail tenants is seen to be the firm's strength. *Kenny Cumming* is a good practitioner. **Clients/Work:** Judicial review of sale of major city centre development site. Acting as Legal Assessor in rent reviews involving interpretation of EC tied house provisions. Judicial Review of grant of road construction consent for large supermarket development.

Archibald Campbell & Harley WS (2ptnrs) A "richly deserved" reputation for tenant work. **Clients/Work:** Acted successfully for Currys Group plc against Wirral Borough Council concerning liquidated penalties which were held to be punitive. Acted for Safeway in Highland & Universal Properties v Safeway Properties Ltd, involving lease "keep open" clauses – going to appeal in the Scottish appeal courts.

Brodies WS Recommended for its work for large landowners as well as for corporate clients. **Clients/Work:** Court of Session Summary trial seeking interpretation of rent review clause applied to two commercial properties. Advising retail sector tenant in dispute re contractual obligation to leave fixtures (air conditioning system) when vacating premises on assignation of commercial lease. Advising Residents Association in dispute with developer re contractual obligation to provide proper roof to 80 properties.

Burness (2ptnrs/1assoc/2ptnrs) Five fee earners spend approximately 30% of their time on contentious property matters. **Clients/Work:** Two £million claims on behalf of major public utility, both involving construction and contamination issues. Claim on behalf of public body re purpose built facility in Falkirk. Multi-million pound claim re agricultural tenancy on behalf of major public sector organisation.

McGrigor Donald Always competent and professional. Contentious property is handled within the commercial litigation department (headed by the firm's managing partner) with 9 fee earners doing some but none specialising. **Clients/Work:** Acting for the Royal Bank of Scotland plc in an action enforcing a standard security. Acting for Trinity Investments Ltd in resisting a judicial review of a planning decision. Acting for receivers Arthur Andersen to enforce a floating security over heritable property.

Semple Fraser (2ptnrs/1assoc) A single minded practice. Predominantly act for landlords but also for some large retail clients. **Clients/Work:** Advising Threadneedle Property Fund Managers for Allied Dunbar Assurance plc as landlords of premises in dispute re repairing obligations and keep open provisions; ICI Paints in disputed dilapidations claim and related issues.

Shepherd & Wedderburn No dedicated department. **Clients/Work:** Aubrey Investments Ltd v DSC Realisations Ltd, a leading case re statutory restrictions affecting a landlord irritating a lease upon insolvency of tenant. Scottish Life Assurance Co Ltd v AGFA-Gavaert Ltd, held that tenant's letter in rent review did not constitute a counter notice.

Bird Semple (3ptnrs/3assts, but not exclusively property litigation) **Clients/ Work:** Acting for Hamilton Estates Ltd against Stirling Council at the Court of Session. The Court found that the Council was not entitled to breach a prelet agreement to lease purpose built office premises.

Gillespie Macandrew (1ptnr/1asst) A "decent" firm. Act predominantly for landlords in both commercial and agricultural sectors (ie. evicting crofters) **Clients/Work:** Moray Estate Development Co; recovery of possession of land subject to agricultural tenancy. Agfa-Gevaert Ltd; dispute on interpretation of rent review clause.

Thorntons (Dundee) (4ptnrs/1asst) Have a reputation as pleasant and easy to deal with. **Clients/Work:** Act for numerous local housing associations and property factors using a computerised rent collection/recovery of possession system. Commercial property litigation for plc developers. Agricultural lease litigation.

NORTHERN IRELAND

None of the firms in this category has a dedicated property litigation practice since there is not sufficient work to justify it. However each firm in our table has a commercial litigation practice and a property practice and therefore handles property litigation issues as they arise.

ALLEN, Martin
Donne Mileham & Haddock,
Brighton (01273) 329833
Specialisation: Property Litigation with experience in a wide range of property related areas including insolvency, professional negligence and construction, in addition to Landlord and Tenant. Now deals primarily with commercial and investment property. Retained by a number of major investment, development and retail companies. In recent years has handled numerous cases relating to commercial leases, (eg. privity, rent reviews, user and keep-open covenants, and repairs) as well as arbitrations, ADR and Lands Tribunal, and on behalf of groups of lessees and property owners and managers.
Career: Qualified 1972. Partner *Donne Mileham & Haddock* 1976. Head of Litigation Department 1982-1994. Marketing Partner 1995 to date.
Personal: Born 18th August 1947. Educated Brighton College 1960-1965. Interests include sailing, naval history, jazz and sport. Lives in West Sussex.

BASTOW, M.
Lyons Davidson, Bristol (0117) 904 6000
Partner and Head of Property Litigation Group.
Specialisation: Experienced in all aspects of property litigation with particular emphasis on landlord and tenant disputes and security enforcement. Work includes dilapidations, forfeiture, 1954 Act renewals, arbitration, possession proceedings and acting for LPA receivers.
Prof. Memberships: Associate of the Chartered Institute of Arbitrators.
Career: Joined *Lyons Davidson* on qualification in 1988. Appointed Partner in 1994. Member of Bristol Housing Lawyers Group, Property Litigation Association and The Legal Aid Area Committee.

BEDFORD, R.J.
Burges Salmon, Bristol (0117) 939 2000

BELCHER, Penny
Eversheds, Leeds (0113) 243 0391
Specialisation: All areas of Property Litigation, Arbitration and Property Dispute Management including Landlord & Tenant disputes, lease renewals, dilapidations, rent reviews, rights of way, boundaries, restrictive covenants. Lands Tribunal , Land Compensation Claims, planning, Judicial Review.
Prof. Memberships: Attorney State Bar of California.
Career: Barrister 1980. Practised as barrister specialising in Property Litigation until 1987. Admitted Attorney State Bar of California 1988. Qualified as solicitor 1993. Joined *Eversheds* 1993. Partner 1997.
Personal: Educated St Hugh's College, Oxford: BA + MA JURISPRUDENCE. Interests include music and theatre, walking, sailing and squash.

BRIGGS, Leona
Osborne Clarke, Bristol (0117) 984 5441
Specialisation: All aspects of property litigation, dealing particularly with commercial landlord and tenant disputes and contested mortgage possession claims.
Prof. Memberships: Law Society and Bristol Law Society.

Career: Articled *Veale Wasbrough*. Joined *Osborne Clarke* on qualification in 1992.
Personal: Lives in Bristol.

COX, Brian
Bobbetts Mackan, Bristol (0117) 929 9001

CUMMING, Kenneth M.
Steedman Ramage WS, Edinburgh (0131) 260 6600
E-mail: kmc@srws.co.uk
Specialisation: General commercial litigation, dispute resolution and advisory work – in particular, Property, Planning and Environmental litigation.
Career: Qualified 1981. At *Dundas & Wilson CS* 1979-1994 (Partner from 1986). Joined *Steedman Ramage WS* as a Partner in 1994.
Personal: Born 8th November 1957.

EASTON, Ewan R.
Maclay Murray & Spens, Edinburgh (0131) 226 5196
See under Litigation (Commercial): 200+ Solicitors, p. 534

EXTON, Julie A.
Veale Wasbrough, Bristol (0117) 925 2020
Partner in Property Services Department.
Specialisation: Practice covers all aspects of contentious property law with particular emphasis on landlord and tenant disputes. Regular speaker at Veale Wasbrough's "PALS" (Property and Legal Support) Seminars.
Prof. Memberships: Law Society and Property Litigation Association.
Career: Joined *Veale Wasbrough* on qualification in 1983. Partner in 1988. Deputy District Judge 1993.
Personal: Born 17.10.57. Lives in Bristol.

FALKNER, J.M.G.
Mills & Reeve, Norwich +44 (0)1603 660155
Agricultural, commercial and residential property and landlord and tenant disputes.
Prof. Memberships: Law Society.
Career: Joined Mills & Reeve 1980. Partner 1988.

HAM, Neil
Burges Salmon, Bristol (0117) 939 2000

HARRISON, Hilary
Eversheds, Birmingham (0121) 233 2001
Specialisation: Main areas of specialisation are dilapidations disputes; Landlord and Tenant, including possession and forfeiture claims and Landlord's unreasonable withholding of consent and issues arising on rent review and opposed lease renewals.
Career: Qualified in 1985 with *Wragge & Co.* Joined *Eversheds* in 1985 becoming an Associate in 1989 and Senior Associate in 1991.
Personal: Born 1960. Attended Presdales Grammar School and Birmingham University. Interests include music and swimming.

HOATH, Helen
Gorna & Co, Manchester (0161) 832 3651
Specialisation: Property litigation; dilapidations; rent reviews; contested business tenancy renewals; specific performance; restrictive covenants; easement disputes; rights to light' Allied London Industrial Properties Ltd v Castleguard Properties Inc 1997 EGCS 18.

Prof. Memberships: Law Society; Association Women Solicitors; Property Litigation Association; Women in Property.
Career: Easingwold School; Worcester College Oxford; Articled *Kramer & Co.* London; *McKenna & Co.*

JENNINGS, Steven
Dibb Lupton Alsop, Manchester (0345) 262728
Specialisation: Property litigation, arbitration and advice covering commercial landlord and tenant work (including rent reviews, dilapidations, contested lease renewal and alienation applications, service charge disputes and forfeiture), restrictive covenants, nuisance, easements, professional negligence and disputes relating to development agreements and the like. Regularly advises arbitrators on legal issues. Frequent speaker at seminars run by the RICS, ISVA and other property related organisations. A member of ARBRIX (the rent review arbitrators club).
Prof. Memberships: Law Society, Chartered Institute of Arbitrators.
Career: Partner with *Gorna & Co*, Manchester 1982-94. Joined *Dibb Lupton Broomhead* as Property partner in 1994. Now Head of Property Litigation *Dibb Lupton Alsop*, Midlands and North West.
Personal: Interests include politics and history.

LLOYD-HOLT, Suzanne
Wragge & Co, Birmingham (0121) 233 1000
Specialisation: Head of Property Litigation Team, specialising in all types of property disputes including dilapidations, rent reviews and site clearance on redevelopment schemes.
Prof. Memberships: French UK Chamber of Commerce – Midlands Branch President, Chartered Institute of Arbitrators-Associate, trained PACT arbitrator.
Career: Qualified in 1974. Partner at *Wragge & Co* from 1988.

LUCAS, Julia
Lawrence Tucketts, Bristol (0117) 929 5252

MORRIS, Peter
Eversheds, Bristol (0117) 929 9555
See under Litigation (Commercial): 200+ Solicitors, p. 524

O'BRIEN, Gary
Eversheds, Birmingham (0121) 233 2001
Specialisation: Head of Property Litigation Team who handles all types of Landlord and Tenant disputes and has particular specialisation in freehold property developments relating to difficult restrictive covenants or major boundary and easement disputes and enforcement of sale and purchase contracts and also clearance of sites for redevelopment schemes.
Career: Qualified in 1985. Joined *Simpson Curtis* in 1987. Partner at *Eversheds* from 1996.
Personal: Born 1959. Attended KEGS Aston and St. John's College, Oxford. Interests include opera and Aston Villa Football Club.

O'FARRELL, Vincent B.
Pannone & Partners, Manchester
(0161) 909 3000
Partner and Head of Department in Commercial Litigation.
Specialisation: Specialises in civil fraud, judicial review, defamation, land disputes, contract and pre-emptive remedies. He is also a notary public.
Career: Vincent was admitted in 1971, when he joined *Howards*, a predecessor to *Pannone & Partners*.
Personal: Leisure interests include theatre, sport and music. Lives in Bury.

O'LOUGHLIN, Philip
Addleshaw Booth & Co, Leeds
(0113) 209 2000
Head of Property Litigation Department, Commercial Property Group.
Specialisation: Practice covers all landlord and tenant and property litigation, in particular rent reviews, dilapidations, property related professional negligence. Work also includes Landlord and Tenant 1954 applications, forfeiture, tenant default.
Career: Articled with *Simmons and Simmons*, qualified 1986; *Withers*, 1987-88; *Crossman Block* 1988-1991; joined the firm 1991; becoming a Partner in May 1995.
Personal: Born 5 May 1960; attended Ipswich School 1971-1978; Cambridge University 1979-1982. Leisure interests include fellwalking, landscape photography, archaeology. Lives near Ilkley.

ORME, J.G.
Osborne Clarke, Bristol (0117) 923 0220
Specialisation: Partner and head of litigation department dealing with commercial litigation, particularly property litigation; banking disputes.
Prof. Memberships: FCI Arb.
Career: Shrewsbury School; Trinity Hall, Cambridge 1973 (1976 MA). Articled *Burges Salmon*. Qualified 1979, assistant solicitor 1979-80. Assistant solicitor *Osborne Clarke* 1980-84; partner 1984.
Personal: Resides Bristol.

PINKNEY, Jason
Eversheds, Nottingham (0115) 950 7000
Specialisation: Main areas of work are possession and forfeiture claims, Landlord and Tenant, recoveries, claims and property related insolvency.
Career: Qualified in 1988 with *Pinsent & Co*. Joined *Eversheds* in 1993 becoming Associate in 1994 and Senior Associate in 1996.
Personal: Born 15.07.64. Attended Bishop Vesey Grammar School and Sheffield University. Interests include cricket, golf and squash.

PUDDICOMBE, Nigel R.
Cartwrights, Bristol (0117) 929 3601
Specialisation: All aspects of property litigation principally acting for lenders and landlords. Clients include breweries, several regional airports, Railtrack, passenger, freight and road transport providers and property companies.
Prof. Memberships: Junior Vice-President, Bristol Law Society. Chairman, Bristol Law Society Civil Courts Committee since 1993.
Career: Qualified 1979. Partner with *Cartwrights* from 1987.
Personal: Born 10th August 1954. Educated Kings College Taunton and Southampton University (LLB 1976). Interests include sport, theatre and gardening. Lives North Somerset.

RANSON, Lee
Eversheds, Manchester (0161) 832 6666
Specialisation: Property litigation – acting for commercial and institutional landlord clients in Retail, local authority and Banking sectors. Specific niche areas include education, leisure and betting and gaming clients.
Prof. Memberships: Law Society.
Career: Qualified – 1990. *Jaques & Lewis* (merged *Eversheds* 1994) 1988 – 1996. Transfered to *Eversheds* Manchester, Jan 1997. Senior Solicitor.
Personal: Born 16.12.64. Educated – Wilmslow Grammer School & Hull University. Married – 2 children. Interests – golf, football, cricket. Lives in Bramhall.

SCANNELL, John
Eversheds, Norwich (01603) 272727
Specialisation: Landlord and tenant – commercial, residential, agricultural. Other property litigation – squatters, adverse possession, title disputes.
Career: University of East Anglia B.Sc Upper Second Class Honours. Articles *Daynes Hill and Perks* 1987-1989. 1989-1992 – non-contentious commercial property/company commercial. 1992-present time – civil litigation, now exclusively property litigation.
Personal: Single. Interests – classical music, jazz guitar, keep fit, food and wine.

SCOTT, Gordon
Edge & Ellison, Birmingham (0121) 200 2001
Specialisation: Head of Property Litigation Unit, which covers the complete spectrum of property-related disputes and includes landlord and tenant, title disputes, easements and covenants, specific performance, judicial review, professional negligence claims and the like. Particular interest in dilapidations claims. Acts for companies across the property sector, including institutional landlords, major retailers,

Housing Associations and development groups.
Prof. Memberships: Member Property Litigation Association. Milk Marque Arbitration Panel.
Career: Joined *Edge & Ellison* as a Partner in 1990 from another local firm, having moved to Birmingham in the early 1980s from *MacFarlanes* and, earlier, *D.J. Freeman & Co*.
Personal: Born 1951. Educated at Whitgift School and Exeter College, Oxford. External interests include rugby, cricket, walking and coping with a large family. Lives in Edgbaston.

SPENCER, Karen
Halliwell Landau, Manchester

STONE, Peter J.W.
Cobbetts, Manchester (0161) 833 3333
Specialisation: Over 20 years experience in litigation for national and regional blue-chip clients. Particular expertise in commercial property litigation (forfeiture, dilapidations, covenants, contested lease renewals, Brewery/Licensed Retailer work) and in defamation (Plaintiff and Defendant) for individual and media clients.
Prof. Memberships: Law Society. Notaries Society.
Career: Educated at Rossall School and Liverpool University (LLB Hons 1st class). Articled at *Cobbetts*, 1974. Qualified 1976, Partner 1979.
Personal: Born 1951. Leisure interests include fellwalking, climbing and scuba diving.

THOMAS, Paul A.
Halliwell Landau, Manchester
(0161) 835 3003
See under Litigation (Commercial): 200+ Solicitors, p. 531

WALKER, Alan
Addleshaw Booth & Co, Manchester
(0161) 934 6000
Specialisation: All aspects of property litigation work, with particular emphasis on landlord and tenant matters, including dilapidations, rent reviews, opposed renewal proceedings, breaches of covenant and associated aspects of property management work.
Prof. Memberships: Law Society. Property Litigation Society.
Career: Magdalene College, Cambridge (M.A., LLM). Articled at *Addleshaw Sons & Latham*1989-1991. Admitted 1991.
Personal: Born 1965. Leisure interests include swimming, walking and theatre.

LOCAL GOVERNMENT

See also: Admin & Public, Education, Employment, Health Care, Housing Associations, Planning, Projects/PFI

RESEARCH: In compiling the tables, we consider all the information available to us, paying particular regard to the market research carried out by our team of ten qualified lawyers. (The researchers' details are set out on page three.) The rankings, therefore, reflect the opinion of the marketplace as revealed by systematic and objective research: see page four. (Our research is audited every year by the British Market Research Bureau.)

OVERVIEW: The fledgling Labour government has inevitably caused a flurry of activity including a White Paper. The emphasis now, as under the previous administration, is on 'public-private partnerships' and there is a growing recognition that 'the private sector is not the enemy.' Genuine policy lawyers are helping local authorities to find innovative ways of bringing in external funds enabling the authority to meet the needs of the community in a manner consistent with its fiduciary duties. Nobody wants another Allerdale case on their hands.

Compulsory Competitive Tendering has now been phased out and is being replaced by the concept of Best Value, which concerns whole service delivery. On the planning side the Development Corporations ceased to exist on 1 July 1998 and development work was handed over to local authority development companies or the Commission for the New Towns.

A real local government lawyer is a policy lawyer as well as a technical lawyer. S/he needs to know procedures, powers and duties and to understand how local authorities work.

This is a client sector in which there is highly competitive pricing so regional firms tend to do well even out of the London Borough Councils, whereas the big City firms with their high overheads are struggling for market share. For this reason Eversheds nationally continue to do well because they can pick up work through their London office and farm it out to cheaper regional offices. They are praised as 'market-leaders' although their 'style is not to everyone's taste.'

Of the London firms Nabarro Nathanson still dominate with Malcolm Iley stepping into the shoes of Carl Hopkins. The niche firms Léonie Cowan & Associates and Jenkins & Hand continue to flourish and the strong and possibly unique local government auditors practice of Rowe & Maw is also doing well. There is little change in the regions where there are few dedicated practitioners in this field. In Scotland there is some change occasioned by the fact that Glasgow City Council have taken their work in-house and contracted it out to Edinburgh City Council.

LEADING FIRMS · LONDON

NABARRO NATHANSON

BERWIN LEIGHTON
SHARPE PRITCHARD

ASHURST MORRIS CRISP
DENTON HALL
LAWRENCE GRAHAM
LÉONIE COWAN & ASSOCIATES
ROWE & MAW
TROWERS & HAMLINS

HIGHLY REGARDED FIRMS

Barnett Alexander Chart
Clifford Chance
D J Freeman
Jenkins & Hand

Herbert Smith
Norton Rose
Titmuss Sainer Dechert
Winckworth & Pemberton

Speechly Bircham

LONDON

Nabarro Nathanson (5ptnrs/10assts) By far the biggest London practice with expertise in education and health law and a PFI practice with 120 local authority clients. *Malcolm Iley* was a city solicitor at Plymouth City Council before entering private practice. He moved last year from Bevan Ashford and now heads the public sector team; he is seen to be marketing the group hard. *Ray Ambrose* is "a particularly good public lawyer." **Clients/Work:** Involved in first PFI schools project, first PFI library project for Bournemouth City Council and first police and magistrate's PFI schemes.

Berwin Leighton (3ptnrs/3assts) Known primarily as a property firm, so local government work centres around major property developments. As well as acting for several local authorities, also act for some private sector clients. *Anna Forge* is respected for her work in infrastructure and planning projects. *Carol McCormack* has a sound reputation but is less high-profile. **Clients/Work:** Advising London Borough of Hackney in connection with proposals for new library, museum, offices and related retail and commercial uses under PFI. Acting for Chester City Council in connection with Phase II proposals for redevelopment of the Forum Centre. Acting for City & County of Swansea property redevelopment and regeneration.

Sharpe Pritchard (4ptnrs/4assts) Well-known for their litigation and parliamentary work. Act in planning and property related matters as well as in judicial review. Known for their agency advisory work for local authorities. *Trevor Griffiths* heads up the team. **Clients/Work:** Representing local authority in Morgan Grenfell v London Borough of Sutton in High Court and Court of Appeal. Acting for consortium of local authorities in R v Yorkshire Purchasing Organisation ex parte British Educational Suppliers. Set of challenges by six local authorities of Director General of Water Services' decision not to exercise his discretion in respect of pre-payment water devices.

Ashurst Morris Crisp (2ptnrs/7assts) Known for property and planning structure work. Had a lot of work for London Docklands Development Corporation and other development corporations which have now ceased to exist and some practitioners questioned their future position. *Tony Curnow*, originally a planning lawyer and known as "Mr Development" does a large amount of local authority housing transfers. He is described as "a steady, solid craftsman". **Clients/Work:** London Borough of Brent – Chalkhill Estate. London Borough of Hackney – Estates Renewal Strategy. London Borough of Sutton – redevelopment of Roundshaw Estate.

Denton Hall (4ptnrs/7assts) Handle local government work in the Planning and Public Law Department. Most of their work is ongoing advice for councils rather than one-off projects. "Made a big reputation a few years ago," they are now known for doing lots of housing work through their Milton Keynes office and are seen on "relatively routine development disposals." Led by *David Danskin*. **Clients/Work:** Inner City Enterprises/Vauxhall Regeneration Company in connection with SRB funding. Barking and Dagenham Council – major regeneration project including SRB-funded initiatives for the Thames Gateway, construction of CTRL, Dagenham Power Station and Barking Reach. Advising Sainsburys in connection with proposed public/private partnership arrangements with Birmingham City Council.

Lawrence Graham (2ptnrs/2assts) The firm has a strong housing practice and also specialises in regeneration work. *Simon Randall CBE* is described as "outstanding." He used to be leader of Bromley Council and "has a genuine interest in housing." *Carl Hopkins*, urban regeneration specialist, joined the firm from Nabarro Nathanson last year. Solicitors from various parts of the firm's practice regularly support the core of dedicated specialists. **Clients/Work:** Completion of large scale voluntary transfers of housing stock to top £1 billion mark and over 65,000 houses. Signature of Heads of Terms for £200 million regeneration of Edmonton Town Centre for London Borough of Enfield. Transfer of four leisure centres for Stevenage Borough Council to Charitable Trust.

Léonie Cowan & Associates (2ptnrs) A "small" practice with a disproportionately large reputation which just keeps on growing. *Léonie Cowen* is "an acknowledged expert" who is seen by all as a true local government specialist. She is "very active and highly regarded" for assisting local authorities with finding new methods of service delivery and achieving "best value." **Clients/Work:** Transfer of Hounslow's leisure, sports and cultural services to group of not-for-profit companies. Economic development project for Redbridge Council. Innovative PFI project for provision of catering services to Lewisham's schools, social services and civic and staff catering.

Rowe & Maw (1ptnr/5assts) "The leading firm" acting in connection with local government district auditors in England, Wales and Northern Ireland. *Tony Child* is a "leading expert in the field, pretty much wedded to local government auditors." *Belinda Schwehr* "has a growing reputation" and is seen as "slightly less hard-edged than Tony Child." **Clients/Work:** Acting for District Auditor in Westminster "Homes for Votes" case. Investigations into circumstances leading to £49million judgment against Welwyn Hatfield DC for deceit. Investigation into financing of Alexandra Palace (Haringey LBC).

Trowers & Hamlins (4ptnrs/7assts) Work mainly on regeneration projects, particularly on the housing side, with work for metropolitan councils particularly prominent. *Ian Doolittle* is now Head of Department and is "a brilliant lawyer, cool and calm in approach." Recently took on an assistant from Ashurst Morris Crisp to develop the team's capacity for urban regeneration development projects. **Clients/Work:** Transfer of London Borough of Islington Leisure Centre to Aquaterra Leisure, a charitable company. Large scale Voluntary Transfer (LSVT) of tenanted housing stock and related assets by Bexley Council to London & Quadrant Bexley Housing Association. Shropshire County Council Transfer of Elderly People's Homes to Coverage Care (Shropshire) Limited.

Barnett Alexander Chart (3ptnrs/5assts) Firm seen as "doing well" in this field although its profile amongst practitioners is not high. Main practice is in externalisation, outsourcing and PFI. Team is headed by *Anthony Fine* ("smart guy") known for his health sector PFI project work. **Clients/Work:** Norfolk and Norwich Hospital PFI; Joint services Command and Staff College PFI; Medium Support Helicopter Training Facility PFI.

Clifford Chance (6ptnrs p/t/15assts p/t) The Local Government group draws on expertise from different practice areas. A significant proportion of the work is advising banks on lending to local authorities and they are known by other practitioners for this rather than for giving advice to the authorities themselves. *Brian Hall* is well-known for his planning work. **Clients/Work:** Advising Corporation of London on City mixed office, residential and retail developments. Advising local authorities on town centre redevelopment prospects including West Dorset District Council and Spelthorne Borough Council. Advising FOCSA Services on a waste to energy incineration project as a central feature in a project being negotiated with Hereford and Worcester County Council.

D J Freeman (4ptnrs/various assts from time to time) Town centre and out of town development work. The firm lost its global Commission for the New Towns work although *Ted Totman* is still working for CNT as strategic corporate adviser. **Clients/Work:** Acting for Fareham Borough Council in regearing of leases of existing town centre shopping development. Acting for Chichester District Council in agreement for development and lease of substantial edge of town site consisting of mixed retail industrial and leisure uses. Acting for Commission for New Towns in agreement with Stevenage Borough Council and consortium of land owners proposing to create a development of 1,600 houses and associated facilities.

Jenkins & Hand (2ptnrs) Two partners who split off from Winckworth & Pemberton to set up their own niche practice specialising in the housing side of local government and acting for registered social landlords or local authorities. The "vivacious" *Catherine Hand* is highly recommended. **Clients/Work:** Acting for LB Tower Hamlets on regeneration scheme in Stepney, advising on model agreement and on creation of company to monitor and supervise regeneration. Acting for Kerrier DC on transfer of entire stock to newly created local housing company in March 1998.

Herbert Smith (3ptnrs) The small team draws specialists from the firm's company, property and litigation departments and advises on powers and vires in conjunction with their administration and public law practice. It advises the Audit Commission as well as local authority clients. "Seen by local authorities as the leading litigation practice." **Clients/Work:** Advising Surrey County Council in relation to waste disposal arrangements. Advising in relation to a streetlighting scheme in London Borough of Brent.

Norton Rose (8ptnrs/13assts) A cross-departmental discipline. Have "made good progress in getting local authority finance work." Their strengths lie in projects, PFI and the structured financing of roads, waste energy and office developments. **Clients/Work:** Acting on the following projects: Croydon Tramlink; Greater Manchester Waste Energy and Sheffield Heart of the City. Total aggregate value of £350 million.

Titmuss Sainer Dechert (5ptnrs/3assts) *Graham McGowan* head of the public sector practice specialises in Local Authority consultancy for major schemes and local government capital finance. He is a "sound steady craftsman." **Clients/Work:** Acting for Hillingdon London Borough Council on redevelopment of St. George's Shopping Centre in Uxbridge. Acting for King's Lynn & West Norfolk Borough Council on the redevelopment and refurbishment of the Vancouver Shopping Centre in King's Lynn.

Winckworth & Pemberton (10ptnrs/11assts) The firm is public sector-oriented and is split into subgroups which correspond to the business sectors within local government. Deal particularly with health authorities, reprovision schemes and private finance in the education sector. *Andrew Murray* heads the Housing and Local Government Department. **Clients/Work:** PFI scheme in Islington. Care provision scheme in Hertfordshire. Urban regeneration scheme in Brent.

Speechly Bircham (3ptnrs p/t/2assts) Traditionally the team worked on large projects but recently focusing on local government IT procurement. Mostly planning and development work. **Clients/Work:** Town centre redevelopment. Acting for London Borough of Croydon on East Croydon Station site. Drafting of IT contracts for Lambeth and Camden.

LEADING INDIVIDUALS · LONDON

CHILD Tony Rowe & Maw
COWEN Léonie Léonie Cowen & Associates
FORGE Anna Berwin Leighton

AMBROSE Ray Nabarro Nathanson
FINE Anthony Barnett Alexander Chart
GRIFFITHS Trevor Sharpe Pritchard
HALL Brian Clifford Chance
HAND Catherine Jenkins & Hand
HOPKINS Carl Lawrence Graham
MCGOWAN Graham Titmuss Sainer Dechert
RANDALL Simon Lawrence Graham
TOTMAN Edward D J Freeman

CURNOW Tony Ashurst Morris Crisp
DANSKIN David Denton Hall
DOOLITTLE Ian Trowers & Hamlins
ILEY Malcolm Nabarro Nathanson
MCCORMACK Carol Berwin Leighton
MURRAY Andrew Winckworth & Pemberton

UP AND COMING

SCHWEHR Belinda Rowe & Maw

LEADERS' PROFILES · LONDON

AMBROSE, Ray
Nabarro Nathanson, London
(0171) 518 3177
Specialisation: Local government and administrative law (powers and duties, statutory interpretation, capital controls, companies). Formerly at GLC and London Residuary Body. Recently advised on 'best value' housing management contract, football stadium development, other regeneration schemes (SRB and others), and partnership structures, Redbridge audit inquiry and transfer of UDC property to EP.
Prof. Memberships: Law Society.
Career: Qualified 1975; Head of Administrative Law and Parliamentary Branch GLC 1985/6; Deputy Director of Legal Services, London Residuary Body 1986-1990. Joined *Nabarro Nathanson* 1991.

CHILD, Tony
Rowe & Maw, London (0171) 248 4282
Specialisation: Practice covers the full range of public and administrative law. Specialist in local government and NHS law. Acts for public bodies and those who deal with them. Adviser to local government and NHS external auditors. Renowned expertise and experience in acting for both applicants and respondents in judicial review and public law proceedings. This includes the first successful challenge in any commonwealth jurisdiction to the adequacy of a government consultation exercise; bringing down the Rate Support Grant (RSG) and ratecapping regime in 1985; overcoming retrospective legislation on RSG; having interest rate swaps declared by the House of Lords to be ultra vires local authorities; 'Bookbinder v Tebbit (No.2)' (1992); 'Allsop v North Tyneside MBC' (1992); 'Burgoine and Cooke v Waltham Forest LBC' (1996) and many more successes. Currently advising the Westminster City Council Auditor in the "homes for votes" case. Previous experience includes 19 years in local government, adviser to both the Association of Metropolitan Authorities and the Association of London Authorities and 8 years as Solicitor to the Audit Commission. Author of many articles and a regular speaker at conferences and seminars. User friendly.
Career: Articled Redbridge London Borough Council; qualified 1971. Assistant Solicitor 1971-1974. Senior Solicitor 1974-1976. Chief Solicitor Greenwich LBC 1976-1979. Assistant Chief Executive and Solicitor 1979-1983; Deputy Chief Executive 1983-1987; Solicitor to Audit Commission 1987-1995; partner *Rowe & Maw* 1995. Education: Ilford County High School; University College, London (LLB First Class Hons). Solicitor (Hons).
Personal: Born 1947. Resides Chelmsford. Interests include football (player/manager Braintree and Bocking United FC), cricket (wicket-keeper, batsman, Redbridge Parks CC), sports generally, crosswords.

COWEN, Léonie
Léonie Cowen & Associates, London
(0181) 964 4177
Specialisation: Local Authority professional work and consultancy, especially public private partnerships, companies, joint ventures, PFI, project finance, Best Value, CCT and quality, social services, education, employment and public procurement. Has advised over 60 local authorities. Recent projects include a transfer of leisure sevices in Hounslow (including a first for libraries), a catering PFI, a sports hall Lottery/PFI, community-led social and economic regeneration companies in England and Wales, an ESCO, transfers of residential homes for older people and £30 million in capital funding for one of these, drafting procurement and service contracts. Contributor to "The Handbook of Local Authority Legal Practice", author of many articles, and regular speaker at conferences and seminars. Member of Local Government Residuary Body (England), director of an NHS trust and an accredited mediator.
Prof. Memberships: Law Society, Assoc. of District Secretaries.
Career: 15 years in local government, latterly as Chief Solicitor to Barnet and Director of Law & Admin./ Deputy Chief Executive at Camden. Founded her own practice in 1989.
Personal: Born 1950. Leisure interests include music and her family.

CURNOW, Tony
Ashurst Morris Crisp, London
(0171) 638 1111
Partner, Head of Public Sector Group.
Specialisation: Advises local authorities and other public sector agencies on regeneration projects. Major schemes include Docklands Highways, Chalkhill Estate for London Borough of Brent, Parkway/M602 inTrafford Park, Hounslow Town Centre, Hackney Estates Regeneration Strategy, London Borough of Sutton's Roundshaw Estate and Surrey Heath

Borough Council's town centre redevelopment at Camberley.
Prof. Memberships: Law Society Planning Panel and Legal Associate RTPI.
Career: Qualified 1979. 11 years in local government. Joined *Ashurst Morris Crisp* 1988, Partner in 1996.

DANSKIN, David
Denton Hall, Milton Keynes
(01908) 690260
Specialisation: Partner, Milton Keynes Office; experience includes property development; major development projects; shopping centres; out of town projects; public sector development advice. Adviser on property aspects of PFI projects and joint ventures; vires issues and capital finance regulation; large scale housing transfers.
Career: Articled *Cripps Harries Willis and Carter*; qualified 1983; joined *Oppenheimers* (now *Denton Hall*) 1983; partner 1989; moved to Milton Keynes office in 1994.
Personal: Born 1957; interests include tennis and golf.

DOOLITTLE, Ian
Trowers & Hamlins, London (0171) 423 8000
Partner, Public Sector. Head of Public Sector.
Specialisation: All aspects of public sector law, especially property and housing law (including housing stock transfers). Specialises in public/private sector partnerships, especially in the context of urban regeneration. Also specialist in environmental law.

FINE, Anthony
Barnett Alexander Chart, London
(0171) 242 4422
Partner in Company & Commercial Department.
Specialisation: Principal areas of work are PFI, Facilities Managements and externalisation, together with corporate finance. In the last 12 months, advised facilities managers in Norfolk and Norwich Hospital PFI and other projects. Firm is a market leader in Local Authority MBO's and has completed over 40 MBO/ MBI/ Development Capital deals in last 5 years. Has advised on externalisation of public sector services, management of change issues and outsourcing. Lectures extensively on subjects such as TUPE and externalisation.

FORGE, Anna
Berwin Leighton, London +44 171 760 1000
Specialisation: General local government law. Primarily acts for local authority clients, also for other public sector bodies and parties dealing with them. Provides advice on capital finance, local government powers and administrative law, interests in companies, compulsory purchase; domestic and European grants, particularly in connection with development, regeneration, leisure or housing schemes. Acts in PFI and other 'partnership' projects. Handles a range of unusual or sensitive cases for local authority clients. Speaks at national conferences and seminars; produces plain guides on local government legal issues.
Prof. Memberships: Law Society.
Career: Qualified 1982. London Borough of Southwark 1983-1989. Joined *Berwin Leighton* in 1989. Partner 1996.
Personal: Born 1951. Leisure interests include ballet, theatre, travel, reading. Two children. Lives in Brighton.

GRIFFITHS, Trevor
Sharpe Pritchard, London (0171) 405 4600
See under Administrative & Public Law, p. 87

HALL, Brian
Clifford Chance, London (0171) 600 1000
See under Planning, p. 643

HAND, Catherine
Jenkins & Hand, London (0171) 222 5002
Partner in Housing and Local Government Department. Set up *Jenkins & Hand* in 1996 with Keith Jenkins as a firm specialising in work for the public and not-for-profit sector.
Specialisation: Work for local government includes advice on local authority powers, CCT, and the creation of local authority companies. Has acted for local authorities and for housing associations on numerous stock transfers, and acted on complex estate regeneration schemes. Advised the DoE on the management agreement for the tenants' right to manage. Also has extensive experience of all aspects of housing association work including private finance, care in the community schemes and constitutional issues.
Career: Qualified 1978. Lecturer in Law at Queen Mary College, London 1978-79 and 1980-84. Lecturer in Law University of Kent 1979-80. In Government Legal Service, Lord Chancellors Department 1984-89. Joined *Winckworth & Pemberton* in 1989, partner 1990. Left to set up new firm 1996.
Personal: Born September 1954. Educated Southampton University 1972-75 (L.L.B 1st Class Hons). Chairman Westminster Medical Research Trust. Trustee of START (a charity for research into skin disease).

HOPKINS, Carl W.V.
Lawrence Graham, London (0171) 395 4661
See under Administrative & Public Law, p. 88

ILEY, Malcolm
Nabarro Nathanson, London (0171) 493 9933
Partner specialising in public sector and local government. Head of Nabarro's public sector team.
Specialisation: Main practice area is public law relating to local government, government departments and public sector powers generally. Experience in local authority outsourcings, asset transfer, regeneration, compulsory purchase, planning, education, competition and PFI, including the consideration of wider European involvement. Currently advising on one of the first "best value" partnership joint ventures. Clients have included London boroughs, district and county councils, government departments, local authority related companies, higher and further education, LAWDAC, and urban development corporations. Currently involved in research concerning the proposed regional development agencies. Media advisor and broadcaster on public sector legal issues. Regular contributor to local government and regional press.
Career: Qualified in 1976. Began career in the private sector, transferred to local government and later became a senior lawyer with Leeds City Council. Appointed City Solicitor and Deputy Chief Executive for Plymouth City Council. Held other senior posts in Lancashire, Sussex and Norfolk. Joined *Nabarro Nathanson* in 1997 as a Partner.
Personal: Born 12 April 1950. College Governor. F.E. Governor, company director,

director of environmental trust and Business in the Community.

MCCORMACK, Carol
Berwin Leighton, London +44 171 760 1000
Partner in Projects and Public Sector Department.
Specialisation: Principal area of work is advising government departments, health bodies, educational establishments, local authorities and other public sector clients on major commercial transactions such as those undertaken through the Private Finance Initiative, town centre redevelopment and refurbishment agreements. Also handles public sector and institutional property work, including grant-related work and the acquisition and disposal of commercial property generally. Presented workshops at Cipfa annual conferences 1991-97, to various local authority valuer associations and co-hosts the *Berwin Leighton* seminars for local government lawyers.
Prof. Memberships: British Council of Shopping Centres, Committee Member of Women in Property.
Career: Articled with *Berwin Leighton* 1983-85 and became a Partner in 1989.
Personal: Born in Middlesbrough 22nd February 1961, attended Selwyn College, Cambridge.

MCGOWAN, Graham
Titmuss Sainer Dechert, London
(0171) 583 5353
Partner in Property Department.
Specialisation: Head of Public Sector unit and member of Property Investment and Development units. Specialises in Local Authority consultancy for major development schemes, town planning and local government finance. Also acts for health and education bodies, as well as private sector organisations. Specialisms include Local Authority Capital Control. Joint author of 'Capital Controls - which way forward?'.
Career: Qualified in 1965. Initially with Richmond upon Thames London Borough Council until 1980 and was Solicitor to the Council/Head of Administration until 1988. 1988-1993 - partner at *Narbarro Nathanson*, 1993-1995 - partner at *Bird & Bird*. 1995-present partner at *Titmuss Sainer Dechert*.
Personal: Born in 1942. Interests include tennis, skiing and travel. Lives in Surrey.

MURRAY, Andrew J.
Winckworth & Pemberton (incorporating Sherwood & Co), London (0171) 593 5000
See under Housing Associations, p. 418

RANDALL, Simon
Lawrence Graham, London (0171) 379 0000
Partner, Head of Local and Public Authority Unit.
Specialisation: Principal area of practice is public sector work advising local authorities on externalisation, charitable trusts, urban regeneration and public procurement, PFI, housing and competitive tendering. Involved in large scale voluntary transfers of housing stock to housing associations and local housing companies. Author of many articles and pamphlets on local government and social issues ranging from the private rented sector, large scale voluntary sector of housing stock, local authority companies, community care and housing finance. Organises many seminars on

health service, housing and local government related matters.

Prof. Memberships: Law Society.

Career: Articled with *Lawrence Graham* and became a Partner in 1970. Member, London Borough of Bromley 1968 - 1994. Chairman London Borough of Bromley Housing Committee 1971-76 and Leader of the Council 1976-81. Member Greater London Council 1981-86. Chairman, London Boroughs Association Housing and Social Services Committee 1978 - 1994. Non-executive Director Bethlem Royal and Maudsley Special Health Authority 1971-94.

Personal: Born 1944. Attended Westminster School and the College of Law, Lancaster Gate. Appointed CBE in June 1991 for housing work in London. Chairman Kelsey Housing Association Ltd and Director Kelsey Care Ltd: formed to provide sheltered and supported housing for those with learning disabilities and the mentally ill. Member of Management Committee of Broomleigh Housing Association Ltd. Secretary, Housing Centre Trust. Member of Editorial Board of Roof magazine. Local Authority Consultancy Services Ltd, Member National Housing Federation Executive Board & Council.

SCHWEHR, Belinda
Rowe & Maw, London (0171) 248 4282
Specialisation: Conducts judicial review proceedings for applicants and respondents and advises on the interaction between public and private law principles for a wide range of clients. Practice ranges from social services law to PFI. Recent work has involved the implementation of statutory functions in the context of scarce resources and the risk of tortious claims for breach of statutory duty after

Gloucestershire and *X v Bedfordshire*, the scope for public law challenge in actions for the recovery of debts arising from statutory charges; hospital discharge disputes; the extent of statutory powers of guardianship in respect of the mentally incapacitated given the possibility of an action for trespass and false imprisonment after *Bournewood*; limitations on the powers of local authorities to contract; the Local Government (Contracts) Act 1997; working with Cherie Booth on an HMSO project to put social services law on the internet, and preparation for the implications of the Human Rights Act for the private and public sector. Advises both local authority and NHS auditors; currently acting for partnerships, and for the proprietor of a clinic regarding his dealings with the Human Fertility and Embryology Authority. A willing advocate. Offers annual advice packages to Social Services Department, involving preventative public law advice for departmental lawyers and Members, and training of care managers.

Prof. Memberships: Administrative Law Bar Association.

Career: Barrister 1985, private practice until 1990 in civil common law chambers; LLM in public law, UCL 1990; university lecturer in public law and a consultant 1990-1997; consultant to author of Community Care Practice and the Law (Jessica Kingsley Ltd 1994); joined *Rowe & Maw* 1997; re-qualified as solicitor 1998; author of many articles on public law issues including a monthly contribution in In-house Lawyer; regular speaker at national conferences, seminars and training sessions. Visiting Fellow, Westminster University.

Personal: Born 1962; Visiting fellow of the University of Westminister; Assistant Editor of

the Administrative Law Report; leisure interests include Having It All.

TOTMAN, Edward
D J Freeman, London (0171) 583 4055
Property Partner.

Specialisation: Principal area of work involves local government and public authorities, including controls on local authority finance and capital expenditure and on company participation, extent of powers, town centre development agreements and joint ventures between public and private sectors. Other main area of work is general commercial property advice and agreements for funding, development, purchase, sale and lettings of all types of commercial property. General legal adviser to the Commission for the New Towns on strategic corporate issues. Development projects include the Glades Centre, Bromley; the Swan Centre, Eastleigh; Chelmsford Shopping Centre and Basildon, Fareham, Chichester and Cwmbran Town Centres. Author of various articles on public and private sector initiatives, local authority capital expenditure controls and 'clawback'. Has chaired and spoken at various conferences and seminars. Legal adviser to The City 2020 Regeneration Initiative 1995/96. Co-author of Section on Joint Venture Agreements in Local Government Precedents and Procedures, published by FT Law & Tax.

Prof. Memberships: Law Society.

Career: Qualified 1970. With Greater London Council 1966-72, Abbey National Building Society 1972-74, Mercantile Credit Company Ltd 1974-79. Joined *D J Freeman* in 1979 and became a Partner in 1981.

Personal: Born 28th June 1942. Attended Wimbledon College, then King's College, London. Leisure pursuits include theatre, reading, swimming, tennis and walking. Lives in Ewell.

The SOUTH and WALES

Bevan Ashford (Plymouth, Exeter) (3ptnrs/4assts) The firm has traditionally had a strong public sector group which was headed by Malcolm Iley before he moved to Nabarros. The team is now headed by a commercial property partner. **Clients/Work:** Town Centre supermarket development for South Devon District Council. South London Science and Technology Park for London Borough of Croydon. Transfer of Careers

Service of three north London boroughs to Prospect.

Morgan Bruce (Cardiff) Peter Burgess left the firm and *Alun Cole,* a public law specialist, now heads the team. The perception in the marketplace is that he is PFI oriented.

Edwards Geldard (Cardiff) (1ptnr/ 2assts) The team led by *Huw Williams* covers local government law from the planning and environmental perspective with particular emphasis on vires work this year. **Clients/Work:** Winding up the Cardiff Bay Opera House Trust and appointed to act for Wales Millennium Centre, the successor project awarded funding by the Millennium Commission and the Arts Council of Wales. Advising on issues relating to constitution of local authority controlled companies.

Eversheds (Cardiff) (7ptnrs/12assts) The practice is broadly based covering property, planning, joint ventures, procurement work, construction and employment. *Eric Evans* is "the name" in the practice although he wears many different hats. His main specialism is in property/PFI-related work for local authorities. **Clients/Work:** Working with Newport County Borough Council re

£1.7 billion investment in South Wales. Providing specialist advice to Welsh Development Agency re common land matters.

Veale Wasbrough (Bristol) (4ptnrs/ 1asst) The team works within the Property Services Department and Company & Commercial Department. They run the Local Government Training Forum, providing training for 'in-house' legal staff. *Basil Smith,* former Chief Executive of Avon County Council and *Simon Baker,* a property lawyer, run the group. **Clients/Work:** Bath Spa Millennium project advising Bath and North East Somerset Council on funding structure and development issues. Advising Bristol City Council on Bristol Harbourside Project, a priority "A" urban regeneration scheme on the DoE's list of local authority PFI projects with millennium funding.

Blake Lapthorn (Fareham) (3ptnrs/ 2assts) Have recruited a local authority procurement specialist to develop the public law practice. Act for 22 local authorities. The main thrust of the work is procurement and PFI. **Clients/Work:** Externalised contracts for local authorities including Brent, Ealing and Croydon.

Dolmans (Cardiff) (5ptnrs/18assts) The pre-eminent firm in the area for local authority insurance-related work, which is "almost a sub-specialism of its own." *Jeffrey MacWilkinson* a senior litigation partner who specialises in professional negligence work, is "well-known in his field." Clients/Work: Favourable settlement of case for Swansea Council involving ransom strip at Whitegates Estate, Swansea. Acting for local authorities in stress-related cases involving employees, and claims brought on behalf of children alleging failure to provide special educational needs. Acting for sixteen Unitary Authorities in Wales dealing with civil litigation.

Underwoods (St. Albans) (2ptnrs/1asst) Two-partner firm doing about 20% local authority work, led by a former London Borough Councillor. Clients/Work: Judicial review of Local Education Authorities' decision on allocation of secondary school places in single sex school. Advising company on judicial review of local authority procedure on CCT in failing to award contract.

MIDLANDS and EAST ANGLIA

Dibb Lupton Alsop (Birmingham) (5ptnrs/1cons/3assts) The firm's local government client base was strengthened by the merger. Major in PFI work. *Anthony Randle* is a specialist in corporate transactional work for local authorities. *Michael Orlik* probably has "more local government experience than anybody else on the list." He is an "ex local government wallah, strong on highways and agreements between developers." Clients/Work: Advising Malvern Hills District Council on establishment of Malvern Hills Science Park. Advising Cheshire Police Authority on rationalisation of accommodation under PFI. Advising Doncaster Metropolitan Borough Council on procurement of North Bridge Relief Road under PFI.

Pinsent Curtis (Birmingham) (6ptnrs/6assts) Known for development and planning work for urban development corporations, local authorities and the Commission for the New Towns. Focusing more on major project work. *Andrew Stacey* and *Martin White* get good reviews. Clients/Work: London Luton Airport – £60m concession-based financing scheme. Acting for Walsall Council on town centre redevelopment. Acting for seven West Midlands councils on innovative £150m refinancing of Birmingham International Airport.

Anthony Collins (Birmingham) (6ptnr/10assts) Seen as a "respectable firm" doing lots of work for housing trusts. Advice on PFI, best value and regeneration. *Martin Knox* is described as "a very bright guy indeed." *Mark Cook* is "excellent" on vires questions, privatisations and CCT. Clients/Work: Major regeneration scheme in West Yorkshire totalling over £100m in public and private investment. Involvement in 6 large scale housing stock transfers with ERCF funding. PFI work in education and housing.

Eversheds (Nottingham, Derby, Birmingham) (1ptnr f/t, 1ptnr p/t/ 7assts) The firm services local authority clients from the commercial sector and is building up PFI work. *Stephen Matthew* in Nottingham is ex-County Solicitor at Shropshire, but "not very high profile." The firm is developing the Birmingham office capability for this work. Clients/Work: Completion of first school PFI project (Colfox School) in November 1997 acting for Dorset County Council. Acting for Lincolnshire County Council in sale of transport division, Lincway.

Wragge & Co (Birmingham) (8ptnrs/6assts) The firm has strengthened its public sector work by recruiting a former Director of Legal and Administrative Services at the City and County of Swansea to head up the Public Sector Group. Clients/Work: Acting on behalf of Hereford and Worcester County Council on a pathfinder PFI project involving the appointment of a private sector partner to provide and service magistrates courts accommodation. Acting on behalf of Solihull MBC in connection with development of Blythe Valley Business Park. Acting§ on behalf of Solihull MBC in connection with development of Blythe Valley Business Park.

Browne Jacobson (Nottingham) 4ptnrs/16assts) The public authority group encompasses both contentious and non-contentious work and carries out defence and advisory work for police and fire authorities as well as local authorities. Specialisms include child abuse, educational cases, statutory nuisance and enforcement work for English Nature. Clients/Work: Representing education departments of 12 local authorities in defending claims brought by pupils and former pupils in relation to alleged failure to diagnose dyslexia and bullying. Following successful defence at a one month trial of a multi-party housing action, instructed in a large number of statutory nuisance actions by Walsall MBC.

Gotelee & Goldsmith (Ipswich) (3ptnrs/2assts) The firm specialises in planning, much of which involves local planning authority clients. Also acts for Westminster City Council on commercial property matters. *Brian Morron* is the local government specialist. Clients/Work: Multimillion pound civil engineering contract for strengthening of northern foundation of Waterloo Bridge for Westminster City Council. Advice on construction contract to Enfield London Borough Council.

Steele & Co (Norwich) (3ptnrs/3assts) "Very much a planning-based firm" but the Public Sector Team covers work across the spectrum of local authority matters. Clients/Work: IMAX Cinema Complex in Waterloo for Lambeth Borough Council. Bromley London Borough Council for non-routine property work.

The NORTH

Eversheds (Leeds) (2ptnrs/1cons/10assts) Many members of the team are ex-local authority. The team acted in the first four PFI deals in local government to reach financial close. *Stephen Cirell* is head of the public sector, local authority and PFI work nationally and "his name is up in headlights." He and *John Bennett* are procurement experts and *David Kilduff* is the waste and energy specialist. Have taken on a consultant from the Chartered Institute of Public Finance to set up a new consultancy offering legal advice on governance, partnerships and best value. **Clients/Work:** Development of the PFI system. Specialist service to develop codes of corporate governance and advise on Nolan principles. Transition of CCT into a system of Best Value.

Masons (Leeds) (2ptnrs/3assts) The firm's well-established reputation for construction work lends a construction/planning flavour to its local authority practice. Also specialise in procurement work. Seen as having expanded recently; they also have a significant presence in Manchester. **Clients/Work:** Acting for Leeds City Council on major dispute concerning South Leeds Stadium. Continuing to act for Leeds City Council on major disputes concerning the pedestrianisation scheme. Advising Harrogate Borough Council on a project for refurbishing Airey Homes.

Pannone & Partners (Manchester) (5ptnrs/5assts) The Public Sector Team works out of several different departments. Have particular experience in dealing with transport issues for local authorities, but not high profile for this work. **Clients/Work:** Advising Greater Manchester Passenger Transport Executive on £130m contract for extension of Manchester Metrolink system.

Acting for the Benefits Agency re north west property aspects of the "PRIME" PFI project, involving 178 properties in the North West. Acting for Rochdale Metropolitan Borough Council in connection with an urban regeneration project in Rochdale, involving refurbishment and new build by a private sector developer.

Pinsent Curtis (Leeds) (6ptnrs/9assts) The team is known for hospital authority projects and enter the tables. The local government work is sourced out of the PFI Group. **Clients/Work:** Cardinal Heenan High School – local authority education PFI project. North Yorkshire County Council – Pathfinder PFI road scheme. London Borough of Hackney – pioneering £75m IT outsourcing project.

SCOTLAND

Brodies WS (4ptnrs) Local government work covers the whole spectrum including judicial review. The four members of the team specialise in waste management regulations, environmental issues and local authority finance; planning; commercial property and transfers of housing stock. **Clients/Work:** Acting for councils in litigation, including contentious aspects of building and contractual matters. Advising on vires of a scheme whereby CCTV operations in a local authority area were transferred to a company set up for that purpose.

Shepherd & Wedderburn WS (3ptnrs/3assts) The team's local authority work includes housing, planning and PFI. *Ian McLeod* is senior litigation partner and he heads the firm's judicial review practice. **Clients/Work:** Major development at Chapel

Kirkcaldy for Fife Council. Acting for various local authorities re forthcoming PFI/Infrastructure projects and in particular new school for East Renfrewshire Council. Advising City of Edinburgh Council on new recreation and leisure facilities.

Bennett & Robertson One of the firm's specialisms is commercial litigation re local authority matters; mainly judicial review in the Court of Session. The "effective" *John Macfie* is court partner.

Burness (6ptnrs/5assts) Specialise in PFI, privatisation and procurement work from the Public Sector Unit. Former leader Annette Pairman has recently left the firm and it remains to be seen what effect this will have on the group. **Clients/Work:** Appointment for the Craigmillar Regeneration Project from City of Edinburgh to advise on development of model for local regeneration company. Advising Oakbank Limited on joint venture between ERDC in Partnership and West Lothian Council for construction of industrial facilities.

Campbell Smith WS (1ptnr) Have lost the Glasgow City Council work since it was taken back in-house and this "may cause them some problems." *John Crawford* ("rated and liked") spends most of his time on this work, which is litigation-based.

Harper Macleod (3ptnrs/2assts) When contract with Stirling District Council ended the team retained general advisory role with

specific responsibility for debt recovery, housing and PFI. Also involved in housing disposals to public/private partnerships. **Clients/Work:** Advising Stirling Council on Public/Private joint venture partnership with John Laing Developments Limited and DePfa-Bank A.G. in respect of the Stirling Thistle Marches Shopping Centre. Devising structure in relation to successful bids by East Ayrshire Council and North Lanarkshire Council for New Housing Partnership Grant.

Simpson & Marwick WS (3ptnrs) "A top litigation firm doing a considerable amount of public work." Act for local authorities and other public bodies such as fire authorities, water authorities etc. in defending public liability claims and bringing claims against third parties. *Michael Wood* is recommended. **Clients/Work:** Currently involved in the e-coli fatal accident inquiry for North Lanarkshire Council's insurer's. Acted for West Lothian Council regarding the e-coli outbreak. Acting in fatal accident inquiries for fire services.

BAKER, Simon
Veale Wasbrough, Bristol (0117) 925 2020
Partner in Property Services Department.
Specialisation: Main areas of practice are commercial property and public administrative law. Work includes property, tendering, joint ventures, developments, landlord and tenant and acquisitions and disposals for the public sector. Other area of expertise is local government work, including CCT, externalisations, regional economic development and planning. Acts for local authorities, development agencies, private and public sector partnerships and developers.
Prof. Memberships: Law Society.
Career: Qualified in 1971. Joined *Veale Wasbrough* in 1972, becoming a Partner in 1973 and Chairman in 1990 until 1998. Council Member of the Law Society of England and Wales from 1989 until 1997. President of Bristol Law Society 1991-92. Director of Solicitors Indemnity Fund Ltd from 1990 until 1997. Director of Western Training and Enterprise Council Ltd since 1993. Director of Western Development Partnership Ltd since 1993.
Personal: Born 15th April 1945. Attended Clare College, Cambridge 1964-68. Lives in Bristol.

BENNETT, John
Eversheds, Leeds (0113) 243 0391
Consultant in Public Sector Unit.
Specialisation: Work covers all aspects of contracting and tendering, including PFI, CCT and EC public procurement. Specialist Editor on Competition for the Encyclopaedia of Local Government Law, and Local Government Precedents and Procedures, co-author of 'Compulsory Competitive Tendering: Law and Practice'; co-author of 'Municipal Trading'; co-author of 'EC Public Procurement: Law and Practice'; co-author of 'Compulsory Tendering for Professional Services'; co-author of over one hundred articles on public sector contracting. Has appeared on TV and addressed numerous conferences and seminars.
Prof. Memberships: Law Society.
Career: Qualified in 1975. Became a Consultant in 1984. Previous appointments include *Malcolm Lynch Solicitors* in Leeds; Head of Public Law Group at Leeds Business School; Solicitor at the Department of Education and Science; Education Assets Board; Senior Contracts Solicitor at Brown & Root (UK) Ltd (Consultant to Esso, Shell, ELF and Mobil); *Peysner & Foley Solicitors* in Sheffield; *John Howell & Co. Solicitors* in Sheffield; and Solicitor for Nottinghamshire County Council.
Personal: Born 11th October 1950. Attended Universities of Nottingham and Sheffield. Leisure interests include wife and family, and outdoor pursuits. Lives in Leeds.

CIRELL, Stephen
Eversheds, Leeds (0113) 243 0391
Partner in Public Sector Unit.
Specialisation: Principal area of practice covers compulsory competitive tendering, externalisation, market testing, municipal trading, European Community Public Procurement the Private Finance Initiative and public sector contracting generally. Other main

area of work is local government law including housing, finance, planning, environmental health, education, social services and highways. Co-author of 'CCT- Law & Practice' (FT 1990), 'Municipal Trading' (FT 1992), 'Competitive Tendering for Professional Services' (FT 1994) and 'Private Finance Initiative for Local Authorities' (FT 1997). Specialist editor to Encyclopaedia of Local Government Law. Specialist correspondent to the Local Government Chronicle and author of numerous articles for professional publications. Lectures frequently on CCT and related matters for commercial course organisers, professional organisations, local authorities and in-house.
Prof. Memberships: Law Society.
Career: Qualified 1984 while with Stockport MBC. Assistant Solicitor, then Principal Solicitor with Dudley MBC 1984-88, then Head of Common Law/Assistant Director at Leeds City Council 1988-93. Joined *Eversheds Hepworth & Chadwick* as a Partner in the Public Sector Unit in October 1993.
Personal: Born 3rd July 1960. Attended University College of Wales Aberystwyth 1978-81. Leisure pursuits include martial arts. Lives in Leeds.

COLE, Alun
Morgan Bruce, Cardiff (01222) 385385
See under Administrative & Public Law, p. 91

COOK, Mark
Anthony Collins Solicitors, Birmingham (0121) 200 3242
Specialisation: Public sector commercial lawyer, with particular experience of "public/private partnerships" in the local government, NHS and education sectors. Advising principally upon service delivery, strategic procurements, facilities management and the Private Finance Initiative, with considerable involvement in EC public procurement, UK competitive tendering legislation and vires issues.
Prof. Memberships: Law Society.
Career: Mark has recently joined from *Pinsent Curtis*, where he was extensively involved in advising upon market testing, externalisations and the Private Finance Initiative in the local government, NHS and education sectors. He has been principally responsible for exploring a legal framework for the "Public Sector Plc" initiative, and contributed to the book of that title published in January 1997.
Personal: Leisure interests - World music, real ale, football and walking. Family details – Married with 2 children.

CRAWFORD, John H.
Campbell Smith WS, Edinburgh (0131) 556 3737

EVANS, Eric
Eversheds, Cardiff (01222) 471147
See under Administrative & Public Law, Planning, Property (Commercial), p. 91,653,709

KILDUFF, David
Eversheds, Leeds (0113) 243 0391
Specialisation: Principal areas of practice primarily concern all aspects of the work of local

government and publicly funded bodies. Emphasis on the commercial and development opportunities in all their forms. Has extensive experience of major development projects both as legal adviser and project manager. Has acted in major procurement and externalisation of services associated with waste management/LAWDCs, highways construction and related services, education, legal and other services. Currently leading the way on public/private partnerships innovations and related funding issues. David is the author of the lead introduction to PFI in the new 'Knights Guide' published by Tolleys. David has led key major projects including the Isle of Wight PFI Waste Project for which he was recently awarded the County Surveyors Plate in recognition of the financial benefits which the project created for the Island. Has spoken at a wide range of conferences and seminars on the PFI, Waste Management services, EU procurement and other issues concerning the public sector.
Prof. Memberships: Law Society: Member of the specialist Law Society Planning Panel.
Career: Qualified in 1982. Appointments include Assistant Chief Solicitor Stockton on Tees, Deputy Secretary Ashford Borough Council then Borough Secretary and Solicitor 1988-1995. Former secretary and honorary legal adviser to the Kent Association of district Councils. Joined *Eversheds* in December 1995.
Personal: Born 26 July 1958. Attended the University of Kent. Married with three children. Lives in Shipley.

KNOX, Martin
Anthony Collins Solicitors, Birmingham (0121) 200 3242
See under Housing Associations, p. 424

MACFIE, John
Bennett & Robertson, Edinburgh (0131) 225 4001

MACLEOD, D. Ian K.
Shepherd & Wedderburn WS, Edinburgh (0131) 228 9900
See under Administrative & Public Law, Employment, Litigation (Commercial), p. 92, 322, 534

MACWILKINSON, Jeffrey
Dolmans, Cardiff (01222) 345531
See under Professional Negligence, p. 676

MATTHEW, Stephen
Eversheds, Nottingham (0115) 950 7000
Specialisation: Joined *Eversheds* in 1995 having previously worked for fifteen years within local government. Before joining *Eversheds*, he was County Secretary and Solicitor of Shropshire County Council. Educated at Farnham Grammar School, the University of Sheffield and the College of Law, London. He specialises in local authority work and is an honorary member of the Association of Council Secretaries and Solicitors. He began his career with South Yorkshire County Council, moved on to Derbyshire County Council and joined Shropshire County Council in 1998 as Assistant County Secretary. Married with three children and lives on the outskirts of Nottingham.

MORRON, Brian
Gotelee & Goldsmith, Ipswich
(01473) 211121
Partner in Commercial Department.
Specialisation: Main areas of practice are local government, planning and employment law. 24 years experience of local authority legal work: ex-Deputy Borough Solicitor at Wandsworth LBC. Chaired Associate Section of the Association of District Secretaries, 1988. Acted as Borough Solicitor to the Royal Borough of Kingston Upon Thames while based in Suffolk. Managed six month contract in 1991 to transfer total housing stock of Suffolk Coastal District Council to a housing association. Currently manages three five year contracts with two other London Borough Councils. Member of Law Society's Planning Panel.
Prof. Memberships: Law Society;
Career: Qualified in 1976. Principal Planning Solicitor, London Borough of Haringey 1978-80, Deputy Borough Solicitor, London Borough of Wandsworth 1983-89. Joined *Gotelee & Goldsmith* in 1989, from 1990 as a partner; from May 1996 as Managing Partner.
Personal: Born 8th March 1949. Attended University of London (LSE), taking an LLB and LLM 1971-2. Executive Committee Member of Suffolk Book League. Lives in Framlingham, Suffolk.

ORLIK, Michael
Dibb Lupton Alsop, Birmingham
(0345) 262728
Partner in Property Litigation Group.
Specialisation: Main area of practice is town and country planning, environmental law, highway law and compulsory purchase. Worked for four local authorities from 1967 to 1989. Currently has a number of local authority and developer clients. Also advises on local authority legislation, powers of local authorities and judicial review.
Has represented numerous clients at local inquiries. Acted in the Skypark planning inquiry, the prosecution of a County Council for obstructing a highway and a lengthy Lands Tribunal case for compensation for compulsory acquisition by a Development Corporation. Author of 'An Introduction to Highway Law' (1993); contributes regular monthly column for the Surveyor. Has lectured on these topics at a number of seminars.
Prof. Memberships: Law Society, Society of Local Authority Chief Executives. Environmental Law Foundation, Education Law Association.
Career: Qualified in 1970. VSO teacher in West Africa 1965-66. Articled clerk and then solicitor with West Sussex C.C. 1967-77. Assistant County Solicitor at Buckinghamshire C.C. 1977-81. Assistant Chief Executive at Dorset C.C. 1981-84. Chief Executive of Surrey Heath B.C. 1984-89. Joined *Needham & James* as a Partner in 1990; firm merged with *Dibb Lupton Broomhead* in 1993.
Personal: Born 21st September 1943. Attended Oxford University 1962-65. Degree in History.

RANDLE, Tony
Dibb Lupton Alsop, Birmingham
(0345) 262728
Partner in Corporate Group.
Specialisation: Practice is exclusively local government and commercial work between the public and private sectors. Heads up DLA's national public/private partnerships group which includes the firm's PFI and local government practices. Has acted for numerous local authorities (Midland and national) on joint ventures, privatisations and externalisations. Led the DLA team advising Coventry City Council on the privatisation of Coventry Airport. Leading 5 pathfinder school PFI projects (including all the pathfinder projects for the Department of Education for Northern Ireland).
Prof. Memberships: Law Society.
Career: Qualified 1987. Partner 1993.
Personal: Born 1962. Exeter University (LLB).

SMITH, Basil
Veale Wasbrough, Bristol (0117) 925 2020
Veale Wasbrough Local Authority Unit.
Specialisation: Appointed by the Local Government Training Forum, an association of 15 Local Authorities to provide training for their 'in-house' legal staff. The training is accredited for the purposes of C.P.D. provision of a comprehensive range of legal, financial, I.T., property and training services through an established consortium made up of Coopers & Lybrand, Donaldsons, The Business School of the University of the West of England and Veale Wasbrough. The consortium is called *Network – working together for local government*. Training for elected councillors. Recently concluded a successful training programme for the councillors of North Somerset Council – a new 'unitary authority'. Approved supplier of legal services to 25 Local Authorities in the South West of England.
Prof. Memberships: Governor of the University of the West of England. Former Clerk to the Avon & Somerset Police Authority. Association of County Chief Executives. Society for Local Authorities Chief Executives. Association of Council Secretaries and Solicitors.
Career: An extensive career in local government, culminating in the appointment as Chief Executive and Clerk of Avon County Council (1989-1995). Formerly County Solicitor of Avon (1982-1989). Currently, Head of Local Government Practice, *Veale Wasbrough*, Bristol.
Personal: Fly fishing, gardening, walking.

STACEY, Andrew J.
Pinsent Curtis, Birmingham (0121) 200 1050
See under Administrative & Public Law, p. 92

WHITE, Martin
Pinsent Curtis, Birmingham (0121) 200 1050
See under Administrative & Public Law, Planning, p. 92, 658

WILLIAMS, Huw
Edwards Geldard, Cardiff (01222) 238239
See under Administrative & Public Law, Planning, p. 92, 658

WOOD, Michael M.
Simpson & Marwick WS, Edinburgh
(0131) 557 1545

MEDIA AND ENTERTAINMENT

RESEARCH: In compiling the tables, we consider all the information available to us, paying particular regard to the market research carried out by our team of ten qualified lawyers. (The researchers' details are set out on page three.) The rankings, therefore, reflect the opinion of the marketplace as revealed by systematic and objective research: see page four. (Our research is audited every year by the British Market Research Bureau.)

OVERVIEW: We have sub-divided the Film and Broadcasting trade into Film Finance, Film & TV Production, and Broadcasting. Film Finance is a new table which highlights firms acting for banks and film financiers. Film & TV Production focuses on work for "producer" clients, including acquiring rights, production/distribution and the borrowing side of finance. Broadcasting includes firms specialising in carriage, regulatory work, content, applications for licences, corporate joint ventures and launching new channels. Some of this work overlaps with Digital Media.

The new film finance table highlights the finance strength of SJ Berwin & Co and Richards Butler. Harbottle & Lewis join Olswang and Marriott Harrison at the top of Film & TV production. Olswang is also at the top of broadcasting and Denton Hall is top in all three sections.

In digital media, Bird & Bird move up to the top band and Liam McNieve and his firm are new entries. Laurie Kaye has left The Simkins Partnership and joined Paisners bringing them into the section.

In music, Russells still stand out at the top and there are four new entries: Hamlin Slowe, Babbington & Bray, Searles and Harrison Curtis. John Cohen joins the theatre tables from music and in publishing, Denton Hall and Taylor Joynson Garrett move up into a band of their own.

Lawrence Harrison and Tim Curtis have also left The Simkins Partnership and set up Harrison Curtis, a niche media practice, which enters the broadcasting, music and theatre tables.

In the South and Wales, the tables have been refined and only those firms which have a specialist media practice remain. Wiggin and Co stand out as the leading firm. In the Midlands and East Anglia, Frances Anderson and her firm move into a band of their own at the top. Sarah Williams, a leader last year, has moved her practice to London. The North remains the same as last year, with niche practitioners handling much of the work. In Scotland, Anderson Strathern and Levy & McRae have entered the tables, and Graham Sibbald of Dundas & Wilson enters as a leading individual.

LONDON

FILM FINANCE/ FILM & TV PRODUCTION/ BROADCASTING

S J Berwin & Co (4ptnrs/7assts make up the Media and Communications Group) *Nigel Palmer* is renowned for being a leading finance lawyer and his production work is

LEADING FIRMS · FILM FINANCE
S J BERWIN & CO
DENTON HALL
RICHARDS BUTLER
BERWIN LEIGHTON
DAVENPORT LYONS
HAMMOND SUDDARDS
OLSWANG

also acknowledged. *Peter McInerney* is rated for a broad range of media work. **Clients/Work:** Acting for Guinness Mahon & Co Ltd on financing of films including "Wilde" and "Chinese Box." Production and financing for Mandalay Entertainment. Advising Radio companies Viva and Golden Rose on regulatory issues. Production work on "Sliding Doors."

Denton Hall (4ptnrs/7assts) *Ken Dearsley* is widely respected for his finance expertise and is also rated for production work. *Michael Ridley* ("amusing," "competent," "hard working") is unanimously regarded as a leader in the broadcasting field. *Adrian Barr-Smith* is respected for general media work but is better known as a sports law specialist. **Clients/Work:** Representing French financier Cofiloisirs in creation of syndicated revolving credit facility for The Film Consortium. Production finance and distribution work for Japanese producer/financier Nippon Film Development and Finance Inc in "Assassin." Represented The Bridge (Sony Pictures and Studio Canal joint venture) in start up operations and acquisition of rights and development deals for over 10 feature films. Advising British Digital Broadcasting on all operational aspects of the new service. Advising on Flextech/BBC joint venture.

Richards Butler (4ptnrs/4assts 100%) *Richard Philipps* is undoubtedly one of the leading finance lawyers and he also does some production work. *Barry Smith* is experienced in production work and is known for having a wide client base. *Stephen Edwards* has a strong reputation for his broadcasting work and is described as "intelligent and easy to work with." **Clients/Work:** Clients include Banque Internationale de Luxembourg; Berliner Bank; Coutts & Co; Banque Paribas; Los Angeles Agency; Channel Four International; North South Productions;

Entertainment Film Distributors; MTV and BBC.

Berwin Leighton (6ptnrs/1asst make up the Media & Hi-Tech Group) Known as an established player in production and broadcasting work, but has its strongest reputation in finance. *Lloyd Evans, Andrew Somper* and *Peter Stone* are noted leaders. **Clients/Work:** Advised Royal Bank of Canada on gap financing films including "Intimate Relations" and "Suspicious Minds." Advising Total Film Group Inc on all production work

LEADING FIRMS FILM AND TV PRODUCTION
DENTON HALL
HARBOTTLE & LEWIS
MARRIOTT HARRISON
OLSWANG
RICHARDS BUTLER
THE SIMKINS PARTNERSHIP
S J BERWIN & CO
DAVENPORT LYONS
THEODORE GODDARD
BERWIN LEIGHTON
HARRISON CURTIS
HENRY HEPWORTH
LEE & THOMPSON
SCHILLING & LOM AND PARTNERS

for "New Swiss Family Robinson" film ($6m). Advising Endemol Entertainment BV on joint venture with Guardian Media Group.

Davenport Lyons The firm's strength is its production work and it is also recognised for finance and broadcasting work . *Leon Morgan* is respected as a leading production and finance lawyer. The firm is the "first choice" for a leading bank. **Clients/Work:** Film/TV finance work for Barclays Bank and The Royal Bank of Scotland. Film and TV production work includes "Jinnah" and "Brookside."

Hammond Suddards (2ptnrs/2assts) The media team is headed by *Brian Eagles* and *Christopher Parkinson,* the latter being known for finance work. The team provide an all-round media service and also act as executive producers. **Clients/Work:** Clients include Baltic Media plc, Barclays Bank plc and Coutts & Co. Films include "Appetite," "Dangerous Obsession" and "Something to Believe In."

Olswang (4ptnrs/8assts 100%) *Mark Devereux* heads the team and is almost unanimously rated as a leader in the finance and production field. *David Zeffman* ("knows the business," "easy to work with") has his strength in broadcasting. *Libby Savill* is also respected. **Clients/Work:** Acted for the management of HAL in setting up new Miramax backed entity in UK. Acted on lottery franchise application for Record Picture Company and others. Acted for Fox on

"Cinderella" and for MGM on "Tomorow Never Dies." Acted for BBC on joint venture with Discovery Communications to create global channel.

Harbottle & Lewis (3ptnrs/5assts) The firm's strength is in production work where it moves up the tables. *Robert Storer* ("brings in clients and gets things done") heads the team and moves up the tables following praise from contemporaries. *Medwyn Jones* was also recommended again. The firm also does broadcasting work. **Clients/Work:**

LEADING FIRMS · BROADCASTING
DENTON HALL
OLSWANG
CLIFFORD CHANCE
RICHARDS BUTLER
D J FREEMAN
GOODMAN DERRICK
HARBOTTLE & LEWIS
WIGGIN AND CO
ASHURST MORRIS CRISP
S J BERWIN & CO
BERWIN LEIGHTON
CAMPBELL HOOPER
DAVENPORT LYONS
FIELD FISHER WATERHOUSE
HENRY HEPWORTH
LOVELL WHITE DURRANT
THE SIMKINS PARTNERSHIP

Acted for Ecosse Films (producers of "Mrs Brown"); for Tiger Aspect (producers of "Mr Bean"); and for Five Girls Ltd (producers of "Spice World - The Movie"). Acting for BSkyB in joint venture with Music Choice Europe Co.

Marriott Harrison (6ptnrs/3assts) Undoubtedly a strong production team. *William Hinshelwood* has a reputation for being a "first class lawyer" who is "approachable." *Richard Moxon* is seen by competitors to handle a lot of work, is highly regarded by clients and moves up in the table. Also recommended is the well-known *Frank Bloom.* Peter Dally has moved to Bird & Bird. **Clients/Work:** Production work on "Bean," "Star Wars Prequel," "The Borrowers" and "The Jackal."

The Simkins Partnership (3ptnrs/2 assts – f/t; 1ptnr, 1asst – p/t) Team includes *Michael Simkins* and *Nigel Bennett.* The firm's strength is in production work for which it moves up the tables. *Anthony Gostyn* is described as "a first class lawyer with first class clients." The firm also does some broadcasting work. Suffered a blow with the departure of three media partners but maintain their strength in film work. **Clients/Work:** Include Channel 4, Coutts Bank, Matrix Films & Television plc.

Theodore Goddard (2ptnrs/6assts) Contemporaries praised the firm for being successful at what it sets out to do. *Peter*

Armstrong and *Jonathan Berger* are respected as leaders. **Clients/Work:** Advising DNA Films on lottery application and subsequently on its arrangements with the Arts Council of England and Polygram. Advised Columbia Pictures on joint venture for new production vehicle for Europe.

Harrison Curtis New niche firm set up by two ex-Simkins partners. Promises to be a major player in the film & TV production field. **Clients/Work:** Include Diplomat Films (Alan Bleasdale's film & TV production company); Zenith Productions and Zone Vision (cable and satellite channel provider).

Henry Hepworth *Michael Henry* is well known and highly regarded as an all-rounder in the media field. He can be "academic," but is an "experienced and very good lawyer." **Clients/Work:** Film & TV production clients include London Films, Skyline Films and Mainstream SA. Broadcasting clients include S4C- the Welsh TV Authority, Gaelic TV Committee and Teilifis Na Gaeligh (Eire).

Lee & Thompson (3ptnrs) Strong on the production side, with unique expertise in music programming. *Jeremy Gawade* ("experienced," "efficient," "good attention to detail") has an impressive reputation among clients. **Clients/Work:** Film production work includes "Spiceworld: The Movie," "Resurrection Man," "The Man with Rain in his Shoes," and "Among Giants." TV production work on "Coming Home" (ITV), "Out of Hours" (BBC) and "No Sweat" (BBC).

Schilling & Lom and Partners (1ptnr/3assts) *Nicholas Lom* heads the team who specialise in non-contentious film, television and music work.

Clifford Chance (13ptnrs/28 assts handle media work – 5ptnrs are f/t). Move up a band in broadcasting. Clients see the group as on the ball and "good on ideas." *Daniel Sandelson* ("excellent, commercial") enters the tables. **Clients/Work:** Acting for British Digital Broadcasting on its application for digital TV licences. Advised Front Row TV on joint venture to set up a pay-per-view movie and sports service. Advising ITN on cross-border investment re pan-European 24 hour news.

D J Freeman (5ptnrs/15assts make up the media and communications dept) **Clients/Work:** Acted on start up of Digital 3 & 4 Ltd re the running and management of their digital terrestrial TV multiplex.

Goodman Derrick Good all-round firm. Move up the tables following consistent praise. **Clients/Work:** Act for Granada, ITV, Channel 4 and the British Board of Film Classification.

Wiggin and Co (3ptnrs/6assts) Undertake non-contentious matters. Eight further lawyers are involved on the contentious side. The firm has a good reputation in this field and moves up the tables. **Clients/Work:** Advised on the film "The Man Who Knew Too Little;" advised Flextech and UKTV on ground-breaking "Millennium" Telewest carriage deal; acted on digital terrestrial tv transmission agreement for SDN.

Ashurst Morris Crisp (1ptnr/7assts) *Tony Ghee* is widely respected. **Clients/Work:** Advising AT Entertainment on channel distribution and programming licensing issues relating to the launch of its digital service in Poland. Acting for Elmsdale Media Ltd in drafting and negotiating VOD movie content supply agreements with three Hollywood studios. Advising Canal+ re licensing of English FA Premier League worldwide TV rights.

Campbell Hooper (3ptnrs/2consts/3 assts) *Carolyn Jennings* heads the Media Department. **Clients/Work:** Advised on the creation and development of new TV production and distribution company called Virgin Century TV Ltd. Advised producers of "Oscar and Lucinda." Representing Orange in their sponsorship of arts activities.

Field Fisher Waterhouse (3ptnrs 60%, total of 14 fee earners involved as required). *Anthony Ballard* ("first class broadcasting lawyer," "remarkably technical") remains a leader. **Clients/Work:** Advising Eurobell on proposals to introduce broadband television services using wireless microwave technology (MVDS). Successfully lobbied for a test and development licence for pioneering field trials of IMS using MVDS technology.

Lovell White Durrant (8ptnrs from various disciplines) **Clients/Work:** Acted for Granada re their involvement with BDB, and

its purchase of YTTV. Acted for The Laser Sales Co Ltd in dispute with the advertiser CIA over purchasing charges.

Peter Dally, ex Marriott Harrison, has moved to **Bird & Bird** where he will concentrate on film production finance and distribution.

LEADING INDIVIDUALS	
FILM FINANCE /FILM & TV PRODUCTION	
BLOOM Frank Marriott Harrison	
DEVEREUX Mark Olswang	
HINSHELWOOD William Marriott Harrison	
MORGAN Leon Davenport Lyons	
PALMER Nigel S J Berwin & Co	
PHILIPPS Richard Richards Butler	
STORER Robert Harbottle & Lewis	
ARMSTRONG Peter Theodore Goddard	
BERGER Jonathan Theodore Goddard	
DALLY Peter Bird & Bird	
DEARSLEY Ken Denton Hall	
GAWADE Jeremy Lee & Thompson	
GOSTYN Anthony The Simkins Partnership	
HENRY Michael Henry Hepworth	
JONES Medwyn Harbottle & Lewis	
MOXON Richard Marriott Harrison	
BARR-SMITH Adrian Denton Hall	
BENNETT Nigel The Simkins Partnership	
EAGLES Brian Hammond Suddards	
EVANS Lloyd Berwin Leighton	
LOM Nicholas Schilling & Lom and Partners	
MCINERNEY Peter S J Berwin & Co	
PARKINSON Christopher Hammond Suddards	
SAVILL Lisbeth Olswang	
SIMKINS Michael The Simkins Partnership	
SMITH Barry Richards Butler	
SOMPER Andrew Berwin Leighton	
STONE Peter Berwin Leighton	

LEADING INDIVIDUALS	
BROADCASTING	
BALLARD Anthony Field Fisher Waterhouse	
RIDLEY Michael Denton Hall	
SANDELSON Daniel Clifford Chance	
ZEFFMAN David Olswang	
EDWARDS Stephen Richards Butler	
GHEE Tony Ashurst Morris Crisp	
JENNINGS Carolyn Campbell Hooper	

DIGITAL MEDIA

Bird & Bird (16ptnrs/18assts handling digital media-related work as required) The firm has a growing reputation in the field with an active client base. *Graham Smith* ("highly rated," "strong reputation") and *David Kerr* ("gets on with it") are leaders. **Clients/Work:** Include Associated Newspapers, Aegean Net, EMAP.

Denton Hall (5ptnrs 55%, 3assts 55% make up a strong team.) *Nicholas Higham's* strength is said to be his wide-ranging inter-

LEADING FIRMS • DIGITAL MEDIA LONDON
BIRD & BIRD
DENTON HALL
OLSWANG
CLIFFORD CHANCE
HARBOTTLE & LEWIS
BIDDLE

est and experience in the field. Team includes *Alan Williams* and *Duncan Calow*. **Clients/Work:** Advising the British Library on its

HIGHLY REGARDED FIRMS
Henry Hepworth
Herbert Smith
Lovell White Durrant
Marriott Harrison
McNeive Solicitors
Mishcon de Reya
The Simkins Partnership

multi-million pound Digital Library Development Project under the Government's Private Finance Initiative.

Olswang (7ptnrs/8assts) Highly rated and provides digital media advice to most of its media clients. *David Zeffman* ("amazingly good") and *Kim Nicholson* ("good on corporate type mixed media") remain leaders. **Clients/Work:** Representing Mecklermedia in first reported case of trade marks on the Internet. Advise Yahoo on its UK activities.

Clifford Chance *David Griffiths* has a strong reputation and the team is "good technically." **Clients/Work:** Work comes from the media, computer and communications group and includes advising on the setting up of certification authorities and on the use and export of encryption technology.

Harbottle & Lewis Regarded as the leading firm in the computer games industry. *Mark Phillips* ("commercial," "pragmatic," "spots issues quickly") is highly rated. **Clients/Work:** Represented Sales Curve Interactive on appeal to Video Appeals Committee against decision of BBFC to refuse certificate under Video Recordings Act 1984 to the computer game Carmageddon. Internet advice to Microsoft Network and Virgin Net.

Biddle (1ptnr 50%/3assts 75%) *Kim Walker* heads the team. **Clients/Work:** Acting for ITN on contracts to manage ITV's web site. Advising Press Association on personalised Internet and mobile phone-based information service. Acting for ITN CD Rom in memory of Princess Diana agreement with Anglia Multimedia.

Henry Hepworth *Michael Henry* has been praised as an experienced "media all-rounder." **Clients/Work:** Represents British Film Institute, Aardman Animations and IMC Digital Media.

Herbert Smith (6ptnrs in the IP group work in digital media) The firm enters the tables this year following the acquisition of the "solid" *Mark Turner* from Garretts. **Clients/Work:** Broderbund PC game publishers. Internet service providers. CD-ROM publishers.

Lovell White Durrant (4 ptnrs including *Lindy Golding*, 10 assts in the computers and communications cross group team). **Clients/Work:** Acting for Discovision in CD manufacturing/licensing litigation. Acting for Barclays Bank on change of Internet service provider. Involved in design, set up and terms for Electronic Program Guides.

Marriott Harrison (2ptnrs 40%/2assts 50%) **Clients/Work:** Advises Mindscape International re computer games including distribution and sales arrangements. Advised Ingames Interactive on deal with SegaSoft. Acted for Digital Animations plc re exploitation of "Steel Legions."

McNeive Solicitors This new firm enters the tables following praise for *Liam McNeive*. Clients describe him as "incredibly bright," "a bit of a maverick." They appreciate his "pragmatic, commercial advice." **Clients/Work:** Advice to AOL and CompuServe on contracts for content acquisition, on-line advertising and web linking deals. Advising Real Media (on-line advertising) on licensing of software. Advice to Good Technology (web site producer).

Mishcon de Reya (2ptnrs/1const/4 assts) Team leader, *Jonathan Cameron*, was recommended again this year. **Clients/Work:** On-line work for newspapers and news agencies. Advice to UK entertainment and cable TV channels.

The Simkins Partnership Robert Hilton has taken over the digital media practice following the departure of *Laurence Kaye* to Paisners.

MUSIC

Russells (6ptnrs commercial, 3ptnrs litigation, 3assts both) The firm remains in a star band of its own – "undoubtedly the most dedicated music practice." Renowned particularly for high profile litigation. *Brian Howard* (litigation) and *Tony Russell* (commercial) remain leaders. **Clients/Work:** Record labels, music publishing companies, individual artists. Setting up new labels, selling and acquiring labels, contract drafting.

Clintons Well-known for high profile trials. *David Landsman*, *David Davis* and *Andrew Sharland* ("good client base," "knows how to run litigation and keep pressure on") are all leaders again.

Eatons (7ptnrs 100%, 3assts 100%) Team is led by *Michael Eaton* ("wonderful," "user-friendly") and *David Glick*. Noted for their commercial work. **Clients/Work:** Handled major independent deal involving restructuring of ZTT records. Set up independent labels for Skint records. Advise Eric Clapton and Bush.

Lee & Thompson (4ptnrs/3assts) Highly respected as one of the stronger firms on the commercial side. *Robert Lee*, *Andrew Thompson* ("good all-round experience") and *Robert Horsfall* were all recommended again. **Clients/Work:** Represent The Spice Girls and handle all their contractual arrangements. Negotiation of All Saints recording agreement with London Records (acting for band's manager). Action instigated by Bunny Wailer and the estate of Peter Tosh (of Bob Marley and the Wailers) against Island Records and the Marley Foundation.

Sheridans (5ptnrs/3assts – ft; 5ptnrs in the litigation dept pt) *Howard Jones* heads the media unit and *Cyril Glasser* is a litigator with music experience. **Clients/Work:** Generally acts for individuals rather than record companies. Clients include Sir Paul McCartney, Kate Bush and Ocean Colour Scene.

Statham Gill Davies (5ptnrs/2assts) **Clients/Work:** Represent Oasis and Suede.

Harbottle & Lewis (3ptnrs/3assts non contentious; 2 ptnrs, 2assts contentious 50%) *Andrew Stinson* ("good understanding of the industry") was described as "intellectual." *Lawrence Abramson* ("can be aggressive," "works very hard") was also recommended again. **Clients/Work:** Merchandising and sponsorship contracts for Spice Girls. Acted for Simon Fuller and 19 Management on termination of Spice Girls' management agreement. Acted for K-Tel v Flute International for breach of copyright resulting in interlocutory injunction for 126 recordings.

The Simkins Partnership (6ptnrs/ 2assts 90% commercial; 2ptnrs/1asst 60% litigation) *Julian Turton* ("impressive intellectual ability," "skilled negotiator," "inspires confidence") and *David Franks* were recommended again this year. **Clients/Work:** Representing Sony Europe on investment in independent labels. Continue to work for the Really Useful Group. Artist clients include Sir Cliff Richard.

Theodore Goddard (3ptnrs/5assts) *Paddy Grafton Green* has a formidable reputation and is known particularly for his tax advice to music clients. *James Harman* ("intellectually superior," "knows his stuff") and *Paul Renney* ("technically very good") are also recommended again. **Clients/Work:** Advising David Bowie on securitisation of royalties. Acted for Universal Music in its joint venture catalogue arrangements with Musicdisc SA. Advised Elvis Costello on distribution contracts with PolyGram Records Inc.

Babbington & Bray Solicitors Limited (2ptnrs 100%, 3assts 100%) A new entry following recommendation from contemporaries. **Clients/ Work:** Include Van Morrison, Texas and Universal Music/MCA Records.

Davenport Lyons *James Ware* heads the music work at the firm. **Clients/Work:** Acted on acquisition of music assets of Word Entertainment. Acted for the Vatican engaging Bob Dylan to appear in concert for 400,000 people in Bologna. Advised on rights and funding of a major new West End musical to be presented in late 1998.

Gentle Jayes *David Gentle* has a good reputation.

Hamlin Slowe (2ptnrs/2assts) *Laurence Gilmore* has a "niche specialism in piracy work and is good at it." **Clients/Work:** Acted for Phonographics Performance Ltd against Maitra in Court of Appeal case; acts for Bruce Springsteen; Acts for Sony Music Entertainment

Denton Hall (1ptnr 100%, 3assts 25-75%) *Robert Allan* heads the team acting for individuals and companies. **Clients/Work:** Acts for EMI plc, Windswept Pacific Music Ltd and Fujipacific Music Inc. Also represents Sony/ATV Music Publishing (UK) Ltd and China Records Ltd.

Harrison Curtis This new niche firm promises to provide strong competition to other larger firms in the music as well as other media fields. **Clients/Work:** Include SINE (a division of Sony Music Entertainment (UK) Ltd) and Island Records Ltd.

Searles Another new two partner firm. *Helen Searle* also joins the table following praise from other practitioners. **Clients/ Work:** Publishing agreement for All Saints. Recording agreement for Finley Quaye. Day to day work for Jamiroquai.

Spraggon Stennett Brabyn (3ptnrs – all full-time music lawyers) Set up in 1995, the firm continues to do good work in the music sector.

Taylor Joynson Garrett (2ptnrs, 2ptnrs/7assts from the IP dept as required) *Paul Mitchell* is known for his work in the publishing and media sectors. **Clients/Work:** Acted for Mechanical-Copyright Society in its alliance with Performing Rights Society on agreement to share facilities and services. Acted for MCPS in joint venture with Phonographic Performance Ltd.

Craig Eadie, formerly the head of the media group at Frere Cholmeley Bishcoff, is now part of **Forsters** – the new firm formed by eleven ex-Freres' partners.

THEATRE

Barry Shaw The well-known *Barry Shaw* is still active and highly regarded in his niche field. **Clients/Work:** Advising on "Sweet Charity," "Damn Yankees," "Wallace & Grommit," "Closer," "Delicate Balance," "The Judas Kiss," "Boy from Oz" (touring Australia), forthcoming "Dr Dolittle."

Campbell Hooper Maintain their strong reputation, despite the retirement of Michael Oliver who is now a consultant. *David Wills* was recommended again and Carolyn Jennings who appears in our broadcasting tables also handles some theatre work. **Clients/ Work:** Production arrangements for Duncan Weldon on "Rent." Work for Theatre of Comedy on Royal Opera at Shaftesbury Theatre and "Brief Lives." Production work on "Hurly Burly" and "Marlene" among others.

Harrison Curtis New niche firm (also in Film & TV production and Music). Aiming to develop a strong practice in this particular field and have already developed a solid client base. **Clients/Work:** Include The Drill Hall Theatre, G&J Productions Ltd and Imagination Entertainments.

Tarlo Lyons *Michael Rose* and an assistant handle theatre work within the firm's entertainment practice. **Clients/ Work:** Continue to work for Cameron Mackintosh. Licensing work for worldwide productions.

Clintons *John Cohen* is particularly well-known for creative contracts. **Clients/ Work:** Representing Andrew Lloyd Webber re "Whistle down the Wind." Representing Tim Rice re "the Lion King."

Harbottle & Lewis (1ptnr/1asst specialise in theatre within this strong entertainment practice). **Clients/Work:** Acting for Pola Jones re major UK tour and West End production of "West Side Story." Acting for ENO re the introduction of new standard form production agreements.

PUBLISHING

Denton Hall *Alan Williams* is particularly highly rated. **Clients/Work:** Defending an action by the Joyce Estate to prevent publication by Picador of a new edition of James Joyce's "Ulysses."

Taylor Joynson Garrett Rated highly for commercial work by clients. The firm is known for its work in the publishing collecting societies field. *Paul Mitchell* is highly regarded by clients. **Clients/Work:** Acting for Macmillan Publishers in the disposal of their Health Service Division to EMAP for £102.3 million. Acting for Macmillan Publishers in acquisition of Heinemann ELT from Reed Elsevier. Acting for Harper Collins in major litigation.

Harbottle & Lewis (4ptnrs/6assts) **Clients/Work:** Acting on behalf of Zone Ltd, publishers of the Manchester United Magazine and books on the Spice Girls. Acting for Penguin Books Ltd on acquisition of children's division of Victor Gollancz.

Henry Hepworth Clients/Work: Granta Books, Smith Gryphon, Carroll & Brown.

Lovell White Durrant Rated as the top firm for commercial work by clients. **Clients/Work:** Advising Robert Fleming on publishing contracts including film rights arising out of the James Bond books and on issues arising out of the Agatha Christie portfolio.

Manches & Co (4ptnrs/6assts 25-50%) **Clients/Work:** Pre-publication clearance for all Which? Magazine titles. Injunctions for Conde Nast to protect the Vogue, GQ and Tatler names. Pre-publication clearance and post-publication defences for Cassells and Victor Gollancz Ltd.

The Simkins Partnership Clients/Work: Sale and purchase of books and magazine titles, book packaging agreements, publishing contracts, printing contracts and book joint ventures.

LEADERS' PROFILES · LONDON

ABRAMSON, Lawrence
Harbottle & Lewis, London (0171) 667 5000
Specialisation: Specialist litigator in all areas of the entertainment and media industries, including music, television, film, publishing and sport.
Prof. Memberships: British Association of Sport and the Law, International Association of Entertainment Lawyers
Career: Education: British School of The Netherlands, University of Manchester, Chester College of Law – LLB 2:1 Professional Career: Trained – *Sheridans*, Solicitor with *Denton Hall* 1988-97, *Harbottle & Lewis* 1996 – to date.
Personal: Married with one child. All sports, music, theatre, travel and entertaining.

ALLAN, Robert
Denton Hall, London (0171) 320 6516
email: rwa@dentonhall.com
Partner in Media and Technology Group.
Specialisation: Works with music industry clients on music publishing, recording contracts, 'due diligence' reviews of music companies and their assets, music business mergers and acquisitions, video licensing, negotiations with rights bodies and other contractual matters, advises users of music, for example, TV programme makers and broadcasters, film production companies and advertisers regarding clearances. Also works on the 'talent' side of the music business, advising on contractual and other issues. Has been published widely in leading professional journals and the trade press. Has lectured at MIDEM and New Music Seminar in New York and to the Beverly Hills Bar Association.
Prof. Memberships: International Association of Entertainment Lawyers (UK Committee Member).
Career: Qualified in 1967. Partner with *Roney & Co.* 1970-1973. Partner with *Simons Muirhead & Allan* 1973-86. Joined *Denton Hall* as a Partner in 1986.
Personal: Born 4th May 1945. Educated at Xaverian College, Brighton. French speaker. Interests include music, skiing, clay pigeon shooting, food and wine.

ARMSTRONG, Peter
Theodore Goddard, London
(0171) 606 8855
Specialisation: Practice covers film, television and theatre. Clients include US studios and ITV companies as well as independent producers and distributors. A director of the British Film Commission.
Prof. Memberships: International Bar Association (Chairman, Intellectual Property and Entertainment Law Committee 1995 to date). British Academy of Film and Television Arts.
Career: Qualified in 1982. Partner, *Bartletts de Reya* and *Mishcon de Reya* 1985-1995. Joined *Theodore Goddard* in 1995 as a partner.
Personal: Born 4 August 1949. Attended University of Cape Town, University College London and New York University.

BALLARD, Tony
Field Fisher Waterhouse, London
(0171) 481 4841
See under Telecommunications, p. 761

BARR-SMITH, Adrian
Denton Hall, London (0171) 320 6501
email: abs@dentonhall.com
Partner in Media and Technology Group.
Specialisation: Main area of practice is sport, covering broadcasting contracts, licensing and merchandising, event regulation, official supplier contracts and disciplinary matters. Also covers media finance, film and T.V. production and distribution. Has acted for the FA Premier League, Commonwealth Games Federation, England and Wales Cricket Board and Scottish Rugby Union. Hon. Legal adviser to Sports Aid Foundation. Consulting Editor 'Law and the Business of Sport' (Butterworths, 1997). Contributor to 'International Media Law' and 'Copinger and Skone James on Copyright'. Tutor at the Film Business School, Madrid. Member of the Panel of Arbitrators of the American Film Marketing Association.
Prof. Memberships: Design & Artists Copyright Society (Honorary Secretary).
Career: Qualified in 1977. Solicitor at *Rubinstein Callingham* 1977-79. Legal Director of Artlaw Services 1980-81; Joined *Denton Hall* in 1982, becoming a Partner in 1986.
Personal: Born 1952. Emmanuel College, Cambridge, 1970-73. Governor of Sports Aid Foundation. Leisure pursuits include cricket, golf and film. Lives in London.

BENNETT, Nigel
The Simkins Partnership, London
(0171) 631 1050
Partner in Media and Entertainment Department.
Specialisation: Main areas of practice cover media finance, production and distribution (particularly in fields of film, television and radio). Experience in advising media groups, producers, distributors, broadcasters and financiers on copyright, financing agreements, production contracts and distribution arrangements world-wide. Other areas of practice include sport, publishing, electronic media work, and alternate dispute resolution.
Prof. Memberships: Law Society, International Bar Association, American Bar Association, Media Dispute Resolution (Founder Member), Editorial Board of International Media Law, Royal Television Society.
Career: Qualified in 1970 with *Rubinstein Nash*. Lecturer in contract and commercial law, College of Law, Lancaster Gate (1971-73). Joined *The Simkins Partnership* in 1973; Partner 1975; Joint Managing Partner 1992-96.
Personal: Born 15th June 1945. Attended Dulwich College 1956-64, Clare College, Cambridge 1964-67. Leisure pursuits include golf, cricket, sailing, walking and the jazz guitar.

BERGER, Jonathan
Theodore Goddard, London
(0171) 606 8855
Specialisation: Main area of practice covers film and television production, finance and distribution. Acts for leading independent producers and distributors. Regular speaker on the film and television industry.
Prof. Memberships: British Academy of Film & Television Arts; Producers Association for Cinema & Television; New Producers Alliance.
Career: Qualified in 1986 with *Bartletts de Reya* and became a partner in *Mishcon de Reya* in 1990 and joined *Theodore Goddard* as a partner in the Media & Entertainment Group in 1995.
Personal: Born 1962. Educated Charterhouse and the University of Kent at Canterbury. Leisure interests include supporting Chelsea FC, cooking and golf.

BLOOM, Frank
Marriott Harrison, London (0171) 209 2000
Media and Entertainment.
Specialisation: Main area of practice is media and entertainment work. Covers all aspects of film, television, cable production, broadcasting, financing and exploitation.
Prof. Memberships: Law Society.
Career: Qualified 1960. Partner *Nicholas Morris* 1965-1984. Left to establish *Frank Bloom & Co.* 1984. Founding partner *Marriott Harrison*.
Personal: Leisure pursuits include theatre, cinema, reading, cooking and travelling. Lives in Walton-on-Thames.

CALOW, Duncan
Denton Hall, London (0171) 242 1212
email: dcc@dentonhall.com
Specialisation: Solicitor specialising in digital media work. Advises content owner, producer and distributor clients on a wide range of projects including Internet and on-line services; CD-Rom, DVD and video games publishing; VOD, ITV, digital television and VR. Written and spoken widely on the legal issues of digital media including contributions to specialist and legal press, national newspapers, BBC2's The Net. Co-author (with Alan Williams and Andrew Lee) of Multimedia: Contracts, Rights and Licensing, FT Law and Tax (1996) and (with Alan Williams and Nicholas Higham) of Digital Media: Contracts, Rights and Licensing, FT Law and Tax (1996).
Career: University of Nottingham; joined *Denton Hall* 1992; qualified 1994.
Personal: Born 1970; leisure interests include art, sport, comedy and politics.

CAMERON, Jonathan
Mishcon de Reya, London (0171) 440 7012
Partner and head of Media and IP Group.
Specialisation: Practice covers the protection and exploitation of intellectual property, in particular in electronic formats in copyright. Acts for Hollywood majors, UK broadcasters, on-line carriers, electronic developers, television and film production companies, computer game manufacturers, software design companies, interactive television, electronic newspapers and hi tech IPR owners; also the Diana Princess of Wales Memorial Fund. Frequent speaker and writer.
Prof. Memberships: Member of the ICC Audio-Visual Committee.
Career: Qualified with *Denton Hall* in 1981. He left to form his own firm in the mid 1980s and joined *Mishcon de Reya* as a partner in 1992.

Personal: Born 26th November 1953. Educated Edinburgh University and Brasenose College Oxford. Lives in West London.

COHEN, John M.R.
Clintons, London (0171) 379 6080
Partner in Entertainment Department.
Specialisation: Main areas of practice are theatre, music and television, negotiating and advising on contracts in relation to all aspects of theatrical production, music recording and publishing, management and television production. Cases handled have included 'Elton John v. Dick James', 'Paul Weller v. Foxton and Buckler', 'Tolhurst v. The Cure', 'Dave Clark v. The Dominion Theatre' and a huge number of non-contentious contracts.
Prof. Memberships: The Law Society.
Career: Qualified 1970. Joined *Clintons* in 1968 and has remained there throughout career, becoming a Partner in 1972.
Personal: Born 14th February 1946. Attended University College London 1964-67. Trustee of Mercury Workshop. Leisure interests include producing musicals. Lives in London.

DALLY, Peter
Bird & Bird, London (0171) 415 6000
Partner in Media Group.
Specialisation: Main area of practice is film and television finance production and distribution. Also handles copyright, competition relating to the film industry and sports broadcasting law. He is the author of "A to Z of Film Business Terminology" published by the Media Business School. Led a team of lawyers at East/West Producers Seminars in London, Warsaw, Prague and Bucharest between 1991 and 1995. Was an Expert at the Film Business School; now Head of Legal Affairs at the Television Business School. Designed and taught the Common Law Module for the European Masters in Audio Visual Management (MEGA) for the Media Business School in 1997 and 1998.
Career: Qualified 1980 with *Denton Hall* and became a Partner in 1986. Partner at *Marriott Harrison* from 1994 to 1998. Recently became a partner at *Bird & Bird*. Before qualifying, worked for Rank Leisure, Chrysalis Records and Mainline Pictures.

DAVIS, David W.
Clintons, London (0171) 379 6080
Specialisation: Media/Entertainment including Music, film and sport. Senior Litigator and Head of Department with *Clintons*.
Career: Instructed during the past 25 years in many of the leading cases in this field representing Rod Stewart, Frank Bruno, The Stone Roses, Pete Townshend, Sony (George Michael), Polygram, Decca, Pavarotti, U2(PRS), Polygram Films International. Also my firm *Clintons* acted in the cases of Elton John, Dave Clark and The Cure.
Personal: Educated at Shooters Hill Grammar School. Admitted to the University of London and subsequently articled to *A. E. Hoffman*. Thereafter, joined David Landsman in 1973. Also lectured in law. Interests include sports, classical music and the arts generally.

DEARSLEY, Ken
Denton Hall, London (0171) 320 6547
email: krd@dentonhall.com
Partner in Media and Technology Group.
Specialisation: Specialises in all aspects of

film financing including tax based financing arrangements, working with the major studios, other film companies, banks and other lending institutions. Wide experience in film and television production and distribution, video distribution, 'due diligence' reviews in the media industry and copyright matters generally.
Prof. Memberships: International Bar Association.
Career: Has been with *Denton Hall* since articles. Qualified in 1974. Became a Partner in 1979.
Personal: Born 1945. Fitzwilliam College, Cambridge 1965-68 (MA Hons in Economics). Leisure pursuits include tennis and music.

DEVEREUX, Mark J.
Olswang, London (0171) 208 8888
Partner and Head of Entertainment Media and Communications Group.
Specialisation: Main area of practice is film and television finance, production and distribution. Responsible for all areas of work covered by entertainment, media and communications. Regular contributor to media trade press.
Prof. Memberships: Law Society, State Bar of California.
Career: Qualified in 1981, joining *Simon Olswang & Co* in the same year and becoming a Partner in 1982.
Personal: Born 2nd August 1956. Attended Lycée Français de Londres 1961-74, then University College London 1975-78. Leisure interests include tennis, skiing, diving and photography. Lives in London.

EADIE, Craig F.
Forsters, London (0171) 863 8333
Partner in Corporate/ Media Department.
Specialisation: Media specialist dealing with corporate and financing work as well as commercial contracts. Former Head of *Frere Cholmeley Bischoff* Media and Communications and Entertainment Group. Author of various articles on media and entertainment. Regular speaker at media seminars.
Career: Qualified in 1980, having joined *Frere Cholmeley* in 1978. Became a Partner in 1986. Founding partner of *Forsters*, August 1998.
Personal: Born in 1955. Educated at Worcester College, Oxford 1973-76 and Aix-Marseilles University 1977-78. Trustee of the Institute of Contemporary British History and Watside Charities. Recreations include bird watching and shooting. Lives in London.

EAGLES, Brian
Hammond Suddards, London
(0171) 655 1000
Partner and Head of Media and Entertainment Unit.
Specialisation: Entertainment, media and sports law; film and media project finance and production, music, merchandising and sponsorship. Also deals with all intellectual property both contentious and non-contentious. He has specific expertise in arbitration and mediation. An accredited CEDR mediator and an arbitrator/mediator for the American Film Marketing Association, the World Intellectual Property Organisation, American Arbitration Association and the Central London County Patents Court. A founder member of Media Dispute Resolution.
Prof. Memberships: International Association of Entertainment Lawyers; Law Society; IBA;

Chartered Institute of Arbitrators; CEDR; British Association of Lawyer Mediators.
Career: Qualified 1960. Assistant Solicitor with *J Sanson & Co* from 1960, and became a Partner in 1961. Partner with *Herbert Oppenheimer Nathan & Vandyk* (1967-1988). Moved to become Partner and Head of Media and Communications Group at *S J Berwin & Co* in 1988. Joined *Hammond Suddards* as a Partner and Head of its Media and Entertainment Unit in May 1994.

EATON, Michael C.A.
Eatons, London (0181) 877 9727
Specialisation: All areas of media and entertainment law, including merchandising, touring, television, film and sport, as well as expertise in corporate law.
Career: Qualified in 1967 and became a Corporate Partner in the city firm, *Stephenson Harwood*. Joined *Dick James Music* in 1977 as Head of Business Affairs to gain further industry experience and was responsible for all business and contractual dealings with a vast roster of clients. Returned to private practice with the formation of *Eaton & Burley* in 1980. In 1990 founded *Eatons*.

EDWARDS, Stephen
Richards Butler, London (0171) 247 6555
Partner in Media and Entertainment Group.
Specialisation: Principal area of practice is broadcasting law including ITC and Radio Authority licence applications; satellite and cable transmission and programme contracts; production financing, distribution and co-production agreements and European regulation. Other main area of work is copyright and media/ entertainment work including copyright collecting society transactions; print and multimedia publishing agreements; talent contracts; copyright tribunal hearings and music industry agreements. Member of Editorial Board of International Media Law. Chairs Hawksmere Conference on 'Rights Clearances for Television Programmes'. Regular speaker at Hawksmere, IBC and other media industry conferences. Author of 'Rights Clearances for Film and Television Production' (PACT, 1997).
Prof. Memberships: British Literary and Artistic Copyright Association, Royal Television Society, Radio Academy.
Career: Qualified in 1976. Joined the BBC in 1978, and was Head of Copyright 1981-1990. Joined *Richards Butler* as a Partner in 1990.
Personal: Born 23rd February 1949. Attended University of the Witwatersrand, Johannesburg 1968-70 and Trinity Hall, Cambridge 1971-73. Leisure pursuits include sailing, cricket and music. Lives in London.

EVANS, Lloyd H.
Berwin Leighton, London +44 171 760 1000
Senior Partner in Corporate Deaptrment.
Head of Media and Hi-Tech Group.
Specialisation: Principal area of practice is media and communications law. Work includes City based securitisation and financing of, and tax shelters for film; telecoms, cable and satellite practice and regulation, sponsorship, interactive technology and all aspects of television, video and theatre. Other areas of practice are international trade law, intellectual property and computer law. Work includes

international asset finance using brands, computer law, copyright and technology licensing. Important matters have included Prudential, Tesco and BAA McArthur Glenn commercial contracts, product liability for major Japanese manufacturers, Telewest Communications product distribution, major South African film tax shelters and film financing with Disney, Lloyds Asset Leasing, Royal Bank of Canada, BNP, Socgen, Bank of America, United News and Media, Republic National Bank of New York, New South Wales Film Commission, Centrespur Group and Scotiabank. Co-author of 'Entertainment Law Precedents' (Longmans) and 'Remedies for Intellectual Sellers of Goods' (Sweet & Maxwell). Has written a number of articles on international competition and copyright. Regular speaker on film finance, securitisation, competition and copyright issues.
Prof. Memberships: Law Society, IBA.
Career: Journalist with Thompson, Camrose and Kemsley Newspapers 1959-64. Group Solicitor, Associated Televison Corporation 1968-79. Joined *Berwin Leighton* as a Partner in 1979.
Personal: Born 3rd February 1941. Educated at Uppingham 1954-59 and The College of Law, Guildford. Interests include shooting, motor racing and underwater photography. Lives in Godalming.

FRANKS, David T.
The Simkins Partnership, London
(0171) 631 1050
Specialisation: Music and Theatre.
Prof. Memberships: The Law Society, IAEL.
Career: Qualified 1973, *The Simkins Partnership* 1974 to date.

GAWADE, Jeremy
Lee & Thompson, London (0171) 935 4665

GENTLE, David
Gentle Jayes, London (0171) 629 3304

GHEE, Tony
Ashurst Morris Crisp, London
(0171) 638 1111
Specialisation: Main practice areas: media and entertainment and telecommunications. Regulatory, corporate and commmercial advice for cable and telecommunications operators and terrestrial and satellite broadcasters and film and television investments. Particular expertise: all aspects of satellite and broadcasting law. Speaks regularly on the convergence of broadcasting and telecoms industries and broadcasting regulation.
Prof. Memberships: IBA, Copinger Society.
Career: Worked: *Blake Dawson Waldron* and TEN television network in Australia. *Denton Hall* and Partner at *AMC* in UK.
Personal: Married.

GILMORE, Laurence
Hamlin Slowe, London (0171) 629 1209
Specialisation: Head of the Entertainment and Intellectual Property Department. Specialised in all aspects of related litigation including copyright, trademark, contract disputes, monopolies and mergers and EC competition law. Practice also covers defamation and passing off actions. Acts for prominent organisations, corporations and individuals

from the world of entertainment.
Prof. Memberships: International Association of Entertainment Lawyers.
Career: Articled at *Davenport Lyons* 1984-86. Assistant solicitor *Taylor Joynson Garrett* 1986-87. Partner, *Hamlin Slowe* since 1988.
Personal: Educated at Preston Manor Grammar School and Trinity Hall, Cambridge. Writes occasional newspaper articles. Leisure pursuits include theatre, music and sport. Born 17th April 1959. Lives in London.

GLASSER, Cyril
Sheridans, London (0171) 404 0444

GLICK, David S.
Eatons, London (0181) 877 9727
Specialisation: Client base ranges from new and emerging artists/bands to major record and publishing companies as well as a number of independent record labels and publishing companies in relation to their various spheres of activities and in particular co-ordinating substantial joint venture and other 'label' structures.
Career: Qualified in 1989 and joined *Eatons* at its inception in 1990.

GOLDING, Lindy
Lovell White Durrant, London
(0171) 236 0066
Specialisation: Contentious and non-contentious intellectual property, multimedia and technology work for media (particularly music, publishing and TV), multimedia and IT clients. Also advises on the IP/IT aspects of transactions for those clients. On the Advisory Panel of Communications Law.
Prof. Memberships: London First Media Industries Group, British Literary and Artistic Copyright Association, International Association of Entertainment Lawyers, Solicitors European Group.
Career: LLB (Hons Adel), LLM (Cantab.), Dip. Intel. Prop. (Bristol). Australian qualified solicitor and barrister 1988. Qualified as an English solicitor 1992. Joined *Lovell White Durrant* 1986. Partner 1996.

GOLDING, Michael
Lovell White Durrant, London
(0171) 236 0066
Specialisation: Intellectual property particularly trade marks and copyright.
Prof. Memberships: INTA, AIPPI, ECTA, ACG, Competition Law Association, Royal Television Society.
Career: BA (Oxon).
Personal: Married to leading digital mixed media and music copyright specialist, Lindy Golding.

GOSTYN, Antony
The Simkins Partnership, London
(0171) 631 1050
Specialisation: Film and television production, finance and distribution agreements. Author of 'Pact Model Contracts' (1991 and 1998 Editions).
Career: Qualified 1975. With Thorn EMI 1976-1982. Partner at *DJ Freeman* 1986-1995. Joined *The Simkins Partnership* as a partner in 1995.

GRAFTON GREEN, Paddy
Theodore Goddard, London
(0171) 606 8855
Specialisation: Work includes advice on (i) copyright issues in relation to recordings, musical compositions and theatrical productions and (ii)

production, distribution, management concert appearance, sponsorship and merchandising agreements. Advice on taxation both within the UK and overseas of income derived by businesses and artists. Cases have included acting as Chairman of BPI Tribunal into chart hyping, and for BMG in the MMC Enquiry into Recorded Music, VPL in its defence of MTV's EC Complaint, for PolyGram in relation to a variety of transactions including its acquisition of ITC, for major companies and artists in structuring international transactions including concert tours (Tina Turner, Michael Jackson and The Rolling Stones) and for David Bowie in relation to the "Bowie Bonds". Lecturer and seminar chairman for IBC Legal Studies and others.
Prof. Memberships: Law Society.
Career: Qualified 1967, having joined *Theodore Goddard* in 1966. Became a Partner in 1973. Member of the firm's Management Committee from 1990-93. Currently the firm's Senior Partner and Head of the Media & Entertainment Group.
Personal: Born 30th March 1943. Attended Ampleforth College 1957-62; holds an MA (Oxon), 1963-65. Leisure interests include music and cricket. Lives in London.

GRIFFITHS, David
Clifford Chance, London (0171) 600 1000
See under Computer Law & I.T., p. 183

HARMAN, James
Theodore Goddard, London
(0171) 606 8855

HENRY, Michael
Henry Hepworth, London (0171) 242 7999
Partner specialising in Media, Communications and Intellectual Property. Publications include Current Copyright Law (Butterworths 1988), Media Industry Documentation (Butterworths 1998), Media Industry Transactions (Butterworths 1998), Media and Entertainment Law Volume 15 of the Encyclopaedia of Forms and Precedents fifth edition reissue (Butterworths 1998), Publishing and Multi-Media Law (Butterworths 1994), Practical Lending and Security Precedents – Security over Intellectual Property Section (Longman 1993), International Agency and Distribution Agreement – UK Section (Butterworths USA 1990), Entertainment Law Volume 15 of the Encyclopaedia of Forms and Precedents (Butterworths 1989), The Film Industry a Legal and Commercial Analysis (Longman 1986), etc.

HIGHAM, Nicholas
Denton Hall, London (0171) 242 1212
email: nach@dentonhall.com
Specialisation: Partner in Media and Technology Group. Main areas of practice are telecommunications, information technology, digital media and copyright. Work includes regulation (14 countries), privatisation (4 countries), outsourcing and system development agreements. Acted on the establishment of the first Trans-European network for telecoms and for satellite operators, and for The British Library on its Digital Library Project for a digital terrestrial broadcaster, and for Internet Service Providers. Author of many articles on regulation, communications and I.T. Regular lecturer on telecommunications, multimedia and I.T.
Prof. Memberships: Associate of Chartered Institute of Patent Agents, International Institute of Communications, Trade Marks Agent, IBA.

Career: Qualified in 1971. Joined *Denton Hall* as a Partner in 1992. Previously at *Linklaters & Paines* 1975-1981, solicitor and Partner at *SJ Berwin* 1981-1992.
Personal: Born 1947. Leisure interests include bridge. Lives in London.

HINSHELWOOD, William
Marriott Harrison, London (0171) 209 2000
Media Entertainment Group.
Specialisation: Main area of practice is film and television production financing and distribution. Acts for a number of prominent production companies (UK and American based) as well as international distributors and other international financing entities.
Career: Qualified in 1981. Partner at *Frank Bloom & Co.*, then Founding Partner of *Marriott Harrison* in 1986.
Personal: Exeter University (LLB) 1973- 76. Leisure interests include classic cars, cricket and wine. Lives outside Ipswich.

HORSFALL, Robert
Lee & Thompson, London (0171) 935 4665

HOWARD, Brian K.
Russells, London (0171) 439 8692
Partner and head of litigation.
Specialisation: Specialises in all media litigation and has handled many of the leading cases in this field for both artists and major record companies, including the disputes between Holly Johnson and ZTT, George Michael and Sony, BMG and Robbie Williams and MCA and Charly Records.
Career: Qualified in 1979 and joined *Russells* in 1982, becoming a partner in 1985.

JENNINGS, Carolyn
Campbell Hooper, London (0171) 222 9070
Head of the Media Department
Specialisation: Specialist in intellectual property rights and contract law with a detailed knowledge of the theatre, film, music, television and merchandising industries. Her practice covers all fields of the entertainment and media business representing independent television companies like Rapido TV and Arrowhead Productions, and companies with extensive media interests like Virgin Century Television Ltd and the Primetime Group of Companies. Other significant clients include The Copyrights Group Limited, Penguin Books Limited and The Terry Mardell Organisation Limited. Also has an extensive practice advising on business immigration both for individuals and major banks based in the UK.
Career: Admitted as a solicitor in 1982 having trained at *Campbell Hooper*.

JONES, Howard
Sheridans, London (0171) 404 0444

JONES, Hugh
Taylor Joynson Garrett, London
(0171) 353 1234
Specialisation: All aspects of publishing law, including copyright and moral rights, publishing contracts and licences, libel, trade marks in publishing and passing off. Regular contributor on legal topics to The Bookseller and The Author. Author of Publishing Law (Routledge, 1996).
Prof. Memberships: Law Society. British Literary and Artistic Copyright Association. Publishing Law Group of Publishers Association. Editorial Committee, Journal of

Communications Law.
Career: Called to the Bar 1976. After 15 years publishing experience (Sweet & Maxwell and Macmillan) joined *Taylor Joynson Garrett* in 1991, and qualified as a solicitor 1992.
Personal: Born 12 January 1950. Educated Eltham College and Ackworth School. Dundee University and LSE. Reform Club. Philharmonia Chorus. Interests music, opera and theatre. Lives in Islington.

JONES, Medwyn
Harbottle & Lewis, London (0171) 667 5000
Partner in Film, Television and Theatre Department.
Specialisation: Main area of practice is television production, financing, distribution and broadcasting. Work includes television commissioning, licensing and financing agreements, programme content (including defamation), broadcasting legislation, crew and other production agreements and union agreements. Also handles film production and financing. Regular lecturer at conferences and seminars.
Prof. Memberships: Law Society, Royal Television Society.
Career: Qualified in 1980. Worked at *Theodore Goddard* 1978-81, then *Walker Martineau* 1981-92 (from 1983 as a Partner). Joined *Cameron Markby Hewitt* as a Partner in 1992 and *Harbottle & Lewis* as a Partner in 1994.
Personal: Born 13th September 1955. Attended Scorton Grammar School, Chester Grammar School, Sheffield University and College of Law. Leisure interests include skiing, regular exercise and good wine. Lives in Richmond.

KAYE, Laurence M.
Paisner & Co, London (0171) 353 0299
Partner in Media Team.
Specialisation: Work includes information and publishing law, IT law, digital media contracts, joint ventures, acquisitions and disposals, I.P. advice for major newspapers, digital media publishers and developers, lobbying work and advice on proposed copyright-related legislation to publishing industry bodies, including European Publishers Council, Newspaper Publishers Association, Directory Publishers Association, IT contracts, trade mark licensing, M&A work, licensing and distribution contracts, and UK and EU competition law. Member of DTI Experts Group on the Directive for the Legal Protection of Databases, Brussels – based Rightsowners Alliance working on the forthcoming EU Copyright Directive and member of Copyright Committee of PPA. Regular writer, lecturer and seminar presenter on digital media issues.
Prof. Memberships: Law Society, IBA's Society for Computers & the Law, British Interactive Multimedia Association.
Career: Qualified in 1975, having joined *Brecher & Co.* in 1973. Left in 1980 to co-found Company and Commercial Department at *Saunders Sobell*. Joined *The Simkins Partnership* in 1994.
Personal: Born 1st September 1949. Attended Haberdashers' Askes School, Elstree, then the Sorbonne, and then Sidney Sussex College, Cambridge. Leisure interests include tennis, jogging, yoga, playing the saxophone, cinema, theatre and family life.

KERR, David
Bird & Bird, London (0171) 415 6000
See under Telecommunications, p. 762

LANDSMAN, David M.
Clintons, London (0171) 379 6080
Partner in Entertainment Department.
Specialisation: Deals with music, TV, video,
sport, merchandising, media and leisure work.
Prof. Memberships: Law Society.
Career: Qualified 1970. Founding partner of *D
M Landsman & Co*, which merged with *Clintons*
in 1990.
Personal: Born 14th March, 1946. Educated at
Haberdashers' Aske's School. Leisure pursuits
include music, reading, sport and family. Lives
in London.

LEE, Robert
Lee & Thompson, London (0171) 935 4665

LOM, Nicholas
Schilling & Lom and Partners, London
(0171) 453 2500
Founder Partner and Head of Entertainment and
Commercial Department.
Specialisation: Main areas of practice – non-
contentious film, television, video, music,
publishing, multimedia and copyright matters.
Career: Qualified in 1982. Articled at *Wright Webb
Syrett* before forming Schilling & Lom in 1984.
Personal: Born 29th April 1949. Attended
Westminster School and Pembroke College,
Cambridge (MA Cantab). Member of the
Groucho Club. Leisure interests include his
children, chess, book collecting.

MCINERNEY, Peter B.G.
S J Berwin & Co, London
+44 (0)171 533 2222
Specialisation: Partner in the Media,
Communications and Sports Group. Specialist
in entertainment and sport industries including
broadcasting, television production, distribution
and finance, merchandising, sponsorship,
advertising and publishing.
Career: Royal National Theatre (1981-1983).
Thames Television (1983-1989). *S J Berwin & Co*
(1989 to date)

MCNEIVE, Liam
McNeive, London (0171) 253 0535

MITCHELL, Paul
Taylor Joynson Garrett, London
(0171) 353 1234
Partner in Intellectual Property Department.
Specialisation: Principal area of practice is
entertainment and media law including copyright
and related work in various areas of the
entertainment and media industry including
music, books, films, television and multimedia.
Other main area involves company law aspects
of the acquisitions and disposals of companies
and joint ventures in the entertainment and
media industry. Editorial Board Member of
'International Media Law'. Contributes articles to
various professional publications and is co-
author of Joynson-Hicks on UK Copyright Law.
Addresses various conferences on topics related
to entertainment and media law.
Prof. Memberships: Law Society.
Career: Qualified in 1976 while with *Joynson-
Hicks* and became a Partner in 1978.
Personal: Born 2nd November 1951. Attended
Canford School 1965-69, then Bristol University
1970-73. Roald Dahl Foundation (Advisory

Board Member). Leisure pursuits include family
life, sailing and walking. Lives in London.

MORGAN, Leon R.
Davenport Lyons, London (0171) 468 2600
Fax: (0171) 437 8216
E-mail: lmorgan@davenport-lyons.co.uk
Partner in Media and Entertainment Department.
Specialisation: Principal area of practice is
media production, finance and distribution
generally and film and television production and
finance in particular as well as literary and music
publishing and multi-media. Also handles
taxation related to the above including planning
for individuals and production/distribution
companies. Helped set up the media lending
division of the Royal Bank of Scotland. Other
major clients include Barclays Bank plc, Bank
Leumi, MVI and Southern Star Circle Plc, Ed
Victor Ltd, The Mersey Television Co. Ltd,
Brookside Productions Ltd and many
individuals including Phil Redmond, Douglas
Adams, Richard Harris and Sylvie Guillem. Is
regularly quoted in industry periodicals.
Prof. Memberships: Law Society.
Career: Qualified and joined *Davenport Lyons*
in 1964. Became a Partner in 1969.
Personal: Born 3rd July 1939. Educated at
Westcliff High School 1951-58. Leisure interests
include film, books, art, theatre, music and
opera. Lives in London.

MOXON, Richard
Marriott Harrison, London (0171) 209 2000
Media/Entertainment Group
Specialisation: Main area of practice is film
and television production and finance including
children's programming together with
involvement in merchandising and character
licensing.
Prof. Memberships: PACT Council, American
Film Marketing Association (Anti-Piracy
Committee), Media Disputes Resolution
(Mediator)
Career: University of Birmingham LLB(Hons.)
1969-1972. Imperial Tobacco Legal Dept. 1975-
1977, *Denton Hall & Burgin* 1977-1984 (partner
1982), Lorimar Productions (Head of Legal &
Business Affairs), 1984-1986, Partner *Marriott
Harrison* 1986 to date.
Personal: Interests: singing, cinema, golf. Lives
Sunbury-on-Thames.

NICHOLSON, Kim
Olswang, London (0171) 208 8731
Partner and Head of IT and Telecommunications
Unit.
Specialisation: Practice covers Corporate
Finance, syndicating equity funding, mergers
and acquisitions, flotation (including dual
listings), takeovers, venture capital funding, all
within the communications industry; also
telecoms and 'on-line' regulatory work and
commercial contracts for exploitation of
products in communications industry.
Career: Qualified 1985. Joined *Olswang* as a
Partner in 1993.
Personal: Born 30.11.60. Educated at
Birmingham University and College of Law,
London. Interests include opera, music, hill
walking, art and antiques.

NYMAN, Bernard
Manches & Co, London (0171) 404 4433
Partner in Manches Media Group.
Specialisation: Principal area of practice is
non-contentious work in publishing (books,
magazines, journals, etc), dealing with
contracts for all aspects of publishing including
electronic publishing, acting for publishers,
authors, literary agents and learned societies.
Also libel reading (i.e pre-publication advice)
and dealing with libel complaints post
publication. Other work is general intellectual
property including advice on copyright, trade
marks and passing off. Also agreements in the
entertainment industry generally (music, film,
video, multi-media merchandising and touring).
Author of the copyright section of 'The
Encyclopedia of Forms & Precedents' (5th Ed,
Vol.21), precedents for Adams: 'Character
Merchandising' (2nd Ed, 1996, Butterworths)
and various articles in 'Entertainment Law
Review'. Currently preparing a contribution to
the forthcoming edition of Copinger & Skone
James on Copyright (Sweet & Maxwell).
Prof. Memberships: Law Society, European
Communities Trade Mark Association, The Media
Society, AIPPI (International Association for the
Protection of Intellectual Property), TIPLO (The
Intellectual Property Lawyers' Association).
Career: Qualified in 1979. Partner at *Rubinstein
Callingham* from 1983. Became Partner at
Manches & Co in 1994 when the two firms merged.
Personal: Born 27th February 1954. Educated
at Royal Liberty School 1965-72 and Sheffield
University 1972-75 (BA in Law). Leisure interests
include jazz, film and theatre. Lives in North
London.

PALMER, Nigel S.
S J Berwin & Co, London
+44 (0)171 533 2222
Head of Media and Communications Group.
Specialisation: Main area of practice is media
and entertainment work, including film
financing, tax shelter financing, merchandising,
film and television production, publishing and
video distribution. Involved in financing of
'Wilde'. Lawyer to 'Thomas the Tank Engine'
company from back bedroom to public
company. Author of Longman's Practical
Commercial Precedents on Merchandising.
Member of Editorial Board of International
Media Law Review.
Prof. Memberships: International Bar
Association, Copinger Society.
Career: Joined *Denton Hall & Burgin* in 1976,
qualifying in 1979. Partner *Denton Hall Burgin &
Warrens* 1983-88. Left to join *S J Berwin & Co.*
as a Partner in 1988. Head of Media and
Entertainment Department.
Personal: Born 12th May 1950. Attended St.
Edward's School, Oxford 1963-67, then Christ
Church College, Oxford 1968-71. Leisure
pursuits include swimming, reading and music.
Lives in Greenwich.

PARKINSON, Christopher
Hammond Suddards, London
(0171) 655 1000
Specialisation: Media finance and
entertainment. Partner specialising in
commercial and financial issues of the media
industries. Clients include advertising agencies,
film production companies, venture capital
houses and related corporations. Structured the
finance for films such as Henry V, Leon the Pig
Farmer and Staggered.

Career: Formerly a Partner with *Gouldens*, solicitors. Joined *Hammond Suddards* as a Partner in October 1995.

PERROT, Robin
Goodman Derrick, London (0171) 404 0606

PHILIPPS, Richard P.S.
Richards Butler, London (0171) 247 6555
Partner in Media Group.
Specialisation: Specialises almost exclusively in film finance work, acting for leading banks and other financial institutions active in the market, distribution companies and major overseas organisations, but also acts for producers.
Career: Qualified 1978. Partner at *Richards Butler* since 1985.
Personal: Born 1952. Educated at Queens' College, Cambridge.

PHILLIPS, Mark D.
Harbottle & Lewis, London (0171) 667 5000
Partner in Company Commercial Department.
Specialisation: Head of both the Publishing Group and the Interactive and New Media Group, specialising in commercial and corporate work for media, leisure and arts industries.
Prof. Memberships: Law Society, Society for Computers and Law.
Career: Qualified in 1986. Worked at *Clifford-Chance* 1984-88. Joined *Harbottle & Lewis* in 1988, became a Partner in 1990.
Personal: Born 3rd April 1961. Attended Manchester Grammar School 1972-78, University College, London 1979-82. Trustee of Performing Arts Lab. School Governor and member of Board of Deputies.

RENNEY, Paul
Theodore Goddard, London
(0171) 606 8855
Email: paulrenney@theodoregoddard.co.uk
Specialisation: Advice on acquisition, protection and exploitation of intellectual property rights in music business, (artists and companies) theatrical productions, general sales promotions, publishing and horseracing; advice on acquisition and disposals of music and publishing companies (including due diligence) and to software clients providing services on, and developing products for, the Internet, and on Data Protection issues.
Prof. Memberships: The Law Society, IAEL (International Association of Entertainment Lawyers); British Italian Law Association.
Career: Qualified 1987 with *Farrer & Co*. Moved to *Theodore Goddard* in 1988; Partner in 1997.

RIDLEY, Michael
Denton Hall, London (0171) 320 6526
email: mfr@dentonhall.com
Partner in Media and Technology Group.
Specialisation: Practice encompasses all aspects of television industry, especially the establishment of new television channels and also includes commissioning, distribution, co-production agreements for films and television, sponsorship agreements, broadcasting regulation, satellite agreements, copyright law, artists' contracts and defamation. Frequently lectures on copyright, television production and broadcasting.
Prof. Memberships: Law Society, Copinger Society, Royal Television Society.
Career: Qualified in 1980. Rights Manager, National Theatre 1980-81. Senior Solicitor

London Weekend Television 1981-89. Joined *Denton Hall* in 1989 and became a Partner in 1990.
Personal: Born 1955; Durham University 1974-77 (BA in Law). Chairman of St Paul's Arts Trust and of Pop Up Theatre Company.

ROSE, D. Michael
Tarlo Lyons, London (0171) 405 2000
Partner in Entertainment, Media & Communications Group. Head of Entertainment Unit.
Specialisation: Principal area of practice is theatre and related work, largely involving stage musicals. Also handles copyright disputes, piracy claims and defamation, as well as most other aspects of entertainment law, with background experience in general company and commercial work. Administration trustee of a large theatre-related charity. Major involvement in contract work (including much international licensing) in respect of over 60 first class stage productions, including such well known musicals as 'Cats', 'The Phantom of The Opera', 'Les Miserables', 'Miss Saigon', 'Five Guys Named Moe', 'Carousel', 'Follies', 'Moby Dick', 'Oliver', 'Martin Guerre', 'Tap Dogs', 'Dances of the Vampires', 'Swan Lake' and 'Cinderella'. Experience also in high profile copyright and employment disputes, as well as some film and TV work. Solicitor to Sir Cameron Mackintosh and his group of companies since 1977. Writes a monthly column in 'The Stage' newspaper on entertainment law; contributes to various other publications including 'Musical Stages' and 'Entertainment Law Review'.
Prof. Memberships: Law Society, International Association of Entertainment Lawyers, Charity Law Association.
Career: Qualified in 1958. Partner in *Randall Rose* from 1960 until merger with *Tarlo Lyons* in 1986.
Personal: Born 27th August 1934. Educated at Rugby School 1948-52 and University College, London 1952-55. Chairman of Allied Cavendish Properties Ltd (30 shareholders) since 1985. Trustee/ director of the Mackintosh Foundation since 1988 and the Theatre Investment Fund Ltd since 1997. Leisure pursuits include golf, theatre, reading and walking. Lives in London.

RUSSELL, Tony
Russells, London (0171) 439 8692

SANDELSON, Daniel
Clifford Chance, London (0171) 600 1000
Specialisation: Specialises in broadcasting, digital convergence, conditional access and new media work with particular emphasis on establishing new broadcasting platforms, digital television and DAB, media regulation, media asset sales and purchases, transborder media investments, and film library work. Major recent transactions include UK DTT, pay-per-view and terrestrial TV franchise bids internationally.
Prof. Memberships: Royal Television Society.
Career: St. Paul's School, London. Oxford University. College of Law. At *Clifford Chance* since 1989, partner since 1986.
Personal: Married, two children. Lives in London.

SAVILL, Lisbeth
Olswang, London (0171) 208 8888
Specialisation: Specialist in the production, financing, distribution and acquisition of feature films and television programmes. Work includes structuring finance therefor, including loans, subsidies, and tax-based leasing deals. Clients

include independent producers, television broadcasters, major US studios and film financiers (including banks).
Career: Obtained Arts/Law degree from University of New South Wales in 1980; began her career as a litigation solicitor in Sydney; followed by international finance work for a major city firm in New York and London 1985-89; and became a partner at *Olswang* in 1991.

SEARLE, H.
Searles, London (0171) 371 0555

SHARLAND, Andrew J.
Clintons, London (0171) 379 6080

SHAW, Barry
Barry Shaw, London (0171) 494 1454
Specialisation: Drafting of documents in connection with theatrical presentations not only in and for the United Kingdom but also overseas. Invariably, but not always, acts for the Producer. Normally involved in the negotiation and preparation of all material documents for clients. Thereafter acts on the further licensing of rights in the ventures. Additionally specialises in music copyright matters, publishing and defamation.
Prof. Memberships: Associated with a large number of subsidised theatres, has sat on numerous boards and is still Secretary of Greenwich Theatre. Is also actively involved with Blackheath FC (Rugby Union) (where he is the Honorary Secretary).
Career: Articled to Oscar Beuselinck and followed him when he rejoined *Wright & Webb* in 1963. Stayed in *Wright & Webb* (which in due course merged with *Syrett & Sons*) until *Wright Webb Syrett* decided to join another firm in 1995 at which point he set up practice on his own.

SIMKINS, Michael
The Simkins Partnership, London
(0171) 631 1050
Specialisation: Negotiating and structuring film and television financing, production and distributions arrangements.
Career: Highgate School; Kings College, London. Articled in Local Government; assistant solicitor with *Iliffe Sweet*; *Gordon Dadds & Co*; *Lovell White Durrant & King*. Founder of *The Simkins Partnership*, 1962.
Personal: Interested in building, architecture, design, furniture, walking and trad jazz.

SMITH, Barry
Richards Butler, London (0171) 247 6555
Partner in Media and Entertainment Group.
Head of Leisure Group
Specialisation: Advises on all aspects of copyright law, film and television production, distribution and financing, cable, satellite and broadcasting regulation, character merchandising, multimedia and other forms of publishing and on music agreements.
Personal: Born 1949. Educated at Queen Mary College, London (LLB), 1972. Qualified 1974.

SMITH, Graham
Bird & Bird, London (0171) 415 6000
See under Computer Law & I.T., Immigration, p. 185, 431

SOMPER, Andrew
Berwin Leighton, London +44 171 760 1000
Specialisation: Principal area of work is divided into two areas: (1) media joint ventures and acquisitions, and (2) film and television

financing and distribution. Acted in 1998 for Endemol Entertainment BV in connection with its UK corporate activities, United Broadcasting and Entertainment on its joint venture with Rapture Television, DreamWorks SKG in relation to structured finance, Walt Disney/Miramax in relation to sale and leasebacks, Barclays Bank, BNP and Royal Bank of Canada in relation to film and television finance, as well as sourcing production finance from the UK, Germany, Canada and the US for a range of production companies.
Career: 1980-1985: Solicitor with *Denton Hall*. 1985-1991: Director of Legal & Business Affairs, Warner Bros Europe. 1991-1995: Managing Director, Audio Visual Holdings Limited. 1995-present: Partner, *Berwin Leighton*.
Personal: Born 14 August 1957. Attended Downing College, Cambridge 1976-1979.

STINSON, Andrew R.
Harbottle & Lewis, London (0171) 667 5000
Partner in Music Department.
Specialisation: Work includes advising artists, songwriters, record producers, record companies, publishing companies and managers on music industry agreements.
Prof. Memberships: Law Society.
Career: Qualified 1981. Partner 1984.
Personal: Born 14 March 1957. Attended Sponne School in Towcester 1969-74, then the University of Wales in Cardiff 1975-78. Lives in London.

STONE, Peter F.
Berwin Leighton, London +44 171 760 1000
Partner in Corporate Department.
Specialisation: Principal area of practice is general commercial work including IT, IP, media and distribution. Also handles UK and EC competition and merger control. Conference speaker on EC merger control and film distribution. Co-author of Practical Commercial Precedents -Entertainment Section (Longmans); EC Merger Control (Japanese Institute of International Business Law); EC Transport Law – a Practitioners Guide (Financial Times).
Prof. Memberships: City of London Solicitors' Company (Member Commercial Law Sub-Committee), American Film Marketing Association (Arbitration Panel Member), Competition Law Association, Solicitors European Group.
Career: Qualified 1968 while with *Wright Webb Syrett*. Director of European Business Affairs Metro-Goldwyn-Mayer 1970-74, then returned to *Wright Webb Syrett* as a Partner. Joined *Berwin Leighton* as a Partner in 1983.
Personal: Born 3rd October 1943. Educated at Kingston Grammar School and Nottingham University (LLB 1965). Lives in London.

STORER, Robert A.
Harbottle & Lewis, London (0171) 667 5000
Partner in Film, Television and Theatre Department.
Specialisation: Main areas of practice are film and television production and finance and copyright issues. Over 20 years' experience representing leading producers including Merchant Ivory Productions Limited and the leading UK completion guarantor. Involved in production and financing of numerous films and television series and programmes, recently

including Mr Bean and Spice World – The Movie. Addressed a number of conferences on media issues.
Prof. Memberships: Law Society, International Bar Association, Director of Association of Independent Producers in early 1980s, Director of Film Finances Ltd 1983-88.
Career: Joined *Harbottle & Lewis* in 1969, qualifying in 1971. Became Partner in 1974.
Personal: Born 29th April 1947. Attended Buxton College 1960-65, then London School of Economics 1965-68. Leisure pursuits include family, golf, tennis and reading. Lives in Barnes, London.

THOMPSON, Andrew J.
Lee & Thompson, London (0171) 935 4665
Partner in the Music Department.
Specialisation: Representing many leading and other recording artists, various record and production companies, individual producers, music publishers, songwriters, agents and managers.
Prof. Memberships: Law Society.
Career: Qualified 1977. Joined *Harbottle & Lewis* in 1978 and became a Partner in 1982. Co-founding Partner of *Lee & Thompson*, from August 1983.
Personal: Born 12th February 1953. Attended London School of Economics and Political Science 1971-74. Lives in London.

TURNER, Mark
Herbert Smith, London (0171) 374 8000
Partner in Intellectual Property and Technology Group
Specialisation: Practice covers a wide range of commercial and intellectual property issues, in the IT and new media industries. Specialist experience in information technology, Internet and online services, CD-Rom and electronic publishing. Clients include many internationally known businesses and organisations. Publications: Co-author of Butterworths 'Encyclopedia of Competition Law', chapter on licensing of intellectual property rights. Co-author of a chapter on complex licensing issues in 'International Technology Transfer' (Kluwer). Correspondent for 'Computer Law and Security Report'. Many articles in national, legal and trade press.
Prof. Memberships: International Chamber of Commerce, Committee on Telecoms and IT. Intellectual Property Institute, Multimedia Committee. International Bar Association. Computer Law Association.
Career: Qualified 1983. *Macfarlanes* 1981-1985. *Denton Hall* 1985-1995 (Partner from 1989). *Garrett & Co.* 1995–1997. Joined *Herbert Smith* as a partner in 1998.
Personal: Born on 3rd September 1956. Educated Latymer Upper School and University College, Oxford (Exhibitioner).

TURTON, Julian M.
The Simkins Partnership, London (0171) 631 1050
Partner in Media and Entertainment and Advertising Departments.
Specialisation: Main area of practice is media and entertainment, with emphasis on the music industry but also including publishing, art, and new media. Other area of practice is advertising and marketing, particularly talent and rights

acquisition documentation. Has represented artists, composers, publishers and record companies, book publishers, media selling operations, advertising agencies, telecoms companies. Editor of 'Neighbouring Rights, Artists, Producers and their Collection Societies', co-editor of 'Impact of Competition Law on the Music Industry' and past contributor to books on 'Merchandising and Sponsorship'and 'Moral Rights'. Author of articles in International Media Law, Entertainment Law Review and Business Magazine. Has lectured to the IBA Berlin Conference in 1996 on new media issues and at commercial seminars on music publishing agreements, on the enforceability of contracts, on new technologies and on performance rights.
Prof. Memberships: President and Committee Member of the International Association of Entertainment Lawyers; Founder Member of Advertising Law International; BAFTA.
Career: Qualified 1980 and joined *The Simkins Partnership* the same year. Articled at *Trower, Still & Keeling*. Became a Partner in 1985.
Personal: Born 23rd July 1952. Attended Bristol University (1974). Leisure interests include family, golf, reading, food and Arsenal F.C. Lives in London.

WALKER, R. Kim
Biddle, London (0171) 606 9301
Partner in Company/ Commercial Department.
Specialisation: Main area of practice is commercial work involving intellectual property, principally as it affects the media and IT industries. Work concerns in particular contractual and commercial issues affecting these industries, including acquisitions, joint ventures, commercial contracts and licences and the ownership, protection and licensing of copyright, trade marks and other intellectual property rights. Also advises on UK and EC competition law and has written and lectured on multimedia, new technologies and the convergence of rights.
Career: Qualified in 1983. Worked at *Freshfields* 1981-5. Joined *Biddle* in 1985, becoming a Partner in 1987. Member of Intellectual Property Sub-committee of the City of London Law Society, Society for Computers and Law.
Personal: Born 15th July 1957. Attended Shrewsbury School 1971-75 and Christ's College, Cambridge, 1976-79. Leisure interests include golf. Lives in Harpenden.

WARE, James
Davenport Lyons, London (0171) 468 2600
Fax: (0171) 437 8216
E-mail: jware@davenport-lyons.co.uk
Specialisation: Copyright & copyright tribunal, music industry, broadcasting, entertainment, merchandising, rights administration, theatre, computer media.
Prof. Memberships: International Association of Entertainment Lawyers. International Managers Federation.
Career: St Johns College, Oxford. Virgin Group, Director. CBS Songs, regional Vice – President, Europe. Partner: *Davenport Lyons* since 1986. Deputy Chairman: Guildford School of Acting. Clients include major figures and corporations in specialist fields of practice.
Personal: Hill walking, rock climbing, music and theatre. Member: Athenaeum, MCC.

WILLIAMS, Alan
Denton Hall, London (0171) 320 6249
email: apw@dentonhall.com
Head of Media and Technology Group.
Specialisation: Work includes digital media, copyright, libel, commercial contract, publishing and film, television and theatre. Co-author with Michael Flint and Clive Thorne of 'Intellectual Property: the New Law'; contributes to Publishing Agreements edited by Charles Clark. Author with Duncan Calow and Andrew Lee of 'Multimedia Contracts, Rights and Licensing' (1st edition 1996) Second edition 1998 with Duncan Calow and Nicholas Higham entitled 'Digital Media: Contracts, Rights and Licensing'. Lectures for Hawksmere and others.
Prof. Memberships: Law Society, Publishing Law Group of the Publishers Association, Editorial Committee of International Media Law.
Career: Qualified in 1969, having joined *Denton Hall* in 1967. Became a Partner in 1972.
Personal: Born 1944. Attended Merchant Taylors' School 1957-63, then Exeter University 1963-66. Clubs include MCC, Groucho, Whitefriars, Omar Khyyam, Magic Circle, Richard III Society, Liveryman of the Worshipful Company of Pewterers. Leisure interests include theatre, music, cricket and walking. Married, one daughter. Lives in London.

WILLS, David
Campbell Hooper, London (0171) 222 9070
Partner in Media and Entertainment Department.
Specialisation: Extensive experience of the law and practice of the theatre. Advises producers, financiers and creative personnel in the West End, on Broadway, off Broadway and all other territories where live theatre is performed. Regularly negotiates production rights, finance agreements, co-production ventures, theatre licences and agreements for the services of creative contributors to theatrical productions. Handles media litigation, e.g., for the George Bernard Shaw estate in the 'My Fair Lady' litigation. Represents writers and performers on stage and screen.
Career: Qualified 1967. Partner at *Campbell Hooper* 1970.
Personal: Trustee of the Mander Mitchenson Theatre Collection. Lives in London and Wiltshire.

ZEFFMAN, David
Olswang, London (0171) 208 8888
Partner and Joint Head of Entertainment, Media and Communications Group.
Specialisation: Principal area of practice involves commercial and corporate aspects of television, music and multimedia businesses. Particular expertise in competition law aspects of entertainment and communications industries. Acted in MMC inquiries into record industry; film distribution; Warner/ Chappell and in BPI/ MCPS Copyright Tribunal Reference.
Prof. Memberships: IBA, IAEL.
Career: Qualified 1983 while with *Frere Cholmeley* and became a Partner in 1989. Appointed Head of Company and Commercial Department, *Frere Cholmeley Bischoff* in 1993. Joined *Simon Olswang & Co* as a Partner in 1994.
Personal: Born 28th February 1958. Attended Haberdashers' Aske's School 1969-76, then Brasenose College, Oxford 1977-80. Lives in London.

The SOUTH and WALES

HIGHLY REGARDED FIRMS
THE SOUTH AND WALES
Wiggin and Co Cheltenham
Morgan Bruce Swansea, Cardiff
Manches & Co Oxford

Wiggin and Co (Cheltenham) (2ptnrs/6 assts) Team described as "impressive." Most work comes from London. **Clients/Work:** Advised Flextech on its £450 million joint venture with the BBC to launch cable, satellite and digital terrestrial channels throughout the UK. Acts for film and TV production companies and satellite and digital service providers.

Morgan Bruce (Swansea, Cardiff) (2ptnrs, 1asst in Swansea; 1ptnr in Cardiff) Contemporaries have noticed an increase in work, particularly in Swansea and the firm moves up as a result. **Clients/Work:** Advise HIT Entertainment Ltd, an international distribution company. Acting for Lluniau Lliw and Fiction Factory in acquiring the rights to the best-selling book, "Rancid Aluminium" by James Hawes. Acted for Aaargh! Animation in the co-production of a "claymation" Christmas special.

Manches & Co (Oxford) (3ptnrs work in conjunction with the London media team to form "Manches Media") Their reputation is mainly for non-contentious advice to publishers. **Clients/Work:** Blackwells, OUP, Internet service providers.

MIDLANDS and EAST ANGLIA

HIGHLY REGARDED FIRMS
MIDLANDS AND EAST ANGLIA
Frances Anderson Birmingham
Edge & Ellison Birmingham
Eversheds Birmingham
Sean Redmond Stafford
Wragge & Co Birmingham
Leathes Prior Norwich

Frances Anderson & Co (Birmingham) Sole practitioner with individual clients in the music, TV, film and multimedia industries. Highly recommended for her "rounded involvement in media and the arts," her "understanding of the politics and background to media issues" and her "commercial acumen." She moves up in the table. **Clients/Work:** Include Birmingham Repertory Theatre, UB40.

Edge & Ellison (Birmingham) (1ptnr 40%, 1assoc 100%, 1assoc 40%) Work relates mainly to entertainment and leisure venues and has a corporate slant. *David Hull* was recommended again. **Clients/ Work:** Contractual advice to Sheffield arena management company, Liverpool Empire and Cardiff International Arena. Advised The Royal Opera House on theatre agreement with The Royal Ballet and Hammersmith Apollo.

Eversheds (Birmingham) (1ptnr/2assts – none f/t) The partner is on the board of West Midlands Business in the Arts. **Clients/Work:** Advises Ragdoll Productions (producers of Teletubbies and Tots TV), Hanrahan Television Ltd, Televideo (sports video producer) and Sound & Picture House (short film producer).

Sean Redmond (Stafford) Sole practitioner handling mainly music work. Described as "well-trained and thorough with an eye for detail," his fellow practitioners feel that he will benefit commercially from his new position as legal and business affairs director of a record label. **Clients/Work:** Represents artists in the pop, folk and jazz fields. Also advises on music publishing on the internet.

Wragge & Co (Birmingham) (2ptnrs/6 assts – none f/t) **Clients/Work:** Publishing, character merchandising, arts funding, television and broadcast regulation.

Leathes Prior (Norwich) (2ptnrs/1asst – none f/t) **Clients/Work:** Advises the music industry on recording contracts, management agreements and copyright.

LEADING INDIVIDUALS
MIDLANDS AND EAST ANGLIA
ANDERSON Frances Frances Anderson
HULL David Edge & Ellison
REDMOND Sean Sean Redmond
SEE PROFILES AT END OF THIS SECTION

The NORTH

Dibb Lupton Alsop (Leeds) (1ptnr/1asst in Leeds; 1ptnr in Manchester) The "highly competent" *Paul Stone* heads the team from Leeds and handles publishing and broadcasting work. **Clients/Work:** Acts for Yorkshire TV and Yorkshire Post Newspapers.

Dickinson Dees (Newcastle-Upon-Tyne) (2ptnrs including *John Pennie*, 1assoc, 2assts – none f/t) **Clients/Work:** Acts for Tyne Tees TV, Border Television plc and Century Radio. Also advise regional publishing companies (Bloodaxe Books) and record labels.

Eversheds (Leeds, Manchester) (1ptnr, 1asst – p/t; 2assts – f/t working between Leeds and Manchester) **Clients/ Work:** Advises Channel 5 Broadcasting on programme and film acquisition and on output agreements with distributors such as MGM. Publishing deal with EMI. Also handles music and multimedia work.

Hart-Jackson & Hall (Newcastle-Upon-Tyne) *Richard Hart-Jackson* has practised in this field for many years and has built up a reputation in the Newcastle area and in London. **Clients/Work:** Contract and contentious advice to British Actors Equity Association, Musicians Union, bands, artists and publishers.

Lea & Company (Stockport) *Stephen Lea* and his assistant were particularly recommended for their music expertise by a London barrister. **Clients/Work:** Independent record companies; artists; songwriters; publishing houses.

McCormicks (Leeds) (5ptnrs/6assts – none f/t). The "charismatic" *Peter McCormick* handles media and entertainment law within the commercial department. His "no-nonsense" approach has been praised by other solicitors. **Clients/Work:** Regular advice to personalities including Paul Merton, Caroline Quentin and Leslie Ash. Three radio franchise bids during 1997. Other clients include BBC Radio Leeds and Yorkshire Television.

Ramsbottom & Co (Blackburn) Described as "having a niche within a niche," *Malcolm Clay* and an assistant handle a variety of work for the circus industry **Clients/Work:** Circus organisers and providers in the UK; international circuses; ice show producers; fairground operators. Work includes licensing, safety regulations and advice on performing animals.

SCOTLAND

Dundas & Wilson CS (4ptnrs, 7assts – none f/t) *Graham Sibbald* has joined the firm from Bird Semple and heads the media team. The work has a corporate slant. **Clients/ Work:** Advises Scottish Radio Holdings on regulatory and corporate matters including their acquisition of Moray Firth Radio Ltd. Also advises Scottish Media Group, Independent Radio Group plc and Scotsman Publications Ltd.

McGrigor Donald (3ptnrs/ 5assts – none f/t) **Clients/Work:** Advising Live TV on the development of their station in Edinburgh. Other clients include BBC Scotland, Carlton TV and Mirror Group Newspapers.

Tods Murray WS (1ptnr/2assts) The well-known *Richard Findlay* works full time in film and TV production, theatre, music, communications and publishing (including internet and CD-Rom advice). **Clients/Work:** Increasing amount of work with the US, acting for clients dealing with Miramax and Columbia Tristar.

Anderson Strathern WS (4ptnrs – 2 f/t/3assts) Known for its sports-based media practice, the firm enters our table this year. *Simon Brown* (previously with Steedman Ramage) is developing the film, TV, music and publishing sides of the practice. **Clients/Work:** Advised In Video Productions Ltd on the sale of part of its business to Delphic Media and Communications Group Ltd. Advised Lynne Kelly re media coverage of her abortion court case. Advised Scottish Rugby Union regarding a U2 concert at Murrayfield.

Bell & Scott WS (3ptnrs) *Andrew Kerr* is heavily involved with the Edinburgh festival fringe society. *Iain Macdonald* is also active in the field. **Clients/ Work:** Producers Association of Cinema and Television; Assembly Theatre; Assembly Film and Television; Kiss 102/105 radio stations.

Levy & McRae Newly recommended this year by fellow practitioners. **Clients/Work:** Include Scottish Television, Grampian Television, The Glaswegian, Border Television and Sky.

Wright Johnston & Mackenzie (3ptnrs, 6assts) Handle a range of entertainment work.

LEADERS' PROFILES • REGIONS

ANDERSON, Frances
Frances Anderson, Birmingham
(0121) 693 3505
Specialisation: Non-contentious work in music, television, film, the arts and multi-media; also information technology.
Prof. Memberships: Law Society; Women in Film and Television; PACT; Society for Computers & Law.
Career: Qualified in 1989 at *Wragge & Co*; set up own practice in 1995.
Personal: Former chairman and currently a director of Birmingham International Film & Television Festival. Company Secretary and a director of the Grand Theatre, Wolverhampton. Company Secretary and a director of the Media Development Agency for the West Midlands.

BROWN, Simon T.D.
Anderson Strathern WS, Edinburgh
(0131) 220 2345
Partner in Corporate Department.
Specialisation: Handles general corporate and commercial work, including acquisitions and disposals, corporate finance, general contract work, agency and distribution agreements and EC law. Specialises in media, entertainment and publishing law, involving film and TV production, financing and distribution contracts, publishing contracts, music industry agreements, sponsorship agreements, intellectual property issues and passing off. Has lectured on media and entertainment law for the Law Society of Scotland and the Institute of Chartered Accountants of Scotland and on copyright and contracts for the Scottish

Publishers' Association. Author of Media and Entertainment Section of "Green's Practice Styles". Contributed Scottish section of 'International Agency and Distribution Law' by Matthew Bender.
Prof. Memberships: Securities Institute (Full Member), English Law Society's European Group, Law Society of Scotland, Society of Writers to Her Majesty's Signet.
Career: Qualified in 1985. Worked for *Dundas & Wilson CS* in Edinburgh 1983-88. Joined *Steedman Ramage WS* in 1989 and became a partner in 1990. Joined *Anderson Strathern WS* as a partner in 1997.
Personal: Born 1960. Attended the University of Edinburgh 1978-83. Enjoys golf, football, literature, travel and family life. Lives in Edinburgh.

CLAY, Malcolm S.
Ramsbottom & Co, Blackburn
(01254) 672222

FINDLAY, Richard M.
Tods Murray WS, Edinburgh (0131) 226 4771
Entertainment Law Partner.
richard.findlay@todsmurray.co.uk
Specialisation: Practices exclusively in entertainment and media law acting for independent film/ television companies, theatre companies (both commercial and subsidised), event managers, a selection of arts and film festivals and over 250 other arts and entertainment organisations.
Prof. Memberships: International Association of Entertainment Lawyers.
Career: Partner *Ranken & Reid* (1979-90); Partner *Tods Murray* (1990); Part-time Lecturer in Film and Business Law – Napier University 1990.

HART-JACKSON, Richard
Hart-Jackson & Hall, Newcastle upon Tyne
(0191) 232 1987
Specialisation: Handles contentious and non contentious media and entertainment work; prepares and negotiates music industry agreements for employers and artistes; heavy emphasis on litigation for musicians and mainstream entertainers. Retained by Musicians Union and British Actors Equity. Successfully acted in leading music industry case – Ray Jackson v EMI Records Limited (1985). Advises and negotiates contracts on behalf of writers/compilers of books and magazines among these being the perpetrators of VIZ Magazine. Arbitrates on and has appeared as an expert witness in media and entertainment disputes.
Prof. Memberships: Law Society: Fellow of the Chartered Institute of Arbitrators.
Career: Qualified in 1968; Partner with *J.W. Mitchell Dodds & Co* 1971-78. Left to establish *Hart-Jackson & Hall* in 1978.
Personal: Born 1943. Leisure interests include – music, sport and family life. Lives in Corbridge, Northumberland.

HULL, David Julian
Edge & Ellison, Birmingham (0121) 200 2001
See under General Corporate Finance, p. 244

KERR, Andrew M.
Bell & Scott WS, Edinburgh (0131) 226 6703

LEA, Stephen
Lea & Company, Stockport (0161) 480 6691

MACDONALD, Iain
Bell & Scott WS, Edinburgh (0131) 226 6703

MCCORMICK, Peter D.G.
McCormicks, Leeds (0113) 246 0622
Senior and Managing Partner.
Specialisation: Substantial area of practice is media and entertainment (allied to extensive portfolio of Sports Law) with considerable experience in both contentious and non-contentious aspects. Advises a number of sporting bodies, clubs and individuals on contractual matters as well as media and entertainment law issues. Clients include Leeds United F.C., a number of sporting personalities, Leslie Ash, Lee Chapman, Billy Pearce, Freddie Trueman, Richard Whiteley and a number of television presenters, actors, actresses and journalists. Advises on all aspects of broadcasting legislation. Has advised on three radio franchise bids. Deals with a number of defamation actions and advice on behalf of leading public figures, including politicians and personalities and handles complaints on broadcasting and press issues. Lectures on media and entertainment. Advises a number of clients in the music industry including performers and managers. Considerable experience of broadcast sponsorship and similar issues. Negotiates contracts for personal benefits, corporate sponsorship and ancillary matters. Has twenty years experience of tax investigation and enquiry work, both Revenue and VAT and serious fraud cases. Resident legal expert on Radio Leeds, Yorkshire Television and the Yorkshire Post. Director of Leeds United Holdings plc.
Prof. Memberships: Member of the Economic, Law and Tax Committee of the Leeds, Bradford and North Yorkshire Chambers of Commerce.
Personal: Chairman of the Yorkshire Young Achiever Awards.President of Harrogate Town F.C.; Member of the Editorial Board, I.P. Business Magazine; Member of the Advisory Board, Sports Law Centre, Anglia University; Head of Sports Law Unit, EuroLink for Lawyers; Vice-President of The Outward Bound Trust; Solicitor to The Duke of Edinburgh's Award; Member of the Legal Working Party of the F.A. Premier League.

PENNIE, John A.
Dickinson Dees, Newcastle upon Tyne
(0191) 279 9000
See under Insolvency, p. 456

REDMOND, Sean
Sean Redmond, Stafford (01785) 211470
Specialisation: Music, acting mainly for artists but also on the "industry" side. Drafting, negotiating and advising on contracts for recording, publishing, management, multimedia, promotion, agency and distribution. Some legal work for designers and fine artists,

and some literary publishing. Has written several articles (for musicians) in two music magazines, and presents occasional seminars.
Career: University of Birmingham 1986 – 89. Trained with *Eversheds*, Birmingham. Qualified 1992. Sole practitioner since 1994.

SIBBALD, Graham I.
Dundas & Wilson CS, Glasgow
(0141) 221 8586
Specialisation: Leader of *Dundas & Wilson* Media Team, major media clients include: Scottish Media Group plc (Scottish Television, Grampian Television, the Herald and Evening Times newspapers);Scottish Radio Holdings plc (Radio Clyde, Radio Forth; and numerous other local radio stations and local newspapers); and The Scotsman Publications Limited (the Scotsman, the European, Evening News newspapers). Major clients in the entertainment sector include: Rangers Football Club PLC, The National Stadium plc and the Scottish Exhibition Centre Ltd. Has most recently advised on several newspaper publishing company and radio station acquisitions and disposals, and on TV and radio broadcasting regulatory matters generally.
Prof. Memberships: Law Society of Scotland.
Career: Edinburgh University. Joined *Dundas & Wilson* as a Partner from *Bird Semple* in 1997.
Personal: Born 1961, married, lives in Glasgow. Interests include film and hillwalking.

STONE, Paul
Dibb Lupton Alsop, Leeds (0345) 262728
Partner, Head of Commercial Litigation, Dibb Lupton Alsop, Leeds Office.
Specialisation: Paul specialises in Corporate/Commercial Litigation including advising on major international disputes involving complex multi-party litigation. He has considerable experience of advising both media clients and corporate/commercial clients on media/marketing law related issues as well as working with PR agencies and other professionals to assist clients in crisis situations. In the past year, the Commercial Litigation Department in Leeds had been involved in a series of defamation, breach of confidence and related disputes including a growing number of cases of trade libel of various types. Paul's team has both pursued and defended a series of complaints to the PCC, BCC and ITC, as well as other associated regulatory bodies such as the ASA. They have, also, been involved in a series of applications to Court for media clients involving challenges to restrictive reporting orders and similar issues.
Career: Born 1960. Read Jurisprudence at Worcester College, Oxford – Upper Second Class Degree. Articled *Charles Russell & Co* 1983-85. Joined *Clifford Chance* (*Clifford Turner*) April 1986. Joined *Dibb Lupton* in Leeds as Partner in the Commercial Litigation Department in October 1993.
Personal: Hill walking, cricket, reading and music.

MEDICAL NEGLIGENCE

RESEARCH: In compiling the tables, we consider all the information available to us, paying particular regard to the market research carried out by our team of ten qualified lawyers. (The researchers' details are set out on page three.) The rankings, therefore, reflect the opinion of the marketplace as revealed by systematic and objective research: see page four. (Our research is audited every year by the British Market Research Bureau.)

OVERVIEW: These are extremely volatile times for medical negligence firms. The axe has already fallen for many defendant firms with the National Health Service Litigation Authority ("NHSLA") provisionally cutting its panel from more than 90 firms to around 18. This decision means that many firms will find it impossible to run a viable defendant practice, while those on the panel have the chance to expand at their expense.

Nowhere is this more apparent than the Midlands where The Lewington Partnership has long had the monopoly on defendant work. Its exclusion from the panel, at least for the moment, leaves a vacuum which looks likely to be filled by Wansbroughs Willey Hargrave and Bevan Ashford, both of which are set to greatly expand and/or open Birmingham offices in the coming year.

Following the NHSLA cuts our defendant tables are obviously smaller than in previous years, however we have left in some non-panel firms which had particularly good reviews and which continue to accept new work from private bodies as well as smaller claims from former trust clients. Some of these firms may also decide to turn their hand to plaintiff work, although the forecast for plaintiff firms is also far from clear.

Legal Aid is currently under review in an attempt to reduce the amount of medical negligence litigation. In Scotland, where Legal Aid is already extremely restricted only a tiny number of plaintiff firms can profitably undertake medical negligence claims; this may well be the picture in England and Wales in a year's time.

LONDON

MAINLY PLAINTIFF

LEADING FIRMS · PLAINTIFF
LEIGH DAY & CO
FIELD FISHER WATERHOUSE
KINGSLEY NAPLEY
PARLETT KENT
EVILL & COLEMAN
PRITCHARD ENGLEFIELD

HIGHLY REGARDED FIRMS
Bindman & Partners
Charles Russell
Pattinson & Brewer

Leigh Day & Co (7ptnrs/5fee earners) Still "in a class of its own" for its "innovative" and "ingenious" approach to claims. The large team is led by *Sarah Leigh* who has been heavily involved in advisory work on the Woolf proposals in the last year and is highly respected for her "wealth of experience." The team also includes the widely praised and "incredibly sensible" *Anne Winyard* and the well regarded *Russell Levy*. **Clients/ Work:** Aids patient who contracted TB in an open ward because hospital not segregating sufficiently; journalist client where failure to diagnose breast cancer; multiple drug resistant TB outbreaks at a London hospital.

Field Fisher Waterhouse (2ptnrs/4assts) Received particular praise for the quality of team leader, *Paul McNeil*. **Clients/Work:** During 1997 recovered over £7 million in damages for victims of medical accidents, several cases being on conditional fee arrangements. Acted on R v Croydon Health Authority and Dowdie v Camberwell Health Authority which both went to Court of Appeal.

Kingsley Napley (4ptnrs/5fee earners) A "pretty hot" firm which includes *Julia Cahill, Christine Marsh* and *Kate Rohde* within its team. **Clients/Work:** Particular interest in acting for plaintiffs with acquired brain injury, whether they be children brain damaged at birth or adults injured in motor vehicle accidents. A high proportion are on behalf of disabled children.

Parlett Kent (5ptnrs/3assts/3other fee earners) The firm has a second office in Exeter where the "superb" *Magi Young* is based, but the main force of this "tremendous" firm is still in London. The team includes *Caroline Jenkins, Elisabeth Jamieson* and *Elizabeth*

Batten, all of whom received strong recommendations. **Clients/Work:** Kirk v South East London Health Authority – failure to diagnose cervical cancer; Cunningham v Kensington, Chelsea & Westminster Health Authority – acted for a woman who had sustained brain damage as a result of psychiatric negligence; Williamson v City & Hackney Health Authority – acted for a woman who had her breast removed without her consent.

Evill & Coleman (8ptnrs/1p/t/4assts who also do personal injury work) *Terry Lee* and his team, including the "very competent" *Liz Martinez*, have acted on several major claims in 1997. **Clients/Work:** Include Smoldon v Whitworth & Nolan; Hurley v Ministry of Defence; Smith v Leicestershire Health Authority.

Pritchard Englefield (2ptnrs/4assts) A team of "solid" practitioners. These include *Grainne Barton* and *Kate Pedler*. **Clients/Work:** Have acted for 70 disabled plaintiffs, often children, in cases involving damages well in excess of £1million in each case. Also Tredget v Bexley Health Authority which established that a father who witnessed the mismanaged birth of his son, who died shortly afterwards, could recover damages for his own psychotic injury.

Bindman & Partners (2ptnrs/2assts) *Claire Fazan's* expanding team received strong praise and may well rise in our tables next year if it can continue to increase its presence. **Clients/Work:** Kelly v JS Birring & Riverside Health Authority – severe brain injury resulting from a road traffic accident and subsequent negligent medical care; West v Enfield & Haringey Health Authority – child with cerebral palsy; several structured settlements for brain injured children.

Charles Russell (1ptnr/3assts) "A small but high quality unit" which, like Bindmans is "growing apace" and may well threaten larger teams in the future. The team is led by *Richard Vallance*. **Clients/Work:** Thomas v Brighton Health Authority; Wells v Wells; Page v Sheerness – all cases which went to the House of Lords

Pattinson & Brewer (2ptnrs/2assts) The team like most of its competitors includes several medically qualified practioners as well as AVMA panel members. **Clients/Work:** Act on

a wide range of claims including those of utmost severity such as brain injury caused at birth. Damages in excess of £2 million recovered for clients during 1997.

MAINLY DEFENDANT

Beachcroft Stanleys (3ptnrs/15assts/7 other fee earners) An "outstanding" team led by *Gay Wilder* which, like the other leading firms here is on the NHSLA panel. Currently acts for over 27 NHS trusts including University Teaching Hospitals. Team includes *John Holmes* and *Anthony Yeaman*. **Clients/Work:** Acted as defence co-ordinating solicitors in the Breast Radiotherapy "RAGE" litigation. Acted for the successful Health Authority Defendants in Clunis v Camden & Islington Health Authority where the Court of Appeal struck out a claim following the killing of Jonathan Zito. Acted for NHS Trust Respondents in L v Bournewood NHS Trust, where the Appeal Court has overturned previous understanding of the law relating to the involuntary admission of patients lacking mental capacity.

Capsticks (12ptnrs/21 assts) Strongly recommended by both fellow practitioners and clients the firm was described as "a leader" which "works hard" and "knows what its doing". *David Mason, Katie Hay, Oliver Longstaff* and *Janice Smith* were all recommended again. **Clients/Work:** Acted

for defendants in the following cases: R v Croydon Health Authority CA – successfully argued that plaintiff's claim for wrongful birth was too remote and unforseeable; Knight v West Kent Health Authority – successful defence of claim that forceps delivery was mismanaged; Frazer v Merton Sutton & Wandsworth Health Authority – successfully argued that the plaintiff's pregnancy was caused by recanalisation of the fallopian tube rather than a failure on the part of the surgeon.

Hempsons (11ptnrs/10assts forming part of a larger Health Care Department) "Excellent firm," "in a class of their own" but can sometimes be "aggressive." Nevertheless, with significant teams in Manchester and Harrogate as well as in London, the firm is clearly a force. Team includes *Bertie Leigh, Janice Barber, Rex Forrester* and *Zoe Harvey*. It also fields several niche specialists including Chris Morris, a dually qualified dentist-solicitor handling dental negligence claims, and Ian Barker, specialising in "white coat crime." **Clients/Work:** Act for 81 NHS bodies – 19 Health Authorities and 62 NHS Trusts – across the country. Within this group the firm has integrated the previous in-house legal team of the Lambeth, Southwark and Lewisham Health Authority. Also acts for a large number of individual practitioners, their representative bodies and for Health Service Managers. Acted on Thomson v Blake-James – a Court of Appeal decision on foreseeability.

Le Brasseur J Tickle (15ptnrs/26assts forming the general Health Care Department) With a large team and client list, the firm is clearly a presence, although felt by some to be increasingly aggressive. *Robert Sumerling* was recommended. **Clients/Work:** Acted for Defendants on Spargo v North Essex Health Authority CA – successful limitation date of knowledge case; Poynter v Hillingdon Health Authority – consent to treatment; Re MB Court of Appeal consent to treatment.

Bird & Bird (10ptnrs/6assts form the firm's Health Group) Not on the NHSLA panel but nevertheless commended by several practitioners and with a sizeable Health Group which includes medical negligence specialists, such as *David Stone*. **Clients/Work:** Acted in several £1m plus settlements for NHS clients in London and South East and regularly advised on urgent matters such as emergency declarations.

BARBER, Janice C.
Hempsons, London (0171) 836 0011
Specialisation: Janice has an enormous
experience of all areas of Healthcare Law,
though she specialises in employment law,
contract law and the law relating to hospital
and general practice. She has undertaken
variously: medico-legal advice to and
representation of defendant Health Authorities,
NHS Trusts and individual practitioners
covering all areas of hospital and general
practice; professional disciplinary and other
Tribunals and statutory Inquiries; defence of
serious criminal charges and employment law,
particularly in relation to hospital practice.
Leading cases Janice has been involved in
include R v. Cox 1992: manslaughter,
euthanasia, acting for the defendant; Howard v.
E Dorset Health Authority 1993: hospital,
negligence, applicability of res ispa loquitur
principle in medical negligence cases, for the
defendant; Thomson v. Blake-James CA 1997:
re. forseeability; WG Dick v. Brookmount
Estates Limited & Ford Sellar Morris
Developments Limited CA 1992: successful
recovery of fees, under Order 14, acting for
Plaintiff, a quantity surveyor; Colley v.
Canterbury Council: House of Lords decision
on planning law and compensation due to
following compulsory purchase order; Stanley
Royd Hospital Inquiry: Salmonella Inquiry, led
to the lifting of Crown Immunity for hospital
kitchens; United Leeds Hospital v. Duncan
Walker 1997: Disciplinary Inquiry under
HSG(95)25 and subsequent appeal to the
Secretary of State.
Career: Janice graduated with a 1st Class
Hons BA at the University of Reading. She was
articled at *Hempsons* and admitted in 1983.
She has been a partner since 1985. She often
conducts seminars and lectures in all the
specialist areas of practice set out above.

BARTON, Grainne
Pritchard Englefield, London
(0171) 972 9720
Partner and Head of Medical Negligence
Department.
Specialisation: Handles exclusively plaintiff
medical negligence matters. Acted in Tredget v.
Bexley Health Authority (nervous shock) in 1994
and Smyth v. Riverside Health Authority
(malaria case) in 1993.
Prof. Memberships: APIL, AVMA, Law
Society, Medical Negligence Panel.
Career: With *Boyes Turner & Burrows* 1987-90.
Qualified in 1989. Joined *Pritchard Englefield* in
1990 and became a Partner in 1993.
Personal: Born 8th October 1963. Educated at
Brunel University 1982-86. Past Honorary
Secretary of TSG. Enjoys singing at weddings.
Lives in Epsom, Surrey.

BATTEN, Elizabeth
Parlett Kent, London (0171) 430 0712/3
Specialisation: Medical negligence specialist
since 1991. Particular interest in oncology, brain
injury, accident and emergency cases and in
psychiatric negligence. Reported case of
'Mahmood v. Siggins'. Has lectured to lawyers
and health professionals on medical
negligence and related topics.
Prof. Memberships: Law Society. Law Society
Medical Negligence panel. AVMA referral panel

member. APIL member.
Career: Admitted 1977. Partner in *Parlett Kent*
from 1993. BA (Cantab) in Economics.

CAHILL, Julia
Kingsley Napley, London (0171) 814 1200
Specialisation: Partner and specialist in
medical negligence and professional
negligence litigation. Cases mainly involve
serious disability or death. Advises on inquests
into death during medical care. Particular
expertise in obstetric negligence claims on
behalf of mother and child. Special interest in
delayed diagnosis of meningitis in children and
delayed diagnosis in adults of cervical cancer,
bowel cancer and breast cancer. Practice also
covers legal negligence involving the pursuit of
claims against legal advisers in medical
negligence cases. Interesting recent cases
include McAllister v. Lewisham and North
Southwark Health Authority [1994] MEDLR.
Increasingly asked to present lectures and
seminars to the legal profession.
Prof. Memberships: Law Society Panel of
Specialist Medical Negligence Solicitors; AVMA
Lawyers Referral Panel; Member APIL, APLA,
ATLA. Secretary to the APIL Medical
Negligence Special Interest Group.
Career: DIP Physiotherapy 1976. Qualified
LL.B 1980. Assistant Director, Action for Victims
of Medical Accidents 1984-1988. Partner *Parlett
Kent & Co.* 1992 - 1994. Joined *Kingsley Napley*
as Partner in September 1994.
Personal: Two children. Lives in Islington,
London.

FAZAN, Claire
Bindman & Partners, London
(0171) 833 4433
Partner in charge of Personal Injury and
Medical Negligence Department.
Specialisation: Medical negligence litigation
on behalf of plaintiffs. Experienced in claims
involving all types of injury. Extensive
experience of claims on behalf of adults and
children who have suffered brain damage and
other permanent and severe disabilities
including those arising from obstetric and
anaesthetic care and failure to diagnose
subarachnoid haemorrhage . Considerable
experience of structured settlements. Advises
in relation to inquests into deaths during
medical care. Experience in respect of
provision and refusal of treatment. Advises
under the Legal Aid Scheme. Co-author of
"Medical Negligence Litigation: A Practitioners
Guide", by Irwin, Fazan & Allfrey [published by
LAG]. Frequently writes and lectures on
medical negligence litigation and associated
topics.
Prof. Memberships: Law Society Medical
Negligence Panel. Association of Personal
Injury Lawyers, AVMA.
Career: Qualified in 1985. Joined *Bindman &
Partners* in 1987 and became a Partner in 1989.
Personal: Born 21st June 1956. Attended
London School of Economics (LLB 1983).

FORRESTER, Rex
Hempsons, London (0171) 836 0011
Partner in Medical and Healthcare Department.
Specialisation: Defendant medical negligence
specialist. Advises and represents NHS
Hospital Trusts and general practitioners, as

well as doctors working in the private sector in
relation to litigation resulting from allegations of
medical negligence arising from all areas of
medical practice. Provides representation and
advocacy before professional disciplinary
tribunals including the GMC, the NHS Tribunal,
and at FHS Appeals. Also represents the
interests of doctors at coronal inquests and
enquiries. Major clients include the Medical
Defence Union Ltd, Brighton Healthcare NHS
Trust and Royal Surrey NHS Trust.
Prof. Memberships: Solicitors' Association of
Higher Court Advocates.
Career: Qualified in New Zealand as a
Barrister and Solicitor in 1986. Senior Assistant
Solicitor with *Hempsons* since 1988, partner
since 1995. Qualified in England & Wales as a
Solicitor in 1991. Obtained Rights of Audience
in the Higher Courts (Civil) in 1994.
Personal: Born 19th September 1962.
Educated at Christ's College, Christchurch,
New Zealand 1976-80, the University of
Canterbury, New Zealand (LL.B 1st Class
Hons, 1985) and Gonville & Caius College,
Cambridge (LL.M, 1986). Interests include
travel, reading and photography. Lives in
London.

HARVEY, C.J. Zoe
Hempsons, London (0171) 836 0011
Partner in Medical & Healthcare Department.
Specialisation: Principal area of practice is
medical and healthcare matters. Handles
litigation relating to all areas of hospital and
general practice. Advises NHS Health
Authorities/ Trusts and practitioners on medico-
legal matters, including professional
disciplinary and tribunal representation. Other
main area of practice is personal injury, with
particular emphasis on medical and
pharmaceutical cases. Major cases include Dr
Sidney Gee v. GMC. Major clients include the
Medical Defence Union Ltd, Lambeth,
Southwark & Lewisham Health Authority, Royal
Surrey Trust and Buckinghamshire Health
Authority.
Prof. Memberships: Law Society, Medico-
Legal Society.
Career: Qualified in 1979. Became a Partner at
Hempsons in 1991.
Personal: Born 16th February 1955. Educated
at St. Annes's College Convent, Sanderstead,
Surrey 1964-73 and Birmingham University
1973-76. Lives in New Malden, Surrey.

HAY, Katie
Capsticks, London (0181) 780 2211
Partner in Medical Litigation Department.
Specialisation: Handles all types of medical
negligence litigation for NHS clients. Has a
particular interest in larger cases, especially
birth injury baby cases. She is an authority on
structured settlements having helped to
pioneer structures in the health service. She
has advised on the drafting of the NHS
Executives Guidance on the subject and has
had articles published on this and other
medico-legal issues. She is responsible for the
firm's in-house training programme.
Prof. Memberships: Law Society, Association
of Women Solicitors.
Career: Qualified in 1988 following articles at
Howard Kennedy. With *Cole & Cole*, Oxford
1988-90. Joined *Capsticks* in 1990. Became a

Partner in November 1992 and a consultant in July 1996.
Personal: Born 24th January 1964. Educated at Reading Abbey School 1976-82, Oxford Polytechnic (BA Hons in Law with History) 1982-85. Interests include running, reading and cinema. Lives in London.

HOLMES, John
Beachcroft Stanleys, London
(0171) 242 1011
Partner in Health Law Group.
Specialisation: Principal area of practice is medical negligence acting for health service bodies in defence claims. Also gives general advice in clinical issues (including risk management), mental health and staff claims. Reported claims include Burton v. Islington Health Authority, Sion v. Hampstead Health Authority, Clunis v. Camden & Islington Health Authority and R v. Bournewood NHS Trust. Acts for Health Service bodies throughout Southern England, mainly in the Thames region, including many major teaching hospitals. The Firm is on the panel for the NHS Litigation Authority (NHSLA).
Prof. Memberships: Law Society.
Career: Qualified in 1984. Joined *Beachcroft Stanleys* in 1986 and became a Partner in 1992.
Personal: Educated at Bristol University 1978-81.

JAMIESON, Elisabeth
Parlett Kent, London (0171) 430 0712/3
Partner
Specialisation: Handles medical negligence (some personal injury) with interest in medical and surgical cases, children injured at birth, obstetrics and gynaecology, psychiatric and fatal cases (including stillbirths).
Prof. Memberships: A.V.M.A, A.P.I.L. Law Society's Medical Negligence Panel.
Career: Qualified in 1987. With *Sinclair Taylor & Martin* 1989-94. *Pritchard Englefield* in February 1994 - 96. From 1996 Partner with *Parlett Kent*.
Personal: Law degree at South Bank Polytechnic. Qualified State Registered Nurse.

JENKINS, Caroline Helen Clare
Parlett Kent, London (0171) 430 0712/3
Senior Partner in Personal Injury Department.
Specialisation: Principal area of practice is medical negligence (plaintiff PI). Particular interest in gynaecological, oncological and obstetrics cases. Also deals with professional negligence. Important cases handled include Gascoine v. Sheridan & Co & Latham (MLR Dec 1994), Kirk v. S.E. London Health Authority, and Leech v. Gloucester Health. Member of Law Society's Medical Negligence Panel from 1995. Author of chapter on Quantum in forthcoming publication - Medical Accidents Handbook.
Prof. Memberships: AVMA, APIL, Law Society, ATLA.
Career: Qualified in 1980. Joined *Parlett Kent & Co* in 1982. Became a Partner in 1983. Now Senior Partner.
Personal: King's College, London University (BA, 1975).

LEE, Terry
Evill & Coleman, London (0181) 789 9221
Partner of Personal Injury Department.
Specialisation: Main areas of practice are catastrophic injuries, medical negligence, brain damage at birth, head injuries, multiple injuries, fatal accident claims and Court of Protection work. He has been involved in a number of significant actions including Brown v. Merton & Sutton Health Authority, Head v. East Anglia Health Authority, Hall v. Pirie and Lambert v. Devon County Council. A further case, Joyce v. Wandsworth Health Authority provided clarification of the judicial approach to causation. Recently, Terry was involved in a sporting injury case which was the first of its kind brought against a rugby referee and which was successful. This was the well-known case of Smoldon v. Whitworth & Nolan. Some of the actions he has conducted include cases where damages well in excess of ú2,000,000 have been awarded and he has also been instrumental in dealing with a number of cases which involve the formation of a structured settlement. Terry acted for Peter Pearse who was brain damaged at birth on 28th December 1970. Mr Pearse recovered damages of over ú2,000,000 and the case was successfully concluded in 1988. He is an assessor to the Personal Injury Panel as well as a member of the Specialised Panel of Personal Injury Solicitors. He is also a member of the Medical Negligence Specialist Panel. He is also co-ordinating solicitors involved in a series of cases where victims have allegedly suffered side effects as a result of the use of corticosteroid medication. Author of articles for legal magazines and a book on injuries of maximum severity. Lectures extensively at conferences and seminars. He is also a referral solicitor to various organisations including AVMA, Spinal Injuries Association, Headway etc.
Prof. Memberships: Association of Personal Injury Lawyers, AVMA (referral solicitor), British Academy of Forensic Science.
Career: Qualified and joined *Evill & Coleman in* 1972. Became a Partner in 1976.
Personal: Born 14th August 1945. Educated at Wimbledon College. Recreations include golf and tennis. Lives in Esher, Surrey.

LEIGH, Bertie
Hempsons, London (0171) 836 0011
See under Health Care, p. 413

LEIGH, Sarah
Leigh, Day & Co, London (0171) 650 1200
Partner in Medical Negligence Department.
Specialisation: Handles primarily major medical negligence cases involving severe disability and death and cases involving mental handicap problems (e.g. Re F in 1989 - a leading case on consent in mental handicap). Has spoken at many conferences and seminars and written several articles.
Prof. Memberships: AVMA, Justice, APIL.
Career: Qualified in 1971. Founder Partner (1974) of *Bindman & Partner*. Left to set up own firm in 1985 (renamed *Leigh Day & Co* in 1988).
Personal: Born 29th July 1942. Trustee of Immigrants Aid Trust. Campaigner for changes in medical negligence litigation system.

LEVY, Russell
Leigh, Day & Co, London (0171) 650 1200
Partner in Medical Negligence Department.
Specialisation: Principal area of practice is plaintiff medical negligence and medical devices (product liability) litigation. Has written numerous articles for various specialist publications and is a regular speaker on medical negligence topics.
Prof. Memberships: AVMA. Secretary and then Co-ordinator of APIL Medical Negligence Special Interest Group 1992-1996. Member of APIL Executive Committee since 1996. Member Lord Chancellor's Department Medical Negligence Working Party 1997, ATLA.
Career: Qualified 1984. Joined *Leigh Day & Co* as a Partner in 1991.
Personal: Born 15th March 1956.

LONGSTAFF, Oliver Robert
Capsticks, London (0181) 780 2211
Specialisation: Principal expertise is medical negligence, acting for NHS Health Authorities and Trusts. Has particular interests in obstetrics and gynaecology and cancer cases. Acted for the successful appellant in R v. Croydon Health Authority. Is a frequent advocate at inquests, and lectures clinicians and risk managers on issues affecting NHS litigation.
Prof. Memberships: Law Society.
Career: Articles at *Hempsons*. Qualified in 1993. Joined *Capsticks* in 1995.
Personal: Born 23rd December 1966. Educated at QEGS Blackburn, Durham University and Newcastle Polytechnic. Marrying September 1998. Musician (Leader, Lawyers' Music Symphony Orchestra).

MARSH, Christine
Kingsley Napley, London (0171) 814 1200
Partner and Head of Medical Negligence and Personal Injury Department.
Specialisation: Handles plaintiff medical negligence. Undertakes Legal Aid work. Emphasis on maximum severity injuries. Has acted in several cases reported in national newspapers. Co-author of 'Fatal Accident Litigation' (Tolley's, 1993). Has lectured and presented seminars. Panel Solicitor on Law Society's Medical Negligence and Personal Injury Panels. AVMA Referral Panel.
Prof. Memberships: APIL, AVMA, Headway, Spinal Injuries Association, Medico-legal Society.
Career: Qualified 1986. Partner at *Bolt Burdon* 1989-92. Joined *Kingsley Napley* as a Partner in December 1992.
Personal: One child. Lives in Oxfordshire. Educated at Royal Latin School, Buckingham 1974-80 and Leicester University 1980-83. Leisure interests include tennis, ski-ing, music and gardening.

MARTINEZ, Liz
Evill & Coleman, London (0181) 789 9221

MASON, David
Capsticks, London (0181) 780 2211
Partner and Director of Clinical Claims.
Specialisation: Principal area of practice is medical negligence with specialisation in obstetrics and neurosurgery cases. Also deals with mental health law. Acted for health authorities in successful defence of a number of reported cases including Rance v. Mid Downs Health Authority; Moore v. Worthing Health Authority, Saad v. Mid Surrey Health Authority, Joyce v. Merton Suttons Wandsworth, de Martell v. Merton and Sutton Health Authority, Muzio v. North West Herts Health Authority, Waters v. West Sussex HA, Corley v. North West Hertfordshire Health Authority and Knight v. West Kent HA. Handles many of the cases in Capsticks where court orders are required relating to future medical care, including Re R (adult): Medical Treatment - one of the leading cases on when care can be withheld. Co-author of "Litigation - A Risk Management Guide for Midwives", published

by the Royal College of Midwives, and articles on medical law for specialist publications. Regular lecturer on medical law and risk management topics, especially obstetrics-related. Honorary legal adviser to College of Health. Defence solicitor representative on steering group of medical negligence working party reporting to Lord Woolf, and now defence solicitor representative and executive Committee Member of the Clinical Disputes Forum. Co-author of the Pre Action Protocol for medical negligence cases.
Career: Called to Bar 1984. Employed Barrister with *Thomas Watts & Co* 1986-1988. Joined *Capsticks* in 1988 as employed Barrister. Requalified as Solicitor and became a Partner in 1990.
Personal: Born 16th October 1955. Attended Winchester College 1969-73, then Oriel College, Oxford 1974-77 (MA in Experimental Psychology). Lives in London.

MCNEIL, Paul
Field Fisher Waterhouse, London (0171) 481 4841
Specialisation: Partner in the Litigation Department of *Field Fisher Waterhouse* specialising in Medical Negligence, Personal Injury and Product Liability, acting mainly for Plaintiffs. Has particular experience in cases involving head and other serious injuries. Publications include "International Product Liability" (1993) co-author. Also lectures on various aspects of medical law.
Prof. Memberships: Law Society Medical Negligence Panel; Association of Personal Injury Lawyers; AVMA.
Career: Qualified 1983. Assistant solicitor, *Amhurst Brown* 1983-1985. Assistant solicitor, *Taylor Joynson Garrett* 1985-1992. Assistant solicitor, *Field Fisher Waterhouse* 1992-1994. Partner since 1994.
Personal: Educated at All Saints' Comprehensive, Huddersfield 1975-1977 and Sheffield University 1977-1980. Leisure pursuits include tennis, running and skiing. Born 26th July 1958. Lives in Putney, London.

PEDLER, Katherine
Pritchard Englefield, London (0171) 972 9720
Specialisation: Plaintiff medical negligence, particularly dental negligence; major cases include spinal surgery and brain injury at birth.
Prof. Memberships: APIL; AVMA; Law Society; Medical Negligence Panel.
Career: Qualified in 1991. Joined *Pritchard Englefield* in 1992 and became a partner in 1996.
Personal: Born 8th December 1959. Interests include theatre, music, design.

ROHDE, Kate
Kingsley Napley, London (0171) 814 1200
Specialisation: Majority of practice is medical negligence litigation on behalf of Plaintiffs. Experienced in claims involving all types of injury. Particular interest in obstetric claims and claims on behalf of children. Also handles education litigation.
Prof. Memberships: AVMA, APIL
Career: Qualified in 1989. With *Compton Carr* 1987 to December 1995, as a partner from 1993. Joined *Teacher Stern Selby* as partner in

1996. Moved to *Kingsley Napley* as a Partner in March 1997.
Personal: Born 3rd November 1963, educated at University College London, lives in London.

SMITH, Janice
Capsticks, London (0181) 780 2211
Partner in Litigation Department.
Specialisation: Principal area of practice is medical negligence with particular interest in cases involving obstetrics, orthopaedics, A&E and cardiology. Also specialises in child protection law as it relates to the NHS. Co-ordinates Capsticks' Risk Management programme and assists NHS Trusts to identify high risk departments and develop incident reporting schemes. Regular lecturer on the Open University Diploma in Risk Management and also lectures on various aspects of medical law.
Prof. Memberships: Law Society and its committees concerning issues of medical negligence.
Career: Qualified in 1985. Assistant Solicitor with *Herbert Smith* 1985-1986. Assistant Solicitor at *Beckman & Beckman* 1987-1990. Joined *Capsticks* in 1990 and became a Partner in 1991.
Personal: Born 24th March 1960. Attended Tunbridge Wells Grammar School for Girls 1971-78, then Leeds University 1978-1981 before taking a year out to work for the Boys Brigade. Vice President of London District Boys' Brigade and Director of Oasis Trust. Lives in Bicester.

STONE, David M.
Bird & Bird, London (0171) 415 6000
Partner. Commercial Litigation Department.
Specialisation: Main area of practice is the health sector, acting for trusts, health authorities and advisory bodies in medical negligence and personal injury claims, employment and defamation matters, risk management, health and admin. law generally. Also handles professional negligence, media law and general commercial litigation. Regular contributor to health press and speaker at health conferences. Editor of Legal Diagnosis and on the Editorial Board of Health Care Risk Report.
Prof. Memberships: Law Society, Medico-Legal Society.
Career: Qualified in 1983. Assistant Solicitor with *Lee Bolton & Lee* 1983-85. Joined *Bird & Bird* in 1985 and became a Partner in 1990.
Personal: Born 1956. Educated at Christ's Hospital, Horsham 1967-74 and Christ's College, Cambridge 1975-78. (Classics). Lives in London.

SUMERLING, R. W.
Le Brasseur J Tickle, London (0171) 836 0099

VALLANCE, Richard A.
Charles Russell, London (0171) 203 5000
Partner in Litigation Department.
Specialisation: An important part of his practice is professional negligence. Began medical negligence work in 1978 with cases concerning children suffering deafness as a result of treatment for burns. Dealt with numerous maternity cases in the early 1980's and was in the forefront of the development of

medical negligence litigation from then on. Also handles commercial litigation. Acted for two of the plaintiffs in the leading case of Naylor v. Preston Area Health Authority, 1987 2 All ER 353. Has lectured on medical negligence to lawyers, doctors and nurses since about 1984 including LAG/ AVMA seminars and conferences and the Law Society Litigation Conference in Birmingham. Contributed a chapter to Powers and Harris's book 'Medical Negligence' (Butterworths) and has written numerous articles. Has appeared on Legal Network TV.
Prof. Memberships: The Law Society and its Committees concerning issues of medical negligence, AVMA & AVMA Lawyers Support Group, Secretary to APIL Medical Negligence Special Interest Group, Medico-Legal Society.
Career: Qualified in 1970. Partner in *Compton Carr* 1972 and, following merger, in *Charles Russell* 1996. Assessor of the Law Society Medical Negligence Panel from July 1994. Appointed mediator in Court of Appeal in 1997.
Personal: Born 26th January 1947. Secondary School Governor. Recreations include squash, tennis, reading, opera and theatre. Lives near Saffron Walden.

WILDER, Gay E.
Beachcroft Stanleys, London (0171) 242 1011
Partner in Health Law Group.
Specialisation: Principal area of practice is defending medical negligence claims for health service bodies. Also advises on all aspects of Health Service law, particularly issues concerning patient care including clinical risk management. Acts for Health Service bodies throughout Southern England, mainly in the Thames Regions. Regular contributor of articles to health publications and *Beachcroft Stanleys* Health Law Bulletin. Editorial Board Member of the 'Medical Law Review'. Frequent speaker at conferences and seminars on medico-legal issues. The Firm is on the panel for the NHS Litigation Authority (NHSLA).
Prof. Memberships: Law Society.
Career: Qualified in 1982. With *Hempsons* 1980-88 (Partner from 1985). Joined *Beachcroft Stanleys* in 1988 and became a Partner in 1989.
Personal: Educated at Reading University 1976-79 (LL.B).

WINYARD, Anne H.
Leigh, Day & Co, London (0171) 650 1200
Specialisation: Partner and specialist in medical negligence. Acts for plaintiffs. Cases mainly involve serious disablities or death, including both adults and children who have suffered brain damage as a result of medical treatment. Publications include chapters in both 'Medical Negligence' (Powers & Harris) and 'Safe Practice in Obstetrics and Gynaecology' (Clements). Regular speaker at medico-legal conferences and seminars.
Prof. Memberships: AVMA, APIL, ATLA.
Career: Qualified 1977. Partner, *Fisher Meredith* 1983-1992. Joined *Leigh Day & Co* as partner in 1992.
Personal: Born 1948.

YEAMAN, Anthony George
Beachcroft Stanleys, London (0171) 242 1011
Partner in Health Law Group.
Specialisation: Principal area of practice is medical negligence, handling claims for Health

Service bodies and advising on all aspects of Health Service law, particularly issues concerning patient care and complaints. Has dealt with multi-party litigation, structured settlements and internal NHS inquiries. Acts for Health Service bodies throughout Southern England, mainly in the Thames region and including many major teaching hospitals. Frequent speaker at conferences and seminars on medico-legal and related issues. The Firm is on the panel for the NHS Litigation Authority (NHSLA).
Career: Qualified in 1988. Assistant Regional Solicitor to former Wessex Regional Health Authority 1988-94. Joined *Beachcroft Stanleys* in 1994.
Personal: Born 11th November 1961. Educated at Middlesex University 1983-85, The College of Law, Guildford 1985-86 and Bournemouth University 1991-93 (DMS).

SOUTH EAST

MAINLY PLAINTIFF

LEADING FIRMS · PLAINTIFF
BOYES TURNER & BURROWS Reading
OSBORNE MORRIS & MORGAN Leighton Buzzard
GADSBY WICKS Chelmsford
THOMSON SNELL & PASSMORE Tunbridge Wells
BLAKE LAPTHORN Portsmouth
WYNNE BAXTER GODFREE & SELWOOD LEATHES HOOPER Brighton

Boyes Turner & Burrows (Reading) (2ptnrs/2assts/1 paralegal) A "fantastic" firm according to one client; "on the ball" according to fellow practitioners – comments which keep it at the top of the rankings. *Adrian Desmond* heads the team. **Clients/Work:** Recovered over £6m in compensation for clients during 1997; act for approximately 400 clients at any one time.

Osborne Morris & Morgan (Leighton Buzzard) (2ptnrs/4 fee-earners) *Tom Osborne* leads the team in this widely respected niche firm. **Clients/Work:** Specialise in cerebral palsy and brain damage claims. Also a large number of inquests.

Gadsby Wicks (Chelmsford) (2ptnrs/3assts/1 legal executive) A firm noted for its strong specialisation: 70% of the work of the firm is medical negligence with another 20% being medical products liability. *Gillian Gadsby* and *Roger Wicks* are the two recommended partners. **Clients/Work:** Concluded a large number of cases during 1997 including one success at trial where damages awarded were in excess of £1m.

Thomson Snell & Passmore (Tunbridge Wells) (1ptnr/4assts forming part of a larger personal injury department) A "competent" team headed by *Andrew Watson*. **Clients/Work:** Miles v West Kent Health Authority – major award in keyhole surgery case; Taylor v West Kent Health Authority – involving causation in breast cancer; Skelton v Lewisham & North Southwark Health Authority – brain damaged child.

Blake Lapthorn (Portsmouth) (2ptnrs/4assts who also do personal injury work) Have a lower profile than their competitors. **Clients/Work:** Victoria Clemo v MOD – settled for overall value structured settlement of £2.5m; Rae v Portsmouth NHS Trust – successful claim on a conditional fee basis where delay in a diagnosis of breast cancer; Floyd v MOD – successfully established defendant's failure to advise plaintiff sufficiently for him to give informed consent to an operation.

Wynne Baxter Godfree & Selwood Leathes Hooper (Brighton) (2ptnrs/2assts) On 1st November 1997 Selwood Leathes Hooper merged with local firm, Wynne Baxter Godfree, but retains its medical negligence team, led by *John Hooper*. **Clients/ Work:** Large number of cerebral palsy and gynaecological claims.

LEADING INDIVIDUALS PLAINTIFF	
DESMOND Adrian Boyes Turner & Burrows	
OSBORNE Thomas Osborne Morris & Morgan	
GADSBY Gillian Gadsby Wicks	
WATSON Andrew Thomson Snell & Passmore	
WICKS Roger Gadsby Wicks	
HOOPER John Selwood Leathes Hooper	

SEE PROFILES AT END OF THIS SECTION

MAINLY DEFENDANT

LEADING FIRMS · DEFENDANT
WANSBROUGHS WILLEY HARGRAVE Winchester
BRACHERS Maidstone
COLE & COLE Oxford

Wansbroughs Willey Hargrave (Winchester) (3ptnrs/14 fee-earners form the Health Department which includes medical negligence work.) With Cole & Cole's exclusion from the NHSLA panel, the firm now stands alone as a leader in the South East. The team, headed by newly recommended *Valerie West* ("sensible and proficient") includes leaders *Anne Bevan* and *Tim Wright*. **Clients/Work:** Acts for over 30 NHS Trusts and health organisations on a wide range of cases from routine retained swab to complex brain damaged baby claims. One case involved an order for withdrawal of treatment to a patient in a persistent vegetative state.

Brachers (Maidstone) (1ptnr/5assts) Also on the NHSLA panel, apparently because of its locality and insurance background. *John Sheath* heads the team. **Clients/Work:** Acts for a large number of trusts in the acute and community health care sector. Acted for the defendant in Dobbie v Medway Health and is coordinating the negotiation of Kent and Canterbury Hospitals smear claims.

Cole & Cole (Oxford) (1ptnr/2assts) Some interviewees expressed surprise that the firm was not selected for the panel and it will continue to run through a large number of older claims while hoping to be reappointed at a later date. *Charles Graham* heads the team. **Clients/Work:** Claims handled in 1997 included a successful application for PVS case which was settled.

LEADING INDIVIDUALS DEFENDANT	
BEVAN Anne Wansbroughs Willey Hargrave	
GRAHAM Charles Cole & Cole	
SHEATH John Brachers	
WEST Valerie Wansbroughs Willey Hargrave	
WRIGHT Tim Wansbroughs Willey Hargrave	

SEE PROFILES AT END OF THIS SECTION

BEVAN, Anne

Wansbroughs Willey Hargrave, Winchester
01962 841 444

Specialisation: Anne specialises in medical negligence work. She has successfully defended many complex High Court actions. Her main interest is in obstetrics and gynaecology and she has been involved in structured settlements of brain-damaged baby claims. She sits on the Medico Legal Committee of the Royal College of Obstetricians and Gynaecologists. She has recently advised many NHS trusts on the question of nurses prescribing drugs. She lectures widely on medico-legal issues.

Career: 1974 Law lecturer; 1979 Called to the Bar; 1982 Lecturer on Health Service management courses / Legal adviser to the Insurance Ombudsman Bureau; 1988 In house lawyer Wessex Regional Health Authority; 1994 Joined *Wansbroughs Willey Hargrave* as a consultant.

DESMOND, Adrian

Boyes Turner & Burrows, Reading
(0118) 959 7711
email: adesmond@b-t-b.co.uk Medical Negligence Group Partner.

Specialisation: Acts for plaintiffs in all types of medical accident cases with special interest in cases of maximum severity, brain, spinal, obstetric and paediatric injury. AVMA referral solicitor since 1984. Assessor to and member of Law Society specialist medical negligence panel since formed. Secretary then co-ordinator of medical negligence special interest group of the Association of Personal Injury Lawyers. Founding member of Richard Grand Society. Acted in many high profile and reported cases. Author of legal and medical articles on issues related to medical negligence. Regular lecturer on the topic and media contributor. Deputy Taxing Master Supreme Court Taxing Office 1994-1998.

Prof. Memberships: AVMA, APIL, SIA, Headway, Patients Association, ATLA, European Brain Injury Society, Richard Grand Society.

Career: Qualified and joined *Boyes Turner & Burrows* in 1980.

Personal: Born 9th January 1955. Educated at Ratcliffe College 1968-73 and Bristol University 1974-77.

GADSBY, Gillian

Gadsby Wicks, Chelmsford (01245) 494929

GRAHAM, C.K.C.

Cole & Cole, Oxford (01865) 262600

Specialisation: Principally defends medical negligence claims, with particular expertise in obstetrics, gynaecology, orthopaedics and neurosurgery. He defended 117 claims bought by HIV & haemophiliacs in 1990-1 and set up an Inquiry into the death of Jonathon Newby in Oxford. He has never lost a medical negligence claim at trial.

Prof. Memberships: Law Society.

Career: Qualified in 1980 and joined *Cole & Cole*, Oxford in 1984. A Partner since 1986.

Personal: Born 24 April 1956. Attended Shrewsbury School and Trinity College, Cambridge, where he gained a First Class Honours Degree in Law. Lives in Oxford and is Undersheriff for Oxfordshire.

HOOPER, John

Wynne Baxter Godfree and Selwood Leathes Hooper, Lewes (01273) 477071

OSBORNE, Thomas R

Osborne Morris & Morgan, Leighton Buzzard (01525) 378177

SHEATH, J.C.

Brachers, Maidstone (01622) 690691

Specialisation: Deals principally with medical negligence and Health Service law particularly inquests, clinical trials and ethical matters. Has had the conduct of successful defence in many high profile decisions including 'Dobbie v. Medway Health Authority', PVS and mental health consent cases.

Prof. Memberships: Kent Medico Legal Society. Chairman Maidstone Local Research Ethics Committee.

Career: Educated at Sir Joseph Williamson's Mathematical School, Rochester. 1963-69. Southampton University 1970-73. *Norton, Rose, Botterell & Roche* 1974-81. Joined *Brachers* in 1981. Partner 1983. Formed medical negligence department which has expanded since Crown indemnity in January 1990. Head of Commercial Litigation Department. Regularly lectures on selected health topics.

Personal: Born 7th May 1951. Married with three teenage children. Lives in Sevenoaks. Interests include music, rugby and running.

WATSON, Andrew S.

Thomson Snell & Passmore, Tunbridge Wells (01892) 510000
Partner and Head of Personal Injury & Medical Negligence Department.

Specialisation: Deals exclusively with medical negligence and personal injury claims. Special areas of expertise are head and spinal injuries. Acted in Dobbie v. Medway Health Authority, Bova v. Spring, Harris v. Bromley Health Authority and Taylor v. West Kent Health Authority.

Prof. Memberships: A.P.I.L.

Career: Qualified in 1975, having joined *Thomson Snell & Passmore* in 1973. Became a Partner in 1981. Legal Aid Area Committee member. Panel solicitor for AVMA, the Spinal Injuries Association and Headway. Member of Law Society's Personal Injury Panel. Member of the Law Society's Medical Negligence Panel.

Personal: Born 29 March 1950. Educated at Oxford (MA 1st Class Honours) 1968-71. Recreations include reading, music, running and cuisine. Lives in Tunbridge Wells.

WEST, Valerie J.

Wansbroughs Willey Hargrave, Winchester (01962) 841444

Specialisation: Specialises in medical negligence litigation and has successfully defended a number of High Court actions. Special interests include obstetrics, paediatrics and neurosurgery claims.

Career: Qualified in 1977. Joined *Wansbroughs Willey Hargrave* in 1977. Became a Partner in 1981. Managing Partner of Winchester, 1996 - present.

WICKS, Roger

Gadsby Wicks, Chelmsford (01245) 494929

WRIGHT, Tim L.

Wansbroughs Willey Hargrave, Winchester (01962) 841444
Consultant in Health Department.

Specialisation: Tim specialises in all aspects of Health Service law. He has extensive experience, including handling the second ever NHS structured settlement. He has particular knowledge of the Mental Health Act, inquests, ethical matters and clinical trials. He recently obtained Court Orders to treat patients without their consent and to withdraw feeding from a PVS patient.

Career: Qualified 1978. With *Woodford & Ackroyd*, Lymington 1984-86 and Wessex Regional Health Authority 1986-94. Joined *Wansbroughs Willey Hargrave* as a Partner in 1994, and is now a consultant.

SOUTH WEST

MAINLY PLAINTIFF

Barcan Woodward (Bristol) (2ptnrs/1asst/1 legal exec. who also do personal injury work) "One of the best firms in terms of quality, experience and caseload." The "outstanding" *Richard Barcan* heads the team. **Clients/Work:** During 1997 acted for plaintiffs on a complex and high value brain damage case which reached the Court of Appeal and the liability aspects of two orthopaedic cases (one total hip replacement, one osteomyelitis).

Over Taylor Biggs (Bristol) (1ptnr/1asst/1 medico-legal assistant) *Christopher Over* is sometimes felt to be "rather aggressive" but the firm was generally well rated. **Clients/Work:** Specialise in cerebral palsy cases and during 1997 achieved a number of settlements in the region of £200,000 – £850,000. Also 20 breast screening cases.

Preston Goldburn (Falmouth) (1ptnr/1 legal executive/1asst who also does child care) Regarded as a good mixed practice led by the "very capable" *Tim Goldburn*. **Clients/Work:** Specialise in gynaecological claims.

Russell Jones & Walker (Bristol) (2 ptnrs/4assts) *Gillian Solly* heads the team (a branch office of the London firm). **Clients/Work:** Mrs N. Robles – the first person to undergo a laproscopic colesectomy in the UK, sustaining significant damage to the liver. Case settled despite an initial denial of liability. During the course of the case the Royal College of Surgeons issued guidelines on laproscopic techniques and the training of surgeons.

Tozers (Exeter) (1ptnr/2'assts/1 nurse) *Laurence Vick* (eccentric) was praised for building a good team. **Clients/Work:** Currently acting for 35 families of children who died or suffered brain damage during heart surgery at the Bristol Royal Infirmary. Also receive instructions nationally in Erb's Palsy claims.

John Hodge & Co (Bristol) (1ptner/2assts-1 part-time) A new entry to our tables this year following several recommendations from both plaintiff and defendant solicitors. The team is headed by the "no nonsense" *Richard England*. **Clients/Work:** Includes paediatric heart operations; oral contraceptive litigation; obstetrics and gynaecological cases.

Veale Wasbrough (Bristol) (1ptnr/2assts) Claims are handled by a specialist team within the firm's personal injury department. The firm is currently applying for a Legal Aid Franchise. **Clients/Work:** Cases dealt with in 1997 include: male aged 62 died after incompatible blood transfusion; male infected by "killer bug" whilst in hospital (one of the few survivors of necrotic fasceitis); incompetently performed breast reduction operation.

Withy King & Lee (Bath) (1ptnr/1 assoc. ptnr) A small but "excellent" team headed by the "technically skilled" *Gerry Ferguson*. **Clients/Work:** Acted for plaintiffs on the following cases: missed pneumococcal septicaemia; failure to diagnose cranio-pharyngioma; wrongful birth.

Wolferstans (Plymouth) (1ptnrs/4assts) A new entry to the tablesand are known for their cerebral palsy, brain injury and congenital hip dislocation cases. *Simon Parford* was recommended. **Clients/Work:** Conditional fee claim for £40k for a client who suffered injury following a prostatectomy; recovered £110k for a woman in her mid-sixties who suffered a partial loss of sight in one eye; acted for the plaintiff in Hedges v Plymouth Hospitals (NHS) Trust (pre-action discovery).

Woollcombe Beer Watts (Newton Abbot) (3ptnrs/3assts who also do personal injury work) Have a reputation as "generalists." Team led by *Derek Reed*. **Clients/Work:** Act for many cerebral palsy cases where foetal distress prior to birth. Also retained swab finally discovered after five operations; metal plate left in arm; breast cancer cases.

Adrian Hickman of Christopher Harrison & Company although "a bit of an eccentric," has a long track record.

Magi Young of Parlett Kent now spends 80% of her time at the new Exeter office of this London firm.

MAINLY DEFENDANT

Bevan Ashford (Bristol) (7ptnrs/14assocs/7

consultants/20assts) By far the predominant defendant firm in the South West servicing clients as far away as the Midlands. Seen as "professional and straightforward". The well-known *Richard Annandale, Paul Barber, Jill Broadhead* and *Andrew Whitefield* constitute an impressive team. **Clients/Work:** Acted on the breast screening cases at Royal Devon & Exeter NHS Trust. Lead advisers (with Beachcroft Stanley) on the *RAGE* Breast Cancer cases. Represented the Hospital trusts in Re "S" – judicial review of rights of women to refuse caesarean section.

Wansbroughs Willey Hargrave (Bristol) (1ptnr/3 fee-earners form part of the Insurance Litigation department) A smaller presence than their Winchester office, but highly praised for having "made a real impact" and in a good position to expand at the expense of other firms not on the NHSLA panel. **Clients/Work:** Defended a £100,000 claim for negligent nursing care of spina bifida patients – settled at £3,500.

Osborne Clarke (Bristol) (1ptnr/1assoc/2assts/2 medical consultants) Failure to be chosen for the NHSLA panel will undoubtedly limit the firm's opportunities, although it will continue to handle smaller claims and is respected for its track record. *Julie Austin* is handling any new work. **Clients/Work:** Act for the United Bristol Healthcare Trust.

ANNANDALE, Richard
Bevan Ashford, Bristol (0117) 923 0111
Specialisation: Partner in the NHS Litigation Department specialising in clinical litigation, medical law and risk management, particularly for hospitals with acute services. He handled a large number of compensation claims arising from a serious and widely publicised radiotherapy incident and succeeded in reaching over 100 settlements without a single writ being issued by using a novel method of mediation and is now involved in a high profile series of claims arising from the national programme of breast screening. He is a member of the Health Authorities' steering group in the actions brought by the pressure group RAGE and is active on working parties responding to the Government's proposals for changes in the field of clinical litigation.
Career: Qualified 1977. Partner since 1993. Director of QRM Healthcare Limited (*Bevan Ashford's* healthcare risk management company) since 1993.
Personal: Educated at Manchester University (LL.B) 1968-71.

AUSTIN, Julie
Osborne Clarke, Bristol (0117) 923 0220

BARBER, Paul
Bevan Ashford, Bristol (0117) 923 0111
Specialisation: As head of the firm's NHS Litigation Department, Paul is widely experienced in all areas of hospital litigation, in particular major obstetric cases. His pre-eminent area of work in recent years has been the handling of multi-party medical negligence actions (such as the haemophiliac HIV, Debedox and Benzodiazipine claims and the Myodil litigation on which he was the lead solicitor for Health Authorities nationally). In addition, Paul has specialist experience of mental health law.
Prof. Memberships: Law Society.
Career: Trained with *Bevan Ashford*. Admitted 1976; Partner 1979.

BARCAN, Richard
Barcan Woodward, Bristol (0117) 963 5237
Specialisation: Practises exclusively in medical negligence and personal injury. Handles Plaintiff work only, including Legal Aid.
Prof. Memberships: AVMA Referral Panel, Law Society Personal Injury Panel, APIL, Bristol Law Society.
Career: Qualified in 1979. Partner with *Gerald Davey & Co* 1985. Founding partner of *Barcan Woodward* in 1992.
Personal: Born 28th November 1951. Attended Westcliff High School for Boys and Liverpool University (LLB 1973). Keen cyclist. Lives in Bristol.

BROADHEAD, Jill
Bevan Ashford, Bristol (0117) 923 0111
Partner in Medical Negligence Department.
Specialisation: Has 22 years experience in the medical negligence field, dealing with a wide variety of cases, particularly obstetric and neurosurgical claims. Actively involved in all the multi-party litigation affecting the NHS. Also has expertise in the law relating to the supervision of registered nursing homes by Health Authorities. Acted in Nash v. Southmead Health Authority, Hall v. Avon Health Authority

(Teaching) and Taylor v Somerset Health Authority. Lectures widely to managers and clinicians within the NHS.
Prof. Memberships: Law Society, Bristol Medico Legal Society.
Career: Qualified in 1978. Joined *Bevan Ashford* in 1976, becoming a Partner in 1986.
Personal: Born 1953. Attended University of Birmingham and St Brandon's School, Clevedon.

ENGLAND, R.P.B.
John Hodge & Co, Bristol (0117) 929 2281
Specialisation: Partner in charge of litigation based at the firm's Bristol office. Specialises in Medical Negligence and Personal Injury Cases. Undertaken Cases Nationwide, including multi party actions, including Benzodiazepine, myodil, and Contraceptives, Paediatric heart operations etc.
Prof. Memberships: Member of the Law Society medical negligence and Personal Injury panels and the Association of Personal Injury Lawyers.
Career: Born 14th February 1951. LLB (Hons) Leeds University 1973. Qualified 1978. Partner *John Hodge*, since 1980.

FERGUSON, Gerry
Withy King, Bath (01225) 425731
Specialisation: Partner specialising in medical negligence and product liability claims for plaintiffs, particularly benzodiazepine/breast implant multi party litigation. Experience of high value claims, cerebral palsy, paraplegia, and psychiatric negligence cases.
Prof. Memberships: Law Society (Personal Injury Specialist Panel / Medical Negligence Specialist Panel), APIL, ATLA, APLA and AVMA (panel member). Legal Aid Area Appeals Committee. Bath and North East Somerset Racial Equality Council, Clinical Society of Bath, MIND Legal Network.
Career: Involved in medical negligence litigation since 1981. Joined *Withy King* in 1989. Legal Aid Franchise Coordinator – Bath area.
Personal: Born 23.7.53. Education: Epsom College; Birmingham University. Married with 2 sons. Lives in Bath. Leisure interests: Motor sport photography.

GOLDBURN, Tim
Preston Goldburn, Falmouth
(01326) 318900

HICKMAN, Adrian
Chris Harrison & Company, Truro
(01872) 241408
Personal and Medical Injuries Specialist.
Specialisation: Emphasis on medical and head injury matters. Acted in 'Hotson v. East Berkshire Health Authority' (loss of chance), 'M v. Plymouth Health Authority' (pre-action discovery), 'Braybrooke v. Parker' (first needs based structured settlement) and 'Jones v. Royal Cornwalls Hospital Trusts' (needle in the baby). George v RCHT. Author of articles published in personal and medical injuries law letter, APIL newsletter AVMA journal and Butterworths Personal Injury bulletin. Lectured for Legal Action Group and at the Law Society's Civil Litigation Conference 1993. Appears regularly on national/local TV and radio stations.
Prof. Memberships: Association of Personal Injury Lawyers.
Career: Although not qualified as a Solicitor,

has specialised in personal injury litigation for 30 years and medical injury litigation for 18 years. Joined *Chris Harrison & Company* in 1994.
Personal: Born 1st March 1949. Founder Member and Chairman of the Headway Cornwall; Member of the Community Health Council. Leisure interests include golf, bird watching and gardening.

OVER, Christopher
Over Taylor Biggs, Exeter (01392) 823811
Founding Partner 1993.
Specialisation: Principal area of practice is medical negligence dealing with claims of all types but particularly catastrophic injury. Represented clients in major medical claims involving substantial damages. Also deals with a wide range of transport cases including route licensing, planning and environmental appeals. Acted in transport cases on European Directives. Contributor to PI text books and Accident Line Book and author of articles in legal publications. Regular conference speaker and broadcasts frequently on local radio and TV.
Prof. Memberships: APIL, AVMA, SIA, Panel Solicitor for RHA and FTA. Law Society Public Relations Board.
Career: Qualified in 1977. Partner for ten years with *Crosse & Crosse* in Exeter: three years as Managing Partner. Founding Partner of *Over Taylor Biggs* in February 1993.
Personal: Born 18th October 1952. Attended King Edwards VI, Camp Hill, and Birmingham University. School Governor and Charity Trustee. Leisure pursuits include walking, badminton, food and drink and travel. Lives near Exeter.

PARFORD, Simon W.
Wolferstans, Plymouth (01752) 663295
Partner in charge of Medical Negligence & Head Injury Unit.
Specialisation: Specialising in Medical Negligence and Head/Brain injury claims, particularly those involving injuries at birth.
Prof. Memberships: Assessor to Law Society Medical Negligence Panel, member of Law Society's Medical Negligence and Personal Injury Panels, AVMA, APIL. ATLA.
Career: Qualified with *Wolferstans* in 1983 and became a partner in 1988.
Personal: Born 12 November 1958. Educated Plymouth College and Birmingham Polytechnic. Leisure pursuits include rugby, wine and photography.

REED, Derek S.
Woollcombe Beer Watts, Newton Abbot
(01626) 202404
Partner in Litigation Department.
Specialisation: Principal area of Practice involves substantial Plaintiff Medical Negligence work with some personal injury content. Has recently specialised in birth injury and cerebral palsy cases. Also very experienced criminal advocate dealing with all aspects of criminal work. Specialist in licensing matters. Has handled numerous substantial cases.
Prof. Memberships: Law Society. Law Society Medical Negligence Panel Assessor. Law Society Medical Negligence Panel and Law Society Personal Injury Panel.
Career: Qualified in 1971 with *Woollcombe Beer Watts* and became a Partner in 1972. Senior Partner since 1997.

Personal: Born 8th September 1946. Attended Liverpool University (LLB 1968). School Governor. Leisure pursuits include golf, sport, walking and gardening. Lives in Ipplepen.

SOLLY, Gillian Catherine
Russell Jones & Walker, Bristol
(0117) 927 3098
Partner in Personal Injury and Medical Negligence Department.
Specialisation: Specialising in medical negligence. Leading a department of 12 solicitors based in London, Birmingham, Manchester, Leeds, Sheffield and Newcastle, (shortly opening in Cardiff). The department covers all of England and Wales. Has a particular interest in laparoscopic surgery and catastrophic injury inluding brain damage at birth. In one such recent case obtained an interim payment of over £500,000. Other main area is personal injury, with particular interest in diseases and accidents in heavy industry.
Prof. Memberships: APIL (former Treasurer), AVMA referral solicitor, Bristol Medico-Legal Society, Bristol Law Society, ATLAS, Law Society's PI Panel Assessor.
Career: Qualified in 1981. Joined *Russell Jones & Walker*, London in 1983 (Partner from 1985). Moved to manage Bristol office in 1994.
Personal: Born 8th August 1957. Educated at Beverley High School for Girls (to 1975) and Warwick University (1975-78). Leisure pursuits include reading, wine and sailing. Lives in Bristol.

VICK, Laurence N.
Tozers, Exeter (01392) 207020

WHITEFIELD, A.T.E.
Bevan Ashford, Bristol (0117) 923 0111
Partner in NHS Litigation Department.
Specialisation: Adviser to Trusts and Health Authorities on legal and ethical issues and clinical risk management. Handles major medical negligence claims, inquests, internal and independent inquiries. Speaker on health law topics, the most recent being the Litigation Culture at the NHS Litigation Authority's conference in Bristol. Other organised events include those by the Royal College of Midwives, the Royal College of Nursing and the Royal Society of Medicine. International conferences include Biotechnology, Ethics and Law in 1995 and Consent Issues in Philedelphia in 1997. Lectures regularly to Trusts on Health Law issues and Risk Management.
Prof. Memberships: Law Society. President of the Tort Law Commission of the U.I.A. International Association of Lawyers.
Career: Admitted 1968. Joined *Bevan Ashford* 1970; Partner 1972. Fellow of Chartered Institute of Arbitrators. CEDR Accredited Mediator.

YOUNG, Magi
Parlett Kent, Exeter (01392) 494 455
London (0171) 430 0713
Specialisation: Medical Negligence Specialist with particular expertise in cases of maximum severity (eg recent award in excess of £2 million). Specialises in acting for children injured at or around birth (eg cerebral palsy and Erbs Palsy) and for people injured as a result of psychiatric negligence. Handles brain injury and spinal injury cases and has particular expertise in obstetric and gynaecology cases. Acts for many people with learning difficulties and has an interest in education and community care provision. Has particular specialism in cases of sexual abuse of patients by health care workers. Also handles personal injury claims including claims against local authorities. Interested in issues of accountability and regularly trains nurses, social workers, doctors and clinical risk managers and lawyers. Also interested in psychological effects of litigation. Undertook research on "Why patients sue doctors" (Lancet 1994) and has trained solicitors on dealing with distressed clients. Acts for clients nationwide particularly in the South East and South West of England and heads *Parlett Kent*'s Exeter office which opened in March 1997.
Prof. Memberships: AVMA referral solicitor, member of Law Society Medical Negligence Panel and Personal Injury Panel. ATLA.
Career: Qualified in 1987 with *Pannone Napier* and *Pannone Blackburn* from 1987 to 1992. Partner from 1991. Joined *Parlett Kent* in 1992 and became a partner in 1993.
Personal: Born 08.12.60. Bristol University (B.Soc. Sci. 1982).

WALES

MAINLY PLAINTIFF

LEADING FIRMS · PLAINTIFF
SMITH LLEWELYN PARTNERSHIP Swansea
HUGH JAMES Bargoed, Cardiff
HUTTONS Cardiff
EDWARDS GELDARD Cardiff
WALKER SMITH & WAY Wrexham

Smith Llewelyn Partnership (Swansea) (2ptnrs/2assts) Huw Llewelyn-Morgan has now left the firm but it is still pre-eminent in Wales. *Peter Llewelyn* remains a leader.

Clients/Work: Roberts v Horsman, Cummins & West Glamorgan Health Authority; Hutton v East Dyfed Health Authority. Peter Llewelyn continues to coordinate the CJD-Growth Hormone Litigation against the government.

Hugh James (Cardiff) (6ptnrs/2assts/ 1 medico-paralegal) The firm's medical negligence practice is spread across six offices with the team leader, *Andrew Davies*, based in Bargoed. **Clients/Work:** Cases handled include cerebral palsy, anaesthetic awareness and orthopaedic negligence, particularly of the lower limbs.

Huttons (Cardiff) (1ptnr/1asst/1 paralegal) The "impressive" *Tim Musgrave* heads the team. **Clients/Work:** During 1997 advised on three substantial birth injury claims.

Edwards Geldard (Cardiff) (1 ptnr/6 assts) **Clients/Work:** Acting on orthopaedic cases including one involving negligent spinal surgery where settlement of £250,000 was achieved. Psychiatric injury where £160,000 was awarded. Failure to diagnose prostate cancer which settled for £145,000.

Walker Smith & Way (Wrexham) (1ptnr/1asst who also do personal injury work) The only listed firm from North Wales. **Clients/Work:** Deals with full range of claims including cancer, cerebral palsy and birth damage cases.

LEADING INDIVIDUALS · PLAINTIFF
DAVIES Andrew Hugh James
LLEWELYN Peter Smith Llewelyn Partnership
MUSGRAVE Tim Huttons

SEE PROFILES AT END OF THIS SECTION

MAINLY DEFENDANT

LEADING FIRMS · DEFENDANT
BEVAN ASHFORD Cardiff

HIGHLY REGARDED FIRMS
Morgan Bruce Cardiff

The bulk of defendant work in Wales continues to be handled by Welsh Health Legal Services headed by the "enormously respected" Anne Louise Ferguson. The rest is dealt with by the following two firms, only the former of which is on the NHSLA panel.

Bevan Ashford (Cardiff) (1ptnr/ 2assocs) Smaller than the firm's Bristol office but praised as "well organised and efficient." *Tessa Shellens* was recommended again this year. **Clients/Work:** Act for Llandough Hospital and Community NHS Trust. Provide ad hoc advice for existing NHS clients. Specialists in complex cases.

Morgan Bruce (Cardiff) (2ptnrs/5assts) Have a long track record. **Clients/Work:** Acts for East Glamorgan NHS Trust, Human Fertilisation and Embryology Authority, Newham Health Services NHS Trust.

LEADING INDIVIDUALS DEFENDANT
SHELLENS Tessa Bevan Ashford

SEE PROFILES AT END OF THIS SECTION

DAVIES, Andrew K.
Hugh James, Bargoed (01443) 822022
Specialisation: His experience in medical negligence work includes obsteric negligence involving injuries of the utmost severity such as brain damage. His work has a broad spectrum however and involves a substantial number of orthapaedic medical negligence cases.
Career: Qualified 1988. Partner 1994.
Prof. Memberships: One of only three solicitors in Wales on the Law Society's Medical Negligence Panel, and is also a member of the Law Society's Personal Injury Panel.

LLEWELYN, Peter
Smith Llewelyn Partnership, Swansea
(01792) 464444

MUSGRAVE, Tim
Huttons, Cardiff (01222) 378621
Partner.
Specialisation: Medical negligence and personal injury, acting for plaintiffs.
Prof. Memberships: AVMA, APIL, Member of Law Society Medical Negligence Panel and AVMA Referral Panel.
Career: Qualified in 1987, with *Thomson Snell & Passmore*, Tunbridge Wells, then *Edwards Geldard* in Cardiff 1988-93. Joined *Huttons* in September 1993.
Personal: Born 1st September 1963. Bristol University 1981-84. Lives in Cardiff.

SHELLENS, Tessa
Bevan Ashford, Cardiff (01222) 462562
Partner in Litigation Department.
Specialisation: Main areas of practice are medical negligence and general NHS advisory work. Has 20 years experience of practice in these areas, with extensive knowledge of advising Health Authorities and Trusts in medical negligence claims, as well as general NHS advisory issues. Also deals with public law, giving general advice to other public bodies in Wales on matters of statutory interpretation and judicial review. Lectures extensively on medical and nursing law throughout England and Wales.
Career: Qualified in 1974. Joined *Bevan Ashford* as a Partner in 1991.
Personal: Born 9th May 1949. Attended Southampton University (BA Hons, History 1970).

MIDLANDS

MAINLY PLAINTIFF

Challinors Lyon Clark (Birmingham) **West Bromwich** (3ptnrs/1assoc/3assts) A "very successful and efficient team" headed by the widely praised *Richard Follis*. Clients/Work: Act on a range of cases from cerebral palsy to dental claims. In 1997 settled a "substantial" number of claims for six figure sums.

Freeth Cartwright Hunt Dickins (Nottingham, Derby) (2ptnrs/3assts) The "outstanding" *Paul Balen* heads the Nottingham team of this "excellent" firm and is regarded as particularly effective in group actions. His fellow partner, *Michael Bird* is

based in Derby. Clients/Work: Dealt with claim by Nottingham H.A. for repayment of damages awarded to a cerebral palsy victim who died eight days after the settlement of her case was approved by the court. Continued work on Norplant multi-party action involving claims by women implanted with a contraceptive device who claim that the information supplied by the manufacturers was deficient.

Anthony Collins (Birmingham) (1ptnr/1assoc/2assts) Seen as doing "good work" in the field, the team is led by the "conscientious" *Anthony Hall*. Clients/Work: M.Guest v Birmingham Health Authority; Joyce and Joyce v Sandwell Healthcare NHS Trust; Jenks v Birmingham Health Authority.

Shakespeares (Birmingham) (1ptnr /2assts – who also do personal injury work) The "very engaging" *Gary Christianson* heads the team at this firm which is regarded as "more characterful than other practices". Clients/Work: Interesting claims in 1997 include: M v Dorricott – a vet with nerves to the left hand disconnected; Hopson v Shropshire H.A. – mishandling of gynaecological surgery; a neonatal death.

Irwin Mitchell (Birmingham) (1ptnr/4assts/6 paralegals) Less noted than the Sheffield office for its medical negligence specialism and felt by some to be more of a personal injury practice. The team is led by

Stuart Henderson. Clients/Work: Acts for plaintiffs in the Royal Orthopaedic Hospital cancer misdiagnosis cases, plaintiff in a severe brain injury case and several cerebral palsy cases.

Newsome Vaughan (Coventry) (1ptnr/1asst who also do personal injury work) A smaller but well regarded team. Clients/Work: Cerebral palsy and cancer misdiagnosis claims.

Thompsons (Birmingham) (2ptnrs/1asst who also do personal injury work). Clients/Work: Cerebral palsy claim which settled for £250,000; fatal misdiagnosis of diabetes (the GP was subsequently convicted of manslaughter); plaintiff who died while taking part in a drug trial.

MIDLANDS

MAINLY DEFENDANT

The Lewington Partnership (4ptnrs/21assts) Some strong views were expressed about this firm but there is no doubt that for the moment it continues to handle the bulk of defendant claims in the Midlands. It is understood that following its exclusion from the NHSLA panel, the firm is undergoing major internal reorganisation and it may yet be appointed in the future. Bevan Ashford

and Wansbroughs Willey Hargrave look set to move into the area to try to claim the work. Clients/Work: O'Driscoll v Dudley H.A. – successfully defended major limitation case. Sherlock v Birmingham H.A. – successfully represented defendant in case of 8 month old severely brain-damaged child.

BALEN, Paul
Freeth Cartwright Hunt Dickins, Nottingham
(0115) 936 9369
Offices also at Derby and Leicester
E-mail: paul.balen@freethcartwright.co.uk
Partner in Civil Litigation Department.
Specialisation: Main areas of practice are medical negligence and product liability. Acts in claims for compensation arising from accidents of all types, co-ordination of group actions and medical negligence claims. Acted in Benzodiazepine litigation and the Allitt victims parents cases and is co-ordinating the Norplant, MMR, 3M hip and breast implant claims. Editorial board member of Health Care Risk Bulletin. Lecturer on medico-legal matters to doctors and lawyers. Is a Radio Nottingham phone-in 'Legal Eagle'. Co-author of Multi-Party Actions (LAG 1995).
Prof. Memberships: Law Society (Personal Injury Specialist Panel and Medical Negligence Specialist Panel assessor) National Secretary of APIL; Referral Solicitor for AVMA. Member of ATLA, ELF, PEOPIL.
Career: Joined *Freeth Cartwright* in 1975. Qualified in 1977. Partner 1980.
Personal: Born 25 February 1952. Attended Nottingham High School 1960-71, then Cambridge University 1971-74. Member of Nottinghamshire Medico-Legal Society. Member of Law Society Working Parties on Group Actions and Conditional Fee Agreements.

BIRD, Michael
Freeth Cartwright Hunt Dickins, Derby (01332) 361000
Offices also at Nottingham and Leicester.
Partner (01.05.97) in Civil Litigation Department.
Specialisation: Main areas of practice are Medical Negligence, Personal Injury and Product Liability. All types of Medical Litigation, but with a particular interest in Anaesthetic cases, including Dental Anaesthesia. Inquest representation. High proportion of Legal Aid work.

Prof. Memberships: APIL, ATLA, AVMA Panel.
Career: Attended Oundle School 1979-84, then University of Nottingham. Joined *Freeth Cartwright* on qualification in 1991. Partner 1997.
Personal: |Born 29th March 1966. Leisure interests include playing in Jazz band (available for bookings) and travel. Married to Helen. (NKY).

CHRISTIANSON, Gary E.
Shakespeares, Birmingham
(0121) 632 4199
Partner in Litigation Department.
Specialisation: Principal area of practice is medical negligence. Handles plaintiff only work, a substantial part of which is legally aided. Broad experience of all types of medical negligence cases including a recent test case on gynaecological surgery and experience of product liability. Also has extensive experience of representation at inquests, including substantial matters of public interest (e.g. Sun Valley poultry fire and M4 Mini bus crash). Has appeared on local radio programmes concerning medical negligence issues. Member of No.6 Area Legal Aid Committee.
Prof. Memberships: Birmingham Medico-Legal Society (Honorary Auditor), Law Society, Birmingham Law Society, Law Society Personal Injury Panel.
Career: Qualified in 1984. Became a Partner at *Shakespeares* in 1988.
Personal: Born 22nd June 1960. Educated at Fhakenham Grammar School 1972-78 and Birmingham University 1978-81. Lives in Wolverhampton.

FOLLIS, Richard T.
Challinors Lyon Clark, Birmingham
(0121) 212 9393
Partner heading Medical Negligence Department.
Specialisation: Handles plaintiff only medical negligence litigation with a substantial proportion of legally aided work. Involved in medical negligence claims since 1979. Now heads a group of 7 solicitors and 2 SRNs and

support staff dealing with all types of medical negligence claims, including obstetric, orthopaedic, psychiatric, oncological, gynaecological, ophthalmological, general surgical and GP liability. Provides representation at inquests. Member of Medico-Legal Training Services Panel. Lectures regularly to both Doctors and Lawyers on medical legal matters.
Prof. Memberships: Law Society, Birmingham Law Society, Birmingham Medico-Legal Society, AVMA Lawyers Support Group. Chairman AVMA Midlands LSG.
Career: Qualified in 1981. Became a Partner in 1984.
Personal: Educated Halesowen Grammar School 1968-74. University College, Cardiff 1976-79. Lives in Belbroughton.

HALL, Antony
Anthony Collins Solicitors, Birmingham
(0121) 200 3242
Specialisation: Acts for both legally aided and privately funded plaintiffs in all aspects of medical litigation, especially obstetric, GP, cancer misdiagnosis, orthopaedic and brain damage claims. Handles personal injury work both legally aided, privately funded and under conditional fee agreements.
Prof. Memberships: Association of Personal Injury Lawyers, Birmingham Medico-Legal Society, Law Society Medical Negligence Panel, Law Society Personal Injury Panel, Referral Panel Solicitor for Action for Victims of Medical Accidents.
Career: Qualified 1986. Assistant solicitor with *Anthony Collins* 1986-89. Associate with a Worcestershire law firm 1989-90. West Midlands Regional Health Authority 1990-92. *Anthony Collins* 1992 onwards (Partner since 1994).

HENDERSON, Stuart
Irwin Mitchell, Birmingham (0121) 212 1828
See under Personal Injury; Mainly Plaintiff, p. 634

EAST ANGLIA

MAINLY PLAINTIFF

Cunningham, John & Co (Thetford) (4ptnrs/5fee-earners who also do personal injury work) Most commentators agreed

that this "dedicated firm" is the leader in East Anglia, if not always the easiest to deal with. The "very shrewd" *Simon John* heads the team. **Clients/Work:** Cases in 1997 included two cerebral palsy claims which settled for £1.3m and £1.275m and a claim for undiagnosed septic arthritis to the hip – £215,000.

Prettys (Ipswich) (1ptnr/1asst) Promoted in our tables this year following praise for its quality. **Clients/Work:** Acted on the following successful claims during 1997: negligent radio surgery to brain – award £112,000; child born following failed sterilisation – award £70,000; child born brain damaged – award £1.2m.

Dawbarns (Wisbech) (1ptnr/1asst who also do personal injury work) Loss of specialist partner Richard Barr who has moved to London has affected the profile of the practice. **Clients/Work:** Currently handling a number of urological and gynaecological claims.

Morgan Jones & Pett (Great Yarmouth) Respected by defendant solicitors who describe partner *David Jones* as an "extremely good plaintiff lawyer.".

EAST ANGLIA

MAINLY DEFENDANT

Mills & Reeve (Norwich/Cambridge) (2ptnrs/7assts) The "quality" team is spread across two offices with the larger force, headed by the "very able" *Howard Weston*, based in Cambridge. *Stephen King* contin-ues to handle 25% medical negligence. **Clients/ Work:** Affiliation to a number of bodies including the Institute of Risk Management and American Academy of Hosptal Lawyers. Publishes a quarterly journal, Vital Signs, for its NHS Trust clients.

Scrivenger Seabrook (St. Neots) (4ptnrs) A well regarded niche practice planning expansion following its appointment to the NHSLA panel. All partners are dedicated to medical negligence. *Mark Scrivenger, Vicki Seabrook* and *John Dyball* were recommended again. **Clients/Work:** Presently act for six NHS Trusts and three Health Authorities. Full range of medical negligence work.

Eversheds (Norwich) (1ptnr/1assoc/1 doctor) Not a major presence but generally well regarded. **Clients/Work:** Currently involved in a number of claims concerning complementary therapy, wrongful detention of patients and consent to treatment.

LEADERS' PROFILES • EAST ANGLIA

DYBALL, John
Scrivenger Seabrook, St. Neots
(01480) 214900

JOHN, Simon G.
Cunningham, John & Co, Thetford
(01842) 752401
Specialisation: Main area of practice is catastrophic injuries. Leads a team of eighteen PI/Medical Negligence lawyers and paralegals. Has particular expertise in head and spinal injuries and medical negligence. Responsible for many awards in excess of £1M. Considerable experience of litigation in Canada and many US States. Lectures on Medical Negligence and PI. Acted for patient in UK 1st NHS Mediation. Author of various articles. Joint Editor of Personal Injury.
Prof. Memberships: AVMA, Headway and SIA referral panels and Law Society Med Neg and Personal Injury panels, APIL, ATLA.
Career: Qualified in 1969 becoming a Partner in 1971 and formed *Cunningham, John & Co* in 1973.
Personal: Born 19th October 1945. Attended Ampleforth College, York.

JONES, David
Morgan Jones & Pett, Great Yarmouth
(01493) 334700

KING, Stephen
Mills & Reeve, Norwich +44 (0)1603 660155
Partner in Health Care Team.
Specialisation: Specialises in professional negligence, including medical negligence. Acts for NHS Trusts and Health Authorities, advising on claims made against them for damages and on insurance arrangements for non-clinical negligence cover. Also covers mental health law, coroners inquests, drug trials, and acts as client partner for health care clients. Has acted in many self-funded structured settlements financing the payment of substantial damages in brain damage cases. Regular lecturer to hospitals on health care law, negligence, risk management and awareness and claims management. Editorial Board Member of Health Care Risk Report (Eclipse Publications), Personal Injury Journal (John Wiley Publications)

SCRIVENGER, Mark John
Scrivenger Seabrook, St. Neots
(01480) 214900

SEABROOK, Vicki
Scrivenger Seabrook, St. Neots
(01480) 214900

WESTON, Howard W.
Mills & Reeve, Cambridge +44 (0)1223 364422
Partner in Health Care Team.
Specialisation: Principal area of practice is medical negligence litigation. Instructed exclusively by defendants, principally NHS Health Authorities and Trusts. Also deals with general NHS, medical and health care issues. Work includes mental health legislation, judicial reviews (including the 'child B' case), injunctions and other related actions. Has acted in major infant brain damage and anaesthetic brain damage cases. Has assisted in co-ordinating Health Authority defences in class actions including the HIV Haemophiliac action and the Myodil action. Currently has conduct of one of the lead cases in the Breast Radiotherapy (RAGE) action.
Career: Qualified in 1966. Joined *Mills & Reeve* as a Partner in 1989.

NORTH WEST

MAINLY PLAINTIFF

Alexander Harris (Altrincham) 4ptnrs/12 fee-earners) A highly respected niche practice dealing with "a huge number of claims" and headed by *Ann Alexander*, perceived as "very good at promoting the interests of patients." *Nicola Castle* was recommended again. **Clients/Work:** During 1997 over £5m was recovered for clients. Recent cases include: Wisniewski v Central Manchester H.A. (Court of Appeal). Bates v Leicester H.A. – limitation case involving adult with brain injury caused more than 30 years ago – succeeded in establishing that plaintiff should be allowed to proceed with his claim. Queen v HM Coroner for Birmingham & Solihull (ex parte Benton) – judicial review re Coroner's decision.

Pannone & Partners (Manchester) (4ptnrs/2assts/7 other fee earners) Received a boost following the acquisition of *Janine Tobias* from Betesh Fox. Now "looking very healthy" and fielding many leading individuals, including *John Kitchingman* who heads the department, *Stephen Jones* and the frequently praised *Jacinta Peake*. who is "the business." **Clients/Work:** R v East Lancashire Health Authority (Ex Parte B) concerning the provision of blood products to haemophiliac children. The Ashworth Inquiry.

Linder Myers (Manchester) (1ptnr/5 fee-earners) Another firm which has benefited from the arrival of former Betesh Fox team members and regarded as "getting stronger." **Clients/Work:** Claim regarding disclosability of witness statements in medical reports. Settlement of parents' claim for over £500,000 following birth of their Downs syndrome child.

Jones Maidment Wilson (Manchester) (2ptnrs/3assts) A new entry to the tables following the arrival of *Olivia Scates* and other medical negligence experts from Hatton Scates Horton which merged with Jones Maidment Wilson last year. **Clients/Work:** Several hundred claims at any one time, specialising in cases of utmost severity. Spinal injury settled for £1.15m. Cerebral palsy case – £900,000. Stillbirth – a five figure sum.

Leigh Day & Co (Manchester) (2ptnrs/3assts who also do personal injury work) Regarded as a London firm which has yet to make its mark in Manchester in terms of volume, although in quality terms "a serious opponent." **Clients/Work:** Failure to diagnose cancer; brain damaged children; failure to diagnose peritonitis; mismanaged delivery.

Lonsdales (Blackpool) (1ptnr/ 4 fee-earners) Better known in Liverpool ("big market share") than Manchester. **Clients/Work:** Specialise in cerebral palsy, brain damage cases. Also oncology cases, Hepatitis group action, orthopaedic and gynaecological claims. About 450 cases at any one time.

Maxwell Entwistle & Byrne (Liverpool) (2 ptners) Team leader *Paul McCarthy* received particular mention, although the firm is not felt to be a major player in this field. **Clients/Work:** Specialises in large catastrophic injury claims.

Russell Jones & Walker (Manchester) Cases include a plaintiff who lost a kidney during an unnecessary hysterectomy, a number of cerebral palsy claims and 'Nicholas Geldard' who died after being transferred

between several hospitals following a brain haemorrhage.

LEADING INDIVIDUALS	
PLAINTIFF	
ALEXANDER Ann Alexander Harris	
KITCHINGMAN John Pannone & Partners	
MCCARTHY Paul Maxwell Entwistle & Byrne	
PEAKE Jacinta Pannone & Partners	
JONES Stephen Pannone & Partners	
SCATES Olivia Jones Maidment Wilson	
TOBIAS Janine Pannone & Partners	

UP AND COMING
CASTLE Nicola Alexander Harris

SEE PROFILES AT END OF THIS SECTION

MAINLY DEFENDANT

LEADING FIRMS • DEFENDANT
HEMPSONS Manchester
HILL DICKINSON Liverpool
GEORGE DAVIES & CO Manchester

Hempsons (Manchester) (7ptnrs/21assts) A "top tier" firm pre-eminent in Manchester for defendant work and headed by the "excellent" *Frances Harrison*. *Frances Comerford* and *Lucy Sealy* ("good at structured settlements") were also recommended again. **Clients/Work:** R v Milling, ex parte West Yorkshire Police Authority – concerned a challenge to the decision of a Medical Assessor. Wisniewski v Central Manchester

HA. Sushal Jindal v Manchester HA – a structured settlement of £700,00 (part of a £1.3 million settlement.)

Hill Dickinson (Liverpool) (5ptnrs/ 11assts who form part of the Health Care team) Have a reputation as being "easy to deal with". *Allan Mowat* heads the department which includes *Anthony Gibbons*. **Clients/Work:** Involvement in the class Benzodiazopine actions. Acting for the North Wales Health Authority on the North Wales Child Abuse Inquiry. Booth v Warrington HA – concerning disclosure of witness statement in expert's report.

George Davies & Co (Manchester) (5ptnrs/3assts) Felt to have "made tremendous strides" and, having won a place on the NHSLA panel, are hoping to expand. *Claire*

Batchelor remains highly recommended. **Clients/Work:** Handling claims involving neurosurgical and obstetrics issues, including several on behalf of brain damaged babies.

LEADING INDIVIDUALS	
DEFENDANT	
BATCHELOR Claire George Davies & Co	
GIBBONS Anthony Hill Dickinson	
HARRISON Frances Hempsons	
MOWAT Allan Hill Dickinson	
COMERFORD Frances Hempsons	

UP AND COMING
SEALY Lucy Hempsons

SEE PROFILES AT END OF THIS SECTION

LEADERS' PROFILES • NORTH WEST • PLAINTIFF & DEFENDANT

ALEXANDER, Ann
Alexander Harris, Altrincham
(0161) 925 5555
Managing Partner and Partner in charge of Medical Negligence Department.
Specialisation: All areas of medical negligence and concomitant issues of public and legal policy. The treatment of children has become a centre of excellence, with a long history of cerebral palsy and anaesthetics cases. To this expertise has been added work with criminal law aspects (representing families of Beverly Allitt's victims), and wider issues including the conduct of inquests (for example, into the death of Robert Benton) and inquiries (for example, into the death of Nicholas Geldard). The practice represents families of victims of BSE/CJD, and is acting for patients suffering harmful consequences following their treatment with LSD. Contributes regularly to television news and current affairs programmes, is an expert frequently consulted by radio reporters and producers, and has been extensively quoted in the press. Lectures on medical negligence issues to legal and medical audiences, and is a visiting Fellow at the Department of Journalism Studies, University of Sheffield.
Prof. Memberships: Law Society, AVMA, ATLA

(Member of Executive Committee Birth Trauma Litigation Group), assessor to Law Society Specialist Medical Negligence Panel. Member of Editorial Board of Health Care Risk Report.
Career: Qualified in 1978 and then became co-founder of *Alexander Harris* in May 1989. First practice in this country specialising exclusively in medical negligence and pharmaceutical product liability. The practice has now added a specialist personal injury department.
Personal: Born 5th November 1954. Attended University College, London (LL.B 1974). Lives in Altrincham, Cheshire.

BATCHELOR, Claire
George Davies & Co, Manchester
(0161) 236 8992
Partner and Head of Healthcare/Medical Negligence Department.
Specialisation: Specialises in Defendant Healthcare related law advising Health Authorities and NHS Trusts. Principal area of work is in the field of medical negligence handling a wide spectrum of claims including complex high value obstetric and neurosurgical claims. Work also involves all areas of NHS advisory work including administrative law,

representation at inquests and advice on risk management strategies.
Prof. Memberships: Law Society and Manchester Medico-Legal Society.
Career: Joined *George Davies & Co.* in 1985. Qualified in 1987 and became a Partner in 1991. Deputy District Judge.
Personal: Educated at Manchester High School for Girls. Bristol University 1980-1983 LLB. Trinity Hall Cambridge 1983-1984 LLM. Leisure interests include the arts, walking and yoga. Lives in Bowdon, Cheshire.

CASTLE, Nicola
Alexander Harris, Altrincham
(0161) 925 5555
Specialisation: Principal area of practice is medical negligence on behalf of Plaintiffs. Specialises in substantial claims involving injury from birth trauma, cerebral palsy and serious head injury. Acted in 'Murphy v. Wirral Health Authority', 'Wiszniewski v. Central Manchester Health Authority' and 'Stephens v. Doncaster Health Authority'. Responsible for the first Structured settlement involving a medical protection society.
Prof. Memberships: The Law Society and member of the Medical Negligence Panel.

Career: Joined *Alexander Harris* in 1991 and qualified in 1993. Made Partner in 1998.
Personal: Born 15th October 1968. Attended Manchester Metropolitan University (LLB 2:1). Leisure pursuits include walking, sailing and outdoor activities generally. Lives in Manchester.

COMERFORD, Frances M.
Hempsons, Manchester (0161) 228 0011
Partner
Specialisation: Main areas of practice are acting on behalf of defendants (health authorities, trusts and practitioners) in medical negligence litigation, involving both hospital practice and general practitioners; risk management; advising private and institutional clients on medical and health care law; court representation including inquests; undertaking the defence of individuals charged with serious criminal offences.
Career: Qualified 1981. Joined *Hempsons* 1990, partner since 1992.

GIBBONS, Anthony
Hill Dickinson, Liverpool (0151) 236 5400
Partner in Health Department.
Specialisation: Principal areas of practice are medical negligence, employment law and NHS advisory work. Handles a large volume of medical negligence cases, particularly brain damage cases of high value. Another significant element of work involves NHS property transactions acting on behalf of major NHS clients in the disposal of surplus property and in particular redundant hospitals. Important cases handled include Booth v. Warrington Health Authority (disclosure of witness statements referred to in experts reports), Ashcroft v. Mersey Regional Health Authority (standard of care of consultants in medical negligence cases) and O'Toole v. Liverpool Health Authority (first self-funded structural settlement case in the medical negligence field). Major clients include North West Regional Health Authority and all NHS trusts in Cheshire and Merseyside. Has given lectures to various NHS clients. Participated as a presenter in Liverpool Law Society course on medical negligence.
Prof. Memberships: Law Society.
Career: Qualified in 1972. Former in-house Legal Adviser with Mersey RHA 1980-90. Joined *Hill Dickinson* as a Partner in 1990. Presently a Partner *Hill Dickinson*.
Personal: Born 10th October 1947. Educated at Xaverian College, Manchester 1959-66 and Nottingham University 1966-69 (Nottingham Co-operative Society Prize 1968, Hill Prize 1969). Leisure pursuits include food, wine and watching sport. Lives in Chester.

HARRISON, Frances A.
Hempsons, Manchester (0161) 228 0011
Partner in Medical & Healthcare Department and Senior Partner in the firm's Manchester office.
Specialisation: Principal area of practice is the law relating to hospitals and general practice. Work includes medico-legal advice to and representation of Health Authorities, NHS Trusts and individual practitioners in medical negligence actions. Advises on ethics in relation to healthcare and also concerning the conduct of and representation at enquiries. Other main areas of practice are defamation

and the law relating to children. Major cases include Whitehouse v. Jordan (HL) [1981], McKay v. Essex Area Health Authority (CA) [1982], Wilsher v. Essex Area Health Authority (HL) [1988] and Naylor v. Preston Area Health Authority (CA) [1987]. Lectures and writes widely. Is a member of ethics and risk management committees within the NHS.
Prof. Memberships: Law Society, Manchester Law Society
Career: Qualified in 1978 and joined *Hempsons*. Became a Partner in 1982. Moved to Manchester in 1990 to lead the firm's Manchester office.

JONES, Stephen L.
Pannone & Partners, Manchester
(0161) 909 3000
Partner in Medical Negligence Department.
Specialisation: Specialised in Medical Negligence work since qualification. Also covers mental health and has a specific interest in psychiatric negligence, presently representing patients at Ashworth Hospital in the Fallon Inquiry due to report in December 1998.
Prof. Memberships: Member of Birmingham Royal Orthopaedic Hospital Cancer Cases Co-ordinating Committee, Member of Law Society Medical Negligence Panel, AVMA Solicitors Referral Panel, MIND Legal Network.
Career: Joined *Pannone & Partners* in 1984, qualified in 1986 and became a Partner in 1992.
Personal: Educated at Manchester Grammar School and Queens College, Cambridge. Leisure interests include amateur football.

KITCHINGMAN, John Michael
Pannone & Partners, Manchester
(0161) 909 3000
Partner in Medical Negligence Department.
Specialisation: Head of department, dealing with all aspects of plaintiff medical litigation for victims of medical accidents with emphasis on cases of maximum severity.
Prof. Memberships: Medical Negligence Special Interest Group, Law Society, AVMA referral panel, ATLA.
Career: Qualified in 1975, became partner in *Pannone & Partners* 1978.
Personal: Fellow of RSA. Leisure pursuits include walking, birdwatching, and travel. Lives in Altrincham.

MCCARTHY, Paul D.
Maxwell Entwistle & Byrne, Kirkby
(0151) 548 7370
Partner and Head of a very large Medical Negligence and Catastrophic Injury Department.
Specialisation: Specialises in medical negligence and catastrophic injury, particularly high value and complex claims. Has a particular interest in claims for compensation for babies brain damaged by negligent mishandling of their birth. Assisted by a partner, an assistant solicitor and a trainee solicitor. Has given a substantial number of lectures to barristers, solicitors and doctors and organised conferences on medical negligence. A speaker and chairman at AVMA National Conference in 1995. Speaker at 3 AVMA Scottish conferences. Chairman of AVMA (North West)

Lawyers Support Group and AVMA referral solicitor. Member of Lord Woolf's advisory committee on medical negligence.
Prof. Memberships: Law Society, Liverpool Law Society. Member of Law Society Medical Negligence, Personal Injury and Mental Health Panels. Assesor for the Medical Negligence Panel. Chairman of Liverpool Law Society's Civil Litigation Committee.
Career: Partner at *Maxwell Entwistle & Byrne* since 1980.
Personal: Born 10th October 1953. Lives in Liverpool. Leisure pursuits include sailing, fell walking, swimming and quizzes.

MOWAT, Allan R.
Hill Dickinson, Liverpool (0151) 236 5400
Specialisation: Head of Health Department at *Hill Dickinson*, specialising in Health Care Law, particularly medical negligence, nursing home registration and advisory work for NHS bodies. Clients include NHS Trusts and Health Authorities, the NHSLA, Medical Defence Union and various insurance companies. Successfully defended the NHS in Benzodiazepine class action.
Prof. Memberships: Law Society, Liverpool Law Society.
Career: Qualified in 1980; in house legal advisor to Mersey Regional Health Authority 1982 - 1990; Partner *Hill Dickinson Davis Campbell* 1990; Appointed Head of Health Department at *Hill Dickinson* 1994.

PEAKE, Jacinta
Pannone & Partners, Manchester
(0161) 909 3000
Senior Executive in Medical Negligence Department.
Specialisation: Specialises in brain injury, including cerebal palsy, laparascopic surgery, cancer cases, orthopaedic and head cases. Past cases include J Coyne v Wigan H.A., J Grieve v Salford H.A. and Re B v Islington H.A.
Prof. Memberships: Member of APIL and AVMA.
Career: Spent 10 years working for North Western RHA undertaking defendant medico legal work, and 13 years undertaking plaintiff medico legal work. Joined *Pannone & Partners* in 1986.
Personal: Leisure interests include cooking and gardening.

SCATES, Olivia
Jones Maidment Wilson, Manchester
(0161) 832 8087
Specialisation: Principal area of practice medical negligence litigation, acting for Plaintiffs. Broad experience of advising in all types of medical negligence cases, including cases of maximum severity. Recent settlements include anaesthetic awareness cases, several cases of delay in diagnosis of cancer and gynaecological cases including failed sterilisation.
Prof. Memberships: Referral Panel Solicitor for Action for Victims of Medical Accidents. Member of Law Society Medical Negligence Panel. Member of Association of Personal Injury Lawyers. (Special interest groups: medical negligence and spinal injuries).
Career: Qualified 1989. Founding partner 1993. Firm has had Legal Aid Franchise since August 1994.
Personal: Born 6.10.63. Educated British School of Brussels. Attended University of Manchester (BSc 1 Hons).

SEALY, Lucy
Hempsons, Manchester (0161) 228 0011
Mainly Defendant
Specialisation: Specialises in Defendant Health Care related law, advising Health Authorities and NHS Trusts. Her main area of work is medico-negligence, including complex high value claims and structured settlements, general advice to Health Authorities and NHS Trusts with a particular interest in child care matters and Court representations, including Inquests.

Prof. Memberships: The Law Society.
Career: Qualified in 1985. Educated at Harrytown Convent of the Nativity, Romiley, Aberystwyth University, and Chester Law College.
Personal: Lives in Altrincham with her husband and two daughters.

TOBIAS, Janine A.
Pannone & Partners, Manchester
(0161) 909 3000
Partner in the Medical Negligence Department.
Specialisation: Deals with all types of medical accidents and cases involving serious injuries including paraplegia, tetraplegia and brain damage. Has given interviews to TV, radio and newspapers both on individual cases and medical negligence generally.
Prof. Memberships: APIL, AVMA referral panel solicitor, Law Society (Personal Injury and Medical Negligence Panels).
Career: Qualified in 1988. Joined *Pannone & Partners* summer 1997.
Personal: Leisure interests include swimming, gym and cycling. Lives in Altrincham.

NORTH EAST

MAINLY PLAINTIFF

LEADING FIRMS · PLAINTIFF

IRWIN MITCHELL Sheffield	
PETER MAUGHAN & CO Gateshead	
HEPTONSTALLS Goole	
STAMP JACKSON AND PROCTER Hull	

HIGHLY REGARDED FIRMS

Hay & Kilner Newcastle-upon-Tyne

Irwin Mitchell (Sheffield) (11ptnrs/6assts, some of whom also do personal injury work) "Superb professionals", "premier firm", "a worthy opponent", "streets ahead of the others" – a selection of the comments which keep the firm at the top of our ranking. The "outstanding" *David Body* who heads the team also received high praise. **Clients/ Work:** Bolitho v City and Hackney Health Authority [HL]; R v North Derbyshire Health Authority exp. Fisher; CJD Litigation Group B Psychiatric Injury.

Peter Maughan & Co (Gateshead) (2ptnrs/2 other fee-earners who also do personal injury work) A niche practice widely recommended for the quality of the team headed by *Peter Maughan*, an "excellent tactician." **Clients/Work:** Brain injury which settled for £700,000. Several cases for premature babies blinded due to over-exposure to oxygen.

Heptonstalls(Goole) (1ptnr/2assts who also do personal injury work) Well regarded in their own locality. **Clients/Work:** Failed sterilisations, misdiagnoses and a number of cerebral palsy cases.

Stamp Jackson & Procter (Hull) (2ptnrs /1assoc/2assts who do both personal injury and medical negligence work). **Clients/ Work:** Recent settlements have included a failed sterilisation, cerebral palsy and a stillborn child.

Hay & Kilner (Newcastle) (3ptnrs/ 2assts) Formerly ranked for both plaintiff and defendant work but now regarded as having more strength in the former, particularly since the firm is not on the NHSLA panel. **Clients/Work:** Acted for a 20 year old girl suffering from Lupus who was treated with the wrong drug and put on a geriatric ward (also a claim by the mother for psychiatric damage). Acted for plaintiff awarded damages of almost £400,000 after a contested hearing.

Angela Curran of Watson Burton is a new entry this year.

LEADING INDIVIDUALS
PLAINTIFF

BODY David Irwin Mitchell	
MAUGHAN Peter Peter Maughan & Co	

UP AND COMING

CURRAN Angela Watson Burton

MAINLY DEFENDANT

LEADING FIRMS · DEFENDANT

CRUTES Newcastle-upon-Tyne
EVERSHEDS Newcastle upon Tyne
WANSBROUGHS WILLEY HARGRAVE Sheffield
HEMPSONS Harrogate
LE BRASSEUR J TICKLE Leeds

HIGHLY REGARDED FIRMS

Samuel Phillips & Co Newcastle upon Tyne
Smith & Graham Hartlepool

Crutes (Newcastle) (4ptnrs/6fee-earners) Highly praised as a specialist team although smaller overall than the other leading firms here. Like them it has been chosen for the NHSLA panel. *Richard Slack*, "a star," is a new entry to our list of leading individuals. **Clients/ Work:** Acting on a £1.4m structured settlement. Several cases settled by alternative dispute resolution.

Eversheds (Newcastle) (3ptners/4assts) A "very experienced" team considered to have "gained expertise from Wilkinson Maughan" following the merger. *Ronald Bradbeer* is the best known lawyer. **Clients/ Work:** Hazel Corns v Darlington Memorial Hospital NHS Trust – a young woman who died as a result of an air bubble entering her blood stream during a routine appendectomy. Anita Osborne v Newcastle Health Authority – successfully defended a claim relating to genetics advice given to the plaintiff.

Wansbroughs Willey Hargrave, (Sheffield) (5ptnrs/16assts who also do a smaller amount of personal injury work) A large and universally recommended team headed by *Diane Hallatt*, "a tough opponent." **Clients/Work:** Brain damaged baby cases (valued between £1m and £2.5m) Paediatric victims' claims and relatives' PTSD claims in the Beverly Allitt incident.

Hempsons (Harrogate) (2ptnrs/22assts forming healthcare/medical negligence teams) Regarded by some as a leader but others feel their main strength is in London. *John Lovel* heads the team. **Clients/Work:** Include claims of utmost severity.

Le Brasseur J Tickle (Leeds) (3ptnrs/ 17assts who also do judicial review and disciplinary work) Perceived as raising their profile in the area although not yet at the top of the field.

Samuel Phillips & Co (Newcastle) (1ptnr/3assts) Currently doing both plaintiff and defendant work with the emphasis on the latter. This may change given their lack of a place on the NHSLA panel. The team is headed by *Barry Speker*. **Clients/Work:** Large number of obstetrics and gynaecological cases. Also mental health work.

Smith & Graham (Durham) (1ptnr /1asst) Generally well liked but perceived as doing less work recently. **Clients/Work:** Not on the NHSLA panel and therefore accepting new instructions on smaller claims only. May expand their plaintiff work.

LEADING INDIVIDUALS
DEFENDANT

HALLATT Diane Wansbroughs Willey Hargrave	
BRADBEER Ronald Eversheds	
SLACK Richard Crutes	
LOVEL John Hempsons	
SPEKER Barry Samuel Phillips & Co	

BODY, David
Irwin Mitchell, Sheffield (0114) 276 7777
Partner in Personal Injury Department.
Specialisation: Main area of practice is
medical negligence on behalf of plaintiffs.
Acted in Maynard v. West Midlands RHA; Davis
v. City and Hackney Health Authority; Aboul-
Hosn v. Governors of National Hospital for
Nervous Diseases, Bolitho v. City and Hackney
Health Authority, Hopkins v. McKenzie, and the
Creutzfeldt-Jacob Disease Litigation. Author of
chapter on 'The Conduct of Proceedings' to
Powers & Harris 'Medical Negligence'. Lectures
regularly to both doctors and lawyers. Chair of
Medical Negligence Special Interest Group of
APIL (1992-1995).
Prof. Memberships: APIL, AVMA.
Career: Qualified in 1981. Worked at *Halls*
1981-91, from 1984 as a Partner. Joined *Irwin*
Mitchell in 1991 as a Partner.
Personal: Born 1st August 1955. Attended
Hereford High School and Corpus Christi
College, Oxford (BA Hons, 1976). Leisure
interests include taking blurred photographs
and still waiting for the revival of the Welsh
rugby team. Lives in Sheffield.

BRADBEER, Ronald
Eversheds, Newcastle upon Tyne
(0191) 261 1661
Senior Partner and Senior Litigation Partner.
Specialisation: Principal area of practice is
medical negligence. Principal legal advisor to
area health authorities and trusts for many
years. Specialised in medical negligence for
over 25 years. Also handles commercial
disputes specialising in commercial contracts,
industrial tribunal cases and construction
matters.
Prof. Memberships: Accredited Mediator with
Centre for Dispute Resolution, Law Society.
Career: Joined *Wilkinson Maughan* in 1960.
Qualified in 1963. Partner in 1967, Managing
Partner in 1993 and Senior Partner in 1997.

CURRAN, Angela
Watson Burton, Newcastle upon Tyne
(0191) 244 4444
Specialisation: Act for Plaintiffs in all types of
medical negligence cases. Special interest in
obstetric cases.
Prof. Memberships: AVMA. APIL,
Career: Joined *Watson Burton* in 1992.
Accredited and experienced mediator.
Personal: Born 22.9.61. Educated at
Newcastle University (BSC 1983) and College
of Law, York. Lives in Chester-le-street. Leisure
time devoted to family, gardening and wine.

HALLATT, Diane
Wansbroughs Willey Hargrave, Sheffield
(0114) 272 7485
See under Health Care, p. 413

LOVEL, John
Hempsons, Harrogate (01423) 522331
Medical Negligence
Specialisation: Medical Negligence. National
Health Service Law. Project Leader (Northern
and Yorkshire) Department of Health. Clinical
Negligence Mediation Pilot.
Prof. Memberships: Law Society.
Career: Shrewsbury School; University College
London - LLB Hons 1971; CEDR accredited
mediator 1996; Trained at Sintons - qualified
1974; Partner at *Maughan & Hall* 1975; Solicitor
with Yorkshire Regional Health Authority 1976;
Legal Adviser to Yorkshire Regional Health
Authority 1989; Head of Yorkshire Health Legal
Services 1990; Partner *Hempsons* 1996.
Personal: Squash, cycling, skiing.

MAUGHAN, Peter J.
Peter Maughan & Co, Gateshead
(0191) 477 9779
Specialisation: Plaintiff Medical Negligence
and personal injury claims. Currently
coordinating all Northern Tobacco Claims
cases in conjunction with Leigh Day & Co.

Prof. Memberships: FCIArb, ADR Group,
ATLA, APIL, APLA, AVMA.
Career: Principal and Senior Partner of Peter
Maughan & Co since 1981.
Personal: Liberal Democrat Councillor and
Parliamentary and Euro-Parliamentary
Candidate. Rotarian. RSPCA Executive
Committee for Newcastle. Married, 3 sons.
Highlands of Scotland - history and language.

SLACK, Richard
Crutes, Newcastle-upon-Tyne
(0191) 281 5811

SPEKER, Barry N.
Samuel Phillips & Co, Newcastle upon Tyne
(0191) 232 8451
Senior Partner and Head of Litigation
Department.
Specialisation: Principal area of work is
medical negligence, personal injury, family and
matrimonial including child care and adoption
and employment law cases. Legal adviser for
Newcastle Health Authority and various NHS
trusts, NSPCC Newcastle upon Tyne and
Barnardo's North East. Regular lecturer on
child care law, mental health law, medical
negligence and employment law. Affiliate of
Institute of Risk Management.
Prof. Memberships: Law Society (Medical
Negligence and Children Panels), Law Society,
Lawyers for Business Users Committee.
Career: Qualified 1971 while with *Leigh Gold &*
Co., then joined *Samuel Phillips & Co.* Became
a Partner in 1973 and Senior Partner in 1987.
Deputy District Judge. Part time Industrial
Tribunal Chairman.
Personal: Born 28th June 1947. Attended
Heaton Grammar School and London
University. Member of Mensa. Leisure pursuits
include golf (Arcot Hall Golf Club), debating
and the Times Crossword. Lives in Newcastle
upon Tyne.

SCOTLAND

MAINLY PURSUER

HIGHLY REGARDED FIRMS
PURSUER

Balfour & Manson Edinburgh
Drummond Miller WS Edinburgh
Fyfe Ireland WS Edinburgh
Lawford Kidd Edinburgh

Nearly all Scottish practitioners spoke of the
difficulties experienced by pursuer (plaintiff) firms due to the limited availability of
legal aid for initial claims investigation. As
a result only a few firms undertake this work
and none are niche specialists of the type

found further south. Instead, medical negligence tends to form part of a general personal injury department. On the defender
(defendant) side, the Scottish Health Central Legal Office handles the majority of
claims directed against Health Boards and
Trusts. Only two other firms do any appre-
ciable amount of defender work.

Balfour & Manson, (Edinburgh) (4ptnrs
/6assts) A "traditional pursuer firm" where
the team is led by the "very experienced"
Alfred Tyler. Clients/Work: Act for the pursuer in McFarlane v Tayside Health Board,
currently on appeal to the House of Lords.

Drummond Miller WS (Edinburgh)
(2ptnrs/ 4 support staff who also do personal
injury work) With an increasing presence in
medical negligence work the firm enters our
tables for the first time, although like others
here it is seen as part of a mixed practice.

Clients/Work: 1997 cases included obstetrics
claims and mis and failed diagnoses.

Fyfe Ireland WS (Edinburgh) (1ptnr/
1associate/1consultant who also do personal injury work) Following the demise of
Gillam Mackie, the old medical negligence
team, headed by the highly praised *Kathrine*
Mackie, has joined Fyfe Ireland where it will
form a specialised unit within the firm.

Lawford Kidd (Edinburgh) (1 ptnr who
also does personal injury work) **Clients/**
Work: Several large cerebral palsy cases and
a claim arising from a baby born dead due to
a mishandled delivery.

LEADING INDIVIDUALS
PURSUER

MACKIE Kathrine Fyfe Ireland WS
TYLER Alfred Balfour & Manson

SEE PROFILES AT END OF THIS SECTION

MAINLY DEFENDER

Shepherd & Wedderburn WS (Edinburgh) (1ptnr/1assoc/1asst who also do personal injury work) *Hugh Donald* was strongly recommended for the quality of his team. **Clients/Work:** Act for the Medical Protection Society representing doctors at disciplinary matters and Fatal Accident Inquiries, including the successful representation of a consultant surgeon at an Inquiry into the death of a young girl who had taken ecstasy and was subsequently refused a liver transplant. Also represent a number of dentists.

Simpson & Marwick WS (Edinburgh) (3-4ptnrs/2assts who also do professional negligence work) "Classed as specialists," and "may have the edge in terms of volume." The team leader *John Griffiths* received unanimous praise. **Clients/Work:** Act for the Medical & Dental Defence Union. Claims include Anderson v Forth Valley Health Board and others (defending a claim brought by parents of two boys born with Duchenne Muscular Dystrophy).

LEADERS' PROFILES · SCOTLAND

DONALD, Hugh R.
Shepherd & Wedderburn WS, Edinburgh
(0131) 228 9900
Chief Executive.
Specialisation: Accredited specialist in medical negligence, representing doctors and dentists in civil claims, inquiries and disciplinary proceedings. Lecturer at a number of conferences on medico-legal subjects. Also aviation representing airline and helicopter operators in both civil claims and accident inquiries.
Career: Qualified in 1975, having joined *Shepherd & Wedderburn WS* in 1973. Became a Partner in 1977. Administrative Head of Litigation Department 1990-94. Appointed Managing Partner in April 1994, and Chief Executive in April 1995.
Personal: Born 5th November 1951. Educated at Edinburgh University. Family Mediator. Chairman, Family Mediation Scotland. Leisure interests include gardening, walking and church. Lives in Edinburgh.

GRIFFITHS, John
Simpson & Marwick WS, Edinburgh
(0131) 557 1545

MACKIE, Kathrine
Fyfe Ireland WS, Edinburgh (0131) 343 2500
Specialisation: Accredited by Law Society of Scotland as specialist in Medical Negligence; currently involved in "Anderson v. Forth Valley Health Board". Also handles broad range of civil litigation involving personal injury and employment.
Prof. Memberships: Law Society of Scotland; Society of Solicitors in the Supreme Courts; Industrial Law Group; Medico-Legal Society of Scotland.
Career: Graduated BA. LLB University of Edinburgh; admitted as Solicitor 1978; became partner 1982; Secretary ILG 1987-97; President SSC 1994-97.
Personal: Married; 1 daughter. Interests include reading, sport and travel.

TYLER, Alfred J.
Balfour & Manson, Edinburgh
(0131) 200 1200
See under Personal Injury; Mainly Plaintiff, p. 638

PARLIAMENTARY & PUBLIC AFFAIRS

RESEARCH: In compiling the tables, we consider all the information available to us, paying particular regard to the market research carried out by our team of ten qualified lawyers. (The researchers' details are set out on page three.) The rankings, therefore, reflect the opinion of the marketplace as revealed by systematic and objective research: see page four. (Our research is audited every year by the British Market Research Bureau.)

OVERVIEW:

Parliamentary Agency: Unlike public affairs, the 1997 general election had little effect on the workload of these firms. Given the government's enthusiasm for transport however, they do expect to see an increase in this type of work. There have been no major projects this year, although the tail end of the Channel Tunnel rail link and Scottish and Welsh devolution are providing a steady source of work.

Given the lengthy qualifying procedure for those wanting to become Roll A parliamentary agents (a fundamental requirement in this area), it is not surprising that there are no new individuals or firms this year. "Only a merger will make a difference" said one of the firms questioned.

Public Affairs: The change in government has resulted in frenzied activity as the various firms advise clients on proposed and likely developments. However, only where the government has made detailed proposals can lawyers comment constructively, and with such a large majority a reduction in lobbying activities is.

LEADING FIRMS • LONDON PARLIAMENTARY AGENCY

DYSON BELL MARTIN (BIRCHAM & CO)
REES & FRERES (LEE BOLTON LEE)
SHERWOOD & CO (WINCKWORTH & PEMBERTON)

SHARPE PRITCHARD

VIZARDS

PARLIAMENTARY AGENCY

Dyson Bell Martin (Bircham & Co) (5ptnrs/3assts) With four Roll A parliamentary agents, their position is unassailable. *Ian McCulloch* was universally praised, and the firm continues to be involved in high profile matters such as the TSB/Lloyds merger. Unlike other firms, they also advise on public affairs. Team includes *Paul Thompson*, *Nick Brown* and *Robert Owen*. Clients/Work: Greater Manchester Passenger Transport Executive (Metrolink system). Hampshire County Council (Rapid Transit Scheme). Acted for Glasgow City Council to promote legislation to relax the lending restrictions on the Burrell collection.

Rees & Freres (Lee Bolton & Lee) A "commercially minded, professional and smart outfit", they are busier than ever thanks to their involvement with transport matters (particularly rail). They also have four Roll A agents, including the "well known and capable" *Joseph Durkin* and "respected" *Peter Lane*. Clients/Work: Thameslink 2000 project.

Sherwood & Co (Winkworth & Pemberton) (4ptnrs/2assts) *Alison Gorlov* is the leading light at this firm which boasts four Roll A agents. They are a "traditional but respected" practice heavily involved in promoting bills, particularly in relation to transport and harbours. *Paul Irving* is "extremely bright." Clients/Work: Corporation of London; Port of London Authority; Railtrack plc and Associated British Ports. Also act for the government in connection with the Channel Tunnel Rail Link.

Sharpe Pritchard (2ptnrs) "Have a smaller practice, but are as good as the rest in terms of quality." Recognised mainly for their work for local authorities, they are "a safe pair of hands." *Michael Pritchard* "knows what he's doing" and though semi-retired is still active. *Alastair Lewis* is proving an able heir apparent. Clients/Work: Promotion of Welsh Highland Railway Transport and Works Act Order; Tamar Bridge Bill, and London Rail Authorities Bill. Act for Association of London Government and Festiniog Railway Company.

Vizards (1ptnr/1asst) Not a mainstream parliamentary firm, but are regarded as worthy of inclusion due to the presence of Roll A parliamentary agent *Ron Perry*. As they are involved primarily in opposing bills, they were unable to provide client/work details.

LEADING INDIVIDUALS • LONDON PARLIAMENTARY AGENCY

DURKIN Joseph Rees & Freres (Lee Bolton & Lee)
GORLOV Alison Sherwood & Co (Winckworth & Pemberton)
LANE Peter Rees & Freres (Lee Bolton & Lee)
McCULLOCH Ian Dyson Bell Martin (Bircham & Co)
PERRY Ronald Vizards
PRITCHARD Michael Sharpe Pritchard
THOMPSON Paul Dyson Bell Martin (Bircham & Co)

BROWN Nick Dyson Bell Martin (Bircham & Co)

IRVING Paul Sherwood & Co (Winckworth & Pemberton)

LEWIS Alastair Sharpe Pritchard

OWEN Robert Dyson Bell Martin (Bircham & Co)

SEE PROFILES AT END OF THIS SECTION

PUBLIC AFFAIRS

Clifford Chance (1ptnr/1asst) *Richard Thomas* runs the firm's dedicated Public Affairs Unit which operates in conjunction with other departments. **Clients/Work:** Advising a food retailer, another retailer and a mortgage company on business practice changes necessary to avoid regulatory intervention.

Dyson Bell Martin (Bircham & Co) (2ptnrs/2assts/2others) *Jonathan Bracken* is the mainstay of public affairs at this parliamentary firm. **Clients/Work:** Acting in connection with the Government's Competition and Government of Wales Bills and Private Members' Bills, the Private Hire Vehicles (London) Bill and Chambers of Commerce Bill.

Lovell White Durrant (Approx 5ptnrs – p/t) *David Tench* "has a good name in the market place" and acts as the firm's public policy consultant. There is also a public policy administrator and a partner co-ordinating work in Brussels. **Clients/Work:** Drafting amendments to Competition Bill which were submitted at committee stage in the Lords. Lobbying the Environment Agency on Packaging Waste Regulations. Advising software trade association on Private Members Bill.

S J Berwin (5ptnrs/8assts – p/t) *Simon Holmes* is the main public policy man, which he does as an adjunct to his EU work. **Clients/Work:** Lobbied competition authorities in connection with Guinness/Grand Met merger. Acted for Betting Office Licensees Association to prevent adoption of EU directive. Represented British Ski Association in fight for the right to work in the Alps.

Radcliffes Ex MP *Sir Gerrard Neale* is a part time consultant and heads the public affairs section at this well regarded, if low profile, firm.

LEADERS' PROFILES · LONDON

BRACKEN, Jonathan
Bircham & Co. (incorporating Dyson Bell Martin), London (0171) 222 8044
Head of Government Relations.
Specialisation: Principal areas of practice are public affairs, lobbying, legislative drafting, parliamentary procedure, research and advice on public policy issues. Over the past year has worked on a number of major Bills including the Competition Bill, Human Rights Bill, Crime and Disorder Bill and National Lottery Bill. Also involved in advising the New South Wales Parliament on the reform of personal injury compensation.
Prof. Memberships: Institute of Public Relations (Government Affairs Group); Administrative Law Bar Association.

BROWN, Nick
Bircham & Co. (incorporating Dyson Bell Martin), London (0171) 222 8044
Specialisation: Specialises in infrastructure legislation, successfully opposed the Crossrail Bill and acted for numerous clients concerned by provisions contained in the Channel Tunnel Rail Link Act. Adviser to charities and trustees. Is presently engaged in promoting a new private sector freight railway in Scotland and England and advising on Thameslink project.
Career: Articled *Bircham & Co* 1979. Qualified as a Solicitor in 1983. Partner and Roll A Agent 1985.
Personal: Attended Westminster School and Jesus College, Oxford. Plays cricket and golf and is a qualified soccer referee. Two children.

DURKIN, Joseph
Rees & Freres, London (0171) 222 5381
Specialisation: Senior partner and specialist in administrative and public law, railways and tramways, highways and harbours, planning, environmental law and compulsory acquisition. 21 years experience of promoting and opposing legislation on behalf of the Central Government, local authorities, major public and private sector transport operators, port authorities, universities and colleges and major national and multinational corporations. Publications include

'Blackstones Guide To The Transport & Works Act 1992' (co-author). Regularly addresses conferences on the parliamentary and legislative process, Royal Charter, harbour law, infrastructure, and Transport & Works projects.
Prof. Memberships: Society of Parliamentary Agents (past president). Law Society.
Career: 1961-70 solicitor in general practice in the City. 1970-73 Government parliamentary draftsman with the Office of the Parliamentary Counsel. Partner, Rees & Freres since 1973, senior partner since 1981.
Personal: Educated at Sheffield University (LL.B). Born 2nd January 1938.

GORLOV, Alison
Winckworth & Pemberton (incorporating Sherwood & Co), London (0171) 222 0441
Specialisation: Senior Parliamentary Partner and Parliamentary Agent. Advises on legislation and legislative drafting, Parliamentary and legislative procedures, constitutional and regulatory matters, transport and other infrastructure (railways, harbours, tramways, utilities), public sector bodies, commercial undertakings. Long experience of acting for central and local Government, major transport undertakers, port authorities, utility undertakers, banks, building societies, charities and educational bodies.
Prof. Memberships: Law Society. Society of Parliamentary Agents.
Career: Joined *Sherwood & Co.* in 1971, qualified in 1975, became a Partner in 1978.

HOLMES, Simon
S J Berwin & Co, London
+44 (0)171 533 2222
Specialisation: European, competition and trade law. Major cases include some of the largest anti-dumping, competition and single market law cases involving lobbying in Brussels, London and other member state capitals.
Prof. Memberships: Recent Chairman, Solicitors' European Group.
Career: 1st Class Honours, Law and Economics from Cambridge. Grande

Distinction, Licence Speciale en Droite Européen, Brussels University.
Personal: Married, 2 daughters. Walking, cycling, tennis, film.

IRVING, Paul
Winckworth & Pemberton (incorporating Sherwood & Co), London (0171) 593 5000
Specialisation: Partner in Parliamentary department. Specialises in drafting, promoting and opposing legislation in Parliament and delegated legislation (including Orders under the Transport and Works Act and the Harbours Act) and in advising on railways, harbours and other infrastructure projects.
Prof. Memberships: Society of Parliamentary Agents (Secretary). Law Society.
Career: Called to the Bar 1986. Requalified as solicitor 1991. Partner at *Sherwood & Co* since 1992.
Personal: Educated at Trinity College, Oxford (MA and D.Phil). Born 7th November 1956.

LANE, Peter
Rees & Freres, London (0171) 222 5381
Specialisation: Partner at *Rees & Freres*. Parliamentary Agent and specialist in public law, transport and infrastructure, and legislative drafting. Experienced in drafting, promoting and opposing legislation, including that for the construction and operation of transport infrastructure projects on behalf of major public sector transport operators, port authorities, local authorities, universities and colleges and major national and multinational corporations. Advises on harbour law, infrastructure and transport and works projects. Publications include 'Blackstone's Guide to the Transport & Works Act 1992' and 'Blackstone's Guide for the Environment Act 1995' (co-author).
Prof. Memberships: Society of Parliamentary Agents. Law Society.
Career: 1977-80, barrister, member of Peter Boydell QC's chambers (*2 Harcourt Buildings*). 1978-80, Lecturer in Laws, Queen Mary College, University of London. 1980-85, Government parliamentary draftsman with the Office of the

Parliamentary Counsel. Since 1985 solicitor at *Rees & Freres*, partner since 1987.
Personal: Educated at Hertford College, Oxford (MA) and University of California, Berkley (LL.M). Born 26th April 1953.

LEWIS, Alastair
Sharpe Pritchard, London (0171) 405 4600
Specialisation: Promotion of and opposition to private and hybrid Bills, Transport and Works orders and Harbour Revision orders.
Acted for a number of petitioners against the Channel Tunnel Rail Link Bill and is promoting a major Bill for the London Boroughs.
Drafted amendments for clients in respect of the most recent Finance Bills and other government legislation.
Prof. Memberships: Society of Parliamentary agents
Career: LL.B Trent Polytechnic, College of Law.
Personal: Football, walking, cycling.

MCCULLOCH, Ian
Bircham & Co. (incorporating Dyson Bell Martin), London (0171) 222 8044
Specialisation: Parliamentary strategy and procedure, tactics and lobbying.
Promoting and opposing primary and subordinate legislation for statutory companies, local authorities, trade associations, transport undertakers, banks, property companies, harbours, charities and sporting and amenity bodies.
Prof. Memberships: Society of Parliamentary Agents (Hon Sec 1989-95; President 1995-98) City of Westminster Law Society (President 1994-95). Law Society. Statute Law Society.
Career: Admitted as a Solicitor 1976. Partner since 1977. Enrolled as a Roll A Parliamentary Agent 1979. Senior Parliamentary Partner since 1992. Senior Partner (1997-).
Personal: Born 13th May 1950. Educated Edinburgh Academy and University of Dundee (LLB Hons. jurisprudence and philosophy).

NEALE, Sir Gerrard
Radcliffes, London (0171) 222 7040
Partner in Public and Parliamentary Affairs Department.
Specialisation: Principal area of practice involves the political positioning of legal or commercial marketing issues affecting national and international companies or institutions. Advises on strategic and tactical planning of public affairs issues.
Prof. Memberships: Law Society, Institute of Directors.
Career: Qualified in 1966. Councillor, Milton Keynes 1973-79 (Mayor 1976-77). Member of Parliament 1979-1992. Joined *Radcliffes & Co* as a Partner in 1991.
Personal: Born 25th June 1941. Attended Bedford School 1948-59. Leisure pursuits include sailing and golf. Lives in London.

OWEN, Robert
Bircham & Co. (incorporating Dyson Bell Martin), London (0171) 222 8044
Specialisation: Main areas of practice continue to be parliamentary and local legislation, town and country planning and environmental law. Over the past year highlights have been: Promoting for the Environment Agency the Wye Navigation Order under the Transport and Works Act 1992 (TWA), and preparing for a three month public local inquiry into objections; promoting for Merseyside Passenger Transport Executive an order under the TWA to authorise the proposed Merseyside Rapid Transit System; acting for objectors in relation to various other orders proposed to be made under the TWA (including Thameslink 2000) for transport infrastructure; co-ordinating a team of five experts giving evidence at a planning appeal for a 100 bed hotel in Canterbury; continuing to act for landowners affected by the proposed Channel Tunnel Rail Link.
Prof. Memberships: Law Society; United Kingdom Environmental Law Association; Society of Parliamentary Agents.
Career: University of London: 1983-1986; College of Law: 1986-1987; Qualified as a solicitor: 1989; Partner with *Bircham & Co.* and *Dyson Bell Martin* since 1991.
Personal: Married with one child. Rugby and running are key leisure interests, together with family pursuits.

PERRY, Ronald
Vizards, London (0171) 405 6302
Partner in Commercial Department.
Specialisation: Principal area of practice is as a Parliamentary Agent. Roll A Agent since 1971. Also deals with commercial property and charities. Contributor to Butterworths' Encyclopaedia of Forms and Precedents.
Prof. Memberships: Law Society, Society of Parliamentary Agents, UKELA.
Career: Joined *Vizards* in 1968, qualified in 1970 and became a partner in the same year.
Personal: Born 24th September 1945. Attended King Edward VI Grammar School, Chelmsford 1957-64, then Leeds University 1964-67. Trustee of the Dunhill Medical Trust. Lives in Wimbledon.

PRITCHARD, Michael
Sharpe Pritchard, London (0171) 222 3551
Partner specialising in parliamentary work.
Specialisation: Main area of practice is parliamentary work, drafting legislation and advising on parliamentary procedure and tactics. Also delegated legislation, Orders, etc., under, amongst others, the Harbours Act and Transport & Works Act. Has been involved with numerous local authority general powers bills, the Cardiff Bay Barrage Act and petitions for protection on the Crossrail Bill and the Channel Tunnel Rail Bill. Author of Parliamentary title of the 'Encyclopaedia of Forms and Precedents'.
Prof. Memberships: Society of Parliamentary

Agents (past President), Law Society.
Career: Joined *Sharpe Pritchard* in 1958, qualified in 1963, became a Partner in 1965 and was senior partner from 1985-1994.
Personal: Born in 1935. Educated at Charterhouse 1948-53 and Balliol College, Oxford 1955-58. Reader in the Church of England. Enjoys walking and music. Lives in Purley.

TENCH, David
Lovell White Durrant, London (0171) 236 0066
Specialisation: Public policy, consumer law. Parliamentary procedure; influencing government policy development.
Prof. Memberships: Solicitor 1952.
Career: Admitted 1952. Government Legal Service 1958-1969; Consumers' Association (legal officer, parliamentary adviser, Director of Legal Affairs) 1969-1994; public policy consultant to Lovell White Durrant 1995-1997.
Personal: Music, literature, avoiding sport. Political reform. Married to a Scot, 5 children.

THOMAS, Richard
Clifford Chance, London (0171) 600 1000
Director, Public Policy Group since 1992.
Specialisation: Helping clients to anticipate, understand and contribute to political and regulatory decision-making and other governmental activities across Whitehall, Westminster and Brussels. Also chairs Marketing and Advertising Group.
Career: Qualified 1973. 1974-92 various public sector appointments, including OFT with high-level contacts with politicians, civil servants and business organisations within UK and internationally.
Personal: LL.B (Southampton) 1970. Member Lord Chancellors' Civil Justice Review (1985-8). Currently member Banking Ombudsman Council and Oftel and ITC Advisory Committees.

THOMPSON, Paul
Bircham & Co. (incorporating Dyson Bell Martin), London (0171) 222 8044
Specialisation: Advice on parliamentary and legislative procedures and tactics, legislative drafting, lobbying and public affairs and the promotion of and opposition to local legislation. Has acted for a wide range of public and private sector bodies including national, local, port and transport authorities, banks and other financial institutions, major plcs, utilities, trade and amenity associations and religious and other charitable bodies. Currently, particularly involved in advising various interests on, and assisting them in relation to, new government legislation, including the detailed arrangements for devolution and other constitutional change, whilst also heavily engaged in the promotion of light rail schemes by Transport and Works Order.
Prof. Memberships: Law Society, Society of Parliamentary Agents.
Career: Called to the Bar 1977. Partner in *Dyson Bell & Co* 1982. Partner and Solicitor at *Bircham & Co and Dyson Bell Martin* since 1990.
Personal: Born 26th March 1954.

PARTNERSHIP

RESEARCH: In compiling the tables, we consider all the information available to us, paying particular regard to the market research carried out by our team of ten qualified lawyers. (The researchers' details are set out on page three.) The rankings, therefore, reflect the opinion of the marketplace as revealed by systematic and objective research: see page four. (Our research is audited every year by the British Market Research Bureau.)

An index to all profiles is on page 67.

OVERVIEW: The major change this year is the elevation of both Ronnie Fox and his firm Fox Williams to take pole positions in the London market. Tony Sacker's team at Kingsley Napley continues its rapid ascension up the ranks and Herbert Smith and newly-merged Ralph Hume Garry are also going up.

There is little change in the regions, although Liverpool firm Cuff Roberts has drawn ahead of a widening field in the North, mainly on the basis of the reputation of Tony Twemlow. McGrigor Donald is new to our Scottish table this year.

Medical partnership lawyers are dealt with separately in the London Tables since neither of the leading firms has a strong general partnership practice. As medical partnerships are subject to a separate regulatory regime it is difficult for non-specialist firms to dabble. However outside London no firms are equally dominant so there is no separate treatment.

LEADING FIRMS • LONDON

FOX WILLIAMS

ALLEN & OVERY
KINGSLEY NAPLEY
ROWE & MAW

EVERSHEDS

HIGHLY REGARDED FIRMS

Bristows
Field Fisher Waterhouse
Herbert Smith
Ralph Hume Garry
Reynolds Porter Chamberlain
Slaughter and May
Wright Son & Pepper

Lovell White Durrant
Macfarlanes
Nabarro Nathanson

Finers

LONDON

Fox Williams (4ptnrs/4assts) Unanimous positive reviews send this firm into the lead for the first time. Known for acting for the 'disgruntled team.' *Ronnie Fox*, founder of the Association of Partnership Practitioners, is widely praised for his "real expertise" and becomes our 'star' practitioner. Co-founder of the firm *Tina Williams* is also recommended. **Clients/ Work:** Represents both sides i.e. firms and the individual. Also well known for contentious work particularly in areas where partnership overlaps with employment issues where new partners are being hired or existing ones fired.

Allen & Overy (2ptnrs/4assts) Work is purely advisory. The department is cross disciplinary with access to experts from other departments including banking and litigation. Firm's high quality reputation stems from *Richard Turnor*, widely praised for his great knowledge. **Clients/Work:** Act mainly for management dealing with non-contentious issues. Typical clients include many of the "Big Five" accountancy firms. This year conducted a major re-financing of a well known property firm.

Kingsley Napley (1ptnr/1asst) The team spends over 50% of time on partnership work and received many favourable comments ("excellent at avoiding unnecessary litigation"). The well-known *Tony Sacker*'s reputation has spread outside London. He has written a widely praised book on partnership law. **Clients/Work:** Deals largely with accountants' (eg. BDO Stoy Hayward), lawyers' and surveyors' partnerships.

Rowe & Maw (1ptnr/2assts) Well-known for non-contentious work. Department anchor man *Richard Linsell* has a long-standing reputation in the field for particular expertise. **Clients/Work:** Involved in high profile merger of two of the big accountancy firms. Achieved important success on a limited liability partnership this year.

Eversheds (1cons/14assts) Broad national practice. John Northam has retired but still acts as a consultant to the firm advising on a number of partnership issues. **Clients/Work:** Advice to various large professional practices; medical, accountancy, legal, property and management consultancy and limited liability partnerships as investment vehicles.

Bristows (1ptnr (John Lace)/3assts) Work carried out by team within corporate department. Contentious and non-contentious work undertaken, dealing with individuals more than firms. **Clients/ Work:** Broad range of partnership work eg. solicitors, accountants and other professionals.

Field Fisher Waterhouse (4ptnrs) Advise professional partnerships although also acts for a number of business partnerships. Two partners also advise on partnership tax. Team is headed by *Colin McArthur*. **Clients/Work:** Include large multi-nationals, 'Big Five' accountancy firms, management consultants and the brewing industry.

Herbert Smith (6ptnrs/10assts) Particularly recommended for when partnership issues become contentious. *David Gold* has a high profile in contentious matters. **Clients/Work:** Commenced representation for a highly publicised merger which could be regarded as the biggest partnership deal of all time.

Ralph Hume Garry (2ptnrs/2assts) *Stephen Ralph* (ex-Boodle Hatfield) has helped create a litigation based practice. Also known for use of ADR and arbitration. **Clients/Work:** Mixture of commercial and private clients. Act for surveyors, solicitors (2-100 partner firms), accountants (small/medium-sized), farming partnerships and a few medical partnerships.

Reynolds Porter Chamberlain (2ptnrs) Reputed to "deal very fairly" in contentious and non-contentious issues. *Stephen Mayer*, a litigator, is recommended. **Clients/Work:**

Mainly professional partnerships and some trading firms.

Slaughter and May (5ptnrs) Primarily handle advisory matters. Specialists are part of company law department. Particular experience in limited liability partnerships in the investment industry. **Clients/Work:** Big Five accountancy firms, leading actuaries and consultant engineers are typical clients.

Wright Son & Pepper (3ptnrs) Do contentious and non-contentious work in the area. Known for being skilled in averting litigation. *Nicholas Wright* is recommended for skill in negotiating break-ups, mergers, demergers, dissolutions, retirement and occasional creation. *David Morgan* deals with solicitors' disciplinary work. **Clients/Work:** Act for regulatory bodies such as the Architects Registration Board, medium sized accountants and solicitors.

Lovell White Durrant (8ptnrs/1asst) Deal with non-contentious partnership issues. Have specialist advisers from different areas of the firm who are involved as and when appropriate. **Clients/Work:** Advise second tier accountants, solicitors' firms, large surveyors and architects on their partnership agreements. Important court case involving the enforcement of client poaching restrictions on a leaving partner.

Macfarlanes Lawyers drawn from across the firm to deal with mainly non-contentious work. "Robust in the way they deal with matters." **Clients/Work:** Experience in banking/ insolvency regarding restructuring dissolved partnerships and other professional partnerships.

Nabarro Nathanson (3ptnrs/5assts) The firm is particularly experienced in property partnerships in an advisory capacity with emphasis on limited structures. **Clients/Work:** Several large property partnerships often focusing on investment in shopping centres.

Finers Have one partner who specialises. Can call on other individuals as and when necessary. **Clients/Work:** Acted for several small/medium partnerships: lawyers, doctors, accountants.

LEADING INDIVIDUALS · LONDON
FOX Ronnie Fox Williams
LINSELL Richard Rowe & Maw
SACKER Tony Kingsley Napley
TURNOR Richard Allen & Overy
GOLD David Herbert Smith
LACE John Bristows
MAYER Stephen Reynolds Porter Chamberlain
MCARTHUR Colin Field Fisher Waterhouse
MORGAN David Wright Son & Pepper
RALPH Stephen Ralph Hume Garry
WILLIAMS Christine Fox Williams
WRIGHT Nicholas Wright Son & Pepper

MEDICAL PARTNERSHIPS

LEADING FIRMS
LONDON · MEDICAL
HEMPSONS
MONIER-WILLIAMS & BOXALLS

Hempsons (4ptnrs/2assts) Work comes their strong medical and healthcare practice. Clearly the leader in this specialist area of partnership law. *Lynne Abbess, Jacqueline Cooper* and *Simon Barnes* maintain their strong position. **Clients/Work:** Represent NHS affiliated GPs and dentists and a few private medical practitioners. Also act for solicitors, accountants and architects. Advise the General Medical Services Committee on policy.

Monier-Williams & Boxalls (1ptnr) *Andrew Hill* is still regarded as a leading medical partnership specialist. **Clients/Work:** Mainly GPs: small private and NHS; also deal with other professional partnerships eg. chartered surveyors.

LEADING INDIVIDUALS
LONDON · MEDICAL
ABBESS Lynne Hempsons
COOPER Jacqueline Hempsons
HILL Andrew Monier-Williams & Boxalls
BARNES Simon Hempsons

LEADERS' PROFILES · LONDON

ABBESS, Lynne M.
Hempsons, London (0171) 836 0011
Partner and joint Head of the Professional Services Department.
Specialisation: Principal area of practice is partnership law, encompassing advice on partnership formation, disputes, termination and associated property matters (in particular NHS GP's cost rent schemes and other surgery developments). Acts for doctors, dentists, solicitors, accountants and other professional partnerships. Advised the BMA/GMSC on policy relating to partnerships and surgery developments affecting all NHS GPs in England and Wales. Author of chapters on partnership in 'The Law and General Practice' and 'When Partners Fall Out' and numerous articles in a variety of professional publications. Frequent lecturer on partnership issues. Legal correspondent for Medeconomics and regular contributor to the Journal 'GP'.
Prof. Memberships: Law Society. Founder member of Association of Partnership Practitioners.
Career: Qualified 1982 while with *Hempsons* and became a Partner in 1985.
Personal: Lives in Kensington, London.

BARNES, Simon M.
Hempsons, London (0171) 836 0011
Partner and joint Head of the Professional Services Department.
Specialisation: Principal area of practice is partnership law. Has extensive experience in handling all areas of such work, acting for solicitors, accountants, patent agents, dentists and especially doctors. Advises on partnership formations, disputes, terminations and all property related matters.
Prof. Memberships: Law Society. Founder member of Association of Partnership Practitioners.
Career: Qualified in 1966. With *Woodham Smith* until 1990 (Partner from 1972 and Senior Partner from 1988). Joined *Hempsons* as a Partner in 1990.
Personal: Born 13th December 1939. Educated at Bradfield College, Berkshire 1953-58 and Corpus Christi College, Cambridge 1959-62. Leisure pursuits include cricket, fly fishing and reading. Member of the Athenaeum. Lives near Tunbridge Wells, Kent.

COOPER, Jacqueline
Hempsons, London (0171) 836 0011
Partner in Professional Services Department.
Specialisation: Partnership law, acting in both partnership formations and disputes mainly for doctors and dentists but also increasingly for other professionals including solicitors, accountants, architects and surveyors. Advising also on related property ownership issues, her background being in property law which she continues to practise enabling her to draw on that experience in the drafting of partnership documentation and settlement of partnership disputes.
Prof. Memberships: Law Society. Founder member of Association of Partnership Practitioners.
Career: Lectures to GPs on property and partnership issues and contributor to magazine 'Financial Pulse' on similar matters. Qualified 1987, solicitor with *Hempsons* and became a Partner in 1992.
Personal: Born 17th April 1962. Lives in London.

FOX, Ronnie
Fox Williams, London (0171) 628 2000
Email:rdfox@foxwilliams.co.uk
Specialisation: Main areas of practice are employment law and partnership law. Specialises in advising partnerships and partners in professional firms. Regularly deals with partnership disputes involving the departure of partners. Chairman of the multi-disciplinary Association of Partnership Practitioners. Master of the City of London Solicitors' Company,

Chairman of the Practice Management Sub-Committee of the IBA; Member of the Law Society Law Management Section Advisory Group; Chairman of Fox Williams Partnership Law Group. Frequently Broadcasts and is the author of numerous articles in the professional and national press on employment, partnership and management topics.
Prof. Memberships: IBA, Law Society, City of London Law Society, Employment Lawyers' Association.
Career: Qualified 1972. Senior Partner at *Fox Williams*.
Personal: Born 27th September 1946.

GOLD, David L.
Herbert Smith, London (0171) 374 8000
See under Litigation (Commercial): 200+ Solicitors, p. 519

HILL, G. Andrew
Monier-Williams & Boxalls, London (0171) 405 6195
Partner specialising in partnership law.
Specialisation: Main area of specialisation is partnership law. Deals with professional partnerships, especially for doctors, drafting partnership deeds and advising both on formation and dissolution and allied problems. Also covers all aspects of wills, trusts and probate.
Prof. Memberships: Law Society, Holborn Law Society (Past President).
Career: Qualified in 1966: *Monier-Williams & Boxalls*.
Personal: Born 15th April 1939. Educated at Winchester and Christ Church Oxford (MA 1962). Lives in East Sheen.

LACE, John D.
Bristows, London (0171) 400 8000
Partner in Company Department.
Specialisation: Main areas of practice are company, corporate finance, partnership, charity and competition law. Extensive experience in mergers, acquisitions, corporate reorganisations and joint ventures, acting particularly for UK and US corporations. Has advised in relation to many partnership agreements, mergers, demergers and disputes, particularly in the accountancy and legal professions.
Prof. Memberships: Law Society.
Career: Qualified in 1973 after articles at *Meade-King & Co* in Bristol. Joined *Bristows* in 1974 and became a Partner in 1978.
Personal: Born 11th September 1947. Educated at Malvern College 1961-66. Enjoys sailing, gardening and photography, and is a member of MCC. Lives in London.

LINSELL, R.D.
Rowe & Maw, London (0171) 248 4282
Direct Dial (0171) 782 8806
Specialisation: Partnership and commercial law. Acts for leading partnerships in all areas of professional practice. The past year has seen a significant increase of work in the areas of mergers and strategic alliances. Also involved in partnership defections and a wide range of partnership disputes. Remains closely involved in the LLP movement. Lectures and writes on these and other professional topics. Also regularly advising on the adoption of improved partnership agreements with particular emphasis on partner retention, profit sharing and succession issues.
Prof. Memberships: IBA, APP.

Career: Jesus College, Cambridge 1966-69; *Rowe & Maw* 1969-1998. Non-executive director of a number of companies.

MAYER, Stephen D.
Reynolds Porter Chamberlain, London (0171) 242 2877
Specialisation: Head of Commercial Litigation. A substantial and increasing area of his practice consists of advice on partnership disputes and their resolution. Clients include professional and commercial partnerships. He is also experienced in employment law.
Prof. Memberships: Law Society; International Bar Association; Media Society.
Career: Educated at St Paul's School and Oriel College, Oxford. Qualified in 1974. Partner of *Reynolds Porter Chamberlain* since 1977.
Personal: Married with 3 children. Leisure interests include erratic golf and slightly less erratic tennis.

MCARTHUR, Colin
Field Fisher Waterhouse, London (0171) 481 4841
Partner in Company and Commercial Department.
Specialisation: Handles all aspects of corporate and partnership law, including establishment, mergers and acquisitions, sales, retirements, dissolutions and joint ventures. Also deals with commercial contracts. Co-author of 'A Director's Guide – Duties, Liabilities and Company Law' (1990), and contributor to 'A Directors Guide to Accounting and Auditing' (1991).
Prof. Memberships: Law Society, I.B.A, Institute of Directors.
Career: Qualified in 1969, having joined *Waterhouse & Co (now Field Fisher Waterhouse)* in 1967. Became a Partner in 1974.
Personal: Born 5th November 1944. Educated at Fettes College 1958-63 and Cambridge University 1963-66. Leisure interests include golf and aphorisms. Lives in London.

MORGAN, David
Wright Son & Pepper, London (0171) 242 5473
Specialisation: Professional matters including advice and representation before disciplinary, other tribunals and appeals to High Court and above, as well as on employment, partnership, fraud and negligence claims generally. Also commercial litigation and courts martial. Specialist also in railway and safety law.
Prof. Memberships: : Chartered Institute of Transport. Institute of Directors.
Career: : Articled *Slaughter and May*. Qualified 1968. *Roche Son & Neale* until 1973. Partner in *R A Roberts* 1973 – 1983. Joined *Wright Son & Pepper* in 1983. Partner since 1987.
Personal: Member of Holborn Law Society Committee and Professional Matters and International Committees, Solicitors European Group, Federation of European Bars Commission on Multi-Disciplinary Partnerships, President of European Federation of Museum and Tourist Railways, Member of Railway Heritage Committee, Deputy President of Transport Trust, Director of various heritage railways and ship companies. Member of the Solicitors Assistance Scheme. Solicitor member of Defendants' Friends (ICA).

RALPH, Stephen
Ralph Hume Garry, London (0171) 831 3737
Specialisation: The firm specialises exclusively in litigation, arbitration and dispute resolution. It

covers the full range of commercial litigation matters specialising in partnership work, in particular solicitors, accountants, surveyors and medical practices. The firm also has particular expertise in insolvency, white collar crime, fraud, asset recovery work and arbitration matters.
Prof. Memberships: Member of Insolvency Practitioners Association, Fellow of the Society of Practitioners of Insolvency, Member of the Insolvency Lawyers Association, Fellow of the Chartered Institute of Arbitrators.
Career: Qualified in 1975. Articled at *Payne Hicks Beach*. Senior Commercial Litigation Partner at *Payne Hicks Beach* until 1992. From 1992 to 1995 Senior Commercial Litigation Partner at *Boodle Hatfield*. 1995 to date Senior Partner at *The Ralph Hume Garry Partnership*. Licensed insolvency practitioner.
Personal: Born 7 April 1946. 1971 BA (Law). 1988 Diploma in Insolvency Law and Administration. 1995 Fellow of the Chartered Institute of Arbitrators. Lives in London and Oxfordshire. Interest include painting, theatre, sport, member of the RAC.

SACKER, Tony
Kingsley Napley, London (0171) 814 1200
Head of Partnership Unit.
Specialisation: Main area of practice is partnership law. Over 20 years experience advising and negotiating in this area. Also deals with charities. Author: "Practical Partnership Agreements" (Jordans).
Prof. Memberships: Association of Partnership Practitioners, City of London Law Society, Westminster Law Society, Association of Charity Lawyers. STEP.
Career: Qualified in 1963. Partner from 1967 at *Egerton Sandler*, which merged with *Kingsley Napley* 1989. Partner at *Kingsley Napley* since 1989. President Westminster Law Society 1987-88. Chairman City of London Law Society 1998 -. Committee Member Association of Partnership Practitioners 1997 -.
Personal: Born 2nd March 1940. Educated at Owens School to 1958. Vice-President of the Union of Liberal & Progressive Synagogues. Recreations include doing communal work. Lives in London.

TURNOR, Richard
Allen & Overy, London (0171) 330 3000
Specialisation: Partner specialising in advising professional partnerships and banks and others who deal with professional partnerships. Also advises wealthy private individuals, their families and trustees in connection with all aspects of tax and estate planning, especially where there is an international aspect, private banks and professional trustees about the related services provided by them to private clients and about trust litigation. Also advises on heritage and cultural property matters.
Prof. Memberships: Member Association of Partnership Practitioners (committee member), IBA Committees on cultural property (Vice-Chairman 1992-94) and trusts and estate planning; member Charity Law Association, Society of Trust and Estate practitioners; Trustee of International Bar Association Educational Trust. Association of Partnership Practitioners (committee member).
Career: Articled *Allen & Overy*, qualified 1980, Partner 1985.
Personal: Oxford University 1977. Born 1956.

WILLIAMS, Christine J.
Fox Williams, London (0171) 628 2000
Partner in Corporate Department.
Specialisation: Within the context of her corporate work, has extensive experience in the area of professional partnerships. Work has included drafting partnership deeds, restructuring partnerships, negotiating mergers of firms, advising on and implementing the incorporation of partnerships. Has also undertaken much work in the area of partnership disputes, including negotiating the departure of partners.
Prof. Memberships: Law Society, City of London Law Society, International Bar Association, Association of Partnership Practitioners.

Career: Qualified in 1977. Partner at *Oppenheimers* 1981-88. Formed and joined *Fox Williams* as a Partner in 1989.
Personal: Born 15th February 1953. Educated at St Anne's College, Oxford 1971-74. Leisure interests include theatre and cinema. Lives in Buckinghamshire.

WRIGHT, Nicholas J.
Wright Son & Pepper, London
(0171) 242 5473
Head of Partnership and Professional Department.
Specialisation: Main area of practice is partnership law. Advises on partnership

disputes and dissolutions, including interventions and practice management of other firms. Member of the Solicitors Assistance Scheme and solicitor member of Defendants' Friends (ICA). Has considerable commercial experience and acts for both UK and overseas corporations.
Prof. Memberships: Law Society.
Career: Qualified in 1970, having joined *Wright Son & Pepper* in 1960. Became a Partner in 1979.
Personal: Born 2nd February 1943. Educated at Charterhouse 1956-60.

The SOUTH

LEADING FIRMS · THE SOUTH

LINNELLS Oxford
TRUMPS Bristol
VEALE WASBROUGH Bristol

HIGHLY REGARDED FIRMS

Burges Salmon Bristol
Osborne Clarke Bristol

Clarkson Wright & Jakes Orpington
Lester Aldridge Bournemouth
Mundays Esher
Slee Blackwell Barnstaple

Payne Marsh Stillwell Southampton
Rawlison & Butler Crawley
Rodgers Horsley Whitemans Guildford

Linnells (Oxford) (2ptnrs/1asst 25 %) Although leader Paddy Gregan has left, the firm has a well-established local partnership practice which keeps it at the top of the table. Bias toward non-contentious work, particularly for veterinary, medical and corporate partnerships. **Clients/Work:** Lawyers, accountants, surveyors, publishing clients.

Trumps (Bristol) (2ptnrs/3assts over 50%) Have a separate partnership unit which specialises in medical partnerships. **Clients/Work:** Act for over 50 GPs and the whole range of professional partnerships ranging from 2-20 partner firms.

Veale Wasbrough (Bristol) (3ptnrs/ 1asst both 40%) Well-known for medical partnership work. **Clients/Work:** Undertake work for a wide range of medical practitioners throughout the South West region. Also dealt with hospital consultants. Advisory work on partnership matters for solicitors, civil engineers, surveyors and architects.

Burges Salmon (Bristol) (7ptnrs – p/t; 6assts – p/t) Particular expertise in farming partnerships stemming from their agricultural and landlord and tenant practices. **Clients/Work:** Other lawyers, accountants, surveyors, engineers and farmers make up their partnership client-base.

Osborne Clarke (Bristol) (4ptnrs) Work handled by corporate and litigation partners; the team has a reputation for sorting out particularly acrimonious disputes without recourse to litigation. Also advise on related tax implications. **Clients/Work:** Mainly professional but also some business partnerships.

Clarkson Wright & Jakes (Orpington) (3ptnrs/1asst all 25 %) Particular reputation for medical partnerships (2-6 partner firms). Said to have cornered market for Kent and South East businesses. Contentious and non-contentious matters handled. **Clients/ Work:** Also act for trading partnerships, architects and surveyors (occasionally).

Lester Aldridge (Bournemouth) (3ptnrs/ 2assts 30-50% of the time) Contentious and

non-contentious matters dealt with, particularly well-known for advising and resolving disputes amongst medical practices (eg. valuation of medical premises). **Clients/Work:** Medical practitioners, trading partnerships (2-12 partners), lawyers, accountants (small/medium).

Mundays (Esher) (2ptnrs) **Clients/Work:** Professional partnerships particularly contentious matters for doctors, solicitors, architects and accountants.

Slee Blackwell (Barnstaple) (1ptnr/ 1asst all 25%) Small provincial firm with a particular speciality in advising medical and veterinary partnerships. Non-contentious only. **Clients/Work:** Small veterinary partnerships of 2/3, beyond that non-professionals make up client base e.g. computer firms, taxi firms and other small businesses.

Payne Marsh Stillwell (Southampton) (1ptnr 50%) Tend to act for partnerships as opposed to individual partners. **Clients/Work:** Include: Doctors and dentists.

Rawlison & Butler (Crawley) (3ptnrs/ 3assts) Commercial litigation department handles partnership disputes. **Clients/Work:** Mainly professional practices including medical practitioners.

Rodgers Horsley Whitemans (Guildford) (1ptnr 50%) Reputation for dental partnership work. **Clients/Work:** Nature of work is non-contentious.

MIDLANDS

HIGHLY REGARDED FIRMS
MIDLANDS

Edge & Ellison Birmingham
Freeth Cartwright Hunt Dickins Nottingham

Edge & Ellison (Birmingham) (2ptnrs/ 2assts all 20%) Practice from within corporate department. **Clients/Work:** Clients are professionals such as lawyers, accountants, surveyors, dentists, funeral directors and insurance companies all predominantly from the Midlands.

Freeth Cartwright Hunt Dickins (Nottingham) (1ptnr) **Clients/Work:** Draft partnership agreements for farmers, doctors, dentists and a number of insurance brokers.

The NORTH

Cuff Roberts (Liverpool) (2ptnrs 25%) The firm moves into top position for the first time this year. *Tony Twemlow*'s "very sensible approach to problems" and ability to make clients "feel they're in safe hands" received much acclaim. Known for dealing with contentious matters and for his ability to avoid litigation. **Clients/Work:** Professional practices.

Kershaw Abbott (Manchester) (1ptnr 30%) Being in a litigation-based practice *Anne Kershaw* handles contentious work such as "hiring and firing" issues. **Clients/Work:** Act largely for solicitors but also for accountants and surveyors.

Cobbetts (Manchester) (1ptnr/1asst) Strong reputation for advisory work to medical partnerships. **Clients/Work:** Drafting commercial and professional partnership agreements in mainly non-contentious matters.

Hill Dickinson (Liverpool) (2ptnrs/1ptnr 30%) *Michael Quinn*(tax background) and Senior Partner *Paul Walton* (litigation background, particularly expert in partnership disputes) do mainly advisory work. **Clients/Work:** Mainly professionals such as solicitors, surveyors and veterinary surgeons.

Mace & Jones (Manchester) (2ptnrs/1asst) Senior Partner and insolvency expert *Graeme Jump* has a well-established reputation in the North. **Clients/Work:** More doctors, lawyers and accountants than commercial partnerships. Mainly non-contentious.

Vaudreys (Manchester) (2ptnrs/2assts) Contentious and non-contentious work; partnership disputes and agreements dealt with. **Clients/Work:** Accountants and joint venture type partnerships. Also have expertise in property-based partnerships.

SCOTLAND

Dundas & Wilson CS (Edinburgh) (2ptnrs) Limited liability partnership(LLP) is a speciality. Mainly non-contentious. Spending 50% time on partnership issues via their Lloyds involvement. **Clients/ Work:** Very often deal with Lloyds members and investment companies.

McGrigor Donald (Glasgow) (3ptnrs) Known for representing partners in contentious matters but also handle non-contentious work eg: restructuring partnership agreements. **Clients/Work:** Professionals: solicitors, architects and accountants (5-10 partner firms) but also handle trading partnerships

Bell & Scott WS (Edinburgh) (3ptnrs/1asst) Partnership matters stem largely from non-contentious issues. **Clients/Work:** For Scott Oswald CA advice on number of general partnership legal matters. Advice in relation to limited partnerships to PLC clients of Mace & Jones. Advising on Scottish Design Agency on all aspects of partnership law.

Fyfe Ireland WS (Edinburgh) (1ptnr 40%) Reputation for advisory work for medical partnerships. **Clients/Work:** Medical, hotel and farming partnerships.

Robson Mclean WS (Edinburgh) (3ptnrs/2assts) Each of the partners specialises in either contentious or non-contentious issues, devoting only a minor proportion of time to the area. **Clients/Work:** Bias toward the non-contentious side, advising the hotel and retail industry.

LEADERS' PROFILES · REGIONS

JUMP, G.K.
Mace & Jones, Manchester (0161) 236 2244
Senior Partner & Partner in Commercial Litigation & Insolvency Department.
Specialisation: Handles a wide range of commercial dispute work including professional negligence. Specialist interests, in addition to Partnership, include Insolvency, Construction Law and Arbitration.
Prof. Memberships: Member of the Association of Partnership Practitioners; President, Manchester Law Society, 1991/92; Honorary Treasurer, Manchester Law Society 1995/98; Founder Member and Honorary Secretary of the Northern Arbitration Association (1990); Associate of the Chartered Institute of Arbitrators since 1987; Past President of the Insolvency Lawyers' Association (1997/98) Fellow of the Society of Practitioners of Insolvency (1998).
Career: Qualified in 1969. Joined *Mace & Jones* in 1971 and became a Partner in 1973. Licensed Insolvency Practitioner since October 1989. Appointed Director of the Solicitors' Indemnity Fund Limited and Insolvency Assessor to the Law Society Post Qualification Casework Committee in 1992.
Personal: Born 22nd February 1945. Married with 'grown up' children. Lives at Willaston, Wirral, Cheshire.

KERSHAW, Anne
Kershaw Abbott, Manchester
(0161) 839 0998
Specialisation: Practises in the field of commercial dispute resolution with particular emphasis on professional partnership disputes and construction disputes.
Prof. Memberships: Member of Association of Partnership Practitioners; Council Member Manchester Financial & Professional Forum; Past President and Council Member of Manchester Law Society; Member of Society of Construction Lawyers; Member of the Legal Aid Area Committee.
Career: Admitted 1975. Practised in North West all working life. Co-founder of *Kershaw Abbott* as niche practice in 1991. Appointed Tax Commissioner in 1995.
Personal: Lives in Ribble Valley with judicial husband and son. Music lover and devoted gardener.

QUINN, Michael J.
Hill Dickinson, Liverpool (0151) 236 5400
Specialisation: Partner in the Commercial Department heading the Private Client Team. Specialist in Partnership Law and advises on estate and tax planning through the use of partnerships, companies and trusts, both onshore and offshore. Speaks fluent French and is the Honorary French Consul in Liverpool.
Prof. Memberships: Society of Estate and Trust Practitioners, Law Society.
Career: Cardinal Allen Grammar School, Liverpool. Christ's College, Cambridge (Latin, Medieval French and Law).
Personal: Art, literature, cinema, opera, current affairs and sport.

TWEMLOW, W.A.

Cuff Roberts, Liverpool (0151) 227 4181
Specialisation: Insolvency, Partnership,
Charities and anything with a 'Chancery' ring to
it. Acted in successful judicial review of VAT
changes affecting the Mail Order Trade in the
Autumn 1996 Budget with (on the Government's
own figures) £350m at stake.
Prof. Memberships: Society of Practitioners in
Insolvency. Insolvency Lawyers' Association.
Association of Partnership Practitioners.
Career: MA (Cantab). Qualified 1968. Assistant
and then Partner (1971) in *Cuff Roberts*.
Chairman of the Young Solicitors Group of the
Law Society (1978). President, Liverpool Law
Society (1995). Managing Partner, *Cuff Roberts*
1998-1994.
Personal: Music, Tennis. Married with three
children. Lives in West Kirby, Wirral.

WALTON, Paul

Hill Dickinson, Liverpool (0151) 236 5400
Senior Partner of Firm. Member of Commercial
and Insurance Litigation Department.
Specialisation: Principal area of practice is
professional negligence acting for insurers of
architects, surveyors, engineers, accountants,
brokers and other professionals. Also plaintiff
work against solicitors and some other
professionals and advice to insurers generally.
Other main areas of practice are partnership
(advising on professional partnership disputes)
and Libel. Important cases handled include
Liverpool L.R.A.T.I v. Sir Frederick Gibberd &
Others (Liverpool R.C. Cathedral litigation);
Christian Brothers v. Eagle Star & Stephensons,
Offshore Reinsurers PCI v. Evandale and Others
(international libel), Rimmer v. Storey (political
libel action) and Comer v. St. Patrick (Occupiers
Liability). Clients include major insurers,
reinsurers and underwriters, dioceses and
religious orders as well as companies and
partnerships.
Prof. Memberships: Law Society, Official
Referees Solicitors Society, Association of
Lawyers for Defence of the Unborn.
Career: Qualified 1969. Became a Partner at
Hill Dickinson Davis Campbell in 1972,
Management Partner in 1989 and Senior Partner
in 1994. Member of Board of Faculty of Law,
Liverpool University, 1996-present. Currently
Senior Partner *Hill Dickinson*.
Personal: Born 18th May 1945. Educated at
Exeter University 1963-66 (Lloyd Parry Prize in
Constitutional Law and Bracton Law Society
Prize) and The College of Law, Guildford 1966-
67. Member of Council of the Catholic Union;
Knight of the Equestrian Order of St Gregory;
Knight of the Holy Sepulchre of Jerusalem.
Activities outside the law include herb growing,
philately, antiques, opera, shooting and anti-
abortion causes. Resides Hoghton, near Preston.

PENSIONS

See also Employee Share Schemes; Employment

RESEARCH: In compiling the tables, we consider all the information available to us, paying particular regard to the market research carried out by our team of ten qualified lawyers. (The researchers' details are set out on page three.) The rankings, therefore, reflect the opinion of the marketplace as revealed by systematic and objective research: see page four. (Our research is audited every year by the British Market Research Bureau.)

OVERVIEW: The most significant development in pensions law over recent years has been the Pensions Act 1995 which came into force in full in April 1997, necessitating a large amount of compliance work in a short space of time. Following the recommendations of the Goode Report a new regulatory body, the Occupational Pensions Regulatory Authority('OPRA')was established to oversee the operation of the Pensions Act. The current Pensions Ombudsman, Julian Farrand, has single-handedly created a fast-track law clarification process, increasing the workload of every practitioner. Specialised pensions litigators are on the increase and it is only a matter of time before a dedicated section appears in this publication.

Some of the larger departments are finding that crossborder work for international pensions plans is on the increase. Pensions law is becoming more complicated. This seems likely to lead to the demise of the 'boutique' firm. The resultant trend is a polarisation of sophisticated work towards the same few large firms and a gap between the firms which are serious and those which are not. This trend spreads also to the regions and Scotland. Conversely, on the individual lawyer level, now that the 'old guard' are retiring, they are being replaced by a spectrum of lawyers with varying skills.

In London, Sacker & Partners, the only niche firm in these tables, maintains its position amongst the leaders. The historical domination of John Quarrell and Stuart James over the other practitioners is perceived to have ended, with no individuals now occupying pole position. The 'Northern Raiders' who have attempted to make inroads into the London market on the basis of their great success in the North have failed to get a serious foothold and are losing staff to the traditional City players.

Genuine specialists outside London are relatively few. In the Midlands Edge & Ellison and Wragges are strong. Further North the market is dominated by the same names: Eversheds, Dibb Lupton Alsop and Addleshaw Booth & Co. In Scotland, Bishop and Robertson Chalmers, Maclay Murray & Spens and Shepherd & Wedderburn are pulling ahead although the proliferation of work means there is room for new firms in the market.

LEADING FIRMS • LONDON

FRESHFIELDS
LINKLATERS
LOVELL WHITE DURRANT
ROWE & MAW
SACKER & PARTNERS

ALLEN & OVERY
CLIFFORD CHANCE
NABARRO NATHANSON
SLAUGHTER AND MAY

HIGHLY REGARDED FIRMS

Baker & McKenzie
Biddle
Cameron McKenna
Hammond Suddards
Travers Smith Braithwaite

Herbert Smith
Simmons & Simmons

Dibb Lupton Alsop
Eversheds
Richards Butler

LONDON

Freshfields (3ptnrs/12assts/1know-how lawyer) The department is widely perceived to be primarily a service department ("resting on its corporate laurels") without the high profile of many of the City firms. However they claim 50% stand-alone pensions work. *Kenneth Dierden* is "technically sound with a practical approach; he deals well with clients and gains their confidence." *David Pollard* is much-praised as an "innovatory, well-informed good all-round" pensions lawyer who "always has an 'Australian case' to back up his view." *Daniel Schaffer*, recently promoted to partner, has an excellent reputation as an "academic lawyer." **Clients/Work:** Acting for Trustees of Railway Pensions Scheme (with over £12b assets) in High Court proceedings arising from South West Trains litigation. Acting for ICI in purchase of $80b part of the business; involving pensions arrangements in over 30 countries, centralised in UK. Acting for Nestlé on a European-wide acquisition, purchased from Dalgety for over £700m and covering over ten jurisdictions.

Linklaters (5ptnrs/15assts) The "impressive" pensions team "have undergone a renaissance recently and are developing a more aggressive feel." One client was impressed by their 'plain English' policy. *Tim Cox* "is an excellent technical lawyer." *Ruth Goldman* has taken over the reigns from the "bright" *Tony Thurnham* who is standing aside this year as Head of Pensions. It is thought that she "will thrive on the management responsibility if given the opportunity." *Claire Petheram*, newly listed as a leader last year and recently made a partner is "a bit of a star." **Clients/Work:** Ongoing advice for eg. BP and Post Office. Acting for members alleged to have received incorrect extra payments in Ferranti case and acting for National Power in the National Grid case.

Lovell White Durrant (5ptnrs/9assts) The jury is out as to the effect of leader Harriet Dawes' retirement, partly because "there are not so many high profile people coming through" although there is consensus that the team is of high quality. They are supported by a well thought of pensions litigation team. *Jane Samsworth* now has a chance to shine as Head of Department. *Russell Strachan* is "underrated", he is "excellent, a consummate professional but does not shout it from the rooftops." *Stephen Ito,* and the "extremely experienced" *John Pearson* are also recommended. Derek Simler has now retired. **Clients/Work:** Pensions aspects of the sale of most of the business of BZW to Credit Suisse First Boston (pensions arrangements covering 15 different jurisdictions). Major High Court action to clarify the benefits to be provided to certain former members of the Principal Civil Service Pension Scheme.

Litigation concerning the use of a pension plan surplus by National Power.

Rowe & Maw (6ptnrs/10assts) Perceived to be at risk of slipping. The "highly respected" and "exceptionally able" *Stuart James* is now Senior Partner and still "doing 90% pensions work" but the perception is that his "time is torn" and his profile diminished. Partners also ranked are *Andrew White* and "effective operator" and "great communicator" *Anna Rogers.* **Clients/Work:** Advising trustees of Provident Mutual Scheme in consideration of merger terms offered by General Accident Scheme following acquisition of Provident Mutual by General Accident. Advising trustees of schemes established for Centrica following the demerger of British Gas into BG and Centrica. Advising P&O in its negotiations with Royal Nedlloyd and Stena on pensions aspects of its joint venture arrangements with the two companies.

Sacker & Partners (15ptnrs/9assts) In the unique and "difficult position" of being a niche pensions firm and traditionally covering the "widest and most elitist range of pensions work." Currently "seem to be going well" but there is debate about the sustainability of their position. They have added to their core pensions work a young team of pensions litigators. "Hard-working" *Mark Greenlees* "has a range of experience" and is currently Chair of the Association of Pensions Lawyers. *Jonathan Seres* is seen less in the marketplace these days; "a brilliant man gone quiet." *Ian Pittaway* has also "not been seen so much in the last year." *Peter Docking, Peter Lester* and *Sarah Tier* are also ranked. **Clients/Work:** Successfully acting for South West Trains in high-profile litigation involving trade unions in which more than £40million was at stake. Invited to give independent legal advice to the Trustee of the Electricity Supply Pension Scheme on the major project of a facility for groups to segregate investment management within the scheme.

Allen & Overy (3ptnrs/10assts) Low-profile pensions department, known to have a good client list but its reputation rests largely on *Derek Sloan,* "one of the grey-haired ones, a consummate old pro." Competitors thought "he would be a more leading individual if he could take his nose away from the grindstone." "Phenomenally busy" but could make use of a bigger team. **Clients/Work:** Disposal by ICI of its bulk chemicals business, involving transfer of pensions rights in over a dozen countries. The establishment of Cable & Wireless Communications by the merger of Mercury/Nynex/Bell Cable Media and Videotron. Disposal by Rexam of its Octagon business.

Clifford Chance (2ptnrs/10assts) Known for corporate support work, they are good at what they do but will miss Chris Johnson now he has retired. *Helen Cox* ("excellent technician") now heads the department. *Nick Sherwin* is "a bright lad,

somewhat undersold." *Joanne Etherton* is "impressive, has an academic approach and is a good communicator." **Clients/Work:** Acting for Deutsche Morgan Grenfell on the pensions aspects of the purchase of part of the NatWest Markets. Acting for Credit Suisse First Boston on the pensions aspects of their purchase of BZW. Acting for Nomura International on the pensions aspects of their £1.2bn purchase of Inntrepreneur pubs from Grand Metropolitan and Fosters.

Nabarro Nathanson (6ptnrs/10assts/2 revenue experts) Large practice which depends on small self-administered schemes rather than larger clients. Traditionally a key player in pensions but the general upheavals at the firm may be having an impact here too. The reputation of the team hinges on *John Quarrell* whose position at the top is now felt to be historical, although he is "always there, a fount of knowledge and loved by clients." *Peter Ford* "appears to be his heir designate" and *John Murray* is also recommended. **Clients/Work:** Bringing into effect of Russian legislative framework for pensions, on which the team has previously advised. Published Guide to UK Pensions Law in November.

Slaughter and May (4ptnrs p/t; 16assts p/t) Generalist team also practises employment and share schemes law. The verdict is "good but need more breadth; intellectually top-rank." *Philip Bennett* is widely praised as "a good technical lawyer" – he is both "extraordinarily able" and "ridiculously hard-working." *Howard Jacobs* wears two hats and also appears as a leader in our employment tables.

Baker & McKenzie (3ptnrs/7assts) "Sound people" with "good clients". People like *Robert West.* In the last year they have taken on a new partner as well as transferring a litigation assistant as a full-time member of the department to co-ordinate pensions litigation. **Clients/Work:** Advising Trustee of South West Trains in the High Court proceedings dealing with the effects of pay restructuring. Advising an airline on worldwide pensions arrangements for staff throughout the world. Advising Hanson Industrial on pensions aspects of sale of electrical products business.

Biddle (4ptnrs/2 litigation ptnrs/6assts/2 litigation assts) Have long reputation in this field, but suffered when Belinda Benney left. There is some perception that they are now "trying hard and doing better." *Hugh Arthur* is "bright and well-liked." *Chris Mullen* is "able technically and rated highly." **Clients/Work:** Acting for Trustees of the National Power Group of the Electricity Supply Pension Scheme in National Power plc v Feldon & others in which a ruling was made for the clients, reversing the prior decision of the Pensions Ombudsman. Advising Trustees of Fisons Pension Fund over the merger terms with Rhine-Poulenc

Pension Fund, leading to proposed creation of £800m fund.

Cameron McKenna (2ptnrs/10assts) The merger brought together Cameron's litigation strength and the McKenna's Financial Services practice. Since John Cunliffe retired, the department is "consolidating." Seen to be active, "looking forwards and well organised." *Nigel Moore* is "a terrific communicator, extremely sensible and commercial and entirely professional." He is supported by a team of "able assistants." **Clients/Work:** Important Industrial Tribunal case, application of TUPE to pensions re contracting out of local government services, in tendering process. Instructed by trustees of the London Electricity Scheme. Ongoing litigation for Ferranti.

Hammond Suddards (3ptnrs/11assts) The firm has "good national coverage" although its approach is a bit "wide." *Jane Marshall* heads the department and is "absolutely sound." *Andrew Powell* is a "practical, robust pensions lawyer of the old school, able and willing to take a positive view about things which is accessible to clients." *Peter Silke* is also recommended. **Clients/Work:** Won beauty parade to act for Financial Services Authority. Acting for Harrison Croftfield on a disposal. Setting up final salary schemes for Welsh Water and Yorkshire Water.

Travers Smith Braithwaite (2ptnrs/4assts) Practitioners have a lot of respect for the "quality people" in this small team. Principal clients tend to be trustees rather than employers. *Paul Stannard* "has earned himself an excellent reputation" and *Stephanie Smith* is spoken of highly. **Clients/Work:** Pioneered contracting out on a money-purchase basis for large final salary schemes of well-known plc clients resulting in savings of £millions. Appointment to OPRA legal panel. Continuing litigation for trustees of the Mirror Group Pension Scheme, the largest of the Maxwell pension schemes.

Herbert Smith (3ptnrs/5assts) Have made a significant comeback and are now "competent but short-handed." In terms of personnel, previously overreliant on *Ian Gault* who has "a growing reputation." **Clients/Work:** Advising De la Rue in relation to the merger of its UK pension schemes. Advising the Institute of Actuaries on the legal aspects of their professional guidance

notes, in particular those drafted to take account of the new requirements under the Pensions Act.

Simmons & Simmons (3ptnrs/5assts/ 1 litigation ptnr/2 litigation assts) A "decent practice" which is "keen" and generally perceived to be "trying hard." Have gained many new pensions fund clients. **Clients/Work:** Advising SmithKline Beecham on introduction of innovative defined contribution arrangement, affecting all 7,000 UK employees. Acting for MoD on privatisation of Devonport Royal Dockyard and Rosyth Royal Dockyard.

Dibb Lupton Alsop (1ptnr/3assts) The London team "rests on National Grid work, mainly corporate support with bolted on Alsop Wilkinson clients." The general feeling is that the team has lost some ground over the last year and is not a genuine specialist; "more commercial litigation with a pensions slant." *Jonathan Fenton* is manager overall of the DLA pensions practice; he is "extremely impressive and has good clients."

Eversheds (3ptnrs/2assts) Another team which has lost ranking over the last year for "not making the impact they ought" despite "some good individuals." The "unconventional" *Robin Ellison* who moved from Hammond Suddards last year is now National Head of Pensions. *Roger Lewis* is also recommended. **Clients/Work:** Ongoing work in relevant litigation on test cases on part-timer pension claims before Court of Appeal and House of Lords. Acting on appeal to the High Court and Court of Appeal against determinations by the Pensions Ombudsman in relation to the surplus of the National Grid Group of the Electricity Supply Pension Scheme.

Richards Butler (1ptnr/2assts) The team – lead by the "charming" *Keith Wallace* – is particularly active in independent trusteeships and advise eight investment managers. **Clients/Work:** Assisting Occupational Pension Defence Union – vehicle for pension scheme trustees. Acting for Railways Pension Arrangements in challenging Inland Revenue attempt to tax sub-underwriting activities. Advising PIA since inception on pensions mis-selling including successfully handling four judicial review attempts. *Belinda Benney* and *Michael Cowley* both retain personal reputations for their work in pensions law.

LEADERS' PROFILES · LONDON

ARTHUR, Hugh
Biddle, London (0171) 606 9301
Partner in Pensions Group.
Specialisation: Handles all areas of pensions law, including advice to major plcs, trustees and individuals. Work includes mergers and acquisitions, corporate and business transfers, litigation and the drafting of complex documentation. Author of numerous articles in specialist pensions publications. Well known speaker at conferences for APL, NAPF, PMI and independently sponsored pensions conferences.
Prof. Memberships: Association of Pension Lawyers, National Association of Pension Funds.
Career: Qualified in 1980. Worked at *Lovell White & King* 1978-84. Joined *Biddle* in 1984, becoming a Partner in 1985.
Personal: Born 6th November 1955. Attended Cardinal Vaughan Memorial School, London 1967-74, then Magdalene College, Cambridge (Open Scholarship in Classics) 1974-77 (MA Law).

BENNETT, Philip F. J.
Slaughter and May, London
(0171) 600 1200
Partner in Pensions/Employment Department.
Specialisation: Main area of practice is
pensions work. Author of 'Pension Fund
Surpluses', March 1989, 1994.
Prof. Memberships: Association of Pensions
Lawyers, Immediate Past Chairman Legislative &
Parliamentary Sub-Committee of the Association
of Pensions Lawyers. Member, Main Committee
of the Association of Pensions Lawyers.
Career: Qualified 1979. Partner 1986. Currently
with *Slaughter and May* in London.
Personal: Born 2 March 1954.

BENNEY, Belinda
Field Fisher Waterhouse, London
(0171) 481 4841
Partner in Pensions Department.
Specialisation: Full-time pensions specialist
since 1986 when switched from private client
work. Since then has covered full range of
pensions work: documentation and rule
drafting, sex discrimination, mergers &
acquisitions, privatisations, severance terms,
application of surplus, trustee duties and
liabilities, asset protection, and all aspects of
pension investment. Frequent speaker at
pensions seminars, Association of Pension
Lawyers and Trustee Training Courses. Author
of 'A Guide to the Pensions Act 1995'
(Butterworths), and the pensions chapter in the
'Administration of Estates' practitioners' manual
published by Tolley's.
Prof. Memberships: National Association of
Pension Funds, Association of Pension
Lawyers, Law Society, Institute of Chartered
Accountants Pensions Sub-Committee.
Career: Qualified in 1981. Worked at
Macfarlanes 1981-85, *Burges Salmon* 1985-86,
Linklaters & Paines 1986-89, *Rowe & Maw*
1989-90 and *Simmons & Simmons* 1990-91.
Joined *Biddle & Co* as a Partner in 1991 before
joining *Field Fisher Waterhouse* in 1996 as head
of the pensions practice.
Personal: Holds an LL.B from the University of
Bristol.

COWLEY, Michael J.
Stephenson Harwood, London
(0171) 329 4422
Partner in Corporate Department and
Employment and Pensions Group.
Specialisation: Pensions covering all aspects
of pensions law, advising banks, public and
private companies, building societies, trustees,
charities and individuals. Also share schemes
and other employee incentives.
Prof. Memberships: Association of Pensions
Lawyers (Member of Legislative and
Parliamentary Sub-Committee), National
Association of Pension Funds, Society of
Pensions Consultants (Member of Financial
Services Regulation Sub-Committee), Share
Scheme Lawyers Group.
Career: Qualified in 1984. Whole career has
been spent with *Stephenson Harwood*, except
for 3 years with the firm's Hong Kong office and
one year with *Burges Salmon*.
Personal: Born 1954. Attended Bryanston
School, then Oxford University (BA in
Philosophy, Politics and Economics). Leisure
pursuits: family, hill walking and reading.

COX, Helen
Clifford Chance, London (0171) 600 1000
Partner in and Head of Pensions Group.
Specialisation: All aspects of pensions law
including scheme documentation;
establishment, merger and winding-up of
schemes; pensions aspects of corporate
transactions, flotations and privatisations.
Prof. Memberships: Law Society, Liveryman
of the City of London Solicitors Company,
Association of Pension Lawyers, (member of
Main Committee) International Pension and
Employee Benefits Lawyers Association.
Career: Qualified 1977. Partner in *Clifford
Chance* 1989.
Personal: Born 25th July 1953. Educated at
University College London (1974 LLB 1st Class
Hons). Leisure interests include travel, cinema,
art and reading. Lives in London.

COX, Tim
Linklaters, London (0171) 456 3692
Partner, Employment & Employee Benefits
Department.
Specialisation: Specialises in mainly pension
law. Work includes drafting pension scheme
documentation, and advising on pensions
matters generally.
Prof. Memberships: Association of Pension
Lawyers: member since 1987; member of
Legislative & Parliamentary Sub-Committee since
1989; Member of Main committee 1991-96.
Career: Articled at *Linklaters & Paines* 1985,
Assistant Solicitor 1987-96, Partner 1996.
Personal: Educated at Sir John Deane's
Grammar School, BA (Law) (Downing College,
Cambridge), BCL (Magdalen College, Oxford).
Born 1960.

DIERDEN, Kenneth N.
Freshfields, London (0171) 936 4000
Partner in Employment, Pensions and Benefits
Department.
Specialisation: Work covers all aspects of the
establishment and operation of pension
schemes (both private and public sector).
Experienced in pensions litigation and has wide
involvement of the pensions aspects of
privatisations. Acts for employers and trustees.
Prof. Memberships: Former Chairman of the
Association of Pension Lawyers. Associate of
the Institute of Taxation. Books and Articles:
Joint editor of Tolley's 'The Guide to the
Pensions Act 1995'. Contributor to Tolley's
'Company Law Handbook' and Tolley's
'Director's Handbook'. Other Relevant
Experience: Former lecturer at the College of
Law. Regular speaker at pensions conferences.
Career: Qualified in 1977. Lecturer at College
of Law 1977/80. Joined *Freshfields* 1980.
Partner 1987.
Personal: Born 1952.

DOCKING, Peter J.
Sacker & Partners, London (0171) 329 6699
Partner in specialist pensions law firm.
Specialisation: Principal area of practice is
pensions law. Covers all aspects including
litigation, sales and purchases, trust law issues
and life office matters. Frequent lecturer and
contributor to pensions and academic journals.
Former Chairman of APL's Education
Committee. Contributor to and Joint Editor of
'EC Pensions Law'.

Prof. Memberships: Association of Pensions
Lawyers, Law Society.
Career: Qualified in 1987. Partner at *Nicholson
Graham & Jones* 1991 to 1996. Joined *Sacker
& Partners* as a partner in 1996.
Personal: Born 1st June 1961. Educated at
Sutton Manor High School for Boys and the
University of Exeter. Leisure activities include
mountaineering, climbing, walking, skiing and
travel.

ELLISON, Robin
Eversheds, London (0171) 919 4500
National Head of Pensions.
Specialisation: Acted in the Maxwell pensions
case. Author of 'Pensions Law and Practice'.
Editor of Pensions Law Reports. Has also
published 'Pensions and Divorce', 'The Pension
Trustee Handbook' and 'Pensions: Europe and
Equality'. Regular broadcaster including
frequent contributions to BBC Radio 4's
'Moneybox'.
Prof. Memberships: NAPF, Association of
Pensions Lawyers, Law Society.
Career: Fellow of Wolfson College, Cambridge
1975-80. Founded *Ellison Westhorp* in 1980,
carrying out exclusively pensions work.
Managing Director of Finance for Housing Ltd
1982-87 and Director of Baltic plc 1985-87.
Consultant for *Hammond Suddards* in 1994.

ETHERTON, Joanne
Clifford Chance, London (0171) 600 1000
Specialisation: All aspects of pensions law
including scheme documentation, pension
scheme mergers and pensions aspects of
corporate transactions, re-organisations and
flotations.
Prof. Memberships: Association of Pension
Lawyers, Law Society, Associate of the
Pensions Management Institute.
Career: Trained *Clifford Chance*, Qualified
1990. University of Warwick, LLB 1987.

FENTON, Jonathan
Dibb Lupton Alsop, London (0345) 262728
Specialisation: Partner and Head of the firm's
national Pensions Group in London.
Experienced in establishment, consolidation,
review and merger of schemes and in scheme
advisory work of all kinds including advice to
industry-wide schemes. He also advises on
transactional work including the pension
scheme aspects of MBOs, MBIs, company
sales, flotations and demergers, on contentious
matters (both at Ombudsman and High Court
level) such as investment and surplus disputes,
acting for independent trustees and advice on
trustee protection and exoneration. Also acts
for insolvency practitioners on pension aspects
of company winding-up. Publications include
'Tolley's Small Self-Administered Pension
Schemes' (1988) and 'Tolley's Pensions
Handbook' (principal co-author 2nd Ed.) 1995.
Prof. Memberships: Association of Pension
Lawyers.
Career: Joined *Oppenheimer Nathan & Vandyk*
in 1981, qualifying in 1983. Assistant solicitor
1983-88. Associate partner of *Oppenheimers*
1988, Partner *Denton Hall* 1989-92. Senior
Associate *Ashurst Morris Crisp* 1992-94. Partner
Alsop Wilkinson since 1994-96, partner in the
merged firm of *Dibb Lupton Alsop* since its
formation in October 1996.
Personal: Educated at Haberdasher's Askes'
School and St John's College, Oxford (MA
Modern Languages).

FORD, Peter

Nabarro Nathanson, London
(0171) 493 9933
Partner in Pensions Department.
Specialisation: Handles all aspects of pensions law, including company sales and purchases, scheme re-organisations and mergers, investment and the preparation of trust documents.
Prof. Memberships: Association of Pensions Lawyers.
Career: Qualified in 1988, having joined *Nabarro Nathanson* in 1986. Became a Partner in 1993.
Personal: Born 8th December 1962. Attended John Fisher School, Purley 1974-81 and the University of Hull 1981-84. Lives in Southfields. London.

GAULT, Ian T.

Herbert Smith, London (0171) 374 8000
Senior Pensions Partner.
Specialisation: Has extensive experience of advising on all aspects of pensions law and practice. Currently on the legislative and parliamentary sub-committee of the Association of Pensions Lawyers, the executive committee of the Pensions Research Accountant's Group and the Council of the Society of Pensions Consultants.
Prof. Memberships: Association of Pensions Lawyers.
Career: Qualified in 1977. Partner at *Herbert Smith* since 1988.
Personal: Educated at Clare College, Cambridge.

GOLDMAN, Ruth T.

Linklaters, London (0171) 456 3686
Partner. Employment and Employee Benefits Group.
Specialisation: Specialises in pensions law and employee benefits. Considerable experience in all main areas of pension law practice including trust law aspects, documentation, mergers and acquisitions, flotations, privatisations, international benefits and industry-wide schemes. Chair of the International Committee of the Association of Pension Lawyers, and Secretary to Steering Committee of International Pension & Employee Benefits Law Association. Articled at *Linklaters & Paines*, and made Partner in 1992.

GREENLEES, Mark B.

Sacker & Partners, London (0171) 329 6699
Partner in specialist pensions law firm.
Specialisation: All aspects of law relating to occupational pension schemes. Represented the male beneficiaries in the 'Coloroll' reference to the European Court. Acted for vendor in what was then the second largest MBO in UK business history. Regular contributor to pensions periodicals; regular speaker at major conferences and seminars. Current Chairman of the Association of Pension Lawyers.
Prof. Memberships: Association of Pension Lawyers.
Career: Qualified in 1979. Joined *Sacker & Partners* in 1977, becoming a Partner in 1982. Current Chairman of APL. Member of the Main Committee of APL 1991-1996. Chairman of Legislative and Parliamentary Committee of APL 1992-1994. Chairman of Legislation Committee of SPC 1991-2. Member of SPC Council.
Personal: Born 18th April 1954. Attended

Berkhamsted 1964-71 and Oxford University 1972-76. Leisure interests include family, old cars and football. Lives near Berkhamsted.

ITO, Stephen

Lovell White Durrant, London
(0171) 236 0066
Specialisation: Principal area of practice is pensions law with a particular emphasis on corporate mergers and acquisitions related work including multi-jurisdiction transactions. Otherwise involved in all aspects of UK pensions law acting mainly for UK, US and EU corporate clients.
Prof. Memberships: Law Society, Association of Pension Lawyers.
Career: Former Barrister (qualified 1984): qualified as a Solicitor in 1992 while with *Lovell White Durrant* and became a Partner in 1995.

JACOBS, Howard

Slaughter and May, London
(0171) 600 1200
Specialisation: Pension scheme restructurings, general pension advice.
Prof. Memberships: City of London Solicitors Company Employment Law Sub-committee.
Career: Winchester College. Pembroke College, Cambridge. *Slaughter and May* since 1975.
Personal: Married, three children. Interests: family and gardening.

JAMES, Stuart C.

Rowe & Maw, London (0171) 248 4282
Senior Partner Pensions Department.
Specialisation: Pensions law and related trust, tax and commercial law matters. Other main area of work is unit trusts and retail financial services. Member of the Pension Law Review Committee 1992-93.
Prof. Memberships: Law Society, Association of Pensions Lawyers (Past Chairman), Reliance Insurance Group (Chairman), M&G Securities Limited, Fellow, Pensions Management Institute.
Career: Articled with *Rowe & Maw*. Qualified in 1967, then joined *Warren Murton & Co.* 1967-77. Returned to *Rowe & Maw* as a partner in 1977
Personal: Born 3rd March 1944. Attended Reed's School 1958-62. Lives in Surrey.

LESTER, C. Peter

Sacker & Partners, London (0171) 329 6699
Partner in specialist pensions only law firm.
Specialisation: Deals with all areas of pensions law with specialist expertise in relation to FURBS and multinational pension provision. Major clients include BBC and the pension funds of leading companies. Regular contributor to pensions periodicals and speaker at major conferences and seminars.
Prof. Memberships: Association of Pension Lawyers. For many years a co-opted member of the Parliamentary Committee of the National Association of Pension Funds.
Career: Qualified in 1968. Partner at *Walker Martineau* 1970-83. Joined *Sacker & Partners* as a Partner in 1983.
Personal: Born in 1944. Educated at Christ's Hospital 1954-62 and Birmingham University 1962-65 (LL.B). Leisure activities include music, theatre and walking. Lives in Hove.

LEWIS, Roger

Eversheds, London (0171) 919 4500
Head of London Pensions Group.
Specialisation: Advises employers and trustees in relation to all aspects of corporate pension arrangements.
Prof. Memberships: Law Society, APL, NAPF.
Career: Qualified 1978. Employed IBM 1966-68, GEC 1968-72 and Commission of the European Communities 1973-75. Joined *Lewis, Lewis & Co.* (now *Eversheds*) in 1976, becoming a Partner in 1979.
Personal: Born 14th April 1945. Attended UCS 1958-63, then Balliol College, Oxford 1963-66 (MA, Physics). Governor of Hebrew University of Jerusalem. Married with two children. Leisure interests include golf, tennis and theatre.

MARSHALL, Jane M.

Hammond Suddards, London
(0171) 655 1000
Partner and Head of Pensions Unit.
Specialisation: Handles all areas of pension law, with particular emphasis on complex advice work and special projects, including scheme mergers, conflicts, privatisation, outsourcing and similar issues affecting the public sector, and pension surpluses. Handled pensions aspects of water privatisation and acted for the trustees in one of the first large surplus refund cases (£50 million). Contributor to professional journals, including Pensions Age, Professional Pensions and Occupational Pensions Quarterly. Lectures at conferences and seminars, and is a speaker on radio and TV. Editor and co-author of 'Pensions: The New Law' (Jordans 1995) and 'Pension Disputes: Prevention and Resolution' (Jordans 1998).
Prof. Memberships: Law Society, Association of Pension Lawyers and International Pensions and Employee Benefit Lawyers Association. Member of the Regulatory Sub-Committee of National Association of Pension Funds. OPAS adviser.
Career: Qualified in 1978. Worked abroad after qualifying. Joined *Lovell White & King* in 1980 to specialise in pensions. Founder partner with pensions specialists *Ellison Westhorp* and became partner with *Hammond Suddards* following its merger with *Ellison Westhorp* in 1994, becoming head of the firm's pension practice.
Personal: Born 17th December 1953. Attended March High School for Girls to 1972, then Dundee University 1972-76 (First Class Honours). Leisure interests include gardening, antiques and local history. Mother of four. Lives in Little Bromley, near Colchester.

MOORE, Nigel

Cameron McKenna, London
(0171) 367 3000
Partner in Tax and Employee Benefits Group.
Specialisation: Main area of practice is pensions. Work includes advising on administration of pension schemes; drafting trust deeds and rules; advising on pension aspects of mergers and acquisitions; advising on mergers of schemes; handling litigation in industrial tribunals (both UK and international), High Court and European Court of Justice. Organises and speaks on trustee training courses. Also handles employment law. Acted in Coloroll's application to the European Court. Speaking experience includes NAPF training courses, APL annual conference and commercial conferences.

Prof. Memberships: Law Society, City of London Solicitors Company, Association of Pension Lawyers (Secretary of International Committee).
Career: Qualified 1986. Articled at *Radcliffes & Co.* 1984-86. Joined *McKenna & Co.* in 1986. Partner 1994.
Personal: Born 13th June 1962. Attended St Albans School 1973-80, Warwick University 1980-83, College of Law Chancery Lane 1983-84 and City of London Polytechnic (MA in Business Law) 1984-86. Leisure interests include golf and football. Lives in Welwyn Garden City.

MULLEN, Chris P.
Biddle, London (0171) 606 9301
Partner in Pensions Department.
Specialisation: Advises companies and scheme trustees on all aspects of pensions law, relating principally to occupational pension schemes. Particular interests include "passport" schemes, FURBS, and advising independent trustees (e.g. one of the independent trustees who took over responsibility for the Maxwell pension schemes after Robert Maxwell's death). Clients include Lloyds, Norcros plc, Costain Group plc, GÇnÇrale des Eaux Group, Oxfam and the NSPCC.
Prof. Memberships: APL, City of London Solicitors Company.
Career: Qualified in 1986 after articles at *Biddle*. Became a Partner in 1990.
Personal: Born 11th September 1960. Educated at Jesus College, Cambridge 1979-82 (BA in Law). Lives in Hertford, Herts.

MURRAY, John
Nabarro Nathanson, London
(0171) 493 9933
Specialisation: Advises employers, trustees and others on all aspects of pensions law; specialises in scheme re-organisation and documentation for approved and unapproved schemes; experienced in pensions litigation and pensions ombudsman enquiries.
Prof. Memberships: Law Society, APL, IPEBLA, former member Association of Pensioneer Trustees Committee 1991-97.
Career: Leeds University (1976 LL.B). Qualified and joined *Nabarro Nathanson* 1979. Partner 1986.
Personal: Born 1953. Resides London.

PEARSON, John
Lovell White Durrant, London
(0171) 236 0066
Partner in Pensions and Employment Group.
Specialisation: Advises employers, trustees and others on all aspects of pensions law and documentation including the establishment, management and termination of occupational pension schemes; reorganisations; offshore schemes; pensions aspects of company sales, purchases and insolvencies; and pensions litigation. Acted for the employers in the Mirror Group Newspapers pensions case (post-Maxwell). Has given pensions seminars, including one in French.
Prof. Memberships: Law Society, City of London Solicitors Company, Association of

Pension Lawyers, International Pension and Employee Benefit Lawyers Association.
Career: Qualified in 1971. Joined *Lovell White Durrant* and became a Partner in 1986.
Personal: Attended King's College, London (LLB 1968).

PETHERAM, Claire
Linklaters, London (0171) 456 3676
Partner, Employment and Employee Benefits Group.
Specialisation: Specialises in all aspects of pension law including pension scheme mergers, pension aspects of commercial transactions, trust law queries relating to pension schemes, investment management issues and plain English documentation.

PITTAWAY, Ian M.
Sacker & Partners, London (0171) 329 6699
Partner in specialist pensions law firm.
Specialisation: Covers all aspects of pension law including acting as trustee, arbitrator and expert witness. Joint author of 'EC Pensions Law' and numerous articles and lectures. Former Chairman and Secretary of APL.
Prof. Memberships: Law Society, Association of Pensions Lawyers, Justice.
Career: Qualified in 1980 and joined *Nicholson Graham & Jones* in 1981. Became a Partner in 1984. Joined *Sacker & Partners* in 1996.
Personal: Born 28th July 1956. Attended the University of Hull 1974-77. Leisure interests include gardening, golf, wine and whisky.

POLLARD, David N.
Freshfields, London London
(0171) 832 7060
Specialisation: Partner in Employment, Pensions and Benefits Department, and group of over 30 lawyers covering the whole range of pensions, employment and benefits work. Acted for trustees in Drexel pension case. Author of book `Employment and Pension Rights in Corporate Insolvency' and contributor of chapters to Tolley's `Employment Law' and Tolley's `Insolvency Law'. Co-Editor Tolley's `Trust Law International' magazine. Editor of `Guide to the Pensions Act 1995' book.

POWELL, Andrew M.
Hammond Suddards, London
(0171) 655 1000
Partner in Pensions Unit.
Specialisation: Handles all aspects of pensions work, including inter alia documentation, deal based work, financial products, mergers and other complex advice work. Contributor to Trust Law International, Accountancy Age, Acquisitions Monthly and others. Co-author of 'Managing a Company Pension Scheme'. Contributor to 'Pensions: The New Law' (Jordans 1995).
Prof. Memberships: Law Society, Institute of Directors, the Society for Advanced Legal Studies.
Career: Qualified in 1980. Articled *Granville West Chivers & Morgan*. Then in-house lawyer covering pensions work for DHSS; adviser to OPB, NHS superannuation fund; responsible for pensions work at *Denton Hall Burgin & Warrens*, before becoming a Partner at *Ellison*

Westhorp in 1990. Joined *Hammond Suddards* in 1994. Former main committee member of Association of Pension Lawyers; member of APL investment sub-committee, IPEBLA and Director of Trustee Corporation Limited.
Personal: Born 26th January 1955. Attended King Henry VIII Grammar School to 1975. Graduated from the University of Wales in 1978; then attended Lancaster Gate College of Law. Lives in Harrow-on-the-Hill.

QUARRELL, John
Nabarro Nathanson, London
(0171) 493 9933
Partner and Head of Pensions Department.
Specialisation: Work covers all aspects relating to occupational and personal pension schemes, including investment legalities, overseas provision, equality issues, litigation matters and dispute resolution. Acts for and advises most leading firms of accountants, many pension providers and a number of firms of pensions consultants and actuaries. Has acted in a large number of leading cases. Author of numerous articles and papers. Lectures at home and abroad. Advises Russian Government.

ROGERS, Anna
Rowe & Maw, London (0171) 248 4282
Partner in Pensions Department.
Specialisation: Specialises in pensions work.
Prof. Memberships: Association of Pensions Lawyers, Fellow and Council Member of Pensions Management Institute.
Career: Qualified in 1985. Became a Partner at *Rowe & Maw* in 1989.
Personal: Born 15th May 1961. Educated at Sheffield High School for Girls 1972-79 and Keble College, Oxford 1979-82. Lives in London. Known as Anna Kelly 1991-96.

SAMSWORTH, Jane M.
Lovell White Durrant, London
(0171) 236 0066
Specialisation: Partner advising on all aspects of pension law and documentation, including establishment, management and termination of occupational pension schemes; reorganisation and scheme mergers; pension aspects of company sales and acquisitions; pension litigation; pensions in insolvency; advising clients in their relations with the regulatory authorities including the preparation of submissions to the Pensions Ombudsman. Co-author of "Guide to the Pensions Act 1995"; regular contributor to seminars and conferences on pension issues.
Prof. Memberships: Fellow Pensions Management Institute; Hon. Secretary of Association of Pension Lawyers and former member of its Legal and Parliamentary and Education and Training Sub-Committees; Member of the Council of OPAS Ltd; Council Member SPC; Law Society; City of London Solicitors.
Career: Qualified 1978. 1978-1993 Greater London Council. 1983 – 1987 British Telecommunications plc; 1987 joined *Lovell White & King* and became a partner in *Lovell White Durrant* in 1991.

SCHAFFER, Daniel
Freshfields, London (0171) 936 4000
Partner in Employment, Pensions and Benefits Group.
Specialisation: Pensions. Advises on all aspects of pensions.
Prof. Memberships: Association of Pension Lawyers (Member of International Committee). Sir John Vinelott Trust Law Committee. Sat on Financial Law Panel working party on "commercial dealings with trustees". Regular speaker.
Career: Joined *Freshfields* in 1988. Part-time tutor in trusts at LSE (1987-88), Merton College, Oxford (1987-90) and Balliol College, Oxford (1988-92).
Personal: Born 13th October 1963. Educated at Haberdashers' Aske's School, Elstree 1971-82, Bristol University 1983-86 (LLB, Simmons Scholar) and Merton College, Oxford 1986-87.(BCL 1st Class). Leisure pursuits include travelling in France. Fluent in French; working knowledge of Spanish.

SERES, Jonathan S.D.
Sacker & Partners, London (0171) 329 6699
Senior Partner of specialist pensions law firm.
Specialisation: Experienced in all aspects of pension schemes, covering establishment, alteration, merger, booklets, related employment law, Financial Services Act work, common investment funds and investment management and custody agreements. Advises employers, trustees, trade unions and charities. Acted in court application to approve merger of Plessey Pension Funds with those of GEC and Siemens. Acted in application to the ECJ in the Coloroll matter (*Sacker & Partners* were acting for the four classes of male beneficiaries). Author of 'Pensions: A Practical Guide' (4th edition 1997, FT Law & Tax,450 pages). Appeared as pensions tax expert on Channel 4's City Programme.
Prof. Memberships: Association of Pension Lawyers, National Association of Pension Funds, Society of Pension Consultants, Law Society.
Career: MA (Oxon). Qualified in 1971, having joined *Sacker & Partners* in 1967. Became a Partner in 1973 and Senior Partner in 1985. Chairman of the Association of Pension Lawyers 1985-88. APL International Sub-Committee 1992-1997. Member of former Government/ Industry Working Party for Personal Pension Schemes.
Personal: Born 13th June 1945. Oxford University PPE (Hons) 1966. Leisure interests include sailing, history and charities. Lives in London.

SHERWIN, Nick
Clifford Chance, London (0171) 600 1000
Partner Tax and Pensions Group
Specialisation: Principal area of practice includes all aspects of pensions law, acting for employers, trustees and product providers. Also advises on employee benefits including share incentive schemes and taxation issues.
Career: Qualified 1986. Partner 1993.
Personal: MA (Cantab), LL.M (U. Penn), A.T.I.I. (Gilbert Buss Medal).

SILKE, Peter D.
Hammond Suddards, London
(0171) 655 1000
Partner in Pensions Unit.
Specialisation: Pensions law specialist. Experienced in all areas of pensions law with particular emphasis on scheme mergers, conflicts, surpluses, drafting and independent trusteeship, transactional work, unapproved schemes and termination of schemes. Has been involved in cases relating to surplus issues and has advised on pensions issues connected with water privatisation. Advises trustees of schemes established by major quoted companies on pensions issues and handles independent trusteeship work arising from the statutory requirements to appoint independent trustees on insolvency. Occasional contributor of articles to professional journals. Contributor to 'Pensions: The New Law' (Jordans 1995).
Prof. Memberships: Law Society; Association of Pensions Lawyers.
Career: Qualified in 1979. With *Lovell White Durrant* 1986-90, then Partner at *Ellison Westhorp* 1991-94. Became a Partner at *Hammond Suddards* in May 1994 on merger with *Ellison Westhorp*.
Personal: Born 2nd December 1949. Educated at Hasmonean Grammar School, London 1961-66, the University of Cape Town 1967-70 (BA, B.Soc.Sc), Birmingham University (M.Soc.Sc, 1973) and York University (BPhil, 1974). Director of the Trustee Corporation Ltd. and Fiscal Services Ltd. Leisure interests include current affairs, specialised philately and reading. Lives in Stanmore, Middlesex.

SLOAN, Derek S.
Allen & Overy, London (0171) 330 3000
Partner and head of Employment, Pensions and Incentives Department.
Specialisation: Practice covers all areas of pensions work including establishing, reorganising, merging and terminating schemes, investment management and custody arrangements, the pensions implications of business sales, reorganisations and insolvencies, funding issues and equal treatment. Regular speaker at conferences.
Prof. Memberships: Law Society, Association of Pension Lawyers, Chairman of APL sub-committee on Pensions Law Reform, Pensions Research Accountants Group.
Career: Qualified 1973, having joined *Allen & Overy* in 1971. Became a Partner in 1977.
Personal: Attended Oxford University 1967-70 (BA Jurisprudence). Born 1948.

SMITH, Stephanie
Travers Smith Braithwaite, London
(0171) 248 9133 or 295 3000
Partner in Pensions Department.
Specialisation: Handles all aspects of pensions law. Regular public speaker.
Prof. Memberships: Association of Pensions Lawyers, Life Assurance Legal Society.
Career: Qualified in 1986. Joined *Travers Smith Braithwaite* in 1993, becoming a Partner in 1994.
Personal: Born 22nd March 1962. Holds an LLB from Queen Mary College, London (1983). Lives in London.

STANNARD, Paul A.C.
Travers Smith Braithwaite, London
(0171) 248 9133 or 295 3000
Partner in Pensions Department.
Specialisation: All aspects of pensions law.
Prof. Memberships: Hon. Secretary Association of Pensions Lawyers(1991 – 1994), Fellow of the Pensions Management Institute.
Career: Qualified 1982. Joined *Travers Smith Braithwaite* as a Partner in 1989.
Personal: Born 1957.

STRACHAN, Russell A.
Lovell White Durrant, London
(0171) 236 0066
Specialisation: Pension law in all its applications, particularly: negotiating scheme reorganisations and mergers, benefit design, sales and acquisitions, conflicts of interest and trustee problems, winding-up, equal pay and contentious issues, investment and regulatory matters, scheme documentation and member communications. Clients include multi-national and UK employers, trustees, insurance companies, investment companies and professional advisors.
Prof. Memberships: Law Society, Association of Pension Lawyers, National Association of Pension Funds.
Career: Articled *Lovell White & King* (now *Lovell White Durrant*); qualified 1970; Partner 1975.

THURNHAM, Tony
Linklaters, London (0171) 456 3690
Partner in Employment & Employee Benefits Group.
Specialisation: Over 20 years' experience in pension matters. Typical matters include pension scheme mergers and restructurings, pension aspects of corporate M&A transactions, trust law aspects of pension schemes, pensions and European law and 'Plain English' pensions documentation. Author of numerous articles; regular speaker at conferences. Qualified 1978. Became a Partner in 1983. Former Chairman of the Association of Pensions Lawyers (1989-90); First Chairman of the International Pension & Employee Benefit Law Association (1987-91). Council Member of National Association of Pension Funds.

TIER, Sarah Jane
Sacker & Partners, London (0171) 329 6699
Partner in specialist pensions law firm.
Specialisation: Deals with all aspects of pensions law including public sector and post-privitisation schemes, scheme mergers, advising trustees and pensions on divorce. Lectures at professional conferences, seminars and workshops. Joint author of 'EC Pensions Law' (Wiley Chancery) and numerous articles in the professional and specialist press.
Prof. Memberships: Law Society, Association of Pensions Lawyers, National Association of Pension Funds.
Career: Qualified in 1986. At *Clyde & Co* 1986-87. Joined *Nicholson Graham & Jones* in 1987 and became a Partner in 1991. Joined *Sacker & Partners* as a partner in 1996.
Personal: Born 21st November 1960. Educated at the University of Southampton 1980-83. Interests include reading and hill-walking. Lives in Hampstead, London.

WALLACE, Keith
Richards Butler, London (0171) 247 6555
Partner specialising in pensions and
professional trusteeship.
Specialisation: Main area of practice covers
pensions and professional trusteeship,
custodianship and investment funds. Acted in
the mineworkers' pensions strike absence
case, 'Cowan v. Charlesworth' (1986), (£100
million); when Bejam employees' benefits were
not honoured by a predator (£5 million) in 1990;
British Telecom disputed pension 'contribution
holiday' (£600 million potential), formation and
authorisation of Britain's first 'Futures' and
'Geared Futures and Options' Unit Trusts 1992-
93 and PIA on introducing regime requiring
financial service industry to compensate for
pension mis-selling (£15bn industry costs)
1994-6. Editor of 'Pension Lawyer' and the
'Trust Deed and Rules Checklist'. Pensions
Commentator of TEN Television Education
Video Service.
Prof. Memberships: Association of Pension
Lawyers (Founding Committee Member), NAPF
Investment Committee (Elected Member 1991-
96), Occupational Pensions Advisory Service
(Council Member & Chairman of Legal Advice
Committee), Association of Corporate Trustees
Pension Committee, Holborn Law Society

(Vice-President 1983-84), Financial Law Panel
(Council and Deputy Chairman), (Financial
dealings with trustees) Working Party.
Career: Qualified in 1971. Partner in *Bird & Bird*
1972-84. Joined *Richards Butler* as a Partner in
1984. Chairman, Maldon Unit Trust Managers
Ltd.

WEST, Robert J.
Baker & McKenzie, London (0171) 919 1000
Partner in Pensions Department.
Specialisation: Principal area of practice
involves advising on all legal aspects of
pensions including trust aspects, litigation,
surpluses, sales and purchases, drafting and
advice to independent trustees. Other area of
work is employee benefits and share schemes.
Acted in South West Trains v. Wightman, The
Times Pension Fund litigation, the Drexel
Pension Scheme litigation and in the sex
discrimination case in the European Court,
Neath v. Hugh Steeper. Contributor on
pensions to Butterworths' Legal Service and
author of articles for Pensions World and
Pensions Management. Addressed many
conferences in UK, USA and Canada.
Prof. Memberships: Law Society, Association
of Pension Lawyers (Member of Main and
Legislative and Parliamentary Committees),
Secretary of International Employee Benefits

Association, Member of the Legal Advice
Committee of the Occupational Pensions
Advisory Service.
Career: Qualified in 1978. Joined *Baker &
McKenzie* in 1982 and became a Partner in
1985.
Personal: Born 1st January 1952. Attended
Maidenhead Grammar School 1963-71 and
Clare College, Cambridge 1971-74. Leisure
pursuits include sports and archaeology. Lives
in Wargrave, Berks.

WHITE, Andrew G.
Rowe & Maw, London (0171) 248 4282
Partner in Pensions Department.
Specialisation: All aspects of law relating to
company and personal pension schemes. Also
handles life insurance, advising insurance
companies on life policies and other products.
Author of 'Pensions Issues in Mergers and
Acquisitions' (FT Law and Tax, 2nd edition
1996); writes a regular monthly article in PLC
Magazine. Frequent speaker at conferences.
Prof. Memberships: Law Society, currently a
member of the Main Committee of the
Association of Pension Lawyers.
Career: Qualified 1974. Joined *Rowe & Maw*
1977, becoming a Partner in 1979.
Personal: Born 1st January 1950. Attended
Manchester Grammar School 1961-68, then
University College, Oxford, 1968-72. Leisure
pursuits include reading. Lives in London.

The SOUTH and WALES

LEADING FIRMS
SOUTH AND WALES

BURGES SALMON Bristol
OSBORNE CLARKE Bristol
EVERSHEDS Cardiff
CLARKS Reading

Burges Salmon (Bristol) (1ptnr/3assts/
1litigation ptnr/1litigation asst) Richard
Leigh, previously named as a leader, has left
the firm; this "must raise some question
marks over their practice." The focus of the
practice is on SERPS and small independent
trusteeships. *Tim Illston* is a "strong all-
rounder with a high profile." **Clients/Work:**
Litigation in the High Court over the
application of surplus on a winding up of a
pension scheme. Setting up a scheme to
mirror the Local Government scheme on
behalf of a recently privatised airport.
Advising two train-operating companies on
the impact of the South-West Trains v
Wightman case on s67 Pensions Act.

Osborne Clarke (Bristol) (2ptnrs/
1cons/1assoc/1asst) The firm historically
occupied top rank in Bristol because of Imperial Tobacco work; it remains very much a
corporate practice. They are thought to be
"going through a transitional phase" with
various personnel changes since last year,
but they are expected to maintain their
profile. Former leader Joachim Steinbach is
working only part-time in pensions as he now
works mainly in education and public law.
The department is now headed by *Mark
Wolmersley*. **Clients/Work:** Appointed to
OPRA's legal advisers panel. Continuing to
act for a number of major pensions clients,
including Imperial Tobacco Pension Fund
and South Western Electricity plc.

Eversheds (Cardiff) (1ptnr 90%/1asst
p/t) The firm does not have a Bristol presence
but has "the only credible pensions lawyer in
Wales" – *Ian Davies* – who is "well-respected
on the far side of the Severn" being
"commercial and pragmatic." **Clients/Work:**
New client, NCM Credit Assurance. Three
Pensions Ombudsman cases. New client,
Bradstock Financial Services as a pensioner
trustee client for which the unit produces
SSAS documentation and general advice.

Clarks (Reading) (1ptnr 70%/1asst)
Based in Reading the firm is not in direct
competition with the other leaders mentioned
in this region. *David Clark* is "quite pro-
active" and known for his independent trustee
work rather than mainstream pensions. Also
provides corporate support. His assistant has
13 years' experience in the industry. **Clients/
Work:** Represented independent trustee in a
reported case regarding forfeiture provisions;
a claim by trustee in bankruptcy to member's
entitlement; K Bull and others v. Hicks and
others In Re: The Trusts of the Scientific
Investment Pension Plan. David Clark acting
as independent trustee alerted OPRA to
failure of trustees of over 400 schemes to
appoint an actuary on incorrect advice given
by life office administering the scheme.

LEADING INDIVIDUALS
SOUTH AND WALES

DAVIES Ian Eversheds
ILLSTON Timothy Burges Salmon
CLARK David Clarks

UP AND COMING

WOLMERSLEY Mark Osborne Clarke

SEE PROFILES AT END OF THIS SECTION

CLARK, David
Clarks, Reading (0118) 958 5321
Partner in Company Department.
Specialisation: Handles all areas of pensions work but has particular experience of advising trustees in conflict situations, advising independent trustees appointed under s23 Pensions Act 1995 and of acting as independent trustee. Also handles corporate insolvency and banking work, advises on the pensions aspects of mergers and acquisitions and advises trustees in bankruptcy on pensions related issues. Acted in 'Clark v. Hicks' (independent trusteeship) and 'Kemble v. Hicks' (independent trustee v. trustees in bankruptcy).
Prof. Memberships: Association of Pension Lawyers.

Career: Qualified in 1983. Admitted as a Solicitor and Barrister in New Zealand in 1979. Worked at *Coward Chance* 1980-84, *Linklaters & Paines* 1984-86 and British Alcan Aluminium plc 1986-88. Joined *Clarks* in 1988, becoming a Partner in 1989.
Personal: Born 20th December 1953. Holds an LLB 1978 and MA (Business Law) 1984. Full time father; mediocre golfer. Lives in Maidenhead.

DAVIES, Ian H.
Eversheds, Cardiff (01222) 471147
Partner in Pensions Unit, Employment, Pensions and Licensing Department.
Specialisation: Handles all aspects of establishing and running pension schemes; documentation; scheme mergers; winding-up;

ownership of surpluses; advice to trustees, acting as independent trustee; and pensions aspects of M&As. Has particular experience of handling multi-scheme mergers. Also handles taxation work, including share option schemes, ESOPs, P.R.P. and business and capital taxation. Has published several articles on pensions and tax issues.
Prof. Memberships: APL.
Career: Qualified in 1984. Joined *Phillips & Buck* (now *Eversheds Cardiff*) in 1982, becoming a Partner in 1988.

ILLSTON, Timothy M.
Burges Salmon, Bristol (0117) 939 2000

WOLMERSLEY, Mark.
Osborne Clarke, Bristol (0117) 927 9209

MIDLANDS and EAST ANGLIA

EDGE & ELLISON Birmingham
EVERSHEDS Derby
WRAGGE & CO Birmingham

EVERSHEDS Birmingham
PINSENT CURTIS Birmingham

BROWNE JACOBSON Nottingham
HEWITSON BECKE + SHAW Northampton

EVERSHEDS Norwich
GARRETTS Birmingham

Edge & Ellison (Birmingham) (4ptnrs/4assts) "A force to be reckoned with" which "makes a big splash." Their independent trustee company is recommended. *Simon Ramshaw* currently heads the national unit. He is described as "a showman, a great character who speaks well and is good with clients" but he is due to become Managing Partner in May 1999. *Richard Davis* is "more of a generalist." *Ian Forrest* is "technical, fair and straight to the point." *Robert Gravill* is also "a quiet steady determined lawyer, rated highly." **Clients/Work:** Appointed, with Government approval, to Royal Devonport Dockyard Pension Scheme, with assets of £600million. Dealing with UK aspects of international demerger project for Dun & Bradstreet. Independent trustee company appointed to OPRA's panel of approved independent trustees.

Eversheds (Derby) (1ptnr/1assoc/1asst) The Derby office has a "distinct practice because of their litigation expertise" and is therefore listed separately from the Birmingham practice. *Giles Orton* "is an out-and-out pensions litigator rather than a main-stream pensions lawyer." He "stands out"

with a national name as "the pensions litigator for the little guy" and the team's reputation rests on him; some criticism that there is no strength in depth. **Clients/Work:** Appointed by the Trustees of Melton Medes (Fletchers) Fund, a £42m fund serving 560 members. Advised an employer on difficulties caused by debt arising on pension scheme winding up under Pensions Act 1995, including the negotiation of compromise of the debt with Trustees of the scheme. Advising the Association of Mirror Pensions on successful complaint to Pensions Ombudsman regarding refusal of Mirror Trustees to release actuarial report.

Wragge & Co (Birmingham) (2ptnrs/3assocs/4assts f/t/1asst p/t) The team only does mainstream pensions work. Praised by clients as "efficient and responsive", they offer a good service. *Vivien Cockerill* stood out this year as receiving widespread praise. She has "the best overall grasp of pensions law." Her "outgoing vivacious character" makes her "the accessible face of Wragges, extra good on the marketing front with clients" combined with being a "good technician with a commercial attitude." *Gerald Hingley* who "built up the department" is also well thought of, "impressive, technically sound." *Sara Hughes* is newly recommended this year as an "assistant who is "excellent, good enough to become a partner." **Clients/Work:** Winning Britannic Assurance as a pensions client, scheme assets approx £750million. Have won 10 out of 14 beauty parades. High volume of work implementing Pensions Act 1995.

Eversheds (Birmingham) (1ptnr/2assocs/2assts) This team does more mainstream pensions work than the Derby office but does not have such a high profile. *Liz Fallon* whilst not having the profile of other leaders is recommended. **Clients/Work:** Increase in appointment of Eversheds Pension Trustees Limited as professional Trustees in non-statutory cases; appointments include Wyko

Group plc and Lumonics Limited. Acting as legal advisors to Law Debenture, independent trustee of Maples Pension Scheme, following receivership of Maples Group. New clients include Pex Plc.

Pinsent Curtis (Birmingham) (2ptnrs/1assoc/2assts/3litigators 50%) Historically strong practice which "did it first in the region." They look after many small self-administered schemes and have a "good historical client base." The house style is one of "attention to detail" and both *Glyn Ryland* and *Daniel Shelley* conform to this style. **Clients/Work:** Successful appeal in the High Court against determination of the Pensions Ombudsman. Continued with £100 million plus scheme merger work. PFI work on public sector and rail sector work.

Browne Jacobson (Nottingham) (1ptnr/1asst) *Kevin Milton* used to be at Wragges, has a "good pedigree and knows his stuff." He does 50% self-generated advice to trustees and independent trustees and 50% corporate support work. **Clients/Work:** Unit concentrated on advice to employers and

COCKERILL Vivien Wragge & Co

GRAVILL Robert Edge & Ellison
HINGLEY Gerald Wragge & Co
ORTON Giles Eversheds
RAMSHAW Simon Edge & Ellison

COLACICCHI Clare Hewitson Becke + Shaw
DAVIS Richard Edge & Ellison
FALLON Liz Eversheds
FORREST Ian Edge & Ellison
RYLAND Glyn Pinsent Curtis
SHELLEY Daniel Pinsent Curtis

CLARKE Trevor Garretts
MILTON Kevin Browne Jacobson
SCOTT Harry Mills & Reeve

HUGHES Sara Wragge & Co

trustees of occupational pension schemes. Firm acts as statutory independent trustee in cases of insolvency and as independent trustee of ongoing schemes.

Hewitson Becke + Shaw (Northampton) (1ptnr/ 2assts/1cons) "A good commercial practice in the second tier." The team is developing a consultancy to advise on alterations to the design of schemes. *Clare Colacicchi* is "excellent." **Clients/Work:** Negotiation of a substantial transfer payment on management buyout of Power Division of Texas Instruments and establishment of a new pensions scheme. Providing ongoing pensions advice relating to the Pensions Act and other issues for the final salary scheme for 1500 employees of a large private hospital. Acting for a major independent trustee in relation to a complaint to the Ombudsman and High Court proceedings.

Eversheds (Norwich) (1ptnr p/t; 1asst p/t) **Clients/Work:** Pensions Act 1995 has resulted in expansion of pensions work dealt with in East Anglia on instructions from both employers and Scheme Trustees, especially in reviewing and updating Scheme Rules and increasing the amount of due diligence work to be carried out on commercial deals and revision of pension provisions following completion of acquisitions.

Garretts (Birmingham) (1ptnr/2assts) The department is run by *Trevor Clarke* "a pensions personality" who "set up the Edge & Ellison practice" and is "robust and commercial as well as being good technically." While he has "a reputation for making waves" he appears to have gone relatively quiet recently. **Clients/Work:** Acting for Finning(UK)Ltd on acquisition of entire issued share capital of H. Leverton Ltd from Unilever UK Holdings Ltd, wholly owned subsidiary of Unilever plc worth over £50,000,000. Advising Cirqual plc on purchase of BWMP (Holdings) Limited for consideration of £36,000,000.

Harry Scott of Mills & Reeve also has a strong personal reputation in Norwich.

LEADERS' PROFILES · MIDLANDS AND EAST ANGLIA

CLARKE, Trevor C.
Garretts, Birmingham (0121) 698 9000
Pensions Partner.
Specialisation: Handles all legal aspects of occupational and personal pension schemes including Revenue unapproved schemes. Particular expertise in privatisation work involving statutory schemes (e.g. LGPS) Scheme mergers and wind-ups. General trouble - shooting. Considerable experience in dealing with Directors small self-administered schemes-recognised by Inland Revenue Pension Schemes Office as pensioner trustee - dealing with 'hospital cases' and up front commission abuses on earmarked policies. General advice to employers, trustees and members. Dealing with 'exit values' from insurance products particularly deposit administration and with profit deferred annuity contracts-reviewing surrender penalties and market value adjustments. Drafting pension deeds and documents; Vetting or drafting Financial Services Act Investment Management Agreements.
Prof. Memberships: Law Society. Full member of the Association of Pension Lawyers (a Founder member in 1984) and the 'Over 21 Club'. Associate of the Chartered Insurance Institute (B'ham Institute Prize Winner). Chartered Insurance Practitioner.
Career: Life and Pensions Consultant before qualifying as a Solicitor. Served Articles with *Edge & Ellison* and became a Partner in 1988. Joined *Simpson Curtis* as a Partner 1990. May 1994 joined *Garretts*. Has been a full time pensions lawyer for over twelve years.
Personal: Aged 49. Bachelor of Laws (2.1) Birmingham. Keen sportsman. Ex First Class Rugby (Moseley). Now windsurfs, and is a fanatical skier and mountain biker. Has daughter Alice aged 8.

COCKERILL, Vivien
Wragge & Co, Birmingham (0121) 233 1000
Specialisation: Acting for trustees and employers in relation to approved and unapproved pension arrangements.
Prof. Memberships: National Association of Pension Fund local group committee, OPAS Adviser.
Career: Articled *Sackers & Partners*. Qualified 1987. Partner at *Wragge & Co* from 1992.
Personal: Born 1961.

COLACICCHI, Clare
Hewitson Becke + Shaw, Northampton (01604) 233233
Specialisation: Specialises pension and trust law. Main areas of pensions practice is advice to trustees and employers relating to the establishment, alteration, merger or termination of occupational pension schemes; questions relating to surpluses and deficits; disputes; including complaints to the Ombudsman.
Prof. Memberships: Association of Pension Lawyers. Member of Council of the Society of Trust and Estate Practitioners.
Career: Qualified 1983. *Macfarlanes* 1981-9. Joined *Hewitson Becke & Shaw* 1989. Became a partner in 1990.
Personal: Born 3 August 1958. Attended Somerville College, Oxford.

DAVIS, Richard G.L.
Edge & Ellison, Leicester (0116) 247 0123
Partner in Pensions Department.
Specialisation: Specialises in occupational pension schemes. Covers documentation, transactional work, scheme mergers, reconstructions and wind ups, insolvency advice and independent trusteeship. Has handled several major scheme mergers.
Prof. Memberships: NAPF; APL; Law Society.
Career: Qualified in 1977. At *Overbury Steward & Eaton* 1978-88. Joined *Eversheds (Wells & Hind)* in 1988 and was a Partner 1989-1997. Joined *Edge & Ellison* in 1997.
Personal: Born 29th April 1952. Attended Leeds University 1970-73.

FALLON, Liz
Eversheds, Birmingham (0121) 233 2001
Partner
Specialisation: Handles all aspects of pensions law including transactional work, scheme reorganisation, advice to insolvency practitioners, establishment of schemes and scheme documentation, independent trusteeship. Has spoken at the Institute of Actuaries Annual Conference and is a regular lecturer for a professional training organisation. Also regularly involved in Trustee training courses.
Prof. Memberships: Law Society, Association of Pension Lawyers, National Association of Pension Funds.
Career: Qualified 1983. Joined *Eversheds* 1981. Became a partner 1997. Heads up pensions team in Birmingham.
Personal: Born 17.2.1959. Attended University of Kent, BA Law and German. Interests include keeping up with 2 young sons and horse riding.

FORREST, Ian
Edge & Ellison, Birmingham (0121) 200 2001
Head of the Pensions Department.
Specialisation: Practice includes the full range of pensions law work including transactional support, documentation, scheme mergers, trusteeship and 'special projects'. Clients include several public companies, a national sports association, charities and insurance companies.
Prof. Memberships: APL, PMI, IPEBLA.
Career: Qualified with *Edge & Ellison* in 1989. Made Associate in 1994 and Partner in 1995.
Personal: Born 2 April 1951. Educated at Loughborough University (1968-71). Law degree gained through part time study.

GRAVILL, Robert
Edge & Ellison, Birmingham (0121) 200 2001
Specialisation: Pensions. The firm has a national pensions practice with partners in Birmingham, London and Leicester and is one of the largest teams of specialist pension lawyers in the country. It acts for over 40 listed public companies, the trustees of many substantial pension funds and most of the leading pension consultancies. Robert is based in the Birmingham office and acts for many of the firms major clients. The four areas he works in are documentation, special project work (such as scheme wind-ups, mergers and surplus exercises) insolvency related pensions issues and trusteeships. He is Managing Director of *Edge & Ellison* Trustees Limited – a large independent provider of trustee services and speaks and writes regularly on pension issues.
Career: Educated Southampton University (LL.B) and College of Law, Guildford.
Personal: Married, lives in Nuneaton and cites his hobbies as walking, skiing and travel.

HINGLEY, Gerald
Wragge & Co, Birmingham (0121) 233 1000
Specialisation: Provides advice and documentation for all aspects of pensions, including the pensions aspects of corporate transactions. Acted for the trustees in the case

of 'Davis v. Richards and Wallington' (1990). Frequent speaker at seminars. Head of *Wragge & Co's* team of pension lawyers.
Prof. Memberships: Association of Pensions Lawyers, Law Society.
Career: Articled *Vizards*. Qualified in 1970. Partner at *Wragge & Co* from 1974.
Personal: Born 2nd July 1943.

HUGHES, Sara
Wragge & Co, Birmingham (0121) 233 1000
Specialisation: Associate in the pensions team. Specialises in legal advice to employers and trustees. Experience covers the Local Government Pension Scheme and the National Health Service Pension Scheme, and recent large scale mergers.
Prof. Memberships: Association of Pension Lawyers
Career: Articled at *Pinsent & Co*. Qualified 1985. Joined *Wragge & Co* in 1985. Associate *Wragge & Co* 1988.
Personal: Born 1961.

MILTON, Kevin
Browne Jacobson, Nottingham
(0115) 950 0055
Specialisation: Advice to trustees, employers and members on the legal aspects of the establishment and operation of occupational schemes. This includes preparing the documentation establishing schemes and altering schemes to meet changing circumstances and legislative requirements.
Prof. Memberships: Association of Pension Lawyers; IPEBLA (International Pension & Employee Benefits Lawyers Association); Law Society; National Association of Pension Funds.
Career: Articled at *Davis, Campbell & Co*. Qualified 1984. Joined *Wragge & Co* in 1987 becoming Associate in 1990. Joined *Browne Jacobson* as Partner in 1995.
Personal: Born 31 March 1960. Married with 2 children. Hobbies – hockey, skiing and scuba diving.

ORTON, Giles A.C.
Eversheds, Derby 01332 360992
Head of Commercial Litigation Department in the East Midlands.

Specialisation: Main area of practice is pensions litigation, conducting disputes over pension schemes, particularly regarding surplus and winding up. Other area of practice is employment: industrial tribunals, wrongful dismissal and restrictive covenants. Acted in 'Falconer v. Aslef and NUR', Imperial Tobacco Mirror Group. Lloyd's Bank Pension Scheme Case. Author of numerous articles on pensions law. Has addressed a wide range of seminars and conferences, also making TV and radio appearances.
Prof. Memberships: Chairman of Pensions Litigation Committee of Association of Pension Lawyers. East Midlands Committee, NAPF.
Career: Qualified in 1983. Worked at *Broomheads* from 1981, becoming an Associate in 1986. Joined *Evershed Wells & Hind* in 1987, Associate 1988 and Partner in 1989.
Personal: Born 18th August 1959. Attended King Edward VII School, Sheffield 1970-77; The Queen's College, Oxford (Hastings Exhibition) 1977-80 and Chester College of Law 1980-81. Derby City Councillor 1988-92.

RAMSHAW, Simon
Edge & Ellison, Birmingham
(0121) 200 2001
Partner in Pensions Department.
Specialisation: Main area of practice is pensions, covering documentation, transactional work, scheme mergers, reconstructions and wind-ups, insolvency advice and independent trusteeship. Has handled several major scheme mergers; is independent trustee to schemes run by a national clothing company, two quoted public companies and a professional practice which is a world leader in its field. Author of various articles for publications issued by pension consultancies, and of a variety of easy-to-read Technical Guides issued by the firm. Regular lecturer for Professional Associations and pension consultancies. Organiser of and speaker at various trustee training courses.
Prof. Memberships: NAPF, APL, IPEBLA, Law Society.
Career: Qualified 1981, working at *Robert Muckle* from 1979 to 1983. Then joined *Edge &*

Ellison, becoming a Partner in 1986.
Personal: Born 28th January 1958. Attended Newcastle upon Tyne University, 1975-78. Member of the *Edge & Ellison* Main Board, Chief Executive of Trustee Company. Active member of local Church. Keen photographer, blues aficionado and guitar player. Lives in Birmingham.

RYLAND, Glyn
Pinsent Curtis, Birmingham (0121) 200 1050
Partner in Pensions Unit, Birmingham
Specialisation: All aspects of UK and Hong Kong pensions law. Scheme set-ups, mergers and wind-ups; statutory compliance advice; FURBS and international aspects; pensions litigation and Ombudsman work; documentation and communication; investment management and custody; pensions on corporate deals, pensions and financial services mis-selling.
Prof. Memberships: Association of Pension Lawyers (Regional Committee Member). Admitted in England and Wales and Hong Kong.
Career: Articles *Eversheds*, Cardiff *(Phillips and Buck)*. Qualified Feb 1988. 1988-December 1991 *Herbert Smith*. January 1992-94 *Johnson Stokes & Master*, Hong Kong. 1994 to present *Pinsent Curtis*. Partner 1995.
Personal: Born 1962.

SHELLEY, Daniel
Pinsent Curtis, Birmingham (0121) 200 1050
Specialisation: All aspects of Pension Law.
Prof. Memberships: Association of Pension Lawyers.
Career: Articles – *Slaughter and May*; *Pinsent Curtis* – Partner 1995.
Personal: Born 1958.

SCOTT, Harry
Mills & Reeve, Norwich +44 (0)1603 660155
Specialisation: Pensions i.e. law and practice relating to occupational pension schemes including documentation, advice and acting as a pension scheme trustee through *Mills & Reeve's* corporate trustee, Francis House Trustees Limited. Full member of the Association of Pension Lawyers.

NORTH WEST

Addleshaw Booth & Co (1ptnr: f/t /1ptnr: p/t/1asst) A "strong commercial practice" with a large client base. They rely on "one or two reasonably large company schemes" as well as transactional work.

David Griffiths is Head of Department. *Francis Shackleton* has "gravitas and long-established contacts." **Clients/Work:** Continuing to advise on pensions aspects of scheme merger for Akzo Nobel. Continuing to advise trustees of Ciba-Geigy Pension Scheme on demerger of pension schemes.

Dibb Lupton Alsop (1ptnr/3assts) "Up there on the basis of their Liverpool reputation where they are absolutely pre-eminent." The Manchester office is not quite as well-established and last year lost Margaret Cox to the Leeds office. Have "super clients." The house style is "cooperative, not point-scoring." *David Wright*, chiefly based in Liverpool, has inherited the mantle. He is "a thoughtful lawyer who is calm with clients and has been operating from a rock-solid pensions practice for years." *Jeremy Harris* is newly recommended this year. **Clients/Work:** Secured pensions work for a

major UK friendly society. Secured pensions work for the UK arm of a major worldwide foods conglomerate. Started to do pensions work for James Fisher & Sons Plc.

Eversheds (1ptnr/3assts/1 litigation ptnr/1 litigation asst) This "good team" concentrates mainly on corporate work, particularly MBOs. *Ronald Graham* is a "dark horse, a quiet type" with a corporate background. **Clients/Work:** Consolidation of nine UK pension schemes for Akzo Nobel to form a single (£115m) fund. Advising bidders for rail franchises in relation to ongoing pension obligations. Advising Bradstock Trustee Services Limited in respect of a number of independent Trusteeship appointments.

Davies Arnold Cooper (1ptnr/3assts) The team does mainly independent trustee work; their company DAC Trustees Limited has been appointed to the panel of OPRA. *Patrick Kennedy* is "enthusiastic, imaginative and good to work with." **Clients/Work:** Acting for Trustees of London Scottish Bank plc Pension Schemes in relation to investment management agreement with their investment advisers. Acting for Trustees of Kemira Coatings Limited Retirement Benefits Plan in relation to legal aspects of their custodianship and investment management arrangements. Representing an insolvency practitioner of Pannell Kerr Forster in pensions-related Personal Investment Authority Ombudsman Application.

Halliwell Landau (1ptnr f/t;1ptnr p/t; 1asst p/t;1litigation ptnr) Do mainly corporate support work and independent trusteeship; "not really a team" since only *Anne Taylor* is full-time. She is a "good marketeer" with an "aggressive style." **Clients/Work:** Advising on the pension scheme of new client

British Regional Airlines. Pro bono work for pensioners' action group relating to the scheme of a large listed company, encompassing not only legal advice but practical advice on lobbying for benefit and other improvements. Large amount of work involving compliance with Pensions Act 1995.

Hammond Suddards (1ptnr/2assts) Small team looking to recruit with a relatively low profile in the region. *Andrew Ashley-Taylor* took over the mantle when Anne Taylor left to go to Halliwell Landau. **Clients/Work:** Litigation and dispute work. Undertaking independent trusteeship of several pensions schemes.

Davies Wallis Foyster (2ptnrs) Perceived as doing mainly corporate support. Have one specialist. **Clients/Work:** Advising on pension aspects of Perkins Engines

Business acquisition by Caterpillar International. Advising receiver of H & K Robertson on pension issues. Pensions support on acquisition of F E Barber Limited.

LEADERS' PROFILES • NORTH WEST

ASHLEY-TAYLOR, Andrew
Hammond Suddards, Manchester
(0161) 830 5000
Specialisation: The law and practice relating to occupational pension schemes and other forms of retirement provision in the UK. Covers a wide variety of pension disciplines for employers, employees and trustees including corporate transactional work, project and merger advice, documentation and pension dispute resolution. Speaks regularly at seminars and writes articles. Qualified mediator for Alternative Dispute Resolution procedures.
Prof. Memberships: Association of Pension Lawyers, Associate of the Pensions Management Institute, Member of the North West Group of the NAPF.
Career: Qualified November 1984 and became an Associate of the Pensions Management Institute in 1990. Worked in private practice to 1988 then joined *Baker & Mckenzie*, London to specialise in Pensions law.
Personal: Golf, travel, cycling, music and theatre.

GRAHAM, Ronald
Eversheds, Manchester (0161) 832 6666
Specialisation: All aspects of Pension Law, including trust documentation and advice (approved and unapproved schemes), sales and acquisitions, scheme mergers, statutory schemes and independent trusteeship.
Prof. Memberships: Full member NAPL, Committee Member NAPF Manchester Group, NWAPL, Law Society.
Career: Qualified 1985 at *Alexander Tatham* (now *Eversheds* Manchester) and became a partner in 1990.
Personal: Attended Kendal Grammar School, Merton College, Oxford (MA in Jurisprudence) and Corpus Christi College, Cambridge (Diploma in Criminology). Interests include theatre, birds and travel. Lives in Hayfield, Derbyshire.

GRIFFITHS, David
Addleshaw Booth & Co, Manchester (0161) 934 6000
Partner in Pensions Department, Commercial Group.
Specialisation: Pensions law, covering advice

to individuals, employers and/or trustees in relation to the maintenance and conduct of occupational pension schemes, scheme mergers and reconstructions, contentious pensions issues and the pensions aspects of mergers and acquisitions. Provides full legal document service.
Prof. Memberships: Association of Pension Lawyers, A.T.T.
Career: Qualified as a solicitor in 1990 with the firm. Associate 1993. Partner 1996.
Personal: Born 15th February 1962. Educated at Bolton School and the University of Edinburgh, (M.A. English Language and Literature). Interests include music, literature, hill-walking and badminton. Lives in Bolton.

HARRIS, Jeremy
Dibb Lupton Alsop, Manchester
(0345) 262728
Specialisation: Full spectrum of pensions work, including pensions aspects of corporate transactions, drafting definitive and other documentation, advisory including Pensions Act 1995, trustee duties.
Prof. Memberships: Member of the Association of Pension Lawyers.
Career: Associate with Dibb Lupton Alsop since 1994. M.A. Oxon (Jurisprudence) 1986. Admitted as solicitor 1990 (formerly barrister called to the bar 1986). Formerly with Engineering Employers Federation 1987-89.
Personal: Born 1964. Married, one son. Regular church-goer. Church work. Cinema/theatre. Cricket. Lives in Cheadle, Cheshire.

KENNEDY, Patrick
Davies Arnold Cooper, Manchester
(0161) 839 8396
Specialisation: All aspects of pensions law and practice, full pensions documentation, including definitive deeds and rules, independent trustees services through Davies Arnold Cooper Trustees Ltd both statutory and ongoing advice to trustees and employers powers and duties, pensions mergers and wind-ups, pension aspects of commercial transactions and representative beneficiary and other pensions litigation.
Prof. Memberships: Director – Davies Arnold

Cooper Trustees Ltd; Full Member – Association of Pension Lawyers; Formerly served on the Committee of the National Association of Pension Funds; Manchester Group and the Barber Committee of the Association of Pension Lawyers.
Career: Highlights of last year: North American owned pension wind-up; representative beneficiary action re: pension fund surplus; major pensions fund merger activity; Davies Arnold Cooper Trustees pension scheme wind-ups and related issues; Pensions Act 1995 and related regulations advice and implementation.

SHACKLETON, Francis
Addleshaw Booth & Co, Manchester
(0161) 934 6000
Partner in Pensions Department, Commercial Group.
Specialisation: Main area of practice is pensions law, handling take-overs and mergers, scheme amalgamations, formation of schemes, documentation, compliance and trusteeship matters. Has lectured and presented seminars on pensions. Currently holds office as Pension Scheme Trustee and as Trustee of private and charitable trusts.
Prof. Memberships: Association of Pension Lawyers, National Association of Pension Funds.
Career: Joined the firm in 1963. Qualified in 1965 and became a Partner in 1969.
Personal: Born 2nd January 1940. Attended Stowe School 1953-58, then St. John's College, Cambridge 1959-62. Governor of Manchester High School for Girls. Lives in Rochdale.

TAYLOR, Anne
Halliwell Landau, Manchester
(0161) 835 3003
Partner and head of Pensions Department.
Specialisation: Specialises in winding-up and merger of pension schemes, advice on the pensions aspects of transfers of business and the impact of the Transfer of Undertakings legislation, dealing with litigious pensions issues including claims against companies, advising on potential breaches of the Pensions Act 1995, actions involving the Pensions Ombudsman. Anne is a director of Halliwell Landau Trustee Limited, an independent

corporate trustee established for the purpose of acting as independent trustee in those situations where it is required or deemed desirable.
Prof. Memberships: NAPF, PMI, APL.
Career: Qualified 5 September 1990.
Personal: Educated at Bradford Girls School. Recreations include sailing, antiques, wine.

WRIGHT, David
Dibb Lupton Alsop, Liverpool
(0345) 262 728
DDI 0151 237 4731
Pensions Partner.
Specialisation: Handles all aspects of pensions law, including advice to industry-wide schemes, plc's, trustees and individuals. Work also includes mergers and acquisitions, corporate and business transfers and pensions litigation. Contributes to pensions periodicals.
Prof. Memberships: Law Society, Association

of Pension Lawyers and an Associate of the Pensions Management Institute (APMI).
Career: Qualified in 1986. Articled with *March Pearson & Skelton*. Joined *Dibb Lupton Alsop* in July 1990. Became Partner in 1995 and now responsible for pensions in the North West. A member of the Legislation Committee of the Society of Pension Consultants and a senior examiner for the PMI.
Personal: Born 19th November 1961. Lives in Orrell, near Wigan.

NORTH EAST

LEADING FIRMS • NORTH EAST
ADDLESHAW BOOTH & CO Leeds
DIBB LUPTON ALSOP Leeds/Sheffield
EVERSHEDS Leeds
HAMMOND SUDDARDS Leeds

HIGHLY REGARDED FIRMS
Dickinson Dees Newcastle upon Tyne
Nabarro Nathanson Sheffield
Walker Morris Leeds
Pinsent Curtis Leeds
Wrigleys Leeds

Addleshaw Booth & Co (2ptnrs/2assts) Seen to be at the top in Leeds. The "extremely energetic and enthusiastic"*Neville Peel* "has a well-known name and is a decent operator." *Rachel Rawnsley* is "competent, sensible and approaches problems commercially." **Clients/Work:** Drafting new set of pension scheme deeds and rules and "opt-out" procedures for member nominated trustees where principal employer of public sector scheme was also sole trustee. Pensions aspects of a complex international and multi-jurisdictional sale of a business, dealing with pension rights across Europe and in the US. Negotiating as independent trustee improved scheme benefits for several hundred members and transfer of all scheme assets and liabilities to a PLC employer's ongoing scheme.

Dibb Lupton Alsop (1ptnr/1cons/ 1assoc/2assts) "Good in parts"; Leeds is rated as better than Sheffield. Current personnel are thought to be "stretched extremely thin" after the loss of Tim Knight from Sheffield. *Margaret Cox* is "a tough negotiator, the person to go to if you want a deal done by midnight tonight." *Martin Lee* has a good reputation. *Kate Payne*, new to our lists, is a lawyer "in the Margaret Cox mould; she will get a deal done quickly." **Clients/Work:** Acting for trustees of Yorkshire Tyne Tees Television Pension Scheme in relation to merger of scheme into Granada Group Pension Scheme. Advising trustee of BASF UK Group Pension Scheme (new client this year) on the set-up of a new

money purchase section of their scheme combined with the conversion of part of the scheme from final salary to money purchase terms. Advising trustees of a £600m scheme in the financial services sector on a merger.

Eversheds (1ptnr/2assts) A stable team, rated in Leeds. *Raymond Ainscoe* is much admired as a "very good technician, quiet and analytical." **Clients/Work:** Drafting of unfunded contractual arrangements and all associated documents for clients. Advice on potential demergers and mergers of group schemes.

Hammond Suddards (1ptnr/3assts) A young team hit by the loss of Richard Archer. *Catherine McKenna* is now running the pensions practice; she is well-regarded although she "doesn't have the same experience as Richard." **Clients/Work:** Establishment of Yorkshire Water Pension Plan. Establishment of new Pension Scheme for United Engineering Forgings Limited for 2000+employees following buy-out from British Steel. Advisers to Northern Electric Group Trustees of the Electricity Supply Pension Scheme.

Dickinson Dees (2ptnrs/4assts) Well-regarded Newcastle firm, not really coming into contact with the Leeds firms. Act for a number of industry-wide schemes. Appointed to OPRA panel. **Clients/Work:** Appointed to national panel of Occupational Pensions Regulatory Authority following nationwide tender exercise. Advising managers of Railways Pension Scheme and associated rail industry pension arrangements.

Nabarro Nathanson (2ptnrs p/t;1asst f/t; 4assts p/t) Reputation is seen to "rest partly on the brand name of the London office." *Margaret Allison* is newly recommended as "a gritty Northerner"who "knows her stuff." **Clients/Work:** Implementing provisions of Pensions Act 1995. Providing audit services to new and existing clients in respect of Pensions Act compliance and updating scheme documentation in light of new regulatory regime.

Walker Morris (1ptnr/1asst) The firm "benefits from being second player to the big names in Leeds; they get lots of conflict and referral work." *Andrew Turnbull* was recom-

mended. **Clients/Work:** Major scheme merger of two schemes, totalling over £600million in assets. Acting as trustee and advising in creation of a major banks qualifying share trust to provide employee benefits.

Pinsent Curtis (1ptnrs/1assts) The team's profile seems somewhat "diminished since Trevor Clarke went to Garretts." **Clients/Work:** Advising on pensions aspects of AM Paper Group Limited deal – the North's largest private equity deal last year. Trustee of Bitmac Ltd Pension & Life Assurance Scheme, including new trust deed and election of member-nominated trustees.

Wrigleys (2ptnrs/1cons p/t) The firm does not set out to service the commercial client, but mainly acts as independent trustee or gives advice to trustees needing independent advice. The department is run by two well-respected partners. The "well thought of" *Richard Archer* took the private client work from Hammond Suddards when he left; *Timothy Knight* is the "best in terms of technicality, very clued up." However neither lawyer has been seen much in the field since the move. **Clients/Work:** Brought in to advise trustees of a PLC which thought it had achieved equalisation but the process was flawed. Acting as trustee to a number of ongoing pensions schemes. Advised on winding up of final salary schemes.

LEADING INDIVIDUALS NORTH EAST
AINSCOE Raymond Eversheds
COX Margaret Dibb Lupton Alsop
LEE Martin Dibb Lupton Alsop
MCKENNA Catherine Hammond Suddards
PEEL Neville Addleshaw Booth & Co
RAWNSLEY Rachel Addleshaw Booth & Co
ARCHER Richard Wrigleys
KNIGHT Timothy Wrigleys
TURNBULL Andrew Walker Morris

UP AND COMING
ALLISON Margaret Nabarro Nathanson
PAYNE Kate Dibb Lupton Alsop

AINSCOE, Raymond
Eversheds, Leeds (0113) 243 0391
Partner in Commercial Department.
Specialisation: Area of practice is pensions. Contributed to Pensions World and Pensions Management. Lectured to Leeds Metropolitan University. Addressed APL, NAPF and PMI conferences.
Career: Qualified 1980 with *Stephenson Harwood*. 1983 joined *Nicholson Graham & Jones*. Joined *Hepworth & Chadwick* 1985. Partner 1987.
Personal: Born 28th April 1954. Attended Bolton School 1965-72, St. Catherine's College, Oxford (BA) 1972-75, B.C.L. 1977. Trustee of Yorkshire Spinal Deformity Trust, Leeds. Leisure pursuits include Italian racing motorcycles. Author of 4 books.

ALLISON, Margaret
Nabarro Nathanson, Sheffield
(0114) 279 4000
Specialisation: Work covers almost every aspect of pension law, including advising trustees and companies on the re-organisation of schemes and the up-dating of scheme documentation. In the last year, has advised on the pension organisations of disposals by several plcs. Enjoys speaking engagements and trustee training.
Prof. Memberships: Full APL member.
Career: Qualified 1987. Specialised in pensions since 1988. Joined *Nabarro Nathanson* 1994 to establish their Sheffield pension team.
Personal: Born 1962. Has lived and worked in Sheffield since 1985. Interests include horses and cats.

ARCHER, J.Richard
Wrigleys, Leeds (0113) 244 6100
Consultant.
Specialisation: Has been involved in pensions work since the early 1980s. Former Head of *Hammond Suddards*' Pensions Unit. Worked on Maxwell case. Former Head of Private Trust Tax and Probate Department: still handles such work. Trustee of several plc Pension Schemes. Has addressed several internal and external seminars. Joint author of Pensions The New Law.
Prof. Memberships: Association of Pension Lawyers, NAPF, Society of Pension Consultants (Yorkshire Committee Member).
Career: Qualified 1969 (Law Society Prizeman). Articled at *Kirbys* 1965-69. Assistant at *Wells & Hind* 1969-71, and at *Linklaters & Paines* 1971-75. Joined *Hammond Suddards* in 1975, becoming a Partner in 1977. Joined *Wrigleys* 1997 as a consultant.
Personal: Born 27th March 1943. Attended Rugby School 1956-61, then Cambridge University 1961-64. Charity Organiser. Leisure interests include running, reading and walking. Lives in Ilkley.

COX, Margaret E.
Dibb Lupton Alsop, Leeds (0345) 262728
Specialisation: Pensions.
Prof. Memberships: Association of Pension

Lawyers.
Career: BA (Oxon). Admitted 1991. Partner: *Dibb Lupton Alsop* since 1994.

KNIGHT, Timothy
Wrigleys, Leeds (0113) 244 6100
Partner.
Specialisation: Principal areas of practice are pensions and private client law. Extensive experience in pensions with a particular emphasis on acting for trustees concerning occupational pension schemes. Also has estate planning, private client and company/commercial experience.
Prof. Memberships: Association of Pension Lawyers (Former Member of Legislative and Parliamentary Committee).
Career: Computer analyst with Rolls Royce 1966-71. Qualified in 1974 while with *Bells* in Farnham. Joined *Dibb Lupton* in 1976 and became a Partner in 1978. Moved to *Wrigleys* 1 May 1997.
Personal: Born 1948. Educated Ampleforth College (Scholar) Worcester College Oxford (Exhibitioner).

LEE, Martin P.W.
Dibb Lupton Alsop, Sheffield
(0114) 283 3247
Specialisation: Consultant for the firm's Pensions Team. A leading practitioner in pensions law in the South Yorkshire area since the early 1980's. Trustee of a number of pension schemes. A director of Fountain Trustee Ltd, the firm's independent pension scheme trustee company.
Career: Qualified 1966.
Personal: Born 24.5.39.

MCKENNA, Catherine
Hammond Suddards, Leeds
(0113) 284 7000
Partner in Pensions Department.
Specialisation: All work relating to occupational pension schemes. General advice work, including documentation, sales and acquisitions, mergers, insolvency advice, FURBS and trusteeship. Regular speaker at seminars and co-author of "Pensions – The New Law" (Jordans).
Prof. Memberships: Association of Pension Lawyers, National Association of Pension Funds, Associate of the Pensions Management Institute, Society of Pension Consultants.
Career: Educated at Nottingham University (LLB Hons) and Chester Law School (2nd class honours). Qualified 1989. Joined *Alsop Wilkinson* in Manchester and moved to *Hammond Suddards*, Leeds in January 1994. Committee member NE NAPF and Chairman NE PMI.
Personal: Born 1964. Interests include socialising, food, wine, watching sport. Lives in Ilkley.

PAYNE, Kate
Dibb Lupton Alsop, Sheffield (0345) 262728
Specialisation: Advises corporate clients and trustees on all aspects of ongoing pension schemes and schemes in winding-up.

Prof. Memberships: Full member of the Association of Pension Lawyers Law Society.
Career: Qualified with *Rowe & Maw[IT-}* and left to join *Ashurst Morris Crisp*. Joined *Dibb Lupton Alsop* in 1995.
Personal: Born 12th May 1962. Educated at Oxford University.

PEEL, Neville
Addleshaw Booth & Co, Leeds
(0113) 209 2000
Partner in Pensions Department, Commercial Group.
Specialisation: Advises employers and trustees regarding all aspects of ongoing occupational pension schemes. Complete service to insolvency practitioners including independent statutory trusteeships. Co-author of 'Pensions and Insurance on Family Breakdown' and 'Pension Schemes Act 1993'.
Career: Qualified in 1967. Previous employment: CEGB, Midlands HQ 1967; Chairman's Staff. CIBA UK 1967-69; Group Secretary and Executive Director of James Neill Holdings plc, Sheffield; Joined the firm as Pensions Partner in 1990.
Personal: Born 27th May 1940. Educated at Manchester University. Lives in Sheffield.

RAWNSLEY, Rachel
Addleshaw Booth & Co, Leeds
(0113) 209 2000
Partner in Pensions Department, Commercial Group
Specialisation: Advises corporate clients and trustees on all aspects of ongoing pension schemes, setting up new schemes, winding up and merging established schemes. Advises insolvency practitioners, including on independent statutory trusteeships. Co-author of 'The Pension Schemes Act 1993' (Sweet & Maxwell). Editor of 'An Introduction to Pensions Law' written and published by the University of Northumbria.
Prof. Memberships: Association of Pensions Lawyers, National Association of Pension Funds.
Career: Qualified with *Allen & Overy* in 1989. Joined the firm in January 1993.
Personal: Born in February 1965. Educated at Cambridge University 1983-86 (MA in Law). Lives in Ilkley.

TURNBULL, Andrew D.C.
Walker Morris, Leeds (0113) 283 2500
Specialisation: Practice covers the full range of pension work and includes creation and administration of schemes, scheme mergers, transactions and wind ups whether acting as an individual independent trustee or through Walker Morris Trustees Limited.
Prof. Memberships: North Eastern Group of the Association of Pension Lawyers.
Career: Qualified 1983. Joined *Walker Morris* after qualification becoming a partner in 1985.
Personal: Born 19th April 1957. Educated at Shrewsbury and Birmingham University. Interests include golf, tennis and keep fit.

SCOTLAND

Bishop and Robertson Chalmers (3ptnrs/1asst) The department has "a different style from the other leaders; smaller in terms of volume and quality;" don't deal with large schemes but are based around smaller schemes and independent trustee work rather than corporate work. The house style is seen as "more traditional" than other firms. *Iain Talman* is "technically sound." *June Crombie* is also recommended. **Clients/Work:** Independent trustee company appointed to board of trustee company on Rosyth Royal Dockyard Pension Scheme, valued at over £300million. Firm serving on OPRA's legal panel.

Maclay Murray & Spens (1ptnr/1assoc/4assts) Previously seen to be "at the top in terms of volume of business and commercial clout," the team is "instructed by the biggest corporate names; listed plcs and multinationals"and has a large number of scheme clients as well as doing lots of transactional work. "Merger king"*Andrew Fleming* is "a main mover and shaker." Former leader Marcus Hellyer has retired and *Peter Trotter* is now at MacRoberts setting up a new practice. In return, however, the

Maclays practice has gained *Sue Beaumont* ("impressive") from MacRoberts plus two of her assistants. She spent some years at Scottish Amicable and is "setting the world alight" with recommendations from London as well as from the local marketplace. **Clients/Work:** Significant new clients: Coates Viyella; £1.1bn assets and Dunn Wilson. Independent legal advice to Trustees of the Bank of Scotland Staff Pension Scheme; £1bn assets.

Shepherd & Wedderburn WS (1ptnr/1assoc/2assts) The "dominant Edinburgh players, acting for corporate big guns."*Andrew Holehouse* who is currently Chair of the Association of Pensions Lawyers in Scotland, has a "commercial approach, takes a view and is easy to deal with."Associate *Louisa Knox* is also "worthy of mention." The two of them "make a particularly effective team, good at responding to challenging situations." **Clients/Work:** Involved in restructuring of public company's group arrangements. Dealing with Pensions Ombudsman complaints.

Burness (Edinburgh: 1ptnr/1assoc/1asst. Glasgow: 1ptnr) Pensions work grew up out of the trusts practice. They are "reasonable corporate players" although smaller than other practices. *Margaret Meehan* is the partner in the Edinburgh office; "elder statesman" *Alister Sutherland* in Glasgow specialises in pensions litigation work, although he combines this with his corporate tax work. **Clients/Work:** Advising Standard Life on difficult/ground-breaking technical matters. Acting for major maritime service company in significant merger and dealing with transfers to and from four pensions schemes. Individual partners are pro-

fessional trustees of professional trusteeships with a total value of over £400m, largest being Scottish Nuclear.

McGrigor Donald (1ptnrs p/t; 3assts p/t) Their work is corporate based and "comparable with Maclays in terms of style of work"although practitioners work part time in pensions. *Ian Gordon* is "extremely able," has "a good balance of corporate and technical expertise" and "gets to the point and has a practical commercial point of view." **Clients/Work:** Joy Manufacturing Holdings – Court of Session litigation on distribution of surplus; Rosyth Royal Dockyard – advising trustees on privatisation issues.

Tods Murray WS A highly regarded firm, building up its pensions practice which although "on the fringes" is newly mentioned this year.

LEADERS' PROFILES · SCOTLAND

BEAUMONT, Sue
Maclay Murray & Spens, Glasgow
(0141) 248 5011

CROMBIE, June
Bishop and Robertson Chalmers, Glasgow
(0141) 248 4672
Specialisation: Pensions law and practice, including independent trusteeships through directorship of Mitre Pensions Ltd.
Prof. Memberships: Member of committee of Scottish Group and full member of the Association of Pension Lawyers.
Career: Qualified 1987, Partner 1991, Partner in pensions unit of business law division. Accredited by the Law Society of Scotland as a specialist in Pensions Law.

FLEMING, Andrew S.
Maclay Murray & Spens, Glasgow
(0141) 248 5011
Partner in Pensions Department.
asf@maclaymurrayspens.co.uk
Specialisation: Main area of practice is pensions, including documentation, merger and winding up of schemes, independent legal

advice to trustees, surplus and deficit questions in schemes and pensions aspects of sales and purchases of companies. Author of articles in 'CA Magazine'. Regular speaker at pensions conferences.
Prof. Memberships: Law Society of Scotland, Association of Pension Lawyers.
Career: Tutor in Private Law, University of Glasgow 1976-84. Worked with *Linklaters & Paines* 1986-89. Joined *Maclay Murray & Spens* in 1989 and became a Partner in 1990.
Personal: Born 26th November 1954. Educated at Kelvinside Academy and Glasgow University 1972-75. Narrow gauge railway enthusiast. Lives in Glasgow.

GORDON, Ian
McGrigor Donald, Glasgow (0141) 248 6677
Partner in Taxation Department. Principal area of practice is employee benefits, including share incentive schemes, option schemes, and employee share ownership arrangements for listed, AIM and Ofex companies. Also advises employees and trustees on pensions law. Work includes establishment of and ongoing advice in relation to approved and unapproved arrangements. Frequent lecturer on pensions

and taxation issues. Has given TV and radio interviews on pension issues.
Prof. Memberships: Association of Pension Lawyers.
Career: Joined *McGrigor Donald* as a trainee in 1979. Qualified in July 1979. One year secondment to *Thomson McLintock CA* in 1983. Became a Partner at *McGrigor Donald* in the same year.
Personal: Educated at Edinburgh University 1975-79. Born 15th August 1957. Lives in Glasgow.

HOLEHOUSE, Andrew N.
Shepherd & Wedderburn WS, Edinburgh
(0131) 228 9900
Partner and Head of Pensions Group.
Specialisation: Deals with all legal aspects of pensions law, including establishment, winding up and ongoing advice for major occupational pension schemes, advice to life offices, pensions aspects of company sales, acquisitions, mergers and flotations, pensions litigation and EC aspects. Also handles employee share schemes. Has written journal articles and regularly speaks at seminars on pensions law.

Prof. Memberships: Chairman Scottish Group Association of Pensions Lawyers, Law Society Pensions Law Accreditation Panel, Law Society Working Party on Pensions Law.
Career: Qualified in England & Wales 1981. With *Rooks Rider*, London 1981-87 (Partner from 1984). Joined *Shepherd & Wedderburn* in 1988. Qualified in Scotland 1989. Became an associate at *Shepherd & Wedderburn* in 1990 and a Partner in 1992.
Personal: Born 8th December 1955. Leisure activities include malt whisky, fine wines, opera, classical music, rugby. Lives in Edinburgh.

KNOX, Louisa
Shepherd & Wedderburn WS, Edinburgh
(0131) 228 9900
Specialisation: Partner in Pensions Group 1998. Deals with all aspects of pensions law, writes journal articles and regularly speaks at seminars.
Prof. Memberships: Committee Member of the Association of Pension Lawyers (Scottish Group), Member of the Association of Pension Lawyers.
Career: Glasgow University (LLB Hons); Qualified 1993; specialised in pensions law since then.
Personal: Hill walking; mountain biking; swimming; socialising – food and drink.

MEEHAN, Margaret
Burness, Edinburgh (0131) 473 6000
Specialisation: Specialises in pensions law and employee benefits. Experience in transactional work, scheme establishment, documentation and trust law advice to employers and trustees. Has written for 'Pension Lawyer' magazine and spoken on BBC Radio on pension matters.

SUTHERLAND, Alister M.
Burness, Glasgow (0141) 248 4933
Specialisation: Partner in the Private Client Department specialising in tax and trust law. Independent professional trustee for a number of pension funds. Has written a number of articles on this area of law for the British Tax Review, Capital Tax News and Private Client Business. Lectures frequently on various pensions, tax and trust law matters and on the law of investment.

TALMAN, Iain J.S.
Bishop and Robertson Chalmers, Glasgow
(0141) 248 4672
Partner in Business Law Division (Head of Pensions Unit).
Specialisation: Accredited by The Law Society of Scotland as a specialist in pensions law. All aspects of pensions law and practice including pensioneer trusteeships, independent trusteeships through directorship of Mitre Pensions Ltd which acts in relation to a number of schemes including the 6,000 member Rosyth Royal Dockyard Pension Scheme. Acted in Mirror Group Pensions and Lilley Group, Clydesdale Group and Capital Foods independent trusteeships cases. Author and speaker.

Prof. Memberships: Law Society of Scotland, Association of Pension Lawyers, Association of Pensioneer Trustees, Local Member of the Scottish Group of the Pensions Management Institute, Actuarial Society of Glasgow (Life and Pensions Group).
Career: Qualified in 1976. Partner in 1978. Past Chairman, Scottish Group of Association of Pension Lawyers, PMI Working Group on Pensions and Divorce, Convener of Law Society Pensions Accreditation Panel, Convener of Law Society Working Party on Pensions.
Personal: Born 18th July 1952. Leisure interests include movies, people, travel and ardent liquors.

TROTTER, Peter A.A.
MacRoberts, Glasgow
(0141) 332 9988
Email: PAAT@macroberts.co.uk
Partner Pensions and Employee Benefits.
Specialisation: Pensions Law (including investment management agreements and acquisitions/disposals) and Employee Share and Management Incentive Schemes (including ESOPs and employee buy-outs).
Prof. Memberships: Associate of Pensions Management Institute (NAPF Prize and Scottish Group Prize 1993), Member of Society of Share Scheme Practitioners and Association of Pension Lawyers, PMI Scottish Group Committee Member.
Career: Joined *MacRoberts* 1998.
Personal: LLB (Birm), LLB (Edin), Dip LP (Strath), APMI.

PERSONAL INJURY

RESEARCH: In compiling the tables, we consider all the information available to us, paying particular regard to the market research carried out by our team of ten qualified lawyers. (The researchers' details are set out on page three.) The rankings, therefore, reflect the opinion of the marketplace as revealed by systematic and objective research: see page four. (Our research is audited every year by the British Market Research Bureau.)

OVERVIEW: Many plaintiff solicitors expressed concern about the "Woolf at the door" and proposed changes to Legal Aid, while on the defendant side the drastic cuts to insurers' panels are putting pressure on many practices. As a result there are far more departures from, than entries to, the tables this year. There has been much talk of proposed mergers and take-overs. In view of the large number of personal injury practices it has not been possible to write about every firm.

LONDON

MAINLY PLAINTIFF

LEADING FIRMS · LONDON PLAINTIFF

LEIGH, DAY & CO
RUSSELL JONES & WALKER
THOMPSONS

PATTINSON & BREWER

HIGHLY REGARDED FIRMS

Evill & Coleman
Hodge Jones & Allen
Rowley Ashworth

Anthony Gold, Lerman & Muirhead
Field Fisher Waterhouse
O.H. Parsons & Partners
Prince Evans

Bolt Burdon
G.L. Hockfield & Co
Lawford & Co
Parlett Kent
Pritchard Englefield
Simmonds Church Smiles
Stephens Innocent
Stewarts

Leigh Day & Co (1ptnr/3assts) Generally very highly respected as a leading player, although some felt that the firm now has a higher profile in other areas such as environmental and product liability work. *Martyn Day* and *Richard Meeran* are leading individuals. **Clients/Work:** Successful claim for American Prosthetics in an amputee case. 'Allender and Allender v

Lawton' – recovery of substantial damages for young woman with total pre-accident amnesia due to brain injury. Substantial recovery of damages in multifatal RTA involving a child. Specialises in horse riding litigation, spinal injury and head injury – including psychiatric injury.

Russell Jones & Walker (9ptnrs/12assts/23other fee-earners) Acknowledged as a major plaintiff firm. *Ian Walker* and *Fraser Whitehead* are leaders. **Clients/Work:** 'Page v Sheerness' [HL] – case on damages and collateral benefits. 'Harvey v Riddell & Avon Insurance Co' – on the interpretation of EC regulations on behalf of paralysed plaintiff. 'Re:O' – substantial claim on behalf of a brain damaged child. Main client base is trade unions.

Thompsons (14ptnrs/4assts) "Not a pushover" and "excellent" were among the comments which kept the firm at the top of our tables. **Clients/Work:** Acts for a wide range of Union clients including Unison, GMB, TGWU, MSF. During 1997 handled test cases of VWF, chronic bronchitis and emphysema against British Coal.

Pattinson & Brewer *Frances McCarthy* remains at the top of her field. **Clients/Work:** Industrial disease cases.

Hodge Jones & Allen (4ptnrs/12fee-earners who also do product liability and medical negligence work) *Patrick Allen* heads the team. Strengthened by the addition of Richard Barr and his team who are currently dealing with high profile product liability cases within the personal injury department. **Clients/Work:** Accidents at work, slipping and tripping, RTAs.

Rowley Ashworth Highly praised by some, although others felt it has lost force

with the retirement of partner Roger Goodier. **Clients/Work:** Undertakes some work for MFSU.

Anthony Gold, Lerman & Muirhead (2ptnrs/4assocs) "Solid stuff but not necessarily high profile." Promoted in the tables this year following several recommendations. Team includes *David Marshall*. **Clients/Work:** 'Russell v Nathan' – plaintiff awarded £55,775 at trial for serious back injuries suffered in road traffic accident. 'Driver v Deas Mallen Souter' – plaintiff who had sustained a whiplash injury awarded £125,000 in an action against his previous solicitors who had allowed his original personal injury claim to be struck out. 'Re:W' – plaintiff who suffered serious psychological damage when taken into care awarded £20,000 in 'pin down' claim.

Field Fisher Waterhouse (2ptnrs/1const/assts) "Know what they're doing", "small but quality work" were some of the views which earned the firm promotion in our tables this year. The team leader, *Rodney Nelson-Jones*, has "achieved a fantastic amount for people with occupational diseases." **Clients/Work:** By the end of 1997 a total of more than £41m had been recovered in over 900 successful asbestos disease claims. In Smith v Dicks Eagle Insulations Ltd recovered record general damages in case of asbestos pleural disease. Also deals with claims arising from transport disasters and fatal accidents.

O.H. Parsons & Partners (7ptnrs/7fee-earners) **Clients/Work:** Clients include Unison, TGWU and GMB. Mainly employers' liability with some RTAs. Specialises in upper limb disorders, occupational stress, lifting accidents, asbestos, emphysema.

Prince Evans (1ptnr/2assts who also do medical negligence work) Generally praised. *Brian Neill* heads the small team. Clients/Work: Specialises in claims involving tetraplegia, paraplegia and brain injury. During 1997/98 concluded at least five claims exceeding £1m of which two exceeded £1.5m.

Bolt Burdon (3ptnrs/7fee-earners) Seen as "aggressive but know what they're doing." Clients/Work: Acts for private clients, about 65% of whom are legally aided with the rest dealt with under conditional fee agreements or private funding. 'Marsh v Home Office' – an award of £65,000 to a prison instructor who suffered PTSD when attacked by two escaping prisoners. 'Kelly v Cairo Waste

Water Consortium' – a successful claim for a plaintiff whose cancer was exacerbated after having been trapped in compressed air in a tunnel. 'Lear v Equipe and another' – claim on behalf of the estate of an Englishman killed in a Parisian road accident.

Pritchard Englefield (3 fee-earners) Perhaps not as prominent as in previous years. Clients/Work: Specialises in catastrophic injuries. Work in 1997 included Purley and Cannon Street rail crashes. Five successful claims for amounts in excess of £250,000.

Martin Howe also has a strong personal reputation.

LEADING INDIVIDUALS · LONDON PLAINTIFF

ALLEN Patrick Hodge Jones & Allen
DAY Martyn Leigh, Day & Co
McCARTHY Frances Pattinson & Brewer
WALKER Ian Russell Jones & Walker
LEE Terry Evill & Coleman
MARSHALL David Anthony Gold, Lerman & Muirhead
MEERAN Richard Leigh, Day & Co
NEILL Bryan Prince Evans
NELSON-JONES Rodney Field Fisher Waterhouse
HOWE Martin Howe & Co
WHITEHEAD Fraser Russell Jones & Walker
WOODS Peter Stephens Innocent

LONDON

MAINLY DEFENDANT

LEADING FIRMS · LONDON DEFENDANT

BARLOW LYDE & GILBERT
BEACHCROFT STANLEYS
BERRYMANS LACE MAWER
DAVIES ARNOLD COOPER
KENNEDYS
VIZARDS
WANSBROUGHS WILLEY HARGRAVE

HIGHLY REGARDED FIRMS

Bannisters Solicitors
Cameron McKenna
Hextall Erskine
Lawrence Graham
Watmores
Edward Lewis
E. Edwards Son & Noice
Greenwoods
Le Brasseur J Tickle
Wedlake Saint

Barlow Lyde & Gilbert (10ptnrs/25assts) An "admirable" and "very solid" team led by *Graham Dickinson*, felt by some to have "turned round" the personal injury department. The team is split into two sub-teams, the first conducting large complex cases and the second handling volume business. Clients/Work: 'Digital v Hampshire County Council'; 'White v QBE'; 'Berryman v London Borough of Hounslow' (CA).

Beachcroft Stanleys (8ptnrs/16assts/ 9 other fee-earners) Unanimously favourable comment was made about this firm which also has a high profile in medical negligence work. *Anthony Cherry*, the team leader is "good to deal with." Clients/Work: Ngcobo & 19 others

v Thor Chemical Holdings Ltd & others – alleged mercury exposure by the defendant's South African subsidiary. Clients include Cornhill Insurance, Guardian Insurance, Norwich Union, IC Insurance and Zurich.

Berrymans Lace Mawer (12ptnrs/28 fee-earners) "Very sensible and efficient" was the general opinion of this substantial team. *Martin Bruffell* is "high profile." Clients/Work: Employers' and public liability including a large number of asbestos and RSI claims. Clients include Royal & Sun Alliance, Guardian, Commercial Union, Generali, NFU Avon, General Accident and Axa Provincial.

Davies Arnold Cooper (Employers' and public liability: 3 ptnrs/16 fee-earners; Motor Group: 1 ptnr/16 fee-earners) No longer felt to be pre-eminent among defendant firms, although still a major player. Has a significant number of leading individuals including the "enormously talented" *Tania Sless* who heads the non-motor department and is a new entry to our tables this year. Other leaders are *David Rogers*, *David McIntosh* and *Margaret Thomas*. Clients/Work: Employers' and Public Liability – heavily involved in construction and asbestos litigation representing a wide range of insurers and lay clients. Successfully resisted a number of RSI cases. Also specialise in sporting and aviation injuries acting on behalf of airlines. Motor Group – act for a number of composite insurers and reinsurers; deal with full spectrum of motor litigation as well as catastrophic injury, European and international litigation.

Kennedys (1ptnr/4fee-earners) The bulk of personal injury work is handled in the Brentwood office (see South East section) but the London team is responsible for claims involving railway companies. Clients/Work: Instructed by the British Railways Board in two test actions involving claims for industrial diseases.

Vizards (13ptnrs/29assts) An "efficient firm" providing a "terrific service for their

clients'" but felt by some to be rather aggressive. Clients/Work: Clients include Royal Sun Alliance, Prudential Assurance, Iron Trades, QBE, Airtours, BAA and Granada.

Wansbroughs Willey Hargrave (3ptnrs/13fee-earners) Perceived by some as stronger outside London, the profile of this firm is likely to change radically if the long-discussed merger with Beachcroft Stanleys finally goes ahead. In the meantime, it is considered to have a "respectable" practice. Clients/Work: Handles claims relating to motor employers' and public liability incidents, acting for around 15 insurers.

Hextall Erskine (Motor Dept. – 1 ptnr/9 fee-earners; Non-motor Dept. – 6 ptnrs/13 fee-earners) Clients/Work: Work includes RTAs and in the non-motor dept a range of industrial and occupational disease including asbestosis, deafness, stress, RSI, travel and sporting injuries. Claims in 1997 included 'Burrows v Vauxhall' (CA) and 'Jameson and another v CEGB.'

Greenwoods (4ptnrs/10assts) A new entry to our lists this year following praise from several commentators. Perceived as "a significant practice" where the team "know what they're doing." The firm is entirely dedicated to insurance-related litigation. Clients/Work: Acts for several large composite insurers, some smaller insurers, the Motor Insurers' Bureau, loss adjusters, brokers, public utilities. Specialises in employers' and public liability claims, significant industrial injury cases, including disease claims, RTAs, particularly MIB claims.

LEADING INDIVIDUALS · LONDON DEFENDANT

BRUFFELL Martin Berrymans Lace Mawer
CHERRY Anthony Beachcroft Stanleys
DICKINSON Graham Barlow Lyde & Gilbert
ROGERS David Davies Arnold Cooper
McINTOSH David Davies Arnold Cooper
SLESS Tania Davies Arnold Cooper
THOMAS Margaret Davies Arnold Cooper

ALLEN, Patrick
Hodge Jones & Allen, London
(0171) 482 1974
Specialisation: Principal area of practice – medical negligence and personal injury work. Member of Steering Committee of Plaintiff lawyers in the Kings Cross Fire and Marchioness litigation and represented many survivors and bereaved in each case. Largest survivor award in Kings Cross litigation – Lipsius £650,000. Ross v Marchioness/ Bowbelle – longest ever taxation in the High Court Taxing Office, established merits of steering committees in multiparty cases and procedure for costs recovery. Since April 1998 with Richard Barr coordinating and managing the Gulf War, MMR and Sheep Dip multi-party claims plus "Romantica" cruise ship and Kerrin Point group claims. Coordinated APIL campaign on small personal injury claims. Contributed to APIL submissions to the Woolf enquiry. Lecturer on legal aid and personal injury practice and costs.
Prof. Memberships: Law Society, Executive Committee of APIL since 1992. Law Society Personal Injury Panel and Medical Negligence Panel and AVMA referral panel. Society of Labour Lawyers. Legal Aid Board. Area 1 Area Committee. Inquest Forum.
Career: Articled *Offenbach & Co.* 74-76. Qualified 1977 and simultaneously set up *Hodge Jones & Allen* with Henry Hodge. Managing partner of *Hodge Jones & Allen* and head of personal injury team.
Personal: Dob 27.5.50. St Catherine's College, Oxford 1969-72. Married to GP, 2 daughters. Lives Camden Town, London. Interests – windsurfing, sailing, hillwalking, opera, theatre.

BRUFFELL, Martin
Berrymans Lace Mawer, London
(0171) 638 2811
Specialisation: Personal injury claims for Defendants with a particular interest in Industrial Disease cases of all types and Employers Liability work generally. Now joint National Head of the large Personal Injury Division and Industrial Diseases Unit at *Berrymans Lace Mawer*. President of FOIL (The Forum of Insurance Lawyers)and a recent contributor to the Law Society's Working Groups on Civil Litigation and Sir Michael Ogden's working Party on the Ogden Tables. On the Editorial Board of JPIL (The Journal of Personal Injury Litigation) and an active and regular speaker on the seminar/conference circuit and an occasional writer of articles. One time contributor to *Binghams'* and *Berrymans'* Motor Claims Cases.
Prof. Memberships: City of London Solicitors' Society, FOIL (President); The Law Society.
Career: Joined *Berrymans* in 1979 and qualified in 1981, becoming a Partner in 1984.
Personal: Born 1955, educated at RGS High Wycombe and Leeds University.

CHERRY, A.J.
Beachcroft Stanleys, London
(0171) 242 1011
Specialisation: Extensive experience in Employers & Products liability, Traveller's Cheque and insurance fraud, risk management, health and safety and industrial disease claims of all types. Lectures both publicly and for clients on employer's liability and ADR.

Immediate past President of the Forum of Insurance Lawyers. Professional organisations at Law Society.
Prof. Memberships: Law Society. Member of Civil Litigation Committee.
Career: Admitted May 1979, articles at *Bates & Partners*, Medico Legal section at ICI Legal Department form 1980 to 1983 (developing an expertise in long-term exposure to chemical and physical agents in the work place through products and the environment), *Stanley Simpson North* (now *Beachcroft Stanleys*) from 1983 to date, a Partner since 1985 (working mostly for insurance companies).

DAY, Martyn
Leigh, Day & Co, London (0171) 650 1200
See under Administrative & Public Law, Environmental Law, Product Liability (Food Law), p. 87, 342, 661

HOWE, Martin
Howe & Co, London (0181) 840 4688

LEE, Terry
Evill & Coleman, London (0181) 789 9221
See under Medical Negligence: Mainly Plaintiff, p. 577

MARSHALL, David
Anthony Gold, Lerman & Muirhead, London
(0171) 940 4000
Specialisation: Principal area of practice – personal injury and medical negligence work. Member of the Law Society's Personal Injury and Medical Negligence Panels. Acted in APIL campaigns on Legal Aid Green and White Papers, Lord Woolf's Report and on the development of Conditional Fees.
Prof. Memberships: Law Society, APIL (Executive Committee Member since 1996 and Treasurer since 1998), South London Law Society (Committee Member since 1995).
Career: Joined *Anthony Gold, Lerman & Muirhead* as a trainee Solicitor in 1985, qualifying in 1987 and becoming a Partner in 1989. Managing Partner 1997.
Personal: Born 5.6.62. Education – Queen's College, Oxford, 1980-1983. Lives in Herne Hill, South London. Honorary Treasurer, Blackfriars Advice Centre. Leisure interests include foreign travel, history and contemporary fiction.

MCCARTHY, Frances
Pattinson & Brewer, London (0171) 400 5100
Partner in Personal Injury Department.
Specialisation: Main area of practice is accidents at work and occupational disease claims. Also handles medical negligence and other areas of personal injury. Has handled successful appeals to the European Court of Justice, on the question of equal treatment in matters of Social Security. Co-author of Know how for Personal Injury Lawyers. Regular lecturer for Legal Action Group and other bodies.
Prof. Memberships: Law Society, Association of Personal Injury Lawyers, Association of Trial Lawyers of America, Environmental Law Foundation.
Career: Qualified in 1981. Joined *Pattinson & Brewer* in 1979, becoming a Partner in 1985. Vice President of APIL, former Vice President of the International Practice Section of ATLA, founder member of ELF. Editorial Board of Journal for Personal Injury Law.

MCINTOSH, David
Davies Arnold Cooper, London
(0171) 936 2222
The Senior Partner in Litigation Department.
Specialisation: Senior partner dealing with commercial insurance and common law litigation dispute resolution concentrating on public liability, and products liability work, including work on behalf of defendants in mass tort and multiple, drug-related litigation, involving 'crisis management' skills in the face of action group or media-orchestrated campaigns, regularly advising UK-based companies on their exposure to the jurisdiction of the US courts under US 'long-arm' statutes; has advised UK and international companies on the EC product liability worldwide; heavily involved in representing insurers and reinsurers and others in international and London market coverage and financial disputes and involvements in the continuing civil litigation and law reform debates.
Prof. Memberships: Member of the Council and Policy Committee of the Law Society of England and Wales, and Vice Chairman of its Civil Litigation Committee, American Bar Association, Society of English and American Lawyers, Chartered Institute of Arbitrators, Executive Officer of the International Association of Defence Counsel, Defence Research and Trial Lawyers Association of America, Arson Prevention Bureau.
Career: Qualified in 1969. Joined *Davies Arnold Cooper* in 1963, becoming Senior Partner in 1977. Member of the Joint Committee of the Senate of the Bar and Law Society which made recommendations to the Lord Chancellor on the proposed US/ UK Reciprocal Enforcements Convention and on allied jurisdictional matters; Member of the Law Society's Working Party which made recommendations in the context of the Lord Chancellor's Review of Civil Justice with regard to personal injury litigation; Member of the International Bar Association and a Chairman of its Committee on Consumer Affairs, Advertising, Unfair Competition and Products Liability. Chairman of the Disaster Litigation Worldwide Programme in Strasbourg in 1989. Member of the Board of Editors of the Journal of Products and Toxic Liability. Member of the Executive Committee of Centre of Advanced Litigation at Nottingham Law School. Member of the Supreme Court Procedures Committee. member of the Editorial Advisory Board of 'The Litigator'.
Personal: Born 10th March 1944. Leisure interests include travelling, playing golf, keeping fit, and principally his family. Lives in London and Loughton.

MEERAN, Richard
Leigh, Day & Co, London (0171) 650 1200
Specialisation: Practice covers environmental, product liability and personal injury claims including actions for damage caused by chemicals, noise, lead paint and asbestos; property devaluation arising from contaminated land, overseas claimants against UK companies (several reported cases); many of these actions being multiparty in nature. Numerous publications in scientific and legal journals and newspapers.
Prof. Memberships: APIL; London Legal Aid Area Committee. Solicitors' Human Rights

Group. International Law Association.
Career: Admitted April 1988. Partner at *Leigh Day* since 1991.
Personal: Born 23/6/61. BSc (London University 1983) LLM Advanced Litigation (Nottingham Law School) 1996

NEILL, Bryan
Prince Evans, London (0181) 567 2001
Specialisation: Partner in charge of Personal & Medical Injury Department. Handles catastrophic injury claims: brain injuries, tetraplegia and paraplegia. Has recovered record UK awards of damages for clients. Numerous £1m+ cases.
Prof. Memberships: Law Society; Association of Personal Injury Lawyers; Association of Trial Lawyers of America; Australian Plaintiff Lawyers Association; Headway; Spinal Injuries Association; International Medical Society of Paraplegia.
Career: Articled *Thompsons*; Qualified 1979; Partner 1982-85; Partner *Prince Evans* 1985-date. Co-author Butterworths 'Structured Settlements – A Practical Guide'.
Personal: Born 1954. LLB (Hons) London University. Resides London.

NELSON-JONES, Rodney
Field Fisher Waterhouse, London
(0171) 481 4841
Partner in charge of Personal Injury Litigation Department.
Specialisation: Personal injury work includes asbestosis, aviation and road accidents. Also handles medical negligence work. Cases have included the M1 Air Crash (Steering Committee Member), Bryce v. Swan Hunter Group (Asbestosis), and Pendergast v. Sam & Dee (medical negligence). Co-author of 'Product Liability – The New Law Under the Consumer Protection Act 1987', 'Medical Negligence Case Law' (2nd ed. 1995) 'Personal Injury Limitation Law' (1994) and 'Computing Personal Injury Damages' (1997). Contributor to 'Structured Settlements – A Practical Guide' and 'Butterworths Personal Injury Litigation Service'.
Prof. Memberships: Law Society.
Career: Qualified in 1975. Worked at *Prothero & Prothero* 1973-77 and *L Bingham & Co* 1977-83. Joined *Field Fisher Waterhouse* in 1983.
Personal: Born on 11 February 1947. Educated at Repton School and Hertford College, Oxford (MA Oxon). Lives in London.

ROGERS, David
Davies Arnold Cooper, London
(0171) 936 2222
Specialisation: Previously head of common law department; all types of personal injury cases ranging from those with a value of £1,000 to £1m; now handling a variety of major claims for insurers particularly those involving foreign jurisdictions.
Prof. Memberships: Member British Maritime Law Association Committee on Passenger Liabilities; member of Law Society Committee responding to Law Commission on damages.
Career: Sloane Grammar School; joined *WH Thompson* in 1967 specialising in personal injury litigation; joined *Holman Fenwick & Willan* in 1970 and as a result of their support qualified in 1975; joined *Davies Arnold Cooper* in 1977; partner since 1979.

Personal: Born 1947; special interest in boating and hill walking.

SLESS, Tania
Davies Arnold Cooper, London
(0171) 936 2222
Specialisation: Employers' Liability, public liability and product liability claims for a wide range of insurers.
Prof. Memberships: A member of FOIL.
Career: Articled *Miley & Miley*, Dublin. Qualified Ireland 1985, England and Wales 1991. *Miley & Miley* 1982-1988. In-house legal department of Prudential Assurance Co Ltd, London 1988-90. *Davies Arnold Cooper* 1990 to date. Partner 1993 Head of EL/ PL department 1994 to date. Author of chapter on 'Irish Damages' in 'Personal Injury Award in EU and EFTA Countries', second edition.
Personal: Reading, cinema, theatre. Resides in Highgate with husband and two sons.

THOMAS, Margaret A.M.
Davies Arnold Cooper, London
(0171) 936 2222
Solicitor in Common Law Department.
Specialisation: Principal area of practice is personal injury litigation with emphasis on industrial accidents and asbestos related claims. Also represents defendants in health and safety prosecutions. Acted in numerous reported asbestos related cases. Clients include insurance companies.
Prof. Memberships: Member Law Society and Association of Women Solicitors.
Career: Qualified in 1977. Articled with *Cole and Cole*, Oxford 1971-75. Clerical Officer and subsequently HM Inspector of Health and Safety with the Health and Safety Executive 1976-81. Joined *Brian Thompson and Partners* as Assistant Solicitor 1981-83 and *Young Jones Hair and Co.* 1983-86. Joined *Davies Arnold Cooper* in 1986.
Personal: Born 26th July 1949. Educated at Oxford High School For Girls 1960-67 and University of Exeter 1968-71. College of Law 1976 and Imperial College of Science and Technology 1979 (Advanced Certificate of Occupational Safety and Health). Leisure interests include playing classical music in various orchestras and chamber groups and singing in choirs large and small.

WALKER, Ian J.
Russell Jones & Walker, London
(0171) 837 2808
Joint Senior Partner in Personal Injury Department.
Specialisation: Has specialised in plaintiff personal injury since 1975. Acted in the then largest CICB award in 1988. Also the then-largest ever court fatal award (£920,000) in 1991. Lead solicitor in the Kings Cross fire cases. Co-Author of 'Tribunal Practice and procedure 1985', 'Know-How for Personal Injury Lawyers 1993 and 1997', and Editor in Chief of the 'Journal of Personal Injury Litigation 1994/5'. Regular lecturer for IBC, Jordans, Euroforum, Hawksmere and others. Assessor for Law Society PI Panel. President of Association of Personal Injury Lawyers. Former co-chair, International Section of Association of Trial Lawyers of America. 1993/5 Co-ordinator for Information Technology Group APIL. Member of Board of Governors, Association of Trial Lawyers of America.

Prof. Memberships: Association of Personal Injury Lawyers, Association of Trial Lawyers of America, Law Society, Holborn Law Society, Medico-Legal Society, Association of Plaintiff Lawyers of Australia, Society for Computers and the Law, London Solicitors Litigation Association.
Career: Qualified in 1974. Joined *Russell Jones & Walker* in 1968, becoming a Partner in 1977.
Personal: Born 15th April 1950. Attended Whitgift School 1961-68. Governor of an independent school. Leisure interests include music, golf, gardening, mountain biking and walking. Lives in Caterham, Surrey.

WHITEHEAD, Fraser
Russell Jones & Walker, London
(0171) 837 2808
Joint Senior Partner Personal Injury Department.
Specialisation: Main areas of practice are personal injury and disease compensation, Health & Safety Law, Trade Union and employment work. Undertakes legal work primarily on behalf of Trades Unions and their members, including industrial accidents and disease, workplace environment issues, Health and Safety law, employment and trade disputes, the law relating to ballots and constitutional law. Also undertakes personal injuries and employment law work on behalf of private individuals and voluntary bodies. Has handled several House of Lords and ECJ cases of significance to collective labour law. Frequently addresses conferences and occasionally writes articles.
Prof. Memberships: APIL, PIP, ATLA, LSLA, I of ER, Law Society, Holborn Law Society. Member of Council of the Law Society.
Career: Joined *Russell Jones & Walker* on qualification in 1975. Became a Partner in 1978.
Personal: Born 14th December 1950. Educated at Pocklington School, Yorkshire 1962-69 and Sheffield University 1969-72. Awarded a Diploma in EEC law from the University of London in 1992. On the Management Committee of the Mary Ward Law Centre, Trustee of the Child Accident Prevention Trust, Secretary Society of Labour Lawyers. Leisure time is devoted to his family, Trade Unions and Labour Party. Lives in London.

WOODS, Peter
Stephens Innocent, London (0171) 353 2000
Partner in Litigation Department.
Specialisation: Main areas of practice are personal injury (including sports injuries) and medical negligence. Acted for many plaintiffs claiming work related upper limb disorders (RSI) from keyboard use. Also handles employment, industrial relations, pensions and insolvency law. Has extensive involvement in acting for Trade Union's employees and pensioners. Acted in British Coal v. British Coal Staff Superannuation Scheme; National Mineworkers & others v. British Coal Corporation and President of the Board of Trade (pit closure decision); and BCCI (SA) in Liquidation. Has addressed numerous seminars and conferences including TUC and APIL.
Prof. Memberships: Personal Injury Panel of Law Society.
Career: Qualified in 1984. Barrister and Solicitor in New Zealand 1985; Solicitor in England 1992. Joined *Stephens Innocent* in 1991, becoming a Partner in 1994.
Personal: Nottingham University (LL.M) 1996. Born 3rd April 1961. Attended University of Canterbury, New Zealand 1979-84 (LLB, BSc).

SOUTH EAST

MAINLY PLAINTIFF

Amery-Parkes (3ptnrs/6assts/ 11 other fee-earners) Now doing mainly plaintiff work although *Alan Hughes* still has a good reputation for defendant. Regarded as a "no-nonsense", "trustworthy" firm. **Clients/ Work:** Predominantly RTAs plus a number of spinal and head injuries for legal expenses insurers.

Blake Lapthorn (3ptnrs/ 11fee-earners who also do medical negligence work) Generally well regarded although some felt the firm's strengths were in other fields such as medical negligence and commercial work. **Clients/Work:** Specialises in catastrophic injuries for clients such as two legal expenses insurers, RAC, Royal College of Nursing, referrals from CABs, Headway and Spinal Injuries Association.

Boyes Turner & Burrows (1ptnr/4fee-earners) A niche firm best known for medical negligence but has built up a respected personal injury practice in the last two years. **Clients/Work:** Specialise in brain and spinal injury claims with an emphasis on cases of maximum severity. In 1997 the team achieved the largest ever CICB award in a case involving brain injury, resulting in a damages figure in excess of £1.6 million.

Osborne Morris & Morgan (6 ptnrs) Regarded as a "specialist" and "pre-eminent in head injury", *Tom Osborne* "does a terrific job." **Clients/Work:** Neurological injuries including cerebral palsy, anaesthetic accidents and head and spinal injuries.

Pattinson & Brewer (3ptnrs/ 7other fee earners) Has the volume of work and profile to remain high up in our table. **Clients/Work:** Specialises in industrial diseases including asbestosis, cancer, RSI, deafness. During 1997 settled Herald of Free Enterprise and currently acting on Marchioness disaster.

Thomson Snell & Passmore (2ptnrs/ 5assts who also do some medical negligence work) A "big name" firm promoted this year on the recommendation of many practitioners. **Clients/Work:** 'Carr v Field' which settled at £2.2m on full liability. Clients include referrals from Headway and National Accident Helpline. Specialises in head injury litigation.

Warner Goodman & Streat (6ptnrs/ 2assts form the civil litigation department) *Edward Voller* stood out at this highly competent firm. **Clients/ Work:** Clients include TGWU and CWU. Specialises in asbestosis, VWF and industrial deafness.

Fennemores (4ptnrs/ 6assts) Most commentators felt this firm had been undervalued last year and it has accordingly been promoted. A "highly regarded" practice which "does a lot of work." **Clients/Work:** Acting for a number of overseas victims of the Watford Junction Rail Crash.

T.G.Baynes & Sons (2ptnrs/4fee-earners who also do medical negligence work) Not a major force, although individual team members received praise. **Clients/Work:** Instructed by two legal expenses insurers and receives referrals from local CABs. Work includes RTAs and head injury claims.

SOUTH EAST

MAINLY DEFENDANT

Davies Lavery "A good firm with a sensible approach." No-one had a bad word to say about this practice which accordingly rose to be equal top of our table.

Kennedys (4ptnrs/22fee-earners, some of whom do plaintiff work) Although generally regarded as a London firm the larger part of Kennedys' personal injury team is based in Brentwood. Perceived as a "hard nosed, tough opponent" on a number of major insurers' panels. *David Scrutton* is a leader. **Clients/Work:** Acts for a broadcasting company and several London bus companies. Handles RTAs, industrial diseases including asbestosis and other chest diseases, industrial accidents. Involved in function evaluation testing.

Bond Pearce (1ptnr/ 9fee-earners) A new entry to the list following praise for this "excellent" practice which has a growing presence in the south east. **Clients/ Work:** Acts for insurance companies, Lloyd's syndicates and those who self-insure. Work includes road traffic, public liability, employers' liability, industrial diseases, product liability and health insurance.

Brachers (1ptnr/2assts) Seen as strongest at partner level. **Clients/Work:** Specialises in employer and public liability defendant work principally for insurers for corporate and local authority bodies. A number of industrial accident claims including asbestosis, RSI, workplace stress and deafness cases. Also handles plaintiff claims via a legal expenses insurer client.

Cole & Cole (3ptnrs/10assts) Undertakes general defendant work with a move recently towards plaintiff work. *Iain Tenquist* remains a leader. **Clients/Work:** Acts for over 30 insurance companies including Cornhill Insurance, General Accident and Norwich Union.

Ensor Byfield (2ptnrs/ 10fee-earners) "A good operation" which received favourable comment. **Clients/Work:** Acts for MOD and several insurers including Zurich, Guardian, Cornhill and Iron Trades. Has a specialised motor claims division. Acted for directors in Lyme Bay canoe tragedy.

A.E.Wyeth & Co (7ptnrs/20fee-earners) Generally seen as a "good solid outfit" with a substantial client base. Handles most claims arising from the Dagenham car plant. *Brian Williams* was recommended again. **Clients/Work:** Clients include various Lloyds syndicates, all Zurich divisions, GAN and local authorities. Recently handling stress-related cases and claims arising from the care of children in local authority homes.

Merricks (1ptnr/5fee-earners) **Clients/Work:** Clients include three major insurers. Claims are balanced between industrial disease (asbestos, deafness, RSI) and RTAs.

SOUTH EAST

PLAINTIFF AND DEFENDANT

Lamport Bassitt (Plaintiff: 1ptnr/6fee-earners; Defendant: 3ptnrs/ 17fee-earners) Described as "competent" and the "best of the group" by some. **Clients/ Work:** Plaintiff: Industrial diseases including asbestosis. Has

a catastrophic injury unit. Acts for TGWU, referrals from consultants and Headway. Defendant: Mainly RTAs but also some employer's liability. Acts for Garwins, Zurich, Royal Sun Alliance, Prudential and Lloyd's syndicates.

Penningtons (1ptnr/4fee-earners) Perceived as biased towards plaintiff work, but have a decent reputation for both. *Christopher Mather* is "excellent" although now sitting as a Recorder and thus less of a presence at the firm. **Clients/Work:** Plaintiff: Referrals from Spinal Injuries Association and Headway. Broad spread of work including sporting injuries. Defendant: A mixture of composite insurers and Lloyd's syndicates. Mainly RTAs.

Buss Murton (3ptnrs/17fee-earners) Felt to be slipping slightly but nevertheless "a decent practice." **Clients/Work:** Plaintiff: Several major legal expenses insurers and Trade Unions. Defendant: Lloyd's syndicates. RTAs, industrial accidents, severe head and spinal injuries.

Cripps Harries Hall (1ptnr/4fee-earners plus 4 other fee-earners who also do SIF work and some medical negligence) Felt by some to be stronger in other areas but otherwise "well thought of." **Clients/Work:** Referrals from local institutions, Headway etc. Pre-

dominantly employers' liability and RTAs.

E.Edwards Son & Noice (3ptnrs/20fee-earners) Despite the size of the team the firm appears to have a low profile among fellow practitioners. **Clients/Work:** Plaintiff: Mainly RTA work for private clients. Defendant: RTA and employers' liability for NIG Skandia, Highway, Pegasus and Northern Star.

Henmans (3ptnrs/8other fee-earners) "Provides a good service." *Mary Duncan* remains a leading individual. **Clients/Work:** Acts for most of the main insurers and legal expenses insurers. Work includes employers' liability, particularly RSI and fatal accidents.

Argles & Court (3ptnrs/ 7fee-earners) Long established firm providing a "good" service. **Clients/Work:** Plaintiff: legal expenses insurers. Defendant: two substantial insurers. Work in 1997 included a £1.1m claim on behalf of a child.

SEE PROFILES AT END OF THIS SECTION

SOUTH WEST

MAINLY PLAINTIFF

Rowley Ashworth (1ptnr/2assts) A "capable, competent and efficient" outfit.

Clients/Work: Acts for members of GMB, TGWU and USDAW.

Russell Jones & Walker (2ptnrs/ 4assts) Generally perceived as a leading plaintiff firm, with a national presence. **Clients/Work:** Representing severely injured infant (secured interim payment of £0.5m for provision of suitable housing). Recovered £180,000 for steel worker (partial amputation of foot as a result of injury to lower limbs). Claims against a healthcare trust arising from the death of Georgina Robinson who was stabbed by a schizophrenic.

Thompsons (3ptnrs/9assts) A "good, aggressive, thoroughly competent" union firm. *Andrew Herbert* remains a leading individual. **Clients/Work:** Mainly handles injuries at work. Recovering £15,000 for neuralgia (injury to face); £40,000 for back injury (chair collapsed); £6,000 for leg injury (employee slipped on wet hospital floor).

Burroughs Day **Clients/Work:** (3ptnrs/ 4assts) Remain active plaintiff practitioners. Plaintiff injured at work when step ladder collapsed (£131,000). Mushroom Workers Lung case (£198,000). Sheet metal press operator's RSI claim (£122,000).

Bishop Longbotham & Bagnall,

(4ptnrs/2assts) Seen as "reliable and efficient." **Clients/Work:** Mainly RTA claims for plaintiffs, but also some employers' liability and factory accidents.

David Gist & Co (5ptnrs/5assts) They "get reasonable work and do it well." Perceived to have a slightly higher profile than previously. **Clients/Work:** Acted for plaintiffs in RTAs to recover £750,000 and £450,000. Represented plaintiff in RTA who allegedly contributed to his injuries by wearing a faulty helmet.

Over Taylor Biggs Has a solid reputation in the south west. "You take notice when they are on the other side" commented one opponent. *Chris Over* was highly recommended and makes a new entry this year.

Slee Blackwell (1ptnr/2 assts- 60%) Have a good reputation for handling routine rather than high profile claims. Deals with a broad range of personal injury matters.

SEE PROFILES AT END OF THIS SECTION

SOUTH WEST

MAINLY DEFENDANT

LEADING FIRMS • SOUTH WEST DEFENDANT

SANSBURY HILL Bristol
WANSBROUGHS WILLEY HARGRAVE Bristol
CARTWRIGHTS Bristol
BEVAN ASHFORD Bristol

HIGHLY REGARDED FIRMS

Frank & Caffin Truro
Ford Simey Daw Roberts Exeter

Sansbury Hill (3ptnrs/13assts) Seen as "good to deal with and know what they're doing." *Michael Guy* is "good – quite aggressive." *Paul Davies* is also a leader. One client commented that the firm had a "cost effective," approach. It remains at the top of the table.

Wansbroughs Willey Hargrave (4ptnrs/18assts) Described as "consistently good" and remains at the top with Sansbury Hill. *Bob Beale* makes an entry this year on the basis of numerous recommendations. Going from strength to strength, it has a huge defendant practice. **Clients/Work:** Defending public utility company against claim by workman seriously injured in work accident. Acting for government department sued by employee for stress at work caused by victimisation and pressure. Acting for the first defendant in five-vehicle motorway pile-up which left the plaintiff motorcyclist with quadriplegia.

Cartwrights (5ptnrs/8assts) Felt by some to have lost direction, but *David Vernalls* is recognised for his expertise. **Clients/ Work:** 'Warren v Middlebrook Mushrooms Ltd' (Court of Appeal decision regarding date of knowledge). 'Steel v Fairfield Mabey Ltd' (case struck out for want of prosecution).

Bevan Ashford (1ptnr/3assts, almost f/t) Better known in Bristol for its medical negligence practice, but maintains a personal injury capacity. **Clients/ Work:** Advising in multiple claim arising from drunk driver crashing into a number of people leaving Keynsham Rugby Club after a Christmas disco. Involved in claims arising from 100-vehicle M4 pile-up. Acting in PTS claims arising from Clapham Rail disaster.

Frank & Caffin (3ptnrs/2assts) One of only two non-Bristol defendant firms listed, this Truro firm is making its presence felt.

Ford Simey Daw Roberts (3ptnrs/4assts) Perceived as having a good insurance practice. **Clients/Work:** Commercial Union; Eagle Star.

LEADING INDIVIDUALS SOUTH WEST • DEFENDANT

DAVIES Paul Sansbury Hill
GUY Michael Sansbury Hill

BEALE Robert Wansbroughs Willey Hargrave
VERNALLS David Cartwrights

SOUTH WEST

PLAINTIFF AND DEFENDANT

LEADING FIRMS • SOUTH WEST PLAINTIFF AND DEFENDANT

BOND PEARCE Plymouth
TOWNSENDS Swindon
VEALE WASBROUGH Bristol
LYONS DAVIDSON Bristol
NASH & CO. Plymouth
STEPHENS & SCOWN Exeter
VEITCH PENNY Exeter
WOLFERSTANS Plymouth

HIGHLY REGARDED FIRMS

Hugh James Bristol
Stones Cann & Hallett Exeter
Tayntons Gloucester
Amery-Parkes Bristol
Bennet Metcalfe Bristol
Boyce Hatton Torquay
Crosse & Crosse Exeter
Davies and Partners Gloucester
Kirby Simcox Bristol
Trobridges Plymouth
Woollcombe Beer Watts Newton Abbot

Bond Pearce (8ptnrs (2 part-time)/37assts) The whole team was praised as "good, sensible and pleasant to deal with." Seen as having experience and depth, they are widely respected. *Jonathan Cooper* is particularly admired.

Clients/Work: Include the Post Office.

Townsends (Plaintiff: 3ptnrs/ 2assts. Defendant: 1 ptnr/1 asst) Specialising in complex, high value spinal and brain injuries, this firm has a strong practice. In particular, *Byron Carron* is "sensible and good." *Brigitte Chandler* is also recommended. **Clients/Work:** Acted for plaintiff soldier in obtaining £1.74m damages from the Ministry of Defence following training accident. Acted for lead defendant in case against Dunlop concerning negligent manufacture of tyres.

Veale Wasbrough (Plaintiff: 1ptnr/7assts. Defendant: 2ptnrs/3assts) Has a solid reputation, particularly for plaintiff work. Considered "good to deal with." **Clients/Work:** TGWU; Royal College of Nursing; The St Paul.

Lyons Davidson (Plaintiff: 2ptnrs/20assts. Defendant: 4ptnrs/7assts (90%)) Has a large personal injury practice. They "work hard and know what they are doing." *Bernard Rowe* is a leading light. **Clients/Work:** 'Hill v William Tompkins Ltd' (sheep dip litigation). Act for Green Flag, Hambros, Royal Sun Alliance.

Nash & Co (3ptnrs/ 5assts) Has an almost exclusively litigation practice, and continues to be well regarded.

Stephens & Scown (4ptnrs/ 1asst) *Simon Middleton* is "respected for plaintiff work and runs a good department." **Clients/Work:** Acted for defendant in case involving Q fever. Acted for plaintiff child suing mother over RTA.

Veitch Penny (Defendant: 3ptnrs/5assts. Plaintiff: 2ptnrs/3assts) More popular with clients than with opponents, particularly the "excellent" *Mike Penny*. **Clients/Work:** On plaintiff side, act for the RAC.

Wolferstans (16ptnrs (4 p/t)/ 19assts (2 p/t)) Has some good, able people, particularly for defence work. "Can be hard nosed."

Hugh James (2ptnrs/2assts) A new entry to the table, it is making its presence felt in the south west, receiving a number of recommendations. **Clients/Work:** Commercial Union; Royal Sun Alliance.

Boyce Hatton (3assts 80%) Known primarily for plaintiff work. **Clients/ Work:** Represented ex-Torquay United football player in claim against another football player and Brentford F.C. for injury caused during a match.

Woollcombe Beer Watts (Plaintiff: 3ptnrs/2assts -50%. Defendant: 1asst – 80%) Handling some interesting group actions, and is generally well thought of. **Clients/ Work:** Acted for 200 plaintiffs pursuing compensation from South West Water for illness following a contaminated water incident. Conducting 35 claims arising from train derailment in Newton Abbot.

LEADING INDIVIDUALS SOUTH WEST PLAINTIFF AND DEFENDANT

CARRON Byron Townsends
CHANDLER Brigitte Townsends
COOPER Jonathan Bond Pearce
MIDDLETON Simon Stephens & Scown
PENNY Michael Veitch Penny
ROWE Bernard Lyons Davidson

WALES

MAINLY PLAINTIFF

LEADING FIRMS • WALES PLAINTIFF

LEO ABSE & COHEN Cardiff
THOMPSONS Cardiff

HIGHLY REGARDED FIRMS

Hugh James Merthyr Tydfil
Walker Smith & Way Wrexham

Huttons Cardiff
Loosemores Cardiff

Leo Abse & Cohen (1ptnr/5fee-earners who also do some medical negligence) "A

leading firm" with "large amounts of work." *Cenric Clement-Evans, Ian Hopkins* and *Robin Williams* remain leaders. **Clients/ Work:** Mainly Trade Union clients including BIFU, GMB, TGWU, BFAWU plus legal expenses insurers. Industrial accidents and disease including a substantial number of industrial deafness claims.

Thompsons (5ptnrs/14assts) Together with Leo Abse felt to be "head and shoulders above the others." *Roger Bent* has moved to full-time consultancy in the last three years leading up to his retirement. **Clients/Work:** Acts for a large number of Trade Unions including GMB, AWU, Unison, ASLEF and the Fire Brigade Union. Recently represented 6000 mineworkers in claims relating to VWF, emphysema and chronic bronchitis. Also 700 asbestos cases throughout Wales and occupational asthma claims.

Hugh James (4ptnrs/ 14fee-earners) A new entry to the rankings in view of the substantial plaintiff work being handled from this office. **Clients/Work:** Acted for lead plaintiffs in group action against British Coal for respiratory disease compensation – negotiated compensation scheme with the government which has secured £26m in compensation to date. Also represented a lead plaintiff in VWF litigation.

LEADING INDIVIDUALS • WALES PLAINTIFF

BENT Roger Thompsons
CLEMENT-EVANS Cenric Leo Abse & Cohen
HOPKINS Ian Leo Abse & Cohen
WILLIAMS Robin Leo Abse & Cohen

WALES

MAINLY DEFENDANT

LEADING FIRMS • WALES DEFENDANT

HUGH JAMES Cardiff
MORGAN BRUCE Cardiff

HIGHLY REGARDED FIRMS

Dolmans Cardiff
Palser Grossman Cardiff

Eversheds Cardiff

Hugh James (10ptnrs/13fee-earners plus other solicitors doing plaintiff work) "A very very professional bunch" who are "definitely

leaders." Team includes *Gareth Williams, Russel Jenkins* and *Michael Jones*. **Clients/Work:** Clients include Royal and Sun Alliance, Commercial Union, Zurich Municipal, Rail Track, Lloyds Syndicated and self-insurers. Work includes employers liability, public liability and road traffic claims. Specialist units deal with claims of maximum severity, disease litigation and actions against Local Authorities.

Morgan Bruce *Simon Cradick* and *Hugh Price* are recommended.

Dolmans (7ptnrs/24fee-earners) Maybe "a bit old-fashioned" but "solid" and "competent." **Clients/Work:** Acts for Zurich Municipal and International, Iron Trades, St Pauls, Guardian, Eagle Star, Lloyds underwriters and 16 new unitary authorities in Wales. Work includes RSI, occupational stress, industrial diseases, public liability.

Palser Grossman (8ptnrs/22fee-earners) A firm which has "expanded massively" in the last year. Highly rated by some, considered "aggressive" by others. Team includes *Ian Hermer*. **Clients/ Work:** Clients include Eagle Star, Zurich, Royal & Sun Alliance, AXA-Provincial and General Accident.

LEADING INDIVIDUALS • WALES DEFENDANT

CRADICK Simon Morgan Bruce
HERMER Ian Palser Grossman
WILLIAMS Gareth Hugh James

JENKINS Russel Hugh James
JONES Michael Hugh James
PRICE Hugh Morgan Bruce

WALES

PLAINTIFF AND DEFENDANT

Douglas-Jones Mercer (4ptnrs/2assts) Particularly rated for defendant work. *Jeremy Wolfe* has acted for insurers for 20 years.

HIGHLY REGARDED FIRMS WALES DEFENDANT AND PLAINTIFF

Douglas-Jones Mercer Swansea
Graham Evans & Partners Swansea

Graham Evans & Partners (2ptnrs/ 4assts) Considered to have "some very good

LEADING INDIVIDUALS • WALES DEFENDANT AND PLAINTIFF

LEWIS Brian Graham Evans & Partners
WOLFE Jeremy Douglas-Jones Mercer

people" including *Brian Lewis*.

MIDLANDS

MAINLY PLAINTIFF

LEADING FIRMS · MIDLANDS PLAINTIFF

FREETH CARTWRIGHT HUNT DICKINS Nottingham
IRWIN MITCHELL Birmingham
ROWLEY ASHWORTH Birmingham
RUSSELL JONES & WALKER Birmingham
THOMPSONS Birmingham, Nottingham

BARRATT GOFF & TOMLINSON Nottingham
NELSONS Nottingham

HIGHLY REGARDED FIRMS

Challinors Lyon Clark West Bromwich

Freeth Cartwright Hunt Dickins (3ptnrs/2assts) "Undoubtedly" a leading plaintiff firm in the Midlands. *Paul Balen* continues to have a high profile. **Clients/Work:** Repre-senting 650 clients suing Airtours after contracting various illnesses in two Turkish hotels. Recovered £475,000 for car crash passenger. Acting for plaintiff who sustained severe head injuries in an RTA (value £1.5m).

Irwin Mitchell (2ptnrs/4assts) Team led in Birmingham by the "excellent" *Stuart Henderson*. **Clients/Work:** Acting in multi-party actions against tour operators arising from mass holiday illness cases. Major head injury cases (£1.75m award and £2m fatal accident award). Representing over 100 plaintiffs in connection with chemical spillage.

Rowley Ashworth Described as "efficient and sensible." Led by the "capable" *David Prain*.

Russell Jones & Walker (4ptnrs including *Jeffry Zindani*/4assts) Perceived by some as "occasionally bombastic", they are generally well regarded. **Clients/Work:** Acted in 'Sharma v CICB' (highest ever general damage award for pain and suffering – £150,000) and 'Colclough v Staffordshire County Souncil' (training obligations for health service employer).

Thompsons (10ptnrs (6 f/t)/23assts) Seen in Birmingham as "good, quick but a bit faceless." The Nottingham office "adopts a realistic attitude." The firm has a number of leading individuals, including the "able" *Sarah Goodman*, "sound" *Anthony Lawton* and "well respected" *Phil King*.

Barratt Goff & Tomlinson (4ptnrs/1assts) A "well organised" and "forceful" exclusively personal injury practice who "move things along smartly and make life difficult for defendants." **Clients/Work:** 'Webber v Bruton' (£1.8m)

LEADING INDIVIDUALS MIDLANDS · PLAINTIFF

GOODMAN Sarah Thompsons
HENDERSON Stuart Irwin Mitchell

BALEN Paul Freeth Cartwright Hunt Dickins
KING Phil Thompsons
LAWTON Anthony Thompsons
PRAIN David Rowley Ashworth
ZINDANI Jeffry Russell Jones & Walker

MIDLANDS

MAINLY DEFENDANT

LEADING FIRMS · MIDLANDS DEFENDANT

BULLER JEFFRIES Birmingham
WILLIAM HATTON Dudley
BROWNE JACOBSON Nottingham
CARTWRIGHT & LEWIS Birmingham
CHAPMAN EVERATT Birmingham
EDGE & ELLISON Birmingham
EKING MANNING Nottingham
EVERATT & COMPANY Evesham
WANSBROUGHS WILLEY HARGRAVE Birmingham
WEIGHTMANS Birmingham

HIGHLY REGARDED FIRMS

Rowley Dickinson Birmingham
Shakespeares Birmingham
Shoosmiths & Harrison Northampton
Willcox Lane Clutterbuck Birmingham

Buller Jeffries (Birmingham) (6ptnrs/14assts) Remains top of the tree thanks to its long-standing reputation. *John Geoffrey* is "a safe pair of hands" and *Derek Adamson* maintains his reputation. **Clients/Work:** Involved in £100m products claim and asbestos class action.

William Hatton (Dudley) (7ptnrs/3assts) Considered "a force to be reckoned with", particularly the "very able" *Timothy Perry*. **Clients/Work:** 'Hitchcock v Hepworth Heating' (plaintiff limited to Scale 1 costs on deafness claim where recovered less than £3,000). 'Haymarket Publications v H.J Systems' (strike out for want of prosecution albeit plaintiff bound to succeed against one or other defendant). 'Bolton v Midland Steel Frames Ltd' (paraplegic plaintiff recovered £700,000, but defendant obtained full indemnity from tyre manufacturer).

Browne Jacobson (Nottingham) (8ptnrs/30assts – some in London. Also do healthcare). Described as "highly experienced and efficient". Very popular with barristers and clients. **Clients/Work:** AGF; Provident Insurance; NFU Mutual.

Cartwright & Lewis (Birmingham) (4ptnrs/4assts) An active and well regarded defendant firm. **Clients/Work:** Axa, Eagle Star. Acted in 'Parsons v Provincial Insurance' (Court of Appeal ruling on the use of juries in alleged fraud/arson cases).

Edge & Ellison (Birmingham) (2ptnrs/9assts) **Clients/Work:** 'Dainty v Colway Tyres' (successfully represented defendant sued for injury sustained at work). 'Willey v LL Jones deceased' (a defendant who suffered a heart attack, lost consciousness and control of his vehicle found not negligent). Also act for AGF.

Eking Manning (Nottingham) (4ptnrs/4assts) A "good, decent firm" although some said they could be "rather aggressive."

Everatt & Company *Catherine Arkell* is much admired and "works well with others." The firm is generally perceived as a solid outfit.

Wansbroughs Willey Hargrave (Birmingham) Seen as "going from strength to strength" and received praise from contemporaries and clients. **Clients/Work:** Royal & Sun Alliance; General Accident; Ecclesiastical.

Weightmans (Birmingham) (7ptnrs/11assts) Led by the "excellent" *Nigel Dace*. **Clients/Work:** Include the Highway Group.

LEADING INDIVIDUALS MIDLANDS · DEFENDANT

ADAMSON Derek Buller Jeffries

ARKELL Catherine Everatt & Company
CHAPMAN Richard Chapman Everatt
DACE Nigel Weightmans
GEOFFREY John Lewis Buller Jeffries
PERRY Timothy William Hatton

MIDLANDS

PLAINTIFF AND DEFENDANT

Newsome Vaughan (Plaintiff: 8assts. Defendant: 1ptnr/4assts) Well thought of: "practical, experienced and helpful." Maintains the top slot.

Amery-Parkes (3ptnrs/3assts) **Clients/Work:** Obtained £1m for victim of RTA and £575,000 for AA patrolman seriously injured while attending breakdown on a motorway hard shoulder.

Flint, Bishop & Barnett (2ptnts/8assts) Has a strong reputation. **Clients/Work:** Acts for TGWU, other trade unions and Lloyd's motor syndicates.

HIGHLY REGARDED FIRMS MIDLANDS PLAINTIFF AND DEFENDANT
Newsome Vaughan Coventry
Amery-Parkes Birmingham
Flint, Bishop & Barnett Derby
Langleys Lincoln

EAST ANGLIA

MAINLY PLAINTIFF

Cunningham, John & Co (5ptnrs/ 6assts) Has "strength in depth and expertise." **Clients/Work:** Acted for injured minor obtaining damages against a driver obeying the speed limit. Recovered £1m for a man seriously injured in head-on collision with an ambulance, and £1.75m for a woman paralysed in a car crash.

LEADING FIRMS • EAST ANGLIA PLAINTIFF
CUNNINGHAM, JOHN & CO Thetford
LEATHES PRIOR Norwich
DAWBARNS Wisbech
METCALFE COPEMAN & PETTEFAR Wisbech
WARD GETHIN King's Lynn
BATES, WELLS & BRAITHWAITE Ipswich

LEADING INDIVIDUALS EAST ANGLIA • PLAINTIFF
CARY Tim Leathes Prior

SEE PROFILES AT END OF THIS SECTION

Leathes Prior (2ptnrs/2assts – p/t) Retain a high profile. *Tim Cary* has "a relaxed style." **Clients/Work:** Hambros.

Metcalfe Copeman & Pettefar (2ptnrs/ 3assts) A "good firm with high quality work."

EAST ANGLIA

MAINLY DEFENDANT

Mills & Reeve (2ptnrs/3assts) Remains the top defendant firm in East Anglia and continues to be well regarded. **Clients/Work:** Acted in 'Stovin v Wise' (House of Lords case on statutory powers). Acts for Norwich Union and NFU Mutual.

Eversheds (4ptnrs/ 8assts) "Makes life superbly easy for barristers" and is very popular with clients. **Clients/Work:** Acts for over 60 insurance companies, a utilities company and a county council.

Prettys (4ptnrs/3assts) Seen as having a strong defendant team. **Clients/Work:** Royal & Sun Alliance, Cornhill, General Accident, Zurich International and the AA.

LEADING FIRMS • EAST ANGLIA DEFENDANT
MILLS & REEVE Norwich
EVERSHEDS Norwich, Ipswich
PRETTYS Ipswich
HEWITSON BECKE + SHAW Cambridge
MERRICKS Ipswich

EAST ANGLIA

PLAINTIFF AND DEFENDANT

Birketts (4ptnrs/5assts) Has a high profile throughout the region. PI accounts for 25% of the firm's workload. **Clients/Work:** Acting in RSI claims involving Financial Times, Hotpoint and Hoover. Also acts for the Communication Workers Union.

Taylor Vinters (3ptnrs/6assts) Attracted tabloid attention this year when it established a new level of award in fatal accident claims. **Clients/Work:** Acted for infant plaintiff in 'Martin and Browne v Grey' (award of £22,500 per annum for loss of mother's services).

HIGHLY REGARDED FIRMS EAST ANGLIA PLAINTIFF AND DEFENDANT
Birketts Ipswich
Buckle Mellows Peterborough
Greenwoods Peterborough
Rogers and Norton Norwich
Taylor Vinters Cambridge

NORTH WEST

MAINLY PLAINTIFF

Leigh, Day & Co (2ptnrs/4fee-earners) A "high profile" and "specialist" team run by the "very solid" *Frank Patterson* and *Geraldine McCool*. **Clients/Work:** Settlement of £1.5m for a child brain damaged in an RTA. CICB settlement of £850,000 for a double amputee IRA victim. Also acts for Communication Workers Union and against the MOD.

Pannone & Partners (5ptnrs/10assts/15other fee-earners) With a long-established reputation in the field there was no lack of praise for the firm's "massive strength" and "consistent standard." Although considered by some to be "the best known and biggest in the area" no individuals were mentioned, suggesting strong teamwork. **Clients/Work:** Tetraplegic case (£2m). Brain damage case (£1.225m). Multi-party actions including Bolton school coach crash in France. Unusual cases included successful action against balloonist Per Lindstrand (Richard Branson's co-pilot). Clients include Hambro, the RAC and private clients covered by legal aid or conditional fee agreements.

Whittles (7ptnrs/24fee-earners) A union-based niche practice (90% of the firm's turnover is from personal injury work). Unanimously praised as "good quality" and "competent." Team leader *Collin Mansfield* is a new entry to the table this year. **Clients/Work:** Clients include the GMB and union members in the retail, baking, social work, heavy engineering and steelwork industries. Specialises in employers' liability including asbestosis, RSI and work-related upper limb disorders. VWF test cases against British Gas and British Rail.

Jack Thornley (3ptnrs/19fee-earners) A union firm which is generally well regarded. **Clients/Work:** Clients include TGWU, USDAW and some private clients. Factory accidents and industrial disease.

Betesh Fox & Co (2ptnrs/17fee-earners) Widely praised as a firm with a substantial profile. **Clients/Work:** CICB structured settlement of £870,000 involving serious brain injury to an infant. Two other structured settlements – one for £350,000, the other for £500,000.

The Paul Rooney Partnership (4ptnrs/5fee-earners who also do medical negligence) Noted for the large volume of legal expenses work handled. **Clients/Work:** Mainly RTAs and industrial disease.

NORTH WEST

MAINLY DEFENDANT

Keogh Ritson (15ptnrs/40fee-earners) "The bees knees" and "leading players," led by a new entry, the "extremely good" *Barry Taziker*. **Clients/Work:** Acts for the majority of the top ten insurers. The department includes a specialist industrial disease unit.

Hill Dickinson (Liverpool – 19ptnrs/39assts; Manchester – 2 ptnrs/3 assts) Seen by some as "a bit aggressive" but by others as "tough but straight." *Anthony Wilson* is a leader. **Clients/Work:** Act for major insurers on VWF, industrial deafness and occupational stress matters. Handling British Gas litigation.

James Chapman & Co (13ptnrs/15assts) A "sensible" defendant firm with a team led by *Kevin Finnigan*, "a wily litigator." **Clients/Work:** Mediated a number of claims with a case value in excess of £1 m. Conducting a number of pioneering claims for insurers involving Vocational Rehabilitation. Over 20 ongoing stress claims including cases arising out of bullying, discrimination and excessive workloads.

Weightmans A "very proactive" practice promoted in our table following several recommendations. *Tony Summers* is "highly respected."

Davies Wallis Foyster (Liverpool – 6ptnrs/21fee-earners; Manchester – 3 ptnrs/6 fee-earners – some of whom also do non-personal injury insurance work). **Clients/Work:** Acts for a number of major insurers handling a range of work from structured settlements to minor whiplash claims. Also covers RTAs, industrial diseases and accidents, employers' and public liability.

Percy Hughes & Roberts (3ptnrs/7fee-earners) Considered by those who knew the firm to be a good, active practice. **Clients/Work:** Acts for the Law Society and major insurers. Handles RTAs, employers' and public liability.

Vaudreys (4ptnrs/16assts) Remains a widely praised firm. **Clients/Work:** Acting for Royal Ordnance in the defence of an employee's claim for catastrophic personal injuries arising out of explosive ordnance disposal work in Kuwait following the Gulf War. Settlement of five test cases where the plaintiffs alleged back injuries as a result of repetitive lifting on a production line.

NORTH WEST

PLAINTIFF AND DEFENDANT

Colemans (3ptnrs/13fee-earners) Perceived as stronger at plaintiff work but "know what they're doing all round." Boast the "young and dynamic" *Roger Coleman* as

LEADING FIRMS • NORTH WEST PLAINTIFF AND DEFENDANT

COLEMANS Manchester
HORWICH FARRELLY Manchester
PERKINS & CO Manchester
SILVERBECK RYMER Liverpool

HIGHLY REGARDED FIRMS

Blackhurst Parker & Yates Preston

LEADING INDIVIDUALS NORTH WEST PLAINTIFF AND DEFENDANT

COLEMAN Roger Colemans

head of the team. **Clients/Work:** Plaintiff: legal expenses insurers and private clients. Defendant: Direct Line, Sabre and other insurers. Saved over £2m on reserves in 1997.

NORTH EAST

MAINLY PLAINTIFF

LEADING FIRMS • NORTH EAST PLAINTIFF

IRWIN MITCHELL Leeds, Sheffield
THOMPSONS Leeds, Newcastle-upon-Tyne
ROWLEY ASHWORTH Leeds
RUSSELL JONES & WALKER Leeds, Sheffield, Newcastle
MARRONS Newcastle upon Tyne
PATTINSON & BREWER York

HIGHLY REGARDED FIRMS

Allan Henderson Beecham and Peacock Newcastle upon Tyne
Browell Smith & Goodyear Newcastle upon Tyne
Philip Hamer & Co Hull
Smith & Graham Hartlepool
Whittles Leeds

Irwin Mitchell (12ptnrs/18assts – none f/t) Very highly regarded in the north east. Five of their lawyers feature as leading individu-

als: *Grahame Codd, John Davis, Michael Napier, John Pickering* and *Andrew Tucker.* **Clients/Work:** Acted in litigation by miners against British Coal (respiratory diseases caused by exposure to allegedly excessive levels of dust). Hodgson v Gallagher & Imperial (conditional fees and press reporting on proceedings in chambers). Brian Ward v Newalls Insulations and Cape Contracts (£750,000 for asbestos disease).

Thompsons The "very able" *Roger Maddocks* "knows the score". The firm continues to be a main player. "They are sensible and know their business," said competitors. Team includes *Pauline Chandler.*

Rowley Ashworth Seen as "strong and busy" and "solid performers."

Russell Jones & Walker (4ptnrs/6assts) "A sensible firm, but not a pushover", its profile in the North is steadily increasing. *Simon Allen* is "a high profile, good guy", admired for his work on the Hillsborough case. **Clients/Work:** Involved in police officers' claim arising from Hillsborough and in Court of Appeal case; "Costello" (remoteness of damage). Obtained £100,000 for police officer exposed to smoke in mock disaster. Acted for family of victim killed when disabled driver mounted pavement.

Marrons Respected by clients and

opponents alike, and admired for its integrity. "A firm you can have dialogue with; they are prepared to negotiate," commented opponents. Team includes some impressive individuals, notably *Patrick Murphy* and *Stephen Porteus.*

Pattinson & Brewer (2ptnrs/1asst) This national firm has a low profile in the north east, but is popular with barristers for whom they "make life easy." **Clients/ Work:** Represented cyclist awarded £300,000 for psychological injury following RTA. Obtained £250,000 for plaintiff with hysterical paraplegia. Acting for plaintiff claiming damages for exposure to asbestos in 1964.

LEADING INDIVIDUALS NORTH EAST • PLAINTIFF

CODD Grahame Irwin Mitchell
DAVIS John Irwin Mitchell
MADDOCKS Roger Thompsons
NAPIER Michael Irwin Mitchell
PICKERING John Irwin Mitchell
TUCKER Andrew Irwin Mitchell
ALLEN Simon Russell Jones & Walker
CHANDLER Pauline Thompsons
MURPHY Patrick Marrons
PORTEUS Stephen Marrons

NORTH EAST

MAINLY DEFENDANT

HIGHLY REGARDED FIRMS NORTH EAST • DEFENDANT

Sinton & Co Newcastle upon Tyne
Crutes Newcastle-upon-Tyne
Deas Mallen Souter Newcastle upon Tyne
Dibb Lupton Alsop Bradford
Hammond Suddards Leeds
Jacksons Stockton-on-Tees
Linsley & Mortimer Newcastle-upon-Tyne
Nabarro Nathanson Sheffield
Wansbroughs Willey Hargrave Leeds
Rollit Farrell & Bladon Hull

Sinton & Co (5ptnrs/5assts) "Unquestionably the leaders in the north east." The team numbers three leading individuals: *James Dias, David Dobbin* and *David Raw.* Considered by clients to be "red hot." **Clients/Work:** Eagle Star; Norwich Union; Guardian; Provident.

Dibb Lupton Alsop (6ptnrs/ 60assts) In common with many of their other offices, the north east is seen as "aggressive and good." *William Evans* and *Peter Anson* are well regarded.

Hammond Suddards (4ptnrs/ 21assts) Generally felt to run cases well, particularly good at trial. **Clients/Work:** 'Cross v Kirklees MBC' (Court of Appeal case dealing with duties of the Highway Authority in clearing snow and ice). Acting for The Chief Consta-

ble and his insurers in relation to PTSD claims by police officers present at the Hillsborough Disaster. 'Radley v Wakefield MBC' (place-

LEADING INDIVIDUALS NORTH EAST •DEFENDANT

DIAS James Sinton & Co
ANSON Peter Dibb Lupton Alsop
DAYKIN Stephen Nabarro Nathanson
DOBBIN David Sinton & Co
DREWE David Crutes
EVANS William Dibb Lupton Alsop
HOTCHIN Samuel Wansbroughs Willey Hargrave
PEACOCK Norman Allan Henderson Beecham and Peacock
RAW David Sinton & Co

ment and maintenance of street lighting).

Jacksons Described as "good from top to bottom." Clients appreciate its specialist knowledge and expertise.

Nabarro Nathanson (3ptnrs/10assts) Has a "steady" northern practice led by

Stephen Daykin. **Clients/ Work:** Acting for British Coal Corporation in respiratory disease litigation. Representing Coal Products in group action by residents of local housing estate alleging that the proximity of a coking plant caused personal injury. Continuing the

VWF litigation in the Court of Appeal.

Wansbroughs Willey Hargrave (5ptnrs/17fee-earners) Described as "excellent and fair and put up a good fight." *Samuel Hotchin* is well thought of. **Clients/ Work:** Royal & Sun Alliance; Eagle Star and EIG.

NORTH EAST

PLAINTIFF AND DEFENDANT

Hay & Kilner (10ptnrs (5 f/t)/5assts (2 f/t)) Seen as a "decent firm." Leading individuals *Peter Pescod* and *Alun Williams* are sensible and good. **Clients/Work:** Royal Sun Alliance; Cornhill; Ecclesiastical. Recovered £1,175,000 for infant plaintiff seriously

LEADING FIRMS • NORTH EAST PLAINTIFF AND DEFENDANT
HAY & KILNER Newcastle-upon-Tyne
LUPTON FAWCETT Leeds
SAMUEL PHILLIPS & CO Newcastle upon Tyne
STAMP JACKSON AND PROCTER Hull

injured after losing control of farm vehicle.

Lupton Fawcett Perceived as "an enlightened firm: pro-active, sensible and constructive." **Clients/Work:** Plaintiff: RAC

LEADING INDIVIDUALS NORTH EAST PLAINTIFF AND DEFENDANT
PESCOD Peter Hay & Kilner
WILLIAMS Alun Hay & Kilner

Legal Services; General Legal Protection; First Assist. Defendant: Provident Insurance, Guardian and ITT London & Edinburgh.

SCOTLAND

MAINLY PURSUER

LEADING FIRMS • SCOTLAND PURSUER
DIGBY BROWN Glasgow
THOMPSONS Edinburgh
BURNSIDE KEMP FRASER Aberdeen

HIGHLY REGARDED FIRMS
Drummond Miller WS Edinburgh
Lawford Kidd Edinburgh
Levy & McRae Glasgow
Allan McDougall & Co SSC Edinburgh
Lefevre Litigation Aberdeen

Digby Brown (11ptnrs/3assocs/ 6assts) A "prominent firm" perceived as expanding rapidly. This growth has been assisted by the addition of a number of solicitors from the former Gillam Mackie. **Clients/Work:** Acts for a major union and legal expenses insurers; also referrals from charities. Work includes RTAs, accidents at work and a specialism in head and spinal injury.

Thompsons (1ptnr/1asst) Consistently described as "aggressive but top notch." All commentators agreed that the firm deserved to be placed top of the list in terms of market share. *Sid Smith* was also praised for his quality work and heavy caseload and is a new entry to the table. **Clients/Work:** Specialises in industrial accidents and diseases.

Burnside Kemp Fraser (2ptnrs/2assts) Little known outside its own locality this niche firm nevertheless received recommendations for two leading individuals,

David Burnside and, a new entry this year, *Sandy Kemp* who is "terrific on the law." **Clients/Work:** Specialises in claims arising out of the offshore oil industry.

Lawford Kidd (2ptnrs/4fee-earners) Another new entry following several recommendations. **Clients/Work:** Acts for unions including AEWU, BALPA and Unison. Handles a number of asbestos related and occupational stress claims. Specialises in cases arising from aircraft disasters.

LEADING INDIVIDUALS SCOTLAND •PURSUER
BURNSIDE David Burnside Kemp Fraser
KEMP Sandy Burnside Kemp Fraser
LEFEVRE Frank Lefevre Litigation
McCULLOCH Grant Drummond Miller WS
SMITH Sid Thompsons
TYLER Alfred Balfour & Manson

SCOTLAND

MAINLY DEFENDER

LEADING FIRMS • SCOTLAND DEFENDER
SIMPSON & MARWICK WS Edinburgh
BIGGART BAILLIE Glasgow
DUNDAS & WILSON CS Edinburgh
HAMILTON BURNS & MOORE Glasgow
PAULL & WILLIAMSONS Aberdeen

HIGHLY REGARDED FIRMS
Shepherd & Wedderburn WS Edinburgh

Simpson & Marwick WS (13ptnrs/30assts) Now considered "the pre-eminent defendant firm" both in terms of resources and market share. *Peter Anderson* received unanimous praise. **Clients/Work:** Handles RSI, industrial diseases and general litigation. Clients include Commercial Union, Eagle Star, ITT London & Edinburgh and General Accident.

Biggart Baillie (2ptnrs/ 3assocs/5assts) A "pretty sound" practice, particularly noted for its industrial disease work. *James Roxburgh* is "highly rated." **Clients/Work:** Clients include Iron Trades Insurance, Railway Claims Ltd, Zurich Municipal, Royal & Sun Alliance and Guardian Royal Exchange. Specialises in industrial disease work, particularly respiratory diseases.

Hamilton Burns & Moore (4ptnrs/3assts/2paralegals) Generally well regarded although some felt the practice was rather dependent on the "very good" *George Moore*. **Clients/Work:** Acts for Direct Line, Norwich Union, Royal & Sun Alliance, Prudential, GA Bonus, Cigna International plus others. Handles a number of industrial accidents and RTAs.

LEADING INDIVIDUALS SCOTLAND • DEFENDER
ANDERSON Peter Simpson & Marwick WS
LYALL Pamela Dundas & Wilson CS
MOORE George Hamilton Burns & Moore
ROXBURGH James Biggart Baillie
TIERNEY James Paull & Williamsons

SCOTLAND

PURSUER AND DEFENDER

Balfour & Manson Received praise for its work and also for *Alfred Tyler*, a "good all rounder" and "solid litigator." Appears in the mainly pursuer table. **Clients/Work:** Special interest in head and spinal injuries.

Anderson Strathern WS (5ptnrs/9fee-earners) Highly recommended for both pursuer and defender work and a new entry to the tables this year. **Clients/Work:** Pursuer: Acting for the Royal College of Nursing in a number of lifting accidents. Defender: Employers' and public liability, industrial accidents and RTAs for Eagle Star and other insurers.

Brodies WS (2ptnrs/ 2assts) Generally well regarded, particularly for defender work. **Clients/Work:** Pursuer: Acts for legal expenses insurers and legally aided private clients. Involved in Girvan v Inverness

Dairies – a leading House of Lords case on the issue of juries in personal injury cases. Defender: Clients include General Accident and Co-op Insurance.

NORTHERN IRELAND

MAINLY PLAINTIFF

Agnew, Andress, Higgins Recognised as having significant institutional clients. Seen as "a premier firm", and consistently described as "extremely competent."

Eammon McEvoy & Co A large provincial practice. *Eammon McEvoy* "has been a force in the provinces for the last 30 years."

Edwards & Co *Aiden Canavan* has a high profile. Seen as a "good operator", he is "always on top of his cases."

NORTHERN IRELAND

MAINLY DEFENDANT

C&H Jefferson (6ptnrs/7assts – not f/t) *Ian Jefferson* heads the firm's defendant practice. *Derek Taylor* "inspires great confidence." **Clients/Work:** Act for RAC and Education Library Boards.

McKinty & Wright (8ptnrs/9assts – p/t) Boasts some well-known leading individuals: *John Cross*, *John Duff* and *Paul Johnston*.

NORTHERN IRELAND

PLAINTIFF AND DEFENDANT

Johnsons (4ptnrs/8assts) *Paul Tweed* is "efficient and easy to deal with but does the job for his client." **Clients/Work:** 'Friel v Friel' (£1.52m RTA case); 'McCauley v Eastern Health & Social Services' (recovered £185,000 for mentally ill patient who set himself on fire after being sold lighter fuel).

Murphy & O'Rawe (4ptnrs/6assts) **Clients/Work:** Handling brain damage claim (£1.5m) for plaintiff. Defending similar claim. Recovered £1.65m for plaintiff in RTA.

O' Reilly Stewart (2ptnrs/6assts) Seen as "a progressive and efficient firm." Leading individual *Brian Stewart* is "active, conscientious, and certainly worth a mention."

SOUTH EAST

DUNCAN, Mary
Henmans, Oxford (01865) 722181
Specialisation: Specialises in personal injury cases for Plaintiffs, and for Defendants and their insurers. Her practice covers the full range of employers liability, product liability, professional indemnity for insurers and she particularly deals with fatal accident claims, industrial disease cases and medical negligence.
Prof. Memberships: Member of the Law Society Personal Injury Panel, AVMA referral panel and FOIL.
Career: Born on 19 November 1958. She was educated at Bicester School and Exeter University, where she acquired an LLB 2:1. Qualified 1983. Practised with *Greenwoods* in 1984 and 1985 and then returned to Henmans where she had been articled, and became a Partner in 1988. Is co-author of "Fatal Accident Claims".
Personal: Married to a Solicitor who practises in London. Two children. Interests include music, sport and family.

HUGHES, David Alan Knoyle
Amery-Parkes, Basingstoke (01256) 356262
Senior Litigation Partner in Personal Injury Department Has specialised in personal injury work since 1961 and deals with complex, high value claims for both Plaintiffs and insurers (road traffic, employers, public liability). Also specialises in insurance related work. Regular speaker at conferences. Co-author of the Judicial Studies Board Guidelines for the Assessment of General Damages in Personal Injury Cases.
Prof. Memberships: Law Society, Law Society Personal Injury Panel Member.
Career: Articled with *Amery-Parkes*, qualifying in 1961, becoming a Partner in 1963.
Personal: Born 21 May 1938. Attended Chigwell School. Leisure interests include music and drama. Lives in Old Alresford, Hampshire.

MATHER, Christopher
Penningtons, Basingstoke (01256) 406300
Consultant in Litigation Department.
Specialisation: Main area of practice is personal injury, handling claims of utmost severity for both defendants and plaintiffs, including where appropriate structured settlements. Also handles admiralty work, mainly dry, and employment law, especially for groups of employees. Chairman of the Steering committees for the Clapham and the Severn Tunnel and Southall rail crashes. Spokesman for Hampshire Law Society involving considerable media involvement. Higher Courts (All Proceedings) Qualification, April 1994. Panel Solicitor Spinal Injuries Association. CEDR accredited mediator.
Prof. Memberships: AVMA, Committee Member of Solicitors Association Higher Courts Advocates. Member of the Law Society Personal Injury Panel.
Career: Qualified in 1973. Joined *Penningtons* in 1994. Assistant Recorder since 1991. Appointed Recorder 1996. Former member of Hampshire and Isle of Wight Valuation Tribunal. Chairman of Hampshire Law Society Public Relations Committee. Part time Special Ajudicator (Immigration and Asylum)

Personal: Born 20th June 1947. Attended Ellesmere College and College of Law. Leisure interests include a small holding. Lives in Romsey, Hants. Founded and organised the Wig & Scapel Society (the Southampton Medico-Legal Society) since 1993.

OSBORNE, Thomas R
Osborne Morris & Morgan, Leighton Buzzard (01525) 378177

SCRUTTON, David T.
Kennedys, Brentwood (01277) 233636
Partner. Senior Partner at Brentwood Office.
Specialisation: Specialises in Personal Injury, particularly occupational diseases. Lectures on the subject. Member of The Law Society and a member of FOIL.
Career: Commenced work with *Barlow, Lyde & Gilbert* in 1961; Admitted 1976. Joined *Kennedys* in 1980. Became a Partner in 1981.
Personal: Leisure interests include antiques and collectibles, music, aviation, motor sport and travel.

TENQUIST, Iain R.
Cole & Cole, Oxford (01865) 262600
Specialisation: Catastrophic injuries, in particular brain injuries; public liability claims, leading the litigation arising from the 60 vehicle pile-up on the M4 in March 1991 involving 10 fatalities; regular contributor of articles to journals; experienced speaker.
Prof. Memberships: Law Society, Forum of Insurance Lawyers.
Career: 1969-76 Magdalen College School, Oxford. 1977-80 King's College, London (LLB). 1980-81 College of Law, Guildford. 1982-5 *Humfrys & Symonds*, Hereford (qualified 1984). 1985 to date *Cole & Cole*.

VOLLER, Edward
Warner Goodman & Streat, Fareham (01329) 288121

WILLIAMS, Brian
A.E. Wyeth & Co, Dartford (01322) 297000
Specialisation: Partner in Insurance Litigation Department. Extensive experience in insurance litigation, in particular road accident, employers liability and public liability personal injury claims, industrial disease claims (e.g. asbestos exposure, noise induced hearing loss); Work related upper limb disorder claims, work related stress claims, product liability, professional indemnity claims and policy disputes. Acted in 'AFZAL & ORS v. FORD MOTOR CO. LTD'.
Prof. Memberships: Law Society; Holborn and Kent Law Societies; Forum of Insurance Lawyers.
Career: Qualified in 1965 whilst at *A.E.Wyeth & Co* and became a Partner in 1965. Appointed Deputy District Judge 1998.
Personal: Born 16th November 1940. Educated at Latymer Upper School, Hammersmith, and College of Law, London. Chairman of Corporate Board of North West Kent College. Lives in Haywards Heath, West Sussex.

SOUTH WEST

BEALE, Robert L.
Wansbroughs Willey Hargrave, Bristol (0117) 926 8981
Specialisation: Bob is head of the firm's Insurance Division nationally, as well as the partner in charge of *Wansboroughs Willey Hargrave*'s Specialised Loss Unit in Bristol. Areas include road traffic accident, employers and public liability, fraud and policy coverage issues. Highlights include the successful defence of two fraudulent arson claims; £1.5m public liability claim for statutory authority.
Prof. Memberships: FOIL.
Career: Educated Exeter University. 1968 *Robins Hay, London*, 1971 qualified. 1971 Assistant solicitor *Burges Salmon*, Bristol. 1974 Joined *Wansborough Willey Hargrave*, 1975 became partner.

CARRON, Byron
Townsends, Swindon (01793) 410800
Partner and Head of Personal Injury Department.
Specialisation: Main area of practice is head injuries and spinal injuries, where damages are usually not less than £100,000 and can be in excess of £1 million. Also handles other injury cases including RTA or industrial accidents. Both plaintiff and defendant work. Has appeared frequently on local TV and radio.
Prof. Memberships: Law Society, Gloucestershire and Wiltshire Law Society, APIL, Personal Injury Panel, Headway (National Bath Bristol & Swindon Groups).
Career: Qualified in 1965. Joined *Townsends* in 1959, becoming a Partner in 1966. Former Chairman of North Wilts Legal Association, Former County Councillor. Vice Chairman of Wilts County Council. Chairman of Finance Committee of WCC, President of Swindon Rotary Club.
Personal: Born 18th March 1942. Attended High School, Swindon and The College, Swindon. Leisure interests include gardening, walking and music. Lives in Swindon.

CHANDLER, Brigitte H.
Townsends, Swindon (01793) 410800
Partner in Personal Injury Department.
Specialisation: Main areas of practice are industrial injury and industrial disease, particularly claims involving inhalation of dangerous dust and fumes, and also including lifting accidents, dangerous machinery and deafness . Wide experience of asbestos claims in every field of work. Has considerable media experience including TV and radio appearances.
Prof. Memberships: Law Society, Gloucestershire and Wiltshire Law Society.
Career: Qualified in 1977. Joined *Townsends* in 1977, becoming a Partner in 1981.
Personal: Born 13th January 1952. Attended Aylesbury High School 1963-70. Manchester University (Upper Second class degree). Leisure interests include theatre and travel. Lives in Swindon.

COOPER, Jonathan J.
Bond Pearce, Plymouth (01752) 266 633
Partner and head of the Health and Safety Group.
Specialisation: Specialises in personal injury

litigation and health and safety issues. Deals with all aspects of occupational health and safety including defending prosecutions and drafting health and safety policies. Very wide experience of industrial disease claims, especially asbestos related. Has handled a number of multi-party actions for industrial disease, including lead poisoning and Styrene contamination. Has written numerous articles on occupational health related matters and was a contributor to a BBC documentary on asbestos claims.
Prof. Memberships: Member of the Law Society Personal Injury Panel.
Career: Qualified in 1984, becoming a partner in 1989.

DAVIES, Paul Roger
Sansbury Hill, Bristol (0117) 926 5341

GUY, Michael
Sansbury Hill, Bristol (0117) 926 5341
Partner specialising in defendant personal injury litigation.
Specialisation: Predominantly employers' liability and major motor claims, Industrial disease (especially RSI). Successfully defended one of the first keyboard RSI cases. Has experience of addressing external conferences and seminars with insurers and major insureds.
Career: Trained with *Wansbroughs Willey Hargrave* 1974-77. Qualified in 1976. Practised with *Sansbury Hill & Co.* 1977-84, as a Partner from 1980. Set up *Macfarlane Guy* in 1984. Assessor for the Law Society's Specialist Personal Injury Panel. Has recently merged Insurance Department of *Macfarlane Guy* with *Sansbury Hill*.
Personal: Born 15th October 1949. Educated at Bristol University 1968-71. Leisure time is devoted to family. Lives in Bath.

HERBERT, Andrew
Thompsons, Bristol (0117) 941 1606
Specialisation: Plaintiff personal injury claims particularly chest diseases including asbestos related claims.
Prof. Memberships: APIL; Bristol Law Society; member of Personal Injury Panel; Assessor for the Law Society Personal Injury Panel.

MIDDLETON, Simon
Stephens & Scown, Truro (01872) 265100
Specialisation: Plaintiff and Defendant personal injury. High volume legal expense and private plaintiff work. Local authority and RTA defendant work. Contributor to: 'Rehabilitation of the Physically Disabled Adult' 2nd edition, Editor, Evans & Chamberlain. 'Journal of Personal Injury Law' editorial board.
Prof. Memberships: APIL, MASS, ATLA, AVMA. Member of the Headway Panel, the Law Society Personal Injury Panel and the Spinal Injuries Panel.
Career: Gresham's School, Norfolk. University of Wales. Calcott Pryce Prize for Evidence.
Personal: Family, writing and golf.

OVER, Christopher
Over Taylor Biggs, Exeter (01392) 823811
Founding Partner 1993.
Specialisation: Principal area of practice is medical negligence dealing with claims of all types but particularly catastrophic injury.

Represented clients in major medical claims involving substantial damages. Also deals with a wide range of transport cases including route licensing, planning and environmental appeals. Acted in transport cases on European Directives. Contributor to PI text books and Accident Line Book and author of articles in legal publications. Regular conference speaker and broadcasts frequently on local radio and TV.
Prof. Memberships: APIL, AVMA, SIA, Panel Solicitor for RHA and FTA. Law Society Public Relations Board.
Career: Qualified in 1977. Partner for ten years with *Crosse & Crosse* in Exeter: three years as Managing Partner. Founding Partner of *Over Taylor Biggs* in February 1993.
Personal: Born 18th October 1952. Attended King Edwards VI, Camp Hill, and Birmingham University. School Governor and Charity Trustee. leisure pursuits include walking, badminton, food and drink and travel. Lives near Exeter.

PENNY, Michael
Veitch Penny, Exeter (01392) 278381
Senior Partner and Head of Defendant Department.
Specialisation: Deals with serious injury cases – road traffic, employers liability and public liability – local authority claims including highway, swimming pool and education cases (E v Dorset part of the X v Bedfordshire series of cases in House of Lords). Has acted in several high profile cases including Herald of Free Enterprise prosecutions and Lyme Bay Canoe Tragedy, resulting in media exposure. Regularly lectures to insurance companies, local authorities and local authority groups. He has also lectured on beach safety in the South West.
Prof. Memberships: Law Society, Devon & Exeter Law Society, Forum of Insurance Lawyers and F.R.S.A.
Career: Qualified in 1971. Trained in London. Worked in a Defendant Practice in Bristol before joining *Veitch Penny* in 1973 and opening the Exeter office which is now the headquarters of a thriving personal injury and insurance practice.
Personal: Born 3rd August 1948. Attended Blundells School, Tiverton and College of Law, Leisure interest include working on his smallholding, rugby and good wines!

ROWE, Bernard V.
Lyons Davidson, Bristol (0117) 904 6000
Partner and Head of Personal Injury and Insurance.
Specialisation: Principal area of practice is personal injury litigation with emphasis on road traffic accidents. Heads a department of 120 personnel, handling personal injury and road traffic litigation throughout the South West for plaintiffs and defendants. Has been involved in numerous substantial personal injury cases, including structured settlements. Experienced lecturer at legal conferences and seminars. Organised 3-day international Conferences on Whiplash injuries and forthcoming conference on Psychological injuries after Road Accidents. Has made television appearances and attended parliamentary meetings for the Motor Accident Solicitors Society in relation to windscreen insurance discs and the Small Claims Court.
Prof. Memberships: Motor Accident Solicitors Society (Chairman 1992-94), Legal Aid Appeal

Committee Member, Law Society, Bristol Law Society (Past Council Member and Training Chairman).
Career: Qualified in 1976. Partner at *Iveson Jarratt* in Hull from 1977. Joined *Lyons Davidson* in 1986 and became a Partner in 1987. Managing Partner 1992-94. Member Judicial Advisory Committee to European Whiplash Association.
Personal: Born 21st December 1951. Educated at Watford Grammar School 1963-70 and Hull University 1970-73 (BA, Politics and Law). Leisure pursuits include driving and fish flying. Lives in Bristol.

VERNALLS, David Francis
Cartwrights, Bristol (0117) 929 3601
Partner in Insurance Department.
Specialisation: Main area of practice is insurance work involving employers liability. Dealing with all aspects of employers liability, including a large number of industrial and agriculture/farming related disease cases. Particular specialisations are deafness, respiratory and other disease claims, limitation of actions, striking out actions for want of prosecution and failure to comply with the RSC. Acted in Cook v. Square D Ltd; Gilbert v. Lanes Storage & Removals Ltd; Gitsham v. CH Pearce & Sons Ltd; Price v. Dannimac Ltd and Beese v. Brosnan Plant and Excavation Contractors Ltd, all heard in the Court of Appeal. Co-ordinator for deafness cases throughout the country for a major employers liability insurance company. Has lectured to a number of insurance companies on industrial disease, limitation and changes in the rules of the High Court and County Court and the new Health and Safety Regulations implementing the European Directives.
Prof. Memberships: Law Society.
Career: Qualified in 1968. Joined *Cartwrights* in 1969 and became a Partner in 1972. Member of Bristol Civil Courts Users Committee.
Personal: Born 1941. Educated at Caerphilly Grammar School 1953-60, then Balliol College, Oxford 1960-63. Leisure pursuits include theatre, reading, swimming and tennis. Lives in Bristol.

WALES

BENT, Roger
Thompsons, Cardiff (01222) 484136
Specialisation: Main area of practice has been personal injuries litigation since admission.
Prof. Memberships: APIL; Cardiff Law Society; member of Personal Injury Panel; ATLA (American Trial Lawyers).

CLEMENT-EVANS, J. Cenric
Leo Abse & Cohen, Cardiff (01222) 383252
Partner in Trade Union Legal Service Department.
Specialisation: Specialises in plaintiff personal injury claims. Work covers fatal accident cases, industrial and other accidents including severe injuries, group deafness and group RSI litigation against a number of employers and other industrial diseases (e.g. dermatitis).
Prof. Memberships: Law Society, Law Society PI Panel, Co-ordinator of Occupational Health Special Interest Group of Association of Personal Injury Lawyers. Lectures on NIHL.
Career: Qualified in 1986. With *Globe Wareing Cropper*, Liverpool 1984-88. Joined *Leo Abse & Cohen* in 1988 and became a Partner in March 1992.

Personal: Born 22nd August 1962. Welsh speaking. Educated at Liverpool College 1970-80, University College of Wales, Aberystwyth 1980-83 and the College of Law, Chester 1983-84. Interests include drama, theatre, cinema, and fitness exercise. Lives in Cardiff.

CRADICK, Simon J.
Morgan Bruce, Cardiff (01222) 385385
Partner in Insurance Department.
Specialisation: Main area of practice is insurance litigation, covering all areas of personal injury work including maximum severity, industrial disease, RSI, factory and road traffic accidents and employers' and public liability claims. Writes a regular bulletin on legal update for all insurance clients. Prepared and lectured on Health and Safety regulations legal costs and industrial disease claims.
Prof. Memberships: Member of Cardiff Law Society, Personal Injury Panel and FOIL.
Career: Qualified in 1984, joined *Morgan Bruce* in 1985 and become a partner in 1988.
Personal: Interests include skiing, walking and playing squash.

HERMER, Ian B.
Palser Grossman, Cardiff Bay (01222) 452770
Defendant personal injury work for leading insurance companies.
Career: Qualified in 1959. Since then has been a partner in his own firm, now an acting consultant with *Palser Grossman*.

HOPKINS, Ian
Leo Abse & Cohen, Cardiff (01222) 383252
Partner in Litigation Department.
Specialisation: Personal injury litigation specialist. Member of Law Society PI Panel and Scheme contact for Law Society's Accident Line. Handles large personal injury claims for both plaintiffs and defendants including a substantial case load of industrial disease claims (particularly occupational asthma and asbestosis). Clients include Trade Unions, Insurance companies and the general public. Supervisor in Legal Aid Board Franchised Legal Aid Department. Member of Steering Committee for Severn Tunnel train crash.
Prof. Memberships: Law Society, APIL, Personal Injury Panel.
Career: Qualified in 1987. Became a Partner at *Leo Abse & Cohen* in 1990.
Personal: Born 20th August 1961. Educated at Aberdare Grammar School and Kingston University 1979-82. Lives in Aberdare.

JENKINS, Russel J.A.
Hugh James, Cardiff (01222) 224871
Specialisation: Partner in the Litigation Department specialising in defendant personal injury work. 27 years experience handling cases for insurers and self-insurers ranging from whiplash to tetraplegic, brain damage, and fatal accident. Also acts for Lloyds syndicates.
Prof. Memberships: Founding member of FOIL (Forum of Insurance Lawyers). Immediate past president of Cardiff Law Society.
Personal: Educated at Cardiff High School and Bristol University (LL.B) 1963-66. Church Warden. Leisure pursuits include watching motor racing and reading. Born 25th October 1944. Lives in Cardiff.

JONES, Michael L.N.
Hugh James, Cardiff (01222) 224871
See under Construction, Education, Litigation (Commercial), p. 212, 292, 525

LEWIS, Brian
Graham Evans & Partners, Swansea
(01792) 655822

PRICE, Hugh
Morgan Bruce, Cardiff (01222) 385385
See under Professional Negligence, p. 677

WILLIAMS, Gareth J.
Hugh James, Cardiff (01222) 224871
Partner in Litigation Department.
Specialisation: Personal injury litigation for insurers. Has acted for insurers for more than 20 years and undertaken the usual range of personal injury work. Also deals with commercial litigation, acting for a number of local companies and partnerships by whom he is regularly instructed to deal with contractual and other disputes. Advises major sports governing body on litigation and constitutional issues.
Prof. Memberships: Law Society; F.O.I.L.
Career: Joined *Hugh James* in 1975 and qualified in 1976. Became a Partner in 1978. First Solicitor in Wales to be appointed a Licensed Insolvency Practitioner. Deputy District Judge from 1991 to date.
Personal: Born 5th September 1951. Educated at Glan Clwyd High School 1962-69 and University College of Wales, Aberystwyth 1969-72 (Morgan Owen Law Prizeman). Leisure pursuits include sport, reading and music. Lives in Cowbridge.

WILLIAMS, Robin
Leo Abse & Cohen, Cardiff (01222) 383252
Partner in Litigation Department.
Specialisation: Principal area of practice covers personal injury claims, employment and Trade Union law. Advises BIFU, GMB and TGWU, various insurance companies, business and private clients. Acts in industrial disease cases including asbestosis, deafness, asthma, RSI and dermatitis. Also handles fatal accident claims, employment injunctions and has extensive experience of all complaints to the Industrial Tribunal including mass dismissal claims, sex discrimination cases, transfer regulations disputes. Has acted in general Chancery and Commercial cases, particularly contested probate actions, winding up petitions and bancruptcy. Lectures on personal injury, employment and Trade Union Law.
Prof. Memberships: Law Society, Personal Injury Panel, APIL (Regional Co-ordinator of the South Wales and West Regional Group).
Career: Qualified in 1980 while with *Leo Abse & Cohen* and became a Partner in 1985.
Personal: Born 15th October 1955. Attended Glanafan Comprehensive School 1966-74 and London School of Economics 1974-77. School Governor. Leisure pursuits include sport (rugby, soccer and badminton), theatre, art, cinema, modern music and reading. Lives in Cardiff.

WOLFE, Jeremy B.
Douglas-Jones Mercer, Swansea
(01792) 650000
Specialisation: Has acted for insurers for 20 years in the usual range of personal injury work including local authority related claims, lifting accidents, R.S.I. and asbestosis claims.
Prof. Memberships: Law Society, Forum of Insurance Lawyers, Member of the Law Society Personal Injury Panel.
Career: Joined *Douglas-Jones & Mercer* in 1976 and qualified in 1978. Became a Partner in 1982.
Personal: Born 29 April 1954. Attended

Redditch County High School and obtained London University (External) LL.B in 1975. Interests include angling, cricket, wine tasting, good foods and gardening.

MIDLANDS

ADAMSON, Derek P.
Buller Jeffries, Birmingham (0121) 212 2620
Specialisation: Personal injury claims particularly fatal accidents, catastrophic injuries, industrial disease and medical negligence. High profile cases have included motorway disasters, asbestos litigation and products' claims. Other principal areas include professional indemnity, fires, construction claims, policy interpretation and defending civil claims against the police.
Prof. Memberships: Law Society, Birmingham Law Society, FOIL.
Career: Articles *Buller Jeffries* 1979-1981. Partner 1985. Deputy District Judge 1993 - 1997
Personal: Born 1956. Birmingham University 1975-78. Leisure Interests: Mainly sport, manager of youth soccer team.

ARKELL, Catherine
Everatt & Company, Evesham (01386) 47191
Senior Partner in Litigation Department.
Specialisation: Acts for defendant insurers in a variety of personal injury claims. Has dealt with serious road traffic claims including paraplegia, head injury, etc, and many disease cases including large volume deafness, asbestos-related, RSI, and hand/arm vibration claims. Has also dealt with large (over £1 million) fire-related claims for insurers. Recent important cases include Rastin v British Steel Plc [1994] (for successful appellant defendants) and Heal v Garringtons Ltd (for defendant's insurers). Contributed to a chapter in 'Hand-arm vibration: A Comprehensive Guide for Occupational Health Professionals' (ed. Pelmear, Taylor & Wasserman).
Prof. Memberships: Law Society.
Career: Qualified in 1979. Became a Partner in *Everatt & Co* in 1980. Now Senior Partner.
Personal: Born 8th November 1954. Educated at Westwood's Grammar School and Bristol University 1973-76. Hon. Legal Advisor to Wychavon Citizen's Advice Bureau.

BALEN, Paul
Freeth Cartwright Hunt Dickins, Nottingham
(0115) 936 9369
See under Medical Negligence: Mainly Plaintiff, Product Liability (Food Law), p. 585, 661

CHAPMAN, Richard
Chapman Everatt, Birmingham
(0121) 633 7440
Partner specialising in defendant personal injury.
Specialisation: Specialises in defendant personal injury. The whole firm acts exclusively for insurers and has no private clients. Has appeared on radio and television.
Prof. Memberships: Law Society, Birmingham Law Society, Birmingham Medico Legal Society.
Career: Qualified in 1970. Founding Partner of *Chapman Everatt & Co.* in May 1992. Birmingham Law Society Council Member since 1979 and President for 1996/97.
Personal: Born 7th October 1945. Educated at Birchfield School 1952-59, then Denstone College 1959-64. Governor of Birchfield School. Leisure interests include all sports, particularly golf and cricket, as well as theatre and cinema. Lives near Wolverhampton.

DACE, Nigel H.
Weightmans, Birmingham (0121) 233 2601
Specialisation: Partner specialising in personal injury work including motor, employers liability, public liability, local authority and professional and medical negligence claims. His practice also covers subsidence and other property claims. Acts for insurance companies and Lloyd's syndicates, at both High Court and County Court level. Very considerable experience of cases involving paraplegic and tetraplegic damage, brain damage and cerebral palsy. Has lectured on behalf of Birmingham Law Society and Worcester Law Society on 'The Practice and Procedure in Personal Injury Claims'.
Prof. Memberships: Birmingham Medico-Legal Society.
Career: Qualified 1973. Trained in London. Partner with *George Green & Co* 1982-96. Partner with *Weightmans* since May 1996.
Personal: Educated at Shrewsbury School 1963-67 and Liverpool University 1967-70. Leisure pursuits include playing golf and tennis, watching most sports, particularly football, and also theatre. Born 6th September 1949. Lives in Hagley, Worcestershire.

GOODMAN, Sarah
Thompsons, Birmingham (0121) 236 7944
Specialisation: Plaintiff personal injury, particularly in major injury and occupational diseases including asbestos litigation. Substantial medical negligence. In the employment field, employee contracts, transfer of undertakings, race, sex and disability discrimination and equal pay.
Prof. Memberships: Member of both the Personal Injury and Medical Negligence Panels.

HENDERSON, Stuart
Irwin Mitchell, Birmingham (0121) 212 1828
Partner in Personal Injury Department.
Specialisation: Particular emphasis on major injury, fatal accident claims and medical negligence. Heads firm's Plaintiff Personal Injury Department in Birmingham. Acted in the Leung case, a 3.4 million record award in personal injury cases in the UK. Has extensive media experience and lectures in-house and externally.
Prof. Memberships: APIL, Law Society.
Career: Qualified in 1992. Joined *Robin Thompson & Partners* in 1979, becoming a Partner in 1992. Partner in *Irwin Mitchell* from January 1995.
Personal: Born 20th February 1958. Attended UCE Birmingham. Leisure interests include tennis, cinema, art, opera and the music of Van Morrison.

KING, Phil
Thompsons, Nottingham (0115) 958 4999
Specialisation: Plaintiff personal injury work, industrial disease cases and professional negligence.

LAWTON, Anthony
Thompsons, Birmingham (0121) 236 7944
Specialisation: Personal injury litigation, employment law, involvement in asbestos cases. Recent judgment on gluteraldhyde asthma case.
Prof. Memberships: Birmingham Law Society; Member of Personal Injury Panel.

LEWIS, Geoffrey J.
Buller Jeffries, Birmingham (0121) 212 2620
Specialisation: Extensive insurance related practice with some plaintiff work as well. Catastrophic injury cases. Fatal Accidents Act claims, Employers' Liability and Property claims. Local authority work and Motor Insurers' Bureau specialist. Policy problems and interpretation. Enjoys unusual or novel accident claims involving points of law.
Prof. Memberships: Law Society, Birmingham Law Society and FOIL.
Career: Articled to Roger Coates at *Buller Jeffries* 1971. Qualified 1973 and partner 1979.
Personal: Born 1949. Graduated 1970 external London University LLB, 2:1 Hons. Leisure interests include running (London Marathon 1996), current affairs, music and DIY.

PERRY, Timothy
William Hatton, Dudley (01384) 211211
Specialisation: Mainly defendant insurance and associated personal injury work. Predominantly deals with employers liability and public liability claims, to include catastrophic injuries and deafness and other industrial diseases.
Prof. Memberships: Law Society and Birmingham Law Society
Career: Educated at Abraham Darby Comprehensive in Telford and then Hull University. After qualifying in 1974, was assistant solicitor at *Brown Jacobson*. Joined *William Hatton* in 1979. Became a partner in 1981.
Personal: Married and lives in Birmingham. Interests include motor sport and football.

PRAIN, David
Rowley Ashworth, Wolverhampton (01902) 771551
Partner in Personal Injury Litigation Department. Charge-out rate is £75 per hour (local County Court rates). Currently Managing Partner.
Specialisation: Over 20 years' experience of all types of injury and disease work on behalf of leading trade unions and private clients.
Prof. Memberships: Law Society, Birmingham and Wolverhampton Law Societies, member of the Law Society's Personal Injury Panel, Association of Personal Injury Lawyers.
Career: Qualified 1973. Articled at *Rowley Ashworth* 1967-72. Re-joined *Rowley Ashworth* in 1975 and became a partner in 1976.
Personal: Born 20th July, 1948. Attended Silcoates School, Wakefield 1960-66; St John's College of Further Education, Manchester 1966-67; Manchester College of Commerce (L.S. Part 1) 1968-69; College of Law, Guildford 1972. Governor of Halesowen College. Leisure pursuits include wood carving, photography, motor sports, gardening and travel. Lives in Kidderminster.

ZINDANI, Jeffry
Russell Jones & Walker, Birmingham (0121) 643 6800
Specialisation: Main area of practice is personal injury acting for a number of Trades Union clients. Acted in the largest noise induced deafness claim for a Police Firearms Officer. Acted in a number of lifting cases, and in particular in the reported case of Colclough v. Staffordshire County Council 1993. Author of Book entitled 'Manual Handling Law and Litigation' (CLT Professional Publishing) and article published in APIL Newsletter Vol 8 issue 1998 entitled 'Unleashing the Manual Handling Tiger'
Prof. Memberships: Member of the Personal Injury Panel Law Society; Member of the Birmingham Medico-Legal Society and APIL.
Career: Qualified in 1989; April 1989 joined *Russell Jones & Walker[IT], in Birmingham, became a partner in July 1994.*
Personal: Born 4th July 1963. Attended Moseley Comprehensive School and UCE. LLB (Hons.); The University of Keele, MA (Industrial Relations).

EAST ANGLIA

CARY, Tim
Leathes Prior, Norwich (01603) 610911

NORTH WEST

COLEMAN, R.J.
Colemans Solicitors, Manchester (0161) 236 5623
Specialisation: Senior Partner and Head of Litigation. Personal specialisation is predominantly high value defendant personal injury work for a number of insurance companies.
Prof. Memberships: Law Society, Manchester Law Society, Forum of Insurance Lawyers.
Career: Birmingham University, Chester College of Law, trained in Manchester. Founder partner of *Janet Scowcroft & Co* in 1984, formed *Coleman & Co* in 1987 and merged the two practices in 1991 to form *Colemans Solicitors*. Also established associated practice of *Coleman & Tilley* in Kingston-upon-Thames in 1988 which merged with *Tarrant Sutton* in 1996 to form *Coleman Tilley Tarrant Sutton*, of which he is Senior Partner.
Personal: Married, two children. Being 40 this year has admitted defeat and succumbed to gardening and dog walking.

FINNIGAN, Kevin P.
James Chapman & Co, Manchester (0161) 828 8000
Specialisation: Heads Personal Injury Department at *James Chapman & Co* dealing with cases of the utmost severity. The cases involve the most severe injuries – brain damage and spinal injuries. The case values well exceed one million pounds. The ethos of the claims handling process is to take a pro-active stance and mediate as many of the claims as early as possible, taking a consensual approach with the Plaintiff's solicitors. Frequently addresses conferences and seminars on the handling of very large claims.
Prof. Memberships: Manchester Law Society. FOIL.
Career: Educated: St Bedes College of Hull University. LLB (Hons) – 1975. Articled at *James Chapman & Co*. Admitted 1978.
Personal: Born: 18.12.53. Married with 3 children. Interests: Hill walking in Ireland, reading and Guinness.

HENTHORN, John L.
Berrymans Lace Mawer, Manchester (0161) 236 2002
Partner in Civil Litigation Department, based at the Manchester Office but also has overall responsibility for the Leeds Office.
Specialisation: Joint head of the firm's Industrial Disease Unit; acts for a number of

major insurance companies dealing with substantial employers' liability accident and disease claims. Lectures and addresses seminars on all aspects of civil litigation.
Prof. Memberships: Law Society, Manchester Law Society.
Career: Qualified in 1970 while at *Lace Mawer* becoming a Partner in 1972. Deputy District Judge since September 1992.
Personal: Born 5th August 1946. Attended Brasenose College, Oxford 1964-67, B.A. (Oxon). Governor, Home Farm Trust (national charity providing full time residential accommodation to adults with learning difficulties). Leisure pursuits include golf (member of the Royal Birkdale Golf Club), tennis, music and bridge. Married with three sons. Lives in Aughton, Ormskirk, Lancashire.

HIGGINS, Bernard
Michael W. Halsall, Newton-le-Willows (01942) 727000

HORNER, Malcolm D.
Rowlands, Manchester (0161) 835 2020
Specialisation: All areas of personal injury litigation including cases of maximum severity and structured settlement. Involved in first structured settlement involving M.I.B. and approved by Court of Appeal. Ad hoc Lecturer.
Prof. Memberships: APIL, member of Law Society Personal Injury Panel. Legal Aid franchisee.
Career: Educated Manchester Grammar School and Nottingham University Law School. Qualified in 1984 and is currently head of the Personal Injury Department at *Rowlands* Solicitors, Manchester.
Personal: Now thirty-something, married with two boys. Living in Altrincham, supporting Manchester United and Broughton Park RUFC.

MANSFIELD, C.P.
Whittles, Manchester (0161) 228 2061

MCCOOL, Geraldine M.
Leigh, Day & Co, Manchester (0161) 832 7722
Specialisation: Main area of practice is aviation for plaintiffs, product liability and MOD claims. Cases have included Lockerbie, British Midland at Kegworth, Piper Alpha and Chinook Mull of Kintyre crash 1994. Co-Author of Longmans Know How PI and Multi Party Actions by LAG.
Prof. Memberships: APIL, ATLA, past Chairman of Young Solicitors Group. Member of Law Society's Personal Injury Panel.
Career: Joined *Leigh Day & Co.* in 1994 as a Partner
Personal: Born 20th April 1961.

PATTERSON, Francis P.
Leigh, Day & Co, Manchester (0161) 832 7722
Specialisation: All areas of personal injury litigation, acting exclusively on behalf of plaintiffs. Handles in particular industrial accidents and industrial disease claims on behalf of trade union clients. Deals with maximum severity damages actions on behalf of plaintiffs with spinal injuries and head injuries. Co-author "PI Know How" – published by Longmans. Co-author "Personal Injury Precedents & Pleadings" – published by Sweet & Maxwell.
Prof. Memberships: Member of the Law Society's Personal Injury Specialist Panel, APIL.

Career: Qualified in 1986, having served articles with *Pannone & Partners*.Became a partner in 1990, and head of personal Injury Litigation in 1993. Partner at *Leigh Day & Co.* from December 1995.
Personal: Born 6th December 1959, graduated from University of Manchester.

PICKERING, John
John Pickering & Partners, Oldham (0161) 633 6667
Specialisation: Specialist in handling asbestos claims for Plaintiffs. Claims handled throughout the country. Much experience in other industrial disease claims, i.e. asthma, white finger, dermatitis, bladder cancer. Also experience in solicitor's and medical negligence claims. Instructed by trade unions for members. Devised Conditional Fee Agreement for trade unions. Pioneered byssinosis, i.e. cotton dust, claims in England. Acted for Plaintiff in recent Leeds neighbourhood asbestos trial of 'Margereson v. J.W. Roberts Limited'. Handled many claims for citizens of Australia and for claimants in Malta with claims to pursue in UK.
Prof. Memberships: APIL. Personal Injury Panel. Legal Aid Franchise.
Career: Qualified 1965. Partner *W.H. Thompson* and *Brian Thompson & Partners* from 1968 until 1979. Founded own firm in Manchester 1979. Now four branches, Oldham, Manchester, Liverpool and Halifax.
Personal: Born 1939.

POPPERWELL, Keith
Geoffrey Warhurst, Manchester (0161) 236 8394
Specialisation: Personal injury claims on behalf of defendant insurers. Responsible for the first UK structured settlement. An advocate of early intervention and rehabilitation in maximum severity cases. Has negotiated settlements in over 150 maximum severity cases.
Prof. Memberships: Law Society.
Career: Senor partner of *Geoffrey Warhurst & Co.* Member of the Working Party for the Establishment of the Rehabilitation UK Disability Assessment Unit. Member of Law Society Working Party on Structured Settlements.
Personal: Married with 3 children. Keen golfer.

POTTER, Hugh
Hugh Potter & Company, Serious Injury Solicitors, Manchester (0161) 832 2255
Specialisation: Mainly brain and spinal cord injury including medical negligence and professional negligence cases. Has growing caseload of English Plaintiffs injured abroad.
Prof. Memberships: Member of The Law Society Personal Injury and Medical Negligence Panels (re-selection applied for), Legal Aid franchise (applied for) and APIL.
Career: Qualified in 1988, became a partner in *Pannone Napier* and *Pannone & Partners* in 1990 and joined *Perkins & Company* as a partner in 1994 and formed *Hugh Potter & Company Serious Injury Solicitors* on 1st May 1998.
Personal: Born 8 June 1962. Fund raiser for Headway and Spinal Injuries Association.

SUMMERS, Tony
Weightmans, Liverpool (0151) 227 2601
Specialisation: All aspects of Personal Injury work with particular interest in Industrial Disease claims, Medical negligence and cases involving catastrophic injury. Insurance Law and Policy interpretation.

Prof. Memberships: Law Society. Member CICAP (Criminal Injury Compensation Appeals Panel) and the CICB.
Career: Liverpool University LLB.

TAZIKER, Barry
Keogh Ritson, Bolton (01204) 532611
Senior Partner.
Specialisation: Insurance policy interpretation. Insurance fraud. Commercial and personal injury litigation, on the instructions of insurers.
Career: Qualified 1970. Partner since 1971.
Personal: Born 11th January 1945. Educated at St Peters' College, Oxford. Open Exhibitioner. Former Chairman of the Area Legal Aid Board. Former President of the local Law Society.

WILSON, Anthony E.
Hill Dickinson, Liverpool (0151) 236 5400
Partner in Insurance Litigation Department.
Specialisation: Main area of practice is defendant personal injury work and professional indemnity cases. Acts on behalf of insurers in road traffic, employers and public liability claims with special interest in serious injury cases. Involved in professional indemnity work for consulting engineers, surveyors and veterinary surgeons. Handled the industrial dispute at Cammell Laird Shipbuilders in 1984, where the strikers had been imprisoned: successfully defended the actions before the Court of Appeal. Lectures to insurers on personal injury claims.
Prof. Memberships: Law Society, Liverpool Law Society and NW representative of FOIL.
Career: Qualified in 1977. Joined *Hill Dickinson Davis Campbell* in 1977, becoming a Partner in 1981. Head of Insurance Litigation Department 1992-94. Management Partner 1994-98. Presently Partner at *Hill Dickinson*.
Personal: Born 23rd December 1951. Attended St Francis Xaviers Grammar School 1963-70, Nottingham University 1970-73 and Chester College of Law 1973-74. Leisure interests include hockey, skiing, tennis and golf. Resides Liverpool.

NORTH EAST

ALLEN, S.J.N.
Russell Jones & Walker, Sheffield (0114) 276 6868
Specialisation: Plaintiff Personal Injury. Involved specifically in Industrial accidents, RSI cases, Asbestos cases, multi-handed fume cases and occupational stress cases. Ran the Hillsborough Police PTSD Litigation which was successful before the Court of Appeal in October 96. Has been involved in 2 of the top 6 RSI settlements ever. Publications: Sol. Journal 1993 and 1994; New Law Journal 1997; PMILL 1996 and 1997; Apil Magazine 1995, 1996, 1997; Legal Times 1996. Regular lecturer on PI and in particular on PTSD, RSI, Stress, Asbestos and procedure. 'PI Update' provider: Law Society Gazette 1996 to date.
Prof. Memberships: APIL. American Trial Lawyers Association. Member of Personal Injury Panel. Local contact point for Headway. Society of Labour Lawyers.
Career: Articled *Farell & Smith*, Sheffield. Qualified 1985. *Brian Thompson & Partners*, Sheffield 1985-89 (Partner 1987). *Russell Jones & Walker* 1989- to date (Partner 1990). Local Managing Partner: Leeds 1996/7. Local Managing Partner: Sheffield 1997. Opened Sheffield office this year. Heads RSI, PTSD and VWF Units and Asbestos within the firm.

Personal: Family. Golf. Photography. Trades Union Movement.

ANSON, Peter
Dibb Lupton Alsop, Sheffield (0114) 2833406
Specialisation: Main area of practice is defendant personal injury with particular reference to mining claims and Construction plant hire claims.
Career: Qualified 1976. Partner 1986.

CHANDLER, Pauline
Thompsons, Manchester (0161) 832 5705
Specialisation: Plaintiff personal injury work with a substantial disease case load bias. Pursued the leading welders lung cases and hundreds of claims for asbestos victims and was involved in the first passive smoking cases.
Prof. Memberships: Member of and assessor for Personal Injury Panel.

CODD, Grahame R.
Irwin Mitchell, Sheffield (0114) 276 7777
Specialisation: Traumatic brain injury and spinal cord injury cases. Tried or settled cases in the last year include 10 claims having combined value of £11.5 million.
Prof. Memberships: APIL – Member of Brain Injury Special Interest Group. Also Member of Spinal Injury Special Interest Group. ATLA. Law Society P.I. Panel Member. HEADWAY, National Head Injuries Assocation, CHIT (Childrens Head Injury Trust). HIRE (Head Injury Re-Education).
Career: Articled *Graysons*, Sheffield; qualified 1981; partner *Graysons* 1983-1986; partner with *Irwin Mitchell* 1986.
Personal: Skiing, tennis, football, electric and acoustic guitar.

DAVIS, John
Irwin Mitchell, Sheffield (0114) 276 7777
Specialisation: Litigation for Plaintiffs (exclusively) in Personal Injury, particularly serious brain and spinal cord injury. Also deals with other types of personal injury litigation. Particular experience of actions against Police and overseas holiday accident litigation. Acted for the Plaintiffs in the reported cases of Hill v South Yorkshire Police, Cropper v South Yorkshire Police, Lumb v South Yorkshire Police, Dennis v Ministry of Defence, Lock v Leicestershire Health Authority. Contributor to various Legal publications.
Prof. Memberships: Law Society, Association of Personal Injury Lawyers, South Yorkshire Medico-Legal Society, American Trial Lawyers Association, Royal Society for the Prevention of Accidents, Deaf Legal Network, Trustee of Sheffield Headway, past committee member of Sheffield Victim Support.
Career: Articled *Lake New & Hurst*, Stockport. Qualified 1983. Partner, *Irwin Mitchell* 1989.
Personal: Born 1957, University of Warwick LLB (Hons). Leisure interests include sport, medieval history, theatre and music. Lives in Sheffield.

DAYKIN, Stephen
Nabarro Nathanson, Sheffield (0114) 279 4000
Partner in Personal Injury Litigation Department.
Specialisation: Areas of practice are industrial disease, employers liability, public liability and health and safety. Has lectured at and chaired seminars on personal injury litigation and health and safety.
Career: Qualified in 1974. Appointed Head of British Coal's Personal Injury Department in 1988. Joined *Nabarro Nathanson* as Partner in charge of Personal Injury Litigation in May 1990.
Personal: Born 6th September 1949. Educated at Newcastle-upon-Tyne University (LLB. 1972).

DIAS, James C.
Sinton & Co, Newcastle upon Tyne (0191) 212 7800
Partner in Personal Injury Department,
Specialisation: Sole area of practice is personal injury (of which 20% is plaintiff and 80% defendant work). Also handles medical negligence. This work is exclusively for plaintiffs on individual referral.
Prof. Memberships: Law Society.
Career: Qualified in 1972 after articles with *John H. Sinton & Co*. Became a Partner in 1974.
Personal: Born 1948. Educated at Austin Friars School, Carlisle 1958-66 and Leeds University 1966-69. President of North of England Medico-Legal Society, Medical Appeal Tribunal Chairman. Leisure interests include sport (cricket, golf, rugby, soccer), theatre, classical music and reading. Lives in Newcastle-upon-Tyne.

DOBBIN, David R.
Sinton & Co, Newcastle upon Tyne (0191) 212 7800
Partner in Litigation Department.
Specialisation: Main areas of practice are personal injury, industrial diseases, employment law and taxi law. Occasional speaker at conferences and seminars.
Prof. Memberships: Law Society, Newcastle Law Society, Past President of North of England Medico-Legal Society.
Career: Worked with *Crutes* 1967-70. Qualified in 1969. Joined *John H. Sinton & Co.* in 1970 and became a Partner in 1972. Became a Recorder in 1995.
Personal: Born 1st December 1944. Educated at Liverpool University 1963-66. Leisure interests include sailing and hill walking. Lives in Newcastle upon Tyne.

DREWE, David M.
Crutes, Newcastle-upon-Tyne (0191) 281 5811

EVANS, William A.
Dibb Lupton Alsop, Sheffield (0345) 262728
Head of Chest Disease Unit and Partner in Insurance Industry Group.
Specialisation: Practice covers defendant personal injury work, particularly industrial diseases. Partner in the Insurance Marine and Aviation Group and Head of the Chest Disease Unit. Author on wide range of insurance and personal injury issues and regular contributor to Insurance Day.
Prof. Memberships: Member of the Forum of Insurance Lawyers, British Insurance Law Association and Chartered Insurance Institute.
Career: Called to the Bar 1977, admitted as a solicitor 1987, partner *Irwin Mitchell* 1988, partner *Dibb Lupton Broomhead* 1994.
Personal: Born 1 June 1954. Attended Worth School, University of Kent and Inns of Court School of Law. Leisure interests include sailing and wine.

HOTCHIN, Samuel G.
Wansbroughs Willey Hargrave, Leeds (0113) 244 1151
Partner in General Insurance Department.
Specialisation: Insurance Litigator. Specialises in personal injury, product liability, and insurance law, including fraudulent claims, policy interpretation and liability.
Career: Qualified and joined *Wansbroughs Willey Hargrave* in 1979. Became a Partner in 1982.

MADDOCKS, Roger
Thompsons, Newcastle-upon-Tyne (0191) 261 5341
Specialisation: Personal injury specialist with particular interest in occupational accident and disease cases. Deals with other types of personal injury cases (and associated professional negligence actions); and with medical negligence claims.
Prof. Memberships: APIL; Newcastle Law Society; member of Personal Injury Panel; Member of Newcastle Court Users Committee.

MURPHY, Patrick
Marrons, Newcastle upon Tyne (0191) 281 1304

NAPIER, Michael
Irwin Mitchell, Sheffield (0114) 276 7777
Senior partner specialising in personal injury.
Specialisation: Personal injury law specialist (plaintiff), latterly via associated firm *Pannone Napier* and concentrating on group personal injury and product liability claims such as Practolol (Eraldin), Opren, and Dalkon Shield IUD. Also major involvement in claims arising from disasters such as Land's End tragedy, Manchester air crash, sinking of the Herald of Free Enterprise, Marchioness disaster, King's Cross fire, Piper Alpha explosion and many others, usually in a leading capacity. Other major non-personal injury cases include X v. United Kingdom (human rights for mental patients, ECHR), Barber v. Guardian Royal Exchange (equal pension rights, ECJ), Michael Foot v. Boundary Commission (electoral constituencies), Blackburn v. Newcastle Health Authority (medical negligence) and Dickinson v. Jones and Alexander (professional negligence). Author of 'Recovering Compensation for Psychiatric Injury' (Blackstone 1995), "Conditional Fees – A Survival Guide" (Law Society Press 1995). 'Psychiatrist & Lawyer-Total Incompatibility?', 'The Medical & Legal Response to Post Traumatic Stress Disorder', 'European Perspectives for Practitioners' and 'Group Litigation- past present and future'. Consultant Editor of Personal & Medical Injuries Law Letter and The Medical Law Review. Frequent lecturer and broadcaster on litigation.
Prof. Memberships: Law Society (Council Member); Chairman Law Society Civil Litigation Committee. Association of Personal Injury Lawyers (Past President); Association of Trial Lawyers of America (Member of Governing Board); Visiting Professor and Chairman of Centre of Advanced Litigation at Nottingham Trent University; Past Chairman of Rampton Hospital Advisory Committee; Member of Mental Health Act Commission 1983-92; Past President of South Yorkshire Medico-Legal Society; Trustee of Pitsmoor Citizens Advice Bureau; Freeman of Cutlers Company, Sheffield.
Career: Qualified in 1970. Articled at *Moss Toone & Deane* 1968-70. Worked with *WH*

Thompson 1970-72, before joining *Irwin Mitchell* in 1972. Partner from 1973.
Personal: Born 11th June 1946. Attended Loughborough Grammar School and Manchester University. Leisure interests include family and mountain biking in Norfolk. Lives in Derbyshire.

PEACOCK, Norman Douglas
Allan Henderson Beecham and Peacock, Newcastle upon Tyne (0191) 232 3048

PESCOD, Peter
Hay & Kilner, Newcastle-upon-Tyne (0191) 232 8345
Partner in Litigation Department.
Specialisation: Main area of practice is personal injury, acting primarily for major insurers in all types of accident/ disease claims. Also acts for health service bodies in defence of medical negligence claims. Handles professional negligence work relating to surveyors, accountants, insurance brokers and architects. Has lectured on medical negligence and special damages.
Prof. Memberships: Law Society, Personal Injury Panel, FOIL (Forum of Insurance Lawyers), FHS Appeals Authority, Deputy District Judge.
Career: Joined *Hay-Kilner* in 1973. Qualified in 1975 and became a Partner in 1976.
Personal: Born 29th June 1951. Educated at Queen Elizabeth Grammar, Darlington 1962-69 and Newcastle University 1969-72. Leisure pursuits include history, politics, landscape gardening, architecture and auction sales. Lives in Ovington.

PICKERING, John
Irwin Mitchell, Sheffield (0114) 276 7777
Specialisation:
Prof. Memberships: Secretary of APIL, Vice Chairman of the Children's Head Injury Trust, ATLA, TLPJ, Law Society, Headway Spinal Injuries Association, AVMA, Justice, Board Member of ATLA Birth Trauma Litigation.
Career: Qualified in 1979 after articles at *Irwin Mitchell*. Became a Partner in the following year. Member of Management Committee.
Personal: Born 23rd July 1955. Educated at Manchester University (LLB Hons, 1976). Member of the Hospital Advisory Board at Thornbury Hospital. Past President of South Yorkshire Medico-Legal Society. Leisure interests include theatre, squash, golf and motor racing. Lives in Sheffield.

PORTEUS, Stephen
Marrons, Newcastle upon Tyne (0191) 281 1304

RAW, David G.
Sinton & Co, Newcastle upon Tyne (0191) 212 7800
Partner in Litigation Department.
Specialisation: Main area of practice is personal injury matters, acting mostly for insurers.
Career: Qualified in 1966, having joined *Sutton Cheshire & Thompson* in 1965. Became a Partner in 1968. Amalgamation with *John H Sinton & Co* in 1971.
Personal: Born 6th October 1943. Educated at Giggleswick School 1951-61, and Durham University 1961-63. Leisure interests include reading, music, philately, watching cricket, rugby and golf. Lives in Rowlands Gill.

TUCKER, Andrew
Irwin Mitchell, Sheffield (0114) 276 7777
See under Product Liability, p. 663

WILLIAMS, Alun C.
Hay & Kilner, Newcastle-upon-Tyne (0191) 232 8345
Partner in Litigation Department.
Specialisation: Has specialised in personal injury work for plaintiffs and defendants since 1979. Also handles health and safety and road traffic work.
Prof. Memberships: Personal Injury Panel, FOIL.
Career: Qualified in 1979. Joined *Hay & Kilner* in 1977, becoming a Partner in 1982.
Personal: Born 7th August 1955. Attended Newcastle University 1973-76. Leisure interests include military history, football, reading and music. Lives in Newcastle-upon-Tyne.

SCOTLAND

ANDERSON, Peter
Simpson & Marwick WS, Edinburgh (0131) 557 1545

BURNSIDE, David
Burnside Kemp Fraser, Aberdeen (01224) 624602
See under Employment Law, p. 321

KEMP, Sandy
Burnside Kemp Fraser, Aberdeen 01224) 624602
See under Employment Law, p. 322

LEFEVRE, Frank Hartley
Lefevre Litigation, Aberdeen (01224) 208208
Founding Partner in Litigation Department.
Specialisation: Main areas of practice are Employment Law and Personal Injury Claims. Also handles all aspects of court practice. Acted in the Piper Alpha disaster in 1988 and handled 33 of the 35 claims in the Ocean Odyssey explosion in 1988. Acted for 6 of the 15 families in the Cormorant Alpha helicopter crash of 1992.
Prof. Memberships: Law Society of Scotland, Aberdeen Society of Advocates (Past President).
Career: Qualified in 1958. Founded *The Frank Lefevre Practice* in 1970. Chairman of Quantum Claims Compensation Specialists Ltd, Britain's first specialist 'no win no fee' company in 1988. Accredited specialist in Employment Law and Solicitor Mediation in 1996. Founded Mid-Line Mediations. Appointed part-time Chairman of Industrial Tribunals (Scotland) 1996.
Personal: Born 4th December 1934. Attended Aberdeen University 1953-58 (MA, LLB). Leisure interests include golf, squash and music. Lives in Aberdeen.

LYALL, Pamela L.
Dundas & Wilson CS, Edinburgh (0131) 228 8000
Specialisation: Partner and Head of Insurance Litigation Group specialising in a broad range of insurance matters including personal injury and professional indemnity. Solicitor-Advocate since March 1996.
Prof. Memberships: The Law Society of Scotland, Society of Solicitor-Advocates.
Career: Attended University of Aberdeen (LLB Hons). Articled *McGrigor Donald*, Glasgow 1980-82; qualified 1982; assistant solicitor

1982; joined *Dundas & Wilson* 1986; partner since 1992.
Personal: Born 1958. Resides Edinburgh. Leisure interests include family, reading, swimming, trying to keep fit and playing the piano very badly.

MCCULLOCH, A. Grant
Drummond Miller WS, Edinburgh (0131) 226 5151
Partner in Litigation Department.
Specialisation: Main area of practice is personal injury, covering all areas of Court of Session reparation including complex medical negligence. Also handles matrimonial work, undertaking only large cases involving complex financial issues. Acted in 'Ross v. Lord Advocate', 'Latter v. Latter', 'Docherty (O'Briens Curator) v. British Steel' and 'Martin v. Chapman'. Part of Tranquilliser Addiction Solicitors Group. Chairman, Scottish Solicitors Myodil Group. Convened several seminars on Family Law, medical and professional negligence. Solicitor-Advocate (civil).
Prof. Memberships: AVMA, APIL, Law Society of Scotland, Society of Solicitors in the Supreme Courts.
Career: Qualified in 1976. Joined *Drummond Miller* in 1974, becoming a Partner in 1979. Accredited Medical Negligence Specialist.
Personal: Born 10th February 1952. Attended Glasgow Academy, then Edinburgh University 1969-74 (LLB, BSc). Temporary Sheriff. President of Law Society of Scotland 1996-1997.

MOORE, George K.
Hamilton Burns & Moore, Glasgow (0141) 353 2121
Specialisation: Litigation for Insurance Companies with particular reference to personal injury, employers and public liability claims. Also specialist in advising on Insurance Company fraud, professional negligence and industrial disease claims. Presently leading a team dealing with the legal aspects of the E-Coli outbreak in Scotland including representing the Insurers of Messrs. John M. Barr & Son.
Prof. Memberships: Member of the Law Society of Scotland, Solicitor to the Supreme Court, Solicitor/Advocate and Member of FOIL.
Career: Admitted as a Solicitor in 1971, founding partner of *Hamilton Burns & Moore* in 1972. Qualified as a Solicitor/Advocate with Rights of Audience in the Court of Session in 1994.

ROXBURGH, James A.R.
Biggart Baillie, Glasgow (0141) 228 8000
Specialisation: Leading defence practioner in industrial (particularly lung) disease cases. Member of Panel of Solicitors advising Law Societys PI Insurers. Represented British regional airlines Logan Air in connection with public inquiry in Shetland into 1996 air crash at Tingwall.
Career: Glasgow University BL 1963, Partner *Biggart Baillie* 1968 – Senior Partner, *Biggart Baillie* 1990 – Engaged for survivors of andrelatives of deceased in Piper Alpha Inquiry 1988 -1990. Represented co-pilot in Cormorant Alpha Inquiry 1992 – 93.
Personal: Married with 2 daughters, 1 son. Leisure interest include skiing, golf, tennis and bridge.

SMITH, Sid
Thompson's, Edinburgh
(0131) 225 4297

TIERNEY, James
Paull & Williamsons, Aberdeen
(01224) 621621
See under Employment Law, p. 323

TYLER, Alfred J.
Balfour & Manson, Edinburgh
(0131) 200 1200
Head of Litigation Department.
Specialisation: Main area of practice is personal injury (with special interest in head and spinal injuries) and medical negligence (with a special interest in birth cases). Also handles general commercial and aviation matters. Has been involved in major multi party actions including the 1986 and Mull of Kintyre Chinook disasters, the Piper Alpha disaster, the Lockerbie disaster and the Brent Spar and Cormorant Alpha helicopter crashes. Represented the pursuer in the House of Lords case of Herd v. Clyde Helicopters and is currently representing the pursuers in the House of Lords appeal of McFarlane v. Tayside Health Board, the failed sterilisation case.
Prof. Memberships: S.S.C, N.P, Association of Personal Injury Lawyers (Scottish Secretary), Spinal Injuries Association, Headway.
Career: Qualified in 1975, having joined *Balfour & Manson* in 1973. Became a Partner in 1978.
Personal: Born 27th January 1951. Educated at Daniel Stewart's College, Edinburgh 1956-69 and Edinburgh University 1969-73. Enjoys golf. Lives in Edinburgh.

NORTHERN IRELAND

BOWDEN, James Ronald
Harrison, Leitch & Logan, Belfast
(01232) 323843 Fax: (01232) 332644
Specialisation: Road Traffic: Employers Liability: Matters which in 1997/98 have included: Serious injury (brain damage and paraplegia); Structured settlements; Repetitive strain injury; Stress in the workplace.
Prof. Memberships: Law Society of Northern Ireland.
Career: Educated at Methodist College, Belfast and Queen's University, Belfast.
Personal: Married: two teenage children.Weekend golfer. Soccer fan.

CANAVAN, Aiden
Edwards & Co, Belfast (01232) 321863

CROSS, John
McKinty & Wright, Belfast (01232) 246751
Specialisation: Defending claims for motor insurers and defending medical negligence suits.
Prof. Memberships: Law Society of Northern Ireland and member of Contentious Business

Committee of the Society.
Career: Qualified 1970. Partner in *McKinty & Wright* 1975. Graduate of Trinity College Dublin (B.A., LL.B).
Personal: Married with 4 children. Leisure interests include Computers and Travel.

DIAMOND, W.Maurice
S.J. Diamond & Son, Belfast (01232) 243726

DUFF, John
McKinty & Wright, Belfast (01232) 246751
Specialisation: Personal injury and general defence work on behalf of insurers.
Prof. Memberships: Law Society of Northern Ireland.
Career: Graduate of Trinity College Dublin 1972. BA (Legal Science). Admitted to the Roll of Solicitors in Northern Ireland 1976. Partner in *McKinty & Wright* 1978.
Personal: Leisure interests include all forms of sport, walking, cinema and reading. Married with 2 children.

EDGAR, Leonard A.
John McKee & Son, Belfast (01232) 232303
Specialisation: All aspects of personal injury and general defence litigation on behalf of insurers.
Prof. Memberships: Law Society of Northern Ireland. FOIL Member.
Career: Educated at Royal Belfast Academical Institution and Queen's University Belfast. Admitted 1980; Partner in *John McKee and Son* 1983; appointed Deputy County Court Judge 1998.
Personal: Sport and family.

GIBSON, C. Michael H.
Tughan & Co, Belfast (01232) 553300
Specialisation: Partner and Head of Litigation Department. Main areas of practice are personal injury, pharmaceutical and asbestos related litigations.

JEFFERSON, H.L. Ian
C & H Jefferson, Belfast (01232) 329545
Specialisation: Senior Partner practising in personal injury work, primarily motor claims, both for Defendants and also Plaintiffs. Clients include major Insurance Companies and Lloyd's Syndicates. Considerable experience of cases involving head injuries including brain damage, spinal injuries and loss of limbs.
Prof. Memberships: Council of the Law Society of Northern Ireland: FOIL: Headway: Spinal Injuries Association.
Career: Qualified Northern Ireland 1971. England 1990.
Personal: Fishing, sailing, hockey and theatre.

JOHNSTON, Paul J.
McKinty & Wright, Belfast (01232) 246751
Specialisation: Personal injury and general defence litigation on behalf of Insurers.

Prof. Memberships: Law Society of Northern Ireland, Law Society of Ireland, The Law Society, FOIL.
Career: Graduated Queen's University Belfast (LLB) 1979. Admitted in Northern Ireland 1981. Partner in *McKinty & Wright* 1986. Admitted in the Republic of Ireland 1993. Admitted in England & Wales 1993.
Personal: Leisure interests include all forms of sport, theatre, cinema and reading. Involved in community and youth work. Married with 3 children.

MCEVOY, Eamonn E.
Eammon McEvoy & Co, Lurgan
(01762) 327734

STEWART, Brian J. C.
O'Reilly Stewart, Belfast (01232) 322512
Partner and head of the Litigation Department.
Specialisation: Specialises in product liability defence work, mainly relating to pharmaceuticals.
Prof. Memberships: Member of the Council of the Law Society of Northern Ireland. Former Chairman of the Belfast Solicitors' Association. Member of the International Association of Defence Council.
Career: Qualified 1978. Admitted to the Republic of Ireland Roll of Solicitors 1991.

TAYLOR, Derek T.
C & H Jefferson, Belfast (01232) 329545
Specialisation: Main area of practice is all aspects of industrial chest disease acting for Defendants including all asbestos-related conditions and occupational asthma. Has some 15 years experience acting for major insurers who have carried EL and PL risks in industry. Other area of expertise is medical negligence. Has some 13 years experience acting for Health Boards in Northern Ireland in all kinds of medical negligence claims. Has acted for the defence in a number of successfully defended and high-profile obstetric cases.
Prof. Memberships: Law Society of NI, NI Medico-Legal Society.
Career: Qualified in 1975. Assistant Solicitor with *Harrison Leitch & Logan* 1975-1977. *L'Estrange & Brett* 1977-1978. Partner with *C&H Jefferson* 1979 to date.
Personal: Born 17th April 1949. Educated Bangor Grammar School, Co. Down and then Queen's University of Belfast 1968-1972. Leisure interests include hill walking and golf. Member of National Trust.

TWEED, Paul
Johnsons, Belfast (01232) 240183
Specialisation: Acts for a number of major Insurance Companies based locally and at Lloyd's. Also has extensive experience in medical negligence and criminal injury/damage claims.
Prof. Memberships: Incorporated Law Society of Northern Ireland (1978). Law Society of England and Wales (1993).

PLANNING

RESEARCH: In compiling the tables, we consider all the information available to us, paying particular regard to the market research carried out by our team of ten qualified lawyers. (The researchers' details are set out on page three.) The rankings, therefore, reflect the opinion of the marketplace as revealed by systematic and objective research: see page four. (Our research is audited every year by the British Market Research Bureau.)

OVERVIEW: The upturn in planning work continued throughout 1997, largely as a result of continued activity in the development market. However, several big names have disappeared from our list this year. Berwin Leighton still have the strongest planning department overall, however Nicholas Taylor is retiring. Taylor was a key figure in Berwin Leighton's success in the field. The widely publicised departure of Garry Hart from Herbert Smith (he has gone to work for the Lord Chancellor) has also caused a stir. He will be a hard act to follow, although David Brock is seen as extremely capable. Ian Gatenby also retired from Cameron McKenna this year.

McGuinness Finch began to develop a reputation for planning work after Helen Norris went there in 1995. This was further enhanced when she was joined by Carl Dyer last year, and the firm has moved up in our table of highly regarded planning practices. Olswang are a new entry this year, having recruited leading specialist Geoffrey Searle.

LEADING FIRMS · LONDON

BERWIN LEIGHTON

S J BERWIN & CO
CAMERON MCKENNA
HERBERT SMITH
NORTON ROSE

ASHURST MORRIS CRISP
CLIFFORD CHANCE
LOVELL WHITE DURRANT
NABARRO NATHANSON

HIGHLY REGARDED FIRMS

Denton Hall
D J Freeman
Gouldens
Linklaters
Simmons & Simmons

Davies Arnold Cooper
McGuinness Finch
Nicholson Graham & Jones
Slaughter and May
Stephenson Harwood
Theodore Goddard

Allen & Overy
Eversheds
Farrer & Co
Field Fisher Waterhouse
Freshfields
Jeffrey Green Russell
Lawrence Graham
Macfarlanes
Masons
Olswang
Taylor Joynson Garrett
Titmuss Sainer Dechert

LONDON

Berwin Leighton (3ptnrs, 10assts, 1const, 1assoc) Still acknowledged as the leading planning firm with a large team and "an enviable client list," despite Nicholas Taylor having stepped down as head of the department. He will become a consultant, advising five or six key clients on a regular basis. *Tim Pugh* ("a true heavyweight") and *Ian Trehearne* ("a good strategist" and "a man to do business with") remain well respected. A new partner, *Tim Hellier*, has been appointed and he joins our list of leaders. *Geoffrey Crighton* was also recommended. However, it was generally felt that the gap between Berwin Leighton and the other firms is narrowing and the next 12 months will be a telling time. **Clients/Work:** Greenwich Millennium Proposals on behalf of English Partnerships. Birmingham Northern Relief Road for Trafalgar House and Italstat. Blue Circle's land holdings in Kent. Continuing to work on a 1.3m sq ft shopping centre development in Bracknell for Legal & General.

S J Berwin & Co (1ptnr, 4assts) The firm's reputation in planning is more or less synonymous with *Pat Thomas* who was described as an "outstanding individual." However, the team has been strengthened by

Simon Ricketts who joined in October 1997 from Lovell White Durrant. He is described as being "immensely effective, a good thinker and organiser – someone who will compliment Pat Thomas." **Clients/Work:** Acted for London City Airport in its application to double the movements at the airport. Acting for British Land on a major City office redevelopment (Plantation Place). Advising Prudential on all planning aspects of the Reading Business Park.

Cameron McKenna (8 fee-earners in total) Team remains strong despite retirement of Ian Gatenby. *Tony Kitson* now heads the team and *Ian Mackay* and *Christopher Williams* have also been recommended to us. Best known for major infrastructure and retail projects. **Clients/Work:** Acting for BAA in the Heathrow Terminal 5 Inquiry; for Berkeley Group on the redevelopment of Gunwharf Quays, Portsmouth; and for Sainsburys on foodstore developments. Other major clients include Brixton Estate, Taylor Woodrow and the Crown Estate Commissioners.

Herbert Smith (4ptnrs, 10assts) Since the departure of Garry Hart, another planning partner has been made up. *David Brock*, described as "a good technician with a sound knowledge of planning law" now heads the team. *Patrick Robinson* was also recommended. **Clients/Work:** Acting for Allied London Properties in their redevelopment proposals at Bracknell Town Centre where there are competing schemes. Acting for Watts Blake Bearne (world's leading ball clay producer) whose application for the extension of a clay quarry in Devon has been called in. Continuing to advise on planning aspects of PFI projects such as the new National Physical Laboratory.

Norton Rose (3ptnrs, 6assts) *Brian Greenwood* heads the department. *Jane Burgess* is in our up and coming section. **Clients/Work:** Obtained planning permission for the Millennium Dome (acting for the New Millennium Experience) and for the Spitalfields Development Group re ABN-Amro Bank headquarters in Spitalfields. Acting for English Heritage on planning strategy for Stonehenge heritage proposals and the Tewkesbury Battlefield Inquiry.

Ashurst Morris Crisp (2ptnrs, 7assts) The team is led by the highly rated *Michael Cunliffe* and includes *Jocelyn Denton* and *Martin Evans* who are also leaders. The assistants include a new recruit from Cameron McKenna and an assistant who returns to Ashursts after a period of secondment with the LDDC. **Clients/Work:** Acted for Union Railways Property re land acquisition and compensation aspects of the Channel Tunnel Rail Link. Advised Royal Ordnance Plc and Trafalgar Property on development of 349 acres of former MoD land in Waltham Park, and Reuters in connection with new offices in Blackwall Yard.

Clifford Chance (1ptnr, 5assts) The Planning and Environment Group is headed by *Brian Hall* who "has his feet firmly on the ground" and is "highly regarded and respected by fellow professionals." *Michael Redman* is also well known. **Clients/Work:** Advising Serco/Laing joint venture on planning and infrastructure aspects of new Joint Services Command and Staff College houses (the first MOD PFI) near Swindon. Advising Richardson Developments re landmark retail and leisure centre in Manchester.

Lovell White Durrant (1ptnr, 2assts) *Michael Gallimore* continues to lead the planning group. He is well regarded and the group is continuing to prosper. Although Simon Ricketts left to join S J Berwin during 1997, he was replaced by a senior solicitor recruited from the London Borough of Enfield. **Clients/Work:** Advising Shearer Property Group, Barclays Bank UK Retirement Fund and John Lewis on a proposed city centre redevelopment in Cambridge (Grand Arcade). Advised Richlone on a challenge to grant of planning permission by local residents. Continuing to advise Prudential on mixed redevelopment in Knightsbridge.

Nabarro Nathanson (3ptnrs including *David Hawkins, Gary Graves* "a highly intelligent and active solicitor," *Norna Hughes*

and *Roger Sherlock,* 3assts.) **Clients/Work:** Advised THI on leisure developments in Bristol and Cheshire (including successfully resisting judicial review). Acted for P&O Developments on two office redevelopment proposals in the West End. Continue to act for Hammerson in efforts to secure consent for extension to Brent Cross Cross Shopping Centre.

Denton Hall (3ptnrs, 6assts) Team led by *Sandra Banks* ("a good technician") and *Stephen Ashworth*, described as "first class" and having "what it takes to make it." *Margaret Casely-Hayford* ("extremely intelligent and forceful") is also recommended. **Clients/Work:** Urban regeneration project in Brighton for Wycote Developments and Sainsburys. Development in Northampton involving 4,500 houses. Further work for Marks & Spencer, Manchester on store damaged by IRA bombing. Acting for M&S and Sainsburys in successful challenge to refusal of extension to out-of-town supermarket (application of sequential test).

D J Freeman (2ptnrs, 1asst) *Moira Fraser* was recommended to us this year, and the "forceful" *Richard Max* is described as a "rising star" and "very enthusiastic and ambitious." A major strength of the practice is advocacy and Richard Max appeared at 12 inquiries last year. **Clients/Work:** The team handles work for both the public and private sectors. Advised Eagle Star on Micheldever Station New Settlement. Acted for NHS Executive on planning aspects of the disposal of surplus hospital sites.

Gouldens (5 fee-earners) Two leaders in *Angela Turner* and *David Cooper*, who has handled around 950 planning inquiries, the majority as advocate. Best known for work on business and retail parks, shopping and leisure developments. **Clients/Work:** David Cooper recently acted as advocate for Flairline in a 78 day inquiry against Westminster City Council and English Heritage, involving listed buildings, conservation areas and their proposed redevelopment. Also acted for Development Securities in judicial review sought by Somerfield of planning permission.

Linklaters (2ptnrs, 1asst f/t, 3assts 70-80%) The team is led by the "highly competent" *Ray Jackson*. **Clients/Work:** Advised LIFFE on its one million sq ft HQ development in Spitalfields. Advised BA on proposed Heathrow Terminal 5 issues such as surface access to the airport, aircraft noise, maintenance facilities and scheduling of night flights. Advised Merrill Lynch on City development opportunities.

Simmons & Simmons (2ptnrs) The team is headed by the "quietly competent" *John Qualtrough*. **Clients/Work:** Advising Asiansky on one million sq ft leisure/retail development on the North Circular Road. Advising Railtrack on planning aspects of new Luton Parkway station. Advising Boots

Properties on town centre redevelopment in Kendal (including archaeological issues).

Davies Arnold Cooper Planning is handled within the Commercial Property Department. Team comprises *Christopher Rees*, who is regarded as a "good commercial lawyer" and a former local government officer. **Clients/Work:** Act for a number of major housebuilders and the Housebuilders Federation.

LEADING INDIVIDUALS · LONDON
GALLIMORE Michael Lovell White Durrant
GREENWOOD Brian Norton Rose
HALL Brian Clifford Chance
KITSON Tony Cameron McKenna
THOMAS Patricia S J Berwin & Co
BROCK David Herbert Smith
CUNLIFFE Michael Ashurst Morris Crisp
GRAVES Gary Nabarro Nathanson
HAWKINS David Nabarro Nathanson
JACKSON Raymond Linklaters
MAX Richard D J Freeman
NORRIS Helen McGuinness Finch
PUGH Timothy Berwin Leighton
TREHEARNE Ian Berwin Leighton
ASHWORTH Stephen Denton Hall
BANKS Sandra Denton Hall
COOPER David Gouldens
CRIGHTON Geoffrey Berwin Leighton
EVANS Douglas Theodore Goddard
GARBUTT John Nicholson Graham & Jones
HILLEBRON Richard Slaughter and May
HUGHES Norna Nabarro Nathanson
JEEPS Barry Stephenson Harwood
MACKAY Ian Cameron McKenna
QUALTROUGH John Simmons & Simmons
REES Christopher Davies Arnold Cooper
ROBINSON E. Patrick Herbert Smith
SEARLE Geoffrey Olswang
SHERLOCK Roger Nabarro Nathanson
STEVENS Peter Jeffrey Green Russell
TURNER Angela Gouldens
WELLS Martin Stephenson Harwood
WILLIAMS Christopher Cameron McKenna
BLANEY Trevor Lawrence Graham
CAMPBELL Gordon Eversheds
CASELY-HAYFORD Margaret Denton Hall
DENTON Jocelyn Ashurst Morris Crisp
DYER Carl McGuinness Finch
EVANS Martin Ashurst Morris Crisp
FRASER Moira D J Freeman
HELLIER Tim Berwin Leighton
JACKSON Andrew Macfarlanes
O'DONOVAN Teige Farrer & Co
REDMAN Michael Clifford Chance
RICKETTS Simon SJ Berwin & Co
SCATES Steven McGrigor Donald
TRUE Justin Titmuss Sainer Dechert

UP AND COMING
BURGESS Jane Norton Rose

McGuinness Finch (2ptnrs, town planner) Niche property firm seen by others as on the way up. *Helen Norris* is particularly highly regarded and *Carl Dyer* has recently strengthened the team.

Nicholson Graham & Jones (3ptnrs, including *John Garbutt*, 3assts handle planning and environment) **Clients/Work:** Continue to handle large amounts of work for Blue Circle, including recent planning application for a new cement works. Advised Levingtons on peat extraction and Essex County Council on judicial review of planning decision on landfill site.

Slaughter and May The Commercial Property Department operates as a single group and all fee-earners handle planning as required. Senior Associate *Richard Hillebron* is a leader and handles planning work almost exclusively. **Clients/Work:** Negotiating planning permission and s106 agreement on a Richard Rogers building in Broadwick Street, Soho.

Stephenson Harwood (1ptnr, 1assoc; 2assts 50%) The planning group is led by *Barry Jeeps* and includes senior associate *Martin Wells*. **Clients/Work:** Defending grant of planning permission and highway agreements for Peel Holdings re Trafford Centre. Redevelopment of Royal Opera House. Alteration and extension to Royal Albert Hall.

Theodore Goddard (1ptnr, 2assts – 100%; 2 ptnrs – 25%) The team is headed by leader *Douglas Evans*, who appears as an advocate at planning inquiries on a regular basis. **Clients/Work:** Acted for Persimmon Homes, who are promoting the release of 800 hectares of green belt land in Hertfordshire. Acted for Cleveland Potash (a subsidiary of Minorco) in securing planning permission for an extension to the UK's only potash mine.

Allen & Overy (8ptnrs, 37 fee-earners in the property dept. handle planning work as required – 2assts specialise) **Clients/ Work:** Emphasis of practice is on PFI and UK power projects. Acting for Premier Prison Services on Lowdham Grange Prison; for SEPUT re Cardiff Bay Retail Park and for

Enron Europe in obtaining consents for construction of a new combined gas cycle turbine power station.

Eversheds (1ptnr, leader *Gordon Campbell*; 2assts) **Clients/Work:** Obtaining consent for residential development of sports field in Wembley for GEC following call-in inquiry. Planning and highways advice on retail/commercial development in Covent Garden for London and Paris Developments. Advice to Church Commissioners on further retail development adjacent to Gateshead Metro Centre.

Farrer & Co Known for acting for landed estates as well as commercial interests. Work includes all aspects of land use, listed building applications and appeals, compulsory purchase and tribunal advocacy. *Teige O'Donovan* handles planning and environmental work exclusively. **Clients/Work:** Arbitration to protect major area of special character; negotiations for complex city centre redevelopment; listed building and heritage work.

Field Fisher Waterhouse (1ptnr 100%, 2assts 50%) Planning work is handled within the Commercial Property Department. **Clients/Work:** Advising ICI on planning aspects of a pipeline replacement and a company hotel. Advising Whitbread on redevelopment of Grade 1 listed former Midland Hotel at St.Pancras station.

Freshfields Planning is handled within the firm's 42 fee-earner property department. **Clients/Work:** Advising Citibank and CSFB on the planning risks of developing their headquarters at Canary Wharf.

Jeffrey Green Russell Planning work is handled by partner *Peter Stevens*. **Clients/Work:** Acted for ABC Cinemas in a variety of matters including listing of one of their buildings, advertising consents etc. Advising on major out of town retail park adjacent to a junction of the M25. Planning inquiry work for leading brewing and leisure company.

Lawrence Graham (4ptnrs, 5assts p/t) *Trevor Blaney* is head of the Town and Country Planning Unit. Joined recently by a specialist in public law and urban regeneration

and a recruit from Nabarros. **Clients/Work:** Trevor Blaney appeared as an advocate at an appeal on behalf of BT and Globus Office World. The decision was a landmark one, as it redefined what is meant by an 'edge of centre' site.

Macfarlanes (2ptnrs, 3assts) The firm maintains a distinct planning practice in addition to its commercial property work and joins the table this year. *Andrew Jackson* heads the planning section. **Clients/Work:** Advising North Thames Regional Office of the NHS Executive on redevelopment of redundant hospital sites in the Green Belt. Advising Axa Sun Life on development of a business park at Droitwich.

Masons (1ptnr, 1assoc) Planning work is handled within the firm's London Property Planning and Environment Group. Known for acting for project consortia and companies in the infrastructure industry as well as other developers and house builders. **Clients/Work:** Advising Berkeley Homes on major development at Hermitage Riverside in Wapping, including public inquiry work. Advising on planning aspects of the English National Stadium project.

Olswang Appear in the planning section for the first time this year, following their recruitment of leading specialist *Geoffrey Searle*. **Clients/Work:** Geoffrey Searle continues to work on multiplex cinema developments. Also advised on proposed factory outlet centre in Peterborough, a docklands development and a CPO objection to a major city centre retail scheme.

Taylor Joynson Garrett (1ptnr, 2assts) **Clients/Work:** Acting for Toyota (GB) in the relocation of their head office to a site in Epsom. Attending major compulsory purchase inquiry in connection with the redevelopment of part of Wantage, Berkshire.

Titmuss Sainer Dechert (3 fee-earners including *Justin True*) Best known for acting for retail developers. **Clients/Work:** Advising Helical Retail and Sears Group Properties on retail park projects. Advising a government department on foodstore development in Cambridgeshire and a developer client on a major residential project in the Midlands.

LEADERS' PROFILES · LONDON

ASHWORTH, Stephen
Denton Hall, London (0171) 242 1212
Specialisation: Partner, Planning and Public Law Group. Experience in planning law, including major development inquiries; judicial review; highway law; compulsory purchase orders; Private Finance Inititative projects. Advises on developing policy issues on retailing; planning benefits; private funding of infrastructure through the planning system; and town centre management.
Prof. Memberships: Member UK Environmental Law Association; Town & Country Planning Association; Urban Land Institute.
Career: Articled *Denton Hall* 1986; qualified

1988; partner 1995; secondment to Sainsbury plc 1992-1994; Harkness Fellowship at Lincoln Institute of Land Policy, Cambridge Massachussets 1995-1996 (researching American approaches to regeneration, provision of infrastructure and public participation in the planning process); Member Department of Transport, Private Sector Panel on Developer Contributions and Highways Agreement; Member DETR, Expert Review Group on Town Improvement Zones.
Personal: Born 1963; leisure activities include cycling, 19th century British history, dry-stone walling, cookery.

BANKS, Sandra
Denton Hall, London (0171) 242 1212
Partner in Planning and Public Law Group.
Specialisation: Main areas of practice are development projects including PFI and planning appeals. Has handled a number of major development projects including factories, offices, landfill sites, a proposed scheme for the redevelopment of Herstmonceux Castle, Leavesden Film Studios and Battersea Power Station, business, research and teaching facilities, golf courses and a major development in East London, involving urban regeneration of 600 acres of largely derelict land. Has acted as advocate before courts and tribunals including

public inquiries, prosecutions and civil claims. Also handles statutory and Parliamentary work, particularly transport and water related and has represented owners affected by recent rail projects, e.g. the Crossrail Bill, and the Channel Tunnel Rail Link Bill. Has lectured for the Law Society and others on public law and judicial review. Author of 'Practical Planning Appeals and Inquiries' for Longman. Examiner for the Joint Examination Board of the Law Society and the Royal Town Planning Institute.
Prof. Memberships: Legal Associate Member of the Royal Town Planning Institute, UKELA, Law Society's Planning Panel, Fellow of the Royal Society of Arts. Member of RTPI Council.

BLANEY, Trevor
Lawrence Graham, London (0171) 379 0000
Specialisation: Senior Planning Partner, specialising in planning law and associated areas, including compulsory purchase and highway's law for both private sector and public authorities. All aspects of planning law undertaken with emphasis on appeal work, particularly advocacy and High Court litigation, including judicial review. Regularly appears as an advocate at planning appeals, local plan inquiries and enforcement appeals. Advocacy undertaken for a wide range of clients. Work also includes negotiating and drafting planning and highways' agreements. Inquiries recently conducted as Advocate on behalf of National Car Auctions, British Telecom, St. George South London Limited, Globus Office World & Crest Strategic Projects Limited. Also acts for Health Authorities and has been instructed in relation to the Claybury Hospital Inquiry which ran for over one year. Is currently instructed by Country & Metropolitan Homes in relation to a major call in Inquiry regarding the redevelopment of a disused RAF base in Gloucestershire for employment use. Has been responsible for the conduct of a number of judicial review proceedings on behalf of NHS Executive, North Thames, Cellnet and London & Regional Properties, the latter in relation to a redevelopment of Crystal Palace. In the Cellnet case he was successful in getting leave to apply to judicial review set aside, a judgment which withstood an appeal to the Court of Appeal.
Prof. Memberships: Law Society's Planning Panel, Legal Associate Member of the Royal Town Planning Institute, United Kingdom Environmental Law Association. Regular contributor to planning publications and lectures widely on planning issues.

BROCK, David M. J.
Herbert Smith, London (0171) 374 8000
Partner in Planning and Environmental Group.
Specialisation: Has a wide ranging planning, environmental and minerals law practice, advising on new settlements, urban regeneration, minerals and waste planning, integrated pollution control, judicial review and parliamentary matters, together with planning and environmental aspects of corporate transactions. Experienced advocate. Contributor to 'Commercial Environmental Law and Liability' (FT Law and Tax).
Career: Qualified in 1980. Partner at *Herbert Smith* since 1989.
Personal: Born in 1954. Educated at Dame Allan's Boys School, Newcastle, Marylebone

Grammar School and University College, London (LL.B). Practising Christian. Enjoys opera, skiing and modern art. Resides near Saffron Walden.

BURGESS, Jane
Norton Rose, London (0171) 283 6000
Senior Assistant Solicitor in the Environmental Services Unit.
Specialisation: All aspects of town and country planning, compulsory purchase and highway related matters, including infrastructure agreements and planning obligations, planning applications and related road closure orders, planning appeals, public inquiries, judicial review and High Court challenges, certificates of lawful use, local plan representations, listed buildings and conservation issues. Contributor to Butterworths Planning Law Service.
Career: Articled in local government. Qualified in 1990. Assistant solicitor at Surrey Council before joining *Norton Rose* in 1992.

CAMPBELL, Gordon
Eversheds, London (0171) 919 4500
Specialisation: Head of Planning and Environmental Group including advocacy at public inquires and in Magistrates' Courts. Particularly involved in environmental and planning aspects of property and corporate transactions. Acts for Funders, Developers, Industrialists and Public Sector bodies (especially in the education sector).
Prof. Memberships: Law Society; UK Environmental Law Association; Law Society Planning Panel; Legal Associate of Royal Town Planning Institute.
Career: Admitted in 1985. Articled at East Yorkshire Borough Council. Latterly, Principal Solicitor to South Bedfordshire District Council. Joined *Jaques & Lewis* (now *Eversheds*) in 1990. Regular speaker and writer on planning and environmental issues.
Personal: Active member of UKELA and other working parties and committees on planning, environmental, urban regeneration and local government issues. Editor of 'Conveying Contaminated Land – Developing Issues'. Author of 'Environmental Liability – A Practitioner's Handbook'. Involved with Disabled Persons interest groups. Member of National Trust and Amnesty International.

CASELY-HAYFORD, Margaret
Denton Hall, London (0171) 242 1212
Partner and non-practising barrister, Planning and Public Law Group.
Specialisation: Practice covers the full range of major project property planning advice (such as housing, multi-purpose stadium and concert venue developments, football league club stadium redevelopment, shopping centres, superstores, hospital development and contaminated land redevelopment proposals, as well as major energy installations). Negotiates planning consents and related agreements, carries out planning audits for funders and developers and co-ordinates and advises on compulsory purchase and land assembly matters and public inquiries covering all regulatory matters related to site development, as well as High Court appeals and judicial review proceedings.
Prof. Memberships: Bar (England and Wales),

Grays Inn, UKELA, Association of Women Barristers, firm's representative on Business in Sport and Leisure.
Career: Called to the Bar by Gray's Inn 1984. Pupillage 4-5 Gray's Inn Square 1985-1987 In house counsel ADC. Joined *Denton Hall* in 1987, partner 1998. Author of 'Practical Planning: Permission and the Application' published by FT Law and Tax December 1995.
Personal: Educated at Streatham Hill High (Girl's Public Day School Trust) and Somerville College, Oxford.

COOPER, David
Gouldens, London (0171) 583 7777
Partner in Planning Department.
Specialisation: Specialises in Local Government work. Has conducted approximately 850 Planning Inquiries on behalf of clients who include ADT; Alton Towers; ARC Properties; Arlington Securities; Arsenal Football Club; Bristol Airport; British Car Auctions; British Aerospace; Citibank; Flairline Properties; GRE Properties; Group Lotus; Hanson Properties Limited; P&O Developments; Pillar Properties; Port Ramsgate; Sally UK; Sir Emmanuel Kay CBE; Sir Robert McAlpine; Southampton Football Group; Tarmac Properties and Virgin, the majority as Advocate. Has also acted on behalf of groups concerned with the conservation of important buildings in London and the Provinces including SAVE Britain's Heritage, the Covent Garden Resident's Association, the Georgian Society and the Victorian Society. He now also has a major practice specialising in Regulatory, White Collar Crime and Fraud.
Prof. Memberships: Law Society Planning Panel, Legal Associate of the Royal Town Planning Institute.
Career: Qualified in May 1967. Gained experience in the planning field with George Wimpey Limited before joining *Gouldens* as a Partner in 1973.
Personal: Born 8th June 1942. Took an LLB(Hons) in 1960. Lives in London SW1.

CRIGHTON, Geoffrey
Berwin Leighton, London +44 171 760 1000
Chartered Town Planner and Senior Associate in Planning & Environment Department.
Specialisation: Planning law specialist involved in retail developments throughout the country and major housing schemes.
Career: Background in local government, having worked for Lancashire and Staffordshire County Councils and Milton Keynes Development Corporation. Joined *Berwin Leighton* in 1980.
Personal: Born in 1943. Educated at the Royal Masonic School (MBA, DipTp, MRTPI).

CUNLIFFE, Michael
Ashurst Morris Crisp, London (0171) 638 1111
Partner and Head of Planning Group.
Specialisation: Planning law acting for both developers and local authorities. Major clients include British Gas, Chelsfield, Thames Water, Trafalgar House and Dartford Borough Council.
Prof. Memberships: Legal Associate of the Royal Town Planning Institute, Member of the Law Society's Planning Panel and Member of the City of London Law Society's Planning and Environmental Law Sub-Committee. Associate Fellow of the Society for Advanced Legal Studies and a Member of the Society's Planning

and Environmental Law Reform Working Group.
Career: Qualified 1974. Joined *Ashurst Morris Crisp* 1983. Partner in 1987.

DENTON, Jocelyn
Ashurst Morris Crisp, London
(0171) 638 1111
Senior Assistant Solicitor in the Planning and Public Sector Groups.
Specialisation: Town and Country Planning and related areas, Compulsory Purchase and Compensation.
Prof. Memberships: Member of the Law Society's Specialist Planning Panel.
Career: Called to the Bar in 1982. Joined *Ashurst Morris Crisp* in 1988 after almost 5 years in local government. Qualified as a Solicitor in 1992.
Personal: Born 19 August 1958. Educated at Queen Mary College, London (LLB Hons. 1981). Enjoys travel, walking, and cookery.

DYER, Carl
McGuinness Finch, London
(0171) 493 9593
Specialisation: Town and Country Planning, especially retail development, cinema work, regeneration and centre development, including project coordination, inquiry and CPO work and all ancillary aspects including Section 106 and other infrastructure agreements.
Prof. Memberships: Law Society.
Career: BA (Hons) Law University of Kent at Canterbury, Anthony London Law Prize, Havant Borough Council (1982-1985), Brighton Borough Council (1985-1986), *Fitzhugh Gates* (1986-1989) Assistant Solicitor, *Norton Rose* (1989-1992) and *Berwin Leighton* (1992-1997), Partner *McGuinness Finch* (1997-).
Personal: Swimming, theatre.

EVANS, Douglas
Theodore Goddard, London
(0171) 606 8855
Specialisation: Advocacy, strategic advice and negotiation of planning permissions and agreements for all forms of property development. Advice on environmental assessment and contaminated land is an important part of the practice. Major clients include national house builders and commercial developers, retailers, institutional developers, power generation companies, waste landfill and incineration companies, utility companies and mining companies. Major cases include :- acting for Thames Water Utilities in the Terminal 5 Inquiry, promoting a 10,000 house development in the green belt ; promoting 3 major "waste to energy" incinerators together with a 51ha landraising site for Hampshire Waste; obtaining planning permission to double the size of the UK's only potashmine for Cleveland Potash; securing planning permission for 650 dwellings on a contaminated site for Fairview Homes; advising two major waste companies on the tendering process for LAWDC disposal using the Private Finance Initiative; presenting objections to numerous Local Plan Inquiries to secure allocations for retail and housing development.
Prof. Memberships: Member of the Law Society Specialist Planning Panel, Legal Associate of the Royal Town Planning Institute, Affiliate Member of the Institute of Waste Management, Member of the City of London Law Society Planning and Environment Sub-Committee and Member of the UK Environmental Law Association. Awarded the Institute of Waste Management Waste

Regulation Award for 1990.
Personal: Leisure interests include: sailing; shooting; and (in this order) staying married!

EVANS, Martin
Ashurst Morris Crisp, London
(0171) 638 1111
Senior Assistant Solicitor in the Planning Group.
Specialisation: Town and country planning and related issues. Particular experience in providing strategic advice on major retail and leisure schemes (both in and out of town) and public inquiries acting both for developer and local authority clients. Major clients include Chelsfield, Reuters, Thames Water, Tesco, British Gas and British Telecom. Also involved in negotiating complex planning and infrastructure agreements on behalf of developers and local authorities.
Prof. Memberships: Law Society, Leisure Property Forum.
Career: Qualified 1989.

FRASER, Moira A.
D J Freeman, London (0171) 583 4055
Head of town and country planning group. Partner in Property Services Department.
Specialisation: Many years specialist experience in planning, CPO and compensation, highway and other infrastructure issues. Emphasis on inquiry work and appeals. Expertise in negotiating and drafting planning and infrastructure agreements. Advises on development plan policies. Acts for public authorities, private sector and amenity groups. Special expertise in large retail.
Personal: The Law Society; UKELA; CBI Property Management Forum; CBI London Region Councillor; Fellow of the Royal Society of Arts; Town and Country Planning Association.
Career: MA (Hons) Cantab. Articled 1977-79 *Norton Rose*, qualified 1979. Joined *D J Freeman*, 1988. Partner 1990.
Personal: Born 1955. Leisure pursuits include golf, art appreciation and family.

GALLIMORE, Michael
Lovell White Durrant, London
(0171) 236 0066
Partner in commercial property department and head of planning group.
Specialisation: Principal area of practice is property development with particular expertise in the planning and environmental aspects of major development and infrastructure projects. Wide experience in office and business park developments, retail schemes, new housing settlements, leisure projects and waste management schemes. Expertise includes negotiations and appeals for planning and associated consents and drafting and negotiation of s.106 agreements and related development/infrastructure agreements. Has acted on numerous judicial review applications and High Court challenges. Experience also on various PFI projects. Acts as an advocate at planning and local plan inquiries.
Prof. Memberships: Law Society Specialist Planning Panel, Law Society Planning and Environmental Law Committee, City of London Law Society Planning and Environmental Law Sub-Committee.
Career: Qualified 1983, Partner 1988.

GARBUTT, John
Nicholson Graham & Jones, London
(0171) 648 9000
See under Environmental Law, p. 343

GRAVES, Gary
Nabarro Nathanson, London
(0171) 493 9933
Specialisation: Partner specialising in all aspects of planning law and practice, including major inquiry work and judicial review.
Prof. Memberships: Member Law Society Planning Panel (1995) and City of London Law Society Planning and Environmental Law Sub-Committee. Legal Associate of RTPI.
Career: Articles: *Russells*; qualified 1983. *Herbert Oppenheimer* (1983-1988); *Lovell White Durrant* (1988-1991); Partner *Nabarro Nathanson* (1991 to date).
Personal: Born 1958. Married with 1 child, resides London.

GREENWOOD, Brian J.
Norton Rose, London (0171) 283 6000
Specialisation: Areas of expertise include planning applications, environmental assessment, negotiation of planning and infrastructure agreements and hearings and appeals. Appears as advocate at appeals. Recent instructions include industrial processes, power stations, landfill, residential and commercial development, listed buildings and conservation areas, motorway service areas and airports. Author of "Butterworths Planning Law Service", co-author of "Environmental Regulation and Economic Growth", editor of "Planning Law Handbook" and "Butterworths Planning Law Guidance".
Prof. Memberships: Chairman, Law Society's Planning and Environmental Law Committee, former Chairman City of London Law Society Planning and Environment Committee; UKELA; Law Society's Specialist Planning Panel.

HALL, Brian
Clifford Chance, London (0171) 600 1000
Specialisation: Head of Planning Unit. Specialises in planning, environmental and Local Government Law.
Career: Qualified in 1980, became Partner in 1988.

HAWKINS, David
Nabarro Nathanson, London
(0171) 518 3261
Partner in Planning Department since 1978.
Specialisation: Covers all aspects of planning and development, particularly large scale commercial developments, public inquiries and judicial review; also administrative law, Parliamentary work and compulsory purchase and compensation. Author of 'Compulsory Purchase' volume of the Encyclopaedia of Forms and Precedents and 'Boynton's Guide to Compulsory Purchase and Compensation'. Addresses seminars regularly.
Prof. Memberships: Law Society; UKELA; IBA; Legal Associate, R.T.P.I.; Law Society Planning Panel.
Career: Member of Planning and Environmental Law Committee of the Law Society, FRSA.
Personal: King's College, London: LLB (Hons).

HELLIER, Tim
Berwin Leighton, London +44 171 760 1000
Specialisation: Wide experience in retail, housing, leisure and office developments, compulsory purchase, comtaminated land, risk management and infrastructure schemes. Acted for AMEC Developments in securing planning permission for the first freight terminal

associated with the Channel Tunnel including 3.5 million square feet of supporting development in the Green Belt. Acted for BAA-McArthur/ Glen (UK) Limited, the factory outlet operator in securing planning approvals for over 1.5 million square feet of retail floorspace.
Prof. Memberships: Law Society, Associate Fellow of the Society of Advanced Legal Studies, UKELA.
Career: Strode Colllege, Egham. Sheffield University LLB(Hons). Law Society Finals, City of London Polytechnic. Qualified 1986; partner *Berwin Leighton* 1997.
Personal: Married with two children. Interests include rugby, running and general fitness, music, his children.

HILLEBRON, Richard
Slaughter and May, London (0171) 600 1200
Specialisation: Specialises in all aspects of Town and Country planning from submission of an application through to decision and appeal if necessary including compulsory purchase, negotiating highways and other agreements with local authorities and Certificates of lawful use or development.
Prof. Memberships: Legal Associate of The Royal Town Planning Institute. Member of The Law Society's Planning Panel. Member City of London Law Society Planning and Environmental Law Sub-Committee.
Career: Qualified 1980.

HUGHES, Norna
Nabarro Nathanson, London
(0171) 493 9933
Partner in Planning Department.
Specialisation: Handles all aspects of planning related work, particularly contentious planning. Also handles rating and Judicial Review, covering business rate appeals and local and central government powers. Represents Costco in all planning matters and in the High Court litigation brought by Tesco, Sainsbury and Safeway, Barking Power Station and listed and post-war buildings. Speaker at RTPI conference on new forms of shopping.
Prof. Memberships: United Kingdom Environmental Law Association.
Career: Qualified in 1989. Joined *Nabarro Nathanson* in 1987, becoming a Partner in 1989. Previously a Barrister specialising in planning, having been called to the Bar in 1982.
Personal: Leisure interests include family, friends, socialising and tennis. Lives in London.

JACKSON, Andrew G.W.
Macfarlanes, London (0171) 831 9222
Specialisation: Planning and environmental law for a range of institutional and health authority clients, public and private companies and landed estates. Advice ranges from general planning strategy to drafting and negotiating highway and planning agreements as well as public inquiry work. Planning advice during the last year has been given on a proposal by an institutional developer to create an extensive business park on a green field site near Droitwich, and to a major property company on a substantial development of land near Chelsea Harbour in London as well as continuing work on the redevelopment of several major redundant hospital sites in the London green belt and on a major edge of town housing and

retail site on the edge of Salisbury, Wiltshire.
Prof. Memberships: Member of the Law Society Planning Panel. Member of the Planning and Environmental Law Sub-committee of the City of London Solicitors Company.
Career: Trinity College, Oxford. MA in Politics Philosophy and Economics. *Macfarlanes* 1975 to present.
Personal: Sport and family. Married with 2 children.

JACKSON, Raymond
Linklaters, London (0171) 456 4884
Partner. Planning & Environmental Unit in the Property Department.
Specialisation: Specialises in all aspects of environmental law including town planning, public health, control of pollution, compulsory purchase and highways. Typical matters have included a wide selection of corporate, privatisation and major property transactions where planning, regulatory and environmental issues have been pertinent. Has had extensive involvement in major public local inquiries for motorways, large redevelopment schemes and compulsory purchase orders. Detailed knowledge of the Compensation Code in respect of claims in the Lands Tribunal and as Parliamentary Agent; considerable experience of Private and Hybrid Bill procedures.
Career: Joined *Linklaters & Paines* in 1985, made Partner in 1988.

JEEPS, Barry
Stephenson Harwood, London
(0171) 329 4422
Partner and Head of Town and Country Planning Group.
Specialisation: Town and country planning. Advised on securing planning permission for the Trafford Centre, Dumplington, Manchester (a major sub-regional shopping centre) which was defended successfully in the House of Lords. Continuing planning advice in relation to London Bridge City (one of the largest urban regeneration projects in the country).
Career: Qualified in 1980 after articles at *Stephenson Harwood*. Became a Partner in 1989.
Personal: Born 1958. Educated at Slough Grammar School 1969-76 and St. Catherine's College, Oxford 1976-79. Leisure pursuits include supporting Tottenham Hotspur F.C.

KITSON, Tony
Cameron McKenna, London
(0171) 367 3000
Partner in Planning Group. Advises on the planning aspects of all sizes and types of property development. Has handled numerous appeals involving retail, office, industrial and residential developments, and appears as an advocate at public local inquiries. Experienced in negotiating and drafting Section 106 Agreements and other development agreements. Advises on all aspects of local authority law and administration, and PFI schemes. Advises on compulsory purchase and compensation, and Transport and Works Act schemes, the clean-up of contaminated industrial sites and disposal for redevelopment. Also provides advice and representation on all rating matters. Speaker at seminars on planning and environmental law, local government law and rating reform. Contributor to Solicitors

Journal, Law Society's Gazette, Journal of Planning and Environmental Law and *McKenna & Co* publications on planning, highways, compulsory purchase and rating.
Prof. Memberships: Law Society, Law Society's Panel of Planning Solicitors. City of London Solicitors Company.
Career: Qualified in 1975. Local authority solicitor before joining *McKenna & Co* in 1988; became a Partner in 1990.
Personal: Born 14th February 1952. Educated at Bancroft's School, Woodford 1963-69 and Warwick University 1969-72. Lives in London.

MACKAY, Ian
Cameron McKenna, London
(0171) 367 3000
Solicitor specialising in all aspects of town planning and development.
Specialisation: Twenty years' experience as planner and planning solicitor of advising planning authorities, developers and public sector agencies on all aspects of town planning and development. Senior member of the Planning Group with particular experience in coordinating large public inquiries throughout the country, including negotiating and drafting complex planning and highway agreements and other planning obligations. Practice also covers highways law and compulsory purchase as well as parliamentary work. Advised the Department of Transport on the Channel Tunnel Rail Link Bill. Major clients include J Sainsbury plc, Try Group plc, Commercial Union Properties Ltd, Pearl Assurance plc, the Crown Estate and Brixton Estate plc.
Prof. Memberships: Law Society, UK Environmental Law Association, City of London Law Society.
Career: Town planner with several local planning authorities, attaining the position of Deputy County Planning Officer. Qualified as a solicitor in 1984. Solicitor (Head of Planning, Highways and Contracts Legal Department), London Borough of Southwark 1986-88. Joined *McKenna & Co* in 1988.

MAX, Richard
D J Freeman, London (0171) 583 4055
Partner in Property Services Department.
Specialisation: Deals with all areas of planning law and practice as well as compulsory purchase and highways work. Offers full and competitive advocacy service to clients for all planning inquiries. Clients include retailers, local authorities, entrepreneurial developers, health authorites, property funds and development companies.
Prof. Memberships: Law Society, Law Society's Planning Panel, Secretary of the City of London Law Society Planning and Environmental Law Sub-Committee, Legal Associate and Council Member of the Royal Town Planning Institute.
Career: Qualified in 1988. Assistant Solicitor at *Macfarlanes* 1988-93. Planning Solicitor, Oxford City Council 1993. At *Radcliffes & Co* 1993-95. Joined *D J Freeman* in April 1995. Made a partner in May 1997.
Personal: Born 1 September 1963. Educated at St Paul's School 1976-82, Oxford Polytechnic 1982-85 and The College of Law, Chester 1985-86. Interests include exhibiting and driving a convertible VW Beetle as well as skiing and cycling. Lives in London.

NORRIS, Helen
McGuinness Finch, London
(0171) 493 9593

O'DONOVAN, Teige
Farrer & Co, London (0171) 242 2022
Called to the Bar 1985. Solicitor Commercial
Property Team.
Specialisation: All aspects of planning and
environmental, including listed building
applications and appeals, parliamentary
petitions, compulsory purchase matters and
tribunal advocacy.
Prof. Memberships: Middle Temple, Law
Society, Law Society's Planning Panel, Legal
Associate RTPI.
Personal: Born 7th January 1961. Educated at
Girton College, Cambridge 1979-82, the
Polytechnic of Central London and the Inns of
Court School of Law. Interests include
architectural art.

PUGH, Timothy
Berwin Leighton, London +44 171 760 1000
Partner; Co-Head Planning and Environmental
Department.
Specialisation: Planning and Environmental
Law. Particular areas of planning-related
expertise: rail and infrastructure projects, urban
regeneration, retail, industrial, warehousing,
waste disposal, land reclamation and housing
projects; compulsory purchase; highway
orders; planning and infrastructure agreements;
Transport and Works Act Orders. Particular
areas of environment-related expertise:
contaminated land; waste disposal;
environmental impact statements; water law;
environmental due diligence; environmental
terms and conditions of contract.
Prof. Memberships: City of London Solicitors
Company, IBA, Society for Advanced Legal
Studies (SAALS). Member: Planning and
Environment Committee of the British Property
Federation; Planning and Environment Law-Sub
Committee of the City of London Law Society;
IBA's Committee on International Environmental
Law; and SAAALS Planning and Environmental
Law Reform Group.
Career: Qualified 1984. Articled at *Donne
Mileham & Haddock* 1982-84. Joined *Berwin
Leighton* 1984; Partner 1990.
Personal: Born 1959. Duffryn High School,
Newport, Gwent; University College, London;
and College of Law, Lancaster Gate. Leisure
interests include skiing, cycling and lying under
old cars. Lives in Hove.

QUALTROUGH, John
Simmons & Simmons, London
(0171) 628 2020
Partner in Property Department.
Specialisation: Advises on all areas of
planning law and practice including appeals;
objections and representations to local plans;
and the drafting and negotiation of planning,
highway and other infrastructure agreements;
highways; compulsory purchase; and
compensation issues. In addition he deals with
commercial property matters where planning is
a significant element, including option
agreements, conditional contracts and sales
coupled with overage/clawback provisions.
Prof. Memberships: Law Society; City of
London Law Society (Committee member of
Planning and Environmental Law Sub-
Committee).
Career: Qualified 1978. Partner at *Simmons &*

Simmons since 1988.
Personal: Born 30th April 1953. Holds a BA
(1974).

REDMAN, Michael
Clifford Chance, London (0171) 600 1000
See under Environmental Law, p. 345

REES, Christopher
Davies Arnold Cooper, London
(0171) 936 2222

RICKETTS, Simon
S J Berwin & Co, London
+44 (0)171 533 2222
Specialisation: Planning and local government
law, advising institutions and developers on
major retail/ business/ residential/ leisure
schemes, including negotiating related
agreements, coordinating appeals and legal
challenges. Extensive experience in compulsory
purchase and related procedures and
Parliamentary work in respect of private and
hybrid Bills.
Prof. Memberships: Member of Law Society,
Member of British Council for Offices Planning
Legislation Committee.
Career: Called to the Bar 1985. Pupillages with
1 Serjeants Inn and 2 Harcourt Buildings.
Member of planning group at *Lovell White
Durrant* 1988 before moving to *S J Berwin* in
1997. Requalified as a solicitor 1991.

ROBINSON, E. Patrick G.
Herbert Smith, London (0171) 374 8000
Specialisation: Commercial property
development and planning work including
negotiated planning consents, Inquiries
(Appeals and Call-In's), judicial review,
compulsory purchase, and general strategic
property and planning advice.
Prof. Memberships: Law Society's Specialist
Planning Panel.
Career: Articled at *Herbert Smith* (1978-80).
Partner 1986. Joint Editor of Blundell & Dobry's
Planning, Applications, Appeals and
Proceedings (5th Ed) 1996.
Personal: Born April 1956. Educated at
University of Nottingham (LLB 1977). Leisure
pursuits include jazz, the Cévennes and family.
Lives in London.

SCATES, Steven
McGrigor Donald, London (0171) 329 3299
Head of London Property Team
Specialisation: Town and country planning
with emphasis on property development.
Experienced advocate. Inquiries (Local Plan,
EIP and appeals), judicial review, master plan
and planning briefs for site assemblies. Land
assembly, options and conditional contracts,
development agreements, consortium and joint
venture arrangements, infrastructure and
construction procurement, contaminated land
and acoustics. Clients include Barratt Homes
Ltd, Bellway Homes Ltd and North Thames
Regional Health Authority. Speaks frequently at
conferences, and is a regular contributor of
articles on planning and property development.
Prof. Memberships: Environmental
Practitioners Group, UKELA.
Career: Reading Borough Council 1978-85.
Partner *Peter Jacobs & Co* 1985-87, and
Sheridans 1987-89. Senior Partner *Scates
Rosenblatt* 1989-94. Partner *Nicholson Graham
& Jones* 1994-98. Partner *McGrigor Donald*
1998.

Personal: Born 17th January 1957. Leisure
pursuits include motorcycling, golf and tennis.
Lives in London.

SEARLE, Geoffrey
Olswang, London (0171) 208 8888
Specialisation: Head of planning: recently
joined *Olswang* to boost their well-respected
property department; has extensive experience
in major development projects in all sectors;
Prof. Memberships: President, British Chapter
FIABCI (The International Real Estate
Federation) 1996-7; President, Environment and
Legislation Committee, FIABCI (1994-8);
Founder Member UKELA;
Career: Qualified in 1968. Local government
1968-73; *Denton Hall & Burgin* 1973-1994
(Partner 1977-94; Managing Partner 1988-92);
sole principal Geoffrey Searle, Planning Solicitor
1994-8; head of planning, property department
Olswang 1998 to date.
Personal: Born June 1945. Fellow of the Royal
Society of Arts, Fellow of the Institute of
Management, Athenaeum Club and City Livery
Club. Leisure interests include walking, family
history, reading and music. Lives in Cotterstock,
Northants (Chairman of the Parish Meeting) and
London.

SHERLOCK, Roger
Nabarro Nathanson, London
0171) 493 9933
Senior Solicitor in Planning Department
Specialisation: Main areas of practice are
planning and compulsory purchase law.
Handles all planning aspects of commercial
and infrastructure development. Other areas of
practice include rating, compensation and
highways. Undertakes advocacy at planning
inquiries and in Lands Tribunal. Author of
articles on rating, compulsory purchase and
highways law.
Prof. Memberships: Legal Associate of RTPI,
Law Society Planning Panel.
Career: Qualified in 1975. Senior lawyer in local
Government 1982-1989. Joined *Nabarro
Nathanson* in 1989.

STEVENS, Peter
Jeffrey Green Russell, London
(0171) 339 7000
Partner 1994. Town Planning Department.
Specialisation: All aspects of planning and
various other central and local government
issues. Work includes highways and
infrastructure, compulsory purchase and
compensation, options and contracts. Makes
regular appearances in the Planning and
Property Development programmes of
Television Education Network.
Prof. Memberships: Law Society. Legal
Associate of RTPI. Member of Law Society's
Planning Panel.
Career: Qualified in 1973. Worked at *Lovell
White & King* 1971-81 before joining *Denton Hall*
in 1981, becoming a Partner in 1988, then
joined *Jeffrey Green Russell* as a Partner in
1994.
Personal: Born 12th March 1948. Attended
Latymer Upper School 1957-67, then
Manchester University 1967-70. Leisure
interests include squash, test cricket, and a
hideaway in rural France. Lives in Wimbledon.

THOMAS, Patricia
S J Berwin & Co, London
+44 (0)171 533 2222
Partner and Head of Planning and
Environmental Group.
Specialisation: Principal areas of practice are
planning and local government law including
highways, land drainage and water matters,
conservation issues (natural and built heritage)
and environment law including compliance and
due diligence audits, advice on IPC
authorisations, water abstraction licences,
pollution and waste cases. Involved in aviation-
related developments. Editor of and main
contributor to 'The Planning Factbook'. Editor of
'Environmental Liability' and 'Water Pollution: Law
and Liability'. Contributed planning law chapter
to 'The Surveyor's Factbook'. Lectures frequently
on planning and environmental topics.
Prof. Memberships: Law Society (member of
Committee on Planning and Environmental
Law), City of London Solicitors' Company
(member of Planning and Environment
Committee), International Bar Association,
Forum UK. Member of Law Society's Specialist
Planning Panel. CBI Property Management
Forum.
Career: Qualified 1974. Planning Solicitor and
Advocate, Greater London Council and London
Borough of Southwark 1975-79. Joined *Denton
Hall Burgin & Warrens* in 1979 and became a
Partner in 1981, then moved to *S J Berwin & Co.*
in 1988 as a Partner and Head of Planning and
Environment Group.

TREHEARNE, Ian
Berwin Leighton, London +44 171 760 1000
Planner and Barrister. Joint Head of Planning
and Environment Department.
Specialisation: Principal area of work is
planning law covering advice and advocacy on
development, including major retail and office
schemes, factory outlet centres, housing,
hotels, utility and waste disposal developments
and local plan inquiries. Specialist active on
conservation, historic building and design
issues. Also environment law advising on
contamination liability and threats and
European Community matters. Advised on
Ludgate development, Euston Centre and
tower, Ebbsfleet Station and 8.5m sq. ft.
development surrounding it, major five-star
hotel in Bloomsbury, 1.6m sq. ft. shopping in
Croydon, the Channel Tunnel Rail Link and
environmental cases such as Dartford and
Welbeck. PFI issues: redevelopment of DSS
estate in Newcastle and Sunderland;
rationalisation and rebuilding of University
College Hospital, United Medical and Dental
Schools and King's College, London.
Numerous conferences and seminars. Lectured
at City University 1982-84.
Prof. Memberships: Royal Town Planning
Institute.

Career: London Borough of Newham, 1972-4,
then joined the London Borough of Islington
1974-77. Joined the London Borough of
Camden in 1979 and moved to *Berwin Leighton*
in 1985. Admitted to Partnership in 1988. Called
to the Bar 1980.
Personal: Born 17th May 1950. Attended
Durham University 1968-71. Leisure pursuits
include sailing, building, books and music.
Lives in London.

TRUE, Justin
Titmuss Sainer Dechert, London
0171) 583 5353
Specialisation: Principal areas of practice are
planning including inquiry work, highways,
environment, local government, CPO work and
judicial review for retailers, housebuilders,
developers, corporate and public sector clients.
Experienced advocate and professional
witness. Drafts planning and infrastructure
agreements.
Prof. Memberships: Royal Town Planning
Institute.
Career: Has a background in Local
Government in London and the Home Counties
between 1974 and 1985. Joined *Titmuss Sainer
Dechert* in 1985. Director of the Association of
Town Centre Management (1994-1997) and
founder member of the Planning Transport and
Development Policy Sub-Group of the
Association. Member of the Planning and
Development Panel of the British Retail
Consortium (1996-1998) and a contributor to
BRC Planning Task Group (1998).
Personal: Born 1955. BA Hons Planning
Studies and Diploma in Town Planning, Oxford
Brooks University. Leisure pursuits include golf,
skiing and cycling. Lives in Surrey.

TURNER, Angela
Gouldens, London (0171) 583 7777
Specialisation: Wide range of planning,
environmental and local government law
including appeals, inquiries, judicial review and
agreements. During 12 years in local
government (Royal Borough of Kensington &
Chelsea), has great experience of planning law
from the local government perspective and
particularly in relation to listed building and
conservation area law and enforcement related
matters. During 13 years in private practice has
an equivalent depth of experience of advising
developers and others on planning strategies
relevant to their proposals. Has acted as
Advocate at Public Inquiries and other tribunals
including the Magistrate and County Courts.
Prof. Memberships: Law Society Planning
Panel; Legal Associate of the Royal Town
Planning Institute; City of London Law Society's
Planning & Environmental Law Sub-Committee;
UKELA Town Planning.
Career: Qualified in 1973. Principal Solicitor,
Royal Borough of Kensington & Chelsea.
Partner at *Gouldens* from 1987.

Personal: Sheffield University (LLB). Co-author
of "Badlands, Essential Environmental Law for
Property Professionals". Many interests.

WELLS, Martin
Stephenson Harwood, London
(0171) 329 4422
Senior Associate in Property Department: Town
and Country Planning Group.
Specialisation: Advises on a wide range of
town planning and related matters, including
agreements, appeals, public inquiries and High
Court challenges. Cases have included
advising on a series of major developments for
the University of Greenwich, Stakis plc, the
Godinton Estate, Wimpey Homes, the Bristol
Port Company, the London Borough of
Hackney, Skandia Property (UK) Limited, Martin
International Holdings plc, Wonder World plc,
the Accor Group, Chiltern District Council and
Den norske Bank ASA and carrying out a study
of public inquiries into waste combustion
installations for the Energy Technology Support
Unit (Department of Trade and Industry).
Prof. Memberships: Legal Associate of Royal
Town Planning Institute, Law Society's Planning
Panel, City of London Law Society's Planning
and Environmental Law Sub-Committee,
UKELA's Planning Law Working Party.
Career: Qualified in 1972. Legal Assistant at
Luton C. B.C. 1965-1971; Solicitor at St Albans
C.C. 1972-73, then Watford B.C. 1973-79;
Principal Planning Administrator, Hertsmere
B.C. 1979-81 and Solicitor to the Council to
1986; Borough Secretary at Runnymede B.C.
1986-87; Assistant Solicitor with *Denton Hall
Burgin & Warrens* 1987-88, joining *Stephenson
Harwood* in 1988. Senior Associate in 1989.
Personal: Born 12th September 1944. Holds
an LLB (Hons) from Exeter University, 1965.
Leisure interests include music and travel. Lives
in Woking, Surrey.

WILLIAMS, Christopher J.C.
Cameron McKenna, London
(0171) 367 3000
Specialisation: Partner in the Planning Group.
Specialising in Town and Country planning
aspects of all sizes and types of property
development, including retail, residential, office,
and industrial development; compulsory
purchase and compensation; planning related
aspects of environmental law, particularly
environmental assessments relating to major
projects; infrastructure projects; advocacy at
public inquiries. Specialist in major
infrastructure projects, including airport and
airport related development. Advising BAA plc
in connection with proposals for a fifth terminal
at Heathrow Airport.
Prof. Memberships: Law Society of England
and Wales.
Career: St John's College, Cambridge
University.
Personal: Born 1962. Resides London. Leisure
interests: skiing, mountaineering.

SOUTH EAST

Brachers (2ptnrs including the highly regarded *Henry Abraham*) Both are on the Law Society Planning Panel and are Legal Associate Members of the RTPI. **Clients/Work:** Local inquiry work for a major housing site of 150 units. Defended a CPO, obtained a Certificate of Lawful Use for a major commercial dock and attended an appeal for a tyre warehouse. Also lodging objections to three major championship golf courses in Kent.

Clarks (5ptnrs, 3assts) *Simon Dimmick* is described as "competent" with "excellent drafting skills." **Clients/Work:** Promotion of 2,500 house Structure Plan development for the University of Reading. Local plan submissions for Blue Circle. Act for several local authorities at county, district and parish levels.

Donne Mileham & Haddock (1ptnr, the "excellent" *Anthony Allen* who spends 60% of his time on planning, 1 asst) The firm also functions as a planning consultancy. **Clients/Work:** Advised Safeway/Gleesons on proposed superstore at Amesbury. Acted for Brighton and Hove Albion Council in opposing a city centre public house. Acting on several major housing developments.

Jameson & Hill Excellent reputation synonymous with *Robert Jameson* who does purely planning work. Particular strength in local planning work. **Clients/Work:** Acted for Uttlesford District Council in the Court of Appeal challenge to the Uttlesford District Plan. Acted for Craven District Council (North Yorkshire) in local plan inquiry. Appeared at Shropshire Minerals Plan Inquiry for Redland Aggregates.

Pitmans (1ptnr, 3assts) Leader *Richard Valentine*, a founder member of the Law Society's Planning Panel, heads the firm's Planning and Environmental Law Group. The group is usually litigation driven, rather than being an adjunct to the Commercial Property Department, and is strong in inquiry work and judicial review. **Clients/Work:** Continuing to act for Somerfield on new sites and judicial review proceedings against other major supermarket operators. Acted on the redevelopment of two town centres and represented McAlpines re a new settlement in Cambridge.

Griffith Smith (1ptnr, *Robert Hinton* 75%, 1asst). **Clients/Work:** Recently acted

for the Port of Shoreham in securing the release of land from an enforcement notice.

Moore & Blatch (3 ptnrs including leader *John Barrington*) Act for landowners as well as housebuilders and developers. **Clients/Work:** Completed negotiations for development of site at Swathling, Hants for 50 dwellings (max) plus relocation of riding school.

Ottaways Partner *Douglas Raine* is experienced in planning work, including advocacy. He acts for individuals, companies and public authorities on a range of matters. Particular specialisation in enforcement and listed building / conservation area issues.

Wollastons (1const, 2ptnrs p/t) Work is principally handled by consultant *James Little*. Strengths include enforcement cases and s.106 agreements. Recent involvement in planning judicial review.

SOUTH WEST

Bevan Ashford (2ptnrs, 1assoc, 1asst) The team consists of partners *David Wood*, who spends 50% of his time on planning work, and *John Bosworth* who is described as "solid and dependable." *Keith Oliver* was recommended this year as an up and coming

planning lawyer. **Clients/Work:** Act for the Secretary of State for Health (South West) re disposal of surplus hospital sites. Advised English Partnerships on planning aspects of the Temple Quay development in Bristol. Acted in successful judicial review proceedings in March 1998 to quash planning permission and conservation area consent granted by Bristol City Council.

Bond Pearce (1ptnr, 1assoc, 2assts) *Marcus Trinick* heads the team, and is "a very sensible person to do business with." Associate *Sarah Holmes* is also a leader. Their major strength is in renewable energy projects and they are instructed by the majority of wind energy developers. **Clients/Work:** Structure and local plan representation programme for the British Wind Energy Association throughout England and Wales. Acting for Associated British Ports on proposed extension to Southampton Container Port. Also act for Plymouth Development Corporation

Burges Salmon (1ptnr, 3assoc including the up and coming *Ian Salter*) Team includes the highly regarded *Patrick Robinson*. Strong in compulsory purchase and minerals planning (three new quarrying clients in past year). Handle their own advocacy (six or

seven times a year). **Clients/Work:** Acted for Orange at a called-in planning inquiry to build a transmitter in an area of outstanding natural beauty. Acted in planning appeal re 10 acre housing development in Chippenham.

Clarke Willmott & Clarke (3ptnrs, 3assts) Seen as having cornered the market in the Taunton area, they are also strong in Bristol. Taunton-based *Nick Engert* is well regarded as an advocate and Bristol-based *John Houghton* is described as a "safe pair of hands." They regularly appear as advocates at planning inquiries and are strong in project management. **Clients/Work:** Public inquiries re food stores at St Ives in Cornwall and Frinton in Essex for Carter Commercial Developments. Advised Secretary of State for Defence on development scheme for former hospital on rural brownfield site. Other key clients include Co-operative Retail Services and the Countryside Commission.

Davies and Partners (1ptnr, leader *Rina Bird*, 3assts) *Katherine Evans* was newly recommended to us this year and there is a new team member from Hammond Suddards. **Clients/Work:** Advising on the proposed redevelopment of the Upper Hayford Air Base to provide 5,000 dwellings and supporting facilities.

Lawrence Tucketts (4ptnrs, 8assts in the Commercial Property Department handle planning when required) *Stephen Pasterfield* who appeared at seven or eight inquiries as an advocate in the past year and an assistant specialise. **Clients/Work:** Acted for Co-operative Retail Services at inquiry for proposed Tesco superstore in Portishead. Acted for Truro Chamber of Commerce in out of town retail 'circus' inquiry. Advised Bristol Rugby Club and Bristol Rovers FC re ongoing planning controversy in relation to Memorial Ground.

Lyons Davidson (1ptnr, town planner, 1asst) The team is led by *Kevin Gibbs*, who has moved into the top band of leading individuals. **Clients/Work:** Advising property company on development of Harlow Business Park. Acting for high street bank on planning problems involved in sale of large residential development site in Bristol. Advising NHS trust on proposed redevelopment of headquarters site in Bristol.

Osborne Clarke (1ptnr, 1asst 40%) Partner, *Andrew Hignett*, is well regarded and appears at planning inquiries as an advocate on a regular basis. **Clients/Work:** Acting for Bath University in the development of their campus.

Alsters Planning work is carried out by *Tom Graham*, who has moved into the top band of leading individuals this year. Strength of the practice is early involvement in projects and project management. **Clients/Work:** Tom Graham acted as advocate at recent superstore inquiry in Trowbridge. Obtaining permission for 350,000 sq ft of warehousing in Bristol. Negotiating permis-

sion for 500 student residences for the University of Southampton.

Cartwrights (1ptnr, *Emrys Parry;* 3assts) Particular strength is compulsory purchase. **Clients/Work:** Acted for Reading Borough Council in settling town centre CPO compensation claims, and Bristol International Airport in connection with a CPO to divert the A38. Attended inquiry concerning proposed development in the greenbelt.

Foot & Bowden *William Jones* spends 70-80% of his time on planning work and Sebastian Head, formerly a barrister at 2 Mitre Court, has recently been recruited. **Clients/Work:** Involvement in planning aspects of Plymouth airport improvements. Application for major industrial/retail site outside Plymouth.

Fynn & Partners (1ptnr, 3 charted town planners) Offer technical as well as legal advice and advocacy. Handle numerous planning appeals each year. A high percentage are enforcement matters. **Clients/Work:** Complex appeal involving planning, listed buildings/conservation areas, and enforcement notice re Purbeck House Hotel and Craigside House Hotel in Swanage.

Lester Aldridge (2 ptnrs – both 50%+, 1asst). Cover a range of work: industrial, retail, and residential. **Clients/Work:** Negotiating planning consent for factory outlet scheme. Successful challenge to Sec of State's refusal to grant permission for supermarket in Somerset. Clients include Dean and Redyhoff and Lloyds Bank.

Sisman Nichols (1ptnr 100%, 1assoc 25%) New entry to the table following *Martin Goodall's* move there from Clarke,

Wilmott & Clarke last year. Handle a range of planning work including judicial review and compulsory purchase.

Stephens & Scown (2ptnrs – 50%, 1const) Substantial amount of mining and quarrying waste management work. **Clients/Work:** Planning inquiry relating to the deposit of waste material near Newton Abbott in connection with the ball clay industry, and advice to a client in the aggregates industry on various road stone plants.

LEADING INDIVIDUALS SOUTH WEST	
BOSWORTH John Bevan Ashford	
ENGERT Nick Clarke Willmott & Clarke	
GIBBS Kevin Lyons Davidson	
GRAHAM Tom Alsters	
HIGNETT Andrew Osborne Clarke	
HOUGHTON John Clarke Willmott & Clarke	
PASTERFIELD Stephen Lawrence Tucketts	
ROBINSON Patrick Burges Salmon	
TRINICK Marcus Bond Pearce	
WOOD David Bevan Ashford	
BEARD Tony Tozers	
BIRD Rina Davies and Partners	
GOODALL Martin Sisman Nichols	
HOLMES Sarah Bond Pearce	
JONES William Foot & Bowden	
PARRY Emrys Cartwrights	

UP AND COMING	
EVANS Katherine Davies and Partners	
OLIVER Keith Bevan Ashford	
SALTER Ian Burges Salmon	

WALES

HIGHLY REGARDED FIRMS WALES
Edwards Geldard Cardiff
Eversheds Cardiff
Aaron & Partners Wrexham
Morgan Bruce Cardiff

Edwards Geldard (1ptnr, 1assoc both 40%) The well regarded *Huw Williams* heads the planning group, which is part of the Commercial Property Department. **Clients/Work:** Planning issues re National Botanic Garden for Wales. Compulsory purchase acquisi-

tions under the Cardiff Bay Barrage Act for Cardiff Bay Development Corporation. Planning aspects of hotel, housing and leisure schemes.

Eversheds (1ptnr 75%, 3assts 100%) The practice is headed by *Eric Evans* and includes *Stephen Manson* who is developing an expertise in PFI projects. **Clients/Work:** Advised the Welsh Development Agency on planning conditions relating to the LG £1.7 billion inward investment project.

Aaron & Partners Branch office in Wrexham gives the firm a presence in North Wales. Planning partner is a Welsh speaker. (for further details see under North West).

Morgan Bruce (2ptnrs, 2assts) Profile for planning work diminished following

departure of Peter Burgess. However, the firm has recently gained a partner from Clifford Chance's Planning and Environment Unit, and a partner from Hugh James in Cardiff. **Clients/Work:** Advising on planning for new infrastructure of Cardiff Wales airport. Acting for local estates management in development of a national chain of homes.

LEADING INDIVIDUALS · WALES	
EVANS Eric Eversheds	
WILLIAMS Huw Edwards Geldard	

UP AND COMING	
MANSON Stephen Eversheds	

MIDLANDS

Edge & Ellison (1ptnr, 2assts) The team is led by highly regarded partner *Martin Damms*. **Clients/Work:** Planning applications for Aldi Stores. Multi-million pound leisure development backed by CPO and involving highway closure and a s106 agreement. Instructions for Allied Domecq including listed building consents and s106 agreements.

Eversheds (1ptnr, 4assts) Team includes well-regarded partner *Rod Bull* and *Anne Tideswell*, formerly of Rowe & Maw. The group does its own advocacy and conducts about 30 inquiries per year. **Clients/Work:** Rod Bull appeared as an advocate at the Shropshire Local Minerals Plan Inquiry. Team acted for Bryant Group in the Battle of Tewkesbury Inquiry. Advised Ford/Jaguar and Coventry City Council on a major industrial park proposal at Whitley, Coventry.

Marron Dodds (4ptnrs, 1asst) The department is headed by *Peter Marron* who is well known in the region and "certainly knows his stuff." **Clients/Work:** Representing major commercial property company at

two Motorway Service Area inquiries. Undertaking advocacy on behalf of several local planning authorities throughout their local plan inquiries. Representing numerous house builders at planning inquiries and local plan inquiries.

Pinsent Curtis (2ptnrs including *Martin White*, 2assts) Strong public sector as well as private sector client base. **Clients/Work:** Acted for West Midlands Development Agency in obtaining planning permission for micro-electronics plant in green belt north of Sutton Coldfield. Thameslink 2000 – acting on behalf of two train operating companies re objections to recent Works Order. Acted for Rover Group on appeal against refusal of planning permission for facilities at Solihull plant.

Wragge & Co (3ptnrs, 2assoc, 2assts) **Clients/Work:** Successful judicial review on behalf of PowerGen of Warwickshire County Council's refusal to enter into a highways agreement (concerning redevelopment of a former power station site). Advising Rapid Transport International on new public transport system for Northampton.

Browne Jacobson (1ptnr, 1const, 3assts) The team has been strengthened by the recruitment of *Brian Smith* from Wilde Sapte. **Clients/Work:** Particularly active on housing matters and have advised numerous housebuilders, such as Lindsey Securities and William Davis on site allocation. Acted for Derby City Council and Mansfield District Council on town centre redevelopments.

Dibb Lupton Alsop **Clients/Work:** One expert in highways law handles planning work with support from 1 asst.

Hewitson, Becke + Shaw (1ptnr, *Peter Taylor*, in Northampton office) Have seen an increase in advocacy work in the past year. **Clients/Work:** Acted for Daventry District Council re Daventry International Rail Freight Terminal. Advised Bedfordia plc on Bedford Borough Council's Local Plan Inquiry.

Martineau Johnson (6ptnrs, 10assts in the Commercial Property Department

handle planning when required) Particular expertise in development of science and technology parks.

Shoosmiths & Harrison (1asst, 2 chartered planners) Focus on strategic and detailed planning, providing a one-stop shop for developers, from identification of sites to sale of units. **Clients/Work:** Recently carried out strategic land identification studies for major housebuilders. Act for Bellway and their strategic land division. Detailed planning proposals on behalf of Coates Viyella.

Freeth Cartwright Hunt Dickins Planning team operates within the firm's Commercial Property Department. Recruited a senior town planner early in 1998. **Clients/Work:** Major planning appeal by CWS re proposed superstore at Stapleford. Work for European Leisure, including planning aspects of two large venue bars in Nottingham. Development at Hippodrome complex in London.

Knight & Sons (1ptnr 20%, 1asst 65%, 1 const) **Clients/Work:** Acting for Morrison Developments on the National Discovery Park, Liverpool, a millennium project linking the docks to the city centre. Also known for minerals and quarrying work – recently advised on the designation of a quarry as a site of special scientific interest.

Wall, James & Davies (1ptnr, 2 planners) **Clients/Work:** Acted for local residents in a judicial review concerning appropriation of public open space. Also act for property developers.

SEE PROFILES AT END OF THIS SECTION

EAST ANGLIA

Hewitson Becke + Shaw The team is led by the "effective" *Peter Brady*, who is particularly strong on advocacy. **Clients/Work:** Advising Homerton College, Cambridge re planning permission for two sites totalling 10

acres for housing development. Advising Shanks & McEwan on planning appeal related to Brogborough waste landfill site outside Bedford. Advised Taywood Homes on 650-house development near Chelmsford.

Mills & Reeve (1ptnr, 2assts) *Beverley Firth* ("very pragmatic and a good all-rounder") is well known in the region. The former Director of Legal Services at Norfolk County Council has recently joined the team. **Clients/Work:** Advised two local airfield operators on enforcement action to curtail activities. Advised Oxford College on planning aspects of major edge of town development.

Eversheds (1ptnr, 2assts) Act for a number of retailers and property developers and

have developed a planning audit service for commercial property clients in transactional work. **Clients/Work:** Negotiated and completed a number of S.106 agreements, including two for residential developments of over 300 units. Successful appeal against terms of a Certificate of Appropriate Alternative Development and pursuit of compensation in Lands Tribunal.

SEE PROFILES AT END OF THIS SECTION

Taylor Vinters (1ptnr, 2assts 50%) *Philip Kratz* has continued to establish himself in the region and is seen as on the way up. **Clients/Work:** Acting for Kings College, Cambridge in negotiations with Cambridge City Council over permitted development rights. Acting for NHM warehousing in pub-

lic inquiry. Acting for major landowner on proposals for large hotel in Cambridgeshire.

Gotelee & Goldsmith (1ptnr, 1const, 1asst) The firm's managing partner, a member of the Law Society's Planning Panel, spends 30% of his time on planning work. He has a niche practice acting for residents

objecting to private airfields. **Clients/Work:** Recently concluded two planning inquiries concerning airfields in Suffolk and Essex. Involved in month long inquiry concerning Elmslett Aerodrome in Suffolk. Obtained planning permission for extension to Michel Roux's restaurant in Bray.

NORTH WEST

LEADING FIRMS • NORTH WEST
HALLIWELL LANDAU Manchester

HIGHLY REGARDED FIRMS
Aaron & Partners Chester
Addleshaw Booth & Co Manchester
Cobbetts Manchester
Eversheds Manchester
Masons Manchester

Davies Wallis Foyster Liverpool

Halliwell Landau (1ptnr, 1asst) *Roger Lancaster* has a good reputation, especially as an advocate, and spends a lot of time on public inquiries. **Clients/Work:** Obtained planning permission on appeal on behalf of North West Regional Health Authority on application to redevelop Calderstones Hospital in Lancashire. Several permissions granted at appeal on behalf of Kwik Fit Properties Ltd relating to B2 development and Sunday Trading. Acted in Modern Homes (Whitworth) Ltd v Lancashire County Council.

Aaron & Partners (2ptnrs 100%, 1ptnr 50%) The team includes *Simon Carter* and

Ian Kinloch who are accomplished advocates. Long-standing expertise in minerals planning, waste disposal and certificates of lawful use. Increasingly involved in built development work.

Addleshaw Booth & Co (2ptnrs, 3assts, 5 other fee-earners in Manchester and Leeds) *Michael Kenworthy* heads the Manchester side of the practice. He has particular experience of preparing planning applications as well as handling advocacy. **Clients/Work:** Redevelopment of All Saints campus for Manchester Metropolitan University. Enforcement notice appeal for Speedlith Photo Litho. Planning advice on the dismantling and re-erection of a listed building for Brunner Mond.

Cobbetts (2ptnrs) *Peter Oldham* is very experienced and well known for his public inquiry work involving major superstores and other commercial developments. **Clients/Work:** Representations at Liverpool UDP Public Inquiry seeking allocation of industrial site for 150,000 sq ft retail warehouse. Advising several clients on latest extension to Manchester's Metrolink. Major planning appeal involving hotel and pub/restaurant development in Cheshire.

Eversheds (7 fee-earners in the north-

ern planning team) Already strong in the north east, are now developing their practice in the north west. **Clients/Work:** Handle work nationally for English Partnerships out of Manchester. Recent advice to United Norwest Co-operatives on compulsory purchase retail development (3 week CPO inquiry).

Masons (1ptnr, 4assts) The team is led by *John Moritz* who is well known in the region and is highly regarded. **Clients/Work:** Advising on the £127m Lowry Centre in Manchester, the Rochdale Canal Restoration project and an urban regeneration partnership scheme in Bradford.

Davies Wallis Foyster (1ptnr/ chartered town planner, 1asst) **Clients/Work:** Obtaining consent for a large office development and advising a client on enforcement.

LEADING INDIVIDUALS
NORTH WEST

LANCASTER Roger Halliwell Landau

MORITZ John Masons
OLDHAM Peter Cobbetts

CARTER Simon Aaron & Partners
KENWORTHY Michael Addleshaw Booth & Co
KINLOCH Ian Aaron & Partners

SEE PROFILES AT END OF THIS SECTION

NORTH EAST

LEADING FIRMS • NORTH EAST
WILBRAHAM & CO Leeds

EVERSHEDS Leeds
WALKER MORRIS Leeds

ADDLESHAW BOOTH & CO Leeds
DICKINSON DEES Newcastle upon Tyne
HAMMOND SUDDARDS Leeds

HIGHLY REGARDED FIRMS
Nabarro Nathanson Sheffield
Ward Hadaway Newcastle upon Tyne

Oxley & Coward Rotherham
Pinsent Curtis Leeds
Rollit Farrell & Bladon Hull

Wilbraham & Co (9 fee-earners all doing pure planning work) *Peter Wilbraham* ("brilliant," "a star") heads the strong team. **Clients/Work:** Major new residential development of 2000 houses in Staffordshire. Proposed motor racing circuit at Durham. All new sewage works for York-

shire Water (permissions negotiated without inquiries – 6 major permissions received within last 12 months).

Eversheds (7 fee-earners between Leeds and Manchester) *Paul Winter* heads the group. **Clients/Work:** Agreements for the film set of "Emmerdale" in the parklands of Harewood House, a Grade 1 listed building. A resumed inquiry into a major landfill proposal in West Yorkshire for the Warmfield Company and related judicial review proceedings.

Walker Morris (3ptnrs, 1asst, 7 other fee-earners handle planning when required) *Andrew Williamson* ("very sound") heads the department. Several regional rivals said that the firm had a good team. **Clients/Work:** Recently concluded an edge of centre supermarket appeal for WM Morrison Supermarkets at Kirkstall involving complex highway issues. Acting for Welcome Break re motorway service area in the Harrogate district.

Addleshaw Booth & Co *Stephen Turnbull* heads the firm's Leeds practice. The former head of Pinsent Curtis' Leeds planning and environmental unit joined in September 1997. A particular specialism of the team is

compulsory purchase. Stephen Turnbull undertakes advocacy at CPO and planning inquiries. He was described as "highly competent" and "a doer." **Clients/Work:** Pursuing objection to CPO for major retail scheme at Wantage on behalf of Sainsburys. Advising Stockton Borough Council re 3rd party challenge of CPO decision by Secretary of State.

Dickinson Dees *Paul Taylor* heads the department, which has been strengthened by the appointment of two chartered town planners in the past year. Areas of particular expertise include minerals and waste disposal. Have seen an increase in non-contentious planning work, particularly major planning applications and negotiation of S106 agreements. **Clients/Work:** Within last 12 months have appeared as advocates at local inquiries into mineral proposals in Northumberland, Durham and Yorkshire.

Hammond Suddards (1ptnr, 2assts, 3 other fee-earners) *David Goodman* heads the department. Handling an increasing amount of electricity generation and transmission work, including appearances at public inquiries and wayleave hearings. **Clients/**

Work: Acting for Eastern Generation Ltd (new client) and the National Grid Company re proposals for major power station at King's Lynn. Advising Elf (another new client) on appeals against refusal of planning permission for filling stations in the South East.

Nabarro Nathanson (3ptnrs, 4 other fee-earners) Particular expertise in minerals planning and waste. Developing a national practice in regeneration projects as well as acting for regional housebuilders. **Clients/Work:** Planning inquiries for major opencast coal operators. Re-structuring and re-developing of chemical sites. Compulsory acquisition and arbitration re sites for major new water treatment infrastructure.

Ward Hadaway (6ptnrs/planning associates (3 ft), 5assts) Strengthened by arrival of 2 more chartered town planners during the past year. **Clients/Work:** Regeneration schemes at Hexham for Matthew Charlton, at East Gateshead for Smith Print Group and Ouseburn for Ouseburn Trust. Acting for English Heritage on development of land adjacent to Whitby Abbey for leisure facilities.

Oxley & Coward Planning practice headed by partner with over 30 years experience of working for public-sector bodies and advising those dealing with them.

Pinsent Curtis (1assoc, 1 other fee-earner) The Leeds office works closely with the larger Birmingham office team. **Clients/Work:** Successful appeal on behalf of ARC re quarry in Scotland. Advising Thornfield Developments re retail development in the Midlands. Advising Samuel Smiths Brewery at Tadcaster re development site in Rochdale.

Rollit Farrell & Bladon (9ptnrs, 10 fee-earners in the property dept – 2ptnrs specialise in planning) "Good solid reputation – have got Hull pretty well sewn up." **Clients/Work:** Lead adviser on the Kingswood development in Hull (new 6,500 home suburb, including 200,000 sq ft retail park and 100 acre business park).

SCOTLAND

LEADING FIRMS · SCOTLAND

ARCHIBALD CAMPBELL & HARLEY WS
Edinburgh
BRODIES WS Edinburgh
DUNDAS & WILSON CS Edinburgh

HIGHLY REGARDED FIRMS

Burness Edinburgh
Maclay Murray & Spens Glasgow
McGrigor Donald Glasgow
Paull & Williamsons Aberdeen
Shepherd & Wedderburn WS Edinburgh

Ledingham Chalmers Aberdeen
McClure Naismith Glasgow

Archibald Campbell & Harley (2ptnrs, 3 other fee-earners) Handle varying amounts of planning work – from 30% to over 75%. *David Cockburn* and *Eric Young* are among Scotland's top planning lawyers. **Clients/Work:** Major client is Scottish Natural Heritage for whom the firm has conducted nine planning inquiries over the past 18 months, including windfarm developments, landfill, CCGT and business park developments and a hydro electricity generating station. Also recently advised ARC Greenways.

Brodies (1ptnr, 1asst) *Neil Collar* has considerable ability." **Clients/Work:** Advising major electricity company on its application to construct a power station (66 day public inquiry). Representing mining company in appeal against refusal of planning permission for an open cast coal mine. Advising major housebuilder on planning application for a 650-house development.

Dundas & Wilson (5 fee-earners) Department is headed by the "extremely able" *Ann Faulds.* Part of team undertaking Scottish Office research project into Development Planning in Scotland. **Clients/Work:** Inquiries into retail, housing, green belt release, roads, listed buildings and open cast mining. Continuing involvement in Dunfermline Eastern Expansion Project and retail proposals including Kinnaird Park in Edinburgh.

Burness (5ptnrs, 3assts, 8 other fee-earners in planning and environmental law group) *Martin Sales* is a leader in the field. Best known for large scale developments in environmentally sensitive areas, particularly minerals developments, and electricity generation. **Clients/Work:** Redland Aggregates/Harris Superquarry project. Magnox project. Advised on £3.5m development of Powderhall Stadium in Edinburgh.

Maclay Murray & Spens (5 fee-earners) Recently joined by partner from Steedman Ramage with experience of retail planning and development issues. **Clients/Work:** Acting for Bondway in judicial review of planning decision by City of Edinburgh Council. Acting for Asda in "ransom strip" litigation against Glasgow City Council.

McGrigor Donald (2ptnrs, 2assts) Planning practice is based in the firm's Litigation Dept. **Clients/Work:** Acting for Trinity Investments re Galashiels superstore (four Court of Session actions to date). Acting for Stewart Milne in planning inquiry concerning Ayr County Hospital (involving demolition of listed building).

Paull & Williamsons (1ptnr (75%), 1assoc, 1const) Have two leaders in *Bruce Smith* and *Jeremy Rowan-Robinson.* Handle housing, industrial and retail work. Particular expertise in regulations affecting fish farming. **Clients/Work:** Housing work for Barretts in Aberdeeen and central belt. Planning inquiry work for Alfred Stuart Properties and Richmond homes.

Shepherd & Wedderburn (4ptnrs, 3 other fee-earners) Group headed by *Colin Innes,* associate in the litigation department, who was newly recommended to us this year. Partner *Kay McCorquodale,* experienced in contentious planning law, is also a leader. Act for public and private sector clients. **Clients/Work:** Instructed by Scottish Power re public inquiry into Powergen's proposal for CCGT power station at Gartcosh, and re impact of Millennium Link Project (to open up Forth, Clyde and Union Canals) on wayleaves.

Ledingham Chalmers (3ptnrs, 2assts – Aberdeen; 1 ptnr – Edinburgh) Planning and environmental law is handled within the Commercial Property Dept. Best known for work for housebuilders. **Clients/Work:** Continue to represent Stewart Milne Group re proposals for a 4,500 house new settlement at Banchory, Aberdeen. Advising Cala Homes on Stirling Local Plan Inquiry and four planning appeals conjoined with it.

McClure Naismith The firm's senior partner, *Gordon Carlisle,* specialises in planning work and is an acknowledged leader with over 30 years experience.

ABRAHAM, Henry
Brachers, Maidstone (01622) 690691
Partner in Planning & Environmental Law
Department.
Specialisation: Experienced in all aspects of
planning applications and appeals,
enforcement proceedings, development plans,
integrated pollution control, all environmental
matters under the EPA 1990, private bills
procedure, compulsory purchase and highway
orders. Occasional contributor to the 'Journal of
Planning & Environment Law'.
Prof. Memberships: UK Environmental Law
Association, Legal Associate Royal Town
Planning Institute, Member of the Law Society's
Specialist Planning Panel.
Career: Qualified in 1983. Joined *Brachers* in
1990 and became a Partner in 1994.
Personal: Born 8th June 1957. St. Dunstan's
College. University of London. Leisure pursuits
include rowing. Lives in London.

ALLEN, Anthony
Donne Mileham & Haddock, Brighton
(01273) 744451
Partner.
Specialisation: Areas of practice, town
planning, environmental and compulsory
purchase law. Partner in charge of the
Environmental Law Unit and *Donne Mileham*
Planning. Has acted in applications and
appeals relating to housing and all types of
commercial development, incinerators, waste
transfer stations, waste to power plants and
mineral extraction, Structure and Local Plan
Policy representations. Author of various articles
on planning topics. Recent seminar topics:
Environmental Law – The European
Background, Environmental Protection Act Part
1 – Integrated Pollution Control, Trading in
Europe – The Environmental Aspects and
Contaminated Land – The New Code.
Prof. Memberships: LMRTPI, International Bar
Association, European Environmental Law Sub
Committee, Environmental Law Foundation,
European Environmental Law Association,
British Nordic Lawyers Association, UK
Environmental Law Association.
Career: MA (Cantab). Qualified in 1970, having
joined *Donne Mileham & Haddock* in 1969.
Became a Partner in 1976. Member of the Law
Society Planning and Environmental Law
Committee.

BARRINGTON, John
Moore & Blatch, Southampton
(01703) 636311
Specialisation: Over 30 years experience of
conducting planning appeals as advocate and
participating in planning promotions and acting
for landowners, local authorities and developers
in connection with options and joint venture
agreements.
Prof. Memberships: Member of the Law
Society's Specialist Town Planning Panel.
Associate Member of Royal Town Planning
Institute.
Career: Qualified in 1957 and after two years
national service joined Moore & Blatch
becoming a partner in 1963.
Personal: Interested in all sports.

BEARD, Tony
Tozers, Exeter (01392) 207020

BELL, Malcolm
Ward Hadaway, Newcastle upon Tyne
(0191) 204 4000
Planning Consultant.
Specialisation: Rural Planning and Rural
Development Control including designated
areas and listed buildings. Awarded PhD for
study of impact of public developments on the
countryside. Specialised in appraisal of rural
policy and planning proposals. Expert on
Access Law and public rights of way. Expert
Witness at Inquiries. Involvement in
development of forestry policy using computer
models. Lectures, writes and broadcasts widely
on countryside topics.
Prof. Memberships: Royal Town Planning
Institute, The Institution of Environmental
Sciences, Fellow of the Royal Agricultural
Societies, Associate of the Institute of
Agricultural Management.
Career: Joint research fellow of Economic and
Social Research Council and Natural
Environment Research Council, based at the
Institute of Terrestrial Ecology. Regional
Professional Services Executive for North East
Region of NFU until 1989. Previously Head of
Countryside Policy at NFU Headquarters and
Planning Advisor to the National Forest.
Personal: Educated at Warwick University (BA
in History and Politics, MA in Social History at
Aston University, PhD). Major cases this year
have included Croft Autodrome Action Group
(inadequate proposals by operators rejected),
wind farm, National Park Development Control
Appeal and many Local Plans.

BERESFORD, Amanda
Addleshaw Booth & Co, Leeds
(0113) 209 2000
Head of Environmental Law; Leeds.
Specialisation: All planning work including
retail, leisure, industrial, residential and
advocacy at Public Inquiries. Also
comprehensive environmental advice including
pollution control, energy, waste, transport,
contaminated land and due diligence. Major
cases include a number of leisure
developments including multiscreen cinemas
and business parks involving contaminated
land issues, also a number of waste and waste
to energy projects and landfill tax issues. Clients
advised include local planning authorities,
major private developers, environmental
regulatory bodies and several NHS Trusts
inward investors and funders. Recognised
authoress and speaker at conferences.
Prof. Memberships: Qualified planner.
Member U.K.E.L.A.
Career: Qualified in 1985 formally a Partner and
head of the Environmental and Planning Unit at
Pinsent Curtis, joined *Addleshaw Booth & Co* in
1997.

BIRD, Rina
Davies and Partners, Gloucester
(01452) 612345

BOSWORTH, John
Bevan Ashford, Bristol (0117) 923 0111
Specialisation: Planning, urban regeneration
and local government law. Advises public and
private sector on all aspects of planning and
compulsory purchase. Special projects have
included regional shopping centres, Canary

Wharf, a new village in South Hampshire,
Temple Quay, Bristol and many new hospital
sites. Advisor to south west branch of
Housebuilders Federation.
Prof. Memberships: Legal Associate of RTPI.
Member of Law Society's Planning Panel.
Career: Qualified 1988. Articled Portsmouth
City Council. Joined *Bevan Ashford* 1995, after
six years working for *Ashurst Morris Crisp*.

BRADY, Peter J.
Hewitson Becke + Shaw, Cambridge
(01223) 461155
Specialisation: Planning, environment and
waste disposal.
Prof. Memberships: Law society's specialist
planning panel.
Career: Leicester University 1973-6 LL.B
(Hons). 1977-79: Cheshire County Council.
1979-81: Hertfordshire County Council. 1981-
84: Northumberland County Council. 1984-88:
Jameson & Hill, Hertford. 1988-90: *Berwin
Leighton*. 1990: *Hewitson Becke + Shaw*.
Personal: Golf.

BULL, Rod
Eversheds, Birmingham (0121) 233 2001
Specialisation: Planning and compulsory
purchase/environmental. Appeared at over 30
inquiries in the last 12 months (majority as
advocate). Major CPO cases for Black Country
Development Corporation at Land Tribunal.
Number of large residential Local Plan and S.78
Inquiries for Bryant Group.
Prof. Memberships: Law Society's Planning
Panel, Legal Associate RTPI, UK Environmental
Law Association, Associate of Institute of
Quarrying.
Career: Educated Rugby, Hull University.
Partner of *Eversheds* leading Planning and
Environmental Team.
Personal: Married, resides Twycross
(Atherstone, Warwick). Interests: walking,
computers and reading.

CARLISLE, Gordon W.R.
McClure Naismith, Glasgow
(0141) 204 2700
Senior Partner specialising in Litigation,
Planning and Environmental, Contract and
Family Law.
Specialisation: Convener of the Planning Law
Committee of The Law Society of Scotland.
Career: Qualified 1963, joined present firm
1965, assumed as Partner 1967, admitted to the
Faculty of Procurators 1969.
Personal: Born 22 November 1937. Graduated
1963 M.A. LL.B., Glasgow University.

CARRUTHERS, Kenneth
Maclay Murray & Spens, Edinburgh
(0131) 226 5196
email: kwc@maclaymurrayspens.co.uk
Specialisation: Specialist in planning and
construction litigation, with in-depth experience
of all aspects of contentious and non-
contentious planning work including pre-
application negotiations, drafting section 75
Agreements, planning inquiries and judicial
challenges.
Career: Heriot Watt University (BSc (Hons)
1983) and Dundee University (LLB 1988, Dip LP
1989). Worked as local government planning
assistant from 1983 to 1986. Member of Royal

Town Planning Institute. Part-time lecturer and tutor in planning law at Heriot Watt University. Legal adviser to Scottish Office funded research projecet on Neighbour Notification.
Personal: Born 1961. Active sailor, skier and golfer.

CARTER, Simon
Aaron & Partners, Chester (01244) 315366
Partner in Planning, Environmental, Minerals and Property Team.
Specialisation: Planning, local government, environmental, minerals and property – including applications, appeals, enforcement, agreements, lawful use and development generally, as well as advocacy. Most aspects of local government law, including highways and compulsory purchase. Author and lecturer on planning. Property development generally.
Prof. Memberships: Law Society, Chartered Institute of Arbitrators, UKELA.
Career: Articled at *Pinsent Curtis*. Qualified 1976. Worked for several local authorities until rejoining private practice with *Aaron & Partners* in 1986, becoming a Partner 1987. Director of AD Waste Ltd. Board Member Housing Association. Director Cewtec .
Personal: Born 1952. Leeds University. Leisure interests include gardening, choral singing and golf.

COCKBURN, David
Archibald Campbell & Harley WS, Edinburgh (0131) 220 3000
Partner in Commercial Property Department.
Specialisation: Specialises in planning and recognised as one of Scotland's leading planning specialists. Handles planning inquiries. Handles a full range of commercial property matters, including purchases, development, sales, leasing (for both landlords and tenants), funding and security work. Contributes book reviews and articles to Law Journal of Law Society of Scotland and Scottish Planning and Environmental Law. Regularly contributes by way of lectures to Law Society Update, Scottish Young Lawyers' Association, Surveyors' bodies, Planning Exchange and Edinburgh University.
Prof. Memberships: Society of Writers to HM Signet.
Career: Qualified in 1966. Worked with Glasgow Corporation 1966-67, then *Breeze, Paterson & Chapman* 1967-70. Joined *Archibald Campbell & Harley WS* in 1970, becoming a Partner in 1971.
Personal: Born 4th February 1943. Attended Edinburgh University 1961-1964. Leisure pursuits include sport and reading. Lives in Edinburgh.

COLLAR, Neil
Brodies WS, Edinburgh (0131) 228 3777
Partner and Head of Planning Law Department, Legal Associate of the Royal Town Planning Institute, LLM for research into use of planning issues 1990.
Specialisation: Handles town and country planning matters – planning applications, appeals and inquiries, planning issues in relation to land acquisition and disposal, Local Authority compulsory purchase, roads etc. Wide experience of private and public sector clients. Recent projects have included public local inquiries into a proposed power station at Gartcosh, proposed housing housing developments around Hamilton, and a proposed open cast coal mine in East Lothian, and the appeal to the House of Lords in relation

to a proposed retail development in Edinburgh. Research for Scottish Office on enforcement and the Permitted Development Order, and for Scottish National Heritage on national parks. Author of 'Planning', published by W.Green & Son and Sweet & Maxwell (Concise Scots Law Series) co-author of "Pollution Control in Scotland" published by T&T Clark and a number of articles in journals. Member of Editorial Board of Scottish Planning and Environmental Law. Has regular planning law columns in Greens Property Law Bulletin. Senior tutor for planning law at University of Edinburgh and speaker on aspects of planning law at several conferences.
Prof. Memberships: Law Society of Scotland, Legal Associate of the RTPI, Society for Computers and Law.
Career: Qualified in 1992, having joined *Brodies WS* in 1990.
Personal: Born 31st March 1967. Educated at the University of Glasgow 1984-88 and 1989-90 (LLB and Diploma) and Liverpool University 1988-89 (LLM). Enjoys playing the saxophone, lacrosse, hockey and softball. Lives in Edinburgh.

CONNAL, R. Craig
McGrigor Donald, Glasgow (0141) 248 6677
Partner in Litigation Department.
Specialisation: Solicitor Advocate. Many years experience of advising on and appearing at Tribunals and Courts in contentious and high profile employment matters. Lectures regularly on employment matters.
Prof. Memberships: Law Society of Scotland.
Career: Contributor, Stair Memorial Encyclopaedia of Scots Law and author of numerous articles.
Personal: Born 7th July 1954. Educated at Glasgow University (LLB, 1st Class Honours 1975). Rugby referee.

DAMMS, Martin
Edge & Ellison, Birmingham (0121) 200 2001
Specialisation: Planning and Environmental Law. Covers full range of contentious and non contentious matters including advising and representing public bodies. Planning applications, appeals, development plan representations, judicial review, negotiating/drafting planning agreements, enforcement action, housing, commercial, retail, leisure and minerals development, highways issues, compulsory purchase proceedings, contaminated land issues and waste regulation, hazardous substances, consents. Advocate.
Prof. Memberships: Law Society. Birmingham Law Society. Member of the Law Society's Planning Panel. Legal Associate R.T.P.I. Member of the Midlands Environmental Business club.
Career: Qualified 1976. In Local Government to 1989. Joined *Edge & Ellison* in 1989. Partner from 1993.
Personal: Born 17th November 1952. Educated at Mexborough Grammar School and University of Birmingham.

DIMMICK, Simon
Clarks, Reading (0118) 958 5321
Specialisation: Town and Country Planning, highways law, environmental work relating to property development. Advice on local authority matters generally. Advocacy. Acts for land owners, developers and local authorities.

Career: Qualified in 1977. 1983-1988 Assistant County Solicitor, Berkshire County Council. Joined *Clarks* in 1988, becoming a Partner in 1989.
Personal: Born 19 January 1952. Educated Kings School, Worcester, and University College, London – LLB 1974. Leisure time interests include family and Church work.

ENGERT, Nick
Clarke Willmott & Clarke, Taunton (01823) 442266
Partner and Head of Planning and Environmental Department.
Specialisation: Main areas of practice are town and country planning, compensation and land development. Regular advocate at Inquiries into local plans, planning appeals, enforcement notices, listed buildings and compulsory purchase orders. Negotiates complex planning agreements. Advises on development schemes and in compensation disputes. Acted in the Exeter Shopping Inquiry in 1987 for Shearwater Holdings Plc and in the Hinkley Point Inquiry for Lady Elisabeth Gass, the principal (and successful) objector to CPO. Currently appearing at Inquiries for several national house building companies. Extensive experience of retail planning and development work (both food and non-food). Extensive advice on major mixed commercial development schemes throughout England and Wales. Regular lecturer on planning and related matters to regional branches of the Royal Town Planning Institute and RICS.
Prof. Memberships: Law Society.
Career: Qualified in 1973. Joined *Clarke Willmott & Clarke* in 1975, becoming a Partner in 1979. Set up the department, incorporating two other partners and eight qualified staff, creating the largest such department in the West.
Personal: Born 28th September 1948. Attended Oundle School and Southampton University. Leisure interests include riding, shooting, tennis, golf, choral singing and wine tasting. Lives in Taunton, Somerset.

EVANS, Eric
Eversheds, Cardiff (01222) 471147
Partner in Commercial Property and Planning Department. (Head of Planning Unit).
Specialisation: Main area of practice is local government and planning. Former Chief Officer in local government. 30 years public sector experience, dealing with all areas of local government. Particular experience in planning and development work. Former Deputy Chief Executive of the Land Authority for Wales. Also deals with compulsory purchase and compensation. Has handled several major compulsory purchase orders, including for the Garden Festival for Wales. Acted in a $4000 million property development in north Cardiff, as well as for the successful purchase of the MOD Married Quarters Estate (£1.7 billion – 57,000 houses). Lead lawyer in the £1.8 billion LG Investment which will create 6,100 jobs, which is Europe's largest inward investment. Speaker at many seminars on roles of public bodies, including public procurement and compulsory competitive tendering. Also head of the Department's Private Finance (PFI) Unit.
Prof. Memberships: Law Society.
Career: Qualified in 1980. Town Clerk, Borough of Blaenau, Gwent 1981-89. Deputy Chief Executive and legal adviser, Land Authority for Wales 1989-92.

Personal: Director of a Local Authority Waste Disposal Company. Leisure pursuits include DIY. Lives in Abertillery.

EVANS, Katherine
Davies and Partners, Gloucester
(01452) 612345

FAULDS, Ann
Dundas & Wilson CS, Edinburgh
(0131) 228 8000
Specialisation: Practises exclusively in planning law and related issues such as roads law and providing advocacy services at public inquiries; clients include Royal Bank of Scotland, Scottish Widows, Carter Commercial Developments Ltd, Stirling Council, Slough Estates, N.C.P. and Local Enterprise Company; Part of the research team appointed by Scottish Office for review of Development Planning in Scotland; extensive retail inquiry experience in both public and private sectors; providing specialist planning advice on PFI projects acting for Water Authorities, Hospital Trust and Airport Authority. Range of work includes advising on development control, enforcement notices, listed buildings, compulsory purchase, local plan inquiries, appeals/ call-in procedures.
Prof. Memberships: Law Society of Scotland, Legal Associate of Royal Town Planning Institute, Member of the Institution of Highways and Transportation; Affiliate of Royal Incorporation of Architects in Scotland.
Career: Attended Strathclyde University (LLB). Articled Central Regional Council, qualified 1989; legal adviser to Planning and Roads Authority before joining *Dundas & Wilson* in 1993; Partner since 1995.
Personal: Born 1956. Resides Edinburgh. Leisure interests include opera, theatre, walking.

FIRTH, Beverley
Mills & Reeve, Cambridge
+44 (0)1223 364422
Specialisation: Partner in the Property Services Department, specialising in all aspects of planning law. Work includes advice on aspects of land development, negotiations with local authorities including planning agreements. Also includes advocacy in planning appeals and in local plan inquiries. Contentious work includes judicial review. Particular environmental expertise in land contamination and waste disposal including clinical waste. Also experience in health and safety. Consultant editor of Longmans Planning and Environmental Law Bulletin. Recent projects include local airfields, new settlements and University campus.

GIBBS, Kevin
Lyons Davidson, Bristol (0117) 904 6000
Partner and Head of Environmental & Planning Group
Specialisation: Main area of practice is Environmental & Planning Law. Has experience in renewable energy projects, particularly CHP projects, environmental due diligence and corporate transactions, environmental authorisations and licensing and advice on all forms of planning applications and appeals including advocacy.
Prof. Memberships: Law Society Planning

Panel, RTPI, Secretary of UKELA South West and member of the Environmental Agency's Regional Environmental Protection Advisory Committee.
Career: Qualified 1990. Local Government Planner from 1980-84; Principal Legal Officer, London Borough of Camden 1984-88. Joined *Lyons Davidson* in 1988 and became Partner and Head of the Group in 1994.

GOODALL, Martin
Sisman Nichols, Bristol (0117) 929 3333
Associate Partner in Planning Law Team.
Specialisation: Twenty years' experience in planning law, including major housing and retail developments. Advocacy at public inquiries in all types of planning appeals,including enforcement and listed building cases, as well as Local Plan inquiries. Practice also covers compulsory purchase and compensation, including major road inquiries. Has particular expertise in legal challenges to planning decisions in the High Court, including many reported cases. Also Judicial Review of other administrative decisions. Has written articles in various publications, including Building Engineer, Solicitor's Journal, The Valuer, Planning, and Journal of Planning and Environment Law. Frequent lecturer on planning law topics.
Prof. Memberships: Member of the Law Society Planning Panel, Legal Associate of Royal Town Planning Institute, United Kingdom Environmental Law Association (South West Branch Chairman), Bristol Law Society (Senior Hon. Secretary), Bristol Chamber of Commerce (former Vice-Chairman of Development, Planning and Traffic Committee). Past Service Member of Association of Council Secretaries and Solicitors.
Career: Qualified 1977. Senior Assistant Solicitor, Hertsmere BC, Hertfordshire 1979 - 82. Solicitor & Deputy Borough Secretary, Waverley BC, Surrey 1982 - 89. Senior Associate, Clarke Willmott & Clarke 1989 - 97. Joined *Sisman Nichols* as Associate in 1997.
Personal: Born 26th March 1948. Lives in Bristol.

GOODMAN, David
Hammond Suddards, Leeds
(0113) 284 7000
 Partner and Head of Planning Department.
Specialisation: Main area of practice is town and country planning handling all aspects of planning issues relating to development, including retailing, residential, office, mineral extraction, waste disposal and leisure uses. Undertakes advocacy at public inquiries. Also deals with environmental law including environmental assessment and environmentally sensitive developments. Has handled a proposal for an overhead transmission line through Cleveland and North Yorkshire, various power generation projects, promotion of clinical waste incinerator proposals, and a football stadium in the North East. Author of articles on planning law. Lectures regularly to RTPI and other professional bodies.
Prof. Memberships: Law Society, Institute of Waste Management Special Interest Group on Incineration, British Wind Energy Association.
Career: Qualified in 1980. Articled at Surrey County Council 1978-80, then Assistant Solicitor

at Oldham Metropolitan B.C 1980-84. Senior Solicitor at Newcastle upon Tyne City Council 1984-88. Joined *Hammond Suddards* in 1988 and became a Partner in 1991.
Personal: Born 15th October 1955. Educated at the Royal Grammar School, Newcastle upon Tyne 1967-74 and Sheffield University 1974-77. Recreations include sport, gardening and theatre.

GRAHAM BA, Tom
Alsters, Bristol (0117) 929 7612
Specialisation: All aspects of planning and environmental law including town and country planning, compulsory purchase, pollution control, and local government law and procedure. Specialises in advocacy, primarily at planning inquiries. Very experienced in drafting planning obligations and related development documentation. Typical recent projects include promoting a 20 year plan for doubling the student population of the University of Southampton through the Southampton City Local Plan, promoting respectively an 'enabling development' policy for sports stadia and a policy for redevelopment of a key City centre site through the Bristol City Local Plan, promoting a 350,000 sq. ft. distribution park in South Gloucestershire and promoting a 30,000 sq.ft. superstore in Trowbridge. Has acted as advocate for the Council at two local plan public inquiries. Is a regular speaker at planning conferences and has written numerous articles. He is the author of 'Contaminated Land' (Jordans 1995).
Prof. Memberships: Law Society, UKELA, Environmental Law Foundation, Law Society Planning Panel.
Career: Qualified in 1984. Started legal career in Local Government. Was chief solicitor at North Hertfordshire D.C. before moving to private practice in the City of London in 1989. Became a partner with *Alsters* in 1995.
Personal: Cycling, motorcycles, keep fit and writing.

HIGNETT, Andrew
Osborne Clarke, Bristol (0171) 984 5373
Specialisation: Retail and Residential Developments, Development of Contaminated Land, Planning Appeals and Local Plan Representations, including advocacy at Public Inquiries.
Career: Qualified 1978. With Local Authorities until 1988, culminating as a Chief Officer in the South West. A planning specialist in private sector since then. Has advised both local authorities and developers in relation to town centre developments including capital spending restrictions. Has acted for both public and private sector clients in relation to planning proposals involving mental health care.

HINTON, Robert
Griffith Smith, Brighton (01273) 324041
Partner in Public Law Department.
Specialisation: Main area of practice is town and country planning, handling all aspects of law, procedure and policy, including local inquiry advocacy. As planning solicitor to Shoreham Port Authority handles complete planning issues in a commercial context. Increasingly dealing with issues of Environmental Law. Also a specialist in the law and practice regarding taxi and private hire licensing, having advised many Taxi Associations and Local Authorities and given

papers for the Law Society Local Government Group and University of Leeds.

Prof. Memberships: Legal Associate of Royal Town Planning Institute. Member of Law Society's panel of solicitors to act in planning cases and Minerals Issues Group.

Career: 27 years employment by local Authorities, the last 12 of these as Chief Executive and Solicitor to a Borough Council. Joined *Griffith Smith* in 1985.

Personal: Born 21st December 1936. Methodist local Preacher. Performs in opera and drama.

HOLMES, Sarah C.

Bond Pearce, Plymouth (01752) 266 633
See under Environmental Law, p. 347

HOUGHTON, John

Clarke Willmott & Clarke, Bristol
(0117) 941 6600
Partner in Planning and Environmental Department.

Specialisation: Wide experience of planning, compulsory purchase, parliamentary and environmental work. Advocate at Section 78 and Local Plan Inquiries. Past projects range through nuclear power Inquiries; gas terminal and pipeline Inquiries; wind farms; DBFO projects; sub-regional and free-standing shopping centres; retail warehouse and foodstore proposals; airport expansion feasibility studies; regeneration of worked-out cement works and quarries; Millennium projects; environmental assessment; contaminated land; waste licensing and SSSI impact mitigation issues.

Prof. Memberships: UK Environmental Law Association.

Career: Educated Cheltenham College and Lincoln College, Oxford (MA Law). Qualified 1973. Partner, *Denton Hall* 1980-1995; Managing Partner *Denton Hall*, Hong Kong 1984-1988; Head of Planning Group, *Denton Hall* 1989-1994; Partner, *Clarke Willmott & Clarke* 1995-present.

Personal: Leisure interests include music, tennis, skiing and walking.

INNES, Colin

Shepherd & Wedderburn WS, Edinburgh
(0131) 228 9900
Specialisation: Planning and Environmental Law. Instructed by Scottish Power Plc in respect of Gartcosh Power Station Inquiry. Instructed by Planning Authority in Leading Case in respect of S50 Agreements.

Career: LL.B (Hons) University of Aberdeen. LL.M (Environmental Law) University of Aberdeen.

JAMESON, Robert

Jameson & Hill, Hertford (01992) 554881
Specialisation: Main area of practice is Town and Country Planning, handling all aspects of planning issues, including retailing, residential, office, mineral extraction, waste disposal, and leisure uses; acting both for private clients and local authorities. Considerable Local Plan experience. Regular advocate at Inquiries into Local Plans. Planning and Enforcement Appeals. In addition, has extensive experience in negotiating complex Planning Agreements.

Career: Qualified in 1971. Started legal career in Local Government. Was Principal Assistant County Secretary at Hertfordshire County Council before co-founding *Jameson & Hill* in

1982. Over 20 years of planning experience.

JONES, William

Foot & Bowden, Plymouth (01752) 675000
Partner in Corporate Services Department.
Specialisation: Main areas of practice are planning and partnerships public authority law. Handles Judicial Review and planning appeals. Author of 'Mineral Development in England and Wales', 'Powers of Local Authorities to Impose Financial Obligations', 'Rights of the Public on Environmental Decision Making in England and Wales' and 'Joint Advisory Editor of Encyclopaedia of Forms and Precedents-Mines and Quarries'. Occasional lecturer on planning appeals at South West Local Government Summer School, on planning law at University of Plymouth as part of Solicitors Continuing Education Programme and for Devon County Council at a Valuers and Surveyors Seminar on compensation provisions of Planning and Compensation Act. Editor of "Cordery on Solicitors: Partnership Structure".

Prof. Memberships: Law Society. Member of the Planning and Environmental Law Committee 1983-1993.

Career: Qualified 1965. Articled with Carmarthenshire Council, before becoming an Assistant Solicitor at Plymouth City Council and an Assistant Town Clerk at the County Borough of Birkenhead. Partner at *Foot & Bowden* since 1972; Notary Public since 1977. Member of working parties and joint author of papers prepared in response to Government consultation on planning and compensation, amendments to the Town and Country Planning Act, simplified planning zones, hazardous substances, derelict land, compulsory acquisition of land, review of old mining permissions, review of planning control, restoration of mineral workings sites with high water tables.

Personal: Company Secretary of Abbeyfield Tamar Extra Care Society, Townsend House. Leisure interests include golf, running and music. Lives in Sheviock, Cornwall.

KENWORTHY, Michael

Addleshaw Booth & Co, Manchester
(0161) 934 6000
Partner in Commercial Property Group.
Specialisation: Specialises in planning, environmental and compulsory purchase matters. Acts for local authorities, utility companies, waste operators, developers and NHS trusts. Advises international companies on environmental due-diligence in land and corporate acquisitions.

Prof. Memberships: Member of the Law Society and UKELA.

Career: University of Keele 1974-1978. Qualified in 1981 with the Council of the City of Chester. Joined the firm in 1986. Partner in 1990.

KINLOCH, Ian

Aaron & Partners, Chester (01244) 315366
Partner in Planning, Environmental, Minerals & Local Government Team.
Specialisation: Planning law – all aspects including advocacy and agreements. Also environmental and local government law including highways, compulsory purchase. Author on planning law and local government topics and lectures. Examiner in planning law for Law Soc/RTPI.

Prof. Memberships: Law Society, RTPI.
Career: Qualified 1967. Various local

government appointments. Joined *Aaron & Partners* in 1993 becoming a Partner in 1994.
Personal: Born 1945. LLM BA LMRTPI. Leisure interests include reading, history and music. Supports Middlesbrough FC. BBC Radio 4 Brain of Britain 1995.

KRATZ, Philip

Taylor Vinters, Cambridge (01223) 423444
Specialisation: All aspects of town and country planning and environmental law. Experienced advocate. Work includes agreements, applications, appeals (including local inquiries), local plan and structure plan representations. Recent experience has included acting in connection with large scale residential proposals in Ely, Cambridgeshire and commercial proposals throughout the country.

Prof. Memberships: Law Society; member of the Law Society's Specialist Planning Panel; Legal Associate member of the Royal Town Planning Institute.

Career: Qualified in 1982. District Solicitor and head of Legal Services with East Cambridgeshire District Council from 1983-1992; Assistant Chief Executive until joining *Taylor Vinters* in May 1995. Head of Planning and Environmental Law Unit.

Personal: Leisure interests include cricket, Jaguar cars and military engineering.

LANCASTER, Roger

Halliwell Landau, Manchester
(0161) 835 3003
Senior Partner and Head of Planning and Environmental Law Department.
Specialisation: Specialises in town and country planning, environmental law and compulsory purchase matters and local government issues, including advocacy at inquiries. Has substantial house building retail and developer clients and also acts for public sector authorities. Regular speaker at conferences and seminars.

Prof. Memberships: Law Society.
Career: Qualified in 1975. Solicitor with Humberside County Council and Birmingham City Council. Joined *Halliwell Landau* as a Partner in 1982. Senior Partner 1995.
Personal: Born in 1951. Educated at Biddulph Grammar School and Leicester University (LLB 1971). Recreations include cricket, squash and gardening.

LITTLE, A. James

Wollastons, Chelmsford (01245) 211211
Consultant in Planning Law.
Specialisation: Author of 'Planning Controls and their Enforcement' and 'Schofield's Election Law' (7th, 8th and 9th editions). Part-time lecturer in Planning Law at Anglia Polytechnic University since 1990.

Career: Qualified in 1973, having been a Barrister 1962-72. Served as a local government officer for more than twenty years. Deputy Clerk of Chelmsford Rural District Council for nine years and Chief Executive of Dunmow Rural District Council for eight years. Solicitor in private practice full-time 1973-86, Senior Partner for the last seven of those years. Sole practitioner and consultant 1989; and Consultant to *Wollastons* since 1990. Member of the General Council of the Bar 1970-72; Chairman of the Society of Local Government Barristers 1967-70. Chairman Social Security Appeal Tribunal 1984-96.

Personal: Degree of Bachelor of Laws at London University; Diploma in Public Administration of London University.

MANSON, Stephen
Eversheds, Cardiff (01222) 471147
Specialisation: Associate specialising in Town and Country Planning, compulsory purchase (including Lands Tribunal work) together with general public sector development and PFI. Former member of Government's Private Finance Panel Executive. Advises a number of local minerals developers on such matters as the current minerals review. Recently involved in advising a major client on potential problems on environmental impact assessment regulations.
Career: Bristol University (LLB Hons). Bristol Polytechnic (LSF First Class Hons).
Personal: Windsurfing.

MARRON, Peter
Marron Dodds, Leicester (0116) 289 2200
Senior Partner in Planning, Development and Public Law Department.
Specialisation: Has twenty-five years' experience of contentious town planning, together with associated work advising the development industry. Also handles public law matters, compulsory purchase and judicial review. Has acted in cases ranging from new village schemes, landfill proposals and many other applications of strategic importance. Has given talks over the years to a number of bodies. Major clients include Barratt Homes, Ideal Homes, Beazer Homes, David Wilson Homes, Wilson Bowden Ltd, Ibstock Bricks Plc, Rolls Royce Plc, Hallam Land Management Ltd and Henry Boot Plc. Individual charge-out rates are based on £125 per hour, negotiable on the basis of complexity and responsibility.
Prof. Memberships: Law Society, Chartered Institute of Arbitrators.
Career: Qualified in 1970. Founded *Marron Dodds* as a Senior Partner in 1978. DOT/ RYA Ocean Yacht Master with commercial endorsement. ACIArb 1990. Fellow of the Royal Society of Arts 1995. Legal Associate of the Royal Town Planning Institute. Member of International Bar Assocation. Member of Law Society's Planning Panel.
Personal: Born 3rd June 1944. Attended Liverpool University (LLB Hons 1966). Leisure interests include the arts and off-shore sailing. Lives in Uppingham, Rutland.

MCCORQUODALE, Kay
Shepherd & Wedderburn WS, Edinburgh (0131) 228 9900
Specialisation: Planning.
Prof. Memberships: Qualified Solicitor Scotland 1988; England 1992.
Career: Articled *Shepherd & Wedderburn WS* 1986-1988; 1988-1990 Assistant Solicitor *Shepherd & Wedderburn WS*; 1990-1992 Assistant Solicitor *Reynolds Porter Chamberlain*, London; 1992-1993 Assistant Solicitor *Shepherd & Wedderburn WS*; 1993 Partner *Shepherd & Wedderburn WS*.
Personal: Education: Nairn Academy; Edinburgh University 1986 LL.B (Hons) Dip. LP, N.P. Born 1964; resides Edinburgh. Interests: theatre, swimming, travel.

MORITZ, John
Masons, Manchester (0161) 234 8234
Specialisation: Worked for several years in local government, gaining invaluable experience in planning, roads and environmental matters. Has advised on a number of major development projects in the North West and nationally. Advises in connection with planning inquiries, compulsory purchase and other road inquiries, landfill, clinical waste incineration, negotiations with Water Authorities and privatised water companies and environmental assessments. Advises local authorities and development corporations in connection with development of all types, including all aspects of urban regeneration and contaminated land. Advises consortia and promoters of schemes under the Government's Private Finance Initiative on the planning and environmental law aspects of projects.
Prof. Memberships: Secretary of North West Branch of UK Environmental Law Association. Member of the Law Society's Planning Panel.
Career: Qualified in 1973. Partner at *Lambert Storey* in 1980. Joined *Masons* in 1990 as a Partner.
Personal: Born in Manchester. LLB Manchester University. Interests leisure, travel, theatre, swimming, viewing and appreciating art and architecture.

OLDHAM, Peter
Cobbetts, Manchester (0161) 833 3333
Partner.
Specialisation: Main area of practice is planning law. Has over 20 years experience of handling planning appeals relating to large retail developments (principally food superstores) and other commercial/ office/ business development schemes, acting for both national retailers and developers. Also handles commercial property development schemes. Acted for Plymouth and South Devon Co-op Soc. Ltd in the 'Planning Gain/ Section 106' case R v. Plymouth City Council, ex parte PSDCS, in High Court and Court of Appeal. Addressed the 'Planning Law and Practice' conference organised by Law and Business Forum in Manchester, 1991.
Prof. Memberships: Law Society, Member of Planning Panel; Legal Associate, Royal Town Planning Institute.
Career: Qualified in 1969. Joined *Cobbetts* in 1967, becoming a Partner in 1973.
Personal: Born 12th April 1945. Attended Manchester Grammar School 1955-63 and the University of Manchester 1963-66. Leisure interests include golf and skiing. Lives in Mellor, Stockport.

OLIVER, Keith
Bevan Ashford, Exeter (01392) 411111
Specialisation: Specialises in Planning, Highways, Compulsory Purchase and Local Government Law, Compensation and Land Tribunal work. Has extensively advised Urban Development Corporations and other bodies on major regeneration and highway projects including establishing exit strategies.
Career: Spent 17 years in Local Government in London and 5 years with *Nabarro Nathanson* before joining *Bevan Ashford* in 1995.

PARRY, Emrys J.
Cartwrights, Bristol (0117) 929 3601
Partner in Commercial Property Section.
Specialisation: Specialises in compulsory purchase, planning and development. Makes and opposes compulsory purchase orders and has acted for a local authority in promotion of CPO for a major town centre redevelopment and Housing Act CPO; for and against planning authorities at appeals; settlement of compensation claims; claims against passenger transport executives, development corporations and local authorities. Clients include local authorities, a major port authority and private clients.
Prof. Memberships: Fellow of the British Institute of Management; Member of the Law Society's Planning Panel.
Career: In local government until 1977. Legal advisor with The Land Authority for Wales 1977-86, then *D J Freeman* 1986-93 (Partner from 1987). Joined *Cartwrights* as a Partner in 1993.
Personal: Born in 1945. Holds a BSc (Econ) (Hons) degree. Chairman, Surrey Heath Housing Association. Leisure interests include golf. Resides in Bristol.

PASTERFIELD, Stephen
Lawrence Tucketts, Bristol (0117) 929 5252
Partner and Head of Planning and Environment Group.
Specialisation: Specialises in planning, handling all issues relating to development including mineral extraction, waste disposal, urban regeneration, retailing, office and residential uses; also compensation and environmental law including waste management licensing, contaminated land, nuisance and water pollution. Acts for Government Departments, Developers, Financial Institutions, Minerals and Waste Operators and Local Authorities as well as private individuals. Very experienced advocate and lecturer on techniques at inquiries. Author of numerous articles. Member of Law Society's specialist Planning Panel and Legal Associate of the Royal Town Planning Institute.
Prof. Memberships: Law Society, Royal Town Planning Institute.
Career: Qualified in 1974. Principal Solicitor, Solihull MBC 1976-79. Deputy City Solicitor, Winchester 1979-1988. Partner at *Lawrence Tucketts* from 1994.
Personal: Born 30th April 1949. Educated Birkenhead School 1960-67. Leisure pursuits include sport of all kinds, especially golf, fishing and horse racing. Lives in Wrington.

RAINE, Douglas
Ottaways, St. Albans (01727) 863131
Specialisation: 35 years experience of local government work with emphasis on planning including advocacy since 1972; involved in a wide variety of projects – housing, commercial, countryside and leisure, minerals and waste, challenges and judicial reviews, for clients of all types from the next-door neighbour to corporate, institutions and public authorities; most enjoys enforcement law and listed building/ Conservation Area issues; Member UKELA and ELF. Increasingly involved in environmental matters, including contaminated land.

ROBINSON, Patrick
Burges Salmon, Bristol (0117) 939 2000

ROWAN-ROBINSON, Jeremy

Paull & Williamsons, Aberdeen
(01224) 621621
(England & Wales) Consultant in Planning and
Environmental Law.
Specialisation: Deals with all aspects of
planning and environmental work, including
appeals, environmental implications of asset
acquisitions and sales, advice on environmental
regulation and environmental litigation. Handles
all aspects of compulsory purchase work,
including objections and compensation claims
and general local government work such as
roads, sewerage and building control. Has
acted in planning appeals relating to housing,
retail, commercial, industrial and mineral
developments. Author, with E Young, of
'Scottish Planning Law & Procedure' (Wm.
Hodge & Co. 1985) and 'Compulsory Purchase
and Compensation: The Law in Scotland' (W.
Green & Son, 1990).
Prof. Memberships: UK Environmental Law
Association, Royal Town Planning Institute
(Legal Associate).
Career: Qualified as Solicitor in England &
Wales in 1966. Assistant Director of Law &
Administration, Cumbria County Council, to
1976. Professor of Planning & Environment Law,
Aberdeen University since 1989. Director of
Aberdeen University Centre for Environmental
Law & Policy from 1994. Member of Scottish
Natural Heritage Main Board from 1998. Joined
Paull & Williamsons in 1992.
Personal: Born 29th March 1944. Gained MA
degree in 1971, LLM in 1981. Legal Associate
RTPI 1982. FRSA 1994. Leisure interests include
sailing and mountaineering. Lives in Aberdeen.

SALES, Martin

Burness, Edinburgh (0131) 473 6000
Specialisation: Martin Sales has for more than
ten years acted for major contractors in the field
of contentious construction and civil
engineering. His arbitration practice includes
acting as legal clerk to arbiters. He also uses his
ADR skills to settle disputes quickly and
efficiently.

SALTER, Ian

Burges Salmon, Bristol (0117) 939 2000

SMITH, Brian

Browne Jacobson, Nottingham
(0115) 950 0055
Partner. Head of Property Department.
Specialisation: Main area of practice is
planning and development. Has over 20 years
post-qualification experience in this field, in
local government, commerce and private
practice. Handles environmental work, dealing
principally with land contamination and
environmental liability in corporate acquisitions
and disposals, funding transactions and
insolvencies. Also deals with local government
law, compulsory purchase and rating.
Prof. Memberships: Member of Law Society
Planning Panel, Legal Associate of Royal Town
Planning Institute, Law Society Advisory Group
on Conservation, Heritage and Rural Issues,
Fellow of the Land Institute.

SMITH, Bruce

Paull & Williamsons, Aberdeen
(01224) 621621
Partner in Planning and Environmental Law
Department.
Specialisation: Main area of practice is

planning. Advises on planning applications,
appeals, enforcement notice appeals, local and
structure plans and the conduct of public
inquiries. Also handles environmental law.
Advises on waste disposal licenses, river
purification issues and other issues arising out
of the Environmental Protection Act. Has acted
in many of the major planning inquiries in
Scotland over the last decade. Lecturer in
planning law at Aberdeen University.
Prof. Memberships: Law Society of Scotland,
Society of Advocates in Aberdeen. Law Society
accredited specialist in Planning Law.
Career: Qualified in 1967. Joined *Paull &
Williamsons* in 1970, becoming a Partner in
1973.
Personal: Born 15th June 1947. Attended
Aberdeen University 1964-67 (LLB). Chairman
of Abernethy Trust which runs four residential
outdoor pursuit centres in Scotland. Leisure
interests include golf, skiing and sailing. Lives in
Aberdeen.

TAYLOR, P.J.A.

Hewitson Becke + Shaw, Northampton
(01604) 233 233
Specialisation: All planning work including
advocacy at planning appeals and local plan
inquiries; Section 106 Agreements; judicial
reviews; enforcements and general planning
law. Acts for companies, private individuals and
local authorities.
Prof. Memberships: The Law Society; Legal
Associate R.T.PI; Member of The Law Society's
Specialist Planning Panel.
Career: Qualified in 1985; *Shacklocks Solicitors*
Mansfield 1985-1986; *Hewitson Becke + Shaw
Solicitors* Northampton 1986 – to date (Partner
since 1989).
Personal: Born 2nd October 1960; Educated at
Brunts Grammar School, Mansfield;
Birmingham University and Chester Law
College. Interests Include: Athletics and
marathon running.

TAYLOR, Paul A.T.

Dickinson Dees, Newcastle upon Tyne
(0191) 279 9000
Partner in Planning Department.
Specialisation: Handles all aspects of
planning including the preparation of
applications, the conduct of appeals (including
advocacy at local inquiries), enforcement
procedures and development plan work. Also
deals with compulsory purchase orders and
land compensation. Experience includes
advocacy at many local inquiries, particularly
involving housing development and open cast
coal extraction.
Prof. Memberships: Law Society, Law Society
Planning Panel. Legal Associate RTPI.
Career: Qualified 1971. Assistant solicitor at
Nottinghamshire County Council 1971-74;
Senior Assistant Solicitor for Leicestershire
County Council 1974-77. Worked for
Hoveringham Group Ltd 1977-82 before joining
*Evershed*sin Newcastle in 1982. Became a
Partner in 1983. Joined *Dickinson Dees* 1994.
Personal: Born 19th August 1947. Holds an
LLB, 1968. Leisure interests include gardening.
Lives in North Shields.

TIDESWELL, Anne

Eversheds, Birmingham (0121) 233 2001
Associate in Planning Team, Property
Department.
Specialisation: All aspects of planning,

including local plan work, planning obligations,
appeals and general advice. Other main areas
of work are highways, including closures and
agreements and compulsory purchase.
Prof. Memberships: Legal Associate RTPI;
Planning panel of Law Society
Career: Articled in Local Government. Qualified
in 1987. Joined *Rowe & Maw* in 1991 as a
Senior Assistant Solicitor.
Personal: Born 1962. Attended University of
Hull 1980-83: LLB Hons.

TRINICK, G. Marcus

Bond Pearce, Plymouth (01752) 266 633
Specialisation: Partner in the Commercial
Property Group specialising in planning and
environmental law. Has appeared as advocate
at over 290 public enquiries and advised on
many planning applications and appeals
concerning minerals, housing, retail, industrial,
energy and tourism developments. International
reputation for his work in renewable energy and
nationally in the waste sector. Has been at the
forefront of the development of the renewable
energy industry advising on more than 70
proposed renewable energy developments and
currently advising on off-shore wind energy
development issues. His work involves projects
in England, Wales, Scotland, Nothern Ireland
and Republic of Ireland as well as elsewhere in
Europe.
Prof. Memberships: Member of the Law
Society Planning Panel, Secretary of British
Wind Energy Association, member of the
European, Republic of Ireland and US Wind
Energy Associations and the UK Environmental
Law Association.
Personal: Qualified in 1983. Joined *Bond
Pearce* in 1990, becoming partner in 1991.

TURNBULL, Stephen

Addleshaw Booth & Co, Leeds
(0113) 209 2000
Specialisation: Specialises in town planning
and local government work; recent cases
include public inquiries into town centre retail
developments, compulsory purchase
promotion and advice for numerous local
authorities; also act for numerous private sector
developers in relation to objections to local
plans and UDPs and planning applications and
appeals including advocacy.
Prof. Memberships: Member of the Law
Society Planning Panel and a Legal Associate of
the Royal Town Planning Institute. Visiting
lecturer in planning law at Leeds Metropolitan
University, and regular speaker at RTPI and
other seminars.
Career: Hull University 1980; admitted 1984;
1984-1986 Basingstoke & Dean Borough
Council; 1986-1989 South Buckinghamshire
District Council; Joined the firm in 1989 and
made a partner in 1995.
Personal: Walking, swimming and football.

VALENTINE, Richard

Pitmans, Reading (0118) 9580224
Specialisation: The co-ordination and
implementation of strategies and tactics
employed in relation to major planning
proposals, particularly in connection with
inquiries and judicial reviews.
Prof. Memberships: Law Society.
Career: Partner: *Stephenson Harwood* 1973-
1977. Partner: *Pitmans* 1977 -.
Personal: Too numerous.

WADE-SMITH, Richard
Wilbraham & Co, Leeds (0113) 243 2200
Specialisation: Partner specialising in infrastructure and energy projects as well as environmental due diligence on corporate and commercial property transactions. Practice covers industrial development, traditional and renewable energy generation, electricity transmission, water and sewage treatment, on-shore gas field, 18km cross-country pipeline and a 55 MW power generation plant; a water abstraction and treatment scheme; an integrated intensive livestock/food production complex; and a number of landfills, and waste water treatment plants. Based on experience gained from acting for US companies he has gained an understanding of US approach to environmental risk assessment and management. As part of the developing trend in the UK he has developed seminars and training programmes to assist UK managers in addressing these issues. Editor of Sweet & Maxwell's Environmental Law Reports.
Prof. Memberships: Member of the Law Society's Specialist Planning Panel.

WALKER, Martin
Edge & Ellison, Birmingham
(0121) 200 2001
Specialisation: Planning and Environmental Law. Advises major developers, house builders, retailers, hotel and leisure chains, waste and mineral operators and also several Waste and Local Planning Authorities. Work includes negotiating/drafting planning and highways agreements, contaminated land, appeals, enforcement, inquiries and judicial review.
Prof. Memberships: Legal Associate RTPI, UKELA, Law Society's Planning Panel, Law Society's Minerals and Waste Issues Group.
Career: Qualified 1984 In Local Government (Cheshire County and Calderdale Borough) to 1988. Worked in Yorkshire "niche" firm until joined *Edge & Ellison* in 1992. Associate from 1994.
Personal: Born 28th September 1959. Educated at Hull University (LL.B) and Leeds Business School (Post Graduate Diploma, Planning and Environmental Law). Book, "Costs in Planning Proceedings" (Longman) and articles published in various journals including JPL.

WHITE, Martin
Pinsent Curtis, Birmingham (0121) 200 1050
Partner in Property Department. Head of Planning and Environment.
Specialisation: Handles planning and related areas including environmental issues, with emphasis on planning appeal work, development plans, issues of planning gain, Section 106 agreements and waste matters. Has acted in appeals relating to major inward investment, airports and business parks, for local Planning Authorities and private sector clients. Also handles local government and public law generally. Involved generally in advice given to local authorities. Author of articles, speaker at conferences and seminars on planning gain and environmental issues.
Prof. Memberships: Law Society (Member of Planning Panel), Legal Associate of Royal Town Planning Institute.
Career: Qualified in 1979. Articled at Solihull Council 1977-79. Joined *Pinsent & Co.* in 1981. Partner in 1987.

Personal: Born 1953. Attended Cambridge University 1972-76; Newcastle Polytechnic 1976-77. Interests include drama and music.

WILBRAHAM, Peter
Wilbraham & Co, Leeds (0113) 243 2200
Specialisation: Acts for public and private sector clients, who are involved in the widest range of development issues. These include Yorkshire Water plc regarding proposed Waste Water Treatment Works; The National Trust relating to Hardwick Hall, Derbyshire and Croome Park, Worcestershire; Land Securities plc on retail proposals; Evans of Leeds Plc and Marley Plc on major residential and industrial proposals. Current major instructions include proposals relating to residential, retail, business parks, industrial, waste disposal, energy, public utility and highway matters.
Prof. Memberships: Honorary Solicitor and Secretary to the Royal Town Planning Institute; a member of the Council of the RTPI and of the Town and Country Planning Summer School and a member of the Law Society's Specialist Planning Panel. Honorary lecturer at Sheffield University. Lectures regularly on planning law issues at professional conferences.
Career: Specialist in planning law for over 25 years. Partner of the late Roger Suddards for most of that time and was responsible for developing a leading provincial planning law practice. Left his former firm *Hammond Suddards* in 1994 to set up his own niche practice in planning and environmental law, which now consists of ten specialist lawyers.

WILLIAMS, Huw
Edwards Geldard, Cardiff (01222) 238239
See under Local Government, Administrative & Public Law, p. 92, 558

WILLIAMSON, Andrew J.
Walker Morris, Leeds (0113) 283 2500
Partner in Planning and Environment Department.
Specialisation: Handles all aspects of planning law with an emphasis on advocacy at s.78 appeals, Local Planning Inquiries, compulsory purchase order and enforcement. Also handles Lands Tribunal and CPA Licensing and Environmental Protection Act authorisation appeals.
Prof. Memberships: Corporate Member of Royal Town Planning Institute, Law Society Planning Panel.
Career: Articled at *Race & Newton* in Burnley 1981-83, then joined *Walker Morris* in 1984 and became a Partner in 1985.
Personal: Born 16th February 1957. Lives in Leeds.

WINTER, Paul E.A.
Eversheds, Leeds (0113) 243 0391
Partner in Property Department.
Specialisation: Main areas of practice are planning and environmental law. Experience includes major town centre schemes, large urban regeneration projects and residential development. Enjoys both the advocacy and the negotiation aspects. Particularly handles environmental aspects of property transactions (especially contaminated land), waste management and development. Handled City Challenge projects, and Mixed Leisure and

Commercial Development, involving the second largest city grant at the time. Contributed 'Contaminated Land' and 'Planning and the Environment' chapters in College of Law Environmental Law Book. Also, contributed contaminated land chapter of the CCH Environment Manual. Part-time lecturer for College of Law, delivered papers at TCPA seminars on 'Sustainability and the Law' and 'Material Considerations'.
Prof. Memberships: Law Society, Town & Country Planning Association (Council & Policy Group member). Member of Specialist Planning Panel of the Law Society. Legal Associate of the Royal Town Planning Institute. Notary Public.
Career: Qualified 1976. Joined *Eversheds Hepworth & Chadwick* as a Partner in 1989. Council Member of the TCPA.
Personal: Born 24th April 1949. Attended Leeds University 1968-72. Leisure interests include music and opera, walking, travelling and reading. Lives in Leeds.

WOOD, David
Bevan Ashford, Bristol (0117) 923 0111
Partner in Commercial Property Department.
Specialisation: Main area of practice is planning and environmental. Handled local authority planning work in Essex 1972-76; specialised in planning and advocacy at Public Inquiries while a Partner in Bristol. Now Head of Planning and Environmental at *Bevan Ashford*. Lead Partner on privatisation of Port of Bristol including the environmental issues and parliamentary procedures arising. Author of an article in 'Urban Regeneration'. Wrote planning law section for NHS Estates 'Estate Code' guidance to land transactions by Health Authorities and Trusts. Lectured for NHS Training Authority, University of the West of England, CBI and others.
Prof. Memberships: Law Society, UK Environmental Law Association.
Career: Qualified in 1969. Worked at *Hatten, Jewers & Mephan* in Basildon, Essex 1969-76. Partner at *Harris & Harris*, Bristol 1976-88, then Partner at *Bevan Ashford* since 1988.
Personal: Born 7th January 1946. Attended Taunton School, Somerset 1957-62.

YOUNG, Eric
Archibald Campbell & Harley WS, Edinburgh
(0131) 220 3000
Consultant in Commercial Department.
Specialisation: Main area of practice is town and country planning law. Also handles environmental law, compulsory purchase and compensation work. Cases have included planning appeals and inquiries and compensation claims. Co-author of 'Scottish Planning Law and Procedure'; author of many other books and articles.
Prof. Memberships: Law Society of Scotland (Solicitor), Honorary Member Royal Town Planning Institute.
Career: Qualified in 1966. Worked in local government 1964-70; lecturer in law at the University of Strathclyde 1970-79, Senior Lecturer in Law, University of Strathclyde 1979-87; Reader in Law, University of Strathclyde 1987-92. Joined *Archibald Campbell & Harley WS* in 1992 as a Partner.
Personal: Born 21st October 1941. Attended University of Edinburgh (MA 1962, LLB 1964). Leisure interests include music, books and gardening. Lives in Dunblane, Perthshire.

PRODUCT LIABILITY

(including Food Law)

RESEARCH: In compiling the tables, we consider all the information available to us, paying particular regard to the market research carried out by our team of ten qualified lawyers. (The researchers' details are set out on page three.) The rankings, therefore, reflect the opinion of the marketplace as revealed by systematic and objective research: see page four. (Our research is audited every year by the British Market Research Bureau.)

OVERVIEW: "Product liability" ranges from advisory and regulatory work to high-profile multiparty litigation. Firms specialise in diverse areas such as pharmaceuticals, engineering, and medical appliances. Sometimes practitioners form part of the medical negligence or personal injury departments of their firms where issues overlap. We have retained a subsection on Food Law where practitioners are particularly specialist but in other cases have highlighted each firm's area of expertise in the text.

There has been little movement in the rankings this year with the main change being the movement of Richard Barr and his team to Hodge Jones & Allen, which results in the firm being ranked for the first time.

It is unclear whether conditional fee agreements will provide adequate funding for product liability litigation. Much will depend on whether insurance companies will cover the defendants' costs in complex cases, particularly those involving a multiplicity of parties. Another possibility is that when the case is in the public interest, Legal Aid will be provided. However where there is only a limited fund available it is doubtful whether this will be practical.

The tobacco litigation has maintained a high profile. At present it is the only group action being run on a conditional fee basis. It is expected to come to trial in 1999 and the result is likely to have a major impact not only on whether tobacco litigation will continue but also whether plaintiff firms will be prepared to risk taking on group actions on conditional fee arrangements. The litigation continues in Scotland and Northern Ireland.

LEADING FIRMS · LONDON

CAMERON MCKENNA

DAVIES ARNOLD COOPER

CLIFFORD CHANCE
FIELD FISHER WATERHOUSE
HODGE JONES & ALLEN
LEIGH DAY & CO
LOVELL WHITE DURRANT
NORTON ROSE
PRITCHARD ENGLEFIELD
SIMMONS & SIMMONS
THEODORE GODDARD

LONDON

Cameron McKenna (8ptnrs/14assts) Remain pre-eminent in the field. Particularly noted for defending multi-party litigation, especially pharmaceuticals. It is also "ahead of the pack on both regulatory and non-contentious" and "very very experienced." Of the many team members named as leading individuals *Christopher Hodges* received particular mention as a "tough opponent" with a "hands on" approach. *Ian Dodds-Smith* has an excellent reputation but is seen as "more of a figurehead." The "tough" *Gary Hickinbottom* is "a very good operator," and has an "enviable reputation." *Mark Tyler* and *Anthony Hobkinson* are also recommended from the firm. **Clients/Work:** Defends claims against manufacturers and suppliers or their insurers; gives advice on reducing product liability risks, risk management, products regulation, product safety and recall; assist clients to develop computerised product liability risk management self-assessment programmes; provide training on product liability risk management.

Davies Arnold Cooper (4ptnrs/7assts) Generally regarded as a "leading player" with an "aggressive" approach to litigation. *Anne Ware,* who heads the team is a "good competent operator" and "tough." Team also includes *Simon Pearl.* **Clients/Work:** Connelly v RTZ (HL) 1997 acting for Rio Tinto plc; co-ordinating Hepatitis C litigation for the NHS Litigation Authority; acting in the Southall Rail Crash Inquiry for English Welsh and Scottish Railways.

Clifford Chance (3ptnrs/5assts) Acknowledged as a presence in product liability work. Act for manufacturers and retailers in the food/beverage industry and has advised on several major product recalls, both national and international. In the medical, healthcare and pharmaceutical industries, the practice acts on diagnostic issues; the group also advises both car manufacturers, particularly Japanese, and component part manufacturers as well as manufacturers in the electrical and telecommunication field. **Clients/Work:** Include Coca Cola, Compaq, Bestfoods UK, CPC (UK) Ltd, HJ Heinz, Public Health Laboratory Service, Safeway Plc, Whitbread Plc.

Field Fisher Waterhouse (1 ptnr within the personal injury department) *Rodney Nelson-Jones* handles the work. **Clients/Work:** Acts for plaintiffs with asbestosis, also claims arising from transport disasters.

Smith v Dicks Eagle Insulations Ltd – recovered record general damages in a case of asbestos pleural disease; member of the solicitors' steering committee for the M1 air crash and Southall train crash

Hodge Jones & Allen (1 ptnr/6 assts/3 scientists) A new entry to the list now that Richard Barr and his team have joined the firm from Dawbarns bringing several major claims with them. **Clients/Work:** Acts for plaintiffs in multi-party actions: sheep dip, Gulf War syndrome and MMR vaccines.

Leigh Day & Co (2 ptnrs/5-6assts) Another new entry to the table following overwhelming recommendation of both the firm and the team leader, *Martyn Day,* respected for his stance in leading the tobacco litigation. **Clients/Work:** Acts for plaintiffs in tobacco litigation, asbestosis and oral contraceptive claims.

Lovell White Durrant (9 ptnrs/28assts) **Clients/Work:** Acts for defendants in tobacco litigation worldwide, particularly in the US. The client base covers a broad range of manufacturers and retailers, and work includes risk management, product recall, mixture of contentious and non-contentious.

Norton Rose (1ptnr/5assts who spend about 10% of their time on product liability work) **Clients/Work:** Include manufacturers of medical products, engineering companies, food and beverage companies, hospitals and insurance companies.

Pritchard Englefield (2ptnrs, one of whom deals with commercial product liability and the other with personal injury related product liability) *Antony Colman* has a "good practice." **Clients/Work:** Cases in 1997 included acting for suppliers of animal housing in which the automated climate control is said to have failed , causing the loss of the animals inside and pipe couplings which burst, resulting in water damage to the interior of a vessel. Also handles personal injury actions arising out of the supply of defective food products, tyres and glass storage jars.

Simmons & Simmons (4ptnrs/8assts) A "quality" firm best known for its involvement in the current tobacco litigation. **Clients/Work:** Acts for defendants in multiparty smoking and health claims, in particular in relation to over 40 conditional actions in England and Wales; acts for a utility company in a major case involving liability and insurance issues arising from claims in relation to the presence of a contaminant in the water supplies; advising as to the liability and safety precautions arising in

relation to asbestos used in buildings.

Theodore Goddard (3ptnrs/5assts spend around 50% of their time on product liability work) Particularly noted for its positive profile in the pharmaceutical field. **Clients/Work:** Cases in 1997 included: acting for MDU in oral contraceptive litigation; defending the subsidiary of a multi-national pharmaceutical company in respect of claims involving the use of a therapeutic product; defending organophosphate claims. Work has a pharmaceutical emphasis – medical products and devices, large product recall for electrical product retailer.

LEADING INDIVIDUALS · LONDON	
DODDS-SMITH Ian Cameron McKenna	
HICKINBOTTOM Gary Cameron McKenna	
HODGES Christopher Cameron McKenna	
TYLER Mark Cameron McKenna	
DAY Martyn Leigh Day & Co	
PEARL Simon Davies Arnold Cooper	
HOBKINSON Anthony Cameron McKenna	
WARE Anne Davies Arnold Cooper	
COLMAN Antony Pritchard Englefield	
NELSON-JONES Rodney Field Fisher Waterhouse	

THE REGIONS

LEADING FIRMS · THE REGIONS
IRWIN MITCHELL Sheffield
ALEXANDER HARRIS Altrincham
FREETH CARTWRIGHT HUNT DICKINS Nottingham
GADSBY WICKS Chelmsford
LEIGH DAY & CO Manchester
LINDSAY ROLAND Poulton-le-Fylde

Irwin Mitchell (Sheffield) (4 ptnrs/3assts) *Andrew Tucker* heads the team at this "top notch" and "very professional" firm which is felt to be in a class of its own in the regions. **Clients/Work:** Represent the families of 22 new variant CJD victims; Silicone breast implants litigation; Capital 3M hip joint litigation.

Alexander Harris (Altrincham) (1 ptnr/ 1asst) *David Harris* ("a player") runs several major product liability cases at this niche practice. **Clients/Work:** Acts on behalf of plaintiffs. Work includes all generic work in LSD multi-party action; investigating claims for "Persona" multi-party action; one of two firms nominated by the Legal Aid Board to carry out preliminary investigations into ECT treatment.

Freeth Cartwright Hunt Dickins (Nottingham) (1 ptnr/2 assts/2 paralegals plus

support from the medical negligence team) The widely praised *Paul Balen,* "extremely knowledgeable" and "technically probably the best product liability lawyer" is the team leader at this firm where the people "really know their stuff." *Richard Beverley* is also recommended. **Clients/Work:** Acts for plaintiffs in Norplant group action where it holds the Legal Aid Board generic contract, has issued over 150 sets of proceedings and co-ordinated information to over 50 other solicitors; MMR and MR childrens' vaccines; breast implants – one of the leading firms in the country dealing with this work nationally with around 2000 clients and provides information to over 150 other firms.

Gadsby Wicks (Chelmsford) (1ptnr 30-40%/1ptnr 20%) Reputation built on involvement in the high profile Myodil litigation, now ended. *Roger Wicks* is recognised as a name in the field. **Clients/Work:** Plaintiff litigation against pharmaceutical and medicine manufacturers. Cases involving Depo-provera contraceptive injections, Septrin and toxic shock syndrome.

Leigh Day & Co (Manchester) (1ptnr/ 1asst) Although the London office has the higher profile, the team of the "highly regarded" *Geraldine McCool* in Manchester is currently doing some significant work in the field. **Clients/Work:** Acts for plaintiffs

in two claims arising from faulty pacemakers and two group actions against the MoD and aircraft manufacturers where catastrophic engine failure caused plane crashes.

Lindsay Roland (Poulton-le-Fylde) (2ptnrs/1asst) Now a two partner firm since the departure of the third partner, Rosalie Houghton at the end of 1997. Regarded as "good to deal with" and "client focused." *Nina Roland* maintains her reputation. **Clients/Work:** Handled a large number of claims involving various pharmaceutical products and currently involved in the largest multi-party action in the country involving cases of environmental pollution causing nuisance and personal injuries.

LEADING INDIVIDUALS THE REGIONS	
BALEN Paul Freeth Cartwright Hunt Dickins	
HARRIS David Alexander Harris	
TUCKER Andrew Irwin Mitchell	
BEVERLEY Richard Freeth Cartwright Hunt Dickins	
MCCOOL Geraldine Leigh, Day & Co	
ROLAND Nina Lindsay Roland	
WICKS Roger Gadsby Wicks	

UP AND COMING	
HOUGHTON Rosalie Houghton & Co	

SCOTLAND

Burness WS (Edinburgh) (2 ptnrs/2assocs who spend 20-80% of their time on product liability) Represent a number of multi-national companies in the pharmaceutical, agrichemical and consumer product fields. *Marsali Murray* is the leading Scottish name.

Simpson & Marwick WS (Edinburgh) (3ptnrs/5assts who spend around 25% of their time on product liability.) Regarded as a "player," particularly in the pharma-ceuticals field. **Clients/Work:** In 1997 handled a number of claims involving pharmaceuticals, motor vehicles and parts, camping equipment.

NORTHERN IRELAND

Elliott Duffy Garrett (Belfast) (2ptnrs/2 assts) Principal focus of the department is the defence of tobacco litigation. **Clients/ Work:** Defence of a claim by a consortium of Northern Irish apple growers against the manufacturer of a leading apple scab fungicide; the defence of proceedings against a leading manufacturer of contraceptives.

O'Reilly Stewart (Belfast) (1ptnr/4 assocs who all spend around 20% of their time in this area) "Well organised" and "tightly run" according to fellow practitioners. *Brian Stewart,* respected for his "long involvement in product liability" heads the team. **Clients/Work:** Manufacturers of organo-phosphates.

BALEN, Paul
Freeth Cartwright Hunt Dickins, Nottingham
(0115) 936 9369
See under Medical Negligence: Mainly Plaintiff, Personal Injury, p. 585, 633

BEVERLEY, Richard
Freeth Cartwright Hunt Dickins, Nottingham
(0115) 936 9369
Partner and Head of Insurance Law.
Specialisation: Specialising in professional negligence, sports and administrative law.
Prof. Memberships: Law Society's Personal Injury Panel. Medical Negligence Panel. Association of Personal Injury Lawyers. Nottinghamshire Medico-Legal Society. Association of Trial Lawyers of America. British Association for Sport and The Law.
Career: Articled with *Withy King & Lee,* Bath. Qualified in 1986. Partner at *Freeth Cartwright* (now *Freeth Cartwright Hunt Dickins*) 1990. LLM Advanced Litigation 1997. CEDR accredited mediator.
Personal: Born 1961. Nottingham University (LL.B). Interests include football and tennis.

COLMAN, Antony
Pritchard Englefield, London
(0171) 972 9720
Partner in Commercial Litigation Department.
Specialisation: Handles wide variety of product liability disputes, with particular experience in relation to industrial machinery as well as consumer products. Fluent German speaker. Author of section on Product Risk Management in Product Liability, Law and Insurance (LLP). Has lectured frequently in England and Germany on product liability and litigation procedure.
Career: Admitted NSW 1980 and England 1986. Partner in *Pritchard Englefield* since 1986.
Personal: Born 1956 in Sydney. BA and LLB from Sydney University. Leisure pursuits include music, tennis, chess.

DAY, Martyn
Leigh, Day & Co, London (0171) 650 1200
See under Administrative & Public Law, Environmental Law, Personal Injury p. 87, 342, 619

DODDS-SMITH, Ian C.
Cameron McKenna, London
(0171) 367 3000
Fax: (0171) 367 2000
Partner and Head of Healthcare Group.
Specialisation: Main area of practice is healthcare related. Deals with the law relating to pharmaceuticals, medical products and devices and products in the cosmetics and food sectors. Specialist in licensing and related regulatory affairs, and on product liability issues. Also covers product liability generally, and personal injury litigation. Has handled many product liability cases, many multi-claimant with international elements including hormone pregnancy tests, oral contraceptives, blood products, benzodiazepines, IUCDs, pesticides and heart valves. Has dealt with several regulatory cases to the E.C.J. including R v. Licensing Authority ex parte Scotia and R v. Licensing Authority ex parte Generics UK and ER Squibb. Author of 'Product Liability for Medical Products' in 'Medical Negligence' (Butterworths) and 'Legal Liabilities in Clinical Trials' in 'Early Phase Human Drug Evaluation'. Joint Editor with Sir Abraham Goldberg of 'Pharmaceutical Medicine and the Law' (The Royal College of Physicians). Author of various articles on regulatory and liability issues. Frequent lecturer in the UK and abroad. Consultant Editor to the Personal and Medical Injuries Law Letter, and to the Regulatory Affairs Journal.
Prof. Memberships: Law Society, American Bar Association, Drug Information Association, Fellow of the Royal Society of Medicine.
Career: Joined *McKenna & Co* in 1974 and qualified in 1976. Became a Partner in 1984. Member of the Royal College of Physicians Working Party on Research at Phase 1 in Healthy Volunteers 1985-86. Member of the Medical Research Council Working Party on legal and ethical issues raised by Research in the Mentally Incapacitated (1988). Temporary Adviser (1987) to W.H.O. on the law relating to clinical trials. Legal adviser to the Clinical Sciences Ethics Committee of the University of London and University College Hospital.
Personal: Born 31st July 1951. Educated at Solihull School and Downing College, Cambridge 1969-72. Recreations include gardening and National Hunt racing. Lives in London.

HARRIS, David N.
Alexander Harris, Altrincham
(0161) 925 5555
Joint Senior Partner and Partner in charge of the Pharmaceutical Product Disaster Litigation Department.
Specialisation: All areas of pharmaceutical product litigation, concentrating on multi party action litigation. Lead Solicitor in Myodil litigation and member of Steering Committees in Opren, Human Insulin, and Hillsborough Disaster. Lead Solicitor in Listeriosis claims against the Government and instructed by families of victims of BSE/ CJD. Lead Solicitor in the investigation of Septrin claims and in the action for underdosing of Radiotherapy at the North Staffordshire District Hospital. Considerable experience in litigation in the USA, including Shiley Heart Valves, Telectronic Pacemakers and Breast Implant claims. Contributes regularly to television news and current affairs programmes and is an expert frequently consulted by radio reporters and producers, and has been extensively quoted in the Press. Lectures on pharmaceutical product and multi party actions to legal and medical audiences. Investigating claims for 'Persona' multi party action. Responsible for all generic work in LSD multi party action. One of two firms nominated by Legal Aid Board to carry out

preliminary investigations into ECT treatment.
Prof. Memberships: Law Society, APIL, ATLA.
Career: Qualified in 1979 and then became co-founder of *Alexander Harris* in May 1989. First practice in this country specialising exclusively in medical negligence and pharmaceutical product liability. The practice has now added a specialist personal injury department. Deputy District Judge on the Northern Circuit since 1988. Assessor to Law Society Personal Injury Panel.
Personal: Born 23rd May 1949. Attended Hull University (LL.B 1972) Lives in Lymm, Cheshire.

HICKINBOTTOM, Gary R.
Cameron McKenna, London
(0171) 367 3000
Specialisation: Partner in the Healthcare group specialising in product liability work with particular reference to medicines and medicinal products. Also handles trade disputes and public law disputes. Important cases include the benzodiazepine litigation, oral contraceptive litigation, minocycline litigation and the ASDA RPM Challenge. Publications include 'Some Practical Problems of Managing Pharmaceutical Product Liability Litigation (with Christopher Hodges published in 'European Pharma Law Centre Position Paper on Product Liability' May 1992). Has also written numerous articles for professional journals.
Prof. Memberships: The Law Society; The City of London Law Society; The Association of Commonwealth Lawyers; The Administrative Law Bar Association; The London Jamaican Capital Case Solicitors' Panel; JUSTICE; The Chartered Institute of Arbitrators (Fellow); The Academy of Experts (Member of Council); Solicitors Association of Higher Court Advocates; National Council for Family Proceedings.
Career: Clerk, *Challinor & Roberts*, Smethwick 1975-1978. Articled clerk, *McKenna & Co* 1979-1981. Assistant solicitor, *McKenna & Co* 1981-1986. Partner, *McKenna & Co* now *Cameron McKenna* since 1986. Solicitor Advocate (All Higher Courts) since 1997. Assistant Recorder (Wales and Chester Circuit) since 1994. Adjudicator for the Parking Appeals Service (the Transport Committee for London) since 1994. Mediator registered with the Academy of Experts since 1991. Central London County Panel of Mediators since 1996. Membership of committees includes: The Law Society Working Party on Group Actions (1994-5); the Academy of Experts Disciplinary Committee (1996 to date); Editorial Board, The Litigator; Editorial Board, Personal Injury.
Personal: Educated at Queen Mary's Grammar School, Walsall 1967-1974, University College, Oxford (MA Hons 1st class) 1975-1978, and Chartered Institute of Arbitrators (Dip IC Arb) 1995-6. Part-time lecturer in law at the Polytechnic of Central London (now University of Westminster) 1980-1981, and at University College, Oxford 1987-1989. Member of Queen Mary's Club, Oxford Society, London Welsh Club, London Welsh Male Voice Choir, Glamorgan Cricket Club (Vice-President), Yr Academi Gymreig. Leisure pursuits include choral singing, opera and ballet, sport and alpine walking. Born 22nd December 1955. Lives in Oxted.

HOBKINSON, Anthony
Cameron McKenna, London
(0171) 367 3000
Partner; Product Liability, and Insurance & Reinsurance Groups.
Specialisation: Has dealt with product liability claims and product recalls in a number of different industries. Acted for the jet engine manufacturers in the British Midland Kegworth disaster and for one of the Joint Ventures in the Piper Alpha oil rig explosion. Experienced in controlling and co-ordinating the defence of multi-jurisdiction claims. Current and recent projects include advising on recall claims involving baby seats, bottles in the brewing industry, car seat-belts and snack foods. Also defending a major gearbox manufacturer following breakdown to a conveyor system. Advising the Association of British Insurers on computer and product issues arising out of Year 2000. Lectures regularly, including seminars to product manufacturers, insurers and the Chamber of Commerce.

HODGES, Christopher J.S.
Cameron McKenna, London (0171) 367 3000
Specialisation: Main areas of practice are product liability, product regulatory and safety law and product recall across a wide range of sectors, including medical devices, pharmaceuticals, automotives and electronics. Editor of 'Product Liability: European Laws and Practice', and 'Product Safety', Chapters in 'Product Liability: Law and Insurance', 'The Textbook of Pharmaceutical Medicine' and various other books. Author of 1995 European Commission Study on the Product Liability Directive.
Prof. Memberships: Law Society, CBI Consumer Affairs Committee and Working Parties on Product Liability and General Product Safety, ABHI Council and Legal Committee, formerly Vice-Chairman of Harrow Health District Ethical Committee, Secretary of International Bar Association Committee S on Product Liability and Consumer Affairs.
Career: Worked at *Slaughter and May* and *Clifford Chance* before becoming Partner at *McKenna & Co* in 1990.
Personal: Born 19th March 1954. Educated at King Edward's School, Birmingham. Academical Clerk at New College, Oxford. Founder member and Trustee of 'The Sixteen'.

HOUGHTON, Rosalie
Houghton & Co, Hereford (01432) 352202
Specialisation: Multi-party actions, product liability, Lead Solicitor in the Oral Contraceptive Pill Group Litigation, HRT Group Litigation, also involved in Copper IUCD Litigation.
Prof. Memberships: AVMA, ATLA, APIL, Law Society, ACFL, and Greystoke Legal Services Medical Negligence Panel.
Career: Marlborough College, University of Kent at Canterbury. Law LL.B (Hons). Guildford Law School. Articled at Forsyte Kerman in London. Founded *Houghton & Co* in November 1997. Regular appearances on radio, TV, and the newspapers. Founding Chairman of the Association of Conditional Fee Lawyers (ACFL).
Personal: Born September 1967.

MCCOOL, Geraldine M.
Leigh, Day & Co, Manchester
(0161) 832 7722
See under Personal Injury; Mainly Plaintiff, p. 635

MURRAY, Marsali C.
Burness, Edinburgh (0131) 473 6000
Specialisation: Partner dealing with commercial litigation and specialising in defender reparation and product liability (including multiple claims) and employment law.

NELSON-JONES, Rodney
Field Fisher Waterhouse, London
(0171) 481 4841
See under Personal Injury; Mainly Plaintiff, p. 620

PEARL, Simon
Davies Arnold Cooper, London
(0171) 936 2222
Partner in Healthcare Unit.
Specialisation: Main areas of practice are medical product liability and negligence. Defends pharmaceutical companies and healthcare professionals and their insurers. Also handles pharmaceutical regulatory work. Co-ordinating solicitor for the NHS in HIV Haemophilia litigation and Hepatitis C litigation. Defended in the whooping cough vaccine test case, Loveday v. Renton. Represented Upjohn in Halcion Regulatory Affairs. Author of Product Liability Insurance chapter in 'Product Liability and Insurance' and of articles in publications including New Law Journal, Product Liability International, International Business Lawyer, Law Society Gazette, Pharmaceutical Marketing and Scrip Magazine. Has spoken widely at conferences.
Prof. Memberships: Law Society. Law Society's Working Party on Group Actions, Medico-legal Society, International Bar Association, American Bar Association, London Litigation Solicitors Association.
Career: Qualified in 1977. Joined *Davies Arnold Cooper* in 1975, becoming a Partner in 1980.
Personal: Born 30th April 1953. Attended Horace Mann School, New York and Birmingham University (LLB(Hons) 1974). Leisure interests include road running, theatre, music and family. Lives in Kimpton, Herts.

ROLAND, K.G.Nina
Lindsay Roland, Blackpool (01253) 357800
Partner. Head of Serious Injuries Department.
Specialisation: Medical negligence and personal injury high value claims and product liability cases. Has been involved in numerous product liability cases, especially against pharmaceutical companies. Regular appearances on TV, radio and national newspapers. Writes weekly legal column for local newspaper.
Prof. Memberships: Law Society, Member of Liverpool Law Society's Bulletin Editorial Committee, Association of Personal Injury Lawyers, ATLA (American Trial Lawyers), International Bar Association, Personal Injury Panel. AVMA.
Career: Qualified 1986. Joined *Goldsmith Williams* in 1990 as a Partner. Founder Partner of *Lindsay Roland Houghton* which commenced practice 1st January 1997, a specialist product liability, medical negligence and serious personal injury niche practice.

STEWART, Brian J. C.
O'Reilly Stewart, Belfast (01232) 322512
Partner and head of the Litigation Department.
Specialisation: Specialises in product liability defence work, mainly relating to pharmaceuticals.
Prof. Memberships: Member of the Council of the Law Society of Northern Ireland. Former Chairman of the Belfast Solicitors' Association. Member of the International Association of Defence Council.
Career: Qualified 1978. Admitted to the Republic of Ireland Roll of Solicitors 1991.

TUCKER, Andrew
Irwin Mitchell, Sheffield (0114) 276 7777
Specialisation: Litigation in respect of products giving rise to injury, particularly pharmaceutical products, medical devices, experience of multi-party litigation both product related and arising from transport disasters and occupational disease. Acted for Plaintiffs in many high profile cases including: Opren, Dalkon Shield, Benzodiazepines, Manchester Aircrash, "Herald of Free Enterprise", Kegworth Aircrash, "Marchioness"/Bowbelle" collision, North Cornwall Water Pollution, Armley Asbestos, Human Growth Hormone/Creutzfeldt-Jacob Disease, Mineworkers V.W.F. and mineworkers respiratory disease.

Prof. Memberships: Law Society, Association of Personal Injury Lawyers, South Yorkshire Medico Legal Society, American Trial Lawyers Association, Secretary to The Environmental Law Foundation.
Career: Articled Wallace Mitchell, Nottingham. Qualified 1985. Partner, Irwin Mitchell, 1988.
Personal: Born October 1960, University of Liverpool, LL.B. Lives North Derbyshire.

TYLER, Mark
Cameron McKenna, London
(0171) 367 3000
Partner in Product Liability and Health & Safety.
Specialisation: Main areas of practice are product liability and health and safety. Co-author of 'Product Safety' and 'Safer by Design'; Consultant Editor of Health and Safety Liability and Litigation; legal reviewer for Croner's Management of Construction Safety. Contributor to 'Buildings and Health: The Rosehaugh Guide to the Design Construction and Management of Buildings', 'A New Balance: A Guide for Property Owners and Developers', 'Environmental Issues in Construction' – CIRIA Special Report, and CIOB Handbook Facilities Management.
Prof. Memberships: Law Society, CBI Health and Safety Panel, CBI Consumer Affairs Panel, Forum of Insurance Lawyers, International Association of Defense Counsel.

Career: Joined McKenna & Co in 1984 and qualified in 1986. Became a Partner in 1992.
Personal: Born 10th October 1960. Educated at Sir William Borlase's Grammar School, Marlow, Worcester College, Oxford and Kings College, London.

WARE, Anne
Davies Arnold Cooper, London
(0171) 936 2222
Specialisation: Specialises in medico-legal and pharmaceutical related litigation; acting for defendants in major multi-party pharmaceutical product liability litigation including the Pertussis litigation, the Benoxaprofen (Opren) litigation and the Benzodiazepine litigation; other areas include environmental and multi jurisdictional litigation; complex medical negligence and medically related personal injury litigation; work related stress; sexual harassment and abuse claims; veterinary, cosmetic and related food product claims.
Career: Admitted 1980; solicitor Davies Arnold Cooper 1980; partner since 1987.
Personal: Born 1954; resides London.

WICKS, Roger
Gadsby Wicks, Chelmsford (01245) 494929

FOOD LAW

These are eventful times for food law specialists. It has been described as a period of uncertainty before the new Food Standards Agency is set up. In Europe progress is slow in harmonising standards despite the desire for free movement of goods. Solicitors reported more litigation, and courts were felt to be harder on defendants due to BSE and E-coli. As the industry becomes more complicated, the number of firms dealing with this work remains small. Clients look for true expertise and a track record. For the niche specialists, the work looks set to continue and there is little change to our tables this year. All firms listed were recognised as 'players' and all are members of the Food Law Group.

LEADING FIRMS LONDON • FOOD LAW
MURRAY & CO
PAISNER & CO
SIMMONS & SIMMONS
TAYLOR JOYNSON GARRETT
WEDLAKE BELL

HIGHLY REGARDED FIRMS
Barlow Lyde & Gilbert
Biddle
Covington & Burling

LONDON

Murray & Co (1ptnr) This small but specialist firm received strong praise from all commentators, as did the "super" *Margaret Murray,* coordinator of the Food Law Group and a high profile figure in this field. **Clients/Work:** Include: Perrier, Best Foods UK, Quaker Oats

Paisner & Co. (1 ptnr/2 assts/2 paralegals) The "excellent" *Craig Baylis* heads a team which is felt to have "good people." Have recently recruited a new assistant who is also an environmental health officer. *Wendy Bernstein* and *Kathryn Gilbertson* are up and coming names. **Clients/Work:** Act for defendants in "sharp end regulatory work", including a potential claim of corporate manslaughter. Clients include: ALPHA Airports Group Plc, Food Hygiene Bureau, Forte Ltd, Gerber Foods International Ltd, Pizza

Hut (UK) Ltd, Whitbread Plc.

Simmons & Simmons (3 ptnrs including *Gareth Davies* /1 asst) **Clients/Work:** Advising various drinks clients in relation to manufacturing under licence and distribution arrangements and contract brewing agreements; advising a Plc in its contract to supply food to Her Majesty's forces worldwide; advising a winery on labels for each company's product.

Taylor Joynson Garrett (1 assoc) *Nick Cody* is seen as having a particular expertise in the field of confectionery. **Clients/Work:** Acts for a major confectioner and provides advice on labelling, trading standards and other regulatory matters.

Wedlake Bell (1ptnr) *Peter Whatmuff* has an excellent reputation in food law and is one of the few lawyers to have a dedicated practice. **Clients/Work:** Acts on behalf of dairy companies. Advises on food market-

ing issues, product development, labelling and trading standards.

Barlow Lyde & Gilbert (3 ptnrs/5 assts who spend up to 50% of their time on product liability) *Gary Freer* undertakes this work from the employment department. **Clients/Work:** Represents one of the parties

LEADING INDIVIDUALS LONDON • FOOD LAW
BAYLIS Craig Paisner & Co
MURRAY Margaret Murray & Co
CODY Nick Taylor Joynson Garrett
DAVIES Gareth Simmons & Simmons
FREER Gary Barlow Lyde & Gilbert
WHATMUFF Peter Wedlake Bell

UP AND COMING
BERNSTEIN Wendy Paisner & Co
GILBERTSON Kathryn Paisner & Co

in the BSE Enquiry as well as a high street chain of fast food restaurants; defends many prosecutions under the Food Safety Act.

Biddle (1ptnr/3assts) A medium sized business law firm with a dedicated food law specialism. Advises producers on pre-

production matters, labelling and prosecutions. **Clients/Work:** Clients include HJ Heinz Company Ltd.

Covington & Burling (1 ptnr/2 assts plus support from its Brussels office) The London office of a US firm whose "main thrust" is

felt to be in pharmaceuticals but also has a presence in food law, particularly regulatory work. **Clients/Work:** Work in 1997 has included labelling and ingredient reviews for confectionery and other foods sold in the EU and elsewhere.

THE REGIONS

LEADING FIRMS
THE REGIONS • FOOD LAW

ANDREW GREGG & CO Bristol
ANDREW M JACKSON & CO Hull
EDGE & ELLISON Birmingham
ELLIOTT & CO Manchester
EVERSHEDS Norwich
SHOOSMITHS & HARRISON Northampton
BEVAN ASHFORD Bristol
EVERSHEDS Birmingham

Andrew Gregg & Co (Bristol) (1ptnr/1asst plus support from 3 other assts) Has a good reputation for product liability work, with *Andrew Gregg* recognised as an expert in the field. **Clients/Work:** Clients include Bradtec Decon. Technologies in connection with its system for deradiation of nuclear affected foods; defend mislabelling claims.

Andrew M Jackson & Co (Hull) (2ptnrs/3assts) The "vastly experienced" *Hugh Smith* has a specialism in vitamins, and the firm has an excellent reputation in the field. **Clients/Work:** Work relates to fish, the effects of prawn glaze regulation and vitamin industry health claims.

Edge & Ellison (Birmingham) (1ptnr/3assts) Practitioners "have a lot of time for" *Steven Edmonds* who heads the team. **Clients/Work:** Defending a high street retailer of electrical appliances in connection

with numerous prosecutions under the Trade Descriptions Act 1968, the Consumer Protection Act 1987, the Consumer Credit Act 1974, the Low Voltage Electrical Equipment Regulations 1995; representing and defending a supermarket chain in connection with investigations and proceedings commenced under Section 12 of the Consumer Protection Act 1987; representing a number of other clients in relation to miscellaneous Trading Standards investigations and prosecutions.

Elliott & Co (Manchester) (1ptnr) The food law work is entirely dealt with by *Barry Holland* who has an "excellent reputation", particularly for meat work. He is currently Chairman of the Food Law Group. **Clients/Work:** Defends major companies on prosecutions brought for out of date products.

Eversheds (Norwich) (4ptnrs/3assts) The team is headed by the widely respected *Owen Warnock.* **Clients/Work:** Successfully defended a prosecution of a major food company over the meat content of a processed meat product; advised on a programme of 'converting' novel alcoholic drink products originating outside the European Union for sale within Europe; advised on EU geographical origin registration, product recalls and advice on health claims in labelling and advertising.

Shoosmiths & Harrison (Northampton) 3ptnrs/2assts) The "outstanding" *Ron Reid* is an eminent name in the field.

Clients/Work: Clients include soft drink manufacturers; major bakers and snackfood producers. Advise on safety issues, product recalls and labelling.

Bevan Ashford (Bristol) (1ptnr/3assts) **Clients/Work:** Provides advice on food law, especially in relation to EC Regulations, health and safety regulations, food hygiene and labelling.

Eversheds (Birmingham) (2ptnrs/5assts) **Clients/Work:** Provide advice on customer complaints and all aspects of product liability and safety including product recalls. On the contentious side the team defends prosecutions brought against clients by Trading Standards.

Roy Tozer is up and coming, and has a broad regulatory practice. He has recently moved from Edge & Ellison to Dibb Lupton Alsop.

LEADING INDIVIDUALS
THE REGIONS • FOOD LAW

EDMONDS Steven Edge & Ellison
GREGG Andrew Andrew Gregg & Co
HOLLAND Barry Elliott & Company
REID Ron Shoosmiths & Harrison
SMITH Hugh Andrew M. Jackson & Co
WARNOCK Owen Eversheds

UP AND COMING

TOZER Royston Dibb Lupton Alsop

SEE PROFILES AT END OF THIS SECTION

LEADERS' PROFILES • LONDON AND REGIONAL PROFILES – FOOD LAW

BAYLIS, Craig
Paisner & Co, London (0171) 353 0299
See under Licensing (gaming, betting & liquor) & Leisure, p. 501

BERNSTEIN, Wendy
Paisner & Co, London (0171) 353 0299
Specialisation: Solicitor in the Litigation Department specialising in all aspects of food safety law, including advising on defending local authority enforcement action; preparing or reviewing due diligence procedures; all aspects of legal compliance and food safety aspects of commercial contracts. Has acted for leading hotel and catering companies.
Prof. Memberships: Food Law Group.
Career: Former South African educated mainly in South Africa. BA (Honours) Jurisprudence from Oxford (St Anne's College). Qualified in 1988. Co-author of 'Food Safety Law and Practice', published by FT Law and Tax.

Personal: Born 1962. Lives in Primrose Hill, London. Married with two children. Interests include family life, reading and cooking.

CODY, Nick
Taylor Joynson Garrett, London
(0171) 353 1234
Specialisation: Advises on a wide range of consumer law issues, including consumer protection, consumer safety and trading standards. Also advises on advertising, sales promotions and related issues. Particular experience in advising clients operating in the food, cosmetics and toy industries.
Prof. Memberships: Member of Food Law Group.
Career: Joined firm in 1967 and has been advising clients on consumer law issues since 1972.
Personal: Leisure – watching cricket and football, walking, local community and family life.

DAVIES, Gareth
Simmons & Simmons, London
(0171) 628 2020
Partner in Commercial Department.
Specialisation: Specialises in the food and drink industry. Scientific and technical adviser to EU Commission (DGVI) on Designations of Geographic Origin and Specific Character. Advises on all matters relating to composition labelling and regulation of food and drink. Has handled various acquisitions and disposals of food processing and distribution businesses, advice and compliance with compositional regulations, labelling regulations and free circulation of products in the EU and relations with the EU Commission, MAFF and local regulatory authorities, including prosecutions. Clients include Booker PLC, E & J Gallo and Ferminich. Contributor (re sale of goods) to Butterworth's 'Encyclopedia of Forms & Precedents'. Lectures regularly on all aspects of food law.

Prof. Memberships: Law Society, Food Law Group (Committee Member).
Career: Qualified in December 1979 (England & Wales) and May 1981 (Hong Kong). Partner at *Simmons & Simmmons* since 1989.
Personal: Born 5th July 1955. Educated at the University of Sheffield 1973-76 (LL.B Hons) and the City of London Polytechnic 1978-81 (MA, Business Law). Leisure interests include sailing, cookery, board games and history. Lives in Burnham-on-Crouch.

EDMONDS, Steven James
Edge & Ellison, Birmingham
(0121) 200 2001
See under Fraud, Health & Safety, p. 404, 408

FREER, Gary
Barlow Lyde & Gilbert, London
(0171) 247 2277
Specialisation: Commercial litigation of all kinds, including consumer, food safety, employment, defamation and professional indemnity.
Prof. Memberships: Food Law Group, Employment Lawyers Association. Trustee, The Divert Trust.
Career: Articles with *Barlow Lyde & Gilbert*, qualified 1986, Partner May 1993.
Personal: Born 16th April 1961, Educated at Nottingham High School and St. Catharine's College Cambridge (M.A.). Interests include hockey (West Hampstead Hockey Club), choral singing and sport of all kinds.

GILBERTSON, Kathryn
Paisner & Co, London (0171) 353 0299
Specialisation: Solicitor in the Business Regulation Unit specialising in all aspects of food safety/health and safety law. Advising and defending clients in respect of local authority enforcement action; drafting and reviewing due diligence protocols; advising on all aspects of legal compliance.
Prof. Memberships: Food Law Group, Chartered Institute of Environmental Health, Society of Food Hygiene Technology.
Career: Educated in Wales. BSc(Hons) Environmental Health from Bristol Polytechnic. Diploma in Health and Safety at Work North East London Polytechnic. Practised as a local authority Environmental Health Officer for 9 years before qualifying as a Solicitor. Admitted 1994.
Personal: Born 1962. Lives in Standon Hertfordshire. Married. Interests include Italian sports cars, fine wine and visiting sites of historical interest.

GREGG, Andrew
Andrew Gregg & Co, Bristol
(0117) 925 8123
Specialisation: All aspects of law concerning food, licensing and health and safety. Acts for wide variety of food and drink manufacturers, processors and retailers. See 'R v. Gateway Foodmarkets Ltd' C.A. TLR 2.1.97.
Prof. Memberships: Secretary Food Law Group, Vice President Bristol Law Society, Council Member Notaries Society.
Career: The Dragon School Oxford, The Kings School Canterbury. Solicitor D.o.A. 1970, Notary Public D.o.A. 1984. For 20 years partner with a leading Bristol firm before setting up own niche practice in 1992.
Personal: Born 12.9.43. Interests include rugby, sailing, motor racing and restoration of vintage cars. Owns and campaigns a 1933 Lagonda. Chairman Bristol and Avon Federation of Clubs for Young People.

HOLLAND, Barry K.
Elliott & Company, Manchester
(0161) 834 9933
See under Licensing (gaming, betting & liquor) & Leisure, p. 509

MURRAY, Margaret
Murray & Co, London (0181) 2884893

REID, Ron F.
Shoosmiths & Harrison, Northampton
(01604) 29977
Specialisation: Main areas of practice are food law, including advice on product liability and Trading Standards matters, consumer and fraudulent claims. Also advises on health and safety, environmental law and liquor licensing. Has set up specialist training department to handle the requirements of national and international companies for in-house training and is a regular speaker at conferences and seminars in his areas of specialisation.
Prof. Memberships: Honorary Member of Executive Committee of Inter-Company Consumer Affairs Association, a trade association of Consumer Care Managers in the food and drinks manufacturing industry. Member of The Food Law Group, Northamptonshire Occupational Safety & Health Association. Secretary to the Food Industry Regional Safety Team. Director of the Radon Council.
Career: Qualified in 1983, having previously been a F.I.L.Ex. Joined *Shoosmiths & Harrison* in 1974. Became a Partner in 1985.

SMITH, Hugh E.
Andrew M. Jackson & Co, Hull
(01482) 325242
Partner in Commercial Litigation Department.
Specialisation: Substantial area of practice involves retail law covering Trading Standards, Health and Safety, Consumer Protection and Consumer Safety. Particular specialism in the vitamin and fish industry. Also specialises in contractual dispute, commercial property disputes, professional negligence, defamation and passing off. Represents finance houses in respect of consumer complaints/recoveries.
Prof. Memberships: Member of the Law Society and the Food Law Group. Also an ADR mediator.
Career: Admitted 1983. Joined present firm in 1989 becoming a Partner in 1991 in charge of the Commercial Litigation Division.
Personal: Born 16.01.59. Attended Nottingham University (LLB Hons).

TOZER, Royston C.L.
Dibb Lupton Alsop, London (0345) 262728
See under Crime: Fraud, p. 405

WARNOCK, Owen
Eversheds, Norwich (01603) 272727
See under Employment Law, p. 314

WHATMUFF, Peter W.
Wedlake Bell, London (0171) 395 3000
Partner in Media, Intellectual Property and Commercial team.
Specialisation: Practice focuses on food law including advertising, labelling and marketing of food, sales promotions, trade marks, passing off, licensing, commercial agreements and environmental work. Has dealt with food law issues for major dairy companies/organisations and for other food companies. Publishes food law newsletter, writes articles for food and legal journals.
Prof. Memberships: Law Society, Food Law Group.
Career: Qualified in 1975. Became a Partner at *Ellis & Fairbairn* in 1984 and a partner at *Wedlake Bell* in 1988.
Personal: Attended Ashville College, Harrogate and the University of East Anglia. Leisure interests include European life and culture, theatre and swimming.

PROFESSIONAL NEGLIGENCE

RESEARCH: In compiling the tables, we consider all the information available to us, paying particular regard to the market research carried out by our team of ten qualified lawyers. (The researchers' details are set out on page three.) The rankings, therefore, reflect the opinion of the marketplace as revealed by systematic and objective research: see page four. (Our research is audited every year by the British Market Research Bureau.)

OVERVIEW: London firms are divided into four specialist areas of professional negligence – Legal (solicitors and barristers), Financial (accountants, financial intermediaries, financial institutions, trust funds and pensions advisers), Insurance (brokers, underwriters and managing agents) and Construction (architects, engineers, project managers, surveyors and valuers).

In London, Barlow Lyde & Gilbert, Cameron McKenna and Reynolds Porter Chamberlain are still the leading firms with the broadest practices. Other firms are listed alphabetically, as many appear in more than one table. Berwin Leighton and Hartfields are new additions this year, largely due to their leading individuals.

The litigation against solicitors and valuers arising out of the late 80's property boom has worked its way through the system, assisted in part by various Court of Appeal and House of Lords judgments which have defined the duty of care owed by professionals. As a result, many firms have seen their work in this area fall off. Furthermore, the lack of building during the last recession means that there are currently few construction claims around; more are expected to materialise in the next few years when the present wave of construction is over.

The growth areas now centre around accountants, financial intermediaries, pensions advisers, insurance brokers, IT consultants and the Millennium problem; nonetheless, the streamlining of insurance panels and the promotion of Alternative Dispute Resolution as a means of case disposal is causing some disquiet.

Most firms act exclusively for either plaintiff or defendant clients with only a few able to do both. However, the lists tend to include a majority of defendant firms as it is these which, by virtue of their presence on insurance panels, have found it easier to build up a specialism in the field.

LEADING FIRMS · LONDON INSURANCE

BARLOW LYDE & GILBERT
CAMERON MCKENNA
CLYDE & CO
REYNOLDS PORTER CHAMBERLAIN
DAVIES ARNOLD COOPER
INCE & CO

HIGHLY REGARDED FIRMS

Fishburn Boxer
Holman, Fenwick & Willan
Rowe & Maw
Elborne Mitchell
Hammond Suddards
Wansbroughs Willey Hargrave
Edward Lewis
Squire & Co

LONDON

LEADERS ACROSS THE BOARD

Barlow Lyde & Gilbert (25ptnrs/42assts) A formidable department which includes *Stuart Hall, David Massa, David Arthur* and *Ian Jenkins,* "one of the top lawyers in this country." Praised for their "common sense and good case management," "high quality staff" and "quick response," they handle all areas of professional negligence, with particular emphasis on accountants' and solicitors' negligence. **Clients/Work:** Act for SIF, major firms of solicitors, most of the Big Five accountants, other accountants, insurance brokers, and other professionals. Recent cases include 'Bank Austria v Coopers & Lybrand' and 'Pacific & General v Hazell and Minet'.

Cameron McKenna (17ptnrs – 6 of whom feature individually in our table) This firm is going from strength to strength and has had no problem replacing its Lloyd's litigation caseload with work for accountants, pensions advisers, trustees, construction and insurance professionals. The much admired "larger than life" *Mark Elborne* moves up to join "tactically astute" *Stephen Tester* as a leading individual, whilst new entry *Vere Wheatley* keeps *Geoff Barrett, Peter Maguire* and *Belinda Schofield* company. **Clients/Work:** Brostoff & Others v Clarke Kenneth Leventhal and Clark Whitehill (claim for £18m+ in respect of fraud of Nick Yound successfully defended); successful defence of Bacon & Woodrow in the largest claim that has ever been made against an actuary (resolved by mediation during 1998); review of minimum accountants professional indemnity wording for the Institute of Chartered Accountants In England and Wales.

Reynolds Porter Chamberlain Has, to some extent, a finger in every pie with high profile individuals such as *Simon Greenley, Alexander Hamer, Barney Micklem* and "outstandingly good" *Paul Nicholas*. SIF work continues to dominate, although there has been an increase in accountants/financial institutions' claims. The firm is respected for its high quality work and people. Clients/Work: Investors Compensation Scheme litigation against 300 solicitors and a building society. Nationwide Building Society v Lewis (salaried partner's liability). Claims handling scheme for middle tier accountants.

FIRMS IN ALPHABETICAL ORDER

The editorial for the other firms listed in the tables follows in alphabetical, rather than ranking order.

LEADING FIRMS • LONDON LEGAL
BARLOW LYDE & GILBERT
REYNOLDS PORTER CHAMBERLAIN
LOVELL WHITE DURRANT
INCE & CO

HIGHLY REGARDED FIRMS
Davies Arnold Cooper
Herbert Smith
Pinsent Curtis
Wansbroughs Willey Hargrave

Beale & Company (6ptnrs/4assts) The firm, including the "solid" *John Ward* and "tough negotiator" *Antony Smith,* handles claims involving (primarily) construction professionals. Clients/Work: Representing engineers in the Great Ormond Street Hospital litigation. Group action by ex BCCI employees against Price Waterhouse. Defending claim by trustees of Natural History Museum concerning mechanical storage services.

Berrymans Lace Mawer (4ptnrs/7assts) *Diana Holtham, Charlotte Capstick* and *Paul Taylor* are the leading lights in this area, assisted by a national team. Clients/Work: Act for all but one of the top ten insurers as well as Lloyd's syndicates and have opened an office in Minster Court. Advice on Year 2000 implications for underwriters and surveyors. Ongoing instruction in DTI investigation. Construction related claims.

Berwin Leighton (2ptnrs/4assts – 2 dual qualified) A new entry this year due to the high profile of *Michael Wilson,* who is "streets ahead in work defending financial institutions." Clients/Work: Claim from

Hong Kong financial institution as consequence of a regulatory fine of £12m (potential loss in excess of £50m); claim from continental bank for dishonest employee affecting nearly 400 accounts and resulting in losses of £30m.

Clyde & Co (3ptnrs/3assts) "Legend in his own time," *Michael Payton* is largely responsible for their continued presence in this table. Clients/Work: Solicitors, accountants, insurance brokers.

Davies Arnold Cooper 10ptnrs/15assts - also do insurance) A quality team that have a high insurance profile, and expertise over all the professions. "Efficient and tough" sums up this group. Clients/Work: Banesto; Galt; Pointwest.

Edward Lewis (9 ptnrs) The team has been strengthened by the arrival of a professional negligence partner from the now merged Oswald Hickson Collier. Clients/Work: Act for Lloyd's Underwriters and some of the leading UK insurance companies.

LEADING FIRMS • LONDON CONSTRUCTION
BEALE AND COMPANY
BERRYMANS LACE MAWER
CAMERON MCKENNA
KENNEDYS
ROWE & MAW
DAVIES ARNOLD COOPER
FISHBURN BOXER
REYNOLDS PORTER CHAMBERLAIN

HIGHLY REGARDED FIRMS
Barlow Lyde & Gilbert
Hextall Erskine
Hartfields
Wansbroughs Willey Hargrave
Williams Davies Meltzer

Elborne Mitchell A firm respected for its insurance expertise. Also handle shipping and aviation related matters.

Fishburn Boxer (13ptnrs/19assts)Team are active in emerging markets such as publishing, media and IT. Continue to be involved with the Lloyd's market. Cover all professions except legal. Clients/Work: Defendant, with particular emphasis on construction and financial.

Freshfields (8ptnrs/10assts) Quality rather than quantity best sums up the work of this team, which concentrates on large, high profile cases, mainly on behalf of plaintiffs. Clients/Work: Act for Polly Peck administrators in £200m claim against Stoy Hayward. Acted for Plaintiff bank suing top 10 City firm. Represented Bank Austria against Price Waterhouse.

Hammond Suddards (4ptnrs/11assts) The London limb of this national firm is led by "sound" ex Alastair Thompson partner

Michael Lent. Are now consolidating after acquiring the Forsyte Saunders Kerman team in 1996. Clients/Work: Legal & General v TGIP (bracket for valuations). Subrogated action against solicitors. Claims involving IT consultants.

Hartfields A niche commercial litigation firm, specialising in insurance related disputes, formed by well regarded ex Alistair Thompson partner, *David Hartfield*. Clients/Work: Acts for accountants, financial intermediaries, licensed conveyancers and construction professionals.

Herbert Smith (14 ptnrs) The firm is seen as having "strength in depth" and, as befits a "premier litigation practice" tends to be involved only in the more high profile, high value complex cases. Clients/Work: Act for Price Waterhouse and Coopers & Lybrand (Singapore) in connection with BCCI and Barings collapses; pension companies; educational establishments; solicitors and construction professionals.

LEADING FIRMS • LONDON FINANCIAL
CAMERON MCKENNA
BARLOW LYDE & GILBERT
HERBERT SMITH
LOVELL WHITE DURRANT

HIGHLY REGARDED FIRMS
Berwin Leighton
Freshfields
Wilde Sapte
Berrymans Lace Mawer
Rowe & Maw
Squire & Co

Hextall Erskine (12ptnrs/5assts) This firm is "on the rise," assisted by the increasingly high profile of the "astute, bright" *Stuart White*. Recent arrivals include a team from the former Jarvis & Bannister and a partner from the former Alastair Thompson & Partners. Clients/Work: Represents barristers, accountants, financial intermediaries, brokers, architects, valuers, surveyors and engineers. Cases include UCB Bank v David J Pinder (business appraisal valuation; reduction of 1/3 for contributory negligence).

Holman Fenwick & Willan (5ptnrs/4assts) Best known as a shipping firm, they also undertake professional indemnity work for insurance professionals. Clients/Work: Defending reinsurance broker against misrepresentation allegations arising from NRG Victory's involvement in the excess of loss spiral. "Hand-holding" of large reinsurance broker in arbitration by insurers alleging material non-disclosure re E&O account.

Ince & Co (8ptnrs/12assts) One of only four London firms on SIF's panel, it is seen, in the main, as "intellectual and commercial," if a bit "traditional." Thought not to have the same volume of E&O work as others but has a good reputation. Led by *Julian Hill*. Clients/Work: Act for large firms of brokers via direct instruction.

Kennedys They still retain top slot for construction related cases. The "dynamic, commercial, bright, tough negotiator" *Nick Thomas* is universally admired. Now managing partner he is less active than before. Clients/Work: Architects indemnifiers, surveyors, financial advisers. Secured Residential Funding plc v Nationwide Building Society; Holbeck Hall Hotel Ltd v Scarborough Borough Council (acting for GEN the site investigation company in the case). Also handle international work.

Lovell White Durrant (15ptnrs/27assts worldwide-none full-time) Tend to get involved only in the more complex, high value, high profile cases, but are seen as "excellent" when they do. Leading individuals are *John Trotter* and new entry *Michael Seymour*. Clients/Work: Defending Clifford Chance in the Canary Wharf litigation, and Theodore Goddard in the Matrix case. Representing the plaintiff liquidators in BCCI v Price Waterhouse and Ernst & Young. Act for BZW in Atlantic Computers case.

Pinsent Curtis (3 ptnrs/ 24 fee-earners) Best known for their SIF work, the London team is led by new entry *David Robinson*. Clients/Work: Case management of the Bristol & West (BW) actions against solicitors, including BW v Fancy & Jackson. BW v SIF and Abbey National v Fallon (dishonesty); BW v May May Merrimans (treatment of MIG in context of lender recovery).

Rowe & Maw (6ptnrs/14assts) This firm received the most compliments, including "clued up," "high quality," "do a better job" and "have to take them seriously." Leading

lights include *Michael Regan* and the "competent" *Sean Connolly*. Clients/Work: Act for Lloyd's and the Companies markets, particularly in pensions, financial institutions, valuations, construction, Year 2000 and fidelity cases. Involved in BBL and one of the largest construction claims ever heard in England.

Squire & Co (6ptnrs/14assts) One of the more colourful firms in this area, its high volume, low value work comes from a couple of insurers. Clients/Work: Gunn v Par Insurance Brokers (broker's negligence)

Wansbroughs Willey Hargrave SIF work forms a substantial part of their practice, particularly in more "run of the mill" cases. Clients/Work: Cover all professionals, including solicitors, surveyors, architects, accountants and insurance brokers. Clients include General Accident.

Wilde Sapte (4ptnrs – 1 in Hong Kong/8assts) The highly regarded *Adrian Mecz* (a new addition this year) is largely responsible for the firm's place in our table with his bankers blanket bonds work. As with other big City firms, they do not have volume work but are involved in some very large multi-party, multi- jurisdictional cases. Clients/Work: Accountants, solicitors, financial institutions and brokers. Represent Deloitte & Touche in various actions, including those brought by Barings and the Omni Group and another against Coopers & Lybrand. Handled $20m claim relating to Columbian bankers bond. Acting for AIG in D&O claims.

Williams Davies Meltzer (5ptnrs) A niche insurance litigation firm. Received a mixed review, although some thought them "on the up." Clients/Work: Act for Lloyd's underwriters, UK/foreign composite insurers, brokers, adjusters, financial institutions in cases involving most professions.

ARTHUR, David
Barlow Lyde & Gilbert, London
(0171) 247 2277
Specialisation: Professional Negligence involving accountants, insurance brokers, solicitors and financial advisors. Also insurance and reinsurance Litigation.
Prof. Memberships: Law Society, International Bar Association, B.I.L.A.
Career: Qualified in 1978. Joined *Barlow Lyde & Gilbert* in 1981. Became a Partner in 1984.

BARRETT, Geoff
Cameron McKenna, London
(0171) 367 3000
Partner in Insurance and Reinsurance Group.
Specialisation: Principal areas of practice involve acting in claims and disputes for Insurers and Reinsurers of accountants, financial advisers, insurance brokers, members' agents, surveyors and loss adjusters and Directors' and Officers' liability cover. Also advises on general insurance and reinsurance

matters including drafting and construction of policy wordings.
Prof. Memberships: Law Society.
Career: Read Law at University College London following which he obtained articles with *Hewitt Woollacott and Chown*, as it then was, in 1979. Was admitted as a solicitor in April 1981 and has been a partner since 1986.

CAPSTICK, Charlotte
Berrymans Lace Mawer, London
(0171) 638 2811
Specialisation: All aspects of professional indemnity insurance and litigation, particularly in the defence of accountants and surveyors.
Career: Joined *Berrymans* on qualifying in 1984 and has since specialised in Professional Negligence work. Became Partner 1988 and now heads Professional Indemnity Department.
Personal: Born 17.10.58. Read Law at St Anne's College, Oxford. Lives in London.

CONNOLLY, Sean
Rowe & Maw, London (0171) 248 4282
Specialisation: Specialises in all areas of contentious non marine insurance and reinsurance work including professional indemnity and product liability insurance matters. Has represented a wide range of professional indemnity merchant banks, accountants, insurance brokers, engineers and surveyors. Involved in the Ramsgate litigation proceedings last year. Is partner in charge of *Rowe & Maw*'s Lloyd's offices comprising some 14 partners and legal staff.
Prof. Memberships: Law Society; International Bar Association; British Insurance Law Association.
Career: University of London (LL.B). Articled *Rowe & Maw* 1982-84. Assistant Solicitor Commercial Litigation Department 1984-86. Solicitor Alexander & Alexander Europe Plc 1986-88. Lloyd's Office *Rowe & Maw* 1988-date.
Personal: Cricket, golf and skiing.

ELBORNE, Mark E.M.
Cameron McKenna, London
(0171) 367 3000
Partner in Insurance and Reinsurance Department.
Specialisation: Principal areas of practice involve acting in claims and disputes for Insurers and Reinsurers of Banks and Financial Institutions, Directors and Officers, Accountants, Financial Advisers and Stockbrokers, Lloyd's Agents and Lloyd's Brokers; advising Insurers and Reinsurers on policy wordings and construction in insurance and reinsurance contracts; acting in major reinsurance arbitration and litigation disputes and advising Reinsurers generally with clients in the London market, Europe, Middle and Far East, USA and Bermuda. Lectured in Bermuda at International Reinsurance Congress and in Hong Kong and London at various conferences on financial institutions insurance, Directors' and Officers' liability cover and on reinsurance.
Prof. Memberships: Law Society, Chartered Institute of Insurers, Society of Insurance Receivers.
Career: Qualified 1983 while at *Cameron Markby Hewitt* and became a Partner in 1988.
Personal: Born 22nd January 1958. School Trustee. Leisure pursuits include golf, swimming, tennis, shooting and opera. Lives near Uppingham, Rutland. Married with 5 children.

GREENLEY, Simon K.P.T.
Reynolds Porter Chamberlain, London
(0171) 242 2877
See under Insurance and Reinsurance: Direct Work, p. 467

HALL, Stuart
Barlow Lyde & Gilbert, London
(0171) 247 2277
Specialisation: Professional Indemnity, especially Accountants, and Commercial Litigation.
Prof. Memberships: English and Hong Kong Law Societies.
Career: Cambridge University; admitted 1975; partner *Dawson & Co* 1976-1985; partner *Barlow Lyde & Gilbert* 1985 to date.

HAMER, Alexander N.
Reynolds Porter Chamberlain, London
(0171) 242 2877
Partner in Insurance and Reinsurance Department.
Specialisation: Main area of practice is insurance and professional liability litigation. Handles litigation for errors and omissions underwriters including accountants, financial advisers and institutions, pension trustees, Directors and Officers, computer consultants, Lloyd's underwriting agents and other professionals. Provides general insurance and policy advice. Regular public speaker on insurance law issues.
Prof. Memberships: Law Society and Institute of Taxation.
Career: Qualified in 1984. Became a partner in *Reynolds Porter Chamberlain* in 1989.
Personal: Born 20th September 1959. Attended Exeter University (LLB Hons 1981). Leisure interests include sailing, windsurfing and music. Lives in Guildford, Surrey.

HARTFIELD, David
Hartfields, London (0171) 405 4440
Partner specialising in professional negligence, insurance and construction work.
Specialisation: Main area of practice is professional negligence, acting for professional indemnity insurers and their insureds in claims against architects, surveyors, engineers, insurance brokers, accountants and licensed conveyancers. Also handles insurance and construction work, acting for (and occasionally against) insurers in respect of policy disputes and for developers in building and contractual disputes.
Prof. Memberships: Law Society.
Career: Qualified in 1972. Previously a Partner at *Alastair Thomson & Partners*. Set up *Hartfields* in 1997.

HILL, Julian
Ince & Co, London (0171) 623 2011
Specialisation: Specialises in marine and non-marine insurance and reinsurance matters. He acts as adviser to the London market on Institute Clauses and at UNCTAD on marine insurance. Editor and co-author of O'May on Marine Insurance and contributor to Halsbury's Laws of England on Admiralty and the Encyclopaedia of Forms and Precedents on Shipping. Marine Insurance Assessor for the examinations of the Institute of Chartered Shipbrokers. Member of the Commercial Court Committee and of the Commercial Court Working Party on the Access to Justice Civil Procedure Reforms.
Career: Was articled at *Ince & Co* and became a partner in 1974.

HOLTHAM, Diana
Berrymans Lace Mawer, London
(0171) 638 2811
Specialisation: Construction litigation with emphasis on professional indemnity claims for engineers and quantity surveyors and other construction related insurance claims.
Prof. Memberships: Official Referees' Solicitors' Association, Society of Construction Law.
Career: : Exeter University 1974-77. Qualified 1980 and joined *Berrymans* in same year. Partner 1986. Head of Construction Department 1992. Co-author of "Berrymans' Building Claims Cases."
Personal: Interests – photography (licentiate of Royal Photographic Society) architecture, housing charities, travel and walking. Lives in Sevenoaks, Kent.

JENKINS, Ian
Barlow Lyde & Gilbert, London
(0171) 247 2277
Specialisation: Insurance, Brokers, Accountants. Directors' and Officers' Liability.
Prof. Memberships: Professional Liability Underwriting Society.
Career: Partner, *Barlow Lyde & Gilbert*, 1974. Elected Senior Partner, 1989. Non -Executive Director of Kiln Holdings Ltd, Crowe Insurance Group Ltd.
Personal: Born 1946. Educated at Denstone College and King's College, London. Leisure interests include family and sailing. Member of Royal Thames Yacht Club. Committee member of Ocean Cruising Club.

LENT, Michael
Hammond Suddards, London Lloyds Office
(0171) 327 3388
Partner in 1983.
Specialisation: Principal area of practice is professional indemnity insurance litigation, acting for insurers of architects, engineers, surveyors, accountants and insurance brokers. Also advises in relation to building contracts. Was involved in the following cases: 'Normid Housing Association v. Ralphs & Mansell', 'Wessex Health Authority v. HLM & others', 'West Faulkner v. London Borough of Newham', 'Lewisham Partnership Investment Ltd v. Morgan'.
Prof. Memberships: Society of Construction Law, Official Referees Solicitors Association, Law Society.
Career: Qualified in 1978. Joined *Alastair Thomson & Partners* in 1981 and became a Partner in 1983. Joined the Lloyds Office of *Hammond Suddards* as a Partner in September 1997.

MAGUIRE, Peter
Cameron McKenna, London
(0171) 367 3000
Partner in Insurance and Reinsurance Group.
Specialisation: Advises on a range of non-marine claims, including policy disputes. Specialises in professional indemnity work, including accountants, consulting engineers, surveyors and miscellaneous professional indemnity matters. Also advising clients on the Year 2000 problem and on policy issues arising out of pension transfer and opt-out claims. Important cases handled include 'Deeny & Others v Littlejohn Frazer' (£250 million claims of Gooda Walker Names struck out, save for claims totalling £7 million). Also acted for the Defendant valuers and agents in 'Holt v De Groot Collis' (duty of care in tort may be wider than in contract), 'Omega Trust Fund v. Wright Son & Pepper and Barker & Co' (effect of disclaimer on alleged duty to syndicate bank; 70% reduction for lenders' contributory negligence) and 'Banque Bruxelles Lambert SA v Eagle Star Insurance Company Ltd & Others' (acting on behalf of John D Wood Commercial Ltd). Major clients include Lloyd's syndicates and insurance companies.
Career: Joined *Hewitt Woollacott & Chown* upon qualification in 1984. Became a Partner at *Cameron Markby Hewitt* in 1989.
Personal: Born 9th December 1957. Educated at Hull University 1976-79. Ardent Charlton Athletic supporter. Lives in Strawberry Hill, Twickenham.

MASSA, David
Barlow Lyde & Gilbert, London
(0171) 247 2277
Specialisation: Professional indemnity specialising predominantly in solicitors' negligence; defamation.
Prof. Memberships: The Law Society; London Solicitors' Litigation Association (LSLA).
Career: Educated at Oxford University; admitted 1962; *Theodore Goddard* 1962-1964; *Knapp Fishers* 1964-1968; *Barlow Lyde & Gilbert* 1968 to date (consultant from May 1998).

MECZ, Adrian
Wilde Sapte, London (0171) 246 7000
Specialisation: Insurance/Reinsurance; All financial institutions and commercial crime

coverage disputes including professional indemnity; New Hampshire Insurance Company v. Philips Electronics North America Corporation.
Prof. Memberships: I.B.A., Section on Business Law, Insurance Committee the American Bar Association, Torts and Insurance Practice Section.
Career: BA. University of Rochester 1975 (USA); J.D. Albany Law School 1978 (USA) Admitted in New York 1979; QLTT 1997

MICKLEM, Charles Thomas
Reynolds Porter Chamberlain, London (0171) 242 2877
Partner in Professional Indemnity Litigation Department.
Specialisation: Professional indemnity litigation specialist. Work relates principally to solicitors, barristers and surveyors. Has addressed various professional indemnity seminars.
Prof. Memberships: Law Society.
Career: Qualified in 1974. Became a Partner in 1977.

NICHOLAS, Paul D.
Reynolds Porter Chamberlain, London (0171) 242 2877
Partner in Insurance and Professional Indemnity department.
Specialisation: Insurance and professional indemnity.
Career: Qualified in 1970, having joined *Reynolds Porter* in 1968. Became a Partner in 1972.
Personal: Born 24th April 1946. Educated at Mill Hill School 1959-63 and Emmanuel College, Cambridge (BA 1967, LLB 1968). Governor of Lockers Park School and Trustee of S.W. Hertfordshire Hospice Charitable Trust.

PAYTON, Michael
Clyde & Co, London (0171) 623 1244
Specialisation: Adviser to Insurers worldwide on most of the major International Insurance problems of recent years, notably (and in no particular order) "PIPER ALPHA"; the invasion of Kuwait; collapse of US Savings & Loans Banks; breast implants; US environmental and pollution claims; break up of the former Yugoslavia and U.S.S.R., Scandinavian credit reinsurance; loss of Sleipner GBS; the kidnap of' 'SHERGAR' the ships 'BRAER', 'ESTONIA', and 'SEA EMPRESS'; Chernobyl related contamination of food crops; and the Lloyd's litigation including Reconstruction and Renewal, in particular the Reinsurance aspects.
Prof. Memberships: Chairman, Solicitors' Indemnity Mutual Insurance Association. Chairman, British Maritime Law Association.
Career: 1984 to date: Senior Partner, *Clyde & Co.*

REGAN, Michael
Rowe & Maw, London (0171) 248 4282
See under Construction & Civil Engineering, p. 200

ROBINSON, David
Pinsent Curtis, London (0171) 418 7000
Specialisation: Main area of practice is professional liability litigation and insurance. Work covers litigation for professional indemnity underwriters including Solicitors Indemnity Fund

for solicitors, barristers, architects, civil and structural engineers and surveyors, insurance brokers and intermediaries. Also handles policy disputes.
Prof. Memberships: International Bar Association, Law Society, Insurance Institute and British Insurance Law Association.
Career: Qualified in 1979 with *Reynolds Porter Chamberlain*. Joined *Pinsent Curtis* (formerly *Pinsent & Co.*) 1982. Became a partner in 1987.
Personal: Born 11 March 1953. Read law at Central London Polytechnic for LLB (Hons). Lives in Chelsea, London. Married with three children. Enjoys fly fishing and shooting.

SCHOFIELD, Belinda
Cameron McKenna, London (0171) 367 3000
Partner in Insurance and Reinsurance Group.
Specialisation: Principal areas of practice are handling professional indemnity claims against accountants, actuaries, Lloyd's agents, financial institutions and insurance brokers and Directors' & Officers' liability acting for insurers and insured. In addition advising on general insurance and reinsurance matters including advising on policy wording construction. Experienced in handling commercial disputes. Speaks at numerous market seminars.
Prof. Memberships: Law Society.
Career: Qualified in 1980 became a partner in *Hewitt Woollacott & Chown* in 1986 which merged with *Cameron Markby* 1989, which merged with *McKenna and Co* in 1997.
Personal: Born 11th June 1956.

SEYMOUR, Michael
Lovell White Durrant, London (0171) 236 0066
See under Litigation (Commercial), p. 521

SMITH, Antony
Beale and Company, London (0171) 240 3474
Partner in Professional Negligence.
Specialisation: Specialises in International and National Construction Dispute Resolution and Litigation. Acted in largest ever claim brought in the Official Referees Division. Regularly defends prosecutions under Health and Safety Law. Writes for Health and Safety at Work Journal. Acts on all types of professional negligence claims including accountants, I.F.A.'s and insurance brokers. Member of O.S.S. panel of solicitors acting on professional negligence actions.
Prof. Memberships: Institution of Occupational Safety and Health; Centre for Dispute Resolution; Law Society; British Insurance Law Association.
Career: Partner with *Beale and Company* since 1985.
Personal: Liverpool University LLB. (Upper Second Class Hons.). Interests include family, football, marathon running and triathlon.

TAYLOR, Paul
Berrymans Lace Mawer, London (0171) 638 2811
Specialisation: Senior Partner and specialist in construction law and professional indemnity. Practice also covers insurance, reinsurance and environmental law. Acts for several major insurers and many professionals, particularly

those involved in the construction industry. Recent cases include a considerable number of international disputes and arbitrations, involving disputes in the Gulf, Southern Africa and the Far East. Currently handling a large number of High Court actions involving construction disputes; these include highways, causeways and/or public buildings (e.g. The British Library). Co-editor of both 'Berryman's Building Claims Cases' and 'Binghams & Berrymans Motor Claims Cases'. Co-author of 'Construction Law and the Environment'. Has written many articles for legal, construction and insurance journals and regularly addresses conferences and seminars both in the UK and abroad. Member of Liability and Insurance Forum of Association of Consulting Engineers, Chairman of a Committee of Institution of Electrical Engineers, member of three FIDIC Committees, and Chairman of one.
Prof. Memberships: International Association of Defence Lawyers; The Society of Construction Law; The Official Referees' Solicitors Association; associate member of FIDIC; liveryman of City Solicitors Company.
Career: Qualified 1969. Joined *Berrymans* 1970, Partner 1973, Senior Partner 1991.
Personal: Educated at King's College, London (LL.B) 1963-66. Leisure pursuits include watching football (Crystal Palace and Wimbledon), photography, chess and three ageing sports cars. Born 25th February 1946. Lives in Tunbridge Wells.

TESTER, Stephen
Cameron McKenna, London (0171) 367 3000
Specialisation: Practises in construction and surveyors' PI, D & O and Contractors All Risk Insurance (both litigation and policy interpretation and drafting). Clients include insurance companies, Lloyds syndicates, insurance brokers and construction companies.
Prof. Memberships: Society of Construction Law.
Career: KCS Wimbledon and St. John's College Cambridge. Qualified 1981. Partner since 1988.
Personal: Interests include family and friends, golf and squash.

THOMAS, Nicholas
Kennedys, London (0171) 638 3688
Senior Partner. Also Partner in associated Northern Ireland practice.
Specialisation: Principal area of expertise is professional indemnity, particularly in the construction field. Acts for architects, surveyors, engineers and contractors, as well as other professionals such as accountants, brokers and authors (defamation). Also covers insurance work generally, including disputes as to whether insurers should respond and which insurers should respond. Acted in 'BBL v. John D. Wood and others', and 'National Trust v. Hayden Young'. Author of 'Professional Indemnity Claims (An Architect's Guide)', published by Architect's Press in 1981. Regularly addresses conferences and seminars, particularly for insurers.
Prof. Memberships: Member of the Law Society, Fellow of the Chartered Institute of Arbitrators. Also qualified as a solicitor in Hong Kong, Northern Ireland and the Republic of Ireland.
Career: Joined *Kennedys* in 1977 and qualified in 1980. Became a Partner in 1981. Became Senior Partner in 1997.

Personal: Born 16th October 1954. Attended Bristol University 1973-76. School Governor. Leisure pursuits include all sports, travel and the arts. Lives near Berkhamsted, Herts.

TROTTER, John
Lovell White Durrant, London
(0171) 236 0066
See under Litigation (Commercial), p. 521

WARD, John J.
Beale and Company, London
(0171) 240 3474
Partner in Construction Department.
Specialisation: Has specialised in construction industry law since 1979, on both UK and overseas projects. Work includes advice on contractual structures, contracts, prevention of disputes, litigation and arbitration, including ICC arbitrations, and professional indemnity work, especially for engineers and surveyors. Also handles health and safety in the construction industry. Work includes advice on duties and obligations under health and safety legislation on systems for compliance and on recent developments (e.g.CDM regulations) as well as defence of prosecutions brought by the Health and Safety Executive against professionals. Advises insurers and brokers on professional indemnity issues, including policy wordings, and specialist applications of professional indemnity policies. Experienced conference speaker and author of articles on a variety of topics.
Prof. Memberships: Law Society, International

Bar Association, International Chamber of Commerce.
Career: Qualified in 1975. Partner with *Beale and Company* since 1977. Now Managing Partner.
Personal: Born 22nd November 1950. Educated at University College, London 1969-72 (LL.B. Hons). Leisure interests include fly fishing, Formula 1 motor racing and football. Lives in Cobham.

WHEATLEY, Vere A.
Cameron McKenna, London
(0171) 702 2345
See under Insurance & Reinsurance: Reinsurance, p. 471

WHITE, Stuart
Hextall Erskine, London (0171) 488 1424
Partner in Insurance Litigation Department.
Specialisation: Main area of practice is professional indemnity, principally construction related, for architects and engineers. Also handles general insurance work, covering insurance disputes, policy wordings and general liability and property litigation. Acted in 'Investors in Industry v. South Bedfordshire D.C.', was involved in 'Crown v. Mowlem' dispute (re final certificates), and was also involved in the personal accident insurance claim following the death of Robert Maxwell. Major clients include insurance companies, mutual insurance associations and Lloyd's syndicates. Has given seminars on a range of topics including architects' liability, product

liability, liability for pollution, drafting of policy wordings, the Housing Grants, Construction and Regeneration Act 1996 and liability of insurers following 'Chapman v. Christopher'. Has addressed the Fire Loss Association of Chartered Loss Adjusters. Regularly contributes to various insurance publications.
Prof. Memberships: Society of Construction Law, British Insurance Law Association, CEDR.
Career: Qualified in 1984. Joined *Hextall Erskine* in 1981, becoming a Partner in 1987.
Personal: Born 1957. Attended The Queen's College Oxford, MA (Hons) 1975-78.

WILSON, Michael G.
Berwin Leighton, London +44 171 760 1000
Specialisation: Professional Indemnity litigation, in particular, claims against domestic and international banks. Direct involvement in many of the leading cases against merchant banks arising as a result of the takeover activity of the late 80s.
Prof. Memberships: Member of the Law Society; City of London Solicitors Company; Asia Pacific Lawyers Association; International Bar Association; Southwestern Legal Foundation; Inter-Pacific Bar Association; Freeman of the City of London; Fellow of the Royal Society of Art.
Career: Articled with *Slaughter and May*; qualified in 1975; Assistant Solicitor 1977-1979; Partner *Berwin Leighton* 1979 to date.
Personal: Golf, tennis, squash, swimming, travel, reading, music.

SOUTH EAST

LEADING FIRMS · SOUTH EAST
BLAKE LAPTHORN Fareham
THOMSON SNELL & PASSMORE Tunbridge Wells
CRIPPS HARRIES HALL Tunbridge Wells

HIGHLY REGARDED FIRMS
Berrymans Lace Mawer Southampton
Donne Mileham & Haddock Brighton
Lightfoots Thame
Merricks Chelmsford

Blake Lapthorn (4ptnrs/6assts) The "outstanding" *David Higham* leads a team which may be developing an edge over the competition. **Clients/Work:** Defendant: solicitors, barristers. Barclays Bank v Dean Wilson and others.

Thomson Snell & Passmore (6ptnrs/4assts) *Trevor May's* team is widely admired.

A firm with a "methodical" and "professional" approach. **Clients/Work:** Defendant:solicitors, accountants, contractors, insurance brokers, architects, engineers, surveyors.

Cripps Harries Hall (5ptnrs, including *Charles Broadie*/14fee-earners) Regarded as "professional and proactive," a firm which "has gained great expertise" since being appointed to the Solicitors' Indemnity Fund in 1994.**Clients/Work:** Defendant: solicitors. Also accountants, architects and surveyors.

Donne Mileham & Haddock (5ptnrs/4assts) Part of an impressive commercial litigation group which includes professional negligence. **Clients/Work:** Plaintiff: Handles negligence actions on behalf of building societies Kent Reliance and Portman; six figure claims against solicitors; against accountants for a seven figure sum in respect of the collapse of a plc in the leisure industry.

Berrymans Lace Mawer (2ptnrs/2assts who also deal with other matters). **Clients/**

Work: Defendant: accountants, surveyors, valuers, engineers.

Lightfoots (2ptnrs/2assts) The "excellent" *Neil Summerfield* leads the team in this small niche practice. **Clients/Work:** Plaintiff: bulk claims for lending institutions and some individuals against surveyors and solicitors.

Merricks (4ptnrs/4assts) Felt by some to have a "hard ball approach," the "very good" *Anthony Sheppard* leads the team. **Clients/Work:** Defendant: solicitors, construction professionals.

LEADING INDIVIDUALS SOUTH EAST
HIGHAM David Blake Lapthorn
BROADIE Charles Cripps Harries Hall
MAY Trevor Thomson Snell & Passmore
SUMMERFIELD Neil Lightfoots
SHEPPARD Anthony Merricks

SEE PROFILES AT END OF THIS SECTION

SOUTH WEST

Bond Pearce (5ptnrs/1asst between two offices) Well respected by fellow practitioners and clients alike as "outstanding in the regions." *Erik Salomonsen* "top drawer" was recommended as was *Richard Challands.* **Clients/Work:** Defendant: solicitors, surveyors, valuers, architects, engineers, accountants, financial services. Act for SIF and a number of professional indemnity insurers including mutual funds, Lloyds syndicates, major composites and large self-insureds.

Wansbroughs Willey Hargrave, (5ptnrs/15assts) Still the leader in the South West for its high profile and quantity of SIF work. *Paul Redfern* and *Paul Rowe,* both "representative of quality at partner level" head the large department dedicated to professional indemnity work. 50% of the office's fee income is derived from this work. **Clients/Work:** Defendant: accountancy, legal and property-related professions, also med-

ical, education, media, computer, banking and finance, facilities management and environmental consultants. Act for 110 insurance companies, Lloyds syndicates and self-insureds.

Cameron McKenna (2ptnrs/5assts) Known primarily for its strong ties with the London market, the firm received praise from clients for its approachability and quality. *Jeremy Barnes* was highly recommended. Act for Lloyds Bank and insurers. **Clients/Work:** Defendant: surveyors, accountants, brokers, bankers, architects. Plaintiff: Claims by building societies.

S J Cornish (2ptnrs/2assts) A "small but tenacious" firm which, thanks to the reputation of the "tough" *Sarah Cornish* has become a successful and reputable niche practice in the unlikely location of Tiverton. **Clients/Work:** Defendant: architects, surveyors, accountants, insurance brokers, financial services advisers. 75% of the firm's work is professional indemnity.

Veale Wasbrough (2ptnrs/5assts as part of a general litigation department). Reputation for construction professional indemnity work for engineers. **Clients/Work:** Plaintiff: act for lending institutions, including Bristol & West and Lloyds Bank. Defendant: engineers, surveyors, valuers.

Burges Salmon (4ptnrs/3assts) An "eminent" and "able" firm. **Clients/Work:** Plaintiff: bulk claims for lending institutions. Clients include: Nationwide Building Society, Royal Sun Alliance, General Accident, Savills, Bar Mutual.

Cartwrights (2ptnrs/1asst) Unusual in acting for both plaintiff and defendant clients. **Clients/Work:** Plaintiff: act for individuals against medical and legal professionals. Defendant: instructed by several composite insurers.

Eversheds (1ptnr/4assts) A lower profile than the Cardiff office for professional negligence (the team here is part of the banking dept) but nevertheless merits a place in our list. **Clients/Work:** Plaintiff: act for lending institutions, mainly against solicitors and accountants. Act for Bank of Ireland, Bristol & West plc, and Legal & General.

Hancock & Lawrence (2ptnrs/2assts dealing with professional negligence as part of a civil litigation team) Have the lion's share of professional indemnity work in Cornwall. **Clients/Work:** Defendant: solicitors, surveyors, accountants.

Lester Aldridge (2ptnrs/2assts) A small but reputable professional indemnity team which has expanded rapidly in the last year. **Clients/Work:** Defendant: accountants, surveyors, architects. Also marine surveyors and mutuals.

Osborne Clarke (1ptnr/3assocs) A new entry to the list this year with an increasing presence in lenders' claims, including involvement with the Bristol and West litigation. **Clients/Work:** Plaintiff: act for lending institutions against solicitors and valuers

Ringrose Wharton & Co (1ptnr/4assts) An "active and effective" niche firm specialising in bulk claims on pensions misselling. **Clients/Work:** Act for financial services advisers. Specialises in acting for and against the life and pensions industry.

WALES

Hugh James (5ptnrs) Promoted in our tables this year following unanimous praise for these "excellent litigators." *Michael Jefferies* is well known. Other members of the team will also act against professionals (esp. solicitors). **Clients/Work:** Plaintiff: Claim for

£2m against an accountant involving complex legal issues about the scope of an auditor's duties; claim for £2m against an accountant in respect of a modern office development;

Morgan Bruce (3ptnrs/5assts) Prominent for the quantity of SIF related work, the team is led by *Richard Hale* and includes *Hugh Price.* **Clients/Work:** Defendant: solicitors, architects, surveyors, accountants.

Eversheds (2ptnrs/7assts) Professional negligence work is handled as part of the general commercial litigation practice acting for lenders. **Clients/Work:** Plaintiff:mainly for lending institutions against solicitors, surveyors, accountants.

Dolmans (5ptnrs/2assts) *Jeffrey MacWilkinson* was recommended again this year for his work against property profes-

sionals. **Clients/Work:** Plaintiff and Defendant: surveyors, accountants, architects, engineers.

Palser Grossman (1ptnr/1const/1asst) Liked by clients for their "sensible and practical approach," *George Grossman* is now working as a consultant. **Clients/Work:** Plaintiff and Defendant: architects, surveyors, solicitors.

MIDLANDS

Browne Jacobson (4ptnrs/7assts) Joint leaders in the Midlands for another year. *Robert Ridgwell* heads the team which is reported to be "great for straightforward cases." Professional indemnity litigation accounts for 14.5% of the firm's total turnover. *Derek Bambury* is also a leader. Clients/Work: Defendant: solicitors,surveyors,accountants,architects, IT consultants, financial advisers.

Pinsent Curtis (5ptnrs/15assts) The "innovative" *Andrew Long* leads a large team

(including *Andrew Paton* - recommended for his use of mediation) which received unanimous praise from practitioners and clients alike. Clients/Work: Defendant: indlude SIF P&U, Rodney Stone Syndicate. workmediated settlement of £10m multiparty claim against solicitor; Cancer Research Fund & Ernest Brown& Co. Defeat of claim by charities alleging duties of care owed to them by solicitor.

Wansbroughs Willey Hargrave (4ptnrs:1 p/t/10assts) Mixed reviews but currently handling over 20 professional negligence claims in excess of £1m. Are panel solicitors for SIF. *Paul Murray* remains a leading light. Clients/Work: Defendant: Cover all traditional professions including solicitors, accountants, architects and surveyors.

Wragge & Co. (3ptnrs/12assts) Specialising in construction, the team (including *Mark Hick*) contains several dual qualified lawyers. Clients/Work: Defendant: construction professionals, accountants, financial advisors.

Dibb Lupton Alsop (1ptnr/1asst) Act for both insurers and professionals. Clients/Work: Defendant: Wide variety of professionals including surveyors, insurance brokers and architects.

Shakespeares (2ptnrs/2assts) *Diana Wareing* leads the small team which aims to offer a more personal service to insurer clients. Clients/Work: Defendant: accountants, brokers, surveyors, architects

THM Tinsdills (4ptnrs/5assts) Following its appointment to the SIF panel the firm has developed a specialised unit. Clients/Work: Defendant: solicitors, construction.

Wright Hassall & Co (5ptnrs/2assts) A well-respected team headed by *Robert McKechnie*, "a force to be reckoned with." Clients/Work: Defendant: Act for all professions except solicitors.

EAST ANGLIA

Mills & Reeve (5-6ptnrs/11assts) Still preeminent, this "pragmatic and high quality"

firm now deals with professional negligence out of two offices. *Guy Hodgson*, "a good technician and tactician" is based in Norwich. Clients/Work: Defendant: all professions, including solicitors.

Eversheds (2ptnrs/2assts who also do "other commercial work") Clients/Work: Plaintiff: act against solicitors, accountants, surveyors. Work in 1997 included a substantial action against two firms of solicitors which settled before trial for in excess of £250,000.

Prettys (3ptnrs/2assts form the civil litigation unit) The firm deals with professional indemnity as part of its general litigation practice. Clients/Work: Defendant: consulting engineers, surveyors, architects, brokers.

NORTH EAST

Wansbroughs Willey Hargrave (4ptnrs/ 12fee-earners – SIF; 2ptnrs/3 fee-earners – other professional negligence) One of the most highly rated of all Wansbroughs'

offices and "top for both quality and volume." *Glenn Miller* heads the large team which includes the "very competent" *Roger Parr*, a new entry this year. Clients/Work: Defendant: solicitors, accountants, construction professionals. Handle approximately 40% of all General Accident's professional indemnity instructions.

Crutes (5ptnrs/3assts who also do a small amount of other work) Malcolm Gregor is now working as a consultant but *John Parker* is a new addition to our tables. Clients/Work: Defendant: solicitors, accountants, surveyors.

Irwin Mitchell (2ptnrs/8assts form part of a larger team, some of whom may also be involved) Viewed as a leading "heavyweight" firm by some, and by others as a "tough opponent" who do well by their clients. The firm has risen in our tables this year due to its increasing presence. *Peter*

Wylde is a leader. Clients/Work: Plaintiff: act against solicitors, accountants, financial advisors, structural engineers. Instructed by a quoted plc in a claim against solicitors following the (reported) striking out of a claim valued at over £1m; a £6.5m claim against a solicitor/director of an international commodities trading company.

Dibb Lupton Alsop (1ptnr/4assts) Promoted in our tables this year following praise for this "up and coming" and "efficient" practice. *David Simon* was again recommended. Clients/Work: Defendant: construction professionals, insurance brokers, accountants, media and computer professionals.

Walker Morris (3ptnrs/4assts) Well perceived. Currently investing heavily in new technology, including Intranet facilities, the firm is seeking to increase its profile. Clients/ Work: Plaintiff: act for lending institutions against solicitors, surveyors, accountants.

Addleshaw Booth & Co. (6ptnrs/7fee-earners about 50% of the time) Not perceived as a major presence in the field, although *Roger Ibbotson* is rated. **Clients/Work:** Plaintiff: act against solicitors, accountants, valuers.

Eversheds (2ptnrs/3assts) A new entry to our list this year following their merger with Wilkinson Maughan. It is still too early to say how much of a market share the restructured practice will be able to capture. **Clients/Work:** Defendant: surveyors, engineers, estate agents, accountants, insurance brokers.

Hammond Suddards (Plaintiff: 3 ptnrs/10 fee earners. Def:1 ptnr) Not a major

presence, the practice is best known for *Edward Coulson*, a "good, solid individual" who does defendant work. Make extensive use of ADR. **Clients/Work:** Act for 10 leading lending institutions against solicitors and property professionals, and a number of institutional clients suing solicitors in connection with shared ownership schemes. For defendants, act for Lloyd's syndicates, composite and mutual insurers.

Hay & Kilner (6ptnrs/3assts as part of the insurance and commercial litigation practice) A well-regarded firm rated primarily for its general litigation practice. *Peter Pescod* is recommended. **Clients/Work:** Plaintiff: act

against solicitors, accountants, valuers. Defendant:accountants, insurance brokers.

LEADING INDIVIDUALS NORTH EAST	
COULSON Edward Hammond Suddards	
IBBOTSON Roger Addleshaw Booth & Co	
MILLER Glenn Wansbroughs Willey Hargrave	
PARKER John Crutes	
PARR Roger Wansbroughs Willey Hargrave	
PESCOD Peter Hay & Kilner	
SIMON David Dibb Lupton Alsop	
WYLDE Peter Irwin Mitchell	

NORTH WEST

LEADING FIRMS · NORTH WEST
JAMES CHAPMAN & CO Manchester
WEIGHTMANS Liverpool

HIGHLY REGARDED FIRMS
Halliwell Landau Manchester
Hill Dickinson Liverpool
Keogh Ritson Bolton
Elliott & Company Manchester

James Chapman & Co (8ptnrs/7assts) Still top ranked for the quantity of SIF work handled by the firm. *John McKenna* is well regarded and *Elisabeth Taylor* received individual praise for her "depth of expertise" and "professional" approach. **Clients/Work:** Defendant: solicitors, architects, surveyors, accountants.

Weightmans (9ptnrs/7assts) Have two

ranked individuals, *Patrick Gaul* and *Frank Maher*. **Clients/Work:** Defendant: solicitors, architects, bankers, surveyors.

Dibb Lupton Alsop (1ptnr/3assts) Involvement in multi-million pound claims and "aggressive marketing" have raised the profile of the firm and as a consequence, its place in our tables. **Clients/Work:** Defendant: architects, surveyors, engineers.

Halliwell Landau (2ptnrs/2assts forming part of the commercial litigation department) A practice beginning to "make a mark" in this field and entering our tables for the first time. **Clients/Work:** Plaintiff: act for lending institutions against solicitors, surveyors, valuers.

Hill Dickinson (8ptnrs/7assts) Regarded as strongest in shipping and general insurance. **Clients/Work:** Defendant: architects, consulting engineers, insurance brokers, veterinary profession, surveyors, advertising agencies, recruitment consultants, manage-

ment consultants, accountants, alternative medicine.

Keogh Ritson (4ptnrs plus several assistants forming part of the insurance department) A practice which received unanimously favourable comments from fellow practitioners. **Clients/Work:** Defendant: insurance brokers, surveyors, engineers, accountants.

Elliott & Co. (2ptnrs/5assts) Perceived as having a lower profile than in the past. **Clients/Work:** Defendant: surveyors, architects, engineers, accountants, insurance brokers, pension advisers, licenced conveyancers.

LEADING INDIVIDUALS NORTH WEST	
MCKENNA John James Chapman & Co	
GAUL Patrick Weightmans	
MAHER Frank Weightmans	
TAYLOR Elisabeth James Chapman & Co	

SCOTLAND

LEADING FIRMS · SCOTLAND
DUNDAS & WILSON CS Edinburgh
SIMPSON & MARWICK WS Edinburgh

HIGHLY REGARDED FIRMS
Balfour & Manson Edinburgh
Biggart Baillie Glasgow
Bishop and Robertson Chalmers Glasgow
Brodies WS Edinburgh
Brechin Tindal Oatts Glasgow
MacRoberts Glasgow
Shepherd & Wedderburn WS Edinburgh

Dundas & Wilson CS (2ptnrs/5 fee-earners) Still joint leaders of the pack, although it remains to be seen whether their market share will be adversely affected by the firm's new connection with Arthur Andersen. *Colin MacLeod* was recommended again this year. The widely respected *Neil Cochran* is already perceived as more involved in admin-

istration these days. **Clients/Work:** Defender: solicitors, barristers, surveyors, accountants, insurance brokers.

Simpson & Marwick WS (3ptnrs/6assts) A substantial team led by *Peter Anderson* which continues to receive praise from both clients and fellow practitioners. *Andrew Renton* was also recommended. **Clients/Work:** Defender: solicitors, surveyors, architects, accountants.

Balfour & Manson (4ptnrs as part of the general litigation department) **Clients/Work:** Defender: solicitors, architects, accountants.

Biggart Baillie (1ptnr/1asst) Partner *James Roxborough* has a good reputation. **Clients/Work:** Defender: solicitors and advocates.

Bishop and Robertson Chalmers (2ptnrs/2assts) The team, headed by *John Welsh*, "a serious operator," handles professional negligence claims as part of its construction practice. **Clients/Work:** Defender: engineers, architects.

Brodies WS (2ptnrs/2assts) Better known for its presence in personal injury and medical negligence, the firm also deals with

claims in this field. *David Williamson* continues to enjoy a good reputation. **Clients/Work:** Pursuer and Defender: Including solicitors, surveyors, architects and accountants.

Brechin Tindal Oatts (2ptnrs/2assts as part of the litigation practice) *Derek Allan* heads the team, which has risen in our tables following favourable comments. **Clients/Work:** Defender: predominantly solicitors; some accountants; some surveyors and design consultants.

LEADING INDIVIDUALS SCOTLAND	
ANDERSON Peter Simpson & Marwick WS	
WELSH John Bishop and Robertson Chalmers	
COCHRAN Neil Dundas & Wilson CS	
MACLEOD Colin Dundas & Wilson CS	
ROXBURGH James Biggart Baillie	
ALLAN Derek John Brechin Tindal Oatts	
RENTON Andrew Simpson & Marwick WS	
WILLIAMSON David Brodies WS	

MacRoberts (8ptnrs/3assts as part of the construction department) Professional negligence work is an offshoot of the firm's strong construction practice. **Clients/Work:** Plaintiff and Defendant: architects, surveyors,

patent work.

Shepherd & Wedderburn WS (2ptnrs/1assts) **Clients/Work:** Defender: Instructed by insurers of a firm of surveyors in three linked claims by a lending institution;

Instructed by insurers of Senior Counsel to defend allegations of negligence against him; Instructed by a major lending institution to pursue a series of claims against a firm of valuers and solicitors.

NORTHERN IRELAND

McKinty & Wright (4ptnrs/8assts who also work in other areas of litigation) Still the

leading professional negligence firm in the province, both for quality and volume. Clients confirmed they were happy with the practice. *Owen Catchpole* has "wide experience." **Clients/Work:** Defendant: all professionals, including a large number of solicitors.

Carson & McDowell (2ptnrs/2assts who also do other commercial litigation work) As SIF panel solicitors the team led by *Brian Turtle* received favourable comment from fellow practitioners. **Clients/Work:** Defendant: solicitors.

C & H Jefferson (4ptnrs) **Clients/Work:** Defendant: solicitors/barristers, accountants, consulting engineers, architects,

surveyors/valuers, insurance brokers.

Cleaver Fulton & Rankin Better known for plaintiff work, the firm is generally well-regarded.

Tughan & Co (2ptnrs/2assts as part of the insurance practice) **Clients/Work:** Plaintiff and Defendant: construction professionals.

LEADERS' PROFILES · REGIONS

ALLAN, Derek John
Brechin Tindal Oatts, Glasgow
(0141) 221 8012
Specialisation: Litigator with particular emphasis in the field of professional negligence acting on behalf of insurance companies in professional indemnity claims.
Prof. Memberships: The Law Society of Scotland. The Scottish Law Agents Society.
Career: Joined *Brechin Robb* as apprentice in 1978. Partner since 1984.
Personal: Golf, Tennis, Walking. Married with two sons.

ANDERSON, Peter
Simpson & Marwick WS, Edinburgh
(0131) 557 1545

BAMBURY, Derek R.
Browne Jacobson, Nottingham
(0115) 950 0055
Specialisation: Accountants and solicitors professional indemnity. Reported cases: County Natwest v. Pinsents, 1994 3 Bank LR, 4. Highlights of the last 12 months: £2.8m claim against accountants arising from corporate finance transaction; £2m claim against accountant in relation to investment of pension fund; £1.9 claim against accountant in relation to Account's Reports on a solicitors practice; £1m claim against solicitors arising from company acquisition.
Prof. Memberships: Member of ICAEW Members Friends Support Panel; Member of Chartered Institute of Insurance.
Career: LLB (King's College London), Admitted 1981 *Browne Jacobson*, Partner 1987 *Browne Jacobson*.
Personal: Sport (football, cricket, golf, racing). Married (Jennie) two children.

BARNES, Jeremy
Cameron McKenna, Bristol (0117) 930 0200
Specialisation: Partner dealing with Insurance and Reinsurance matters with emphasis on

Defendant Professional Indemnity work. Extensive experience with financial services claims (including Pensions misselling), accountants, brokers, architects and engineers.
Career: Qualified 1989. Partner 1995.
Personal: Born 1964. Married with 3 children.

BROADIE, Charles
Cripps Harries Hall, Tunbridge Wells, Kent (01892) 506160
Specialisation: Heads the team that carries out work for the Solicitors Indemnity Fund. Extensive experience in professional indemnity work.
Prof. Memberships: Member of Law Society and local Law Society. Member of the Legal Aid Area Committee in Brighton.
Career: Education: Bradfield College; Sidney Sussex College, Cambridge University (1966 BA – now MA, 1968 LLB – now LLM); Universite de Nancy, France. Articled *Field Roscoe*, London; Qualified 1969; *Hedleys*, London 1970-1972; Secretariat of the European Commission of Human Rights, Strasbourg 1972-1974; Assistant solicitor *Cripps Harries Hall*, Tunbridge Wells, 1974-1976; Partner from 1976.
Personal: Reading, foreign languages, walking, local church.

CATCHPOLE, Owen
McKinty & Wright, Belfast (01232) 246751
See under Construction, Defamation and Litigation (Commercial), p. 210, 283, 536

CHALLANDS, Richard
Bond Pearce, Plymouth (01752) 266 633
Partner in the Insurance Group.
Specialisation: Specialises in professional indemnity and insurance litigation. Handles work on behalf of accountants, brokers, solicitors, barristers and engineers. Also deals with policy and coverage disputes and has wide experience of claims involving fraud.
Prof. Memberships: Member of the International Bar Association Insurance Group

and the British Insurance Law Association.
Career: Qualified 1975. Joined *Bond Pearce* in 1973, becoming partner 1980.

COCHRAN, Neil
Dundas & Wilson CS, Edinburgh
(0131) 228 8000
Specialisation: Built-up extensive practice in litigation matters for insurance companies in the commercial field covering all matters relating to breach of contract, property claims and produce liability. Developed a practice handling litigation and contentious matters for the principal clients of the Firm. Acts for insurance companies in professional indemnity cases for solicitors, accountants, engineers, surveyors, and also in fire and personal injury claims.
Prof. Memberships: Member British Insurance Law Association.
Career: Attended University of Edinburgh (LLB). Articled *Lindsays WS*; qualified 1972; Partner *Robert White & Co* 1974; Partner *Bonar Mackenzie* 1977; Partner *Dundas & Wilson CS* since 1984; appointed Chairman at *Dundas & Wilson* 1996.
Personal: Born 1948; married; two children. Resides North Berwick. Leisure interests include golf. Has also been recommended as a Leader in the Field of Personal Injury: Mainly Defendant and Litigation (Commercial).

CORNISH, Sarah
S J Cornish, Tiverton (01884) 243377
Founding partner of niche litigation firm.
Specialisation: Specialises in professional indemnity and insurance litigation defending claims against a wide range of professionals including accountants, architects, brokers, engineers and surveyors. Also acts for insurers in insurance litigation and policy coverage disputes.
Career: Qualified in 1982 with *Hewitt Woolacott & Chown*. Left *Bond Pearce* where a partner in 1991 to set up own practice.

COULSON, Edward
Hammond Suddards, Leeds
(0113) 284 7000
Specialisation: Acting for insurers professional negligence claims against accountants, architects and consulting engineers, licensed conveyancers, insurance brokers and others and insurance related disputes.
Career: Bryanston School 1968-72. St John's College, Cambridge 1973-76.
Personal: Literature, gardening, walking.

GAUL, Patrick
Weightmans, Liverpool (0151) 227 2601
Specialisation: Professional negligence, solicitors and doctors in particular. Regularly lectures on variety of topics in civil litigation, especially medical negligence. Very substantial civil practice.
Prof. Memberships: Law Society.
Career: Oxford University BA Jurisprudence.

GROSSMAN, George
Palser Grossman, Cardiff Bay
(01222) 452770
Specialisation: Defendant insurance litigation, predominently professional negligence claims against accountants, surveyors and architects; also commercial and construction litigation.
Career: Cardiff High School; University College, London (LLB Hons.) University of Poiters (Diploma in French Studies); Deputy District Judge; Past President Cardiff Law Society; past Chairman South Wales Area Committee of C.A.B.
Personal: Resides Cardiff. Music, charities for the blind, tennis.

HALE, Richard
Morgan Bruce, Cardiff (01222) 385385
Partner in Professional Indemnity Department. Particular emphasis on claims against solicitors arising out of non-contentious practice.
Career: Qualified in 1971. Joined *Morgan Bruce* in 1969, becoming a Partner in 1974.
Personal: Born 19th July 1947. Attended University College London 1965-68. Lives in Cardiff.

HICK, Mark
Wragge & Co, Birmingham (0121) 233 1000
Specialisation: Leads Professional Indemnity Team. Defends cases against Accountants, Surveyors, Actuaries and many other professionals. Cases includes £100 million claim arising from construction of factory, £15 million insurance brokers professional indemnity claim; acting in £10 million venture capitalists professional indemnity claim.
Prof. Memberships: The Chartered Insurance Institute. The British Insurance Law Association. The Liabilities Society.
Career: Called to the Bar 1979. Admitted as Solicitor 1985. Partner at *Wragge & Co* from 1991.
Personal: Born 1957.

HIGHAM, David
Blake Lapthorn, Fareham (01489) 579990
Specialisation: Head of Civil Litigation at *Blake Lapthorn. Blake Lapthorn* Civil Litigation Department comprises 37 lawyers in London and Hampshire. Personal specialisation is professional negligence particularly lawyers and surveyors. Has particular expertise in cases involving professional fraud and professional conduct issues for solicitors. Lectures on claims handling and claims avoidance. Recent leading cases include Barclays Bank v. Dean Wilson CA 1998.
Career: First career as submarine officer in the Royal Navy. Joined *Blake Lapthorn* as Articled Clerk in 1976, qualifying in 1979. Partner in 1980. Appointed head of Civil Litigation in 1991. LLM in Advanced Litigation at Nottingham Trent University 1996.

HODGSON, Guy
Mills & Reeve, Norwich +44 (0)1603 660155
Specialisation: Partner and head of the firm's insurance group of 35 lawyers covering professional indemnity, general liability and health risks. Specialises in professional indemnity risks for insurers, mutual funds and professional firms. Acts for all professions dealing with claims brought against them and any related insurance issues. Joined *Mills & Reeve* to develop their professional indemnity practice after gaining a number of years experience working in the London market. Regular speaker on professional indemnity matters.
Prof. Memberships: British Insurance Law Association. IBA. Law Society.

IBBOTSON, Roger
Addleshaw Booth & Co, Leeds
(0113) 209 2000
Partner in the Litigation and Dispute Resolution Group.
Specialisation: Since qualification has practised exclusively in the field of litigation specialising in professional negligence and personal injury cases.
Prof. Memberships: Member of the Committee of Leeds Law Society. President Leeds Law Society 1996/97. Member of the Law Society Council 1998.
Career: University of Manchester 1963; qualified with *Burton & Burton*, Leeds 1966; joined Booth & Co 1966: partner 1970.
Personal: Trustee Spooner Charitable Trust and Leeds Girls High School Trust.

JEFFERIES, Michael
Hugh James, Cardiff (01222) 224871
See under Construction & Civil Engineering, Litigation (commercial), p. 212, 525

LONG, Andrew P.
Pinsent Curtis, Birmingham (0121) 200 1050
Partner in Insurance Litigation and Head of Financial Services Litigation.
Specialisation: Professional indemnity defendant work, specialising in acting for solicitors and for the financial services industry. Author, speaker and leading expert on pension mis-selling claims. Acts for mutuals, Lloyd's Underwriters, insurers and the financial services industry.
Career: Qualified in 1980, National Coal Board 1981-1986. Joined *Pinsent & Co.* in 1986 becoming a Partner in 1989.
Personal: Born 1955. Educated at Exeter School and Pembroke College, Oxford. Interests include bridge, family and village sport.

MACLEOD, Colin
Dundas & Wilson CS, Edinburgh
(0131) 228 8000
Specialisation: Partner in Insurance Litigation Group; main areas of practice are professional negligence, acting for insurers in claims against various professionals and commercial litigation, particularly banking related litigation. Recent cases include Sharp v Thomson; Retail Parks Investments v Royal Bank; Beneficial Bank v McConnachie and Style Financial Services Ltd v Bank of Scotland.
Prof. Memberships: Member of the Law Society of Scotland.
Career: Attended University of Edinburgh (LLB (Hons)). Articled *Dundas & Wilson CS* 1977-1979; qualified 1979; Partner since 1983.
Personal: Born 1955. Resides Edinburgh. Leisure interests include travel, sport and family. Has also been recommended as a Leader in the Field of Litigation (Commercial).

MACWILKINSON, Jeffrey
Dolmans, Cardiff (01222) 345531
Partner in Litigation Department.
Specialisation: Senior litigation Partner specialising in personal injury and professional negligence. Handles both plaintiff and defendant work in relation to professional negligence. Remaining litigation work is defendant based which includes employers liability, building cases, and civil actions against the police. Major clients include various insurance companies and local authorities as well as Police authorities.
Prof. Memberships: Law Society, Chartered Institute of Arbitrators, FOIL.
Career: Qualified in 1966. Partner with *Dolmans* since 1972. Deputy District Judge since 1991.

MAHER, Frank
Weightmans, Liverpool (0151) 227 2601
Specialisation: Professional Indemnity primarily for solicitors, but also accountants, bankers, engineers, surveyors, valuers. Numerous major fraud investigations, financial services claims, construction litigation and policy wording disputes. Acting for solicitors in 'Alford v West Bromwich Building Society' and others. Home income scheme group action.
Prof. Memberships: Law Society – past involvement nationally and locally. Former Chairman of National Committee of Young Solicitors Group, member of civil litigation, council membership and professional and public relations committees of the Law Society and general committee of Liverpool Law Society. Joint working partner of the Bar Council and Law Society on the Civil courts – sub committee chairman.
Career: Liverpool University LLB. Educational Foundation Prize.

MAY, Trevor N.
Thomson Snell & Passmore, Tunbridge Wells
(01892) 510000
Partner and head of Professional Indemnity/Professional Negligence Department.
Specialisation: Deals exclusively with professional indemnity and professional negligence claims. Special Areas of Expertise are solicitors, accountants, surveyors and engineers.
Career: Joined *Thomson Snell & Passmore* on qualification and became a partner in 1972. Past President Tunbridge Wells, Tonbridge and District Law Society, Part-time Chairman of

Industrial Tribunal, Chairman of Monitoring Panel for Law Society Trainees.
Personal: Born 8/11/1945. Recreations include history, reading, the theatre, and walking.

MCKECHNIE, Robert
Wright Hassall & Co, Leamington Spa (01926) 886688

MCKENNA, John
James Chapman & Co, Manchester (0161) 828 8000
Specialisation: Professional Indemnity cases on behalf of Insurers and Indemnifiers.
Prof. Memberships: The Law Society and The Manchester Law Society.
Career: Admitted – January 1966. Senior Partner – 1976 to date.

MILLER, Glenn
Wansbroughs Willey Hargrave, Leeds (0113) 244 1151
Partner in Insurance Litigation Department.
Specialisation: Experienced in handling general insurance and reinsurance disputes, and policy coverage issues. Head of the firm's Specialised Loss Unit, which investigates and advises on arson, fraud and theft. Also advises accountants, intermediaries and solicitors on professional negligence matters relating to corporate transactions.
Career: 1981 *Clifford Chance*. Qualified 1983. Joined *Wansbroughs Willey Hargrave* 1989. Became Partner in 1993.

MURRAY, Paul C.
Wansbroughs Willey Hargrave, Birmingham (0121) 631 4099
Partner in Professional Indemnity and Insurance Department.
Specialisation: Handles all aspects of professional negligence work, acting for solicitors, estate agents, surveyors, accountants, IFAs, venture capitalists and architects. He is also experienced in advising on general liability matters, particularly policy and coverage disputes.
Career: Qualified 1980. Joined *WWH* 1981. Became Partner in 1986.

PARKER, John C.
Crutes, Newcastle-upon-Tyne (0191) 281 5811

PARR, M. Roger
Wansbroughs Willey Hargrave, Leeds (0113) 244 1151
Specialisation: Since 1978, Roger has handled professional indemnity, defective title and restrictive covenant claims exclusively. He acts on behalf of solicitors, architects, accountants, and surveyors, and handles construction-related claims. He also has experience of intellectual property and partnership disputes.
Career: 1971 Qualified. 1970 Joined *WWH*, Leeds.

PATON, Andrew J.
Pinsent Curtis, Birmingham (0121) 200 1050
See under Alternative Dispute Resolution, p. 113

PESCOD, Peter
Hay & Kilner, Newcastle-upon-Tyne (0191) 232 8345
Partner in Litigation Department.
Specialisation: Main area of practice is

personal injury, acting primarily for major insurers in all types of accident/ disease claims. Also acts for health service bodies in defence of medical negligence claims. Handles professional negligence work relating to surveyors, accountants, insurance brokers and architects. Has lectured on medical negligence and special damages.
Prof. Memberships: Law Society, Personal Injury Panel, FOIL (Forum of Insurance Lawyers), FHS Appeals Authority, Deputy District Judge.
Career: Joined *Hay-Kilner* in 1973. Qualified in 1975 and became a Partner in 1976.
Personal: Born 29th June 1951. Educated at Queen Elizabeth Grammar, Darlington 1962-69 and Newcastle University 1969-72. Leisure pursuits include history, politics, landscape gardening, architecture and auction sales. Lives in Ovington.

PRICE, Hugh
Morgan Bruce, Cardiff (01222) 385385
Partner and Head of Insurance Department.
Specialisation: Main areas of practice are professional negligence and personal injury for insurance clients. Has handled many maximum severity claims including quadriplegic and serious head injury. Professional negligence work for solicitors, brokers, engineers, surveyors and accountants. Author of article on Structured Settlements; regularly lectures on Woolf changes and to RICS on adequacy of professional indemnity cover. Trained ADR mediator.
Prof. Memberships: President of Cardiff Law Society 1998-99; member of Personal Injury Panel and FOIL.
Career: Articled at *Hardwickes* (now *Morgan Bruce*) and qualified in 1975; partner in 1978. Deputy District Judge 1988-97.

REDFERN, Paul W.L.
Wansbroughs Willey Hargrave, Bristol (0117) 926 8981
Partner in Professional Indemnity and Insurance Department.
Specialisation: Principal area of practice is professional indemnity, acting for a wide range of professions including surveyors, architects, accountants, brokers, financial intermediaries and developing schemes with insurers and brokers for the "new" professions. Acted for E&O underwriters in the Lloyd's litigation. Also acts for insurers in insurance litigation and policy coverage disputes. Recently set up a scheme covering defamation, negligence and other risks for members of the Periodical Publishers Association and a negligence scheme for members of the British Institute of Facilities Management.
Career: Qualified in 1978, having joined *Wansbroughs Willey Hargrave* in 1976. Became a Partner in 1981.

RENTON, Andrew L.
Simpson & Marwick WS, Edinburgh (0131) 557 1545

RIDGWELL, Robert
Browne Jacobson, Nottingham (0115) 950 0055
Specialisation: Defendant Professional Indemnity work, particularly on behalf of surveyors, financial/insurance intermediaries and solicitors. Has particular expertise in advising Underwriters on coverage issues.

Prof. Memberships: ACI Arb.
Career: Educated at Lincoln School and Queens College, Cambridge. Joined *Browne Jacobson* 1980. Specialising in defendant Professional Indemnity work since 1986. Partner since 1984.
Personal: Church warden. Married, with teenage family.

ROWE, Paul N.C.
Wansbroughs Willey Hargrave, Bristol (0117) 926 8981
Partner and Head of Professional Indemnity Litigation Department in Bristol.
Specialisation: Main area of practice is professional negligence. Handles claims for all professions including solicitors, surveyors, accountants, architects, financial intermediaries and insurance brokers.
Career: Qualified in 1970. Joined *Wansbroughs Willey Hargrave* in 1971, becoming a Partner in 1976.

ROXBURGH, James A.R.
Biggart Baillie, Glasgow (0141) 228 8000
See under Personal Injury: Mainly Defendant, p. 637

SALOMONSEN, V. Erik
Bond Pearce, Exeter (01392) 211 185
Partner and Head of the Insurance Group.
Specialisation: Specialises in professional indemnity, defending claims against a wide range of professionals, including medical professionals. Work includes wide range of employers and public liability claims including work in the farming industry and for local authority and health trusts. Undertakes defence of environmental claims and prosecutions, frequently as advocate. Panel solicitor for mutual funds, Composites and Lloyds underwriters. Lectures on all aspects of insurance and liability issues at conferences and seminars and has given a number of radio and television interviews on related topics.
Prof. Memberships: An accredited mediator, a member of the British Insurance Law Association and the International Bar Association, immediate past President of the Plymouth Medico-Legal Society.
Career: Qualified in 1975. Joined *Bond Pearce* in 1975, becoming a partner 1979.

SHEPPARD, Anthony
Merricks, Chelmsford (01245) 491414
Specialisation: Professional Indemnity including solicitors (on SIF panel) and construction related litigation.
Prof. Memberships: Law Society. Institute of Arbitrators. Society of Construction Law. Official Referees Solicitors Association.
Career: Southampton University Law Degree. Qualified April 1976. Articled at *Richards Butler*, London.
Personal: Shooting.

SIMON, J. David
Dibb Lupton Alsop, Leeds (0345) 262728
Specialisation: Professional indemnity insurance for defendants' insurers for all types of professionals (other than solicitors). Particular emphasis on architectural and geotechnical problems.
Career: Joined predecessor of firms of *Dibb Lupton Alsop* in 1971. Qualified in 1974. Partner in 1975. Head of Professional Indemnity at *DLA* (and predecessors) since 1985.
Personal: Born 1950.

SUMMERFIELD, Neil
Lightfoots, Thame
(01844) 212305 or 212574/5
Specialisation: Professional Negligence work
with particular emphasis on claims against
solicitors and surveyors on behalf of lending
institutions.
Career: Qualified 1985. *Lightfoots*, Solicitors,
1983 to date. Became Litigation Partner 1989.
Personal: Born 18th February 1959. University
of East Anglia. LL.B (Hons).

TAYLOR, Elisabeth
James Chapman & Co, Manchester
(0161) 828 8000
Specialisation: Professional Indemnity cases
on behalf of Insurers and Indemnifiers.
Prof. Memberships: The Law Society and The
Manchester Law Society.
Career: Educated University of Bristol (LLB)
1971. Admitted – April 1974. Joined *James
Chapman & Co* – 1976, Partner – 1979.

TURTLE, W. Brian W.
Carson & McDowell, Belfast (01232) 244951
See under Employment, Litigation
(Commercial), p. 325, 536

WAREING, Diana M.
Shakespeares, Birmingham
(0121) 632 4199
Specialisation: Defendant Professional
Indemnity work, particularly on behalf of
accountants, surveyors and insurance
brokers/intermediaries.
Prof. Memberships: BILA and FOIL.
Career: Includes: Assistant Solicitor at
Linklaters & Paines from 1975 to 1979.
Partner at *Duggan Lea & Co.* (now
Shakespeares) from 1980 to date.
Has dealt with Defendant Professional
Indemnity work since 1979.

WELSH, John
Bishop and Robertson Chalmers, Glasgow
(0141) 248 4672
See under Construction & Civil
Engineering, p. 215

WILLIAMSON, David
Brodies WS, Edinburgh (0131) 228 3777
See under Employment, Litigation
(Commercial), p. 323, 525

WYLDE, Peter R.
Irwin Mitchell, Sheffield (0114) 276 7777
Specialisation: Professional negligence
claims arising from commercial transactions,
mergers and acquisitions and commercial
litigation. Leads *Irwin Mitchell's* Professional
Negligence unit which handles claims across a
wide spectrum of professional disciplines (in
particular, solicitors, accountants, valuers,
financial advisors, architects) also covers
commercial and residential property
transactions, private client matters, personal
injury and other types of civil litigation. Currently
handling a £4m group action for a faming co-
operative in respect of auditors' negligence, a
claim in excess of £5m against a
solicitor/director of an international commodities
trading company, several fraud/negligence
actions against solicitors in excess of £0.5m.
Prof. Memberships: National Network for
Mediation; Association of Northern Mediators;
Law Society.
Career: Qualified 1983. *Irwin Mitchell* Partner
1985. Educated at Royal Grammar School,
Newcastle Upon Tyne and Sheffield University.
Head of *Irwin Mitchell* Litigation Department
(Corporate Services). Head of Professional
Negligence Unit.
Personal: Leisure interests include cycling,
squash and theatre.

PROJECTS/PFI

RESEARCH: In compiling the tables, we consider all the information available to us, paying particular regard to the market research carried out by our team of ten qualified lawyers. (The researchers' details are set out on page three.) The rankings, therefore, reflect the opinion of the marketplace as revealed by systematic and objective research: see page four. (Our research is audited every year by the British Market Research Bureau.)

OVERVIEW: This year we have two tables for London, one for project finance and a second for PFI/PPP. Many firms appear in both although a few appear in only one table, notably Berwin Leighton, newly promoted to leading firm status for PFI. Rankings of individual firms differ between the two tables. Herbert Smith appears in the third band of leading firms for project finance but at the top of the PFI table as a consequence of its early focusing and involvement in the area. Similarly Lovell White Durrant is higher in the PFI table reflecting the firm's initial concentration on UK rather than overseas projects.

To succeed as a world player in project finance requires a combination of factors. Exposure to many different types of project, a large throughput of projects, time on each of the three sides of the table and a network of overseas offices, both where the projects are located and in the financial centres to tap the various sources of funding. Few firms can claim to satisfy all these requirements. The result, as in many other areas of the law, is an exclusive circle that most firms will never break into.

Even those firms which argued that they should be in the top band for project finance agreed that Allen & Overy, Clifford Chance and Linklaters should be there with them. Freshfields is the closest UK competition. However this is an area where a firm's *international* presence is what counts, not the location of its head office. A table based on a firm's international capacity rather than the reputation of its London office would give greater prominence to the American firms, although some do already appear.

This year we have included a separate table of non-UK firms which are active in project finance around the world but not ranked in the London tables. The list is unranked.

Regions: As a rule regional firms concentrate on the domestic market to a far greater degree than City firms. They are also more likely to act for the public sector than for funders or project companies. A quick glance at the Clients/Work in the following editorial confirms this. There is some evidence that the top City firms are increasing their hold over the market at the expense of the regional and weaker London firms. Why? Because whilst regional firms appear cheaper they are often reinventing the wheel when apparently more expensive London lawyers can do the job more quickly having already been over the arguments and knowing what the funders will accept.

Having said that, there are a number of successful regional firms. The best known are Eversheds (the market leader in education and local authority PFIs) and Pinsent Curtis. Dibb Lupton Alsop, Morgan Bruce and Addleshaw Booth & Co also have national reputations.

For the Scottish firms the main competition is not the City practices except on the banking side where the London firms are still the dominant force.

LEADING FIRMS · LONDON PROJECTS

ALLEN & OVERY
CLIFFORD CHANCE
LINKLATERS

FRESHFIELDS
MILBANK, TWEED, HADLEY & MCCLOY
NORTON ROSE

ASHURST MORRIS CRISP
CAMERON MCKENNA
DENTON HALL
HERBERT SMITH
SLAUGHTER AND MAY
WHITE & CASE
WILDE SAPTE

HIGHLY REGARDED FIRMS PROJECTS

Baker & McKenzie
Lovell White Durrant
Shearman & Sterling
Simmons & Simmons

S J Berwin & Co
Coudert Brothers
Masons
Taylor Joynson Garrett
Trowers & Hamlins

LONDON

Allen & Overy 30 ptnrs (17 in London) and 70 other lawyers have worked on major projects in some 32 countries during the last year, from London and 19 overseas offices (which now include Albania!). "Doing phenomenally well and nice people." The firm at or near the top of everyone's lists. A&O's "dynamic duo," *Graham Vinter* ("someone who always lives up to his reputation") and *Anne Baldock* ("extraordinarily good") continue to have the highest of profiles. Other members of the team include *Jonathan Horsfall Turner* ("we like him because he makes everyone else feel young"), *Brian Harrison, Anthony Humphrey* and *David Sedgley* ("the rising star"). Andrew Trehair has now left for warmer climes. **Clients/Work:** US$2.5bn Oman LNG project involving the construction of the world's largest LNG trains. The £286m financing of the Sutton Bridge power project by way of two concurrent 25 year bond issues, one in the UK market and one in the US. Advising the North of Scotland Water Authority on the Inverness & Fort William Sewerage Project, the first PFI sewerage project to reach financial close. Advising the project company on the A1-M1 link road.

Clifford Chance (150 lawyers including 30 partners (12 in London) are members of the firm's World-wide Projects Group.) 1997 saw the firm advise on over 200 projects with a combined value exceeding US$95bn so it is not surprising that some interviewees described CC as "over stretched, with people rushing from project to project". But this volume and quality of projects make them undisputed leaders. Seven partners and 20 assistants are making a big effort to get into PFI and are "always on market." The big names include: *Rodney Short, Michael Bray, Tim Soutar* ("has the knack of getting people to enjoy working for him"), *Chris Wyman* ("probably the best CC have"), *Margaret Gossling, Anthony Bankes-Jones, John East, Paul Simpson* and *Peter Blake*. **Clients/Work:** For the arrangers, JP Morgan, Chase, BCI and UBS on restructuring and financing of the Omnitel GSM telecoms Project in Italy. Advising the sponsors on all aspects of the 1200MW Saltend power station. Advising Cruciform Services Ltd on the development of a training and research centre to house the new Wolfson Institute for Medical Research and the merged UCL and Royal Free medical schools.

Linklaters (18ptnrs) Historically acted for project sponsors/bidders, the firm is now as likely to be seen acting for funders and is a leader in PFI as well as one of the top global projects practices. A new development is the establishment of a dedicated project bonds team. The "incredibly clever people" they field include *Bruce White* whose tough,

"no bullshit" approach to negotiations goes down well with clients ("after Moses, Bruce is God's main legal spokesman") and *David Weber*. Whilst renowned for their robust support of clients, if you get *Stuart Salt* or *Clive Ransome* "you're on a home run." With some of the others "it can be a bruising experience." *Jeremy Gewirtz* (a "star of his generation") is up & coming. **Clients/Work:** Advising on the Sutton Bridge power project, involving the first bond financing of a UK IPP. The Rion-Andirion Bridge project in Greece. The Laibin B power project in China. Advising the arranging banks lending to the SPV on the £122m Darford & Gravesham NHS Trust, the first acute hospital project to reach financial close. Advising AMEC and Building & Property Group on new DGH at Cumberland Infirmary in Carlisle, including a £85m bond issue

Freshfields The Global Project Finance Group (which also does PFI) keeps 45 partners busy (20 of them in London) "The firm knocking loudest on the door of the top band." Many interviewees thought the firm was not pushing project finance as aggressively as it could. Apparently even when not trying hard *Kent Rowey's* group was named project finance team of the year by two respected business journals. *Nick Bliss* "always has a complete overview" and the projects team, which includes *Edward Evans*, is "wonderful at logistics, perfectly co-ordinated and don't waste time with unnecessary paperwork." **Clients/Work:** Advising Electricité de France and GEC Alsthom, the project sponsors, on the Laibin B BOT 2 x 360MW coal fired power plant in the PRC. Advising the lenders, EBRD, OPIC and JEXIM in the oil and gas project financing of Sakhalin island in the Russian Far East. Acting for PPM, the successful consortium, on the DSS Project PRIME, "the Mother of all PFI Deals." Advising Financial Security Assurance on the £239m M6/M74 Scottish DBFO road scheme, successfully combining commercial bank financing with bond financing

Milbank, Tweed Hadley & McCloy (4ptnrs/13assts) "So focused on project finance it's virtually a mainline narcotic for them." Milbank's world-wide reputation gives the London office credibility beyond its size. Lawyers include *Phillip Fletcher* and *Jane Templeton-Knight,* who moves up one band. **Clients/Work:** Saudi Yanbu Petrochemical Company on the US$3.22bn Yanpet Expansion project, the largest ever petrochemical financing in the world. Representing the lead arrangers, Credit Lyonnais, ING Leasing, Société Générale and KfW in the US$400m senior bank financing to support satellite projects for the European space launch consortium, Arianspace. Advising ABN AMRO and Barclays Capital on the US$250m financing of the Lisheen zinc mine in County Tipperary, Rep. of Ireland.

Norton Rose (26ptnrs/37assts, 14/36 in PFI) "Flavour of the month" in the domestic UK market, principally for independent power projects and scoring well on all the league tables. Popular with the banks. Besides London (with 16 ptnrs), lawyers are based in Bahrain, Moscow, Paris and Singapore. *Jeffery Barratt* and *Jon Ellis* move up one band. "A great team," described as "bloody nice bunch to deal with," but "there is no evidence yet that they will become more than they already are." Lack a major international network, particularly in the US and, following the breakdown of the firm's 22-year association with Johnson Stokes & Master, in Hong Kong. *David Coulter* was recommended for PFI. **Clients/Work:** Acting for UBS on the Saltend 1200MW power project. Advising the credit agencies on the Oman LNG project. Scotia Water Consortium on four Scottish projects, combined value £220m. Taylor Woodrow Construction for the £100m Sheffield "Heart of the City" project.

Ashurst Morris Crisp (14ptnrs/25assts) Could be a force to be reckoned with if they really want to become one, but not in the magic circle yet. Whilst the firm suffers from the lack of an extensive overseas network and the massed ranks of its main competitors, they have had a good year in PFI and move up to become a leader. *Mark Elsey* "gives a jolly good service," as does *Jan Sanders* who "does a great job". **Clients/Work:** Autolink Concessionaires (M6) plc on a 100km DBFO contract which reached financial close, including the £250m of bond financing. Advising Marubeni on its first investment in an IPP in India (and as EPC contractor) in the 330MW naptha fired powers project in Tamil Nadu. Acting for BZW, 3i and Innisfree as equity and mezzanine investors in relation to the £220 million Norfolk and Norwich general hospital project.

Cameron McKenna (38ptnrs/55assts – 27/40 in London) "Unbeatable" when advising on strategic electricity issues but in the broader area of project finance they will have to do a lot more to break in. *Fiona Woolf* and *Richard Price* are the best known individuals. **Clients/Work:** Advising Nile Independent Power Ltd on the development of a 240MW hydro project near the Bujagali Falls in Uganda. Advising a consortium of US and Polish construction companies and South African toll road operators on their successful tender for the Gdansk Town leg of the A-1 motorway. Advising the successful consortium (Securicor/Costain) on the Bridgend DBFO project.

Denton Hall (35ptnrs/16assts, 13/13 in PFI) Excellent in specialist areas (particularly energy, water and rail) rather than across the board. Lacks the banking profile of its major competitors but not the skills or people. In PFI the firm gained a lot of exposure acting for the Highways Agency on the first two tranches of DBFO roads. Some interviewees found the negotiations "a little sticky", but as one banker pointed out "the deals got done, money's been advanced and that's the ultimate test." *Ellen Gates* ("a superlative draftsman who deserves recognition for the groundbreaking DBFO contract"), *James Dallas* and *Ed Marlow* are the established names, whilst *Matthew Jones* (on the banking side) is by all accounts "a complete star". **Clients/Work:** Instructed by Venkatesh Coke & Power Ltd in connection with a coke/power co-generation project in Tamil Nadu, India. Advising the Chinese Government (as part of an Asian Development Bank team) on the Chengdu Water Project, the first water treatment facility under China's BOT programme. Advising a Tarmac plc lead consortium on the Dartford and Gravesham PFI hospital project, the first PFI project in the health sector to reach financial completion.

Herbert Smith (39ptnrs in the UK and overseas) *Andrew Preece* "understands why something is an issue for the other side" and leads a team (described as "delightful to deal with") going from strength to strength. Having taken an early decision to get involved in PFI when other lawyers were not sure whether it would work, the firm is now the market leader although the competition is stiffening. *Nick Tott* and *Jason Fox* have been particularly important in establishing the firm's reputation. *Mark Newbery* (managing partner of the Singapore office) is another respected player. With less international offices than the magic circle, they are concentrating on China, India and francophone Africa. **Clients/Work:** China Travel (Service) Holdings Ltd on a concession and JV for the development of 6 toll roads in Shandong Province. Jindal Tractebel on its 260MW IPP. Advising London and Continental Railways on the financing and development of the Channel Tunnel Rail Link and the Eurostar business. Advising the NHS on the £214m Norfolk and Norwich NHS Trust.

Slaughter and May "Always first class, but not a projects firm." Even if they wanted to be one, the firm has too few overseas offices to mount a major campaign at establishing a first-rate global projects practice. As usual, there is no specific department however, 28 partners, including *Martin Roberts, St.John Flaherty* ("typical Slaughters"), *Ian Goldie* ("ditto"), *Chris Saunders* and *Paul Stacey* have particular expertise. **Clients/Work:** Acting for the banks on the £2bn multi-source financing of an LNG project at Qalhat, Oman. Advising the EIB on an ECU 370 million loan in relation to the Rion-Antirion Bridge in Greece. Acting for the project companies on the building and upgrading of the basic telephone system in four regional areas of Hungary.

White & Case (5ptnrs/15assts) A real power internationally, as large as Milbank's

in London but a few years behind in market profile. The London office has also led on projects in the Far East, South & Central Asia and the Carribbean. Moving up to become a leader. *Margaret Cole* and *John Bellhouse* are the best known individuals. **Clients/Work:** Acting for the sponsors in connection with the development of the Higau copper/gold mine in Indonesia. International legal advisers to the Cross Israel Highway Authority for Phase 1 of the first BOT toll road project in Israel. Representing the developers of a 116MW electric/70MW thermal co-generation facility in Poland.

Wilde Sapte (10ptnrs/20assts) Always tend to score highly in competitions and have closed a good number of deals. What effect will the Andersens debacle have on the firm's future? Until now the focus has been on the UK, the merger might have given them a real global presence. *Mary Bonar* is well thought of and *Stan Gniadkowski* "does a jolly good job." *Bruce Johnston* has "a firm grasp on project finance structures and issues" but can be too firm a protagonist. **Clients/Work:** ECGD on the US$1.56bn Bhadravati and the US$1.4bn Vizag power projects in India, and the US$1bn Athens Ringroad. Laing and Serco on the £230m Norfolk & Norwich Hospital project. RBC Dominion Securities/AMBAC on the £130m Seafield/River Almond/Esk Valley sewerage project

Baker & McKenzie (4ptnrs/17assts) A substantial London office with the reputation and size to take on the big ticket projects. Active in transport, power, mining and petrochemicals but did not receive many comments this year. **Clients/Work:** Autostrada Wielkopolska SA, the successful project company on the 360km A2 motorway from Swiecko to Strykow. For the lead arranger on the 330MW gas-fired Rades power project in Tunisia. Dresdner Bank, as arranger and lead manager on a DM1.65bn silicon chip wafer manufacturing facility Advanced Micro Devices, Inc.

Lovell White Durrant (13prtnrs/16assts) PFI has been a primary focus and a successful one. *Mike Matheou* must have been busy. He received more recommendations than any other individual in the PFI sector, including the following testimonial from one of the City's notorious rottweillers. "He does a better job of protecting his client than anyone I have ever come across." *Gavin McQuater* is also well regarded and *Mark Darley* is 'up & coming.' **Clients/Work:** Advising a government promoter on the development of Colombo as a global hub port. Acting for Nissho Iwai in a US$70m facility to finance rocket production in the Ukraine for the first project for the commercial launch of satellites from a floating platform. Acting for the senior lenders on the Norfolk & Norwich NHS Trust DBFO project.

Shearman & Sterling (4ptnrs/16assts UK qualified with 30 more US lawyers) Last year the firm took a big part of Milbank's London team, who have hardly been seen since (*Kenneth MacRitchie* and *Nicholas Buckworth*). Expect this situation to change rapidly. Internationally, one of the strongest projects firms. **Clients/Work:** Advising Intergen as the preferred bidder on three out of five build operate power projects in Turkey. Advising European Company for Mobile Services, a JV of France Telecom Mobile, Motorola and Orascom, in the US$500m financing to fund the purchase of 15 year GSM licence in Egypt.

Simmons & Simmons The 18 partners and 36 assistants based in London (13ptnrs/26assts), Hong Kong, Paris, Lisbon and Abu Dhabi "know what they're doing," and are now being pulled together into a Major Projects Group. During 1997 they were involved in 40 projects with an aggregate value in excess of US$14.2bn. Particularly strong in the rail sector and making a name in MoD PFIs. **Clients/Work:** Advising The Law Debenture Trust Corporation plc in relation to the upstream phase of the US$3bn Qatargas LNG project. Advising the Electricity Generating Authority of Thailand on power purchase arrangements. Completing the £100m Medium Support Helicopter Aircrew Training Facility, the first PFI project awarded by the MoD.

S J Berwin & Co (2ptnrs/3assts) *Geoff Haley* enjoys a reputation as a hard working lawyer. His talented team includes the up & coming *Mark Johnson*. **Clients/Work:** The Government of Barbados on the development of Barbados Airport. The Government of Jordan on the Disi Mudawara water pipeline. Acting for Amey, Coopers & Lybrand and Barclays on the Northern Birmingham Mental Health Trust.

Coudert Brothers (5ptnrs/4assts) A firm with an extensive reach and particularly

strong in Asia and the CIS. **Clients/Work:** Representing Sakhalin Energy Investment Company and its shareholders, Marathon Oil, Mitsui & Co, Shell Petroleum NV and Mitsubishi, in connection with the US$348m EBRD, OPIC and J-Exim led project financing of offshore oil and gas fields in the Russian Far East. Acting for the producer companies on a US$1.5bn pipeline in Russia and Kazakstan.

Masons (5ptnrs/4assocs/6assts, 15/8/17 in PFI) "More than competent but still on the learning curve," coming at it from the construction/property side rather than project finance. "They need to sit in the funders seat more often." **Clients/Work:** Advising the successful consortium on the £150m Nottingham Light Rail project. Anglian Water International on their bid for the £67m Chengdu Water treatment BOT project in China. Acting for Aqumen, the preferred bidder on the £100m S Tees PFI Hospital project.

Taylor Joynson Garrett (9ptnrs/6assts – of which 2 partners are full time) "Not a firm with projects written all over it but what they do they do well." **Clients/Work:** Advising the project company and sponsors in relation to the syndication of the api ENERGIA project, the first Italian IPP to be syndicated. Advising developers of renewable energy projects in Northern Ireland. Advising a consortium of London University Colleges, including the School of Oriental and African Studies, on the £6/8m Bloomsbury CHP project

Trowers & Hamlins 12ptnrs and 12assts based in London, Oman, Dubai and Abu Dhabi. "An automatic choice in the Middle East." The firm has links with law firms in Jordan, Yemen, Qatar, Egypt, Saudi Arabia and Bahrain. **Clients/Work:** Charus, the lead promoter of a consortium forming the

US$3bn Sohar Aluminium Smelter Company in Oman. Jordanian Ministry of on the implementation policy for BOOT/BOO. Borealis A/S on a US$1.5bn polyethylene production JV with state owned Abu Dhabi National Oil Company.

NON UK FIRMS ACTIVE OVERSEAS

Blake Dawson Walden AUS
Chadbourne & Parke US
Clayton Utz AUS
Cleary, Gottlieb & Hamilton US
Cravath, Swaine & Moore US
Davis Polk & Wardell US
Debevoise & Plimpton US
Dewey Ballantine US
Freehill Hollingdale & Page AUS
Fulbright & Jawoski US
Hunton & Williams US
Gide Loyrette Nouel French
Kelley, Drye & Warren US
Latham & Watkins US
Mallesons Stephens Jaques AUS
Mayer, Brown & Platt US
McDermott, Will & Emery US
Orrick, Herrington & Sutcliffe US
Paul, Hastings, Janofsky & Walker US
Paul, Wiess, Rifkind, Wharton & Garrison US
Reid & Priest US
Simpson Thacher & Bartlett US
Skadden, Arps, Slate, Meagher & Flom US
Squire Sanders & Dempsey US
Sullivan & Cromwell US
Stikeman, Elliott Canadian
Vinson & Elkins US
Winston & Strawn US

PFI ONLY

Berwin Leighton (6ptnrs/6assts) A real breadth of experience in PFI means the firm moves up to become a leader. Starting to act for funders as well as public and private sector clients. *Simon Allan* is respected in the field. *Tom Lyon* has become a consultant, whilst *Carol McCormack* joins the list as up and coming. **Clients/Work:** Acting for UCL on the Cruciform project. Acting for the Wellhouse NHS Trust. Advising AMEC on the Longbenton project to provide new accommodation for 7,000 staff of the Benefits Agency on Tyneside.

Bird & Bird (5ptnrs/10assts) "A fine, specialist IT and telecoms outfit." *Roger Bickerstaff* is well known in his sector. **Clients/Work:** Acting for the MoD on its £500m deal with EDS to harmonise the Armed Forces' pay, pension and administration IT systems. Advising the Employment

LEADING FIRMS · LONDON · PFI

HERBERT SMITH
LINKLATERS

ALLEN & OVERY
CLIFFORD CHANCE
DENTON HALL
FRESHFIELDS
LOVELL WHITE DURRANT

ASHURST MORRIS CRISP
BERWIN LEIGHTON
CAMERON MCKENNA
WILDE SAPTE

HIGHLY REGARDED FIRMS · PFI

Bird & Bird
Masons
Norton Rose
Simmons & Simmons
Slaughter and May

Beachcroft Stanleys
S J Berwin & Co
Nabarro Nathanson

Lawrence Graham
Macfarlanes
Rowe & Maw

Service on the procurement of new IT infrastructure and business process re-engineering. Advising the Foreign & Commonwealth Office on the procurement of a global telecommunications service.

Beachcroft Stanleys (6ptnrs/11assts) Having acted for the NHS since 1948 they

have a head start in health PFIs. A frequent comment was. "if *Barry Francis* could do all the work they'd be a strong practice but...." The real test is whether they can breakout of the health sector. **Clients/Work:** Taylor Woodrow on the £40m South Bucks NHS Trust project. For Jarvis FM on the UCL

Cruciform Research Building. Chelsea & Westminster Healthcare NHS Trust in its IT PFI procurement.

Nabarro Nathanson (25 lawyers regularly do PFI work. "Good First Division rather than Premiership" with some "sound corporate lawyers who understand how to structure a deal." Commended for not "over lawyering things." Bias towards public sector clients and particularly successful in local government PFIs. **Clients/Work:** Surrey CC and Epsom and Ewell BC on the development of a new "lifestyle centre" at Epsom. Royal Borough of Kingston-on-Thames' new riverside development. Maidstone BC on leisure development schemes involving economic regeneration and structures.

Lawrence Graham A new entrant, recommended for smaller projects and local authority work.

Macfarlanes (4ptnrs/4assts) Noted particularly for their work in the health sector. *John Moore* has a substantial track record in the field. *John Skelton* was also recommended. **Clients/Work:** West Middlesex University NHS Trust on the redevelopment of the hospital. Acting for a Mowlem led consortium on the redevelopment and operation of Manchester Magistrates

Courts. Acting for a Tarmac/Group 4 consortium on with the redevelopment and operation of GCHQ.

Rowe & Maw (Core team of 3ptnrs/4assts) Well known in property related PFIs. **Clients/Work:** Advising the LASER consor-

tium, the preferred bidder to redevelop the National Physical Laboratory. Oxford CC on a proposal to redevelop the Oxford Castle site. Advising Compass Management and Leasing Inc. as joint facilities managers for Project PRIME.

LEADING INDIVIDUALS · LONDON · PFI	
BALDOCK Anne Allen & Overy	**PREECE Andrew** Herbert Smith
BLISS Nick Freshfields	**TOTT Nicholas** Herbert Smith
FOX Jason Herbert Smith	**VINTER Graham** Allen & Overy
MATHEOU Michael Lovell White Durrant	**WHITE Bruce** Linklaters
COULTER David Norton Rose	**MARLOW Ed** Denton Hall
ELSEY Mark Ashurst Morris Crisp	**MCQUATER Gavin** Lovell White Durrant
GATES Ellen Denton Hall	**SEDGLEY David** Allen & Overy
GNIADKOWSKI Stan Wilde Sapte	
ALLAN Simon Berwin Leighton	**LYON Thomas Stephen** Berwin Leighton
BICKERSTAFF Roger Bird & Bird	**MOORE John** Macfarlanes
FRANCIS Barry Beachcroft Stanleys	**NOBLE Perry** Freshfields
HALEY Geoff S J Berwin & Co	**PRICE Richard** Cameron McKenna
JOHNSTON Bruce Wilde Sapte	**SKELTON John** Macfarlanes

UP AND COMING · LONDON · PFI	
DARLEY Mark Lovell White Durrant	**MCCORMACK Carol** Berwin Leighton
JOHNSON Mark S J Berwin & Co	**SANDERS Jan** Ashurst Morris Crisp
JONES Matthew Denton Hall	

SEE PROFILES AT END OF THIS SECTION

LEADERS' PROFILES · LONDON

ALLAN, Simon L.
Berwin Leighton, London +44 171 760 1000
Specialisation: Head of PFI team and specialist in major developments and infrastructure related projects. Major projects include development of the Ludgate complex for Rosehaugh Stanhope, the Treasury Building PFI project for HM Treasury, Longbenton PFI project for the project vehicle, Kings College/UMDS PFI project again for the project vehicle, construction of the new Parliamentary Building over Westminster tube station and development of the Channel Tunnel Rail Link domestic and international passenger station at Ebbsfleet.
Career: Qualified in 1979, assistant solicitor with *Kenneth Turner Brown* (1979-81) and *Ashurst Morris Crisp* (1981-88). Partner with *Berwin Leighton* since 1988.
Personal: Family of four children. Hobbies include reading, music and wine.

BALDOCK, Anne
Allen & Overy, London (0171) 330 3000
Specialisation: Project Finance: All aspects of major projects work including acting for banks, sponsors and multi-laterals, recent deals include Sutton Bridge Power Project – Eurobond and 144A offering (representing project company) Docklands Light Railway – Project Bond (representing inderwriters) road, rail, prison and hospital PFI transactions (representing project companies or lenders). Also recently involved in various power, road, mining and infrastructure projects in Russia, Croatia and the African continent.
Specialisation: PFI: All aspects of major projects and PFI work including acting for banks, sponsors and multi-laterals. Has worked in all major PFI sectors including road, rail, prison, MOD property and Local Authority.

Notable deals include Channel Tunnel Rail Link (acting for lenders), the majority of the private prison transactions (including the first in Scotland) acting for sponsors, Docklands Light Railway – Project Bond (representing underwriters) and London Luton Airport (local authority PFI) acting for lenders.
Career: Articled at *Allen & Overy*; Qualified 1984; Partner 1990; Secondment with major US bank 1986-88.
Personal: Born 1959, graduate of LSE.

BANKES-JONES, Anthony
Clifford Chance, London (0171) 600 1000
Partner.
Specialisation: Specialising in projects, project finance, securitisation and banking, including structured financings, clearing systems and general financial work and energy, oil and gas, natural resources.
Career: Articled *Slaughter and May*; Partner *Clifford Chance* since 1985.
Personal: Educated at Lambrook, Bracknell, Berks; Marlborough College, Wiltshire – major upon scholarship; Worcester College, Oxford (BA Jurisprudence). Born 1952.

BARRATT, Jeffery
Norton Rose, London (0171) 283 6000
Partner, Head of Global Projects Group.
Specialsation: All areas of banking, financing and capital markets debt instruments, in particular project related financings. Involved in many complex infrastructure and other project financings in the UK and worldwide, acting for banks, sponsors, project companies, export credit agencies and multilateral agencies. On The Editorial Board of Butterworths Financial Law and Practice.
Career: Qualified 1973, joined *Norton Rose*

1976, Partner 1979. Established and ran Bahrain office 1979-82. Training Partner 1987-91. Headed South East Asian Project Finance Group, based in Hong Kong 1993-95. Chairman Partnership Committee 1997.

BELLHOUSE, John
White & Case, London (0171) 726 6361
Specialisation: Advising on a major international infrastructure projects, with a particular emphasis on construction contracts. Recent transactions include: leading the team acting for the developer of the Esenyurt Power Plant in Turkey; advising the sponsor of a hydroelectric scheme in Uganda; sitting as an arbitrator in a dispute between two Italian construction companies.
Career: Admitted England and Wales in 1971; admitted Hong Kong 1983; Partner *McKenna & Co* 1976-94; Partner *White & Case* 1994 – to date; Executive Partner, London Office, *White & Case* 1998 – to date.

BICKERSTAFF, Roger
Bird & Bird, London (0171) 415 6000
See under Computer Law & I.T., p. 182

BLACK, Alan
Linklaters, London (0171) 456 5948
Partner 1983. Head of Global Projects.
Specialisation: Main area of practice has been international projects. Extensive experience of acting for governments, sponsors and lenders on major projects for transport, airports and aviation, oil, gas, and derivative products, and projects involving concessions granted by governments to private developers in both civil law and common law countries.
Career: Qualified 1976. Attended Kings College, London.

Personal: Born 1952. Leisure activities include golf and the opera.

BLAKE, Peter M.W.
Clifford Chance, London (0171) 600 1000
Specialisation: Projects and project financing. Acting for banks and sponsors on energy and infrastructure projects financed on a limited resource basis. Also acting for corporations in the energy field. A member of the International Bar Association and the International Nuclear Law Association. LLB (Hons) University College London 1973. Partner 1979. Leisure pursuits include skiing and sailing.

BLISS, Nick
Freshfields, London (0171) 936 4000
Specialisation: Project finance and PFI. He led the Freshfields teams which acted for Road Management Group in the (March 1996) A1(M) and A419/A417 DBFO Road Projects: the first UK monoline insured eurobond infrastructure financing and, subsequently, the M6 DBFO Road monoline insured eurobond infrastructure financing, acting for FSA the monoline insurer. He has been heavily involved in projects in a number of other areas of PFI (prisons, health and MOD projects). He has also been involved in a variety of other major international projects financings, acting for Xenel in the Hub River Power Project and for US Eximbank in the Uch and Saba Pakistani power projects. His most recent project of note was acting for the leading institutions to the N4 South African Maputo Corridor Toll Road Project (February 1998): the first infrastructure project financing in South Africa.
Prof. Memberships: Law Society, International Bar Association.
Career: Barnard Castle School, Corpus Christi College, Cambridge.
Personal: Rowing, cycling, back surgery, childcare and other strenuous pursuits.

BONAR, Mary
Wilde Sapte, London (0171) 246 7000
Partner in Banking Department.
Specialisation: Member of Major Projects Group and Head of Rail Group. Main areas of practice are project finance and rail. Experience infrastructure, power, Public Private Partnerships and industrial projects and rail industry. Clients including governments, major banks, ECAs and major corporate sponsors. Lectures and writes on project finance and rail industry.
Prof. Memberships: Liveryman, Worshipful Company of Carmen and City of London Solicitors Company; Women Solicitors Association. Member Chartered Institute of Transport.
Career: LLB. Admitted in 1971. Solicitor and Partner (from 1973) at *Gamlens* Lincolns Inn 1971-89. Joined *Wilde Sapte* as Partner in 1989.
Personal: Born 28th July 1947. Educated at St Bernard's Convent High School, Westcliff, Essex 1958-65, University College, London 1965-68 and The College of Law, Lancaster Gate 1970-71. Princes Youth Trust Business Adviser. Lives in the City of London.

BRAY, Michael
Clifford Chance, London (0171) 600 1000, Milan (0039)2 7600 8040
See under Banking, p. 136

BUCKWORTH, Nicholas
Shearman & Sterling, London
(0171) 920 9000
Partner in Project Finance Department.
Specialisation: Advising project developers and financial institutions on all aspects of the structuring, negotiation, development and financing of major infrastructure projects particularly in the power and transportation sectors. Currently involved in advising on projects in Turkey, the Middle East and North Africa, as well as in Hungary, Italy and the United Kingdom. Regular participant in industry conferences and in client focused presentations and working groups.
Career: Qualified in 1986. With *Clifford Chance* 1984-94. Partner *Milbank, Tweed, Hadley & McCloy* 1994- November 1996. Partner, *Shearman & Sterling* November 1996.
Personal: Born 2nd February 1961. Educated at Dundee University (LL.B Hons, 1983). Leisure activities include skiing, squash, golf, music and cinema.

COLE, Margaret B.
White & Case, London (0171) 726 6361
Specialisation: International and project finance, representing both borrowers and lenders, in the U.S. and particularly in emerging markets. Oil, gas, mining, corporate and financial transactions, bank finance and investment funds.
Prof. Memberships: Admitted as a solicitor in England and Wales (1996), member of New York Bar (1984), admitted in various jurisdictions in Australia.
Career: LL.B. Sydney University, LL.M, Harvard Law School. Partner at *White & Case* since 1995. 1991-1995 Principal Counsel at IFC. Prior to 1991, partner in banking and finance group of *Freehill, Hollingdale and Page* in Australia.

COULTER, David
Norton Rose, London (0171) 283 6000
Specialisation: PFI, Project Finance, Public Sector Finance and Banking – PFI Projects in last year have included Hereford and Worcester and Greater Manchester waste to energy plants; Sheffield "Heart of the City" Project; Scottish Water Projects at Seafield and Almond Valley, Dalmuir, Tay and Levenmouth; MOD Bulldog Replacement Project; the New Millennium Experience.
Prof. Memberships: Law Society, Law Society of Scotland, City of London Solicitors Company.
Career: Mainholm Academy, Ayr to 1979; Edinburgh University LLB (1984), DIPLP (1985); Admitted Scotland (1986), Notary Public (Scotland) (1986); Admitted England & Wales (1989).
Personal: Sailing, hillwalking and travel. Married (Catriona Rose) – one daughter Fiona.

DALLAS, James
Denton Hall, London
(0171) 242 1212 jad@dentonhall.com
Chairman of Denton Hall.
Partner in Energy and Infrastructure Group.
Specialisation: Experienced in oil and gas work, including project finance; gas, electricity and rail privatisation and regulation in the UK and internationally; private finance initiative projects in the UK. Regular speaker at conferences on privatisation and regulation issues. Editor of the *Utilities Law Review*.
Prof. Memberships: Law Society; UK Oil

Lawyers Group; Centre for the Study of Regulated Industries (committee member).
Career: Qualified 1979 while articled with a City firm. Joined *Denton Hall* in 1985, became a Partner in 1986 and Chairman 1996.
Personal: Born 1955. Attended Eton College and St Edmund Hall, Oxford 1973-76 (MA Jurisprudence).

DARLEY, Mark
Lovell White Durrant, London
(0171) 236 0066
Specialisation: The principal area of practice is PFI and International Project Finance, with a particular emphasis on financing. Throughout his career Mark Darley has been involved in all forms of structured and revenue dependent financing, including factoring asset back securitisations, trade finance and buy-outs, as well as projects both in the UK and overseas. Recent transactions include advising the arranging banks on the Norfolk & Norwich Hospital PFI Project, advising the arranging bank in connection with a project at Beirut Airport, advising the arrangers in connection with a further hospital PFI transaction, advising the bidders in connection with a power project in Saudi Arabia and port and railroad developments in the Middle East.
Prof. Memberships: The Law Society.
Career: Educated at Bradford Grammar School and Manchester University (2:1 Hons); qualified 1986; partner at *Lovell White Durrant* in 1996.
Personal: Born 1961; resides London. Leisure interests shooting and fishing.

EAST, John
Clifford Chance, London (0171) 600 1000
Specialisation: Asset/ Project Finance, principally ship, property and aircraft financings, as well as lease financings in London from 1972 – 91 (1983 – 1985 in Singapore). Also handled project finance in transport infrastructure, and for power and petrochemical projects in various Asian countries, and previously in North sea oil and gas financings. Member of the core management group of the Finance and Project Area.
Career: Qualified 1972. Partner 1976. Managing partner Singapore 1983 – 85. Senior Partner Hong Kong 1991- present.

ELLIS, Jonathan
Norton Rose, London (0171) 283 6000
Specialisation: Projects work, acting for banks, project companies, export credit agencies and multilateral agencies on varied types of projects in the UK and internationally.

ELSEY, Mark
Ashurst Morris Crisp, London
(0171) 638 1111
Specialisation: Acting for governments, sponsors, contractors and lenders in relation to UK and international infrastructure projects. Head of the firm's Projects Group and a member of the Transport Funding Committee of London First.

EVANS, Edward T.H.
Freshfields, London (0171) 936 4000
See under Banking, p. 137

FLAHERTY, St. John
Slaughter and May, London
(0171) 600 1200
Specialisation: Banking, project finance.

Prof. Memberships: The Law Societies of England and Hong Kong.

FLETCHER, Phillip
Milbank, Tweed, Hadley & McCloy, London
(0171) 448 3000
Partner (Project Finance Group).
Specialisation: Specialising in the development and financing of major infrastructure projects, including power plants, pipelines, roads and satellites. Has represented parties in relation to projects in Europe, the US and Asia, including: the Orion Satellite Project, and recent Arianespace Satellite financings; Yanpet Petrochemicals Project; Saudi Arabia; the Birecik and Marmara Ereglisi power projects, Turkey; the Tapada Power Plant, Portugal; the Medway Power Project, UK; the Teverola, Ferrara, Serene, Lomellina and Rosen Power Plants, Italy; and the IEC cogeneration projects 144A debt insurance, U.S.. Lecturer at conferences on negotiation of project documentation.
Career: Has been with *Milbank, Tweed* since 1983 and was resident in the firm's Hong Kong office in 1987 and 1988.
Personal: Born 16th September 1957. Educated at Georgetown University School of Foreign Service (B.S. 1979), Fletcher School of Law & Diplomacy (MA, 1983) and the University of California, Berkeley (JD, 1983).

FOX, Jason
Herbert Smith, London (0171) 374 8000
Partner, Projects Group.
Specialisation: Advising the public sector, corporates and banks on all aspects of the structuring, development and financing of projects in a variety of sectors including oil and gas, aviation, property and public infrastructure. Main area of practice is advising on PFI projects. Regular participant in industry conferences on the PFI.
Career: Qualified in 1987 with *Herbert Smith* and became a partner in 1994. Seconded to the Private Finance Panel Executive - February to September 1994. Editor (jointly with Nicholas Tott) of The Private Finance Initiative Handbook (Jordans, due for publication Autumn 1998).

FRANCIS, Barry
Beachcroft Stanleys, London
(0171) 242 1011
Specialisation: PFI, major facilities management projects and other commercial transactions in the health and other public sectors including public sector/private sector joint ventures, facilities management contracts and procurement and administrative law advice. Current projects include major hospital building and services projects (PFI). Head of *Beachcroft Stanleys'* Projects Group and Joint Chairman of the Health Law Group. Regular speaker at conferences and seminars. Contributor to a range of specialist publications. A member of the Editorial Board of 'The PFI Report'.
Prof. Memberships: Law Society
Career: Admitted 1977, at *Beachcroft Hyman Isaacs* (now *Beachcroft Stanleys*) Associate 1979-80, Partner 1980 to date.
Personal: Born 14th March 1953. Educated at Enfield Grammar School and University of Bristol. Interests include travel, history and food. Lives in North London.

GATES, Ellen
Denton Hall, London (0171) 242 1212
Specialisation: Partner in the Energy and Infrastructure Group. Energy, natural resources and infrastructure projects, including project finance and private finance initiative projects; negotiating and drafting commercial contracts for UK and international energy, transport, and water projects.
Prof. Memberships: IBA, UK Energy Lawyers Group, American Bar Association.
Career: Qualified 1977 (Texas) 1992 (England). At *Vinson & Elkins* (Texas) 1978-1984. *Slaughter and May* 1985-1987, *Vinson & Elkins* (London) 1987-1990. Joined *Denton Hall* in 1991. Became a partner in 1993.
Personal: Born 22 January 1952. Educated Trinity University, Texas (Geology 1974 BA), University of Texas School of Law (1977 JD), Cambridge University (1978 LLB). Interests include walking, architectural history, reading.

GAYFORD, Robert M.
Taylor Joynson Garrett, London
(0171) 353 1234
Specialisation: International Banking and Finance. Head of Banking Department at *Taylor Joynson Garrett* and a member of the Projects Group. Specialises in project finance, asset finance and secured and unsecured lending. Has advised on the financing of power generation projects in the UK and abroad including the first independent power project in the UK. Also advised the project company and sponsors on the api Energia IGCC project financing, one of the first IPP's in Italy.
Prof. Memberships: Law Society, International Bar Association.
Career: The Royal Bank of Canada: Head of Group Legal Department 1985-1988. Standard Chartered Merchant Bank Limited: Project Finance Division 1983-1985. *Norton Rose*, London and Bahrain 1975-1983. Education: Marlborough College, Southampton University.
Personal: Married: two children. Leisure interests: sport and travel.

GEWIRTZ, Jeremy
Linklaters, London (0171) 456 5900
Specialisation: UK and international projects. Extensive experience acting for government, sponsors and lenders, particularly in the power and transportation sectors. Recent transactions include acting for the lead managers on the bond financing of the Sutton Bridge power project and for the sponsors in relation to two TOR generation projects in Turkey. Also recently involved in various power projects in Europe (Spain. Portugal) and the Middle East (Egypt, Yemen).
Prof. Memberships: Member of New York Bar; Law Society.
Career: Articled at *Linklaters*; qualified 1989; became Partner 1998. Educated at Oxford University and University of Pennsylvania.

GNIADKOWSKI, Stan
Wilde Sapte, London (0171) 246 7000
Specialisation: Specialises in property and project development work. As a necessary adjunct to that practice he also advises on non-contentious construction law matters. Usually acting for developers, land owners or institutions his practice covers all development related matters including rights of light, adjoining owners' issues and pre-let agreements. Stan led the team which acted for Octagon Healthcare, the project co on the Norfolk & Norwich Hospital PFI project, the largest and most complex to achieve financial close, achieved in January 1998. He is now appointed to represent the newly formed Laing Hyder on the series of PFI projects they intend to undertake. They are currently short listed on three school projects as well as bidding in the health, emergency and court sectors. He is on the National Audit Office panel of legal advisers.
Prof. Memberships: British Council for Offices, Investment Property Forum, Microscope Ball Committee.
Career: After Articles in local government followed by a year with a development corporation, joined the legal department of *John Laing PLC* with whom he worked from 1984 to 1987. Joining City solicitors, *D J Freeman*, in 1987 he became a partner the following year and played a significant part in the development of *D J Freeman*'s property practice. In January 1997, left *D J Freeman* to become a senior equity partner at *Wilde Sapte* where continues to advise on major property and project development matters.
Personal: Single. Interests include photography, motor racing (watching not participating) and the cinema.

GOLDIE, Ian
Slaughter and May, London
(0171) 600 1200
Specialisation: Energy and Natural Resources. Infrastructure Projects. Recent Projects include: 1996 – £260m DLR-Lewisham Extension Project. 1997 – US$460m Kaltim Prima Coal Project, Indonesia. 1998 – US$250m Pecem IPP Project, Brazil.
Prof. Memberships: Section on Energy and Natural Resources, International Bar Association. Institute of Petroleum.
Career: Jesus College, Cambridge. BA, MA.

GOSSLING, Margaret
Clifford Chance, London (0171) 600 1000
Partner in Projects Group.
Specialisation: Advising lenders and sponsors on all aspects of major infrastructure projects in Europe and Asia, particularly in the power and oil and gas sectors. Also experienced in general banking and bank mergers (e.g. the Manufacturers Hanover/ Chemical merger and the Chase/ Chemical merger).
Career: St. Anne's College, Oxford 1980-1983 (MA Hons), Articled *Coward Chance*; qualified 1986; Partner 1993.
Personal: Married, resides London.

HALEY, Geoff
S J Berwin & Co, London
+44 (0)171 533 2222
Infrastructure Department.
Specialisation: Partner undertaking commercial, construction law and project finance activities in the UK and overseas. Specialist in PFI with expertise in the fields of energy, water treatment, transportation, private power generation, waste to energy schemes, accommodation, urban renewal, healthcare and education. Major PFI projects include the Channel Tunnel Rail Link; Gas distribution network in Greece; DBFO Road Programme; 3 Embassies; 4 airports; 6 hospital PFI projects; Keele University; Waltham Forest College; water project and solar power station in Jordan.
Career: *Universities:* London University, College of Law, Henley Management College, Chartered Institute of Marketing. *Degrees and*

Qualifications: 1966 BL, 1988 MBA, 1989 DM.
Professional Career: Year qualified: 1971.
Summary of Professional Career: Deputy Group
legal adviser – Costain Group plc. Partner –
Theodore Goddard. Partner and head of
Infrastructure Department – *S J Berwin & Co.*
Consultant to the European Commission and
the European Bank for Reconstruction and
Development; expert consultant to UNCTAD
and UNIDO, former adviser to No. 10 Policy
Unit, adviser to International Energy Authority,
adviser to the high level finance panel of ECIS.
Lectures extensively both home and abroad.

HARRISON, Brian
Allen & Overy, London (0171) 330 3000
Specialisation: One of the senior partners in
Allen & Overy's highly regarded international
projects practice. He has a broad client base
advising banks, sponsors and multi-laterals on
major international power and infrastructure
projects. In the last year, he has been involved in
projects based in Central and Eastern Europe,
the Middle East and the UK in transactions
valued at over US$ 3 billion.
Career: Auckland University (1975, LLB),
qualified New Zealand 1976, England 1985;
assistant solicitor, *Johnson Stokes & Master*,
Hong Kong 1980-1983; assistant solicitor *Allen
& Overy*, London and Dubai 1983-1985; Partner
New York and London 1987.
Personal: Born 1953. Interests include
yachting and motorcycling.

HASLAM, Peter
Norton Rose, London +852 2843 2276
Hong Kong + 852 2843 2276
Specialisation: Partner, resident in the Hong
Kong office, where the firm operates in
association with the Hong Kong firm of *Johnson
Stokes & Master.* Since joining *Norton Rose* in
London on qualification in 1981, has advised on
most types of banking work, both in the UK and
more recently in Hong Kong. Specialises in
project and acquisition finance and has been
involved in a number of recent significant
infrastructural projects in Hong Kong (such as
Black Point, Western Harbour, Route 3, the air
cargo handling franchise for Hong Kong's new
international airport, the freight forwarding
centre at the airport and the River Trade
Terminal) and elsewhere.

HORSFALL TURNER, Jonathan
Allen & Overy, London (0171) 330 3000
Specialisation: Partner dealing with
syndications, securitisations, project finance,
capital markets, privatisations, debt
restructurings, bank and financial institution
acquisitions and disposals and general banking.
Career: Articled *Allen & Overy*, qualified 1970,
Partner 1973.
Personal: Cambridge University (1968 MA).
Born 1945.

HUMPHREY, Anthony R.
Allen & Overy, London (0171) 330 3000
Specialisation: Partner specialising in
financing transactions and with broad
experience in company and corporate finance
matters; has extensive experience in all aspects
of financing, particularly tiered or structured
debt/equity financings including international
project financings, acquisition financings and

other complex multi-sourced financings; has
advised on transactions worldwide including the
North Sea, North America, the Gulf, the Far East
and Australia.
Prof. Memberships: Member, Section on
Energy and Natural Resources Law of the
International Bar Association.
Career: Articled Allen & Overy, qualified 1975,
Partner 1981.
Personal: Durham University (1972 BA).
Born 1951.

JOHNSON, Mark
S J Berwin & Co, London
+44 (0)171 533 2222
Specialisation: Innovative PFI/ PPP projects
and project finance techniques in municipal
services, healthcare, education, transportation
and government accommodation and facilities.
Founding member of Manchester PFI Taskforce
and active in new bond financing of municipal
infrastructure.
Prof. Memberships: Project Finance
Association (Secretary), International Bar
Association (Sub-Committee on International
Projects), Society of Construction Law,
Docklands Business Club, Associate Fellow of
Institute for Advanced Legal Studies.
Career: Cheadle Hulme School, Cheshire;
Brasenose College, Oxford (MA): University of
Amsterdam (LLM); College of Law, Guildford.
Cert. Project Finance. Articled *Theodore
Goddard* 1992. European Commission DGIV
1992, Klein Goddard Paris 1993. Lloyds of
London 1994.
Personal: Great public houses of Cheshire,
Karaoke and the collected works of the
Bee Gees.

JOHNSTON, Bruce
Wilde Sapte, London (0171) 246 7000
Partner, Project Finance Group.
Specialisation: Major international and
national projects. Recent PFI and public-private
partnership projects include Norfolk and
Norwich Hospital, Highland Sewerage,
Fazakerley Prison, Law Hospital, Seafield
Sewerage, Agecroft Prison and Barnet Hospital
in the UK and the Athens Ringroad in Greece.
Frequent speaker at conferences and author of
articles.

JONES, Matthew
Denton Hall, London
(0171) 242 1212 mnj@dentonhall.com
Specialisation: Partner in Banking and
Finance Group, specialising in banking,
structured finance and PFI. Member of Denton
Hall team on PFI projects including Highways
agency DBFO Roads (M1-A1, M40, South
Midlands Network and A13), Essex County
Council A130 and Dartford and Gravesham
Hospital. Joint Editor, International Banking and
Financial Law.
Prof. Memberships: European Society for
Banking and Financial Law.
Career: University of Southampton 1983-86.
Qualified as a solicitor with *Denton Hall* in 1989,
partner 1996.
Personal: Born 1965. Married with one child,
lives in London. Plays keyboards in firm's band.

LYON, Thomas Stephen
Berwin Leighton, London +44 171 760 1000
Consultant in Finance Department.
Specialisation: Principal area of practice is
P.F.I. work. Experienced in leasing, asset
finance and structured finance in all their
branches as well as corporate tax and banking.
Regular conference speaker and author of
articles.
Prof. Memberships: Finance and Leasing
Association.
Career: Qualified in 1965. Assistant solicitor at
Woodham Smith Borradaile & Martin 1965-68.
Joined *Berwin & Co* in 1968 and became a
Partner in 1970.
Personal: Born 26th November 1941.
Educated at University College School 1954-59
and Wadham College, Oxford 1959-62. Leisure
interests include music, reading and walking.
Lives in London and Yorkshire.

MACRITCHIE, Kenneth
Shearman & Sterling, London
(0171) 448 3000
Partner in Project Finance Group.
Specialisation: Advising clients in negotiating
and structuring commercial agreements for
major infrastructure projects. Projects include
transport infrastructure; mining; power; oil and
gas and telecommunications. Recent
transactions comprise advising on
privatisations, including the coal industry in the
U.K; on UK Private Finance Initiative including
the Channel Tunnel Rail Link Project and on
major independent power, telecom and oil and
gas financings in the U.K., Europe and Asia.
Clients include international banks and project
developers.
Prof. Memberships: Law Society, Law Society
of Scotland.
Career: Qualified in 1976. Partner, *Clifford
Chance 1991-94. Milbank, Tweed, Hadley &
McCloy* in 1994 -1996. Joined *Shearman &
Sterling* as a partner, 1996.

MARLOW, Ed
Denton Hall, London (0171) 242 1212
Specialisation: Partner in Banking and
Financial Markets Group, Company and
Commercial Department. Head of *Denton Hall's*
UK PFI practice. Main areas of work cover all
aspects of limited resource (project) finance,
banking and building society work. In addition to
PFI, includes advice on funding and Treasury
activities, including PIBs, capital markets and
hedging, bilateral and syndicated borrowings,
commercial lending and general building society
law including mergers and conversions. Regular
speaker at conferences on lending techniques.
Prof. Memberships: Law Society, City of
London Solicitors Company, Freeman of
City of London.
Career: Qualified in 1980 with *Herbert
Oppenheimer Nathan Vandyk.* Moved to Heron
Corporation plc in 1987. Joined *Denton Hall* in
1988. Partner 1989.
Personal: Born 18th December 1954. Attended
Christ's College, Cambridge 1974-77.

MATHEOU, Michael S.
Lovell White Durrant, London
(0171) 236 0066
Specialisation: Working in the firm's Project
Finance Unit advising on overall structure and
risk allocation. Heavily involved in work under
the PFI across a range of sectors including
transport (M1/A1 DBFO Road; Manchester

Metrolink; Croydon Tramlink), Healthcare (New Royal Infirmary of Edinburgh, Edith Cavell Hospital, Peterborough; South Buckinghamshire NHS Trust), Government Accommodation (DSS PRIME) and IT (TAFMIS Project; "Prestige" Ticketing Project). Also working on a range of infrastructure projects internationally including BOT Waste Water Project in Oman, Bauxite mine and harbour development in Guyana and Oil refinery and petro-chemicals project in India.
Prof. Memberships: Law Society.
Career: *Lovell White Durrant*, London and Hong Kong since 1980, Partner 1989. LLB (Hons) Nottingham University.

MCCORMACK, Carol
Berwin Leighton, London +44 171 760 1000
See under Local Government, p. 553

MCCORMICK, Roger
Freshfields, London (0171) 936 4000
Specialisation: Project Finance (all sectors, all countries).
Prof. Memberships: International Bar Association.
Career: Partner of *Freshfields* since 1981. Head of Project Finance 1991-1997.
Personal: Born 1951, Educated M.G.S. and Oxford.

MCQUATER, Gavin
Lovell White Durrant, London
(0171) 236 0066
Specialisation: Project finance. Handles UK (including a number of private finance initiative) projects and international limited recourse transactions, across a range of industries including transport, water and general infrastructure, dealing with contracting authorities, sponsors and financial institutions. Advises on transaction structuring, such as bankable risk allocation and the tender process. Experience of a wide spread of joint ventures, business set ups, corporate reorganisations and M&A transactions.
Prof. Memberships: Law Society.
Career: Qualified with *Lovell White & King* in 1979; partner since 1985; 1990-1994 in Hong Kong office; now head of firm's project finance unit.

MOORE, John E.
Macfarlanes, London (0171) 831 9222
Partner in Property Development.
Specialisation: Has acted since qualification for Institutional Investors, including Insurance Companies and Pension Funds, in connection with the investment and development of land, and agricultural law. Represents tenants as well as landlords in relation to their agricultural holdings and Public Bodies (including NHS Trusts) in relation to agricultural tenancy rights on surplus land when considering developments and PFI proposals. Lectures on agricultural law.
Career: Joined *Macfarlanes* in 1970. Qualified 1973. Partner in 1979.

NEWBERY, Mark
Herbert Smith, Singapore (65) 536 7990
See under Energy – Electricity, p.332

NOBLE, Perry
Freshfields, London (0171) 936 4000
Specialisation: Project finance and banking. Mainly transportation and telecommunications projects. Acted for London Transport on funding aspects of the Jubilee Line extension and led

the team acting for London Transport on the letting of the concession under PFI for the Croydon Tramlink light rail project. Recently acted for the winning consortium bidding for the Taiwan High Speed Rail Project. Acted for Mercury One2One on the recent £1.6 billion syndicated facility and for Bouygues Telecom on its Fr15bn facility.
Prof. Memberships: Law Society.
Career: Letchworth Grammar School, North East London Polytechnic, Bristol University (LL.M Commercial Law).
Personal: Married, no children but pregnant wife. All sport, particularly cricket. Dog walking and cinema.

PHILLIPS, Richard A.R.
Freshfields, London (0171) 936 4000
Specialisation: Work includes asset and project finance, commercial law, corporate law, mergers and acquisitions, joint ventures, disposals and privatisations. Has a specialist industry focus of railways and has a wide experience of high profile corporate, project and finance work within this industry.
Prof. Memberships: Law Society, Chartered Institute of Transport, City Solicitors' Company.
Career: Qualified in 1981. Joined *Freshfields* in 1985, becoming a partner in 1989.
Personal: Born 1955, lives in London.

PHILLIPS, Robert
Cameron McKenna, London
(0171) 367 3000
Partner in Projects Group.
Specialisation: Principal area of practice is advising on transactions involving private/public sector participation with particular emphasis on major infrastructure and capital projects. Work covers specialist contract drafting, work with other consultants of a risk profile, and negotiating terms of project documents required for limited recourse financed infrastructure schemes. Major projects include independent power projects in Sub Saharan Africa, Portugal, Morocco, Malaysia and India; road and/or rail schemes in the UK., Poland, and Portugal and, in particular, advising the Department of Transport on the High Speed Channel Rail Link. Regular speaker at international conferences and has been retained by the World Bank to assist in development courses for the introduction of competition for public/private sector partnerships.
Prof. Memberships:
Major Projects Association.
Career: Partner at *McKenna & Co.* since 1979, including period as Senior Resident Partner in Hong Kong 1983-88. Admitted as a Solicitor, Hong Kong, 1983 and as a Barrister and Solicitor, State of Victoria, Australia, 1986.
Personal: Born 15th May 1947. Lives in Walton-on-Thames, Surrey.

PREECE, Andrew
Herbert Smith, London (0171) 374 8000
Partner and Head of International Projects Group.
Specialisation: Has considerable experience in major projects work including project finance, lease finance and general commercial work, with particular expertise in oil and gas and infrastructure matters, both domestic (including numerous transactions effected under the Private Finance Initiative) and international, and in complex project, lease and property financings.
Prof. Memberships: Law Society, International

Bar Association, UK Energy Lawyers Group, Finance & Leasing Association.
Career: Qualified in 1970. Became a Partner at *Herbert Smith* in 1977.
Personal: Educated at Selwyn College, Cambridge.

PRICE, Richard
Cameron McKenna, London (0171) 367 3000
Specialisation: Head of corporate department at *Cameron McKenna*, advising on mergers and acquisitions, joint ventures and strategic alliances particularly those involving a cross border aspect. Particular areas of speciality include defence, IT, rail and waste management. Also specialising in Private Finance Inititative and major projects.
Prof. Memberships: The Law Society.
Career: Qualified 1977. Articled at *McKenna & Co.* Partner from 1985. Personal: Born 27.5.1953. Educated at Cowbridge Grammar School and Leeds University. Lives in Richmond.

RANSOME, Clive
Linklaters, Hong Kong +852 28 42 4820
Partner in the Project & Asset Finance Department, Hong Kong Office.
Specialisation: Has worked on a number of major projects, project financings and structured financings in the UK, Europe and Asia. These include the Channel Tunnel (acting for the arranging banks), Northern Ireland's power privatisation (for NIGFN), the Pego power project in Portugal (acting for National Power, EdF and Endesa), the Tanjing JaTi 'B' power project in Indonesia (acting for NSBC and the lenders), the TelecomAsia telecommunications project in Bangkok (acting for KFW and other lenders), the Sikap power project in Malaysia (acting for KFW and other lenders) power, telecommunications projects and road projects in the PRC, Thailand and Indonesia, the Ravvafield financing in India, the Star refinery in Thailand, and other oil and commodities – based financing facilities in favour of borrowers in the region. Also a number of general banking and capital market transactions.

ROBERTS, Martin J.D.
Slaughter and May, London
(0171) 600 1200
Specialisation: Has been involved in more than fifty oil & gas and energy-related projects (acting for purchasers, sellers, sponsors and financiers) since the mid 1970's and more recently Power Station and other infrastructure projects (including road and rail) in the UK and overseas. Has acted for both sponsors and Banks on major PFI projects.
Prof. Memberships: The Law Society, City of London Solicitors Company, International Bar Association.
Career: *Slaughter and May* 1967, qualified in 1969 and became Partner 1975.
Personal: Born 20 March 1944, attended Shrewsbury School and Trinity Hall, Cambridge.

ROWEY, Kent
Freshfields, London (0171) 936 4000
See under Energy – Electricity, p. 333

SALT, Stuart
Linklaters, London (0171) 456 5912
Partner in the Project & Asset Finance Group.
Specialisation: Main area of practice has been international projects. Extensive experience of acting for governments, sponsors and lenders on major projects in the power and energy sectors.

SANDERS, Jan
Ashurst Morris Crisp, London
(0171) 638 1111
Specialisation: Projects (and general corporate work). Acted for Consort Healthcare (Durham) Limited, sponsor of New DGH, Durham, Barclays Development Capital, Innisfree and 3i as equity provider to Norfolk and Norwich and Building and Property Group, subcontractors on DSS Longbenton.
Career: Beal Grammar School for Girls, University College, London, articled *Withers* Partner *Ashurst Morris Crisp* 1994.
Personal: Married with two children.

SAUNDERS, Chris
Slaughter and May, London
(0171) 600 1200
Specialisation: Main areas of practice include joint ventures, projects, banking and project finance, primarily in power, energy and telecommunications.
Career: Qualified with *Slaughter and May* 1979. Partner 1986.

SEDGLEY, David
Allen & Overy, London (0171) 330 3000
Specialisation: Project Finance.
Career: Articled *Allen & Overy*, qualified 1989. Partner 1995.
Personal: Born 1964.

SHORT, Rodney
Clifford Chance, London (0171) 600 1000
Specialisation: Project Finance. Acting for sponsors, lenders and/or MLAs in limited resourse financing of infrastructure and industrial/energy projects on a world wide basis. Also expert in general banking law such as syndicated loans and corporate restructurings. Important transactions handled include acting for sponsors on Indian 'fast track' IPP, for lenders on Spanish IPP, for sponsors on the Portuguese gas system and for lenders on Venezuelan petrochemical projects. A frequent conference speaker on subjects of project finance and banking law.

SIMPSON, Paul
Clifford Chance, London
(0171) 600 1000 Partner.
Specialisation: Partner in Projects Group specialising in development and financing of infrastructure projects, including those in the power, oil and gas, mining and transport sections. Recent projects include Sattend IPP in the UK and Sevlax IPP in Italy.
Career: Qualified 1980. LLB (Hons) Edinburgh. *Clifford Chance* since 1983. Partner since 1989.

SKELTON, John
Macfarlanes, London (0171) 831 9222
Partner in Company, Commercial and Banking Department.
Specialisation: A partner specialising in banking and corporate law, a particular area of expertise is in major infrastructure projects and project finance. He advised in relation to the DBOF project for Bridgend Prison, the Docklands Light Rail extension to Greenwich and Lewisham and the proposed redevelopment of West Middlesex Hospital. He is part of the twelve strong Macfarlanes PFI team which includes partners from other specialist areas, namely Jeremy

Courtenay-Stamp from the commercial section, John Moore from the property section and Mark Baldwin a corporate tax specialist – the team has advised on a range of PFI projects acting for both purchasers and the project company as well as project sponsors in their capacity as service providers and providers of debt and equity finance.

SOUTAR, Tim
Clifford Chance, London (0171) 600 1000
Specialisation: Partner specialising in the commercial and financial aspects of large scale industrial and infrastructure projects, primarily in the power, energy (including refinery and petrochemicals) and transport sectors, multilateral and export credit financing. Recent transactions include: Sual (Philippines), Tanjung Jati B (Indonesia), and Zhuhai and Zhabei (PRC) power plants, and the Star Refinery project and BERTS combined transport system, both in Thailand. Also handles banking work, bilateral, syndicated, and other aspects of debt finance, secured and unsecured. Contibutor to 'Project Finance' (IFR) and 'Loans to China' (IFR).
Prof. Memberships: Member of UK Power Sector Working Group.
Career: BA Jurisprudence, St Catherine's College Oxford, Diploma in Chinese Law, University of East Asia, Macau (1987), Partner *Clifford Chance* 1988.

STACEY, Paul
Slaughter and May, London (0171) 600 1200
Qualified with *Slaughter and May* 1983. Partner 1990. Main areas of practice include electricity-related work, banking and project finance. Member of The Law Society. Born 1959.

TAYLOR, Michael
Norton Rose, London (0171) 283 6000
See under Energy – Oil and Gas, p. 333

TEMPLETON – KNIGHT, Jane
Milbank, Tweed, Hadley & McCloy, London
(0171) 448 3000
Specialisation: Partner in Project Finance Group, specialising in the development and financing of major infrastructure projects including mining, oil and gas pipeline, transport infrastructure, satellite and power plant finance: represented parties in relation to infrastructure projects in Europe, North America, Asia and Africa including: Croydon Tramlink; Lisheen Zinc Mine, Ireland; Sea Launch satellite system; New Tagus Bridge, Portugal; Pego and Tapada Power Stations, Portugal; Rosen Power Station, Italy; the Serene group of power stations, Italy; Second Severn Bridge; Newport gold heap leaching project in Uzbekistan; South East London waste-to-energy plant; The Kasese Cobalt Mine, Uganda. Other transactions have included management buy-out and buy-ins as well as cross-border acquisitions.
Career: Durham University, BA Honours (upper second), 1985. University of Newcastle -upon-Tyne, Solicitors Final Examination, 1986. *Allen & Overy*, London – Qualified 1989. Associate 1989-December 95. *Milbank, Tweed,Hadley & McCloy*, London – January 1995 senior associate, October 1996, elected partner.

TOTT, Nicholas P.
Herbert Smith, London (0171) 374 8000
Specialisation: Principal areas of work include all forms of financing and banking work with particular emphasis on asset finance, leasing,

project financing and Private Finance Initiative (PFI) Projects. Seconded to the Private Finance Panel Executive for fifteen months with responsibility for PFI Projects in Scotland, Northern Ireland and the Ministry of Defence. Publications include a chapter "Public Finance in the UK" in Leasing Finance (Euromoney 1997, 3rd Edition.) Editor (jointly with Jason Fox) of The Private Finance Inititative Handbook (Jordans, due for publication Autumn 1998).
Prof. Memberships: Law Society; City of London Solicitors' Company.
Career: Qualified Scotland (1985), England and Wales (1991). Partner 1992.
Personal: Born 8th May 1960. Educated at Edinburgh University. Leisure pursuits include Golf and Skiing.

VINTER, Graham D.
Allen & Overy, London (0171) 330 3000
Specialisation: Partner specialising in all aspects of project finance.
Career: Articled *Allen & Overy*, qualified 1982, Partner 1988. Author of "Project Finance: a Legal Guide" (2nd.ed., 1998).
Personal: Oxford University (BA 1979). Ludwig-Maximilians University, Munich (1977-78). Elected member of Mole Valley District Council (1988). Born 1956.

WEBER, David
Linklaters, London (0171) 456 5870
Partner, Project and
Project Finance Department.
Specialisation: Long and successful track record of structuring, negotiating and documenting complex projects and bringing them to successful financial closing. Has acted for sponsors and lenders on the development and financing of projects in the UK, Europe, Asia and Africa. Has particular expertise in projects involving multi-sourced financing from commercial banks, export credit agencies, and multi lateral lending agencies and capital markets, including the $1.8bn Hub Power Station Project, Pakistan, and the proposed DM1bn Mochovske Nuclear Power Station Project, Slovakia. His projects have also included projects whose location spans more than one country and he is therefore familiar with solving the special problems of multi-jurisdictional projects. (Anglo-French Channel Tunnel; $4bn Chad – Cameroon Pipeline). Other major projects include several limited-recourse oil development financings and project financings in the transportation and telecommunications fields.

WHITE, Bruce
Linklaters, London (0171) 456 5988
Partner, Project Finance Group.
Specialisation: Focuses on UK PFI projects. Recent projects include arranging finance for the Fazakerley Prison project, advising the sponsors on the new Scottish ATC centre and advising lenders and/or bidders on other PFI projects.
Personal: Attended University of Dundee, LL B, DIP LP 1984. Qualified 1986. Partner in 1995.

WOOLF, Fiona
Cameron McKenna, London (0171) 367 3000
See under Energy – Electricity, p. 334

WYMAN, Chris
Clifford Chance, London (0171) 600 1000
Partner. Main area of practice is project financing in the power, infrastructure and natural resources sectors.

The SOUTH and WALES

Masons (Bristol) (3ptnrs/3assts) With the arrival of *Iain Fairbairn* and Cathryn Vickers from Bevan Ashford, Masons' projects group has both doubled in size and become more rounded, adding public sector experience to their existing private sector reputation. **Clients/Work:** Advising on Hereford Hospital and the South Gloucester IT Partnership project.

Morgan Bruce (Cardiff) (8ptnrs/1assoc/5assts) The dominant PFI firm in Wales. The PFI group is headed by Alun Cole, formerly a legal adviser to the Home Office and the Welsh Office. **Clients/Work:** Advising the Cardiff Bay Development Corporation on the largest PFI project in Wales. Advising Gwent Constabulary on the Ystrad Mynach 31 Cell Accommodation Unit. Advising Symonds, the main subcontractor and a member of the PPM consortium on the DSS PRIME project.

Veale Wasbrough (Bristol) (5ptnrs/4assts) 3 strands to the PFI practice: MoD projects; PACE; and local authority work. The focus is on procurement authorities. **Clients/Work:** Advising on the £400m pa, 15 year partnering agreement regarding the Naval Recruiting and Training Agency, a flagship MoD PFI. Advising Bristol CC on the £180m plus Bristol Harbourside city centre regeneration project. Advising on the procurement of 15,000m″ new office accommodation for DETR and the planning inspectorate.

Bevan Ashford (Bristol) (3ptnrs/7assts) The loss of PFI specialists Iain Fairbairn and Cathryn Vickers is a major blow but the firm is expected to have a continuing role in PFI. The former head of construction is the new head of the group. **Clients/Work:** Acting for Glan Y M″r NHS Trust on a £54m project, the largest health scheme in Wales. Acting for Newbury College on a pathfinder project to provide new teaching accommodation with an innovative income generating aspect. Acting for Invicta Leisure developing a £6m health and tennis centre at Brighton University.

Burges Salmon (Bristol) (3ptnrs/6assts) Increasingly making its presence felt in PFI and enters the lists for the first time. **Clients/Work:** Retained to advise the MoD on PFI/partnering projects for a five year period. Advised the MoD on the Defence Fixed Telecommunications System, the largest MoD PFI signed to date. Adviser of senior debt to PFI consortia in hospital sector.

The MIDLANDS and EAST ANGLIA

Dibb Lupton Alsop With the numbers to take on the largest projects Dibbs have had some real successes. Described as "solid and pretty good" the firm's national 75 strong PFI team is co-ordinated from Birmingham by *Tony Randle*. Unusually for a regional practice funding work plays a significant role. **Clients/Work:** Advising the MoD on the £500/750m redevelopment of Colchester barracks. Advising the Department of Education for Northern Ireland on all their pathfinder projects. Advising Cheshire Police Authority on the rationalisation and procurement of accommodation.

Pinsent Curtis (5ptnrs/5assts) "Good core expertise." Have a national reputation, mainly acting for public sector clients. *Patrick Twist* and *Cameron Woodrow* are the best known PFI lawyers in the region. **Clients/Work:** Advising 7 local authorities on the £150m refinancing and restructuring of Birmingham Airport, a PPP. Acting on a £60m concession based financing of London Luton Airport. Acting on a £850m waste management concession for Hampshire Waste Services.

Eversheds (Nottingham) (1ptnr/8assts) The Leeds office may get all the publicity but the "user friendly" *Stephen Matthew* and his team usually lead on the education and police projects. **Clients/Work:** Completing the first school PFI project for Dorset CC, and Staffordshire, Norfolk, Essex County Councils and Enfield on other school PFI projects. Acting for GNRT, the company developing Greater Nottingham's Light Rapid Transit system.

Mills & Reeve (4ptnrs/4assts) Successful in picking up NHS work, the firm is now moving into education and LA projects. The majority of projects are in the £10/15m range, mainly acting for sponsors. **Clients/Work:** Acting for West Berks Priority Care Services NHS Trust on a new community hospital project. Instructed by Southend Community Care Services NHS Trust. Acting for the University of Westminster on a substantial residential accommodation project.

Wragge & Co (4ptnrs/6assts) A late entrant to PFI, the firm also has a substantial general projects practice undertaking energy and transport related projects. **Clients/Work:** Acting for Travel West Midlands as part of the consortium on the DBFO Midlands Metro Line. Advising PowerGen on its £340m National Freight Distribution Park. Derbyshire CC on a £25-30m magistrates court project. Tarmac on a bid for the A130 road scheme.

Edge & Ellison (2ptnrs/2assocs/1asst) Focusing on leisure and healthcare. **Clients/Work:** Acting for the successful bidder to provide services to South Bucks NHS trust. Acting for the preferred bidder for a 20 year concession to provide catering services and refurbishment works to Queen's Medical Centre in Nottingham. Advising Birmingham Millennium trust on PFI issues for its proposed £120m development in the heart of Birmingham.

THE NORTH

Addleshaw Booth & Co (Manchester/Leeds 24ptnrs/15assts) One of the "natural leaders in the North," who "know what they're doing." *Keith Johnston* heads the overall projects group *Tim Wheldon* is also well known. The majority of work is for promoters. **Clients/Work:** South Manchester University Hospitals NHS Trust on a £90m prioritised project. South Yorkshire Passenger Transport Executive, Doncaster MBC and Rail Track on a £25m new passenger transfer interchange at Doncaster. Leeds Community and Mental Health Services Teaching NHS Trust – reached financial close on two and advising on a further 11 schemes.

Eversheds (Manchester/Leeds) (4ptnrs/6assts) "You can't question their expertise in education and local authority PFIs." The other firms, including the big boys in London, are still trying to catch *Stephen Cirell* and his team up. Less well positioned for in bidder/funder work and for other sectors of PFI. **Clients/Work:** Acting on the first four pathfinder local government PFIs identified by the 4Ps. Advising Hereford & Worcester on the largest local authority PFI to date, a £400m waste management project. Advising on the innovative refurbishment of Stoke-on-Trent's schools, a project involving subcontracting work back to the council and a joint venture.

Pinsent Curtis (Leeds) (9ptnrs/6assts in Leeds, supported by 12 associates and partners in London and Birmingham) Headed by *Arthur Lovitt* in Leeds. Strong in the public sector but lacking depth in other areas. **Clients/Work:** Acting on the North Durham Acute Hospitals NHS trust £96m development of a new district general hospital (reached financial close on 31 March 1998). Advising North Yorkshire CC on 3 pathfinder road schemes. Advising Cardinal Heenana High School on a pathfinder development of a new voluntary-aided school in Leeds.

Dickinson Dees (Newcastle) "A force to be reckoned with" and the beneficiary of fierce regional loyalty in their Newcastle fiefdom. Moving up to become a Leader, as does *Simon Lewis*, on the back of closing Carlisle Hospital. Also active in transport and local authority work. *Alison Fellows* is up & coming and on secondment to the private finance unit of the NHS Executive in Leeds. **Clients/Work:** Acting for Carlisle Hospitals NHS Trust on the £86m Cumberland Infirmary Redevelopment project, the 2nd DGH to reach financial close and the first to get bond funding.

Masons (Manchester/Leeds) (5ptnrs/4assocs/5assts) "You can't knock Masons." A high quality outfit with a reputation for acting for bidding consortia although now breaking out of their compartmentalisation as just contractors' lawyers. **Clients/Work:** Acting for Sir Robert McAlpine and Trevor Osbourne Group on Norfolk Police HQ. Acting for the DSS Contributions Agency in the Newcastle Estate Development Project.

Acting for the Lowry Trust on the Lowry Centre, Salford.

Irwin Mitchell (5ptnrs/2assst) Specialising in sports/leisure projects, mainly for public sector clients. **Clients/Work:** Advising on the Sheffield bid (now preferred bidders) for the BOO contract for the £57m headquarters of the UK Sports Institute. Acting for Sheffield City Trust on the £15m National Ice Centre project. Both these projects have lottery funding. Advising the promoters of Football World.

Wansbroughs Willey Hargrave A firm that enjoyed a head start in PFI as they were already advisers to a number of Trusts. **Clients/Work:** Hospital entrance/concourse redevelopment. Transfer of staff residential accommodation to a housing association

Garretts (Leeds) *Frank Suttie* leads the national PFI practice, however since leaving Pinsent Curtis he has been far less visible. **Clients/Work:** Advising Nottingham Trent University on a project to provide conference and student accommodation and related facilities. Advising Merseyside Passenger Transport Executive on a light rapid transport system for Liverpool. Advising on the Derbyshire Police Authority Divisional HQ project.

SCOTLAND

Dundas & Wilson CS (5ptnrs/2assts (core team) supported by another 3 ptnrs/20 assts). Active in every sector of PFI and "never a pain to deal with." Led by the pragmatic *Michael McAuley* and *Alan Campbell*, a new entrant to the leaders' list. *Robert Pirrie* is also highly regarded. **Clients/Work:** Acting for two of the three Scottish Water Authorities (East of Scotland Water Authority and West of Scotland Water Authority). Acting for the University of Edinburgh in the £170m new Royal Infirmary project. Acting for the funders for the preferred bidder for the £70m Falkirk Schools project.

MacRoberts (3ptnrs/4assts) "Flexible, rigorous and determined to get it right." *David Henderson* has successfully made the transition from construction lawyer to PFI expert and leads the team. A new banking recruit has fixed what was previously thought to be the only weak link. A slight tilt towards bidder work exists as a consequence of the firm's client base. **Clients/Work:** Appointed by Falkirk Council to act in a £60m PFI project for five new schools. Acting for the Royal Infirmary of Edinburgh (with LWD) on a £200m project. Financial close for the Gleeson/Canmore consortium for Inverness Airport PFI.

Burness (5ptnrs/5assts) Have made big inroads over the last year. PFI is dealt with by the Construction & Engineering Department headed by *Anthony Read* ("sharp and knowledgeable. Doesn't take unreasonable positions") The effective team includes recent recruits from MacRoberts and McGrigors. **Clients/Work:** Acting for Ballast Wiltshire on the Falkirk Council Schools project, the first in Scotland. Acting for the DSS on project PRIME (£4.6bn). Acting on the Strathclyde Police New Force Training and Recruitment Centre.

McClure Naismith *Steven Brown* and his group learned their trade on health projects and learned it well. The question is, following the health review, will they be able to diversify into other areas? **Clients/Work:** Acting for Hairmyres & Stonehouse NHS Trust on a £67.5m DGH, financially closed in April 1998. Acting for the preferred bidder in the £11m Derby Divisional Police Headquarters project. Acting for the preferred bidder in the £14m West Lothian College project.

McGrigor Donald (12ptnrs/13assts) A collection of good individuals rather than a fully integrated team. Overall, slightly lacklustre when judged by McGrigor's usual high standards. *David Bankier* and *Brandon Nolan* are the two established names, whilst *Donna Stevenson* is up & coming. **Clients/Work:** Acting for Morrison Construction Group plc in the provision of accommodation at Clarendon College, Nottingham, a listed building, involving National Heritage Fund financing. Acting for the Law Hospital NHS trust in the procurement of a new £250m DGH. Acting for the DoE for Northern Ireland on the construction of Westlink Motorway, Belfast.

Shepherd & Wedderburn (7ptnrs/8assts) "Coming on nicely." *Paul Hally's* focused team has received a big boost with the arrival of *David Nash*, a new recruit from the Scottish Office where he had been specialising in PFI. Expected to climb higher in the lists. **Clients/Work:** Completion of the M6 DBFO. Acting for the Scottish Prison Service on the Kilmarnock prison project. Acting for Chesterton Scotland Ltd on the Falkirk College PFI project to provide a new college facility in Stirling.

Tods Murray (4ptnrs/4assts) *William Simmons* and his firm are new entrants to the lists. Recommended on both sides of the border for their co-ordinated, "get the job done," approach. Active in health, water and local government, acting for public and private sectors and funders. **Clients/Work:** Scottish aspects of Project PRIME. Dundee Waste to Energy plant, the first major local authority PFI to be completed in Scotland. Advising Barclays Bank on Hairmyres and Stonehouse Hospitals Project, the first major hospital project in Scotland to reach financial close.

Maclay Murray & Spens (7 fee earners) Are best known for "putting the kilt on projects run from England". Lacking a focus following last year's departure of Robert Pirrie to D&W, although *Michael Livingston* looks like he could be up to the challenge. **Clients/Work:** Advising the North of Scotland Water Authority on its £45m procurement of new sewage treatment works for Inverness and Fort William, the first such scheme to reach financial close in Scotland.

Henderson Boyd Jackson (3ptnrs/1assoc/3assts) "Starting to crop up more often." The firm's Capital Projects Group is active in education, defence housing and health, but is best known for social housing projects (20% of the workload). **Clients/Work:** Mainly act on the private sector side. Act for Jarvis plc, Gleeson and Miller.

LEADING INDIVIDUALS
SCOTLAND

BROWN Steven McClure Naismith
HENDERSON David MacRoberts

BANKIER David McGrigor Donald
CAMPBELL Alan Dundas & Wilson CS
HALLY Paul Shepherd & Wedderburn WS
MCAULEY Michael Dundas & Wilson CS
NOLAN Brandon McGrigor Donald
READ Anthony Burness
SIMMONS William Tods Murray WS

UP AND COMING

LIVINGSTON Michael Maclay Murray & Spens
NASH David Shepherd & Wedderburn WS
PIRRIE Robert Dundas & Wilson CS
STEVENSON Donna McGrigor Donald

SEE PROFILES AT END OF THIS SECTION

LEADERS' PROFILES · REGIONS

BANKIER, David A.
McGrigor Donald, Glasgow (0141) 248 6677
Partner in Property Department.
Specialisation: Main area of practice is commercial property law, with an increasing emphasis on funding of property developments and investments, joint ventures and public/private sector initiatives in commercial property. Acted in the site assembly and development and later completed a £70 million syndicated bank lending facility to finance phase 1 of the Broomielaw Development, Glasgow. Recently has acted in the sale of the 1st phase, one of Scotland's largest office disposals, and the development of a major £25 million headquarters building as a further phase. Advised the £160m acquisition of Glasgow's St. Enoch Centre, the largest retail acquisition in Scotland so far. Presently advising North Lanarkshire Council as successors to Cumbernauld Development Corporation in the major redevelopment of Cumbernauld Town Centre. More recently has branched into PFI, as head of the firm's capital projects unit, and is advising on the ú120 million new Law District General Hospital.
Career: Qualified in 1977, having joined *McGrigor Donald* in 1970. Became a Partner in 1978.
Personal: Born 24th March 1949. Educated at Edinburgh University (LLB 1970). Leisure interests include art history, Scottish contemporary paintings, sailing and skiing. Lives in Glasgow.

BROWN, Steven
McClure Naismith, Edinburgh
(0131) 220 1002
Specialisation: Project finance and PFI. Advises public sector, private sector consortia and banks. Practice covers many PFI sectors and holds overseas appointments on BOO/BOT schemes in power generation, and water and sewerage. Represented Grampian Health Board in the innovative Stonehaven Hospital PFI procurement, Bank of Scotland in the Stirling College PFI project and the NHS Trust at the new Hairmyres District General Hospital. Part of the team advising the consortium on the South Bucks hospital project. All of these projects have achieved financial closure. Currently advising on health, education, local authority and transport projects. Active in the UK renewable energy industry.
Prof. Memberships: Society of Writers to HM Signet, Law Society of Scotland.
Career: Qualified in 1980. Partner in *McClure Naismith* since 1986, now Head of Projects Group.
Personal: Born 20 November 1956. Educated at Irvine Royal Academy 1969-74, University of Edinburgh 1974-78. Lives near Edinburgh. Leisure pursuits include family, computers, music, golf. Chairman of a charity for adults with learning difficulties.

CAMPBELL, Alan
Dundas & Wilson CS, Edinburgh
(0131) 228 8000
Specialisation: With a background in corporate law, now concentrates exclusively upon project work including PFI. With several ongoing current projects, notable completed projects include: project leader for *Dundas & Wilson* team advising preferred bidder for the New Law Hospital PFI Project, the UK's second and the largest NHS bond issue (ú136m); project leader for *Dundas & Wilson* team advising Highlands and Islands Airports Limited in the new Inverness Airport Terminal PFI Project; leading acquisition of the private hospital known as Health Care International, Clydebank from the receivers on behalf of Abu Dhabi Investment Company; acting for Scottish Hydro-Electric plc in its power stations projects at each of Fellside (BNFL Sellafield), Seabank (British Gas, Nr Bristol) and Keadby (Norweb).
Career: Edinburgh University LLB (Hons) Dip LP. Qualified 1986. Partner 1992. Head of Infrastructure Group.

CIRELL, Stephen
Eversheds, Leeds (0113) 243 0391
See under Local Government, Adminstrative & Public Law , p. 91, 557

FAIRBAIRN, Iain
Masons, Bristol (0117) 924 5678
(with effect from 7 October 1998)
Head of Commercial Department.
Specialisation: General commercial advice on both sides of public/private joint ventures, facilities management contracts and procurement and vires issues, with specialisation in project finance, particularly for NHS Trusts and other public bodies under PFI, currently including MOD and prioritised NHS

acute schemes
Prof. Memberships: Law Society.
Career: 1977-1982 *Slaughter and May* Assistant Solicitor. 1982-1996 *Bevan Hancock/Bevan Ashford*. 1996-1998 *Bevan Ashford* Head of Commercial Department. October 1998, Partner *Masons*.
Personal: Sailing, Skiing, Hill Walking.

FELLOWS, Alison
Dickinson Dees, Newcastle upon Tyne
0191 279 9000
PFI projects. Head partner acting for Carlisle Hospital NHS Trust on PFI project for the redevelopment of the Cumberland Infirmary. Followed by 6 omonths secondment to Private Finance Unit of NHS Executive to assist with ongoing projects.
Career: Cambridge University 1980-83. *Field Fisher Waterhouse* 1985-88. *Dickinson Dees* 1988 to date. Married to Tim Care also a partner at Dickinson Dees. Son Charlie aged 3.

HALLY, Paul W.
Shepherd & Wedderburn WS, Edinburgh
(0131) 228 9900
See under General Corporate Finance, Insolvency, p. 257, 458

HENDERSON, David
MacRoberts, Glasgow (0141) 332 9988
Partner in Construction and Projects Department.
Specialisation: Main area of practice is construction and engineering law with emphasis on PFI and other infrastructure projects. Currently involved in a variety of PFI projects in the healthcare, education, roads and wastewater sectors. Led legal team for successful consortium at Highland sewerage project. Joint author of annotated version of CDM Regulations. Advised on Scots law aspects of 1998 edition of GC Works Contracts. Co-author of forthcoming 'MacRoberts on Building Contracts'.
Prof. Memberships: Associate of Chartered Institute of Arbitrators (ACIArb).
Career: Qualified in 1979, having joined *MacRoberts* in 1977. Became Partner in 1983. Accredited by Law Society of Scotland as Specialist in Construction Law (1994).
Personal: Born 18th July 1955. Educated at Kilmarnock Academy and Edinburgh University. Lives in Giffnock, Glasgow.

JOHNSTON, Keith T.
Addleshaw Booth & Co, Manchester
(0161) 934 6000
Partner in Corporate Finance Group.
Specialisation: Principal area of practice is corporate finance (see separate entry). Other main areas of work include partnerships and joint ventures between public and private sector parties relating to economic development, regeneration and infrastructure initiatives, advice to public sector bodies on transactional and constitutional matters, PFI work and advice to private sector and public sector parties on grant assistance.
Prof. Memberships: Law Society. Chairman: North West Company Secretaries' Forum. Head of Projects Group at the firm.
Career: Qualified in 1976. Became a Partner in 1981. 1991-94 Member of board of *Norton Rose*

M5 Group. Board member of *Addleshaw Booth & Co*.
Personal: Born 3rd July 1952. Attended Bootle Grammar School 1963-70, then London University 1970-73 (External). Governor of The Grange School, Hartford, Cheshire. Leisure pursuits include badminton (Manchester League), chess and tennis. Lives in Hale, Cheshire.

LEWIS, Simon
Dickinson Dees, Newcastle upon Tyne
0191 279 9000
See under Construction & Civil Engineering, p. 212

LIVINGSTON, Michael B
Maclay Murray & Spens, Glasgow
(0141) 248 5011
See under Financial Services (FSA, Compliance etc), p. 389

LOVITT, Arthur
Pinsent Curtis, Leeds (0113) 244 5000
Specialisation: Partner in Property Department. Head of PFI, Leeds. Involved in major property developments (various retail leisure, office and business park schemes). PFI and Public Sector Partnership work includes: representing, as lead partner, North Durham Acute Hospitals NHS Trust on their PFI scheme which achieved financial close on 31/3/98 (the fifth major NHS scheme in the country to achieve financial close); also advised upon the St James's and Seacroft University Hospital NHS Trust PFI Scheme, Bradford Superdome, Royal Armouries, Leeds and the disposal of the first part of the Epsom Cluster for the Secretary of State for Health.
Prof. Memberships: Round Table (former Chairman of Leeds Round Table).
Career: Bradford Grammar School and Nottingham University (LLB 2:1). Qualified with *Daynes Hill & Perks* (now *Eversheds*) in Norwich. Three years in Commercial Property Department of *Linklaters & Paines*. Joined *Simpson Curtis* in 1990. Partner in 1994.
Personal: Walking and travel.

MATTHEW, Stephen
Eversheds, Nottingham (0115) 950 7000
Specialisation: Stephen Matthew joined *Eversheds* in 1995 having previously worked for fifteen years within local government. Before joining *Eversheds*, Stephen was County Secretary and Solicitor of Shropshire County Council. Stephen was educated at Farnham Grammar School, the University of Sheffield and the College of Law, London. He specialises in local authority work and is an honorary member of the Association of Council Secretaries and Solicitors. He began his career with South Yorkshire County Council, moved on to Derbyshire County Council and joined Shropshire County Council in 1998 as Assistant County Secretary. Stephen is married with three children and lives on the outskirts of Nottingham.

MCAULEY, Michael
Dundas & Wilson CS, Glasgow
(0141) 221 8586
Specialisation: Partner in Construction and Engineering Group specialising in PFI and non-

contentious construction and engineering matters. Currently advising East of Scotland Water Authority in relation to the Almond Valley and Seafield Project and the Esk and Levenmouth Projects; advising Glasgow City Council on Secondary School Rationalisation.
Prof. Memberships: The Law Society of Scotland, the International Bar Association.
Career: Attended University of Glasgow (LLB Hons, DipLP). Articled *McGrigor Donald*; qualified 1989; assistant solicitor *McGrigor Donald* 1989-1992; Senior Commercial Executive at John Brown Engineering Limited 1992-1995; Associate at *Dundas & Wilson CS* 1995-1997. Partner since 1997.
Personal: Born 1956. Resides Helensburgh. Leisure interests include cycling and interior design.

NASH, David
Shepherd & Wedderburn WS, Edinburgh
(0131) 228 9900
Specialisation: PFI Commercial Contracts. Current projects: Daldowie & Shieldwall Sewage PFI; East Renfrewshire PFI; Scottish Children's Reporters Administrations PFI. Past projects: M8 DBFO: M6 DBFO: New Scottish Office, Victoria Quay: Skye Bridge.
Prof. Memberships: Law Society of Scotland.
Career: School: George Watson University College, Edinburgh. Edinburgh University – Hons MA, LLB (1969-1976). 1983-98 – Scottish Office Legal Department.
Personal: Music, travel, skiing.

NOLAN, Brandon
McGrigor Donald, Glasgow (0141) 248 6677
Specialisation: All aspects of contentious and non-contentious matters relating to construction law. Worked on Skye Bridge Project and on subsequent PFI infrastructure projects in Scotland, England and Northern Ireland. On the contentious side has conducted the advocacy in a number of substantial arbitrations. A frequent speaker at commercially organised seminars.
Prof. Memberships: Associate of the Chartered Institute of Arbitrators; Society of Construction Law; International Bar Association; Official Referees Solicitors Association.
Career: Qualified 1980 with *McGrigor Donald & Co* (as it was then). Became a partner in 1987. Head of the Construction and Engineering Unit at *McGrigor Donald*.
Personal: Born 4th November 1955. Educated at Glasgow University 1974-1978. Leisure interests include visiting a gym and films.

PIRRIE, Robert
Dundas & Wilson CS, Edinburgh
(0131) 228 8000
Specialisation: Private equity; PFI/ infrastructure projects (education and local authority). Adviser to lenders on Falkirk schools PFI project; adviser to Glasgow City Council on its schools modernisation PPP project; adviser to Falkirk College on completed Stirling Education Centre PFI project; adviser to Telford College on campus redevelopment PPP project.
Prof. Memberships: Law Society of Scotland; Member of Company Law Committee; Writer to the Signet.
Career: Kelvinside Academy; Glasgow University LLB (Hons) 1978. Qualified 1981. Partner *Maclay Murray & Spens* 1985-1997; Partner *Dundas & Wilson CS* and head of

Private Equity and Corporate and Commercial 1997 to date.

RANDLE, Tony
Dibb Lupton Alsop, Birmingham
(0345) 262728
See under Local Government, p. 558

READ, Anthony J.M.
Burness, Edinburgh (0131) 473 6000
Specialisation: Advising the public sector, bidders and banks on all aspects of the structuring, development and financing of projects. Main area of practice is advising on PFI projects. Current PFI projects include acting for Strathclyde Police on new training and recruitment centre, Perth & Kinross Council on office accommodation project and preferred bidder on Falkirk Schools Pathfinder Project. Regular speaker at conferences.

SIMMONS, William G.
Tods Murray WS, Edinburgh
(0131) 226 4771
william.simmons@todsmurray.co.uk.
Specialisation: Work includes infrastructure projects and PFI, corporate finance, mergers and acquisitions, banking and general commercial work including joint ventures.
Prof. Memberships: Law Society of Scotland.
Career: Qualified 1981 *Bishop & Co*. Joined *Dorman Jeffrey & Co* 1983 (Partner 1984). Joined *Tods Murray* as a Partner in 1986.
Personal: Born 1958. Attended Hutchesons Boys Grammar School 1967-1975 and Glasgow University 1975-79 (LL.B Hons). Leisure: hill walking and skiing.

STEVENSON, Donna
McGrigor Donald, Glasgow (0141) 248 6677
See under Property (Commercial), p. 723

SUTTIE, Frank
Garretts, Leeds (0113) 244 5000
London (0171) 649 9238
Specialisation: Private Finance Initiative and other project finance/ privatisation work. Advised in three of the Government's prioritised health PFI projects and currently advises in similar projects in health, education and for Government Departments. Specialises in procurement strategies, commercial contract negotiation, bid evaluations, client approval procedures and funding issues. Is a contributor to a major forthcoming text on the private finance initiative.
Prof. Memberships: Law Society. Admitted as a Solicitor 1985.
Career: Kirkcaldy High School. University of Stirling. University of London.

TWIST, G. Patrick A.S.
Pinsent Curtis, Birmingham (0121) 200 1050
See under Banking, p. 147

WHELDON, Timothy
Addleshaw Booth & Co, Leeds
(0113) 209 2000
See under General Corporate Finance, p. 251

WOODROW, Cameron
Pinsent Curtis, Birmingham
(0121) 200 1050
Specialisation: Major projects; public-private partnerships (including PFI); privatisations; corporate restructuring; joint ventures; acquisitions and disposals; project management. Major transactions have included the pre-franchising reorganisation of the Central Trains Operating Unit of British Rail; the ú150 million restructuring and refinancing of Birmingham International Airport; a US$150 million joint venture for LucasVarity; the ú70 million concession based financing of London Luton Airport; and the acquisition by GEC Alsthom/Tarmac of the Central Infrastructure Maintenance Unit of British Rail. Significant experience in advising both public bodies (including local authorities) and major private sector clients in the transport, automotive and engineering sectors. Expertise in commercial, company, contract and public law.
Prof. Memberships: Law Society.
Career: BA (Jurisprudence), Brasenose College, Oxford. *Freshfields* 1983-1993 (qualified 1986). Partner *Pinsent Curtis* 1993 to date. Birmingham head and national practice co-ordinator for major projects. Awarded "PFI Team of the Year" by Legal Business for Birmingham Airport restructuring.
Personal: Married. Two children. Resides Edgbaston. Common Purpose graduate.

PROPERTY (COMMERCIAL)

RESEARCH: In compiling the tables, we consider all the information available to us, paying particular regard to the market research carried out by our team of ten qualified lawyers. (The researchers' details are set out on page three.) The rankings, therefore, reflect the opinion of the marketplace as revealed by systematic and objective research: see page four. (Our research is audited every year by the British Market Research Bureau.)

OVERVIEW: Any firm that has not had a good year needs seriously to reconsider its marketing strategy. Without exception practitioners around the country told us that they were busier than they had been since right before the start of the last property slump. No one could accuse solicitors of being bullish about future prospects though. An optimistic property lawyer is someone who expects the good times to last beyond December 1998, with only one interviewee in the entire British Isles predicting similar levels of activity continuing into the new Millennium.

In London, Linklaters maintain their position at the head of the tables. As one competitor put it "What is particularly impressive about Linklaters' property practice is that you don't think of Linklaters as a property firm but it is still unarguably the best." Nabarros moves down another notch. Of particular note this year were Gouldens and McGuinness Finch. The latter firm achieved exceptional commendation in both our telephone and written surveys.

No single firm stands out in the South East. However within their local market many were highly rated. In the South West, Burges Salmon was seen to be slightly ahead of the rest but by no means dominant. The picture was almost unchanged in Wales and the Midlands. Eversheds and Mills & Reeve have however established a lead in East Anglia, whilst Hammond Suddards is a new entrant in the North West on the basis of strong recommendations by every surveyor we spoke to in Manchester although no lawyer mentioned them. In the North East, Eversheds have fallen behind over the last year whilst Garretts have done particularly well and McGuinness Finch enter the lists for the first time on several recommendations.

Whilst Dundas & Wilson and McGrigor Donald remain the leading Scottish firms, Maclay Murray & Spens and Shepherd & Wedderburn are so close " you could almost throw a tablecloth over them." The property market in Northern Ireland is as buoyant as that on the mainland with work gravitating more towards the top four firms and, amongst smaller firms, Mills Selig is said to be doing particularly well.

LEADING FIRMS · LONDON

LINKLATERS

ASHURST MORRIS CRISP
BERWIN LEIGHTON
CLIFFORD CHANCE
NABARRO NATHANSON

S J BERWIN & CO
HERBERT SMITH
LOVELL WHITE DURRANT

NATIONAL SURVEY
Top Ten Firms UK-wide

This table differs from the other tables in this section in two respects. It is derived from the results of a *written* survey of buyers of legal services in FTSE All Share companies and leading property lawyers. Secondly the survey asked respondents to rank firms and individuals on a *national* basis.

The table below is based on the first 150 questionnaires returned and lists the ten firms with the most recommendations in descending order.

1 Linklaters
2 Berwin Leighton
2 Nabarro Nathanson
4 Ashurst Morris Crisp
5 Clifford Chance
6 Eversheds
7 Herbert Smith
8 Lovell White Durrant
9 McGrigor Donald
10 Addleshaw Booth & Co

LONDON

Linklaters (24ptnrs/39assts) "They always bring something extra to the party." An outstanding client base and enormous corporate back-up coupled with "a great range of skills" make them the undisputed leading property practice in the UK. In our written survey the firm received as many first place nominations as Nabarros, Berwin Leighton and Clifford Chance combined. Not that their lofty position has gone to their heads. As a partner in a tiny competitor explained; "There's no arrogance when you're dealing

HIGHLY REGARDED FIRMS 100+ FEE-EARNERS
Allen & Overy
Cameron McKenna
Denton Hall
D J Freeman
Freshfields
Norton Rose
Simmons & Simmons
Titmuss Sainer Dechert
Dibb Lupton Alsop
Eversheds
Lawrence Graham
Macfarlanes
Richards Butler
Rowe & Maw
Slaughter and May
Travers Smith Braithwaite
Wilde Sapte

with Linklaters' property lawyers, even as a small firm. They roll up their sleeves and try to sort problems out." Department Head, *Robert* "Lord" *Finch* (known for his "relentless, almost bullying"negotiating style) came out as the UK's leading property lawyer in our written survey. Other well known names are *Martin Elliott* ("the hardest working partner at Linklaters and scarily organised") and *Jeffrey Bailey* ("charming and efficient"). *James Harbach*, a senior assistant and "a really great bloke who does the work of a partner" is newly included as an up & coming. The "brilliant" David Lloyd has now retired. The only cloud on the horizon is the approaching (albeit still fairly distant in some cases) retirement of the "cabal of larger than life characters" who built up the firm's reputation. Will the assistants coming through be up to the mark? **Clients/Work:** Retained on the development of new LIFFE headquarters. Lendlease – Bluewater Park portfolio. Acting on the huge disposal by Ropemaker of its Mayfair and Knightsbridge property portfolio.

Ashurst Morris Crisp (12ptnrs/45assts) Perhaps the strongest recommendation was Linklaters' choice of Ashursts to act for them on their move to new offices. "Superb, pragmatic property people" who scored lots of

brownie points by keeping a handle on all the Docklands transactions – "an amazing achievement." Clients praised them as "highly competent technically, excellent on contractual issues and good at covering all the loopholes." *Laurence Rutman* is "one of the top property lawyers around" but is expected to announce his retirement shortly. Whilst *Ian Nisse* has "a terrific following" he is now the firm's managing partner so fee-earning time is seriously reduced. The "excellent" *David Albert* was also recommended. **Clients/Work:** Newly instructed by NatWest, appointed to work on the NatWest Tower. Acting for Simmons & Simmons on their move to CityPoint. Instructed on the winding down of London Docklands, involving 1000 property disposals before the Corporation closed down.

Berwin Leighton (18ptnrs/30assts) Niche property firm with burgeoning profile seen as strong on the banking, secured lend-

HIGHLY REGARDED FIRMS 30-100 FEE-EARNERS
Gouldens
Maxwell Batley
Field Fisher Waterhouse
Forsyte Saunders Kerman
Manches & Co
Nicholson Graham & Jones
Olswang
Boodle Hatfield
Finers
Fladgate Fielder
Mishcon de Reya
Paisner & Co
Speechly Bircham
Trowers & Hamlins
Wedlake Bell

ing, investment side. Received some seriously good recommendations on the quality of the practice ("fight hard for their clients but pleasant to deal with") and "its stunningly good people." However there is a question mark hanging over their ability to resource work at the right level and they are said to be recruiting heavily. *Philip Bretherton* is "tip-top." *Laurie Heller* "has a certain aura about him" and is a "much admired, excellent practitioner." *David Taylor,* Head of Department, is "a slick operator" considered to be the leading light at Berwin Leighton and a "mover in the system." *Malcolm Brummer* is a "bright guy indeed and gets deals done." *Peter Rudolph* was also recommended. **Clients/Work:** Acting for English Partnerships, owner of Millennium Dome site, on creation and development of site and sale of Millennium village and superstore site. Acting for new client Legal & General on redevelopment of Barrington House involving surrender from Linklaters and preletting to Flemings of 280 000 sq.ft and 25-year lease at rent of £50 per

sq ft ie a rent of £12.5m. For Prudential Portfolio Managers the "swap"of 250 Euston Road in return for four central London properties: total asset value £400m.

Clifford Chance (17ptnrs/55assts) Some saw them as "on a par with Linklaters." Perceived to "take a practical commercial approach to dealmaking"and are particularly seen on property funding work. There is said to be some inconsistency in the personnel fielded by the department. *Tony Briam* ("nice to deal with") has now stepped down as Head of Property and "able lawyer" *Teddy Bourne* ("no histrionics. He understands the objectives") has taken on that mantle. *Robert Macgregor* is "clever and clients like him."*Rupert Hill* is "extremely good and extremely nice." *Tony Briam* and *Iain Morpeth* are also highly rated. **Clients/Work:** Advising Canary Wharf Group Ltd on number of large transactions including £555m securitisation, world's largest single development securitisation. Advising Burford on complex purchase for £210m of Trocadero Centre and London Pavilion at Piccadilly Circus from Trocadero Group. Advising Littlewoods Organisation plc on the disposal of 19 stores to Marks & Spencer for £192.5m within 7 working day deadline of receipt of instructions.

HIGHLY REGARDED FIRMS UNDER 30 FEE-EARNERS
McGuinness Finch
Coudert Brothers
Fenners
Forsters
Glovers
Hamlin Slowe
Julian Holy
Park Nelson
Stepien Lake Gilbert & Paling
Teacher Stern Selby
Thomas Eggar Church Adams

Nabarro Nathanson (35ptnrs/100assts) Nabarros' decline, whilst not precipitous or irreversible, is nevertheless highly visible and much remarked upon. It attracts criticism because expectations of a firm at the top of the profession are so high. It is attributed in part to the firm's unsuccessful attempt to diversify away from core areas. There are other factors. Whilst the people at the top were agreed to be "phenomenal," some of the others "are not really good enough." There were complaints that the firm is too aggressive. "They always draft the most aggressive document, send you the most aggressive mark up and take the most aggressive position." Having said all of that the firm does have a terrific client list and "some extremely proficient and expert people." The best known are *Geoffrey Lander* (an "effective marketeer"), *John Samson* ("a terrific lawyer"), *Graham Lust* and *David Wright.*

Clients/Work: Acting for GE Capital on acquisition of 191 commercial properties amounting to 2.8m sq ft from MEPC for approx £300m. Acting for Hammerson Plc on establishment of The Oracle Ltd Partnership, Hammerson's joint venture with an overseas investor, and development and investment in The Oracle Shopping Centre, Reading, value approx £215m. Advising Heron Property Corporation on three London office developments totalling 300,000sq ft and a value of approx £150m.

SJ Berwin & Co (8ptnrs/27assts) Some practitioners commented that the practice had traditionally been thin on clients ("just the one great client; British Land") but has been expanding its network of clientele over the last year and has therefore "come on enormously." Can be aggressive and has no leaders in our lists. **Clients/Work:** Acquisition of GUS property portfolio. Acquisition of 950 betting shops for Corals. Acquisition

of 19 stores from Littlewoods. New clients: Dixons, Oasis Stores plc, Axa Investment Managers SA, Royal & Sun Alliance, Chelsfield, BZW and Banker's Trust.

Herbert Smith (15ptnrs/48assts) Generally competent with some excellent individuals – constructive partners (including *Patrick Robinson* and *Christopher Harrison*) who "get deals done and mould assistants in that pattern" working for "super" clients. They are seen by some as gaining ground. However their property work is viewed in the market-place as a spin-off from other activities and experience of assistants is variable. *Chris Tavener* and *James Barnes* received many recommendations to enter our lists. **Clients/Work:** Bank relocations eg.relocation of Credit Agricole Lazard Financial Products Bank from the former Telegraph Buildings on Fleet Street to the Moorfields development. Letting of Globe House on Embankment by Hammer-

son to BAT Industries Plc for its new corporate HQ at an annual rent of c £7m. £300m merger of the medical schools of Guy's, St Thomas' and King's College (all represented by Herbert Smith).

Lovell White Durrant (12ptnrs/38assts) "Impressive and a delight to deal with" although "not always exciting." "Top quality" department head *Bob Kidby* has "gone out and got business on his own then spun that off into other parts of the firm." *Simon MacDonagh* is a "leading practitioner" who is seen about a lot. *Michael Stancombe* is "committed." **Clients/Work:** Purchase and leaseback of the ICI Headquarters buildings in Millbank for over £100m. Acting for the Prudential in the purchase of a further interest in the Bluewater Shopping Centre, being the Multiplex cinema site pre-let to Hoyts. Also for the Prudential, advising on the largest letting in the West End this year, of 30 Berkeley Square to BT.

HIGHLY REGARDED
100+ FEE-EARNERS

Allen & Overy (8ptnrs/37assts) Known for "clever, original, financed property work" and for "clear straightforward drafting – they aim to get the deal done and don't look for problems." **Clients/Work:** Acting for Bass on the sale of their estate of 1428 rented and managed pubs to Elba, a vehical formed by BT Capital Partners and a management group. Acting for a subsidiary of Herm's International on the rental of a prime retail space in Manchester. Acting for Hypobank on the financing for the development of the Citibank building in Canary Wharf.

Cameron McKenna (24ptnrs/48assts) In terms of property, the merger seems to be a case of 2+2 = 4. They are however "enjoyable to come up against and usually pretty impressive." *Roger Martin* is a "well-known and well-respected chap," as is *Nicholas Brown*. **Clients/Work:** Acquisition of Kingsland Industrial Park, Basingstoke on behalf of Brixton Estate. Acquisition of a block of property at Arundel Great Court, The Strand, comprising the Howard Hotel and Arthur Andersens's London offices on behalf of Moorland Estates Blackstone. Letting 33 Old Broad Street in the City to Halifax on behalf of Argyll Property Asset Managers.

Denton Hall (13ptnrs/28assts) A broad based, "user friendly" practice best known in the retail sector, although the firm also has a sizeable amount of investment and development work. The Milton Keynes office (3ptnrs/13assts) is seen as the "6th floor of Chancery Lane." *Diana Courtney* is "always sensible to deal with." **Clients/Work:** Acting for a major Far Eastern organisation in the purchase of Albion Wharf / Bridge Wharf Battersea for residential development. Subletting of Ebbgate House from Barclays

to Dresdner Bank AG. Many new stores for Marks & Spencer including a new megastore in Manchester following the 1996 bombing.

D J Freeman (21ptnrs/32assts) For a while the firm looked as if it would become a parable on how hard it is to build a reputation and how easily it can be lost. "And then they rallied rather well." A "can do" practice, rightly praised for its "admirable approach to technology and modern documentation." *Paul Clark* is "a lovely academic lawyer, whose reputation is built on creativity." **Clients/Work:** Purchase of a 6 acre, 123 unit shopping centre in Sale, Cheshire for Warner Estates plc. Acting for Benchmark plc on 2 major portfolio acquisitions in Belgravia and Knightsbridge. Sale of a £12m shopping centre at Caerphilly for Boots Properties.

Freshfields (10ptnrs/31assts) Despite one client's eulogy for the firm ("At the end of a transaction it's pretty rare for someone to phone up and say how good your lawyers were. It happens when you use Freshfields.") they do not have a profile as a leading property practice, except for "tax based deals and securitisations." *Geoffrey le Pard,* "a decent property lawyer," heads what is, however, definitely more than a service department. **Clients/Work:** Project PRIME – acting for the successful consortium (Partnership Property Management) in the largest property transfer ever undertaken in the UK from the Department of Social Security. Acting for tenants at Canary Wharf – Citibank (51,095 sq.m) and CSFB (25,547 sq.m). Welcome Break, an innovative securitisation for Bankers Trust.

Norton Rose (7ptnrs/30assts) Property may not be the main thrust of the firm's business but they get high profile work and approach it in a "flexible and innovative manner." **Clients/Work:** Acted for Spitalfields

Developments Ltd on a £250m/700,000 sq ft sale/development for LIFFE. Acted for Pillar Property PLC on the acquisition of land at Capability Green Business Park for a 630,000 sq ft office development. Advisers to the New Millennium Experience Company Ltd on the Millennium Exhibition at Greenwich.

Simmons & Simmons (16ptnrs/36assts) A firm on the up with an improving profile. Increasingly seen in "meaty transactions – and not just for RailTrack." *Alan Butler* "sees the big picture." **Clients/Work:** Despa's £100m funding of the redevelopment of 90-100 Wood Street, EC2. Abu Dhabi Investment Authority's £215m joint venture with Hammerson to develop the Oracle in Reading. £150m securitisation for Principal Healthcare Finance.

Titmuss Sainer Dechert (13ptnrs/31assts) *Steven Fogel* is one of the "notable exceptions to the generalisation that property lawyers lack charisma." An unusual spread of work, with 50% of the practice representing commercial tenants, particularly retail tenants, rather than the property industry. **Clients/Work:** Acting for the French retailer, Etam Development, on the property aspects of its £90m takeover of UK listed Etam plc. Helical Retail's £50m forward sale of 2 retail parks to Legal & General. Advising the British Shoe Corporation on the property aspects of the sale of Dolcis, Shoe Express and Shoe City.

Dibb Lupton Alsop (11ptnrs/8assts/6assocs) A stretched team regularly seen on large portfolio transactions. **Clients/Work:** MEPC/GE Capital disposal Portfolio £300m; Property aspects of Greenwich Healthcare PFI including ground breaking litigation; Hampton Trust plc: acquisition of site for Birmingham's tallest building.

Eversheds (11ptnrs/21assts) The property practice has been described as being "high volume, low cost." Interviewees' experience with the weaker Eversheds offices appeared to flavour their views of the firm as a whole. Recognised to be gaining market share – which may have provoked some of the adverse opinion. Nationally the firm as a whole came a high sixth in our written survey, ahead of Herbert Smith and LWD. **Clients/Work:** Acquisition of Coopers & Lybrands HQ at Embankment Place, part of BP Pension Fund's Knightsbridge and Mayfair Estates and Lion Plaza (formerly the NatWest Triangle) for overseas investors.

Lawrence Graham (23ptnrs/37assts) Joined by the property department of Forsyte Saunders Kerman. FSK had "an amazing client list" so it should be a strong merger. Putting a brave face on the loss of half of Legal & General's £3bn property portfolio to Berwin Leighton. The firm was given the choice of which portion of the work it wanted to keep and opted for the retail half. **Clients/Work:** Legal & General's sale of Arundel Great Court. Hermes' £33m forward purchase and lease back of Hatfield Business park in Hartfordshire. Universities Superannuation Scheme's purchase of a site for a factory outlet shopping centre in Hampshire.

Macfarlanes (9ptnrs/24assts) A department of "sound and easy to deal with" lawyers with an increasing amount of investment work. **Clients/Work:** Redevelopment

of Hobart House as a joint venture between Mountcity Investments and the Grosvenor Estate. The purchase for Legal & General's Industrial Property Investment Fund of 17 industrial estates. Acquisition of a 225,000sq ft distribution warehouse for Comet.

Richards Butler (11ptnrs/18assts) Pretty solid and "a decent bunch to work with." Well known for their work in the leisure sector, especially for Rank. **Clients/Work:** Refinancing the infamous Point West building for the Development Bank of Singapore and Overseas Union Bank. £150m sale and leaseback between British Land and Tank Group involving 20 leisure properties. Sumitomo Life Realty's £55m sale of two trophy buildings in the City at Angel Court.

Rowe & Maw (7ptnrs/16assts) Despite a good client base and some "excellent" partners, including the "super efficient" *James Black,* widely thought not to be coping with market pressure as well as some. The departure of David Gidney to Bristol has not helped. **Clients/Work:** EMI Group plc's disposal of the HMV and Dillons businesses to HMV Media Plc. Horserace Totalisation Board's acquisition of 130 betting offices from Coral Bookmakers and Ladbrokes. Acquisition and management of The Orchards shopping centre in Haywards Heath.

Slaughter and May (7ptnrs/28assts) It must be a difficult existence in the shadow of Slaughter's mighty corporate department. No matter how complex the transactions you

do, or the quantity, everyone sees you as a "mere service department." The deals *Graham White* and the others have been involved with suggest they are more than that. **Clients/Work:** Guardian Properties and Morgan Grenfell Asset Management's acquisition of Castle Meadow Retail Park from Boots Properties. Costain Group PLC's sale of its interest in the Spitalfields development and advising on the acquisition and office development by LIFFE. Worldwide sale of 370 properties in connection with the sale by Unilever plc of its fragrances and specialty chemicals division to ICI Plc.

Travers Smith Braithwaite (11ptnrs/23assts) Not seen in the market as much as before. Widely, if perhaps unfairly, described as a service department. **Clients/Work:** The Odyssey Trust Company Ltd's 23 acre waterfront leisure development in Belfast – one of the 12 landmark lottery projects. Clearwater Estates' £80m cruise liner terminal complex at Greenwich. Swan Hill (Whitley) Ltd's £60m factory outlet development in Hampshire.

Wilde Sapte (5ptnrs/17assts) *Stan Gniadkowski* retains his high profile. This firm is a new entrant on the back of some strong recommendations. **Clients/Work:** Amresco UK's £26.4m purchase of 13 properties from Land Securities. ABN Amro Leasing's subsidiary, Lease Plan UK Ltd, on the pre-let of its new UK HQ premisics in Slough. Helical Properties' sale of its 14 acre Coronation Park site in West London.

HIGHLY REGARDED 30-100 FEE-EARNERS

Gouldens (8ptnrs/14assts) Former Head of Department retired in April 1997. The team has grown by three assistants since last year. They are seen to have "a strong team" with some "go-getting younger lawyers coming through." They are "doing well" in "their own idiosyncratic way." **Clients/Work:** Acting for Ashtenne Ltd on its £79m float to become Ashtenne Holdings plc. Instructed by new client GTC. Continuing to act for largest client Pillar Property plc, including forward funding for £73m retail park development of Broughton Park, Chester, to be undertaken by Development Securities plc.

Maxwell Batley (8ptnrs/8assts) Property accounts for approx 40% of the firm's workload. Seen to be "first class people"who are "coming on a storm" and are "way ahead of the competition." Head of Department was described by one interviewee as "a wonderful property lawyer." **Clients/Work:** Acquisition of a half-share in the £170m Shires Shopping Centre in Leicester for Hermes Property Asset Management. International development project in Kenya acting for Atlantis Projects Ltd. Ongoing redevelop-

ment work for Manchester City Centre. New client; BP Investment Pension Fund, Ropemaker Properties.

Field Fisher Waterhouse (15ptnrs/15assts) Have a respected practice in licensed property and building up leisure property work. Their lead partner is "thorough and technically good." **Clients/Work:** Acting for British Railways Board in handling property aspects of remainder of British Rail privatisation programme involving several hundred properties. Won contract by competitive tender to continue to provide estate management work for DfEE's HQ estate. Advising on acquisition of new Mayfair head offices for UK subsidiary of NGC Corporation.

Manches & Co (10ptnrs/11assts) A large and "decent" practice; lawyers in the department are "capable and can be aggressive." **Clients/Work:** Have advised Liberty on redevelopment of their Regent Street store plus disposal of all regional retail outlets. Acting for Prime Commercial Group on the purchase of 3 major shopping centres from Land Securities – total value £50m plus. Acting for MEPC on joint venture and financing arrangements for science and technology park outside Cambridge.

Nicholson Graham & Jones (11ptnrs/

12assts) Property accounts for approx 30% of the workload of the firm. We received conflicting reports on their property practice: but some thought them "extremely proficient." **Clients/Work:** Acting for Heron Corporation in its acquisition of a portfolio of seven properties from Hypo Property Services Ltd. Acting for Pearl Assurance plc on the purchase of a Leisure Site at Brighton Marina from Brighton Marina Commercial Ltd. Acting for Regalian Properties PLC.

Olswang (5ptnrs/12assts) The new kid on the block, Olswangs are not traditionally known for their property work but have "taken an overall strategy to choose areas of work and concentrate on them" one of which is property for which they are gaining a "strong reputation." *David Kustow* is highly regarded as "user-friendly." **Clients/Work:** The acquisition of 5 shopping centres on behalf of Capital and Regional Properties plc for £147m. Sale of 250 Euston Road on behalf of Minerva plc for £105m. Sale of a mixed portfolio of 34 properties for MEPC plc for £103m.

Boodle Hatfield (11ptnrs/8assts) The firm is primarily known for its work for Grosvenor Estate, which is its key client. Variously described as "a delight to deal with, pleasant and efficient." Clients/Work: Acting for ELP Properties in purchase of 40 properties from General Accident for over £62m. Acting for Treasury Holdings who formed two Ltd partnerships to acquire a £77m portfolio of 11 properties, including Tolworth Tower near Kingston, from Hermes financed by GE Capital Corporation. Acting for The Grosvenor Estate in acquisition of the Walks Shopping Centre, Basingstoke (£70m).

Finers (13ptnrs/11assts) Have taken on five new property partners in the last year to develop the department. They are "seen around a lot, have a proactive approach and some good people." Many practitioners who had met them on the other side questioned their "unnecessarily aggressive" style. Others, however, noticed the "beginnings of a charm offensive." Clients/Work: Acting for Marylebone Warwick Balfour Group PLC in development of West India Quay, second largest development in Docklands since Canary Wharf. Acting for Pizza Hut & KFC in the acquisition of new units at Alton Towers & Chessington World of Adventure.

Fladgate Fielder (13ptnrs/7assts) The firm is moving into new premises in October in its effort to become "a more dynamic West End firm." Four of the property partners have recently moved to Charles Russell taking their clients with them, which may have an impact. Clients/Work: Acting for Capital & Regional Out of Town Ltd on development of SnoWorld Leisure Park Milton Keynes(£35 m). Acting for Terrace Hill Group plc in successful tender to Thanet District Council for redevelopment of Ramsgate harbour. Acting for Sun Microsystems on acquisition of land adjacent to M3 in Hampshire for development of new HQ in United Kingdom.

Mishcon de Reya (10ptnrs/2cons/11assts) Provide advice on Landlord & Tenant, development, construction, taxation and planning law. Clients/Work: Acting for City Acre Property Investment Trust on conditional disposal of 2 major buildings in City for redevelopment at price of £87.5m. Acting for Rialto Homes Plc in acquisition of 13 acre Guinness Distillery site at Wandsworth Bridge for Norman Foster residential/commercial development. Acting for Glaxo Wellcome Pension Fund in disposal of an office portfolio for £37m.

Paisner & Co (12ptnrs/28assts) Reasonable and have "some quality people." Clients/Work: Acting for The Great Universal Stores PLC(GUS) in connection with joint venture between The British Land Company PLC and GUS and work arising from property portfolio of 982 properties with an aggregated value of £900m. Acting for BL & Universal Plc in the first year of its operation in the disposal to various purchasers of over 300 investment properties with value in excess of £100m.

Speechly Bircham (12ptnrs/7assts) Merged in May of last year with Bailey Shaw & Gillett. Have "always been a player," they are "good to deal with and have some rather good clients and good performers." Clients/Work: Acting for Scottish Life Assurance Company on disposal of a mixed portfolio of 33 English properties. Acting for Lincoln Assurance on acquisition of Barton Arcade in Manchester, comprising 47 retail/office units within a listed structure. Continuing to act on Phase 1 of its major redevelopment in Marylebone High Street.

Trowers & Hamlins (6ptnrs/6assts) "Highly regarded" particularly for their Housing Association work. Clients/Work: Acquisition of 5 stores across the country for Crabtree & Evelyn in high profile locations.

Wedlake Bell (5ptnrs/3assts plus 1 p/t asst) Have a longstanding reputation for property and secured lending. Clients/Work: Disposal of Cowley Business Park for Kyle Stewart Properties Ltd. Acquisition of a portfolio of properties for S.G. Whitaker Ltd. Disposal of Brocket Hall on behalf of the Trustees of the Brocket Estate.

HIGHLY REGARDED UNDER 30 FEE-EARNERS

McGuinness Finch (10ptnrs) A small, idiosyncratic, partner-only firm with some "impressive people who are good at getting deals done." A client list and standing disproportionate to the firm's size. Specialise in out of town retail developments Clients/Work: Acting for Lutterworth Partnership (Asda Group plc and The Church Commissioners for England) on development of distribution building for occupation by Shell UK Ltd. Acting for FT Patten Properties Ltd on development of Automated Processing Centre in Chester for occupation by Post Office. Acting for Akeler Midlands Ltd with development of call centre for occupation by Mercury One2One Ltd.

Coudert Brothers (6ptnrs/7assts) This firm has acquired *Richard Woof's* Debenham & Co, a firm with a strong reputation in its own right for shopping centre developments. Clients/Work: Dusco/Capital Shopping Centres development of an extension to the Victoria Shopping Centre, Nottingham. Hilstone Corporation Ltd's acquisition of Tooting Bec Hospital. Fairview Homes Ltd's acquisition of Kennedy Tower.

Fenners (2ptnrs/1asst) Able opponents if "rather lacking in depth of resources." *John Fenner* is "one of the property world's characters" and "you have to be on your toes if John's on the other side." Clients/Work: Acquisition and sale of Blackfriars House, EC4 to be redeveloped as an hotel. £35m town centre redevelopment of Lower Precinct, Coventry for Arrowcroft Ltd. Redevelopment of The Gateway, Croydon (£100m) for Arrowcroft Ltd.

Forsters (5ptnrs/18assts) The property arm of Frere Cholmeley Bischoff which spun off when Frere's merged with Eversheds. *Sophie Hamilton* has "initiative."

Clients/ Work: Purchase of three properties from AMP and the redevelopment of a retail and leisure scheme in Belfast for Guardian Properties. Sale of Wardour Street, W1 and relocation to Theobald's Court for Warner Bros. Acquisition of a 50% interest in Dartford Trade Park from Allied London Properties for Clerical Medical Group.

Glovers (1ptnr/2assts) "Impressive" property practice. **Clients/Work:** Exchange of Master Building Agreement for the Royal Victoria Dock North in favour of Highpine Ltd from LDDC. Sir Robert McAlpine Group's purchase of St Andrews Retail Park, Birmingham. UCL's acquisition of a site in Penton Rise and Pentonville Road.

Hamlin Slowe (6ptnrs/4assts) Reputation for being "fine to deal with." **Clients/**

Work: Property diligence for the sale of NPC to Cendant Corporation for £801m. Sale of Embankment Place for Greycoat plc for £212.5m. Sale of Middleton Shopping Centre for Dwyer Estates plc for £27m.

Julian Holy (6ptnrs/1assts) "The man with the big handshake." The majority of interviewees not only respected Julian Holy's dedication and professionalism but positively enjoyed working with him. "He gets things done incredibly quickly and never tries to stitch you up. Unbelievably commercial."

Park Nelson (8ptnrs/4assts) Recommended for the ability of two partners who combine charm, intellect and hard work. **Clients/Work:** Development, investment and retail.

Stepien Lake Gilbert & Paling (4ptnrs/4assts) Lost a few people but those

that remain, including *Tim Lake*, are "decent blokes with a great sense of humour." Last year the firm was involved in approx. £750m of property transactions.

Teacher Stern Selby (7ptnrs/6assts) The majority of the firm's clients are overseas/offshore with an increasing emphasis on Israeli investors.

Thomas Eggar Church Adams (2ptnrs/1assocs/6assts in London, 11ptnrs/1assoc/13assts throughout the South East) The new name for Church Adams Tatham following its merger with Thomas Eggar Verrall Bowles. A property oriented practice widely known for its work for Railtrack. **Clients/Work:** £22m deed of grant for Railtrack. Development of Leeds railway station for Railtrack. Major portfolio sale for a life company.

ALBERT, David
Ashurst Morris Crisp, London
(0171) 638 1111
Partner in Commercial Property Department.
Specialisation: All aspects of Commercial Property, with particular emphasis on joint ventures, development and investment work. Acts for funds, developers, property companies, public authorities and occupiers.
Career: Qualified in 1969. Joined *Ashursts* 1976; became partner in 1978.

BAILEY, Jeffrey
Linklaters, London (0171) 456 4756
Partner 1980. Property Department.
Specialisation: Property Law specialist. Significant involvement for overseas clients (particularly German and Dutch) on inward investment into UK real estate.
Career: Member of the Court of Common Council of the Corporation of London.
Prof. Memberships: Attended Neath Grammar School, attained LLB (Hons) from University of Wales 1971. Qualified in 1974.
Personal: Born 1949. Leisure pursuits include collecting 18th and 19th century porcelain.

BARNES, James C.
Herbert Smith, London (0171) 374 8000
Partner in Commercial Property Department.
Specialisation: He has a broad range of experience in commercial property and property related matters with a particular emphasis on development projects, property joint ventures, property finance and security and, latterly, on schemes promoted under the UK Government's Private Finance Initiative.
Career: Queen's University, Belfast (LLB); qualified 1980; partner *Herbert Smith* 1989.
Personal: Sport – skiing, sailing, marathon running.

BLACK, J.A.
Rowe & Maw, London (0171) 248 4282
Specialisation: All commercial property work particularly institutional investment and development funding. Recent transactions include the forward purchase of a new headquarters building in Sheffield pre-let to a

newly privatised building society; the forward funding of a large office building in Reading and the disposal of a surplus warehouse building for an overseas client, first creating a saleable investment by letting the building to be extended by the Landlord and the subsequent sale of the property to an institution, with the extension in course of construction.
Career: Qualified May 1977, Partner *Braby & Waller*, Partner *Rowe & Maw* since 1989.

BOURNE, Teddy
Clifford Chance, London (0171) 600 1000
Head of Property.
Specialisation: Partner dealing with commercial property; particular experience in joint ventures; office, industrial and retail development; head office leases; portfolio acquisitions and disposals; inward investment from France and Germany in UK commercial property; property aspects of corporate transactions. Specialises in a broad range of commercial property work including investment, development, leasing, buying, selling and joint venturing. Chairman of the Investment Property Forum's Working Party on streamlining commercial property transactions 1994-1997, and principal author of the IPF Code of Practice on "Readiness for Sale".
Career: Articled *Linklaters & Paines*; qualified 1972; Assistant Solicitor *Clifford Chance* 1972-81; Partner *Clifford Chance* 1981.
Personal: Educated Brentwood School; King's College, London (1969 LL.B Hons). Born 1948; resides Hampstead. Leisure: Kendo, fencing, tennis, cross-country skiing, cinema.

BRETHERTON, Philip
Berwin Leighton, London +44 171 760 1000
Partner in Property Department.
Specialisation: Main areas of practice are commercial property, property development, and P.F.I. projects.
Prof. Memberships: Law Society.
Career: Qualified in 1974. Worked at *Slaughter and May* 1972-78, then *Simmons & Simmons* 1978-94, from 1979 as a Partner. Joined *Berwin Leighton* as a Partner in 1994.
Personal: Born 22nd March 1950. Attended

King's School Gloucester 1954-67, then Trinity College Oxford 1968-71. Leisure interests include opera, collecting 78s, tennis, skiing and bridge. Lives in Maidenhead.

BRIAM, Tony
Clifford Chance, London (0171) 600 1000
Partner.
Specialisation: Work covers all commercial property law, particularly advice on the acquisition, development and letting of Town Centre Retail Schemes. Has advised a number of local authorities (most recently Corporation of London) in relation to the disposal of City Centre properties. Acts for project companies in relation to property aspects of IPPS. Other work includes acquisition and disposal of investment property and acts for major Japanese companies investing in property in the UK.
Career: Admitted 1974. Partner 1981.
Personal: MA Cantab.

BROWN, Nicholas A.
Cameron McKenna, London
(0171) 367 3000
Partner and Manager of Property Group.
Specialisation: Handles property development and investment work for national and international property companies, institutions and retailers. Work includes acquisition and disposal of investment properties, acquisition funding and disposal of office and retail properties and development sites, and leases of all types of commercial property, both completed and in course of construction, and subsequent management of investments. Examples of matters handled are the acquisition of a development site for 1,000,000 square feet of commercial development and 600 homes; development of supermarkets; the acquisition, development, letting and disposal of a 180,000 square foot office building at Kings Road, Reading; the acquisition of a business park site for a 500,000 square foot head office development for an international company; development of a 275,000 square foot retail park; and the property aspects of the Channel Tunnel Rail Link.
Prof. Memberships: City of London Law

Society, Land Law Committee/Investment Property Forum.
Career: Qualified in 1974 after articles at *McKenna & Co*. Became a Partner of *McKenna & Co* in 1980 and Head of the Property Group in 1991, Solicitor to the Leathersellers' Company.
Personal: Born 21st November 1949. Educated at Bristol University 1968-71 (BA in History, Economics and Politics).

BRUMMER, Malcolm H.
Berwin Leighton, London +44 171 760 1000
Partner in Property Department.
Specialisation: Principal areas of activity comprise banking and other commercial property transactions. Acted in 1980s for bank syndicates on Broadgate development, Bank of America on first UK mortgage-backed Eurobond issue, Alliance & Leicester on first building society commercial participation mortgage scheme and P & O on £300 million financing of the Meadowhall development, Sheffield; and in the 1990s for all 55 banks led by National Westminster on £1 billion reconstruction and refinancing of Rosehaugh Stanhope Group; Tesco on £170m and £420m joint ventures with British Land; and Peel Holdings on the financing of the Trafford Centre in Manchester.
Prof. Memberships: Member Law Society.
Career: Qualified in 1972. Partner in 1975. Head of Property Department 1983-90. Chairman of Finance Committee 1988-93. Chairman of Firm 1990-94.
Personal: Born 21st March 1948. Educated at Haberdashers Aske's, Elstree 1959-65 and Downing College, Cambridge 1966-69. Leisure interests include opera, stamps and family. Lives in London.

BUTLER, Alan J.
Simmons & Simmons, London
(0171) 628 2020
Partner 1977. Property Department.
Specialisation: Broad-based commercial property practice with emphasis on bank and institutional funding, institutional investment and development financing transactions. Acts for banks, institutions and property companies in connection with property transactions. Clients past and present include NatWest Investment Bank, Security Pacific, Chase Manhattan, BNP, Swiss Bank Corporation, Banque Paribas, Mitsubishi Estate Company, DESPA, the Abu Dhabi Investment Authority, Land Securities, MEPC and some of the UK's largest property companies.
Prof. Memberships: Law Society.
Career: Qualified in 1973 while at *Simmons & Simmons* and became a Partner in 1977.
Personal: Born 26th April 1947. Attended St. Edmund Hall, Oxford 1966-69 Lives in Oxshott, Surrey.

CLARK, Paul E.
D J Freeman, London (0171) 583 4055
Partner, Head of Property Services Department.
Specialisation: Commercial property – especially landlord and tenant, shopping centres, development projects and PFI. An advocate of plain English. Author of the leasebook – a new concept in leasing multi-let property. Lectures and writes, principally on landlord and tenant issues.

Prof. Memberships: Law Society, City of London Solicitors Company (member land law sub-committee), British Council of Shopping Centres, Anglo American Real Property Institute.
Career: Qualified in 1970. *Rubinstein Nash & Co* 1968-72 *Linklaters & Paines* 1972-83. *DJ Freeman* 1984, Partner in 1985, Head of Property in 1990. UK member of European Board of DePfa-Bank. Member of Advisory Board, Oxford Institute of Legal Practice.
Personal: Born 18th March 1946. Educated at Bemrose Grammar School, Derby 1957-64. Manchester University 1964-67 (LLB Hons). Leisure pursuits include music, reading and the church. Lives in Hitchin.

COURTNEY, Diana
Denton Hall, London (0171) 320 6260
Partner in Commercial Property Department.
djc@dentonhall.com
Specialisation: Work covers all commercial property law, particularly advice in relation to investment property/ development funding, acting for occupiers of offices, shops, leisure and industrial property, landlord and tenant advice (including major disputed rent reviews), harbour property work and corporate support. Has lectured on a wide variety of landlord/tenant subjects.
Prof. Memberships: The City Property Association (council member and past president), British Council for Offices, British Property Federation, Anglo American Real Property Institute. CWIL (Association of Women Solicitors and Barristers).
Career: Qualified in 1961, joining *Oppenheimers* in 1961. Partner 1966; joined *Denton Hall* in 1988. Non-Executive Director of Bradford & Bingley Building Society since 1993. Fellow of RSA.

ELLIOTT, Martin J.H.
Linklaters, London (0171) 456 4478
Specialisation: Partner and specialist with over 18 years' experience in commercial property work. Transactions involving offices, shops, warehouses and industrial premises, acting for property companies, funds and end-users on sales, purchases, lettings, developments, rent reviews and joint ventures. Main specialist area is development and investment work.

FENNER OBE, John Ronald
Fenners, London (0171) 430 2200
Senior Partner in Commercial Property and Town Planning Department.
Specialisation: Many years experience of commercial property acquisitions, sales, developments, funding, joint venture agreements, property tax, major lettings and building contract advice, all relating to office, industrial and retail developments, including regional shopping centres. Has handled acquisitions of development sites for a major national food retailer, various PLC's and local authority schemes (town centres). Represents a wide range of commercial clients including banks and overseas investors. Expertise in urban regeneration.
Prof. Memberships: Law Society.
Career: Qualified in 1960. Became a Partner of *Lionel Leighton & Company* in 1962. Founder Partner of *Berwin Leighton* in 1970, Managing Partner 1980-84, Chairman of Partners 1984-90

and a Senior Partner 1990-94. Founder and Senior Partner of *Fenners* in 1994. Chairman of the British Urban Regeneration Association (BURA) 1991. Chairman British Friends of Israel Philharmonic Orchestra Foundation 1993-97. Chairman Housing Investment Group 1996.
Personal: Born 7th December 1935. Attended Tonbridge School 1949-53, then University College, London 1953-56. Leisure interests include opera, skiing, tennis, community service and politics. Lives in London.

FINCH, Robert G.
Linklaters, London (0171) 456 4768
Partner. Commercial Property Department.
Specialisation: Has been involved in a wide variety of City based and regional transactions throughout the country, involving buying, selling, financing, developing and leasing properties of all types. Has also been involved in the development of and/or investment into property in the USA, the Middle East and Continental Europe.
Prof. Memberships: Is a member of The Law Society and sits on the Court of the City of London Solicitors' Company. Is also a Governor of several schools and a non-executive director of Corney & Barrow.

FOGEL, Steven
Titmuss Sainer Dechert, London
(0171) 583 5353
Senior Partner and member of the Property Department. Leader of the firm's Property Industry Group.
Specialisation: Advises UK and non-UK organisations on all property, and landlord and tenant matters, especially advising on the structure of property transactions and, in particular, preparing complex funding and rent review provisions. Active mainly in the private sector for owner and occupiers but also in the public sector.
Prof. Memberships: Member Investment Property Forum, British Council of Shopping Centres; Anglo-American Real Property Institute; Lambda Alpha International; associate member of Chartered Institute of Arbitrators, member of Board of Advisers, the Centre of Property Law, University of Reading (1997).
Career: *Cohen & Meyohas*, Paris 1973-1974; Qualified 1976; articled *Titmuss Sainer & Webb* 1974-1976; partner 1980; Head of Property Department 1990-1998; Senior Partner (1998), Blundell law lecturer, 1985 and 1996; member of Law Commission Working Party on U.C. PACT (Property Arbitration on Court Terms) landlord and Tenant-LCWP 95 HMSO, 1985-1986; member of RICS working party on Landlord and Tenant Act 1954 (1993-); member Joint Working Party of Law Society and RICS on commerical leases; legal adviser to Property Committee of British Retail Consortium and acted for them in the passage through parliament of the Landlord & Tenant (Covenants) Act 1995; member of RICS Commercial Property Panel; member British Property Federation Customer Focus Working Party; director of Spiro Institute (1992-); trustee "Motivation" wheelchair charity (1992-). Treasurer and now non-voting governor of Anglo American Real Property Institute.
Personal: Born 1951. Educated at Carmel College and King's College London; LLB (Hons) Hickling prize 1972; LLM 1973; ACI Arb 1991; Leisure activities – Jazz, cycling, skiing, cinema and creative writing. Married to Joan, they have three children, Frances, George and Jonathan. Lives in London.

GNIADKOWSKI, Stan
Wilde Sapte, London (0171) 246 7000
Specialisation: Specialises in property and project development work. As a necessary adjunct to that practice he also advises on non-contentious construction law matters. Usually acting for developers, land owners or institutions his practice covers all development related matters including rights of light, adjoining owners' issues and pre-let agreements. Most recently he has advised Helios properties on the sale of a factory outlet centre at Clacton, and forward funded industrial developments at Watford and Park Royal. Development acquisitions have been made for Greycoat PLC in the City at Equitable House and in the West End at 76-88 Wardour Street. He led the team that advised City and West End on their recapitalisation by Security Capital Global Realty, following which 7 Clifford Street, London, W1 was acquired and fully let, the ITN Building has been the subject of a purchase and leaseback and 7-9 Portland Place has been let.
Prof. Memberships: British Council for Offices, Investment Property Forum, Microscope Ball Committee.
Career: After Articles in local government followed by a year with a development corporation, joined the legal department of *John Laing PLC* with whom he worked from 1984 to 1987. Joining City solicitors, *D J Freeman*, in 1987 he became a partner the following year and played a significant part in the development of *D J Freeman*'s property practice. In January 1997, left *D J Freeman* to become a senior equity partner at *Wilde Sapte* where he continues to advise on major property and project development matters.
Personal: Single. Interests include photography, motor racing (watching not participating) and the cinema.

HAMILTON, Sophie C.
Forsters, London (0171) 863 8333
Specialisation: Broad based commercial property practice including acquisition and funding (clients include Clerical Medical); acting for occupiers on major relocations (this year including Dresdner Kleinwort Benson to Ebbgate House and Warner Bros. to Theobolds Court); leisure (including multiplex cinemas for Warner Village); institutional work (appointed solicitor to the Goldsmith's Company); private trusts and residential developers (Hutchison Whampoa and Cala).
Career: Educated St Mary's School, Calne; Marlborough College; Clare College, Cambridge. Qualified 1979; Partner 1985; Head of Property Dept 1991-1994 (all at *Frere Cholmeley Bischoff*); founding partner of *Forsters* 1998.
Personal: Married, lives in London, enjoys theatre, cinema, reading and cooking.

HARBACH, James
Linklaters, London (0171) 456 4445
Specialisation: Senior assistant specialising in commercial property and structured finance. Acts for developers, occupiers and financiers on construction and development projects; joint ventures; the provision of bank and project bond finance; and the securitisation of property and non-property interests.

HARRISON, Christopher H.
Herbert Smith, London (0171) 374 8000
Specialisation: Institutional property investment. The sale of the Ministry of Defence Married Quarters Estate. The redevelopment of the Brent Cross Shopping Centre. Head of Property Department.
Career: Harrow School. Articled *Halliley & Morrison*. Joined *Herbert Smith* 1969.
Personal: Cricket, walking (preferably with dog), being with family, Philippa, Oliver and Claudia.

HELLER, Laurie
Berwin Leighton, London +44 171 760 1000
Partner in Commercial Property Department.
Specialisation: Main area of practice is general commercial property with special emphasis on property development, forward funding and joint venture arrangements. Also handles general commercial law. Recent matters have included the acquisition, development and letting of the Royal Bank of Canada Centre, Queen Victoria Street EC4; the acquisition and other aspects of the refurbishment of 99 City Road, London EC1 for Inmarsat and acting for Development Securities PLC on the development of Shire House and Milton House, Silk Street, London EC2. Clients include PDFM Ltd, St. Martins Property Corporation Ltd, Prudential Assurance Co. Ltd, Legal & General Assurance and the Royal Bank of Canada. Editor of and contributor to Sweet & Maxwell's 'Practical Commercial Precedents' and 'Commercial Property Development Precedents'. Frequent contributor to *The Estates Gazette* and other property based journals. Regular contributor to BBC Select/ Legal Network Television. Charge-out rate is £260.00 per hour.
Prof. Memberships: City of London Law Society Property Sub-Committee.
Career: Qualified in 1959. At *Titmuss Sainer & Webb* 1959-63 (Partner from 1962. Partner at *Leighton & Co* 1963-70. Founder and Senior Partner of *Berwin Leighton* from 1980.
Personal: Born 14th April 1934. Educated at Battersea Grammar School 1945-52 and Sidney Sussex College, Cambridge 1953-56 (Legal Tripos, 1st Class Hons). Leisure activities include reading, writing and pontificating as well as skiing and gardening. Lives in London.

HILL, Rupert
Clifford Chance, London (0171) 600 1000
Specialisation: Partner specialising in Commercial Property work with special emphasis on investment acquisitions and disposals acting for large institutions. Work also includes acquisition funding of office, retail and leisure development sites throughout the UK, and in Ireland.
Career: admitted 1978, Law MA Oxon, became Partner in *Clifford Chance* in 1986.

KIDBY, Robert J.
Lovell White Durrant, London (0171) 236 0066
Specialisation: Property related financing, PFI, secured lending, institutional sales/ purchases/ management, property joint ventures and development projects including shopping centres, offices, airports and hotels. Has lectured extensively on property development and property investment to audiences in England, Europe and Japan.
Career: Qualified as a Solicitor in 1977 and has specialised in commercial property work ever

since. Currently managing partner of the property department at *Lovell White Durrant*.

KUSTOW, David
Olswang, London (0171) 208 8888
Specialisation: All aspects of commercial property law – investment, development retail centre and funding transactions. Head of Property at *Olswang* during a year that has seen significant expansion in the *Olswang* property practice both in terms of additional personnel and considerable expansion in the client base/ turnover. Acts for a variety of quoted and unquoted property companies, including large private investment vehicles and property based funds. Also serves the property requirements of various companies in the advertising and media sectors, particularly those involved in film, satellite and cable. Notable transactions recently undertaken include a single investment property disposal for a consideration of £105 million, the property aspects of a re-organisation of assets with values exceeding £200 million, the property aspects of a flotation and the acquisition of a number of investment/ development properties for a single client, over a 12 month period, for an aggregate consideration exceeding £150 million.
Prof. Memberships: A member of the International Real Estate Federation (FIABCI); A Director of NFTS Ealing Studios Limited (The National Film and Television School operating company for Ealing Film Studios); Co-Chair of the Property Sub-Committee of the British Film Institute.
Career: Admitted 1973; 1970-1991 – *Brecher &Co* (Partner since 1975); 1991-1998 – *Olswang* (Partner and Head of Property Group).
Personal: Married to teacher of children with learning difficulties. Has two children. Principal leisure interests include reading (particularly modern history), travel, music and the cinema.

LAKE, Tim
Stepien Lake Gilbert & Paling, London (0171) 655 0000
Partner.
Specialisation: Large scale development work (commercial and residential) including joint venture and consortia arrangements with all attendant property finance issues. Acts for listed and unlisted developers and equity investors.
Career: Qualified December 1980. Set up own practice in 1985 and subsequently merged his practice with *Birkbeck Montagu's*. A founding partner of *Stepien Lake Gilbert & Paling* in 1991.
Personal: Born December 1955. Educated Radley and Exeter University. Interests include shooting, tennis, golf and skiing. Lives in Oxfordshire.

LANDER, Geoffrey
Nabarro Nathanson, London (0171) 518 3254
Partner and Head of Commercial Property Industry Group since 1994 and Managing Director of the Corporate Occupiers Group.
Specialisation: Acts for corporate occupiers (Chase Manhattan Bank, JP Morgan and HSBC), investors (Hanover Property Unit Trust and BBC Pension Trust Limited) and property companies (Capital & Counties plc). Conference speaker. Published a number of articles. Chargeout rate £350 per hour.
Prof. Memberships: President of the British Council for Offices. Chairman of the Board of NACORE Europe and member of the Board of

the UK Chapter. Board Member of the American Chamber of Commerce.

LE PARD, Geoffrey
Freshfields, London (0171) 936 4000
Specialisation: Handles all aspects of commercial property including landlord and tenant, investment, development, planning and finance.
Career: Qualified in 1981. Joined *Freshfields* in 1981, becoming a Partner in 1987. Head of Property Department since 1993.
Personal: Born 30th November 1956. Attended Purley Grammar School 1968-70, Brockenhurst Grammar School 1970-75, Bristol University 1975-78 and Guildford College of Law 1978-79. Lives In Dulwich.

LUST, Graham
Nabarro Nathanson, London
(0171) 493 9933
Property Finance specialist.
Specialisation: Extensive experience in commercial property investment and development transactions for major property institutions, public property companies and public sector organisations including Central Government Departments. Has developed innovative forms of property financing documentation for inward investors including tax based property financings for multinational clients.
Prof. Memberships: Law Society.
Career: Qualified in New Zealand in 1974, and in England in 1979. Became a Commercial Property Partner in 1980. Head of Property Finance Group.
Personal: Born 1950.

MACDONAGH, Simon M.P.
Lovell White Durrant, London
(0171) 236 0066
Specialisation: Commercial property acquisition, development and financing for developers, financial institutions and local authorities with particular expertise in hotel acquisition and management and commercial joint ventures.
Prof. Memberships: Member of the British Property Federation, the Anglo-American Real Property Institute and the British Council for Offices.
Career: Qualified as a Solicitor in 1979; joined *Lovell White & King* (now *Lovell White Durrant*) in 1980; Partner in 1985.

MACGREGOR, Robert
Clifford Chance, London (0171) 600 1000
Specialisation: Handles a broad range of commercial property transactions. Has acted for buyers, sellers, investors, developers, occupiers and local authorities in relation to office, retail, hotel, leisure and infrastructure projects both in the UK and abroad. Recent experience includes forwards fundings and forward purchases of offices in London, Hong Kong and Dublin; tax-based and construction loan financings (acting for borrowers); equity sharing joint ventures; and a number of large office pro-lettings.
Prof. Memberships: Member of the Anglo American Real Property Institute; the British Council for Offices and the Institute of Directors.
Career: Qualified 1985. Articled at *Titmuss Sainer Dechert*. Joined *Clifford Chance* in 1990. Partner *Clifford Chance* 1992.

MARTIN, Roger
Cameron McKenna, London
(0171) 367 3000
Partner in Commercial Property Group.
Specialisation: Main area of practice is development funding and investment work. Also experienced in landlord and tenant work, redevelopment of town centres and development or purchase of city office schemes.
Prof. Memberships: Law Society, City of London Law Society, British Council for Offices.
Career: Qualified in 1976. Joined *Cameron Markby Hewitt* in October 1979. Partner in Commercial Property 1982.
Personal: Born 3rd October 1952. Attended Cambridge University, BA 1973, MA 1976. Leisure pursuits include sport, family and travel. Lives in London.

MORPETH, Iain C.S.
Clifford Chance, London (0171) 600 1000
Specialisation: Partner in Commercial Property Department. Handles international and domestic transactions including investment and development projects, property joint ventures, leasing, equity and debt financing, structured and tax based finance including Islamic finance. Contributing author 'Joint Ventures in Property: Structures and Precedents' (1993 Sweet & Maxwell). LLB in 1978. Partner in 1988.

NISSE, Ian
Ashurst Morris Crisp, London (0171) 638 1111
Partner in Commercial Property Department.
Specialisation: Commercial Property matters with an emphasis on development projects, investment transactions and joint ventures. Clients for whom he is the lead partner include British Telecom, Chelsfield, Church Commissioners for England, Hemingway and Pearson.
Career: Became a partner at *Ashursts* in 1987.

ROBINSON, E. Patrick G.
Herbert Smith, London (0171) 374 8000
Specialisation: Commercial property development and planning work including all aspects of planning (see entry under Planning section). Established track record in all aspects of property work, with an emphasis on corporate relocations, site assembly and development cases.
Prof. Memberships: Law Society's Specialist Planning Panel.
Career: Articled at *Herbert Smith* (1978-80). Partner 1986. Joint Editor of Blundell & Dobry's Planning, Applications, Appeals and Proceedings (5th Ed) 1996.
Personal: Born April 1956. Educated at University of Nottingham (LLB 1977). Leisure pursuits include jazz, the Cévennes and family. Lives in London.

RUDOLF, Peter.D.
Berwin Leighton, London +44 171 760 1000
Specialisation: Property development, particularly retail and office, and investment. Recent transactions include the acquisition and development of The Mall, Cribbs Causeway (Prudential Assurance); redevelopment and letting of Barrington House, Gresham Street, London EC4 (Legal & General); acquisition and development of Serpentine Green regional shopping centre, Peterborough (Tesco);

acquisition and development of major shopping extension at Milton Keynes (London and Amsterdam Properties); redevelopment of Albert Dock, Liverpool (Arrowcroft).
Prof. Memberships: Law Society.
Career: Bedford School; St Johns, Cambridge – MA 1st Class Honours.
Personal: Participation in sports especially squash and triathalons.

RUTMAN, Laurence D.
Ashurst Morris Crisp, London (0171) 638 1111
Head of Property Department 1974-1998.
Specialisation: Led negotiations relating to Millennium site at Greenwich, Canary Wharf, Albangate, Paddington Basin, 1 Curzon Street and numerous transactions for the public and private sector. Principal external adviser to London Docklands Development Corporation throughout its existence.

SAMSON, John
Nabarro Nathanson, London (0171) 493 9933
Specialisation: Property joint ventures. Development and funding. Portfolio tenders and investment advice. Provides consultancy and second opinions on property law.
Prof. Memberships: Law Society.
Career: Partner at *Nabarro Nathanson* since 1972. Editor Property Law Bulletin since 1985. Blundell Memorial lecturer in 1992. Regularly lectures both at conferences and at companies' offices.

STANCOMBE, Michael F.
Lovell White Durrant, London
(0171) 236 0066
Specialisation: Investment, financing and development (acting for both institutions and developers). Management of major portfolios; joint ventures and indirect investment vehicles. Also acts for a major retail group on new developments.
Prof. Memberships: Member of the British Council for Offices and Investment Property Forum. Representative Member of the British Property Federation, City Property Owners Association and Westminster Property Owners Association.
Career: Articled at *Durrant Piesse* (now *Lovell White Durrant*); qualified 1979; Partner 1982.

TAVENER, Chris
Herbert Smith, London (0171) 374 8000
Partner in Commercial Property Department.
Specialisation: Deals with a full range of commercial property work for developer and institutional clients. Particular expertise in landlord and tenant work.
Career: Became a Partner of the firm in 1982.
Personal: Born in 1948. Educated at RGS, Guildford and Christ Church, Oxford. Leisure time devoted to golf, skiing, music and family. Lives in Islington and (whenever possible) North Norfolk.

TAYLOR, David
Berwin Leighton, London +44 171 760 1000
Head of Property Department.
Specialisation: Main areas of practice are commercial property development and investment. Broad commercial practice including acquisition development and joint ventures with specialist involvement for local authority and public sector clients. Recent transactions include significant purchases for the Prudential, Development Projects for AMEC,

British Land and Kingspark. In addition, clients include AA, CLS Holdings, Godfrey Bradman and Akeler.
Career: With *Lovell White & King* from 1974 to 1979. Joined *Berwin Leighton* in 1980 and became a Senior Associate in 1987. Became Head of Property Department 1996.
Personal: Born 5th August 1956. Educated at Shooters Hill Grammar School. Leisure interests include classic cars. Lives in Smarden.

WHITE, Graham P.
Slaughter and May, London (0171) 600 1200
Specialisation: Experienced in all aspects of commercial property work, including landlord and tenant matters, structured and tax-based finance, commercial property investment, secured lending and development work. *Slaughter and May's* extensive corporate client list means the Commercial Property Department is frequently involved in major private company sales and purchases and he has been responsible for the property aspects of a large number of such deals. Recently acted for Unilever plc on the disposal of its fragrances and speciality chemicals division, co-ordinating a large team of overseas lawyers dealing with

over 300 properties worldwide. This year, also fulfilled a similar role for Williams plc on the disposal of its paints division. Regular contributor to Property Week and The Estates Gazette. He is also a member of the committee producing a set of standard conditions for commercial property transactions based on the Standard Conditions of Sale.
Prof. Memberships: City of London Law Society Land Law Sub-Committee; The Law Society.
Career: Qualified in 1980 after articles at *Slaughter and May*. Became a Partner in 1987.
Personal: Born 1955. Educated at Haberdashers' Aske's, Elstree and St. Catherine's College, Oxford.

WOOF, Richard
Coudert Brothers, London (0171) 203 2248
Specialisation: Real estate investment, development and financing, covering a wide spectrum of properties – offices, shopping centres, retail warehouses, business parks, factories and hotels. In particular acting on the development of many enclosed shopping centres, including Thurrock Lakeside; Eldon Square, Newcastle; Queensgate Centre,

Peterborough and The Glades, Bromley.
Prof. Memberships: British Property Federation; British Council of Shopping Centres; Society for Computers and Law; Clarity.
Career: Educated at King's College, Taunton and The College of Law. *Debenham & Co.* – assistant solicitor (1964-1967), partner (1967-1974) senior partner (1974-1997); *Coudert Brothers* – partner (1997-1998). Commercial property editor of The Law Society' Gazette (1975-1993).

WRIGHT, David
Nabarro Nathanson, London (0171) 493 9933
Partner in Property Department.
Specialisation: Dealing exclusively with commercial property with emphasis on development projects and institutional investment; extensive experience of leading teams in acquisition, disposal and leasing of major property portfolios.
Career: Qualified 1971.
Personal: Born 1946. Attended Bishop Vesey's Grammar School, Sutton Coldfield then Bristol University 1965-68. Leisure: golf, gardening.

SOUTH EAST

HAMPSHIRE/KENT/ SURREY/EAST & WEST SUSSEX

HIGHLY REGARDED FIRMS
SOUTH EAST – HAMPSHIRE/KENT/ SURREY/EAST & WEST SUSSEX

Blake Lapthorn Fareham
Bond Pearce Southampton
Donne Mileham & Haddock Brighton
Paris Smith & Randall Southampton
Stevens & Bolton Guildford
Thomas Eggar Church Adams Chichester, Horsham, Reigate, Worthing

Cripps Harries Hall Tunbridge Wells
Rawlison & Butler Crawley
Sherwin Oliver Portsmouth
Shoosmiths & Harrison Southampton
Thomson Snell & Passmore Tunbridge Wells

Coffin Mew & Clover Portsmouth
Dean Wilson Brighton
Moore & Blatch Southampton
Penningtons Basingstoke, Newbury

Blake Lapthorn (5ptnrs/11assts) A regional heavyweight and "good at most things." Well resourced offices in Southampton and Fareham handle the full range of property work. **Clients/Work:** Allday Stores, Lidl UK Properties GmbH and Whitbread Plc.
Bond Pearce (7ptnrs/10assts) The merged firm of Bond Pearce and Hepherd Winstanley & Pugh. A large dedicated property team combining HW&P's retail and development practice with BP's landlord and

institutional client base. A respected firm with some talented people and expected to go from strength to strength. *Nigel Pugh* has a high reputation and is "good to deal with." *Tim Baily* joins the 'up & coming' lists on the back of his work for Associated British Ports. **Clients/Work:** ABP's proposal to extend the Southampton container port on to its 600 acre Dibden Bay site. Representing the Crown Estate in the Teesside Development Corporation's Stockton regeneration scheme. BAT's new lease of a 100,000 sq. ft office and warehouse premises in Southampton.
Donne Mileham & Haddock (9ptnrs/ 2assts) *Michael Bailey* and his team are known for getting the high profile projects in the Brighton area (acquisition of Brighton Marina, the West Pier, acting for Brighton & Hove Albion in its hunt for a new home, etc.). "Always professional" the firm is developing a specialism in high-tech industries. Recruited two new property partners. **Clients/Work:** Thompsons CSF on the development of a high specification simulation centre. Sunley Estates Plc's acquisition of Sovereign Harbour site at Eastbourne. Continuing to act on the expansion of Daewoo's automotive design and engineering complex at Worthing.
Paris Smith & Randall (4ptnrs/4assts) "Efficient and a pleasure to deal with." Good clients. Good people. An all round good firm with a strong local base and new offices. They received more positive comments than any other firm in the area. **Clients/Work:** Act for government departments including the DoT and the Benefits Agency. Leisure and marina management. Norwegian Cruise Lines, Alldays, Vosper Thornycroft.
Stevens & Bolton (4ptnrs/2assocs /2assts) A small operation that has carved a

large niche. **Clients/Work:** Advising Energy Systems Ltd on the acquisition of hydro-electric schemes and landfill gas generation plants. Hayes Distribution Services Ltd's £6m purchase of North & South Installations Ltd including the acquisition of 6 commercial properties. BOC Distribution Services Ltd on a distribution agreement with Victoria Wine Ltd involving the purchase of new premises.
Thomas Eggar Church Adams (10ptnrs/20assts across 5 offices including London) Despite its image as a private client firm, it has some large property clients. The merger with Church Adams should give commercial property a higher profile. **Clients/Work:** Disposal and acquisition of franchises in Bournemouth and Southampton for the Hendy Lennox Group. All Gleeson Homes property work. Advising on the incorporation of the Glanmore Property Fund.
Cripps Harries Hall (7ptnrs/4assts) Growing rapidly and known for its work for institutions, residential and general developers. Corporate support is increasingly important, now 30% of total work. **Clients/Work:** Berkeley Homes (Kent) Ltd, Britannia Life Ltd and MJ Gleeson Group plc.
Rawlison & Butler (4ptnrs/2assts) A compact firm with a good standing in commercial property. "Thorough and easy to deal with." **Clients/Work:** Crest Nicholson Plc. Swarovski UK Ltd. Duracell Batteries Ltd.
Sherwin Oliver (3ptnrs/5 fee earners) Regarded as effective and high quality. **Clients/Work:** Hoare Hughes Group. Fatty Arbuckles Ltd. Fullers Group of Companies.
Shoosmiths & Harrison (2ptnrs/ 2assts) Not part of the "Southampton mafia." *Graham Bennett* (ex Wilde Sapte)

has a good name. **Clients/Work:** Advising the Roehampton Institute of Higher Education on the property reorganisation and financing of 5 new halls of residence; advised NBTY Inc on the acquisition of Holland & Barrett's property portfolio; advising HJ Heinz UK Ltd on the acquisition and disposal of property interests.

Thomson Snell & Passmore (7ptnrs/2assts) A traditional, steady firm with a well established commercial property arm. **Clients/Work:** Sale of substantial development land in the Ashford area for a leading

water company. Acquisition of large urban landholdings in the Medway area for a local authority as part of a scheme of urban regeneration.

Coffin Mew & Clover (4ptnrs/3assts) A new entrant, the firm is well known for acting for local developers in the Portsmouth area. **Clients/Work:** University of Portsmouth. Entrepreneurial developers in the Portsmouth area.

Dean Wilson (3ptnrs/2assts) A Brighton firm rather than a regional practice but highly regarded. **Clients/Work:** Acting upon the

property portfolio of Nissan UK Ltd. Acting upon major letting of office building in Telford to Inland Revenue for the owner. Acting for major property investor in buying landmark office building in Brighton.

Moore & Blatch (7ptnrs/5assts) Known for their work with developers.

Penningtons (5ptnrs) The leading firm in North Hampshire. **Clients/Work:** Sale of WTI Training Group's Midlands training centre in Derby. Acting for Progress Software Ltd on the lease of part of the Black & Decker HQ building at Slough.

BERKS/BUCKS/ GREATER LONDON/ OXON

HIGHLY REGARDED FIRMS SOUTH EAST – BERKS/BUCKS/ GREATER LONDON/OXON	
Denton Hall Milton Keynes	
B.P. Collins & Co Gerrards Cross	
BrookStreet Des Roches Witney	
Clarks Reading	
Harold Benjamin & Collins Harrow	
Linnells Oxford	
Pitmans Reading	
Cole & Cole Oxford	
Colemans Maidenhead	
Laytons Hampton Court	
Willmett & Co Windsor	

Denton Hall (3ptnrs/6assts/7 other fee earners) "Co-operative and a pleasure to deal with." The Milton Keynes office was born out of the privatisation of the Milton Keynes Development Corporation. Acting for the Commission for New Towns (CNT), the firm was conflicted from working for many local businesses. Also act for well known national institutions and retailers. **Clients/Work:** Construction of a theatre/art gallery for Milton Keynes with lottery funding. New specialist practice using IT UD strategy for bulk processing of remortgage packages for mutual building society.

B.P. Collins & Co (5ptnrs/3assts) "Effi-

cient." Handle property work outsourced by PLCs and the UK branches of US and Japanese corporations. **Clients/Work:** £16m portfolio sale. Purchase of 4 superstores in St Petersburg and an island in the Falklands.

BrookStreet Des Roches (5ptnrs/5assts) A young firm that continues to attract new partners (the latest is Paddy Gregan who is also joined by Richard Smith from Dallas Brett). Predominantly act for commercial tenants. **Clients/Work:** Booker plc. Blockbusters. The National Grid Company.

Clarks (6ptnrs/4assts) Appointed two new partners to strengthen the team. **Clients/Work:** Numerous deals for 20 NHS trusts; acquisition of a new HQ and offices for an international engineering company; acquisition of a new HQ for BMW Financial Services (GB) Ltd.

Harold Benjamin & Collins (5ptnrs/3assocs/1asst) Developers (residential/commercial/industrial) are the engine room of this "competent" practice. **Clients/Work:** Frogmore Estates plc/Groveworld Ltd's acquisition of land for a residential/commercial development in Islington. Acting for Dartford BC as landowner in a proposed major leisure scheme. Acquisition of an inner city brown field development site for a commercial/residential development.

Linnells (5ptnrs/1assoc/3assts) A good firm but losing people (last year they had 7ptnrs and 5assts). **Clients/Work:** Clients include Blackwell Group, major Oxford colleges and Berkeley Homes.

Pitmans (4ptnrs/11assts) A straight forward firm with a good reputation in planning and development work. *James Burgess* is well thought of. **Clients/Work:** BICC PLC. Alfred McAlpine Homes. Netcape.

Cole & Cole (6ptnrs/6assts) Although seen by some as "inconsistent," the firm has a sizeable and growing client base. **Clients/Work:** Letting of a hi-tech scheme of buildings comprising 8,264sq m at Milton Park. Sale of Supergas Ltd's property assets to British Gas. Managing Thames Valley Police Authority's property portfolio.

Colemans (1ptnr) Good and detail orientated. **Clients/Work:** Acted on behalf of Courtaulds Textiles plc. Acquisition of a 7.5 acre site at Manton Wood Enterprise zone, Worksop. Sale of office development in London for £3.4 m on behalf of private company. Transfer of agricultural land into trust on behalf of private client, value £2m.

Laytons (4ptnrs/4assts) Housebuilding and land development. Part of a practice with offices in London and Manchester. **Clients/Work:** Project Solicitors to Cambourne, the new settlement near Cambridge comprising 750,000 sq ft of industrial, commercial, retail and leisure facilities. Assignment of lease providing 60,000 sq ft net of additional space for the headquarters of QVC (the shopping Channel), on Chelsea Bridge.

Willmett & Co (2ptnrs/2assts) A firm with a sensible and practical approach. **Clients/Work:** Virgin, Sue Ryder charity shops and Innovex on their HQ in Marlow.

BEDS/HERTS/ESSEX

HIGHLY REGARDED FIRMS SOUTH EAST – BEDS/HERTS/ESSEX	
Kenneth Elliott & Rowe Romford	
H. Montlake & Co Ilford	
Wollastons Chelmsford	
Ellison & Co Colchester	
Hawkins Russell Jones Hitchin	
Pictons St. Albans	
Tolhurst Fisher Southend-on-Sea/Chelmsford	

Kenneth Elliott & Rowe (5ptnrs/2assts) An efficient firm with experienced staff. **Clients/Work:** Acquisition and disposal of retail parks in south London, Essex and Bucks. Assembly of a town centre development scheme in West London. Relocation of a major manufacturer from its existing 300,000 sq ft factory to new facilities.

H. Montlake & Co (3ptnrs) "The best client base in Essex," handling investment, development and the whole gamut of property work. *Mike Bonehill* is a new and larger than life entrant to the list of 'Leading Individuals.'

Wollastons (2ptnrs/3assts) A disciplined outfit who are respected for the

LEADING INDIVIDUALS SOUTH EAST	
BAILEY Michael David Donne Mileham & Haddock	
BENNETT Graham Shoosmiths & Harrison	
BONEHILL Mike H. Montlake & Co	
BURGESS James Pitmans	
PUGH Nigel Bond Pearce	

UP AND COMING	
BAILY Tim Bond Pearce	

SEE PROFILES AT END OF THIS SECTION

efficient way they run their business. The majority of the work is for local and regional businesses. **Clients/Work:** Major FE college camps extension (with a PFI element); town centre retail redevelopment project; contaminated land transactions, for both residential and commercial use.

Ellison & Co (3ptnrs/2assts) **Clients/Work:** Acquisition by DFDS plc of a shipping warehouse operation in Immingham;

restructuring and finance of Colne Housing Association in Colchester; acting for Essex Wildlife Trust, one of the largest landowners in the county.

Hawkins Russell Jones (3ptnrs/1asst, 1ptnr p/t) **Clients/Work:** Freehold and leasehold commercial property of all kinds.

Pictons (9ptnrs/2assts) Have a business-

like approach. **Clients/Work:** £3.37m development in Buckinghamshire. Acquisition of a £1.25m storage and distribution warehouse in Hertfordshire.

Tolhurst Fisher (3ptnrs/2assts in Southend and Chelmsford) "A super firm" and a new entrant following a number of recommendations.

LEADERS' PROFILES · SOUTH EAST

BAILEY, Michael David
Donne Mileham & Haddock, Crawley (01293) 605000
Partner in Property Department.
Specialisation: Specialises in commercial property. Work includes handling the development of new sites, construction work, joint ventures, landlord and tenant, sales and purchases of businesses and land transactions for charities and educational bodies. Provides solicitor expert reports on conveyance practice. CAB Tutor 1974-84, Sussex University and Brighton College of Technology part time lecturer 1967-80.
Prof. Memberships: Law Society, Associate of School of Urban and Regional Studies, Sussex University.
Career: Qualified in 1965. Assistant and partner at *Gates & Co* in Brighton 1966-71. Partner at *Whitley Hughes & Luscombe* Crawley from 1973. Firm merged with *Donne Mileham & Haddock* in 1986.
Personal: Educated at Varndean Grammar School, Brighton and College of Law. Positions held include President Sussex Law Society from 1995, Treasurer/Trustee of the Webb Memorial Trust (an educational charity), member of Legal Aid Area Committee from 1975, Chairman 1990/1. Member Know How Housing Team to Eastern Europe. Lives in Burgess Hill.

BAILY, Tim G.
Bond Pearce, Southampton (01703) 332 001
Specialisation: Associate in the Commercial Property Group. Specialises in commercial property, development, investment and commercial landlord and tenant.
Career: Qualified 1987, becoming Associate 1997.

BENNETT, Graham
Shoosmiths & Harrison, Southampton (01489) 881010
Specialisation: Commercial Property - all aspects including privatisations (Chatham Docks and Southend Airport), insolvency (Tudor Grange Group), funding (1 Cockspur St, Trafalgar Square) and charities (Central Board of Finance of Church of England). Joint author 'Housing Act 1988 - A Practical Guide'. Recent transactions include advising the Central Board of Finance on the consequences of The Turnball Report, East Hampshire Housing Association in respect of the development of its head office, the Roehampton Institute, London on the structuring and financing of five new halls of residence, the restructuring of the property interests of Industrial Rubber plc as part of its MBO and HJ Heinz in connection with its acquisition of Frank Coopers marmalade.
Prof. Memberships: Law Society; Society of Practitioners of Insolvency; Charity Law Association.
Career: Articled *Ashurst Morris Crisp*, assistant *Clifford-Turner*, Partner *Wilde Sapte*, 1994 Partner *Shoosmiths & Harrison*.
Personal: Golf, cricket and riding.

BONEHILL, M.J.
H. Montlake & Co, Ilford (0181) 553 1311
Specialisation: Commercial Property, Property Development.
Prof. Memberships: Member of the Law Society. Former President of the West Essex Law Society.
Career: City of London School. University College London.
Personal: Chairman of the National Youth Theatre of Great Britain. Life Governor of the Imperial Cancer Research Fund.

BURGESS, James C.A,
Pitmans, Reading (0118) 9580224
Specialisation: Considerable experience in commercial property matters, including acquisitions, sales, joint venture agreements, funding, investment and developments. He also has significant knowledge pertaining to residential development, land assembly and acquisition.
Prof. Memberships: Law Society.
Career: He qualified in 1982 and joined *Pitmans* in 1989.
Personal: Born 1957. Educated Radley College. Leisure interests: Tennis, skiing and fishing.

PUGH, Nigel
Bond Pearce, Southampton (01703) 632211
Partner in the Commercial Property Group.
Specialisation: All types of commercial property transactions. Specialising in institutional funding, commercial leases, site acquisition, retail development in town, out of town and edge of town, multiple town centre purchases, construction work, joint ventures, landlord and tenant, statutory agreements, retail parks, student accommodation schemes. Clients include public quoted companies, banks, receivers, a large number of southern based (including London) developers, further education colleges.
Prof. Memberships: Law Society, Society of Notaries Public, Solicitors European Group.
Career: Qualified in 1970. Articles in the City. Joined *Hepherd Winstanley & Pugh* in 1973 as a Partner and *Bond Pearce in 1998 on merger.*
Personal: Director of the Southampton and Fareham Chamber of Commerce and Industry since 1978. Member of the Southampton University Court. Honorary Solicitor of the Southampton Surveyors and Auctioneers and Valuers Association.

SOUTH WEST

Burges Salmon (10ptnrs/27assts) "In front by a nose with a strong regional practice" and a national perspective. They are perceived as "workwinning at tender, putting their name about," and having a "go-ahead, big presence." They have recently taken on partner from Rowe & Maw to grow the development practice. *Robin Battersby* is "one of the old school, a figurehead." *Bob Smyth* receives praise as "one of the best." *Stuart King* and *John Dunn* are both recommended for the first time. **Clients/Work:** Continuing to act for BG Properties, Bristol 2000 and the

Harbourside Centre (formerly the Centre for the Performing Arts) with redevelopment of Bristol Harbourside. Acquisition, development, sale and lease back of over 300,000 square feet national distribution centre at Severnside for Matthew Clark plc. Legal due diligence for FirstGroup plc into planning, construction, title, environmental and managed estate aspects of their acquisition of the majority shareholding in Bristol International Airport plc.

Bond Pearce (6ptnrs/2assocs) Deals with a wide range of investment, development and management. *David Gunn* is highly-regarded as "an active, enthusiastic

and energetic property lawyer." Provide a niche interim development funding package to clearing banks and other institutional lenders. **Clients/Work:** Acting for South West Water Plc on the acquisition of the landfill business of Terry Adams Ltd. Continuing work for the Highways Agency and notably acting on land acquisitions relating to Second Severn Crossing.

Osborne Clarke (6ptnrs/17assts) This "traditional Bristol practice" rebranded itself as a dynamic city-centre firm 18 months ago. Property is a big chunk of their work and they have a "good quality, solid practice handling large clients." **Clients/Work:** DIRAC House for Institute of Physicists. Sale of London Life HQ to KPMG for over £3m.

Veale Wasbrough (6ptnrs/2assts) The practice is seen to be "reasonably strong although not front-runners." They are known for a regional work base which rests on health-related work. They have a good profile and run good property law seminars. *Tim Smithers* is known for his strength on the planning and environmental side of property work. *Nigel Sommerville* is Senior Partner. He is "extremely sound and a bright lawyer." **Clients/Work:** Bristol Business Park – development including prefunding construction letting and disposal. Harbourside Development – acting for Bristol City Council on major redevelopment of leisure facilities offices and housing on a 65 acre city centre site. Development of Portishead, acting for South West public authority on development of 2000 residential units with business units a district centre and marina.

Bevan Ashford (4ptnrs/6assocs/4assts) The practice has a public sector emphasis depending to a large extent on hospital work. "Number of good individuals" including "sound player"*Peter Scott* and *Andrew Rothwell*. **Clients/Work:** Advice on the establishment of a regional distribution centre for Lidl UK Assets GmbH. Completion of

lease/acquisition negotiations worth £11m for Scorpio Inns. Completing £1.2m deal for purchase of Abbey Stadium in Swindon for BS Group plc.

Clarke Willmott & Clarke (5ptnrs/9assts) The property practice is seen to be "up and coming and growing." The firm is "generally big in the West Country." *Ian Macaulay* is highly regarded. **Clients/Work:** Acquisition of over £15m worth of properties from Eastern Electricity by Hanson Properties. Disposal to Powerhouse Retail Ltd of over 60 leasehold interests acting for vendor, Hanson Plc. Property aspects of three MBOs for Bridport Plc.

Crawford Owen (3ptnrs/2assocs/2assts) This "tiny but good quality practice" has "a strong specialist niche team" doing "a good chunk of institutional work." *Martin Davies Jones* has a good reputation although he is close to retirement. **Clients/Work:** Acting for Bristol and West Plc on their new HQ on Temple Quay. Continuing work for Hanson. MEPC – almost the major client.

Michelmores (3ptnrs/4assts) *Andrew Maynard* & *Peter Lowless* are recommended. **Clients/Work:** Sale of a championship golf club: St Mellion International Golf and Country Club. Acquisition, development and letting of three out-of-town retail centres. Advising institutional lender on the funding of the acquisition of an industrial estate.

Lyons Davidson (2ptnrs/2assocs/1asst) Known primarily for its development practice, specialist units deal with high volume estate conveyancing and repossession sales, securities work and healthcare property. *Timothy Davidson* leads the team. **Clients/Work:** Acting for the University of the West of England in leasing more than 140,000 sq.ft. of student accommodation in the Centre of Bristol converted from former redundant secondary office space.

Wansbroughs Willey Hargrave (3ptnrs/15assts) Have moved to a brand new office space and have recently taken "a quantum leap in terms of property exposure." Seen to be "going places." *Michael Bothamley* is newly recommended. **Clients/Work:** Site assembly, development, letting and investment sale relating to a town centre insurance company relocation. Letting and property management work, land assembly and development work relating to the next phase of a 120,000 sq ft shopping centre.

Cartwrights (2ptnrs/6assts) Known as licensing specialists, the team is led by *Ian Dunn*. **Clients/Work:** Handled two major property auctions for British Railways Board – one comprising 96 properties; the other 61. Appointed by Railtrack plc to handle commercial property work on a national basis.

Davies and Partners (4ptnrs/3assts A further 5ptnrs and 7assts specialise in large residential developments) A "buoyant" practice on the fringe of Bristol in a business park. **Clients/Work:** Industrial lettings, out of

town retail developments, acquisition and management of investment property for individuals and plcs.

Lawrence Tucketts (4ptnrs/8assts) The practice is "edging up," perceived as fairly big, covering all sectors with lots of retailing clients. **Clients/Work:** Acting for Beaufort Homes in Bristol Harbourside project including two substantial acquisitions. Acting for C&J Clark International in acquisitions programme in England and Wales. Handling University of West of England's disposal of Redland campus.

Lester Aldridge (6ptnrs/1asst) Niche units for marina developments, rest and nursing homes and hotels and licensed premises. Known more for their strong planning practice than their property work. **Clients/Work:** Current substantial transactions for the Meggitt PLC Group. Dealing with the whole of the property portfolio for a national assurance company, the Teachers Assurance Group. Currently acquiring property in excess of £4m.

Trumps (1ptnr/1asst) The practice has a "good reputation acting for developers." The firm has moved offices and has a "confident fresh image." **Clients/Work:** Bristol Harbourside Development – acting for JT Group in its development of 103,000 sq.ft. of leisure space; Acting for Brandon Hire plc in its major expansion of retail and out of town outlets in the South of England; Acting for Sun Life Pensions Management on acquisition and leasing back of pension portfolio properties.

Boyce Hatton (4ptnrs/4assts: 1p/t) **Clients/Work:** Stage 2 of Barton Development Torquay (500 units). Contract arrangements regarding land at Ivybridge, Devon of 11acres of residential land. Documentation regarding residential development at Dartmouth – 50 units.

Bretherton Price Elgoods (4ptrs, 1p/t/3assts) Particular experience in development work, investment sales and acquisitions. **Clients/Work:** Partner headed up team of lawyers in £66m development in Spain. Acting for film studio involving new multi-m pound developments in Cheltenham.

Charles Russell (2ptnrs) Acting for Business Expansion Schemes companies. **Clients/Work:** Acted on Bovis Homes flotation. Acted for non-UK based investors on purchase of properties to the value of in excess of £10m and disposal of 568 acre mixed use development site at Grange Park, Northampton.

Eversheds (2ptnrs/1assoc/3assts) "Big on the leisure side, dealing with licensed property work." Seen to be trying to grow their presence in Bristol with newly increased office space. **Clients/Work:** Acting for Oddbins as lead property lawyers in their national expansion programme. Acting for Carlsberg-Tetley where the team has been appointed to provide mainstream property advice for England and Wales. Acting for Burger King as lead property lawyers.

Foot & Bowden (3ptnrs/5assts) Team has wide expertise enabling it to deal with a range of transactions. **Clients/Work:** Act for University of Plymouth in relation to all of its property related work; Acted for the Plymouth Development Corporation; Acted for Samuel Greenaway with the disposal of the Crown Hotel and the acquisition of the Lugger (Public house).

Hancock & Lawrence (3ptnrs 2 f/t; 3assts) **Clients/Work:** Advising Falmouth College of Arts in first example of PFI involving higher education sector in England and Wales.

Kitsons (practising as 'Ursula Bagnall & Co' in Totnes) Property accounts for approx one fifth of the firm's turnover.

Laceys (4ptnrs/1asst) Large amount of general Landlord & Tenant work, estate development and sale and purchase of hotels and other businesses.

Porter Dodson (6ptnrs: 3 p/t/4assts: 2 p/t) Team has considerable experience in land option agreements for commercial development with planning conditions, retail sales, farm business tenancies etc. **Clients/Work:** Sale of development land to supermarket with occupation leaseback, landswap and related JCT Design and Build contracts. Commercial land swaps with surrenders of

agricultural tenancies and refinancing operations involving buyouts.

Rickerby Watterson (7ptnrs/4assts) Based in Cheltenham. Property work accounts for nearly 40% of the firm's turnover. **Clients/Work:** For a national brewer, two block disposals of 150 licensed retail premises. Advising County Council on sale of its LAWDC. Acting in a consortium of land owners in multi m pound option arrangement with Bryant Homes for complex residential development.

Steele Raymond (5ptnrs/1assoc/1asst) This Bournemouth firm does out of town and town centre development work including site acquisition on behalf of retail clients. **Clients/Work:** Multi-million pound construction project for student accommodation in Bournemouth. Acquisition of housing stock, share equity properties and homeless accommodation by Housing Association from Local Authority.

Townsends (6ptnrs-full-time/2ptnrs-part-time/2assts-full-time/2assts-part-time) Known primarily as a personal injury firm but provides property services to its business clients. **Clients/Work:** Clients include Vodafone Ltd; Haydon Development Co. Ltd; Legal & General Assurance Society Ltd(pension scheme property purchases).

Trethowan Woodford (4ptnrs/7assts) **Clients/Work:** Include: Harcros Timber &

Building Supplies Ltd/ Jewson Ltd. James Hay Pension Trustees Ltd; Barrett Homes Ltd.

Wolferstans (6ptnrs/2assts) Property work handled out of the commercial department. Plymouth firm. **Clients/Work:** Advising on new national watersports and sailing centre on a former MoD site. Purchase of hotel, golf and leisure complexes.

LEADING INDIVIDUALS
SOUTH WEST

GUNN David Bond Pearce
MAYNARD Andrew Michelmores
SMITHERS Tim Veale Wasbrough
SMYTH Robert Burges Salmon

BATTERSBY Robin Burges Salmon
DAVIDSON Timothy Lyons Davidson
DAVIES JONES Martin Crawford Owen
DUNN Ian Cartwrights
LOWLESS Peter Michelmores
MACAULAY Ian Clarke Willmott & Clarke
ROTHWELL Andrew Bevan Ashford
SCOTT Peter Bevan Ashford
SOMMERVILLE Nigel Veale Wasbrough

UP AND COMING

BOTHAMLEY Michael Wansbroughs Willey Hargrave
DUNN John Burges Salmon
KING Stuart Burges Salmon

SEE PROFILES AT END OF THIS SECTION

LEADERS' PROFILES · SOUTH WEST

BATTERSBY, Robin S.
Burges Salmon, Bristol (0117) 939 2000

BOTHAMLEY, H.L. Michael
Wansbroughs Willey Hargrave, Bristol
(0117) 926 8981
Specialisation: Head of Property at *Wansboroughs Willey Hargrave*. Acts for a range of national and regional developers, retailers and institutions. Has particular expertise in development work where current projects include a number of retail and leisure schemes. Also acts for several major residential portfolio investment companies.
Career: Durham University. 1980 joined *Wansborough Willey Hargrave*. Partner with *Wansborough Willey Hargrave* 1986.

DAVIDSON, Timothy J.
Lyons Davidson, Bristol (0117) 904 6000
Partner in Property Department.
Specialisation: Principal area of practice is property development and investment work. This includes acquisitions and disposals of land for commercial or residential development purposes, planning, highway and drainage agreements, letting, funding and disposal of completed developments. Types of development include offices, retail, shopping centres, business and industrial parks and residential estates. Also handles general commercial conveyancing for a range of business clients and landlord and tenant work. Has been involved in several major town centre retail development schemes and the sale of a portfolio of commercial properties with a value

of in excess of £80 million. Clients include developers, several local authorities, NHS Trusts and Further Education Colleges.
Prof. Memberships: Law Society, Bristol Law Society.
Career: Qualified in 1971. Partner at *Lyons Davidson* since 1972. Under-Sheriff of Bristol.
Personal: Born 27th June 1948. Educated at Downside School (to 1966). Lives in Bristol.

DAVIES JONES, Martin
Crawford Owen, Bristol (0117) 984 9000

DUNN, Ian H.
Cartwrights, Bristol (0117) 929 3601
Specialisation: Handles all aspects of acquisition and disposal of commercial property, particularly block property transactions in the leisure, licensing and transport sector. Specialisation includes conditional acquisition and disposal of development land; estate management work and business lettings; block property auctions; secured lending for instititions, breweries and other commercial lenders.
Career: Qualified in 1981, joined *Cartwrights* 1988 and became a Partner in 1990. Bristol City Councillor from 1983-1986.

DUNN, John
Burges Salmon, Bristol (0117) 939 2000

GUNN, David J.
Bond Pearce, Exeter (01392) 211185
Partner and head of the Commercial Property Group.

Specialisation: Has specialised in Commercial Property work since qualifying dealing with development, investment and funding including joint ventures. Has a particular interest in waste management, acting for a number of waste disposal companies in connnection with site acquisition/disposal and management, and minerals work involving, in particular, the acquisition of mines and quarries. As a french speaker has worked on property and other commercial transactions involving french companies or organisations.
Prof. Memberships: Member of the Law Society, Association Des Juristes Franco-Britanniques.
Career: Qualified in 1982. Joined *Bond Pearce* in 1980, becoming partner in 1987.

KING, Stuart
Burges Salmon, Bristol (0117) 939 2000

LOWLESS, Peter
Michelmores, Exeter (01392) 436244

MACAULAY, Ian
Clarke Willmott & Clarke, Bristol
(0117) 941 6600
Specialisation: Funding, development and institutional work. Within last year: range of loans, development agreement for lead office letting, complex option for large area, a transfer of over 20 properties (including large development site in East Anglia), another transfer of over 30 properties. Assisted Land Registry computerised search project in Bristol.
Prof. Memberships: Law Society. Vice Chair

Property Committee of Bristol Law Society.
Career: Qualified in 1980. Joined Bristol office of *Clarke Willmott & Clarke* in 1994 as a Partner, after practice in the City and in Bristol.
Personal: Walking.

MAYNARD, Andrew E.
Michelmores, Exeter (01392) 436244

ROTHWELL, Andrew C.
Bevan Ashford, Exeter 01392 663347
Partner in Commercial Property Department.
Specialisation: Specialises in commercial property. Main areas of practice include project finance, commercial industrial property, and development. Has experience in public sector work with Government Agencies, Local Authorities and NHS Trusts.
Career: Qualified in 1980. Employed in various

local government posts. Joined *Bevan Ashford* in 1989 and became a Partner in 1991. Company Secretary of Advoc, the International Network of law firms.
Personal: Born on 1st May 1956. Studied law at the London School of Economics. Leisure interests include farming, football, cricket, golf and squash. Shareholder in Manchester United Plc.

SCOTT, Peter
Bevan Ashford, Bristol (0117) 923 0111
Head of Commercial Property Department.
Specialisation: Covers a wide range of property work including commercial development work, P.F.I contractual work in the Education and Health sectors, property support on corporate transactions and disposal of substantial surplus sites.
Prof. Memberships: Law Society.

Career: *Norton Rose* 1969-72; *Boodle Hatfield* 1972-75. Joined *Bevan Ashford* 1975; Partner 1977.

SMITHERS, Tim M.D.
Veale Wasbrough, Bristol (0117) 925 2020
See under Energy & Utilities, p. 337

SMYTH, Robert J.
Burges Salmon, Bristol (0117) 939 2000

SOMMERVILLE, Nigel
Veale Wasbrough, Bristol (0117) 925 2020
Partner in Property Services Department
Specialisation: Property Development; land acquisition; planning; property finance. Expert witness on property issues in professional negligence cases.
Prof. Memberships: The Law Society
Career: Marlborough College; Trinity College Cambridge (MA); qualified as solicitor October 1968.

WALES

Edwards Geldard (5ptnrs/7assocs/3assts) On the Welsh Development Agency panel of lawyers. See themselves as leading regional firm, have establishment work. You "cannot knock *Rowland Davies*' ability as a property lawyer." He is regarded as "a formidable opponent." *Katherine Gates* is a senior associate who enters the lists for the first time this year and is doing a lot of regeneration work as Davies' number two. **Clients/Work:** Continuing involvement in the £1.7billion inward investment by the Korean LG group. Continued land assembly for the Millennium Stadium and the negotiation of development documentation for the adjoining commercial developments, for Welsh Rugby Union. Continuing development at Cardiff Gate Business Park.

Eversheds (7ptnrs/12assts) Interestingly, the commercial property department is perceived as "streets ahead in size"compared to the competition although actual numbers disprove this. Leader *Alan Meredith* mainly works for the Welsh Development Agency;

he is a "good competent chap." *Eric Evans* is also recommended for the first time. **Clients/Work:** Acting on behalf of WDA with construction of a bespoke factory for Acer Deriferals (UK) Ltd at St Mellons Cardiff – 180,000sq.ft. (first Taiwanese investment into Wales). Acting for Matsushita Electronic Components (UK) Ltd in development of a major new facility at Baglan Industrial Estate.

Morgan Bruce (10ptnrs/19assts) Predominantly known for their health trust work. Merged with Guthrie Francis at the end of last year. One of their partners now services Gwent clients, doing health-trust work and investment property work.Their Swansea office is "the most significant." They "have worked hard at increasing the size, depth and extent of their work." *Rob James* is recommended. **Clients/Work:** Acting on behalf of Acer Peripherals Inc. to advise on acquisition of an industrial site at Wentloog Cardiff. Planning and regulatory work in TBI's bid for purchase of Bristol Airport. Acting on behalf of ABP in its £20m development of South Wales Docks (Barry).

Berry Smith (2ptnrs/2assts/2cons) Work for a number of local developers. The department "depends on *Roger Berry* ("Mr Development") as an individual." He is seen as "the viable alternative to Eversheds" because of his personal qualities. **Clients/Work:** Currently acting for developers doing land assembly for projected theme park at North of Newport which would be the second biggest single inward investment to Wales. Millennium Stadium Retail/Leisure Developments for Brunswick/ Taylor Woodrow.

Hugh James (9ptnrs/20assts) Known primarily for their Housing Association work. *David Roberts* is now Senior Partner

and is "pre-eminent in Housing Association-related property work in Wales; carved a niche for himself." He is always quoted as a personality but "one property lawyer does not make a commercial property practice" and the firm is not known for its strength in depth. **Clients/Work:** First letting on a large industrial park in Bristol area to major international company. Acquisition of large residential/small retail site on outskirts Cardiff; 800 houses, some retail development and consortium agreement with number of developers.

Palser Grossman (2ptnrs/2cons/2assts) Work for a number of well-known local developers. "An interesting firm, growing rapidly" and "hungry for work." They "have some good quality clients but are not yet a match for the others."

Beor Wilson & Lloyd (2ptnrs/2assts) Small practice, but recommended.

Robertsons (4ptnrs/3assts) A niche practice doing "primarily developers' property work."*Martell Williams* has gained a strong reputation in the region.

Dolmans (3ptnrs/2assts) A "solid firm" with "one or two good individuals."

BERRY, Roger John
Berry Smith, Cardiff (01222) 345 511
Specialisation: Full range of commercial property work including investment and development with particular emphasis on landlord and tenant. Also joint ventures and banking.
Career: Qualified 1978. Articled *Broomheads & Neals*(Sheffield). At *Simpson Curtis* (Leeds)1978-1981 and *Phillips & Buck* now *Eversheds*, Cardiff 1981-1986. Established *Berry Smith* 1986.
Personal: Born 19.3.1952, Colne, Lancashire. Educated at Sedbergh School and Emmanuel College, Cambridge (MA). Interests; football and cycling.

DAVIES, Rowland
Edwards Geldard, Cardiff (01222) 238239
Partner in Commercial Property Department.
Specialisation: Work includes development work, urban regeneration, investment and acquisitions and disposals. Acted for the Cardiff Bay Barrage Scheme and undertook the land assembly for the Millennium Stadium, Cardiff. Is a Consultant to Cardiff University Legal Practice Course.
Prof. Memberships: Law Society and Cardiff and District Law Society.
Career: Qualified in 1978. Joined *Edwards Geldard*, becoming a Partner 1981.
Personal: Born 27th August 1953. Attended Cardiff High School 1964-71 and Downing College, Cambridge 1972-5. Leisure interests include art, music, literature, cinema, theatre and gardening. Lives in Cardiff.

EVANS, Eric
Eversheds, Cardiff (01222) 471147

GATES, Katherine
Edwards Geldard, Cardiff (01222) 238239
Specialisation: Senior Associate in Commercial Property Department. Work includes Commercial development and leisure. Investment portfolios and housing land acqusitions on behalf of public and private sectors. Acted in the Celtic Gateway

International Technology Business Park, Cardiff Bay.
Prof. Memberships: Law Society and Cardiff and District Law Society. Women in Property.
Career: Qualified in 1987. Joined *Edwards Geldard* as an Associate becoming a Senior Associate in 1996. Previously spent eight years at *Osborne Clarke*.
Personal: Interests include travelling, walking and rugby. Property advisor to Prince's Youth Business Trust.

JAMES, Robert W.
Morgan Bruce, Cardiff (01222) 385385
Specialisation: Principal area of practice is large scale public and private development work. Advising on joint ventures, disposals for administrative receivers, secured lending, licensed trade (brewing) leases and construction contracts.
Prof. Memberships: One of the first accredited mediators under the Law Society/ RICS PACE scheme for the renewal of business leases.
Career: Qualified 1978.
Personal: Born 8th August, 1953. Educated Wrekin College Wellington and Jesus College Oxford. Spare time pursuits include: Rugby, Cricket and Theatre. He is a Committee Member of Cardiff-Stuttgart Association. *Morgan Bruce* liaison partner for the Association of European Lawyers.

MEREDITH, Alan
Eversheds, Cardiff (01222) 471147
Partner. Head of Commercial Property Department.
Specialisation: Work includes property joint ventures between private and public sector and general commercial conveyancing. Also handles urban regeneration in the public sector, acting for both public and private sector bodies. Has given seminars on contaminated land for the Chartered Surveyors Study Group and has co-authored with his environmental partner, Martin Warren, a book entitled "Contaminated Land - Managing Liabilities".
Prof. Memberships: Law Society, Country Landowners Association.

Career: Qualified in 1976. Joined *Phillips & Buck* (now *Eversheds*)as a Partner in 1982. Currently Head of Commercial Property Department.
Personal: Born 8th January 1952. Attended University of Wales, Aberystwyth. Member of Management Committee of Swansea Cricket and Football Club. Trustee of Dragons Rugby Trust. Member of Board of ERC Ltd (European Rugby Cup Limited). Leisure interests include golf, rugby and reading. Lives in Cowbridge near Cardiff.

ROBERTS, David Lloyd
Hugh James, Cardiff (01222) 224871
Partner in Commercial Property Department.
Specialisation: Work includes site assembly and acquisition, including option work, agreement and grant of lease and forward sale agreements in relation to office, retail and industrial developments. Undertakes large scale land acquisition for a large volume house builder, as well as loan documentation. Specialises in Housing Association stock transfers and other social housing initiatives. Acted in the transfer of Glyn Taff Estate from Taff Ely BC to Newydd Housing Association (the first and only Pt. IV Housing Act 1988 transfer in Wales).
Prof. Memberships: Legal Advisor to Sports Council of Wales Drugs Abuse Advisory Committee.
Career: Qualified in 1974. Joined *Hugh James* in 1972, becoming a Partner in 1975. Member of British Athletics Team 1974-78. Competed at European and Commonwealth Championships. Member of Hawkes Club and Achilles Club.
Personal: Born 5th June 1949. Attended Grove Park Grammar School, Wrexham 1960-68; Selwyn College, Cambridge 1968-72 (MA, LLB) and Guildford College of Law. Member of firm's Board of Management. Leisure interests include golf, tennis and family. Lives in Cardiff.

WILLIAMS, Martell
Robertsons, Cardiff (01222) 237777

MIDLANDS

Wragge & Co (18ptnrs/32assts) It is often said that "Wragges is the City firm" in Birmingham. This is a quality outfit with a "powerful property practice". They "have the edge and are more conspicuously successful than rivals in being partner-led and client-driven." *David Askin* is recommended as is *Robert Caddick* who is "fair and proficient and always good to have on the other side." *Mark Dakeyne* now "has his finger back on the pulse." Partners are said to be "interested in doing the work," and it is done at partner and associate level. **Clients/Work:** Acting on a development agreement for MEPC Ltd for 125 Colmore Row, current Lloyds Bank HQ, and concurrent investment purchase of Victoria Square House (probable project value over £75m). Acting for Kingspak

Developments Ltd on purchase of Brighton Marina in a joint venture vehicle. Development agreement for Castlemore Securities in a joint venture with Eagle Star for 500,000sq.ft. redevelopment of the Hampshire Centre, Bournemouth.

Eversheds (9ptnrs/29assts) The practice is large so has good client coverage and is respected for being "commercially minded." *Adrian Bland* is now Senior Partner and has been replaced as Head of Department. There is some feeling that the practice has suffered because he "was a major player." **Clients/Work:** Amec Developments Ltd – 38 acre office campus forming part of Birmingham Great Park acquired from NHS for 400,000 sq.ft. office development. English Partnerships – broad range of regeneration, gap funding and development work including two Enterprise Zones and three Urban Vil-

lages. St Modwen Properties Plc – acting on purchase etc of Cannock Shopping Centre.

Edge & Ellison (12ptnrs/19assts) Have a historical reputation for being "streetwise, friendly commercial guys." Leicester practice is stong and complements the Birmingham office. Said to be a "reasonable practice; a solid team of partners although no stars." **Clients/Work:** Acting for Enterprise Plc mixed use development scheme for Wolverhampton Town Centre (£60m). Redevelopment of former Continental Tube Factory, Darlaston for Barberry House Properties plc (£30m). Acting for Folkes Properties in letting of 250,000 sq.ft Britannia Park Development Corporation Automotive Component Park.

Pinsent Curtis (9ptnrs/5assocs/15assts) "Act for the old money." Seen more as a service department which "has good people to make it work but is not given the support in-house to raise its profile." Perceived as "good solid people" with good marketing. *Barry Brice* heads the practice. **Clients/Work:** Disposal of Fosse Plaza retail scheme (£55m+), acting for Castlemore. Acting for I.M.Properties in acquisition of investment portfolio of Yorkshire Property Holdings Ltd (£30m+). Acting for West Bromwich Building Society on property due diligence on the acquisition from Century Life Plc of a mixed commercial and residential mortgage book for circa £90m. Approximately 2200 properties involved.

Martineau Johnson (6ptnrs/10assts) Seen as being "significantly ahead of the rest of the highly regarded firms." However thought to lack the 'critical mass' that would make them leaders. They are associated with the educational sector, university science parks etc. **Clients/Work:** Advising retail enterprise agency in site acquisition and redevelopment involving PFI/PPP funding. Group reorganisation involving 25 properties for Dutch multinational group.

Dibb Lupton Alsop (7ptnrs/7assts) Act for commercial lenders on acquisitions. National skills groups deal with areas such as retail, leisure, development, institutional funding, property, investment, health and education. **Clients/Work:** Acting for Hampton Trust Plc on acquisition of City Centre site for tallest building in Birmingham.

Knight & Sons (8ptnrs/4assocs) A well-regarded brewery-based practice in the potteries. **Clients/Work:** Acting for major retail client in multi-site funding and forward sale package valued at approximately £45m for sites located in Stoke on Trent, Walsall and Hull. Acting for Newstead Properties Ltd in a multi million pound refinancing of substantial property portfolio located in Midlands and NW regions. Acting in a property PFI with overall transaction value in the region of £250m.

Lee Crowder (4ptnrs/10assts) The firm was a new entry to the lists last year and is rapidly rising. It has recently moved into the city centre from Edgbaston and competitors say this is now "beginning to pay off." Act for King Edwards School, major land-owners in and around Birmingham, so are ubiquitous in property deals. *Joel Kordan* is their rising star. **Clients/Work:** Acting for freeholders of a development site in Birmingham incorporating total buildings in excess of 275,000 sq ft with development value of £16m. Acting for vendor in disposal of major warehouses for £11m. Acting for freeholder in staggered disposal of site to be developed as business park exceeding 100 acres with an undeveloped value of over £15m.

Hewitson Becke + Shaw (17ptnrs/ 30assts/1assoc) Property management work enhanced by agriculture specialism and expanding development division. **Clients/Work:** Acting for large property-owning companies handling all aspects of property portfolios and including major British plc owning over 300 properties.

Higgs & Sons (6ptnrs/3assts) A "hard-hitting Black Country firm."

Manby & Steward (5ptnrs/4assts) A "Black Country firm with local influence."

Needham & James (5ptnrs/1asst) The firm's property client base is owner-manager developers. They pick up some material

work. **Clients/Work:** Work for The National Grid Company and Conoco.

Band Hatton (2ptnrs/1assoc/1cons/ 1asst) **Clients/Work:** Handling property portfolio for head office of Allied Irish Bank(GB) in Uxbridge. Acting for Com Tel Ltd, handling their head office property portfolio. Acting for a major local charity.

Freeth Cartwright Hunt Dickins (9ptnrs/3assocs/6assts) Commercial property constitutes about 25% of this Nottingham-based firm's practice. **Clients/Work:** Continuing involvement with Castle Wharf Development in Nottingham. Continued involvement with the Nottingham General Hospital Site. Advising on a significant number of major transactions for the Nottinghamshire County Council Superannuation Fund.

Harvey Ingram Owston (6ptnrs/2assocs/ 5assts) Known as a strong retail team. **Clients/Work:** Advising Leicester City Challenge Ltd with sale of parts of Bede Island North, Leicester. Acting for Stead & Simpson Ltd in acquisition of 69 retail shoe shops from Shoe Express. Advising Heart of National Forest Foundation in acquisition of former colliery site for development as visitors centre.

Shoosmiths & Harrison (6ptnrs/7assts) Mainly an insurance practice with property accounting for about 12% of workload.

Wright Hassall & Co (5ptnrs/3assts) Acts for developers and builders and has a particular strength in housing associations work. The firm appointed two new commercial property partners in the last year. **Clients/Work:** British Waterways Board. Moreland plc. Chase Midland plc.

LEADERS' PROFILES · MIDLANDS

ASKIN, David J.
Wragge & Co, Birmingham (0121) 233 1000
Specialisation: All types of commercial property development, letting, funding, sales, especially town centre redevelopments, offices, retail/business parks and private/public sector joint ventures. Acts for developers, local authorities and investor-purchasers. Heavyweight experience on complex schemes.
Career: Educated Bilston Grammar School; St Catharine's College, Cambridge (1967 MA Law); (1968 LLM). Articled *Wragge & Co*; qualified 1970; partner 1973; Director Worfield Golf Club plc.

Personal: Born 1946. Lives Newport, Shropshire. Interests include cricket, golf and fishing.

BLAND, Adrian D.
Eversheds, Birmingham (0121) 233 2001
Partner.
Specialisation: Development, urban regeneration, investment, finance.
Career: Joined *Eversheds* 1978. Partner 1987. Head of Property 1989. Senior Partner 1997.
Personal: Born 03.04.56 Kendal, Cumbria. Educated Kendal Grammar School, Birmingham University, LLB (Hons).

BRICE, Barry
Pinsent Curtis, Birmingham (0121) 200 1050
National head of property.
Specialisation: Specialises in property development and investment. Major projects in last 12 months include: Development, letting and disposal of Fosse Plaza Retail Park, Leicester. Acquisition from British Coal Corporation of some 350 acres of land near the M42 motorway in Warwickshire to be developed as major industrial park; Acting upon an acquisition and development of retail park at Sutton Coldfield; Acting for Stanifer Hotels Limited upon joint venture with Holiday Inn in

relation to development and management of new hotels throughout the UK.
Career: St John's College, Oxford. Qualified in 1975 at *Pinsent Curtis* (then *Pinsent & Co*). Partner 1980. National head of property 1995.

CADDICK, Robert J.
Wragge & Co, Birmingham (0121) 233 1000
Specialisation: Property development (especially major projects, limited partnerships and public/private sector joint developments).
Career: Articled *Wragge & Co.* Qualified 1975. Partner at *Wragge & Co* from 1981.
Personal: Born 1951.

DAKEYNE, Mark L.
Wragge & Co, Birmingham (0121) 233 1000
Partner.
Specialisation: Commercial property development, particularly large industrial and retail/leisure schemes. Also handles the property portfolios of large corporates.
Career: Articled in London and spent four years after qualification in 1983 with *Herbert Smith*. Joined *Wragge & Co* in 1987 and became a Partner in 1990. Head of Property Group since 1993.
Personal: Born 1958.

KORDAN, Joel
Lee Crowder, Birmingham (0121) 236 4477
Specialisation: All areas of commercial property development including lettings, sales, funding and joint venture agreements, with particular emphasis on largescale industrial and retail schemes. Also, large residential property development practice. Clients include developers, retailers, contractors and housebuilders.
Career: Articled *Wragge & Co.* Qualified 1990. Partner at *Lee Crowder* since 1997.
Personal: Born 1961, USA. Attended King Edward VI Five Ways Grammer School, Birmingham and London School of Economics (B.Sc. (Econ)).

EAST ANGLIA

LEADING FIRMS • EAST ANGLIA

EVERSHEDS Ipswich, Norwich
MILLS & REEVE Norwich

HIGHLY REGARDED FIRMS

Birketts Ipswich
Hewitson Becke + Shaw Cambridge

Few & Kester Cambridge
Gotelee & Goldsmith Ipswich
Greenland Houchen Norwich
Greenwoods Peterborough
Leathes Prior Norwich
Prettys Ipswich
Taylor Vinters Cambridge

Eversheds (16ptnrs/18assts in Norwich and Ipswich) "They have depth of resource and don't mess you around." Too large to survive solely on the East Anglian market, 50% of the work comes from outside the region. Building up an informal relationship with Clifford Chance. "We do the due diligence which they can't do economically." **Clients/Work:** Securitisation of £100m property portfolio for Nursing Home Properties Plc, followed by purchase and leaseback of a further 60 nursing homes. Tarmis plc's acquisition of 43 care homes. Masterworks Development Corporation's acquisition and sub-lease of a building in the City for a hotel.
Mills & Reeve (10ptnrs/17assts) A long-

established, technically driven and "generally excellent" firm. Three teams are dedicated to NHS trusts, colleges & universities and East Anglian businesses. *Tony Cowper* is "a maverick but he's outstandingly able." **Clients/Work:** Act for half of all Cambridge Colleges and 50 other higher education institutions nationally. For the developer on the construction of a 70,000 sq ft HQ in the Midlands for a multinational. Multi party redevelopment of Bradford City Centre.
Birketts (6ptnrs/4assts) Ipswich based but solid. The partners have a good reputation and "if you deal with them you know they'll be sensible." **Clients/Work:** Acquisition of packages of Public Houses for regional and local brewers. Development work for Sanctuary Housing Association. Act for Willis Corroon Group plc
Hewitson Becke + Shaw (9ptnrs/7assts) An efficient and reputable firm which tends to act for developer clients and hightech/biotech companies moving into the area. 50% of the practice is within Cambridgeshire, with the rest in the Midlands and North London. **Clients/Work:** Acquiring residential sites for national housebuilders. Advising on property investment portfolios. Property management for national retailers, banks, builders merchants and public house owners.
Few & Kester (4ptnrs/1asst) A fine, well established if "slightly old fashioned" local firm. **Clients/Work:** Colleges, housing associations and local councils.

Gotelee & Goldsmith (2ptnrs/4assts) Very much an Ipwich and East Anglian firm. **Clients/Work:** Local authorities. London Boroughs. Small private companies.
Greenland Houchen (4ptnrs) Known for their work for local builders, developers and housing associations. **Clients/Work:** Include Broadland Housing Association Ltd (£17 m refinancing of in excess of 1,000 units) and Peddars Way Housing association Ltd. (acquisition of let property portfolio of 71 units for £1.25 m).
Greenwoods (2ptnrs/2assts) An impressive practice that serves its clients well. Usually acts for occupiers rather than investors/landlords. **Clients/Work:** Act for the Highways Agency from North London to Lincolnshire and from Staffordshire to Essex. EMAP plc. Thomas Cook plc.
Leathes Prior (3ptnrs/4assts) A good regional firm.
Prettys (2ptnrs/2assts) **Clients/Work:** PFI scheme at a London hospital. Quasi blight scheme. Disposal of a supermarket development site in Attleborough, Norfolk to Budgens.
Taylor Vinters (6ptnrs/5asts) Reputation for being an approachable forward looking practice. **Clients/Work:** The University of Cambridge and 11 colleges. Bradford Property Trust. Redland Aggregates.

LEADING INDIVIDUALS
EAST ANGLIA

COWPER Tony Mills & Reeve

SEE PROFILES AT END OF THIS SECTION

LEADERS' PROFILES • EAST ANGLIA

COWPER, Tony
Mills & Reeve, Cambridge
+44 (0) 1223 364422
Specialisation: Partner with responsibility for commercial property and development and redevelopment issues.
Prof. Memberships: Law Society Member

Career: Director of a former residential property BES company. Acted in setting up one of the Cambridge Colleges. Client partner to some of the largest property owning educational institutions in the country. Responsible for setting up Cambridge Science Park and all subsequent legal work associated with it.

Currently acting in connection with two more Science/Business Parks including site set-up, subsequent lettings and sales. Acting in connection with the development of a new town.
Personal: Golf.

NORTH WEST

Addleshaw Booth & Co (18ptnrs/33assts) The big, establishment practice with a large institutional following (approx 70% of the firm's client base). The large and well respected department includes *Diana Craven* and *Susie Diggines*. *David Tully* retains a reputation in commercial property although he is also known for his private client work. **Clients/Work:** Barlows plc's acquisition of a nationwide development and investment portfolio from Rowlinson Securities. AAH plc's relocation of all regional and HQ offices to a purpose built complex in the Midlands. AMEC's forward funding of an Asda Store Development within the Hulme Regeneration Scheme.

Cobbetts (15ptnrs/20assts) One of the old school and "not as keen to cut the competition's throat" as some. Half the firm's turnover comes from commercial property work. Secured lending and property finance is carried out by the banking team. *Steve Benson* leads the retail and leisure team and was recommended for his thoroughness and desire to get the deal done. **Clients/Work:** Maple Grove Developments Ltd's acquisition of a site at Stone Cross for redevelopment as warehouses. CRS Ltd's development of leisure park adjacent to the CRS's Sandbrook Park HQ. HBG Ltd's (formerly GA Properties Ltd) acquisition at Manor Park, Runcorn for office development.

Dibb Lupton Alsop (11ptnrs/24assts) Doing extremely well, with four people being mentioned as leaders. The Manchester office alone acted on £1bn worth of deals in 1997. As one extremely satisfied client put it " they understand why every line is in a lease." Despite Dibbs' reputation for being hard nosed, most practitioners found them easy to deal with. *Roy Beckett* has built up a balanced and respected team which includes *Philip Rooney* (described as "the best property lawyer in Liverpool" by one of his competitors), *Mark Beardwood* ("approachable. He gets your drift straight away") and *Anita Weightman*. **Clients/Work:** £75m acquisition of Hayward Distribution Park for BP Pension Fund, a new and London based client. Sale of Trafford Retail Park for CWS within a 20 day time frame. Sale of Abbey National's Property Investment Fund Portfolio for +£50m.

Eversheds (5ptnrs/16assts) "You can't ignore Eversheds in property." *Stephen Sorrel* is the arch business getter. Also well known are *John Moody* and the up and coming *Tessa Leonard*. The only negative comment is a widely held perception that they "pass work down to a junior level too fast." **Clients/Work:** Great Northern Warehouse and G-Mex district of central Manchester to provide a new convention centre, civic square, retail, leisure and office accommodation. Renewal/regeneration of Manchester city centre following the IRA bombing. English Partnerships' 23 acre/ £150m Temple Quay development in Bristol.

Halliwell Landau (8ptnrs/18assts) A strong and strengthening team, particularly on the development side. *Geoffrey Marks*, head of the department, has "been around forever and seen pretty much everything." *Stephen Goodman* is said to have a flourishing practice. Described as "boisterous and a little dogmatic," he always manages to get the deal done. **Clients/Work:** WAXY Hartlepool Ltd's £54.5m sale of Middleton Grange shopping centre to Pillarcaise Partnership. WD Ltd's £32m/250,000 sq. ft. development of the Kingsgate shopping centre, Huddersfield. Baltic Plc's acquisition of Manchester's landmark listed Grand Hotel.

Bullivant Jones & Co (6ptnrs/12assts) A national reputation and a retail client list that far larger firms would kill for. The best known partners are *Pamela Jones* ("technically gifted") and *Michael Stephens*. **Clients/Work:** Acquisition, development, letting and sale of Great Northern Retail Park, Huddersfield; the Menai Retail Park, Bangor; a site in Stockport including largest B&Q Warehouse in country.

Davies Wallis Foyster (10ptnrs/12assts) Active in straight commercial property and for entrepreneurial clients in retail, office, industrial and leisure. Equally strong in Liverpool and Manchester. *Guy Wallis*, "absolutely charming," has a good presence in Manchester and in Liverpool. **Clients/Work:** Major letting of office space for Manchester Airport. St Modwen Group's £4.5m sale of Gerard Cross, Ashton-in-Makerfield. Advising in the £40m sale of South East shopping centre.

Field Cunningham & Co (3ptnrs/2assts) Traditionally known for housebuilding although 50% of the practice is in the commercial sector, principally retail and leisure. *Peter Ashworth* (a non executive director of Barretts) "knows his business inside out" and is the firm's driving force, the only criticism of him being that he can be "over zealous." *David Stratton* was also recommended. **Clients/Work:** Barratt Developments plc in sale of 50% interest in Barratt International Resorts Ltd to Macdonald Hotels plc; Farrho Developments Ltd in 120,000 sq ft development in Oldham Centre; Thornfield Developments Ltd in 23,000 sq ft development at Parrs Wood High School Didsbury Manchester inc multiscreen cinema, bowling alley, restaurants, health and fitness facility.

Slater Heelis (4ptnrs/2assocs/4assts) "Rock solid if uninspiring." **Clients/Work:** Bruntwood Estates Ltd's purchase of York House and West Riverside, Manchester and Ashburner House, Old Trafford. Pentith Ltd purchases and leases of Pizza Express properties in Chase and Beverley. Aldi Stores Ltd purchase of new sites for supermarkets in Congleton and Wrexham.

Vaudreys (6ptnrs/6assts) An extremely high profile practice considering their size. **Clients/Work:** United Assurance plc's portfolio disposals. Acting for the Inland Revenue in the first office PFI deal to be completed. Awarded work for PACE in the NW and the NE.

Bermans Best known for their brewery practice.

Cuff Roberts (6ptnrs/2assts) Solid, traditional and reputable. "Always do a good job. You know you're never going to get rubbish from them." Act predominantly for retail clients. **Clients/Work:** Acquisition of Columbus Quay site for landmark waterfront residential development for Tay Homes (North West) Ltd and subsequent sales.

Hammond Suddards (2ptnrs/9assts) Not often mentioned by fellow practitioners, but the firm and partner *Liam Buckley* were referred to by many of the Manchester surveyors we interviewed. **Clients/Work:** Acting for Royal Bank of Scotland providing £4m development finance to GA Properties for Daresbury Court, Runcorn. Development of 2 CCGT power station projects at Anglesey and Fleetwood for Canatax Energy Ventures/GE Power Systems Incorporated. Allied London Properties plc's £12m acquisition of Market Walk shopping centre, Newton Abbot.

Hill Dickinson (7ptnrs/3 other fee earners) Setting themselves up to break into the big league by taking over a Chester firm to add to the developer side of the practice. Act for large pension funds on a national basis as well as commercial clients, builders and the public sector. **Clients/Work:** Merchant Navy Pension Funds' development of the Pinners Hall, EC2. Refurbishment and letting of office premises to the MoD and SoS for Employment for BICC Group Pension Trust Ltd.

Jones Maidment Wilson (3ptnrs/3assts f/t, 1 p/t) Reputable but low profile. **Clients/Work:** Development, investment and landlord & tenant.

Napthen Houghton Craven (3ptnrs/3assts) "A firm on the way up," and in the fortunate position of acting for rapidly expanding clients. **Clients/Work:** Yates Brothers Wine Lodges PLC on the acquisitions and management of their portfolio. Conlon Construction's developments of investment properties and joint ventures including 34 acres of industrial property.

Weightmans (2ptnrs/6assts) Highly thought of and seen to be expanding beyond property as a core practice area. **Clients/Work:** Lidl (UK) GmbH on a £6m sale and leaseback. Neptune/ Swallow Hotel and leisure development at Queen Sq, Liverpool. Columbus Quay development, Liverpool.

Aaron & Partners (3ptnrs/2assts) A quality practice in Chester. **Clients/Work:** Sale of an operational quarry; leases of chemical works; joint venture development work for a local authority involving industrial and employment sites.

Barker Booth & Eastwood Always professional. The firm was praised for being thoughtful and for conducting "quality negotiation."

Berrymans Lace Mawer (7ptnrs/5assts) Always highly regarded. Recruited an assistant and partners in planning and environment. **Clients/Work:** Landmark development on the Liverpool waterfront. For the landlord on the redevelopment and pre-letting of a shopping arcade in Southport.

Brabner Holden Banks Wilson (6ptnrs/7assts) Based in Liverpool and Preston. A large part of the work is for housing associations. **Clients/Work:** Knowsley MBC's sale of a site for Liverpool FC's Football Academy. Estate work for North West Brewery Company.

Bremner Sons & Corlett (4ptnrs/1asst) **Clients/Work:** Work for Housing Associations, Agricultural Property and Friendly Societies.

Chaffe Street (2ptnrs/2assts) A strong corporate practice which feeds the property side. **Clients/Work:** NM Rothschild & Sons' provision of loan facilities to Fairbank Estates to fund its Trafford Park development. Flowcrete PLC's acquisition of new HQ office and factory premise at Sandbach.

Elliott & Co (3ptnrs/2assts) Have recruited one new assistant this year. **Clients/Work:** Acquisition of NW site for major residential developer £2.5m. Acquisition of 10 retail units(rental value each £100k-£200k)for Scottish Power Retail division.

Gorna & Co (4ptnrs/3assts) **Clients/Work:** Investment property portfolio sale £6.3m. £40m refinance purchase for a housing association. Sale of office investment in Manchester £5.1m.

Kuit Steinart Levy (4ptnrs/8assts) Busy within their section of the market and respected by the other local firms. Merged with Hammelburger Marks. **Clients/Work:**

Acted on behalf of the shareholders of Stationery Box Ltd in the disposal of a nationwide chain of 118 shops. Acted on behalf of a group of private investors in the disposal of commercial properties in excess of £20m.

Pannone & Partners (4ptnrs/3assts) Considered decent people to work with. **Clients/Work:** GMPTE Metrolink extension. DSS on Project PRIME (178 properties). Realty Estates' acquisition of Gateway House, Manchester.

Walker Smith & Way (6ptnrs/1asst/1assoc.) A reputable property practice.

LEADING INDIVIDUALS
NORTH WEST

ASHWORTH Peter Field Cunningham & Co
BECKETT Roy Dibb Lupton Alsop
JONES Pamela Bullivant Jones & Company
MARKS Geoffrey Halliwell Landau
MOODY John Eversheds
STRATTON David Field Cunningham & Co
TULLY David Addleshaw Booth & Co

BENSON Stephen Cobbetts
BUCKLEY Liam Hammond Suddards
CRAVEN Diana Addleshaw Booth & Co
DIGGINES Susan Addleshaw Booth & Co
GOODMAN Stephen Halliwell Landau
ROONEY Philip Dibb Lupton Alsop
SORRELL Stephen Eversheds
STEPHENS Michael Bullivant Jones & Company
WALLIS Guy Davies Wallis Foyster

UP AND COMING · NORTH WEST

BEARDWOOD Mark Dibb Lupton Alsop
LEONARD Tessa Eversheds
WEIGHTMAN Anita Dibb Lupton Alsop

SEE PROFILES AT END OF THIS SECTION

LEADERS' PROFILES · NORTH WEST

ASHWORTH, P.H.
Field Cunningham & Co, Manchester (0161) 834 4734
Senior Partner.
Specialisation: Acts for major developers and housebuilders throughout the North. Responsible for the acquisition of land for approximately 1400 houses annually. Involved with large retail and leisure developments throughout the United Kingdom including superstores, cinemas, bingo clubs and bowling alleys. Deals with numerous joint ventures with other developers and financiers for residential and commercial developments. Handles the funding of major commercial developments. Non-executive Director of Barratt Developments plc.
Career: Qualified March 1961. Articled at *Field Cunningham & Co.* and became a Partner in 1962.
Personal: Born 23rd January 1938. Educated at Arnold School Blackpool. Lives in Hale, Cheshire.

BEARDWOOD, Mark
Dibb Lupton Alsop, Liverpool (0345) 262728
Specialisation: Handles a broad range of commercial property transactions for a variety of clients, including property investors and developers, occupiers of retail, office, manufacturing and distribution space. Transactions include property development and funding, joint ventures, landlord and tenant. Also acts for a number of institutions within the higher and further education sectors providing a broad range of advice but including VAT planning for major property developments. Currently advising the contracting authorities on two major PFI schemes.
Career: Educated at St. Anselm's College, Birkenhead and Oxford University. Articled at *Linklaters & Paines*. Qualified 1985. Partner *Dibb Luton Alsop* 1990. Head of Liverpool Property Department 1998.

BECKETT, Roy
Dibb Lupton Alsop, Manchester (0345) 262728
Specialisation: Property development and investment and structured finance for institutions and property companies.
Prof. Memberships: Law Society and Interact.
Career: Qualified 1983. Joined *Alsop Wilkinson* 1987 becoming partner in 1989. Head of Manchester Property Department in 1992 (*Dibb Lupton Alsop* 1996).
Personal: Born 1958. Lives Bowdon, Cheshire. Leisure interests include skiing, squash, tennis and overseas travel.

BENSON, Stephen
Cobbetts, Manchester (0161) 833 3333
Specialisation: Commercial property in the Retail and Leisure sector. Acts for household name retailers and licensed premises operators in the pub, restaurant and hotel sector.
Prof. Memberships: Law Society. Associate member of American Bar Association.
Career: Educated at Manchester University

and Chester College of Law. Qualified 1980.
Personal: Born 1955. Married with 3 children. Lives in Knutsford. Leisure interests, exercise, member of Morgan sports car club and Chairman of Patrons of Manchester City Art Gallery.

BUCKLEY, Liam
Hammond Suddards, Manchester
(0161) 830 5000
Partner - Commercial Property
Specialisation: Specialises in Commercial Property Finance and Development, Property Investment and Joint Ventures. Member of the firms Energy / Utilities Grouping dealing particularly with power station development. Recent transactions include the sale of Manchester Arndale Centre, acting for P & O Properties Limited.
Career: Articled *Last Suddards*; Qualified 1987. Partner *Hammond Suddards*.
Personal: Born 1961. Resides Calverley, Leeds. Enjoys music, golf and skiing. Member of Northcliffe Golf Club.

CRAVEN, Diana
Addleshaw Booth & Co, Manchester
(0161) 934 6000
Partner in the Commercial Property Group.
Specialisation: Wide ranging commercial property interests but specifically including development schemes, land reclamation, property partnerships and joint ventures and funding agreements. Clients include Government agencies, plc developers, banks and companies with substantial property portfolios.
Career: With *Herbert Smith* 1972-1977 including articles. Moved to Manchester in 1977 and became a Partner in 1981.
Personal: Interests include professional and managerial level womens groups, gardening and travel when time permits.

DIGGINES, Susan C.
Addleshaw Booth & Co, Manchester
(0161) 934 6000
Partner in Commercial Property Group.
Specialisation: Main area of practice is commercial property work covering retail/office development, portfolio sales/acquisitions investment and joint venture schemes. 1996 - led property team acting for United Utilities in much publicised disposal of retail arm of NORWEB.
Career: Qualified 1984.

GOODMAN, Stephen L.
Halliwell Landau, Manchester
(0161) 835 3003
Specialisation: Head of Property Department. Stephen is particularly active in development transactions and advises on the structure of property transactions, including land assembly, development agreements, funding arrangements, joint ventures and statutory agreements.
Career: Articled *Bennett & Co*; qualified 1985; Assistant *Nabarro Nathanson* 1986-1989; Partner *Gorna & Co*; Partner *Halliwell Landau* 1993.
Personal: Born 1961. Resides Chester. Keen golfer and Evertonian.

JONES, Pamela
Bullivant Jones & Company, Liverpool (0151) 227 5671
Senior Partner in Commercial Conveyancing Department.
Specialisation: Main areas of practice are retail and commercial property.
Prof. Memberships: Law Society.
Career: Qualified in 1977. Joined *Bullivant Jones & Company* in 1973, becoming a Partner in 1978 and Senior Partner in 1994.
Personal: Born 7th January 1951. Attended Holyhead Comprehensive 1962-68. Leisure interests include reading and gardening. Lives near Tarporley, Cheshire.

LEONARD, Tessa
Eversheds, Manchester (0161) 832 6666
Specialisation: Commercial development in particular business parks and leisure schemes handling both development and disposal. Also specialises in development agreements and joint ventures between the public and private sector. Recent urban regeneration projects include: acting for English Partnerships in providing public sector funding to revitalise Manchester City Centre after the 1996 IRA bomb; acting for English Partnerships in the acquisition of the Royal William Yard, Plymouth. Recent/current projects/developments include: acting for AMEC Developments in relation to investment sales and lettings at Cheadle Royal business park; acting for Kirklees Henry Boot Partnership in relation to a major retail scheme in Huddersfield.
Prof. Memberships: Association of Women Solicitors.
Career: Manchester High School for Girls; Birmingham University; articled *Halliwell Landau*, achieving Partnership; joined *Eversheds (Alexander Tatham)* 1990, Partner 1993.
Personal: Resides Wilmslow, married with one son. Leisure: DIY, theatre, wine, books.

MARKS, Geoffrey
Halliwell Landau, Manchester
(0161) 835 3003
Specialisation: Former Head of Property Department. Deals with full range of property work including development and investment work and all property aspects of property secured lending.
Prof. Memberships: Associate of Chartered Institute of Arbitrators.
Career: Articled *AH Howarth & Co*; qualified 1963; partner *AH Howarth & Co* (now *Howarth Goodman & Co*) 1965-74; partner *Maurice Rubin & Co* 1974-84; partner *Halliwell Landau* 1984.
Personal: Born 1941; resides Prestwich. Educated at Arnold School, Blackpool. Recreations include theatre and opera.

MOODY, John
Eversheds, Manchester (0161) 832 6666
Partner in Commercial Property Department.
Specialisation: Work covers all aspects of commercial property with a particular emphasis on investment and management work. Involved in several high profile residential and commercial developments and advises several FTSE 100 companies on their strategic property

requirements. Contributes articles to professional journals and local press. Lectures at Preston Polytechnic and to professional bodies on property joint ventures.
Prof. Memberships: Law Society.
Career: Articled 1973-75 at *Ingham Clegg & Crowther* in Preston and became a Partner in 1980. Joined *Yates Barnes* in 1989, then moved to *Eversheds Alexander Tatham* in 1990. Became Head of Commercial Property Department in 1990 and Managing Partner in 1993. Following the merger of *Eversheds* offices in Leeds and Manchester became Deputy Managing Partner of these offices.
Personal: Born 19th February 1950. Attended Nottingham High School 1961-69, then Jesus College, Cambridge 1969-72. Leisure pursuits include golf (Cambridge Blue 1970-71 and 71-72 and County Golfer), theatre, overseas travel, mowing the lawn and terrorising the cat. Lives in Bowdon, Cheshire.

ROONEY, Philip
Dibb Lupton Alsop, Liverpool (0345) 262728
Specialisation: Commercial property; advises a wide range of investors, funders, developers and occupiers on all manner of property related projects; acts for local authorities, urban regeneration bodies and other public and quasi public sector organisations on the exploitation of their public property assets.
Prof. Memberships: Law Society.
Career: After graduating from Oxford University, joined the firm in 1978, partner in 1984. Head of Liverpool Property Department 1992-1998; appointed national head of Property and Construction Group 1998.
Personal: Married; 3 children. Enjoys classical music, sport, theatre.

SORRELL, Stephen
Eversheds, Manchester (0161) 832 6666
stephen.sorrell@eversheds.co.uk Partner and Head of Department: Commercial Property - Eversheds - Leeds and Manchester.
Specialisation: Commercial property development (industrial, office, leisure and retail) and urban regeneration. Acts as strategic legal adviser to English Partnerships (the Government's Urban Regeneration Agency) and has advised English Partnerships ii relation to a number of its major inward investments such as Siemens (£1.4 billion investment) in the North East as the co-ordinating lawyer for the public sector participants in the £145 million regeneration of the G-Mex District of Manchester City Centre and in Bristol in connection with the Temple Quay Site and in Plymouth in relation to the Royal William Yard. He advises private sector developers such as AMEC Developments Limited (Cheadle Royal, the 80 acre business park in South Manchester and Ashton Moss in East Manchester), MEPC plc and several local authorities in particular regard to public and private sector joint venture arrangements to procure urban development.
Prof. Memberships: Law Society and International Bar Association.
Career: Training, *Abson Hall* (Manchester and Stockport) Solicitor and Partner, *Abson Hall*, Partner in *Eversheds* from 1989 to present.
Personal: Born 5th October 1959. Educated Marple Hall Grammar School, Manchester University and Chester College of Law. Leisure interests include cinema, music and a passion for Manchester City FC. Lives in South Manchester and is married with 2 children.

STEPHENS, Michael
Bullivant Jones & Company, Liverpool
(0151) 227 5671

STRATTON, D.
Field Cunningham & Co, Manchester
(0161) 834 4734
Partner.
Specialisation: Undertakes a wide range of commercial conveyancing transactions. Has specialised in major developments of all types, with particular emphasis on retail and office development, both town centre and out of town. Widespread experience of joint venture, institutional funding and secured lending work, as well as acquisition and disposal of major investment portfolios. Has been involved with the Fishergate Centre, Preston; Cockhedge Centre, Warrington; Clapham Junction Centre; Concourse Centre, Skelmersdale and the Galleria Centre, Hatfield.
Prof. Memberships: Law Society
Career: Articled with Warrington Borough Council. Qualified in 1971. Worked for Christian

Salvesen Properties as Group Legal Adviser. Joined *Halliwell Landau* in 1979 and became Deputy Senior Partner. Joined *Field Cunningham & Co.* in 1996.
Personal: Born 16th May 1947. Educated at Altrincham Grammar School for Boys and Colwyn Bay Grammar School, then Leeds University 1965-68. Lives in Bowdon, Cheshire.

TULLY, David J.
Addleshaw Booth & Co, Manchester
(0161) 934 6000
Partner in Private Client Group.
Specialisation: Principal area of practice covers all aspects of commercial property work. Also acts for landed estates advising on tax schemes. Chairman of Law Society Joint Committee with RICS producing Model Rent Review Clauses 1979-85. Lectured for College of Law on Model Rent Review Clauses.
Prof. Memberships: Law Society, Manchester Law Society.
Career: Qualified 1964 while with the firm and became a Partner in 1969.

Personal: Born 13th March 1942. Governor Manchester Grammar School. Vice-President St. James's Club, Manchester. Leisure pursuits include fishing, shooting and golf. Lives in Hale, Cheshire.

WALLIS, Guy St J.
Davies Wallis Foyster, Liverpool
(0151) 236 6226

WEIGHTMAN, Anita
Dibb Lupton Alsop, Manchester
(0345) 262728
Specialisation: Development finance and secured lending. Portfolio acquisitions and disposals. Capital raising (sale and leaseback). Leisure development (A3, D2 Users).
Prof. Memberships: Law Society. Manchester Law Society.
Career: Westholme School, Blackburn. University of Newcastle Upon Tyne. College of Law, Chester.

NORTH EAST

LEADING FIRMS · NORTH EAST

ADDLESHAW BOOTH & CO Leeds

DIBB LUPTON ALSOP Leeds
DICKINSON DEES Newcastle upon Tyne
EVERSHEDS Leeds
WALKER MORRIS Leeds

PINSENT CURTIS Leeds

HIGHLY REGARDED FIRMS

Garretts Leeds
Hammond Suddards Leeds

Eversheds Newcastle upon Tyne
Gosschalks Hull
Irwin Mitchell Sheffield
Nabarro Nathanson Sheffield
Read Hind Stewart Leeds

Andrew M. Jackson & Co Hull
Gordons Wright & Wright Bradford
Jacksons Stockton-on-Tees
McGuinness Finch Leeds
Robert Muckle Newcastle-upon-Tyne
Rollit Farrell & Bladon Hull
Ward Hadaway Newcastle upon Tyne
Watson Burton Newcastle upon Tyne

Archers Stockton-on-Tees
Attey Bower & Jones with Dibb and Clegg Doncaster
Denison Till Leeds
Oxley & Coward Rotherham
Stamp Jackson and Procter Hull

Addleshaw Booth & Co (18ptnrs/33assts) "A good conscientious sensible firm." The practice has a fine and well-deserved reputation for "good sound commercial lawyers." Local surveyors say there is "less personality involved than at other leading firms." *John Pike* is rated. *Tim Tonkin* has an "aggressive

style" but is spoken of highly. Clients say he "cuts through the technicalities and gives answers rather than creating more problems."
Clients/Work: Acting for the Carnbane House Group on development of a retail leisure scheme in Northern Ireland building some 210,000sq.ft.of space. Acting for Halifax plc on 25-year lease of City offices (200,000 sq.ft). Acting for Stadium on development of a retail/leisure scheme in Liverpool building (500,000 sq.ft.)
 Dibb Lupton Alsop (6ptnrs/16assts) Thought to be "increasingly taking a market share" having experienced some time "in the doldrums" after the merger. *Neil McLean* is known as a "troubleshooter who is prepared to get his hands dirty" and is "commercial, good at cutting through the technicalities." *Martin Grabiner* is praised as a "quality lawyer" who is "very aware of the details."
Clients/Work: Acting for The Burton Group Plc in sale of investment portfolio of 29 properties. Acting for Leven Properties Ltd in acquisition of major investment portfolio. Acting for Sears Property Developments Ltd in acquisition of three major development sites in London, East Anglia and South Wales.
 Dickinson Dees (12ptnrs/26assts) The firm is absolutely dominant in the Newcastle marketplace, a "large fish in a small pond." *Neil Braithwaite* has just become the new Managing Partner. He is "well-suited to the North-East" with his "traditional" approach.
Clients/Work: Rolls Royce Power Ventures – development of substantial portfolio of gas turbine power stations in South. Bellway – joint venture, major urban regeneration project of over 200 acres (former Ipswich Airfield).
 Eversheds (Leeds) (8ptnrs/20assts) "Well-established" team may feel loss of *Andrew Latchmore* who is now in a more

management role. Clients rate him "highly and enjoy having him on the frontline." However *John Foster* is now Head of Department and according to some clients "an ample replacement for Andrew" although others think he has "yet to prove himself."
Clients/Work: Acquisition by Thrall Car, US railway carriage builder of the former ABB works in York, major piece of inward investment into the region. Two substantial NHS Trust PFI jobs for new care facilities for EMI patients for brain injury rehabilitation. Enterprise Zone disposals acting for the developer, a public/private sector partnership, including an Enterprise Zone investment package and an Enterprise Zone letting acting for a major space user.
 Walker Morris (10ptnrs/15assts) The property team has a "good following with banks and local developers" although it is limited by being local. *Michael Kempley* is seen as the "mainspring of the department, but there is a perception that he is "winding down." However, the department includes two newly rated individuals: *David Duckworth* who is "an extremely safe pair of hands and a quality operator." *Judith Pike* has also impressed. **Clients/Work:** Appointed as legal advisors to Priority Sites Ltd, a joint venture between the Royal Bank of Scotland plc and English Partnerships. Acting on behalf of Evans of Leeds Plc with several schemes including a 60 acre business park at York. Acting as lead solicitors co-ordinating four other firms for Rosedale Property Holdings Ltd in obtaining long term finance facilities secured on portfolios of properties in the UK.
 Pinsent Curtis (11ptnrs/3assocs/11assts) The old Simpson Curtis property practice was based on an established practice of old retainers and senior establishment figures. The merged firm has "a comfortable client base" and the lawyers are respected as "good

technicians." *Nigel McLea* is "Head Boy" in the department; an extremely bright lawyer, "clients stick to Nigel like glue." **Clients/Work:** Acting for Secretary of State for Health in phased development of over 100 acres of land at Epsom, Surrey for 1500 dwellings and associated amenities. Acting for Thorpe Park(Leeds)Ltd in development of new business park in North of over 310 acres. Acting for Trinity Developments Ltd on a multi-million pound redevelopment of local authority site at Broad Street, Halifax.

Garretts (3ptnrs/7assts) The "new boys around" known for property-linked corporate work. While they do not have the size they have "good people and nice transactions." There is said to be a bit of a personality cult around *Michael Sleath*, who has the "world's biggest Christmas card list." He is able to carry off his role as Mr Marketeer because he is "practical, sensible, commercial and very experienced." *Paula Dillon* also received favourable mention. **Clients/Work:** Advising Halewood Supplier Park on multi-let 1m sq.ft. industrial park adjoining the Ford factory in Halewood,Liverpool. Acting for developer of Calder Island, Wakefield on all aspects of 400,000 sq.ft. mixed development.

Hammond Suddards (5ptnrs/11assts) The widespread perception in the marketplace is that commercial property is more of a service function. There are no recommended individuals in our lists and the team is felt to have lost some significant people. **Clients/Work:** Advising English Partnerships in acquisition of former ABB railway works in the City of York and on letting of substantial part to Thrall Car Manufacturing Company. Advising Yorkshire Electricity plc on sale of City West Office Park, Leeds for a substantial sum.

Eversheds (Newcastle) (13ptnrs/11assts) Merged with Wilkinson Maughan last year which means they have greater numbers but still have a way to go to challenge Dickinson Dees in property. **Clients/Work:** Act for Tyne and Wear Development Corporation and English Partnerships. Act for a number of house builders (Barratt, Beazer, Wimpey). Act for several inward investors into the region (ADI Ltd from Taiwan, Seika Corporation from Japan, video Products Groups Ltd from the USA).

Gosschalks (6ptnrs/2assocs/2assts) Particularly known for conveyancing of licensed premises. Property is the main fee-earning practice area of the firm. Also have "some good individuals." **Clients/Work:** Acted for Nomura in connection with multi million pound sale of 800 public houses to Grovebase Properties Ltd (now Wellington Finance plc). Do work for Granada Travel Lodges and Forte(UK)Ltd.

Irwin Mitchell (6ptnrs/8assts) The firm experienced "rapid growth from nowhere a few years ago" and is now known as "a reasonable regional player." The general feeling

is that the firm is "one to watch and is trying to cross the gulf between the leaders and the highly regarded firms." **Clients/Work:** Acting for Suon Cambridge Ltd on funding and development of its £100m Cambridge Research Park with plans to develop up to 600,000 square feet. Acting for Thorntons plc on more than one hundred retail transactions/lettings in the last year. Acting for Hallam Land Management Ltd and Henry Boot Developments Ltd on acquisition and proposed mixed retail/leisure/business park development of up to 500,000 square feet at Fylde Lancashire.

Nabarro Nathanson (5ptnrs/26assts) Said to be an unusual combination; they have not got the all-round strength of the leaders but in certain areas they are a step above. The practice "fluctuates with the fortunes of the London office to which it is conclusively stapled." **Clients/Work:** Landlord and Tenant management and disposals for A.G.Stanley: FADS and Homecare Shops. Acquisition of share capital of company owning premises let to Salford University.

Read Hind Stewart (6ptnrs/1asst) Known as having "some good individuals." The practice received a large number of positive recommendations partly because of *Andrew Flounders* who is regarded as quality and is "their best weapon." **Clients/Work:** Clients include: Tameside Park Ltd – major industrial Estate at Tameside Greater Manchester; Caddick Group – Bradford City Centre Redvelopments; Knowsley Development Partnership – regeneration project.

Andrew M. Jackson & Co (9ptnrs/5assts) Have penetrated the Hull market and are highly regarded for their work. *Ian Wilkinson* heads the department. **Clients/Work:** Sale of 14 properties for £9.5m for Northern Foods Pension Fund. Acting for various clients on sale and purchase of retail parks worth over £100m. Acting for Associated British Ports in lease of land for £350m power station.

Gordons Wright & Wright (6ptnrs/6assts) Previously a traditional practice with a strong local client base. However they are now "reinventing themselves in a way that does not alienate their existing clients; with a young team giving pro-active advice." **Clients/Work:** A series of acquisitions for Wm Morrison Supermarkets PLC. Development of a new factory on a nine acre site off the M62 for Carrington Wire Group. Sale and leaseback of large Cashmere Works site in Bradford for Dawson International PLC.

Jacksons (4ptnrs/3assts) The firm has a good following in Hull. Known for being "efficient in their dealings." They act for Northern Electric among others. **Clients/Work:** Tees and Hartlepool Port Authority. Middlesbrough Council.

McGuinness Finch (10ptnrs/2assts) Received a number of excellent recommendations this year and enter the tables new this year.

Robert Muckle (2ptnrs/2assocs/8assts) Less broadly-based than some practices; they do a lot of banking property work. They have "one or two good players with some decent clients." **Clients/Work:** Dysart Developments Ltd – development and construction of 280,000 square foot factory outlet at Walker Riverside on behalf of Dresser. Cecil M Yuill Ltd – acquisition of Princess Mary Maternity Hospital, Jesmond for conversion into luxury town houses/apartments complex. Acted for City and Northern Projects Ltd on acquisition etc on 7 industrial units.

Rollitt Farrell & Bladon (9ptnrs/2assts) Property is one fifth of the practice's workload **Clients/Work:** Redevelopment of former office premises into a hotel scheme including provision of collateral warranties. Housing stock refinancing for major Housing Association.

Ward Hadaway (8ptnrs/6assts) **Clients/Work:** Instructed on DSS Prime Disposal, value approximately £200m. Acting on property matters for Northern Rock Building Society in their conversion to PLC status. Acting for developers within "Grainger Town Initiative" on major redevelopments in Newcastle.

Watson Burton (6ptnrs/1assoc) The commercial property department is divided into commercial development, residential development, landlord and tenant and housing association law. **Clients/Work:** Acted as part of a team in acquisition of substantial industrial and commercial property portfolio comprising a number of industrial estates in UK for £75m. Negotiating and advising Higher Education Corporation on multiphase new Campus development with a projected cost of £60+m.

Archers (2ptnrs f/t/2ptnrs p/t/2assts p/t) **Clients/Work:** Cameron Hall Developments Ltd; Hexham Auction Mart Co. Ltd; Springhealth Leisure Ltd.

Attey Bower & Jones with Dibb and Clegg (3ptnrs/7assts) **Clients/Work:** Sematic UK Ltd; industrial unit purchase. Spring Choice Care Homes; sale. Donbac.

Denison Till (3ptnrs) Well-regarded. Act for significant number of middle-ranking, small scale commercial property dealers.

Oxley & Coward A niche firm specialising in advice to NHS Trusts, including transfers of NHS property and acquisitions of land and buildings. **Clients/ Work:** Advice on shopping development schemes in hospitals. Building a new private hospital unit in the grounds of a trust, with the trust providing services to the unit for a charge.

Stamp Jackson & Procter (1ptnr/ 1asst) They "have good people, know what they are doing and act as property specialists."

LEADERS' PROFILES • NORTH EAST

BRAITHWAITE, Neil
Dickinson Dees, Newcastle upon Tyne
(0191) 279 9000
Head of Property Department.
Specialisation: Handles Urban Regeneration, Development Agreements and property joint ventures, Enterprise Zone transactions, historic house rescues. Recent projects include: Barking Reach development for Bellway plc; Enterprise Zone schemes at Sunderland and Tyne Hill; Development Agreement for Sunderland AFC Stadium for Tyne and Wear Development Corporation; Agreements to transfer 6 major development sites from Tyne and Wear Development Corporation to English Partnerships; Development Agreement to secure the preservation of Stoneleigh Abbey, Warwickshire; Agreements on behalf of The Phoenix Trust to secure the preservation of historic buildings; International Centre for Life - Millennium Fund development in Newcastle.
Career: Trinity College, Cambridge M.A. Law Society Finals. *Joynson Hicks* 1976-1978. *Clifford Chance* 1978-1980. *Dickinson Dees* 1980 to date. (Partner 1981 onwards - Head of Property from 1990-1991). Managing partner from 1998.

DILLON, Paula
Garretts, Leeds (0113) 207 9000
Specialisation: Specialises in commercial property. Particularly well regarded for development and development finance, acting for developers, lenders, tenants and PFI participants. Recognised as a lawyer who will make deals happen. Skilled negotiator with ability to reconcile potentially conflicting interests. Current projects include acting for Intercity JIS Limited in acquiring, developing and letting 1 million square feet of industrial space and a 100-acre business park in the North West.
Prof. Memberships: Law Society
Career: University of Manchester. Qualified 1986.
Personal: Walking, cycling, skiing. Married with no children or pets.

DUCKWORTH, David J.
Walker Morris, Leeds (0113) 283 2500
Specialisation: Property Development and Secured Lending, PFI. Head of property - *Walker Morris*.
Career: Darwen Grammar School.
Personal: Sport and Sailing.

FLOUNDERS, Andrew J.
Read Hind Stewart, Leeds (0113) 246 8123
Specialisation: Head of Property Department. Acts primarily for developers.
Prof. Memberships: Law Society.
Career: Educated – Benton Park Grammer School and Manchester University. Qualified - *Read Hind Stewart* 1983 and Partner since 1984.

Personal: Born 1958. Married with two sons and lives in Calverley. Fascinated by all sports and still plays football. Round Table.

FOSTER, John
Eversheds, Leeds (0113) 243 0391
Partner in Property Development Department.
Specialisation: Property Development including site assembly, construction, pre-letting, funding and investment sales and complicated participation or profit sharing arrangments. Enterprise Zones a speciality. Wide experience in public and private sector partnership, grants and PFI, and leisure.
Prof. Memberships: Law Society.
Career: MA Oxford. Articles with *Macfarlanes*. 1983 joined *Eversheds*, becoming a partner in 1985.
Personal: Interests – Munros.

GRABINER, Martin
Dibb Lupton Alsop, Leeds (0345) 262728
Specialisation: All types of commercial property work with emphasis on development and financing and joint venture arrangements involving both the private and public sector (including PFI Projects) and portfolio acquisition and disposal in respect of varied types of property (including office, industrial, retail and higher education) acquisiton and sales. In addition - commercial property and commercial work in relation to infrastructure and transport (in particular canals and railways).
Career: 1984-86 First In-house Solicitor for the Wickes Group of Companies, London. 1986-88 Partner – *Boodle Hatfield*, London. 1989 to date Partner – *Dibb Lupton Broomhead* and *Dibb Lupton Alsop*, Leeds. Education: St Paul's School, London; Trinity College, Cambridge (MA).
Personal: Born 1953; resides North Yorkshire. Married with five children. Leisure: Organic husbandry and early classical music and member of the Leeds Library.

KEMPLEY, Michael
Walker Morris, Leeds (0113) 283 2500
Specialisation: Retail property with emphasis on department store acquisitions in anchor tenant situations in shopping centres. In addition acquisition of retail space in the high street for multiple operators.
Prof. Memberships: LL.B and Member of British Council of Shopping Centres.
Career: Qualified 1960. At *Booth & Co.* 1960 to 1965 and subsequently with *Scott Turnbull & Kendall* until, and after, their merger with *Walker Morris*.
Personal: Educated Mount St Mary's College and Leeds University. Lives in Harewood, Yorkshire.

LATCHMORE, Andrew
Eversheds, Leeds (0113) 243 0391
Partner and National Managing Partner responsible

for all services delivered to clients by the firm.
Specialisation: Has a wide range of experience in commercial property development work on retail office and industrial schemes acting for developers, funders, owners and tenants. Specialist interest in the education sector. Has acted in a number of development projects for educational establishments and for banks funding such projects. This has included innovative tax driven lease transactions to raise capital. Acted for MEPC plc on a number of schemes including a mixed office retail and hotel development in Leeds, for Hammerson UK Properties plc in the major refurbishment and extension of Freshney Place shopping centre, Grimsby, and for the University of York and P&O Developments in the creation of a joint venture company to develop the York Science Park and the anchor letting of a 100,000 square foot building to Smith & Nephew Research. Has written several articles for legal journals and has lectured at a number of RICS and *Eversheds* seminars.
Prof. Memberships: Law Society, Leeds Law Society (Honorary Secretary 1984-90).
Career: Qualified in 1975. Became a Partner at *Eversheds (then Hepworth & Chadwick)* in 1978.
Personal: Born 9th February 1950. Educated at Oundle School 1963-69 and Leeds University 1970-73. Leisure pursuits include golf, tennis, skiing, music and walking. Lives in Leeds.

MARKS, Christopher
Hammond Suddards, Leeds
(0113) 284 7000
Specialisation: All aspects of property development and investment, urban regeneration, public sector, grant and funding agreements, joint ventures and dealing with the property aspects of inward investment projects and major infrastructure projects. Landlord and tenant advice, licensed premises, acquisitions and disposals, secured lending on properties. Pipeline leases and gas exploration and development.
Career: Education; North East London Polytechnic (BA (Hons) Law 1979), Wolfson College, Cambridge (LLM (Cantab)) 1980. Career history: 1980-1982 *Waltons & Morse*; 1983-1988 *Edge & Ellison* - solicitor associate; 1988 joined *Hammond Suddards*; Partner 1989.

MCCLEA, Nigel
Pinsent Curtis, Leeds (0113) 244 5000
Head of Property, Leeds
Specialisation: Specialises in large scale commercial projects, property in public and private sectors (with particular focus on education and health). Major leisure projects: Jorvik Viking Centre, York; The Oxford Story, Oxford; The Pilgrim Way, Canterbury; Royal Armouries Museum, Leeds; Relocation of Sunderland Football Club.
Career: Qualified 1975. Partner in *Simpson*

Curtis (now *Pinsent Curtis*) 1978. Fellow of the Royal Society of Arts, Manufacturers and Commerce.
Personal: Born 1951. Educated at Ashville College, Harrogate and Queen's College, Cambridge.

MCLEAN, Neil
Dibb Lupton Alsop, Leeds (0345) 262728
Specialisation: Head of Property Group in Leeds. Commercial Property. Principal areas of specialisation are property development and retail work. Acts for a wide range of national clients in all aspects of development portfolio management and acquisitions and disposals.
Career: Qualified 1977, Partner 1981.

PIKE, John D.
Addleshaw Booth & Co, Leeds
(0113) 209 2000
Head of Commercial Property Group (includes Commercial Property, Environmental, Construction, Planning and Property Litigation).
Specialisation: Main area of practice is commercial property work, covering development, banking, environmental, investment and joint venture matters. Environmental law experience includes contaminated land remediation, waste and lender risk. Numerous articles in property and environmental journals.
Career: Joined the firm in 1969. Qualified 1972. Partner 1976.
Personal: Born 4th October 1947. Jesus College Cambridge (MA: Hons). De Montfort University (MA: Environmental Law). Governor Moorlands School, Leeds. Director: Leeds

Environmental Business Forum. Interests include sports and family. Lives in Wetherby.

PIKE, Judith Mary
Walker Morris, Leeds (0113) 283 2500
Specialisation: Specialist in secured lending and property finance matters, and leasing work predominantly retail and office. Highlights include: advising lenders on the provision of facilities to the leisure industry and to residential developers. The acquisition of ten out of town retail sites on behalf of a major retailer. Advising a major Plc in corporate relocation in London with a base rent in excess of £1m.
Prof. Memberships: Law Society.
Career: Skipton Girls High School; King's College University of London; Articled *Lee Bolton & Lee*, Westminster. 1987-1990 *Allen & Overy*; *Walker Morris* 1990 to present. Partner at *Walker Morris* 1993 to present.
Personal: Married with two children. Interests include walking, mountaineering and family.

SLEATH, Michael R.
Garretts, Leeds (0113) 207 9000
Partner in Property department.
Specialisation: Handles all areas of commercial property, but particularly commercial property development and licensed properties. Spent two years assembling Meadowhall and dealing with its planning and onward disposal.
Prof. Memberships: Law Society, Committee Member of Leeds Law Society.
Career: Qualified in 1977. Worked at *Simpson Curtis*; Legal Department of Asda Group plc 1978-81; and returned to *Simpson Curtis* in

1981, becoming a Partner in 1982. Joined *Garretts* in 1994 as a Partner.
Personal: Born 6 December 1952. Attended Northampton Grammar then Southampton University 1971-74. Married with two children. Lives in West Yorkshire.

TONKIN, Tim
Addleshaw Booth & Co, Leeds
(0113) 209 2000
Specialisation: Practice covers full range of commercial property work, with particular emphasis on office, retail and leisure developments. Recent experience includes acting on a number of property joint ventures.
Career: Qualified 1977. With *Herbert Smith* 1974-1982. Joined the firm in 1982 and became partner in 1984.
Personal: Born 1951. Educated at Truro School and Exeter College Oxford. Lives in Leeds. Interests include his allotment and Sheffield Wednesday F.C.

WILKINSON, Ian
Andrew M. Jackson & Co, Hull
(01482) 325242
Partner in Commercial Property Department.
Specialisation: Specialises in out of town retail parks, acting primarily on behalf of tenants. Other area of expertise is pension fund investments.
Career: Joined *Payne & Payne* in 1965. Qualified in 1968. Joined *Andrew M. Jackson* in 1973 and became a Partner in 1974.
Personal: Born 25th June 1944. Attended Beverley Grammar School 1955-62, then Southampton University 1962-65. Enjoys sport, reading and walking. Lives in Beverley.

SCOTLAND

DUNDAS & WILSON CS Edinburgh
MCGRIGOR DONALD Glasgow
MACLAY MURRAY & SPENS Glasgow
SHEPHERD & WEDDERBURN WS Edinburgh
ARCHIBALD CAMPBELL & HARLEY WS Edinburgh
BIRD SEMPLE Glasgow
SEMPLE FRASER WS Glasgow
STEEDMAN RAMAGE WS Edinburgh

Dundas & Wilson CS (12ptnrs/34assts) A firm with "huge firepower but thoughtful about how they use it." Traditionally the institutions' firm to McGrigors' developer practice but the distinction is blurring. *Donald Shaw* is "an interesting character" with a forceful style. *David Steel* "keeps things simple and is always prepared to listen." *Hamish Hodge, Philip Dacker* (head of property finance group) and *Brian Leggat* were also recommended. **Clients/Work:** Buchanan Partnership (AMP/Slough Estates) letting of Buchanan Galleries. TBI plc's anchor letting to Debenhams in the Overgate Centre,

Dundee. The lease to Eaton Shared Services of Tay House, Glasgow.

McGrigor Donald (13ptnrs/29assts) Great tacticians but more confrontational than D&W. Have a wealth of talent and experience including *Thomas Anderson* ("a sit down and sort it out lawyer who sees around corners"), *David Bankier* ("one step down from God!"), *Donna Stevenson* ("a rocket scientist. Sees and takes every point possible") and *Alison Newton* who possesses that rare combination of technical and deal making skills with an infectious personality. **Clients/Work:** Kumagai Gurmi's disposal of 3 buildings at 1 Atlantic Quay, Glasgow. Acquisition of West Register (Property) Ltd from a leading Scottish institution. Acting for Pillar Property Investments on the development of a 160,000 sq ft HQ building for BTplc.

Maclay Murray & Spens (37 fee-earners) The arrival of *Robin Garrett* ("doesn't waste time playing legal ping pong with irrelevant matters") added new vigour to an already lively property group which is close to being in the top band. The talented team are *Iain Macniven* ("highly capable"), *Ian Quigley* ("technically zealous"), *Malcolm Fleming* ("a lawyer of the old

Biggart Baillie Glasgow
Brodies WS Edinburgh
Burness Edinburgh
Dickson Minto WS Edinburgh
Fyfe Ireland WS Edinburgh
Miller Samuel & Co Glasgow
Paull & Williamsons Aberdeen
Thorntons WS Dundee
Tods Murray WS Edinburgh
Alexander Stone & Co Glasgow
Alex Morison & Co WS Edinburgh
Boyds Glasgow
Davidson Chalmers WS Edinburgh
Ledingham Chalmers Aberdeen
MacRoberts Glasgow
The Morton Fraser Partnership Edinburgh
Bishop and Robertson Chalmers Glasgow
Harper Macleod Glasgow
Henderson Boyd Jackson WS Edinburgh
Leslie Wolfson & Co Glasgow
Wright, Johnston & Mackenzie Glasgow

school but an effective one") and the up & coming *Jennifer Johnson* ("hard but fair"). **Clients/Work:** Sale of Sauchiehall Centre, Glasgow, the Howgate Centre, Falkirk and

Edinburgh Fort Retail Park. Friends' Provident's acquisition of Craigleith Retail Park.

Shepherd & Wedderburn WS (8ptnrs/ 6assocs/29assts) A firm that retains a traditional image but having "given itself a good shake" combines it with a pro-active approach. Rapidly catching up with the top two. The best known leaders are chalk and cheese in temperament. *David Smith* "does things conventionally, there's no pomposity about the man; he cuts straight through to the real issues and is exceptionally easy to deal with." His antithesis, *Nicholas Ryden,* is a lawyer of "almost legendary volatility – particularly if he thinks you're a twit" but is "quite brilliant, with a frightening eye for detail." Some of his peers "love him to bits." *James Dobie,* "an exceptional lawyer," is up and coming. **Clients/Work:** Pillar Property PLC's purchase and funding of Kinnaird and The Fort retail parks. Midland Bank PLC/First Direct call centres at Hamilton International Technology Park, Lanark and Cartsburn, Greenock.

Archibald Campbell & Harley WS (9ptnrs/9assts) "We reckon we're good enough" says *David Cockburn* (a lawyer who "doesn't mince his words or get side tracked by irrelevancies"). Enough of our interviewees agreed for the firm to move up into the 'Leading Firms' bracket. A renowned retail practice which also has broad experience with developers and landlords. *Drew Wallace* is seen by some to be a "hard nosed deal maker." **Clients/Work:** Ongoing development of the Academy Centre, Inverness for MFI. Ashtenne Holdings plc's acquisition of three property companies for the Whithorn Group. Purchase of options and land at Gilston, Polmont for Frogmore Developments Ltd.

Bird Semple (4ptnrs/17fee earners) "Bouncing back." Acting on Braehead and other major projects has given *Graeme Sunter's* group a high profile again after a few years in the doldrums. **Clients/Work:** Braehead Letting phase for Capital Shopping Centres. Grampian Care – ongoing programme of sale and leasebacks. Sale and retail/leisure development of the Palace Grounds in Hamilton for South Lanarkshire Council.

Semple Fraser WS (8ptnrs/9assts/ 2assocs) "A bit different." To clients they are "in a league of their own in their presentation, style and quality." Several other solicitors saw them less favourably and described them, for example, as too "clever." *Paul Haniford* is "a charming and impressive operator." *Heather Nisbet* is up and coming. Made up two commercial property partners this year. **Clients/ Work:** Svenska Handelsbanken's disposal of Tay House, Glasgow. Schroders' acquisition of retail investment in Princes St, Edinburgh. Chesser Properties Ltd's disposal of Chesser House, Edinburgh.

Steedman Ramage WS (7ptnrs/13 fee earners) Robin Garrett was a big loss but the firm and *Sandy Reid* still have a lot to offer. Retains a reputation for being pro-active and immensely strong in the retail sector (although more fee income is now derived from their development practice). Acquired Henderson Boyd Jackson's Glasgow team adding two partners and two assistants. **Clients/Work:** Acquisition of new department stores at Inverness and Dundee for Debenhams plc. Helical Retail's acquisition, funding and pre-letting of a development site at Buchanan St, Glasgow. Portman Commercial's £55m property portfolio funding packages for acquisition etc.

Biggart Baillie (7ptnrs/4assocs/12assts) **Clients/Work:** Wilcon Homes, the developer in the Dunfernline East project, a 900 acre, £1bn development with a 20 year timetable. Clydesdale Banks lease of Clydesdale Bank Plaza, Edinburgh.

Brodies WS (9ptnrs/18assts) A pillar of the Edinburgh establishment – "rock solid." *Dale Strachan's* views "carry a lot of weight." Strachan is described as "a good operator who knows how to turn the heat on." *Keith Griffiths* was also recommended. **Clients/Work:** Property aspects of the Stock Exchange acquisition of Fiscal Properties plc and the disposal of the entire Scottish porfolio. Acting for the preferred bidder, PPM, on the Scottish aspects of Project PRIME. Sale of Abbotsinch Retail Park for Sydney & London Properties Ltd.

Burness (7ptnrs/16assts) Not quite the force they were although still extremely competent. *Ian Wattie* ("easy to deal with and sensible") heads a team which includes *David Reid* and the up and coming *Ewan Thomson.* **Clients/Work:** Sun Life +£100m portfolio investment acquisition. Ladbroke Racing's acquisition of Scottish property interests of Coral. Stannifer Developments acquisition, development, letting and disposal at Inverness Retail Park.

Dickson Minto WS (1ptnr/3assts) Received strong commendations from users of legal services, not just from its own clients but from those on the other side of transactions. *Philip Andersen* was praised for his highly commercial, "say what you mean and do what you say" approach and for being "positive, to the point of brashness." **Clients/Work:** Acquisition of a distribution/manufacturing network of properties in the UK, Europe, Southern Africa and Asia. Refinancing of a £21m portfolio of industrial properties. Lease of the firm's new office in Blythswood Sq, Glasgow.

Fyfe Ireland WS (6ptnrs/7assts) "Competent people to deal with." *Alistair Wilson* is a "sensible guy who gets what he wants without drawing any more blood than he needs." **Clients/Work:** Acquisition and ongoing management of The Forge, Parkhead Shopping Centre, Glasgow for ND

Properties Inc. and Chesterfield Properties; development and letting of major leisure scheme at Fountainpark, Edinburgh for THI Ltd.; Secured re-finance of 5 industrial estates for Helaba.

Miller Samuel & Co (4ptnrs) "Lack the bodies for the really big deals." Concentrate on development work and giving a personal service. *Iain Doran,* "the great debunker," always cuts to the chase. **Clients/Work:** Acting for Vico Property Group on the acquisition of the £20m Portland Gate leisure and retail development in Kilmarnock. Acquiring the Pollok shopping centre in Glasgow for Retail Property Holdings. Acting for Capital and Regional Properties on redevelopment of the £30m Blythswood Retail Park, Renfrew.

Paull & Williamsons (9ptnrs/7assts) A large fish in a small pond. *Leslie Dalgarno* has "sewn up" the Aberdeen market and now crops up all the time. Recommended as a deal maker. **Clients/Work:** Acquisition of the former Post Office, No. 1 George Sq, Glasgow – potential tenants include Harvey Nichols. Appointed to act for the Halliburton group of companies. Acting on the £17m Beach Development.

Thorntons WS (3ptnrs/2assts) The preeminent firm in Tayside. *Stewart Brymer* is "one of the good guys, bright, commercial and highly thought of by all the major central belt firms." **Clients/Work:** Edge Properties plc, Bett Brothers plc and Granchester Group plc. Edge Investments' purchase and development of the 15.5 acre Forge Retail Park.

Tods Murray WS (8ptnrs/15assts) A sound practice, if "a little staid". **Clients/Work:** Advised on: the sale of Bank of Scotland pension scheme Scottish property portfolio; Madford Developments (Scotland) Ltd in acquisition and forward funding of development site in Glasgow (over £2.6m); Rotch Property, London in acquisition and leaseback of Halls of Residence at The Robert Gordon University, Woolman Hill, Aberdeen (over £6m).

Alexander Stone & Co (3ptnrs/1asst) A small, property specialist that "punches well above its weight." *Lionel Most* and his partners "ably" act for landlords, retail tenants and 'third sector clients'.

Alex Morison & Co WS Good but small.

Boyds (3ptnrs/2assts) A small but respected outfit. **Clients/Work:** Include Safeway Stores plc; Monsoon Holdings Ltd.; Comet Group plc.

Davidson Chalmers WS (3ptnrs/1assoc/4assts) A firm with a good client base and a growing practice.

Ledingham Chalmers (10ptnrs/9 other fee earners) *John Curran* is "not a time waster" and "understands the necessity of ensuring that both sides get what they want." Good reputation in Aberdeen. **Clients/Work:** Cala-Morrison in the first four lettings of the Clydesdale Bank Plaza development in Edinburgh. Morrison Developments Ltd on acquisition, forward funding etc of development in Aberdeen. George Craig Group Ltd's letting at the Aberdeen Beach Leisure Development.

MacRoberts (7ptnrs/6assocs/3assts) A solid but low profile practice. **Clients/Work:** GA Properties Ltd's development of new office facilities for the Inland Revenue in Glasgow and Edinburgh. Eagle Taverns Ltd's purchase of 9 pubs from Scottish & Newcastle. Princes Square Development Ltd's letting of shopping centre in East Kilbride.

The Morton Fraser Partnership (4ptnrs/9assts) "They get the job done." **Clients/Work:** Acting for Scottish & Newcastle on a refinancing. A nursing home operator's acquisition of 6 homes. United

Distillers disposal of Balmenach Distillery.

Bishop and Robertson Chalmers (3ptnrs/1assoc/3assts) **Clients/Work:** Bett Properties. Instructed from time to time to act for Royal Bank of Scotland. Various colleges/universities.

Harper MacLeod (3ptnrs/4assts) Under *Mark Dewar's* effective guidance, property has become the fastest growing part of the firm. **Clients/Work:** Arlington Securities PLC's purchase of 60 acres for the development of the Glasgow Business Park. Clerical Medical Investment Group Ltd/Britel Fund Trustees Ltd's acquisition of Princes Square Specialty Shopping Centre, Buchanan St, Glasgow. Completion of pre-letting at Stirling Thistle Marches Shopping Centre.

Henderson Boyd Jackson WS (7ptnrs/11assts) Steaming ahead until the Glasgow office jumped ship. Expected to bounce back. **Clients/Work:** British Land Company Plc's acquisition of a property portfolio from GUS. Royal Bank of Scotland's funding of a West Coast shopping centre. Highfield Group Ltd's acquisition of a property portfolio from St Andrew Homes Ltd, the nursing homes division of Vaux plc.

Leslie Wolfson & Co Good at what they do but "not movers and shakers."

Wright, Johnston & MacKenzie (4ptnrs/5assocs/3assts) An old school firm with a respectable practice.

LEADERS' PROFILES · SCOTLAND

ANDERSON, Philip T.
Dickson Minto WS, Edinburgh
(0131) 225 4455
Partner in the Property Department
Specialisation: Retail, industrial, offices, healthcare and leisure. Also deals with investment, finance, development and landlord and tenant.
Prof. Memberships: Law Societies (Scotland and England).
Career: Born 1959. Inverness Royal Academy followed by Glasgow University.
Personal: Interests include fishing, observing golf and motor biking.

ANDERSON, Thomas D.
McGrigor Donald, Glasgow (0141) 248 6677
Specialisation: Joint Ventures; Property Finance; Development work generally but with emphasis on hotel development work and shopping centre development; forward funding agreements; leases generally but with particular specialism in turnover arrangements.
Prof. Memberships: Law Society of Scotland.
Career: 1971-75 Edinburgh University (LLB Hons); 1980-89 *Biggart Baillie & Gifford*, Partner (Commercial Property/ Corporate); 1989 to date *McGrigor Donald*, Partner (Commercial Property).
Personal: Two daughters, aged 15 and 17. Leisure interests include golf, duplicate bridge and skiing.

BANKIER, David A.
McGrigor Donald, Glasgow (0141) 248 6677
Partner in Property Department.
Specialisation: Main area of practice has an increasing emphasis on funding of property developments and investments, joint ventures and public/private sector initiatives in commercial property. Acted in the site assembly and development and later completed a £70 million syndicated bank lending facility to finance phase 1 of the Broomielaw Development, Glasgow. Recently has acted in the sale of the 1st phase, one of Scotland's largest office disposals, and the development of a major £25 million headquarters building as a further phase. Advised in the £160m acquisition of Glasgow's St. Enoch Centre, the largest retail acquisition in Scotland so far. Presently advising North Lanarkshire Council as successors to Cumbernauld Development Corporation in the major redevelopment of Cumbernauld Town Centre. More recently has branched into PFI, as head of the firm's capital projects unit, and is advising on the £120 million new Law District General Hospital.
Career: Qualified in 1977, having joined *McGrigor Donald* in 1970. Became a Partner in 1978.
Personal: Born 24th March 1949. Educated at Edinburgh University (LLB 1970). Leisure interests include art history, Scottish contemporary paintings, sailing and skiing. Lives in Glasgow.

BRYMER, Stewart
Thorntons WS, Dundee (01382) 229111
Partner in Commercial Department.
Specialisation: Main areas of practice are commercial property, especially general property development work and leasing and investment. Has acted in relation to a number of large out of town non-food retail parks. Increasing involvement in rent review arbitrations. Chairman of the Editorial Review Board of 'The Conveyancing Manual'.
Prof. Memberships: The Law Society of Scotland.
Career: Qualified in 1979 and joined *Thorntons WS* in the same year. Became a Partner in 1983. Received Law Society accreditation as a specialist in commercial leasing law 1993 and renewed 1998. Notary Public.
Personal: Born 30th January 1957. Attended Morgan Academy 1969-75 and Dundee University 1975-79 (1st Class Hons). Leisure pursuits include golf, fishing and choral singing. Lives in Dundee.

COCKBURN, David
Archibald Campbell & Harley WS, Edinburgh
(0131) 220 3000
Partner in Commercial Property Department.
Specialisation: Handles a full range of commercial property matters, including purchases, development, sales, leasing (for both landlords and tenants), funding and security work. Also advises on planning matters.

Contributes book reviews and articles to Law Journal of Law Society of Scotland and Scottish Planning and Environmental Law. Regularly contributes by way of lectures to Law Society Update, Scottish Young Lawyers' Association, Surveyors' bodies, Planning Exchange and Edinburgh University.
Prof. Memberships: Society of Writers to HM Signet.
Career: Qualified in 1966. Worked with Glasgow Corporation 1966-67, then *Breeze, Paterson & Chapman* 1967-70. Joined *Archibald Campbell & Harley WS* in 1970, becoming a Partner in 1971.
Personal: Born 4th February 1943. Attended Edinburgh University 1961-1964. Leisure pursuits include sport and reading. Lives in Edinburgh.

CURRAN, John W.
Ledingham Chalmers, Aberdeen
(01224) 408408
Specialisation: Senior Commercial Property Partner.
Specialisation: Advises listed and unlisted property companies on land acquisition, planning procedures and financing for residential and commercial property development. Accredited by The Law Society of Scotland as a specialist in Planning Law.
Career: Qualified 1975. With *Edmonds & Ledingham* 1972-1990 (Partner from 1977) and with merged firm *Ledingham Chalmers* since 1991.
Personal: Born 15th February 1951. Educated at Aberdeen Grammar School and Aberdeen University. Interests include football, squash, golf and reading.

DACKER, Philip A.
Dundas & Wilson CS, Edinburgh
(0131) 228 8000
Specialisation: Specialises in Commercial Property, Property Finance, Development and Investment. Occasional speaker at seminars.
Prof. Memberships: Law Society of Scotland; International Bar Association; Institute of Directors; Society of Writers to H.M. Signet.
Career: Attended University of Edinburgh (LLB, NP, WS). Articled *J & F Anderson WS*, 1970-1972; assistant solicitor *Alexander Hendry & Son*, 1972-1973; assistant solicitor *Dundas & Wilson*, 1973-1976; Partner at *Dundas & Wilson* since 1976; Managing Partner 1991-1996; Head of Property Finance Group since 1996.
Personal: Married. Resides Edinburgh. Leisure pursuits include powerboating, family and walking.

DALGARNO, Leslie S.
Paull & Williamsons, Aberdeen
(01224) 621621
Specialisation: Head of Commercial Property Department, advising private and public property companies and financial institutions on all aspects of property acquisition, development funding and disposal throughout the whole of Scotland. Acted on all aspects of the acquisition and planning and financial matters in relation to No.1 George Square, Glasgow, a major retail, leisure and lifestyle development in the city centre of Glasgow.
Prof. Memberships: Law Society of Scotland and member of Investment Property Forum.
Career: Graduated from Aberdeen University in 1971, LL.B. with Distinction. Joined Messrs. *Paull & Williamsons* as Trainee in 1971,

becoming a Partner in the Commercial Property Department in 1977. Head of Department since 1986. Notary Public.
Personal: Born 19th March 1950. Educated at Robert Gordon's College and Aberdeen University. Leisure pursuits include golf and football. Lives in Aberdeen.

DEWAR, Mark A. M.
Harper Macleod, Glasgow (0141) 221 8888
Specialisation: Commercial leasing, property investment and property development. Acted in purchase, redevelopment and ongoing letting of Princes Square Speciality Shopping Centre, Buchanan Street, Glasgow, development and letting of Stirling Thistle Marches Shopping Centre, Stirling, site acquisition and development of Glasgow Business Park and acquisition and funding of redevelopment for retail purposes of former George Hotel site, Buchanan Street, Glasgow.
Prof. Memberships: Law Society of Scotland accredited Specialist in Commercial Leasing.
Career: Trained at *McGrigor Donald*, Glasgow; Associate *McGrigor Donald* 1989; Partner *Harper Macleod* 1996.
Personal: Born 1959. Educated at Marr College, Troon and University of Glasgow. Married; two children. Interests include golf, football and hillwalking. Lives in Troon.

DOBIE, James A.
Shepherd & Wedderburn WS, Edinburgh
(0131) 228 9900
Specialisation: Property Development and institutional investment with particular emphasis on retail developments. Acted for Freeport Leisure plc in development of first factory outlet centre in Scotland, and for Pillar Property plc in retail park developments. Acted for New Edinburgh Limited on a number of lettings and onward sales at Edinburgh Park. Also involved in specialist telecommunication property acquisitions for Orange plc.
Prof. Memberships: Law Society of Scotland.
Career: Educated at Edinburgh University. Joined *Shepherd & Wedderburn WS* 1988 as trainee, became partner in 1995.
Personal: Born 14/08/64. Leisure interests: football, literature, wine and East African culture.

DORAN, Iain A.
Miller Samuel & Co, Glasgow
(0141) 221 7934
Partner in Commercial Property Department.
Specialisation: Main area of practice is commercial property development, including site assembly, pre-letting, forward and other funding arrangements and sales of investment. Also acts as legal clerk to arbitrators, arbiters and experts regarding legal disputes arising in rent reviews. Is accredited as a specialist in commercial leasing by the Law Society of Scotland.
Prof. Memberships: Law Society of Scotland, The Chartered Institute of Arbitrators.
Career: Qualified in 1981. Joined *Miller Samuel & Co.* in 1982 and became a Partner in 1983.
Personal: Born 6th November 1957. Educated at Edinburgh University 1975-79. Lives in Glasgow.

FLEMING, Malcolm F.
Maclay Murray & Spens, Glasgow
(0141) 248 5011
mff@maclaymurrayspens.co.uk
Specialisation: Partner specialising in the

transfer and leasing of commercial property. Has in-depth experience of rent reviews. Co-author of "Drafting and Negotiating Commercial Leases in Scotland". Author of "Dilapidations in Scotland".
Prof. Memberships: Member of Royal Faculty of Procurators.
Career: Cambridge University (BA 1964) and Edinburgh University (LL.B 1966).
Personal: Born 1943.

GARRETT, Robin J.
Maclay Murray & Spens, Glasgow
(0141) 248 5011
E-mail: rjg@maclaymurrayspens.co.uk
Partner in Commercial Property Department.
Specialisation: Main area of practice is development work for developers and occupiers, including site assembly, planning, letting and disposals. Also handles general acquisitions, including freehold purchases and assignations of leases. Has lectured and led groups at various seminars.
Prof. Memberships: Writer to the Signet.
Career: Qualified in 1983. Previously partner with *Steedman Ramage*. Joined *Maclay Murray & Spens* 1997.
Personal: Born 2nd April 1959.

GRIFFITHS, Keith M.
Brodies WS, Edinburgh (0131) 228 3777
Specialisation: Commercial Property with particular emphasis on advising national multiple retailers on their Scottish property portfolio.
Career: Qualified 1979. Employed at *W & J Burness* 1977-1982; joined *Steedman Ramage* in 1982, Partner 1984-1996; joined *Brodies* as a Partner in 1996.
Personal: Born 1956. Interests include hillwalking, hockey, golf and theatre.

HANIFORD, Paul S.
Semple Fraser WS, Glasgow (0141) 221 3771
Fax: (0141) 221 3776/3859 E-Mail:
psh@semplefraser.co.uk
Specialisation: Property investment and development; also landlord and tenant work customarily offering advice to a non-Scottish client base.
Prof. Memberships: Society of Writers to HM Signet, Law Society of Scotland.
Career: Articled *Fyfe Ireland & Co WS* 1978-1980; legal assistant *Moncrieff Warren Paterson* 1980-1; legal assistant *Bird Semple* 1981-3; partner 1983-90; founding partner *Semple Fraser* 1990. Member: President's Committee, Glasgow & Renrewshire Branch of British Red Cross.
Personal: Born 26 November 1955. Educated at Glasgow Academy and Glasgow University (MA-LL.B). Interests include skiing, squash, tennis and travel. Lives in Glasgow.

HODGE, James (Hamish) S.
Dundas & Wilson CS, Edinburgh
(0131) 228 8000
Specialisation: Consultant in Commercial Property Group. For 30 years has dealt exclusively with all aspects of commercial property with emphasis on investment, development, rent review and landlord/ tenant matters; extensive experience in particular in the acquisition/ development of shopping centres and portfolio purchases. Recent deals include acquisition of Tenant's interest and reletting of Menzies' store in Princes St, Edinburgh to Next at £1m rental, acquisition/ development of £35m office development in Edinburgh for Standard

Life, forward letting of units on Dumfries Retail Park development for Helios Properties plc.
Prof. Memberships: Law Society of Scotland; The Society of H.M. Writers to the Signet.
Career: Attended University of Edinburgh (LLB). Qualified in 1966; Notary Public in 1967; Partner *Dundas & Wilson* since 1968. Member of the Law Society of Scotland Commercial Leasing Accreditation Panel.
Personal: Born 1942. Lives in Edinburgh. Leisure interests include golf (Bruntsfield Links Golfing Society, Blairgowrie Golf Club), curling and motorsport.

JOHNSON, Jennifer D.
Maclay Murray & Spens, Edinburgh
(0131) 226 5196
Specialisation: Head of commercial property department. Practice covers all areas of commercial property including property investments and development, security work and leasing. Handled the purchase and sale of six shopping centres in the last three years.
Prof. Memberships: W.S Society. Notary Public.
Career: Edinburgh University. Qualified 1979. Partner in *Maclay Murray & Spens* in 1988.

LEGGAT, J.Brian
Dundas & Wilson CS, Edinburgh
(0131) 228 8000
Specialisation: Partner in Commercial Property Group and Head of Education Group. Main areas of practice include property investment, landlord and tenant leasing, leisure, leisure development, PFI projects.
Prof. Memberships: Law Society of Scotland, The Society of Writers to H.M. Signet, Member of Investment Property Forum (Committee member of IPF Scottish Education Committee).
Career: Attended University of Edinburgh (LLB). Qualified at *Lindsay Duncan & Black WS* in 1971; assistant *Dundas & Wilson* 1971-1973; Partner *Dundas & Wilson CS* since 1973. Head of Commercial Property 1983-1993. Chairman of Partnership 1993-1996. Governor, The Edinburgh Academy.
Personal: Born 1948. Leisure interests include rugby, golf, sailing, curling, riding and music.

MACNIVEN, Iain G.
Maclay Murray & Spens, Glasgow
(0141) 248 5011
igm@maclaymurrayspens.co.uk
Specialisation: Commercial property partner with extensive experience of all aspects of commercial property work, including acquisitions and sales, leasing and development work and general portfolio management. Acts for a wide variety of institutions, investors, developers and local authorities.
Career: Glasgow University (MA 1975, LL.B 1977).
Personal: Born 1953.

MOST, Lionel D.
Alexander Stone & Co, Glasgow
(0141) 332 8611
Head of Commercial Leasing Division
Specialisation: Main area of practice is commercial leasing, and all aspects of property and development work where the main issue is leasing. Law Society of Scotland Accredited Specialist in Commercial Leasing. Occasional

Arbiter and Expert Witness in Commercial Leasing Disputes. Part time lecturer at the University of Glasgow in conveyancing for LL.B degree. External Examiner in Conveyancing and Property Law (Honours) at the University of Strathclyde. Periodic lecturer for CPD seminars.
Prof. Memberships: Law Society of Scotland (Member of Business of Conveyancing Committee).
Career: Joined *Alexander Stone & Co* in 1977 as apprentice, qualified in 1979, becoming a partner in 1983.

NEWTON, Alison
McGrigor Donald, Glasgow (0141) 248 6677
Specialisation: Acting in the following in 1998:- Advised Dumfries & Galloway Council on first externalisation of care for the elderly in Scotland (11 homes and ancillary services). Leisure development, acting for Barwood and Wilcon Homes Limited at Fife Leisure Park, Dunfermline. Retail development, acting for Dawn Devlopments Limited at Irvine Retail Park. Acquiring all units for Tom Cobleigh plc in Scotland. Developed and let and now selling Loch Lomond Factory Outlet Centre and developing and letting Morrisons Factory Outlet Centre in Tillicoultry
Prof. Memberships: Law Society of Scotland. Member of Committee of Scottish Branch of British Council of Shopping Centres.
Career: 1980-84 Dundee University (LLB, DIPLP). 1984-86 Trainee, *McGrigor Donald*. 1986-90 Assistant. 1990 - 94 Associate. 1994 to date – Partner Commercial Property.
Personal: Lives and plays in Glasgow, showjumps competitively, skis enthusiastically and reads avidly.

NISBET, Heather M.
Semple Fraser WS, Glasgow
(0141) 221 3771
E.mail : hmn@semplefraser.co.uk
Specialisation: Property development and investment including specifically acting as chief Scottish solicitor for major food retailer in relation to site acquisitions and sole Scottish solicitor acting for multinational major cinema operator in relation to acquisitions of new leasehold opportunities (on development and lease agreements). In addition, convenor of the firm's Property Tax Group with a specialisation in VAT as it applies to land and property.
Prof. Memberships: Law Society of Scotland.
Career: Traineeship: *Headrick Ingles Glen & Co* 1983-1985, Legal Assistant: *Bird Semple and Crawford Heron* 1986-1989, Associate: *Bird Semple Fyfe Ireland* 1989-1990, Partner: *Semple Fraser* 1992 to date.
Personal: Born 1962. Educated Kirkcudbright Academy and Edinburgh University.

QUIGLEY, Ian S.
Maclay Murray & Spens, Edinburgh
(0131) 226 5196
isq@maclaymurrayspens.co.uk
Specialisation: Partner dealing in all aspects of commercial property work, including development and leasing pre-funding and development finance.
Prof. Memberships: Writer to the Signet and Notary Public.
Career: Glasgow University (LL.B 1969).
Personal: Born 1946.

REID, David R.
Burness, Edinburgh (0131) 473 6000
Specialisation: Deals primarily with large commercial and institutional clients, advising on property developments, high street retailing and commercial leases. He is involved very heavily with major joint ventures and pre-funded developments. Also frequently consulted for opinions on property disputes. Major clients include The Post Office, Grosvenor Developments Ltd, Sun Life Assurance Society plc, St Andrews University, Johnson Group Cleaners plc and TSB Bank. Spent some time as a conveyancing tutor at Edinburgh University.

REID, Sandy
Steedman Ramage WS, Edinburgh
(0131) 260 6600
Specialisation: Development, letting, purchase/ sale, investment and joint ventures. Experience includes acquisition, development and letting of major shopping centres; mixed use developments both in and out of town; large portfolio transactions. Recent transactions include acting for Marks and Spencer in acquisition and regearing of Gyle Shopping Centre, Edinburgh; for J Sainsbury in sale and leaseback of Scottish/ Irish distribution centre; and for Helical Retail in acquisition, pre-letting and funding of development of George/Commercial Hotels complex in Glasgow.
Prof. Memberships: Law Society of Scotland. Society of Writers to H.M.Signet.
Career: Educated Robert Gordon's College, Aberdeen 1966-1972; Aberdeen University 1972-1975. Joined *Steedman Ramage* 1975, qualified 1977; Partner 1980; Senior Partner 1993.
Personal: Born 15th September 1954. Married, 2 sons. Leisure activities include music and sport.

RYDEN, Nicholas C.
Shepherd & Wedderburn WS, Edinburgh
(0131) 228 9900
Partner in Commercial Property Department.
Specialisation: Work includes all aspects of commercial property, banking, non-contentious construction matters, PFI Projects. Occasional lecturer at Law Society PQLE courses; gives papers to AARPI and RICS in Scotland.
Prof. Memberships: WS Society, Law Society of Scotland, Anglo American Real Property Institute, (Governor) Investment Property Forum.
Career: Joined *Shepherd & Wedderburn* in 1974. Qualified in 1976, becoming a Partner in 1978.
Personal: Born 20th March 1953. Attended Fettes College and Aberdeen University.

SHAW, Donald G.B.
Dundas & Wilson CS, Edinburgh
(0131) 228 8000
Specialisation: Partner dealing primarily with major development, institutional investment, planning and construction; head of 60 plus lawyers in Commercial Property Group; divisional leader of commercial property and construction law groups. Current examples of work include Buchanan Galleries shopping centre, Glasgow; and Hyundai semiconductor facility in Fife; advising RICS on written Rent Review guidance for expert/arbitration determinations for all Scottish members and BPF standard lease clauses.

Prof. Memberships: Law Society of Scotland.
Career: Attended University of Aberdeen (LLB).
Articled *Shepherd & Wedderburn*; qualified
1979; Partner *Dundas & Wilson* since 1985;
Deputy Managing Partner since 1995.
Personal: Leisure interests include music,
history, psychology, art, wine and travel.

SMITH, David A.
Shepherd & Wedderburn WS, Edinburgh
(0131) 228 9900
Partner in Commercial Property Department.
Specialisation: Main areas of practice are
development projects, leases, collateral
warranty documentation and opinion work.
Occasional speaker at conferences and
seminars.
Prof. Memberships: Law Society of Scotland,
Society of Writers to the Signet.
Career: Joined *Shepherd & Wedderburn* in
1969. Partner in 1974.
Personal: Born 17th November 1947.
Edinburgh University 1966-69. Leisure pursuits
include veterans' hockey, golf, hill walking and
gardening. Lives in Edinburgh.

STEEL, David A.
Dundas & Wilson CS, Glasgow
(0141) 221 8586
Specialisation: Partner specialising in
commercial property with emphasis on
investment, development and landlord and
tenant matters; property issues in PFI projects;
accredited specialist on commercial leases.
Acted on behalf of Ravenseft Properties Limited
(part of Land Securities PLC) in the funding,
development and letting of Almondvale and
Livingston (opened August 1996).
Prof. Memberships: Law Society of Scotland;
Scottish Law Agents Society.
Career: Attended University of Glasgow (LLB).
Articled *MacKenzie Roberton*; qualified 1973;
assistant solicitor with *McLean & Stewart* 1973-
1975; assistant solicitor with *Breeze Paterson &
Chapman* 1975-1976; Partner 1976-1995;
joined *Dundas & Wilson* as Partner 1995.

STEVENSON, Donna
McGrigor Donald, Glasgow (0141) 248 6677
Specialisation: Partner in Property

Department. Member of *McGrigor Donald's*
'Capital Projects Unit' with extensive experience
in PFI transactions, particularly within the health
sector. Donna's background is in property
development, including tax driven transactions.
Career: Educated at Glasgow University.
Joined *McGrigor Donald* 1986 as trainee,
assumed as partner in 1995.
Personal: Leisure interests: hill-walking, tennis
and reading.

STRACHAN, K.P.Dale
Brodies WS, Edinburgh (0131) 228 3777
Specialisation: Commercial Property Partner
dealing with Development, Construction Law
and Practice, Tenant Representation and
Property PFI.
Prof. Memberships: Society of Writers to Her
Majesty's Signet. International Bar Association.
Career: George Heriot's School. University of
Aberdeen (1977 LLB). Qualified 1979. Assistant
Solicitor *Brodies* 1979-83; Partner since 1983.
Personal: Family, fishing, skiing, motorcycling,
flying. Married to Ghillie (1982). Two sons, (1988
& 1991).

SUNTER, Graeme
Bird Semple, Glasgow (0141) 221 7090
Specialisation: Specialising in commercial
development, environmental issues associated
with commercial property and liquor, licensing.
Recent transactions include the development
and letting of Braehead Shopping Centre in
Glasgow for Capital Shopping Centres plc,
which when complete, with a construction cost
of in excess of 200 million pounds will be one of
Scotland's single largest property
developments. Lloyds Bank Pension Fund,
various, including £5m purchase and Merchant
Navy Pension Fund, two disposals in excess of
£3m and a £2.2m purchase.
Career: Graduated LLB Edinburgh University
1975. Trainee solicitor *Wright & Crawford*,
Paisley 1975-77. Assistant solicitor *Walker &
Laird*, 1977-80. Partner *Walker & Laird* 1980-85.
Joined *Bird Semple* as an assistant 1985.
Became a partner in the Commercial Property
Department 1987.

THOMSON, Ewan
Burness, Edinburgh (0131) 473 6000
Specialisation: Commercial property law,
principally development, property investment
and landlord/ tenant with emphasis on retail.
Client portfolio includes Diageo, DSS,
Kingfisher, PPM PRIME, Standard Life and
Vickers. In 1997/98 involved in Burness team
advising DSS on Scots Law aspects of Project
PRIME.

WALLACE, Andrew
Archibald Campbell & Harley WS, Edinburgh
(0131) 220 3000
Specialisation: Partner specialising in
commercial property, leasing, investment and
development acquisition with particular
emphasis on investment and industrial property.
Career: Strathclyde University (LLB Hons),
qualified in 1985, joined *Archibald Campbell &
Harley WS* same year. Appointed Partner in 1988.
He has been a regular lecturer to surveyors and
the WS Society on leasing and related subjects.

WATTIE, J.Ian
Burness, Edinburgh (0131) 473 6000
Specialisation: Commercial Property Law,
principally development, property investment
and landlord/tenant. Advised Shoprite on their
rapid expansion in the early 1990s and eventual
£45m disposal to Kwik Save. Institutional client
portfolio includes DSS, The Miller Group
Limited, The Post Office, MEPC and Sun Life. In
1996/1998 has led *Burness* team in advising
DSS on Scots Property Law aspects of Project
PRIME, largest office accommodation PFI
project to date. Currently advising developer
client on major city centre leisure schemes.

WILSON, Alistair J.
Fyfe Ireland WS, Edinburgh (0131) 343 2500
Specialisation: Concentrates on commercial
property law, acting extensively for investors,
retailers, finance providers and developers, with
considerable experience of providing strategic
commercial advice in substantial property
transactions and in negotiating the necessary
documentation. Has particular experience of
cross-border property transactions involving
conflict of laws.

NORTHERN IRELAND

Carson & McDowell (2ptnrs/1assoc/
4assts) "An excellent reputation." The flag is
carried by *Alan Reilly* who is "extremely
good, head and shoulders above the others"
and had a "meticulous style."

Elliott Duffy Garrett (3ptnrs/4assts)
Now act for British Land and Land
Securities. *Laurence Mahood* acts mainly for
landlords; he is "impressive." *Christine
Hamilton* is newly recommended as an up
and coming. **Clients/Work:** Acquisition of
The Arches retail park for British Land.

L'Estrange & Brett (4ptnrs/4assts)
Involved in almost all property PFI projects
in Northern Ireland. They "have a couple of
good people"of whom *Alan Hewitt* is "head
and shoulders above the others."
Clients/Work: Actively involved on behalf of
major national supermarket chain in its
acquisition and development of property
portfolio in N Ireland. Acting for local regen-

eration body, Laganside in development of
Waterfront Hall, BT Tower and The Hilton
Hotel on banks of River Lagan.

Tughan & Co (3ptnrs/4assts f/t, 2/1 p/t)
Competitors "come across them regularly."
Phyllis Agnew is "involved in lots of major
property developments." **Clients/Work:**
Commercial property development. Acquisition and sale of investment property for
institutional and private investors. PFI work
for public and private sector clients.

Cleaver Fulton & Rankin (5ptnrs: 4p/t;
6assts: 3p/t) A "very old" firm whose property department seems big in numbers but
they have provincial firms in Bangor and
Armagh. Not seen around as much recently.
Neil Faris has a "more academic" style than
other leaders. **Clients/Work:** Acting for USS
in acquisition of Forestside Shopping Centre
from Sainsburys; Acting for BT in Riverside
Tower major new HQ at Lanyon Place

Waterside, Belfast; Acting in acquisition of Northern Ireland's largest chain of nursing homes/private residential homes.

Johns Elliott (4ptnrs/2assts) Acts for landlords and developers of major shopping centres in N Ireland. **Clients/Work:** Clients include MEPC UK Ltd, Scottish Widows and Northern Ireland Housing Executive.

McKinty & Wright (1ptnr p/t, 2ptnrs f/t/ 2assts) Known to "have some good clients." Work for many retail occupiers. **Clients/Work:** Acting for Marks & Spencers in acquisition of 2 new properties; in Belfast and Newry. Acting for Morrisons on their largest development, the Carrick Fergus Maritime Area, sponsored by Department of the Environment and Carrick Fergus Borough Council.

Mills Selig (5ptnrs: 2 p/t;1cons/1assoc/ 2assts) Up to 60% of firm's turnover comes from property work. The department "has an excellent name"and is known as the "most aggressive team in terms of growth." Stratton Mills is said to be retiring, and will be greatly missed. They have recently taken on an associate partner from Cleaver Fulton & Rankin. **Clients/Work:** Acting for purchaser of Brookmount Buildings, Belfast; a major property investment of shop and office space. Acting for developer at Dungannon, a major provincial development for a national food retailer. Acting for the developer in the sale of a major office block at the corner of Donegall Square, Belfast, sold as new headquarters of Ulster Bank.

C&J Black (2ptnrs) Historically strong, but now known for acting for a couple of major clients, including the Norwich Union.

Hewitt & Gilpin Mainly residential, not much commercial work.

Johnsons Not known particularly for commercial work; although they "have a good caseload. Not seen much on the other side of big deals.

Kearney Sefton Are seen around regularly although one of their major clients has just sold off lots of properties so their workload may be diminished.

LEADERS' PROFILES · NORTHERN IRELAND

AGNEW, B.E. Phyllis M.
Tughan & Co, Belfast (01232) 553300
Parter and Head - Property and Commercial Department.
Specialisation: Main area of practice is commercial property development including property finance, bank and institutional funding, institutional investment, joint venture arrangements and PFI projects.
Prof. Memberships: Law Society of Northern Ireland, IBA, SIP and European Lawyers Group.
Career: Qualified 1981. Assistant Solicitor at *Tughan & Co.* 1981 - 1988. Partner since 1988.

FARIS, Neil C.
Cleaver Fulton & Rankin, Belfast
(01232) 243141
Specialisation: Commercial Property with special emphasis on Environmental Law. Practice also covers issues of Administrative and Public Law and European Union/Competition Law with special reference to Northern Ireland.
Prof. Memberships: Member: UKELA, IAEL, Competition Working Party.
Career: Qualified in 1977 and Partner and Head Consultancy Department.
Personal: Born 1950, educated in Belfast and at Trinity College Dublin and University of Cambridge.

HAMILTON, Christine A.
Elliott Duffy Garrett, Belfast (01232) 245034

HEWITT, V. Alan
L'Estrange & Brett, Belfast (01232) 230426
Senior Partner and Head of Commercial Property Department.
Specialisation: Main area of work: Commercial Property.
Prof. Memberships: Law Society of Northern Ireland. (Council Member 1991-; Chairman Professional Indemnity Insurance Committee 1995-97; Chairman, Professional Conduct Committee, 1997-) Law Reform Advisory Committee for Northern Ireland. International Bar Association.
Career: Qualified 1967. Partner in *L'Estrange & Brett* since 1969. Senior Partner since 1994.
Personal: Born 1941. Education: Queen's University, Belfast (L.L.B.), University of Michigan (L.L.M.).

MAHOOD, Laurence
Elliott Duffy Garrett, Belfast (01232) 245034
Specialisation: Commercial property development, letting and investment, acquisitions and disposals. Recent projects included acting for the developer of a major new shopping centre, refurbishment and extension of an exisitng centre and the first themed leisure development in Northern Ireland.

Prof. Memberships: Law Society of N.Ireland. Representative on joint Law Society/RICS Forum.
Career: LIB Queens University, Belfast 1976. Admitted solicitor 1978. Law Society Silver Medal awarded. Admitted partner 1982.
Personal: Contributing author to "Butterworth's Property Law in Europe".

REILLY, Alan J.
Carson & McDowell, Belfast (01232) 244951
Specialisation: Acquisition and disposal of Commercial Property and all types of interests therein. Development of Retail Property (including site assembly - project management). Rent reviews for both Landlord and Tenant. This year: sold two shopping centres in country towns, sale and leaseback of anchor stores in two other shopping centres in countrry towns sold to chain of shops, purchased shopping centre and industrial estate in Belfast, disposal of office block and retail investment property in Belfast.
Career: M.A. (CANTAB). Whole career with *Carson & McDowell* (qualified 1976, partner 1978).
Personal: Married with two daughters.

SHIPPING AND MARITIME LAW

See also Commodities, Insurance and Reinsurance, Transport (Road and Rail)

RESEARCH: In compiling the tables, we consider all the information available to us, paying particular regard to the market research carried out by our team of ten qualified lawyers. (The researchers' details are set out on page three.) The rankings, therefore, reflect the opinion of the marketplace as revealed by systematic and objective research: see page four. (Our research is audited every year by the British Market Research Bureau.)

OVERVIEW: Contentious work is divided into Wet or 'Admiralty' (collision, salvage, total loss, etc.) and Dry or 'Marine' (charterparties, bills of lading, cargo and MOA). We also include separate tables for firms specialising in Yachts and Finance work.

In London, there is no change at the top of the 'Dry' list, but further down the table, Constant & Constant and Lawrence Graham move up a band. Amongst the niche firms, Bentleys, Stokes & Lowless continues to rise and new firm Curtis Davis Garrard makes an entry, as does David Charity's firm Stockler Charity. Holman Fenwick & Willan move up to join Ince & Co at the top of the 'Wet' table, while the 'Finance' and 'Yachts' tables remain the same.

In terms of leading individuals, quite a few have retired this year and others have moved firms. We also have some new faces although it still remains the case that most of those on our list are the elder statesmen of shipping.

Not surprisingly, given the relatively small pool of firms outside London with shipping expertise, there are no changes to our tables this year, save for the inclusion in the South of leading individual Nicola Ellis' firm.

LONDON

LARGE FIRMS

Ince & Co (Wet: 9ptnrs/9assts. Dry:38 ptnrs/45assts). A "professional firm with a great reputation." Everyone agreed that they have a dominant slice of the London market. "Star" *Richard Williams* is "the best lawyer around." *Richard Sayer* is also greatly admired although less active now due to his role as managing partner. Six other leaders feature in the list. **Clients/Work: Wet:** Acted for owners of "Orapin Global" re collision with "Evokios" and consequent oil spillage into the Malacca straits. Acted for owners of "Nissos Amorgos" and "Olympic Sponsor" which both ran aground in the Maracaibo Triangle. Acted for owners of "ICL Vikraman" which sank with significant loss of life after collision with "Mount 1." **Dry:** Acted for cargo and terminal owners re total loss of "Trade Daring" during loading. Represented the owners in the "Indian Grace/Indian Endurance" case (House of Lords dismissed claim for £2.6m leaving owners liable only for £7,200) and "The Aegean Sea" (US $60m

pollution and cargo claims arising from vessel running aground in Spain).

Clyde & Co (Wet: 18ptnrs/17assts. Dry: 29 ptnrs/31assts.) "A well structured firm." Suffered a blow this year with the loss of leading individual Tony Rooth and retirement of Peter Morgan and Michael Harrisson. However, the firm still has six leading individuals including the "amazingly bright" *Simon Fletcher.* "He's the person rivals would go to." **Clients/Work: Wet:** Acted in the "Sea Empress" and "MC Carla." **Dry:** Act for Société Générale in litigation arising from the collapse of the Blue Flag Shipping Empire, and for NYK over the loss of containers of cyanide off the Chilean coast. Also act in the Dubai Aluminium dispute.

Holman, Fenwick & Willan (Worldwide Wet: 10ptnrs/15assts. Dry: 40ptnrs/46 assts) "Tough and tenacious," with a reputation for efficiency. Received numerous recommendations for their "commerciality" which has resulted in their promotion up the 'wet' table this year. *Archie Bishop* is greatly admired for his wet work. Seven other partners appear in our list including client favourite *Hugh Livingstone.* **Clients/Work: Dry:** "Bukjta Russksaya;" "Eurus"(scope of indemnities

LEADING FIRMS · LONDON
LARGE FIRMS · DRY

INCE & CO

CLYDE & CO
HOLMAN, FENWICK & WILLAN

HILL TAYLOR DICKINSON

HIGHLY REGARDED FIRMS · DRY

Richards Butler
Stephenson Harwood

Clifford Chance
Constant & Constant
Lawrence Graham
Norton Rose
Sinclair Roche & Temperley

Barlow Lyde & Gilbert
Herbert Smith

LEADING FIRMS · WET

HOLMAN, FENWICK & WILLAN
INCE & CO

CLYDE & CO

HILL TAYLOR DICKINSON

HIGHLY REGARDED FIRMS · WET

Bentleys, Stokes & Lowless
Constant & Constant
Holmes Hardingham
Richards Butler
Shaw and Croft
Stephenson Harwood
Waltons & Morse

LEADING FIRMS
LONDON · YACHTS

BERRYMANS LACE MAWER
HOLMES HARDINGHAM

DIBB LUPTON ALSOP

under charterparties). **Wet:** "Nagasaki Spirit" (level of award for salvor taking oil pollution measures). "Samaina" (collision with Greek warship). Acting for Environmental Agency re striking of the Thames Barrier by a sand dredger.

Hill Taylor Dickinson (Wet/Dry:10-ptnrs/20assts) With five leading individuals, including *John Evans*, the firm is popular, with interviewees from all over the country singing their praises. Favourable comments included: "straight, user-friendly, easy to deal with, commercial, down to earth and sensible." Unusually, no negative comments at all were made. **Clients/Work: Dry:** "Ocean Blessing." **Wet:** "Nagasaki Spirit;" "Apostolis" (Court of Appeal); "Sea Empress" (acting for charterers and insurers).

Richards Butler (Wet/Dry: 20ptnrs/24 assts). The general feeling amongst practitioners is that this firm has recovered its footing and is on its way back up. "They have good partners, excellent assistants and are fun to deal with, courteous, solid and straightforward." In particular *Andrew Taylor* is seen by clients as "very thorough, commercial and a safe pair of hands" whilst *Lindsay East* is "one of London's leading dry litigators." **Clients/Work:** Acted in "Giannis NK;" "Griparion;" "Sagheera;" Steamship Mutual; Lexmar v Nordisk and Vosnoc v Transglobal (first case involving interpretation of section 12 of the Arbitration Act 1996)

Stephenson Harwood (Wet: 3ptnrs/7assts. Dry: 6ptnrs/14assts. Finance: 9ptnrs/13 assts) Have some good people, particularly the "experienced" *Steven Lowe,* "major player" *David Slade* and new entry, the much admired *Robin Slade*. Respected more for their wet work, they have benefitted from lateral hires and continue to expand. Clients appreciate their "efficiency and pragmatism." **Clients/Work: Dry:** Acted in "Guiseppe di Vittorio" (demise charterers); Ali Shipping Corporation v Shipyard Trogir (confidentiality of arbitration proceedings); A/S D/S Svendborg v Wansa (mareva injunctions). **Wet:** Acted for owners of "Nakhodka" which broke in two causing pollution in Japan (US$150m claims); involved in "Mount 1"/"ICL Vicraman" collision in Malacca Straits (total loss of vessel and 26 crew), and acted for Cenargo Navigation Ltd following abandonment and salvage of "Merchant Patriot." Finance: Acting for World Bank affiliate International Finance Corporation on US$120m long term debt and equity financing of 10 chemical tanker new-buildings for PT Laju Tanker Tbk; Cenargo Group in US$201m syndicated loan financing and re-financing deal, and Awilco on merger with PGS (nominal value US$860m).

Clifford Chance (Wet/Dry: 7ptnrs/18 assts. Finance: 3ptnrs – 1f/t; 8assts) "Provide a Rolls Royce service. John Bassindale has retired but they still have the "superb" *Tony Vlasto*. **Clients/Work: Wet:** Act for the owners of "Evoikos" (oil spill), "Vikartindur" (total loss in Iceland) and "Albion Two" (sank with total loss of crew). **Dry:** Act for Kvaerner Kleven in dispute with NCV Ltd re construction of 6 reefer vessels and charterers re dispute with the owners of "Halki" (construction of Arbitration Act 1996). **Finance:** Acted for Residensea (new luxury floating apartment concept). Acted for Kvaerner on $500m sale of Cunard (including the QE2) to Carnival Corporation.

Constant & Constant (18ptnrs/8assts) Described as "commercial" they have a surprisingly high profile for a relatively small firm. This is attributable primarily to "good people who know what they are doing." *Tim Llewelyn* enters our leading individuals table this year on the basis of client recommendations. *Richard Olsen* and *Anthony Miller* also received favourable mentions. The firm moves up as a result. **Clients/Work:** Sanwa v Choyang Star (collision); "Vikartindur" (grounding). Acted for CP Ships in its purchase of Contship Container Line and Lykes Lines.

Lawrence Graham (6ptnrs/8assts) Making steady advances up the table due largely to their extensive former Iron Curtain practice. They are "hard nosed, shrewd, persistent and remarkable." Leader *Mike Lax* is "like a space machine – incredibly organised and efficient." Generally, the firm is seen to be one of the toughest opponents and were variously described as "tenacious, clever and prompt." **Clients/Work:** Acting for Republic of Ukraine over recent UK legislation affecting Ukraine owned ships. Representing Gesco in dispute with Anglo-Georgian Shipping re joint venture, and Latvian Shipping Company in dispute with Gdansk Shipyard arising from breach of $170m six ship building contract.

Norton Rose (Dry: 12ptnrs/29assts world-wide. Finance: 12ptnrs/23assts world-wide. Not all f/t) Generally considered to be "on the way back to being the force they were" in shipping. Are particularly strong in ship finance where *John Shelton* and *Jeremy Gibb* continue to have high profiles. *Christopher Hobbs* makes an entry this year. **Clients/ Work: Dry:** Defending Sembawang in shipbuilding case; involved in "Romantica" (loss of passenger ship off Cyprus); representing Stena in dispute concerning operation of Holyhead port. Finance: Acted for MeesPierson N.V in US$195m syndicated loan; US$60m syndicated loans to companies associated with Golden Union Shipping Company S.A. Also $100m US public offering of secure loan notes.

Sinclair Roche & Temperley (Wet/Dry: 3ptnrs/7assts; Finance: 10ptnrs/14assts) Felt by some to be slipping after losing some of their wet team last year and selling their Singapore office to Watson Farley. But

LEADING INDIVIDUALS • LONDON DRY/WET	
BISHOP Archie Holman, Fenwick & Willan	VLASTO Tony Clifford Chance
SAYER Richard Ince & Co	WILLIAMS Richard Ince & Co
BUCKLEY Michael Waltons & Morse	ROOTH Anthony Watson, Farley & Williams
CRUMP Richard Holman, Fenwick & Willan	SLADE David Stephenson Harwood
EVANS John Hill Taylor Dickinson	TAYLOR Andrew Richards Butler
GOSLING James Holman, Fenwick & Willan	TAYLOR Timothy Hill Taylor Dickinson
OLSEN Richard Constant & Constant	WALLIS Robert Hill Taylor Dickinson
BARDOT Andrew Bentleys, Stokes & Lowless	LAX Michael Lawrence Graham
BURCH Michael Bentleys, Stokes & Lowless	LEACH Ben Sinclair Roche & Temperley
BUSH Philip Jackson Parton	LIVINGSTONE Hugh Holman, Fenwick & Willan
CROFT Roger Shaw and Croft	LLEWELLYN Tim Constant & Constant
DE LA RUE Colin Ince & Co	LOWE Charles Holman, Fenwick & Willan
DONITHORN Michael Holman, Fenwick & Willan	LUX Jonathan Ince & Co
EAST Lindsay Richards Butler	PARTON Nicholas Jackson Parton
EVERS Ralph Clyde & Co	SLADE Robin Stephenson Harwood
FISHER Nicholas Fishers	STRONG Malcolm Ince & Co
FLETCHER Simon Clyde & Co	THORP Clive Clyde & Co
HEBDEN David Thomas Cooper & Stibbard	WEISS Oliver Ince & Co
HOBBS Christopher Norton Rose	WILSON James Ince & Co
HODGSON Derek Clyde & Co	WILSON Robert Holman, Fenwick & Willan
BROWN Anthony More Fisher Brown	LOWE Steven Stephenson Harwood
BROWNE Benjamin Clyde & Co	LUCAS Charles Middleton Potts
CHARITY David Stockler Charity	MEAD Ray Barlow Lyde & Gilbert
CROPPER Stephen Hill Taylor Dickinson	MILLER Anthony Constant & Constant
DONOGHUE Andrew Middleton Potts	MORGAN Julian Edwin Coe
GINSBERG Roy Waltons & Morse	ROBINSON Nicholas Herbert Smith
HARRIS Graham Richards Butler	THOMAS Anthony Clyde & Co
HEALEY Robin Ince & Co	THWAITES Ken Berrymans Lace Mawer
JOHNSON Andrew Hill Taylor Dickinson	WINTER Glenn Holmes Hardingham

SEE PROFILES AT END OF THIS SECTION

generally are seen as strong as ever on the dry and finance sides. *Ben Leach* and *Charles Foster* continue to be "well regarded" and *Ian Gaunt* is a new entry in finance. **Clients/Work:**

Finance: Acted for agents in Osprey Maritime Ltd US$944m term loan facilities, Chase Manhattan Bank in Stena AB US$500m revolving credit facility and Carnival Corporation in connection with US$1.1 billion cruise ship order and US$500m acquisition of the Cunard cruise line."

Barlow Lyde & Gilbert (3ptnrs/6assts) Seen as players in the market by virtue of their general insurance reputation. The team includes the respected *Ray Mead.* **Clients/ Work:** Acted for charterers of "Tokio Express" following collapse of stows of containers during severe weather off Land's End. Represented owners of "Askania Nova" re $10m cargo claim. Act for UK P&I Club, Skuld; Lloyd's Claims Office.

Herbert Smith (5ptnrs/20assts) Their appearing in this field is no surprise, given their expertise and involvement in every contentious area of law. *Nicholas Robinson* is particularly rated. **Clients/Work:** Represented a major Chinese cargo insurer in a contested salvage appeal, a major British bank following collapse of Adriatic Tankers Group and a Greek managed shipowner concerning dispute with French bank.

Watson Farley & Williams (26ptnrs/ 53assts) Known primarily for their finance work, although this may change with the addition of leading dry man, the "first class" *Tony Rooth* who is "an intimidating opponent." *Alastair Farley* and *Martin Watson* are "extremely personable and technically able." **Clients/Work:** Finance: Advised Celebrity Cruise on $1.3 billion amicable take-over by Royal Caribbean Cruise; The Pegasus Group on its bond offer of $145m in ship mortgage notes, and The Kvaerner Group on the $190m sale of cruise vessel to NCL Cruises Ltd.

Wilde Sapte (5ptnrs/10assts) Highly regarded for asset finance, the firm naturally features in the ship finance list. Team includes *Robert Dibble.* **Clients/Work:** US LILO financings for Lloyds Leasing and Capital Bank high speed ferries; Airtours Cruise Ship financing; Natwest Shell tanker financing.

Berrymans Lace Mawer (2ptnrs/2assts – not f/t) Known mainly for the yachting work carried out by *Ken Thwaites.* **Clients/Work:** Include: Lombard, Independent Insurance Co, Lloyd's Claims office and Claims & Recoveries Bureau Ltd.

NICHE FIRMS

Bentleys, Stokes & Lowless (9assts/ 13assts) Move up this year following glowing praise. They are seen as good all-rounders and are "straightforward, honest and competent." The "no nonsense, commercial" *Andrew Bardot* "has got what it takes and makes the client feel confident." *Michael Burch* is also recommended. **Clients/Work:** "Giannis NK" (House of Lords); "Happy Fellow" (Court of Appeal) and Surzor v Koros.

Holmes Hardingham (Wet/Dry: 11ptnrs – 5f/t; 13assts – 6f/t) Mixed views about this niche practice. Generally seen to have a solid spread of expertise." All agreed that *Glenn Winter* " is very commercial and doesn't

waste time with silly points." **Clients/ Work:** "Lalazar" (Standard Chartered Bank v PNSC) re ante-dated bills of lading. Acting for salvors of "Sand Kite" (vessel collided with Thames Barrier).

Jackson Parton (12ptnrs/5assts) Headed by the "larger than life " *Philip Bush*, it has some good talented individuals and tends to be "justifiably aggressive" **Clients/Work:** Acted in "The Silimna." Also handles cargo claims and charterparty disputes for British Steel.

More Fisher Brown (9ptnrs/7assts-75% shipping) An "excellent, punchy, bright and aggressive" firm with a reputation for commercial shipping litigation. The practice is headed by the "determined" *Tony Brown.*

Shaw and Croft (7 ptnrs/4assts – not all f/t) *Roger Croft* was recommended again as a leading individual. Felt to "punch above their weight," particularly in wet cases although they are also respected for their dry work.

Elborne Mitchell Less visible lately, since the retirement of leading individual Ray Clarke, but still thought to be a good firm.

Middleton Potts (8ptnrs/8assts) This "interesting, tight operation" mainly does dry work. Generally regarded as efficient and thorough. *Andrew Donaghue* and *Charles Lucas* are recommended. **Clients/Work:** Acted for Portnet in Bouygues v Ultisol (factors governing stays of proceeding in multi-party litigation); the "Trade Nomad" (construction of maintenance clause in standard Sheltime 4 form and the "Taria" (payment provision of the Norwegian Sale form).

Thomas Cooper & Stibbard (Wet: 4ptnrs/4assts. Dry: 9ptnrs/4assts) Generally admired for its handling of the Spanish fishing vessels/EC case which is seen as really increasing its profile. The team is led by *David Hebden.* **Clients/Work: Dry:** "Henriette Tholstrup," "Vergina," "Lyme Bay" and "Factortame." **Wet:** "European Emerald," "Red Falcon/ Volvox Hansa" and "Bos 400."

Waltons & Morse (5ptnrs/3assts) *Roy Ginsberg* is the best known name in this firm. **Clients/Work:** Includes: "River Gurara."

Curtis Davis Garrard (3ptnrs/6assts) Established in September 1996 as a breakaway from Watson, Farley & Williams, this niche firm, based at Heathrow Airport's Terminal 4, is making its presence felt in the dry arena. **Clients/Work:** Louis Dreyfus Armateurs; Egon Oldendorff; Stena Drilling

Fishers (2ptnrs/4assts) Only small, but extremely good was the majority opinion about this firm. "They could out-litigate anyone in the top firms" according to one practitioner. *Nicholas Fisher* is "excellent." **Clients/Work:** Cool Carriers AB; BP Chemicals Trading Ltd and Hapag-Lloyd AG.

Lewis Moore & Co (3ptnrs/4assts) This niche firm is recognised as a good, solid practice and is definitely "on the scene." **Clients/Work:** "Ocean Enterprise;" Velos v Harbour Insurance: UDO plc takeover of LDO Holdings Ltd and Geoprint Ltd

Stockler Charity (2ptnrs/3assts) Known for leading individual *David Charity* who is "outstanding," they carry out wet and dry work. **Clients/Work:** Cho Yang Shipping Ltd v Coral (UK) Ltd; Global Container Lines Ltd v State Black Sea Shipping Company.

Waterson Hicks (3ptnrs/5assts) The loss of Nigel Waterson has not gone without comment and the general consensus is that the firm is undergoing a bit of a transition.

Clients/Work: Acted for charterers in the "Agamemnon" (notice of readiness)

Williamson & Horrocks (2ptnrs/4assts p/t) Not making as much of an impact as in recent years, but still a presence. **Clients/Work:** Acted in "Daylam." Act for Tsavliris, Pentow, British Marine Mutual and the Shipowners' Club.

LEADERS' PROFILES · LONDON

BARDOT, A.
Bentleys, Stokes & Lowless, London (0171) 782 0990
Specialisation: Qualified 1980. Partner 1982. Principal areas of practice: all aspects of 'dry' shipping and insurance related litigation and arbitration and non contentious matters, including sale and purchase and M.O.A. matters. French speaker.
Prof. Memberships: London Maritime Arbitration Association supporting member. Baltic Exchange member.

BISHOP, Archie
Holman, Fenwick & Willan, London (0171) 488 2300
Senior Partner.
Specialisation: Main area of practice is Admiralty law, with an emphasis on collision, salvage, oil pollution and marine insurance. Legal advisor to International Salvage Union. Contributes a variety of articles to specialised marine publications. Regular speaker at conferences and seminars.
Prof. Memberships: Law Society; British Maritime Law Association; City of London Solicitors Company; Royal Institute of Navigation; Average Adjustors Association; Secretary, Admiralty Solicitors Group.
Career: Deck officer with P&O Line 1954-60. Joined Holman Fenwick & Willan 1960, became a Partner in 1971 and Senior Partner in 1989. Appointed Examiner in Admiralty 1996.
Personal: Born 21st July 1937. Thames Nautical Training College HMS Worcester 1952-54. British First Mates Foreign Going Certificate 1959, Solicitor 1971. Leisure pursuits horse riding, golf, art and music. Lives in Farnham.

BROWN, Anthony
More Fisher Brown, London (0171) 247 0438

BROWNE, Benjamin
Clyde & Co, Guildford (01483) 555555
Partner in Marine Casualty Department.
Specialisation: Specialises in all aspects of marine casualties, in particular oil pollution, salvage, collision, general average, transhipments and disputes arising from contracts for carriage of goods by sea. Has handled numerous salvage cases both in Lloyd's Open Form Salvage Agreement "No Cure – No Pay" and in other fora. Advises marine cargo, hull and P+l insurers, shipowners, charterers and oil companies on shipping problems. Has a special interest in the Middle East where he helped establish the firm's Middle East Regional Office in Dubai. Has delivered a number of papers on salvage, collision and other maritime legal subjects to various audiences worldwide. Has spoken on oil pollution at many conferences and seminars and has had a number of pieces on oil pollution damage compensation published recently.
Prof. Memberships: Middle East Association, Middle East Legal Practitioners Forum, British

Middle East Law Council.
Career: Qualified in 1978 while at Lovell White & King. With Morrell Peel & Gamlen in Oxford 1979-81. Joined Clyde & Co in 1981 and became a Partner in 1985. Resident Partner in the firm's new Middle East Office for 13 months in 1989 and 1990.
Personal: Born 18th May 1953. Educated at Eton College 1966-71 and Trinity College, Cambridge 1972-75 (MA). Married with 3 children.

BUCKLEY, Michael
Waltons & Morse, London (0171) 623 4255

BURCH, M.
Bentleys, Stokes & Lowless, London (0171) 782 0990
Specialisation: Admiralty Law especially Collision and Salvage. Investigations into causation of all types of marine casualty.
Prof. Memberships: Law Society; Admiralty Solicitors' Group; Royal Institute of Navigation; Nautical Institute; Honourable Company of Master Mariners.
Career: Deck Officer with Port Line and the Bowater Steamship Company 1952-1961; entered legal profession 1962; Solicitor and Partner 1968; joined Bentleys, Stokes & Lowless 1988. Head of Admiralty Department.
Personal: Born 1934; School of Navigation; Warsash 1951-52; Master's Foreign Going Certificate 1961; leisure interests: playing and listening to music; reading; protection of environment. Resides Cambridge and on the Suffolk Coast.

BUSH, Philip
Jackson Parton, London (0171) 702 0085
Specialisation: Formerly an equity partner with Richards Butler, Philip Bush has been influential in the rapid rise of Jackson Parton's reputation and profile in London's shipping law sector. Primarily renowned as a lilitigator specialising in sale and purchase, charterparty and bill of lading matters, he also acts regularly in Bank/ Borrower workout situations and advises a number of owners, charterers, operators and traders in non-contentious commercial and strategic issues. His promotion of commercially sensible swift dispute resolution has resulted in several appointments as mediator. He is now accepting arbitration appointments.

CHARITY, David E.
Stockler Charity, London (0171) 404 6661
Partner in Litigation Department.
Specialisation: Maritime arbitration and litigation. Extensive experience advising shipowners, charterers and protection and indemnity associations and conducting associated litigation. Numerous reported decisions, the most recent of which is Global Container Lines v. Black Sea Shipping etc. (1997). Co-author of 'Legal Aspects of the Gulf War' (1991) and has written numerous articles for legal and shipping periodicals. Lectures regularly at conferences and seminars.

Prof. Memberships: Law Society, Supporting Member of London Maritime Arbitrators Association.
Career: Articled with Holman Fenwick & Willan 1964-66, qualified in 1966 and became a Partner in 1972. Left in 1992 to become one of the Founding Partners of niche shipping practice Stockler Charity.
Personal: Born in 1941. Attended Kingswood School 1954-60, then London School of Economics 1961-64. Leisure pursuits include mountaineering and music. Lives in Tunbridge Wells.

CROFT, Roger
Shaw and Croft, London (0171) 645 9000
Senior Partner specialising in admiralty law and insurance law.
Specialisation: Principal area of practice is admiralty and insurance law. Work includes collision, salvage, pollution, environmental damage and total loss. Other main area of practice is fraud and money laundering. Acted in the 'Goring' (House of Lords) and 'Mare' (Court of Appeal) cases. Clients include major shipowners, salvors, insurers and P&I clubs.
Prof. Memberships: Law Society, City of London Solicitors Company, London Maritime Arbitrators Association, Royal Institute of Navigation, Average Adjusters Association, Admiralty Solicitors Group.
Career: Joined the Royal Navy in 1962. Electronic Engineer from 1967. Qualified in 1978. Senior Partner at Shaw and Croft from 1992.
Personal: Born 19th May 1946. Educated at Wallington County Grammar School and London University. Interests include golf, cricket, music, gardening and reading.

CROPPER, Stephen
Hill Taylor Dickinson, London (0171) 283 9033
Partner and Group Leader in Shipping and Insurance Department.
Specialisation: Principal area of practice is investigation of marine casualties and insurance coverage. Work inludes investigating liability for collisions, salvage, total loss of vessels on behalf of owners and underwriters (both H&M and P&I and involving also coverage disputes). Other area is P&I claims on behalf of owners and P&I clubs. Work includes investigation and defence of claims against shipowners by third parties. Has dealt with many large collisions and total losses of vessels in all parts of the world involving loss of life and cargo, pollution and considerations of limitation of liability. Major clients include hull and machinery underwriters in the UK, mainland Europe and Japan, owners and managers all over the world and major P&I clubs. Has addressed conferences in England, Japan, Australia and New Zealand and had articles published in Lloyd's List and other publications.
Prof. Memberships: Law Society, British Maritime Law Association, Maritime Law Association (US), Maritime Law Association of

Australia & N.Z, Association of Average Adjusters, L.M.A.A.
Career: Qualified in 1974. Joined *Hill Taylor Dickinson* in 1978 and became a partner in 1982.
Personal: Born 10th May 1947. Educated at Derby School 1958-66 and St. John's College, Oxford 1966-69. Leisure activities include golf, skiing, gardening and travelling in France. Lives in London.

CRUMP, Richard W.
Holman, Fenwick & Willan, London
(0171) 488 2300
Partner in Commercial Litigation Department.
Specialisation: Practice encompasses all areas of shipping litigation, including charterparty disputes, cargo claims, ship sale disputes, joint venture and pool agreement disputes and related commercial litigation. Has spoken at seminars in Athens and Bombay.
Prof. Memberships: Law Society Member.
Career: Qualified in 1981 having joined *Holman Fenwick & Willan* in 1979. Became a Partner in 1987.
Personal: Born 6th September 1957. Educated at St. Paul's School, London 1970-74, Oriel College, Oxford 1975-78 and College of Law, Guildford 1979. Lives in London.

DE LA RUE, Colin M.
Ince & Co, London (0171) 623 2011
Specialisation: With others in the firm he has acted in most major oil pollution incidents worldwide in the last 15 years – including the Haven, Aegean Sea, Braer, Sea Empress and Nissos Amorgos cases – and on a day-to-day basis advises shipowners, oil companies, P & I Clubs, marine underwriters and others on the commercial ramifications of the subject. Extensive experience of claims under compensation conventions and industry schemes. Has spoken on marine pollution and disaster response at seminars and conferences in many countries around the world.
Prof. Memberships: British Maritime Law Association Pollution Sub-Committee; elected titulary member of the Comit, Maritime International for work in drafting the Guidelines on Oil Pollution Damage adopted by the CMI Conference in 1994.
Career: Bar Finals 1977; admitted as solicitor 1980; partner *Ince & Co* 1986; head of firm's pollution group; General Editor of 'Liability for Damage to the Marine Environment' (Lloyd's of London Press, 1993) and co-author of a forthcoming book on the law and practice of marine pollution; Visiting Lecturer in Shipping Law at the City University Business School in London 1986-96.
Personal: Born 11th October 1953. Education: Elizabeth College, Guernsey and Pembroke College, Cambridge (modern languages and law). Married with two children. Lives in Woodbridge, Suffolk. Spare time activities include involvement in various charities and local community affairs, also golf, tennis, natural history and music.

DIBBLE, Robert K.
Wilde Sapte, London (0171) 246 7000
Partner. Manager of Asset Finance Group and Head of Ship Finance Group.
Specialisation: Ship and aircraft finance, trade and countertrade. Acts mainly for banks but also for various owners and operators. Speaks good Russian and French.

Career: Retired voluntarily from the Royal Navy in rank of Commander in 1977. *Linklaters & Paines* 1978-81. *Wilde Sapte* 1981 (Partner 1982).

DONITHORN, Michael G.
Holman, Fenwick & Willan, London
(0171) 488 2300
Partner in Commercial Litigation Department.
Specialisation: Principal area of practice is marine litigation. Specialises in commercial disputes arising from casualties. Particular experience of bulk and liner trades, P&I insurance and liability insurance generally. Other areas of practice are marine insurance and international sale of goods. Clients include major P&I clubs, liner operators, time charter operators, bulk vessel owners, gas carrier owners and market underwriters. CEDR Accedited Mediator.
Prof. Memberships: Law Society, BMLA, LMAA (supporting member), Member of Baltic Exchange.
Career: Called to the Bar 1974. Practiced at the Bar 1974-76. Lawyer for West of England P&I Club 1976-78. Joined *Coward Chance* 1978. Admitted Solicitor 1980. Partner at *Coward Chance* (subsequently *Clifford Chance*) 1984-94. Joined *Holman Fenwick & Willan* as a Partner in 1994.
Personal: Born 27th January 1951. Educated at Cannock Grammar School 1962-69, Balliol College, Oxford 1969-72 (BA Hons, Modern History 1972, MA 1979) and the College of Law, Chancery Lane 1972-74. Leisure pursuits include farming. Lives in Surrey.

DONOGHUE, Andrew Charles
Middleton Potts, London (0171) 600 2333
Partner in Shipping Litigation Department.
Specialisation: Main areas of practice are charterparty, bill of lading and ship sale & purchase disputes together with problems arising under contracts for the international sale of goods. Acts primarily for P&I Clubs, Defence Associations and individual shipowners, charterers and commodity houses. Major recent cases handled include Aectra Refining & Marketing Inc. v. Exmar N.V. and the Bouygues v. Caspian et al litigation.
Prof. Memberships: The Baltic Exchange; Supporting Member LMAA.
Career: M.A. Degree in Jurisprudence, Lincoln College, Oxford 1973; articled clerk and assistant solicitor *Richards Butler & Co* 1974-1980. With *Middleton Potts* since 1980.
Personal: Born 15th November 1951. Leisure interests: mountaineering, naval and ancient history.

EAST, Lindsay T.
Richards Butler, London (0171) 247 6555
Partner. Head of Shipping and Insurance Group.
Specialisation: Main area of practice is shipping and insurance. Acts for owners and charterers direct or through their insurers (P&I and defence clubs) in all contractual disputes, charterparty, bill of lading, MOA, and building contracts. Particular expertise in drafting and advising on club rules and shipbuilding disputes. Also handles general marine and non-marine insurance, acting for cargo insurers and reinsurers and war-risk underwriters. Cases have included 'Antaios', 'Antares', 'Antonis P. Lemos', Standard Steamship v. Gann, 'Aditya Vaibhav', 'Aegean Maritime v. Flender Werft' and 'Sagheera'. Speaker at and chairman of various seminars.

Prof. Memberships: Baltic Exchange.
Career: Qualified in 1973, having joined *Richards Butler* in 1971. Became a Partner in 1977.
Personal: Born 24th March 1949. Attended Skinners School to 1966, then Worcester College, Oxford 1967-70. Leisure interests include cricket, opera and travel. Lives in Rickmansworth, Herts.

EVANS, John C.
Hill Taylor Dickinson, London
(0171) 283 9033
Specialisation: Shipping and insurance litigation.
Career: Llandovery College; University College of Wales, Aberystwyth (1972 LLB).
Personal: Resides Stebbing.

EVERS, Ralph
Clyde & Co, London (0171) 623 1244
Specialisation: International shipping and insurance work with an emphasis on cargo recovery claims. He acts for cargo insurers and their representatives in England and worldwide.

FARLEY, Alastair
Watson, Farley & Williams, London
(0171) 814 8000
afarley@wfw.com
Specialisation: Partner in the Shipping Group, specialising in international finance, commercial shipping, ship finance and general corporate work. Head of International Shipping Group.
Career: Qualified 1971; founding and senior partner *Watson, Farley & Williams* 1982; non-executive director,Close Brothers Group plc and Stirling Shipping Company Limited; Court of Assistants, Worshipful Company of Shipwrights; Liveryman, City of London Solicitors Company.
Personal: Born 1946; MA Jesus College,Cambridge; resides Milland, Hampshire.

FISHER, Nicholas
Fishers, London (0171) 709 7203
Partner specialising in commercial shipping litigation, insurance and reinsurance litigation.
Specialisation: Handles commercial shipping litigation, including significant client base in container, reefer and tanker operations. Also insurance and reinsurance litigation involving brokers' PI claims.
Prof. Memberships: London Maritime Arbitrators Association (Supporting Member), Baltic Exchange, The City of London Solicitors' Company.
Career: Qualified in 1979. Partner at *Richards Butler* 1984-88. Founding Partner of *More Fisher Brown* 1988-93. Founded *Fishers* in May 1993.
Personal: Educated at Glyn Grammar School, Epsom, then Clare College, Cambridge (MA).

FLETCHER, Simon
Clyde & Co, Guildford (01483) 555555

FOSTER, Charles
Sinclair Roche & Temperley, London
(0171) 452 4000
Specialisation: Ship finance; problem shipping loans and related work-outs.
Career: M.A. (Cantab); and articles: *Frere Cholmeley & Co*; *Sinclair Roche & Temperley*1972-76 (Junior Partner); Chief Executive Officer, GATX International Finance

Inc. (Subsidiary of GATX Corporation of Chicago) 1976-81; *Sinclair Roche & Temperley* 1981-97 (Equity Partner 1985; Consultant since 1995).

GAUNT, I.J.
Sinclair Roche & Temperley, London
(0171) 452 4000
Specialisation: All aspects of ship ownership and ship finance, asset and project financing, and banking.
Career: Education: Hulme Grammar School; Selwyn College, Cambridge (MA Law 1975). Career: Called to the Bar 1973; Assistant Parliamentary Counsel, 1976-1978; *Sinclair Roche and Temperley*, since 1979, and partner since 1981; solicitor, 1980; Far East Managing Partner, 1994 – 1997.
Personal: Born 1951; resides London. Interests: music, theatre, tennis.

GIBB, Jeremy S.P.
Norton Rose, London (0171) 283 6000
Partner in Banking Department.
Specialisation: Principal area of practice is asset finance, especially for ships and aircraft. In the shipping field has over 10 years experience in the City of London, acting for financiers and owners of all types of vessels, including cruise ships and offshore vessels. Also deals with acquisition finance, especially acquisition and disposal of leasing companies. Has handled major FPSO structured financing as well as numerous structured and vanilla tax-based leasing deals.
Prof. Memberships: Law Society, Connecticut Maritime Association.

GINSBERG, Roy
Waltons & Morse, London (0171) 623 4255

GOSLING, James C.
Holman, Fenwick & Willan, London
(0171) 488 2300
Partner in Admiralty Department.
Specialisation: Principal areas of practice are salvage, collision, total loss and wreck removal, acting mainly for salvors, shipowners, hull underwriters and P & I Clubs. Also handles marine insurance, general shipping and commercial law MOA disputes, charterparty disputes and cargo claims. Important cases have included "Scandanavian Star", "Europa" collision with "Inchon Glory", "Belgrave" and "Smit Tak B.V. v. Selco Salvage". Clients include several leading salvage companies, ship owners, hull underwriters, ship managers, insurance brokers and one southern hemisphere tycoon. Is on the editorial board of the *International Maritime Law*. Has lectured on Admiralty Law in Mexico and Venezuela in Spanish, and in London and Piraeus.
Prof. Memberships: Member of the Instituto Ibero-Americano De Derecho Maritimo.
Career: Qualified in 1980. Partner in 1988.
Personal: Born 28th June 1955. Educated at Ampleforth College, York and at St.Catharine's College Cambridge. Leisure interests include rugby, skiing, tennis, sailing, rowing, motor cycling, antiques and crosswords. Speaks French and Spanish.
Lives near Saffron Walden.

HARRIS, Graham
Richards Butler, London (0171) 247 6555
Specialisation: Wide experience of dispute resolution in the shipping and transportation industries including shipbuilding, sale and purchase, charterparty, bill of loading through transport documentation and insurance disputes.
Career: Qualified October 1981 (IT+)Norton, Rose *then* Richards Butler. *Partner at* Richards Butler *1988*.
Personal: Born 28th September 1956. Educated at King's School, Canterbury and Oriel College Oxford (MA Jurisprudence, First Class Hons). Lives in London.

HEALEY, Robin
Ince & Co, London (0171) 623 2011
Specialisation: Specialises in charterparty, cargo claims, sale of goods and Admiralty work, marine and non-marine.
Career: Qualified in 1971. Became a partner in 1980. Admitted in Hong Kong 1980. Member of the Council of the Law Society representing International Practice 1998.

HEBDEN, David G.
Thomas Cooper & Stibbard, London
(0171) 481 8851
Senior Partner.
Specialisation: Main area of practice is Admiralty and Marine Insurance Law. Work includes shipping and maritime law, collision, salvage, shipping safety, rules and regulations, and emergency response team management. Also management adviser to shipping and marine insurance industries. Handles day to day shipping problems, including criminal offences at sea, discipline and passenger ship operations. Edited and prepared Laws of Oleron. Author of numerous articles on shipping matters and safety at sea. Has addressed a variety of conferences and seminars.
Prof. Memberships: Law Society, British Maritime Law Association, Admiralty Solicitors Group, Honourable Company of Master Mariners.
Career: Qualified 1971, having joined *Thomas Cooper & Stibbard* in 1964. Became a Partner in 1973 and Senior Partner in 1992. FG Master's Certificate of Competency 1962; BMLA Committee on Salvage 1992.
Personal: Born 2nd March 1937. Attended Barnard Castle School 1948-52; HMS 'Worcester' 1952-54; School of Navigation, Southampton University 1962-64. ISM Lead Auditor 1997.

HOBBS, Christopher
Norton Rose, London (0171) 283 6000
Specialisation: Partner in the shipping litigation group, commercial litigation department, specialising in charterparty and bill of lading disputes; has major casualty experience in connection with lost passenger and merchant vessels, together with insurance aspects arising; also experienced in oil and commodity disputes; offshore work, shipbuilding and ship repair disputes, banking and insolvency; regular speaker at international conferences on shipping law. Recent cases include: representing Texaco as charterers and cargo-owners in the "SEA EMPRESS" grounding; representing owners and their P&I clubs in relation to the losses of "OCEANOS" and "MELETE"; representing steel traders Trans

World on multi-jurisdictional dispute; representing Enron in the CATS and J-Block litigation. Clients include Almare, Athenian Tankers, Coeclerici, Hyundai, Mitsui, Neste and Varnima.
Career: Articled *Norton Rose*; qualified 1986; assistant solicitor *Herbert Smith* 1990-1991; assistant solicitor *Norton Rose* 1991; partner 1995; Commission in 3rd Royal Tank Regiment as tank troop commander 1980-1983.

HODGSON, Derek
Clyde & Co, London (0171) 623 1244
Specialisation: Shipping/marine/insurace. Experienced in representing shipowners/P&I clubs/Hull underwriters and charterers in High Court actions and Arbitrations. Particular speciality in Thailand, Greece, South America and Africa.

JOHNSON, Andrew
Hill Taylor Dickinson, London
(0171) 283 9033
Partner in Shipping and Maritime Law Department.
Specialisation: Main area of practice is shipping litigation, covering charter parties, bills of lading, collision and salvage. Co-author of 'A Guide to the Hamburg Rules'; contributor to 'Marine Claims'.
Prof. Memberships: Law Society.
Career: Qualified in 1984, having joined *Hill Dickinson* in 1980. Became a Partner in 1987.
Personal: Born 5th February 1955. Lives in London.

LAX, Michael D.
Lawrence Graham, London (0171) 379 0000
Partner in Shipping Department.
Specialisation: Deals with a range of shipping and maritime law matters. Work includes international trade litigation and arbitration, charter party disputes, cargo claims, marine insurance disputes, oil pollution claims, ship finance, sale and purchase, and shipbuilding contracts.
Career: Qualified in 1977. B.A. (Dunedin).
Personal: Born 22nd December 1952. Member of Cannons Sports Club. Lives in Wallington.

LEACH, Ben
Sinclair Roche & Temperley, London
(0171) 452 4000
Partner, Head of Litigation
Specialisation: Main area of work is 'dry' shipping litigation of all types, including charterparty disputes, cargo claims, marine insurance and general average, sale and purchase disputes and new building disputes. Also specialises in mortgage enforcement and 'work out' situations, including negotiations with third party claimants, problems with crew and ITF and other practical aspects. Also a specialist in commodity law (see separate listing under 'Commodities: Physicals').
Prof. Memberships: Law Society, LMMA Supporting Members Committee
Career: Articled to *Richards Butler* in 1969, qualified as a solicitor in 1971, joined *Sinclair Roche & Temperley* in 1975 and became a partner in 1978.
Personal: Born 24th October 1945. Attended Leeds University 1965-68. Accredited CEDR mediator.

LIVINGSTONE, Hugh J
Holman, Fenwick & Willan, London
(0171) 488 2300
Specialisation: Partner in commercial litigation department. Specialising in all types of marine litigation on behalf of shipowners, charterers and insurers (P & I and market), as well as sellers and buyers of ships.
Career: Educated University of Cape Town (BA LLB) and University College London (LL M). Admitted 1976 (South Africa), 1985 (England and Wales) and 1986 (Hong Kong). Partner in *Holman Fenwick & Willan* 1986. Resident Partner in Hong Kong office 1986-1988 and subsequently at London office.

LLEWELLYN, Tim
Constant & Constant, London
(0171) 261 0006
Specialisation: Admiralty, P & I and Defence work, in particular matters arising from shipping casualties and accidents. Litigation in the High Court, and arbitration.
Prof. Memberships: Law Society, London Maritime Arbitrators Association (supporting member).
Career: Attended Bristol Cathedral School (1950-1955), University of Southampton School of Navigation (1956), Navigating Officer (1957-1968), Extra Master Certificate (1968), Senior Lecturer in Maritime Studies, City of London Polytechnic (1970-1974). Joined *Constant & Constant* in 1975, Partner 1978-1996. Consultant 1996 to date.
Personal: Sailing, reading.

LOWE, Charles R
Holman, Fenwick & Willan, London
(0171) 488 2300
Partner in Admiralty Department.
Specialisation: Admiralty law. 27 years specialisation in collision, salvage, total loss, wreck removal, fixed and floating installation damage, oil pollution claims, disputed claims on H & M underwriters and the whole ambit of admiralty (wet) practice on a 100% specialisation basis. Numerous salvage and collision casualties handled last year.
Career: Malvern College (1958-1964), Christs College Cambridge (1964-1967). MA Cantab. Admitted 1971. Joined *Holman, Fenwick & Willan* 1971. Joined partnerhsip 1978. Opened Hong Kong office as first resident partner 1978-1982.
Personal: Born 1945. Divorced. Two children. Resident Herts. Leisure activities – sailing, scuba diving, fly-fishing & tying, horse riding worldwide and wildlife.

LOWE, Steven
Stephenson Harwood, London
(0171) 329 4422
Partner in Litigation Department.
Specialisation: Commercial shipping and insurance litigation and arbitration, both domestic and international (US, several European countries, ICC arbitration etc), including newbuilding/sale and purchase disputes (frequently involving complex issues of naval architecture or marine engineering), charterparty, ship management, banking and oil trading disputes, insurance coverage issues (especially P&I, marine hull and reinsurance), advising on policy wordings and drafting policy/Club Rule changes.
Prof. Memberships: BMLA
Career: Joined *Holman Fenwick & Willan* August 1970, qualified November 1972, Partner January

1976; Joined *Stephenson Harwood* 1989.
Personal: Born 1946. Cambridge University (Classics and Law) 1966-9; married, one son/cat/hamster (and infinite stick insects). Enjoys (intermittently) books, music, wine, and (on rare occasions) golf.

LUCAS, Charles David
Middleton Potts, London (0171) 600 2333
See under Commodities: Physicals, p. 178

LUX, Jonathan
Ince & Co, London (0171) 623 2011
See under Alternative Dispute Resolution and Commodities: Physicals, p. 113, 178

MEAD, Ray
Barlow Lyde & Gilbert, London
(0171) 247 2277
Partner in Shipping Department.
Specialisation: Main area of practice is shipping and international trade; also handles general commercial litigation. Author of numerous articles. Occasional lecturer.
Prof. Memberships: London Maritime Association, London Maritime Arbitration Association.
Career: Qualified in 1975. Joined *Barlow Lyde & Gilbert* in 1990 as a Partner.
Personal: Born 1st February 1951. Attended Latymer Upper School 1962-70, then Birmingham University 1971-74. Leisure interests include sport, arts and family. Lives in Hurtspier Point West Sussex.

MILLER, RD*, Anthony R.
Constant & Constant, London
(0171) 261 0006
Admiralty Partner in Shipping and Maritime Law.
Specialisation: Has handled salvage, collision, pollution damage to offshore structures and wreck removal cases since 1966. Also handles charterparty, marine insurance, P&I and ports work. Acted in the 'Amoco Cadiz' case. Author of various articles on salvage and other marine topics. Reviews books for the Chartered Institute of Arbitrators. Lt Cdr, (Retired) Royal Naval Reserve. Has command experience in Mine Counter Measure vessels. Qualified as a naval diver. Lectured at ABA, LLP seminars, client seminars in Chile and International Tug and Salvage Conventions.
Prof. Memberships: Law Society, Nautical Institute.
Career: Qualified in 1965, Joined *Constant & Constant* in 1966. Admiralty Partner.
Personal: Born 11th January 1942. Attended Wellington College 1955-58, then the Tabor Academy USA 1959 and Law Society's School of Law 1964. Governor of Haberdashers Askes' Schools, Elstree. Leisure pursuits include computers, carpentry, sailing and gardening. Lives in Sandhills, Surrey.

MORGAN, Julian A.L.
Edwin Coe, London (0171) 691 4000
Partner in Shipping Group.
Specialisation: Shipping work covers sale and purchase, joint ventures, P and I club work and FD&D work. Also handles arbitration. Editor of 'Shipping Case Cards'. Lectures to P&I clubs on shipping and related topics.
Prof. Memberships: Law Society, London Maritime Arbitrators Association (supporting member).
Career: Called to the Bar 1977. Worked at

West of England P&I club 1979-85 before joining *Watson Farley & Williams*. Admitted as a solicitor in 1988. Joined *Edwin Coe* as a Partner in 1991.
Personal: Born 28th September 1955. Leisure interests include skiing, swimming, golf and foreign languages. Lives in London N6.

OLSEN, Richard F.
Constant & Constant, London
(0171) 261 0006
Partner in Shipping Department.
Specialisation: Principal area of practice is Admiralty work. Specialist since 1970 in collision, salvage, marine insurance, pollution and shipping accidents generally. Regular conference speaker at, amongst others, the International Bar Association and International Tug and Salvage Conventions.
Prof. Memberships: International Bar Association, Association of Average Adjusters (Subscriber), London Maritime Arbitrators' Association (Supporting Member), City of London Admiralty Solicitors Group.
Career: Qualified in 1969. *Constant & Constant* 1970-72.(Assistant Solicitor) *William A. Crump & Son* 1974-1986 (Partner). *Stephenson Harwood* 1986-1997 (Partner). Partner with *Constant & Constant* since 1997. Royal Naval Reserve Officer 1967-87.
Personal: Born 1943. Attended Mill Hill School 1956-61, Worcester College, Oxford 1962-65 and the Scandinavian Institute of Maritime Law at Oslo University 1972-73. Leisure pursuits include sailing, skiing, photography, wine and reading.

PARTON, Nicholas
Jackson Parton, London (0171) 702 0085
One of the founding partners.
Specialisation: Cargo claims, charterparty disputes, collision and salvage, general average, casualty investigations and international trade. Particularly experienced in Francophone Jurisdictions.

ROBINSON, J. Nicholas
Herbert Smith, London (0171) 374 8000
Partner, Head of Shipping Litigation Department.
Specialisation: Handles all aspects of 'wet' and 'dry' litigation including insurance, charterparty bills of lading and insolvency disputes. Specialises in injunctive relief and multi-jurisdictional disputes. Major reported cases handled include 'Babanaft' (1988), 'Star Texas' (1992) and 'Bazias 3&4' (1992).
Prof. Memberships: Law Society, London Maritime Arbitrators' Association, Solicitors' European Group.
Career: Qualified 1976. Admitted Hong Kong 1984. Partner with *Holman Fenwick & Willan* 1982-89 (Hong Kong 1984-86). Joined *Herbert Smith* in 1989 and currently heads the Shipping Litigation Group.
Personal: Born 6th August 1951. Attended Exeter University 1969-72. Supporting member of LMAA.

ROOTH, Anthony
Watson, Farley & Williams, London
(0171) 814 8000
trooth@wfw.com
Specialisation: Tony Rooth recently joined *Watson, Farley & Williams* to help expand their shipping litigation practice, particularly of the shipowners, P&I and defence insurers. Formerly

with *Clyde & Co*, Tony has specialised in shipping and marine insurance law for over 20 years. His particular expertise is in charterparty and bill of lading disputes and P&I insurance. He is joint editor of the Gard P&I Handbook. His main geographical focus is Scandinavia, Continental Europe and Mediterranean countries, in particular Greece and Turkey.

RUSSELL, Mark A.
Stephenson Harwood, London
(0171) 329 4422
Partner and Head of Shipping
Specialisation: All aspects of non-contentious shipping law, acting for lenders and shipowners.
Career: Qualified at *Simmons & Simmons* in 1983. *Sinclair Roche & Temperley* 1984-1995 (partner in 1989). Joined *Stephenson Harwood* as a partner in 1995.

SAYER, Richard J.
Ince & Co, London (0171) 623 2011
E-mail: richard.sayer@ince.co.uk Partner covering maritime law. Senior partner.
Specialisation: Main areas of practice are admiralty (collision, salvage and other casualties), charter party disputes, sale and purchase litigation and maritime fraud. Acted for owners of numerous headline casualties including 'The Braer' following the Shetland disaster in 1993. Also a member of the four-man FERIT (Far East Regional Investigation Team) established by all the major Far East insurance associations to investigate the incidence of maritime fraud in the South China Sea in the 1970s.
Prof. Memberships: Chairman (since 1991) of the City of London Admiralty Solicitors Group (Secretary 1972-91), Chairman of the BMLA Salvage Sub-Committee, member of the Baltic Exchange, supporting member of the Association of Average Adjusters, and of the Maritime Arbitrators Association, member of the Admiralty Court Committee since 1986, and member of the Lloyd's Form Working Party. Appointed Examiner in Admiralty 1996.
Career: Qualified in 1966, having joined *Ince & Co.* in 1962. Became a Partner in 1970. Was admitted in Hong Kong in 1979 and spent five months there opening the firm's Hong Kong office. Became Senior Partner in 1995.
Personal: Born 7th May 1943. Attended Framlingham College 1956-61. Leisure interests include golf, cricket and jazz. Lives in London.

SHELTON, John H.
Norton Rose, London (0171) 283 6000
Specialisation: Shipping finance, acting for owners, lenders, lessors, builders, and others.
Prof. Memberships: The Law Society, The Baltic Exchange.
Career: Articled at *Pinsent & Co*, Birmingham, joined *Norton Rose* on qualifying in 1981. Became partner 1987.
Personal: Married, four children. Principal interests: fatherhood.

SLADE, David L.
Stephenson Harwood, London
(0171) 329 4422
Senior Partner
Specialisation: Main area of practice is shipping finance, shipbuilding contracts and sale and purchase of ships, acting mainly for banks,

ship-owners, shipbuilders and shipbrokers. Also deals with disputes under shipbuilding contracts and sale and purchase contracts.
Prof. Memberships: Law Society, Worshipful Company of Shipwrights.
Career: Qualified in 1966. Joined *Stephenson Harwood* as a Partner in 1985.
Personal: Born on 3rd July 1941. Educated at St. Peter's, York 1954-60, then Emmanuel College, Cambridge 1960-63 and 1966. (MA 1966 LLM 1966) Formerly a member of the Territorial Army (Airborne Artillery). Holder of T.D.

SLADE, Robin J.
Stephenson Harwood, London
(0171) 329 4422
Specialisation: An admiralty specialist, he has built up and heads an eight strong team specifically dedicated to handling all types of admiralty work and which includes six ex-mariners, four with Master's Certificates and one young Chief Engineer. He and his group have in-depth experience of handling significant major casualties and is one of the few such groups in the City of London. He has been involved in many well known casualties including Penlee Lifeboat Disaster, "EUROPEAN GATEWAY" and "HERALD OF FREE ENTERPRISE" (all major public enquiries), "INDEPENDENTA", "KOWLOON BRIDGE", "KHARK 5" and, in the last two years "SEA PRINCE" and "NAKHODKA". Also, in the last year he has been instructed on a number of substantial collisions, salvage and P&I cases. He is experienced in negotiating and drafting wreck removal contacts.
Career: Qualified 1974, first became a partner in 1976 and joined SH as a partner in 1995.
Personal: Born 9 September 1946. Educated at St. Peters, York. Attended School of Navigation, Warsash. Married. One Daughter. Interests include skiing, sailing, collecting pictures, theatre, eating and drinking.

STRONG, Malcolm
Ince & Co, London (0171) 623 2011
Specialisation: Sale and purchase and finance of ships including related corporate, insurance, charterparty and other aspects. Was partner in the 'Niobe' (House of Lords case on sale of ships in 1995).
Prof. Memberships: Law Society. Supporting member London Maritime Arbitrators' Assocation.
Career: Cambridge University (Sidney Sussex College) MA., LL.M. Partner in *Ince & Co.* since 1970.
Personal: Married with one daughter. Interests: music, cinema, theatre, rugby and cricket.

TAYLOR, Andrew D.
Richards Butler, London (0171) 247 6555
Partner in Shipping Unit.
Specialisation: Specialises in charter disputes, cargo liabilities, marine insurance, P&I clubs and sale and purchase. Co-author of "Voyage Charters" – Lloyds of London Press.
Career: Qualified in 1980. Partner at *Richards Butler* since 1983.
Personal: Born 1952. Educated at Lincoln College, Oxford (MA).

TAYLOR, Timothy
Hill Taylor Dickinson, London
(0171) 283 9033
Partner in Shipping and Insurance Department.
Specialisation: Principal area of practice is insurance and shipping litigation. Cases of interest include the 'Stena Nautica' (1982) 'Piper Alpha' (1989), the 'Bowbelle' (1990) and the 'Wondrous' (1992).
Prof. Memberships: Chairman Marine Insurance Standing Committee, British Maritime Law Association; British Insurance Law Association; Association of Average Adjusters; London Maritime Arbitrators' Association; International Bar Association.
Career: Qualified in 1978 while with *Hill Dickinson & Co.* and became a Partner in 1982. CEDR Accredited Mediator.
Personal: Born 22nd June 1954. Attended Clifton College. Member of the MCC. Leisure pursuits include golf. Lives in Walton-on-the-Hill.

THOMAS, Anthony
Clyde & Co, Guildford (01483) 555 555
Partner in Shipping and Litigation Department.
Specialisation: Main area of practice is shipping litigation. Has considerable experience in litigation in the Commercial Court in London, London Arbitration and proceedings overseas. Handles cargo claims and marine insurance disputes. Acted in the Herald of Free Enterprise case for cargo interests against P&O. Author of numerous articles. Has spoken at a number of lectures around the world.
Prof. Memberships: Law Society.
Career: Qualified in 1976, joining *Clyde & Co.* the same year. Partner 1981.
Personal: Born 27th May 1952. Attended Leamington College 1963-70, then Manchester University 1970-73. Leisure interests include sport, art and architecture. Lives in Grayshott, Surrey.

THORP, Clive
Clyde & Co, London (0171) 623 1244
Partner in Shipping Department.
Specialisation: Main areas of practice are charterparties, commodities, oil, Mareva injunctions, Anton Piller sequestration, payment of judgment debts, sovereign immunity and demurrage arbitrations. Also handles enforcement of judgments. Acted in 'Sonangol v. Lundquist', privilege against self-incrimination; and 'Griparion' on indemnity costs. Lectures on Mareva injunctions, demurrage and shipbroker commissions.
Prof. Memberships: Baltic Exchange.
Career: Qualified 1976. Worked at *Holman Fenwick and Willan* 1976-79, joining *Clyde & Co.* in 1979. Became Partner in 1982. Member of Law Society Committee on Arbitration.
Personal: Born 28th August 1950. Attended Malvern College 1963-68, Hull University 1969-72 and College of Law. Common Councillor. Legal Officer for Association for Research into Stammering in Childhood.

THWAITES, Ken
Berrymans Lace Mawer, London
(0171) 638 2811
Specialisation: All aspects of work relating to yachts and other pleasure craft. Primarily litigation, including collision, salvage, personal injury, recovery and insurance disputes but also non-contentious work, in particular drafting policy wordings and yacht building agreements.
Prof. Memberships: The firm is a member of

the British Marine Industries Federation and an associate of the Yacht Brokers, Designers and Surveyors Association.
Career: Educated at Dover Grammar School. LLB(Hons) Degree from London University. Qualified as a solicitor with *Ingledew Brown Bennison & Garrett* in 1976 and dealt with yacht claims there from 1977. Has headed the yacht department of *Berrymans* since the two firms became associated in December 1996.
Personal: Married with one daughter. Interests include motor racing, clay pigeon shooting and foreign travel.

VLASTO, Tony
Clifford Chance, London (0171) 600 1000
Partner in International Maritime, Trade and Insurance Group.
Specialisation: Head of Admiralty Practice Group, specialising in particular in all aspects of casualty work; covering also a wide range of general maritime work including charterparty and bill of lading disputes, marine insurance litigation/arbitration and sale and purchase disputes.
Career: LLB 1972; Qualified 1975; Partner *Clifford Chance* 1981. Member of the Baltic Exchange, BMLA. City of London Admiralty Solicitors' Group; supporting member of the London Maritime Arbitrators Association and the Association of Average Adjusters; Steering Committee member of the London Shipping Law Centre.

WALLIS, Robert H.
Hill Taylor Dickinson, London
(0171) 283 9033
Specialisation: Admiralty law, particularly Collision, Salvage, Wreck Removal, Total Loss, Pollution Claims, Limitation of Liability and Marine Insurance Litigation.
Prof. Memberships: Law Society and Solicitors' European Group, British Maritime Law Association, CMI Sub-Committee on LoF 95, International Bar Association, Asia-Pacific Lawyers' Association.
Career: Leicester University LLB 1972, qualified 1975, Partner with Elborne Mitchell 1976-1988, joined *Hill Taylor Dickinson* as Partner 1988.
Personal: Born 1950, married with two children. Interests include golf, tennis and rugby.

WATSON, Martin A.
Watson, Farley & Williams, London
(0171) 814 8000
mwatson@wfw.com Partner in Shipping Group.
Specialisation: Main area of practice is ship finance, covering international finance, commercial leasing, banking, asset finance

and corporate restructuring.
Career: Founding Partner of *Watson, Farley & Williams* 1982.
Personal: Educated at St Catharine's College, Cambridge (BA).

WEISS, Oliver A.R.
Ince & Co, London (0171) 623 2011
Qualified 1976. Partner 1984. Fluent French speaker. Practice includes dispute resolution whether through court or arbitration of matters involving International Trade, Carriage of Goods by Sea, Charterparty, Bills of Lading, Ship Sale & Purchase and Marine Insurance. Instructed in marine total loss investigations either for owners or hull underwriters. Acted for hull underwriters in successful defence of owner's claim in *Marel* 1992 1 Lloyd's Rep 402 and 1994 1 Lloyd's Rep 624.

WILLIAMS, Richard W.
Ince & Co, London (0171) 623 2011
Partner handling chartering, carriage of goods by sea, commodities and insurance.
Specialisation: Acts regularly for shipowners, charterers, cargo interests, P&I and other underwriters. Major cases include 'Nanfri', 'Scaptrade', 'Galatia', 'Atlantic Emperor', 'Lefthero', 'Gregos' and 'Houda'. Drafted documents for a UN Agency. Co-author of Limitation of Liability of Maritime Claims (3rd Ed. 1998) and numerous articles on shipping topics. Regular speaker at conferences worldwide and long-standing member of Lloyd's of London Speakers Panel and Maritime Training Programme.
Prof. Memberships: Law Society, Average Adjusters' Association, London Maritime Arbitrators Association.
Career: Articled with *Ince & Co.*, qualified in 1973 and became a Partner in 1978.
Personal: Born 13th June 1948. Gained LLB at UCW Aberystwyth 1966-69, then LLM at University College, London 1971. Leisure pursuits include travel, suffering Welsh rugby, archaeology and learning to play the guitar. Lives in Surrey.

WILSON, James R.K.
Ince & Co, London (0171) 623 2011
Specialisation: James initially worked mainly on the charterparty and cargo claims side of the firm's business. In recent years however, he has concentrated on the 'wet' side of the practice and has been increasingly involved in marine casualties, including the 'Braer' and 'Sea Empress', where the breadth of his admiralty experience has been of great value. His client base is drawn from across the maritime industry and includes owners, Clubs and marine underwriters.

Career: James graduated from Cambridge with an Honours Degree in Law. He joined *Ince* in 1983 and on the completion of his Articles he joined *Ince & Co's* Hong Kong office for 3 years. He became a partner in 1991.
Personal: Out of the office James is a keen sportsman and enjoys golf, squash and shooting.

WILSON, Robert G.
Holman, Fenwick & Willan, London
(0171) 488 2300
Partner in Commercial Litigation Department.
Specialisation: Principal area of practice is shipping and maritime law. Work covers commercial legal advice, handling and resolving disputes, negotiations, conducting litigation and arbitration: including newbuildings, conversion and repair (ship/offshore), MOA, pools, charters, bills of lading, P&I and Defence Club work, marine insurance (including total losses), international trade, especially tankers and the oil trade. Also deals with insurance, commercial and banking law where related to shipping and trading interests. Reported litigation he has acted in includes "Delfini" (Court of Appeal – title to sue), "Kyzikos" (House of Lords – laytime), "Evpo Agnic" (Court of Appeal – arrest), "Arta"(Court of Appeal – shipbrokers negligence), "Apj Priti" (Court of Appeal – safe berth) and "Padre Island" (House of Lords – P&I club/ third party claims).
Prof. Memberships: Law Society, London Maritime Arbitrators Association (supporting member).
Career: Qualified in 1977, having joined *Holman Fenwick & Willan* in 1975. Became a Partner in 1982.
Personal: Born 8th February 1952. Educated at Watford Grammar School 1962-69 and Corpus Christi College, Cambridge 1970-74 (MA Maths, History; Law). Interests include family, golf and travel. Lives in Hadley Wood, Herts.

WINTER, Glenn
Holmes Hardingham, London
(0171) 283 0222
Specialisation: Main areas of specialisation are charterparty disputes and defending bulk liquid cargo claims. Major cases handled include 'The Mito' (1987), ' The Stena Pacifica' (1990), 'The Holstencruiser' (1992) and 'The Stolt Sydness' (1996).
Career: Attended Keble College, Oxford and the University of Illinois. Qualified in 1982. Founding Partner of *Holmes Hardingham*.
Personal: Born 7th May 1956. Married with two children.

The SOUTH and EAST ANGLIA

LEADING FIRMS • FINANCE
THE SOUTH AND EAST ANGLIA

BOND PEARCE	Plymouth, Southampton
DAVIES, JOHNSON & CO	Plymouth
FOOT & BOWDEN	Plymouth
GRANT & HORTON	Plymouth
DONNE MILEHAM & HADDOCK	Brighton
DALE & CO	Felixstowe
JOHN WESTON & CO	Felixstowe

LEADING FIRMS • YACHTS
THE SOUTH AND EAST ANGLIA

GRANT & HORTON	Plymouth
DONNE MILEHAM & HADDOCK	Brighton
NICOLA ELLIS & CO	Plymouth

Bond Pearce (Plymouth, Southampton) (4ptnrs/2assts) Have a reputation for good quality work and a solid team. **Clients/Work:** Standard P&I Association; P&O European Ferries; Geest Line; UK P&I Club.

Davies, Johnson & Co (Plymouth) (3 ptnrs/2assts) *Johnny Johnson* received numerous unprompted mentions and is considered to be the main player in the South East. The firm is seen as "commercial and good to deal with." Clients liked them for their "extreme competency and good value." **Clients/ Work:** Involved in the "Darya Tara" case.

Foot & Bowden (Plymouth) (2ptnrs/ 3assts – wet/dry) Active in shipping. Can sometimes have an aggressive style. **Clients/ Work:** Acted for the pilot in the "Sea Empress" case. Act for Brown and Root; Royal Sun Alliance and Norwich Union.

Grant & Horton (Plymouth) (2ptnrs/ 2assts) Led by *Nicholas Horton* now Robert Leigh has left private practice. **Clients/Work:** Involved in "Factortame;" represented shipyard in Pendennis Shipyard Ltd v Magrathea (Pendennis) Ltd, and defended Master and First Officer of "CITA" following vessel's grounding in relation to MSA prosecution.

Donne Mileham & Haddock (Brighton) (1ptnr/1asst) *Michael Bloomfield* is "making strides to establish himself as a major player in the south." **Clients/Work:** Acted for Transpacific Towage, Manila in US$2m LOF salvage, Thomas Miller P&I in US$1.2m cargo claim re "Sally Euroway," and West of England P&I Club in US$4m "Al Qamar El Saudi El Misri"/ "Berge Duke" collision in Suez Bay.

Dale & Co (Felixstowe) *Michael Dale* handles dry and wet work. **Clients/Work:** Include: Port of Ipswich and Reclaim Ltd.

John Weston & Co (Felixstowe) (1ptnr/ 1asst – also do transport). *John Weston* is an efficient and good practitioner. **Clients/ Work:** Wilful misconduct of carriers under CMR Convention case in Bavaria and local case concerning duty of care owed to employee using terminal handling equipment.

Nicola Ellis & Co (Plymouth) *Nicola Ellis* has been recommended primarily for her yachting work.

LEADING INDIVIDUALS
THE SOUTH AND EAST ANGLIA

HORTON Nicholas	Grant & Horton
JOHNSON Jonathan	Davies, Johnson & Co
DALE Michael	Dale & Co Solicitors
WESTON John	John Weston & Co
BLOOMFIELD Michael	Donne Mileham & Haddock
ELLIS Nicola	Nicola Ellis & Co

The NORTH

LEADING FIRMS • DRY/FINANCE
THE NORTH

EVERSHEDS	Newcastle-upon-Tyne
HILL DICKINSON	Liverpool
RAYFIELD MILLS	Newcastle-upon-Tyne
DIBB LUPTON ALSOP	Liverpool
ANDREW M. JACKSON & CO	Hull
MILLS & CO	Newcastle-upon-Tyne

HIGHLY REGARDED • WET
THE NORTH

Andrew M. Jackson & Co	Hull
Hill Dickinson	Liverpool
Rayfield Mills	Newcastle-upon-Tyne

Eversheds (Newcastle-upon-Tyne) (5ptnrs, 2f/t; 5assts, 3 f/t) *Chris Hilton* is "the best – measured and sensible with no drama." *Lex Dowie* also received numerous mentions. The team is generally felt to be down to earth to suit their clients. **Clients/Work:** Involved in the "Ettrick" (ship-building Commercial Court case).

Hill Dickinson (Liverpool) (6ptnrs/ 6assts) Seen as pleasant to work with. *David Wareing, John Maxwell* and *Peter Jackson* are particularly admired. **Clients/Work:** Handled "River Gurara" and "Arctic Trader"

Rayfield Mills (Newcastle-upon-Tyne) (8ptnrs/4assts) *Stephen Mills* is "very business like" and the firm is highly rated by both regional and London firms, as well as clients. "They offer a commercial, prompt and efficient service and understand our business." *Richard Rayfield* is well respected. **Clients/Work:** Acted in the "Bukhta Russkaya;" representing Mobil Export Corporation in large Commercial Court action.

Dibb Lupton Alsop (Liverpool) (3ptnrs/4assts) A sensible outfit and *David Mawdsley* "knows his stuff." *Raymond Phillips* and *Martin Hill* also received recommendations. **Clients/ Work:** Acted in "Arabesque" (policy repudiation for non disclosure) and "Karin B."

Andrew M Jackson & Co (Hull) (**Dry:** 1ptnr/2assts. **Wet:** 1ptnr/1asst. **Finance:** 1ptnr/1asst) Headed by the "thoroughly competent" *Silas Taylor*, they are admired by practitioners and clients country-wide. **Clients/Work:** Represented the owners of the "Rojen" in Admiralty & Commercial Court in multi-party case where the ship had knocked over a dock crane which then damaged other property.

Mills & Co (Newcastle-upon-Tyne) Respected shipping firm, with two highly rated individuals, *Geoffrey Mills* and *Alistdair Brown*.

LEADING INDIVIDUALS
THE NORTH

HILTON Chris	Eversheds
HILL Martin	Dibb Lupton Alsop
MAWDSLEY David	Dibb Lupton Alsop
MAXWELL John	Hill Dickinson
PHILLIPS Raymond	Dibb Lupton Alsop
RAYFIELD Richard	Rayfield Mills
TAYLOR Silas	Andrew M. Jackson & Co
WAREING David	Hill Dickinson
BROWN Alistdair	Mills & Co
DOWIE Lex	Eversheds
JACKSON Peter	Hill Dickinson
MILLS Geoffrey	Mills & Co
MILLS Stephen	Rayfield Mills

SCOTLAND

Henderson Boyd Jackson WS (2ptnrs/4assts) The "main players" in Scotland. *James Lowe* is "particularly good to work with." *Duncan Maclean* was also recommended again. **Clients/Work:** Britannia P&I, Amerada Hess; BP shipping and Briggs Marine. Continued defence of claims against Braer Corporation and insurers.

Maclay Murray & Spens (Wet/**Dry:** 2ptnrs/1asst. Finance: 1ptnr/2assts) Highly regarded for their shipping and finance work. **Clients/Work:** Ship Mortgage Finance Co plc; Skuld: Clyde Shipping Ltd; West of England: Bilboroughs; Lithgows Ltd.

Mackinnons (5ptnrs/2assts) "Straightforward and easy to deal with." *Keith MacRae* was recommended. **Clients/Work:** Skuld; Gard; Britannia Shipowners Mutual; Standard Steamship; Aberdeen Harbour Board; Peterhead Bay Authority; Dolphin Drilling.

LEADERS' PROFILES · REGIONS

BLOOMFIELD, Michael
Donne Mileham & Haddock, Brighton
01273 329833
Specialisation: Ship and boat collisions, salvage, cargo claims, sale and purchase, personal injury claims. Represented clients in Admiralty Court claim against boatyard for negligent repairs to vessels engines (The "Sigrid").
Prof. Memberships: Law Society.
Career: BSc Maritime Studies; ex Merchant Navy Deck Officer. Admitted as solicitor 1980 after articles *Sinclair Roche Temperley*. With *Richards Butler* 11 years until 1995 when joined *Donne Mileham & Haddock*.
Personal: Sailing.

BROWN, Alistdair B.
Mills & Co, Newcastle-upon-Tyne
(0191) 233 2222

DALE, Michael
Dale & Co Solicitors, Felixstowe
(01394) 284118

DOWIE, Lex
Eversheds, Newcastle upon Tyne
(0191) 261 1661
Partner in Shipping and International Trade Department.
Specialisation: Main area of practice involves contentious and non-contentious 'dry' shipping work, including charterparties, bills of lading, shipbuilding and ship repair, international sale of goods and related finance. Other main area of work is insurance and reinsurance involving marine and non-marine litigation and policy/contract drafting.
Prof. Memberships: British Insurance Law Association.
Career: Called to the Bar in 1975. Qualified as a Solicitor in 1978, while at *Holman Fenwick & Willan*. Legal Adviser for Coastal States Petroleum (UK) Ltd 1981-83, then Claims Manager for RK Carvill & Co. Ltd (Lloyd's Brokers) 1983-88. Returned to private practice with *Taylor Joynson Garrett* 1988-90. Joined *Eversheds* in 1990 and became a Partner in 1991.
Personal: Born 26th November 1951. Attended Glasgow Academy 1961-70 and Gonville and Caius College, Cambridge 1970-74.

ELLIS, Nicola
Nicola Ellis & Co, Plymouth (01752) 227428

HILL, Martin
Dibb Lupton Alsop, Liverpool (0345) 262728
Specialisation: Insurance coverage disputes subrogation and defence of liability claims. Acts for a number of major insurers.
Prof. Memberships: Committee member of Liverpool Underwriters Association and associate member of Manchester Marine Insurance Association.
Career: Qualified 1977. Partner with *Hill Dickinson & Co* and then *Hill Dickinson Davies Campbell* until 1993. Practice of *Alsop Wilkinson* from 1993.
Personal: Born 12.5.1953. Sixth generation solicitor. Personal interests include rebuilding and racing vintage and classic cars and working on the bench.

HILTON, Chris J.
Eversheds, Newcastle upon Tyne
(0191) 261 1661
Partner in Shipping Department.
Specialisation: Shipping and maritime law. Has over 25 years experience in London and Newcastle, including 15 years managing a mutual FD & D association. Experienced in all aspects of maritime law ('wet' and 'dry') and is an arbitrator. Also handles insurance work. Acted in 'Vimeira (H.L.)', 'Hitachi v. Viafiel (C.A.)', 'Manila Nos. 1 & 2 (C.A.)' and 'Cindy (Federal Supreme Court of Nigeria)'. Member of the drafting committee of BIMCO, on the 'Shipman' and 'Crewman' contracts.
Prof. Memberships: Law Society, Chartered Institute of Arbitrators (Fellow).
Career: Qualified 1975. Joined *Eversheds* as a Partner in 1976. Member of the BMLA Committee on Carriage of Goods by Sea.
Personal: Cambridge University 1968-71, Adelaide University in 1972. Leisure interests include golf.

HORTON, Nicholas
Grant & Horton Marine Solicitors, Plymouth
(01752) 265265
Partner specialising in marine work.
Specialisation: Full legal service to insurance and marine industries with particular specialism in yachts – in the UK and internationally; litigation and commercial contract work; marine insurance; sale and purchase; build and refit contracts; international litigation.
Prof. Memberships: British Marine Industries Federation, Royal Ocean Racing Club, Royal Western Yacht Club.
Career: Qualified 1986. *Ingledew Brown Bennison & Garrett* 1984-88. Partner *Davies*

Grant & Horton 1990-97; Co-founder of *Grant & Horton*, Marine Solicitors, May 1997.
Personal: Born August 1960, Merton College, Oxford 1979-82. Leisure: Sailing and family. Lives Plymouth.

JACKSON, Peter W.
Hill Dickinson, Manchester (0161) 2788800
Partner in Marine Department and Head of Hill Dickinson's Manchester office.
Specialisation: Main areas of practice are marine, goods in transit and insurance litigation. Work includes cargo claims, for both cargo and liability insurers, particularly international road haulage claims; ship related cargo claims for cargo interests; salvage; and monitoring foreign litigation. Also handles marine insurance work, particularly marine insurance policy interpretation for underwriters. Acted in 'ICI plc v. MAT transport', 'ITT v. Birkart', the 'Breydon Merchant' F & W Freight, the 'Los Angeles' and 'Microfine v. Transferry Shipping'. Individual charge-out rate is approximately £120 per hour, inclusive of mark-up.
Prof. Memberships: Liverpool Underwriters Association, Manchester Marine Insurance Association, London Maritime Arbitrators Association.
Career: Qualified in 1985, having joined *Hill Dickinson Davis Campbell* in 1983. Became a Partner in 1989.
Personal: Born 3rd April 1961. Attended St Edward's College, Liverpool 1972-79, then Exeter College, Oxford 1979-82. Leisure interests include football (Vice Chairman of South Liverpool FC, former Chairman of Football Supporters Association). Lives in Liverpool. Email number Jacko@Hill Dicks.com.

JOHNSON, Jonathan
Davies, Johnson & Co, Plymouth
(01752) 226020
Partner specialising in Shipping and Maritime Law.
Specialisation: Shipping and maritime law since 1976, also handles commercial litigation work.
Prof. Memberships: LMAA (Supporting), BMIA
Career: Qualified in 1976. Worked at *Richards Butler* London and Hong Kong 1976-92, became Partner in 1980. Joined *Davies Grant & Horton* in 1992 as Partner. Founded *Davies, Johnson & Co* May 1997.
Personal: Born 31st March 1951. Attended Nottingham University, taking LLB in 1972. Lives in Plymouth.

LOWE, James A.G.
Henderson Boyd Jackson WS, Edinburgh
(0131) 226 6881
Principal Maritime Partner.
Specialisation: Handles sale and purchase agreements, ship building and financing, ship registration as well as admiralty work, such as collisions, salvage, marine pollution, ship building and repair contract disputes. Author of "Maritime Securities" in the Stair Memorial Encyclopedia and various articles for the legal, marine and fishing industry press. Has presented papers at Law Society Maritime Law courses and to marine insurers on aspects of the Marine Insurance Act 1906.
Prof. Memberships: Law Society of Scotland, Honourable Company of Master Mariners, Writer to the Signet, British Maritime Law Association, Nautical Institute.
Career: Ship's Officer 1966-1980. Gained Master Mariners Certificate in 1976. Joined *Boyd Jameson WS* and qualified as a Solicitor in 1985. Became a Partner in 1986. Joined *Henderson Boyd Jackson* 1993 upon the merger of *Boyd Jameson* and *Henderson & Jackson* in 1993.
Personal: Born 14th April 1949. Educated at Edinburgh University 1980-84. Enjoys golf, shooting and fishing. Lives in Edinburgh.

MACLEAN, A. Duncan
Henderson Boyd Jackson WS, Edinburgh
(0131) 226 6881
Specialisation: All aspects of contentious admiralty work including collisions, salvage, marine pollution, personal injury claims, insurance disputes, ship building and repair disputes and general commercial disputes. Various aspects of "dry" work. Acts for P&I Clubs and marine insurers and also acts for various sectors of the fishing industry. Has presented papers to marine insurers on Marine Insurance Act 1906 and various other legal issues relevant to their operation.
Prof. Memberships: Law Society of Scotland, British Maritime Law Associaton, Writer to the Signet.
Career: Qualified 1988. Senior solicitor *Brodies WS* until 1994. Joined *Henderson Boyd Jackson* in 1994. Became a Partner in 1996.
Personal: Born: 1966. Lives in Edinburgh. Married with two daughters. Educated: Edinburgh University 1983-1987. Interests: Sports, the outdoors.

MACRAE, Keith G.
Mackinnons, Aberdeen (01224) 632464
Partner in Maritime and Litigation Department.
Specialisation: Acts for marine insurers, covering hull and machinery and P&I. Has particular experience in fishing vessel insurance and claims. Practice split between hull/ admiralty work (collisions, salvage, total loss and casualty investigation) and P&I claims (in particular personal accident/ employers liability claims from accidents on oil rigs and ships). Also handles oil pollution cases. Work includes on-site investigation on- and off-shore. Has a substantial case load in the Sheriff Court and Court of Session, acting for Defenders in personal injury claims and for Pursuers in ship repair and ship builders negligence claims and contractual disputes. Gave a paper to Law Society of Scotland's Second Maritime Law Seminar. Presents seminars on Marine Insurance to clients.
Career: Qualified in 1982. Joined *Mackinnons* in 1980, becoming a Partner in 1983.
Personal: Born 23rd May 1953. Attended Aberdeen University 1971-76 (MA(Hons)) and 1977-80 (LLB). Honorary Norwegian Consul in Aberdeen; Honorary Danish Vice-Consul in Aberdeen. Leisure interests include football, rock and jazz music and travelling. Lives in Catterline.

MAWDSLEY, David H.
Dibb Lupton Alsop, Liverpool (0345) 262728
0114 272 0202 (International)Partner in Marine Department.
Specialisation: All aspects of shipping and insurance law, including collision, salvage, general average, bill of lading and charterparty disputes, carriage of passengers and goods by sea, conditions of carriage, shipbuilding and ship finance documentation, marine insurance.
Prof. Memberships: Liverpool Underwriters' Association, Manchester Marine Insurance Association, London Maritime Arbitrators' Association, Association of Average Adjusters.
Career: Qualified in 1969. Partner with *Dibb Lupton Alsop* (and predecessor firms) since 1973.
Personal: Educated at Liverpool Institute High School and Liverpool University. Interests include fell walking, classical music, and all aspects of transport.

MAXWELL, M. John
Hill Dickinson, Liverpool (0151) 236 5400
Partner in Marine Department.
Specialisation: Specialises in shipping litigation, in particular on behalf of Shipowners, P&I Associations and Port Authorities. Marine accidents and casualty investigations for UK and foreign clients, collision, salvage, cargo claims and personal injury investigations, including in relation to Ro-Ro/passenger ferries. Charterparty and commercal disputes and Arbitrations.
Prof. Memberships: London Maritime Arbitrators Association
Career: Qualified 1969. Partner in Marine Department of *Hill Dickinson* since 1976. Notary Public.
Personal: Education: Sedbergh School. Liverpool University.

MILLS, Geoffrey G.
Mills & Co, Newcastle-upon-Tyne
(0191) 233 2222

MILLS, Stephen
Rayfield Mills, Newcastle-upon-Tyne
(0191) 261 2333

PHILLIPS, Raymond J.
Dibb Lupton Alsop, Liverpool (0345) 262728
Partner in Litigation Department.
Specialisation: Specific areas of practice include carriage of passengers and goods by sea and road, fire, toxic tort, crisis and disaster management, shipbuilding and repair.
Prof. Memberships: Liverpool Underwriters' Association, Manchester Marine Insurance Association, London Maritime Arbitrators Association.
Career: Qualified 1970. Partner with *Dibb Lupton Alsop* (and predecessor firms) from 1973.
Personal: Educated Liverpool Institute High School and Birmingham University. Interests include sailing, skiing, fell walking, chess and bridge.

RAYFIELD, Richard
Rayfield Mills, Newcastle-upon-Tyne
(0191) 261 2333

TAYLOR, Silas W.
Andrew M. Jackson & Co, Hull
(01482) 325242
Partner and Head of Admiralty and Shipping Department.
Specialisation: Main area of practice is marine casualty work. Acts on behalf of all main P&I clubs in collisions, salvage and major personal injury cases. Particular expertise in legal matters relating to the fishing industry. Also deals with disputes in respect of towage, pilotage, shipbuild and repair, etc. and claims under hull and machinery insurance. Has spoken on maritime law at conferences arranged by the Nautical Institute. Has contributed articles to 'Lloyd's Maritime and Commercial Law Quarterly', and the Nautical Institute's 'Seaways'.
Career: Qualified and joined *Andrew M. Jackson* in 1975. Became a Partner in 1980.
Personal: Born 3rd February 1953. Educated at Bedford Modern School 1964-71 and Hull University 1971-74. Leisure pursuits include fishing, badminton and bowling.

WAREING, W. David
Hill Dickinson, Liverpool (0151) 236 5400
Partner.
Specialisation: Representing shipowners and P & I Associations particularly with reference to crew and stevedore accident and occupational disease claims, also acting on behalf of liability underwriters in relation to pleasure craft accidents.
Prof. Memberships: Liverpool Underwriters Association, Manchester Marine Insurance Association, Liverpool Law Society General Committee Member.
Career: Qualified 1978 with *Hill Dickinson & Co.* Partner from 1982.

WESTON, John
John Weston & Co, Felixstowe
(01394) 282527

SPORTS LAW

See also Media & Entertainment and Advertising & Marketing

RESEARCH: In compiling the tables, we consider all the information available to us, paying particular regard to the market research carried out by our team of ten qualified lawyers. (The researchers' details are set out on page three.) The rankings, therefore, reflect the opinion of the marketplace as revealed by systematic and objective research: see page four. (Our research is audited every year by the British Market Research Bureau.)

OVERVIEW: The same three firms as last year remain at the top in London: Denton Hall because of the expertise of Adrian Barr-Smith; Farrer & Co for the experience of Charles Woodhouse and rising star, Karena Vleck, and Townleys for its niche practice and volume of work. Freshfields and Nicholson Graham & Jones have moved up the tables due to the popularity of Raj Parker at the former and Warren Phelops at the latter. Christine Bowyer-Jones of Moorhead James and Caroline Temperton of Charles Russell enter the tables on recommendation from their contemporaries. Ashurst Morris Crisp and Harbottle & Lewis also enter the lists. Outside London, Maurice Watkins of James Chapman, Peter McCormick of McCormicks and Richard Alderson of Edge & Ellison are the best known personalities in the sports field.

Work in the field ranges from intellectual property, corporate, broadcasting and sponsorship to disciplinary and regulatory advice to personal injury.

LEADING FIRMS · LONDON

DENTON HALL
FARRER & CO
TOWNLEYS

BIRD & BIRD
HERBERT SMITH

CHARLES RUSSELL
EDWARD LEWIS
FRESHFIELDS
MAX BITEL, GREENE
NICHOLSON GRAHAM & JONES

HIGHLY REGARDED FIRMS

Clintons
Collyer-Bristow
Russell Jones & Walker

Epstein Grower & Michael Freeman
Harbottle & Lewis
Lawrence Graham
Memery Crystal
Moorhead James
Wedlake Bell

Ashurst Morris Crisp
Davies Arnold Cooper
Field Fisher Waterhouse
Hammond Suddards
John Bowden Trainer & Co
Keene Marsland
Lovell White Durrant
Mishcon de Reya
Payne Hicks Beach
The Simkins Partnership
Simmons & Simmons
Theodore Goddard

LONDON

Denton Hall (4ptnrs/3assts) Including arguably *the* leading sports lawyer, *Adrian Barr-Smith* ("clearly at the top," "effective," "great clients"). Practice is complemented by the planning department whose clients include Chelsea Football Club. **Clients/Work:** Ongoing work for FA Premier League. Acting for England and Wales Cricket Board re Cricket World Cup 1999. Acting for Manchester 2002 Ltd re Commonwealth Games.

Farrer & Co (5ptnrs/1asst) The "eminent" *Charles Woodhouse* heads the department and he remains at the top of the field. *Karena Vleck* ("impressive," "active") is highly thought of and moves up the tables. **Clients/Work:** Acting for BAF re application to strike out Diane Modahl's claim. Assisting Central Council of Physical Recreation and British Olympic Association re formation of Sports Dispute Resolution Panel. Acting for UK Athletics 98 Ltd in acquisition of assets from BAF.

Townleys (4ptnrs/16assts) Founded in 1983, this is the only firm to specialise solely in sports law. *Nicholas Couchman* and *Stephen Townley* are two of the best known personalities in the firm. *Jonathan Higton* is also highly regarded. *Darren Bailey* has moved into the leaders table. **Clients/Work:** Successfully representing Formula One against subsidiary of Sony in computer games infringement case. Advising UK Sports Council re choice of venue for UK Sports Institute. Report on European Sponsorship market for European Commission.

Bird & Bird (1ptnr/3assts including *Justin Walkey,* and *Felicity Reeve* who moves up into the leaders) **Clients/Work:** Represents Greg Rusedski and Stefan Edberg re sponsorship, endorsement, appearances and tax planning. Advises the Football Association on all commercial matters, including new kit arrangements and the new national stadium. Acts for the Interpublic Group of Companies.

Herbert Smith (5ptnrs from the litigation and company depts) Strong reputation across the board for commercial, broadcasting, litigation and disciplinary matters. *Mark Gay* ("great technical knowledge") is particularly recommended for his work for the FA and the IAAF, and has been in the public eye recently acting for the ASA in the Hamilton Bland Enquiry. **Clients/Work:** Acted for West Ham United on recent reorganisation. Acted for Pilkington plc re sponsorship of Pilkington Cup. Advised on creation of new British American Racing Formula One team.

Charles Russell (3ptnrs/2assts, with *Patrick Russell* spending the most time on this area – about 70%). *Robin Bynoe* and *Caroline Temperton* (new entry) spend only a small proportion of time in this field but have been particularly recommended. **Clients/Work:** Advising the Jockey Club re horse and jockey doping issues and defending Jockey Club decisions in court. Also acts for Hurlingham Polo Association.

Edward Lewis (3ptnrs/3assts) Including *Michael Breen* (best known for his work for Damon Hill) and *Brian Moore* (former Harlequins, England and British Lions player and known particularly for the insurance and personal injury slant to his sports work). **Clients/Work:** Damon Hill's new contract with Jordan Grand Prix Ltd. Bridgend Rugby Club's incorporation and successful offer for shares. Action between players from Gloucester and Rosslyn Park Rugby Union clubs for alleged assault.

Freshfields (1ptnr/2assts, more as required) "Clear-thinking" *Raj Parker* is primarily an insurance lawyer, but also has an excellent reputation in the sports field. **Clients/ Work:** Advising the FA re the Premier League Inquiry into the improper use of agents in football transfers and financial irregularities including 'bungs'. Acting for the FA in disciplinary proceedings against Bruce Grobbelaar and Hans Segers following their acquittal on criminal charges. Also involved in arbitration for the Olympics in Sydney in 2000.

Max Bitel, Greene *Nicholas Bitel* is "one of the established names in this field." **Clients/Work:** Include Wimbledon Championships, Ryder Cup 1999, London Marathon and George Graham (ex-Arsenal manager).

Nicholson Graham & Jones (4ptnrs/ 4assts) *Warren Phelops* ("bright," "talks a good game," "active") moves up the tables. **Clients/Work:** English First Division professional rugby clubs joint venture with RFU. Acted on behalf of Mohammed Al Fayed re investment in Fulham Football Club. Restructuring and finance raising for London Welsh RFC.

Clintons (2ptnrs/2assts) *Philip Stinson* has "great industry knowledge" and is developing a sports practice in conjunction with Clintons' established media practice. **Clients/Work:** Acts mainly for individuals including players, agents and sponsors. Recently handled separation agreements for footballers; tax issues for racing drivers and a youth millennium project.

Collyer-Bristow (1ptnr/1asst) *Alan Burdon-Cooper* has acquired a new assistant to help particularly on the IP and sponsorship aspects of sports law. **Clients/Work:** Sale of The Sponsorship Group to IPG. Advising on the London Triathlon. Acts for many top sports agencies.

Russell Jones & Walker (4ptnrs/2assts

– all p/t) *Paul Kitson* heads the national sports unit and is known for personal injury actions as well as commercial and sponsorship work. **Clients/Work:** Acted for Victor Ubogu re the Simon Fenn ear biting incident. Acts for the Professional Footballers Association (PFA). Represents individual sports personalities in football, rugby and snooker.

Epstein Grower & Michael Freeman (2ptnrs/4assts) The well-known *Mel Goldberg* heads the team. **Clients/Work:** Hans Segers; Darren Pitcher; Stan Collymore.

Harbottle & Lewis (4ptnrs/2assts) A new entry this year following recommendation from other practitioners. **Clients/Work:** Advising Ryder Cup Committee re alteration of the team selection procedure and subsequent dispute with Miguel Martin. Acting for Loftus Road in negotiation of Wasps' sponsorship and kit agreements. Advising Audi Sport re their British Touring Car Team agreement with Volkswagen.

Lawrence Graham (3ptnrs including *Charles Ouin*/3assts) **Clients/Work:** Cardiff Arms Park; Barry Hearn; Football Licensing Authority.

Memery Crystal *Peter Crystal* and *Lesley Gregory* handle sports law within the company/commercial dept. **Clients/Work:** Lennox Lewis. Wembley National Stadium – football sponsorship. Clipper Ventures – Ofex float and sponsorship of yacht race.

Moorhead James (3ptnrs) *Benedict Moorhead* remains well respected and *Christine Bowyer-Jones* joins the table for the first time having been recommended for her "knowledge and clarity."

Wedlake Bell (2ptnrs: 1 p/t: 1asst p/t) *Jonathan Cornthwaite* handles mainly sports-related broadcasting issues. **Clients/ Work:** Report to Department of Culture, Media & Sport on major spectator sports. Sponsorship agreement for Surrey County Cricket club. Advice to Racecourse Holdings Trust on merchandising programme.

Ashurst Morris Crisp (6ptnrs/12assts - none f/t) **Clients/Work:** Sponsorship agreements for Wimbledon Tennis Championship, Professional Cricketers Association and Dunlop Slazenger. Represented Jim McKenzie re his dismissal as chief executive of the World Professional Billiard and Snooker Association.

Davies Arnold Cooper (1ptnr/2assts – p/t) **Clients/Work:** Kieron Brady v Sunderland FC. Ian Knight v Gary Bennett & Chester City. McCord v Swansea City & J. Cornforth.

Field Fisher Waterhouse Richard Bagehot has retired which may weaken the sports practice, but this may be offset by the merger with Allison & Humphreys which has introduced some sports/broadcasting work. **Clients/Work:** Advises Amsport (insurance provider for sports professionals). Advised Ebbw Vale RFC and Welsh

international Mark Jones in disputes with Welsh Rugby Union. Advised in the WRU Golden Share Dispute.

Hammond Suddards (4ptnrs including *Brian Eagles*/ 6assts – none f/t) **Clients/ Work:** Acting for Umbro in sponsorship litigation with Steve McManaman and in sponsorship deals with Alan Shearer, Michael Owen and David Seaman. Advised NM Rothschild & Sons Ltd as sponsor to Sunderland AFC's flotation. Advising directors of Bournemouth FC re insolvency of the club.

John Bowden Trainer & Co *Nick Trainer* is a sole practitioner deriving his reputation from his work for Terry Venables. **Clients/Work:** Mainly represents individuals. Recently acted for footballer Marcus Gale against Wimbledon and for Jamie Stewart at his FA drugs hearing.

Keene Marsland (2ptnrs/1asst – both p/t) **Clients/Work:** Formation of Boxing Charity and other work for British Boxing Board of Control. Reconstitution of womens' tour and contracts for the Solheim Cup for the European Ladies Golf Association.

Lovell White Durrant (3ptnrs/9assts – none f/t) Sports work is handled in conjunction with the intellectual property department. **Clients/Work:** Advising Mars re sponsorship of English and Scottish football teams at World Cup 98. Acting for the Sports Council re their bids to build the National Stadium at Wembley. Establishing a national youth football tournament.

Mishcon de Reya (2ptnrs) **Clients/Work:** Successful appeal on behalf of Diane Modahl against doping allegations. Concluding agreements for West Indies Cricket Board on the licensing of rights to broadcast tours. Advising West Indies

Cricket Board and United Cricket Board of South Africa on staging of World Cup 1999.

Payne Hicks Beach (1ptnr/other assts as required) The partner handling sports law here is a former international yachtsman. **Clients/Work:** Acts for Olympic medal winner, Lawrie Smith, re sponsorship agreements. Advises Edward Warden-Owen re America's Cup campaigns. Represents Spirit of Britain Ltd.

The Simkins Partnership Sports work is handled from the various media depart-

ments. **Clients/Work:** Sports agencies; national regulatory bodies; rugby clubs.

Simmons & Simmons (9ptnrs/19assts – none f/t) **Clients/Work:** Advising Charterhouse Development Capital re acquisition of its 37% stake in Sheffield Wednesday FC. Advises Williams Grand Prix Ltd in litigation. Advising the MCC re sponsorship issues at Lords. Also developing a sports/immigration law specialism.

Theodore Goddard Clients/Work: ISL Marketing AG; British Horseracing Board.

LEADERS' PROFILES · LONDON

BAILEY, Darren
Townleys, London (0171) 713 7000
Partner.
Specialisation: Representation of domestic and international sports governing bodies on a wide range of issues including doping, general disciplinary matters, constitutional structures, liability, insurance issues and the application of risk management programmes. Also advises on commercial issues in sport, including sponsorship and television, freedom of movement and competition matters (domestic and European) and defamation in sport. Successfully represented the International Tennis Federation in High Court proceedings bought by Mats Wilander and Karel Novacek; successfully represented the promoter of Rugby World Cup in defamation proceeding against Business Age Magazine. Editor Sports Law Administration and Practice.
Prof. Memberships: Officer of the British Association for Sport and the Law, The Law Society.
Career: Stoneham School: Windsor and Maidenhead College, University of Birmingham, Partner in 1998. (F.A. Coach 1992).
Personal: Former footballer turned Coach with a keen interest in all sports.

BARR-SMITH, Adrian
Denton Hall, London (0171) 320 6501
email: abs@dentonhall.com
Partner in Media and Technology Group.
Specialisation: Main area of practice is sport, covering broadcasting contracts, licensing and merchandising, event regulation, official supplier contracts and disciplinary matters. Also covers media finance, film and T.V. production and distribution. Has acted for the FA Premier League, Commonwealth Games Federation, England and Wales Cricket Board and Scottish Rugby Union. Hon. Legal adviser to Sports Aid Foundation. Consulting Editor 'Law and the Business of Sport' (Butterworths, 1997). Contributor to 'International Media Law' and 'Copinger and Skone James on Copyright'. Tutor at the Film Business School, Madrid. Member of the Panel of Arbitrators of the American Film Marketing Association.
Prof. Memberships: Design & Artists Copyright Society (Honorary Secretary).
Career: Qualified in 1977. Solicitor at *Rubinstein Callingham* 1977-79. Legal Director of Artlaw Services 1980-81; Joined *Denton Hall* in 1982, becoming a Partner in 1986.
Personal: Born 1952. Emmanuel College, Cambridge, 1970-73. Governor of Sports Aid Foundation. Leisure pursuits include cricket, golf and film. Lives in London.

BITEL, Nicholas
Max Bitel, Greene, London (0171) 354 2767

BOWYER-JONES, C.M.
Moorhead James, London (0171) 831 8888
Partner in Litigation Department.
Specialisation: Main areas of practice are litigation and employment. Advises on a wide range of sports related matters including doping control issues and health and safety. Acts for the UK Sports Council and the English Sports Council. Also lectures.
Prof. Memberships: British Association for Sport and The Law, Employment Lawyers Association, Law Society.
Career: Qualified 1985. Co-founded *Moorhead James* in 1992.
Personal: Born in 1959. Educated Howells School, Denbigh and St Hilda's College, Oxford.

BREEN, Michael M. G.
Edward Lewis, London (0171) 404 5566
Specialisation: Partner, Corporate and Commercial Department, *Edward Lewis*. As head of the firm's Sports Unit, generally recognised as one of the UK's leading sports lawyers, advising on all related areas of the law including commercial contracts, intellectual property issues, merchandising rights and sponsorship agreements. Strong profile in the athletics sector where he has acted for Linford Christie and Colin Jackson and in professional motor racing where he acts for Damon Hill and has acted for the Grand Prix Drivers Association. Other recent instructions include the England Rugby Football Union, Harlequins RUFC and the swimmer and world record holder, Mark Foster. Acted on the First Sino-British soccer meet in Beijing, China.
Prof. Memberships: Member of the British Association for Sport and Law; Holborn Law and Law Society Member; Member of the Fundraising Committee for the Down's Syndrome Association.
Career: Articled *Robert Gore and Co*; qualified 1988; Assistant Solicitor *Robert Gore and Co* 1988-1989; Partner *Robert Gore and Co* 1989-1993; Partner *Edward Lewis* 1993 to date.
Personal: Born 1962, married, lives in Wormley, Surrey. Rathmore Grammar School, Belfast; University College of Wales, Aberystwyth (LL.B. Hons); College of Law, Guildford. Leisure interests include motor racing and classic sports cars; sport and fitness, particularly rugby and skiing; oenology.

BURDON-COOPER, Alan R.
Collyer-Bristow, London (0171) 242 7363
Specialisation: Sponsorship in sports, arts and TV; licensing and merchandising. During the past year he has advised: The Prudential, in connection with the acquisition of rights to and the organisation of the Prutour; Esprit Marketing Limited in relation to the London Triathlon; Xerox Limited in connection with their sponsorship of the Rugby World Cup 1999; Hyder plc in connection with their sponsorship of the Millennium Stadium in Cardiff.
Prof. Memberships: Member of the Executive Committee of the Institute of Sports Sponsorship.
Career: Articled at *Collyer-Bristow*, qualified 1968, partner 1969.
Personal: Born 1942. Educated at Oundle School (1955-61), Emmanuel College, Cambridge (1964 MA LLB). Governor of the Rose Bruford College of Speech and Drama. Liveryman of the Worshipful Company of Dyers. Leisure pursuits include music, sport and gardening. Lives near Hemel Hempstead.

BYNOE, Robin
Charles Russell, London (0171) 203 5000
Email: robinb@cr_law.co.uk
Partner in Intellectual Property Group.
Specialisation: Main area of practice is information technology, including multimedia and media work, including merchandising, sponsorship, film production and distribution, video and other publishing and franchising. Deals with sports authorities and sporting litigation. Co-author of the book 'Franchising' (FT Law and Tax: 1995). Author of numerous articles, including for the American Bar Association, Franchise Law Journal, Corporate Counsel, and the Journal of Brand Management. Presents numerous in-house and commercial conferences.
Prof. Memberships: British Association of Sport and the Law, INTA.
Career: Qualified in 1973, having joined *Jaques & Co.* (now *Eversheds*) in 1971. Joined *Charles Russell* as a partner 1996.
Personal: Born 1st June 1948. Attended Oxford University 1967-70. Founder member of Felix the Wrestler. Lives in London.

CORNTHWAITE, Jonathan P.
Wedlake Bell, London (0171) 395 3122
Head of Intellectual Property.
Specialisation: Sports law, including broadcasting, media, copyright, trade and service marks, passing off, designs, technology licensing, pharmaceuticals and publishing. Also covers competition law, including restrictive practices, unfair competition, UK and EU

competition and anti-trust regulations. Has handled major television contracts for leading sporting associations in tennis and rugby football. Author of 'Intellectual Property and the Internet' and 'Marketing Law that Matters'; also publishes updates on intellectual property law.
Prof. Memberships: Law Society, City of Westminster Law Society, Competition Law Association, The Intellectual Property Lawyers' Association, The Licensing Executives' Society.
Career: Qualified in 1979. Joined *Wedlake Bell* in 1987, becoming a Partner in 1989.
Personal: Born 19th June 1954. Attended St Paul's School and the Universities of Oxford and Cambridge. Leisure interests include history, philately, tennis and languages. Lives in Strawberry Hill, Twickenham.

COUCHMAN, Nicholas
Townleys, London (0171) 713 7000
Partner and Head of Sports Marketing and IP Group.
Specialisation: Contract and intellectual property aspects of sports marketing in over 15 sports (particularly football and rugby union), including sponsorship contracts, character marketing, personality endorsement agreements, the development and protection of sports brands, and advertising law. Particular specialism in sports rights piracy, counterfeiting and 'ambush marketing' (prevention and litigation), and advising on protection and licensing of sports brands. Also involved in development of new sponsorship projects in music, culture and the media. Clients include/ have included major sports events (e.g. Rugby World Cup, European Rugby Cup, Royal Ascot, Formula 1), corporate sponsors (Carlsberg-Tetley, Times Newspapers, Nationwide Football League), sports organisations (the England and Wales Cricket Board, the English and UK Sports Councils), clubs (Spartak Moscow) and several communications/ sponsorship agencies. Author 'Ambush/ Parasitic Marketing and Sport' and numerous trade press articles. Regular lecturer at sports media law conferences.
Career: Qualified 1990. Partner *Townleys* 1992.
Personal: Born 1965. Attended Devonport High School and Nottingham University. French speaker.

CRYSTAL, Peter
Memery Crystal, London (0171) 242 5905
See under Corporate Finance: 1-125 Fee Earners, p. 228

EAGLES, Brian
Hammond Suddards, London
(0171) 655 1000
See under Media & Entertainment: Film, p. 565

GAY, Mark E.
Herbert Smith, London (0171) 374 8000
Partner in Commercial Litigation Department.
Specialisation: Has substantial experience in both the contentious and non-contentious aspects of sports law. Considerable expertise in advising various sporting bodies on constitutional issues.
Career: Qualified in 1988. Became a Partner at *Herbert Smith* in 1995.
Personal: Educated at Lady Margaret Hall, Oxford.

GOLDBERG, Mel
Epstein Grower & Michael Freeman, London
(0171) 723 3040
Partner and Head of Sports Division.
Specialisation: Has represented numerous international football players and clubs, Olympic Gold medallists and several world champions in boxing, squash, tennis and athletics. Has arranged the transfers of several million pound football players from one club to another, and the transfer of European International footballers to the UK. Drafted the Constitution of the International Squash Players Association (ISPA) and was Vice-Chairman of the British Olympic Travel Association to the Moscow Olympic Games in 1980. Has written several articles for leading sports magazines both in the USA and the UK, and has appeared on several television programmes both in the UK and in the USA. Has spoken on the subject of sports law at seminars and conferences.
Prof. Memberships: Sports Lawyers Association (USA) and British Association for Sport & Law (Manchester).
Career: Qualified in 1963. Founded own firm under the style of *Douglas Goldberg & Co* in 1968 before working in the USA. On his return became a Consultant with *Bird & Bird* in the City. Now a Partner with *Epstein Grower and Michael Freeman*. Listed in 'Who's Who in the Law'.
Personal: Educated at St. John's College, Cambridge 1957-60 (MA Hons. in Law 1960). Past President of Hampstead Rotary Club. Leisure interests include tennis, squash and swimming. Lives in London. Married, 3 children.

GREGORY, Lesley
Memery Crystal, London (0171) 242 5905
Specialisation: Corporate and Commercial matters, including corporate finance, acquisitions and disposals, Official List and AIM, capital raising, joint ventures and commercial sports law, including licensing, sponsorship, merchandising and catering contracts. Acted for Wembley Stadium in the negotiations for Littlewood's sponsorship of the F.A. Cup Final and the England Team. Acted for Charlton Athletic F.C.; advised on contractual arrangements to acquire Rights to the Monte Carlo Tennis Tournament; involved in advising Wembley on the new National Stadium.
Prof. Memberships: The Law Society, Women in Management, CISCO and the British Association for Sport and Law.
Career: Articled *Courts & Co*. Qualified 1983; solicitor *Memery Crystal* 1983-1988; Partner since 1988.
Personal: Born 1960; resides London.

HIGTON, Jonathan
Townleys, London (0171) 713 7000
Partner.
Specialisation: All television and related media sports matters, in particular sports rights acquisition, representation and distribution agreements throughout the World.
Career: Called to the Bar 1984. Joined *ITV Sport* in 1987 with responsibility for all the ITV Network's sports agreements, including FA and the first exclusive Football League television agreement. Joined *Townleys* 1991. Responsible for all television and related issues both domestically and internationally for sports clients and specialist sports television

distributors/agents. Has advised on projects including Rugby World Cup, Davis Cup, Fed Cup, 5 – Nations Rugby, Heineken Cup, Asian Football Programme, Table Tennis World Championships, International Cricket and worldwide distribution of both domestic and international football and other domestic and international sports rights and programming.
Personal: Born 1958. Attended Wycliffe College, Reading University and the University of Westminster.

KITSON, Paul
Russell Jones & Walker, London
(0171) 837 2808
Specialisation: Plaintiff personal injury specialist. Has successfully pursued numerous claims for injuries on the sports field for footballers and rugby players. Has spoken at seminars and conferences on sports law and regularly writes for sports magazines and legal journals.
Prof. Memberships: Committee member of British Association of Sport & the Law; Member of the Association of Personal Injury Lawyers; Member of Law Society Personal Injury Panel.
Career: Partner with *Russell Jones & Walker* since 1992.

MOORE, Brian C.
Edward Lewis, London (0171) 404 5566
Specialisation: Insurance Litigation partner specialising in general commercial disputes, negligence claims and sports related matters in the areas of professional negligence, product and public liability, employers' liability and personal injury. His personal injury expertise has been put to increasing use in Rugby Union where fellow players, referees and clubs have become open to the threat of legal action as a result of the 'professionalisation' of the sport and the implications of the Ben Smolden case.
Prof. Memberships: FSA.
Personal: Well known for his 'leisure' interests having played Rugby Union for Harlequins and represented England at all senior and full international levels, gaining 64 caps and 3 grand slams in all. Otherwise known as 'The Pit Bull'. His other interests remain wine, opera and art.

MOORHEAD, Benedict R.K.
Moorhead James, London (0171) 831 8888
Founding Partner and sports law specialist.
Specialisation: More than ten years experience as a specialist in sports law. Advises on a range of sports-related matters including merchandising agreements, sponsorship, doping control issues, sports stadia and sports medicine. Acts for the English Sports Council, the U.K. Sports Council, the Sports Council Trust, National Sports Medicine Institute and other governing bodies, and is legal advisor to various sports clubs, racing teams and charities. Has written articles on sponsorship in sport. Also lectures.
Prof. Memberships: Law Society, Statute Law Society, British Association for Sport and the Law.
Career: Qualified in 1983 while at *Blyth Dutton* and became a Partner of the firm in 1987 and of *Lawrence Graham* in 1991. Founded *Moorhead James* in 1992.
Personal: Born in 1958. Attended Marlborough College and holds a BA in Law (1981). Chairman of Wellesley House and St Peter's Court Educational Trust. Plays cricket, golf, tennis and skiis. Lives in London and Kent.

OUIN, Charles

Lawrence Graham, London (0171) 379 0000
Specialisation: Partner in the Company and Commercial department specialising in commercial contracts and general corporate work. Practice covers sales of businesses and companies, MBOs, venture capital, corporate restructuring, joint ventures and tenders. Also deals with public sector contracts and externalisations. Advised the Government on the establishment of the National Lottery.
Career: Qualified 1973. Assistant solicitor, *Holloway Blount & Duke* 1973-76. Partner, *Blyth Dutton* 1976-92. Partner, *Lawrence Graham* since 1992. Non-executive director of William Sinclair Holdings Plc.
Personal: Educated at Sherborne School and the College of Law. Leisure pursuits include sailing, fishing, architecture and theatre.

PARKER, Raj D.

Freshfields, London (0171) 936 4000
See under Insurance & Reinsurance: Reinsurance, p. 469, 520

PHELOPS, Warren

Nicholson Graham & Jones, London (0171) 648 9000
Specialisation: Business issues relating to sport: in particular, corporate finance (including flotations, takeovers, mergers and acquisitions), corporate structuring and strategy, company, commercial and media (including television, sponsorship and merchandising).
Prof. Memberships: Sits on executive committee of Institute of Sports Sponsorship. Law Society, ESCA, British Association of Sport and the Law, the Royal Television Society.
Career: *Slaughter and May*: trainee solicitor, March 1990-1992; Assistant Solicitor, March 1992-June 1993. *Nicholson, Graham and Jones*: Assistant Solicitor, June 1993 to date. Partner and Head of Sports Group, January 1996 to date.
Personal: Fanatical sports player (rugby, football, cricket (for any teams that will have him), squash and tennis) and watcher, especially rugby (Wasps), football (Arsenal) and cricket (Middlesex).

REEVE, Felicity

Bird & Bird, London (0171) 415 6000
Partner in Company Department and Sports Group.
Specialisation: Advises on the commercial exploitation of sports related rights: in particular, event staging and promotion, ambush marketing, sponsorship, and licensing. Increasingly involved in sports related acquisitions, financings and joint ventures. Other area of practice is general commercial law principally multimedia or intellectual property related.
Prof. Memberships: Law Society.
Career: Qualified in 1993 whilst at *Macfarlanes*. Joined *Bird & Bird* in 1994 and became a partner in 1998.
Personal: Born 1968. Educated at School of St Helen and St Katherine and Lady Margaret Hall, Oxford. Lives in London.

RUSSELL, Patrick

Charles Russell, London (0171) 203 5018
Partner in Litigation Department.
Specialisation: Acts for sporting regulatory authorities and clubs in the regulatory and disciplinary field. Experienced in public law, judicial review and restraint of trade. Also handles contentious work related to the London insurance and reinsurance market. Acted in judicial review decisions for the Jockey Club and The Law Society, and in ex parte A.H, Aga Khan, and Swindon Town FC.
Prof. Memberships: Law Society, British Association for Sport and Law.
Career: Joined *Charles Russell* in 1976 and qualified in 1979. Became a Partner in 1980. Director of the Solicitors Indemnity Mutual Insurance Association Ltd. Contributing Editor, 'Cordery on Solicitors'.
Personal: Born 11th May 1952. Educated at Ampleforth College 1965-70 and University College, Oxford 1971-74. Recreations include golf, sailing, tennis and motorcycling. Lives near Towcester, Northants.

STINSON, Philip

Clintons, London (0171) 379 6080
Partner in Entertainment Department.
Specialisation: The law as it applies to marketing and broadcasting with particular reference to the business of sport. Clients include sponsorship and other marketing consultants and agencies, television production companies, sponsoring and sponsored organisations, governing bodies and organisers of major charitable and other events. Often advises in-house legal departments of sponsoring organisations. Author of articles in British Association for Sport and Law Journal and in numerous trade journals. "Highly Recommended" as a sports law practitioner in Legal Business Magazine. Author of section on Sport in Practical Commercial Precedents.
Prof. Memberships: Member of Advisory Board and Officer of the British Association for Sport and Law.
Career: Articled and qualified with *Richards Butler* 1988-91. Joined *Collyer-Bristow* in 1991, Partner 1995. Joined *Clintons* as a partner in 1996.
Personal: Born 16th May 1962. Educated at Marlborough College and Worcester College, Oxford. Enjoys real tennis, football and the arts. Lives in London.

TEMPERTON, Caroline

Charles Russell, London (0171) 203 5000
Specialisation: Main area of practice trade marks and in particular disputes relating to comparative advertising such as Macmillan Magazines Limited v RCN Publishing Company Limited; copyright; designs; trade secrets and related litigation; entertainment, media and sports related disputes.
Prof. Memberships: Associate member of ITMA. British Association of Sport and Law.
Career: Qualified in 1991 at *Wragge & Co*, Birmingham. Joined *Jacques & Lewis* (now *Eversheds*) in 1992 and *Freshfields* in 1995. Joined *Charles Russell* as a senior assistant in 1996. Attended Oxford University and Chester College of Law.
Personal: Born 6 May 1965. Lives in London. Scuba diving and vintage cars.

TOWNLEY, Stephen

Townleys, London (0171) 713 7000
Partner and Founder.
Specialisation: Main area of practice covers sports marketing. Assists and advises on the creation, management and exploitation of sports marketing rights, including sponsorship, television, new media and merchandising. Has been involved in this capacity with the Rugby World Cup, Olympic Games, Soccer World Cup, Tour de France and Davis Cup. Co-author of 'Sponsorship Sport Art and Leisure' and various other publications. 1995 *Townleys* appointed official legal rights consultants to GAISF (General Association of International Sports Federations). General Counsel to the International Tennis Federation.
Prof. Memberships: IBA (former Chairman of Sports Committee), International Committee SLA, ANZSLA, Sponsorship Association (Founder), European Sponsorship Consultants Association (Co-founder). 1995 Arbitrator – Court of Arbitration for Sport, Switzerland.
Career: Qualified in 1978, having articled at *Ingledew Brown Bennison & Garrett*. Company Secretary and legal adviser for Hawker Siddley Diesels 1978-79, then in-house counsel to the Société Monégasque de Promotion Internationale West Nally SA 1979-83. Founded *Townleys* in 1983.
Personal: Born 15th December 1952. Took an LLM in 1975. Leisure interests include basketball, tennis and game fishing. Lives in London and Grosmont.

TRAINER, Nick

John Bowden Trainer & Co, London (0181) 482 1003

VLECK, Karena

Farrer & Co, London (0171) 242 2022
Partner in the Commercial team.
Specialisation: Principal area of practice is sports law providing specialist advice for sports governing and representative bodies, individual sports people, sports charities and sponsors. Disciplinary procedures and rules, sports doping cases, formations and advice on constitutions both corporate and unincorporated, merchandising, sponsorship, representation agreements. Other areas of practice are intellectual property generally, charity law and company and commercial law. Appointed Director of UK Athletics 98, the interim governing body for athletics in the UK. Acted for the British Athletic Federation in relation to Diane Modahl and Paul Edwards. Other clients include the Central Council of Physical Recreation, the British Paralympic Association and the All England Netball Association.
Prof. Memberships: Committee Member of British Association for Sport and Law.
Career: Qualified in 1992 after articles at *Farrer & Co*. Partner 1998.
Personal: Born 10th March 1967. Educated at Millfield School, Street, Somerset 1983-85 and St John's College, Cambridge 1986-89. Lives in London.

WALKEY, Justin

Bird & Bird, London (0171) 415 6000
Partner in Company Department and Head of Sports Group.
Specialisation: In-depth knowledge covers the media, sports and entertainment industries. Particular expertise includes sports marketing (creation, protection and exploitation of events; sale and purchase of events; constitutional and disciplinary matters; TV, video, film and publishing rights deals; sponsorship; licensing and merchandising) and individual representation (general business management, tax planning, endorsement and appearance contracts). Founder of Sportslink Worldwide. Other area of practice is general corporate and commercial law, both nationally and internationally, primarily in the areas of media and communications to include digital media,

telecommunications, broadcasting, advertising, publishing and promotion. Recent high profile work in football for the FA in the staging and marketing of Euro'96 and the New National Stadium.
Prof. Memberships: Law Society, Licensing Executives Society.
Career: Qualified in 1984. Joined *Bird & Bird* the same year and became a partner in 1987.
Personal: Born 1957. Attended Sherborne School, then the University of Westminster. Lives in London.

WOODHOUSE, Charles
Farrer & Co, London (0171) 242 2022
Partner in the Commercial team.
Specialisation: Sports law. Honorary Legal Adviser, Commonwealth Games Council for England and Legal Adviser to numerous sports governing bodies, representative bodies and charities. Has advised on the formation, structure and constitutions of many governing bodies, also on disciplinary procedures and rules, handling sport doping cases, eligibility issues and sponsorship and licensing agreements. Co-author of the Palmer Report 'Amateur Status and Participation in Sport' (1984). Has written and

spoken at numerous conferences on sports law topics, including the Law Asia 1993 Conference in Sri Lanka on "The role of the lawyer in sport" and UK Sports Council 1996 Conference on ethical issues in drugs and sport.
Career: Joined *Farrer & Co* in 1964. Qualified 1966, became a Partner in 1969.
Personal: Born 6th June 1941. Attended Marlborough College, McGill University, Montreal and Peterhouse, Cambridge. Leisure interests include cricket and golf. Director, Santos USA Corp. Chairman, Rank Pension Plan Trustee Ltd. Trustee, LSA Charitable Trust. President Guildford Cricket Club. Chairman Sports Dispute Resolution Panel. President, British Association for Sport and Law.

The SOUTH

HIGHLY REGARDED FIRMS
THE SOUTH

Trethowan Woodford Southampton

Alsters Bristol
David Jeacock Swindon
Matthew McCloy & Partners Newbury
Osborne Clarke Bristol
Pickworths St. Albans
Stones Cann & Hallett Exeter

Trethowan Woodford (Southampton) *Keith Wiseman* has ongoing work for the FA and is particularly busy this year with the World Cup.
   Alsters (Bristol) (2ptnrs/1asst) **Clients/Work:** Representing all first division professional rugby players in the EPRUC and

RFU negotiations. Also advises county cricketers, league footballers and golf clubs.
   David Jeacock (Swindon) Principal, *David Jeacock*, specialises in disciplinary and doping control issues. **Clients/Work:** Works in the athletics sector and in disabled sport.
   Matthew McCloy & Partners (Newbury) *Matthew McCloy* specialises in equine law and is known for his work for jockeys.
   Osborne Clark (Bristol) (2ptnrs/2assts) *Andrew Braithwaite* is developing a "solid practice." **Clients/Work:** Restructuring of the PGA's disciplinary procedure. Infringement action for Ryder Cup Ltd. Stock exchange listing for Bolton Wanderers FC.
   Pickworths (St. Albans) (1ptnr/1asst – p/t) **Clients/Work:** Involved in Senna manslaughter trial in Italy. Act for David

LEADING INDIVIDUALS • SOUTH

BRAITHWAITE Andrew Osborne Clarke
COURTENAY-STAMP Bronwen Stones Cann & Hallett
JEACOCK David David Jeacock
MCCLOY Matthew Matthew McCloy & Partners
WISEMAN Keith Trethowan Woodford

SEE PROFILES AT END OF THIS SECTION

Coulthard and Dario Franchitti.
   Stones Cann & Hallett (Exeter) 4ptnrs/3assts in the personal injury and travel team handle sports-related injuries) *Bronwen Courtenay-Stamp* is particularly well-known for her niche ski-ing injuries practice. **Clients/Work:** Handle plaintiff and defendant accident cases. Act for all major travel insurers including Countrywide Assistance and Alpha Assistance.

MIDLANDS and EAST ANGLIA

HIGHLY REGARDED FIRMS
MIDLANDS AND EAST ANGLIA

Edge & Ellison Birmingham
Greenland Houchen Norwich
German & Soar Nottingham

Edge & Ellison (Birmingham) (1ptnr/1asst plus consultant Sir Bert Millichip) *Richard*

Alderson ("safe pair of hands") has "by far the highest profile and the largest practice in the Midlands." **Clients/Work:** Flotations of Aston Villa and Leicester City FC. Complaint to the European Commisssion on behalf of the Football League re loss of UEFA Cup place. Administration of British Athletics Federation.
   Greenland Houchen *Trevor Nicholls* spends 75% of his time on sports related work, mainly football. **Clients/Work:** Advises FA Premier League working party. Acted for Norwich City since 1983, but they

now have an in-house solicitor so this work has decreased.
   German & Soar *John Gardiner* handles the sports-related work.

LEADING INDIVIDUALS
MIDLANDS AND EAST ANGLIA

ALDERSON Richard Edge & Ellison
NICHOLLS Trevor Greenland Houchen
GARDINER John German & Soar

SEE PROFILES AT END OF THIS SECTION

The NORTH

James Chapman & Co (Manchester) *Maurice Watkins* ("unparalleled experience in the football field") moves up to the top band. He was recently invited to Brazil to participate in an international conference concerning football as a business and the new Pelé law. *Nicholas Marshall* is increasingly active in the field. **Clients/Work:** Acting for Manchester United in its joint venture with Granada and Sky in forming MUTV and in a sponsorship deal with Sharp. Advising Leicester City FC on its acquisi-

tion by Soccer Investments plc. Advising Formula 3 team on its contract with an engine supplier.
   McCormicks (Leeds) *Peter McCormick* heads the team and is known to have great clients. *Richard Cramer* has particular expertise in rugby league. **Clients/Work:** Advised Australian Rugby League in dispute with Rugby Football League re World Cup.
   George Davies & Co (Manchester) Team includes *John Hewison* and *Mark Hovell*. **Clients/Work:** Professional Footballers Association; Cricket Association; Basketball Association.

LEADING FIRMS • THE NORTH

JAMES CHAPMAN & CO Manchester
MCCORMICKS Leeds
GEORGE DAVIES & CO Manchester
GORNA & CO Manchester
WALKER MORRIS Leeds

HIGHLY REGARDED FIRMS

Addleshaw Booth & Co Manchester
Zermansky & Partners Leeds

   Gorna & Co (Manchester) *Michael Morrison* handles sports work in conjunction with media and employment work. **Clients/Work:** Represented Leicester City FC in arbitration against Wolverhampton Wanderers FC re transfer of Zeljko Kalac. Acted for various FC managers in the negotiation and documentation of their contracts. Represented Joe Royle (Everton FC) and other managers in claims arising from their dismissal.

Walker Morris (Leeds) *Chris Caisley* heads a team of 3 assts. **Clients/Work:** Represents ASICS, David Batty and Super League Europe Ltd.

Addleshaw Booth & Co (Manchester) The sport and entertainment unit is part of the commercial dept. **Clients/Work:** Advising Robert H Lowe plc re licensing of World Cup 1998 clothing. Advising Adidas re Prince Naseem's sponsorship contract. Also act for Allsports and Umbro.

Zermansky & Partners (Leeds) (4ptnrs) **Clients/Work:** Working for Rugby Football League for over 50 years. Also advises Tai Chi organisation, British Amateur Rugby League Association and individuals in sports administration and management.

LEADING INDIVIDUALS THE NORTH
MCCORMICK Peter McCormicks
WATKINS Maurice James Chapman & Co
CAISLEY Christopher Walker Morris
CRAMER Richard McCormicks
HEWISON John George Davies & Co
HOVELL Mark George Davies & Co
MORRISON Michael Gorna & Co

UP AND COMING
MARSHALL Nicholas James Chapman & Co

SCOTLAND

LEADING FIRMS · SCOTLAND
ANDERSON STRATHERN WS Edinburgh
HENDERSON BOYD JACKSON WS Edinburgh
ALEX MORISON & CO WS Edinburgh
BURNESS Glasgow
BENNETT & ROBERTSON Edinburgh
HARPER MACLEOD Glasgow

Anderson Strathern WS (4ptnrs/2assts p/t) *John Kerr* and his firm move up the tables following a successful year. **Clients/Work:** Sponsorship and product endorsement agreements for Scottish Rugby Union. Successful petitions on behalf of member of Scottish Amateur Boxing Association who had been wrongfully suspended. Incorpora-

tion of Scottish Games Association as limited liability company.

Henderson Boyd Jackson WS (1ptnr/1asst) *Alistair Duff* maintains his reputation as a leader in the field, acting particularly for individuals. **Clients/Work:** Successful judicial review of British Ice Hockey Association decision on behalf of a player. Advising GW Weir over South African incident. Advice to numerous international rugby players.

Alex Morison & Co WS (ptnr *Alan Grosset* and 2assts p/t) **Clients/Work:** Stirling County RFC Incorporation. Scottish Gymnastics Incorporation. Boroughmuir RFC contract work.

Burness (3 ptnrs/3 assts) *Andrew Sleigh* heads the team. **Clients/Work:** Sponsorship of Scottish National team and home matches. Successfully prosecuted the SRU's case against Christophe Lamaison following the

French international game in Paris this year. Advising Derek Paterson in contract dispute with West Hartlepool RC.

Bennett & Robertson *David Bennett* and his firm have been newly recommended by other Scottish firms.

Harper Macleod (3ptnrs including *Stephen Miller*/1asst) **Clients/Work:** Advises Glasgow Hawks RFC. Taken judicial review proceedings against Scottish Football Association.

LEADING INDIVIDUALS SCOTLAND
DUFF Alistair Henderson Boyd Jackson WS
GROSSET Alan Alex Morison & Co WS
KERR John Anderson Strathern WS
BENNETT David Bennett & Robertson
SLEIGH Andrew Burness
MILLER Stephen Harper Macleod

LEADERS' PROFILES · REGIONS

ALDERSON, Richard A.
Edge & Ellison, Birmingham (0121) 200 2001
Partner and Head of Sports Unit.
Specialisation: Sole area of practice is sport administration and associated commercial activities, advising governing bodies on television, sponsorship, discipline and constitutional matters. Also works for industry, covering sport and event sponsorship and broadcast sponsorship. Acts for The Football League, British Athletic Federation and other sports bodies. Working in this sector since 1987.
Prof. Memberships: British Association for Sport and the Law.
Career: Qualified in 1976 with *Edge & Ellison*, becoming a Partner in 1981.
Personal: Born 17th July 1951. Attended Bristol University 1970-73. Trustee of St Giles' Hospice (Special interest: charity shops). Leisure interests include tennis and Aston Villa. Lives in Birmingham.

BENNETT, David A.
Bennett & Robertson, Edinburgh
(0131) 225 4001

BRAITHWAITE, Andrew
Osborne Clarke, Bristol (0117) 923 0220
See under Intellectual Property, p. 486

CAISLEY, Christopher
Walker Morris, Leeds (0113) 283 2500
Chairman of the firm and Head of Commercial Litigation Department and Sports Law Group.
Specialisation: Main area of practice is sports law. Work includes contract negotiations and disputes, personality merchandising, licensing agreements, and acting for sports personalities, clubs and associations. Other area of practice is commercial litigation. Cases have involved acting for the RFL in defence of High Court proceedings brought for relief against an alleged unfair restraint of trade by an international rugby player, bringing into question the entire system for the transfer of players between countries; the prosecution of actions by football league managers against their former clubs subsequent to dismissal; and applications for declaratory relief by Football League players for release from their contracts. Chairman of Bradford Bulls RLFC and of The Super League, creating regular contact with the media.
Prof. Memberships: The Rugby Football League, The British Association for Sport and the Law.
Career: Qualified in 1978, becoming a Partner in 1979. Member of the *Walker Morris* International Committee; also Practice Development Partner. Former member of the RFL Board of Directors.
Personal: Born 2nd June 1951. Attended Grange Boys Grammar School, Bradford. Vice-

Consul for the Netherlands Yorkshire and Derbyshire. Leisure interests include running, reading and an interest in most sports. Lives in Lancashire.

COURTENAY-STAMP, Bronwen
Stones Cann & Hallett, Exeter
(01392) 666 777
See under Travel, Tourism & Package Holidays, p. 778

CRAMER, Richard G.
McCormicks, Leeds (0113) 246 0622
Partner.
Specialisation: Substantial experience in sports law and in particular Rugby League, Rugby Union and Football, dealing with both contentious and non-contentious aspects. Acts for Keighley Cougars RLFC, Wakefield Trinity RLFC, and a number of top rugby league players such as Gary Schofield. Recently acted for the Australian Rugby League in its dispute with the Rugby Football League in respect of the 1995 World Cup. More recently appointed to act for the Association of First and Second Division Rugby League clubs in their attempt to obtain a new independent broadcasting contract. Attracted international recognition when acting for Keighley Cougars in the case against the Rugby League following the Rupert Murdoch deal. Dealt with the acquisition of the West

Yorkshire Ice Hockey Super League Franchise for, Leeds Sporting plc, owners of Leeds United F.C. Also deals with high value commercial litigation matters and insolvency cases, both personal and corporate, acting for a number of insolvency practitioners.

DUFF, Alistair M.
Henderson Boyd Jackson WS, Edinburgh
(0131) 226 6881
Litigation/Sports Partner.
Specialisation: Handles all types of sports work including damages actions between players, team contracts with players, commercial agreements regarding sponsorship/merchandising and other related matters. Has published numerous articles for journals on sporting matters and is regularly quoted in the national press.
Prof. Memberships: Law Society of Scotland, Writer to the Signet, Committee Member and on the Advisory Board for the British Association for Sport and the Law.
Career: Qualified Solicitor since January 1982 and Litigation Partner since 1987. Joined *Henderson Boyd Jackson* as a Litigation Partner in 1992 and has specialised in Sports Law since 1994.
Personal: Personal: Born 2 November 1956. Educated at George Watsons College, Edinburgh, Hamilton College, New York USA (Scholarship) and Aberdeen University 1976-79. Has completed 13 marathons including New York, Boston and Mount Everest and has taken part in 3 climbing trips to the Himalayas. Ambition – to climb K2. Married to a doctor, has 2 young children and lives in Edinburgh.

GARDINER, John
German & Soar, Nottingham
(0115) 916 5200
Partner in Litigation Department.
Specialisation: Main area of practice is sports law. Has acted for a number of well-known sporting figures in soccer, rugby league, rugby union and tennis, over contract disputes, injury claims and the liability of the coach for injury suffered. Also handles advocacy, medical negligence, child care and, recently, education. Author of numerous articles in the local and trade press. Has received his Higher Courts Criminal Proceedings qualification.
Prof. Memberships: Law Society, AVMA, British Association for Sport and the Law, Law Society's Panel of Child Care Specialists.
Career: Qualified 1970 Articled at *Perry Parr & Ford* 1964-69, then joined *Seviers* in Derby until 1971. Joined *German & Soar* in 1971, becoming a Partner in 1973.
Personal: Born 26th April 1946. Attended Becket School, Nottingham. Leisure interests include rowing, badminton, walking, cycling and writing. Lives in Beeston, Nottingham.

GROSSET, Alan G.
Alex Morison & Co WS, Edinburgh
(0131) 226 6541
Specialisation: Sports Law. Legal advisor to the Scottish Sports Association and numerous other sports governing bodies, representative bodies and charities. Has advised on constitutional issues for governing bodies and sports clubs as well as disciplinary procedures and sponsorship agreements. Centrally involved in the campaign for rate relief for

amateur sports clubs in Scotland and led the successful valuation appeal 'Lasswade RFC and Others v. Lothian Regional Assessor'. Has written and spoken at several conferences on sports law topics including the 1992 Barcelona Sport and the Law Conference on "Nations without Countries and Sport". In 1997/98 has acted in governing body and Premier Division rugby club incorporations.
Prof. Memberships: Law Society of Scotland, Society of Writers to Her Majesty's Signet; British Association for Sport and the Law.
Career: Educated Royal High School and Edinburgh University. Joined *Alex Morison & Co* in 1965, qualified 1967, became a partner in 1970.
Personal: Born 18 January 1942. Leisure interests include tennis and golf, past Chairman Scottish Sports Association; past President Scottish Lawn Tennis Association; past Captain Duddingston Golf Club Limited; currently Vice-Chairman of the Scottish Sports Council and the Scottish Director of the Sports Dispute Resolution Panel Ltd.

HEWISON, John
George Davies & Co, Manchester
(0161) 236 8992
Partner in Commercial Department and Managing Partner.
Specialisation: Principal area of practice is sports law, representing sportsmen (mainly professional footballers) in relation to employment contracts, management agreements, taxation disputes and sponsorship contracts. Also handles general company, commercial and EC law. Director of PFA Financial Management Limited and PFA Enerprises Ltd. Clients include the Professional Footballers Association, PFA Financial Management Ltd and numerous professional footballers. Has also advised the Cricketer's Association, and the Basketball Players Association. Defended Alan Shearer against FA charge for alleged kicking incident. Speaker on trades unions in sport at conferences on player power and on the future of sports entertainment.
Prof. Memberships: Law Society, British Association for Sport and the Law.
Career: Qualified in 1973. Assistant and then Partner (1978) with *George Davies & Co* since qualification.
Personal: Born 16th November 1948. Educated at Manchester Grammar School 1960-68 and Nottingham University 1968-71 (LL.B). Plays golf and follows most sports, particularly football and cricket. Lives in Lymm, Cheshire.

HOVELL, Mark
George Davies & Co, Manchester
(0161) 236 8992
Specialisation: Partner in the Commercial Department specialising in sports law. Acts for various professional footballers on contractual, employment, taxation and insolvency related matters. Advises the Professional Footballers Association and the Basketball Players Association on commercial and trade union related matters.
Prof. Memberships: British Association for Sport and Law. Licensed Insolvency Practitioner.
Personal: Educated at UMIST (BSc Hons Management Science) 1986-1989. Leisure pursuits include football, golf, squash and skiing. Born 7th January 1968. Lives in Manchester.

JEACOCK, David
David Jeacock, Swindon (01793) 854111
Sole principal specialising in sports law.
Specialisation: Main area of practice is sports law, concentrating on constitutional and drug related issues, but including intellectual property issues arising out of sport. Also handles company and commercial matters. Major clients include sports governing bodies. Formerly Secretary to British Athletics Federation Drug Advisory Committee. Currently General Secretary of and Legal Adviser to British Athletics League and Legal Adviser to the Sportshall Athletic Federation. Drugs Officer for British Wheelchair Sport Foundation and International Stoke Mandeville Wheelchair Sports Federation.
Prof. Memberships: Law Society, British Association for Sport & Law.
Career: Qualified in 1970. Deputy Legal Adviser to Burmah Castrol 1973-81. Group Solicitor to Fisons PLC 1981-83. Established own practice in 1984.
Personal: Born in 1946. Educated at Exeter College, Oxford 1964-67. Member Swindon Harriers. Lives in Wootton Bassett.

KERR, John N.
Anderson Strathern WS, Edinburgh
(0131) 220 2345
Specialisation: Handles general corporate and commercial work, including acquisitions and disposals, corporate finance, general contract work agency and distribution and EU law. Specialises in Sports Law. Acts as lead partner for Scottish Rugby Union as well as other governing bodies and clubs; involved with constitutional issues, sport sponsorship and product endorsement, discipline and drug related issues as well as the provision of new facilities.
Prof. Memberships: Founder member of Financial and Legal Advisory Panel of the Scottish Sports Council; Law Society of Scotland; Society of Writers to Her Majesty's Signet; Member of British Association of Sport and Law.
Career: LL.B (Hons) Edinburgh 1978; Qualified 1980, Partner in *Strathem & Blair* in 1984 and became partner in merged *Anderson Strathern* in 1992.
Personal: Born 1956. Lives in Edinburgh. Enjoys sport at all levels.

MARSHALL, Nicholas
James Chapman & Co, Manchester
(0161) 828 8000
Specialisation: A partner in the Company/Commercial Department handling a wide range of matters. Main area of practice is sports related including licensing and merchandising, sponsorship agreements, event regulation and media agreements. Also advises on company and corporate finance matters for sports clients including football club flotations and advises sports persons on a variety of matters, including the protection and exploitation of their intellectual property rights. Also involved in overseas soccer transfers.
Career: Qualified in 1988. Joined *James Chapman & Co.* in 1995 and became a partner in 1996.
Personal: Born 22nd January 1964. Attended the University of Reading.

MCCLOY, Matthew
Matthew McCloy & Partners, Newbury
(01635) 551515
Senior Partner specialising in bloodstock and equine law.
Specialisation: Handles all aspects of legal work relating to bloodstock (i.e. racehorses)

and horses generally including litigation, commercial, disciplinary tribunals, sales and purchases, breeding, ownership, etc. Also deals with sports, media and sponsorship law. Covers sports disciplinary and sponsorship work (including drug related cases), television rights (negotiation and contract) and sponsorship (negotiation and contract). Important cases handled include Naughton v. O'Callaghan and R v. The Jockey Club ex parte His Highness the Aga Khan. Clients include various bodies in racing e.g. The Jockey's Association, Federation of Bloodstocks Agents, breeding societies, etc. Also acts for the World Professional Billiards and Snooker Association and other sports bodies. Has had various articles published in magazines and newspapers, has appeared on television many times and given a number of lectures (e.g. Asian Racing Conference in Manila, 1993). Charge-out rate is £150 per hour.
Prof. Memberships: Law Society.
Career: Qualified in 1974. Member of the Horseracing Advisory Council 1982-93. Society of International Thoroughbred Auctioneers since 1980 and the International Cataloguing Standards Committee since 1982. Member of the Racing Development Committee since 1992 and Director of the British Horseracing Board from 1995-1998.
Personal: Born 7th May 1948. Educated at Radley College 1962-68 and Sandhurst 1968-70. Leisure interests include riding, fishing, shooting and gardening. Lives in Newbury.

MCCORMICK, Peter D.G.
McCormicks, Leeds (0113) 246 0622
Senior and Managing Partner.
Specialisation: Substantial area of practice is Sports Law (allied to portfolio of media and entertainment) with considerable experience in both contentious and non – contentious aspects. Acts for Leeds United Football Club and is a Director. Dealt with the multi-million pound sale of the Club to Caspian Group plc (now Leeds Sporting Plc) and continues to advise the Club and its associated/subsidiary companies and Leeds Sporting Plc. Acts for a number of other sports clubs and bodies and professional sportsmen. Also has expertise in horse-racing, particularly disciplinary hearings and appeals; the only British lawyer to have appeared before the Jockey Club of Germany. Also handles matters relating to Rugby (Union and League), athletics, cricket, boxing, shooting (advises renowned Yorkshire Shoot) and motor racing. Clients include Jenny Pitman, Freddie Trueman, Howard Wilkinson, Gordon Strachan, George Graham, Gary McAllister, David Batty, Lee Chapman, Castleford RLFC, Wakefield Trinity RLFC, Keighley Cougars RLFC, Otley RUFC, Henry Wharton and a number of other personalities and the Football Supporters Association. Negotiates contracts for personal benefits, corporate sponsorship and ancillary matters including broadcasting and deals with a substantial workload of intellectual property matters (registration, protection and enforcement). Advised on IP enforcement in Euro '96 tournament for UEFA and World Cup 1998. Deals with litigation cases including defamation and complaints relating to broadcasting and the Press. Acted in the Leeds United/Stuttgart UEFA Disciplinary Hearing in Zurich. Also has twenty years experience of tax investigation and enquiry work, both Revenue and VAT and serious fraud cases. Handles

increasing amount of commercial work acting for DFS Furniture Company plc, the F.A. Premier League, Iceland Frozen Foods plc, Polypipe plc, The Duke of Edinburgh's Award, Hays plc and others. Columnist with the Yorkshire Post. Writes for a number of publications. Lectures widely. Awarded the Higher Courts (Criminal Proceedings) Qualification in 1994. Resident legal expert on Radio Leeds, Yorkshire Television and the Yorkshire Post. Member of the Legal Working Party of the FA Premier League.
Prof. Memberships: Member of the Economic, Law and Tax Committee of the Leeds, Bradford and North Yorkshire Chambers of Commerce.
Personal: Vice President of the Outward Bound Trust. Chairman of the Yorkshire Young Achiever Awards. President of Harrogate Town F.C.; Member of the Editorial Board, I.P. Business Magazine; Member of the Advisory Board, Sports Law Centre, Anglia University; Head of Sports Law Unit, EuroLink for Lawyers; Solicitor to The Duke of Edinburgh's Award; Member of the Legal Working Party of the F.A. Premier League.

MILLER, Stephen C.
Harper Macleod, Glasgow (0141) 221 8888
Partner in Commercial Litigation Department.
Specialisation: Main area of practice is employment and sport. Acted in McGuire -v- Scottish Football Association (Judicial Review). Managerial clients include Tommy McLean, Iain Munro, Alex McLeish, Jock Brown and Eamonn Bannon. Handled Paul Gascoigne's Scottish legal affairs. Acts for Agent who became first Scottish Licensed Players' Agent. Assisted in re-draft of Scottish Rugby Union's Disciplinary Procedures. Frequent lecturer.
Prof. Memberships: Born 5th January 1965. Attended Aberdeen University 1983-88, LLB (Hons) DipLP. Leisure interests include football, tennis, cycling and calligraphy. Lives in Glasgow.

MORRISON, Michael
Gorna & Co, Manchester (0161) 832 3651
Specialisation: Vast experience in wide range of Sport related business including Employment Law (contentious and non-contentious), Endorsement and Sponsorship Agreements, exploitation and protection of Intellectual Property Rights, Media Law including Publishing and Defamation, and Administrative Law. Involved mainly in Professional Football, has acted for clubs, Players and Agents dealing with a variety of work including Contracts, Claims, Commercial Agreements, Arbitrations and Disciplinary Tribunals. Has acted for the majority of Managers of Premier League and Football League Clubs for more than 25 years in the negotiation and documentation of Contracts, in the pursuit and settlement of Unfair and Wrongful Dismissal Claims and in Disciplinary proceedings. Other sports include Rugby (both codes), swimming, golf and tennis.
Prof. Memberships: Law Society, British Association for Sport and Law, Manchester Law Society, Employment Lawyers Association.
Career: Educated at Cardinal Langley School at St Ambrose College, joined Gorna & Co in July 1967. Admitted 1974. Partner 1976.
Personal: Married 1971 with 2 sons. Enthusiastic but incompetent golfer, passionate Manchester United supporter, member of the Variety Club of Great Britain.

NICHOLLS, Trevor
Greenland Houchen, Norwich (01603) 660744
Specialisation: Sports law and administration in the context of professional football. Member of The F.A. Premier League Legal Working Party.
Prof. Memberships: British Association for Sport and the Law.
Career: Qualified 1971. Partner 1972. Senior Partner 1988.
Personal: Born 2nd May 1935. Educated Norwich School. Formerly in the Colonial Police before a second career in the law. Lives in Norfolk.

SLEIGH, Andrew F.
Burness, Glasgow (0141) 248 4933
Specialisation: Has acted as external legal advisor to The Scottish Football Association and for Clansmen Sporting Club/ T. Gilmour, Scotland's leading boxing promoter. Particular expertise in constitutional and administrative law aspects of governing body activities.

WATKINS, Maurice
James Chapman & Co, Manchester (0161) 828 8000
Partner in Commercial Department.
Specialisation: Sports law specialist. Solicitor for Manchester United Football Club since 1976 and, since flotation, Manchester United PLC. Also an adviser to the Football Association Premier League and other Premier and Football League clubs on various matters. Member of the Premier League Legal Working Party. Premier League representative on Association of European Union Premier Football Leagues. Also solicitor to a number of first-class sportsmen and administrators. Director of Manchester United Football Club plc and Manchester United PLC. Has handled numerous high-value soccer transfers at home and abroad. Represents clubs and players before UEFA and FA Disciplinary bodies and International and League Compensation Tribunals and negotiates TV, sponsorship and advertising contracts. Former lecturer in law at Manchester University. Extensive media experience on football related matters.
Prof. Memberships: Chairman of the British Association for Sport and the Law.
Career: Qualified in 1966. Solicitor for the Co-operative Insurance Society 1966-68. Joined James Chapman & Co as a Partner in 1968.
Personal: Educated at Manchester Grammar School 1952-60 and University College, London (LLB and LLM). Secretary of Manchester Homeopathic Clinic and trustee of The Football League Limited Players Retirement Income Scheme. Interests include cricket, soccer and tennis. Lives in Cheshire.

WISEMAN, Keith St. J.
Trethowan Woodford, Southampton (01703) 321000
Senior Partner.
Specialisation: Sports Law in general and Football in particular. Child Care work (member of Children Panel since its inception).
Career: Qualified 1970. Partner 1973. Under-Sheriff of City of Southampton. Coroner for City of Southampton and New Forest.
Personal: Born 23 May 1945. Oxford University Tennis Blue. County Tennis player. Vice Chairman of Southampton Football Club. Chairman of The Football Association. Rotary member.

TAX (CORPORATE) AND VAT

RESEARCH: In compiling the tables, we consider all the information available to us, paying particular regard to the market research carried out by our team of ten qualified lawyers. (The researchers' details are set out on page three.) The rankings, therefore, reflect the opinion of the marketplace as revealed by systematic and objective research: see page four. (Our research is audited every year by the British Market Research Bureau.)

OVERVIEW: No lawyer likes their department to be described as a "service department" but to a large extent the standing of a tax department depends on the overall strength of the firm. To attract the best minds, tax departments need a high and constant throughput of quality work. The top five firms in London have the largest corporate departments so it is no surprise that they have the leading tax practices. Tax departments and key players do attract work in their own right, sometimes significant amounts, but one or two brilliant individuals do not make a leading practice.

There is nothing to show between the three leading firms except numbers. Clifford Chance and Allen & Overy are seen to be closing the gap but most agree they still have a little way go.

Corporate tax is less well developed in the regions, particularly in Scotland, but it is a growing area. Pinsent Curtis led the way in Birmingham and Leeds, whilst Hammond Suddards and the other large regional firms are now muscling in on the action, often by poaching each others teams.

VAT continues to be a growth area, albeit one where the accountants have the upper hand. Lovell White Durrant has been particularly successful in establishing itself as a leader although most firms have a capability. London firms which were recommended for VAT only and not mentioned for direct tax are listed on page 749. Our main tax tables are a composite of the firms' standing in VAT and direct tax.

An index to all profiles is on page 67.

LEADING FIRMS · LONDON

FRESHFIELDS
LINKLATERS
SLAUGHTER AND MAY

ALLEN & OVERY
CLIFFORD CHANCE

HIGHLY REGARDED FIRMS

Ashurst Morris Crisp
Herbert Smith
Lovell White Durrant
Macfarlanes
Norton Rose
Simmons & Simmons

S J Berwin & Co
Cameron McKenna
Theodore Goddard
Travers Smith Braithwaite
Watson, Farley & Williams
Wilde Sapte

Berwin Leighton
Clyde & Co
Denton Hall
Dibb Lupton Alsop
Field Fisher Waterhouse
Hammond Suddards
Nabarro Nathanson
Olswang

LONDON

Freshfields (14ptnrs/19assts in London with a further 17 lawyers throughout Europe) "Seen everything, done everything, know (almost) everything." *Richard Ballard* (noted for his "sheer intellectual firepower" and "for making a big impression in a short time") heads a department ranked number one in Euromoney's International Tax Review ahead of the big six accounting firms. The all important strength in depth includes *Roger Berner* ("consistently good"), *Francis Sandison* (recreating himself as a VAT specialist heading a unit with 4 other fee earners), *Sarah Falk* ("fantastic, sensible and creative"), *Stephen Hoyle* ("a commercial negotiator with a clear idea of tax problems – other lawyers enjoy working opposite him"), the up & coming *Murray Clayson* and six other recommended names. **Clients/Work:** Red-

land PLC in defence of the £1.8bn takeover by Lafarge. LVMH in relation to the merger between Guinness and Grand Met. MCI Communications ($20bn proposed merger wth BT, then on the competing bids by WorldCom and GTE).

Linklaters (11ptnrs/20assts in London, 2ptnrs/2assts in both New York and Paris, 1ptnr in Bangkok) "Technically excellent but not as colourful as Freshfields or Slaughters." *Tony Angel*, head of the department, "has the knowledge and experience to make the complex appear simple." Other leaders include *Guy Brannan, Mike Hardwick* ("a pleasant chap and excellent too"), *Mark Kingstone, Nikhil Mehta* ("comes across well"), *Tom Scott, Simon Clark* (one of the firm's 2 VAT experts – the other is the up & coming *Martin Lynchehan*) and *Yash Rupal*. **Clients/Work:** Demerger of Billiton from Gencor and new issue and listings. Pacifi-

corp/Energy Group. Undertaking a major partial exemption appeal for a company in the financial sector.

Slaughter and May (6ptnrs/circa 20assts) A reputation out-stripping the firm's size, in tax as in other areas. Whilst the high gearing (twice that of Linklaters and Freshfields) is seen as a weakness by other firms, it is described as a strength by Slaughters. And whatever the firm may lack in numbers it makes up in quality. *Stephen Edge* ("the legal world's Richard Branson: a bearded genius with a gift for publicity") remains the pre-eminent lawyer practising corporate tax. What Edge has that makes him so out of the ordinary is "a genuinely innovative mind and seemingly boundless and infectious enthusiasm." What he doesn't have is time. *Howard Nowlan* is almost as highly rated, described as "a superb lawyer; he has an encyclopedic knowledge of tax law but isn't weird with it." Other notable individuals are *Graham Airs, Tony Beare* ("a good chap to work with or against") and *Fiona Ferguson*. The firm also has 2 ex-Inland Revenue investigators. Clients/Work: The Grand Met/Guinness merger. The Reed Elsevier/Kluwer merger (which collapsed at the last minute). Continued work on the Hoechst appeal, now going to the ECJ.

Allen & Overy (6ptnrs/24assts) "As good as the best – if you get the right person." The least high profile of the large firms has taken a strategic decision to ratchet itself up in heavyweight tax partners and foot soldiers. Although financing work constitutes only 25% of the department's turnover, the perception persists that the practice is not as broad based as the others. *Patrick Mears* "a really decent chap with tremendous experience" heads the department which includes *Miles Walton* ("a skilful operator"), *David Lewis* and *Michael McGowan* ("explains esoteric points clearly"). This years new recruit is *Brenda Coleman* ("lucid and oozing common sense"). *Gill Gowtage* is up & coming in VAT. Clients/Work: Disposal by ICI of its polyesters and films businesses. Takeover by Yorkshire Holdings plc of Yorkshire Electricity. Secured financing of Canary Wharf. Flotation of Thompson Holidays.

Clifford Chance (20ptnrs/50assts worldwide, 14/32 in the UK) Strong in numbers, with many lawyers who would stand out as exceptional in any company, but taken as a whole still lacking the consistency and breadth of the top three. *Douglas French* ("a fair man and a pleasure to deal with") moves up a band. Others are *Michael Ehrlich, Jonathan Elman* ("exceptionally bright"), *Peter Elliott, Ross Howard, David Harkness* ("a solid and dependable adviser"), *Michael Wistow* ("sound and knowledgeable") and the up & coming *Etienne Wong*. Clients/Work: Advising the Burton Group plc on its demerger of Debenhams Department Stores. Advising Credit Suisse First Boston on its acquisition of the UK and European equities, equity capital markets and M&A advisory businesses of BZW from Barclays Bank Plc.

Ashurst Morris Crisp (4ptnrs/9assts) "Solid but not massively exciting." Three partners make the leader's list with a good amount of quality work coming through the door, particularly of the MBO kind. Stephen Machin has joined KPMG. The group is now headed by *John Watson*, a venture capital specialist. The other players are the "charming" *Sue Crawford* and *Ian Johnson*. Two lawyers concentrate on VAT work. Clients/Work: Acting for Legal & General Ventures on the

£600m buy-out of BTR's Polymer Products group. Advising Autolink Concessionaires (M6) plc on the £250m financing of the M6 Motorway extension. Acting for Chelsfield plc on the £90m acquisition of the Westbury hotels (London/New York).

Herbert Smith (4ptnrs/9assts) The team, "all of a high standard," are led by the "softly spoken but shrewd" *David Martin*. Other names are *Neil Warriner*, newly recommended for VAT and *Ross Fraser*. Lost Brenda Coleman to A&O. Clients/Work: Securitisation of embedded value insurance business for NPI. Advice to the regional electricity companies on the new pooled electricity supply scheme. Restructuring proposals for London & Continental.

Lovell White Durrant (6ptnrs/8assts) "Some of the most down to earth tax lawyers in London." Bulk of work (50/65%) is M&A related, but *Don Kelly* and the others also do property, project finance, investment etc. *Greg Sinfield* runs a high profile specialist indirect tax team. Clients/Work: Xerox's £1bn acquisition to increase its control of Rank Xerox to 100%. Barclays disposal of BZW to CSFB. Acting for Vickers on its disposal of Rolls Royce Motors to VW.

MacFarlanes (3ptnrs/4assts) "A solid department that more than pulls its weight." *Nigel Doran* has built up a respected practice in a short space of time. The team includes the "bright" *Ashley Greenbank* and the "exceedingly bright" *Mark Baldwin*. Whilst the weight of Mark's reputation is in VAT, he was also recommended for his corporate tax expertise. Clients/Work: Disposal of the UK and French healthcare businesses of Compagnie Générale des Eaux for £1.1bn to Cinven investors. Demerger of Saatchi & Saatchi businesses out of Cordiant plc. Establishment of Legal & General Industrial Property Fund.

Norton Rose (5ptnrs/10assts) A smaller team, but well established and regarded. Anchored in finance. *Christopher Norfolk* has "a tremendous and richly deserved reputation." *John Challoner* "makes you feel confident when he's on your side." *Isla Smith* is "effective if sometimes a little conservative in her thinking." Clients/Work: Advising Guinness in relation to its merger with Grand Met. Tax-based financing of telecommunications equipment to be used by the Orange group. Advising Spitalfields Development Group on the sale/development of land at Spitalfields to LIFFE.

Simmons & Simmons (6ptnrs/8assts in London) Joined by 2 new partners including *Edward Troup* (returning from his sojourn as special adviser to Ken Clarke at the Treasury and concentrating on the strategic side of things). The loss of Stephen Coleclough continues to provoke comment – "after all, a laid back tax lawyer is a rare animal" – but still a strong team that "never appears stretched." Trying to do more tax consultancy work of

pure transactional work. *Paul Hale* is well thought of, as is *Peter Nias*, an "effective communicator." Clients/Work: Acting for Bass Brewers Ltd on the Disposal of its 50% interest in Carlsberg-Tetley PLC to Carlsberg A/S. Advising Gallaher Group Plc on its US$3bn demerger from American Brands Inc. Major transfer pricing negotiations successfully completed for a pharmaceutical client.

SJ Berwin & Co (5ptnrs/9assts) A progressive and aggressive firm with a growing body of expertise. Leaders on limited partnerships with a fine reputation in property, venture capital and related areas. Clients sing *Simon Rose's* praises to his rivals, whilst *Heather Corbin* is another new entrant. Clients/Work: Acting for the partners in the Phoenix Partnership on the sale of Phoenix Securities corporate finance businesses to Donaldson Luftkin & Jenrette Inc. Acting for British Land PLC on the structuring of a joint venture with Rank Group PLC. Full taxation structuring advice to Phildrew Ventures and the purchaser on the MBO of the transport division of Hogg Robnson plc.

Cameron McKenna Respected people "who do the business" but not of the highest profile. Clients/Work: Restructuring First Ireland Investment Trust Ltd to narrow the discount at which it was trading to net asset value. Advising The Money Store, a US mortgage company, on the securitisation of its mortgage portfolio. Advising CBS on tax structuring for the Winter Olympics in Nagano.

Theodore Goddard (3ptnrs/5assts) *Tim Sanders,* "a delightful chap with a real breadth of knowledge" leads a decent practice that is "ticking over nicely." Clients/Work: Acting for Signet Group plc on their capital reorganisation and reduction. Advising Standard Chartered bank and the Brent Walker Bank Syndicate on the £700m disposal of the William Hill Group. Acting for Destec Energy in the Indian Queens power station leasing transaction.

Travers Smith Braithwaite (4ptnrs/7assts) Much of the firm's reputation in tax is bound up with *Alasdair Douglas*, now senior partner and spending only 20% of his time on tax matters. *Richard Stratton* is the other personality. Clients/Work: Tax planning on £1bn of MBOs, 8 flotations and on the private equity film finance for 'C15 – The Professionals' the film version of the 1970s TV series.

Watson, Farley & Williams (5prtns in London, Paris, Moscow and New York) "Two powerful individuals but not a throbbing practice." Pretty hot in asset financing rather than transactional work. *Christopher Preston* has "a wealth of experience in both direct and indirect tax," whilst *Oonagh Witty* is "more than able," if sometimes "a touch abrasive." Clients/Work: Acting for a plc on the judicial review of a decision by Customs & Excise to charge excise duty. Taking over the appeal to the High Court for a financial institution.

Wilde Sapte (6ptnrs/6assts) The bleed at Wilde Sapte continues. Following the departure of Russell Jacobs to an accountants, Andy Collins (not in our tax lists), "a top chap in asset finance," now heads a department lacking in big personalities but the remaining team are competent. **Clients/Work:** HMG (Dept. of the Environment) on the sale of the Housing Corporation Housing Association loan portfolio to NatWest. Bank of Scotland on the Securitisation of its first Shared Appreciation Mortgage™ loan portfolio. The Eastern Group in connection with the US lease financing of Peterborough power station.

Berwin Leighton (3ptnrs/3assts & 1 Tony Bunker) 40% property, 40% corporate. *John Overs'* team are well regarded in property matters. **Clients/Work:** Sale of British Shoe subsidiaries by Sears. Acquisition of the Irish food retailing businesses of Associated British Foods plc for £641m. Faro Seafood Customs Duty case at the European Court of Justice.

Clyde & Co A bit thin on the ground except for the "excellent" *Susan Ball,* "a focused and lucid tax lawyer."

Denton Hall (2ptnrs/2assts) The firm and *Jane Harger* are new entrants, with particular expertise in energy, media and telecoms related work. **Clients/Work:** Acting for APAX Ventures on Ginger Group's acquisition of Virgin Radio. Advising Dixons on the structure of its JV with Cellnet. Advising an insurance company on a transfer-pricing dispute regarding the insurance premium for a portfolio transfer.

Dibb Lupton Alsop (4ptnrs/5assts) Part of a large and respected national practice headed by an ex-Coopers partner. Handle international tax, corporate reorganisations, media and electronic commerce, leasing transactions as well as the normal M&A work.

Field Fisher Waterhouse (3ptnrs/ 2assts) Do not have a high profile in the field although *Nicholas Noble* has a reputation for financial products and financial security transactions. Advise many Japanese and Chinese companies. **Clients/Work:** Advising on the introduction of intermediary relief from stamp duty and stamp duty reserve tax for market-making intermediaries, stock lending and repo activities, and on tax aspects of financial products.

Hammond Suddards (1ptnr/4assts) *Chris Haan* leads the London tax department

that includes a French tax lawyer. Tax lawyers are also based in Manchester and Leeds, with the three centres operating as a single unit. **Clients/Work:** Demerger of Creative Publishing plc from Fine Art Developments plc. Acting for FKI plc on its £131m takeover of Bridon plc. Acquisition of Hero Drinks from Hero AG by Cott UK.

Nabarro Nathanson (3ptnrs/4assts) "A mixed bag." Losing Chris Cox to Beachcroft Stanleys has not helped. *Peter Kempster,* a chartered accountant, and recommended for property finance remains, as does *Michael Cant,* someone who "fully deserves his VAT and stamp duty reputation." **Clients/Work:** The Dartford and Gravesham PFI project. The AMP/Pearl Assurance and Chelsfield

joint venture. The formation of The Reading Oracle joint venture.

Olswang (2ptnrs/1assts) Only three fee earners (including *Kay Butler*) but all competent. The group handles film financing (approx. 20% of turnover) as well as the more usual corporate, property and employee benefits work. **Clients/Work:** Restructuring a £500m property investment fund for UK and US investors. Conducting a dispute with the Revenue on the deductibility of legal fees. Representing the British Film industry in negotiations with the Revenue on a new statement of practice.

Christopher Cox has moved from Nabarro Nathanson to Beachcroft Stanleys.

VAT ONLY

Ann L. Humphrey (1ptnr/1asst (p/t)) A sole practitioner specialising in VAT (60%), but also handles corporate tax work. Consultancy for firms with no in-house tax expertise. **Clients/Work:** Advice on the VAT liability of supplies of telecommunications services and air time to UK customers; the UK VAT treatment of car leasing and hire purchase; the liability to UK withholding tax in connection with a $15m issue of floating rate notes by a UK bank.

Mainprice & Co (1ptnr/2barristers/1asst) Do absolutely nothing but VAT with "a distinctly West End approach." *Hugh Mainprice* helped to draft the original VAT legislation. Undoubtedly one of the more interesting characters of the VAT world he has a solid client following.

Speechly Bircham (4ptnrs) When *John Avery Jones* "does his stuff he's as good as anyone" but not thought to be the active force he was. **Clients/Work:** Ashtead plc – agreed offer for Sheriff Holdings plc; reconstruction of PA Consulting Group's share capital.

Titmuss Sainer Dechert (3ptnrs/6assts) *Malachy Cornwall-Kelly* has a strong reputation in VAT as well as for Customs & Excise. *Mark Stapleton* is newly recommended for his "great technical ability and no nonsense approach." **Clients/Work:** Advice to Sears plc in conjunction with the sale of its shoe division disposals. A high profile international football transfer. Variety of complex property development projects.

LEADERS' PROFILES • LONDON

AIRS, Graham J.
Slaughter and May, London
(0171) 600 1200
Specialisation: Principal area of practice is corporate tax. Particular experience of privatisations, securitisations, mergers and acquisitions. Author of chapter on EC Direct Tax Measures in Tolley's Tax Planning.
Prof. Memberships: Member of The Law Society's Revenue Law Committee, The Law Society, European American Taxation Institute.
Career: Qualified in 1978 after articles at *Slaugher and May* and stayed at firm until 1980. Partner in *Airs Dickinson* 1980-1984. Returned to *Slaughter and May* 1984 and became a Partner in 1987.
Personal: Born 8 August 1953. Married Stephanie 1981. Educated Newport Grammar, Emmanuel College Cambridge.

ANGEL, Anthony L.
Linklaters, London (0171) 456 5636
Partner 1984. Head of Tax Department.
Specialisation: Over 19 years' experience in corporate tax work, especially capital markets, structured and international finance, mergers and acquisitions and international tax structuring. Responsible for the development of the firm's capital markets tax practice and many new financial products. Typical matters include domestic and international mergers and acquisitions, structured finance work and capital raising and complex market and derivative transactions. Member of the International Bar Association, Executive Committee of Capital Markets Forum. Qualified 1978.

AVERY JONES C.B.E., John
Speechly Bircham, London (0171) 353 3290
See under Trusts & Personal Tax, p. 784

BALDWIN, Mark
Macfarlanes, London (0171) 831 9222
Partner in Corporate Tax Group.
Specialisation: Handles all areas of indirect tax work, principally VAT, but also excise duties and customs duty. As well as general planning advice, he conducts litigation and has represented clients in the VAT and Duties Tribunal. He also practises in other business tax fields, principally property finance, development and investment, collective investment schemes and insurance. Has written articles on indirect tax topics in a number of journals. He is the European case note contributor to Devoil Indirect Tax Intelligence. Regular conference speaker.
Prof. Memberships: Law Society, VAT Practitioners Group.
Career: Qualified in 1987 Assistant Solicitor at *Freshfields* between 1987 and 1995, when he returned to *Macfarlanes* becoming a partner in May 1997.
Personal: Born 24 January 1963. German speaker.

BALL, Susan
Clyde & Co, London (0171) 623 1244
Partner and Head of Tax Department.
Specialisation: Main area of practice is corporate tax. Work covers tax aspects (including Stamp Duty) of corporate reorganisations, mergers, acquisitions and corporate disposals. Also handles taxation aspects of inward and outward investment for the UK and of new issues and flotations. Other area of practice is taxation of employees, including share schemes, ESOPs and employee benefits. Conducts occasional external and internal lecturing. Member of the Law Society Revenue Law Committee 1982-89 and Corporation Tax sub-committee 1995-. Co-Author of 'Gammie and Ball-Tax on Company Reorganisations' and 'Masters and Ball-Taxation of Expatriate Employees' (to be published 1999). Has written frequently on taxation topics.
Prof. Memberships: Law Society, City of London Solicitors Company, Law Society of New South Wales.
Career: Qualified in 1973. Worked at *Linklaters & Paines* 1971-89 (Partner 1981-89). Assistant

Solicitor at *Blake Dawson Waldron* in Sydney 1989-91; admitted in New South Wales in 1989. Joined *Clyde & Co.* as Deputy Head of Tax Department in 1993.
Personal: Born 3rd November 1948. Holds an MA (Oxon) from St Hugh's College, Oxford 1967-70.

BALLARD, Richard M.
Freshfields, London (0171) 936 4000
Partner and Head of Tax Department.
Specialisation: Specialises in corporate finance (including mergers, demergers, reconstructions and cross border transactions); tax-based and structured financing of all types, including cross border transactions; capital markets work including structured bond issues, hybrid instruments, repackaging and securitisation; derivatives transactions of all types; experience in Inland Revenue enquiries and in Commissioners and court litigation. Contributor to 'Tolley's Tax Planning' and 'Tolley's Company Law' and frequent contributor to tax journals and to various *Freshfields* publications.
Career: Qualified 1978. Became a Partner at *Freshfields* in 1984.
Personal: Born 1953. Attended Queens' College, Cambridge.

BEARE, Tony
Slaughter and May, London (0171) 600 1200
Specialisation: Corporate Tax. Qualified 1987. Partner 1994. Main area of practice is corporate tax and, in particular, structured finance, corporate finance and capital markets.
Prof. Memberships: The Law Society.
Personal: Born 30 November 1959. Educated at Durban High School, Haberdashers' Aske's, Elstree and St. Catharine's College, Cambridge and St Edmund Hall, Oxford.

BERNER, Roger F.
Freshfields, London (0171) 936 4000
Partner in Tax Department.
Specialisation: Head of International Tax Group. Main specialisations are cross border

corporate finance, including acquisitions, mergers, joint ventures and restructurings.
Prof. Memberships: The Law Society; City Solicitors' Company.
Career: Joined *Freshfields* 1976; Partner *Stevens & Bolton* 1982-90; Partner *Freshfields* 1993.
Personal: Born 16th March 1952. 1974 Clements Inn Prize. Main interests include music, books and sport.

BRANNAN, Guy C.H.
Linklaters, London (0171) 456 5690
Partner in Tax Department.
Specialisation: Specialises in corporate tax matters. Main areas of practice include mergers and acquisitions, reorganisations and reconstructions, capital markets and finance transactions, EC tax law and tax litigation. Member of the permanent Tax Commission on the Union Internationale des Avocats. Member of the American Bar Association (Taxation Section). Co-editor of Taxation of Companies and Company Reconstructions.

BUTLER, Kay
Olswang, London (0171) 208 8888
Partner, Head of Tax Unit.
Specialisation: Spans the spectrum of tax work including acquisitions and disposals, corporate reorganisations, partnership refinancing, capital and industrial building allowances, sale and lease backs, film investment, employee incentives, devising new financing products, and VAT and other tax disputes. She has lobbied the EC Commission, the Inland Revenue and HM Customs and Excise for changes in the law. She was also the only legal representative on the British Screen Advisory Counsel's committee which negotiated the statement of practice concerning the new relief for investment in film with the Inland Revenue.
Prof. Memberships: Law Society; VAT Practitioners Group.
Career: Qualified 1987 at *Oppenheimers*; Assistant Solicitor *Richards Butler* 1988-1990; *S.J. Berwin & Co* 1990-95, becoming a partner in 1993. Joined *Olswang* in 1995 as Head of Tax.
Personal: Interests include perfecting my golf swing and entertaining my young daughter and even younger black labrador.

CANT, Michael
Nabarro Nathanson, London
(0171) 493 9933
Partner in Corporate Tax Department.
Specialisation: Specialises in Corporate Tax, particularly VAT and Stamp Duties.
Prof. Memberships: Law Society, VAT Practitioners Group.
Career: Qualified in 1984. Joined *Turner Kenneth Brown* as an Assistant in 1988.
Personal: Born 19th September 1958. Attended Leeds Polytechnic 1976-79, then Guildford Law School 1980. Leisure interests include golf. Lives in Haslemere, Surrey.

CHALLONER, John
Norton Rose, London (0171) 283 6000
Partner in Commercial Tax Department.
Specialisation: Principal area of practice is corporate taxation. Extensive experience in relation to the taxation of company

acquisitions, property developments, UK corporate restructurings, collective investment schemes and dealing with the complex VAT and other tax issues relating to international ventures. Author of Sale and Leaseback chapter in Longman's Tax Planning and Precedents. Frequent speaker at conferences and seminars.
Prof. Memberships: International Fiscal Association.
Career: Qualified 1977 while with *Nelson & Steele* in Stoke-on-Trent. H.M. Inspector of Taxes 1979-84. Joined *Norton Rose* in 1984 and became a Partner in 1988.
Personal: Born 9th August 1952. Attended Wilmslow School and Exeter University. Lives in Saffron Walden.

CLARK, Simon H.T.
Linklaters, London (0171) 456 4902
Partner. Property Department, in charge of Property Tax Unit.
Specialisation: Has over 11 years' experience in this area of law. Has given tax advice on numerous landmark real estate transactions. Articled at *Linklaters & Paines* and qualified in 1981, Solicitor in Tax Department 1981-83, Solicitor in Property Department 1983-88. Made Partner in 1988.

CLAYSON, Murray J.
Freshfields, London (0171) 936 4000
Specialisation: International tax, corporate structuring especially cross-border, financing, banking, securities, capital markets, derivatives, structured finance.
Prof. Memberships: Chartered Institute of Taxation (FTII). Member of International Tax Sub-Committee. International Fiscal Association: member of British Branch Committee and Technical Sub-Committee.
Career: Sidney Sussex College, Cambridge (MA, LL.M). Partner 1993.

COLEMAN, Brenda
Allen & Overy, London (0171) 330 3000

CORBEN, Heather
S J Berwin & Co, London
+44 (0)171 533 2222
Partner in Tax Department
Specialisation: General corporate taxation, with a particular emphasis on mergers and acquisitions, joint ventures, corporate structuring, and property transactions, including VAT.
Prof. Memberships: The Law Society, Associate of The Chartered Institute of Taxation.
Career: Articled *Norton Rose*; qualified 1987. Partner *S J Berwin & Co* 1997.
Personal: Born 1959. Attended Manchester University 1977-80.

CORNWELL-KELLY, Malachy
Titmuss Sainer Dechert, London
(0171) 583 5353
International Trade and Customs Division.
Specialisation: Negotiates and handles disputes with Customs and Excise and IBEA on all VAT, customs and excise duty matters. Work covers investigation cases, tariff classification, valuation and transfer pricing issues, origin, duty preference, export rebates, CAP questions, import and export licensing, anti-

dumping duties, and appeals to and appearances before the VAT and Duties Tribunal and the European Court. Cases have included agricultural levy disputes and CAP export refunds, tariff classification, origin disputes, customs duty panel, VAT liability, Single Market excise liabilities, collateral insurance rights, judicial review of Customs & Excise and United Nations trade sanctions. Author of 'European Community Law', 2nd edition, a regular column in The In-House Lawyer and The Practical Tax Lawyer, and articles in Taxation, The Law Society's Gazette and Exporting Today. Frequent conference speaker.
Prof. Memberships: Law Society VAT and Duties Committee, VAT Practitioners Group, Customs Practitioners Group, Institute of Indirect Taxation, Law Society representative on Joint Customs Consultative Committee.
Career: Qualified in 1971. Worked at Customs and Excise Solicitor's Office 1972-77, then *Richards Butler* 1977-83. Joined the Law Society as Revenue Law Committee Secretary in 1983 before becoming Director of Tax Investigations for the Parliamentary Ombudsman in 1988. Joined *Titmuss Sainer & Webb* (now *Titmuss Sainer Dechert*) in 1993.
Personal: Born 11th May 1947. Attended King's College, London, 1965-68 (LLB), then College of Law, London, 1968-69, Ecole Nationale d'Administration, Paris, 1975. Secretary of the Tax Law Review Committee at the Institute for Fiscal Studies 1993-95, chairman of the VAT and Duties Tribunal and deputy special commissioner. Leisure interests include cider and beer making and collecting Customs memorabilia. Lives in Sevenoaks, Kent.

COX, Christopher
Beachcroft Stanleys, London
(0171) 242 1011
Specialisation: Corporate tax matters of all descriptions, including VAT, particularly concerning commercial property - development agreements, joint ventures, property unit trusts and securitisation, PFI, finance leasing, overseas aspects. Co-author of CGT on Businesses (Sweet & Maxwell, 1992).
Prof. Memberships: VAT Practitioners Group Property Sub - Committee.
Career: St. Edward's School, Oxford; Hertford College, Oxford. Qualified 1970. *Coward Chance* 1970-77, *Spicer and Pegler* 1981-84, *Nabarro Nathanson* 1984-97, partner 1986-97. Partner *Beachcroft Stanleys* since 1997.
Personal: Married, 2 daughters.

CRAWFORD, Sue
Ashurst Morris Crisp, London
(0171) 638 1111
Partner in Tax Department.
Specialisation: Principal area of practice is corporate tax with particular emphasis on corporate reorganisatons, mergers, de-mergers, and acquisitions including cross-border transactions. Also specialises in oil and gas tax; property taxation and taxation of financial institutions/transactions (including tax based structured financing), extending to securitisation, leasing and enterprise zones.
Career: Articled *Coward Chance (Clifford Chance)*; qualified 1984. Partner *Ashurst Morris Crisp* since 1994.
Personal: Educated at Wycombe Abbey School; Girton College Cambridge University.

DORAN, Nigel J.L.
Macfarlanes, London (0171) 831 9222
Partner in Corporate Tax Group.
Specialisation: Corporate tax specialist. Work includes mergers and acquisitions, joint ventures, MBO's, MBI's, corporate finance, international, employment, investment funds, banking and property. Important transactions include the demergers of Royal Doulton and Saatchi & Saatchi, sale by Allders plc of Allders International, sale by Lonrho plc of London Metropole and sale of J O Hambro Magan to NatWest Markets. Regular speaker at tax conferences, author of 'Taxation of Corporate Joint Ventures' (Butterworths) and joint author of "Collective Investment Schemes: the Law and Practice" (FT Law and Tax).
Prof. Memberships: City of London Law Society (Revenue Law Subcommittee), Chartered Institute of Taxation, Association of Certified Accountants, Chartered Institute of Bankers.
Career: Qualified in 1984 having joined *Macfarlanes* in 1982. Became a Partner in 1988.
Personal: Born 11th March 1950. Educated at Trinity College, Glenalmond 1963-69 and St. Edmund Hall, Oxford 1969-73. Leisure interests include golf and modern languages. Lives in Twickenham.

DOUGLAS, Alasdair F.
Travers Smith Braithwaite, London (0171) 248 9133 or 295 3000
Specialisation: Head of Corporate Tax Department and Managing Partner of firm. Main areas of work are corporate finance, mergers, acquisitions, reconstructions and investigation work. Career: Qualified 1977. Partner 1985. Managing Partner 1995.

EDGE, Steve
Slaughter and May, London (0171) 600 1200
Partner in Corporate Tax Department.
Specialisation: Principal area of practice is corporate taxation with a particular emphasis on corporate finance and asset finance. Expertise in financial instruments, cross border financial transactions and securitisations and other capital markets work. One of the first UK tax lawyers to concentrate on tax and other financial aspects of big ticket leasing and other asset and major project financings. Advises mainly UK and US multinationals and investment banks. Experience of privatisations and Inland Revenue investigations. Contributes to a number of publications on corporate tax.
Career: Qualified in 1975 while with *Slaughter and May* and became a Partner in 1982.
Personal: Born 29 November 1950. Attended Canon Slade Grammar School, Bolton 1962-69, then Exeter University 1969-72. Lives in London.

EHRLICH, Michael
Clifford Chance, London (0171) 600 1000
Partner. Specialises in tax on financial and property transactions including corporation tax and VAT.
Career: Articled *Dawson & Co.*; qualified 1977; Partner *Clifford Chance* since 1986.
Personal: Educated at Bedales School; Southampton University; Warwick University (BSc Mathematics; MSc). Born 1948.

ELLIOTT, Peter
Clifford Chance, London (0171) 600 1000
Partner.
Specialisation: Principal area of practice is corporate tax with particular emphasis on cross border structures and transactions and corporate and international finance. Frequent speaker/ chairman at taxation related seminars, author of numerous articles in professional publications, and a member of the editorial board of the EC Tax Review (Intertax) published by Kluwer and of Corporate Tax Review published by Key Haven. Member of the International Bar Association and heads the firm's International Tax Group.
Career: Solicitor 1975. Partner 1980.

ELMAN, Jonathan
Clifford Chance, London (0171) 600 1000
Partner.
Specialisation: Taxation of Corporate and Financing Transactions.
Career: Solicitor 1987. Partner 1994.

FALK, Sarah
Freshfields, London (0171) 936 4000
Partner in Tax Department.
Specialisation: Main area of practice is corporate tax. Work covers corporate tax planning and corporate finance.
Prof. Memberships: Law Society.
Career: Qualified 1986, having joined *Freshfields* in 1984. Became a Partner in 1994.
Personal: Born 1962. Attended Sidney Sussex College, Cambridge, 1980-83.

FERGUSON, Fiona
Slaughter and May, London (0171) 600 1200
Specialisation: Banking, Structured Finance, M&A, Conversion of Building Societies.
Career: MA Cambridge.
Personal: Flying, sailing, playing piano.

FRASER, R.D.A.
Herbert Smith, London (0171) 374 8000
Specialisation: Main practice areas include insurance company mergers and acquisitions (highlights of the last year include advising on the NPI securitisation of embedded value transactions and on the acquisition by Windsor Life of the UK life business of GAN); investment funds (recent transactions include the unitisation of Kleinwort Overseas Investment Trust) and cross-border reorganisations and mergers.
Career: London School of Economics; College of Law; qualified 1973; partner *Herbert Smith* 1982.

FRENCH, Douglas
Clifford Chance, London (0171) 600 1000
Partner in Corporate Tax.
Specialisation: Specialises in tax; particularly tax related to corporate and commercial transactions.
Career: Articled *Freshfields*; qualified 1981; Partner *Clifford Chance* since 1988.
Personal: Educated at Walbottle High School, Newcastle; Oxford (MA Law) ATII. Born 1956, married, two sons.

GOWTAGE, Jill
Allen & Overy, London (0171) 330 3000
Specialisation: VAT and other indirect taxes (customs/excise) deals with specific transactions, general advice, investigations and litigation in financial, corporate, property and charity sectors. Also writes and lectures on VAT.
Prof. Memberships: Law Society (Member of VAT and Dukes Sub-Committee). VAT Practitioners' Group.
Career: LL.B, (University of Birmingham); Barrister (Lincoln's Inn); Senior Legal Advisor Solicitor's Office H.M Customs and Excise; VAT Senior Manager KPMG; Head of Indirect Tax *Allen & Overy*

GREENBANK, Ashley
Macfarlanes, London (0171) 831 9222
Specialisation: Partner in the Corporate Tax Group specialising in UK and cross-border tax aspects of corporate finance transactions, mergers and acquisitions and venture capital work.
Prof. Memberships: Law Society.
Career: King Edwards School Birmingham, Selwyn College Cambridge MA (1985), Lincoln College Oxford BCL (1989). Qualified 1988. Articles at *Freshfields* (1986-1988) Assistant solicitor *Freshfields* Tax Department (1989-1994). Assistant solicitor *Macfarlanes* Company Commercial and Banking Department (1994-1997). Partner 1997.

HAAN, Christopher
Hammond Suddards, London (0171) 655 1000
Partner and Head of Tax Unit.
Specialisation: Structured and project finance, both domestic and cross-border, corporate taxation of mergers and acquisitions and reconstructions both domestic and cross-border, taxation of financial instruments and financial institutions (including insurance companies) generally.
Prof. Memberships: The Law Society, a Fellow of the Royal Society for the Arts and Director of the Local Investment Fund.
Career: Partner at *Herbert & Gowers* 1969-71, Partner at *Linklaters & Paines* 1974-81, Partner/Senior Partner at *S J Berwin & Co* 1982-92, Partner at *Coudert Brothers* 1992-94, Partner at *Hammond Suddards since 1995*.

HALE, Paul D.
Simmons & Simmons, London (0171) 628 2020
Partner in Corporate Tax Department.
Specialisation: Main area of practice is corporate tax and value added tax. Work includes mergers and acquisitions, stock exchange listings, project finance, structured finance and property transactions. Also handles taxation of collective investment schemes, including unit trusts, investment trusts and offshore funds. Author of various articles.
Prof. Memberships: Law Society, City of London Solicitors' Company, VAT Practitioners Group, International Bar Association.
Career: Qualified 1985, having joined *Simmons & Simmons* in 1983. Became a Partner in 1990.
Personal: Born 1st August 1959. Attended Winchester College 1973-77, then Worcester College Oxford 1977-81. Leisure interests include family life, gardening, tennis and bridge. Lives in Amersham.

HARDWICK, Michael J.
Linklaters, London (0171) 456 5658
Partner in Tax Department.
Specialisation: Specialist in corporate taxation, with particular experience advising on tax issues in relation to privatisations, corporate reorganisations, disposals, acquisitions, takeovers, mergers, joint ventures and flotations. Qualified in 1984, having joined *Linklaters & Paines* in 1982. Became a Partner in 1991. Born 1958.

HARGER, Judith
Denton Hall, London (0171) 242 1212
Specialisation: jbh@dentonhall.com. Partner in Tax Department. Specialises in corporate and financial taxation, including international and cross-border structures and transactions. Main areas of practice are mergers and acquisitions, joint ventures, tax-driven reorganisations, inward investment into UK/Europe and multi-national group tax planning.
Career: St. Anne's College, Oxford (MA Jurisprudence).
Personal: Leisure interests include family, theatre and gardening.

HARGREAVES, Colin
Freshfields, London (0171) 832 7352
Specialisation: All aspects of corporate tax. In particular asset and project finance, structured financing arrangements, and some corporate finance.
Prof. Memberships: Law Society. City of London Law Society (member, CLLS Revenue Law Sub-Committee).
Career: Uppingham School; Leeds University; Qualified 1988; Partner *Freshfields* 1996.
Personal: Sailing (member, Burnham Overy Staithe Sailing Club).

HARKNESS, David
Clifford Chance, London (0171) 600 1000
Specialisation: Partner specialising in corporate tax including mergers and acquisitions, corporate restructurings, joint ventures, international tax planning, financing transactions and securitisations.
Career: Colchester Royal Grammar School; Sheffield University (1985 LLB); Articled *Clifford Chance*; qualified 1989; Partner 1996.
Personal: Born 1963; resides London.

HIGGINBOTTOM, Louise
Norton Rose, London (0171) 283 6000
Partner in Tax Department.
Specialisation: Corporate and asset finance.
Prof. Memberships: Law Society, Associate of Institute of Tax, Member of Corporation Tax Sub-committee of Revenue Law Committee of Law Society, IBA, ABA.
Career: Joined *Norton Rose* 1981. Qualified 1983. Partner 1991.
Personal: Born 17th August 1958. Attended Southampton University 1977-80.

HOYLE, Stephen L.
Freshfields, London (0171) 936 4000
Partner 1988. Tax Department.
Specialisation: Main area of practice is the taxation of insurance business and tax-based financing.
Personal: Born 17.9.1955. Attended St

Catherine's College Oxford 1973-76, Gonville & Caius College Cambridge, 1976-77, and Northwestern Law School, Chicago, 1977-78.

HUMPHREY, Ann
Ann L. Humphrey, London (0171) 378 9370
Fax: 0171 378 9360 E-mail:
annlhumphrey@dial.pipex.com
Specialisation: Wide-ranging tax experience during fifteen years in the City, particular emphasis on VAT. Tax litigation experience at all levels, from VAT Tribunal or Special Commissioners up to the Court of Appeal.
Prof. Memberships: Member of the Law Society's Revenue Law Committee and its VAT and Duties Sub-Committee and of Custom's VAT Land and Property Liaison Group, and the VAT Practitioners Group.
Career: Admitted as a solicitor in 1977. Master's degree in Law. Master of Business Administration. Until May 1993 corporate tax partner in City firm, *Richards Butler*. In July 1993 set up her own practice, concentrating on VAT and corporate tax. The firm's work is around 40% corporate tax, and 60% VAT. The firm expanded in 1997 and moved to new custom-built offices at Tower Bridge.
Personal: French and Japanese speaker. Deputy Social Security Commissioner. Board member of a housing association.

JOHNSON, Ian L.
Ashurst Morris Crisp, London (0171) 638 1111
Partner in Tax Department.
Specialisation: Involved in advising on the taxation implications of a wide range of corporate transactions advising both overseas and UK clients.
Prof. Memberships: Associate of the Chartered Institute of Taxation.
Career: Graduated in law from Edinburgh University.

KELLY, Donald C.
Lovell White Durrant, London
(0171) 236 0066
Specialisation: Corporate tax partner specialising in all aspects of business tax including taxation implications of mergers, acquisitions and joint ventures (particularly cross-border), UK equipment leasing and property transactions and North Sea oil tax.
Prof. Memberships: Law Society, City of London Solicitors' Company.
Career: Articled *Lovell White & King* (now *Lovell White Durrant*); qualified 1980; partner 1986; specialised in UK corporate tax since qualification.

KEMPSTER FCA, Peter
Nabarro Nathanson, London
(0171) 493 9933
Specialisation: Corporate taxation with particular emphasis on property finance and cross-border transactions.
Prof. Memberships: Law Society: Fellow of The Chartered Institute of Taxation: Fellow of The Institute of Chartered Accountants in England & Wales.
Career: Qualified as Chartered Accountant with *Arthur Andersen* in 1981 and as solicitor with *Nabarro Nathanson* in 1987. Partner 1987; Head of Tax Department 1991-1996; Property Finance Department since 1996. Council

Member of The Chartered Institute of Taxation.
Personal: Born 1956. Durham University 1975-78.

KINGSTONE, Mark
Linklaters, London (0171) 456 5714
Partner. Tax Department.
Specialisation: Specialises in mergers and acquisitions, funds and corporate reconstruction work. Co-author of 'Taxation of Companies and Company Reconstructions'.
Career: Articled at *Linklaters & Paines*, qualified in 1988, and became Partner in 1995. Graduated from Oxford University with a first class honours in Jurisprudence.
Personal: Born 1962.

LEWIS, David E.
Allen & Overy, London (0171) 330 3000
Specialisation: Partner dealing with corporate tax and all aspects of UK and international corporate tax work including both UK and cross border mergers and acquisitions and group reorganisations and reconstructions, specialising also in banking and capital markets transactions.
Prof. Memberships: Member Law Society Revenue Committee, Chairman of the Stamp Duty Sub-Committee of the Law Society Revenue Law Committee; Member Corporation Tax Sub-Committee of The Law Society Revenue Law Committee.
Career: Articled *Allen & Overy*, qualified 1976, Partner 1982.
Personal: Exeter University 1973. Born 1952.

LING, Timothy A.
Freshfields, London (0171) 936 4000
Partner in Tax Department.
Specialisation: All aspects of corporate tax, and particularly UK and cross-border mergers and acquisitions, reconstructions, joint ventures, demergers, private company acquisitions and disposals, new issues.
Prof. Memberships: Law Society and City of London Law Society.
Career: Qualified in 1973. Became partner in *Freshfields* 1977. Head of Tax Department 1985-91. Member of Law Society Revenue Law Committee 1981-91.
Personal: Born 17th September 1948. Educated The King's School, Canterbury and The Queen's College, Oxford (MA). Leisure interests include sailing and music. Member of Royal Harwich Yacht Club.

LYNCHEHAN, Martin
Linklaters, London (0171) 456 5716
Specialisation: Tax Partner specialising in structured finance, VAT and M&A.
Career: Articled *Oppenheimers/ Richards Butler*. Qualified 1989. *Richards Butler* 1989-93; *Linklaters* 1993- date. 1993 -1995 Secretary to VAT Land and Property Consultative Committee; 1994-97 VAT Practitioners' Group Technical Committee Member; 1997-date VAT Practitioners' Group Finance Bill Committee Member.

MAINPRICE, Hugh
Mainprice & Co, London (0171) 730 8705
Specialisation: Value Added Tax and Insurance Premium Tax. Has appeared in more VAT tribunal cases for appellants than anyone else in the UK commencing with the case of Rentokil v C & E Commrs 1973 VATTR 31 heard on the 4th April 1973 and since then has been involved in over 50 cases in the Higher

Courts including the House of Lords.
Prof. Memberships: Law Society, Chartered Institute of Taxation; Ordem dos Advogados, Portugal, Royal Geographical Society.
Career: Called to the Bar, Gray's Inn in 1961, became a Solicitor in 1978. Employed in the Colonial Legal Service from 1950 to 1964. Joined the Solicitors Office *HM Customs & Excise* in 1965 and, as a Senior Legal Assistant participated in the drafting of the original VAT legislation. Resigned from the *Customs* in March 1972 to set up his own legal/consultancy practice on VAT. Was the first person to be awarded a fellowship of the Chartered Institute of Taxation for a thesis on VAT. Author of 'Concise Guide VAT' (1972); 'Mainprice & Willson on VAT' (1973); 'Mainprice on VAT' (Butterworths) (1978); 'Practical VAT Planning' (Tolleys) (1983); 'VAT Disputes' (CCH) (1986). Wrote and edited the original CCH 'British VAT Reporter' (1984). Original editor of the News letters 'VAT Intelligence' (Gee & Co) and 'Practical VAT' (Legal Studies & Services). Author of numerous articles in Accountancy Age, British Tax Review, Taxation and Tax Practitioner. Has made frequent broadcasts on Television and Radio.
Personal: Born 24 April 1928. Educated at Sherborne and London University. Interests include music, photography and travel.

MARTIN, David
Herbert Smith, London (0171) 374 8000
Specialisation: Partner heading the firm's tax section advising on all kinds of business-related tax matters and has played a significant role in many high-profile transactions including company reorganisations, demergers, disposals and acquisitions of companies and businesses; has also been involved in many finance leasing transactions and other financing methods as well as advising on several substantial tax litigation matters.
Career: Qualified 1979;
partner *Herbert Smith* 1986.
Personal:
Educated at St John's College, Cambridge.

MCGOWAN, Michael T.
Allen & Overy, London (0171) 330 3000
Specialisation: Specialises in general corporate tax, with emphasis on structured finance and securitisation transactions. Recent deals have included: advising on the UK tax aspects of the acquisition and financing of the Ministry of Defence Married Quarters Estate; advising the US bidders on the UK tax aspects of the 1996 contested takeover of Northern Electric plc and the 1997 recommended takeover of Yorkshire Electricity; advising the managers in respect of the 1997 secured Eurobond offering by Canary Wharf.
Career: Articled and qualified as a solicitor at Clifford Chance: 1987-90. Assistant solicitor, *Linklaters & Paines* 1990-95 (including two years in New York 1993-94, part of which was spent on secondment at *Sullivan & Cromwell*). Assistant solicitor *Allen & Overy* 1995-97. Partner *Allen & Overy* 1997 - .
Personal: Born 21st September 1963. Educated Newcastle-under-Lyme High School and Magdalen College, Oxford (MA BCL). Married with two daughters. Interests: reading, listening to music, walking, being a parent.

MEARS, Patrick M.
Allen & Overy, London (0171) 330 3000
Specialisation: Practice covers the corporate tax aspects of transactions in a wide range of areas. His experience covers, in particular, the giving of UK tax advice in the fields of domestic and cross-border mergers and acquisitions, domestic and cross-border corporate reorganisations, flotations, domestic and international banking, asset and structured finance, PFI, securitisations, capital markets issues and securities trading and lending. He lectures on topical corporate tax issues.
Prof. Memberships: Member of the City of London Law Society's Revenue Law Sub-Committee.
Career: Articled *Allen & Overy*; qualified 1982; partner 1988.
Personal: Born 1958. London School of Economics 1979.

MEHTA, Nikhil V.
Linklaters, London (0171) 456 5686
Partner. Tax Department
Specialisation: Specialises in corporate taxation with particular emphasis on international finance, derivatives, cross-border structures and joint ventures. Head of the India Business Group. Also deals with projects, privatisations, cross border structures, international joint ventures and international finance. Practised tax law in Bombay, India from 1977-80, Legal Assistant in Inland Revenue Solicitor's Office 1981-83. Joined *Linklaters & Paines* in 1983, becoming a Partner in 1989.

NIAS, Peter
Simmons & Simmons, London
(0171) 628 2020
Partner in Tax Department.
Specialisation: Main areas of practice are corporate, commercial and international taxation. Work includes cross border transactions (in particular mergers, acquisitions, reorganisations), transfer pricing and thin capitalisation, finance leasing, and structured finance transactions.
Prof. Memberships: Law Society. Member of Law Society International Tax Sub-Committee, the Chartered Institute of Taxation International Tax Sub-Committee and ICC UK Tax Committee.
Career: Qualified in 1979. Joined *Simmons & Simmons* in 1976, becoming a Partner in 1982 and Head of Tax Department in 1992.
Personal: Born 24th November 1953. Attended Manchester University 1973-6. LLB. Leisure interests include family and outdoor life, clay and game shooting, music and tennis. Lives in Great Horkesley.

NOBLE, Nicholas R.
Field Fisher Waterhouse, London
(0171) 481 4841
Partner and Head of Tax Department.
Specialisation: Practice covers the taxation of UK and international transactions, in particular companies and company reorganisations, securities and transactions in securities. Co-author of 'Butterworths Company Reorganisations: Tax and Tax Planning' and 'Butterworths International Taxation of Financial Instruments and Transactions' and joint editor of and contributor to 'Butterworths Tax Planning Service'.
Prof. Memberships: ATII.
Career: Qualified in 1979 having joined *Field Fisher Waterhouse* in 1977. Became a partner in 1984.

Personal: Born 1st October 1953. Educated at Winchester College and Durham University. Recreations include fencing, walking and reading.

NORFOLK, Edward Christopher
Norton Rose, London (0171) 283 6000
Partner in Commercial Tax Department.
Specialisation: Principal area of work involves advising on tax aspects of mergers and acquisitions, corporate structuring (domestic and international), banking and oil and gas. Author of 'Taxation Treatment of Interest and Loan Relationships' (Butterworths, 3rd Ed. 1997). Member of Editorial Committee 'Practical Law for Companies'. Frequent speaker at conferences and seminars.
Prof. Memberships: Law Society (Member, Revenue Law Committee), Chartered Institute of Taxation (FTII), International Bar Association, International Fiscal Association.
Career: Articled at *Longmores* in Hertford, then joined *Gabb & Co.* in Abergavenny. Joined *Norton Rose* in 1975 and became a Partner in 1979.
Personal: Born 8th August 1948. Attended St. John's School, Leatherhead 1962-66, then Southampton University 1966-69. Leisure pursuits include skiing and fishing. Lives in Wimbledon.

NOWLAN, Howard M.
Slaughter and May, London
(0171) 600 1200
Specialisation: Corporate tax - general, restructurings, demutualisations, transfer pricing.
Career: MA Oxon.

OVERS, John H.
Berwin Leighton, London +44 171 760 1000

PORTER, Sue
Freshfields, London (0171) 936 4000
Specialisation: Specialises in Corporate Taxation, particularly in the finance/ capital markets area, including structured finance, securitisation, derivatives, banking and bond issues and general corporate tax advice. Acts for banks, building societies and corporates. Contributor, Tolley's Tax Planning.
Career: Qualified 1984.
Partner 1992 in Tax Department.

PRESTON, Christopher A.L.
Watson, Farley & Williams, London
(0171) 814 8000
Email: cpreston@wfw.com
Partner in Finance Group.
Specialisation: Main area of practice covers leasing and asset finance/ structured finance, company taxation and international tax planning. Also specialises in VAT and customs duties, including both contentious and non-contentious matters and appearing before the VAT tribunal.
Prof. Memberships: Law Society (Member of Revenue Law Committee and Chairman of VAT & Duties Sub-Committee), Institute of Tax, VAT Practitioners Group (Founder Member). Fellow of the Institute of Taxation.
Career: Admitted 1975. Joined *Watson, Farley & Williams* as a partner in 1982.
Personal: Born 9th October 1950.

LEADERS' PROFILES • LONDON continued

ROSE, Simon
S J Berwin & Co, London
+44 (0)171 533 2222
Specialisation: VAT and indirect taxes in property and commercial transactions, private equity and offshore funds, including venture trusts and investment trusts; VAT litigation.
Prof. Memberships: Law Society, Institute of Indirect Taxation, VAT Practitioners Group.
Career: Articled *Lovell White Durrant* 1990-92; Qualified 1992; Joined *S J Berwin & Co* 1994.
Personal: Born 1968: Exeter University 1986-89 LLB (Law), London University 1996-98 LLM (Taxation).

ROSS, Howard
Clifford Chance, London (0171) 600 1000
Partner, Tax Group.
Specialisation: All aspects of corporate and commercial tax, in particular transfer pricing, tax disputes, oil and gas taxation and international corporate tax planning.
Career: Qualified 1971, Partner: 1981.
Personal: LLB London School of Economics. Admitted to Israel Bar, 1974.

RUPAL, Yash
Linklaters, London (0171) 456 5646
Partner, Tax Department.
Specialisation: Specialises in general corporate tax with particular emphasis on structured finance/ product development, derivatives and other financial instruments. Recent deals have included: acting for Liberty Life on its global offering of convertible bonds - the first ever global convertible issue by a South African issuer; acting for several leading investment banks in developing tax efficient financing structures; acting for Orange plc on its recent restructuring, syndicated loan facility and global offering.

SANDERS, Tim
Theodore Goddard, London
(0171) 606 8855
Specialisation: All corporate and banking related tax matters including cross-border financial structuring. Co-author of Tolleys Tax Indemnities and Warranties. Contributor to Tolleys Company Law.
Prof. Memberships: Law Society; Fellow of the Chartered Institute of Taxation.
Career: Llandovery College (Thomas Phillips Scholar), Thames Valley G.S., London University (LLB). Joined *Theodore Goddard* from *Allen & Overy* in 1991, Partner in 1992. Head of Corporate Tax Department.
Personal: Born 1959. Qualified 1984. Married with 2 children. Interests include rowing, golf and gardening. Lives in Epsom.

SANDISON, Francis G.
Freshfields, London (0171) 936 4000
Partner in Tax Department.
Specialisation: Main area of practice is corporate tax, and VAT. Cases have included Collard v. Mining and Industrial Holdings (H.L. 1989), R v. HM Treasury, ex parte Daily Mail and General Trust (ECJ 1988); Smithkline Beecham's merger with Beecham and Varity's merger with Lucas. Co-author of 'Whiteman on Income Tax' (3rd edition, 1988). Chairman of the Law Society's Corporation Tax Sub-Committee; member, Tax Law Review

Committee.
Prof. Memberships: Law Society, City of London Law Society (Distinguished Service Award 1997), Addington Society, VAT Practitioners' Group.
Career: Qualified in 1974. Assistant Solicitor at *Freshfields* 1974-80, Partner in *Freshfields'* Tax Department from 1980.
Personal: Born 1949. Educated Charterhouse and Magdalen College Oxford. Leisure interests include fishing, wine and reading. Lives in Surrey.

SCOTT, Thomas A.
Linklaters, London (0171) 456 5692
Partner in Tax Department.
Specialisation: Specialist in the corporate taxation aspects of mergers, domestic and cross-border acquisitions, re-structuring and financings, with almost 20 years experience in this area. Attended Magdalen College, Oxford University (MA Hons). Lecturer in Law, Lincoln College, Oxford in 1980. Qualified in 1983 at *Linklaters & Paines*, becoming a Partner in 1989. Publications include 'Tolley's Tax Planning and Tolley's Company Acquisitions Handbook'.

SINFIELD, Greg
Lovell White Durrant, London
0171) 236 0066
Specialisation: VAT and other indirect taxes (customs/excise duty, insurance premium tax) relating to commercial, financial services and property sectors. Investigation and litigation regarding indirect tax including judicial review, condemnation proceedings and appeals to the VAT and Duties Tribunal and the higher courts. Represents clients in VAT Tribunal and appeared in the High Court as a junior in 'Customs & Excise v. P&O' in February 1996. Writes articles on VAT matters and lectures in the UK and Europe on the above.
Prof. Memberships: Law Society, VAT Practitioners' Group.
Career: Called to the Bar 1981. Customs & Excise Solicitor's Office 1983-1988. *Durrant Piesse* 1988. Qualified as a Solicitor 1989. Partner in *Lovell White Durrant* 1993. Solicitor advocate 1994.

SMITH, Isla M.
Norton Rose, London (0171) 283 6000
Partner in Taxation Department.
Specialisation: Principal area of practice is the tax aspects of financing transactions, including leasing and asset finance, banking, structured finance and securitisation, project finance and international corporate tax structuring. Other main areas of practice are corporate restructuring, company acquisitions and disposals. Has dealt with a substantial number of tax based aircraft, ship, rolling-stock and project financings and cross border leasing transactions. Clients include banks, bank leasing companies, airlines, shipping companies, rolling stock companies, multinational groups of companies, financial intermediaries and arrangers. Author of chapters in the ICAEW 'Taxation Service' and Longman's 'Practical Tax Planning'. Speaker at a number of conferences.
Prof. Memberships: Law Society, City of London Law Society, Chartered Institute of

Taxation, International Fiscal Association, International Bar Association, Finance and Leasing Association.
Career: Admitted as an Attorney of the Supreme Court of S.Africa in 1974. Qualified as a solicitor in England & Wales in 1980. Became a Partner at *Norton Rose* in 1985.
Personal: Born 17th February 1952. Educated at Westville Girls' High School, Natal, S.A. 1960-68, the University of Pretoria and the University of Natal, Durban 1969-72. Leisure pursuits include keeping up with two children, aerobics, music, tennis and skiing. Lives in Wimbledon.

STAPLETON, Mark
Titmuss Sainer Dechert, London
(0171) 583 5353
Partner, Tax and Private Client Department
Specialisation: Advises on UK and international direct and indirect taxation issues, in particular VAT. Specialises in property sector work such as commercial property developments, joint ventures and overseas aspects. Also, taxation of corporate mergers and acquisitions works and onshore and offshore investment funds.
Prof. Memberships: Associate of the Institute of Taxation (1989-), National Secretary of the VAT Practitioners Group.
Career: Articled at *Turner Kenneth Brown*. Qualified in 1988. Solicitor at *Turner Kenneth Brown* until 1993. Joined *Titmuss Sainer Webb* (now *Titmuss Sainer Dechert*) 1993. Appointed partner at *Titmuss Sainer Dechert* 1996-. Has written articles for the Tax Journal and appears on videos for both Television Education Network and Legal Network television. Conference speaker for Henry Stewart Conferences.
Personal: Born 1964. Educated at King Edward VI Grammar School, Chelmsford. Graduated from Nottingham University (LLB). Resides in London. Interests include tennis, football, cinema and theatre.

STAVELEY, Ben W.
Freshfields, London (0171) 936 4000
Specialisation: Specialisations include the tax treatment of capital markets, derivatives and securities transactions and the tax position of banks and other financial institutions.
Career: Education - Magdalene College, Cambridge. Became Partner 1987.

STRATTON, Richard J.
Travers Smith Braithwaite, London
(0171) 248 9133
Partner in Corporate Tax Department.
Specialisation: Handles corporate tax matters. Specialist in funds and investment structures including onshore and offshore funds, limited partnerships, venture capital trusts, property based structures and structured finance. Recent articles - Venture Capital Trusts chapter in Tolleys Tax Plannning; articles concerning CREST and SDRT in "PLC" magazine.
Career: Qualified in 1983. Partner at *Travers Smith Braithwaite* since 1989.

TAYLOR, David
Freshfields, London (0171) 936 4000
Partner in Tax Department.
Specialisation: Main area of work is corporate tax including banking, asset and structured finance, and some corporate finance.

Prof. Memberships: Law Society, City of London Solicitors' Company.
Career: Qualified in 1984.
Personal: Born 26th July 1959. Attended Cambridge University 1977-80 and 1981-82. Lives in Hampshire.

THOMPSON, Michael
Freshfields, London (0171) 936 4000
Partner in Tax Department.
Specialisation: Advises on most UK tax aspects of corporate transactions. Has a particular specialisation in oil and gas taxation and a second specialisation in structuring the financing of all types of receivable through securitisation techniques. Acts for a number of oil and gas companies and banks. Chairs the Law Society's sub-committee on oil taxation and is a member of the UK Oil Industry Taxation Committee.
Prof. Memberships: Law Society .
Career: Qualified in 1979. Became a partner at *Freshfields* in 1985.
Personal: Born 18th June 1954. Educated at Bradford Grammar School and Trinity College, Cambridge.

TROUP, Edward
Simmons & Simmons, London
(0171) 628 2020
Specialisation: Corporate tax, including financing and corporate transactions. Advises on tax policy and strategic tax planning.
Prof. Memberships: Law Society, Institute of Taxation, Institute for Fiscal Studies, International Fiscal Association.
Career: MA, MSc (Oxon).
Personal: Cinema, cycling, opera, Anglo-Saxon history, sleep.

WALTON, Miles
Allen & Overy, London (0171) 330 3000
Partner in Corporate Tax Department.
Specialisation: Deals with all areas of

corporate tax with a particular interest in tax for banks, structured finance, asset finance and corporate funding. Co-author of 'Taxation and Banking' (Sweet & Maxwell). Has written various articles for legal journals and spoken at a number of seminars and conferences on corporate tax.
Prof. Memberships: Law Society, Institute of Taxation (Associate).
Career: Qualified in 1980. With *Slaughter and May* 1980-83. Joined *Wilde Sapte* in 1983 and became a Partner in 1984. Joined *Allen & Overy* in 1997.
Personal: Born 15th July 1955. Educated at Ratcliffe College, Leicester 1968-73, Brasenose College, Oxford (MA) 1974-77 and Chester College of Law 1977-78. Leisure interests include saxophone, wine, scuba diving and clocks. Lives in London.

WATSON, John G.
Ashurst Morris Crisp, London
(0171) 638 1111
Partner in Tax Department.
Specialisation: Fund work, enterprise zones, venture capital, international tax, all corporate deals and leasing. Legal adviser to the EZPUTA. Leads IFMA Steering Committee on all aspects of PFPVs. Contributor to Tolleys Tax Planning and other textbooks.
Career: Barrister 1975-1978; *Neville Russell* 1978-1983. Joined *Ashurst Morris Crisp* in 1983. Partner in 1989.
Personal: Born 23 April 1951. Christs College Cambridge (1970-1973). Exhibition and MA in mathematics.

WARRINER, Neil
Herbert Smith, London (0171) 374 8000
Specialisation: Partner dealing with corporate tax matters generally with particular expertise in indirect taxes (VAT, stamp duty) and the tax aspects of transactions in the energy and property industries. Recent major transactions

include the redevelopment of Brent Cross Shopping Centre, the opening of the electricity supply market to greater competition and the disposal by Chevron of its UK downstream business to Shell UK.
Career: The Law Society; The City of London Solicitor's Company; UKOITC.
Prof. Memberships: St Peter's College, Oxford; qualified 1987; partner *Herbert Smith* 1994.
Personal: Keen golfer.

WHITTY, Oonagh A.
Watson, Farley & Williams, London
(0171) 814 8000
email: owhitty@wfw.com
Specialisation: Partner in the finance group, specialising in tax aspects of asset/ structured finance and international tax.
Career: Qualified 1981; Partner *Watson Farley & Williams* 1987.
Personal: Born 1954; resides London; attended Imperial College, London University (BSc).

WISTOW, Michael John
Clifford Chance, London (0171) 600 1000
Specialisation: Tax Partner specialising in finance transactions including securitisation, leasing, and tax-based structured and property financings.
Career: Manchester University; Trained *Clifford Chance*; Qualified 1990; Partner 1997.

WONG, Etienne
Clifford Chance, London (0171) 600 1000
Specialisation: Specialises in indirect taxes such as VAT and stamp duty, and advises on all aspects of corporate tax related to property, telecommunications, Internet, media and financial transactions.
Career: Qualified 1990.
Personal: Educated at Uppingham School and Bristol University (LLB). Interests include writing music and screenplays.

The SOUTH, EAST ANGLIA and WALES

HIGHLY REGARDED FIRMS
THE SOUTH, EAST ANGLIA AND WALES

Burges Salmon Bristol
Eversheds Norwich
Mills & Reeve Cambridge
Osborne Clarke Bristol
Wiggin and Co Cheltenham

Blake Lapthorn Fareham
Clarke Willmott & Clarke Taunton
Thomas Eggar Church Adams Chichester

Burges Salmon (Bristol) (1ptnr/3assts) "Pleasant and able." *Tim Illston* splits his time with pensions work. **Clients/Work:** Sale of Glosford Holdings Ltd to Wescol Group plc. £21m reorganisation of a family farming company. Share scheme for Science Systems.

Eversheds (Norwich) (1ptnr/1asst/1 chartered accountant) Work includes employee benefits as well as VAT and corporate tax.

Clients/Work: Acting on Textron's takeover of Ransomes plc. Acting for the vendor on the sale of Howard Long International to Albert Fisher Group plc. Acting for Nursing Home Properties plc on a £100m securitisation issue.

Mills & Reeve (Cambridge) (1ptnr/2assts) *Ted Powell* (ex Freshfields), newly promoted to partner, and his businesslike team handle M&A, commercial property and VAT often with a crossborder aspect. **Clients/Work:** Major VAT planning project for a higher education client. Tax planning and structuring for a £10m MBO. VAT structuring advice for a Millennium project.

Osborne Clarke (Bristol) (2ptnrs/2assts) Majority of the work is transaction based, especially involving owner managed businesses. Also leasing, financing and property related matters. Staffed by a posse of ex Slaughter's lawyers including *Philip Moss*. **Clients/Work:** Successful appeal to the Special Commission on the refusal of a CGT clearance. MBO of Masstock Arable led by NatWest Ventures.

Wiggin and Co (Cheltenham) (2ptnrs/2assts) Spawned from Freshfields private

client department many years ago, the firm is unusual for a small regional practice in having a strong international aspect. 50% of the firm's work has an international tax element. *Rod Marlow* is the best known lawyer. **Clients/Work:** Tax structuring – domestic and international companies, transactional work; tax planning for entrepreneurs (and offshore trusts); VAT, share option schemes.

Blake Lapthorn (Fareham) (1ptnr/2assts) With *Niall Murphy* (a chartered accountant and barrister before qualifying as a solicitor) the firm has gained some capacity

LEADING INDIVIDUALS
THE SOUTH, EAST ANGLIA AND WALES

MOSS Philip Osborne Clarke
ILLSTON Timothy Burges Salmon
MARLOW Rod Wiggin and Co
POWELL Ted Mills & Reeve

UP AND COMING

MURPHY Niall Blake Lapthorn
POPPLEWELL Nigel Clarke Willmott & Clarke

SEE PROFILES AT END OF THIS SECTION

and heavy weight tax experience. **Clients/Work:** Corporate re-organisation of the Warings Group. Advising on cross border finance leasing of equipment. Advising on tax driven VAT capital gains and national insurance structures.

Clarke Willmott & Clarke (Taunton)

(1ptnr) Although the firm does not have a separate tax department, *Nigel Popplewell* is establishing a reputation in the area. **Clients/Work:** Advising on a capital allowance claim regarding contract work worth £35m. Establishing stock dividend schemes as part of pre-sale tax planning for a

private client selling companies. Undertaking a successful VAT Tribunal against Customs.

Thomas Eggar Church Adams (Chichester) (1ptnr/1asst/2 tax managers) Coming at things from the context of the private family owned company acting for proprietor/shareholders.

MIDLANDS

Pinsent Curtis (7ptnrs/2assocs/3assts) The leading and largest tax practice in the Midlands although some of the fee earners specialise in employee benefits (David Pett) and as senior partner Julian Tonks cannot spend much time at the coal face. The core corporate tax team includes *Ian Hyde*, *Catherine Robins* and *Elizabeth Morgan*. **Clients/Work:** Acting for the major shareholders and the company on the flotation of Gremlin Interactive. Acting for the management team on the £84m MBO of Bristol Street Group from Britax International plc. Establishing one of the largest landfill tax

environmental bodies in the country for a national waste company.

Wragge & Co (1ptnr/3assocs/3assts) "Hard but fair." A reasonably sized tax group by London standards and a large one for the regions. Work covers cross border, inward investment and property as well as transactional matters. The team includes *Peter Smith* and the 'up & coming' *Kevin Lowe*, a recent recruit from Eversheds. **Clients/Work:** Acting for taxpayer in Privy Council Tax Appeal from Hong Kong (Cosmotron Manufacturing Ltd v CIR). Acting for Castlemore Securities Ltd structuring Hampshire Centre LP, a property development joint venture. Acting for Richard Ellis on the structuring and implementation of its incorporation.

Dibb Lupton Alsop (1ptnr/1assoc/1asst) Recruited *Gregory Morris* (a former accountant and "a sound tax lawyer") and his team from Edge & Ellison.

Eversheds (1ptnr/3assts) *Philip Harrison* ("gifted individual") is based in Nottingham, chairs the firm's National Business Tax Group. Three centres have particular tax

strength; London for stamp duty and financial services, Leeds for financial structures and Nottingham for entrepreneurial companies. Recently appointed three newly qualified assistants and an accountant who has partner status, but lost an assistant and a senior associate. **Clients/Work:** Advised Downing Corporate Finance Limited on structures for enterprise zone trusts; advised Clarendon College in relation to the tax aspects of the refurbishment of the Adams Building (PFI project).

The NORTH

Pinsent Curtis (Leeds) (2ptnrs/1assoc/2assts) The best known tax practice outside London was established by *Judith Greaves* and includes the "excellent" *John Christian*, an "extremely good tax lawyer." **Clients/Work:** Advising on the structured financing of cross-border JV and acquisition. Advising HSBC Private Equity on the North's largest private equity deal in '97, a £145m debt and equity investment in AM Paper. Advising on tax structuring of a UK joint venture.

Addleshaw Booth & Co (Leeds, Manchester) (2ptnrs/3assts) Stronger in

Manchester than Leeds with two well know partners, *Richard Hayes* and *Ed Jenkins,* with the latter perceived as the driving force. *John Toon* made a good impression in the Leeds office, holding the breach until Janet Jones arrived as a lateral hire from Dickson Minto. **Clients/Work:** Advising Flexitallic Group Inc. on the acquisition of the Worldwide flexitallic business of T&N plc for US$70m. Advising HSBC Private Equity and acquisition vehicle on the MBI of Abbey Hospitals. Acting for Carclo Engineering Group plc on the acquisition of Silleck Davall, a division of EIS Group plc.

Hammond Suddards (Leeds, Manchester) (Leeds – 1ptnr/ 2assts; Manchester – 3assts, one of whom will become a partner in November) A substantial part of Hammond's tax expertise is based in Manchester and Leeds, including the "always pleasant and professional" *Mark Simpson*. An indirect tax team was established in 1996 and is based in Manchester. **Clients/Work:** Disposal of ARM Utility Services Ltd to Sketchley plc. Reorganisation and flotation of Ultraframe plc. Acting for the management team in MBO of Tenmat from T&N plc.

Dickinson Dees (Newcastle upon Tyne) (1ptnr/2assts) *Tony Hennessey,* "a fine lawyer," heads the firm's tax unit, the only one of note in the North East. **Clients/Work:** Advising the shareholders and optionholders of Richmond Ice Cream in the reverse takeover by Treats plc. Advising shareholders on the flotation of Northern Recruitment Group plc. Advising Vaux Group plc in relation to the disposal of the St. Andrews' Homes nursing homes business.

Eversheds (Leeds, Manchester) (1ptnr/2assts) A courteous and effective team that will miss Richard Hutchinson who has left to join Coopers. *David Jervis* is "someone you can progress things with."

Walker Morris (Leeds) (1ptnr/3assts) The tax unit, headed by *Simon Concannon,* forms part of the corporate and commercial department. Work also includes tax based litigation and employee benefits. **Clients/**

Work: Acted for Leeds & Holbeck Building Society on a complex derivative financing. Tax led takeover of Bradford City Football Club. Tax status monitor for a listed venture capital trust.

SCOTLAND

HIGHLY REGARDED FIRMS
SCOTLAND

McGrigor Donald Glasgow

Maclay Murray & Spens Glasgow

MacRoberts Glasgow

McGrigor Donald (1ptnr/1assoc/2assts) The firm is unique in Scotland, having enough lawyers to be called 'a group.' *Ian Gordon* is ably supported by the "perennially charming" *Susan Hoyle,* someone who

"understands the issues and legal intricacies." **Clients/Work:** Section 110 reconstruction Saracen Value Trust. Share arrangements on the flotation of Core Group plc.

Maclay Murray & Spens (1ptnr) *Martyn Jones* is practical and effective and still going strong. Actively recruiting.

MacRoberts (2 fee earners) *Isobel d'Inverno*, a chartered accountant by qualification, has made the firm "a bit of a force in tax." **Clients/Work:** Institutional buy out of PSL Group – advisers to Natwest Equity Partners Limited; MBO of Smith & McLaurin Limited – advisers to MBO

team; PFI – Highlands and Islands Airport (advisers to Project).

LEADING INDIVIDUALS
SCOTLAND

D'INVERNO Isobel MacRoberts

GORDON Ian McGrigor Donald

JONES Martyn Maclay Murray & Spens

UP AND COMING

HOYLE Susan McGrigor Donald

LEADERS' PROFILES · REGIONS

CHRISTIAN, John M.S.
Pinsent Curtis, Leeds (0113) 244 5000
Partner in Corporate Tax Department.
Specialisation: Corporate and property tax, including corporate finance, reconstructions and demergers, asset finance, treasury and financing, property taxation, employee incentives, VAT, collective investment schemes and public bodies.
Prof. Memberships: VAT Practitioners Group. Member of the Corporation Tax Sub-Committee of Law Society Revenue Law Committee. Fellow of the Chartered Institute of Taxation.
Career: Qualified 1985. *Freshfields* 1983-89. Joined *Simpson Curtis* in 1990, becoming a Partner in 1991.

CONCANNON, Simon
Walker Morris, Leeds (0113) 283 2500
Partner in Corporate Department,
Head of Tax Unit.
Specialisation: Principal area of practice is corporate and property tax. Work includes restructuring, leasing, structured bank financing, MBOs, venture capital funding, employee remuneration schemes and VAT planning. Also handles tax disputes including dealing with the Inland Revenue Special Compliance Office, Special Investigation Section, and Stamp Office, the Contributions Agency and Customs & Excise. Major clients include Empire Stores PLC, Greenwoods (Menswear) Limited, Kalon Group PLC, the Leeds & Holbeck Building Society, Vaux Group PLC, Capital for Companies VCT PLC and IMS Group PLC.
Career: Qualified in 1990. With *Clifford Chance* 1990-94. Joined *Walker Morris* in 1994 and became a Partner in 1996.
Personal: Born 1966. Educated at Hertford College, Oxford 1984-87 and the College of Law, Chester 1987-88. Lives in Ilkley.

D'INVERNO, Isobel
MacRoberts, Edinburgh (0131) 226 2552
isobeld@macroberts.co.uk
Director – Corporate Tax.
Specialisation: Main area of practice is

corporate taxation work. Includes corporate acquisitions, disposals, re-organisations, EIS and Reinvestment Relief issues, PFI's and VAT on commercial property and corporate transactions. Has addressed seminars on PFI tax and company re-organisations, as well as lecturing on VAT and corporate work. VAT examiner for Chartered Institute of Taxation.
Prof. Memberships: Institute of Chartered Accountants (England & Wales), Chartered Institute of Taxation, VAT Practitioners Group, Member of Tax Law Committee of Law Society of Scotland.
Career: Trained as Chartered Accountant with *Ernst & Whinney* in London. Practised with *Ernst & Young* from 1980 and *Arthur Young* from 1985 as Tax Specialist. Joined *Brodies WS* as VAT and Corporate Tax Specialist in June 1991. Joined *MacRoberts* in August 1997.
Personal: Educated at St Andrew's University (MA Russian Language and Literature 1979). Gained ACA 1983, then ATII 1984. Non-executive member of the National Board for Nursing, Midwifery and Health Visiting for Scotland.

GORDON, Ian
McGrigor Donald, Glasgow (0141) 248 6677
Partner in Taxation Department.
Specialisation: Principal area of practice is employee benefits, including share incentive schemes, option schemes, and employee share ownership arrangements for listed, AIM and Ofex companies. Also advises on corporate acquisitions and reconstructions. Frequent lecturer on taxation issues.
Prof. Memberships:
Association of Pension Lawyers.
Career: Joined *McGrigor Donald* as a trainee in 1979. Qualified in July 1979. One year secondment to *Thomson McLintock CA* in 1983. Became a Partner at *McGrigor Donald* in the same year.
Personal: Educated at Edinburgh University 1975-79. Born 15th August 1957. Lives in Glasgow.

GREAVES, Judith
Pinsent Curtis, Leeds (0113) 244 5000
See under Employee Share Schemes, p. 297

HARRISON, Philip J.
Eversheds, Nottingham (0115) 950 7000
Partner in Tax Department.
Specialisation: Work includes tax aspects of corporate and property transactions, tax disputes, employee taxation and personal tax planning for business clients (especially planning for the sale of unquoted companies). Acts for a sponsor of enterprise zone trusts. Also handles profit-related pay and employee share incentives, including revenue approved and unapproved schemes and ESOPs (both onshore and offshore). Responsible for the tax and employee incentive aspects of the privatisation of Harland and Wolff Shipyard in 1989. Acted for the taxpayer in Mairs v. Haughey (arising from the H&W privatisation) up to his victory in the House of Lords in 1993. Head of Tax for *Eversheds* throughout the Midlands and divides time between Birmingham and East Midlands practices.
Prof. Memberships: Law Society, Society of Trust and Estate Practitioners.
Career: Qualified in 1986. Articled with *Evershed & Tomkinson* 1984-86. Became an Associate with *Evershed Wells & Hind* in 1989 and a Partner in 1991.
Personal: Born 22nd November 1960. Attended King Edward VI School, Lichfield 1972-79; Emmanuel College, Cambridge 1979-82 (BA 1982, MA 1986) and 1983-84 (LLM); College of Law, Chester 1982-83. Leisure interests include family, reading, walking and old cars. Lives in Nottingham.

HAYES, Richard
Addleshaw Booth & Co, Manchester (0161) 934 6000
Partner in Commercial Tax Department, Commercial Group.
Specialisation: Head of Commercial Tax Department providing specialist tax services to the firm. Specialises in employee share schemes including ESOPs, option schemes

and long term incentive schemes for both public and private companies.
Prof. Memberships: Law Society, Manchester Law Society;
Society of Share Scheme Practitioners.
Career: Qualified in 1972. Joined the firm in 1973, becoming a Partner in 1975. Treasurer of the Manchester Incorporated Law Library Society.
Personal: Born 31st October 1947. Attended Trinity Hall, Cambridge (MA 1969, LLB 1970). Chairman of the Manchester Midday Concerts Society. Leisure interests include railways, opera, classical music and sheep. Lives in Chapel-en-le-Frith.

HENNESSY, Tony
Dickinson Dees, Newcastle upon Tyne (0191) 279 9000
Specialisation: A broad range of corporate tax work, including all tax aspects of mergers, acquisitions, corporate reorganisations and flotations together with employee share scheme and remuneration planning work, asset financing and leasing and VAT planning.
Career: Called to the Bar 1979. Practised corporate tax in both a City of London practice and in a major provincial firm before being appointed as head of the corporate tax group at *Dickinson Dees* in 1992.
Personal: Educated St. Mary's College Crosby and University College Oxford (MA). Leisure interests include rugby, hill walking and 18th century music.

HOYLE, Susan
McGrigor Donald, Glasgow (0141) 248 6677
Specialisation: Main area of practice is corporate tax law, dealing with acquisitions and disposals, group reorganisations and MBO's. Also deals with employee share schemes.
Prof. Memberships: The Chartered Institute of Taxation.
Career: Qualified in October 1986. Worked for Ernst & Young and Coopers & Lybrand. Joined *McGrigor Donald* in 1995.
Personal: Educated Glasgow University.

HYDE, Ian R.
Pinsent Curtis, Birmingham (0121) 200 1050
Specialisation: Corporate and property taxation including tax efficient structures for joint ventures, demergers, reconstructions and property development. Ian also advises on VAT planning taxation of intellectual property and tax based investment structures.
Prof. Memberships: VAT Practitioners Group. Consulting Editor to Butterworths Encyclopaedia of Forms and Precedents.
Career: BA Oxford University (1987). *Rowe & Maw* (1988 - 1992). *Pinsent Curtis* (1992 - date).

ILLSTON, Timothy M.
Burges Salmon, Bristol (0117) 939 2000

JENKINS, Edmund
Addleshaw Booth & Co, Manchester (0161) 934 6000
Partner, in Commercial Tax Department, Commercial Group.
Specialisation: Practice covers all areas of business and property tax and includes advising upon the tax aspects of mergers and acquisitions, reorganisations and

restructurings, exiting strategies for persons selling their business and MBOs and other venture capital transactions. Acts for a mixture of quoted and private companies, individuals and venture capital houses.
Career: Called to the bar 1985. Re-qualified as a Solicitor 1991. At *Clifford Chance* 1989-1994 and *Halliwell Landau* 1994-1996 (Partner from 1995). Joined the firm as a Partner in 1996.
Personal: Born 31.1 63. Educated at Princethorpe College and Liverpool University. Interests include playing squash, golf and Italian wines. Married with two daughters and a son. Lives in Hale, Cheshire.

JERVIS, David M.
Eversheds, Leeds (0113) 243 0391
Specialisation: Main areas of practice are Corporate Tax, including sale and purchase of companies and businesses, group reorganisations, management buy-outs, employee share schemes including long term incentive plans and international schemes, VAT planning and tax efficient employee remuneration. Speaks on tax matters at seminars.
Prof. Memberships: Member of the Institute of Taxation.
Career: Paralegal with *Minter Ellis Morris Fletcher* in Brisbane. Qualified 1992 with *McKenna & Co.* Joined *Eversheds* 1994.
Personal: Born 21st September 1966. Garforth Comprehensive School in Leeds and University of Kent at Canterbury. Lives in Leeds. Interests include house renovation and outdoor pursuits.

JONES, Martyn
Maclay Murray & Spens, Glasgow (0141) 248 5011
mhj@maclaymurrayspens.co.uk
Specialisation: Partner, head of tax department and formerly senior tax lecturer at Glasgow University. Advises on VAT on property, capital allowances and capital gains. Co-author of "Revenue Law in Scotland". Much respected for his analysis, writings and lectures on the potential taxation implications of a devolved Scottish Parliament.
Prof. Memberships: Member of the Tax Law Committee of the Law Society of Scotland and its income tax and VAT sub-committees.
Career: Glasgow University (LL.B 74).
Personal: Born 1952.

LOWE, Kevin
Wragge & Co, Birmingham (0121) 233 1000
Specialisation: Pre-sale tax planning for vendors and purchasers; extracting value from owner-managed and family companies and businesses; corporate tax planning generally. Moving to *Wragge & Co.* allowed a focus on these areas and several significant tax planning instructions have already been completed.
Prof. Memberships: Law Society, Chartered Institute of Taxation (Vice-Chairman of West Midlands Branch).
Career: Sheffield University 1986 - 1989; *Eversheds* 1990 - 1997 (Associate 1996); *Wragge & Co.* 1998 (Associate).
Personal: A 'social' sportsman and ex-athlete.

MARLOW, Rod
Wiggin and Co, Cheltenham (01242) 224114
Partner.
Specialisation: Company, tax and financial services matters, for UK and international companies and trusts.
Prof. Memberships: Law Society, International Bar Association.
Career: Qualified in 1977. *Lovell White Durrant* 1975-80. Joined *Wiggin and Co* in 1980, becoming a Partner in 1982.
Personal: Born 30th September 1949. Attended Uppingham School 1964-69, and Magdalene College, Cambridge 1970-73. Lives in Amberley, Gloucestershire.

MORGAN, Elizabeth
Pinsent Curtis, Birmingham (0121) 200 1050
Specialisation: Corporate tax including corporate finance, corporate reorganisations, mergers and acquisitions, management buy-outs and flotations. Tax planning for private companies and their shareholders. Co-writes the Corporate Tax section for Practical Tax Lawyer.
Career: Cambridge University 1984 - 1987 (BA). Worked for *Pinsent Curtis* since qualification in 1994.

MORRIS, Gregory
Dibb Lupton Alsop, Birmingham (0345) 262728
Specialisation: Main areas of practice are corporate tax, business tax, capital gains tax, employee share based incentive schemes and VAT. Provides tax planning advice to companies and individuals.
Prof. Memberships: Institute of Chartered Accountants.
Career: Qualified 1984. *Arthur Young* (tax department) 1984-86, *TI Group Plc* (tax department) 1986-87, *Wolsely Plc:* Group Financial Accountant 1987-89, *Edge & Ellison* 1989-1997, *Dibb Lupton Alsop* 1997 to present.
Personal: Born 1955. Educated St. Philip's Birmingham, Oscott College, Birmingham and, eventually, University of Birmingham. Lives in Sutton Coldfield.

MOSS, Philip G.S.
Osborne Clarke, Bristol (0117) 984 5359
Partner in Tax Department.
Specialisation: All taxes for the corporate client, both domestic and international, with additional emphasis on the owner-managed business.
Prof. Memberships: Solicitor and Associate of the Chartered Institute of Taxation.
Career: *Speechly Bircham* (1983-85); *Slaughter & May* (1985-89); *Osborne Clarke* (1990 - Partner 1991).

MURPHY, Niall
Blake Lapthorn, Fareham (01489) 579990
Specialisation: Taxation aspects of corporate, reorganisations and reconstructions; mergers and acquisitions, joint ventures and international tax planning; taxation issues in property development and investment, the design and drafting of employee share schemes: Reorganisation and sale of Warings Construction Group; Kerry Group acquisition of Dalgety Food Ingredients and sale of Milling Division; Acquisition of Webbs Foods; and Acquisition of Sowester.
Prof. Memberships: ICAEW, ATII, Solicitor.
Career: Accountant with Binder Hamlyn (1980-

1986), Solicitor *Nabarro Nathanson* (1987-1991), Senior Solicitor *Wilde Sapte* (1991-1992); sole practice (1992-1995); Solicitor *Blake Lapthorn* (1996), Partner (1998).

POPPLEWELL, Nigel

Clarke Willmott & Clarke, Taunton
(01823) 445209

Specialisation: All areas of corporate and property tax (including VAT). Corporate acquisitions, disposals and reorganisations. Disputes with the Inland Revenue and Customs and Excise including representation before VAT Tribunals and Tax Commissioners. Recent cases/ matters include advice on capital allowances in respect of a £35m aviation contract, successfully concluding a number of Inland Revenue investigations with the Special Compliance Office, and successfully representing clients in a 9 day VAT tribunal.

Prof. Memberships: Law Society, Chartered Institute of Taxation, VAT Practitioners Group.

Career: Studied natural sciences at Cambridge. After obtaining a degree, spent 7 years playing professional cricket for Somerset and taught biology and chemistry during the winters. In 1985 retrained as a lawyer, starting with *Clarke Willmott & Clarke* in 1987 and becoming a partner in 1993.

POWELL, Ted

Mills & Reeve, Cambridge
+44 (0)1223 364422

Specialisation: All aspects of corporate and commercial tax including VAT and employee benefits. Specialist areas include tax planning for universities and other charities. Recent work - tax structuring for a major Millennium project; advising buyout team on large utilities MBO; advising on UK end of a take

over by a US Limited Partnership of a UK sales promotion business.

Prof. Memberships: Law Society; VAT Practitioners Group; Fellow of Royal Society of Arts.

Career: Merton College, Oxford, 1973-1976. Fellow in History, Downing College, Cambridge 1982-89; Trainee at *Freshfields* 1991-93; assistant Solicitor in Tax Department, 1993-95. Joined *Mills & Reeve* 1995. Became partner 1997.

Personal: Married with two children. Ex-professional interest in medieval history. Author of book on King Henry V.

ROBINS, Catherine

Pinsent Curtis, Birmingham (0121) 200 1050
Partner in the Corporate Tax Department.

Specialisation: All areas of corporate tax work including advising on the tax aspects of corporate finance and M & A transacations, flotations, management buy-outs and corporate reorganistions. Writes the corporate tax section for Practical Tax Lawyer.

Prof. Memberships: Member of the Income Tax Sub-Committee of the Law Society Revenue Law Committee.

Career: Bristol University 1983-1986 (LLB). Qualified in 1989. Joined *Pinsent Curtis* from *Allen and Overy* in 1990. Became a Partner in 1996.

SIMPSON, Mark C.

Hammond Suddards, Leeds
(0113) 284 7000
Partner in Corporate Tax Department.

Specialisation: Deals with the tax aspects of all types of corporate transaction, including corporate and asset finance and banking matters, employment tax including share

schemes, ESOP's and PRP, and VAT with particular reference to property transactions. Also undertakes tax planning for business proprietors (tax mitigation on investment and disposals including MBO's). Has written articles for various publications including 'Mortgage Finance Gazette' and 'PLC' and has spoken at a number of conferences and seminars.

Prof. Memberships: Law Society, VAT Practitioners Group.

Career: Qualified in 1985. With *Freshfields* until joining *Hammond Suddards* in 1991.

Personal: Educated at Churston Grammar School, Brixham, Devon 1971-78, Downing College, Cambridge 1978-82 (MA, LL.B) and Chancery Lane Law College 1982-83. Lives in Harrogate.

SMITH, Peter

Wragge & Co, Birmingham (0121) 233 1000
See under Employee Share Schemes, p. 297

TOON, John

Addleshaw Booth & Co, Leeds
(0113) 209 2000

Specialisation: To a significant and increasing degree practice focuses on the tax advice for property transactions for a mix of retail, developer, institutional and public sector clients. Also heavily involved in the tax apects of a broad range of corporate and commercial transactions.

Prof. Memberships: Law Society, Chartered Institute of Taxation, VAT Practitioners Group.

Career: Qualified as a solicitor in 1991; Joined *Addleshaw Booth & Co.* in January 1995.

Personal: Married with two children. Enjoys golf, theatre and gardening.

TELECOMMUNICATIONS

See also Computer Law & IT; Media & Entertainment (Digital Media)

RESEARCH: In compiling the tables, we consider all the information available to us, paying particular regard to the market research carried out by our team of ten qualified lawyers. (The researchers' details are set out on page three.) The rankings, therefore, reflect the opinion of the marketplace as revealed by systematic and objective research: see page four. (Our research is audited every year by the British Market Research Bureau.)

An index to all profiles is on page 67.

OVERVIEW: A comprehensive telecoms practice must offer regulatory and transactional advice and be supported by a strong corporate department. The global nature of the telecoms industry means that a leading telecoms practice will also have strong international connections. For this reason, UK telecoms work is firmly London based. In order to reflect the international character of this work we have introduced a new International Practices (non-UK) list which includes respected American telecoms practices.

There has been substantial movement in the tables. Clifford Chance are still accepted as a pre-eminent name in the field, but there was a strong feeling that other firms also deserved to be in the highest category. Allen & Overy, Bird & Bird, Baker & McKenzie and Simmons & Simmons join them in the top band of leading firms. While each firm approaches telecoms work from its own unique perspective, they all have sufficient strength in most of the defined areas to warrant a place at the top.

Coudert Brothers, Freshfields and Rakisons were deemed to have fallen slightly behind their competitors. Outside London only Eversheds in Leeds and Wiggin & Co in Cheltenham have recognised telecoms practices.

LEADING FIRMS · LONDON

ALLEN & OVERY
BAKER & MCKENZIE
BIRD & BIRD
CLIFFORD CHANCE
SIMMONS & SIMMONS

ASHURST MORRIS CRISP
COUDERT BROTHERS
DENTON HALL
LINKLATERS

HIGHLY REGARDED FIRMS

Charles Russell
Freshfields
Lovell White Durrant
Olswang

Field Fisher Waterhouse
Rakisons
Sidley & Austin
Taylor Joynson Garrett

LONDON

Allen & Overy (9 corporate ptnrs, 6 finance ptnrs 13 corp assts, 12 fin assts) Promoted this year to the leading band of firms. Considered to have a "good strong practice," especially in financing, and are "aggressive and keen on price." The team includes the "sensible and pragmatic" *Ian Ferguson*, and *Claire Wright* who has been promoted from up and coming. **Clients/Work:** Advising Cable & Wireless and Cable and Wireless Communications on the £5bn merger of Mercury, Bell Cable Media, Nynex CableComms and Videotron. Advising the Turkish Government on restructuring of their telecoms sector and the privatisation of Türk Telekom. Advising Telkom SA on restructuring.

Baker & McKenzie (2ptnrs/4assts in core team, plus 5 other ptnrs) *Peter Strivens* heads the department, but keeps a lower profile than the "supportive and enthusiastic" *Stephanie Liston*, who has "a broad perspective on telecoms." They are seen to draw strength from the international capability of

the firm. **Clients/Work:** Advised Energis on joint venture with Deutsche Telekom and France Telecom. Advised on the IPO of Polish Telecoms operator. Advise Iridium.

Bird & Bird (15ptnrs/13assts) Have had a good year in the telecoms field, but there is a feeling that a lack of international strength may hamper long term development. The "linchpin" of the department is *David Kerr*, who is described by a client as "professionally expert and easy to get on with. He has a flexible mind and outlook, and anticipates what we need." **Clients/Work:** Advised British Gas Transco on the disposal of its telecoms assets to ICL; advised a leading telecoms operator on an important case relating to entitlement to withdraw a telephone number allocated to a customer; advised on joint venture for digital interactive TV services.

Clifford Chance (12ptnrs/40assts) While maintaining their high profile and excellent work, it was universally felt that they were no longer out on their own at the top. *Liz Hiester* is well-known generally and *Tim Schwarz* is known for his finance expertise. Undertake telecoms work in relation to

privatisation, financing, liberalisation and licensing work. **Clients/Work:** Acting on privatisation of TeleDanmark; financing advice for PTC (Polish GSM operator); acting for the Organisation of Eastern Caribbean States on the liberalisation of the Caribbean telecoms sector.

Simmons & Simmons (14ptnrs/21assts) Making a great push in this area, and have been elevated from the third band of leading firms to the top. They have built "a strong team in a short time," which is supported by a solid corporate practice. *Tom Wheadon* has a "commercial feel for the industry," and *Chris Watson* is "great on the competition side of telecoms." Their cable work, in particular, has been singled out for recommendation. **Clients/Work:** General Cable plc; OLO Group; International Facilities licence group (comprising 34 of the 46 applicants for the first IF licences).

Ashurst Morris Crisp (8ptnrs/15assts in Communications, Media and Technology) A well-known satellites practice, which is the province of the highly experienced *Stewart White*. *Tony Ghee* has also been recommended again even though he has been focusing more on the media side this year. **Clients/Work:** Advised Thuraya Satellite on equity raising and procurement of satellite based mobile phone system; acted for Baring Bros in relation to the formation of CWC; Virgin Communications.

Coudert Brothers (2ptnrs/4 assts) May suffer from the loss of Michael Rhodes, although the "knowledgeable" *Colin Long* is still widely admired as a doyen in the industry. **Clients/Work:** Advised WorldCom on merger with MCI and acquisition of Compuserve Network Services; advised Telenor on investment in Ukraine.

Denton Hall (2ptnrs/3assts as specialists, plus 6 others in team) Respected telecoms practice with strong international connections. *Nicholas Higham* knows about telecoms from the IT perspective. Specialists in regulation, privatisation, commercial deals and satellite work. **Clients/Work:** Acting for the governments of Bulgaria, Estonia and The Bahamas on privatisation of their national operators, involving reforming the legal and regulatory framework etc; advising Hutchison on its network operations; advising six new applicants for UK International Facilities Licences and/or PTO licences.

Linklaters (12ptnrs/5assts) *Robyn Durie* is regarded as a knowledgeable telecoms lawyer, approaching the subject from an IP background. The firm has particular strength in corporate transactions and financing involving telecoms companies. **Clients/Work:** Advised BT on deals with MCI and Cegetel; advised on flotation of Telecom Italia; advised China Telecom on its Hong Kong/New York listing.

Charles Russell (6ptnrs/6assts in Media and Communications group) Described by clients as "a friendly and approachable firm giving sound advice." The "robust" *Mark Moncreiffe* is "strong commercially" and "able to deal with complex issues under pressure." **Clients/Work:** Advised Freepages Group plc (UK) on

NASDAQ listing, investing in RequesT Ltd, and on the joint venture with VNU.

Freshfields (14ptnrs/20assts in Telecoms & Media) *Rachel Brandenburger* is a well respected competition lawyer who also specialises in the telecoms field. **Clients/Work:** Acted for MCI Communications on its lapsed proposed merger with BT; Belgacom; Acted for Omnitel Pronto Italia in relation to the establishment and financing of a cellular telephone system in Italy.

Lovell White Durrant (4ptnrs, 8assts in Computers, Communications and Media unit) *Heather Rowe* is well respected as a telecoms lawyer with a banking background. **Clients/Work:** Acted on a number of global telecommunications outsourcing agreements and general telecoms service agreements for both suppliers and customers; act for a major UK cable company in respect of regulatory, contractual and other contentious matters.

Olswang (3ptnrs/6assts) The Communications Group operate a respected telecoms practice. **Clients/Work:** Advising Ionica Plc on its global share offering and dual listing in London and on NASDAQ; Paging Network Inc in its negotiations in respect of UK spectrum allocation; Torch Telecoms Ltd on regulatory work.

Field Fisher Waterhouse (7ptnrs/ 17assts) Enter the tables following the merger with Allison & Humphreys. Good reputation especially for building networks and infrastructure. *Tony Ballard* enters the list for the first time, and is described as "the leading expert on wireless matters." **Clients/Work:** Act for Colt Telecommunications Group Plc (one of the UK's top five public telecoms operators); advised Eurobell Holdings Plc on obtaining spectrum in the 40ghz band and obtaining licences and general corporate/commercial advice.

Rakisons (3ptnrs/4assts) Making a big push in this area. Team includes the "business orientated" *Chris Hoyle* (negoti-

ated one of the first OLO interconnect agreements with BT). **Clients/Work:** Focuses on out-sourcing and licensing work. Clients include: IDT; Easynet; Singapore Telecom.

Sidley & Austin (2ptnrs/5assts) Have the back-up of a large US practice, but have not made a major impact on the UK market. The telecoms practice is spearheaded by *John Edwards*. **Clients/Work:** AT&T Colt; European Commission.

Taylor Joynson Garrett (3ptnrs/4assts) Recommended for their cable work. *Edward Mercer* has "acute telecoms expertise and commercial nous." **Clients/Work:** Outsourcing for Rank and Reckitt & Colman; creation of new trade association for the calling card services industry; commenting on the Licensing and Interconnection Directives into UK law for CCA (Cable Communications Association).

LEADERS' PROFILES • LONDON

BALLARD, Tony
Field Fisher Waterhouse, London
(0171) 481 4841
Partner
Specialisation: Main area of practice covers television and film. Commercial and regulatory work for television network and service providers in both public and private sectors, including established broadcasters and new entrants in the satellite, cable, multimedia and general telecoms fields; also for providers of infrastructure for satellite and terrestrial networks. Major feature film production and distribution. Other areas of practice include competition, copyright and administrative law. Arbitrator on International Arbitration panel of American Film Marketing Association and trained mediator for alternative dispute resolution. Frequent speaker at conferences.
Prof. Memberships: International Bar

Association, Law Society, BLACA, CLIP, RTS and Chairman of UK branch of European Centre for Space Law.
Career: Qualified in 1974, having joined *Allison & Humphreys* in 1971. Became a Partner in 1975. Merged with *Field Fisher Waterhouse* in 1998.
Personal: Born 21st August 1945. MA (Cantab) 1964-68. Fellow of Royal Anthropological Institute. Leisure interests include astrophysics and painting. Lives in London and Suffolk.

BRANDENBURGER, Rachel
Freshfields, London (0171) 936 4000
Brussels (00) 32 2 230 0820
Partner, Head of Freshfields Communications and Media Group.
Specialisation: Has led many projects in front of the UK and EU regulatory authorities, including the European Commission, the Office

of Telecommunications, the Independent Television Commission and the Department of Trade and Industry and the European Commission. Communications work has included advising international telecommunications operators, mobile operators and cable franchise operators in the UK, continental Europe and the USA. Through this work, she has experience of mergers and strategic alliances and privatisations, as well as licensing, interconnection and other regulatory issues in the communications sector. Also has a range of media clients including broadcasters, programme providers and newspaper publishers. Regular contributor to legal and industry publications on communications and media and speaker at conferences and seminars.
Career: Articled with *Freshfields*; qualified in 1979; became a partner in 1988.

Personal: Born 2nd April 1954. Educated at North London Collegiate School 1961-72 and St Hilda's College, Oxford 1973-76 (MA Jurisprudence).

DURIE, Robyn
Linklaters, London (0171) 456 3256
Partner, Corporate Department, Communications Group.
Specialisation: Wide experience in broadcasting, telecommunications, commercial regulatory, and intellectual property and information technology work over the past 15 years.Qualified 1977 – Australia, 1987 – England & Wales. Became a Partner, 1990. Publications include 'Australian Halsbury Commentary on Broadcasting and Telecommunications', co-author of 'Broadcasting Law & Practice' and 'Whale on Copyright' (Third Edition). Editor of the 'Telecommunications & Computer Law Journal'.

EDWARDS, John
Sidley & Austin, London (0171) 360 3600
Specialisation: Telecommunications, broadcasting and information technology law including corporate and commercial transactions in the sector as well as regulatory advice including UK and EC competition law aspects.
Prof. Memberships: Law Society. City of London Solicitors' Company.
Career: 1970 to 1994 *Clifford Turner/Clifford Chance.* 1994 to date *Sidley & Austin*; Managing Partner of London office.

FERGUSON, Ian
Allen & Overy, London (0171) 330 3000
Specialisation: Advises on all aspects of telecommunications in the UK and internationally, including regulation, strategic investments, privatisations, mergers and acquisitions, joint ventures and on contracts for the supply of telecommunications systems, equipment and services. Also specialises in information technology, advising on all aspects including, in particular, outsourcing, e-commerce and electronic banking arrangements.
Prof. Memberships: IBA.
Career: Articled *Allen & Overy*, qualified 1985, Partner 1992.
Personal: Born 11th September 1959. Educated at Sevenoaks School and Southampton University 1982 (LLB). Interests include photography and travel.

GHEE, Tony
Ashurst Morris Crisp, London
(0171) 638 1111
See under Media & Entertainment: Film & Broadcasting, p. 566

HIESTER, Liz
Clifford Chance, London
(0171) 600 1000
Partner. Principal area of practice is telecommunications and related converging industry areas including information technology and broadcasting.

HIGHAM, Nicholas
Denton Hall, London (0171) 242 1212
email: nach@dentonhall.com

Specialisation: Partner in Media and Technology Group. Main areas of practice are telecommunications, information technology, digital media and copyright. Work includes regulation (14 countries), privatisation (4 countries), outsourcing and system development agreements. Acted on the establishment of the first Trans-European network for telecoms and for satellite operators, and for The British Library on its Digital Library Project for a digital terrestial broadcaster, and for Internet Service Providers. Author of many articles on regulation, communications and I.T. Regular lecturer on telecommunications, multimedia and I.T.
Prof. Memberships: Associate of Chartered Institute of Patent Agents, International Institute of Communications, Trade Marks Agent, IBA.
Career: Qualified in 1971. Joined *Denton Hall* as a Partner in 1992. Previously at *Linklaters & Paines* 1975-1981, solicitor and Partner at *SJ Berwin* 1981-1992.
Personal: Born 1947. Leisure interests include bridge. Lives in London.

HOYLE, Christopher
Rakisons, London (0171) 367 8000
Head of the Telecommunications and Information Technology Department.
Specialisation: Main areas of practice are telecommunications and information technology work, both regulatory and commercial. Obtained the first UK ISR licence. Negotiated the first reseller OLO interconnection agreement with BT. Significant in obtaining many UK international facilities licences in the first tranche of applications. Has negotiated various telecommunications joint ventures and interconnection agreements. Currently working on various interconnection agreements around Europe, switch partition and co-location agreements, international settlement agreements and outsourcing agreements for telecommunications services. His department has a significant presence in the UK and Europe and acts for investors in submarine cable systems, facilities based carriers, satellite service providers, PITs, mobile data providers, resellers, Governments regarding privatisation of their telecoms industry, terminal manufacturers, internet service providers, and value added service providers, both domestically and internationally.
Prof. Memberships: Federal Communications Bar Association, Contributor to Telecommunications and Space Journal.
Career: Qualified 1983. Partner with *Rakisons* since 1995.
Personal: Born 13th October 1959. Holds an LLB (Hons) Cantaur, LLM (Hons) Cantab and Dip IPL (London). Leisure interests include rugby and the theatre. Lives in London.

KERR, David
Bird & Bird, London (0171) 415 6000
Partner in Company Department.
Specialisation: Main area of practice is corporate and commercial work involving deals in the telecommunications, digital media and information technology sectors. Has extensive experience of major transactions in these areas, including acquisitions, joint ventures, project finance, privatisation and outsourcing agreements. Frequent speaker at conferences

on telecommunications and information technology.
Prof. Memberships: Communications Lawyers Association, IBA, Law Society.
Career: Qualified in 1985. Joined *Bird & Bird* in 1985, becoming a Partner in 1987.
Personal: Born 1960. Attended Jesus College, Cambridge (MA Hons, 1982). Lives in London.

LISTON, Stephanie
Baker & McKenzie, London (0171) 919 1000
Partner in Corporate/Commercial Department.
Specialisation: Communications work includes advising upon, drafting and negotiating communications related contracts and commercial transactions and providing EC and UK regulatory advice in connection with telecommunications and broadcasting activities.
Career: Qualified in England and Wales in 1994. Admitted to the District of Columbia Bar in 1988. Admitted to the State Bar of Texas 1985. Associate with *Fulbright & Jaworski*, in London, Houston, Texas, and Washington, D.C.: 1987-89. Senior Attorney with *MCI Communications Corporation* 1990-92. *Freshfields'* Company Department 1992-95. Joined *Baker & McKenzie* – London in 1995.
Personal: Born 15th March 1958. Attended The Colorado College (BA in History/Political Science 1980), University of San Diego Law School 1980-82 and University of Notre Dame London Law Centre 1982-83 (Juris Doctor 1983). Attended Trinity Hall, Cambridge University (LL.M. in English Law – 1st Class – 1984). Lives in Hampstead.

LONG, Colin
Coudert Brothers, London (0171) 203 2248
Partner in Corporate/Commercial Department.
Specialisation: Main area of practice is the corporate, commercial and regulatory aspects of communications. Also advises on competition law and intellectual property issues. Has advised on a number of leading telecom deals and cases, such as establishment of Mercury One-2-One (Corporate); Merger of WorldCom/MCI (Regulatory/Merger Control); EC Studies on Multimedia, Interconnection (Regulatory/Competition Rules); Successful litigation against the Director General of Telecommunications; Study for a Global Mobile Satellite Services Operator (Regulatory). Author of Telecommunications Law & Practice (Sweet & Maxwell Second Edition 1995); author of numerous articles, and a regular speaker.
Prof. Memberships: Law Society, International Bar Association, (Joint Chairman Communications Law Committee), Society for Computers and Law.
Career: Qualified in 1970. Joined *Coudert Brothers* in 1990 as a Partner.
Personal: Born 4th June 1946. Attended Epsom College 1959-64, then Bristol University 1964-7. Leisure interests include swimming, skiing, golf and tennis. Lives in London.

MERCER, Edward
Taylor Joynson Garrett, London
(0171) 353 1234
Head of IT/Telecommunications Group.
Specialisation: Main area of work covers the regulatory competition and commercial aspects of running telecommunications systems worldwide. Particular expertise in the regulatory field, interconnect, procurement

agreements and in relation to the cable industry. Related work covers wayleaves, construction contracts and street works. Has particular knowledge of the regulation of conditional access. Acted in a number of private placements and involved in regulatory aspects of flotation work associated with cable companies in the UK. Acts for cable and telecomms trade association and operators' groups. Contributor to the Law Society Gazette, Annual Media Law Review and trade magazines. Frequent lecturer at seminars on cable and telecommunication issues in the UK and Europe.

Prof. Memberships: Law Society, Association of Council Secretaries and solicitors.

Career: Qualified 1980. Head of Legal Section Adur District Council 1980-83, then Borough Solicitor, Rossendale Borough Council 1983-85. Secretary to Cable Authority 1985-89. Joined *Allison & Humphreys* in 1989, becoming a Partner in 1990. Partner *Taylor Joynson Garrett* 1996.

Personal: Born 1st February 1956. Attended King Edward's Five-Ways School 1967-74, then Trinity College, Cambridge 1974-77. Leisure pursuits include clay pigeon shooting, acting and badminton. Churchwarden. Lives in Lewes.

MONCREIFFE, Mark

Charles Russell, London (0171) 203 5000
Partner in Company/Commercial Department, Head of Media and Communications Group.

Specialisation: Acts principally for companies active in the UK and international telecommunications and media market. Is involved in regulatory and transactional work in this area.

Prof. Memberships: Law Society.

Career: Qualified in 1978. Joined *Charles Russell* in 1984 and became a Partner in 1985.

Personal: Born 23rd March 1953. Attended Uppingham School 1966-70, Queens' College, Cambridge, 1971-4, and Université Libre de Bruxelles 1974-5. Leisure interests include varied outdoor sports.

ROWE, Heather

Lovell White Durrant, London
(0171) 236 0066

Specialisation: Non-contentious information technology and multimedia work, including matters relating to the Internet, telecommunications, electronic banking, electronic data interchange and lending and security re companies in the computer and telecommunications areas. Editor newsletters of Committee R (technology) of the IBA; Chairman UK editorial board 'Droit de l'Informatique et des Telecoms'; consultant editor, 'IT Law Today' and 'Computer Law and Security Report'; correspondent 'Computer and Telecommunications Law Review'; contributor 'Communication Law' and 'Banking Technology'; editorial Board Butterworths Journal of International Banking and Financial Law: editorial board 'Virtual Finance'.

Prof. Memberships: Vice-Chairman Committee R (technology), IBA; Chairman ICC International Working Party on Data Protection and Privacy; Member ICC UK Computing, Telecommunications and Information Policies Commission; member International Telecommunication Users Group and Telecommunications Users Association.

Career: Articled *Wilde Sapte*, London: Qualified 1981 with *Wilde Sapte*; Assistant

Solicitor, *S J Berwin & Co*: Assistant Solicitor, *Lovell White Durrant*; Partner 1988.

SCHWARZ, Tim

Clifford Chance, London (0171) 600 1000
Partner in Media, Computer and Communications Group.

Specialisation: Specialising in international telecoms and informatics projects: telecoms privatisations, BOT agreements, telecoms financings, etc. Has worked on telecoms and informatics projects on the ground in Albania, Bulgaria, Burundi, Congo, Czech Republic, Hungary, Kenya, Latvia, Lithuania, Poland, Romania, Russia, Slovak Republic, Slovenia, Turkey, Uganda, Ukraine, West Bank/Gaza.

Career: Partner, *Clifford Chance*, May 1997. Main telecoms lawyers, World Bank Legal Department, 1995-97. Solicitor, *Clifford Chance*, 1989-95. Seconded to OFTEL's Legal Department, 1989-90. Trainee solicitor, *Clifford Chance*, 1987-89.

Personal: BA Jurisprudence, Oxford University, 1981. BCL, Oxford University, 1982. Première et deuxième licences en droit européen, ULB, Brussels 1984-86.

STRIVENS, Peter

Baker & McKenzie, London (0171) 919 1000

Specialisation: Partner and the Head of the Telecommunications Practice Group. Work includes advice on licensing and regulatory issues in the UK and other jurisdictions, investments and joint ventures in the telecommunications industry and advising on a wide range of industry issues, including contractual negotiations and disputes. He has extensive experience of cross-border transactions and privatisation investments in Central and Eastern Europe and is currently working on telecommunications privatisations in Poland and Lithuania. He gives frequent conference presentations on telecommunications issues and has written the UK and International Chapters of "Baker & McKenzie – Telecommunications Laws in Europe", Butterworths 1998. He qualified in 1984 with *Baker & McKenzie* and became a Partner in 1990.

Career: Educated at St Johns College, Johannesburg, University of Witwatersrand (1971-1975) and Balliol College, Oxford (1979-1981).

Personal: Born 15 December 1954. Leisure activities include painting, tennis and looking after a growing family. Lives in London.

WATSON, Chris

Simmons & Simmons, London
(0171) 628 2020
Head of Telecommunications

Specialisation: Telecoms; Competition; European Union and Trade Law. Recent major cases/ matters: Prohibition of BT/ BSkyB joint marketing campaign by Oftel; Prohibition of BT Reconnect Offer by Oftel; Acquisition of Imminus Limited by General Cable Plc; Acquisition of 50% interest in Yorkshire Cable by General Cable Plc from Singapore Telecom; Merger of General Cable with Telewest Plc; Issue of International facilities licences by Oftel – advice to 35 of 46 applicants, advising principally in relation to community and competition law; Advice to CCA on Fair Trading Condition and drafting submissions to Oftel; Advice to CCA on Reform of Competition Law and drafting submissions to DTI; Advice to Rapture TV

Limited on carriage terms and start up arrangements; Member of Steering Committee of Broadcasting Policy Research Project of Regulatory Policy Institute Oxford University; Appointed as legal adviser, to the panel of experts advising the National Audit Office on its review of Oftel's use of its competition regulation powers in the Licensing regime; Advice to Viatel Inc on all European aspects of its recent (April 1998) successful joint debt and equity issue which raised over US$1 billion for a project in eight separate European jurisdictions; Advice on a similar project for a different client; Advice to Econophone/ ATL on the UK regulatory and EC aspects of Econophone's successful February 1998 US$300 million debt financing; Advice to ACC Corporation in relation to its European subsidiaries in its merger with Teleport Communications Group, Inc; Recommended as legal adviser by The World Bank on international projects. Speaking Engagements: Speaker at Regulatory Policy Institute on Competition and Telecommunications 16 v 97; Speaker in Amsterdam at Techlaw Conference on Competition and Telecommunications 23 v 97; speaker in Manila (at IPBA Conference) on Competition and Telecommunications in the UK 31 viii 97; Speaker in London at LEGG Conference on International Telecommunications Competition & Accounting Rates 17 xi 97; Speaker in Madrid at (Spanish Association of Telecommunication Law & Information Technologies Seminar) on Oftel and the Development of Competitive Telecoms in the UK 11 xii 97; Speaker in Londson (CLT Training Course) on the Interconnection 21 i 98; Speaker in London (Presentation for One2One) on Interconnection 18 & 19 ii 98; Speaker in London at (Euroforum Conference) on Regulating Digital Broadcasting in London 20 ii 98.

Prof. Memberships: Solicitor, England and Wales. Avocat à la Cour (Member of Paris Bar).

Career: Education: Marlborough College 1970-74, New College Oxford 1976-79; MA (Modern Languages); College of Law, Guildford 1980 (CPE) and 1981 Law Society Finals. Career History: Joined *Simmons & Simmons* 1981; admitted as a solicitor in 1983; partner 1988; founded *Simmons & Simmons* Paris Office 1988; qualified and admitted as an Avocat à la cour Paris in 1993; Managing Partner, Paris Office 1991 to 1994; Head of International telecoms, *Simmons & Simmons* London 1995 to date. Languages: French, German, Italian (all spoken), Spanish, Portuguese, Russian (reading only).

Personal: Leisure interests: Chablis growing; fly fishing; bird watching; hockey (Honourable Artillery Company); cricket; music and books.

WHEADON, Tom

Simmons & Simmons, London
(0171) 628 2020

Specialisation: His specialisation is in the law, regulation and policy of telecommunications. In that field, he is regarded in Legal Directories as a "Leading Individual" and as one of the 25 Best Business Lawyers in the UK. Recent work has included work for the Government and the Industry on International Facilities Liberalisation, the introduction of the Network Charge Control Regime, the three most recent re-negotiations of BT's Standard Interconnect Agreement and a number of wet and dry international infrastructure projects. He advises a wide range of clients in this field and is a regular conference speaker and contributor of

articles to specialist journals.
Prof. Memberships: Law Society and International Bar Association.
Career: Southampton University, Guildford Law School, admitted as a solicitor in England and Wales in 1989. 1987-1989: Trainee Solicitor, *Ashurst Morris Crisp*. 1989-1995: Assistant Solicitor, *Ashurst Morris Crisp*. 1995-1996: Corporate and Regulatory Affairs Solicitor, Videotron Corporation Ltd. 1996 to date: Partner, Communications at *Simmons & Simmons*.
Personal: Married to Kate with three sons, Fred, Henry and George.

WHITE, Stewart
Ashurst Morris Crisp, London
(0171) 638 1111
Partner and Head of Telecommunications Group.
Specialisation: All aspects of law and regulation of media and communications including policy and strategy in the UK and in relation to the European Union, Middle East, Latin America, Asia, the India sub-continent and Africa.
Prof. Memberships: Editor and contributor to numerous specialist material and guest lecturer on telecommunications law at Queen Mary College, London.
Career: Admitted NSW 1976 and UK 1979. Partner *Blake Dawson Waldron* Sydney 1983-1988. Practised in UK since June 1988. Joined *Ashurst Morris Crisp* as Head of Media and Communications in 1994.

WRIGHT, Claire M.
Allen & Overy, London (0171) 330 3000
Specialisation: Main area of specialisation is telecommunications, advising on telecommunications related projects both in the UK and internationally including telecommunications regulation, strategic investments, joint ventures and privatisations. Seconded to the Network Competition Department of Oftel in 1994. Subsequently has acted for Cable & Wireless in connection with the merger of Mercury Communications, NYNEX CableComms and Bell Cablemedia, Swisscom in connection with strategic investments in India and Malaysia and Telekom SA in South Africa in connection with the introduction of a strategic equity partner. She has also advised on telecommunications privatisations in the Czech Republic, in Belgium, Turkey, Moldova, Lithuania and Jordan. Currently is advising in connection with the telecommunications privatisation in Pakistan and Estonia and on the auction of third generation mobile spectrum for the Radiocommunications Agency.
Prof. Memberships: TMA, City of London Solicitors Company.
Career: Articled *Allen & Overy*, qualified 1988, seconded to Oftel in 1994, Partner 1996.
Personal: Born, 6th December, 1962. Attended University College London. Leisure interests include golf.

THE REGIONS

Eversheds (Leeds) (1ptnr/4assts) The work of the Leeds based national practice competes with the City firms, although the work is more commercial and regulatory than corporate or project based. Act for both users and buyers of systems and services. *Neil Brown* heads the team, and spends about 50% of his time on telecoms. **Clients/Work:** Network development work for Energis; Mitel Telecom Ltd; commercial work and network building for Cable & Wireless.

Wiggin & Co (Cheltenham) Niche media and communications practice with international connections. **Clients/Work:** Mainly undertake cable broadcasting and satellite work.

John Watkinson works for InterConnect Communications Ltd in Chepstow. Despite not being in private practice, he appears in the list of leading telecoms practitioners because he is regarded as "something of a guru in the telecoms industry."

INTERNATIONAL PRACTICES (NON UK)

The American firms have a longer tradition of experience in telecoms work and operate in a sophisticated market. Most of the firms which are based in New York (such as **Skadden, Arps, Slate, Meagher & Flom**) tend to act on the finance and transactional side, although **Coudert Brothers** and **Debevoise & Plimpton** are two New York firms which are also respected regulatory advisors. The firms based in Washington DC are more likely to be niche practices which focus on regulatory work. **Goldberg Goddles Weiner & Wright** is a small niche practice devoted to telecoms work. **Squire Sanders & Dempsey** has a comprehensive international practice. It is known for the work it does for the US government, but has also done the privatisation work for the governments of the Czech Republic and Honduras. **Morrison & Foerster** is originally from San Francisco and "has an impressive regulatory practice."

BROWN, Neil
Eversheds, Leeds (0113) 2430391
Profile: Telecommunications Partner. Head of *Eversheds* Telecoms and Energy Utility Groups.
Specialisation: Main area of practice is work of a commercial/regulatory nature for clients in Telecoms and Energy industries. Telecoms work includes regulatory advice, industry specific commercial agreements, network and infrastructure development, and some international projects. Telecom clients include Orange, Martin Dawes, Torch, PSI Net, Eskom Telecommunications (South Africa) and St. Olav (Poland). In the Energy sector he has recently handled 4 major independent power projects, 2 for Yorkshire Electricity and 2 for major industrial buyers of power. Well-known also as an adviser on canals and inland waterways.
Prof. Memberships: International Bar Association (Communications and Utilities Committees).
Career: Joined *Breeze & Wyles*, Hertford 1981. Qualified 1983 and left to join *Watson Burton*, Newcastle. Moved to *Eversheds* in 1986. Partner 1988.
Personal: Born 17th January 1957. Attended Richard Hale, Hertford 1969-77, then Warwick University 1977-80. Leisure pursuits include supporting Newcastle United F.C., performing magic, the theatre and languages (Spanish and French). Lives near Ilkley.

WATKINSON, John
InterConnect Communications, Chepstow
(01291) 620425
Director.
Specialisation: Main areas of practice are European Telecommunications and Radiocommunications law and regulation: licenses: Interconnect agreements: contracts: privatisation. Key projects have included a review of telecommunication regulation and

laws throughout the EC, Central Europe and North America, advising the Governments of Austria, Poland, Bulgaria, Latvia, Macedonia, Morocco, Mauritius, Norway, Ukraine, Slovak Republic, Czech Republic, Bosnia and Caisse Française de Developpement France on telecommunication and radiocommunication issues. Frequent contributor to seminars and conferences on these matters. Joint author of

UK Telecommunications Approval Manual and of European Approval Manual. Course Leader at the Institute of Directors on 'The Director and the Law'.
Career: Qualified in 1986. Previously Barrister at Law 1972-86. MP for West Gloucestershire 1974-79; Parliamentary Private Secretary Home Office, 1976-79. Member of Public Accounts Committee 1976-79; Member of Council of

Europe 1976-79; Member of Western European Union 1976-79. Rapporteur Legal Affairs Committee 1978-79, Defence and Armaments Committee 1978-79. Reporter for BBC Money Programme 1979-83. Director and Head of Legal and Regulatory Services for InterConnect Communications Limited (ICC) from 1985.
Personal: Born in January 1941. Attended Oxford University 1960-63.

TRANSPORT (ROAD AND RAIL)

RESEARCH: In compiling the tables, we consider all the information available to us, paying particular regard to the market research carried out by our team of ten qualified lawyers. (The researchers' details are set out on page three.) The rankings, therefore, reflect the opinion of the marketplace as revealed by systematic and objective research: see page four. (Our research is audited every year by the British Market Research Bureau.)

OVERVIEW: The section divides into Road and Rail. Road is then sub-divided into Carriage/Commercial and Regulatory (Disciplinary and Licensing).

Carriage: This heading relates to carriage of goods and related disputes (including CMR disputes). It covers claims for loss or damage to cargo and insurance claims for carriers/forwarders or insurers. Most firms with carriage experience are able to deal with intermodal disputes which may include carriage of goods by rail or sea.

Commercial: Only a small number of firms are heavily involved in this area which includes contract advice to vehicle operators, hauliers, freight forwarders and distributors.

The carriage and commercial tables are combined and the major changes in London involve Waltons & Morse. Both the firm and Chris Dunn move up to the top band following praise from clients for their good service, competitive fees and friendly approach.

Regulatory (Disciplinary and Licensing): Covers criminal and disciplinary proceedings for matters such as tachograph and overloading offences or contravention of construction and use regulations. Also includes licensing of goods and passenger operators and related public inquiries.The majority of firms have understandably not disclosed client names as clients do not wish to gain unnecessary publicity for criminal/disciplinary matters.

In the London tables, Wedlake Saint have moved into a top band on their own, having been singled out by clients and practitioners nationwide as "a cut above the rest" in terms of quality and quantity of work. Jeremy Fear and his firm also move up following strong countrywide recommendations. There is little change to the tables in the regions. In Manchester, Jonathan S Lawton has merged with The Wake Dyne Partnership to form Wake Dyne Lawton which joins the list.

Rail: An area which is subject to continuous change following privatisation. Firms which acted for the major players during the privatisation remain in the tables if they have moved on to other projects or are still acting for the same clients. A new wave of firms are now acting for the privatised rail companies. Denton Hall and Tom Winsor move up the tables as they have a good spread of the new clients. Dibb Lupton Alsop are a new entry recommended particularly by major franchisee clients. Hollingworth Bissell (a 2 partner firm of ex BR lawyers) is also a new entry.

ROAD: CARRIAGE/COMMERCIAL

LONDON

Clyde & Co (1 ptnr/2 assts 70% (London); 3 ptnrs/4 assts – 100% (Guildford)). A trade association recommends them to its members and has never had a dissatisfied customer. Clients are impressed with the good service. *David Hall* ("major player", "very commercial and able") is known to have a good following. *Anthony Thomas* is highly regarded for his cargo insurance claims work. *Maire Ni Aodha* is recommended as up and coming. **Clients/Work:** Carriage/ Commercial.

Hill Dickinson Universally regarded as a leading firm in the field. *Julia Marshall* is a "determined" lawyer, praised for her commercial sense and protection of her clients. *Kay Pysden* is also recommended. **Clients/Work:** Carriage.

Holmes Hardingham (4 ptnrs/1 asst/1 legal exec 70%) The firm has a solid reputation and is highly respected both technically and commercially. Praised for focusing on the real issues. *Adrian Hardingham* is described as "one of the best in the field." *Andrew Messent* is an "academic and knowledgeable lawyer" with good commercial sense. *Tim Knight* and *Jane Hobbs* are also recommended. **Clients/Work:** Carriage: Spectra v Hayesoak acting for underwriters re interpretation of RHA conditions (Ct. of Appeal). Lacey's Footwear v Bowler acting for liability insurers of Bowler (road haulier) re interpretation of wilful misconduct provisions of CMR convention (Ct. of Appeal).

Waltons & Morse (2 ptnrs/2 assts 100%; 1 asst 50%) Have the potential to present serious competition to the larger firms, particularly because of their competitive fees. Described by clients as "top rank" and "extremely competent" with a "specialist team of lawyers providing a one to one service from start to finish". *Chris Dunn* has established a star reputation for being "thorough, professional and meticulous – leaving no stone unturned before recommending a course of action". He and the firm move up to the top band. *Ian Charles-Jones* also has a good following. **Clients/Work:** Carriage/Commercial: Successful Ct. of Appeal defence against claim by Sphere Drake Insurance plc for goods damaged by fire in transit from UK to Italy. Acted on subrogated cargo insurer's claim against carriers and a security firm arising out of armed hijack in Northern Ireland.

Berrymans Lace Mawer (*Stuart Armstrong* and 1 asst, both 50%) **Clients/Work:** Carriage: Cargo claims relating in particular to damaged machinery and food arriving in the UK at incorrect temperatures.

Davies Arnold Cooper (1 ptnr/1 asst spend 60% of their time dealing with transit matters as part of the firm's marine transport department). *Ken Silk* is "a fine lawyer who deals with cases on a no nonsense basis." **Clients/Work:** Carriage.

Hill Taylor Dickinson (1 ptnr 20%/1 asst 40%) Particularly noted for intermodal disputes, stemming from their shipping expertise. *Kevin Sach* does the work. **Clients/Work:** Carriage.

The SOUTH

Davies Lavery (Maïdstone) (2 ptnrs) Excellent reputation nationwide as a "specialist niche practice." *Magdalene Lavery* is respected for her legal and commercial expertise. **Clients/Work:** Carriage: Spectra v Hayesoak re interpretation of RHA conditions (Ct. of Appeal). Levco Ltd v Rolenco Ltd & Ors. re interpretation of CMR conditions.

Burges Salmon (Bristol) (4 ptnrs 30%/3 assts 40%) *Richard Wynn-Jones* is well-known and respected by his contemporaries. **Clients/Work:** Commercial: Acquisition of share in Bristol Airport for FirstGroup plc. Acting in connection with bids for Sheffield Supertram and the Rio de Janeiro metro.

Bond Pearce (Plymouth) (2 assts) Part of the shipping and aviation practice. **Clients/Work:** Carriage.

Prettys (Ipswich) *Roland Sharp* heads the dept. **Clients/Work:** Carriage. Goods and transit disputes. Warehouse and logistics agreements.

The NORTH

LEADING FIRMS
ROAD: CARRIAGE · THE NORTH
DIBB LUPTON ALSOP Liverpool
HILL DICKINSON Liverpool/Manchester
ANDREW M. JACKSON & CO Hull
DICKINSON DEES Newcastle upon Tyne
EVERSHEDS Leeds

Dibb Lupton Alsop (Liverpool) *Martin Hill* handles road transport work from the Liverpool office. **Clients/Work:** UK and international insurers and underwriters. Practice includes policy drafting and recovery work.

Hill Dickinson (Liverpool/Manchester) (1 ptnr/1 asst both 50% – Manchester) (1 asst 50% – Liverpool) *Peter Jackson* is renowned nationally for his specialist knowledge in the transit field particularly under the CMR convention. Recommended as "number one in the North". *Caroline Henning* has been in the field for a while and moves to the third band from up and coming. **Clients/Work:** Carriage: Acted for insurers in Spectra v Hayesoak (Ct of Appeal).

Andrew M. Jackson & Co (Hull) (1ptnr/1 asst 25%) The firm's reputation hangs on *Dominic Ward* who was described as "strong technically and a good negotiator with up-to-date knowledge." **Clients/Work:** Carriage.

Dickinson Dees (Newcastle) (5 ptnrs from the commercial/competition group) Clients describe them as "an able team". **Clients/Work:** Carriage: Go-Ahead's acquisition of Brighton Transport.

Eversheds (Leeds/Manchester) (10 ptnrs, 17 assts in the northern road logistics and distribution team) Headed by *Jonathan Guest,* the team draws on expertise from the commercial, banking/finance litigation and property departments. **Clients/Work:** Commercial: Advising Lynx on its Euro-Express CMR conditions for distribution throughout Europe. Act for NFC plc, Hayes plc and UCI Freight.

LEADING INDIVIDUALS
ROAD: CARRIAGE · NORTH
JACKSON Peter Hill Dickinson
GUEST Jonathan Eversheds
HILL Martin Dibb Lupton Alsop
WARD Dominic Andrew M. Jackson & Co
HENNING Caroline Hill Dickinson

SEE PROFILES AT END OF THIS SECTION

ROAD: REGULATORY, DISCIPLINARY AND LICENSING

LONDON and SOUTH EAST

LEADING FIRMS
ROAD: REGULATORY LONDON AND SOUTH EAST
WEDLAKE SAINT London
DONNE MILEHAM & HADDOCK Brighton
MOORE & BLATCH Southampton
JEREMY FEAR & CO Enfield
PELLYS Bishop's Stortford

HIGHLY REGARDED FIRMS
Hawkins Russell Jones Stevenage
Kenneth Elliott & Rowe Romford
Griffith Smith Brighton

Wedlake Saint (London) (2 ptnrs/1 legal exec) Move up into a top band on their own following praise from clients who rate them extremely highly. ("Big players and good at it", "star firm"). *Alice Knott* is described as "highly effective" and *Barry Prior* is a "good advocate – very approachable". **Clients/Work:** FTA and Confederation of Passenger Transport UK members.

Donne Mileham & Haddock (Brighton) (2 ptnrs/1 asst – all 50%) **Clients/Work:** 25 Public Inquiries in the last year.

Moore & Blatch (Southampton) *David Thompson* has been recommended for his advocacy.

Jeremy Fear & Co (Enfield) (*Jeremy Fear* has 1 asst) Instructed as an agent by a number of leading provincial firms and described as "*the* transport lawyer in London." He has moved up the tables as a result. Also recommended for his knowledge of the London Borough of Transport Scheme and for his advocacy. **Clients/Work:** Magistrates Court and transport tribunals.

Pellys (Bishop's Stortford) (1 ptnr 85%/1 asst 50%) A small but well-known firm. *Roland Pelly* is known for his work for PCVs.

Hawkins Russell Jones (Stevenage) *Robin Cooper* handles transport work together with crime and employment. He has particular interest in PCVs, LGVs, plated weights, drivers' hours, security of loads and EC regulations.

Kenneth Elliott & Rowe (Romford) (1ptnr/1asst/1transport manager) **Clients/Work:** Licensing, public inquiries and appeals to transport tribunal.

Griffith Smith (Brighton) (1 ptnr) Specialism in private hire licensing for taxis.

LEADING INDIVIDUALS
ROAD: REGULATORY LONDON AND SOUTH EAST
FEAR Jeremy Jeremy Fear & Co
KNOTT Alice Wedlake Saint
PRIOR Barry Wedlake Saint
PELLY Roland Pellys
THOMPSON David Moore & Blatch
COOPER Robin Hawkins Russell Jones

SEE PROFILES AT END OF THIS SECTION

SOUTH WEST and WALES

LEADING FIRMS
ROAD: REGULATORY SOUTH WEST AND WALES
CARTWRIGHTS Bristol
CARTWRIGHTS ADAMS & BLACK Cardiff
OVER TAYLOR BIGGS Exeter

Cartwrights (Bristol) (3ptnrs/3assts) *Geoffrey Jones* ("knowledgeable", "easy to talk to", "very persuasive when he puts forward an argument") is known for his public inquiry work. **Clients/Work:** Include Firstbus plc, West Midlands Travel, Tesco Distribution and Road Haulage Association.

Cartwrights Adams & Black (Cardiff) (2 ptnrs 33% including *Geoffrey Williams*. **Clients/Work:** John Raymond Transport Ltd and Sheddick Transport.

Over Taylor Biggs (Exeter) (1ptnr/1asst) *Christopher Over* ("competent, forceful and astute") has a national reputation and moves up into a band of his own. The firm handles drivers' hours, licensing, overloading and vehicle defects. **Clients/Work:** Defending companies charged in transport related multiple fatalities under Health and Safety at Work Act in Truro Coach crash. Defending company charged in South Wales court with 70 tachograph offences and achieving full acquittal.

LEADING INDIVIDUALS
ROAD: REGULATORY SOUTH WEST AND WALES
OVER Christopher Over Taylor Biggs
JONES Geoffrey Cartwrights
WILLIAMS Geoffrey Cartwrights Adams & Black

SEE PROFILES AT END OF THIS SECTION

MIDLANDS

LEADING FIRMS
ROAD: REGULATORY • MIDLANDS
CARLESS DAVIES & CO Halesowen
ROTHERAS Nottingham
IRONSIDES Northampton

Rotheras (1ptnr 100%/2 ptnrs 50%, 1 ptnr 35%) *Ian Rothera* has an outstanding national reputation for his experience and ongoing work in this field. **Clients/Work:** RHA and FTA.

Carless Davies & Co (1 ptnr/1 asst/1 const) **Clients/Work:** RHA and FTA. *Michael Carless* has a national reputation.

Ironsides (1 ptnr/1 asst 50%) *Peter Mair*

was recommended particularly for his advocacy.

LEADING INDIVIDUALS
ROAD: REGULATORY • MIDLANDS
CARLESS Michael Carless Davies
ROTHERA Ian Rotheras
MAIR Peter Ironsides

SEE PROFILES AT END OF THIS SECTION

EAST ANGLIA

LEADING FIRMS
ROAD: REGULATORY • EAST ANGLIA
BARKER GOTELEE Ipswich
GOTELEE & GOLDSMITH Ipswich

Barker Gotelee (2 ptnrs 50%) *Michael Gotelee* and his firm have received nationwide recognition and praise and the firm has moved up as a result. **Clients/Work:** Panel solicitors for the RHA.

Gotelee & Goldsmith *Jonathan Ripman* is known for his experience in this field and has contributed to publications

such as Roadway and Commercial Motor.

LEADING INDIVIDUALS
ROAD: REGULATORY • EAST ANGLIA
GOTELEE Michael Barker Gotelee
RIPMAN Jonathan Gotelee & Goldsmith

SEE PROFILES AT END OF THIS SECTION

NORTH WEST

LEADING FIRMS
ROAD: REGULATORY • NORTH WEST
BACKHOUSES Blackburn
WAKE DYNE LAWTON Chester
BLACKHURST PARKER & YATES Preston
CHARLES STANSFIELD & CO Wilmslow
AARON & PARTNERS Chester

Backhouses *John Backhouse* maintains his reputation, while his son, *James Backhouse* has developed a following of his own and enters our tables. **Clients/Work:**

Shane Raymond Nuttall (t/a Redland Coaches) v Vehicle Inspectorate. Birkett & Naylor v Vehicle Inspectorate. Criminal proceedings against Bird (Alan).

Wake Dyne Lawton *Jonathan Lawton* merged his "national road transport practice" with The Wake Dyne Partnership in June this year. He was described by one interviewee as "the leading practitioner nationwide." He has higher Court advocacy rights and appears in the Crown Court.

Blackhurst Parker & Yates *Michael Waller* is particularly known for PCV work.

Charles Stansfield & Co The "effective" *Charles Stansfield* works with an ex-traffic policeman representing motorists and

transport companies. **Clients/Work:** RHA and FTA panel solicitors

Aaron & Partners (1 ptnr/1 asst) **Clients/Work:** RHA panel solicitors.

LEADING INDIVIDUALS
ROAD: REGULATORY • NORTH WEST
BACKHOUSE John Backhouses
LAWTON Jonathan Wake Dyne Lawton
STANSFIELD Charles Charles Stansfield & Co
WALLER Michael Blackhurst Parker & Yates

UP AND COMING
BACKHOUSE James Backhouses

SEE PROFILES AT END OF THIS SECTION

NORTH EAST

LEADING FIRMS
ROAD: REGULATORY • NORTH EAST
FORD & WARREN Leeds
JOHN O'NEILL & CO Newcastle
BYWATERS Wetherby

Ford & Warren (2 ptnrs/ 2 assts 25-50%) The leading practice in the north. *Stephen Kirkbright* is described as an "exceptional lawyer." *Gary Hodgson* is praised for his ability to "get to grips with cases and get good results".

John O'Neill & Co *Roger Hird* and his firm act for hauliers throughout the country.

Bywaters (2 ptnrs including *Mike Snell* who is known for his advocacy work) The

firm was particularly recommended by a client. **Clients/Work:** RHA panel solicitors.

LEADING INDIVIDUALS
ROAD: REGULATORY • NORTH EAST
KIRKBRIGHT Stephen Ford & Warren
HODGSON Gary Ford & Warren
HIRD Roger John O'Neil & Co
SNELL Mike Bywaters

SEE PROFILES AT END OF THIS SECTION

SCOTLAND

LEADING FIRMS
ROAD: REGULATORY • SCOTLAND
JEFFREY AITKEN SOLICITORS Glasgow

Jeffrey Aitken Solicitors *Michael Whiteford* remains the only recommended specialist in Scotland. He is known for his public inquiries and acts for haulage and bus operators.

LEADING INDIVIDUALS
ROAD: REGULATORY • SCOTLAND
WHITEFORD Michael Jeffrey Aitken

SEE PROFILES AT END OF THIS SECTION

NORTHERN IRELAND

Martin & Brownlie (1 asst 50%) Isobel Brownlie, a leading individual last year, has

left the firm and been appointed a County Court Judge. Her workload has been taken over by a fairly junior solicitor.

LEADING FIRMS
ROAD: REGULATORY • N.IRELAND
MARTIN & BROWNLIE Belfast

ARMSTRONG, Stuart
Berrymans Lace Mawer, London
(0171) 638 2811
Specialisation: Main areas of practice are cargo and goods in transit claims (charterparties, bills of lading, CMR and domestic road haulage, Warsaw Convention) and related cargo and G.I.T. liability insurance disputes. Acts for cargo underwriters, recovery agents, hauliers' liability underwriters, freight forwarders and hauliers.
Prof. Memberships: London Maritime Arbitrators' Association (supporting member). Association of Average Adjusters (annual subscriber).
Career: Articled with *Ingledew Brown*, qualified in 1983 and became a Partner in 1985. Joined *Berrymans* in December 1996.
Personal: Born 1958. Educated at The King's School, Canterbury 1971-76 and Southampton University 1976-79 (LLB Hons). Leisure interests include golf and chess.

BACKHOUSE, James
Backhouses, Blackburn (01254) 677311
Specialisation: Commercial Transport Law including: Defending prosecutions brought by the Vehicle Inspectorate, Police and Trading Standards, Environment Agency, Health & Safety Executive; Operators and Vocational Licensing including Inquiries, Environmental, Maintenance and Financial; Employment all issues; Health & Safety all issues. Current cases include 'Nuttall v. Wing' House of Lords, 'R v. Hennessey' Appeal against conviction (Court of Appeal) of causing death by dangerous driving. Currently dealing with a number of causing death cases arising out of passenger and goods transport industry. Has also lectured on Article 177 references to the ECJ, involvement in two such references. Experience in rebated diesel cases, including Vat & Duties Tribunal. Currently involved in defending alleged illegal transportation of arms to Nigeria prosecution.

BACKHOUSE, John
Backhouses, Blackburn (01254) 677311
Specialisation: Road Transport law and licensing of goods and passenger vehicles. A higher courts advocate in criminal cases. Appears in the Transport Tribunal, European Court, High Court and Court of Appeal Criminal Division. Takes licensing cases in the Traffic Courts. On Appeal to Court of Appeal last year, conviction of George and Roberts for Death by Dangerous Driving quashed, a wheel-loss case. Birkett Hayton v DPP Section 97 on (1)(A)(iii) Transport Act. DPP v Nuttall T/A Redline on permitting. Has appeared in European Court of Justice in 2 cases on Tachograph law.
Prof. Memberships: Law Society. Higher Courts Advocate (CRBYE).
Career: 2 years military service then advocacy doing transport law work for the last 37 years.
Personal: Married with a daughter and two sons, one a solicitor and the other a trainee solicitor.

CARLESS, Michael Joseph
Carless Davies & Co, Halesowen
(0121) 550 2181

CHARLES-JONES, Ian
Waltons & Morse, London (0171) 623 4255

COOPER, Robin
Hawkins Russell Jones, Stevenage
(01438) 222 223
Partner and Head of Criminal Law Department
Specialisation: All aspects of road traffic law but with particular emphasis on Construction and Use Regulations, PCV's, LGV's, plated weights, driver's hours, security of loads, EC Regulations etc plus extensive employment law expertise.
Career: Admitted 1977, whilst in public service. Joined *Hawkins Russell Jones* in 1981 and became a Partner in 1982.
Prof. Memberships: Law Society.
Personal: Born 18th September 1947. Educated at Luton Grammar School. Obtained LL.B(Hons) London University (external). Active Rotarian, keen on music, languages and travel. Lives in a Bedfordshire market town.

DUNN, Chris
Waltons & Morse, London (0171) 623 4255

FEAR, Jeremy
Jeremy Fear & Co, Enfield (0181) 367 4466

GOTELEE, Michael
Barker Gotelee, Ipswich (01473) 611211
Specialisation: Road Haulage and Public Service vehicle licensing, vehicle operation, prosecutions, disciplinary and environmental public inquiries, accidents, drivers' hours, CMR and employment. The firm covers other commercial aspects for businesses, tax, land, planning, pollution and waste.
Career: Qualified 1963. Since 1966 has acted for a wide range of operators and RHA and FTA members.
Personal: Born 1938. Interests are old vehicles, sailing and walking.

GUEST, Jonathan
Eversheds, Leeds (0113) 243 0391
Specialisation: Road transport law, logistics and distribution contracts, national and international carriage by road, rail and air, CMR, BIFA, sector based joint ventures and multi modal contracts.
Career: Qualified 1982, Partner 1986.

HALL, David
Clyde & Co, London (0171) 623 1244
Partner in Non-Marine Transit and Insurance Departments.
Specialisation: Main area of practice is non-marine carriage of goods including national and international road carriage, warehousing, insurance, sales and purchases of goods and freight forwarding. Also experienced in reinsurance disputes, marine charterparty disputes and carriage of goods by sea, especially recovery against sea-carriers. Addressed conferences on standard trading conditions and the impact of arson on insurers. Acts for British International Freight Association, Trade Association for Freight Forwarders.

HARDINGHAM, Adrian
Holmes Hardingham, London
(0171) 283 0222
Partner in Cargo Claims Department.
Specialisation: Principal areas of practice are transport and shipping law, encompassing international and domestic carriage of goods by road, sea and air. Other main area of work is marine insurance, particularly cargo risks. Major cases handled include Buchanan v. Babco (H.L.) (1978), Silber v. Islander Trucking (1985), ITT v Birkart (1988), the 'Rewia' (1991), and Spectra v Hayesoak (1997). Major clients include UK and overseas underwriters, traders, freight forwarders, hauliers and insurance recovery agents. Contributor of various articles on the CMR Convention in Lloyd's Maritime & Commercial Law Quarterly.
Career: Qualified 1978. Founding Partner of *Holmes Hardingham*.
Personal: Attended University College, Oxford. Holds private pilot's licence.

HENNING, Caroline
Hill Dickinson, Liverpool (0151) 236 5400
Specialisation: Solicitor (formerly a Barrister) working from Liverpool office specialising in marine, goods in transit and insurance litigation. Particularly marine cargo claims and road haulage claims, bill of lading and charter party disputes, Air carriage claims.
Prof. Memberships: Honourable Society of Middle Temple, WISTA.
Career: Called to bar 1993. Joined *Hill Dickinson Davis Cambell* Marine Department in 1993. Presently Solicitor with *Hill Dickinson*.
Personal: Wadham College, Oxford. Inns of Court School of Law. Leisure pursuits include food, wine and films. Lives in Liverpool but supports Newcastle United.

HILL, Martin
Dibb Lupton Alsop, Liverpool (0345) 262728
Specialisation: Insurance coverage disputes subrogation and defence of liability claims. Acts for a number of major insurers.
Prof. Memberships: Committee member of Liverpool Underwriters Association and associate member of Manchester Marine Insurance Association.
Career: Qualified 1977. Partner with *Hill Dickinson & Co* and then *Hill Dickinson Davies Campbell* until 1993. Practice of *Alsop Wilkinson* from 1993.
Personal: Born 12.5.1953. Sixth generation solicitor. Personal interests include rebuilding and racing vintage and classic cars and working on the bench.

HIRD, Roger
John O'Neill & Co, Newcastle
(0191) 222 1808

HOBBS, Jane
Holmes Hardingham, London
(0171) 283 0222
Transport: Road-Carriage/Commercial
Specialisation: Main areas of practice are carriage of goods by road and sea and related insurance issues. Handles a wide range of cases involving domestic road haulage and CMR, including freight forwarding and warehousing. Insurance work includes advising on policy disputes and handling subrogated claims on behalf of underwriters. Experienced in pursuing and defending bill of lading and charterparty cargo claims.
Career: Attended Merton College, Oxford 1985–1988. Qualified 1991. Joined *Holmes Hardingham* in 1992 and became a partner in 1997. Contributor to 'Multimodal Transport' (LLP 1997).

HODGSON, Gary
Ford & Warren, Leeds (0113) 243 6601
Specialisation: Partner in Commercial Law Department. Main area of expertise – HGV transport. Particularly experienced on operators licensing and regulatory matters. Extensive defence experience before magistrates courts and crown courts throughout England and Wales on full range of road traffic prosecutions. Particular specialisation in drivers' hours and records offences and European regulations. Extensive appearances throughout England and Wales on prosecutions arising from 'lost wheels' mystery. Recommended solicitor for the Road Haulage Association and Freight Transport Association. Specialisation in consultancy advice to transport companies on internal systems for monitoring safety and general operation. Consultancy work for businesses in the Haulage industry seeking BS5750 and ISO9000 accreditation. Regularly lectures to trade associations on road transport matters. Co-author of Commercial Motor Legal Bulletin. Regular contributor to the Trade Press.
Career: Qualified 1977. Joined *Ford & Warren* in 1978. Became Partner in 1985.

JACKSON, Peter W.
Hill Dickinson, Manchester (0161) 2788800
Email number Jacko@Hill Dicks.com.
Partner in Marine Department and Head of Hill Dickinson's Manchester office.
Specialisation: Main areas of practice are marine, goods in transit and insurance litigation. Work includes cargo claims, for both cargo and liability insurers, particularly international road haulage claims; ship related cargo claims for cargo interests; salvage; and monitoring foreign litigation. Also handles marine insurance work, particularly marine insurance policy interpretation for underwriters. Acted in 'ICI plc v. MAT transport', 'ITT v. Birkart', the 'Breydon Merchant' F & W Freight, the 'Los Angeles' and 'Microfine v. Transferry Shipping'. Individual charge-out rate is approximately £120 per hour, inclusive of mark-up.
Prof. Memberships: Liverpool Underwriters Association, Manchester Marine Insurance Association, London Maritime Arbitrators Association.
Career: Qualified in 1985, having joined *Hill Dickinson Davis Campbell* in 1983. Became a Partner in 1989.
Personal: Born 3rd April 1961. Attended St Edward's College, Liverpool 1972-79, then Exeter College, Oxford 1979-82. Leisure interests include football (Vice Chairman of South Liverpool FC, former Chairman of Football Supporters Association). Lives in Liverpool.

JONES, Geoffrey N.D.
Cartwrights, Bristol (0117) 929 3601
Specialisation: Senior Partner practising transport law with over 25 years experience in relation to all aspects of bus and lorry licensing and related public inquiries, road use public inquiries and judicial review challenges to Local Authorities. Also specialises in employment and industrial relations law with experience of all aspects of employment and industrial relations matters in contracts, service agreements and disciplinary procedures; multi-applicant industrial tribunals; TURA in tribunals; commercial transactions and advice and legal action in relation to industrial action.

Personal: Educated at Bristol University, 1956-1959. Former Lecturer at the College of Law. Trustee, Southmead Hospital Research Foundation. Lives in Bristol.

KIRKBRIGHT, Stephen
Ford & Warren, Leeds (0113) 243 6601
Partner in Business Law Department.
Specialisation: Main area of practice is transport. Experienced since 1970 in all aspects of road transport with particular specialisation in HGV and PSV transport, nationally and internationally. Has experience of operator licensing, criminal road traffic problems, civil claims arising out of road traffic accidents, goods in transit, and CMR claims. Acts as legal adviser to Road Haulage Association and recommended solicitor to the Freight Transport Association and Irish Road Haulage Association. Has sat on consultative committees at the Department of Transport on new legislation. Involved in leading authorities before the Transport Tribunal on finance, for HGV and PSV operators, particularly Rosswood, RHA v John Dee Limited, and JJ Adam Limited. Handled the leading cases on 'causing and permitting' (Kelly v Shulman and Redhead Freight v Shulman); and on 'using' (Travel-gas Midlands Ltd v Reynolds and others). Regular contributor to trade press. Principal editor of Commercial Motor Legal Bulletin. Regularly addresses conferences and meetings for RHA and FTA. Makes regular appearances on Radio and Television on transport issues.
Prof. Memberships: Fellow of the Chartered Institute of Transport.
Career: Qualified in 1968. Joined *Ford & Warren* in 1966 becoming a Partner in 1970. Currently Head of Business Law and member of Managing Board of *Ford & Warren*. Born 18 October 1941. Attended Sheffield University 1961-64 and College of Law 1965-66.
Personal: Leisure interests include music (plays guitar and piano) and painting. Lives in Wakefield.

KNIGHT, Tim
Holmes Hardingham, London (0171) 283 0222
Partner in Cargo Claims Department.
Specialisation: Main area of practice is carriage of goods by road, covering national and international carriage by road, warehousekeeping, related insurance matters and terms and conditions of business. Also experienced in carriage by sea work, including bill of lading claims, and carriage by air and rail.
Career: Joined *Ingledew Brown* in 1986, qualifying in 1988. Joined *Holmes Hardingham* in 1989. Became Partner in 1993.
Personal: Born 17th March 1964. Attended University of Kent 1983-85. Leisure pursuits include golf and squash. Lives in Enfield.

KNOTT, Alice C.
Wedlake Saint, London (0171) 405 9446
Specialisation: A Partner in the firm's transport law department. Main areas of practice include goods vehicle and PSV operating licencing matters. Conducting public inquiries before the Traffic Commissioner; The defence of Road Traffic Act prosecutions; Personal injury actions both road traffic accidents and employer's liability matters. Major cases have involved multi-defendant prosecutions in respect of EEC and domestic drivers hours/records matters and civil litigation arising as a result of major

motorway accidents.
Prof. Memberships: Memberships include The Law Society, The Road Operations Committee of the Confederation of Passenger Transport, The Freight Transport Association, The Chartered Institute of Transport.
Career: Born 30.12.63. Attended Benenden School 1976-1981. Exeter University 1982-85.
Personal: Horse riding, swimming and tennis.

LAVERY, Magdalene
Davies Lavery, Maidstone (01622) 688171
Specialisation: International and internal transit including CMR. Freight forwarders liability and policy disputes.
Prof. Memberships: Law Society.
Career: LLB Kings College, London. Upper Second Class.

LAWTON, Jonathan
Wake Dyne Lawton, Tattenhall, Chester (01829) 773100
Specialisation: Road traffic law specialist since 1972, with particular emphasis on commercial operations. Also handles employment law matters, health and safety, and some environmental work. Regular contributor to a number of trade publications, including Croners. Joint honorary legal adviser to the UK Warehousing Association. Freeman of the City of London. Gives frequent lectures and seminars on road haulage law, health and safety and employment.
Prof. Memberships: Heavy Transport Association.
Career: Qualified in 1962. Solicitor-Advocate (Higher Courts Criminal) 1997.
Personal: Born 18th February 1935. Cambridge University 1956-59.

MAIR, Peter
Ironsides, Northampton (01604) 234800
Specialisation: Main areas of practice are Transport Law, Goods and Passenger Vehicle Licensing and road traffic law generally. Handles specialist Advocacy before Traffic Commissioner, the Transport Tribunal and Magistrate's Court. Has represented several high profile UK and European companies in the past twelve months. Acts for RHA and FTA members regularly. Other specialisms include advice on wide range of Health & Safety issues and representation of companies faced with criminal prosecutions. Also experienced in Food Law and Liquor Licensing. Trained mediator for ADR.
Prof. Memberships: Law Society, ADR Group.
Career: Admitted 1971. Partner with *Ironsides*.
Personal: Aged 53. Educated at Oundle School. Qualified MCC coach. Rotarian and After Dinner Speaker.

MARSHALL, Julia
Hill Dickinson, London (0171) 695 1000
Partner in Marine & Cargo Department (London).
Specialisation: Advice and litigation in the field of insurance (marine and non-marine) and goods in transit inter-modally. Has a particular interest in the emerging rail freight industry. Drafts and advises Underwriters on policy wordings and advises merchants and carriers on conditions of trading. Has been involved in a number of leading decisions relating to CMR, e.g. Cicatiello and others v Anglo European Shipping Services Ltd and others, which successfully argued the first armed hijack defence under CMR Article 17.2. Founder of

ELLSA (European Lawyers for Land, Sea and Air), a specialist European group ensuring expedient international assistance in shipping, transit, insurance and most commercial areas.
Prof. Memberships: LL.B 1974 : F.C.I.Arb 1995. Supporting Member of the London Maritime Arbitrators Association. Member of the Rail Freight Group.
Career: Admitted 1977 after first training and working in the medical field. Proprietor of own firm 1981. May 1994 merged with and became a partner in the current firm of *Hill Dickinson*.

MELBOURNE, William
Clyde & Co, Guildford (01483) 555555.

MESSENT, Andrew
Holmes Hardingham, London
(0171) 283 0222
Partner in Cargo Claims Department.
Specialisation: Main area of practice is claims arising from the carriage of goods by sea, road and air, and related insurance issues. Co-author of 'CMR: Contracts for the International Carriage of Goods by Road' (1995, 2nd Edition). Contributor to 'International Carriage of Goods by Road (CMR)' (1987).
Career: Qualified 1975. Worked with *Ingledew Brown* until 1976, then took up a lecturing post until 1985. Returned to IBBG, becoming a Partner in 1987, and moved to *Holmes Hardingham* as one of the founding Partners in 1989.
Personal: Born 1951. Attended Wimbledon College, then Gonville & Caius College, Cambridge.

NI AODHA, Maire
Clyde & Co, London (0171) 623 1244
Specialisation: Domstic and international road haulage, freight forwarding, warehousekeeping and shipping. Advising industry and insurers.
Career: Qualified Irish solicitor and admitted in England and Wales.

OVER, Christopher
Over Taylor Biggs, Exeter (01392) 823811
Founding Partner 1993.
Specialisation: Principal area of practice is medical negligence dealing with claims of all types but particularly catastrophic injury. Represented clients in major medical claims involving substantial damages. Also deals with a wide range of transport cases including route licensing, planning and environmental appeals. Acted in transport cases on European Directives. Contributor to PI text books and Accident Line Book and author of articles in legal publications. Regular conference speaker and broadcasts frequently on local radio and TV.
Prof. Memberships: APIL, AVMA, SIA, Panel Solicitor for RHA and FTA. Law Society Public Relations Board.
Career: Qualified in 1977. Partner for ten years with *Crosse & Crosse* in Exeter: three years as Managing Partner. Founding Partner of *Over Taylor Biggs* in February 1993.
Personal: Born 18th October 1952. Attended King Edwards VI, Camp Hill, and Birmingham University. School Governor and Charity Trustee. leisure pursuits include walking, badminton, food and drink and travel. Lives near Exeter.

PARKER, Michael
Clyde & Co, Guildford (01483) 555555

Specialisation: Retained by the Cold Storage and Distribution Federation and the British International Freight Assocation, advising on all areas of transport law with an increasing involvement in EC law aspects and Customs investigations. Also acting for many members of the CIDF and BIFA and their Liability Underwriters.
Career: Qualified in 1979, joining *Clyde & Co*, Guildford in 1981. Partner since 1984.
Personal: Cardinal Vaughan Memorial School. Magdalene College, Cambridge. MA (Hons) (Cantab) Scholar Honoris Causa 1973-6.

PELLY, Roland des Voeux
Pellys, Bishop's Stortford (01279) 758080
Senior Partner specialising in transport and drivers hours laws.
Specialisation: Principal area of practice is transport and drivers hours laws, operational scheduling, investigations and reports to operators to ensure full legal and best practice compliance for operators as well as advising on specialised contracts of employment and licensing requirements. Also handles planning, employment and crime. Appears in the Magistrates Court, Crown Court and before traffic commissioners. Joined with specialist brokers to the industry to launch The Transport Operators Protection Scheme, legal expenses insurance designed to give maximum protection and legal support to the transport industry. Joint author of 'The Practical Guide to Drivers Hours and Records Rules'. Lectures regularly on drivers hours to various regional committees of coach and bus operators associations.
Prof. Memberships: Confederation of Passenger Transport UK (formerly Bus and Coach Council).
Career: Qualified in 1967. Established *Pellys* in 1971. Currently Senior Partner.
Personal: Born 13th February 1943. School Governor. Lives in Stansted.

PRIOR, Barry A.
Wedlake Saint, London (0171) 405 9446
Partner and Head of firm's Transport Law team of 5 fee-earners and para-legals.
Specialisation: Main area of practice is road transport law for goods and passenger vehicles; work covers operators licensing, defence of prosecutions, personal injury (road traffic and employers' liability), contract drafting, and commercial litigation associated with the industry. Also handles carriage of goods and passengers claims, including CMR/ Domestic contracts and local authority tendering bus contracts. Cases have included litigation arising from many major motorway multi-vehicle accidents, public inquiries into operators licenses and major driver's hours/records prosecutions. Contributor to 'Commercial Motor Magazine', the 'Journal of the British Association of Removers' and 'Coach and Bus Week'.
Prof. Memberships: Law Society, Chartered Institute of Transport, Freight Transport Association, Confederation of Passenger Transport, Law Society Personal Injury Panel.
Career: Qualified in 1969. Joined *Wedlake Saint* as a Partner in 1985.
Personal: Born 24th October 1943. Attended Lawrence Sheriff School, Rugby 1956-63, then Sheffield University 1963-66. Fellow of the

Chartered Institute of Transport; Affiliate Member Institute of Road Transport Engineers; Council Member of CPT UK. Lives in Marlow, Bucks.

PYSDEN, Kay
Hill Dickinson, London (0171) 214 7900
Specialisation: Advice, Litigation and Arbitration in the fields of uni and multi modal transport including disputes of jurisdiction and law and ship arrest. Advising on appropriate terms and conditions of freight operators and insurers on policy wording. Has been involved in a number of leading decisions eg. in the area covering RHA – 'Spectra v. Hayesoak' on bailment and construction of limitation provisions and CMR – 'Texas Instruments and Ors v. Nason Europe & Ors' being one of the first High Court actions where the carriers right to limit liability was disallowed due to a finding of wilful default under article 29.1, and BIFA tons – Rhone Prulenc Rorer Ltd v. TGA Ltd + Ors (CA) where due incorporation of terms was considered.
Prof. Memberships: Supporting member of the London Maritime Arbitrators Association, Panel Member of the Conciliation Panel of the London Maritime Arbitrators Association, Member of the Advisory Body of Legal Matters of FIATA and FIATA's representative on the CMI working party for uniformity of the law of the Carriage of Goods by Sea.
Career: Admitted 1987 having been educated at Tormead School, Guildford and gaining an LLB Hons Degree at University College London. Partner in 2 previous firms, having joined *Hill Dickinson Davis Campbell* in 1997 as a Partner. Currently Partner *Hill Dickinson*.
Personal: Lives in Claygate, Surrey.

RIPMAN, Jonathan
Gotelee & Goldsmith, Ipswich
(01473) 211121
Head of Litigation Department.
Specialisation: Main area of practice is road haulage work, including public enquiries, tachographs, overloading, general haulage problems in both Magistrates and Crown Courts, terms of business, trading conditions. Also experienced in debt recovery (computerised debt recovery service), employment advice (especially directors' and senior managers' contracts), environmental law and European legislation. Articles published in Roadway, Motor Transport, Commercial Motor, East Anglian Daily Times and Evening Star.
Prof. Memberships: LawNet, LawNet (Europe) – affiliated to EuroJuris, Suffolk & North Essex Law Society (Public Relations Officer), Communications Advisory Board.
Career: Joined *Gotelee & Goldsmith* in 1978. Qualified 1981. Partner 1984. Head of Litigation Department. Two years working experience in road haulage industry 1976-1978.
Personal: Born 13th June 1953. Attended Rugby School 1966-72, then St. Catharine's College, Cambridge 1973-75. School Governor, Woodbridge School. Chairman P.A.C.T. (Suffolk-based children's charity). Leisure pursuits include walking, sport and family. Lives in Woodbridge, Suffolk. Member of M.C.C.

ROTHERA, Ian
Rotheras, Nottingham (0115) 910 0600
Head of Transport Department.
Specialisation: Specialises in HGV and PCV Law, defence of prosecutions in Magistrates and Crown Courts, Construction & Use

offences, drivers' hours and tachographs, operator's licence applications, disciplinary and environmental public inquiries, Transport Tribunal appeals. Panel solicitor for the RHA and the FTA. Founder Member of the Association of Road Transport Lawyers. Member of Nottinghamshire Chamber of Commerce Transport Committee. Deputy Coroner for Nottinghamshire.

SACH, Kevin
Hill Taylor Dickinson, London
(0171) 283 9033
Transport: Carriage by Sea and Road/Commercial.
Specialisation: International carriage of goods by sea and road; charterparty disputes; marine insurance.
Prof. Memberships: Law Society.
Career: Born 1959. Merton College, Oxford – BA Hons French and German. Solicitors' Finals, College of Law, Lancaster Gate. Qualified with *Hill Dickinson & Co* (now *Hill Taylor Dickinson*) in 1986. Associate Partner 1989. Partner in *Hill Taylor Dickinson* 1991.
Personal: Married with three children. Football fanatic. Resides Witham, Essex.

SHARP, Roland
Prettys, Ipswich (01473) 232121
Specialisation: Significant part of practice is carriage of goods by road – national and CMR. Acts for insurers as well as carriers and associated businesses on business terms, distribution, warehousing and logistics aspects and related transport matters.
Prof. Memberships: Association of Road Transport Lawyers, Felixstowe Port Users Association.
Career: Qualified 1986 and worked at *Masons* until joining *Prettys* in 1992.
Personal: Born 10th March 1958. Attended Wellington College (1970-75) and Leeds University (1976-79). Leisure pursuits include sailing and golf.

SILK, Ken
Davies Arnold Cooper, London
(0171) 936 2222

SNELL, Michael
Bywaters Topham Phillips Solicitors, Wetherby (01937) 580300

STANSFIELD, Charles
Charles Stansfield & Co, Wilmslow
(01625) 539695

THOMAS, Anthony
Clyde & Co, Guildford (01483) 31161
See under Shipping & Maritime Law, p. 732

THOMPSON, David C.
Moore & Blatch, Southampton
(01703) 636311
Specialisation: Undertakes public enquiries in relation to goods vehicle licensing, the operation of transport businesses, operating centres and disciplinary hearings. Also acts in defending prosecutions for breaches of Road Traffic Law, covering a wide area in central/Southern England representing drivers and operating companies charged with offences in the magistrates and crown court. The firm provides advocacy services both in magistrates court and at public enquiries before the traffic commissioner. Deals with environmental issues and contract disputes arising out of carriage of goods. The firm acts for many leading haulage companies across the South and has defended a major tachograph prosecution in the UK which involved offences committed both in the UK and Europe.
Prof. Memberships: David Thompson is a member of Association of Road Transport Lawyers and a member of the Road Hauliers Association, the Law Society's Personal Injury Panel and the Association of Personal Injury Lawyers.
Career: He was formerly prosecuting solicitor for Manchester City Council. Joined *Moore & Blatch* in 1982 and became a Partner in the firm in 1989.
Personal: Enjoys all sports activities in particular football, cricket and rugby.

WALLER, Michael
Blackhurst Parker & Yates, Preston
(01772) 253601

WARD, Dominic
Andrew M. Jackson & Co, Hull
(01482) 325242
Partner in 1992.
Specialisation: Disputes involving carriage of goods by sea and road including advising transport intermediaries. International trade disputes, other contractual disputes involving marine or transport related matters.

Career: Qualified 1987.
Prof. Memberships: AIJA, SEG.
Personal: Born 30.3.63 in London. Education to age 14 in Germany. Speaks German. Interests include rugby, golf, badminton, cinema, books, and travel.

WHITEFORD, Michael G.
Jeffrey Aitken Solicitors, Glasgow
(0141) 221 5983
Specialisation: Road Transport Law. Practice covers representation at operator licence public inquiries before the Traffic commissioner, industrial tribunals and defending in prosecutions in the Scottish courts. Acts for many leading haulage and bus operators.
Prof. Memberships: Law Society of Scotland. Association of Road Transport Lawyers and the Royal Faculty of Procurators in Glasgow.
Career: Qualified 1971. Joined *Jeffrey Aitken* and has been a partner since 1972.
Personal: Born 15th December 1946. Educated Glasgow University.

WILLIAMS, Geoffrey
Cartwrights Adams & Black, Cardiff
(01222) 465959
Partner in Litigation Department.
Specialisation: Has 19 years of experience of representing operators of heavy goods and public service vehicles in Magistrates Courts, at Public Inquiries and before the Transport Tribunal. Also prosecutes for The Law Society in the Solicitors Disciplinary Tribunal and handles some defence work. Has rights of audience in the Higher Courts in civil proceedings. Lectures for transport organisations such as the Freight Transport Association.
Prof. Memberships: Law Society.
Career: Qualified in 1978. Joined *Cartwrights Adams & Black* in 1976, becoming a Partner in 1980.
Personal: Born 29th April 1954. Attended Trent Polytechnic, Nottingham 1972-75 and College of Law Chester 1975-76.

WYNN-JONES, Richard
Burges Salmon, Bristol (0117) 939 2000

RAIL

LONDON

LEADING FIRMS
RAIL: LONDON

FRESHFIELDS
LINKLATERS
SIMMONS & SIMMONS

DENTON HALL
FIELD FISHER WATERHOUSE

CLIFFORD CHANCE
DIBB LUPTON ALSOP
HERBERT SMITH
SLAUGHTER AND MAY
WILDE SAPTE

HIGHLY REGARDED FIRMS

Eversheds
Hollingworth Bissell
Norton Rose
Pinsent Curtis
Theodore Goddard
Wright Son & Pepper

Freshfields (22 ptnrs from various departments) Rated for their impressive client base. *Richard Phillips* is described as "imaginative, keen and a good negotiator". **Clients/Work:** Acting for English, Welsh and Scottish Railways on the acquisition of Railfreight Distribution. Acting for London Underground on its Power, Telecoms, Ticketing and Northern Line resignalling projects (over £1 billion). Acting for the Taiwan High Speed Rail Consortium (world's largest railway infrastructure project – over £20 bn).

Linklaters (12 ptnrs including *Philip Heyes*/30 assts from various departments) Rated for providing good quality advice. **Clients/Work:** Advising overseas governments on privatisations (Australia, Kenya, Pakistan). Completing refinancing of Channel Tunnel. Act for OPRAF.

Simmons & Simmons Described as "prominent players". *Gareth Davies* is notable in rail finance. **Clients/Work:** Railtrack.

Denton Hall Highly rated as an "active" rail practice, the firm has moved up the tables. *Tom Winsor* ("high flyer") is known as a great self-publicist, but is also a "brilliant, hard-working lawyer". **Clients/Work:** Acting for Virgin Rail Group on £2m upgrade of West Coast Main Line. Acting for South Wales & West Railway on successful appeal against Railtrack re access and timetabling matter. Acting for TOC on first arbitration against Railtrack re track access and performance regime.

Field Fisher Waterhouse *Nicholas Thompsell* ("enthusiastic") is rated for his broad experience and the firm move up the table. **Clients/Work:** Advised British Rail on the 5 outstanding non-passenger franchise privatisations. Advised Regional Railways North East on the £120m acquisition and leasing of a new fleet of 16 class 333 trains. Represent South West Trains.

Clifford Chance Active on the acquisitions side of the market. *Jeremy Brownlow* ("nice to deal with", "good commercial grasp") is highly rated as a good all-rounder. **Clients/Work:** Financing for banking and leasing clients.

Dibb Lupton Alsop (6 ptnrs/7 assts from various departments) A new entry this year recommended for rolling stock work. **Clients/Work:** Acquisition of rolling stock worth £100-400m for Connex Rail.

Herbert Smith (4 ptnrs) The work has a corporate bias. **Clients/Work:** Advising London & Continental Railways on all matters relating to its Eurostar operations, the construction and financing of the Channel Tunnel Rail Link and its proposed corporate reorganisation. Advising Eurotunnel on restructuring its £9bn debt financing.

Slaughter and May *Simon Phillips* handles some work for the Rail Regulator.

Wilde Sapte (11 ptnrs/12 assts from various departments) Highly regarded for financing of rolling stock and for tax advice.

Mary Bonar is particularly recommended. **Clients/Work:** Acting for Virgin Rail Group on successful acquisition of franchise of Inter City West Coast. Acting for Export Development Corp. of Canada in £250m financing of E, W & S Railways locomotives.

Eversheds *Max Harnden* (ex-Frere Cholmeley Bishcoff) has depth of experience following eight years in the legal dept of BR.

Hollingworth Bissell (2 ptnrs) Niche practice set up last year. Both are ex-BR lawyers who were heavily involved in the privatisation. Rated for their broad knowledge of the industry.

Norton Rose (10 ptnrs/14 assts drawn from corporate finance, banking, leasing and tax – p/t). **Clients/Work:** Represent Angel, Forward Trust and Porterbrook (ROSCOS). Acting for financier or lessor in several major UK rolling stock aqcuisitions in 1997.

Pinsent Curtis (4 ptnrs 15%) **Clients/Work:** Advising Connex South Eastern and Central on day to day matters.

Theodore Goddard (2 ptnrs 35%-65%/10 assts from various departments as and when required).

Wright Son & Pepper **Clients/Work:** Advising 11 heritage railways with an emphasis on regulatory, health and safety, licensing, franchising, access agreements and public inquiries.

Simon Wethered of Charles Russell has a good personal reputation.

LEADING INDIVIDUALS
RAIL: LONDON

BROWNLOW Jeremy Clifford Chance
DAVIES Gareth Simmons & Simmons
HEYES Philip Linklaters
PHILLIPS Richard Freshfields
WINSOR Tom Denton Hall

THOMPSELL Nicholas Field Fisher Waterhouse

BONAR Mary Wilde Sapte
HARNDEN Max Eversheds
PHILLIPS Simon Slaughter and May
WETHERED Simon Charles Russell

SEE PROFILES AT END OF THIS SECTION

THE REGIONS

HIGHLY REGARDED FIRMS
RAIL: THE REGIONS

Burges Salmon Bristol
Eversheds Leeds
Osborne Clarke Bristol
Wragge & Co Birmingham

Burges Salmon (Bristol) (2 ptnrs/11 assts as required) Reputed to be an active firm with good clients. *Richard Wynn-Jones* is well known and respected nationwide. **Clients/Work:** Acting for St. Paul International Insurance/Great Western Trains on Southall rail accident. Acting for G W Holdings on acquisition of 70 new vehicles. Acting for Great Eastern Railway in relation to closure of part of a light maintenance depot in London.

Eversheds (Leeds/Birmingham) The rail team is part of the national transport practice referred to in the Road section. **Clients/Work:** OPRAF, English & Scottish Railways Limited, National Express.

Osborne Clarke (Bristol) (3 ptnrs/5 assts from various departments – 25%) *Clive Watts* has been recommended as "excellent" by clients and contemporaries and enters the tables. **Clients/Work:** Acting for Prism Rail re manufacture and supply agreements for 43 new trains. Also advising on manufacture and supply of barrier gates.

Wragge & Co (Birmingham) (4 ptnrs including *Michael Whitehouse*/6 assts) **Clients/Work:** Acting for Travel West Midlands re Midlands Metro Line. Acting for PowerGen on a £340m project to provide distribution space for logisitics operators and a rail freight terminal.

LEADING INDIVIDUALS
RAIL: THE REGIONS

WATTS Clive Osborne Clarke
WYNN-JONES Richard Burges Salmon
WHITEHOUSE Michael Wragge & Co

SEE PROFILES AT END OF THIS SECTION

BONAR, Mary
Wilde Sapte, London (0171) 246 7000
Partner in Banking Department.
Specialisation: Head of Rail Group. Main areas of practice are rail law, project finance and asset finance. Experience commercialisation of rail industry, financing of rail infrastructure (including using Public Private Partnerships) and rolling stock; in domestic market specialises in track access, regulation and franchising. Clients include major banks, lessors, ECAs, governments, franchise groups and other corporates. Lectures and writes on rail industry and project finance.
Prof. Memberships: Liveryman, Worshipful Company of Carmen and City of London Solicitors Company; Women Solicitors Association. Member of Chartered Institute of Transport.
Career: LLB. Admitted in 1971. Solicitor and Partner (from 1973) at *Gamlens* Lincolns Inn 1971-89. Joined *Wilde Sapte* as Partner in 1989.
Personal: Born 28th July 1947. Educated at St Bernard's Convent High School, Westcliff, Essex 1958-65, University College, London 1965-68 and The College of Law, Lancaster Gate 1970-71. Princes Youth Trust Business Adviser. Lives in the City of London.

BROWNLOW, Jeremy
Clifford Chance, London (0171) 600 1000
See under Corporate Finance: 250+ Fee Earners, p. 226

DAVIES, Gareth
Simmons & Simmons, London
(0171) 628 2020
Specialisation: Specialises in commercial law in particular relating to railways. He played a leading role in advising on the legal steps to be taken to restructure British Rail and in creating the framework to handle safety, environment, competition, liability and operational matters as well as facilitating future renewal of and investment in Britain's rail network. Led and managed the team of lawyers acting for Railtrack Plc in creating the matrix of contracts to give effect to this new regime. Advised on the legal arrangements for the financing and implementation of a number of major new rail projects including ThamesLink 2000 and West Coast Mainline and has been closely involved with drafting and negotiating the contracts for these projects. Advises on crossborder rail transactions relating to "Freight Super Highways" in the EU. Also handles PFI and other projects work. Clients include Railtrack Plc. Contributor (re sale of goods and joint ventures) to Butterworth's 'Encyclopaedia of Forms and Precedents'.
Prof. Memberships: Law Society, Food Law Group (Committee Member).
Career: Qualified in December 1979 (England & Wales) and May 1981 (Hong Kong). Partner at *Simmons & Simmmons* since 1989.
Personal: Born 5th July 1955. Educated at the University of Sheffield 1973-76 (LL.B Hons) and the City of London Polytechnic 1978-81 (MA, Business Law). Leisure interests include sailing, cookery, board games and history. Lives in Burnham-on-Crouch.

HARNDEN, Max
Eversheds, London (0171) 919 4500
Specialisation: Specialises in commercial and legal issues relating to the Rail industry, in particular the contractual matrix relating to the privatisation restructuring.
Career: Qualified 1988. Worked for the British Railways Board (BRB) where he was integrally involved in shaping and executing BRB's parliamentary and commercial strategy. In 1996 joined *Frere Cholmeley Bischoff* which merged with *Eversheds*, London August 1998.

HEYES, Philip
Linklaters, London (0171) 456 3320
Specialisation: Partner specialising in corporate finance, UK and international transportation law, rail privatisation and privatisations.
Career: Qualified 1988. Made Partner 1995.

PHILLIPS, Richard A.R.
Freshfields, London (0171) 936 4000
Specialisation: His work includes asset and project finance, commercial law, corporate law, mergers and acquisitions, joint ventures, disposals and privatisations. Richard has a specialist industry focus of railways and has a wide experience of high profile corporate, project and finance work within this industry.
Prof. Memberships: Law Society, Chartered Institute of Transport, City Solicitors' Company.
Career: Qualified in 1981. Joined *Freshfields* in 1985, becoming a partner in 1989.
Personal: Born 1955, lives in London.

PHILLIPS, Simon J.
Slaughter and May, London (0171) 600 1200
Specialisation: Corporate finance, M&A, general corporate.
Career: Educated Winchester College and Queens' College, Cambridge. Joined *Slaughter and May* 1982. Partner since 1991.

THOMPSELL, Nicholas P.
Field Fisher Waterhouse, London
(0171) 481 4841
Specialisation: Corporate/Commercial lawyer. Particular interests include transport /travel (especially rail) and privatisation/PFI. Acts for South West Trains in relation to commercial /regulatory aspects of its rail operations. Advised Regional Railways North East on rolling stock leasing. Acted for British Railways Board in relation to numerous disposals. Acted for The Thomas Cook Group Limited in various transactions. Acted for an airline in relation to BA Franchise. Advised on various PFI schemes. Advised on the privatisation of HMSO and the Paymaster Agency.
Prof. Memberships: Law Society. City of London Law Society, Rail Study Association, Association of Partnership Practitioners.
Career: School: Bablake School, Coventry. University: King's College, London (LLB, AKC). Law School: College of Law, Chester. Articled *Slaughter and May*. Assistant Solicitor *Slaughter and May* 1987 – 92. Assistant Solicitor *Field Fisher Waterhouse* 1992, becoming a partner in 1993.
Personal: Trying to keep up with daughters' interests in music and computers.

WATTS, Clive
Osborne Clarke, Bristol (0117) 923 0220
See under General Corporate Finance, p. 240

WETHERED, Simon
Charles Russell, London (0171) 203 5000
Specialisation: Procurement, supply agreements, joint ventures, commercial law, insolvency, charities.
Prof. Memberships: Law Society, Charity Law Association, Insolvency Practitioners Association, Society of Practitioners of Insolvency.
Career: Clifton College, Bristol and Worcester College, Oxford. Qualified in 1970 with *Simmons and Simmons*. Partner *Dibb Lupton Alsop* 1978-1998. Partner *Charles Russell* 1998 -
Personal: Wine, opera, sailing, keeping fit. Liveryman of the Distillers Company. Member City Law Club. The Athenaeum. Married with three children.

WHITEHOUSE, Michael
Wragge & Co, Birmingham (0121) 233 1000
Specialisation: Head of Projects Group; Transport (rail, metros, railports), privatisations, PFI and project work and corporate finance.
Prof. Memberships: Committee member of Rail Freight Group, Chamber of Commerce Rail Forum.
Career: Articled *Slaughter and May*. Qualified 1977. Partner at *Wragge & Co* from 1987. Railfreight Group non-executive director; Chamber of Commerce Regional Rail Forum member.
Personal: Born 1952.

WINSOR, Tom
Denton Hall, London (0171) 242 1212
email: tw@dentonhall.com Partner in Energy and Infrastructure Group and Head of Railways Group.
Specialisation: Specialises in energy and infrastucture including international upstream oil and gas law, project finance, electricity, regulation, privatisation and railways.
Prof. Memberships: Member of Law Society of England and Wales, Law Society of Scotland, Society of Writers to HM Signet, IBA (Business Law and Energy and Natural Resources Law Sections), University of Dundee Petroleum and Mineral Law Society (president 1988-89), Society of Scottish Lawyers in London (president 1987-89), UK Energy Lawyers Group, member, Advisory Panel, Centre for the Study of Regulated Industries, published 'Taylor and Winsor on Joint Operating Agreements' textbook, honorary lecturer at Centre for Petroleum and Mineral Law and Policy, University of Dundee, frequent conference speaker, widely published on energy, regulation and railways topics.
Career: Apprenticeship with *Thorntons & Dickies WS*; assistant solicitor with *Thorntons & Dickies WS* 1981-82, admitted Scotland 1981, Notary Public 1982, self employed solicitor 1982-83, assistant solicitor *Dundas & Wilson CS* 1983-84, assistant solicitor *Norton Rose* 1984-91, qualified England 1991, joined *Denton Hall* 1991, partner 1991. On secondment as Chief Legal Adviser and General Counsel to the Rail Regulator 1993-95.
Personal: Born 7 December 1957. Educated Grove Academy, Dundee, Edinburgh University (1979 LLB), Dundee University (1983 Diploma in Petroleum Law, postgraduate dissertation on pipeline financing).

WYNN-JONES, Richard
Burges Salmon, Bristol (0117) 939 2000

TRAVEL

RESEARCH: In compiling the tables, we consider all the information available to us, paying particular regard to the market research carried out by our team of ten qualified lawyers. (The researchers' details are set out on page three.) The rankings, therefore, reflect the opinion of the marketplace as revealed by systematic and objective research: see page four. (Our research is audited every year by the British Market Research Bureau.)

LONDON

TRAVEL, TOURISM, PACKAGE HOLIDAYS

Overview: Firms in this sub-section deal with work ranging from regulatory compliance work with CAA, ATOL, ABTOT and IATA dominating; litigation with personal injury and consumer claims foremost but with scope for some heavyweight commercial claims and arbitrations; commercial work from advising on brochure production, ticket and general conditions to producing best practice policies for tele-sales and defence of trading standards prosecutions.

This year has seen much interest in the outcome of the MMC Inquiry into the travel industry which has implications for all holiday related businesses and many firms have reported a very busy year. As with last year the leading firms continue to be Field Fisher Waterhouse and Nicholson Graham & Jones and their star players Peter Stewart and Cynthia Barbor still dominate. Booth & Blackwell became Kingsford Stacey Blackwell in December 1997 and their travel practice is improved by their increased access to 'know-how'. For regulatory work the acknowledged leader is Richard Venables at Lane & Partners with Richard Gimblett at Barlow Lyde & Gilbert impressing this year. Away from London, Mason Bond and their personable star Stephen Mason are continuing to service big name national clients with good all round expertise.

Field Fisher Waterhouse (2ptnrs ; 3assts) "Specialist firm – good at what they do," and "know the industry." *Peter Stewart* ("succinct") and the less well known *Simon Chamberlain* have "together with NGJ, by far the biggest share of the market." Clients/Work: Involved in the MMC Inquiry. Advising on the introduction of new industry products. Accepting referral of instructions from a major City firm which sought this firm's expertise in licensing matters.

Nicholson Graham & Jones (3ptnrs ; 3assts) "Active in the market" known to be "fair to deal with." Clients rated them. *Cynthia Barbor* and *Tim Robinson* ("a true expert") head up this well regarded practice. Clients/Work: Include Thomson Tour Operations Ltd, ABTA and Kuoni.

Norton Rose (1ptnr 50%; 4assts 50 % Litigation Department) Good on financial aspects. Highly thought of lead partner *Patrick Farrell* is an "extremely good communicator." Clients/Work: Acted for Lunn Poly in large judicial review of holiday insurance charges linked to package holiday discount deals. Involved in the MMC Inquiry. Britannia Airways.

Lane & Partners (1ptnr/1asst) The "leading regulatory lawyer" *Richard Venables* is "the man for domestic licensing work." Venables admits his workload is aviation biased but he has a significant tour operator caseload as well. Clients/Work: KLM(UK) and a number of UK and foreign airlines. Acting in a significant aviation arbitration. General regulatory work relating to the CAA and ABTA.

Piper Smith & Basham (1ptnr 70-80%, 1ptnr 40%, 2assts 50%) "Active" and seeking to expand, leading light *Ian Skuse* has "been in the market a long time." Clients/Work: Involved in a heavyweight dispute with the CAA. Assisting in creation of new charter airline. Advising airline with major regulatory difficulties.

Barlow Lyde & Gilbert (3ptnrs/6assts) *Richard Gimblett* is a leading individual within this firm noted for its regulatory expertise. Clients/Work: Advice to the tour operating industry (through FTO) on recent CAA proposals for change to ATOL regime regarding the introduction of requirement for personal indemnities from company directors. Other regulatory work through FTO.

Herbert Smith (3ptnrs 10%; 2assts) Cross-departmental developing team, keen to increase their profile. **Clients/Work:** Continue to act for First Choice in corporate and litigious matters including the first group action by tourists against a tour operator.

Acting for Northern Leisure in nightclub acquisitions. Representing Queensborough Holdings.

Kingsford Stacey Blackwell (3ptnrs; 2 p/t; 2assts 25-50%) Formerly Booth & Blackwell. New to the rankings, *Trevor Sears* is

local counsel for IATA dealing with all work and specialising in travel agency insolvency matters. The firm merged in December 1997. **Clients/Work:** Include IATA, British Airways, Lufthansa.

LEADERS' PROFILES · LONDON

BARBOR, Cynthia M.
Nicholson Graham & Jones, London
(0171) 648 9000
Partner in Litigation Department and Joint Head Travel and Leisure Law Unit.
Specialisation: Main area of practice is travel and leisure law. Has over fifteen years experience in acting for major UK and international tour operators, travel agents, ground handlers, insurers, hotels, airlines and trade associations, advising on substantial litigation, commercial agreements and regulatory issues. Also handles general commercial litigation, including insurance and personal injury actions. Writes regularly for Travel Trade Gazette and other travel publications. Speaks frequently on travel law at UK and international conferences.
Prof. Memberships: Law Society, Institute of Travel and Tourism, Incentive Travel and Meetings Association.

CHAMBERLAIN, Simon
Field Fisher Waterhouse, London
(0171) 481 4841
Specialisation: Partner in the Aviation, Travel & Tourism Department specialising in commercial, corporate and regulatory work within the aviation and travel industries.
Career: Qualified in 1977. *Richards Butler & Co.* 1973-81. British Airways Plc 1981-1990. *Rowe & Maw* 1990-1994. Partner at *Field Fisher Waterhouse* since 1994.
Personal: Educated at Downside School. Born 8th August 1953. Lives in East Sussex.

FARRELL, Patrick
Norton Rose, London (0171) 283 6000
Partner in Commercial Litigation Department
Specialisation: Advises tour operators, travel agents and airlines on claims handling, contractual disputes of all descriptions, brochure terms and conditions, bonding arrangements and regulatory matters. Also acts for airlines (including start ups) and financiers advising on domestic and European regulatory matters. Acts regularly in aircraft finance litigation.
Prof. Memberships: MRAES, Vice Chairman of the Royal Aeronautical Society Air Law Group, Chairman of the UK ICC Commission on Air Transport, Member of Institute of Travel and Tourism, IBA, LSLA, CLLS (Chairman of the CLLS Aeronautical Law Sub-Committee).

GIMBLETT, Richard
Barlow Lyde & Gilbert, London
(0171) 247 2277
See under Aviation: Aviation Insurance Litigation, p. 130, 132

ROBINSON, Tim S.H.
Nicholson Graham & Jones, London
(0171) 648 9000
Partner in Litigation Department, joint Head Travel and Leisure Law Unit.
Specialisation: Travel, Tourism and Leisure law. Acts for tour operators, travel agents, hotel groups, insurers, airlines and trade associations. Also handles general commercial litigation, libel and media acting for newspaper and magazine publishers. Writes for Travel Trade Gazette and major travel and tourism publications, the national press, TV and radio. Speaks at travel industry conferences in the UK and worldwide.
Prof. Memberships: Institute of Travel and Tourism, Media Society, Incentive Travel and Meeting Association, Board Director of Pacific Asia Travel Association (UK and worldwide), European Tour Operators Association.
Career: Qualified 1977. Joined *Nicholson Graham & Jones* 1979. Partner 1982.
Personal: Born in 1953. Attended St Edmund Hall, Oxford 1971-73. Leisure interests include music, reading, riding and classic cars.

SEARS, Trevor P.R.
Kingsford Stacey Blackwell, London
(0171) 447 1200
Specialisation: Local counsel to the International Air Transport Association (IATA) and consultant to airlines with particular regard to their relationship with travel agents. Licensed Insolvency Practitioner and speaker at airline and travel seminars, radio and T.V. Acting for several airlines in connection with current IATA Trust cases.
Prof. Memberships: MSPI
Career: Qualified 1972. Joined *Booth and Blackwell*. Partner 1974. Senior Partner prior to merger with *Kingsford Stacey* 1997.
Personal: Born 1948. Educated at Epsom College. Lives in Surrey. Interests include travel, music, hockey and people.

SKUSE, Ian G.
Piper Smith & Basham, London
(0171) 828 8685
Partner and Head of Travel and Litigation.
Specialisation: Acts for large and small travel

agents, tour operators, airlines and for business travel agents. Practice covers claims, corporate and commercial work of all kinds including negotiations with Regulators including ABTA, CAA, IATA and Trading Standards Officers. extensive experience in managing commercial agreements concerning all aspects of the travel business, both leisure and business. Excellent track record at managing litigation of all kinds in the Courts and with trade association and Regulators. Expert guidance offered through the regulatory framework of ATOL Licensing, Code of Conduct matters and Airline Regulation. A regular columnist for Business Travel World and the Independent on Sunday and founder member of the consultancy group, Travel Resources.
Prof. Memberships: Institute of Travel and Tourism, CIMTIG.
Career: Qualified in 1980. *Piper Smith & Basham* in 1983 . Partner since 1987.

STEWART, Peter J.
Field Fisher Waterhouse, London
(0171) 481 4841
Partner and Head of Aviation Travel and Tourism Department.
Specialisation: Practice covers commercial areas (contentious and non-contentious) concerning the travel industry. Non-contentious work includes contractual arrangements between travel companies and their suppliers, compliance with regulatory requirements, joint ventures and business sales/purchases. Contentious work includes disputes with suppliers, other travel companies and customers. Author of 'A Practical Guide to Package Holiday Law and Contracts' (third edition 1993) and regular articles for ITT journal and other trade papers. Regularly lectures for IBC and ITT at travel industry conferences.
Prof. Memberships: IFTTA, ITT.
Career: Qualified 1982, having joined *Field Fisher Waterhouse* in 1980. Became a Partner in 1985.
Personal: Born 3rd February 1956. Attended Campbell College in Belfast 1969-73, then Pembroke College Cambridge 1974-77. Leisure interests include golf, tennis and music. Lives near Sevenoaks, Kent.

VENABLES, Richard
Lane & Partners, London (0171) 242 2626
See under Aviation: Aviation Regulatory Commercial, p. 131

THE REGIONS

Mason Bond (Leeds) (3ptnrs/1asst) Acknowledged as the leading firm in the regions. "Courteous and effective litigator" *Stephen Mason* is co-author of "Holiday Law" and member of the Law Society's Civil Litigation Committee. *Claire Ingleby* heads the non-contentious side. Despite the Leeds location, they have a number of London-based clients which enables them to compete with London firms on costs. **Clients/Work:** Defending tour operators in trading standards prosecutions relating to 'fluid pricing' policies. Increasing amount of public liability defence work. Acting for large number of tour operators, travel agents and trade associations.

Eversheds (Middlesbrough, Newcastle upon Tyne) (2ptnrs 50%; 1asst, 1asst 50% and 2 other assts as required) Known name *Melanie Pears* is the main specialist in this office dealing with consumer claims, commercial work, licensing and customer care work. **Clients/Work:** Drafting terms and conditions for brochures, booking and ticket conditions. Handling relations with Trading Standards and potential prosecutions. Compliance audits and related litigation assistance.

Stones Cann & Hallett (Exeter) (2ptnrs/1asst) Personal Injury and Travel department in this niche practice known for PI skiing accident work but covering other aspects of sports and travel accident litigation. *Bronwen Courtenay-Stamp* continues to be recognised as a leader in this small but growing field. **Clients/Work:** Major legal expenses insurers and other insurers and loss adjusters. Inspection and advice following fatal accident in the French Alps. Operation of a 24 hour legal helpline.

Buss Murton (Tunbridge Wells) (1ptnr 60%; 2assts) Small niche practice. **Clients/Work:** Insurance related work on adventure holidays. Overseas road accident work. Legal expenses insurance claims.

Clairmonts (Glasgow) (2ptnrs up to 20%; 2assts up to 20%) Travel Holiday Law is not the major area of practice but significant enough to merit a good reputation for the work done. **Clients/Work:** Travel agents, tour operators, other travel companies dealing with contractual disputes, trading standards and advertising advice.

Shakespeares (Birmingham) (1ptnr 40%; up to 4assts 40%) *The* experts in all aspects of waterways related law. **Clients/Work:** Acting for two trade associations including Inland Waterways Association. Continuing work on the River Wye public inquiry. Advising generally in relation to British Waterways Board proposal for trust status.

Tozers (Exeter) (1ptnr 60%; 2ptnr 15-30%; 2-4assts 15%) Have carved a well regarded niche providing a package of cross-departmental legal services for the owners of holiday parks and leisure attractions. **Clients/Work:** Acting for British Holiday and Home Parks Association Ltd and its members ranging from small caravan parks to large holiday operators. Revising standard agreement for purchasing of holiday caravans. General legal advice in environmental, planning, consumer litigation and licensing work.

Ford Simey Daw Roberts (Exeter) (1ptnr ; 2ptnrs 50%; 1asst 20%) Moving into the 'highly regarded' slot this year by virtue of their growing client list and respected for an increased profile. **Clients/Work:** Operating a helpline for members of West Country Tourist Board. Acting for a number of trade associations. Devon Farms holiday company.

LEADERS' PROFILES • REGIONS

COURTENAY-STAMP, Bronwen

Stones Cann & Hallett, Exeter
(01392) 666 777
Specialisation: Heads the Personal Injury, Travel and Insurance Team. Particularly concentrates on Travel and Tourism Litigation and Sports Law in connection with skiing. Provides an on call 24 hour service for several client companies who may require immediate specialist advice and can and does organise attendance at the scene of ski accidents of a serious nature where that proves necessary. Gives lectures and writes articles for both the Travel Industry and Lawyers.
Prof. Memberships: A Member of the Law Society Personal Injury Panel and of the Association of Personal Injury Lawyers.
Career: Educated in the North East of England. Law Degree at Exeter University, First Class Honours in Law Society Finals. Articled at *Stones* spending the majority of her qualified career dealing with Personal Injury, Travel, Tourism and Skiing Law.
Personal: Married with one child. Enjoys foreign travel and watersports. A very keen snow skier.

INGLEBY, Claire

Mason Bond, Leeds (0113) 242 4444
Partner in Travel Law Department.
Specialisation: Main area of work is drafting contractual and other documentation for tour operators. Has drafted booking conditions for many major operators and prepares supplier's contracts, agency agreements, newspaper/operator contracts for reader offers, promotional agreements and conditions and brochure wording. Also handles litigation on behalf of tour operators, defends consumer claims, deals with Trading Standards enquiries and prosecutions and represents operators before the ABTA Code of Conduct Committee. Provides advice on all areas of law affecting tour operators. Firm acts on behalf of more than 100 tour operators of varying sizes. Also represents travel agents, newspapers and a trade association. Author of a number of articles for the 'Travel Law Journal' and one for 'The Legal Executive'. Has lectured for the University of Northumbria and addressed the annual conference of ABTOF in 1994, 1995 and 1996. Conducts in-house seminars for tour operators on a number of subjects.
Prof. Memberships: Law Society.
Career: Joined *Mason Bond* on qualification in 1990. Became a Partner in 1994.
Personal: Born 5th December 1965. Exeter University 1984-87. Leisure activities include hill walking. Lives near Skipton, North Yorkshire.

MASON, Stephen M.

Mason Bond, Leeds (0113) 242 4444
Partner in Travel Law Department.
Specialisation: Advises tour operators and travel agents. Work includes defending claims brought by consumers, advocacy, dealing with trading standards departments, conducting seminars, drafting booking conditions and supplier contracts. Also handles commercial aspects of travel law, including commercial disputes and litigation, copyright, trademarks and passing off. Acted in 'Bowerman and Wallace v. ABTA 1995 CA', and in many first instance travel law cases reported in Current Law. Joint Editor of the 'Travel Law Journal'. Has addressed numerous seminars on travel law topics advertised by the University of Northumbria, held at the Institute of Advanced Legal Studies, London; and also teaches Civil Advocacy. Higher Courts (Civil Proceedings) Qualification 1994. Used these Rights of Audience to defend a major tour operator successfully against a large claim in the High Court, January 1997 and to appear in the Divisional Court in Dudley v. Inspirations East Ltd 1997. Joint Author 'Holiday Law' Sweet & Maxwell (2nd ed.) 1998; Member of the Law Society Civil Litigation Committee since 1997.
Prof. Memberships: Law Society, International Federation of Travel and Tourism Advocates.
Career: Qualified 1974. Senior Partner since 1986.

Personal: Married, 3 children. Attended Bradford Grammar School to 1967, and Cambridge University to 1971. Leisure interests include travel, acting and supporting Leeds United FC. Lives in Ilkley, West Yorkshire.

PEARS, Melanie
Eversheds, Middlesbrough (01642) 247456

Associate.
Specialisation: Acts as adviser to many household name travel sector clients. Work involves client compliance audits, drafting of terms and conditions, consumer complaint handling, intellectual property disputes and general commercial matters. Has written for the Travel Law Journal and has presented papers at

many recent IBA conferences.
Career: Qualified in 1994. Originally trained as a barrister, after which she worked in industry for Shell and then in publishing, before joining *Eversheds* 1989.
Personal: Born 10th February 1965.

HOTELS AND LEISURE

Overview: Leading firms in this sector are rated in this section not simply because they handle commercial property deals for clients in the hotel/leisure industry. Specialists have acquired in-depth industry knowledge which is why the best lawyers have often come from the industry.

Firms in this area are not in direct competition with each other. On the whole, it is personalities who dominate and our rankings are influenced by how well those personalities are supported within their firms. For example Douglas Wignall of Douglas Wignall & Co is a perfect example of an industry grown specialist offering a particular type of expertise (in his case hotel management contracts). Many of the leading firms reported a busy year for the full range of hotel and leisure companies.

The major players this year remain S J Berwin for their strong corporate acquisitions work and Clifford Chance for their impressive client list. Garretts have ascended this year primarily because of the arrival of Andrew Little and his expertise from Field Fisher Waterhouse.

All the firms mentioned are situated in London.

S J Berwin & Co (2ptnrs 55-70%; 6assts 55-70% in commercial property department). Five other fee earners less involved in commercial and other departments – "strong in this market." Surveyors thought them "pretty sharp" and "exceedingly diligent." "Leading man," "hardworking" *David Ryland* was thought hard to get hold of but he "will do anything for clients and they love him ... thorough and bright." *Bryan Pickup* is known for his leisure-related work. **Clients/Work:** Acting for Ladbrokes in the £376m acquisition of Coral. Sale of Plaza on Hyde Park Hotel. Acting for British Land in £161m joint venture with the Rank Group PLC.

Clifford Chance (3ptnrs active commercial and financial departments and 3ptnrs less active from other departments; 4-20assts.) Know their way around the industry. Get into the top slot because of the level of work and standard of clients. This year has been a busy one for lead partner *Andrew Carnegie* ("professional and thorough") "his clients get good service." **Clients/Work:** Include Arcadian, Burford Group plc, Jarvis Hotels plc.

Denton Hall (5ptnrs up to 90%; 2assts ,

with up to 6 others when necessary.) Handling of a range of leisure and hotel related work for a number of quality hotel development clients who have been active in acquisitions this year. Also known for cinema work. **Clients/Work:** Advising Parkview International, providing advice on the redevelopment of Battersea Power station as a leisure and entertainment complex, including residential, post-production facilities and two hotels. Advised Festival Leisure Park Limited on £50m leisure facilities. Acting for Virgin Cinemas Limited in relation to their Multiplex Cinemas at Cardiff, Birmingham, Slough and Manchester.

Field Fisher Waterhouse (4ptnrs/ 7assts in the dedicated hotel and leisure department plus 1 partner 50% in another department.) Almost all thought the loss of Andrew Little must have left a gap. However if they have suffered they do not appear to be troubled now. Whilst they no longer have a big name, they still have substantial clients and handle large deals. **Clients/Work:** Luminar PLC. Advising Marriott in relation to the acquisition of the former Midland Hotel at St Pancras station – part of the Kings Cross regeneration project. David Lloyd Leisure PLC dealing with site assembly, planning advice and development agreements for three new health clubs in UK. Acting for Whitbread in the vast majority of their Beefeater and Travel Inn acquisitions and their "stand alone" hotels.

Linklaters (1ptnr 75% & 1ptnr 40%; 1 senior assistant 75% in Commercial Property Dept.) *Patrick Plant* is "straightforward and practical," "good on big ticket work," "very able" and "an international practitioner." Leading industry clients thought Plant "user friendly" and surveyors were impressed with his experience at Forte. Hotel and Leisure deals represented approximately 10% of the department's disclosed deals this year but the significant Bass plc deals raise the profile. **Clients/Work:** Bass plc £279m sale of 130 Gala Bingo Clubs. RF Hotels acquisition of Cardiff Bay and Balmoral Edinburgh hotels. Mandarin Hotel acquisition of the Hyde Park Hotel probably the biggest acquisition in London this past year.

Lovell White Durrant (6ptnrs/7assts varying degrees of hotel and leisure work) No specific department but firm is prominent because of Granada work. Acted on the deal of the year (the Granada disposal).

Clients/Work: Include: Granada/Forte, Stakis, Cine-UK, Warner Bros.

Richards Butler Work is handled by the Property Department. "Good overall." Ex-Rank man *Richard Nicoll* heads up this work within the department. **Clients/Work:** Acted for the Rank Group in £150m sale and lease-back with British Land. Acted in high profile leisure developments throughout the UK for clients including Odeon Cinemas and Warner Holidays.

Eversheds (1ptnr 95%; 1assoc ; 1asst) Good in parts but not well known in the market. **Clients/Work:** Handling complete rewrite of ticket conditions, brochure booking descriptions and training telesales personnel. Trading Standards work. Cruise market clients and cruise ship charter operators.

Garretts (1ptnr 1ptnr 30-40% and 3assts varying %.) Acquisition of industry leader *Andrew Little* from Field Fisher Waterhouse with his outstanding reputation for hotel management agreements has moved the firm up the rankings. **Clients/Work:** For TBI plc acting in the negotiation of management and operating contracts with Hilton International for a major new UK city centre hotel development. For a major Middle Eastern Trading Group acting in the negotiation of the management and operating agreements with Kempinski Hotels SA for a major UAE hotel project.

Norton Rose (1ptnr 50%; 4assts 50%) "Good firm, commercial... clued up on the market." **Clients/ Work:** Represented The Thomson Travel Group in the MMC Inquiry; represented Lunn Poly in judicial review.

Stephenson Harwood (2ptnrs 50%, 5ptnrs 50%; 7assts used as and when necessary) A "commercial" and "helpful" team. **Clients/Work:** Accor Group (Sofitel, Novotel, Ibis, Formule 1, Luncheon Vouchers). Acting for Capital Corporation on the £25m acquisition of the Cromwell Mint Casino. Acting for Robert Fleming & Co on a £33m loan to finance six Health & Fitness Clubs.

Allen & Overy (2ptnrs including *Roger Davies*) "Excellent at the big stuff " but some doubt cast on whether they can truly be called specialists in this field. "Such hotel work as they do is really incidental to their general commercial practice." **Clients/Work:** Queens Moat House on sale of large hotel portfolio. Thomson Travel Group. Acting for a number of leisure companies, hotel owners and developers.

Freshfields There is no specific team in this area and they have not been as active this year in hotel or leisure work. *Mark Wheelhouse* is acknowledged to have a degree of specialist knowledge.

Paisner & Co (3ptnrs/3assts f/t. 4ptnrs plus various assistants as required) Some leading surveyors rate the firm highly. Leading industry clients have described *David Levy* as the "guru" with "a keen eye on the business." **Clients/Work:** Include Bass Taverns Limited, First Leisure Corporation plc, Forte (UK) Ltd.

Douglas Wignall & Co (1principal) *Douglas Wignall* runs this "specialised" firm. Unanimously praised as "the man for smaller jobs." Reputation is for hotel management agreements. **Clients/Work:** Securum, Intercontinental, Sheraton. Work includes acquisitions and disposals in the UK.

Simmons & Simmons (3ptnrs between 50-75% up to 7assts) "Quite prominent and very commercial." Many deals currently underway; their client base keeps them in the running. **Clients/Work:** Include Bass plc, Abu Dhabi Investment Authority, Brent Walker Group PLC.

Joelson Wilson & Co (1ptnr 40%; 1property asst) Small firm which handles overseas work and has a leading reputation in the gaming licensing industry. **Clients/Work:** Casinos, quoted companies.

LEADING INDIVIDUALS · UK HOTELS AND LEISURE

CARNEGIE Andrew Clifford Chance	
LITTLE Andrew Garretts	
PICKUP Bryan S J Berwin & Co	
PLANT Patrick Linklaters	
RYLAND David S J Berwin & Co	
WIGNALL Douglas Douglas Wignall & Co	

LEVY David Paisner & Co	
NICOLL Richard Richards Butler	

DAVIES Roger Allen & Overy	

UP AND COMING

WHEELHOUSE Mark Freshfields

SEE PROFILES AT END OF THIS SECTION

LEADERS' PROFILES · UK · HOTELS AND LEISURE

CARNEGIE, Andrew
Clifford Chance, London (0171) 600 1000
Specialisation: Partner in commercial property practice specialising in commercial property (in particular relating to the hotel and leisure industry), property finance and insolvency: in recent years has acted on many high profile hotel transactions particularly in respect of the purchase and financing of a number of large central London hotels; has also been involved in a number of international transactions involving cross border legal work.
Career: Dollar Academy; University of Newcastle upon Tyne; College of Law (1983 Law). Articled *Cartmell Shepherd*; qualified 1986; *Cameron Markby* (now *Cameron Markby Hewitt*) 1986-88; solicitor *Clifford Chance* 1988-96; partner 1996.
Personal: Born 1962. Resides London. Leisure: fishing, shooting, hill walking.

DAVIES, Roger
Allen & Overy, London (0171) 330 3000
Specialisation: Areas of practice include hotel sale and purchase and management contracts, oil and gas and international joint ventures and commercial contracts.
Career: Articled *Allen & Overy*, qualified 1972, Partner 1976, Partner in charge of Dubai office 1980-83
Personal: Fitzwilliam College, Cambridge 1969. Born 1946.

LEVY, David N.
Paisner & Co, London (0171) 353 0299
Specialisation: Partner in Property Department specialising in all types of commercial property work including planning. He acts in particular for the leading companies in the hotel and leisure fields and over 20 years has dealt with the acquisition and disposal of many hundreds of hotels, restaurants and leisure properties of all types. Also has specialist involvement with Motorway Service Areas.
Prof. Memberships: Law Society. Business In

Sport & Leisure. British Israel Law Association.
Career: Educated at Wanstead County High School and Hertford College Oxford. Qualified in 1972. Became a partner at *Paisner & Co* in 1976.
Personal: Born 1948. Resides Finchley, London. Married with 2 children.

LITTLE, Andrew
Garretts, London (0171) 438 5174
Partner specialising in hotels and leisure industry related work.
Specialisation: Main area of practice involves advising clients in the hotel industry. Work includes purchases and sales of hotel and leisure businesses, negotiating hotel management agreements and operating leases, advising on financing of hotels and leisure projects, negotiating joint venture and development agreements and advising on franchising and time-sharing arrangements. Also advises banks on restructuring schemes for hotels, and in negotiating loan and security documents. An adviser to the British Hospitality Association. Frequently lectures at seminars and conferences for the hotel industry.
Prof. Memberships: Law Society, International Bar Association, Hotel Catering & International Management Association, British Association of Hotel Accountants.
Career: Qualified in 1973. With *Lawrence Graham* 1971-76, then a Partner at *Fox & Gibbons*, Dubai and London 1976-84. Vice President and General Counsel, Holiday Inns International 1985-89. Partner at *Field Fisher Waterhouse* 1990-1997. Joined *Garretts* 1997.
Personal: Born 25th November 1948. Educated at Uppingham School, Exeter University and Guildford College of Law. Leisure pursuits include sailing, golf, theatre, and travel in India. Lives in London W11. Hurlington Club, St. Mawes Sailing Club.

NICOLL, R.C.
Richards Butler, London (0171) 247 6555
Partner and Head of Property

Specialisation: All aspects of commercial property investment and development and acts for a broad range of investors, developers and end users of commercial and residential properties in the UK and internationally. Advises extensively on the acquisition and development of a number of new high-profile leisure projects for major clients including Odeon Cinemas, Rank Leisure, Warner Holidays and Oasis Villages.
Prof. Memberships: Law Society
Career: Qualified 1974, joined *Richards Butler* in 1972.
Personal: Born 1950. Leisure interests include Lawyers Fishing Club, rugby and sports generally. Member of MCC.

PICKUP, Bryan J.
S J Berwin & Co, London
+44 (0)171 533 2222
Partner in Property Department.
Specialisation: Main area of practice is leisure. Handles the sale, purchase and funding of leisure businesses such as golf clubs, hotels, bingo clubs, cinemas, arenas and sports facilities. Acted in the acquisition by SMG of London Docklands Arena and a joint venture for ice hockey use, the funding and acquisition by Sun Life Assurance Society plc of 4 leisure parks and the flotation of Holmes Place plc.
Prof. Memberships: Business in Sport & Leisure
Career: Qualified in 1981. Joined *S J Berwin & Co.* in 1988 as a Partner.
Personal: Born 15th April 1953. Attended Whitgift School Croydon 1961-69 and Fitzwilliam College, Cambridge 1970-74. Leisure interests include golf and hockey. Lives in Wimbledon.

PLANT, Patrick
Linklaters, London (0171) 456 4718
Specialisation: Partner specialising in commercial property, hotel and leisure.
Career: Articled *Wilsons*, Salisbury, qualified

1986, partner *Linklaters & Paines* since 1994. **Personal:** Born 1962.

RYLAND, David S.
S J Berwin & Co, London
+44 (0)171 533 2222
Specialisation: Hotel & leisure sales and purchases, structured finance transactions, management contracts, joint ventures and the establishment of collective investment schemes. Transactions dealt with in the last year relating to the hotel and leisure industry include the purchase of the Washington Hotel and the Green Park Hotel, the sales of the Plaza on Hyde Park, the Newport Hilton, the Bulmer Lawn Hotel and the Linton Lodge Hotel, the acquisition by Ladbroke of the Coral Group, the negotiation of a management contract relating to Sheraton Belgravia and the restructuring of property interests relating to the Great Western Hotel, the establishment of MWB Leisure Fund II, the forward funding of various leisure parks in the UK, and the establishment of various tax efficient collective investment vehicles for the unitisation of real estate.
Prof. Memberships: Member of the British Council of Shopping Centres, Legislative Committee.
Career: *Clifford Chance* 1981-1988; *S J Berwin & Co* 1988-date. Dulwich College: 1965-1972

Exeter College Oxford University: 1973-1977 (first in Mods and Greats). Frequent lecturer and writer of articles on property investment related matters.
Personal: Married. Interests include sport, music and cinema.

WHEELHOUSE, Mark
Freshfields, London (0171) 936 4000
Specialisation: Main area of practice is commercial property work with particular emphasis on the property aspects of business deals and acquisitions. Acts for a major leisure operator and advised the sponsoring banks on the flotation of two major hotel groups in 1996.
Prof. Memberships: Law Society; City of London Solicitor's Company.
Career: Attended Queen Elizabeth Grammar school, Wakefield 1975-1980 and King's College, London 1981-1984. Qualified and joined *Freshfields* 1987. Partner 1996.
Personal: Born 1962. Lives; Beaconsfield.

WIGNALL, Douglas
Douglas Wignall & Co, London
(0171) 583 1362
Principal.
Specialisation: Main area of practice is hotels and leisure. Work includes hotel and resort

developments in UK and Europe, international hotel management contracts, acquisition and disposal of hotels, advising on all aspects of hotel operational matters. Also handles general commercial law, covering all forms of commercial contracts, franchise, distribution and other agency agreements, and joint venture agreements. Has been involved in hotel and/or resort projects in most countries in Western Europe, Africa, Middle East and Russia. Major clients include ITT Sheraton Corporation, Morrison International Developments Ltd and Blakes Hotel Ltd. Has lectured and written articles on hotel management contracts. Individual charge-out rate is £175 per hour.
Prof. Memberships: Law Society, International Bar Association, Member of British Middle East Law Council, Member of the Company of Scriveners.
Career: Qualified in 1974. Worked in industry for approximately 10 years including Legal Counsel with Sheraton Management Corporation between 1981-84. Set up *Douglas Wignall & Co* in 1984.
Personal: Born 15th April 1950. Attended Brentwood School 1957-68, Leeds University 1968-71, and Guildford Law College 1971-72. Leisure interests include squash and music; member of Hurlingham Club. Lives in London W6.

TIMESHARE

LEADING FIRMS • UK
TIMESHARE
TODS MURRAY WS Edinburgh
STONES CANN & HALLETT Exeter
HEDLEYS London
ROWE & MAW London

HIGHLY REGARDED FIRMS
Paisner & Co London

Tods Murray WS (Edinburgh) (2ptnrs p/t 2assts 50%) Nothing but praise for "doyen" *David Anderson* – "first class" "knowledgeable." This firm is the acknowledged leader in this specialisation within a specialisation. **Clients/Work:** Acted in $18m Global Development sale of EU business to Signature Resorts Inc. Dealing with the implementation of the EU directive to regulate sales and the conse-

quent implications for the timeshare industry. Acting on testcase rating appeal relating to the rating of timeshare resorts.

Stones Cann & Hallett (Exeter) (1ptnr/ 1asst and up to 4assts 50%) "Active firm" described as relative newcomers to this area with consumer rather than timeshare operator emphasis. *Timothy Bourne* rated for his consumer representation. **Clients/Work:** Two major timeshare exchange organisations. Significant number of owners associations. Some timeshare developers.

Hedleys (London) "Only involved in one timeshare development and so may not have a broad spread of expertise to offer." *Colin Jenkins* ("knows his onions," "competent, knowledgeable") has been in the industry for years.

Rowe & Maw (London) (2ptnrs 50%; 3assts 30-40%) Have lost Nicholas Benson and Martin Briggs, both to in-house positions, so many query whether this firm is still a player. However investment in

resources would appear to be keeping their big clients happy and they have certainly not seen a drop off in work. The timeshare team is part of the Aviation, Transport and Leisure Department. **Clients/Work:** LSI merger with Signature and LSI's acquisition of Global Anfi Del Mar and their $40m receivables financing with Finova Capital Corp – the first of its kind in Europe. Regulatory and resort management issues.

Paisner & Co (London) (1ptnr 30% 2assts 10-30%) **Clients/Work:** Marriott Vacation Club International and other international investment clients. Dealing with DTI over new EU regulatory implementation difficulties.

LEADING INDIVIDUALS
UK • TIMESHARE
ANDERSON David Tods Murray WS
JENKINS Colin Hedleys
BOURNE Timothy Stones Cann & Hallett

SEE PROFILES AT END OF THIS SECTION

LEADERS' PROFILES • UK • TIMESHARE

ANDERSON, David S.
Tods Murray WS, Edinburgh (0131) 226 4771
Email: david.anderson@todsmurray.co.uk
Specialisation: All aspects of Timeshare and Leisure related work throughout the UK and Europe; 1975 devised legal structure for first UK timeshare project; advises developers, banks, management companies, trade bodies and other suppliers of services to timeshare industry; legal advisor and secretary to Timeshare Council; author of numerous articles.
Prof. Memberships: Law Society of Scotland
Career: Qualified *Tods Murray* 1972; Partner 1974.
Personal: Born 1948. Attended Perth Academy and Edinburgh University (1970 LLB). Leisure – golf.

BOURNE, T.H.S.
Stones Cann & Hallett, Exeter
(01392) 666 777
Partner
Specialisation: All aspects of timeshare law. Acts for and has advised Banks, Developers, Hotel Groups, Owners Associations, the main timeshare exchange organisations and national timeshare organisations. Author of articles for the Law Society and Estates Gazette, International Banking and Financial Law Journal, New Law Journal and Travel magazines. Lectures on timeshare law to the Institute of Bankers and several universities.
Prof. Memberships: The Law Society, Institute of Management.

Career: Qualified 1981. Partner *Stones* 1983.
Personal: Born 22nd March 1945. Educated Clifton College and HM Royal Marines. Lives in Exeter.

JENKINS, Colin
Hedleys, London (0171) 638 1001
Specialisation: Timeshare; author of "Practical Timeshare and Group Ownership" & timeshare title of the Encyclopaedia of Forms & Precedents (Butterworths); legal adviser to the European Timeshare Federation; member of the Board of Management of the Timeshare Council (UK).

TRUSTS AND PERSONAL TAX

RESEARCH: In compiling the tables, we consider all the information available to us, paying particular regard to the market research carried out by our team of ten qualified lawyers. (The researchers' details are set out on page three.) The rankings, therefore, reflect the opinion of the marketplace as revealed by systematic and objective research: see page four. (Our research is audited every year by the British Market Research Bureau.)

OVERVIEW: Most practitioners in London were aware of the leading players, but in the regions firms tended not to know about each other's work. In order to make our assessment we relied in part on written representations from the firms. Most trusts work is carried out within private client departments and the nature of the work means that specific details of clients and matters are generally highly confidential. Most firms recommended here undertake a full range of trusts work for a variety of clients. We do not list the type of work each firm undertakes, but where a firm has a particular emphasis or specialism we highlight this in the text. Due to the large number of firms, we do not write about all of them. For further details, readers should refer to the A-Z section. In London, Charles Russell have consolidated their position following the acquisition of the Norton Rose private client department last year, and they move up to the top band. Niche firm Currey & Co (together with partner Nicholas Powell) also move up following praise from their peers. Speechly Bircham and Bircham & Co received strong recommendations and go up a band each. New firm, Forsters, replaces Frere Cholmeley Bishcoff in the lists (following the disbanding of the latter, the private client department and those partners who did not join Eversheds formed Forsters).

In the South East, Blake Lapthorn in Portsmouth and Henmans in Oxford enter the lists. In the South West, Steele Raymond in Bournemouth is a new entry and Coodes in St Austell moves up a band. In East Anglia, Willcox & Lewis in Norwich (new niche private client firm set up by Michael Willcox and Ian Lewis) is a new entry. In Scotland, the private client partners from Dundas & Wilson and Burness have set up a new firm, Turcan Connell, which replaces the larger firms in the table.

LONDON

Allen & Overy (4ptnrs/15assts) Have alongside an archetypal City practice, an excellent private client deaprtment. *Richard Turnor* ("very able indeed, intelligent and extremely good at commercial partnerships") and *Clare Maurice* are the most prominent members of the team. Clients/Work: Advising a Mexican Bank re an international asset-holding structure using the UK as a location for the trust. Advising wealthy entrepreneurs on tax implications of business flotation. Acquisition of UK landed estates for non-domiciled individuals.

Boodle Hatfield (5ptnrs/3assts) *Richard Moyse* was highly recommended by his peers. The "very clever" *Kate Howe* also stands out. The department was joined this year by two new partners from Camerons and Winckworth & Pemberton bolstering the tax, trusts and contentious skills of the department, and compensating for the loss of one other partner to the Bar. Clients/Work: Tax planning for large complex landed estates, private companies, high net worth individuals and families worldwide. Increasing work for entrepreneurial individuals with tax and succession issues. Acting for foreign investors establishing businesses in the UK and Europe.

Charles Russell (7ptnrs 70-90%/5assts 80-100% in Private Capital Department; 4 ptnrs 70-100%, 2assts in Private Property Department. 7 Legal Execs both depts) The arrival of the Norton Rose team increased the size and profile of the department. The firm has concentrated on consolidating that advantage with increasing international work this year. They have moved up to the top band as a result. Described by competitors as "a good practice – held in the highest regard." *Michael Macfadyen* is described as "helpful and firm," while the "understated" *David Long* is a "safe pair of hands" who "really knows his law." *Catriona Syed* "adds strength to the team." Clients/Work:

Ingram v IRC – acting for the taxpayer in the Court of Appeal. Acting for trustees of the Dent-Brocklehurst Estate re sale of Poussin work to Getty Museum. Acting for the Dorneywood Trust.

Farrer & Co (11ptnrs/2assoc/7assts , 7 legal execs also act as trust managers and probate administrators) The department is led by *Henry Boyd-Carpenter* and includes *Mark Bridges* who works with "a sense of controlled urgency." **Clients/Work:** Creating international holding structures for the 'super rich.' Off-shore practice deals with inward tax and international issues. Acting for substantial Middle Eastern business proprietors.

Lawrence Graham (8ptnrs/8assts) Described as "a sensible straight firm." The "brilliant" and "pragmatic" *Martyn Gowar* remains a clear leader in the field. **Clients/Work:** Taking on the estate of Diana, Princess of Wales and acting for a number of the UK's most prominent families. Off-shore institutional work and the management of approximately £100m in-house investment business. Contentious trust issues.

Macfarlanes (7ptnrs/12assts) Described as "incredibly good" with "superb people." Expert *Michael Hayes* is considered " a real heavy-weight intellectual." *John Rhodes* is "impressive." John Dilger is now a consultant and works three days a week. **Clients/Work:** Acting for the eldest son of a major UK estate-owning family re streamlining the family tax position to produce an income from the various trusts. Advising trustees of a number of off-shore trusts involved in acrimonious application for financial assistance. Assisting a number of on and off-shore trusts involved in Inland Revenue investigations.

Withers (10ptnrs general/6ptnrs specialist areas/28assts) Huge private client department with some big names. Known for their assertive style. Increase in pure international work. Team includes *Robin Paul* specialising in probate, *Stephen Cooke*, *Anthony Thompson* and *John Riches*. Michael Carpenter and Peter Duffield are no longer with the firm. **Clients/Work:** Increase in domestic and international contentious probate work, including acting in 'The Midland Bank Trustee (Jersey) Limited v FPS.' Advising on the protection and preservation of individual and family assets. Acting for the clients of Swiss banks re tax planning for significant estates including creation of trusts and private trust companies in off-shore jurisdictions.

Currey & Co (7ptnrs/4assts) Described as a "very clever specialist firm." It has remained a niche practice and is respected by contemporaries for its established client base and quality of work. It moves up a band as a result. The "brilliant" *Nicholas Powell* heads the team. **Clients/Work:** Acting for traditional landed estates and wealthy individuals providing complex estate planning, trusts and taxation advice. Also wills and probate work.

Speechly Bircham (1ptnr 75%/ 5ptnrs/ 2cons/6assts) *Richard Kirby* is head of the department which benefits from "the awesome and brilliant tax lawyer" *John Avery Jones C.B.E.* recommended for his "quick grasp of essential facts." **Clients/Work:** Victory in the landmark expatriate tax case – Willoughby. The launch of the 'Home Loan Plan' as a way of helping individuals remain in their homes in a tax efficient way. Continue to act for Lord Lloyd Webber, The Howard de Walden Estate and the Vestey family.

Bircham & Co (5 ptnrs/3 cons/3 assts/9 trust and probate mangrs)The practice has been expanding gradually over the past few years and is well respected by competitors.

Peter Goodwin is "extremely competent." **Clients/Work:** Estate planning for UK residents.

Nicholson Graham & Jones (1ptnr/ 2ptnrs 50%/ 2assts) The "extremely good" *Eliza Mellor* ("clever" and "a good sense of humour") and "big name speaker" *Michael Jacobs* handle most of the private client work. **Clients/Work:** Acting for international entrepreneurs and titled and non-titled wealthy families requiring long-term strategic planning and tax structures. Employee-related trust arrangements involving overseas and on-shore trusts. Advising the heir to a major international industrial fortune.

Payne Hicks Beach (6ptnrs/1assoc/ 1asst, 11 non-solicitor trust managers) *Graham Brown* ("traditional and bright") is senior partner and head of the department, which includes *Chris Jarman*. **Clients/Work:** International tax and trusts practice involving foreign law, tax regimes and double tax treaties.

Taylor Joynson Garrett (8ptnrs/8assts in private client dept). Considered to have a "good off-shore practice." *Michael Stanford-Tuck* ("good speaker" and "good with clients") remains a leader. Recently gained a senior solicitor from Boodle Hatfield. **Clients/Work:** Global reorganisation of off-shore tax planning structure for high net worth family. Administration of global estate of Japanese citizen involving co-ordination of probate procedures in US, France, Switzerland, Jersey, UK and Japan. Tax planning for dual nationality family (US/UK) including royalty income.

Forsters (3ptnrs/8assts) A new firm with a private client department drawn from the Frere Cholmeley practice. *David Willis*, *John Drewitt* and *David Robinson* remain leaders in the field. **Clients/Work:** Acting for wealthy individuals and their families in tax planning, settlements and landed estates. Assisting in the efficient disposal of heritage assets and particularly a private collection of Dutch masters. Also advise non-domiciled individuals.

Hunters (10 partners of which 3 are full-time, the other 7 spend varying amounts of time) "General practitioners of the old school,"the firm specialises in private client work. Team includes *John Kennedy, Mark Tod* and *Michael Skrine* ("a safe pair of hands"). **Clients/Work:** Probate and heritage work. Some offshore work and traditional landed estate families. Acting for high net worth individuals.

Lee & Pemberton (7ptnrs/3assts/6 trust managers, legal execs and tax specialist) Well respected by contemporaries for their traditional practice and move up a band. **Clients/Work:** Landed estate families; heritage property; high net worth individuals; trust formation and administration, including off-shore work; tax planning; probate.

Collyer-Bristow (2ptnrs/4assts) **Clients/Work:** Reconstruction of UK and off-shore trusts. Increasing amount of contentious probate matters. Acting for the trustees in the settlement of a family dispute involving substantial property assets held in trust.

Dawson & Co (5ptnrs/3assts/3 trust managers) Department led by *Joseph Richardson* ("conscientious and traditional," "good both technically and with clients"). **Clients/Work:** Specialises in taxation, acting for landed estates and offshore clients.

Paisner & Co (5ptnrs/5assts) Have their own trust company, Paicolex, in Zurich with subsidiaries in the BVI and Jersey. **Clients/Work:** On the non-contentious side, international work has increased. On the contentious side, recent work includes a contested will dispute in excess of £3 million.

Simmons & Simmons (4ptnrs/9assts/9assts less than 50%) The departure of David Wey to a US firm has left the "exceedingly good" *Caroline Garnham* in charge and she joins our list of leaders. **Clients/Work:** Acting for large UK estates in the disposal of prominent properties. Advising high net worth individuals, particularly non-UK domiciles, on tax planning.

Titmuss Sainer Dechert (2ptnrs/4assts) **Clients/Work:** Represent 16 of the "Sunday Times Rich List families." Establishing a strong international practice, particularly in Canada, focusing on capital tax issues.

Trowers & Hamlins (5ptnrs/2assts) **Clients/Work:** Pre-immigration tax planning and offshore settlements for foreign clients. Major trust partition with beneficiaries and trustees resident in three different jurisdictions.

Wedlake Bell (6ptnrs/5assts) **Clients/Work:** Cross-border issues involving estate devolution, inheritance and asset protection for UK and non-UK individuals and families. Advising on a wide range of taxation issues, including CGTA, trust taxation and

Inland Revenue investigations.

Cumberland Ellis Peirs (2 f/t ptnrs/1 p/t ptnr/3assts) Practitioner saw them as "charming and delightful" to deal with. **Clients/Work:** Handling every aspect of a client's financial affairs from tax advice to wills preparation. Active Financial Services department giving independent advice.

Gouldens (2ptnrs/3assts) **Clients/Work:** Advising the executors of Matthew Harding. Advising a wealthy Lebanese family in relation to off-shore asset protection structures. Also act for private banks, trust companies and wealthy UK and foreign individuals.

Linklaters (1ptnr/1const/4assts/2 probate assts). Described as an "effective team." **Clients/Work:** Tax and estate planning including the creation of trusts. International trust and asset protection structures and issues arising from the ownership of shares

in private and public companies. Acting for UK and overseas clients (US, Hong Kong, Switzerland, EU and Middle East) undertaking probate and Chancery litigation.

Masons (1ptnr/3assts) **Clients/Work:** Acting for UK and overseas clients in trust, tax and succession matters. Advising a well-known and highly successful author. Dealing with contentious trust and probate matters, including one trust fund in excess of £50m.

Maxwell Batley (1 ptnr/3 assts) Seen as an "assertive" team.

Russell-Cooke, Potter & Chapman (2ptnrs/4assts/4 probate/trust administrators/1const) **Clients/Work:** Contentious and non-contentious probates. Cross border estates. Wills, trusts and tax.

Witham Weld (6 ptnrs/4assts) Known for their work for premier Roman Catholic clients and institutions.

LEADERS' PROFILES • LONDON

AVERY JONES C.B.E., John
Speechly Bircham, London (0171) 353 3290
Specialisation: Taxation of all kinds.
Prof. Memberships: Member of Treasury appointed Tax Law Rewrite Steering Committee, Law Society (Member and past Chairman of Revenue Law Committee), Chartered Institute of Taxation (Past President), International Fiscal Association, Institute for Fiscal Studies, International Academy of Estate & Trust Law, International Bar Association. Steering Committee of the tax law simplification project/consulting.
Career: Partner in *Speechly Bircham* since 1970, Senior Partner since 1985, Deputy Special Commissioner of Income Tax and part-time Chairman of VAT and Duties Tribunals, Editor of British Tax Review, Member of the Editorial Board of Simon's Taxes, Chairman of the Board of Trustees of the International Bureau of Fiscal Documentation.

BOYD-CARPENTER C.V.O., Henry
Farrer & Co, London (0171) 242 2022
Partner in General Private Client and Financial Services team.
Specialisation: Main areas of practice are general private client work, wills, settlements, probate, settled land, landed estates and charities.
Prof. Memberships: Law Society, Holborn Law Society.
Career: Joined *Farrer & Co* in 1962. Qualified in 1966, became a Partner in 1968. Private Solicitor to the Queen since 1995, Solicitor to the Duchy of Cornwall 1976-1994.
Personal: Born 11th October 1939. Educated at Charterhouse 1953-58 and Balliol College, Oxford 1959-62. School Governor and Charity Trustee. Enjoys reading, music, hill walking and gardening. Lives in Ascot, Berkshire.

Personal: Born 1940, educated at Rugby School and Trinity College, Cambridge.

BRIDGES, Mark T.
Farrer & Co, London (0171) 242 2022
Partner, Head of International Private Client Team.
Specialisation: Handles tax and trust matters, particularly for non-domiciled and non-resident individuals.
Prof. Memberships: Law Society, Member of STAR Group and Trust Law Committee.
Career: Joined *Farrer & Co* in 1978. Qualified in 1980, became a Partner in 1985. Solicitor to the Duchy of Lancaster 1998.
Personal: Born 25th July 1954. Educated at Cambridge University 1973-77. Special Trustee of Middlesex Hospital, Treasurer of Bach Choir, Council Member of Royal School of Church Music. Recreations include sailing and music. Lives in London.

BROWN, Graham S.
Payne Hicks Beach, London
(0171) 465 4300
See under Charities, p. 158

COOKE, Stephen

Withers, London (0171) 936 1000
Partner in Private Client Department.
Specialisation: Main area of practice is tax and asset management planning for the private client, both in the UK and offshore. Speaker at seminars on a wide range of trust, tax and related issues. Contributor to 'Tax Cases Analysis' and co-author of 'Inheritance Tax on Lifetime Gifts' (1987).
Prof. Memberships: City of London Law Society, International Fiscal Association, Society of Trust and Estate Practitioners.
Career: Qualified in 1971, having articled with *Clay Allison & Clark*, Nottinghamshire. Awarded the Law Society SH Clay prize. Joined *Withers* in 1971; Partner in 1973.
Personal: Born 30th July 1946. Attended Stamford School 1956-64 and Leicester School of Architecture. Chairman of the London Handel Society Ltd. Leisure interests include art, music, cricket, gardening and tennis. Lives in Well, Basingstoke.

DOLMAN, Robert A.

Wedlake Bell, London (0171) 395 3000
Specialisation: Specialises principally in private client tax and trusts both in UK and offshore.
Prof. Memberships: Law Society: STAR group.
Career: Qualified in 1971; Partner with *Baileys, Shaw and Gillett* until 1985; Partner with *Wedlake Bell* 1986 to date (Senior Partner from 1994).
Personal: Born 15 October 1945: Educated at Felsted and Oxford University. Chairman of Family Assurance Society. Chairman of the Jesters Club. Lives in West Sussex; interests are court games and theatre.

DREWITT, John

Forsters, London (0171) 863 8333
Specialisation: Advises on landed estates, estate planning, trusts, capital taxation; also deals with charities and the Court of Protection. Acts as *homme d'affaires* and professional trustee for a wide range of private clients. Experienced in Variation of Trust and other Court applications.
Prof. Memberships: Country Landowners Association, Royal Horticultural Society, STEP.
Career: Qualified 1961. Joined *Frere Cholmeley* 1971 (Partner 1975). Consultant with *Forsters* from August 1998.
Personal: Born 1937. Education at Oundle School. Interests include opera, architecture, horseracing, farming.

GARNHAM, Caroline

Simmons & Simmons, London
(0171) 628 2020
Specialisation: Capital Gains Tax and Inheritance Tax for individuals and trusts, succession and estate planning for individuals and trusts, cross border tax and estate conflict resolution for individuals and trusts, offshore trust dispute resolution, creation and reorganisation.
Prof. Memberships: Fellow of the Chartered Institute of Tax – committee member of Capital Taxes Sub Committee. Member of Society of Trusts and Estates Practitioners – member of Technic Committee and International Committee. Solicitor.
Career: BSc Exeter University. Solicitor, qualified 1981. Head of Private Capital Group

and Partner *Simmons & Simmons*. Fellow of the Chartered Institute of Tax. F.T.I.I
Personal: Hunting, tennis, singing. Married with two children, homes in London and Gloucestershire.

GOODWIN, Peter

Bircham & Co. (incorporating Dyson Bell Martin), London (0171) 222 8044
Specialisation: Estate planning for UK families and non-UK domiciliaries; advice on UK and non-UK trusts.
Prof. Memberships: Law Society; Westminster Law Society; STAR Group; STEP.
Career: Qualified as solicitor (1968). Partner: *Freshfields* (1974-1990). Partner: *Bircham & Co.* (1990 to date).
Personal: Born October 1943. Shrewsbury School (1957-62). Worcester College, Oxford (1962-65). Member of Committee of 1930 Fund for District Nurses.

GOWAR, Martyn

Lawrence Graham, London (0171) 379 0000
Senior Partner and Partner in Tax Department.
Specialisation: Specialises principally in Private Client Tax, acting for large landed estates, trustees (particularly offshore trusts), and private clients with business interests. Also inter-generational transfers of family businesses and general tax work, income tax, capital gains tax and inheritance tax advice generally, including income tax on structured settlements and tax on insurance policies. Editor of Butterworths Encyclopaedia of Forms and Precedents (Vol. 30 on Partnership) and contributor to Simon's Taxes on the tax and trust treatment of demerger shares issues and enhanced scrip dividends. Has lectured widely over the last 20 years.
Prof. Memberships: Law Society; Chartered Institute of Taxation (Associate 1976, Fellow 1981); Executive Council member of International Academy of Estate and Trust Law. Member Addington Society.
Career: Joined *Lawrence Graham* in 1967, qualifying in 1970 and becoming Partner in 1973 and Senior Partner in 1997. Member of numerous revenue law committees including the Tax Committee of the Association of Corporate Trustees (1987 to 1996) and the Capital Taxes Committee of the Chartered Institute of Taxation. Also Clerk to the Governors of Wellington College and Clerk to the Trustees of the Hamlyn Trust. A trustee of the Laura Ashley Foundation and the Council of St. Paul's Cathedral Choir School. Fellow of the Royal Society of Arts.
Personal: Born 11th July 1946. Educated at King's College School, Wimbledon and Magdalen College, Oxford 1964-67. Lives in Elstead, Surrey and enjoys golf, cricket and gardening.

HAYES, Michael

Macfarlanes, London (0171) 831 9222
Partner and Head of Tax and Financial Planning Department.
Specialisation: Specialises in private client tax planning. Work includes tax and estate planning, both national and international, for high net worth individuals, their trusts and closely held companies. Also wills and probate. Other area of practice is charities, including formation of charitable trusts and companies; establishing subsidiary trading vehicles; and negotiations with Charity Commission and

Inland Revenue. Joint editor of Contentious Matters Division of Butterworths Wills Probate and Administration Service; Contributor to Tolley's "Administration of Estates." Has spoken at numerous national and international conferences.
Prof. Memberships: Law Society, City of London Law Society, Society of Trusts and Estates Practitioners, Committee Member of the Law Society, Wills and Equity Committee, Association of Pension Lawyers, Association of Contentious Trust and Probate Specialists. Member of Camelot Winners Advisory Panel.
Career: Qualified in 1968 while with *Macfarlanes*. Became a Partner in 1974. Head of Tax and Financial Planning since 1991.

HOWE, Kate

Boodle Hatfield, London (0171) 629 7411
Specialisation: Private client taxation, including planning for the landed estate and international tax planning for UK and non-UK residents and domiciliaries; UK and offshore trust advice; commercial property taxation, particularly VAT.
Prof. Memberships: Law Society. STEP (Society of Trust & Estate Practitioners)
Career: Articled at *Boodle Hatfield* in 1987. Has lectured widely on Tax Planning and contributed to 'Legal Network Television.'
Personal: Attended the London School of Economics (LLB). Lives in London.

JACOBS, Michael

Nicholson Graham & Jones, London
(0171) 648 9000
Head of Private Client Department.
Specialisation: Tax on M & A transactions; employee share schemes; international tax, trusts, charities, and public sector bodies. Author of 'Tax on Take-overs' (7 editions) and 'Rewarding Leadership' (published by CISCO, February 1998); contributor to 'Tolley's Tax Planning' and 'Tolley's VAT Planning.' Consultant editor of Tolley's Trust Law International.
Prof. Memberships: Trust Law Committee (Founder Member and (1994-97) Secretary); Share Scheme Lawyers Group (Founder Member and Vice-Chairman); Employee Share Scheme Committee (Chairman) CISCO; STEP; IFA; IFS; Charity Law Association.
Career: Articled at *Nicholson Graham & Jones* 1970; Partner 1976. Head of Tax Department 1981.

JARMAN, Chris

Payne Hicks Beach, London
(0171) 465 4300
Partner in Tax, Trust & Probate Department.
Specialisation: Deals with a wide range of domestic and international trust, estate and tax planning for both old and new money clients, whether based in the U.K. or abroad; advice to "private" and institutional charities; property-related VAT advice for charity, commercial and land-owning clients; and commercial property advice to landowners seeking to realise potential development value. Member of Law Society's Revenue Law Committee and Capital Taxes Sub-Committee. Member of two-man Law Society team which procured significant changes to the Trusts of Land and Appointment of Trustees Act 1996 as it went through the House of Lords.
Prof. Memberships: Law Society; Holborn Law Society; STEP; Charity Law Association; Charities Property Association.
Career: Called to the Bar in 1976, qualified as

solicitor 1980. Member of *Freshfields* Private Client Department 1978-84, joined *Payne Hicks, Beach* in 1984 (Partner in 1986).
Personal: Born 1954, educated at Sherborne School and Magdalene College, Cambridge. Leisure interests include singing and music generally, and "social" cricket and golf; cycles approx. 2,800 miles per year commuting from South London.

KENNEDY, John
Hunters, London (0171) 412 0050
Specialisation: Private client work including landed estates, national heritage property, inheritance tax planning and trusts.
Prof. Memberships: Law Society, STEP.
Career: Sherborne School. Emmanuel College, Cambridge (M.A. 1967).
Personal: Cricket, skiing, gardening.

KIRBY, Richard C.
Speechly Bircham, London (0171) 353 3290
Partner 1973.
Specialisation: Main area of practice is private client work, handling estate and tax planning for UK and non-UK domiciliaries and trusts. Also charity law and administration. Has written numerous articles for national newspapers and specialist taxation periodicals.
Prof. Memberships: Law Society.
Career: Head Private Client and Charity Team 1980. Solicitor Worshipful Company of Pewterers 1981 (Freeman 1991).
Personal: Born 18th September 1946. Educated Sevenoaks School 1960-65 and Jesus College, Oxford 1965-68 MA. Member Council Mental After Care Association 1982 (Hon. Treasurer 1987-). Member Carlton Club. Enjoys reading, theatre and swimming. Lives in Dulwich.

LONG, David
Charles Russell, London (0171) 203 5096
Partner in Private Client Department.
Specialisation: Handles a wide range of trusts, wills, probate, estate planning and charity law. Especially interested in international succession problems and contentious probate. Has broadcast on radio and television on wills and lectured on Powers of Attorney.
Prof. Memberships: Law Society, Holborn Law Society (President 1992-93, Chairman Trust Section), Charity Law Association, STEP. Member of joint committee of The Law Society with the Court of Protection and Public Trust Office 1993-7.
Career: Joined *Charles Russell* in 1972 and became a partner in 1974. Hon. Solicitor Royal Philharmonic Society. Hon. Auditor the Law Society, 1994-98.
Personal: Born 3rd March 1946. Educated at King Edward's School, Birmingham and Balliol College, Oxford 1964-67.

MACFADYEN, Michael R.
Charles Russell, London (0171) 203 5000
Partner in Private Client Department.
Specialisation: Main areas of practice are private client (national and international), tax planning, charities, trusts, probate and Court of Protection.
Prof. Memberships: Law Society, City of London Solicitors Company, Society of Trusts and Estates Practitioners, Charity Lawyers

Association.
Career: Qualified in 1966. Joined *Norton Rose* in 1961, becoming a Partner in 1970. Joined *Charles Russell* 1997.
Personal: Born 1943. Attended Marlborough College 1956-61. Leisure interests include golf, cricket and walking. Lives in Henley-on-Thames.

MAURICE, Clare M.
Allen & Overy, London (0171) 330 3000
Specialisation: Partner specialising in advising UK and non-UK domiciled individuals and families on how to structure their assets both on shore and internationally. She has special experience advising on the UK taxation of offshore structures and Inland Revenue investigations into such activities. She also acts for grant-making and operational charitable organisations advising on all aspects of their activities.
Career: Articled *Allen & Overy*; qualified 1978, partner 1985, Special Trustee of St Bartholomew's Hospital, Director English Touring Opera Limited.
Personal: Educated Sherborne School for Girls. Birmingham University (1975 LL.B). Born 1954. Resides London.

MELLOR, Eliza
Nicholson Graham & Jones, London (0171) 648 9000
Partner in Private Client Department.
Specialisation: Has over twenty years experience working for UK and overseas-based clients on matters ranging from UK income, capital gains and inheritance tax advice to structuring international families estate planning and trust litigation. Has lectured abroad on the use of trusts.
Prof. Memberships: Law Society; Technical & International Committees of STEP; International Academy of Estate & Trust Lawyers. International Tax Planning Association.
Career: Qualified in 1974. Became a Partner of *Nicholson Graham & Jones* in 1985.
Personal: Educated at City of Worcester Grammar School for Girls and Cambridge University. Lives in London.

MOYSE, Richard M.
Boodle Hatfield, London (0171) 629 7411
Partner in charge of Private Client/ Tax and Financial Planning Department.
Specialisation: Main areas of practice are tax, trusts and financial planning (with an international emphasis), post-mortem tax planning and probate. Specialist fields are capital taxation, trusts, succession, heritage property, contentious trusts and probates. Experienced in the use of trusts in different jurisdictions for estate planning, asset protection and avoidance of forced heirship situations. Has experience in handling large international trusts with conflicts of law, family disputes and succession problems. Has made numerous contributions to professional and in-house publications. Extensive lecturing experience, especially on capital taxation and international tax planning in the UK and abroad, to audiences such as the International Academy of Estate and Trust Law and the International Bar Association.
Prof. Memberships: Law Society, International Academy of Estate and Trust Law, International

Tax Planning Association, International Bar Association, STAR Group.
Career: With *Lawrence Graham* from 1969-73. Qualified in 1970. Joined *Boodle Hatfield* in 1973 and became a Partner in 1974. Member of the Revenue Law Committee of the Law Society and Chairman of Capital Taxes Sub-Committee. Vice President (Europe) of the International Academy of Estate and Trust Law. Member of the 1994 Principal Private Residence Relief Working Party and 1997 Transfer of Assets Abroad Working Party.
Personal: Born 29th September 1943. Educated at Plymouth College 1948-62, then St. John's College, Oxford 1962-65. Married with four children. Leisure pursuits include travel, cricket, music, genealogy, fly fishing and painting. Lives in London.

PAUL, Robin
Withers, London (0171) 936 1000
Partner in Private Client Department.
Specialisation: Main area of practice is probate and succession. Head of Probate Group, advising executors and beneficiaries on all aspects of probate and post death tax planning, often with an international element. Also deals with trusts, tax and estate planning and heritage property. Co-author of 'The Lawyers Factbook' (Administration of Estates section), 'Practical Will Precedents' and Tolley's 'Administration of Estates' '(Chapter on Business and Agricultural Property). Departmental Editor for International Estates section of Journal of International Trust and Corporate Planning. Contributor to various legal journals and to Sweet & Maxwell's `Practical Tax Planning with Precedents' and the Succession section of 'Practical Commercial Law.' Has lectured at various conferences on wills and succession, with particular emphasis on international aspects.
Prof. Memberships: STEP, Law Society, Westminster Law Society.
Career: Qualified in 1977, having joined *Withers* in 1975. Became a Partner in 1982.
Personal: Born 19th December 1952. Educated at Malvern College, then Brasenose College, Oxford 1971-74. Lives in London.

POWELL, Nicholas R.D.
Currey & Co, London (0171) 828 4091

RHODES, John
Macfarlanes, London (0171) 831 9222
Partner Tax and Financial Planning Department.
Specialisation: Particular areas of interest include UK Inheritance and Capital Gains Tax. UK and offshore trusts, the law of domicile and international trust and estate planning.
Prof. Memberships: Law Society, Society of Trust and Estate Practitioners.
Career: Qualified in 1970 while with *Macfarlanes*. Became a Partner in 1975.

RICHARDSON, Joseph Charles
Dawson & Co, London (0171) 421 4800
Partner in Private Client Department.
Specialisation: Main area of specialisation is taxation. Covers all areas, particularly capital taxation planning (CGT and IHT) and all aspects of settlements (offshore, variation, etc) and heritage property. Also deals with a range of general private client work for high net worth individuals and families (both old and new money) and some charity work. Acts for a number of major landed estates and offshore

clients. Has lectured on IHT and agricultural tenancies, and has specialised recently in CGT reinvestment relief.
Prof. Memberships: Law Society, Society of Trusts and Estates Practitioners.
Career: Qualified in 1974. Partner in *Dawson & Co* since 1976.
Personal: Born 21st October 1949. Educated at St Olave's and St Peter's Schools, York 1959-68, then Durham University 1968-71 (BA in Law). Former Chairman of Selectors, Squash Racket Association (currently Chairman of Disciplinary Panel). Leisure interests are mainly sporting and include cricket, golf and squash. Married with three children and lives near Basingstoke, Hants.

RICHES, John
Withers, London (0171) 936 1000
Specialisation: Partner in Private Client Department. Main practice areas are estate and capital tax planning for U.K. and non U.K. domiciled individuals. Clients include entrepreneurs, private banks and offshore trustees. Has lectured at major conferences in U.K. and overseas and contributes to professional journals and professional training videos.
Prof. Memberships: Council Member of STEP serving on the Technical and Education Committees.
Career: Qualified in 1985. Worked with two major regional firms before joining *Simpson Curtis* in 1990. Partner *Simpson Curtis/ Pinsent Curtis* 1992-96, Partner of *Withers* since May 1996.
Personal: Born 1961. Squash, theatre, walking. Active member of local church.

ROBINSON, David J.R.
Forsters, London (0171) 863 8333
Partner.
Specialisation: Private client specialist, with particular expertise in estate planning, capital taxation and heritage property.
Prof. Memberships: Holborn Law Society and City of London Law Society.
Career: Qualified in 1981. With *Glover & Co* 1982-85. Joined *Frere Cholmeley* in 1985 and became a Partner in 1989. Founding Partner of *Forsters* August 1998.
Personal: Born in 1955. Educated at Westminster School and Pembroke College, Cambridge. Leisure interests include collecting books, music, art and travel.

SKRINE, A.M.A.
Hunters, London (0171) 412 0050
Specialisation: Main areas of practice include probate trusts and estate planning.
Prof. Memberships: Law Society. Society of Trusts and Estates Practitioners.
Career: Qualified 1970. Joined *Hunters* in 1965 and became partner in 1971.
Personal: Born 1944. Educated at Lancing College 1958-1963. Leisure interests include tennis, skiing and gardening.

STANFORD-TUCK, Michael
Taylor Joynson Garrett, London (0171) 353 1234
Partner in Tax and Personal Planning Department.
Specialisation: Principal area of practice is

international trust and tax planning, acting for high net worth individuals, mainly those who are non-UK domiciled. Work includes protection of assets, structuring cross-border investments, asset enhancement, diversification and protection. Also deals with domestic private client work, encompassing UK based estate and tax planning, landed estates, heritage property, contentious and non-contentious probate and chancery litigation. Has administered a major multinational estate, principally in Japan involving detailed assessment of Japanese estate tax and capital gains tax law. He also undertakes trust restructuring for high net worth families relocating to or investing in the UK and has handled high profile contentious and non-contentious chancery proceedings under the Settled Land Act 1925. Experienced lecturer and author of various articles.
Prof. Memberships: Law Society, City of London Solicitors Company, Freeman of the City of London, Society of Trust and Estate Practitioners, Bermuda Society (Committee Member), Star Group.
Career: Qualified in 1972. With *Lovell White & King* 1972-75. Partner with *Appleby Spurling & Kempe* (Bermuda) 1975-84. Admitted Barrister and Attorney Supreme Court of Bermuda 1978. Joined *Taylor Joynson Garrett* as a Partner in 1985.
Personal: Born 3rd November 1946. Educated at Radley College 1960-65 and Southampton University 1965-68. Leisure activities include golf, gardening, skiing and country sports. Lives in Newbury, Berks.

SYED, M. Catriona
Charles Russell, London (0171) 203 5000
Specialisation: International and domestic private client work, including tax and estate planning for UK and non-UK domiciliaries; trusts; charity law and practice; trust aspects of commercial transactions.
Prof. Memberships: STEP Technical Committee member; Charity Law Association; City of London Solicitors Company; Law Society.
Career: Practised at the Chancery Bar 1983-1986. *Norton Rose* 1986-97. Joined *Charles Russell* (partner 1997).
Personal: Lives in London. Leisure interests include theatre, opera, fine wine, walking, travel and reading.

THOMPSON, Anthony J.
Withers, London (0171) 936 1000
Partner in Private Client Department.
Specialisation: Main areas of practice are tax planning, asset structuring, trusts and probate. Acted in Hambro & Others v. Marlborough & Others (application under the Settled Land Act for an order to resettle the Blenheim Parliamentary Estates). Clients include proprietors of landed estates, proprietors of businesses (particularly in the property industry) and offshore trustees. Has lectured at IBC conferences and contributed to Television Education Network. Editor of Trusts Section of Private Client Business.
Prof. Memberships: Law Society, Society of Trust and Estate Practitioners. Member of

Advisory Committee of FTSE International Private Client Indices.
Career: Qualified in 1968. Partner of *Withers* since 1970. Head of Private Client Department 1980-87. Managing Partner 1987-93.
Personal: Born 29th May 1943. Educated at Haberdashers Aske's School 1956-60 and Trinity College, Cambridge 1961-65. Chairman of Governor Glenesk School. President of Horsley Cricket Club. Recreations include golf and amateur dramatics. Lives near Guildford.

TOD, Mark
Hunters, London (0171) 412 0050
Specialisation: Private clients with particular expertise in trusts and estates, tax planning and heritage property and maintenance funds.
Prof. Memberships: The Law Society, Holborn Law Society, Society of Trust and Estate Practitioners.
Career: Qualified in 1971 having joined *Waterhouse & Co.* in 1968. Partner 1977. Partner and head of Private Client Department, *Field Fisher Waterhouse* 1989 to 1996. Joined *Hunters* as a partner 1996.
Personal: Born 1946. Educated at University College School, Hampstead and Oriel College, Oxford. Married with two children. Leisure interests include walking, theatre and watching cricket. Lives in London.

TURNOR, Richard
Allen & Overy, London (0171) 330 3000
Specialisation: Partner specialising in advising wealthy private individuals, their families and trustees in connection with all aspects of tax and estate planning, especially where there is an international aspect. Also advises private banks and professional trustees about the related services provided by them to private clients and about trust litigation, and professional partnerships and banks and others who deal with professional partnerships. Also advises museums and other institutions on heritage and cultural property matters.
Prof. Memberships: Member IBA Committees on cultural property (Vice-Chairman 1992-94) and trusts and estate planning; member Charity Law Association, Society of Trust and Estate practitioners; Trustee of International Bar Association Educational Trust; Association of Partnership Practitioners (Committee Member).
Career: Articled *Allen & Overy*, qualified 1980, Partner 1985.
Personal: Oxford University 1977. Born 1956.

WILLIS, David. C.
Forsters, London (0171) 863 8333
Senior Partner of Forsters.
Specialisation: Trusts (UK and Offshore), estates and personal taxation together with some family law work.
Prof. Memberships: Society of Trusts and Estate Practitioners; Country Landowners Association; Solicitor's Family Law Association.
Career: Oxford University (MA). Qualified initially as a barrister before becoming a solicitor. Partner in *Frere Cholmeley Bischoff* 1978-1998. Founding partner of *Forsters* August 1998.

SOUTH EAST

Boodle Hatfield (3ptnrs/1asst/1 legal exec) *Sue Laing* heads the department and, following particular recommendation, moves up the tables into a band of her own. Acquired another private client partner from the now defunct firm Morrell Peel & Gamlen. **Clients/Work:** Acting for landed estates and wealthy families in complex on and off-shore tax planning. Probate and trust management. Continuing to act for Oxford Colleges and the University.

Cripps Harries Hall (6ptnrs/3assts) *Simon Leney* is the well-known partner in this strong private client firm. This year has seen the formation of a trust corporation to handle the increasing amount of trustee work and the setting up of an Inheritance Disputes unit. One partner sits as Head of the Law Society Probate Section. **Clients/Work:** Advising both domestic and overseas individuals with a strong investment business emphasis and continued expertise in estate and tax planning work.

Thomas Eggar Church Adams (4ptnrs/13assts) "Strong" firm, praised for their "good style." *Robert Ash* and *Richard Thornely* ("fair-minded and logical") remain respected and *Amanda King-Jones* joins the list of leaders. **Clients/Work:** Hold around 500 trusts under administration. In-house trust company upgraded to full Trust Corporation status. Corporate arrangement to manage 150 trusts for minors arising from payment of death in service benefits.

Thomson Snell & Passmore (5ptnrs including *James Krafft*/9assts/2 legal execs/6

investment fund managers) **Clients/Work:** Emphasis on offshore trusts work. Developing specialist services for the elderly.

Adams & Remers (3ptnrs/4 trust managers) **Clients/Work:** Provide lifetime legal support to major estates. Tax dept specialises in Lloyds affairs.

Blandy & Blandy (1ptnr/4assts). The private client dept has a new head (ex-Nabarros) who has introduced more London-based clients to the firm. **Clients/Work:** The Stratfield Saye Estate; The Englefield Estate; Lady Samuel.

Cole & Cole (4ptnrs/8assts, 3assts). Known for agricultural related work. One of the partners writes for the Financial Times on private tax. **Clients/Work:** Acting for a number of high profile clients both here and abroad. Advising newly monied clients following business disposal and flotations.

Iliffes Booth Bennett (2ptnrs/4assts) **Clients/Work:** Clients range from local families to wealthy estates and institutions. Increasing focus on provision for the elderly and disabled through discretionary trusts. Referrals from the Alzheimers Disease Society.

Moore & Blatch (2ptnrs/1asst in the "wealth management" department.)

Blake Lapthorn (2ptnrs/5assts) Department also includes 4 qualified financial advisers. New to the list this year.

Donne Mileham & Haddock (1ptnr/9 legal execs and others handling probate, trusts, tax and investment services) **Clients/Work:** The investment, trust and tax department advises individuals, trustees and business clients.

Paris Smith & Randall (1ptnr/1asst, 1 ex-KPMG acct advises on personal tax)

Brachers (2ptnrs/1asst) **Clients/Work:** Specialise in advising entrepreneurs, farmers and high net worth individuals. The firm administers 200 trusts.

Burstows (1ptnr/8 fee-earners – not solicitors) The department is divided into contentious probate and trust matters on one side and advice to UK domiciliaries owning assets outside the UK on the other. **Clients/Work:** Include: A range from accountancy firms to pharmaceutical companies.

Henmans (2ptnrs/2assts) New entry this year. Recent work includes reorganisation of family trusts, deeds of variation, work for elderly and disabled clients and setting up an heirloom settlement.

SOUTH WEST

Anstey Sargent & Probert (2ptnrs; 1ptnr 70%, 1ptnr 60%/3assts/5 legal execs) Described as "traditional" and "hugely knowledgeable." *Adrian Miller* ("his clients really rate him") heads this "healthy" department with "senior player" *Alex Elphinston* handling many old money clients and an increasing number of entrepreneurs. New fund management team set up this year to handle the increasing investment business. **Clients/Work:** Act for substantial land

owning clients, agricultural interests and the trust department of a national bank.

Bond Pearce (2ptnrs/1ptnr 40%/3assts) *Jonathan Nicholson* ("modest and excellent") heads the department. The merger with Hepherd Winstanley & Pugh in May 1998 is likely to strengthen the department. **Clients/Work:** Advise entrepreneurs from across the south of England in multi-jurisdictional matters often involving complex foreign probate issues.

Burges Salmon (3ptnrs including *Martin Mitchell* and *Charles Wyld*/6 assts)

Known for their tax planning work. **Clients/Work:** Review of standard trust documentation for a major American bank for use by their clients worldwide. Structural reorganisations for wealthy land owners.

Charles Russell (3ptnrs 60-90%) **Clients/Work:** The Cheltenham office of the London firm handles trusts for wealthy clients in the South West.

Osborne Clarke (2ptnrs/7assts (f/t)/3assts (p/t)) Team includes *Sandra Brown, John Sharpe* and *Stephen Pallister.* **Clients/Work:** Personal tax/trust work for the

"Bailey Newspaper Group" shareholders.

Wiggin and Co (4ptnrs f/t; 2ptnrs p/t; 3assts f/t; 1asst p/t) A "high profile" international practice led by *Michael Fullerlove.* The competitor's choice for referrals. **Clients/Work:** Emphasis on international tax planning and asset protection.

Wilsons Solicitors Large private client department including *John Emmerson* ("good reputation for landed estates – relates well to clients") and *Peter Fitzgerald* ("good senior lawyer"). Described by peers as a "class act," the firm is best known for offshore trusts and complex estate planning.

Clarke Willmott & Clarke (6ptnrs/ 4assts) The private client dept works closely with the asset management team and the planning dept to provide an integrated service. **Clients/Work:** Recently secured an agreement from an investment group to compensate a client for poor advice concerning the sale of an investment product.

Hooper & Wollen (3ptnrs/1asst) Increasing focus on advice to the elderly. *Nigel Wollen* is a "top notch operator."

Lawrence Tucketts (1ptnr/1asst) **Clients/Work:** Clients include landowners, directors and professionals. Court of Protection work is on the increase.

Lester Aldridge (5ptnrs including *Barry Glazier*/1assoc/4assts) **Clients/Work:** Earl and Countess of Suffolk and Berkshire; Earl and Countess of Sandwich. Also act for trust company, Southern African. Provide willwriting service for Teachers Assurance.

Steele Raymond (1ptnr/2assts) New entry this year. **Clients/Work:** Act for well-known entertainment personalities. Work includes settlements of agricultural property and advising non-domiciled clients re UK tax aspects of asset holding.

Stones Cann & Hallett Stones merged with Cann & Hallett on 1 May 1998, increasing its all-round strength. **Clients/Work:** Continue to handle trusts and estate planning for local farmers, landowners and businessmen.

Veale Wasbrough (1ptnr/2assts) **Clients/Work:** Estate planning work for individuals, private companies and owner-managed businesses. Increasing experience in nursing home fee planning resulting in the creation of family trusts.

Cartwrights (1ptnr/1asst) **Clients/Work:** Advising a major life insurance company on the development of a new will-based trust product. Developing asset preservation trusts. Advising local private wealthy individuals and commercial clients on inheritance and tax planning matters.

WALES

Beor Wilson & Lloyd (2ptnrs 50%/1asst 75%) Recognised practice.

Bevan Ashford (1 cons 1ptnr/1 legal exec) **Clients/Work:** On National Lottery Winners Advisory Panel.

Edwards Geldard (1ptnr/ 2assoc/1asst) "Sound" department. **Clients/Work:** Administration of multi-million pound estates, tax planning for wealthy British entrepreneurs and private clients.

Eversheds (1ptnr/1asst) **Clients/Work:** The Cardiff and Bristol offices offer tax and trusts advice as support to the company and commercial dept. Noted especially for their work for the elderly and their trust documentation service.

MIDLANDS

Hewitson Becke & Shaw (3ptnrs/3assts/2 legal execs) One of the largest depts outside London, with a specialist investment services unit. **Clients/Work:** Handle probate, trust creation and administration, Court of Protection work and tax planning projects for farmers and landowners.

Martineau Johnson (4ptnrs/3assts/5 legal execs) *Hugh Carslake* ("very good") heads the largest private client department in Birmingham, which has grown following the arrival of Eversheds and Edge & Ellison personnel. **Clients/Work:** Tax planning and estate organisation for landed families and some industry wealth. Trust creation and administration.

Lee Crowder (2ptnrs/5assts) **Clients/Work:** Clients include charities, King Edward School Foundation and Bass plc.

Wragge & Co (1ptnr/5assts) *Louise Woodhead* ("very able") leads the team. **Clients/Work:** Clients include owners and directors of companies and landowners. Tax restructuring for entrepreneurs including offshore planning.

Freeth Cartwright Hunt Dickins (3ptnrs/2assts) **Clients/Work:** The trusts team handles over 200 trusts and recently set up a Charitable Foundation. The probate team act for substantial estates.

Herbert Wilkes Capital tax planning for high net worth individuals and specialist advice for the elderly. Focusing on clients of local banks, building societies and businesses.

Higgs & Sons (3ptnrs/3assts) Estate and tax planning advice for company proprieters and high net worth individuals.

Roythorne & Co (1ptnr/2assts) **Clients/Work:** Dealing with self administered pension schemes. Probate including agricultural and business relief with multi jurisdictional assets. Trust creation and administration.

Shakespeares (3ptnrs/ 13 fee-earners in the private client dept) Focus on charities work. Also have a dedicated investment management dept.

Willcox Lane Clutterbuck (2ptnrs/1 asst/1 legal exec/1 trust manager) A growing trusts and charities practice. **Clients/Work:** Act for the Birmingham Institute for the

Deaf, the Birmingham Hospital Saturday Fund and Solihull College.

LEADING INDIVIDUALS
MIDLANDS

CARSLAKE Hugh Martineau Johnson	
WOODHEAD Louise Wragge & Co	

EAST ANGLIA

LEADING FIRMS · EAST ANGLIA

EVERSHEDS Norwich
HEWITSON BECKE + SHAW Cambridge
MILLS & REEVE Norwich
BANKES ASHTON Bury St. Edmunds
GREENE & GREENE Bury St. Edmunds
PRETTYS Ipswich
TAYLOR VINTERS Cambridge
WARD GETHIN King's Lynn

HIGHLY REGARDED FIRMS

Cozens-Hardy & Jewson Norwich
Hood Vores & Allwood Dereham
Steele & Co Norwich
Willcox & Lewis Norwich

Eversheds (6ptnrs/2assts between Norwich and Ipswich) **Clients/ Work:** Capital tax planning for family companies and trusts involving substantial assets. Advising in conjunction with US lawyers re family

settlements, following changes in tax laws.

Hewitson Becke + Shaw (2ptnrs/1 asst) *Peter Ewart* heads the team (including five directors of investment services, settlements, funds and legal execs) from Cambridge and all offices work closely together. The client base consists mainly of farmers and landowners. The firm has a new investment services unit.

Mills & Reeve (12ptnrs/11 assts in the private client and tax planning dept). *Justin Ripman* heads the team and is also on the panel of advisers to the lottery. **Clients/Work:** Recently created a maintenance fund in conjunction with a claim for conditional exemption from inheritance tax enabling the family to retain a landed estate. Set up of companies to take advantage of re-investment relief to purchase farms.

Bankes Ashton (4ptnrs/8assts) **Clients/Work:** Due to merge with Graham & Oldam, so will also have a presence in Ipswich. Integrated tax planning, portfolio management and income tax service in addition to probate and trusts practice.

Prettys (2ptnrs/3 fee-earners – non-solicitors) **Clients/Work:** Domestic and international probate matters especially mixed UK and French estates. Acting for estranged daughter of French domicile and successfully claiming her entitlement to her estate under French law. Winding up estate of US domiciled editor of UK magazine.

Willcox & Lewis (2ptnrs/ 2assts) A niche private client firm formed in October 1997 by *Michael Willcox* (previously head of private capital group at Eversheds) and *Ian Lewis* (previously private client partner at Nabarros). **Clients/Work:** Advise high net worth individuals, trustees and charities. The work has an international emphasis with clients in Europe and the US.

LEADING INDIVIDUALS
EAST ANGLIA

EWART Peter Hewitson Becke + Shaw
LEWIS Ian Willcox & Lewis
RIPMAN Justin Mills & Reeve
WILLCOX Michael Willcox & Lewis

NORTH EAST

LEADING FIRMS · NORTH EAST

DICKINSON DEES Newcastle upon Tyne
ADDLESHAW BOOTH & CO Leeds
ANDREW M. JACKSON & CO Hull
EVERSHEDS Newcastle upon Tyne/Leeds
LUPTON FAWCETT Leeds
PINSENT CURTIS Leeds
WRIGLEYS Leeds
BROOKE NORTH Leeds
GORDONS WRIGHT & WRIGHT Bradford
IRWIN MITCHELL Sheffield
WARD HADAWAY Newcastle upon Tyne

HIGHLY REGARDED FIRMS

Armitage Sykes Hall Norton Huddersfield
Askews Redcar
Harrowell Shaftoe York
Latimer Hinks Darlington
Rollit Farrell & Bladon Hull
Walker Morris Leeds

Dickinson Dees (7 ptnrs/6assts/2 accountants, 9 tax managers/10 legal execs all) Large, respected department including *Adrian Gifford* (head of team, acts for many wealthy individuals), *George Lyall* (an ex-accountant) and *Alexander Dickinson.* **Clients/Work:** Act for major private landowners and wealthy families, particularly in the north of England (have often acted for four or five generations and play a key role in the administration of their affairs). Also new clients from the business community.

Addleshaw Booth & Co (2ptnrs including *Paul Howell*/7assts) **Clients/ Work:** Review of complex family trust worth in excess of £150 million. Parallel trust arrangement for two directors resulting in capital gains tax saving in excess of £1 million. Devised innovative IHT saving plan using business property relief to save several hundred thousand pounds.

Andrew M Jackson & Co (2ptnrs/1 trust administrator/1asst) A well regarded niche firm. Head of Private Client Department, *Kevin Webster*, is an ex-Eversheds man. Trusts and personal tax accounts for

approx. 25% of firm's finance. **Clients/Work:** Administration of estates worth £22m. Administering approx. 150 trusts, some worth £1m. Enduring power of attorney and care fee planning for the elderly.

Eversheds (5ptnrs/6assts/4 other fee earners)The Newcastle office has expanded considerably with the addition of the Wilkinson Maughan private client team. The Leeds office, led by *Peter Chadwick*, also has considerable experience. **Clients/Work:** Inheritance tax planning using gifts, trusts and offshore structures. Computerised probate and trust charter system linked with local and national stockbrokers, accountants and financial advisers.

Lupton Fawcett (3 ptnrs/6assts, 8 legal execs) Partner *John Eaton* is well regarded for investment work ("excellent"). Seen as having "good quality smaller clients." Work is split between Leeds and Harrogate offices. **Clients/Work:** On and offshore trusts and tax work. Also specialists in handling cases for the elderly including long term care and nursing fees.

Pinsent Curtis (1ptnr–*Nigel Binks*/ 2consts/1assoc) **Clients/Work:** Tax and trustee advice re sale of private company by offshore trustees (£21m). Pre-flotation tax planning involving stock dividends and trusts (£35m). Reconstruction of UK trusts and formation of new trusts (£7m).

Wrigleys (6ptnrs/9assts/4 trust mngrs) "Charismatic, high profile" *Matthew Wrigley*, the founding partner, has again been recommended. He has a particular interest in heritage property. **Clients/ Work:** Have acquired much of Hammond Suddards workload.

Brooke North (2ptnrs/2assts) **Clients/ Work:** Acted for the taxpayer in Couch v Caton, a share valuation/tax case in the Court of Appeal.

Gordons Wright & Wright (2ptnrs/ 4assts – 2 p/t)). Increasing their profile and looking to expand.

Irwin Mitchell (2ptnrs/3ptnrs p/t; 1asst) Have a good reputation for the quality of work. **Clients/Work:** Will writing services for 1500 clients of two financial institutions. Trust and inheritance tax planning for high net worth individuals. Applications to the Court of Protection for personal injury victims with substantial damages.

Ward Hadaway (3ptnrs/3assts) Known to maintain a commitment in private client work. **Clients/ Work:** Advise landowners, farmers, owner-managed businesses, trustees of UK and foreign trusts and entrepreneurs.

NORTH WEST

Berrymans Lace Mawer (1ptnr/2assts/ 1ptnr in London). *David Bishop* heads the team in Liverpool. **Clients/ Work:** Dealing with trusts for clients following Labour election victory. Setting up discretionary trusts to take advantage of reliefs.

Brabner Holden Banks Wilson (2ptnrs/4assts Liverpool; 1ptnr Preston). *Mark Feeny* heads the team which has increased in size with the acquisition of the private client department of Weightmans.

Cobbetts (2ptnrs/3assts/4 legal execs) **Clients/Work:** Focus on entrepreneurs and private tax and trusts for business clients.

Halliwell Landau (1ptnr/4assts). *Geoffrey Shindler* heads the department. **Clients/ Work:** Awarded a long term contract to supply legal services to Barclays Bank Trust Co Ltd.

SCOTLAND

Brodies WS (10ptnrs including *Andrew Dalgleish*/2assts/3 accountants/4 trust managers) Large private client department. Remains committed to trusts and private tax work and have a policy of integrating this work with their commercial services. **Clients/Work:** Particular interest in inheritance tax planning and the farming market.

Maclay Murray & Spens (19 fee-earners in the private client dept) *Ian Stubbs* remains respected for his estates work and another partner is the director of Scottish Widows. **Clients/Work:** Act for private individuals, trusts and private estates.

Murray Beith Murray WS (5ptnrs including *Hugh Younger*/4assts/4 accountants/ 4 trust managers) **Clients/ Work:** The client base is developing from traditional estates and farm owners to wealthy individuals. Focus on tax and financial planning through the Financial Services dept.

Tods Murray WS (3ptnrs including *David McLetchie*/ 3assts)

Turcan Connell WS (8ptnrs/9assts/15 trust and tax account managers) A new specialist private client firm formed by partners from Dundas & Wilson and Burness. It includes leaders *Douglas Connell*, *George Menzies* and *Hubert Ross* and is already seen as a major player in the field.

Anderson Strathern WS (7ptnrs/ 2assts) Have a large department and volume of work and move up the table as a result. **Clients/Work:** Setting up of excluded property offshore trusts for non-UK domiciliaries. Establishing a string of new trading companies for CGT reinvestment relief. Trust reorganisation for a landed client.

Ledingham Chalmers (4ptnrs/3assts/4 paralegals/1 financial services mngr) **Clients/Work:** Emphasis on tax and estate planning for landowners and also specific advice to the elderly.

MacRoberts (2ptnrs including *David MacRobert*/2assts advise on trusts and charities). **Clients/Work:** Continue to advise high net worth individuals on tax planning and administration.

The Morton Fraser Partnership (1 ptnr/1 asst) Private client work including trusts/personal tax (representing a third of the firm's workload) is dealt with by the Morton

Fraser Milligan arm of the partnership. *Scott Rae* is the rated partner.

Shepherd & Wedderburn WS (5ptnrs including *Robin Fulton*/20 fee-earners). **Clients/Work:** A traditional private client practice which is gradually shifting its

emphasis from established clients to "new money clients." In conjunction with the corporate dept, there is an increase in the provision of complex tax advice.

NORTHERN IRELAND

LEADING FIRMS
NORTHERN IRELAND

C & J BLACK Belfast

CARSON & MCDOWELL Belfast

CLEAVER FULTON & RANKIN Belfast

S.J. DIAMOND & SON Belfast

ELLIOTT DUFFY GARRETT Belfast

HEWITT & GILPIN Belfast

JOHNSONS Belfast

L'ESTRANGE & BRETT Belfast

WILSON NESBITT Belfast

C & J Black (1 ptnr 40%/1 cons.) Small but well regarded practice including partner *Elma McCaw*.

Carson & McDowell (1ptnr/2assts) **Clients/Work:** Advised on several discretionary trusts to preserve IHT position prior to 1998 Budget. Acting for foreign domiciliary concerning will of UK assets.

Cleaver Fulton & Rankin (3 ptnrs -*Joy Scott*, *Alastair Rankin* and *Peter Rankin*/1 asst) **Clients/Work:** Creation of lifetime trusts by a minor settlor suffering from mental incapacity. Administration of large heritage property estate. Administration of estate involving appointment of assets to offshore trust.

Other ranked firms of note include **S.J. Diamond & Son**, with recognised leader *Anne Copeland* and assistants and **Johnsons**,

with *Herbert McCracken* and two assistants. **L'Estrange & Brett's** team of two partners and two assistants includes *Alan Hewitt*. **Wilson Nesbitt** has a relatively large department including recognised partner *Gilbert Nesbitt*.

LEADING INDIVIDUALS
NORTHERN IRELAND

COPELAND Anne S.J. Diamond & Son

HEWITT Alan L'Estrange & Brett

MCCAW Elma C & J Black

MCCRACKEN Herbert Johnsons

NESBITT Gilbert Wilson Nesbitt

RANKIN Alastair Cleaver Fulton & Rankin

RANKIN Peter Cleaver Fulton & Rankin

SCOTT Joy Cleaver Fulton & Rankin

LEADERS' PROFILES · REGIONS

ASH, Robert
Thomas Eggar Church Adams, Chichester (01243) 786111
Specialisation: Main areas: Personal finance planning, trust and personal tax.
Prof. Memberships: STEP and Law Society.
Career: Qualified 1967-. Partner in *T.E.C.A.* since 1972. Founder Director of Thesis.

BINKS, Nigel
Pinsent Curtis, Birmingham (0121) 200 1050

BISHOP, David C.
Berrymans Lace Mawer, Liverpool (0151) 236 2002
Head of Private Client and Pensions.
Specialisation: Main areas of specialisation are trusts and tax planning for individuals and private companies including offshore arrangements; all aspects of occupational pensions and charities. Notary Public.
Prof. Memberships: Law Society, Chairman, Liverpool Branch Society of Trust and Estate Practitioners, International Tax Planning Association, ass. Association of Pension Lawyers.
Career: Qualified 1972 Partner *Laces & Co* (now *Berrymans Lace Mawer*) 1974. Head of Private Client Department 1995.
Personal: Born 6th April 1947. Educated Sedbergh School 1960-65, Caius College, Cambridge 1966-69. Lives in Formby.

BROWN, Sandra
Osborne Clarke, Bristol (0117) 923 0220
Specialisation: Partner managing the tax and trust department; tax and estate planning with particular reference to the foreign element; trusts including offshore trusts; charities.

Prof. Memberships: STEP, Notary Public.
Career: Articled *Burges Salmon*; qualified 1983. Assistant solicitor; associate *Osborne Clarke*; partner 1989.
Personal: Resides Bristol.

CARSLAKE, Hugh
Martineau Johnson, Birmingham (0121) 200 3300
Partner in Private Client Department.
Specialisation: Main area of practice covers tax planning, trusts and estate planning and ecclesiastical law. Acts for the owners of landed estates and private individuals in their personal and trustee capacities. Registrar for and legal adviser to the Diocese of Birmingham.
Prof. Memberships: Law Society, STEP. Ecclesiastical Law Association (ELA).
Career: Qualified in 1973, having joined *Martineau Johnson* in 1972. Became a Partner in 1974, Notary Public in 1981, Head of Private Client Department in 1991 and Diocesan Registrar in 1992.
Personal: Born 15th November 1946. Attended Rugby School, 1960-65, then Trinity College, Dublin, 1966-70. Chairman of the Barber Institute of Fine Arts (University of Birmingham); Council Member of the Birmingham and Midland Institute; Member of the Council of the University of Birmingham; Trustee of the Worcester Cathedral Appeal Trust. Council Member of the Notaries society. Leisure interests include family, music and gardening. Lives in Warwickshire.

CHADWICK, Peter
Eversheds, Leeds (0113) 243 0391
Specialisation: Over 20 years specialising in

Trusts and Estate Planning, Probate and Wills, Landed Estates and Charity Law.
Prof. Memberships: Law Society, CLA, Charity Law Assocation.
Career: Qualified 1975. Partner with *Eversheds* (formerly *Heyworth & Chadwick*) since 1978. Non-executive director *Next plc* 1980-1986.
Personal: Born 1951. Educated Oundle School and Newcastle upon Tyne University. Trustee various charities. Hobbies: fly-fishing, mountaineering and music.

CONNELL, Douglas
Edinburgh (0131) 228 8111
See under Charities, p. 164

COPELAND, E.Anne
S.J. Diamond & Son, Belfast (01232) 243726

DALGLEISH, Andrew M.C.
Brodies WS, Edinburgh (0131) 228 3777
Specialisation: Main areas of practice are capital tax planning, trusts (private client, commercial and public), wills and executries. Co-author Barr Biggar Dalgleish and Stevens, Drafting Wills in Scotland; contributor to Withers, International Trust Precedents; Lawrence, International Personal Tax Planning Encyclopaedia; Norrie & Scobbie, Trusts; and George, International Charitable Giving.
Prof. Memberships: Law Society of Scotland, Society of Trust and Estate Practitioners, Association of Pension Lawyers (associate).
Career: Qualified 1975. Partner *Brodies* 1978.
Personal: Born 1951, resides Edinburgh.

DICKINSON, Alexander
Dickinson Dees, Newcastle upon Tyne
(0191) 279 9000
Specialisation: Partner advising on Trusts, Wills, Probate, Tax Planning, Heritage Property Landed Estates and Charity Law.
Prof. Memberships: Law Society, STEP.
Career: Qualified 1989, Partner 1997.
Personal: Lives in Northumberland.

EATON, John C.J.
Lupton Fawcett, Leeds (0113) 280 2000
Financial Services Partner
Specialisation: 32 years specialisation in financial, tax, trust, and investment matters for Private Clients. Author, 'Midland Guide to Inheritance and Investment of Inherited Moneys.' Regular contributor to financial, legal, and business journals, broadcaster and speaker at legal and financial seminars.
Prof. Memberships: Law Society – Law Society Financial Services Subcommittee – S.B.A. – Institute of Financial Planning – Solicitors for Independent Financial Advice – Association of Solicitor Investment Managers – Securities Institute – Society of Trusts & Estates Practitioners – Fellow, Institute of Directors.
Career: Qualified 1965. President Bradford Law Society 1984. Senior Partner, *Eaton & Co.*, Bradford until 1988, then Financial Services partner at *Lupton Fawcett*, Leeds. Won 1997 HIFAL Award for Best Financial Services Firm.
Personal: Born June 1943. Educated at Charterhouse and Trinity Hall Cambridge. Cambridge Footlights 1961-64. Keen musician. Trustee of various charities.

ELPHINSTON, Alexander
Anstey Sargent & Probert, Exeter
(01392) 411221
Specialisation: Partner in Private Client Department. Tax planning for individuals through wills and trusts: particular involvement in attorneyship and court of protection work as well as living wills. Also Trustee of and advisor to various Charities.
Prof. Memberships: Member of the Law Society: Secretary of STEP (West of England).
Career: Qualified with *Waterhouse* in London, before moving to Devon, joining *Anstey Sargent & Probert* in 1987.
Personal: Born 6th June 1955. Repton School and Durham University. Married with three young children: interests include theatre, cricket, jazz and jigsaw puzzles. Trustee and governor of local school.

EMMERSON, John C.
Wilsons Solicitors, Salisbury (01722) 412412
Partner in Tax Planning Department.
Specialisation: Main area of practice is tax planning (UK and international), trust law and charitable trusts. Cases handled have included Ampthill Peerage Claim(1976), 'Raikes v. Lygon' (1988) and 'Hatton v. IRC' (1992). Author of articles in British Tax Review and other publications. Has experience of speaking at tax seminars.
Prof. Memberships: Law Society, International Tax Planning Association, Society of Tax and Estate Practitioners.
Career: Qualified 1967. Former Head of Private Client Department at *McKenna & Co.* up to 1991, when the Department moved out of London to *Wilsons*, Salisbury, Wiltshire. Partner, 1991.
Personal: Born 1937. Attended Merchant

Taylor's School, then Magdalen College Oxford 1958-61. Governor of Salisbury College. Trustee of Wiltshire Community Foundation. Fellow of the Woodard Corporation. Leisure interests include fly-fishing. Lives in Wylye, near Salisbury, Wiltshire.

EVANS, Michael
Burges Salmon, Bristol (0117) 939 2000

EWART, P.W.
Hewitson Becke + Shaw, Cambridge (01223) 461155
Prof. Memberships: Society of Trust & Estate Practitioners. Charity Law Association.

FEENY, Mark R.
Brabner Holden Banks Wilson, Liverpool (0151) 236 5821
Head of Probate and Trust Department.
Specialisation: Deals with trusts, estate and tax planning and contentious probate and related matters.
Prof. Memberships: Law Society. Liverpool Law Society. Society of Trust and Estate Practitioners.
Career: Qualified in 1981. Partner 1983.
Personal: Deputy Sheriff for Counties of Merseyside, Lancashire and Greater Manchester. Chairman Merseyside Housing Association. Born 16.10.55.

FITZGERALD, Peter R.
Wilsons Solicitors, Salisbury (01722) 412412
Partner in Farms and Estates Department.
Specialisation: Specialises in agricultural estates including stately homes, chattels, heritage law, agricultural law and tax. Firm represents some 280,000 acres of agricultural land. Author of occasional articles on heritage and taxation matters and occasional speaker at conferences and seminars.
Prof. Memberships: CLA, HHA.
Career: Qualified in 1969. Partner at *Fladgate Fielder* 1975-95. Joined *Wilsons* as a Partner in 1995.
Personal: Educated at Canford School and Trinity College, Oxford (MA). Lives near Wincanton, Somerset.

FULLERLOVE, Michael Reame
Wiggin and Co, Cheltenham
(01242) 224114
Specialisation: Private client work for high net worth individuals, both in the U.K. and elsewhere. A large part of his practice involves international asset and tax structuring on work inbound and outbound to and from the USA.
Prof. Memberships: The Law Society; International Tax Planning Association; STEP.
Career: University of Birmingham: LLB. Magdalen College, Oxford: B.C.L.Articles and Assistant Solicitor: *Freshfields*, City of London.
Personal: Born 1948. Gardening and Genealogy.

FULTON, Robin D.
Shepherd & Wedderburn WS, Edinburgh
(0131) 228 9900
Partner and head of private client department.
Specialisation: Specialist areas taxation, trusts and estates, partnerships and charity law.
Prof. Memberships: Qualified Solicitor Scotland 1979.
Career: *Shepherd & Wedderburn*; qualified 1979; Assistant Solicitor 1979-1982, Partner 1982; Scottish Editor 'Sergeant & Sims on

Stamp Duties' and 'Foster's Inheritance Tax;' senior tutor in wills, trusts and executries, Edinburgh University Diploma in Legal Education.
Personal: Born 1956; resides Edinburgh. Interests: sport generally but particularly squash, tennis, golf, skiing and food and wine.

GIFFORD, Adrian C.
Dickinson Dees, Newcastle upon Tyne
0191 279 9000
Head of Private Client Department.
Specialisation: Advises major landowners and businessmen on their personal affairs.
Prof. Memberships: STEP.
Career: Qualified in 1977. Became Partner at *Dickinson Dees* in 1979.
Personal: Born 1946. Educated at Merchant Taylors School and St Andrew's University. Lives in Northumberland.

GLAZIER, Barry
Lester Aldridge, Bournemouth
(01202) 786161
Partner in Private Client Department.
Specialisation: Corporate and personal tax, particularly for family-owned businesses, as well as landed estates, onshore and offshore trusts, and charities. Appointed Managing Partner in 1994.
Career: Articled *Penningtons*, London; qualified 1966; Solicitor *Clifford Turner* 1966-1971; Partner *Lester Aldridge* since 1972; President of Dorset Chamber of Commerce and Industry 1992-1993, President Bournemouth & District Law Society 1991-1992; Director and Company Secretary, Dorset Training and Enterprise Council; chairman of Eurolegal 1991-1995; Chairman of Hurstpierpoint Lawyers' Society.
Personal: Born 1941; resides Wimborne Minster. Educated at Hurstpierpoint College (1950-1960); St Peter's College, Oxford (1960-1963 BA, 1968 MA Oxon); Notary Public. Recreations include concerts and opera, piano playing, walking, ornithology, gardening.

HEWITT, V. Alan
L'Estrange & Brett, Belfast (01232) 230426
See under Property (Commercial), p. 724

HOWELL, Paul J.
Addleshaw Booth & Co, Leeds
(0113) 209 2000
Specialisation: Head of the firm's Private Client Group. Main areas of expertise are in UK and offshore personal tax planning and trusts, formation of charities and National Heritage Schemes.
Prof. Memberships: Memberships: Society of Estate and Trust Practitioners. Country Land Owners Assocation.
Career: Liverpool University 1974; admitted in 1977; joined the firm in 1990 as a partner.
Personal: Tennis, skiing, sailing, windsurfing and bridge.

KING-JONES, Amanda
Thomas Eggar Church Adams, Chichester
(01243) 786111
Partner and Head of Private Client Division.
Specialisation: Main areas of practice are personal tax and financial planning probate and trusts. Also deals with the affairs of the elderly.
Prof. Memberships: Law Society and Society of Trust and Estate Practitioners.

Career: Joined *T.E.V.B.* 1981. Qualified 1983. Partner 1987. Co-Author of Probate Practice Manual (Sweet & Maxwell).
Personal: Educated at Roedean School 1969-77. Exeter University (LLB) 1978-1981.

KRAFFT, James A.
Thomson Snell & Passmore, Tunbridge Wells (01892) 510000
Partner and Head of Private Client Department.
Specialisation: Main areas of practice are general private client work, personal financial planning, tax planning, wills, settlements, powers of attorney and probate.
Prof. Memberships: Law Society and Society of Trust and Estate Practitioners.
Career: Qualified in 1971, Articled and practised in London before joining *Thomson Snell & Passmore* in 1976.
Personal: Born 1st May 1944. Educated at Downside School and St. Catherine's College, Oxford. Leisure interests include golf, tennis, bridge, reading and psychology. Lives in Langton Green, Kent.

LAING, Sue
Boodle Hatfield, Oxford (01865) 798744
Specialisation: Handles UK Capital, Income and Corporation Tax planning for landed estates, individuals, trusts, partnerships and private companies; the creation, running and termination of UK and overseas trusts; the interaction of UK and foreign taxes via double tax treaties or UK unilateral relief; the taxation of and transactions within the UK or involving UK entities; UK and overseas taxation of complex trust/corporate structures; and long-term planning for individuals, particularly with a foreign element.
Prof. Memberships: STEP.
Career: Qualified 1978; Partner in *Boodle Hatfield* 1981; Established Oxford office as first Resident Partner, 1994. Regular contributor to various tax publications and "Legal Network Television."
Personal: Born 1954. MA (Oxon) 1978. Lives near Oxford.

LENEY, Simon
Cripps Harries Hall, Tunbridge Wells, Kent (01892) 506160
Specialisation: Head of Private Client Department. Handles creation/ use of settlements and will trusts; trusteeship and executorships; wills and administration of estates; powers of attorney and attorneyships; inheritance tax and estate planning; charity law; Inheritance (Provision for Family and Dependants) Act claims and other trust or inheritance disputes or claims; in the last year appointed to represent high net worth estate in high profile professional trustee fraud case.
Prof. Memberships: Member of Securities Institute, Director of Solicitors Benevolent Association, member of Society of Trust and Estate Practitioners (STEP), Notary Public.
Career: Educated at Sherborne School, Dorset. Articled at *Donne Mileham and Haddock*; Qualified 1977; Salaried partner 1979; Equity partner 1982; Head of Private Client Department 1989; joined *Cripps Harries Hall* 1994; Head of Private Client Department 1996 to date.
Personal: Married with two children. Interests include rugby, vintage and classic cars, home and garden.

LEWIS, Ian G.
Willcox & Lewis, Cambridge (01954) 261 444
Specialisation: Estate planning, trusts (UK and offshore) and domicile. Also charity law and practice.
Prof. Memberships: Law Society, Society of Trusts and Estates Practitioners, and elected Academician of International Academy of Estate and Trust Law.
Career: Qualified 1972. Partner *Kenneth Brown Baker Baker*, *Turner Kenneth Brown* and *Nabarro Nathanson* (1974-1997) following mergers. Established niche private client practice acting for high net worth individuals in 1997.
Personal: Educated Dartford Grammar School and St Catherine's College, Oxford. Recreations include sailing, hill walking, reading and music.

LYALL, George
Dickinson Dees, Newcastle upon Tyne (0191) 261 1911
Specialisation: Personal Tax Partner and Private/Charitable Trust Specialist. Provides advice on domicile and related issues to UK expatriates in Northern Europe, including appeals of EC rulings and International Estate Planning.
Prof. Memberships: English and Scottish Solicitor, CA, NP and TEP.
Career: 1976-1982 Edinburgh University – B.Com, LLB and Dip.LP. 1982-1985 Scottish Court Solicitor and Notary Public. 1985-1994 Chartered Accountant and Senior Tax Manager at Arthur/Ernst & Young. March 1994 Joined *Dickinson Dees*.
Personal: Married to Roz with three sons.

MACROBERT, David J.C.
MacRoberts, Glasgow (0141) 332 9988
Partner and head of Trust Department.
Specialisation: Specialist areas include wills, trusts, inheritance tax, capital gains tax, income tax, executries, power of attorney, charities and investments.
Career: Glenalmond College; Dundee University (1975 LLB). Trainee *Brechin Robb*; qualified 1977; assistant solicitor *MacRoberts* 1977-19801; partner 1980; former senior tutor Glasgow University; former external examiner in finance tax and investment Edinburgh University, Diploma in Legal Practice; member Revenue Committee Law Society of Scotland; Capital Taxes Sub Committee of Chartered Accountants of Scotland. Trustee of Scottish Civic Trust.
Personal: Born 1953; resides Paisley. Leisure: skiing, sailing, shooting, fishing, gardening; member: Royal Gourock Yacht Club, Royal Western Yacht Club, Western Club, Western Club, RSAC.

MCCAW, Elma
C & J Black, Belfast (01232) 550060
Specialisation: Probate, Inheritance Tax Planning, Discretionary Trusts, Wills, Deeds of Family Arrangement.
Prof. Memberships: Member of the Incorporated Law Society of Northern Ireland, Belfast Solicitors' Association.
Career: LL.B. (Second Class Honours first Division), Queens University, Belfast. Qualified as a Solicitor in 1976. Partner in *C & J Black*, Solicitors since 1982.

MCCRACKEN, Herbert L.
Johnsons, Belfast (01232) 240183
Specialisation: Head of Private Client Department dealing with Conveyancing, Probate, Wills and Trusts, Tax Planning and all aspects of Property Law including planning.
Prof. Memberships: Law Society of Northern Ireland.
Career: Educated: Banbridge Academy, Queens University, Belfast.

MCLETCHIE, David W.
Tods Murray WS, Edinburgh (0131) 226 4771
david.mcletchie@todsmurray.co.uk
Specialisation: Trusts Estates, Personal Tax and Financial Planning.
Prof. Memberships: Law Society of Scotland: STEP, WS Society, Notary Public.
Career: Apprentice solicitor *Shepherd & Wedderburn WS* 1974-76. Joined *Tods Murray* 1976. Partner 1980. Head of department dealing with administration of estates and trusts, wills, charities, personal tax and financial planning.
Personal: Born 1952. Educated George Heriots School, Edinburgh; Edinburgh University LLB (Hons) 1974. Leisure: politics, golf, football.

MENZIES, George M.
Turcan Connell WS, Edinburgh (0131) 228 8111
Specialisation: Extensive experience in Trust Law and Succession including the use of trusts in tax and estate planning and the preservation and passing on of family businesses. Also experienced in offshore tax planning, asset protection trusts and inward investment to the United Kingdom. Acts as trustee of several pension trusts, and charitable trusts.
Career: Current Directorships: Scottish Council (Development & Industry) (Vice – President); Greencastle Farming Plc: Endeavour Training (Scotland); Newcastle Building Society Scottish Advisory Board Member.

MILLER, Adrian W.M.
Anstey Sargent & Probert, Exeter (01392) 411221
Partner in charge of Private Client Department.
Specialisation: Family and financial planning for individuals and landed estates, tax trusts and attorneyship, equity and offshore, advance directives, charities and friendly society work.
Prof. Memberships: Law Society, Vice Chairman STEP (West of England).
Career: Joined *Anstey Sargent & Probert* in 1974 from *Gregory Rowcliffe & Co.*
Personal: Born 7th November 1947. Radley College and Corpus Christi College, Oxford: Jurisprudence. Chief personal interest is his family and their home and garden in mid-Devon where he is church warden. His family Scottish sporting estate and French holiday property absorb the rest of his leisure time.

MITCHELL, A.W. Martin
Burges Salmon, Bristol (0117) 939 2000

NESBITT, H.W. Gilbert
Wilson Nesbitt, Belfast (01232) 323864
Specialisation: Specialises in capital taxation, trust, wills, probate, housing association,

residential building work and commercial property.
Prof. Memberships: Notary Public, Managing Partner Wilson Nesbitt since 1982.
Career: LLB Queen's University Belfast (1973), MA Ohio University (1976), qualified 1978, Partner *Wilson Nesbitt* 1982.
Personal: Born 10 October 1951. Leisure interests include snowboarding, waterskiing and tennis.

NICHOLSON, Jonathan B.
Bond Pearce, Plymouth (01752) 266 633
Specialisation: Partner in the firm's Private Client Group with over 25 years experience in wills, probate, trusts and personal tax. Also specialises in charity law and is solicitor to several major charities.
Prof. Memberships: Member of the Society of Trust and Estate Practitioners (Chairman of West of England branch) and the Association of Charity Lawyers.
Career: Graduate of Trinity College, Dublin, qualified in 1968 and joined the University of Zambia as lecturer in law, returning to the UK in 1971. Joined *Meade King* in Bristol and was solicitor to the Bristol Municipal Charities. Moved to *Bond Pearce* in 1983, becoming partner in 1985.

PALLISTER, Stephen
Osborne Clarke, Bristol (0117) 923 0220

PORTER, John Neil
Burges Salmon, Bristol (0117) 939 2000

RAE, Scott A.
The Morton Fraser Partnership, Edinburgh (0131) 550 1000
Specialisation: Tax, Trusts, Estate Planning.
Prof. Memberships: Solicitor, W.S., N.P., T.E.P.
Career: LL.B. (Hons 1st) Edinburgh University – 1966. Partner with *Morton Fraser* since 1970. Current appointments:- Convener Law Society of Scotland Tax Law Committee; Secretary, The International Academy of Estate and Trust Law; Collector, W.S. Society; Member VAT Tribunal (Scotland).
Personal: Born 17.12.44

RANKIN, Alastair J.
Cleaver Fulton & Rankin, Belfast (01232) 243141
Specialisation: Chancery and Equity, Probate, Taxation, Trusts and Estates, Wills.
Prof. Memberships: Member of Council The Law Society of Northern Ireland since 1985: Treasurer 1991-1995; Junior Vice-President 1995-96; President 1996-97. Senior Vice-President 1997-98.
Career: Qualified as Solicitor 1977. Partner 1980. Part-time Lecturer on Wills, Revenue and Administration of Estates since 1988 at the Institute of Professional Legal Studies, Queens University of Belfast. Part-time Chairman Pensions Appeal Tribunals for Northern Ireland.
Personal: Born 5 September 1951. Educated Trinity College Dublin (BA Dublin University). Member, Society of Trust and Estate Practitioners.

RANKIN, Peter J.
Cleaver Fulton & Rankin, Belfast (01232) 243141
Specialisation: Corporate Law, Acquisitions, Charities, Trusts, Real Estate.
Prof. Memberships: Law Society of Northern Ireland.

Career: Qualified as Solicitor 1968. Partner in 1970.
Personal: Educated Trinity College, Dublin (B.A., LL.B. Dublin University).

RIPMAN, Justin
Mills & Reeve, Norwich +44 (0)1603 660155 + 44 (0)1223 364422
Partner
Specialisation: Specialises in tax and estate planning with particular emphasis on trust and tax issues affecting landed estates.

ROSS, Hubert J.
Turcan Connell WS, Edinburgh (0131) 228 8111
Specialisation: Specialises in advising family companies and businesses, entrepreneurs and high net worth individuals on all aspects of personal and corporate taxation. Having worked for seven years as a merchant banker, he brings an understanding of finance as well as taxation to bear. He liaises with Firm's Guernsey office when acting for non-residents, non-domiciliaries and offshore groups of companies.

SCOTT, Joy D.
Cleaver Fulton & Rankin, Belfast (01232) 243141
Partner in Private Client Department.
Specialisation: Private client work including trusts, wills, tax planning and property law. Also acts for a number of charities. Has lectured on mortgage and conveyancing practice at the Institute of Legal Studies, Belfast.
Prof. Memberships: Law Society of Northern Ireland, International Bar Association.
Career: Articled to *Carson & McDowell*. Qualified 1978. Worked with Solicitors Branch of Department of the Environment from 1979 to 1984. Joined *Cleaver Fulton & Rankin* in 1984 and became a Partner in 1987.
Personal: Educated at Bloomfield Collegiate School, Belfast and Queen's University Belfast 1971-1975. Leisure interests include the theatre, gardening, travel, skiing and church work. Lives in greater Belfast area.

SHARPE, John W.
Osborne Clarke, Bristol (0117) 923 0220
Partner in Tax and Trust Department.
Specialisation: Work includes UK and international personal taxation, trusts, wills, succession, probate, off-shore tax planning, heritage property and maintenance funds, charitable trust and companies, agricultural law and landed estates. Makes regular appearances at seminars in various locations.
Prof. Memberships: Law Society, Society of Trust and Estate Practitioners.
Career: Qualified in 1974. Solicitor at Macfarlanes 1974-79. Joined *Osborne Clarke* in 1979, becoming a Partner in 1980. Director of Bath & Wessex Opera Ltd, Jackdaws Educational Trust Ltd and the Oldham Foundation.
Personal: Born 17th March 1949. Attended Lancing College, Sussex 1962-67, Keble College, Oxford 1967-70 and College of Law, Lancaster Gate 1971-72. Leisure interests include music, tennis, walking and golf. Lives in Bath.

SHINDLER, Geoffrey A.
Halliwell Landau, Manchester (0161) 835 3003
Partner in Trust and Estate Planning Department.
Specialisation: Specialises in trusts, personal

taxation with specific reference to inheritance tax and capital gains, and wills and probate. Regular contributor to Practical Tax Lawyer. Regular conference speaker.
Prof. Memberships: Chairman Society of Trust and Estate Practitioners (STEP); International Bar Association; American Bar Association Real Property, Probate and Trust Law Section; Institute for Fiscal Studies; Securities Institute; Trust Law Committee; Academician International Academy of Estate and Trust Law; Member Editorial Board Tolley's Trust Law International.
Career: Qualified in 1969. Articled at *March Pearson*. Joined *Halliwell Landau* as a partner in 1986. Honorary Associate of Centre for Law and Business, Manchester University; Director of Amos Nelson Ltd, Roach Packing Case and Timber Co Ltd and United Optical Ltd.
Personal: Born 1942. Attended Bury Grammar School and Cambridge University (MA LLM Cantab). Leisure interests include Marylebone Cricket Club, Lancashire CCC, Manchester United FC, St James's Club and Portico Library; Non-professional theatre director. Lives in Prestwich, Manchester.

STUBBS, Ian M.
Maclay Murray & Spens, Glasgow (0141) 248 5011
ims@maclaymurrayspens.co.uk
Specialisation: Private client partner specialising in personal tax planning, trusts, partnership law, agricultural property and forestry investment. Also a qualified chartered accountant.
Prof. Memberships: Member of Institute of Chartered Accountants of Scotland. Fellow of the Chartered Institute of Taxation. Sits on the Council of the Law Society of Scotland and a member of the Tax Law Committee. Member of the Society of Trust and Estate Practitioners.
Career: Glasgow University (LL.B 1965), CA 1968, FTII 1991.
Personal: Born 1943.

THORNELY, Richard
Thomas Eggar Church Adams, Horsham (01403) 214500
Partner in Private Client Department.
Specialisation: Main areas of practice are personal tax planning, wills, probate and trusts, charities and the affairs of the elderly.
Prof. Memberships: Law Society, S.T.E.P.
Career: Qualified in 1981. Joined current firm in 1992 and became a Partner in 1993.
Personal: Born 20th January 1957. Educated at Rugby School 1969-74 and Trinity Hall, Cambridge 1975-78. Governor of Queen Alexandra Hospital Home, Worthing and Honorary Solicitor to various charities. Recreations include mountaineering and music. Lives in Horsham.

VOREMBERG, Rhoderick P.G.
Wilsons Solicitors, Salisbury (01722) 412412
Specialisation: Main area of practice is strategic tax and trust planning for farmers and landowners, including planning for substantial development land disposals. Also advises extensively on Charity Law and is solicitor to Salisbury Diocesan Board of Finance and other private and national charities including The National Rifle Association and National Motor Museum.
Prof. Memberships: STEP, ALA, CLA, HHA.
Career: Rugby School and Magdalene

College, Cambridge (MA 1978). Qualified in 1980 with *Burges Salmon*, Bristol (Assistant Solicitor to 1982). Partner at *Wilsons* since 1985. Head of Private Client Departments since 1995.
Personal: Married with 3 children (9-13). Amateur silversmith. Captain of the English Eight (Match Rifle) since 1993 and has represented England and Great Britain in match rifle competitions on numerous occasions since 1979.

WEBSTER, Kevin S.
Andrew M. Jackson & Co, Hull
(01482) 325242
Specialisation: Head of Tax, Trust & Probate Department. Specialises in estate planning, creation and administration of trusts, complex Wills and probate and charity law.
Prof. Memberships: Associate member of Chartered Institute of Taxation and member of Society of Trust and Estate Practitioners.
Career: Admitted 1986.
Personal: Interests include supporting York City

WILLCOX, Michael
Willcox & Lewis, Norwich (01508) 480 100
Specialisation: Emphasis on international private client matters. Also handles financial services work. Elected Academician (1984) International Academy of Estate and Trust Law San Francisco USA.
Prof. Memberships: Law Society.
Career: Qualified in 1970. Worked at *Kenneth Brown Baker Baker* 1972-83 in charge of private client department. Partner at *Turner Kenneth Brown* 1983. Worked at *Willcox & Co* 1984-93; firm merged with *Eversheds* in 1993. Established *Willcox & Lewis* May 1997.
Personal: Born 13th May 1945. Attended Manchester University 1963-66 (LLB (Hons)). Lives in Norwich.

WOLLEN, Nigel J.
Hooper & Wollen, Torquay (01803) 213251
Partner in Probate, Tax and Trust Department.
Specialisation: Qualified 1969. Partner 1971. Specialises in personal family and financial planning including landed estates and non-residents.
Prof. Memberships: Law Society, STEP.
Career: Qualified in 1969, having joined *Hooper & Wollen* in 1965. Assistant Solicitor at *Herbert Smith* 1970-71; Partner at *Hooper & Wollen* from 1971.

Personal: Born 16th August 1945. Attended Marlborough College 1959-64. Vice Admiral of Royal Torbay Yacht Club. Leisure interests include sailing and skiing. Lives in Torquay.

WOODHEAD, Louise S.
Wragge & Co, Birmingham (0121) 233 1000
Specialisation: Main areas of practice include trusts, estate planning and tax planning, with emphasis on exit planning for owners of businesses and charities.
Prof. Memberships: Law Society; STEP; Charity Law Association.
Career: Qualified in 1983. Became a partner in 1994. Head of private client group.

WRIGLEY, Matthew
Wrigleys, Leeds (0113) 244 6100
See under Charities, p. 166

WYLD, Charles
Burges Salmon, Bristol (0117) 939 2000

YOUNGER, Hugh P.
Murray Beith Murray W.S. Edinburgh
(0131) 225 1200
Specialisation: Specialist in Trust and Tax Law and Estate Planning.
Prof. Memberships: Solicitor, Step.
Career: Qualified 1981.

SOLICITORS'
A-Z of Firms

CHAMBERS & PARTNERS

AARON & PARTNERS Grosvenor Court, Foregate St, Chester, CH1 1HG **Tel:** (01244) 315366 **Fax:** (01244) 350660 **DX:** 19990 **Ptnrs:** 10 **Asst solrs:** 10 **Other fee-earners:** 6 **Contact:** Simon Carter **Notaries public:** *2 Commercial law practice covering property, litigation & company commercial with niche specialisms including corporate finance, planning, environment, minerals & waste, transport & warehousing, employment, insolvency, construction and agriculture. Associate Offices in France and Switzerland.*

WORKLOADS			
Corporate & Commercial	35%	Commercial Litigation	20%
Property & Agriculture	15%	Minerals & Waste	10%
Planning & Environmental	10%	Transport	5%
Insolvency	3%	Private Client	2%

ABERDEIN CONSIDINE & CO

8 & 9 BON-ACCORD CRESCENT, ABERDEEN, AB11 6DN
Tel: (01224) 589700 **Fax:** (01224) 572575 **DX:** 46 ABERDEEN

The Firm: A leading North East firm with 12 branch offices. One of the largest property firms in Scotland also with strong commercial, criminal, matrimonial and civil law departments. Specialised mortgage recovery and asset management departments.

Other Offices:

415 Union St (Property) Aberdeen AB11 6DA; *Tel:* (01224) 589589; *Fax:* (01224) 589456.

413 Union St (Office) Aberdeen AB11 6DA; *Tel:* (01224) 589444; *Fax:* (01224)589456.

Station Square, Aboyne AB34 5HX; *Tel:* (013398) 86020; *Fax:* (013398) 87187.

5 Bridge St, Ballater AB35 5QP; *Tel:* (013397) 55344; *Fax:* (013397) 56180.

8 Dee St, Banchory AB31 5ST; *Tel:* (01330) 824646; *Fax:* (01330) 824854.

225 North Deeside Rd, Culter AB14 0UJ; *Tel:* (01224) 734734; *Fax:* (01224) 735475.

115 Victoria St, Dyce AB21 7AX; *Tel:* (01224) 723737; *Fax:* (01224) 724867.

57 Bridge St, Ellon AB41 9AA; *Tel:* (01358) 721893; *Fax:* (01358) 724104.

43 West High St, Inverurie AB51 3QQ; *Tel:* (01467) 621263; *Fax:* (01467) 625195.

42 Queen St, Peterhead AB42 1TQ; *Tel:* (01779) 475365; *Fax:* (01779) 478780.

13-15 Evan St, Stonehaven AB39 2EQ; *Tel:* (01569) 766166; *Fax:* (01569) 766110.

51 Victoria Rd, Torry AB11 9LS; *Tel:* (01224) 878161; *Fax:* (01224) 8727333.

Managing partner:	Harvey Aberdein
Senior partners:	Harvey Aberdein
	Iain Considine

WORKLOADS	
Conveyancing and real estate	40%
Civil court	20%
Criminal	20%
Commercial	15%

CONTACTS	
Civil Court	Colin Forbes
Commercial	Jacqueline Law
Conveyancing	Robert Fraser
Criminal	Peter Shepherd
Investment	Gordon Storry
Mortgage Recovery & Asset Management	
	Harvey Aberdein
Probate/Executry	Iain Considine

A S LAW Myrtle Parade, Liverpool, L7 7EL *Tel:* (0151) 707 1212 *Fax:* (0151) 707 2458 *DX:* 28953 Liverpool 2 *Ptnrs:* 4 *Asst solrs:* 3 *Other fee-earners:* 6

ABSON HALL 30 Greek Street, Stockport, SK3 8AD *Tel:* (0161) 480 1221 **Fax:** (0161) 480 4246 **DX:** 22603 Stockport **Ptnrs:** 11 **Asst solrs:** 6 **Other fee-earners:** 7 **Contact:** Mr James P Horan *Established North West firm best known for commercial and personal injury litigation, commercial property and family.*

WORKLOADS			
Litigation including personal injury			40%
Family, children, divorce			20%
Property	15%	Company, commercial	10%
Crime	5%	Licensing	5%
Private client	5%		

ACTONS 2 King St, Nottingham, NG1 2AX *Tel:*(0115) 9100 200 **Fax:** (0115) 9100 290 **DX:** 10001 **Ptnrs:** 10 **Asst solrs:** 12 **Other fee-earners:** 12 **Contact:** Mr C.P. Billyeald *Established firm with reputation for insolvency work. Experience in company/ commercial property, civil litigation, insurance claims, criminal law and private work.*

WORKLOADS			
Insolvency	25%	Personal injury	22%
Commercial litigation	20%	Company/ commercial	16%
Crime	7%	Residential conveyancing	4%

ADAM COCHRAN 6 Bon Accord Square, Aberdeen, AB9 1XU *Tel:* (01224) 588913 *Fax:* (01224) 581149 *DX:* AB1 Aberdeen *Ptnrs:* 3 *Asst solrs:* 2

ADAMS 24 Palmerston Place, Edinburgh, EH12 5AL *Tel:*(0131) 225 8813 *Ptnrs:* 5

ADAMS & REMERS

TRINITY HOUSE, SCHOOL HILL, LEWES, BN7 2NN
Tel: (01273) 480616 **Fax:** (01273) 480618 **DX:** 3100 LEWES 1 **Email:** ADAMS-REMERS.CO.UK

The Firm: Adams & Remers is one of the UK's oldest firms and prides itself on providing a high quality service for institutional, corporate and private clients. The practice's principal office is an imposing building in the County Town of Lewes – a centre of excellence providing a high degree of expertise under one roof.

Principal Areas of Work:

General Description: *Work includes:* company/commercial law and all aspects of general civil litigation. Commercial property work is undertaken for institutions, pension funds, health authorities, landed estates and trusts. Private client work includes estate planning, trusts, probate, investment management and taxation.

Senior partner:	Kevin Ardagh
Number of partners:	5
Assistant solicitors:	6
Other fee-earners:	24

WORKLOADS	
Private Client	60%
Commercial Litigation/Insolvency	30%
Commercial	10%

ADDLESHAW BOOTH & CO

SOVEREIGN HOUSE, PO BOX 8, SOVEREIGN STREET, LEEDS, LS1 1HQ
Tel: (0113) 209 2000 **Fax:** (0113) 209 2060 **DX:** 12004 LEEDS **Email:** JRU@ADDLESHAW-BOOTH.CO.UK

100 BARBIROLLI SQUARE, MANCHESTER, M2 3AB
Tel: (0161) 934 6000 **Fax:** (0161) 934 6060 **DX:** 14301 MANCHESTER **Email:** INFO@ADDLESHAW-BOOTH.CO.UK

Addleshaw Booth & Co is *the* firm of the North providing commercial advice and legal solutions to a wide range of clients in the corporate, financial, public and private sectors regionally, nationally and internationally.

The Firm: Addleshaw Booth & Co formed in 1997 and has over 900 staff members including 86 partners. The firm acts for 92 PLCs and for 35 of the 71 building societies in England & Wales, including the top ten building societies. The Manchester office has the Investors in People award with the Leeds office currently working towards it.

Principal Areas of Work: A wide range of commercial legal services is provided to a client base which includes public companies, private businesses, banks, building societies, financial institutions and high net worth individuals. The firm is organised into the following groups:

Banking and Financial Services: Has extensive expertise in banking and building society law, asset finance and litigation for financial institutions. In 1997, banking deal value exceeded £2.4 billion. The group also has a large insolvency practice which deals with all aspects of corporate and personal insolvencies for lenders, insolvency practitioners and creditors.

Commercial Property: The largest combined property and property financing group across the North with national recognition for work in retail parks, industrial, commercial, office and leisure developments, management and financing and development and investment work for institutions. The group also has acknowledged expertise in construction, planning, property litigation and environmental law.

Commercial: Provides an unparalleled level of support for clients on all their day-to-day business needs across intellectual property, European and competition law, commercial contracts, employment, pensions, share schemes and tax issues.

Corporate Finance: Advises on all aspects of corporate finance activity including Yellow Book and Blue Book work, buy-outs, buy-ins, mergers and acquisitions, reconstructions, joint ventures, stock exchange listings and placings and takeovers. The firm has particular expertise in dealing with high value corporate finance work and holds a nationally recognised position. In 1997 the firm advised on in excess of £2 billion worth of corporate finance transactions – the equivalent of one deal for each business day including some of the largest in the region. The firm has recently been named as the joint 'number 1' in the UK for the number of deals advising equity houses on venture capital-backed deals.

Litigation and Dispute Resolution: Offers an innovative range of solutions for commercial clients involved in national and international business disputes. The group provides litigation services in all civil courts as well as dispute resolution. The group also serves an expanding client base of insurer clients particularly in the areas of personal injury and professional indemnity litigation.

Private Client: Offers private clients a full range of services on wills, charities, trust and tax law and planning. The group also has a family law unit with extensive expertise in high value financial settlements.

Recovery Management: Uses state-of-the-art computer technology, advising on all aspects of debt recovery including credit management, mortgage repossessions and shortfall recovery.

Managing partner:	Mark Jones
Senior partner:	Paul Lee
Marketing Director:	Carolyn Roberson
Number of ptnrs:	86
Number of fee-earners:	443
Total staff:	932

CONTACTS	
Banking & Financial Services	John Priestley
Commercial	Malcolm Pike
Commercial Property	John Pike
Corporate Finance	Andrew Needham
Litigation/Dispute Resolution	John Gosling
Private Client	Paul Howell
Recoveries Management	Anthony Ruane

The firm also has a national reputation in PFI and Public Sector work, with a cross-group team specifically focused on this area. Coupled with this, the firm's market-facing units provide expertise in market sectors such as sport & media, utilities and pharmaceuticals and healthcare.

AGNEW, ANDRESS, HIGGINS

92 HIGH STREET, BELFAST, BT1 2DG
Tel: (01232) 320035 **Fax:** (01232) 249380

Number of partners:	3
Assistant solicitors:	2
Other fee-earners:	1

The Firm: Established 1985. Agnew Andress Higgins is a progressive practice that provides a comprehensive legal service to both Union and private clients. It has also developed a substantial litigation department with experience of personal injury, public liability and road traffic cases, particularly in employers liability cases. Agnew Andress Higgins act mainly for Plaintiffs and has an established Union based clientele. It has also built up a considerable Defence practice acting in relation to Professional Negligence work.

Principal Areas of Work:

Personal Injury: *Work inludes:* industrial injury, industrial disease and road traffic accident claims.

Defence Practice: *Work inludes:* specialist department is dedicated to defending professional negligence claims.

Private Client: *Work inludes:* conveyancing, wills, matrimonial and commercial leasing.

Litigation: J.A.Agnew S.N.F.Andress Sandra Duffy

Private Client: R.J.Higgins Josephine Doyle

AITKEN NAIRN WS 7 Abercromby Place, Edinburgh, EH3 6LA **Tel:** (0131) 556 6644 **Fax:** (0131) 556 6509 **DX:** 18 Edinburgh **Email:** aitkennairn@ednet.co.uk **Ptnrs:** 6 **Asst solrs:** 3 **Other fee-earners:** 3 **Contact:** Mr W.D. Muirhead *Specialisms include estate agency, pursuer and defender personal injury, commercial property, family law and debt collection.*

WORKLOADS			
Litigation	36%	Private client	32%
Residential property	26%	Commercial property	6%

AKIN GUMP STRAUSS HAUER & FELD L.L.P.

ONE ANGEL COURT, LONDON, EC2R 7HJ
Tel: (0171) 796 9600 **Fax:** (0171) 796 9610 **DX:** 132323 FINSBURY PARK

Managing partner:	L Keith Hughes
Number of partners:	5
Assistant solicitors:	5
Other fee-earners:	0

CONTACTS	
Corporate	John Edwards
Corporate	Stephen Hatfield
Insurance	Patrick Devine
Project Finance	Kaamil Ansar

The Firm: Founded in 1945, Akin, Gump, Strauss, Hauer & Feld, L.L.P., a leading international law firm, numbers 700 lawyers with offices in London, Moscow, Brussels, Washington, New York, Los Angeles, Philadelphia, Dallas, Houston, Austin and San Antonio.

Principal Areas of Work:

Capital Markets: The London office's primary focus is the representation of both issuers and underwriters in capital markets transactions. In 1995 the firm completed the first major global securities offering by a Russian company and in 1996 completed a second convertible bond offering. Recent and current offerings have included debt and equity issues involving diverse industries such as media and telecommunications, as well as sovereign issues.

Corporate Finance and Securities: The firm represents issuers, underwriters and institutional investors in public and private offerings of securities in both the US and global markets. The firm's experience includes offerings of debt, equity and convertible securities; warrants; industrial development, municipal and other public bonds; and interests in public and private investment funds.

Project Finance: Transactional work has focused on project finance and privatization matters, where we represent lenders, developers, underwriters, pipelines, endusers, independent sovereign states, consortia and other parties. In the area of international privatization, the firm has represented clients seeking to establish the fiscal, legal, technical and regulatory frameworks to support and attract market-oriented financial sector reform and development.

Oil, Gas and Energy: The firm represents clients in all types of energy transactions throughout the world, before such entities as federal agencies involved in energy regulation and policy and various international and foreign tribunals. The group's practice includes work in the drafting and negotiation of study groups, bidding groups, operating groups and other forms of association for the conduct of international oil and gas operations. In addition, the firm represents clients before relevant governmental entities within host countries during the bidding, negotiation and performance of exploration and production contracts.

AKIN GUMP STRAUSS HAUER & FELD, L.L.P.

Continues overleaf

Insurance: The firm represents insurers, reinsurers and brokers, as well as financial institutions, companies and regulatory and government bodies in connection with insurance sector transactions, insurance regulation and the development of complementary insurance/financial products. The firm provides advice on such matters as the formation of new insurers, subsidiaries, branches and distribution agencies; compliance with local regulatory requirements; and cessation of business. In addition, the firm advises on the drafting and interpretation of environmental liability policies; D&O construction and liability clauses; and life, health, disability and pensions contracts. The firm also advises on the development of insurance and capital markets instruments and connected legal and regulatory implications.

ALAN J. BAILLIE 37 Union Street, Dundee, DD1 4BS *Tel:* (01382) 202444 *Fax:* (01382) 202208 *DX:* DD68 *Ptnrs:* 2 *Asst solrs:* 1 *Other fee-earners:* 1

ALEXANDER HARRIS

ASHLEY HOUSE, ASHLEY ROAD, ALTRINCHAM, WA14 2DW
Tel: (0161) 925 5555 **Fax:** (0161) 925 5500 **DX:** 19866 ALTRINCHAM 1 **Email:** DOCS@ALEXHARRIS.CO.UK
Internet: HTTP://WWW.ALEXHARRIS.CO.UK

The Firm: Specialists in health-related work in the UK and USA, including medical negligence, pharmaceutical product liablility and personal injury. Founded in 1989 by Ann Alexander and David Harris, the firm's fee-earners include a US-qualified lawyer. Close links have been developed with practices in California, Florida and elsewhere in North America and Canada. Clients include UK citizens injured during visits to the US and Canada, and plaintiffs claiming against US-based manufacturers. The firm receives an increasing volume of referrals from non-specialist solicitors.

Principal Areas of Work:

Medical Negligence department deals with all aspects of medico-legal matters, with emphasis on brain damage, anaesthesia, general surgery, radiation damage and general surgery in addition to all aspects of dental negligence.

Pharmaceutical Product & Disasters department deals with adverse drug reactions and faulty medical devices, including Myodil, Persona, LSD, Septrin, radiotherapy and pacemakers. It has expertise in multi-party claims, and has represented victims of the Hillsborough disaster and the serial murderer, Beverly Allit.

Personal Injury department includes two members of the Law Society Personal Injury Panel and handles cases from the spectrum of road and industrial accidents as well as industrial disease. It has expertise in tourist accidents claims, particularly in North America.

Managing partner:	Ann Alexander
Senior partner:	David Harris
Number of partners:	5
Assistant solicitors:	7
Associates:	3
Other fee-earners:	11

WORKLOADS	
Plaintiff medical negligence	65%
Plaintiff personal injury	20%
Pharmaceutical product liability, medical devices and disasters	15%

CONTACTS	
Medical negligence	Ann Alexander
Personal injury	David Harris
Pharmaceutical product liability	David Harris

ALEXANDERS

203 TEMPLE CHAMBERS, TEMPLE AVENUE, LONDON, EC4Y 0DB
Tel: (0171) 353 6221 **Fax:** (0171) 583 0662 **DX:** LDE 264 CHANCERY LANE **Email:** INFO@ALEXANDERS-SOLICITORS.CO.UK

The Firm: The firm is a specialist private client practice.

Principal Areas of Work:

Estate & Tax Planning: (*Contact:* Mark Buzzoni)
Probate & Trust: (*Contact:* Graham D Ogilvie)
Property & Agricultural: (*Contact:* Elisabeth A Jupp)
Family & Matrimonial: (*Contact:* Martyn J Daldorph)
Personal Injury & Medical Negligence: (*Contact:* Richard D O'Halloran)

Senior partner:	Graham Ogilvie
Number of partners:	5
Assistant solicitors:	3
Other fee-earners:	2

WORKLOADS	
Litigation	45%
Tax & Trust	45%
Property	10%

ALEXANDER STONE & CO 4 West Regent Street, Glasgow, G2 1RW **Tel:** (0141) 332 8611 **Fax:** (0141) 332 5482 **Email:** mailbox@alexanderstone.co.uk **Ptnrs:** 5 **Asst solrs:** 3 **Contact:** Lionel Most or Philip Rodney; *Specialist practice with emphasis on commercial and commercial property work.*

WORKLOADS			
Non Leasing Commercial Property			38%
Commercial Leasing	28%	Corporate	15%
Commercial Litigation	14%	Private Client	4%
Other	1%		

ALEX MORISON & CO WS

ERSKINE HOUSE, 68 QUEEN STREET, EDINBURGH, EH2 4NN
Tel: (0131) 226 6541 **Fax:** (0131) 226 3156 **DX:** 38 EDINBURGH

162 ST. JOHNS ROAD, EDINBURGH, EH12 8AZ
Tel: (0131) 316 4422 **Fax:** (0131) 539 7600

51 FREDERICK STREET, EDINBURGH, EH2 1LH
Tel: (0131) 226 6000 **Fax:** (0131) 226 2540

AFTON HOUSE, 26 WESTNILE STREET, GLASGOW, G1 2PF
Tel: (0141) 221 3123 **Fax:** (0141) 221 4228 **DX:** 386 GLASGOW

The Firm: The practice which was started in 1854 is now based in Edinburgh and Glasgow providing services in a variety of fields to commercial clients and individuals both within and outwith Scotland. There are particular strengths in the areas of commercial property, corporate law, litigation, private house building and private client work.

The firm has a wide ranging client base including major UK companies operating in such fields as telecommunications and construction as well as Banks, Building Societies, other financial institutions, insurance companies, property investors and developers.

The firm is also a member of the Libralex Group of European lawyers and is thus well placed to provide legal service to the high standard of expertise and commitment, for matters which require cross-border expertise.

The firm's ethos is the adoption of a common sense practical approach to all legal matters and it undertakes agency work on behalf of other firms of solicitors in all of its areas of expertise.

Principal Areas of Work:

The Commercial Property Department continues to be one of the fastest growing areas of the firm dealing with all aspects of investment, leasing and development work with particular strengths in the areas of industrial and retail.

The Commercial/Corporate Department provides comprehensive advice for business clients on all company and partnership matters and has particular expertise in company re-organisations, buy-outs, mergers and acquisitions and all kinds of business and asset purchases. There are significant areas of specialism in AIM work, medical partnerships and sports law.

The firm's expanded Litigation team provides advice on a range of commercial disputes including building contracts, sale and supply of goods and contractual matters. A particular speciality is reparation claims for negligence and other breaches of duty.

The firm is also widely recognised for its experience in employment law, and debt recovery as also insolvency work.

Private client litigation covers contractual disputes, claims for damages and personal injury claims with a notable expertise in medical negligence. The full range of family law services are provided.

The Residential Property, sales and letting activities are handled from the Frederick Street Office in Edinburgh through which a full range of financial services can also be offered to private clients including advice on mortgages and insurances.

The Private Client Department provides a full range of advice on trusts, wills and executries, investment and tax planning.

The firm's Institutional Department provides advice for financial institutions on debt recovery, mortgage arrears, repossession and third party recovery issues.

The firm's dedicated Department for builders deals with all the needs of housebuilders in Scotland from those operating on larger estates to smaller more specialised sites and provides advice on planning and environmental law.

Chairman:	R.W. Flockhart
Number of partners:	16
Assistant solicitors:	16
Other fee-earners:	20

WORKLOADS	
Litigation	23%
Commercial Property/Corporate	21%
Institutional	18%
Residential/Estate Agency	15%
Private Client	12%
Builders	11%

CONTACTS	
Builders	Robin Flockhart
Commercial Corporate	Alan Grosset
Commercial Property	Norman Smith
Institutional	Roddy McIntyre
Litigation	Julian Osborne
Private Client	Ewen Dyce
Residential Property	Ross Hadden

ALFRED SEVIER & SONS

8-9 ST MARY'S GATE, DERBY, DE1 3JF
Tel: (01332) 347611 **Fax:** (01332) 291364 **DX:** 11506 DERBY 1

The Firm: The practice was founded by Alfred Sevier over 50 years ago and specialises in personal injury litigation of all types including industrial accidents, road accidents, medical negligence and industrial diseases. There is also a non-contentious department. The firm has partners who are members of the Law Society Personal Injury and Medical Negligence Panels and acts on behalf of major union and insurance company clients.

Senior partner:	R.J.R. Sevier
Number of partners:	3
Other fee-earners:	6

ALISTAIR MELDRUM & CO 8-9 Genotin Terrace, Enfield, EN1 2AF **Tel:** (0181) 367 0064 **Fax:** (0181) 366 8578 **DX:** 90609 Enfield **Ptnrs:** 2 **Asst solrs:** 2 **Other fee-earners:** 3 **Contact:** Mr Alistair Meldrum *Criminal practice, handling minor to major matters including drug importation, 24 hour police station attendance, legal aid work undertaken.*

WORKLOADS			
Criminal law	80%	Family law	20%

ALLAN HENDERSON BEECHAM AND PEACOCK 7 Collingwood Street, Newcastle upon Tyne, NE1 1JE **Tel:** (0191) 232 3048 **Fax:** (0191) 261 7255 **Ptnrs:** 5 **Asst solrs:** 4 **Other fee-earners:** 7 **Contact:** Sir Jeremy H. Beecham *Providing a high quality service in the areas of personal injury, crime, matrimonial, and conveyancing to both private and trade union clients.*

ALLAN JANES 21-23 Easton Street, High Wycombe, HP11 1NU **Fax:** (01494) 442315 **DX:** 4402 High Wycombe **Email:** ajanes@globalnet.co.uk **Ptnrs:** 7 **Asst solrs:** 4 **Other fee-earners:** 4 **Contact:** Mr Ray Taylor *Specialises in company/commercial; commercial property; commercial and private litigation; wills, tax, trusts and probate; residential property and family; liquor and betting licensing; employment.*

WORKLOADS			
Commercial property/ company			26%
Matrimonial/ family			19%
Crime	13%	Probate, trusts & wills	12%
Private litigation	11%	Residential property	11%
Commercial/ private litigation	8%		

ALLAN MCDOUGALL & CO SSC 3 Coates Crescent, Edinburgh, EH3 7AL **Tel:** (0131) 225 2121 **Fax:** (0131) 225 8659 **DX:** 32 Edinburgh **Ptnrs:** 9 **Asst solrs:** 7 **Other fee-earners:** 7 **Contact:** Mr John George *The firm has a long history in civil litigation, particularly pursuers personal injury, medical negligence and matrimonial and family law.*

WORKLOADS			
Litigation	68%	Private client	24%
Commercial property	6%	Corporate	2%

ALLEN & FRASER 78 Dean St, London, W1V 6BE *Tel:* (0171) 437 4001 *Fax:* (0171) 439 0650 *DX:* 44714 Soho Square *Ptnrs:* 3 *Asst solrs:* 1 *Other fee-earners:* 2

ALLEN & OVERY

ONE NEW CHANGE, LONDON, EC4M 9QQ
Tel: (0171) 330 3000 **Fax:** (0171) 330 9999 **DX:** 73 **Internet:** WWW.ALLENOVERY.COM

The Firm: Allen & Overy is one of the UK's leading international law firms. Founded in 1930 it has 200 partners and over 2,200 staff working in 19 major centres on three continents serving businesses, financial institutions, governments and private individuals where there is a need for decisive legal advice on complex transactions. Internationally, Allen & Overy has an Association with two leading continental firms, Gide Loyrette Nouel in France, and Loeff Claeys Verbeke in the Benelux countries.

Principal Areas of Practice:

Corporate: The firm provides a comprehensive service covering all aspects of company and commercial law including public takeovers, mergers and acquisitions, disposals, Stock Exchange flotations, international equity offerings, joint ventures and strategic alliances, corporate restructuring and management buy-outs. Specialist practice groups also deal with privatisations, building societies, energy law, environmental law, insurance, media & communications, financial services, construction, EC & competition, intellectual property and information technology.

Banking: The firm advises financial institutions and borrowers on all types of financing transactions in the UK and overseas including acquisition finance, project finance, property finance, trade finance, restructurings including debt for equity swaps and all forms of structured finance, asset finance (including aviation and shipping), securitisations, risk reduction techniques and derivatives and all forms of international finance.

International Capital Markets: The firm advises in relation to capital markets transactions by issuers from all over the world (including developing countries as well as those with developed economies). These include eurobond issues, euro-equity offerings, equity linked issues, securitisations and derivatives. The firm also has a highly regarded US law practice which now numbers 10 partners and over 40 US qualified lawyers. The practice advises on a wide range of transactions with a significant or dominant US element.

Litigation: The firm's litigation and dispute resolution practice deals with all forms of commercial dispute including aviation, banking and finance, commercial fraud and crime, construction, defamation, DTI enquiries, employment, environmental law, EC & competition, information technology, intellectual property, product liability, professional negligence, property, shipping and trade sanctions.

Private Client: The firm's large practice provides comprehensive advice to wealthy individuals, entrepreneurs and senior directors, trustees, families, museums, universities and charities worldwide.

Project Finance: The firm has one of the leading project finance practices advising all parties in major projects in the UK, Europe (including Central and Eastern Europe), South East Asia and China, and elsewhere, acting for lenders, project owners and sponsors, governments, public authorities, contractors, developers and investors. In 1997 alone, the firm advised on projects in some 32 countries and 14 industrial sectors. For last year total project costs for power, telecom, infrastructure, PFI and natural resources projects were

Managing partner:	John Rink
Senior partner:	Bill Tudor John
UK	
Number of partners:	132
Assistant solicitors:	441
Other fee-earners:	171
International	
Number of partners:	68
Assistant solicitors:	224
Other fee-earners:	73

CONTACTS	
Banking	David Morley
Building Societies	Peter Holland
Business Reconst & Insolvency	Gordon Stewart
Communications	Richard Cranfield
Construction	John Scriven
Corporate and Commercial	Guy Beringer
Derivative Products	Jeff Golden
EC and Competition Law	Mark Friend
Employment, Pens. & Incentives	Derek Sloan
Energy	Roger Davies
Environmental	Owen Lomas
Financial Services	Paul Phillips
Housing Associations	David Morley
Information Technology	Ian Ferguson
Insurance	Ian Stanley
Intellectual Property	Colleen Keck
International Capital Markets	Richard Sykes
Litigation	Andrew Clark
MBOs	Alan Paul
Media & Entertainment	Andrew Morton
Mergers/Acquisitions/Takeovers	Alan Paul
Pharmaceutical & Med. Prods.	Colleen Keck
Private Clients	Richard Turnor
Private Finance Initiative	Anne Baldock
Privatisation	Peter Holland
Projects & Project Finance	Graham Vinter
Property (Commercial)	Gideon Hudson
Securitisation	David Krischer
Tax (Corporate)	Patrick Mears
VAT & Indirect Tax	Jill Gowtage

US$21.5bn, US$8.2bn, US$24.3bn, US$5.4bn and US$17.4bn respectively.

Property: The firm provides a full commercial property service to landowners, institutions, property companies, developers, contractors, investors and banks on areas including building contracts, commercial leases and underlettings, development agreements, housing association law, joint ventures, planning procedures and appeals, redevelopments, short and long term funding and site acquisition.

Taxation: The firm provides a comprehensive corporate tax service including advice on employee benefits and share schemes, and VAT and other indirect taxation.

Overseas Offices: Beijing, Brussels, Budapest, Dubai, Frankfurt, Hong Kong, Madrid, Milan, Moscow, New York, Paris, Prague, Rome, Singapore, Tirana, Tokyo, Turin and Warsaw.

Foreign Languages: English, Arabic, Bengali, Cantonese, Czech, Danish, Dutch, Finnish, French, German, Greek, Hebrew, Hindi, Hungarian, Italian, Japanese, Malay, Mandarin, Persian, Polish, Punjabi, Russian, Spanish, Swedish, and Urdu .

ALLINGTON HUGHES 10 Grosvenor Rd, Wrexham, LL11 1SD *Tel:* (01978) 291000 *Fax:* (01978) 290493 *DX:* 26651 *Ptnrs:* 9 *Asst solrs:* 2 *Other fee-earners:* 10

ALSTERS

30A COLLEGE GREEN, BRISTOL, BS1 1TB
Tel: (0117) 929 7612 **Fax:** (0117) 927 2889 **DX:** 7826 BRISTOL 1

The Firm: Alsters was established in 1984 and has seen significant growth in the last few years as a direct result of its commercial property/company commercial successes. The firm's Sports Unit is nationally recognised for its work with a large number of high profile sportsmen and women.

Principal Areas of Work:

Commercial Property: *Work includes:* site assembly, joint ventures, acquisitions, sales and investment work. Also specialist expertise in redevelopment proposals – option to purchase, conditional contract etc. The department includes a dedicated Planning and Environmental Unit.

Company/Commercial: *Work includes:* business start-ups, acquisitions, mergers, de-mergers and disposals, employment contracts, terms and conditions and general commercial agreements.

Sport: *Work includes:* all aspects of sports law, both contentious and non-contentious, including inter alia matters in relation to discipline, contracts, constitutions, liability, asset management, sponsorship, intellectual property, copyright trade marks and ground development.

Recruitment: The firm consistently seeks to attract high calibre professionals in the above areas of work. Applications with CV to David Powell.

Senior partner:	David Powell
Number of partners:	6
Assistant solicitors:	6
Other fee-earners:	3

WORKLOADS	
Commercial Property	45%
Company/Commercial	25%
Sports	15%
Litigation	10%
Other	5%

CONTACTS	
Commercial Property	T. Graham
Company/Commercial	P. Albery
Litigation	P. McKnight
Sports	D. Powell

AMERY-PARKES

LAW COURTS CHAMBERS, 33 CHANCERY LANE, LONDON, WC2A 1EN
Tel: (0171) 404 7100 **Fax:** (0171) 404 6588 **DX:** 162 LON CHANCERY LANE WC2

The Firm: Founded in 1892 the firm now has offices in four major centres. Whilst principally known for its personal injury and accident litigation work (both for plaintiffs and defendants), the firm also has a large private client practice in all locations. In Basingstoke, there is a large conveyancing practice, both residential and commercial as well as a substantial PI department. There is also a developing defendant PI section. The Birmingham office also has a substantial PI department, dealing with both plaintiff and defendant work. In addition, there is a common law department dealing with all aspects of matrimonial, criminal and child care work, as well as Mental Health Act tribunals. Bristol office again has a substantial PI department, as well as a conveyancing department, dealing with residential and commercial matters. In London there are significant departments dealing with company commercial, commercial litigation, employment law and probate, trust and tax.

At Basingstoke there are 7 partners. *Contact:* Steven Slough. Birmingham office has 6 partners. *Contact:* Damian Knowles. Bristol office has 2 partners. *Contact:* John Crocker. London office has 5 partners. Contact: William Davis.

Foreign Connections: In London the firm has French and Spanish speakers and international work is undertaken. The firm has an associated office in Paris.

Agency Work: Agency work is handled in all offices.

Senior partner:	Damian Knowles
Number of partners:	21
Assistant solicitors:	11
Other fee-earners:	37

WORKLOADS	
Accident claims recovery/ personal injury	60%
Conveyancing, commercial and domestic	15%
Commercial and general litigation	10%
Corporate	10%
Probate trust and tax	5%

CONTACTS	
Commercial Litigation	Darryl Greer
Common Law	Tony Thomas, Nigel Mears
Conveyancing	Peter Black, Ros Goulstone
Corporate	William Davis
Personal injury	Alan Hughes, Celia Sohpal
Probate, trust and tax	Anne Lewis

AMHURST BROWN COLOMBOTTI

2 DUKE STREET, ST. JAMES'S, LONDON, SW1Y 6BJ
Tel: (0171) 930 2366 **Fax:** (0171) 930 2250 **DX:** 412

The Firm: Amhurst Brown Colombotti is a medium sized commercial practice with considerable international experience. Clients receive a great deal of personal attention from partners who combine practical business experience with legal skills. The firm's expertise includes company formations and flotations, mergers and acquisitions, cross-border transactions, joint ventures, information and computer technology (including the Internet), entertainment (including film financing and music), financial services, commercial and residential property transactions, trust and private client work, commercial litigation, matrimonial and immigration.

International Connections: The firm has offices in Poland and associates in Italy, Spain, the United States of America, Russia, India, Denmark, Brazil and Pakistan.

Foreign Languages: French, Italian, Spanish, German, Polish and Russian.

Managing partner:	P.F.G. Amandini
Senior partner:	P.D. Smithson
Number of partners:	17
Assistant solicitors:	8
Other fee-earners:	5

WORKLOADS	
Commercial Property	30%
Litigation	30%
Company Commercial	25%
Private Clients	10%
International	5%

ANDERSEN & CO Boswell Cottage, 19 Southend, CR0 1BE *Tel:* (0181) 680 3131 *Fax:* (0181) 688 7058

ANDERSON FYFE

90 ST. VINCENT STREET, GLASGOW, G2 5UB
Tel: (0141) 248 4381 **Fax:** (0141) 204 1418 **DX:** GW 138

The Firm: Established over 150 years ago, Anderson Fyfe provides commercial services dedicated to all aspects of business, company and employment law, while its private client division provides a comprehensive portfolio of services to individuals. Against this background of tradition the practice is responsive and flexible to the changing needs of its clients.

Principal Areas of Work:

Business Law: (*Contact:* David Chaplin). The firm's commercial division provides a service dedicated to all aspects of business and company law from company formation, financing and growth to acquisitions, investment and sales. For existing businesses, the firm handles joint ventures, distribution agreements, agency and licensing, franchises and commercial contracts, intellectual property and trade protection, employment audits and the preparation of service contracts for senior personnel. The firm also has strong litigation and debt recovery departments.

Private Client: (*Contact:* Christopher Wilkin). The private practice division looks after individual clients' investments, trusts, tax, wills and executry matters as well as residential conveyancing.

Commercial Conveyancing: (*Contact:* Kenneth Meldrum). The firm also carries out all aspects of commercial conveyancing, including land acquisition and development, opencast coal mining, quarrying and planning appeals, and housing association work.

Litigation: (*Contact:* Roddy McIlvride). The firm has an extensive commercial and public sector litigation department and has been instructed in a number of leading Scottish cases in the Court of Session and House of Lords. Roddy McIlvride is a solicitor advocate with rights of audience in the Court of Session and the House of Lords.

Employment: (*Contact:* Tom McEntegart). The firm also has a department specialising in employment law which advises both employers and employees in such matters as the preparation of service contracts and the negotiation of severance packages as well as representing clients at Industrial Tribunals.

Managing partner:	David H. Chaplin
Number of partners:	6
Assistant solicitors:	7
Other fee-earners:	8

WORKLOADS	
Litigation and recovery	29%
Corporate/ business law/ insolvency	26%
Private client/trust/executry	23%
Commercial and domestic conveyancing	22%

CONTACTS	
Business Law	D H Chaplin
Commercial Conveyancing	K T Meldrum
Domestic Conveyancing	Lesley Forrest
Employment Law	T McEntegart
Litigation	R R McIlvride
Private Client Services	CG A Wilkin

ANDERSON MACARTHUR & CO Old Bank of Scotland Buildings, Stornoway, HS1 2BG *Tel:* (01851) 703356 *Fax:* (01851) 702766 *Ptnrs:* 3 *Asst solrs:* 1 *Other fee-earners:* 2

ANDERSONS Boswell Cottage, 19 Southend, CR0 1BE *Tel:* (0181) 680 3131

ANDERSON STRATHERN WS

48 CASTLE STREET, EDINBURGH, EH2 3LX
Tel: (0131) 220 2345 **Fax:** (0131) 226 7788 **DX:** 3 EDINBURGH

The Firm: This prominent Edinburgh practice offers a comprehensive range of services to business and private clients throughout Scotland and beyond. Anderson Strathern is a highly competitive, full service firm with a client base which includes major national and international companies, local authorities, financial institutions, property investors and developers, insurance companies and a number of substantial landowning interests. Clients include: Eagle Star, the Royal College of Nursing, Napier Univeristy, the National Trust for Scotland, the Scottish Rugby Union and the Coal Authority.

As a member of The Association of European Lawyers, the firm is strongly placed to provide advice on any matters which require cross border expertise and makes full use of an advanced communications and management system. The partnership combines legal expertise, commercial awareness, strength in depth and value for money.

Types of work undertaken: The corporate department undertakes mergers and acquisitions, MBOs and MBIs, business start-ups and institutional finance, joint ventures and insolvency. It also has considerable experience of advising on intellectual property matters, commercial contracts (including computer contracts), competition matters and European law. The Firm has specialist experience in Media and Entertainment, Publishing, Sports and Leisure and Education. Anderson Strathern covers all aspects of commercial property work including planning, construction law and environmental law. The firm has particular expertise in Housing Association lending and acquisition work, landlord and tenant law, property acquisition and financing and development work with two partners accredited specialists in commercial leasing law.

The litigation department is renowned for its liability insurance work and health service law with one partner an accredited specialist in employment law and another in medical negligence. Two are solicitor advocates with rights of audience in the highest Scottish civil courts.

The firm maintains, and intends to develop, its position as one of the foremost practices in rural/agricultural and private client work. The rural department provides a full service on all agricultural and heritage matters, with two partners accredited specialists in agricultural law.

Private client work covers trusts, tax planning, insurance, financial planning and investments, residential conveyancing and mortgage advice.

In addition to its commitment to existing areas of practice, the firm is developing a series of firm wide units which focus on particular client requirements. These draw on a wide range of expertise to build the optimum team for every client requirement. Areas covered include Liability Insurance, the Financial Sector, Employment and Land Ventures – which offers advice on commercial diversification projects to land owners – and intellectual property.

The use of new technology is central to the efficiency of a modern law firm. Anderson Strathern has consistently kept abreast of the latest developments in legal software with the belief that an investment in technology and in training pays dividends in the provision of an effective service. The firm also recognises the importance of investing in its people, having recently committed to the IIP standard, and runs a detailed in-house training programme, covering both legal and management issues.

Managing partner:	Robin M. Stimpson
Chairman:	Alan S. Menzies
Number of partners:	26
Assistant solicitors:	27
Other fee-earners:	39

CONTACTS	
Agricultural/ rural/ sporting	Alasdair Fox
Agricultural/ rural/ sporting	Robin Stimpson
Commercial property	David Hunter
Commercial property	Alan Menzies
Company/ commercial	John Kerr/Simon Brown
Litigation	Robert Fife/ Ruari MacNeill
Private client	John Blair, Robin Watt

ANDREW BRYCE & CO 7 Queen St, Coggeshall, Colchester, CO6 1UF *Tel:* (01376) 563123 *Fax:* (01376) 563336 *Ptnrs:* 1

ANDREW GREGG & CO 6 Queen Square, Bristol, BS1 4JE **Tel:** (0117) 925 8123 **Fax:** (0117) 925 5567 **Ptnrs:** 1 **Asst solrs:** 5 **Contact:** Mr Andrew Gregg *Established general practice specialising in licensing, health & safety, food law and white collar crime.*

ANDREW M. JACKSON & CO Essex House, Manor Street, Hull, HU1 1XH **Tel:** (01482) 325242 **Fax:** (01482) 212974 **DX:** 11920 **Email:** lawyers@amj.co.uk **Ptnrs:** 23 **Asst solrs:** 24 **Other fee-earners:** 23 **Contact:** John Hammersley *Established in1874, Andrew M. Jackson & Co has developed a thriving practice with an excellent reputation for providing an extensive range of specialised legal services.*

WORKLOADS			
Commercial property	34%	Litigation	20%
Shipping	15%	Company	11%
Family	10%	Private client	10%

ANDREW KEENAN & CO Nickleby House, Charles Dickens Terrace, Maple Road, London, SE20 8RE *Tel:* (0181) 659 0332 *Fax:* (0181) 659 3689 *DX:* 34860 Penge *Ptnrs:* 1 *Asst solrs:* 1 *Other fee-earners:* 4

ANNE HALL DICK & CO 157 Kilmarnock Road, Shawlands, Glasgow, G41 3JE *Tel:* (0141) 636 0003 *Fax:* (0141) 636 0303 *DX:* 501146 Shawlands *Ptnrs:* 3 *Asst solrs:* 1

ANN L. HUMPHREY The Boathouse Office, 57a Gainsford Street, London, SE1 2NB **Tel:** (0171) 378 9370 **Fax:** (0171) 378 9360 **Email:** annlhumphrey@dial.pipex.com **Ptnrs:** 1 **Other fee-earners:** 1 **Contact:** Ann L. Humphrey *Niche tax practice with substantial experience in VAT and corporate tax planning which has recently moved to purpose-built offices at Tower Bridge.*

WORKLOADS			
VAT	60%	Corporate Tax	40%

ANSELM ELDERGILL Solicitors Chambers, 169 Malden Road, London, NW5 4HT *Tel:* (0171) 284 1006 *Fax:* (0171) 916 2553 *Ptnrs:* 1

ANSTEY SARGENT & PROBERT

4-6 BARNFIELD CRESCENT, EXETER, EX1 1RF
Tel: (01392) 411221 **Fax:** (01392) 218554 **DX:** 8308 EXETER

The Firm: A major regional practice which advises a wide range of business clients whilst maintaining a strong private client department. Specialist areas include company and commercial work, insolvency, planning and commercial property, leisure sector, wills attorneyships and tax planning, personal injury, litigation, matrimonial and child care. The Budleigh Salterton and Cowick Street, Exeter offices handle conveyancing, wills and litigation. The Firm is a member of the Quality Law Group (QLG).

Other Offices: 44 Cowick Street, Exeter, EX4 1AP *Tel:* (01392) 410030 *Fax:* (01392) 422597 *DX:* 89853 Exeter

Council Chambers, Budleigh Salterton, EX9 6RL *Tel:* (01395) 442223 *Fax:* (01395) 446374 *DX:* 122841 Budleigh Salterton.

Senior partner:	J.C.N. Robinson
Chief Executive:	Richard Smith
Number of partners:	17
Assistant solicitors:	10
Other fee-earners:	16

CONTACTS	
Commercial Property/Leisure	Geoffrey Trobridge
Company/Commercial	Richard Coombs
Computers & I.T./Employment	Edmund Probert
Insolvency	Stephen Lawson/Justin Day
Investment/Asset Management	John Crowley
Litigation/Personal Injury	Angus McNicol
Matrimonial/Child Care	Paul Willoughby
Planning	Isabel Diver
Private Client/Tax Planning	Adrian Miller

ANTHONY COLLINS SOLICITORS St Philip's Gate, 5 Waterloo Street, Birmingham, B2 5PG **Tel:** (0121) 200 3242 **Fax:** (0121) 212 7442 **DX:** 13055 Birmingham 1 **Email:** acs@acollins-sol.co.uk **Ptnrs:** 11 **Consultants:** 3 **Other fee-earners:** 42 **Contact:** Beryl MacDonald *A proactive niche market practice providing services primarily to the voluntary sector including housing and local government, charities, commercial property, business law, litigation, licensing, personal injury and medical negligence.*

WORKLOADS			
Housing & Local Government			31%
Litigation	17%	Private Client	12%
Business Law	11%		
Personal Injury/Medical Negligence			10%
Commercial Property	9%	Charities/Church Law	5%
Licensing	5%		

ANTHONY GOLD, LERMAN & MUIRHEAD

NEW LONDON BRIDGE HOUSE, 25 LONDON BRIDGE STREET, LONDON, SE1 9TW
Tel: (0171) 940 4000 **Fax:** (0171) 378 8025 **DX:** 39915 LONDON BRIDGE SOUTH **Email:** AGOLD@AGOLD.LAW.CO.UK

43 STREATHAM HILL, LONDON, SW2 4TP
Tel: (0181) 678 5500 **Fax:** (0181) 674 8004 **DX:** 58604 STREATHAM

The Firm: Founded by the present senior partner, Anthony Gold, in 1963, Anthony Gold, Lerman & Muirhead is a progressive and expanding practice which offers affordable specialist skills to both businesses and individuals. The firm's lawyers' intellectual calibre and commitment to achieving the best possible result for their clients is second to none.

Principal Areas of Work:
Company and Commercial: *(Contact:* Anthony Gold). Dealing with the acquisition and disposal of companies and unincorporated businesses, all general commercial agreements including joint ventures, agency and distribution, intellectual property matters and employment.
Commercial Dispute Resolution: *(Contact:* Sarah Ahmed). Advising in connection with, and conducting, an enormous variety of claims in all divisions of the High Court and in the County Court, both of a national and international content, with expertise in arbitration and ADR.
Family and Divorce: *(Contact:* Mark Harper). Specialising in financial cases, including Inheritance Act cases, with experience of international family disputes and abductions. The department is highly ranked, and one of the largest in London. Mark Harper was on the National Committee of the Solicitors' Family Law Association for six years. Partner,

Managing partner:	David Marshall
Senior partner:	Anthony Gold
Number of partners:	12
Assistant solicitors:	9
Other fee-earners:	12

CONTACTS	
Admin/ public/ property litign	Robin Levett
Commercial conveyancing	Howard Lerman
Commercial litigation	Sarah Ahmed
Corporate and commercial	Anthony Gold
Family law	Mark Harper, Kim Beatson
Medical negligence	David Marshall, Jon Nicholson
Personal injury	David Marshall, Jon Nicholson
Professional negligence	Sarah Ahmed

Kim Beatson, is an accredited sole lawyer mediator and Mark Harper is also a mediator.

Landlord & Tenant/Property Disputes: *(Contact:* Robin Levett). Conducting all types of landlord and tenant claims arising out of dilapidation and service charge disputes, possession, forfeiture and lease renewals. Property related work includes actions relating to mortgagees' duties and disputes as to equitable interests.

Medical Negligence: *(Contact:* David Marshall). Specialising in actions exclusively for plaintiffs against NHS trusts and doctors. David Marshall and Jon Nicholson are members of the Medical Negligence Panel.

Personal Injury: *(Contact:* Jon Nicholson). Specialising in the full range of actions for plaintiffs, including complex and high value cases. All the firm's specialist solicitors are members of APIL and Jon Nicholson and David Marshall are also Personal Injury Panel members.

Professional Negligence: *(Contact:* Sarah Ahmed). Acting for commercial and individual plaintiffs in claims against solicitors, accountants, surveyors and financial advisers.

Public Law: *(Contact:* Robin Levett). Specialising in judicial review of the decisions of local and public authorities, the department has a high reputation in this field.

Property: *(Contact:* Howard Lerman). Handling acquisitions, development and financial work for retailers, investors, landlords and homebuyers.

Wills & Probate: *(Contact:* Mark Politz). Specialising in drafting wills, including tax planning, the administration of estates and trusts and investment advice.

ARCHERS Barton House, 24 Yarm Road, Stockton on Tees, TS18 3NB *Tel:* (01642) 673431 *Fax:* (01642) 613602 *Ptnrs:* 9 *Asst solrs:* 8 *Other fee-earners:* 10

ARCHIBALD CAMPBELL & HARLEY WS 37 Queen Street, Edinburgh, EH2 1JX **Tel:** (0131) 220 3000 **Fax:** (0131) 220 2288 **DX:** 181 Edinburgh **Email:** administrator@achws.co.uk **Ptnrs:** 14 **Asst solrs:** 12 **Other fee-earners:** 9 **Contact:** Andrew Wallace *Known for commercial property and planning. Rapidly growing corporate practice. Other specialist units: banking, debt recovery, employment, environment, litigation, private client.*

WORKLOADS			
Commercial property	43%	Private clients	31%
Litigation	12%	Corporate/ commercial	9%
Planning/ environmental	5%		

ARGLES & COURT 12 Mill Street, Maidstone, ME15 6XU *Tel:* (01622) 656500 *Fax:* (01622) 656690 *DX:* 51965 Maidstone 2 *Ptnrs:* 17 *Asst solrs:* 5 *Other fee-earners:* 24

ARMITAGE SYKES HALL NORTON 72 New North Rd, Huddersfield, HD1 5NW **Tel:** (01484) 538121 **Fax:** (01484) 518968 **DX:** 711270 Huddersfield 9 **Ptnrs:** 7 **Asst solrs:** 6 **Other fee-earners:** 10 **Contact:** Neville Sheard. *Wide range of services for commercial and private client.*

WORKLOADS			
Company/ commercial	45%	Litigation	35%
Private client	20%		

ARNHEIM & CO

No 1 LONDON BRIDGE, LONDON, SE1 9QL
Tel: (0171) 939 1660 **Fax:** (0171) 939 1661 **DX:** 122963 LONDON BRIDGE 2 **Email:** FIRSTNAME_LASTNAME@EUROPE_NOTES.PW.COM
Internet: HTTP://WWW.ARNHEIM.CO.UK

Set up in association with Price Waterhouse, the initial focus of the practice has been to provide legal advice and assistance on all aspects of corporate transactions. The firm has also established specialisms in other areas to harness the opportunities arising from its association with Price Waterhouse and introductions by its own lawyers; these include banking and finance, energy, financial services, HR/employment, intellectual property, IT/outsourcing, communications/broadcasting and property.

The Firm: Arnheim & Co. was established in March 1996 by Chris Arnheim since when it has grown to over 40 lawyers including 13 partners. The firm is a member of the European network of correspondent law firms of Price Waterhouse with more than 500 lawyers in 25 jurisdictions and enjoys considerable demand from multinationals for the co-ordinated provision of high quality, multi-territory, multi-disciplinary professional services. Since its establishment, Arnheim & Co's strategy has been to recruit, develop and market the legal expertise necessary to compete with leading law firms and to provide solutions to the legal aspects of complex business problems.

At the time of going to press Arnheim & Co is in merger discussions with the Coopers & Lybrand correspondent law firm, Tite & Lewis.

Client base: The firm's client base is drawn from introductions by its own lawyers, through Price Waterhouse correspondent law firms and from Price Waterhouse. Around 50 per cent of Arnheim & Co's workload has been for Price Waterhouse clients both in the UK and overseas. Joint projects have been undertaken with Price Waterhouse offices in Europe, North America and the Pacific Rim. The firm has recruited lawyers with experience of working for leading corporates and whose strengths are not just technical legal analysis, but also practice development, transaction management and client service.

Types of work undertaken: Whilst the primary focus of the firm remains on corporate transactions (M&A, venture capital, refinancing, strategic alliances, cross-border) Arnheim&Co includes lawyers with expertise in a wide range of specialisations including banking and finance, energy, financial services, HR/employment, intellectual property, IT/outsourcing, communications/broadcasting and property.

Senior partner:	Chris Arnheim
Number of partners:	14
Assistant solicitors:	29
Other fee-earners:	3

WORKLOADS	
Corporate/ Banking and Finance	50%
Financial Services	15%
HR/Employment	15%
Intellectual Property	8%
IT/Outsourcing/Communications/Broadcasting	8%
Property	4%

CONTACTS	
Banking & Finance	Samantha Hampshire
Communications & Broadcasting	Jonathan Kembery
Corporate Transactions	Chris Arnheim
Financial Services	Martin Cornish
HR/Employment	Tim Johnson
Intellectual Property	James Hodgson
International	Paul Downing
IT/Outsourcing	Sandra Honess
Property	Helen Black
Venture Capital	Leon Flavell/Patrick Martin

Arnheim & Co.
Correspondent Law Firm of Price Waterhouse

ARNOLD & PORTER

25 BUCKLERSBURY, LONDON, EC4N 8DA
Tel: (0171) 329 4329 **Fax:** (0171) 653 9829

The Firm: Arnold & Porter is a United States law firm with over 400 lawyers. The head office is in Washington DC. The London office is a multinational partnership which includes English and U.S. lawyers. A variety of work is handled in London, reflecting the diverse nature of the firm's U.S. practice. The full resources of the U.S. office can be called upon to assist clients.

Principal Areas of Work:

General Description: The office opened in mid-1997 and handles work mainly in the areas of competition, capital markets, energy, privatisation, EU, corporate transactions and arbitration/litigation.

Other Offices: Washington DC, New York, Denver, Los Angeles and representative offices in Istanbul, Budapest and Moscow. The firm has access to a global network of practitioners who have at some point participated in a long-established foreign associates programme operated by the firm for over 50 years.

Senior partner:	Robert H. Winter
Administrative partner:	James D. Dinnage
Number of partners:	2
Assistant solicitors:	3
US associates:	2

ARNOLD THOMSON 205 Watling Street West, Towcester, NN12 6BX **Tel:** (01327) 350266 **Fax:** (01327) 353567 **DX:** 16932 Towcester **Ptnrs:** 1 **Asst solrs:** 4 **Other fee-earners:** 1 **Contact:** Mr M.A. Thomson. *A niche agriculture firm, formed in 1990 to serve the increasingly complex needs of the farming and landowning community.*

WORKLOADS			
Sales, purchases and development work			35%
Trusts/ tax and probate	20%	Agricultural tenancies	15%
Civil litigation	10%	Partnerships	10%
Quotas	10%		

ARTHUR COX

STOKES HOUSE, 17-25 COLLEGE SQUARE EAST, BELFAST, BT1 6HD
Tel: (01232) 230007 **Fax:** (01232) 262650 **DX:** 2012 NR BELFAST 2 **Email:** BELFAST@ARTHURCOX.IE

The Firm: Arthur Cox – Northern Ireland was established in 1996, following the merger of the Belfast office of Arthur Cox, one of the largest practices in the Republic of Ireland, with the long established law firm of Norman Wilson & Co which has particular strengths in the areas of corporate banking, commercial, property and employment law. The firm merged in December 1997 with Martin & Brownlie to give added strength to its employment and litigation departments. The firm is in a unique position to provide a range of cross-border services from its Belfast and Dublin Offices.

Principal Areas of Work:

Banking/Financial Services: (*Contact partner:* Angus Creed). The firm is established as one of the leading practices in all aspects of banking and secured lending.

Company/Commercial: (*Contact partner:* John Fish). Includes all types of company/commercial law matters, mergers and acquisitions, joint ventures, agency and distribution agreements with particular emphasis on cross-border transactions.

Competition/European: (*Contact partner:* John Meade). Competition and EU regulatory advice with particular reference to cross-border transactions.

Commercial Property: (*Contact partner:* Rowan White). Covers a significant range of property and commercial property related transactions including commercial development for private and public companies and financial institutions.

Litigation/Employment: (*Contact Partner:* Peter Martin). A wide range of litigation services with particular reference to employment and commercial litigation.

Other Offices: Dublin, New York.

Contact partner:	John Fish
UK	
Number of partners:	5
Assistant solicitors:	7
Other fee-earners:	6
International	
Number of partners:	34
Assistant solicitors:	42
Other fee-earners:	31

WORKLOADS	
Banking/financial services	30%
Property	30%
Company/commercial law	20%
Litigation (including employment)	20%

ASHTON BOND GIGG Pearl Assurance House, 5 Friar Lane, Nottingham, NG1 6BX **Tel:** (0115) 947 6651 **Fax:** (0115) 947 5244 **DX:** 10002 **Ptnrs:** 7 **Asst solrs:** 3 **Other fee-earners:** 8 **Contact:** Lorraine Wheatley *High profile practice with corporate, commercial and private clients. Handles commercial litigation (shareholder/ partnership disputes), commercial, corporate, insolvency, commercial conveyancing, tax and trusts.*

WORKLOADS			
Commercial Litigation	50%	Corporate Commercial	20%
Property	20%	Private Client	10%

ASHTON MORTON SLACK 35-47 North Church Street, Sheffield, S1 2DH **Tel:** (0114) 275 2888 **Fax:** (0114) 270 0029/273 0108 **DX:** 10530 **Ptnrs:** 12 **Asst solrs:** 4 **Other fee-earners:** 23 **Contact:** Mr J.C. Rose. *A general practice best known for its personal injury, employers' liability, commercial and domestic conveyancing. Caters for a full range of clients including legally-aided individuals.*

WORKLOADS			
Personal Injury	50%	Commercial	15%
Conveyancing	15%	Other	13%
Probate & Tax	7%		

ASHURST MORRIS CRISP

BROADWALK HOUSE, 5 APPOLD ST, LONDON, EC2A 2HA
Tel: (0171) 638 1111 **Fax:** (0171) 972 7990 **DX:** 639 **Email:** ENQUIRIES@ASHURSTS.COM **Internet:** WWW.ASHURSTS.CO.UK

The Firm:

- Major international legal practice headquartered in London
- Rated third by the Hambro Company Guide as a leading quoted company adviser [see *The Company Guide* May Quarter 1998]
- A business partner committed to giving clients competitive advantage
- Specialist sector knowledge keeps clients at the cutting edge of their industry
- Complete coverage of the principal areas of commercial law
- Offices in London, Brussels, Frankfurt, Paris, Singapore, Tokyo and liaison office in New Delhi. In addition we have associated offices with Negri-Clementi, Montironi & Soci in Italy.
- AMC's clients are from the business sector particularly banking, brewing, computing, healthcare, media, energy and telecommunications and from both the public sector and local government as well as stockbrokers, accountants, investment banks and surveyors

AMC operates in all the principal areas of commercial law including:

Company and Commercial: Advising clients on international mergers and acquisitions, corporate finance, EU and competition law, reconstruction, insolvency, IP/IT insurance, and employment.

Banking: Advising lenders, issuers, borrowers, and advisers in the fields of corporate debt derivatives, bond issues, acquisitions, project finance, management buy-outs, and trade finance.

Property and Planning: Working with landlords, developers, tenants and public authorities, offering general property, planning, environmental law and litigation advice.

Litigation: Including building and development issues, EU and competition law, product liability, insolvency and professional negligence.

Tax: Covering all aspects of cross-border work including international buy-outs, collective investment schemes, demergers, securitisations and debt trading.

Other Offices:

Brussels – Avenue Louise 375, 1050 Brussels
Frankfurt – Ulmenstraße 22, 60325 Frankfurt-am-main, Germany
Paris – 22 rue de Marignan, Paris, 75008
Singapore – 6 Battery Road, #15-08, Singapore 049909
Tokyo – Kioicho Building, 8th Floor, 3-12 Kioicho, Chiyoda-Ku, Tokyo 102 and our liaison office in **New Delhi** – 6 Aurangzeb Road, D1, New Delhi, 110011.

Associated offices: Milan – Studio Legale Associato, Via Monte Napoleone, 12, 20121 Milan. Rome – Via S. Maria in Via, 12, 00187 Rome. Verona – Via Scrimiari, 10, 37129 Verona.

Senior partner:	Andrew Soundy
UK	
Number of partners:	75
Assistant solicitors:	235
Other fee-earners:	132
International	
Number of partners:	13
Assistant solicitors:	42
Other fee-earners:	5

WORKLOADS	
Company	45%
Property	25%
Litigation	15%
Banking	10%
Tax	5%

CONTACTS	
Banking and International Finance	Justin Spendlove
Buy-Outs	Charlie Geffen
Communications, Media and Technology	Chris Ashworth
Competition	Nigel Parr
Construction	Christopher Vigrass
Corporate Finance	David Macfarlane
EC	Julian Ellison
Employment	Caroline Carter
Energy	Michael Johns
Environment and Product Liability	John Evans
Environmental	Helen Loose
General Corporate	Geoffrey Green
Insurance	Jeremy Hill
Intellectual Property	Ian Starr
IT	Mark Lubbock
Litigation	Edward Sparrow
Planning	Michael Cunliffe
Projects	Mark Elsey
Property	Simon Cookson
Property Litigation	Michael Madden
Reconstruction and Insolvency	Nick Angel
Share Schemes	Paul Randall
Sport	Roger Finbow
Tax	John Watson

ASKEWS 4-6 West Terrace, Redcar, Cleveland TS10 3BX **Tel:** (01642) 475252 **Fax:** (01642) 482793 **DX:** 60020 Redcar **Email:** info@askews.com **Ptnrs:** 3 **Other fee-earners:** 7 *General practice known for child care and matrimonial, personal injury, probate and trusts.*

WORKLOADS			
Litigation	34%	Family Law	32%
Property & Probate	29%	Business	5%

ATTEY BOWER & JONES WITH DIBB AND CLEGG 82 Cleveland Street, Doncaster, DN1 3DR **Tel:** (01302) 340400 **Fax:** (01302) 323710 **DX:** 12558 **Email:** attbow@aol.com **Ptnrs:** 26 **Asst solrs:** 9 **Other fee-earners:** 73 **Contact:** Mr Peter Hannam *General commercial and family practice with offices in Doncaster (3), Rotherham, Barnsley, Mexborough, Wath, Goldthorpe and Thorne.*

BABBINGTON & BRAY SOLICITORS LIMITED 42 Southwick St, London, W2 1JQ *Tel:* (0171) 724 4707 **Fax:** (0171) 724 6641 **Ptnrs:** 2 **Asst solrs:** 3 **Contact:** George Babbington *Small firm known for its entertainment practice specialising in music industry work.*

BABINGTON & CROASDAILE 9 Limavady Road, Waterside, Londonderry, BT47 1JV *Tel:* (01504) 349531 *Fax:* (01504) 345785 *DX:* 3060 Nr Londonderry 1 *Ptnrs:* 5 *Asst solrs:* 5 *Other fee-earners:* 3

BACKHOUSES 23 Wellington St (St. John's), Blackburn, BB1 8DE **Tel:** (01254) 677311 **Fax:** (01254) 676075 **DX:** 17976 Blackburn **Ptnrs:** 3 **Other fee-earners:** 1 **Contact:** Mr J.A. Backhouse *Expertise in law relating to the transport industry, both HGV and coach/ passenger travel.*

WORKLOADS	
Road transport law (bus/coach/haulage offences)	50%
Transport licensing (driver/vehicle/operator)	25%
Contract disputes, CMR etc	10%
Employment/environmental/health & safety litigation	10%
Personal injury litigation	5%

BADHAMS THOMPSON 95 Aldwych, London, WC2B 4JF *Tel:* (0171) 242 4154 *Fax:* (0171) 404 0009 *DX:* 14 Ch.Ln. *Ptnrs:* 8 *Asst solrs:* 10 *Other fee-earners:* 4

BAIRD & COMPANY 2 Park Place, Kirkcaldy, KY1 1XL *Tel:* (01592) 268608 *Fax:* (01592) 203369 *DX:* 10 Kirkcaldy *Ptnrs:* 10 *Asst solrs:* 6 *Other fee-earners:* 2

BAKER & MCKENZIE

100 NEW BRIDGE STREET, LONDON, EC4V 6JA
Tel: (0171) 919 1000 **Fax:** (0171) 919 1999 **DX:** 233 **Email:** LONDON.INFO@BAKERNET.COM **Internet:** HTTP://WWW.BAKERNET.COM

Baker & McKenzie is the world's leading multinational law firm. The London office is an established City firm with a strong domestic and foreign client base. It provides a full range of legal services to corporations, financial institutions, governments and entrepreneurs.

The Firm: Baker & McKenzie was founded in 1949. The firm has grown by anticipating trade and capital flows around the world. Today Baker & McKenzie has more than 59 offices in 34 jurisdictions.

Its strategy is to provide for its clients the best combination of local legal and commercial knowledge and international expertise and resources. The firm is sensitive to the need to provide not only legal excellence but also a user friendly service which is efficient, transparent and value for money. To this end the firm implements a variety of client care and quality management programmes.

Baker & McKenzie is uniquely well placed to blend advice on the law and practice of a number of jurisdictions to help the client achieve its objectives: their lawyers work in national, European and international practice groups in their areas of expertise. Many lawyers have the benefit of work experience in the firm's overseas offices.

Principal Areas of Work:

● International and domestic banking and finance; swaps and derivatives; privatisations; domestic and cross-border corporate and commercial transactions; the structuring of multinational groups; international equity and debt offerings; venture capital; privately financed projects.

● International tax and trust planning; VAT and import/export questions; litigation, arbitration and ADR; civil fraud; insolvency;

● European Union and competition law; energy; environmental; intellectual property; biotechnology; information technology; on-line services and electronic commerce; telecommunications, entertainment and media; employment and pension matters; insurance; construction and engineering; commercial property and the legal aspects of lobbying.

Other Offices:

Almaty, Amsterdam, Baku, Bangkok, Barcelona, Beijing, Berlin, Bogotá, Brasilia, Brussels, Budapest, Buenos Aires, Cairo, Caracas, Chicago, Dallas, Frankfurt, Geneva, Hanoi, Ho Chi Minh City, Hong Kong, Houston, Hsin Chu, Juarez, Kiev, Lausanne, Madrid, Manila, Melbourne, Mexico City, Miami, Milan, Monterrey, Moscow, Munich, New York, Palo Alto, Paris, Prague, Rio de Janeiro, Riyadh, Rome, St Petersburg, San Diego, San Francisco, São Paulo, Santiago, Singapore, Stockholm, Sydney, Taipei, Tijuana, Tokyo, Toronto, Valencia, Warsaw, Washington DC, Zurich.

Managing partner:	Nigel Carrington
UK	
Number of partners:	55
Assistant solicitors:	110
Other fee-earners:	67
International	
Number of partners:	796
Assistant solicitors:	1496
Other fee-earners:	874

WORKLOADS	
Corporate/ finance/ EC/ tax/ commercial	48%
Litigation/ construction	23%
Employment/ pensions/ immigration	15%
Intellectual property	8%
Commercial property	6%

CONTACTS	
Banking and Finance	Chris Hogan
Central & Eastern Europe	Peter Magyar
Civil Fraud	Nick Pearson
Commercial	Michael Herington
Construction	Jeremy Winter
Corporate Finance	Gabriel Fisher
EC, Competition & Trade	Lynda Martin Alegi
Employee Benefits	Michael Ingle
Employment	Fraser Younson
Energy	Hugh Stewart
Environment	Alison Flood
Immigration	Michael Ingle
Information Technology	Don Jerrard, Harry Small
Insolvency	Nick Pearson
Insurance	Michael Herington, David Fraser
Intellectual Property	Don Jerrard, Michael Hart
Litigation and Arbitration	Gerald Cooke
Pensions	Robert West
Privatisations	Tim Gee
Projects	Mike Webster
Property	Michael Smith
Securities	Michael Caro, Tim Gee
Structured and Project Finance	Peter Gaines
Swaps and Derivatives	Schuyler Henderson
Tax	James macLachlan
Telecommunications	Peter Strivens
VAT, Customs and Excise	Andrew Hart
Venture Capital	Helen Stroud

BALDOCKS St Mary's House, 59 Quarry St, Guildford, GU1 3UD *Tel:* (01483) 573303 *Fax:* (01483) 300337 *DX:* 2409 Guildford 1 *Ptnrs:* 8 *Asst solrs:* 8 *Other fee-earners:* 6

BALFOUR & MANSON

54-66 FREDERICK STREET, EDINBURGH, EH2 1LS
Tel: (0131) 200 1200 **Fax:** (0131) 200 1300 **DX:** 4 EDINBURGH **Email:** ENQUIRY@BALFOUR-MANSON.CO.UK

The firm: One of the leading Scottish litigation practices, Balfour & Manson also has substantial commercial, private client and property client bases. The practice provides a comprehensive range of legal, financial and general advice from a wide variety of departments with in-depth expertise for Scottish, English and foreign clients and solicitors. The principal departments are litigation, commercial/corporate, private client and property.

Principal Areas of Work:

Litigation: (Head of Department: Fred Tyler). The firm has a strong litigation department which handles all aspects of litigation, with particular expertise in acting in personal injury, professional negligence and contractual claims, in multi-party actions and in family law with considerable experience in international child abduction. Additionally, this department handles commercial work, including insurance, intellectual property disputes, tribunal work, planning and building contracts.

Commercial/Commercial Property: (Head of Department: John Hodge). This department handles purchase, lease, sale and security work for clients of all types and sizes but particularly provides services for medium sized private companies.

Private Client: (Head of Department: Brenda Rennie). This department advises clients from within and without Scotland providing insurance services; tax work; finance and investment advice; and wills, trusts and executries. This department offers a unique support for elderly and infirm clients and their families.

Property: (Head of Department: Kenneth Robertson) Services include estate agency; house purchase and sale; residential leasing and repossession work.

Foreign Languages: French and German

Managing partner:	Anne Pacey
Chairman:	Andrew Gibb
Number of Partners:	16
Number of Associates:	4
Assistant Solicitors:	16
Other fee-earners:	24

WORKLOADS	
Litigation	50%
Private Client	20%
Property	20%
Commercial/Commercial Property	10%

CONTACTS	
Commercial property	J. Hodge
Corporate	A. Keatinge
Domestic property	K. Robertson
Domestic property	A. Pacey
Employment	M. Neilson
Family law	A. Gibb
Financial services & tax	M. Burns
Litigation	F. Tyler
Litigation	S. Kennedy
Litigation	I. Leach
Private client	B. Rennie

BAND HATTON

1 COPTHALL HOUSE, STATION SQUARE, COVENTRY, CV1 2FY
Tel: (01203) 632121 **Fax:** (01203) 229038 **DX:** 11207

The Firm: A long-established practice, founded in 1896, Band Hatton offers a high quality legal service to both business and private clients, utilising up-to-date technology and working methods, while maintaining traditional values and a commitment to a personal and approachable service. The firm enjoys a strong reputation in the commercial field, in particular for its commercial property work. The litigation practice is expanding rapidly in the areas of commercial, employment and matrimonial law. Band Hatton is a member of LawNet, the Federation of Independent Law Firms, and LawNet Europe, and adheres to the LawNet Quality Management Standard "Quality in Law".

Contact partner:	Philip Costigan
Number of Partners:	4
Associate Partners:	2
Other Assistant Solicitors:	4
Other Fee-earners:	5

CONTACTS	
Commercial property	Philip Costigan
Other commercial/corporate	Haydn Jones
Private client litigation	Paul Wright
Private client non-contentious	Simon Rock

BANKES ASHTON 81 Guildhall Street, Bury St. Edmunds, IP33 1PZ **Tel:** (01284) 762331 **Fax:** (01284) 764214 **DX:** 57200 Bury St Edmunds **Ptnrs:** 8 **Asst solrs:** 10 **Other fee-earners:** 7 **Contact:** David Wybar *Legal services for private clients, commercial clients and agricultural business – contact: David Wybar. Investment management services – contact: Michael FitzRoy.*

WORKLOADS			
Tax planning/wills/probate	29%	Agricultural	12%
Litigation	11%	Commercial property	10%
Investment management	10%	Residential conveyancing	10%
Company and commercial	9%	Matrimonial	7%
Debt recovery	2%		

BANNATYNE, KIRKWOOD, FRANCE & CO 16 Royal Exchange Square, Glasgow, G1 3AG *Tel:* (0141) 221 6020 *Fax:* (0141) 221 5120 *Ptnrs:* 4 *Asst solrs:* 3 *Other fee-earners:* 1

BANNERS Marsden Chambers, 2 Marsden Street, Saltergate, Chesterfield, S40 1JY *Tel:* (01246) 209773 *Fax:* (01246) 231188 *DX:* 12370 Chesterfield 1 *Ptnrs:* 7 *Asst solrs:* 3 *Other fee-earners:* 8

BANNISTERS SOLICITORS

6 – 7 GREAT JAMES STREET, LONDON, WC1N 3DA
Tel: (0171) 242 3413 **Fax:** (0171) 831 6088 **DX:** 165 (CH.LN.)

The Firm: Bannisters has grown from being founded as a niche practice in 1983 to become a thriving and mainstream insurance firm. The practice changed its name in 1997 as part of marking a fresh emphasis on the long term development of its position as a premier service provider to the Company Insurance Market first and foremost.

Bannisters remains remarkable amongst firms of its size in being able to offer such a depth and breadth of service to an exclusive insurer client base. The success of Bannisters has been built upon the consistent delivery of high quality results for insurers, upon an understanding of the needs that drive the insurance industry and upon a proactive attitude.

Bannisters offers distinct specialisms in product liability, professional indemnity, property damage, construction, fraud and policy matters. The firm is a panel solicitor for the major company insurers and there is a very strong and well known personal injury department.

Bannisters has resolute determinations and a clear agenda for its own position as a well respected and innovative insurance firm.

Senior partner:	Alan Bannister
Number of partners:	5
Assistant solicitors:	6
Other fee-earners:	7

WORKLOADS	
Insurance litigation	100%

CONTACTS	
Personal Injury	Crispin Kenyon/Steven King/ Paul Greenhalgh
Policy/General Insurance Litigation	
	Alan Bannister/Richard Houseago

BARBARA CARTER 117 Vicarage Road, King's Heath, Birmingham, B14 7QG *Tel:* (0121) 441 3238 *Fax:* (0121) 441 2191 *Ptnrs:* 1 *Asst solrs:* 0 *Other fee-earners:* 1

BARCAN WOODWARD 31 North Street, Bedminster, Bristol, BS3 1EN *Tel:* (0117) 963 5237 *Fax:* (0117) 966 8582 *DX:* 98975 Bedminster (Bristol) *Ptnrs:* 4 *Asst solrs:* 4 *Other fee-earners:* 2

BARKER, BOOTH & EASTWOOD 346 Lytham Rd, Blackpool, FY4 1DW *Tel:* (01253) 362500 *Fax:* (01253) 341032 *DX:* 27651 *Ptnrs:* 9 *Asst solrs:* 2 *Other fee-earners:* 3

BARKER GOTELEE 41 Barrack Square, Martlesham Heath, Ipswich, IP5 3RF **Tel:** (01473) 611211 **Fax:** (01473) 610560 **DX:** 124722 MARTLESHAM HEATH **Email:** bg@barkergotelee.co.uk **Ptnrs:** 3 **Asst solrs:** 9 **Other fee-earners:** 3 **Contact:** Richard Barker *Specialises in commercial work for business, farmer and landowner.*

BARLOW LYDE & GILBERT

BEAUFORT HOUSE, 15 ST. BOTOLPH STREET, LONDON, EC3A 7NJ
Tel: (0171) 247 2277 **Fax:** (0171) 782 8500 **DX:** 155 **Email:** GBBLGCPW@IBMMAIL.COM **Internet:** WWW.BLG.CO.UK

SUITE 893, LIME STREET, LONDON, EC3M 7DQ
Tel: (0171) 782 8051 **Fax:** (0171) 782 8053

The Firm: Barlow Lyde & Gilbert is one of the leading commercial city practices, having been established in 1841. The firm remains the leader in the field of insurance and reinsurance law and professional indemnity. The firm's well established areas of practice in commercial litigation, corporate law, construction, aviation, shipping, employment, environmental law, information technology, product liability and banking continue to expand.

Principal Areas of Work:

Commercial Litigation: The firm is well known for its substantial commercial litigation practice, handling commercial disputes around the world.

Reinsurance: The reinsurance division, the largest of its kind in Europe has been involved in many of the major market disputes and crucial landmark cases in the last 15 years such as the House of Lords cases: *Axa Re v Field* and *Hill v M&G Re.*

Professional indemnity: The professional indemnity division, again the largest of its kind, specialises in claims against solicitors, accountants, surveyors, directors and officers, management consultants and financial institutions. It also advises clients in their dealings with professional disciplinary bodies, SFO, DTI and other regulatory bodies.

General Insurance: The general insurance division offers a comprehensive service to composites, mutuals and self assureds to include policy coverage and wording disputes, property claims, bloodstock, contingency, product liability, medical negligence, employers, motor and public liability. The firm was recently involved in the House of Lords case *Digital v Hampshire County Council.*

Senior partner:	Ian Jenkins
Number of partners:	71
Assistant solicitors:	113
Other fee-earners:	64

CONTACTS	
Aviation	Ian Awford
Banking	Graham Wedlake
Commercial Litigation	Richard Dedman
Commercial Property	Malcolm Rogerson
Competition and EU	David Strang
Construction	Kevin Perry
Corporate & Finance	John Longdon
Employment	Gary Freer
Environment	Nicholas Hughes
Information Technology	Richard Dedman/ David Strang
Insurance Litigation	Roger Doulton
Personal Injury	Graham Dickinson
Professional Indemnity	David Arthur
Reinsurance	Colin Croly
Shipping	Ray Mead
Tax	Gary Richards

Continues overleaf

Shipping: The shipping division advises clients on both dry and wet work including charter parties, bills of lading, marine insurance and all types of marine casualty.

Aviation: The aviation division advises and assists in connection with legal issues affecting all areas of aviation and space coverage, and is well known for its work in air disaster investigations and claims handling.

Construction: The construction division is actively involved in the civil engineering and building sectors in the construction industries both in the UK and overseas, acting for contractors, sub-contractors and employers in the private and public sectors, for professional consultants and insurers.

Environmental Liability: The environmental liability group provides clients with a comprehensive environmental legal service, specialising in liability and regulatory matters.

Company/Commercial: The corporate and finance division handles the full range of corporate work which includes management buyouts and joint ventures, flotations, reconstructions, corporate finance, corporate capital, regulatory investigations, taxation, insolvency law and EU and competition law. A recent development has been the addition of a unit specialising in banking.

Commercial Property: The commercial property division is well established and deals primarily with banks, life companies, pension funds and developers.

Employment: The employment group provides clients with a comprehensive service, including representation at industrial tribunals advising on board room disputes and keeping clients up-to-date on this ever changing area of law.

The firm recognises the need to develop new products and services to meet the requirements of the business and publishes several in-house journals: the Insurance Law Quarterly; the Directors' and Officers' Liability Review; the Pollution and Environmental Risk Digest; the Employment Law Review and the Construction Law Briefing. Other publications of note are the reinsurance division's *Reinsurance Practice and the Law* and *All Risks Property Insurance*. One of the firm's partners founded and still edits the Butterworth's Merger Control Review and also edits the Merger chapter of Tolley's Company Law.

Other Offices: Hong Kong, Lloyd's (London)

BARLOWS

55 QUARRY STREET, GUILDFORD, GU1 3UE
Tel: (01483) 562901 **Fax:** (01483) 573325 **DX:** 2407 GUILDFORD **Email:** ENQUIRIES@BARLOWS.CO.UK

The Firm: Barlows has established a substantial commercial practice in recent years whilst continuing to offer a full range of private client services. A significant factor in the growth of the commercial work has been the success of the department in attracting business from firms in London which are looking for city expertise at provincial prices.

Principal Areas of Work:

Commercial and Commercial Litigation: (*Contact Partner:* Christine Goodyear) The range of work in the commercial department includes business formation, shareholders' agreements, sales, mergers and acquisitions, company reorganisation, partnership affairs, insolvency and related work, commercial and trading agreements, service agreements, and all aspects of employment law. In the last few years some substantial contracts for the public sector have been undertaken. A company secretarial service is offered. The firm is practised in handling commercial agreements involving other countries in the European Union, and has developed personal links with firms of a similar size abroad. Barlows has a notary public on the staff.

Commercial Property: (*Contact Partner:* Mike England) This department specialises in the full range of commercial property work, including property development, town and country planning, leases, licenses and tenancy agreements, site use and environmental implications, Landlord & Tenant Act matters and sales, purchases and options.

General Litigation: (*Contact Partner:* David Foster and Helen Goatley) The firm has a sizeable caseload in defendant personal injury and liability work. There are three lawyers on the Law Society's Personal Injury Panel and one on the Medical Negligence Panel. A Legal Aid Franchise was achieved in 1994. Agency work is undertaken in Guildford County Court, Guildford District Registry and Staines County Court. Whilst both general and commercial litigation is a substantial part of the firm's work, Barlows is also committed to the role of mediation and launched an Alternative Dispute Resolution Centre based at the Guildford and Chertsey offices in 1996. Other services include debt recovery, insolvency and property litigation.

Private Client Services: (*Contact Partner:* Tim Adams) The private client department continues to undertake probate, trusts and tax work and private client property.

Family Litigation: (*Contact Partners:* Tony Jenkins and Michael Goodridge) This department undertakes a wide range of personal and family matters including divorce,

Managing partner:	David Knox
Senior partner:	Tony Jenkins
Number of partners:	12
Assistant solicitors:	22
Other fee-earners:	6

WORKLOADS	
Private client	41%
Commercial/commercial litigation	22%
General litigation & personal injury	15%
Commercial property	12%
Family litigation	10%

CONTACTS	
Commercial	Christine Goodyear
Commercial	Denise Herrington
Commercial litigation	Hamish Cameron Blackie
Employment	Christine Goodyear
Employment	Mike England
Employment	Hamish Cameron Blackie
Family	Tony Jenkins
Family	Mike Goodridge
General/commercial litigation	David Foster
General/commercial litigation	Helen Goatley
Mediation	David Foster
Medical Negligence	Helen Goatley
Personal Injury	David Foster
Probate	Tim Adams
Probate	Murray Campbell
Property	Gordon Reid
Property	William Norris
Property	Mike England
Property	Helen Archibald

co-habitation and pre-nuptial agreements, adoption and childcare. One solicitor is a long-term honorary legal advisor to RELATE, and the firm also has members in the Solicitors Family Law Association.

Nature of clientele: Clients include major national companies, a substantial property developer in the social housing sector, insurance companies, local authorities, family businesses, national and local charities, all types of business from plc to sole trader, and the majority of the independent schools in the area and further afield.

Other Offices: 30 Church Street, Godalming, Surrey GU7 1EP*Tel:* (01483) 417121
Elliott House, Gogmore Lane, Chertsey, Surrey KT16 9AF*Tel:* (01932) 568245

BARNETT ALEXANDER CHART

60 GRAYS INN ROAD, LONDON, WC1X 8LT
Tel: (0171) 242 4422 **Fax:** (0171) 242 1102 **DX:** 42 LDE

The Firm: Barnett Alexander Chart is a commercial law firm with recognised strengths in corporate and litigation work. The firm has enjoyed a period of continuous growth since the early 90's. Although advising principally on UK domestic issues, the firm also operates internationally, particularly in Europe and North America. There is a concentration of specialist skills in niche areas.

Number of partners:	11
Assistant solicitors:	12
Other fee-earners:	3

CONTACTS	
Corporate finance	Edward Marston
Commercial	Dean Harper
PFI/Public sector	Anthony Fine
Sports	Peter Talibart
Finance litigation	Peter Moody
Insurance litigation	David Ostroff
Commercial litigation	Colin Isenberg
Insolvency	Danny Davis
Intellectual property	Peter Moody
Employment	Peter Talibart
Commercial property	John Chart
Licensing	Neil Shestopal

Principal Areas of Work:

Corporate Finance: The firm is well known for its corporate finance work, in particular venture capital transactions, together with mergers, acquisitions and disposals of companies, management buy-ins and buy-outs, project finance, share issues and shareholder agreements.

Commercial: The firm has extensive experience in a wide range of commercial agreements, including international trading terms, joint ventures and partnerships, licensing, distribution and agency, computer hardware and software contracts, facilities management.

PFI/Public Sector: The firm has a leading public sector practice in externalisation, outsourcing and PFI, advising local authorities, government agencies, suppliers and facilities managers including work on major infrastructure projects. The firm also advises on procurement issues.

Sports: The firm advises on all aspects of sports law, sponsorship, marketing, management of events, TV and media, representing sporting associations, clubs, individuals, agents and managers.

Financial Litigation: Expertise covers banking issues, debt and asset recovery, financial services, commercial frauds and insolvency, including injunctive relief and worldwide tracing of assets.

Insurance Litigation: The firm conducts duty of care and insurance related litigation; advising both insurers and plaintiffs, together with ADR and mediation.

Commercial Litigation: The firm has wide experience of contract and negligence litigation, arbitration, construction and engineering disputes, warranty claims, shareholder and partnership disputes and defamation.

Insolvency: The firm provides a full range of insolvency advice, both corporate and personal, acting for insolvency practitioners and creditors, including banks and directors.

Intellectual Property: The firm advises on both contentious and non contentious IP matters, including copyright, design right, patents and trademarks across a wide range of industries from manufacturing to entertainment. Confidential information and restraint of trade, are areas of particular expertise.

Employment: The firm is a leading employment law adviser, dealing with all aspects, both contentious and non-contentious, including pan-European projects. The firm's public sector work means extensive experience of Transfer of Undertakings and Acquired Rights. The firm also provides dedicated immigration advice, particularly to corporations.

Commercial Property: The firm advises on hotel and retail development, the acquisition and disposal of commercial property, the ownership and use of business premises including shops, offices, warehouses and factories, rent reviews, planning law, property taxation, environmental issues and the law for estate agency.

Licensing: The firm has a specialist licensing unit, dealing with all aspects of liquor licensing, advising hotels, restaurants, leisure facilities and trade bodies.

Other offices: Hammersmith.

Languages Spoken: French, German, Italian.

Recruitment and Training: Contact Peter Talibart.

BARNETT SAMPSON High Holborn House, 52-54 High Holborn, London, WC1V 6RL **Tel:** (0171) 831 7181 **Fax:** (0171) 269 5141 **DX:** 254 LDE **Ptnrs:** 5 **Asst solrs:** 1 **Other fee-earners:** 2 **Contact:** Ms Elspeth Chapman *An effective approach to commercial law, family law, litigation, including substantial group actions, particularly in the financial services field, and property.*

WORKLOADS			
Financial Services/Commercial Litigation/ Administrative Law			40%
Family	35%	Company/Commercial	15%
Commercial Property	5%	Private Client	5%

BARRATT GOFF & TOMLINSON The Old Dairy, 67a Melton Road, West Bridgford, Nottingham, NG2 5GR **Tel:** (0115) 981 5115 **Fax:** (0115) 981 9409 **DX:** 719903 West Bridgford **Ptnrs:** 4 **Asst solrs:** 1 **Other fee-earners:** 5 **Contact:** Mrs Jill Barratt *Specialists in maximum severity injuries but also undertaking the full range of personal injury work including medical and professional negligence.*

WORKLOADS	
Personal Injury (plaintiff: 95%; defendant: 5%)	100%

BARRIE WARD & JULIAN GRIFFITHS 5 Clarendon Street, Nottingham, NG1 5HS *Tel:* (0115) 9412622 *Fax:* (0115) 924 0485 *DX:* 711344 NOTTM 16 *Ptnrs:* 3 *Asst solrs:* 2 *Other fee-earners:* 3

BARRY SHAW 118-120 Wardour Street, London, W1V 3LA *Tel:* (0171) 494 1454 *Fax:* (0171) 494 1455 *Ptnrs:* 1

BARTRAM & CO 1st Floor, 302 Bath Road, Hounslow, TW4 7DN **Tel:** (0181) 814 1414 **Fax:** (0181) 814 1515 **Ptnrs:** 1 **Asst solrs:** 1 **Other fee-earners:** 3 **Contact:** Peter Bartram. *Specialist immigration and asylum law practice based near Heathrow Airport (opposite Hounslow West tube). Private and legal aid work undertaken.*

BATES & PARTNERS Baryta House, 29 Victoria Avenue, Southend-on-Sea, SS2 6AR *Tel:* (01702) 349494 *Fax:* (01702) 332437 *DX:* 2800 Southend *Ptnrs:* 13 *Asst solrs:* 4 *Other fee-earners:* 44

BATES, WELLS & BRAITHWAITE

CHEAPSIDE HOUSE, 138 CHEAPSIDE, LONDON, EC2V 6BB
Tel: (0171) 551 7777 **Fax:** (0171) 551 7800 **DX:** 42609 (CHEAPSIDE 1)

The Firm: Bates, Wells & Braithwaite was originally established to meet the needs of smaller business clients, and has subsequently developed a strong reputation for a wide range of litigation and family and matrimonial work, as well as a pre-eminence in charity law.

Principal Areas of Work:

Company and Business Law: The department handles a wide range of company/commercial work including take-overs, joint ventures, management buy outs, commercial contracts and corporate tax advice.

Litigation: A strong department handles a wide range of commercial litigation, and has particular expertise in employment, administrative law, entertainment, social work law, libel and personal injury. The firm is also known for its activities in the vital areas of human rights and civil liberties.

Charity Law: The department is active across the whole of the voluntary sector and represents some of the best-known national and international charities and foundations. It provides a national advisory service to solicitors and has produced a number of specialist publications.

Family Law: This well known and highly regarded department specialises in family law mainly financially based but also including complex children and cohabitee law often with an international element. Lawyers in the department are specialist mediators.

Property: This recently expanded department handles the full range of commercial property matters including development, purchase of freeholds and leaseholds for occupation and investment, the granting of leases, mortgages and planning advice.

Immigration and Nationality Law: This department advises both the individual client and large and small corporations on immigration matters.

Foreign Connections: As early as 1971, the firm was instrumental in establishing the PARLEX Group of European Lawyers. This Group is now represented throughout Europe, is registered as the first European Economic Interest Group, uses English as its common language, and offers an excellent facility through which to transact cross-frontier business.

Senior partner:	Andrew Phillips
Number of partners:	21
Assistant solicitors:	18
Other fee-earners:	17

WORKLOADS	
Charity	20%
Family	20%
Litigation	20%
Property	20%
Company/ commercial	10%
Immigration	10%

CONTACTS	
Administrative Law	John Trotter
Charity law	Andrew Phillips, Stephen Lloyd, Fiona Middleton
Company/ commercial	Hugh Craig, David Robinson
Employment	William Garnett
Family law	Frances Hughes, Pauline Fowler
Immigration	Philip Trott
Litigation	Martin Bunch
Property	Anthony Cartmell, Nick Ivey

BATTENS (WITH POOLE & CO)

CHURCH HOUSE, YEOVIL, BA20 1HB
Tel: (01935) 423685 **Fax:** (01935) 706054 **DX:** 100503

The Firm: Battens was established almost 300 years ago but in recent years has grown to be one of the larger firms in the South West, with 25 partners and 7 offices situated in Somerset and Dorset, all linked on an IT network. In the past year the firm has merged with Poole & Co, a respected private client practice of similar age and status, and restructured its business into five Divisions in order to develop its client focus and to manage its financial and operational performance.

The Divisions are: **Private Client Legal:** property, trusts, attorneyships, wills and probate **Private Client Services:** investment management, financial planning, tax and trust administration **Commercial:** agriculture, employment, commercial property, corporate, partnership, planning, charities **Litigation:** matrimonial, child care, personal injury, civil litigation

These Divisions are assisted by the **Management Division** which provides support on financial management, personnel, IT, marketing and operations generally.

The partners have a substantial interest in **Dryfield Trust Plc,** an authorised institution under the Banking Act.

The firm has members on the following Law Society panels – planning, child care, personal injury. There are two in-house stockbrokers plus three investment managers who are accredited by the Law Society.

Clients include a variety of private individuals, plc and smaller companies, institutions, partnerships and sole traders. Battens provides clients with quality, value for money legal and financial planning services.

Other Offices:
Crewkerne: **Tel:** (01460) 74401; **Fax:** (01460) 73988; **DX:** 43401 Crewkerne
Dorchester: **Tel:** (01305) 250 560; **Fax:** (01305) 260876; **DX:** 8705 Dorchester
Shaftesbury: **Tel:** (01747) 852343; **Fax:** (01747) 852684; **DX:** 46003 Shaftesbury
Sherborne: **Tel:** (01935) 814811; **Fax:** (01935) 816436; **DX:** 49151 Sherborne
Taunton: **Tel:** (01823) 331066; **Fax:** (01823) 332046; **DX:** 32116 Taunton
Weymouth: **Tel:** (01305) 774666; **Fax:** (01305) 760423; **DX:** 8753 Weymouth

Chairman:	Ray Edwards
Number of partners:	25
Assistant solicitors:	21
Other fee-earners:	16

WORKLOADS	
Private Client Legal	40%
Litigation	31%
Commercial	16%
Private Client Services	13%

CONTACTS	
Directors:	
Commercial	Melanie Shuldham
Litigation	Graham Hughes
Management	Andy Marshall
Private Client Legal	Jeanie Bogaardt
Private Client Services	Mervyn Ellis

T.G. BAYNES & SONS 208 Broadway, Bexleyheath, DA6 7BG *Tel:* (0181) 301 2525 *Fax:* (0181) 304 1475 *DX:* 31801 Bexleyheath *Ptnrs:* 13 *Asst solrs:* 9 *Other fee-earners:* 13

BEACHCROFT STANLEYS

20 FURNIVAL STREET, LONDON, EC4A 1BN
Tel: (0171) 242 1011 **Fax:** (0171) 831 6630 **DX:** 45 LONDON, CHANCERY LANE **Email:** BEACHCROFT@BEACHCROFT.CO.UK
Internet: HTTP://WWW.BEACHCROFT.CO.UK

Beachroft Stanleys continues to meet its strategic objectives to remain a market leading practice in the health and insurance sectors. They are committed to developing their commercial practice and by identifying that their strengths lie in advertising and marketing, construction, education, retail and water/utilities, the firm ensures that its focus remains clear and achievable.

Feedback from clients acknowledges their depth of expertise, track record and reputation, friendly and personable staff and their dependability under pressure.

The firm's role is to enable clients to achieve a competitive edge within their own industry or service sector. They endeavour to understand the issues that are important to their clients which enables them to identify opportunities to add value and save costs to the service they provide.

The firm has introduced sophisticated practice and case management systems which have significantly improved the production of financial information and client reports enabling clients to establish budgetary controls.

Principal Areas of Work: The firm is structured into the following 9 departments:

Commercial Litigation provides its services to the Firm's industry and service sector clients. The Department handles a wide range of commercial disputes in the courts, arbitration tribunals and is increasingly involved in alternative dispute resolution such as mediation.

Commercial Property provides a full range of specialisations in property managment, property investment and finance, dispute resolution and property litigation, planning and environment and construction. The Department has an excellent reputation for working well with surveyors and other property intermediaries.

Corporate Finance is principally concerned with M&A, disposals, listings, new issues, capital restructurings, and joint ventures for a variety of clients in the UK and overseas.

Continues overleaf

Senior partner:	Rt Hon The Lord Hunt of Wirral MBE
Chief Executive:	Patrick Maddams
Number of partners:	42
Assistant solicitors:	77
Total staff:	339
Other fee-earners:	66

WORKLOADS	
Commercial	38%
Health	31%
Insurance	31%

CONTACTS	
Advertising and Marketing	Simon Hodson
Commercial Litigation	Rebecca Whiting
Commercial Property	John Phelps
Construction	Lawrence Bruce
Corporate Finance	Simon Hodson
Education	Julian Gizzi
Employment	Elizabeth Adams
European Community	Julie Nazerali
Health Litigation	Gay Wilder
Information Technology	Barry Francis
Insurance Litigation	Rt. Hon. The Lord Hunt of Wirral MBE
Intellectual Property	Jonathan Radcliffe
Projects	Barry Francis
Retail	Laurence Markham
Tax & Trust	Paul Solon
Water (Utilities)	James Beshoff

The **Education** Department is recognised as a leading practice acting for some of the major universities. The Department is noted for its high calibre institutional work and for the handling of funding matters for both the HEFC and the FEFC.

Employment undertakes work for clients both in the public and private sectors. In the public sector the Department acts for health service bodies, local authorities and educational establishments. Within the private sector it acts for employers covering the full range of contentious and non-contentious matters including High Court and Tribunal Actions and all forms of discrimination and industrial relations' matters.

As an acknowledged market leader in its field the **Health Litigation** Department carries out a vast range of work including medical defence work and a variety of advisory work on patient care issues. The **Health Law Group** provides clients with the full range of legal services including medical negligence, property, employment, planning and environmental, IT & IP, and PFI.

Insurance Litigation deals with all claims and risk management issues and is acknowledged as a market leading practice, regularly instructed by 4 out of the top 10 general insurers as well as reinsurers, Lloyds syndicates and governing bodies. The Department provides a cross range of services including personal injury and claims arising from motor accidents, policy coverage disputes and product liability including specialist knowledge on major international product liability claims.

The multi skilled **Projects** Department works almost exclusively in the PFI market. The department has completed or is advising on a range of projects in the health, defence, IT, education and local authority arena.

All tax matters are handled by the **Tax & Trust** Department, its particular strength is in its ability to offer an integrated legal and accounting service.

Applicants for training contracts should apply in writing by 1 August, two years prior to commencement of training. A brochure and application form is available from the Director of Training.

The firm organises regular in-house seminars for both clients and non-clients on issues that are identified as being of major concern and interest to them. It also holds "roadshows" and on-site seminars for both clients and non-clients.

The firm publishes a number of bulletins including Health, Insurance, EU, Education, Employment and Intellectual Property and Information Technology.

BEALE AND COMPANY

GARRICK HSE, 27-32 KING ST, COVENT GARDEN, LONDON, WC2E 8JD
Tel: (0171) 240 3474 **Fax:** (0171) 240 9111 **DX:** 51632 COVENT GARDEN **Email:** BEALE@DIAL.PIPEX.CO

The Firm: Beale and Company is a long established firm (founded in 1837) which provides a comprehensive range of services to commercial clients. The main areas of the firm's practice are construction and insurance. The firm has a strong international practice. The firm provides high quality legal advice combined with a practical and commercial approach.

Principal Areas of Work:

Construction: (*Contact Partner:* John Ward). The firm provides legal advice and, where necessary, representation, in relation to projects in the UK and throughout the world, to Employers, Contractors and professionals, on all aspects of civil and structural engineering contracts, related insurance and bond provisions and collateral warranties, and on joint ventures, corporate structures, partnerships, DBFO forms of contract and other forms of contract, on disputes and dispute resolution, and on and in negotiations, litigation, arbitration and other alternative forms of dispute resolution.

Engineers: (*Contact Partner:* Rachel Barnes). This is a special section of the firm's construction practice. The firm are the solicitors for the Association of Consulting Engineers and have acted for more than thirty of the top fifty firms of consulting engineers in the UK. The firm acts for engineers and others prosecuted under Health and Safety legislation.

Insurance: (*Contact Partner:* Christopher Cullen). The firm acts for insurers and their insureds in handling professional indemnity and public liability claims and on risk management and other ways of reducing or preventing claims. The firm advises insurers on policy wording, coverage issues and disputes between insurer and insured.

Litigation: (*Contact Partner:* Anthony Smith). The firm handles a wide range of other commercial litigation, including disputes in the fields of banking, intellectual property, supply of goods and services and employment. The firm handles a large amount of international litigation and are Privy Council Agents.

Company and Commercial: (*Contact Partner:* Michael Archer). The firm advises on all aspects of company commercial transactions, including acquisitions and disposals of usinesses, setting up joint ventures, corporate finance arrangements, restructuring of

Managing partner:	John Ward
Senior partner:	John Ward
Number of partners:	8
Assistant solicitors:	7
Other fee-earners:	9

WORKLOADS	
Construction	35%
Insurance	35%
Litigation	15%
Company and Commercial	10%
Private Client	5%

companies and partnerships and establishing commercial contractual relationships such as distribution, agency and licensing networks, advice on information technology and intellectual property and on directors' duties and liabilities, employment problems and claims, partnership disputes and corporate compliance.

Private Client: (*Contact Partner:* Rachel Barnes). The firm advises private clients, domiciled and non-domiciled, on tax planning, formation of trusts, wills and probates.

Foreign/International Connections The firm is a member of a European network of correspondent law firms. The firm also has correspondent law firms in Bombay, Calcutta, Dhaka, Kampala, Karachi, Mombasa, Nairobi and Port Louis. One of the firm's consultants works in Bangladesh.

Recruitment and Training The firm recruits on average three graduate trainees each year. Currently there are five graduate trainees in the firm.

BEAUMONT AND SON Lloyds Chambers, 1 Portsoken St, London, E1 8AW **Tel:** (0171) 481 3100 **Fax:** (0171) 481 3353 **DX:** 551 **Ptnrs:** 14 **Asst solrs:** 23 **Other fee-earners:** 14 **Contact:** Mr James Edmunds *Areas of practice include aviation, insurance and reinsurance, litigation. Commercial matters including financing with a significant although not exclusive aviation emphasis.*

WORKLOADS	
Aviation, insurance and reinsurance, litigation claims	75%
Commercial leasing, banking and asset finance	15%
Conveyancing and private client	5%
Marine, hull claims, collision, liabilities, salvage	5%

BECKMAN & BECKMAN 20 Balcombe Street, London, NW1 6NB **Tel:** (0171) 724 1435 **Fax:** (0171) 724 7017 **DX:** 41717 Marylebone 2 **Ptnrs:** 5 **Asst solrs:** 1 **Other fee-earners:** 1 **Contact:** Norman I Beckman. *Known for its close involvement with clients it covers, with expertise, a wide range of commercial, property and private work.*

BEITEN BURKHARDT MITTL & WEGENER 13 Devonshire Square, London, EC2M 4TH **Tel:** (0171) 392 9100 **Fax:** (0171) 392 9101 **Ptnrs:** 2 **Associate lawyers:** 3 **Other fee-earners:** 2 **Contact:** Mr Stephan Grauke *Specialised areas: Cross-border mergers, acquisitions and joint ventures, corporate finance, corporate and commercial; media law.*

BELL LAMB & JOYNSON 6 Castle St, Liverpool, L2 0NB *Tel:* (0151) 227 2626 *Fax:* (0151) 227 5937 *DX:* 14110 *Ptnrs:* 13 *Asst solrs:* 4 *Other fee-earners:* 8

BELL LAX LITIGATION Mill House, 2 High Street, Sutton Coldfield, Birmingham, B72 1XA **Tel:** (0121) 355 0011 **Fax:** (0121) 355 0099 **DX:** 15736 Sutton Coldfield **Email:** peter_a_lax@link.org **Ptnrs:** 2 **Asst solrs:** 5 **Other fee-earners:** 4 **Contact:** Ms Heather Bell *Niche litigation practice specialising exclusively in resolving commercial disputes, accident and insurance claims. Also expertise in aviation and defamation matters.*

WORKLOADS	
Commercial disputes	75%
Accident and insurance work	25%

BELL & SCOTT WS 16 Hill Street, Edinburgh, EH2 3LD **Tel:** (0131) 226 6703 **Fax:** (0131) 226 7602 **DX:** 114 Edinburgh 1 **Email:** maildesk@bellscott.co.uk **Ptnrs:** 9 **Asst solrs:** 5 **Other fee-earners:** 10 **Contact:** Mr Bruce Anderson, Managing Partner *Property development law specialists – commercial and residential – with complementary corporate, litigation and private client services for owner-managed businesses.*

WORKLOADS			
Commercial Property	55%	Litigation	20%
Private Client	15%	Corporate	10%

BELMORES Goodchild House, 27 Castle Meadow, Norwich, NR1 3DS *Tel:* (01603) 617947 *Fax:* (01603) 630086 *Ptnrs:* 5 *Asst solrs:* 3 *Other fee-earners:* 6

BELTRAMI & CO 93 West Nile Street, Glasgow, G1 2FH *Tel:* (0141) 221 0981 *Fax:* (0141) 332 9892 *DX:* GW8 *Ptnrs:* 2 *Asst solrs:* 4 *Other fee-earners:* 1

BENNETT & ROBERTSON 16 Walker Street, Edinburgh, EH3 7NN *Tel:* (0131) 225 4001 *Fax:* (0131) 225 1107 *DX:* ED5 Edinburgh *Ptnrs:* 12 *Asst solrs:* 15 *Other fee-earners:* 6

BENTLEYS, STOKES & LOWLESS

INTERNATIONAL HOUSE, 1 ST. KATHARINE'S WAY, LONDON, E1 9YL
Tel: (0171) 782 0990 **Fax:** (0171) 782 0991 **DX:** 1074

The Firm: Bentleys, Stokes & Lowless is traditionally associated with the maritime and insurance sectors.

Principal Areas of Work:

Admiralty: Specialist advice and representation is offered in relation to: salvage, pollution, total loss, groundings, unsafe port claims, damage claims, collisions and public, official and casualty inquiries and investigations.

Shipping, Insurance & Litigation: The department advises on a wide range of marine and insurance related matters, including charterparty/Bill of Lading contracts, marine, cargo and aviation insurance, cargo claims, road transport, commodity contracts, commercial contracts, ship sale and purchase, construction, building and general litigation.

Foreign Languages: French, Spanish and Italian.

Senior partner:	A. Bardot
Number of partners:	9
Assistant solicitors:	8
Other fee-earners:	4

WORKLOADS	
Shipping, marine & non-marine insurance	100%

CONTACTS	
Admiralty	M Burch
Charterparty/ marine insurance	A D Bardot, W J Chetwood

BEOR WILSON & LLOYD Calvert Hse, Calvert Terrace, Swansea, SA1 6AP *Tel:* (01792) 655178 *Fax:* (01792) 467002 *DX:* 39550 *Ptnrs:* 6 *Asst solrs:* 2 *Other fee-earners:* 2

BERG & CO

SCOTTISH MUTUAL HOUSE, 35 PETER STREET, MANCHESTER, M2 5BG
Tel: (0161) 833 9211 **Fax:** (0161) 834 5566 **DX:** 14379 **Email:** HELP@BERG.CO.UK

The Firm: Occupying modern offices at the heart of Manchester's commercial district, Berg & Co is a highly-motivated, proactive, commercial and forward thinking firm serving the needs of business clients both in the UK and internationally.

Principal Areas of Work:

Company and Commercial: *(Contact Partner:*R.L. Berg). Work includes:formations, mergers and acquisitions, joint ventures, disposals, development and venture capital finance, share option schemes, insolvency and liquidation, intellectual property and competition law. A full range of employment personnel services is also provided.

Litigation: *(Contact Partner:*C. Khan). *Work includes:*contract claims, retention of title, shareholders' actions, freeze orders and injunctions. Also insolvency and intellectual property. *(Contact Partner:* Peter Woolf). *Work includes:*Contract claims, matrimonial finance, consumer credit and consumer hire, professional negligence and debt collection.

Commercial Property: *(Contact Partner:*G. Rechnitzer). *Work includes:*acquiring, financing, developing and disposing of commercial and investment property, including advice on taxation, planning and related insurance matters.

Employment: *(Contact Partner:*Stephanie Klaas). Advice on all aspects of workforce issues eg: negotiation of senior employees' severance packages, rationalisation of business including redundancies and transfer of undertakings.

Nature of Clientele: Clients include public (including listed) and private companies, educational institutions, financial institutions, partnerships and individual entrepreneurs seeking an innovative and practical approach to legal services.

Foreign Connections: The firm has an extensive range of contacts in Europe, the USA and the Far East which enable it to progress its clients' affairs beyond UK boundaries. Languages spoken include French and German.

Managing partner:	Reuben Berg
Senior partner:	Reuben Berg
Number of partners:	9
Assistant solicitors:	10
Other fee-earners:	5

CONTACTS	
Commercial leasing	P.G. Woolf
Commercial litigation	C. Khan
Commercial property	G. Rechnitzer
Consumer credit	P.G. Woolf
Corporate and commercial	R. L. Berg, S.A. Foster
Human resources	R. L. Berg
Human resources	S. Klass
Insolvency	S. Fulda
Matrimonial finance	P.G. Woolf

BERMANS Pioneer Buildings, 65-67 Dale St, Liverpool, L2 2NS *Tel:* (0151) 227 3351 *Fax:* (0151) 236 2107 *DX:* 14116 *Ptnrs:* 10 *Asst solrs:* 7 *Other fee-earners:* 41

BERNARD CHILL & AXTELL The First House, 1a The Avenue, Southampton, SO17 1AH *Tel:* (01703) 228821 *Fax:* (01703) 211300 *DX:* 38508 Southampton 3 *Ptnrs:* 7 *Asst solrs:* 2 *Other fee-earners:* 7

BERRY & BERRY 11 Church Road, Tunbridge Wells, Kent, TN1 1JA **Tel:** (01892) 526344 **Fax:** (01892) 511223 **DX:** 3908 **Email:** Berry_Berry@compuserve.com **Ptnrs:** 8 **Asst solrs:** 8 **Other fee-earners:** 7 **Contact:** Mrs Zai Koder *Branch Office: Tonbridge. General practice includes civil, personal injury, employment, criminal, matrimonial/family, commercial, conveyancing, tax and probate. Three legal aid franchises. Lawnet member.*

WORKLOADS			
Civil litigation	35%	Matrimonial & family	20%
Property	20%	Probate	15%
Criminal litigation	10%		

BERRYMAN & CO

PARK HOUSE, FRIAR LANE, NOTTINGHAM, NG1 6DN
Tel: (0115) 941 7574 **Fax:** (0115) 941 9623 **DX:** 10004 NOTTINGHAM 1 **Email:** LEGAL@BERRYMAN.CO.UK **Internet:** WWW.BERRYMAN.CO.UK

The Firm: Established in 1896 this dynamic partnership has continued to expand in each of the principal areas of work, especially the insurance litigation and commercial departments.

Principal Areas of Work:

Commercial/Corporate Company/Commercial matters, Corporate Finance, Employment, Insolvency, IT, Intellectual Property, Commercial Property/Development, Planning and Environment, Litigation

Insurance Litigation Defendant insurance litigation for major Insurers, Loss Adjusters and Local Authorities

Private Client Family, Wills, Probate, Estate Planning, Residential Conveyancing, Personal Injury

Crime and Immigration All aspects of personal and corporate crime

Other Associated Office: Berryman Davies Lavery – Birmingham. Joint venture with Davies Lavery, London and Maidstone

Managing partner:	Charles Harrington
Senior partner:	Andrew Morton
Number of partners:	14
Assistant solicitors:	11
Other fee-earners:	13

WORKLOADS	
Commercial/Corporate	33%
Insurance Litigation	25%
Private Client	24%
Crime	18%

CONTACTS	
Commercial/Corporate	R. Brackenbury/D. James
Insurance Litigation	A. Morton/R. Halliday
Private client	C. Harrington/M. Smith
Crime	S. Varley

BERRYMAN DAVIES LAVERY King Edward House, 135a New Street, Birmingham, B2 4QQ **Tel:** (0121) 689 8900 **Fax:** (0121) 689 8901 **DX:** 13043 Birmingham **Email:** Berryman@DaviesLavery.co.uk **Ptnrs:** 8 **Asst solrs:** 2 **Other fee-earners:** 2 **Contact:** Claire McKinney *A specialist niche Practice providing a quality service to the Insurance industry. Other associated offices: Berryman & Co in Nottingham, Davies Lavery in London and Maidstone.*

WORKLOADS	
Insurance Litigation	100%

BERRYMANS LACE MAWER

SALISBURY HOUSE, LONDON WALL, LONDON, EC2M 5QN
Tel: (0171) 638 2811 **Fax:** (0171) 920 0361 **DX:** 33861 FINSBURY SQ. **Email:** GBBLMALL@IBMMAIL.COM

CASTLE CHAMBERS, 43 CASTLE STREET, LIVERPOOL, L2 9SU
Tel: (0151) 236 2002 **Fax:** (0151) 236 2585 **DX:** 14159 LIVERPOOL 1 **Email:** GBBLMALL@IBMMAIL.COM

KING'S HOUSE, 42 KING STREET WEST, MANCHESTER, M3 2NU
Tel: (0161) 236 2002 **Fax:** (0161) 832 7956 **DX:** 14302 MANCHESTER 1 **Email:** GBBLMALL@IBMMAIL.COM

Berrymans Lace Mawer has an established position as one of the largest and strongest litigation practices in the U.K. The firm is also able to provide a comprehensive legal service to the insurance market and to commercial, professional and private clients in the U.K. and overseas. It has built upon its huge reputation in the insurance field and its commercial expertise continues to develop in strength in both its contentious and non contentious practises with a 20% growth in the last year.

The Firm: There are seven offices in England situated in London EC2 and EC3, Birmingham, Leeds, Liverpool, Manchester and Southampton. Each office is able to offer the complete range of expertise to all of the firm's clients.

The firm's client base covers UK and foreign commercial organisations, including major insurance companies, consulting engineers, contractors, architects, surveyors, quantity surveyors, accountants, barristers, solicitors, health trusts, private hospitals, government departments and agencies, local authorities, police authorities, privatised services and commercial and private clients.

Principal Areas of Work: The firm is administratively divided into four business groups all of which are represented in each of the firm's offices. They are:

Insurance Liability Group: consisting of Personal Injury, General Liability and Agency work.

Specialist Divisions Group: consisting of Construction, Environment, Insurance/Reinsurance, Marine, Medical Law and Professional Indemnity.

Commercial Group: consisting of Company Commercial, Commercial Litigation, Commercial Property, Employment, EU & Competition and Recovery Insurance work.

Private Client Group: covering all aspects of Private Client work, Family Law and Domestic Conveyancing. Each office provides an agency service for representation at local courts.

For further information or a copy of a brochure please contact David Hunt, the Marketing Manager, on 0171 638 2811.

Overseas office: Dubai.

Associated overseas offices: Paris (as Bertagna Gruia Berrymans), Athens, Brussels, Bucharest, Dusseldorf, Madrid, Singapore, Stuttgart. Berrymans Lace Mawer is a member of the BLM EEIG and the Association of European Lawyers.

Worldwide	
Number of Partners:	84
Fee Earners:	276
Total Staff:	610

WORKLOADS	
Insurance Liability Group (including personal injury, general liability and agency work)	60%
Specialist Divisions Group (including Construction, Environment, Insurance, Re-insurance, Marine, Medical Law and Professional Indemnity)	20%
Commercial Group (Company Commercial, Commercial Litigation, Commercial Property, Employment, EU & Competition and Recovery)	15%
Private Client Group (all aspects of private client work, family law and domestic conveyancing)	5%

CONTACTS	
Birmingham	Chris Wiggin
Leeds	John Henthorn
Liverpool	David Evans
London EC2	Paul Taylor
London EC3	David Wilkinson
Manchester	Nigel Roden
Southampton	Martin Bruffell
Dubai	Nigel Truscott

BERRY, REDMOND & ROBINSON 19 The Boulevard, Weston-super-Mare, BS23 1NR
Tel: (01934) 619000 *Fax:* (01934) 614148 *DX:* 84015 Weston-super-Mare *Ptnrs:* 6 *Asst solrs:* 5 *Other fee-earners:* 4

BERRY SMITH Brackla House, Brackla Street, Bridgend, CF31 1BZ *Tel:* (01656) 645525
Fax: (01656) 645174 *DX:* 38004 Bridgend *Ptnrs:* 6 *Asst solrs:* 5 *Other fee-earners:* 3

S J BERWIN & CO

222 GRAYS INN ROAD, LONDON, WC1X 8HB
Tel: +44 (0)171 533 2222 **Fax:** 0171 533 2000 **DX:** 255 LONDON CHANCERY LANE WC2 **Email:** INFO@SJBERWIN.COM

SQUARE DE MEEÂS 19, BTE 3, B-1050, BRUSSELS, BELGIUM
Tel: +32 2 511 5340 **Fax:** +32 2 511 5917

The Firm: Founded in 1982, S J Berwin & Co's rapid growth and success is best explained by its ability to handle complex corporate and commercial transactions, coupled with a creative approach to clients' problems, a speedy response and close involvement in their strategic decision making.

Clients: S J Berwin & Co acts for clients ranging from major multi-national business corporations and financial institutions to high net worth individuals. The firm is especially favoured by entrepreneurial business clients who find the firm particularly well attuned to their outlook and needs. Increasingly, the firm is focusing on industry sectors including pharmaceuticals and biotechnology, media, communications and information technology, sport and leisure. Internationally, the firm operates through its own network of overseas law firms and is also the English member of Interlaw.

Training: In order to maintain its commitment to organic growth and development, they will recruit up to 30 ambitious, commercially minded individuals to begin training in September 2000. Apply to Helen Turnbull, Head of Training.

Principal Areas of Work: The firm is well known for its corporate work and offers a full range of corporate finance services including mergers and acquisitions, capital markets, private equity, management buy-outs and securities regulation, coupled with an active international banking practice, including insolvency and reconstruction. National and international taxation advice, including the structuring of international transactions and property development, is provided by the tax group. Estate planning and asset protection advice is given to private clients in the UK and overseas. The charities group advises on all aspects of charity law, including advice on large fund-raising and lottery-assisted projects.

The firm has a strong European dimension. Its EU, competition and trade law practice is conducted through the London and Brussels offices and advises on domestic and EU mergers and acquisitions, competition, anti-trust and anti-dumping, regulatory work and judicial review proceedings. The firm has been named 'Competition Team of the Year' in the Annual Legal Business Awards.

All aspects of commercial property work are handled for a wide range of clients, including property companies, developers, institutions, retailers and hoteliers. Specialist groups advise on public and private funding programmes for major infrastructure projects, construction and local government finance issues. A highly regarded planning and environment team is an integral part of this growing and expanded practice.

The firm's litigation practice handles a broad range of substantial international and domestic commercial litigation as well as mediation and arbitration which is undertaken by the specialist ADR Services Unit. In addition, the practice includes a specialist property litigation group and an advocacy group.

An active insolvency group handles the whole spectrum of insolvency work, from corporate insolvency and bankruptcy to reconstructions. International trade mark, copyright and patent litigation, international trade mark registration and the identification, exploitation and protection of intellectual property rights are undertaken by a specialist intellectual property group.

Other areas of commercial work include film financing and animation production work and communications as well as commercial contracts, frequently with an international dimension, including franchising, agency distributorship, joint venture and trading agreements and information technology.

Other Offices: Brussels, Frankfurt

Senior partner:	David Harrel
UK	
Number of partners:	72
Assistant solicitors:	118
Other fee earners:	70
International	
Number of partners:	1
Assistant solicitors:	2
Other fee earners:	4
Total Staff (UK & International):	548

WORKLOADS	
Company/Commercial	50%
Commercial Property	20%
Litigation	17%
EU/Competition	10%
Tax	3%

CONTACTS	
ADR	David I Shapiro
Advocacy	Richard Slowe
Banking	Gillian Smith
Brussels	David Cox
Charities	Moira Protani
Construction	Ian Insley
Corporate Finance	Robert Burrow, Matthew Hudson
Employment	Nicola Walker
Environment	Mark Brumwell
EU/Competition	Stephen Kon
Insolvency	Stephen Maffey
Intellectual Property	Jeremy Schrire, Ray Black
Investment Funds	Josyane Gold
Leisure	Bryan Pickup
Litigation	Tim Taylor
Media, Communications & I.T.	Nigel Palmer
Pharmaceuticals	Jeremy Schrire
Planning	Pat Thomas
Projects	Gillian Smith, Simon McLeod
Property	Stephen Willson
Property Litigation	Michael Metliss, Vivien King
Securities	Charles Abrams
Sport	Jonathan Metliss, Peter McInerney
Tax	David Hinds, Michael Trask
Trade Marks	John Olsen

S J Berwin & Co

BERWIN LEIGHTON

ADELAIDE HOUSE, LONDON BRIDGE, LONDON, EC4R 9HA
Tel: +44 171 760 1000 **Fax:** +44 171 760 1111 **DX:** 92 **Email:** INFO@BERWINLEIGHTON.COM **Internet:** WWW.BERWINLEIGHTON.COM

The Firm: Berwin Leighton is a major City firm, highly regarded for its property, finance and corporate expertise. Founded in 1970, we are a modern, growing practice with a clear client service focus and an expanding blue chip client base. Our strategy is to build on our high quality reputation in our chosen specialisms. The firm puts a premium on commercial, as well as technical advice, client relations and quality transactional care. We are entrepreneurial, tenacious and innovative.

Principal Areas of Work:

Property: Berwin Leighton's property department is one of the country's leading commercial property practices. It represents institutions, investors, developers, retailers, banks and government bodies in the full range of commercial property activity. The planning group is a clear market leader and our construction and environment groups enjoy similar reputations. A unique combination of the firm's property skills and its project finance and public sector experience, has been the driving force behind the firm's emergence as a market leader in Private Finance Initiative work.

Finance: The finance department brings together Berwin Leighton's experience in banking, debt financing, equipment leasing and property financing and also includes the firm's highly regarded tax group. The department advises lenders and borrowers in major financing projects in the UK and overseas.

Corporate: The corporate department represents medium-sized public and private companies and corporate finance houses, in mergers, acquisitions, corporate recoveries and flotations. Its clients are principally drawn from the property, retail, IT, media, telecommunications and finance sectors. The department has a strong private equity team that acts for venture capital houses and management teams. The department also acts for major international corporations, particularly in the USA, South Africa, Israel and Scandinavia, seeking either investment opportunities, or financing, in the UK and Europe. As part of the corporate department, the commercial group comprises a dedicated team of specialists, who have established a rapidly growing presence in media, telecommunications, IT and intellectual property, reflecting the convergence of these disciplines.

Litigation: The litigation department handles a wide range of commercial litigation instructions in construction, banking and property disputes and has been at the forefront of the move towards introducing and using methods of alternative dispute resolution. The financial institutions group represents insurers in relation to claims under the Bankers' Policy and acts for both banks and insurers in professional indemnity claims, as well as banks in non-insurance contentious matters.

Brussels Berwin Leighton's Brussels office is the base of the firm's EC law practice which provides specialist advice to our public and private sector clients in the areas of competition and public procurement, employment, environment, transport and telecommunications.

Recruitment and Training: Berwin Leighton has a comprehensive programme for trainee solicitors, recruiting 20 trainees each year. Further details, including a copy of our recruitment literature, are available on request.

Other offices:

Brussels 13B Avenue de Tervuren 1040 Brussels Belgium *Tel*: +322 732 3144 *Fax*: +322 732 3979

Managing partner:	R.J. Jones
UK	
Number of partners:	73
Assistant solicitors:	123
Other fee-earners:	48
International	
Number of partners:	1
Assistant solicitors:	1
Other fee-earners:	2

WORKLOADS	
Property (including planning)	42%
Company/commercial (including corporate finance)	28%
Litigation	18%
Finance (including tax)	12%

CONTACTS	
Banking	Marc Palley
Commercial Property	David Taylor
Construction	Terry Fleet
Construction Litigation	Michael Blackburne
Contentious Property	Roger Cohen
Corporate	John Bennett
EC and Competition	Velia Leone
Employment	Robert Eldridge
Environment	Andrew Waite
Financial Institutions	Michael Wilson
Insolvency	Keith Bordell
Intellectual Property	Peter Stone
Litigation	Michael Goldmeier
Media	Andrew Somper
Planning	Ian Trehearne
Private Equity	Fabrizio Carpanini
Private Finance Initiative	Simon Allan
Private Litigation	Roger Cohen
Property Finance	Simon Kildahl
Public sector	Anna Forge
Tax	John Overs

BETESH FOX & CO 17 Ralli Courts, West Riverside, Manchester, M3 5FT **Tel:** (0161) 832 6131 **Fax:** (0161) 832 8172 **DX:** 14359 **Ptnrs:** 9 **Asst solrs:** 14 **Other fee-earners:** 20 **Contact:** Stephen Fox *Handles company/commercial, crime, PI, professional negligence, litigation, commercial fraud and forensic services.*

WORKLOADS	
Commercial & civil litigation and insurance law	27%
Commercial fraud, serious crime, forensic services	27%
Personal injury	27%
Company/ commercial and property	18%

BEVAN ASHFORD

35 COLSTON AVENUE, BRISTOL, BS1 4TT
Tel: (0117) 923 0111 **Fax:** (0117) 929 1865 **DX:** 7828 BRISTOL 1 **Email:** NJK@BEVANASHFORD.CO.UK

WATERLOO HOUSE, FITZALAN COURT, NEWPORT ROAD, CARDIFF, CF2 1EL
Tel: (01222) 462562 **Fax:** (01222) 461388 **DX:** 33011 CARDIFF **Email:** NJK@BEVANASHFORD.CO.UK

CURZON HOUSE, SOUTHERNHAY WEST, EXETER, EX4 3LY
Tel: (01392) 411111 **Fax:** (01392) 250764 **DX:** 8301 EXETER **Email:** ROUS@BEVAN-ASHFORD.CO.UK

1 CHANCERY LANE, LONDON, WC2 1LF
Tel: (0171) 421 4400 **Fax:** (0171) 421 4422 **DX:** 1058 CHANCERY LANE **Email:** D.WIDDOWSON@BEVANASHFORD.CO.UK

MUTLEY HOUSE, 23 PRINCESS STREET, PLYMOUTH, PL1 2EX
Tel: (01752) 256888 **Fax:** (01752) 256012/250508 **DX:** 8273 PLYMOUTH 2 **Email:** PLYMOUTH.GTNW@BEVAN-ASHFORD.CO.UK

41 ST JAMES STREET, TAUNTON, TA1 1JR
Tel: (01823) 284444 **Fax:** (01823) 270869 **DX:** 32115 TAUNTON **Email:** STJAMES.ID@BEVAN-ASHFORD.CO.UK

GOTHAM HOUSE, TIVERTON, EX16 6LT
Tel: (01884) 242111 **Fax:** (01884) 259303 **DX:** 49002 TIVERTON **Email:** POST.CJCP@BEVAN-ASHFORD.CO.UK

The Firm: Bevan Ashford is one of the largest regional practices in the country. It has a network of offices serving clients across the South of England, the Midlands and Wales. Clients range from multinational corporations and institutions to smaller businesses, partnerships and individuals.

Bevan Ashford founded ADVOC, a network of similar independent commercial legal firms which now extends across 40 cities in Europe, the Middle East and Asia which enables Bevan Ashford to service the requirements of its clients internationally.

The firm's predominant strengths lie in corporate transactions, commercial property, planning and environmental law, commercial litigation and employment matters, IT, intellectual property and media law.

The firm is now one of the leading providers of PFI Advice. It currently represents over 49 Capital Schemes in a number of sectors. The firm also acts for a number of Local Authorities, Development Corporations, and Colleges of Further Education.

In addition, some offices have developed particular niches:

Bristol is the largest office in the firm and is well known for its national practice for National Health Service bodies and, consequently, strong departments in the fields of medical litigation, commercial property, construction, planning, PFI, environmental law and employment law.

Cardiff has a long established reputation in acting for local businesses and has developed a strong NHS practice in Wales. Bevan Ashford's west country offices operate cross office departments with each office having its own particular strengths.

Exeter is a commercial centre with strong departments in company and commercial, commercial property, construction, planning, environmental law, PFI, commercial litigation, employment law, and defendant insurance work as well as providing a full range of private client services.

The **Plymouth** office deals with major corporate clients and is active in education, pensions, media law, planning, environmental, commercial property, commercial litigation and employment law.

Taunton and **Tiverton** combine a full range of general commercial work, with high quality private client services. Taunton's particular strength lies in company and commercial, commercial property and plaintiff personal injury and together with the Tiverton office provides a centre of excellence for agricultural law. Tiverton is widely respected for its strength in agricultural law, personal taxation and estate planning.

The **London** office services client's corporate headquarters and public sector clients in and around the London area, as well as providing facilities for international clients.

IT is well established throughout the firm; this provides access to knowledge systems, other fee-earners, and increasingly clients. Bevan Ashford is achieving its ambition to compete successfully in national markets, providing comprehensive commercial services to corporate and public sector clients, appreciative of the cost benefits of a regional practice.

Management Board Chairman: Nick Jarrett-Kerr	
Number of partners:	60
Assistant solicitors:	105
Other fee-earners:	84

WORKLOADS	
NHS Litigation	26%
Company/Commercial	25%
Property	25%
Commercial Litigation	18%
Private Client	6%

CONTACTS	
Bristol	Nick Jarrett-Kerr
Cardiff	Nick Jarrett-Kerr
Exeter	Simon Rous
London	David Widdowson
Plymouth	George Wilkinson
Taunton	Ian Daniells
Tiverton	Christopher Palmer

INVESTOR IN PEOPLE

■ **BEVAN** ■
ASHFORD
SOLICITORS

BEVERIDGE ROSS & PREVEZER

10-11 NEW STREET, LONDON, EC2M 4TP
Tel: (0171) 626 1533 **Fax:** (0171) 929 4982 **DX:** CDE 828

The Firm: Established since the early 1980s, Beveridge Ross & Prevezer is a well-regarded City firm, which has attracted a strong property, corporate, commercial and private client base. The firm is best known for commercial property, company/ commercial, commercial litigation (including insolvency and large debt recoveries), computer law, white collar crime, matrimonial, franchise and trade finance. The firm also has strong overseas connections in India, China, Hong Kong, Sweden, and Africa, as well as the usual European countries. Acting for a number of household names Beveridge Ross & Prevezer has grown on its reputation of being one of the youngest firms in the City, and for being able, as a result of its size, to give a personal and individual service to its clients at partner level.

Managing partner:	Mark Prevezer
Senior partner:	Mark Prevezer
Number of partners:	9
Assistant solicitors:	3
Other fee-earners:	2

BEVIRS 36 Regent Circus, Swindon, SN1 1UQ *Tel:* (01793) 532363 *Fax:* (01793) 619585 *DX:* 38618 Swindon 2 *Ptnrs:* 10 *Asst solrs:* 6 *Other fee-earners:* 8

BEVISS & BECKINGSALE Law Chambers, Holyrood Street, Chard, TA20 2AJ *Tel:* (01460) 61494 *Fax:* (01460) 63821 *DX:* 43300 *Ptnrs:* 8 *Asst solrs:* 5 *Other fee-earners:* 6

BIDDLE

1 GRESHAM ST, LONDON, EC2V 7BU
Tel: (0171) 606 9301 **Fax:** (0171) 606 3305 **DX:** 1008 LONDON CHANCERY LANE **Email:** LAW@BIDDLE.CO.UK **Internet:** WWW.BIDDLE.CO.UK

Biddle is a highly progressive City business law practice with a particularly strong reputation in the corporate, pensions, IT, media, litigation and insolvency fields. The firm has a new and entrepreneurial management team (the managing partner and senior partner are in their early forties) and in the last two years there has been a 20% increase in fee-earning staff and associated expansion into two further office sites based near the firm's prime Gresham Street location. This has seen a very significant turnover increase for the firm.

The Firm: Already well-regarded for its integrity and professionalism, Biddle's strategy is to provide a genuine City-based alternative for commercial clients who are looking for a first-class service. New instructions come from an exceptionally wide client base, reflecting the firm's reputation for all round excellence as well as in its specialist areas. They include institutions, major pension funds, banks, leading insolvency practitioners, listed companies, television companies, newspapers, insurers, publishers and major casinos.

The firm's hallmark is the ability to advise on and implement precise and imaginative legal solutions to clients' business objectives in a user friendly manner.

Membership of LOGOS, a group of independent law firms with offices throughout the European Union, enables Biddle to offer a high quality international service to its clients. The firm also has strong US and Middle-East connections.

Principal Areas of Work:

Company and Commercial: The focus of the corporate department is transaction oriented including, in particular, M & A and buy-out work. There has also been significant involvement in Stock Exchange and AIM flotations and a variety of joint ventures. The department has had its best business year ever from its new custom designed offices adjacent to 1 Gresham Street.

Media and Entertainment: The firm acts for a wide range of media clients and is particularly well known for its work for television news organisations, newspapers, publishers and international news agencies. Our work regularly involves advising on legal and commercial issues relating to the internet, on-line publishing and electronic commerce.

Defamation: In defamation, the firm continues to be involved in a large number of the headline cases. Biddle advises the main book publishing companies in London on libel, copyright and contractual matters arising out of the new media. Biddle recently acted for Vanity Fair in defence of the libel claim brought by Fayed and for Chris Patten concerning his publishing contract with HarperCollins.

Litigation: The firm's litigation department remains heavily involved in the Maxwell litigation and has a wide-ranging work load of other complex cases both here and abroad. The last year has seen a particular emphasis on banking, construction, professional negligence, warranty and trust litigation cases and an increasing involvement in ADR.

Pensions: In the pensions field, the firm has an outstanding reputation for the depth of its expertise and the quality of its advice across the whole spectrum of pensions law, including

Managing partner:	Desmond O'Connell
Senior partner:	Martin Winter
Number of partners:	34
Assistant solicitors:	36
Other fee-earners:	16

WORKLOADS	
Corporate/commercial	33%
Litigation	20%
Media & IT	14%
Pensions	14%
Property	8%
Insolvency	7%
Employment	4%

CONTACTS	
Company/Commercial	Martin Winter & Roger Fink
Construction	David Lancaster
Corporate Finance	Martin Lane
Employment	Geoff Tyler
Food Law	Julian Harris
Gaming	Julian Harris
Insolvency	Christopher Mallon
Intellectual Property & Digital Media	Kim Walker
IT	Brian Palmer
Litigation	David Lancaster
Media	David Hooper
Pensions	Hugh Arthur
Private Client	David Biddle
Professional Indemnity	David Lancaster
Property	Peter Watson
Taxation	Mark Cawthron

Continues overleaf

negotiations on the pensions aspects of corporate acquisitions and disposals, advice on pensions reconstructions and insolvency-related work for independent trustees. Biddle is a member of the OPRA panel of legal advisers.

Licensing: The firm sponsored the International Gaming Conference in London and the gaming department successfully represented clients in a leading case under the Gaming Act 1968.

Employment: The firm's employment department handles all aspects of UK and European employment law and HR practices. It is frequently involved in high profile cases, for example, those involving senior executives' compensation on wrongful dismissal (Clark v BET) and on transfers under TUPE (Adams -v- Lancashire County Council). The department has particular expertise in Anton Piller and injunctive relief to recover and prevent the wrongful use of confidential information and in the enforcement of restrictive covenants. The department also carries out investigations where an employer suspects fraud or other misconduct and advises on how such matters should be handled and on the recovery of misappropriated assets.

Insolvency: The firm's insolvency department has continued to attract major insolvency work, representing the country's leading insolvency practitioners in a wide range of insolvency matters but in particular in international financial sector insolvencies. It has also established a considerable reputation in fraud and asset tracing through experience gained in BCCI and other major cases.

Private Finance and Equity: Biddle's strong private client and corporate tax departments complement all areas of the firm's work and represent a wide range of international and UK high net worth individuals and trusts.

Commercial Property: The firm's commercial property group has been extensively involved in major office, retail, leisure and investment property transactions for a variety of clients and continues to expand its highly regarded environmental law practice.

BIGGART BAILLIE Dalmore House, 310 St. Vincent Street, Glasgow, G2 5QR **Tel:** (0141) 228 8000 **Fax:** (0141) 228 8310 **DX:** 9 Glasgow **Email:** info@biggartballie.co.uk **Ptnrs:** 20 **Asst solrs:** 32 **Other fee-earners:** 18 **Contact:** Campbell Smith *Acts for major industrial, financial and commercial enterprises across Scotland.*

WORKLOADS			
Commercial property	34%	Corporate	30%
Litigation	23%	Private client	13%

BINDMAN & PARTNERS

275 GRAY'S INN RD, LONDON, WC1X 8QF
Tel: (0171) 833 4433 **Fax:** (0171) 837 9792 **DX:** 37904 KING'S CROSS

The Firm: Founded in 1974, Bindman & Partners are specialists in civil liberties and human rights issues. The firm has the resources to handle major litigation, and considerable experience and expertise in the following areas. A large amount of legal aid work is handled.

Principal Areas of Work:

Defamation and Media Law: (*Contact:* Geoffrey Bindman). Wide experience in representing individuals, newspapers, TV companies and other media organisations.

Administrative Law: (*Contact:* Stephen Grosz). *Work includes:* judicial review, environmental protection, discrimination and police powers.

Employment: (*Contact:* Robin Lewis). The firm represents mainly employees, but also some corporations, trade unions, voluntary agencies and pressure groups, on matters including discrimination and equal pay claims.

Crime: (*Contact:* Neil O'May). Work ranges from major fraud cases and serious crimes to minor offences.

Housing: (*Contact:* Saimo Chahal). The firm handles landlord and tenant law, especially for tenants.

Family: (*Contact:* Felicity Crowther). An extensive matrimonial and family practice includes legally-aided clients.

Children: (*Contact:* Katherine Gieve). *Work includes:*wardship, adoption, care-proceedings, child abduction, custody and access disputes.

Medical Negligence & Personal Injury: (*Contact:* Claire Fazan). The firm has an established expertise in medical negligence and other personal injury cases.

Immigration and Nationality: (*Contact:*Alison Stanley). Immigration expertise includes work permits, EC, comparative and international migration.

Senior partner:	Geoffrey Bindman
Number of partners:	15
Assistant solicitors:	10
Other fee-earners:	7

CONTACTS	
Civil Litigation	Geoffrey Bindman
Civil Litigation	Stephen Grosz, Clive Romain, Nick Braithwaite
Criminal Law	Neil O'May, Adrian Clarke
Criminal Law	Michael Schwarz,Sharon Persaud
Criminal Law	Judi Kemish
Employment	Robin Lewis
Family Law	Felicity Crowther
Family Law	Katherine Gieve
Housing	Saimo Chahal, Sue James
Housing	Stephen Brown, Barbara Wyatt
Immigration	Alison Stanley, Graham Smith
Medical Negligence	Claire Fazan
Personal Injury	Terry Donovan

BIRCHALL BLACKBURN

CRYSTAL HOUSE, BIRLEY STREET, PRESTON, PR1 2AQ
Tel: (01772) 561663 **Fax:** (01772) 202438 **DX:** 713290

The Firm: Birchall Blackburn has two main offices in Preston and Manchester, supported by a network of satellite offices in Central and East Lancashire, allowing clients ready access to a comprehensive range of legal services. Founded in 1950 to provide a full range of legal service for corporate, institutional and private clients, Birchall Blackburn is one of the most progressive firms in the North West with a growing reputation within the commercial field. The firm has specialist departments which include commercial and company law, commercial property, commercial and civil litigation, licensing and the leisure sector, family law, corporate and personal insolvency and debt recovery and private client work. Close partner contact is central within the service which combines commercial awareness and experience with a pragmatic down to earth approach. Legal aid work is also undertaken and the firm are holders of the Legal Aid Franchise.

Other Offices: Waldorf House, 5 Cooper Street, Manchester M2 2FW (Tel 0161-236-0662) (Fax 0161-236-0687)

Managing partner:	J. David Blackburn
Senior partner:	J. David Blackburn
Number of partners:	12
Assistant solicitors:	21
Other fee-earners:	16

BIRCHAM & CO. (incorporating DYSON BELL MARTIN)

1 DEAN FARRAR ST, WESTMINSTER, LONDON, SW1H 0DY
Tel: (0171) 222 8044 **Fax:** (0171) 222 3480 **DX:** 2317 VICTORIA SW1

The Firm: Established for many years in London SW1, this firm combines a balanced private client and commercial practice. The firm also practises as Parliamentary Agents under the name Dyson Bell Martin, and in 1995 was enlarged by merger with the Piccadilly firm, Stoneham Langton & Passmore.

The practice has always carried out a wide variety of work and, in addition to its substantial private client work, it played a prominent role in establishing and advising railway companies in the 19th Century. It has been linked since its foundation with the leading UK eye hospital and also acts for a significant number of charities engaged in heritage, education and training, the relief of poverty and hospitals and medical affairs generally. Commercial clients include established multinational companies and new businesses operating in a range of fields.

The firm places a strong emphasis on maintaining close contact between clients and the partners responsible for their cases.

Recent developments have included a marked expansion in the volume of corporate finance work undertaken, notably concerning flotations. In addition, the private client department, one of the largest of any central London firm, is closely linked to a growing investment management division established in 1995. The firm's work in leasehold reform has grown strongly over recent years as has the civil litigation practice.

Principal Areas of Work:

Private Client: Private client services include all aspects of financial planning for the individual including wills, trusts and tax compliance for individuals and trustees. In the area of tax planning the firm acts increasingly for foreign nationals both within the U.K. and internationally. The department also includes a substantial probate practice.

Charities: Charity clients range from major national charities to family charitable trusts, the firm advising on all aspects, including formation, administration and promotion. All 'commercial' aspects of charities' activities are covered e.g. acquiring and disposing of businesses and undertakings, fund-raising and commercial participation/commercial arrangements with third parties. The firm's reputation in this field is reflected by its membership of the National Council for Voluntary Organisations Panel of Approved Lawyers.

Investment Management: Bircham Investment Management (BIM) offers private clients a comprehensive investment management service. Funds under management are growing steadily and the department is a sponsored member of the CREST settlement system using the firm's nominee company. BIM aims to provide a seamless service between private client legal services and investment management, managing private client, trust and charity funds on a discretionary and advisory basis.

Property activities for private clients include all aspects of landed estates, both urban and rural, such as estate management, agricultural and other tenancies and town and country planning. The firm also has a leading practice in the leasehold reform field. Matrimonial and family law matters are dealt with and civil litigation services are provided, covering such areas as personal injury and medical negligence.

Senior partner:	Ian McCulloch
Executive Committee Chairman:	Nick Brown
Number of partners:	21
Assistant solicitors:	16
Other fee-earners:	36

WORKLOADS	
Private client/charities	30%
Parliamentary/public affairs	21%
Litigation	20%
Property	16%
Company/Commercial	10%
Investment Management	3%

CONTACTS	
Charities	Simon Weil
Company/Commercial	John Turnbull
Employment	Ian Adamson
Investment Management	Christopher Jones-Warner
Litigation	George Josselyn
Parliamentary/Public Affairs	Robert Owen
Private Client	Peter Goodwin
Property	John Stephenson

BIRCHAM & CO.

SOLICITORS

INCORPORATING DYSON BELL MARTIN, PARLIAMENTARY AND PUBLIC AFFAIRS

Continues overleaf

Company and Commercial: Company and commercial services include corporate finance (in particular flotations on the Official List, AIM and OFEX), company acquisitions and disposals, partnerships and joint ventures and all types of commercial agreements. The department undertakes a substantial amount and variety of employment work and also gives advice on intellectual property matters.

Commercial Property: Commercial property expertise covers all the main areas, in particular investment, retail, landlord and tenant, development schemes, project management, funding loan arrangements and site acquisitions and disposals.

Litigation: All aspects of commercial litigation are handled, including building litigation, property disputes and insurance litigation as well as matrimonial work for private clients.

Parliamentary Public Affairs: Bircham & Co.'s parliamentary and public affairs department, which practises under the name of Dyson Bell Martin, advises on all aspects of the law-making process, whether at a European, national or local level. This includes advice on influencing government policy and resulting legislation, advice on transport infrastructure and other major public works, public enquiries and promoting and opposing private and local legislation.

Foreign Connections: As a member of the Private Association of Lawyers in Europe, Bircham & Co. has associated firms in twenty European cities.

BIRCH CULLIMORE Friars, White Friars, Chester, CH1 1XS **Tel:** (01244) 321066 **Fax:** (01244) 312582 **DX:** 19985 Chester **Ptnrs:** 8 **Asst solrs:** 2 **Other fee-earners:** 7 **Contact:** Mr. N. Cummings *A general private client practice founded 200 years ago, offering a full range of legal services to both private and business clients. Also have a respected and growing agricultural practice. Now expanding on the commercial side.*

WORKLOADS	
Private Client	38%
Residential/ Commercial Conveyancing	29%
Litigation/ Matrimonial	16%
Ecclesiastical/ Charities/ Agriculture	8%
Trust Administration	8%

BIRD & BIRD

90 FETTER LANE, LONDON, EC4A 1JP
Tel: (0171) 415 6000 **Fax:** (0171) 415 6111 **DX:** 119 LONDON **Internet:** HTTP://WWW.TWOBIRDS.COM

The Firm: A broadly-based commercial law firm, best known for its intellectual property and technology expertise, particularly in the areas of communications, information technology, digital media and technology transfer.

Principal Areas of Work:

Banking: *(8 Partners).* Advice to lenders and borrowers on all aspects of banking and insolvency law including project finance, asset and property finance, securitisation, acquisition finance, bank regulation, banking technology, debt rescheduling, insolvency, derivatives and banking litigation.

Brands and Trade Marks: *(7 Partners).* A dedicated brands and trademarks group provides specialist advice on the full range of strategic, contractual and litigation issues associated with this field.

Commercial Litigation: *(5 Partners).* This department undertakes all forms of UK and international commercial disputes including sale of goods, computer and telecommunication disputes, product liability, property litigation, insurance, defamation, professional negligence, sport, employment, shipping, international trade, arbitration and ADR work.

Commercial Property: *(5 Partners).* Comprehensive service in relation to all land transactions including property finance and development for a wide range of companies, organisations and individuals.

Communications: *(17 Partners).* Substantial practice advising on international infrastructure projects, regulation of the industry, provision of service, use of apparatus, interconnection of systems, and competition law issues.

Corporate: *(21 Partners).* Full range of legal services including mergers & acquisitions, joint ventures, MBI's and MBO's, restructuring, flotations and the related tax issues.

EC: *(3 Partners).* European community law forms an integral part of Bird & Bird's client services. Advice is provided through the Brussels office and concentrates in particular on competition enforcement and legislative developments within each of the firm's specialist sectors.

Digital Media: *(18 Partners).* Full range of commercial advice including joint ventures and financing; rights acquisition and clearance; publishing; electronic distribution and payment; marketing; telecommunications, broadcasting and commercial use of the Internet.

Employment: *(4 Partners).* Advice on contracts of employment, requirements of UK and EC law, TUPE on outsourcing, mergers & acquisitions, employee incentive schemes, termination and the enforcement of fiduciary duties and contractual obligations by injunction.

Senior partner:	David Harriss
UK	
Number of partners:	39
Assistant solicitors:	59
Other fee-earners:	23
International	
Number of partners:	2
Assistant solicitors:	3

WORKLOADS	
Company	44%
Intellectual Property	32%
Litigation	11%
Property	11%
Private Client	2%

CONTACTS	
Banking	Trystan Tether
Brands & Trade Marks	Morag Macdonald
Commercial Litigation	Duncan Quinan
Commercial Property	Robert Scott
Communications	David Kerr
Corporate	Charles Crosthwaite
Digital Media	David Kerr
EC	Simon Topping
Employment	Penelope Christie
Environment	Robert Scott
Health	David Stone
Information Technology	Hamish Sandison
Intellectual Property	Trevor Cook
PFI	Roger Bickerstaff
Pharmaceuticals	Trevor Cook
Sport	Justin Walkey
Tax	Richard Ward

Environment: *(2 Partners).* Advice and assistance on waste on land, atmospheric pollution, noise, water, hazardous substances and product liability issues, particularly in relation to mergers & acquisitions and property transactions.

Health: *(11 Partners).* Over 40 years' experience in this field. Comprehensive service handling, amongst other things, medical negligence claims, property and PFI matters. The firm advises a wide range of NHS Trusts and other healthcare organisations.

Information Technology: *(18 Partners).* Lawyers with technical backgrounds and in-house IT industry experience provide a full range of advice to IT users and suppliers in the public, private and utilities sectors, on IT procurement, outsourcing, electronic trading, IT disputes and PFI projects.

Intellectual Property: *(12 Partners).* Extensive experience in all aspects of this field, but best known for conducting patent actions and other substantial litigation with a heavy technical content.

PFI: *(6 Partners).* The firm has expertise in IT, telecommunications and property-related PFI transactions, having already advised on a number of major projects in these fields for a variety of public-sector bodies. The firm drafted the government's model-form PFI Agreement for IT-related projects.

Pharmaceuticals: *(7 Partners).* Substantial practice handling a wide range of matters for clients in the pharamaceuticals, biotechnology and medical devices sectors, in particular corporate finance, intellectual property, product liability and regulatory issues.

Sport: *(2 Partners).* Advice and assistance on the full range of sports marketing and administration work with extensive domestic and international transactional experience for governing bodies, rights purchasers, sports businesses, teams and individuals; including UK and EC competition law and tax.

Tax: *(1 Partner).* Advice on all aspects of the firm's main practice areas including the creation of tax efficient structures for commercial, corporate and public sector transactions (including tax based financings).

Nature of Clientele: Bird & Bird services a wide spectrum of organisations from multi-nationals and institutions to smaller companies and private individuals. A significant proportion of its clients are high-technology companies.

Recruitment: *Partner:* Graham Camps. Six trainee solicitors and a significant number of assistant solicitors are recruited annually. The firm's Law Society accredited training programme is co-ordinated by a university law lecturer.

Other Offices:

EU Office: 209A Avenue Louise, 1050 Brussels, Belgium
Tel:(322) 644 3616 *Fax:*(322) 644 2486 *Contact:* Simon Topping

Hong Kong: 20/F Printing House, 18 Ice House Street, Central, Hong Kong
Tel: (852) 2530 0960 *Fax:* (852) 2523 3138 *Contact:* Vivien Crook.

BIRD SEMPLE

249 WEST GEORGE STREET, GLASGOW, G2 4RB
Tel: (0141) 221 7090 **Fax:** (0141) 204 1902 **DX:** GW10 GLASGOW **Email:** ENQUIRIES@BIRDSEMPLE.CO.UK **Internet:** WWW.BIRDSEMPLE.CO.UK

NAPIER HOUSE, 27 THISTLE STREET, EDINBURGH, EH2 1BS
Tel: (0131) 459 2345 **Fax:** (0131) 459 5600 **DX:** ED 271 EDINBURGH 1

The Firm: Bird Semple is one of Scotland's leading law firms. To meet the challenges of a dynamic and changing marketplace the firm has established two specialist industry sector groups: Bird Semple Property and Construction and Bird Semple TechMedia. The firm also has a thriving private client group.

Bird Semple Property & Construction provides a full range of services to the property sector including investment, disposal and letting advice, property finance, construction and engineering and advice in relation to property disputes. The Property & Construction Group also has employment, environment and PFI expertise to complement the skills of the core property specialists. The firm's reputation as well as experience has been enhanced by its involvement in some of the largest and most successful property deals to take place in Scotland in recent years.

Bird Semple TechMedia offers a full range of legal solutions to the technology, media and new media sectors. The group has corporate, litigation, intellectual property and employment specialists and advises companies, whose core business is in these sectors or organisations involved in these sectors, on issues ranging from stock exchange listings and MBOs to licensing agreements and employment contracts.

A cost effective approach to the law is vital in today's marketplace. The provision of services such as alternative dispute resolution, mediation and arbitration are all aimed at reducing the costs often associated with litigation and disputes.

Continues overleaf

Managing partner:	Gordon Hollerin
Senior partner:	Keith Deighton
Number of partners:	17
Assistant solicitors:	39
Other fee-earners:	6

CONTACTS	
Commercial Property	Graeme Sunter
Construction and Engineering	Fenella Mason
Corporate	Jack Gardiner
Debt Recovery	Joan Devine
Defamation	Derek Currie
Dispute Resolution	Gordon Hollerin
Employment	Derek Currie
Insolvency	Joan Devine
Inward Investment	Jack Gardiner
PFI	Jack Gardiner
Private Client	Lawrence Marshall
Property Disputes	Gordon Hollerin
Property Finance	Jack Gardiner
TechMedia	Norman Oliver

Litigation: The firm is recognised for its pioneering work in the area of alternative dispute resolution and Gordon Hollerin is an accredited mediator and the firm are founder members of the Centre for Dispute Resolution.

Construction and Engineering Unit: The Construction and Engineering Unit led by Fenella Mason has developed a reputation as one of Scotland's leading advisers for contentious and non-contentious advice in this area advising a number of leading construction clients. The firm's expertise in this area has involved the team in a variety of PFI projects.

Property Finance Unit: With many financial institutions having established dedicated teams to deal in the funding of property transactions, there is an increasing demand for lawyers specialising in complex and innovative property funding structures. Bird Semple has established a Property Finance Unit which is dedicated to structuring deals which meet the needs of both the property and financial sectors.

Inward Investments: A number of Bird Semple's clients are foreign investors whose inward investments have been handled by Jack Gardiner and Bill Ferrie. The firm currently acts for several foreign clients both in a UK and European context.

Defamation: The firm's defamation practice is thriving with the emphasis very much on prevention rather than cure. The firm acts for many of Scotland's leading newspaper titles.

Debt recovery: Debt recovery is an unfortunate reality of today's business environment. Bird Semple offers a value for money service which uses technology to manage high volumes of instructions.

The services described here are by no means exhaustive. Details of the full range of commercial and private client services are available on the firm's web site. www.birdsemple.co.uk

If you are interested in these or any other services the firm can provide, please contact the relevant partner.

BIRKETT LONG

ESSEX HOUSE, 42 CROUCH ST, COLCHESTER, CO3 3HH
Tel: (01206) 217300 **Fax:** (01206) 572393 **DX:** 3603 COLCHESTER **Email:** MAIL@BIRKETTLONG.CO.UK
Internet: HTTP://WWW.BIRKETTLONG.CO.UK

RED HOUSE, COLCHESTER ROAD, HALSTEAD, CO9 2DZ
Tel: (01787) 272200 **Fax:** (01787) 472398 **DX:** 41450

The Firm: A progressive practice, Birkett Long provides a wide range of services to commercial and private clients. Clients include major companies, local authorities, family businesses, education, medical and public sector bodies and institutions, insurance companies, property investors, landowners and farmers. Every client has a contact partner.

Managing partner:	Chris Holmes
Senior partner:	Tony Frost
Number of partners:	16
Assistant solicitors:	8
Other fee-earners:	20

WORKLOADS	
Litigation – Commercial	25%
Private Client	25%
Litigation – PI and Private	20%
Property	20%
Company and Business	10%

Principal Areas of Work:

Company and Business Law: Acquisitions and disposals, joint ventures and commercial contracts in the UK and elsewhere (several European languages spoken), PFI projects, education, health, employment, computer law and intellectual property.

Litigation: Commercial, property, professional negligence, personal injury, debt collection, IT, ADR mediation net.

Family Law: Disputes arising from family breakdowns, financial, care, custody and inheritance claims.

Property: Commercial and residential, town and country planning and environmental law, appeals and inquiries.

Private Client: Wills, probate, trusts, estate planning, tax, investment and pensions.

Agriculture: Property, estate and tax planning and management, landlord and tenant, town and country planning and environmental.

CONTACTS	
Commercial Litigation & PI	Adrian Livesley
Commercial Property	Susan Masters
Company & Commercial Law	Wanda Domhof
Computer Law & Intellectual Property	Nigel Mason
Education	Philip George
Employment	Jane Eatock
Family Law	Chris Holmes
Planning/Environment	Mike Jones

BIRKETTS 24-26 Museum St, Ipswich, IP1 1HZ *Tel:* (01473) 232300 *Fax:* (01473) 230524 *DX:* 3206 Ipswich *Ptnrs:* 21 *Asst solrs:* 7 *Other fee-earners:* 38

B.M. BIRNBERG & CO 103 Borough High St, London Bridge, London, SE1 1NN *Tel:* (0171) 403 3166 *Fax:* (0171) 378 1856 *DX:* 39903 London Bridge South *Ptnrs:* 2 *Asst solrs:* 11 *Other fee-earners:* 8

BISHOP LONGBOTHAM & BAGNALL Rodney Hse, 5 Roundstone St, Trowbridge, BA14 8DH *Tel:* (01225) 755656 *Fax:* (01225) 753266 *DX:* 43106 *Ptnrs:* 11 *Asst solrs:* 10 *Other fee-earners:* 16

BISHOP AND ROBERTSON CHALMERS

2 BLYTHSWOOD SQUARE, GLASGOW, G2 4AD
Tel: (0141) 248 4672 **Fax:** (0141) 221 9270 **DX:** GW 11 **Email:** MAIL@BISHOPS-LAW.CO.UK **Internet:** HTTP://WWW.BISHOPS-LAW.CO.UK

22 AINSLIE PLACE, EDINBURGH, EH3 6AJ
Tel: (0131) 220 3355 **Fax:** (0131) 220 3777 **DX:** ED.215

The Firm: One of the largest firms in Scotland, with offices in Glasgow and Edinburgh, this firm has a commercial focus. The non-commercial needs of clients can also be met by the Private Client Division. Employing the latest technology systems and reacting swiftly to commercial, social and legal developments both at home and in Europe, the firm displays a forward-looking approach tailored to its clients' needs.

Bishop and Robertson Chalmers operates in three divisions; business law which has units specialising in corporate, commercial property, pensions, European Community law and environmental law; litigation which has specialist construction law, insolvency and employers/public liability units and private client/trusts.

Principal Areas of Work:

Business Law Division: The practice is well known for its work in the corporate law field, including corporate restructuring, take overs, mergers, management buy-outs, and advising banks and insurance companies; intellectual property law; media law; insolvency law; pensions law, including benefit design, establishment of schemes, acquisitions and disposals, insolvency wind-ups, redundancies, trusteeships (advising trustees or providing trustee services either individual or through our company, Mitre Pensions Ltd) and all aspects of general advice in pensions law and practice. Accreditations as specialists have been awarded by The Law Society of Scotland to Russell Lang in insolvency law and Iain Talman and June Crombie in pensions law.

The firm has devoted considerable resources to developing expertise in European Community Law and can offer commercial clients concise assistance on competition law and the effect of environmental legislation. Clients can benefit from the firm's ability to identify legislation in progress and lobby the client's view point, to advise on the effects of legislation as it is implemented and to provide litigation services at the European Court of Justice and the Court of First Instance in Luxembourg.

The firm is associated with UAB Bishop and Robertson Chalmers, a firm incorporated in Lithuania in 1995 with an office in Vilnius, Lithuania. With its business law experience at an international level, the firm provides a comprehensive legal service to allow trade to flow smoothly between Lithuania and other countries.For commercial property work there is a team with a wealth of practical experience. Among the range of services available are: purchases, sales, leasing, securities, town and country planning, property investment, property development, licensing and environmental advice.

Litigation Division: The division has experience in all fields of litigation whether in Court of Session, Sheriff Court, or the criminal courts. Tom Marshall in the Edinburgh Office is a Solicitor Advocate and is a fellow of the Chartered Institute of Arbiters. Accreditations as specialists by The Law Society of Scotland have been awarded to John Welsh in construction law and as a solicitor mediator, and David Whyte in employment law. The range of services available include: arbitration, contract disputes, construction law, alternative dispute resolution, damage claims, employment law, industrial relations, licensing, matrimonial law, personal and property claims, insolvency, bankruptcy and debt recovery.

Private Client Division: The division covers all aspects of law affecting the individual, including purchase and sale of residential property, wills, inheritance tax planning, trusts, financial management and independent financial and investment advice. As authorised by Law Society of Scotland, the firm also offers independent financial and investment advice.

Other Offices: 22 Ainslie Place, Edinburgh, EH3 6AJ. *Tel:* 0131 220 3355. *Fax:* 0131 220 3777.

Associated Office: UAB Bishop and Robertson Chalmers, Sermuksniu GTV 1-7 2001 Vilnius Lithuania. *Tel:* +370 2 61 48 75. *Fax:* +370 2 62 41 47

Foreign Languages: French, German.International connections and associated offices: Member of IAG International. Associated offices throughout Western and Eastern Europe, Northern and Central America and Hong Kong.

Managing partner:	James A. Millar
Senior partner:	John A. Welsh
Number of partners:	19
Assistant solicitors:	21
Other fee-earners:	24

WORKLOADS	
Litigation	32%
Corporate/commercial	26%
Commercial property	18%
Private client/trusts	13%
Insolvency and asset recovery	11%

CONTACTS	
Commercial property	Kenneth Ross (Glasgow)
Commercial property	James Warnock (Edinburgh)
Corporate	James Millar (Glasgow)
Corporate	Rodger Murray (Edinburgh)
Debt recovery	David Whyte (Glasgow)
EC law	Iain Taylor (Glasgow)
Employment	David Whyte (Glasgow)
Environmental	Kenneth Ross (Glasgow)
Insolvency	Russell Lang (Glasgow)
Litigation	Alastair Lockhart (Glasgow)
Litigation	Tom Marshall (Edinburgh)
Pensions	Iain Talman (Glasgow)
Private client	Helen Stirling (Glasgow)

BISHOP & SEWELL

90 GREAT RUSSELL STREET, LONDON, WC1B 3RJ
Tel: (0171) 631 4141 **Fax:** (0171) 636 5369 **DX:** 278 CHANCERY LANE

The Firm: Established in 1979 to provide the range and expertise of services of a larger city practice with an emphasis on establishing a personal partner/client relationship. Clients include international banks, public and private companies, trusts, charities and high net-worth private clients. The firm is a general practice and its case load includes the following work: banking, insolvency, company/commercial (including franchising, mergers and acquisitions and management buy-outs), commercial and residential conveyancing, litigation (commercial, construction and general civil work), employment, trusts, family law, wills and probate, and agency work.

Senior partner:	Stephen Bishop
Number of partners:	6
Assistant solicitors:	3
Other fee-earners:	2

CONTACTS	
Commercial Litigation	T Tribius
Company/Commercial	J Sewell/R Williams
Conveyancing	S Bishop
Family/Private Client	M Gillman

BLACKADDER REID JOHNSTON

30 & 34 REFORM STREET, DUNDEE, DD1 1RJ
Tel: (01382) 229222 **Fax:** (01382) 201132 **DX:** DD2 DUNDEE

The Firm: Blackadder Reid Johnston is one of the largest firms in Tayside, offering the complete range of legal services. Each department has a team of experienced solicitors. Two of the partners are accredited employment law specialists.

Principal Areas of Work:

Private Client: (*Contact Partner:* Dennis Young). Provides a comprehensive estate and tax planning service, including in-house financial, accounting and taxation services. Services include trusts, executry, charity and Power of Attorney administration.

Commercial/corporate: (*Contact Partner:* Sandy Meiklejohn). In the corporate and commercial fields the firm advises all types of businesses on setting up, mergers, acquisitions and reconstructions. The firm's expertise in handling commercial property and security transactions is widely sought after, as is its licensing law unit.

Litigation: (*Contact Partner:* Lindsay Foulis). The firm handles employment and family law matters, personal injury and reparation claims, tribunal representation, criminal proceedings and a full range of commercial litigation and debt collection services.

Residential Property: (*Contact Partner:* Donald Hutcheson). The firm operates a successful Estate Agency and conveyancing service throughout its property shop and branch network, supported by its independent mortgage and insurance broking unit.

Other branch offices: Kirriemuir and Carnoustie.

Managing partner:	Donald Hutcheson
Senior partner:	Dennis Young
Number of partners:	13
Assistant solicitors:	9
Other fee-earners:	16

WORKLOADS	
Conveyancing	36%
Private client	21%
Litigation	16%
Commercial	13%
Financial services	11%
Other	3%

CONTACTS	
Private client	Dennis Young
Commercial	Sandy Meiklejohn
Litigation	Lindsay Foulis
Residential property	Donald Hutcheson

BLACKHURST PARKER & YATES 9 Cannon Street, Preston, PR1 3QD *Tel:* (01772) 253601 *Fax:* (01772) 202085 *DX:* 17113 Preston 1 *Ptnrs:* 5 *Asst solrs:* 6 *Other fee-earners:* 3

BLACKS Hanover House, 22 Clarendon Road, Leeds, LS2 9NZ *Tel:* (0113) 243 3311 *Fax:* (0113) 242 1703 *DX:* 26414 *Ptnrs:* 8 *Asst solrs:* 5 *Other fee-earners:* 7

BLAIR ALLISON & CO Fountain Court, Steelhouse Lane, Birmingham, B4 6EE *Tel:* (0121) 233 2904 *Fax:* (0121) 236 8913 *DX:* 23534 *Ptnrs:* 3 *Asst solrs:* 3 *Other fee-earners:* 1

BLAIR & BRYDEN 27 Union Street, Greenock, PA16 8DD *Tel:* (01475) 888777 *Fax:* (01475) 781836 *DX:* GR2 Greenock-1 *Ptnrs:* 15 *Asst solrs:* 12 *Other fee-earners:* 12

BLAKE LAPTHORN

NEW COURT, 1 BARNES WALLIS ROAD, SEGENSWORTH, FAREHAM, PO15 5UA
Tel: (01489) 579990 **Fax:** (01489) 579126 **DX:** 132290 FAREHAM 5

Blake Lapthorn is a major regional practice providing a complete legal service for both commercial and private clients.

Work for commercial clients is undertaken from our purpose built commercial law centre situated adjacent to the M27 between Portsmouth and Southampton and from our Southampton city centre office. Our commercial clients range from family-owned companies to multi-nationals located in Hampshire, West Sussex, East Dorset, South Wiltshire and beyond. Our North Harbour Office along the M27 corridor undertakes work for private clients from within the surrounding area ranging from tax and financial planning, wills and probate, matrimonial and family to criminal defence work.

Commercial: The firm's Commercial Department has developed expertise in a number of specialist areas including corporate finance, construction law, pensions, insolvency and information technology. The overall size of the department gives it the critical mass necessary to undertake the largest of jobs and the firm has a growing reputation for handling large commercial transactions. It acted for two of the train operating units in the British Rail privatisation. Other specialist areas include employment law, commercial and regulatory crime, licensing and corporate tax.

Commercial Property: The Commercial Property Department is one of the largest in the region and acts for a number of household names in connection with its property portfolio. The work ranges from routine volume work to multi million pound single transactions. The firm also has a substantial domestic conveyancing unit retained by private clients, banks and building societies.

Litigation: The firm's Litigation Department is one of the most substantial in the South outside London. It has particular skills in professional indemnity work and medical negligence and personal injury claims. It has a large and successful commercial litigation team and a volume debt collection practice. The firm also has a well regarded London agency practice.

Throughout our 125 year history Blake Lapthorn has always had its clients' interests to the fore. The firm is committed to employing and developing high quality staff supported with the latest information technology to meet our clients' needs.

Brochures describing the work that the firm undertakes are available upon request.

Senior partner:	David W. Russell
Number of partners:	42
Assistant solicitors:	80
Other fee-earners:	53

WORKLOADS	
Commercial/commercial conveyancing	41%
Civil litigation	35%
Private client	18%
Crime/matrimonial	6%

CONTACTS	
Banking	Kathryn Shimmin
Charity law	Colin Barlow
Civil litigation	David Higham
Company/ commercial	Caroline Williams
Company/ property	Carey Blake
Construction	Peter Barber
Criminal law	John Mitchell
Debt collection	Nicholas Poole
Education	Sarah Palmer
Employment	Max Craft
Environmental/ planning	Colin Barlow
Financial planning	David Russell
Information technology	Chris McClure
Insolvency	Nicholas Keitley
Licensing law	Walter Cha
Pension law	Graham Withers
Residential property	Michael Profit
Tax	Niall Murphy

BLAKEMORES Station Tower, Station Square, Coventry, CV1 2GR **Tel:** (01203) 525858 **Fax:** (01203) 228440 **DX:** 11228 Coventry **Ptnrs:** 12 **Asst solrs:** 11 **Other fee-earners:** 19 **Contact:** Mr. Gerard Whitehouse. *Other offices: Ashby, Birmingham, Leamington Spa, Stratford, Tetbury, Tamworth. General practice known for Commercial, PI, Property and Private Client work.*

WORKLOADS			
Property	26%	Litigation	14%
Family	13%	Private Client	10%
Insurance	7%		

BLAKESLEY RICE MACDONALD Gray Court, 99 Saltergate, Chesterfield, S40 1LD *Tel:* (01246) 555111 *Fax:* (01246) 271207 *DX:* 12358 *Ptnrs:* 8 *Other fee-earners:* 4

BLANDY & BLANDY

1 FRIAR ST, READING, RG1 1DA
Tel: (0118) 958 7111 **Fax:** (0118) 956 8220 **DX:** 4008 READING **Email:** LAW@BLANDY.CO.UK **Internet:** HTTP://WWW.BLANDY.CO.UK

The Firm: Founded in 1733, Blandy & Blandy is the oldest established legal practice in Reading. Despite its longevity, the firm is modern and progressive in outlook, whilst remaining friendly and approachable. The firm's work is organised into specialist departments providing a full range of legal services to both business and individual clients.

Principal Areas of Work:

Commercial Group: The firm's Commercial Group was established in 1993 as an "umbrella" for the firm's commercial services. Emphasis is placed on providing a practical and pro-active service and clients can expect a high degree of partner involvement.

Corporate and Commercial: The department deals with a wide range of non-contentious commercial work and has particular expertise in the area of mergers and acquisitions and other corporate transactional work, as well as in IT and intellectual property law. All aspects of employment law, both contentious and non-contentious are dealt with. One of the partners sits as a part-time chairman of industrial tribunals and the firm is accordingly well placed to advise on industrial disputes and TUPE issues.

Litigation: The firm has built a particularly strong reputation for litigation. Particular specialisms have been developed in relation to insurance litigation and betting, gaming and liquor licensing and the department is regularly involved in heavy licensing work. A computerised debt collection service is offered.

Commercial Property: All aspects of commercial conveyancing work are handled including landlord and tenant, development and planning.

Private Client Group: The firm has an enviable reputation for its private client work and its clients range from individuals to large landed estates.

Trusts, probate and tax planning: The department's specialisms include trusts and tax planning work as well as the preparation of wills and probate. The firm has particular expertise in handling work for landed estates.

Conveyancing: The department's workload includes estate development, planning matters, work for housing associations as well as routine residential conveyancing.

Family Law: The firm has an extensive and highly regarded matrimonial and family law practice. The firm is able to offer the services of trained mediators and has expertise in child-care and child support work.

Civil litigation: A full range of civil litigation work is dealt with including personal injury claims, probate litigation and bankruptcy. The firm holds a legal aid franchise and legal aid is available in appropriate cases.

Recruitment & Training: The firm attaches great importance to recruitment and training. Applications in writing, with CV, to Philip Tranter.

Further information on the firm can be found on its website: http://www.blandy.co.uk

Senior partner:	R.G. Griffiths
Number of partners:	11
Assistant solicitors:	8
Other fee-earners:	13

WORKLOADS	
Corporate & Commercial	23%
Family	19%
Private Client	19%
Residential Property	16%
Litigation	14%
Commercial Property	9%

CONTACTS	
Child care	Brenda Long
Commercial property	Kate Taylor
Corporate & commercial	Philip Tranter
Employment	Richard Griffiths
Family	Andrew Don
Intellectual Property	Philip Tranter
Licensing	Sue Dowling
Litigation	Philip D'Arcy
Personal injury	Marie de Viell
Private client	Graham Benwell

BLASER MILLS WINTER TAYLORS Park House, 31 London Road, High Wycombe, HP11 1BZ *Tel:* (01494) 450171 *Fax:* (01494) 441815 *DX:* 4429 High Wycombe *Ptnrs:* 18 *Asst solrs:* 23 *Other fee-earners:* 10

BLICK & CO Sophia House, 32-35 Featherstone Street, London, EC1Y 8QX **Tel:** (0171) 253 6250 **Fax:** (0171) 251 3519 **Ptnrs:** 7 **Asst solrs:** 2 **Other fee-earners:** 1 **Contact:** Mr Robert Blick *Highly regarded commercial practice with international bias with departments specialising in maritime and family law and offering specialist services to commercial clients.*

WORKLOADS			
Shipping	40%	Family law	30%
Company	20%	Commercial and Property	
Litigation etc	10%		

BLYTHE LIGGINS

EDMUND HOUSE, RUGBY ROAD, LEAMINGTON SPA, CV32 6EL
Tel: (01926) 831231 **Fax:** (01926) 831331 **DX:** 11872 **Email:** BLYTHELIGGINS.CO.UK

The Firm: Blythe Liggins prides itself on its progressive approach, combining efficiency with professional excellence and strong, clear management. The service is personal and the partners place emphasis on getting to know their clients individually and their businesses. The firm offers expertise in all major areas of the law.

Principal Areas of Work:

Company and Commercial: *(Contact Partner:*David Lester). *Work includes:* Acquisitions and disposals, company formation and business planning, partnerships, insolvency and debt collection, licensing and competition law.

Commercial Litigation: *(Contact Partner:*Richard Thornton). *Work includes:* High Court and County Court litigation, including employment law, personal injury, insurance, consumer law, intellectual property and building disputes.

Commercial and Residential Property: *(Contact Partner:*Patrick Riley). *Work includes:* Town and country planning, commercial and domestic property, purchase and sale advice, and landlord and tenant matters.

Private Client: *(Contact Partner:*Paul Waterworth). *Work includes:* Matrimonial and family law, tax and financial planning and pensions, estate planning, and wills, probates and trusts.

Nature of Clientele: The firm acts for large companies, multinationals, finance houses, educational establishments, charities, small businesses and private individuals.

Managing partner:	J.M. Labrum
Senior partner:	P.J. Riley
Number of partners:	11
Assistant solicitors:	4
Other fee-earners:	9

WORKLOADS	
Litigation	40%
Property	30%
Company & commercial	20%
Private client	10%

CONTACTS	
Civil litigation	Richard Thornton
Commercial property	Patrick Riley
Company/ commercial	David Lester
Domestic property	John Labrum
Employment	Richard Moon
Family litigation	Paul Waterworth
Private client	Donald Hunter

BOBBETTS MACKAN

17 BERKELEY SQUARE, CLIFTON, BRISTOL, BS8 1HB
Tel: (0117) 929 9001 **Fax:** (0117) 922 5697 **DX:** 37011 CLIFTON (BRISTOL)

The Firm: Committed to providing quality, independent, efficient and cost-effective legal services. Provides a contemporary service based upon an established reputation. Organised in specialist teams, it aims to ensure that the service offered meets the clients' needs, be they "lay clients" or referral and agency work for the profession. Advocacy services, including higher courts, are available. Member of LawGroup UK – an independent grouping of quality law firms subject to an annual, external quality audit.

Principal Areas of Work: Civil Litigation including personal injury, employment, medical and professional negligence with expertise in Judicial Review and Public Law. Family & Childcare including divorce, complex financial matters and children. Criminal Defence including fraud and Courts Martial. General Practice including conveyancing, leasing and business advice.

Agency Work: Civil Litigation: *(Contact John Peake).* Criminal defence: *Contact Tony Miles.* Family and Childcare: *(Contact Sally Mitchell).*

Managing partner:	Anthony Miles
Senior partner:	Anthony Grove
Number of partners:	5
Assistant solicitors:	15
Other fee-earners:	19

WORKLOADS	
Civil litigation	35%
Criminal defence	35%
Matrimonial, care, children	20%
Non-contentious	10%

CONTACTS	
Criminal Defence	Anthony Miles
Employment	Kevin Wood
Family & Childcare	Sally Mitchell
Non-contentious	Anthony Grove
Personal Injury	John Peake

BOGUE AND MCNULTY 3 Carlisle Gardens, BT14 6AT *Tel:* (01232) 351502 *Fax:* (01232) 742185

BOLITHO WAY 13/18 Kings Terrace, Portsmouth, PO5 3AL **Tel:** (01705) 820747 **Fax:** (01705) 862831 **DX:** 2205 Portsmouth 1 **Email:** office@bolithoway.com **Ptnrs:** 6 **Asst solrs:** 4 **Other fee-earners:** 2 **Contact:** Mr J Cregan *Focuses on litigation, company, commercial and intellectual property.*

WORKLOADS			
Matrimonial/Family/Child Care			20%
Crime	20%	Company/commercial	17%
Civil/Commercial litigation	15%	Personal injury	10%
Private client	10%	Intellectual property	8%

BOLT BURDON

16 THEBERTON STREET, ISLINGTON, LONDON, N1 0QX
Tel: (0171) 288 4700 **Fax:** (0171) 288 4701 **DX:** 122237 UPPER ISLINGTON **Email:** BOLTBURDON@BOLTBURDON.CO.UK

1 PROVIDENCE PLACE, ISLINGTON, LONDON, N1 0NT
Tel: (0171) 288 4800 **Fax:** (0171) 288 4801 **DX:** 122237 UPPER ISLINGTON **Email:** BOLTBURDON@BOLTBURDON.CO.UK

The Firm: Bolt Burdon is a modern professional business committed to providing swift practical advice and the highest levels of service.

Principal Areas of Work:

Business Clients: Bolt Burdon understands its clients' business needs and provides a complete – and above all – pro-active business service. The Firm has particular expertise in commercial property, commercial litigation and partnership disputes and formations.

Personal Clients: A cradle to grave service including financial services (pensions, investments, mortgages – the Firm has six qualified IFAs), wills, tax planning, matrimonial and residential conveyancing.

Personal Injury, Medical Negligence, Professional Negligence:
Three specialist teams acting for plaintiffs. The Firm has members of personal injury and medical negligence specialist panels and a legal aid franchise.

Managing partner:	Lynne Burdon
Number of partners:	10
Assistant solicitors:	27
Other fee-earners:	20

INVESTOR IN PEOPLE

BONAR MACKENZIE WS

9 HILL STREET, EDINBURGH, EH2 3JT
Tel: (0131) 225 8371 **Fax:** (0131) 225 2048/9065 **DX:** 7 EDINBURGH

The Firm: One of Scotland's longest established firms providing a full range of legal services with an emphasis on personal attention and a high level of direct partner involvement. The firm has an impressive client base, acting for various well known financial institutions, High Street retailers and other PLCs. The firm is committed to providing a high quality professional service at competitive fee levels and is always pleased to meet prospective clients to discuss their requirements and terms of engagement.

The firm is highly regarded for its expertise and efficiency in Debt Recovery and Repossessions having gained considerable experience acting for various Banks and Building Societies for many years.

Senior partner:	Anthony Petrie
Number of partners:	12
Assistant solicitors:	4
Other fee-earners:	7

CONTACTS	
Commercial Conveyancing	Anthony Petrie
Debt Recovery	Robert Clephane
Estate Agency	Stephen Murray
Residential Conveyancing	Stephen Murray
Wills & Trust	Alistair Bowman

BOND PEARCE

BRISTOL BRIDGE HOUSE, REDCLIFF STREET, BRISTOL, BS1 6BJ
Tel: (0117) 929 9197 **Fax:** (0117) 929 9198 **Email:** XVST@BONDPEARCE.COM

DARWIN HOUSE, SOUTHERNHAY GARDENS, EXETER, EX1 1LA
Tel: (01392) 211 185 **Fax:** (01392) 435 543 **DX:** 8321 EXETER **Email:** XDJG@BONDPEARCE.COM

BALLARD HOUSE, WEST HOE ROAD, PLYMOUTH, PL1 3AE
Tel: (01752) 266 633 **Fax:** (01752) 225 350 **DX:** 8251 PLYMOUTH **Email:** XJET@BONDPEARCE.COM **Internet:** WWW.BONDPEARCE.COM

KINGS PARK ROAD, SOUTHAMPTON, SO15 2UF
Tel: (01703) 632 211 **Fax:** (01703) 720 700 **DX:** 38517 SOUTHAMPTON 3 **Email:** AJA@BONDPEARCE.COM

The Firm: Already recognised as a major commercial player in southern England, its merger on 1 May 1998 with leading Southampton law firm Hepherd Winstanley & Pugh, and its new Bristol office positions Bond Pearce as one of the country's top ten regional law firms.

Commercially aware, progressive and innovative, the firm's culture places strong emphasis on tailoring its services to meet individual client requirements. Bond Pearce is amongst the largest law firms nationally to have met the stringent demands of ISO9001 and is well advanced towards achieving Investors in People accreditation. Equally important is Bond Pearce's investment in the development of new specialisations, practice areas and skills for all staff and not least communications – its services are provided within the framework of the very latest in office facilities and modern technology.

Whilst the firm's offices are spread across southern England, Bond Pearce acts on behalf of commercial and institutional clients throughout the UK. A national client base enhanced through the firm's commitment to providing a specialist service across a wide range of sectors including: Aviation, Construction, Education, Regulatory Services, Health, Insolvency, Insurance, Lenders and Venture Capitalists, Retail, Shipping, Waste and Energy.

Internationally, Bond Pearce is generating an increasing volume of cross-border work through overseas clients and contacts.

Principal Areas of Work: Litigation remains an important part of the practice and Bond Pearce is particularly well known for its work in the fields of professional indemnity, insurance, personal injury, corporate recovery, construction law, employment, landlord & tenant, insolvency and intellectual property. The key litigation strength brought in from the merger is a litigation team that acts for national and local retailers, advising in areas such as customer complaints, consumer credit, security issues, employment matters, food law, licensing, trading standards and Sunday trading. This team has acted in a number of cross border matters and actions in the European Court of Justice. Bond Pearce accepts all types of agency work and provides mediation and other ADR services in association with CEDR and the ADR Group. The firm established the South West Centre for Mediation in 1996.

The Commercial Property Group encompasses a variety of property work, especially retail, commercial and industrial park development, dealing with a wide range of investment, development, management and construction issues. The firm's strong planning and environmental unit remains at the forefront of work relating to renewable energy and waste management. The Corporate Group has built its reputation acting for management teams, lending institutions and investors across southern England in MBOs, MBIs, IBIs, acquisitions, disposals and mergers. Commercial work is handled by a specialist team advising on the full spectrum of commercial agreements, often with an international element. Work includes advice on intellectual property rights, research and development agreements, licensing, joint ventures and competition law. Bond Pearce recognises that commercial clients need much more than just legal advice – the firm works closely with clients, providing a level of service, commitment and practical understanding one would expect from an in-house legal team.

The Corporate Recovery and Banking Team, including three licensed insolvency practitioners, has established a national reputation acting for financial institutions and insolvency practitioners.

The Personal Legal Services Group handles the personal legal affairs of the firm's clients including wills, trusts, tax advice, powers of attorney, conveyancing, family and matrimonial law.

Contact Partners:	Bristol:	Victor Tettmar
	Exeter:	David Gunn
	Plymouth:	Julian Trahair
	Southampton:	Tony Askham
Number of Partners:		53
Assistant Solicitors:		92
Other Fee-earners:		69

WORKLOADS	
Litigation	50%
Commercial, Banking & Insolvency	22%
Property	20%
Personal Legal Services	8%

CONTACTS	
Banking & Insolvency	Victor Tettmar
Construction	Christine Hanley
Corporate Finance, Commercial & Tax	Roger Acock
Employment	Simon Richardson/Nikki Duncan
Insurance & Professional Indemnity	Erik Salomonsen
Intellectual Property	Tom Phipps/Julian Hamblin
International	Nick Page
Litigation	Tony Askham
Mediation & ADR	Andrew Tobey
Personal Injury	Mark Thompson
Personal Legal Services	Jonathan Holyhead
Property, Planning & Environment	David Gunn
Regulatory Services & Pensions	Geoffrey Clarkson
Shipping	Nick Page

Bond Pearce
Incorporating Hepherd Winstanley & Pugh

BOODLE HATFIELD

61 BROOK STREET, LONDON, W1Y 2BL
Tel: (0171) 629 7411 **Fax:** (0171) 629 2621 **DX:** 53

The Firm: Founded over 275 years ago, Boodle Hatfield has grown into a leading Central London commercial and private client practice, with a second office in Oxford. Its main departments are property, tax and financial planning, corporate and litigation, although some activities – such as employment law – are cross-departmental. The firm aims to establish close working relationships with its clients, to provide practical, expert and cost-effective advice and to deliver an excellent, personal service.

Principal Areas of Work:

Property: The department has extensive experience in commercial and residential property work, having been involved in town centre, business park and leisure developments as well as large-scale urban estate transactions and associated landlord and tenant matters. Its capabilities include town and country planning, construction and environmental law. It acts for developers, owners, funders, occupiers and UK-based and international investors.

Tax and Financial Planning: The department has a leading reputation for its expertise in tax planning for large complex estates, private companies and high net worth individuals and families, often in an international context. This includes inheritance, capital gains and income tax planning, advice on VAT, the establishment of UK and overseas trusts and corporate structures, contentious trusts and probate, pensions and charity work.

Corporate: The department advises on start-ups (including companies establishing themselves in the UK), mergers, acquisitions and disposals, management buyouts and buy-ins, joint ventures, banking, investment agreements, listings and the issue of securities, commercial agreements (including computer contracts), employment law and immigration. Its specialist Anglo-German practice is headed by a bilingual, dual-qualified English lawyer.

Litigation: The department is active in all kinds of commercial matters, with particular knowledge of agrochemical issues and also has notable experience in property and construction litigation; employment; and in matrimonial and family law.

International Connections: Much work has an international element, especially in North America, Germany and France, where the firm has well-established links with substantial firms.

Recruitment and Training: The firm has openings for assistant solicitors in each department. Four or five trainees are recruited per year; some spend six months on secondment to ICI, Shell International or Llewelyn Zietman (the firm's specialist Intellectual Property associate). Application forms are available from the Recruitment Administrator.

Other Office: 6 Worcester Street, Oxford OX1 2BX Tel: (01865) 790744 Fax: (01865) 798764 DX: 4329 Oxford

Opened in 1994, the Oxford office now has 6 resident partners and has recently doubled its office space to meet increased demand. It specialises presently in private client work encompassing tax, trusts and financial planning, wills and probate; charities; pensions; and in commercial, agricultural, educational and residential property. All other services are available on demand.

Senior partner:	Peter Scoble
Number of partners:	25
Assistant solicitors:	16
Other fee-earners:	17

CONTACTS	
Anglo-German service	Chris Putt
Commercial Litigation	Simon Fitzpatrick
Commercial Property	Tim Manning (London)
	Peter Webber (Oxford)
Construction	Howard Russell
Corporate	Andrew Drake
Employment	Russell Brimelow
Environment	Edward Sutherland
Family	Michael Tulloch
	Vivien Gifford
Private Client, Trusts	Richard Moyse (London)
	Sue Laing (Oxford)
Property Litigation	Michael Tulloch
Tax	Kate Howe (London
	Alan Ciechan (Oxford)
Town & Country Planning	Lucy Slater

BOODLE

HATFIELD

BORLAND MONTGOMERIE KEYDEN Apsley House, 29 Wellington Street, Glasgow, G2 6JA *Tel:* (0141) 221 8004 *Fax:* (0141) 221 8088 *DX:* 55 Glasgow *Ptnrs:* 13 *Asst solrs:* 5 *Other fee-earners:* 6

BOWER & BAILEY Anchor House, 269 Banbury Road, Summertown, Oxford, OX2 7JF *Tel:* (01865) 311133 *Fax:* (01865) 311722 *DX:* 40669 Summertown *Ptnrs:* 16 *Asst solrs:* 21 *Other fee-earners:* 3

BOWER COTTON

36 WHITEFRIARS STREET, LONDON, EC4Y 8BH
Tel: (0171) 353 3040 **Fax:** (0171) 583 2869 **DX:** 94 LONDON

The Firm: founded in 1818, this is a commercially orientated practice with a relatively young partnership. It provides an extensive range of legal services including all aspects of company/ commercial work such as acquisitions and disposals, joint ventures, corporate tax, company reconstructions, licensing, franchising, aviation and employment. The firm has a large number of overseas based commercial clients. The firm specialises in energy with special emphasis on the retail petrol industry. Bower Cotton also provides advice on litigation, insolvency, all forms of property issues plus family and private client matters.

Foreign Connections: the firm has established links with Switzerland, Spain, France and the USA.

Foreign Languages: French and Spanish.

Recruitment and Training: applications should be addressed to Robert Perrin. The firm provides a full programme of in-house continuing legal education.

Managing partner:	**Guy Vincent**
Senior partner:	**Paul Simms**
Number of partners:	8
Assistant solicitors:	4
Other fee-earners:	5

WORKLOADS	
Commercial Property	29%
Company/ commercial	25%
Private client and other	24%
Litigation	22%

CONTACTS	
Company/ commercial	Paul Simms
Employment	Guy Vincent
Family	Michael Conlon
Litigation	Andrew Couch
Private client	Paul Shaerf
Property	Michael Parker

BOYCE HATTON 12 Tor Hill Rd, Castle Circus, Torquay, TQ2 5RB *Tel:* (01803) 295343 *Fax:* (01803) 214876 *DX:* 59000 *Ptnrs:* 6 *Asst solrs:* 1 *Other fee-earners:* 17

BOYDS

THISTLE HOUSE, 146 WEST REGENT STREET, GLASGOW, G2 2RZ
Tel: (0141) 221 8251 **Fax:** (0141) 226 4799 **DX:** 120 GLASGOW **Email:** MAIL@BOYDSLAW.COM **Internet:** WWW.BOYDSLAW.COM

The Firm: Boyds Solicitors are very much a part of the business scene in Glasgow. Their client range runs from some substantial companies which are household names through to smaller businesses run by sole traders and entrepreneurs. They are committed to providing quality commercial advice thereby satisfying their clients. International contacts and trade are a growing source of the business with the firm being a member of the Law Exchange International.

Principal Areas of Work:

Commercial Property: Commercial leases, purchases and sales, development and management work, security work.

Corporate: Mergers and acquisitions, buy outs, buy ins, corporate finance, commercial contracts and insolvency advice.

Litigation: Employment, construction disputes, landlord tenant disputes, repossession work, general contractual disputes, debt recovery and matrimonial.

IT Law and IP Law: Contractual issues, copyright, design disputes, advice on the internet.

Private Client: Independent financial advice (also provided to corporate clients) on pensions, key man etc. and house purchase and sales with relevant mortgage advice.

Managing partner:	**Robert Gall**
Senior partner:	**David Boyce**
Number of partners:	6
Assistant solicitors:	10

WORKLOADS	
Commercial property development/funding	50%
Corporate/ commercial	20%
Litigation	20%
Private client	10%

CONTACTS	
Commercial Property	David Boyce
Corporate	John McMuldroch
IT & IP Law	John McMuldroch
Litigation	Robert Gall
Private client	Lynn Sweeney

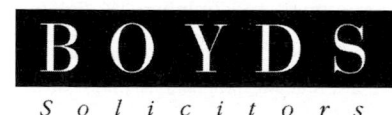

BOYES TURNER & BURROWS

10 DUKE ST, READING, RG1 4RX
Tel: (0118) 959 7711 **Fax:** (0118) 957 3257 **DX:** 54741 READING 2 **Email:** BTB@COMPUSERVE.COM **Internet:** WWW.BTB-SOLICITORS.CO.UK

The Firm: Boyes Turner & Burrows is a leading Thames Valley firm which successfully combines high quality commercial and individual client services. It occupies modern air-conditioned offices in Reading, is fully computerised and employs over 80 staff. The firm is committed to providing fast, effective advice.

Principal Areas of Work:

Banking and Insolvency: Headed by a LIP the firm acts for all the major insolvency practices as well as clearing banks and other financial institutions in both corporate and personal insolvency and securities work.

Corporate/Commercial: The firm acts for many substantial businesses based in the Thames Valley including UK subsidiaries of multi-nationals. Advice includes business formation, acquisitions & disposals, partnerships and joint ventures, inward investment and corporate restructuring, general business law advice, commercial and trading agreements including distribution and licensing, competition law, company secretarial work.

Debt Collection: Fully computerised system providing competitive rates and handling bulk recoveries for major trading companies as well as financial institutions.

Employment: Preparation of employment contracts, advice on disciplinary issues, industrial tribunal representation, restraint of trade, wrongful dismissal, sex and race discrimination.

Family: Divorce and separation, financial provision, children, emergency procedures (members of SFLA).

Intellectual Property: Ownership and exploitation of IPR, licensing, IPR disputes, computer contracts (software and hardware), product liability. Clients include engineering, electronics and computer companies as well as software houses.

Litigation: Contract disputes, shareholder and partnership disputes, negligence claims, property disputes, mortgage repossessions, landlord and tenant. Agency work undertaken.

Medical Negligence: A specialist team acts exclusively for the victims of medical accidents (AVMA and Law Society referral solicitors, members APIL)

Personal injury: RTAs; work related injuries, CICB/A, Personal Injury Panel; SIA referral panel and Headway. Maximum severity claims (members APIL and Accident Line).

Private Client: Wills, trusts, probate, personal tax planning and residential conveyancing.

Property: Sales and leases of commercial property, commercial and residential development projects, commercial lending, landlord and tenant.

Planning: Planning advice for property development projects as well as appeals and planning enforcement.

Nature of Clientele: The firm acts for a number of major Thames Valley based businesses across a broad spectrum of activity, but with strong connections in the hi-tech, electronics and engineering sectors. It also acts for banks, public authorities as well as start-ups and newly established subsidiaries of foreign parents.

Boyes Turner & Burrows has steadily grown across the whole range of its practice and has doubled its number of lawyers over the past five years. It has a strong commitment to client satisfaction.

Recruitment and Training: The firm restricts the number of trainee solicitors recruited to ensure that the best training is given to those taken on every year. The firm takes its training responsibilities seriously, for both trainee solicitors and assistant solicitors, and operates an in-house training programme. (*Staff Partner:* Adrian Desmond. *Training Partner:* Michael Farrier).

Senior partner:	Peter Daniel
Number of partners:	12
Assistant solicitors:	17
Other fee-earners:	15

WORKLOADS	
Corporate/Commercial (including insolvency)	25%
Commercial Property and Planning	20%
Litigation (including employment)	20%
Medical Negligence/Personal Injury	20%
Private Client	10%
Family	5%

CONTACTS	
Banking and insolvency	Chris Branson
Commercial	Bill Gornall-King
Corporate	Roy Butler
Debt Collection	Mike Robinson
Employment	Michael Farrier
Intellectual property/IT	Bill Gornall-King
Litigation	Mike Robinson
Marketing	Georgina Froud
Medical negligence	Adrian Desmond and Susan Brown
Partnership Secretary	John Brunnen
Personal injury	Nicola Heales
Private client	Ashley Wilkin
Property	Peter Daniel
Town and country planning	Anthony Cooley

B.P. COLLINS & CO

COLLINS HOUSE, 32-38 STATION RD, GERRARDS CROSS, SL9 8EL
Tel: (01753) 889995 **Fax:** (01753) 889851 **DX:** 40256 GERRARDS CROSS

The Firm: B.P. Collins & Co. was established in 1965, and has expanded significantly to become one of the largest and best known legal practices at the London end of the M4/ M40 corridors. At its main office in Gerrards Cross, the emphasis is on commercial work, with particular strengths being company/ commercial work of all types and including information technology, commercial property and litigation.

Principal Areas of Work at Gerrards Cross Office:

Company/ Commercial: (*Contact Partner:*David Stanning. *5 Partners*). The activities of the company/commercial department cover all aspects of business life and include substantial company acquisitions and disposals, management buy-outs, information technology/IP, business transfers, shareholders' agreements, agency, distribution and franchise agreements and employment matters. Colin Cork is the specialist insolvency partner and James Allen is the specialist IT partner.

Litigation: (*Contact Partner:*Nicholas Hallchurch. *4 Partners*). *Work includes:*Corporate disputes, information technology matters, entertainment, construction and intellectual property disputes. The firm also has an established reputation for employment and personal injury work.

Commercial Property: (*Contact Partner:*Justin Samuel. *7 Partners*). The property department handles the sale, purchase and leasing of all types of commercial property, including offices, shops, factories, warehouses, hotels and nursing homes. It also deals with landlord and tenant legislation, (residential, business or agricultural) planning matters, and acts for developer clients in relation to residential projects. One partner specialises in agricultural matters.

Private Client: *(Contact Partner:*David Wilkinson. *1 Partner*). Conveyancing, probate, wills, trusts and tax planning services are offered to the private client. Members of S.T.E.P.

Other Offices: Beaconsfield and Chalfont St. Peter.

Senior partner:	Brian Collins
Number of partners:	14
Assistant solicitors:	11
Other fee-earners:	9

WORKLOADS	
Commercial property	35%
Company and commercial	20%
Litigation	20%
Private client	10%
Residential conveyancing	10%
Matrimonial	5%

CONTACTS	
Company and commercial	David Stanning
Litigation	Nick Hallchurch
Commercial property	Justin Samuel
Matrimonial	Sue Andrews
Private client	David Wilkinson
Residential conveyancing	Mike Arundel

BRABNER HOLDEN BANKS WILSON

1 DALE ST, LIVERPOOL, L2 2ET
Tel: (0151) 236 5821 **Fax:** (0151) 227 3185 **DX:** 14118 LIVERPOOL **Email:** BRABNERHOLDEN@GCONNECT.COM
Internet: HTTP://WWW.RUDEX2.COM/BRABNER-HOLDEN.HTML

6-8 CHAPEL STREET, PRESTON, PR1 8AN
Tel: (01772) 823921 **Fax:** (01772) 201918 **DX:** 17118

The Firm: One of the top Northwest firms, Brabner Holden Banks Wilson was formed in 1990 by the merger of Brabner Holden in Liverpool and Banks Wilson in Preston, bringing together the experience, talent and prestige gained by the two firms over their 200+ year histories. Brabner Holden Banks Wilson is fully committed to a client-centred approach. Each of their retained clients, from large Plcs to private individuals, is assigned a Client Relationship Manager reponsible for delivering a prompt, efficient and friendly service. The firm acts throughout the UK for public and private companies, local and national institutions, local authorities, housing associations, brewers, newspapers and radio clients.

Principal Areas of Work:

Corporate: Highly regarded for all corporate work, the firm advises on acquisitions, disposals, buy-outs, buy-ins, demergers, venture capital, joint ventures, corporate finance, private finance for housing associations, distributorships, agencies and franchising. The firm has a growing list of cutting-edge multimedia clients.

Commercial and Agricultural Property: The department has expertise in handling acquisitions, leases, development and sales. Universally recognised as the leading firm in the North for housing association work, Brabner Holden Banks Wilson also acts for local authorities and a number of breweries both locally and nationally.

Litigation: The litigation team are renowned for their expertise in employment law, media and defamation work, as well as contractual disputes, construction litigation, intellectual property actions, landlord and tenant and competition law. The department also has a national specialism in environmental protester legislation. Brabner Holden Banks Wilson operates a computerised debt collection service.

Private Client: Brabner Holden Banks Wilson provide tax planning, trust administration, probate and conveyancing advice to an impressive base of high net-worth clients. The firm also has a strong reputation as a charity law practice.

Managing partner:	Michael Brabner
Senior partner:	Lawrence Holden
Number of partners:	18
Assistant solicitors:	26
Other fee-earners:	17

WORKLOADS	
Corporate	26%
Probate & trust/ tax planning	21%
Private client property & litigation	19%
Commercial property	18%
Commercial litigation	16%

CONTACTS	
Commercial litigation	Amanda Webster, Andy Cross
Commercial property	Ross Shine, Keith Housley
Corporate	Tony Harper, Mike Livesey
Employment	Andy Cross
Housing assocs & charities	Lawrence Holden
Intellectual property	John Schorah
Media & defamation	Mark Manley
Private client	Mark Feeny, George Erdozain

BRABNER
HOLDEN
BANKS
WILSON

SOLICITORS

Continues overleaf

Foreign Connections: The firm is a member of Eurolegal, a network of law firms providing access to specialist legal advice across the European Community.

Recruitment & Training: Recruiting three trainee solicitors annually, the firm is fully commited to a comprehensive training programme for all its staff. Every employee has a Quality Culture card, identifying the key points in their strategy for delivering exceptional quality. Brabner Holden Banks Wilson was the first legal practice on Merseyside and one of the first in Britain to achieve the prestigious Investor In People award.

BRABY & WALLER (DEBT RECOVERY DIVISION OF IRWIN MITCHELL SOLICITORS)

48-50 ST. JOHN ST, LONDON, EC1M 4DP
Tel: (0171) 250 1884 **Fax:** (0171) 490 1416 **DX:** 87 CH.LN. **Email:** BRABY&WALLER@IRWINMITCHELL.CO.UK
Internet: WWW.BRABYWALLER.CO.UK

The Firm: Braby & Waller was founded in the 19th century and developed as a City of London commercial practice with particularly close connections in the building materials, manufacturing, finance and supply industries. The firm merged with Irwin Mitchell in May 1998 and has adopted the Irwin Mitchell name for corporate work. The Braby & Waller name has been retained to launch a new national debt recovery service building on the firm's expertise and reputation in this area.

Principal Areas of Work: As noted above the Braby & Waller name will now be associated with national debt recovery work on a national and international basis.

Debt Recovery: (*Contact:* Barry Hogg, London; Stephen Hunter, Sheffield). The Braby & Waller debt recovery department has historically been one of the largest in London and is well respected for the quality of its work. Following the merger of the practice with Irwin Mitchell this service has been expanded with the inclusion of a department based in Sheffield enabling the firm to offer even more resource in this area. The firm acts for major national and international manufacturers, distributors, communications providers lenders and professional firms.

BRACHERS

SOMERFIELD HOUSE, 59 LONDON ROAD, MAIDSTONE, KENT ME16 8JH
Tel: (01622) 690691 **Fax:** (01622) 681430 **DX:** 4806 MAIDSTONE 1 **Email:** NAME@BRACHERS.CO.UK **Internet:** HTTP://WWW.BRACHERS.CO.UK

The Firm: Brachers is a major regional firm with an established London office at 12 New Fetter Lane, EC4, and a subsidiary multi lingual credit management operation. It has developed a substantial practice in the healthcare sector reflected in its NHSCA panel appointment, employment, both defendant and plaintiff insurance work, debt recovery and insolvency and others. From this has sprung a wider but closely networked corporate finance and commercial practice for which the firm has recruited specialists from the City.

The firm retains close links with Kent's agricultural community and meets a need for services in agricultural law.

As befits a firm more than 100 years old, it has a well established private client department which is focused on tax and trust work. This is supported by a successful investment department which has been appointed as a share shop in several privatisations and maintains City links relevant to the firm's company and corporate finance work.

Managing partner:	Geoffrey G. Dearing
Number of partners:	19
Assistant solicitors:	26
Other fee-earners:	34

CONTACTS	
Company/Commercial	Stuart Butler-Gallie
Debt collection and Insolvency	Geoffrey Dearing
Litigation	John Sheath
Private Client and Financial Services	Simon Palmer
Property and Planning	Geoffrey Burr

BRADLEYS 19 Castle St, Dover, CT16 1PU *Tel:* (01304) 204080 *Fax:* (01304) 215092 *DX:* 6300 Dover *Ptnrs:* 7 *Asst solrs:* 2 *Other fee-earners:* 10

BRECHIN TINDAL OATTS

48 ST. VINCENT STREET, GLASGOW, G2 5HS
Tel: (0141) 221 8012 **Fax:** (0141) 221 7803 **DX:** 96 GLASGOW

The Firm: Brechin Tindal Oatts was created on 1st February 1997 on the merger of two prominent Glasgow law firms, to advise on a wide range of commercial and corporate matters. Brechin Tindal Oatts have particular expertise in insurance litigation (the firm's membership of Insurolaw – European Insurance Lawyers Group – allows access to international expertise) and in employment law; the firm recently launched the Employment Law Consultancy, which provides a specialist employment law service to the legal and other professions. In addition, the firm has a wealth of expertise in advising Housing Associations and Co-operatives, large and small. Niche specialisms are being developed in charity law and timeshare.

Principal Areas of Work:

Corporate: (*Contact:* Stephen MacGregor). The firm advises on all aspects of corporate law including company formations, acquisitions, re-structuring and disposal, business start up/buy out, banking and finance, commercial contracts, partnerships, franchising, service contracts and intellectual property.

Commercial property: (*Contact:* Alan Borthwick). A range of commercial property work is undertaken including property development, property investment, leasing (landlord and tenant), acquisitions and disposals, social housing, farms and estates, hotels and leisure, commercial renting, securities and planning.

Litigation: (*Contact:* Dorothy Hatfield). The firm undertakes a wide range of civil and commercial litigation and has an Edinburgh office primarily servicing court of session work. The firm advises many leading insurers, and has a particular specialty in professional indemnity insurance. In addition, the litigation department deals with contractual disputes, product liability actions, licensing, debt recovery, insolvency and corporate recovery work. The firm also deals with family law matters and offers a mediation service in this area.

Private client: (*Contact:* Susan Lang). A comprehensive service is provided for private clients including residential conveyancing, bulk employee relocation, personal investments, tax and financial advice, wills, trust and executry work.

Foreign Languages: Spanish, French, German.

International Connections: Through membership of Insurolaw, the firm has associations with law firms in most European jurisdictions.

Managing partner:	W.S. Young
Number of partners:	15
Assistant solicitors:	14
Other fee-earners:	13

BREEZE & WYLES 114 Fore Street, Hertford, SG14 1AG **Tel:** (01992) 558411 **Fax:** (01992) 582834 **DX:** 57901 Hertford **Ptnrs:** 7 **Asst solrs:** 6 **Other fee-earners:** 6 **Contact:** J.H.A. Williams *Known for commercial and domestic conveyancing, the firm handles litigation (especially personal injury), probate, employment and planning law. Progressive firm with four offices.*

WORKLOADS	
Domestic conveyancing	44%
Litigation – general/ family	29%
Commercial/ company conveyancing	12%
Probate wills	11%
Planning	4%

BREMNER SONS & CORLETT 1 Crosshall Street, Liverpool, L1 6DH *Tel:* (0151) 227 1301 *Fax:* (0151) 227 1300 *DX:* 14119 Liverpool 1 *Ptnrs:* 10 *Asst solrs:* 2 *Other fee-earners:* 7

BRENDAN KEARNEY KELLY & CO 4 Clarendon Street, Derry, BT48 7EX *Tel:* (01504) 266935 *Fax:* (01504) 371845 *Ptnrs:* 5 *Asst solrs:* 1 *Other fee-earners:* 1

BRETHERTON PRICE ELGOODS

123 PROMENADE, CHELTENHAM, GL50 1NW
Tel: (01242) 224433 **Fax:** (01242) 574285 **DX:** 7403 CHELTENHAM 1 **Email:** BPE@BPE.CO.UK

The Firm: Formed in 1989 by the merger of two strong commercial practices, Bretherton Price Elgoods serves a wide range of business, corporate and institutional clients locally and nationally through its three divisions:

Corporate & Commercial Services: (*Contact Partner:* John Workman). The practice advises on all commercial matters, including corporate finance, AIM, Offex and insolvency, as well as handling substantial building and civil engineering transactions, contractual disputes, insurance, intellectual property, personal injury and employment law. The Commercial Property team has a strong reputation in retail park schemes, dealing with funding, site acquisition, obtaining planning permission, negotiation and concluding of lettings and sales. BPE has particularly strong connections with Spain and Estonia.

Managing partner:	Malcolm Price
Senior partner:	David Oldham
Number of partners:	12
Assistant solicitors:	10
Other fee-earners:	19

WORKLOADS	
Litigation	25%
Corporate/commercial	23%
Volume re-mortgages etc	20%
Commercial property	17%
Work for insurance companies	15%
Private client/misc	10%

Continues overleaf

Volume Services to Institutional Clients: (*Contact Partner:* David Oldham). The pratice undertakes substantial work for building societies, insurance companies and unions, including conveyancing, repossession sales and personal injury litigation
Private Client Services: (*Contact:* Natalie Claridge). After joining forces with a specialist conveyancing firm last year, the partnership has a very active domestic conveyancing department and also handles probate, trust, tax and related matters.
Other Offices: 11 Guilford Street, London, WC1 1DT *Tel:* (0171) 404 0456

BRETHERTON
PRICE
Total solutions in Law **ELGOODS**
Solicitors

BRETHERTONS

16 CHURCH ST, RUGBY, CV21 3PW
Tel: (01788) 579579 **Fax:** (01788) 570949 **DX:** 11672 RUGBY **Email:** CLIENTCARE@BRETHERTONS.CO.UK

The Firm: Brethertons offers a wide range of legal services from both Rugby and Banbury. The firm is a legal aid franchise holder and there is a 24-hour helpline for legal advice.

Foreign languages: French, Spanish and Gujerati.

Other offices:

Domestic Property Department: 26 Regent Street, Rugby CV21 2PN
Tel: (01788) 551611
Fax: (01788) 551597
Brethertons Auld and Jardine: 30 High Street, Banbury, Oxfordshire, OX16 8ER
Tel: (01295) 270999
Fax: (01295) 257575
DX: 24239 Banbury
Domestic Property Department: 30 High Street, Banbury, Oxfordshire OX16 8ER
Tel: (01295) 270056
Fax: (01295) 277648
DX: 24239 Banbury

Managing partner:	C.B. Cooper
Senior partner:	P. Smith
Number of partners:	10
Assistant solicitors:	6
Other fee-earners:	14

CONTACTS	
Agriculture/ planning	Paul Smith
Commercial litigation	Shaun Jardine
Company/ commercial	Cliff Cooper
Computer and IT law	Andrew Katz
Crime and road traffic	Rod Ross
Domestic conveyancing	Alan Hooper
Family	Elizabeth Randall
Pers. injury/ civil lit.	Richard Pell
Trusts and probate	Chris Pratt

BREWER HARDING & ROWE 1 The Square, Barnstaple, EX32 8LX *Tel:* (01271) 342271 *Fax:* (01271) 377685 *DX:* 34957 Barnstaple *Ptnrs:* 8 *Asst solrs:* 4 *Other fee-earners:* 6

BRIAN KOFFMAN & CO Queen's Chambers, 5 John Dalton St, Manchester, M2 6ET *Tel:* (0161) 832 3852 *Fax:* (0161) 833 2547 *Ptnrs:* 2 *Asst solrs:* 4 *Other fee-earners:* 6

BRIDGE MCFARLAND SOLICITORS 19 South St. Mary's Gate, Grimsby, DN31 1JE *Tel:* (01472) 311711 *Fax:* (01472) 311500 *DX:* 13507 Grimsby *Ptnrs:* 10 *Asst solrs:* 5 *Other fee-earners:* 16

BRIDGEWOOD HOPKINSON & WOZNY 75 Bridge Street, Manchester, M3 2RH *Tel:* (0161) 833 4111 *Fax:* (0161) 839 3780 *DX:* 14356

BRIFFA & CO

BUSINESS DESIGN CENTRE, UPPER ST, ISLINGTON GREEN, LONDON, N1 0QH
Tel: (0171) 288 6003 **Fax:** (0171) 288 6004 **Email:** BRIFFA@BRIFFA.COM **Internet:** HTTP://WWW.BRIFFA.COM

The Firm: A highly regarded specialist intellectual property practice. Briffa & Co's underlying principle is to offer the expertise of a big firm coupled with the personal service from a committed team of lawyers.

The Work: Resolving all disputes relating to intellectual property rights including copyright, registered and unregistered design rights, trade marks, patents, confidential information and trade libel. The firm has a particular reputation for copyright and design work.

The Clients: The firm has an extensive national and international client base representing many of the major industry sectors.

The Fees: Full cost advice and information given at outset. Budgets always fixed for substantial litigation.

Number of partners:	1
Assistant solicitors:	4
Other fee-earners:	1

WORKLOADS
Intellectual property protection and enforcement
100%

CONTACTS	
Intellectual Property	Margaret Briffa/Laura Bence

BRIFFA & Co.
intellectual property lawyers

BRISTOWS

3 LINCOLN'S INN FIELDS, LONDON, WC2A 3AA
Tel: (0171) 400 8000 **Fax:** (0171) 400 8050 **DX:** 269 LONDON/CHANCERY LANE **Email:** INFO@BRISTOWS.CO.UK **Internet:** WWW.BRISTOWS.COM

The Firm: Bristows is a law firm dedicated to serving businesses with interests in technology or intellectual property, ranging from pharmaceuticals, electronics, IT and telecommunications to brands, multimedia and entertainment. They are a market leader in this area and act for many major corporations. With over 150 years of experience in this field, they have earned an enviable international reputation and have developed one of the largest intellectual property practices in Europe; yet they remain a friendly niche firm compatible with the needs of new and growing companies.

Bristows are a young partnership in a long established firm committed to excellence in their chosen fields. With the continuing recruitment of lawyers and scientists of the highest quality, they aim to stay at the forefront of specialist firms advising businesses with a strong technology or intellectual property base.

The firm has a substantial number of lawyers who first trained as scientists and who are readily able to understand sophisticated technology. This factor sets them apart from their competitors and has generated unparalleled expertise in litigation and corporate and commercial transactions in which intellectual property or an understanding of technology plays a significant part. Their litigation expertise also extends to commercial disputes of all kinds, including product liability and employment matters.

Bristows is able to field teams of lawyers to handle litigation and transactions demanding multidisciplinary skills, often with an international or cross-border flavour. This is an increasingly important aspect of their business, particularly in the light of European integration and its effect on the development of intellectual property and competition law.

Bristows has lawyers who are experienced in corporate and commercial law and in all forms of transaction from take-overs and mergers to joint ventures and technology spin-offs from universities. They also have significant complementary practices in real property, tax, competition, charity, employment and environmental law.

Languages Spoken: French, German, Italian, Polish, Greek, Spanish, Dutch, Punjabi, Cantonese.

Recruitment and Training: Bristows recruits outstanding trainee solicitors each year. The long-term prospects are excellent; many of the present partners trained with the firm. Although a scientific background is particularly useful in intellectual property, applicants with good degrees in any subject are encouraged to apply. A comprehensive in-house training programme is organised. Some trainees spend a few months on secondment to IBM, Gillette and other leading companies. Application forms and a recruitment brochure are available.

Managing partners:	Sally Field and John Lace
Number of partners:	19
Assistant solicitors:	37
Other fee-earners:	26

WORKLOADS	
Intellectual property (inc. related EC and anti-trust)	52%
Company/ corporate finance/ commercial	15%
Computer and IT	15%
Commercial litigation	10%
Commercial property	5%
Charities/ professional institutions/ partnership/ environmental	3%

CONTACTS	
Charities & Professional Institutions	John Lace
Commercial litigation	David Brown, Kevin Appleton
Commercial property	Michael Rowles, Alexandra Lethbridge
Company	Paul Cooke, John Lace
Computers and IT	Philip Westmacott, John Allcock
Corporate finance	Paul Cooke, Mark Hawes
EC and anti-trust litigation	Pat Treacy
Employment	Kevin Appleton
Environmental	Richard Burnett-Hall
Intellectual Property: biotechnology & pharmaceuticals	Tim Powell, Penny Gilbert
Intellectual Property: brands/trademk	Sally Field, Paul Walsh
Intellectual Property: commercial/comp	Pat Treacy, Matthew Warren
Intellectual Property: general	Edward Nodder
Intellectual Property: patents	Ian Judge, David Brown
Media	Paul Walsh
Partnership	John Lace
Tax	Miranda Cass

BROBECK HALE & DORR INTERNATIONAL

HASILWOOD HOUSE, 60 BISHOPSGATE, LONDON, EC2N 4AJ
Tel: (0171) 638 6688 **Fax:** (0171) 638 5888 **Email:** INFO@BHDUK.COM

The Firm: Founded in 1990 by two major U.S. law firms with offices throughout the United States, Brobeck Hale and Dorr International are leading legal advisors to emerging technology companies and the financial intermediaries (investment banks and venture capitalists) who deal with such companies.

Principal Areas of Work: Corporate finance – Mergers and acquisitions – Venture capital – Intellectual property – High technology – Biotechnology – Company/Commercial

Other Offices:

Hale and Dorr offices: Boston and Wellesley, Massachusetts; Washington DC.

Brobeck, Phleger & Harrison offices: San Francisco, Los Angeles, Palo Alto, San Diego and Newport Beach, California; Austin, Texas; Denver, Colorado; New York, New York.

Managing partner:	David M. Ayres
Senior partner:	David M. Ayres
Number of partners:	4
Associates:	7

BRODIES WS

15 ATHOLL CRESCENT, EDINBURGH, EH3 8HA
Tel: (0131) 228 3777 **Fax:** (0131) 228 3878 **DX:** ED10 EDINBURGH-1 **Email:** MAILBOX@BRODIES.CO.UK **Internet:** HTTP://WWW.BRODIES.CO.UK

Brodies is a broadly based practice providing the full range of services to commercial and private clients in the UK and overseas.

The Firm: The core legal services provided are corporate, property, litigation, trust and tax, employment, planning, environmental and private client. The firm's business clients range from small businesses and entrepreneurs to large PLCs and local authorities. Private clients cover a similarly wide range from crofters to landed estate owners.

Principal Areas of Work:

Corporate: The Corporate Department is able to advise on all areas of corporate and commercial law. It is particularly well known for the privatisation work it has done and has an excellent reputation for PFI work, mergers, acquisitions, corporate finance, banking and franchising, as well as VAT and corporate tax. An intellectual property group provides advice to an increasing number of clients.

Commercial Property: Commercial property expertise ranges from acquisition, development and disposal of commercial land and buildings for institutional investors, developers and landlords, to leasing of all space requirements including retail and licensed property matters. Property advice is also provided in agricultural and forestry matters and as a consultancy service to local government and other public authority bodies.

Tax, Planning and Environment: The firm's corporate tax and VAT specialism provides advice to all the other areas of the firm. The planning department and environmental law group operate in the same way and work particularly closely with the firm's property and litigation services.

Litigation: In civil and commercial litigation, Brodies' expertise is in banking, corporate, insurance, reparation and property work including building contracts. Professional negligence, partnership, employment, intellectual property, shipping and licensing litigation services are also provided. The firm has an excellent reputation in personal injury litigation and family law. A substantial debt recovery service is provided. The firm has five solicitor-advocates with extended rights of audience in the Court of Session, House of Lords and Judicial Committee of the Privy Council and three Law Society Accredited Specialists in Employment Law and a part-time Chairman of Industrial Tribunals.

Private Client: Brodies' large private client practice offers a comprehensive residential and rural property service incorporating both the conveyancing and estate agency aspects. The firm's surveyors are particularly experienced in landed estate, farming and town house properties. The firm is well known for its expertise in agricultural law, sporting estates and forestry as well as personal financial planning, inheritance tax advice and trust work.

Brodies aims to combine knowledge, skill and experience with commercial realism to provide a practical problem-solving service for clients. The management and development of the firm are focused towards this.

Brochures and newsletters are available on request by contacting Brodies' Marketing Executive, Stuart Gristwood.

Managing partner:	William Drummond
Senior partner:	J. Ronald Gardiner
Number of partners:	26
Assistant solicitors:	46
Other fee-earners:	29

WORKLOADS	
Commercial litigation	25%
Commercial property	25%
Corporate	15%
Private client	15%
Rural	12%
Land and estates	8%

CONTACTS	
Banking	Linda Kinniburgh
Construction Law	Moira Clark
Corporate	Alistair Campbell
Corporate Tax & VAT	Alan Barr
Employment	Joyce Cullen
Environment	Charles Smith
Franchising/I.P. (non-contentious)	Julian Voge
Intellectual Property (contentious)	David Walker
Litigation	Susan Craig
Planning	Neil Collar
Private Client	David Houldsworth
Property	Dale Strachan
Trust & Tax	Andrew Dalgleish

BROOKE NORTH

CROWN HOUSE, GREAT GEORGE STREET, LEEDS, LS1 3BR
Tel: (0113) 283 2100 **Fax:** (0113) 283 3999 **DX:** 713100 LEEDS, PARK SQUARE

The Firm: An ISO 9001 approved practice with a long-standing reputation for handling the national and international affairs of a wide range of commercial concerns. There is an emphasis on UK and international company and commercial work, commercial litigation, insolvency, commercial property and property management, employment, offshore trusts and strategic tax planning and environmental law. Commercial acumen and quality of service are the watchwords of the practice. The firm is a founder member of QLG, a national organisation of selected law firms in major UK cities. Agency work undertaken.

Other Offices: Branch Office: London. *Tel:*(0171) 404 4305. *Fax:* (0171) 405 1191.

Other Connections: Carter Jones McDonald, Isle of Man and Ray Pilley, Gibraltar.

Managing partner:	Gordon Watson
Number of partners:	14
Assistant solicitors:	7
Other fee-earners:	8

CONTACTS	
Commercial litigation	Richard Stockdale/Richard Parr
Commercial property	Rodney Dalton
Company/ commercial	Hugh Middlemass
Employment law	Richard Parr/Sara C M Morgan
Insolvency	Stuart Frith/ Steven Frieze
Managing Partner	Gordon Watson
Tax and trusts	Gordon Watson

BROOKSTREET DES ROCHES 1 Des Roches Square, Witan Way, Witney, OX8 6BE **Tel:** (01993) 771616 **Fax:** (01993) 779030 **DX:** 40205 Witney **Ptnrs:** 7 **Asst solrs:** 6 **Other fee-earners:** 2 **Contact:** Nigel Street or Ken Brooks *Principal areas of work are company commercial and commercial property with a particular specialism in commercial retail, environmental matters and related litigation.*

WORKLOADS			
Commercial property	50%	Commercial litigation	25%
Company	20%		

R.M. BROUDIE & CO 1-3 Sir Thomas St, Liverpool, L1 8BW *Tel:* (0151) 227 1429 *Fax:* (0151) 236 5161 *DX:* 14248 *Ptnrs:* 2 *Asst solrs:* 5 *Other fee-earners:* 12

BROWELL SMITH & GOODYEAR Transport House, John Dobson Street, Newcastle upon Tyne, NE1 8TW **Tel:** (0191) 221 1611 **Fax:** (0191) 221 1465 **Ptnrs:** 5 **Asst solrs:** 9 **Other fee-earners:** 19 **Contact:** P.A. Browell *Providing the highest quality personal injury, matrimonial, crime and conveyancing services to both private clients and the trade union movement.*

WORKLOADS			
Personal Injury	70%	Private Client	30%

BROWN COOPER

7 SOUTHAMPTON PLACE, LONDON, WC1A 2DR
Tel: (0171) 404 0422 **Fax:** (0171) 831 9856 **DX:** 35731 BLOOMSBURY **Email:** POST@BROWNCOOPER.DEMON.CO.UK

The Firm: Brown Cooper provides a distinctive, high quality but cost-effective service for commercial clients. Matters are invariably supervised by an experienced partner. As well as bringing to bear extensive experience in the fields of corporate commercial (*Contact:* Nigel Urwin) and property transactions (*Contact:* Michael Coyne) and litigation, the firm has in depth knowledge of industries including film and television, upstream oil and gas, publishing and printing, fashion, hotel and restaurant, and travel. The impressive litigation team (*Contact:* Robin Cooper) has particular expertise in VAT litigation, insurance, medical negligence, employment, crossborder debt recovery, libel and media litigation as well as domestic and international arbitration.

Languages Spoken: Italian, French, German.

Senior partner:	Robin Cooper
Number of partners:	4
Assistant solicitors:	6
Other fee-earners:	3

BROWNE JACOBSON

44 CASTLE GATE, NOTTINGHAM, NG1 7BJ
Tel: (0115) 950 0055 **Fax:** (0115) 947 5246 **DX:** 10007 NOTTINGHAM **Email:** INFO@BROWNEJ.CO.UK

ALDWYCH HOUSE, 81 ALDWYCH, LONDON, WC2A 4HN
Tel: (0171) 404 1546 **Fax:** (0171) 836 3882 **DX:** 37960 KINGSWAY **Email:** LON@BROWNEJ.CO.UK

Browne Jacobson is a substantial commercial and institutional law firm which has a practical approach providing first-class client service.

The Firm: Already acknowledged as a leading regional practice offering a comprehensive range of services, the firm has continued to develop a nationwide reputation for quality and has a growing international presence. It operates from the heart of the country in Nottingham and also has an office in the City of London. The international development is driven primarily through London and Paris where the firm has an associated office.

Browne Jacobson has experienced and enthusiastic teams which adopt an integrated problem solving approach for all their clients. This is coupled with a firm-wide philosophy of being dedicated to providing value for money without compromising quality.

Principal Areas of Work: Browne Jacobson specialises in corporate and commercial work, commercial property, commercial litigation, insurance and private client work.

    Company/Commercial: The firm provides a broad spectrum of company, commercial and corporate finance work including: flotation's and new issues, mergers and acquisitions, MBOs/MBIs, venture capital, banking, commercial contracts (including joint ventures, franchising, agency and distribution agreements), corporate tax, pensions, share schemes, employment, intellectual property and information technology.

    Commercial Property: Commercial property work includes dealing with industrial and commercial property acting for investors, developers, local authorities, housing associations, major retailers and other commercial clients. The firm also covers all aspects of construction law, landlord and tenant, and can advise on planning and environmental issues.

    Litigation: As a founder member of the Centre for Dispute Resolution, the firm seeks alternatives to litigation wherever possible. Commercial litigation work includes employment disputes, intellectual property, construction, debt collection, licensing, trading standards and acting for general commercial clients to resolve their commercial disputes quickly and effectively.

Continues overleaf

Managing partner:	Derek Bambury
Number of partners:	36
Assistant solicitors:	62
Other fee-earners:	51

WORKLOADS	
Insurance & personal injury litigation	30%
Corporate/commercial	27%
Professional indemnity	18%
Commercial & other litigation	17%
Taxation/trusts	4%
Other	4%

CONTACTS	
Commercial litigation	Peter Ellis
Commercial property	Brian Smith
Company/ commercial	Peter Hands
Corporate finance/banking	Rob Metcalfe
Employment	Edward Benson
Environmental and planning	Brian Smith
Health law	Carole Ayre
Intellectual property and information technology	
	Peter Ellis
Pensions	Kevin Milton
Personal injury	Gareth Edwards
Professional indemnity	Robert Ridgwell
Public and administrative law	Nick Parsons
Taxation/trusts	Maryvonne Hands

Health: The firm's health law team acts for health authorities and NHS Trusts in commercial, property, and litigation matters including clinical negligence litigation.

Insurance: The firm has a large and experienced insurance group acting for major insurers on a national basis. The group handles personal injury (including sports-related injuries), employers' liability and professional indemnity claims against solicitors, surveyors, accountants and engineers. Browne Jacobson has a strong local authority department which specialise in providing primarily this type of advice but couples it with a strong understanding of the specific client's needs.

Private Client: Private client work handled includes all aspects of personal taxation, trusts, wills, probate and administration.

The firm includes fluent French, Spanish, Malay, and Italian speakers.

BROWN & WOOD, A Multinational Partnership

PRINCES COURT, 7 PRINCES STREET, LONDON, EC2R 8AQ
Tel: (0171) 778 1800 **Fax:** (0171) 796 1807

The Firm: Founded in 1914, Brown & Wood has developed a major global securitisation practice and provides legal services to major participants in the world's capital markets.

Principal Areas of Work:

U.S. Securities and Corporate Law: Work includes: advising on all aspects of U.S. securities laws, including 144A issues, SEC registrations, exempt transactions, stock exchange listings, depositary receipt programmes, Investment Company Act matters and other regulatory considerations.

Securitisation: Work includes: securitisation of a wide variety of assets, including mortgages, credit card receivables, future flows, lease receivables, trade receivables etc; collateratised loan obligations.

Structured Finance: Work includes: assisting with English law structured finance transactions and products, including asset-backed transactions of all types, repackagings and other forms of secured lending.

Investment Funds: Work includes: offshore investment funds and pooled investment vehicles, including some of the most innovative structures of recent years.

Tax: Work includes: cross-border financing transactions and unique expertise in the complex interaction of the U.S. tax system with the U.K. and other European systems.

Other Offices:

Brown & Wood LLP One World Trade Center, New York, NY 10048-0557
Tel: +1 212 839 5300; *Fax:* +1 212 839 5599

10877 Wilshire Boulevard, Suite 1402, Los Angeles, CA 90024-4341
Tel: +1 310 443 0200; *Fax:* +1 310 208 5740

555 California Street, Suite 5000, San Francisco, CA 94104-1715
Tel: +1 415 772 1200; *Fax:* +1 415 397 4621

815 Connecticut Avenue, NW, Suite 701, Washington, DC 20006-4004
Tel: +1 202 973 0600; *Fax:* +1 202 223 0485

China World Tower, Suite 2315, Jian Guo Men Wai Avenue, Beijing 100004, China
Tel: +8610 6505 5359; *Fax:* +8610 6505 5360

Bank of China Tower, 1 Garden Road, Central, Hong Kong
Tel: +852 2509 7888; *Fax:* +852 2509 3110

Tokyo Representative Office, Kioicho Building, 6th Floor, 3-28 Kioicho, Chiyoda-Ku, Tokyo 102, Japan *Tel:* +813 5276 0045; *Fax:* +813 5276 0049

Senior partner:	Christopher B Mead
Number of partners:	5
Assistant solicitors:	13
Other fee-earners:	4

CONTACTS	
Investment Funds	William Morrison
Securitisation	Michael Durrer
Structured Finance	Margaret Boswell
Tax	R.J. Ruble
U.S. Securities and Corporate Law	Christopher Mead

BRUNTON MILLER Herbert House, 22 Herbert Street, Glasgow, G20 6NB *Tel:* (0141) 337 1199 *Fax:* (0141) 337 3300 *DX:* GW21 *Ptnrs:* 8 *Asst solrs:* 3 *Other fee-earners:* 4

BRUTTON & CO West End House, 288 West Street, Fareham, PO16 0AJ *Tel:* (01329) 236171 *Fax:* (01329) 289915 *DX:* 40809 *Ptnrs:* 5 *Asst solrs:* 11 *Other fee-earners:* 1

BUCKLE MELLOWS 45-51 Priestgate, Peterborough, PE1 1LB *Tel:* (01733) 568175 *Fax:* (01733) 562064 *DX:* 12312 P'Boro 1 *Ptnrs:* 10 *Asst solrs:* 8 *Other fee-earners:* 15

BULLER JEFFRIES 36 Bennetts Hill, Birmingham, B2 5SN **Tel:** (0121) 212 2620 **Fax:** (0121) 212 2210 **DX:** 13051 Birmingham 1 **Email:** buller-jeffries@link.org **Ptnrs:** 7 **Asst solrs:** 11 **Other fee-earners:** 8 **Contact:** Mr Geoffrey Lewis *Specialists in personal injury work and all aspects of insurance claims and law. Commercial and domestic department. Also at Coventry.*

WORKLOADS	
Personal injury and insurance related litigation	95%
Commercial and domestic conveyancing, wills and probate	5%

BULLIVANT JONES & COMPANY

STATE HOUSE, 22 DALE ST, LIVERPOOL, L2 4UR
Tel: (0151) 227 5671 **Fax:** (0151) 227 5632 **DX:** 14120 LIVERPOOL **Email:** MAIL@BULLIVANTJONES.CO.UK

The Firm: The firm was established in 1970, and has since come to be held in high regard, particularly in the field of commercial property and property related litigation. It places a high emphasis on quality of service and commitment to retained clients.

Principal Areas of Work: The firm deals with all matters relating to commercial property, with a particular emphasis on the retail sector. In addition, it handles property and retail related litigation together with a wide range of employment, commercial and private client work.

Senior partner:	Pamela Jones
Number of partners:	10
Assistant solicitors:	17
Other fee-earners:	3

Bullivant Jones & Company

BUNKERS 7 The Drive, Hove, BN3 3JS *Tel:* (01273) 329797 *Fax:* (01273) 324082 *DX:* 59257 Hove *Ptnrs:* 6 *Asst solrs:* 5 *Other fee-earners:* 13

BURD PEARSE 21 Fore St, Okehampton, EX20 1AJ *Tel:* (01837) 52416 *Fax:* (01837) 54540 *DX:* 82500 *Ptnrs:* 3 *Asst solrs:* 4 *Other fee-earners:* 3

BURGES SALMON

NARROW QUAY HOUSE, NARROW QUAY, BRISTOL, BS1 4AH
Tel: (0117) 939 2000 **Fax:** (0117) 902 4400 **DX:** 7829 **Email:** GBBSSTEL@IBMMAIL.COM **Website:** WWW.BURGES-SALMON.CO.UK

The Firm: Burges Salmon is a large single office firm which has added an impressive range of regional, national and international clients to its extensive client list. The firm has doubled in size in the last five years through organic growth. The firm attributes its success to: enthusiasm and energy; enterprise and entrepreneurialism; experience and expertise; efficiency and effectiveness; and excellence and equality. These hallmarks are displayed by all the firm's legal and support teams, singling Burges Salmon out as quality business advisers for the new millennium.

To learn more about Burges Salmon and the way client relationships are handled, call any of the work contacts in the box opposite. To learn more about their recruitment process and high quality training, contact Bob Llewellin.

Principal Areas of Work: The firm delivers a full range of services either through its traditional practice groups or by specialist units according to the needs of each client. These units include: banking and insolvency; building societies; charities; construction and engineering; employment and employee benefits and pensions; environment; financial services; housing associations; minerals and mining; planning; rent review; telecommunications and transport and distribution.

Corporate practice group: Handles a growing number of flotations, Stock Exchange work, a full range of company and corporate finance transactions and all associated UK and EU business law. The expanding international practice of this group extends to inward investment, UK offshore and international tax planning and asset protection. The group has a national reputation for unit trust and financial services work and a significant presence in the fields of employment and agribusiness.

Commercial property group: Handles the full range of property transactions including all aspects of planning, environment, funding, building procurement, management, lettings and construction, engineering and other disputes. It has become involved in a number of prestige schemes and in portfolio acquisitions and disposals for property investors in addition to its flourishing corporate support work.

Banking/insolvency group: Deals with all aspects of banking, securities, and investment work and corporate insolvency.

Commercial litigation practice group: Provides a full litigation service for the firm's business clients with particular expertise in intellectual property, professional negligence, employment, insolvency, white collar crime, insurance and partnership disputes. The team includes experts on arbitration and ADR.

Agricultural practice group: Covers the complete range of UK and EU agricultural law, both contentious and non-contentious and extends to the provision of high quality advocacy services.

Private client group: Deals with a wide range of trust and tax issues including the provision of estate and tax planning, financial planning, heritage preservation, UK and offshore trusts, immigration and emigration, family and matrimonial breakdown, charities, high value residential conveyancing and staff relocation.

Recruitment and Training: The firm recruits law, non-law and mature graduates, and offers both in-house training and residential courses with the Norton Rose M5 Group. Vacation experience is also available. Apply two years in advance; forms from R.D.Llewellin.

Managing partner:	Guy Stobart
Senior partner:	David Marsh
Number of partners:	40
Assistant solicitors:	106
Other fee-earners:	39

CONTACTS	
Agribusiness	Roger Hawes
Agriculture	William Neville
Arbitration	Adrian Llewelyn Evans
Asset finance	Sandra Forbes
Charities	Charles Wyld
Construction	Marcus Harling
Corporate banking	Sandra Forbes
Corporate finance	Christopher Godfrey
Corporate tax	Tim Illston
Dispute resolution	Adrian Llewelyn Evans
Employment	George Dyson
Environment	Robert Smyth
EU/competition	Laura Claydon
Financial services	Christopher Godfrey
Housing associations	Stephen McNulty
Information technology	Simon Coppen
Insolvency	Guy Stobart
Insurance	Christopher Jackson
Intellectual property	Simon Coppen
Mergers and acquisitions	Alan Barr
Pensions	Tim Illston
PFI and partnering	Marcus Harling
Planning and land use	Patrick Robinson
Private Client	Martin Mitchell
Product liability	Adrian Llewelyn Evans
Professional indemnity	Paul Haggett
Property	Stuart King
Property development	David Gidney
Property finance	Catherine Elliot
Property litigation	Neil Ham
Rail	Nick Olley
Trade and industry	Richard Wynn-Jones
Transport and distribution	Richard Wynn-Jones
Unit trusts	Christopher Godfrey
Venture capital	Roger Hawes

BURGES SALMON
SOLICITORS

BURLEY & GEACH 8 Swan St, Petersfield, GU32 3AE *Tel:* (01730) 262401 *Fax:* (01730) 265182 *DX:* 100402 *Ptnrs:* 8 *Asst solrs:* 6 *Other fee-earners:* 6

BURNESS

50 LOTHIAN ROAD, FESTIVAL SQUARE, EDINBURGH, EH3 9WJ
Tel: (0131) 473 6000 **Fax:** (0131) 473 6006 **DX:** 73 EDINBURGH **Email:** EDINBURGH@BURNESS.CO.UK

Burness is one of Scotland's premier commercial law firms with offices in Edinburgh and Glasgow.

The Firm: Burness has a strong UK and overseas client base and the firm's success reflects the high concentration of expertise among its lawyers and its direct and commercial approach.

The firm operates in specialist groups which are formed to meet the corporate, commercial property, construction and litigation business needs of clients.

The Edinburgh office has recently moved to the landmark building in the heart of the city's new financial district. This follows last year's doubling in size of the Glasgow office.

Principal Areas of work:

Company/Commercial: Burness has a substantial and diverse corporate and commercial core practice involving acquisitions and disposals of companies and businesses, capital markets, corporate finance, venture capital investment, banking, joint ventures and general corporate advice. John Rafferty and his team have secured the firm's position amongst the leading firms for AIM work in Scotland and frequently acts alongside English and foreign law firms on the Scottish aspects of major financings. Andrew Sleigh continues to give momentum to the firm's corporate finance practice in Glasgow.

Banking: The firm's banking practice has received a significant boost with the appointment of two new partners – corporate banking partner, Scott Wilson, in Glasgow and consumer finance specialist, Alan Soppitt, in Edinburgh.

Projects/PFI: The firm continues its exceptional success in PPP/PFI. Anthony Read and his team continue to grow their reputation as leading players in this field, with very strong accommodation sector experience through projects such as a new training centre for Strathclyde Police; Project PRIME for the Department of Social Security (largest UK PFI project to date – o4.6 billion) and new offices for Perth & Kinross Council. The firm is also active in the education and healthcare sectors, winning Scotland's first schools project in Falkirk and three NHS trust projects.

Commercial Property: The firm's success in the commercial property sector continues to grow with a strong client base of developers, retailers, leisure specialists and investors, as well as a very substantial practice for PFI/public sector clients.

Inward Investment: Through Paul Pia (currently Chairman of The Japan Society of Scotland), the firm has one of the strongest inward investment practices in Scotland acting for corporations in continental Europe, North America and the Pacific Rim.

Litigation: The firm continues to deal with a large number of international and commercial arbitrations, commercial litigation cases and judicial review procedures and to extend its defender product liability work. Employment work is also a growing area of expertise in both Edinburgh and Glasgow.

Other Offices: 242 West George Street, Glasgow G2 4QY. *Tel:* (0141) 248 4933. *Fax:* (0141) 204 1601. Email: glasgow@burness.co.uk

Managing partner:	**Kenneth Ross**
Chairman:	**John Rafferty**
Number of partners:	25
Assistant solicitors:	32
Other fee-earners:	19

WORKLOADS	
Corporate/commercial/construction	46%
Commercial property	35%
Litigation	18%
Private client	1%

CONTACTS	
Banking	Scott Wilson/Christopher Scott
Commercial Litigation	Dr Martin Sales/Bruce Logan
Commercial Property	Ian Wattie/Andrew Sobolewski
Construction/Engineering/PFI	Anthony Read
Corp.Fin/Company/Commercial	John Rafferty/
	Andrew Sleigh
Employment	Marsali Murray/Shona MacLean

BURNETT & REID

15 GOLDEN SQUARE, ABERDEEN, AB10 1WF
Tel: (01224) 644333 **Fax:** (01224) 632173 **DX:** 19 ABERDEEN **Email:** BURNETT-REID@LINK.ORG

The Firm: Aberdeen's longest established firm, founded in 1754, has traditionally specialised in landed estate management and agricultural holdings. The client base has however expanded and broadened so that the firm now covers most fields of law with expertise also having been aquired in relation to: corporate/commercial law, trust and tax planning, family/matrimonial law, and child law.

Principal Areas of Work:

Corporate/Commercial: Company formations, acquisitions, disposals and mergers. Commercial Contracts. Company secretarial services. Commercial Property: sales, purchases, leasing and security including licensed premises.

Agricultural/Landed Estates: Specialist and general advice to the farming and land-owning community including purchase/sale of farms and landed estates, leasing of agricultural holdings, Milk Quota, and management/factoring of landed estates.

Residential Property: Covering all aspects of purchase/sale (including Estate Agency) of all types of residential property. Leasing of residential property with full factoring service.

Litigation: Covering all types of civil disputes with specialist advice in matrimonial/family and child law.

Private Client/Executry/Trust: Covering all aspects of private client work with specialist advice on taxation, investments, life assurance, pensions, wills and inheritance tax planning.

Senior partner:	Alastair O. Robertson
Managing partner:	Michael D. McMillan
Number of partners:	9
Assistant solicitors:	7
Other fee-earners:	11

WORKLOADS	
Residential property and estate agency	23%
Trust/Executry/Private	21%
Agriculture/Landed Estates	16%
Corporate/Commercial	16%
Litigation (including Matrimonial/Family/Child Law)	16%

CONTACTS	
Agricultural Law	Alastair Robertson
Corporate/Commercial	Angus Matheson
Executry and Trust	Eilidh Scobbie
Land Management	John Sutherland
Litigation/Family Law	Joan Catto
Private Client	Stan Cusiter/Roger Lawrence
Residential Property	Fraser Leslie

BURNETTS 6 Victoria Place, Carlisle, CA1 1ES *Tel:* (01228) 552222 *Fax:* (01228) 522399 *DX:* 63005 Carlisle *Ptnrs:* 16 *Asst solrs:* 5 *Other fee-earners:* 13

BURNSIDE KEMP FRASER 4 Queens Terrace, Aberdeen, AB10 1XL *Tel:* (01224) 624602 *Fax:* (01224) 624011 *DX:* 78 Aberdeen *Ptnrs:* 3 *Asst solrs:* 2 *Other fee-earners:* 1

BURROUGHS DAY 14-16 Charlotte St, Bristol, BS1 5PT *Tel:* (0117) 929 0333 *Fax:* (0117) 927 2342 *DX:* 7825 *Ptnrs:* 13 *Asst solrs:* 13 *Other fee-earners:* 22

BURSTOWS 8 Ifield Road, Crawley, West Sussex RH11 7YY **Tel:** (01293) 603603 **Fax:** (01293) 603666 **DX:** 57100 CRAWLEY **Email:** post@burstows.co.uk **Ptnrs:** 15 **Asst solrs:** 19 **Other fee-earners:** 17 **Contact:** Mr Don Burstow, Senior Partner *Legal services for business and private clients. Offices also in Brighton and Horsham.*

WORKLOADS		
Private Client		33%
Corporate/Commercial including Employment and Commercial Property		27%
Litigation	19%	Insolvency	12%
Personal Injury	9%	

BURT BRILL & CARDENS 30 Old Steyne, Brighton, BN1 1FL *Tel:* (01273) 604123 *Fax:* (01273) 570837 *DX:* 2709 *Ptnrs:* 5 *Asst solrs:* 5 *Other fee-earners:* 6

BURTON COPELAND

51 LINCOLN'S INN FIELDS, LONDON, WC2A 3LZ
Tel: (0171) 430 2277 **Fax:** (0171) 430 1101 **DX:** 37981 KINGSWAY

The Firm: Established in 1982 specialising in criminal law, especially commercial fraud. In 1991 the firm opened a thriving London office.

Principal Areas of Work: The firm's commercial fraud department, with five experienced former members of the Commercial Fraud Squad, is located in both the Manchester and London offices (*Contact Partner:* Ian Burton). The London office deals almost exclusively with "white collar" crime including major SFO, Inland Revenue and Customs & Excise prosecutions. Extradition and general criminal defence work is also undertaken. The Manchester office, which also handles a large juvenile and general criminal caseload, complements its commercial fraud work with a wide range of commercial services. The firm provides property and litigation expertise.

Foreign Languages: French, German.

Manchester Office: Royal London Hse, 196 Deansgate, Manchester, M3 3NE. *Tel:* (0161) 834 7374. *Fax:* (0161) 839 0364 *DX:* 14362 Manchester 1.

Managing partner:	Maurice Mason
Senior partner:	Ian R. Burton
Number of partners:	20
Assistant solicitors:	14
Other fee-earners:	21

WORKLOADS	
Commercial fraud	45%
Crime	45%
Litigation/ private client	10%

CONTACTS	
Commercial fraud	I.R. Burton
Criminal	M.P. Mackey
Motoring	N. Freeman
Private client	M.C. Mason

BURY & WALKERS Britannic Hse, Regent St, Barnsley, S70 2EQ **Tel:** (01226) 733533 **Fax:** (01226) 207610 **DX:** 12251 **Ptnrs:** 12 **Asst solrs:** 6 **Other fee-earners:** 9 **Contact:** Mr M. P. Burke at 4 Butts Court, Leeds LS1 5JS *Known for commercial conveyancing, commercial litigation, landlord and tenant. Also matriminial and child care, probate and trust, general litigation.*

WORKLOADS	
Litigation (including commercial litigation)	40%
Private (property, wills, probate and tax)	34%
Commercial 26%	

BUSS MURTON

THE PRIORY, TUNBRIDGE WELLS, TN1 1JJ
Tel: (01892) 510222 **Fax:** (01892) 510333 **DX:** 3913 TUNBRIDGE WELLS **Email:** INFO@BUSSMURTON.CO.UK

The Firm: Buss Murton was formed in 1985 from the merger of two of Kent's oldest firms, and today it combines business experience going back over 275 years with a modern and forward-thinking approach. The firm is a general practice and, whilst family and private client matters remain important areas of work, its company/ commercial and commercial litigation departments have expanded rapidly in recent years.

Principal Areas of Work:

Company/ Commercial: Work covers the full spectrum of business activity including formation of companies and partnerships, acquisitions, mergers and disposals, commercial contracts of all kinds, employment, EC law, intellectual property, environmental law and insolvency.

Property: Involved in all types of commercial and residential matters ranging from highly complex and heavy weight developments to bulk residential work on behalf of institutions.

Personal Injury: Handles all types of plaintiff and defendant personal injury and medical negligence work including legal expenses, insurance and union funded matters. Specialist sub-section deals with R.T.A. claims.

Personal litigation: Has a strong matrimonial, childcare and family following alongside its general coverage of all other types of personal litigation. Criminal work is not undertaken.

Private Client: A large private client department which has generated a well-established following, handles all aspects of wills, probate, trusts, estate management and tax planning.

Financial Services: Specialist department advises corporate and private clients on: sources of finance, investments, life assurance, pensions.

Agriculture: A separate agricultural department has been formed to service an extensive farming client base. The department covers every aspect of farming including the specialist areas of alternative uses of land, planning law, environmental law and farm sales.

Other Offices: The main offices at Tunbridge Wells are complemented by a branch network at Cranbrook, Hawkhurst, Tenterden and Staplehurst.

Recruitment and Training: The firm recruits two or three trainee solicitors every year. The nature and scope of the matters handled provide an excellent training base. It is our policy to retain staff following successful completion of training contracts. Applications in writing should be addressed to Philip Davis.

Managing partner:	Robert Sedgwick
Senior partner:	John Cherrill
Number of partners:	21
Assistant solicitors:	8
Other fee-earners:	32

WORKLOADS	
General Litigation	30%
Company and commercial property	20%
Private Client & Financial Services	20%
Commercial Litigation	12%
Residential Conveyancing	10%
Family	8%

CONTACTS	
Agriculture	Robert Madge
Commercial Litigation	Mark Agombar
Commercial Property	David Phillips
Company/Comm & Environment	Robert Sedgwick
Corporate Finance	Robert Sedgwick
Employment	Helen Wynn
Family	Patrick Palmer
Financial Services	Geoffrey Craig
Legal Expenses Insurance Lit	Rhonda Hesling
Pensions	Keith Goodman
Personal Injury	John Hedley
Private Client	John Toth
Resd Property & Housing Assoc.	David Phillips

BUSS MURTON
SOLICITORS

INVESTOR IN PEOPLE

A QUALITY SERVICE
Approved by The Legal Aid Board

BUTCHER & BARLOW 2 Bank Street, Bury, BL9 0DL *Tel:* (0161) 764 4062 *Fax:* (0161) 797 2912 *DX:* 20506 *Ptnrs:* 8 *Asst solrs:* 4 *Other fee-earners:* 6

CADWALADER, WICKERSHAM & TAFT

55 GRACECHURCH STREET, LONDON, EC3V 0EE
Tel: (0171) 456 8500 **Fax:** (0171) 456 8600 **Internet:** WWW.CADWALADER.COM

The Firm: Founded in New York in 1792, this firm is one of the leading Wall Street practices, specialising in the financial services sector including corporate, securities and finance work, capital markets, financial restructuring, real estate financing, commercial loan and banking services, litigation, tax and private client work. The recently established London office focuses particularly on capital markets, derivatives, structured finance, insurance, financial restructuring , tax and corporate law.

Principal Areas of Work:

Capital Markets: *Work includes:* all forms of debt, equity and hybrid financing, including derivatives, securitisation, structured finance, real estate financing and re-financing.

Managing partner:	Robert O. Link Jr.
Senior partner:	John F. Fritts
Number of partners:	5
Other fee-earners:	12

CONTACTS	
Capital Markets	James Starky, John Walker
Financial Restructuring and Corporate	
	Andrew Wilkinson, James Roome
Tax and Private Client	Russell Jacobs

Financial Restructuring: *Work includes:* contentious and non-contentious insolvency and workouts, with a particular specialisation in the insurance, re-insurance and distressed debt sectors and all forms of corporate structuring and reconstructions.

Corporate: *Work includes:* all forms of corporate and corporate finance activities, with a particular regard to international mergers and acquisitions, joint ventures and corporate reconstructions.

Tax and Private Client: *Work includes:* all forms of domestic and international corporate taxation, with a focus on cross border structured financing arbitrage, and planning opportunities for corporate and high net worth individuals.

Recruitment: The firm is keen to consider high quality candidates to practise in the aforementioned areas.

Other Offices: New York, Washington D.C., Los Angeles, Charlotte.

CAMERON MCKENNA

MITRE HOUSE, 160 ALDERSGATE STREET, LONDON, EC1A 4DD
Tel: (0171) 367 3000 **Fax:** (0171) 367 2000 **DX:** 724 **Email:** INFO@CMCK.COM **Internet:** HTTP://WWW.CMCK.COM

The Firm: Experience, resource, focus and enterprise – the hallmark of Cameron McKenna.

Cameron McKenna has a wealth of experience and the depth of resource to handle the largest assignments. More than that, the firm's focus on industry expertise marks it out as a world class leader in many areas and, being as enterprising as its clients, Cameron McKenna is determined to make things happen, giving a business lead, not just a legal opinion.

Clear communication is the key – the firm speaks with authority and gets straight to the point. It is open about fees, who is responsible for the client's overall relationship with the firm and who is on the team on any particular transaction.

Principal Areas of Work: Cameron McKenna is a major full service City and international commercial law firm, with particular strengths in the banking and finance, corporate, construction, infrastructure projects, energy, healthcare and bioscience, insurance and property sectors. It advises businesses and governments throughout the world.

Cameron McKenna has a broad and balanced corporate finance practice for both public and private companies, as well as M&A, MBO and MBI work, financial restructurings, privatisations and corporate tax. The firm acts for some 90 UK and international banks and, with its experience in the financing of infrastructure projects, is regarded as one of the pre-eminent firms in banking and asset and project finance, including PFI work. Its outstanding insurance and reinsurance practice is founded on a close involvement with the insurance market over the last 60 years.

Its property practice is one of the strongest, with high profile clients in the institutional, development and retail areas; it is ranked as a leader in environmental law, financial services regulation, health & safety at work, immigration, pensions, planning and product liability; and has strong specialist expertise in such topics as advertising and marketing, anti-trust and competition law, EC law, employment, fraud, information technology, multimedia and telecommunications, intellectual property, press disputes and securitisation.

Cameron McKenna has significant firm-wide litigation resources covering the whole practice with experience in dispute management, arbitration and mediation allied to specific industry expertise.

Industry expertise is a factor which marks out Cameron McKenna. The firm is a leader in advising clients in a range of industries including construction, energy (oil & gas, electricity, power generation and water), financial services, life sciences (particularly pharmaceuticals and biotechnology), transport (aviation, railways, roads and ports) and waste management.

Cameron McKenna helps clients internationally, either through its own offices or through well-established contacts, particularly in Europe, the CIS, Asia-Pacific and the USA.

More information is available from either the Senior or the Managing Partner, or from any of the contact partners listed.

Other Offices: Aberdeen, Bristol; Brussels; Budapest, Prague, Warsaw; Moscow, Almaty, Tashkent; Hong Kong; Washington DC, San Francisco.

Managing partner:	Robert Derry-Evans
Senior partner:	Bill Shelford
UK	
Number of partners:	149
International	
Number of partners:	31
Assistant solicitors:	118
Other fee-earners:	37

CONTACTS	
Aviation	Tim Brymer
Banking and international finance	Duncan Aldred
Central Europe	Robert Windmill
Charities	Andrew Crawford
CIS	Elena Kirillova
Construction	Ann Minogue
Corporate finance	Sean Watson/Arfon Jones
Corporate tax	Mark Nichols
Defamation, trade libel, media complaints	
	Tim Hardy
EC law/competition/anti-trust	
	Richard Taylor/Nick Paul
Employment	Simon Jeffreys/Anthony Fincham
Energy	Fiona Woolf/Penelope Warne
Environment	Pamela Castle
Financial services regulation	Simon Morris
Health & safety	Mark Tyler
Hong Kong	Julian Ogley
Immigration	Julia Onslow-Cole
Infrastructure projects/PFI	Frank Dufficy/
	Robert Phillips
Insolvency	John White
Insurance and reinsurance	Anthony Hobkinson
IP/advertising & marketing	Stephen Whybrow/
	Guilherme Brafman
IT/telecoms	John Armstrong
Life sciences	Ian Dodds-Smith/Julian Thurston
Litigaton, arbititration and dispute management	
	Tim Hardy
M&A	Richard Price/Mike Rich
Pensions	Nigel Moore
Planning	Tony Kitson
Product liability & integrity	Chris Hodges/
	Anthony Hobkinson
Property	Charles Romney/Nick Brown
Transport	Richard Price/Trevor Butcher
Venture capital	Anthony Lewis
Water	Richard Temple

cameron mcKenna

CAMERONS

218 STRAND, TEMPLE BAR, LONDON, WC2R 1AZ
Tel: (0171) 353 5572 **Fax:** (0171) 936 2296 **DX:** 217 CH.LN. **Email:** STRAND@CAMERONS.CO.UK

1 PETERBOROUGH ROAD, HARROW, HA1 2YW
Tel: (0181) 423 6666 **Fax:** (0181) 864 4904 **DX:** 4213 HARROW 1 **Email:** HARROW@CAMERONS.CO.UK

THE MALTINGS, OAKHILL, NR BATH, BA3 5AS
Tel: (01749) 841184 **Fax:** (01749) 841185 **DX:** 43009 SHEPTON MALLET **Email:** JVB@CAMERONSB.PIPEX.COM

The Firm: Camerons is a progressive firm whose primary aim is to provide the best advice and to maintain complete integrity in all its dealings. The firm traces its roots to the 19th century. From its offices in the Strand (opposite the Law Courts), Harrow and Bath the firm provides an extensive range of legal services to business and private clients.

Principal Areas of Work:

Commercial: The department advises on corporate finance and banking, mergers and acquisitions, corporate taxation, restructuring, utilities and energy, international projects and joint ventures, employment and intellectual property.

Church and Charity Law: One of the leading firms on church law and charity law, the department advises many charities, foundations, schools and colleges.

Property: The department advises on all aspects of commercial and domestic property, planning, environment and developments.

Litigation: In addition to commercial and property litigation, the firm has specialists in building and construction, employment, family, personal injury and intellectual property.

Private Client: All personal legal work is undertaken including tax advice and wills, trusts and administration of estates.

Other Areas of Work: Expertise is also available in Australian law and the law of the Russian Federation.

Foreign Connections: The firm is associated with A Khromtsov & Partners, Moscow, Russian Federation. The firm also has strong connections in Australia, Hong Kong, the People's Republic of China, Singapore and Indonesia where it has acted on a number of minerals, exploration, energy industry infrastructure and financial services projects.

Senior partner:	D.M. Tuft
Practice Manager:	Philip Humphrys ACIB
Number of partners:	10
Assistant solicitors:	5
Other fee-earners:	6

CONTACTS	
Banking	John Ricks
Charity Law	Michael Stewart
Church law	John Beaumont
Commercial litigation/ADR	David Sims
Commercial property/planning	John Ricks
Corporate/international	Lewis Jackson
Employment/intell. property	Philip Ross-Smith
Family law and divorce	Ian Lloyd
Tax	Jack Harper FCA FTII

CAMPBELL HOOPER

35 OLD QUEEN ST, LONDON, SW1H 9JD
Tel: (0171) 222 9070 **Fax:** (0171) 222 5591 **DX:** 2365 VICTORIA **Email:** CH@CAMPBELL-HOOPER.CO.UK

The Firm: Campbell Hooper is a medium-sized firm with an established base of commercial and individual clients. The firm is a member of Proteus, a European network of independent law firms providing an integrated service.

Principal Areas of Work:

Company/ Commercial: (*Contact:* Martin Wright). Multi-disciplinary teams provide a comprehensive service to domestic and overseas business clients. From start-ups and venture capital to mergers, acquisitions and company restructuring. Particular expertise in telecommunications, IT contracts, banking, finance, financial services and business immigration.

Commercial Property: (*Contact:* Stephen Siddall). Extensive experience in commercial and residential development and funding work to include office, retail, leisure and town centre developments with specialist construction advice. Expertise extends to investment, landlord and tenant, planning and environmental law.

Media: (*Contact:* Carolyn Jennings). Extensive experience in film, TV, theatre, broadcasting, recording and music publishing and collective agencies; video, cable and satellite TV, character and other merchandising and publishing, trademarks and intellectual property. Clients include writers, performers, and creative personnel, many leaders in their field.

Litigation: (*Contact:* Jonathan Whitehead). A strong team handles a variety of work including intellectual property, building contracts, landlord and tenant, insolvency, contractual disputes and libel.

Employment: (*Contact:* William Granger). Advises and trains employers and senior management on contracts, policies, acquisition and removal of personnel, together with the full range of tribunal disputes.

Private Client: (*Contact:* Alex Cuppage). Handles conveyancing, estate planning, establishment and administration of charities, wills, trusts, settlements, probate and personal taxation.

Family and Matrimonial: (*Contact:* Sarah Anticoni). Solicitors Family Law Association members. Promotes a constructive and conciliatory approach to resolving all issues relating to divorce, separation, finance and children.

Managing partner:	Martin Wright
Number of partners:	18
Assistant solicitors:	19
Other fee-earners:	11

WORKLOADS	
Commercial litigation (including construction & employment)	27%
Commercial property	21%
Company	20%
Media/Entertainment	18%
Private client	14%

CONTACTS	
Company	M.J. Wright
Construction	D.A. Salmon
Domestic conveyancing	A. Gill
Employment	W.D. Granger
Family	S.T. Anticoni
Immigration	S.T. Anticoni
Litigation	J.W. Whitehead
Media	C.S. Jennings
Property	J.S. Siddall
Trust and estate planning	A.G. Cuppage

CAMPBELL SMITH WS

21 YORK PLACE, EDINBURGH, EH1 3EN
Tel: (0131) 556 3737 **Fax:** (0131) 473 7700 **DX:** 51 EDINBURGH

The Firm: Campbell Smith WS is a broadly-based firm which expanded recently on merging with two smaller legal practices. A range of services is provided for both commercial and private clients, including full estate agency services.

Principal Areas of Work:

Commercial: *(Contact:*Neil Ferguson). The firm provides advice on all aspects of commercial law for a range of businesses, from public companies to sole traders. All aspects of commercial property work are undertaken including that relating to agricultural businesses and licenced premises.

Litigation: *(Contact:*John H. Crawford). The firm undertakes civil litigation on behalf of public authorities, commercial clients and private clients, with personal injury litigation a particular strength.

Private Client: *(Contact:*David Henderson or Eric J. Scott). The range of services includes residential conveyancing, matrimonial and family work, taxation advice, trusts, wills, estate administration and executry work.

Estate Agency Services: Full estate agency services are provided including inspections and valuations, preparation of particulars, marketing and viewing arrangements.

Education: *(Contact:*Eric J. Scott). The firm is able to provide particular advice in relation to recorded children with special educational needs.

Senior partner:	J.H. Crawford
Number of partners:	5
Assistant solicitors:	3
Other fee-earners:	4

WORKLOADS	
Property; conveyancing (commercial and domestic)	45%
Court including matrimonial and litigation	35%
Trust	19%
Financial	1%

CONTACTS	
Commercial	D.N. Ferguson/ David Henderson
Education	Eric Scott
Litigation	John H. Crawford
Private client	David Henderson/ Eric Scott

CAMPBELL SMITH W.S.

SOLICITORS

CANTER LEVIN & BERG 46-48 Stanley St, Liverpool, L1 6AL *Tel:* (0151) 474 5757 *Fax:* (0151) 474 5763 *DX:* 14122 *Ptnrs:* 12 *Asst solrs:* 15 *Other fee-earners:* 21

CAPSTICKS

77-83 UPPER RICHMOND ROAD, LONDON, SW15 2TT
Tel: (0181) 780 2211 **Fax:** (0181) 780 1141 **DX:** 59461 PUTNEY .

This firm is one of the leading legal advisers to the National Health Service. It handles litigation, commercial and property work for NHS Trusts and health authorities, as well as other public sector bodies and insurers.

The Firm: Founded in the late 1970s to act on behalf of the NHS, CAPSTICKS has invested heavily in developing an outstanding level of expertise through a modern infrastructure of research, training and data management. It also operates stringent quality controls and has held the ISO 9001 standard of quality assurance for professional firms since 1994. The firm's innovative approach and standards of excellence have helped it to attract an exceptionally able team of lawyers.

CAPSTICKS has won a number of accolades for excellence. The firm won the Lawyer/HIFAL award "Law Firm of the Year (the best medium-sized firm)" in 1997 and the TSB Business of Law award in 1994. Its diploma course in risk management (now in its seventh year) is accredited by the Open University.

Principal Areas of Work: The firm's work is divided between the clinical negligence, property and commercial and litigation and advisory departments.

The clinical negligence department handles a large volume of cases, ranging from small claims to disasters arising from obstetric accidents, which comprise some of the largest PI claims in this country. Part of CAPSTICKS' research has been into how such accidents may be avoided and this work forms a large part of the firm's *pro bono* programme.

Health service management requires compliance with an ever-growing volume of regulations and CAPSTICKS has concentrated its resources to deal with these matters. This work is intellectually challenging and the advisory department guides clients through some of the most sensitive decisions taken in the NHS, such as decisions to close major hospitals or departments, from which judicial reviews may well follow. The advisory department is supported by an expert system which enables lawyers to have on-line access to CAPSTICKS' database of previous advice, articles and precedents derived from more than 20,000 NHS cases.

The property and commercial department advises on many PFI projects and has already completed several schemes. Innovative work is also being carried out in the primary care field including advising on new primary care pilot schemes and on joint ventures between Health Authorities and

Senior partner:	Brian Capstick
Number of partners:	16
Assistant solicitors:	29
Other fee-earners:	21

WORKLOADS	
Clinical Negligence	50%
Litigation and advisory	25%
Property and commercial	25%

CONTACTS	
Clinical Negligence	Brian Capstick
Litigation and advisory	Peter Edwards
Property and commercial	Hilary Blackwell

Continues overleaf

Local Authorities. The commercial department has particular expertise in the procurement of computer and other services to the NHS, including the European Union Rules and our commercial litigators have been recovering substantial sums of monies lost through fraud on the NHS.

The firm maintains its own data processing company (which also looks after about 30 other legal practices) and has one of the most advanced IT applications in private practice.

CAPSTICKS sees its future in further expansion in the health service and the public sector, through development of all its areas of expertise and innovative services.

CARLESS DAVIES & CO 140 Stourbridge Road, Halesowen, B63 3UL *Tel:* (0121) 550 2181 *Fax:* (0121) 550 9954 *DX:* 14506 Halesowen *Ptnrs:* 2 *Asst solrs:* 1 *Other fee-earners:* 2

CARNSON MORROW GRAHAM 18 Main Street, Bangor, BT20 5AE *Tel:* (01247) 457911 *Fax:* (01247) 450679

CARRICK CARR & WRIGHT

NORWICH HOUSE, SAVILE STREET, KINGSTON UPON HULL, HU1 3ES
Tel: (01482) 325385/590000 **Fax:** (01482) 327584 **DX:** 11935 HULL

APPLETON HOUSE, 3A WEDNESDAY MARKET, BEVERLEY, HU17 0DG
Tel: (01482) 869342 **Fax:** (01482) 867796 **DX:** 28321 BEVERLEY

106 MICKLEGATE, YORK, YO1 1XZ
Tel: (01904) 686631 **Fax:** (01904) 686621 **DX:** 61511 YORK 1

Best known for its Debt Recovery, Accident Claims, Commercial Litigation and Company/Commercial Work. Also handles Commercial Property; Conveyancing, Family and Private Client Matters, Medical Negligence.

Managing partner:	Jonathan Carr
Senior partner:	John Wright
Number of partners:	7
Assistant solicitors:	3
Other fee-earners:	15

CARRICK READ INSOLVENCY

TRAFALGAR HOUSE, 29 PARK PLACE, LEEDS, LS1 2SP
Tel: (0113) 243 2911 **Fax:** (0113) 244 2863 **DX:** 14085 LEEDS

NORWICH HOUSE, SAVILLE STREET, HULL, HU1 3ES
Tel: (01482) 211160 **Fax:** (01482) 585798 **DX:** 119935 HULL

SALISBURY HOUSE, LONDON WALL, LONDON, EC2M 5PS
Tel: (0171) 216 5560 **Fax:** (0171) 628 7525

The Firm: Carrick Read Insolvency is the merged insolvency departments of Read Hind Stewart, Garwood Devine and Druces and Attlee forming a specialist insolvency practice operating from offices in Hull, Leeds and London. The firm is backed by the combined resources of three offices and more than 140 staff. The partners are all licensed insolvency practitioners and the practice acts on behalf of liquidators, receivers, administrators, trustees and those on both sides of the insolvency procedure.

Managing partner:	Christopher Garwood
Number of partners:	3
Assistant solicitors:	11
Other fee-earners:	16

WORKLOADS	
Insolvency	100%

CARSON & MCDOWELL

MURRAY HOUSE, MURRAY STREET, BELFAST, BT1 6HS
Tel: (01232) 244951 **Fax:** (01232) 245768 **DX:** 403 NR BELFAST **Email:** LAW@CARSON-MCDOWELL.COM

The Firm: Founded in 1852, the firm has considerable reputation in Northern Ireland and beyond for its experience in all aspects of Corporate and Commercial Practice, Commercial Property, Corporate Finance, Insolvency, Employment, Commercial Contracts, Civil Litigation and Arbitration. We also have a particular reputation in Professional Negligence Defence, both medical and legal. Outside the province, we have strong relationships with leading firms in Dublin, London and the regional centres, often operating as the NI link in projects for inward investment. The firm has recently strengthened its expertise in the field of PFI.

Principal Areas of Work:

Company & Commercial: (Michael Johnston, David Jamison) Our corporate department offers a complete service, covering all areas of practice involving close co-operation with other professionals. We have established links with a number of firms in The City of London through working in concert with them on many transactions. We have acted in the privatisation of Northern Ireland Public Utilities.

Commercial Property: (Alan Reilly, Jeremy Hill) Our commercial property department deals with the purchase, development, management and sale of business property, from the single shop unit to the City Centre office building. We provide a complete package, including site assembly, project management, developments by way of lease, mortgage and onward investment sale. We are equally experienced in residential development.

Commercial Security: (Roger Nixon) An established commercial security department which has built sound relationships with financial institutions in the province and beyond. We have extensive experience with the various forms of security which are available. We will also deal with investigation of property title land searches and enquiries, companies office file searches, property insurance cover and appropriate legal registrations and statutory notices.

Litigation: (Brian Turtle, Peter Davison, Ken Gouk) Our practice has many years of experience, not only in the traditional court system but also in the area of Equal Opportunity Tribunal, Employment Tribunal and Lands Tribunal, Planning Applications and Building Arbitrations. We provide a similar level of assistance in the specialised fields of law such as Professional Negligence, Marine Law, Defamation and Carriage of Goods. We have extensive experience in those areas of the law which are unique to Nothern Ireland such as The Criminal Damage Legislation, Fair Employment Law, and the licensing of the sale of intoxicating liquor and bookmakers' premises. In the business field we handle all types of commercial litigation, from simple debt collection (our debt collection system now has its own dedicated computer base) through to normal contractual claims, intellectual property and employment problems to the major commercial dispute which may involve domestic and European law. In addition, we will deal with the many and varied problems which inevitably arise from corporate insolvency.

Senior partner:	W.B.W. Turtle
Number of partners:	8
Assistant solicitors:	13
Other fee-earners:	10

WORKLOADS	
Civil litigation	35%
Commercial property	30%
Company/ commercial	30%
Private client	5%

CONTACTS	
Civil litigation	Brian Turtle
Commercial lit./Arbitration	Peter Davison
Commercial property	Alan Reilly
Commercial security	Roger Nixon
Company/Commercial	Michael Johnston
Employment	Brian Turtle
PFI	Michael Johnston
Professional negligence	Ken Gouk

CARTER HODGE

18 HOGHTON ST, SOUTHPORT, PR9 0PB
Tel: (01704) 531991 **Fax:** (01704) 537475 **DX:** 20102 **Email:** INFORMATION@CARTERHODGE.CO.UK **Internet:** WWW.CARTERHODGE.CO.UK

The Firm: Carter Hodge is a general practice offering a wide range of services to business and private clients. Tracing its origins from 1889 the Firm has modern and progressive outlook from its involvement with Legal Aid Franchising, Investors in People and Practice Management Standards to the award winning Financial Services Department.

The Firm is regulated by The Law Society in the conduct of investment business.

Principal Areas of Work: Litigation (High Court work, commercial litigation, PI and professional negligence), Family, Company/Commercial, Property, Private Client, Criminal.

Other Offices: Ainsdale, Birkdale, Heswall and St. Helens.

Managing Partner:	Stephen Holmes/
	Mark Robinson/David Rigby
Number of Partners:	7
Assistant Solicitors:	6
Other Fee-earners:	10

CONTACTS	
Commercial conveyancing	Stephen Holmes
Criminal	Nick Archer
Financial services	Stephen Holmes
General litigation	Mark Robinson
Matrimonial	Lynne Coventry
Personal injury	Mark Robinson
Probate & trust	David Byard
Residential conveyancing	Stephen Holmes

CARTER LEMON 11 Breams Building, London, EC4A 1HB *Tel:* (0171) 405 7554 *Fax:* (0171) 242 3926 *DX:* 25 London *Ptnrs:* 9 *Asst solrs:* 2 *Other fee-earners:* 4

CARTMELL SHEPHERD Viaduct House, Carlisle, CA3 8EZ *Tel:* (01228) 531561 *Fax:* (01228) 401490 *DX:* 63006 *Ptnrs:* 12 *Asst solrs:* 14 *Other fee-earners:* 13

CARTWRIGHT CUNNINGHAM HASELGROVE & CO 282-284 Hoe Street, Walthamstow, London, E17 9PL *Tel:* (0181) 520 1021 *Fax:* (0181) 520 5107 *DX:* 32007 Walthamstow *Ptnrs:* 10 *Asst solrs:* 14 *Other fee-earners:* 11

CARTWRIGHT & LEWIS 100 Hagley Road, Edgbaston, Birmingham, B16 8LT **Tel:** (0121) 452 1989 **Fax:** (0121) 456 3977 **DX:** 707293 Edgbaston **Ptnrs:** 11 **Asst solrs:** 8 **Other fee-earners:** 10 **Contact:** Mr Anthony Rich *Known for commercial litigation. Has one of the largest personal injury departments in the West Midlands.*

WORKLOADS			
Personal injury	49%	Property	20%
Family	9%	Commercial litigation	7%
Crime	6%	Probate/ trusts	5%
Company/ commercial	4%		

CARTWRIGHTS

MARSH HOUSE, 11 MARSH STREET, BRISTOL, BS99 7BB
Tel: (0117) 929 3601 **Fax:** (0117) 926 2403 **DX:** 7851 BRISTOL **Email:** INFO@CARTWRIGHTS.COM

The Firm: Cartwrights is recognised as a leading national firm in the fields of transport, leisure and licensing and has one of the largest insurance departments in the South West. The firm is also known for its expertise in employment, property and company commercial work. Lawyers increasingly work together in market sector groups to meet the needs of a wide range of businesses from start ups to quoted PLCs.

Principal Areas of Work:

Commercial: (*Contact:*Chris Mitchell). Regularly handles large scale commercial transactions. The department comprises specialist units dealing with company/commercial, commercial property, compulsory purchase and planning, commercial litigation, employment, computer & IT law, and transport. The firm's employment unit offers a complete service to employers, combining legal, human resource and industrial relations skills in a seamless package supplemented by practical training services.

Leisure and Licensing: (*Contact:*Tim Davies). A complete nationwide and EU-wide service to clients operating in the food and drink retailing, licensed trade, bingo, casino, cinema and leisure sectors including many high street names. A section of the department specialises in food hygiene, packaging and labelling matters.

Insurance: (*Contact:*David Vernalls). Work includes investigating and handling insurance litigation claims, criminal prosecutions under health and safety and road traffic legislation, inquests and public inquiries. The department is organised into specialist units including Health and Safety, Occupational Diseases, Motor, Employers' Liability, Public Liability, Property Risks and Product Liability.

Private Client: (*Contact:* Andrew Blair). Work includes civil litigation particularly professional negligence, medical negligence and conveyancing.

Nature of Clientele: Over 20 FTSE 100 companies including major UK leisure and brewery companies, supermarket chains and insurance companies; local authorities including regional airports, port authorities; construction companies; computer companies; entrepreneurs; local businesses of all sizes; loss adjusters, self-insuring PLCs and private individuals.

Recruitment: Recruitment of professional staff is dealt with by Christopher Eskell. Applications for a training contract should be made two years in advance. A brochure and application form are available on request.

Foreign Connections: Cartwrights has established contacts with law firms in Europe, USA, the Far East and Australia. The firm is a member of Eurolink for Lawyers. French, German and Welsh spoken.

Managing partner:	Christopher Eskell
Senior partner:	Geoffrey Jones
Number of partners:	16
Assistant solicitors:	27
Other fee-earners:	22

WORKLOADS	
Commercial	34%
Insurance	33%
Licensing and leisure	26%
Private	7%

CONTACTS	
Commercial litigation	Nigel Puddicombe
Commercial property	Ian Dunn
Compulsory purchase/planning	Emrys Parry
Construction	Nigel Williams
Corporate	Chris Mitchell
Employment	Geoffrey Jones
Food safety, consumer protection	Michael Parrott
Health & safety	Christopher Eskell
Insurance/personal injury	David Vernalls
IT/computer	Nigel Williams
Licensing and leisure/gaming	Tim Davies
Local authorities	Emrys Parry
Private client	Andrew Blair
Transport	Geoffrey Jones

CARTWRIGHTS
SOLICITORS

CARTWRIGHTS ADAMS & BLACK

36 WEST BUTE STREET, CARDIFF, CF1 5UA
Tel: (01222) 465959 **Fax:** (01222) 480006 **DX:** 200751 CARDIFF BAY

The Firm: Established in 1988 when Adams & Black merged with the Cardiff Office of Cartwrights. The firm has maintained its high reputation with regard, in particular, to Defendant Personal Injury, transport, professional conduct and licensing. The firm continues to practice from its Cardiff Bay Offices in the heart of one of Europe's most exciting Developments.

Principal Areas of Work:

Personal Injury: Specialist Industrial Disease Department. Almost exclusively Defendant Employer's Liability Personal Injury serving heavy industry. Includes some Defendant RTA and Public Liability.

Professional Conduct: With the Partner in charge having higher rights of audience in the Civil Courts, this Department is expanding quickly. Work includes prosecution and Defence.

Commercial Department: Focusing on commercial conveyancing, trade agreements and all aspects of company law.

Commercial Litigation: Handles all aspects of High and County Court Work for Corporate Clients. Includes construction, arbitration etc.

Licensing: Countrywide for established brewing clients, hotels, individual licences and retail outlets.

Transport: We operate countrywide conducting all advocacy for a large number of hauliers, the FTA and RHA.

Prosecution: Conducted on behalf of a number of Clients who retain their rights to private prosecution.

Employment: All aspects, mainly for employers including representation before Industrial Tribunals, Contracts of Employment, service occupancies, discrimination.

Other: Private client work to include probate, domestic conveyancing and immigration.

Recruitment and Training: The firm is always keen to consider quality candidates from the UK or overseas. Applications with a CV to Mr Christopher Childs.

Managing partner:	Lyndon Brain
Senior partner:	Lyndon Brain
Number of partners:	7
Assistant solicitors:	1
Other fee-earners:	5

CONTACTS	
Commercial Department	Mrs SGT Parnell
Commercial Litigation	A S Jones
Employment	C Childs
Licensing	C Childs
Other	Mrs SGT Parnell
Personal injury	JL Brain
Professional Conduct	G Williams
Prosecution	C Childs
Transport	G Williams

CHADBOURNE & PARKE

REGIS HOUSE, 45 KING WILLIAM STREET, LONDON, EC4R 9AN
Tel: (0171) 337 8000 **Fax:** (0171) 337 8001

The Firm: Chadbourne & Parke LLP is an international law firm with its main office in New York City and additional offices in Washington, Los Angeles, Moscow, Hong Kong and Singapore. In London, the firm conducts its practice through Chadbourne & Parke, a multi-national partnership which includes registered foreign lawyers and solicitors. They have reciprocal relationships with firms in Almaty, Melbourne, Minsk and Tokyo. They provide a full range of legal services on corporate, project finance and energy, litigation, intellectual property, domestic and international tax, employment law and ERISA, environmental, insurance and reinsurance, trusts and estates, government contracts, and corporate finance matters.

Their London office provides a range of legal services, with a particular focus on project finance, product liability, corporate finance, international tax, and insurance and reinsurance matters. Solicitors and attorneys in their London office participate in the firm's project finance practice and provide a base for servicing our U.S. and non U.S. clients in infrastructure development and financing throughout the world.

Contact partner:	William Greason
Number of partners:	5
Associates:	3

CHAFFE STREET

BROOK HOUSE, 70 SPRING GARDENS, MANCHESTER, M2 2BQ
Tel: (0161) 236 5800 **Fax:** (0161) 228 6862 **DX:** 14431 MANCHESTER

The firm provides a full range of specialist commercial legal services; namely company/ commercial work, commercial property, corporate recovery and commercially orientated litigation.

The services available include flotations, acquisitions and disposals, mergers, management buy-outs, banking law, venture and investment capital, project and asset financing, corporate finance, insolvency, intellectual property, competition law, employment law, pensions, aircraft, commercial property and environmental law.

Managing partner:	R.H. Street
Senior partner:	R.H. Street
Number of partners:	14
Assistant solicitors:	6
Other fee-earners:	7

WORKLOADS	
Company/ commercial	65%
Commercial property	25%
Commercial litigation	10%

CHALLINORS LYON CLARK Guardian House, Cronehills Linkway, West Bromwich, B70 8SW *Tel:* (0121) 553 3211 *Fax:* (0121) 553 2079 *DX:* 713650 West Bromwich 6 *Ptnrs:* 21 *Asst solrs:* 22 *Other fee-earners:* 20

CHAMBERS & CO Jonathan Scott Hall, Thorpe Road, Norwich, NR1 1UH *Tel:* (01603) 616 155 *Fax:* (01603) 616 156

CHAPMAN EVERATT 8 Temple Street, Birmingham, B2 5BT **Tel:** (0121) 633 7440 **Fax:** (0121) 633 7262 **DX:** 13025 Birmingham **Ptnrs:** 5 **Asst solrs:** 3 **Other fee-earners:** 2 **Contact:** Richard Chapman *Specialist Defendant personal injury/employers' liability/ practice.*

WORKLOADS	
Defendant Personal Injury	100%

CHARLES LUCAS & MARSHALL 28 Bartholomew St, Newbury, RG14 5EU *Tel:* (01635) 521212 *Fax:* (01635) 37784 *DX:* 30802 *Ptnrs:* 17 *Asst solrs:* 8 *Other fee-earners:* 20

CHARLES RUSSELL

8-10 NEW FETTER LANE, LONDON, EC4A 1RS
Tel: (0171) 203 5000 **Fax:** (0171) 203 0200 **DX:** 19 LONDON/CHANCERY LANE **Internet:** WWW.CR-LAW.COM

Charles Russell is a prominent London law firm which is committed to advising both corporate and private clients.

The Firm: Founded over two centuries ago, it is based in the heart of legal London, in EC4, and has additional offices in EC3, Cheltenham and Guildford. As the UK member of the American Law Firm Association and the London member of the Association of European Lawyers, the firm has a network of close professional contacts throughout the world.

The firm has grown rapidly in recent years becoming increasingly well known in the field of business whilst retaining its long established reputation for private client and family work. So, although the firm remains one of a handful of City firms to whom discerning individuals turn for advice, it also acts for numerous listed companies and institutions.

Principal Areas of Work: Whilst the firm advises corporate clients in a wide range of industries on commercial and litigious matters, the following distinct markets constitute those for which Charles Russell is best known:

Media & Communications, insurance, commercial property and charities.

Industry groups are supported by a number of specialist teams which include employment and employee benefits, corporate finance, tax, EC/competition, intellectual property, computer law and planning.

> **Commercial/corporate:** Includes stock market flotations, mergers and acquisitions, venture capital financing, banking, institutional funding arrangements, management buy-outs and buy-ins, business start-ups and corporate rescues. Advice is also given on commercial contracts of all kinds, agency and distribution agreements, partnership matters and all aspects of corporate tax.
>
> **Litigation:** The litigation team deals with a full range of matters, both in the UK and overseas, with a special emphasis on commercial disputes, contentious IP, sports regulation, Judicial Review, pharmacy law and medical and professional negligence.

Managing partner:	Patrick Russell
Senior partner:	Laurie Watt
Number of partners:	62
Assistant solicitors:	65
Other fee-earners:	35

WORKLOADS	
Private Capital/Family	27%
Litigation (commercial)	18%
Commercial Property	17%
Media & Communications	11%
Other Corporate & Commercial	10%
Insurance/Reinsurance	9%
Charities	8%

CONTACTS	
Charities	Michael Scott
Commercial Property	Michael Bennett
Computer Law	David Berry
Corporate & Commercial	James Holder
Employment	David Green
Family	Peter George
Insurance/Reinsurance	Stephen Carter
Intellectual Property	Robin Bynoe
Litigation	Richard Vallance
Media & Communications	Mark Moncreiffe
Pensions and Employee Benefits	Andrew Hudson
Planning	Geoffrey Jordan
Private Capital	W. Paul Harriman
Private Property	Hugh Jackson
Sport	Patrick Russell
Tax	George Duncan

Commercial Property: Charles Russell's commercial property group advises investors, developers and occupiers. In addition to handling the acquisition/disposal of industrial, commercial and retail property, the team devises and negotiates financing agreements. It also handles landlord and tenant arrangements and all aspects of management for commercial property.

Media & Communications: The group provides an integrated service to the converging industries which include telecommunications, information technology, multimedia, film, music, entertainment and sport.

Insurance: From its specialist insurance office, the firm advises international insurance/reinsurance companies and consultants, Lloyd's syndicates, mutuals, brokers, underwriting agents and run-off managers on both contentious and non-contentious matters.

Charities: The firm has a long established, varied and expanding charities practice comprising a team of specialists who provide a full range of legal services.

Private Capital: Charles Russell is home to one of the UK's leading private client and family practices. The family team deals with issues relating to marriage, its breakdown, separation, divorce, residence, contact and child abduction, often involving legal and financial disputes in differing international jurisdictions. Furthermore, the firm advises wealthy individuals, successful entrepreneurs, professionals and institutions, both in the UK and internationally, on tax, trust, estate restructuring, probate, including contentious probate, trust administration, agriculture and property transactions and management. Literature and briefing notes are available on request.

Other Offices: Killowen House, Bayshill Road, Cheltenham, GL50 3AW. *Telephone*: (01242) 221122 *Contact* Francis Rundall. The Old Magistrates Court, 71 North Street, Guildford, GU1 4BJ. *Telephone*: (01483) 252525 *Contact* Roger Pierce.

CHARLES STANSFIELD & CO 96 Water Lane, Wilmslow, SK9 5BB *Tel:* (01625) 539695 *Fax:* (01625) 535863

CHARSLEY HARRISON

RIDING COURT, RIDING COURT ROAD, DATCHET, SLOUGH, SL3 9LF
Tel: (01753) 586000 **Fax:** (01753) 582233 **DX:** 42267 SLOUGH WEST

The Firm: Formed by the merger in 1973 of two long established and well respected Thames Valley practices, Charsley Harrison is a modern, forward-thinking firm geared to meet the needs of both commercial and private clients. The practice has developed rapidly in recent years to represent a wide range of business clients throughout the UK, the EC, the USA and the Pacific Basin and has established links with commercial lawyers in the major cities of the USA, Australia and throughout Europe. Unfettered by the high accommodation and staffing costs of city centre firms the practice is able to ensure a high degree of partner involvement in the day to day matters of clients, and a prompt, efficient and professional service.

Principal Areas of Work:

Company and Commercial: (*Contact:* Phillip Jones). A comprehensive service both domestically and internationally encompassing corporate finance, competition, acquisitions and disposals, mergers, MBOs and joint ventures, distribution and agency agreements, intellectual property rights, taxation, insolvency and employment law matters.

Litigation: (*Contact:* Kate McCulloch). All aspects of litigation for both corporate and private clients in the UK and abroad before a wide range of courts and tribunals. Work includes general contractual and commercial disputes, misrepresentation, employment matters, insolvency and banking-related litigation, personal injury, professional negligence and defamation.

Property: (*Contact:* Simon Doyle). Extensive experience of property transactions including purchase, sale, leasing and mortgaging of commercial and retail property, estate development, planning and environmental advice, licensing, site assembly, joint ventures and agricultural property.

Private Client: (*Contact:* Giles Shedden). The firm has a long tradition in providing a friendly and efficient service to individuals in all aspects of their private legal affairs. Work includes wills, tax and estate planning, personal and family finance, investment management, pensions, saving schemes and school fees planning, charity law and Court of Protection work. A full service is also provided in relation to matrimonial and family law including childcare and adoption.

Other Offices: Windsor, Slough and Ascot. Associated firm in the Netherlands.

Senior partner:	Simon Doyle
Number of partners:	6
Assistant solicitors:	2
Other fee-earners.	8

Notaries Public	
Phillip Jones	(01753) 586 000
Giles Sheddon	(01753) 851 591
Peter Beech	(01753) 517600

WORKLOADS	
Company/ commercial	35%
Property	33%
Litigation	18%
Probate/ trust	5%

CONTACTS	
Company/ commercial	Phillip Jones
Litigation	Kate McCulloch
Probate/ trust	Giles Shedden
Property	Simon Doyle

CHATTERTONS 28 Wide Bargate, Boston, PE21 6RT **Tel:** (01205) 351114 **Fax:** (01205) 356018 **DX:** 26803 **Ptnrs:** 9 **Asst solrs:** 14 **Other fee-earners:** 11 **Contact:** Mr Peter L. Cropley, Senior Partner *General practice known for property work, insolvency, commercial, agricultural and planning law, litigation and private client work. Other offices at Horncastle and Sleaford Lincolnshire.*

WORKLOADS			
Litigation	44%	Property	24%
Trust/Tax/Probate	17%	Company/Commercial	8%
Insolvency	5%	Pension	1%
Planning	1%		

C & H JEFFERSON

NORWICH UNION HOUSE, 7 FOUNTAIN STREET, BELFAST, BT1 5EA
Tel: (01232) 329545 **Fax:** (01232) 244644 **DX:** 439 NR.BELFAST

The Firm: Established in 1898, C& H Jefferson is one of the leading practices in Northern Ireland with an excellent reputation for its comprehensive legal and agency services.

Principal Areas of Work:

Litigation: The firm is one of the largest litigation practices in Northern Ireland, specialising in all areas of defence and commercial litigation and has corporate membership of FOIL.

Commercial: The firm has a strong commercial department embracing commercial property transactions; banking and securities, company formations, sales, acquisitions and reconstructions; partnerships; insolvency; debt recovery; agency work for leading firms in Great Britain and elsewhere, maritime law and defamation.

Employment: The firm has a vibrant employment law practice with a dedicated team, particularly acting for employers, with extensive expertise in discrimination law (sex, religion and disability), and advising on contracts of employment.

Private Client: We provide a full range of services commensurate with a long established practice including conveyancing; wills and administration of estates; tax planning and trusts and family law.

Foreign Languages: Spanish, Italian and French.

Managing partner:	H.L.I. Jefferson
Number of partners:	8
Assistant solicitors:	10
Other fee-earners:	4

WORKLOADS	
Litigation	65%
Commercial	20%
Employment	10%
Private Client	5%

CONTACTS	
Commercial	Kenneth Rutherford
Employment	Mark Tinman
Litigation	Gareth Jones
Private Client	David Lennon

CHRIS HARRISON & COMPANY

GODOLPHIN HOUSE, 7/8 CATHEDRAL LANE, TRURO, TR1 2QS
Tel: (01872) 241408 **Fax:** (01872) 273848 **DX:** 81212 TRURO

The Firm: Chris Harrison & Company is a niche practice with 2 departments.

Principal Areas of Work: Domestic and Commercial Conveyancing, Business and Residential Leases, Partnership Law, Probate and Wills.

Chris Harrison, the Principal of the firm, has over 17 years experience in these areas.

Personal Injury and Medical Negligence: The firm employs 2 executives, one of whom has now completed 30 years in the legal profession. Whilst acting in all types of personal injury claims there is an emphasis towards head injury matters with the firm being on Headway's list of recommended solicitors. In medical negligence matters the firm acts exclusively for the victims of medical injury with one of our executives being a member of the Cornwall Community Health Council.

Managing partner:	Chris Harrison
Number of partners:	1
Other fee-earners:	4

CONTACTS	
Personal injury/medical neg.	Adrian Hickman (Executive)
Personal injury/medical neg.	Claire Wallens (Executive)
Priv./comm. conveyancing etc	Chris Harrison (Principal)
Priv./comm. conveyancing etc	Peggy Morris (Executive)

CHRISTIAN FISHER

42 MUSEUM STREET, BLOOMSBURY, LONDON, WC1A 1LY
Tel: (0171) 831 1750 **Fax:** (0171) 831 1726 **DX:** 35737 BLOOMSBURY

The Firm: Christian Fisher was set up in 1985 and specialises in civil liberties and human rights work. The firm has a long standing reputation for undertaking high profile test cases in these areas and a commitment to delivering high quality legal aid work. It has a franchise in personal injury, crime, housing, employment and immigarion.

Principal Areas of Work:

Human Rights Cases: The firm expects to bring many test cases on the new Human Rights Act. Past cases have included the lead Court of Appeal case on damages against the police (Hsu). Cases on suing the police for negligence (Osman in the ECHR and Reeves in the House of Lords), judicial review of regulations withdrawing benefit from asylum seekers (ex parte B), deaths in custody (Wayne Douglas) many judicial reviews of government and miscarriage of justice cases.

Number of partners:	3
Assistant solicitors:	6
Other fee-earners:	3

Personal Injury: The firm has a particular profile in the areas of construction, environmental and transport safety and a substantial case load in these areas. It has acted in the Lockerbie and Marchioness Disasters and is currently the lead firm in the Steering Committee representing the victims of the Southall Train Crash. It also has a developing medical negligence practice.

Crime: Major criminal trials including fraud, political crime and miscarriages of justice.

Employment: Particularly race and sex discrimination and trades union cases.

Housing: For tenants – disrepair and homelessness

Immigration: A track record in acting for asylum seekers.

CHURCH BRUCE HAWKES BRASINGTON & PHILLIPS 51-54 Windmill St, Gravesend, DA12 1BD *Tel:* (01474) 560361 *Fax:* (01474) 328315 *DX:* 6800 Gravesend *Ptnrs:* 6 *Asst solrs:* 3 *Other fee-earners:* 6

C & J BLACK Linenhall House, 13 Linenhall Street, Belfast, BT2 8AA *Tel:* (01232) 550060 *Fax:* (01232) 234125 *DX:* 431 NR Belfast 1 *Ptnrs:* 3 *Asst solrs:* 1 *Other fee-earners:* 1

CLAIRMONTS 9 Clairmont Gardens, Glasgow, G3 7LW *Tel:* (0141) 226 3020 *Fax:* (0141) 221 0127 *DX:* 512212 Glasgow

CLAREMONT SMITH

125 HIGH HOLBORN, LONDON, WC1V 6QF
Tel: (0171) 405 8811 **Fax:** (0171) 831 0973 **DX:** 372 LONDON CHANCERY LANE

The Firm: The origins of Claremont Smith can be traced back in Central London to February 1814. It is best known for its work in the fields of pensions and commercial property acting as it does in relation to all legal affairs of one of the UK's larger pension funds.

Principal Areas of Work: Pensions; commercial property; telecommunications law; European and competition law; commercial litigation; trade associations; personal injury litigation and employment law.

Managing partner:	Roger D. Smith
Senior partner:	Roger D. Smith
Number of partners:	10
Assistant solicitors:	3

CLARICOAT PHILLIPS

140 BARNSBURY ROAD, LONDON, N1 0ER
Tel: (0171) 226 7000 **Fax:** (0171) 833 4408

The Firm: John Claricoat and Hilary Phillips were both in private practice before joining the government service. She initially joined DES in 1970 for 3 years, he the Charity Commission in 1966. They were senior lawyers there until they set up as Claricoat Phillips Associates in 1994. Jordan's have published their Charity Law A-Z, Key Questions Answered and they have written many articles for charity and legal periodicals. They act as consultants both to lay clients and their professional advisers.

Number of partners:	2

CLARKE WILLMOTT & CLARKE

THE WATERFRONT, WELSH BACK, BRISTOL, BS1 4SB
Tel: (0117) 941 6600 **Fax:** (0117) 941 6622 **DX:** 78247 BRISTOL 1

The Firm: Clarke Willmott & Clarke is one of the leading firms in the South West. The firm combines close partner contact with commercially aware advice to meet a range of commercial and private needs.

High quality, creative advice is provided promptly and economically through integrated teams of specialists. The firm's lawyers concentrate on long-term commercial benefits and work closely with clients to ensure that these are identified within well managed relationships.

Clients range from major Plcs and multinationals to prominent landowners and farmers. Building societies and insurance companies are also represented alongside associations, institutions and individuals.

Principal Areas of Work:

Company/Commercial: (*Contact:* Robert Hunt (Bristol)). Public and private company and commercial transactions including takeovers, hive-downs, joint ventures, shareholder agreements, restructuring, acquisitions and sales of unincorporated undertakings, commercial and distribution agreements and the associated employment issues.

Commercial Property: (*Contact:* Ian Macaulay (Bristol) and Roger Seaton (Taunton Blackbrook)). Considerable experience in acquisitions, sales, joint ventures, development agreements and landlord and tenant.

Planning: (*Contact:* John Houghton (Bristol) and Nick Engert (Taunton Blackbrook)). This expanding team has acquired a national reputation in all matters relating to town and country planning and land development. Advice on planning applications and enforcement notices, Section 106 agreements and representation before Public Inquiries.

Environmental Law: (*Contact:* John Houghton (Bristol) and Tim Hayden (Taunton Blackbrook)). One of the few firms in the South West offering specialisation in both contentious and non-contentious matters. Prosecution and defence work for both statutory bodies and private clients and advice on non-contentious issues, particularly contaminated land and waste disposal.

Private Client: (*Contact:* Stuart Thorne (Taunton)). The firm prides itself on the quality and range of services offered to the private client including personal tax planning, asset management, wills, trusts and probate, administration of estates, family, matrimonial and residential conveyancing.

Agriculture: (*Contact:* Tim Russ (Yeovil)). The firm has a long tradition in support of the farming and agricultural community in the South West and is particularly active in the area of agricultural tenancies and milk quotas.

Litigation: (*Contact:* David Sedgwick (Bristol)). A wide range of general commercial litigation including commercial contracts, building disputes, employment disputes, defamation, intellectual property and professional negligence.

Personal Injury: (*Contact:* Peter Livingstone (Yeovil)). A specialist team which has gained a national reputation for its practical handling of personal injury, medical negligence and other damage claims for both defendant and plaintiff.

Insolvency/Debt Collection: (*Contact:* Stephen Allinson LIP (Taunton Blackbrook) for insolvency or Jane Dunlop (Yeovil) for computerised debt collection).

Licensing: (*Contact:* Tim Hayden (Taunton Blackbrook)). Advice relating to licensed premises, breweries, and individual owners and licensees, betting and gaming, and registered and proprietary clubs.

Foreign Connections: Clarke Willmott & Clarke has strong links with lawyers and other professionals throughout Europe. Languages spoken include French, German, Spanish, Russian, Italian, Dutch and Cantonese.

Recruitment and Training: The firm annually recruits approximately 10 trainee solicitors. Please contact Alan Burnhams, the Director of Human Resources at the Yeovil office.

Other Offices: The firm's other principal offices are Taunton (01823) 337 474, Taunton Blackbrook (01823) 442 266 and Yeovil (01935) 401 401.

Managing Partner:	Tony Monds
Executive Chairman:	Michael Clarke
Number of partners:	35
Assistant solicitors:	61
Directors:	4
Other fee-earners:	82

WORKLOADS	
Private Client including Residential Conveyancing	
	35%
Commercial Litigation and Contentious	29%
Commercial Property	20%
Personal Injury	11%
Corporate	5%

CONTACTS	
Agriculture	Tim Russ
Asset Management	Peter Nellist
Commercial Litigation/ADR	David Sedgwick
Commercial Property	Roger Seaton
Corporate	Robert Hunt
Employment	Kevin Jones
Environmental	John Houghton
Family	Felicity Shakespear
Heath and Safety	Martin Pettingell
Insolvency and Debt Collection	Stephen Allinson LIP
Lender Services	Robert Morfee
Licensing	Tim Hayden
Personal Injury	Peter Livingstone
Planning	Nick Engert
Private Capital	Stuart Thorne
Professional Indemnity	Tim Russ
Residential Property	Angela Thompson
Tax	Nigel Popplewell

CLARK HOLT 1 Sanford Street, Swindon, SN1 1QQ *Tel:* (01793) 617444 *Fax:* (01793) 617436 *DX:* 38606 Swindon *Ptnrs:* 3 *Asst solrs:* 3 *Other fee-earners:* 2

CLARK RICKETTS One Lincoln's Inn Fields, London, WC2A 3AU **Tel:** (0171) 404 1551 **Fax:** (0171) 404 2662 **Ptnrs:** 2 **Asst solrs:** 1 *A practice specialising in all aspects of aviation law, acting for financiers, lessors, airlines and operators.*

WORKLOADS	
Aviation (commercial, regulatory and aviation related litigation)	100%

CLARKS

GREAT WESTERN HOUSE, STATION RD, READING, RG1 1SX
Tel: (0118) 958 5321 **Fax:** (0118) 960 4611 **DX:** 54700 READING 2 **Email:** INMAIL@CLARKS-SOLICITORS.CO.UK
Internet: WWW.CLARKS-SOLICITORS.CO.UK

Clarks is highly regarded as a leading provider of commercial services in the Thames Valley area.

The Firm: Operates from a single office, representing one of the largest concentrations of solicitors in the South East, outside London. It is a recognised leader in several specialist areas as well as having broad commercial depth. The only firm in the Thames Valley to have been ranked in a recent independent survey of FTSE250 companies, clients include multinational and listed companies. The firm also has a large number of relationships with public sector bodies and not-for-profit organisations especially health, education and local government.

Focus is on quality service, strong client relationships and a continual training programme to sustain legal excellence. Every solicitor at Clarks develops specialist expertise in at least one area but not at the expense of broader commercial experience. The firm believes it is important to cultivate legal skills which combine specialist interests with an appreciation of the context in which they are applied. A partner is assigned to each client to provide a personal point of contact at all times. Broader relationships may develop with a range of specialists from different disciplines and bespoke teams are created as necessary to tackle larger projects.

The firm has developed Case Plans and Client Protocols to satisfy the needs of clients. Case Plans provide a project snapshot showing timetable, key events and estimated costs. They are regularly reviewed as part of the firm's strategy of acting in partnership with its clients. Client Protocols clearly define the basis of an ongoing relationship and the manner in which services are provided. They underline the firm's commitment to quality and to achieving its client's objectives.

Clarks' strong training culture is extended to clients. Several practical programmes have been developed aimed at enhancing management performance through greater knowledge of the relevant law and procedures. Clarks' lawyers are called on to deliver training all over the country.

Principal Areas of Work:

The Thames Valley has the stongest economy in the UK outside London and Reading is the region's dynamic commercial capital. Clarks' depth and range of experience reflect its single office culture and its many years presence in this vibrant area.

Company/Corporate Finance: The firm has one of the strongest and best resourced corporate practices in the area and can manage substantial and specialist transactions. It has strong professional contacts – locally, in the City and elsewhere – but the strength of Reading as the regional financial and professional centre means increasingly that deals of this nature can be led from the Thames Valley.

Commercial Property: A large commercial property team acts for owners, developers, investors and funders. Clarks provides a comprehensive property service including PFI projects. The firm offers a highly skilled planning consultancy and handles planning applications and appeals. Another team handles environmental issues and related litigation.

Employment: Of particular importance is the employment law and employee benefits team which has an enviable reputation, not just within the Thames Valley. This is one of the fastest growing areas of business as clients find that employee relations are more and more regulated by national and EU laws. The firm is one of the few outside of London with a specialist pensions practice including provision of independent trustee services.

Litigation: The firm remains one of the leading regional commercial litigation practices. It has unrivalled specialist expertise including hands-on experience of successful Alternative Dispute Resolution.

There are specialist teams for banking, insolvency and construction. In addition, the firm's presence in the centre of silicon valley has resulted in strong intellectual property and IT work.

The firm is noted for its specialist knowledge of certain sectors such as Transport and Logistics, the Motor Industry, Healthcare, Construction, IT and various manufacturing industries.

Clarks has a long-standing European network and can manage transactions on a pan-European basis.

The firm's work includes a high quality private client service, benefitting both business executives and private individuals for whom Clarks is the firm of choice for their property and personal matters.

Managing partner:	Michael Sippitt
Number of partners:	15
Assistant solicitors:	19
Other fee-earners:	16

CONTACTS	
Banking and Finance	David Few
Commercial and European	Peter James
Commercial Property	Tom Howell
Company & Corporate Finance	Richard Lee
Construction	David Rintoul
Corporate Recovery	David Few
Dispute Resolution & Litigation	Antony Morris
Employment Services	Helen Beech
Environment	Derek Ching
Health and Medical Services	Tom Howell
Information Technology	Peter James
Intellectual Property	Peter James
Pensions	David Clark
Planning	Simon Dimmick
Public Sector	Simon Dimmick
Residential Property	Mary Robertson
Wills, Trusts and Tax Planning	Peter Clark

CLARKSON WRIGHT & JAKES

VALIANT HOUSE, 12 KNOLL RISE, ORPINGTON, BR6 0PG
Tel: (01689) 871621 **Fax:** (01689) 878537 **DX:** 31603 ORPINGTON

The Firm: Established in 1875, Clarkson Wright & Jakes is a substantial commercial practice whose aim is to offer a personal service tailored to clients' specific needs. The firm, a member of LawNet, undertakes a wide range of legal work, and offers notarial services and the expertise of units specialising in employment, partnership, doctors' matters and French law. The firm has been recognized as an Investor in People.

Principal Areas of Work are:

(1) **Company & Commercial:** (*Contact Partner:* Michael North). *Work includes:* company and business acquisitions and sales, MBOs and MBIs, franchise, agency, distribution and other commercial agreements, conditions of sale, terms of business, partnership especially for doctors, business start ups.

(2) **Employment:** (*Contact Partner:* Claire Singleton). *Work includes:* contracts of employment and other employment documentation, claims in the Industrial Tribunals and civil courts for dismissal, discrimination and breach of contract.

(3) **Commercial Property:** *Work includes:* acquisition, mortgage and disposal of freehold and leasehold shops, factories and other properties, landlord and tenant matters (including lease renewals and surrenders).

(4) **Commercial Litigation:** (*Contact Partner:* Leslie Seldon). *Work includes:* company, commercial and partnership disputes, construction disputes, arbitration, landlord and tenant matters, defamation, professional negligence, passing off actions and contractual disputes, licensing, debt collection and mortgage repossessions.

(5) **Personal Injury Litigation:** (*Contact Partner:* David Greenhalgh). *Work includes:* motor, employers' and public liability claims, industrial disease and professional indemnity claims; medical negligence.

(6) **Private Client:** (*Contact Partners:* Peter Giblin and Amanda Custis ATII). *Work includes:* residential property, wills and trusts, tax planning, enduring powers of attorney, winding-up of estates and executorships, Court of Protection and matrimonial.

Foreign Languages: French, Italian and Spanish.

Managing partner:	Andrew C. Wright
Senior partner:	Leslie Seldon
Number of partners:	9
Assistant solicitors:	1
Other fee-earners:	13

WORKLOADS	
Private client	25%
Personal injury litigation	20%
Commercial litigation	15%
Commercial property	15%
Company/ commercial (including notarial)	15%
Employment	10%

CONTACTS	
Commercial	Michael North
Commercial Litigation	Leslie Seldon
Personal Injury	David Greenhalgh
Private Client	Peter Giblin/Amanda Custis

CLARK & WALLACE 14 Albyn Place, Aberdeen, AB10 1RZ *Tel:* (01224) 644481 *Fax:* (01224) 635237 *DX:* 8 Aberdeen *Ptnrs:* 9 *Asst solrs:* 4 *Other fee-earners:* 2

CLAUDE HORNBY & COX

35-36 GREAT MARLBOROUGH STREET, LONDON, W1V 2JA
Tel: (0171) 437 8873 **Fax:** (0171) 494 3070 **DX:** 37211 PICCADILLY

The Firm: The practice has specialised in criminal law since its foundation over 70 years ago. In addition there is a thriving civil department.

Principal Areas of Work:

Crime: All aspects of criminal law are covered. Cases range from homicide, drugs and terrorist offences, and corporate fraud on a multi-million pound scale to driving offences and shoplifting. Both privately-paid and legally-aided defence work is undertaken. The practice will also accept instructions to prosecute. The partners regularly represent Defendants in Court Martial cases tried in the UK and abroad.

Other Areas of Work: General civil litigation in the High Court and the County Court, family law, wills, immigration, personal injury, employment; and both commercial and domestic conveyancing. The practice offers representation before Professional Disciplinary Tribunals.

Clientele: The firm can provide advice for individuals and small businesses on a wide range of subjects.

Recruitment: Two trainee solicitors are recruited each year. Training is given in both the criminal and civil sections of the firm. Applications to the Training Partner, Michael Butler.

Senior partner:	Richard Hallam
Number of partners:	2
Assistant solicitors:	6
Other fee-earners:	5

WORKLOADS	
Criminal litigation	70%
Civil litigation (High Court & County Court)	10%
Matrimonial	7%
Personal injury	6%
Disciplinary proceedings (prof. bodies)	4%
Conveyancing	3%

CONTACTS	
Civil litigation	Mohammed Mir/Nikki Powell
Criminal litigation/Disciplinary proceedings	
	Richard Hallam/Michael Butler/Christopher Green

CLAYTONS PO Box 38, 22 Rothesay Rd, Luton, LU1 1PT *Tel:* (01582) 724501 *Fax:* (01582) 405815 *DX:* 5909 *Ptnrs:* 3 *Asst solrs:* 5 *Other fee-earners:* 5

CLEARY, GOTTLIEB, STEEN & HAMILTON City Place House, 55 Basinghall Street, London, EC2V 5EH **Tel:** (0171) 614 2200 **Fax:** (0171) 600 1698 **Ptnrs:** 7 **Asst solrs:** 19 **Other fee-earners:** 12 **Contact:** Manley O'Hudson, Jnr. *A leading international firm engaged in the general practice of law in major cities around the world.*

WORKLOADS	
Corporate	100%

CLEAVER FULTON & RANKIN

50 BEDFORD STREET, BELFAST, BT2 7FW
Tel: (01232) 243141 **Fax:** (01232) 249096 **DX:** 421 NR BELFAST

The Firm: Cleaver Fulton & Rankin is one of Northern Ireland's foremost legal practices, located in the centre of Belfast. Founded in 1893, the firm has continued the tradition of providing clients with a thorough understanding of the legal context of their undertakings and offers sound and practical advice. In recent years the firm has experienced sustained growth and offers an extensive range of legal services with a special emphasis on litigation, company and commercial activities, work for educational and charitable bodies, public and institutional authorities and all categories of private client work.

Principal Areas of Work:

Company and Commercial: (*Contact:* Peter Rankin, Patrick Cross or Jenny Ebbage). The whole range of company work is undertaken, including incorporation, take-overs, liquidations and receiverships and company secretarial services.

Commercial Property: (*Contact:* Jim Houston or Patrick Cross). All aspects of acquisition, development and investment. The practice's property lawyers assist clients in all aspects of business start-ups and in lease renewal or rent review.

Litigation: (*Contact:* Patrick O'Driscoll, Rosalie Prytherch, Brendan Fox or Geoffrey Macartney). The firm has a highly respected reputation for providing experienced and able assistance in litigation matters, including the specialist areas of commercial litigation, employment law, defamation, product liability, licensing, intellectual property and construction law.

Private Client: (*Contact:* Alastair Rankin, Joy Scott or William Cross). An extensive service to private clients entails giving advice on a variety of legal matters and maintaining close working relationships with other professionals including accountants, stockbrokers and estate agents. Matrimonial law and aspects of children's law are also covered.

Consultancy: (*Contact:* Neil Faris). The firm has established a team to service the specialised needs of clients in legal consultancy and legal advisory work in Northern Ireland including public law and judicial review. Training seminars are organised for clients and their employees on the impact of new legislation.

Employment and Labour: *Contact:* Rosalie Prytherch or Patrick Cross). The firm handles all aspects of employment including tribunals, TUPE and Northern Ireland's special discrimination legislation.

Agency: The firm specialises in providing agency services to lawyers in other jurisdictions – contact the partner or associate in the relevant area.

Contact partner:	N.C. Faris
Number of partners:	11
Assistant solicitors:	12
Other fee-earners:	12

WORKLOADS	
Commercial property	25%
Company/ commercial	25%
Litigation	25%
Private client	15%
Employment	10%

CONTACTS	
Accident and injury claims	P. O'Driscoll/W. Cross
Admiralty & marine	W. Cross
Banking securities and finance	P. Rankin/ Jenny Ebbage
Charity law	Alastair Rankin/ Peter Rankin
Commercial conveyancing	J. Houston/ P. Cross
Commercial litigation	P. O'Driscoll/ B. Fox
Company acquisitions/ mergers	P. Rankin/ Jenny Ebbage
Company management/secretarial	Jenny Ebbage
Construction and building	B. Fox
Criminal damage compensation	William Cross
Debt collection	G. Macartney
EC law and competition	Neil Faris/B Fox
Employment and labour	P. Cross/ R. Prytherch
Environmental law	Neil Faris
Franchising	Patrick Cross/ B. Fox
Insolvency	P. Cross
Intellectual property	B. Fox
Licensing law	Patrick Cross
Matrimonial	William Cross
Private client	Joy Scott/ Alastair Rankin
Wills/ trusts/ estate planning	Alastair Rankin

CLEMENT JONES 49 High Street, Holywell, CH8 7TF *Tel:* (01352) 713353 *Fax:* (01352) 713838 *DX:* 21722 Holywell *Ptnrs:* 9 *Asst solrs:* 7 *Other fee-earners:* 21

CLIFFORD CHANCE

200 ALDERSGATE STREET, LONDON, EC1A 4JJ
Tel: (0171) 600 1000 **Fax:** (0171) 282 7071 **DX:** 606 LONDON **Internet:** HTTP://WWW.CLIFFORDCHANCE.COM

The Firm: Since its 1987 merger, Clifford Chance has rapidly developed into a genuinely global firm, advising many of the world's leading financial institutions and corporations, as well as governments and multilateral agencies. The firm provides a full range of legal services from offices in 24 major business and financial centres around the world. Over two thirds of its business is sourced from outside the UK.

The firm operates as a single worldwide partnership; this ensures a consistently high level of quality across its offices and this provides a solid platform for the delivery of an integrated service to our clients worldwide.

The firm provides a comprehensive range of legal services relating to: international and domestic banking and securities, corporate and commercial work, commercial property and construction, contentious business, shipping and taxation.

Principal Areas of Work: They are organised into a number of broad service areas most of which are divided into smaller working groups. Their clients' needs frequently require multi-disciplinary teams and our structures are flexible to reflect that.

Corporate and Commercial: The firm is well-known for their corporate work, especially mergers and acquisitions, flotations (UK and international), leveraged and management buy-outs, insolvency, insurance, energy, oil and gas and government privatisations. They have expertise in EC and national competition and trade law. The firm also handles a wide range of commercial contracts with a strong involvement in information technology, telecommunications, media, the environment, employee share plans, employment and pensions, services relating to patents, designs, trade marks, copyright, trade secrets and the preparation and negotiation of exploitation agreements.

Finance: They have one of the foremost international finance practices in the world, acting for a wide range of commercial banks, investment banks and corporations, as well as regulatory agencies, supranational bodies, governments and government agencies. They are noted for their core banking, capital markets, projects and asset finance, securitisation, derivatives and regulatory practices and they are a leader in developing new financial techniques.

Contentious Business: The firm has a major dispute resolution practice which operates worldwide and undertakes all types of English and international commercial disputes. While the vast majority of disputes are resolved without formal proceedings, they undertake litigation in all English Courts and other jurisdictions worldwide. They undertake arbitration in all major arbitration centres and also handle other forms of resolution such as mediation. Their litigation lawyers also undertake enquiries, insolvency matters and all types of investigation. Groups of contentious business lawyers undertake work in many specialist fields across all the firm's areas of work.

Tax: They handle tax aspects of major corporate and financial transactions including M & A, financings, leasing, financial instruments, property, fund management and trust planning.

Commercial Property: They have a leading commercial property practice handling a variety of property related transactions whether international or UK based. Their clients include corporations, institutions, pension funds, local and public authorities, individuals and banks, whether in the role of investor, developer, landowner, occupier, borrower, funder or lender. The areas of work they undertake include investment, development projects, leasing, preletting and shell and core lettings, joint ventures, institutional funding, secured lending, property securitisation, property insolvency and security enforcement, portfolio acquisition, disposal and investigation, property aspects of corporate transactions, town planning and planning enquiries, environmental, infrastructure, transport and power projects and construction.

Clientele: The firm's strength comes from the aggregation of their talents and the breadth and depth of their specialisations. Their clients are therefore offered the highest standards of legal expertise. They also provide a close working relationship with lawyers whose approach is both practical and imaginative. Clients are drawn from many different industries and countries. They act for businesses, financiers and governments throughout the world and their lawyers accordingly have capabilities in many jurisdictions.

Recruitment: The firm continues to expand and career prospects across a range of legal disciplines are excellent. Approximately 205 trainee lawyers are expected to be recruited in 1998. Candidates may come from the law or other disciplines. They seek those who are good communicators and problem solvers with commercial as well as legal knowledge and understanding. Long-term prospects are excellent. Applications should be made between August and October, two years in advance, to Anne Niblock. Overall, at Clifford Chance they aim to

Managing partner:	Tony Williams
Senior partner:	Keith Clark
UK	
Number of partners:	180
Assistant solicitors:	683
Other fee-earners:	165
International	
Number of partners:	91
Assistant solicitors:	593
Other fee-earners:	83

CONTACTS	
Advertising and marketing	Richard Thomas
Asset/project finance	Geoffrey White
Banking	Michael Bray, Robert Palache
Building societies	Jonathan Beastall, Nick Jordan, Howard Ross
Capital markets	David Dunnigan, Stephen Roith
Collective investment schemes	James Barlow
Commodities	Ed Patton, Tim Plews
Company/commercial	David Childs, Peter Charlton, Graham Smith
Computer law and IT	Christopher Millard, David Griffiths
Construction	Alan Elias, John Beechey, Tim Steadman
Corporate finance	David Childs, Peter Charlton
Derivatives	Habib Motani, Tim Plews
EC & competition	Jim Wheaton, Alex Nourry
Employee benefits	Robin Tremaine
Employment law	Chris Goodwill, Chris Osman
Energy and utilities	Tony Bankes-Jones
Environmental law	Christopher Napier, Robin Griffiths, Brian Hall
Finance Projects	Tony Bankes-Jones, Margaret Gossling, Rodney Short, Chris Wyman
Financial services	Tim Herrington
Hotels & leisure	Teddy Bourne, Andrew Carnegie
Housing association finance	Robert Smith
Insolvency	Mark Hyde, David Steinberg
Insurance and reinsurance	Katherine Coates, Terry O'Neill, Stephen Lewis, Leon Boshoff
Int. commercial arbitration	John Beechey
Intellectual property	David Perkins
International financial mkts	Tim Plews
Litigation (commercial)	Tony Willis, Chris Perrin
Litigation (property)	Wendy Miller, John Pickston
Local government	Brian Hall
Media & entertainment	Mark Poulton, Daniel Sandelson
Multimedia	Daniel Sandelson, David Griffiths, Christopher Millard
Pensions	Helen Cox
Planning	Brian Hall
Property (commercial)	Teddy Bourne
Public international law	Jeremy Carver
Public Policy	Richard Thomas
Publishing	Michael Smyth
Retail	Michael Howell, Michael Edwards
Securitisation	Robert Palache, Chris Oakley
Shipping & maritime law	Chris Perrin
Sovereign debt rescheduling	Cliff Godfrey
Tax (corporate)	Douglas French, Howard Ross
Telecommunications	Liz Hiester, Christopher Millard, Tim Schwarz

CLIFFORD CHANCE

Chambers & Partners

be forceful and effective in the interests of their clients. They see themselves as combining innovation, creativity and commercial awareness with an unstuffy style and an empathy with client problems. A brochure for clients or prospective trainee solicitors is available on request.

Other Offices: *Europe:* Amsterdam, Barcelona, Brussels, Budapest, Düsseldorf, Frankfurt, Madrid, Milan, Moscow, Padua, Paris, Prague, Rome, Warsaw; *Asia:* Bangkok, Hong Kong, Shanghai, Singapore, Tokyo; Hanoi, Ho Chi Minh City; *Middle East:* Dubai; *North America:* New York.

Languages: All known business and commercial languages.

CLIFFORD CHANCE

CLIFFORD & CO 24-26 Great Suffolk Street, London, SE1 0UE **Tel:** (0171) 928 9401 **Fax:** (0171) 261 0142 **Ptnrs:** 2 **Asst solrs:** 1 **Contact:** Mr Frank Clifford *Specialists in Personal Injury litigation for Plaintiffs only. National coverage. Legal aid and private funding undertaken. Established 1965.*

WORKLOADS	
Personal injury	100%

CLINTONS

55 DRURY LANE, LONDON, WC2B 5SQ
Tel: (0171) 379 6080 **Fax:** (0171) 240 9310 **DX:** 40021 COVENT GDN. 1 **Email:** INFO@CLINTONS.CO.UK

The Firm: Clintons is widely recognised as one of the foremost firms in the worlds of entertainment, sport and the media. The firm also has an extensive general commercial practice, with acknowledged strengths in property and litigation.

Principal Areas of Work:

Entertainment, Sport and the Media: The firm acts for a wide range of clients from well known individuals to major corporations. Specialist advice is provided in the businesses of music, theatre, television, advertising and marketing, merchandising and film and publishing, and generally in the protection and exploitation of intellectual property rights.

Corporate and Commercial: The firm provides advice in all aspects of the commercial world including new ventures, corporate restructuring, international taxation, employment, liquidation and receivership.

Property: Clintons handles all types of property transaction from commercial developments to residential conveyancing. The firm has a special expertise in secured lending, and includes banking and other lending institutions as its clients. The property team is led by two partners and works closely with external property specialists.

Litigation: Clintons is recognised for the strength of its practice in this area. The firm has a formidable reputation for the excellence of the service that it provides and for its ability to deal with heavyweight and high profile litigation. The firm deals with a wide range of contentious work including in entertainment, sport and the media, and in banking, employment, personal injury and matrimonial matters. The firm also has a dedicated unit dealing with all aspects of asset financing and acts in connection with major corporate fraud and related matters.

Private Client: Clintons advises on all aspects of arrangements for private individuals, including offshore settlements, tax, wills, probate, trusts and matrimonial finance. The work undertaken includes advice relating to the links between the business and personal assets of private individuals and the firm works closely with other professional advisers in the establishment of tax efficient and practical personal arrangements for the benefit of its clients.

Debt Recovery: The firm has a sophisticated computer based debt recovery department dealing with both high volume corporate collection and individual case by case matters.

International Connections: The firm has considerable overseas connections, particularly in the USA, continental Europe, Ireland, Israel and in the Channel Islands, Cayman and the Bahamas.

Senior partner:	John Cohen
Number of partners:	13
Assistant solicitors:	6
Other fee-earners:	13

CONTACTS	
Advertising and Marketing	Philip Stinson
Corporate/Commercial	John Seigal
Employment	John Seigal
Film and Television	David Landsman
Litigation	David Davis, Andrew Sharland
Matrimonial	Tim Bienias
Multimedia	James Jones
Music	David Landsman, Peter Button, Andrew Myers
Property	Lawrence Middleweek, Michael Goldman
Publishing	Sally Hamwee
Sport	Philip Stinson, Jacqueline Brown
Tax, Trusts and Private Client	Sally Hamwee
Theatre	John Cohen

CLINTONS
S O L I C I T O R S

CLYDE & CO

51 EASTCHEAP, LONDON, EC3M 1JP
Tel: (0171) 623 1244 **Fax:** (0171) 623 5427 **DX:** 1071 **Email:** SANDRA.HAWKING@CLYDE.CO.UK

The Firm: Clyde & Co is a major international law firm, particularly strong in trade, shipping, transport, insurance, reinsurance, corporate and finance matters. The practice is fast growing and has a strong international reputation. Many of the lawyers travel widely on client business, working closely with the Clyde & Co overseas offices and correspondent lawyers. The firm's international business is serviced from offices in London, Guildford, Cardiff and regional offices in France and Greece, the Far East, Middle East and Latin America with an associate office in St. Petersburg.

Principal Areas of Work:

Shipping and Marine Insurance: The firm has an international reputation in this field, acting for shipowners, charterers, shipbuilders, cargo owners and insurers. Areas handled include salvage and collision, carriage of goods, charterparty disputes, marine insurance, bills of lading, general average, pollution, ship finance, sale and purchase, shipbuilding and ship repair disputes.

Insurance Litigation (non-marine and general): The firm advises on insurance policies of all kinds including: E&O, D&O, construction risks, credit and political risks, product liability, jewellers block and specie insurance, film and entertainment, bloodstock, financial institutions, transport and aviation.

Insurance (non-contentious): The firm advises on corporate and business transactions in London and world markets, insurance regulation and insurance products.

Reinsurance: The firm specialises in the drafting and interpretation of reinsurance contracts and the pursuit, defence and resolution of reinsurance claims.

Company Commercial: The firm's corporate department provides top quality commercial advice and handles a wide range of corporate and commercial transactions including flotations; takeovers and mergers; company refinancing and restructuring; demergers; partnerships; venture captial arrangements; MBOs and MBIs; IPOs, joint ventures and inward investment. It regularly advises UK and international insurance companies and companies operating in the Lloyd's market and has had a significant involvement in the introduction of corporate capital to Lloyd's. The department also advises on all types of commercial contracts including distribution and agency arrangements, manufacturing and supply agreements, licensing arrangements.

Banking: The firm's banking group advises on a broad range of international and domestic financing transactions and regulatory issues. The group acts for both international and domestic banks, merchant banks, financial institutions and securities houses and has particular expertise in advising the insurance industry on banking matters.

Commercial & Corporate Litigation: The firm conducts litigation and arbitration before Courts and tribunals in the UK and worldwide through its overseas offices and correspondent lawyers, regarding disputes arising from banking, commodities, trading, commercial contracts, sale of goods, debt recovery, corporate crime, fraud, professional indemnity, product liability and personal injury.

International Trade, Commodities & Finance incl. Asset Finance: The firm advises a wide range of clients on asset finance, commodities, countertrade and project finance.

IT & Telecommunications: The firm acts for suppliers and users of IT equipment and services and can advise on a broad range of issues related to the IT and telecommunications industries.

Energy: The firm represents oil producing and exploration companies, oil traders, refineries and petrochemical producers on all aspects of their operations worldwide. The work includes: joint ventures, exploration and production agreements and statutory regulation.

Employment: The firm advises on terms of employment and employment policies, restrictive covenants, wrongful and unfair dismissal, discrimination cases and termination packages.

EC & Competition Law: The firm advises UK and foreign companies on regulation and competition law, state aids, free movement of goods and capital and insurance.

Aviation: The firm advises on all areas of corporation and litigious aspects of the aviation industry and its insurers.

PFI: The firm's company and commercial, banking, construction, EC, litigation, IT and Healthcare departments work together on all PFI, CFQ and other public sector projects.

Property & Construction: The firm represents UK and international developers, contractors, consultants and funders in the procurement and disposal of private and public sector commercial developments. Advice is given on all litigious aspects of the construction industry with an emphasis on arbitration and ADR.

Senior Partner:	Michael Payton
Practice Partner:	Tony Thomas
UK	
Number of partners:	79
Assistant solicitors:	106
Other fee-earners:	58
International	
Number of partners:	17
Assistant solicitors:	27
Other fee-earners:	7

WORKLOADS	
Insurance/ reinsurance	30%
Marine	30%
Company, commercial, banking, property	20%
International trade	10%
Other commercial litigation	10%

CONTACTS	
Aviation	Simon Poland/Jane Andrewartha
Banking	David Page
Commercial litigation	Jonathan Wood/ Corinna Cresswell
Company/commercial	David Page/Anthony Garrod
Construction	Niamh Burke
Corporate litigation	Conrad Walker
EC & Competition Law	Stuart Macdonald
Employment	Paul Newdick/Chris Duffy
Energy	Peter Felter
Ins. Lit. (non-marine/general)	Michael Payton/ Rod Smith
Insolvency	Jonathan Wood/Paul Newdick
Insurance (marine)	Nigel Chapman/John Dunt
Insurance (non-contentious)	Stephen Browning/ David Salt
IT & Telecommunications	Anthony Garrod
Medical negligence	John Mitchell
Personal injury	Angela Horne
PFI	Stuart Macdonald
Product Liability	John Blacker/Chris Harris
Professional indemnity	Peter Farthing
Property	Robert Pilcher/Aidan Heathcote
Reinsurance	Nigel Brook/Paul Bugden
Ship finance	Simon Poland
Shipping	Tony Thomas/Brian Nash
Tax	Susan Ball
Trade & Commodities	Andrew Wells/David Best
Transport	Michael Parker/David Hall

Tax: The firm's highly regarded tax specialists advise on all aspects of corporate and personal taxation, including company reorganisations, employee renumeration packages and equity incentive schemes/estate planning and asset protection and offshore trusts and settlements.

Transport: The firm advises on carriage of goods, CMR and insurance and trading conditions.

Nature of Clients: Clyde & Co acts for insurance companies, shipping and financial services firms, major oil companies, banks, property developers, public companies and multinationals.

Other Offices: Guildford, Cardiff, Hong Kong, Singapore, Dubai, Caracas, Paris and Piraeus.

Associate Office: St. Petersburg.

COBBETTS

SHIP CANAL HOUSE, KING ST, MANCHESTER, M2 4WB
Tel: (0161) 833 3333 **Fax:** (0161) 833 3030 **DX:** 14374 MANCHESTER 1

The Firm: Cobbetts is one of the largest independent firms in the North West and offers a comprehensive range of legal services to its largely blue chip client base.   The firm is committed to meeting the individual needs of a wide range of commercial concerns and maintains a substantial private client department. It is particularly well-known for its commercial property and planning work having the largest Commercial Property Division in the North West; and has a flourishing Corporate/Commercial Division.   The practice has well established European connections and is a member of Eurolegal.

Principal Areas of Work:

Commercial Property: All types of property-related transactions, including secured lending, development, planning plus environmental and auctions work.

Litigation: High Court and County Court litigation, including emergency injunctions, industrial tribunals, intellectual property, personal injury and motor accident claims, building and construction disputes, possession cases for mortgagees, landlord and tenant, Factories Act and Health and Safety legislation, insurance, consumer credit, debt recovery, defamation, insolvency, and enforcement of security.

Corporate and Commercial: Company formations, acquisitions and disposals, corporate reorganizations, management buy-outs, joint ventures, flotations on the Stock Exchange, corporate finance and tax, banking, EC law and intellectual property, trading agreements, employment law and pensions.

Private Client: Wills, probate, trusts and settlements, pensions, domestic and estate conveyancing, family and matrimonial law, all aspects of tax and general financial planning, insurance, tax appeals and share valuations.

Licensing and Leisure Industry: Licensing applications, finance raising, employment problems and staff contracts, and advice on EC regulations.

Nature of Clientele: The firm serves most of the major breweries operating in the North West and has a flourishing owner managed business client base as well as being particularly strong in the retail and leisure sectors.

Recruitment and Training: The firm recruits at least six trainee solicitors every year. Applications by letter and CV to Simon Jones.

Languages Spoken: French, German, Italian, Spanish.

Managing partner:	Michael Shaw
Senior partner:	Anthony Fielden
Number of partners:	33
Solicitors:	32
Other fee-earners:	24

WORKLOADS	
Commercial Property	32%
Company/ commercial	28%
Litigation	26%
Private Client	9%
Debt coll ection	5%

CONTACTS	
Banking and Finance	Robin Higham
Commercial	Roger Hawes
Commercial Property	Anthony Fitzmaurice
Construction	Henry Stone
Corporate finance	Robert Turnbull
Debt Recovery	Richard Webb
Employment & Pensions	Judith Watson
Environmental	Simon Jones
Insolvency	Mark Whittell
Intellectual property	Robert Roper
IT & Computer Contracts	Robert Roper
Licensing	Hamish Lawson
Litigation	Mark Whittell
Matrimonial	David Pickering
Media	Philip Atkinson
Planning	Peter Oldham
Private client (including Trusts)	Alan Sturrock

COFFIN MEW & CLOVER

17 HAMPSHIRE TERRACE, PORTSMOUTH, PO1 2PU
Tel: (01705) 812511 **Fax:** (01705) 291847 **DX:** 2207 PORTSMOUTH

The Firm: A major regional firm providing a comprehensive service to both commercial and private sectors throughout south Hampshire and nationally for certain niche markets. Operating from a total of seven strategically located offices, the firm is structured into two divisions – Business Services and Private Clients.

Business Services are offered from major office premises in the centre of Southampton (for the City and its environs) and just off the M27 at Fareham (for the Portsmouth, Fareham, Gosport conurbation). Four core departments (Corporate & Commercial, Commercial Property, Litigation, and Social Housing) form the backbone of the division. Within that formal structure there are a number of sub departments and units which serve the needs of particular market niches.

Corporate and Commercial: A rapidly expanding department capable of dealing with a wide range of matters from Formation through Acquisition, Merger, Sale, Restructuring of organisations (including Insolvency and Liquidation) and all aspects of Commercial Contracting, including Conditions of Sale and Purchase, Franchising and Agency and Distribution arrangements.

Commercial Property: A traditional strength of the firm with long established connections both directly with local developers and land owners and with other professionals such as land agents, surveyors and property management companies.

Litigation: This department handles a broad range of Commercial Insolvency and Insurance Litigation, Company and Partnership Disputes and Professional Negligence. Specialities include Employment, Property, Housing and Debt Recovery.

Social Housing: This department acts for a large number of Housing Associations and has established a formidable reputation and client base reaching far beyond its immediate local environment.

Specialist Niche Units include: Consumer Finance and Insurance, Construction, Healthcare, Marine and Intellectual Property.

The Business Services Division acts for national clients in addition to substantial local organisations in both Public and Private Sectors.

Private Client Services: Seven strategically located offices in the major centres of population along the coast of Hampshire all offer services to Private Clients. The division comprises six departments – Crime, Family, Financial Services, Personal Injury, Probate & Trust and Residential Property.

Family: One of the largest matrimonial practices in the south, with a particular reputation and expertise for handling cases where complex property and financial matters are involved; and a substantial Childcare practice with three lawyers on the Children Panel.

Financial Services: A centralised department employing industry experts with the facility to provide advice to clients at any of the firm's offices.

Crime: A well established criminal practice with a substantial volume of work undertaken in the local Magistrates and Crown Courts, and with criminal advocates based at several locations.

Personal Injury: A long established team dealing with personal injury claims ranging from minor to those of the utmost severity and with a particular expertise in claims on behalf of members of the Armed Forces.

Probate and Trust: A large centralised department for the whole firm operating out of the Fareham office and offering advice on Wills, Administration of Estates, Enduring Power of Attorney, Court of Protection, Trusts, and Financial Services.

Residential Property: A very large workload of residential conveyancing is handled by this department.

Managing partner:	David Baker
Number of ptnrs:	20
Number of fee-earners:	79
Total staff:	185

CONTACTS	
Business Services	
Co-ordinating Partner	Malcolm Padgett
	(01329) 825617
Commercial contracting	Nick Gross
Commercial litigation	Charles Holt
Consumer finance & insurance	Malcolm Padgett
Construction	Huw Morgan
Corporate/Commercial	Nick Gross
Employment	Jon Bridges
Healthcare	Philip Yetman
Insolvency	Nick Gross
Intellectual property	Sarah McNab
Marine	Charles Holt
Property	Don Neil
Social housing	Jennifer Bennett
Private Client Services	
Co-ordinating Partner	Pauline Johnson
	(01703) 334661
Crime	Bill Meads
Family	Pauline Johnson
Financial services	Laurie Fenwick
Mental health	Geraldine Johns
Personal injury	Keith Hayward
Probate & trust	Roger Hancock
Residential property	Courtney Kenny

COLE & COLE Buxton Court, 3 West Way, Oxford, OX2 0SZ *Tel:* (01865) 262600 *Fax:* (01865) 721367 *DX:* 96200 Oxford West *Ptnrs:* 35 *Asst solrs:* 43 *Other fee-earners:* 49

COLE & CO St Andrew House, 141 West Nile Street, Glasgow, G1 2RN **Tel:** (0141) 353 0007 **Fax:** (0141) 353 1110 **DX:** GW15 Glasgow 1 **Email:** rlc@coleandco.co.uk **Ptnrs:** 1 **Asst solrs:** 2 **Contact:** Ron Cole *Commercial property practice established in 1996 by experienced former property partner of a large national firm.*

WORKLOADS			
Commercial Property	95%	Residential Property	5%

COLE & CO 23 Tombland, Norwich, NR3 1RF *Tel:* (01603) 617078 *Fax:* (01603) 630050 *DX:* 5220 Norwich *Ptnrs:* 5 *Asst solrs:* 4 *Other fee-earners:* 1

COLEMANS 27 Marlow Road, Maidenhead, SL6 7AE *Tel:* (01628) 631051 *Fax:* (01628) 22106 *DX:* 6405 Maidenhead *Ptnrs:* 7 *Asst solrs:* 8 *Other fee-earners:* 1

COLEMANS SOLICITORS

ELISABETH HOUSE, 16 ST. PETER'S SQUARE, MANCHESTER, M2 3DF
Tel: (0161) 236 5623 **Fax:** (0161) 228 7509 **DX:** 14380 **Email:** INFO@COLEMANS-SOLS.CO.UK

The Firm: Established in the early 80's, Colemans is a young, forward-thinking commercial law firm, practising from offices in Manchester and Walsall in the West Midlands. The Walsall office was opened to cater for local demand for road traffic accident, personal injury and private client work. Over recent years it has expanded to include company and commercial, commercial property, franchising and commercial litigation.

Principal Areas of Work:

Commercial Litigation: (*Contact Partner:* Roger Coleman). A wide range of civil disputes is handled for both plaintiffs and defendants, including commercial contract disputes, property litigation, employment matters and landlord and tenant disputes.

Commercial Property: (*Contact Partner:* Andrew Himelfield). The firm deals with development work, landlord and tenant, retail and industrial premises, agricultural land, secured lending, freehold acquisition/disposal on behalf of various blue-chip, national and international clients.

Company/ Commercial: (*Contact Partner:* Pauline Cowie). Comprehensive proactive and strategic legal advice is offered on acquisitions and disposals, shareholders agreements, joint ventures, commercial contracts, terms and conditions of trade, agency and distribution.

Debt Recovery: (*Contact:* Sue Paterson). The firm operates a fully computerised debt recovery service and advises clients on all aspects of their credit control.

Family: (*Contact:* Lynn Levesley). The department opened in January 1998 and handles all aspects of family law including divorce and separation with an emphasis on child care.

Franchising: (*Contact Partner:* Pauline Cowie). The firm has particular expertise in all aspects of franchising, acting for both franchisors and franchisees on a national and international level. Colemans is an Affiliate Member of the British Franchise Association, and is one of the few specialist practices in the country with this accreditation.

Insurance Litigation: (*Contact Partner:* Roger Coleman). The department has grown steadily in the past year with particular emphasis on high value personal injury claims and professional negligence claims.

Personal Injury: (*Contact Partners:* Sarah Barr/John Hesketh/David Stevenson). The firm has a specialist uninsured loss recovery department which is one of the largest in its field, acting for motor fleets and legal expenses schemes nationwide. The practice has access to a nationwide panel of associated experts to enable it to handle claims anywhere in the country. John Hesketh, David Stevenson and David Erwin are members of the Law Society's Personal Injury Panel. The department is experienced in handling claims for medical negligence and fatal accidents including representation at inquests.

Private Client: (*Contact Partner:* Alison Roberts). The department handles residential conveyancing, building estate work, probate, Court of Protection and wills.

Managing partner:	Roger Coleman
Senior partner:	Roger Coleman
Number of partners:	7
Assistant solicitors:	8
Other fee-earners:	23

CONTACTS	
Commercial litigation	Roger Coleman
Commercial property	Andrew Himelfield
Company/ commercial	Pauline Cowie
Debt recovery	Sue Paterson
Family	Lynn Levesley
Franchising	Pauline Cowie
Insurance	Roger Coleman
Private Client	Alison Roberts
Uninsured loss recovery/PI	John Hesketh/ Sarah Barr (Manchester)
Uninsured loss recovery/PI	David Stevenson (Walsall)

COLES MILLER 44-46 Parkstone Road, Poole, BH15 2PG *Tel:* (01202) 673011 *Fax:* (01202) 675868 *DX:* 07609 *Ptnrs:* 14 *Asst solrs:* 10 *Other fee-earners:* 21

COLLYER-BRISTOW

4 BEDFORD ROW, LONDON, WC1R 4DF
Tel: (0171) 242 7363 **Fax:** (0171) 405 0555 **DX:** 163 CH.LN.   **Email:** CBLAW@COLLYER-BRISTOW.CO.UK
Internet: HTTP://WWW.COLLYER-BRISTOW.CO.UK

The Firm: Collyer-Bristow is an imaginative and innovative firm based in Bedford Row. It was established in 1760 but its environment and approach is progressive and friendly. The firm acts for a wide range of institutional clients, public and private companies, charities, businesses, professional partnerships and private clients. An association with a group of European practices and membership of Eurolink have assisted in developing valuable continental links. The bright modernised offices now contain a professionally run Art Gallery where regular and varied exhibitions are held.

Principal Areas of Work:

General Description: The firm has a strong commercial property practice and an expanding corporate and commercial department. The litigation and family law departments have excellent reputations within the profession and from August 1998 the firm will be incorporating the highly regarded matrimonial firm of S. Rutter & Co, adding strength to its existing family law practice. The sport entertainment and marketing practice is developing, and the firm remains committed to providing a comprehensive personal service for its private clients, both in the UK and offshore.

Company/Commercial: The department continues to grow and its work includes company formations, mergers, acquisitions, sales, buy-outs, reorganisations and all the related range of contractual and commercial advice, including an expertise in advice to company directors.

Commercial Property: The department acts for many investment companies, property developers and financial institutions on freehold and leasehold sales and disposals, office development schemes, major shopping centre developments, agricultural matters, planning and other related work. Residential and domestic transactions are also handled and the firm has developed a speciality in leasehold enfranchisement advice.

Litigation: This strong team has experience in property-related and construction litigation and arbitration, judicial review work, commercial and contractual disputes, professional negligence, defamation and employment law, and in representation before professional tribunals. The firm is now also developing a strong personal injury and medical negligence practice.

Intellectual Property: The firm has a growing reputation in this field, particularly for handling contentious trademark and patent disputes.

Private Client: Unlike most Central London firms, Collyer-Bristow has maintained and expanded its private client practice, for whom it handles tax planning, trusts, financial and investment advice within the UK and offshore, wills and the administration of estates, and charities.

Family: This is one of the leading matrimonial practices in the country. Its reputation extends across the entire range of family work, including divorce, custody and financial disputes, wardship and cohabitation. The department is increasingly involved in international work such as forum-shopping, child abduction and the recognition of decrees and is one of the appointed firms on the Lord Chancellor's child abduction panel.

Employment: A specialist team, acting for employers and employees, handles a wide range of employment and boardroom disputes, industrial tribunal applications, executive service contract advice, and the preparation of employment terms and conditions.

Sport, Entertainment and Marketing: The firm has a substantial practice in this field, acting for sponsorship, promotions and merchandising consultancies, advertising and marketing agencies, governing bodies, sponsors, sports photographers and publishers, film and video producers and distributors.

Agency Work: The agency litigation department provides a service for more than 100 firms outside the capital and overseas. (*Contact:* Matthew Marsh).

Recruitment and Training: For those candidates who do not believe that biggest necessarily means best, the firm offers a refreshing alternative; trainee solicitors work closely with partners on a wide variety of work in a friendly atmosphere – opportunities that only a smaller firm can provide. Applicants should have a good academic background, an assured and lively personality, a positive approach and preferably some computer literacy and linguistic ability. CV and references to John Saner.

Senior partner:	Roger Woolfe
Number of partners:	17
Assistant solicitors:	10
Other fee-earners:	15

WORKLOADS	
Litigation	25%
Matrimonial and family	21%
Property (commercial)	20%
Private client	18%
Commercial	12%
Sport entertainment and marketing	4%

CONTACTS	
Company/commercial	Paul Sillis/John Bailey
Employment	Keith Corkan
Family/matrimonial	Michael Drake
Intellectual Property	Christopher Rennie-Smith
Litigation	Joanna Kennedy
Personal Injury/Medical Negligence	Barrie Barker
Private client	John Saner
Property	Roger Woolfe
Sport, entertainment & marketing	Alan Burdon-Cooper

COMERTON & HILL Murray House, 4 Murray Street, Belfast, BT1 6DN *Tel:* (01232) 234629 *Fax:* (01232) 233908 *DX:* 415 NR BELFAST 1 *Ptnrs:* 4 *Asst solrs:* 1 *Other fee-earners:* 3

CONDIES 2 Tay Street, Perth, PH1 5LJ *Tel:* (01738) 440088 *Fax:* (01738) 441131 *DX:* 25 Perth *Ptnrs:* 7 *Asst solrs:* 7 *Other fee-earners:* 3

CONFREYS 219 Mackintosh Place, Roath, Cardiff, CF2 4RP **Tel:** (01222) 458080 **Fax:** (01222) 497080 **Ptnrs:** 1 **Asst solrs:** 0 **Other fee-earners:** 1 **Contact:** Neil Confrey. *Specialist niche practice in mental health law, particularly in representing individuals before the Mental Health Review Tribunal.*

WORKLOADS	
Mental health law	100%

CONSTANT & CONSTANT

SEA CONTAINERS HOUSE, 20 UPPER GROUND, BLACKFRIARS BRIDGE, LONDON, SE1 9QT
Tel: (0171) 261 0006 **Fax:** (0171) 401 2161 **DX:** 1067 LONDON CITY EC3 **Email:** TWOCONSTANTS@DIAL.PIPEX.COM

The Firm: Established in 1911, Constant & Constant is a leading international law firm, providing commercial law services from offices in London and Paris. Advice is given on a large variety of business activities including establishment of an enterprise, expansion into new areas, negotiation of contracts, raising finance and resolving disputes. Whilst resources and strong technical knowledge enable the firm to deal with substantial matters at a level associated with larger firms, Constant & Constant offer a personal and long term approach to the legal requirements of clients, whether they be private individuals, government agencies, financial institutions, private companies or PLCs.

Principal Areas of Work:

Maritime: The most established area of the practice, with an international reputation as specialists advising in matters ranging from cargo claims to marine casualties, from ship finance to competition law.

Taxation: Legal services in both corporate and personal taxation, advising on all areas of direct and indirect tax, but with a particular emphasis on cross-border issues.

Corporate and Commercial: UK and international corporate affairs, from business structuring to a wide range of commercial contract issues.

Private Client: Services in connection with such matters as wills, trusts, probate, financial planning, nationality and immigration, and family law.

Media and Entertainment: The department's all-round commercial perspective, together with an excellent working knowledge of the industry, enables a quality service on media and related issues, such as contracts, intellectual property, regulatory matters and corporate affairs.

Banking and Finance: Areas of expertise include asset financing, project and corporate finance, property acquisition and development finance, documentary credits and derivatives.

Property: Expanded significantly over the past 25 years, the department deals with all aspects of residential sale and purchase, landlord and tenant and property investment.

Employment: Whether in the context of disputes at an individual level or in the form of industrial action, the firm advises on all aspects of employment law, acting for both employers and employees.

Construction: International and domestic advice, contract drafting and litigation/arbitration in all aspects of construction and civil engineering matters.

Senior partner:	Jonathan Ecclestone
UK	
Number of partners:	26
Assistant solicitors:	7
Other fee-earners:	7
International	
Number of partners:	3
Assistant solicitors:	2
Other fee-earners:	0

CONTACTS	
Banking & Finance	Nigel Emerson
Company/commercial	André Harries/Ian Taylorson
Construction	Tim Reynolds
Employment	John Dickinson
Maritime	Anthony Miller/Graham Crane
Media & Entertainment	Ian Taylorson
Property & Private Client	Richard Wilson/ Denis Dowling
Taxation	Andrew Terry

COODES

8 MARKET STREET, ST. AUSTELL, PL25 4BB
Tel: (01726) 75021 **Fax:** (01726) 69103 **DX:** 81250 **Email:** COODES@LINK.ORG

The Firm: Coodes was founded over 250 years ago and is one of the largest Cornish practices. Its main office is in St. Austell with other offices at Truro, Newquay, Liskeard, Launceston and Callington. The firm has substantial contacts with the agricultural and commercial community throughout Cornwall. It has solicitors who are members of the Law Society's Personal Injury and Child Care Panels and with rights of audience in the higher courts. The firm has been awarded a Legal Aid Franchise and Investors in People.

Principal Areas of Work: Private client, crime, commercial and domestic conveyancing, civil litigation, family work. Within these departments the firm has specialists in agriculture, employment law, professional negligence, personal injury and licensing.

Managing partner:	R.J.E. French
Senior partner:	J.A. Coode
Number of partners:	9
Assistant solicitors:	4
Other fee-earners:	17

CONTACTS	
Agriculture	Robert Foulkes
Civil litigation	Michael Drynan
Conveyancing	Roger French
Crime	Michael Gregson
Employment	Jeremy Harvey
Family	Michael Drynan
Probate/ trusts	Jonathan Coode

COOLE & HADDOCK

5 THE STEYNE, WORTHING, BN11 3DT
Tel: (01903) 213511 **Fax:** (01903) 237053 **DX:** 3717 WORTHING

14 CARFAX, HORSHAM, RH12 1DZ
Tel: (01403) 210200 **Fax:** (01403) 241275 **DX:** 57600 HORSHAM

The Firm: Established in Horsham in 1898 and Worthing in 1960, Coole & Haddock built its reputation initially on an extensive private client base mainly in Sussex. This is now complemented by expanding commercial and litigation departments which offer a comprehensive service to businesses over a wider area.

Commercial/commercial property – Iain Swalwell; Commercial and civil litigation/employment – Stephen Loosemore; Property litigation – Peter Byfield; Residential conveyancing – Paul Burke and Peter Graves; Probate and trusts – Christina Bennett; Matrimonial/child care – Richard Ager; Debt recovery – Stephen Loosemore; Crime – Nigel Desoutter

Managing partner:	W.Paul Burke
Senior partner:	F.N.F. Haddock
Number of partners:	11
Assistant solicitors:	7
Other fee-earners:	6

COOPER SONS, HARTLEY & WILLIAMS Portland Tower, Portland Street, Manchester, M1 3PT **Tel:** (0161) 236 0321 **Fax:** (0161) 228 7767 **DX:** 14484 – Manchester 2 **Ptnrs:** 12 **Asst solrs:** 8 **Other fee-earners:** 5 **Contact:** Mr. M.G. Morris. *Broad mix of commercial and private client work including litigation, property and employment. Well established matrimonial and probate/trust departments.*

WORKLOADS			
Property and private client	30%	Litigation	25%
Matrimonial	25%	Corporate	10%
Others	10%		

COPLEYS Red Hse, 10 Market Hill, St. Ives. Huntingdon, PE17 4AW *Tel:* (01480) 456191 *Fax:* (01480) 67171 *DX:* 46402 *Ptnrs:* 5 *Asst solrs:* 1

CORBETT & CO Churcham House, 1 Bridgeman Road, Teddington, TW11 9AJ **Tel:** (0181) 943 9885 **Fax:** (0181) 977 3122 **Email:** mail@corbett.co.uk **Ptnrs:** 1 **Asst solrs:** 2 **Other fee-earners:** 1 **Contact:** Edward Corbett. *Specialise in UK and international construction projects and disputes, including ADR and arbitration.*

WORKLOADS	
International Construction projects/disputes	50%
UK Construction projects/disputes	50%

COUDERT BROTHERS

20 OLD BAILEY, LONDON, EC4M 7JP
Tel: (0171) 203 2248 **Fax:** (0171) 248 3001/3002 **DX:** LDE 49

The Firm: Coudert Brothers in London is a multi-national partnership of registered foreign lawyers and solicitors. It is part of a worldwide network of offices established in 24 cities in 15 countries around the world. Coudert Brothers is one global partnership and the London office therefore provides the facilities of a full service London law firm as well as access to the international network of Coudert Brothers. The London office has sixteen partners, twelve of whom are solicitors and three of whom are US attorneys.

The offices of Coudert Brothers are established in the major financial centres of the world including offices in Europe, Central Asia, North America and the Asia Pacific region. The major offices in Europe are established in Paris, London, Brussels, Moscow, St. Petersburg, Almaty and Berlin.

The North American offices are established in New York, Washington, Los Angeles, San Francisco, San Jose, Palo Alto, Denver and Montreal. The Asia Pacific offices are established in Bangkok, Beijing, Ho Chi Minh City, Hanoi, Hong Kong, Jakarta, Singapore, Sydney and Tokyo.

The firm has associated offices in Mexico City and Budapest. The firm's Moscow office was the first established by a foreign law firm in 1988 and is now one of the largest in Moscow servicing all the states of the former Soviet Union. Coudert Brothers opened an office in Kazakhstan in 1998.

LONDON OFFICE: This office specialises in international investment, trade and finance with particular expertise in corporate finance, mergers and acquisitions, joint ventures; capital markets, banking and project finance, international tax and trust planning; telecommunications and media law; energy privatisation and infrastructure projects; and arbitration and litigation.

Senior partner:	Steven Beharrell
Number of partners:	16
Assistant solicitors:	13
Other fee-earners:	9

WORKLOADS	
Corporate finance	30%
Litigation/ arbitration	20%
Banking/ project/ structured finance	15%
Capital markets/ funds	10%
Energy/ telecoms/ multimedia	10%
Real property	10%
Tax	5%

CONTACTS	
Arbitration	Bridget Wheeler
Banking and finance	Alexander Janes
Corporate finance	Steven Beharrell
Energy	Steven Beharrell
Funds	Alasdair Gordon
Litigation	Bridget Wheeler
Project finance	Peter O'Driscoll
Real property	Philip Burroughs
Telecommunications	Colin Long

COUDERT BROTHERS
INTERNATIONAL LAWYERS

COURTS & CO

15 WIMPOLE ST, LONDON, W1M 8AP
Tel: (0171) 637 1651 **Fax:** (0171) 637 0205 **DX:** 42722 OXFORD CIRCUS NORTH

The Firm: Courts & Co is a 'niche' firm, specialising in company and commercial work. The firm provides an in-depth, personal service to companies and their directors working closely with their business advisers, particularly their accountants. The firm's policy is to combine the highest level of technical expertise with a close understanding of the client's business and commercial requirements.

Principal Areas of Work: A large part of the firm's work consists of advising on the purchase and sale of businesses, corporate mergers and reorganisations, as well as a full range of business and commercial matters including taxation and intellectual property work. The firm handles commercial conveyancing, heavy commercial litigation (including environmental and town and country planning matters), employment work (both litigious and non-litigious) mainly for employers; and estate planning, trusts and probate work.

Nature of Clientele: Clients include private and public companies, professional partnerships and individual entrepreneurs in all areas of business; charities and trusts. Much of the firm's work is for overseas clients.

Senior partner:	Bill Holmes
Number of partners:	5
Assistant solicitors:	3
Other fee-earners:	3

WORKLOADS	
Company, commercial and tax	40%
Commercial litigation	30%
Conveyancing/trusts,wills & probate	30%

CONTACTS	
Company/commercial	Ian Paterson, Patrick Gilmour
Conveyancing/probate & trusts	Bill Holmes
Litigation	Michael Krantz, Frank Ryan

COVINGTON & BURLING

LECONFIELD HOUSE, CURZON STREET, LONDON, W1Y 8AS
Tel: (0171) 495 5655 **Fax:** (0171) 495 3101

The Firm: Covington & Burling was founded in Washington DC in 1919 and now has approximately 325 lawyers, including 30 lawyers and solicitors in the London and Brussels offices, as well as a correspondent office in Paris with over 40 lawyers.

Principal Areas of Work: Major practice areas in London include intellectual property, communications and technology issues, regulation of food, drugs, and other consumer products, corporate and securities law, international taxation, litigation and arbitration, competition and trade, and legislative issues.

The London Office: The London office established a multi-national partnership in 1993 and now has 8 solicitors, in addition to U.S. and German lawyers. The office maintains extensive collections of EU and national legal resources. London is also a focal point for multi-jurisdictional issues for Covington & Burling lawyers, who may call, as required, upon the Firm's informal network of international local counsel contacts in over thirty countries throughout Western and Eastern Europe, Australasia, Africa, and the Americas.

Languages: English, French, German, Italian, Portuguese, Spanish.

Managing partner:	Richard Kingham
Senior partner:	Charles E. Lister
Number of partners:	5
Assistant solicitors:	17
Other fee-earners:	6

WORKLOADS	
Intellectual Property	30%
Corporate & Commercial	20%
Medicines and Consumer Product Regulation	20%
International Taxation	15%
General litigation & Arbitration	10%
Other	5%

COZENS-HARDY & JEWSON Castle Chambers, Opie St, Norwich, NR1 3DP *Tel:* (01603) 625231 *Fax:* (01603) 627160/ 612690 *DX:* 5214 *Ptnrs:* 9 *Asst solrs:* 7 *Other fee-earners:* 12

CRANE & WALTON 113-117 London Rd, Leicester, LE2 0RG *Tel:* (0116) 255 1901 *Fax:* (0116) 255 5864 *DX:* 17012 *Ptnrs:* 10 *Other fee-earners:* 6

CRANSWICK WATSON 7 Greek Street, Leeds, LS1 5RR **Tel:** (0113) 245 2450 **Fax:** (0113) 243 2430 **DX:** 12013 **Ptnrs:** 11 **Asst solrs:** 5 **Other fee-earners:** 6 **Contact:** Mr David Gill *A commercial firm specialising in developing owner-managed businesses.*

WORKLOADS			
Private client	25%	Commercial property	20%
Commercial litigation	15%	Company/ commercial	15%
Family/ matrimonial	15%	Defendant personal injury	10%

CRAWFORD OWEN 43 Queen Square, Bristol, BS1 4QR *Tel:* (0117) 984 9000 *Fax:* (0117) 925 1296 *DX:* 78232 Bristol *Ptnrs:* 3 *Asst solrs:* 2

CRIPPS HARRIES HALL

SEYMOUR HOUSE, 11-13 MOUNT EPHRAIM ROAD, TUNBRIDGE WELLS, KENT, TN1 1EN
Tel: (01892) 506160 **Fax:** (01892) 544878 **DX:** 3954 TUNBRIDGE WELLS **Email:** RECEPTION@BROOKE.CRIPPSLAW.COM

The Firm: Cripps Harries Hall enjoys a dominant position in its marketplace, reflected in the specialist lists in all recent editions of *Chambers and Partners' Directory*. The firm attributes this to four key factors. First, it takes time to understand its clients and the issues confronting them. Second, it is attracting ever more new clients with its claim to provide 'London style skills at out-of-London prices'. Third, the firm's strong commitment to the highest standards of service. Fourth, a high level of partner involvement in clients' work, relative to many large firms.

Over the past twelve months the growth of the firm continued at a rapid pace, evidenced by an increase in turnover of more than 25% over the previous year. The firm is on target to sustain a similar growth rate this year. Cripps Harries Hall is now the largest firm in Kent and East Sussex. In Spring 1998 the firm acquired an additional office in Tunbridge Wells for its Commercial Division, adding significant capacity for further growth.

The broad spectrum of commercial and institutional clients for which the firm acts is drawn from an increasingly wide area. The corporate & commercial and commercial property teams are winning a steady stream of new clients in competition with leading London firms. The extensive collection of services offered to these clients are all provided with a combination of commercial awareness, responsiveness, good value and enthusiasm.

A long-held commitment to high standards led to the establishment of a formal quality assurance programme over five years ago. Internal procedures are in place to meet the performance standards required by institutional and commercial clients. The firm has sophisticated IT systems and has established secure, direct electronic links with appropriate clients.

The number of solicitors in the firm increased steadily over the past year, and includes several who made the move from London firms. The firm is actively recruiting more top calibre solicitors in several specialist areas. The firm recruits eight trainee solicitors annually and is proud of the high proportion of its current solicitors that trained with the firm.

In summary, Cripps Harries Hall is progressing steadily towards being regarded as the leading law firm in the South East outside London.

Principal Areas of Work: Contributing to the firm's growth over the past year were unprecedented volumes of corporate & commercial, commercial litigation and commercial property work. The firm has a strong reputation, in particular, for its skills in such fields as company share acquisitions and sales, MBOs and MBIs, formation and dissolution of companies, corporate finance, commercial property and employment. The commercial litigation practice of the firm is growing fast by meeting the needs of discerning businesses and institutions. For example, mediation has enabled several clients to avoid costly and protracted litigation. The firm is also well known for property development and insolvency work.

In private client work, the firm has a wealth of experience and is fast developing a reputation in managing the affairs of wealthy private clients to rival the top London firms in this field. The private client practice is long established and strengthened by the finance and investment services division, believed to be the most comprehensive such operation of any firm of solicitors in the country. The total of clients' funds under management is over £200 million and rising sharply. 1997 saw the launch of a service known as *Private Office* making the firm the first in the country to compete in the private banking market.

Other Offices: 14 Buckingham Street, London WC2N 6DF, Crowborough, Heathfield. Associated offices: Berlin, Frankfurt, Madrid, Munich, Paris, Rotterdam.

Managing partner:	Jonathan Denny
Senior partner:	Andrew Fermor
Number of partners:	28
Assistant solicitors:	40
Other fee-earners:	50

WORKLOADS	
Commercial litigation	25%
Corporate & commercial property	24%
Finance and investment services	20%
Private client	14%
Residential/agricultural conveyancing	12%
General litigation	5%

CONTACTS	
Commercial Litigation	Roger Byard
Commercial Property	Andrew Fermor
Construction Litigation	Peter Ashford
Corporate and Commercial	Trevor Carney
Corporate Finance	Caroline Farrant
Debt Collection	Russell Simpson
Dispute Resolution/Arbitration	John Mulcare
Employment	Katie McCarthy
Environment	Michael Stevens
Estate Planning	Gary Rogerson
Family Law	Jacqui Kempton
Housing Associations	Mike Vos
Insurance Litigation	Gavin Tyler
Intellectual Property	Christopher Langridge
Investment Management/Advice	David Lough
Land Use & Agriculture	John Mulcare
Licensing	Russell Simpson
Personal Injury	Duncan Wright
Planning	Trevor West
Professional Negligence	Charles Broadie
Property Litigation	Carol Wakeford
Residential Conveyancing	Phyllida de Salis
Residential Property Development	Michael Ellis
Sports Law	Christopher Hall
Tax Planning	Gary Rogerson
Trusts and Charities	Simon Leney
Wills and Probate	Peter Raymond

CRIPPS HARRIES HALL

CROCKERS OSWALD HICKSON

10 GOUGH SQUARE, LONDON, EC4A 3NJ
Tel: (0171) 353 0311 **Fax:** (0171) 583 1417 **DX:** 52

The Firm: Formed from two long-established City firms, Crockers and Oswald Hickson Collier, both with reputations built in the field of insurance; the latter forms the core of the corporate and commercial work of the combined firm. Oswald Hickson Collier's international reputation for libel, slander and copyright work strengthens an already substantial practice in defamation at Crockers. The combined firm's links with insurers also provide significant work in the areas of personal injury claims and general litigation. In addition, the firm provides a wide range of legal services in property and company and commercial law. Private clients are welcomed and there is a thriving private client department. The firm is always happy to hear from high-calibre assistant solicitors. The firm usually recruits two trainee solicitors each year.

Principal Areas of Work:

Media: The department offers advice on libel, slander, copyright, passing-off, contempt of court, reporting restrictions, PACE applications, pre-publication and pre-broadcasting advice and breach of confidence, as well as on libel insurance and publishing and licensing agreements.

Company/ Commercial: The department handles a broad range of commercial work, including private company sales and acquisitions, joint ventures and employment law, predominantly for clients in the insurance industry.

Litigation: The department deals with all non-media litigation and the principal areas of activity are professional indemnity, employers' liability, personal injury and motoring claims and general commercial litigation.

Property: The department handles all types of commercial property work including development and landlord and tenant as well as domestic conveyancing.

Private Client: The department deals with trusts, wills, probate, personal tax and related areas of work. The estates of both UK and foreign Lloyd's Names are handled by the department. Nature of Clientele: The firm acts for international, national and provincial newspaper groups as well as some of the larger magazine and book publishers, television companies, syndication agencies and picture libraries. It also acts for a major property development company and, reflecting its historical connection with the insurance industry, it also numbers amongst its clients several insurance companies, as well as numerous Lloyd's Brokers and Underwriting Agents. The partnership sees itself as an effective and competitive commercial firm, prominent in publishing and insurance law, providing a personal service second to none.

Joint Senior partners:	Simon Kingston and Rupert Grey
Number of partners:	9
Assistant solicitors:	18
Other fee-earners:	9

WORKLOADS	
Defamation and Media	44%
Personal Injury and General Litigation	30%
Property	15%
Company and Commercial	8%
Private Client	3%

CONTACTS	
Company/ commercial	Katy Jones
Defamation/ copyright	Rupert Grey, Richard Shillito
Personal injury/ motoring	Peter Norman
Private client	Alan Macfadyen
Property	Simon Kingston, Diana Cornforth

CROFTONS Television House, Mount Street, Manchester, M2 5FA **Tel:** (0161) 834 4391 **Fax:** (0161) 839 1743 **DX:** 18572 Manchester 7 **Ptnrs:** 5 **Asst solrs:** 2 **Other fee-earners:** 7 **Contact:** Mr Jeff Palmer *Substantial volume of commercial and personal injury work. Well known as specialists in Housing Association work and Co-operative Society law.*

WORKLOADS	
Housing associations	30%
Co-operative societies	20%
Private client (probate/ conveyancing/ litigation)	20%
Commercial/company	15%
Personal Injury	15%

CROMBIE WILKINSON Clifford House, 19 Clifford Street, York, YO1 1RJ **Tel:** (01904) 624185 **Fax:** (01904) 623078 **DX:** 61501 **Ptnrs:** 8 **Asst solrs:** 5 **Other fee-earners:** 8 **Contact:** Andrew Faulkes. *A long established firm offering a wide range of services to private and commercial clients. Other offices Selby and Malton.*

WORKLOADS	
Property (Residential/Commercial)	32%
Family/Matromonial/Children Work	30%
Wills/Trust/Probate	14%
Litigation/Personal Injury/Medical Negligence	11%
Crime	6%
Commercial	4%
Agricultural	3%

CROSSE & CROSSE 14 Southernhay West, Exeter, EX1 1PL *Tel:* (01392) 258451 *Fax:* (01392) 278938 *DX:* 8313 *Ptnrs:* 11 *Asst solrs:* 9 *Other fee-earners:* 11

CRUTES 7 Osborne Terrace, Newcastle-upon-Tyne, NE2 1RQ **Tel:** (0191) 281 5811 **Fax:** (0191) 281 3608 **DX:** 62553 Jesmond **Ptnrs:** 20 **Asst solrs:** 25 **Other fee-earners:** 25 **Contact:** James Bowyer *Main areas of work are civil litigation (all aspects and particularly personal injury), commercial and private client work. Other Offices at Carlisle, Middlesbrough & Carlisle.*

WORKLOADS	
Insurance/Personal Injury	58%
Private Client	15%
Insurance/Professional Indemnity	13%
Health Related Work	7%
Commercial	4%
Employment	3%

CUFF ROBERTS

100 OLD HALL STREET, LIVERPOOL, L3 9TD
Tel: (0151) 227 4181 **Fax:** (0151) 227 2584 **DX:** 14126 LIVERPOOL 1 **Email:** E-MAIL@CUFFROBERTS.CO.UK

The Firm: Cuff Roberts was established in 1861. In 1982 Cuff Roberts merged with North Kirk and in 1987 the combined firm merged again with Banks Kendall. Well known and respected for its expertise in commericial property, the mergers of the 1980s strengthened and developed the company commercial and litigation departments.

The firm now carries on a commercial practice in the Company Commercial, Commercial Property, Commercial Litigation and Debt Recovery fields, but has retained a commitment to the provision of private client services to enable the owners, directors and senior management of its corporate clientele to be provided for fully.

Principal Areas of Work:

Company Commercial: *(Work includes)* Charity Law, Commercial lending, Corporate Finance, Insolvency, Partnership, Drafting and reviewing commercial contracts, Sale and purchases of companies and businesses, Sports law.

Commercial Property: *(Work includes)* All aspects of commercial property with particular emphasis on retail properties including acquisitions, disposals, leasing, property development and estate conveyancing.

Commercial Litigation: *(Work includes)* Contentious and non-contentious construction work, including arbitration and mediation (having a dual qualified solicitor/quantity surveyor and a CEDR accredited mediator in the firm). Defamation, Defence of specialist prosecutions (e.g. Environmental Protection and Environment Acts, Health and Safety at Work Act, Food Act), Employment, Environment, Licensing, Planning, Professional negligence, Property litigation, Sports law.

Debt Recovery: *(Work includes)* All aspects of debt recovery with particular expertise in consumer credit, agricultural and insolvency debts. Fully computerised system allows rapid & efficient processing of large and small batches of cases at highly competitive rates. Fixed charges for all common debt recovery steps. Full litigation support.

Private Client: *(Work includes)* Probate, Trusts, Tax planning, Family, Domestic conveyancing.

Foreign/International Connections: The firm has established contacts with law firms in a large number of European and worldwide countries.

Recruitment and Training: The firm usually requires candidates with a good law degree, preferably with computer and keyboard skills, but CPE qualifiers are considered on merit.

Senior partner:	B.B Wright
Executive Board: Ted Birch, David Rawlinson, Ian Black	
Practice Director:	Declan O'Neill
Number of Partners: 19	
Number of Assistants: 12	

WORKLOADS	
Commercial Litigation	24%
Commercial Property	24%
Private Client	24%
Company Commercial	19%
Debt Recovery	9%

CONTACTS	
Commercial Litigation	Ann Heseltine
Commercial Property	Roger Calvert
Company Commercial	Sue Russell
Debt Recovery	Jonathan Hogg
Private Client	Carol Mason

A NATIONAL GROUP OF LAW FIRMS

CUFF ROBERTS
— SOLICITORS —

CULBERT AND MARTIN 7 Donegall Square West, Belfast, BT1 6JB *Tel:* (01232) 325508 *Fax:* (01232) 438669 *DX:* 498 NR Belfast 1 *Ptnrs:* 2 *Asst solrs:* 1 *Other fee-earners:* 1

CUMBERLAND ELLIS PEIRS

COLUMBIA HSE, 69 ALDWYCH, LONDON, WC2B 4RW
Tel: (0171) 242 0422 **Fax:** (0171) 831 9081 **DX:** 250 CH.LN.

The Firm: Formed in 1989 by a merger of two long-established Central London practices, the firm has attracted considerable company/commercial and commercial property work and has a substantial litigation department; it also continues to provide the full range of private client services. The firm's philosophy is to combine high quality advice with a positive, personal service, at reasonable cost.

Principal Areas of Work:

Company/Commercial: A wide variety of work is handled, including takeovers, buy-outs, flotations, intellectual property and employment law for businesses of all sizes.

Litigation: The firm is active in High Court, County Court and Tribunal work (both commercial and private), including personal injury, landlord and tenant, and debt recovery, and is particularly strong in employment and matrimonial law.

Property: The department acts for institutions and companies in a wide variety of commercial property work. A separate section deals with residential conveyancing.

Private Client: The department handles all aspects of a client's personal affairs, including probate, wills, trusts, tax planning and landed estates.

Financial Services: All aspects of independent financial advice, including tax-efficient investments, pension and pre-retirement planning, life assurance, school fees, mortgages and health and income protection.

Nature of Clientele: The firm acts for public and private companies, institutions, charities (particularly City Livery companies) and a large number of private individuals.

Managing partner:	Lionel Judd
Senior partner:	Roger Hollinshead
Number of partners:	12
Assistant solicitors:	7
Other fee-earners:	9

CONTACTS	
Commercial property	Robert Maclean
Company/commercial	Iain Mitchell
Financial services	Lionel Judd/Colin Studd
Litigation	Neil Turner
Private client	Roger Hollinshead
Residential conveyancing	Robert Maclean

CUMBERLAND ELLIS PEIRS
SOLICITORS

Chambers & Partners

CUNNINGHAM, JOHN & CO Fairstead House, 7 Bury Road, Thetford, IP24 3PL **Tel:** (01842) 752401 **Fax:** (01842) 753555 **DX:** 124810 **Ptnrs:** 9 **Asst solrs:** 9 **Other fee-earners:** 22 **Contact:** Simon John. *Known for Commercial (PLC clients), Personal Injury and Medical Negligence. L.S. Panels Members: Family/Crime, Tax, Agriculture, Private, USA Connections.*

WORKLOADS			
Personal Injury	26%	Conveyancing	20%
General Litigation	17%	Medical Negligence	14%
Commercial	10%	Matrimonial	8%
Private Client	5%		

CUNNINGHAMS Suite 2c, 11 Peter Street, Central Buildings, Manchester, M2 5QR **Tel:** (0161) 833 1600 **Fax:** (0161) 833 1060 **Ptnrs:** 2 **Asst solrs:** 2 **Other fee-earners:** 6 **Contact:** Mr Martin Cunningham *Specialists in criminal defence work, including white collar crime. Legal aid work undertaken. Particular expertise in the area of commercial fraud, sexual offences and drug related crime.*

WORKLOADS	
Criminal defence work	95%
Welfare and general green form advice	5%

CUNNINGHAM TURNER 10 Richmond Terrace, Blackburn, BB1 7BE *Tel:* (01254) 59292 *Fax:* (01254) 264142 *DX:* 15256 Blackburn 2 *Ptnrs:* 4 *Asst solrs:* 2 *Other fee-earners:* 0

CURREY & CO 21 Buckingham Gate, London, SW1E 6LS *Tel:* (0171) 828 4091 *Fax:* (0171) 828 5049 *DX:* 2300 Victoria *Ptnrs:* 7 *Asst solrs:* 3 *Other fee-earners:* 4

CURTIS DAVIS GARRARD Lancaster House, Northumberland Close, Heathrow Airport, TW19 7LN **Tel:** (0181) 400 2400 **Fax:** (0181) 400 2420 **Email:** cdg@cdg.co.uk **Ptnrs:** 3 **Asst solrs:** 6 **Other fee-earners:** 1 **Contact:** Mr Ian Garrard *Commercial litigation and arbitration firm. Specialists in the shipping, offshore (oil & gas), banking and energy sectors.*

WORKLOADS			
Shipping	35%	Energy	25%
Offshore	25%	Banking	15%

CURWENS

CROSSFIELD HOUSE, GLADBECK WAY, ENFIELD, EN2 7HT
Tel: (0181) 363 4444 **Fax:** (0181) 367 1301 **DX:** 90601 ENFIELD **Email:** LAW@CURWENS.CO.UK

The Firm: Substantial General Practice in North London, Essex and Hertfordshire serving a wide range of Business and private Clients with particular strengths in Commercial Litigation, Company and Commercial work, Mergers & Acquisitions, Landlord & Tenant, Trust and Property.

Offices at:

College House College Road Cheshunt Herts EN8 9BL
Tel: (01992) 631 461 *Fax:* (01992) 639332DX 30150 Cheshunt

58 High Street Hoddesdon Herts EN11 8ET
Tel: (01992) 463 727 *Fax:* (01992) 446830DX 80651 Hoddesdon

17 High Street Royston Herts SG8 9AA
Tel: (01763) 241 261 *Fax:* (01763) 242125DX 37300 Royston

29 Highbridge Street Waltham Abbey Essex EN9 1BZ
Tel (01992) 712 549 *Fax:* (01992) 769987DX 54301 Waltham Abbey

Senior partner:	Wyndham James
Number of partners:	12
Assistant solicitors:	9
Other fee-earners:	11

CONTACTS	
Company & Commercial	John Riddett
Landlord & Tenant	Robert Pearson
Litigation	Alan Carter
Mergers & Acquisitions	Peter Poole

Curwens
Solicitors

M.B. CUTTLE & CO Bridge Street Chambers, 72 Bridge St, Manchester, M3 2RJ **Tel:** (0161) 835 2050 **Fax:** (0161) 831 7986 **Ptnrs:** 5 **Asst solrs:** 2 **Other fee-earners:** 10 **Contact:** Mr. R.G. Williamson *One of the largest and most experienced criminal firms in Manchester. The firm also handles personal injury, civil litigation, commercial and domestic conveyancing.*

WORKLOADS			
Crime	60%	Accident	15%
Children/ family	15%	Contract	5%
Employment	5%		

DALE & CO SOLICITORS 10 Victoria Street, Felixstowe, IP11 7ER *Tel:* (01394) 284118 *Fax:* (01394) 276097

DARBYS

SUN ALLIANCE HOUSE, 52 NEW INN HALL STREET, OXFORD, OX1 2QA
Tel: (01865) 247294 **Fax:** (01865) 793411 **DX:** 4304 OXFORD **Email:** LAW@DARBYS.CO.UK

This Oxford general practice serves business and private clients in a variety of fields. It has notable strengths in company law, commercial property, family and crime.

The Firm: Darbys was established in 1919 in part of its current offices. The practice enjoyed steady organic expansion over the years and has always had a strong reputation for property and private client work. More recently the firm has also focused increasingly on company and commercial work. In 1990 it took over neighbouring premises to accomodate its growth and in 1992 it further strengthened its company and commercial expertise by recruiting a partner in the field from a major firm in the City.

The firm believes its expansion is due in large part to a strong core of loyal clients. These include Oxford colleges, private companies and other businesses. Among the clients are Professional Staff Plc, Oxford United Football Club, Oxford University Press and Chancellors Group of Estate Agents. The practice is established and reliable, with strength and depth in the areas in which it has chosen to specialise. It also benefits from links with other firms of solicitors though its membership of LawNet.

Recent developments at the firm include the continued expansion of the company and commercial department, each member of which has worked in the City of London. In 1996 the firm was granted a legal aid franchise in every department in which application was made.

The firm is fully departmentalised and is currently undertaking a major information technology network program, involving all fee-earners and secretaries, and has recruited a full-time IT manager.

Agency work is carried out in most fields.

Principal Areas of Work:

Company/ Commercial:*Work includes:* acquisitions and disposals, shareholder agreements, commercial agreements and intellectual property issues. Company reorganisations and boardroom matters are also dealt with. The department has acted in a large number of local transactions, many of them multi-million pound deals. The department also advised on the UK aspects of the flotation of one of its major clients in NASDAQ, the US stock exchange, in an intital public offering of more than £29m, and more recently on the sale of a specialist electronics company for £23m.

Commercial property and conveyancing: All aspects are handled, and the firm has acted on an increasingly large number of acquisitions.

Criminal: This department is one of the largest in Oxford and has a legal aid franchise with devolved powers. The department is supplemented by a growing immigration practice with national reputation.

Family and Litigation: The family and litigation department both enjoy good reputations dealing with a wide variety of matters. Again a legal aid franchise with appropriate developed powers exists.

Over the next five years Darbys intends to undergo a continued expansion notably by developing its company and commercial work and expanding its client base.

Senior partner:	Sturge Taylor
Number of partners:	9
Other fee-earners:	29

WORKLOADS	
Commercial property and conveyancing	22%
Litigation	21%
Criminal and immigration	19%
Matrimonial	16%
Company, commercial and IP	12%
Trusts and probate	10%

CONTACTS	
Commercial property and conveyancing	
	Sturge Taylor, Michael Clifton,
	Nick Hedges, Rupert Curtis
Company, commercial and IP	Stephen Dyde,
	Nick Hedges
Criminal and immigration	Jim Astle, Michael Geeson
Litigation	Paul Lowe
Matrimonial	Catherine Eddy, Victoria Smith
Trusts and probate	Jayne Dimmick

M C DARLINGTON Diocesan Registry, Church House, 90 Deansgate, Manchester, M3 2QH
Tel: (0161) 834 7545 *Fax:* (0161) 839 0092

DARLINGTON & PARKINSON 78 Pitshanger Lane, Ealing, London, W5 1QX **Tel:** (0181) 601 9910 **Fax:** (0181) 566 8285 **DX:** 99631 Acton 2 **Ptnrs:** 6 **Asst solrs:** 5 **Other fee-earners:** 6 **Contact:** Kenneth Grant *The firm is a substantial legal aid practice, specialising in criminal, matrimonial, and child-related work.*

DAVENPORT LYONS

1 OLD BURLINGTON STREET, LONDON, W1X 2NL
Tel: (0171) 468 2600 **Fax:** (0171) 437 8216 **DX:** 37233 PICCADILLY 1 **Email:** DL@DAVENPORT-LYONS.CO.UK

The Firm: Davenport Lyons is a long established firm in the west end of London. The firm is particularly well known, and generally acknowledged as a leader, in the entertainment and media fields and also has an excellent reputation in company and commercial work providing a service normally associated with larger city firms. The firm has wide experience in providing comprehensive legal services to corporate and commercial clients across a broad spectrum of market sectors. Those markets include the media in all its forms (film, television, radio, music, theatre, publishing and the newspaper industry), the retail sector, advertising, the hotel, sport and leisure industries, computers and information technology as well as property investment and development. The firm prides itself on an unusual blend of high quality legal expertise and commercial sensitivity to clients' needs. This service is provided with speed and efficiency and at a competitive price. The firm has always recognised the importance to clients of partner attention. It has wide and long-standing contacts in the international sphere particularly with US and EU businesses and lawyers.

Principal Areas of Work: The firm provides legal services to a wide range of corporate and individual clients and has expertise in a number of particular specialised fields:

Company and Commercial: (*Contact Partners:* Anthony Fiducia, Michael Hatchwell). Advice on formations, reorganisations, acquisitions, venture capital, business start ups, joint ventures and corporate tax planning. The firm is particularly well known for its work for growing companies up to and including Stock Exchange quotations.

Employment: (*Contact Partners:* Anthony Fiducia, Michael Hatchwell, Kathryn Pavey). The firm provides specialist and comprehensive advice in all areas of employment law and presents and defends cases in the Industrial Tribunal, the County Court and the High Court.

Media: (*Contact Partner:* Leon Morgan). The firm's wide and continually expanding experience in these fields is reflected in its client list which includes substantial television companies, talent and sales agencies, banks and other financiers, advertising and media agencies. The firm has wide experience of international issues.

Copyright, Music and Entertainment: (*Contact Partner:* James Ware). The firm has a strong reputation in the UK and US and acts for many leading music publishing corporations and individual musicians advising on recording contracts, copyright and the problems of performers and artists. The firm covers every aspect of the entertainment market and advises on the impact of EU legislation.

Litigation: (*Contact Partners:* Kevin Bays, David Gore, Kathryn Pavey). Commercial litigation is a long-established, substantial and successful element of the practice servicing the firm's corporate and entertainment clients.

Defamation: (*Contact Partners:* Kevin Bays, Philip Conway, Robin Shaw). A leader in this field, the firm's clients include a large number of national newspapers, book and magazine publishers and Private Eye. The firm represents both plaintiffs and defendants.

Property: (*Contact Partners:* Graham Atkins, John Downing, Richard Kelsey, Paul McCombie). A strong commercial property department acts for major developers, property investors, lending institutions and high profile multiple retailers in a broad range of substantial property and property related matters. The firm also provides a first class specialist residential property service.

Liquor Licensing: (*Contact Partners:* Philip Conway, Kathryn Pavey). The firm has developed its liquor licensing work for its large numbers of clients in restaurant and night-club businesses.

Private Client: (*Contact Partners:* John Burrell, Judith Spells). This department provides a full service to private clients, both domestic and overseas, including matrimonial matters, wills, the administration of estates, personal tax, and trusts work.

Sport: (*Contact Partner:* Kevin Bays). The firm has a well established practice advising promoters of sporting events and individual sportsmen in connection with protecting and enhancing their interests.

Davenport Lyons is a growing, efficiently managed, user friendly firm able to satisfy the legal requirements of clients from private individuals to the largest of corporations.

Senior partner:	Leon R. Morgan
Number of partners:	15
Assistant solicitors:	15
Other fee-earners:	11

WORKLOADS	
Company commercial	25%
Litigation	23%
Entertainment/ media	22%
Commercial property	18%
Private client	12%

CONTACTS	
Company/commercial	Anthony Fiducia, Michael Hatchwell
Defamation	Kevin Bays, Philip Conway, Robin Shaw
Employment	Anthony Fiducia, Michael Hatchwell, Kathryn Pavey
Media	Leon Morgan
Liquor Licensing	Philip Conway, Kathryn Pavey
Litigation	Kevin Bays, David Gore, Kathryn Pavey
Copyright/Music/Entertainment	James Ware
Private Client	John Burrell, Judith Spells
Property	Graham Atkins, John Downing, Richard Kelsey, Paul McCombie
Sport	Kevin Bays
International Coordinator	Michael Hatchwell

DAVID BIGMORE & CO 36 Whitefriars Street, London, EC4Y 8BH **Tel:** (0171) 583 2277 **Fax:** (0171) 583 2288 **DX:** 213 LDE **Email:** db@dbigmore.demon.co.uk **Ptnrs:** 1 **Asst solrs:** 1 **Other fee-earners:** 1 **Contact:** David Bigmore *Niche practice specialising in both British and international franchising. Also advises on a broad range of corporate and commercial matters (with particular emphasis on mergers and acquisitions) and commercial litigation and commercial property work.*

WORKLOADS	
Franchising (and related work)	75%
Other corporate and commercial	25%

E. DAVID BRAIN & CO 8 Church Street, St. Austell, PL25 4AT *Tel:* (01726) 68111 *Fax:* (01726) 61433 *DX:* 81252 St. Austell *Other fee-earners:* 5

DAVID CHARNLEY & CO Phoenix House, 102-106 South Street, Romford, RM1 1RX *Tel:* (01708) 766155 *Fax:* (01708) 730743 *DX:* 4614 Romford *Ptnrs:* 1

DAVID DU PRÉ & CO

90-92 PARKWAY, REGENTS PARK, LONDON, NW1 7AN
Tel: (0171) 284 3040 **Fax:** (0171) 485 1145 **DX:** 57070

The Firm: Established in 1991 by David du Pré, a former matrimonial barrister who qualified as a solicitor in 1980 and held senior positions in two leading City firms before setting up his own matrimonial practice. He is a member of the Solicitors Family Law Association, the International Society of Family Law, the Family Mediators Association, and the U.K. College of Family Mediators.

Principal Areas of Work: Matrimonial, family and co-habitation law including: separation and parental responsibility agreements, divorce petitions, financial applications including emergency applications and cases where there is an international dimension including child abduction. Mediations arranged.

Senior partner:	David du Pré
Number of partners:	1
Assistant solicitors:	1

WORKLOADS	
Family/matrimonial/divorce	100%

CONTACTS	
Family/matrimonial/divorce	David du Pré

DAVID GIST & CO 21/23 Clare Street, Bristol, BS1 1TZ **Tel:** (0117) 927 9111 **Fax:** (0117) 927 9101 **DX:** 7880 Bristol **Ptnrs:** 5 **Associates:** 2 **Asst solrs:** 5 **Other fee-earners:** 12 **Contact:** Ms Susan Brewster *David Gist & Co deals mainly with Plaintiff Personal Injury claims, predominantly those arising from motor accidents, and also an increasing number of medical negligence and industrial accident claims. Other offices located in Redfield and Worle.*

DAVID GRAY & COMPANY Old County Court, 56 Westgate Road, Newcastle upon Tyne, NE1 5XU **Tel:** (0191) 232 9547 **Fax:** (0191) 230 4149 **DX:** 61036 Newcastle upon Tyne **Email:** lawyers@davidgray.co.uk **Ptnrs:** 6 **Other fee-earners:** 16 **Contact:** Mr Graham Anderson – Practice Director *At David Gray & Company we aim to be the solicitors of choice for all. Providing full, efficient and effective access to justice and the law especially for those prejudiced by economic, social and cultural circumstances.*

WORKLOADS			
Crime	20%	Family	20%
Immigration	20%	Others	20%
Civil	10%	Mental Health	10%

DAVID JEACOCK 16 Church St, Wootton Bassett, Swindon, SN4 7BQ **Tel:** (01793) 854111 **Fax:** (01793) 853600 **Ptnrs:** 1 **Contact:** Mr David Jeacock *A small personal practice which enjoys working with its clients principally in commercial and sporting matters.*

WORKLOADS			
Company/ commercial	50%	Sports law	30%
Private and general	20%		

DAVID LEVENE & CO Ashley House, 235-239 High Road, Wood Green, London, N22 4HF *Tel:* (0181) 881 7777 *Fax:* (0181) 889 6395 *DX:* 35658 Wood Green 1 *Ptnrs:* 7 *Asst solrs:* 22 *Other fee-earners:* 31

DAVID MYLAN 49 Glebe Road, London, N8 7DA *Tel:* (0181) 347 7270 *Fax:* (0181) 347 7270

DAVID PHILLIPS & PARTNERS 202-268 Stanley Rd, Bootle, L20 3EP *Tel:* (0151) 922 5525 *Fax:* (0151) 922 8298 *DX:* 18806 Bootle *Ptnrs:* 8 *Asst solrs:* 3

DAVID PRICE & CO 5 Great James Street, London, WC1N 3DA *Tel:* (0171) 916 9911 *Fax:* (0171) 916 9910 *Ptnrs:* 1 *Asst solrs:* 2 *Other fee-earners:* 1

DAVID & SNAPE Wyndham House, Wyndham Street, Bridgend, CF31 1EP *Tel:* (01656) 661115 *Fax:* (01656) 660545 *DX:* 38001 Bridgend *Ptnrs:* 7 *Asst solrs:* 4 *Other fee-earners:* 3

DAVIDSON CHALMERS WS 10 Castle Terrace, Edinburgh, EH1 2DP *Tel:* (0131) 228 9191 *Fax:* (0131) 228 9003 *DX:* 408 Edinburgh *Ptnrs:* 4 *Asst solrs:* 3 *Other fee-earners:* 2

DAVID TRUEX AND COMPANY

212 STRAND, LONDON, WC2R 1AP
Tel: (0171) 583 5040 **Fax:** (0171) 583 5151 **DX:** 252 (CH.LN) **Email:** MAIL@DAVIDTRUEX.COM **Internet:** WWW.DAVIDTRUEX.COM

The Firm: Family law specialist firm founded by American-born David Truex, who is also qualified as an Australian barrister and solicitor. Senior consultants Henry Brookman (also dual qualified in England and Australia) and Catherine Banks conduct most of the firm's Australian and English litigation, assisted by two paralegal staff. David Truex's work focuses on cross-jurisdictional cases involving forum disputes, international enforcement and consultancy on the application of foreign laws and international treaties. The firm's video conferencing facilities are particularly useful in international cases. All solicitors are members of the Solicitors Family Law Association.

Principal Areas of Work: Most of the firm's work is in the English family law jurisdiction, including a large international agency practice with referrals from foreign lawyers, law societies and embassies. The firm has considerable experience in contested international custody disputes including Hague Convention child abduction matters. Particular expertise is claimed in complex financial disputes where off-shore assets are in issue.

International: With two dual-qualified solicitors the firm is retained by English and foreign lawyers to provide expert consultancy on cross-jurisdictional family law issues, particularly with respect to recognition and enforcement of foreign orders in England and Wales. The firm is highly experienced in dealing with questions of forum and resolving international forum disputes. Strong links are maintained with selected law firms and government agencies in Australia, New Zealand, the United States, Germany, France, Spain and Asia.

Principal:	David Truex
Number of partners:	1
Senior Consultants:	2
Other fee-earners:	2

WORKLOADS	
English family law	60%
International family law (including consultancy & agency)	40%

CONTACTS	
Family Law	David Truex, Catherine Banks and Henry Brookman.

DAVIES AND PARTNERS

ROWAN HOUSE, BARNETT WAY, BARNWOOD, GLOUCESTER, GL4 3RT
Tel: (01452) 612345 **Fax:** (01452) 611922 **DX:** 55253

The Firm: Davies and Partners is forward-thinking and objective in approach. The firm handles a large amount of commercial property, estate conveyancing, company and commercial, commercial litigation, and secured lending work and has also developed a strong personal injury and medical negligence practice.

Principal Areas of Work:

Land Development: (*Contact Partner:* Barrie Davies). The firm handles all aspects of development land, from initial site acquisition to individual unit transfers and ancillary documentation, planning applications and appeals, building contracts and freehold and leasehold matters.

Company/Commercial: (*Contact Partner:* Thomas Brennan). The firm has extensive experience in the whole range of company and commercial work, including corporate finance, mergers, acquisitions and restructuring, MBOs, publicly-quoted companies, company and partnership formation, joint ventures, shareholders' agreements, banking, financial services and franchising; intellectual property, including international, EC and UK competition implications.

Commercial Property: (*Contact Partner:* Peter Mitchell). The firm handles all aspects of commercial property including industrial, office and retail premises for both Landlords and Tenants and all associated funding, development and property management issues.

Commercial Litigation: (*Contact Partner:* Geoffrey Hand). *Work includes:* building contracts, judicial review, landlord and tenant, employment, insurance, professional negligence, public liability, economic torts, corporate insolvency, unlawful trading, licensing, debt collection and banking litigation.

Personal Injury and Medical Negligence: (*Contact Partner:* Robert Ashton). The firm handles extensively both plaintiff and defendant personal injury work. Medical negligence work is plaintiff-orientated. Two fee earners are members of the Law Society Personal Injury Panel.

Other Areas of Work: All aspects of corporate and personal tax and financial planning, agricultural law (including land acquisition and disposal, agricultural holdings, grazing agreements, share farming agreements, EC implications and business tenancies) and private client work (including residential conveyancing, re-mortgaging, wills, trusts and estate management, and distribution and winding-up of estates).

Other Offices: Bristol, Birmingham.

Senior partner:	D.B. Davies
Number of partners:	19
Assistant solicitors:	26
Other fee-earners:	13

CONTACTS	
Commercial litigation	Geoffrey Hand
Commercial property	Peter Mitchell
Company/commercial	Tom Brennan
Land development	Barrie Davies
Personal Injury and Medical Negligence	
	Robert Ashton
Private client	Richard Maisey

DAVIES ARNOLD COOPER

6-8 BOUVERIE STREET, LONDON, EC4Y 8DD
Tel: (0171) 936 2222 **Fax:** (0171) 936 2020 **DX:** 172 **Email:** DACLON@DAC.CO.UK

85 GRACECHURCH STREET, LONDON, EC3V 0AA
Tel: (0171) 936 2222 **Fax:** (0171) 410 7998 **DX:** 172 **Email:** DACLON@DAC.CO.UK

60 FOUNTAIN STREET, MANCHESTER, M2 2FE
Tel: (0161) 839 8396 **Fax:** (0161) 839 8309 **DX:** 14363 MANCHESTER **Email:** DACMAN@DAC.CO.UK

MILBURN HOUSE, DEAN STREET, NEWCASTLE-UPON-TYNE, NE1 1LE
Tel: (0191) 230 5115 **Fax:** (0191) 230 0296 **DX:** 60311 GATESHEAD **Email:** DACNEW@DAC.CO.UK

The Firm: Established in the City in 1927, Davies Arnold Cooper has offices in London, Manchester, Newcastle, a London Insurance Market office, Madrid and an associate office in Brussels. They have long established contacts with leading law firms throughout the world.

Davies Arnold Cooper are well known for their practical and commercial approach. The firm's campaigning and pioneering style, coupled with its involvement in most of the high-profile litigation cases in the past ten years, reinforces its' position as one of the UK's leading law firms.

The firm is organised in a client focused structure with core sectors covering Insurance, Financial Services, Construction, Property, Pharmaceutical, Healthcare and Technology serviced by specialist skill groups. Their primary areas of specialisation are:

Alternative Dispute Resolution (ADR): (*Contact:* Nick Sinfield). The firm have been key influencers in the evolution of the ADR process, one of their partners was an Assessor on the Woolf Committee and they are a founder member of the Centre for Alternative Dispute Resolution (CEDR). They have hands-on experience of using the ADR process in major UK and international cases.

Banking: (*Contact:* Chris Sykes). The Banking Group advises UK and international banks and financial institutions on funding transactions of all kinds. They provide expertise in secured, unsecured, bilateral, syndicated and club deals with particular emphasis on property finance, acquisition finance, corporate banking and secondary debt market transactions.

Commercial Property, Planning & Environment: (*Contact:* Nick Collins). The Group advise on all aspects of commercial property including development (residential and commercial), funding, joint ventures, option agreements, lease negotiation, large portfolio purchases and sales, creation of retail, industrial and residential estates and business parks. They act for investment companies in acquisitions and sales, and are actively involved with landlords and tenants in the management of their portfolios.

Areas of expertise include commercial lettings, compulsory purchase, residential and commercial development, housing, joint venture agreements, landlord and tenant, option agreements, environmental, planning, portfolio purchases and sales, property finance, property recovery and insolvency, investment.

The Planning & Environmental unit deals with planning and compulsory purchase for developers and landowners and has been involved in high profile environmental compliance actions. They advise businesses and organisations who are affected by European and UK "green" legislation such as waste disposal, marine, contaminated land, construction and nuisance.

Construction: (*Contact:* Daniel Gowan). The Construction and Engineering Group advises worldwide on arbitration, litigation and mediation, contract formation, procurement, major projects and all aspects of construction and engineering insurance.

They act for international organisations in construction, engineering, oil, petrochemicals, structural and civil engineering and have recent involvement in key projects in Trinidad, Hong Kong, Ethiopia, Thailand, Australia and the Middle East.

Corporate Insurance and Reinsurance: (*Contact:* Chris Croft/Ambereen Salamat). The Group has specialised expertise in acquisitions, disposals, mergers and joint ventures in the insurance sector. They advise on portfolio transfers and all issues relating to mutuals, as well as commercial contracts entered into by life and non-life companies, Lloyd's Market entities and brokers, financing and financial structures, securitisation, competition law issues and all aspects of regulation of insurance and reinsurance companies, Lloyd's entities and brokers. They are involved with the authorisation of insurance companies worldwide and the establishment of corporate capital vehicles at Lloyds.

EU/Competition: (*Contact:* Marjorie Holmes). The European Group is multi-disciplinary and provides a comprehensive service to businesses affected by EU competition law and other directives and regulations. They also advise companies tendering for European funded projects under the EC Phare and Tacis programmes.

Healthcare and Pharmaceutical Product Liability and Mass Tort: (*Contact:* Anne

Managing partner:	Laurence Messer
Senior partner:	David McIntosh
UK	
Number of partners:	56
Assistant solicitors:	129
Other fee-earners:	65
International	
Number of partners:	1
Assistant solicitors:	8
Other fee-earners:	0

WORKLOADS	
Litigation	77%
Corporate	12%
Property/Banking	11%

DAVIES
ARNOLD
COOPER
SOLICITORS

Ware). The Group deals with all areas of healthcare and pharmaceutical product liability, litigation, regulatory work, medical negligence and claims advice including agrochemicals and veterinary products.

They have been involved in most of the major pharmaceutical product liability litigation in the UK and have wide experience of the challenging problems that arise with high profile cases, particularly the extra-legal dimensions of crisis management and media relations.

They also deal with all types of claim arising from the use of products and have expertise in mass tort litigation where multiple claims are brought relating to the same product or incident. Davies Arnold Cooper is one of the leading practices in the development of multi-party action procedures in the UK.

Insolvency and Insurance Insolvency: (*Contact:* Nigel Montgomery). The Insolvency Group handles receiverships and administrations and works closely with major banks on rescues and reorganisations. They act for partners in most of the major accounting firms in their capacity as administrative receivers, administrators, liquidators and supervisors of voluntary arrangements and for purchasers of assets out of insolvency situations. The Group specialises in solvent liquidations of investment trusts and Schemes of Arrangement for insurance and reinsurance companies.

Insurance Litigation: (*Contact:* Nick Sinfield). The firm has one of the largest insurance practices in the UK and have acted in many of the major cases in the insurance sector over the last decade. They have substantial expertise in regulatory and corporate litigation in the insurance market.

Intellectual Property and Media: (*Contact:* Catrin Turner). The Intellectual Property Group has expertise in all aspects of contentious and non-contentious intellectual property and media law and has recently been involved in major anti-piracy programmes and grey goods disputes.

Defamation: (*Contact:* Keith Mathieson). As part of their Intellectual Property and Media Group, defamation specialists advise on all aspects of media and publishing law including trade libel, copyright, confidentiality, contempt of court, reporting restrictions and passing off. Clients include a wide range of newspaper, magazine and book publishers, broadcasters, libel insurers, companies and private individuals.

International Commercial Disputes Resolution: (*Contact:* Akbar Ali). The firm are leaders in the resolution of disputes by institutional or ad hoc arbitration and they have been involved in many high profile arbitration references in the banking, construction, marine and pharmaceutical industries.

Major Projects and Private Finance Initiative: (*Contact:* Akbar Ali). Davies Arnold Cooper are at the leading edge of PFI and currently advise on schemes worth over £400m. Their focus is on banking, funding, construction, healthcare, property, corporate, employment, intellectual property and information technology. They work closely with financiers, consortia, public and private sector organisations from initial planning through procurement to the construction and management of the project.

Marine: (*Contact:* Marjorie Holmes). The Marine Group advises on all aspects of the marine transport industry in the UK, Europe and worldwide. In the commercial shipping sector, they lead the use of alternative dispute resolution (ADR) on all matters relating to marine and transport insurance, with a particular speciality in handling CMR claims.

They act for marine insurers and reinsurers including shipowners, charterers, oil companies, protection and indemnity clubs, drydock owners, shipbuilders and salvors.

Oil and Gas: (*Contact:* John Bolton). They act for multinational companies in relation to oil, gas and electricity generating projects as well as refinery construction and pipeline projects worldwide and specialise in arbitration and litigation of energy related disputes and utility related insurance.

Pensions: (*Contact:* Michael Fletcher/Patrick Kennedy). The Pensions Group advises on establishing, merging, reorganising and winding up occupational pension schemes, pension issues arising on acquisitions and disposals of business, independent trusteeship services through a separate trustee company, independent trustees, E&O underwriters on mis-selling of schemes, employer and trustee powers.

Employers' and Public Liability: (*Contact:* Tania Sless). Davies Arnold Cooper are one of the UK's leading practices in Employers', Public and Product Liability claims. They act for major retailers, airlines and building companies, NHS Trusts, large composite insurers and foreign insurance companies, particularly Japanese and Italian, operating in the UK and worldwide.

They have developed a specialist expertise in disease related litigation, particularly asbestos and Work Related Upper Limb Disorder claims.

Motor: (*Contact:* Malcolm Henké). The Motor Group acts for leading composite insurers, reinsurers and direct insurers as well as catastrophically injured Plaintiffs. They undertaken arbitrations, inquests, County and High Court litigation, Court of Appeal and House of Lords' cases. They have expertise across Europe and in dealing with transatlantic litigation, particularly involving European nationals injured in the USA and American

**DAVIES
ARNOLD
COOPER**
SOLICITORS

Continues overleaf

nationals injured in Europe.

Professional Indemnity and D&O: (*Contact:* Nicholas Sinfield/Kenneth McKenzie). The firm represent insurers and insureds in claims against barristers, solicitors, accountants, architects, engineers, underwriting agents, stockbrokers, merchant banks, investment advisers, financial institutions, Lloyd's agents, directors, officers and regulatory organisations. They advise insurers on coverage issues in professional indemnity risks and on bringing subrogated claims against other professional advisers.

Property Insurance Litigation: (*Contact:* Nick Young). The Property Insurance Group acts for insurers on all types of property insurance disputes. They defend insurers on claims made against them and prosecute subrogated claims on their behalf and on coverage issues on property related risks.

Reinsurance: (*Contact:* Michael Dobias). The Reinsurance and Financial Risks Group has been the leading exponent of reinsurance law worldwide for more than 25 years, advising clients from a broad spectrum of Lloyd's and London Market reinsurers and reinsured, and the international market. They also provide a comprehensive service to financial risk underwriters..

Other Offices: In the UK, they have offices in Manchester and Newcastle. In Europe, in Madrid and an associate office in Brussels. They have close links with major law firms in all important overseas jurisdictions, particularly the United States and Japan. Their London Market Office provides an on-the-spot service to the Lloyd's insurance market.

Languages Spoken: French, German, Greek, Italian, Spanish, Russian, Flemish, Gujerati, Punjabi, Urdu, Swedish and Japanese.

Recruitment and Training: Davies Arnold Cooper recruits 21 trainee solicitors a year. Applications to Rita Siwoniku, in the firm's London office. No minimum degree required although a good 2:1 strongly preferred.

DAVIES, JOHNSON & CO Mayflower House, Armada Way, Plymouth, PL1 1LD *Tel:* (01752) 226020 *Fax:* (01752) 225882 *DX:* 8254 Plymouth *Ptnrs:* 4 *Asst solrs:* 2

DAVIES LAVERY Palace Court, 17 London Road, Maidstone, ME16 8JE **Tel:** (01622) 688171 **Fax:** (01622) 672847 **DX:** 51971 Maidstone 2 **Ptnrs:** 4 **Asst solrs:** 11 **Other fee-earners:** 11 **Contact:** Magdalene Lavery

WORKLOADS	
Insurance Litigation	70%
Property and Commercial	20%
Transit	10%

DAVIES WALLIS FOYSTER

5 CASTLE STREET, LIVERPOOL, L2 4XE
Tel: (0151) 236 6226 **Fax:** (0151) 236 3088 **DX:** 14128 LIVERPOOL-1 (0161) 228 3702 **Email:** ENQUIRIES@DWF-LAW.COM

HARVESTER HOUSE, 37 PETER STREET, MANCHESTER, M2 5GB
Tel: (0161) 228 3702 **Fax:** (0161) 835 2407 **DX:** 14313 MANCHESTER-1 (0161) 228 3702**Email:** ENQUIRIES@DWF-LAW.COM

The Firm: Rapid growth in recent years has seen Davies Wallis Foyster emerge as one of the North West's leading commercial law practices. The firm's success is based upon four core values which underpin its philosophy, namely: commitment to understanding clients' needs, efficient service delivery, technical expertise and competitive fees. DWF's client base ranges from national developers, major PLCs and financial institutions to private companies and government and public sector organisations.

Principal Areas of Work:

Corporate: (*Contact:* Mark O'Connor). Corporate law is one of the firm's key areas of expertise, particularly flotations, acquisitions and disposals, buy-outs, joint ventures, franchising, venture capital and commercial lending. The corporate team also handles: computer contracts, marketing and intellectual property agreements, European Union law (*contact:* Andrew West) and pensions (*contact:* Gerald Power) as well as any private client work (*contact:* Paul Liddle) arising from commercial contacts.

Commercial Property: (*Contact:* Andrew Green). The firm's property department is one of the largest in the North West, handling property development work for a large number of national retailers, brewers and property developers. Planning, compulsory purchase and environmental practices are also expanding, resulting in close ties with public sector authorities.

Commercial Litigation: (*Contact:* Andrew Gregory). DWF has a strong reputation in commercial litigation – especially in the areas of banking, brewing and asset finance recovery. These specialisms are complemented by a high profile presence in the areas of employment and contentious and non-contentious construction law.

Insurance Litigation: (*Contact:* Ian Titchmarsh). The practice also encompasses a major

Managing partner:	Jim Davies
Number of partners:	43
Total staff:	261

WORKLOADS	
Litigation	46%
Corporate	36%
Property	18%

CONTACTS	
Corporate	Mark O'Connor
Insurance	Ian Titchmarsh
Litigation	Andrew Gregory
Property	Andrew Green

insurance litigation department which handles defendant work for many of the UK's major insurance companies and which has seen rapid expansion in recent years. The work of the department ranges from personal injury litigation and the defence of substantial policy claims to advice on the drafting and interpretation of insurance policies.

Licensing: (*Contact:* Nick Dickinson). DWF's licensing department is one of the UK's largest, processing licensing applications and providing licensing training for national supermarket chains, off-licences brewers and the entertainment and leisure industry in general.

Banking & Insolvency: (*Contact:* Mike Jennings). DWF's Banking Unit has brought together considerable banking and insolvency experience with complementary litigation and property skills to provide banking clients with a truly specialist resource.

Employment: (*Contact:* Andrea McWatt). DWF's Employment Team acts for a number of national organisations providing contractual and health and safety advice as well as industrial tribunal representation.

Recruitment: The practice serves clients throughout the UK, providing a comprehensive range of commercial legal services. The firm is committed to the recruitment of high calibre solicitors for all its legal specialisms and recruits up to 8 trainees solicitors annually. Brochures are available upon request.

DAVIS BLANK FURNISS 90 Deansgate, Manchester, M3 2QJ *Tel:* (0161) 832 3304 *Fax:* (0161) 834 3568 *DX:* 14311 Manchester *Ptnrs:* 10 *Asst solrs:* 10 *Other fee-earners:* 9

DAWBARNS 1-2 York Row, Wisbech, PE13 1EA **Tel:** (01945) 461456 **Fax:** (01945) 461364 **DX:** 41351 **Ptnrs:** 8 **Asst solrs:** 6 **Other fee-earners:** 12 **Contact:** David Chapman *Undertakes a wide range of work including specialist family law, personal injury (including medical negligence), company/commercial/construction departments. Office at King's Lynn.*

WORKLOADS			
Civil – Other	37%	Family Law	28%
Civil – Multi-Party	15%	Conveyancing	8%
Probate, Wills etc	6%	Commercial	4%
Criminal	3%		

DAWSON & CO

2 NEW SQUARE, LINCOLN'S INN, LONDON, WC2A 3RZ
Tel: (0171) 421 4800 **Fax:** (0171) 421 4848 **DX:** 38 **Email:** LEGAL@DAWSON-AND-CO.CO.UK

The Firm: A medium-sized firm which handles a substantial volume of all types of litigation, property and property development, and tax planning work.

It also acts for many large agricultural estates with their attendant trust and settled land work, a number of charities and large Housing Associations.

Other main areas of work include probate, matrimonial and company and commercial work, minerals, royal charters and international asset management.

Senior partner:	Kenneth Wood
Number of partners:	17
Assistant solicitors:	9
Other fee-earners:	14

WORKLOADS	
Litigation (inc. family)	39%
Property	22%
Tax	16%
Probate/Trusts	15%
Company	8%

DAWSON CORNWELL & CO 16 Red Lion Square, London, WC1R 4QT **Tel:** (0171) 242 2556 **Fax:** (0171) 831 0478 **DX:** 35725 **Email:** mail@dawsoncornwell.co.uk **Ptnrs:** 8 **Asst solrs:** 4 **Other fee-earners:** 2 **Contact:** Ms Rhiannon Lewis. *Leading family law practice, with eight matrimonial specialists including international children expert, all members of SFLA. Also probate, property, litigation.*

WORKLOADS			
Family and matrimonial	73%	Conveyancing	12%
Wills, trusts and probate			10%
Litigation and miscellaneous			4%

DEAN WILSON

96 CHURCH STREET, BRIGHTON, BN1 1UJ
Tel: (01273) 327241 **Fax:** (01273) 770913 **DX:** 2706 BRIGHTON **Email:** THE LAWYERS@DEAN-WILSON.CO.UK

The Firm: Dean Wilson offers a comprehensive range of services to both commercial and private clients, with particular expertise in relation to property development, employment law and licensing matters. The partners include a former Local Authority Planning Committee Chairman, a former Chairman of Industrial Tribunals, a Recorder, a member of the Personal Injuries Panel, a member of the Childrens Panel, and a member of the Society of Trust & Estate Practitioners.

Principal Areas of Work:

Corporate and Commercial: (*Contact Partner:* David Barling). The firm can advise on all aspects of corporate, commercial and financial matters, including company and partnership formation, restructuring, acquisitions and disposals, and insolvency. Expertise is offered in employment law, and licensing law relating to pubs, clubs, restaurants and gaming. A full range of commercial property work is undertaken including estate development, planning work, commercial leasing and commercial conveyancing.

Landlord and Tenant: The firm specialises in all aspects of landlord and tenant law both residential and commercial. A substantial amount of litigation of this type is dealt with (*Contact Partner:* Nick Perkins). The firm are honorary solicitors to the Association of Residential Letting Agents, and also to the Southern Private Landlords Association. Leasehold enfranchisement is fully covered (*Contact Partner:* Joanna Ward).

Litigation: (*Contact Partner:* Ian Wilson). A range of civil and criminal litigation is undertaken including civil engineering and construction disputes, marine disputes, personal injury actions, professional negligence actions, employment disputes including applications for restraint of trade and non-competition injunctions, industrial tribunals, licensing matters and debt recovery.

Private Client: Private client service includes wills, probate, administration of estates, trusts and tax planning (*Contact Partner:* Georgina James), residential conveyancing and leases (*Contact:* Joanna Ward), charity law (*Contact:* Georgina James), family law matters including separation, divorce, welfare of children and property disputes (*Contact Partner:* Linda Wall) and criminal law (*Contact:* Imogen Bell).

Financial Services: The firm is authorised to carry out discrete investment business. (*Contact:* John Atkinson or Karen Hooker).

Managing partner:	Dudley J. Dean
Senior partner:	Dudley J. Dean
Number of partners:	7
Assistant solicitors:	4
Other fee-earners:	6

WORKLOADS	
Domestic conveyancing/probate	24%
Commercial property	15%
General litigation	15%
Landlord & tenant	15%
Employment	13%
Company/commercial	10%
Matrimonial	5%
Planning	3%

CONTACTS	
Commercial, commercial property, landlord & tenant (non-contentious)	D. Barling
Domestic conveyancing/ probate	G. James
Employment	I. Wilson
Landlord & tenant litigation	N. Perkins
Leasehold enfranchisement	J. Ward
Matrimonial	L. Wall
Planning	D. Barling

DEAS MALLEN SOUTER Eldon Chambers, 23 The Quayside, Newcastle upon Tyne, NE1 3DE *Tel:* (0191) 221 0898 *Fax:* (0191) 232 0930 *DX:* 61085 *Ptnrs:* 9 *Asst solrs:* 3 *Other fee-earners:* 1

DEBEVOISE & PLIMPTON IFC 14th Floor, 25 Old Broad Street, London, EC2N 1HQ **Tel:** (0171) 786 9000 **Fax:** (0171) 588 4180 **Ptnrs:** 4 **Associates:** 7 **Asst solrs:** 1 **Other fee-earners:** 1 **Contact:** David Smalley *An international firm specialising in capital markets, financings, telecommunications, privatisations mergers and acquisitions, investment funds, international arbitrations and commercial litigation. New York, Washington DC, Paris, Moscow and Hong Kong.*

DEBORAH MILLS ASSOCIATES Tamsin House, 4 Chapel Street, Marlow, SL7 1DD *Tel:* (01628) 487 711 *Fax:* (01628) 481 678 *Ptnrs:* 2 *Asst solrs:* 2 *Other fee-earners:* 3

DEIGHTON GUEDALLA Top Floor, 30-31 Islington Green, London, N1 8DU *Tel:* (0171) 359 5700 *Fax:* (0171) 359 9909 *DX:* 58251 Islington *Ptnrs:* 2 *Asst solrs:* 1 *Other fee-earners:* 2

DENISON TILL Goodbard House, Infirmary Street, Leeds, LS1 2JS *Tel:* (0113) 246 7161 *Fax:* (0113) 246 7518 *DX:* 26426 Leeds (Park Square) *Ptnrs:* 14 *Asst solrs:* 4 *Other fee-earners:* 14

DENNIS FAULKNER & ALSOP Beethoven House, 32 Market Square, Northampton, NN1 2DQ *Tel:* (01604) 620161 *Fax:* (01604) 230178 *DX:* 701725 Northampton 5 *Ptnrs:* 9 *Asst solrs:* 4 *Other fee-earners:* 2

DENTON HALL

5 CHANCERY LANE, CLIFFORD'S INN, LONDON, EC4A 1BU
Tel: (0171) 242 1212 **Fax:** (0171) 404 0087/ 320 6161 **DX:** 242 **Email:** INFO@DENTONHALL.COM **Internet:** HTTP://WWW.DENTONHALL.COM

The Firm: Denton Hall is one of the largest firms in London with 116 partners, more than 300 other lawyers and nearly 800 staff in total in our offices around the world. Based in the City of London with a satellite office in Milton Keynes, our practice has grown and diversified rapidly in recent years.

Denton Hall is a full service practice serving UK and international clients. We provide the full range of legal corporate and commercial legal services required by companies, financial institutions, governments and non-profit making bodies.

Internationally, Denton hall has an extensive Asian network, with offices in Beijing, Hong Kong, Singapore and Tokyo. The firm also has offices in Brussels, New York and Moscow. Denton Hall is a founder member of the Denton International Group of Law Firms, an alliance with Heuking Kühn Lüer Heussen Wotjek in Germany, Lind & Cadovius in Denmark, Lambert Grohmann Stolizka Rîhsner in Austria, Saläs Vincent & Associés in France, de Besche & Co in Norway and Bufete Lupicinio Rodríguez in Spain.

Principal Areas of Work: Denton Hall is one of the most up to date and progressive firms in London, occupying a leading position in many areas of law. We are particularly well-known in the areas of energy, media and technology, infrastructure projects, privatisations, corporate and financial services, commercial property, retail, planning and public law, environment, intellectual property, litigation and arbitration.

The firm advises in all aspects of corporate and international law, including public issues, mergers and acquisitions, joint ventures, banking, competition, tax, insurance, insolvency, corporate fraud, pensions and employment.

Other Offices: Beijing, Brussels, Hong Kong, Milton Keynes, Moscow, New York, Singapore, Tokyo.

Associated Offices: Barcelona, Berlin, Chemnitz, Cologne, Copenhagen, Dresden, Düsseldorf, Frankfurt, Hamburg, Madrid, Munich, Oslo, Paris Potsdam, Vienna.

Recruitment and Training: The Firm recruits around 30 trainee solicitors every year. Please apply by letter and CV, two years in advance, to Virginia Glastonbury.

The firm also welcomes applications from qualified solicitors and other fee earners at all levels of experience, which should be sent to Paul Green.

Managing partner:	Jonathan Tatten
Chrairman:	James Dallas
UK	
Number of partners:	92
Assistant solicitors:	137
Other fee-earners:	98
International	
Number of partners:	21
Assistant solicitors:	33
Other fee-earners:	43

WORKLOADS	
Company and commercial	38%
Litigation and arbitration	26%
Property and planning	22%
Media and technology	14%

CONTACTS	
Banking & financial markets	Anthony Bonsor
Commercial property	Martin Quicke, Roger Sutcliffe
Company/ commercial	Tony Grant
Competition & EC	David Aitman
Employment & immigration	Stephanie Dale
Energy	Malcom Groom
Environmental law	Jacqui O'Keeffe
Financial Markets	Robert Finney
Insolvency	Michael Steiner
Intellectual property	Clive Thorne
Litigation & arbitration	Cindy Leslie, Liz Tout
Media & entertainment	Ken Dearsley, Alan Williams
Planning	Sandra Banks
Project finance	James Dallas
Tax	Jane Douglas
Telecommunications	Nicholas Higham
Transport	Tom Winsor

DENTON HALL

MEMBER OF THE DENTON INTERNATIONAL GROUP OF LAW FIRMS

DEVONSHIRES

SALISBURY HOUSE, LONDON WALL, LONDON, EC2M 5QY
Tel: (0171) 628 7576 **Fax:** (0171) 256 7318 **DX:** 33856 FINSBURY SQUARE

The Firm: City based, Devonshires provides high quality legal services for public and private sector clients including banks, building societies, other commercial investors, general commercial clients, housing associations, local authorities, non-profit making bodies and entrepreneurs. It is a leading housing law firm and now represents over 130 social landlords. Since 1988 it has negotiated funding transactions raising over £1.8 billion for social housing. Reflecting the success of its practice the firm has trebled in size in the last six years. It is expanding into work for local authorities. The firm has a thriving commercial property department acting for pension funds and other investors. A rapidly expanding litigation practice handles matters including fraud, insolvency, commercial disputes, partnership disputes and general contract. It has handled conditional fee cases in insolvency and has a growing reputation in art/antiquities recovery litigation. A recently established employment unit provides support services to personnel/human resources officers.

Principal Areas of Work: Bulk property transfers, development site conveyancing, shared ownership and right to buys, for institutions, development corporations and local authorities; planning and construction law; housing management, repossession, disrepair and CCT; domestic and international commercial litigation; asset recovery; white collar crime; corporate, including acquisitions, equity issues and joint ventures; general litigation for institutions and debt collection; employment law; banking and capital markets.

Managing partner:	Nigel Hardy
Senior partner:	Julian Roberts
Number of partners:	16
Assoc/Assist Slrs.:	10
Other fee-earners:	17

CONTACTS	
Commercial Litigation	Philip Barden
Corporate/Commercial	Gareth Hall
Housing Management	Jane Mogollon/
	Nicholas Billingham
Local Authorities	Julie Bradley
Low Cost Home Ownership	Michael Phillips/
	Jane Nunnerley
NHS trusts	Duncan Brown/David Brittain
Planning and Construction	Nigel Hardy
Property	Allan Hudson/Duncan Brown
Property Security	Julie Bradley
Religious Charities	John Dodd
Social Housing Finance	Andrew Cowan

DEWAR HOGAN

46 BOW LANE, CHEAPSIDE, LONDON, EC4M 9HR
Tel: (0171) 246 2929 **Fax:** (0171) 489 0590

The Firm: Dewar Hogan specialises exclusively in contentious property matters and property litigation relating to commercial and residential property. All of its members were formerly with leading London law firms and have many years of experience. Clients of the practice include property companies, property funds, public authorities, banks and private investors. The practice accepts referrals from other firms of solicitors on a fee sharing basis.

Principal Areas of Work: Disputes between landlords and tenants, lenders and borrowers and clients and their professional advisers.

Managing partner:	R.D. Hogan
Senior partner:	R.D. Hogan
Number of partners:	2
Assistant solicitors:	2
Other fee-earners:	1

WORKLOADS	
Property litigation	100%

CONTACTS	
Property litigation	Ronald Hogan, John Cox

DEWEY BALLANTINE

1 UNDERSHAFT, LONDON, EC3A 8LP
Tel: (0171) 456 6000 **Fax:** (0171) 456 6001

Dewey Ballantine is one of the major US based law firms. It has had a significant international practice for some years, particularly in Central Europe, Latin America and Asia. The international presence was further developed in 1996 when the firm substantially expanded its London office which, with the addition of English qualified partners and assistants, now offers English as well as New York law advice, with a particular emphasis on capital markets, project financing in emerging markets, structured finance and cross border leasing, mergers and acquisitions.

The Firm: Having its origins in New York in 1909, where the firm is based, the firm also has substantial offices in Washington D.C. and Los Angeles. Internationally, in addition to its London office, the firm has Central European offices in Warsaw, Prague and Budapest and an office in Hong Kong. The firm is also active in the Middle East. Dewey Ballantine has a highly diversified practice, with regular clients including multinational companies, commercial and investment banks, governmental organisations, energy companies, telecommunications service providers and insurance companies. The breadth of the practice is reflected in the London office activity which combines a significant capital markets practice focusing on emerging markets (involving both debt and equity issues) with project finance, structured finance (including securitisation), tax related cross-border leasing and financial products (two of the London partners being tax specialists) and privatisation, mergers and acquisitions and other transactional work, particularly in Central and Eastern Europe (including Russia).

London Managing Partner:	Stuart Odell
Number of Resident Partners:	8
Number of Resident Fee-earners:	25
Total Resident Staff:	58

CONTACTS	
Capital Markets	Camille Abousleiman
Central and Eastern Europe	Stephen Jones
Leasing	Stuart Odell
Project Finance	James D. Simpson, Jr.
Structured Finance and Securitisation	
	Douglas Colliver
Tax	Fred Gander

S.J. DIAMOND & SON Corry House, 7-19 Royal Avenue, Belfast, BT1 1FB *Tel:* (01232) 243726 *Fax:* (01232) 230651 *Ptnrs:* 3 *Asst solrs:* 4 *Other fee-earners:* 1

DIANE HINCH

28 GROSVENOR STREET, LONDON, W1X 9FE
Tel: (0171) 917 9680 **Fax:** (0171) 917 6002 **Email:** DHINCH@COMPUSERVE.COM

The Firm: Established as a niche practice in United States immigration law, the firm specialises in business-related visas, from non-immigrant working visas to permanent residence and U.S. citizenship. The U.S. office is located in Orange County, California, just south of Los Angeles.

Nature of Clientele: Clients from the following industries are represented: computer hardware and software, aerospace, electronics and engineering, entertainment, including film and music video production companies, biomedical and financial services.

Other Office: California, U.S.

Membership of EEIGs and International Associations: International Bar Association, Inter-Pacific Bar Association, Los Angeles Bar Association, Orange County Bar Association and British-American Chamber of Commerce, Orange County.

Managing partner:	Diane Hinch
Senior partner:	Diane Hinch
Number of partners:	1

WORKLOADS	
US immigration	100%

DIBB LUPTON ALSOP

125 LONDON WALL, LONDON, EC2Y 5AE
Tel: (0345) 262728 **Fax:** 0171 600 1650 **DX:** 33866 LONDON FINSBURY SQUARE

WINDSOR HOUSE, TEMPLE ROW, BIRMINGHAM, B2 5LF
Tel: (0345) 262728 **Fax:** (0121) 212 5794 **DX:** 13022 BIRMINGHAM 1

ARNDALE HOUSE, CHARLES STREET, BRADFORD, BD1 1UN
Tel: (0345) 262728 **Fax:** (01274) 783000 **DX:** 712510 BRADFORD 10

65 RUE STEVIN, BRUSSELS 1000,
Tel: 00 32 2230 4454 **Fax:** 00 32 2230 2012 **DX:** 10005 BDS (BELGIUM)

16TH FLOOR, KAILEY TOWER, 14-16 STANLEY STREET, CENTRAL HONG KONG,
Tel: + 852 2 524 2003 **Fax:** + 852 2 810 1345

117 THE HEADROW, LEEDS, LS1 5JX
Tel: (0345) 262728 **Fax:** (0113) 245 2632 **DX:** 12017

6 DOWGATE HILL, LONDON, EC4R 2SS
Tel: (0345) 262728 **Fax:** (0171) 3291785 **DX:** 799 LONDON CITY

101 BARBIROLLI SQUARE, MANCHESTER, M2 3DL
Tel: (0345) 262728 **Fax:** (0161) 2354111 **DX:** 14304 MANCHESTER 1

FOUNTAIN PRECINCT, BALM GREEN, SHEFFIELD, S1 1RZ
Tel: (0345) 262728 **Fax:** (0114) 270 0568 **DX:** 708580 SHEFFIELD 10

INDIA BUILDINGS, WATER STREET, LIVERPOOL, L2 0NH
Tel: (0345) 262728 **Fax:** (0151) 236 9208 **DX:** 14103

7TH FLOOR, NO 2 MINSTER COURT, MINCING LANE, LONDON, EC3R 7XW
Tel: (0345) 262728 **Fax:** (0171) 7966784 **DX:** 33866 LONDON FINSBURY SQUARE

The Firm Dibb Lupton Alsop is one of the top ten law firms in the country in terms of turnover. It is the only truly national firm and combines a strong regional network of offices in Birmingham, Bradford, Leeds, Liverpool, Manchester and Sheffield with major offices in the City of London. Dibb Lupton Alsop also has an important overseas presence with established offices in Hong Kong and Brussels, together with a growing volume of work in Europe and the Far East handled by their UK-based lawyers.

The extensive network of offices enables a speedy response to clients' needs and maintains the delivery of premium quality services throughout the country. The structure, which includes industry-focused business groups, means they have the ability to field specialist teams of experts to provide the solutions to all requirements. Many of these experts have previously worked in-house in their respective industries and thus have an intimate understanding of the commercial imperatives as well as the legal issues involved.

Committed to adding value to clients' businesses by delivering the highest standards of professional advice and expertise, and to retaining and recruiting the highly-motivated and highly-skilled professionals required to ensure this level of service, Dibb Lupton Alsop is run according to the same business principles that drive their clients. The firm also submits to the same economic principles as its clients by its belief in good value for money as well as service excellence being as important in legal services as in any other business sector.

Principal Areas of Work:

Insurance, Marine & Aviation (*Contact:* Kevin McLoughlin). The Insurance, Marine & Aviation Group handles insurance claims from the routine to the catastrophic. It offers specialist expertise in regulatory and commercial work for insurers and self-insured enterprises; wet and dry shipping work on behalf of ship owners, insurers and P + I Clubs; medical negligence; litigation and commercial agreements in respect of general aviation and airline work together with services to product manufacturers and airport authorities. The Group has a substantial team of lawyers dedicated to serving the needs of insurers and brokers.

Banking Group (*Contact:* Mark Vickers). The Banking Group undertakes acquisition finance, syndications, structured finance, cross-border financing, project finance, secured lending, building society finance, housing association funding, the financing of Public/Private Partnerships, receivables financing, reconstructions, securitisation, capital markets and take privates. The Group also advises on compliance, regulatory and strategic issues, and liaises closely with the firm's corporate finance, tax, corporate recoveries, insolvency and finance litigation lawyers.

Litigation Group (*Contact:* Neil Micklethwaite). The Litigation Group deals with all aspects of commercial and corporate disputes for PLCs, private companies, professional firms, banks and financial institutions. It includes specialist teams in Finance and Banking Litigation, Commercial Regulation, Financial Regulation and Communications &

Managing partner:	Nigel Knowles
Senior partner:	Roger Lane-Smith
Number of partners:	223
Associates:	133
Assistant solicitors:	226

WORKLOADS	
Corporate	18%
Insurance	18%
Property & Construction	18%
Litigation	16%
Corporate Recovery & Insolvency	8%
Human Resources	7%
Communications & Technology	6%
Business Services	5%
Banking	4%

CONTACTS	
Banking Group	Mark Vickers
Business Services Group	Mary Barlow
Communications and Technology Group	
	David Barrett
Corporate Group	Andrew Darwin
Corporate Recovery & Insolvency Group	
	Peter Cranston
Human Resources Group	David Bradley
Insurance, Marine & Aviation Group	
	Kevin McLoughlin
Litigation Group	Neil Micklethwaite
Property & Construction Group	Philip Rooney

Continues overleaf

Technology Litigation. In the rapidly changing environment affecting litigation services the Group's approach is to reduce the uncertainties inherent in commercial disputes by effective case management and innovative solutions.

Communications & Technology Group (*Contact:* David Barrett). The Communications & Technology Group provides an integrated business service to suppliers and users of technology, communications information and electronic commerce providers, publishers, cable operators, advertising agencies, innovators, broadcasters, telecommunications operators, the media and those wishing to protect or exploit their brand. The Group comprises 4 specialist units: IT & Telecommunications, Media & Communications, Intellectual Property and EU Competition. The establishment of a Brussels office in April 98 will greatly enhance the Group's standing in its specialist areas.

Corporate Group (*Contact:* Andrew Darwin). The Corporate Group is involved in four principal sectors; corporate finance, venture capital, commercial and corporate tax. It also includes private capital and commercial regulatory teams. The combination of a City corporate/commercial practice with a strong regional reputation makes the group a substantial force in its markets, combining high levels of technical skills and experience with accessibility, value for money and commercial acumen.

Corporate Recovery & Insolvency (*Contact:* Peter Cranston). The Corporate Recovery & Insolvency Group is one of the largest practices in the country and deals with all types of insolvency procedures for both corporates and individuals. It offers clients a complete service including asset disposals, property sales, investigation work, litigation and international asset recovery. The Group is continually expanding the range of services offered to clients, developing new ways of dealing with the problems that arise in modern corporate recovery and insolvency work.

Property & Construction (*Contact:* Philip Rooney). The Property & Construction Group handles all aspects of the acquisition, financing, development, letting and disposal of commercial property as well as residential property development. The Group also includes property litigation, planning and construction specialists to provide an integrated service to those clients requiring it. National skill groups deal with areas such as retail, leisure, development, institutional funding, property investment, health and education. The Construction team provides comprehensive legal services, including contentious and non-contentious advice. Team members have extensive track records in all aspects of building and engineering work and are well-equipped to understand clients' commercial objectives. Experience extends to procurement, one-off and standard documentation, major projects and P.F.I. and B.O.T. type projects.

Human Resources Group (*Contact:* David Bradley). The Human Resources Group provides employment law and pensions advice together with training in all HR Legal areas. The Group acts for employers and senior executives and trustees of pension schemes. The Employment Team delivers advice and solutions to all employee issues from recruitment through to termination and beyond including change management programmes. Particular strengths are in contractual change, senior executive issues, discrimination and Immigration. A full and expert advocacy service is provided in house. The Pensions team acts for companies and trustees providing a full range of services including dispute resolution and is one of the largest teams in the UK.

Business Services Group (*Contact:* Mary Barlow). Dibb Lupton Alsop's Business Services Group provides solutions to collections and processing requirements including debt collection, repossessions and recoveries. It offers a one-stop shop for debt recovery and debt management, and has one of the most advanced computerised debt collection systems in the marketplace. It also offers a special on-line mortgage repossession and conveyancing facility which has been developed for building societies, banks and other secured lenders. The Group, based in Bradford, provides a service aimed at maximising the return for clients and achieving this in the swiftest possible time and always to the benefit of their bottom line.

Nature of Clientele: Dibb Lupton Alsop serves PLCs, private companies, banks and financial institutions, charities and public sector organisations. It has specialist knowledge of a wide range of business and industry sectors including insurance, transport, building societies and banking, IT and telecommunications, hotels and leisure, engineering, property and construction, textiles, sports, public authorities and financial services.

Languages Spoken: German, French, Spanish, Portuguese, Danish, Turkish, Korean, Swedish, Japanese, Italian, Greek, Hindi, Dutch.

DICKINSON DEES

ST. ANN'S WHARF, 112 QUAYSIDE, NEWCASTLE UPON TYNE, NE99 1SB
Tel: 0191 279 9000 **Fax:** 0191 279 9100 **DX:** 61191 **Email:** LAW@DICKINSON-DEES.CO.UK **Internet:** WWW.DICKINSON-DEES.COM

The Firm: Dickinson Dees is the largest firm of solicitors in the North East region, with a total staff of over 300. The practice offers both commercial and private client services. Specialist services include development and construction, banking and commercial lending, corporate tax, pensions, employee incentives, public procurement, commercial and EC law (based locally and in Brussels), health sector, environmental and planning, local authority and public sector work, employment, information technology, social housing and agriculture. The firm has an associated office in Brussels.

For further information contact Graham Wright, Senior Partner or John Flynn, Business Development Partner.

Senior partner:	Graham Wright
Number of partners:	46
Assistant solicitors:	56
Other fee-earners:	54

CONTACTS	
Commercial property	Geoff Hockaday
Company & commercial	Nigel Bellis
Litigation	Glenn Calvert
Private client	Adrian Gifford

DICKINSON MANSER 5 Parkstone Rd, Poole, BH15 2NL **Tel:** (01202) 673071 **Fax:** (01202) 680470 **DX:** 07602 **Ptnrs:** 7 **Asst solrs:** 5 **Other fee-earners:** 7 **Contact:** Lewis H. Parkyn *General practice. Clients include small businesses, private individuals and PLCs. Legal Aid Franchise. Members of LawGroup UK. Agency work undertaken.*

WORKLOADS			
Litigation	33%	Probate & trusts	33%
Property/commercial	33%		

DICKSON MINTO WS

ROYAL LONDON HOUSE, 22-25 FINSBURY SQUARE, LONDON, EC2A 1DS
Tel: (0171) 628 4455 **Fax:** (0171) 628 0027

The Firm: Established in 1985, the firm has grown substantially and handles corporate transactions throughout the UK. As a result of the concentration of numbers of specialist lawyers the firm has the resources to deal with transactions of all sizes and complexity for its wide range of corporate clients, including private companies, listed companies and financial institutions.

Dickson Minto has acted in some of the largest MBOs and MBIs in Europe, frequently involving other jurisdictions such as the USA, South America, Australasia and the Far East. The firm has acted in financial buy-outs/ins of over £10bn and acts for a number of leading banks and institutions. Its experience in this field has led to it becoming involved in a significant number of substantial listings and public company takeovers and mergers, and it is now one of the few firms registered as a sponsor with the Stock Exchange.

Principal Areas of Work: In addition to its Mergers and Acquisitions function, the firm has specialist resources in the areas of banking, EU and competition law, pensions law, intellectual property and taxation. The firm has wide experience in dealing with and co-ordinating transactions involving other advisers and through its well-established contacts with foreign lawyers in international transactions.

Dickson Minto continues to expand and, through its emphasis on the recruitment and intensive training of high quality staff, it has been able to maintain and continues to provide a flexible service, responsive and dedicated to the needs of all corporate clients.

Other Offices: 11 Walker Street, Edinburgh EH3 7NE (*Tel:* (0131) 225 4455 *Fax:* (0131) 225 2712)

Managing partner:	Bruce W. Minto
Senior partner:	Alastair R. Dickson
Number of partners:	12

WORKLOADS	
Company/commercial/corporate finance	85%
Banking	15%

CONTACTS	
Banking	Michael J. Barron
Company/commercial/corporate finance	
	Alastair R. Dickson

DIGBY BROWN The Savoy Tower, 77 Renfrew Street, Glasgow, G2 3BZ **Tel:** (0141) 566 9494 **Fax:** (0141) 566 9500 **DX:** GW17 **Ptnrs:** 10 **Asst solrs:** 8 **Other fee-earners:** 7 **Contact:** Jim Wright *An established practice specialising in pursuer and defendant personal injury work. Offices also in Edinburgh and Dundee.*

WORKLOADS			
Pursuer Litigation	58%	Insurance	33%
Conveyancing	8%		

DIXON, COLES & GILL Bank House, Burton Street, Wakefield, WF1 2DA *Tel:* (01924) 373467 *Fax:* (01924) 366234 *DX:* 15030 *Ptnrs:* 2 *Asst solrs:* 2 *Other fee-earners:* 2

D J FREEMAN

43 FETTER LANE, LONDON, EC4A 1JU
Tel: (0171) 583 4055 **Fax:** (0171) 353 7377 **DX:** 103 **Email:** MARKETING@DJFREEMAN.CO.UK **Internet:** DJFREEMAN.CO.UK

The Firm: D J Freeman has developed a client orientated approach to the provision of legal services. Its services are primarily structured around client market sector groups rather than legal disciplines. Multi-disciplinary teams mixing company commercial, litigation, property and tax lawyers operate in its insurance, media and communications and property services departments. A strong commercial litigation department provides a range of litigation services to major corporate clients and in-house legal teams. It has a high profile in employment and corporate reconstruction and insolvency work and its developing practices of public international law and intellectual property law, particularly in branding and merchandising rights, has strengthened the practice.

The firm has developed organically rather than through merger, and aims to combine the highest standards of client service with the constant development of the knowledge of the businesses of the clients and the markets in which they operate. It has pioneered the use of computers in litigation support and document management systems.

Principal Areas of Work:

Commercial Litigation: (*Contact:* Sally Hine). *Work includes:* complex international disputes and asset recovery, information technology disputes, intellectual property, in particular trade marks, branding, merchandising and fashion, employment, copyright, defamation and contempt of court, insolvency, financial services including banking, leasing, shareholder remedy and regulatory work and public international law, including border disputes.

Insurance and reinsurance: (*Contact:* David Kendall). *Work includes:* insurance and reinsurance dispute resolution, including arbitration, litigation and ADR, Lloyd's, insurance industry regulation, corporate finance, insurance company insolvency and restructuring, agency, run-off and marine and non-marine claims including professional indemnity and product and environmental liability claims.

Media and Communciations: (*Contact:* Tony Leifer). *Work includes:* libel, copyright, regulatory and other litigation, company commercial and corporate finance services to the broadcasting, film, entertainment, publishing, print, IT and communications industries.

Property Services: (*Contact:* Paul Clark). *Work includes:* property development projects, property investment and dealing, new business leases, equity participation mortgages, secured loans, property management, landlord and tenant, construction litigation, property taxation, corporate finance work for property companies, foreign investment in UK property, PFI projects, town and country planning and construction matters including collateral warranties, and environmental issues. The firm is a member of the British Council of Shopping Centres, the British Property Federation and the British Council for Offices and the Property Investment Forum.

International Connections: D J Freeman has particularly strong connections in Germany through its association with Westphal Voges Krohn of Hamburg, Berlin and Rostok.

Nature of Clientele: D J Freeman represents a wide range of UK and international corporate clients, including property investment, development and construction companies, financial institutions, insurance companies, accountants and other professionals, local and other public authorities, the manufacturing, fashion, leisure and media industries, major retailers and professional and trade associations.

Senior Partner:	Colin Joseph
Chief Executive:	Jonathan Lewis
Number of partners:	47
Assistant solicitors:	57
Other fee-earners:	25

WORKLOADS	
Property services	43%
Insurance services	24%
Commercial litigation	21%
Media & communications	12%

CONTACTS	
Construction	Anthony Edwards
Employment	Jane Moorman
Insurance	David Kendall
Insurance Insolvency	Vivien Tyrell
Intellectual Property	Alexendar Carter-Silk
Litigation	Sally Hine
Media and Communications	Tony Leifer
Planning	Moira Fraser
Property	Paul Clark
Property Finance & PFI	Caroline Janzen
Property Litigation	Christine Derrett
Public International Law	Tim Daniel
Public Sector	Ted Totman
Retail Property	Monica Blake
Taxation	Chris Comyn

DOBERMAN HORSMAN College Chambers, 92-94 Borough Road, Middlesbrough, TS1 2HL **Tel:** (01642) 230130 **Fax:** (01642) 230133 **DX:** 60508 **Ptnrs:** 4 **Asst solrs:** 3 **Other fee-earners:** 5 **Contact:** Ms R Matharu *A general practice specialising in civil litigation and commercial work.*

WORKLOADS	
Personal injury and medical negligence	50%
Commercial litigation	20%
Commercial work and commercial property	20%
Others	10%

DOLMANS

17 WINDSOR PLACE, CARDIFF, CF1 4PA
Tel: (01222) 345531 **Fax:** (01222) 398206 **DX:** 33005 CARDIFF

The Firm: With roots going back over 180 years and a presence in South Wales since 1893, Dolmans is a large Cardiff firm providing commercial legal services to corporate, public sector and individual clients. The partnership was restructured in 1970, with the Cardiff practice retaining and continuing under the name of Dolmans and has, since then, expanded to meet client needs. It considers the supervision of assistant solicitors by the partners to be of primary importance in ensuring a thorough quality service to its clients.

Principal Areas of Work:

Litigation: The firm is well known for its experience and expertise in the field of litigation, becoming the dominant firm in the region for insurance and public sector defendant work with the majority of instructions coming from local authorities and constabularies, either direct or through insurers or others. Its workload covers employer's and public liability, personal injury and landlord and tenant work and includes private sector work. Dolmans is well respected also in the field of plaintiff litigation and a specialist team was established 5 years ago to deal with motor claims. It is now the leading firm in the region for plaintiff motor claims litigation. Its insurance workload has increasingly become national.

Property, Commercial and Private Client: Dolmans has a strong reputation for property, commercial and private client work. This includes commercial and domestic conveyancing, property development, landlord & tenant and institutional mortgages; business start-ups, company formation, partnership agreements, take-overs, insolvency, finance, employment and contract. It also deals with matrimonial and family law, trusts, wills, probate and taxation.

Other Office: 18A Merthyr Road, Whitchurch, Cardiff CF4 1DG. *Tel:* (01222) 692979. *Fax:* (01222) 624415. DX 69191 Whitchurch, Cardiff.

Senior partner:	Adrian Oliver
Managing partner:	Ralph Lewis
Number of partners:	11
Assistant solicitors:	15
Other fee-earners:	16

CONTACTS	
Agency	David Boobier
Company & Commercial	Ralph Lewis
Employment	John Wilkins
Insolvency	John Wilkins
Institutional Defendant Litigation	Jeffrey MacWilkinson
Landlord & Tenant	Ralph Lewis
Licensing	John Wilkins
Matrimonial	Randolph Jones
Motor Claims Plaintiff Litigation	Philip Bradley
Private & Commercial Litigation	David Boobier
Private Client & Small Company	Roger Morgan
Property	Moy Lewis
Wills, Trusts and Probate	Roger Morgan

DONALD RENNIE WS 7 Blinkbonny Cresent, Edinburgh, EH4 3NB *Tel:* (0131) 476 7007 *Fax:* (0131) 476 7008 *DX:* 539943 Edinburgh 19 *Ptnrs:* 1

DONNS SOLICITORS PO Box 41, 201 Deansgate, Manchester, M60 1DZ *Tel:* (0161) 834 3311 *Fax:* (0161) 834 2317 *DX:* 14312 *Ptnrs:* 8 *Asst solrs:* 1 *Other fee-earners:* 69

DONNELLY & WALL Callender House, 58/60 Upper Arthur Street, Belfast, BT1 4GP *Tel:* (01232) 233157 *Fax:* (01232) 329743 *Ptnrs:* 4 *Asst solrs:* 3 *Other fee-earners:* 2

DONNE MILEHAM & HADDOCK

100 QUEENS ROAD, BRIGHTON, BN1 3YB
Tel: 01273 329833 **Fax:** 01273 747500 **DX:** 2703 BRIGHTON 1

The Firm: Donne Mileham & Haddock, well established as one of the leading firms in the South East, is one of only a few providing a comprehensive range of services to business and institutional clients comparable with the City. Client focused teams operate from the firms twin commercial centres at Brighton and Crawley. The firm also offers a full range of high quality private client services.

Principal Areas of Work:

Corporate/Commercial: (*Contact Partner:* Derek Sparrow). An experienced team handles a comprehensive range of high value projects on a regular basis including: company/partnership formations, takeovers, mergers and acquisitions, MBOs, Stock Exchange flotations, franchises, intellectual property work and commercial contracts. The firm acts on behalf of high profile national and international clients and small businesses.

Employment: (*Contact Partner:* Simon Bellm). The firm has extensive experience in acting for employers, employees and TUs on such matters as service contracts, redundancies and unfair dismissals, disciplinary and grievance procedures, discrimination, pensions and incentive schemes.

Litigation: (*Contact Partner:* Tim Aspinall). The firm is well known for its litigation expertise and is skilled in handling particularly large and complicated cases. It has a number of specialist litigation teams: commercial, property, information technology, intellectual property, construction, professional negligence, and insurance and reinsurance. The firm is a leader in shipping law and is well known for personal injury and family work. In addition, foreign litigation matters are handled by a team with practical experience of working abroad.

Commercial Property: (*Contact Partner:* Martin Allen). Leading specialists in commercial conveyancing, planning, construction and property litigation head teams in each of these fields, now combined as "DM&H Commercial Property Services". This department handles all forms of freehold and leasehold transactions and has particular expertise in site assembly and development, development funding and joint ventures, planning and environmental law, institutional secured funding and property litigation. Major clients include developers and investors, as well as a full range of businesses and institutions.

Other Areas of Work: The Firm offers a full range of private client services, including domestic conveyancing, financial and investment services, wills, probate and trusts and family, personal injury and medical negligence.

Managing partner:	**Tim Aspinall**
Chairman:	**Derek Sparrow**
Number of partners:	33
Assistant solicitors:	24
Other fee-earners:	40

CONTACTS	
Agricultural law	Marion Wilcock/Anne Milne
Charities	Michael Long
Commercial litigation	Tim Aspinall
Commercial Property	Martin Allen/Michael Bailey
Company/comm.	Derek Sparrow
Computer law	Tim Aspinall/Justin Ellis
Constr./Engin.	Michael Bailey/Emma Simons
Corporate finance	Dennis Edmonds
Criminal law	Roger Hartwell/Ray Blount
Ecclesiastical law	Michael Bailey
Education	Michael Bailey/Martin Allen
Employment law	Simon Bellm
Environmental law	Tony Allen
Family law	David Stevens/Sue Taylor
Financial services	Rod Gentry
Franchising	Derek Sparrow
Healthcare	Michael Long
Housing Associations	Michael Bailey/Tina George
Insolvency	Stephen King
Intellectual prop.	Tim Aspinall/Justin Ellis
Licensing & leisure	Roger Hartwell
Personal injury	Richard Pollins/Sue Millership
Planning	Tony Allen
Private client	Roger Hartwell
Property Litigation	Martin Allen
Residential Property	Clive Smith/Nick Warde
Shipping	Michael Bloomfield/Alistair Rustemeyer

DORSEY & WHITNEY Veritas House, 125 Finsbury Pavement, London, EC2A 1NQ **Tel:** (0171) 588 0800 **Fax:** (0171) 588 0555 **Ptnrs:** 4 **Asst solrs:** 6 **Contact:** Peter E. Kohl *Corporate finance (asset securitisation, Eurobonds, other international securities, offerings, capital markets transactions), Mergers and Acquisitions, Joint Ventures, Contract Negotiation and Tax and Energy Law. (English and U.S. law).*

DOUGLAS-JONES MERCER 147 St. Helens Rd, Swansea, SA1 4DB **Tel:** (01792) 650000 **Fax:** (01792) 458212 **DX:** 39556 **Email:** post@djm.law.co.uk **Ptnrs:** 13 **Asst solrs:** 8 **Other fee-earners:** 12 **Contact:** Mr Jeremy Wolfe *A high street practice with specialist departments in commercial, defendant and plaintiff personal injury, family, crime, conveyancing and probate law. The firm has a branch office network. The firms' commercial department is currently undergoing a period of growth.*

WORKLOADS			
Commercial	20%	Conveyancing & probate	20%
Crime	20%	Defendant & plaintiff P.I.	20%
Family	20%		

DOUGLAS & PARTNERS 116 Grosvenor Road, St. Pauls, Bristol, BS2 8YA *Tel:* (0117) 955 2663 *Fax:* (0117) 954 0527 *Ptnrs:* 5 *Asst solrs:* 5 *Other fee-earners:* 7

DOUGLAS WIGNALL & CO 44 Essex Street, Strand, London, WC2R 3JF **Tel:** (0171) 583 1362 **Fax:** (0171) 583 0532 **DX:** 48 (Ch.Ln.) **Email:** doug@easynet.co.uk **Ptnrs:** 1 **Contact:** Douglas Wignall *Work includes international hotel and resort developments, international hotel management agreements, acquisition and disposal of hotels, general commercial law, commercial and residential conveyancing.*

WORKLOADS	
Hotels & Leisure	75%
Commercial & Residential Conveyancing	15%
Other Company/Commercial	10%

DOWNS

156 HIGH STREET, DORKING, SURREY, RH4 1BQ
Tel: (01306) 880110 **Fax:** (01306) 876266 **DX:** 57300 DORKING

The Firm: Downs is one of Surrey's largest firms. Specialists exist in all key areas of law servicing a wide-ranging client base, both nationally and internationally.

Services for the Business Client:

Commercial Property: (*Contact Partners:* Iain MacLeod and Michael Debens).
Company/Commercial: (*Contact Partner:* Christopher Shipley).
Commercial Litigation: (*Contact Partner:* Christopher Millar).
International: (*Contact Partner:* David Freeman).

Services for the Private Client:

Conveyancing: (*Contact Partner:* Celia Perry).
Trusts, Wills, Probate and Tax: (*Contact Partner:* Timothy Hughes).
Matrimonial and Child Care: (*Contact Partner:* Anne Trier).
Accidents and Personal Injury: (*Contact:* Andrew Christmas).

Senior partner:	David Rea
Number of partners:	11
Assistant solicitors:	9
Other fee-earners:	6

WORKLOADS	
Commercial Property	20%
Company/Commercial	20%
Litigation	20%
Trusts/Probate	20%
Conveyancing	10%
Matrimonial	10%

DOWSE & CO 23-25 Dalston Lane, London, E8 3DF *Tel:* (0171) 254 6205 *Fax:* (0171) 923 1497 *Ptnrs:* 5 *Asst solrs:* 3 *Other fee-earners:* 4

DRUCES & ATTLEE

SALISBURY HOUSE, LONDON WALL, LONDON, EC2M 5PS
Tel: (0171) 638 9271 **Fax:** (0171) 628 7525 **DX:** 33862 FINSBURY SQUARE **Email:** INFO@DRUCES.COM **Internet:** WWW.DRUCES.COM

The Firm: A City firm since 1767 with a strong commercial base, providing a wide range of legal services to the property and corporate sectors, and high net worth individuals. Strong traditional values of client care based on integrity, knowledge and reliability, are underpinned by a modern and dynamic approach to providing legal solutions. The firm specialises in advising investors in commercial property, and those in the financial services and hotel, pub & leisure trades. It is well established in advising high net worth individuals on the deployment and protection of assets, and on matrimonial and family law issues. The firm's insolvency arm operates under the name of Carrick Read Insolvency Solicitors and has offices in London, Hull and Leeds. Druces & Attlee is a founder member of Druces International, linking law firms in 11 countries in Europe.

Principal Areas of Work:

Commercial Property Investment
Finance & Investments
Hotel Pub & Leisure
Insolvency
Private Capital/ Matrimonial

Recruitment and Training: The firm aims to expand its core practice areas through recruitment at all levels. A trainee is taken on every six months, for four 6-month placements (private capital, litigation, property and company commercial). Additional trainee places may be available for strong applicants interested in the firm's core practice areas. All applications should be forwarded to Richard Monkcom, Staff Partner.

Senior partner:	John Edwardes Jones
No of partners:	15
Assistant solicitors:	16
Other fee earners:	8
Total no of fee-earners:	39
Total no of staff:	76

WORKLOADS	
Commercial property	35%
Company/ Commercial/ Financial Services	25%
Private Client	15%
Commercial and Property Litigation	10%
Family/ Matrimonial	10%
Insolvency	5%

CONTACTS	
Commercial property	Chris Hamer
Commercial/ Property Litigation	Richard Sherrin
Company/ Commercial	Charles Atlee
Employment	Richard Monkcom/ Toby Stroh
Family/ Matrimonial	Kathryn Peat
Financial Services	Philip Mitchell
Hotel, Pub & Leisure	Jon Redding
Insolvency	Simeon Gilchrist
International	Toby Stroh
Private Capital	Roy Campbell

DRUMMOND MILLER WS 32 Moray Place, Edinburgh, EH3 6BZ *Tel:* (0131) 226 5151 *Fax:* (0131) 225 2608 *DX:* 104 Edinburgh *Ptnrs:* 20 *Asst solrs:* 16 *Other fee-earners:* 12

DUKES ARNOLD DU FEU 19 / 20 Easton Street, High Wycombe, HP11 1NT *Tel:* (01494) 511900 *Fax:* (01494) 511505

A.H. DUNCOMBE & COMPANY 98 High Street, Thame, OX9 3EH **Tel:** (01844) 261026 **Fax:** (01844) 217448 **DX:** 80553 **Email:** lawyers@duncombe.co.uk **Ptnrs:** 3 **Other fee-earners:** 2 **Contact:** Dr J Good *Exclusively commercial practice with an established reputation in company/commercial and computer law, contentious and non-contentious intellectual property.*

DUNDAS & WILSON CS

SALTIRE COURT, 20 CASTLE TERRACE, EDINBURGH, EH1 2EN
Tel: (0131) 228 8000 **Fax:** (0131) 228 8888 **DX:** 553001 EDINBURGH 18

180 STRAND, LONDON, WC2R 2NN
Tel: (0171) 344 0344 **Fax:** (0171) 438 2518 **DX:** 137 LONDON CHANCERY LANE

SUTHERLAND HOUSE, 149 ST VINCENT STREET, GLASGOW, G2 5NW
Tel: (0141) 221 8586 **Fax:** (0141) 221 8687 **DX:** GW345 GLASGOW

MADELEINE SMITH HOUSE, 6/7 BLYTHSWOOD SQUARE, GLASGOW, G2 4AD
Tel: (0141) 221 9880 **Fax:** (0141) 221 9804 **DX:** GW178 GLASGOW

The Firm: Having merged with Dorman Jeffrey in September last year, Dundas & Wilson is now the largest Corporate and Commercial Law Firm in Scotland, with offices in Edinburgh, Glasgow and London, and is a member of the Andersen Worldwide international network of law firms. The Firm offers an unprecedented spread and depth of specialist skills in the Corporate and Commercial areas and is organised into industry facing groups, enabling it to provide clients with added value through the relevant detailed industry knowledge.

The size and quality of the client base (including 8 FTSE 250 Companies) and the size and complexity of deals distinguish the Firm from all law firms outside the very leading group in the City of London. The growth of the Firm in past years has continued and there are now 56 Partners (including 4 based in London) and a total of 216 lawyers. This has enabled the concentration of quality resources in key industry areas and has resulted in significant expansion in each of them.

Furthermore, the Firm has worked closely with lawyers in Garretts, its associated law firm in England in a wide variety of national and international transactions, particularly in the areas of commercial property, banking, corporate, technology, infrastructure and environment.

Together with Garretts, the combined U.K. practice has a turnover of £50 million, over 100 partners and a further 270 qualified lawyers and a unique spread of integrated offices throughout the United Kingdom. The U.K. legal practice is one of the top 20 U.K. practices, measured by size and turnover.

Membership of the Andersen Worldwide international network of law firms gives the firm access to vast resources globally in training and education as well as the latest information technology and support systems. It also increases the width and depth of the services the firm can provide to its clients, allowing them access to professional services and support on a world wide basis.

Managing partner:	Chris Campbell
Chairman:	Neil Cochran
Number of partners:	56
Other fee-earners:	160

WORKLOADS	
Corporate/ Commercial	44%
Commercial Property	29%
Banking	17%
Litigation	10%

CONTACTS	
Banking	Michael Stoneham
Commercial Litigation	Lorna Sibbald
Commercial Property	Donald Shaw
Construction and Engineering	Alistair McLean
Corporate & Commercial	Robert Pirrie
Corporate Finance	David Hardie
Corporate Recovery/ Insolvency	Ian Cuthbertson
Education	Brian Leggat
Human Capital Services (Employment/Pensions etc.)	Eilidh Cameron
Infrastructure	Alan Campbell
Insurance Litigation	Pamela Lyall
Private Equity	Robert Pirrie
Technology	Laurence Ward

DUNDONS 261 Lavender Hill, London, SW11 1JD *Tel:* (0171) 228 2277 *Fax:* (0171) 924 2759 *DX:* 58556 *Ptnrs:* 2 *Asst solrs:* 4 *Other fee-earners:* 3

DUNNINGS 130 High Street, Honiton, EX14 8JR *Tel:* (01404) 41221 *Fax:* (01404) 44976 *DX:* 48800 Honiton

---

DUTHIE HART & DUTHIE 517-519 Barking Rd, Greengate, Plaistow, London, E13 8PT **Tel:** (0181) 472 0138 **Fax:** (0181) 470 7628 **DX:** 52407 Canning Town **Ptnrs:** 5 **Asst solrs:** 14 **Other fee-earners:** 15 **Contact:** Mr. S. Murphy *Established general practice with reputation for particular expertise in Criminal Law. Franchised by the Legal Aid Board.*

WORKLOADS			
Criminal litigation	60%	Matrimonial	12%
Personal injury and general common law			10%
Conveyancing	8%		
Mental health	5%	Probate	5%

DUTTON GREGORY Trussell House, 23 St. Peter Street, Winchester, SO23 8BT *Tel:* (01962) 844333 *Fax:* (01962) 863582 *DX:* 2515 Winchester *Ptnrs:* 15 *Asst solrs:* 6 *Other fee-earners:* 15

EAMMON MCEVOY & CO 22 Church Place, Lurgan, BT66 6EY *Tel:* (01762) 327734 *Fax:* (01762) 321760 *Ptnrs:* 3 *Asst solrs:* 6

EASTLEYS The Manor Office, Victoria St, Paignton, TQ4 5DW *Tel:* (01803) 559257 *Fax:* (01803) 558625 *DX:* 100603 Paignton *Ptnrs:* 8 *Asst solrs:* 9 *Other fee-earners:* 8

EATONS

22 BLADES COURT, DEODAR RD, PUTNEY, LONDON, SW15 2NU
Tel: (0181) 877 9727 **Fax:** (0181) 877 9940

The Firm: Eatons specialise in all aspects of entertainment work with particular emphasis on legal and commercial advice in connection with music and all related areas such as recording, publishing, video, management, merchandising and television arrangements for a full range of emerging and established artists as well as independent and major companies. The combined qualifications of the partners encompass many years of industry and private practice experience.

Contacts:

Company Commercial: Michael Eaton/Elisabeth Hale
Litigation: Jeremy Wakefield/Martin Dacre
Media & Entertainment: David Glick/Martin Dacre/Tim Smith/Adam Van Straten
Property: Elisabeth Hale/Jeremy Wakefield

Managing partner:	Martin Dacre
Senior partner:	Michael Eaton
Number of partners:	7
Assistant solicitors:	2
Other fee-earners:	1

EATON SMITH MARSHALL MILLS Britannia Buildings, St. Peter's Street, Huddersfield, HD1 1BB **Tel:** (01484) 821300 **Fax:** (01484) 821444 **DX:** 712956 **Ptnrs:** 12 **Asst solrs:** 4 **Other fee-earners:** 12 **Contact:** Christopher J. Turner *One of the largest practices in Kirklees. The firm handles a substantial volume of both commercial and private client work, including legal aid.*

WORKLOADS			
Commercial & other litigation	24%		
Matrimonial & Family	16%	Personal Injury	15%
Commercial Property	12%	Company/Commercial	12%
Wills Trusts & Probate	10%	Conveyancing	9%
Licensing	2%		

EDDOWES WALDRON & CASH 12 St. Peter's Churchyard, Derby, DE1 1TZ *Tel:* (01332) 48484 *Fax:* (01332) 291312 *DX:* 17501 *Ptnrs:* 6 *Asst solrs:* 3

EDGE & ELLISON

RUTLAND HOUSE, 148 EDMUND ST, BIRMINGHAM, B3 2JR
Tel: (0121) 200 2001 **Fax:** (0121) 200 1991 **DX:** 708610 BIRMINGHAM 17 **Email:** JAMES.RETALLACK@EDGE.CO.UK
Internet: WWW.EDGE.CO.UK

18 SOUTHAMPTON PLACE, LONDON, WC1A 2AJ
Tel: (0171) 404 4701 **Fax:** (0171) 831 9152 **DX:** 37984 LONDON/KINGSWAY

REGENT COURT, REGENT STREET, LEICESTER, LE1 7BR
Tel: (0116) 247 0123 **Fax:** (0116) 247 0030 **DX:** 17006 LEICESTER

The Firm: Edge & Ellison is one of the UK's leading law firms; its aim is to focus its combined skills, experience, commitment, personalities, strength in depth and locations to add value to its clients' needs and provide a major firm service at a highly competitive 'regional' based cost. In response to the rapidly changing market for legal services the firm recently launched The Way Forward, a radical three-year programme of business re-engineering. The objectives are three-fold, to achieve pre-eminence in the Midlands; to double the size and turnover of the London office; to treble the volume of transatlantic business. These objectives will be achieved via a number of initiatives including innovative coaching and IT initiatives, new client and service projects and a range of new products focused on client and sectoral needs.

Senior Partner:	James Retallack
Managing Partner:	Gil Hayward
Managing Partner Elect:	Simon Ramshaw
Partner, Client Development:	Ian Reaves
Number of Partners:	78
Assistant Solicitors:	117
Other Fee-earners:	72

WORKLOADS	
Litigation	34%
Company/ commercial	31%
Commercial property	25%
Pensions & Employment	10%

Principal Areas of Work:

Asset Finance: A dedicated team advising clients operating in the equipment leasing, hire purchase and finance sectors. Clients include major clearing banks, leasing companies and financial institutions. Work handled includes receivables financing, factoring and invoice discounting and all forms of operating and finance leasing in the medium to larger sectors including shipping, aircraft and project finance.

Banking & Insolvency: This department is able to advise on financial transactions, from inception to insolvency and recovery. The department has considerable experience and a well-deserved reputation for providing teams of lawyers tailored to the needs of administrative receivers, administrators and liquidators, banks and finance houses.

Commercial: Advising UK and overseas clients on trading arrangements, agency and distributorship agreements and Financial Services Act implications, as well as the impact of legislation emanating from Brussels. Sponsorship agreements, computer contracts and sports law is also a feature of this department.

Commercial Property: A substantial core department advises on all aspects of commercial property including development, investment, buying, selling and leasing of commercial, retail, industrial, leisure and residential property. The firm also deals with landlord and tenant law including business leases, rent reviews and investment schemes.

Continues overleaf

The firm has specialist planning and construction units.

Competition: The Competition Unit deals with all aspects of UK and EC competition law including dealing with EC Merger Regulation applications, merger references under the Fair Trading Act and the impact of competition law on commercial transactions. The Unit has recently extended its expertise to the impact of the EC Directives in the area of public procurement and competitive tendering by public authorities.

Computer Law: A team with knowledge of and experience in drafting and negotiating a range of agreements relating to the provision of computer hardware and software and computer-related products and services. Types of agreement produced or advised upon have varied according to clients' requirements but include turnkey agreements, bespoke software agreements, hardware supply or leasing agreements, source code deposit agreements and bureau facilities agreements.

Construction: A dedicated Unit advises on all aspects from contractual arrangements to litigation and dispute resolution. Acting on behalf of developers, contractors, professionals, housing associations, purchasers and tenants the team advises on preparing and drafting terms of professional appointments, terms of warranty agreements for funders, purchasers and tenants and forms of building contracts and amendments to such contracts. The team has special expertise in arbitration and High Court litigation.

Corporate Finance: Advising on Stock Exchange, Take-over Panel and international corporate as well as development capital transactions. Mergers, acquisitions and disposals for both public and private companies, and management buy-outs and buy-ins are very much at the heart of this department.

Debt Recovery: A dedicated credit control unit with the ability to take prompt and efficient action to stop debts becoming bad debts, providing a computerised but personal service to clients, tailored to aid their credit control requirements and to offer a response from initial instruction within one day. The unit also reviews documentation to ensure that terms and conditions of payment are in line with business objectives and enforceable.

Employment: A dedicated employment group is devoted exclusively to employment law and employment-related problems. As well as continually monitoring legislative and judicial changes, the team advises on avoidance of employment problems and the best and most cost-effective way of dealing with them. Members of the team regularly appear at industrial tribunals throughout the country. Much of the team's work includes preparation of terms and conditions through to drafting of complex equal opportunities procedures, executive service agreements and staff handbooks.

Energy & Natural Resources: The firm acts for a number of major quarrying companies. Over the years it has developed a widely-based practice in waste disposal and waste management which includes the generation of heat and power from waste and other aspects of power generation.

Environmental: Work includes evaluating liabilities in buying or developing contaminated land; corporate due diligence and advising on warranties and indemnities in relation to mergers and acquisitions; advising on and preparing corporate environmental policies and environmental management systems.

Healthcare: Our Healthcare Group has advised both Trust Hospitals and private hospitals, healthcare and nursing homes, on a variety of matters including sales and purchases, the financing and operation of residential care and nursing homes, regulatory work, employment, employer and employee liability, research and development. We also act for clients who supply goods and services to the healthcare sector.

Insurance & Personal Injury: A specialist unit, well known in the insurance market for providing a commercial and quality service principally to insurers, underwriters, authorities, public utilities and other corporate bodies in relation to their litigation. This includes personal injury claims (whether arising from employers, public and motor liability obligations or medical negligence), commercial disputes (including product liability and professional negligence) and policy coverage issues involving non-disclosure, misrepresentation or fraud. In addition, members of the unit advise on issues of health and safety and risk management.

Intellectual Property: Negotiating, drafting and advising on a variety of agreements relating to the exploitation of intellectual property rights (e.g. licences and assignments of patents and know how, copyright, design or trade marks). The department carries out the due diligence investigations of potential target companies, trade and service mark searches and applications and advice on disputes concerning ownership or infringement of intellectual property rights.

International: The firm is committed to providing clients with the information, advice and assistance they need in doing business around the world, a team advises on specific regulations and directives that affect individual business sectors and commercial agreements. The firm has close associations with like-minded lawyers in Pittsburgh, Atlanta, San Diego and New York, also in Brussels, Paris, Amsterdam, Dusseldorf, Frankfurt, Berlin, Madrid and Milan.

Licensing: Enjoying a long standing national reputation in the licensing field, a dedicated team advises and makes applications on behalf of pub and club owners, breweries, owners of stadia and sponsors of events, also theatres, sports facilities, snooker halls, amusement arcades and casinos. Work undertaken ranges from new licence applications to protection orders and transfers. The team has in depth expertise in the Gaming Acts and dealing with local authorities regarding obtaining and keeping public entertainment licences.

Litigation: No organisation seeks litigation, but sometimes it becomes inevitable. The firm has a strong litigation department accustomed to acting promptly and with authority to resolve disputes where practicable or take and progress or defend proceedings through all courts, where necessary or appropriate. Work includes contract disputes, partnership and shareholder disputes, professional negligence claims, intellectual property litigation and injunctions. The firm acts in the legislative areas of health and safety, environmental law, consumer protections, trade descriptions and consumer credit and has a dynamic advocacy unit.

Marketing & Media Services: The firm acts for the largest marketing services group in the world as well as assisting entertainment and media business managers in theatres, opera and music-based organisations. Advice given includes intellectual property, including agreements covering advertising, film production and finance, commissioning of artistes and composers, publishing and recording contracts, distribution or licence arrangements, merchandising, sponsorship and protection of confidential information and rights ownership.

Pensions: The firm has one of the largest teams of pensions lawyers outside London. Although dealing purely with legal issues, the work is wide-ranging – from SSAS facility to dealing with major documentation and scheme restructuring projects. In addition to providing a full pensions legal service, the team also works on a one-off project basis with those clients who already have a detailed and in-depth pension knowledge. A trustee facility is available and the department runs tailored trustee training courses.

Planning: Work includes all aspects of planning applications, appeals inquiries and Local Plans proceedings and the drafting of deeds relating to planning obligations. The advice given relates to the wider issues including the environmental impact on planning and compulsory purchase proceedings and the acquisition and sale of property generally and the planning team works closely with the firm's environmental unit.

Property Litigation: The team advises on landlord and tenant disputes involving actions, forfeiture and re-entry, exclusion orders, possession and dilapidations claims, breaches of contract, specific performance and residential and service tenancies.

Retail: The firm has a specialist team of lawyers who act on a regular basis for retailers of all types and sizes, from listed public companies to family businesses, supermarket chains to corner shops, national charities, breweries, off licences, post offices and newsagents. Work includes negotiating leases, buying and selling premises and businesses, Landlord & Tenant Act renewals and negotiations, rent reviews, dispute resolution, debt recovery, in-store franchising, 'original tenant' liability, deeds storage, licensing, employment issues, debt recovery and close liaison with retail agents.

Sports Law: The firm acts for a leading premier division football club, as well as several major sports governing bodies. The team deals with regulatory and disciplinary matters, negotiating contracts with sponsors, television and promotional firms, equipment suppliers, advertising and other commercial activities including intellectual property rights. The firm has direct experience of legislation affecting sports clubs including sports ground licensing and safety procedures. Other commercial aspects include advising sports organisations on membership and constitutional difficulties and assuming the 'spokesman' role if required.

Foreign Connections: The firm enjoys strong long-standing links with like minded firms throughout Europe and the USA.

Recruitment and Training: The firm has a comprehensive training programme for trainee solicitors and qualified members of staff, many of the courses being run in the purpose built training suite in the Birmingham office. Approximately 22-25 trainee solicitors are recruited each year and trainees can serve their articles in any of the firm's offices. If you are interested in exploring opportunities with the firm at trainee or qualified level, please contact Graham Smith, Partner in Charge of Training and Recruitment.

Responding to client demands – delivering an innovative, technically excellent service – means everyone within the firm being the best at what they do. The Way Forward will create a continuous learning culture throughout the firm providing the highest standards of service delivery to our clients.

CONTACTS	
Advocacy	Steve Edmonds
Asset finance	Angela Davis
Banking	Angela Hardman
Commercial	Michael Luckman
Commercial Property	David Goldsmith, Mark Newcombe
Competition	Paul Hughes
Computer law	Caroline Egan, Robert Hamill
Construction	David Lloyd Jones, Jonathan Hosie
Corporate finance	David Hull, Simon Gordon
Debt recovery	Bob Partridge
Employment	Veronica Dean
Energy & natural resources	Rory Tait
Engineering	Fred Honnor
Environmental	Gwyn Williams
Financial Services	Stuart Fleet
Healthcare	Paul Cliff
Insolvency	John Sullivan
Insurance and P.I.	Chris Davies
Intellectual property	Michael Luckman
Licensing	Andrew Potts, Stephanie Perraton
Litigation	Digby Rose, Jayne Willetts
Marketing services	Nick Allen
Media & Entertainment	David Hull
Pensions	Ian Forrest
PFI	Richard Baizley
Planning	Martin Damms
Property litigation	Gordon Scott
Quarry aggregates	Roger Collier
Retail	Ian Withers, Simon Boss
Sports law	Richard Alderson
Tax	Neil Pearson

Edge & Ellison
S O L I C I T O R S

EDMONDS BOWEN & COMPANY 4 Old Park Lane, London, W1Y 3LJ **Tel:** (0171) 629 8000 **Fax:** (0171) 221 9334/495 6382 **DX:** 37217 Piccadilly **Ptnrs:** 5 **Asst solrs:** 1 **Other fee-earners:** 5 *The practice handles company/commercial, litigation, entertainment, employment, property and private client matters.*

WORKLOADS			
Company/Commercial	25%	Litigation	25%
Media/Entertainment	25%	Propety/Private Client	25%

EDMONDSON HALL 168 High Street, Newmarket, CB8 9AJ **Tel:** (01638) 560556 **Fax:** (01638) 561656 **DX:** 50521 Newmarket **Ptnrs:** 2 **Asst solrs:** 2 **Other fee-earners:** 2 **Contact:** Mark Edmondson *Specialises in bloodstock law, acting within the racing and breeding industry. Also general equine law expertise. Strong litigation practice.*

WORKLOADS	
Commercial & Bloodstock Litigation	45%
Property (Commercial & Domestic)	35%
Family	10%
Company Commercial & Charities	5%
Employment	5%

EDWARD FAIL BRADSHAW & WATERSON

402 COMMERCIAL ROAD, STEPNEY, LONDON, E1 0LG
Tel: (0171) 790 4032 **Fax:** (0171) 790 2739 **DX:** 300701 TOWER HAMLETS

The Firm: One of the oldest established firms in East London, Edward Fail have had a reputation as specialists in criminal law since the 1920s. A merger in 1961 with the general practice of Bradshaw & Waterson (founded in 1887) brought a wide range of legal services to the firm and the merged practices have over a century of experience of dealing with the family and business problems of the area.

Principal Areas of Work: The firm has a particularly strong reputation in the area of criminal law and deals with the whole spectrum of criminal offences, including serious crime, petty crime and white collar fraud. The firm also has thriving departments in family law and litigation.

Managing partner:	John Lafferty
Senior partner:	Edward Preston
Number of partners:	5
Assistant solicitors:	4
Other fee-earners:	10

CONTACTS	
Civil litigation	John Lafferty
Criminal	Edward Preston
Family	Maeve O'Higgins

EDWARD HARRIS & SON Heathfield House, 91 Heathfield, Swansea, SA1 6EL **Tel:** (01792) 652007 **Fax:** (01792) 641533 **DX:** 39597 Swansea 1 **Email:** 100325,2655@compuserve.com **Ptnrs:** 2 **Asst solrs:** 2 **Other fee-earners:** 5 **Contact:** Edward Harris *General practice specialising in agricultural/countryside law, common land law and manors, estate planning, immigration, professional negligence and crime.*

EDWARD LEWIS

VERULAM GARDENS, 70 GRAY'S INN ROAD, LONDON, WC1X 8NF
Tel: (0171) 404 5566 **Fax:** (0171) 404 2244 **DX:** 1027 LONDON CHANCERY LANE WC2 **Email:** MAIL@EDLEWIS.MHS.COMPUSERVE.COM
Internet: HTTP://WWW.EDWARDLEWIS.CO.UK

The Firm: Edward Lewis is a progressive and growing firm which has established a reputation for taking a practical, creative and business orientated approach to the provision of commercial legal advice to domestic and international clients. The firm has strong European connections and provides multilingual legal services to foreign and UK clients.

In all of its key areas of specialisation, Edward Lewis provides a highly competitive, cost effective and professional service which is directed towards achieving its clients' commercial objectives. The partners are committed to delivering a high quality, personalised service, which all contemporary, successful businesses now demand and which is reflected in the calibre and range of individuals and organisations which instruct the firm.

The Edward Lewis business philosophy is supported by a commitment to the recruitment and training of like-minded professional and support staff and by ongoing investment in information technology which serves to ensure an effective and efficient service.

Principal Areas of Work: Edward Lewis advises the private and public business sectors on matters relating to the key areas of insurance litigation, company and commercial law, commercial litigation and property. Specialists in these main areas will often work together in integrated teams to advise clients on deals and actions which call for expertise across a broad spectrum of the law. All of the firm's partners have developed niche areas of practice and expertise and are able to advise clients who are active in specific business and industry sectors, where lawyers have to combine precise legal advice with the intrinsic understanding and experience of how a particular market sector operates.

The main areas of law on which advice is provided include: insurance litigation; banking and corporate finance; venture capital; personal injury; professional and medical negligence; public and employers' liability; company and commercial law; property – including planning, landlord and tenant, investment, development and residential; professional indemnity; defamation; employment law; intellectual property; sports; trusts; health and safety; construction; insolvency; cross-border transactions and disputes; EC and UK competition law.

The firm acts for some of the most highly respected, successful organisations and individuals across a range of sectors including: the commercial and domestic insurance and reinsurance markets; banking; media and telecommunications; publishing; politicians; retailing; healthcare; sports; property development, management and investment; transport; private trusts; national and international holding groups and trading companies.

Chairman:	Tony Collins
Number of partners:	20
Assistant solicitors:	32
Other fee-earners:	23

WORKLOADS	
Insurance Litigation	64%
Commercial Property	14%
Commercial Litigation	11%
Corporate	11%

CONTACTS	
Banking and Corporate Finance	
	J.Fellerman, M.Thomas
Commercial Litigation	B.Murphy, A.Irvine, A.Yates
Commercial Property	J. Dening, M. Kutner
Company and Commercial	M.Breen, M. Thomas
Construction	S. Quinn, A.Yates
Employment/Defamation	B.Murphy
European	B. Lewis
Health care	J.Fellerman
Insolvency	M.Thomas, A.Irvine
Insurance Litigation	T.Collins, B.Lewis
Intellectual Property	B.Murphy, M.Breen
Landlord and Tenant	J.Dening
Medical Negligence	K.West
Personal Injury	T.Collins, B.Moore
Product Liability	B.Moore
Professional Negligence	B.Moore, R. Osborne
Public and Employers' Liability	J.Rutter, K.West
Retail	J.Dening, D.Giacon
Sports Law	M.Breen

During 1998/99, Edward Lewis plans to continue expanding across all areas of its practice through both generic growth and the strategic recruitment of specialist practitioners. Close attention will be given to ensuring that its clients continue to receive the business orientated, professional service for which the firm is recognised.

New client enquiries are welcomed and should be directed to the firm's marketing department in the first instance which will notify the appropriate partners.

EDWARDS & CO 28 Hill Street, Belfast, BT1 2LA *Tel:* (01232) 321863 *Fax:* (01232) 332723 *DX:* 410 NR Belfast *Ptnrs:* 3

EDWARDS GELDARD

DUMFRIES HOUSE, DUMFRIES PLACE, CARDIFF, CF1 4YF
Tel: (01222) 238239 **Fax:** (01222) 237268

ALED HOUSE, LAKESIDE BUSINESS VILLAGE, ST DAVIDS PARK, DEESIDE, CH5 3XL
Tel: (01244) 538190 **Fax:** (01244) 538191

ST MICHAELS COURT, ST MICHAELS LANE, DERBY, DE1 9HQ
Tel: (01332) 331631 **Fax:** (01332) 294 295

72 ST JAME'S STREET, NOTTINGHAM, NG1 6FJ
Tel: (0115) 924 0631 **Fax:** (0115) 924 0431

The Firm: Edwards Geldard is one of the leading regional law firms. The firm's offices are located in Cardiff, Deeside, Derby and Nottingham. Whilst continuing to expand the traditional areas of work in the company and commercial, commercial property, litigation and private client departments, the firm has, in recent years, acquired particular expertise in a variety of 'niche' areas of legal work. These include mergers and acquisitions, corporate finance and banking, intellectual property, public law, planning and environmental law, energy law, rail and transprt law, construction contracts and building arbitration, employment law, insolvency, trusts and tax, secured lending and property litigation.

The firm's growth in recent years has been characterised by an expansion of its work for major Stock Exchange listed clients and for City of London based organisations and by the growing reputation of its work for public sector bodies.

Principal Areas of Work:

The following services are offered from each office. Initial enquiries can be directed to the most convenient office:

Company/ Corporate	Intellectual Property	E U Law
Environmental Law	Secured Lending	Construction & Engineering
Banking & Insolvency	Tax, Trusts & Estate Administration	Commercial Contracts/ Utilities
Employment	Commercial Property	Property & Development
Planning & Public Law	Commercial Litigation	Personal Injury Private Client

Languages Spoken: French, German, Ukranian, Polish, Spanish, Italian & Welsh.

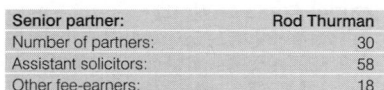

Senior partner:	Rod Thurman
Number of partners:	30
Assistant solicitors:	58
Other fee-earners:	18

WORKLOADS	
Company/ Commercial	32%
Property	30%
Litigation	26%
Other	12%

E. EDWARDS SON & NOICE

9-15 YORK ROAD, ILFORD, IG1 3AD
Tel: (0181) 514 9000 **Fax:** (0181) 514 9009 **DX:** 200850 ILFORD 4 **Email:** EESN@LINK.ORG

292-294 PLASHET GROVE, EAST HAM, LONDON, E6 1DQ
Tel: (0181) 514 9000 **Fax:** (0181) 552 1864 **DX:** 4702 EAST HAM

108 HIGH STREET NORTH, EAST HAM, LONDON, E6 2HU
Tel: (0181) 514 9000 **Fax:** (0181) 470 7970 **DX:** 4702 EAST HAM

THE ASDA CENTRE, TOLLGATE ROAD, BECKTON, LONDON, E6 4JP
Tel: (0181) 514 9000 **Fax:** (0171) 473 0156 **DX:** 4702 EAST HAM

The Firm: A progressive firm with a number of prestigious clients in the Insurer, Trade Union and Legal Expense Insurer Sectors. The firm is long recognised as a quality supplier of legal services in the private sector having been one of the first tranche of firms awarded a Legal Aid Franchise in 1994. Currently participating as a pilot firm in the Boards Civil and Assistance Contracting Pilot. A well resourced practice able to compete with City practices. Committed to quality initiatives and offering a wide range of expertise underpinned by a commitment to meeting the needs of all clients in terms of efficiency, quality and value for money. The firm was visited by The Lord Chancellor in July of 1996 by recommendation from The Lord Chancellor's Department and The Legal Aid Board to view in particular their Quality Procedures, Training Initiatives and File Review Procedures. A Legal Aid Franchise has been awarded in all available areas.

Principal Areas of Work:

Personal Injury: (*Contact:* Christopher Crook). Members of the Personal Injury Panel. Specialisation in road accident and industrial injury. We act as Plaintiff for individuals and a very large volume of our work is referred to the firm by Legal Expense Insurers and Trade Unions. The firm acts for a number of major Insurance clients.

Medical Negligence: (*Contact:* Philippa Barton).

Family: (*Contact:* David Emmerson or Rebecca Wigglesworth). A large expanding practice with the emphasis on mediation to solve financial and children issues.

Injunctions: (*Contact:* Tony Roe or Rebecca Wigglesworth). No appointment needed for injunction service dealing in domestic violence, racial attacks and unlawful eviction.

Crime: (*Contact:* Barry Linnane). From routine Magistrate Court matters to major fraud, high profile cases.

Commercial Property: (*Contact:* Charles Newman and Hilary Green). Clients receive a high degree of personal attention from the partners.

Private Client: (*Contact:* Charles Newman). Defamation, sports and media, Commercial conveyancing.

Domestic conveyancing: (*Contact:* Linda Storey).

Planning: (*Contact:* Peter Ivermee). Planning appeals, negotiation and applications.

Licensing: (*Contact:* Peter Ivermee). New Public House and Restaurant applications, Transfers and extension of hours.

Housing: (*Contact:* Gordon Turner). Disrepair, homelessness and unlawful eviction.

Immigration and Nationality: (Contact: Rita Sethi). Refugee, family re-union and work permits.

Agency Work: (*Contact:* David Emmerson). For all London and West Essex Courts.

Senior Partner:	Charles F. Newman
Practice Director:	Ken Wimberg
Number of partners:	9
Assistant solicitors:	22
Other fee-earners:	22

WORKLOADS	
Personal injury and negligence	55%
Commercial and domestic conveyancing	15%
Others	15%
Family	10%
Crime	5%

CONTACTS	
Commercial property	Charles Newman
Crime	Barry Linnane
Domestic conveyancing	Linda Storey
Employment	Gordon Turner
Family	David Emmerson
Housing	Gordon Turner
Immigration	Rita Sethi
Injunctions	Rebecca Wigglesworth
Licensing	Peter Ivermee
Medical negligence	Philippa Barton
Personal injury	Christopher Crook
Planning	Peter Ivermee
Quality Systems	Ken Winberg
Sports and media	Charles Newman
Wills & Probate	Alan Cleverley

EDWIN COE

2 STONE BUILDINGS, LINCOLN'S INN, LONDON, WC2A 3TH
Tel: (0171) 691 4000 **Fax:** (0171) 691 4111 **DX:** 191 LONDON CHANCERY LANE WC2 **Email:** MAIL@EDWINCOE.COM

The Firm: Edwin Coe is an established commercial firm in Lincoln's Inn offering a comprehensive partner-led service. Emphasis is placed on both quality and speed of response to clients' needs and achieving objectives efficiently and cost effectively. The client base is world-wide and includes a variety of large and small public and private companies as well as institutions, charities and unincorporated associations. Some sovereign states instruct the firm. Advice is also provided to individuals in both professional and private roles.

Edwin Coe makes a point of acquainting itself with the business of its clients and aims to give clear and practical advice. A number of standard works have been written by partners of the firm on different areas of the law, including insolvency and the responsibilities of company directors. In addition, the firm regularly holds seminars on legal issues for its clients and contacts. Larger firms continue to refer work to Edwin Coe.

Principal Areas of Work:

Corporate: The firm's corporate group acts for clients in all areas of company and commercial law and deals with a diverse range of mainstream corporate activities including mergers and acquisitions. The group has a growing reputation in offshore, international and banking matters as well as being established in the areas of charities and social housing.

Litigation: Services offered include arbitration, asset protection and recovery, banking, commercial litigation, factoring, fraud, insurance claims, intellectual property, landlord and tenant protection, professional and disciplinary tribunals and professional negligence claims. The employment team advises on service contracts, remuneration, relocation, wrongful dismissal, discrimination and redundancy, including representation at industrial tribunals. Edwin Coe provides general litigation support including a debt collection service, and accepts High Court litigation agency work from other solicitors.

Property: Clients include property investors and developers, insurance companies, banks and retailers. The group undertakes banking security work, property development, landlord and tenant, licensing, mortgages and debentures, planning, investment acquisitions, property portfolios and rent review advice.

Private Client: Specialises in the commercial development and management of the affairs of high net worth individuals and the creation and management of domestic and foreign trusts, charities, estate planning and administration, tax planning and wills.

Insolvency: The firm's insolvency team is headed by a licensed practitioner and has strong connections with banks and accountants. It gives advice to both corporate and individual clients on all aspects of administration, liquidation and receivership.

Marine and Aviation: The specialist team undertakes contentious and non-contentious work covering all aspects of international trade, and has correspondent lawyers throughout the world.

Other languages spoken: French, German, Russian, Polish, Mandarin, Cantonese, Italian.

Senior partner:	John Tomlins
Number of partners:	17
Assistant solicitors:	13
Other fee-earners:	13

WORKLOADS	
Corporate	28%
Litigation	24%
Property	18%
Private Client	16%
Insolvency	8%
Marine and Aviation	6%

CONTACTS	
Corporate	Michael Edwards
Insolvency	Christopher Berry
Litigation	David Greene
Marine and Aviation	Julian Morgan
Private Client	John Shelford
Property	John Tomlins

Edwin Coe

SOLICITORS

EKING MANNING 44 The Ropewalk, Nottingham, NG1 5EL *Tel:* (0115) 953 2532 *Fax:* (0115) 953 2533 *DX:* 10010 *Ptnrs:* 10 *Asst solrs:* 9 *Other fee-earners:* 2

ELAINE MAXWELL & CO 26 Sun Street, Lancaster, LA1 1EW **Tel:** 01524 840810 **Fax:** 01524 840811 **Ptnrs:** 1 **Asst solrs:** 1 **Other fee-earners:** 1 *A niche firm, dealing solely with education law and community care, acting for clients nation-wide. Elaine Maxwell has worked in the field since 1990, acting for schools, universities, parents and students, offering expert legal advice in this highly specialised area.*

WORKLOADS	
Special Educational Needs	70%
Student Work	20%
Other Education & Community Care	10%

ELBORNE MITCHELL

ONE AMERICA SQUARE, CROSSWALL, LONDON, EC3N 2LB
Tel: (0171) 320 9000 **Fax:** (0171) 320 9111 **DX:** 1063 **Internet:** WWW.ELBORNES.COM

The Firm: Ever since the firm was founded in 1968, the work of Elborne Mitchell has been firmly focused on shipping, insurance and international trade. The firm is experienced in dealing with issues and problems in these core business sectors, giving commercial advice on business operations as well as handling shipping and insurance claims and litigation. The firm is a forward-looking group of lawyers, ready to give constructive and independent advice to clients worldwide.

Principal Areas of Work:

Insurance and Reinsurance: (Fee-earners: 10). The firm is well known for its knowledge and experience in a wide range of insurance and reinsurance matters, from the drafting of policies to the investigation of insurance frauds and the litigation of complex disputes in the insurance and reinsurance markets. Insurance claims work includes professional negligence and product liability claims and Lloyd's litigation.

Shipping and International Trade: (Fee-earners: 7). Shipping and the specialist area of admiralty law have always formed an important part of the firm's practice. Its experience extends to public investigations under the Merchant Shipping Act as well as to salvages, ship collisions and total loss claims. The firm has a team of lawyers concerned with the import and export of goods and methods of financing their purchase and sale. They can assist with the special problems arising from carriage of goods by air, sea, rail and road, and the firm's work extends to the insurance aspects of international trade.

Commercial Litigation: (Fee-earners: 3). Areas of work include litigation and arbitration of disputes concerning commodities and futures contracts, commercial debt recovery, business disputes, commercial defamation and injunctions.

Company/ Commercial: (Fee-earners: 5). The firm can assist with the structuring of business operations whether the client is based in the UK or overseas. It advises on the formation of companies and partnerships, and on any questions of DTI requirements, EC competition law, immigration requirements, contracts of employment and tax implications. The firm advises on problems arising from the failure and insolvency of commercial undertakings, particularly in the fields of insurance, shipping and international trade.

International Connections: While the firm does not have offices overseas, it enjoys close professional relations with firms of lawyers in most parts of the world. Advice on foreign law and local conditions can be obtained quickly, and clients' interests abroad are protected by qualified representatives answering directly to Elborne Mitchell.

Recruitment: The firm recruits two trainee solicitors every year. It looks for intelligent and articulate lawyers with a good general education. Applications should be made on application forms available from Michelle Jepson.

Managing partner:	Alasdair Gillies
Senior partner:	Andrew Pincott
Number of partners:	11
Assistant solicitors:	8
Other fee-earners:	6

WORKLOADS	
Insurance & reinsurance	60%
Shipping	15%
Company/ commercial	13%
Commercial litigation	12%

CONTACTS	
Commercial	Philip Greig
Commercial litigation	Tim Brentnall
Professional negligence	Jolyon Patten
Reinsurance	Andrew Pincott
Shipping	Peter Tribe

ELIZABETH CAIRNS Knowle Hill Farm, Ulcombe, Maidstone, ME17 1ES *Tel:* (01622) 858191 *Fax:* (01622) 858004 *Ptnrs:* 1

ELLIOT MATHER SMITH The Courtyard, 49 Low Pavement, Chesterfield, S40 1PB *Tel:* (01246) 231288 *Fax:* (01246) 204081 *DX:* 12362 Chesterfield *Ptnrs:* 12 *Asst solrs:* 5 *Other fee-earners:* 12

ELLIOTT & COMPANY

CENTURION HOUSE, DEANSGATE, MANCHESTER, M3 3WT
Tel: (0161) 834 9933 **Fax:** (0161) 832 3693 **DX:** 14346 **Email:** MAIL@ELLIOTT-LAW.CO.UK

The Firm: A well-established independent firm, founded in Manchester in 1968, Elliott & Company offers a comprehensive and commercially aware service to its client base, both in the UK and overseas.

Principal Areas of Work:

Litigation: (*Contact Partner:* John Groome). The firm specialises in contentious work and has particular experience in insurance law, handling work ranging from professional indemnity, employer and public liability cases to fire and disaster claims and international claims. A wide variety of commercial litigation is undertaken, including construction disputes, product liability, insolvency work, debt recovery, personal injury claims, and consumer problems.

Company/ Commercial: (*Contact Partner:* Katharine Mellor). A full range of commercial services is available. *Work includes:* corporate finance matters, mergers and acquisitions, franchising, computer law, aviation law, intellectual property work, and employment law.

Licensing: (*Contact Partner:* Barry Holland). The specialist licensing department has handled the licensing of the new Trafford Centre in Manchester.

Property: (*Contact Partner:* Tim Chapman). *Work includes:* commercial and residential conveyancing and agricultural law. The firm has significant experience in retail property and in the fields of planning and environmental law.

International Connections: The firm is a founder member of the Euro-American Lawyers Group, which provides instant access to expert advice throughout Europe and America.

Senior partner:	Katharine Mellor
Number of partners:	10
Assistant solicitors:	16
Other fee-earners:	8

CONTACTS	
Aviation Law	Katharine Mellor
Commercial litigation	Fiona Miller
Commercial property	David Walton
Company commercial	Katharine Mellor
Construction	Mike Woolley
Employment law	Fiona Miller
Insurance litigation	John Groome/Graham Hughes
Intellectual property	Robert Jones
Licensing	Barry Holland
Motor litigation	Clare Edwards
Personal injury	Julian Holt/Neal Samarji
Private client	Tim Chapman
Professional negligence	John Groome

ELLIOTT DUFFY GARRETT

7 DONEGALL SQUARE EAST, BELFAST, BT1 5HD
Tel: (01232) 245034 **Fax:** (01232) 241337 **DX:** 400 NR BELFAST

The Firm: Established 1973 Elliott Duffy Garrett is well regarded for its role in serving the business community in Northern Ireland, and for its links with international clients. A wide range of commercial legal services is offered with particular emphasis on company law, commercial property and planning, litigation and insolvency.

Principal Areas of Work:

Company Law: A full service is provided with particular emphasis on corporate finance, mergers and acquisitions, joint ventures, management buy-outs, secured lending and related banking work, inward investment and venture capital services.

Commercial Property and Planning: Work includes commercial property development, letting and investment acquisitions and disposals, planning and environmental law.

Employment Law: Specialist advice provided in relation to all aspects of employment and anti-discrimination law and practice.

Litigation: Work includes product liability, construction law, professional negligence, insurance, insolvency and general litigation.

Foreign/International Connections: The firm has a formal association with A & L Goodbody, one of Dublin's principal law firms, through the A & L Goodbody (NI) Association.

Managing partner:	Michael P. Lynch
Senior partner:	J.Brian Garrett
Number of partners:	11
Assistant solicitors:	7
Other fee-earners:	5

WORKLOADS	
Commercial property	25%
Commercial litigation	20%
Company/ commercial	20%
Labour/ employment	20%
Private client	10%
Insolvency	5%

CONTACTS	
Commercial property	W. Laurence Mahood
Company/ commercial	Jacqueline Kerr
Employment Law	Harry Coll
Insolvency	Michael Wilson
Litigation	Michael P. Lynch
Private client	Barry E. Thompson

ELLIS-FERMOR & NEGUS Market Place, Ripley, DE5 3BS *Tel:* (01773) 744744 *Fax:* (01773) 570047 *DX:* 16873 Ripley *Ptnrs:* 9 *Asst solrs:* 4 *Other fee-earners:* 6

ELLIS JONES Sandbourne House, 302 Charminster Road, Bournemouth, BH8 9RU *Tel:* (01202) 525333 *Fax:* (01202) 535935 *DX:* 122752 Bournemouth 10 *Ptnrs:* 6 *Asst solrs:* 5 *Other fee-earners:* 21

ELLIS MOXON 22 Market Place, Burslem, Stoke-on-Trent, ST6 4AY *Tel:* (01782) 577700 *Fax:* (01782) 575363 *DX:* 22305 Burslem *Ptnrs:* 7 *Asst solrs:* 1 *Other fee-earners:* 3

ELLISON & CO Headgate Court, Head Street, Colchester, CO1 1NP *Tel:* (01206) 764477 *Fax:* (01206) 764455 *DX:* 3601 Colchester *Ptnrs:* 13 *Asst solrs:* 4 *Other fee-earners:* 15

ELLIS WOOD Langdales, New Garden House, 78 Hatton Garden, London, EC1N 8JR *Tel:* (0171) 242 1194 *Fax:* (0171) 831 9480 *DX:* 248 Ch.Ln. *Ptnrs:* 3 *Asst solrs:* 2 *Other fee-earners:* 1

ENSOR BYFIELD

EQUITY COURT, 73-75 MILLBROOK ROAD EAST, SOUTHAMPTON, SO15 1RJ
Tel: (01703) 483200 **Fax:** (01703) 212127 **DX:** 49665 SOUTHAMPTON 2 **Email:** INFO@ENSORBYFIELD.COM

The Firm: Ensor Byfield is a business focused law firm in Southampton, committed to supporting local and national companies in all aspects of their business activities, from start up to the realisation of their objectives. With specialists in all areas of commercial law likely to be required by most businesses, the firm handles a wide range of commercial work. The London office services the firm's international and City based clients. A brochure is available on request.

Principal Areas of Work: The practice provides a full range of legal services and acts in a number of areas including banking, TV and radio, transport, aviation, insurance litigation, music, motor racing, football, tennis, retailing, property development, management and investment. The firm has a small private client department.

Company/Commercial: Department meets commercial needs including listed company work, mergers, company development and restructuring, raising finance, MBOs/MBIs, acquisitions and disposals. Also offers contractual advice in the computer, entertainment and sporting fields, together with debt collection, employment matters and general commercial litigation.

Insurance Litigation: Pre-eminent in the southern region, this department provides first rate advice to insurers in all areas of claims.

Commercial Property: Department offers considerable experience in most areas of commercial property transactions with particular reference to office, retail and investment properties.

Other offices: No 1 Great Cumberland Place, London W1H 7AL *Tel:* (0171) 224 8080 *Fax:* (0171) 224 8848

Senior Partner:	Rod Evans
Chief Executive:	Christopher Crowcroft
Number of partners:	9
Assistant solicitors:	4
Other fee-earners:	15

WORKLOADS	
Insurance litigation	45%
Company/ commercial	35%
Commercial property	10%
Commercial litigation	9%
Private client	1%

CONTACTS	
Commercial litigation	M. Wilson
Commercial property	T. Southorn
Company/ commercial	J. Byfield/J. Harrison
Corporate finance	J. Harrison
Defendant insurance litigation	R. Evans
Private client	L. Thomas
Residential property	L. Thomas

EPSTEIN GROWER & MICHAEL FREEMAN

ONE GREAT CUMBERLAND PLACE, LONDON, W1H 8DQ
Tel: (0171) 723 3040 **Fax:** (0171) 723 2988 **DX:** 44433 MARBLE ARCH **Email:** W1LAW@AOL.COM

The Firm: An expanding firm, founded in 1991, Epstein Grower & Michael Freeman is dedicated to the provision of pro-active service to a wide range of commercial clients as well as specialising in certain niche areas. It regards the partners' negotiating skills as the key to its success on behalf of clients.

Principal Areas of Work:

Litigation: (*Contact Partners:* Howard Epstein, Michael Freeman). The Firm specialises in heavy commercial litigation and has particular experience in insurance law (emanating from its defence of Lloyd's Names), professional negligence and partnership disputes. Further, in the criminal field, the Firm handles commercial fraud.

Property: (*Contact Partner:* Edmund Grower). The Firm has great depth of experience in both commercial and residential conveyancing, `acting for commercial investors, dealers and developers, institutional lenders and private clients.

Sport: (*Contact Partner:* Mel Goldberg). The Firm represents a number of well-known sports stars and has vast experience in all aspects of work concerning such clients.

Intellectual Property: (*Contact Partner:* Howard Epstein). The Firm's exploitation of hi-technology from its inception has led to in-depth knowledge of this specialised area, both contentious and non-contentious.

Recruitment: The Firm places a high priority on recruitment and training, and invites applicants for September 1999 onwards.

Contact partner:	Howard Epstein
Number of partners:	4
Assistant solicitors:	3
Other fee-earners:	4

WORKLOADS	
Litigation	60%
Conveyancing	20%
Sport & Commercial	20%

ERIC ROBINSON & CO 18 West End Rd, Bitterne, Southampton, SO18 1DN *Tel:* (01703) 425000 *Fax:* (01703) 446594 *DX:* 52750 Bitterne *Ptnrs:* 10 *Asst solrs:* 12 *Other fee-earners:* 15

ERSKINE MACASKILL & CO 4 Gayfield Square, Edinburgh, EH1 3NW **Tel:** (0131) 557 1520 **Fax:** (0131) 557 5970 **DX:** 191 Edinburgh **Contact:** (Sarah Erskine). *Specialist matrimonial and child law practice. Also undertakes conveyancing, judicial review and criminal defence work.*

WORKLOADS			
Matrimonial/Child Law	45%	Criminal Defence Work	22%
Conveyancing	20%	Judicial Review Work	8%
Others	5%		

EVANS BUTLER WADE 165 Greenwich High Road, London, SE10 8JA **Tel:** (0181) 858 8926 **Fax:** (0181) 858 8131 **Ptnrs:** 4 **Asst solrs:** 4 **Other fee-earners:** 1 **Contact:** Mr C. Evans *Specialists in housing association developments and management work, employment work, and family work, especially in relation to same-sex relationships.*

WORKLOADS			
Social Housing (Management)			30%
Social Housing (Property)			30%
Domestic Conveyancing	10%	Employment	10%
Family	10%	Other	5%
Personal Injury	5%		

EVANS DODD

5 BALFOUR PLACE, MOUNT STREET, LONDON, W1Y 5RG
Tel: (0171) 491 4729 **Fax:** (0171) 499 2297 **DX:** 44644 MAYFAIR

Principal Areas of Work:

General Description: Established in 1975 as a commercial practice with a strong international bias.

Company and Commercial: (*Contact:* Geoffrey Dodd). All aspects of company and commercial work including public and private corporate law, acquisitions, new issues, joint ventures, banking and finance, aircraft acquisitions, financing and tax planning.

Commercial Property: (*Contact:* Joseph Hyde). Commercial property acquisitions, sales, leases and financing. Domestic property work also undertaken.

Litigation: (*Contact:* Jeremy Hershkorn). All types of commercial litigation and disputes.

Managing partner:	Geoffrey Dodd
Senior partner:	Geoffrey Dodd
Number of partners:	7
Assistant solicitors:	1
Other fee-earners:	2

WORKLOADS	
Company/ commercial	50%
Litigation	25%
Property	15%
Taxation	10%

EVERATT & COMPANY 104 High Street, Evesham, WR11 4EU **Tel:** (01386) 47191 **Fax:** (01386) 48515 **DX:** 16167 **Ptnrs:** 4 **Asst solrs:** 2 **Other fee-earners:** 1 **Contact:** Miss Catherine Arkell *A specialist practice acting for major insurance companies in both employers' liability and road traffic claims.*

WORKLOADS	
Personal injury (mainly for defendant's insurers)	80%

EVERSHEDS

SENATOR HOUSE, 85 QUEEN VICTORIA STREET, LONDON, EC4V 4JL
Tel: (0171) 919 4500 **Fax:** (0171) 919 4919 **Email:** GRADREC@EVERSHEDS.CO.UK **Internet:** WWW.EVERSHEDS.COM

The Firm: Eversheds, the national law firm, has 12 offices throughout England and Wales and five offices internationally.

Principal Areas of Work: Eversheds are industry leaders in the property and litigation fields and operate over 30 specialist groups of lawyers with expertise in the following business areas:

Arbitration	Alternative Dispute Resolution	Banking
Building Societies	Commercial law	Commercial litigation
Commercial property	Competition	Computer/IT
Construction	Consumer credit	Corporate finance
Corporate tax	Debt recovery	Employment
Environment	EU Law	Education
Entertainment	Financial Services	Franchising
Insolvency	Insurance	International Law
Intellectual property	Licensing	MediaPartnerships
Pensions	Personal injury	PFI
Planning	Public sector	Residential property
Shipping		

Nature of Clients: Its client base consists of major national and international public corporations, acting for over 100 plcs, local and public and private authorities.

Foreign Connections: The firm also has offices in Brussels, Copenhagen, Paris, Moscow, Monaco and associated offices elsewhere. It also liaises with firms throughout Europe, USA and the Far East.

Recruitment: Eversheds recruits approximately 95 trainee solicitors each year. Apply to any office for a trainee solicitors' brochure and application form.

Training: Eversheds has a full-time Director of Training and a well-established programme of in-house training at all levels.

Chairman:	Keith James
UK	
Number of partners:	322
Assistant solicitors:	455
Other fee-earners:	533
International	
Number of partners:	5
Assistant solicitors:	12

WORKLOADS	
Company/commercial	33%
Litigation	30%
Property	24%
Employment	7%
Other	6%

Continues overleaf

London: Senator House, 85 Queen Victoria Street, London EC4V 4JL
Managing Partner: Peter Scott Tel: (0171) 919 4500 Fax: (0171) 919 4919

Birmingham: 10 Newhall Street, Birmingham B3 3LX
Managing Partner: Ian Jollie Tel: (0121) 233 2001 Fax: (0121) 236 1583

Bristol: 11-12 Queen Square, Bristol, BS1 4NT
Managing Partner: David Vokes Tel: (0117) 929 9555 Fax: (0117) 929 2766

Cardiff: Fitzalan House, Fitzalan Road, Cardiff CF2 1XZ
Managing Partner: David Vokes Tel: (01222) 471147 Fax: (01222) 464347

Derby: 11 St. James Court, Friar Gate, Derby DE1 1BT
Managing Partner: John Sarginson Tel: (01332) 360992 Fax: (01332) 371469

Ipswich: Churchgates House, Cutler Street, Ipswich IP1 1UR
Managing Partner: Colin Brown Tel: (01473) 284428 Fax: (01473) 233666

Leeds: Cloth Hall Court, Infirmary Street, Leeds LS1 2JB
Managing Partner: David Ansbro Tel: (0113) 243 0391 Fax: (0113) 245 6188

Manchester: London Scottish House, 24 Mount Street, Manchester M2 3DB
Managing Partner: John Moody Tel: (0161) 832 6666 Fax: (0161) 832 5337

Teesside: Permanent House, 91 Albert Road, Middlesbrough TS1 2PA
Managing Partner: Nigel Robson Tel: (01642) 247456 Fax: (01642) 240446

Newcastle: Milburn House, Dean Street, Newcastle-upon-Tyne NE1 1NP
Managing Partner: Nigel Robson Tel: (0191) 261 1661 Fax: (0191) 261 8270

Norwich: Holland Court, The Close, Norwich NR1 4DX
Managing Partner: Colin Brown Tel: (01603) 272727 Fax: (01603) 610535

Nottingham: 1 Royal Standard Place, Nottingham NG1 6FZ
Managing Partner: John Sarginson Tel: (0115) 950 7000 Fax: (0115) 950 7111

INTERNATIONAL:

Brussels: 75 Avenue de Cortenberg, 1000 Brussels *Partner:* John Grayston Tel: (32) 2 737 9340 Fax: (32) 2 737 9345

Copenhagen: Ostergade 27, DK-1100 Copenhagen, Denmark (Associated Office) *Partner:* Mikael Lunoe Tel: (45) 33 155033 Fax: (45) 33 155077

Paris: Frere Cholmeley 42 Avenue de President Wilson, 75116 Paris, France Tel: 33 1 4434 7100 Fax: 33 1 4434 7111

Monaco: Frere Cholmeley Bischoff 24 Boulevard Princess Charlotte, Monte Carlo, 98000 Monaco Tel: 3 77 9310 5510 Fax: 3 77 9310 5511

Moscow: ALM Advocates Bureau in Association with Frere Cholmeley Bischoff Block B, Ulitsa Delegat Skaya 3, 103473 Moscow, Russia Tel: 7 501 258 5058 Fax: 7 501 258 5060

EVERY & PHILIPS The Laurels, 46 New St, Honiton, EX14 8BZ *Tel:* (01404) 43431 *Fax:* (01404) 45493 *DX:* 48800 Honiton *Ptnrs:* 9 *Asst solrs:* 7 *Other fee-earners:* 8

EVERY & PHILIPS 37-41 Hight Street, Belfast, BT1 2AB *Tel:* (01232) 234800 *Fax:* (01232) 243391

EVILL & COLEMAN 113 Upper Richmond Road, Putney, London, SW15 2TL *Tel:* (0181) 789 9221 *Fax:* (0181) 789 7978 *DX:* 59451 *Ptnrs:* 8 *Asst solrs:* 4 *Other fee-earners:* 8

FAEGRE BENSON HOBSON AUDLEY

7 PILGRIM STREET, LONDON, EC4V 6DR
Tel: (0171) 450 4510 **Fax:** (0171) 450 4544 **DX:** 401 LONDON **Email:** LAWYERS@FAEGRE.CO.UK

The Firm: Faegre Benson Hobson Audley is a multinational partnership of English and American lawyers in London, formed between Faegre & Benson LLP and Hobson Audley Hopkins & Wood to provide English business law services to U.S. clients and American business law services to English clients. Faegre &Benson LLP is a firm of more than 275 lawyers with offices in Minneapolis, Minnesota; Denver, Colorado; Des Moines, Iowa; and Frankfurt, Germany. Hobson Audley Hopkins & Wood is a firm of more than 35 solicitors in London.

London Office: English business law services are provided in corporate and commercial, intellectual property, information technology, employment, litigation and property matters. American business law advice on U.S. corporate law and commercial transactions, including acquisitions, incorporations, joint ventures, distribution agreements, product liability and immigration, is provided in London and through the U.S. offices of Faegre & Benson LLP.

Language Spoken: French, German, Portugese, Spanish.

Managing partner:	Gerald Hobson
Managing Partner:	Gale Mellum

WORKLOADS	
Corporate Finance/ M&A	30%
Company/Commercial	25%
Litigation	15%
Property	12%
Employment	10%
Financial Services	8%

THE FAMILY LAW CONSORTIUM

2 HENRIETTA STREET, LONDON, WC2E 8PS
Tel: (0171) 420 5000 **Fax:** (0171) 420 5005 **DX:** 40012 COVENT GARDEN **Email:** FLC@TFLC.CO.UK **Internet:** WWW.TFLC.CO.UK

The Firm: Founded in September 1995 by leading practitioners in the field of family law and family breakdown, this is England's first practice to combine solicitors, mediators and counsellors. It models many of the intentions and principles behind the Family Law Act. Many solicitors refer their clients to the practice for family law work and mediation. All mediators and counsellors are fully accredited. Each of the various services provided by the practice is independent of the others. Details of the costs are available in advance.

Legal advice: covers all aspects of family law with particular emphasis on middle and higher income financial cases, often involving complex and/or offshore assets, and on children cases, again with a number involving international aspects.

Mediation: is conducted by co-mediators, combining lawyer mediators and non-lawyer mediators but sole mediation is also available. Many referrals are from family law solicitors acting for a party or from mediation organisations.

Counselling: is available for individuals or couples.

Preliminary Interviews: are specifically available at reduced rates to discuss which service may be more appropriate and any preliminary concerns.

Number of partners:	3
Assistant solicitors:	2
Total Mediators:	6
Other fee-earners:	3

FARLEYS

22-27 RICHMOND TERRACE, BLACKBURN, BB1 7AQ
Tel: (01254) 606000 **Fax:** (01254) 583526 **DX:** 13604 BLACKBURN 3

Other offices in Accrington and Burnley.

The Firm: Established in 1957, Farleys is a broad-based practice encompassing a number of specialised departments in its offices in Blackburn, Accrington and, from 1996, Burnley. The firm has built up a reputation in the North West of England for providing a high level of service both to private clients and to an increasing number of well-known commercial clients. In 1996 Farleys gained Legal Aid Franchises for both Family and Criminal departments.

Principal Areas of Work:

Commercial: A very successful and growing department covering all aspects of company and commercial work, with a growing expertise in entrepreneurial and manager-owned businesses.

Personal Injury/General Litigation: The firm handles personal injury, both medical and professional negligence, employment matters and environmental disputes. Members of the Personal Injury Panel and the Mental Health Review Tribunal Panel.

Family/Matrimonial: One of the largest family law departments in the North West dealing with all aspects of Family Law, especially Care Proceedings and substantial Ancillary Relief matters. Legal Aid Franchise.

Criminal: One of East Lancashire's busiest and most effective Criminal practices, dealing with all matters including the most serious.

Property: All aspects of private client property transactions.

Private Client: An extensive range of services offered in the area of Wills, Probate, Trustee and Executorship.

Senior partner:	A. N. Holden
Number of partners:	10
Assistant solicitors:	23
Other fee-earners:	21

WORKLOADS	
Civil litigation	30%
Conveyancing & probate	20%
Criminal	20%
Family	20%
Company	10%

CONTACTS	
Company/Commercial	Chris Porter/Nigel Holden
Crime & Environment	Paul Schofield/Andrew Church-Taylor
Family/Matrimonial	Kathryn Hughes/Ann Bamford
Personal Injury/Litigation	Mike Corrigan/Steve McNeill/Kieran O'Connor
Property & Private Client	Nigel Holden/Chris Porter

FARRER & CO

66 LINCOLN'S INN FIELDS, LONDON, WC2A 3LH
Tel: (0171) 242 2022 **Fax:** (0171) 831 9748 **DX:** 32 CHANCERY LANE

The Firm: Farrer & Co is one of the UK's leading law practices. It provides a range of specialist advice to private, institutional and corporate clients. The firm has long been recognised for the quality of its service, both technical and personal. This has been achieved by consistently recruiting team players possessing flair and intellect coupled with a desire to exceed clients' expectations. The client base is world wide and the clients are frequently leaders in their fields.

To meet the increasingly specialised demands of clients, the firm is divided into small flexible teams which have evolved out of the more traditional departmental structure of private client, property, litigation and commercial work. Its breadth of expertise is reflected in the fact that it has an outstanding reputation in fields as diverse as matrimonial law, offshore tax planning, employment, heritage work, charity law and defamation.

Principal Areas of Work:

Private Client: The firm is recognised as an established leader in the services it provides to its private clients. Core work includes tax planning, heritage property, wills and the administration of estates, probate and trusts. Agricultural estates and private property specialists advise on property matters, while clients also benefit from the firm's strong reputation in management and employment practices. The matrimonial team is pre-eminent and advises on family disputes arising from marriage breakdown or inheritance claims, family provision and child-related issues.

Work for institutions is focused on a highly successful and expanding charities team. In addition to charity law, teams advise these clients on taxation, employment, sponsorship and intellectual property issues. The firm has long had a reputation for advising sports industry clients and this is now matched by its work for museums, galleries and educational organisations.

Commercial: A full range of work is undertaken for commercial clients, with notable expertise in the media industry. Specialisations include employment and pensions, mergers and acquisitions, intellectual property, banking and FSA. The commercial property team manages all types of work for clients, while the litigation team has advised on almost every type of business dispute: contract, fraud, insolvency, construction, asset recovery, libel, government inspections and prosecutions.

Recruitment: Six trainee solicitors are recruited annually; a 2(1) degree is preferred, not necessarily in law. Considerable involvement is encouraged and prospects are excellent. Applications should be submitted by the summer two years in advance (forms available on request). All employment enquiries to be addressed to the personnel manager.

Foreign languages spoken: French and German.

Managing partner:	Robert Clinton
Senior partner:	Richard Griffiths
Number of partners:	39
Assistant solicitors:	42
Other fee-earners:	25

CONTACTS	
Agriculture	Simon Pring
Banking and FSA	Jonathan Bayliss
Charities	Judith Hill
Civil litigation	Adrian Parkhouse
Commercial litigation	Richard Parry
Commercial property	Raymond Cooper
Company/Commercial	James Thorne
Defamation and media	Robert Clinton
Education	Henry Boyd-Carpenter
Employment	Geoffrey Richards
Family	Fiona Shackleton/Richard Parry
Heritage/cultural property	Judith Hill
Intellectual property	Peter Wienand
Landlord & tenant	Raymond Cooper
Pensions	Elizabeth Potter
Sport and leisure	Charles Woodhouse
Tax – trusts and estates	Henry Boyd-Carpenter/ Mark Bridges
Town and country planning	Raymond Cooper

FAULKNERS

ARGYLL HOUSE, BATH STREET, FROME, BA11 1DP
Tel: (01373) 465051 **Fax:** (01373) 467414 **DX:** 43802 FROME

The Firm: Established in the early 1900s, Faulkners is a general practice offering a wide range of legal services to both private and commercial clients. Urgent matters are dealt with out of hours and home visits are available to clients experiencing mobility problems. Legal aid work is undertaken. The four offices within the practice are linked by land lines to a computer network, allowing the establishment of specialist departments within the firm as a whole.

Principal Areas of Work:

General Description: *Work includes:* company/commercial, licensing, insolvency, debt collection, agriculture, residential conveyancing, property development, commercial property, employment, planning, consumer disputes, professional negligence, landlord and tenant, property disputes, criminal work, family and matrimonial, wills, probate, trusts and tax.

Nicholas Rheinberg, the East Somerset Coroner, is a member of the Law Society's Personal Injury Panel as is Ben Whelan and with three partners and an Assistant Solicitor together with support staff involved in personal injury, this is a particular strength of the firm, as is matrimonial and child care work, with Patricia Wayman a member of the Law Society's Children Panel. The firm is represented on the Bath and Mendip Police Station and Court Duty schemes.

Other Offices: Midsomer Norton, Paulton and Radstock, *Tel:* (01761) 417575.

Senior partner:	A. Sheppard
Number of partners:	10
Assistant solicitors:	1
Other fee-earners:	7

CONTACTS	
Agricultural	A. Sheppard
Civil litigation	N.L. Rheinberg
Civil litigation	T. Williams
Commercial and residential conveyancing	S. Emery
Company/commercial	N.L. Rheinberg
Company/commercial	A. Sheppard
Crime	D. Holden White
Employment	J. Hollis
Matrimonial and child care	P. Wayman
Probate and trusts	A. Sheppard

FENNEMORES

200 SILBURY BOULEVARD, CENTRAL MILTON KEYNES, MK9 1LL
Tel: (01908) 678241 **Fax:** (01908) 665985 **DX:** 84757 MILTON KEYNES – 3 **Email:** INFO@FENNEMORES.COM **Internet:** WWW.FENNEMORES.COM

5 SPENCER PARADE, NORTHAMPTON, NN1 5AA
Tel: (01604) 250525 **Fax:** (01604) 231254

The largest firm based in Milton Keynes, Fennemores reflects the dynamic business culture of the new city.

The Firm: Fennemores was the first legal practice established in Milton Keynes. It has grown in line with the expansion of the city around it, to over 200 staff. In the mid-1980's the growth of industry and commerce in Milton Keynes led Fennemores to adopt an increasingly commercial emphasis. It now serves businesses throughout the region.

The business client base of the practice reflects the diversity of the region's industry and includes listed companies, UK arms of multinationals and owner-managed businesses. Fennemores is particularly experienced in meeting the needs of the distribution, hi-tech, motor and property development industries that flourish in Milton Keynes.

Clients: Include Alps Electric (UK), Aston Martin Lagonda, Binney & Smith Europe (Crayola & Revell), DRS, Hawtal Whiting, Pharmacia & Upjohn and Scania (GB).

Fennemores offers quality service and excellent value for money. It is innovative and technically capable, commercially aware whilst maintaining the highest professional standards. Heavy investment in IT results in unparalleled speed of response and flexibility.

Principal Areas of Work: Company Commercial; Commercial Property; Commercial Litigation; Private Client (including conveyancing, matrimonial, wills & probate); Personal Injury; Debt Services

Senior partner:	Christopher Hilton-Johnson
Number of partners:	15
Assistant solicitors:	11
Other fee-earners:	48

CONTACTS	
Commercial litigation	Charles Clay
Commercial property	Raymond Sothcott
Corporate finance	Chris Robinson
Debt recovery	Guy Brooks
Employment	Andrew Peck
Private client	Andrew Ray

FENNERS

180 FLEET STREET, LONDON, EC4A 2HD
Tel: (0171) 430 2200 **Fax:** (0171) 430 2218 **DX:** CHANCERY LANE LDE 256

The Firm: Fenners is a City-based firm specialising in company/commercial law, commercial property, town planning and residential property development and offers a leading capability in urban regeneration. The firm has a broad client base including public and private companies, financial advisers, banks and other institutions.

Principal Areas of Work:
Commercial Property: (*Contact Partners:* John Fenner and Jeremy Taylor). Investment acquisitions and disposals, site assembly and development (retail, office and industrial), regional and city centre schemes involving both the public and private sectors, institutional funding and forward sale agreements, commercial lettings for landlords and tenants, building agreements, secured lending for borrowers and lenders.
Corporate and Commercial Law: (*Contact Partner:* Robert Fenner). New issues on the Official List and the Alternative Investment Market, corporate finance, corporate reorganisations, management buy-outs, venture capital investments, mergers and acquisitions, joint ventures, intellectual property, employment law and employee share option schemes.
Planning: (*Contact Partner:* John Fenner). Redevelopment schemes (both commercial and residential), urban regeneration schemes, planning agreements for infrastructure work, planning gain and use restrictions, planning appeals and inquiries.
Residential Property Development: (*Contact Partner:* Jeremy Taylor). Site assembly and acquisition, management schemes, sales, town planning matters, road, sewer and other similar agreements.
Property Finance: (*Contact Partner:* Jeremy Taylor). Portfolio reconstructions, development finance and property joint venture schemes.

Foreign Languages: French, German, Italian, Portuguese, Hebrew.

Managing partner:	Robert Fenner
Senior partner:	John Fenner
Number of partners:	3
Assistant solicitors:	4

WORKLOADS	
Commercial property	50%
Corporate/ commercial	35%
Residential property	15%

CONTACTS	
Commercial property	John Fenner/Jeremy Taylor
Corporate/ commercial	Robert Fenner
Planning	John Fenner
Property finance	Jeremy Taylor
Residential property	Jeremy Taylor

FENWICK ELLIOTT

353 STRAND, LONDON, WC2R 0HS
Tel: (0171) 956 9354 **Fax:** (0171) 956 9355 **DX:** 178 LDE **Email:** RECEPTION@FENWICKELLIOTT.CO.UK

The Firm: Fenwick Elliott is a niche commercial law firm which specialises in construction, engineering and energy law. The firm provides a cost effective service, drawing on a wealth of expertise to provide commercially aware and practical advice. Robert Fenwick Elliott and Tony Francis are joint editors of the Construction Industry Law Letter, and Robert Fenwick Elliott is the author of "Building Contract Litigation" and "Building Contract Disputes: Practice and Precedents". Various of the Partners are members of the Official Referees Solicitors Association (ORSA) and ORSA accredited adjudicators and regularly lecture in the firm's specialist area. The firm has a monthly column in Building Magazine. The firm's practice is both domestic and international.

Principal Areas of Work:

Contentious: The firm handles large volumes of litigation and arbitration from routine loss and expense claims to the unique. The firm has particular expertise in Alternative Dispute Resolution (ADR) and adjudication procedures, and in the preparation of claims and delay analysis.

Non-Contentious: The firm handles contract drafting and advice from major complex developments to standard form sub-contracts, including experience of BOT type schemes.

Client Base: The firm acts nationally and internationally for developers, institutional investors, local authorities, utilities, main contractors, specialist sub-contractors, architects, engineers, surveyors, and private clients. Further, the firm acts for various foreign Government Corporations. Most of the firm's clients are well known in the construction industry.

Foreign Languages: French, Urdu.

Senior partner:	Robert Fenwick Elliott
Number of partners:	5
Assistant solicitors:	7
Other fee-earners:	3

WORKLOADS	
Contentious Construction (including ADR and Arbiration)	60%
Non-Contentious Construction	30%
Other related work	10%

FEW & KESTER Chequers House, 77-81 Newmarket Rd, Cambridge, CB5 8EU *Tel:* (01223) 363111 *Fax:* (01223) 323370 *DX:* 122893 Cambridge 4 *Ptnrs:* 9 *Asst solrs:* 4 *Other fee-earners:* 7

FIELD CUNNINGHAM & CO

ST. JOHN'S COURT, 70 QUAY ST, MANCHESTER, M3 3EJ
Tel: (0161) 834 4734 **Fax:** (0161) 834 1772 **DX:** 728855 MANCHESTER 4

The Firm: Established in 1867, Field Cunningham & Co is a successful 'niche' commercial property practice specialising in development work and associated commercial and property litigation. It places a high emphasis on providing a high level of personal service and commitment within a commercial environment.

Principal Areas of Work:

Commercial Property: The firm deals with all aspects of commercial property, with particular emphasis on development work in the retail, residential, office, leisure and commercial sectors, development funding, and joint ventures. Activities include work in associated planning, environmental and Lands Tribunal matters. An increasing volume of property secured lending work is being undertaken on behalf of Banks. In addition to its commercial development and re-development work the firm acts for national and local house-builders – the volume of new house sales undertaken is approximately 1 per cent annually of all UK private housing starts.

Commercial Litigation: Especially in property and construction-related and environmental matters, also intellectual property, employment and general commercial disputes.

Company/commercial: Private company sales and purchases, joint ventures, MBOs, business start-ups, partnerships, intellectual property and employment.

Recruitment: The firm normally takes one law graduate (2:1 required) annually. Applications by covering letter and CV. See *Leading Individuals* (Commercial Property – North West).

Senior partner:	Peter Ashworth
Number of partners:	4
Assistant solicitors:	2
Other fee-earners:	10

WORKLOADS	
Commercial property	78%
Commercial litigation	15%
Company commercial	5%
Private client	2%

FIELD FISHER WATERHOUSE

41 VINE STREET, LONDON, EC3N 2AA
Tel: (0171) 481 4841 **Fax:** (0171) 488 0084 **DX:** 823 LONDON **Email:** INFO@FFWLAW.COM **Internet:** HTTP://WWW.FFWLAW.COM

The Firm: Field Fisher Waterhouse is a City-based firm with a substantial UK and international corporate practice. It has a reputation of providing an excellent all-round service to an impressive list of clients drawn from a variety of sectors. In January 1998 the firm merged with Allison & Humphreys to create a one-stop service to clients in the communications and media sector. The merger has also increased the firm's corporate finance, pensions and litigation practices. The firm prides itself on its collegiate atmosphere, its constructive approach to career development and its creative and commercial approach to law.

Principal Areas of Work:

Banking and Finance: Asset financing and leasing, capital markets, currency and interest swaps, derivatives, FSA advice, international and domestic lending, collective investment funds and products, insolvency and receiverships, securitisation.

Communications and Media: Commercial, corporate and regulatory advice to telecommunications companies, broadcasters and film companies.

Corporate Finance: Capital raising and debt financing, M&As, management buy-outs, joint ventures, PFI projects, privatisations and corporate re-organisations.

Commercial Law: Advertising and sales promotion, construction, distribution and agency, partnerships, sponsorship.

Commercial Property: Development planning and financing, secured lending, golf courses and recreational properties, hotels and licensed premises, industrial complexes, office and store developments, pipeline conveyancing, telecommunications infrastructure, and commercial and residential leasing.

EC and Competition Law: All aspects of EC and UK competition law and single market regulation.

IP/IT: Copyright and designs, franchising, passing-off, patents, trade marks, trade secrets, computer contracts, outsourcing projects, the Internet and anti-piracy.

Commercial Litigation: Administrative law, contractual disputes, travel and tourism disputes, construction and development, defamation, EC law, insurance, international trade, professional negligence and discipline, and property.

Medical Litigation: Asbestosis, disaster law, pharmaceutical accidents, medical negligence, industrial accidents and disease and product liability.

Tax: Tax planning for UK and multinational companies, taxation of financial instruments, employee benefits and share schemes, VAT, and estate planning.

Travel and Tourism: Clients include travel agents and tour operators, hotels, restaurants, caterers and leisure complexes, airlines and other carriers.

Other Areas of Work: The firm is well known for its expertise in a number of industry sectors including: advertising; aviation; energy; franchising; health; hotels and leisure; rail; shipbuilding and ship finance; sport; and travel and tourism. Many of our lawyers undertake secondments with clients, thereby gaining an in-depth understanding of the sectors in which our clients are involved as well as providing clients with an added value service. The firm is also well known for its work in charity law, employment law, liquor licensing and pensions.

Nature of Clientele: The firms has a wide-ranging client base which includes commercial and industrial companies (many of them household names), banks and other financial institutions, governments, trade associations, professional partnerships, and charities.

Foreign Connections: The firm has an office in Brussels. It acts for numerous overseas clients and has particularly strong connections in China, France, Germany, Italy, Japan, Korea, Scandinavia and the US. The firm works closely with overseas firms in these and other countries. It also employs overseas lawyers. Languages spoken at the firm include Danish, French, German, Italian, Japanese, Korean, Mandarin, Spanish and Swedish.

Recruitment: It is expected that the firm will continue its organic growth, recruitment of laterals and strategic mergers with niche firms. At least ten trainees are recruited annually. A structured training programme is carried for both trainees and young solicitors. A variety of literature about the firm and the specialist services it provides is available on request.

Managing partner:		John Price
Senior partner:	•	Paul Honigmann
Number of partners:		58
Assistant solicitors:		71
Other fee-earners:		54

CONTACTS	
Aviation	Simon Chamberlain
Banking/Capital Markets and Derivatives	Jon Fife/ Guy Usher
Charity	Catherine Allison
Commercial Property	John Pedder
Communications	Tony Ballard
Competition	Charles Whiddington
Construction	Caryn Mackenzie
Corporate Finance	Tim Davies
Employee Benefits	Graeme Nuttall
Employment	Steven Lorber
Energy and Pipelines	Howard Coffell
Financial Services/Funds	Kirstene Baillie
Franchising and Distribution	Mark Abell
Hotels and Leisure	Paul Houston
Immigration	Heather Prescott
Int. Trade and Projects	John Wilson
Intellectual Property	Mark Abell
IT/Internet	Michael Chissick
Licensing	Peter Glazebrook
Litigation (Commercial)	Mark Lowe
Litigation (IP/IT)	Nick Rose
Media	Ellen Fleming
Medical Litigation	Rodney Nelson-Jones
Partnership	Colin McArthur
Pensions	Belinda Benney
Planning and Environmental	Richard Webber
Private Client	Heather Fuff
Professional Discipline	Paul Honigmann
Rail	Nicholas Thompsell
Shipbuilding/Finance	John Wilson
Tax (Corporate)	Nicholas Noble
Travel and Tourism	Peter Stewart

FIELDINGS PORTER Silverwell House, Silverwell Street, Bolton, BL1 1PT *Tel:* (01204) 387742 *Fax:* (01204) 362129 *DX:* 24144 *Ptnrs:* 11 *Asst solrs:* 13 *Other fee-earners:* 12

FIELD SEYMOUR PARKES 1 London Street, Reading, RG1 4QW *Tel:* (0118) 9391011 *Fax:* (0118) 9502704 *DX:* 4001 *Ptnrs:* 7 *Asst solrs:* 10 *Other fee-earners:* 17

FINERS

179 GREAT PORTLAND ST, LONDON, W1N 6LS
Tel: (0171) 323 4000 **Fax:** (0171) 580 7069 **DX:** 42739 OXFORD CIRCUS NORTH **Email:** MRALLI@FINERS.CO.UK

The Firm: Finers is a leading practice in the West End offering a full range of services to a broad client base of a commercial, institutional and private nature. It is highly regarded for the quality of its legal advice. On an international scale Finers is the only UK law firm to be a member of the Network of Leading Law Firms (NLLF) and an active member of the International Law Group (ILG). As a young, dynamic and progressive firm Finers is able to apply innovative solutions to problems as part of its service and commitment to its clients. Excellent levels of client care are underpinned by Finers distinctive business acumen and awareness of client needs in the sectors in which they operate. A high participation of partners guarantees involvement at the most senior level. This ensures optimum performance in the best interests of clients at all times.

Principal Areas of Work:

Commercial Property: (*Contact:* Melvyn Orton). This is an extremely active department, advising household name clients, developers, investment companies and national retail and restaurant chains in connection with developments, joint ventures, sales, purchases and leases of offices, shops, and industrial premises in the UK and abroad. The firm also advises on planning, construction and licensing matters. The department has groups specialising in Development, Retail, Trading, Investment and Financing.

Corporate and Commercial: (*Contact:* Peter Jay). The department handles all types of public and private company work, including acquisitions, mergers and flotations as well as Corporate Tax with particular expertise in APEX and AIM markets. It also covers Intellectual Property, Information Technology, Insolvency, Partnership and Employment Law.

Litigation: (*Contact:* Christopher Butler). This department deals with all types of disputes ranging from major international commercial contracts to employment disputes. Whilst most matters are resolved in English Courts, members of the department are experienced in Arbitration and all forms of alternative dispute resolution both in the UK and also in foreign jurisdictions. There is a particular expertise in Construction, Defamation, Family and Matrimonial Law, Restraint of Trade, Property Litigation, Professional Negligence, Insurance, Freight and Dry Shipping, Intellectual Property and Licensing. The firm also acts as Privy Council agents for Commonwealth Appeals.

Private Client: (*Contact:* Jeffrey Cohen). This department handles Residential Property and Conveyancing, Wills, Probate, Immigration, as well as Tax and Personal Finance.

International: (*Contact:* Michael Simmons). The firm is an active member of the International Lawyers' Group (ILG), a well-established association of international law firms and the Network of Leading Law Firms. The firm is therefore in a position to recommend firms in foreign jurisdictions or indeed work with clients' chosen advisors. There is particular interest in the US, European work including Eastern Europe, Middle East, South Africa, India and Malaysia.

Other: The firm operates a number of cross discipline groups in Employment Law, Construction Law, Intellectual Property, Professional Practice, Landlord and Tenant, and Retail Services.

Recruitment and Training: Finers have a carefully structured annual recruitment programme characterised by the quality of its in-house training. Write, enclosing CV, to Philip Rubens.

Managing partner:	Richard Gerstein
Number of partners:	35
Assistant solicitors:	20
Other fee-earners:	10

WORKLOADS	
Property	44%
Litigation	33%
Corporate/Commercial	17%
Private Client	6%

CONTACTS	
Commercial Litigation	Philip Rubens
Construction Law	Jonathan Collins
Corporate/Commercial	Peter Jay
Employment Law	Anthony Barling
Finance	Paul Millett
Freight & Dry Shipping	Paul Bugden
Immigration	John d'Ardenne
Information Technology	Anthony Barling
Insolvency	Richard Curtin
Insurance	Paul Bugden
Intellectual Property	Mark Elmslie
International	Michael Simmons
Leasehold Enfranchisement	John Hewitt
Licensing	Ian Gerrard
Litigation	Christopher Butler
Matrimonial	Christopher Butler
Partnership	Michael Simmons
Personal Injury	Leon Marks
Planning	Nichola Armstrong
Professional Negligence	Richard Gerstein
Property	Melvyn Orton
Property Development	David Battiscombe
Property Finance	Paul Sheeter
Property Investment	Melvyn Orton
Property Litigation	John Hewitt
Property Retail	Katherine Miller
Property Trading	Sam Charkham
Tax	Stephen Arthur
Trusts	Robert Craig
Wills & Probate	Jeffrey Cohen

FINERS SOLICITORS

FINN, GLEDHILL 1-4 Harrison Rd, Halifax, HX1 2AG **Tel:** (01422) 330000 **Fax:** (01422) 342604 **DX:** 16022 Halifax **Ptnrs:** 8 **Asst solrs:** 2 **Other fee-earners:** 5 **Contact:** Michael Gledhill *An all-round practice with an emphasis on commercial work.*

WORKLOADS		
Commercial (property, landlord and tenant, finance, company, etc)		30%
Civil litigation (commercial and other)		18%
Conveyancing	12%	Crime	10%
Divorce and Matrimonial	10%	Probate and trust	9%

FISHBURN BOXER

60 STRAND, LONDON, WC2N 5LR
Tel: (0171) 925 2884 **Fax:** (0171) 486 3256 **DX:** 8 CH.LN.

61 St. Mary Axe., London EC3A 8AA. Fax: (0171) 204 0030.

The Firm: Fishburn Boxer is a progressive, medium-sized firm with attractive, centrally located offices in the Strand and in the heart of the City at St Mary Axe. The firm has modern computer and database facilities, an extensive library and research resources.

Principal Areas of Work: General Description: The firm handles substantial High Court litigation, commercial work in insurance, reinsurance and professional indemnity for Lloyd's of London and insurance companies, commercial and residential conveyancing, company and tax work. The firm also provides specialist insurance services to the London insurance market.

    Insurance: *Work includes:* all types of insurance and reinsurance disputes, claims, professional indemnity, setting up insurance schemes, drafting policy wordings and undertaking pre-risk surveys.

    Litigation: *Work includes:* commercial, High Court, building contract disputes, slander and libel, personal injury, employment, and intellectual property.

    Company/commercial property: *Work includes:* company formations, acquisitions and disposals of shares and assets, takeover agreements, joint ventures, service agreements, management buy-outs, shareholders' agreements, loan documents and insolvency and property letting and leasing, landlord and tenant.

Nature of Clientele: Fishburn Boxer has a wide, primarily corporate, client base. It also acts for individuals in employment, conveyancing, estate and tax planning.

Languages spoken: French, German, Spanish, Portuguese and Russian.

Recruitment and Training: Trainee solicitors are recruited annually. Regular in-house seminars and training sessions are held for all staff.

Senior partner:	Andrew Davis
Number of partners:	13
Assistant solicitors:	16
Other fee-earners:	13

WORKLOADS	
Litigation	95%
Corporate and commercial	5%

CONTACTS	
ADR	Alison Wallace
Claims handling	Richard Clegg
Commercial litigation	Andrew Davis
Construction	Mark Klint
Corporate	Michael Bowden
Employment	Alison Wallace
Insurance & reinsurance	Stephen Leonard
Personal injury	Christopher Lowney
Private client	Michael Bowden
Professional indemnity	Sheona Wood
Property	Michael Bowden

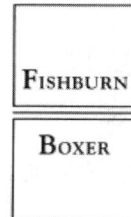

FISHBURN

BOXER

FISHER MEREDITH

2 BINFIELD ROAD, STOCKWELL, LONDON, SW4 6TA

CRIME, MENTAL HEALTH, IMMIGRATION
Tel: (0171) 622 4468 **Fax:** (0171) 498 0415 **DX:** 37050 OUT OF HOURS: (0171) 487 0006

FAMILY
Tel: (0171) 924 9124 **Fax:** (0171) 924 9906 OUT OF HOURS: (0171) 487 0006

CONVEYANCING, WILLS AND PROBATE, HOUSING, WELFARE BENEFITS, COMMUNITY CARE, EDUCATION, EMPLOYMENT
Tel: (0171) 564 2900 **Fax:** (0171) 787 0005 OUT OF HOURS: (0171) 487 0006

The Firm: Founded by Eileen Meredith Pembridge and another in 1975, Fisher Meredith now consists of six partners and 67 other staff. It has always been a High Street practice doing a large amount of legal aid work but is departmentalised for increased efficiency and to meet specialisation needs. The firm remains firmly committed to personal litigation and legal aid work and is still expanding. Fisher Meredith now has departments specialising in (a) family work of all types including children's advocacy and domestic violence, (b) a substantial amount of criminal law, (c) actions against the Police (d) mental health work (e) non-contentious work including conveyancing, wills and probate, (f) community care and education, (g) immigration, (h) welfare benefits, (i) housing law and (j) employment. Eileen Pembridge is the Law Society Council member for London South, member of the Courts & Legal Services Committee and a former Chair of the Law Society's Family Law Committee. The firm has a franchise in family, crime, housing, immigration, welfare benefits, mental health and actions against the police.

Principal Areas of Work:

    Family: (*Contact:* Eileen Pembridge/Janette Butler. *Fee-earners:* 13 including 2 on Children's Panel). Covers divorce, complex ancillary relief, cohabitation, inheritance, injunctions and all types of children's cases, public and private.

    Crime: (*Contact:* Stephen Hewitt. *Fee-earners:* 15). A large and thriving department offering an efficient, careful and caring service.

    Police Cases: (*Contact:* David Tyme. *Fee-earners:* 6). An efficient and dedicated service, covering also Prisoners Rights.

    Community Care/Education: (*Contact:* Pat Wilkins. *Fee-earners:* 3). A fast expanding department geared to prompt and efficient responses.

Senior partner:	Eileen Pembridge
Number of partners:	6
Assistant solicitors:	28
Other fee-earners:	10

WORKLOADS	
Crime	51%
Family (including Children)	30%
Civil	14%
Conveyancing	4%
Wills & probate	1%

CONTACTS	
Children	Janette Butler
Community Care/Education	Patricia Wilkins
Conveyancing	Ros Widgery
Crime	Stephen Hewitt
Family	Eileen Pembridge
Housing	David Foster
Immigration	Douglas Noble
Police actions	David Tyme
Welfare benefits	Stefano Ruis
Wills & probate	Michael Statham-Fletcher

Continues overleaf

Immigration: (*Contact:* Douglas Noble. Fee-earners: 4). A dedicated source covering all aspects from asylum to judicial review.

Residential and Commercial Conveyancing: (*Contact:* Rosalind Widgery/Joy Bailey. *Fee-earners:* 3). A friendly and prompt service from senior solicitors.

Wills: (*Contact:* Michael Statham-Fletcher. Fee-earners:1). The department offers a moderately priced and fast service on all aspects of wills, tax planning and on non-contentious probate.

Mental Health: (*Contact:* Rebecca Ellison. Fee-earners:2 both on MHRT Panel). A prompt and caring service, covering also Court of Protection.

Housing law: (*Contact:* David Foster. Fee-earners: 2). All aspects of housing law for tenants and other residential occupiers.

Welfare benefits: (*Contact:* Stefano Ruis. Fee-earners: 1). All social security appeals, housing benefit review boards and judicial reviews.

Employment: (*Contact:* David Tyme. Fee-earners: 1).

Nature of Clientele: The firm's clients are mostly individuals engaged in personal transactions or litigation.

Languages Spoken: French, Spanish, German and Italian.

Agency Work: Fisher Meredith accept instructions in its areas of expertise.

Charges: For legal aid work, the charges are as fixed by the LCD. For private clients, the firm charges £100-180 per hour, as of early 1998.

FISHERS 9-13 Fenchurch Buildings, London, EC3M 5HR **Tel:** (0171) 709 7203 **Fax:** (0171) 709 7204 **Email:** FISHCITY@COMPUSERVE.COM **Ptnrs:** 2 **Asst solrs:** 3 **Other fee-earners:** 2 **Contact:** Mr Nicholas Fisher *City firm providing specialised services in the areas of commercial shipping, insurance, re-insurance and international trade.*

WORKLOADS	
Commercial shipping and international trade litigation	70%
Professional indemnity and insurance litigation	25%
Drafting shipping and insurance documentation	5%

FITZHUGH GATES

3 PAVILION PARADE, BRIGHTON, BN2 1RY
Tel: (01273) 686811 **Fax:** (01273) 676837 **DX:** 2727 BRIGHTON 1

The Firm: Founded in 1806, Fitzhugh Gates is a general practice offering legal services to both private and commercial clients. The firm offers substantial expertise in commercial and domestic conveyancing, and has specialist practitioners in matrimonial law, licensing, employment and personal injury. Agency work is undertaken in the nearby County Court and licensing in the Magistrates Court.

Senior partner:	Anthony Druce
Number of partners:	9
Assistant solicitors:	2
Other fee-earners:	10

Principal Areas of Work:

Commercial Property: (*Contact Partner:* Tony Foot). The practice advises on the full range of company law, including business start-up, acquisition and disposal. An active department has specialists in housing association work, nursing homes, residential property, petrol service stations and the licensing trade.

Domestic Conveyancing: (*Contact Partner:* Andrew Matthias). All types of domestic conveyancing are undertaken. Quotations are provided when required and the firm maintains close links with other professionals, including surveyors and architects.

Litigation: (*Contact Partner:* Anthony Druce). Litigation work includes general commercial disputes, employment law, contentious family/matrimonial work, personal injury and medical negligence cases. The firm has a legal aid franchise for personal injury and family work.

Private Client: (*Contact Partner:* Robert Watson). The department undertakes all aspects of private client work, including wills, trusts, probate, independent financial advice and estate administration.

Other Offices: The firm has a branch office in Shoreham-by-Sea.

FLADGATE FIELDER

HERON PLACE, 3 GEORGE ST, LONDON, W1H 6AD
Tel: (0171) 486 9231 **Fax:** (0171) 935 7358 **DX:** 9057 WEST END

The Firm: Fladgate Fielder is one of the leading business law practices in the West End of London with a pedigree that can be traced back over 200 years. The firm offers legal advice of the highest quality in a non-bureaucratic environment; its clients include UK, Continental European, North American and Israeli listed companies and institutions, major private companies and entrepreneurs.

Pivotal to the firm's success are the following factors; namely its standard of excellence in client service, the calibre of its expertise, its innovative and commercial approach to the solution of problems and the combination of efficiency and cost effectiveness to reach the optimum result.

Principal Areas of Work:

Corporate Listings and flotations, AIM quotations, mergers and acquisitions, venture capital, MBOs, UK and cross border corporate and commercial transactions, employment, immigration, computer and intellectual property law, banking, partnership law and company secretarial work.

Property: Acquisition and disposal, funding, construction and development, investment, secured lending, landlord and tenant, housing associations, joint ventures, portfolio management, residential estate conveyancing, town and country planning, environmental issues, and enterprise zone development.

Litigation: General commercial litigation, professional negligence, asset recovery, corporate recovery, landlord and tenant, intellectual property, libel, matrimonial, construction disputes, building and product liability, and insurance litigation.

Tax: All aspects of taxation including corporate and business taxes as well as off-shore and international aspects, personal tax planning, wills, probate, charities and land estate matters.

Foreign connections: Fladgate Fielder has an expanding international dimension based on multi-lingual lawyers working in London. The firm has Anglo American, German, Israeli and French Desks and is able to conduct business in German, French and Hebrew.

Senior partner:	Howard Keen
Chairman:	Paul Leese
Number of partners:	30
Assistant solicitors:	21
Other fee-earners:	15

WORKLOADS	
Property	39%
Corporate/commercial	31%
Litigation	23%
Tax	7%

CONTACTS	
Anglo-American	Nicolas Greenstone
Anglo-French	Nicolas Greenstone
Anglo-German	Andrew Kaufman
Anglo-Israeli	Avram Kelman
Commercial Contracts	Charles Boundy
Corporate	Nicolas Greenstone
Employment	Jessica Learmond-Criqui
Immigration	Jessica Learmond-Criqui
Libel	Simon Ekins
Litigation	Paul Leese
Property	Allen Cohen
Tax	Andrew McKenzie
Town Planning	Daniel Drukarz

FLETCHERS Scarborough House, 30-32 Bridlesmith Gate, Nottingham, NG1 2GQ *Tel:* (0115) 959 9550 *Fax:* (0115) 959 9597

FLINT, BISHOP & BARNETT Royal Oak House, Market Place, Derby, DE1 2EA *Tel:* (01332) 340211 *Fax:* (01332) 347107 *DX:* 11504 *Ptnrs:* 19 *Asst solrs:* 12 *Other fee-earners:* 8

STEPHENSON FLINT & HOLMES Bank House, 287/289 Chapel Street, Salford, M3 6BX *Tel:* (0161) 834 9214 *Fax:* (0161) 833 0647 *DX:* 14373 Manchester 1 *Ptnrs:* 5 *Asst solrs:* 2

FLYNN & MCGETTRICK 24-26 Arthur Street, Belfast, BT1 3EF *Tel:* (01232) 244212 *Fax:* (01232) 236490 *Ptnrs:* 3 *Asst solrs:* 3

FOLLETT STOCK Malpas Road, Truro, TR1 1QH *Tel:* (01872) 241700 *Fax:* (01872) 225052 *DX:* 81225 Truro *Ptnrs:* 3 *Asst solrs:* 1

FOOT & BOWDEN

FOOT & BOWDEN BUILDING, 21 DERRY'S CROSS, PLYMOUTH, PL1 2SW
Tel: (01752) 675000 **Fax:** (01752) 671802 **DX:** 118102 PLYMOUTH 2 **Email:** E-MAIL@FOOT-BOWDEN.CO.UK
Internet: WWW.FOOT-BOWDEN.CO.UK

PYNES HILL, RYDON LANE, EXETER, EX2 5AZ
Tel: (01392) 203980 **Fax:** (01392) 203981 **Email:** E-MAIL@FOOT-BOWDEN.CO.UK

The Firm: Foot & Bowden was founded in 1908 and has well established national and international links with other law firms. It is staffed with a number of lawyers from major international law firms and prides itself on the quality and speed of service provided to clients. A London presence and two regional offices, combined with a growing national and international client base, enables the firm to provide a first class service at reduced cost. Fees, which are agreed with clients, are structured to be fair and flexible so as to give clients full value for money.

Main Areas of Work:

Company/Commercial/Commercial Property: The firm's work in this area has increased and new partners have been recruited to reflect the larger workload.

Admiralty: The firm handles a broad range of shipping work, including charterparty, bill of lading, marine insurance claims, ship construction and finance, casualties, commodities and offshore energy matters.

Media and defamation work: Has expanded in line with client demand and the firm now has a recognised national strength in this department, particularly as the industry is undergoing a greater change than has been apparent for many decades. Similarly, the firm's employment department is expanding.

Banking: Is also a recognised specialist area of work that has grown during the course of the last 5 years, (primarily as a result of client demand), and its department is headed by a partner with between 3 and 4 assistants.

ADR: Whenever possible the firm uses ADR or arbitration to settle disputes to save costs, time, damaged relationships and resources.

Private Client and Advocacy: Family work – with an emphasis on the needs of children – is a recognised strength of the firm.

Nature of Clientele: Includes British Airways, Northcliffe Newspapers, Lloyds Bank Plc, Wrigley's, British Gas, P&I Clubs, major insurers (e.g. Eagle Star and Commercial Union).

Managing partner:	Jane Lister
Senior partner:	William Jones
Number of partners:	21
Assistant solicitors:	18
Other fee-earners:	19

WORKLOADS	
Commercial	60%
Private client	40%

CONTACTS	
Advocacy	Roger Page, Plymouth
Banking	Robin Brown, Plymouth
Commercial Litigation	Patrick Power, Plymouth
Commercial Property	Cindy Rai, Plymouth
Company/Commercial	Simon Gregory, Exeter
Company/Commercial	Mark Lewis, Plymouth
Employment	Jon Loney, Plymouth
Environment	Mike Horwood, Plymouth
Family	Margaret Bonner, Plymouth
Insurance	Charles Hattersley, Plymouth
Media	Tony Jaffa, Plymouth
Personal Injury	Philip Carpannini, Plymouth
Planning	Sebastian Head/William Jones, Plymouth
Private Client	Robert Dennerly, Plymouth
Shipping/Ship Const/Maritime	Charles Hattersley, Plymouth
Tax Planning	Tim Emerson, Plymouth

FORBES & PARTNERS

RUTHERFORD HOUSE, 4 WELLINGTON STREET, ST. JOHNS, BLACKBURN, BB1 8DD
Tel: (01254) 54374 **Fax:** (01254) 52347 **DX:** 17952

The Firm: Established over 100 years ago, Forbes & Partners is a general practice with a mixed commercial and private client base. A substantial amount of legal aid work is undertaken.

Principal Areas of Work: The practice handles a wide variety of work, including company/commercial, agriculture, civil and commercial litigation, debt recovery, employment, criminal prosecutions, family and matrimonial work, housing, immigration, licensing, wills, probate and trusts, and financial services.

Other Offices: Blackburn (3), Accrington (2), Clitheroe, Preston and Chorley.

Senior partner:	Peter Scholes
Number of partners:	16
Assistant solicitors:	41
Other fee-earners:	30

WORKLOADS	
Company and commercial	30%
Insurance litigation	30%
Crime	20%
Private client	20%

FORD SIMEY DAW ROBERTS 8 Cathedral Close, Exeter, EX1 1EW *Tel:* (01392) 274126 *Fax:* (01392) 410933 *DX:* 8316 Exeter *Ptnrs:* 17 *Asst solrs:* 9 *Other fee-earners:* 9

FORD & WARREN

WESTGATE POINT, WESTGATE, LEEDS, LS1 2AX
Tel: (0113) 243 6601 **Fax:** (0113) 242 0905 **DX:** 706968 LEEDS

The Firm: Ford & Warren is a major commercial firm in the North of England. The size and strength of the firm enables expert teams of lawyers to be put together helping clients achieve their business objectives.

Senior partner:	Keith Hearn
Number of partners:	12
Assistant solicitors:	29
Other fee-earners:	31

Organisationally it has four departments.

Business Law Department: The business law department provides a full range of management advice to employers. The Managing Partner, Keith Hearn, is in this department as Head of Employment Law along with Peter Reeve, Head of Corporate. The employment team deal with issues right across the board from Tribunal claims, fraudulent Directors, trade union disputes and injunctions.

Corporate law encompasses mergers, acquisitions, MBO's, MBI's and commercial contracts along with intellectual property issues.

Commercial Law Department: Provides a full range of contentious and non-contentious services. From property litigation, planning and environment and contruction through to transport public inquiries. This department handles major commercial litigation in close liaison with the Business Law Department. Head of Department, Stephen Kirkbright and Partner Gary Hodgson have enormous expertise in transportation issues. Jeremy Rowland deals with insolvency issues and Joanne McKenzie the debt recovery side of things. Ted Brown takes care of education and charities; Peter McWilliams handles brewery and licensing issues. Paul Anderson handles commercial property, Mark Lawson deals with construction issues and Chris Charlesworth commercial litigation and professional negligence issues.

Claims Department: Blaise Smith and Nick Collins run strong teams acting for major insurance companies through the country. Litigation includes employers liability, road traffic, fire and insurance fraud claims. As well as the defendant claims team, the department has a plaintiff team who have unrivalled expertise in high profile multi-plaintiff claims, including the Tenerife air crash, Bradford stadium fire, Zeebrugge ferry sinking and the Hillsborough stadium disaster. Our medical negligence team goes from strength to strength.

Private Client Department: This department caters for all the needs of the private client from matrimonial law to estate planning. David Wightman has a long established reputaion acting for major land owners and heritage property. Nigel Dixon deals with probate and trust issues, John Robson residential conveyancing and relocation and Jo McConville handles matrimonial issues.

FOREMAN LAWS 25 Bancroft, Hitchin, SG5 1JW **Tel:** (01462) 458711 **Fax:** (01462) 459242 **DX:** 7102 Hitchin **Email:** lawyers@foremanlaws.co.uk **Ptnrs:** 8 **Asst solrs:** 5 **Other fee-earners:** 3 **Contact:** Mr Martin J. Foreman *Strong commercial, property development and construction base, alongside full range of private client services. Well-developed use of IT.*

WORKLOADS			
Company	25%	Commercial Property	20%
Civil Litigation	15%	Probate & Trusts	15%
Residential	15%	Family	10%

FORSTERS 67/68 Grosvenor Street, London, W1X 9DB **Tel:** (0171) 863 8333 **Fax:** (0171) 863 8444 **DX:** DX: 82 988 **Email:** mail@forsters.co.uk **Ptnrs:** 12 **Other fee-earners:** 58 *Twelve partners of Cholmeley Bischoff, including the entire property and private client departments, partners in corporate, media and litigation, and four consultants, have set up a new independent practice, Forsters.*

Managing Partner:	Paul Roberts
Senior Partner:	David Willis

FORSYTE SAUNDERS KERMAN

79 NEW CAVENDISH ST, LONDON, W1M 8AQ
Tel: (0171) 637 8566 **Fax:** (0171) 436 6088 **DX:** 99 LN.

Senior Partner:	Paul Di Biase
Chief Executive:	Jonathan Freedman
Number of partners:	21
Assistant solicitors:	12
Other fee-earners:	12

WORKLOADS	
Commercial property	58%
Litigation	21%
Company/ commercial	13%
Private client	8%

CONTACTS	
Commercial property	Catherine Diggle
Company/ commercial	Peter Carter
Litigation	Howard Zetter
Private client	Michael Lewis

The Firm: Forsyte Saunders Kerman is an independent medium-sized firm, whose spread and depth of commercial work reflects its effective approach and commitment. This is a commitment to understanding and achieving clients' business objectives. This is reflected in the quality of the firm's clients which would be the envy of many larger firms. It is large enough to handle substantial and sophisticated projects, yet small enough to encourage individual development. It makes the same commitment to its training programme and its lawyers. Forsyte Saunders Kerman is particularly highly regarded for its top quality commercial property and corporate work; it has a substantial High Court litigation practice (including a specialist property litigation team) and an active private client department. The firm is managed on truly corporate lines with a Board headed by a Chairman and a Chief Executive.

Principal Areas of Work:

Property: *(Contact: Catherine Diggle. 10 Partners).* The department handles the whole range of property transactions in the private and public sectors including city centre and other commercial developments, planning, investment acquisitions and disposals, owner/occupier sales and purchases, retail property transactions and property transactions for the leisure industry. The department includes a unit which specialises in acting for petrol station operators and another unit which specialises in all property transactions required by residential developers and housebuilders.

Company and Commercial: *(Contact: Peter Carter. 4 Partners).* The department's activities encompass the full range of corporate and commercial work. Clients include quoted and unquoted companies, partnerships and sole proprietors with a special emphasis on entrepreneurial and management-owned businesses. Its main areas of work are corporate finance including acquisitions and disposals of both public and private companies, management buy-outs and buy-ins and all forms of commercial work including intellectual property, media-related agreements, joint ventures and competition. It also has expertise in consumer credit, asset finance and niche banking, building society, security and financial services work.

Litigation: *(Contact: Howard Zetter. 5 Partners).* The department is experienced in giving a swift practical service to the business and private client in a way which is sensitive to clients' needs and priorities. It handles a wide range of commercial and civil litigation and is particularly well-known for: property-related disputes, construction actions and arbitrations, inter company and partnership disputes, employment and family work.

Private Client: *(Contact: Michael Lewis. 2 Partners).* The department advises individuals, trusts and executors in business, professional, or public life including overseas nationals whose United Kingdom interests need to be protected or promoted. It provides a wide range of services relating to tax, wills and trusts and is particularly noted for tax planning and asset protection for wealthy individuals and business proprietors.

FOSTER BAXTER COOKSEY

6-10 GEORGE STREET, SNOW HILL, WOLVERHAMPTON, WV2 4DN
Tel: (01902) 311711 **Fax:** (01902) 311102 **DX:** 702433 WOLVERHAMPTON 5

Managing partner:	Graham Sower
Senior partner:	Peter Lawley
Number of partners:	15
Assistant solicitors:	8
Other fee-earners:	19

CONTACTS	
Commercial property	Simon Bowdler
Corporate services	James Hayes
Employment	Graham Sower
Insolvency	Robert Brown
Legal audits	Robert Brown
Litigation	Nigel Sellar
Private client	Ian Fallon

The Firm: Formed by the merger of four well-established Midlands firms, Foster Baxter Cooksey now has over one hundred staff and serves a broad spectrum of private and business clients. The firm has particular expertise in corporate work, commercial property, intellectual property and civil litigation.

Specialist areas: Alternative Dispute Resolution; Building Societies; Corporate Finance; Insolvency; Partnership.

Other Offices: Telford and Willenhall.

Recruitment & Training: The firm recruits three trainee solicitors (with at least a 2.1 degree) each year. Applicants should write to Kim Carr, Training Partner, with a full CV.

FOSTERS 60 London Street, Norwich, NR2 1JY *Tel:* (01603) 620508 *Fax:* (01603) 624090 *DX:* 5225 Norwich-1 *Ptnrs:* 10 *Asst solrs:* 13 *Other fee-earners:* 10

FOX & GIBBONS

2 OLD BURLINGTON STREET, LONDON, W1X 2QA
Tel: (0171) 439 8271 **Fax:** (0171) 468 1297 **DX:** 37244 PICCADILLY 1 **Email:** LAW@FOX-AND-GIBBONS.COM
Internet: HTTP://WWW.FOX-AND-GIBBONS.COM

The Firm: Established in 1959, Fox & Gibbons is the longest established British law firm in the Middle East and has the largest number of offices there.

Principal Areas of Work:

Company/Commercial/Major Projects: (*Contact:* Paul Sheridan). All types of company/commercial law and major projects such as energy, infrastructure and water projects and privatisations; agency, distribution and franchise agreements, charities, company formations, joint ventures and mergers and acquisitions including venture capital buy-ins, buy-outs, etc., competition law, computers and information technology, EC law through its own office and through its membership of EuroAdvocaten (a formal group of European lawyers), estate planning – wills and probate, financial services, food law, immigration, intellectual property, licensing, pensions, public companies and offerings, public international law (treaties and international organisations) and trade – domestic and international.

Banking and Corporate Finance: (*Contact:* Robert Sprawson). *Work includes:* trade finance, letters of credit, bills of exchange, syndicated loans, sub-participations, project financing, asset financing, secured lending, fund raising, debt and equity funding and corporate financial reconstructions, general banking matters, formation of branches and subsidiaries of financial institutions.

Property and Construction Finance: (*Contact:* Madeleine Smallwood). The department has particular expertise in commercial and residential developments including hotel and leisure developments (including gaming establishments), office and retail centres for UK-based and international clients and for the Health Sector, Public Utilities and Statutory Undertakings. In addition, it has been involved in the acquisition and management of many substantial country and sporting estates, agricultural and farming properties, and stud-farming and racing establishments. Construction work includes projects in the UK and abroad acting for major domestic and international contractors, employers and professionals and negotiating all forms of construction related documentation.

Commercial Litigation/Employment Law: (*Contact:* Rachel Harrap). Services offered include resolution of contentious commercial disputes in the Courts and Tribunals, in commercial arbitrations, both UK-based and international, and through alternative dispute resolution including resolution of cross-border transactions, shipping disputes, construction and engineering disputes, insolvency, banking claims and product liability disputes. Employment Law services include transfer of undertakings, contracts of employment, ESOPs, senior executive packages on appointment and termination, boardroom disputes, restraint of trade, enforcement of restrictive covenants, confidentiality and ancillary injunctive relief, due diligence on employment warranties on mergers and acquisitions, discrimination, unfair dismissal, redundancy and compromise agreements.

Taxation: (*Contact:* Desmond Parte). *Work includes:* tax planning in corporate structuring and re-structuring, international tax planning, trusts, wills and inheritance tax planning, VAT advice, taxation issues relating to residence or domicile, tax implications of doing business in the UK, tax planning for the bloodstock industry, establishment and administration of offshore companies and trusts.

Foreign connections: Several languages spoken by members of the firm, many of whom have worked abroad. The five offices in Dubai, Abu Dhabi, Oman, Cairo and Turkey make it the largest firm in the Middle East of all London law firms. In addition, it is the only London law firm with its own office in Gibraltar. The firm is a member of EuroAdvocaten, a formal grouping of lawyers, which has fellow members in Germany, Holland, France, Greece, Italy, Belgium, Luxembourg, Ireland, Spain, Portugal, Norway, Denmark and Austria. The firm also has associated offices in Kuwait, Lebanon, Yemen, Saudi Arabia and India.

Managing partner:	Robert Sprawson
Senior partner:	Robert Gibbons
Number of partners:	7
Assistant solicitors:	6
Other fee-earners:	10
Internationally	
Number of partners:	4
Assistant solicitors:	26
Other fee-earners:	7

WORKLOADS	
Company/Commercial	35%
Property and Construction	30%
Commercial Litigation and Employment	15%
Banking/Corporate Finance	10%
Taxation	10%

CONTACTS	
Banking & Corporate Finance	R Sprawson
Commercial Litigation & Employment	R Harrap
Company/Commercial	P Sheridan
Property and Construction	M Smallwood
Taxation	D Parte

FOX WILLIAMS

CITY GATE HOUSE, 39-45 FINSBURY SQUARE, LONDON, EC2A 1UU
Tel: (0171) 628 2000 **Fax:** (0171) 628 2100 **DX:** 33873 FINSBURY SQ. **Email:** MAIL@FOXWILLIAMS.CO.UK

The Firm: Fox Williams provides the highest quality corporate and commercial legal services coupled with a commitment by the partners to their clients' businesses. Since its formation, the firm's energetic approach and rapid, effective, responsive service have resulted in steady growth in both business and reputation. Fox Williams is particularly well-known for its mergers and acquisitions, employment law and partnership work.

Principal Areas of Work:

Corporate: (*Contact Partner:* Paul Osborne). The firm undertakes a wide range of international and domestic transactional and corporate finance work including public company takeovers and mergers, acquisitions and disposals of private companies and businesses, capital raising transactions, flotations, MBOs and venture capital. General corporate work includes business start-ups, restructurings, film financing, banking and financial services work, insolvency and corporate rescue and tax.

Commercial: (*Contact Partner:* Stephen Sidkin). The businesses of UK and international clients benefit from positive and informed commercial advice on distribution and agency agreements, franchising, terms of trading, product liability, data protection legislation and all aspects of the protection and exploitation of intellectual property rights, licensing of technology, computer hardware and software agreements, and UK and EC competition law.

Employment: (*Contact Partner:* Mark Watson). Fox Williams is well-known for its expertise in calculating and negotiating payments on termination of employment. Employment lawyers deal with every aspect of employment from drafting service agreements to enforcing restrictive arrangements. Advice is given on laws prohibiting discrimination on the grounds of sex, race and disability.

Property: (*Contact Partner:* Bryan Emden). Work undertaken includes dealing with substantial property portfolios involving auctions, sales and leasebacks of retail, office and industrial premises; advising on environmental and planning matters, secured lending, VAT and estate management. Development companies are also advised on site purchase and sale schemes as well as associated joint venture projects.

Litigation: (*Contact Partner:* Lindsay Hill). A strong team handles a broad range of substantial UK and international litigation and arbitration and is committed to achieving fast and commercially effective solutions. It has specialist expertise in resolving intellectual property and financial services issues. Its work also involves solving disputes relating to trading, shareholder and joint venture arrangements.

Other Areas of Work: Fox Williams' partnership group is well-known for its work for both firms and individual partners in a variety of professions. In addition the firm has considerable experience in advising on legal issues arising from on-line commerce and the use of the Internet.

Nature of Clientele: Clients range from multinational corporations and major public companies to family businesses and individual entrepreneurs. Fox Williams acts for banks and other financial institutions, regulatory authorities, accountants and other professionals, including overseas lawyers.

Senior partner:	Ronnie Fox
Number of partners:	13
Assistant solicitors:	20
Other fee-earners:	6

WORKLOADS	
Employment	32%
Corporate	31%
Litigation	16%
Commercial	12%
Property	9%

CONTACTS	
Commercial	Stephen Sidkin
Commercial Property	Bryan Emden
Corporate & Financial Services	Tina Williams
Corporate Rescue & Insolvency	Robin Tutty
Corporate Tax	Vishvas Kanji
Discrim & Business Immig	Jane Mann
Employment	Mark Watson
IT and Internet Law	Nigel Miller
Litigation: Comm & Fin Services	Lindsay Hill
Litigation: Comm & Intell Prop	Simon Taylor
M&A and Corporate Finance	Paul Osborne
Partnership	Ronnie Fox

FOY & CO

PO BOX 111, 63 HALLGATE, DONCASTER, DN1 3DQ
Tel: (01302) 327136 **Fax:** (01302) 367656 **DX:** 12563 DONCASTER

CHURCH STEPS, ALL SAINTS SQUARE, ROTHERHAM, S60 1QD
Tel: (01709) 375561 **Fax:** (01709) 828479 **DX:** 12601 ROTHERHAM

15 PEAKS MOUNT, CRYSTAL PEAKS, SHEFFIELD, S20 7HZ
Tel: (0114) 251 1702 **Fax:** (0114) 251 1750 **DX:** 717230 SHEFFIELD 28

102 BRIDGE STREET, WORKSOP, S80 1HZ
Tel: (01909) 473560 **Fax:** (01909) 482760 **DX:** 12207 WORKSOP

The Firm: Established Legal Practice offering a wide range of domestic and commercial services including conveyancing, litigation, matrimonial and family, criminal and motoring, Wills and Probate, all commercial matters.

Managing partner:	Paul Evans
Senior partner:	Stephen J. Paramore
Number of partners:	7
Assistant solicitors:	8
Other fee-earners:	15

FRANCES ANDERSON Unit 608b, The Big Peg, The Jewellery Quarter, 120 Vyse Street, Birmjngham, B18 6NF *Tel:* (0121) 693 3505 *Fax:* (0121) 753 3515 *Ptnrs:* 1

FRANCIS HANNA & CO Central Chambers, 75-77 May Street, Belfast, BT1 3JL *Tel:* (01232) 243901 *Fax:* (01232) 244215 *DX:* 473NR Belfast *Ptnrs:* 3 *Asst solrs:* 9 *Other fee-earners:* 2

FRANCIS J IRVINE & CO 86 Great Victoria Street, Belfast, BT2 7BD *Tel:* (01232) 246451 *Fax:* (01232) 331735 *Ptnrs:* 2 *Asst solrs:* 1 *Other fee-earners:* 1

FRANK & CAFFIN

PRINCES HOUSE, PRINCES STREET, TRURO, TR1 2EY
Tel: (01872) 273077 **Fax:** (01872) 242458 **DX:** 81201 TRURO

The Firm: Frank & Caffin is a well-established firm which was founded over a hundred years ago. The firm has a legal aid franchise.

Principal Areas of Work:

Company/ Commercial: (*Contact Partner:* B. Henderson Smith). The department advises on company acquisitions, partnership formations, property transactions and licensing. Further expertise is offered in matters relating to employment law and agriculture.

Litigation: (*Contact Partner:* M. Chanter). The firm undertakes a broad range of litigation, including insurance company work, contractual disputes, professional negligence, property litigation, landlord and tenant problems and family matters.

Private Client: (*Contact Partner:* R.A. Bland). A comprehensive service is offered to the private individual. This includes conveyancing independent financial advice, wills, probate and trusts.

Senior partner:	T.H. Rowse
Number of partners:	7
Assistant solicitors:	2
Other fee-earners:	5

WORKLOADS	
Civil litigation	37%
Conveyancing/ private client	36%
Company commercial	15%
Matrimonial	10%

FRANKS, CHARLESLY & CO Hulton House, 161/166 Fleet Street, London, EC4A 2DY *Tel:* (0171) 353 1588 *Fax:* (0171) 583 0647 *DX:* 152 Chancery Lane *Ptnrs:* 13 *Asst solrs:* 4 *Other fee-earners:* 8

FREEMANS 7 St Mary's Place, Newcastle-upon-Tyne, NE1 7PG *Tel:* (0191) 222 1030 *Fax:* (0191) 222 1819 *DX:* 61100 Newcastle-upon-Tyne

FREETH CARTWRIGHT HUNT DICKINS

WILLOUGHBY HOUSE, 20 LOW PAVEMENT, NOTTINGHAM, NG1 7EA
Tel: (0115) 936 9369 **Fax:** (0115) 936 9370 **DX:** 10039 NOTTINGHAM **Email:** POSTMASTER@FREETHCARTWRIGHT.CO.UK

NORMAN HOUSE, FRIARGATE, DERBY, DE1 1NU
Tel: (01332) 361000 **Fax:** (01332) 207177

Freeth Cartwright Hunt Dickins is a major Midlands Practice offering services to both commercial and private client across the entire legal spectrum. Although based in Nottingham, Derby and Leicester, the Firm has a wide range of clients throughout the UK and many of its clients have strong international connections.

The Firm: Freeth Cartwright Hunt Dickins has grown rapidly in recent years and now ranks as one of the leading East Midlands' firms offering comprehensive legal services in the public and private sectors.

Whilst aiming to provide the very best service possible in all areas, the Firm also prides itself on its wish and ability to understand the businesses of its clients and to demonstrate to them that with a properly developed relationship it can significantly add value. We believe that major legal practices should be in "partnership" with their clients, not merely reacting to clients' specific instructions and dealing with problems after they have arisen. We aim to combine first-class legal expertise with a thorough knowledge of our clients' business. All our lawyers are encouraged and trained to be both practical and commercial in their approach to the provision of legal services.

Types of work undertaken: The Firm's commercial practice covers a broad spectrum of corporate, commercial and financial work from small day to day transactions to significant mergers and acquisitions, some with an international content.

Our corporate and commercial team provides the full range of services specialising in MBOs, MBIs, the re-organisation and financing of businesses, mergers, acquisitions and joint ventures. The Firm also has a significant capability in specialist areas including pensions, competition, EC law, corporate tax and sport and entertainment law. We have a specialist intellectual property unit dealing with both contentious and non-contentious work including a comprehensive international trademark registration service and significant work in the telecommunications and IT sectors. Two partners are exclusively involved in the area of corporate crime, advising companies and their directors following prosecution by statutory and public authorities and dealing with all aspects of corporate fraud.

With one of the largest commercial property departments in the Midlands, the Firm acts for developers of industrial, residential and commercial property, institutional lenders and investors, privatised utilities, housing associations and commercial landlords and tenants. We have dedicated units covering planning, environment issues and construction.

The emphasis in Dispute Resolution is on risk management and risk avoidance. We have specialist groups in employment, landlord and tenant, construction litigation, professional negligence and insurance. The Firm also undertakes significant insolvency, recovery and litigation work for major banks and accountants. We act for Lloyds underwriters, insurers and indemnity institutions. The Firm has particular expertise in medical negligence and product liability under the leadership of Paul Balen who enjoys an established national reputation in the field. The group has significant experience in co-ordinating high profile group actions, both in the UK and overseas.

Emphasising the Firm's range of services, the private client units provide expertise in family and childcare matters, housing litigation, immigration, personal injury, residential conveyancing and wills and probate.

The Firm plans to continue growth through organic development, by pursuing pro-active strategic and marketing policies and by investing in high calibre people, from trainee solicitors to partners.

Senior Partner:	Ian Payne
Chief Executive:	Colin Flanagan
Number of partners:	45
Assistant solicitors:	59
Other fee-earners:	64

WORKLOADS	
Dispute Resolution	31%
Commercial property	26%
Private Client	23%
Corporate and commercial services	20%

CONTACTS	
Administrative/Public Law	Richard Beverley
Banking	Paul Thorogood
Charities	Nigel Cullen
Company/Commercial	Ian Worthington
Competition	Philip Raven
Construction	Guy Berwick
Corporate Crime	Michael Thurston
Corporate Finance	Karl Jansen
Employment	David Potter
Family	Hugh Young
Housing Associations	Gary Reynolds
Immigration	Sue Miles
Information Technology	Andrew Margiotta-Hills
Insolvency	Graham Greenfield
Intellectual Propety	Helen Driscoll
Licensing	Malcolm Radcliffe
Litigation (Commercial)	Richard Bullock
Litigation (Property)	Martin Lee
Pensions	John Heaphy
Personal Injury	Jane Goulding
Planning	Ian Tempest
Private Client	Nigel Cullen
Product Liability	Paul Balen
Professional Negligence	Richard Beverley
Property (Commercial)	George Taylor
Sports	Simon Taylor

FRERE CHOLMELEY BISCHOFF 4 John Carpenter Street, London, EC4Y 0NH **Tel:** (0171) 615 8000 **Fax:** (0171) 615 8080 **DX:** 140 London Chancery Lane WC2 **Email:** mail@freres.com **Ptnrs:** 42 **Asst solrs:** 58 **Other fee-earners:** 46 **Contact:** Teresa Harman
On 1 August 1998 Frere Cholmeley Bischoff and Eversheds, one of the UK's largest national law firms, merged their City practices. 12 Freres partners have established Forsters, an independent practice. See Eversheds and Forsters for further information.

FRESHFIELDS

65 FLEET STREET, LONDON, EC4Y 1HS
Tel: (0171) 936 4000 **Fax:** (0171) 832 7001 **DX:** 23 **Email:** EMAIL@FRESHFIELDS.COM **Internet:** HTTP://WWW.FRESHFIELDS.COM

Freshfields is a major international law firm and market leader in international transactions with over 1000 lawyers around the world. It provides full legal services to national and international corporations, financial insititutions and governments through offices in Europe, Asia and New York. This service has been strengthened in 1998 by its strategic alliance with the leading German law firm, Deringer Tessin Herrmann & Sedemund. Together they are able to offer clients an international network operating out of 19 offices in 14 countries.

In the European Union the two firms provide comprehensive coverage in all the major European jurisdictions as well as having one of the largest and most highly regarded European law practices in Brussels.

In Asia the firm's network of offices allows it to work effectively throughout the region and it has one of the strongest local presences of any international law firm. In China alone it has advised on more than 200 joint ventures and other investments during the last 18 months.

International contacts:

Freshfields:
Bangkok – James Lawden (+662 679 6123)
Barcelona – Toni Valverde (+349 3 301 9758)
Beijing – Douglas Markel (+8610 6410 6338)
Hanoi – Tony Foster (+844 8247 422)
Ho Chi Minh City – Mark Fraser (+848 8226 680)
Hong Kong – Ruth Markland (+852 2846 3400)
Madrid – John Byrne (+349 1 319 1024)
Milan – Laurie McFadden/Giovanni Lega (+39 2 625 301)
New York – Ailsa Urwin (+1 212 765 8685)
Paris – James Vaudoyer (+33 1 44 56 44 56)
Rome – Neil Falconer (+39 6 844 681)
Singapore – Roger Dyer (+65 535 6211)
Tokyo – Charles Stevens (+81 3 3584 8500)

Freshfields Deringer (joint offices):
Brussels – John Davies (+32 2 230 0920)
Moscow – Jacky Baudon (+785 0085 Codes: +7501 or +7095)

Deringer Tessin Herrmann & Sedemund:
Berlin – Helmut Bergmann (+49 30 20 17 44 0)
Cologne – Ludwig Leyendecker/Joachim Pfeffer (+49 2 21 20 50 70)
Frankfurt – Karsten Müller-Eising (+49 69 170 990)

Senior Partner:	Anthony Salz
Chief Executive:	Alan Peck
Managing Partner:	Ian Terry
Managing Partner (Asia):	Ruth Markland
Number of partners:	132
Assistant solicitors:	384
Other fee-earners:	175

CONTACTS	
Arbitration	Nigel Rawding
Asset finance	Tim Lintott
Banking	Simon Hall
Commercial property	Geoff Le Pard
Communications & media	Rachel Brandenburger
Construction & engineering	Sally Roe
Corporate	Gavin Darlington
Employment, pensions & benefits	Peter Jeffcote
Energy	Jon Rees
Environment	Paul Bowden
EU/Competition	Nick Spearing
Financial services	Guy Morton
Insolvency	Peter Bloxham
Insurance	Philip Richards
Intellectual property	Hugh Stubbs
International tax	Roger Berner
Investment funds	Anthony McWhirter
Joint ventures	Ian Hewitt
Litigation	Josanne Rickard
Mergers & acquisitions	Barry O'Brien
Project finance	Kent Rowey
Securities	Stephen Revell
Tax	Richard Ballard

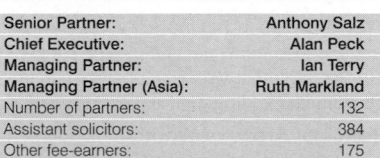

FURLEY PAGE FIELDING & BARTON

39 ST. MARGARET'S STREET, CANTERBURY, CT1 2TX
Tel: (01227) 763939 **Fax:** (01227) 762829 **DX:** 5301 CANTERBURY

The Firm: One of the largest practices in East Kent, tracing its roots back to 1725. Although old established, the firm is committed to modern business practice. Lawyers are organised in specialist groups and offer a level of service that competes at a regional level. The firm is associated with the French commercial law firm, ADES in Lille.

Principal Areas of Work include:

Commercial: The firm acts for a number of national and international PLCs, insurers, and a wide range of smaller private companies. Work includes Commercial Property, Franchising, Distribution, Environmental and Commercial Contracts. The firm also handles work for charitable and educational institutions. Agriculture has also been a long standing area of practice.

Litigation: The Department has groups specialising in Personal Injury (including Medical Negligence), Commercial and Building, Landlord & Tenant, Employment and Matrimonial. Agency work is regularly undertaken.

Debt Recovery: A specialist computer supported service operating Debt Recovery at fixed rates.

Private Client: Comprehensive Tax Planning, Domestic Conveyancing, Probate, Court of Protection and Wills.

Financial Services: An in-house department offering Investment, Life Assurance, Pensions and other financial advice. Also at Whitstable: 01227 274241.

Senior partner:	V.E. Barton
Number of partners:	16
Assistant solicitors:	6
Other fee-earners:	20

WORKLOADS	
Litigation	38%
Trust and estates	25%
Commercial	20%
Residential Conveyancing	13%
Financial services	1%

CONTACTS	
Company/commercial	C B Wacher
Employment	J S Gauton
Litigation	P W Hawkes
Private Client	H M Barrett

FYFE IRELAND WS

ORCHARD BRAE HOUSE, 30 QUEENSFERRY ROAD, EDINBURGH, EH4 2HG
Tel: (0131) 343 2500 **Fax:** (0131) 343 3166 **DX:** ED 23 **Email:** MAIL@FYFEIRELAND.COM **Internet:** WWW.FYFEIRELAND.COM

The Firm: Fyfe Ireland is a dynamic law firm providing a comprehensive range of legal services to commercial and private clients. It is particularly well regarded in the commercial property field but with a solid corporate practice and an expanding litigation presence covering commercial litigation and increasingly reparation.

Principal Areas of Work:
Commercial Property: All aspects of work are undertaken both on behalf of tenants, landlords, institutions and lenders. There is particular experience of cross-border security transactions.

Private Client: The normal range of private client service is undertaken with particular strengths in inheritance tax planning, trusts and succession.

Corporate: A very wide base of private company work is complemented by public company and investment trust expertise. There is also sound experience of intellectual property and private finance work. The department works closely with the commercial property department. Teams of lawyers are allocated to issues cross-departmentally.

Litigation: A broad base of general commercial litigation in both the Court of Session and Sheriff Courts in Scotland is provided. There is good experience in building contract disputes and following upon recruitment into the department there is a growing base of reparation and employment related work. Substantial repossession work is undertaken for lenders.

Recruitment: The firm us always keen to consider quality candidates from the UK. Any applications with an appropriate CV should be sent to Steven Kerr.

Other Office: 1 Dyers Buildings, London, EC1N 2SX *Tel:* (0171) 814 9200. *Fax:* (0171) 814 9196.

Senior partner:	Andrew Cubie
Number of partners:	12
Assistant solicitors:	30
Other fee-earners:	17

WORKLOADS	
Commercial Property	37%
Private Client	24%
Corporate	23%
Litigation	16%

CONTACTS	
Commercial Property	Steve Kerr
Corporate	Stephen Gibb
Litigation	Drew Taylor
Private Client	Greig Honeyman

FYNN & PARTNERS

70 RICHMOND HILL, BOURNEMOUTH, BH2 6JA
Tel: (01202) 551991 **Fax:** (01202) 295403 **DX:** DX 7608 BOURNEMOUTH **Email:** TRAINING@FYNNPARTNERS.CO.UK
Internet: HTTP://WWW.FYNNPARTNERS.CO.UK

The Firm: Fynn & Partners was formed in 1995 as the demerged Bournemouth office of Penningtons. It contains what was previously the environmental, licensing and planning department of Penningtons, with a national reputation, supported by a commercial property department with extensive expertise in leisure/licensed property matters. The firm generally covers all aspects of company and commercial law, with a growing private client practice.

Managing partner:	Alan Arnold
Number of partners:	6
Assistant solicitors:	4
Other fee-earners:	6

GABB & CO 32 Monk St, Abergavenny, NP7 5NW *Tel:* (01873) 852432 *Fax:* (01873) 857589 *DX:* 43752 Abergavenny *Ptnrs:* 14 *Asst solrs:* 6 *Other fee-earners:* 3

GADSBY WICKS 35/37 Moulsham Street, Chelmsford, CM2 OHJ *Tel:* (01245) 494929 *Fax:* (01245) 495347 *DX:* 89707 Chelmsford 2 *Ptnrs:* 2 *Asst solrs:* 2 *Other fee-earners:* 3

GALLEN & CO Olympic House, 142 Queen Street, Glasgow, G1 3BU *Tel:* (0141) 204 1175 *Fax:* (0141) 204 4494

GAMLINS 31-37 Russell Road, Rhyl, LL18 3DB *Tel:* (01745) 343500 *Fax:* (01745) 343616 *DX:* 17352 RHYL *Ptnrs:* 11 *Asst solrs:* 16 *Other fee-earners:* 12

GAMON ARDEN & CO Church House, 1 Hanover Street, Liverpool, L1 3DW *Tel:* (0151) 709 2222 *Fax:* (0151) 709 3095 *Ptnrs:* 2 *Other fee-earners:* 2

GARRETTS

180 STRAND, LONDON, WC2R 2NN
Tel: (0171) 344 0344 **Fax:** (0171) 438 2518 **DX:** 127 LDE

1 VICTORIA SQUARE, BIRMINGHAM, B1 1BD
Tel: (0121) 698 9000 **Fax:** (0121) 698 9050 **DX:** 13017 BIRMINGHAM 1

BETJEMAN HOUSE, 104 HILLS ROAD, CAMBRIDGE, CB2 1LH
Tel: (01223) 355977 **Fax:** (01223) 535327 **DX:** 88010 CAMBRIDGE

1 CITY SQUARE, LEEDS, LS1 2AL
Tel: (0113) 207 9000 **Fax:** (0113) 207 9001 **DX:** 26444 LEEDS PARK SQUARE

BANK HOUSE, 9 CHARLOTTE STREET, MANCHESTER, M1 4EU
Tel: (0161) 228 0707 **Fax:** (0161) 228 1926 **DX:** 14349 MANCHESTER 1

ABBOTS HOUSE, ABBEY STREET, READING, RG1 3BD
Tel: (0118) 949 0000 **Fax:** (0118) 9490049 **DX:** 54711 READING 2

The Firm: Garretts is a young and dynamic law firm which provides commercial advice to UK and foreign companies. Founded in 1993, it now has offices in London, Reading, Leeds, Manchester, Birmingham and Cambridge. Its associated firm in Scotland, Dundas and Wilson, has offices in Edinburgh and Glasgow.

Garretts is able to provide a full service to clients from each of its offices on a national and international basis. Multi-jurisdictional transactions are facilitated through its membership of the Andersen Worldwide international network of law firms. This is one of the world's fastest growing legal networks with over 1000 lawyers in over 30 countries.

As well as offering advice in all the areas expected of traditional commercial law firms (see below), Garetts aims to offer clients increased choice in the way that legal services are delivered. There is the opportunity for Garretts to work closely with colleagues at Arthur Andersen to provide integrated professional advice – but only where client needs require this. Whatever the delivery mechanism, Garretts' philosophy is to offer a practical and cost effective service of the highest quality.

Garretts has grown by attracting quality lawyers UK wide and is still recruiting. It prides itself on commitment to training and to its people. 1997 saw the arrival of Garretts' first ever graduate intake. (It intends to recruit some 35 trainee solicitors annually by the year 1999.) Garretts also operates an overseas secondment programme for newly qualifieds and above, again facilitated through member firms of the Andersen Worldwide international legal network. In addition, a programme of training on business management skills for Garretts lawyers is currently being developed in conjunction with various business schools for implementation in the near future.

Garretts aims to continue its growth strategy by ongoing investment in people, technology and information. Together with Dundas & Wilson, it currently ranks in the UK's top 20 law firms by size and fee income.

Legal services include: Banking, insurance and finance; Collective investment schemes; Commercial litigation; Corporate and commercial; Corporate recovery and insolvency; EC and competition; Human capital services (including share scheme advice, employment, employee benefits and pensions law); Intellectual Property, New media and IT law; International trade; Private client advice; Property, planning and contruction; Public sector services including advice on PFI and infrastructure projects.

Work contacts:

Banking and financial services: Peter Richards Carpenter (London), Ian Akitt (Leeds), Susan Molloy (Manchester)

Corporate and Commercial: David Bolton (London), Paul Finlan (Birmingham), Gerry Fitzsimons (Cambridge), Sean Lippell (Leeds), Steve Devlin (Manchester), Adrian Phillips (Reading)

Collective Investment Schemes: Simon Atiyah (London)

Commercial Property: Adrian Watson (Birmingham), Mike Sleath (Leeds), Dean Copley (Manchester), Debra Kent (Reading)

Construction: Raymond Joyce (Birmingham)

Human Capital Services (incl employment and share schemes): Paul McCarthy (London), Guy Lamb (Leeds), Paula Cole (Manchester), Andrew Fishleigh (Reading)

IT/IP: Andrew White (London), Richard Bonner (Leeds), Jason Austin (Manchester), Alison Harrington (Reading)

Managing partners:	Julia Chain (London)
	and Chris Campbell (regions)
Number of partners:	46
Assistant solicitors:	123

WORKLOADS	
Corporate	43%
Property/Construction	19%
Human Capital Services	15%
Litigation	9%
Intellectual Property/Info Technology	8%

CONTACTS	
Banking	Peter Richards-Carpenter
Corporate	David Bolton
Corporate finance	Simon Atiyah
EEC Law	Philip Ruttley
Employment & Benefits	Paul McCarthy
Environmental	Keith Barnett
Financial services	Peter Richards-Carpenter
Information technology	Alison Harrington
Insurance	James Greig
Intellectual property	Alison Harrington
Litigation	Andrew Fishleigh
Media/Entertainment	Alison Harrington
Pensions	Trevor Clarke
Planning	Debra Kent
Professional negligence	Andrew Fishleigh
Property	Keith Barnett

Continues overleaf

Public Sector/PFI: Nick Painter, Frank Suttie (Leeds), Greg McMahon (Manchester)

Tax: Anthony Betts (Leeds), Shabnam Qasim (Manchester)

EC and Competition: Philip Ruttley (London), Darrell Smith (Leeds), Phil McDonnell (Manchester)

Private clients: Judith Powell (London)

Litigation: Raymond Joyce (Birmingham), David Harlock (Leeds), Carolyn Jackson-Smith (Manchester), Andrew Fishleigh (Reading)

GARSTANGS 115A Chancery Lane, London, WC2A 1PP **Tel:** (0171) 242 4324 **Fax:** (0171) 242 4329 **Ptnrs:** 5 **Asst solrs:** 7 **Other fee-earners:** 12 **Contact:** Richard Cornthwaite/Paul Graham. *A radical specialist practice with substantial expertise in the fields of white-collar crime, extradition and ancillary civil and public interest litigation.*

WORKLOADS			
Criminal/ civil litigation	60%	Criminal general	30%
Company/ commercial	10%		

GATELEY WAREING

EQUITY HOUSE, 7 ROWCHESTER COURT, WHITTALL STREET, BIRMINGHAM, B4 6DD
Tel: (0121) 236 8585 **Fax:** (0121) 233 1874 **DX:** 24904 B'HAM 4

KNIGHTSBRIDGE HOUSE, LOWER BROWN STREET, LEICESTER, LE1 5NL
Tel: (0116) 255 5544 **Fax:** (0116) 255 1144 **DX:** 10829 LEICESTER

The Firm: Gateley Wareing is one of the leading independent firms of solicitors serving the needs of owner-led businesses across the Midlands. The firm's aim is to remain a medium sized company providing a specialised service to the owner-led business sector and to develop its niche areas of practice at its offices in Birmingham and Leicester.

Principal Areas of Work:

Corporate Services: Advice is given on company formations, acquisitions and disposals, mergers, management buy-outs, corporate finance, flotations, bank financing and corporate taxation. Company secretarial services are provided along with the drafting of commercial documents and advice on intellectual property matters.

Litigation: Business disputes of all types are handled including contract and partnership disputes, professional negligence, intellectual property, landlord and tenant, shareholder disputes, redundancy and unfair dismissal. The department also deals with betting, gaming and liquor licence work and provides a computerised debt collection service.

Commercial Property: The firm advises on the purchase, sale and leasing of commercial property, land acquisition for residential and commercial development, advice to landlords and tenants, planning and building contract work, mortgages and bridging finance.

Construction: The firm provides a comprehensive service to all aspects of the construction industry, which includes advising on the appropriate form of contract documentation, dealing with contractual problems and handling disputes, whether by litigation or arbitration.

Banking and Insolvency: The firm has a dedicated department which specialises in banking and insolvency law and related areas. Work includes loan facility and security documentation, recoveries and debt restructuring, advising on priority issues and compliance with regulatory requirements. Advice is given to clients on corporate strategy and directors' responsibilities, and insolvency practitioners on such matters as their appointment, the rights of creditors and the preservation and recovery of assets.

Housing Associations: The firm has a particular and established expertise in housing association projects having acted for a substantial number of housing associations for many years.

Private Client and Trusts: Clients are advised on personal tax and estate planning, will drafting and estate administration, and specialist advice is provided to a range of charitable institutions.

Family Law: The firm advises on all aspects of family law including potential or actual matrimonial break-ups, property, children, child abduction, matrimonial problems with an international aspect and inheritance and taxation issues.

Nature of Clientele: The firm has specialist expertise in providing services to owner-led businesses. Other clients include banks, housing associations, venture capitalists, property developers, professional partnerships, charitable institutions and individuals.

Recruitment & Training: Trainee solicitors are taken on yearly. Applications from non-law graduates are welcomed. A curriculum vitae should be sent to Neil Handel.

Senior partner:	Brendan McGeever
Number of partners:	13
Assistant solicitors:	27
Other fee-earners:	15

WORKLOADS	
Corporate Services	25%
Banking and Insolvency	24%
Commercial Property/Housing Associations	18%
Construction	15%
Civil Litigation	8%
Trusts and Charities	6%
Family	4%

CONTACTS	
Banking and Insolvency	
	Eugene Jordan/Brendan McGeever
Civil Litigation	Brendan McGeever/Simon Spencer
Commercial Property	John Beckett/Craig Mitchell
Construction	Peter Davies/Andrew Hickman
Corporate Services	Michael Ward/Craig Ferguson/
	Paul Hayward/Andrew Madden
Family	Michael Vale
Housing Associations	Craig Mitchell/Neil Handel
Trusts and Charities	Stephen Gateley/Mark Reid

GENTLE JAYES 26 Grosvenor Street, London, W1X 0BD *Tel:* (0171) 629 3304 *Fax:* (0171) 493 0246 *DX:* 44618 MAYFAIR *Ptnrs:* 3 *Asst solrs:* 2 *Other fee-earners:* 2

GEORGE DAVIES & CO Fountain Court, 68 Fountain Street, Manchester, M2 2FB *Tel:* (0161) 236 8992 *Fax:* (0161) 228 0030 *DX:* 14316 Manchester 1 *Ptnrs:* 14 *Asst solrs:* 9 *Other fee-earners:* 5

GEORGE GREEN & CO

195 HIGH ST, CRADLEY HEATH, WARLEY, B64 5HW
Tel: (01384) 410410 **Fax:** (01384) 634237 **DX:** 20752

The Firm: Established in 1897 and based in the heart of the Black Country, George Green & Co. is acknowledged as providing the business community with a real alternative to City firms whilst retaining its commitment to the provision of legal advice to its private clientele.

Principal Areas of Work:

Company/ Commercial: (*Contact Partner:* Richard Cliff or Guy Green). *Work includes:* start-ups, acquisition and mergers, reconstructions, corporate finance, MBOs, flotations, partnerships, commercial agreements, joint ventures and taxation.

Commercial Litigation: (*Contact Partner:* Neil Cutler or Richard Green). *Work includes:* contract disputes, debt collection, employment, intellectual property, building disputes, landlord and tenant, planning disputes, insolvency, defamation, European law and emergency injunctions. The work involves both High Court and County Court actions, in addition to arbitrations and industrial tribunal hearings.

Claims Litigation: (*Contact Partner:* Neil Cutler). *Work includes:* advice to plaintiffs on matters relating to insurance law, motor accident claims, accidents at work, agricultural accidents, medical claims, property and occupier's liability, public and employer's liability claims, and health and safety prosecutions.

Property Development/ Planning: (*Contact Partner:* Cheryl Leyser). *Work includes:* acquisitions and disposals of land and buildings, leasing, building and development contracts, taxation, property finance, commercial/ residential estate development and planning.

Private Client: (*Contact Partner:* Neill Robb). *Work includes:* wills, probate, estate planning, trusts, charities, pensions, matrimonial law, domestic conveyancing, personal taxation and general criminal work.

Other Offices: Halesowen.

Managing partner:	JO'N Robb
Senior partner:	R.M. Cliff
Number of partners:	9
Assistant solicitors:	8
Other fee-earners:	13

GEORGE IDE, PHILLIPS

LION HOUSE, 79 ST. PANCRAS, CHICHESTER, PO19 4NL
Tel: (01243) 786668 **Fax:** (01243) 787566 **DX:** 30306 CHICHESTER **Email:** MAILDESK@GEORGEIDE.CO.UK
Internet: HTTP://WWW.GEORGEIDE.CO.UK

BELMONT LODGE, BELMONT STREET, BOGNOR REGIS, PO21 1LE
Tel: (01243) 829231 **Fax:** (01243) 825553 **DX:** 31204 BOGNOR REGIS **Email:** MAILDESK@GEORGEIDE.CO.UK
Internet: HTTP://WWW.GEORGEIDE.CO.UK

Principal Areas of Work: Litigation with a strong bias towards personal injury and medical negligence. The Personal Injury Department concentrates on Plaintiff work and represents many of the major Legal Costs Insurers. The firm was a founder member of MASS (Motor Accident Solicitors Society), and Anthony Goff is a member of APIL. The firm participates in Accident Line.

They undertake many other forms of litigation including family, child care, mental health, crime, building disputes, professional negligence and most other types of civil litigation. They have members of the Children, Personal Injury and Mental Health Panels, Duty Solicitor Scheme, hold a Legal Aid Franchise in all areas except Welfare Benefit and Debt and can offer family mediation.

Both offices undertake a full range of non contentious services with strengths in Commercial Conveyancing, Landlord and Tenant work, Company and Commercial. The Firm has a strong Probate, Wills and Trust and Private Client department.

Other Offices: 166 Pagham Road, Nyetimber, Bognor Regis, West Sussex. *Tel:* (01243) 265513; *Fax:* (01243) 265514.

Senior partner:	Clive Phillips
Number of partners:	11
Assistant solicitors:	5
Other fee-earners:	14

WORKLOADS	
Personal Injury/Medical Negligence	50%
Non Contentious	30%
Other Litigation	20%

CONTACTS	
Children	Fraser Poole, Renella Squires
Commercial	Robert Enticott, Clive Phillips
Conveyancing	Ursula Watt, Chris Powell
Crime	Ian Oliver, Ian Mellor
Employment	Julian Bobak
Family	Fraser Poole, Renella Squires
General Litigation	Julian Bobak
Medical Negligence	Julian Bobak, Philip Lea
Mental Health	Ian Oliver
Personal Injury	Anthony Goff, Fraser Poole
Trust & Probate	Chris Powell, Ursula Watt

GEORGE, JONAS & CO

CITADEL, 190 CORPORATION STREET, BIRMINGHAM, B4 6QD
Tel: (0121) 212 4111 **Fax:** (0121) 212 1770 **DX:** 13013

The Firm: The firm specialises in crime, libel, personal injury law, including medical negligence and civil actions against the police. Its longstanding reputation of dealing with the most serious criminal trials has been extended in recent years into white collar crime and fraud trials, particularly being instructed by professionals. Agency commissions undertaken.

Senior partner:	S.M. Jonas
Number of partners:	2
Assistant solicitors:	3
Other fee-earners:	8

WORKLOADS	
Crime	75%
P.I.	25%

GEORGE MATHERS & CO 23 Adelphi, Aberdeen, AB1 2BL *Tel:* (01224) 588599 *Fax:* (01224) 584147

GEPP & SONS 58 New London Rd, Chelmsford, CM2 0PA **Tel:** (01245) 493939 **Fax:** (01245) 493940 **DX:** 3306 Chelmsford **Ptnrs:** 14 **Asst solrs:** 8 **Other fee-earners:** 11 **Contact:** Jonathan Douglas-Hughes *General practice, handling agriculture, commercial, criminal, insurance, litigation, matrimonial, personal injury, probate and trust, commercial and residential property and shrievalty.*

WORKLOADS			
Litigation	31%	Criminal Law	21%
Matrimonial	13%	Trust & Probate	10%
Domestic Conveyancing	9%	Property	8%
Other	5%	Commercial	3%

GERMAN & SOAR Fenchurch House, 12 King St, Nottingham, NG1 2AZ **Tel:** (0115) 916 5200 **Fax:** (0115) 910 1290 **DX:** 10040 **Ptnrs:** 7 **Asst solrs:** 4 **Other fee-earners:** 6 **Contact:** Mr J. Gardiner *Known for child care, matrimonial, crime, personal injury, conveyancing, probate. Also experienced in sports law, medical negligence, defamation, commercial litigation.*

GHERSON & CO

1 GREAT CUMBERLAND PLACE, LONDON, W1H 7AL
Tel: (0171) 724 4488 **Fax:** (0171) 724 4888 **Email:** GHERSON@MACLINE.CO.UK **Internet:** HTTP://WWW.GHERSON.COM

The Firm: Established in 1988, now in its tenth year, this is one of the few specialist practices providing in-depth advice on UK immigration law, British nationality law, and European Union freedom of movement of persons. Roger Gherson is a well-known solicitor with many years' experience in the field of immigration law. He is complemented at the firm by Sally Thompson and Anne Morris. The firm is committed to solving the most challenging problems.

Principal Areas of Work: Particular expertise in employment and work permits for a wide range of employers, banks, financial institutions, software houses, year 2000 problem companies, film production companies and other business related immigration (including executive relocation, and the admission of entrepreneurs, investors, sole representatives, writers, artists and composers). In addition to a strong corporate caseload, the firm also deals with: EC Associate nationals, EC related immigration issues, an increasing number of cases under the same sex concession; the acquisition of settlement and citizenship; complex nationality issues; family reunion; students and other temporary categories; appeals to Adjudicators and the Immigration Tribunal against the refusal of entry clearance, further leave to remain, threatened deportation, etc; judicial review to the High Court.

Clientele: Wide corporate and private client base including other firms of solicitors. The firm is one of the few corporate immigration practices to offer a Legal Aid service.

Foreign Connections: Extensive links overseas particularly in China (including Hong Kong), South Africa, USA and the Indian Sub-Continent.

Associate Office: 2303-7 Dominion Centre, 43-59 Queens Road East, Wan Chai, Hong Kong. Tel: 00 852 280 23210. Fax: 00 852 282 42051.

Managing partner:	Roger Gherson
Senior partner:	Roger Gherson
Number of partners:	1
Assistant solicitors:	1
Other fee-earners:	2

WORKLOADS	
UK immigration/ nationality law/ EU freedom of movement	100%

CONTACTS	
Immigration and nationality	Roger Gherson

GILFEDDER & MCINNES 34 Leith Walk, Edinburgh, EH6 5AA *Tel:* (0131) 553 4333 *Fax:* (0131) 555 3712 *Ptnrs:* 6 *Asst solrs:* 5 *Other fee-earners:* 2

GILL AKASTER Scott Lodge, Milehouse, Plymouth, PL2 3DD **Tel:** (01752) 500111 **Fax:** (01752) 563403 **DX:** 120026 Plymouth 12 **Ptnrs:** 12 **Asst solrs:** 4 **Other fee-earners:** 8 **Contact:** Malcolm Pillar *Particular knowledge of fisheries law. Also offices at Lockyer St Plymouth and Marlborough Road Plymouth*

WORKLOADS			
Matrimonial & family	25%	Residential property	22%
Civil litigation	20%		
Company & commercial, including Commercial Property			15%
Probate, trusts, tax	13%	Crime	5%

GILLESPIE MACANDREW WS

31 MELVILLE STREET, EDINBURGH, EH3 7JQ
Tel: (0131) 225 1677 **Fax:** (0131) 225 4519 **DX:** 113 EDINBURGH **Email:** MAIL@GILLESPIEMACANDREW.CO.UK

The Firm: Gillespie Macandrew WS has a long tradition of advising substantial private and commercial clients and estate/ agricultural landowners. The firm is a past winner of the TSB/Law Society of Scotland Business of Law Award and continues to invest in technology, training and new client service opportunities. The firm is a member of the Private Association of Lawyers in Europe founded in 1974 with associate offices throughout Europe.

Principal Areas of Work:

Corporate: (*Contact Partner:* Derek A.J. McCulloch). The firm undertakes all aspects of company/ commercial work and business support services through a team of 6 commercial lawyers. Corporate formations and acquisitions, joint ventures and employment law. UK and European trade, distribution, licensing and agency. Sponsorship and merchandising. Renewable energy projects, fish farming and agri-business. The firm is one of two panel members to Edinburgh Business Development assisting developing businesses.

Commercial Property: (*Contact Partner:* Derek A.J. McCulloch). Office retail and industrial property. All aspects of land development, investment and construction law. Planning and environment law. Licensed property. Commercial lending and securities.

Private Client: (*Contact Partner:* Simon A. Leslie). The practice maintains a strong private client base, and divides its specialist service into the following areas: wills, trusts and inheritance tax planning; income tax; securities and investment fund management; and executries, curatories and both UK and offshore trust administration.

Investment/Fund Management: (*Contact Partner:* Thomas K Murray). Comprehensive range of investment services from full discretionary management to execution only. Brochure and Rate Card available on request.

Agriculture/ Estate: (*Contact Partner:* Randall L. Nicol). The department offers expertise in this area, with emphasis on advice to estate and farm landowners. Areas of expertise include fishing, sporting estates, forestry, mineral exploitation and quotas.

Residential Property: (*Contact Partner:* Barbara Finlayson). This department offers clients a full estate agency, conveyancing and factoring service in respect of domestic properties. The firm has close links with several lending bodies. Relocation enquiries welcome.

Litigation: (*Contact Partner:* Ian Turnbull). Civil litigation undertaken in fields of commercial and property disputes with particular interest in employment and construction matters, debt recovery, and matrimonial.

Number of partners:	9
Assistant solicitors:	11
Other fee-earners:	12

WORKLOADS	
Private client and Investment	40%
Commercial client	30%
Agriculture/estate	20%
Litigation	5%
Residential/domestic	5%

CONTACTS	
Agriculture/estate	Randall Nicol
Commercial dept	Derek McCulloch
Investment/fund management	Thomas Murray
Litigation	Ian Turnbull
Private client	Simon Leslie
Residential property	Barbara Finlayson

GILLS Equity Chambers, 5 Hortus Road, Southall, UB2 4AJ *Tel:* (0181) 893 6869 *Fax:* (0181) 893 6396 *DX:* 52256 Southall 2 *Ptnrs:* 2 *Asst solrs:* 2 *Other fee-earners:* 2

GIRLINGS 158 High Street, Herne Bay, CT6 5NP *Tel:* (01227) 373874 *Fax:* (01227) 365897 *DX:* 32303 Herne Bay *Ptnrs:* 16 *Asst solrs:* 4 *Other fee-earners:* 56

GLAISYERS

10 ROWCHESTER COURT, PRINTING HOUSE ST, BIRMINGHAM, B4 6DZ
Tel: (0121) 233 2971 **Fax:** (0121) 236 1534 **DX:** 24933 BIRMINGHAM 4 **Email:** ADVICE@GLAISYERS.CO.UK
Internet: HTTP:WWW.GLAISYERS.CO.UK

The Firm: Glaisyers specialises in criminal, family law and child care and also handles personal injury, consumer law, debt recovery, general contract, landlord and tenant, conveyancing, trust and probate, estate planning, licensing, mental health, housing law and welfare benefits. Close to all courts. All types of agency work undertaken.

Managing partner:	Charles P. Royle
Senior partner:	Charles P. Royle
Number of partners:	11
Assistant solicitors:	8
Other fee-earners:	12

A QUALITY SERVICE
Approved by The Legal Aid Board

GLANVILLES 16 Landport Terrace, Portsmouth, PO1 2QT *Tel:* (01705) 827231 *Fax:* (01705) 753611 *DX:* 2211 *Ptnrs:* 17 *Asst solrs:* 14 *Other fee-earners:* 13

GLAZER DELMAR 223-229 Rye Lane, Peckham, London, SE15 4TZ *Tel:* (0171) 639 8801 *Fax:* (0171) 358 0581 *DX:* 34258 Peckham *Ptnrs:* 3 *Asst solrs:* 7 *Other fee-earners:* 5

GLENISTERS

TELEVISION HOUSE, 269 FIELD END ROAD, EASTCOTE, RUISLIP, HA4 9LS
Tel: (0181) 868 4343 **Fax:** (0181) 429 3606 **DX:** 35150 EASTCOTE

The Firm: Established in 1906, Glenisters aims to provide innovative solutions to many of the problems which face its commercial, corporate, institutional and individual clients.

Principal Areas of Work:

Banking and finance: A dedicated banking and finance Unit responds quickly to the needs of the Firm's lending clients in the areas of professional indemnity, mortgage arrears recovery and repossessions, sales and lettings and loan administration.

Corporate Services: Work includes commercial litigation, intellectual property and company law.

Employment Law and Business Immigration: Advice on all employment matters and business immigration, including all Home Office categories of entry to the U.K.

Family Law: Advice on divorce and separations, financial ancillary matters and mediations.

Property: Commercial and residential conveyancing, advice on construction and planning matters and Landlord and Tenant.

Private Client: Work includes Wills and probate, administration of estates, trusts and settlements, tax and financial services.

Senior partner:	Michael O'Brien
Number of partners:	5
Assistant solicitors:	3
Other fee-earners:	15

WORKLOADS	
Banking and Property	50%
Commercial Litigation	25%
Private Client and Family Law	15%
Company Commercial	5%
Employment/Business Immigration	5%

CONTACTS	
Banking and Finance	Gavin Dowell
Employment	Sharmila Mehta
Litigation	Mark Faith
Private client	Michael O'Brien
Property	Robert Moseley

GLOVERS

115 PARK STREET, LONDON, W1Y 4DY
Tel: (0171) 629 5121 **Fax:** (0171) 491 0930 **DX:** 44438 MARBLE ARCH

The Firm: Glovers is an established firm which specialises in the following principal areas of work:

Commercial Property: (*Contact:* John Barber). The firm has an acknowledged reputation in commercial property, development and in commercial landlord and tenant matters. Work includes development agreements, acting for major retailers, developers, maufacturers and investors, planning negotiations, selling and leasing of commercial developments, rent reviews and all other aspects of landlord and tenant law.

Company/ Commercial: (*Contact:* Stephen Clow). *Work includes:* company formations, M.B.O.'s, purchases and sales, corporate finance work and joint ventures, marketing agreements and the drafting of conditions of sale.

Banking & Finance: (*Contact:* Jeremy Simmonds/ Catherine Cava). The firm acts for a number of UK and overseas banks on a wide variety of banking matters, including secured lending and the restructuring of loans and charges.

Commercial Litigation: (*Contact:* Tony Bourne/ Edward Vaughan). The department is proactive in its approach to litigation, but does not ignore the value of forceful and structured negotiations in the litigation process. Work includes landlord and tenant matters, commercial disputes, banking cases, insolvency and professional negligence. Glovers in one of the four original firms reponsible for implementation of ADR practices in this country and has its own ADR unit.

Construction: (*Contact:* David Miles). The firm acts for one of the UK's leading construction companies and has wide experience in advising on construction contracts, collateral warranties and compex building disputes.

Employment: (*Contact:* Peter Pitt). The firm covers all areas of employment law, both contentious and non-contentious, discrimination, transfer of undertakings and compromise agreements.

Professional Negligence: (*Contact:* Stephen Twaites). Litigation arising out of property and banking disputes, white collar fraud and claims against solicitors and surveyors.

Private Client: (*Contact:* Frances Dewhurst). A comprehensive service is offered to all individuals in all matters relating to wills and personal financial and tax planning. UK and offshore trusts are also areas with which we are familiar.

Senior partner:	Jeremy Simmonds
Number of partners:	11
Assistant solicitors:	9
Other fee-earners:	4

CONTACTS	
Banking	Jeremy Simmonds
Commercial litigation	Tony Bourne
Commercial property	John Barber
Company/ commercial	Stephen Clow
Construction	David Miles
Private client	Frances Dewhurst

GODFREY DAVIS & WAITT Westminster Bank Chambers, 49-51 High St, Ramsgate, LT11 9RP *Tel:* (01843) 585321 *Fax:* (01843) 325636 *DX:* 30603 *Ptnrs:* 1 *Asst solrs:* 1

GODLOVES Russell House, 15 St. Pauls Street, Leeds, LS1 2LZ *Tel:* (0113) 225 8811 *Fax:* (0113) 2258844 *DX:* 14078 Leeds Park Square *Ptnrs:* 12 *Asst solrs:* 6 *Other fee-earners:* 5

GOLDKORN DAVIES MATHIAS

6 COPTIC STREET, BLOOMSBURY, LONDON, WC1A 1NH
Tel: (0171) 631 1811 **Fax:** (0171) 631 0431 **DX:** 35705 BLOOMSBURY **Email:** GDMLAW@COMPUSERVE.COM

The Firm: Established in its present form in 1989 by amalgamation. Goldkorn Davies Mathias is a progressive practice that provides a comprehensive legal service to both commercial and private clients. It has a substantial reputation for defence of serious fraud and white collar crime and handles major litigation.

Principal Areas of Work: Includes the prosecution and defence of actions in all divisions of the High Court and in the County Court, including Advocacy in the High Court and Court of Appeal.

Personal injury: Work includes traffic, accidents and industrial injury. The practice is prepared to carry out work on a conditional fee basis.

Property: Work includes commercial and residential property, conveyancing of all types.

Commercial: Work includes commercial and employment contracts, partnerships, sports agreements.

Major crime: Work includes defence of alleged serious and VAT fraud and white collar crime.

Managing partner:	Michael Davies
Number of partners:	4
Other fee-earners:	2

WORKLOADS	
Litigation	35%
Major Criminal work	35%
Conveyancing	28%
Commercial	10%

CONTACTS	
Commercial	Roy Mathias
Conveyancing	Michael Davies
Crime	John Perry
Litigation	Geoffrey Goldkorn

GOLDS

8 NEWTON TERRACE, GLASGOW, G3 7PJ
Tel: (0141) 300 4300 **Fax:** (0141) 300 4350 **DX:** GW40 **Email:** GOLDS@GOLDS.CO.UK

The Firm: Golds Solicitors concentrates on company and commercial work; banking, building society and commercial finance work; housing association; commercial property matters and litigation.

Principal Areas of Work:

Corporate and Commercial Work: (Ellis Simpson) Wide range of activities including sales and purchases of companies, restructurings and management buy-outs. The practice has particular expertise in banking work, including asset finance, sophisticated securitisation and insolvency matters. Golds also offers a complete service to commercial lenders from the drafting of original documentation to volume processing and litigation services. A comprehensive range of intellectual property work is also carried out.

Commercial Property: (Brian Meldrum) All aspects of sales, acquisitions and leases for a broad range of clients including investors, developers and builders, multiple retailers and institutional lenders.

Commercial Litigation & Employment: (Frances Eccles) Includes a wide range of commercial matters including trade disputes, contract disputes, property litigation, security work and debt recovery. Golds offers specialist services in insolvency, employment and insurance litigation.

Housing Association: (Ellis Simpson) Golds has established a prominent practice involving loan transactions for Housing Associations and housing stock transfers.

Managing partner:	Jonathan Edwards
Senior partner:	Stephen Gold
Number of partners:	7
Assistant solicitors:	13
Other fee-earners:	22

WORKLOADS	
Specialist Corporate Conveyancing	38%
Commercial Property	27%
Commercial Litigation	25%
Corporate & Commercial	10%

CONTACTS	
Client Services Manager	Louise Irvine

GOLDSMITH WILLIAMS 42-44 Stanley Street, Liverpool, L1 6AL *Tel:* (0151) 231 1292 *Fax:* (0151) 231 1369 *DX:* 14186 Liverpool *Ptnrs:* 3 *Asst solrs:* 1 *Other fee-earners:* 20

GOODGER AUDEN 2/4 Lichfield Street, Burton-on-Trent, DE14 3RB *Tel:* (01283) 544323 *Fax:* (01283) 535448 *DX:* 10704 *Ptnrs:* 8 *Asst solrs:* 6 *Other fee-earners:* 10

GOODMAN DERRICK

90 FETTER LANE, LONDON, EC4A 1EQ
Tel: (0171) 404 0606 **Fax:** (0171) 831 6407 **DX:** 122

The Firm: Goodman Derrick was founded in 1954 by Lord Goodman. It has a broad commercial practice focusing on commercial and corporate finance, property and litigation work with an excellent reputation for media work in television, publishing and related industries.

Principal Areas of Work:

Media/Media Litigation: (*Contact Partner:* Patrick Swaffer). *Work includes:* contentious and non-contentious work for television broadcasters and independent producers; much work in the fields of video/film classification, newspapers, publishers, advertising and other areas of the media and arts. On the litigation side, defamation, copyright, judicial review and broadcasting-related disputes are particular areas of note.

Property: (*Contact Partner:* Michael Collins). *Work includes:* all aspects of commercial property transactions, especially work for retail companies, investors, property development, funding, leases, planning and agricultural holdings. In addition, the firm handles some high-quality residential work.

Commercial Litigation: (*Contact Partner:* Tim Langton). *Work includes:* a broad range of commercial disputes, professional negligence, banking, insurance, insolvency, employment, fraud, intellectual property and property litigation.

Corporate: (*Contact Partner:* David Edwards). *Work includes:* acquisitions and disposals and related tax aspects, joint ventures, business start-ups, shareholders' agreements, management buy-outs rights issues, share offers, mergers and reorganisations, commercial agreements and the licensing of intellectual property.

Private Clients/Charities: (*Contact Partner:* Diana Rawstron). *Work includes:* establishment and drafting, tax and financial planning, wills and estates, probate, and trusts.

Nature of Clientele: Goodman Derrick has an impressive client list acting for many public figures, public and private companies, charities, large retail chains, property companies and developers, television companies, broadcasters and independent producers, publishers and newspapers, and trade associations.

Recruitment: Applications by letter and CV to Mr. Nicholas Armstrong, Recruitment Partner.

Senior partner:	John Roberts
Number of partners:	14
Assistant solicitors:	10
Associates:	3
Other fee-earners:	12

WORKLOADS	
Media	30%
Corporate	26%
Commercial litigation	22%
Property	17%
Charities/ private client	5%

CONTACTS	
Banking/Insolvency	Charles Morrison
Charities/Private client	Diana Rawstron
Commercial litigation	Tim Langton
Company Commercial	David Edwards
Construction	Susan White
Corporate	John Roberts
Defamation	Patrick Swaffer/Jeffery Maunsell
Employment	Noel Deans
Insurance	Charles Morrison/Tim Langton
Media	Patrick Swaffer/Paul Herbert
Property	Michael Collins
Publishing	Jeffery Maunsell/Nicholas Armstrong
Tax	Ian Montrose

GOODMAN RAY 450 Kingsland Road, Dalston, London, E8 4AE **Tel:** (0171) 254 8855 **Fax:** (0171) 923 4345 **DX:** 46807 Dalston **Ptnrs:** 4 **Asst solrs:** 2 **Other fee-earners:** 3 **Contact:** Peggy Ray *Specialist family law with criminal law department. Strong reputation for child-related work. All partners are members of the Law Society Children Panel.*

GORDON & SMYTH 420 Sauchiehall Street, Glasgow, G2 3JS *Tel:* (0141) 332 5705 *Fax:* (0141) 332 6036 *DX:* GW33

GORDON DADDS

80 BROOK STREET, MAYFAIR, LONDON, W1Y 2DD
Tel: (0171) 493 6151 **Fax:** (0171) 491 1065 **DX:** 131

The Firm: Founded in 1921, Gordon Dadds offers specialist areas of expertise to clients. Although best known for its family and private client work, through its merger in 1996 with the niche commercial practice of Jepson Goff, Gordon Dadds now provides to the commercial client a comprehensive service from a coordinated team drawn from the departments in the firm.

Principal Areas of Work:

Family Law: (*Contact:* Douglas Alexiou). Combining determination with sensitivity, the firm handles complex financial cases, frequently with international aspects, contact to children, wardship and adoption, and divorce and separation agreements. Emergency procedures, such as dealing with child abduction are also handled as are injunction proceedings and problems arising from cohabitation.

Company/Commercial: (*Contact:* Michael Jepson). The department offers a personal and efficient service which provides effective and practical solutions for clients. Areas of expertise include project finance, venture capital and joint ventures, asset finance and leasing, mergers and reorganisations, hotel acquisitions and management and commercial agreements.

Litigation: (*Contact:* Hugh Elder). The litigation department handles all forms of commercial litigation as well as company directors' disqualification, defamation, employment, inheritance, personal injury, professional negligence, property (including landlord and tenant) matters and road traffic cases (civil and criminal).

Managing partner:	Roger Peters
Senior partner:	Douglas Alexiou
Number of partners:	11
Assistant solicitors:	6
Other fee-earners:	4

WORKLOADS	
Family law	32%
Company/Commercial	20%
Private client	18%
Litigation	15%
Property	15%

CONTACTS	
Company/Commercial	Michael Jepson
Family law	Douglas Alexiou
Litigation	Hugh Elder
Private client	Roger Peters
Property	David Goff

Private Client: (*Contact:* Roger Peters). Advice is given in the fields of tax and estate planning and administration, with particular regard to overall personal considerations as well as to strictly legal matters. Assignments include administration of estates and post death tax planning, advice on tax returns, drawing up and executing wills and financial management. The firm has built up a range of expertise in acting for charities.

Property: (*Contact:* David Goff). The property department has extensive experience in dealing with a wide range of commercial activities including development, acquisitions, capital enhancement, offices, leasing, building contracts, retail, trading estates, hotels, complexes, joint ventures and mortgages and lending.

Foreign Languages: French and Greek.

Recruitment: The firm recruits two high-calibre graduates a year as trainee solicitors. Applications should be received by July, two years before articles commence. Please address applications to Miss Sue Bland.

GORDONS WRIGHT & WRIGHT

14 PICCADILLY, BRADFORD, BD1 3LX
Tel: (01274) 202202 **Fax:** (01274) 202100 **DX:** 11716 BRADFORD **Email:** MAIL@GWW.CO.UK

The Firm: Gordons Wright & Wright is one of Yorkshire's largest legal firms. It acts for a wide range of commercial organisations including plcs. Particular strengths are corporate work, employment, licensing, commercial property, personal injuries and family. Key industrial sectors served include retail, electronics and textiles.

The firm also provides a full service to private clients. It has obtained a Legal Aid Franchise.

Gordons Wright & Wright continues to expand and in 1996 acquired a further 7,500 sq ft of office space in Bradford.

Other Offices: 6-14 Devonshire Street, Keighley, West Yorkshire BD21 2AY.*Tel:* (01535) 667731. *Fax:* (01535) 609748. *DX:* 21454 Keighley.

4 Park Road, Bingley, West Yorkshire BD16 4JA.*Tel:* (01274) 568347. *Fax:* (01274) 569813. *DX:* 21101 Bingley.

Managing partner:	Tim Ratcliffe
Senior partner:	Richard Wilson
Number of partners:	17
Assistant solicitors:	18
Other fee-earners:	16

WORKLOADS	
Commercial property	28%
Litigation	25%
Private client	25%
Company/commercial	11%
Family	11%

GORNA & CO

VIRGINIA HOUSE, CHEAPSIDE, KING ST, MANCHESTER, M2 4NB
Tel: (0161) 832 3651 **Fax:** (0161) 834 8572 **DX:** 14339

The Firm: Essentially a commercial firm, Gorna & Co has a national reputation for its work in commercial property development. The practice has a nationwide clientele and provides its corporate and commercial clients with the full range of commercial advice.

Principal Areas of Work: In addition to commercial property, development and disposal work, the practice handles a broad spectrum of corporate and commercial matters, including corporate finance work, mergers, acquisitions and disposals and franchising. A variety of contentious work is undertaken, including commercial litigation, commercial property litigation, personal injury claims, medical negligence cases, intellectual property protection, employment law and debt recovery.

Other Areas of Work: In addition, extensive private client services are available, ranging from wills, trusts and probate to tax planning. There is particular expertise in inheritance tax work.

Nature of Clientele: The firm represents the interests of a number of well-known medium-sized and large companies, including property companies, as well as Friendly Societies, Housing Associations and Health Authorities and Trusts throughout the country. The firm also has an expanding sports law practice and is particularly renowned for its work as solicitors for the League Managers Association.

Managing partner:	Peter Doyle
Senior partner:	Michael Morrison
Number of partners:	8
Assistant solicitors:	9
Other fee-earners:	5

CONTACTS	
Commercial litigation	Helen Hoath
Commercial property	Stephen Hindmarsh
Company and commercial	Tony Lomax
Trusts and probate	Tony Hall

GOSSCHALKS

QUEENS GARDENS, HULL, HU1 3DZ
Tel: (01482) 324252 **Fax:** (01482) 590290 **DX:** 11902 HULL 1 **Email:** INFO@GOSSCHALKS.CO.UK

Gosschalks is a prominent general Practice based in Hull where it is one of the largest legal practices. It features strongly in work on a regional and national basis and there is a strong emphasis on Commercial and Licensing work.

The Firm: The firm has a national reputation for its expertise in Licensing and is the exclusive Licensing legal firm for a number of major national Clients in this field. The senior partner, Les Green, is Co-Editor of Patersons Licensing and he is acknowledged to be "arguably the Country's leading Licensing Lawyer".

The firm also has a large number of partners who are recognised as specialists in their own field. Of particular note are those in the Commercial Property, Company/Commercial, Civil and Commercial Litigation, Family Law and Crime Departments. Founded over l00 years ago the firm has a long history of serving the local community, business and otherwise, in its Crime and Private Client Departments. A Legal Aid Franchise has been granted in all areas for which it was applied. The firm's move in l994 to substantial purpose built City Centre Offices facilitates the continued expansion and further upgrading of technology.

Principal Areas of Work:

The Civil Litigation Department: (*Contact:* Liam Barlow/Bruce Wilkie) handles a wide range of matters and is well known for acting for a large number of nationally known Insurance Companies. Although a large part of the Department's work is defence based, it also acts for a number of private Clients on a Plaintiff basis in all areas of personal injury and also specialises in medical negligence cases. This specialist medical negligence Department has grown substantially over the last 2 years as a result of deliberate targeting and reputation

The Commercial Litigation Department: (*Contact:* Tony Clark) acts for Corporate and Commercial Clients in a wide range of disputes and seeks commercial solutions through either litigation or alternative dispute resolution processes. There is particular expertise in dealing with Landlord and Tenant disputes for Licensing Clients.

The Commercial Property Department: (*Contact:* Dick Llewellyn/Richard Gooch) handles the whole range of property transactions in the commercial field for Corporate and Private Clients. Particularly known for its conveyancing of licensed premises it also has a substantial reputation for its general commercial conveyancing work. Domestic conveyancing on a large scale is also carried out (Contact Neil Johnson).

The Family/Matrimonial Department: (*Contact:* Ian Lanch) activities encompass the whole range of disputes within this field. The Department acts for Clients both on a Private and Legally Aided basis but with particular regard to the Private Client and high value financial settlement cases. Wills, Trusts and Probate are also handled for Clients of the firm.

The Licensing Department: (*Contact:* Les Green/Clare Johnson) acts for a large number of nationally known Corporate Clients as well as a large number of Private Clients. As mentioned above Les Green has a national reputation for his ability and knowledge within the licensing field.

The Company/Commercial Department: (*Contact:* Simon Lunt/Bruce Raper) handles the whole range of Company transactions in the Private and Public Sector. Clients include both quoted and unquoted Companies, Partnerships and Sole Proprietors. Acquisitions, Management buyouts, Commercial Contracts and all types of general Corporate work are conducted.

The Defence Advocacy Department: (*Contact:* Bill Waddington) acts for Companies, Partnerships and Individuals. Representation is provided at all stages of proceedings from the initial investigation to the conduct of trials. It is one of the largest Departments of its type within the region, with particular emphasis on defending Trading Standards/Health & Safety prosecution.

The Employment Department: (*Contact:* Simon Steen) advises both Employer and Employee, with particular emphasis on representation of the Employer, offering immediate advice and representation throughout up to and including Tribunal work.

Managing partner:	Ian Lanch
Senior partner:	Les Green
Number of partners:	25
Assistant solicitors:	21
Other fee-earners:	21

WORKLOADS	
Commercial property	31%
Civil/commercial litigation	25%
Family/private client/probate	16%
Company/Commercial	12%
Licensing	9%
Crime/Defence Advocacy	7%

CONTACTS	
Civil litigation	Bruce Wilkie/Liam Barlow
Commercial litigation	Tony Clark
Commercial property	Dick Llewellyn/Richard Gooch
Company/Commercial	Simon Lunt/Bruce Raper
Crime/Defence Advocacy	Bill Waddington
Domestic conveyancing	Neil Johnson
Employment	Simon Steen
Family	Ian Lanch
Licensing	Les Green/Clare Johnson
Private Client	Hugh Williamson

GOTELEE & GOLDSMITH

31-41 ELM ST, IPSWICH, IP1 2AY
Tel: (01473) 211121 **Fax:** (01473) 230387 **DX:** 3220 IPSWICH

The Firm: Gotelee & Goldsmith is firmly established as one of Suffolk's leading practices and provides a complete range of legal services for both commercial and private clients – including local authorities, major companies and small and medium-sized businesses. Litigation has long been a strength of the firm but as a result of the considerable expansion of its commercial client base Gotelee & Goldsmith is now equally well known for its local authority and commercial work. The firm is an active member of LawNet and pioneered the LawNet Quality Standard.

Principal Areas of Work:

Company/Commercial: Broad range of company and commercial services including company/partnership formation, MBOs, acquisition or sale of companies and businesses, corporate finance, tax matters, trading agreements, licensing, company receiverships and liquidations, insolvency work, franchising and intellectual property.

Commercial Litigation: Commercial claims and disputes, construction litigation, insurance company litigation, intellectual property and professional negligence. Established expertise in road haulage and advising hauliers on UK and EU legislation governing over-loading, construction and use, drivers' hours, tachographs and vehicle maintenance. Volume debt collection for extensive corporate client base.

Employment Law: Full service for both contentious and non-contentious work including advice on contracts of employment, discrimination, redundancy and unfair dismissal.

Commercial Property: Particular expertise in purchase, sale or leasing of industrial sites, office buildings, commercial and residential development projects, building contracts, joint ventures, planning matters and tax.

Agricultural Services: Property law, tax planning, agricultural tenancy law and milk quotas.

Local Authority/ Environmental: Extensive experience of acting for a number of local authorities. Also compulsory purchase and planning appeals both for and against local authorities, health and safety, pollution, noise and environmental matters.

Civil & Criminal Litigation: Family law and child care, criminal law and civil litigation including personal injury and insurance work.

Private Client: Residential conveyancing, wills, trusts, administration of estates, tax, and caring for the elderly and infirm.

Other Offices: 6 Church Street, Hadleigh, Suffolk IP7 5DU. *Tel:* (01473) 822102.

Foreign Languages: French and Italian.

International Connections: As a member of LawNet Europe Gotelee & Goldsmith is associated with over 600 firms throughout Europe.

Managing partner:	B. Morron
Number of partners:	10
Assistant solicitors:	11
Other fee-earners:	14

WORKLOADS	
Company/commercial	20%
Family/criminal litigation	20%
Private client	20%
Civil litigation	15%
Commercial property	15%
Commercial litigation	10%

CONTACTS	
Agricultural services	Peter Crix
Civil litigation	Jonathan Ripman
Commercial litigation	Jonathan Ripman
Commercial property	Mary Dolley
Company/commercial	Jonathan Rands
Criminal litigation	Hugh Rowland
Empl./env./local authority	Brian Morron
Family	Martin Ward
Personal injury	Timothy Humpage
Private client	Peter Crix

Gotelee & Goldsmith
solicitors

GOUGHS 28 Church St, Calne, SN11 0HX *Tel:* (01249) 812086 *Fax:* (01249) 816378 *DX:* 44800 *Ptnrs:* 12 *Asst solrs:* 6 *Other fee-earners:* 3

GOULDENS

22 TUDOR STREET, LONDON, EC4Y 0JJ
Tel: (0171) 583 7777 **Fax:** (0171) 583 3051 **DX:** 67 **Email:** INFO@GOULDENS.COM **Internet:** HTTP://WWW.GOULDENS.COM

Based in the City of London, Gouldens' leading corporate practice provides a range of legal services to major UK and international commercial clients.

The Firm: Gouldens has grown steadily over the past decade and established a first class reputation in the corporate field. Gouldens consistently appears in the league tables of the Top 20 (and most consulted) UK legal advisers (viz: ranked 15th in Corporate Money's League Table of the Top 30 Law Firms (by deal value) on deals announced in 1998 year to date (March 1998); ranked in *KPMG's New Issue Statistics for July to December 1997* (summary of London flotations between 1 January 1994 and 31 December 1997) **8th** (by solicitor to the company) **and 10th** (by solicitor to the issue); and ranked in *In-House Lawyer's review of M&A activity in 1997* (April 1998) (16th and 15th Most Consulted Adviser by value and number of deals done, respectively). The firm's corporate clients operate in many different areas including banking, capital markets, corporate finance, insurance, healthcare, retailing, mining, waste management, international trade, telecommunications, information technology, property development and construction. Gouldens assists clients achieve their business objectives effectively and cost efficiently whilst maintaining the highest levels of technical legal excellence. The firm seeks to recruit (and retain) solicitors and trainees who wish to accept the challenge of responsibility in an atmosphere where not only technical expertise but flair, originality and enthusiasm are highly regarded and rewarded. Its system of training is unique. Up to twenty trainee solicitors are recruited each year.

Principal Areas of Work: Gouldens divides its work into the main practice areas described below. There are also a number of specialist areas staffed by multi-skilled teams such as construction, environment, insolvency, insurance and reinsurance, communications, media and technology, intellectual property, employment, employee benefits and pensions, regulatory matters, fraud and white collar crime as well as project finance pursuant to the Private Finance Initiative.

Company/Commercial: The firm's company and commercial department has a strong reputation in the City and advises, amongst others, major public companies and institutions on all aspects of commercial activity including corporate finance, public company takeovers and flotations, mergers and acquisitions, joint ventures, venture capital, management buy-outs, information technology, international agreements and franchise and distribution networks and agreements, as well as providing specialist support in areas such as EU and competition law, intellectual property and pensions and employee benefits.

Banking and Capital Markets: The firm's banking and capital markets department advises borrowers, lenders, issuers, lead managers and trustees on corporate debt, syndicated lending, capital market issues and structured, asset and project finance. The firm advises a number of clients who are active in the secondary debt markets.

Property and Planning: The firm's property and planning departments advise developers, institutional investors, surveyors, and other professionals on the financing, planning implications, tax structuring, and implementation of major developments.

Litigation, Insurance and Reinsurance, and Insolvency: The firm handles a wide variety of domestic and international commercial disputes relating to construction, defamation, employment, financial and corporate matters, insolvency, insurance and reinsurance and intellectual property and has a strong reputation in the field of patent and trade mark disputes. The insurance and reinsurance practice is broadly based, advising Lloyds and other London market insurers on many classes of risk including professional indemnity and directors' and officers' liability. The firm's insolvency group advises insolvency practitioners and lenders on corporate recovery and insolvency.

EU and International: As well as dealing with high profile EU legal and trade issues, the firm has developed a significant international practice, particularly in the CIS and Central Europe, advising major companies and institutions on infrastructure projects, privatisations and joint ventures as well as governments on a number of issues including the development of new banking, securities, and foreign investment-related legislation. Gouldens is also active in the Far East with a strong base of Japanese clients.

Languages spoken: Dutch, French, German, Greek, Hebrew, Italian, Japanese, Romanian, Russian, Spanish, Welsh.

Managing partner:	Charters Macdonald-Brown
Senior partner:	Patrick Burgess
UK	
Number of partners:	35
Assistant solicitors:	66
Other fee-earners:	30
International	
Number of partners:	2
Assistant solicitors:	4

WORKLOADS	
Company/Commercial (including corporate tax)	42%
Property (including planning)	23%
Litigation (including IP)	20%
Banking/Capital Markets	12%
Personal/International Tax Planning	3%

CONTACTS	
Banking/Capital Markets	Tom Budd
CIS/Central Europe	James Campbell
Commercial litigation	Charters Macdonald-Brown
Commercial property	Clare Deanesly
Communications, media & technology	
	Simon Chalkley
Company/ commercial	Max Thorneycroft
Construction	Craig Shuttleworth
Corporate finance	Russell Carmedy
Corporate tax	Patrick Harrison
Employment	Martin Piers
Environment	Clare Deanesly
EU and international	Charters Macdonald-Brown
Far East/Japan	Max Thorneycroft
Fraud/white collar crime	David Cooper
Insolvency	Barry Donnelly
Insurance/reinsurance	Ian Lupson
Intellectual property	Charters Macdonald-Brown
Pensions/Employee Benefits	John Papadakis
Personal/Int'l Tax Planning	Jennet Davies
Project Finance/PFI	Russell Carmedy
Regulatory	Barry Donnelly

GOWMANS 65 Hyde Road, Paignton, TQ4 5BT **Tel:** (01803) 546100 **Fax:** (01803) 528351 **DX:** 100600 Paignton **Ptnrs:** 4 **Asst solrs:** 7 **Other fee-earners:** 7 **Contact:** Mr David Boddam-Whetham *General practice covering all main areas of law, with specialists in personal injury, family and child care.*

GRAEME CARMICHAEL 9 Paget Road, Ipswich, IP1 3RP **Tel:** (01473) 252159 **Fax:** (01473) 214778 **Ptnrs:** 1 *Specialist family lawyer. See under family law section.*

WORKLOADS			
Public Law (Children)	60%	Divorce/Ancillaries	20%
Private Law (Children)	20%		

GRAHAME STOWE, BATESON 5-7 Portland St, Leeds, LS1 3DR **Tel:** (0113) 246 8163 **Fax:** (0113) 242 6682 **DX:** 12022 **Ptnrs:** 9 **Asst solrs:** 10 **Other fee-earners:** 10 **Contact:** Grahame Stowe *A general practice handling all areas of litigation work but with particular emphasis in criminal and mental health and matrimonial law.*

WORKLOADS			
Matrimonial	40%	Crime	20%
Conveyancing	15%	Civil litigation	10%
Mental health	10%	Personal injury	5%

GRAHAM EVANS & PARTNERS Moorgate House, 6 Christina Street, Swansea, SA1 4EP **Tel:** (01792) 655822 **Fax:** (01792) 645387 **DX:** 39573 Swansea **Ptnrs:** 9 **Asst solrs:** 4 **Other fee-earners:** 10 **Contact:** Simon Howell *Also at: 110 Clase Road, Morriston, Swansea. Tel: (01792) 310402 DX: 56758 Morriston.*

GRAHAM & OLDHAM Electric House, Lloyds Avenue, Ipswich, IP1 3HZ **Tel:** (01473) 232425 **Fax:** (01473) 230505 **DX:** 3221 Ipswich **Ptnrs:** 13 **Asst solrs:** 9 **Other fee-earners:** 21 **Contact:** Paul Whittingham *Practice linked closely with Europe. Specialist departments providing a full range of legal services. Legal aid franchise and ISO 9001.*

WORKLOADS			
Personal Injury/Litigation	37%	Private Client	18%
Company Commercial	15%	Crime	15%
Family	15%		

GRAHAM & ROSEN 8 Parliament St, Hull, HU1 2BB *Tel:* (01482) 323123 *Fax:* (01482) 223542 *DX:* 11925 *Ptnrs:* 8 *Asst solrs:* 5 *Other fee-earners:* 9

GRANT DEWAR

180 WEST REGENT STREET, GLASGOW, G2 4RW
Tel: (0141) 572 1900 **Fax:** (0141) 572 1909 **DX:** GW 32, GLASGOW

The Firm: Grant Dewar are a recent amalgamation of the firms of Grant & Company and Downie Aiton, with a strong commercial/private client base, a substantial litigation practice with a particular specialisation in Contract Disputes, Personal Injury claims, debt recovery, Judgement Enforcements and Professional Negligence claims.

Principal Areas of Work:

Commercial: An experienced department both in Company Law, Partnerships, Commercial Property, commercial and employment contracts and computerised debt recovery.

Litigation: A broadly based department which undertakes Contract Disputes, Industrial Tribunals, Professional Negligence, Family Law and all other types of court related work.

Personal Injury: Grant Dewar act on behalf of a number of corporate organisations who provide a litigation service for customers in the recovery of loss as a result of Road Traffic Accidents and Personal Injury. A specialised team/department is dedicated to this area of the law.

Private client: Property law, creation of trusts, wills, executrices, financial services, tax planning and life insurance.

Property: Domestic house purchase and sales.

Other Offices: 48 West Regent Street, Glasgow (0141) 572 1900

Number of partners:	4
Assistant solicitors:	4
Other fee-earners:	4

CONTACTS	
Commercial	Andrew F. Dewar/ Ronald N. Brown
Litigation	Hugh J Grant
Personal Injury	Norman Lindsay
Private Client	Ronald Brown/ Andrew F. Dewar

GRANT & HORTON MARINE SOLICITORS Lynher Building, Queen Anne's Battery, Plymouth, PL4 0LP **Tel:** (01752) 265265 **Fax:** (01752) 265260 **DX:** 8262 Plymouth 2 **Ptnrs:** 2 **Asst solrs:** 3 **Other fee-earners:** 1 **Contact:** Mr Nicholas Horton *Specialists in the insurance and marine industries dealing with national and international work with particular expertise in the yacht/super-yacht field.*

WORKLOADS			
Insurance	30%	Commercial	30%
Admiralty	25%	Personal Injury	15%

GRANVILLE-WEST 23 Commercial Street, Pontypool, Torfaen, NP4 6XT *Tel:* (01495) 751111 *Fax:* (01495) 753858 *DX:* 44250 Pontypool *Ptnrs:* 10 *Asst solrs:* 4 *Other fee-earners:* 8

GRAYS Duncombe Place, York, YO1 7DY **Tel:** (01904) 634771 **Fax:** (01904) 610711 **DX:** 61505 **Ptnrs:** 8 **Asst solrs:** 1 **Other fee-earners:** 3 **Contact:** Mr. F.A. Lawton. *Best known for trusts and taxation, charities, agriculture, and property work.*

WORKLOADS	
Private Client and Charity	42%
Agricultural, Commercial and Residential Property	32%
Litigation	18%
Family	5%

GRAYSONS 6 Paradise Square, Sheffield, S1 1TB *Tel:* (0114) 272 9184 *Fax:* (0114) 276 8664 *DX:* 10509 Sheffield *Ptnrs:* 12 *Asst solrs:* 9 *Other fee-earners:* 9

GREATHEAD & WHITELOCK 3-5 Hamilton Terrace, Pembroke, SA71 4DF *Tel:* (01646) 682101 *Fax:* (01646) 621248 *Ptnrs:* 5

GREEN & CO 2-4 Atkinson Street, Manchester, M3 3BH *Tel:* (0161) 834 8980 *Fax:* (0161) 834 8981 *Ptnrs:* 1 *Asst solrs:* 5 *Other fee-earners:* 1

GREENE & GREENE 80 Guildhall Street, Bury St. Edmunds, IP33 1QB *Tel:* (01284) 762211 *Fax:* (01284) 705739 *DX:* 57205 *Ptnrs:* 8 *Asst solrs:* 3 *Other fee-earners:* 10

GREENLAND HOUCHEN

38 PRINCE OF WALES RD, NORWICH, NR1 1HZ
Tel: (01603) 660744 **Fax:** (01603) 610700 **DX:** 5217 NORWICH

The Firm: A long established general practice which seeks to offer at its three offices a full range of legal services. The partners include in their clientele builders and developers, housing associations, members of the local farming community and other commercial and corporate enterprises, as well as the private client. All aspects of litigation are undertaken with a significant legal aid element.

Managing partner:	Anita C. Piper
Senior partner:	Trevor Nicholls
Number of partners:	10
Assistant solicitors:	2
Other fee-earners:	4

GREEN SHEIKH & CO (FORMERLY GREEN DAVID CONWAY & CO)

45 CRAWFORD PLACE, LONDON, W1H 2BY
Tel: (0171) 258 0055 **Fax:** (0171) 724 0385 **DX:** 41726 MARYLEBONE 1 **Email:** GSC@NETCOMUK.CO.UK

The Firm: Established in 1972, the firm provides a comprehensive but personal service over a broad range of commercial work to UK and international private, corporate and institutional clients. The firm has established significant connections in Africa, Asia and the Middle East.

Principal Areas of Work:
    Litigation: (*Contact:* D.J. Green).
    Media and Intellectual Property: (*Contact:* D.J. Green or P.J. Leathem).
    Corporate and Commercial: (*Contact:* S.R. Sheikh or C. Halperin).
    Property: (*Contact:* S.R. Sheikh or H.D. Posener).
    Insolvency: (*Contact:* H.D. Posener).
    Tax and Trusts: (*Contact:* D.J. Green or S.R. Sheikh).
    Hotels & Leisure and Healthcare: (*Contact:* S.R. Sheikh or P.L. Belcher).

Senior Partners:	Douglas J. Green
	and Saleem R. Sheikh
Managing Partner:	Saleem R. Sheikh
Number of partners:	6
Assistant solicitors:	6
Other fee earners:	7

GREENWOOD KYLE 1 Finkle Street, Kendal, LA9 4AE **Tel:** (01539) 721613 **Fax:** (01539) 726137 **DX:** 63401 Kendal **Ptnrs:** 2 **Asst solrs:** 2 **Other fee-earners:** 2 **Contact:** Mr. S. Barton *A broadly based practice dealing with all aspects of property, agricultural, matrimonial, criminal and private client law.*

WORKLOADS	
Domestic and commercial property	35%
Criminal	25%
Matrimonial and civil litigation	25%
Probate	15%

GREENWOODS 20 Bedford Square, London, WC1B 3HL *Tel:* (0171) 323 4632 *Fax:* (0171) 631 3142

GREENWOODS

30 PRIESTGATE, PETERBOROUGH, PE1 1JE
Tel: (01733) 555244 **Fax:** (01733) 347988 **DX:** 12306 PETERBOROUGH 1 **Email:** SHAMILL@GREENWOODS.CO.UK
Internet: WWW.GREENWOODS.CO.UK

IN ASSOCIATION WITH:, CRIVELLO CARLSON MENTKOWSKI STEEVES s.c., MILWAUKEE, WISCONSIN, 53203, USA, 53203

The Firm: Greenwoods is a leading regionally-based law firm ideally positioned to serve clients in East Anglia and the East Midlands. Approximately 45 minutes from London, the firm offers a comprehensive range of legal services to commercial and private clients. Although located in Peterborough, the client base includes companies and organisations that are of a national and international stature as well as those that are local and regional. Greenwoods' success is based on the philosophy of providing a blend of successful, experienced and dedicated lawyers whose prime objective is to provide the client with the best possible commercial advice.

Principal Areas of Work:

Company/Commercial: The Company & Commercial Department provides the full range of corporate services but has a particularly strong reputation for the acquisitions and disposals of businesses and companies. The department advises on competition law and advertising law, as well as having considerable experience working with the DTI and the MMC. It has an established and well known reputation in the media field. Commercial Dispute Resolution advises on commercial disputes finding solutions through Court procedures and mediation techniques. Recent work ranges from the defence of a multi-national breach of contract claim to board room and partnership disputes, property litigation and professional negligence claims. In relation to insolvency work, the firm advises insolvency practitioners, companies, partnership and individuals on rescue procedures, security appraisals and disposals of businesses.

Intellectual Property: Intellectual Property handles a wide range of contentious and non-contentious work including patent infringement actions in the Patents Court, High Court actions for trade mark infringement, passing off and copyright infringement. The firm presently acts in patent related proceedings in the Irish High Court and in ICC arbitration proceedings in Paris as well as negotiating licences of right. During the year the firm advised a US client for a Europe wide patent licensing programme.

Construction: The Construction Law Department has a reputation as a centre of excellence on all non contentious and contentious aspects of building, construction and engineering matters. The three construction partners, backed by two assistant solicitors, one of whom has 18 years experience as a Chartered Civil Engineer, have over 60 years experience between them in construction law.

Employment: The Employment and Employee Benefits Department has four fee earners and boasts three full members of the Employment Lawyers Association and an associate member of the Association of Pension Lawyers who is also an associate of the Pensions Management Institute. The department is very active in the provision of training both to clients in-house and at public seminars.Greenwoods reputation was founded on a strong and experienced litigation base that still applies today including family law and licensing.

Personal Injury: The Personal Injury Department goes from strength to strength. Its principal clients consist of major insurers, legal expense insurers, liability adjustors and a trade union. The department acts for both Plaintiffs and Defendants. Its fee earners have increased to seven to deal with its substantial growth.

Property: The Property Department deals with all types of transactions connected with agricultural, commercial, and residential property, including planning matters. Added to this, Greenwoods has a partner-led, dedicated team that specialises in housing law.

Probate: The Probate Department offers advice on taxation, trusts, probate and wills.

Greenwoods generally recruit up to four trainees annually. A minimum 2(2) degree is required, not necessarily in law. Apply by handwritten letter (plus typed CV) to Rosemary Gearing.

A brochure of the firm's services is available on request or if you wish, you may browse their web site: www.greenwoods.co.uk

Managing partner:	Shelagh Smith
Senior partner:	David Weekes
Number of partners:	17
Assistant solicitors:	14
Other fee-earners:	20

WORKLOADS	
Commercial Services	38%
Property	22%
Construction	16%
Insurance	12%
Private Client	12%

CONTACTS	
Agricultural	Nick Plumb
Commercial dispute resolution	Nigel Long
Commercial property	Stephen Illingworth
Company/commercial	Shelagh Smith
Construction	Martin Wood
Employment	Robert Dillarstone
Family	Jane Proctor
Housing law	Michael Taylor
Insolvency	James Maxey
Intellectual property	Philip Sloan
Personal injury	David Weekes
Probate	Michael Beresford

GREGORY, ROWCLIFFE & MILNERS

1 BEDFORD ROW, LONDON, WC1R 4BZ
Tel: (0171) 242 0631 **Fax:** (0171) 242 6652 **DX:** 95

The Firm: Gregory, Rowcliffe & Milners is a progressive firm with an established reputation in quality private client advice, litigation services, corporate and business law.

The firm has its roots going back to 1784. It consists of a well established private client, company/commercial and litigation practice with strongly developed Anglo-German connections, (with fluent German-speakers at all levels throughout the firm); and long standing links with a number of organisations concerned with Anglo-German trade.

Principal Areas of Work:

Company/ Commercial: (*Contact:* John Anderson). The department has excellent international links with Europe, especially Germany, the USA and the Far East, and represents national and multi-national concerns, providing practical legal and taxation solutions to business problems and objectives over a broad spectrum of commerce and industry.

Litigation: (*Contact:* Christopher Harper). The firm provides a full range of litigation services to institutional, business and private clients in respect of administrative law (especially judicial review applications against public bodies), commercial, employment and property disputes, family law (including matrimonial disputes), personal injury and claims relating to trusts and wills. The firm is noted for the international (especially German) aspect of its commercial and family litigation. It also has an extensive and well regarded London agency practice.

Private Client: (*Contact:* Peter Scott). The firm has expertise in inheritance and tax-planning (both resident and offshore) including the preservation of listed buildings and works of art, the creation of charitable trusts, and the administration of estates, often with an international dimension.

Property: (*Contact:* David King). All aspects of commercial, industrial, agricultural, residential and investment conveyancing including estate management, planning and tax planning.

Managing partner:	John Anderson
Number of partners:	12
Assistant solicitors:	2
Other fee-earners:	9

WORKLOADS	
Litigation	36%
Private client	23%
Company/ commercial	21%
Property	19%

CONTACTS	
Anglo German	Lesley Pendlebury Cox
Company/ Commercial	John Anderson
Employment	John Sharpe
Family/ matrimonial	Fenella Pringle
Litigation	Christopher Harper
Private client	Peter Scott
Property	David King
Tax	Peter Scott

GRIFFITH SMITH 47 Old Steyne, Brighton, BN1 1NW *Tel:* (01273) 324041 *Fax:* (01273) 384 000 *DX:* 2701 Brighton-1 *Ptnrs:* 11 *Asst solrs:* 5 *Other fee-earners:* 17

GRIGOR & YOUNG 1 North Street, Elgin, IV30 1UA **Tel:** (01343) 544077 **Fax:** (01343) 548523 **DX:** 520656 **Ptnrs:** 6 **Asst solrs:** 4 **Other fee-earners:** 4 **Contact:** W.P Mennie *Sale, purchase, leasing and factoring of farms, limited partnerships leases, commercial and residential conveyancing, liquor licensing, family and child law.*

WORKLOADS	
Court and related work/ matrimonial	27%
Domestic conveyancing	23%
Executry and trust	18%
Company, commercial and agricultural	15%
Estate agency	9%
Private client and other	8%

GRINDEYS Glebe Court, Stoke on Trent, ST4 1ET **Tel:** (01782) 846441 **Fax:** (01782) 416220 **DX:** 21053 **Email:** grindeys@aol.com **Ptnrs:** 13 **Asst solrs:** 14 **Other fee-earners:** 24 **Contact:** Paul Godfrey *Grindeys is a long established firm. Strengths in company/commercial work, commercial litigation, commercial property and personal injury litigation. ISO 9001 accredited.*

WORKLOADS	
Company/Commercial	35%
Commercial Property	20%
Insurance/Commercial Litigation	20%
Private Client	20%
Employment	5%

GROSS & CO.

84 GUILDHALL STREET, BURY ST. EDMUNDS, IP33 1PR
Tel: (01284) 763333 **Fax:** (01284) 762207 **DX:** 57203

23 BENTINCK STREET, LONDON, W1M 6AB
Tel: (0171) 935 5541 **Fax:** (0171) 935 6638

The Firm: Established in W. Suffolk for over 150 years, this progressive firm offers a specialist immigration service and has a fast-expanding commercial practice as well as a traditional general practice. The firm has an unusually international clientele, as well as sizeable private companies, small businesses and private clients. It is a member of the NIS Group of Independent Solicitors. The firm has an office in London W1 to service its London and international clients.

Principal Areas of Work:

Immigration and Nationality law: The majority of work is in the field of business immigration. Assistance is also given in US and Canadian immigration law, and a consultancy service is offered to other solicitors through the ImmLaw service (brochure available).

Company/ Commercial: Expertise in most areas of commercial practice, including commercial property, for a wide range of business clients.

Litigation: All types of litigation including commercial, civil, matrimonial and legal aid. Agency work undertaken.

Private Client: Conveyancing, wills/ estate planning.

Foreign Connections: The firm has overseas associate offices in USA, Canada, South Africa, India, Spain, Russia and Hong Kong.

Languages Spoken: French, German and Russian.

Senior partner:	G.D. Kirk
Number of partners:	6
Assistant solicitors:	1
Other fee-earners:	7

WORKLOADS	
Immigration and nationality law	20%
Company/ commercial	15%
Wills and probate	15%
Civil litigation	12%
Commercial property & Agriculture	10%
Matrimonial	10%
Residential conveyancing	10%
Employment	8%

CONTACTS	
Civil litigation	N. Amor
Commercial property & Agriculture	J. Cobbold
Company/ commercial	G. Kirk
Employment	N. Amor
Immigration/ nationality law	G. Kirk
Matrimonial	K. Pender
Residential conveyancing	A. Gordon-Stables
Wills and probate	A. Day

GULBENKIAN HARRIS ANDONIAN

181 KENSINGTON HIGH STREET, LONDON, W8 6SH
Tel: (0171) 937 1542 **Fax:** (0171) 938 2059 **DX:** 47204 KENSINGTON

The Firm: Whilst the firm engages in a wide range of commercial work (including litigation) it is best known for its expertise in immigration and nationality law which is undertaken for both commercial and private clients.

Principal Areas of Work:

Immigration and Nationality Law: (*Contact Partner:* Bernard Andonian or Peter Wyatt). *Work includes:* nationality applications, all aspects of UK immigration and advice (business and private), refugee and asylum work and obtaining work permits. The firm has experience in US immigration, Hong Kong, Eastern Europe (including Russia), Middle East, Sri Lanka and South Africa. The firm is a founder member of the European Immigration Lawyers group. Paul Gulbenkian and Bernard Andonian are both part-time Immigration Adjudicators.

Matrimonial and Family Law: (*Contact Partner:* Paul Gulbenkian or Bernard Andonian). Comprehensive services are provided including advice on separation, divorce, wardship, custody, adoption and all related financial, property and taxation matters. The senior partner is one of the founder members of the Solicitors Family Law Association.

Other Areas of Work: In addition, the firm handles commercial litigation, commercial and domestic property transactions, defamation, intellectual property and probate and trust.

Nature of Clientele: A largely international client base including multinationals as well as small to medium sized companies and private individuals.

Languages Spoken: French, Chinese, Spanish, Danish, Swedish, Farsi, Armenian and Arabic.

Senior partner:	Paul Gulbenkian
Number of partners:	10
Assistant solicitors:	3
Other fee-earners:	3

WORKLOADS	
Immigration	70%
Matrimonial	20%
General	10%

CONTACTS	
General	Paul Gulbenkian
Immigration	Bernard Andonian
Immigration	Peter Wyatt
Matrimonial	Bernard Andonian
Matrimonial	Paul Gulbenkian

R. GWYNNE & SONS Edgbaston Hse, Walker St, Wellington, TF1 1HF *Tel:* (01952) 641651 *Fax:* (01952) 247441 *DX:* 23107 *Ptnrs:* 9 *Asst solrs:* 13 *Other fee-earners:* 14

HACKING ASHTON

BERKELEY COURT, BOROUGH ROAD, NEWCASTLE-UNDER-LYME, ST5 1TT
Tel: (01782) 715555 **Fax:** (01782) 715566 **DX:** 20954

The Firm: Hacking Ashton provides a comprehensive legal service to commercial clients, with particular expertise in property development, intellectual property and construction matters, and also handles a wide range of private client work.

Principal Areas of Work:

Company/ Commercial: (*Contact:* Robert Ashton). Advice is offered with regard to company formations, acquisitions, disposals, franchising, take-overs, mergers, joint ventures, capital restructuring and financing, service and consultancy agreements, employment law, agency and distribution agreements, partnership and banking.

Litigation: (*Contact:* Malcolm Hacking). The firm specialises in work with a highly technical content, particularly intellectual property (including patents, trademarks, copyright, licensing, franchising and character merchandising), and building construction conciliation and arbitration. The department also undertakes personal injury cases (including medical negligence) and debt collection services.

International Law: (*Contact:* Robert Ashton). Advice is available on establishing overseas businesses, distributorship and agency agreements, EC legislation, restrictive trade practices legislation, foreign litigation, currency financing and commercial documentation.

Commercial Property: (*Contact:* Tom Gregory). The firm deals with sales and purchases of property, estate and commercial development, leasing, landlord and tenant law, mortgages and representation at public enquiries, planning appeals and tribunals.

Agricultural Law: (*Contact:* Tom Gregory). The firm handles all aspects of agricultural law including tenancies, quotas, tax planning and sale/ purchase of land. It also deals in equine business in all its aspects.

Private Client: (*Contact:* Lindsey Howland). The department advises on residential conveyancing, tax planning, family and matrimonial law, wills, trusts and probate.

Foreign Connections: The firm has established an impressive network of international connections, and is associated with overseas firms with offices in Paris, Milan, Geneva and Hamburg. The firm also supplies legal advice in Eastern Europe, the Far East, the Americas and Africa, with correspondent offices in Holland, New York, Canada, Hong Kong, Tokyo, India, Brazil and Mexico.

Managing partner:	Thomas Gregory
Senior partner:	Robert F. Ashton
Number of partners:	7
Assistant solicitors:	4
Other fee-earners:	9

WORKLOADS	
Commercial property	35%
Commercial litigation	30%
Company/ commercial	20%
Private client	10%
Agricultural	5%

CONTACTS	
Agricultural	T.R. Gregory
Commercial	R.F. Ashton
Commercial litigation	D.V.Potts
Commercial property	T.R. Gregory
Commercial property	C.A. Whittles
Company work	R.F Ashton
Construction	M.R. Hacking
Debt Collection	I. Bould
Domestic Conveyancy	A. Phillips
Employment	R.F. Ashton
Personal injury	B. White
Probate/ private client	L.G. Howland
Tax	R.Storey

HADENS (FORMERLY HADEN STRETTON SLATER MILLER) Leicester Buildings, Bridge Street, Walsall, WS1 1EL *Tel:* (01922) 720000 *Fax:* (01922) 720023 *DX:* 12122 Walsall *Ptnrs:* 16 *Asst solrs:* 8 *Other fee-earners:* 18

HALL & HAUGHEY 90 Mitchell Street, Glasgow, G1 *Tel:* (0141) 221 4800 *Fax:* (0141) 248 4802

HALLETT & CO

11 BANK ST, ASHFORD, TN23 1DA
Tel: (01233) 625711 **Fax:** (01233) 643841 **DX:** 30202 ASHFORD

The Firm: Hallett & Co is one of the oldest firms in the county and has a long history of advising local families, businessmen and farmers. It has particular expertise in agricultural matters including field sports, employment and commercial law and in tax and trusts.

Principal Areas of Work:

Property: *Work includes:* freehold and leasehold properties, holiday homes, housing associations, tenancy and lease agreements, compulsory purchase, Town and Country Planning applications and appeals, planning enquiries and general conveyancing work, in particular a substantial amount of estate development work.

Company/Commercial: *Work includes:* business start-up, franchising, joint ventures, commercial and employment contracts, company acquisition and disposal.

Commercial Litigation: *Work includes:* employment and redundancy disputes, unfair dismissal, consumer law, partnerships, building disputes, landlord and tenant, licensing applications and appeals, debt recovery and carriage of goods.

Private Client: *Work includes:* matrimonial and family law, personal injury, insurance claims, employment law, criminal law, wills, probate and trusts, tax planning and professional negligence. Legal aid work is undertaken.

Managing partner:	Richard Rix
Senior partner:	E.M. Skilbeck
Number of partners:	8
Assistant solicitors:	5
Other fee-earners:	15

Agriculture: *Work includes:* buying and selling agricultural land, planning applications and appeals, quotas and subsidies, company formations and partnerships, share farming agreements, tied cottages and Agricultural Holdings legislation.

Other Offices: New Romney, Lydd.

Foreign Languages: French.

HALLINAN, BLACKBURN, GITTINGS & NOTT 26 Buckingham Palace Road, London, SW1 OQP *Tel:* (0171) 834 3135 *Fax:* (0171) 828 3367 *Ptnrs:* 1 *Asst solrs:* 2 *Other fee-earners:* 3

HALLIWELL LANDAU

ST. JAMES'S COURT, BROWN ST, MANCHESTER, M2 2JF
Tel: (0161) 835 3003 **Fax:** (0161) 835 2994 **DX:** 14317 **Email:** INFO@HALLIWELLS.COM

The Firm: Halliwell Landau is one of Manchester's leading commercial law firms. The firm has an impressive client list and provides a comprehensive range of commercial legal advice to support their business activities. The partnership has a reputation for combining experience, commercial awareness and a willingness to consider new approaches and ideas. The firm's philosophy of entrepreneurial awareness with close attention to detail and dedication to high professional standards has become the hallmark of its work.

Principal Areas of Work:

Corporate: This is one of the largest departments in the region, advising on mergers, acquisitions, disposals, MBOs/MBIs, banking law and corporate finance.

Commercial Property: One of the leading commercial property advisers in the North West advising on a range of commercial property issues including the acquisition and disposal of properties, site assembly and negotiation of leases.

Commercial Litigation: Advises on all aspects of commercial litigation including property litigation, banking and recovery work, professional negligence.

Planning and Environmental: Widely acknowledged as one of the most respected planning appeal practices in the country, advising some of the region's top companies and local and national developers.

Construction and Bonds: Advises on all facets of construction law including bonds and guarantees, which play a crucial role in construction agreements.

Employment Law: Advises clients on both contentious and non-contentious aspects of legislation.

Trusts and Estate Planning: Acknowledged as one of the leaders in the field in the north west advising senior business executives and individuals of high net worth on income and estate planning, the creation of trusts and administration of investments. Also advises trustees and charities.

Intellectual Property: This department's advises on traditional categories of patents, copyright, trademarks and registered designs as well as advice on any form of intangible rights.

Insolvency and Corporate Recovery: Principally directed at supporting banks and insolvency practitioners on specialised insolvency matters. Also advises companies and directors on the legal aspects of restructuring, reorganising and refining.

Insurance Litigation: A rapidly growing department advising on general insurance issues, policy disputes, indemnity and warranty issues. All types of defendant personal injury work.

Pensions: Advises companies, trustees and others on all aspects of pensions law including current issues, mergers, acquisitions, documentation, wind ups, litigation and provision of independent trustee services through Halliwell Landau Trustees Limited.

Senior partner:	Roger Lancaster
Number of partners:	43
Assistant solicitors:	62
Other fee-earners:	22

WORKLOADS	
Corporate and banking	24%
Commercial litigation	20%
Commercial property	17%
Insolvency	12%
Insurance litigation	12%
Intellectual property	4%
Planning and environmental law	4%
Trust and estate planning	4%
Employment	3%

CONTACTS	
Commercial litigation	Paul Thomas
Commercial property	Geoff Marks
Corporate	Alec Craig
Corporate tax	Adam Pappworth
Employment	Stephen Hills
Insolvency	Andrew Livesey
Insurance litigation	Chris Phillips
Intellectual property	Jonathan Moakes
Pensions	Anne Taylor
Planning & environmental law	Roger Lancaster
Trusts and estate planning	Geoffrey Shindler

A. HALSALL & CO 47-48 Hamilton Square, Birkenhead, L41 5BD *Tel:* (0151) 647 6323 *Fax:* (0151) 647 9818 *DX:* 17853 *Ptnrs:* 7 *Asst solrs:* 1 *Other fee-earners:* 1

HAMILTON BURNS & MOORE 13 Bath Street, Glasgow, G2 1HY *Tel:* (0141) 353 2121 *Fax:* (0141) 353 2181 *DX:* 47 Glasgow *Ptnrs:* 6 *Asst solrs:* 6 *Other fee-earners:* 4

HAMLIN SLOWE

ROXBURGHE HOUSE, 273-287 REGENT ST, LONDON, W1A 4SQ
Tel: (0171) 629 1209 **Fax:** (0171) 491 2259 **DX:** 53803 OXFORD CIRCUS NORTH **Email:** ADMIN@HAMLINS.CO.UK

This medium sized London practice is property-orientated with a substantial commercial client base.

The Firm: Founded in 1906 undertakes a wide variety of work but has particular expertise in commercial property, commercial, secured lending, intellectual property, entertainment and media matters. The Firm's clients include several public companies and many large and well-known private companies.

Principal Areas of Work:

Property: The Property Department (Brian Casey) has a long and established reputation in; financing, acquisition, letting and disposal of shop, office and industrial property as well as handling development, town and country planning, compulsory purchase and landlord and tenant matters.

Secured Lending: The Secured Lending Department (Keith Roffey) acts for lenders in; professional negligence, possession, mortgage documentation, arrears, sales, insolvency, consumer credit and unsecured loss recovery matters. The Department has developed on-line computer systems for mortgage and arrears recovery.

Litigation, including Media, Entertainment and IP: The firm is known for the strength of its Litigation Department (Laurence Gilmore) which supports the non-litigious departments, handles heavy commercial litigation, matrimonial and personal injury matters and includes the Entertainment, Media and Intellectual Property Department which has an outstanding reputation in the entertainment sector, particularly in the areas of copyright infringement. It handles all aspects of entertainment law for clients who include copyright societies, music publishers, record companies, record producers, composers, authors, recording artists, and film and video production companies. The Department also advises on matters of; defamation, libel, information technology, multi-media, trade marks, passing off and design right.

Company/Commercial: The Company and Commercial Department (Gordon Oliver) deals with; mergers, acquisitions, disposals, franchising, employment and partnership matters. The Department also advises on share and rights issues, public flotations, corporate reorganisations, liquidations and joint ventures. This Department encompasses a division which specialises in advising the Leisure Industry and has an Asset Planning Division (Nick Giles) which handles personal taxation, inheritance tax planning, pensions, trusts, wills and probates.

Hamlin Slowe has a strong client base of both large and small clients. The firm's Brochure describing the Services that the firm has to offer is available upon request.

Managing partner:	B.M. Casey
Number of partners:	21
Assistant solicitors:	6
Other fee-earners:	8

WORKLOADS	
Litigation Services	30%
Property Services	30%
Entertainment/Intellectual property	15%
Company and commerical	12%
Secured lending	10%
Asset Planning	3%

CONTACTS	
Asset Planning	Nick Giles
Company and commercial	Gordon Oliver
Litigation including Entertainment, Media and Intellectual Property	Laurence Gilmore
Property services	Brian Casey
Secured lending	Keith Roffey

HAMMOND SUDDARDS

7 DEVONSHIRE SQUARE, CUTLERS GARDENS, LONDON, EC2M 4YH
Tel: (0171) 655 1000 **Fax:** (0171) 655 1001 **DX:** 33885 FINSBURY SQUARE

2 PARK LANE, LEEDS, LS3 1ES
Tel: (0113) 284 7000 **Fax:** (0113) 284 7001 **DX:** 26441 **Email:** ENQUIRIES@HAMMONDSUDDARDS.CO.UK

TRINITY COURT, 16 JOHN DALTON STREET, MANCHESTER, M60 8HS
Tel: (0161) 830 5000 **Fax:** (0161) 830 5001 **DX:** 14347 MANCHESTER 1

SUITE 688 LLOYD'S, 1 LIME STREET, LONDON (LLOYDS), EC3M 7HA
Tel: (0171) 327 3388/3399 **Fax:** (0171) 621 1217 **DX:** 807 LONDON/CITY

PENNINE HOUSE, 39-45 WELL STREET, BRADFORD, BD1 5NU
Tel: (01274) 764400 **Fax:** (01274) 730484 **DX:** 11796

AVENUE LOUISE 250, 1050 BRUSSELS BELGIUM,
Tel: 00 32 2 627 7676 **Fax:** 00 32 2 627 7686

The Firm: One of the UK's major commercial practices, Hammond Suddards offers comprehensive legal services to a wide range of national and international clients. In addition to its offices in London, Leeds, Manchester and Bradford, the firm has a specialist EC law office in Brussels and an insurance practice based in Lloyd's of London. The firm has around 520 lawyers, with a total staff of over 1,170.

Principal Areas of Work:

Banking: (*Contact:* Gwendoline Griffiths) A broad range of banking work is carried out both for financial institutions (including UK clearing banks and leading building societies) and for borrowers. Particular areas of expertise are acquisition finance, commercial lending both secured and unsecured, project finance, property finance, trade finance and syndications.

Commercial Dispute Resolution: (*Contact:* Mike Henley) *Work includes:* All commercial claims and disputes for the firm's corporate clients ranging from straightforward claims to substantial contested actions. The firm has particular expertise in Alternative Dispute Resolution (ADR) and arbitration.

Construction and Engineering: (*Contact:* Mark Hilton) One of the largest bespoke construction practices in the UK, the firm acts for major employers and contractors both nationally and internationally on all aspects of construction law in both contentious and non-contentious matters. The team has considerable experience of ADR which is of increasing significance to the construction industry.

Corporate Finance: (*Contact:* Richard Burns) *Work includes:* Public company takeovers, flotations and listing work generally, mergers and acquisitions, disposals, MBOs/MBIs, venture capital and joint ventures. This work is carried out in the UK and overseas for both UK and overseas companies and institutions. The firm presently provides corporate services to over 35 PLCs and specialist services to many others. In 1997 the firm completed corporate transactions with an aggregate transaction value in excess of £3 billion.

Employment: (*Contact:* Tim Russell) One of the largest employment practices in the UK, work includes advising on all areas of contentious and non contentious employment issues, including service agreements, restrictive covenants, compensation packages, transfer of undertakings, discrimination, disciplinary procedures, redundancies and boardroom, union, individual or group disputes.

Financial Services and Corporate Tax: (*Contact:* Christopher Haan) *Work includes:* Advice on tax planning at all levels, employee share option schemes and offshore tax. This unit incorporates particular derivatives expertise offering advice on both standard and new derivatives products. Specialist documentation unit executes all types of derivatives documentation including ISDA, IFEMA, ICOM and PSA/ISMA.

Insolvency and Corporate Recovery: (*Contact:* Chris Jones) *Work includes:* Advice to insolvency practitioners and banks on all aspects of their work as receivers, liquidators, trustees, administrators and supervisors. The firm also advises companies and partnerships experiencing serious financial difficulties. Much of the work is international.

Insurance: (*Contact:* Andrew McDougall) *Work includes:* Employers' liability, public liability, product liability, motor claims and professional indemnity work. The Lloyds of London office has a particular reputation for professional indemnity claims as well as coverage disputes and policy wording, insurance products and specialist areas such as political risks and reinsurance. The firm acts for most leading UK insurance companies and many of the Lloyds syndicates.

Intellectual Property: (*Contact:* Larry Cohen) All aspects of intellectual property rights including litigation and licensing, except applications work. This includes patents, trademarks, copyright and trade secrets. The firm also handles all aspects of film, music, television, sports and publishing work. The firm has specific experience in the fields of

Managing partner:	Chris Jones
Senior partner:	John Heller
Worldwide	
Number of partners:	89
Assistant Solicitors:	219
Other fee earners:	223

WORKLOADS	
Litigation	42%
Corporate	20%
Insolvency and corporate recovery	19%
Property and planning	19%

Continues overleaf

information technology and telecommunications, pharmaceutical and agrochemicals regulatory law, and crucially in the application of EU law to IP issues. It provides a leading edge service to suppliers and users of high technology in the public and private sectors.

Lender Services: (*Contact:* Lucci Dammone) The unit co-ordinates the provision of extensive services for many of the UK's leading lending institutions. Additionally, the unit incorporates a specialist section which is able to effectively and efficiently deal with very large volumes of litigation cases and conveyancing transactions utilising sophisticated information technology.

Pensions: (*Contact:* Jane Marshall) One of the largest and most experienced teams in the UK, Hammond Suddards handles the legal aspects of all kinds of pension arrangements, ranging from large occupational schemes to product development work for providers and unapproved top up schemes. Work includes advising employers and trustees, pension surpluses, conflicts, scheme mergers and reorganisations, pension disputes and litigation, insolvency and corporate transactions. They edit and are co-publishers of the Pensions Law Reports.

Property: (*Contact:* Chris Marks) *Work includes:* Purchases, sales and option agreements, office developments, acquisition and disposal of industrial premises, mineral extraction, quarrying and tipping agreements, negotiations, preparation and renewal of leases, city centre redevelopments and retail park development. Planning work includes: planning applications, planning audits, appeals and advocacy, planning applications, planning audits, appeals and advocacy, planning and enforcement, highway orders, compulsory purchase and advice in relation to listed buildings.

EU Law: (*Contact:* Konstantinos Adamantopoulos) A full European law service including competition law, anti-dumping, merger control, environmental law, existing and proposed legislation and regulations. Advice is also given on EC loans and grants, free movement of goods, people, services and capital, and intellectual property.

Nature of Clientele: Hammond Suddards acts for public companies and large private companies, banks, building societies, insurance companies and other large organisations and for subsidiaries and divisions of UK and overseas multinationals.

Foreign Connections: Brussels office; specialist India Business practice; In-house fluency in: Cantonese, Dutch, Finnish, French, German, Greek, Gujarati, Hebrew, Indi, Indonesian, Italian, Japanese, Lithuanian, Marathi, Persian, Portuguese, Punjabi, Serbo Croat, Spanish, Turkish.

Recruitment and Training: The firm recruits around 20 trainee solicitors each year. Applications (in the form of a CV and covering letter) should be sent to Ben Reeves, the Graduate Recruitment Manager, at the London office.

London: 7 Devonshire Square, Cutlers Gardens, London, EC2M 4YH
Tel: (0171) 665 1000 Fax: (0171) 665 1001 DX: 33885 Finsbury Square

Leeds: 2 Park Lane, Leeds LS3 1ES
Tel: (0113) 284 7000 Fax:(0113) 284 7001 DX: 26441

Manchester: Trinity Court, 16 John Dalton Street, Manchester M60 8HS.
Tel: (0161) 830 5000 Fax: (0161) 830 5001 DX: 14347 Manchester 1

Lloyds of London: Suite 688 Lloyd's, 1 Lime Street, London EC3M 7HA.
Tel:(0171) 327 3388/3399 Fax:(0171) 621 1217 DX: 807 London/City

Bradford: Pennine House, 39-45 Well Street, Bradford, BD1 5NU
Tel:(01274) 764 400 Fax:(01274) 730 484 DX: 11796

Brussels: Avenue Louise 250, 1050 Brussels, Belgium
Tel:(00) 322 627 7676 Fax:(00) 322 627 7686

HANCOCK & LAWRENCE The Old Mansion House, Quay Street, Truro, TR1 2HD *Tel:* (01872) 272333 *Fax:* (01872) 240390 *DX:* 81200 Truro *Ptnrs:* 8 *Asst solrs:* 3 *Other fee-earners:* 4

HANSELL STEVENSON 13 Cathedral Close, Norwich, NR1 4DS *Tel:* (01603) 615731 *Fax:* (01603) 633585 *DX:* 5204 *Ptnrs:* 8 *Asst solrs:* 13 *Other fee-earners:* 17

HARBOTTLE & LEWIS

HANOVER HOUSE, 14 HANOVER SQUARE, LONDON, W1R 0BE
Tel: (0171) 667 5000 **Fax:** (0171) 667 5100 **DX:** 44617 MAYFAIR **Email:** HAL@HARBOTTLE.CO.UK **Internet:** WWW.HARBOTTLE.CO.UK

The Firm: Harbottle and Lewis is recognised for the unique breadth of its practice in entertainment and media, including newer industries such as digital mixed media. It has a substantial practice in mainstream commercial and specialist property investment and development. The firm's aviation practice has also developed an outstanding reputation.

Principal areas of Work:

The *music industry* specialists concentrate on recording contracts, music publishing agreements, video agreements, merchandising and sponsorship agreements, licensing, and tour and distribution agreements.

The *film, television and theatre* department covers work such as feature films, television production, cable, satellite, video, radio, theatrical production and management, book and magazine publishing.

The *digital mixed media* group acts for clients in all areas of media related industries. Interactive digital media clients include media game hardware providers and software publishers. The group's expertise in internet and domain name issues is recognised and Harbottle & Lewis is the leading firm in the UK in the field of computer games.

Governing bodies, clubs, promoters and sports persons are represented by members of the *sport* group who advise on constitutional and regulatory matters and handle issues relating to sponsorship, promotion and venue agreements, player contracts, broadcasting, endorsements, merchandising, licensing of intellectual property rights and immigration.

The firm's *company and commercial* lawyers' work includes mergers and takeovers, flotations, finance, joint ventures and management buy-outs, employment law, insolvency, competition/antitrust law and commercial agreements of all kinds.

The *aviation* group deals with airline regulation and competition, aircraft acquisition, and all other legal aspects of the aviation business. Harbottle & Lewis is regarded as a leading firm in the field of aviation law.

A team of lawyers is primarily concerned with contract, *intellectual property* issues, including copyright, trade mark, passing off and domain name disputes, defamation, media issues, matrimonial work, and property litigation, as well as general and *commercial litigation*.

Members of the *advertising* group provide advice on the codes of conduct, all commercial contracts and copyright, brand protection, as well as libel and defamation advice through its copy checking service. It also provides general corporate, commercial, employment and litigation advice.

The firm's *property* specialists handle commercial development and investment work. A substantial part of the department's work involves arts, heritage, leisure and sporting properties. Their expertise includes environmental and planning law.

The *tax* group provides UK and international tax support to other departments as well as acting for clients in their own right. The firm has expertise in all aspects of commercial tax, as well as dealing with tax planning for individuals and trusts, wills and probate.

Other specialist groups consisting of lawyers from different parts of the firm pool specific industry and legal expertise in areas such as *IT, fashion, franchising, employment, radio, charities and immigration*.

Managing partner:	Colin Howes
Senior partner:	Michael Bowler
Number of partners:	15
Assistant solicitors:	50
Other fee-earners:	9

WORKLOADS	
New Media & Entertainment	35%
Corporate/Commercial	20%
Litigation	20%
Property	15%
Aviation	10%

CONTACTS	
Advertising	Alice Rayman
Aviation	Dermot Scully
Charities	Robert Reilly
Corporate/commercial	Colin Howes
Defamation	Gerrard Tyrrell
Digital Mixed Media	Mark Phillips
Employment law	Marian Derham
Film	Robert Storer
Immigration	Susanna Riviere
Insolvency	Samantha Phillips
Intellectual Property	Gerrard Tyrrell
Litigation	Michael Bowler
Music	Andrew Stinson
Property	Alan Patten
Radio	Marian Derham
Sport	Robert Mitchell/Paul Cairns
Tax, trust, probate	Linda Courtney
Theatre	Sean Egan
TV	Medwyn Jones

HARDING EVANS Queen Chambers, 2 North Street, Newport, NP9 1TE *Tel:* (01633) 244233 *Fax:* (01633) 246453 *DX:* 33202 *Ptnrs:* 8 *Asst solrs:* 5 *Other fee-earners:* 2

HARDWICK STALLARDS

CENTURION HOUSE, 37 JEWRY STREET, LONDON, EC3N 2EX
Tel: (0171) 423 1000 **Fax:** (0171) 481 3002 **DX:** 822 LONDON/CITY **Email:** MAIL@HARDWICK.CO.UK

The Firm: Recently formed through the merger of City firms Hardwick & Company and Stallards, its clientele consists principally of entrepreneur-managed businesses and a number of listed companies. The partner-led approach provides an in-house style of service and an emphasis on business experience.

Principal Areas of Work:

Company and Commercial:(*Contact:* Alan Williams). A broad range of corporate and commercial work, including intellectual property, partnerships, acquisitions and disposals,

Managing partner:	Simon J Hardwick
Senior partner:	Keith M Robinson
Number of partners:	11
Assistant solicitors:	5
Other fee-earners:	6

Continues overleaf

joint ventures, commercial contracts, and general commercial advice.

Corporate Finance:(*Contact:* Keith Robinson). Stock Exchange work, AIM and OFEX flotations, debt/equity issues, venture capital investment, institutional funding and secured lending, MBOs and MBIs, and corporate reconstructions.

Commercial Property:(*Contact:* Simon Hardwick). Commercial development and investment work for private and public companies, overseas investors, financial institutions and individual entrepreneurs, together with all aspects of landlord and tenant work, estate management and work for local authorities.

Litigation:(*Contact:* Rhodri James). Dealing with most kinds of disputes which arise in the course of operating a business; particular experience in the areas of landlord and tenant, construction contracts, factoring and banking, together with personal injury work.

Employment:(*Contact:* Jacques Smith). Contentious and non-contentious work, including advice in connection with general and sports contracts, organisational aspects, disqualification of directors, and restrictive covenants, together with related disputes.

Shipping:(*Contact:* Rupert Steer). Advice on contentious and non-contentious shipping matters, including charterparties, bills of lading, commodities, insurance and re-insurance, salvage, towage and collisions.

Overseas: The firm has a Caribbean Representative Office in Barbados, principally advising shipping and insurance clients in connection with English law.

HAROLD BENJAMIN & COLLINS

HILL HOUSE, 67-71 LOWLANDS ROAD, HARROW, HA1 3EQ
Tel: (0181) 422 5678 **Fax:** (0181) 864 0322 **DX:** 4243 HARROW 1 **Email:** ENQUIRIES@HBEN.CO.UK

The Firm: The firm was established in 1953 and is widely known for development and commercial conveyancing and building litigation. The firm is excellently located in central Harrow, an area increasingly convenient for a rapidly expanding base of property and other commercial clients, both regional and national. It has growing litigation and corporate departments. The firm's policy of investment in key people, its fine offices and IT expansion has promoted strong growth particularly in the last 5 years.

Principal Areas of Work:

Property Department: Development, commercial and residential conveyancing; town planning and environmental law; commercial leasehold premises work acting for both landlords and tenants; retail premises; commercial mortgage work for institutional lenders.

Litigation Department: Building and property litigation; personal injury and medical negligence; employment law; general litigation.

Corporate/Commercial Department: Wide range of corporate clients with broad spread of work including acquisitions, joint ventures, intellectual property, partnership, general commercial contracts, agency distribution, finance and competition law.

Private Client Department: A full service of family law; wills and probate; residential conveyancing, especially substantial properties.

Senior partner:	Roger Lane
Number of partners:	8
Assistant solicitors:	7
Other fee-earners:	4

WORKLOADS	
Commercial property	51%
Private client, family and probate	19%
Litigation	15%
Corporate	14%

HAROLD G. WALKER & COMPANY Lansdowne House, Christchurch Road, Bournemouth, BH1 3JT *Tel:* (01202) 555691 *Fax:* (01202) 294118 *DX:* 7609 *Ptnrs:* 9 *Asst solrs:* 6 *Other fee-earners:* 3

HAROLD MICHELMORE & CO 15-21 Market Street, Newton Abbot, TQ12 2RN **Tel:** (01626) 332266 **Fax:** (01626) 331700 **DX:** 59103 **Ptnrs:** 6 **Asst solrs:** 4 **Other fee-earners:** 4 **Contact:** Christopher Thomas *General practice known for agricultural, commercial, employment, PI and family litigation. Good European connections and languages.*

HARPER MACLEOD The Ca'd'oro, 45 Gordon Street, Glasgow, G1 3PE **Tel:** (0141) 221 8888 **Fax:** (0141) 226 4198 **DX:** GW86 **Email:** maildesk@harpermacleod.co.uk **Ptnrs:** 10 **Asst solrs:** 14 **Other fee-earners:** 9 **Contact:** Prof. Lorne D. Crerar *Four principal departments operate multi-disciplinary practice groups specialising in banking, construction, employment, licensing, natural resources, public sector & housing and sport.*

WORKLOADS			
Litigation	30%	Property	30%
Corporate & Commercial	20%	Recoveries	20%

HARRIS & CARTWRIGHT

WINDSOR CROWN HOUSE, 7 WINDSOR RD, SLOUGH, SL1 2DX
Tel: (01753) 810710 **Fax:** (01753) 810720 **DX:** 42268 SLOUGH (WEST) **Email:** STEPHEN_FULLER@HARRCART.CO.UK

The Firm: Established at the beginning of this century, Harris & Cartwright is a progressive and enlightened firm building on its accumulated knowledge and experience to provide a high quality, responsive and cost-effective service to all its clients. With two offices in Slough (one dedicated to Company/Commercial work) and others in nearby Langley and Burnham the firm is one of the largest in the Thames Valley.

Principal Areas of Work:

Company & Commercial: (*Contact Partner:* Stephen Fuller). A rapidly expanding department, now accounting for approximately one-third of total fee income, assists business clients across the full spectrum of problems faced from start-up to flotation and beyond. Services include commercial conveyancing, business sales, takeovers, mergers and acquisitions; partnership formations and agreements; commercial negotiations; company secretarial and administrative matters; commercial litigation; insolvency and receivership; employment; terms and conditions of sale; service contracts and similar agreements.

Litigation: (*Contact Partner:* Christopher Gooderidge). The firm offers an efficient and cost effective service for the resolution of disputes. A wide range of work encompasses Medical Negligence, Personal Injury, Family and Crime. All members of the department specialise in the work they undertake and are, variously, members of: The Law Society's Children, Personal Injury, and Medical Negligence Panels; The AVMA Referral Panel; The APIL Medical Negligence Special Interest Group; MASS and ATLA. The practice has considerable experience in dealing with High Court, County Court and statutory tribunal litigation.

Private Client: (*Contact Partner:* Paul Norris). The work of the department covers all matters relating to the personal and financial affairs of private clients. Services include computerised residential and commercial conveyancing and advice on planning, development, advice to landlords and tenants of commercial, residential and agricultural property; probate, wills, trusts and estate administration; financial guidance and tax planning; establishment and administration of trusts and charities, and Powers of Attorney; financial services including advice on investment, insurance and pensions.

Other Offices:

18 Church Street, Slough, SL1 1PT
Tel: (01753) 810710 *Fax:* (01753) 532886

272 High Street, Langley, Slough SL3 8HD
Tel: (01753) 548011 *Fax:* (01753) 580931

71 High Street, Burnham, Slough SL1 7JX
Tel: (01628) 663041/2 *Fax:* (01628) 667898

Foreign Languages: French and German.

Senior partner:	P.M. Norris
Number of partners:	7
Assistant solicitors:	11
Other fee-earners:	14

CONTACTS	
Commercial Litigation	Raj Dhokia
Commercial Property	Paul Norris
Corporate/commercial	Stephen Fuller
Crime	Mark Moorcraft
Debt Collection	Mathew Lorimer
Employment	Raj Dhokia
Family	Punam Denley
Landlord & Tenant	Andrew Grant
Medical Negligence	Christopher Gooderidge
Personal Injury	Kent Pattinson
Residential Conveyancing	Dan Walters
Wills, Probate, Trusts	June Snook

Harris & Cartwright

● *Solicitors*

HARRIS & HARRIS 14 Market Place, Wells, BA5 2RE **Tel:** (01749) 674747 **Fax:** (01749) 676585 **DX:** 44900 Wells **Ptnrs:** 6 **Asst solrs:** 2 **Other fee-earners:** 7 **Contact:** Mr. T.F. Berry. *Firm with specialists in commercial, family law, construction, ecclesiastical, insolvency and mental health. Also, office in Frome and Consultant in France.*

HARRISON BUNDEY & CO. 219-221 Chapeltown Road, Leeds, LS7 3DX **Tel:** (0113) 237 4047 **Fax:** (0113) 237 4685 **Ptnrs:** 9 **Asst solrs:** 6 **Other fee-earners:** 6 **Contact:** Ruth Bundey *An inner city high street practice specialising in crime, civil liberties, immigration and family, childcare, inquests and personal injury.*

HARRISON CURTIS 40 Great Portland Street, London, W1N 5AH **Tel:** (0171) 637 3333 **Fax:** (0171) 637 3334 **Email:** mail@harrisoncurtis.co.uk **Contact:** Lawrence Harrison or Tim Curtis *A small firm offering high quality advice to a broad range of media and entertainment clients. Expertise in music, film, television, theatre, advertising, design and marketing, new media and sports law.*

WORKLOADS	
Media and Entertainment	80%
Company Commercial	10%
Sport	10%

HARRISON, LEITCH & LOGAN Victoria House, 54 – 58 Chichester Street, Belfast, BT1 4HN **Tel:** (01232) 323843 **Fax:** (01232) 330187 **DX:** 401 NR Belfast **Ptnrs:** 4 **Asst solrs:** 4 **Other fee-earners:** 4 **Contact:** Jonathan Hool *Personal Injury and Commercial Litigation, Company, Commercial Property, Banking, Insolvency and Private Client.*

WORKLOADS	
Litigation	60%
Conveyancing and commercial	40%

HARROWELL SHAFTOE

1 ST. SAVIOURGATE, YORK, YO1 2NQ
Tel: (01904) 620331 **Fax:** (01904) 655855 **DX:** 61506 YORK

The Firm: A long established firm with a modern outlook. Harrowell Shaftoe has long acted for companies and family firms in the York, North Yorkshire region. Known particularly for its well established private client practice but with substantial development in recent years in company, commercial and litigation work. The firm is committed to quality and is a member of the national network of quality law firms, Law Group UK. The firm has a legal aid franchise in seven categories.

Principal Areas of Work:
  Company/ Commercial
  Commercial Property
  Commercial Litigation
  Private Client
  Family Law
  Personal Injury
  Crime

Recruitment and Training: The firm recruits trainees each year.

Other Offices:

Harrowell Shaftoe, Moorgate House, Clifton Moor, York.
Tel: (01904) 690111. *Fax:* (01904) 692111

Harrowell Shaftoe, Westow House, The Village, Haxby, York.
Tel: (01904) 760237. *Fax:* (01904) 761555. *DX:* 61460 Haxby

Senior partner:	John F. Yeomans
Number of partners:	11
Assistant solicitors:	8
Other fee-earners:	11

WORKLOADS	
Litigation	40%
Private client work	35%
Company commercial work	25%

CONTACTS	
Agency work	Robert Onyett
Commercial litigation	John Yeomans
Commercial property	Kevin Millar
Company/ commercial	James Scott
Crime	Jackie Knights
Family Law	John Reynard
Medical negligence	Mark Tempest
Personal injury	Mark Tempest
Private client	William Miers

HART BROWN 20 Bedford Road, Guildford, GU1 4TH **Tel:** (01483) 887766 **Fax:** (01483) 887752 **DX:** 2412 Guildford 2 **Ptnrs:** 17 **Asst solrs:** 32 **Other fee-earners:** 15 **Contact:** Alan Preskett *Largest firm based wholly within Surrey. General practice. Other offices in Guildford, Godalming, Cranleigh, Cobham, Farnham and Woking.*

WORKLOADS			
Family	22%	Commercial	21%
Residential property	20%	Civil litigation	15%
Crime	11%	Private client	11%

HARTFIELDS

ACADEMY COURT, 94 CHANCERY LANE, LONDON, WC2A 1DU
Tel: (0171) 405 4440 **Fax:** (0171) 405 4350 **DX:** 431 LONDON/CHANCERY LANE

The Firm: Hartfields was established on 1st September 1997. Almost all of the partners and staff were previously with the well-respected firm of Alastair Thomson & Partners. It is a specialist litigation practice operating in specific areas.

Principal Areas of Work: Insurance law and policy advice; professional negligence; other liability insurance; building disputes; and commercial disputes.

Clients: Clients include public and private companies, insurers, professional practices and housing developers.

Senior/managing partner:	David Hartfield
Number of partners:	3
Assistant solicitors:	2
Other fee-earners:	2

WORKLOADS	
Professional negligence	50%
Other liability insurance	20%
Building disputes	10%
Commercial disputes	10%
Insurance law	10%

HART-JACKSON & HALL 3a Ridley Place, Newcastle upon Tyne, NE1 8JQ **Tel:** (0191) 232 1987 **Fax:** (0191) 232 0429 **DX:** 61003 **Ptnrs:** 3 **Contact:** Richard Hart-Jackson *Known for entertainment law. Also handles civil and personal injury litigation, property, family and business law.*

WORKLOADS			
Commercial	30%	Family/ Childcare	25%
Litigation	20%	Property	20%
Other	5%		

HARTLEY & WORSTENHOLME 20 Bank St, Castleford, WF10 1JD *Tel:* (01977) 732222 *Fax:* (01977) 603105 *DX:* 700134 Castleford *Ptnrs:* 8 *Asst solrs:* 10 *Other fee-earners:* 5

HARTNELL & CO 20 Cathedral Yard, Exeter, EX1 1HB **Tel:** (01392) 421777 **Fax:** (01392) 421237 **DX:** 8388 Exeter **Ptnrs:** 1 **Asst solrs:** 4 **Contact:** Norman Hartnell *Family law practice. For caring specialist help in times of crisis.*

WORKLOADS	
Family	100%

HARVEY INGRAM OWSTON 20 New Walk, Leicester, LE1 6TX **Tel:** (0116) 254 5454 **Fax:** (0116) 255 4559 **DX:** 17014 Leicester 2 **Email:** hio@hio.co.uk **Ptnrs:** 26 **Asst solrs:** 24 **Other fee-earners:** 36 **Contact:** Stephen Woolfe *Firm provides a broad range of business and private client services and has specialist teams. Two satellite offices in suburbs.*

WORKLOADS			
Litigation	30%	Property	27%
Commercial	20%	Trusts	13%
Private Clients	10%		

HASTIES 51 South Bridge, Edinburgh, EH1 1PP *Tel:* (0131) 556 7951 *Fax:* (0131) 558 1596 *DX:* 16 Edinburgh *Ptnrs:* 3 *Asst solrs:* 3 *Other fee-earners:* 3

HATCH BRENNER 4 Theatre Street, Norwich, NR2 1QY **Tel:** (01603) 660811 **Fax:** (01603) 619473 **DX:** 5237 Norwich **Ptnrs:** 9 **Asst solrs:** 3 **Other fee-earners:** 10 **Contact:** Alan Dobbins. *Property, commercial, civil litigation (including employment and personal injury), family and crime. Legal Aid Franchise, Personal Injury and Children Panels.*

HATCHER ROGERSON 25 Castle Street, Shrewsbury, SY1 1DA *Tel:* (01743) 248545 *Fax:* (01743) 242979 *DX:* 19725 Shrewsbury *Ptnrs:* 10 *Asst solrs:* 4 *Other fee-earners:* 18

HATTON SCATES & HORTON 5-7 Byrom Street, Manchester, M3 4PF **Tel:** (0161) 833 0020 **Fax:** (0161) 833 4186 **Contact:** Olivia Scates *The firm has recently amalgamated with* **Jones Maidment Wilson**. *Known for its expertise in plaintiff personal injury with 75% of the work being medical negligence including cases involving injuries of the utmost severity.*

WORKLOADS			
Medical negligence	75%	Personal injury	20%
Judicial review/Other	5%		

HAWKINS RUSSELL JONES 7-8 Portmill Lane, Hitchin, SG5 1AS *Tel:* (01462) 628888 *Fax:* (01462) 631233 *DX:* 7100 *Ptnrs:* 16 *Asst solrs:* 6 *Other fee-earners:* 19

HAWLEY & RODGERS 19-23 Granby St, Loughborough, LE11 3DY *Tel:* (01509) 230333 *Fax:* (01509) 239390 *DX:* 19602 *Ptnrs:* 12 *Asst solrs:* 8 *Other fee-earners:* 8

HAY & KILNER

MERCHANT HOUSE, 30 CLOTH MARKET, NEWCASTLE-UPON-TYNE, NE1 1EE
Tel: (0191) 232 8345 **Fax:** (0191) 221 0514 **DX:** 61019 NEWCASTLE UPON TYNE

The Firm: Established in 1946, Hay & Kilner is one of the North East's major legal practices, dealing with a full range of work on behalf of commercial organisations, institutions and private clients. The firm is a member of LawNet.

Principal Areas of Work:

Commercial: company, commercial, takeovers and mergers, management buyouts, investments and securities, banking, building societies, employment, computer contracts, intellectual property, partnership law, licensing and leisure, insolvency, commercial property, leasing, tax, planning and construction.

Litigation: personal injury, insurance, medical negligence, commercial litigation, employment disputes, landlord and tenant, product liability, professional negligence, construction disputes, debt collection, defamation, criminal law; Alternative Dispute Resolution.

Private Client: domestic conveyancing, family and matrimonial, inheritance, tax, wills, probate and trust and residential property

Other Offices: Wallsend and Gosforth.

Senior partner:	John Kilner
Number of partners:	23
Assistant solicitors:	8
Other fee-earners:	10

CONTACTS	
Commercial litigation	Martin Soloman
Commercial property	Colin Dickinson
Company/commercial	Nick James
Construction	Martin Soloman
Employment	Neil Dwyer
Family law	Ken Carlisle
Insolvency	Neil Harrold
Insurance	Peter Pescod/Ros Sparrow
Medical negligence	David Bradshaw
Personal injury	Alun Williams
Private Client	Keith Hateley

HEDLEYS 15 St Helen's Place, Bishopsgate, London, EC3A 6DJ *Tel:* (0171) 638 1001 *Fax:* (0171) 588 7547 *DX:* 598 *Ptnrs:* 2 *Asst solrs:* 1

HEGARTY & CO 48 Broadway, Peterborough, PE1 1YW *Tel:* (01733) 346333 *Fax:* (01733) 62338 *DX:* 16850 Peterborough *Ptnrs:* 8 *Asst solrs:* 9 *Other fee-earners:* 16

HEMPSONS

33 HENRIETTA STREET, COVENT GARDEN, LONDON, WC2E 8NH
Tel: (0171) 836 0011 **Fax:** (0171) 836 2783 **DX:** 40008 COVENT GARDEN **Email:** LONDON-HEMPSONS@BTINTERNET.COM

CLARENDON HOUSE, 9 VICTORIA AVENUE, HARROGATE, HG1 1DY
Tel: (01423) 522331 **Fax:** (01423) 500733 **DX:** 11965 HARROGATE 1 **Email:** HARROGATE-HEMPSONS@BTINTERNET.COM

PORTLAND TOWER, PORTLAND STREET, MANCHESTER, M1 3LF
Tel: (0161) 228 0011 **Fax:** (0161) 236 6734 **DX:** 14482 MANCHESTER 2 **Email:** MANCHESTER-HEMPSONS@BTINTERNET.COM

The Firm: Hempsons is well-known for its particular expertise in the field of medical and healthcare law, partnership work and charity law. The firm has long provided a comprehensive range of services to the professions and charities; clients include health authorities, NHS trusts, healthcare organisations, professional bodies, Royal Colleges and individual professionals.

Principal Areas of Work:

Medical Litigation: The firm has long been renowned for its expertise in this field and handles matters relating to medical and dental negligence (all areas of hospital and general practice), defendant personal injury litigation, quantum of damages, class actions, disciplinary cases for professional organisations or their members, codes of professional practice and medical crime. Hempsons is one of the national firms on the NHS Litigation Authority's restricted panel of healthcare solicitors to act in defence of medical negligence claims.

Healthcare Law: The firm advises a range of healthcare organisations on all aspects of law and ethics, mental health and community care law, administrative law and NHS regulatory law.

Partnership: Advice to doctors and other professionals on the formation of partnerships and partnership agreements; the accession and retirement of partners; the dissolution of partnerships and partnership disputes.

Commercial Litigation/Defamation: Advice in relation to all forms of UK commercial disputes including litigation in respect of employment, insurance, arbitration, ADR work, product liability and sale of goods matters. Defamation work is carried out for local authorities and many substantial commercial undertakings.

Commercial Property: The department handles commercial, institutional, professional property, including acquisitions and developments, grant, renewal and termination of leases, rent reviews and the Cost Rent Scheme for general practitioners including funding proposed surgery developments.

Charity Law: A complete service to charities, large and small, including: formation and restructuring of charities, advice to trustees and management on legal duties and powers, updating constitutions, employment issues, dealings with the Charity Commission and the Inland Revenue, financial and commercial activities, trading subsidiaries; fundraising and appeals; disputed legacies.

Commercial Work and PFI: This team specialises in the commercial problems of NHS Trusts and Health Authorities, charities and professional clients. The firm is developing a strong reputation in Private Public Partnership/PFI with its work for NHS Trusts, with 4 significant completions in the past year.

Employment: The firm has a lively and proactive team of employment lawyers providing solutions to HR problems in the NHS, for employers and professionals, and our charity clients. Hempsons has particular experience in all types of discrimination work and Paragraph 190 Appeals.

Managing partner:	Janice Barber
Senior partner:	Bertie Leigh
Number of partners:	28
Assistant solicitors:	66
Other fee-earners:	21

WORKLOADS	
Medical litigation	38%
Healthcare	15%
Partnership	15%
Commercial property	12%
Charity	10%
Commercial litigation/ defamation	10%

CONTACTS	
Charity	Ian Hempseed
Commercial Litigation	Hilary King
Commercial Property	Graham Lea (London)
Commercial Property	Alan Burns (Manchester)
Commercial Property	John Haigh/ Louise Holroyd (Harrogate)
Defamation	Mark Shaw
Employment	Val Cook (London)
Employment	Pat Jones (Manchester)
Employment	Kerry Devlin (Harrogate)
Healthcare	Bertie Leigh (London)
Healthcare	Ann Meadowcroft (Manchester)
Healthcare	John Lovel (Harrogate)
Medical Litigation	John Taylor (London)
Medical Litigation	Frances Harrison (Manchester)
Medical Litigation	John Lovel (Harrogate)
Partnership	Simon Barnes/Lynne Abbess
PPP/PFI	Tim Young

HEMPSONS SOLICITORS

HENDERSON BOYD JACKSON WS

19 AINSLIE PLACE, EDINBURGH, EH3 6AU
Tel: (0131) 226 6881 **Fax:** (0131) 225 1103 **DX:** ED27

The Firm: Strong systems, quality recruitment and an emphasis on client care have allowed the firm of Henderson Boyd Jackson to grow into one of Scotland's leading law firms with an ever expanding client base. HBJ is now widely acknowledged as being at the forefront of commercial legal practice and has increased in size by 30% per annum over the last five years. This growth is testament to the firm's commitment to providing quality service, economically, to commercial clients, based principally in Scotland.

Over the last three years however, the firm has developed a cross border capability which has been maximised since establishing an office in the South East of England. The maintenance of close working relationships with clients has served to ensure high levels of client retention across the broad spectrum of the firm's activities.

While the firm has experienced rapid growth in its traditional markets of commercial and corporate law, commercial property and admiralty work the firm continues to develop in areas which include Intellectual Property and, significantly, the emerging sector of Commodity Law which includes personal injury and mortgage service work; instructions currently being received from a number of the major financial institutions.

The firm predicts that its current rate of growth will continue to hold should the now established principles of client care and considered pricing be maintained. The client list is impressive and includes fully listed companies, AIM listed organisations, family businesses and professional partnerships.

Principal Areas of Work:

Corporate: The Corporate partners continue to be involved in the full spectrum of transactions including MBOs, MBIs, joint ventures, start ups, acquisitions and disposals. With an ever increasing number of full stock exchange and AIM listings to their credit the Department is clearly a growth areas for the firm. The demand for expertise in the law of Intellectual Property is accelerating and HBJ's Corporate Department have ensured that ample resource has been put in situ to manage the needs of clients in this field. The Corporate Department's clients include a number of the country's leading plcs.

Commercial Property: The Commercial Property Department has grown by almost 50% in the last three years while turnover has virtually doubled. The department continues to be involved in all aspects of Commercial Property transactions and also benefits from a specialist licensing division. Clients include development, trading and investment companies, as well as a number of internationally recognised tenants.

Litigation: The Litigation Department was further augmented during 1997 with a view to significant development in 1998. The appointment of a new partner, and two new assistants will enable the firm to expand its service provision which currently comprises debt recovery, insolvency, building arbitration and personal injury.

Maritime: The firm's Maritime Department is the recognised leader in its sector. The Department continues to provide expertise in all aspects of Maritime Law from the drafting of ship building contracts and ship sale and purchase agreements to collisions, salvage, pollution, personal injury and port and harbour operations.

Other Offices:

158 West Regent Street, Glasgow, G2 4RL
Tel: (0141) 248 1124 *Fax:* (0141) 248 1123

Winter Hill House, Station Approach, Marlow, SL7 1NT
Tel: (01628) 488877 *Fax:* (01628) 488532

Managing partner:	Malcolm McPherson
Number of partners:	20
Assistant solicitors:	35
Other fee-earners:	25

WORKLOADS	
Corporate	30%
Commercial property	25%
Litigation	25%
Maritime	10%
Private client	10%

CONTACTS	
Commercial property	Struan Leishman
Corporate	Ross Blyth
Litigation	Maggie Keith
Maritime	Jim Lowe
Private client	Ross MacKay

HENMANS

116 ST. ALDATES, OXFORD, OX1 1HA
Tel: (01865) 722181 **Fax:** (01865) 792376 **DX:** 4311 OXFORD 1

The Firm: Henmans has expanded by 40% over the last 5 years. Continual investment in additional skills and extension of its IT systems and premises has produced a powerful set of resources. With swift and accurate advice as the starting point, the firm's policy is to get close to its clients, to take the initiative and to deliver forward planning and guidance, whether to corporations, institutions or individuals.

Principal Areas of Work:

Corporate and Commercial Services: A full range of corporate expertise is provided for private and listed companies, including flotations, MBOs, corporate finance and company sales/purchases. Commercial services (contract negotiation, often in a European context, publishing and IT agreements, copyright etc.) are backed by the firm's substantial risk management and dispute resolution resources. The emphasis is always on positive, cost effective advice.

Employment: (*Contact:* Colin Henney: see "Leader" entry). Both employer and employee work undertaken including Industrial Tribunal and High/County Court litigation; advice on employment contracts and other industrial relations matters.

Professional negligence: A team of eight solicitors in this department specialises in defendant professional indemnity work on behalf of solicitors and other professionals.

Personal Injury/Employers' Liability/Medical Negligence: (*Contact:* Anthony Henman & Mary Duncan: see "Leader" entry). The department has a leading reputation for both plaintiff and defendant work. Most of the major insurance companies are represented. Two partners are on the panel of solicitors recommended by Action for Victims of Medical Accidents.

Agricultural/Land department: A comprehensive service is provided for farmers and land owners throughout the Midlands, Southern England and Wales.

Commercial property: All aspects of site assembly, funding and disposal. Particular expertise in green field development work; planning.

Probate: Specialist team dealing with all aspects of wills, succession, trusts and tax. Three solicitors are Members of the Society of Trust and Estate Practitioners.

Family: The department deals in particular with complex financial matters arising from separation and divorce, frequently where there is a family owned business including mediation. Members of the Solicitors Family Law Association.

Charities: In addition to administration of charity property, assistance is provided with legal aspects of fund raising, legacy administration, trading subsidiaries etc, to a growing list of national charities as well as long-standing local charity clients. One partner is a member of the Charity Law Association.

Other Office: 6 Oxford Street, Woodstock, Oxfordshire, OX20 1TW. *Tel:* (01993) 811396. *Fax:* (01993) 813184. *DX:* 53700 Woodstock.

Managing partner:	Sam Eeley
Senior partner:	Anthony Henman
Number of partners:	15
Assistant solicitors:	17
Other fee-earners:	17

WORKLOADS	
Company/commercial/empl./com. property	20%
Personal injury and medical negligence	20%
Professional negligence	20%
Agricultural law	15%
Family	10%
Private client	10%
Charities	5%

CONTACTS	
Agricultural/land law	Roger Henman
Charity	Peter Jeffreys
Commercial litigation	Peter Steer
Commercial property	Jeremy Ramsdale
Company/commercial	Malcom Sadler
Employment	Colin Henney
Family	Maureen Clarke
Medical negligence	Mary Duncan
Personal injury	Anthony Henman
Probate/tax planning	Alexandra Houston
Professional negligence	Francis Dingwall

HENRY HEPWORTH

5 JOHN STREET, LONDON, WC1N 2HH
Tel: (0171) 242 7999 **Fax:** (0171) 242 7998 **Email:** HH@MEDIALAW.CO.UK

The Firm: Henry Hepworth is a specialist media and intellectual property practice with a distinctive high-quality client base which is active across the entire spectrum of the visual, print, copyright and intellectual property industries.

Principal Areas of Work: The firm advises solely in the areas of media, communications and intellectual property. It has two departments, a non-contentious department active in film, television and multimedia and a contentious department which services the print and visual industries advising in defamation and other litigious matters. The firm also provides advice and assistance to other UK and international firms on media/intellectual property matters. In addition to a traditional fee structure the firm offers a fixed fee retainer service.

Number of partners:	3
Assistant solicitors:	2
Other fee-earners:	1

WORKLOADS	
Defamation and Contentious matters	60%
Non Contentious matters	40%

CONTACTS	
Defamation and Contentious matters	
	Brian Hepworth/Jason McCue
Non Contentious matters	Michael Henry

HENRY HYAMS & CO 7 South Parade, Leeds, LS1 5QX *Tel:* (0113) 243 2288 *Fax:* (0113) 242 9714 *DX:* 12028 *Ptnrs:* 8 *Asst solrs:* 5 *Other fee-earners:* 10

HENRY MILNER & CO

COUNTY HOUSE, 14 HATTON GARDEN, LONDON, EC1N 8AT
Tel: (0171) 831 9944 **Fax:** (0171) 831 9941 **DX:** 53305 CLERKENWELL

The Firm: Henry Milner has specialised exclusively in criminal defence work for 23 years. His practice offers a personal and experienced service, handling serious and complicated criminal cases of all types.

Principal Areas of Work: Work handled by the firm includes white collar crime (including VAT fraud), mortgage frauds, drugs importation cases involving Customs and Excise, robbery, kidnapping, murder and blackmail. Mr Milner also specialises particularly in High Court bail applications.

Managing partner:	Henry F. Milner
Senior partner:	Henry F. Milner
Number of partners:	1
Other fee-earners:	1

HEPTONSTALLS

7-15 GLADSTONE TERRACE, GOOLE, DN14 5AH
Tel: (01405) 765661 **Fax:** (01405) 764201 **DX:** 28831 GOOLE

9-11 ROPERGATE END, PONTEFRACT, WF8 1JU
Tel: (01977) 602804 **Fax:** (01977) 602805 **DX:** 22255 PONTEFRACT

The Firm: Heptonstalls, with its Goole and Pontefract offices, is a major provider of legal services in Yorkshire and North Lincolnshire. The firm aims to ensure that clients receive an efficient personal and friendly service whatever their legal needs.

Principal Areas of Work:

Personal Injury and Medical Negligence: *(Contact Partner:* John Burman). This department has a leading regional reputation for plaintiff claims arising from medical treatment, road traffic accidents, industrial accidents and disease, defective products and related matters. Special interests include obstetrics and gynaecology, head and spinal injuries, and traumatic brain injury. John Burman is on the AVMA Medical Negligence Referral Panel and is one of two members of the Law Society Medical Negligence and Personal Injury Panels.

Commercial/Agriculture: *(Contact Partner:* Malcolm Walker). Advice on a wide range of business and commercial law including employment and and commercial litigation. The firm has extensive experience in advising agricultural businesses on such areas as land law, conservation, agricultural tenancies and other aspects of land management.

Private Client: *(Contact Partner:* Roger Beattie). The firm advises on property, tax and family finance, wills, probate and trusts, landlord and tenant disputes, family and matrimonial law, and welfare benefits.

Other Offices: 1 Vicar Lane, Howden, Yorkshire. DN14 7BP. *Tel:* (01430) 430209.

Senior partner:	Roger Beattie
Number of partners:	6
Assistant solicitors:	12
Other fee-earners:	8

WORKLOADS	
PI/Medical negligence	35%
Property/Common law/Civil	25%
Trusts & probate & tax	16%
Criminal	12%
Matrimonial	12%

CONTACTS	
Agriculture	M.G. Walker
Commercial/Property	R. Beattie
Criminal	A.S. Pinchbeck
Employment	A.S. Pinchbeck
Medical negligence	J. Burman
Personal injury	J. Burman
Tax/Probate and Trust	M.G. Walker
Welfare and Family	C. Luckett

HERBERT MALLAM GOWERS 126 High St, Oxford, OX1 4DG *Tel:* (01865) 244661 *Fax:* (01865) 721263 *DX:* 4321 Oxford *Ptnrs:* 6 *Asst solrs:* 4 *Other fee-earners:* 2

HERBERT SMITH

EXCHANGE HOUSE, PRIMROSE STREET, LONDON, EC2A 2HS
Tel: (0171) 374 8000 **Fax:** (0171) 374 0888 **DX:** 28 **Email:** HSMAIL@HERBERTSMITH.COM **Internet:** HTTP://WWW.HERBERTSMITH.COM

The Firm: Herbert Smith is a premier international law firm operating from the City of London, Brussels, Paris, Hong Kong and Singapore. Herbert Smith is able to co-ordinate a global service of the highest order for its clients.

Founded in 1882 Herbert Smith now has over 700 lawyers supported by 700 other staff. The firm advises major corporate organisations, governments, financial and other institutions and commercial concerns of all types, around the world and in all spheres of business activity. Herbert Smith lawyers devote their skills to anticipating and avoiding legal problems, enabling the firm's clients to achieve commercial success. The firm's commitment to excellence is underlined by a rigorous professional development programme which ensures that our lawyers keep ahead of changes in law and practice.

Types of work undertaken: Herbert Smith provides a comprehensive range of legal services across all areas of corporate and commercial life. The firm is consistently highly placed in legal league tables and rankings. Frequently, our role puts us at the centre of industries which are reshaping and we are well known for our innovative work on ground-breaking deals and restructurings. The firm has a long-standing reputation for advice on mergers, acquisitions and takeovers and is highly regarded for its expertise in corporate finance. In recent years Herbert Smith has developed an increasingly significant role in the arena of international finance and banking, particularly in the specialised field of international capital markets.

Herbert Smith is widely acknowledged as a leading adviser on international energy law, and the firm is regularly involved in restructurings, privatisations and complex transactions around the world. Many such deals reflect our strength in international projects and project finance where the firm's expertise also extends to developments and infrastructure projects of many kinds and on which it advises clients throughout the world.

Other areas of corporate expertise include: competition law; corporate recovery; employment; European law; insurance; investment funds; media; telecommunications; pensions and share schemes; tax; and trusts and charities.

Herbert Smith enjoys a formidable reputation for its expertise in both domestic and international litigation and arbitration – a pre-eminent position it has held for several decades. In this it is the breadth of the firm's practice which distinguishes Herbert Smith from its competitors. Areas of specialism include: administrative and public law; banking; civil fraud; construction; defamation; employment; energy; environment; information technology; insurance and reinsurance; intellectual property; public and private international law; professional indemnity; regulatory and compliance cases; shipping; and sport. Herbert Smith has experience before every type of court and tribunal and conducts arbitrations in all parts of the world. It is the firm's consistent aim to add value to our client's business as a whole and not to concentrate alone on the narrow issues in dispute. We use alternative dispute resolution procedures in appropriate cases and several of our partners are accredited mediators.

The firm's planning and development expertise is well recognised, following its involvement in a number of the high-profile projects of recent years. Herbert Smith is also highly regarded in the field of institutional investment – buying, selling and managing national portfolios on behalf of some of the UK's leading property investors.

Senior partner:	Edward Walker-Arnott
Worldwide:	
Number of Partners:	145
5Assistant Solicitors:	343
Other Fee-earners:	219

CONTACTS	
Banking	Clive Barnard
Capital Markets	Dina Albagli
Commercial Litigation	Harry Anderson
Commercial Property	Christopher Harrison
Construction and Engineering	Michael Davis
Corporate	Richard Bond
Corporate Finance	Caroline Goodall
Corporate Recovery	Stephen Gale
Defamation	David Natali
EC and Competition	Jonathan Scott
Employee Incentives	Colin Chamberlain
Employment	John Farr
Energy	Alan Jowett
Environment	David Brock
Insurance	Marian Pell
Insurance Litigation	David Higgins
Intellectual Property	Bill Moodie
International Commercial Arbitration	Julian Lew
International Fraud	Sonya Leydecker
International Project Finance	Andrew Preece
	Nicholas Tott
Investment Funds	Nigel Farr
Media	Charles Plant
Mergers and Acquisitions	Stephen Barnard
Pensions	Ian Gault
Planning and Development	Patrick Robinson
Shipping	Nicholas Robinson
Tax	David Martin
Telecoms	Tim Bellis
Trusts and Charities	John Wood
Utilities Regulation	Elizabeth McKnight
Venture Capital and MBOs	David Paterson

HERBERT SMITH

HERBERT WILKES

41 CHURCH ST, BIRMINGHAM, B3 2RT
Tel: (0121) 233 4333 **Fax:** (0121) 233 4546 **DX:** 13047

The Firm: Established over 60 years ago, Herbert Wilkes has developed into a modern commercial practice offering a wide range of legal services to business, industry and private individuals.

Principal Areas of Work:

Company and Commercial: (*Contact Partner:* Gareth O'Hara). The department handles all aspects of company formation, acquisitions and disposal, corporate finance, management buy outs and corporate restructuring.

Litigation: (*Contact Partner:* Nigel Wood). The firm deals with the full range of commercial litigation services including High Court, County Court and matters arising from EC legislation. It also provides a specialised commercial debt collection service. Other work includes commercial contract disputes, personal injury, employment matters and health and safety at work.

Property: (*Contact:* Adele McDermott). The practice undertakes and advises on domestic and commercial conveyancing, property development, shops, offices, factories, leases, planning matters, joint ventures and landlord and tenant matters.

Private Client: (*Contact Partner:* Anna Dunford). The firm offers advice to individuals regarding wills, settlements, probate, inheritance tax, personal taxation and pensions. The firm also provides a service to private clients on matters of employment, personal injury, consumer legislation, family matters and divorce, criminal work and licensing.

Nature of Clientele: Business and industrial clients nationally as well as long-standing private clients.

Foreign Connections: The firm has professional links in the major European cities particularly in relation to property buying in Europe. Links with France and Germany are particularly strong.

Other Office: 10 Coleshill Road, Hodge Hill, Birmingham B36 8AA. *Tel:* (0121) 784 8484. *Fax:* (0121) 783 4935 DX:27434.

Managing partner:	Anna Dunford
Senior partner:	Nigel Wood
Number of partners:	16
Assistant solicitors:	22
Other fee-earners:	18

WORKLOADS	
Litigation (including insolvency)	36%
Corporate and commercial	27%
Conveyancing	25%
Tax/ trust/ probate	12%

CONTACTS	
Building contracts	Peter Tugwell
Civil litigation	Nigel Wood
Commercial conveyancing	Adele McDermott
Corporate/commercial	Gareth O'Hara
Debt recovery	Kevin Curran
Employment	Steven Hopkins
Insolvency	David Cleary
Large scale voluntary transfer	Peter Ewin
Medical Negligence	Nick Tubb
Personal injury	Maxine Kelly
Public authority & Housing associations	
	Richard Jaffa
Tax/trust	Anna Dunford

HEWITSON BECKE + SHAW

42 NEWMARKET ROAD, CAMBRIDGE, CB5 8EP
Tel: (01223) 461155 **Fax:** (01223) 316511 **DX:** 133155 CAMBRIDGE 8 **Email:** MAIL@HEWITSONS.COM (FOR ALL OFFICES)
Internet: WWW.HBSLAW.CO.UK (FOR ALL OFFICES)

7 SPENCER PARADE, NORTHAMPTON, NN1 5AB
Tel: (01604) 233233 **Fax:** (01604) 627941 **DX:** 12401 NORTHAMPTON

STUART HOUSE, CITY ROAD, PETERBOROUGH, PE1 1QF
Tel: (01733) 897979 **Fax:** (01733) 898060 **DX:** 12344 PETERBOROUGH 1

53 HIGH STREET, SAFFRON WALDEN, CB10 1AR
Tel: (01799) 522471 **Fax:** (01799) 524742 **DX:** 200300 SAFFRON WALDEN

The Firm: Hewitson Becke + Shaw traces its origins back to 1865. The firm has an extensive company and commercial practice, a thriving private client base and a growing body of public sector clients.

Principal Areas of Work:

Commercial Property: (*Contact Partner:* Alan Brett). The firm handles a large volume of commercial property work, from the construction of major commercial and residential developments and science parks to small retail and industrial units. The firm is increasingly used by major concerns abroad, including Hong Kong. Work includes the acquisition, development and letting of all manner of commercial sites. The firm has particular expertise in complex funding mechanisms and joint ventures.

Company/Commercial: (*Contact Partner:* Bridget Kerle). Work includes mergers and acquisitions, company structuring and restructuring, venture and development capital investment, management buy-outs/buy-ins, rights issues, Stock Exchange flotations, European Union and International law, merger control, OFT/ Commission investigations, joint ventures, pensions, employee share option and incentive schemes, partnerships and insolvency. The firm acts for a significant number of public limited companies as well as owner-managed businesses and is doing an increasing amount of UK-related work from an expanded US client base.

Intellectual Property: (*Contact Partner:* Ian Craig). The firm advises on all aspects of obtaining, exploiting and enforcing intellectual property rights, with particular expertise in computer hardware and software, biotechnology, pharmaceutical, film, music and book publishing industries.

Managing partner:	Alan Brett
Senior partner:	Ian Barnett
Number of partners:	50
Assistant solicitors:	40
Other fee-earners:	37

WORKLOADS	
Litigation	36%
Commercial property	26%
Company/ commercial	22%
Private client	16%

CONTACTS	
Agriculture	Ian Barnett
Commercial litigation	John Shephard
Commercial property	Alan Brett
Company/ commercial	Bridget Kerle
Construction	Tim Richards
Debt services	Steve Martin
Employment	Nick Sayer
Intellectual property	Ian Craig
Investment Services	Andrew Lowin
Planning and environmental	Peter Brady
Private client	Peter Ewart
Property funding	Alan Brett
Residential property	David Sabberton

Continues overleaf

Private Client: (*Contact Partner:* Peter Ewart). Work includes administration of estates, trusts, tax, wills, enduring powers of attorney, pensions, charities, residential property advice, landed estates, court of protection and matrimonial.

Litigation: (*Contact Partner:* John Shephard). The services are provided through eight groups each consisting of staff dedicated to one of the following areas of specialisation: banking, commercial contract law/ equity, construction, employment, intellectual property, personal injury, crime and family. The firm acts nationally for several major clearing banks.

Employment: (*Contact Partner:* Nick Sayer). Work includes service contracts, pensions, dismissal, redundancy, compensation for unfair dismissal, profit sharing and share option schemes and general employee benefits. The firm is a member of the Employment Lawyers Association and six members of the firm are individual members of the Association.

Agriculture: (*Contact Partner:* Ian Barnett). Work includes the granting of development options by landowners, joint venture and share farming agreements, farm partnerships, taxation and environmental matters, sales and tenancies and mineral exploitation. The firm has a significant following of landed estates and farming clients.

Bloodstock: (*Contact Partner:* David Hollest). The firm advises on all aspects of bloodstock law with particular emphasis on property transactions and general litigation.

Planning and Environmental: (*Contact Partner:* Peter Brady). Work includes planning appeals and local plan inquiries, advising developers, investors, local authorities, conservation and amenity groups, and individuals. The firm has two members of the Law Society's Specialist Planning Panel.

Residential Property: (*Contact Partner:* David Sabberton). Work includes sales, purchases and mortgages of freehold/ leasehold houses/ flats for private clients and institutions as well as builders and developers.

Investment Services: (*Contact Director:* Andrew Lowin). Work includes a comprehensive range of services for individuals, company executives, private trustees, pension fund trustees and charities.

Debt Services: (*Contact Director:* Steve Martin). Work includes consultancy, outsourced credit control, pre-legal service, debt recovery.

Hewitson Becke+Shaw
SOLICITORS

HEWITT & GILPIN Thomas House, 14-16 James Street South, Belfast, BT2 7GA *Tel:* (01232) 323254 *Fax:* (01232) 331741 *Ptnrs:* 6 *Asst solrs:* 2

HEXTALL ERSKINE

28 LEMAN STREET, LONDON, E1 8ER
Tel: (0171) 488 1424 **Fax:** (0171) 481 0232 **DX:** 562 CITY

The Firm: A long-established practice – the firm continues to build upon its known expertise in commercial and insurance related civil litigation. Litigation clients include leading UK composites, Lloyd's syndicates, corporations and foreign based companies. The practice also covers a wide range of non-contentious work.

Principal Areas of Work:

Insurance: *Work includes:* all aspects of litigation including professional indemnity (especially surveyors & valuers, brokers, architects, accountants, barristers, engineers, tour operators, sheriffs, bailiffs, directors and officers), insurance and reinsurance disputes, product liability, employers' liability, all aspects of health and safety, public authority work, motor, contractors' all risks, fire and property, policy wordings and general advice.

Commercial Litigation: *Work includes:* employment, construction and general commercial litigation, debt recovery. Founder member of CEDR – a partner is a qualified mediator.

Company Commercial: All aspects of company and commercial law are handled including formation, sale and purchase of companies, flotations, joint ventures, trade disputes and employment matters.

Commercial Property: The department handles funding and acquisitions, joint ventures, planning and tax-related aspects over a wide range of commercial and industrial property.

Private Client: The main areas of expertise are personal tax planning, wills, trusts and estate planning and pension scheme guidance for the self-employed and company directors, matrimonial and residential property.

Member of FOIL – Federation of Insurance Lawyers
Member of STEP – Society of Trust & Estate Practitioners.
Member of Solicitors' Family Law Association and Family Mediators Association.

Senior partner:	John Bundy
Number of partners:	21
Assistant solicitors:	10
Other fee-earners:	25

WORKLOADS	
Insurance related	83%
Other commercial litigation	5%
Private client	5%
Property	4%
Company commercial	3%

CONTACTS	
ADR	Anna Dalglish
Commercial litigation	David Hadfield
Commercial property	Stephen Chapman
Company/Commercial	Anthony Millson
Construction & engineering	Jill Heaton
Employers' & public liability	Neil Thomas
Employment litigation	Anne Lumsden
Family	Anne Lumsden
Insurance litigation	William Jarvis/John Startin
Motor	Richard Cheveley
Policy wordings	Stuart White/William Jarvis
Product liability	William Jarvis
Professional indemnity	Stuart White/Alastair Cornforth
Property risks	Jill Heaton
Reinsurance	Robert Wilson/William Jarvis/John Startin
Wills, probate & tax planning	Anthony Millson

Recruitment & Training: The firm recruits four trainee solicitors a year. Applications by letter and CV to Stuart White.

Foreign Connections: The firm has close working relationships with lawyers in the United States and on the Continent and has ready access to advice on foreign law in most jurisdictions.

HICKMAN & ROSE

144 LIVERPOOL ROAD, LONDON, N1 ORE
Tel: (0171) 700 2211 **Fax:** (0171) 609 6044 **Emergencies: (**01459) 138106 **DX:** 122234 UPPER ISLINGTON **Email:** HICKMAN@DIRCON.CO.UK

The Firm: Established in 1991, Hickman & Rose is a rapidly growing practice specialising in all aspects of the criminal justice system. It runs intensive training programs for professional staff on a regular basis. This firm has the expertise to take on complex and difficult one-off matters, while tackling smaller problems efficiently and cost-effectively.

Principal Areas of Work:

Crime *Work includes:* Murder, manslaughter, drugs and firearm conspiracies, as well as a substantial magistrates and youth court practice.

Serious fraud *Work includes:* Serious and international fraud, computer crime, and high value bank instuments.

Actions against police A specialist department is devoted to bringing actions against the police for misconduct, assaults, wrongful arrests.

Prisoners rights A dedicated unit works on prisoners rights, including multi party actions in the case of prison assualts, and judicial reviews.

Mental Health A growing team works on behalf of those detained under the Mental Health Act and those affected by Community Care legislation.

Number of partners:	5
Assistant solicitors:	15

WORKLOADS	
Crime	70%
Prisoner Rights	10%
Serious Fraud	10%
Actions Against the Police	5%
Mental Health	5%

CONTACTS	
Actions Against the Police	Hope Liebersohn
Crime	Liz Sergeant
Mental Health	Louise Smith
Prisoner Rights	Daniel Machover
Serious Fraud	Ben Rose

HIGGS & SONS Blythe House, 134 High Street, Brierley Hill, DY5 3BG *Tel:* (01384) 342100 *Fax:* (01384) 342000 *DX:* 22751 Brierley Hill *Ptnrs:* 20 *Asst solrs:* 15 *Other fee-earners:* 10

HILL BAILEY GROUP Wells House, 15-17 Elmfield Rd, Bromley, BR1 1QP *Tel:* (0181) 290 1177 *Fax:* (0181) 464 3328 *DX:* 94703 Bromley 3 *Ptnrs:* 11 *Asst solrs:* 10 *Other fee-earners:* 26

R. & J.M. HILL BROWN & CO 3 Newton Place, Glasgow, G3 7PU *Tel:* (0141) 332 3265 *Fax:* (0141) 332 2613 *DX:* 512207 Glasgow- Sandyford Place *Ptnrs:* 6 *Asst solrs:* 1 *Other fee-earners:* 1

HILL DICKINSON

PEARL ASSURANCE HOUSE, 2 DERBY SQUARE, LIVERPOOL, L2 9XL
Tel: (0151) 236 5400 **Fax:** (0151) 236 2175 **DX:** 14129 LIVERPOOL 1 24 HOUR EMERGENCY NUMBER: (01426) 179 605
Email: LAW@HILLDICKS.COM

34 CUPPIN STREET, CHESTER, CH1 2BN
Tel: (01244) 896600 **Fax:** (01244) 896601 **DX:** 19991 CHESTER 24 HOUR EMERGENCY NUMBER: (01426) 179 605

SUN COURT, 66/67 CORNHILL, LONDON, EC3V 3NB
Tel: (0171) 695 1000 **Fax:** (0171) 695 1001 **DX:** 98940 CHEAPSIDE 2 24 HOUR EMERGENCY NUMBER: (01426) 179 605

50 FOUNTAIN STREET, MANCHESTER, M2 2AS
Tel: (0161) 278 8800 **Fax:** (0161) 278 8801 **DX:** 14487 MANCHESTER 2 24 HOUR EMERGENCY NUMBER: (01426) 179 605

Founded in 1810, Hill Dickinson is now one of the largest commercial law firms in the North West, providing a portfolio of specialist legal advice to both the domestic and international market. It is fundamental to the Hill Dickinson philosophy to care for clients, whilst delivering a highly professional, cost effective service. Their ISO 9001 accreditation reflects a demonstrated and on-going commitment to client care.

The Firm: The practice has a strong and marked reputation in the insurance, litigation, company commercial, commercial property, marine and transport domain, and provides specialists to deal with an increasingly wide range of legal requirements. The firm has a total of 400 staff, including more than 60 Partners. Operations have been substantially extended over recent years with offices now in Liverpool, Manchester, Chester and the City of London. All offices have full conference facilities, on-line communication links, an extensive reference library and access to a number of electronic legal data sources.

Principal Areas of Work: With a wealth of specialist advisers, the firm undertakes a wide range of legal work in the commercial and private domain and is structured into specialist groups.

Insurance: One of the largest departments of its kind in the country, Hill Dickinson acts for most major insurers and, through them, a large proportion of their corporate and individual policy holders. The department has the capacity and resources to deal with a wide range of litigation issues, including the most complex of "test" or multi-party actions, and to react quickly to incidents or claims requiring immediate legal assistance.

Health: The firm has one of the UK's largest medico-legal practices, acting on behalf of health authorities, NHS trusts and other health service bodies. The firm is a member of the panel of solicitors maintained by the National Health Service Litigation Authority and was the first in the country licensed to provide health/medical negligence elements within training contracts.

Property & Construction: The Hill Dickinson property and construction team provides legal advice across the full range of property matters, including construction and engineering projects. They act for retailers, manufacturers, service providers, developers, investors, contractors and public sector clients. They have experience in retail, office, industrial, leisure and residential projects and provide specialist advice in relation to environmental and planning issues.

Commercial: The commercial group advises on a broad range of matters as diverse as intellectual property, European law, franchising, employment, pensions and PFI. They are one of the leading commercial litigation firms in the North West and where litigation is inevitable the commercial litigation team provides full support.

Corporate: Lawyers in the corporate group provide advice on all aspects of corporate law including company formation, mergers, acquisitions, management buy-outs and buy-ins, venture capital, flotation and insolvency.

Marine & Cargo: Recognised as one of the leading specialist shipping solicitors in the UK, Hill Dickinson has provided advice to both national and international clients since 1810. The department also has well established experts handling cargo and transit matters and consequently has the resources to offer a truly comprehensive service.

Private Client: The firm retains a strong private client base, providing specialist advice on for example, tax and estate planning, wills, trusts, probate and financial planning matters. Literature, outlining in detail, all aspects of the firms' activities, is available on request and they are pleased to have a preliminary discussion on any specific requirement.

Foreign languages: Italian, French, German, Spanish, Welsh, Portugese, Russian, Greek, Cantonese

Managing partner:	David Wareing
Senior partner:	Paul Walton
Number of partners:	65
Assistant solicitors:	53
Other fee-earners:	66

WORKLOADS	
Litigation (inc insurance/construction/ professional negligence)	50%
Commercial property, planning and environmental	15%
Shipping	15%
Company, commercial, pensions, tax, intellectual property, PFI	10%
Health/medical negligence	10%

CONTACTS	
Commercial	Elizabeth Mackay
Corporate	Andrew Smithson
Health	Allan Mowat
Insurance	Mike McKenna/Simon Parrington
Marine & Cargo	John Hulmes/Julia Marshall
Private Client	Mike Quinn
Property/Construction	David Swaffield/David Chinn

HILL TAYLOR DICKINSON

IRONGATE HOUSE, DUKE'S PLACE, LONDON, EC3A 7LP
Tel: (0171) 283 9033 **Fax:** (0171) 283 1144 **DX:** 550 **Email:** ENQUIRY@HTD-LONDON.COM

City-based Hill Taylor Dickinson is a commercial firm servicing the business and financial community in the United Kingdom and internationally.

The Firm: Hill Taylor Dickinson is based in the City of London. The firm also has offices in Dubai, Greece and Hong Kong.

The firm has expanded considerably in the 1990s and now comprises 27 partners and 158 people world-wide. The three overseas offices have been established and new areas of business have been developed (see below). This growth has been achieved by organic growth within the firm complemented by external recruitment (including at partner level), particularly directed towards the development of new business areas.

Clients range from major international corporations to owner managed businesses. Critical to the success of the firm's relationship with all of them is close partner involvement and understanding of their operations and markets.

Principal Areas of Work: Hill Taylor Dickinson's practice is entirely commercial.

The firm's **transactional** work includes **company/commercial** and **financing** – for example, venture capital, leasing and asset finance, ship building and finance, corporate buy-outs and buy-ins – as well as **commercial property**. Its clients include banks and other financial institutions, both City based and overseas, insurers, employers' organisations and a wide variety of corporate clients, notably in the leisure, manufacturing and publishing sectors.

The **insolvency** department has been involved in many complex and high-profile cases. The department deals with both corporate and personal insolvency, including receiverships and corporate reconstruction and recovery. Its clients include banks, accountants and corporate clients.

The **personal injury**, **ITF** and **employment** department acts mainly for employers, insurers, owners and P&I clubs in shipping and transport and a wide variety of industries. It deals with mass and individual claims. The department's work includes preventative and practical advice, including the drafting of accident reporting documents and procedures, drafting contractual clauses and employment contracts, safety policies and a whole spectrum of employment and personal injury claims.

Hill Taylor Dickinson's expertise in **shipping** – an area in which it acts for shipowners, P&I clubs, insurers, as well as major oil companies – makes it one of the foremost practices in this field. The shipping department handles the full range of commercial problems arising out of international trade and transport, including major maritime casualties, disaster litigation, pollution claims, charterparty disputes and cargo claims.

The firm has also significantly increased its practice in **commodities** disputes in recent years. Its clientele in this area includes trading houses and a number of trade associations.

The **insurance and reinsurance** division acts for underwriters, insurance companies, brokers and assureds. London – both Lloyd's and the companies market – is a major source of the division's work, but the firm derives its clients from all over the world. Hill Taylor Dickinson's reputation in marine insurance is well established and the firm has a team specialising in non-marine areas of insurance and reinsurance.

Hill Taylor Dickinson is a progressive and dynamic firm seeking to provide an effective personal service to both national and international clients and a commercial approach to legal problems and their resolution.

Senior partner:	John Pople
Number of partners:	23
Assistant solicitors:	19
Associate Partners:	12
Other fee-earners:	12

WORKLOADS	
Shipping and Commodities	50%
Commercial Transactional	17%
Insurance and Reinsurance	14%
Insolvency	12%
Personal Injury	7%

CONTACTS	
Commercial Property	Richard Taylor
Commodities	Jeff Isaacs
Company/Commercial	Tim Railton, Malcolm Entwistle
Insolvency	Mike McCarthy
Insurance	Tim Taylor, Robin Williams, Tim Burton
Personal Injury	Maria Pittordis
Shipping	John Evans, Stephen Cropper
Shipping	Robert Wallis, Andrew Johnson

Hill
Taylor
Dickinson
solicitors

HILLYER MCKEOWN

BELL TOWER WALK, ST WERBURGH STREET, CHESTER, CH1 2DY
Tel: (01244) 345551 **Fax:** (01244) 342824 **DX:** 22153 CHESTER NORTHGATE

The Firm: The merged practice of Philip Jones, Hillyer & Jackson and Hilton Blythe Porteous. Specialising in Company, Commercial and Insolvency matters. The established and fast growing Insolvency department deals with major Accountancy firms country wide. The merger of the two firms which took place in May 1998 further crystallised the expanding Company Commercial department. In addition there is a fast growing Personal Injury department with two members of the Law Society's Personal Injury Panel. The firm is also a member of the Children Panel and undertakes work on a wide basis for Guardians Ad Litem. A further principal area of work relates to landlord and tenant matters which is dealt with on a national basis. The firm also has Legal Aid Franchises and a wide commercial and private client litigation department. The private client work includes wills, trusts, administration of estates, tax, financial planning, residential property, family matters and matrimonial disputes.

Other Offices:

9 Hunter Street, Chester CH1 2AQ.
2 Church Road, Bebington, Merseyside L63 7PH.
90-92 Telegraph Road, Heswall, Merseyside L60 0AQ.

Senior partner:	J.W. Hillyer
Number of partners:	10
Assistant solicitors:	3
Other fee-earners:	6

WORKLOADS	
Insolvency	18%
Personal Injury	17%
Company Commercial	14%

CONTACTS	
Commercial Litigation	John Hillyer
Company Commercial	Phil McKeown
Insolvency	Mark Davies
Personal Injury	Nigel Tomlinson

HOBSON AUDLEY HOPKINS & WOOD

7 PILGRIM STREET, LONDON, EC4V 6DR
Tel: (0171) 450 4500 **Fax:** (0171) 450 4545 **DX:** 401 LONDON **Email:** LAWYERS@HOBSONAUDLEY.CO.UK **Internet:** WWW.HOBSONAUDLEY.CO.UK

The Firm: A City firm specialising in business law, with a broad range of international and UK corporate clients. The firm is the product of the merger in March 1996 of the strong corporate law and commercial litigation practice of Hobson Audley with the specialist intellectual property, information technology and commercial litigation expertise of Hopkins & Wood. Prior to the merger, Hopkins & Wood was already a leader in the intellectual property, information technology and telecommunications fields, whilst Hobson Audley had established a reputation for corporate finance work, ranking highly in the league tables for new issues. Hobson Audley Hopkins & Wood combines strength in corporate law, litigation and commercial property with specialist areas such as employment, intellectual property, IT, multimedia and electronic commerce. The firm's commercial property group offers specialist advice in the areas of development, finance, institutional investment and urban regeneration at a level commensurate with that offered by the largest City firms. The firm's broad range of legal skills is coupled with an international perspective and an awareness of business needs.

Principal Areas of Work:

Company: The firm provides a full range of corporate law services to public and private companies, investors and buy-out teams. Transactional work includes mergers and acquisitions, MBOs, Stock Exchange work, venture capital finance, banking and debt financing.

Commercial: The firm advises on joint ventures, distribution and agency, franchising, UK and EU competition law, international trade, terms of business, general contract law.

Litigation and Dispute Resolution: Prior to their merger, both Hobson Audley and Hopkins & Wood had strong reputations for litigation and had handled numerous substantial actions, arbitrations and appeals up to the House of Lords. The merged firm combines these strengths with additional and recent experience in ADR and mediation.

Commercial Property: The Commercial Property Group has a depth of experience in the private and public sectors, with a strong bias towards development, finance, property joint ventures and institutional investments.

Intellectual Property: Copyrights, design right and registered designs, patents, trademark and service mark infringement actions, passing off, trade libel and comparative advertising, protection and misuse of confidential information, franchising, know-how and show-how, technology transfer agreements, disputes and arbitration.

Information Technology: The firm acts for a well established client base ranging from multi-nationals to small businesses in the high technology, computing, multimedia, publishing, telecommunications and biotech fields and advises on IT contract negotiation, telecommunications, electronic commerce, multimedia and interactive software contracts.

Employment: Employment contracts, disciplinary matters, maternity rights, discrimination, health and safety issues, redundancy, employment legislation relating to transfer of businesses, contentious employment matters including termination arrangements, unfair and wrongful dismissal claims and industrial action.

Managing partner:	Gerald Hobson
Number of partners:	17
Assistant solicitors:	18
Other fee-earners:	6

WORKLOADS	
Commercial Litigation (incl. IP)	36%
Corporate Finance/Company Commercial	32%
Commercial Property	17%
Information Technology	7%
Banking, financial services, insolvency	4%
Employment	4%

CONTACTS	
Commercial	David Walter, Robert Bond
Commercial Property	Godfrey Bruce-Radcliffe
	Simon Smith
Company	Max Audley Rupert Connell
	David Walter, Anthony Brockbank
Employment	Gerald Hobson, Caroline Whiteley
Information Technology	Robert Bond, David Walter
Insolvency Services	Rupert Connell, Malcolm Robson
Insurance	Berry Holding-Parsons, Roger Hopkins
Intellectual Property	Andrew Joyce, Claire Poll
Litigation & Dispute Resolution	Gerald Hobson,
	Roger Hopkins, Malcolm Robson, Andrew Joyce

Insolvency Services: Contentious and non-contentious aspects of corporate insolvency law and practice in areas such as receiverships, company voluntary arrangements, liquidations, administrations, cross-border insolvencies and directors' responsibilities.

Insurance: The firm is experienced in the unique problems of the London Market. It advises on liability claims on behalf of errors and omissions insurers, directors' and officers' liability insurance, reinsurance, policy drafting, coverage disputes and IT developments in the London Market, professional indemnity claims on behalf of institutions including leading building societies.

Nature of Clientele: The firm's client base is drawn principally from the UK, continental Europe and North America. Clients are involved in manufacturing, high technology, computing, telecommunications, publishing, marketing services, healthcare, oil and gas, oil field services, banking, the financial services and securities industries, building societies and property investment and development.

Foreign Connections: In August 1997, the firm formed a Multinational Partnership with Faegre & Benson LLP of Minneapolis under the name of Faegre Benson Hobson Audley. Association with Faegre & Benson LLP has enhanced the firm's international contacts with the introduction of a number of substantial US corporations whose UK interests are now represented by Faegre Benson Hobson Audley.

Foreign Languages Spoken: French, German and Italian.

G.L. HOCKFIELD & CO 41 Reedworth Street, Kennington Rd, London, SE11 4PQ **Tel:** (0171) 735 0489 **Fax:** (0171) 820 1707 **DX:** 33252 **Ptnrs:** 4 **Asst solrs:** 2 **Other fee-earners:** 2 **Contact:** James Garvey *Principal areas of work are housing litigation and claimant personal injury, medical and other professional negligence work.*

WORKLOADS	
Housing	48%
Personal injury	37%
Professional negligence (including medical negligence)	12%
Micellaneous areas	3%

HODGE JONES & ALLEN

TWYMAN HOUSE, 31-39 CAMDEN ROAD, LONDON, NW1 9LR
Tel: (0171) 482 1974 **Fax:** (0171) 267 3476 **DX:** 57050 CAMDEN TOWN **Email:** HJA@HODGE-JONES-ALLEN.CO.UK

The Firm: Hodge Jones & Allen was established in 1977 and has expanded rapidly, especially since moving to new premises in September 1997. The firm has a particular reputation for legal aid work. It has been involved in a number of high profile and leading cases, notably cases involving racial discrimination and personal injury cases arising from the King's Cross fire and the Marchioness disaster. Following a merger with Richard Barr and his multi-party team from Dawbarns of Norfolk, the firm is handling 3 major group claims including Gulf War Syndrome.

Principal Areas of Work:

Personal Injury: (*Contact Partner:* Patrick Allen). The PI team acts for plaintiffs, particularly those who have been injured in road accidents, tripping cases, accidents at work, as a result of medical negligence and claims against the police. Patrick Allen is a member of the executive committee of the Association of Personal Injury Lawyers and the Law Society personal injury and medical negligence panels. Three other solicitors are members of the PI panel. The multi-party unit led by Richard Barr is handling 3 group actions – Gulf War Illness, MMR childhood vaccines and Organophosphate sheep dip. In each action, the firm holds a generic contract with the Legal Aid Board. The police claims unit led by Tina Salvidge deals with unlawful arrest, assault, malicious prosecution and false imprisonment. It is handling the compensation claims for the Bridgewater Four.

Housing: (*Contact Partner:* Wendy Backhouse). The housing team deals with disrepair, homelessness claims including applications for judicial review, possession cases and all aspects of landlord and tenant work, principally on behalf of tenants. Wendy Backhouse is chair of the Housing Law Practitioners' Group.

Non-contentious and Employment: (*Contact Partner:* Charles Pigott). This unit deals with all types of employment and discrimination claims for employees and voluntary/statutory sector employers. It also deals with non-contentious employment and property work. All members of the unit undertake their own advocacy.

Family: (*Contact Partner:* Lynn Roberts). The family team covers all aspects of family work including property disputes following separation or divorce, conflicts over children, care proceedings and applications for emergency injunctions. Five members of the team are on the child care panel and two on the Lord Chancellor's Department's Child Abduction Panel. All solicitors belong to the Solicitor's Family Law Association. Mediation is now offered by accredited family mediators.

Criminal: (*Contact Partner:* Nigel Richardson). The team deals with the full range of magistrates court and crown court work. Solicitors are on local police station and court duty

Managing partner:	Patrick Allen
Senior partner:	Henry Hodge
Number of partners:	13
Assistant solicitors:	22
Other fee-earners:	15

WORKLOADS	
Crime	28%
Personal injury and medical negligence	27%
Family	20%
Housing and landlord and tenant litigation	14%
Employment and general litigation	7%
Non-contentious property	4%

CONTACTS	
Civil claims against the police	Tina Salvidge
Crime	Nigel Richardson
Discrimination	Henry Hodge
Family and children	Lynn Roberts
Housing litigation	Wendy Backhouse
Medical negligence	Nicky Moony
Mental Health Tribunals	Louise Coubrough
Multi-party (pi/med neg/product liability)	
	Richard Barr/Patrick Allen
Personal injury	Patrick Allen
Property/corporate	Charles Pigott

Continues overleaf

solicitor schemes. Representatives are available to attend police stations at all hours. Solicitors can be contacted outside office hours via the emergency phone number (01459) 111192.

Other Areas of Work: (*Contact Partner:* Charles Pigott). Corporate and contractual advice (constitutions, applications for charitable status, restructuring) for charities and housing associations.

Nature of Clientele: Most clients are individuals who live in the north London area. A significant number of clients come from all over the country as a result of the firm's national reputation in various areas (eg multi-party cases). Some clients are housing associations, local authorities, voluntary and statutory bodies and local businesses.

Recruitment and Training: The firm runs a structured and popular training scheme for trainee solicitors. The annual intake is presently three. Interviews take place in October for training places the following September.

HOLLINGWORTH BISSELL

EAST SIDE OFFICES, KINGS CROSS STATION, LONDON, N1 9AP
Tel: (0171) 904 4678 **Fax:** (0171) 904 4680

The Firm: Hollingworth Bissell is a two partner firm providing legal services (both general and specialist rail related) to the railway industry.

Principal Areas of Work:

Commercial – General: Sales and acquisitions of companies and businesses, joint ventures, shareholders' agreements, reorganisations, procurement contracts, advice on intellectual property rights, computer contracts, agency contracts, conditions of trading and advice on the legal aspects of advertising, including the running of sales promotions.

Commercial – Rail Specific: Agreements for access to rail facilities, connection agreements, agreements for railway services, traffic agreements, advice on licence conditions and franchise agreements, station redevelopments and interaction with third party operators.

Property: Landlord and tenant and general commercial property advice.

HOLMAN, FENWICK & WILLAN

MARLOW HOUSE, LLOYDS AVENUE, LONDON, EC3N 3AL
Tel: (0171) 488 2300 **Fax:** (0171) 481 0316 **DX:** 1069 LONDON CITY EC3

The Firm: Holman, Fenwick & Willan has a global reputation for excellence in its chosen fields. The Firm has a network of offices throughout the world in London, Paris, Rouen, Nantes, Piraeus, Hong Kong and Singapore. Its network of offices enables the firm to assist its clients at a local and regional level and the firm has considerable experience in guiding litigation in numerous jurisdictions. The firm's style is to maintain a close commitment to its clients and a deep understanding of their business and commercial requirements.

Holman, Fenwick & Willan has one of the world's largest Admiralty and Marine Litigation practices with a wealth of experience and expertise in the field. The firm's Senior Partner, Archie Bishop, is an Examiner in Admiralty. The firm maintains a 24 hour emergency service geared to immediate response to maritime casualties worldwide.

The firm also deals with broader commercial litigation and international arbitration together with international trade and commodity disputes. The firm has a thriving Non-Marine Insurance and Reinsurance practice.

The firm undertakes litigation, arbitration and dispute resolution in the following areas: collision, salvage, marine pollution, charterparties, bills of lading, ship repair, ship sale and purchase, ship building and finance, personal injury, marine insurance, offshore oil exploration, commodities, international sale of goods, insurance, reinsurance, banking, insolvency, energy, environment and professional negligence.

Holman, Fenwick & Willan also undertakes a substantial amount of non-contentious work particularly related to the needs of the maritime and international trading and financial community. This includes Ship and Asset Finance, Commercial and Corporate advice, Insolvency, EC and Competition law, Banking, Insurance, Property and Energy work.

Senior partner:	W.A. Bishop
Number of partners:	50
Assistant solicitors:	41
Trainee Solicitors:	14
Other fee-earners:	24

WORKLOADS	
Shipping (admiralty and marine litigation)	50%
Commercial litigation/international trade	20%
Corporate/marine finance and related non-contentious work	15%
Reinsurance	15%

CONTACTS	
Admiralty	Archie Bishop
Commercial Litigation	Jonathan Fine
Commodities/Intl. Trade	Patricia Francies
Corporate	Brian Robinson
Corporate & Financial Litigation	Simon Congdon
EC & Competition Law	Philip Wareham
Energy	Nick Hutton
Insolvency	Noel Campbell
Marine Litigation	Greg Gray
Non-Marine Insurance/Reinsurance	John Duff
Personal Injury	Alan Walls
Property	Ian Narbeth
Ship & Asset Finance	Stephen Drury

HOLMAN, FENWICK & WILLAN

HOLME ROBERTS & OWEN LLP Mellier House, 26a Albemarle Street, London, W1X 3FA **Tel:** (0171) 499 8776 **Fax:** (0171) 499 7769 **Ptnrs:** 2 **Asst solrs:** 1 **Other fee-earners:** 2 **Contact:** Mr Bruce Kohler *The London office of Denver-based HRO serves clients in the cable television, telecommunications, beverages and professional sports industries.*

HOLMES HARDINGHAM

22-23 GREAT TOWER STREET, LONDON, EC3R 5AQ
Tel: (0171) 283 0222 **Fax:** (0171) 283 0768 **DX:** 636 **Email:** HOHA@COMPUSERVE.COM

The Firm: Holmes Hardingham is a commercial and maritime law firm with an international practice, concentrating on litigation and arbitration related to shipping and transportation.

Principal Areas of Work: The firm focuses on shipping law, with all 11 partners and 17 other fee-earners handling a variety of shipping-related matters including: international trade and carriage of goods by sea, road and air, commodity sale disputes, commercial and Admiralty litigation and arbitration, oil and gas exploration, marine insurance, collision and salvage, ship sale, purchase and finance, and yachts and pleasure craft.

Managing partner:	David Johnston
Senior partner:	Anthony Holmes
Number of partners:	11
Assistant solicitors:	11
Other fee-earners:	6

HOLMES MACKILLOP 109 Douglas Street, Glasgow, G2 4HB *Tel:* (0141) 226 4942 *Fax:* (0141) 204 0136 *Ptnrs:* 6 *Asst solrs:* 3 *Other fee-earners:* 5

HOOD VORES & ALLWOOD The Priory, Church St, Dereham, NR19 1DW *Tel:* (01362) 692424 *Fax:* (01362) 698858 *DX:* 45050 *Ptnrs:* 5 *Asst solrs:* 2 *Other fee-earners:* 5

HOOPER & WOLLEN Carlton House, 30 The Terrace, Torquay, TQ1 1BS **Tel:** (01803) 213251 **Fax:** (01803) 296871 **DX:** 59204 Torquay (2) **Email:** lawyers@hooperwollen.co.uk **Internet:** www.hooperwollen.co.uk **Ptnrs:** 10 **Asst solrs:** 4 **Other fee-earners:** 9 **Contact:** Mrs P. C. Bear *Specialising in conveyancing, family, child care, litigation, PI, probate, trust, investment management, commercial, company. Agency instructions accepted.*

HORNBY, BAKER JONES & WOOD 26 Bridge Street, Newport, NP9 4SB *Tel:* (01633) 842812/262848 *Fax:* (01633) 267847 *DX:* 33209 Newport *Ptnrs:* 4 *Other fee-earners:* 1

HORWICH FARRELLY

NATIONAL HOUSE, 36 ST ANN STREET, MANCHESTER, M60 8HF
Tel: (0161) 834 3585 **Fax:** (0161) 834 3630 **DX:** 14322 MANCHESTER 1 **Email:** HORFAR@AOL.COM

The Firm: Since its formation in 1969, Horwich Farrelly has grown to become one of the North West's leading niche practices.

The firm specialises in Insurance litigation, Commercial litigation, Conveyancing and Employment Law whilst also carrying out a wide variety of private client work.

Sound legal and commercial advice, excellent service and an intuitive understanding of their clients needs, forms the basis of the firms success.

Investment in people and the recruitment process has given Horwich Farrelly a significant advantage. It has ensured that prospective, as well as current clients, benefit from an array of legal skills, delivered by people who are easy to talk to.

Managing partner:	Nigel Yates
Senior partner:	Stephen Boylan
Number of partners:	10
Assistant solicitors:	6
Other fee-earners:	26
Total Staff:	110

HOUGHTON & CO Penn House, 10 Broad Street, Hereford, HR4 9AP **Tel:** (01432) 352202 **Fax:** (01432) 355513 **DX:** 17237 Hereford 1 **Email:** houg-sol@wbsnet.co.uk **Contact:** Mrs R. Houghton *The firm's reputation stems from Rosalie Houghton's Oral Contraceptive Pill Group Litigation. Founding members of the Association of Conditional Fee Lawyers – ACFL.*

WORKLOADS	
Medical Negligence	100%

HOWARD KENNEDY

19 CAVENDISH SQUARE, LONDON, W1A 2AW
Tel: (0171) 636 1616 **Fax:** (0171) 499 6871 **DX:** 42748 OXFORD CIRCUS NORTH **Email:** POSTMASTER@HK.HIWAY.CO.UK
Internet: WWW.HK.HIWAY.CO.UK

The Firm: Established in the mid-1930s, Howard Kennedy is a well-regarded firm. Primarily a commercial practice, the firm offers a wide range of services for its clients, which include public companies, public authorities, entrepreneurial businesses and private individuals. The firm provides an international service to clients and professional advisers. All the major European languages are spoken. Howard Kennedy is a registered Sponsor of the London Stock Exchange.

Principal Areas of Work:

Corporate/Commercial: (*Contact:* Alan Banes). The department deals with a high calibre of corporate and corporate finance work which includes Stock Exchange flotations, public share offerings on the London Stock Exchange and the Alternative Investment Market including those under the Enterprise Investment Scheme, Venture Capital Trusts, mergers and acquisitions, reconstructions and amalgamations, Stock Exchange Yellow Book, The City Code on Take-Overs and Mergers, venture capital and private equity. The department also advises on shareholder disputes in conjunction with the litigation department. The department combines a high degree of technical know-how and personal partner-led service, and frequently deals with the large city firms. Commercial services include commercial contracts, employment law, agency, distribution and franchising agreements, share option and incentive schemes, consumer protection legislation, corporate taxation and EC law.

Intellectual Property (IP) and Information Technology (IT): (*Contact:* John Fleming). The department's work covers a wide range of IP, IT and technology matters, including: patents, copyright, design rights and trade marks; computer hardware, software and networking issues; internet and multimedia; drafting and negotiating agreements relating to technology.

Litigation: (*Contact:* Craig Emden). A broad range of disputes is handled, for both commercial and private clients, domestic and international. *Work includes:* commercial arbitration, mediation, ADR, and disputes relating to: company and partnership matters, shareholders, commercial contracts, negligence, insolvency, property, including landlord and tenant actions, professional negligence, employment, banking, insurance related matters, intellectual property and debt recovery. Private litigation includes matrimonial problems, family law, personal injury claims, defamation, inheritance and trust related disputes and immigration.

Commercial Property: (*Contact:* Paul Springall). A strong and experienced department includes a number of partners who handle large-scale commercial and residential developments and investments. Besides acting for banks, property developers and investors this department acts for several major retail, leisure, restaurant and hotel chains. The department has considerable expertise in office, industrial and all other types of property as well as in the related specialities of secured lending, planning, licensing, compulsory purchase, compensation, housing law and tenancy problems. Expertise extends to VAT and other tax-related aspects of property transactions. Clients include several listed companies and many smaller companies in the commercial property field.

Construction: (*Contact:* Irvinder Bakshi). All aspects of work, from the non-contentious to arbitration and litigation are covered, both domestically and internationally. Clients range from governments, local authorities, institutions and individual businesses.

Pensions and Employee Benefits: (*Contact:* Graham Chrystie). The group advises on all aspects of pensions with emphasis on advising pension scheme trustees. Clients range from trustees, institutions, companies, employees, pension consultants. The firm is a member of the International Benefit Lawyers Network.

Trust and Estate Planning: (*Contact:* Roger Seaton).The department's work includes: estate planning, wills, trusts including offshore arrangements, probate, personal taxation, financial services, domestic conveyancing and charities.

International: (*Contact:* Anthony Slingsby). International clients with business or investment projects in the UK and overseas are advised by the firm's multi-lingual team. UK clients with overseas interests or activities have the benefit of a large network of overseas legal correspondents.

International Trade & Finance Group: (*Contact:* Philip Leacock). Serves major international clients with largely transactional work, encompassing, in particular, international trade and finance, bank lending and syndications, international joint ventures, infrastructure and capital projects, project finance, commodities, derivatives and their regulation, international arbitration and dispute resolution. Clients range from multinational corporations to individual entrepreneurs. Its members constitute one of the most experienced London based teams.

Senior partner:	Trevor J. Newey
Number of partners:	29
Assistant solicitors:	19
Other fee-earners:	14

WORKLOADS	
Property	42%
Corporate/Commercial	30%
Litigation	24%
Trust and Estate Planning	4%

CONTACTS	
Company/ commercial	Alan Banes
Construction	Irvinder Bakshi
Intellectual Property and Information Technology	
	John Fleming
International	Anthony Slingsby
Litigation	Craig Emden
Pensions and Employee Benefits	Graham Chrystie
Project finance	Philip Leacock
Property	Paul Springall
Trust and Estate Planning	Roger Seaton

HOWARTH GOODMAN 8 King Street, Manchester, M60 8HG *Tel:* (0161) 832 5068 *Fax:* (0161) 833 2917 *DX:* 14308 Manchester 1 *Ptnrs:* 4 *Asst solrs:* 4 *Other fee-earners:* 10

HOWE & CO 27a Bond Street, Ealing, London, W5 5AS *Tel:* (0181) 840 4688 *Fax:* (0181) 840 7209 *Ptnrs:* 1 *Asst solrs:* 3 *Other fee-earners:* 9

HOWELL & CO

1341 STRATFORD ROAD, HALL GREEN, BIRMINGHAM, B28 9HW
Tel: (0121) 778 5031 **Fax:** (0121) 777 3967 **DX:** 714513 HALL GREEN 2

The Firm: Established in 1979. Howell & Co provides a comprehensive legal service to both commercial and private clients. The firm deals with property law dealing both with residential and commercial conveyancing and litigation specialising in white collar crime, large scale frauds including Inland Revenue, Customs and Excise and Serious Fraud Office cases and dealing with the Metropolitan Police Commercial Fraud Department and Regional Fraud Squad cases.

Principal Areas of Work:

White Collar Crime: Defence work in relation to Inland Revenue, Customs and Excise and Serious Fraud Offence prosecutions. Also defence work in relation to commercial frauds prosecuted by the Metropolitan Police Commercial Fraud Department and Regional Fraud Squads. The firm acts for Solicitors, Accountants, Surveyors, other professional people and non professional people.

Crime (non White Collar): Magistrates' Court and Crown Court work. The firm has acted in numerous murder cases and recently acted for a professional person accused of gross negligence manslaughter. The firm also defends prosecutions relating to importation and supplying of drugs.

Litigation: The work includes litigation in the County Court, High Court and other Tribunals for both private clients and commercial clients.

Private Cients: Work includes drafting of Wills, Probate and Administration of Estates.

Property and Conveyancing: Work includes residential and commercial conveyancing for both private and commercial clients including major National developers dealing with both the conveyance of plots and the purchase of development land.

Number of partners:	2
Assistant solicitors:	4
Other fee-earners:	7

WORKLOADS	
Crime	70%
Litigation	15%
Conveyancing	10%
Other	5%

HOWELLS

427-431 LONDON ROAD, SHEFFIELD, S2 4HJ
Tel: (0114) 249 6666 **Fax:** (0114) 250 0656 **DX:** 10584

THE AVERY BUILDINGS, 15-17 BRIDGE STREET, SHEFFIELD, S3 8NL
Tel: (0114) 249 6666 **Fax:** (0114) 249 1455 **DX:** 10584

42 SPITAL HILL, SHEFFIELD, S4 7LG
Tel: (0114) 249 6666 **Fax:** (0114) 249 6700 **DX:** 10584

The Firm: Established in 1979 to specialise in protecting the rights of individuals, the firm has grown to be one of the country's largest Legal Aid practices with Legal Aid quality franchises in all franchised areas of work.

Principal Areas of Work:

Criminal Law: *Work includes:* all criminal matters with particular expertise in public order offences, serious fraud, juveniles and youth, Road Traffic Law, miscarriages of justice and cases involving mentally disordered defendants.

Family Law: *Work includes:* all aspects of matrimonial and children law with particular expertise in domestic violence, financial relief of matrimonial breakdown, private and public law children cases, adoption and education advice and representation.

Civil and Community Law: *Work includes:* accident claims, industrial disease claims, medical negligence and actions against the police. Specialist advice and representation provided in housing, employment and equal opportunities law, immigration, mental health and welfare benefits.

Managing partner:	Libby Jones
Number of partners:	11
Assistant solicitors:	16
Other fee-earners:	17

WORKLOADS	
Civil Litigation	33%
Crime	33%
Family	33%

HOWES PERCIVAL

OXFORD HOUSE, CLIFTONVILLE, NORTHAMPTON, NN1 5PN
Tel: (01604) 230400 **Fax:** (01604) 620956 **DX:** 12413 NORTHAMPTON **Email:** LAW@HOWES-PERCIVAL.CO.UK
Internet: WWW.HOWES-PERCIVAL.CO.UK

The Firm: A major commercial practice, with offices in the East Midlands and East Anglia, Howes Percival provides a pragmatic, commercially sensitive range of legal services to clients throughout the United Kingdom. The firm's success is based on an emphasis on high quality, value for money advice co-ordinated by a specific contact partner with specialist knowledge of the industry sector and appropriate legal expertise.

Principal Areas of Work: The firm handles all aspects of company/ commercial law including MBOs and MBIs, commercial litigation, commercial property and general corporate work. All aspects of employment law matters are handled by a specialist team based at the Northampton office. Other areas of specialist expertise include banking law, corporate finance and taxation, insolvency and debt recovery.

Other Offices:

Provincial House, 37 New Walk, Leicester LE1 6TU
Tel: (0116) 247 3500 *Contact:* Jit Singh

252 Upper 3rd Street, Grafton Gate East, Central Milton Keynes MK9 1DZ
Tel: (01908) 67282 *Contact:* Brandon Ransley.

The Guildyard, 51 Colegate, Norwich, Norfolk NR3 1DD.
Tel: (01603) 762103 *Contact:* Alan Kefford.

Overseas associated offices in Brussels, Gibraltar, The Hague, Oslo and Los Angeles.

Languages Spoken: Danish, French, German, Hindi, Italian, Norwegian, Punjabi and Spanish.

Senior partner:	Michael Percival
Number of partners:	26
Assistant solicitors:	17
Other fee-earners:	32

CONTACTS	
Commercial litigation	Sara Wilkinson
Commercial property	Roger Burnell
Company/ commercial	Brandon Ransley
Employment	Debra Holliman

HUGH JAMES

ARLBEE HOUSE, GREYFRIARS RD, CARDIFF, CF1 4QB
Tel: (01222) 224871 **Fax:** (01222) 388222 **DX:** 33000

Nature of Firm: Hugh James is one of the largest firms in Wales with a UK wide reputation for its commercial and insurance litigation practice and commercial property work. The firm has a rapidly growing commercial practice and has established a reputation for insolvency work.

Other Offices: In addition to its main Cardiff office, the firm has an office in Bristol and a network of offices throughout South East Wales to include Merthyr, Treharris, Bargoed, Talbot Green and Blackwood.

Principal Areas of Work:

Company & Commercial: This is one of the firm's fastest growing departments with experience in a wide range of matters including business start-ups, venture capital, mergers and management buy-outs; commercial contracts; patents and trademarks; stock exchange work and partnerships. (*Contact:* Mr Felix Macintosh).

Commercial Property: The firm acts for Housing for Wales and numerous housing associations, financial institutions, national developers, local authorities and private clients. A full range of property-related matters is covered to include planning work and secured lending. (*Contact:* Mr David Roberts).

Commercial Litigation: The firm has one of the leading provincial litigation practices acting for a large number of national and international insurers and also dealing in construction, employment, insolvency, professional indemnity and general commercial litigation. (*Contact:* Mr Gareth Williams).

Private Client: The firm remains committed to the individual client. Services include plaintiff personal injury claims, family work, conveyancing, wills and probate and criminal defence work. Legal aid work is undertaken. Several of the partners are fluent Welsh-speakers. (*Contact:* Ms Cherry Wright).

Foreign Connections: The firm acts for international clients as well as those with overseas interests. Associations have been formed with legal practices in Nantes, Madrid, Dusseldorf, Rome, Milan and Naples.

Agency: All types of agency work are accepted. (*Contact:* Mr Alun Jones).

Recruitment and Training: The firm recruits about five trainee solicitors every year. Applications by letter and CV should be made to Ms Sian Buck. The firm has a Director of Continuing Education, Ms Christine King, and a well-developed programme of in-house lectures and seminars. Brochures are available on request.

Managing partner:	Cherry Wright
Senior partners (Joint):	David Roberts
	and Geoffrey Adams
Number of partners:	42
Assistant solicitors:	34
Other fee-earners:	94

WORKLOADS	
Commercial litigation, incl construction, insolvency, insurance	55%
Commercial property	15%
Company/ commercial	15%
Private client	15%

CONTACTS	
Agency	Alun Jones
Commercial litigation	Gareth Williams
Commercial property	David Roberts
Company & commercial	Felix Macintosh
Private client	Cherry Wright

HUGH JAMES
SOLICITORS

HUGH POTTER & COMPANY, SERIOUS INJURY SOLICITORS Grampian House, 4th Floor, 144 Deansgate, Manchester, M3 3ED *Tel:* (0161) 832 2255 *Fax:* (0161) 834 5198.

HUMPHREYS & CO.

14 KING ST, BRISTOL, BS1 4EF
Tel: (0117) 929 2662 **Fax:** (0117) 929 2722 **DX:** 78239 **Email:** LAWYERS@HUMPHREYS.CO.UK

Principal Areas of Work: Commercially orientated practice with emphasis on commercial litigation including particularly intellectual property and reinsurance work; also company and commercial work, property, construction, entertainment, insolvency, insurance, professional negligence, personal injury and competition law.

Senior partner:	R.A. Humphreys
Number of partners:	4
Assistant solicitors:	6
Other fee-earners:	1

HUMPHRIES KIRK

GLEBE HOUSE, NORTH STREET, WAREHAM, BH20 4AN
Tel: (01929) 552141 **Fax:** (01929) 556701 **DX:** 49700 WAREHAM **Email:** HUMPHRIES.KIRK@DIAL.PIPEX.COM

The Firm: Humphries Kirk is one of the most innovative firms in the South which manages to retain a successful balance between catering for substantial commercial clients and the traditional private client. Humphries Kirk was one of the first firms to qualify for ISO 9001 in this region.

Principal Areas of Work:

Company/ Commercial: Intellectual property, mergers and acquisitons (including international).

Commercial Litigation: All work from Industrial tribunal work up to High Court and International litigation.

Banking and Financial Law: The firm acts for a number of substantial German financial institutions and also for several German savings banks.

Agricultural: The firm is the recognised lead solicitors for the National Farmers Union in Dorset.

Other Areas of Work: Full range of private client services.

Foreign Connections: The firm has associated offices in Versailles, France and Cologne, Germany and is the founder member of the International Legal Association known as *Humphries Kirk Wagner Jean.* The firm maintains a network of relationship lawyers world-wide.

Other Offices: Swanage, Dorchester, Poole, Bournemouth and London (Consulting rooms).

Languages Spoken: French, German, Spanish, Italian.

Senior partner:	M.J. Greenleaves
Number of partners:	8
Assistant solicitors:	10
Other fee-earners:	13

WORKLOADS	
Conveyancing	27%
Litigation	24%
Trusts & Probate	23%
Commercial	12%
Matrimonial	7%
Criminal	4%
Personal Injury	3%

HUNT & COOMBS 35 Thorpe Rd, Peterborough, PE3 6AG *Tel:* (01733) 565312 *Fax:* (01733) 552748 *DX:* 12302 *Ptnrs:* 8 *Asst solrs:* 12 *Other fee-earners:* 6

HUNTERS

9 NEW SQUARE, LINCOLN'S INN, LONDON, WC2A 3QN
Tel: (0171) 412 0050 **Fax:** (0171) 412 0049 **DX:** 61

The Firm: Although founded in the early 18th century, the firm is a thriving modern partnership, serving a broadly-based private and institutional clientele.

Principal Areas of Work:

General Description: The firm has a long-established reputation in private client, charity, banking security, and matrimonial work; and an increasing emphasis on commercial property, company/commercial law, employment and litigation.

Private Client: (*Contact:* John Kennedy. *8 Partners, 3 Asst. Solrs.*) *Work includes:* trusts, tax planning, tax returns, heritage and agricultural property, wills, probate and conveyancing.

Charities: (*Contact:* Paul Almy. *2 Partners1 Asst. Solr.*) *Work includes:* acting for major charities; registrations, schemes, trading arrangements, and housing associations.

Banking Security Work: (*Contact:* Hugh Woodeson. *2 Partners and an assistant.*) *Work includes:* security work for banks.

Matrimonial: (*Contact:* Hugh Woodeson. *2 Partners*) *Work includes:* all aspects, but particularly cases with a substantial financial element.

Commercial Property: (*Contact:* Michael Skrine. *4 Partners and an assistant.*) *Work includes:* acquiring and selling property investments, and business tenancies.

Company/Commercial Law and Employment: (*Contact:* Paul Almy. *2 Partners.*) *Work includes:* private companies, partnerships, commercial contracts, acquisitions and disposals, employment, contracts and staff handbooks, unfair and wrongful dismissal, redundancy, service occupancies, equal opportunity and race discrimination.

Litigation: (*Contact:* Henry Hood. *2 Partners.*) *Work includes:* wide range of High Court/County Court work; breach of contract; landlord and tenant disputes, and enforcement of security.

Foreign Connections: Close relationship with firms in Australia.

Recruitment and Training: *Partner:* Paul Almy. One trainee solicitor with a good degree is recruited annually. Fortnightly seminars. Wide spread of work and direct client contact.

Senior partner:	H.A. Woodeson
Number of partners:	11
Assistant solicitors:	4
Other fee-earners:	9

HUTTONS 16-18 St Andrews Crescent, Cardiff, CF1 3DD **Tel:** (01222) 378621 **Fax:** (01222) 388450 **DX:** 33065 **Ptnrs:** 5 **Asst solrs:** 6 **Other fee-earners:** 7 **Contact:** Mr S.M.C. Hutton *A specialist litigation practice with particular expertise in criminal law, civil (including medical negligence), family and child care law.*

WORKLOADS			
Crime			40%
Personal Injury/Medical Negligence			18%
Family	15%	Civil Litigation	12%
Commercial	6%	Child Care	5%
Private Client	4%		

IAIN SMITH & COMPANY 18-20 Queen's Road, Aberdeen, AB15 4ZT **Tel:** (01224) 645454 **Fax:** (01224) 646671 **DX:** 4 Aberdeen **Email:** info@iainsmith.com **Ptnrs:** 10 **Asst solrs:** 12 **Other fee-earners:** 10 **Contact:** Peter A. Macari (Managing Partner) *An Investor in People. Specialist expertise in corporate, insolvency, family and employment law and debt recovery.*

WORKLOADS			
Litigation/Family Law	35%	Corporate/Commercial	25%
Conveyancing – Domestic	20%	Wills & Executives	10%
Conveyancing – Commercial			5%
Insolvency			5%

IAN DOWNING 8 The Crescent, Plymouth, PL1 3AE *Tel:* (01752) 226224 *Fax:* (01752) 26213

ILIFFES BOOTH BENNETT

LOVELL HOUSE, 271 HIGH STREET, UXBRIDGE, UB8 1AQ
Tel: (01895) 230941 **Fax:** (01895) 811926 **DX:** 45105 UXBRIDGE

THE BURY, CHURCH STREET, CHESHAM, BUCKS, HP5 IJE
Tel: (01494) 778822 **Fax:** (01494) 773951 **DX:** 50302 CHESHAM

23 HIGH STREET, INGATESTONE, CM4 9DU
Tel: (01277) 354065 **Fax:** (01227) 355191 **DX:** 120375 INGATESTONE

135-137 HIGH STREET, SLOUGH, SL1 1DN
Tel: (01753) 516533 **Fax:** (01753) 516821 **DX:** 3431 SLOUGH

The Firm: With offices in Middlesex, Berkshire, Buckinghamshire and Essex, this firm is one of the largest practices in the South East outside central London.

Its principal aim is to deliver efficient and effective legal services to an extensive business and private client community. It has particular strengths in commercial property and litigation, private client work, personal injury litigation and family and criminal law.

Principal Areas of Work:

Commercial: Purchase and sale of retail, office and industrial property, property development, lease negotiations and renewals. Agricultural property dealing. Secured lending work for banks and financial institutions.

Company Law: Company sales and acquisitions, restructuring and mergers. Terms and conditions of business, company secretarial services, company formations. Franchise agreements.

Litigation: Commercial contract disputes, debt recovery, personal injury, and landlord and tenant disputes.

Family Law: Divorce and separation including financial and children issues care proceedings and adoption.

Private Client: Preparation of wills, probate, estate administration, taxation advice and trusts.

Domestic Conveyancing: Full estate agency service, freehold and leasehold property conveyancing and preparation of leases and tenancy agreements.

Employment: Unfair dismissal, redundancy, discrimination at work, contracts of employment and pensions.

Criminal Law: 24 hour emergency cover, attendance at police stations, defence in criminal proceedings, juvenile offences and motoring offences.

Foreign Languages: French, Urdu, Punjabi, Gujerati, Hindi.

Managing partner:	Steven Booth
Number of partners:	17
Assistant solicitors:	20
Other fee-earners:	33

WORKLOADS	
Commercial and agricultural property	21%
Family/ matrimonial	20%
Crime	16%
Personal injury & civil litigation	15%
Company/ commercial and commercial litigation	11%
Residential conveyancing	10%
Wills, probate, tax, etc.	7%

CONTACTS	
Civil litigation	Rosemary Jeffries (01494) 778822
Commercial litigation	Andrew Olins (01895) 230941
Commercial property	Susan Mawson (01895) 230941
Company/commercial	Susan Mawson (01895) 230941
Crime	Tom Brownlow (01895) 230941
Family	Shon Roberts (01895) 230941
Personal injury litigation	Tony Wiseman (01895) 230941
Residential conveyancing	M. Silverman (01494) 778822
Wills and probate	Gillian Murray (01494) 778822

ILIFFES
BOOTH
BENNETT
SOLICITORS

INCE & CO

KNOLLYS HOUSE, 11 BYWARD STREET, LONDON, EC3R 5EN
Tel: (0171) 623 2011 **Fax:** (0171) 623 3225 **DX:** 1070 LONDON CITY EC3 **Email:** FIRSTNAME.SURNAME@INCE.CO.UK

Ince & Co has a worldwide reputation in maritime and insurance law. It handles, on a global basis, cases covering all aspects of international trade.

The Firm: Ince & Co is based in the City of London with offices in Hong Kong and Singapore serving the Far East and Pacific Rim and in Piraeus serving the Greek shipping community and the eastern Mediterranean. Close links with a network of leading international lawyers complements the firm's service to clients around the world.

A feature of the firm's service is that clients deal with the same partner from initial advice to trial. Appropriate efforts are made to avoid the expense of litigation, including the use of alternative dispute resolution (ADR). Ince & Co has a reputation for clear legal analysis and tenacious imaginative litigation. The firm thrives through the ability of its fee-earners to understand and meet its clients' commercial interests.

Principal Areas of Work: Ince & Co specialises in litigation relating to all aspects of international trade, shipping and insurance. Ince & Co's insurance practice covers all aspects of UK and international insurance: marine, aviation, non-marine and reinsurance.

The partners include some of the most notable City lawyers in this field, who have advised on many of the issues, both litigious and non-contentious, confronting all sectors of the world's insurance industry. Over the past 15 years, the firm has participated in the majority of the leading insurance cases which have been instrumental in determining many points of principle. The firm is often instructed in drafting and regulatory matters.

Since before the *Torrey Canyon* in 1967, Ince & Co has been involved in the aftermath of many of the major international maritime casualties. This includes acting on the most significant pollution casualties worldwide in recent years: the *Exxon Valdez, Haven, Aegean Sea, Braer* and *Sea Empress* oil spills. The firm also acted for the owners on the *Piper Alpha* oil rig disaster, advising on technical and insurance problems as well as personal injury and loss of life; the capsizing of the *Herald of Free Enterprise* and the collision between the *Marchioness* and the *Bowbelle* in relation to the loss of life and personal injury claims.

The firm operates a 24-hour emergency response service 365 days a year and is geared to a rapid response in the event of a maritime, aviation or energy related casualty. A feature of the firm's ability to respond to high-profile emergencies is the availability of partners who are trained in the management of the media. The Ince & Co team is also complemented by several experienced ex-mariners.

Ince & Co undertakes banking, construction work, commercial conveyancing, and has a thriving professional indemnity litigation department. Ince & Co's developing corporate practice covers the full range of company matters and the firm has a growing involvement in the former Soviet Union and eastern Europe.

Recruitment: Ince & Co recruits between seven and ten trainee solicitors annually. Early responsibility is encouraged under close supervision by partners. The majority of trainee solicitors stay on after qualification.

Senior partner:	Richard Sayer
Number of partners:	54
Other fee-earners:	102

WORKLOADS	
Insurance/ reinsurance	40%
Shipping & international trade/commodities	40%
Company, commercial, property	10%
Professional indemnity	10%

CONTACTS	
Admiralty	James Wilson, Richard Sayer, Chris Beesley
Aviation	Anthony Fitzsimmons, Mike Pollen
Construction	David Sheehan, Chris Jefferis
Corporate	Nick Gould, David Coupe
Dry shipping	Richard Williams
Energy	David Steward, Chris Sprague
Environment and pollution	Colin de le Rue, Ian Chetwood
EU law	Denys Hickey, Anthony Fitzsimmons
Insurance & reinsurance	Peter Rogan, Julian Hill
International trade & commodities	Stuart Shepherd, Clare Calnan
Personal injury	Chris Sprague
Professional indemnity	David Rutherford, Andrew Ottley, Charlotte Davies
Property and private client	Albert Levy
Ship finance	Malcolm Strong, Tony Suchy
Shipbuilding	Mike Pollen, David Steward

INGHAM CLEGG & CROWTHER Guild Chambers, 4 Winckley Square, Preston, PR1 3JJ
Tel: (01772) 250931 *Fax:* (01772) 823150 *DX:* 17106 Preston 1 *Ptnrs:* 13 *Asst solrs:* 12
Other fee-earners: 18

IRONSIDES

ARNCLIFFE HOUSE, 9 SPENCER PARADE, NORTHAMPTON, NN1 5AH
Tel: (01604) 234800 **Fax:** (01604) 232624 **DX:** 12402 NORTHAMPTON 1

MACAULAY HOUSE, 10 FRIAR LANE, LEICESTER, LE1 5QD
Tel: (0116) 251 5253 **Fax:** (0116) 251 2005 **DX:** 10827 LEICESTER 1

OAKHAM OFFICE, 76 HIGH STREET, OAKHAM, LE15 6AS
Tel: (01572) 724455 **Fax:** (01572) 756267 **DX:** 28335 OAKHAM

The Firm: Ironsides' three offices provide a broad general service at reasonable cost to both private and commercial clients. In recent years there has been a growing emphasis on commercial work.

Principal Areas of Work:

Commercial Work: (*Contact Partner:* James Coningsby in Leicester, Ralph Harris in Northampton). *Work includes:* all elements of business, company and partnership law, employment law, intellectual property, EC law, restrictive practices in trade and employment, road haulage, transport and liquor licensing.

Private Client: (*Contact Partner:* Peter Mair in Northampton, Bill Tyler in Leicester). Work includes: family law, mediation, divorce, custody and access, division of assets, residential conveyancing, drafting of wills, setting up and administration of trusts, powers of attorney, tax planning and personal financial advice.

Litigation: (*Contact Partner:* Chris McKinney in Leicester, Paul Guppy in Northampton). *Work includes:* disputes between companies, debt recovery, employment law cases, personal injury negligence cases for individuals and corporate clients, including medical negligence, and construction cases.

Financial Planning: (*Contact Partner:* Parry Leggett). Work includes: personal and corporate investment, pension, insurance and tax planning advice.

Senior partner:	Peter Mair
Number of partners:	11
Assistant solicitors:	9
Other fee-earners:	11

WORKLOADS	
Insurance litigation	21%
Company/ commercial	19%
Probate	16%
Conveyancing	15%
Civil litigation	12%
Family Law	10%
Court & Advocacy	4%
Financial Planning	4%

CONTACTS	
Civil litigation	C. McKinney
Company/ commercial	R. Harris
Conveyancing	W. Tyler
Court and Advocacy	P. Mair
Family Law	A. Kiddle
Financial Planning	P. Leggett
Insurance litigation	P. Guppy
Probate	C. Osborne

IRWIN MITCHELL

ST. PETER'S HOUSE, HARTSHEAD, SHEFFIELD, S1 2EL
Tel: (0114) 276 7777 **Fax:** (0114) 275 3306 **DX:** DX 10513 **Email:** ENQUIRIES@IRWINMITCHELL.CO.UK
Internet: WWW.IRWINMITCHELL.CO.UK/IRWINMITCHELL

The Firm: Irwin Mitchell, with offices in Sheffield, Birmingham, Leeds and London, is particularly known for commercial law, commercial litigation, insurance, family, personal injury and disaster law. The recent merger with London practice Braby & Waller has strengthened the firm's presence in the City. A nation wide debt recovery service has been launched under the Braby & Waller name (see entry for Braby & Waller).

Principal Areas of Work:

Corporate Services: Company/Commercial/ EU: (*Contact:* Kevin Cunningham. *Fee-earners:* 33). Services offered include mergers, buy-outs and acquisitions; formation of companies and partnerships; education and charities; commercial contracts; joint ventures; banking; insolvency; intellectual property; high-tech; licensing; corporate finance and taxation; sports law; computers & IT and pensions. The EU unit offers guidance on European and International law.

Corporate Services: Commercial Property: (*Contact:* Kevin Docherty. *Fee-earners:* 32). This department covers all areas of property transactions including joint venture agreements, development projects, development funding, construction, building contracts and planning. The department has specialist retail, development and commerical units within it.

Corporate Service: Commercial Litigation: (*Contact:* Peter Wylde. *Fee-earners:* 59). *Work includes:* commercial and financial disputes, intellectual property, insolvency, employment, professional negligence, insurance, sale of goods, product liability, building contracts and property disputes.

Business Crime: (*Contact:* Kevin Robinson. *Fee-earners:* 2). The firm is well-known in this field for handling the Matrix-Churchill 'arms to Iraq' affair, and also provides advice on criminal law generally.

Insurance: (*Contact:* Joe Simpson. *Fee-earners:* 158). The firm handles both contentious and non-contentious insurance work in the form of advising on policy conditions and insurance litigation, acting for insurers in defending claims particularly in the fields of employers' liability, product liability and public liability. The firm also operates a large legal expenses unit.

Managing partner:	Howard Culley
Senior partner:	Michael Napier
Number of partners:	75
Assistant solicitors:	104
Other fee-earners:	261

WORKLOADS	
Corporate services	34%
Insurance litigation services	32%
Plaintiff personal injury litigation	22%
Private client	12%

CONTACTS	
Business crime	Kevin Robinson
Commercial litigation	Peter Wylde
Commercial property	Kevin Docherty
Company/ commercial	Kevin Cunningham
Corporate services	Michael Jelly
Employment	Barry Warne
Family and matrimonial	Martin Loxley
Insurance	Joe Simpson
Intellectual property	James Love
Personal injury	John Pickering
Police prosecution	Mike Whitworth
Residential conveyancing	Steve Martin
Wills and trusts	Paul Hirst

Continues overleaf

Debt Collection and Credit Control: (*Contact:* Peter Wylde. *Fee-earners:* 21). The firm operates a computerised debt collection service. They deal with credit investigations and reports and representation at creditors' meetings.

Personal Injury: (*Contact:* John Pickering. *Fee-earners:* 89). Mainly acting for plaintiffs, the firm has a national and international reputation for personal injury litigation.

Disaster Law: (*Contact:* Michael Napier). The firm offers a specialist service covering: defective products, adverse drug reactions, large-scale and multiple accidents and international disasters. Major involvement in claims arising from disasters include: Manchester Air Crash, sinking of "Herald of Free Enterprise", "Marchioness" disaster, King's Cross Fire, "Piper Alpha" explosion, and Land's End tragedy.

Private Client Services: Family Law: (*Contact:* Martin Loxley. *Fee-earners:* 12). The full range of matrimonial and family services are offered.

Private Client Services: Conveyancing: (*Contact:* Steve Martin. *Fee-earners:* 9). Acting on behalf of private individuals, clearing banks and others, the firm operates a fully computerised conveyancing service with close partner involvement.

Private Client Services: Trust and Probate: (*Contact:* Paul Hirst. *Fee-earners:* 7). The trust and probate team deals with wills, personal taxation, trusts and probate on behalf of private individuals and business clients requiring personal advice for their directors or employees.

Police Prosecutions: (*Contact***: Mike Whitworth. Fee-earners: 20)**

Nature of Clientele: Clients range from the private individual and the family business to public companies and institutions on a national and international scale.

Other Offices: Birmingham, Leeds, London.

Foreign Connections: Well established links with lawyers in the USA and most other foreign jurisdictions. Particular expertise in transatlantic and Far Eastern work.

ISADORE GOLDMAN 125 High Holborn, London, WC1V 6QF *Tel:* (0171) 242 3000 *Fax:* (0171) 242 9160 *DX:* 124 *Ptnrs:* 10 *Asst solrs:* 3 *Other fee-earners:* 2

ISON HARRISON & CO Duke House, 54 Wellington Street, Leeds, LS1 2EE **Tel:** (0113) 284 5000 **Fax:** (0113) 284 5020/40/50 **DX:** 12076 **Ptnrs:** 9 **Asst solrs:** 21 **Other fee-earners:** 31 **Contact:** Heather Waites *Expanding general practice with strong civil litigation.*

WORKLOADS			
Personal injury	30%	Civil litigation	19%
Crime			15%
Commercial & residential conveyancing			11%
Other	10%	Children's	5%
Matrimonial	5%	Trust, Probate & Wills	5%

JACKAMAN, SMITH & MULLEY 7 Northgate St, Ipswich, IPU 3BU *Tel:* (01473) 255591 *Fax:* (01473) 230796 *DX:* 3229 *Ptnrs:* 10 *Asst solrs:* 2 *Other fee-earners:* 12

JACKSON & CANTER

32 PRINCES ROAD, LIVERPOOL, L8 1TH
Tel: (0151) 708 6593 **Fax:** (0151) 708 5850 **DX:** 14156 FREE PHONE: 0800 132746

The Firm: The firm, a franchised legal Aid practice with I.I.P. Accreditation and runner-up in the HIFAL Client Care Award 1996, aims to provide a quality legal service to the private client.

Principal Areas of Work:

Criminal Work: (*Contact Partner:* Stephen Rogers). There is a well organised criminal department which already undertakes regular agency work for other practices in the area.

Civil Litigation and Injury Work: (*Contact Partner:* Chris Topping). Two of the partners are members of the Personal Injury Panel. The firm deals with all types of personal injury work including medical negligence and road traffic accident work.

Family Work: (*Contact Partner:* Keith Robinson). Two of the partners are members of the Children Panel. Divorce and related family problems are also dealt with.

Mental Health: (*Contact Partner:* Christopher Topping). The firm has 2 Mental Health specialists who are members of the Mental Health Panel.

Immigration: (*Contact Partner:* Andrew Holroyd). The firm has a wide experience in dealing with immigration and nationality work.

Help for the Small Business: (*Contact Partner:* Andrew Holroyd). The firm aims to give straightforward advice for those starting up new businesses.

Other Offices: Liverpool City Centre, Garston, Scotland Road and the Dingle.

Agency Work: General litigation in the Liverpool County Court and the District Registry and in the Liverpool City Magistrates' Court.

Managing partner:	Andrew Holroyd
Senior partner:	Andrew Holroyd
Number of partners:	6
Assistant solicitors:	7
Other fee-earners:	13

WORKLOADS	
Crime	33%
Civil litigation and personal injury	30%
Family	15%
Housing and landlord & tenant	10%
Immigration	5%
Welfare benefits	5%

CONTACTS	
Civil litigation	Chris Topping
Criminal	Steve Rogers
Family	Keith Robinson
Housing	Simon Ward
Immigration	Andrew Holroyd
Mental Health	Chris Topping
Small businesses	Andrew Holroyd

JACKSON PARTON

18 MANSELL STREET, LONDON, E1 8AA
Tel: (0171) 702 0085 **Fax:** (0171) 702 0858 **Telex:** 8812084 SEALAW G

The Firm: Jackson Parton is a medium-sized niche City practice specialising in shipping, commodity, insurance and related commercial litigation and arbitration. The firm founded in 1992 has flourished ever since.

Principal Areas of Work: (*Contact Partner:* Nicholas Parton). The firm offers expertise in the full range of P&I and FD&D work, including charter disputes, cargo claims, pollution and general average. Other work includes sale and purchase, shipbuilding, mortgage enforcement disputes, marine insurance matters, commodity disputes, grounding, collision and salvage cases.

Foreign Languages: Arabic, French, Dutch, Greek, Italian, Japanese, Norwegian, Persian (Farsi) and Spanish.

Managing partner:	Graham Jackson
Senior partner:	Graham Jackson
Number of partners:	12
Assistant solicitors:	4
Other fee-earners:	3

WORKLOADS	
Commercial shipping: owners, charterers, cargo owners & insurers	70%
Admiralty: collision and salvage	30%

CONTACTS	
Admiralty	Brian Roberts
Commercial shipping	Nicholas Parton

JACKSONS

INNOVATION HOUSE, YARM ROAD, STOCKTON-ON-TEES, TS18 3TN
Tel: (01642) 643643 **Fax:** (01642) 873737 **DX:** 715796 STOCKTON **Email:** GENQUIRY@JACKSONS.LAW.CO.UK
Internet: HTTP://WWW.JACKSONS.LAW.CO.UK

THE TERRACE, ST PETERS WHARF, ST PETERS BASIN, NEWCASTLE UPON TYNE, NE6 1TZ
Tel: (0191) 265 2626 **Fax:** (0191) 265 3030 **DX:** 60960 BYKER

The Firm: Jacksons offers a full range of legal services with a wealth of experience in insurance litigation, company/commercial and commercial property, employment law and private client matters.

The firm has invested heavily in new technology, having provided every member of staff with a Pentium Processor workstation. In addition, Jacksons is connected by e-mail both internally and externally. It has also developed ProNet North, an e-mail network for lawyers in the north east and the first of its kind anywhere in the UK. It also has its own website which was developed in-house, and which is regularly updated.

The firm's insurance litigation department offers expertise in disease work for defendants as well as traumatic injury, property damage and road traffic accidents. The client list includes eight out of the UK's top ten insurers.

The firm has a national reputation for its experience in employment law and offers specialist representation at industrial tribunals throughout the UK, as well as in the Employment Appeal Tribunal.

The company/commercial department covers the full range of services for the corporate client, including company formations, share issues, joint ventures and corporate insolvency. The commercial property team specialises in commercial leasing and conveyancing for builders and major developers. The commercial litigation team offers expertise in insolvency, professional negligence, contract disputes, corporate debt collecting and insurance recovery work.

Jacksons have been at the forefront of alternative dispute resolution and have pioneered mediation techniques as founder members of ADR Net Limited.

Managing partner:	Bill Goyder
Senior partner:	Kevin Fletcher
Number of Partners:	18
Assistant Solicitors:	15
Other Fee-earners:	17
Total Staff:	156

WORKLOADS	
Insurance litigation	53%
Commercial litigation	12%
Private Client	10%
Company/commercial and commercial property	9%
Other Commercial	9%
Employment	7%

CONTACTS	
Commercial litigation	Robin Bloom
Commercial property	Geoff Skeoch
Company/commercial	Tina Hartley
Employment	Kevin Fletcher
Insolvency	Stephen Wiles
Insurance litigation	Richard Clarke

JACK THORNLEY Deansgate Court, 244 Deansgate, Manchester, M3 4BQ *Tel:* (0161) 832 8999 *Fax:* (0161) 832 0306 *DX:* 14385 Manchester *Ptnrs:* 6 *Asst solrs:* 9 *Other fee-earners:* 13

JACQUELINE EVERETT & CO 26 Ellora Road, Streatham, London, SW16 6JS *Tel:* (0181) 664 6042 *Fax:* (0181) 677 3037

JAMES & CO 99 Manningham Lane, Bradford, BD1 3BN **Tel:** (01274) 729900 **Fax:** (01274) 721100 **Email:** Jamesco@ukimmigration.co.uk **Internet:** www.ukimmigration.co.uk **Ptnrs:** 1 **Other fee-earners:** 2 **Contact:** Charles James. *Specialist immigration firm. Charles James started in immigration in 1981. Marriage, business, dependent relatives, political asylum.*

JAMES CHAPMAN & CO

76 KING STREET, MANCHESTER, M2 4NH
Tel: (0161) 828 8000 **Fax:** (0161) 828 8018 **DX:** 14492 MANCHESTER 2 **Email:** JMC.@CHAPMAN-JAMES.PRESTEL.CO.UK

The Firm: James Chapman & Co was established 100 years ago and from its earliest days concentrated on insurance and indemnity work. It has maintained this specialisation and also handles corporate and commercial work, commercial and residential conveyancing and probate work.

Clients of the Firm include many major insurance companies and substantial corporate entities. The Firm is one of the leading Practices in the Insurance and Indemnity field in the North West with the capacity to deal with claims of any size. With 59 fee earners involved solely in this work, the Firm can handle an individual claim or a series of claims. The Firm recruits 4 Articled Clerks a year, as well as additional Assistant Solicitors.

Principal Areas of Work

The Firm consists of departments handling Insurance and Indemnity work on behalf of Defendants (client contact: John McKenna), Personal Injury on behalf of Defendants and Insurers (client contact: Kevin Finnigan), Company and Commercial work (client contact: Maurice Watkins), Property and Probate (client contact: Peter Marsden). The Firm also specialises in Sports Law (client contact: Maurice Watkins).

The Insurance and Indemnity department undertakes a wide variety of work including Personal Injury and Professional Indemnity claims, building and construction claims, product liability and fire claims, motor claims, employers and public liability claims. The department's lawyers also advise on disputes arising from the interpretation of insurance policies. Professional Indemnity matters are handled on behalf of Solicitors, Surveyors, Architects, Accountants and a broad variety of other professional groups.

The Company/Commercial department provides services to a variety of clients from listed public companies to smaller owner-run businesses. The service includes advice on sales and acquisitions, intellectual property and a whole range of general commercial matters including a specialisation in Sports Law headed by Maurice Watkins (a Director of Manchester United Plc). This field of work covers sponsorship, advertising and merchandising.

The Conveyancing department advises clients on all aspects of residential conveyancing as well as on commercial matters including shops, offices and other business premises.

James Chapman & Co intends to sustain the high quality provision of Insurance and Indemnity services that has been its hallmark since the Firm was founded, as well as developing its expertise in other areas. In recent years the Practice has expanded steadily and it believes it will maintain this growth. The Firm's policy is to increase the number of qualified staff not only to meet the increase in demand for its services, but also to ensure that all clients receive a cost effective service.

Managing partner:	Peter Whitehead
Senior partner:	John McKenna
Number of partners:	24
Assistant solicitors:	22
Other fee-earners:	21

WORKLOADS	
Defendant Insurance/Indemnity	80%
Company work	10%
Conveyancing Residential/Commercial & Probate	5%
Plaintiff Personal Injury	5%

CONTACTS	
Comp/Commercial & Sports Law	Maurice Watkins
Personal injury	Kevin Finnigan
Professional indemnity	John McKenna
Property/Private Client	Peter Marsden

JAMES & GEORGE COLLIE 1 East Craibstone Street, Bon Accord Square, Aberdeen, AB11 6YQ *Tel:* (01224) 581581 *Fax:* (01224) 580119 *DX:* 43 Aberdeen *Ptnrs:* 6 *Asst solrs:* 5 *Other fee-earners:* 8

JAMES KENDALL Saint Martins House, 210-212 Chapeltown Road, Leeds, LS7 4HZ *Tel:* (0113) 294 5059 *Fax:* (0113) 294 5001

JAMESON & HILL 72-74 Fore Street, Hertford, SG14 1BY *Tel:* (01992) 554881 *Fax:* (01992) 551885 *DX:* 57908 Hertford *Ptnrs:* 4 *Asst solrs:* 3 *Other fee-earners:* 5

JANE COKER & PARTNERS Emma House, 214 High Road, London, N15 4NP **Tel:** (0181) 885 1415 **Fax:** (0181) 885 2882 **DX:** 55604 Sth Tottenham **Ptnrs:** 3 **Asst solrs:** 2 **Contact:** Ms Jane Coker *Highly regarded for its immigration law practice, children and family work. Expertise in housing, police actions and education also acknowledged.*

JAY BENNING & PELTZ

ONE GREAT CUMBERLAND PLACE, LONDON, W1H 7AL
Tel: (0171) 636 9043/ 872 3600 **Fax:** (0171) 631 4207/ 872 8086 **DX:** 44425 MARBLE ARCH **Email:** POST@MARBLE-ARCH.LAW.CO.UK
Internet: HTTP://WWW.MARBLE-ARCH.LAW.CO.UK

The Firm: Husband and Wife Team, Barry Jay and Gillian Benning established Jay Benning & Co in 1961. They merged with Stephen von Peltz, who has been in practice since 1968, to form Jay Benning & Peltz in 1994. Whilst firmly established as a mainstream capital city practice with global links, Jay Benning & Peltz nonetheless retains the personal touch which it knows is vital to its clients. It strives, not simply to advise on the law or to solve problems, but also to be constantly alert to possible opportunities for its clients, anticipating demands and prompting fresh ideas. Providing a broad range of expertise, coupled with considerable experience in every legal discipline, Jay Benning & Peltz is a full service law firm with the resources to match. Gillian Benning is a member of the Solicitors' Assistance Scheme.

Principal Areas of Work:

Company and Commercial: Jay Benning & Peltz has for many years specialized in company law, commercial law and corporate finance work and employment related matters, acting for a wide range of corporate clients and providing a legal perspective on all matters requiring general business and financial advice.

The firm deals with:

● Mergers and Acquisitons of companies and businesses; capital issues; security transactions; banking and security documentation; management and leveraged buy-ins and buy-outs; corporate reorganisations and restructuring

● Competition and commercial law; formation and enforcement of commercial contracts; copyright, trademarks, patents and other intellectual property matters

● Legal support and advice to lenders, insolvency practitioners and borrowers relating to the conduct of administrations, receiverships, creditor arrangements, liquidations and realisations

● Employment law services to employers and individuals, with advice relating to employment, pensions, share options, incentive schemes, service agreements, individual and collective disputes

● Matters concerning direct or indirect taxation arising on transactions, often in conjunction with external financial advisers.

Property: Jay Benning & Peltz advises owner-occupiers, landlords and tenants on their diverse requirements and also acts for investors in property and property developers. Advice is given on all aspects of the acquisition, financing and disposal of freehold and leasehold property and portfolios both for UK & overseas organisations. The commercial property lawyers work with others on the firm on corporate acquisitions, disposals and reorganisations to ensure that the property aspects are fully considered.

The work includes lease renewals and surrenders, rent review negotiations, general landlord and tenant matters, property management, joint ventures, development and funding agreements and title investigations and certificates of title.

The firm also has wide ranging experience, acting for borrowers and lenders in all aspects of the taking of or realisation of security over property including mortgages and charges, debentures, facility letters, guarantees, priority arrangements, disposals on behalf of insolvency office holders and sales by mortgagees in possession.

Leasehold Reform and Enfranchisement: Jay Benning & Peltz have one of the country's leading experts in this field who also sits on a Government advisory panel investigating the further amendments proposed for this area by the present Governmnent.

Residential Property Litigation Team: A dedicated team established by the firm to meet the need occasioned by the regime for recovery of service charges introduced by the Housing Act 1996.

Insolvency: Historically, Jay Benning & Peltz through its managing partner, Gillian Benning, has been involved in all aspects of insolvency work, developing a wide range of contacts in other professions. One of the partners, Paul Saffron, is a licensed insolvency practitioner.

The firm is in constant demand to act for insolvency practitioners, forcreditors, for debtors and also for directors of troubled companies. It has a wide and long-standing experience of all the rescue and reconstruction procedures as well as the more conventional insolvency processes. It deals regularly with insolvent partnerships, with particular emphasis on professional partnerships and individual insolvencies, with instructions coming from all corners of the market.

Technical expertise is supplemented by a clear understanding of the commercial problems confronting the firm's clients on a day to day basis.

Managing partner:	Gillian Benning
Number of partners:	11
Consultants:	3
Assistant solicitors:	4
Other fee-earners:	7

WORKLOADS	
Property	30%
Company & commercial	20%
Litigation	20%
Family	10%
Insolvency	10%
Private client	5%
Reisidential Property Litigation	5%

CONTACTS	
General	Gillian Benning
Residential Property Litigation Team	Andrew Georgiou

Continues overleaf

Litigation: Civil and commercial litigation are areas for which Jay Benning & Peltz has earned a strong reputation. The firm undertakes the whole range of contentious work. The firm is frequently called upon to apply emergency procedures both outside and within the jurisdiction of the UK and is used to dealing with serious and complex problems.

A key area of specialisation is in matters where criminal proceedings are contemplated, particularly in the field of business crime. Lawyers at Jay Benning & Peltz are adept at dealing with such matters and all the attendant problems.

Family: Jay Benning & Peltz provides comprehensive advice and legal support on all family or domestic matters and problems associated with relationship breakdowns, including divorce, matrimonial finance and property, arrangements for children, adoption, wardships and injunctions and cases involving off-shore assets and overseas jurisdictions.

The firm believes in a conciliatory approach to divorce and financial problems. Its goal is negotiated settlements although in some cases in order to secure a fair outcome litigation pursued firmly is necessary.

Private Client: Jay Benning & Peltz deals with residential conveyancing, probate and trust administration, and with all aspects of personal finance, including wills, tax planning, investment management, general tax advice and powers of attorney. It is also able to obtain independent advice on all types of investment.

Foreign/International Connections: Stephen Peltz has developed over the past twenty years extensive commercial and property connections in South East Asia, Central and East Africa.

The firm also has extensive contacts in the United States of America and Israel. The firm has an associate office in Hamburg.

Recruitment and Training: Jay Benning & Peltz has adopted a policy of recruiting the best trainees, encouraging whenever possible those individuals to remain with the firm on qualification. The firm also welcomes consultancy arrangements with leading lawyers. The firm has obtained authorisation from the Law Society to allocate continuing professional credit to courses which are organised in-house for its own staff, non-fee paying guests and clients.

J.B. WHEATLEY & CO 119 Camberwell Road, SE5 OHB *Tel:* (0171) 701 2983 *Fax:* (0171) 703 1621 *Ptnrs:* 5 *Asst solrs:* 12 *Other fee-earners:* 6

JEFFREY AITKEN SOLICITORS Inter-City House, 80 Oswald Street, Glasgow, G1 4PU *Tel:* (0141) 221 5983 *Fax:* (0141) 226 4538 *Ptnrs:* 5 *Asst solrs:* 1 *Other fee-earners:* 6

JEFFREY GREEN RUSSELL

APOLLO HOUSE, 56 NEW BOND STREET, LONDON, W1Y OSX
Tel: (0171) 339 7000 **Fax:** (0171) 499 2449 **DX:** 44627 MAYFAIR **Email:** JGR@JGRLAW.CO.UK **Internet:** HTTP://JGRWEB.COM

The Firm: Jeffrey Green Russell is a medium-sized commercial law firm based in Bond Street, London W1.

Technology and Communications: The firm is committed to technology and human resources development, both of which have made a significant contribution to its success. The firm has a local area network running Novell Netware. Staff at all levels have PCs running Windows for Workgroups as the desktop GUI and lawyers have Gateway 2000 Pentium PCs. All PCs are capable of internal and external e-mail via the Internet; scheduling and diary (Novell Groupwise); word processing (WordPerfect 6.1); document management and know-how retrieval (Soft Solutions); desktop fax; spreadsheets (Microsoft Excel 5); Internet research; and access to the Hildebrandt marketing database, the back-office accounting system and other specialised programs. The firm uses the DPS automatic document assembly and case management system for large scale insurance claims litigation and property sales matters. It incorporates direct e-mail capability to clients.

Principal Areas of Work:

Company/Commercial: (*Contact:* Tony Coles). A broad spectrum of services focus on commercial and financial activity. Corporate work includes formations, mergers, acquisitions, MBOs, joint ventures, reorganisations and share issues. Other areas of expertise are commercial work (including computer contracts and the Internet), banking and finance, intellectual property and franchising, and corporate taxation.

Litigation: (*Contact:* Phillip Cohen). Quick, positive, effective action is the hallmark of this department in general commercial litigation, insurance disputes, including professional negligence and product liability, personal injury and legal expenses insurance, property litigation, employment matters, debt collection and insolvency, and commercial fraud including computer and technology-related offences.

Managing partner:	C. Whitfield-Jones
Senior partner:	C. Whitfield-Jones
Number of partners:	26
Assistant solicitors:	25
Other fee-earners:	7

CONTACTS	
Company/ commercial	Anthony Coles
Insurance litigation	Bryan Lincoln
Leisure & licensing	Julian Skeens
Litigation	Phillip Cohen
Private client	Phillip Harris
Property	Clive Whitfield-Jones

Property: (*Contact:* Clive Whitfield-Jones). The department offers a full range of services including planning, development work, property finance, investment, dealing (including portfolio break-ups and auction work) and landlord and tenant law.

Licensing and Leisure: (*Contact:* Julian Skeens). A strong department caters for the special demands of the leisure industry, offering a comprehensive service representing clients in courts throughout the country. The firm deals with bingo, nightclubs and discos, pubs, off licences, restaurants and catering, hotels, cinemas, amusement arcades and gaming.

Personal Finance: (*Contact:* Phillip Harris). The department provides a specialist service dedicated to the protection and enhancement of clients' personal wealth. The range of services includes wills and probate, estate and financial planning, trusts and settlements, administration of estates and overseas tax arrangements.

Nature of Clientele: Clients cover a spectrum of commerce, finance and industry, ranging from small businesses to multi-national corporations. Activities include banking, finance, the Internet, technology, leisure, restaurants, the licensed trade, brewers, insurance, airlines and property development.

Foreign Connections: The firm is a member of ACL International, an association of commercial lawyers worldwide. For further information contact the International Partner, David Judah.

JEFFREYS & POWELL 4 Lion Street, Brecon, LD3 7AU *Tel:* (01874) 622106 *Fax:* (01874) 623702 *Ptnrs:* 4 *Asst solrs:* 2

GEOFFREY WARHURST 21 Newton Street, Manchester, M1 1HH *Tel:* (0161) 236 8394 *Fax:* (0161) 236 0640

JENKINS & HAND Clutha House, 10 Storey's Gate, London, SW1P 3AY *Tel:* (0171) 222 5002 *Fax:* (0171) 222 5004 *DX:* 99924 Victoria *Ptnrs:* 2

JEREMY FEAR & CO 5a St. Onge Parade, Southbury Road, Enfield, N17 6SB *Tel:* (0181) 367 4466 *Fax:* (0181) 367 3481 *Asst solrs:* 1

JOELSON WILSON & CO

70 NEW CAVENDISH STREET, LONDON, W1M 8AT
Tel: (0171) 580 5721 **Fax:** (0171) 580 2251 **Email:** INFO@JOELSON-WILSON.CO.UK

The Firm: Established in 1957, Joelson Wilson & Co provides a personal and individual approach and a highly commercial service to its clients. Traditionally known for its strong company/commercial, commercial litigation and commercial property practice, the firm has an established reputation for its work in the leisure industry in the UK and overseas. Solicitors in its specialised licensing department appear in Licensing Courts throughout the entire country. The firm's employment law unit has a growing reputation. There is a strong international element to the firm's practice. It is the UK member of European Lawyers Network (EEIG) working closely with the other member firms in Amsterdam, Brussels, Frankfurt, Paris and Stockholm.

Senior Partner:	Paul Wilson
Managing Partner:	Paul Baglee
Number of partners:	5
Assistant solicitors:	5
Other fee-earners:	4

WORKLOADS	
Company/Commercial	35%
Licensing (liquor/gaming/betting/entertainment)	30%
Commercial Litigation and Employment	24%
Property	11%

JOHN BATTERS & CO Craigie Hall, 6 Rowan Road, Glasgow, G41 5BS *Tel:* (0141) 427 6884 *Fax:* (0141) 427 7909 *Ptnrs:* 1

JOHN BOWDEN TRAINER & CO 20/21 Tooks Court, Cursitor Street, Chancery Lane, London, EC4A 1LB *Tel:* (0171) 334 9192 *Fax:* (0171) 334 9193 *DX:* 33 LDE *Ptnrs:* 2 *Asst solrs:* 2

JOHN BOYLE AND CO The Square, 5 West End, Redruth, TR15 2SB *Tel:* (01209) 213507 *Fax:* (01209) 219470 *DX:* 81758 Redruth *Ptnrs:* 3 *Asst solrs:* 3 *Other fee-earners:* 4

JOHN FORD SOLICITORS Third Floor, Sun Court House, 18-26 Essex Road, London, N1 8LN *Tel:* (0171) 288 1066 *Fax:* (0171) 288 1099

JOHN GAUNT & PARTNERS Omega Court, 372 Cemetery Road, Sheffield, S11 8FT **Tel:** (0114) 266 8664 **Fax:** (0114) 266 0101 **DX:** 709063 Sheffield **Email:** gauntlaw@compuserve.com **Ptnrs: 3 Asst solrs: 1 Other fee-earners: 1 Contact:** John R.T. Gaunt. *Specialist commercial practice, particularly for the licensed and leisure industries.*

WORKLOADS			
Liquor licensing	50%	Commercial property	20%
Landlord and tenant (contentious/ non-contentious)			20%
Commercial litigation			10%

JOHN HODGE & CO 27/31 Boulevard, Weston-super-Mare, BS23 1NY *Tel:* (01934) 623511 *Fax:* (01934) 418210 *DX:* 8403 *Ptnrs:* 10 *Asst solrs:* 3 *Other fee-earners:* 10

JOHN LEWIS SOLICITOR ADVOCATE

NORTH MUSKHAM PREBEND, CHURCH STREET, SOUTHWELL, NG25 0HQ
Tel: (01949) 851 513 **Fax:** (01949) 851 514 **DX:** 11630 SOUTHWELL **Email:** ADVOCATE@JOHN-LEWIS.COM

The Firm: John Lewis is a Solicitor Advocate with Higher Rights of Audience in all civil courts in the UK and he is also a Registered Trade Mark Attorney. He undertakes contentious and non-contentious work covering all aspects of intellectual property law, media law and defamation, and commercial disputes with a technical aspect, especially where emergency injunctions are being sought. He appears in all civil courts and also in proceedings for invalidity and revocation, oppositions and official objections in the Trade Marks Registry and in proceedings at the Patent Office. Instructions are accepted on a project basis or at an hourly rate, directly from companies, firms and individuals, from Trade Mark and Patent Attorneys, from solicitors, and from in-house legal departments.

Principal Areas of Work:
Intellectual Property: *Work includes:* Trade marks, patents, copyright, designs, passing off, trade secrets and confidential information.
Media Law: *Work includes:* Trade libel and malicious falsehood, libel, slander, entertainment.
Commercial: *Work includes:* Computer software, IT, multimedia, internet, licensing.
Litigation: *Work includes:* Mareva orders, Anton Piller orders, Chancery procedures, cases with an insolvency aspect, cross-border and international disputes.

Other Offices: 80 Fleet Steet, London, EC4Y 1EL. Tel: (0171) 936 3877; Fax: (0171) 822 2828.

WORKLOADS	
Intellectual Property (including IP litigation, tribunals and non-contentious work incl. licensing)	
	85%
Litigation (non-IP)	10%
Commercial (non-IP)	5%

CONTACTS	
All aspects	John Lewis, MA, MITMA

Intellectual Property Attorney

JOHN MCKEE & SON

55 ROYAL AVENUE, BELFAST, BT1 1FD
Tel: (01232) 232303 **Fax:** (01232) 230081 **DX:** 470 NR BELFAST

The Firm: John McKee & Son was established in 1887 and is a well known family firm in the Belfast and North Down areas which, despite its long history, adopts a progressive and modern approach. The firm is best known in the field of litigation, where its personal injury work for insurance companies is particularly well-regarded. The firm has a large commercial practice, and specialises in insolvency, all aspects of commercial property and corporate work, employment work and debt recovery, including mortgage repossession, and consumer credit, acting mainly for corporate clients and insolvency practitioners.

Contacts: Commercial litigation: *Melanie Jones;* Commercial Property/Corporate: *Lex Ross;* Employment: *Avril McCammon*; Insolvency: *Lex Ross*; Personal injury: *Leonard Edgar;* Private client: *Albert Jordan*

Senior partner:	Lex Ross
Number of partners:	5
Assistant solicitors:	4
Other fee-earners:	2

WORKLOADS	
Litigation	50%
Commercial	40%
Private client	10%

JOHN O'NEILL & CO 19 Ridley Place, Newcastle, NE1 8JN *Tel:* (0191) 222 1808 *Fax:* (0191) 230 0096 *Ptnrs:* 2 *Other fee-earners:* 4

JOHN PICKERING & PARTNERS

9 CHURCH LANE, OLDHAM, OL1 3AN
Tel: (0161) 633 6667 **Fax:** (0161) 626 1671 **DX:** 23616

6 ST ANN'S PASSAGE, 29/31 KING STREET, MANCHESTER, M2 6BE
Tel: (0161) 834 1251 **Fax:** (0161) 834 1505 **DX:** 718161

19 CASTLE STREET, LIVERPOOL, L2 4FX
Tel: (0151) 227 1214 **Fax:** (0151) 258 1262 **DX:** 14222

The Firm: Established in 1979, John Pickering & Partners is a personal injury firm, acting only for Plaintiffs.

The firm has a special interest and expertise in acting for people disabled by industrial diseases and are specialists in asbestos disease claims, having referrals from doctors, trade unions, specialist advice agencies.

The firm has pioneered asbestos factory neighbourhood injury litigation in the U.K. and in 1995 won the first case of environmental injury to be tried in England.

In April 1998, John Pickering & Partners won a landmark group action against British Gas for victims of vibration white finger.

The firm has clients throughout England and Wales and also in Ireland, Australia, Canada, U.S.A., New Zealand and South Africa.

In addition to personal injury, industrial accidents and disease claims, the firm also takes on medical negligence claims.

Number of partners:	6
Assistant solicitors:	2
Other fee-earners:	2

CONTACTS	
Oldham:	John Pickering, James Thompson
Manchester:	Anthony coombs, Carol Ann Hepworth, Geraldine Coombs
Liverpool:	Patrick Walsh, Catherine Higgins, Darryl Nolan

JOHNS ELLIOT

11 LOMBARD STREET, BELFAST, BT1 1RG
Tel: (01232) 326881 **Fax:** (01232) 248236 **DX:** 419 NR BELFAST **Email:** INFO@JOHNSELLIOT.COM **Internet:** HTTP://WWW.JOHNSELLIOT.COM/

The Firm: Johns Elliot is a leading City firm offering a wide range of legal services, with particular emphasis on commercial and corporate matters. The firm was established in 1837.

Each client has contact with a single partner who bears responsibility for the conduct of that client's business, although individual aspects will be dealt with by specialist lawyers.

Principal Areas of Work:

Company/ Commercial Property: *Work includes:* company formations, reconstructions and acquisitions, and all aspects of commercial property, from initial planning applications to satisfying the requirements of the developers' financiers.

Employment Law: An increasingly problematic area for commercial clients, legal advice is given at an early stage to assess the potential impact of legislation, evolve efficient working practices and ensure good industrial relations are established and maintained.

Litigation: A major part of the firm's practice, this department deals with construction, commercial litigation and debt collection, and is also involved in defamation actions for newspapers and local broadcasting networks.

Managing partner:	**Maurice Butler**
Senior partner:	**Maurice Butler**
Number of partners:	8
Assistant solicitors:	2
Other fee-earners:	4

WORKLOADS	
Company/commercial	45%
Litigation	25%
Other	15%
Probate and tax	15%

CONTACTS	
Company/ commercial	Maurice Butler
Litigation	Ronald Robinson
Private client	David Leitch

THE JOHNSON PARTNERSHIP Cannon Courtyard, Long Row, Nottingham, NG1 6JE *Tel:* (0115) 941 9141 *Fax:* (0115) 947 0178 *DX:* 10082 *Ptnrs:* 8 *Asst solrs:* 5 *Other fee-earners:* 13

JOHNSONS 50-56 Wellington Place, Belfast, BT1 6GF *Tel:* (01232) 240183 *Fax:* (01232) 249239 *DX:* 405 NR Belfast *Ptnrs:* 4 *Asst solrs:* 8

JOHNSTON & HERRON George Johnston House, Bank Street, Lochgelly, KY5 9QN *Tel:* (01592) 780421 *Fax:* (01592) 782726 *Ptnrs:* 2 *Asst solrs:* 1 *Other fee-earners:* 3

JOHN WESTON & CO 10 Victoria Street, Felixstowe, IP11 7ER **Tel:** (01394) 282527 **Fax:** (01394) 276097 **DX:** 31467 Felixstowe **Email:** johnwest@sprynet.co.uk **Ptnrs:** 1 **Other fee-earners:** 2 **Contact:** Mr John Weston *A specialist firm dealing exclusively with marine and transportation matters.*

WORKLOADS	
Marine and Transportation	100%

JONATHAN STEPHENS & CO Ty Cornel, 11 Castle Parade, Usk, NP5 1AA *Tel:* (01291) 673344 *Fax:* (01291) 673575 *DX:* 32552 Usk *Ptnrs:* 1

JONES & CASSIDY 220 Ormeau Road, Belfast, BT7 2FY *Tel:* (01232) 642290 *Fax:* (01232) 642297 *Ptnrs:* 2 *Asst solrs:* 1 *Other fee-earners:* 3

JONES, DAY, REAVIS & POGUE

BUCKLERSBURY HOUSE, 3 QUEEN VICTORIA STREET, LONDON, EC4N 8NA
Tel: (0171) 236 3939 **Fax:** (0171) 236 1113

Senior partner:	Stephen E. Fiamma
Number of partners:	4
Associates:	19
Other fee-earners:	3

The Firm: Tracing its origins to 1893 in Cleveland, Ohio, Jones Day's reach and practice have developed in response to the globalisation of capital, trade, and technology, as well as to the changing needs of the Firm's clients. Today, Jones Day encompasses more than 1,200 lawyers resident in 20 worldwide locations, and ranks among the world's largest and most geographically diverse law firms. The Firm is notable for the breadth of its representation of major industrial corporations, providing significant legal services to over half of the *Fortune 500* companies. It is organised into four major practice Groups: Business Practice, Government Regulation, Litigation, and Tax.

The London Office: Jones Day has had an office in London since 1986. With 23 lawyers, it has one of the largest presences in London among US-based firms. The Office offers both US and English law advice in dispute resolution, tax, structured finance, and mergers and acquisitions. Its practice integrates with the strengths and clients of the Firm worldwide.

Principal Areas of Work:

Mergers & Acquisitions: An important part of the work of the London Office involves advice and assistance to US, British and other companies acquring businesses, investing, or forming joint ventures in the United Kingdom, other European locations, and the US. Almost all of this work is cross-border in nature. The Office handles English law issues which typically arise in the context of an acquisition or divestiture of a UK company of business assets, such as employment law taxation, real property transfers, environmental issues, and competition law.

Taxation: The members of the London Office Tax Group advise both US-based and non-US-based enterprises in connection with tax aspects of international transactions and investments. They offer US and UK tax expertise, with particular emphasis on the tax dimensions of cross-border mergers and acquisitions. The Office has an outstanding practice in tax-based structured finance transactions, in which it is a recognised leader.

Corporate Finance and Securities Law: The London Office is involved in a variety of financing and banking transactions, including leveraged acquisition financing, securitisations, and other secured and unsecured financial transactions. London lawyers are also called upon for advice concerning US and UK securities law matters, particularly in the case of British companies making equity or debt offerings in the US and the listing of securities on the London Stock Exchange.

Litigation and Arbitration: The London Office represents clients in English High Court litigation, English and other European arbitration proceedings, and alternative dispute resolutions in a broad range of substantive areas of law. The Litigation Group also frequently advises on the many complex issues that arise in cross-border litigation and arbitration, including questions of jurisdiction, conflicts of law, pre-trial investigations, discovery, and enforcement of judgements. Jones Day's London-based lawyers are experienced in matters that include fraud and white-collar crime, disputes arising out of international trade, commodities, shipping, energy, insurance, employment, product liability, tax, and other general contractual and tortious actions.

Foreign Languages: German, French, Italian, Turkish, Hindi, Telugu, Tamil, Urdu, Kannada, and Punjabi.

Other Offices: Atlanta, Brussels, Chicago, Cleveland, Columbus, Dallas, Frankfurt, Geneva, Hong Kong, Irvine, Los Angeles, New York, Paris, Pittsburgh, Riyadh, Taipei, Tokyo, Washington DC & New Delhi (associated office).

JONES MAIDMENT WILSON 5 Byrom Street, Manchester, M3 4PF **Tel:** (0161) 832 8087 **Fax:** (0161) 835 3123 **DX:** 14372 **Ptnrs:** 13 **Asst solrs:** 18 **Other fee-earners:** 4 **Contact:** Bill Jones *Firm has five departments: Crime, Family & Welfare Benefits, Company/Commercial, Litigation, Private Client & financial Services. Strong legal aid.*

WORKLOADS			
Litigation/crime	34%	Company/commercial	30%
Family	19%	Private client	17%

JONES MYERS GORDON Pearl Chambers, 22 East Parade, Leeds, LS1 5BZ *Tel:* (0113) 246 0055 *Fax:* (0113) 246 7446 *DX:* 14080 Leeds Park Square *Ptnrs:* 3 *Asst solrs:* 2 *Other fee-earners:* 1

JOY MERRIAM & CO 67 Burdett Road, London, E3 4TN *Tel:* (0181) 980 7171 *Fax:* (0181) 981 7981 *DX:* 55652 Bow *Ptnrs:* 2 *Asst solrs:* 4

J.R. JONES 56A The Mall, Ealing, W5 3TA *Tel:* (0181) 566 2595 *Fax:* (0181) 579 4288 *DX:* 5134 Ealing *Ptnrs:* 4 *Asst solrs:* 8 *Other fee-earners:* 7

JULIAN HOLY 31 Brechin Place, London, SW7 4QD *Tel:* (0171) 370 5443 *Fax:* (0171) 244 7371 *DX:* 35765 South Ken. *Ptnrs:* 8 *Asst solrs:* 1 *Other fee-earners:* 2

KANAAR & CO

6-8 JAMES STREET, LONDON, W1M 5HN
Tel: (0171) 495 6060 **Fax:** (0171) 495 3770 **DX:** 9022 WEST END

The Firm: Kanaar & Co is a general practice firm specialising in all aspects of media and entertainment law. The bulk of its clients are from the entertainment industry. Traditionally, the firm's focus has been music and copyright matters but is becoming increasingly involved in TV, Film, Publishing and the Visual Arts. The Senior Partner, Nicholas Kanaar, has over 30 years experience of acting for clients in the media and entertainment industry.

Principal Areas of Work:

Litigation: Considerable experience in all types of litigation, in particular intellectual property disputes and entertainment related fields such as defamation. Nicholas Kanaar's experience includes acting in the landmark case of Schroeder v McCaulay (1974) to the recent notable cases of Godfey v Lees & Others (1995) and ZYX Music GmbH v King & Others (1995).

Contract: The firm undertakes all forms of company/commercial work, specialising in the exploitation of copyright in all formats.

General: The firm also handles residential and commercial conveyancing, personal injury, employment, matrimonial and private client matters.

Managing partner:	Nicholas Kanaar
Senior partner:	Nicholas Kanaar
Number of partners:	10
Assistant solicitors:	14
Other fee-earners:	6

WORKLOADS	
Litigation	40%
General (incl. prop., copyright, empl., matrim., private client)	35%
Contract	25%

CONTACTS	
Contract	N. Kanaar
Conveyancing	B. Martelli
Copyright	N. Kanaar
Litigation	N. Kanaar, John Simmons, S. Morrisey

KAUFMAN KRAMER SHEBSON 21 Dorset Square, London, NW1 6QW *Tel:* (0171) 262 4511 *Fax:* (0171) 262 8603 *DX:* 41716 Marylebone 2 *Ptnrs:* 8 *Asst solrs:* 4 *Other fee-earners:* 1

KEARNEY SEFTON Franklin House, 12 Brunswick Street, Belfast, BT2 7GE *Tel:* (01232) 232940 *Fax:* (01232) 332865 *Ptnrs:* 3 *Asst solrs:* 4

KEEBLE HAWSON MOORHOUSE Old Cathedral Vicarage, St. James' Row, Sheffield, S1 1XA *Tel:* (0114) 272 2061 *Fax:* (0114) 270 0813 *DX:* 10527 *Ptnrs:* 22 *Asst solrs:* 8 *Other fee-earners:* 18

KEELY BEEDHAM

28 DAM STREET, LICHFIELD, WS13 6AA
Tel: (01543) 420000 **Fax:** (01543) 258469 **DX:** 19005

The Firm: A commercial law practice specialising in the provision of a wide range of legal services to companies and businesses. The firm is composed predominantly of commercial lawyers and provides a level of expertise and service generally expected of large City firms. The firm is involved in commercial and company work, commercial property work, employment law, intellectual property law, banking and insolvency and commercial litigation. There are also departments dealing with matrimonial disputes, personal injury claims and trust and probate services.

Commercial Litigation: (*Contact:* Andrew McGauley).

Commercial/Company: (*Contact:* John Primmer).

Property: (*Contact:* John Parkes).

Managing partner:	Andrew Beedham
Senior partner:	Stephen Keely
Number of partners:	9
Assistant solicitors:	7
Other fee-earners:	9

WORKLOADS	
Company/ commercial	45%
Conveyancing	17%
Other	17%
Commercial conveyancing	11%
Personal injury	7%
Commercial litigation	3%

KEENE MARSLAND 37 Artillery Lane, Bishopsgate, London, E1 7LT *Tel:* (0171) 375 1581 *Fax:* (0171) 375 0318 *DX:* 179 London City *Ptnrs:* 7 *Asst solrs:* 3 *Other fee-earners:* 2

J. KEITH PARK & CO Claughton House, 39 Barrow Street, St. Helens, WA10 1RX *Tel:* (01744) 730933 *Fax:* (01744) 451442 *DX:* 19451 *Ptnrs:* 5 *Asst solrs:* 32 *Other fee-earners:* 75

KEMP & CO Saddlers House, Gutter Lane, London, EC2V 6BR **Tel:** (0171) 600 8080 **Fax:** (0171) 600 7878 **Email:** info@comlegal.com **Ptnrs:** 2 **Other fee-earners:** 4 **Contact:** Mr Richard Kemp *'A law firm for the .com world' servicing computer, information and communications work.*

WORKLOADS			
Commercial	40%	Competition	20%
Corporate	20%	Intellectual Property	20%

E. & L. KENNEDY 72 High Street, Belfast, BT1 2BE *Tel:* (01232) 232352 *Fax:* (01232) 233118 *Ptnrs:* 3

KENNEDYS

LONGBOW HOUSE, 14-20 CHISWELL ST, LONDON, EC1Y 4TY
Tel: (0171) 638 3688 **Fax:** (0171) 638 2212 **DX:** 46628 BARBICAN

50 MARK LANE, LONDON, EC3R 7QT
Tel: (0171) 638 3688 **Fax:** (0171) 702 9757 **DX:** 514 LONDON/CITY

EWING HOUSE, 130 KINGS ROAD, BRENTWOOD, CM14 4EA
Tel: (01277) 233636 **Fax:** (01277) 219175 **DX:** 5020 BRENTWOOD

ASSOCIATED OFFICE:, 64-66 UPPER CHURCH LANE, BELFAST, BT1 4QL
Tel: (01232) 240067 **Fax:** (01232) 315557 **DX:** 490 NR BELFAST 1

One of the leading litigation firms within the City, Kennedys is primarily known as an insurance driven commercial litigation practice. The firm is also recognised for its skills in the non-contentious commercial field, particularly within the insurance, construction and transport industries.

The Firm: Kennedys has grown rapidly in recent years and has become a major player in the insurance litigation sector. With the recent addition of solicitors from the London office of Elliott & Co., the firm's expertise in this area has been considerably enhanced. The firm has a strong client base in Europe and has French and German lawyers based in-house. Kennedys is also active in the USA and the Far East. Many Partners are qualified to practise in Hong Kong and, since the opening of the associated office in Belfast in 1996, six Partners are qualified to practise in Northern Ireland and two Partners are qualified to practise in the Republic of Ireland.

Principal Areas of Work: This is a City practice acting for a wide range of clients both nationally and internationally. The firm is one of the leading defendant insurance ligation firms with expertise built up over a considerable number of years.

The practice is structured to allow specialised litigation teams handle the whole spectrum of insurance work including personal injury, professional indemnity, banking and finance, reinsurance, medical negligence, product liability, directors' and officers' liability and employers' and public liability.

The firm's construction work is renowned; its expertise stemming from over 25 years' close links with the construction industry. Work carried out includes the drafting and negotiating of building contracts, resolution of contractual and site disputes and the commencement, conduct and settlement of formal proceedings (litigation, arbitration and ADR) worldwide.

Considerable expertise has also been built up in transport work and Kennedys now has an experienced team handling railway litigation matters from personal injury and employment law to health and safety and environmental issues.

The expanding commercial department handles all the traditional commercial work of a City practice including mergers and acquisitions, joint venture agreements, financing transactions and cross-border advice for non-UK clients.

The commercial property department deals with a wide range of property transactions, including commercial and leisure developments, secured lending for institutions and development finance.

Senior partner:	Nick Thomas
Chairman:	Stephen Cantle
Number of partners:	40
Assistant solicitors:	51
Other fee-earners:	40

WORKLOADS	
Insurance litigation	83%
Company/commercial	6%
Employment	6%
Construction (non-contentious)	3%
Commercial property	2%

CONTACTS	
Banking	Eric Sumner
Commercial property	Richard Harris
Company/commercial	James Shaw
Construction (contentious)	Nick Thomas
Construction (non-contentious)	James Shaw
Employment	Andrew Gilbert
Insurance	Steve Cantle
Medical negligence	Janet Sayers
Personal injury	David Scrutton (Brentwood)
Pharmaceutical/Prod. Liability	Shane Sayers
	(Mark Lane)
Railway Litigation	Andrew Gilbert
Reinsurance	Nick Williams

Kennedys

Legal advice in black and white

Kennedys has a growing employment practice acting for insurance companies, railway companies and other large commercial concerns. The Healthcare Department is also expanding, acting for the NHSLA and hospitals and their insurers, and advising on medical negligence, employment issues and commercial matters. A further developing area of work within Kennedys is the banking and insolvency practice.

The Brentwood office specialises in defendant personal injury work for insurers, including disaster and fatal accidents, industrial disease and motor claims work. The Belfast and Mark Lane offices provide the same wide-ranging legal work as the main Chiswell Street office.

As a result of sustained expansion the Firm is always keen to consider applications from qualified lawyers who are competent, confident and commercially driven. Fluency in a major European language, especially French or German, is a positive asset, as is experience or a genuine interest in insurance-related law. Trainee Solicitor places are available from September 2000 and all graduate recruitment enquiries as well as placements, paralegal work and general job applications should be sent to Marcus Franks, Director of Personnel.

Kennedys perceives itself as a resourceful and competitive commercial litigation practice with strong insurance links and wide international connections. The firm continues to expand to meet the needs of international businesses. It has a practical and personal approach to the individual requirements of all its clients.

Associated Offices: Paris, New York, San Francisco, Belfast, New Delhi, Karachi, Hong Kong.

KENNETH BUSH Evershed House, 23/25 King Street, King's Lynn, PE30 1DU *Tel:* (01553) 692737 *Fax:* (01553) 691729 *DX:* 57802 King's Lynn *Ptnrs:* 13 *Asst solrs:* 4 *Other fee-earners:* 7

KENNETH CURTIS & CO 88 Aldridge Road, Perry Barr, Birmingham, B42 2TP *Tel:* (0121) 356 1161 *Fax:* (0121) 356 2973 *DX:* 21502 *Ptnrs:* 3 *Asst solrs:* 3 *Other fee-earners:* 1

KENNETH ELLIOTT & ROWE

162-166 SOUTH STREET, ROMFORD, RM1 1SX
Tel: (01708) 757575 **Fax:** (01708) 766674 **DX:** 4602 ROMFORD **Email:** LAW@KER.CO.UK

The Firm: One of the larger law firms in Essex, Kenneth Elliott & Rowe has enjoyed a period of constant expansion despite the recession. In addition to providing advice on corporate law, insolvency and commercial law from its London office, the firm's Romford office has specialist expertise in such areas as insolvency (where the firm has the only qualified licensed insolvency practitioner solicitor in Essex), employment, personal injury, childcare, licensing and transport, as well as conducting private client work. 1997 saw the firm opening a Docklands office.

Principal Areas of Work:

Commercial Property: (*Contact:* Chris Dixon). A high percentage of work is foreign sourced. The firm has extensive experience of estate development and investment acquisition for a number of major clients. The firm also represents major multiple retailers and local authorities. The firm has particular expertise in commercial landlord and tenant litigation.

Licensing: (*Contact:* Beverley Hamblin) Specialists in gaming, liquor and entertainment licensing.

Transport: (*Contact:* Adam Carr) Specialists in road haulage, transport and carriage of goods. Jim Duckworth, an acknowledged expert in this field and author of Road Transport Law, is a consultant to the practice.

Company/ Commercial: (*Contact:* Mark Dixon). Advises on all aspects of company and commercial work, specialising in business start ups and financing, asset security, sales and purchases of assets and shares and employment.

Mark Dixon is a licensed insolvency practitioner and member of the Insolvency Lawyers Association. The insolvency department advises insolvency practitioners, directors, creditors and debtors in all aspects of insolvency law and practice.

Film production: (*Contact:* Mark Sadler). The firm advises lo-no budget film start up companies on all aspects of film production, usually on a deferral basis. Members of the department have practical experience of getting these types of companies and the films they produce off the ground.

Managing partner:	C. Dixon
Number of partners:	11
Assistant solicitors:	8
Other fee-earners:	17

WORKLOADS	
Common law	35%
Commercial property	25%
Licensing/Transport	15%
Insolvency	10%
Private client	10%
Employ ment	5%

CONTACTS	
Commercial property	Chris Dixon
Common law	Edward Woodcraft
Employment	James Stonebridge
Film Production	Mark Sadler
Financial services	David Rogers
Insolvency	Mark Dixon
Licensing	Beverley Hamblin
Matrimonial	Rebecca Gardiner
Private client	David Farr
Transport	Adam Carr

Continues overleaf

Social and Family Law: (*Contact:* Edward Woodcraft). The firm is socially conscious, is franchised by the Legal Aid Board and has members on both the Child Care and Personal Injury Panel of the Law Society. The Firm undertakes a substantial number of plaintiff medical negligence claims.

Nature of Clientele: The firm undertakes work for substantial financial institutions, local authorities, public companies, retail chains, commercial and industrial estate developers and overseas investment clients including state owned enterprises. There is a strong link with Gulf countries, particularly Lebanon, and also with India and the People's Republic of China.

Languages: French, German, Greek, Hindi, Gujerati, Russian, Turkish, Punjabi, Cantonese, Mandarin, Urdu, Arabic, Bengali, Spanish.

Other Offices:

109 Baker Street, London W1M 1FE. *Tel:* (0171) 224 0522; *Fax:* (0171) 224 0546. DX: Marylebone 2

24 Market Way, Chrisp Street, London E14 6AG. *Tel:* (0171) 515 1078; *Fax:* (0171) 515 0099.

KENT JONES AND DONE

CHURCHILL HOUSE, REGENT ROAD, STOKE-ON-TRENT, ST1 3RQ
Tel: (01782) 202020 **Fax:** (01782) 202040 **DX:** 20727 HANLEY **Email:** EMAIL@KJD.CO.UK

The Firm: Whilst the origins of the practice go back to the nineteenth century, the firm has developed rapidly in recent years to become the dominant corporate practice in the region outside Birmingham providing a wide range of specialist and general commercial advice. Corporate finance, commercial litigation, commercial property and planning and environmental are among its particular strengths. The firm adopts a progressive and down to earth approach to its work.

In the past four years, nine new partners in their early/mid thirties have been appointed. Recent developments include the appointment of Adrian Ross as managing partner, Graham Neyt as head of litigation, Philip Medford as head of property and Peter Ellis as head of corporate.

Among the prominent matters with which the firm has recently been involved are; acting on behalf of Alchemy Partners in relation to two public to private buyouts comprising the £10.4m cash offer for Stone based Instem plc, Skuyfeat's recommended offer for Bristol based UK Safety plc and also the £9m buyout and re-financing of Ashbury Confectionery Ltd; a category A action against the Coal Authority due to proceed to trial in Summer 1998 which is of significant local and national importance; the obtaining of planning permission for a residential/business park development in Leicestershire; and advising in relation to competition law aspects of an EC investigation.

Principal Areas of Work:

Corporate Department: (*Contact Partner:* Peter Ellis). The department handles the full range of corporate finance work, including deal initiation and negotiation, acquisitions, banking, disposals, management and leveraged buy-outs, management buy-ins, reorganisations, mergers/demergers and stock exchange transactions. An increasing amount of work is being undertaken for venture capitalists. The commercial unit advises on conditions of trading, agency and distribution, know-how licensing, copyright design and trademark protection, joint ventures, anti-competition and monopolies, franchising, EC law, partnerships, insolvency and entertainment law. The firm also has established employment and pensions units which specialise in the following areas: service agreements and terms and conditions of employment, share option and profit share schemes, unfair and wrongful dismissal, anti-competition/restrictive covenants, industrial disputes, redundancy, labour relations strategy, health and safety, conditions of work and pension schemes.

Property Department: (*Contact Partner:* Philip Medford). The department advises developers, landowners, landlords, tenants and housing associations. Services include: freehold and leasehold acquisitions and disposals, property aspects of company take-overs and disposals, residential/commercial estate developments, building contracts/collateral warranties, compulsory purchase and compensation, business rates, VAT on property, housing association site acquisitions, agricultural property and share farming agreements, sporting rights and forestry. On development matters the department offers a unique "one-stop" service of site appraisal/acquisition, obtaining planning permission, site marketing, sale negotiation and disposal.

Litigation Department: (*Contact Partner:* Graham Neyt). The department handles disputes through the High Court and Appeal Courts, Lands Tribunal, Industrial Tribunals, County Courts and arbitration, providing advocacy where necessary. Established

Managing partner:	Adrian Ross
Senior partner:	A.A. Reeves
Number of partners:	15
Assistant solicitors:	13
Other fee-earners:	15

CONTACTS	
Banking/security	Peter Ellis
Commercial litigation	Graham Neyt
Commercial property/leases	Derek Morris
Commercial/EC	Adam Kelly
Construction	Adam Kelly
Corporate Finance	Edward Dawes
Debt	Martin Cork
Development	Philip Medford
Employment	Peter Gavin
Entertainment	A.A. Reeves
Housing Associations	Derek Morris
Insolvency	Peter Ellis/Adrian Ross
Insurance	Adrian Ross
Intellectual property	Michael Servian
Minerals/agriculture	David Burrows
Pensions	Roderick Ramage
Planning/environmental	Grant Anderson
Private client/personal	Michael Gee
Subsidence	Graham Neyt
Taxation/charities	Jim Moore
Trading/competition	Adam Kelly

KJD
Kent Jones and Done

experience includes: commercial contractual disputes (often multi-jurisdictional) equipment and building failures, distributorship and agency disputes, landlord and tenant disputes, dilapidations claims, and other property litigation, insurance, corporate warranty claims, company shareholder disputes, intellectual property protection (copyright, passing off and trademarks), professional negligence actions and private international disputes. The department has a well established specialism in relation to coal mining subsidence claims and also operates a computerised debt recovery service.

Planning and Environmental Department: (*Contact Partner:* Grant Anderson). The department has built up a team of specialist lawyers providing legal advice on all aspects of the law and practice relating to planning, property development and environmental law. Advice is provided on planning applications and appeals, compulsory purchase (including major highway schemes), the promotion of planning schemes through Parliament, objections to proposed developments and the preparation of site planning appraisal reports. Environmental matters handled by the department include pollution control, waste disposal, contaminated land, statutory and civil nuisance, health and safety legislation and environmental audits. Close contacts are maintained with the mining and quarrying industry.

Nature of Clientele: The client base is broad, ranging from small to medium sized private companies to public companies and subsidiaries of multi-nationals. Their activities vary from manufacturing, distribution and retailing to the financial sector and media and entertainment. The firm also acts for housing associations and some individuals.

International Connections: The firm has long standing relationships with leading law practices in the USA, Europe and the Middle East, Australia and the Far East.

Foreign Languages: French, German and Afrikaans.

KJD
Kent Jones and Done

KEOGH RITSON

GOULD HOUSE, 59 CHORLEY NEW RD, BOLTON, BL1 4QP
Tel: (01204) 532611 **Fax:** (01204) 362 944 **DX:** 25851 BOLTON 2 **Email:** EMMA@KEOGH02.KEOGH-RITSON.LAW.CO.UK

Keogh Ritson is one of the North West's leading litigation practices providing a comprehensive legal service to the insurance industry and to professional, commercial and private clients on a regional and national basis.

The Firm: is committed to providing their clients with the highest quality of service and prides itself on its commercial ability to provide creative, practical and responsive solutions to their client's business problems together with that all important personal touch.

The firm's commitment to IT remains undiminished both in terms of internal communications within the firm and external communications with clients as demanded with The Millennium approaching.

Keogh Ritson have achieved the BS EN ISO 9001:1994 accreditation for their insurance litigation department and the commercial department is currently working towards achieving certification. The firm as a whole is now seeking to achieve the Investors In People Award.

Principal Areas of Work: Keogh Ritson is well known for its substantial defendant insurance litigation department. This specialist department has an excellent reputation in the insurance market for its personal injury defence work. The department deals with all aspects of defendant personal injury work ranging from minor RTA cases to cases of the utmost severity. The firm acts for the majority of the major composite insurers in the UK along with many Lloyds Syndicates.

The commercial department represents clients ranging from privately owned companies to national businesses in transactions including acquisitions, disposals, mergers, joint ventures with a rapidly growing reputation in employment law and environmental law.

The commercial litigation department acts for both insurer and private commercial clients dealing with professional negligence claims, building cases, computerised debt recovery and contractual/commercial disputes of any nature.

There is also a private client department which handles such matters as probate, wills and domestic conveyancing to support the clients of the firm.

Senior partner:	Barry Taziker
Management partner:	Don Clarke
Number of partners:	20
Assistant solicitors:	33
Other fee-earners:	22

WORKLOADS	
Insurance litigation	75%
Company/commercial work	15%
Commercial litigation	10%

CONTACTS	
Commercial litigation	Peter Unsworth
Commercial property	David Johnson
Company/ commercial	Alan Robins
Employment	Alan Lewis
Insurance litigation	David Tyson
Private client	Rachel Semor
Professional indemnity	Nicola McLoughlin

KERSHAW ABBOTT

QUEEN'S CHAMBERS, 5 JOHN DALTON STREET, MANCHESTER, M2 6FT
Tel: (0161) 839 0998 **Fax:** (0161) 839 1019 **DX:** 14348 MANCHESTER 1

The Firm: Based in the centre of the Manchester business community, Kershaw Abbott is a modern and progressive practice serving commercial and insurance clients. Work of quality is handled in an effective and individual manner by partner led teams, conscious always to provide a cost effective service.

Principal Areas of Work: The firm is best known for its work in the fields of construction, professional partnership disputes, commercial and insurance litigation. A specialist service is also offered in the areas of employment and insolvency.

Contact partners:	Anne Kershaw and Christopher Abbott
Number of partners:	5
Assistant solicitors:	3
Other fee-earners:	2

KETCHEN & STEVENS WS 55-57 Queen Street, Edinburgh, EH2 3PA *Tel:* (0131) 226 4081 *Fax:* (0131) 220 1612 *DX:* 61 Edinburgh *Ptnrs:* 7 *Asst solrs:* 11 *Other fee-earners:* 11

KIDD RAPINET 14 & 15 Craven Street, London, WC2N 5AD *Tel:* (0171) 925 0303 *Fax:* (0171) 925 0334 *DX:* 2 Ch.Ln. *Ptnrs:* 37 *Asst solrs:* 9 *Other fee-earners:* 11

KIDSTONS & CO 1 Royal Bank Place, Buchanan Street, Glasgow, G1 3AA **Tel:** (0141) 221 6551 **Fax:** (0141) 204 0507 **DX:** 56 Glasgow **Email:** mail@kidstons.co.uk **Ptnrs:** 6 **Asst solrs:** 4 **Other fee-earners:** 8 **Contact:** Calum Jones *A long established practice with particular expertise in litigation (employment and personal injury), insolvency, and commercial property.*

WORKLOADS			
Litigation (including employment)			25%
Taxation & trust			20%
Commercial property	15%	Corporate	15%
Insolvency	15%	Domestic property	10%

KIERAN & CO 20 The Cross, Worcester, WR1 3PZ *Tel:* (01905) 28635 *Fax:* (01905) 521803 *DX:* 16265 *Ptnrs:* 1

KIMBELL & CO

352 SILBURY COURT, SILBURY BOULEVARD, MILTON KEYNES, MK9 2HJ
Tel: (01908) 668555 **Fax:** (01908) 674344 **DX:** 31408 **Email:** RECEP@KIMBELL-MK.CO.UK

The Firm: Established in 1986 by former City solicitors, Kimbell & Co aims to offer corporate clients practical, commercial advice. The firm has particularly strong links with the brewing, distribution and high-tech industries and also with the financial services sector.

Principal Areas of Work:

Corporate: The firm has built a reputation for buy-outs and mergers and acquisitions, as well as general corporate finance work.

Commercial: Services include acquisition finance and banking, securities and associated loan documentation.

Commercial Litigation: Specific experience is offered in property related matters, insolvency, recovery, employment, intellectual property and competition law.

Commercial Property: Expertise covers large commercial developments, acquisitions and disposals, construction and landlord and tenant, with particular experience in the retail sector.

Services to the brewing/licensed trade sector: A specialist knowledge of related issues has been developed through working for major national brewers.

International Connections: Close contacts have been developed with European law firms in order to provide a full range of services to clients with interests outside the UK.

Senior partner:	Stephen Kimbell
Number of partners:	6
Assistant solicitors:	7
Other fee-earners:	3

WORKLOADS	
Corporate	37%
Litigation	29%
Commercial property	18%
Securities	16%

CONTACTS	
Brewing/Banking	Peter Holden
Commercial Litigation	Richard Brown
Commercial Property	Timothy Clark
Corporate	Stephen Kimbell/Jonathan Hambleton

KING & GOWDY 298 Upper Newtownards Rd, Belfast, BT4 3AJ *Tel:* (01232) 659511 *Fax:* (01232) 671550 *Ptnrs:* 5 *Other fee-earners:* 1

KINGSFORD STACEY BLACKWELL

14 OLD SQUARE, LINCOLN'S INN, LONDON, WC2A 3UB
Tel: (0171) 447 1200 **Fax:** (0171) 831 2915 **DX:** 141 CHANCERY LANE **Email:** KSB@KINGSFORDS.CO.UK

The Firm: Kingsford Stacey Blackwell is a progressive, commercial law firm, based in Lincoln's Inn. The firm prides itself on its approachable Partner-led broad range of services. Technical expertise is matched by practical, commercial advice and competitive fees.

Senior partner:	Jonathan Wood
Number of partners:	18
Assistant solicitors:	22
Other fee-earners:	14

WORKLOADS	
Litigation	36%
Property	26%
Private Client and Residential	13%
Other	10%
Company Commercial	8%
Licensing	7%

Principal Areas of Work:

	Contacts:
Commercial Litigation	*Charles Rankmore*
Airline and Travel	*Trevor Sears*
Insolvency	*Trevor Sears*
Commercial Property	*Robert Sweet*
Company/Commercial	*Robert Neville*
Licensing	*Robert Edney*
Employment	*Marie van der Zyl*
Private Client	*Susan Floyd*
Factoring	*Dedan Gilroy*
Landlord and Tenant	*Kenneth Smith*
Family	*Nina Ingram*
Residential Property	*Richard Martin*
Agency	*Minhaj Saiyid*

Foreign Connections: The firm is the English member of Consulegis a worldwide grouping of International Lawyers.

The firm offers a specialist London Agency Service.

Other Offices: Lincoln House, High Street, Harpenden, Hertfordshire, AL5 2SX. *Tel:* (01582) 766866 *Fax: (01582) 712424. DX:* 80454 Harpenden

KINGSFORD STACEY BLACKWELL
SOLICITORS

KINGSLEY NAPLEY

KNIGHTS QUARTER, 14 ST JOHN'S LANE, LONDON, EC1M 4AJ
Tel: (0171) 814 1200 **Fax:** (0171) 490 2288 **DX:** 22 CH.LN.

The Firm: The firm was established over 50 years ago by the late Sir David Napley and rapidly gained a reputation for its civil, commercial and criminal litigation practice. It is now one of the foremost firms in this field, with considerable experience in handling complex and weighty cases, often with an international element.

Managing partner:	Paul Terzeon
Senior partner:	John Clitheroe
Number of partners:	32
Assistant solicitors:	15
Other fee-earners:	17

WORKLOADS	
Commercial litigation	33%
Criminal litigation	30%
Commercial property	16%
Family	11%
Company commercial	10%

Principal Areas of Work: The firm is unusual in Central London in being able to provide advice and assistance across a broad field, including criminal litigation. Whilst its contentious work is well known, a significant proportion of the firm's work is derived from commercial property, company/commercial, taxation and allied work.

Commercial Litigation: The department's work encompasses commercial and civil litigation, professional misconduct, defamation, immigration, employment, and building and landlord and tenant disputes. With the increasing complexity of cases, very often there are both civil and criminal implications and the department is experienced in handling both aspects. Two of the partners also undertake licensing work.

Criminal Litigation: The work covers a broad spectrum including corporate and City fraud, DTI and Inland Revenue investigations and money-laundering and asset tracing enquiries. Much of the work is international. The firm also advises in extradition matters, general crime and road traffic cases. Members of the firm appear regularly before various regulatory and professional bodies, both prosecuting and defending.

Family: The firm is well known for its family and matrimonial work. Cases range from all issues concerning childcare, through to cohabitation and complex financial matters on divorce.

Company/ Commercial: The department advises on joint ventures, partnerships, finance, taxation, flotations, rights issues, takeovers, insolvency and liquidation, and general business issues.

Property: All aspects of conveyancing of commercial freehold and leasehold property undertaken, together with a small amount of residential property work.

Medical Negligence: The department is one of the largest in London. All types of medical negligence work are undertaken and there is an emphasis on cases involving injuries of maximum severity, in particular, cerebral palsy. The firm also handles personal injury work.

CONTACTS	
Commercial litigation	David Speker
Commercial property	Francis Weaver
Company commercial	Tony Sacker
Criminal litigation	Christopher Murray
Employment	Richard Fox
Family	Pamela Collis
Immigration	Lesley Kemp
Licensing	Michael Caplan
Medical negligence	Christine Marsh

Commercial Immigration: This is one of the largest dedicated immigration departments since Elspeth Guild and her immigration team joined the firm. Primarily specialises in business and employment related immigration with wide expertise in all aspects of UK immigration and nationality issues.

Nature of Clientele: Varied: from large public companies to all types of successful businesses and individuals.

Foreign Connections: French, German and Spanish are spoken.

KIRBY SIMCOX 1 John Street, Bristol, BS1 2HS **Tel:** (0117) 927 7361 **Fax:** (0117) 927 2868 **DX:** 7833 Bristol 1 **Ptnrs:** 7 **Asst solrs:** 12 **Other fee-earners:** 8 **Contact:** Mr J.P. Godwin *A broadly-based general practice with a local and national contentious and commercial bias.*

WORKLOADS	
Civil litigation, P.I. and Family	49%
Criminal defence	22%
Commercial & conveyancing & Residential	20%

KIRK JACKSON 97 Chorley Rd, Swinton, Manchester, M27 2AB **Tel:** (0161) 794 0431 **Fax:** (0161) 794 4957 **DX:** 28201 **Ptnrs:** 7 **Asst solrs:** 4 **Other fee-earners:** 1 **Contact:** Michael Brunert *All round legal practice best known for building/construction litigation and foreign work.*

WORKLOADS			
Construction litigation	22%	Insurance litigation	14%
Commercial property	12%	Family	10%
General commercial litigation	10%		
International employment and miscellaneous			10%
Probate and trusts	10%	Domestic conveyancing	7%
Personal injury	5%		

KIRKLAND & ELLIS International Financial Centre, Old Broad Street, London, EC2N 1HQ **Tel:** (0171) 816 8700 **Fax:** (0171) 816 8800 **Ptnrs:** 3 **Asst solrs:** 6 **Other fee-earners:** 1 **Contact:** Mr Samuel Haubold *An international firm advising on arbitration, litigation, corporate finance and commercial matters.*

KITSONS (practising as 'Ursula Bagnall & Co in Totnes)

2 VAUGHAN PARADE, TORQUAY, TQ2 5EF
Tel: (01803) 296221 **Fax:** (01803) 296823 **DX:** 59203 TORQUAY

The Firm: Established in 1826, Kitsons is a general practice serving private and commercial clients. The firm handles legal aid work and holds a Legal Aid Franchise. It is also a Member of "Accident Line", "A.P.I.L." and "A.M.V.A"

The firm became an 'Investor in People' in March 1998.

Principal Areas of Work:

Commercial Property: *Work includes:* Town and country planning, landlord and tenant, mortgages and commercial lending, sale and purchase and letting of all types of commercial properties and businesses including hotels.

Company/ Commercial: *Work includes:* All aspects of company and commercial work including intellectual property, franchising, licensing and leisure, partnership and employment law matters. The firm advises on EC law.

Private Clients: *Work includes:* Wills, trusts, tax administration of estates, charities and financial services, including investment advice.

Property: *Work includes:* Domestic conveyancing, mortgages, landlord and tenant, rights of access, drainage etc., housing development schemes.

Litigation: *Work includes:* Insolvency, debt collection, personal injury, medical negligence, liquor licensing, building disputes, contractual disputes, general commercial litigation, alternative dispute resolution ("ADR"), family and child care work. Fee-earners are also members of Specialist Panels in respect of Child Care and Personal Injury.

Foreign Languages: French and German.

Foreign Connections: The firm has established strong links with legal practices in Belgium, France and Germany.

Other Offices:

Ashburton: 2 North Street, Ashburton, Devon TQ13 7QD
Tel: (01364) 652468 *Fax:* (01364) 652027. Contact: Philip Palmer

Newton Abbot: 14 Devon Square, Newton Abbot, Devon TQ12 2HR. DX: 59118 Newton Abbot *Tel:* (01626) 203366 *Fax:* (01626) 203360. Contact: Peter Reade.

Ursula Bagnall & Co,16 High Street, Totnes, Devon, TQ9 SSD.DX: 81511 Totnes *Tel:* (01803) 865361 *Fax:* (01803) 862482. Contact: Ursula Bagnall.

Managing partner:	Peter Reade
Number of partners:	9
Assistant solicitors:	5
Other fee-earners:	11

WORKLOADS	
Litigation	38%
Private Client	26%
Property	22%
Commercial	14%

CONTACTS	
Commercial Property	Lloyd Hale/Graham Forward
Commercial Property	Peter Reade
Company/Commercial	Graham Forward/Peter Reade
Litigation	Robert Newman/Ursula Bagnall/ Andrew Perkins
Litigation (Personal Injury)	Ursula Bagnall/ Michael Penfold
Private Clients	Mrs Lynn Smith/John Ireland
Property	Lloyd Hale/Peter Reade

KITSONS
SOLICITORS

KNIGHTS Regency House, 25 High Street, Tunbridge Wells, TN1 1UT **Tel:** (01892) 537311 **Fax:** (01892) 526141 **DX:** 3919 Tunbridge Wells **Email:** knights@atlas.co.uk **Ptnrs:** 2 **Other fee-earners:** 4 **Contact:** Mr M. D. M. Knight *Litigation practice, specialising in country sports and countryside law, defamation, trespass, judicial review and crime.*

WORKLOADS			
Civil litigation	80%	Criminal litigation	20%

KNIGHT & SONS

THE BRAMPTON, NEWCASTLE-UNDER-LYME, ST5 0QW
Tel: (01782) 619225 **Fax:** (01782) 717260 **DX:** 711120 NEWCASTLE UNDER LYME 7

TOOTAL HOUSE, 19-21 SPRING GARDENS, MANCHESTER, M2 1EB
Tel: (0161) 281 4000 **Fax:** (0161) 281 4010

The Firm: Knight & Sons was founded in 1767. In the late 18th century the clients of the firm were the major landowners and men of affairs of the North Midlands. The firm still acts for many of the older businesses and families of the area. The practice has expanded to include a wide range of businesses from throughout the country. As one of the leading firms in the West Midlands, the firm's horizons stretch beyond this country across Europe. The firm provides expert practical advice in a friendly manner and atmosphere. The firm has grown substantially reflecting its success in recent years. This growth is due to several factors – a willingness to respond to the changing needs and demands of business, a continuing improvement in the range and quality of skills and services the firm has to offer and an ability to attract high quality staff. In the Autumn of 1997 the firm successfully opened a branch office in Manchester. There is one factor in particular which sets the firm apart and which has demonstrably helped in retaining clients and winning business and that is the quality of the relationships which the firm enjoys with its clients.

Principal Areas of Work:

Corporate and Commercial: There is a high level of ability in all types of corporate and commercial work and particular expertise in corporate finance, MBOs, intellectual property, EC and competition, computer law and complex commercial transactions.

Commercial Property: The firm has a strong and growing reputation in commercial property work, reflected in its success in winning nationally based tenders. There is particular expertise in mines and minerals, development work, the handling of large property portfolios and landlord and tenant.

Commercial Litigation: The firm's rise in the field of litigation has been rapid and successful, particularly relating to insolvency, property and disputes with a highly technical content. The firm is also a member of ADR Net, the alternative dispute resolution service, and has six trained mediators in this field.

Private Client: The firm has considerable strength in depth and is very highly regarded, with particular expertise in trusts and taxation.

Particular Specialisations: The firm has formed specialist units to concentrate on areas where particular expertise and knowledge is needed: Agriculture; Licensed Trade; Environmental and Planning; Employment; Construction; Intellectual Property; Mines and Minerals.

Managing partner:	Derek John Miller
Senior partner:	Anthony Peter Bell
Number of partners:	19
Assistant solicitors:	20
Other fee-earners:	20

WORKLOADS	
Commercial property	40%
Corporate & commercial	23%
Commercial litigation	22%
Private client	15%

CONTACTS	
Agriculture	Brona Simmonds
Banking	Cindy Quirk
Charities	Kate Smith
Commercial property	Karl Bamford
Commercial/Competition	Steve Elder
Construction	Stephen Belshaw
Corporate Finance	Nick Davenport
Development	Richard Lashmore
Employment	Isabel Hancock
Insolvency	Derek Miller
Intellectual property	James Bird
Licensing	Richard Jones
Litigation	Alan Shackleton
Mines and Minerals	Paul Calladine
Planning and environment	Andrea Bruce
Taxation	Henry Davenport

KNOWLES BENNING 2 George Street West, Luton, LU1 2BX *Tel:* (01582) 736861 *Fax:* (01582) 457092 *DX:* 5923 Luton *Ptnrs:* 10 *Asst solrs:* 8 *Other fee-earners:* 4

KROLL, RUBIN & FIONELLA LLP Asia House, 31-33 Lime Street, London, EC3M 7HR *Tel:* (0171) 621 1142 *Fax:* (0171) 283 6391 *Ptnrs:* 10 *Asst solrs:* 40

KUIT STEINART LEVY 3 St. Mary's Parsonage, Manchester, M3 2RD *Tel:* (0161) 832 3434 *Fax:* (0161) 832 6650 *DX:* 14325 *Ptnrs:* 15 *Asst solrs:* 9 *Other fee-earners:* 11

LACEYS 5 Poole Road, Bournemouth, BH2 5QL **Tel:** (01202) 557256 **Fax:** (01202) 551925 **DX:** 7605 Bournemouth **Ptnrs:** 8 **Asst solrs:** 4 **Other fee-earners:** 6 **Contact:** Mr Wise. *General practice known for commercial property, commercial litigation and private client work. Other offices in Winton and Parkstone.*

WORKLOADS			
Commercial Property	30%	Litigation	30%
Private Client	30%		

LAMB BROOKS Victoria Hse, 39 Winchester St, Basingstoke, RG21 7EQ *Tel:* (01256) 844888 *Fax:* (01256) 840427 *DX:* 3000 Basingstoke *Ptnrs:* 12 *Asst solrs:* 7 *Other fee-earners:* 11

LAMPORT BASSITT

46 THE AVENUE, SOUTHAMPTON, SO17 1AX
Tel: (01703) 634931 **Fax:** (01703) 222346 **DX:** 38529 SOUTHAMPTON 3 Video Conferencing: 01703 330936
Email: EMAIL@LAMPORTBASSITT.CO.UK **Internet:** HTTP://WWW.LAMPORTBASSITT.CO.UK

The Firm: The firm operates an expanding and predominantly commercial practice, and places particular emphasis on technical ability and specialisation. The firm is a niche practice aiming to provide high quality services within specialist areas. The firm makes full use of modern technology. Most senior fee-earners are highly experienced in their chosen fields. The firm is ISO 9001 registered.

Principal Areas of Work:

Commercial: A wide range of corporate, employment, insolvency, planning, property, and liquor, betting and gaming licensing work.

Litigation: The firm is involved in the full range of litigation work including building disputes, commercial contracts, debt collection, employment disputes, intellectual property matters, maritime law, property disputes, professional negligence, and has a large personal injury department. Agency work undertaken.

Private Client: Residential property, personal tax, probate, trusts, wills and matrimonial.

Nature of Clientele: Clients include substantial UK and overseas-based listed and private companies from a wide area of industry and commerce, insurance companies, trade unions and trade associations.

Recruitment: A minimum of two trainee solicitors is recruited each year. Enquiries to Mr. D.H. Cooksley, Practice Manager.

Senior partner:	A.J. Lightfoot
Number of partners:	9
Assistant solicitors:	14
Other fee-earners:	11

WORKLOADS	
Litigation	70%
Company/ commercial	21%
Private client	9%

CONTACTS	
Commercial	S.P. Kelly
Litigation	R.G.B. Solomon
Private Client	J.E. Excell

LAMPORT BASSITT
solicitors

LANE & PARTNERS

15 BLOOMSBURY SQUARE, LONDON, WC1A 2LP
Tel: (0171) 242 2626 **Fax:** (0171) 242 0387 **DX:** 134442 BLOOMSBURY **Email:** INFO@LANE.CO.UK **Internet:** HTTP://WWW.LANE.CO.UK

The Firm: Lane & Partners was established in 1974 and is a firm with strong international connections. Before joining it a number of the partners worked for leading City firms. Lane & Partners concentrates on providing a partner-led service at competitive rates to commercial clients, covering all the main areas of law of relevance to them. It is well-known for its work in the areas of international arbitration, construction, and aviation and travel law.

Principal Areas of Work:

Company and Commercial Law: The firm advises clients on all aspects of company and commercial law, including mergers and acquisitions, joint ventures, Stock Exchange requirements, the Financial Services Act, insolvency and employment law and UK and EC competition law.

Intellectual Property: The firm advises in respect of patent, trade mark and copyright matters, including licensing, franchising, merchandising and all aspects of infringement.

Litigation: The firm is active in all aspects of commercial litigation with particular emphasis on actions in the Commercial Court.

Arbitration: The firm has an active international arbitration practice, with particular emphasis on major construction disputes. It is involved in many ICC Court of Arbitration cases in the capacity of legal advisers to a party or with a member of the firm acting as an arbitrator.

Commercial Property: The firm is involved on behalf of commercial clients in all aspects of property work including the acquisition of freehold and leasehold properties for occupation, investment or development, the sale and management of properties, planning law and appeals and environmental law.

Construction: The firm advises on all aspects of construction law, including the negotiation and preparation of construction contracts, the interpretation of the standard forms used by the industry and the preparation and handling of claims.

Aviation and Travel: The firm advises UK and foreign airlines and tour operators and travel agents. Advice is also given on aviation insurance and liability cases and on aircraft acquisition and leasing transactions.

Nature of Clientele: As well as acting for UK companies, the firm has a considerable number of foreign clients, particularly Swedish, American and Japanese companies. In size, they range from well-known multinationals to small private companies. Their businesses are equally diverse, stretching from international construction and heavy engineering to cosmetics, computers and tour operating.

Senior partner:	Terence Lane
Contact partner:	William Morton
Number of partners:	12
Assistant solicitors:	7
Other fee-earners:	3

WORKLOADS	
Litigation	25%
Company/commercial	20%
Property (commercial)	20%
Construction and arbitration	17%
Aviation and travel	12%
Intellectual property and marketing	6%

CONTACTS	
Aviation & travel	Richard Venables
Company and commercial	Keith Gallon/
	William Morton
Construction and arbitration	Terence Lane/
	Colin Hall
Intellectual property and marketing	Michael Varvill
Litigation	Ludovic de Walden/Piers Lane
Property	Richard Hardman/Mark Barber

Foreign Connections: The firm has associated offices in Washington D.C., Los Angeles, Tokyo, Dusseldorf, Hamburg, Brussels, Milan, Paris, Stockholm, Lahore, Toronto, Mexico City, Seoul, Oslo, Zurich, Geneva, Vienna and Singapore.

Languages Spoken: French, Italian and Swedish.

Recruitment: One trainee solicitor is taken on per annum.

LANGLEY & CO

66-67 CORNHILL, LONDON, EC3V 3NB
Tel: (0171) 397 9650 **Fax:** (0171) 929 6316 **DX:** 760 LONDON/CITY

The Firm: Langley & Co was established in 1993 and specialises exclusively in employment law. Its principals are Dale Langley, Jill Andrew and Nick Ralph who between them have over 40 years' experience, and all of whom were previously with major City firms. The firm deals with all aspects of employment law for corporate clients including contentious and non-contentious matters and also acts for individuals in employment disputes. It aims to provide a highly personalised and responsive service geared to the needs of clients. It is pleased to offer competitive fee quotations and also has a range of fixed price services including the conduct of and representation at Industrial Tribunals. Other services which the firm currently provides include bespoke employment law training courses for clients and the legal profession.

Number of partners:	3
Assistant solicitors:	2
Other fee-earners:	5

WORKLOADS	
Employment	90%
General commercial advice	10%

LANGLEYS

QUEENS HOUSE, MICKLEGATE, YORK, YO1 6WG
Tel: (01904) 610886 **Fax:** (01904) 611086 **DX:** 61533 YORK 1 **Internet:** HTTP://WWW.LANGLEYS.CO.UK

34 SILVER ST, LINCOLN, LN2 1ES
Tel: (01522) 531461 **Fax:** (01522) 510476 **DX:** 11010 LINCOLN

NEWPORTE HOUSE, DODDINGTON ROAD BUSINESS PARK, LINCOLN, LN6 3JZ
Tel: (01522) 888 555 **Fax:** (01522) 888 556 **DX:** 700678 LINCOLN

The Firm: Langleys is a progressive and modern firm, well established with City centre offices in Lincoln and York. The firm historically offered clients an all-round service, with a distinct emphasis on litigation. Langleys largest and most important area of work is accident claims, they have a large department specialising in this work based at both their Lincoln and York offices. With eighteen dedicated fee earners this specialist department acts for most of the major insurance companies and many loss adjusters. Langleys have gained an excellent reputation in this area.

Ten years ago Langleys opened in York and subsequently they have undergone rapid expansion. The practice is now grouped into specialist departments, which include childcare, family law, a common law department, conveyancing and wills & probate.

Langleys have a specialist company commercial team involving corporate, employment, banking, commercial litigation and commercial conveyancing specialisms. The firm has a legal aid franchise and is committed to quality work provided by specialist lawyers.

To meet the growing demand for their services, last year Langleys opened new offices at Newporte House, Doddington Road Business Park, Lincoln, to cater exclusively for the insurance claims, banking, and company commercial clients. These offices benefit from high technology facilities and easy access to the city by-pass and ample car parking. Langleys, with its structured ten year business plan aims to continue development in all areas of their business activities whilst continuing to provide a first class comprehensive service to private clients, with a particular emphasis on quality controls and are currently working towards an "Investors in People" accreditation.

Principal Areas of Work:

Insurance Claims Department: This department has a large specialist team acting for most of the major insurance companies and loss adjustors. The department has an increasing reputation for their proactive and commercial approach.

Company Commercial and Banking Department: The work of this department includes the sale and acquisition of businesses, joint ventures, mergers, partnerships, formation, structure and funding of companies, banking, insolvency, employment and commercial litigation.

Domestic Conveyancing: Dealing with all aspects of conveyancing, mortgages, surveys and every other issue of moving house.

Senior partner:	J. R. Morgan
Managing partners:	M.D. Williamson &
	P.R. Cragg
Number of partners:	11
Assistant solicitors:	18
Other fee-earners:	22

WORKLOADS	
Accident/Insurance (defendant)	41%
Accident/Insurance (plaintiff)	16%
Domestic Conveyancing	12%
Commercial	6%
Matrimonial	6%
Commercial Conveyancing	4%
Other	3%
Wills etc	3%
Agency and Miscellaneous	2%
Criminal	2%
Debt Collection	2%
Surveys and Valuations	2%
Common Law	1%

CONTACTS	
Accident (defendant)	D. Thompson/S. King
Accident (plaintiff)	C. Jones/Ian Pryer
Agency	D. Tonge
Commercial	R. Taylor
Commercial Conveyancing	M.D. Williamson/
	D. Macharaga
Criminal	Nick Darwin/J. Bowling
Debt Collection	Karen Bedford
Domestic Conveyancing	S. Crabtree/A. Abbot
Employment	John White/Roger James
Matrimonial	P. Lowe/P. Hardy
Tax and Finance	D. Glayzer
Wills, Trust and Probate	J. Petch/M. Rogers

Continues overleaf

Family and Matrimonial Department: The Family law department has a team of dedicated lawyers who provide expert advice on family law and welfare benefit and whose reputation for child care, maintenance and domestic violence is particularly strong and growing.

Plaintiff Personal Injury Department: The department advises on road traffic claims, injuries caused by crime and medical negligence cases.

Other Areas of Work: These include debt collection, tax planning, wills, probate, trusts and criminal work. The firm also has estate agency departments at both Lincoln and York with qualified surveyors and valuers.

LANYON BOWDLER 23 Swanhill, Shrewsbury, SY 1 1NN *Tel:* (01743) 236400 *Fax:* (01743) 354994 *DX:* 19721 Shrewsbury

---

LARBY WILLIAMS 53 Mount Stuart Square, Cardiff, CF1 6DR **Tel:** (01222) 472100 **Fax:** (01222) 472011 **DX:** 200750 Cardiff Bay **Ptnrs:** 2 **Asst solrs:** 2 **Other fee-earners:** 1 **Contact:** Miss Frances Williams *Larby Williams was established in December 1997 by two experienced family law practitioners, with offices in Cardiff Bay and the market town of Cowbridge. Family and child care form a niche part of the practice with one partner a member of the Law Society Children Panel. The firm also provides a general service to private and small business clients with an emphasis on licensing, agricultural and probate matters.*

WORKLOADS			
Family Law	55%	Property/Probate	25%
Commercial/Agricultural			20%

LARCOMES 168 London Rd, North End, Portsmouth, PO2 9DN *Tel:* (01705) 661531 *Fax:* (01705) 671043 *DX:* 42401 *Ptnrs:* 7 *Asst solrs:* 5 *Other fee-earners:* 10

LATHAM & WATKINS

ONE ANGEL COURT, LONDON, EC2R 7HJ
Tel: (0171) 374 4444 **Fax:** (0171) 374 4460

The Firm: Latham & Watkins is a multi-national partnerhip with nine US and five international offices. The lawyers in the London office practice English and U.S. law and represent a cross-section of the firm's transactional and regulatory expertise. As client needs dictate, London-based lawyers can also call upon the collective expertise of over 850 Latham & Watkins lawyers practising worldwide in disciplines encompassing virtually every aspect of business-related law.

The London Office: The work undertaken by the London office is approximately 80% finance (primarily project finance) and 20% corporate.

Languages Spoken: German, Urdu and Japanese.

Other Offices: Los Angeles, New York, Chicago, San Diego, Orange County, New Jersey, Washington DC, San Francisco, Palo Alto, Hong Kong, Moscow, Singapore and Tokyo.

Managing partner:	Joseph Blum
Senior partner:	David Miles
Number of partners:	6
Assistant solicitors:	10
Other fee-earners:	1

LATIMER HINKS 5-8 Priestgate, Darlington, DL1 1NL *Tel:* (01325) 381600 *Fax:* (01325) 381072 *DX:* 69282 Darlington 6 *Ptnrs:* 8 *Asst solrs:* 7 *Other fee-earners:* 15

LAWFORD & CO

WATCHMAKER COURT, 65 ST. JOHN'S STREET, LONDON, EC1M 4HQ
Tel: (0171) 353 5099 **Fax:** (0171) 353 5355 **DX:** 53311 CLERKENWELL

The Firm: Established in 1952, Lawford & Co is a medium-sized practice with offices in the City and the principal regions, well known for its expertise in litigation. The firm offers clients the personal attention of a small firm as well as the breadth of legal knowledge offered by a large nationwide practice.

Principal Areas of Work:

Personal Injury: (*Contact:* Graham Humby) The personal injury department receives instructions from a wide range of trade unions, professional associations, institutional clients and legal expenses insurers. The firm has particular expertise in representing Plaintiffs following accidents at work and has dealt with some of the largest UK financial awards and settlements in recent years. The firm employs 33 fee earners in England and Wales and has an association with Lawford Kidd in Scotland to provide national coverage.

Managing partner:	Clive Robertson
Senior partner:	Graham Humby
Number of partners:	11
Assistant solicitors:	22
Other fee-earners:	12

WORKLOADS	
Personal Injury	60%
Education	15%
Employment	15%
Civil Litigation/Commercial Property/ Company Commercial	10%

Employment: (*Contact:* Joy Drummond) The firm has a large and thriving employment department representing predominantly trade union members and private clients. The department currently consists of three partners and six assistant solicitors and has specialists in all aspects of employment law.

Education: (*Contact:* Clive Robertson) The firm acts for a number of institutions in further and higher education as well as schools, advising and acting in matters such as property acquisition and financing, commercial contracts and company formation, student and staff issues and corporate governance. The firm regularly acts in emergency applications to the Courts.

Commercial Property: (*Contact:* Larraine Phillips) The firm is involved on behalf of commercial clients dealing with all aspects of property work. This includes the acquisition of freehold and leasehold properties for investment or development, occupation, sale and management as well as dealing with the full range of planning and environmental law and appeals.

Aviation: (*Contact:* Tony Hows) The firm acts for aircraft owners and pilots in the general aviation sector as well as Pilot Associations in the UK and overseas. Work includes aircraft purchase, wet/dry leases, aircraft accidents, inquiries and inquests, loss of licence claims, CAA, JAA and FAA Regulations and prosecutions, insurance claims and pilot related employment matters.

Nature of Clientele: Clients include Trade Unions and Employee Associations, Universities, Higher Education Institutions and schools. Legal Expenses Insurers and small to medium-sized companies and private clients.

Other Offices: Richmond, Manchester and Nottingham.

Associated Office: Lawford Kidd & Co, Edinburgh

LAWFORD KIDD 12 Hill Street, Edinburgh, EH2 3LB **Tel:** (0131) 225 5214 **Fax:** (0131) 226 2069 **DX:** ED 159 EDINBURGH **Ptnrs:** 3 **Asst solrs:** 4 **Other fee-earners:** 2 **Contact:** Mr David Sandison **Specialisation:** *Personal Injury Litigation for Trade Union clients; Medical Negligence, Court of Session Litigation; Private Client Department.*

LAWGROUP UK Orbital House, 85 Croydon Road, Caterham, CR3 6PD *Tel:* (01883) 341341 *Fax:* (01883) 340066 *DX:* 36806 Caterham *Ptnrs:* 1600 *Asst solrs:* 3000 *Other fee-earners:* 5000

THE LAW OFFICES OF MARCUS J. O'LEARY

CENTENNIAL COURT, EASTHAMPSTEAD ROAD, BRACKNELL, RG12 1YQ
Tel: (01344) 303044 **Fax:** (01344) 300808 **Email:** MOLEARY@MJOL.CO.UK **Internet:** HTTP://WWW.MJOL.CO.UK

The Firm: Rapidly expanding niche practice specialising in information technology and intellectual property matters. Comprising established practitioners in these fields, the practice is modern, progressive and provides an excellent cost effective service to all of its clients.

Principal Areas of Work:

Information Technology: Experienced practitioners with in-house experience can offer a full range of advice to high technology companies and other companies using high technology products.

Intellectual Property: All copyright, design, patent, biotechnology, trade mark, passing off and confidential information issues handled quickly and efficiently with regard to the client's best interest.

Internet/Multimedia: The firm acts for well known international companies active in this specialist area. Good quality leading edge advice is assured.

Music, media and entertainment: Advice and contracts for musicians, composers, and film makers.

Advertising: The firm has extensive experience in dealing with advertisements and promotions in different media formats both nationally, internationally and on the Internet.

Competition Law: Advice on UK and EC Competition law is available in relation to all matters dealt with by the firm.

Company/Commercial: The firm provides a full range of legal services including mergers and acquisitions, joint ventures, MBO's and MBI's restructuring, flotations, particularly in connection with high technology companies.

Litigation: Can be undertaken by the firm in connection with any of the matters listed above.

Clientele: Mainly well known international high technology companies.

Recruitment: A small number of very highly qualified and experienced assistant solicitors will be needed each year.

Foreign languages: French, German, Spanish, Hindi and embryonic Japanese.

Number of partners:	4
Assistant solicitors:	1
Other fee-earners:	1

WORKLOADS	
IT/IP/Internet/Multimedia	75%
Advertising/Media/Entertainment	10%
Company/Commercial	10%
Litigation	5%

CONTACTS	
Advert./Media/Entertainment	Marcus O'Leary/Celia Nortcliff
Company/Commercial	Rupert Wright/Paul Milton
Internet/Multimedia	Marcus O'Leary/Celia Nortcliff
IT/IP	Paul Milton/Marcus O'Leary/Celia Nortcliff
Litigation	Celia Nortcliff

LAWRENCE GRAHAM

190 STRAND, LONDON, WC2R 1JN
Tel: (0171) 379 0000 **Fax:** (0171) 379 6854 **DX:** 39 CHANCERY LANE **Email:** INFO@LAWGRAM.CO.UK **Internet:** HTTP://WWW.LAWGRAM.COM

The Firm: Lawrence Graham is one of the leading law firms in London. Its principal office is located at 190 Strand, London opposite the Law Courts; its established shipping practice operates from a separate office in St. Mary Axe. The firm has an association with Rosenman & Colin, a major New York law firm, Koo & Partners, in Hong Kong, Koraboimpex & Co. in Varna, Bulgaria, E. Kanaan & Co in Beirut and Maritime Business and Legal Services, Mariupol, Ukraine. It was also the founding member of ABLE (Associated Business Lawyers in Europe) with associated firms in Antwerp, Brussels, Hamburg, Madrid, Paris and Stockholm. The firm handles all aspects of legal work with particular strengths in: corporate and commercial law including corporate finance; commercial property; commercial, insurance, property and shipping litigation; and tax planning and private client.

Principal Areas of Work:

Commercial Property: (17 Partners). Work includes: All commercial property matters, conveyancing, leaseholds, new developments, business parks and shopping centres, urban regeneration, construction and building law, planning, environmental, property finance and securitisation and property litigation. The firm acts for some of the largest institutional investors in property and some of the most progressive property developers. There is a local public authority unit which advises on contracting out and externalisation of services including large scale transfers to housing associations.

Company and Commercial: (20 Partners).The department acts for banks, stock brokers and other financial institutions. *Work includes:* corporate finance transactions, flotation and Stock Exchange work, investment fund work, Financial Services Act regulation, banking, pensions, intellectual property and competition law, insolvency and energy law, EC law and many types of commercial contracts, including employment and share option schemes. The department also advises on all aspects of law affecting sporting and leisure industries. The department has a large US client base.

Insurance/Commercial/Litigation: (13 Partners). Work includes:a balance of commercial litigation in conjunction with the company and commercial department, insurance and reinsurance matters including personal injury work, product liability, medical negligence and ADR.

Shipping: (6 Partners). Work includes: the full range of maritime law including charterparties, contractual matters, marine insurance, collision and salvage, international law and financing.

Tax and Financial Management: (10 Partners). Work includes: UK and international taxation advice, employee share schemes and cross-border and other tax efficient structuring of commercial transactions. Offshore trusts, estate planning and probate, investment services and asset management, personal litigation, matrimonial and private property work including agricultural work.

Recruitment and Training: Applications for trainee solicitors should be made by letter and CV to Mrs Diane Austin. Training is considered of major importance and in-house training programmes are undertaken. The firm also has a social club and a fitness centre.

Managing partner:	Bill Richards
Senior partner:	Martyn Gowar
Number of partners:	67
Assistant solicitors:	66
Other fee-earners:	54

WORKLOADS	
Litigation/shipping	37%
Commercial property	27%
Company/commercial	26%
Tax & Financial Management	10%

CONTACTS	
ADR	Alan Hart/Victoria Jordan
Advertising & Marketing	Michael Smyth/Andrew Dobson
Banking and Financial	Paul Walker/Richard Elphick
Capital Markets	Charles Wilkinson/Michael Storar
Collective Investments	Charles Wilkinson/Nicholas Heather/Victoria Younghusband
Construction	Alan Hart
Employment	Yvonne Gallagher
Environmental	Caroline May
EU/Competition	Anthony Woolich
Housing Associations	Simon Randall/Nicholas Turner
Insolvency	John Verrill
Insurance (Corporate & Regulatory)	Robert Smith
IP and IT	Jonathan Riley
Litigation (Commercial)	Andrew Dobson/Pam Bryan
Litigation (Insurance)	Michael Edwards
Litigation (Property)	Penny Francis/Jane Fox Edwards
Local Government	Simon Randall
Medical Negligence	Catherine Percy/Elizabeth Carr
Mergers & Acquisitions	Michael Storar
Oil & Gas	John Verrill/Michael Combes
Pensions	Robert Smith
Personal Injury	Elizabeth Carr
Planning	Trevor Blaney
Product Liability	Michael Edwards
Professional Indemnity	Catherine Percy/Victoria Jordan
Property (Commercial)	Michael Duffy/Paul Kinsella
Reinsurance	Nicholas Bradley
Shipping	Michael Lax/Roger Cooper
Sport and Leisure	Charles Ouin/Jonathan Riley
Tax (Corporate)	Robert Field/Michael Murphy
Tax (Personal), trusts and probate	Tim Thornton Jones/Andrew Young
Urban Regeneration	Carl Hopkins
VAT/Customs & Excise	Robert Field

LAWRENCE JONES Sea Containers House, 20 Upper Ground, Blackfriars Bridge, London, SE1 9LH **Tel:** (0171) 620 1311 **Fax:** (0171) 620 0860 **DX:** 44304 Southwark **Email:** law.jones@dial.pipex.com **Ptnrs:** 15 **Asst solrs:** 4 **Other fee-earners:** 6 **Contact:** Michael Offer. *City firm with strong international client base. Work areas include company, commercial, banking, property, transport, shipping, aviation, insurance, immigration, environment.*

WORKLOADS			
Banking/property	42%	Company/commercial	32%
Commercial disputes	26%		

LAWRENCE TUCKETTS

BUSH HOUSE, 72 PRINCE STREET, BRISTOL, BS99 7JZ
Tel: (0117) 929 5252 **Fax:** (0117) 929 8313 **DX:** 7830 BRISTOL **Email:** CONNECT@LAWRENCE-TUCKETTS.CO.UK

The Firm: A progressive, expanding commercial practice, the firm acts as business advisers to a wide variety of clients, corporate and unincorporated, whilst maintaining a strong private client department. Particular strengths are in company and commercial work, litigation, property, planning and environmental, litigation for financial institutions, insolvency and employment law.

Lawrence Tucketts offers a fresh, focused approach to providing commercial solutions to legal problems. The firm's geographical location provides it with a competitive cost base which is attractive to national organisations with regional networks.

Practice groups and specialist teams deliver tailored services providing flexible and objective support for management teams, underpinned by financial certainty on costs. Quality of Service: The firm's ability to deliver a cost effective service on time is clearly demonstrated by its achievement of ISO 9001, the International Standard of Quality Assurance; the first law firm in the South West to be approved. Lawrence Tucketts has been formally recognised as an Investor in People organisation. Member of European Law Firm

Foreign Languages: French, German, Spanish and Italian.

Senior partner:	Tim Pyper
Number of partners:	17
Assistant solicitors:	32
Other fee-earners:	15

WORKLOADS	
Litigation	43%
Commercial property and planning	23%
Commercial and corporate	18%
Private client	16%

CONTACTS	
Commercial and corporate	David Pester
Commercial litigation	Richard Flowerdew
Commercial property	Edward Cooke
Employment	Alana Weeks
Insolvency and recoveries	Judith Brown
Personal injury	Stephen Duddell
Planning and environmental	Stephen Pasterfield
Private client	Kerry Gwyther
Waste management	Edward Cooke

EUROPEAN LAW FIRM
★ ★ ★ ★ ★ ★ ★ ★ ★ ★ ★ ★

LAWRENCE WOOD 23 Prince of Wales Road, Norwich, NR1 1BG *Tel:* (01603) 616112 *Fax:* (01603) 760538 *DX:* 5221 Norwich *Ptnrs:* 4 *Asst solrs:* 2

LAWSON COPPOCK & HART 18 Tib Lane, Cross St, Manchester, M2 4JA *Tel:* (0161) 832 5944 *Fax:* (0161) 834 4409 *DX:* 14370 *Ptnrs:* 8 *Asst solrs:* 3 *Other fee-earners:* 3

LAW SOUTH

66 GUILDFORD STREET, CHERTSEY, KT16 9BB
Tel: (01932) 560902 **Fax:** (01932) 571250

Nature of Group: Law South is a group of ten independent law firms in major centres throughout the South East of England. Formed in 1988, the Group's major objective is the establishment of inter-firm networks to provide collective resources for training, marketing and pooled legal expertise, thus ensuring a consistently high standard of service throughout the region. Quality projects leading to ISO9001, Legal Aid Franchising and Investors in People are implemented, and all member firms have one or more external accreditation.

Member Firms:
Barlows: (Guildford and Surrey)
Blake Lapthorn: (Portsmouth, London and Hampshire)
Brachers: (Maidstone & London)
Donne Mileham & Haddock: (Brighton and East Sussex)
Girlings: (Canterbury and East Kent)
Leigh Williams: (Bromley and North Kent)
Thomas Eggar Church Adams: (London, Chichester, Worthing, Horsham and Reigate)
Thomson Snell & Passmore: (Tunbridge Wells and Mid-Kent)
White & Bowker: (Winchester and Hampshire)
Wilsons: (Salisbury, and Wiltshire/Dorset)

Dir. of Administion:	Christina Myers
Number of partners:	223
Assistant solicitors:	163
Other fee-earners:	236

LAYTONS

CARMELITE, 50 VICTORIA EMBANKMENT, BLACKFRIARS, LONDON, EC4Y 0LS
Tel: (0171) 842 8000 **Fax:** (0171) 842 8080 **DX:** 253 CHANCERY LANE **Email:** LAYTONSL@LAYTONS.COM

Laytons is a commercial firm with three primary fields of focus – corporate and commercial law, construction law and land development – each comprising a range of complementary specialist skills.

The Firm: The Firm's four offices in London, Bristol, Hampton Court and Manchester work autonomously but share their respective specialist skills and form specific teams whenever appropriate. International legal service is provided partly within the UK offices and partly through a network of overseas associates.

The Firm is strongly client-led, building close working connections with clients and encouraging ongoing contact between the client's personnel and all members of the team assigned to the client. Strong emphasis is placed on understanding the client's business so as to give advice of high technical quality which is commercially effective and achieves results.

A creative, energetic, practical approach allied to technical expertise, a commitment to achieve the client's objectives, high-quality service and client care are hallmarks of the Firm's approach. Teamwork, mutual support and openness characterise its internal ethos.

Principal Areas of Work: The Firm integrates a range of complementary specialist skills to provide a complete service relevant to its target markets.

The work of its company/commercial group includes domestic and cross-border mergers, acquisitions and joint ventures, Stock Exchange work, venture capital and other corporate finance, bank lending, corporate tax, commercial contracts, EU law, competition work, international trade, product liability, advertising and public relations work. Intellectual property (both contentious and non-contentious) matters are an important part of the Firm's commercial work for a varied range of clients in the manufacturing, electronic publishing, data and computer industries.

The Firm's construction law group is recognised as a national leader. It offers non-contentious advice, contract preparation and collateral warranty advice as well as specialist dispute resolution skills, including arbitration and litigation.

The land development group provides an overall service for both commercial and residential property development, including portfolio management, property tax, planning advice, hearings and infrastructure agreements. It advises on land warehousing, joint ventures, acquisition and licensing of landfill sites and power generation from waste. The Firm also has expertise in environmental issues including contaminated land projects, environmental claims and contracts and tendering for provision of environmental services.

The Firm's litigation and dispute resolution group deals with UK and international commercial litigation and arbitration disputes, insurance litigation, professional negligence, product liability, personal injury, land and environment disputes, debt recovery and regulatory crime. It works closely with the non-contentious practice teams.

Employment and human resource issues of all kinds, including pensions and incentives advice, are dealt with by a specialist unit, and a corporate recovery team, which includes two licensed insolvency practitioners, deals with all types of recovery and insolvency-related matters.

Charities and private client matters form an integral part of serving the clientbase and are dealt with by two units, one serving charities and providing estate planning, trust and administration services, the other with family law matters.

Principal Offices:

Bristol – Saint Bartholomews, Lewins Mead, Bristol BS1 2NH. Tel: (0117) 929 1626.

Hampton Court – 76 Bridge Road, Hampton Court, East Molesey, Surrey KT8 9HF. Tel: (0181) 481 7000.

Manchester – 22 St. John Street, Manchester M3 4EB. Tel: (0161) 834 2100.

LEA & COMPANY Bank Chambers, Market Place, Stockport, SK1 1UN *Tel:* (0161) 480 6691 *Fax:* (0161) 480 0904 *DX:* 19651 *Ptnrs:* 2 *Other fee-earners:* 3

Senior Partner:	David Hillyer
Chief Executive Ptnr:	Richard Kennett
Number of partners:	28
Assistant solicitors:	31
Other fee-earners:	20

WORKLOADS	
Company/commercial	37%
Commercial property/land development	20%
General litigation	17%
Building litigation	10%
Employment	9%
Other including private client/trusts	4%
Insolvency	3%

CONTACTS	
Advertising	Neale Andrews
Commercial litigation	Richard Harrison
Company/commercial	Richard Kennett
Construction	John Redmond
Employment	James Davies
Environment	Simon Day
European/product liability	Patrick Kelly
Family	Christine Barker
Insolvency	Anthony Harris
Land development	Chris Taylor
Private client/charities	Ian Burman
Real property	David Hillyer
Tax	Marc Selby

LEATHES PRIOR

74 THE CLOSE, NORWICH, NR1 4DR
Tel: (01603) 610911 **Fax:** (01603) 610088 **DX:** 5205 NORWICH

The Firm: Leathes Prior is the largest independent law firm in Norfolk with 17 partners and over 100 employees in 4 offices. The firm's established position requires that the broadest range of services are available to clients. However, more recently, the firm has been developing a growing reputation in commercial work, with acknowledged leadership in a number of specialist areas. Leathes Prior's independence and structure means that the firm provides a highly competitive and responsive, partner led service, able to satisfy the vast majority of demands from commercial clients. With its affiliation to EU-LEX and extensive foreign language skills, the firm acts for numerous clients with overseas interests.

Principal Areas of Work: Leathes Prior's commercial department draws in partners with specialist skills ranging from company formation, property, planning, intellectual property, EC law, employment and litigation. In addition, they have a well established reputation in franchising, insolvency and insurance/personal injury cases. To provide a one-stop shop, the firm also provides full financial planning services for both commercial and private clients. Among private clients, Leathes Prior has a considerable reputation in matrimonial, criminal and civil liberty issues and has gained a legal aid franchise.

Foreign Connections: Founder member of the EU-LEX International Practice Group; Languages include French, Spanish, German, Dutch, Russian etc

Offices: Norwich, North Walsham, London.

Number of partners:	17
Assistant solicitors:	13
Other fee-earners:	15

CONTACTS	
Charitable trusts/ Private Client	William Riley
Civil liberties/ immigration/P.I.	Tim Cary
Commercial property	Gavin Wilcock
Corporate/ commercial	Paul Warman
Crime	Trevor Beckford
Employment/ litigation	Martin Plowman
Franchising/ IP	Jonathan Chadd
Insolvency/ banking	Mark Oakley
International	Jonathan Chadd
Matrimonial/ family	Ros Thickett, Ian Denning
Planning/ environmental	Angela Fahy

LEBOEUF, LAMB, GREENE & MACRAE

NO 1, MINSTER COURT, LONDON, EC3R 7AA
Tel: (0171) 459 5000 **Fax:** (0171) 459 5099 **DX:** 520 LONDON/CITY

The Firm: LeBoeuf, Lamb, Greene & MacRae is a multinational partnership affiliated with LeBoeuf, Lamb, Greene & MacRae L.L.P., a United States law firm with over 625 lawyers in 15 domestic and 6 international offices. The lawyers in the London office include English solicitors and U.S. lawyers and represent a cross-section of the firm's clientele in corporate, litigation and regulatory matters. Close coordination is maintained between the lawyers in the London office and those in other LeBoeuf offices so that the full resources of the firm may be called upon to assist clients in virtually every aspect of the law.

Principal Areas of Work:

General Description: The London office principally serves clients in the insurance/reinsurance, banking, energy, aviation and marine industries. A full range of legal services, including civil litigation, U.S., U.K. and E.C. insurance regulation, corporate/commercial, property, energy/utilities/project finance, insolvency and banking regulation, are provided.

Insurance and Reinsurance: (*Contact Partners:* James F. Johnson, 4th; Peter J. Sharp; L. Charles Landgraf). U.S., U.K. and E.C. corporate, regulatory and litigation matters of all types.

Civil/Commercial Litigation: (*Contact Partners:* Peter J. Sharp; Christopher A. Gooding). Litigation, arbitration and alternative dispute resolution of all types, including transnational and in particular U.S./U.K. disputes.

Energy/Utilities/Project Finance: (*Contact Partners:* Alan Jones; Garry Pegg). Electricity, oil and gas transactional and advisory matters; regulatory advice; privatisations and major international project work.

Corporate/Commercial: (*Contact Partners:* Alan Jones; Charles Ashton; Anthony Richmond). Corporate mergers and acquisitions, joint ventures and general corporate finance/commercial advice.

Banking: (*Contact Partners:* Peter J. Sharp; Paul Flood). Litigation and general banking advisory matters.

Insolvency: (*Contact Partners:* James F. Johnson, 4th; Peter J. Sharp). All matters involving insolvencies in the U.S., U.K. and E.C. including in particular insurance insolvency.

Commercial Property: (*Contact Partner:* Nicholas I. Shepherd). All aspects of commercial property investment and transactions.

Foreign Offices: LeBoeuf, Lamb, Greene & MacRae L.L.P. has offices in the United States in New York, Washington D.C., San Francisco, Albany, Boston, Denver, Harrisburg, Hartford, Houston, Jacksonville, Los Angeles, Newark, Pittsburgh, Portland, Salt Lake City, and elsewhere in Brussels, Moscow, Almaty and Tashkent Bishkek together with working arrangements with local lawyers in numerous other jurisdictions.

Managing partner:	James F. Johnson, 4th
Senior partner:	James F. Johnson, 4th
Number of partners:	8
Assistant solicitors:	24
Other fee-earners:	6

LE BRASSEUR J TICKLE

DRURY HOUSE, 34-43 RUSSELL STREET, LONDON, WC2B 5HA
Tel: (0171) 836 0099 **Fax:** (0171) 831 2215 **DX:** 37985 KINGSWAY WC2

6-7 PARK PLACE, LEEDS, LS1 2RU
Tel: (0113) 234 1220 **Fax:** (0113) 234 1573 **DX:** 14086 LEEDS PARK SQUARE

The Firm: Le Brasseur J Tickle have continued to expand the provision of legal services with further acquisitions during 1997/8, most notably that of the niche commercial practice North & Co along with other indidvidual appointments. Further expansion in the corporate commercial and IT sectors are planned for this year.

Principal Areas of Work:

Healthcare: The firm acts for NHS Trusts, Health Authorities, medical mutuals and defence organisations, as well as private sector hospitals and their insurers, insurance companies, medical partnerships and associated professional regulatory bodies. i) *Contentious and Regulatory:* Clinical & dental negligence, class actions and steering group committee members, risk management, criminal, disciplinary and regulatory law and professional ethics, mental health and community care law, administrative and child care law. ii) *Commercial Law and PFI:* EU public procurement and PFI projects, development and construction contracts, energy and utilities supply agreements and outsourcing arrangements, facilities management, information systems and maintenance agreements, environmental and clinical waste disposal arrangements and insurance coverage issues, joint ventures, corporate governance and partnership law. iii) *Property:* Transfers from the Secretary of State to Trusts, acquisitions and disposal of Trust property and assets, acquisition of health centres andother primary care units, leasing and landlord and tenant matters.

Corporate Law: The firm handles a wide range of corporate matters, including the acquisition and disposal of companies and businesses, corporate restructuring, venture capital and management buyouts/ins, public placings on the alternative investment market (AIM), secured lending and debt restructuring.

Commercial: The commercial group advise on and structure and negotiate a wide range of commercial agreements and joint ventures, both domestic and international, including telecommunications (satellite broadcasting) and computer contracts, distribution and agency agreements, franchise arrangements, EU law, environmental law, construction and intellectual property matters. Further expansion of this Department has taken place during 1997/8 with the acquisition of a small niche corporate law practice. The firm's International practice, primarily in the "US" has also continued to expand.

Property: The property group handles all aspects of commercial property work on behalf of property companies and developers, ranging from prime retail development sites to light industrial, manufacturing and business premises.

Litigation: The firm handles a wide range of domestic and international disputes including insurance, corporate disputes, product liability, construction and engineering disputes, partnerships, professional negligence, defamation claims, emergency injunctions and proceedings before the European Court and the Privy Council.

Employment: The firm has a strong employment team who advise on all aspects of the field and the firm has acted in several landmark cases both before the domestic courts and tribunals and the European Court. Whilst primarily acting as advisers to institutional clients the firm also regularly represents individuals typically in Executive roles. The firm has particular experience in acting for the Health Sector in this field and advises on issues arising out of the Whitley Council regulations.

Insurance: In addition to the firms professional indemnity practice and the provision of insurance services to the UK health sector, the Insurance Group provides legal services to a wide range of UK and International corporate policyholders, particularly from the US, advising on the regulation, law and practice of Lloyd's of London and the London Insurance Market and represents policyholders in UK coverage litigation and international and domestic arbitrations.

Personal Injury: A very strong unit with several partners having extensive experience in a wide range of personal injury claims and product liability class actions, including the benzodiazapine and hepatitis blood bank litigation.

Environmental: The firm advises on environmental due diligence in corporate transactions, liability issues arising from the sale and purchase of contaminated land and legal and contractual issues concerning the disposal of waste and in particular the disposal of clinical waste.

Personnel Changes: *London Office:* In conjunction with the continued expansion of the professional and medical negligence teams, the firm's Commercial team has been strengthened by the addition of the 3 partners of North & Co and their staff. They are particularly experienced in the fields of commercial property and corporate work, including AIM placings.

Senior partner:	Robert Sumerling
Number of partners:	26
Assistant solicitors:	32
Other fee-earners:	6

CONTACTS	
Commercial Law	Michael Scanlan (London)
	Nick Rawson (Leeds)
Corporate Law	Jonathan North (London)
Employment	Alex Leslie, Simon Dinnick (London)
	Kate Williams (Leeds)
Environmental	Geoffrey Sparks (London)
Healthcare – Commercial Law	Geoffrey Sparks
Healthcare – Contentious & Regulatory	
	Stephen Janisch (London), Nick Rawson (Leeds)
Insurance	Michael Scanlan (London)
Litigation	Simon Dinnick, Michael Scanlan (London)
Personal Injury	Christian Dingwall (London),
	Kate Williams (Leeds)
PFI	Geoffrey Sparks (London)
Property	Simon Wakefield (London),
	Michael Thorniley-Walker (Leeds)

Leeds Office: The rapid growth has continued, with the most notable staff additions being the recruitment of experienced health care solicitors from other firms in the region, extending the expertise that already existed in this field.

LEDINGHAM CHALMERS

5 MELVILLE CRESCENT, EDINBURGH, EH3 7JA
Tel: (0131) 200 1000 **Fax:** (0131) 200 1080 **DX:** ED275 EDINBURGH

1 GOLDEN SQUARE, ABERDEEN, AB10 1HA
Tel: (01224) 408408 **Fax:** (01224) 408402 **DX:** AB15 ABERDEEN

6 FRASER STREET, INVERNESS, IV1 1DW
Tel: (01463) 713071 **Fax:** (01463) 713755 **DX:** IN4 INVERNESS

Ledingham Chalmers unique distinction is its network of offices in three major Scottish locations – Edinburgh, Aberdeen and Inverness – and in three key overseas locations – Baku (Azerbaijan), Istanbul (Turkey) and Stanley (Falkland Islands). The firm has a growing reputation for developing close working relationships with business clients and providing innovative solutions. Instructions are welcomed from lawyers both in Scotland and in other jurisdictions. The overseas offices regularly receive instructions from UK and US law firms.

The Firm: Ledingham Chalmers is a full service law firm which places emphasis on careful selection and continuous development of its qualified and unqualified personnel. The aim is to provide a stimulating and supportive environment which in turn provides a quality service to both business and private clients.

Principal Areas of Work: Areas of current expansion within the domestic practice, which is conducted from offices in Edinburgh, Aberdeen and Inverness, are corporate finance, oil and gas (both North Sea and overseas) and commercial property development. The Baku office is focused primarily on the developing energy sector and the Istanbul office provides advice on investment in Turkey and the region. The Falkland Islands office is already advising clients involved in the early stages of offshore oil development.

The main services provided from the Scottish offices are:
Corporate/Commercial (including Oil and Gas)
Commercial Property (including Agriculture)
Litigation (including Employment)
Private Client (including Residential Property)

Developments: In 1998 the firm appointed a Director of Human Resources and a Director of Finance to enhance its management team. Both appointments are at partner level and contribute to the firm's strategic planning process.

Overseas Offices: Stanley, Falkland IslandsIstanbul, TurkeyBaku, Azerbaijan Republic

Managing partner:	**David Laing**
Number of partners:	25
Assistant solicitors:	32
Other fee-earners:	30

WORKLOADS	
Commercial property	27%
Company/ commercial	27%
Residential property	23%
Litigation	15%
Private client	8%
Banking	5%

CONTACTS	
Agriculture	Allan Collie (Aberdeen)
Commercial property	John Curran (Aberdeen)
Corporate/commercial	John Rutherford (Aberdeen)
International and finance	Gavin Farquhar (Edinburgh)
Litigation	Steven Love (Edinburgh)
Oil and gas	Robert Ruddiman (Aberdeen)
Private Client	Erlend Flett (Aberdeen)

LEDINGHAM CHALMERS
SOLICITORS

LEE BOLTON & LEE

1 THE SANCTUARY, WESTMINSTER, LONDON, SW1P 3JT
Tel: (0171) 222 5381 **Fax:** (0171) 222 7502 **DX:** 2301 VICTORIA **Email:** 106102.1723@COMPUSERVE.COM

The Firm: Established at 1 The Sanctuary in 1855, Lee Bolton & Lee is a well established Westminster practice incorporating both commercial, charity, education and private client work. The firm offers extensive experience and advice across a wide spectrum of activities and is associated with a firm of solicitors and parliamentary agents, Rees and Freres, to provide a specialist service in parliamentary, public and administrative law.

Principal Areas of Work:
Private client: *(Contact:* M.J.G Fletcher). The firm provides expert advice on a full range of private client matters including domestic property, personal taxation and individual financial planning, wills, trusts, probate and the administration of estates. In addition, a separate department handles all aspects of family and matrimonial law.

Ecclesiastical, Education and Charities. *(Contact:* P.F.B. Beesley). As well as general advice on ecclesiastical matters and disciplinary proceedings, the firm advises three diocesan bishops as Registrars. In the education sphere, advice is provided on all matters from establishing a new school to day-to-day operational and employment matters. The firm's charity practice is linked, but not confined to, its educational and ecclesiastical work and covers all aspects of charity creation, registration and administration including trusts, tax and charitable property.

Corporate Services: *(Contact:* A.O.E. Davies/G.J. Fountain/M.D.G.Collins).Advice is provided for clients ranging from established organisations to emerging businesses and

Senior partner:	**A.O.E. Davies**
Number of partners:	16
Assistant solicitors:	7
Other fee-earners:	13

CONTACTS	
Charities	P.F.Beesley, A.C.James
Commercial property	G.J.Fountain
Company/ commercial	A.O.E.Davies
Ecclesiastical/Education	P.F.Beesley, N.J.Richens
Litigation	J.P.Sergeant
Parliamentary	J.A.Durkin
Private client	M.J.G.Fletcher
Public law	P.R. Lane, M.A.R. Peto
Railway property	J.Taplin, K.E. Wallace, P. Robinson

Continues overleaf

entrepreneurs on every aspect of commercial life from company formations, reconstructions, mergers, MBOs, joint ventures, Stock Exchange work, employment law and pensions, banking and financial services, funding, planning and development work is handled for banks, institutional clients, investors and developers.

Litigation: *(Contact:* J.P.Sergeant).A thriving litigation department handles a range of matters including general commercial contracts, employment disputes, computer litigation, professional and medical negligence, property building and landlord and tenant disputes, defamation, insurance and personal injury claims. The firm has long standing relations with numerous public bodies and has developed a considerable expertise in the area of judicial review proceedings.

LEE CROWDER

39 NEWHALL STREET, BIRMINGHAM, B3 3DY
Tel: (0121) 236 4477 **Fax:** (0121) 236 4710 **DX:** 13034

The Firm: Although Lee Crowder is one of the oldest firms in the country (and certainly the oldest firm in Birmingham), in outlook it is one of the most dynamic and rapidly expanding medium sized firms in the region. The firm has grown by leaps and bounds over the last few years and there is no sign of a slow down in the rate of expansion. It is the firm's intention to continue its growth by recruiting only the highest quality fee earners at all levels. The firm is committed to providing an excellent service to its clients at a competitive rate with an emphasis on partner involvement and to maintain and enhance its reputation, both regionally and nationally.

Principal Areas of Work:

Company/Commercial: The department acts for a broad range of clients, both large and small, including publicly quoted companies and deals with specialist corporate and commercial work as well as acting in corporate finance transactions. Principal activities involve acquisitions, mergers and disposals, joint ventures and shareholder agreements, non-contentious insolvency, venture capital and commercial agreements.

Commercial Litigation Department: The firm handles a broad range of litigation with particular specialisation in insolvency/director's disqualification, property litigation and employment.

Commercial Property Department: The firm acts for both commercial and residential property developers, institutions, investors, retailers, housing associations and landed estates. Clients range from individual and owner/managed businesses to publicly quoted companies.

Private Client Department: The firm is now a major player in the regional market dealing with all aspects of estate and tax planning, charity advice and has particular expertise in financial services.

Senior partner:	Stephen Gilmore
Number of partners:	14
Consultants:	2
Assistant Solicitors:	24
Other fee earners:	7

WORKLOADS	
Company/Commercial	30%
Litigation	30%
Property	30%
Private Client	10%

LEEDS DAY 6 Bedford Road, Sandy, SG19 1EN *Tel:* (01767) 680251 *Fax:* (01767) 691775 *DX:* 47801 Sandy *Ptnrs:* 11 *Asst solrs:* 8 *Other fee-earners:* 22

LEE & PEMBERTONS

45 PONT ST, LONDON, SW1X 0BX
Tel: (0171) 589 1114 **Fax:** (0171) 589 0807 **DX:** 38166 KNIGHTSBRIDGE

The Firm: Established in the late 18th century, Lee and Pembertons is a successful Knightsbridge firm, noted for its substantial property and private client work. In recent years the firm has expanded its practice to offer the full range of corporate and commercial legal services. It has established a reputation for providing a partner led personal service to clients, and there is a commitment to client care and quality management at all levels.

Principal Areas of Work:

Property: (*Contact:* Damian Greenish). *Work includes:* acquisitions and disposals of commercial, residential and agricultural properties, agricultural tenancies and farming partnerships, landlord and tenant and Rent Act law, property development, construction law, town and country planning and leasehold enfranchisement.

Private Client: (*Contact:* Andrew Stebbings). *Work includes:* creation, administration and termination of all types of trusts (in particular charitable trusts), wills, probate and the administration of estates, financial services and tax planning, Lloyd's memberships, pensions and life insurance.

Commercial: (*Contact:* Richard Roney). *Work includes:* company formations, acquisitions, sales, mergers and liquidations, purchases and financing of businesses and

Managing partner:	Giles Pemberton
Senior partner:	Richard Roney
Number of partners:	21
Assistant solicitors:	18
Other fee-earners:	12

WORKLOADS	
Property	40%
Private client	35%
Litigation	15%
Commercial	10%

CONTACTS	
Commercial	Richard Roney
Litigation	John Roney
Private client	Andrew Stebbings
Property	Damian Greenish

partnerships, oil and gas projects, service agreements, banking, insurance, gaming and clubs, environmental law, EC law and regulations affecting businesses.

Litigation: (*Contact:* John Roney). *Work includes:* commercial, landlord and tenant, company, building and intellectual property disputes, planning appeals, insolvency, defamation, professional negligence, personal injury, matrimonial and family law; immigration and nationality matters; alternative dispute resolution.

Languages Spoken: French, Italian, Spanish, German, Swedish and Cantonese.

Recruitment: Two trainee solicitors are recruited annually. A full training programme is available including in-house video. Applications with CV to Diana Graves.

LEE & PRIESTLEY

12 PARK SQUARE, LEEDS, LS1 2LF
Tel: (0113) 243 3751 **Fax:** (0113) 246 7357 **DX:** 14074 LEEDS PARK SQUARE

With offices in Leeds and Bradford, this practice provides the full range of corporate and commercial services. The corporate team is handling an increasing volume of acquisitions and disposals and has particular expertise in management buy-outs and buy-ins. Commercial matters covered include agency, distribution, franchise and supply agreements.

The firm has a strong and rapidly expanding employment and commercial litigation practice and also handles all aspects of commercial property and insolvency work.

The firm is well know for the quality of its personal injury and civil litigation work, family and childcare law.

Lee & Priestley also has expertise on a wide range of private client matters, including wills, tax and trusts and acts for a number of charities.

Lee & Priestley is now seeing tangible benefits and growth resulting from a programme of heavy investment in people able to bring skills to the firm. The range and quality of services offered has seen a significant increase and the firm aims to move further up the league table of regional firms in the coming years.

The firm is achieving considerable growth in Leeds, whilst maintaining its position as one of the leading firms in Bradford. The commercial clients of the firm include a number of PLCs and a large range of small to medium size enterprises. In addition, it serves a large number of private clients in the Yorkshire area. Lee & Priestley sees its dedication to client relationships as the reason for its success.

Managing partner:	John Priestley
Senior partner:	John Priestley
Number of partners:	15
Assistant solicitors:	9
Other fee-earners:	24

CONTACTS	
Child care and education law	Charles Prest
Commercial litigation and employment	Iain Jenkins
Commercial property	Robert Sheard, Robert Hall
Conveyancing	James Priestley
Corporate and commercial	Jonathan Oxley, Bruce Copsey, Morgan Williams
Family Law	John Taylor, Andrea Dyer
Insolvency	Nigel Whitfield
Personal injury, medical negligence and litigation	Brian Walker, Sonia Hume-Dawson
Professional Negligence	Michael Rakusen
Residential Care	Rachel Hall
Trust & Probate	Henry Beckwith

LEES LLOYD WHITLEY Castle Chambers, 43 Castle Street, Liverpool, L2 9TJ *Tel:* (0151) 227 3541 *Fax:* (0151) 227 2460 *DX:* 14164 Liverpool *Ptnrs:* 11 *Asst solrs:* 8 *Other fee-earners:* 43

LEES & PARTNERS 44/45 Hamilton Square, Birkenhead, L41 5AR *Tel:* (0151) 647 9381 *Fax:* (0151) 666 1445 *DX:* 17856 Birkenhead *Ptnrs:* 8 *Asst solrs:* 5 *Other fee-earners:* 17

LEE & THOMPSON Green Garden House, 15-22 St. Christopher's Place, London, W1M 5HD *Tel:* (0171) 935 4665 *Fax:* (0171) 486 2391 *Ptnrs:* 8 *Asst solrs:* 2

LEFEVRE LITIGATION 70 Carden Place, Aberdeen, AB10 1UP **Tel:** (01224) 208208 **Fax:** (01224) 626917 **DX:** AB79 **Ptnrs:** 3 **Asst solrs:** 2 **Contact:** Mr Frank H. Lefevre *Specialist litigation practice, particularly known for employment, mediation and personal injury work.*

WORKLOADS			
Personal Injury	60%	Criminal	20%
Commercial & Other	10%	Employment Law	10%

LEIGH, DAY & CO

PRIORY HOUSE, 25 ST. JOHN'S LANE, LONDON, EC1M 4LB
Tel: (0171) 650 1200 **Fax:** (0171) 253 4433 **DX:** 53326 CLERKENWELL **Email:** MAIL@LEIGHDAY.DEMON.CO.UK

INTERNATIONAL HOUSE, 82-86 DEANSGATE, MANCHESTER, M3 2ER
Tel: (0161) 832 7722 **Fax:** (0161) 839 2329 **DX:** 718178 MANCHESTER 3

The Firm: A leading firm specialising in all aspects of complex personal injury work and multi-party actions. Winner of the Lawyer/HIFAL Law firm of the Year Award 1996.

Principal Areas of Work:

Environmental Department: Specialising in claims as a result of exposure to pollution (radiation, chemicals, pesticides, sewage in the sea) together with industrial disease and nuisance claims. Cases include the childhood leukaemia cases around Sellafield, and cases against the tobacco industry.

Medical Negligence Department: Concentrates on cases involving serious disabilities or death. Also specialises in medical devices such as artifical heart valves, pacemakers and silicone breast implants.

Accident Litigation Department: This department deals with a full range of personal injury claims including road traffic accidents, accidents at work and product liability claims. There is a special expertise in horse riding accidents, actions against the MOD and aviation disasters.

Administrative Law Department: The department's clients include local authorities and objectors concerning plan making, development control, enforcement and appeals. It undertakes a large number of judicial reviews.

Senior partners:	Sarah Leigh, Martyn Day
Number of partners:	14
Assistant solicitors:	13
Other fee-earners:	9

CONTACTS	
Accident	Jenny Kennedy (London)
Accident	Geraldine McCool (Manchester)
Administrative Law	Richard Stein
Environmental	Martyn Day
Medical negligence	Sarah Leigh

LEMON & CO

CHELSEA HOUSE, 1 LITTLE LONDON COURT, ALBERT STREET, SWINDON, SN1 3HY
Tel: (01793) 496341 **Fax:** (01793) 511639 **DX:** 400912 SWINDON 6 **Email:** LEMONCO@STAR.CO.UK

34 REGENT CIRCUS, SWINDON, SN1 1PY
Tel: (01793) 527141 **Fax:** (01793) 614168 **DX:** 400912 SWINDON 6 **Email:** LEMONCO@STAR.CO.UK

The Firm: Founded in 1914, they are one of the largest and longest established firms in Swindon, providing an extensive range of services for businesses and private clients and are dedicated to client care. They are one of the few Swindon firms specialising in commercial law. They have participated in complex property and corporate transactions in recent years.

Principal Areas of Work:

Company/Commercial: Company formations, acquisitions and disposals, mbo/mbi, employment contracts and conditions, shareholders and partnership agreements, j.v. agreements, intellectual property, franchise, agency and distribution agreements, commercial property and all aspects of landlord and tenant law.

Litigation: All matters.Specialists in family, criminal, child care, personal injury, employment and commercial litigation.

Private Client: Estate planning, wills, charity law, management of trusts and settlements, probate work, administration of estates and financial and tax advisory services. Our specialist conveyancing department is widely acknowledged for providing a quality service.

Company Relocation: The specialist unit undertakes employee relocation conveyancing for national relocation companies and is known for meeting their exacting standards.

Senior partner:	Richard Fry
Number of partners:	9
Assistant solicitors:	4
Other fee-earners:	4

WORKLOADS	
Private client	40%
Litigation	32%
Company/ Commercial	28%

CONTACTS	
Commercial litigation	Clive Bell
Commercial property	Martin Evans
Company/ Commercial	Nial Ledingham
Employment	Clive Bell
Family	Stephen Moss
Personal injury	Tim Dixon
Private client	Deirdre Moss
Residential Property	David Halfhead

LEO ABSE & COHEN

40 CHURCHILL WAY, CARDIFF, CF1 4SS
Tel: (01222) 383252 **Fax:** (01222) 345572 **DX:** 33002

The Firm: Leo Abse & Cohen has an outstanding reputation in Litigation with specialist services in personal injury, insurance litigation, medical negligence, commercial and general litigation, employment, family and serious crime. In addition, the firm has a strong property section and deals with an increasing amount of company commercial matters.

Managing partner:	Ian Hopkins
Senior partner:	John Sherratt
Number of Partners:	7
Associate Partners:	14
Assistant Solicitors:	27
Other Case Workers:	17

LEONARD GRAY 72-74 Duke St, Chelmsford, CM1 1JY **Tel:** (01245) 251411 **Fax:** (01245) 490728 **DX:** 3309 Chelmsford 1 **Ptnrs:** 6 **Asst solrs:** 2 **Other fee-earners:** 7 **Contact:** Mr Richard Randall *The firm has specialised departments noted for Children/Family Law, Agricultural Law and Personal Injury work.*

LÉONIE COWEN & ASSOCIATES

30 KINGSWOOD AVENUE, QUEENS PARK, LONDON, NW6 6LR
Tel: (0181) 964 4177 **Fax:** (0181) 964 0311 **Email:** LEONIE.COWEN@LCOWEN.CO.UK

The Firm: Founded in 1989, the firm specialises in local government and administrative law. Léonie Cowen spent 15 years at senior level in local government and is an accredited mediator.

Principal Areas of Work:

Powers: Vires especially after Allerdale.

Public Private Partnerships/Joint Ventures/Trading: Including sport and leisure, arts, culture and libraries service transfers to new not-for-profit bodies, management buy-outs, municipal and cross-border trading.

Local Authority Companies: The Part V framework and its impact, company structures.

PFI/Project Funding/Local Authority Finance: The capital finance regime, audit issues and relationships with external auditors, interest rate swaps.

Social Services (esp. Community Care): Transfer of residential homes for older people/adults, and capital funding for development and refurbishment.

Best Value CCT/Procurement: Implementation of quality systems and public procurement.

Employment: TUPE, local authority terms and conditions (including sensitive senior level cases), superannuation schemes and pensions.

Education: Services to education authorities and governing bodies.

Charities: Setting-up and management of charities and other non-profit bodies.

Corporate: Business transfers, joint ventures, shareholders agreements.

Commercial Property: Acquisition, funding, management and disposal of property for public authorities, housing associations, businesses and investors.

Number of partners:	1
Other fee-earners:	1

WORKLOADS	
Local government law	80%
Charities	10%
Commercial property	5%
Corporate	5%

CONTACTS	
Charities	Léonie Cowen/Andrew Riddell
Commercial property	Andrew Riddell
Corporate	Léonie Cowen/Andrew Riddell
Local government law	Léonie Cowen

LESLIE WOLFSON & CO 19 Waterloo Street, Glasgow, G2 6BQ *Tel:* (0141) 226 4499 *Fax:* (0141) 221 6070 *DX:* 106 Glasgow *Ptnrs:* 4 *Asst solrs:* 1 *Other fee-earners:* 3

LESTER ALDRIDGE

RUSSELL HOUSE, OXFORD ROAD, BOURNEMOUTH, BH8 8EX
Tel: (01202) 786161 **Fax:** (01202) 786110 **DX:** 7623 BOURNEMOUTH 1 **Email:** ENQUIRIES@LESTER-ALDRIDGE.CO.UK

The Firm: Lester Aldridge is one of the largest law firms in central Southern England. It is a progressive and innovative practice which has adopted a corporate style management structure. The firm is market led with an emphasis on the development of specialist units offering expert advice on specific aspects of the law from lawyers who are familiar with a particular industry. Lawyers are encouraged and trained to adopt a commercial approach, seeking legal solutions to business problems.

Principal Areas of Work:

Company and Commercial:*Work includes:* business acquisitions, disposals and joint ventures, commercial contract, intellectual property, trading contracts, international trade, and EC law.

Litigation: The firm has a large litigation department with substantial overseas experience. *Work includes:* commercial disputes, computer and intellectual property litigation, emergency procedures, shareholder and partnership disputes, arbitration and health and safety. Private Client litigation units include Family law and personal injury.

Insurance: The department handles professional indemnity insurance (including marine insurance) acting for general insurers, Lloyd's Underwriters and re-insurers.

Commercial Property:*Work includes:* residential and commercial estate development, mortgage and leasing of all types of property, planning and environmental law and landlord and tenant. Niche units for marina developments, rest and nursing homes, and hotels and licensed premises.

Employment:*Work includes:* contracts of employment and service agreements, contract and labour disputes, unfair dismissal and redundancy.

Insolvency: The firm has a strong insolvency team providing a service to insolvency practitioners across the country and banks.

Banking and Asset Finance: The firm has one of the largest asset finance units in the country dealing with small and medium ticket transactions for UK bank owned and independent finance houses. The unit includes specialist litigators and a computerised recovery of goods service. The banking unit advises banks and other lenders on lending and recovery techniques.

Debt Services: Lester Aldridge offers a highly efficient computerised bulk debt collection service.

Private Client Services: The firm has a strong private client department advising individuals and trusts on tax and estate planning including setting up and administrating non-resident trusts.

Investment Services: The firm also advises companies and individuals on investments, pensions and life assurance, and offers discretionary management services. The unit now manages approximately £50m on behalf of clients.

Recruitment and Training: The firm recruits at least four trainee solicitors every year. Apply by letter and CV to Norman Dunnington at Russell House, Oxford Road, Bournemouth, BH8 8EX.

Foreign Connections: The firm has many connections in Southern Africa. A Southern African desk services clients wishing to trade with Southern Africa or vice versa. The firm's existing European links with major law firms in the EC are under-pinned by a number of lawyers fluent in French, Spanish, German, Dutch and Afrikaans. The firm is a member of Eurolegal.

Managing partner:	**Barry Glazier**
Chairman:	**Colin Patrick**
Number of partners:	29
Assistant solicitors:	19
Other fee-earners:	30

WORKLOADS	
Litigation	35%
Banking and finance	16%
Commercial property	16%
Trusts, tax and wills	14%
Corporate	10%
Investment services	5%
Residential property	4%

CONTACTS	
Asset finance	Pip Giddins
Banking	Graham Jeffries
Care homes	Peter Grose
Commercial property	Bob Robertson
Computer law and IT	Richard Byrne
Construction	Richard Byrne
Consumer credit	Pip Giddins
Contentious probate	Geoff Thomas
Corporate	David Ashplant
Corporate immigration	Stuart Southgate
Debt Services	Andrew Corke
EC and international trade	David Ashplant
Employment	Susan Evans
Environment	Jonathan Howe
Family	Stephen Foster
Health & safety	Richard Byrne
Hotels & licensed premises	Oonagh McKinney
Insolvency	Malcolm Niekirk
Insurance Litigation	Michael Giddins
Intellectual property	David Ashplant
International probate	John Maddocks
International tax planning	Barry Glazier
Investment services	Steve Dean
Landlord and tenant	Bob Robertson
Licensing	Colin Patrick
Litigation	Jeremy Allin
Marina & leisure development	Jonathan Howe
Partnerships & joint ventures	Susan Cowan
Pensions	Keith Hooper
Personal injury	Karen Thompson
Planning	Roger Woolley
Private finance initiative	Roger Woolley
Probate/estate administration	David Parkhouse
Professional indemnity	Michael Giddins
Property litigation	Richard Byrne
Residential conveyancing	Tony Roberts
Southern Africa	Stuart Southgate
Trusts and UK tax planning	Barry Glazier

L'ESTRANGE & BRETT

7-9 CHICHESTER STREET, BELFAST, BT1 4JG
Tel: (01232) 230426 **Fax:** (01232) 246396 **DX:** 424 NR BELFAST 1 **Email:** LANDBRETT@DNET.CO.UK

The Firm: One of the largest firms in Northern Ireland, L'Estrange & Brett is primarily a commercial firm, with strong national and international links in the British Isles, the rest of Europe and North America.

Principal Areas of Work:

Corporate Law: (*Contact Partner:* John Irvine). L'Estrange & Brett acts for a wide range of corporate clients and regularly provides advice on matters such as business start-ups and incorporation, acquisitions and disposals, mergers, joint ventures and share issues work. The firm also has a strong presence in the corporate finance market and frequently advises clients on regulatory and compliance matters under the Financial Services Act.

Commercial Law: (*Contact Partner:* Richard Gray). Clients are advised on all legal aspects of their business activities, including sales and marketing, distribution, franchising, competition law, intellectual property and computer law.

Projects/PFI: (*Contact Partner:* John Irvine). The firm has developed a significant practice in this area, acting for both public and private sectors on a number of projects in Northern Ireland across a variety of sectors.

Commercial Property: (*Contact Partner:* Alan Hewitt). One of the largest departments in the firm, L'Estrange & Brett's commercial property solicitors deal with an extensive range of work, including sales, purchases, tenancies, charges, planning and environmental aspects and property management.

Litigation: (*Contact Partner:* Adam Brett). The main focus of the firm's litigation department is commercial litigation and employment law, and it is regularly involved in IP and construction disputes, in addition to more general commercial work. Advice is also provided on personal injury matters.

Banking/ Financial Services: (*Contact Partner:* Brian Henderson). One of the most rapidly developing areas of the practice, the service builds on the firm's close links with large commercial practices in the City of London and Dublin. Work covered includes securitisation, asset and finance leasing and debt rescheduling and reorganisation.

Other Areas of Work: The firm can also provide expertise on insolvency and EU law in addition to providing a general private client service.

Senior partner:	Alan Hewitt
Number of partners:	9
Assistant solicitors:	10
Other fee-earners:	4

WORKLOADS	
Commercial property	37%
Corporate and commercial law	35%
Litigation (including employment law)	23%
Private client	5%

LEVI & CO 33 St. Pauls Street, Leeds, LS1 2JJ *Tel:* (0113) 244 9931 *Fax:* (0113) 244 6789 *DX:* 12033 Leeds *Ptnrs:* 8 *Asst solrs:* 4 *Other fee-earners:* 9

LEVISON MELTZER PIGOTT

9-13 ST ANDREW STREET, LONDON, EC4A 3AF
Tel: (0171) 556 2400 **Fax:** (0171) 556 2401 **DX:** 200 LONDON CHANCERY LANE

The Firm: Levison Meltzer Pigott is a specialist divorce and family law firm formed very recently on 1 June 1998. The three partners had worked together for almost 13 years in a medium size Central London general practice. The firm deals with all areas of divorce and family law, including advising on pensions, the rights of unmarried couples and all the changes that have been or will be made under the Family Law Act 1996.

Jeremy Levison is a founder member of the International Academy of Matrimonial Lawyers and currently vice-president of its European section. His contacts with family lawyers worldwide assists in the significant proportion of cases that have an international dimension. Claire Meltzer regularly broadcasts on television and radio, particularly on the subject of pensions and divorce, and has written numerous articles and papers on matters of divorce and family law. Simon Pigott has lectured for the College of Law, was one of the first family law mediators trained by the Family Mediators Association, was its Chair between 1995 and 1997 and is currently Vice-Chair of the United Kingdom College of Family Mediators.

Each of the partners is an Associate of the American Bar Association (Family Section) and all the firm's solicitors are members of the Solicitors Family Law Association.

Contacts:	Jeremy Levison, Claire Meltzer, Simon Pigott
Number of Partners:	3
Assistant Solicitors:	2

WORKLOADS	
Family/Matrimonial/Finance	60%
Children	30%
Co-habitation	10%

LEVY & MCRAE 266 St Vincent Street, Glasgow, G2 5RL **Tel:** (0141) 307 2311 **Fax:** (0141) 307 6857/8 **DX:** GW149 Glasgow **Ptnrs:** 4 **Asst solrs:** 3 **Other fee-earners:** 9 **Contact:** Peter Watson *Specialist areas include, media law, aviation, international claims and litigation, personal injury, fatal and public accident inquiries, civil and criminal litigation, Inland Revenue and Customs and Excise investigation, employment law, partnership & company law, defamation and libel.*

THE LEWINGTON PARTNERSHIP

MIDLAND HOUSE, 132 HAGLEY ROAD, EDGBASTON, BIRMINGHAM, B16 9NN
Tel: (0121) 454 4000 **Fax:** (0121) 456 3631 **DX:** 707290 EDGBASTON 3 **Email:** HEALTHLAW@LEWINGTON.BYTENET.CO.UK

ST THOMAS HOUSE, ST THOMAS STREET, WINCHESTER, SO23 9HE
Tel: (01962) 866615 **Fax:** (01962) 855317 **DX:** 2517 WINCHESTER

TEMPLE COURT, CATHEDRAL ROAD, CARDIFF, CF1 9HA
Tel: (01222) 786440 **Fax:** (01222) 786441 **DX:** 33099 CARDIFF

The Firm: The firm was founded in 1993 and has grown and developed to become one of the major firms advising the NHS, the insurance industry and public authorities. The firm's success can be measured in terms of growth. When the practice started trading on 1 July 1993 there were just over 40 NHS clients and 46 staff. In 1998 The Lewington Partnership can boast an NHS client list of over 100 with a staff complement of over 100, 47 of whom are fee earning lawyers.

The firm specialises in defendant clinical negligence and personal injury work; employment, estates and property matters and commercial litigation and advice. Specialist expertise includes:

Public Private Partnerships	Mental Health Law
Child Care Law	Healthcare and Medical Ethics
Risk and Claims Management	Medical Advice and Representation.
Administrative and Public Law	Corporate Governance

The Lewington Partnership is confident that they have the leading all round healthcare law team in the country serving the NHS from bases in Winchester and Cardiff as well as their head office in Birmingham.

Snr/Managing partner:	Tony Lewington
Number of partners:	8
Associates:	11
Assistant solicitors:	17
Other fee-earners:	11

CONTACTS	
Administrative and Public Law/Community Care	
	Sheila Waddington
Clinical neg. and Health Care Law	Stuart Knowles
Commercial Law	Sheree Peaple
Commercial Property	Tom Cassidy
Employment law	Kate Levy
Personal injury	Howard Jacks

LEWIS MOORE & CO. Craven House, 121 Kingsway, London, WC2B 6PA **Tel:** (0171) 831 6300 **Fax:** (0171) 405 4485 **Ptnrs:** 3 **Other fee-earners:** 4 **Contact:** Mr L. Moore *This firm specialises in marine litigation as well as ship sale and purchase. Also handles commercial property work.*

WORKLOADS	
Shipping and commercial	75%
Property	25%

LEWIS SILKIN

WINDSOR HOUSE, 50 VICTORIA STREET, LONDON, SW1H 0NW
Tel: (0171) 227 8000 **Fax:** (0171) 222 4633 **DX:** 2321 VICTORIA **Email:** INFO@LEWISSILKIN.COM

The Firm: The success of Lewis Silkin is the result of the emphasis the firm gives to clients and its staff. The firm promotes valued relationships with its clients and believes that to deliver commercially relevant advice it is vital to understand its clients' business.

To provide the range of services demanded, Lewis Silkin is organised into three departments – Corporate, Litigation and Property and is developing expertise and services for the converging industries including communications, technology, leisure and marketing services. A particular quality of the firm is the way members of these departments work and inter-relate to ensure a first class service.

Principal Areas of Work:

Corporate: (*Contact:* Trevor Watkins). Undertakes corporate and commercial work which has become increasingly sophisticated embracing project financing, outsourcing and service provision agreements, hi-tech and IT projects, franchising agreements, joint ventures, employee benefits and share schemes in addition to a wide range of general commercial contracts.

Corporate Finance: (*Contact:* Clare Grayston). Provides a comprehensive range of corporate finance services including acquisitions and mergers, flotations, takeovers, MBO's, MBI's, joint ventures, venture capital schemes, restructuring, financing and banking.

Commercial Litigation: (*Contact:* Tom Coates). Embraces a number of specialist groups and has become known for its success in winning and resolving disputes which include a string of high profile victories.

Commercial Property: (*Contact:* Len Goodrich). Provides advice and support to a number of blue-chip clients. Particular emphasis is given to the retail and leisure industries. It acts on acquisitions and disposals, funding developments, planning and environmental law and landlord and tenant.

Construction: (*Contact:* Helen Garthwaite). Offers clients a highly specialised and comprehensive service including both contract drafting, negotiation and advice, and arbitration and dispute resolution. It advises on project finance, security-taking and on day-to-day contract administration issues.

Lead partner:	Roger Alexander
Number of partners:	27
Assistant solicitors:	33
Other fee-earners:	25

WORKLOADS	
Corporate finance / commercial	25%
Commercial property/Construction/Social housing	
	24%
Commercial litigation	23%
Employment	9%
Advertising/Media/Defamation	7%
Intellectual property/IT	7%
Insurance and other	5%

CONTACTS	
Advertising	Stephen Groom
Commercial litigation	Tom Coates
Commercial property	Len Goodrich
Company commercial	Trevor Watkins
Construction	Helen Garthwaite
Corporate finance	Clare Grayston
Defamation	Roderick Dadak
Employment	Mike Burd
Insurance	Dennis Wilkins
Intellectual property	Stephen Groom
Services to lenders	Richard Waller
Social housing	Gillian Bastow

Employment: (*Contact:* Mike Burd). The team has become amongst the most highly regarded in London and continues to develop both its contentious and non-contentious practice.

Insurance: (*Contact:* Dennis Wilkins). Specialises in professional indemnity claims against construction professionals, surveyors, financial advisers and professionals in the media and advertising worlds.

Intellectual Property: (*Contact:* Stephen Groom) Focuses on supporting marketing, media and communications clients on contentious and non-contentious aspects of copyright, trade marks and IP. The team has been strengthened with additional expertise in defamation (*Contact:* Roderick Dadak) and is developing an increasing profile for its IT work.

Marketing Services: (*Contact:* Stephen Groom). The firm is an acknowledged leader in advertising law and provides a comprehensive service to clients in advertising, design, PR, sales promotion, media and direct marketing.

Services to Lenders: (*Contact:* Richard Waller). Handles conveyancing, repossessions, professional negligence and general corporate and property advice to residential lenders. Some of these services are delivered through the Farnham office.

Social Housing: (*Contact:* Gillian Bastow) Specialises in funding and development schemes, property management and constitutional advice to the housing sector.

Nature of Clientele: Lewis Silkin acts for a diverse range of national and international corporate clients ranging from large corporations and PLC's to entrepreneurs. A large number of our clients are from the creative and hi-tech industries such as advertising, design, publishing, computers and media as well as those in leisure, retail, property, residential lending, construction and utilities.

Foreign Connections: The firm has links with firms throughout the world, including the United States and is the UK representative of the Global Advertising Lawyers' Alliance (GALA) an international association of corporate communications lawyers, which now incorporates the European Advertising Lawyers' Association (EALA).

LIDDELL ZURBRUGG

15-17 JOCKEY'S FIELDS, LONDON, WC1R 4BW
Tel: (0171) 404 5641 **Fax:** (0171) 831 8460 **DX:** 0061 CH.LN.

The Firm: Liddell Zurbrugg specialises in insurance and personal injury litigation, both on behalf of insurers and private clients within the UK and other European countries.

Principal Areas of Work: The firm also specialises in serious injury work particularly head injury; Clients include a number of Lloyd's syndicates and insurance companies, both UK and foreign including legal expense insurers. Several languages are spoken fluently and the firm has established connections in most European countries with particular emphasis on France, Spain, Portugal, Belgium, Switzerland and Germany. The firm includes a Spanish lawyer whose main area of work consists of personal injury claims in Spain and giving evidence before English Courts in relation to spanish law. In addition, he deals with general litigation, property transactions, child abduction and custody cases. The firm deals with with high profile litigation work including substantial claims for malicious prosecution and miscarriage of justice.

Managing partner:	Michael Zurbrugg
Senior partner:	Michael Zurbrugg
Number of partners:	4
Other fee-earners:	12

LIGHTFOOTS

THE OLD RED LION, 1-3 HIGH STREET, THAME, OX9 2BX
Tel: (01844) 212305 or 212574/5 **Fax:** (01844) 214984 **DX:** 80550 THAME

The Firm: This progressive firm, the first nationally to gain and be re-awarded the 'Investors in People' award, provides sound advice on most aspects of English corporate and private client law. It also holds a legal aid franchise.

Principal Areas of Work:

Commercial services include: company/ commercial, commercial property, employment, tax, property litigation and specialist debt collection, mortgage repossession, professional negligence and pharmaceutical departments.

Private client work includes: wills, probate, trusts, residential conveyancing, other general civil litigation and specialist personal injury and family law departments.

The firm also has a thriving Estate Agency and a property letting and management business, trading under the name of Vermons.

Foreign Languages Spoken: French, Hindi, Gujarati .

Senior partner:	Martin Hector
Number of partners:	5
Assistant solicitors:	7
Other fee-earners:	15

WORKLOADS	
Commercial litigation	35%
Domestic Conveyancing	18%
Commercial	15%
Family	15%
Trusts and Probate	7%
Commercial Conveyancing	5%
Employment	5%

LINDER MYERS Phoenix House, 45 Cross Street, Manchester, M2 4JF **Tel:** (0161) 832 6972 **Fax:** (0161) 834 0718 **DX:** 14360 **Email:** law@lindermyers.co.uk **Ptnrs:** 10 **Asst solrs:** 16 **Other fee-earners:** 18 **Contact:** Mr Bernard F. Seymour *Commercial and Litigation practice.*

WORKLOADS			
Company/ commercial	25%	Personal injury	25%
General litigation	15%	Medical negligence	13%
Matrimonial	12%	Private client	10%

LINDSAY ROLAND

3 ALL HALLOWS ROAD, BISPHAM, BLACKPOOL, FY2 0AS
Tel: (01253) 357800 **Fax:** (01253) 357801 **DX:** 703319 – POULTEN-LE-FYLDE

The Firm: The practice specialises exclusively in Medical Negligence/Personal Injury cases of utmost severity and Product Liability/Multi-Party Action claims.

Principal Areas of Work:

Product Liability/Multi-Party Actions: The firm has been granted a contract by the Legal Aid Board in the third generation oral contraceptive claims against the manufacturers. The solicitors have extensive experience in other such actions including HRT, Myodil, Hepatitis C and HIV virus, anticonvulsant medication, Seprin, infant drinks, radiotherapy claims and Hillsborough Disaster.

Medical Negligence: Specialises in cases of utmost severity, especially brain and spinal injuries, obstetric and gynaecology claims. Also anaesthetic and general surgery, Accident & Emergency, prescription, failure to diagnose, radiation and general medical negligence cases.

Personal Injury: Represents Plaintiffs who have suffered serious injuries in road traffic, industrial and other accidents and disease cases.

Number of partners:	2
Assistant solicitors:	2
Other fee-earners:	11

LINDSAYS WS

11 ATHOLL CRESCENT, EDINBURGH, EH3 8HE
Tel: (0131) 229 1212 **Fax:** (0131) 229 5611 **DX:** 25 EDINBURGH

The Firm: Lindsays is a medium-sized Edinburgh firm founded around 1815 whose objective is to provide a partner-led personal service with an emphasis on quality. Although historically regarded as a primarily private client firm Lindsays also has thriving commercial and litigation practices. To complement these legal services Lindsays has developed a significant presence in the residential property market through its estate agency service. Lindsays was one of the first legal practices in Scotland to recognise the benefit to its clients of adopting written quality procedures and has gained approval under the quality standard ISO 9001.

Principal Areas of Work:

Commercial Property: (*Contact Partner:* David Reith). All aspects are covered: purchases, sales, leasing, secured lending, other asset finance, asset recovery and building contracts particularly in relation to disputes. Other more specialised areas of expertise are education, intellectual property, especially licensing agreements, liquor licensing, including the purchase and sale of licensed premises, company formations and secretarial services, take-overs and acquisitions, the formation and management of charitable trusts and companies and road haulage.

Litigation: (*Contact Partner:* Alistair Mackie). A comprehensive debt recovery service is offered as is advice on employment law, contractual disputes, damages claims, arbitration and matters falling within the jurisdiction of the Scottish land courts. The members of the department are also experienced in dealing with personal litigation and can offer advice in connection with divorce and other family disputes and motoring offences.

Residential Conveyancing: (*Contact Partner:* Bob Arbuthnott). The department assists with all aspects of buying and selling residential property and is authorised to arrange mortgages and insurance.

Private Client: (*Contact Partner:* Brian Robertson). In addition to traditional private client work involving the preparation of wills, acting for and as executors in winding up estates, setting up and administering trusts, this department now offers an in-house Investment Management service which has some £30,000,000 under management. Complementary income tax, tax planning and other independent financial advice is also available.

Nature of Clientele: In addition to the private client, the firm regularly acts for hoteliers, retailers, landed estates, building societies, institutions (academic and financial), charities and heritage trusts.

Other Offices:

163a Bruntsfield Place, Edinburgh EH10 4DG *Tel:* (0131) 228 6993
77 Main Street, Davidsons Mains, Edinburgh EH4 5AD *Tel:* (0131) 312 7276

Senior partner:	R.J. Elliot
Number of partners:	13
Assistant solicitors:	10
Other fee-earners:	16

WORKLOADS	
Commercial	29%
Private client	29%
Residential conveyancing	22%
Litigation	20%

CONTACTS	
Asset finance	Alasdair Cummings
Banking	Alasdair Cummings
Building arbitration	Alan Mackay
Charitable companies	David Reith
Commercial contracts	Nora Kellock
Commercial property	David Reith
Crofting/ agriculture	Roy Shearer
Education	Roy Shearer
Employment	Douglas Tullis
Executry and wills	Callum Kennedy
Intellectual property	Nora Kellock
Investments	Rodger Urquhart
Liquor licensing	Nora Kellock
Litigation	Alistair Mackie
Personal financial planning	John Elliot
Residential property	Bob Arbuthnott
Trusts and tax planning	Brian Robertson

LINKLATERS

ONE SILK STREET, LONDON, EC2Y 8HQ
Tel: (0171) 456 2000 **Fax:** (0171) 456 2222 **DX:** 10 CDE

Linklaters is one of the world's largest international law firms, which operates from the UK and major financial centres around the globe.

The Firm: Linklaters' development has been in response to the commercial needs of its clients – major corporations, banks, financial institutions and governments. Since its formation over 150 years ago Linklaters has had offices in the heart of the City of London. With the growth in global financial markets, cross-border transactions and project finance, the firm has developed internationally with offices in Bangkok, Brussels, Frankfurt, Moscow, Paris, Hong Kong, Singapore, Tokyo and New York. Linklaters also has representative offices in Washington and São Paulo.

Linklaters aims to achieve preeminence in its chosen areas of practice through a firm-wide commitment to excellence and through the experience, helpfulness and creativity of its people. Its goal is to understand, meet and, wherever possible, exceed the expectations of its clients by delivering a first class service and by continually investing in its people and in the training, know-how and technology necessary to support them.

Types of Work Undertaken: Unusually for a City law firm, Linklaters combines core businesses – all of which are leaders in their fields – in corporate, international finance, commercial property and litigation.

The firm's corporate practice is largely concerned with financial and commercial transactions and advice on company matters including share offerings, takeovers and mergers, company reconstructions and privatisations. Specialist groups also advise on UK and offshore investment funds, regulatory compliance, insurance, competition and EC, project and asset finance, corporate recovery and insolvency and employment and employee benefits.

Linklaters is the established world leader in international capital markets work and a leading firm in syndicated bank lending. It serves both corporate and banking clients on securities issues (under UK, US, French and other laws), and bank lending, as well as structured financings and all categories of derivative products. It also advises on all types of commercial property transactions, including investments, developments and business lettings. The firm has specialists who advise on planning, environmental and local government issues, construction contracts and property investment structures.

The firm's litigation practice encompasses most types of contentious business arising in a financial, commercial or industrial context. As well as court, tribunal and arbitration work, it also handles investigations, document handling and debt recovery.

In addition, Linklaters has specialist departments in the fields of intellectual property and information technology, tax and trusts.

Other Offices: Bangkok, Brussels, Frankfurt, Moscow, Paris, Hong Kong, Singapore, Tokyo, New York.

Representative Offices: Washington, São Paulo

Managing partner:	Terence Kyle
Senior partner:	Charles Allen-Jones
UK	
Number of partners:	156
Assistant solicitors:	441
Other fee-earners:	19
Total staff:	1573
International	
Number of partners:	65
Assistant solicitors:	159
Other fee-earners:	23

WORKLOADS	
Corporate	40%
Commercial property	15%
International finance	15%
Litigation	15%
Tax	8%
Intellectual property	5%
Trusts	2%

CONTACTS	
Banking	Haydn Puleston Jones
Capital Markets	Stephen Edlmann
Commercial Property	Robert Finch
Competition/ EC	David Hall
Construction and Engineering	Marshall Levine
Corporate	Anthony Cann
Corporate Recovery/Insolvency	Robert Elliott
Employment/Employee Benefits	Raymond Jeffers
Environment	Beverley Adam
Financial Mkts & Derivatives	Paul Nelson
Intellectual Property & Information Technology	
	Jeremy Brown
International Finance	Stephen Edlmann
Investment Funds	Paul Harris
Litigation	Brinsley Nicholson
Planning and Local Government	Ray Jackson
Project and Asset Finance	Alan Black
Securities	Michael Canby
Tax	Tony Angel
Trusts	Nigel Reid

LINNELLS

GREYFRIARS COURT, PARADISE SQUARE, OXFORD, OX1 1BB
Tel: (01865) 248607 **Fax:** (01865) 728445 **DX:** 82261 OXFORD 2 **Email:** LAW@LINNELLS.CO.UK

The Firm: Established over 90 years ago, Linnells is now one of the largest provincial firms in the South-East. It is a broad based practice with the emphasis on providing first class advice in a friendly and accessible manner. The partners regard commitment to their staff as paramount and the firm has the Investor in People Award. Last year saw the implementation of a professional management structure ensuring the business is run effectively and efficiently for the benefit of both staff and clients.

Principal Areas of Work: 'Linnells Commercial' comprises three main areas:

Commercial Property is still one of the firm's greatest strengths, with the team handling complex and high value transactions. The Company and Commercial team deals with all types of transactions from company formations through to mergers, acquisitions and share sales. The firm has strong links with other law firms within the EU and regularly deals with European issues. The Charities Unit is thriving and the team now acts for several national charities. Intellectual property and IT work is on the increase and the firm also specialises in aviation and tourism law. The Commercial Litigation and Dispute Resolution team continues to expand. Last year saw considerable development in employment, construction, professional negligence and asset management work. Linnells continues to be a leader in alternative dispute resolution and has a number of trained mediators. The firm is a founder member of ADR Net.

The Private Client Department is a major part of the firm and comprises three main teams. The Litigation Team has long had a reputation for family and divorce work as well as expertise in childcare law. It also handles a large amount of personal injury work (plaintiff) and landlord and tenant litigation as well as licensing matters. The Criminal Unit is now one of the largest in Oxfordshire and it also has a very busy Immigration and Nationality Unit. Linnells has a Legal Aid franchise and has the procedures in place to handle conditional fees.

The Residential Property team acts for a variety of developers, building societies and relocation companies as well as private clients. Probate, Wills and Trusts team continue to play a key role in the firm's private client work. The team also handles Court of Protection work.

Nature of Clientele: The firm's clients include well-known private companies and plcs, county councils, several leading charities, breweries, motor dealers, property developers, building companies, high technology companies, publishers and university institutions. It also has a large private client base, many of whom are drawn from the University community.

Other offices: Bicester, Milton Keynes and Newport Pagnell.

Managing partner:	Jonathan Lloyd-Jones
Senior partner:	Martyn Ess
Number of partners:	21
Assistant solicitors:	26
Other fee-earners:	17

WORKLOADS	
Private Client Litigation	33%
Private Client	26%
Commercial Litigation	16%
Commercial Property	14%
Company/Commercial	11%

CONTACTS	
Aviation and Tourism	Glenvil Smith
Charities	Joss Saunders
Child Care	Tony Hughes
Commercial Litigation	Jonathan Lloyd Jones
Commercial Property	John Deech
Company/Commercial	Joss Saunders
Construction	Jonathan Lloyd-Jones
Crime	Warwick Clarke
EC and International	Euan Temple
Employment	James Whiter
Family	Christine Plews
Immigration	Philip Turpin
Insolvency	Jonathan Lloyd-Jones
Intellectual Property	Joss Saunders
Landlord & Tenant Litigation	Carol Oster
Personal Injury	Jeremy Irwin-Singer
Probate and Trusts	Martyn Ess
Residential Property	Anne Cowell

LINSKILLS SOLICITORS Harrington House, Harrington Street, Liverpool, L2 9QA **Tel:** (0151) 236 2224 **Fax:** (0151) 236 0151 (Criminal) **DX:** 14215 **Ptnrs:** 1 **Asst solrs:** 8 **Other fee-earners:** 19 **Contact:** Mr M.B.Heller (Practice Manager) *Legal aid franchise in crime, family, welfare and personal injury. Branch office (Welfare Advice Centre) 195 Kensington, Liverpool L7 2RF Tel: (0151) 260 1001 Fax: (0151) 261 1936*

WORKLOADS			
Criminal	65%	Personal injury	10%
Road traffic accident	6%	Conveyancing	5%
Civil litigation	5%	Welfare	5%
Matrimonial	4%		

LINSLEY & MORTIMER

69-75 THE SIDE, NEWCASTLE-UPON-TYNE, NE1 3DD
Tel: (0191) 232 4192 **Fax:** (0191) 261 6949 **DX:** 61043 NEWCASTLE

The Firm: Established over 45 years ago from a litigation base, the firm in the last 10 years has expanded into commercial and insolvency work. All matters are directly supervised by partners.

Principal Areas of Work:

Private Client/ Commercial: *Contact:* Richard Chadeyron.
Personal Injury Litigation: *Contact:* Alan Simpson.
Commercial Litigation, Insolvency & Professional Negligence: *Contact:* Toby Scott.

Nature of Clientele: Insurers, adjusters, private companies.

Senior partner:	R, Chadeyron
Number of partners:	3
Assistant solicitors:	2
Other fee-earners:	2

WORKLOADS	
Civil litigation	85%
General commercial	10%
Private client	5%

LISTER CROFT HARROW DARNTON Victoria Chambers, 40 Wood Street, Wakefield, WF1 2HL *Tel:* (01924) 881000 *Fax:* (01924) 387404 *DX:* 15010 Wakefield *Ptnrs:* 8 *Asst solrs:* 4 *Other fee-earners:* 5

LIVINGSTONE BROWNE 84 Carlton Place, Glasgow, G5 9TD *Tel:* (0141) 429 8166 *Fax:* (0141) 429 1337 *DX:* 60 Glasgow

LLEWELYN ZIETMAN Temple Bar House, 23-28 Fleet Street, London, EC4Y 1AA **Tel:** (0171) 842 5400 **Fax:** (0171) 842 5444 **DX:** 209 Chancery Lane **Email:** llz@compuserve.com **Ptnrs:** 12 **Asst solrs:** 11 **Other fee-earners:** 18 **Contact:** Ms Julie Evans *A niche practice specialising in commercial litigation and commercial law, with emphasis on intellectual property, IT and fraud related matters.*

WORKLOADS			
Commercial Litigation	50%	Intellectual Property	50%

LLOYD COOPER 7A Grafton Street, London, W1X 3LA **Tel:** (0171) 629 4699 **Fax:** (0171) 355 3796 **DX:** 37208 Piccadilly **Ptnrs:** 4 **Asst solrs:** 3 **Other fee-earners:** 2 **Contact:** P.R. Lloyd Cooper *A commercial practice best known for its work in insurance and commercial litigation, company/commercial and commercial property.*

WORKLOADS			
Insurance and reinsurance litigation			50%
Company and commercial			25%
Commercial property	15%	Commercial litigation	10%

LOCHNERS TECHNOLOGY SOLICITORS Craven House, Station Road, Godalming, Surrey GU7 1EX **Tel:** (01483) 414588 **Fax:** (01483) 416065 **Email:** lochners@compuserve.com **Ptnrs:** 2 **Asst solrs:** 2 **Para legal:** 1 *Specialists in technology-related law and associated areas of the law including patents, trademarks, copyrights, designs, confidential information and information technology.*

LOCKHARTS

TAVISTOCK HOUSE SOUTH, TAVISTOCK SQUARE, LONDON, WC1H 9LS
Tel: (0171) 383 7111 **Fax:** (0171) 383 7117 **DX:** 122015 TAVISTOCK SQUARE 2

The Firm: A firm of solicitors which specialises in medical law and which provides expert legal advice to all the professions; particularly doctors, dentists, solicitors, accountants, architects and surveyors. Established in 1995 by Andrew Lockhart-Mirams, who has worked in the medical field for over 25 years, the firm provides an in-depth experience of Partnership agreements and disputes; property development and secured lending; all aspects of litigation, with particular emphasis on Judicial Review proceedings; employment law; representation of professionals in disciplinary proceedings; and administrative, Health and Safety and NHS Regulatory Law.

Number of partners:	3
Assistant solicitors:	3
Trainee Solicitors:	1

LONSDALES 342 Lytham Road, Blackpool, FY4 1DW *Tel:* (01253) 345258 *Fax:* (01253) 348943 *DX:* 27652 Blackpool *Ptnrs:* 3 *Asst solrs:* 2 *Other fee-earners:* 6

LOOSEMORES Alliance House, 18-19 High St, Cardiff, CF1 2BP *Tel:* (01222) 224433 *Fax:* (01222) 373275 *DX:* 33008 *Ptnrs:* 10 *Asst solrs:* 11 *Other fee-earners:* 8

LOUDONS WS 29 St Patrick Square, Edinburgh, EH8 9EY **Tel:** (0131) 662 4193 **Fax:** (0131) 662 1910 **DX:** ED 294 Edinburgh 1 **Ptnrs:** 2 **Asst solrs:** 1 **Other fee-earners:** 4 **Contact:** Mr Alasdair Loudon *Specialist practice with very strong reputation for its family law expertise, particularly financial claims and settlements.*

WORKLOADS	
Family Law (incl Child Law)	100%

LOVELL WHITE DURRANT

65 HOLBORN VIADUCT, LONDON, EC1A 2DY
Tel: (0171) 236 0066 **Fax:** (0171) 248 4212 **DX:** BOX 57 **Email:** INFORMATION@LOVELLWHITEDURRANT.COM
Internet: HTTP://WWW.LOVELLWHITEDURRANT.COM

Lovell White Durrant is a leading international law firm based in the City of London. The breadth of the firm's legal practice and depth of its specialist skills enable it to offer a comprehensive service to financial, corporate and government clients around the world.

The Firm: Lovell White Durrant's pioneering approach to the development of its international practice is shown in the history of its expansion overseas, with the establishment of offices in Brussels (1972), New York (1977), Hong Kong (1982), Paris (1990), Tokyo (1990), Prague (1991), Beijing (1992), Ho Chi Minh City (1994), Chicago (1995), Moscow (1997) and Singapore (1998).

Lovell White Durrant has an excellent reputation for its advice on EU law, helped by the strength of its Brussels office. Through the Prague, Moscow and London offices, the firm is also ideally placed to work with clients who have interests in the developing economies of Central & Eastern Europe and Russia.

In Asia there is a strong demand for the combined service available from the five Lovell White Durrant offices in the region. The firm's stature in Asia is shown in its membership of the influential Pacific Rim Advisory Council, an association of major law firms undertaking work in the region.

In North America, Lovell White Durrant is the only major UK based firm to have an office in Chicago as well as New York. The Chicago office has grown rapidly since its launch in 1995 and focuses primarily on work in the insurance and reinsurance sector where, in conjunction with other Lovell White Durrant offices in Europe and Asia, a sizeable dual US/UK jurisdictional service has been built. Through established relationships with other leading law firms, the firm is also active in other regions of the world, including the Latin American, African, Scandinavian and South Asian countries.

Principal Areas of Work: Banking and capital markets, corporate finance, property and litigation are central to the firm's practice. The size and international strengths of the firm enable it to put together expert teams of lawyers with direct experience of advising on some of the largest and most complex transactions and cases of recent years, both in the UK and elsewhere in the world.

In addition to these core areas of practice, Lovell White Durrant is recognised as one of the market leaders in insurance and reinsurance, business restructuring and asset recovery, pensions and employment law. Tax, competition law, intellectual property, telecoms, utilities, commodities, international trade, construction and engineering are also particular strengths of the firm. Lovell White Durrant places great emphasis on helping clients to achieve their business objectives by providing legal advice that is both imaginative and commercially aware. It is also known for nurturing its working relationships with clients both large and small and consistently achieves very high ratings for client satisfaction in independent research.

Further Information: A comprehensive list of specialist brochures, client notes and newsletters is available from Janet Frangs. Prospective trainee solicitors should contact Lynda Neal for details of the recruitment programme. Further information is available from any Lovell White Durrant office or via the firm's Internet web page at http://www.lovellwhitedurrant.com

Managing partner:	Lesley MacDonagh
Senior partner:	Andrew Walker
Worldwide	
Number of Partners:	165
Assistant Solicitors:	393
Other Fee-earners:	243
Total number of people worldwide:	1,580

CONTACTS	
Advertising/Consumer law	Andrew Skipper
Arbitration/ADR	Mark Huleatt-James
Asset finance	Robin Hallam
Banking	John Penson
Broadcasting	Jennifer McDermott
Business restructuring	Nicholas Frome
Capital markets	David Hudd
Commercial	Andrew Skipper
Commodities	David Moss
Computers/IT	Quentin Archer
Construction and engineering	Nicholas Gould
Corporate finance/M&A	Hugh Nineham
Defamation	Jennifer McDermott
Employee benefits	Louise Whitewright
Employment	Andrew Williamson
Energy	Michael Stanger
Entertainment	Lindy Golding
Environmental	Ruth Grant
EU and competition	Simon Polito
Financial services	Richard Stones
Fraud and asset recovery	Keith Gaines
Insurance and reinsurance	John Powell
Intellectual property	Michael Golding
Litigation	Russell Sleigh
Lloyd's	Leah Dunlop
MBO/ Venture capital	Allan Murray-Jones
Media law	Jennifer McDermott
Pensions	Jane Samsworth
Planning	Michael Gallimore
Product liability	John Meltzer
Professional indemnity	John Trotter
Project finance	Gavin McQuater
Property	Robert Kidby
Public policy	Neil Fagan
Regulatory investigations	Graham Livingstone
Shipping and international trade	Philip Quenby
Tax	Daniel Friel
Telecommmunications	Heather Rowe
VAT	Greg Sinfield

LOXLEYS Bishopsgate House, 5-7 Folgate Street, London, E1 6BX **Tel:** (0171) 377 1066 **Fax:** (0171) 377 5004 **DX:** 131418 Bishopsgate **Email:** mail@loxleys.demon.co.uk **Ptnrs:** 5 **Asst solrs:** 6 **Other fee-earners:** 2 **Contact:** Graeme Harris *A general property, commercial, probate and trust practice, liquor and entertainment licensing a speciality. Strong connections with Europe and India.*

LUCAS & WYLLYS 5 South Quay, Great Yarmouth, NR30 2QJ **Tel:** (01493) 855555 **Fax:** (01493) 330055 **DX:** 41100 **Ptnrs:** 6 **Asst solrs:** 3 **Other fee-earners:** 11 **Contact:** David Ellis *A general practice with specialists in matrimonial, commercial, personal injury, criminal, conveyancing and wills and probate.*

WORKLOADS			
Civil	24%	Conveyancing	24%
Criminal	21%	Matrimonial	17%
Probate	11%	General	3%

LUMB & MACGILL Prudential Buildings, 11 Ivegate, Bradford, BD1 1SQ **Tel:** (01274) 730666 **Fax:** (01274) 723453 **Ptnrs:** 5 **Asst solrs:** 1 **Other fee-earners:** 5 **Contact:** Kerry Macgill *Specialists in criminal, care and licensing work. Legal aid and Mental Health Tribunal.*

WORKLOADS			
Crime	85%	Child care	15%

LUPTON FAWCETT Yorkshire Hse, Greek St, Leeds, LS1 5SX **Tel:** (0113) 280 2000 **Fax:** (0113) 245 6782 **DX:** 12035 Leeds **Ptnrs:** 14 **Asst solrs:** 25 **Other fee-earners:** 47 **Contact:** Kevin Emsley *A broadly based practice. Clients include both large Plcs, owner managed businesses and private individuals.*

WORKLOADS			
Personal Injury			35%
Company commercial and Commercial property			18%
Private Client	16%	Commercial Litigation	14%
Debt Collection	9%	Insolvency	6%
Advocacy	1%		

LYONS DAVIDSON

BRIDGE HOUSE, 48-52 BALDWIN ST, BRISTOL, BS1 1QD
Tel: (0117) 904 6000 **Fax:** (0117) 904 6001 **DX:** 7834

The Firm: Lyons Davidson continues it's growth in the South West and now has offices at Bristol, Birmingham and Plymouth. The firm with a total staff of 250 focuses on Insurance Litigation, Corporate, Commercial and Property work. The firm, which has been accredited with IIP, provides it's staff, through training contracts with the University of the West of England, with extensive training on all issues of the law.

Senior partner:	Pete Fergie
Number of partners:	16
Assistant solicitors:	38
Other fee-earners:	82

Principal Areas of Practice:

Commercial Property: (*Contact Partners:* Tim Davidson and John Hicks). Clients include major companies, developers, investors, banks, financial institutions, retailers and local authorities. The department is well-known for its development practice and has substantial experience across the whole range of property transactions. Specialist units deal with high-volume estate conveyancing and re-possession sales, securities work and healthcare property.

Environment and Planning: (*Contact Partner:* Kevin Gibbs). Advice on planning, environmental and waste law is provided to the firm's public and private sector clients by a specialist team with backgrounds and professional qualifications in applied science, town planning and local government.

Company/Commercial: The full range of corporate services is provided including company sales and acquisitions, management buy-outs, partnerships, flotations, EC law, intellectual property, banking and securities, receiverships and liquidations. Lyons Davidson Trustee Company offers an independent trustee service and works in tandem with the Pensions and Employment Law Group.

Company/Commercial & Intellectual Property: (*Contact Partner:* Richard Squire).

Insolvency: (*Contact Partner:* Paul Hardman).

Pensions: (*Contact Partner:* Sarah Gray).

Commercial Litigation: All aspects of civil and commercial litigation are undertaken including contract, construction, professional negligence, employment, intellectual property, real and leasehold property, banking and insolvency disputes. There is also an expanding licensing practice and the department operates its own advocacy unit.

Commercial Claims: (*Contact Partner:* Peter Fergie).

Property litigation: (*Contact Partner:* Martin Bastow).

Professional Negligence: (*Contact Partner:* Peter Fergie).

Medical Negligence and Healthcare: (*Contact Partner:* Nigel Montgomery). Lyons Davidson has an expanding Healthcare Law department which provides advice to NHS Trusts and other Healthcare providers in all fields of legal need. It offers an outstanding level of expertise and experience and its lawyers include a former medical registrar and former nurses. The Department has extensive experience in advising on cases of medical negligence.

Insurance Litigation and Injury Claims Service: The department provides expert advice and representation to Plaintiffs (P) and Defendants (D) on all aspects of personal injury and insurance claims. In-house continued expansion is attributed to the emphasis on immediate access to specialist knowledge for all of the 79 fee earners through a highly developed internal network. The department has 3 in-house Accident Investigation Engineers, a medical report booking service and offers training facilities for its Liability and Legal Expense Insurer clients.

Continues overleaf

Insurance Claims: (*Contact:*(P) Bernard Rowe, (D) Trevor Still).

Road Traffic Accident Claims: (*Contact Partner:* Bernard Rowe (P), Trevor Still (D)).

Occupiers' and Employers' Liability: (*Contact Partner:* Nigel Montgomery).

Insurance Policy Disputes & Insurance Fraud: (*Contact Partner:* John Gore).

Family: (*Contact Partner:* James Myatt) The department offers a full and comprehensive range of service on all matrimonial and domestic matters. Work includes all financial aspects of divorce and separation, child care (in particular child abduction), domestic violence, cohabitation and welfare benefits. Believed to be the first of its kind in Bristol, the department also offers a counselling service to its clients.

Private Client: (*Contact Partner:* James Myatt) This established department offers a comprehensive range of services on all matters relating to the individual. Expert advice from experienced and STEP qualified personnel includes all financial aspects of personal taxation, estate administration, will writing, trusts Court of Protection, and services for the Elderly.

Training and Recruitment: The Firm recruits up to seven trainee solicitors each year. Applications should be made by hand written letter and C.V. to Mr John Hicks.

Other Offices: Plymouth, Birmingham.

MACARTHUR STEWART 87 High Street, Fort William, PH33 6DG *Tel:* (01397) 702455 *Fax:* (01397) 705949 *Ptnrs:* 7 *Asst solrs:* 10 *Other fee-earners:* 10

MACDONALD OATES Square House, The Square, Petersfield, GU32 3HT *Tel:* (01730) 268211 *Fax:* (01730) 261232 *DX:* 100400 *Ptnrs:* 7 *Asst solrs:* 6 *Other fee-earners:* 1

MACE & JONES

DRURY HOUSE, 19 WATER STREET, LIVERPOOL, L2 0RP
Tel: (0151) 236 8989 **Fax:** (0151) 227 5010 **DX:** 14166 LIVERPOOL **Email:** LWD@MACEANDJONES.CO.UK

30 SHERBORNE SQUARE, HUYTON, L36 9UR
Tel: (0151) 480 7000 **Fax:** (0151) 449 1953 **DX:** 15453 HUYTON **Email:** LWD@MACEANDJONES.CO.UK

98 KING STREET, KNUTSFORD, WA16 6EP
Tel: (01565) 755488 **Fax:** (01565) 652711 **DX:** 22959 KNUTSFORD **Email:** LWD@MACEANDJONES.CO.UK

14 OXFORD COURT, BISHOPSGATE, MANCHESTER, M2 3WQ
Tel: (0161) 236 2244 **Fax:** (0161) 228 7285 **DX:** 18564 MANCHESTER 7 **Email:** LWD@MACEANDJONES.CO.UK

The Firm: A leading regional practice in the North West, Mace & Jones remains a full service firm while enjoying a national reputation for its commercial expertise, especially in employment, litigation/insolvency, corporate and property. The firm's clients range from national and multi-national companies and public sector bodies to owner-managed businesses and private individuals, reflecting the broad nature of the work undertaken. Sound practical advice is given always on a value for money basis.

Contacts:

Commercial litigation	*Craig Blakemore*
Commercial property	*Tim Williams*
Company/Commercial	*Alan Thompson*
Employment	*Martin Edwards*
Insolvency	*Graeme Jump*
Personal injury	*Stewart McCulloch*

Managing partner:	Lawrence Downey
Senior partner:	Graeme Jump
Number of partners:	24
Assistant solicitors:	33
Other fee-earners:	20

WORKLOADS	
Commercial Litigation/Insolvency	20%
Commercial property	20%
Company/Commercial	20%
Employment	20%
PI/Private Client/Family	20%

MACE & JONES
SOLICITORS

MACFARLANES

10 NORWICH STREET, LONDON, EC4A 1BD
Tel: (0171) 831 9222 **Fax:** (0171) 831 9607 **DX:** 138 **Email:** CYR@MACFARLANES.COM **Internet:** HTTP://WWW.MACFARLANES.COM

Macfarlanes is a leading City firm, with a wide range of practice. This, and its emphasis on and investment in training, have helped it to recruit the best lawyers who thrive in an environment which the larger City firms cannot offer. Macfarlanes is at the forefront in many practice areas, and is instructed by leading participants in many industrial and commercial sectors who appreciate the distinctive benefits of working with a cohesive City firm. The scale of some of the firm's work is equal to that at the biggest City firms.

The Firm: Throughout the firm's practice there is extensive international involvement. Many clients are overseas-based or owned, and many transactions extend beyond the UK.

Types of work undertaken: Macfarlanes has a strong reputation in the traditional City domain of corporate finance work. It is placed highly in flotation and management buy-out league tables and in mergers and acquisitions work, including takeovers. The firm's related specialist areas, such as intellectual property, corporate tax, banking and employee benefits, mean that Macfarlanes can provide its broad range of commercial clients with the high quality of legal services demanded by them, both in relation to corporate transactional work and at the clients' operational level. The firm has a particularly strong reputation for advertising and marketing work as well as investment funds and financial services.

Work for the property sector covers all transactions involving the ownership, development, investment in and financing of land. Commercial property investment and development transactions are at the core of the work of the Property Department whose reputation and profile continues to rise as the quality of its work and of the transactions in which it is involved are more widely recognised.

Advice is also given on residential and agricultural property, with specialist groups for planning and environmental work, enterprise zone matters and the retail, leisure and health sectors. Much work includes landlord and tenant issues. The firm has substantial experience in property-related insolvencies, including LPA receiverships.

Macfarlanes' wide range of litigation and other dispute resolution work includes: leading employment law cases; acting for insured and insurer, especially in advertising and surveying cases; IP cases and disputes over computer hardware and software; financial services regulatory issues and enquiries; Lloyd's-related work; sovereign debt, securities and other banking disputes; judicial review, breach of contract and professional negligence claims.

Macfarlanes is one of the leading UK firms in advising private clients and their family trusts, both domestically and internationally. Tax planning, including the creation and administration of trusts, the preparation of wills and administration of estates are central to this work. The firm forms and advises many charitable companies and trusts. The international element is very important both for UK-based families and for overseas taxpayers seeking advice on tax and trust law. The firm is frequently instructed at the request of many of the largest US law firms and private banks for this work. Partners have been appointed by courts in the UK and abroad to be trustees in place of existing trustees.

Other specialist areas of work, mainly for commercial clients, fall outside historic categories and often involve lawyers from several departments, for example Private Finance Initiative projects.

Other office: Brussels

Senior Partner:	Vanni Treves
Managing Partner:	Roger Formby
Number of partners:	51
Assistant solicitors:	88
Other fee-earners:	62

WORKLOADS	
Company/ commercial	46%
Property	22%
Litigation	18%
Tax and financial planning	14%

CONTACTS	
Acquisitions & disposals	Peter Turnbull
Advertising	William King
Agricultural	John Moore
Banking	Tony Evans
Corporate finance	Robert Sutton
Corporate property	Chris Field
Employee benefits	Douglas Shugar
Employment	Tony Thompson
Enterprise zones	Chris Field
Financial services	Bridget Barker
General commercial and I.P.	William King
Health care	John Moore
Investment funds	Bridget Barker
Lending	Tony Evans
Litigation	Tony Thompson
MBOs/MBIs, financial purchases	Kevin Tuffnell
Pensions	Douglas Shugar
PFI	Jeremy Courtenay-Stamp
Planning & environmental work	Andrew Jackson
Private Client	Michael Hayes
Property development	Chris Field
Property investment	Chris Field
Residential property	John Hornby
Retail property	Richard Reuben
Unit Trusts	Tim Cornick

MACKAY SIMON

58 QUEEN STREET, EDINBURGH, EH2
Tel: (0131) 240 1400 **Fax:** (0131) 240 1401 **DX:** ED 243

The Firm: The firm (formerly Mackay WS) was established in 1988 by Malcolm Mackay with the sole aim of providing a specialised employment law service. Since then Shona Simon has been assumed as a partner and a number of other fee earners are employed in different areas of the speciality. The firm continues to practice only in employment law.

Principal Areas of Work: Malcolm Mackay is mainly involved in dealing with collective employment matters such as business transfers; business reorganisation; redundancies and other multiple claims. Shona Simon specialises in discrimination and equal pay. Other fee earners deal primarily with unfair dismissal; drafting of contracts and service agreements; working time and other miscellaneous employment matters. In addition to carrying out legal work for clients, Mackay Simon also hold client seminars covering different aspects of employment law.

Academic work: Malcolm Mackay and Shona Simon lecture regularly at academic institutions, conferences and seminars on different aspects of employment law. They have co-written a book on the subject to be published by Greens in July this year. They co-edit the Green's Employment Law Bulletin and regularly write on employment matters for the Journal of the Law Society of Scotland. Other colleagues within the firm are also involved in lecturing and writing. Professor Vic Craig of Heriot Watt University is a Consultant with the firm. Mackay Simon place a great emphasis on achieving the correct balance between the academic and practical aspects of employment law.

Clients and geographical area: Mackay Simon act for large number of businesses from the very small to the very large throughout the UK. Although the firm is based in Edinburgh, solicitors from Mackay Simon appear regularly in Industrial Tribunals throughout the United Kingdom. The firm is also involved in trade union work, particularly for two of the main teaching unions in Scotland, and is instructed regularly by the Equal Opportunities Commission. Work for individuals is also undertaken. The firm acted for the applicant/pursuer in the ECJ referral in *Brown v Rentokil.*

Objectives: All at Mackay Simon recognise that employment law is a complex subject but that it must be applied in a sensible and realistic way. The firm's general approach is characterised by a recogntion that many disputes can be resolved without resort to litigation if a rational approach is taken. However, if litigation is necessary representation is almost always provided in-house.

Number of partners:	2
Assistant solicitors:	5
Other fee-earners:	4

WORKLOADS	
Employment	100%

CONTACTS	
Employment	Malcolm R. Mackay

MACKINNONS

21 ALBERT STREET, ABERDEEN, AB25 1XX
Tel: (01224) 632464 **Fax:** (01224) 632184 **DX:** AB 34 **Email:** MACKINNONS@SOL.CO.UK

379 NORTH DEESIDE ROAD, CULTS, ABERDEEN, AB15 9SX
Tel: (01244) 868687 **Fax:** (01224) 861012 **DX:** AB34 **Email:** MACKINNONS@SOL.CO.UK

The Firm: Progressive six-partner practice specialising in shipping and commercial law with substantial private client department providing a full range of legal services. The firm is very experienced in all aspects of marine and admiralty law including marine insurance, collisions, salvage, litigation and personal injury as well as acting in the defence of prosecutions under the full range of Merchant Shipping, Pollution and Fisheries Legislation. The firm acts for numerous P&I clubs and fishing mutuals providing a hands-on service aboard ships, fishing boats and oil rigs. Mackinnons has a substantial marine and commercial practice dealing with purchase, sale, finance and chartering of fishing boats, offshore oil supply and stand-by vessels, and other vessels.

Managing partner:	Charles M. Scott
Senior partner:	Dennis N. Yule
Number of partners:	6
Assistant solicitors:	3
Other fee-earners:	2

MACKINTOSH & WYLIE P.O. Box 31, 23 The Foregate, Kilmarnock, KA1 1LE *Tel:* (01563) 525104 *Fax:* (01563) 537100 *DX:* 7 Kilmarnock *Ptnrs:* 6 *Asst solrs:* 2 *Other fee-earners:* 2

MACKRELL TURNER GARRETT Inigo Place, 31 Bedford St, London, WC2E 9EH *Tel:* (0171) 240 0521 *Fax:* (0171) 240 9457 *DX:* 40037 Covent Garden 1 *Ptnrs:* 17 *Asst solrs:* 10 *Other fee-earners:* 7

MACLAY MURRAY & SPENS

151 ST. VINCENT STREET, GLASGOW, G2 5NJ
Tel: (0141) 248 5011 **Fax:** (0141) 248 5819 **DX:** GW 67 **Email:** LAWYER@MACLAYMURRAYSPENS.CO.UK

Maclay Murray & Spens is committed to offering all of its clients the highest quality – commercial advice at canny Scottish prices. We exist to service the needs of our clients, be they private or commercial, and not the other way round.

The development and growth of the Brussels office reflects our commitment to meet the needs of an extensive client base, while our London office provides an ideal platform for Scottish clients doing business in the City, and for London based clients looking for a premier law firm without City overheads.

Understanding clients and their business is the focus of the firm's approach. This has lead to the development of well-organised expert departments in fields such as pensions, intellectual property, taxation, banking, fraud, construction, employment and PFI.

The firm recognises that many transactions require hand-picked teams made up of lawyers with differing skills from differing departments if the specific needs of the client and the transaction are to be fully met. To this end, the firm ensures that all departments and units are closely linked to give the client the best possible service.

Other Offices:

3 Glenfinlas Street, Edinburgh EH3 6AQ
Tel: (0131) 226 5196 *Fax:* (0131) 226 3174

10 Foster Lane, London EC2V 6HH.
Tel: (0171) 606 6130. *Fax:* (0171) 600 0992

Scotland Europa Centre, 35 Square de Meeus, B-1000, Brussels, Belgium
Tel: 00 32 2 502 9184 *Fax:* 00 32 2 502 9544

Foreign Languages: French, German, Italian, Norwegian

Managing partner:	Michael J. Walker
Senior partner:	Ronald Graham
Number of partners:	39
Associate solicitors:	23
Assistant solicitors:	51
International partners:	1

WORKLOADS	
Company/ commercial	40%
Commercial property	28%
Litigation	17%
Private client	15%

CONTACTS	
Banking	Robert Laing
Commercial property	Jennifer Johnson
Company/Commercial	Magnus Swanson
Employment	Mark Hamilton
Environmental	Andrew Primrose
EU	Michael Dean
Fraud and financial services	Richard Clark
Intellectual Property	Fiona Nicolson
Litigation	Ewan Easton
Pensions	Andrew Fleming
Private client	Donald White
Tax	Martyn Jones

Maclay Murray & Spens
Solicitors

EDINBURGH · GLASGOW · LONDON · BRUSSELS

MACLEOD & MACCALLUM P.O. Box No.4, 28 Queensgate, Inverness, IV1 1YN *Tel:* (01463) 239393 *Fax:* (01463) 222879 *DX:* 12 Inverness *Ptnrs:* 10 *Asst solrs:* 3 *Other fee-earners:* 10

MACPHEE & PARTNERS St Mary's House, Gordon Square, Fort William, PH33 6DY **Tel:** (01397) 701000 **Fax:** (01397) 701777 **DX:** FW 531408 **Email:** manager@macpheelaw.demon.co.uk **Website:** http://www.scotlaw.co.uk/mcp/ **Ptnrs:** 3 **Asst solrs:** 4 **Other fee-earners:** 3 **Contact:** Duncan MacPhee *Largest practice in area. Winner 1997 TSB Law Society of Scotland Business of Law Awards (small firms). Crofting Law specialism.*

MACROBERTS

152 BATH STREET, GLASGOW, G2 4TB
Tel: (0141) 332 9988 **Fax:** (0141) 332 8886 **DX:** GW70 **Email:** MAILDESK@MACROBERTS.CO.UK **Internet:** HTTP://WWW.MACROBERTS.CO.UK

27 MELVILLE STREET, EDINBURGH, EH3 7JF
Tel: (0131) 226 2552 **Fax:** (0131) 226 2501 **DX:** ED207 **Email:** MAILDESK@MACROBERTS.CO.UK

The Firm: MacRoberts is a leading commercial law firm offering a comprehensive range of legal services to corporate, commercial, public sector and private clients. Established almost 150 years ago, MacRoberts, through its offices in Edinburgh and Glasgow, provides quality legal services in a prompt, efficient and friendly manner. The Firm is committed to delivering the highest standards of professional advice and expertise.

Principal Areas of Work:

Corporate: All aspects of corporate and commercial law including: incorporations, reorganisations, take-overs and mergers, management buy-outs and joint ventures (UK and international); loan debenture and equity finance, syndications, consumer credit; banking flotations, Stock Exchange requirements, new issues, placings and other issues, employee share schemes and pension schemes; receivership, administration, liquidation and bankruptcy; partnership agreements; EC law; commercial contracts, including agency distribution and finance agreements; entertainment law; privatisations.

Commercial Property: Corporate and private clients are advised on all aspects of heritable and leasehold property matters including: acquisition, sale and leasing of commercial and industrial property; commercial, industrial and housing development, investment and finance; commercial and personal secured loans; environmental law; agricultural law, including forestry; company relocation schemes; timeshare and leisure developments; planning law; licensing and gaming law.

Construction: Advice in connection with drafting of construction contracts, professional appointments, collateral warranties; building and engineering disputes and arbitration.

Corporate Tax & VAT: Including tax & VAT aspects of corporate acquisitions, disposals and reorganisations, commercial property transactions and PFI projects.

Employment: Employment and service contracts, disciplinary and grievance procedures, other procedural rules, employment policies including health & safety, sex and race discrimination, equal pay; trade union disputes; all forms of employment tribunals.

Intellectual Property & IT: Franchising, patents and patent licensing, copyright, trademarks and know-how agreements; data protection; computer contracts.

Litigation and Arbitration: The department acts for and advises on all aspects of: civil litigation in both Sheriff Courts and the Court of Session; building and engineering disputes and arbitration; insurance and other commercial litigation; rating and valuation; planning; professional negligence; liquidation, administration, receivership and bankruptcy; product liability; debt recovery; reparation claims; intellectual property disputes; licensing.

PFI & Capital Projects: One of the largest practices in Scotland, clients include NHS Trusts, local authorities, bidding consortia and banks in a wide range of sectors including healthcare, education, roads, wastewater and office accommodation.

Private Client: Specialist advice to individuals, trustees and executors in relation to tax planning and mitigation; preparation of tax returns; investment advice; establishment and administration of trusts; wills; administration of estates; preparation of Powers of Attorney; financial services; acquisition, sale and leasing of estate and domestic property; setting up and administration of curatories.

Foreign Languages: French, German, Greek, Dutch, Italian, Norwegian.

International Connections & Associated Offices: Member of ADVOC, an international network of independent lawyers, providing access to legal services throughout Europe and Asia.

Managing partner:	John Macmillan
Number of partners:	25
Assistant solicitors:	47
Other fee-earners:	10

CONTACTS	
Banking	Norman Martin
Charities	David MacRobert
Commercial property	Laurence Fraser, Allan Mackenzie
Construction	David Henderson, Lindy Patterson
Corporate	Ian Dickson, Norman Martin
Corporate tax and VAT	Isobel d'Inverno
Employment	John Macmillan, Raymond Williamson
Energy Law	Ian Dickson
Environmental & Planning	Jamie Grant
EU & Competition	David Flint
Intellectual property/IT	David Flint
Licensing and gaming	John Loudon
Litigation & Arbitration	Richard Barrie, Neil Kelly
PFI & Capital Projects	Michael Murphy, David Henderson
Private Client	David MacRobert

MADDEN & FINUCANE 88 Castle Street, Belfast, BT1 1HE *Tel:* (01232) 238007 *Fax:* (01232) 439276 *DX:* 434 NR Belfast *Ptnrs:* 4 *Asst solrs:* 8 *Other fee-earners:* 22

MAGRATH & CO

52-54 MADDOX STREET, LONDON, W1R 9PA
Tel: (0171) 495 3003 **Fax:** (0171) 409 1745 **DX:** 9009 WEST END **Email:** MAGRATH@MAGRATH.FTECH.CO.UK
Internet: HTTP://WWW.MAGRATH.CO.UK

The Firm: Founded in 1990, Magrath & Co is a progressive and commercially orientated niche law firm which continues to enjoy rapid growth. The firm's lawyers have extensive experience in their fields, and are dedicated to providing prompt, expert advice which meets and anticipates their clients' requirements.

Principal Areas of Work:

Immigration: (*Contact:* Chris Magrath). The firm's dedicated immigration department covers the full range of immigration issues but advises primarily on commercial immigration including global expatriation planning, work permits, applications and appeals. The firm has particular experience in US-UK immigration matters and produces a regular bulletin each quarter to provide legal updates on immigration and employment law.

Employment Law: (*Contact:* Helen Jerry). The firm's employment department deals with all aspects of employment law including contentious employment disputes, mass redundancies, consultation and industrial action, contract drafting and discrimination issues.

Corporate Fraud: (*Contact:* Gary Summers). The firm is experienced in a wide variety of 'white collar' crime, and can also advise in cases of investigation by agencies such as the Serious Fraud Office, DTI, Inland Revenue and Customs & Excise. Additionally the firm handles a wide range of criminal allegations of a more general nature.

Civil Litigation: (*Contact:* Nick Goldstone). The firm is instructed by a wide range of clients on a variety of commercial and entertainment related issues. Although increasingly geared towards the corporate sector, the firm welcomes private clients on both a fee paying and legally aided basis.

Entertainment Law: (*Contact:* Alexis Grower). Advice on music and literature publishing, recording, production and management agreements; financing, production, distribution and marketing of TV, film, theatre and commercials. Also: merchandising and sponsorship agreements; sports-related advice; and gaming & betting law.

Other areas of work: All aspects of company and commercial law and commercial property (*Contact:* David Ashton).

Nature of Clientele: The firm acts for a large number of major multinationals, together with other public companies, owner-managed businesses and private individuals throughout Britain, the US and Europe.

Foreign Connections: The practice is affiliated to New York-based Gibney Anthony & Flaherty, and to Munich-based David Hole and has links with other legal and professional services firms throughout the rest of the world's major commercial centres. Chris Magrath is also a qualified US Attorney, admitted to the New York State Bar.

Managing partner:	David Ashton
Senior partner:	Chris Magrath

WORKLOADS	
Immigration/ employment	40%
Crime	25%
Civil litigation	14%
Entertainment	12%
Commercial	6%
Property	3%

CONTACTS	
Civil litigation	Nick Goldstone
Commercial	David Ashton
Corporate fraud/Crime (general)	Gary Summers
Employment	Helen Jerry/Chris Magrath
Entertainment	Alexis Grower
Immigration	Chris Magrath
Property	David Ashton

MAIDMENTS

ST JOHNS COURT, 74 GARTSIDE STREET, MANCHESTER, M3 3EL
Tel: (0161) 834 0008 **Fax:** (0161) 832 4140

The Firm: Maidments is one of the country's leading criminal law practices with a significant reputation in the defence of Serious Crime and Commercial Fraud. The firm can be considered as a truly national criminal law firm and aims to continue its expansion through the opening of further offices in the country's major centres of criminal law practice. The firm is renowned for its tenacious and skilful defence of cases of Serious Crime and Commercial Fraud. The practice has offices in Manchester, London, Birmingham, Liverpool, Bolton and Sale.

Principal Areas of Work:

Crime: The practice undertakes a substantial volume of cases before Magistrates and Crown Courts in the North West, Merseyside, the Midlands, London, the South East and throughout the country. Representation of clients is undertaken on both a Legal Aid and private fee paying basis. The firm has been awarded the crime category franchise by the Legal Aid Board.

Serious Crime: The firm has undertaken representation in many notable cases throughout the country including Serious Crime cases of murder, conspiracy, robbery and prison mutiny. The practice has a substantial reputation in the defence of drug supply and importation cases.

Number of partners:	10
Assistant solicitors:	7
Other fee-earners:	44

WORKLOADS	
Commercial Fraud	40%
Criminal	30%
Serious Crime	30%

CONTACTS	
Company Fraud	Allan Maidment (London & Manchester)
Criminal	Alison Glynn (Manchester)
Lennox Manifold (Birmingham) James Parry (Liverpool)	
Jane Potter (Bolton) Lindsay Sutton (Sale)	
Serious Crime	Allan Maidment (London & Manchester), Mahan Manu (Birmingham)

Continues overleaf

Commercial Fraud: Work in Commercial Fraud is led by Allan Maidment and has involved many significant cases of Commercial Fraud including banking and insurance fraud, advance fee fraud, long firm fraud, DTI and Customs and Excise cases. Numerous referrals of this type of work are received from solicitors and other professionals.

Other Offices:

36 Young Street, Manchester M3 3FT. (0161) 834 0008

150 Regent Street, London W1R 5FA. (0171) 432 0456

177 Corporation Street, Birmingham B4 6RG. (0121) 200 2221

6 Stanley Street, Liverpool L1 6AF. (0151) 236 8100

113 Deansgate, Bolton BL1 1HB. (01204) 455 455

27 Cross Street, Sale, Cheshire M33 7FT. (0161) 969 8111

MAINPRICE & CO

80 EBURY STREET, LONDON, SW1W 9QD
Tel: (0171) 730 8705 **Fax:** (0171) 730 8706 **Email:** MAINPRICE-CO@EASYNET.CO.UK **Internet:** HTTP://WWW.MAINPRICE.CO.UK

Number of partners:	5

The Firm: Established in 1972, Mainprice and Co is the oldest practice that specialises exclusively in VAT. The firm was founded by Hugh Mainprice in 1972 after he left the Solicitor's Office of HM Customs and Excise in 1972 where he had assisted in drafting the original VAT legislation. It has acted for more clients before the VAT Tribunals, the High Court, the Court of Appeal and the House of Lords than any other firm in the UK and its clients have included many of the largest firms in the country as well as small firms and private individuals. In March 1998 the Firm uniquely represented two different clients in two VAT appeals heard on the same day in the European Court of Justice in Luxembourg. The Firm's consultants are all, individually, recognised as specialists in VAT law and the firm does not advise or provide legal services in any other matter other than Value Added Tax.

Languages spoken: French, Italian, Swahili.

Associated Office: Quarteira, Portugal.

MAITLAND WALKER

22 THE PARKS, MINEHEAD, TA24 8BT
Tel: (01643) 707777 **Fax:** (01643) 700020 **DX:** 117408 MINEHEAD **Email:** MAITWALK@COMPUSERVE.COM

Number of partners:	1
Assistant solicitors:	2
Other fee-earners:	2

WORKLOADS	
Competition/IP Law	40%
Commercial Litigation	30%
EC/Trade Law	20%
General Commercial	10%

The Firm: Established in 1996 by Julian Maitland-Walker, the firm has expanded rapidly to become one of the leading niche EC and Competition law practices. The firm acts for a wide range of commercial clients, individual traders, companies and trade associations. In addition, a consultancy service is offered as a facility to other law firms in both the UK and abroad in specialist EC and Competition law matters. The firm aims to provide the quality of service offered by City firms at a lower cost and to build a close personal relationship with clients to meet all their needs in the area of commercial legal advice.

Principal Areas of Work:

EC/Trade Law: advice on all aspects of EC law including freedom of movement and fredom of establishment, specialist advice on all aspects of national and international trade, operational logistics, anti-dumping investigations, state aids and public procurement.

Commercial Litigation: Group actions involving breach of EC Competition law in the brewery and petrol retailing sectors together with a range of other commercial disputes.

Competition/IP Law: advising on the application of Competition law to distribution, agency, franchising and other commercial agreements, representing clients before the EC Commission and the UK Competition Authorities in anti-trust investigations. Advising on know-how, trademark, copyrights, performing and broadcasting rights and other related intellectual property rights.

General Commercial: advice on mergers and acquisition transactions, joint ventures, banking and insurance law, commercial agreements, environmental law and commercial property transactions.

Consultancy Services: the firm offers a unique consultancy service to other law firms both in the UK and abroad providing specialist advice on competition and trade law and other areas of EC law. This enables other law firms to offer the services of Julian Maitland-Walker as an integral part of its services to clients through an "in-house" consultancy facility.

Other Offices: London Office: Tel 0171 222 9070 (in association with Campbell Hooper)

Languages Spoken: French, German, Italian

MALCOLM LYNCH

19 HIGH COURT LANE, THE CALLS, LEEDS, LS2 7EU
Tel: (0113) 242 9600 **Fax:** (0113) 234 2080 **DX:** 12100 LEEDS 1 **Email:** LAW@MALCOLMLYNCH.COM **Internet:** WWW.MALCOLMLYNCH.COM

The Firm: The firm is a niche company/commercial practice well known for its work for clients developing products and services for a sustainable future.

It has advised clients in the renewable energy industry for several years.

Its corporate finance work encompasses public share issues and bank security documentation for financial institutions and there is a strong focus on social and ethical investment.

The firm has a strong reputation in charity law and a large proportion of its clients are charities. Local government and housing associations also form a significant part of its client base.

Managing partner:	Malcolm Lynch
Senior partner:	Malcolm Lynch
Number of partners:	2
Assistant solicitors:	1
Other fee-earners:	3

WORKLOADS	
Charity Law	30%
Commercial Property	30%
Company/Commercial	30%
Employee Share Schemes and ESOP's	5%
Employment Law	5%

MALKINS Inigo House, 29 Bedford St, Covent Garden, London, WC2E 9ED **Tel:** (0171) 379 3385 **Fax:** (0171) 379 3137 **DX:** 40034 Covent Gdn. 2 **Ptnrs:** 12 **Asst solrs:** 1 **Other fee-earners:** 2 **Contact:** Kevin Bichard *Work includes commercial property, corporate work, commercial litigation and private client. Significant overseas connections particularly in the Far East.*

MALLINICKS ATTORNEYS 25 Savile Row, London, W1X 1AA **Tel:** (0171) 333 2700 **Fax:** (0171) 439 0566 **Email:** attorneys@mallinicks.co.uk **Ptnrs:** 6 **Asst solrs:** 1 **Contact:** Mr Justin Hardcastle *Telecommunications, exchange control and investment, intellectual property, joint ventures in South Africa, immigration, private client services, litigation, arbitration.*

MANBY & STEWARD

MANDER HOUSE, MANDER CENTRE, WOLVERHAMPTON, WV1 3NE
Tel: (01902) 578000 **Fax:** (01902) 424321/713564 **DX:** 10403

GEORGE HOUSE, ST JOHN'S SQUARE, WOLVERHAMPTON, WV2 4BZ
Tel: (01902) 578000 **Fax:** (01902) 311886 **DX:** 702431

BLOUNT HOUSE, HALL COURT, TELFORD TOWN CENTRE, TF3 4NQ
Tel: (01952) 291525 **Fax:** (01952) 291921 **DX:** 707202

1 ST LEONARD'S CLOSE, BRIDGNORTH, SHROPSHIRE, WV16 4EL
Tel: (01746) 761436 **Fax:** (01746) 766764 **DX:** 23202

The Firm: With a head office in Wolverhampton and offices in Telford and Bridgnorth, Manby & Steward provide an extensive range of services for the Business and Private client. They are progressive, established and have a structure of specialist groups, which are partner led. They aim to provide practical advice responsive to clients' requirements.

In 1997 Manby & Steward merged with Woolley Beavon solicitors of Wolverhampton.

Nature of Clientele: The firm acts for a broad range of private clients, businesses and companies, developers, builders and housing associations.

Foreign Languages: French, Portuguese, Spanish, Hindi, Punjabi and Japanese.

Contacts:

Agriculture	*Stephen Corfield*
Commercial litigation	*Clive Williams*
Commercial property	*Kevin Styles*
Company/ commercial	*Gavin Southall*
Planning law	*Niall Blackie*
Private client	*David Shepherd*

Managing partner:	Clive H.G. Williams
Senior partner:	John Thorneycroft
Number of partners:	14
Assistant solicitors:	15
Other fee-earners:	21

WORKLOADS	
Commercial conveyancing	33%
Litigation	25%
Residential conveyancing	19%
Company/ commercial	14%
Private client	9%

MANCHES & CO

ALDWYCH HOUSE, 81 ALDWYCH, LONDON, WC2B 4RP
Tel: (0171) 404 4433 **Fax:** (0171) 430 1133 **DX:** 76 **Email:** MANCHES@MANCHES.CO.UK

The Firm: Manches & Co is a full service City firm at the forefront in a number of specialist legal practice areas and industrial sectors. Manches & Co has arrived at its current position among London's leading firms through organic growth and strategic merger. This has enabled it to consolidate its expertise in corporate and commercial, property, litigation and banking and to expand in specialist areas such as employment, intellectual property (comprising media and publishing) information technology, insurance (including Lloyd's) and family law. Manches & Co recognises that the legal market is client driven and aims to offer clients premium service and niche expertise at competitive prices. To this end, the firm emphasises a plain speaking, straightforward, value-for-money approach and is run along corporate lines, with all non-legal functions handled by the Chief Executive.

Principal Areas of Work:

Company and Commercial: (*Contact Partner:* Alasdair Simpson). *Work includes:* M&A, venture capital, corporate reorganisations, AIM flotations, joint ventures and partnerships, service agreements, share options and other executive incentive schemes, competition law, franchising, commercial tax and employment.

Property: (*Contact Partner:* Louis Manches). *Work includes:* all aspects of commercial property, including investment and development work for institutions and property companies, social housing, secured lending and joint ventures, retail property and construction.

Litigation: (*Contact Partner:* James Foster). *Work includes:* commercial dispute resolution with particular expertise in construction and property, banking, insolvency, insurance, product liability, breach of contract and intellectual property. Cross-department groups focus on employment, publishing tax, computers and environmental law.

Intellectual Property: (*Contact Partner:* Peter Stevens) *Work includes:* Advertising, Sales Promotions, Marketing and Trade Description Law, Biotechnology, Computer Law, Copyrights, Film, Television and Entertainment product and services, Multimedia Exploitation, Passing off, Publishing, Defamation and UK and EC Competition.

Family: (*Contact Partner:* Jane Simpson). *Work includes:* divorce, children, financial provision, separation agreements, adoption, guardianship, affiliation proceedings, and jurisdiction crossing.

Employment: (*Contact Partner:* Alasdair Simpson). *Work includes:* executive remuneration and benefits, termination package, staff manual, discrimination policies, unfair and wrongful dismissal claims in the Industrial Tribunal, County and High Court.

Tax: (*Contact Partner:* Stephen Goldstraw). *Work includes:* mergers and acquisitions, joint ventures, flotation planning, profit extraction, leasing, management buy-outs, employee benefits, property tax, VAT planning, stamp duty planning, partnership tax, off-shore trading arrangements, insurance and tax, company pension schemes and tax appeals.

Personal Estate Planning: (*Contact Partner:* Susan Midha). *Work includes:* estate planning, preparation of wills, establishment of trusts, administration of estates and charities.

Recruitment and Training: There are currently 17 trainee solicitors. The firm's Director of Education and Training has responsibility for directing and monitoring each individual's training, and a programme of regular internal lectures has been evolved to assist in this process. CV's should be sent to Ms Philippa Firth at the London office or Mr David Tighe in Oxford.

Senior partner:	A.J. Simpson
Number of partners:	46
Assistant solicitors:	54
Other fee-earners:	23

WORKLOADS	
Corporate	22%
Commercial litigation	20%
Commercial property	20%
Family law	12%
Intellectual property	8%
Banking and insolvency	7%
Employment	4%
Social housing	4%
Personal estate planning	3%

CONTACTS	
Banking	Mark Douglas
Commercial property	Louis Manches
Commercial tax	Stephen Goldstraw
Commercial/I.T.	Peter Stevens
Corporate	Melvin Pedro
Employment	Alasdair Simpson
Environment	George Gandy
Family law	Jane Simpson
Insolvency	Lorinda Peasland
Insurance	Peter Angel/Charles Gordon
Intellectual property	John Rubinstein
Litigation	James Foster
Media	Paul Woolf
Personal estate planning	Susan Midha
Publishing	Bernard Nyman
Social housing	Richard Frost

MANDER HADLEY & CO' 1 The Quadrant, Coventry, CV1 2DW *Tel:* (01203) 631212 *Fax:* (01203) 633131 *DX:* 11204 *Ptnrs:* 12 *Asst solrs:* 3 *Other fee-earners:* 7

MAPLES TEESDALE

21 LINCOLN'S INN FIELDS, LONDON, WC2A 3DU
Tel: (0171) 831 6501 **Fax:** (0171) 405 3867 **DX:** 192 LONDON **Email:** ENQ@MAPLESTEESDALE.CO.UK

The Firm: Maples Teesdale can trace its origins to 1782. The firm aims to provide a first class service to business and private clients and value for money. The firm's clients range from a government department and blue chip household name companies to smaller companies and private individuals.

Principal Areas of Work:

Commercial Property: The department deals with all aspects of commercial property work including acquisitions and disposals, landlord and tenant matters, secured lending, large scale developments, funding agreements, joint ventures and auctions.

Litigation: The department handles a broad spectrum of commercial litigation ranging from simple debt collection to complex contractual, company and partnership disputes and insolvency matters. It also handles all aspects of property-related litigation and disputes including landlord and tenant matters, management problems, reconstruction/redevelopment, eviction actions, forfeiture work, rent collection, rent reviews, lease renewals, service charge disputes, dilapidations claims, disputed options to break, planning enquiries, secured loan realisations and restructurings and professional negligence arising from the provision of property-related services. In addition, it deals with all aspects of building contracts and consultants' appointments.

Commercial: The department advises on the formation, acquisition, sale and merger of companies and partnerships, capital structures, shareholders' agreements, loan and equity finance and participation, joint ventures, employment, terms of business and a wide variety of commercial contracts.

Private Client: The department advises on all aspects of family affairs including the preparation of wills, financial and tax planning, the formation and administration of trusts, the administration of estates, matrimonial matters and the formation of and advice to charities.

Residential Property: A full range of residential property services is provided to private clients and the department also undertakes the purchase, sale and lettings of agricultural land and estates.

Senior partner:	Richard Read
Number of partners:	11
Assistant solicitors:	6
Other fee-earners:	10

CONTACTS	
Commercial	Richard Read
Commercial property	Mark Bryan
Litigation	Paul Matcham
Private client	Hugh Wilson
Residential property	Edward Bliss

MAPLES
TEESDALE
SOLICITORS

MARGARET BENNETT

CHARLTON HOUSE, 5A BLOOMSBURY SQUARE, LONDON, WC1A 2LX
Tel: (0171) 404 6465 **Fax:** (0171) 240 5492 **DX:** 35740 BLOOMSBURY 1 **Email:** EXCLUSIVE@DIVORCE.UK.COM

Established in 1990 as the first law firm practising exclusively in Family Law (uniquely with in-house divorce counselling, as well), Margaret Bennett Solicitors, provides outstanding experience in this specialist field.

The Firm: The Senior Partner, Margaret Bennett, is Chairman of the Family Law Committee of the International Bar Association, a founder member and former Vice-President of the International Academy of Matrimonial Lawyers, founder of the Intercountry Adoption Lawyers' Association, a Deputy District Judge, Principal Registry of the Family Division, High Court, London and a frequent speaker at national and international conferences. The consultant, John D. Bieber, is the author of *If Divorce is the Only Way* published by Penguin Books. The consultant counsellor is Lady Patricia Harris, co-founder (1980) of the Divorce Conciliation and Advisory Service. All Solicitors within the firm are members of the SFLA.

Principal Areas of Work: Practising exclusively in family law requires a high level of understanding as well as expertise. Divorce is a very distressing experience. The firm offers its own in-house counselling service for clients who need help with the emotional burden of marital breakdown, creating a better awareness of client needs and how their problems may best be resolved.

Where children are involved time may be of the essence. Such cases are handled with the utmost sensitivity, the child's needs being paramount. The senior partner is a member of the Lord Chancellor's Panel of Solicitors on Child Abduction, the firm having sound expertise in cases under The Hague and European Conventions on the Civil Aspects of International Child Abduction.

The firm's work in this area is facilitated by a close association with professional firms around the world. In complex international cases working closely with a client's other professional advisers often achieves the best and most creative results.

Senior and Managing Partner:	
	Margaret H. Bennett
Number of partners:	5
Assistant solicitors:	2
Associate:	1
Other fee-earners:	1

WORKLOADS	
Family law	100%

CONTACTS	
Family law	Margaret H. Bennett

Margaret Bennett Solicitors prides itself on being innovative. This involves being able to put together a team for any client problem, enabling it to handle the most urgent and substantial of cases. It also means meeting the challenges of contemporary life, such as UK and intercountry adoption and the growing tendency of couples to cohabit outside marriage. Selective with their clientele Margaret Bennett Solicitors can devote the time and attention to each matter that it deserves.

Foreign Languages: French, German and Italian

MARGRAVES

OLD COURT CHAMBERS, LLANDRINDOD WELLS, LD1 5EY
Tel: (01597) 825565 **Fax:** (01597) 825220 **DX:** 200154 LLANDRINDOD **Email:** LAW@MARGRAVES.CO.UK **Web Site:** www.wyenet.co.uk/margraves

The Firm: Margraves is an established niche practice specialising in wills, trusts, probate, estate and inheritance tax planning. The principal of the firm, Clive Margrave-Jones, has devoted his professional life to this field as a practitioner, visiting university lecturer and an established author and editor of eight publications in this and related fields.

The area of agricultural law is covered by Christopher Rodgers, the author of numerous texts. Margraves also receives instructions on a consultancy basis from solicitors, accountants, IFA's and other professions.

Senior partner:	Clive Margrave-Jones
Number of partners:	1
Assistant solicitors:	3

WORKLOADS	
Private client	90%
Agricultural law	10%

CONTACTS	
Agricultural law	Christopher Parker Rodgers
Private client	Clive Margrave-Jones

MARRIOTT HARRISON

12 GREAT JAMES STREET, LONDON, WC1N 3DR
Tel: (0171) 209 2000 **Fax:** (0171) 209 2001 **DX:** 0001 LONDON CHANCERY LANE **Email:** EMAIL@MARRIOTTHARRISON.CO.UK

This central London firm provides a range of commercial and corporate services, with particular emphasis on media law and tax.

The Firm: Most of the partners have been partners in major London firms which they had left with a commitment to provide a high-quality personalised service to clients. The majority of the founding partners specialised in the media industry and although the firm has grown with strong expertise in corporate, commercial, tax and litigation matters, specialisation in the ever more complex media industry remains the hallmark of the practice.

Types of work undertaken:

The Media Group: The media group deals with all aspects of production of software in its widest sense (films, television, music and sound recordings, CDi, CD-ROM, computer games, computer programs and the like) through to their delivery to the consumer. This involves in-depth knowledge of intellectual property rights and copyright as well as regulatory matters relating to broadcasting, cable and satellite operations. Sports representation includes involvement in Formula One motor racing. Clients include multinational media corporations, cable channels and operators, major US studios, banks, film distributors, UK studios, leading computer games publishers, film and television production companies and creative talent.

Company and Commercial: Company and commercial expertise is provided in such areas as mergers, acquisitions and disposals, management buy-outs and venture capital, restructuring, banking, financial services, Eastern Europe, technology, software and intellectual property. The department also advises on a wide variety of commercial agreements and arrangements. The group is particularly strong in venture capital and corporate acquisitions both within and without the firm's media industry clients which it increasingly supports in a broad range of complex commercial transactions, including television and radio licence applications.

The Tax Department: The tax department advises on a range of international commercial activities and has an established facility for setting up offshore structures. It has a reputation for providing clear practical advice and for developing innovative structures to meet client's commercial and tax objectives.

The Litigation Group: The litigation group is widely experienced in commercial litigation with particular expertise in media-related cases and general intellectual property matters. Considerable work is undertaken in co-operation with US lawyers in international litigation involving intellectual property rights. There is a substantial proportion of interlocutory work seeking injunctive relief.

Managing partner:	Frank Bloom
Number of partners:	14
Assistant solicitors:	7
Consultants:	3
Other fee-earners:	1

WORKLOADS	
Company/commercial/tax	50%
Media	35%
Litigation	10%
Property	5%

CONTACTS	
Commercial/Tax	Stephen Mullens
Company	Jon Sweet
Litigation	Peter Curnock
Media	William Hinshelwood
New Media/Music	Tony Morris
Property	Vivienne Elson

MARRON DODDS

1 MERIDAN SOUTH, MERIDAN BUSINESS PARK, LEICESTER, LE3 2WY
Tel: (0116) 289 2200 **Fax:** (0116) 289 3733 **DX:** 710910 LEICESTER MERIDIAN

32 FRIAR LANE, LEICESTER, LE1 5RA
Tel: (0116) 262 8596/ 253 8585 **Fax:** (0116) 251 8322/ 253 0212 **DX:** 10830 LEICESTER 1

The Firm: The commercial practice of Marron Dodds is conveniently located a very short distance from Junction 21 of the M1 Motorway. The firm has an established reputation in the areas of planning development and environmental law and specialist advice is provided in all areas of commercial property, company/commercial, commercial litigation and employment law. In the city centre there is a legal aid franchised practice providing extensive representation in the local criminal courts and a 24 hour police station attendance service; and a range of services are provided for the individual client with an emphasis on personal injury litigation, medical negligence, matrimonial disputes, care proceedings and welfare law.

Senior partner:	Peter Marron
Number of partners:	14
Assistant solicitors:	11
Other fee-earners:	12

WORKLOADS	
Commercial and public law	45%
Criminal litigation	35%
Civil litigation and matrimonial	20%

Contacts:

Civil litigation	*Vera Stamenkovich*
Commercial property	*Nick Robinson*
Company/commercial	*Kevin Sumner*
Criminal litigation	*Brian Dodds*
Family/matrimonial	*Manjit Obhi*
Planning	*John Edmond*

MARRONS 58 Jesmond Road West, Newcastle upon Tyne, NE2 4PQ *Tel:* (0191) 281 1304 *Fax:* (0191) 212 0080 *DX:* 62555 Jesmond *Ptnrs:* 3 *Asst solrs:* 3 *Other fee-earners:* 3

MARSDEN HUCK 3 Ribblesdale Place, Preston, PR1 3NA *Tel:* (01772) 254048 *Fax:* (01772) 204367 *DX:* 17158 Preston 1

MARSHALL & GALPIN Vanbrugh House, 20 St. Michael's Street, Oxford, OX1 2EA *Tel:* (01865) 792300 *Fax:* (01865) 793616 *Ptnrs:* 11 *Asst solrs:* 14 *Other fee-earners:* 3

MARSH, FERRIMAN & CHEALE Southfield House, 11 Liverpool Gardens, Worthing, BN11 1SB *Tel:* (01903) 228200 *Fax:* (01903) 228201 *DX:* 3701 Worthing 1 *Ptnrs:* 6 *Asst solrs:* 4 *Other fee-earners:* 10

MARSONS SOLICITORS

AMADEUS HOUSE, 33-39 ELMFIELD ROAD, BROMLEY, BR1 1LT
Tel: (0181) 313 1300 **Fax:** (0181) 466 7920 **DX:** 121100 BROMLEY 9 **Email:** BROMLEY@MARSONS.CO.UK

4-5 MARKET PLACE, BEXLEYHEATH, DA6 7DU
Tel: (0181) 303 0168 **Fax:** (0181) 298 9181 **DX:** 130386 BEXLEYHEATH 4 **Email:** BXHEATH@MARSONS.CO.UK

A very successful and award winning practice.

- Kent Company of the Year 1998
- Winner – The Law Firm Management Award 1998
- Winner – The Legal Executive Award 1998

Gross turnover increased by 300% in five years and staff numbers doubled to 115 in four years.

Chief Executive:	B.J. Marson
Practice Director:	Sue Marson
Finance Director:	David Goulden
Human Resources:	Debbie Viner
Number of partners:	7
Assistant solicitors:	9
Other fee-earners:	55

Principal Areas of Work: Contacts:

Social Housing or Property Litigation *Kevin Lee;* Commercial Property *Stephen Chubb;* Professional Negligence *Jennifer White;* New Homes Development *Jayne Dempster;* Private Client *Caroline Landes;* Personal Injury *Elizabeth King;* Company/Commercial *Natalka Solowski;* Mortgage Lenders *Brian Marson;* Property *Brian Marson;* Title Insurance *Brian Marson;* Crime *Georgina Earle-Hutton.*

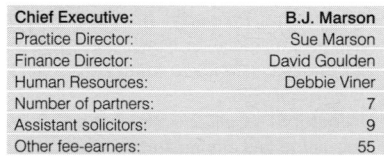

INVESTOR IN PEOPLE

MARTINEAU JOHNSON

ST. PHILIPS HOUSE, ST. PHILIPS PLACE, BIRMINGHAM, B3 2PP
Tel: (0121) 200 3300 **Fax:** (0121) 200 3330 **DX:** 13031 **Email:** MARTJOHN@MARTJOHN.CO.UK

The Firm: Martineau Johnson is one of the four biggest independent single establishment firms in the provinces with 33 partners and over 100 fee earners. Tracing its roots back to 1828 the firm has in recent years adopted a policy of basing its practice on the specific needs of clients and commercial sectors. While primarily a commercially based firm, Martineau Johnson boasts market leadership in Private Client and Education sector work.

Principal Areas of Work:

Banking: (*Contact:* Ian Baker). Acting for banks in funding and financial reconstruction work.

Charities: (*Contact:* Michael Fea). Formation, financial and administration advice for trustees and beneficiaries.

Commercial Agreements: (*Contact:* Geraldine Tickle). Joint ventures, franchising and conditions of sale and purchase.

Commercial Litigation: (*Contact:* Andrew Spooner). Civil litigation and arbitration of most kinds are conducted.

Commercial Property: (*Contact:* Joanna Lawson-King). Sales and purchases, leases and option agreements of commercial, industrial, office and investment property, including acting for institutional investors.

Company: (*Contact:* Richard Wrigley). Sales and purchases of shares in and assets of limited companies.

Construction: (*Contact:* Paul Mountain). Contentious and non-contentious construction and civil engineering work is handled for principally developer but also contractor and sub-contractor clients.

Construction Litigation: (*Contact:* Andrew Spooner). Arbitration and other proceedings arising out of building contracts.

Corporate: (*Contact:* Michael Winwood). There are a number of listed company clients for whom Stock Exchange work is undertaken, as well as for companies going to the market.

Corporate Finance: (*Contact:* Richard Wrigley). Management buy-outs and buy-ins.

Debt: (*Contact:* Andrew Adams). Volume debt collection work of all kinds.

Development and Special Projects: (*Contact:* Barry Sankey). Sales and purchases and options relating to land to building and development projects.

EC & Competition: (*Contact:* Geraldine Tickle). Competition law including merger control, MMC enquiries, EU complaints, pricing, trading conduct, and its application to distribution, joint ventures, franchising and licensing.

Ecclesiastical: (*Contact:* Hugh Carslake). The firm acts as Registrar to the Birmingham Diocese.

Education: (*Contact:* Nicola Hart). Retained solicitors to 12 Universities and about 20 Colleges of Further Education.

Employment: (*Contact:* Ian Marshall). Advising clients on all aspects, contentious and non-contentious, including discrimination and equal rights.

Insolvency: (*Contact:* Brian Aikman). Acting for administrators, receivers, liquidators and trustees in bankruptcy and for creditors affected by debtors' financial difficulties.

Intellectual Property: (*Contact:* William Barker). Copyright, trade marks, passing off and patent advice for owners and users of such rights.

Licensing: (*Contact:* Andrew Spooner). Obtaining liquor licenses and advising on the law in that area.

Pensions: (*Contact:* Simon Laight). Acting for pension fund trustees in relation to formation and administration.

Tax – Private: (*Contact:* Matthew Hansell). Advising private clients on their tax planning and administration of returns.

Tax – Corporate: (*Contact:* Yvonne Redfern). Advising on all aspects of corporate taxation.

Town & Country Planning: (*Contact:* Barry Sankey). Advising business and investor clients on law in this area, and its relationship to development transactions and environmental questions.

Trusts, Settlements, & Wills: (*Contact:* Hugh Carslake). Advising private clients on personal financial planning and arrangements through the creation of these instruments as well as the administration of estates.

Venture Capital: (*Contact:* Roger Blears). The firm has a particular specialism in the financing of technology based companies having been the first solicitors firm to sponsor such a company onto the Stock Exchange.

Managing partner:	David Gwyther
Senior partner:	Michael Shepherd
Number of partners:	33
Assistant solicitors:	46
Other fee-earners:	34

WORKLOADS	
Property	22%
Litigation	17%
Corporate	15%
Private client	15%
Commercial agreement & Utilities	8%
Banking & Insolvency	7%
Intellectual property	6%
Education	5%
Employment	5%

CONTACTS	
Banking	Ian Baker
Charities	Michael Fea
Commercial agreements	Geraldine Tickle
Commercial litigation	Andrew Spooner
Commercial property	Joanna Lawson-King
Company	Richard Wrigley
Construction	Paul Mountain
Corporate	Michael Winwood
Corporate finance	Richard Wrigley
Debt	Andrew Adams
Development and special projects	Barry Sankey
EC and competition	Geraldine Tickle
Ecclesiastical	Hugh Carslake
Education	Nicola Hart
Insolvency	Brian Aikman
Intellectual property	William Barker
Licensing	Andrew Spooner
Pensions	Simon Laight
Tax – corporate	Yvonne Redfern
Tax – private	Matthew Hansell
Town and country planning	Barry Sankey
Trusts, settlements and wills	Hugh Carslake
Venture Capital	Roger Blears

MARTINEAU JOHNSON
SOLICITORS

Foreign Connections: The firm is a member of an international legal association and has fellow member firms with which it enjoys close connections in the major trading centres of the world.

Recruitment & Training: Up to 5 trainee solicitors are recruited annually. Training and prospects are excellent, most of the present partners having served articles with the firm. Application forms are available from Diane Price, Human Resources Director.

MARTIN-KAYE

HAZLEDINE HOUSE, CENTRAL SQ., TELFORD CENTRE, TELFORD, TF3 4JL
Tel: (01952) 291757 **Fax:** (01952) 291759 **DX:** 28073

Principal Areas of Work:

Company and commercial *Contact:* Stuart J. Haynes
Intellectual property
Technology transfer
Franchising
Commercial conveyancing *Contact:* Barry Stimpson
Landlord and tenant *Contact:* Robert Hughes
Commercial and general litigation *Contact:* Graham W. Davies
Debt collection Personal injury *Contact:* Christopher Cann
Probate and trusts *Contact:* Roderick M. Kirby
Agricultural and charity law *Contact:* Barry Stimpson
Employment law *Contact:* Andrew E. Wylde
Financial services *Contact:* Bryan Cash

Managing partner:	Andrew J.L. Green
Senior partner:	Graham Davies (Chairman)
Number of partners:	8
Assistant solicitors:	2
Other fee-earners:	10

WORKLOADS	
Commercial	40%
Property	40%
Probate and Trust	20%

Foreign connections: The firm has extensive experience in business abroad and was a founder member of I.A.G. International, a European Group of professional advisors.

Nature of clientele: A broad base of private and commercial clients, including well known multi national companies. Agency and legal aid work undertaken.

Recruitment and training: The firm recruits on a regular basis and provides first-class all round training for trainee solicitors in each of the firms departments. (*Contact:* Mrs Maguire).

MARTIN TOLHURST PARTNERSHIP 7 Wrotham Rd, Gravesend, DA11 0PD *Tel:* (01474) 325531 *Fax:* (01474) 560771 *DX:* 6801 Gravesend *Ptnrs:* 8 *Asst solrs:* 4 *Other fee-earners:* 7

MARTIN PROWEL, EDWARDS & DAVIES Hallinans House, 22 Newport Road, Cardiff, CF2 1TD *Tel:* (01222) 496316 *Fax:* (01222) 498566 *DX:* Cardiff 33037 *Ptnrs:* 5 *Asst solrs:* 4 *Other fee-earners:* 2

MASON BOND King Charles House, King Charles Croft, Leeds, LS1 6LA **Tel:** (0113) 242 4444 **Fax:** (0113) 246 7542 **DX:** 26409 **Ptnrs:** 5 **Asst solrs:** 1 **Other fee-earners:** 5 **Contact:** Mr Stephen Mason *Specialise in tour operator, travel and holiday law. Also handles childcare, family and criminal law.*

WORKLOADS			
Travel Industry	70%	Child care work	20%

MASON & MOORE DUTTON Kirkton House, 4 Hunter St, Chester, CH1 2AS **Tel:** (01244) 348881 **Fax:** (01244) 351513 **DX:** 22151 **Ptnrs:** 7 **Asst solrs:** 2 **Contact:** Mr Rory Lea *Established 1890 General practice known for agriculture and matrimonial work. Also private client work, commercial work for SME's, general litigation and liquor licensing. Legal Aid Franchise.*

MASONS

30 AYLESBURY STREET, LONDON, EC1R 0ER
Tel: (0171) 490 4000 **Fax:** (0171) 490 2545 **DX:** 53313 CLERKENWELL **Email:** INFO@MASONS.COM **Internet:** WWW.MASONS.COM

The Firm: Masons has offices in London, Bristol, Manchester, Leeds, Brussels, Dublin, Hong Kong, Guangzhou (PRC), Singapore and Glasgow° and associated offices across Scandinavia and in Cairo. The firm works regularly in continental Europe, the Middle East, the Pacific Rim, Africa and the Indian subcontinent. Masons provides a broad range of legal services and is well known for advising the construction, engineering, and information technology industries. While the firm's main specialities include large scale (often international) dispute resolution and advice on major infrastructure projects generally, Masons also offers a full range of commercial, legal risk management, tax and financial planning and charity services.

Principal Areas of Work:

Construction and Engineering: Masons is involved, in the UK and internationally at every stage of the construction process on projects as diverse as airports, tunnels, motorways, rail transport systems, marinas, water systems, reservoirs, hospitals and oil rigs. This can be in the context of joint ventures, BOT and PFI schemes or for individual companies. Structuring, negotiating, drafting and advising generally on contracts, associated documentation and project finance are major fields of activity. The firm handles national and international disputes whether in the context of arbitration, litigation or ADR including ICC, LCIA and other institutional and non-institutional arbitration work. The firm's Construction and Civil Engineering department is divided into sectors as follows: building; civil engineering; international arbitration; power; process, oil and gas; transportation and water.

Information & Technology: A strong and experienced team for the information and technology industries, both national and international; suppliers and users. Work involves resolving a wide range of disputes – the largest team in the UK dealing with IT project-based disputes. Masons also undertakes drafting and negotiation of agreements for the supply and procurement of software systems and information; advising on software development, licensing and distribution; and establishing and protecting rights in technology and advising on all aspects of the millennium date change problem. Specialisms include outsourcing, joint marketing ventures, system supply and procurement, channel distribution, data protection and international data flows. With the convergence of computing and telecommunications, an experienced team is now servicing the online services and new media sectors (covering both content- and technology-related work). Masons' own advanced and distinctive use of IT/IS gives particular insight in this area.

Commercial Dispute Resolution: Advice is given in relation to commercial disputes in a wide range of areas including construction and engineering, technology, intellectual property, international trade, insurance, fraud and general commercial matters. Dispute resolution techniques include the traditional methods of litigation and arbitration and, increasingly, Alternative Dispute Resolution procedures. Masons pioneered the application of information technology to the effective management of complex litigation matters and continues to be at the forefront of such use.

Project and Asset Finance: Masons' Project and Asset Finance Group advises on the financing requirements and the effective management of both domestic and overseas infrastructure and industrial projects, including those arising from the government's Private Finance Initiative; the financing of ships, aircraft, plant and machinery; cross-border and tax based leasing; sales aid or vendor leasing; Local Authority leasing; vehicle leasing; 'big' and 'middle' ticket equipment leasing; construction, trade and commercial finance; financial instruments and derivatives; and corporate banking.

Property Litigation: Advice is given on the full range of property disputes and property management, including landlord and tenant matters such as rent reviews, dilapidations and repossessions. This involves acting for a wide range of businesses with extensive and strategically important property portfolios such as those in the leisure and drinks sectors.

Corporate & Commercial: The firm advises on all aspects of corporate and commercial work particularly corporate finance, privatisations, concession arrangements, mergers and acquisitions, buy-outs and venture capital. A core area of activity is advising on national and international joint ventures, partnerships and other strategic and operational alliances.

India: Masons' India Unit, established in 1987, was the first such unit abroad. It acts for a wide range of international companies doing business in India and Indian companies doing business in the EU. Its Indian qualified lawyers advise on matters in Delhi, Bombay, Calcutta, Madras and Bangalore. It is involved in applications to Government authorities; BOT/ BOO's in the energy sector and construction and civil engineering; and for a wide range of industrial sectors; transfer of technology and licensing; acquisitions; collaborations and arbitration and litigation.

Worldwide Managing Partner:	Anthony Bunch
UK Managing Partner:	Peter Wood
Senior Partner:	John Bishop
Number of partners:	74
Assistant Solicitors:	157
Other fee-earners:	69

CONTACTS

Asset Finance and Leasing	Nigel Weiss, London
Banking	Christopher Brown, London
Building	Mark Collingwood, Bristol
Civil Engineering	Laurence Fryer, London
Commercial Dispute Resolution	
	Raymond Werbicki, London
	Edward Davies, Manchester
	Adam Harris, Bristol
	Mark Richards, Leeds
	Robert Lewington, Hong Kong
Construction & Engineering	
	Andrew Hibbert, Manchester
	Martin Harman, London
	Mark Collingwood, Bristol
	Dean Lewis, Hong Kong
	Keith Hartley, Leeds
	Dudley Solan, Dublin
	Iain Black, Singapore
	Vincent Connor, Glasgow
Consulting	Gail Swaffield, London
Corporate & Commercial	Russell Booker, London
	Richard Bates, Hong Kong
Debt recovery	Richard Williams, London
Employment	Michael Ryley, London
Environmental	Bonnie Martin, Bristol
	Mark Richards, Leeds
	John Moritz, Manchester
	Peter Stockdale, London
EU law	Barbara Linehan, Brussels
	Mark Lane, London
Health & Safety	Susan Fink, London
India	Arun Singh, London
Information & Technology	Andrew Smith, Manchester
	Adam Harris, Bristol
	Shekagh Gaskill, Leeds
	Robert McCallough, London
Insolvency	Richard Williams, London
International Arbitration	Phillip Capper, London
Oil and Gas	Neil Bogle, London
Planning	John Moritz, Manchester
	Bonnie Martin, Bristol
	Peter Stockdale, London
Power	Martin Roberts, London
Process	Peter Cassidy, London
Project Finance and PFI	Steven Bond,
	Steven Janes, London
Property	Colin Rowe, Manchester
	Beverley Pike, Bristol
	Guy Jordan, London
Property Litigation	Anne Molyneux, London
	Bonnie Martin, Bristol
Tax & Financial Planning	Peter Instone, London
Transportation	Martin Harman, London
Water	Mark Lane, London

EU Law: A multi-discipline unit co-ordinated from London and Brussels gives advice on the impact of EU law on corporate risk management issues and transactions particularly in those industries or areas of domestic law where EU law is having a significant impact, e.g. construction and engineering, information technology, transborder data flows and data protection, the energy industries, the environment, health and safety, employment, competition law, and public procurement law.

Planning: As with Masons' other Practice Areas, the planning function is operated as a compliment to the Firm's principal strengths and focuses within the construction, engineering and property development industries. As such, planning lawyers advise within teams involved with major project, infrastructural and PFI development activities. The Firm advises across the regulatory regime from 'planning to negotiation' to the preparation and conduct of inquiries relating to statutory plans, appeals and compulsory purchase. The environmental aspect of planning is an increasingly important areas of work.

Environmental: Masons' environmental law service is focused towards Masons' key business sectors including construction and engineering, property and infrastructure development, energy, transportation, water and waste. By drawing upon the skills and experience of all other areas of the firm's expertise it offers a fully integrated approach particularly in the areas of the assessment and management of risk.

Health and Safety: Health and safety services extend from assisting in planning for the impact of legislative requirements on business activities through to prosecutions and other contentious matters.

Property: Masons' property-related services are channelled into five initiatives: (a) activities allied to the principal focuses of the Firm involving major project, infrastructural and PFI development; (b) commercial property development; (c) commercial and residential investment (including inward investment); (d) property management for investors and businesses (the Firm provided property and planning advice to a host of businesses within another of its key business sectors, the IT world); (e) a specialist house building and housing service.

Tax and Financial Planning: Masons offers a comprehensive service with a significant international element, covering tax (planning and appeals), trusts (UK and overseas), wills, and probate, administration of estates, charity (creation and advice).

Employment: Masons deals with all legal aspects of employer and employee relations, including employee documentation, industrial tribunal and other employment-based proceedings, the resolution of individual and collective disputes, employee benefits, TUPE related issues and immigration.

Consulting: Masons offers consultancy services in the field of legal risk management, including legal risk audits and dispute pre-emption advice particularly for in-house legal departments. Building on the firm's reputation in using IT, advice is also given on IT strategy, system specification and specialist technologies such as hypertext, imaging and document assembly.

Insolvency: Masons acts for insolvency practitioners generally and also advises company management and individuals on insolvency matters.

Debt Recovery: The firm operates a fully computerised debt recovery service covering all stages of the process from correspondence through to court proceedings and enforcement if necessary.

UK Offices: The firm operates on a national basis and serves clients from offices in London, Bristol, Manchester, Leeds and Glasgow°.

Overseas Offices: Masons' **Hong Kong** office provides an all round commercial service to clients in Hong Kong and other parts of the Far East with particular emphasis on construction and engineering projects, commercial litigation, company commercial and property and China related advice. The firm has an office in **Guangzhou**, China which offers general commercial advice particularly on joint venture agreements with PRC entities as well as servicing clients in the construction and engineering fields throughout China. The **Singapore** office opened last year in response to the needs of Major Projects clients the office concentrates on all aspects of Major Project work, including construction, financing, I.T. and cross-border dispute resolution across S.E. Asia. Masons is the first overseas law firm to open an office in Ireland with the launch of an office in **Dublin**. The office is an extension of the firm's worldwide construction and engineering practice area. For details on its **Brussels** office, please refer to main classification: EU Law. Masons has extensive contacts and associations with law firms and consultants on a worldwide basis.

Recruitment and Training: The firm usually recruits 15-17 trainee solicitors each year. Apply by Masons' application form with covering letter to Richard Laudy, London office.

Other Offices:
Bristol: *Contact:* Mark Collingwood. *Tel:* (0117) 924 5678
Manchester: *Contact:* Andrew Hibbert. *Tel:* (0161) 877 3777
Leeds: *Contact:* Keith Hartley. *Tel:* (0113) 233 8905

Continues overleaf

Glasgow°: *Contact:* Vincent Connor. *Tel:* (0141) 314 3968
Brussels: *Contact:* Barbara Linehan. *Tel:* (32) 2 646 0260
Dublin: *Contact:* Dudley Solan. *Tel:* +353 (0)1 638 3838
Hong Kong: *Contact:* Robert Lewington. *Tel:* 2521 5621
Guangzhou: *Contact:* Martin McCann. *Tel:* 86 208 778 2788
Singapore: *Contact:* Iain Black. *Tel:* +65 339 8577

° associated

MATTHEW ARNOLD & BALDWIN

PO BOX NO. 101, 20 STATION RD, WATFORD, WD1 1HT
Tel: (01923) 202020 **Fax:** (01923) 215050 **DX:** 4508 WATFORD **Email:** INFO@MABLAW.CO.UK **Internet:** WWW.MABLAW.CO.UK

The Firm: Best known for its commercial work, the firm has grown to be one of the leading commercial practices in the Northern Home Counties. Clients range from private individuals to international groups. The firm also has a strong reputation for its private client work and holds a Legal Aid Franchise. They are a member of LawNet and they have good European connections from the Eurojuris network. Partners and staff have a commitment to quality and the firm holds the LawNet Quality Standard, which in 1999 becomes accredited to ISO 9002.

Principal Areas of Work:

Corporate Finance/ Company Commercial: (*Contact Partner:* Chris Green). A full commercial service including acquisitions and disposals, corporate and bank lending. MBOs and MBIs, joint ventures, shareholder, agency and distribution agreements. They are particularly used to working with and understanding the needs of in house legal departments.

Commercial Property: (*Contact Partner:* Richard Hanney). Extensive experience of commercial property matters including new developments, large industrial sites, leasehold and freehold acquisitions and disposals, associated planning and environmental issues and building contracts.

Commercial Litigation and Banking: (*Contact Partner:* Steven Mills). The firm acts in matters ranging from major commercial disputes to debt collection, with a particular reputation for banking litigation, insolvency and for obtaining pre-emptive remedies.

Personal Injury: (*Contact Partner:* Ian Sankey). They have a growing reputation for speed and effectiveness in medical negligence and severe disability cases. They have been quoted for their expertise in recent train crash claims.

Employment: (*Contact Partner:* Alan Piper). A dedicated Team draws upon the experience of human resources professionals and an Industrial Tribunal Chairman, to provide a comprehensive service.

Intellectual Property and Information Technology Law: (*Contact Partner:* Clare Stothard). They have created a multi-discipline unit to service the needs of both listed and small businesses in all areas of intellectual property law and information technology law. They cover both contentious and non-contentious issues such as software licensing.

Insolvency: (*Contact Partner:* Gavin Jones). A specialist unit has been created in the last year headed by partner and Licensed Insolvency Practitioner Gavin Jones to service the growth in banking and financial work.

Licensing: (*Contact Partner:* Alan Piper). Specialist expertise from clubs & pubs, to large stadiums in joint use by Rugby and Football Clubs with their different licensing regimes.

Family: (*Contact Partner:* Christine Ramsey). Substantial expertise in matrimonial and family matters with a strong reputation for their advocacy.

Trusts & Personal Tax, Wills & Probate: (*Contact Partner:* Iain Donaldson). A specialist estate planning service and a comprehensive wills, trusts, tax, and probate service. The emphasis is on wealth protection, particularly for business people and carers of those affected by mental incapacity. The Team also undertakes appointments by Courts and an increasing amount of contentious work.

Residential Conveyancing: (*Contact Partner:* David Marsden). The largest dedicated residential conveyancing department in the area, widely acknowledged for the personal interest it takes in the success of clients' transactions and for the commercial soundness of its advice.

Senior partner:	John M. Baldwin
Number of partners:	15
Assistant solicitors:	11
Other fee-earners:	18

WORKLOADS	
Company Commercial	22%
Commercial Litigation, Debt collection & Banking	
	18%
Commercial Property and Agricultural	12%
Family and Childcare	12%
Residential Conveyancing	12%
Tax, Trusts and Probate	8%
Insolvency	6%
Intellectual Property & Information Technology	5%
Personal Injury	5%

CONTACTS	
Company Commercial	Chris Green
Commercial litigation and banking	Steven Mills
Debt collection	Ian Sankey
Commercial property	Richard Hanney
Family	Christine Ramsey
Resi. convey. & estate devel.	David Marsden
Tax, Trusts & Probate	Iain Donaldson
Insolvency	Gavin Jones
IT/Intellectual Property	Clare Stothard
Employment	Alan Piper
Personal injury	Ian Sankey

MATTHEW MCCLOY & PARTNERS Toomer's Wharf, Newbury, RG14 1DY **Tel:** (01635) 551515 **Fax:** (01635) 550228 **DX:** 30806 **Ptnrs:** 2 **Asst solrs:** 2 **Contact:** Andrew Chalk. *A general practice dealing with commercial work and litigation. Recognised specialists in bloodstock and sports, media and sponsorship law.*

MATTILA SOLICITORS 10a Electric Avenue, London, SW9 8JX *Tel:* (0171) 274 7821 *Fax:* (0171) 326 0241 *DX:* 58768 Brixton *Ptnrs:* 1 *Asst solrs:* 2

MAURICE COHEN & CO

309 KENTISH TOWN ROAD, LONDON, NW5 2TJ
Tel: (0171) 267 2967 **Fax:** (0171) 267 0839 **DX:** 46475 KENTISH TOWN

The Firm: Maurice Cohen & Co is well established in the niche area of immigration law and has rapidly gained repute particularly in the field of political asylum. Notably in the last year it has appealed to the Court of Appeal in relation to an Iranian Asylum Seeker claiming political asylum on the basis of his sexual orientation and is currently acting in many similar cases. The firm additionally has substantial expertise in all areas of business immigration and handles all types of immigration work. The firm prides itself on the efficient, professional and personal attention given to all clients.

Managing partner:	M. Cohen
Senior partner:	M. Cohen
Number of partners:	1
Assistant solicitors:	2

WORKLOADS	
Immigration	95%
Litigation	5%

MAX BARFORD & CO 16 Mount Pleasant Road, Tunbridge Wells, TN1 1QU **Tel:** (01892) 539379 **Fax:** (01892) 521874 **DX:** 3918 **Email:** alert@mbarford-u-net.com **Ptnrs:** 5 **Asst solrs:** 5 **Other fee-earners:** 3 **Contact:** Mr M. Barford

WORKLOADS			
General litigation	32%	Criminal	25%
Children work	16%	Conveyancing	14%
Personal injury	8%	Other	5%

MAX BITEL, GREENE 1 Canonbury Place, London, N1 2NG **Tel:** (0171) 354 2767 **Fax:** (0171) 226 1210 **DX:** 51852 Highbury **Ptnrs:** 5 **Asst solrs:** 2 **Other fee-earners:** 2 **Contact:** Mr. Max Bitel *General commercial practice handling company, commercial litigation and property, and insolvency. Sports law practice acting for sporting bodies.*

WORKLOADS			
Property	40%	Litigation	25%
Company/Commercial	15%	Insolvency	10%
Sports	10%		

MAX GOLD & CO Ruskin Chambers, Scale Lane, Hull, HU1 1LW *Tel:* (01482) 323579 *Fax:* (01482) 327686 *DX:* 11939 Hull *Ptnrs:* 4 *Asst solrs:* 13 *Other fee-earners:* 17

MAXWELL BATLEY

27 CHANCERY LANE, LONDON, WC2A 1PA
Tel: (0171) 405 7888 **Fax:** (0171) 242 7133 **DX:** 190 **Email:** MAXWELLBATLEY@MAXWELLBATLEY.COM **Internet:** WWW.MAXWELLBATLEY.COM

The Firm: Maxwell Batley is a major commercial practice which has established a strong reputation for professional expertise and a commercially orientated approach. Importance is attached to developing a commercial understanding of each client's business and the markets within which a client operates, ensuring a business-like and practical approach is adopted. Direct partner involvement is maintained with each client. The firm has achieved a reputation for providing prompt and cost effective advice, often of an innovative nature, and consequently Maxwell Batley is seen as providing a genuine alternative to the larger commercial law firms.

Principal Areas of Work: Maxwell Batley avoid rigid departmental divisions, which can often inhibit flexibility. Importance is attached to lawyers of different disciplines working together on transactions as a team. The main practice areas are as follows:-

Banking: (*Contact Partner:* Fraser McColl) The firm has extensive expertise in working with banks and other financial institutions, as well as their customers, in all types of banking and financial transactions. The work includes project finance, acquisition finance, syndicated lending, mezzanine finance and advice on regulatory matters, and trade finance.

Company/Commercial: (*Contact Partner:* Ian McIntyre, Fraser McColl) Work includes mergers and acquisitions, loan capital, general commercial advice, compliance, venture capital, MBO's, MBI's, PFI, local authority and competitive tendering, distribution and marketing agreements, information technology, insolvency and European law.

Corporate Finance: (*Contact Partner:* Christopher North) Work undertaken includes flotations, takeovers, placings, rights issues and reconstructions.

Litigation: (*Contact Partner:* Philip Knights) The firm handles large claims for its institutional, corporate and private clients. There is an emphasis on property related disputes, but the firm has wide experience in company, commercial, professional negligence, insolvency and general insurance works (including employers and product liability claims). Over the last year, a unit has been developed dealing specifically in employment issues, for employers and employees, spanning advice on contracts and policies concerning discrimination, European law and pensions as well as litigation.

Senior partner:	Michael Cassidy
Managing partners:	Raymond Levine,
	Fraser McColl
Number of partners:	15
Assistant solicitors:	8
Other fee-earners:	7

WORKLOADS	
Property (Commercial)	40%
Company/Commercial	21%
Litigation	21%
Banking	10%
Private Client	8%

CONTACTS	
Banking	Fraser McColl
Company/Commercial	Ian McIntyre/Fraser McColl
Corporate Finance	Christopher North
Litigation	Philip Knights
Matrimonial	David Sterrett
Property (Commercial)	Candice Blackwood
Property (Residential)	John O'Gorman
Tax and Estates	Frank O'Shea
Trusts/Pensions	Frank O'Shea

Continues overleaf

Property: (*Commercial Contact Partner:* Candice Blackwood, *Residential Contact:* John O'Gorman) The commercial property group deals with all aspects of buying, selling, developing, financing, leasing and managing commercial property. A number of innovative large scale transactions have been handled in recent years. These have included development finance transactions and setting up creative structures to deal with joint ownership of property and joint ventures. Advice is given on the use of various types of corporate and non-corporate vehicles, ensuring the right balance between risk, control and taxation is achieved in the structure adopted.

The group has a number of major institutional clients. It also acts extensively for developers, smaller investors and occupiers. Their ability to handle this work in a speedy and cost-effective way is enhanced by their experience of complex and high value transactions. The group is also involved on major development schemes outside the UK. The firm also offers a comprehensive residential conveyancing service, acting for corporate and private clients and off-shore companies and for banks providing finance for residential conveyancing transactions.

Private Client: (*Contact Partner:* Frank O'Shea) The firm is committed to serving their private clients and provide a full service for trusts, wills, probate, the administration of estates and tax planning in the UK and offshore clients personal and family business interests. This work group also serves charities and pension schemes and has a new matrimonial law section dealing with divorce, financial and property matters, care and custody of children, cohabitation and all aspects of family law. In conjunction with their residential property section and employment law unit the firm provides a comprehensive service for all private clients.

MAXWELL ENTWISTLE & BYRNE 14 Castle Street, Liverpool, L2 0SG *Tel:* (0151) 227 4545 *Fax:* (0151) 236 5067 *DX:* 14192 *Ptnrs:* 10 *Asst solrs:* 9 *Other fee-earners:* 19

MAXWELL MACLAURIN 100 West Regent Street, Glasgow, G2 2QB *Tel:* (0141) 332 5666 *Fax:* (0141) 332 6757 *Ptnrs:* 8 *Asst solrs:* 3 *Other fee-earners:* 1

MAYCOCK'S

BROADGATE HOUSE, 7 ELDON STREET, LONDON, EC2M 7LS
Tel: (0171) 375 0586 **Fax:** (0171) 375 0587 **Email:** MAYCOCK@GJE.CO.UK

The Firm: The firm was established in 1993 and specialises in the law relating to the exploitation and enforcement of intellectual property rights and in the field of information technology. The firm's clients range from those involved in biotech and pharmaceuticals, through chemicals and engineering to character merchandising. The firm works closely with patent and trade mark attorneys, Gill Jennings & Every, in offering clients a complete IP service.

Senior partner:	John d'A. Maycock
Number of partners:	1
Assistant solicitors:	1
Other fee-earners:	1

WORKLOADS	
Intellectual property	100%

MAYER BROWN & PLATT

BUCKLERSBURY HOUSE, 3 QUEEN VICTORIA STREET, LONDON, EC4N 8EL
Tel: (0171) 246 6200 **Fax:** (0171) 329 4465 **Internet:** HTTP://WWW.MAYERBROWN.COM

Mayer, Brown & Platt is a large, long-established commercial practice encompassing the full range of general corporate and financial matters.

The Firm: Founded in 1881, Mayer, Brown & Platt is one of the oldest and largest law firms in the United States. The London office was opened in 1974. In 1996 the London office became a multi-national partnership and now practises English law.

The London office undertakes all types of sophisticated corporate, commercial and financing work. Its clients consist of major UK, US and foreign public companies and financial institutions. In recent years, the activity of the London office has increased substantially as its involvement in international mergers, acquisitions and structured finance transactions has increased. In the US, the firm is probably best known for its representation of major commercial banks (in particular in connection with complex financing transactions and innovative financial products), and its appellate litigation practice (particularly in the US Supreme Court).

Principal Areas of Work: The principal areas of the firm's practice may be categorised as follows: corporate and securities, finance and banking, derivatives, litigation, taxation, real estate, bankruptcy and reorganisation, anti-trust and trade regulation, franchising, ERISA, employee benefits and executive compensation, emerging markets (Russia, Central Asia, Latin America, Africa), environmental law, white-collar crime, insurance and reinsurance,

Senior partner:	Richard A. Cole
Resident lawyers: 30	
Total lawyers: 748	

WORKLOADS	
CIS	33%
Corporate	33%
Finance	33%

CONTACTS	
UK Partners	E Bettelheim, R Colel Coles, J Gordon
	N Khodadad, D Petkovic, M Uhrynuk, N Wright

international trade, investment and finance, international joint ventures, government relations, natural resources, public law and finance, regulated industries, trusts, estates and foundations, labour, ecclesiastical, healthcare and pro bono work.

Lawyers within the firm have experience in every context of legal problem-solving, negotiation, arbitration, trial and appellate litigation, legislation and regulation.

The work of the London office includes domestic and international financings, banking, capital markets and derivatives, trade finance, project finance, work-outs and restructuring, joint ventures, international securities transactions, corporate reorganisations and mergers and acquisitions. The firm has an extensive practice in the former Soviet Union, with various representative offices and is involved in major joint venture and financing transactions in a variety of industry sectors in the region including mining and natural resources.

Other Offices: Berlin, Chicago, Houston, Cologne, Los Angeles, New York, Washington DC

Representative Offices: Almaty, Asgabat, Bishkek, Moscow, Tashkent

Correspondent Offices: Paris (Lambert Armeniades & Lee), Mexico City (Jauregui, Navarrete, Nader y Rojas SC)

MAY, MAY & MERRIMANS

12 SOUTH SQUARE, GRAY'S INN, LONDON, WC1R 5HH
Tel: (0171) 405 8932 **Fax:** (0171) 831 0011 **DX:** 225 LONDON **Email:** MMM@LINK.ORG

The Firm: Founded in 1786, May, May & Merrimans is best known for its private client work, offering a high-quality personal service to individuals and families, many of whom are the owners of substantial residential and agricultural estates and commercial property. The firm brings the same quality of service to its corporate clients and undertakes a broad range of company and commercial business.

Principal Areas of Work:

Private client: Specialist advice includes estate planning, will drafting, the creation and variation of all types of settlements including offshore and charitable trusts, and personal and estate taxation. A considerable volume of probate work is handled, often involving large estates which may include overseas property.

Property: A full range of property work is undertaken ranging from new town sites to mineral excavations, office and shop leases, agricultural tenancies, estate sales and substantial domestic conveyancing transactions.

Litigation: The litigation element of the practice deals with most types of contentious civil law, including landlord and tenant issues, negligence claims, employment, defamation and general commercial disputes.

Matrimonial: This department handles all aspects of family law, including marriage breakdown and related financial issues, disputes involving children and Inheritance Act claims.

Company and Commercial: The firm can assist in the formation of companies and partnerships, in the sale and acquisition of existing enterprises and in all matters which arise in the course of running a business or private company, including share issues, the drafting of contracts and employment questions.

Senior partner:	Christopher Walsh
Number of partners:	11
Assistant solicitors:	5
Other fee-earners:	2

WORKLOADS	
Private client (tax, trust, probate)	50%
Property (domestic/agricultural/comm.)	30%
Litigation/ matrimonial	15%
Company/ commercial	5%

CONTACTS	
Civil Litigation	Sarah Gillette
Company/commercial	Alexandra Sarkis
Family/ matrimonial	Susan Black
Private client	Giles Gostwick
Property	Sandy Schofield

MAYO & PERKINS

20 GILDREDGE RD, EASTBOURNE, BN21 4RP
Tel: (01323) 730543 **Fax:** (01323) 737214 **DX:** 6900

The Firm: Founded in 1910, Mayo & Perkins is a modern general practice which has particular expertise in litigation, family law, commercial and domestic property, and trust and probate work. The main office is in Eastbourne with branch offices in Hailsham and Hampden Park.

Principal Areas of Work:

Litigation: (*Contact Partner:* B. Davis). Work handled includes commercial litigation, personal injury claims and debt recovery, building disputes, breaches of contract and criminal proceedings, family and child care, employment and housing.

Property: (*Contact Partner:* K.D. Minto). Both residential and commercial conveyancing are undertaken.

Company/ Commercial: (*Contact Partner:* P.K. Jelly). A wide variety of work includes company acquisitions and sales, partnership and loan documentation and tax implications.

Private Client: (*Contact Partner:* J.R.M. Clarke). The firm advises on wills, trusts and probate, including probate disputes, financial and tax planning including capital investment, life assurance, pensions and mortgages.

Managing partner:	Simon Dodds
Senior partner:	Ronald Naylor
Number of partners:	13
Assistant solicitors:	6
Other fee-earners:	9

WORKLOADS	
Litigation	35%
Private Client	24%
Company/Commercial	21%
Property	20%

CONTACTS	
Company/ commercial	P.K. Jelly
Litigation	B. Davis
Private client	J.R.M. Clarke
Property	K.D. Minto

MCARTHUR STANTON Royal Bank Buildings, 35 High St, Dumbarton, G82 1LU *Tel:* (01389) 762266 *Fax:* (01389) 742282 *DX:* 500590 *Ptnrs:* 7 *Asst solrs:* 2 *Other fee-earners:* 1

MCCANN & GREYSTOKE 38 Church Lane, Canston House, Belfast, BT1 4KH *Tel:* (01232) 246 098 *Fax:* (01232) 330 795

MCCASH & HUNTER P.O. Box 17, 25 South Methven Street, Perth, PH1 5ES *Tel:* (01738) 620451 *Fax:* (01738) 631155 *DX:* 4 Perth *Ptnrs:* 5 *Asst solrs:* 4 *Other fee-earners:* 4

MCCLENAHAN CROSSEY & CO 41 New Row, Coleraine, BT52 1AE *Tel:* (01265) 43491 *Fax:* (01265) 42377

MCCLOSKEY & CO

FOUNTAIN HOUSE, 19 DONEGALL PLACE, BELFAST, BT1 5AB
Tel: (01232) 240310 **Fax:** (01232) 240312 **DX:** 495 NR BELFAST 1

The Firm: McCloskey & Co is a long established and predominantly defendants litigation practice. Litigation clients include U.K. Insurers, Lloyds Syndicates and Government Bodies.

Principal Areas of Work: The firm is one of Northern Ireland's leading insurance litigation practices. It has expertise in professional negligence, public liability, employers liability, product liability, road traffic claims and all other areas of insurance litigation. It has developed a particular expertise in dealing with the defence of fraudulent fire claims.

Contacts:

Other Defence Litigation	H. McGrattan
Professional Negligence	J. McGuigan

Senior partner:	Joseph McGuigan
Number of partners:	2
Assistant solicitors:	2

WORKLOADS	
Other Defence Negligence	40%
Professional Negligence	40%
General	20%

MCCLURE NAISMITH

292 ST VINCENT STREET, GLASGOW, G2 5TQ
Tel: (0141) 204 2700 **Fax:** (0141) 248 3998 **DX:** 64 GLASGOW **Email:** 100321.3327@COMPUSERVE.COM

49 QUEEN STREET, EDINBURGH, EH2 3NH
Tel: (0131) 220 1002 **Fax:** (0131) 220 1003 **DX:** 135 EDINBURGH

POUNTNEY HILL HOUSE, 6 LAURENCE POUNTNEY HILL, LONDON, EC4R 0BL
Tel: (0171) 623 9155 **Fax:** (0171) 623 9154 **DX:** 764 CDE LONDON

The Firm: McClure Naismith is a commercially focused law firm dedicated to providing the highest quality legal services to its clients in Scotland, England and internationally. The firm is actively involved in privatisations particularly in the sectors of transport, energy and utilities and regularly handles inward investment, principally from the United States, Japan and Europe. The London office provides a full range of English Law advice in the fields of corporate/commercial (including project finance, banking and intellectual property), property and commercial litigation.

Principal Areas of Work:

Corporate/Commercial: (*Contact Partner:* Kenneth Chrystie) The firm advises on all aspects of corporate and commercial law. Specialist advice is offered on company formation and finance, management buy-outs, mergers & acquisitions, banking, intellectual property, licensing and distribution agreements, franchising, computer hardware and software agreements, contracts in the entertainment business, employment issues, insolvency, competition law and mining contracts. The department's industrial expertise embraces coal mining, transport, pharmaceuticals, distilling and electronics.

Project Finance and PFI: (*Contact Partner:* Steven Brown) The firm provides project finance advice to companies promoting infrastructure projects principally in the energy and water industries, both in the UK and overseas. The firm also represents a range of public sector organisations, construction consortia and banks in developing projects under the Private Finance Initiative, with experience in the health, water, energy and education sectors.

Commercial Property: (*Contact Partners:* Michael Brown, Glasgow and Caroline Docherty, Edinburgh). The practice handles all aspects of property development work for institutional, corporate and private clients including: site acquisition, leasing and sale; factory, shop and office developments; funding arrangements; building contracts; residential estate work; tax driven schemes; assured tenancy arrangements; private sector rented housing and management contracts; joint venture agreements and ancillary contracts. The firm advises landlords and tenants on all aspects of commercial, agricultural and

Senior partner:	G.W.R. Carlisle
Number of partners:	21
Assistant solicitors:	47
Other fee-earners:	10

WORKLOADS	
Commercial Property	25%
Corporate/Commercial	25%
Litigation	25%
Banking/Finance	10%
Private Client	10%
Intellectual Property	5%

CONTACTS	
Commercial property	Michael Brown
Consumer credit	Frank Johnstone
Corporate/ commercial	Kenneth Chrystie
Litigation (Edinburgh)	William Walker
Litigation (Glasgow)	Alan Thompson
London	Robin Shannan
Private client	Gordon Shearer
Project Finance/PFI	Steven Brown

residential leasing. The department also has teams specialising in environmental law, secured lending, and asset finance.

Litigation: (*Contact Partners:* Alan Thomson, Glasgow and William Walker, Edinburgh). The firm undertakes all types of litigation in all courts, tribunals and inquiries throughout Scotland, including Scotland's Supreme Court, the Court of Session, Edinburgh. It also undertakes ADR and Arbitration. Advice is provided to commercial and private clients on a wide range of problems and disputes. Its principal areas of practice include: asset recovery; construction; employment; matrimonial; insolvency; debt recovery and credit control; intellectual property; personal injuries; professional negligence and general insurance; licensing, planning and environmental; and property.

Consumer Credit: (*Contact Partner:* Frank Johnstone). One of the foremost departments of its kind in Scotland, clients include many of the country's leading finance houses, leasing companies, banks and credit card companies. The firm advises the Consumer Credit Trade Association. The service includes high volume debt recovery, asset recovery, the drafting of credit documentation and advice on current and contemplated legislation. The firm also advises on data protection issues.

Employment: (*Contact Partner:* Alan Thomson, Glasgow). In this significant area of practice, the firm principally advises employers in relation to all aspects of employment law including all statutory claims in relation to employment as well as wrongful dismissal and other common law claims. Representation is undertaken in all types of cases before industrial tribunals and the Sheriff Court.

Intellectual Property: (Contact Partner: Kenneth Chrystie). As well as negotiating licence agreements for client companies world-wide the firm is instructed in a wide range of intellectual property disputes including patent infringements, breach of copyrights, trade mark issues and passing off actions.

Private Client: (*Contact Partner:* Gordon Shearer, Glasgow, and Caroline Docherty, Edinburgh). The practice offers specialist advice on tax estate planning, wills, trusts, executries, curatories, tax planning, insurance, pensions, investment portfolios and the purchase, sale and leasing of residential property.

Foreign Languages: French, Danish.

International Connections & Associated Offices: Member of the World Law Group with representative offices in Europe, the USA and the Far East.

MCCORMACKS

122 MILE END ROAD, LONDON, E1 4UN
Tel: (0171) 790 4339 **Fax:** (0171) 790 5846 **Email:** SOLICITORS@MCCORMACKS.CO.UK

49 QUEEN VICTORIA STREET, LONDON, EC4N 4SE
Tel: (0171) 329 0001 **Fax:** (0171) 248 2588 **Email:** SOLICITORS@MCCORMACKS.CO.UK

The Firm: Founded in 1988 McCormacks rapidly established a fierce reputation in criminal law. The successful founding office is still based in the heart of London's east end. The firm also runs a well-regarded and matrimonial department and an expanding Property & Probate office. The firm's City of London branch specialises in high-end criminal casework.

The firm is unusual of its type. All casework is conducted by solicitors. As a matter of policy the firm long ago decided against the employment of paralegal staff to conduct casework, setting itself apart from most competitors. The firm is noted as being technologically advanced. The firm includes members of the British Academy of Forensic Sciences.

Principal Areas of Work:
Criminal Law: (*Contact:* Andrew Palazzo) A large proportion of the firm's work is criminal law – both privately funded and legally aided. A broad spectrum of work is covered from road traffic to major crimes of violence, importation of drugs, major fraud, terrorism, extradition and Customs & Excise work. McCormacks fraud work includes successful defence in specialist cases involving the Serious Fraud Office and the City of London Fraud Investigation Group. The City of London Office criminal department specialises in major VAT, excise and drugs importation cases.

Family Law: (*Contact:* Christine Dean) Covers all areas including childcare and ancillary relief. It advises on Welfare Law. The firm is able to assist individuals in matters concerning Local Education Authorities.

Property & Probate: (*Contact:* Malcolm Brereton) All aspects of residential and business conveyancing including licensing. Probate service.

Litigation: Based in the City of London Office this work is restricted to actions against the police and prison authorities.

Senior partner:	Ugo Palazzo

WORKLOADS	
Criminal litigation	68%
Family litigation	16%
Property	16%

CONTACTS	
Actions Against Police	Leslie Cuthbert
Crime	Andrew Palazzo
Family	Christine Dean
Property	Malcolm Brereton

MCCORMICKS

BRITANNIA CHAMBERS, 4 OXFORD PLACE, LEEDS, LS1 3AX
Tel: (0113) 246 0622 **Fax:** (0113) 246 7488 **DX:** 26427 LEEDS PARK SQUARE **Email:** MCCORMICKS@BTINTERNET.COM

The Firm: McCormicks is a high profile, progressive and highly regarded firm which has expanded by planned organic growth to attain a reputation for expertise in a number of fields. It has offices in Leeds and Harrogate and associated offices throughout Europe. It offers a comprehensive range of legal services, both to its national and international corporate clients as well as to many notable private clients. It has been described in a survey of the law firms in Yorkshire and Humberside by the Yorkshire Post as "A law firm in the top rank" and by Yorkshire Television as "one of the region's top law firms".

The firm is admired for its continued ability to operate successfully in the company and commercial field, whilst at the same time maintaining its commitment to the private client. The average age of the partners is 35 and the firm has a reputation for a vibrant and dynamic atmosphere.Currently, company/commercial and litigation account for 70% of the fee income, criminal (serious fraud, tax cases and complex criminal matters) 15% and matrimonial, private client and conveyancing 15%.

Partners hold the Higher Courts Qualification, memberships of the Law Society's Personal Injury and Child Care Panels and Fellowship of the Chartered Institute of Arbitrators; partners are also trained and experienced in Mediation and Alternative Dispute Resolution. The firm is a member of the Law Society's Accident Line scheme. Both the Leeds and Harrogate practices were the first in the region to be awarded Legal Aid Franchises. The firm has strengthened it's corporate recovery department dealing with all aspects of insolvency work with personnel having worked on the Maxwell and BCCI cases.

Principal Areas of Work: Commercial litigation, company and commercial, corporate and white collar crime including VAT and Inland Revenue investigation work and tribunals, debt collection and mortgage repossesion, employment, European law, family law, intellectual property, media and entertainment, sports law (one of the premier practices in the country), insolvency, personal injury, general crime (especially road traffic), private client, defamation, charity law.

Foreign Connections: Associated offices in France, Germany, The Netherlands, Belgium, Eire, Spain, Italy, Portugal and Gibraltar; members of "Eurolink for Lawyers". Fluent French, German, Italian and Spanish spoken.

Other Office: Harrogate : Wharfedale House, 37 East Parade, Harrogate, North Yorkshire HG1 5LQ *Tel:* (01423) 530630 *Fax:* (01423) 530709 *DX:* 11974 Harrogate 1. *Resident Partner:* Geoffrey A. Rogers.

Managing partner:	Peter D.G. McCormick
Senior partner:	Peter D.G. McCormick
Number of partners:	7
Assistant solicitors:	9
Other fee-earners:	15

WORKLOADS	
Company/commercial & litigation	70%
Criminal	15%
Matrimonial, private client & conveyancing	15%

CONTACTS	
Commercial litigation	Neil Goodrum
	Richard Cramer
Company/commercial	Peter McCormick
	Clive Lawrence
Debt collection	Richard Cramer
	Mark Burns
Defamation	Peter McCormick
	Clive Lawrence
Employment	Neil Goodrum
	Richard Cramer
European Law	Richard Moran
Family/matrimonial	Mark Burns
	Geoff Rogers
Insolvency	Richard Cramer
	Roger Hutton
Intellectual property	Clive Lawrence
	Richard Moran
Media and entertainment law	Peter McCormick
	Clive Lawrence
Personal injury	Neil Goodrum
	Claire Reid
Serious fraud	Clive Lawrence
	Geoff Rogers
Sports law	Peter McCormick
	Richard Cramer

MCCOURTS 53 George IV Bridge, Edinburgh, EH1 1EJ *Tel:* (0131) 225 6555 *Fax:* (0131) 225 5054 *Ptnrs:* 3 *Asst solrs:* 4 *Other fee-earners:* 2

MCGRATH & CO

4TH FLOOR, KING EDWARD HOUSE, 135A NEW STREET, BIRMINGHAM, B2 4QJ
Tel: (0121) 643 4121 **Fax:** (0121) 624 1060

The Firm: MCGRATH & CO, *Manjit Singh* very experienced Immigration Solicitors (Head of the Department) and his Deputy, *Tauhid Pasha*, Solicitor lead this large franchised department comprising of two Solicitors, one Legal Executive, two Trainee Solicitors, three experienced Immigration Advisors and one Trainee Immigration Advisor. The Department is known for its quality immigration work.

Clients: Solid Legal Aid Practice. Large refugee case work. Clients from all communities and all parts of the world.

Principal Areas of Work: All areas of personal immigration work. Includes Political Asylum, Immigration Appeals, Judicial Reviews. Offer a 24 hour emergency call out service for those detained on basis of their immigration status.

All the main languages of the Indian sub-continent are spoken in the department. Experienced Immigration Advisor and Legal Executive, Shabir Akhtar conducts regular village visits in Pakistan.

Some business immigration is undertaken (Work Permits).

Senior partner:	G.J. McGrath
Number of partners:	7
Assistant solicitors:	14
Other fee-earners:	57

CONTACTS	
Crime	Errol Robinson
Employment	Chris Johnson
Family	Valerie Osborne
Housing	Rosaleen Kilbane
Immigration	Philip Turpin
Personal injury	Steve Bennett
Welfare benefits	Monica Wasiak

MCGRIGOR DONALD

PACIFIC HOUSE, 70 WELLINGTON STREET, GLASGOW, G2 6SB
Tel: (0141) 248 6677 **Fax:** (0141) 204 1351 **DX:** GW 135 **Email:** MARKET@MCGRIGORS.COM **Internet:** HTTP://WWW.MCGRIGORS.COM

The Firm: McGrigor Donald is a corporate and commercial law practice operating throughout the United Kingdom. With our well established London office, the firm has developed specialist teams offering advice to clients under both English and Scottish law, and the ability to provide a cross border service is increasingly attractive to clients in Scotland, England, Wales and internationally with UK-wide interests.

McGrigor Donald's offices in Edinburgh, Glasgow and London are complemented by an office in Brussels, headed up by Michael Renouf. The practice is also a member of Globalaw.

The firm's approach is to operate in every case as a constructive and effective force in achieving the commercial objectives of clients. Its style in handling legal work is widely recognised as direct and forthright. Clients range from small businesses to major companies and institutions, operating in such fields as banking, construction, energy, food and drink, technology and the public sector, the health sector, leisure, retailing and transport.

1997 saw continued investment in a new practice management system and the continuation of a training programme for all fee earners focusing on the management of business development.

Principal Areas of Work:
The firm is structured into 4 departments (company, property, litigation and taxation) with specialist units working within and across these departments. The firm's key strengths are in corporate finance, technology, property, construction and capital projects all of which have experienced a significant increase in activity throughout 1997.

The corporate finance team handled a wide variety of work dealing with larger and more complex transactions, many with a cross border or international element. A new partner, David Crone (formerly of Pinsent Curtis) joined the team, based in Edinburgh. The year culminated in the team being short listed for the Legal Business 97 Awards – Corporate Finance Team of the Year.

The firm's technology team dealt with an increasing workload, particularly from international clients, acting in a range of deals including flotations, acquisition of technology and technology companies, protection strategies and enforcement of IP rights.

The Property department acted in some of the most important property deals ever done in Scotland – deals justifiably regarded as commercial landmarks for the property industry UK-wide. Three new partners within the department – Melanie White's assumption as a partner and the appointments of Steven Scates (formerly of Nicholson Graham and Jones) and Mark Johnstone (formerly of Reynolds Porter Chamberlain) further strengthened the team's ability to provide a cross border service to clients.

The firms's construction unit has seen a significant increase in construction drafting work due to an upturn in property/development deal driven work and the firm's extensive involvement in PFI/PPP throughout the UK. At the same time the team dealing with disputes has expanded substantially to deal with the volume of litigation which it is conducting in the Court of Session and the Official Referees Court as well as at arbitration.

The firm's capital projects/PFI team has brought the number of projects which have reached financial close to a total of 5. The unit is currently working intensively on projects at various stages ranging from and including water and sewerage, housing, a district hospital and a college of education.

Other areas of significant activity include inward investment where the firm has been successful in advising in a series of major investments into Scotland, including Cadence Design Systems Inc.

The firm is committed to solicitor advocacy, with a partner appearing regularly in the Court of Session – the Scottish equivalent of the High Court. Other lawyers frequently provide an advocacy service at planning inquiries, arbitrations and other types of hearings.

Other Offices:
Erskine House, 68-73 Queen Street, Edinburgh EH2 4NF. *Tel:* (0131) 226 7777. *Fax:* (0131) 226 7700.

63 Queen Victoria Street, London EC4N 4ST. *Tel:* (0171) 329 3299. *Fax:* (0171) 329 4000.

9 Rond-Point Schuman, Box 13, B-1040 Brussels, Belgium. *Tel:* (+322) 233 37 47. *Fax:* (+322) 233 37 40.

Managing partner:	Kirk Murdoch
Senior partner:	Fred Shedden
Number of partners:	48
Assistant solicitors:	85
Other fee-earners:	42

WORKLOADS	
Company (including banking)	34%
Property	32%
Litigation	26%
Taxation (including private client)	8%

CONTACTS	
Banking	John Macfarlane
Construction law	Brandon Nolan
Corporate finance	Morag McNeill
Employment law	Jim Young
Environmental law	Patricia Hawthorn
Financial Services	Frank Doran
Inward Investment	Colin Gray
IP/Technology	Shonaig Macpherson
Litigation	James Taylor
Pensions & employee benefits	Ian Gordon
Planning	Craig Connal
Project Finance	David Bankier
Property development/investment	Ian Lyall
Public Sector	Niall Scott
Taxation	Allan Nicolson

MCGUINNESS FINCH 9 Stratford Place, London, W1N 9AE *Tel:* (0171) 493 9593 *Fax:* (0171) 629 2839 *DX:* 9076 West End *Ptnrs:* 12 *Asst solrs:* 4 *Other fee-earners:* 1

MCKAY & NORWELL WS 5 & 7 Rutland Square, Edinburgh, EH1 2AS *Tel:* (0131) 229 2212 *Fax:* (0131) 228 4538 *DX:* 138 Edinburgh *Ptnrs:* 7 *Asst solrs:* 11 *Other fee-earners:* 11

MCKENZIE BELL 19 John St, Sunderland, SR1 1JG **Tel:** (0191) 567 4857 **Fax:** (0191) 510 9347 **DX:** 60719 **Email:** mckbell@dial.pipex.com **Ptnrs:** 6 **Asst solrs:** 5 **Other fee-earners:** 2 *Known for licensing, conveyancing, litigation, debt collection, employment, company and commercial work, trust and charity law and crime.*

MCKINTY & WRIGHT

EAGLE STAR HOUSE, 5-7 UPPER QUEEN STREET, BELFAST, BT1 6FS
Tel: (01232) 246751 **Fax:** (01232) 231432 **Email:** POST@MCKINTY-WRIGHT.CO.UK

The Firm: McKinty & Wright is a Belfast-based firm with a client-oriented, commercial and litigation practice. Although the firm offers specialist expertise on matters peculiar to Northern Ireland, it has a wide client base outside the province, including international and multi-national companies. It is also pleased to include amongst its clients many leading insurance companies, Lloyds syndicates and insurance intermediaries.

Principal Areas of Work: McKinty & Wright offers a wide range of services to the commercial and insurance client, from routine advice to insolvency, property, insurance matters and litigation. The firm's litigation department has extensive experience in all aspects of commercial litigation with specialised expertise in personal injury, construction, professional negligence, defamation, insurance and general commercial litigation. The firm also has departments handling insolvency, employment, licensing, corporate finance, property and general commercial advice. McKinty and Wright strives to provide an efficient and cost effective service to all its clients and to maintain a close working relationship.

Senior partner:	John Cross
Number of partners:	11
Assistant solicitors:	12
Other fee-earners:	4

CONTACTS	
Commercial property	Ivan Frazer
Company/commercial	Eric Boyd
Litigation	Paul Johnston

MCLELLANS

OLD CROSS HOUSE, OLD CROSS, HERTFORD, SG14 1RB
Tel: (01992) 300800 **Fax:** (01992) 300844 **DX:** 57921 HERTFORD

The Firm: McLellans is a niche practice specialising in commercial property, licensing and employment law for the licensed trade and is one of the leading leisure practices in the Northern Home Counties. Six fee earners are experienced advocates (including three former barristers).

Principal Areas of Work:
Commercial Property: The firm provides a full commercial property service that is particularly focused on complex property acquisition for leisure industry clients.
Licensing: The firm has a dedicated Liquor Licensing Department which handles advocacy from within its own ranks throughout England and Wales.
Employment: The firm advises on all aspects of employment and disciplinary matters and handles advocacy in the Industrial Tribunal and Employment Appeal Tribunal, particularly in relation to licensed trade employment matters.

Nature of Clientele: Clients include a national pub chain and a regional brewer.

Managing partner:	Christine McLellan
Senior partner:	Nigel Mahoney
Number of partners:	4
Assistant solicitors:	5
Other fee-earners:	1

WORKLOADS	
Commercial Property	45%
Licensing	25%
Employment	15%
Property Litigation	10%
Matrimonial	5%

CONTACTS	
Commercial Property	S. Locke
Employment	N. Mahoney
Licensing	K. Healy
Property Litigation	S. Heath

MCMANUS & KEARNEY Law Society House, 106 Victoria Street, Belfast, BT 1 3JZ *Tel:* (01232) 243658 *Fax:* (01232) 332151

MCMILLAN KILPATRICK S.S.C. 12 Alloway Place, Ayr, KA7 2AG *Tel:* (01292) 264696 *Fax:* (01292) 610647 *DX:* 1 Ayr *Ptnrs:* 6 *Other fee-earners:* 2

MCNEIVE 26 Cowper Street, London, EC2A 4AP *Tel:* (0171) 253 0535 *Fax:* (0171) 253 0537

MEADE-KING

24 ORCHARD STREET, BRISTOL, BS1 5DF
Tel: (0117) 926 4121 **Fax:** (0117) 929 7578 **DX:** 7812

The Firm: An expanding, dynamic practice Meade-King advises commercial and corporate clients whilst maintaining a strong private client department. Committed to quality assurance and a strategic programme of investment in staff, the firm provides speedy and realistic advice to the business community.

Principal Areas of Work:

Company and Commercial: Business start-up, joint venture and franchising, commercial property, employment, partnership agreements and commercial contracts.

Insolvency: Corporate and personal insolvency, advice to receivers, administrators, liquidators and trustees in bankruptcy as well as individuals and companies in financial difficulty.

Property: Acquisition, development and disposal of commercial property. Portfolio management. Expert in the retail sector.

Litigation: Commercial litigation, contract disputes and professional negligence. Arbitration work, particularly in building and property disputes. Credit management and debt recovery work.

Corporate Defences: Expertise in food safety law, health and safety, trading standards and advertising standards work.

Charities: Formation and administration of all types of trusts, management of trusts and advice to trustees. Experienced in the particular challenges of working with volunteers and professional staff.

Managing partner:	Peter Watkin
Number of partners:	7
Other fee-earners:	15

CONTACTS	
Charities	P.J. Watkin
Commercial	J.N.G. Hawkins
Corporate Defences	J.H. Kelly
Insolvency	C. Harris
Litigation	A.J. Chivers
Private Client	R.J. Boulding

Meade ■ King
SOLICITORS

MEMERY CRYSTAL

31 SOUTHAMPTON ROW, LONDON, WC1B 5HT
Tel: (0171) 242 5905 **Fax:** (0171) 242 2058 **DX:** 156 CHANCERY LANE **Email:** MC@MEMERY-CRYSTAL.CO.UK
Internet: WWW.MEMERY-CRYSTAL.CO.UK

The Firm: The emphasis in this thriving London firm is on commercial business and corporate issues. The firm is committed to providing its clients with practical and commercially viable advice with a strong sense of commitment. The Partners all have backgrounds in large City practices and have come together with the same belief that only through direct partner involvement can the best possible legal service be given, based on skills and experience built up over many years.

Memery Crystal is a niche practice operating in corporate finance, commercial litigation and property. Within these areas specialist groups deal with company/commercial matters, sports law, tax, insolvency, construction, insurance, corporate crime and regulatory law, employment and property litigation.

Clients include listed and private companies, partnerships, individuals and trusts. As a member of the International Lawyers Network, the firm has strong links with lawyers in all major business centres.

Memery Crystal is always pleased to receive applications from well-qualified, high-calibre, assistant solicitors. In addition, the firm usually recruits two or three trainee solicitors each year.

Principal Areas of Work:

Corporate Finance: (*Contact:* Lesley Gregory): The Corporate Finance Department covers the full range of commercial business. It is well known for advising listed companies on all matters and small to medium sized companies on entry to the full market, AIM and OFEX, as well as all aspects of capital raising, acquisitions and disposals, management buy-ins, management buy-outs and joint ventures. The department also handles general commercial work, distribution agreements, service and consultancy agreements, share option schemes and employment matters. The department has a substantial sports law practice, covering licensing, sponsorship, ticketing and catering contracts. The department incorporates the taxation practice, advising on U.K. corporate and personal tax, including stamp duty, V.A.T. and tax planning both in the U.K. and internationally.

Commercial Litigation: (*Contact:* Harvey Rands): The Litigation Department has specialist groups dealing with company and financial law and regulations, employment, litigation and arbitration in commercial shipping, professional indemnity, insurance and construction law, Directors' and Officers' liability, criminal prosecutions, regulatory proceedings and defamation. The insolvency group advise on corporate and international insolvency matters, including receivership, administration, liquidation, investor and

Senior partner:	Peter M. Crystal
Managing partner:	Jonathan P. Davies
Number of partners:	10
Assistant solicitors:	15
Other fee-earners:	10

WORKLOADS	
Corporate Finance	40%
Litigation	40%
Property	10%
Property litigation	10%

CONTACTS	
Corporate Finance	Lesley Gregory
Employment	Andrew Newman
Insolvency	Bernard Clarke
Litigation	Harvey Rands
Property	Douglas Robertson
Property litigation	Dan Pfeiffer
Sports Law	Peter M. Crystal
Tax	Dr Kameel Khan

Continues overleaf

depositor recovery, tracing remedies, civil aspects of commercial fraud and gaming and licensing. The employment group advise on employment and labour law, including service and employment contracts, disciplinary and grievance procedures, termination disputes, equal opportunity and discrimination.

Property Litigation: (*Contact:* Dan Pfeiffer): Property Litigation is undertaken in relation to all aspects of landlord and tenant law for both commercial and residential property including recovery of arrears, possession of properties, breach of covenant, dilapidations, 1954 Act, lease renewal and landlord and tenant disputes.

Property: (Contact: Douglas Robertson): The Property Department acts on the acquisition, disposal, letting and development of industrial and leisure premises, shops and offices and on residential conveyancing. It also advises on construction contracts and town and country planning.

Memery Crystal sees itself as a progressive and growing firm, able to deal with all the requirements of small to medium sized companies and specialist requirements of larger companies. Memery Crystal is committed to establishing long term relationships with its clients, providing a cost effective, personal, partner lead service.

Brochures describing the firm and its specialist groups are available on request.

MERRICKS

8 LION STREET, IPSWICH, IP1 1DQ
Tel: (01473) 231331 **Fax:** (01473) 230041 **DX:** 3264 IPSWICH 1 **Email:** IPSWICH@MERRICKS.CO.UK

207-208 MOULSHAM STREET, CHELMSFORD, CM2 0LG
Tel: (01245) 491414 **Fax:** (01245) 263829 **DX:** 89702 CHELMSFORD 2 **Email:** CHELMSFORD@MERRICKS.CO.UK

LANCASTER HOUSE, 67 NEWHALL STREET, BIRMINGHAM, B3 1LX
Tel: (0121) 233 0062 **Fax:** (0121) 233 9880 **DX:** 13145 BIRMINGHAM 1 **Email:** BIRMINGHAM@MERRICKS.CO.UK

The Firm: Merricks is predominantly a litigation practice with particular expertise in construction and insurance matters, servicing clients throughout the country from its offices in Ipswich, Chelmsford and Birmingham. It also handles marine and transit, commercial property and employment work.

Senior partner:	A.K. Sheppard
Number of partners:	14
Assistant solicitors:	18
Other fee-earners:	12

Principal Areas of Work:

Insurance: (*Contact Partner:* Andrew Hunn). Merricks has a long and close relationship with clients in the insurance markets. Work includes a substantial volume of personal injury and industrial disease work, property damage, Contractors' All Risks, fraudulent claims and policy disputes.

Professional Indemnity: (*Contact Partner:* Anthony Sheppard). Acting for leading players including Solicitors Indemnity Fund and construction related professionals.

Construction/Engineering: (*Contact Partner:* Rupert Cowen). An expert team handles: contractual claims, payment of certificates, liability disputes, contract drafting and interpretation, Duty of Care Warranties, joint venture agreements and insurance claims.

Marine and Transit: (*Contact Partner:* Mariel Monk). Areas handled include cargo and charterparty disputes, cargo claims and recoveries, marine insurance, collision and salvage, international trade, CMR and domestic road haulage, freight forwarding, warehouse keeping, Road Traffic Act defences and vehicle operators licences.

Commercial Property: (*Contact Partner:* Mike Alexander). Investment Property work of all description undertaken including property management, commercial development, commercial conveyancing and landlord and tenant.

Employment: (*Contact:* Sean Stanton-Dunne). All aspects of employment law in both the contentious and non-contentious fields covered.

WORKLOADS	
Construction	20%
Defendant personal injury	20%
Other insurance litigation (eg recoveries, liability, fraud)	20%
Professional indemnity	20%
Commercial property	8%
Marine and transit	6%
Other	6%

MERRIMAN WHITE

3 KING'S BENCH WALK, INNER TEMPLE, LONDON, EC4Y 7DJ
Tel: (0171) 936 2050 **Fax:** (0171) 583 1783 **DX:** 1015 LONDON CHANCERY LANE

The Firm: A long-established compact City firm with an additional office in Guildford. It undertakes litigation, property and commercial work for business clients of all sizes, including major companies in building and publishing, and offers a range of specialist services for NHS Trusts and other organisations in the healthcare industry. Also provides a wide spectrum of property, tax, estate and matrimonial services to private clients.

Managing partner:	Jeremy Wolff
Senior partner:	Raymond St. J. Murphy
Number of partners:	2
Assistant solicitors:	13
Other fee-earners:	4

Other Offices: Merlaw House, 12 The Mount, Guildford GU2 4HN. *Tel:* (01483) 574466. *Fax:* (01483) 506910. *DX:* 2457.

METCALFE COPEMAN & PETTEFAR 8 York Row, Wisbech, PE13 1EF **Tel:** (01945) 464331 **Fax:** (01945) 476695 **DX:** 41350 **Ptnrs:** 12 **Asst solrs:** 9 **Other fee-earners:** 8 **Contact:** David Rutter *General practice with expertise in retail law, personal injury and commercial conveyancing. Other offices at Peterborough, King's Lynn and Thetford.*

METCALFES

46-48 QUEEN SQUARE, BRISTOL, BS1 4LY
Tel: (0117) 929 0451 **Fax:** (0117) 929 9551 **DX:** 7835 BRISTOL **Email:** INFO@METCALFES.CO.UK **Internet:** WWW.METCALFES.CO.UK

The Firm: Established for over 250 years, Metcalfes enjoys an excellent reputation for its work on behalf of both commercial and private clients. It is particularly noted for its personal injury and commercial litigation expertise.

Principal Areas of Work:

Company/Commercial: *Work includes:* MBOs, banking, acquisitions and disposals, intellectual property and charities.

Commercial Litigation: *Work includes:* construction, insolvency, employment, banking, professional negligence, company and partnership disputes and debt recovery.

Personal Injury & Insurance Litigation: *Work includes:* defendant work for major insurers, plaintiff work for private clients, industrial injury and disease, motor and medical negligence.

Property: *Work includes:* a wide range of transactions on behalf of corporate and private clients, construction and development conveyancing and self build projects.

Private Client: *Work includes:* trusts, probate, wills, tax planning and personal finance.

Languages Spoken: French, Spanish, German, Punjabi, Urdu, Arabic, Italian, Turkish, Greek.

The firm was the first legal practice in Bristol to receive the Investor in People Award.

Senior partner:	David Boniface
Number of partners:	7
Assistant solicitors:	13
Other fee-earners:	7

WORKLOADS	
Personal Injury and Insurance Litigation	40%
Commercial Litigation	15%
Company/ Commercial including Banking	15%
Private Client	15%
Property	15%

CONTACTS	
Commercial Litigation	David Boniface
Company/Commercial	Tony Forster
Employment	Anthony Heath
Medical Negligence	Gary McFarlane
Personal Injury	Kay McCluskey
Property	Anthony Smith

MICHAEL HUTCHINGS Sandhayes, Corsley, Warminster, BA12 7QQ *Tel:* (0468) 105777 *Fax:* (01373) 832785 *Ptnrs:* 1

MICHAEL W. HALSALL 2 The Parks, Newton-le-Willows, WA12 0NZ *Tel:* (01942) 727000 *Fax:* (01942) 717555 *DX:* 713120 Newton-le-Willows 2 *Ptnrs:* 3 *Asst solrs:* 4 *Other fee-earners:* 15

MICHELMORES 18 Cathedral Yard, Exeter, EX1 1HE *Tel:* (01392) 436244 *Fax:* (01392) 215579 *DX:* 8304 *Ptnrs:* 13 *Asst solrs:* 5 *Other fee-earners:* 15

MIDDLETON POTTS

3 CLOTH STREET, BARBICAN, LONDON, EC1A 7LD
Tel: (0171) 600 2333 **Fax:** (0171) 600 0108 **DX:** 46621 **Email:** MAIL@MIDDLETONPOTTS.CO.UK

The Firm: Middleton Potts was founded in 1976 by six partners, all of whom had previously been with a well-established City practice, and has grown steadily over the past two decades. The firm acts for shipping, commodity, financial, commercial and industrial clients from all over the world. It has four principal areas of work, as described below, and where a matter requires the involvement of lawyers from more than one discipline the client partner will ensure close co-ordination between the disciplines and provide continuity and a regular point of contact between the client and the firm.

Principal Areas of Work:

Shipping/Commodities Litigation: The firm's commodities practice has long been one of the most respected in the City, and the department contains several of the best known names in this field. Cases involving all types of commodities are handled, the main clients being international trading houses. The shipping practice also has a long-established and solid reputation and there are 16 partners and assistants who do this work. The cases handled are primarily charterparty and bill of lading disputes, though salvage, wreck removal and pollution cases are also undertaken. The main clients are P&I and Defence Clubs, shipowners, charterers and their insurers, and companies in the off-shore energy field.

Corporate/Commercial/Banking/Insurance: This department has also achieved considerable success, enjoys work of the highest calibre and often acts in transactions where

Senior partner:	Christopher Potts
Number of partners:	18
Assistant solicitors:	11
Other fee-earners:	8

WORKLOADS	
Shipping/Commodities Litigation	55%
Corporate/Commercial/Banking/Insurance	25%
Commercial Litigation	15%
Property	5%

CONTACTS	
Shipping/Commodities Litigation	Christopher Potts, David Lucas, Andrew Donoghue, Russell Ridley, Robert Parson
Corporate/Commercial/ Banking/Insurance	David Godfrey, David Rabagliati, Stephen Morrall
Commercial Litigation	Derek West, Patrick Hann
Property	Karin Horsley

Continues overleaf

the largest City firms are on the other side. The department handles international and domestic banking and financial matters of all kinds (including ship and project finance transactions), insurance and reinsurance work, the establishment by foreign entities of branches and subsidiaries in the UK, regulatory, compliance and administrative work, the preparation of standard documentation, acquisitions and disposals of shares and assets, corporate reorganisations, joint ventures, ship sales and purchases, international construction contracts and other major industrial, commercial and infrastructure projects (including schemes under the Private Finance Initiative), tax matters and a very broad spectrum of corporate and general commercial matters (including employment law, pensions law, insolvency and intellectual property work).

Commercial Litigation: This expanding group handles commercial disputes of all kinds and conducts both High Court litigation and domestic and international arbitration proceedings. The main areas of work are: insurance and reinsurance, construction and technical disputes, banking and financial services litigation; insolvency; commercial fraud; tracing actions and cross-border litigation and disputes in relation to real property, intellectual property, employment and corporate matters.

Property: The areas handled by this department include the acquisition, funding, development and disposal of freehold and leasehold office and residential premises, industrial sites and other commercial property units and portfolios, planning matters, the general management of property interests, and general commercial transactions related to property.

Foreign Connections: With a very strong international focus to the practice, Middleton Potts has developed close contacts with clients, lawyers and other professionals from different jurisdictions throughout the world. Many of its lawyers speak at least one, and some speak several, of the following languages: French, German, Hebrew, Italian, Norwegian, Polish, Portuguese, Spanish and Turkish.

Nature of Clientele: The client base covers a very broad spectrum and includes: commodity trading houses; shipowners and charterers; P&I clubs; oil majors and traders; major international banks, insurance companies and other financial institutions; freight forwarders and transportation companies; airlines; multi-national manufacturing and trading corporations; property companies; international construction companies and project joint ventures; foreign state enterprises.

Recruitment and Training: The firm places a high priority on recruitment, education and development of trainees and young assistant solicitors whom it considers to be the most important source of potential future partners. In order to attract the highest calibre of candidates, the firm offers remuneration competitive with the best on offer in the City of London. Applications should be made by letter, accompanied by a full CV, to Miss Hazel Alton.

MIDDLEWEEKS Swan Buildings, 20 Swan Street, Manchester, M4 5JW *Tel:* (0161) 839 7255 *Fax:* (0161) 839 7243 *Ptnrs:* 3 *Asst solrs:* 2 *Other fee-earners:* 8

MILBANK, TWEED, HADLEY & MCCLOY Dashwood House, 69 Old Broad Street, London, EC2M 1QS **Tel:** (0171) 448 3000 **Fax:** (0171) 448 3029 **Ptnrs:** 4 **Asst solrs:** 12 **Other fee-earners:** 2 **Contact:** Mr Phillip Fletcher. *Has acknowledged expertise in advising governments, lenders and sponsors in financing international infrastructure projects under English and New York law.*

WORKLOADS			
Project Finance	70%	Banking/capital markets	20%
Leasing	10%		

MILES PRESTON & CO

ELDON CHAMBERS, 30 FLEET STREET, LONDON, EC4Y 1AA
Tel: (0171) 583 0583 **Fax:** (0171) 583 0128

The Firm: Miles Preston & Co is a specialist matrimonial and family law practice formed in May 1994, the three founding partners having previously worked together for over 10 years in a large Central London general practice. The firm deals with all aspects of matrimonial and family law including divorce and separation, cohabitation and pre-marriage agreements, all issues relating to children and the full range of emergency procedures. Many of the cases involve the resolution of complex financial issues usually concerning substantial assets, some with an international dimension. The practice aims to adopt a firm, effective and fair approach to the conduct of its cases and to offer a high quality and cost efficient service to its clients. All its solicitors are members of the Solicitors' Family Law Association.

Foreign: The practice has close contacts with a number of other family lawyers worldwide. In addition Miles Preston has been President of the International Academy of Matrimonial Lawyers which has as its members 280 prominent international family lawyers practising in various countries around the world.

Managing partner:	**Miles Preston**
Senior partner:	**Miles Preston**
Number of partners:	3
Assistant solicitors:	2

WORKLOADS	
Family & Matrimonial	90%
Cohabitation/ Paternity disputes	10%

CONTACTS	
Cohabitation/ paternity	Julia Stancyzk
Family and matrimonial	Siobhan Readhead

MILLAR SHEARER & BLACK 40 Molesworth Street, Cookstown, BT80 8PH *Tel:* (01648) 762346 *Fax:* (01648) 766761 *DX:* 3272 Nr Cookstown *Ptnrs:* 5 *Asst solrs:* 4 *Other fee-earners:* 14

MILLER & COMPANY 75-79 Regent St, Cambridge, CB2 1BE **Tel:** (01223) 366741 **Fax:** (01223) 460429 **DX:** 5816 Cambridge **Ptnrs:** 3 **Asst solrs:** 3 **Other fee-earners:** 5 **Contact:** Ms Kathleen English *A general practice with one of the largest and most experienced matrimonial and childcare departments in Cambridge.*

MILLER GARDNER

497 CHESTER ROAD, MANCHESTER, M16 9HF
Tel: (0161) 877 4777 **Fax:** (0161) 877 5777 **DX:** 25751 OLD TRAFFORD **Email:** MILLER.GARDNER@ZEN.CO.UK

The Firm: Established in 1991. Miller Gardner is a specialist niche Practice servicing the needs of private clients in the main. Its two main areas are in crime, including commercial fraud and personal injury. Commercial and domestic conveyancing has recently been offered as an additional service with the acquisition of a small Practice dealing exclusively with conveyancing. A small number of private commercial clients are also accommodated principally by a Senior Partner. The Firm has a Legal Aid Franchise in all main categories of work.

Principal Areas of Work:

Crime: Work includes commerical fraud, drug trafficking and the more serious cases. Additionally, the firm provides a 24 hour service at Police Stations for clients arrested and handles run of the mill criminal work in addition.

Personal Injury: Work is taken on principally for Plaintiffs involved in road traffic accidents, accidents at work, tripping and increasingly involving medical negligence. No Win/No Fee (C.F.A.) as well as after the events legal Insurance is offered in addition to Legal Aid.

Conveyancing: The Firm has a dedicated department dealing with domestic and commercial conveyancing.

Commercial Work: This is also handled for a number of corporate clients and sole traders and partnerships.

Expansion: The firm is in negotiations at present for the merger with another substantial Practice offering additional personal injury expertise and family.

Number of partners:	3
Assistant solicitors:	4
Other fee-earners:	6

WORKLOADS	
Crime	45%
Personal Injury	30%
Conveyancing	10%
Other Litigation	10%
Commercial	5%

CONTACTS	
Crime	Mr Geoffrey B Miller
Litigation	Mr Rodney M Gardner
Personal Injury	Miss Jeanette Miller
Private Client	Mr Rodney M Gardner

MILLER HENDRY 10 Blackfriars Street, Perth, PH1 5NS *Tel:* (01738) 637311 *Fax:* (01738) 638685 *DX:* 21 Perth *Ptnrs:* 16 *Asst solrs:* 11 *Other fee-earners:* 10

MILLER SAMUEL & CO

RWF HOUSE, 5 RENFIELD STREET, GLASGOW, G2 5EZ
Tel: (0141) 221 7934 **Fax:** (0141) 221 5376 **DX:** 161 GLASGOW

The Firm: Founded in 1973, Miller Samuel is a well established city centre firm which provides a comprehensive legal service to commercial clients with particular expertise in property development and leasing. The firm has developed a thriving litigation practice which complements the commercial work including landlord and tenant litigation and employment law. It also handles a substantial amount of debt recovery, personal injury and matrimonial work. Its range of services include all private client fields.

Principal Areas of Work:

Commercial Property/ Corporate: (Contact: Iain A. Doran). Corporate property development, commercial leasing, investment, funding, construction, etc., service with specialist rent review arbitration/ expert services. Private company work and general commercial contracts also handled.

Litigation: (Contact: Robert P. Kerr). Contract disputes, employment, debt collection, recovery of possession of heritable property, finance leasing, consumer credit, arbitration, industrial injury claims, road traffic accident claims, matrimonial and food law.

Private Client: (Contact: Michael Samuel). A comprehensive service is provided offering clients advice on the administration of estates, tax planning, charities and wills. This department also deals with the purchase and sale of residential property.

Managing partner:	P. Michael Samuel
Senior partner:	P. Michael Samuel
Number of partners:	11
Assistant solicitors:	4
Other fee-earners:	10

WORKLOADS	
Commercial litigation, employment and reparation	50%
Commercial property and corporate	40%
Personal including residential, conveyancing, wills, trusts	10%

CONTACTS	
Commercial litigation	R.P. Kerr
Commercial litigation	Marie McDonald
Commercial property/corporate	I. Doran, D.C. Lamb
Commercial property/corporate	K.T. Gibson/ John McQuillan
Debt recovery	R.P. Kerr, Marie MacDonald
Employment law	Robert P. Kerr
Matrimonial	Laura M Doherty
Reparation	Robert P. Kerr
Residential conveyancing	P.M. Samuel/E.L. Laverty
Wills, trusts	P.M. Samuel

MILLS & CO Milburn House, Dean Street, Newcastle-upon-Tyne, NE1 1LE *Tel:* (0191) 233 2222 *Fax:* (0191) 233 2220 *Ptnrs:* 5 *Asst solrs:* 1

MILLS & REEVE

FRANCIS HOUSE, 112 HILLS ROAD, CAMBRIDGE, CB2 1PH
Tel: +44 (0)1223 364422 **Fax:** +44 (0)1223 355848 **DX:** 122891 CAMBRIDGE 4 **Email:** DMO@MILLS-REEVE.COM

FRANCIS HOUSE, 3-7 REDWELL STREET, NORWICH, NR2 4TJ
Tel: +44 (0)1603 660155 **Fax:** +44 (0)1603 633027 **DX:** 5210 NORWICH **Email:** RMJ@MILLS-REEVE.COM

The Firm: Mills & Reeve is one of the UK's largest law firms outside London and the largest in the Eastern Region with 50 partners, 200 lawyers and a total strength of over 400.

The firm offers a full range of corporate, commercial, property, litigation and private client services, in particular focusing on being:

● an advisor to Eastern Region businesses and their owners;
● a competitive supplier of high volume legal services for insurers and other financial institutions;
● a national specialist in the sectors of: Agriculture; NHS Trusts; Higher Education.

For all the firm's clients their aim is to:

● provide creative solutions to their problems;
● be innovative in devloping new products and service to meet their needs;
● meet consistently the high standards of delivery and quality of service they expect.

Principal Areas of Work:

Corporate and Property: The corporate and property teams handle matters as diverse as the businesses they advise. As well as substantial corporate, commercial, property and dispute resolution teams in both offices, they have specialised teams in intellectual property, tax, employment, pensions, insolvency, construction and engineering, PFI, planning and environmental matters and licensing. The firm is able to provide clients with a complete service including advocacy in-house at all levels of the civil and criminal courts and the use of alternative dispute resolution.

Insurance: The insurance team is one of the most substantial outside London, embracing all liability risks and with specialist professional indemnity teams.

Agriculture: Mills & Reeve enjoy a well established national reputation in agriculture and related agri-business. Their agriculture team is expanding its range of advice to clients at all points on the food chain. They also have one of the largest landed estate and private client practices outside London advising a wide range of land owners, entrepreneurs and business people on personal tax planning both in the UK and offshore.

Health: NHS Trusts and Health Authority work continues to expand over a wide geographical basis throughout the UK The firm acts for over 60 NHS bodies and are currently advising on over 20 PFIs within the healthcare sector.

Education: Significant growth continues to be achieved in work for educational institutions where they act for over 50 universities and colleges. A full range of work is undertaken including PFI schemes and tax efficient funding schemes.

Senior partner:	Jonathan Barclay
Managing partners:	Mark Jeffries
	& Duncan Ogilvy
Number of partners:	50
Assistant solicitors:	77
Other fee-earners:	70

WORKLOADS	
Agriculture, tax and estate planning	20%
Corporate	20%
Insurance	18%
Health & Universities	17%
Property	15%
Private Client	10%

CONTACTS	
Agriculture	William Barr & Matthew Arrowsmith-Brown
Corporate	Mark Jeffries
Health	Raith Pickup & Stephen King
Insurance	Guy Hodgson
Private Client	Roger Bamber
Property	Beverly Firth
Universities	Glynne Stanfield

MILLS SELIG

20 CALLENDER STREET, BELFAST, BT1 5BQ
Tel: (01232) 243878 **Fax:** (01232) 231956 **DX:** 459 NR BELFAST **Email:** MILLS-SELIG@MSN.COM

The Firm: Founded in 1959, Mills Selig has since developed to become a major force both in Northern Ireland and beyond, providing a comprehensive range of services to its predominantly corporate clientele.

The firm's traditional strengths are in commercial property and corporate/corporate finance work but it is also developing a strong presence in litigation, particularly defamation, commercial litigation, product liability and employment law. Placing a strong emphasis on high quality service and developing close working relationships with clients, each client has an assigned Partner to act as a contact point with overall knowledge of the client's affairs.

Principal Areas of Work:

Commercial Property: Acting for developers of retail, industrial, commercial and residential property, institutional lenders and investors and commercial landlords and tenants.

Company and Commercial: Complete range of company and commercial services with particular expertise in merger and acquisition of companies and businesses, joint ventures both locally and internationally and corporate finance. Specialist knowledge of retail, pharmaceuticals, energy, textiles, food industries, agrichemicals and franchising.

Litigation: Full range of civil litigation and tribunal services, with particular expertise in commercial litigation, defamation, product liability, professional indemnity, employment, construction, criminal damage and property litigation.

Private Client: Residential conveyancing, wills, trusts, estate planning and probate.

Senior partner:	W. Stratton Mills
Number of partners:	6
Associate partners:	2
Assistant solicitors:	3
Consultants:	1
Other fee earners:	4

WORKLOADS	
Commercial Property	40%
Company and Commercial	30%
Litigation	25%
Other	5%

CONTACTS	
Comm. Litigation	Paul Spring, Brian Ham, Adam Curry
Comm. Property	Stratton Mills, Brian Ham, Ivan Selig
Company/Commercial	R. Fulton, B. McCann, I. Selig
Corporate Finance	Richard Fulton
Defamation	Paul Spring
Employment	Bill McCann
Environment and Planning	Michael Burns
Insolvency	John Kearns
Private Client	Jeremy Mills
Product Liability	Paul Spring

MINCOFFS

KENSINGTON HOUSE, 4-6 OSBORNE ROAD, NEWCASTLE-UPON-TYNE, NE2 2AA
Tel: (0191) 281 6151 **Fax:** (0191) 281 8069 **DX:** 62550

The Firm: The firm was established in 1948.

Principal Areas of Work:

General Description: Commercial property, corporate transactions and litigation represent the principal areas with particular experience in licensing, planning and professional negligence claims.

The firm's philosophy is to provide clients with a partner led service with experienced and enthusiastic support staff.

The firm holds a Legal Aid Franchise and has received the Investors in People Award.

Please contact the Managing Partner for any further information.

Managing partner:	Austen Science
Number of partners:	6
Assistant solicitors:	7
Other fee-earners:	11

MINTER ELLISON

20 LINCOLN'S INN FIELDS, LONDON, WC2A 3ED
Tel: (0171) 831 7871 **Fax:** (0171) 404 6722 **Internet:** HTTP://WWW.MINTERS.COM.AU

The Firm: A long established Australian based multinational firm, Minter Ellison has offices and associated firms throughout Australia and Asia and in London. The firm established its London office in 1974, making it the longest established Australian law firm in the UK. The London office provides advice to UK and European law firms, UK and European companies, financial institutions and private investors on all aspects of Australian law.

Principal Areas of Work:

Australian Law: Company and takeover laws; regulation of the Australian securities industry; mergers and acquisitions; international finance; legal and tax implications of Australian financial transactions; telecommunications and information technology; joint ventures and commercial contracts; establishment of new businesses in Australia; general commercial advice; defence and government contracting; employment laws and practices; foreign investment in Australia; insurance laws; Australian based litigation, arbitration and dispute resolution; intellectual property; and taxation. The firm also offers access to expertise in New Zealand law through its associated firm Rudd Watts & Stone.

English & European Law: Lawyers in the London office are able to advise the firm's clients who are carrying on business in the UK and other parts of Europe. The main areas of practice are general corporate and commercial advice, takeovers and acquisitions, telecommunications and information technology, banking and finance, commercial contracts, business laws, taxation, financial services, employment law and competition law.

The firm also maintains close contact with specialist advisers in leading English law firms.

International Transactions: The London office offers expertise in structuring and negotiating international agreements and has made a significant contribution to the successful implementation of business ventures in Europe, Australia and Asia.

Other Offices: Sydney, Melbourne, Brisbane, Canberra, Hong Kong.

Associated Firms: Adelaide, Perth, Auckland, Wellington, Singapore, Jakarta.

Resident Partners:	Michael Whalley
	Robert Hanley
Number of partners (worldwide):	156
Fee-earners (London):	5
Fee-earners (worldwide):	728

WORKLOADS	
Commercial	25%
Corporate	25%
Mergers/ acquisitions	25%
Banking	10%
Tax	10%
International	5%
Other	5%

MISHCON DE REYA

21 SOUTHAMPTON ROW, LONDON, WC1B 5HS
Tel: (0171) 440 7000 **Fax:** (0171) 404 5982 **DX:** 37954 KINGSWAY **Email:** POSTMASTER@MISHCON.CO.UK **Internet:** WWW.MISHCON.CO.UK

Mishcon de Reya is a high profile and dynamic commercial practice based in central London. The firm's reputation has been built on its commercial litigation, defamation, entertainment, media and family work. It is increasingly highly regarded for its corporate and commercial property expertise as the firm's ability to attract high quality instructions in these practice areas continues to grow. The firm's deep understanding of its clients' needs underpin every area of its practice.

The Firm: Mishcon de Reya provides legal services to a wide range of corporate and individual clients. The firm was established as Victor Mishcon & Co. in 1929 and continues to grow rapidly. In response to strong client demand, the firm continues to build on its expertise in non-contentious work in line with its business strategy. Over the past year the firm has significantly expanded its corporate and commercial property capability with the addition of numerous highly respected partners and solicitors from City firms. Over the last two years the number of solicitors in the firm has increased by 24%. In the same period, whilst maintaining its strong litigation practice, fee income from corporate and comercial property work has increased from 30% to represent almost 50% of total fee income. The firm has a youthful and dynamic culture and continues to attract the highest quality lawyers.

Principal Areas of Work: The firm has traditionally been organised into litigation, corporate and commercial, property, media and entertainment, family and private client departments. However, in line with industry sectors and client requirements, specialist units combine lawyers from various departments.

Corporate: The firm's services to corporate clients include new business start-ups, management buy-outs, mergers, acquisitions and disposals, flotations, joint ventures, venture capital and general corporate advice.

Commercial: Commercial work includes advice on general contract negotiation, international trade, financing and secured lending, trade finance, employment and industrial relations and protection and exploitation of intellectual property rights.

Corporate Tax: The Corporate Tax Department advises on all aspects of corporate and international tax, tax planning and offshore arrangements.

Property: The firm's enlarged property department acts for publicly quoted property companies, pensions funds, banks, house builders, retailers and restaurant chains as well as private investors and other property users. Work undertaken includes major site assemblies, sale and purchase of investment portfolios, joint venture structuring and secured lending, landlord and tenant disputes, planning agreements, construction contracts, pre-lets and plot sales.

Litigation: The litigation department works nationally and internationally and advises on both corporate and media matters. The corporate division covers trade finance disputes, bank recoveries, fraud investigations, white-collar crime, employment disputes, directors' contracts, minority shareholder actions, insolvencies, insurance disputes, property and construction contracts, partnership disputes, tax investigations and commercial issues. Employment advice is given on contract disputes, wrongful and unfair dismissal, European employment law, disciplinary hearings, immigration and work permits, tax and advice on drafting personnel policies and equal opportunities advice. Contentious media disputes on which we advise include defamation, breach of confidence/privacy issues, contempt and intellectual property. Consideration is always given to Alternative Dispute Resolution and all our litigators are mediation trained.

Media: The firm's specialist media group maintains its film, television and music base and has expanded into new media, particularly as advsiers to online information providers. In the past year this expertise has expanded into product and personality licensing.Mishcon de Reya's services to private individuals include divorce and separation, cohabitation disputes, property and financial settlements, children's cases, adoption and international child abduction. The firm has particular expertise in international high net worth cases and those involving a media aspect. It also offers guidance in private client matters such as probate, trust, estate and succession law as well as tax planning advice.

The firm provides *pro bono* legal advice to a number of organisations including Artwork, Board of Deputies of British Jews, City Ballet of London, Diamond Dance, Jamaican Council for Human Rights, Liberty, The Fabian Society and The Mary Ward Legal Centre. A leading medium-sized practice run openly by young partners, the firm has an excellent reputation built over many years. It is chaired by John Jackson, a senior business figure and chairman of Ladbroke Group plc.

Further details of the firm's services are available from their marketing department.

Chairman:	John Jackson
Number of partners:	32
Assistant solicitors:	50
Other fee-earners:	25

WORKLOADS	
Litigation	40%
Property	26%
Corporate (including entertainment)	22%
Family/Private Client	12%

CONTACTS	
Banking and Finance	Richard Tyler
Corporate	Kevin Gold, Patrick Heffernan
Defamation	Karen Sanig
Employment	Rowena Herdman-Smith
Family	Sandra Davis, Maggie Rae
Fraud	Gary Miller, Kasra Nouroozi
Immigration	Kamal Rahman, Philip Barth
Insolvency Recovery	Michael Gleeson
Litigation	Tony Morton-Hooper, Anthony Julius
Media and Intellectual property	Jonathan Cameron Mimi Curran
Private client	Christopher Allen
Property	Philip Freedman
Tax	Brian Slater

MITCHELLS ROBERTON George House, 36 North Hanover Street, Glasgow, G1 2AD **Tel:** (0141) 552 3422 **Fax:** (0141) 552 2935 **DX:** Glasgow 77 **Ptnrs:** 12 **Asst solrs:** 6 **Other fee-earners:** 9 **Contact:** Irene Nicolson *Established for over 250 years, with a strong private client base and vibrant company/commercial, property and litigation departments.*

WORKLOADS			
Private Client	30%	Company/Commercial	25%
Property	25%	Litigation	20%

MONIER-WILLIAMS & BOXALLS

71 LINCOLN'S INN FIELDS, LONDON, WC2A 3JF
Tel: (0171) 405 6195 **Fax:** (0171) 405 1453 **DX:** 37975 KINGSWAY

The Firm: Monier-Williams & Boxalls originated in 1790 and has developed a comprehensive range of services for business clients and for private individuals.

The firm has been well known since the last century for its expertise in the Wine Trade and has a unique reputation in related intellectual property law. It has also acquired and developed particular expertise in Employment Law, Professional Partnerships, Charity and Surrogacy Law.

The firm's clients include major public companies, banks, multiple retailers, insurance companies, educational establishments and well known charities. The approach is one of providing a personal service, with close involvement of partners, both in its specialised areas of work and in its wider general practice.

The firm's foreign connections include acting for agencies of the French, Spanish and Mexican governments.

Foreign Languages: Spanish, French and Gujarati.

Number of partners:	9
Other fee-earners:	4

CONTACTS	
Charity law	Michael Dunn
Company and Commercial	John Randel
Employment	Pamela Davies
Litigation	Gerald Neylan
Medical Partnerships	Andrew Hill
Property	Christopher Hughes
Surrogacy	Christine Bryon
Wine Trade Matters	David Sills

H. MONTLAKE & CO 197 High Rd, Ilford, IG1 1LX *Tel:* (0181) 553 1311 *Fax:* (0181) 553 3066 *DX:* 200859 Ilford 4 *Ptnrs:* 6 *Other fee-earners:* 1

MOORE & BLATCH

11 THE AVENUE, SOUTHAMPTON, SO17 1XF
Tel: (01703) 636311 **Fax:** (01703) 332205 **DX:** 38507 SOUTHAMPTON 3

The Firm: Moore & Blatch is one of the major law firms in central Southern England with a commercial office in Southampton and a private client office in Lymington. The firm has five departments including an investment department in the Lymington office. Particular areas of strength are company, commercial litigation, commercial property, private client, wealth administration and town planning and estate development.

Principal Areas of Work:

Company: (*Contact Partner:* Roger Bailey. *Fee-earners:* 4). This department specialises in corporate transactions, including share and business acquisitions, MBOs and public offers and has been involved in bringing companies to AIM. Advice on company law, directors' responsibilities, insolvency, competition and EC law, partnership, employment and commercial matters.

Personal Injury and Insurance: (Contact Partner: David Thompson. *Fee-earners:* 18). This department handles all aspects of personal injury work, including industrial disease, medical negligence and road traffic injuries for both plaintiffs and defendants. Within the department is a specialist serious injury team. The department also advises insurers on all aspects of insurance law.

Litigation: (*Contact Partner:* Robert Miles. *Fee-earners:* 7). The department provides a range of litigation services including employment law, health and safety legislation, insolvency work, banking litigation, substantial trade and construction disputes, professional negligence and debt collection. In addition the firm undertakes admiralty work.

Property: (*Contact Partner:* Steve Ingram. *Fee-earners:* 10). The department handles the acquisition, disposal and management of commercial property, joint ventures, loan work and social housing schemes. The department also handles volume residential conveyancing schemes, landlord and tenant work and residential and commercial land development and planning.

Planning and Development: (*Contact Partner:* John Barrington. *Fee-earners:* 4). Work includes planning agreements, planning appeals and inquiries and judicial reviews on behalf of developers, landowners and local authorities.

Private Client: (*Contact Partner:* David Rule. *Fee-earners:* 17). The department provides a complete wealth administration service for private client families and work includes tax and estate planning, investments, wills, trusts, charitable trusts, probate and retirement

Managing partner:	Michael Caton
Senior partner:	Robert Miles
Number of partners:	15
Assistant solicitors:	17
Other fee-earners:	28

WORKLOADS	
Private Client (Tax/Trust/Probate)	35%
Insurance & Personal Injury	33%
Property	17%
Litigation	10%
Company	5%

CONTACTS	
Commercial property	Steve Ingram
Company	Roger Bailey
Insolvency	Peter Jeffery
Insurance	David Thompson
Intellectual property	Leanne Prowse
Litigation	Robert Miles
Private client	David Rule
Town planning	John Barrington

Continues overleaf

finance, family law, general civil litigation and property. The department includes M.S.I. (Dip), A.T.I.I. and A.C.I.B. qualified specialists and has five members of S.T.E.P.. The firm is a full member of the Association of Solicitor Investment Managers.

Intellectual Property: (Contact Partner: Leanne Prowse. *Fee-earners:* 2). The firm handles all matters relating to intellectual property rights and undertakes trade mark registrations. Work includes transfer of intellectual property rights, licensing, infringement actions, related contracts, including computer software, franchising, agency and distribution.

Housing Associations: (Contact Partner: Michael Caton. *Fee-earners:* 5). A broad range of services is provided by the firm ranging from finance and development to the recovery of rent arrears and the provision of conveyancing services.

Lender Services: (Contact Partner: Steve Ingram. *Fee-earners:* 5). The firm provides a wide range of legal services to both residential and commercial lenders including both secured and unsecured lending. Work includes drafting lending documentation, asset recovery, repossession litigation, professional negligence litigation and conveyancing services to mortgage lenders.

Transport Law: (Contact Partner: David Thompson. *Fee-earners:* 2). The firm acts for and advises shipping companies, ferry operators and road haulage companies and has considerable expertise of representing these companies at public and transport enquiries. In addition the firm advises on related environmental issues.

Nature of Clientele: The firm acts for public and private companies, insurance companies, financial institutions, partnerships and individuals.

In 1997 the firm won the silver award in the Lawyer-Hifal awards for the best financial services firm.

MOORHEAD JAMES

21 FLEET STREET, LONDON, EC4Y 1AA
Tel: (0171) 831 8888 **Fax:** (0171) 936 3635

The Firm: Moorhead James is a commercial practice offering a comprehensive range of services to clients ranging from private individuals to multinational businesses.

Principal Areas of Work:

Corporate & Commercial: *Work includes:* formations, flotations, corporate restructuring, franchising and licensing, sports and leisure, banking, corporate finance, education, EU law and aviation.

Property: The department advises on all aspects of commercial and residential conveyancing, environmental law, construction and development and oil and gas, landlord and tenant.

Litigation: This includes High Court and County Court Actions, landlord and tenant and other property disputes, employment matters, debt collection, professional negligence and insolvency.

Matrimonial: All aspects of divorce, financial settlements, cohabitation.

Private Client: *Work includes:* tax planning, charities, wills and probate.

Overseas Associated Offices: Frankfurt, Rome, Milan, Paris, Hong Kong, Beijing, Prague, Budapest.

Foreign Languages: French, German, Cantonese.

Senior partner:	Ben Moorhead
Number of partners:	6
Assistant solicitors:	1

WORKLOADS	
Company and commercial/ international	40%
Property and secured lending	35%
Litigation, matrimonial, landlord and tenant, employment and immigration	25%

CONTACTS	
Company/ commercial	Ben Moorhead
Company/ commercial	David James
Corporate finance	Ben Moorhead
Corporate finance	David James
Employment	Christine Bowyer-Jones
Litigation	Christine Bowyer-Jones/Wayne de Nicolo
Matrimonial/Family	Susan Leon
Offshore tax planning	R. Moorhead
Oil and gas	Julian Bishop
Property	Julian Bishop/Susan Leon
Sports and leisure	Ben Moorhead

MORE & CO 19 Dublin Street, Edinburgh, EH1 3PG *Tel:* (0131) 557 1110 *Fax:* (0131) 557 8882 *Ptnrs:* 3 *Asst solrs:* 15 *Other fee-earners:* 3

MORECROFT URQUHART 8 Dale Street, Liverpool, L2 4TQ *Tel:* (0151) 236 8871 *Fax:* (0151) 236 8109 *DX:* 14142 *Ptnrs:* 14 *Asst solrs:* 6 *Other fee-earners:* 23

MORE FISHER BROWN 1 Norton Folgate, London, E1 6DA *Tel:* (0171) 247 0438 *Fax:* (0171) 247 0649 *DX:* 131-415 Bishopsgate *Ptnrs:* 9 *Asst solrs:* 7 *Other fee-earners:* 1

MORGAN BRUCE

BRADLEY COURT, PARK PLACE, CARDIFF, CF1 3DP
Tel: (01222) 385385 **Fax:** (01222) 385300 **DX:** 33014 CARDIFF

167 FLEET STREET, LONDON, EC4A 2JB
Tel: (0171) 822 8000 **Fax:** (0171) 822 8222 **DX:** 261

11 GOLD TOPS, NEWPORT, NP9 4UJ
Tel: (01633) 244988 **Fax:** (01633) 246130 **DX:** 33226 NEWPORT (SOUTH WALES)

PRINCESS HOUSE, PRINCESS WAY, SWANSEA, SA1 3LJ
Tel: (01792) 634634 **Fax:** (01792) 634500 **DX:** 39581 SWANSEA 1

Established over 160 years ago, Morgan Bruce provides the full range of commercial legal services to corporate, public sector and individual clients throughout England and Wales.

The Firm: Founded in Wales in 1836, Morgan Bruce has four offices in Cardiff, London, Newport and Swansea. Its office in the heart of London enables the firm to provide clients in Wales and England with City-based expertise at competitive rates.

Principal Areas of Work: The firm provides services to public and private companies, banks, building societies, professional partnerships and sole traders.

The firm is divided into three commercial divisions which span all four offices. The company and commercial department offers a comprehensive service, undertaking Stock Exchange work, mergers, acquisitions and disposals, corporate finance and management buy-outs.

The commercial property department has widespread experience in industrial and harbourside developments, housing and flat development, extensive transactional work for public authorities, land assembly for landfill, hospital-related transactions, housing associations, landlords and tenants and a specialised knowledge of the property needs of the leisure and brewing industries.

The substantial litigation and insurance departments include units specialising in the construction industry and protection of intellectual property, and solicitors who have rights of audience in the High Court.

The firm has provided services to the public sector for many years and has established connections with universities and other higher education institutions, health authorities and NHS Trusts, charities, local authorities, an urban development corporation, departments of government, cultural institutions and statutory bodies.

A number of special interest groups have been developed to provide advice on banking law, construction, employment law, environmental law, European law, fraud, intellectual property and competition issues, housing associations, health, the private finance initiative and professional indemnity.

Sectors of specialisms include the energy industry, building society law, liquor, licensing and gaming, public administration legal issues, relocation of company staff, media law and computerised debt collection service, while a dedicated department provides a comprehensive litigation service to insurance companies. Defendant work covers every aspect of personal injury, public liability and property damage claims.

Other specialist litigation departments deal with professional negligence and indemnity, landlord and tenant and property litigation.

The private client department specialises in the full range of private and personal matters, including property, estates administration, tax, wills and trusts.

Foreign Connections: The firm has strong international links and is a founder member of the Association of European Lawyers and has established connections with law firms in North America and the Far East. Languages spoken include Bemba, French, German, Greek, Italian, Mandarin, Spanish, Welsh, Punjabi, Hebrew, Portuguese and Polish.

Managing partner:	Guy Clarke
Senior partner:	John Bowen
Number of partners:	59
Assistant solicitors:	78
Other fee-earners:	34

WORKLOADS	
Property	25%
Commercial litigation	23%
Company	22%
Insurance	21%
Landlord & tenant	5%
Family	2%
Private client	2%

MORGAN JONES & PETT 95 St. Georges Road, Great Yarmouth, NR30 2NR *Tel:* (01493) 334700 *Fax:* (01493) 334710 *DX:* 41102 *Ptnrs:* 2 *Asst solrs:* 1 *Other fee-earners:* 4

MORGAN, LEWIS & BOCKIUS

4 CARLTON GARDENS, PALL MALL, LONDON, SW1Y 5AA
Tel: (0171) 747 5500 **Fax:** (0171) 839 3650/930 8456 **DX:** 37224 PICCADILLY 1 **Internet:** HTTP://WWW.MLB.COM

The Firm: Founded in Philadelphia in 1873, Morgan Lewis & Bockius LLP is one of the oldest and largest law firms in the US with over 300 partners and 900 lawyers. As one of the first major US law firms to develop a multi-city practice, Morgan Lewis & Bockius LLP is a leading international law firm able to draw on a wide diversity of capabilities and substantive experience. As a multi-national partnership the firm has a commitment to utilise technology in order to provide a superior service to clients. E-mail, voice messaging and state-of-the-art data communications enable lawyers throughout the firm to work together pooling resources and talents on single projects despite geographical separation. Many of the firm's lawyers have attained positions of recognition in their respective fields of expertise.

London Office: Established in 1981, the London office specialises in international and cross-border mergers and acquisitions, financings and tax planning for corporations and individuals and acts as a focal point for many of the international and cross-border business transactions which are handled by the firm in Europe and the Middle East. Such financing work includes broad expertise in loan, equity and guarantee financings from national and multilateral financing institutions such as the World Bank, the International Finance Corporation, the Overseas Private Investment Corporation, the Export-Import Bank and other such institutions. In addition this includes the full range of English company/ commercial; commercial litigation; property; tax; trusts; food and drug regulatory work and other ancillary practice areas. In January 1994 the London office became a multi-national practice of Registered Foreign Lawyers and Solicitors recognised by The Law Society.

Areas of Practice: Worldwide, the firm handles a vast diversity of legal work including antitrust; arbitration and ADR; banking and financial services; bankruptcy and reorganisation law; business and corporate law; construction; customs law; energy; environmental law; executive compensation and employee benefits; food, drug and cosmetics law; foreign direct investment in the US; Government contract and regulation; immigration; insurance law; intellectual property and technology; international financings and trade; litigation; mergers and acquisitions; personal and private client law; product liability; securities law; trademark and copyright law and transport law.

Other Offices: Philadelphia, Washington, New York, Los Angeles, Miami, Harrisburg, Pittsburgh, Princeton, Brussels, Frankfurt, Tokyo, Singapore, Jakarta.

UK	
Number of partners:	9
Other lawyers:	14
Other fee-earners:	4
Worldwide	
Number of partners:	315
Other lawyers:	594
Other fee-earners:	243

WORKLOADS	
Corporate/Commercial	40%
Litigation	18%
Trusts	18%
Tax	13%
Employment	6%
Conveyancing	5%

CONTACTS	
Conveyancing	Stephen Turner
Corporate/Commercial	Robert Rakison/Tom Benz
Employment	Malcolm Mason
Litigation	Bob Goldspink/Steven Loble
Pharmaceutical	Anthony Warnock-Smith
Tax and Trusts	Charles Lubar/David Way

Morgan, Lewis & Bockius

REGISTERED FOREIGN LAWYERS & SOLICITORS

MORRISON & FOERSTER 21-26 Garlick Hill, London, EC4V 2AU *Tel:* (0171) 815 1150 *Fax:* (0171) 815 1159 *Ptnrs:* 1

MORTON FISHER

CARLTON HOUSE, WORCESTER ST, KIDDERMINSTER, DY10 1BA
Tel: (01562) 820181 **Fax:** (01562) 820066 **DX:** 16301/16302

The Firm: Morton Fisher has six offices covering a wide geographical area throughout Worcestershire. The firm serves the needs of the local community, specialising in company/ commercial work for business, agricultural law, and private client work. The firm handles a substantial amount of litigation, including matrimonial work, commercial litigation, planning, property and estate administration. Members of the firm are on the Law Society's Children Panel, the Personal Injury Panel and the Mental Health Review Tribunal Panel. It holds the Legal Aid Franchise.

Other Offices: Worcester, Stourport-on-Severn, Bromsgrove, Bewdley, Cleobury Mortimer.

Contacts: Agricultural *J.S.C. Quinn*; Charity *D.C. Bishop*; Child care *Miss K.Brake*, *Mrs G. Trenchard*; Commercial litigation and planning *T.M.L. Jones;* Debts *N. Robertson Smith*; Health *J.S.C. Quinn*; Matrimonial *Miss K. Brake*; Medical negligence *N. Robertson Smith*, *B.A Cairns*, *C.G.A. Stanley*; Personal injury *C.G.A. Stanley*, *N. Robertson Smith*, *B.A.Cairns*, *M.V.Burton*

Managing partner:	J.S. Quinn
Senior partner:	T. Morgan
Number of partners:	19
Assistant solicitors:	24
Other fee-earners:	24

WORKLOADS	
Civil litigation	30%
Family	25%
Commercial	15%
Probate/Trusts	15%
Residential conveyancing	15%

THE MORTON FRASER PARTNERSHIP

15 & 19 YORK PLACE, EDINBURGH, EH1 3EL
Tel: (0131) 550 1000 **Fax:** (0131) 550 1002 **DX:** 119 EDINBURGH

The Firm: Morton Fraser Commercial (Managing Director, Craig Bowman). All business client services are provided including commercial litigation. The corporate division deals with formation, administration, and reconstruction of companies, flotations, mergers and acquisitions and management buyouts, pensions, international trade, competition law, intellectual property and computer law, insolvency and banking law, with particular specialisms in asset finance and equipment leasing. The commercial property group undertakes all aspects of commercial property work including purchase, sale and leasing, planning, property development and investment, lending and securities and cross-border transactions, and is complemented by the firm's experience in the areas of environmental law and liquor licensing. Commercial litigation handles all types of litigation, tribunals, arbitration and ADR, with particular experience in debt recovery, security realization, employment and shipping. The Case Management unit specialises in the provision of bulk commodity legal services to institutional clients at low unit cost using the most up to date case management software.

Morton Fraser Milligan – (Managing Director, Linda Urquhart). This business provides all private client services including litigation, residential conveyancing, rural conveyancing and advice on agriculture, wills, executries, taxation, trusts, investment, financial planning.

Morton Fraser International – (Managing Director, Gordon Kerr). A new business unit, established to provide a comprehensive international legal and relocation service to corporate clients with particular emphasis on business migration, employment law and employee benefits worldwide.

Morton Fraser Relocation – (Managing Director, Gordon Kerr). A comprehensive relocation service operating from Birmingham and Edinburgh for corporate clients involved in moving employees within the UK.

Other Offices:

Morton Fraser Relocation, Fountain House, Great Cornbow, Halesowen, West Midlands. Tel: 0121-585 3400. Fax: 0121-585 5056;

Morton Fraser International, Hart House, 6 London Road, St Albans, HERTS. Tel: (01727) 840275).

Foreign Languages: French, German.

International Connections & Associated Offices: A representative office at Bte. 3, Square de Meeus 19, 1050, Brussels (Tel: 32 2 511 5823, Fax: 32 2 502 7604) and a member of Interlaw. Strong overseas connections are maintained with France, Japan, Korea, Australia, USA, Germany, Norway, Sweden, Italy and Holland.

Managing partner:	Gordon Kerr
Senior partner:	John Wightman CBE
Number of partners:	20
Assistant solicitors:	29
Other fee-earners:	46

WORKLOADS	
Private clients	35%
Commercial property	22%
Corporate	16%
Commercial litigation	14%
Family/Private client litigation	13%

CONTACTS	
Morton Fraser Commercial	Craig Bowman
Morton Fraser International	Jackie Cameron
Morton Fraser Milligan	Linda Urquhart
Morton Fraser Relocation	Gordon Kerr

MOWAT DEAN & CO WS 45 Queen Charlotte Street, Leith, Edinburgh, EH6 7HD *Tel:* (0131) 555 0616 *Fax:* (0131) 553 1523 *Ptnrs:* 4 *Asst solrs:* 3 *Other fee-earners:* 1

MOWLL & MOWLL 34 & 36 Castle Street, Dover, CT16 1PN *Tel:* (01304) 240250 *Fax:* (01304) 240040 *DX:* 6302 Dover *Ptnrs:* 8 *Asst solrs:* 3 *Other fee-earners:* 8

MULLIS & PEAKE Marshalls Chambers, 80A South Street, Romford, RM1 1QS *Tel:* (01708) 762326 *Fax:* (01708) 747145 *DX:* 4604 Romford *Ptnrs:* 9 *Asst solrs:* 3 *Other fee-earners:* 7

MUNDAYS

CROWN HOUSE, CHURCH ROAD, CLAYGATE, ESHER, KT10 0LP
Tel: (01372) 809000 **Fax:** (01372) 463782 **DX:** 36300 ESHER **Email:** HUB@MUNDAYS.CO.UK **Internet:** HTTP://WWW.MUNDAYS.CO.UK/LAW/

31 RUE MONTOYER, BOX 2, B-1040, BRUSSELS,
Tel: +32 2 502 2752 **Fax:** +32 2 512 5344

HAMILTON HOUSE, 1 TEMPLE AVENUE, LONDON, EC4Y 0HA
Tel: (0171) 437 8080 **Fax:** (0171) 437 8180

Mundays is a comprehensive legal practice that is particularly strong in the commercial field, with notable franchising, mergers and acquisitions, corporate finance, retail pharmacy, intellectual property and European/competition law practices. Based in Esher in Surrey, the firm has widespread connections.

The Firm: Established in 1960, Mundays has acquired a diverse client base that includes major international and national companies as well as smaller local businesses and individuals.

As part of the firm's commitment to providing quality services, each client is encouraged to look upon a particular partner as its principal contact in the firm. Each specialised department has a department head who is responsible for overseeing case management. Departments work with each other flexibly in cases where more than one is involved. At the outset of every new matter, clients are advised on Mundays' terms of business and the basis upon which fees are to be charged.

Principal Areas of Work:

The **Corporate Department** handles a range of high quality transactions and contracts including acquisitions and disposals of companies, joint ventures and public company work. The department also has experience in capital markets as well as in specialised areas such as employee share schemes. In the past year it has handled over 30 major transactions with a value exceeding £80m.

The **Commercial Department** has a specialist financial services unit that gives advice to banks and other lenders as well as to borrowers. Its expertise covers equity and venture capital, secured lending transactions and matters arising from the Financial Services Act. The department also has units dealing with distribution matters and employment law. In addition, it gives advice on general aspects of commercial law such as contractual disputes and mergers.

The complete range of property transactions is handled by the **Commercial Property Department**, including commercial leasehold transactions for both landlords and tenants, sale and purchase of unincorporated businesses as going concerns and town and country planning matters.

Mundays also has departments focusing on intellectual property, IT, litigation, licensing and partnership law.

Franchising: As one of the leading franchising practices in the UK, Mundays handles a variety of work concerning franchise agreements, franchise funding agreements, franchise disputes, international franchising and specialised aspects of property transactions in franchises.

The firm was instrumental in establishing The Franchise Lawyers European Group, whose members have offices in many countries both inside and outside the European Union. One of the Partners, Manzoor Ishani, is the author of a number of books on franchising matters and a regular contributor to Business Franchise Magazine, Franchise World, Business Money, Enterprise Magazine and numerous other journals. He is also an active lecturer in Britain and abroad, as is Ray Walley, another Partner who specialises in intellectual property work.

International: Mundays also has an office in Brussels.

A European and international unit within the commercial department has wide experience in European Community and other foreign legislation.

Managing partner:	Ray Walley
Senior partner:	Peter Munday
Number of partners:	14
Assistant solicitors:	6
Other fee-earners:	6

WORKLOADS	
Company and commercial (including franchising and IP)	35%
Residential property, matrimonial, tax and probate	24%
Commercial property	23%
Commercial litigation	18%

CONTACTS	
Commercial Property	Simon Withers
Corporate/Commercial	Peter Munday
Franchising	Manzoor Ishani
Intellectual Property/IT	Ray Walley
Litigation	Fiona McAllister
Pharmacy	Simon Withers
Private Client	Richard Ashby/Mehboob Dharamsi
Private Client	Karen Barham

MUNRO & NOBLE 26 Church Street, Inverness, IV1 1HX *Tel:* (01463) 221727 *Fax:* (01463) 225165 *DX:* IN 15 *Ptnrs:* 8 *Asst solrs:* 4 *Other fee-earners:* 5

MURPHY & O'RAWE Scottish Provident Building, 7 Donegall Sq West, Belfast, BT1 6JF **Tel:** (01232) 326636 **Fax:** (01232) 243777 **Ptnrs:** 4 **Asst solrs:** 7 **Other fee-earners:** 4 **Contact:** Betty O'Rawe and Patrick Eastwood *Broadly based practice, known for its insurance litigation expertise.*

WORKLOADS	
Litigation (defence and plaintiff)	80%
Commercial and conveyancing	20%

MURRAY BEITH MURRAY W.S.

39 CASTLE STREET, EDINBURGH, EH2 3BH
Tel: (0131) 225 1200 **Fax:** (0131) 225 4412 **DX:** ED40, EDINBURGH **Email:** MAILDESK@MURRAYBEITH.CO.UK

This progressive Edinburgh-based practice offers an extensive range of services to private and business clients, with specialities including asset management and tax planning, agricultural law and land purchase, and advising young and growing entrepreneurial businesses.

The Firm: Established in 1849, Murray Beith Murray actively seeks to combine its traditional strength of a dedicated client service with modern management and innovative use of technology.

Murray Beith Murray's client base includes national and international companies, property investors and developers, financial institutions and private investors and a significant number of land owning interests. The firm's aim is to create, enhance and protect the wealth of its clients.

The firm's services are provided through three separate divisions, namely private client, asset management and commercial.

Principal Areas of Work: Murray Beith Murray's core business is private client work and the firm is regarded as one of the leading private client legal firms in Scotland. This division provides a comprehensive range of legal, financial and administrative services, including wills and estate planning, trusts, taxation and executries. In the area of property law it offers a full service on agricultural law and rural property matters alongside a residential conveyancing service.

The asset management division offers a full financial planning service including a comprehensive, independent overview of a client's investment and financial needs. Advice is given on a wide range of financial planning issues, including protection of the family, school fees planning, insurance, pensions advice for retirement planning and investment.

Measured by funds under management, Murray Beith Murray is one of the largest solicitor investment managers in the United Kingdom. It provides a full range of investment management and administration services on both a discretionary and advisory basis.

The commercial division offers an extensive range of legal services to assist companies from start-up, through the early years to flotation and beyond. An efficient, competitive and personal service is combined with excellent financial contacts, deal-making skills and information-technology systems.

Services include the acquisition, development and realisation of commercial property of all kinds, together with advice on regulatory planning and environmental issues. These are supported by a litigation service, which includes amongst its specialities, work in the areas of professional negligence claims and insolvencies.

Managing partner:	F. Adam J. More
Senior partner:	William Berry
Number of partners:	9
Assistant solicitors:	12
Other fee-earners:	22

WORKLOADS	
Private Client	44%
Asset Management	32%
Commercial	24%

CONTACTS	
Asset Management	W. R. Gemmell
Commercial Property	F. A. J. More
Corporate	W. A. Finlayson
Litigation	N. J. Pollock
Private Client	H. P. Younger

MURRAY & CO Trac House, 34 Francis Grove, Wimbledon, London, SW19 4DT *Tel:* (0181) 2884893 *Fax:* (0181) 2884894 *DX:* 300120 Wimbledon Central *Ptnrs:* 2 *Other fee-earners:* 2

MYER WOLFF & MANLEY 15/16 Bowlalley Lane, Hull, HU1 1YE **Tel:** (01482) 223693 **Fax:** (01482) 225089 **DX:** 11904 **Ptnrs:** 5 **Asst solrs:** 5 **Other fee-earners:** 8 **Contact:** Timothy F. Durkin *A Legal Aid and private client practice specialising in criminal law, child care, matrimonial and mental health Tribunal work.*

WORKLOADS		
Crime		47%
Family (including child care and mental health)		21%
Personal injury/ claims	13%	Matrimonial	10%
Conveyancing/ probate	9%		

NABARRO NATHANSON

50 STRATTON STREET, LONDON, W1X 6NX
Tel: (0171) 493 9933 **Fax:** (0171) 629 7900 **DX:** 77 LONDON CHANCERY LANE WC2 **Internet:** HTTP://WWW.NABARRO.COM

THE ANCHORAGE, 34 BRIDGE STREET, READING, RG1 2LU
Tel: (0118) 950 4700 **Fax:** (0118) 950 5640 **DX:** 4068 READING

SOUTH QUAY, VICTORIA QUAYS, WHARF STREET, SHEFFIELD, S2 5SY
Tel: (0114) 279 4000 **Fax:** (0114) 278 6123 **DX:** 712550 SHEFFIELD-20

209A AVENUE LOUISE, 1050 BRUSSELS, BELGIUM.
Tel: 00 322 626 0740 **Fax:** 00 322 626 0749

Nabarro Nathanson is one of the country's leading commercial practices providing the full range of legal services to national and international clients.

The Firm: Nabarro Nathanson is a focused commercial practice, with more than 100 partners and some 300 fee-earners. The firm has recently undergone a period of growth that has seen major infrastructure changes, significant increases in fee earning and a new emphasis on client relationships. The firm is recognised as a leading player in many areas of the law including the corporate sector, property, IT, pensions, public sector, planning, property litigation and PFI. More than 25 per cent of the firm's work is with clients based overseas.

In 1999 the firm will move its London office to new premises between the City and the West End where it can optimise investments in IT and other support systems. There is also a new focus on training and development from which all members of Nabarro Nathanson now benefit.

The firm is always looking for individuals who can make a contribution to its success. Recent growth provides opportunities for qualified solicitors across a range of specialisms. There are also vacancies for trainee solicitors – mostly in London but also in the firm's Reading and Sheffield offices. Candidates must have an upper second degree, although not necessarily in law. Long-term prospects are excellent. Contact Jane Squire for application information.

Details of all the firm's activities are demonstrated on its web site – www.nabarro.com

Principal Areas of Work: Nabarro Nathanson's strength and diversity is a reflection of its varied, and growing, client base. Clients' needs are addressed through a range of industry sector groupings that run alongside traditional legal departments. These groupings comprise commercial property, energy, computers, communications and electronic publishing, pensions, insurance and financial services, public and private projects, corporate finance and a National Centre for Law in Industry which services the needs of the manufacturing sector.

The corporate department covers mergers and acquisitions, flotations, venture capital and management buyouts, EU law, intellectual property, tax, energy and insurance. The firm is also a leader in banking transactions for domestic and international banks and other major financial institutions.

Nabarro Nathanson has long been one of Britain's leading property law firms specialising in development, portfolio management, property finance, large scale acquisitions and investments and overseas property. Separate departments deal with property litigation, construction law work, and public sector matters (including planning, PFI and CPO). Other areas where the firm has significant strengths are IT (based in Reading), tax, health and community care, personal injury, charities and pensions. Nabarro Nathanson also has a high reputation for its general litigation and corporate insolvency work.

The breadth of work undertaken is matched by the quality of service provided – Nabarro Nathanson prides itself in being a highly commercial and forward-thinking practice with friendly, high-quality, professional staff.

Other Offices:

209A Avenue Louise 1050 Brussels Phone: (+32) 2 626 0740 Fax: (+32) 2 626 0749

In Association with Cabinet Lipworth
130 Rue de Faubourg St Honore 75008 Paris
Phone: (00) 33 1 53 75 41 41Fax: (00) 33 1 53 75 14 12

Associated Offices: Dubai, Hong Kong

Senior partner:	David Bramson
Number of partners:	111
Assistant solicitors:	237
Other fee-earners:	85

CONTACTS	
Banking	John Belton
Charities	Jonathan Burchfield
Construction	Roger Wakefield
Corporate/Commercial	David Wightman,
	Clive Lightburn, Rosemary Martin-Jones
Electricity	Robert Tudway
Employment	Valmai AdamsKeith Pugh
Environment	Mike Renger
EU/Competition	Cyrus Mehta
Health	David Anderson
Health & Safety	Gareth Watkins
Information Technology	Tony Bailes
Insolvency	Michael Prior
Intellectual	Guy Heath
International Tax	Malcolm Finney
Litigation	Peter Sigler,
	Ian MacPherson, Peter Sheppard
Minerals	John Blackwell
National Centre for Law in Industry	Gareth Watkins
Oil and Gas	Mark Saunders
Pensions	John Quarrell
Personal Injury	Steve Daykin
PFI	Malcolm Iley, Tim Shaw
Planning	David Hawkins
Property	Geoffrey Lander
Property	Jim Kinnier-Wilson
Property Litigation	Iain Travers
Public Sector	Malcolm Iley
Sheffield	Susan McKenna
Shipping	George Brown
Sports	Michael Hales
Tax	Malcolm Finney
Trusts/Private Client	Jim Edmondson
Venture Capital	Rhidian Jones

NALDER & SON Farley House, Falmouth Rd, Truro, TR1 2AT *Tel:* (01872) 241414 *Fax:* (01872) 242424 *DX:* 81204 Truro *Ptnrs:* 12 *Asst solrs:* 6 *Other fee-earners:* 19

NAPIER & SONS 1/9 Castle Arcade, Belfast, BT1 5DF *Tel:* (01232) 244602 *Fax:* (01232) 330330 *Ptnrs:* 6 *Asst solrs:* 3 *Other fee-earners:* 2

NAPTHEN HOUGHTON CRAVEN

7 WINCKLEY SQUARE, PRESTON, PR1 3JD
Tel: (01772) 883883 **Fax:** (01772) 257805 **DX:** 714572 PRESTON 14

The Firm: Created on the merger in 1990 of two of Preston's leading firms, Houghton Craven & Dicksons and Napthens. Since the merger, the firm has continued to expand, concentrating on the development of specialist departments, partner managed and led, and designed to provide a speedy response for all clients with particular emphasis on commercial work. Whilst the practice is based in the North West, the firm's clients are spread throughout the country and much of the firm's work is carried out on a national level.

Principal Areas of Work: The firm provides a wide range of legal services for commerce industry and private clients. Best know for its commercial property and corporate work, the firm has developed a thriving department specialising in employment law and also specialises in commercial, personal injury and road traffic accident litigation.

Other particular areas of specialisation are agricultural, planning and compensation and education.

Senior partner:	Peter J. Hosker
Number of partners:	13
Assistant solicitors:	6
Other fee-earners:	15

NASH & CO. Beaumont House, Beaumont Park, Plymouth, PL4 9BD *Tel:* (01752) 664444 *Fax:* (01752) 667112 *DX:* 8250 Plymouth *Ptnrs:* 7 *Asst solrs:* 7 *Other fee-earners:* 1

NATHAN, SILMAN

OSPREY HOUSE, 78 WIGMORE ST, LONDON, W1H 9DQ
Tel: (0171) 935 0898 **Fax:** (0171) 486 4803 **DX:** 9019 WE **Email:** MJNATHAN@LINK.ORG

The Firm: A commercial practice serving the needs of the established corporate client, the entrepreneur and the individual. The practice style is based on personal, partner-led service, with prompt and accurate advice being enhanced by sound commercial judgement. Best known for its niche retail specialisation, the firm's client base includes market leaders in that sector as well as in the property development and investment and construction industries.

Principal Areas of Work: The firm is recognised as having developed a particular expertise in retail property and related work and acts for a number of 'household name' retailers, with specialist seminars on topical issues being held regularly for clients and others. The firm is also known for its commercial property expertise (with a particular emphasis on development and joint-ventures), company/commercial, banking and commercial and property litigation.

Managing partner:	Michael J. Nathan
Senior partner:	Geoffrey Silman
Number of partners:	4
Assistant solicitors:	2
Other fee-earners:	2

CONTACTS	
Commercial property	S Lewis
Company/commercial	M Nathan
Litigation	Georgia Christofoli
Retail	G Silman

THE NATIONAL SOLICITORS' NETWORK

CONQUEST LEGAL MARKETING, 156 CROMWELL ROAD, LONDON, SW7 4EF
Tel: (0171) 244 6422 **Fax:** (0171) 370 6893 **DX:** 44109 GLOUCESTER ROAD

Nature of Group: The National Solicitors' Network (TNSN) was formed by Conquest Legal Marketing in 1991 to provide institutional, corporate and private clients with legal services of the highest quality.

The Firms: The Network embraces more than 250 independent solicitors' practices with 400 offices spread throughout England and Wales. Member firms range from two partner practices to a 37 partner commercial firm. As the largest solicitors' network in the UK, the Network provides an influential voice for its members. A full-time management and marketing team is based in London and there is a panel of regional representatives.

The Group: The Network generates and distributes substantial levels of profitable work to member firms. Agreements have been formed with building societies, insurance companies, banks, centralised lenders, major employers, an international charity and several NHS trusts. A national County Court agency service was set up in 1993 and has delivered significant benefit to participating firms. In addition to the generation of fee-earning work, there is a commitment to practice development and quality initiatives. A full range of services includes quality and training seminars and consultancy, information technology advice, negotiated discounts on professional indemnity top-up premiums and other benefits and discounts including marketing materials, office supplies and printwork services.

The Future: The Network's representative role is increasing as issues such as competitive tendering, franchising of legal services and the adoption of minimum practice standards become the norm. For more details and an application form please write to the address above.

Managing partner:	Richard Berenson
Operations:	Robin Richard
Membership:	Angela Willis
Number of partners:	1627
Other fee-earners:	2734

NEEDHAM & GRANT 14 Lincoln's Inn Fields, London, WC2A 3BP *Tel:* (0171) 242 5866 *Fax:* (0171) 831 8254 *Ptnrs:* 5 *Asst solrs:* 4 *Other fee-earners:* 2

NEEDHAM & JAMES 25 Meer Street, Stratford upon Avon, CV37 6QB *Tel:* (01789) 414 444 *Fax:* (01789) 296 608 *DX:* 16202 Stratford upon Avon *Ptnrs:* 12 *Asst solrs:* 10 *Other fee-earners:* 10

NEIL F. JONES & CO

3 BROADWAY, BROAD STREET, BIRMINGHAM, B15 1BQ
Tel: (0121) 643 1010 **Fax:** (0121) 643 1969 **DX:** 701215 EDGBASTON 4 **Email:** INFO@NEILFJONES.CO.UK

The Firm: Founded in 1980 the firm specialises in contentious and non-contentious construction matters, commercial disputes and a substantial amount of professional indemnity insurance work. Clients include major PLCs, professional practices, insurance companies and public bodies and the firm has gained national recognition.

We provide a swift, quality service focusing on client care and proactive advice and regularly hold free client seminars outlining recent changes and we also produce publications concerning relevant legal topics.

Neil F Jones & Co acts for and advises all sides of the building and engineering industries including public and private employers, contractors, sub-contractors and professionals (eg architects, engineers and surveyors), and their insurers.

Senior partner:	Jeffrey Brown
Number of partners:	5
Assistant solicitors:	6
Other fee-earners:	5

CONTACTS	
Construction (contentious)	Jeffrey Brown, Kevin Barrett, Simon Baylis, Ian Yule, Mark Arrand
Commercial litigation	Ian Yule, Mark Arrand
Construction (non-contentious)	Kevin Barrett, Simon Baylis
Insurance	Jeffrey Brown, Ian Yule, Mark Arrand

NEIL F. JONES & CO
S O L I C I T O R S

NEILL CLERK & MURRAY 3 Ardgowan Square, Greenock, PA16 8NG *Tel:* (01475) 724522 *Fax:* (01475) 784339 *DX:* 7 Greenock *Ptnrs:* 6 *Asst solrs:* 3

NEIL MYERSON SOLICITORS

THE COTTAGES, REGENT ROAD, ALTRINCHAM, CHESHIRE, WA14 1RX
Tel: (0161) 928 2065 **Fax:** (0161) 941 3719 **Email:** NEILMYERSON@COMPUSERVE.COM

The Firm: Established in 1982, Neil Myerson Solicitors is a rapidly expanding and progressive firm that provides a comprehensive legal service to both commercial and private clients. It has also developed a substantial personal injury, medical negligence and housing practice.

Principal Areas of Work:

Company Commercial: Corporate Finance, Commercial Property, Commercial Litigation, Company Formation, Commercial and Competition, Information Technology and Intellectual Property, Employment Law, Pensions and Taxation.

Private Client: Financial Services, Residential Conveyancing, Probate and Wills and Family and Divorce.

Personal Injury/Housing: Personal Injury Litigation, Medical Negligence, Litigation and Housing Disrepair cases.

Other Departments/Activities: The firm has its own Costs Drafting Department and has a Notary Public.

Recruitment: The firm is always keen to consider quality candidates at all levels. Application with CV to Neil Myerson.

Other Offices: 2-6 Greenhills Rents, Cowcross Street, London, EC1M 6BN. Tel: 0171 336 7555. Fax: 0171 251 5606 (as Winter Myerson).

Senior partner:	Neil Myerson
Number of Partners:	4
Assistant Solicitors:	12
Other Fee Earners:	20
Notary Public:	1

WORKLOADS	
Company Commercial	55%
Personal Injury/Housing	40%
Private Client	5%

NEIL MYERSON
SOLICITORS

NELSON & CO St. Andrew's House, St. Andrew's Street, Leeds, LS3 1LF **Tel:** (0113) 227 0100 **Fax:** (0113) 227 0113 **DX:** 713103 Leeds **Ptnrs:** 9 **Asst solrs:** 9 **Other fee-earners:** 12 **Contact:** David Parkin – practice manager *A corporate and private client practice. Particular specialisation in personal injury, commercial property, professional negligence, property litigation and debt recovery.*

NELSONS Pennine House, 8 Stanford Street, Nottingham, NG1 7BQ **Tel:** (0115) 958 6262 **Fax:** (0115) 958 4702 **DX:** 10096 **Ptnrs:** 23 **Contact:** Christine Pudge *Broad based practice known for commercial, private client and crime including business crime. Recently opened office in Derby.*

WORKLOADS		
Commercial		31%
Crime (including businesss crime)		31%
Family	11% Personal Injury	11%
Private client		10%
Civil (immigration and welfare)		6%

NESS GALLAGHER 358 Brandon Street, Motherwell, ML1 1XA *Tel:* (01698) 254644 *Fax:* (01698) 262012 *Ptnrs:* 2 *Asst solrs:* 3

NEWSOME VAUGHAN

GREYFRIARS HOUSE, GREYFRIARS LANE, COVENTRY, CV1 2GW
Tel: (01203) 633433 **Fax:** (01203) 256496 **DX:** 18854 COV.2

The Firm: Newsome Vaughan is a dynamic Civil Litigation practice which has enjoyed rapid growth in recent years, whilst maintaining its reputation in private client and corporate work

Principal Areas of Work: The firm specialises in personal injury litigation (Plaintiff and Defendant), medical negligence, civil litigation, mortgage repossessions, housing associations, company/commercial, commercial property, and general private client work.

Overseas Connections: The firm is a member of Law Group International.

Contacts: Civil Litigation *Alan Lodge;* Commercial Property *Rupert Griffiths;* Company/Comercial *David Vaughan;* Estate Development *Rupert Griffiths;* Housing Associations *Paul Saunders;* Insurance Litigation *Peter Jones;* Matrimonial *Alan Markham;* Medical Negligence *Brigitte Goff;* Mortgage Possession *Paul Saunders;* Personal Injury Litigation *Alan Lodge;* Private Client *Ian Grindal;* Professional Negligence *Alan Lodge.*

Senior partner:	Peter Jones
Number of partners:	5
Assistant solicitors:	9
Other fee-earners:	8

WORKLOADS	
Litigation	67%
Commercial/Business	20%
Private Clients	13%

NICHOLAS MORRIS

70-71 NEW BOND STREET, LONDON, W1Y 9DE
Tel: (0171) 493 8811 **Fax:** (0171) 491 2094 **DX:** 82967 MAYFAIR **Email:** MAIL@NICHOLASMORRIS.CO.UK
Internet: WWW.NICHOLASMORRIS.CO.UK

The Firm: Established over 35 years ago, the firm of Messrs. Nicholas Morris was from the beginning in the forefront of Entertainment, Film, Music and Media Law.

Representing top music groups, international stars of stage and screen, record companies, publishers, managers and agents, the firm is also keen to help and advise new bands, writers and composers; the firm also has an expertise and links with the sporting world.

The firm has a highly competent team of lawyers dealing with business affairs, commercial property, employment, family law, immigration, partnerships, company/commercial, insolvency, Wills and trusts, High Court litigation and most other forms of court proceedings including before the Privy Council.

Foreign Connections: The firm has international connections extending to the Far East, the United States, Europe, S.Africa and the Middle East.

Visit their Web site at: http://www.nicholasmorris.co.uk

Managing partner:	G. de Mornay Davies
Number of partners:	3
Assistant solicitors:	1
Other fee-earners:	5

WORKLOADS	
Entertainment	45%
Litigation	20%
Property, Wills	20%
Commercial	10%

CONTACTS	
Business Affairs, Property	G de Mornay Davies
Company, Commercial	J.Charles
Entertainment	L.Lowy/M.Smith/J.Levy/ J.Elford
Family Law	Simon Baldwin-Purry
Litigation	M.Jaques
Probate	G. Davies

NICHOLLS & CO 2 Aylsham Road, Norwich, NR3 3HQ *Tel:* (01603) 499999 *Fax:* (01603) 499998 *Ptnrs:* 2 *Other fee-earners:* 1

NICHOLSON GRAHAM & JONES

110 CANNON STREET, LONDON, EC4N 6AR
Tel: (0171) 648 9000 **Fax:** (0171) 648 9001 **DX:** 58 LONDON CHANCERY LANE **Email:** INFO@NGJ.SPRINT.COM **Internet:** WWW.NGJ.CO.UK

Nicholson Graham & Jones is a broad-based commercial practice in the heart of the City of London. This year it celebrates its 140th anniversary.

The Firm: During the 1990s the firm has doubled in size and has expanded its specialist capabilities. The firm provides a cost-effective, responsive and commercial legal service driven by the needs of its clients. The 1995 merger with Brecher & Co is proving to be an outstanding success. The firm's plans for growth have taken two very significant steps forward this year. A leading team of six construction lawyers from Bristows Cooke & Carpmael headed by James Hudson has joined the firm to create a new Construction and Engineering Department led by David Race. This department provides a wide range of services to the construction and property industries. The inolvency unit has been enhanced by the arrival of insolvency specialists, Paul Oughton and Tony Griffiths (and their two assistants) from Hill Taylor Dickinson.

Nature of Clientele: NGJ acts for a wide range of clients, many of whom have international interests. The firm is a founder member of GlobaLex, an international alliance of law firms with offices across the USA, Europe and the Far East and has an office in Brussels. The network is committed to the provision of integrated international legal services to its clients. Clients include listed and privately owned companies, institutions, the public sector and entreprenuers.

Principal Areas of Work:

General Description: There are five departments: corporate commercial, litigation, property, construction and engineering and private client. The development of the firm is increasingly based on cross-departmental groups focused on particular industry or business sectors or legal disciplines. Specialist units advise in the fields of sports, employment, environment and travel and leisure law, where legal expertise is combined with a wide understanding of the industries.

Corporate Commercial: The firm is particularly well known for its corporate work, including flotations, mergers and acquisitions, corporate finance and all UK, EU and international business transactions. Banking, insolvency, venture capital, UK and EC competition, intellectual property, sport and sponsorship law are areas of specialist expertise within the corporate department.

Litigation: The litigation department has extensive experience in commercial dispute resolution, both domestic and internationally, through ADR, arbitration and the courts. Specialist areas include financial services and banking, insolvency, employment, travel and leisure in addition to a wide range of general commercial, corporate and property litigation.

Property: The property department handles all types of transactions including financing, development, acquisitions, disposals and town planning.

Construction & Engineering: The new construction and engineering department is one of the largest and strongest in the country advising on contentious and non-contentious construction matters. A unique range of services is offered covering project/contract work through to litigation, arbitration and alternative dispute resolution including adjudication, mediation and conciliation.

Private Client The private client department advises on all aspects of estate and individual tax planning, frequently with an international element, specialising in international trust and tax advice, probate and acting for charities.

Recruitment & Training: This thriving firm wishes to hear from high quality lawyers, and recruits up to ten trainee solicitors each year. Apply by handwritten letter (with CV and names of referees) to Gail Harcus.

Managing partner:	Michael Johns
Number of partners:	52
Assistant solicitors:	35
Other fee-earners:	24

WORKLOADS	
Litigation	29%
Property	25%
Corporate and Commercial	22%
Construction and Engineering	10%
Banking	9%
Private client	5%

CONTACTS	
Banking	Richard Talbot
Commercial	Ian Green
Commercial Litigation	Tony Walker
Competition	Peter Bond
Construction and Engineering	David Race
Corporate finance	Richard Herbert
Corporate tax	Richard Woolich
Election law	Piers Coleman
Employment	Tony Walker
Healthcare and Pharmaceuticals	Owen Waft
Insolvency	Shashi Rajani
Intellectual Property	Sarah Kirk
Planning and environment	John Garbutt
Private client	Eliza Mellor and Michael Jacobs
Property	Richard Smith
Property Finance	Paul Salsbury
Property Litigation	Richard Franklin
Public sector	John Garbutt
Shipping and aviation finance	Austen Hall
Sport & sponsorship	Warren Phelops
Travel & leisure	Tim Robinson
Venture capital	Nicola Solomons

NICHOLSONS 23 Alexandra Rd, Lowestoft, NR32 1PP **Tel:** (01502) 532300 **Fax:** (01502) 568814 **DX:** 41204 **Ptnrs:** 6 **Asst solrs:** 3 **Other fee-earners:** 7 **Contact:** Mrs Tonia Baker *Long-established firm known for company/ commercial, debt recovery, insolvency, litigation, divorce and conveyancing.*

WORKLOADS		
Divorce, matrimonial, housing		24%
Company, commercial, partnership		21%
Civil litigation and agency 17%	Domestic property	17%
Probate, trust and wills		13%
Liquidation, bankruptcy, VAT		6%
Criminal litigation		2%

NICOLA ELLIS & CO 5 St Lawrence Road, Plymouth, PL4 6HR *Tel:* (01752) 227428 *Fax:* (01752) 670312 *Ptnrs:* 1

NIGHTINGALES 12 St. John St, Deansgate, Manchester, M3 4DX *Tel:* (0161) 832 6722
Fax: (0161) 832 7293 *DX:* 14330 *Ptnrs:* 6 *Asst solrs:* 2 *Other fee-earners:* 2

NORTON ROSE

KEMPSON HOUSE, CAMOMILE STREET, LONDON, EC3A 7AN
Tel: (0171) 283 6000 **Fax:** (0171) 283 6500 **DX:** 85 LONDON/1064 CITY **Internet:** HTTP://WWW.NORTONROSE.COM

The Firm: Norton Rose continues to excel as the finance and business firm uppermost in its chosen markets – corporate finance, asset finance, project finance, acquisition finance, development finance and financial litigation.

The firm's offices are in London, Bahrain, Brussels, Hong Kong, Moscow, Paris, Piraeus and Singapore. In addition Norton Rose has significant experience in advising clients in Scandinavia, Central Eastern and Southern Europe and throughout the Middle East, East Asia and Sub-Saharan Africa.

Their clients are international banks, financial institutions and funds, multi-national corporate businesses, major public and private companies in the firm's various domestic markets, government departments and agencies, statutory undertakings and sovereign states.

Norton Rose provides expert services to a select number of international industry and market sectors. The firm is clearly established as an acknowledged leading professional adviser in banking, insurance, shipping, aviation, railways, construction, energy, media and telecoms. Clients rely upon Norton Rose's in-depth understanding of industry issues, commitment to industrial expansion and ability to develop new techniques to accelerate commercial advantage.

For each sector Norton Rose provides banking and corporate clients with asset finance, equity and structured financial advice, development, acquisition, consolidation and restructuring services, contractual, tax and employee relations advice, regulatory and competition advice, real and intellectual property services, and, where necessary, risk management, arbitration, litigation, workouts and insolvency advice.

Their specialist teams in corporate finance, capital markets, project finance and commercial litigation build long term relations with clients both internationally and in their various domestic markets.

Principal Areas of Work:

Corporate Finance: The firm's corporate finance teams advise on public and private company mergers and acquisitions, privatisations, international joint ventures, inward investments, collective investment media, venture capital and general commercial work.

Capital Markets: Their capital markets teams advise banks and other financial institutions on international and domestic equity issues, securities trading, bonds, convertibles, derivatives, swaps, options, and asset, property and development finance securitisations.

Project Finance: The firm's project finance teams act for banks, contractors, sponsors, ECAs and mezzanine finance interests. They advise on all financial issues, inter-creditor agreements, risk management, receivables and trading issues, securitisation and restructuring, land, environmental, property and construction matters. Projects include energy, oil and gas, water, telecoms, infrastructure and transportation.

Commercial Litigation: Their commercial litigation teams undertake a high proportion of multi-jurisdictional and international disputes. Clients are advised on risk management, arbitration and alternative dispute resolution, litigation, regulatory disputes, work outs and insolvency.

Other: Other specialist teams cover competition and EC law, state aid, public procurement and international trade and utilities regulation; employment law, employee benefits, pension and employment-related immigration matters; international, corporate and commercial taxation; property development, investment and management, planning and the environment.

During the past year Norton Rose has advised, amongst others, on significant matters for Guinness, The New Millennium Experience Company, HSBC, Ciba, CERN, Lukoil, LIFFE, P&O, Total, Orange and all three Roscos. In February 1988 their property and construction teams won their respective 1997 Legal Business Teams of the Year Awards for their work on major London developments at Spitalfields and the Millennium Dome.

The firm's team structure enables partners and assistants to work closely together on related types of work. This provides a more in-depth and pro-active level of service to clients, improves know-how and quality of training, and gives better support and career development for trainee solicitors and junior assistants. As the firm expands it creates excellent career prospects, including opportunities to work overseas both before and after qualification.

Recruitment: Norton Rose recruits 70 trainee solicitors every year. It encourages high quality graduates of any discipline to apply: intellectual ability, personality, determination,

Managing partner:	Roger Birkby
Senior partner:	David Lewis
UK	
Number of partners:	95
Assistant solicitors:	249
Other fee-earners:	139
International	
Number of partners:	28
Assistant solicitors:	55
Other fee-earners:	14

WORKLOADS	
Banking and Asset Finance	30%
Corporate finance	30%
Litigation	25%
Property, planning & environmental	10%
Misc	5%

CONTACTS	
Aviation	Peter Thorne
Banking	Jamie Logie, Stephen Parish
Capital markets	Gilles Thieffry
Commercial litigation & arbitration	Peter Rees
Competition and EC	Martin Coleman
Construction	Peter Hall
Corporate finance	Simon Sackman
	Barbara Stephenson
Energy	Michael Taylor
Human resources	Stuart Lippiatt
Insurance	Chris Robinson
Intellectual property	Richard Barratt
Media & telecommunications	Keith Hyman
Project finance	Jeff Barratt
Property planning & environmental	Peter Burrows
Railways	Gordon Hall
Shipping	Peter Martyr
Taxation	John Challoner, Isla Smith

Continues overleaf

and the ability to get on with others are more highly prized than degree subject matter. The firm has always been a pioneer of training and personal development. It has a training programme dedicated specifically to trainee solicitors. Highly competitive salaries are offered, as well as other benefits including sports club, regular social events, and a staff restaurant. Recruitment brochures and application forms are available from Annabel Newell, Graduate Recruiter.

Norton Rose remains one of the most genuinely pleasant places to work. There is a cohesiveness and camaraderie in the firm that is hard to find elsewhere. This provides real benefits for the firm's clients. The ability to field teams of lawyers who work effectively together and who enjoy the development and achievement of long term relationships with their clients is clearly welcomed.

Other offices: Hong Kong, Singapore, Bahrain, Brussels, Paris, Piraeus, Moscow.

OFFENBACH & CO 60 Great Marlborough Street, London, W1V 2BA **Tel:** (0171) 434 9891 **Fax:** (0171) 734 2575 **DX:** 89260 Soho Square **Ptnrs:** 5 **Asst solrs:** 6 **Other fee-earners:** 3 **Contact:** Mr Bernard Carnell. *Known for crime including commercial fraud and drug related matters. Also civil litigation, entertainment, property, licensing, company and commercial, family, matrimonial and obscene publications.*

WORKLOADS			
Criminal defence	80%	Commercial and civil	20%

OGLETHORPE STURTON & GILLIBRAND 16 Castle Park, Lancaster, LA1 1YG **Tel:** (01524) 67171 **Fax:** (01524) 382247 **DX:** 63500 Lancaster **Ptnrs:** 8 **Asst solrs:** 4 **Other fee-earners:** 6 **Contact:** Andrew Penny. *Well established family firm, specialising in agricultural property and private client work, together with associated commercial, litigation and criminal practice.*

WORKLOADS			
Private client	34%	Litigation	28%
Commercial	13%	Commercial property	12%
Agriculture	10%	Other	3%

OLSWANG

90 LONG ACRE, LONDON, WC2E 9TT
Tel: (0171) 208 8888 **Fax:** (0171) 208 8800 **DX:** 37972 KINGSWAY **Email:** OLSMAIL@OLSWANG.CO.UK
Internet: HTTP://WWW.OLSWANG.CO.UK

The Firm: Olswang does things differently. Established in 1981, it has an impressive growth record fuelled by strong client demand, an insistence on excellence, a deep commercial understanding of its core markets, and its application of modern management practices. Originally Olswang's reputation was based on its strong media and entertainment practice but this has broadened considerably in recent years to embrace corporate finance, technology, communications, intellectual property, litigation and commercial property – for growing and large companies affected by digital convergence and the Information Age. Today, Olswang is recognised for its youthful culture, foresight, commercial pragmatism and focus.

Principal Areas of Work: Olswang has groups for corporate, litigation, property and entertainment, media and communications work, but the main thrust of the practice is the specialist units which combine lawyers from each of these disciplines.

The **Corporate Group** is the largest and fastest growing group. While half its time is spent on media and communications-related companies, it also has an impressive and growing list of clients from other business sectors. Work includes mergers and acquisitions, flotations, financings, MBOs, venture capital and joint ventures.

There is an **IT and Telecommunications Unit** and an **Electronic Business Unit**, which have lawyers from all disciplines advising on the corporate, commercial, regulatory, litigation and property issues which affect clients in, or doing business with, the telecommunications and IT industries.

There are three partners in the **Corporate Tax Unit** whose expertise covers international, corporate, property, on-line and VAT issues. The **Advertising Unit** provides corporate, commercial and litigation advice to major advertising agencies and advertisers.

The **Entertainment, Media and Communications Group** provides commercial advice to both content developers (film, TV, multimedia and music companies, independent producers and publishers) and carriers (terrestrial broadcasters, cable and satellite operators and telecommunications companies).

The **Litigation Group** includes the firm's highly acclaimed Media Litigation and **Defamation Unit** – advising traditional and electronic publishers and high profile plaintiffs. Also within litigation is the **Employment Unit**, comprising four dedicated lawyers specialising in restrictive covenants and trade union issues and a growing **commercial**

Managing partner:	John Akerman
Senior partner:	Simon Olswang
Number of partners:	33
Assistant solicitors:	52
Other fee-earners:	20

WORKLOADS	
Company/commercial	33%
Entertainment/media	27%
Litigation	20%
Property	20%

CONTACTS	
Advertising and marketing	Jonathan Goldstein
Banking	Graeme Levy
Cable and satellite	David Zeffman
Commercial Litigation	David Stewart
Corporate	Adrian Bott
Defamation	Geraldine Proudler
Electronic Business	Victor Timon
Employment	Julia Palca
Entertainment	Mark Devereux
Film Finance	Lisbeth Savill
Insolvency	Graeme Levy
Intellectual property	Andrew Inglis
IT	Kim Nicholson
Multimedia	John Enser
Planning	Geoffrey Searle
Property	David Kustow
Property litigation	Marcus Barclay
Publishing	Selina Potter
Retail Property	John Akerman
Tax	Kay Butler
Telecommunications	Kim Nicholson

litigation practice covering disputes such as shareholder disputes, insurance issues and telecommunications litigation.

Although there are over 25 lawyers at Olswang with experience in intellectual property, the **Intellectual Property Unit** serves as a focus and advises on both contentious and non-contentious matters in the media, technology, manufacturing and service sectors.

There are two commercial property teams: the **retail property team** advises major high street retailers and niche retailers and the **investment property team** advises institutional investors, listed property companies and large corporate tenants. Olswang also has a dedicated **Property Litigation Unit** which works closely with the property teams and the firm's **insolvency** lawyers.

International: Serving the global media, entertainment, telecommunications and information industries, Olswang has been advising both domestic and international companies on international commercial and legal matters for many years.

Booklets, newsletters and other publications are available on request, or via Olswang's web site.

ORCHARD

99 BISHOPSGATE, LONDON, EC2M 3YU
Tel: (0171) 392 0200 **Fax:** (0171) 392 0201

The Firm:

Established only three years ago, Orchard has quickly made its name as one of the newest, most vibrant firms in the Square Mile. Built on the expertise of a highly experienced team, it is just one of the reasons why Orchard has already won the business of many major banks and international corporations. Orchard is commited to working in partnership with its clients.

Principal Areas of Work:

Commercial Litigation	*Simon Malcolm*
Corporate Finance	*Susan Breen*
Mergers and Acquisitions	*Nick Davis*
Financial Services	*David Orchard*
Banking	*David Orchard*
Commercial Contracts	*Nick Davis*
Commercial Property	*Roger Coral*
Employment and Employee Benefits	*Simon Malcolm*
IT/IP	*Paul Taylor*
Corporate Insolvency	*David Orchard*

Managing partner:	**David Orchard**
Number of partners:	8
Assistant solicitors:	11
Other fee-earners:	4

WORKLOADS	
Company Commercial	35%
Commercial Litigation	30%
Commercial Property	15%
Employment	15%
IT/IP	5%

O'REILLY STEWART O'Reilly Stewart House, 114-116 Royal Avenue, Belfast, BT1 1DL **Tel:** (01232) 322512 **Fax:** (01232) 323003 **DX:** 3700 NR Belfast **Email:** oreillystewart@dnet.co.uk **Ptnrs:** 2 **Asst solrs:** 8 **Other fee-earners:** 6 **Contact:** Orla Cole *Emphasis on personal injury litigation and commercial property. Agency work undertaken for English firms in defence litigation and company/commercial matters. Also building society work, licensing, employment and family.*

WORKLOADS			
Litigation	50%	Company/ commercial	20%
Conveyancing	20%	Building society work	5%
Licensing & gaming	5%		

ORMEROD HEAP & MARSHALL

GREEN DRAGON HOUSE, 64-70 HIGH STREET, CROYDON, CR0 9XN
Tel: (0181) 686 5000 **Fax:** (0181) 680 0972 **DX:** 2619 CROYDON **Email:** ORMERODS.CO.UK **Internet:** WWW.ORMERODS.CO.UK

The Firm: With its origins in 1896 the firm is now a progressive amalgamation of a number of niche practices with state of the art I.T. back up. It caters for commercial and private clients. Its Managing Director is Sir John Wickerson, past President of The Law Society.

Principal Areas of Work:

Commercial Department: mergers and acquisitions; advice on Rule 9 takeover offers; business start ups; joint ventures; contract negotiations in E.E.C. and elsewhere; employment agreements and disputes; commercial conveyancing; commercial litigation, particularly on computer disputes generally and year 2000 specifically.

Private Client: work includes wills, probate, trust and tax planning; financial services (the firm is regulated by the Law Society in the conduct of investment business).

Personal Injury: a specialist department is dedicated to corporate clients and private individuals.

Employment: expertise in dealing with contract, unfair dismissal and Industrial Tribunal cases.

Professional Disciplinary actions: the firm has a specialist team dealing with professional misconduct cases of all kinds.

Senior partner:	John Wickerson
Number of partners:	12
Assistant solicitors:	8
Other fee-earners:	11

WORKLOADS	
Commercial	60%
Personal injury	20%
Litigation	10%
Private client	10%

CONTACTS	
Commercial	Stephen Marshall
Employment	Janet Borrow
Litigation	Simon Cook
Personal Injury	Ian Heap
Private Client	Peter Woods
Professional discipline	John Williams

OSBORNE CLARKE

50 QUEEN CHARLOTTE ST, BRISTOL, BS1 4HE
Tel: (0117) 923 0220 **Fax:** (0117) 927 9209 **DX:** 7818 BRISTOL – 1 **Email:** INFO@OSBORNE-CLARKE.CO.UK **Internet:** WWW.OSBORNE-CLARKE.CO.UK

HILLGATE HOUSE, 26 OLD BAILEY, LONDON, EC4M 7HS
Tel: (0171) 600 0155 **Fax:** (0171) 248 9934 **DX:** 466 LONDON CHANCERY LANE WC2

APEX PLAZA, FORBURY ROAD, READING, RG1 1AX
Tel: (0118) 925 2000 **Fax:** (0118) 925 0038 **DX:** 117882 – READING, APEX PLAZA

Osborne Clarke is widely held to be the dominant commercial law firm in the South of England. Based in Bristol, it is also a major force in its chosen national practice areas – corporate finance, employment, venture capital, IT telecoms and media – where it competes head on with the largest City and national firms. The firm is also particularly well-endowed with prominent sector specialists in litigation, commercial property, corporate banking, tax, environment and pensions. It has a growing international client base in the US and Europe, particularly in Denmark and in Germany.

The Firm: Recent growth has been exceptional, evidenced by the doubling of fee income over three years. 1997 saw the value of the firm's corporate deals rocket to over £2 billion and the launch of a new office in the Thames Valley – the firm's third key location in the South of England – to service the corporate finance, venture capital, IT and employment markets. Despite its success, however, Osborne Clarke retains its original values.

The firm is:
- dedicated to deserving the loyalty of its clients and its people;
  - successful in attracting and retaining the best people in the market by satisfying their aspirations for interesting and rewarding careers;
  - a communicator of business solutions in plain language;
  - innovative and highly committed to meeting the challenge of change;
  - a leading user of IT within the legal market; commercial and professional in all its dealings;
  - active in supporting the communities in which it works and lives.

Principal Areas of Work: Osborne Clarke services a wide range of sectors. Currently, it advises companies in: advertising and marketing, banking, distribution, energy and utilities, facilities management, financial services, healthcare, higher education, IT, insolvency, leisure, life assurance, manufacturing, media and entertainment, packaging, petrol retailing, the public sector, professional services, rail transport, real estate, retailing, telecoms, venture capital and waste disposal.

Other Offices: Barcelona, Brussels, Cologne, Copenhagen, Frankfurt, Hamburg, Milan, Paris, Rotterdam

Managing partner:	Leslie Perrin
Senior partner:	Chris Curling
Number of partners:	50
Assistant solicitors:	118
Other fee-earners:	41

WORKLOADS	
Corporate	30%
Litigation	22%
Commercial Property	15%
Human Resources	15%
IT, Telecoms and Media	12%
Tax and Trust	6%

CONTACTS	
Advertising & Marketing	Tim Birt (London)
Commercial Property	Simon Speirs (Bristol)
	Jane Lougher (London)
Corporate Banking	Margaret Childs (Bristol)
Corporate Finance	Simon Beswick (Bristol)
	Andrew Saul (London)
	Richard Smerdon (Thames Valley)
Corporate Tax	Philip Moss (Bristol)
Danish Matters	Roy Lambert and Per Troen (London)
Employment	Nicholas Moore (London)
	Julian Hemming (Bristol)
	Danielle Kingdon (Thames Valley)
German Matters	Adrian Taylor (Frankfurt)
	Chris Curling (Bristol)
	Stuart Miller (London)
Insolvency	Patrick Cook (Bristol)
	Richard Baines (London)
IT, Telecoms and Media	Simon Rendell (London)
	Andrew Braithwaite (Bristol)
	Russell Bowyer (Thames Valley)
Litigation	Clare Robinson (Bristol)
	Adrian Lifely (London)
Tax and Trusts	Sandra Brown (Bristol)

OSBORNE MORRIS & MORGAN Danbury House, West Street, Leighton Buzzard, LU7 7DD *Tel:* (01525) 378177 *Fax:* (01525) 851006 *DX:* 90804 Leighton Buzzard *Ptnrs:* 6 *Asst solrs:* 4 *Other fee-earners:* 4

OSBORNES 68 Parkway, London, NW1 7AH **Tel:** (0171) 485 8811 **Fax:** (0171) 485 5660 **DX:** 57053 Camden Town. **Ptnrs:** 6 **Asst solrs:** 12 **Other fee-earners:** 5 **Contact:** Angus Andrew. *Well-established high street firm delivering quality legal services in specialist fields. Holds Legal Aid Franchise and BSI Certification.*

WORKLOADS			
Housing and Civil Litigation	25%	Matrimonial & Family	25%
Personal Injury Litigation	25%	Res and Commercial Property	15%
Wills and Probate	10%		

OSWALD GOODIER & CO 10 Chapel St, Preston, PR1 8AY **Tel:** (01772) 253841 **Fax:** (01772) 201713 **DX:** 714571 Preston 14 **Ptnrs:** 3 **Other fee-earners:** 1 **Contact:** Mark Belderbos *A general practice, handling work for religious orders and charities as well as substantial amounts of trust and probate work.*

WORKLOADS	
Charity, Trust & Probate	30%
Residential Property & Landlord & Tenant	30%
Commercial Property/Company	18%
Personal Injury & Other Litigation	11%
Matrimonial & Family 7% Other	4%

OTTAWAYS 1 St. Peter's St, St. Albans, AL1 3DJ *Tel:* (01727) 863131 *Fax:* (01727) 840009 *DX:* 6102 *Ptnrs:* 5 *Asst solrs:* 2 *Other fee-earners:* 2

OURY COLHOUN & CO 54 Jermyn Street, St James, London, SW1Y 6LX *Tel:* (0171) 629 8844 *Fax:* (0171) 629 8855

OVERBURY STEWARD & EATON 3 Upper King St, Norwich, NR3 1RL *Tel:* (01603) 610481 *Fax:* (01603) 632460 *DX:* 5208 Norwich *Ptnrs:* 7 *Asst solrs:* 6 *Other fee-earners:* 14

OVER TAYLOR BIGGS 1 Oak Tree Place, Manaton Close, Matford Business Park, Exeter, EX2 8WA **Tel:** (01392) 823811 **Fax:** (01392) 823812 **DX:** 300350 Exeter 5 **Ptnrs:** 3 **Asst solrs:** 4 **Other fee-earners:** 3 **Contact:** Mr Christopher Over *New firm formed to offer partner only service from business park on outskirts of Exeter. Company commercial, property and litigation work.*

WORKLOADS			
Commercial property	25%	Company/ corporate	25%
Medical negligence/ personal injury			20%
Transport			20%
Construction litigation			10%

OWEN WHITE

SENATE HOUSE, 62-70 BATH RD, SLOUGH, SL2 3SR
Tel: (01753) 536846 **Fax:** (01753) 691360 **DX:** 3409 **Email:** LAW@OWENWHITE.COM

The Firm: This long-established practice occupies modern offices in the heart of the Thames Valley. It handles work of a predominantly commercial nature and has secured a reputation as one of the leading specialist firms in the area of British and International franchising.

Principal Areas of Work:

Franchising and Licensing: The department offers practical advice based on many years' experience both in the UK and worldwide. Anton Bates is a recognised specialist and legal adviser to the British Franchise Association, to which the firm is affiliated.

Company/Commercial: The firm advises on all aspects of a company's trading activities, with an emphasis upon information technology and computer law, European, EC and competition law.

Commercial Property and Development: Work ranges from the acquisition and disposal of warehouses, factories, offices and building and development sites, to the sale and purchase of shops and businesses.

Housing: The firm has gained a strong reputation in representing major housing associations at all stages of development and acquisition.

Litigation: Owen White has an expanding commercial litigation and insolvency department. The firm's range of experience also includes: industrial relations problems, medical negligence and personal injury claims. Richard Keen is a member of the Personal Injury Panel and a qualified mediator.

Employment: Work includes advising both employers and employees. Representation at Industrial Tribunals.

Other Areas of Work: Private client services focus on: wills, probate, tax planning, residential conveyancing.

Managing partner:	Richard Keen
Number of partners:	5
Assistant solicitors:	7
Other fee-earners:	7

WORKLOADS	
Litigation (inc. Employment)	40%
Commercial property development	20%
Company/commercial	20%
Franchising/licensing	10%
Housing	10%

CONTACTS	
Commercial property & development	Nick Barnard
Company/commercial	Jane Masih
Employment	Richard Keen
Franchising and licensing	Anton Bates
Housing	Nick Barnard
Litigation	Richard Keen

OXLEY & COWARD

34/46 MOORGATE ST, ROTHERHAM, S60 2HB
Tel: (01709) 510999 **Fax:** (01709) 512999 **DX:** 12600 ROTHERHAM **Email:** MAILBOX@OXCOW.CO.UK

The Firm: Oxley & Coward evolved from a general practice by concentrating on certain core markets: Information Technology, business (including agriculture), the National Health Service and private client. The firm capitalises on its geographical location by offering clients a personal flexible service across the country, on a costs base far below that of its larger rivals in London and Leeds. Oxley & Coward's lawyers receive an intensive commercial training, with trainees, solicitors and partners alike spending time working in-house with clients. The firm's IT work in particular has a significant international element, and it has forged links with specialist IT lawyers in the United States, Europe, India and Australia.

Principal Areas of Work: Oxley & Coward's IT client list includes some of the IT industry giants and "household name" companies. All types of IT-related work are undertaken, from outsourcing to software development and distribution. The firm is actively involved in legal aspects of the "Year 2000 problem" (it conducted one of the first major millenium compliance disputes, and has assisted a number of major businesses in carrying out large-scale Year 2000 systems and contract audits) and has advised on a number of IT contracts relating to the deregulation of the electricity industry. Oxley & Coward partners are regular speakers at conferences and seminars.

The firm undertakes a full range of work for business clients in the Midlands and North East, including sales and acquisitions, shareholders agreements and corporate reorganisations, agency/distributorship agreements, and the drafting of trading terms and conditions, especially for novel products and services. There is emphasis on TUPE and other employment issues relating to business transfers and in particular outsourcing, as well as advice for employers on contentious matters. Oxley & Coward has considerable expertise in advising GP practices and the proprietors of care homes. The licensing section acts for a number of major brewing and leisure concerns, and the firm's courts team supports the service to business clients in defending traffic, product and regulatory prosecutions.

Oxley & Coward acts for more than 30 health authorities and NHS trusts. In supporting this client base through the sweeping changes in the NHS since 1990, the firm has transferred around £700 million of NHS property, and provides specialist advice on NHS estate management and asset development/disposal. Oxley & Coward has advised on a wide range of other ventures in this now highly commercial sector, including the exploitation of intellectual property rights.

Oxley & Coward provides a comprehensive legal service to private clients across the UK, ranging from tax and estate planning (including the creation and administration of private trusts) to divorce and family/child law, especially cases with a foreign element. There an active plaintiff PI practice with a marked emphasis on industrial accidents and illnesses, and a very busy criminal courts section. The firm considers its private client services to be crucial in the support of its business client base, particularly in advising owners of private businesses on divorce.

Managing partner:	Henry Everatt
Number of partners:	10
Assistant solicitors:	9
Other fee-earners:	9

WORKLOADS	
Private Client	40%
Business	30%
Information Technology	25%
NHS	5%

CONTACTS	
Business	Rosemary Downs
Information Technology	John Yates
NHS	James Ogley
Private Client	Henry Everatt

A QUALITY SERVICE
Approved by The Legal Aid Board

INVESTOR IN PEOPLE

PAGAN MACBETH

8 MANOR PLACE, EDINBURGH, EH3 7DD
Tel: (0131) 220 3334 **Fax:** (0131) 220 0004 **DX:** ED 189 **Email:** JBCLARKE@PAGAN.CO.UK

The Firm: The Practice specialises in the provision of comprehensive business law advice. It has associated offices throughout Europe and is particularly noted for sports/media law, insolvency law, corporate finance, commercial property development and work on compulsory competitive tendering.

Other Offices:

12 St. Catherine Street, Cupar, Fife, KY15 4HN.
Tel: (01334) 657000. Fax: (01334) 655063. DX: 560543 CUPAR.

Buchan House, Carnegie Campus, Queensferry Road, Dunfermline, Fife, KY11 5PL.
Tel: (01383) 626666. Fax: (01383) 626111. DX: DF 48

Senior partner:	John Clarke
Number of partners:	4
Assistant solicitors:	2
Other fee-earners:	4

WORKLOADS	
Commercial Property	30%
Corporate	30%
Sports/Media law	20%
Insolvency	10%
Franchising	5%
Partnership	5%

PAGAN OSBORNE 12 St. Catherine Street, Cupar, KY15 4HN *Tel:* (01334) 653777 *Fax:* (01334) 655063 *DX:* 560543 *Ptnrs:* 12 *Asst solrs:* 7 *Other fee-earners:* 9

PAISNER & CO

BOUVERIE HOUSE, 154 FLEET ST, LONDON, EC4A 2DQ
Tel: (0171) 353 0299 **Fax:** (0171) 583 8621 **DX:** 198 **Email:** INFO@PAISNER.CO.UK

The Firm: Established over 60 years ago, Paisner & Co is a broadly-based commercial firm acting for national and international clients across a wide range of sectors and in particular leisure, retail and mail order, health, communications, manufacturing, high-technology, property development, insurance and financial services. Clients include Forte, Great Universal Stores, Psion, ALPHA, First Leisure, European Telecom, Estates & Agency Holdings, Courts, BL Universal, Ascot Holdings, Tie Rack, Allied London Properties, Armour Trust, Huntleigh Technology and AON.

Principal Areas of Practice:

Corporate and corporate finance: The firm advises on a broad range of areas including acquisitions and disposals, reconstructions, mergers and takeovers of public and private companies; flotations, public offerings and private placements; management buy-outs/buy-ins; joint ventures and development capital; leasing and asset finance and banking and insolvency.

Commercial: The firm advises on all types of commercial issues including distributorship and agency agreements, marketing and sponsorship, management agreements, health and insurance related work and biotechnology. The firm also deals with all aspects of EU and UK competition law.

Intellectual Property: The firm handles a wide variety of IP work, particularly IT contracts, franchising and trademark registration work as well as general IP licensing and litigation.

Tax: The firm provides a comprehensive corporate and international tax service.

Property: The firm provides a full commercial property service to some of the UK's largest property portfolio owners/managers as well as developers. The firm has a well respected property litigation group and a construction/engineering group which advises employers, contractors and professionals on a range of projects. The group has experience in dispute resolution, both nationally and internationally through ADR, arbitration and the courts.

Litigation: The firm's litigation practice handles commercial disputes of all kinds (whether arising in the UK or abroad) leading to court, tribunal or arbitration. A dedicated group deals with food law, licensing and business protection issues. Associated areas of expertise include health and safety and trading standards.

Employment and Pensions: The firm advises employers and employees on all contentious and non-contentious aspects of employment law and on all aspects of occupational pension schemes.

Trusts and Estate Planning: The firm advises individuals and trustees on the full range of tax and financial matters including tax planning, trusts, offshore arrangements and charities. The firm is also recognised for its expertise in contentious probate work.

Insurance/Reinsurance: The firm deals with international and UK reinsurance and insurance dispute resolution, arbitration and litigation; the formation, acquisition and disposal of insurance companies, brokers, agents and captives; corporate reorganisations and regulatory and compliance work.

Foreign Connections: The firm has formed an EEIG with Uettwiller Grelon, Gout, Canat & Associes (UGGC), a French legal practice with a branch in Brussels. Additionally, Paisner & Co has established close working relationship with other overseas law firms particularly in the European Union, North America, Israel and South Africa.

Senior partner:	Harold Paisner
Number of partners:	44
Assistant solicitors:	47
Other fee-earners:	34

WORKLOADS	
Company/Commercial	33%
Commercial property	24%
Litigation	20%
Trusts & Estate planning	9%
Insurance/Reinsurance	8%
Employment	6%

CONTACTS	
Banking/Insolvency	Stephen Marshall/ Stephen Nelson
Charities	Anne-Marie Piper
Company/Commercial	Jonathan Kropman
Construction	Hugh Nicholls/Terry de Souza
Corporate finance	Stephen Rosefield/Keith Stella
Corporate tax	Amanda Rowland
Employment	Stephen Levinson
EU/UK competition law	Adrian Magnus
Intellectual property/ Information Technology	Linda Fazzani
Leasing	Keith Stella
Liquor Licensing	Craig Baylis
Litigation	David Parkin
Pensions	Norman Russell
Property	Geoff Hayhurst
Reinsurance/insurance	Jonathan Sacher
Trademarks	Debrett Lyons
Trusts and estate planning	Martin Paisner

PALMER COWEN

16 BERKELEY ST, LONDON, W1X 5AE
Tel: (0171) 491 7810 **Fax:** (0171) 491 0071 **DX:** 37219 PICCADILLY

The Firm: Founded in 1981 this progressive Mayfair practice offers a full commercial and private client service with strong overseas connections.

The firm continues to expand both at home and abroad. An office in Bahrain co-ordinates work throughout the Gulf States and the firm is also a founder member of Law Link providing the firm's clients with prompt access to high quality legal advice throughout Europe, the Middle East and the Indian Sub-Continent.

Principal Areas of Work

Company/Commercial: (*Contact: Martin Varley, Sunil Sheth*) The department advises commercial clients ranging from emerging businesses to quoted companies. Services offered include acquisitions and disposals, restructuring, corporate finance, joint ventures, partnerships,communications law, taxation, employment matters, distribution and agency agreements, trading terms and general commercial agreements.

Litigation: (*Contact: Anthony Cowen, Alistair Langford*) Traditionally a strong element of the practice, handling a varied caseload regularly involving matters of a high profile and topical nature. The work covers all aspects of commercial litigation, negligence and personal injury, matrimonial, defamation, employment and building disputes.

Property: (*Contact: Nicholas Plaut, John Clementson*) The department deals with the full range of domestic and commercial property matters, planning and construction law. Particular strengths include secured lending, portfolio, leisure and retail work.

Private Client: (*Contact: Andrew Miller*) The needs of private clients represent an important cornerstone of the firm's practice. The work of this department includes estate planning and administration, immigration, wills, trusts, probate and personal taxation. A significant amount of offshore work is undertaken.

Recruitment & Training: Three trainees are recruited annually and it is planned that they will spend 6 months in each of the Company/Commercial, Private Clients, Property and Litigation departments. The firm looks for an engaging personality with both a creative and sensible approach to work. CVs to Stuart Evans or Andrew Miller. A brochure about Palmer Cowen is available upon request.

Senior partner:	A. Cowen
Number of partners:	10
Other fee-earners:	17

WORKLOADS	
Company/Commercial	42%
Litigation	24%
Property	24%
Private Client	10%

PALMER WHEELDON

DAEDALUS HOUSE, STATION RD, CAMBRIDGE, CB1 2RE
Tel: (01223) 355933 **Fax:** (01223) 460266 **DX:** 5807 **Email:** PWSOLS@CAMLAW.WIN-UK.NET

The Firm: A progressive organisation which has achieved considerable growth both in commercial and private client work in recent years. Its strength is in advising the middle business sector. The Firm's clients include some household names. In 1997 the commercial team handled a number of high profile transactions including moving an AIM Company to the full stock market list. The Firm is committed to the personal development of its staff and the use of technology.

Principal Areas of Work:

Company and Commercial: Company sales and acquisitions; MBO's and MBI's; corporate finance; insolvency and partnership.

Commercial litigation: Contract disputes; contentious employment work; professional negligence and debt recovery including handling high volume debt work for a large public utility.

Commercial property: Sales and purchases of land for property developers and a local authority.

Private Client: Tax, Trust, Wills and Probate.

Agriculture: Contentious agricultural work and farm sales and purchases.

Recruitment: The firm recruits up to 2 trainee solicitors every year. Apply in writing to Rosemary Green, Director of Human Resources.

Agency Work: Agency work is undertaken in Cambridge County Court and District Registry.

Managing partner:	Ian P. Mather
Senior partner:	Philip Speer
Number of partners:	8
Assistant solicitors:	8
Other fee-earners:	8

WORKLOADS	
Non commercial litigation (PI & family)	22%
Commercial litigation	21%
Commercial	18%
Commercial property	14%
Domestic property	14%
Private client	11%

CONTACTS	
Agricultural	Jane Lichtenstein
Commercial	Philip Speer
Commercial litigation	Ian Mather
Insolvency	Philip Speer, Ian Mather
Personal injury	Ruth Booy
Private Client	Lindsay Menenger
Property	Nick Toovey

PALSER GROSSMAN Discovery House, Scott Harbour, Cardiff Bay, CF1 5PJ *Tel:* (01222) 452770 *Fax:* (01222) 452328 *DX:* 33064 Cardiff 1 *Ptnrs:* 15 *Asst solrs:* 15 *Other fee-earners:* 19

PANNONE & PARTNERS

123 DEANSGATE, MANCHESTER, M3 2BU
Tel: (0161) 909 3000 **Fax:** (0161) 909 4444 **DX:** 14314 MANCHESTER 1 **Internet:** WWW.PANNONE.COM

The Firm: Pannone & Partners is one of the largest practices in the North West. It has strengths not shared by firms of a similar size in the ability to service all types of work for both personal and commercial clients with the firm's strength and size being split evenly between the two.

Principal Areas of Work:

Corporate & Commercial: A comprehensive range of corporate services are available including all aspects of business start up and formation, banking and finance, commercial contracts, company law and competition law. This department also contains specialists offering expertise in Public Sector, Intellectual Property and Advertising & Marketing.

Commercial Property: This department undertakes the full range of commercial property transactions including purchases, sales, mortgages, planning, development, leases, joint ventures and portfolio management.

Commercial Litigation: This progressive and successful department is acknowledged by its competitors to be tough, knowledgeable and effective. Experienced in litigating in all courts and tribunals, their watchword is commerciality. It also houses the Debt Collection Unit.

Employment: This team carries out work for both employers and employees, drafting contracts and conducting their own advocacy.

Forensic: An important service not found in many other law firms dealing with white collar crime and regulatory breaches.

Construction: An entirely separate team who only carry out construction work of both contentious and non-contentious nature.

Insolvency: This team aims to give prompt considered practical advice from which clients can derive financial and commercial benefit.

Licensing: Headed by Tony Lyons, whose former practice, Copeland Lyons, was one of only two in the UK specialising solely in liquor and entertainment licensing law. The department represents a wide range of clients.

Personal Injury: This department is consistently accredited as the strongest PI team in the North West, with a demonstrable national and international reputation for the quality of its work, the size of settlements obtained and expertise in handling multi-party and complex claims. The department also handles many hundreds of claims each year arising out of less serious accidents.

Medical Negligence: This dedicated team of medical negligence specialists act for clients throughout the country seeking redress for sometimes catastrophic injuries received during medical treatment. Members of this department do not undertake any other form of PI work thereby guaranteeing a high degree of specialism.

Family: With nine specialist lawyers this is one of the foremost family law departments in the country. They are accustomed to handling not only divorce and separation cases, but also substantial ancillary financial matters and all aspects of disputes involving children, including contested adoption.

Private Client: A large department dealing with residential conveyancing, tax planning, wills and estates and Court of Protection work. The staff provide a caring and efficient service when undertaking your most personal transactions.

International Services: We are founder members of the Pannone Law Group, Europe's first integrated international law group taking the form of a European Economic Interest Grouping. Its lawyers recognised the need to offer creative, imaginative and practical advice on a Pan-European basis. PLG maintains offices in: Andorra, Belgium, Canada, France, Germany, Italy, Portugal, Netherlands, Spain, Switzerland, Sweden and the UK. We recognise the importance of communication between different cultures and often transact business in French, German, Swedish and Danish.

Recruitment & Training: The firm offers eight training contracts each year with a programme of in-house lectures and seminars. The firm encourages trainees to stay on qualification. Application forms are available from Julia Hearn.

Quality: Pannones were the first law firm to achieve BS5750 accreditation, now ISO9001, and also hold several Legal Aid Franchise certificates.

Philosophy: "We pride ourselves on our ability to work in partnership with our clients and to offer practical and cost effective solutions, meeting clients' needs."

Managing Partner:	Joy Kingsley
Senior Partner:	Rodger Pannone –
	President of the Law Society 1993-94
Number of Partners:	45
Assistant Solicitors:	33
Other Fee-earners:	48

WORKLOADS	
Commercial Litigation	29%
Personal Injury	18%
Corporate	16%
Family	12%
Commercial Property	10%
Medical Negligence	8%
Private Client	7%

CONTACTS	
Corporate and commercial	Soren Tattam
Commercial property	Andrew Simpkin
Commercial litigation	Vincent O'Farrell
Employment	Christine Bradley
Construction	Gareth Jessop
Business Crime	Paul Taylor
Insolvency	Paul Johnson
Intellectual property	Laurie Heizler
Public sector	Steven Grant
Licensing	Tony Lyons
Debt collection	Simon McCrum
Private client	Hugh Jones
Personal injury	Carol Jackson
Family	Catherine Jones
Medical negligence	John Kitchingman
Financial services	Tony Ashton
French property	Lindsay Kinnealy

PANNONE
& PARTNERS

SOLICITORS

PARDOES 6-9 King Square, Bridgwater, TA6 3DG *Tel:* (01278) 457891 *Fax:* (01278) 429249 *DX:* 80602 *Ptnrs:* 10 *Asst solrs:* 8 *Other fee-earners:* 19

PARIS SMITH & RANDALL

NUMBER 1 LONDON ROAD, SOUTHAMPTON, SO15 2AE
Tel: (01703) 482482 **Fax:** (01703) 631835 **DX:** 38534 SOUTHAMPTON 3 **Email:** PARISOL@PARISOL.CO.UK **Internet:** WWW.PARISOL.CO.UK

The Firm: Paris Smith & Randall has been established for 175 years in the centre of Southampton. Particularly noted for its commercial property and company/ commercial services, the firm also has strong litigation, matrimonial and private client teams.

Principal Areas of Work:

Company/ Commercial: (*Contact Partner:* Andrew Heathcock). This department has a particularly high reputation in company and insolvency matters.

Property: (*Contact Partner:* Mark Howarth). The department handles a wide range of property work including management of commercial and residential property portfolios, secured lending, retail premises, development and investment property. The firm also acts for the Public Sector and Housing Associations as well as company's relocation packages.

Litigation: (*Contact Partner:* Clive Thomson). The firm is particularly strong in commercial and personal injury cases, and handles a wide range of litigation. The firm is located close to the Central Law Courts and undertakes all categories of agency work.

Private Client: (Family: *Contact Partner:* Richard Smith. Tax & Estate Planning: *Contact Partner:* Crispin Jameson) these departments are both leaders in the region. The firm is well known for its work in the family field with an emphasis on divorce and weighty financial relief claims. It has set up a family mediation centre and has a Child Care Specialist. Trust and general tax planning advice form part of a broad range of work for the 6 strong Tax & Estate Planning Department. This also includes personal estate management, pension, probate, financial services and immigration and nationality.

Employment: (*Contact Partner:* Malcolm Ross). The department is involved in representing and advising corporate, statutory, and individual clients on all aspects of employment law.

Number of partners:	14
Assistant solicitors:	17
Other fee-earners:	15

WORKLOADS	
Commercial property	24%
Company and commercial	20%
Litigation	14%
Family law	13%
Tax & estate planning	13%
Residential property	10%
Employment	6%

CONTACTS	
Child Care	Justin Belcher
Company and commercial	Andrew Heathcock
Employment	Malcolm Ross
Family	Richard Smith
Insolvency	Malcolm Le Bas
Litigation	Clive Thomson
Mediation	Neil Davies
Probate/ tax/ trusts	Crispin Jameson
Property	Mark Howarth
Public Sector Unit	Daisy Churchill

PARKER BULLEN

45 CASTLE STREET, SALISBURY, SP1 3SS
Tel: (01722) 412000 **Fax:** (01722) 411822 **DX:** 58001

8 NEWBURY STREET, ANDOVER, SP10 1DW
Tel: (01264) 400500 **Fax:** (01264) 355957 **DX:** 90304

The Firm: Formed by merger in 1987, the Firm's turnover, profits and Plc client list have grown substantially. With further increases forecast the Firm is poised to grow organically or by acquisition of other practices.

Principal Areas of Work: In addition to routine legal activities, particular specialities include High Court Litigation, Debt Recovery and Insolvency, Personal Injury, Defamation, Matrimonial & Family, Employment, Squatters, Licensed Trade, Employment, Squatter Eviction, Education, Charities & Trusts and full Company & Commercial services encompassing MBOs, Franchising and Intellectual Property.

Clients: Lloyds/TSB Group, Gibbs Mew Plc, Norcros Plc, Triton Plc, Icon Clinical Research Ltd, the Comtel Group of Companies, The Rural Development Commission and Bryanston School.

Managing partner:	**Chris Nichols**
Senior partner:	**Nicholas Bourne**

CONTACTS	
Agricultural Property	Nicholas Bourne
Commercial Property	Tim Crarer, Chris Nichols
Company & Commercial	Mark Lello
Education, Employment	Richard Le Masurier
High Court, Debt Collection	James Welsh
High Court, PI, Housing	Colin Carnegy
Licensed Property	Tim Crarer
Private Client	Robert Sykes, Robin Hiscocks

PARKINSON WRIGHT Haswell House, St. Nicholas Street, Worcester, WR1 1UN **Tel:** (01905) 726789 **Fax:** (01905) 21363 **DX:** 716 257 **Ptnrs:** 10 **Asst solrs:** 5 **Other fee-earners:** 10 **Contact:** D.G. Wright *Known for personal injury work, family and childcare law, crime, conveyancing and advice to business clients. Offices: Droitwich, Evesham.*

WORKLOADS			
Family law	28%	General litigation	27%
Conveyancing	20%	Criminal law	15%
Business client work	5%	Wills and probate	5%

PARK NELSON

1 BELL YARD, LONDON, WC2A 2JP
Tel: (0171) 404 4191 **Fax:** (0171) 405 4266 **DX:** 186 CH.LN.

The Firm: Park Nelson is one of the oldest firms of solicitors in the country and it celebrated its two hundreth anniversary in 1996. It has provided two Presidents of the Law Society. It continues to grow in the modern world with its many and notable clients but in a controlled way. The partners are determined that the firm at all times remains "partner led", that clients always have access to partners and that partners have day to day supervision and control the work of the firm. Its reputation is that of a long established firm of integrity and reputation, responsive to its clients' needs, with acknowledged areas of skill particularly in commercial property (including funding and development), construction law, consumer credit law, employment, insurance litigation and private client services. The firm has strong international connections and work throughout the world including the United States, southern Africa, the far east and Australia and the former Soviet Union states, but particularly in western Europe and especially France and Ireland. The firm has associated offices in Dublin, Paris, Rome and Milan. Three of its partners are admitted as solicitors in the Republic of Ireland.

Principal Areas of Work:

Commercial Property: (*Contact Partner:* Eugene O'Keeffe). The firm has particular expertise in handling developments, funding agreements and commercial leases in the retail field. In addition it provides expertise in planning, compulsory purchase and environmental law.

Company Commercial: (*Contact Partner:* Timothy Ford). Most aspects of company work and a high degree of skill and experience in employment law, commercial law and matters (particularly joint ventures with a foreign element), intellectual property, finance, banking and credit and consumer law.

Litigation/Construction: (*Contact Partner:* John Kings). In-depth experience in contentious and non-contentious construction law and commercial litigation. Other areas of specialisation include landlord and tenant, employment law and sports law.

Private Client Services: (*Contact Partner:* John Bishop). The work of this department reflects in legal terms the private banking concept in banking by covering all personal property, tax, matrimonial and family law, probate and trust work (especially cross border trusts) which the firm undertakes for individuals and families.

International and European Law: (*Contact Partner:* Richard Fairbairn). Advice is provided for French diplomats, French companies establishing branches or subsidiaries in the UK, and UK clients purchasing French property.

Agency: Agency work is handled.

Foreign Connections: The firm has associated offices in Dublin, Paris, Rome and Milan.

Managing partner:	Timothy Ford
Senior partner:	Eugene O'Keeffe
Number of partners:	16
Assistant solicitors:	11
Other fee-earners:	9

WORKLOADS	
Commercial property	44%
Litigation/Construction	27%
Private Client Services	15%
Company/Commercial	14%

CONTACTS	
Commercial property	Eugene O'Keeffe
Company Commercial	Timothy Ford
Litigation/Construction	John Kings
Private Client Services	John Bishop

PARK WOODFINE 1 Lurke St, Bedford, MK40 3TN **Tel:** (01234) 400000 **Fax:** (01234) 401111 **DX:** 716007 Bedford 5 **Email:** admin@Parkwoodfine.co.uk **Ptnrs:** 10 **Asst solrs:** 8 **Other fee-earners:** 14 **Contact:** Garry Dannan *A general practice handling commercial and residential property, commercial matters, matrimonial, civil and criminal litigation. Other offices in Northampton, Rushden, Flitwick and London.*

WORKLOADS			
Litigation	25%	Family	23%
Property	20%	Commercial	11%
Criminal	11%	Probate	6%
Financial services	4%		

PARLETT KENT

SIGNET HOUSE, 49-51 FARRINGDON RD, LONDON, EC1M 3JB
Tel: (0171) 430 0712/3 **Fax:** (0171) 430 1796 **DX:** 53308 CLERKENWELL

PORTLAND HOUSE, LONGBROOK STREET, EXETER, EX4 6AB
Tel: (01392) 494455 **Fax:** (01392) 491199 **DX:** 134052 – EXETER 15

The Firm: Established in the 1950's Parlett Kent is a firm noted for its expertise in a wide range of personal injury litigation most particularly in recent years obtaining a reputation for medical negligence litigation. The firm has in house para-medical support and specialises in complex medical negligence cases. It is committed to applying it's expertise to cases of merit regardless of venue or quantum of case. The Firm has legal aid franchises in respect of personal injury litigation and undertakes private work including Conditional Fee Agreement cases. All 5 partners are members of the Law Society's Medical Negligence Panel, the Association of Personal Injury Lawyers, the AVMA referral Panel and Magi Young and Julie Say are members of the Law Society's Personal Injury Panel. Caroline Jenkins and Magi Young are members of the Association of Trial Lawyers of America. The firm opened an office in Exeter in March 1997 where they specialise in Medical Negligence and personal Injury Litigation.

Principal Areas of Work:

Medical Negligence: This Department deals with cases of the utmost severity (accidents at birth, brain injuries and spinal injuries) as well as a wide range of both High Court and County Court claims. The firm has particular expertise in cases of obstetric and psychiatric negligence as well as cases arising out of failures to diagnose and treat cancer. It also specialises in claims against the legal profession arising out of mishandling of medical negligence claims. Members of the practice regularly lecture lawyers, doctors, nurses, Health Service Managers and social workers on medical negligence and risk management.

Personal Injury: This Department deals with a full range of personal injury claims, including road traffic accidents and accidents at work, for both Plaintiff and Defendants. Two of the partners are members of the Personal Injury Panel.

Other Areas of Work: Conveyancing, Wills, Trusts, Probate, Taxation and Family.

Languages Spoken: French, Urdu, Punjabi

Recruitment: At least one trainee solicitor is recruited annually. The firm has an Equal Opportunities policy and all posts are advertised.

Senior partner:	Caroline Jenkins
Number of partners:	5
Assistant solicitors:	4
Other fee-earners:	4

WORKLOADS	
Medical negligence	70%
Conveyancing and general non-contentious	10%
Personal injury	10%
Matrimonial	5%
Professional negligence	5%

CONTACTS	
Exeter Office	Magi Young
Family	Elizabeth Batten
Medical negligence	Caroline Jenkins
Personal Injury	Julie Say
Private Client	Maggie Leiper

PARROTT & COALES 14 Bourbon St, Aylesbury, HP20 2RS *Tel:* (01296) 482244 *Fax:* (01296) 433723 *DX:* 4100 Aylesbury *Ptnrs:* 7 *Asst solrs:* 6 *Other fee-earners:* 9

O.H. PARSONS & PARTNERS Sovereign Hse, 212-224 Shaftesbury Avenue, London, WC2H 8PR *Tel:* (0171) 379 7277 *Fax:* (0171) 240 1577 *Ptnrs:* 4 *Asst solrs:* 5 *Other fee-earners:* 4

PATRICIA U. HYLAND 6 Callender Street, Belfast, BT1 5BN **Tel:** (01232) 324035 **Fax:** (01232) 438150 **DX:** 465 NR, Belfast 1 **Ptnrs:** 1 **Asst solrs:** 1 *Matrimonial law, Children's Order cases, civil, conveyancing litigation. Probate. Also at: 1005 Upper Newtonards Road, Dundonald, Belfast BT16 0RN*

PATTINSON & BREWER

30 GREAT JAMES STREET, LONDON, WC1N 3HA
Tel: (0171) 400 5100 **Fax:** (0171) 405 7239 **DX:** 394

The Firm: The firm of Pattinson and Brewer was founded in about 1892. It has long been a leading trade union practice, having connections going back to the Taff Vale case in 1901 and the formation of the TGWU in 1921. It has a proud commitment to plaintiff personal injury and disease work, and a well-established reputation in the fields of equal opportunities, and medical and professional negligence. It has developed a leading profile in the field of employment law. The firm has a strong team of general litigators and a very experienced property department.

Other Offices:

8-12 New Road, Chatham, Kent ME4 4QR. *Contact:* John Couch.
Tel: (01634) 830080. *Fax:* (01634) 830813. *DX:* 6711.

Transport House, Victoria Street, Bristol BS1 6AY. *Contact:* Janet Chidgey.
Tel: (0117) 927 3233. *Fax:* (0117) 927 3272. *DX:* 78148.

1 Bridge Street, York YO1 6WD. *Contact:* Kevin Hughes.
Tel: (01904) 670077. *Fax:* (01904) 655052. *DX:* 61565 York.

Recruitment: The firm presently recruits one to two trainee solicitors each year, and looks for an interest in plaintiff-orientated work.

Managing partner:	John Davies
Chairman:	John Couch
Number of partners:	17
Assistant solicitors:	10
Other fee-earners:	32

WORKLOADS	
Personal injury	59%
Employment/ labour law	18%
Medical negligence	10%
General litigation	6%
Conveyancing/ commercial	5%
Criminal	2%

PAUL DAVIDSON & TAYLOR Chancery Court, Queen Street, Horsham, RH13 5AD *Tel:* (01403) 262 333 *Fax:* (01403) 262 444 *DX:* 57617 Horsham

---

PAUL KLINGER & CO Reading, *Tel:* (01189) 257 512

PAULL & WILLIAMSONS

INVESTMENT HOUSE, 6 UNION ROW, ABERDEEN, AB10 1DQ
Tel: (01224) 621621 **Fax:** (01224) 640446 **DX:** 35 ABERDEEN **Email:** IH@PAULL-WILLIAMSONS.CO.UK
Internet: HTTP://WWW.PAULL-WILLIAMSONS.CO.UK

The Firm: One of the largest firms in Aberdeen, Paull & Williamsons have enhanced their legal services to meet the increased pace of economic activity in the North East of Scotland in recent years. Moreover the client benefits from an efficient internal cross-referral system which provides immediate access to other departments on other areas of the law. The firm also conducts seminars for clients on matters of concern to them, including employment, industrial relations and the effects of new legislation.

Principal Areas of Work:

Corporate Services: (*Contact Partner:* Sidney Barrie). The firm has a long reputation for serving commercial clients in the North East and has close links with the local financial community. The department handles all types of corporate and commercial transactions including business start-ups, partnerships and incorporation; company administration; takeovers and acquisitions; disposals; management buy-outs; insolvency, receivership, liquidation and administration; commercial contracts, licensing and intellectual property; shipping and vessel finance; venture capital financing and investment.

Commercial Property Services: (*Contact Partner:* Leslie S Dalgarno). The department has recently expanded its operations and now has considerable experience in commercial property developments throughout Scotland. Valuable connections are maintained with other professionals in the commercial property field, such as surveyors, architects and project managers. The firm offers a comprehensive service covering the acquisition and development, leasing and funding of both office and industrial developments. In addition proven experience has been demonstrated in the fields of retail development, major residential development, licensed premises, agricultural and sporting estates, and woodland and aquacultural development. Planning applications, whether at first instance or at appeal stage, are also handled by the firm.

Private Client Services: (*Contact Partners:* George Alpine and David O.M. Geddie). The first practice in Aberdeen to open a separate estate agency office, the department now operates from large premises in the heart of the city. The service includes advice on valuation, marketing strategy, mortgages, insurance, contracts of sale and purchase and the

Senior partner:	Bruce Smith
Number of partners:	29
Assistant solicitors:	30
Other fee-earners:	8

Continues overleaf

handling of enquiries prior to sale. The firm also attends to the client's personal financial requirements in tax planning, succession, trusts, insurance and personal financial management. This expertise extends to cover agricultural partnerships and estate work.

Litigation: (*Contact Partner:* James K. Tierney). The firm has the experience to deal with all areas of contentious work either prior to formal litigation or arbitration or through representation in the courts and tribunals. The department's work ranges from matters which might face the commercial client, including commercial contracts, employment matters, credit control, Health and Safety at Work, and insolvency to matters of personal concern, such as matrimonial disputes and employment problems. Having developed expertise in the negotiation, pursuit and defence of personal injury claims, the firm has also recently achieved a significant reputation in advising clients and their insurers following major disasters and representing them at subsequent public inquiries.

Other Offices:

New Investment House, 214 Union Street, Aberdeen AB10 8QY.
e-mail: nih@paull-williamsons.co.uk
13 North Bank Street, Edinburgh EH1 2LP

THE PAUL ROONEY PARTNERSHIP 19-23 Stanley Street, Liverpool, L1 6AA **Tel:** (0151) 227 2851 **Fax:** (0151) 255 0455 **DX:** 14183 **Ptnrs:** 7 **Asst solrs:** 2 **Other fee-earners:** 36 **Contact:** Mr Paul Rooney *Established in 1977, a specialist civil and criminal litigation firm dealing mainly with personal injury claims including factory accidents, industrial diseases, medical and professional negligence, sports injuries and road traffic accidents.*

WORKLOADS	
Road traffic accidents/personal injury	85%
Crime	10%

PAYNE HICKS BEACH

10 NEW SQUARE, LINCOLN'S INN, LONDON, WC2A 3QG
Tel: (0171) 465 4300 **Fax:** (0171) 465 4400 **DX:** 40 CH.LN. **Email:** [CONTACT]@PAYNE-HICKS-BEACH.CO.UK

The Firm: Well-known and respected Inns of Court firm, established in the early eighteenth century. Although the firm draws strength from its long traditions, the character of the firm is an entirely modern one which has been created by the present partners' own chosen specialisations, several of which have been the object of favourable comment in journals in the last few years.

Principal Areas of Work: The firm is organised into five departments.

Tax, Trust and Probate: (*Contact:* Graham Brown). These are areas of specialisation for which the firm has a reputation as one of the best in London. The range of work undertaken is wider than traditionally associated with private client work, and extends from heritage and agricultural work and property development taxation, to advising entrepreneurs and senior directors, charities, and to off-shore and continental transactions.

Corporate/ Commercial: (*Contact:* Guy Green/Max Hudson). This department deals with the full range of corporate and business law acting for public and private companies and a range of individual entrepreneurs. The international section deals with many clients and correspondents abroad, and has strong connections both within the European Community and elsewhere, including North America and Japan. *Work includes:* acquisitions and mergers, banking, competition law, employment law, EC law, intellectual property including computers and franchising, management buy-outs, marketing and sale of goods law, new issues and partnership agreements.

Commercial Litigation: (*Contact:* Peter Stockwell/ Richard Butcher). The firm has a strong commercial litigation department handling a broad range of work including commercial disputes requiring urgent injunctive relief, arbitration, intellectual property, commercial, landlord and tenant and town and country planning. There is also particular experience in representing clients before regulatory enquiries. Specialised areas of work include advising clients in yacht racing and design and construction, building contract work, partnership disputes and all other aspects of insolvency for both corporate and individual clients.

Family Law: (*Contact:* David Leverton/ Ian Airey). This department is well known for its specialisation in all aspects of family law including divorce and separation, adoption, custody and wardship, and financial claims. Personal injury actions are also handled.

Property and Conveyancing: (*Contact:* David Fitzgerald/ Andrew Crawford).

Commercial Property: This section deals with all aspects of property transactions, leases, secured lending, management of investment property, development work including joint ventures and planning agreements.

Residential and Agricultural Conveyancing: This section deals with residential conveyancing, farm and forestry transactions, agricultural property and staff loan schemes.

Senior partner:	Graham Brown
Managing partner:	David Leverton
Number of partners:	18
Number of associates:	2
Assistant solicitors:	8
Other fee-earners:	22

WORKLOADS	
Private client	33%
Commercial litigation	13%
Commercial property	12%
Corporate/commercial	10%
Matrimonial and family law/ litigation	10%
Residential/agricultural property	10%
Tax (business and corporate)	10%
General, miscellaneous	2%

CONTACTS	
Commercial litigation	Peter Stockwell
Commercial property	David FitzGerald
Corporate/commercial	Guy Green
Employment/Sports	Richard Butcher
Family/Matrimonial	David Leverton
General conveyancing	Andrew Crawford
Intellectual property	Richard Butcher
Probate	Alastair Murdie
Tax/trust	Graham Brown

Foreign Connections: The firm has associates in Paris with a network of other correspondents internationally. Several of the partners conduct legal work in French, German or Danish.

Recruitment and Training: There are usually two or three vacancies for trainee solicitors every year. The minimum educational requirement is a good degree, but emphasis is placed on personality as well as academic achievements. Applications should be made by letter (with CV and references) to the Recruitment Partner. The firm is also always interested to receive appplications from high quality solicitors seeking to move from the City.

PAYNE MARSH STILLWELL 6 Carlton Crescent, Southampton, SO15 2EY *Tel:* (01703) 223957 *Fax:* (01703) 225261 *DX:* 38514 Southampton 3 *Ptnrs:* 7 *Asst solrs:* 2 *Other fee-earners:* 5

PEDEN & REID 22 Callender Street, Belfast, BT1 5BU *Tel:* (01232) 325617 *Fax:* (01232) 247 343 *DX:* 389 NR Belfast *Ptnrs:* 4 *Asst solrs:* 3

PELLYS The Old Monastery, Windhill, Bishop's Stortford, CM23 2ND *Tel:* (01279) 758080 *Fax:* (01279) 657578 *DX:* 50401 *Ptnrs:* 6 *Asst solrs:* 5 *Other fee-earners:* 9

PENNINGTONS

BUCKLERSBURY HOUSE, 83 CANNON STREET, LONDON, EC4N 8PE
Tel: (0171) 457 3000 **Fax:** (0171) 457 3240 **DX:** 98946 CHEAPSIDE 2

The Firm: The major departments of the firm are: corporate and commercial, litigation, property, private client (including family). Penningtons has particular strengths in the areas of intellectual property, commercial litigation, commercial property, family law, dispute resolution, the administration of trusts and agricultural work. Overseas activity includes specialist knowledge of and experience in Italy, France, South Africa, Hong Kong and the Far East, the USA, India and Pakistan, the Russian Federation, the CIS and the FSU. The firm is founding member of the European Law Group, an association of twelve commercial law firms in the EU, Norway and Switzerland, and is a member of the Law Society Solicitors European Group. Penningtons has in-house lawyers qualified in several overseas jurisdictions.

Principal Areas of Work: The firm is organised into a number of service areas, most of which operate in smaller working groups. These cross-departmental groups cover specific areas of law and industry sectors such as insolvency, intellectual property, environmental, ADR, shipping, construction, planning, immigration, employment, publishing, personal injury, tax and pensions.

  The corporate department: offers a full range of legal skills and experience in corporate finance, management buy-outs and buy-ins, mergers and acquisitions and joint ventures. The department is equipped to deal with multi-disciplinary and cross-border transactions and regularly undertakes work in overseas jurisdictions. Clients for whom the department acts range from governments, multi-national companies, banks, public companies, stockbrokers and financial institutions to entrepreneurs, other professionals, private companies and individuals.

  The commercial department: advises on most aspects of commercial law, including intellectual property (where it has particular expertise in publishing, technology transfer, information technology and computer law), distribution, agency and supply, competition law, inward investment and establishment in the UK, immigration and nationality, banking, joint ventures, company and business acquisitions and disposals, pensions and employees' benefit schemes and tax.

  The litigation department: acts for clients in all types of business disputes, national and international, including construction and engineering disputes, employment matters, insolvency work, insurance, partnership disputes, personal injury claims, professional indemnity claims, secured lending recoveries, share sale and purchase disputes, trade arbitrations and including all aspects of commercial property and landlord and tenant matters. Members of the department are familiar with ADR techniques in addition to litigation and arbitration. The shipping group is part of this department. It provides a world wide international commercial and corporate shipping and arbitration services from the firm's London and Paris offices, relating to marine insurance, salvage and collisions, general average, marine pollution, charterparty disputes, carriage of goods and bill of lading disputes, ship finance, sale and purchase, ship building and repair disputes. The group has extensive experience of major marine casualties, total losses and the contractual issues arising out of such incidents, including personal injury and loss of life claims.

Managing partner:	Lesley Lintott
UK and International	
Number of partners:	38
Assistant solicitors:	39
Other fee-earners:	46

WORKLOADS	
Litigation (including shipping)	33%
Property	29%
Corporate/commercial	24%
Private client (including matrimonial)	14%

CONTACTS	
ADR	Henry Brown
Agricultural	Michael Fellingham, Julian Chadwick
Banking	Geoffrey Walkley
Commercial Property	Roger Loveland
	Anthony Bussy
	John Ewens
	John Mathe
	Tom Rossiter
	Catriona Smith
	Biddy Walker
	Martin O'Donoghue
Construction	Roger Loveland, Sue Dixon
Corporate and Commercial	Ron Allsopp
	Franco Bosi, Charles Brooks, Robin Peile
	Mark Telfer, Richard Tyson
Corporate Recovery	Noel McMichael, Sue Dixon
	Tracy Gane
Employment	Paul Hadow
Environmental	John Math, Peter Allan
Family	Susan Philipps, Richard Price
Insolvency	Noel McMichael
Intellectual Property	Geoffrey Walkley
Litigation	Paul Hadow, Tracy Gane
	Julian Calnan, Jonathan Rouse, Michael Felce
Matrimonial	Susan Philipps
Medical Negligence	Chris MatherDavid Raine
Personal Injury	Chris MatherDavid Raine
Planning	Roger Bullworthy
Private Client	Lesley Lintott, Michael Fellingham
	Julian Chadwick
Professional Negligence	Chris Mather, Michael Felce
Relocation/housing ass'ns	Andrew Templeman
	Jonathan Rouse
Residential Property	Anthony Bussy
	Andrew Templeman
Shipping	Peter AllanGreg O'Neill

Continues overleaf

The property department: represents companies, institutions and individuals, both UK and overseas, seeking property advice – investors, developers, funders and occupiers. Its members have wide experience in dealing with investment sales and purchases, funding agreements, development schemes, landlord and tenant matters, agricultural investments, as well as smaller commercial property work. Specialist town and country planning, environmental and construction law advice is also provided.

The private client department: provides a wide range of services, in particular all aspects of personal tax planning (including offshore), wills, trusts and the administration of estates.

The family department: deals with all areas of family law including separation, divorce, the welfare of children, child abduction and adoption and property disputes between partners. Specialists within the department are members of the Solicitors Family Law Association and the Family Mediators Association.

Europe: A full European service is provided by Penningtons in association with the member firms of the European Law Group. Specialist advice is available on such matters as EU competition law, Italian and French law from Penningtons' City office.

Languages: French, German, Spanish, Italian, Urdu, Punjabi, Gujerati, Russian and Chinese.

Other Offices: Basingstoke, Godalming, Newbury, Paris.

PERCY HUGHES & ROBERTS

19 HAMILTON SQUARE, BIRKENHEAD, L41 6AY
Tel: (0151) 647 6081 **Fax:** (0151) 666 1080 **DX:** 17862 **Email:** PHR@LINK.ORG

The Firm: Percy Hughes & Roberts is a highly focused well established law firm. The firm was founded in 1919, and whilst retaining traditional values, we have continued to develop and expand, placing an emphasis on creating a dynamic culture suitable to the needs of both commercial and private clients.

Principal Areas of Work: Percy Hughes & Roberts is committed to investing substantial resources in developing centres of expertise. These specialities include:-

Litigation: The Litigation Department acts for major insurance companies and is one of the North West's leading insurance litigation practices. The litigation team has expertise in employers liability, product liability, industrial disease, road traffic claims, and all other areas of insurance litigation. A specialist unit deals with fraudulent and contrived motor claims. Advocacy forms a regular part of the firm's practice, providing regular Solicitors advocacy before professional tribunals, industrial tribunals and licensing matters. Agency work is also carried out.

Commercial Property: The Commercial Property Department provides specialist services to include town centre regeneration; residential and commercial urban renewal; shop, office and hotel development; leisure and license to premises developments, and services for agricultural and equestrian property. The department provides the highest standards of service and a positive and practical approach to business problems.

Employment: Tribunal representation is provided for unfair dismissal and discrimination cases for both employers and employees. Drafting of employment contracts and other employment documents is undertaken.

Professional Services: The Professional Services Unit offers a discreet and thorough service advising and assisting in a wide range of professional problems. There is particular expertise in matters of discipline and conduct issues and problems with professional bodies. Advocacy before professional tribunals and committees is an intricate part of the service.

Private Client: The full range of private client services are offered to include Wills, Trusts, Probate, Residential Conveyancing, Matrimonial Family Law Issues with particular expertise in Child Law matters.

Managing partner:	Jackie Smith
Senior partner:	Peter Johnson
Number of partners:	7
Assistant solicitors:	5
Other fee-earners:	10

CONTACTS	
Commercial Litigation	Jackie Smith
Commercial Property	Janet McBurney
Employment and Private Client	Mark Bland
Professional Services	Jonathan Goodwin

PERKINS & CO 1 King Street, Manchester, M2 6AW *Tel:* (0161) 834 7770 *Fax:* (0161) 834 8399 *DX:* 710304 Manchester 3 *Ptnrs:* 4 *Asst solrs:* 3 *Other fee-earners:* 3

PERRIS NICOL & DENVIR 798 Newport Road, Rumney, Cardiff, CF5 8DH *Tel:* (01222) 796311 *Fax:* (01222) 779261 *DX:* 118475 Rumney Cardiff *Ptnrs:* 3 *Asst solrs:* 4 *Other fee-earners:* 2

PETER CARTER-RUCK AND PARTNERS

INTERNATIONAL PRESS CENTRE, 76 SHOE LANE, LONDON, EC4A 3JB
Tel: (0171) 353 5005 **Fax:** (0171) 353 5553 **DX:** 333 CH.LN. **Email:** LAWYERS@CARTER-RUCK.CO.UK **Internet:** WWW.CARTER-RUCK.CO.UK

The Firm: Peter Carter-Ruck and Partners is a well-established medium sized firm of Solicitors, which is particularly well-known for its media expertise and its high profile defamation practice. The firm also undertakes most other types of litigation such as intellectual property, employment and general commercial litigation in addition to non-contentious work, including property and trusts. The firm's media work covers all aspects of advice in the area with emphasis on speed and efficiency of service to clients and taking a direct and practical approach to achieving clients' objectives. The firm maintains a 24 hour 7 days a week service.

Senior Partner:	Andrew Stephenson
Senior Consultant:	Peter F. Carter-Ruck
Number of partners:	15
Assistant solicitors:	5
Other fee-earners:	5

Principal Areas of Work:
Media and Defamation: (*Contact Partners:* Andrew Stephenson, Alasdair Pepper, Nigel Tait, Charlotte Watson, Ruth Collard, Cameron Doley and Christopher Hutchings). All aspects of media activity are covered from book, radio, newspaper report and article reading, TV programme clearances for libel and contempt together with all types of media litigation.
Intellectual Property: (*Contact Partners:* Guy Martin and Lee Penhaligan). This department covers copyright, passing off and trade mark work, with both non contentious work, including publishing, film and theatrical contracts, and contentious work.
Litigation: (*Contact Partner:* Nigel Tait.) The department has extensive experience in general commercial litigation, in particular in solicitors' negligence claims, and also undertakes employment advice and litigation.
Trusts and Property: (*Contact Partner:* Lee Penhaligan) The department provides a full commercial and residential conveyancing service and has experience in all aspects of Trust law.
Commercial: (*Contact Partners:* Nigel Tait and Guy Martin) The department has particular experience in drafting commercial, intellectual property and employment experience in accordance with related agreements. The firm is also authorised to handle appeals to the Judicial Committee of the Privy Council in its capacity as Privy Council agents.

Foreign Connections: The firm has appointed agents in over 50 countries which enables it, for example, to provide definitive copyright advice in cases involving international publication.

Other associated offices in Aldershot, Glasgow, Manchester, Munich, Paris, Rome, San Francisco.

PETER EDWARDS & CO Murrayfield House, The Kings Gap, Merseyside, Hoylake, L47 1HE *Tel:* (0151) 632 6699 *Fax:* (0151) 632 0090

PETERKINS 100 Union Street, Aberdeen, AB10 1QR **Tel:** (01224) 626300 **Fax:** (01224) 626123 **DX:** AB3 **Ptnrs:** 23 **Asst solrs:** 10 **Other fee-earners:** 10 **Contact:** Neil Hunter **Also at:** 227 Sauchiehall Street, Glasgow G2 3EX *Tel:* (0141) 331 1050 *Fax:* (0141) 332 6847 *DX:* GW3. *Corporate/commercial and general practice with associated European offices including Brussels.*

WORKLOADS			
Residential Property	38%	Corporate & Commercial	18%
Private Client	15%	Litigation	13%
Commercial Property	12%	Miscellaneous	4%

PETER LIELL 40 Osborne Road, Potters Bar, EN6 1SF *Tel:* (01707) 665540 *Fax:* (01707) 665560 *Ptnrs:* 1

PETER MASTERS & CO 85 Regent Street, Cambridge, CB2 1AW *Tel:* (01223) 462700 *Fax:* (01223) 461080 *DX:* 5811 Cambridge *Ptnrs:* 1

PETER MAUGHAN & CO 15A Walker Terrace, Gateshead, NE8 1EB *Tel:* (0191) 477 9779 *Fax:* (0191) 477 7997 *DX:* 60323 Gateshead *Ptnrs:* 2 *Other fee-earners:* 2

PETER, PETER & WRIGHT 8 Fore Street, Holsworthy, EX22 6ED *Tel:* (01409) 253262 *Fax:* (01409) 254091 *DX:* 118650 Holsworthy *Ptnrs:* 12 *Asst solrs:* 3 *Other fee-earners:* 16

PETER RICKSON AND PARTNERS

6 WINCKLEY SQUARE, PRESTON, PR1 3JJ
Tel: (01772) 556677 **Fax:** (01772) 202445 **DX:** 714570 PRESTON 14 **Email:** INFO@PRP.E-MAIL.COM

THE STOCK EXCHANGE BUILDING, 4 NORFOLK STREET, MANCHESTER, M2 1DP
Tel: (0161) 833 3355 **Fax:** (0161) 833 1042 **DX:** 14318 MANCHESTER 1 **Email:** INFO@PRP.E-MAIL.COM

UNION CHAMBERS, 63 TEMPLE ROW, BIRMINGHAM, B2 5LS
Tel: (0121) 631 3304 **Fax:** (0121) 643 0787 **DX:** 13026 BIRMINGHAM 1 **Email:** BIRMINGHAM@PRP.E-MAIL.COM

The Firm: The practice is one of the best-known in the North West dealing with insurance litigation. There are also substantial commercial litigation, commercial property and corporate services departments. In 1993 a Birmingham office was opened to provide a specialist personal injury service in the Midlands.

Principal Areas of Work:

Insurance Litigation: (*Contact Partners:* Steve Hackett, Preston. Jean Hindmoor, Manchester. David Wallen, Birmingham). The firm acts for most of the major insurance companies and is one of the North West's leading specialist practices. The insurance litigation department handles employers' liability, public and product liability and road traffic claims. There is a specialist team dealing with disease claims. In addition, the department advises extensively on policy interpretation.

Commercial Litigation: (*Contact Partner:* Peter Moore, Manchester). All types of business and contractual disputes, partnership litigation, intellectual property, construction and arbitration, landlord and tenant actions and debt collection.

Corporate Services: (*Contact Partner:* Paul Lockett, Manchester). Acquisitions, disposals, mergers, joint ventures, capital restructuring, flotations, commercial agreements, employment law and intellectual property and a full company secretarial service including in-house incorporation.

Commercial Property & Private Client: (*Contact Partner:* Diana Robertson, Preston). Freehold acquisitions and disposals, leases of commercial, industrial and retail sites. For house builders, a comprehensive service in relation to land acquisitions and development and residential plot sales. The private client services include wills and probate, domestic conveyancing and matrimonial advice.

Managing partner:	Fraser Haddleton
Senior partner:	Peter Rickson
Number of partners:	19
Assistant solicitors:	11
Consultants:	2
Other fee-earners:	26

WORKLOADS	
Insurance Litigation	69%
Commercial Litigation	11%
Corporate Services	10%
Commercial Property and Private Client	10%

PETERS & PETERS

2 HAREWOOD PLACE, HANOVER SQUARE, LONDON, W1R 9HB
Tel: (0171) 629 7991 **Fax:** (0171) 499 6792 **DX:** 44625

This specialist West End practice (founded in 1938) is best known as one of the leading firms in the area of white-collar crime and commercial litigation, both domestic and international. It also has specialisms in international business law and intellectual property.

The Firm: Peters & Peters concentrates not only on the quality of the service it provides, but also on its technical expertise and practical know-how. It aims to be innovative and to provide solutions to problems that cut across the traditional boundaries of legal disciplines. The firm believes it was one of the first practices to develop such a multi-disciplinary approach; consequently, a high proportion of partners and staff have built up a very considerable level of expertise.

Much of the practice's work is high profile and it is frequently international in scope. The firm has built up close working relationships with law firms overseas. As a result it regularly receives instructions by way of referral and invitations to speak at international conferences and seminars as well as to contribute to business and legal journals throughout the world. Members of the firm have received requests to serve on government committees and to advise foreign regulators and international organisations.

Principal Areas of Work: Commercial litigation – an area in which the firm's practice has expanded rapidly in recent years. Expertise covers the whole range of contentious work including civil fraud, contractual disputes, employment law and defamation, as well as personal and corporate bankruptcy and related insolvency matters. The firm has a wealth of experience in the application of emergency procedures both outside and within the jurisdiction of the UK. Because of the firm's particular mix of specialisms, it is often asked to deal with civil litigation matters where criminal proceedings are also contemplated, with all the complications of parallel litigation. Often such cases include the further complexities of private or public international law.

Managing partner:	Raymond Cannon
Senior partners:	Monty Raphael,
	Raymond Cannon
Number of partners:	11
Assistant solicitors:	7
Other fee-earners:	13

WORKLOADS	
Business crime	60%
Civil litigation	35%
Commercial/Commercial conveyancing	5%

CONTACTS	
Business crime	Monty Raphael
	Keith Oliver
	Louise Delahunty
	Julia Balfour-Lynn
	Jo Rickards
	Michelle O'Neill
	David Corker
	Peter Binning
Commercial litigation	Sarah Hannam
	Kathryn Garbett
Intellectual Property/Franchising	Raymond Cannon

The practice's longstanding experience in business crime is one of its key strengths. This has been built up over a great variety of cases in which it has acted for large organisations in both an investigative and a preventive role, as well as for individual defendants. The caseload encompasses all forms of corporate fraud, as well as cross-border issues, extradition and mutual assistance as well as forensic tax and revenue work. Expertise includes VAT and Customs infractions, insolvency crime, securities offences and the regulatory activities of government and financial services institutions.

The firm also undertakes domestic and international business matters offering advice in the field of business law, corporate dealings, commercial relationships including agency, distribution, intellectual property, franchising and licensing, particularly in matters relating to the European Union and North America. The firm also provides a service to corporate and private clients in commercial conveyancing and conducts agency work in all its specialist areas.

Peters & Peters aims further to develop its specialisms in the UK and overseas, with particular emphasis on commercial litigation.

PETTMAN SMITH

79 KNIGHTSBRIDGE, LONDON, SW1X 7RB
Tel: (0171) 235 1288 **Fax:** (0171) 235 2683 **DX:** 38168 KNIGHTSBRIDGE **Email:** PS@PSLAW.CO.UK **Internet:** WWW.PETTMAN-SMITH.COM

The Firm: A modern commercial practice, established in 1982, which has since grown considerably. The firm seeks to provide practical and commercially viable solutions to legal and business problems in a friendly, professional manner. The practice is particularly noted for its work in intellectual property.

Principal Areas of Work:
Commercial Litigation: (*Contact:* Jonathan Sachs). A comprehensive service includes commercial fraud, employment disputes and property and building contract litigation.
Commercial Property: (*Contact:* Ann Glaves-Smith). The firm handles development work from acquisition to sale, mortgage and other bank security work.
Intellectual Property: (*Contact:* Nicola Berridge). Both contentious and non-contentious work is handled. Actions include copyright, patents, trademarks, passing-off and counterfeit goods. The firm has particular experience in interlocutory proceedings. Non-contentious work includes software licensing and character merchandising.
Company/Commercial: (*Contact:* Michael Pettman). Company acquisitions and mergers, joint ventures and shareholders' agreements. Venture capital funding and technology-related work. Company reorganisations and restructuring. Business acquisitions and disposals. Management buy-outs and investments. Financial services work including disciplinary and regulatory work. Shareholder and partnership disputes. Insolvency advice, personal and corporate. Company formation and administration. Commercial agreements in particular intellectual property licensing agreements. Software licencing and development and hardware contracts. Service and consultancy agreements. Other commercial advice.
Taxation: (*Contact:* Michael Pettman). International tax planning is a particular strength, and immigration and nationality questions are also handled.

Nature of Clientele: Clients include major public companies, small businesses and entrepreneurs. There is a substantial client base in America and the Middle East.

Managing partner:	Ann Glaves-Smith
Senior partner:	Michael Pettman
Number of partners:	7
Assistant solicitors:	4
Other fee-earners:	2

WORKLOADS	
Company and commercial	33%
Litigation	33%
Property	33%

CONTACTS	
Commercial litigation	Alexandra Adam
Commercial property	Ann Glaves-Smith
	Marie-Garrard Newton
Company and commercial	Michael Pettman
Intellectual property	Jonathan Sachs

PHILIP CONN & CO

7TH FLOOR, LINCOLN HOUSE, 1 BRAZENNOSE STREET, MANCHESTER, M2 5FJ
Tel: (0161) 833 9494 **Fax:** (0161) 834 4540 **Email:** PHILIPCONNCO@BTINTERNET.COM

The Firm: Philip Conn & Co was founded in 1975 solely as a commercial practice. It has now established a reputation for having one of the strongest intellectual law practices outside of London with an equal emphasis on contentious and non-contentious work. A multi-disciplinary approach is taken, and scientists are recruited to meet the needs of intellectual property. Clientele ranges from multi-national public companies to medium sized and owner managed companies.

The practice undertakes an increasing amount of merger and acquisition and other company work, including, most recently, a sale of a client's business for £50m and a NASDAQ flotation. This is in addition to joint venture work which is often technology based. The next training vacancy is 1998.

Foreign Connections: The firm has strong links with lawyers, patent attorneys and firms in the EU, USA and Australasia in particular, and extensive experience in the conduct of litigation and intellectual property licensing overseas.

All correspondence should be addressed to the Managing Partner.

Managing partner:	A. Ian Morris
Number of partners:	4
Assistant solicitors:	3
Other fee-earners:	5

WORKLOADS	
Corporate/Commercial	40%
Intellectual property (contentious and non-contentious)	40%
Commercial conveyancing/employment/other	10%
Commercial litigation	10%

CONTACTS	
Conveyancing	N Greene
Corporate	T J Osborn
Intellectual Property	A I Morris
IP Litigation & Employment	A P Gibson

PHILIP HAMER & CO

9-11 SCALE LANE, HULL, HU1 1PH
Tel: (01482) 326666 **Fax:** (01482) 324432 **DX:** 11933 HULL

KING MEWS, 1 FRANCES STREET, DONCASTER, DN1 1JR
Tel: (01302) 344929 **Fax:** (01302) 344928 **DX:** 28692 DONCASTER 2

WATERSIDE BUSINESS PARK, LIVINGSTONE ROAD, HESSLE, HU13 0EJ
Tel: (01482) 627866 **Fax:** (01482) 626169 **DX:** 716156 HULL 16

VICTORIA HOUSE, 143/145 THE HEADROW, LEEDS, LS1 5TA
Tel: (0113) 244 2332 **Fax:** (0113) 244 0223 **DX:** 14081 LEEDS PARK SQUARE

PHILIP HAMER LIMITED, 35 TOWNHEAD STREET, SHEFFIELD, S1 2EZ
Tel: (0114) 252 1050 **Fax:** (0114) 252 1055 **DX:** 10591 SHEFFIELD 1

The Firm: Philip Hamer & Co is one of the fastest growing and most technologically advanced legal firms in the Yorkshire region. The firm is committed to quality and is registered by the BSI to the ISO 9000 quality standard. Specialist departments within the firm ensure that the right balance of skills, knowledge and expertise are applied to each project undertaken. The firm has an in-house maintained Web Site – www.hamers.com

Principal Areas of Work:

Accident and Personal Injury: (*Contact*: Jim Wyatt). The firm has an increasing reputation for personal injury work and deals with a wide range of cases including medical negligence and multi-plaintiff action. The senior team members are on The Law Society Specialist Personal Injury Panel.

Company & Commercial: (*Contact*: Alastair Watt, Paul Worthy). The Department has recently relocated to a modern out of town development overlooking the Humber Bridge.

Litigation: (*Contact*: Andrew Kingston). The department handles all High Court and County Court disputes relating to the sale and transport of goods, building and construction. In addition the firm offers a computerised debt collection service.

Matrimonial: (*Contact*: Peter Harris). The department is renowned for its expertise in all aspects of this field and has members on The Law Society Children Panel.

Private Client: (*Contact*: Paul Landau, Tim Booth).

Senior partner:	Philip Hamer
Number of partners:	6
Assistant solicitors:	26
Other fee-earners:	23

CONTACTS	
Civil litigation	Andrew Kingston
Company and commercial	Alastair Watt
Conveyancing (domestic)	Tim Booth
Matrimonial	Peter Harris
Personal injury	Jim Wyatt
Wills and probate	Paul Landau

PICKERING & BUTTERS

19 GREENGATE STREET, STAFFORD, ST16 2LU
Tel: (01785) 603060 **Fax:** (01785) 607500 **DX:** 14551 STAFFORD 1 **Email:** SOLS@P-AND-B.DEMON.CO.UK

The Firm: A progressive and developing practice. The range of specialisms belies its provincial position.

Principal Areas of Work:

Commercial: *Work includes:* corporate governance, agreements, acquisitions and disposals of property and businesses, environmental, employment, intellectual property, business recovery and insolvency.

Personal Injury: *Work includes:* plaintiff and defendant.

Private Client: *Work includes:* property, wills, trusts and probate, tax planning, and financial services.

Civil Litigation: *Work includes:* commercial litigation and road haulage, police disciplinary hearings, intellectual property and insolvency.

Recruitment: The firm is always keen to receive applications from quality candidates. Applications with CV to Christopher Lee.

Other Offices:

Market Square, Rugeley, Staffs. WS15 2BN.
Tel: 01889 803080; *Fax:* 01889 803081

Managing partner:	Roger Price
Number of partners:	10
Assistant solicitors:	7
Other fee-earners:	11

WORKLOADS	
Private Client	27%
Commercial	23%
Civil Litigation	19%
Personal Injury	18%
Family	7%
Criminal	6%

CONTACTS	
Civil Litigation	Jill Benbow
Commercial	Don White
Criminal	Alan Bentley
Family	John Trubshaw
Personal Injury	Jan Boulter
Private Client	David Worrall

PICKWORTHS

55 MARLOWES, HEMEL HEMPSTEAD, HP1 1LE
Tel: (01442) 261731 **Fax:** (01442) 230356 **DX:** 8809 HEMEL HEMPSTEAD

6 VICTORIA STREET, ST. ALBANS, AL1 3JB
Tel: (01727) 844511 **Fax:** (01727) 844277 **DX:** 6143 ST ALBANS

28 STATION ROAD, WATFORD, WD1 1EG
Tel: (01923) 227292 **Fax:** (01923) 236807 **DX:** 51504 WATFORD 2

The Firm: Pickworths is a leading Hertfordshire practice, registered for ISO 9001, offering a comprehensive range of services to commercial and private clients.

Principal Areas of Work:

Company/ Commercial: (*Contact:* Peter Goodman). Advice is provided on all aspects of commercial, financial and business law including the restructuring of companies, shareholders agreements, acquisitions and disposals, refinancing, management buy-outs, contract discussions, terms and conditions, intellectual property, debt collection, employment contracts and disputes, general office procedures and Health and Safety Regulations.

Litigation: (*Contact:* David White). A comprehensive range of commercial litigation services form a substantial part of Pickworths business and the firm has a long established reputation in this field. *Work includes:* breach of contract, emergency injunctions and relief, personal injury and negligence claims for plaintiffs and insurance companies, insolvency and corporate recovery of business debts. The Watford office holds a Legal Aid Franchise for Matrimonial and Personal Injury Work.

Commercial Property: (*Contact:* Glenda Ferneyhough). Advice is given on: acquiring 'greenfield' sites, buying and selling premises, commercial leases and property management.

Planning & The Environment: (*Contact:* David Forbes).The firm has a specialist in-house team dealing with all planning matters including local planning enquiries, enforcement notices, established use certificates, submission of planning applications, compensation for compulsory purchase and appeals to the Department of the Environment. David Forbes is the author of two published books on planning law.

Advocacy: (*Contact:* Fred Lamb). Criminal, County Court and High Court advocacy is undertaken. The firm has a specialist in mental health cases, an active Road Traffic Department and also deals with all liquor licensing, regulatory cases and road haulage etc.

Employment: (*Contact:* Ian Tottman). Comprehensive advice for both employers and employees on resignation, dismissal and redundancy, and representation at Industrial Tribunals. In addition a full service dealing with the drafting and preparation of contracts of employment.

Senior partner:	D. Forbes
Number of partners:	6
Assistant solicitors:	6
Other fee-earners:	4

WORKLOADS	
Litigation	30%
Property/planning	25%
Commercial/sports law	20%
Advocacy & Crime	15%
Employment, wills and probate	10%

CONTACTS	
Advocacy & Crime	F. Lamb
Commercial	P.J. Goodman
Employment	I.T. Tottman
Litigation/matrimonial	D.R. White
Planning	D.S. Forbes
Property	G. Ferneyhough
Sports law	P.J. Goodman

Continues overleaf

Sports Law: (*Contact:* Peter Goodman). Pickworths is one of the country's leading practices in motor racing, acting for teams, drivers and organisers involved in Formula 1, Formula 3000, Formula 3, Touring Car Championships and various other classes. The firm has also acted for manufacturers of exotic road going cars.

Private Client: (*Contact:* Patricia Hollings). *Work includes:* residential conveyancing, matrimonial/ child care, wills and probate.

PICTONS

KEYSTONE, 60 LONDON RD, ST. ALBANS, AL1 1NG
Tel: (01727) 798000 **Fax:** (01727) 798002 **DX:** 122730 ST. ALBANS 10

30-32 BROMHAM ROAD, BEDFORD, MK40 2QD
Tel: (01234) 273273 **Fax:** (01234) 353110 **DX:** 5614

1 THE WATERHOUSE, WATERHOUSE STREET, HEMEL HEMPSTEAD, HP1 1ES
Tel: (01442) 242441/250111 **Fax:** (01442) 248569 **DX:** 8800

CARLTON COURT, 66 ALMA STREET, LUTON, LU1 2PL
Tel: (01582) 410114 **Fax:** (01582) 402736 **DX:** 130465 LUTON 10

ASHTON HOUSE, 409 SILBURY BOULEVARD, CENTRAL MILTON KEYNES, MK9 2LJ
Tel: (01908) 663511 **Fax:** (01908) 661800 **DX:** 31411

13 TOWN SQUARE, STEVENAGE, SG1 1BP
Tel: (01438) 350711/342400 **Fax:** (01438) 359255 **DX:** 6006

24 THE AVENUE, WATFORD, WD1 3NS
Tel: (01923) 237631 **Fax:** (01923) 226135 **DX:** 4505

The Firm: Pictons was established 1967 and grew rapidly during the 1970s and 1980s into a seven office firm spanning Herts, Beds and Bucks. Since 1993 the firm has been organised on a departmental basis across the branch network. Pictons are committed to providing a service to all clients which combines the highest levels of professionalism with practical actionable advice in an environment which is approachable, supportive and efficient. The firm offers a depth and breadth of service whether in a single discipline or across a range of specialist areas by providing teams tailored to meet either a specific transaction or general client brief. Pictons operate to written quality standards and in 1996 made a commitment to "Investors in People". Departments offering Legal Aid services were amongst the first to receive Legal Aid franchises in 1994.

Principal Areas of Work:

Commercial: The department's core strengths are in Mergers, Acquisitions, Buy-ins, Buy-outs, Share and Asset sales/purchases, Venture capital, Banking and Finance (mainly sescurity work), Commercial Property, and all aspects of landlord and tenant work including the grant and renewal of leases.

Commercial Litigation: The principle areas of work covered by the Commercial Litigation team include contract, landlord and tenant and shareholder disputes, directors liability, professional negligence and intellectual property.

Sport: A number of international sports celebrities, players agents and national organisations are represented by the Sports unit. The emphasis is mainly on Football and Rugby although other sporting areas are covered.

Insolvency: Pictons Insolvency team primarily advises and acts for IPs although some work is carried out for companies and privately owned businesses.

Employment: The employment unit acts for both large and small businesses dealing with the full range of employment related issues including race relations, sex and disability discrimination.

Financial Services: Created to offer business and private clients independent and impartial financial advice the firm's Investment and Financial Services department provides advice in all areas of business and personal finance including loans, investments, pensions, life assurance and general insurance matters.

Domestic Conveyancing: In addition to a substantial volume of private client transactions the department undertakes bulk conveyancing work for lending and other institutions and includes a relocation service.

PI and Medical Negligence: This team forms the largest section of the firms Civil Litigation department. There is a member of Accident Line at every office. At the Milton Keynes branch there is particular emphasis on claims in respect of brain injury and damage.

Family: Throughout the firm Pictons have practitioners dedicated to Family Law including the specialist areas of Pensions and Child Abduction. Four solicitors are members of The Children Panel.

Managing partner:	Gerard Sampson
Chairman/Senior partner:	Christopher Brown
Number of partners:	34
Assistant solicitors:	32
Other fee-earners:	44

WORKLOADS	
Commercial, property and company	25%
Crime	22%
Commercial litigation/ personal injury	18%
Family	16%
Domestic conveyancing	15%
Probate/ trusts/ tax planning	4%

CONTACTS	
Civil Litigation/PI	Sue Jarvis (Milton Keynes)
Commercial Litigation	David Fagan (St Albans)
Corporate and Commercial	Roger Talbot (St Albans)
Crime	David Healey (Luton)
Domestic Conveyancing	Chris Tate (Luton)
Employment	Antony Arbuthnot (St Albans)
Family	Adrienne Dunphy (Hemel Hempstead)
Insolvency	Bryan Green (St Albans)
Investment & Financial Planning	
	Neil Caisley (St Albans)
Probate Trusts and Wills	Elizabeth Harrold (Hemel Hempstead)
Sport	Peter Baines (St Albans)

Criminal: The Criminal department covers the entire spectrum of criminal work. The work is almost exclusively legally-aided although some privately funded work is undertaken particularly in the areas of white-collar fraud and road-traffic offenses.

The Litigation and Criminal departments accept, through all offices of the firm, agency work at Magistrates and County courts for other firms.

Brochures detailing the services of the firm are available on request.

PINSENT CURTIS

3 COLMORE CIRCUS, BIRMINGHAM, B4 6BH
Tel: (0121) 200 1050 **Fax:** (0121) 626 1040 **DX:** 703167 BIRMINGHAM 12 **Email:** JOHN.PRATT@PINSENT-CURTIS.CO.UK

41 PARK SQUARE, LEEDS, LS1 2NS
Tel: (0113) 244 5000 **Fax:** (0113) 244 8000 **DX:** 26440 LEEDS PARK SQUARE **Email:** MALCOLM.LLOYD@PINSENT-CURTIS.CO.UK

DASHWOOD HOUSE, 69 OLD BROAD STREET, LONDON, EC2M 1NR
Tel: (0171) 418 7000 **Fax:** (0171) 418 7050 **DX:** 1195-6 FINSBURY CIRCUS **Email:** GRAEME.BRISTER@PINSENT-CURTIS.CO.UK

The Firm: Leading UK national law firm large publicly listed client base, consistently ranked in The Company Guide top group of legal advisers to listed companies. Growing international focus and sole UK membership of US/European network of legal firms.

In the past year, Pinsent Curtis has recruited more than 20 new partners several from City firms to work throughout the firm. With a national reputation in many areas of law such as employment and employee share schemes, where its lawyers are authors of definitive reference works, the firm was the first to appoint a "Big Six" accounting firm partner as its financial director and among the first to appoint dedicated client service partners to ensure consistent delivery of quality service.

Principal Areas of Work: Six main practice areas – commercial, corporate, employment, litigation, property and tax and pensions – supported by a number of specialist national groups covering EU and UK Competition law, banking and finance, building societies, financial services, regulatory issues, professional indemnity, IP and IT, franchising, major projects including an award-winning PFI team, construction, environment and planning.

Corporate: One of the largest national Corporate Finance departments of any UK firm, regularly ranked among leading advisers in independent surveys. Three specialist operating groups – stock exchange; private equity and banking and finance. In 1997, the department nationally advised on transactions totalling in excess of £5.8 billion.

Commercial: Multi-disciplinary specialist department advising on commercial contracts, complex IP and IT issues, millennium compliance, franchising, EU & UK competition notably EC Merger Regulation notification.

Employment: The 21 dedicated lawyers makes this among the largest UK employment practices. Independently recognised as the leading UK adviser on TUPE and discrimination law, as well as being at the forefront of interpreting UK and EU employment legislation. Runs bespoke training for blue chip clients.

Litigation: With 120 lawyers, this is one of the largest national litigation teams with considerable specialist City expertise and international experience. Specialises in commercial contract disputes, corporate acquisitions and disposals, corporate recovery, libel and defamation, financial services issues, product liability disputes and shareholder and director disputes. A pioneer in Alternative Dispute Resolution with several trained mediators. Sizeable Professional Indemnity team advising major clients including the Solicitors' Indemnity Fund and major insurers. Has taken a lead on pensions misselling and professional negligence in financial services selling.

Property: Large Commercial Property department advising clients with property interests throughout the UK. Specialises in portfolio management, property development and investment, planning and environment, secured lending, mines and minerals, property litigation and construction and engineering.

Tax: Dedicated tax team ranking in size and quality alongside leading City practices with a number of nationally-recognised experts in corporate tax and employee share schemes. UK and international clients advised on all areas of corporate tax, restructuring, offshore trusts, VAT, employee share schemes, personal tax planning and charities.

Recruitment and Training: The firm runs an extensive in-house national training scheme for lawyers and managers at all levels interwoven with a programme of targeted external seminars and residential courses.

Overseas Offices: Brussels.

Foreign Languages: Chinese (Cantonese), Dutch, French, German, Greek, Hebrew, Hindi, Italian, Japanese, Shona, Spanish, Swedish, Ukrainian, Urdu, Welsh.

Senior partner:	Julian Tonks
Number of partners:	124
Assistant solicitors:	130
Other fee-earners:	123

WORKLOADS	
Litigation & professional indemnity	38%
Corporate/commercial	34%
Property	19%
Tax	9%

CONTACTS	
Commercial	Stephen Chandler
Corporate	Alan Greenough
Employment	John McMullen
Litigation	Nigel Kissack
Property	Barry Brice
Tax	David Pett

PIPER SMITH & BASHAM 31 Warwick Square, London, SW1V 2AF *Tel:* (0171) 828 8685
Fax: (0171) 630 6976 *DX:* 110 Ch.Ln. *Ptnrs:* 5 *Asst solrs:* 4 *Other fee-earners:* 4

PITMANS

47 CASTLE STREET, READING, RG1 7SR
Tel: (0118) 9580224 **Fax:** (0118) 9585097 **DX:** 40102 **Email:** PBETTERTON@PITMANS.COM

The Firm: Pitmans is one of Thames Valley's leading commercial practices, offering a comprehensive legal service to local, national and international businesses. In recent years the partnership has grown and with it, the breadth of skills and specialisations offered. Pitmans' membership of InterAct Europe 1993 EEIG has proved to be invaluable to the success and growth of the practice.

Principal Areas of Work:

Company/Commercial: (*Contact Partner:* John Hutchinson. *Fee-earners:* 14). The company/commercial department is one of the largest in the South East, outside London. It handles a wide variety of work including company formations, mergers and acquisitions, management buy-outs, institutional investment agreements, trading agreements, employment issues, share option schemes and financial services. It advises overseas clients on questions of location and handles work overseas for British clients. The department also offers specialist reports tailored to the needs of individual clients on developing European law affecting them and is able to review legal frameworks in other countries.

Corporate Security and Insolvency: (*Contact Partner:* David Archer. *Fee-earners:* 9). A specialist department is dedicated to corporate security and insolvency work.

Intellectual Property: (*Contact Partner:* Philip Weaver. *Fee-earners:* 4). The intellectual property department has gone from strength to strength and acts for a large number of the international computer and software companies both in the Thames Valley and overseas. The department offers a wide range of services both of a contentious and non-contentious nature in the patent, copyright, trademark, know-how and entertainment sectors.

Commercial Property: (*Contact Partner:* Christopher Avery. *Fee-earners:* 16). A significant percentage of Pitmans' work is in the commercial property sector. The firm is renowned for its work in land acquisitions, joint venture arrangements and particularly for its expertise in planning and public enquiries. The department's clients include one of the largest landowners in the country, a number of substantial PLCs, local authorities and health authorities. It also has a department specialising in the sale of new homes for residential developers.

Environmental Law: (*Contact Partner:* Richard Valentine. *Fee-earners:* 3). The environmental law department has integrated well with the existing commercial property, general commercial and planning work. This department offers a wide range of services within this complex area of law with particular emphasis on the new laws developing in the European Community.

Litigation: (*Contact Partner:* Susan O'Brien. *Fee-earners:* 24). The litigation department has wide experience in all areas of commercial litigation, especially in the hi-technology, construction and finance industries and in international trade. It regularly works with other departments to provide a team approach for larger litigation matters. A debt collection service is available to clients. Criminal, and matrimonial litigation is not undertaken.

Planning: (*Contact Partner:* Richard Valentine. *Fee-earners:* 3). Nearly all the commercial property partners have specialist knowledge of planning law, and a broad range of expertise covers: development strategy, agreements with Highway and Planning Authorities, major planning appeals and judicial reviews of planning decisions.

Other Areas of Work: Pitmans undertakes a substantial amount of other non-contentious business, such as residential conveyancing, trust and probate work, wills, family settlements and personal tax planning.

Nature of Clientele: Clients range from large PLCs to newly-established businesses, and from private clients to local authorities. They are located throughout the country and worldwide. Pitmans is a founder member of an EEIG, with associated law firms in Amsterdam, Copenhagen, Hamburg, Madrid, Munich, Oslo and Paris.

Managing partner:	Christopher Avery
Senior partner:	Tony Jones
Number of partners:	13
Assistant solicitors:	20
Other fee-earners:	29

WORKLOADS	
Company/commercial	23%
Litigation	23%
Property (commercial)	20%
Residential development	11%
Planning and environmental	8%
Intellectual property	7%
Insolvency	5%
Private client	3%

CONTACTS	
Commercial property	Christopher Avery
Company commercial	John Hutchinson
Environmental	Richard Valentine
Insolvency	David Archer
Intellectual property	Philip Weaver
Litigation	Sue O'Brien
Planning	Richard Valentine
Private client	Tony Jones

POPPLESTON ALLEN

37 STONEY STREET, THE LACE MARKET, NOTTINGHAM, NG1 1LS
Tel: (0115) 953 8500 **Fax:** (0115) 953 8501 **DX:** 10100 NOTTINGHAM

The Firm: Established in May 1994 by two nationally-renowned solicitors, Jeremy Allen and Susanna Poppleston. Poppleston Allen is a niche practice specialising exclusively in licensing matters.

Principal Areas of Work: Poppleston Allen deals with liquor, public entertainment, and betting and gaming licensing. First class legal expertise is provided from the conception stages of a project through acquisition, regular renewal, upgrading and transfer of licences, to dealing with particular problems at licensed premises.

The firm's client base is wide and not restricted to its immediate area, and its consequent experience of the policies and quirks of licensing authorities covers every county in England and Wales. It offers unrivalled expertise in the niche area of discotheques and clubs, as well as dealing with pubs, bars and off-licences.

Poppleston Allen currently acts for Bass Leisure Entertainment, European Leisure, Kingfisher Leisure, Luminar Leisure, Pizza Express, Rank Entertainment, Scottish & Newcastle and a number of developers. It is also able to market the specialist practice to other law firms who themselves lack a dedicated licensing department.

Senior partner:	J. Allen
Number of partners:	2
Assistant solicitors:	4
Other fee-earners:	5

WORKLOADS	
Licencing (liquor, public entertainment, betting and gaming	100%

CONTACTS	
Licensing	J.R. Allen, S. Poppleston

PORTER DODSON Central House, Church Street, Yeovil, BA20 1HH **Tel:** (01935) 424581 **Fax:** (01935) 706063 **DX:** 100501 Yeovil **Email:** PD.YEOVIL@PD.TelMe.com **Ptnrs:** 25 **Other fee-earners:** 72 **Other staff:** 160 **Contact:** Mr Tom George *General Practice with particular experience in agricultural, commercial, personal injury, tax and trusts and private client work. Other offices located in Taunton, Bridgwater, Wellington, Langport, Sherborne, Sturminster Newton and Blandford Forum.*

WORKLOADS			
Litigation	44%	Property/Commercial	34%
Probate, tax and trusts	22%		

PORTRAIT SOLICITORS IN ASSOCIATION WITH DENTON HALL 1 Chancery Lane, London, WC2A 1LF **Tel:** (0171) 320 3888 **Fax:** (0171) 430 1242 **DX:** 69 **Ptnrs:** 2 **Asst solrs:** 3 **Other fee-earners:** 1 **Contact:** Miss Judith Portrait or Mr Dominic Flynn *Specialist private client and charity practice.*

POTHECARY & BARRATT

TALBOT HSE, TALBOT COURT, GRACECHURCH ST, LONDON, EC3V 0BS
Tel: (0171) 623 7520 **Fax:** (0171) 623 9815 **DX:** 590 CITY

The Firm: A long-established firm with particular expertise in charity and ecclesiastical law, trusts, commercial property, planning and company law and insolvency. It also deals with probate matters and family law.

Other Office: White Horse Court, North Street, Bishop's Stortford, Hertfordshire CM23 2LD. *Tel:* (01279) 506421. *Fax:* (01279) 657626. *DX:* 50402 Bishop's Stortford.

Managing partner:	T. B. Warren
Senior partner:	D. Mobsby
Number of partners:	8
Assistant solicitors:	5
Other fee-earners:	4

POWELL & CO 77 Woolwich New Road, Woolwich, London, SE18 6ED *Tel:* (0181) 854 9131 *Fax:* (0181) 855 4174 *Ptnrs:* 2 *Asst solrs:* 1 *Other fee-earners:* 5

POWELL SPENCER & PARTNERS

290 KILBURN HIGH RD, LONDON, NW6 2DD
Tel: (0171) 624 8888 **Fax:** (0171) 328 1221 **DX:** 123862 KILBURN 2

The Firm: Powell Spencer & Partners is one of London's foremost legal aid practices, with a strong reputation for its work in the areas of criminal, family, matrimonial, personal injury, medical negligence and civil liberties litigation. The firm offers a community-based service and has adapted its offices to meet the requirements of clients with disabilities and undertakes home visits.

Principal Areas of Work:

Litigation: A specialist range of litigation is undertaken, namely criminal defence, personal injury and medical negligence, child care, family and matrimonial work; welfare benefits advice.

Contact:

Criminal	*Greg Powell*
Child Care	*Mike Tait*
Matrimonial and Family	*Toby Hales*
Personal Injury and Medical Negligence	*John Gillman*
Welfare Benefits Advice	*Sue Davies.*

Managing partner:	G. Powell
Senior partner:	G. Powell
Number of partners:	6
Assistant solicitors:	5
Other fee-earners:	15

WORKLOADS	
Criminal defence	60%
Civil family	18%
Personal injury	18%
Welfare benefits	4%

CONTACTS	
Civil family	Toby Hales
Criminal defence	Greg Powell
Personal injury	John Gillman
Welfare benefits	Sue Davies

PRESTON GOLDBURN The Old Brewery Yard, High Street, Falmouth, TR11 2BY *Tel:* (01326) 318900 *Fax:* (01326) 311275 *DX:* 81169 *Ptnrs:* 3 *Asst solrs:* 1 *Other fee-earners:* 1

PRETTYS Elm House, 25 Elm Street, Ipswich, IP1 2AD *Tel:* (01473) 232121 *Fax:* (01473) 230002 *DX:* 3218 *Ptnrs:* 15 *Asst solrs:* 16 *Other fee-earners:* 27

PRICE & SON 33 Hill Lane, Haverfordwest, SA61 1PS *Tel:* (01437) 765331 *Fax:* (01437) 768663 *DX:* 98279 Haverfordwest *Ptnrs:* 4 *Asst solrs:* 0 *Other fee-earners:* 2

PRINCE EVANS

77 UXBRIDGE RD, EALING, LONDON, W5 5ST
Tel: (0181) 567 3477 **Fax:** (0181) 840 7757 **DX:** 5100 EALING

The Firm: Prince Evans is a well established, broadly based London practice able to provide practical and specialist advice to both commercial and private clients. Prince Evans has a reputation for a robust and energetic approach with the highest commitment to customer care.

Principal Areas of Work:

Housing and Public Sector: The largest area of the firm's practice and one of the largest departments dedicated to this sector in the UK. The firm acts for over 80 housing associations, numerous local authorities and other institutions involved in this sector and has considerable experience of private sector/public sector partnership arrangements particularly as regards housing and increasingly in the field of community care.

Banking and Finance: An expanding area of practice particularly with regard to housing finance. The firm has acted for numerous borrowers in a range of transactions from bilateral loans to group borrowing arrangements and capital market issues. It also acts for an increasing number of banks lending in this sector, and advises clients on all aspects of Banking Law including treasury management and related issues.

Company/Commercial: The firm has developed considerable expertise, and deals with a variety of company and commercial transactions including company formations, acquisitions, and takeovers, lettings and disposals both for occupation and, in particular, for investment companies; service and commercial agreements, employment contracts and partnership matters.

Property: The firm handles all matters dealing with residential and commercial property including acquisitions, disposals, construction, development and planning advice public/private sector joint ventures; new initiatives, advising on the management of property and the complete range of landlord and tenant matters.

Litigation: General commercial disputes, construction disputes, property disputes, insolvency, employment, contentious probate and intellectual property. The firm has developed a particular reputation for effective housing management advice including all aspects of advocacy and court work and in the field of employment and industrial tribunal work.

Managing partner:	Trevor Morley
Senior partner:	Louis Robert
Number of partners:	7
Assistant solicitors:	20
Other fee-earners:	12

WORKLOADS	
Property	45%
Litigation	20%
Banking & Finance	15%
Personal Injury/Medical Negligence	10%
Private Client	10%

CONTACTS	
Banking	T.E. Morley
Child care	P. Eldin-Taylor
Company/Commercial	T.E. Morley
Construction	R.J. Jennings
Crime	P. Eldin-Taylor
Employment law	R.J. Jennings
Housing & Public Sector	L.J. Robert
Landlord and Tenant	R.J. Jennings
Litigation	R.J. Jennings
Medical negligence	B. Neill
Personal injury	B. Neill
Private client	T.B. Lemon
Property	L.J. Robert
Tax	T.B. Lemon

Personal Injury and Medical Negligence: The firm undertakes work in all aspects of this field with particular emphasis on cases involving major disability, notably spinal and brain injuries. Prince Evans has on several occasions obtained record U.K. damages for plaintiffs in such cases and has pioneered the development of the concept of structured compensation.

Private Client: A wide range of work which includes UK tax and financial and estate planning; wills, trusts and probate. Prince Evans also advises on all aspects of matrimonial and family law, child care and criminal law.

PRITCHARD ENGLEFIELD

14 NEW ST, LONDON, EC2M 4TR
Tel: (0171) 972 9720 **Fax:** (0171) 972 9722 **DX:** 88 LONDON **Email:** PO@PRITCHARDENGLEFIELD.CO.UK

The Firm: Pritchard Englefield, which can trace its origins to 1848, is a well-known City of London law firm practising primarily in general commercial law. The firm is committed to working in and with Europe and is one of the leading law firms in the areas of Anglo-German and Anglo-French trade. Approximately half the firm's partners are fluent in a second European language, and the practice was given the Silver award for Best European Law Firm in The Lawyer HIFAL Awards 1996. Particular emphasis is placed on mergers and acquisitions, property, corporate and tax advice including offshore structures and trusts, commercial and civil litigation, banking law, employment law and all aspects of commercial law. The firm has a broad client base including substantial foreign and UK-based corporations, investors, banks and private individuals.

Managing partner:	Stuart McInnes
Senior partner:	Michael Cohn
Number of partners:	21
Assistant solicitors:	13
Other fee-earners:	20

Principal Areas of Work:

Company/Commercial: David Glass
Banking: Anthony Harris
Litigation: Michael Cohn
Property: David Levene
IP: Peter Groves
Medical Negligence/PI: Grainne Barton
Employment: Belinda Avery
Private client: David King-Farlow
Family: Marian Joseph
German: David Ratcliffe/John Rhodes
French: David Glass

Other Offices:

Frankfurt; Hong Kong
Member of Pannone Law Group EEIG and International Lawyers' Group

Foreign Languages: German, Italian, French, Spanish.

Recruitment and Training: Accepting only trainees fluent in at least one European language other than English.

PRITCHARD ENGLEFIELD
SOLICITORS

PRYCE & CO 6 East Saint Helen Street, Abingdon, OX14 5EW **Tel:** (01235) 523411 **Fax:** (01235) 533283 **DX:** 35853 Abingdon **Ptnrs:** 3 **Asst solrs:** 5 **Contact:** Mr. S.P.B. Capel *Established 1820s. General practice with particular experience in agriculture, company, property and personal injury work. Also at 1 Church Street, Wantage, Oxon.*

WORKLOADS			
Probate, Wills, Trusts	24%	Agriculture	22%
Personal Injury	14%		

PULLIG & CO Bridewell House, 9 Bridewell Place, London, EC4V 6AP *Tel:* (0171) 353 0505 *Fax:* (0171) 936 2548 *DX:* 123 Chancery Lane *Ptnrs:* 4 *Asst solrs:* 1 *Other fee-earners:* 5

PUNCH ROBSON 35 Albert Road, Middlesbrough, TS1 1NU **Tel:** (01642) 230700 **Fax:** (01642) 218923 **DX:** 60501 Middlesbrough **Email:**commercial@punchrobson.co.uk **Ptnrs:** 13 **Asst solrs:** 6 **Other fee-earners:** 9 **Contact:** Ian G. Cox, Practice Manager *Deals with a range of legal matters including family, personal injury, crime, conveyancing, employment and commercial. Established 1877.*

PUTSMANS Britannia House, 50 Great Charles Street, Birmingham, B3 2LT *Tel:* (0121) 237 3000 *Fax:* (0121) 236 7361 *DX:* 702312 Birmingham 10 *Ptnrs:* 14 *Asst solrs:* 8 *Other fee-earners:* 23

PYE-SMITHS The Hall, 4 New St, Salisbury, SP1 2QJ **Tel:** (01722) 412345 **Fax:** (01722) 412321 **DX:** 58006 **Ptnrs:** 3 **Asst solrs:** 7 **Other fee-earners:** 13 **Contact:** Mrs J. Cameron *General family and commercial practice which includes crime, marine law and forfeiture proceedings.*

R.D.BLACK & CO. 31 Old Jewry, London, EC2R 8DQ *Tel:* (0171) 600 8282 *Fax:* (0171) 600 8228 *Ptnrs:* 1 *Asst solrs:* 4

RADCLIFFES

5 GREAT COLLEGE STREET, WESTMINSTER, LONDON, SW1P 3SJ
Tel: (0171) 222 7040 **Fax:** (0171) 222 6208 **DX:** 113 LONDON CHANCERY LANE WC2 **Email:** RADCLIFFES@RADCLIFFES.CO.UK
Internet: WWW.RADCLIFFES.CO.UK

The Firm: Radcliffes (formerly Radcliffes Crossman Block) is a thriving commercial law firm providing clients, including owner managed business, institutions, public authorities, Plcs and private individuals with the full range of legal services in the UK and overseas. As the sole English member of Commercial Law Affiliates (the world's largest affiliation of medium-sized independent law firms), we have the unique ability to offer multi-jurisdictional services across more than 70 countries. Radcliffes has strong links with Radcliffes Trustee Company SA, which offers services from both Geneva and Jersey and provides a vital tool for international tax planning. With regard to recruitment, 3 trainees are required each year. A recruitment brochure is available on request and application is by CV with letter to the recruitment partner.

Principal Areas of Work:

Company Commercial: A solid reputation in the traditional areas of company, commercial and corporate law with a particular strength in mergers and acquisitions, disposals, corporate finance, full Stock Exchange listings as well as placings on AIM, joint ventures and strategic alliances. Advice is provided on all areas of EC and competition law together with employment, pensions and an established reputation in public affairs.

Litigation and Dispute Resolution: The department handles disputes on behalf of clients in both domestic and overseas markets relating to general contract and tort, insurance law, employment law, arbitration, international trade and carriage of goods, property and landlord and tenant law, banking and professional negligence.

Property Investment, Development and Occupation: Clients include institutions and property companies as well as companies involved in property transactions in the course of their normal business. Legal services include: acquisition and disposal of investment property, granting of leases, legal aspects of property management, land acquisition and site assembly, environmental and planning requirements, building contracts, forward funding and financing agreements, tax planning and VAT implications.

Tax and Private Client, including Family Law and Residential Property: The firm is committed to serving the needs of the private client and advises business owners, senior executives, trustees and individuals – both UK and non UK domiciliaries – on a range of matters, including tax and estate planning, financial planning, succession, trusts, family law and residential property.

The firm also operates various specialist groups which concentrate their activities in particular business sectors. The principal groups are: Information Technology and Telecommunications, Health, Charities & Education and Leisure plus specialist overseas groups representing Italy, South Africa and America.

Associated Office: Nice.

Managing partner:	**Richard Price**
Senior partner:	**Lyddon Simon**
Number of partners:	36
Assistant solicitors:	22
Other fee-earners:	27

CONTACTS	
Banking/financial institutions	Rupert Lescher
Charities	Paul Voller/Guy Greenhous
Commercial property	Charles Farrer
Company Commercial	Roland Gillott
Corporate finance	Rupert Lescher
Employment	Michael Elks
European Union law	Roland Gillott
Family law	Roger Cobden-Ramsay
Financial services	Philip Maddock
Health	Andrew Parsons
Immigration	Tim Newsome
Intellectual property	Philip Peacock
IT and Telecommunications	Roland Gillott
Italy	Michael Nathanson
Leisure	Robert Sear
Litigation: Commercial	Michael Elks
Litigation: Property	Robert Highmore
Publishing & Multimedia	Robin Baron
South Africa	Lyddon Simon, Tim Newsome
Tax & private client	Stephen Lewin

RADCLIFFES

RAEBURN CHRISTIE & CO 16 Albyn Place, Aberdeen, AB9 1PS **Tel:** (01224) 640101 **Fax:** (01224) 638434 **DX:** 2 Aberdeen **Ptnrs:** 12 **Asst solrs:** 14 **Other fee-earners:** 8 **Contact:** Mr R.G. Christie *Commercial firm with particular strength in commercial litigation, employment, commercial property, licensing and private client matters.*

WORKLOADS			
Commercial & corporate	40%	Litigation	30%
Private client	30%		

RAKISONS

CLEMENTS HOUSE, 14/18 GRESHAM STREET, LONDON, EC2V 7JE
Tel: (0171) 367 8000 **Fax:** (0171) 367 8001 **DX:** 206 LONDON **Email:** RAKISONS@RAKISONS.CO.UK

The Firm: Rakisons, founded in 1979, is an English law firm with an international practice offering a complete legal service for financial, commercial and industrial clients.

Principal Areas of Work:

Telecommunications and IT: All aspects of telecoms and IT including outsourcing; obtaining telecom licences; interconnection; carrier agreements; regulatory advice; software and hardware licensing and distribution agreements.

Corporate: Takeovers and mergers; joint ventures and shareholders agreements; reorganisation and restructuring of companies; asset acquisition and disposals; management and leveraged buy-outs; venture capital finance; company formations and establishment of businesses; Stock Exchange aspects of share and security transactions; partnerships: formation and dissolution; flotations on AIM; company and partnership disputes. Insolvency related transactions.

Commercial: Agency distribution, licensing and franchising agreements; leasing and finance agreements; terms and conditions of trade; service contracts, consultancy agreements and related employment matters; patents, trademarks and other intellectual property matters; computer contracts; corporate funding; banking law; commercial disputes.

Commercial Litigation: Commercial litigation; arbitrations; corporate and partnership litigation; defamation; intellectual property litigation; obtaining and discharge of injunctions; securities and derivatives; insurance and re-insurance litigation; enforcement of security and related banking litigation; commercial debt recovery; Inland Revenue and Customs and Excise Back-Duty Investigations. Insolvency related litigation.

Commercial Property: Commercial industrial and residential development; investment; acquisitions, disposals and leases; dealing; auctions and tenders; funding and security documentation; planning; building contracts; property taxation; landlord and tenant law; portfolio management; hotel, leisure and licensed premises; environmental law.

Employment: All aspects of employee/employer relations including disciplinary matters; redundancy; termination packages; maternity; discrimination; TUPE related issues, collective disputes; Tribunal and High Court litigation (including Tribunal representation).

Foreign Connections: Languages spoken include French, German, Spanish, Portuguese, Italian and Hebrew. Rakisons has an extensive network of regional and international contacts making it possible to service clients throughout the world.

Managing partner:	Tony Wollenberg
Senior partner:	Tony Wollenberg
Number of partners:	11
Assistant solicitors:	16
Other fee-earners:	2

WORKLOADS	
Corporate/ commercial	30%
IT/Telecommunications	25%
Litigation/Employment	25%
Property/Environment	15%
Employment	5%

CONTACTS	
Corporate	Joel Adler
Employment	David von Hagen
Litigation	Tony Wollenberg
Property	Brendan Patterson
Telecommunications	Christopher Hoyle

RALPH HUME GARRY

SWAN HOUSE, 37-39 HIGH HOLBORN, LONDON, WC1V 6AA
Tel: (0171) 831 3737 **Fax:** (0171) 831 5757 **DX:** 174 LONDON CHANCERY LANE **Email:** RALPHHUMEGARRY@COMPUSERVE.COM
Internet: HTTP://OURWORLD.COMPUSERVE.COM/HOMEPAGES/RALPHHUMEGARRY

The Firm The practice placed in the centre of the legal world between the High Court and the Old Bailey specialises exclusively in litigation and dispute resolution. Partnership law, fraud and insolvency are notable areas of expertise.

The partners have come together from other law firms where they were all senior litigation specialists with many years of experience in all forms of dispute resolution. The firm has been established to serve the needs of existing clients and contacts and to provide for changes to the system of litigation and arbitration in England and Wales.

The firm attaches particular importance to achieving an early resolution to disputes which is both commercial and cost effective in cases where such an approach is appropriate. It concentrates on detailed analysis of the dispute by identifying the issues, the evidence and the merits of parties' respective positions before advising on appropriate strategies.

Stephen Ralph, the senior partner, is a licensed insolvency practitioner. He also sits as an arbitrator in relation to partnership matters. John Hume is a Solicitor Advocate. Peter Garry and David Grant are Accredited Mediators. Christopher Hough is a Chartered Engineer and an Accredited Adjudicator.

Principal Areas of Work: The firm acts across a broad spectrum of commercial litigation and dispute resolution, including arbitrations. The partners have conducted a number of high profile white collar fraud trials and regulatory investigations, DTI inquiries and SFO prosecutions relating to allegations of fraud, insider dealing and multiple share applications. The partners have also represented company directors facing disqualification and represented clients before professional disciplinary tribunals and other self-regulating bodies.

Continues overleaf

Managing partner:	Peter Garry
Senior partner:	Stephen Ralph
Number of partners:	6
Assistant solicitors:	3

WORKLOADS	
Commercial Litigation including Arbitration and ADR	100%

CONTACTS	
Alternative dispute resolution	Peter Gary and David Grant
Arbitration	Stephen Ralph
Commercial litigation	Any Partner
Company boardroom and shareholder disputes and take-over litigation	John Hume
Construction and engineering	Christopher Hough
Inland Revenue and Customs & Excise prosecutions	John Hume and David Grant
Insolvency	David Grant
Insurance	Any Partner
Intellectual property, media and entertainment	Peter Garry
Partnership	Stephen Ralph and Simon Blandy
Pensions	Peter Garry
White collar fraud and regulatory	John Hume and David Grant

The firm acts for banks, insolvency practitioners and borrowers on matters including enforcement of securities, tracing of assets, actions on preferences and avoidance of prior transactions, recovery of assets and examination of directors under the Insolvency Act 1986.

The firm also acts for professional firms, groups of partners or individuals on problems relating to dissolution, expulsion, internal disputes and restructuring of partnerships. It has also assisted client partnerships and their bankers in financial reviews, often involving negotiations with landlords and other creditors and re-financing, and negotiations concerning the interests of individual partners.

The firm is instructed in insurance disputes including professional indemnity, product liability, claims and policy interpretation and issues arising out of the Lloyds of London dispute. It acts in boardroom, shareholder and employment disputes as well as those arising out of joint venture agreements. Construction disputes include loss and expense, defects and professional negligence claims in relation to major building and civil engineering projects.

The firm also deals with pension disputes, acting for beneficiaries, pension fund trustees and their advisers.

The firm also advises a wide range of clients on contentious intellectual property issues, including those which are media and entertainment related. The firm has extensive experience of injunction applications and having obtained and executed Anton Piller orders, it is able to provide supervising solicitors in relation to such orders.

Foreign/International Connections: The firm has close ties with law firms in Europe (notably in France, Switzerland, Germany and Liechtenstein), North America, Australasia and the Pacific rim. Instructions can be taken in French and German.

Ralph Hume Garry

RAMSBOTTOM & CO 25-29 Victoria St, Blackburn, BB1 6DN *Tel:* (01254) 672222 *Fax:* (01254) 681723 *DX:* 15251 *Ptnrs:* 6 *Asst solrs:* 5 *Other fee-earners:* 5

RATCLIFFE DUCE & GAMMER 49 & 51 London Street, Reading, RG1 4PS **Tel:** (0118) 957 4291 **Fax:** (0118) 939 3143 **Ptnrs:** 9 **Asst solrs:** 6 **Other fee-earners:** 6 **Contact:** A.D. Chancellor-Weale *Best known for its family/ matrimonial, personal injury and private client work.*

RAWLISON & BUTLER

GRIFFIN HOUSE, 135 HIGH STREET, CRAWLEY, RH10 1DQ
Tel: (01293) 527744 **Fax:** (01293) 520202 **DX:** 120750 CRAWLEY 8 **Email:** INFO@RAWLIS.CO.UK

The Firm: A leading regional practice. Rawlison & Butler is an ambitious and growing firm serving clients predominantly in the south-east of England offering a comprehensive service from its office close to London-Gatwick. Rawlison & Butler's success reflects its reputation as a responsive and creative organisation providing legal advice focussed on the needs and ambitions of its clients. The firm offers a comprehensive range of legal services. There is an international dimension to the firm's practice with an emphasis towards the EU, North America and Asia Pacific. Clients range from owner-managed businesses to listed companies, multinational corporations and local government authorities. The firm is organised on a departmental basis with partners responsible for practice groups that draw on the experience of lawyers from across the firm's formal departmental structure. Rawlison & Butler strive to achieve the highest standards by a commitment to investing in its people and organisation. This is reflected in the firm embracing the latest technology and the continued development of its know-how resources. Private client services are provided from the Horsham office. Rawlison & Butler is keen to recruit driven high calibre qualified lawyers with a proven record of high academic achievement and professional success. The firm also has an active trainee solicitor programme.

Principal Areas of Work: Particular areas of expertise include:- corporate transactions; purchase and sale of businesses; corporate finance, commercial property; planning and residential development; commercial contracts; employment law; intellectual property; commercial litigation; probate, and tax planning.

Brochures outlining the services offered by Rawlison & Butler are available on request.

Other offices:

15 Carfax, Horsham, West Sussex, RH12 1DY.
Tel: (01403) 252492; *Fax:* (01403) 241545. *DX:* 57602 Horsham

Managing partner:	James Chatfield
Senior partner:	Robin Skinner
Number of partners:	8
Assistant solicitors:	12
Other fee-earners:	13

WORKLOADS	
Commercial property	30%
Company commercial (including employment)	25%
Commercial litigation	24%
Private client	21%

CONTACTS	
Commercial Litigation	Clive Lee (Crawley)
Commercial Property	Robin Skinner and Clive Prior (Crawley)
Corporate & Commercial	James Chatfield (Crawley)
Corporate Finance	Tim Sadka (Crawley)
Employment	Louise Dabbs (Crawley)
Family	Robert Worthing (Horsham)
Insolvency	Richard Homewood (Crawley)
Planning	Carl Burton (Crawley)
Private client	Digby Armstrong (Horsham)

RAWSTHORNS St. George's Chambers, 4 Fishergate Walk, Preston, PR1 2LH *Tel:* (01772) 254251 *Fax:* (01772) 203858 *DX:* 25261 Preston 2 *Ptnrs:* 8 *Asst solrs:* 1 *Other fee-earners:* 7

RAYFIELD MILLS 3 Collingwood Street, Newcastle-upon-Tyne, NE1 1JE *Tel:* (0191) 261 2333 *Fax:* (0191) 261 2444 *Ptnrs:* 8 *Asst solrs:* 4

RAYNER DE WOLFE

31 SOUTHAMPTON ROW, LONDON, WC1B 5HJ
Tel: (0171) 405 1212 **Fax:** (0171) 405 1191 **DX:** 143 LONDON CHANCERY LANE WC2 **Email:** RDW@RAYNERDEWOLFE.CP.UK

Rayner De Wolfe acts mainly for commercial clients and high-net-worth individuals. Its Holborn base was chosen partly because it provides convenient access for the purpose of its particularly active international practice and its proximity to the City.

The Firm: The firm can trace its origins to 1938. A merger of Rayner & Co and De Wolfe & Co in 1983 resulted in an enlarged principal office and enhanced development of the commercial client base. This includes banks, insurance companies, airlines and publishers, as well as family businesses. Among the larger companies for whom it acts are Air France and Alitalia, London & Manchester Group Plc and the international De Agostini Publishing Group. Banking clients include Credit Suisse and Lloyd's Bank TSB.

The practice is a founder member of INTERLEGES, a formal association of independent law firms which has now successfully grown to more than 20 members, providing representation in every member state of the European union, as well as in North America, the Middle East and Central and Eastern Europe. The senior partner of the firm, Stephen Rayner, is chairman of the Law Society's Committee on Relations with Central and Eastern Europe.

While large enough to meet the needs of major corporate clients, Rayner De Wolfe provides a highly personal and cost-effective service, with all cases being handled or supervised by partners, who stay in close contact with their clients, their businesses and their problems. There is great emphasis on client care and the firm believes that it was amongst the first to issue client care guides and formal terms of business.

Principal Areas of Work: The company/commercial department is particularly active in merger and acquisition work and joint ventures, as well as intellectual property and taxation. Expertise in banking law, including security documentation and structuring debt equity arrangements, is well provided. The department's work for the financial services industry includes retail financial services compliance. Additionally, the department handles EU, the Middle East and Central Eastern Europe matters and offshore transactions. It is frequently involved in international commercial arrangements, through the firm's offices and its associated offices worldwide.

Commercial property activities include acting for domestic and offshore investors in UK real estate, development projects, planning and licensing. A specialist property service is provided for private clients, for all types and values of property.

The litigation and dispute resolution department deals almost exclusively with matters of a commercial nature and sees its forte as handling actions of considerable factual and documentary complexity. Particular areas of operation are banking, intellectual property, insolvency, property and international litigation. It also deals with white-collar fraud, professional negligence, arbitration and travel industry matters. It has important specialisations, in addition, in family law (particularly complex financial situations) and employment law.

Rayner De Wolfe aims for expansion in all its departments, particularly in the commercial and banking areas. The existing emphasis on international and banking work will increase.

Managing partner:	Stephen Rosen
Senior partner:	Stephen Rayner
Number of partners:	10
Assistant solicitors:	3
Other fee-earners:	8

WORKLOADS	
Corporate/ commercial	32%
Commercial litigation	28%
Commercial Property	27%
Family Law	9%
Employment	4%

CONTACTS	
Air law/ travel law	E P Graham
Banking	S A Rosen
Commercial litigation	S A Rosen
Corporate/ commercial	S A Rayner
Employment	A S Finlay
Family Law	Eileen Graham
Immigration & nationality	M L Yugin
Intellectual property	J D North
International litigation	J Lederman
Private client	A S Finlay
Property	M L Yugin

RAYNER DE WOLFE
SOLICITORS

R.D.BLACK & CO. 31 Old Jewry, London, EC2R 8DQ **Tel:** (0171) 600 8282 **Fax:** (0171) 600 8228 **Ptnrs:** 1 **Asst solrs:** 4

WORKLOADS			
Commodities	40%	Shipping	40%
Commercial Litigation	20%		

READ HIND STEWART

TRAFALGAR HOUSE, 29 PARK PLACE, LEEDS, LS1 2SP
Tel: (0113) 246 8123 **Fax:** (0113) 244 2863 **DX:** 14085 **Email:** RHSLAW@RHS-LAW.CO.UK **Internet:** WWW.RHS_LAW.CO.UK

The Firm: Read Hind Stewart was established in 1987 and has now developed into a major practice in the commercial centre of Leeds.

Principal Areas of Work: The practice undertakes commercial work and has particularly strong corporate, commercial property, commercial litigation and employment departments. European law is a specialisation, specifically German law-related matters.

Recruitment: As a developing practice, Read Hind Stewart is continually looking for outstanding candidates. Please contact David Hymas, Managing Partner.

Managing partner:	David Hymas
Number of partners:	14
Assistant solicitors:	11
Other fee-earners:	24

WORKLOADS	
Commercial property	35%
Company/ commercial	25%
Commercial litigation	23%
Employment	9%
Debt recovery	8%

REDFERN & STIGANT 57 Balmoral Road, Gillingham, ME7 4PA *Tel:* (01634) 575511 *Fax:* (01634) 855152 *DX:* 6607 Gillingham *Ptnrs:* 7 *Asst solrs:* 3 *Other fee-earners:* 8

REES & FRERES 1 The Sanctuary, Westminster, London, SW1P 3JT **Tel:** (0171) 222 5381 **Fax:** (0171) 222 4646 **DX:** 2301 Victoria **Ptnrs:** 16 **Asst solrs:** 7 **Other fee-earners:** 13 **Contact:** Joe Durkin *Specialise in commercial property, public, parliamentary and local government law, transport infrastructure projects, planning, compulsory acquisition and commercial litigation.*

REES PAGE 30-36 Lichfield Street, Wolverhampton, WV1 1DN *Tel:* (01902) 5777777 *Fax:* (01902) 577735 *DX:* 10405 Wolverhampton *Ptnrs:* 15 *Asst solrs:* 6 *Other fee-earners:* 10

REID MINTY

19 BOURDON PLACE, BOURDON STREET, MAYFAIR, LONDON, W1X 9HZ
Tel: (0171) 318 4444 **Fax:** (0171) 318 4445 **DX:** 44615 MAYFAIR **Email:** LAWYERS@REIDMINTY.CO.UK

The Firm: Founded in 1980, the firm's reputation is built on litigation, but is now expanding into all commercial fields of law.

Principal Areas of Work:

Commercial Litigation: *Work includes:* contractual disputes, intellectual property, banking litigation, container and transport law, shareholder and partnership disputes, insolvency, defamation, employment law and injunctions.

Professional Negligence: The firm handles cases concerning solicitors, surveyors and accountants and is a member of a specialist panel.

Personal Injury: *Work includes:* trade union and private plaintiff work, member of specialist panel.

Commercial Property: The full range of work is undertaken.

Company/Commercial: Full range of work undertaken including M & A, joint ventures, MBO's, investor schemes and other commercial contracts.

Health Authority: Special Hospital and Secure Unit specialisation.

Sports Law: Expertise for players, teams and governing bodies.

Nature of Clientele: Fully quoted PLCs, banks, multinational corporations, full range of general commercial and private clients, health authorities, investment trusts, trade unions and private individuals.

Foreign Connections: The firm is the only UK member of the European Business Lawyers network, and has recently opened an office in Bahrain to service increasing work from the Gulf States. Strong US contacts and clients.

Managing partner:	Andrew Reid
Senior partner:	Andrew Reid
Number of partners:	11
Assistant solicitors:	5
Other fee-earners:	29

CONTACTS	
Commercial litigation	S J Moss
Company/Commercial/Sports	J R Ebsworth
Container leasing	S J Moss
Defamation	N Neocleous
Employment/Health Authority	A Irons
Horseracing	A S Reid
Insolvency	S J Moss
Personal injury	S E Brown
Property	M J Gunson

REUMERT & PARTNERS

ONE KNIGHTRIDER COURT, LONDON, EC4V 5JP
Tel: (0171) 236 4406 **Fax:** (0171) 236 4599 **Email:** RP@REUMERT.CO.UK

The Firm: Founded more than one hundred years ago, Reumert & Partners is one of the largest law firms in Denmark. The firm is consulted by a wide range of domestic and international clients in the fields of industry, trade, banking, finance, transport and insurance. Reumert & Partners is today a full service law firm with the highest level of expertise within all areas of law.

The London Office: Through the London office which was established more than a decade ago, the firm has built a successful international practice with a particular focus on UK clients and London based transactions. The London office assists clients in contentious as well as non-contentious matters within the firm's main areas of practice.

Principal Areas of Work:

Mergers & Acquisitions: Company and business acquisitions, mergers, management buy-outs, management buy-ins, corporate restructuring, joint-ventures.

Corporate Finance: Stock-exchange flotations, public and private offerings of debt and equity securities, securities regulation and general corporate law.

Banking and Finance: Financial services, corporate lending, taking of security, syndications, asset and project financing, financial leasing, foreclosures and borrower defaults, the financial sector and its regulation.

Maritime, Aviation and Transport Law: All legal aspects of the transport industry, including contracts and liability matters, insurance and financing, sale and purchase, contracts of affreightment, shipbuilding contracts.

Insurance, Tort and Negligence: Indemnity, liability and rights of recourse within all commercial insurance areas, reinsurance, policy drafting, liability questions in contract and tort, regulatory matters.

Industrial Property and Competition Law: Patents, trademarks, designs and copyrights, marketing rights, competition law and licences, computer law, agency and distributor agreements.

EU Law: All aspects of EU regulation and harmonisation measures.

Property, Construction and Environmental Law: Property acquisition and divestiture, property development and investment, property financing, building and construction contracts, environmental legislation.

Insolvency: Receiverships, corporate re-organisations, compulsory and voluntary winding-up proceedings.

Litigation and Arbitration: All types of litigation before the Danish courts, Danish and international arbitration and mediation. All partners handle litigation and arbitration work within their own area of expertise. The partners act as arbitrators in Denmark and abroad.

Other Offices: Copenhagen.

Senior partner:	Thomas Albrechtsen, LL.M.

WORKLOADS	
Banking and finance	40%
Corporate and commercial	40%
Litigation & Arbitration	10%
Shipping & Insurance	10%

CONTACTS	
London	Thomas Albrechtsen, L.L.M.

REYNOLDS DAWSON 34 John Adam Street, Charing Cross, London, WC2N 6HW
Tel: (0171) 839 2373 *Fax:* (0171) 839 2344 *Ptnrs:* 2 *Asst solrs:* 2 *Other fee-earners:* 4

REYNOLDS PARRY-JONES & CRAWFORD 10 Easton St, High Wycombe, HP11 1NP
Tel: (01494) 525941 *Fax:* (01494) 530701 *DX:* 4407 *Ptnrs:* 7 *Asst solrs:* 8 *Other fee-earners:* 4

REYNOLDS PORTER CHAMBERLAIN

CHICHESTER HOUSE, 278-282 HIGH HOLBORN, LONDON, WC1V 7HA
Tel: (0171) 242 2877 **Fax:** (0171) 242 1431 **DX:** 81 CHANCERY LANE **Email:** RPC@RPC.CO.UK

The Firm: Reynolds Porter Chamberlain is one of the country's leading insurance and litigation practices. The firm also has a thriving commercial practice providing a wide range of legal services to both UK and international businesses, institutions, and private individuals. It has strong overseas connections and is a founder member of TerraLex, an international association of law firms across over 100 jurisdictions.

Principal Areas of Work:

Insurance/Reinsurance: The department meets the needs of insurance and reinsurance companies and Lloyd's underwriters. It handles general insurance and reinsurance market litigation and is also particularly noted for its professional indemnity work, acting for the insurers of accountants, architects, barristers, brokers, engineers, financial advisers, solicitors and other professionals. It also has a substantial practice acting for the insurers of Directors and Officers, banks and financial institutions. Its office in Leadenhall Street provides close proximity to the surrounding insurance market.

Corporate: The corporate department acts for publicly quoted companies, multinational corporations, private companies, trade associations and partnerships. Work includes: acquisitions and mergers, share issues, corporate finance, banking, yellow book work, insolvency, franchise and distribution, information technology, competition law and financial services regulations.

Commercial Litigation: *Work includes:* contractual disputes, defamation, information technology, product liability, agency and franchising, insolvency, personal injury, partnership and property disputes.

Intellectual Property: Patents, trademarks, designs and copyright disputes and licensing are handled for the professions and for industries ranging from pharmaceutical companies to computing, publishing and entertainment companies.

Employment: *Work includes:* contracts, restrictive covenants, misuse of confidential information and trade secrets, employee benefits, pensions and Industrial Tribunal hearings.

Education: The firm acts for teachers' professional associations, universities and schools and advises on all aspects of education law including the further and higher education sectors.

Tax: *Work includes:* UK and international tax planning, offshore trusts, foundations and corporations and the tax implications of property transactions and investments in the UK.

Property: The property department acts for both publicly quoted property companies and investment funds as well as general trading companies in commercial property transactions. Areas of work include investment, site acquisitions, joint ventures, development, town and country planning and landlord and tenant law.

Construction: *Work includes:* advice on building contracts and related documentation and a substantial amount of arbitration and litigation.

Private Client: The firm offers a considerable range of services to private clients, including financial services, personal taxation, wills, trusts, probate and immigration.

Family: *Work includes:* all aspects of matrimonial and family law and the department is well known for its high profile wardship cases for local authorities and the Lord Chancellor's Department.

Nature of Clientele: Clients include multinational corporations, publicly quoted companies, private companies, property developers, professional and trade associations, insurance and reinsurance companies, underwriters, mutuals, private individuals and partnerships.

Recruitment & Training: The firm recruits six trainee solicitors a year. Bursaries are available. Application forms are available from Miss Sally Andrews.

Senior partner:	Alan Toulson
Number of partners:	42
Assistant solicitors:	68
Other fee-earners:	47

WORKLOADS	
Insurance/Reinsurance	25%
Professional Indemnity	25%
Commercial Litigation	10%
Construction	10%
Corporate	10%
Property	10%
Intellectual Property	5%
Private Client/ Family	5%

CONTACTS	
Commercial Litigation	Stephen Mayer
Commercial Property	Edward Meerloo/David Haywood
Company/Commercial	Alan Toulson
Construction	Charles Gardner
Corporate Finance	Tim Anderson
Defamation	Liz Hartley
Employment	Geraldine Elliott
Family	Jeffrey Freeman
Insolvency	Justin Westhead
Insurance/Reinsurance	Simon Greenley
Intellectual Property	Andrew Hobson
Personal Injury	Duncan Harman-Wilson
Private Client	Colin Russell
Professional Indemnity	Paul Nicholas
Tax & Pensions	Charles Suchett-Kaye

Reynolds Porter Chamberlain
solicitors

RICHARD BUXTON 40 Clarendon Street, Cambridge, CB1 1JX *Tel:* (01223) 328933 *Fax:* (01223) 301308 *Ptnrs:* 1

RICHARD HALL & PARTNERS 145 Albert Road, Middlesbrough, TS1 2PP **Tel:** (01642) 218444 **Fax:** (01642) 210498 **DX:** 60511 Middlesbrough **Email:** RVMHall@aol.com **Ptnrs:** 3 **Asst solrs:** 2 **Other fee-earners:** 1 **Contact:** Mr Richard Hall *General practice handling company/ commercial, private client and civil litigation matters with particular expertise in licensing law.*

RICHARD MONTEITH 34 Portmore Street, Portadown, BT62 3NG *Tel:* (01762) 330780
Fax: (01762) 350271 *Ptnrs:* 1

RICHARDS BUTLER

BEAUFORT HOUSE, 15 ST. BOTOLPH STREET, LONDON, EC3A 7EE
Tel: (0171) 247 6555 **Fax:** (0171) 247 5091 **DX:** 1066 CITY/18 LONDON **Email:** LAW@RICHARDSBUTLER.COM

Richards Butler's international law practice now has a presence in twelve countries around the world and continues to grow within both developed and emerging markets.

The Firm: Richards Butler experienced another year of significant growth in revenues in 1997/98. It has opened new offices in Piraeus, Islamabad and Doha. Its São Paulo office now has an independent presence in Brazil and has increased its size significantly during this period.

The firm is City based and services the needs of its large international clients which are concentrated in the market sectors of banking and financial services, insurance, media, entertainment, leisure and sports, information technology and telecommunications, shipping, international trade and commodities and property. 65% of the firm's work has an international dimension.

Principal Areas of Work: Richards Butler advises in all major areas of commercial law, including:

Corporate and Commercial – advising clients on domestic and international mergers and acquisitions, joint ventures and inward investment; EU and competition law; intellectual property and information technology; insurance company regulatory requirements; tax issues in the UK and other jurisdictions; all aspects of international finance and banking including financial services and other regulatory requirements; project finance including asset-based financing and cross-border leasing; media and entertainment law, both regulatory and transactional; anti-piracy and copyright protection; corporate recovery and insolvency including cross-border matters; employment and industrial relations; pensions and unit trust issues; and advice on contracts in all areas of energy law.

Property – advising on all aspects of property, environmental and planning law including investment and financing of land and commercial property; VAT; planning requirements for local authorities; construction and contract negotiation; financing and claim preparation; and advice on licensing of hotels and leisure premises including liquor licensing, betting, gaming, late-night licensing and multi-leisure site licensing.

Commercial Litigation – advising on all matters requiring dispute resolution skills including litigation at all Court levels. As one of the largest litigation practices in the UK, the group has expertise in all major litigation areas including financial services/regulatory and banking; all aspects of media and information technology; insurance; employment; and general corporate litigation. The group has substantial experience in arbitration and mediation techniques. The group has acted, and is acting, in many of the major commercial disputes in the City.

Shipping – advising on all aspects of shipping, including charter party disputes, bill of lading claims; ship sale and purchase; drafting of, and disputes concerning, shipbuilding contracts; marine insurance and reinsurance; the drafting of, and litigation concerning, all aspects of mutual insurance (such as P&I and Defence Clubs); salvage, collision and major casualties (the firm has a 24 hour casualty response line); all aspects of ship finance acting both for banks and borrowers; trade and commodities, including the buying and selling of hard and soft commodities; and trade finance.

Other offices: Abu Dhabi, Beijing, Brussels, Doha, Hong Kong, Islamabad, Muscat, Paris, Piraeus, São Paulo and Warsaw.

Senior partner:	**Tim Archer**
Chief Executive:	**Chris Schulten**
UK	
Number of partners:	62
Assistant solicitors:	84
Other fee-earners:	72
International	
Number of partners:	32
Assistant solicitors:	64
Other fee-earners:	20

WORKLOADS	
Corporate/Commercial/Banking/Finance	43%
Shipping/International Trade & Commodities/Insurance	23%
Litigation (Commercial)	20%
Property (Commercial)	14%

CONTACTS	
Admiralty	Richard Harvey
Aviation and Aircraft Finance	Jeff Sherwood
Banking	Nola Beirne
Commercial and EC	Stephen Sayer
Commercial Litigation	Roger Parker
Competition Law	Katherine Holmes
Construction and Engineering	Roger Parker
Corporate	Christopher Jackson
Employment	Georgina Keane
Energy	Stephen Sayer
Environmental Law	John Aylwin
Financial Services	Simon Gleeson
Information Technology	Ken Ollerton
Insolvency	Jon Yorke
Insurance and Reinsurance	Mark Connoley
Intellectual Property	David Marchese
Licensing	Elizabeth Southorn
Local Government	John Austin
Media and Entertainment	Stephen Edwards
Pensions and Unit Trusts	Keith Wallace
Property	Richard Nicoll
Ship Finance	Adam Morgan
Shipping	Lindsay East
Tax	Leslie Powell
Trade and Commodities	David Pullen

RICHARDS BUTLER
INTERNATIONAL LAW FIRM

PETER RICHBELL & CO 3 Mill Lane, Broomfield, Chelmsford, CM1 7BQ *Tel:* (01245) 440500 *Fax:* (01245) 443297 *Ptnrs:* 2

RICHMONDS SOLICITORS 35 Potter Street, Worksop, S80 2AG **Tel:** (01909) 474321 **Fax:** (01909) 483852 **DX:** 12202 Worksop. **Ptnrs:** 4 **Asst solrs:** 16 **Other fee-earners:** 7 **Contact:** Mrs C.E. Boulds. *Wide range of work with specialist departments in PI, probate, matrimonial and commercial.*

WORKLOADS			
Matrimonial	19%	Litigation	16%
Domestic Conveyancing	15%	Personal Injury	15%
Commercial Property	12%	Wills Trust Probate	11%
Company Commercial	7%	Financial Services	5%

RICKERBY WATTERSON

ELLENBOROUGH HOUSE, WELLINGTON STREET, CHELTENHAM, GL50 1YD
Tel: (01242) 224422 **Fax:** (01242) 518428 **DX:** 7415 CHELTENHAM **Email:** RW@RICKERBY.CO.UK

The Firm: Rickerby Watterson is a leading Gloucestershire firm with an established commercial law practice and a strong private client base.

Principal Areas of Work:

Corporate: The firm acts in the sale and purchase of businesses, re-structuring and re-financings, shareholder agreements, and raising finance and venture capital.

Commercial: Work includes advising on partnership and joint venture agreements, agency and distribution agreements, UK and EC competition law, and intellectual property. The firm advises on all aspects of employment law for both employer and employee.

Insolvency: A specialist group advises office holders, creditors and business proprietors on all aspects of insolvency legislation.

Property: Commercial property experts advise clients on acquisitions, funding, development and disposal, environmental and planning work, landlord and tenant matters, and licensing. The firm also has an active residential property team.

Private Client: The firm has a substantial private client practice offering asset management and advice in such areas as capital tax planning, trusts, investments, mental incapacity and care for the elderly.

There is close co-operation between the various groups to ensure that specialist skills throughout the firm are delivered to clients in a co-ordinated and structured manner.

Nature of Clientele: The firm mainly acts for plcs and owner-managed companies, local subsidiaries of national and multi-national plcs, companies in commercial property, leisure companies and operators allied to the licensed trade, educational establishments, and high net worth individuals.

Managing partner:	Mark Fabian
Senior partner:	John Clarke
Number of partners:	18
Assistant solicitors:	12
Other fee-earners:	15

WORKLOADS	
Property	38%
Private Client/Asset Management	23%
Company Commercial	18%
Company Litigation	10%
Employment	4%
Insolvency	4%
Family	3%

CONTACTS	
Asset Management	Mark Hartley
Company Commercial	Richard Knight
Company Property	David Massey
Corporate Litigation	Nick Worthington
EC & Competition Law	Anne Compton
Education	John Clarke
Employment	John Clarke
Family Law	Carolyn Green
Insolvency & Realisation	Derek Jones
Licensed Trade	Robin Beckley
Private Client	Mark Hartley
Residential Property	Tim Davies

Rickerby Watterson
SOLICITORS

RINGROSE WHARTON & CO. 5 Queen Square, Bristol, BS1 4JQ *Tel:* (0117) 922 6233 *Fax:* (0117) 922 6983 *DX:* 78153 Bristol *Ptnrs:* 1 *Asst solrs:* 6 *Other fee-earners:* 2

ROBERT LIZAR 159 Princess Road, Moss Side, Manchester, M14 4RE *Tel:* (0161) 226 2319 *Fax:* (0161) 226 7985 *Ptnrs:* 3 *Asst solrs:* 2 *Other fee-earners:* 1

ROBERT MUCKLE

NORHAM HOUSE, 12 NEW BRIDGE STREET WEST, NEWCASTLE-UPON-TYNE, NE1 8AS
Tel: (0191) 232 4402 **Fax:** (0191) 261 6954 **DX:** 61011

The Firm: Robert Muckle is one of the leading commercial law firms in the North East of England. It primarily works with corporate clients based in the northern region who are competing in both local and worldwide markets. The firm has grown rapidly and is well known for all areas of its corporate legal work including mergers, acquisitions, disposals and management buy-outs, intellectual property, employment, property development, construction and planning, banking law, loan finance, insolvency and commercial litigation. It places great store on understanding the long term objectives of its clients' companies; on providing workable solutions to their problems and on giving a responsive service to fast-moving businesses.

Recruitment and Training: Excellent career prospects for the right people. Vacancies: approximately 4 per year. Apply to Ian Gilthorpe, Managing Partner.

Managing partner:	Ian Gilthorpe
Senior partner:	Hugh Welch
Number of partners:	12
Assistant solicitors:	24
Other fee-earners:	10

WORKLOADS	
Commercial	38%
Commercial Property	33%
Commercial Litigation	29%

CONTACTS	
Commercial	Hugh Welch
Litigation	Roddy Gordon
Property	Jonathan Combe

ROBERTSON & CO, TECHNOLOGY LAW PRACTICE 18 Broomhouse Road, London, SW6 3QX **Tel:** (0171) 731 4626 **Fax:** (0171) 731 4598 **Email:** DRCR@techlaw.co.uk **Contact:** Mr Ranald Robertson *Specialist legal support to users and suppliers on computing, software and internet issues. Benefits include speedy access to senior IT/computer law experience at a reasonable and affordable cost.*

ROBERTSONS 6 Park Place, Cardiff, CF1 3DP *Tel:* (01222) 237777 *Fax:* (01222) 390996 *DX:* 33039 Cardiff *Ptnrs:* 10 *Asst solrs:* 3 *Other fee-earners:* 4

ROBIN INCE Suite 3, Third Floor, Grampian House, 144 Deansgate, Manchester, M3 3ED *Tel:* (0161) 839 2550 *Fax:* (0161) 819 5005

ROBINSONS 83 Friar Gate, Derby, DE1 1FL *Tel:* (01332) 291431 *Fax:* (01332) 291461 *DX:* 11544 Derby 1 *Ptnrs:* 12 *Asst solrs:* 8 *Other fee-earners:* 10

ROBSON MCLEAN WS 28 Abercromby Place, Edinburgh, EH3 6QF *Tel:* (0131) 556 0556 *Fax:* (0131) 556 9939 *DX:* 162 Edinburgh *Ptnrs:* 8 *Asst solrs:* 17 *Other fee-earners:* 9

RODGERS & BURTON

15-17 CHURCH RD, BARNES, LONDON, SW13 9HG
Tel: (0181) 878 4854 **Fax:** (0181) 876 8228 **DX:** 59702 BARNES **Email:** KK@RANDB.LAW.CO.UK

The Firm: The firm was founded in 1835, and has had a presence in Barnes since 1952. The firm occupies offices overlooking Barnes Common and has recently merged with another local firm Messrs Ashbys.

Principal Areas of Work: Whilst being a general High Street practice, Rodgers & Burton offers certain specialist advice in servicing landlords and Housing Associations. In particular, they offer experience in landlord and tenant litigation, housing association law and finance, disposals and acquisitions of property, lease back financing of acquisitions, shared ownership schemes, planning appeals, construction contracts and disputes.

Other Areas of Work: Rodgers & Burton also have fee earners with experience in employment law, personal injury, debt recovery and a busy matrimonial department. The firm offers an Agency Service in Wandsworth, West London and Brentford County Court.

Senior partner:	David Moore
Number of partners:	3
Assistant solicitors:	2
Other fee-earners:	4

WORKLOADS	
Private & Commercial Conveyancing	52%
Civil Litigation	36%
Matrimonial	12%

CONTACTS	
Conveyancing/Wills & probate	Kathryn Kinnear
Landlord and tenant	David Moore
Matrimonial	Gillian Tyndall
Personal Injury/Employment/Debt Recovery	
	Mark Woloshak

RODGERS HORSLEY WHITEMANS Castle House, Castle Street, Guildford, GU1 3UL *Tel:* (01483) 302000 *Fax:* (01483) 301242 *DX:* 2445 Guildford 1 *Ptnrs:* 3 *Asst solrs:* 3 *Other fee-earners:* 1

ROEBUCKS 12 Richmond Terrace, Blackburn, BB1 7BG *Tel:* (01254) 668855 *Fax:* (01254) 680838 *DX:* 15254 Blackburn 2 *Ptnrs:* 6 *Asst solrs:* 5 *Other fee-earners:* 4

ROGERS AND NORTON 5-7 Willow Lane, Norwich, NR2 1EU *Tel:* (01603) 666001 *Fax:* (01603) 629663 *DX:* 5226 Norwich *Ptnrs:* 7 *Asst solrs:* 7 *Other fee-earners:* 14

ROGERS & WELLS LLP

CITY TOWER, 20TH FLOOR, 40 BASINGHALL STREET, LONDON, EC2V 5DE
Tel: (0171) 628 0101 **Fax:** (0171) 628 6111

The Firm: For more than a century, Rogers & Wells has been providing clients with creative and effective representation in domestic and international transactions and major litigations. Rogers & Wells serves the world's leading financial institutions, industrial companies and businesses in virtually every sector of the economy as well as individuals and government entities. The firm's international work, comprising nearly half of the practice, spans the globe.

The London Office: In addition to matters referred from the national offices, the London office concentrates primarily on the areas of:

    Finance: *Work involves* advising foreign clients in raising capital in the US market and US companies in raising capital overseas; participating in global transactions as issuers' and underwriter's counsel; representing major international financial institutions and corporate and government issuers; international fund transactions both US registered and offshore.
    Acquisitions: Work covers the full range of legal advice required by foreign clients making acquisitions in the US and abroad and US clients making acquisitions abroad.

Managing partner:	Daniel Bushner
Senior partner: Laurence E. Cranch (New York)	
Number of partners:	2
Assistant solicitors:	13
Other fee-earners:	1

WORKLOADS	
Securities/corporate	65%
Banking	15%
Funds	10%
Mergers and Aquisitions	10%

CONTACTS	
Corporate finance	Daniel Bushner

Service includes counselling on tax, antitrust, ERISA, real estate and environmental and government regulation issues.

Tax: *Work includes:* domestic and international tax considerations for sophisticated mergers and acquisitions, business and investment partnership structuring, securities offerings and other financings and real estate investments; transfer pricing issues for foreign and US clients; taxation of investment partnerships; development of new financial products in the tax-exempt and taxable markets; municipal financings; tax controversy practice.

Intellectual Property: The full range of legal services involving patents, copyrights and trademarks, extending to both corporate transactions for the acquisition of technology and litigation for defence or protection of intellectual property.

International Trade: *Work includes* representing foreign and US manufacturers, importers and exporters in all phases of antidumping and countervailing duty investigations, other trade investigations and litigation, customs matters, international transactions and government relations.

Other Offices: New York, Washington DC, Paris, Frankfurt, Hong Kong.

ROITER ZUCKER

5-7 BROADHURST GARDENS, SWISS COTTAGE, LONDON, NW6 3QX
Tel: (0171) 328 9111 **Fax:** (0171) 644 8900 **DX:** 38850 SWISS COTTAGE **Email:** ROITERZUCKER@BTINTERNET.COM

The Firm: Roiter Zucker carries out all types of commercial work, and is particularly well-known for its intellectual property work. RZ's IP department deals with all aspects of intellectual property – patents, trade marks, copyright, industrial design and confidential information.

The firm has a strong base in medicine and pharmaceuticals and an excellent reputation for its patent litigation. It has acted in many leading cases in this area, often acting for generic companies and has an enviable record for defeating ill-founded monopolies.

Clients: Many of Roiter Zucker's clients first came to the firm as small businesses, and the firm has in many instances taken companies from start up through public company status to full stock exchange listing.

The firm is small, but highly skilled. It is used to working in the international arena, and can draw on expert advice worldwide.

Number of partners:	7
Assistant solicitors:	3
Other fee-earners:	6

WORKLOADS	
Litigation including contentious IP work	45%
Commercial: IP/pharmaceutical/competition	35%
Company	10%
Property	10%

CONTACTS	
Contacts	Warren Roiter, Anna McKay

ROLLIT FARRELL & BLADON

WILBERFORCE COURT, HIGH STREET, HULL, HU1 1YJ
Tel: (01482) 323239 **Fax:** (01482) 326239 **DX:** 715756 HULL 15 **Email:** MAW@ROLLITS.CO.UK

The Firm: One of the principal firms in the Yorkshire region offering a comprehensive legal service. Highly regarded as a commercial practice. Expertise in corporate and commercial law is unrivalled in East Yorkshire.

Principal Areas of Work:

Company/ Commercial: Company acquisitions and disposals, flotations, share issues, fund raising, joint ventures, MBOs, finance and credit agreements, insolvency, equipment leasing and financing agreements, intellectual property, franchising, competition law, restrictive practices and EU law.

Commercial and Residential Property: Commercial conveyancing, town & country planning, environmental law, landlord and tenant and Housing Association work.

Litigation: Commercial litigation, employment law, insurance litigation, intellectual property disputes, licensing, matrimonial, building contract disputes, debt recovery and professional indemnity.

Private Client: Tax planning, settlements, wills, estate administration, enduring powers of attorney, domestic conveyancing and Court of Protection work.

Other Offices:

Rowntree Wharf, Navigation Road, York YO1 9WE. *Tel:* (01904) 625790.
26 & 28 Lairgate, Beverley HU17 8ER. *Tel:* (01482) 882278.
4 Bondgate, Helmsley YO62 5BS. *Tel:* (01439) 770207.

Managing partner:	S. J. Trynka
Senior partner:	D.M. Scanlan
Number of partners:	28
Assistant solicitors:	15
Other fee-earners:	25

WORKLOADS	
Company and Commercial	25%
Litigation (including employment)	21%
Property	21%
Private Client	15%
Insurance Litigation	11%
Planning and Development	7%

CONTACTS	
Commercial Litigation	George Coyle
Company and Commercial	James Brennand
Employment	Pauline Molyneux
Environmental	Steve Hawkins
Insolvency	Richard Field
Insurance Litigation	Peter Maharry
Planning	John Downing
Private Client	David Bowes
Property	Martyn Justice

ROOKS RIDER

CHALLONER HOUSE, 19 CLERKENWELL CLOSE, LONDON, EC1R 0RR
Tel: (0171) 689 7000 **Fax:** (0171) 689 7001 **DX:** 53324 CLERKENWELL **Email:** LAWYERS@ROOKSRIDER.CO.UK

Rooks Rider is a long-established London firm servicing UK and international businesses and the people behind them. The firm's particular expertise is in the field of tax, and partners ensure that tax planning is considered in all areas of practice.

The Firm: The firm is the highly successful result of amalgamation (in 1976) of two complementary legal practices. Riders had offered a wide range of services to high profile wealthy individuals since 1761, whereas Rooks had practised as a City firm dealing with corporate transactions. This complementary skills base has enabled the firm to develop and grow with its clients into a personable practice which specialises in advising business and the people behind business: entrepreneurs and high-net-worth individuals.

Principal Areas of Work: A high quality comprehensive and personal service is offered to business and individual clients in the fields of company and commercial law, partnerships, joint ventures, commercial and residential property and planning, civil litigation (including employment, intellectual property, construction and professional negligence), onshore and offshore tax planning, probate, matrimonial and charity law. The firm prides itself in offering creative advice with a practical approach to achieving the client's ambitions and has an increasing international practice.

The firm has particular strengths in relation to business and company transactions (contacts: Christopher Cooke and Nicholas Jacob), landlord and tenant and property development (Clare Foinette and Michael Pinkerton), and intellectual property litigation (Richard Walker). Skilled employment advice (litigious and non-litigious) is offered to both employers and employees.

The firm has concentrated on servicing both entrepreneurs individually and the corporate requirements of its clients, and advises company shareholders and directors as well as high-net-worth foreigners. The firm has developed, and is particularly well known for, its offshore tax planning speciality, using trusts and corporate structures in a wide range of overseas centres. Partners travel to most low tax centres and lecture on trusts and taxation as far afield as Hong Kong.

Its traditional private client base has expanded considerably, advising in relation to landed estates, wills, trusts, probate and tax planning. This enables the firm to provide an extensive service to all high-net-worth individuals, be they UK, foreign nationals or expatriates and entrepreneurs in particular.

Rooks Rider has a significant matrimonial practice having advised in 1997 in the largest settlement ever made by a UK court.

The firm has recently developed a service with the needs of professional and business women particularly in mind.

It is part of the Leasehold Advisory Group (together with a firm of surveyors and an independent financial adviser) offering a specialist service in relation to the Leasehold Reform, Housing and Urban Development Act 1993.

The firm publishes a newsletter and a variety of brochures including a general brochure with details of all the firm's services which is available on request.

The firm is always seeking to recruit high-calibre qualified staff. In addition, two trainee solicitors are recruited annually. All enquiries to the personnel officer.

Managing partner:	Richard Walker
Senior partner:	Christopher Cooke
Number of partners:	11
Assistant solicitors:	18
Other fee-earners:	9

WORKLOADS	
Company/ Commercial	42%
Litigation	23%
Private client	19%
Property	16%

CONTACTS	
Company/Commercial	Nicholas Jacob
Litigation	Richard Walker
Private client	Christopher Wright
Property	Clare Foinette

ROOKS RIDER SOLICITORS

ROOTES & ALLIOTT 27 Cheriton Gardens, Folkestone, CT20 2AR *Tel:* (01303) 851100 *Fax:* (01303) 851150 *DX:* 4903 *Ptnrs:* 6 *Asst solrs:* 2 *Other fee-earners:* 3

ROSENBLATT 9-13 St Andrew Street, London, EC4A 3AE *Tel:* (0171) 955 0880 *Fax:* (0171) 955 0888 *DX:* 493 London Chancery Lane *Ptnrs:* 6 *Asst solrs:* 10 *Other fee-earners:* 4

ROSLING KING

2-3 HIND COURT, FLEET ST, LONDON, EC4A 3DL
Tel: (0171) 353 2353 **Fax:** (0171) 583 2035 **DX:** 154

The Firm: Rosling King is a commercial firm which successfully competes with the largest City practices in its areas of expertise whilst offering close contact with its clients. It was originally founded on a base of institutional property clients but its client base now includes a significant number of banks and lenders as well as other major financial institutions and insurance companies. The last year has seen further growth in the firm's involvement in insurance, re-insurance and banking law.

The Firm tackles substantial jobs. In doing so it aims to maintain a high level of personal contact between clients and partners. This enables the Firm to achieve a thorough understanding of clients' business objectives.

Rosling King is accustomed to servicing the needs of overseas clients doing business in the UK. Through its professional associates around the world and its own experience in international business, it also assists UK clients doing business abroad.

Principal Areas of Work:

Banking/Finance: work includes: advising banks, building societies and other lending institutions on the drafting of loan documentation, new loans, the acquisition of loan books and generally in the structuring and enforcement of loans and securities.

Civil Fraud: work includes: advice for banks, building societies and other lending institutions on structures to prevent fraud, analysis of problems and recovery advice.

Company/Commercial: work includes: acquisitions and disposals, mergers, MBOs, partnerships, insolvency, employment law, intellectual property, EEC and UK competition law for institutions and companies in the UK and abroad.

Commercial Litigation/Dispute Resolution: work includes: acting principally for institutional and substantial clients on professional indemnity claims, insurance, loss recovery, repossessions, personal injury, property and construction including mediation, arbitration and ADR.

Construction Law: work includes: all aspects of building contract documentation, professional appointments, warranties, bonds and advice thereon for the property lending and insurance industries.

Environmental Law: work includes: advice on environmental assessment, liability and compliance for institutions and property companies, land owners, the construction industry and professionals.

Insurance: work includes: insurance/reinsurance policy wording and interpretation advice, litigation, arbitration and ADR resolution of coverage disputes, general liability, personal injury, professional indemnity, property, construction and environmental related matters. Clients include Lloyds syndicate, UK and internationally based insurers and reinsurers as well as insurance professionals.

Property: work includes: a full service for the property industry and clients include leading institutions, public and private development and investment companies as well as banks and insurance companies.

Sports Law: work includes: advice for sports personalities and organisations including sponsorship and agency contracts, constitutional and tribunal law, employment, finance and property work.

Foreign Connections: The practice has associations with firms in Berlin, Brussels, Düsseldorf, Edinburgh, Hong Kong, Madrid, Milan, New York, Paris, Singapore, Stockholm and Zurich and strong connections with overseas lawyers and accountants in many other cities as well as a range of overseas clients.

Senior partner:	Owen Rafferty
Number of partners:	15
Assistant solicitors:	24
Other fee-earners:	21

WORKLOADS	
Litigation/Insurance	50%
Property/Construction/Environmental	30%
Company Commercial/Banking/Sports	20%

CONTACTS	
Banking/Finance	Owen Rafferty/John Pearson
Civil Fraud	Owen Rafferty/Georgina Squire
Company Commercial	Graham Clark
Construction	John Beagley
Environmental	Andrew Hardman
Insurance	Georgina Squire/Michael Green
Litigation	Georgina Squire/Annabel Crumley
Property	Owen Rafferty/Malcolm MacFarlane
Sports Law	John Beagley

ROSS & CONNEL 10 Viewfield Terrace, Dunfermline, KY12 7JH *Tel:* (01383) 721156 *Fax:* (01383) 721150 *DX:* DF 11 *Ptnrs:* 5 *Asst solrs:* 1 *Other fee-earners:* 1

ROSS & CRAIG

12A UPPER BERKELEY STREET, LONDON, W1H 7PE
Tel: (0171) 262 3077 **Fax:** (0171) 724 6427 **DX:** 44416 MARBLE ARCH **Email:** RECEPTION@ROSSCRAIG.COM

The Firm: Established in the 1950's with an emphasis on commercial client work, acting for public and private companies, businesses and individual entrepreneurs but with strong teams in respect of private client matters, family, personal injury, trusts, financial planning and bankruptcy.

Principal Areas of Work:

Commercial Property: Development projects, acquisitions, portfolio break-ups, structuring joint venture schemes of varying complexity with associated planning and funding requirements conducted through tax efficient procedures. Clients number major developers retailers and hotel operators. Particular niche in banking security.

Company/Commercial: Includes a full range of corporate and commercial transactions, with ancillary employment, shareholder and director agreements, floatation, institutional and other funding schemes. Some of our specialist areas include intellectual property, computer contracts, media, entertainment, film and TV funding and production documents.

Litigation: Commercial disputes, landlord and tenant litigation and property disputes, employment law, intellectual property, complex personal injury work, professional negligence, insolvency and liquidations.Environmental Law: The specialist Land Regeneration Unit enjoys high level connections with relevant professionals and government departments. It provides services in a consultancy capacity and as a principal adviser on legal and risk management recognised as "leaders in the field".

Family Law: As well as usual areas of advice, this team has special expertise in dealing with cohabiting partners and in advising on the financial issues in a practical way.

Nature of Clientele: Clients range from internationally known companies to small businesses and individuals.

Foreign Connections: The firm has close links with lawyers in Europe, America, Middle East, Far East and much off-shore and EU compliancy work.

Managing partner:	David Leadercramer
Senior partner:	Leonard Ross
Number of partners:	9
Consultants/assistant solicitors:	11
Other fee-earners:	3

WORKLOADS	
Property (inc. environmental)	50%
Company/commercial	20%
Litigation	18%
Family	9%
Private client	3%

CONTACTS	
Company/commercial	Ian Bloom
Environmental	Martin Polden
Family/private client	Frances Sieber
Litigation	David Leadercramer
Property	Daniel Polden

ROSS HARPER & MURPHY WS 163 Ingram Street, Glasgow, G1 1DW **Tel:** (0141) 552 6343 **Fax:** (0141) 552 8150 **DX:** 190 Glasgow **Ptnrs:** 16 **Asst solrs:** 31 **Other fee-earners:** 28 **Contact:** Cameron Fyfe *Large criminal and civil litigation practice.*

WORKLOADS			
Criminal	40%	Civil	35%
Conveyancing	20%	Welfare Rights	5%

ROTHERAS

2 KAYES WALK, STONEY STREET, THE LACE MARKET, NOTTINGHAM, NG1 1PZ
Tel: (0115) 910 0600 **Fax:** (0115) 910 0800 **DX:** 10028 NOTTINGHAM

The Firm: Est in 1857, Rotheras has built its reputation upon a quality service to clients and is known particularly for its commercial and litigation work. The firm is organised into specialist departments, each headed by partners who have considerable experience in their particular field. It acts for institutions, trade associations, companies, small businesses and has a thriving private client department.

Principal Areas of Work:

Corporate and Commercial: Work includes: company formations, share issues, acquisitions, commercial agreements, employment contracts, intellectual property, commercial property including landlord and tenant, compulsory purchase, leases, town and country planning.

Litigation: Civil litigation of all kinds including a significant personal injury department for both Plaintiff and Defendant clients, including medical negligence with P.I. Panel members; contentious intellectual property matters, employment disputes, contractual disputes including construction. The last two years have seen a considerable growth in employment law with a new partner appointed who sits as a part-time Chairman of Industrial Tribunals.This department also includes a special Road Transport section advising clients in connection with operator licensing, traffic prosecutions, insurance related work, carriage of goods and all aspects of road transport.

Private Client Department: Handles all aspects of personal taxation, trusts, wills, probate and administration as well as family and matrimonial law. One of its partners is a member of the Child Care Panel.

Other Areas of Work: The firm also offers advice in ecclesiastical matters. One of its partners is the Diocesan Registrar for the Diocese of Southwell. It is also able to advise educational institutions on all aspects of contentious and non-contentious education law.

Managing partner:	Mike Butler
Senior partner:	Chris Hodson
Number of partners:	9
Assistant solicitors:	3
Other fee-earners:	6

WORKLOADS	
General litigation (inc PI/ transport/comm. lit)	40%
Company commercial and employment	20%
Probate, trusts and tax	15%
Family (inc. childcare)	10%
Property	10%
Other	5%

CONTACTS	
Commercial litigation	Mr R.B. Hammond
Company, commercial & planning	Mr C.C. Hodson
Ecclesias./Education	Mr C.C. Hodson
Employment	Mr. M. Butler
Family and matrimonial	Miss C. Bianchina
Personal injury	Mrs J.E. George
Property	Mrs A.J. Redgate
Transport	Mr P.I. Rothera
Wills, trusts, probate, tax	Mr J.D. Allen

ROWBERRY MORRIS Morroway House, Station Road, Gloucester, GL1 1DW **Tel:** (01452) 301903 **Fax:** (01452) 411115 **Ptnrs:** 6 **Asst solrs:** 4 **Other fee-earners:** 3 **Contact:** Conrad Sheward *Progressive firm with strong litigation bias – particularly personal injury, professional negligence, family, crime and employment. Also property and charity work.*

WORKLOADS			
Litigation	50%	Family	20%
Property &Trust	20%	Crime	5%
Employment	5%		

ROWBERRY MORRIS & CO 17 Castle Street, Reading, RG1 7SB *Tel:* (0118) 958 5611 *Fax:* (0118) 959 9662 *DX:* 40125 Reading *Ptnrs:* 8 *Asst solrs:* 3 *Other fee-earners:* 4

ROWE & MAW

20 BLACK FRIARS LANE, LONDON, EC4V 6HD
Tel: (0171) 248 4282 **Fax:** (0171) 248 2009 **DX:** 93 **Email:** ROWEANDMAW@ROWEANDMAW.CO.UK **Internet:** WWW.ROWEANDMAW.CO.UK

The Firm: Rowe & Maw is one of the UK's leading commercial law firms, with offices in London, including one at Lloyd's, and in Brussels. Founded over 100 years ago, Rowe & Maw has grown to become one of the top commercial law firms in London. With 70 partners and a legal staff in excess of 200, the Firm is large enough to provide the broad range of services required by their clients, yet is still able to provide an individual, personalised service, led by our partners. Their reputation is built upon delivering commercial and pragmatic advice with the client's objectives the key consideration.

Principal Areas of Work: The firm's main strength has always been in advising companies and businesses across their range of activities, both in their day-to-day business and on special projects. Their client list includes top UK and international companies. They are equally familiar with acting for small and medium sized businesses, be they owner-managed or listed entities.

Rowe & Maw's corporate group provides the wide spectrum of services needed to meet today's requirements in such operations as buying and selling businesses, public company takeovers, management buy-outs, flotations and other equity and debt financings, joint ventures and major projects. They have experience of a wide range of transactions, both domestic and cross border. With commerce becoming increasingly global, the firm is well placed to meet their clients' international requirements which are supported cost-effectively by the competition law office in Brussels and a network of overseas firms which deliver the same quality of service and speed of response that Rowe & Maw provides.

In addition to their mainstream corporate practice, the Firm has a number of other strengths. They are widely acknowledged as one of the top firms in the fields of construction, property, litigation, pensions, insurance, employment, intellectual property, environment, aviation, partnership and public law.

A Quality Service: Rowe & Maw is committed to providing a top quality service, based upon an understanding of businesses and their commercial requirements. Great emphasis is placed upon managing work cost effectively and efficiently on behalf of clients. A client contact partner is always allocated to each client. Their responsibilty is to co-ordinate all of the services provided and to ensure that clients are kept fully informed at all stages.

Recruitment: The firm seeks approximately 20 high-calibre graduates to train with it for articles each year.

Managing partner:	Andrew Carruthers
Senior partner:	Stuart James
UK	
Number of partners:	70
Assistant solicitors:	113
Other fee-earners:	68
International	
Number of partners:	3
Assistant solicitors:	2
Other fee-earners:	1

WORKLOADS	
Corporate	37%
Litigation	22%
Property	12%
Pensions	9%
Construction	8%
Intellectual property	7%
Employment	4%
Private client	1%

CONTACTS	
Aviation & Transport	M Henrick
Banking & Projects	N Morrison
Commercial Property	J Toomey
Construction Litigation	M Regan
Corporate Finance	S Bottomley
Employment	J Roskill
Environment	H Devas
EU/Competition Law	S Baxter
Insolvency	D Allen
Insurance	S Connolly
Intellectual Property	S Gare
Litigation & Dispute Resolution	A McDougall
Mergers and Acquisitions	P Maher
Partnership	R Linsell
Pensions	S James
Private Client	R Powles
Public and Administrative	T Child
Tax	P Steiner

ROY PYBUS 254 Smithdown Road, Wavertree, Liverpool, L15 5AA *Tel:* (0151) 475 4400 *Fax:* (0151) 475 4411

ROWLANDS

3 YORK STREET, MANCHESTER, M2 2RW
Tel: (0161) 835 2020 **Fax:** (0161) 835 2525 **DX:** 14475 MANCHESTER 2

The Firm: One of the largest firms in Manchester, Rowlands traces its roots back to 1885. A general practice, the firm has a network of branch offices throughout Greater Manchester.

Principal Areas of Work:

Litigation: (*Contact Partner:* Malcolm Horner). *Work includes:* personal injury claims arising from accidents whether at work, on the road or caused by medical or professional negligence; also landlord and tenant disputes, criminal cases and motoring offences, debt recovery and insolvency problems. Legal aid work is undertaken.

Family & Matrimonial: (*Contact Partner:* Sidney Oxley). *Work includes:* specialist advice concerning custody and access, child care, maintenance injunctions and property settlements, affiliation orders and disputes between cohabitees.

Private Client: (*Contact Partner:* Philip A Bellamy). *Work includes:* domestic conveyancing, wills, probate, trusts, administration of estates and taxation advice.

Company/ Commercial & Commercial Property: (*Contact Partner:* Philip A. Bellamy). *Work includes:* advice on formation, acquisition, employment matters and all aspects of commercial property work. Liquor and gaming licences.

Other Offices: Stockport, Droylsden, Sale, New Moston and Urmston.

Managing partner:	Ronald Taylor
Senior partner:	Philip A. Bellamy
Number of partners:	11
Assistant solicitors:	14
Other fee-earners:	16

WORKLOADS	
Litigation	46%
Family & Matrimonial	24%
Private Client	18%
Company/Commercial & Commercial Property	12%

CONTACTS	
Commercial property	Philip A. Bellamy
Company and commercial	Ron Taylor
Family and matrimonial	Sidney Oxley
Litigation	Malcolm Horner
Private client	Philip A. Bellamy

ROWLEY ASHWORTH

247 THE BROADWAY, WIMBLEDON, LONDON, SW19 1SE
Tel: (0181) 543 2277 **Fax:** (0181) 543 0143 **DX:** 300003 WIMBLEDON SOUTH

The Firm: Established in 1829, Rowley Ashworth is a specialised partnership known for its particular expertise in the field of employment law and personal injury compensation claims on behalf of trade unions and their members.

Principal Areas of Work: The work handled covers claims for personal injury, industrial accidents, traffic accidents and industrial disease. The firm is also experienced in residential and commercial conveyancing, wills and probate.

Other Offices: Birmingham, Exeter, Wolverhampton, Leeds and Liverpool.

Memberships: London Litigation Solicitors Association; Industrial Law Society. Many fee earners are members of APIL and Law Society P.I. panel.

Managing partner:	David Prain
Number of partners:	19
Assistant solicitors:	39
Other fee-earners:	20

CONTACTS	
Conveyancing	Andrew Struthers
Employment & labour law	Michael Short
Personal injury	John Moore
Wills, probate	Andrew Struthers

ROWLEY DICKINSON

HALIFAX HOUSE, 93-101 BRIDGE STREET, MANCHESTER, M3 2GX
Tel: (0161) 834 4215 **Fax:** (0161) 834 5153 **DX:** 14332 M1

65 CHURCH STREET, BIRMINGHAM, B3 2DP
Tel: (0121) 233 2298 **Fax:** (0121) 236 9155 **DX:** 13018 BIRMINGHAM

The Firm: Rowley Dickinson is a strong medium sized firm of solicitors with 14 partners.

The practice offers a wide range of legal services but has particular skills in the areas of corporate, property and personal injury law.

The emphasis is very much on a personal approach with a high partner to client ratio. Clients attracted to the practice apart from Insurance Companies and Property Developers, include many owner managed businesses who require a variety of cost effective legal services such as debt collecting and employment/contract law.

Managing partner:	A. Fitzpatrick
Senior partner:	K. Simpson
Number of partners:	14
Assistant solicitors:	7
Other fee-earners:	10

ROYDS TREADWELL

2 CRANE COURT, FLEET STREET, LONDON, EC4A 2BL
Tel: (0171) 583 2222 **Fax:** (0171) 583 2034 **DX:** 102 CHANCERY LANE **Email:** INFO@ROYDS.LAW.CO.UK

The Firm: Royds Treadwell is a substantial and long established partnership. Our aim is to give the client prompt partner attention at reasonable cost whilst providing a high degree of specialisation in each department.

Principal Areas of work:

Company/Commercial: The department deals in company formations, disposals, acquisitions, shareholder agreements, joint ventures, MBOs and has particular expertise in intellectual property, insolvency, banking, construction and advising directors.

Property: The department deals with all aspects of commercial property together with landlord & tenant, and other property related matters. The department also has a wide practice in residential conveyancing.

Litigation: The department deals with the full range of litigation matters. It has considerable expertise in the areas of insolvency, banking, debt recovery, fraud and international asset recovery. It has specialists in family, criminal, landlord & tenant law, intellectual property, professional negligence and licensing work. The firm carries out Privy Council work and acts for the Government of Mauritius. The department in addition specialises in personal injury work and are Members of The Law Society Personal Injury Panel.

Employment: This is a specialist unit bringing together the expertise of the firm's various departments through one point of contact.

Private Client and Tax: The work of this department includes wills, trusts, probate, pensions, specialist financial services including tax, investment advice and estate planning.

Foreign Connections: The firm has strong links in France, the Channel Islands, the Far East, Mauritius, Ireland and the USA.

Languages Spoken: French, German.

Other Offices: Morden, Surrey.

Senior Partner:	Arthur Alexander
Number of partners:	15
Assistant solicitors:	7
Other fee-earners:	8

WORKLOADS	
Litigation and employment	40%
Company	20%
Private client and tax	20%
Property	20%

CONTACTS	
Company/Commercial	Peter Wootton
Employment	Richard Woodman
Litigation	Stewart Wilkinson
Personal injury	James Millar Craig
Private client	Christopher Wright
Privy Council	Richard Woodman
Property	Adam Maberly
Tax	Arthur Alexander

ROYTHORNE & CO 10 Pinchbeck Rd, Spalding, PE11 1PZ *Tel:* (01775) 724141 *Fax:* (01775) 725736 *DX:* 26701 Spalding *Ptnrs:* 18 *Asst solrs:* 10 *Other fee-earners:* 27

RUDLINGS & WAKELAM 1 Woolhall Street, Bury St Edmunds, IP33 1LA **Tel:** (01284) 755771 **Fax:** (01284) 762404 **DX:** 57202 Bury St Edmunds **Email:** rudlings-wakelam.co.uk **Ptnrs:** 5 **Asst solrs:** 5 **Other fee-earners:** 8 **Contact:** Julia Wakelam *Specialists in child care/family and matrimonial, personal injury and employment (particularly discrimination) law. Also handles agricultural, company/ commercial, civil litigation, probate and conveyancing (both commercial and domestic).*

RUPERT BEAR MURRAY DAVIES

UNION CHAMBERS, 11 WEEKDAY CROSS, NOTTINGHAM, NG1 2GB
Tel: (0115) 924 3333 **Fax:** (0115) 924 2255

The Firm: Rupert Bear Murray Davies is a firm of solicitors specialising in matrimonial and family law. It was established by Rupert Bear who has been a matrimonial lawyer in Nottingham for 29 years. The firm comprising the former staff and family law practice of Eversheds, Nottingham has now been supplemented by Murray Davies who has himself in excess of 16 years experience in family law as a partner in another Nottingham firm. It also has contacts with accountants, valuers, pension advisors, insurance brokers and other professionals who may be required to assist in resolving financial matters resulting from the breakdown of a relationship.

Principal Areas of Work: *Work includes:* cohabitation agreements and pre-marriage arrangements, separation and divorce, the legal status of children and the resolution of any dispute arising in relation to children, and financial arrangements relating to all aspects of family relationships, including elderly clients.

Managing partner:	Murray Davies
Senior partner:	C Rupert Bear
Number of partners:	3
Assistant solicitors:	4
Other fee-earners:	1

WORKLOADS	
Matrimonial/Public Child Law	93%
Conveyancing	7%

CONTACTS	
Matrimonial	C.Rupert Bear/Murray Davies
Mediation	Sarah Heathcote/Catherine Stevens
Public Child Law	Russell Tolley

RUSSEL & AITKEN 22 & 24 Stirling Street, Denny, FK6 6AZ *Tel:* (01324) 822194 *Fax:* (01324) 824560 *DX:* 1171 *Ptnrs:* 12 *Asst solrs:* 9 *Other fee-earners:* 9

RUSSELL-COOKE, POTTER & CHAPMAN

8 BEDFORD ROW, LONDON, WC1R 4BU
Tel: (0171) 405 6566 **Fax:** (0171) 831 2565 **DX:** 112 CHANCERY LANE

2 PUTNEY HILL, PUTNEY, LONDON, SW15 6AB
Tel: (0181) 789 9111 **Fax:** (0181) 780 1194 **DX:** 59456 PUTNEY

BISHOP'S PALACE HOUSE, KINGSTON BRIDGE, KINGSTON-UPON-THAMES, KT1 1QN
Tel: (0181) 546 6111 **Fax:** (0181) 541 4404 **DX:** 31546 KINGSTON

The Firm: Russell-Cooke is an energetic, professionally-managed firm which has developed a reputation for specialist expertise in a number of areas without sacrificing its collective breadth of experience. After more than a century in Lincoln's Inn, the firm moved its headquarters to Bedford Row in late 1997 in order to accommodate rising numbers of solicitors and improve meeting room and training facilities. The majority of staff continue to be based in its Putney office.

With overheads lower than those of competing firms based solely in Central London, the firm has been able to make substantial reinvestment in technology, facilities and human resources; it has an experienced Director of Training and has recently installed its second generation of PCs in a firm-wide network. The firm's distinctive culture has produced cohesive and committed legal teams which are encouraged to develop and maintain long-term relationships with clients.

Principal Areas of Work:

Include

Commercial Property	Commercial Litigation
Company Commercial	Private client
Trusts, Wills and Probate	Family
Medical Negligence and Personal Injury	Crime
Child Care	Conveyancing including French property

Within these areas the firm encourages specialisation. The firm has an unusually large client base (in excess of 10,000 clients instructing within the last three years). The requirements of these clients, who tend to have an ongoing relationship with the firm, mean that the range of services provided by the firm is unusually broad. The firm continues to be successful because its cost base is appropriate, it has young partners and staff and it has for many years subspecialised to match the best competing expertise in the areas in which it operates.

Managing partner:	John Gould
Senior partner:	Michael Maskey
Number of partners:	20
Assistant solicitors:	26
Other fee-earners:	23

WORKLOADS	
Property	30%
Family/Child Care/PI Litigation/other	25%
Probate Wills & Trusts	15%
Commercial Litigation	10%
Company/Commercial	10%
Criminal Law	10%

CONTACTS	
Child Care	John Hackett
Commercial & Construction Litigation/ADR	
	Francesca Kaye
Commercial property	Peter Dawson
Company/Commercial	Jonathan Thornton
Conveyancing	Nigel Coates
Criminal matters	Ian Ryan
Family Law	Camilla Thornton
Medical Negligence	Mike Danby
Personal Injury	Isabel Chaplain
Probate and Wills	Richard Frimston
Trusts	Michael Best

RUSSELL-COOKE

SOLICITORS

RUSSELL JONES & WALKER

SWINTON HOUSE, 324 GRAY'S INN ROAD, LONDON, WC1X 8DH
Tel: (0171) 837 2808 **Fax:** (0171) 837 2941 **DX:** 202 **Email:** 101317.2022@COMPUSERVE.COM **Internet:** WWW.RJW.CO.UK

The Firm: Russell Jones & Walker, founded in London in the 1920's has grown rapidly in the last 10 years expanding from 100 to over 350 staff and partners, establishing regional offices in Newcastle, Sheffield, Leeds, Manchester, Birmingham and Bristol. Cardiff will open in 1998. The emphasis on people has enabled the firm to develop an impressive range of specialist services of particular value to individuals and those who represent them.

Principal Areas of Work:
Personal Injury: (*Contact Partners:* Ian Walker/ Fraser Whitehead). The firm is one of the leading plaintiff personal injury practices. A total of over 90 lawyers deal with a wide range of plaintiff personal injury work including compensation for industrial injury, disasters, chemical poisoning and environmental pollution, road traffic accidents, disease and disablement and criminal assault.
Employment: (*Contact Partner:* Edward Cooper). The firm has a large specialist employment department with a highly respected reputation within the industry, dealing with all aspects of individual and collective plaintiff employment law, both litigious and non litigious and including contracts, discrimination, dismissal issues, transfers and pensions.
Criminal Law and Investigations: (*Contact Partner:* Rod Fletcher). The firm has a reputation as one of the leading criminal law practices within the UK advising and representing clients on all aspects of criminal law with a particular focus on white collar crime and commercial fraud.

Senior partner:	John M. Webber
Chief Executive:	Mark Feeney
Number of partners:	38
Assistant solicitors:	56
Other fee-earners:	54

WORKLOADS	
Personal injury	64%
Crime and Fraud	9%
Defamation	8%
Employment	8%
Medical Negligence	5%
Professional Negligence, Commercial Litigation,	
General Litigation	4%
Property, Family and Probate	2%

CONTACTS	
Commercial litigation	Barton Taylor
Criminal	Rod Fletcher
Employment	Edward Cooper
Family, Wills, Probate and Trusts	Oliver Gravell
Medical Negligence	Gillian Solly
Personal injury	Ian Walker, Fraser Whitehead
Property	Peter Klim

Continues overleaf

Litigation: (*Contact Partner:* Barton Taylor). The commercial litigation department advises on all aspects of commercial litigation including professional negligence, defamation, intellectual property and insolvency. Specialist groups focus on copyright and sports law but the department is particularly regarded for its libel expertise having successfully acted against all national daily and Sunday newspapers and most radio and TV companies.
Medical Negligence:(*Contact Partner:* Gillian Solly). The firm has a first class reputation for resolving medical negligence cases. The department is a rapidly expanding area of the practice. The department has an exceptional success rate. All types of plaintiff medical negligence work is undertaken with particular expertise in claims involving young children, representation at inquests and alternative dispute resolution in litigation including mediation.

Other Areas of Work: In addition to the specialist areas of work listed above the firm has expertise in the following areas:

Commercial and residential conveyancing, landlord and tenant contracts, public and administrative law, public inquiries, family matrimonial law and other private client services including wills, probate and trusts.

Other Offices: Birmingham, Bristol, Manchester, Leeds, Sheffield, Newcastle and Cardiff (opening 1998).

RUSSELL JONES & WALKER
SOLICITORS

RUSSELL & RUSSELL Churchill House, Wood Street, Bolton, BL1 1EE *Tel:* (01204) 399299 *Fax:* (01204) 389223 *DX:* 24146 Bolton 1 *Ptnrs:* 12 *Asst solrs:* 13 *Other fee-earners:* 16

RUSSELLS

REGENCY HOUSE, 1-4 WARWICK ST, LONDON, W1R 6LJ
Tel: (0171) 439 8692 **Fax:** (0171) 494 3582 **DX:** 37249 PICCADILLY 1

The Firm: Founded by its present senior partner in 1974, Russells is best known for its experience and reputation in the entertainment industry.

Principal Areas of Work: Although recognised as one of the leading firms in the entertainment industry, with six commercial partners the firm also advises on general commercial matters. Three litigation partners also handle all types of litigation including breach of copyright, defamation, property disputes and divorce. It is also active in commercial and residential property, wills and probate.

Managing partner:	R.A.W. Page
Senior partner:	A.D. Russell
Number of partners:	9
Assistant solicitors:	3
Other fee-earners:	2

RUSSELLS GIBSON MCCAFFREY 13 Bath Street, Glasgow, G2 1HY **Tel:** (0141) 332 4176 **Fax:** (0141) 332 7908 **Ptnrs:** 4 **Asst solrs:** 2 **Other fee-earners:** 1 *General practice with particular expertise in family law.*

RUSTONS & LLOYD Beaufort House, 136 High Street, Newmarket, CB8 8NN **Tel:** (01638) 661221 **Fax:** (01638) 661732 **DX:** 50501 **Ptnrs:** 7 **Asst solrs:** 2 **Other fee-earners:** 13 **Contact:** Mr Michael Drake *General practice specialising in blood-stock related matters.*

S. RUTTER & CO

SUITE 420, SALISBURY HOUSE, FINSBURY CIRCUS, LONDON, EC2M 5QQ
Tel: (0171) 628 8641/4 **Fax:** (0171) 374 8070 **DX:** 33869 FINSBURY SQUARE

The Firm: Established in 1931 S. Rutter & Co is best known for its experience and reputation in complex and substantial financial disputes in matrimonial matters, including in particular work involving an international element. The firm also places special emphasis upon High Court litigation of all types (including commercial litigation, employment, landlord and tenant, personal injury, professional negligence and debt recovery) and general company matters. The practice has a department dealing with commercial and residential conveyancing, wills and probate. From August 1998 the firm is merging with the highly regarded Holborn firm Collyer-Bristow

Managing partner:	D.A. Hart-Leverton
Senior partner:	G.M. Rutter
Number of partners:	2
Assistant solicitors:	2
Other fee-earners:	3

SACKER & PARTNERS

29 LUDGATE HILL, LONDON, EC4M 7JQ
Tel: (0171) 329 6699 **Fax:** (0171) 248 0552 **DX:** 63 CH.LN.

The Firm: Sacker & Partners was established in 1966 and is the largest specialist pensions law practice in the UK.

Principal Areas of Work: All the fee earners practise exclusively in pensions law (and related areas of employment law). The full range of pensions work is undertaken, including pensions litigation, international aspects of pensions provision, and merger and acquisition work. Clients are employers (including leading public companies), trustees (including professional trustees) and trade unions. Referral work from other law firms (for example pensions advice on transactions) is an important part of the practice. The practice also has expertise in independent trusteeship through its company Independent Trustee Limited.

Senior partner:	Jonathan Seres
Number of partners:	15
Assistant solicitors:	15
Other fee-earners:	1

WORKLOADS	
Pensions	100%

CONTACTS	
Pensions	Ian Pittaway/Peter Lester/
	Chris Close/Mark Greenlees

SALANS HERTZFELD & HEILBRONN HRK

CLEMENTS HOUSE, 14-18 GRESHAM STREET, LONDON, EC2V 7NN
Tel: (0171) 509 6000 **Fax:** (0171) 726 6191 **DX:** 196

Salans Hertzfeld & Heilbronn is among the leading law firms in Europe, with 272 fee-earners (including 52 partners) based in London, Paris, New York, Warsaw, Moscow, St Petersburg, Kiev and Almaty. The firm's London office is situated in the City and provides a full range of services to both domestic and international clients. It is particularly well known for its work in the banking/finance sector and the motor vehicle industry. Its employment department enjoys a strong reputation.

The Firm: Salans Hertzfeld & Heilbronn HRK is the London office of the merged practices of Paris-based Salans Hertzfeld & Heilbronn and London-based Harris Rosenblatt & Kramer. The firm is a multi-national partnership and consists of English solicitors and registered foreign lawyers. The firm includes lawyers of more than a dozen nationalities qualified to practise law in all of the jurisdictions in which the firm is present. The diverse skills, professional qualifications, national backgrounds and linguistic abilities of its lawyers provide the firm with the ability to handle matters requiring local expertise as well as skills in cross-border transactions.

Principal Areas of Work: The London office acts for a wide range of domestic and international businesses, including UK and foreign banks, finance houses, building societies, international financial institutions and investment funds.

The banking department has an established reputation for its work both in the UK and overseas (including the emerging markets of Eastern Europe and the former Soviet Union). Its services include advising upon a wide variety of loans (including syndicated loans), lease and security documentation, terms and conditions for trade, asset-based and project finance and arrangements for development capital and investment funds in the UK and overseas. The department has specialist knowledge of motor vehicle stocking finance, lease and hire purchase arrangements, consumer credit documentation, portfolio securitisations and insolvency.

The commercial litigation department has particular expertise in banking and recoveries litigation and professional negligence. The work includes general commercial and banking litigation, professional negligence claims, landlord and tenant disputes, debt recovery and consumer credit, insolvency and LPA receiverships.

The corporate department offers a full domestic corporate and commercial service as well as advice on corporate structuring and privatisations in emerging markets. The practice includes structuring, documenting and negotiating domestic and cross-border mergers and acquisitions, licensing agreements, agency, distribution and franchise arrangements, joint venture agreements and IT, IP and computer services contracts.

The property department acts for developers, contractors, financiers, operators and investors on projects in the UK and abroad. The work embraces all aspects of acquisitions, disposals, development and financing of commercial properties.

The employment department is widely recognised as a leader in its practice area. It is headed by Barry Mordsley, who sits as a part-time Chairman of Industrial Tribunals, is a member of the Employment Lawyers' Association and was on the Law Society Employment Law Committee. The department deals with both contentious and non-contentious work, providing advice on such matters as contracts of employment, restrictive covenants, employee benefits, unfair dismissals, redundancies and discrimination cases.

A dedicated out of town office deals with volume recoveries and title perfection for leading banks, finance houses and building societies.

Other Offices: Paris, New York, Warsaw, Moscow, St Petersburg, Kiev and Almaty.

Managing partners (UK):	Roger Abrahams
	Robert Starr
UK	
Number of partners:	10
Assistant solicitors:	30
Other fee-earners:	15
International	
Number of partners:	52
Assistant solicitors:	220

WORKLOADS	
Banking & Finance/Corporate	50%
Litigation	25%
Employment	15%
Commercial Property	10%

CONTACTS	
Banking and Finance	Stephen Finch
	George Macdonald
Banking Recoveries	Caroline Havers
Commercial Arbitration	Lionel Rosenblatt
Commercial Property	Roger Abrahams
Corporate and Commercial	Stephen Finch
Emerging Markets	Robert Starr
	Philipp Windemuth
Employment	Barry Mordsley
General Commercial Litigation	Jeffrey Elton
Insolvency	Alison Gaines
Professional Negligence	Lionel Rosenblatt

SHH
SALANS HERTZFELD & HEILBRONN HRK

SAMUEL PHILLIPS & CO

GIBB CHAMBERS, 52 WESTGATE ROAD, NEWCASTLE UPON TYNE, NE1 5XU
Tel: (0191) 232 8451 **Fax:** (0191) 232 7664 **DX:** 61028 **Email:** ADMIN@SAMUELPHILLIPS.CO.UK

The Firm: A long-established firm offering a comprehensive range of legal services to private and business clients. In particular, the firm has many years' experience in medico-legal matters, and acts for a number of NHS Trusts.

Principal Areas of Work:

Company and Commercial: (*Contact Partner:* Stephen Doberman). *Work includes:* partnerships and joint ventures, acquisitions, formations, reconstructions, commercial contracts, intellectual property, advising on funding, tax and insurance requirements, licensing and services to overseas companies.

Property: (*Contact Partner:* Stephen Doberman). The work covers all aspects of commercial and residential property including investment, funding, planning and residential building estates.

Litigation: (*Contact Partner:* Barry Speker). Work dealt with includes: medical negligence, employment, commercial disputes, building contract disputes, debt collection, tribunal representation, crime, immigration and personal injury matters.

Other Areas of Work: The firm also deals with all family and matrimonial matters particularly in relation to child care and adoption as well as wills, probate and tax planning, and has a large criminal department. Members of Law Society Panels: Medical Negligence, Personal Injury, Children, Mental Health. Legal Aid Franchise in all areas.

Managing partner:	Barry N. Speker
Senior partner:	Barry N. Speker
Number of partners:	4
Assistant solicitors:	8
Other fee-earners:	6

WORKLOADS	
Medical negligence and related medico-legal work	30%
Crime	20%
Family and child care	20%
Property	15%
Civil litigation	10%
Employment	5%

CONTACTS	
Child care	Barry Speker, Robert Gibson
Company/ Commercial	Stephen Doberman
Crime	Stuart Grant
Employment	Robert Gibson, Barry Speker
Family law	Barry Speker
Immigration	Barry Speker
Medical negligence	Barry Speker
Personal injury	Robert Gibson
Property	Stephen Doberman

SANSBURY HILL 6 Unity Street, Bristol, BS1 5HH **Tel:** (0117) 926 5341 **Fax:** (0117) 922 5625 **DX:** 7821 Bristol **Ptnrs:** 5 **Asst solrs:** 8 **Other fee-earners:** 5 **Contact:** Mr M. Guy *Specialist Defendant personal injury firm. Also crime.*

WORKLOADS			
Civil litigation	80%	Criminal	15%
Non-contentious	5%		

SAUNDERS & CO 71 Kingsway, London, WC2B 6ST *Tel:* (0171) 404 2828 *Fax:* (0171) 4042929 *DX:* 37995 Kingsway *Ptnrs:* 4 *Asst solrs:* 9 *Other fee-earners:* 12

SAVAGE CRANGLE 15 High Street, Skipton, BD23 1AJ **Tel:** (01756) 794611 **Fax:** (01756) 791395 **DX:** 21751 **Email:** law@savage-crangle.co.uk **Ptnrs:** 5 **Other fee-earners:** 5 **Contact:** Peter Crangle *General practice known for Commercial, Agricultural, Housing, P.I. and Private Client Work.*

WORKLOADS	
Commercial/Agricultural/Housing	70%
Private Clients	20%
Personal Injury	10%

SCHILLING & LOM AND PARTNERS

ROYALTY HOUSE, 72-74 DEAN ST, LONDON, W1V 6AE
Tel: (0171) 453 2500 **Fax:** (0171) 453 2600 **DX:** 89265 (SOHO SQUARE 1) **Email:** LEGAL@SCHILLINGLOM.CO.UK
Internet: WWW.SCHILLINGLOM.CO.UK

This Firm: Specialising in media and entertainment, this London firm provides legal advice for corporate and individual clients in television, film, music, fashion, sport and related industries. The firm also undertakes commercial litigation, company and commercial work and family matters.

The company acts for broadcasters, publishers, record companies, film producers and a number of media corporate clients. It also acts for many celebrities and high-profile individuals who are the subject of constant press attention.

The firm has an enviable reputation for robust but practical litigation. Its in depth knowledge of the various media industries within which it principally works provides it with both a better understanding of the needs of its clients, and also a distinct advantage in legal disputes.

In its entertainment work, the firm is innovative and commercial. Again its high degree of specialisation ensures that it negotiates the best deal available by having an intimate knowledge of the industry. This also allows us to be fully aware of the needs of its clients, to whom it is both approachable and empathetic.

Principal Areas of Work:

Litigation Defamation, copyright, breach of confidence, contractual disputes, family and employment.

Senior partner:	Keith Schilling

WORKLOADS	
Defamation	25%
Film, Television & Music	20%
Intellectual Property	20%
Company Commercial	15%
Family	15%
Sport	5%

CONTACTS	
Commercial Litigation & Libel	Jonathan Coad
Company Commercial	Shelley-Anne Salisbury
Family	Tina Smithson
Film and Television	Nicholas Lom
Intellectual Property & Sport	Eddie Parladorio
Media & Defamation Litigation	Mark Thomson
Music	Iain McKane

Entertainment Entertainment work includes production, financing, and distribution agreements, sales agency agreements, cable and satellite agreements, television co-production agreements and agreements with individual directors, producers, actors, writers and composers. Option agreements for film and television rights, copyright licensing and assignments, and video exploitation agreements are also dealt with.

Industry Specialities Services to the music industry include preparing and negotiating recording agreements, publishing agreements, and general commercial and management and merchandising agreements.

There is also specialist family law expertise for all aspects of family law, including divorce and custody issues.

As to the theatre, the firm provides agreements for playwrights, artists, directors and designers, as well as for investors. It also provides production agreements and actors and actresses' contracts.

Literary matters dealt with include publishing agreements, writers' agreements, options and proof-reading for libel and copyright infringements.

Company and commercial services include company takeovers, asset sales and purchases, management buyouts, mergers and company restructuring, licensing agreements, distribution agreements, employment contracts, partnership deeds, joint ventures, shareholders' agreements, terms and conditions of business, franchise agreements, concession agreements, merchandising licenses, computer software licenses and distribution agreements.

The firm provides specialist advice to the fashion industry, and acts for a number of high profile fashion clients. The firm also provides a comprehensive array of legal services for a number of high profile sporting clients.

SCOTT-MONCRIEFF, HARBOUR & SINCLAIR Signet House, 49/51 Farringdon Road, London, EC1M 3JB *Tel:* (0171) 242 4114 *Fax:* (0171) 242 3605 *DX:* 53336 Clerkenwell *Ptnrs:* 4 *Asst solrs:* 2 *Other fee-earners:* 1

SCRIVENGER SEABROOK 26 New Street, St. Neots, PE19 1AJ **Tel:** (01480) 214900 **Fax:** (01480) 474833 **DX:** 100315 St Neots **Ptnrs:** 4 **Other fee-earners:** 1 **Contact:** Vicki Seabrook *The firm deals exclusively in defendant, medical negligence and general healthcare work with a small percentage of personal injury.*

WORKLOADS			
Medical negligence	95%	Personal injury	5%

SEAN REDMOND The Moat House, 133 Newport Road, Stafford, ST16 2EZ *Tel:* (01785) 211470 *Fax:* (01785) 229684 *Ptnrs:* 1

SEARLES The Chapel, 26A Munster Road, London, SW6 4EN **Tel:** (0171) 371 0555 **Fax:** (0171) 371 7722 **Ptnrs:** 3 **Asst solrs:** 1 **Other fee-earners:** 1 **Contact:** Helen Searle, Tim Northrop or Christy McNaughtan *Entertainment and IP specialists in the record, publishing, television, and design industries to include both contentious and non-contentious matters.*

WORKLOADS	
Music industry (both classical and popular)	70%
Film and television	20%
Sponsorship, P.R. and advertising	10%

SEARS TOOTH 50 Upper Brook Street, London, W1Y 1PG *Tel:* (0171) 499 5599 *Fax:* (0171) 495 2970 *DX:* 44643 Mayfair *Ptnrs:* 4 *Asst solrs:* 2 *Other fee-earners:* 1

SEDDONS 5 Portman Square, London, W1H 0NT **Tel:** (0171) 486 9681 **Fax:** (0171) 935 5049 **DX:** 9061 West End **Email: Postmaster@seddons.co.uk Ptnrs:** 14 **Asst solrs:** 6 **Other fee-earners:** 5 **Contact:** Harvey Ingram *Broad-based commercial practice with strong aviation, company/commercial, employment, entertainment, litigation (including shipping and commodities) property and sports departments. Prague Office.*

WORKLOADS	
Litigation	35%
Property	35%
Company and Commercial (including Employment and Entertainment)	30%

SEDGWICK, DETERT, MORAN & ARNOLD

5 LLOYD'S AVENUE, LONDON, EC3N 3AX
Tel: (0171) 929 1829 **Fax:** (0171) 929 1808 **Email:** EMAIL@SDMA.COM **Internet:** WWW.SDMA.COM

The Firm: Sedgwick, Detert, Moran & Arnold is America's third largest firm specialising in commercial litigation, including insurance and product liability law. Founded in 1933, the Firm has a total of 265 attorneys with offices in San Francisco, Los Angeles, Orange County, Chicago, New York and Zurich.

London Office: This office was opened in 1985 and became one of the first multinational partnerships in 1992. With an emphasis on directors and officers liability, fidelity, professional indemnity, entertainment and property claims, as well as international arbitrations, the office acts for a number of major international corporations, insurers and reinsurers.

Managing partner:	A. C. Barker
Number of partners:	3
Assistant solicitors:	1
Other fee-earners:	3

WORKLOADS	
Insurance Litigation	40%
Arbitration	20%
Commercial Litigation	20%
Non-contentious Insurance	20%

SEMPLE FRASER WS

130 ST VINCENT STREET, GLASGOW, G2 5HF
Tel: (0141) 221 3771 **Fax:** (0141) 221 3776/3859 **DX:** GW 337 **Email:** INFO@SEMPLEFRASER.CO.UK

10 MELVILLE CRESCENT, EDINBURGH, EH3 7LU
Tel: (0131) 623 8777 **Fax:** (0131) 623 7201 **DX:** ED 447 **Email:** INFO@SEMPLEFRASER.CO.UK

The Firm: Established in 1990, Semple Fraser is a specialist commercial law practice with a very strong reputation for its commercial property work and a concomitant expertise in corporate matters. The business of clients is closely supervised by a partner with a clear understanding and appreciation of individual client circumstances and requirements. The firm is organised on the basis of Special Sector Groups made up of lawyers who share expertise in different *complimentary* areas of law and industry. These groups keep abreast of business and legal developments in their sector in order to develop optimum and innovative responses to complex commercial transactions.

Principal Areas of Work:

Commercial Property: (*Contact Partner:* Alister Fraser (Edinburgh) and Angus MacRae (Glasgow)). *Work includes:* property development and investment, leasing, property taxation (VAT), planning and environmental law, construction, property related insolvency, retail, nursing homes, leisure and recreation schemes and enterprise zone developments.

Company and Commercial: (*Contact Partner:* Stuart Russell (Glasgow) and Kathleen Stewart (Edinburgh)). *Work includes:* business start-up, acquisition and disposal, take-overs, mergers and acquisitions, corporate finance, management buy-outs and buy-ins, institutional investment, banking, insolvency and reconstruction and corporate rescue.

Commercial Litigation: (*Contact Partner:* Alison Gow (Edinburgh) and Stuart Macfarlane (Glasgow)). *Work includes:* all aspects of commercial litigation, especially property related disputes and employment matters. The litigation group has extensive experience of Court of Session work. *The firm has recently expanded by opening an office in Edinburgh. With the introduction of a Scottish Parliament this gives the firm a presence in Scotland's capital city and seat of government.*

Other Languages: German, French, Dutch.

Managing partner:	Alister Fraser
Senior partner:	David Semple
Number of partners:	13
Assistant solicitors:	14
Other fee-earners:	6

WORKLOADS	
Commercial property	40%
Company/commercial	25%
Litigation	25%
Banking	10%

CONTACTS	
Banking	Kathleen Stewart
Commercial property	Angus MacRae/Alister Fraser
Company/commercial	Kathleen Stewart/Stuart Russell
Litigation	Stuart Macfarlane/Alison Gow

SENIOR CALVELEY & HARDY 8 Hastings Place, Lytham St. Annes, FY8 5NA *Tel:* (01253) 733333 *Fax:* (01253) 794430 *Ptnrs:* 4 *Asst solrs:* 3

SHACKLOCKS 19 The Ropewalk, Nottingham, NG1 5DU **Tel:** (0115) 941 0789 **Fax:** (0115) 947 5561 **DX:** 10076 **Ptnrs:** 11 **Asst solrs:** 6 **Other fee-earners:** 8 **Contact:** Robin Wilson – Senior Partner *Leading regional practice. Work includes commercial, property, litigation, debt collection, employment, intellectual property, licensing, EC law and private client services.*

WORKLOADS			
Commercial	28%	Private Client	17%
Litigation	16%	Licencing	12%
Other	11%	Employment	8%
Personal Injury	8%		

SHADBOLT & CO

CHATHAM COURT, LESBOURNE ROAD, REIGATE, RH2 7LD
Tel: (01737) 226277 **Fax:** (01737) 226165 **Email:** SHADBOLTLAW.CO.UK **Internet:** WWW.SHADBOLTLAW.CO.UK

The Firm: Shadbolt & Co is a specialist commercial law practice providing a high quality service to business clients in the United Kingdom and internationally. The firm acquired its outstanding reputation advising clients involved in the field of major projects and in the construction and engineering industries. It now works in a wide range of practice areas including corporate, property, employment and aviation. The firm offers a cost-effective and imaginative commercial service backed by an unusual degree of experience. Most partners and fee-earners have a background of working in large City of London firms.

Principal Areas of Work:

Construction and Engineering: The firm handles a wide range of contentious and non-contentious work relating to the construction and engineering industries in the UK and internationally. Recent disputes have been handled in Taiwan, Uganda, China, Hong Kong and Egypt.

Major Projects: The firm advises a variety of clients on the commercial and legal aspects of major projects including reveiwing and drafting contract documentation. The firm is used to working in collaboration with financial and other advisers on major projects both in the United Kingdom and elsewhere in the world.

Corporate: The firm has particular expertise in company sales and purchases, corporate finance, reorganisations and joint ventures. The firm also undertakes a wide variety of other high quality commercial work, including franchising, intellectual property, computer contracts, European law, competition and advice on general commercial agreements of all kinds.

Commercial Dispute Resolution: The firm's work includes litigation, arbitration and other forms of dispute resolution in relation to international and domestic business disputes. The firm is experienced in ADR techniques.

Commercial Property: In their commercial property practice they are able to provide specialist advice on development and commercial property matters of all kinds, particularly in the fields of sales and purchases, property financing and landlord and tenant law.

International Activities: Their clients are from many different countries. Many of them operate internationally. They provide a comprehensive service to assist them on projects or transactions outside their home country.

Employment Law: The firm acts for many substantial employers. They represent their clients in the Courts and industrial tribunals and deal with employment and related matters such as health and safety. They keep their clients up to date with developments under both European and UK law.

Aviation: The firm's work includes all aspects of international aviation operations including liabilities, insurance, airport planning, air traffic control and environmental and regulatory questions.

Nature of Clientele: Clients include well-known names in the construction industry. The Firm's clientele has a strong international bias and clients come from a variety of countries.

Recruitment and Training: The firm has an on-going recruitment programme for trainee solicitors and for qualified candidates with particular experience and expertise in the construction and engineering industry. Considerable importance is attached to in-house training and the continuing education programme for its solicitors.

International Connections & Associated Offices: The firm has offices in Hong Kong and Paris and it enjoys excellent working relationships with lawyers from many different countries.

Managing partner:	**Richard Shadbolt**
Senior partner:	**Richard Shadbolt**
Number of partners:	11
Assistant solicitors:	9
Other fee-earners:	4

WORKLOADS	
Disputes	60%
Construction and engineering (non-contentious/major projects)	20%
Corporate/other	20%

CONTACTS	
Aviation	Tim Unmack
Construction and Engineering	Simon H. Delves
Corporate	Andrew J. Trotter
Disputes resolution/Litigation	Peter L. Sheridan
Employment	Helen J Boddy
Major projects	Elizabeth J. Jenkins
Property	Sean Ryan

SHAKESPEARES

10 BENNETTS HILL, BIRMINGHAM, B2 5RS
Tel: (0121) 632 4199 **Fax:** (0121) 643 2257 **DX:** 13015

The Firm: As one of Birmingham's larger and broader based firms of Solicitors, Shakespeares provides comprehensive legal advice to a wide range of clients including PLCs, banks, owner-managed businesses, private individuals, universities, schools and colleges, insurance companies and charities.

The firm is recognised for its commitment to the quality of its service, having ISO9001 accreditation, and is committed to obtaining an Investors in People award. As one of Birmingham's larger leading law firms, over the past year Shakespeares has consolidated and strengthened its position as a key regional player reflected in a number of key long-term strategic decisions. The firm has made some considerable changes in personnel. Retirements and other changes have produced a more balanced list of partners. Simultaneously, the firm has injected young blood into the partnership, through promotions from within the firm and external recruitment of high quality specialists. However, the firm still remains a partner-orientated practice, ensuring access to senior expertise as and when required, and still aims to offer a flexible and personal approach.

Principal Areas of Work:

Company and Commercial: (*Contact:* Jill Kennedy. *Fee-earners:* 22, including employment unit and Business Lit team). Shakespeares company and commercial advice extends to a broad range of areas including company structure, corporate finance, general contractual work and other commercial activities, such as licensing and franchising, distribution and agency agreements and insolvency. The firm also has a considerable specialism in Employment Law, acting for both employers and employees. The firm also offers business litigation including alternative dispute resolution.

Litigation: (*Contact:* John M. Buckingham. *Fee-earners:* 32). Shakespeares has a substantial Litigation department covering a broad range of legal services. The thrust of the work in the Department is for Business Insurance companies, Banks, institutional clients and local authorities. Defendant personal injury work is undertaken for a number of insurance company clients. The firm also has a large computerised Debt Recovery Department and also handles matters such as intellectual property, construction cases and professional indemnity claims. Shakespeares also handles litigation matters for individuals including medical negligence, matrimonial disputes and crime, particularly white collar fraud.

Property: (*Contact:* Paul R M Reading. *Fee-earners:* 6). A comprehensive range of property services are provided for financial institutions, property developers and housing associations, as well as private individuals. Leasing and financing of commercial property are handled, as well as joint ventures and taxation matters for a broad range of businesses from owner-managed businesses to PLCs.

Private Client: (*Contact:* Clare Laird. *Fee-earners:* 14). The firm offers a broad range of private client services including Wills, Probate Trusts, Enduring Powers of Attorney and Tax Planning advice. Additionally, Shakespeares has a dedicated Investment Management Department – currently with £45 million under investment. Shakespeares has a specialist charity team handling all matters relating to Charity Law and associated areas such as property, employment and general commercial advice. The charity team is led by Gary De'Ath who is one of the leading specialists in the area.

Managing partner:	Andrew Argyle
Senior partner:	Charles B. Flint
Deputy Senior partner:	John Buckingham
Number of partners:	17
Assistant solicitors:	32
Other fee-earners:	16

WORKLOADS	
Litigation	58%
Property	15%
Private client	14%
Commercial	10%
Other	3%

CONTACTS	
Banking Litigation	Stephen Jones
Business Litigation	Mark Beesley
Charities	Gary De'Ath
Company and Commercial	Jill Kennedy
Crime	Stephen Daly
Debt Collection	Rohit Deepak
Education	Anthony Jones
Employment	Mike Hibbs
Family Law	Nicola Walker
Insurance Litigation	John Buckingham
Investment Management	Graham Englefield
Medical Negligence	Gary Christianson
Private Client	Clare Laird
Professional Indemnity	Diana Wareing
Property	Paul Reading

SHARMAN & TRETHEWY 1 Harpur St, Bedford, MK40 1PF **Tel:** (01234) 303030 **Fax:** (01234) 409040 **DX:** 5604 **Email:** SharmanLaw@aol.com **Ptnrs:** 6 **Asst solrs:** 7 **Other fee-earners:** 9 **Contact:** Mr Ian Codrington *Established 1809. Handles all areas of practice including commercial, conveyancing, probate, civil and criminal litigation. Agency work undertaken. Also at Ampthill; Tel: (01525) 750 750*

WORKLOADS	
Litigation	49%
Probate, wills, trusts and tax	21%
Company & commercial property	15%
Residential conveyancing including mortgage sales	14%
Other	1%

SHARPE PRITCHARD

ELIZABETH HOUSE, FULWOOD PLACE, LONDON, WC1V 6HG
Tel: (0171) 405 4600 **Fax:** (0171) 242 2210 **DX:** 353

Nature of Firm: A well established practice in the fields of litigation for the public and private sectors; with conveyancing, trusts, tax and some company and commercial. Also well known parliamentary agents.

Principal Areas of Work:

General Description: A general practice with a strong emphasis on litigation for a wide variety of clients; particularly public and local authorities and professional clients. Expanding property and planning department.

Litigation: (*Contact:* Ashley Badcock). All areas covered particularly construction, environmental and property related litigation, personal injury including medical negligence; local and public authority related litigation – judicial review; commercial and defamation; employment; insolvency and debt collection; Chancery, child care and family.

Parliamentary: (*Contact:* Michael Pritchard). A substantial practice for public and local authorities, promotion and opposition of bills for a variety of clients.

Property and commercial: (*Contact:* Romaine Snashall). A wide variety of property-related work, conveyancing, trusts, tax and some company/ commercial. Expanding development work for local authorities. Town and country planning work undertaken.

Contracts: (*Contact:* Stephen Millen). The firm undertakes drafting and negotiation of contracts for works, services and supplies and advises on EU and UK public procurement, and joint ventures and private finance transactions.

Nature of Clientele: Public and local authorities, professional, private and small corporate, housing trusts, charities etc.

Foreign Connections: Italian and French spoken.

Agency Work: Substantial agency practice in all areas; urgent work undertaken – contact Mr. Richards.

Recruitment and Training: Three trainee solicitors a year are taken on. They should have good academic qualifications and the ability to work as part of a well-knit team. Applications with a C.V. should be made in September of each year to Ashley Badcock.

Charges: On application.

Senior partner:	Ashley Badcock
Number of partners:	11
Assistant solicitors:	8
Other fee-earners:	17

WORKLOADS	
Civil litigation	44%
Contracts	18%
Property Trusts/Tax	17%
Parliamentary	15%
Planning	6%

CONTACTS	
Civil litigation	A. Badcock
Contracts	S. Millen
Parliamentary	M. Pritchard
Planning	J. Sharland
Property and commercial	R. Snashall

SHARP & PARTNERS 6 Weekday Cross, Nottingham, NG1 2GF *Tel:* (0115) 959 0055 *Fax:* (0115) 959 0099 *DX:* 10019 *Ptnrs:* 9 *Asst solrs:* 7 *Other fee-earners:* 6

SHAW AND CROFT

115 HOUNDSDITCH, LONDON, EC3A 7BU
Tel: (0171) 645 9000 **Fax:** (0171) 626 3639 **DX:** 824

The Firm: Established in 1980 as a specialist shipping and commercial law practice, the firm has grown steadily in these fields, while developing expertise in related areas.

Principal Areas of Work:

Shipping and Maritime Law: (*Contact Partner:* Roger Croft). The firm handles every aspect of contentious shipping work, including collisions, salvage, charter parties, bills of lading, cargo damage, pollution, and shipbuilding disputes.

Ship Finance and Corporate: (*Contact Partner:* Richard Coles). Sale and purchase, finance and registration of ships, yachts and fishing vessels, company acquisitions and disposals, joint ventures, agency and employment law.

Commodities: (*Contact Partner:* Bob McCunn). Work handled includes international sale of goods (particularly oil, grain and other commodities) together with other international commercial transactions.

Insurance: (*Contact Partner:* Jonathan Kenyon). Litigation and advice on all aspects of the insurance markets in London and abroad, particularly marine insurance, P&I, Brokers E and O, reinsurance.

Property: (*Contact Partner:* Roger Colton). Acquisition and disposal of commercial and residential property, landlord and tenant, probate.

Nature of Clientele: Shipowners, charterers, P and I Clubs and Insurers, salvage companies, banks, commodity traders, oil companies, ship managers, shipbuilders, insolvency practitioners, property developers and investors.

Senior partner:	Roger Croft
Number of partners:	10
Assistant solicitors:	5
Other fee-earners:	13

WORKLOADS	
Shipping Litigation	36%
Admiralty	27%
Insurance (Marine and Non-Marine)	11%
Ship Finance, Corporate & other non-contentious	11%
Commercial Litigation	10%
Commodities	5%

CONTACTS	
Admiralty	Roger Croft/Hamish Edgar
Commercial litigation	Nicholas Taylor
Commodities	Bob McCunn
Insurance	Jonathan Kenyon
Personal Injury	Hamish Edgar
Property	Roger Colton
Ship Finance/Corporate	Richard Coles
Shipping litigation	Giles de Bertodano
Shipping litigation	Roland Jackson

Continues overleaf

Foreign Connections: The firm has particularly strong connections with France, Greece, Eastern Europe, N. Africa and the Middle East. French, Spanish, German, Greek, Italian and Afrikaans are spoken. A worldwide network of correspondent lawyers in all major shipping and commercial centres is actively maintained.

SHEAN DICKSON MERRICK 14/16 High Street, Belfast, BT1 2BS **Tel:** (01232) 326878 **Fax:** (01232) 323473 **DX:** 460 Nr Belfast **Ptnrs:** 4 **Asst solrs:** 3 **Other fee-earners:** 2 **Contact:** Mr David Moffett *Experienced in licensing matters, the practice also includes company/ commercial, litigation and private client work.*

WORKLOADS			
Commercial/ company	25%	Licensing	20%
Private client	20%	Personal Injury	15%
Commercial litigation	10%	Employment	10%

SHEARMAN & STERLING 9th Floor, 199 Bishopsgate, London, EC2M 3TY *Tel:* (0171) 920 9000 *Fax:* (0171) 920 9020 *Ptnrs:* 9

SHEPHERD & WEDDERBURN WS

SALTIRE COURT, 20 CASTLE TERRACE, EDINBURGH, EH1 2ET
Tel: (0131) 228 9900 **Fax:** (0131) 228 1222 **DX:** 553049 EDINBURGH 18 **Email:** MAIL.DESK@SHEPWEDD.CO.UK **Internet:** WWW.SHEPWED.CO.UK

155 ST. VINCENT STREET, GLASGOW, G2 5NR
Tel: (0141) 566 9900 **Fax:** (0141) 565 1222 **DX:** GW 409, GLASGOW-1

75 CANNON STREET, LONDON, EC4N 5BN
Tel: (0171) 489 9900 **Fax:**

The Firm: Shepherd & Wedderburn is one of the largest commercial legal firms in Scotland with a complement of approximately 280 people. It provides a full range of legal services to corporate, commercial, public sector and private clients.

The aim at Shepherd & Wedderburn is to work in partnership with clients, demonstrating the firm's commitment to clients' business objectives and flexibility in response to their commercial requirements. The development of staff is central to this approach to business. The firm believes that only by investing heavily in its staff can it offer clients the best possible service from highly skilled and enthusiastic professionals.

The proof of the success of this philosophy is to be found in the extensive range of services the firm provides to its clients including many quoted and public sector organisations.

Principal Areas of Work:

Corporate & Commercial: In the corporate and commercial fields the firm provides a full range of services, although it has developed a particular expertise in advising the financial sector (in particular corporate finance and banking) and in Stock Exchange-related work including new issues of securities for investment trusts. The corporate commercial department is also noted for its work in mergers and acquisitions (including MBOs and MBIs), Eurobond issues, insolvency, energy law, commercial contracts, employment law and intellectual property.

Commercial Property: The firm prides itself on its reputation in all aspects of commercial property work, including investment purchases, sales and development and leasing transactions. It also acts regularly in the acquisition and sale of hotels and other leisure interests.

Litigation: In the litigation field, the firm handles all types of disputes before the Scottish courts and represents clients in arbitrations, public enquiries and administrative tribunals. It offers specialist advice on employment law, family law, building/construction contracts and professional indemnity claims.

Private Client: For the private client, the firm provides personal tax and estate planning advice, trust and executry administration, and a full service in the acquisition and disposal of forestry, sporting and agricultural interests and in residential property transactions.

In addition the firm has built considerable expertise in PFI/Infrastructure related work, Pensions, Technology and in the Housing Association and Healthcare sectors.

Chief Executive:	Hugh Donald
Number of partners:	30
Number of fee-earners:	136
Total staff:	280

CONTACTS	
Banking securities & finance	Iain Meiklejohn
Commercial law	James Saunders
Commercial property	Patrick Andrews
Companies/corporations	James Will
Construction/building	James Dobie
Contract	Liz McRobb
Devolution	David Nash
Employment	Sheila Gunn
Energy	James Saunders
Health	Hugh Donald
Housing Association	Alison Campbell
I.T/intellectual property	James Saunders
Insolvency/bankruptcy	Paul Hally
Litigation/arbitration	Ian MacLeod
Mergers & acquisitions	James Will
Pensions	Andrew Holehouse
PFI/Infrastructure	David Nash
Private client	Robin Fulton

SHEPSTONE & WYLIE (UK)

5TH FLOOR, 44-48 DOVER STREET, LONDON, W1X 3RF
Tel: (0171) 344 7600 **Fax:** (0171) 344 7555

The Firm: Shepstone & Wylie is a substantial South African firm of attorneys and is associated with Maitland & Co. in Europe.

The London Office: Work undertaken by the London office includes shipping, commodities, banking, corporate and commercial work, corporate finance, transnational tax, business and investment planning, immigration and intellectual property.

Languages Spoken: French, German, Afrikaans.

Other and Associated Offices: *Shepstone & Wylie:* Durban, Pietermaritzburg, Richards Bay. *Maitland & Co:* London, Luxembourg, Geneva, the Isle of Man, Paris

Contact partner:	John Herholdt
No of partners – London:	5
Assistant solicitors – London:	4
Other fee-earners – worldwide:	250

SHERIDANS

14 RED LION SQUARE, LONDON, WC1R 4QL
Tel: (0171) 404 0444 **Fax:** (0171) 831 1982 **DX:** 270 **Email:** GENERAL@SHERIDANS.CO.UK

The Firm: Sheridans has a substantial international practice, is particularly noted for its work in all branches of the entertainment, media and communications industries and offers a wide range of litigation services. The firm also has a growing reputation for its work in company/commercial and property law.

Principal Areas of Work:

Entertainment & Media: (*Contact:* Howard Jones). *Work includes:* legal services relating to recording artistes, publishing and record companies, intellectual property, theatre, TV, copyright, merchandising, books, video, the press and related areas.

Litigation: (*Contact:* Cyril Glasser). The department has considerable experience in litigation involving commercial, entertainment, media, computer and public law work; matrimonial and immigration law and some criminal work. It also specialises in defamation and employment cases, banking litigation, and obtaining emergency orders.

Company/Commercial: (*Contact:* Ian Watson). *Work includes:* the raising of finance, setting up of companies, negotiation of joint ventures, management buy-outs, demergers, acquisitions and disposals, reorganisations, insolvency and employment, intellectual property law, trademarks, copyright, and general commercial work.

Property and Planning: (*Contact:* Peter Jacobs). Work in the commercial sphere includes secured lending, property development, building schemes, property financing, investments and planning. The department also handles residential conveyancing, licensing, wills and probate.

Nature of Clientele: The clientele includes major recording artistes and companies, television production companies, classical music composers, publishers; a substantial private client base as well as corporate clients.

Foreign Connections: The work undertaken in the entertainment, media and communications field, and the commercial field generally, requires extensive overseas contact, with the result that the firm is well-versed in dealing with foreign lawyers and professional advisers.

Recruitment and Training: The firm recruits three trainee solicitors every year. Applications should be made with a CV and an accompanying letter to Cyril Glasser during August 1998 (for September 2000).

Managing partner:	Cyril Glasser
Number of partners:	17
Assistant solicitors:	7
Other fee-earners:	7

WORKLOADS	
Commercial and other litigation	40%
Entertainment and media	35%
Property and planning	15%
Company/commercial	10%

CONTACTS	
Commercial litigation	Cyril Glasser
Company/commercial	Ian Watson
Computers and IT	Michael Thomas
Employment	Ruth Harvey
Entertainment and media	Howard Jones
Matrimonial and immigration	Richard Gifford
Property/ planning/ probate	Peter Jacobs

SHERRARDS

35 MARKET PLACE, ST. ALBANS, AL3 5DN
Tel: (01727) 840271 **Fax:** (01727) 836775 **DX:** 6100 ST. ALBANS

2ND FLOOR, 45 GROSVENOR ROAD, ST. ALBANS, AL1 3EW
Tel: (01727) 832830 **Fax:** (01727) 832833 **DX:** 6100 ST. ALBANS

The Firm: Sherrards was founded in 1880 and has become one of the major providers of Corporate and Commercial advice in the area. Sherrards has an expert team of Personal Injury Panel Specialists. It is also renowned for its expertise in Employment law.

Contacts:
Commercial litigation (including Employment): *Simon Braun*
Commercial property: *Alasdair McMillin*
Conveyancing: *Andrew Moore*
Corporate/Commercial: *Melvin Dawe*
Crime: *Angela Edge*
Matrimonial: *Anna Low*
Personal injury: *John Holtom*
Private client: *John Brian*
Wills, trusts, estate planning: *Alex Drake*

Managing partners:	Alasdair McMillin
	Mr John Brian
Number of partners:	2
Assistant solicitors:	10
Other fee-earners:	4

WORKLOADS	
Litigation (including Personal Injury and Employment)	36%
Private Client	34%
Company Commercial (including Commercial Property)	30%

SHERWIN OLIVER

NEW HAMPSHIRE COURT, ST PAULS ROAD, PORTSMOUTH, PO5 4JT
Tel: (01705) 832200 **Fax:** (01705) 865884 **DX:** DX 2268 PORTSMOUTH

THE OLD MANOR HOUSE, WICKHAM ROAD, FAREHAM, PO16 7AR
Tel: (01329) 822611 **Fax:** (01329) 822612 **DX:** 40816 FAREHAM

The Firm: Sherwin Oliver Solicitors is one of the leading commercial law practices in South Hampshire, providing a wide range of legal services to the business community. The firm is a member of LawNet.

Principal Areas of Work:
Company commercial: The firm advises on acquisitions, mergers, expansion and restructuring of businesses, contracts, conditions of sale and purchase, licensing, franchising and all aspects of commercial law.

Commercial property: This department handles a wide range of property transactions, with a particular speciality in commercial and residential development, work management and landlord and tenant matters.

Corporate recovery: One of the largest specialist corporate recovery and insolvency departments on the South Coast specialises in all aspects of corporate and personal insolvency, realisation of assets and LPA receiverships.

Commercial litigation: All forms of commercial litigation are handled by this department, including contract disputes, landlord and tenant, construction disputes, insurance claims and debt recovery. The department is acting for two national business organisations in bringing claims against the Government in the European Commission of Human Rights.

Employment law: This specialist department advises national and local businesses on all aspects of the law, including trade union negotiations and industrial relations. It also acts for senior employees and members regularly appear in Industrial Tribunals nationwide.

Franchising and intellectual property: The firm is an affiliate member of the British Franchise Association and has a substantial reputation for work in this speciality and in contentious and non contentious intellectual property matters, particularly in the field of computer law.

Tax, trusts & probate: This department deals with all aspects of wills and probate. It also establishes and administers trusts, and advises upon tax planning.

International connections: Sherwin Oliver Solicitors is a member of LawNet Europe and Eurojuris which provide access to a network of 650 associated firms in 19 countries.

Foreign languages: French and German

Managing partner:	Nigel Steward
Number of partners:	12
Assistant solicitors:	12
Other fee-earners:	9

WORKLOADS	
Company commercial	30%
Commercial litigation	25%
Commercial property	25%
Corporate recovery/Insolvency	10%
Employment	5%
General	5%

CONTACTS	
Commercial litigation	Christopher Brockman
Commercial property	Andy Peck
Company/commercial	Nigel Craig
Computers/IT	Nigel Craig
Corporate recovery/Insolvency	David Oliver
Employment law	John Taylor
Franchising/I.P.	Geoffrey Sturgess
Tax, trusts & probate	Clive Saunders

SHIELD & KYD 5 Bank Street, (PO Box 61), Dundee, DD1 9LB *Tel:* (01382) 224112 *Fax:* (01382) 200109 *DX:* 17 Dundee *Ptnrs:* 12 *Asst solrs:* 3

SHOOSMITHS & HARRISON

THE LAKES, BEDFORD ROAD, NORTHAMPTON, NN4 7SH
Tel: (01604) 543000 **Fax:** (01604) 543543 **DX:** 712280 **Email:** NORTHAMPTON@SHOOSMITHS.CO.UK **Internet:** WWW.SHOOSMITHS.CO.UK

COMPTON HOUSE, ABINGTON STREET, NORTHAMPTON, NN1 2LR
Tel: (01604) 543000 **Fax:** (01604) 542245 **DX:** 712280

LOCK HOUSE, CASTLE MEADOW ROAD, NOTTINGHAM, NG2 1AG
Tel: (0115) 906 5000 **Fax:** (0115) 906 5001 **DX:** 10104

REGENTS GATE, CROWN STREET, READING, RG1 2PQ
Tel: (0118) 949 8765 **Fax:** (0118) 949 8800 **DX:** 4009

BLOXAM COURT, CORPORATION STREET, RUGBY, CV21 2DU
Tel: (01788) 573111 **Fax:** (01788) 536651 **DX:** 11686

RUSSELL HOUSE, 1550 PARKWAY, SOLENT BUSINESS PARK, WHITELEY, FAREHAM, SOUTHAMPTON, PO15 7AG
Tel: (01489) 881010 **Fax:** (01489) 881000 **DX:** 124693 WHITELEY

52-54 THE GREEN, BANBURY, OX16 9AB
Tel: (01295) 267971 **Fax:** (01295) 267751 **DX:** 24204

The Firm: Shoosmiths & Harrison is regarded as one of the most progressive and innovative national law firms. Gross fee income in 1997/98 was in excess of £31m, achieved through acting for a wide range of client organisations including internationally known blue chip companies, financial institutions, large private companies, public sector organisations, SMEs and partnerships. Additionally, a thriving private client practice concentrates principally on providing services to directors, executives and staff of business clients and other high net worth individuals.

The practice comprises six main sectors: Business Services, Property Services, Banking, Personal Injury, Private Client and Property Direct. In particular, the firm has an outstanding reputation in the Commercial, Financial Institutions and Insurance worlds.

A number of industry teams exist which draw together legal specialisms and industry-specific knowledge. Perhaps most well known are the Transport, Food, New Homes, Construction and Marine teams.

With offices in six strategic locations, clients can access large local resources backed by additional national strength and expertise when required. All offices are integrally linked through wide area computer and telecommunications networks and videoconferencing, providing clients with access to the resources of the whole firm comprising over 950 personnel.

Shoosmiths & Harrison actively encourages and assists clients to instigate service agreements which clearly set out the service standards demanded of their lawyers and the agreed charging basis including, where possible, an estimate or fixed fee quotation. This helps to build the trust and respect which is essential to establishing mutually beneficial business relationships.

Corporate: *Contact:* Nigel Thorne
Employment: *Contact:* Peter Ellis
Intellectual Property: *Contact:* John Hill
EC/International: *Contact:* Kit O'Grady
Computer: *Contact:* Karen Harrison
Debt Recovery: *Contact:* Richard Gwynne
Insolvency: *Contact:* Neil Bradshaw, Andrew Pickin
Lending Arrears (Commercial): *Contact:* Chris Cox
Lending Arrears (Domestic): *Contact:* Andrew Tubbs
New Homes: *Contact:* John Peet
Construction: *Contact:* David Bispham
Planning: *Contact:* Chris Waumsley
Environmental Health: *Contact:* Ron Reid
Environmental: *Contact:* Grania Thompson
Commercial Property: *Contact:* Nigel Haynes
Banking and Commercial Lending: *Contact:* John Temple
Personal Injury: *Contact:* John Spencer
Defendant PI: *Contact:* Michael Murray
Food Law: *Contact:* Ron Reid
Transport: *Contact:* Jane Raca
Property Direct: *Contact:* Andrew Tubbs
Commercial Finance: *Contact:* Nick Bradley
Domestic Property: *Contact:* David Inch
Private Client, Trust, Tax, Wills: *Contact:* David Endicott
Family: *Contact:* Suzanne Kingston
Financial Services: *Contact:* Keith Halford

Managing partner:	Graham New
Number of partners:	69
Assistant solicitors:	105
Other fee-earners:	268

WORKLOADS	
Insurers	39%
Business services	29%
Property services	23%
Private client	9%

SHOOSMITHS&HARRISON
SOLICITORS

SHORT RICHARDSON & FORTH 4 Mosley St, Newcastle upon Tyne, NE1 1SR
Tel: (0191) 232 0283 **Fax:** (0191) 261 6956 **DX:** 61037 **Ptnrs:** 5 **Asst solrs:** 5 **Contact:**
Mr M.C. Short *A mainly commercial firm best known for employment law and commercial property.*

WORKLOADS			
Employment law	35%	Civil litigation	22%
Commercial property	22%	Company and commercial	18%
Private client	3%		

SHULMANS 21 York Place, Leeds, LS1 2EX *Tel:* (0113) 245 2833 *Fax:* (0113) 246 7326
DX: 706958 Leeds Park Square *Ptnrs:* 7 *Asst solrs:* 8 *Other fee-earners:* 13

SIDLEY & AUSTIN

1 THREADNEEDLE STREET, LONDON, EC2R 8AW
Tel: (0171) 360 3600 **Fax:** (0171) 626 7937 **DX:** 580 LONDON CITY **Email:** LFELMINGHAM@SIDLEY.COM **Internet:** WWW.SIDLEY.COM

This leading international law firm gives advice in all major areas of commercial activity. Its London practice comprises principally English solicitors with particular expertise in banking, structured finance, information industries, taxation, corporate finance, property and corporate law.

The Firm: Sidley & Austin was founded in Chicago in 1866 and established in London in 1974 where it operates as a multinational partnership. It has offices in eight centres of commerce across the globe. Clients include many of the world's leading institutions, banks and businesses.

The London practice aims to maintain the firm's tradition of furnishing high quality, cost-effective advice in a collegiate environment. It has adopted a strategy of matching its clients' requirements with customised advice, emphasising long-term client relationships.

Lawyers in the office have extensive European practice experience and can assist clients with matters within the European Union and elsewhere. Teams of lawyers are quickly mobilised, and carefully managed, to assist clients wherever their needs arise. The English lawyers are supported by US-qualified lawyers resident in London and in the other offices of the firm and by relationships with leading independent law practices around the world.

Types of Work Undertaken: Expertise in banking and structured finance covers such areas as banking regulations, domestic and international lending, single bank and syndicated facilities, project finance, trade finance and capital markets. Asset securitisation is a particular strength and work in this field is carried out for originators, underwriters, credit enhancers, liquidity banks and credit rating agencies. The London office works closely with lawyers in the firm's US offices in adapting US financing techniques to European and other non-US assets and markets.

The firm's information industries expertise covers all aspects of telecoms, IT, IP and media, and includes software development, electronic publishing, electronic banking and satellite services. Extensive knowledge of domestic and international regulations underpins the firm's advice in these matters. Taxation advice is provided by the London office regarding both domestic and international transactions, including mergers and acquisitions, joint ventures, corporate finance, banking and structured finance, commercial property and asset finance.

Advice on corporate finance and commercial matters includes mergers, acquisitions and takeovers, joint ventures, flotations company formations, inward investment and employment law. The firm's wide-ranging knowledge of the telecommunications, utilities and other regulated industries gives it special expertise concerning the privatisation of state-owned enterprises.

Property and property finance expertise includes debt and equity based financing, development arrangements, acquisitions and disposals and institutional investment work.

Managing partner:	John Edwards
Resident Partners:	10
Assistant Solicitors:	26
Other Fee-earners:	9

CONTACTS	
Banking regulation	Graham Penn/Sarah Smith
Banking, trade & project finance	Howard Waterman
Capital Markets	Jane Borrows
Corporate	Mark Pinder
Information Industry	John Edwards/Gill Andrews
Intellectual Property	Peter Langley
Property	Julian Goodman
Structured finance	Jane Borrows/Graham Penn/ Robert Plehn/Sarah Smith
Tax	Drew Scott
US matters	Robert Plehn

SILKS

BARCLAYS BANK CHAMBERS, 27 BIRMINGHAM ST, OLDBURY, WEST MIDLANDS, B69 4EZ
Tel: (0121) 511 2233 **Fax:** (0121) 552 6322 **DX:** 20876 OLDBURY 2

The Firm: Founded by the present senior partner in 1953 Silks have expanded into a practice having substantial company clients including public companies, without losing sight of its original roots in criminal, matrimonial work and domestic conveyancing.

Principal Areas of Work:

Criminal: Long established practice defending clients in local Magistrates' Courts and Crown Courts.

PI & Civil Litigation: Broad range of litigation work with recent membership at both offices on Accident Line panel with Partners and support staff specialising in personal injury claims.

Conveyancing: Domestic and Commercial. Sales and purchases of domestic, commercial and industrial properties, leases and tenancy agreements.

Matrimonial/Child Care/Welfare: Members on Children panel regularly representing children and parents in Magistrates' and County Courts. Experienced matrimonial lawyers and trained welfare advisers.

Company and Commercial: Company formations, sales and purchase of companies and businesses, shareholder agreements, service agreements and general commercial advice.

Wills and Probate: Including advice on inheritance tax and planning.

Employment & Licensing: One Partner has twenty years experience representing clients, including a retail plc, in Tribunals throughout the UK and advising on contractual claims and general employment matters.

Crime: *Contact:* T.J. Bytheway. *3 Partners.*

Employment: *Contact:* J.B. Burn. *1 Partner.*

Nature of Clientele: Clients include private individuals, small and medium-sized companies, and three PLCs.

Agency Work: Crime: *Contact T.J. Bytheway;* Matrimonial: *Contact T.J. Bytheway.*

Languages Spoken: Hindi, Urdu, Punjabi.

Managing partner:	J.B. Burn
Senior partner:	J.G. Silk
Number of partners:	6
Assistant solicitors:	2
Other fee-earners:	12

WORKLOADS	
Conveyancing	29%
Others	29%
Family/Matrimonial	13%
Company & commercial	12%
Trust & probate	9%
Personal Injury	8%

CONTACTS	
Commercial property	K A H Jones
Company & commercial	J G Silk
Crime	T J Bytheway
Employment	J B Burn
Litigation	J B Burn
Matrimonial	T J Bytheway
Residential property	K A H Jones

SILVERBECK RYMER

HEYWOODS BUILDING, 5 BRUNSWICK STREET, LIVERPOOL, L2 0UU
Tel: (0151) 236 9594 **Fax:** (0151) 227 1035 **DX:** 14189 LIVERPOOL **Email:** SILVER_RYMER@MSN.COM

THORNWOOD HOUSE, COUNTY SQUARE, NEW LONDON ROAD, CHELMSFORD, CM2 0RG
Tel: (01245) 293910 **Fax:** (01245) 351661 **DX:** 89723 CHELMSFORD 2

The Firm: Silverbeck Rymer was founded in 1946 and is a niche firm focusing on Civil Litigation. Primarily, it services the insurance industry.

For over a decade, Silverbeck Rymer's litigation work has grown organically year on year. This has required an increase in staffing levels, larger premises, and in 1997 the opening of a second office.

The firm has a strong business focused Partnership which sustains its competitive advantage by accurate and thorough research providing a comprehensive understanding of client needs.

Silverbeck Rymer has retained a strong and prestigious client base over many years, and is constantly increasing its market share of business.

Principal Areas of Work: Silverbeck Rymer is a leading specialist firm in the field of litigation, and over a number of years, it has developed particularly close links with the insurance industry. Its range of services is constantly being developed to meet changing client needs. Dedicated departments are in operation to retain focus and enhance the specialism of skills.

Silverbeck Rymer represents over 20 major insurance companies, including major main line and legal expense insurers for whom it acts in either Plaintiff or Defendant Litigation. It also represents its insurance clients in defended road traffic and liability claims and insurance fraud. One of its primary focus areas is acting for legal expense insurers in the area of plaintiff personal injury litigation in all liability areas, contractual disputes, debt recovery and actions in tort.

Also, the firm has a technical personal injury unit which is headed up by the Senior Partner. This is one of the fastest growing departments within the firm and exists to answer insurance company clients requirements for expertise in catastrophic and serious personal injury claims. The firm has a panel of prestigious evidential experts and has strong connections with the Senior Bar.

Senior partner:	James Rymer
Managing partner:	Patricia Ewen
Number of partners:	6
Assistant solicitors:	29
Associates:	4

WORKLOADS	
Plaintiff Litigation	42%
Defendant Litigation	35%
Catastrophic personal injury	18%
Commercial Litigation	5%

CONTACTS	
Catastrophic Personal Injury and Insurance Fraud	
	James Rymer
Defendant Insurance	Charles Rymer
Plaintiff Personal Injury and Commercial Litigation	
	Patricia Ewen

Continues overleaf

Silverbeck Rymer prides itself on thorough file management and planning across all departments of the firm which keeps cases on track. This is particularly relevant in the technical personal injury litigation department. Matters are handled with skill, efficiency and cost effectiveness within parameters and protocols agreed with clients.

Finally Silverbeck Rymer has a large personal injury department dedicated to the industrial sector. Amongst its clients is a large national organisation which was created to improve the position of miners and other emplyees who have suffered employment-related injury or illness. Silverbeck Rymer practises from prestigious listed buildings in both the heart of Liverpool's business community and in Chelmsford Essex.

SILVER SAVORY SMITH

15-17 CASTLE STREET, CAMBRIDGE, CB3 0AH
Tel: (01223) 562001 **Fax:** (01223) 518310 **DX:** 88009 CAMBRIDGE 1

The Firm: This young successful firm offers a specialist range of legal services and is widely recognised as a leading advocacy practice. The firm obtained a Legal Aid Franchise in January 1995. They deal almost exclusively in litigation. Their main emphasis is placed upon child-care, criminal law, family law and civil, where the specialisation is in personal injury, contract, employment, and actions against the police.

Sen & Manag partner:	Raphael Silver
Number of partners:	3
Assistant solicitors:	5
Other fee-earners:	2

Child care: *Contact:* Raphael Silver; **Crime**: *Contact:* Alex Savory; **Matrimonial**: *Contact:* Suzanne Smith

THE SIMKINS PARTNERSHIP

45-51 WHITFIELD ST, LONDON, W1P 6AA
Tel: (0171) 631 1050 **Fax:** (0171) 436 2744 **DX:** 7 CH.LN **Email:** SIMKINS@SIMKINS.COM **Internet:** HTTP://WWW.SIMKINS.COM

The Firm: The Simkins Partnership is a commercial law firm providing a wide range of legal services with a particular focus on the media, entertainment, marketing and leisure industries.

The firm was established in 1963, since when its film and music law work have steadily developed to form the core of one of the largest and most broadly-based media practices in Europe. The Simkins Partnership is also a leading firm in related areas such as theatre, television, advertising and marketing, sport, publishing, digital media and photography.

The firm's various specialist groups are complemented by general departments; the corporate, litigation, property and private client departments act for a wide range of individual and corporate clients, again with an emphasis on digital media and entertainment.

Great emphasis has always been placed on the firm's network of contacts, both at home and overseas, and the firm maintains close links with relevant trade associations and other industry bodies. The firm is the UK member of Advertising Law International, a worldwide network of law firms specialising in advertising and marketing law, and over the years has assembled a network of contacts with media law firms throughout the world.

Principal Areas of Work:

Media and Entertainment: Including film and television production, distribution and finance, cable, video, theatre, music, radio, sport, publishing, digital media and photography.

Advertising and Marketing: The firm advises major advertisers and many of the largest UK advertising agencies on a wide range of issues including domestic and international copy clearance, regulatory matters and artist and client contracts.

Corporate: The corporate department advises on all types of transaction in its field and has extensive experience in corporate finance and the disposal and acquisition of businesses and companies, particularly in the media and entertainment sector.

Property: The property department is experienced in all types of property work including the management, acquisition and disposal of substantial portfolios.

Litigation: The department is broadly divided into media litigation and commercial. The media group covers intellectual property, defamation and disputes involving the specialist media departments. Commercial litigation includes employment, property, travel and international trade and commodities.

Family: The family department is one of the leading practices in its field and advises clients on all aspects of family law. Because of the firm's focus the department is particularly experienced in advising entertainers and other high profile individuals.

Private Client: The private client department advises on such matters as wills, trusts, domestic conveyancing and personal taxation. Additionally, there is a substantial volume of immigration and nationality work for both private individuals, performing artists and corporate clients.

Senior partner:	Michael Simkins
Number of partners:	22
Assistant solicitors:	10
Other fee-earners:	5

WORKLOADS	
Media & Entertainment	60%
Other	40%

CONTACTS	
Advertising	Charles Swan
Commodities	Nick Fenner
Competition	Tony Quick
Corporate	Paul Walker
Digital Media	Robin Hilton
Employment	Roger Billins
Family	Howard Stacey
Film	Nigel Bennett
Immigration & work permits	Vanessa Hall-Smith
Litigation:General	Roger Billins
Litigation:Media	Dominic Free
Music	Julian Turton
Photography	Charles Swan
Private client	Bob Rutteman
Property	Cyrus Fatemi
Publishing	Julian Turton
Sport	Nigel Bennett
Television & Video	Antony Gostyn
Theatre	David Franks
Travel	Nicola-Jane Taylor

THE SIMKINS PARTNERSHIP
SOLICITORS

SIMMONDS CHURCH SMILES

13 BEDFORD ROW, LONDON, WC1R 4BU
Tel: (0171) 242 9971 **Fax:** (0171) 405 0874 **DX:** 101 LONDON **Email:** SCS@LINK.ORG

The Firm: A respected, medium-size Holborn firm with branches in Tunbridge Wells and (as 'Corsellis') in Wandsworth. Founded in 1842, it has a comprehensive practice with a wide client base. The firm has international contacts, particularly in New Zealand and Hong Kong, and experience in Privy Council work. Partners of the firm are members of the Law Society's Personal Injury and Medical Negligence Panels. One partner is a Solicitors' Family Law Association trained mediator.

Principal Areas of Work: The firm has a high reputation for its skill and experience, with particular emphasis on company and commercial work (including commercial property), plaintiff personal injury (including claims against the Ministry of Defence) and professional negligence (including medical, dental and solicitors), employment, matrimonial and probate/ trust work.

Senior partner:	William R. Bennett
Number of partners:	11
Assistant solicitors:	2
Other fee-earners:	10

WORKLOADS	
Civil Litigation and Family	35%
Company/Commercial/Employment	25%
Property and Environment	20%
Trust, Probate and Tax	20%

SIMMONS & SIMMONS

21 WILSON STREET, LONDON, EC2M 2TX
Tel: (0171) 628 2020 **Fax:** (0171) 628 2070 **DX:** 12 **Email:** SIMMONS-SIMMONS.COM

The Firm: Simmons & Simmons is an international law firm providing advice worldwide to corporations, governments and other institutions through its network of offices and other associations and alliances. The firm was founded over 100 years ago in 1896. Since that time the firm's growth has been continuous. Since the early 1960s the firm has been committed to developing an international practice. Offices were opened in 1962 in Brussels, in 1979 in Hong Kong, in 1988 in Paris, in 1990 in New York, in 1992 in Lisbon, in 1993 in Milan, in 1994 in Abu Dhabi, in 1995 in Shanghai and in 1997 in Rome. In 1997 the firm also established an International Securities Unit with US firm Fried, Frank, Harris, Shriver & Jacobson which combines English and US lawyers, working together in teams, to provide a full international securities law service. The firm also has strong international practices serviced from its overseas offices and through its alliances advising clients in, for example, Japan, Australia, India, Thailand, Korea, Taiwan, Sweden, Germany, Spain, Poland and Brazil.

The firm has 157 partners, with 32 partners overseas and a total staff worldwide of over 1,400. Its mission is to use their legal skills to help clients achieve their commercial and business objectives. The firm has a culture of business management and development in which every member of the firm is involved. The firm prides itself on being human, open and continually seeking to improve itself.

Quality of service delivery is recognised to be at the heart of good legal practice. The firm has developed its own unique project management system which ensures legal advice is delivered as efficiently and effectively as possible within budget. It has also invested heavily in technology. It is the first City firm to have linked its offices using a data communication link which will enable common access to and transfer of complex information above and beyond basic word processing and e-mail information.

Languages spoken in the firm include English, French, German, Spanish, Italian, Swedish, Portuguese, Dutch, Greek, Mandarin, Japanese, Russian, Czech, Slovakian, Polish, Cantonese, Afrikaans, Hungarian, Latvian, Hindi, Arabic and Vietnamese.

Principal Areas of Work: As a leading international law firm, Simmons & Simmons has particular expertise in mergers & acquisitions, privatisations, venture capital, international equity, corporate finance, major projects and PFI, financial services, capital markets products, repackagings, securitisations, corporate treasury and bank lending.

It is also able to provide a strength and depth of quality advice in commercial law, EC and competition, intellectual property, communications and media law, development and construction work, property and planning, environmental law, energy, biotechnology, railways, all forms of dispute resolution, employment and pensions advice and taxation. Other areas of expertise include insolvency, structured finance, unit trusts, insurance, commodities, asset finance, entertainment, sports, shipping and advice on private capital to individuals.

Managing Director:	Alan Morris
Senior Partner:	Bill Knight
Worldwide	
Number of partners:	157
Assistant solicitors:	388
Other fee-earners:	213

WORKLOADS	
Corporate Finance and Company	41%
Commercial/Intellectual Property/EC	15%
Property	14%
Litigation	12%
Banking and Capital Markets	10%
Tax	7%
Environmental	1%

CONTACTS	
Banking	Graham Rowbotham/Gordon Stewart
Capital Markets	David Dickinson/John Russell
Collective Investment Schemes	Iain Cullen
Commercial Law	Edwin Godfrey/Jeremy Sivyer
Commodities	Jonathan Melrose
Computer Law	Rowan Freeland
Construction	Robert Bryan
Corporate	Jerry Walter
Corporate Finance	William Charnley
EC & Competition	Peter Freeman/Martin Smith
Employment	Janet Gaymer
Energy	Jerry Walter/Andrew Campbell
Environmental	Stephen Tromans/Kathryn Mylrea
Financial Services	Richard Slater
Immigration	Hilary Belchak
Insolvency	John Houghton
Insurance	Christopher Braithwaite/Jane Newman
Intellectual Property	Kevin Mooney/Helen Newman
Litigation (commercial)	Paul Mitchard/Philip Vaughan
Litigation (property)	Carol Hewson
Major Projects	Ken Woffenden
Media	Helen Newman
Pensions	Charles Scanlan
Pharmaceuticals	Kevin Mooney
Planning	Stephen Elvidge
Private Client	Caroline Garnham
Privatisation	Roger Butterworth
Property (commercial)	Alan Butler
Securitisation	James Bresslaw
Shipping	Quentin Bargate
Tax (corporate)	Peter Nias/Heather Savage
Telecoms	Christopher Watson/Tom Wheadon
Venture Capital	Alan Karter

SIMONS MUIRHEAD & BURTON

50 BROADWICK STREET, SOHO, LONDON, W1V 1FF
Tel: (0171) 734 4499 **Fax:** (0171) 734 3263 **DX:** 44738 SOHO SQ **Email:** SMAB@DIRCON.CO.UK

The Firm: Simons Muirhead & Burton, founded in 1972 in Covent Garden as a human rights and criminal practice, is now established in Soho to service the expanding media side of its client base. The firm, which aims to provide a quality service at competitive rates, undertakes work for commercial and private clients and operates the legal aid system in all its practice areas.

Principal Areas of Work: Simons Muirhead & Burton's core businesses are in media law, both contentious and non-contentious, and in its wide-ranging criminal law practice.

Media and Entertainment: (*Contact:* Simon Goldberg). Particularly films, television, theatre and publishing.

Civil Litigation: (*Contact:* Razi Mireskandari). Specialising in media, defamation and intellectual property.

Criminal Defence Work: (*Contacts:* Corporate Fraud – David Kirk. General Crime – Anthony Burton and Steven Bird)

Corporate Investigations: (*Contact:* David Kirk)

Immigration and Nationality: (*Contact:* Larry Grant).

Privy Council: (*Contact:* Angela Horne). Civil and criminal cases.

Civil Liberties and human rights cases: (*Contact:* Larry Grant). The firm also undertakes company and commercial work, commercial and residential conveyancing, employment and charity law.

The firm has opened an office in Wandsworth, principally to undertake general criminal work (*Contact:* Steven Bird).

Agency Work: 1. The location of the firm enables it to service cases in the High Court and all central London courts and tribunals.
2. The firm also acts as Privy Council agents.

Senior partner:	Anthony Burton
Number of partners:	9
Assistant solicitors:	6
Other fee-earners:	9

WORKLOADS	
Criminal litigation	43%
Media law	16%
Civil litigation	14%
Immigration	12%
Conveyancing	8%
Company and commercial law	7%

CONTACTS	
Civil litigation	R. Mireskandari
Commercial fraud	D.N. Kirk
Company and commercial	S.M. Goldberg
Conveyancing	D.G. Michaels
Crime	A.C. Burton & S. Bird
Immigration	L.A. Grant
Investigations	D.N. Kirk
Media/entertainment	S.M. Goldberg

SIMPSON & MARWICK WS

18 HERIOT ROW, EDINBURGH, EH3 6HS
Tel: (0131) 557 1545 **Fax:** (0131) 557 4409 **DX:** 161 EDINBURGH

The Firm: Simpson & Marwick is a civil litigation practice specialising in personal injury, professional negligence and commercial litigation. From offices in Edinburgh, Glasgow, Aberdeen and Dundee the firm represents clients in Courts throughout Scotland. The firm has particular expertise in defender reparation work and provides a partner-led service to a wide range of clients involved in the insurance industry throughout the UK. Defence organisations, pharmaceutical companies, oil companies and several prominent professional bodies are also numbered amongst the firm's corporate clients. In recent years the firm has grown considerably, particularly in Glasgow and Aberdeen, and has developed new areas of specialisation including healthcare law and building contract litigation. The firm's team of litigators is one of the largest and most experienced in the country.

Principal Areas of Work:

Personal Injury: Most partners are experienced in handling claims ranging from catastrophic injury to industrial diseases, accidents at work and road traffic cases.

Professional Indemnity: The firm acts for a range of professionals including architects, surveyors, accountants, engineers and other solicitors.

Medical Negligence: The healthcare law team comprises two partners, one with extensive experience in the NHS and one who was formerly a qualified GP.

Major Accident Actions: These include the Piper Alpha disaster inquiry and subsequent litigation, the Chinook, Brent Spar and Cormorant Alpha helicopter crashes and the Pan Am litigation following the Lockerbie crash.

Public and Employer Liability: Many insurers and Scottish local authorities instruct the firm in claims resulting from fire, flood, property and environmental damage. Advice is also provided to local authorities and insured companies in relation to health and safety issues and a range of employment law matters.

Other Offices:
93 West George Street, Glasgow, G2 1PB. *Tel:* (0141) 248 2666 *Fax:* (0141) 248 9590
Contact: Paul Wade
1 Carden Place, Aberdeen, AB10 1UT. *Tel:* (01224) 624924 *Fax:* (01224) 626590
Contact: Robert Leith
15 South Tay Street, Dundee, DD1 1NU. *Tel:* (01382) 200373 *Fax:* (01382) 200370
Contact: John MacEachern

Senior partner:	John Miller
Chairman:	Gordon Keyden
Number of partners:	15
Assistant solicitors:	23
Other fee-earners:	14

WORKLOADS	
Personal injury	35%
Professional negligence	30%
Commercial litigation	10%
Construction law	10%
Healthcare Law	10%
Property/private client	5%

CONTACTS	
Commercial litigation	Peter Anderson/Andrew Renton
Construction law	Andrew Renton
Family law	John Thomson
Health & Safety	Robert Leith/Gordon Keyden
Healthcare law	Dr Pamela Abernethy/ John Griffiths
Insurance law	Gordon Keyden/Douglas Russell
Local government	Michael Wood/Kate Shaw
Oil industry	Douglas Russell/Robert Leith
Personal injury	Gordon Keyden/Michael Wood
Private client	John Miller
Professional negligence	Dr Pamela Abernethy/ Peter Anderson
Residential property	Richard Loudon

SIMPSON MILLAR

101 BOROUGH HIGH STREET, LONDON BRIDGE, LONDON, SE1 1NL
Tel: (0171) 407 1851 **Fax:** (0171) 378 1881 **DX:** 39902 LONDON BRIDGE SOUTH

This firm specialises in personal injury litigation, acting on behalf of the victims of accidents. It also provides employment and medical negligence expertise to institutions and individuals. The firm has its headquarters in London and branch offices in Leeds, Bristol, Birmingham and Kendal.

The Firm: The firm was founded in the early 19th Century and has never moved from its birthplace at the foot of London Bridge. It originally served businesses around the historic port of London and to this day retains some of its original clients. Now a national firm with a spread of regional offices it remains committed to serving trades unions and their members as well as developing further commercial and individual clients.

The principal departments are: personal injury (contact Anthony Wontner-Smith or Peter Watson), medical negligence (contact Anna Corsellis), employment (contact Alistair Denham or Gill Sage), private client (contact Terry Yates).

Principal Areas of Work: All aspects of personal injury and disaster work are dealt with. Cases frequently handled include accidents sustained at work and road traffic accidents. Expertise is offered in industrial disease, post-traumatic stress disorder, noise induced deafness, repetitive strain injury and asbestos-related diseases. The firm has successfully pursued claims arising out of the disasters such as the Bradford City football stadium fire, the capsizing of the Herald of Free Enterprise, the Dunkeswick air crash in Yorkshire, the Cannon Street rail crash and the use of Thalidomide. Members of the firm are on the Law Society's Personal Injury Panel and the Association of Personal Injury Lawyers. The firm carries out a significant amount of conditional fee work for private clients and legally aided clients.

Medical negligence claims ranging form cerebral palsy and fatal accidents to mis-diagnosed fractures have been dealt with successfully. The firm has developed close links with Action for Victims of Medical Accidents and advises regularly not only on civil claims but also on NHS complaints procedures and mediation.

All aspects of employment and industrial relations law are dealt with, including drafting and interpretation of service contracts and Trades Union rules. Employment litigation services are also offered. The firm has recently been involved with ground breaking litigation concerning discrimination on the grounds of disability under the Disability Discrimination Act; it has acted for the sufferers of conditions such as asthma, epilepsy, diabetes and those with visual and physical impairments. A full training package is available for victims and for companies wishing to update their equal opportunities policies.

Private client work includes residential conveyancing, wills and probate, and family law.

Other Offices:

39 St Paul's Street, Leeds, LS1 2JG *Tel:* (0113) 2451554 *Fax:* (0113) 244 2369 *DX:* 14098 Leeds Park Square

20 Church Road, Lawrence Hill, Bristol, BS5 9JA *Tel:* (0117) 9559800 *Fax:* (0117) 9557915

Sloane Street, Birmingham B1 3BX *Tel: (0121) 233 2263 Fax:* (0121) 233 2265

Senior partner:	A. Wontner-Smith
Number of partners:	11
Assistant solicitors:	21
Other fee-earners:	8

WORKLOADS	
Personal injury	91%
Conveyancing	2%
Employment	2%
Other	2%
Probate, trust management & wills	2%
Matrimonial	1%

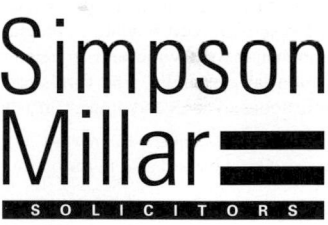

SIMPSON THATCHER & BARTLETT 99 Bishopsgate, 21st Floor, London, EC2M 3YH
Tel: (0171) 422 4000

SINCLAIR ROCHE & TEMPERLEY

ROYEX HOUSE, 5 ALDERMANBURY SQUARE, LONDON, EC2V 7LE
Tel: (0171) 452 4000 **Fax:** (0171) 452 4001 **DX:** 119510 FINSBURY SQUARE

The Firm: Sinclair Roche & Temperley is a major international law firm specialising in shipping, trade and transport. Founded in the City of London in 1934, the firm today also has offices in Hong Kong, Singapore, Shanghai and Bucharest. Sinclair Roche & Temperley provides high quality specialised legal advice to the international business community. Following the firm's alliance in January 1998 with Singapore-based banking and corporate law firm, Colin Ng & Partners, the firm has strengthened its presence in key Asian markets, in particular in Indonesia, Singapore and China.

Principal Areas of Work: In London, the Firm's principal practice areas include ship, asset and project finance, shipping and commercial litigation, arbitration and ADR, marine casualty and insurance, commodities, aviation, company/commercial, corporate finance, commercial property, oil and gas, insolvency and European Community law. In Hong Kong, the firm's practice comprises primarily shipping, litigation, company/commercial, commodities, arbitration and asset finance work. In Singapore, the firm handles shipping, litigation and arbitration and offshore asset and corporate finance. Sinclair Roche & Temperley is the leading Maritime law firm in Shanghai and has also developed an active practice in banking and inward investment.

All litigation partners have considerable expertise in shipping, in which the firm has a strong reputation, particularly relating to charterparty work, shipbuilding, ship sales and mortgage enforcement. The specialist maritime casualty department handles problems arising from major marine disasters and other marine environmental cases throughout the world.

In the area of asset finance, the firm's clients are predominantly European and Scandinavian financial institutions, shipowners, airlines, insurance companies and other commercial trading companies, including those involved in offshore oil and gas exploration.

The company/commercial department handles a significant volume of international and UK acquisitions, disposals and joint ventures. Members of the department have been increasingly active in advising on investment and privatisation projects in the developing markets of Central and Eastern Europe and the CIS. In Romania, the firm is extensively involved in investment advice and joint venture work as well as privatisation. The London office has a growing reputation in transport and leisure related company/commercial work and in active fund management.

The firm's aviation practice advises banks, leasing companies, manufacturers and airlines on the law and practice relating to the purchase, financing and leasing of aircraft, engines and components worldwide and in relation to registration, certification, route licensing and aviation law generally. The firm's tax unit is engaged in advising on the international tax implications of asset and project finance transactions and company/commercial matters.

The firm has established expertise in the areas of commercial property law, environmental law, privatisation and also in European Community law, especially competition issues.

Managing partner:	Jeff Morgan
UK	
Number of partners:	27
Assistant solicitors:	35
Other fee-earners:	27
International	
Number of partners:	10
Assistant solicitors:	16
Other fee-earners:	10

WORKLOADS	
Litigation	44%
Ship and project finance	26%
Company/commercial	10%
Marine casualty and insurance	8%
Commercial property	5%
Aviation	4%
EC	1%

CONTACTS	
Aviation and tax	David Relf
Commercial property	Martin Whitworth
Company/commercial	Kevin Dean
EC law	Alfred Merckx
Litigation	Ben Leach
Marine casualty and insurance	Joe Atkinson
Ship and project finance	
	George Hodgkinson and Ian Gaunt

SINCLAIR TAYLOR & MARTIN 9 Thorpe Close, Portobello Road, London, W10 5XL *Tel:* (0181) 969 3667 *Fax:* (0181) 969 7044 *DX:* 47601 Ladbroke Grove *Ptnrs:* 5 *Asst solrs:* 4 *Other fee-earners:* 4

SINGLETONS

THE RIDGE, SOUTH VIEW ROAD, PINNER, HA5 3YD
Tel: (0181) 866 1934 **Fax:** (0181) 429 9212 **Email:** ESSINGLETON@LINK.ORG

The Firm Founded in 1994 by well-known competition/ intellectual property solicitor, Susan Singleton, Singletons provides highly specialised advice on EC/ UK competition law, intellectual property, computer/ IT and commercial and EC law to well known public companies and others at competitive rates. Susan Singleton is author of a number of books including "EC Competition Law" and "EU Intellectual Property Law" (Financial Times 1996) and "Year 2000: Law and Liability" (Sweet & Maxwell 1998) and is editor of IT Law Today, Trading Law and Comparative Law of Monopolies.

The firm is a member of the Technology Law Practice, which is made up of similar technology law firms connected electronically and, when required, operating as a "virtual firm", without high overheads.

Managing partner:	E.Susan Singleton
Number of partners:	1

WORKLOADS	
Commercial law/ EC	30%
Competition law	30%
Intellectual property law	25%
Computer/ IT law	15%

CONTACTS	
All categories	Susan Singleton

SINTON & CO 5 Osborne Terrace, Newcastle upon Tyne, NE2 1QL *Tel:* (0191) 212 7800 *Fax:* (0191) 281 3675 *DX:* 62551 Jesmond *Ptnrs:* 10 *Asst solrs:* 5 *Other fee-earners:* 11

SISMAN NICHOLS 11 Elmdale Road, Clifton, Bristol, BS8 1SL *Tel:* (0117) 929 3333 *Fax:* (0117) 929 2200 *DX:* 37032 Clifton *Ptnrs:* 4 *Asst solrs:* 4 *Other fee-earners:* 6

S J CORNISH Twyford House, Kennedy Way, Tiverton, EX16 6RZ *Tel:* (01884) 243377 *Fax:* (01884) 243388

SKADDEN, ARPS, SLATE, MEAGHER & FLOM LLP 1 Canada Square, Canary Wharf, London, E14 5DS *Tel:* (0171) 519 7000 *Fax:* (0171) 519 7070 *Ptnrs:* 6 *Asst solrs:* 19 *Other fee-earners:* 6

SLATER HEELIS

71 PRINCESS ST, MANCHESTER, M2 4HL
Tel: (0161) 228 3781 **Fax:** (0161) 661 0048 **DX:** 14334

The Firm: The firm was founded in 1773 and the city offices occupy modernised Georgian premises in the centre of Manchester. Fee earners have access to computer and word processing networks.

Principal Areas of Work: General Description: Slater Heelis has been involved in the commercial life of Manchester for over 200 years and is now one of the leading firms in the North West, conducting an extensive commercial practice in the region and nationally on a broad client base. The firm has a strong all-round team which is friendly but highly professional, handling complex high quality work. The firm has expanded considerably in recent years and further expansion is anticipated in the corporate, property and litigation departments.

Company/Commercial: (*Contact Partner:* Christopher Dunn). The work of this department includes listed and other public company work, mergers, re-organisations, acquisitions and disposals of companies and businesses, management buy-outs and all aspects of legal services to all sizes of businesses.

Commercial Property: (*Contact Partner:* Steve Kinsey). *Work includes:* commercial conveyancing and development, support in relation to corporate and commercial transactions, landlord and tenant, planning and housing association work.

Residential Property: (*Contact Partner:* Jarlath Walsh). General domestic conveyancing.

Litigation: (*Contact Partner:* Kevin Jaquiss). The emphasis is on commercial litigation, involving preparations for trial and injunction applications where necessary in substantial High Court actions. There is a significant employment law and industrial tribunal practice. The firm is also well known for its personal injury litigation.

Private Client: (*Contact Partner:* Nick Shaw). The firm has a significant private client practice dealing with all aspects of family law, wills and tax planning, and all aspects of estates and trusts.

Matrimonial and Family: (*Contact Partner:* Mike Hamlin). The firm has a long-standing reputation in family law, personal injury, and other common law claims.

Banking and Insolvency: (*Contact Partner:* Egan Brooks). The firm handles live banking and recovery work, and acts for liquidators and receivers frequently on major receiverships.

Agency Work: All types of agency work are undertaken. *Contact:* Kevin Jaquiss, litigation partner in the Manchester office.

Nature of Clientele: Clients include industrial and property PLCs and numerous other business organisations including UK subsidiaries of multinationals together with government departments and co-operative societies. The firm acts as North Regional solicitors to a major clearing bank, as well as for other banks and financial institutions.

Other Offices: Lloyds Bank Building, 1 Tatton Rd, Sale, Greater Manchester M33 1XR. *Tel:* (0161) 969 3131. *Contact:* Jarleth Walsh.

Recruitment and Training: Six vacancies exist for articles with the firm commencing in 2000. Applicants should possess the academic and personal qualities necessary to deal with the challenging nature of the firm's work, a sense of commitment and the ability to work as part of a team, able to relate quickly to the needs of clients. Trainee solicitors are placed with each partner or senior solicitor to whom they are allocated for periods between four and six months, and after the first placement there is consultation over subsequent placements.

Senior partner:	E.R. Brooks
Number of partners:	20
Assistant solicitors:	23
Other fee-earners:	10

WORKLOADS	
Company/commercial	28%
Litigation	27%
Property	18%
Insolvency/banking	16%
Employment	6%
Private client	5%

CONTACTS	
Banking and insolvency	Egan Brooks
Company/commercial	Christopher Dunn
Housing association	Mike Gaskell
Litigation	Kevin Jaquiss
Matrimonial/ family	Mike Hamlin
Private client	Nick Shaw
Property (commercial)	Steve Kinsey
Property (domestic)	Jarlath Walsh

Slater Heelis
SOLICITORS

Continues overleaf

The training is largely practical, working on client matters from the outset with instruction in that context. Responsibility is given and supervision exercised according to developing ability. The firm seeks to recruit future solicitors from its trainees. Fifteen of the firm's partners were trained with the firm. Applications should be made by letter to Christopher Dunn at the Manchester office, and accompanied by a full CV.

SLAUGHTER AND MAY

35 BASINGHALL STREET, LONDON, EC2V 5DB
Tel: (0171) 600 1200 **Fax:** (0171) 600 0289 **DX:** 11 LONDON CITY EC2 **Internet:** WWW.SLAUGHTERANDMAY.COM

The Firm: Slaughter and May is one of the pre-eminent law firms in the world. It has a diverse and extensive international practice dealing with a wide range of corporate, commercial and financial work for UK, overseas and international clients.

The Approach: Slaughter and May aims to provide a professional service of the highest quality. The firm has a distinctive approach to the practice of law and encourages all its lawyers to gain a wide experience in commercial and financial matters so that they offer not only a depth of legal expertise but also versatility and a breadth of commercial experience. Slaughter and May is noted for its positive approach combining technical excellence, commercial awareness and an ability to provide practical, constructive solutions.

Internationally: International work is fundamental to the firm's practice both in London and in its overseas offices and Slaughter and May's lawyers travel widely. The firm has established close working relations with the leading independent law firms around the world so that the best local advice and service is available to each client wherever this is required.

Principal Areas of Work: Slaughter and May's practice covers a broad spectrum of corporate, commercial and financial work. Clients include industrial and commercial companies from all business sectors, banks, financial institutions and professional firms as well as governments, public bodies and other organisations. The principal areas of practice comprise:

Corporate and Corporate Finance: covering securities issues, flotations, mergers and acquisitions and corporate and commercial transactions generally including privatisation-related work.

Banking and Capital Markets: including international debt and equities issues and derivatives; international and domestic lending, structured finance and project and asset finance; and insolvency and asset-tracing work.

Financial Regulation: dealing with the regulatory aspects of corporate finance, fund management, securities and derivatives as well as supervision and regulation of banks, building societies and friendly societies, insurance companies and Lloyd's.

Litigation and Arbitration: dealing with a wide range of commercial proceedings and disputes including hearings before the High Court, the House of Lords and the Privy Council, domestic and international arbitrations, formal enquiries, investigations and inter-jurisdictional disputes.

Intellectual Property: advising on all aspects of the creation and ownership of intellectual property rights including the acquisition, development and licensing of computer systems and programs.

Property: including all types of commercial property transactions as well as advice on construction and engineering projects in the UK and overseas.

Environment: providing specialist advice on a broad spectrum of environmental issues.

Tax: advising on the tax aspects of corporate transactions and activities, including development of tax-efficient structures and instruments.

EC and Competition: providing advice from London and Brussels on UK and EC competition law, particularly in relation to acquisitions and mergers and joint ventures.

Pensions and Employment: including employee share benefit schemes, industrial conflicts, sex discrimination and equal pay problems and pensions and employment aspects of company acquisitions, disposals and takeovers.

Recruitment and Training: approximately 75 trainee solicitors are recruited every year. Candidates must have a good academic record. Financial assistance is available for the CPE and LPC in the form of a maintenance grant plus tuition and examination fees. For further information on Vacation Schemes and career opportunities for graduates and qualified lawyers, please write to Neil Morgan, Head of Personnel.

UK	
Number of partners:	91
Assistant solicitors:	270
Other fee-earners:	119
International	
Number of partners:	16
Assistant solicitors:	51
Other fee-earners:	23

WORKLOADS	
Corporate and financial	66%
Commercial litigation	10%
Property (commercial)	7%
Tax	6%
Pensions and employment	5%
EC and competition law	3%
Intellectual property	3%

CONTACTS	
Asset finance	Tom Kinnersley
Banking	Richard Slater
Capital markets	David Frank
Corporate finance	Michael Pescod
EC and competition	Malcolm Nicholson
Environment	Dermot Rice
Financial Regulation	Ruth Fox
General corporate/commercial	Nigel Boardman
Insolvency	Jonathan Rushworth
Intellectual property	Chris Hickson
Investment funds	Colin Hall
Litigation and arbitration	Richard Grandison
Pensions and employment	Edward Codrington
Project finance & energy	Martin Roberts
Property	Peter Langley
Tax	Steve Edge

SLAUGHTER AND MAY

SLEE BLACKWELL 10 Cross Street, Barnstaple, EX31 1BA *Tel:* (01271) 372128 *Fax:* (01271) 344885/22505 *DX:* 34952 Barnstaple *Ptnrs:* 9 *Asst solrs:* 8 *Other fee-earners:* 13

A.E. SMITH & SON

FROME HOUSE, LONDON ROAD, STROUD, GL5 2AF
Tel: (01453) 757444 **Fax:** (01453) 757586 **DX:** 58801 STROUD

STOKESCROFT, COSSACK SQUARE, NAILSWORTH, GL6 0DZ
Tel: (01453) 832566 **Fax:** (01453) 835 441 **DX:** 123329 NAILSWORTH **Email:** AE.SMITH.AND.SON@FARMLINE.COM

The Firm: Founded about 1835 the firm operates from offices in Stroud and Nailsworth. As well as dealing with a very wide range of commercial and private client work, the firm has particular experience in the fields of agricultural law, trusts and probate, property and estate development, advocacy, mental health and education (particularly special educational needs). The firm has a Legal Aid Franchise in Matrimonial & Family, Mental Health, Crime and Personal Injury. The firm also has connections with European lawyers.

Managing partner:	T.J. Mugford
Number of partners:	5
Assistant solicitors:	4
Other fee-earners:	1

CONTACTS	
Nailsworth Office	Tim Mugford
Stroud Office	John Bridges

SMITH FORTS 30 Great Underbank, Stockport, SK1 1ND *Tel:* (0161) 480 4043 *Fax:* (0161) 474 7491 *DX:* 19658 Stockport 1 *Ptnrs:* 7 *Asst solrs:* 11 *Other fee-earners:* 7

SMITH & GRAHAM Church Square Chambers, Hartlepool, TS24 7HE **Tel:** (01429) 271651 **Fax:** (01429) 231274 **DX:** 60651 **Ptnrs:** 6 **Asst solrs:** 10 **Other fee-earners:** 5 **Contact:** Dougal Swan *Other offices in Durham and Peterlee. The firm focuses on company/ commercial, civil litigation, medical negligence, licensing, leisure, crime, conveyancing, probate and family law. Established in 1888. Legal Aid franchise.*

WORKLOADS	
Commercial, property and licensing	25%
Crime	20%
PI and medical negligence	20%
Private client	18%
Litigation	17%

SMITH LLEWELYN PARTNERSHIP 18 Princess Way, Swansea, SA1 3LW **Tel:** (01792) 464444 **Fax:** (01792) 464726 **DX:** 92051 Swansea 3. **Ptnrs:** 5 **Asst solrs:** 7 **Other fee-earners:** 7 **Contact:** Mark Harvey *Undertakes all work but is also one of the largest plaintiff, personal injury and medical negligence practice in South Wales.*

WORKLOADS			
Medical Negligence	25%	Personal Injury	25%
Family	15%	Non Contentious	10%
Other	8%	Welfare	7%

THE SMITH PARTNERSHIP College Chambers, Uttoxeter New Road, Derby, DE22 3WZ *Tel:* (01332) 296888 *Fax:* (01332) 382301 *DX:* 11528 Derby *Ptnrs:* 13 *Asst solrs:* 28 *Other fee-earners:* 48

SMYTH BARKHAM

29 FLEET STREET, LONDON, EC4Y 1AA
Tel: (0171) 353 4777 **Fax:** (0171) 353 4666

The Firm: Smyth Barkham was formed on 1st May 1997 by Joyce Smyth and Caroline Barkham who moved from Theodore Goddard where they jointly spent over 25 years in practice. The Firm specialises in giving advice to high net worth Private Clients including entertainers, musicians, members of the aristocracy, entrepeneurs, trustees and beneficiaries.

Number of partners:	2
Assistant solicitors:	2

Principal Areas of Work:

Estate Planning and tax advice.

Offshore and onshore protection of assets.

Structuring of family affairs for tax savings and protection of family members.

Trusts for tax savings, asset protection and family protection.

Advice to Trustees and beneficiaries of trusts.

Formation of private and public Charities.

Advice to Charity Trustees and beneficiaries.

Advice to those newly divorced or widowed regarding their change in circumstances.

SONNENSCHEIN

ROYEX HOUSE, ALDERMANBURY SQUARE, LONDON, EC2V 7HR
Tel: (0171) 600 2222 **Fax:** (0171) 600 2221 **Email:** LONDON@SONNENSCHEIN.COM

The Firm: Established in Chicago in 1906, Sonnenschein, Nath & Rosenthal is a full service international law firm with more than 450 lawyers in eight offices. The London office opened in 1994 and has both English lawyers and lawyers licensed to practise in New York and Illinois. The firm provides high quality creative representation to clients through its unified office network and the application of advanced technology to legal service.

Principal Areas of Work:

Company and Commercial: Acquisitions and disposals, securities offerings, joint ventures, financings, loan documentation and general commercial matters.

Commercial Litigation: Including High Court, County Court, international commercial arbitration and alternative dispute resolution.

Employment: High Court and Tribunal litigation, transaction advice, contract and policy drafting, immigration.

Commercial Property: Including secured lending and commercial landlord and tenant work.

Insurance/Reinsurance: Formations, joint ventures, captives, coverage, new products, commercial and professional liability claims, international treaty disputes, financial institutions and credit risks, legal audits, commutations and insolvency.

Food and Cosmetics: Advising manufacturers, suppliers, distributors, importers and advisers to the food and cosmetics industries on food and cosmetics regulation and compliance issues in the UK and EU.

Other Offices: Chicago, Kansas City, Los Angeles, New York, San Francisco, St Louis and Washington D.C.

Managing partner:	Peter Borrowdale
Number of partners:	5
Assistant solicitors:	5
Other fee-earners:	4

CONTACTS	
Arbitration	David Hacking
Commercial Litigation and Employment	
	Colin Harvey
Commercial Property	Rupert Jones
Company/Commercial	Peter Borrowdale/
	Antoinette Jucker
Corporate Finance and Banking	Jonathan Griffiths
Food and Cosmetics	Hilary Ross
Insurance/Reinsurance	Peter Schwartz

SPARLING BENHAM & BROUGH 3 West Stockwell St, Colchester, CO1 1HQ **Tel:** (01206) 733733 **Fax:** (01206) 564551 **DX:** 3607 **Email:** Mail@sparlings.co.uk **Ptnrs:** 9 **Asst solrs:** 4 **Other fee-earners:** 3 **Contact:** John Hawkins, Robert Jacklin, Martyn Carr *General practice established over 100 years with offices in Colchester, Frinton-on-Sea and Manningtree.*

WORKLOADS	
Litigation	35%
Probate and trusts	35%
Company and commercial	10%
Conveyancing	10%
Family and matrimonial	10%

SPEECHLY BIRCHAM

BOUVERIE HOUSE, 154 FLEET ST, LONDON, EC4A 2HX
Tel: (0171) 353 3290 **Fax:** (0171) 353 4825/4992 **DX:** 54 **Email:** SPEECHLY@SPEECHLY.CO.UK

The Firm: A City of London firm, Speechly Bircham's principal activities are in specialist areas of commercial law, with recognised strengths in corporate, property and litigation work. In addition, the firm has a highly regarded tax, private client and charity practice.

The firm provides a partner-led service which is structured to meet each client's individual needs and characterised by a strong commitment to high standards of professionalism and quality. Each client will have access to a partner who is responsible for the overall supervision of the client's business with the firm. Where required, the expertise of specialist practice groups is drawn upon, thereby providing a complete advisory service.

Speechly Bircham's clients include fully listed and other quoted companies, a wide range of private companies, institutions, banks, charities and professional firms, as well as trusts, families and individuals. From its strong UK base the firm also advises many overseas clients on UK legal issues and corporate transactions. It also advises UK clients doing business overseas by working with a well-established network of correspondent law firms, with particularly strong connections in continental Europe, North America, the Caribbean and South Africa.

Principal Areas of Work: The firm has a number of specialist practice groups, several of which are acknowledged by independent surveys to rank among the leading advisers in their field.

Corporate/Commercial: The firm's *Corporate Finance* group advises on all aspects of equity and debt capital raisings, whilst *Mergers and Acquisitions* experience ranges from the sale of family companies to corporate acquisitions, take-overs and divestments, cross-border acquisitions and joint ventures. The firm's *Banking and Finance* team acts across a range of credit transactions and regulatory matters.

The *Financial Services* group deals with regulatory and compliance issues and has an established reputation for its collective investment schemes work. The *Venture Capital* group acts on a broad range of financings and buy-outs.

The firm's internationally recognised *Corporate Tax* specialists advise on the domestic and international tax aspects of transactions, corporate structures and other activities.

Managing partner:	Mark Musgrave
Number of partners:	40
Assistant solicitors:	27
Other fee-earners:	28

WORKLOADS	
Corporate	30%
Litigation	25%
Property	25%
Private client	20%

CONTACTS	
Banking & Finance	Nick Janmohamed
CDR	Stephen Dobson
Charities	John Ward
Construction	Tim Raper
Corporate Finance	Michael Lingens
Corporate Tax	John Avery Jones
Employment and Employee benefits	Alan Julyan
Financial Services	Mervyn Couve
IT	Tom Shaw
Mergers & Acquisitions	Michael Lingens
Pensions	Xenia Frostick
Planning & Environment	Brian Convery
Private Clients	Richard Kirby
Property Investment and Development	
	Charles Palmer
Property Litigation	Graham Ling
Retail Property	Mark Hodgkinson
Venture Capital	Stephen Armstrong

The firm's *Information Technology* group combines expertise in information technology and telecommunications, and has considerable international experience.

Employment: Speechly Bircham has a recognised team of *employment* specialists who are active in both contentious and non-contentious work and work closely with the firm's experts in *pensions* and *employee benefits*.

Commercial Dispute Resolution: The *Commercial Dispute Resolution* group advises on all forms of national and international commercial disputes with a particular emphasis on banking, telecommunications, asset recovery and regulatory challenge work.

Commercial Property: Speechly Bircham aims to provide an integrated property service, which draws upon the expertise of the *Construction* group, *Development, Planning and Environment* teams and the *Property Litigation* group, all of which are consistently ranked among the leading advisers in their fields. In particular, the firm's *Property Investment* lawyers have an established reputation in advising on all aspects of property investment, development and management. The firm also advises prominent clients in the *Retail Property* sector.

Private Client: The firm's substantial and highly-rated *Private Client* practice advises individuals and families on all matters of personal wealth management. It has considerable experience of planning and implementing tax strategies, including setting up off-shore structures to protect assets from tax, exchange controls and other risks faced by clients operating in the international environment. In addition, Speechly Bircham is one of the UK's leading advisers to the *Charities* sector.

SPEECHLY BIRCHAM

SPICKETTS Gelliwastad House, 4 Gelliwastad Rd, Pontypridd, CF37 2AU *Tel:* (01443) 407221 *Fax:* (01443) 485789 *DX:* 44350 *Ptnrs:* 6 *Asst solrs:* 2 *Other fee-earners:* 3

SPIRO GRECH & CO Clifton House, 8 Four Elms Road, Roath, Cardiff, CF2 1LE *Tel:* (01222) 222255 *Fax:* (01222) 450162 *Ptnrs:* 2 *Asst solrs:* 2 *Other fee-earners:* 4

SPRAGGON STENNETT BRABYN 225 Kensington High Street, London, W8 6SA *Tel:* (0171) 938 2223 *Fax:* (0171) 938 2224 *Ptnrs:* 3 *Asst solrs:* 0 *Other fee-earners:* 1

SPRECHER GRIER

LINCOLN HOUSE, 300 HIGH HOLBORN, LONDON, WC1V 7JH
Tel: (0171) 544 5555 **Fax:** (0171) 544 5565 **DX:** 0041 **Email:** INFO@SPRGR.CO.UK **Internet:** WWW.SPRGR.CO.UK

The Firm: Sprecher Grier is a highly-motivated commercial law firm founded on the philosophy of providing pro-active, practical and results-oriented advice over a broad spectrum of commercial legal work. The firm has particular expertise in banking, corporate recovery and insolvency work for a client base which includes financial institutions, professional practices and major companies and has established an excellent reputation since its formation in 1984.

Senior Partners:	David Sprecher and Ian Grier
Number of partners:	7
Assistant solicitors:	3
Other fee-earners:	2

Principal Areas of Work:

Company/Commercial: (*Contact:* David Sprecher or Emma Shipp). The department has a strong reputation for handling all forms of acquisitions disposals and joint ventures including complex reconstructions. *Work includes:* mergers and acquisitions, MBOs, computer software agreements, employment contracts, banking and security documents and advice on a wide range of commercial matters.

Insolvency and Debt Recovery: (*Contact:* Ian Grier or Edward Judge). The firm is widely recognised as one of the UK's leading specialists in this area, and operates by combining effective legal advice with practical business action. Work involves advising insolvency practitioners on the technicalities of the law, assisting with liquidations, receiverships or petitions for administration orders and voluntary arrangements. Corporate rescue and restructuring is also an area of expertise. The debt recovery team offers speed and efficiency to obtain the best possible solution for clients.

Commercial Litigation: (*Contact:* Ian Grier or Peter Loosley). A wide range of contentious business is handled, focusing on the need to achieve a fast and cost-effective result for clients. *Work includes:* banking litigation, building and construction disputes, intellectual property matters (especially design and copyright), service contracts, disputes involving employment agencies and recruitment consultants, and property related actions.

Commercial Property: (*Contact:* Lesley Goring or Angela Robinson). A focus on broad business issues underlies advice on the acquisition and disposal of business premises, commercial Landlord and Tenant and disposal of property on behalf of financial institutions and insolvency practitioners.

SQUIRE & CO 49-50 St. Johns Square, London, EC1V 4JL **Tel:** (0171) 490 3444 **Fax:** (0171) 250 4087/4115 **DX:** 46617 Barbican **Email:** squires@squires.co.uk **Ptnrs:** 7 **Asst solrs:** 4 **Other fee-earners:** 9 **Contact:** Nicholas Squire *Professional indemnity, and all classes of liability business; insurance investigations; insurance and reinsurance disputes; construction; civil fraud; alternative dispute resolution; commercial litigation and arbitrations.*

SQUIRE SANDERS & DEMPSEY LLP Royex House, Aldermanbury Square, London, EC2V 7HR **Tel:** (0171) 776 5200 **Fax:** (0171) 776 5233 **Ptnrs:** 3 **Asst solrs:** 3 **Contact:** Joseph Markoski *International transactions, mergers and acquisitions, joint ventures, privatisations, corporate finance, capital markets, securities, infrastructure, project and asset financing, telecommunications, multimedia.*

STAFFORD YOUNG JONES

THE OLD RECTORY, 29 MARTIN LANE, LONDON, EC4R 0AU
Tel: (0171) 623 9490 **Fax:** (0171) 929 5704 **DX:** 176 LONDON

The Firm: Stafford Young Jones is a long established City of London practice serving the needs of both corporate and individual clients to a high professional standard, using modern methods and technology where appropriate whilst maintaining a friendly and personal service.

Managing partner:	Helen Wenham
Senior partner:	P.B. Adams
Number of partners:	11
Assistant solicitors:	3
Other fee-earners:	2

Principal Areas of Work:

Family law:(*Contact:* Paul Adams). Paul is a member of the SFLA and the firm is a member of the Relate Quality Partnership Scheme. Advice on all aspects of family law, including: separation and divorce; arrangements for children's residence and education; arrangements for contact with children; separation agreements and financial settlements.

Housing Association work:(*Contact:* Pamela Yelland). The firm acts for a considerable number of registered social landlords in the area of housing and landlord and tenant litigation.

Employment Law: (*Contact:* Paul Adams). Advice given to both employer and employee on a full range of employment issues.

General Litigation: (*Contact:* Andrew Strong). Experienced in all claims, including contractual and consumer disputes and personal injury litigation, acting for both Plaintiffs and Defendants; commercial litigation, particularly property litigation. Computerised and cost effective debt recovery for individual and corporate clients.

Wills and Probate: (*Contact:* Christopher Munday). Preparation of wills and living wills; Enduring Powers of Attorney; Inheritance Tax planning; administration of estates; advice to executors and beneficiaries on probate and succession law; variation of estates and the obtaining of grants of representation in England to the estates of foreign nationals.

Trusts & Personal Tax Planning: (*Contact:* Neil Fulton). Formation, management and administration of trusts; asset management and financial planning; Court of Protection work. The firm offers a Nominee Company service which is a sponsored member of CREST.

Residential Property: (*Contact:* Francis Backman). A fast and efficient service in the purchase and sale of freehold and leasehold property, short term letting and remortgages with specialist advice in the area of insolvency.

Commercial Property: (*Contact:* Martin Gaston). A comprehensive service acting for corporate and individual clients advising buyers and sellers, landlords and tenants and borrowers and lenders in the acquisition, disposal and management of commercial property with specialist advice in the area of insolvency.

Company and Commercial: (*Contact:* Terry Chandler). Advice on the formation, acquisition and disposal of commercial ventures and associated matters. Acting for financial institutions in the areas of lending and borrowing.

Recruitment and Training: The firm has a maximum number of 3 trainee solicitors. Prospective trainees should write to Paul Adams enclosing a CV.

Languages spoken: French, German and Portuguese.

STAFFURTH & BRAY York Road Chambers, Bognor Regis, PO21 1LT *Tel:* (01243) 864001 *Fax:* (01243) 860708 *DX:* 31212 *Ptnrs:* 5 *Asst solrs:* 4 *Other fee-earners:* 9

STAMP JACKSON AND PROCTER 5 Parliament Street, Hull, HU1 2AZ *Tel:* (01482) 324591 *Fax:* (01482) 224048 *Ptnrs:* 8 *Asst solrs:* 10 *Other fee-earners:* 12

STANLEY TEE & COMPANY High Street, Bishop's Stortford, CM23 2LU *Tel:* (01279) 755200 *Fax:* (01279) 758400 *DX:* 50404 Bishop's Stortford *Ptnrs:* 12 *Asst solrs:* 11 *Other fee-earners:* 6

STATHAM GILL DAVIES 55 New Cavendish Street, London, W1M 1RE *Tel:* (0171) 487 5565 *Fax:* (0171) 487 4409 *Ptnrs:* 8 *Asst solrs:* 2 *Other fee-earners:* 1

STEEDMAN RAMAGE WS

6 ALVA STREET, EDINBURGH, EH2 4QQ
Tel: (0131) 260 6600 **Fax:** (0131) 260 6610 **DX:** ED 95 **Email:** INFO@SRWS.CO.UK

AFTON HOUSE, 26 WEST NILE STREET, GLASGOW, G1 2PF
Tel: (0141) 242 6600 **Fax:** (0141) 242 6610 **DX:** GW14 **Email:** INFO@SRWS.CO.UK

The Firm: Steedman Ramage is one of Scotland's leading commercial practices offering broad experience in all of its departments and is currently best known for the quality of its commercial property services but with continued growth in other commercial areas.

Principal Areas of Work:

Commercial Property: (*Contact Partner:* Sandy Reid). The department is noted in particular for its involvement in the retail world and specialises in major land developments, all other types of property development, investment and funding, commercial leasing (for landlord and tenant), joint ventures, freehold and leasehold sales and purchases, property related aspects of cross-border corporate or commercial deals, planning, commercial finance and security work, relocation schemes and housing associations.

Corporate: (*Contact Partner:* James Blair). The department has a wide ranging practice with extensive experience in sales, acquisitions and mergers, management buy-outs, distribution agreements, European law, media and entertainment, insolvency, franchising, share schemes, intellectual property, joint ventures, publishing and all types of commercial contracts. The department has particular experience in all aspects of property finance and in property joint ventures (both UK and international).

Litigation: (*Contact Partner:* Kenneth Cumming). Practice areas include: commercial litigation generally and commercial property litigation in particular and other contractual disputes, mediation, arbitration, copyright and intellectual property, personal and corporate insolvency, employment and industrial tribunal work, debt recovery, personal injury and medical negligence, defamation, planning and environmental law, judicial review, interdict and reparation.

Construction: (*Contact Partner:* Mark Finlay). All aspects of construction and engineering work including contracts, appointments, warranties and all forms of dispute resolution.

Foreign Languages: French, German, Italian.

International Connections & Associated Offices: Member of International Bar Association, Union Des Avocats Europeen, Union Internationale Des Avocats.

Chairman:	Sandy Reid
Number of partners:	13
Assistant solicitors:	15
Other fee-earners:	7

CONTACTS	
Banking and Finance	Iain MacKinnon, James Blair
Commercial Litigation	Kenneth Cumming, Victoria Craig
Commercial Property	Sandy Reid, Iain McHardy
Construction	Mark Finlay
Corporate/Commercial	James Blair, Scott Kerr
Employment	Scott Kerr, Victoria Craig
Environment	Kenneth Cumming, David Ratter
EU and Competition	Scott Kerr
Housing Associations	Gregor Mair
Insolvency	Gregor Mair, Victoria Craig
IP and IT	Scott Kerr
Licensing	Victoria Craig
Media and Entertainment	Scott Kerr, James Blair
Planning	Sandy Reid, Kenneth Cumming
Retail	Iain McHardy, Iain McLean

SOLICITORS

STEELE & CO 2 The Norwich Business Park, Whiting Rd, Norwich, NR4 6DJ *Tel:* (01603) 627107 *Fax:* (01603) 625890 *DX:* 5218 *Ptnrs:* 14 *Asst solrs:* 12 *Other fee-earners:* 53

STEELE RAYMOND

RICHMOND POINT, 43 RICHMOND HILL, BOURNEMOUTH, BH2 6LR
Tel: (01202) 294566 **Fax:** (01202) 552285 **DX:** 7643 BOURNEMOUTH 1 **Email:** MAIL@STEELERAYMOND.CO.UK

The Firm: Steele Raymond was formed in 1979 and has expanded rapidly since that date, building up a wide range of business clients both in this country and abroad. The firm advises on all areas of company, commercial and business law, but also has a substantial private client practice.

Principal Areas of Work: General Description: *Work includes:* company and business sales and purchases, company formations and reorganisations, partnership matters, intellectual property, EC law, competition law, commercial contracts (including computer contracts), aviation, commercial property matters, town and country planning, environmental law, insolvency and commercial litigation, personal injury, professional and medical negligence, education law. The firm has a partner with a particular interest in canine law.

Nature of Clientele: The firm advises a wide range of clients including individuals, partnerships, housing associations, higher, further and other educational bodies, insolvency practitioners and private and public companies and insurance companies.

Other Offices: 31 West St, Wimborne, Dorset BH21 1JT. *Contact:* Mr. John Andrews. All areas of work are undertaken, other than criminal matters.

Agency Work: The firm undertakes work, other than criminal work, on an agency basis. *Contact:* Simon Outten or John Andrews.

Recruitment and Training: The firm has vacancies for a trainee solicitor and normally has vacancies for specialised staff in various parts of its practice. Strong emphasis is placed on training at all levels.

Foreign Connections: Increasingly the firm's work involves an overseas element, and strong contacts have been developed with legal firms overseas, especially in other EC countries and North America. Steele Raymond has achieved ISO 9001 accreditation for its complete range of services and holds a Legal Aid Franchise.

Managing partner:	David Steele
Chairman:	John Raymond
Number of partners:	12
Assistant solicitors:	7
Other fee-earners:	6

WORKLOADS	
Litigation	28%
Company and commercial	27%
Commercial property	25%
Education	10%
Private client	10%

CONTACTS	
Aviation/ medical negligence	John Andrews
Commercial litigation	Simon Outten
Commercial property	John Daniels/Bill Oliver
Company & comm.	Paul Longland/David Steele
Education	Bill Oliver
Employment	Simon Outten/Peter Rolph
Insolvency, Landlord & tenant	Julian Fenn
Partnership	John Raymond
Personal injury	John Andrews/Peter Rolph
Private client	Paul Causton
Residential developments	Sue Middleton
Taxation	Paul Causton

STEELE RAYMOND

STEPHEN RIMMER & CO 28 Hyde Gardens, Eastbourne, BN21 4PX *Tel:* (01323) 644222 *Fax:* (01323) 733034 *DX:* 6906 *Ptnrs:* 9 *Asst solrs:* 4 *Other fee-earners:* 8

STEPHENS INNOCENT 21 New Fetter Lane, London, EC4A 1AP *Tel:* (0171) 353 2000 *Fax:* (0171) 353 4443 *Ptnrs:* 7 *Asst solrs:* 13 *Other fee-earners:* 6

STEPHENSON HARWOOD

ONE, ST PAUL'S CHURCHYARD, LONDON, EC4M 8SH
Tel: (0171) 329 4422 **Fax:** (0171) 606 0822 **DX:** 64 CHANCERY LANE WC2

Stephenson Harwood is a major City firm with a considerable reputation for contentious and non-contentious expertise in the corporate/commercial, banking and financial services, shipping, property and private client fields. Putting a premium on technical excellence, responsiveness and commercial pragmatism, the firm delivers top quality results on time. Clients are served through an international network of offices and associations.

The Firm: Stephenson Harwood has a 160-year-old tradition of delivering a personal service to clients which include multinational corporates, public and private companies, large financial institutions, institutional investors, government and public bodies, insurance companies, professional partnerships and individuals. With an international capability, the firm's size and flexibility enable it to provide a closely-tailored response to clients' needs. It combines transactional flair, clear-cut advice and decisive action with a working atmosphere that clients appreciate. And in sectors where industry knowledge is the key, the firm's understanding of clients' businesses and markets means that it can provide even sharper and more precisely targeted advice. The firm focuses on finding innovative legal solutions and structures that meet clients' business objectives in a cost-effective way. It believes in looking after clients rather than simply processing their work, which includes ensuring that they are advised by the individual lawyers they have come to know and rely on. In all that it does, Stephenson Harwood is a client-centered practice.

Principal Areas of Work: Advising on a broad spectrum of corporate/commercial transactions, Stephenson Harwood has a well-established expertise in corporate finance. Specialised groups also offer extensive experience of fund management and the launching of funds; the regulatory aspects of the financial services market; intellectual property and IT; infrastructure projects; EU/competition matters; and employment and pensions issues. A dedicated group advises on all related tax questions.

Stephenson Harwood has a very high profile litigation and arbitration practice. Handling an extensive range of substantial commercial disputes, the firm is widely recognised for its expertise in complex fraud, asset tracing, money laundering, professional indemnity and insurance cases. It has established a pre-eminent reputation for its handling of regulation and corporate investigation work. It is also highly experienced in the successful deployment of ADR techniques.

The firm's established banking practice covers commercial lending and syndications, as well as more specialised areas such as trade and project finance, bringing an innovative and versatile approach to the wide range of transactions and issues on which it advises. The firm also has a considerable reputation for its insolvency work.

In the property field, Stephenson Harwood covers all aspects of commercial property (including tax issues), with a particular expertise in property investment; planning; property finance; office and retail development; management; urban regeneration; and PFI transactions.

The international shipping group is a full-service practice advising on finance, marine accidents (including collision and salvage) and commercial issues (such as P&I and marine insurance, and international trade). It also acts for clients in disputes.

Stephenson Harwood remains one of the few leading City law firms to undertake private client, family and matrimonial work. It has particular experience helping non-domiciled/non-resident clients.

Overseas Offices: Brussels, Guangzhou, Hong Kong, Madrid, Piraeus, Singapore. Associated with FIDAL, Société d'Avocats, France; Žurić i Partneri, Croatia; Elias Sp. Paraskevas Attorneys at Law 1933, Greece, Al Sarraf & Al Ruwayeh, Kuwait.

UK	
Number of partners:	60
Assistant solicitors:	95
Other fee-earners:	51
International	
Number of partners:	11
Assistant solicitors:	31
Other fee-earners:	20

CONTACTS	
Banking and Capital Markets	Tony Stockwell
Charities	Ann Phillips
Commercial Litigation	John Fordham
Commercial Property	Colin Mackenzie-Grieve
Company/Commercial	Tony Scales
Construction Litigation	Steven Wait
Corporate Finance	Judith Shepherd
Corporate Investigations/Asset-Tracing	
	John Fordham
Corporate Tax	John Carrell
Employment	Kate Brearley
Environment	David Cuckson
EU and Competition	Antony Mair
Family and Matrimonial	Jonathan Walsh
Fraud and Regulation/Business Crime	
	Tony Woodcock
Funds and Financial Services	Andrew Sutch
Information Technology	John Enstone
Infrastructure Projects & Privatisation	
	Colin Fergusson
Insolvency	Geoff Woolf
Insurance Insolvency	Peter Fidler
Insurance/Reinsurance Litigation	James Crabtree
Intellectual Property and Patent Agency	Tibor Gold
International Arbitration	Robin Neill
Pensions and Benefits	Michael Cowley
Private Client	Mark Baily
Private Finance Initiative	
	Peter Walters/David Cuckson
Professional Indemnity	Roland Foord
Project Finance	Tony Stockwell
Property Development	Marcel Haniff
Property Finance	Richard Light
Property Litigation	Ken Duncan
Shipping Admiralty	Robin Slade
Shipping Dry Litigation	Andrew Keates
Shipping Finance	Mark Russell
Town and Country Planning	Barry Jeeps
Trade and Project Finance	Tony Stockwell

STEPHENSONS 26 Union St, Leigh, WN7 1AT *Tel:* (01942) 608942 *Fax:* (01942) 679778 *DX:* 22504 *Ptnrs:* 17 *Asst solrs:* 30 *Other fee-earners:* 88

STEPHENS & SCOWN

25-28 SOUTHERNHAY EAST, EXETER, 2603
Tel: (01392) 210700 **Fax:** (01392) 274010 **DX:** 8305 EXETER **Email:** SOLICITORS@STEPHENS-SCOWN.COM

The Firm: Stephens & Scown is one of the largest firms in the South West with its head office in Exeter and three other offices in Cornwall, in St. Austell, Truro and Liskeard. It is a well established commercial and private client practice with an increasing number of national and international clients. Stephens & Scown was one of the first firms to be granted a legal aid franchise and currently holds franchises in nine categories. Three solicitors at the Exeter office have rights of audience in the higher courts. The firm has three solicitors who are members of the Law Society's Planning Panel, four on the Personal Injury Panel and four on the Child Care Panel.

Agency Work: All types of work undertaken.

Charges: Fees are normally charged on an hourly basis. Quotations are given for residential conveyancing but fixed fees can be agreed in advance for certain types of work including debt recovery.

Principal Areas of Work: The firm is divided into 7 main departments: Commerce, Litigation, Personal Injury, Magistrates Court & Crown Court, Family Law, Property and Private Client. Within these main departments are groups concentrating on more specialist areas of legal practice, including Banking, Corporate Finance, Employment, Debt, Agriculture, Planning and Environmental, Waste Disposal, Minerals, Domestic Conveyancing and Land Development. All departments are organised on a practice-wide basis.

Commerce: The firm handles all aspects of company and commercial work. Specialisms include sales and acquisitions, business start-ups and planning, joint ventures, company formations and reorganisation. Services include "Businesslink", an advice service for small and starter businesses. The firm is experienced in European matters and has a close association with the European Law Department of Exeter University.

Litigation: Activities include a substantial amount of banking work, particularly insolvency and repossessions with a high-turnover, low-cost debt collection system as well as dealing with building and construction disputes. There is also a specialist employment law unit providing employment law advice and handling industrial tribunal cases.

Personal Injury: The personal injury and medical negligence departments deal with a substantial workload of institutional and private work for both plaintiffs and defendants.

Magistrates Court and Crown Court: The firm has the largest criminal practice in Exeter and East Devon, including a large youth court practice, and has a significant presence in Cornwall.

Family: This department is one of the largest in the country, handling all aspects of family law ranging from large financial disputes to heavyweight public law/child care cases and more recently mediation.

Property: This includes the general sale and purchase of commercial property, property development and tenancy agreements. Stephens & Scown is one of the leading agricultural practices in the west country with work including tenancy law, milk quota regulations, tax planning and pollution claims. The firm is well-known for its expertise in the law relating to mineral extraction and waste disposal work, and other environmental issues. There is an important Land Development Unit.

Private Client: Three partners handle wills and probate and the firm also administers trusts and provides other financial advice.

Nature of Clientele: The firm has a wide client base ranging from major plcs and a full range of general commercial clients and institutions to smaller firms and individuals.

Languages Spoken: French, Spanish, German.

Recruitment: The firm recruits four trainee solicitors each year. There are annual vacancies for assistant solicitors and executives.

Other Offices:

St. Austell: 3 Cross Lane, Cornwall PL25 4AX
Tel: (01726) 74433 *Fax:* (01726) 68623 *DX:* 81251 St. Austell

Truro: Richmond Villa, 37 Edward Street, Cornwall TR1 3AJ
Tel: (01872) 265100 *Fax:* (01872) 279137 *DX:* 81203 Truro

Liskeard: 17 Dean Street, Cornwall PL14 4AB
Tel: (01579) 342745 *Fax:* (01579) 346771 *DX:* 81654 Liskeard

Senior partner:	Roger Keast
Chief Executive:	Richard Hoskin FCA
Number of partners:	33
Assistant solicitors:	26
Other fee-earners:	27

WORKLOADS	
Property	26%
Litigation	21%
Family	16%
Personal Injury	14%
Commerce	13%
Financial/Probate	5%
Magistrates Court/Crown Court	5%

CONTACTS	
Agriculture	Martin Clayden, Richard Jones
Commerce	Jonathan Church, Guy Curry
Debt collection	Brian Doyle, Mark Stubbs
Employment	Nigel Moore, Ian Pawley
Family	Peter Payne, Michael Lowry
Financial/Probate	Ian Pawley, Alan Williamson
Insolvency	Matthew Wald, Jonathan Church
Litigation	Chris Harper, Mark Stubbs
Magistrates/Crown Court	Stephen Nunn
Personal injury	Simon Middleton, Brian Doyle
Planning/Environment	Richard Hull, Ian Lamond
Property	Michael Beadel, Jonathan Hoggett

STEPIEN LAKE GILBERT & PALING

4 JOHN STREET, LONDON, WC1N 2EH
Tel: (0171) 655 0000 **Fax:** (0171) 655 0055 **DX:** 9 CHANCERY LANE

The Firm: The firm was founded in April 1991 formerly being the property department of one of the oldest firms in the City. The firm's major activities are in the commercial property field and this covers all aspects of commercial and residential development, banking, secured lending, investment, property finance and joint ventures.

Nature of Clientele: The firm acts for a number of banks, major commercial and residential developers and a number of UK and overseas investors. The firm also acts for a number of UK property investment funds and high net worth individuals.

Recruitment and Training: Recruitment Partner: M.W. Thomas.

Senior partner:	K.J. Stepien
Number of partners:	4
Other fee-earners:	4

CONTACTS	
Banking/Funding	K.J. Stepien
Development	T.M.D. Lake, M.W.Thomas
Investment	K.J. Stepien, S.P. Paling
Retail/Offices	S.P. Paling

STEVENS & BOLTON

1 THE BILLINGS, WALNUT TREE CLOSE, GUILDFORD, GU1 4YD
Tel: (01483) 302264 **Fax:** (01483) 302254 **DX:** 2423 GUILDFORD 1 **Email:** MAIL@STEVENS-BOLTON.CO.UK

The Firm: Stevens & Bolton is one of Surrey's largest firms, and is well known for its extensive commercial practice in Guildford. It has experienced litigation and commercial property departments, an established reputation in the field of company law, and is able to combine specialist taxation advice with its other areas of practice. The firm also has a strong private client office in Farnham, which has been particularly successful at attracting business away from City firms.

Principal Areas of Work:

Company/Commercial: (*Contact Partner:* Richard Baxter). The department is experienced in corporate finance and transactional work, including acquisitions and disposals of companies and businesses, management buy-outs, company restructurings, venture development capital and other business finance. A broad spectrum of other commercial matters is dealt with including computer law, intellectual property, employment, franchising, competition law and trading agreements.

Commercial Property and Planning: (*Contact Partner:* Michael Laver/James Mitchell). This department is equipped to handle a wide range of freehold and leasehold transactions, including funding and security issues, rent reviews, planning, taxation and environmental matters. The firm also provides a comprehensive service for developers, agricultural clients and residential property matters.

Litigation: (*Contact Partner:* Richard King). Work is predominantly UK/international contract disputes and professional negligence claims with particular growth in disputes handled in the IT, civil engineering, finance and leasing sectors. Specialist expertise is available on shareholder and partnership disputes, international trade, commercial property, insolvency and insurance matters, with separate units handling employment, debt recovery and personal injury work. Family law matters are dealt with by a unit with experience in complex financial cases, including those with an international element.

Private Client: (*Contact Partner:* Nicholas Acomb). The firm has a strong reputation in this area, advice ranging from wills and probate to personal tax planning including UK and offshore trusts. The firm also handles more complex institutional trust work, often for overseas clients. Charity work is also handled by this department.

Clientele: UK and overseas clients include listed public companies, large private companies, partnerships and individuals.

Other Offices:

5 Castle Street, Farnham, Surrey GU9 7HT.
Tel: (01252) 725040. *Fax:* (01252) 723501. *DX:* 32800 Farnham.

Managing partner:	Michael Laver
Senior partner:	Michael Hunter
Number of partners:	15
Assistant solicitors:	17
Other fee-earners:	4

WORKLOADS	
Company/ commercial	27%
Litigation	25%
Commercial property	20%
Private client	13%
Other property	11%
Family/matrimonial	4%

CONTACTS	
Commercial litigation	Richard King
Commercial property	Michael Laver/James Mitchell
Company/ commercial	Richard Baxter
Computer Law/IP	Tudor Alexander
Employment	Paul Lambdin
Family/ matrimonial	Caroline Gordon-Smith
Insolvency	Paul Lambdin
Personal Injury	Janet Waine
Personal tax & trust	Nicholas Acomb
Planning & environmental	Catherine Davey
Residential property	Andrew Bussy
Wills & probate	Michael Hunter

STEWARTS

63 LINCOLN'S INN FIELDS, LONDON, WC2A 3LW
Tel: (0171) 242 6462 **Fax:** (0171) 831 6843 **DX:** 369 LONDON

The Firm: A practice specialising in litigation, company/commercial and insolvency work. The litigation departments have particular expertise in head and spinal injuries, medical negligence and professional negligence acting for both plaintiffs and defendants and their insurers. The firm handles litigation and company/commercial work with a strong international element and is a member of a world-wide network of law firms.

Managing partner:	Graham Fisher
Number of partners:	8
Assistant solicitors:	12
Other fee-earners:	4

STEWART & WATSON 59 High Street, Turriff, AB53 7EL *Tel:* (01888) 563773 *Fax:* (01888) 563227 *Ptnrs:* 8 *Asst solrs:* 7

STIBBE SIMONT MONAHAN DUHOT

66 GRESHAM STREET, LONDON, EC2V 7NH
Tel: (0171) 600 4400 **Fax:** (0171) 600 4411

The Firm: The firm operates as a truly multinational partnership of Dutch, Belgian and French lawyers. The history of the constituent parts of the firm goes back to the beginning of the century. The firm has well over 100 partners and 400 fee earners. It is one of the leading law firms in each of its three home jurisdictions.

Principal Areas of Practice: The firm is a full service law firm with an internationally oriented general commercial practice and special emphasis on mergers and acquisitions, banking, securities, corporate and structured finance, project finance, real estate, telecommunications, intellectual and industrial property, environmental law, administrative law, insolvency, litigation and arbitration; the firm distinguishes itself from many other large law firms in Continental Europe because of its specialised tax practice.

Other Offices: Principal offices in Amsterdam, Brussels and Paris; branch office in New York.

Senior Partners:	Allard C. Metzelaar/
	Hans Marseille

WORKLOADS	
Banking, finance, securities	50%
Mergers and acquisitions	45%
Miscellaneous	5%

CONTACTS	
M & A/Finance	Allard C. Metzelaar
Tax	Hans Marseille

STITT & CO 4 Paper Buildings, Temple, London, EC4Y 7HA **Tel:** (0171) 583 4834 **Fax:** (0171) 353 6801 **DX:** 1052 **Ptnrs:** 5 **Contact:** Andrew Jeffrey *Specialises in property (including development and investment) and litigation (including Bar-related cases) family, libel, wills and probate, landlord and tenant.*

STOCKLER CHARITY

2-3 CURSITOR STREET, CHANCERY LANE, LONDON, EC4A 1NE
Tel: (0171) 404 6661 **Fax:** (0171) 404 6717 **DX:** 445 LONDON **Email:** STOCKCHARY@AOL.COM

The Firm: Stockler Charity is a highly-regarded niche City of London practice formed in October 1992. It specialises in commercial litigation and arbitration, in particular in the 'wet' and 'dry' maritime, insurance and commodity trading fields. Since its inception, the firm has grown steadily in these areas. One of the firm's assistant solicitors is also a Master Mariner. It has associated offices throughout Europe, being the U.K. representative of Ars Legis, as well as a worldwide network of correspondent lawyers. French and German are spoken. The firm's client network is international in nature and includes major commodity traders (particularly dealing in oil, steel and sugar), shipowners/managers, charterers, P&I Clubs, cargo interests/underwriters, hull and machinery underwriters and salvors.

Number of partners:	3
Assistant solicitors:	2
Other fee-earners:	2

CONTACTS	
Commercial litigation	W.T. Stockler
Commodity trading litigation	G. Brunton
Marine litigation/arbitration	D.E. Charity

STONE KING

13 QUEEN SQUARE, BATH, BA1 2HJ
Tel: (01225) 337599 **Fax:** (01225) 335437 **DX:** 8001 BATH **Email:** NAME@STONEKING.DEMON.CO.UK

The Firm: Established in 1785, Stone King has a substantial commercial and private client practice in the West Country. It is known nationally for its Charity and Education expertise and has a growing reputation for intellectual property and employment law. It is well known for its matrimonial and family work. In 1997 it merged with the Bath firm Macfarlane Guy, increasing its expertise in the fields of Crime and Commercial Litigation.

Nature of Clientele: The firm's work is divided between private clients and, in the commercial sphere, medium to substantial businesses, schools, other large charities, and landed estates.

Other Office:

28 Ely Place, London EC1N 6RL. *Tel:* (0171) 242 0242 *Fax:* (0171) 405 4786.

Number of partners:	8
Assistant solicitors:	9
Consultants:	3
Other fee-earners:	12

WORKLOADS	
Commercial and Charities	40%
Private client litigation	33%
Private client	27%

STONES CANN & HALLETT

NORTHERNHAY PLACE, EXETER, EX4 3QQ
Tel: (01392) 666 777 **Fax:** (01392) 666 770 **DX:** 8306 EXETER **Email:** SC&H@TNSN.COM

TRINITY COURT, SOUTHERNHAY EAST, EXETER, EX1 1PG
Tel: (01392) 666 777 **Fax:** (01392) 666 770 **DX:** 8306 EXETER **Email:** SC&H@TNSN.COM

8 STATION ROAD, OKEHAMPTON, EX20 1DZ
Tel: (01837) 52804 **Fax:** (01837) 52840 **DX:** 82502 OKEHAMPTON

The Firm: Stones Cann & Hallett is one of the largest practices in Exeter offering a range of services to both corporate and private clients. Established last century, the firm has a progressive outlook with all offices linked by modern communications systems. It has a Legal Aid Franchise

Principal Areas of Work: The firm has a particularly strong reputation in commercial litigation, property, construction, charity law, company/commercial, insolvency, timeshare, housing associations and personal injury claims with a speciality in international ski law and holiday claims. Niche areas are:

Housing Associations: (*Contact:* Nick Dyer): expertise in site acquisition throughout the south and south west; shared ownership schemes; HAMA and Care in the Community schemes with local authorities and health trusts; funding of housing schemes; and repossession work.

Personal Injury: (*Contact:* Bronwen Courtenay-Stamp): with four members on the Personal Injury Panel and Robin Challans also a member of FOIL (The Forum of Insurance Lawyers), the department has longstanding experience of this type of work with particular specialisation in international skiing law and holiday claims, and defence litigation for major insurers.

Timeshare: (*Contact:* Tim Bourne): this department acts for many of the leading timeshare development companies throughout the UK and beyond, setting up agreements with Owners' Committees and advising other countries on compliance with international regulations.

Construction: (*Contact:* Peter Buechel): this expanding department has an established reputation acting for employers, funds, professionals and their insurers, contractors and sub-contractors at all levels in relation to both non-contentious matters and disputes. Experienced in Arbitration and Court proceedings as well as other dispute resolution techniques.

Private Client: (*Contact:* David Howell-Richardson): personal tax; financial planning; agricultural work; and a strong Family Team with representation on the Children Panel and as a member of the Relate Quality Partnership.

Stones Cann & Hallett opened The Law Shop, the region's first legal retail outlet in September 1997. The Law Shop has extended opening hours including Saturdays, and offers legal advice at convenient times and in relatively informal surroundings.

Foreign connections: the firm co-founded Omni Juris, an EEIG registered in Paris with members throughout Europe, and maintains contact with Legal Netlink, an American group of independent law firms with affiliates in Japan and Korea. Languages spoken: French, German, Spanish, Maltese and Tagalog (Philippines).

Managing partner:	WH Winterbotham
Number of partners:	16
Assistant solicitors:	9
Other fee-earners:	11

WORKLOADS	
Commercial, including Housing Associations:	36%
Trusts & Probate	16%
Civil litigation	15%
Family	15%
Residential property	11%
Criminal	7%

CONTACTS	
Agriculture	Paul Tucker
Charity Law	Helen Honeyball
Commercial Litigation	Paul Keeling
Commercial Property	Christopher Rundle
Company/Commercial	Tony Lloyd
Construction/Civil Engineering	Peter Buechel
Crime	Peter Seigne
Defence Insurers	Robin Challans
Employment	Kate Gardner
Family	David Howell-Richardson
Housing Association	Nick Dyer
Insolvency	Paul Keeling
Leisure/Timeshare	Tim Bourne
Plaintiff Personal Injury	James Browne
Site Development & Residential Property	
	Hugh Winterbotham
Skiing & Travel Personal Injury	
	Bronwen Courtenay-Stamp
Wills/Trusts/Probate/Tax	Michael Harris

STONES PORTER

26 FARRINGDON STREET, LONDON, EC4A 4AQ
Tel: (0171) 248 9991 **Fax:** (0171) 236 4025 **DX:** 1056

The Firm: Stones Porter is well known for its property, litigation and banking work and acts for a wide range of major companies and institutions. Most of the partners are property related specialists.

Principal Areas of Work:

Property: *Work includes:* planning, development, building contracts, joint ventures, town centre developments, shopping centres, business parks, retail parks, leisure parks, property management and leases and funding.

Company/Commercial: *Work includes:* share and loan issues, venture capital investments, Stock Exchange listings, joint ventures, management buy-outs and buy-ins, share options, structured finance, corporation tax, partnership agreements, contracts of employment, terms and conditions of trading, agency agreements, intellectual property, computer agreements, EC law, competition law and banking securities.

Litigation: *Work includes:* breach of contract, misrepresentation, professional negligence, intellectual property, employment law, landlord and tenant disputes, building contract disputes, professional indemnity insurance, planning proceedings and disciplinary tribunals.

Property Finance: The firm acts for a number of the clearing banks and advises other financial institutions on all aspects of banking including asset finance, secured and unsecured lending, security documentation and guarantees. The Property Finance group also deals with more complicated limited partnerships and securitisation.

Insolvency: *Work includes:* receivership, administration, voluntary arrangements, business sales, winding-up, bankruptcy, debt recovery and property possession actions.

Private Client: *Work includes:* tax planning, settlements and trusts, wills and probate, estate administration, Court of Protection and personal insolvency.

Nature of Clientele: The firm has considerable experience in acting for banks, institutions, manufacturing and distribution companies, retailers and property investment companies and developers.

Managing partner:	Robin Assael
Number of partners:	9
Assistant solicitors:	8
Other fee-earners:	7

WORKLOADS	
Commercial property	53%
Litigation	30%
Company/commercial	12%
Private client	5%

CONTACTS	
Banking realisations	Heather Leeson
Commercial Property	Jonathan Morshead/ Stephen Garford
Company/commercial	Hugh Edmunds
Insolvency	Stephen O'Brien/Terry Green
Litigation	Roger Hanson
Private client	Nicola Dudley
Property Finance	John Clark/Stephen O'Brien/ Terry Green
Retail Property	Robin Assael

STRINGER SAUL

17 HANOVER SQUARE, LONDON, W1R 9AJ
Tel: (0171) 917 8500 **Fax:** (0171) 917 8555 **DX:** 42701 OXFORD CIRCUS (NORTH)

The Firm: Stringer Saul is a commercial law firm with a commitment to the provision of a quality service. The firm has particular strength in company and commercial work and has a well established reputation in the pharmaceutical and biotechnology areas. Listed below are the principal areas of practice with contact names.

Principal Areas of Work:

Commercial Property and Planning: (*Contact:* Bill Harrup).

Corporate Advice including: Insolvency, reconstruction and recovery (*Contact:* David Smith). Company secretarial services (*Contact:* Norman Ziman).

Corporate Finance; Mergers and Acquisitions: (*Contact:* David Smith).

Employment: (*Contact:* Ruth Hickling).

General Commercial Litigation: (*Contact:* Martin Russell).

Intellectual Property and Information Technology (contentious and non-contentious): (*Contact:* Gary Howes).

Pharmaceuticals and Biotechnology: (*Contacts:* Diana Sternfeld/Gary Howes).

Secured Lending: (*Contact:* Martin Ackland).

Taxation: (*Contact:* Paul Yerbury).

Nature of Clientele: The firm's clients range from multinational public companies to small owner managed businesses, including companies in the pharmaceutical and biotechnology sectors, finance, leisure, publishing, the media, property and mining. The firm's clients include Flare Group, Medeva, Nycomed-Amersham, Pharmacia & Upjohn, Probus Estates, Reunion Mining, SmithKline Beecham, SkyePharma and Wolters Kluwer.

Foreign Connections: Stringer Saul has strong connections with overseas lawyers and accountants and regularly acts for overseas clients.

Executive partner:	Diana Sternfeld
Number of partners:	15
Assistant solicitors:	9
Other fee-earners:	1

WORKLOADS	
Company/Commercial	41%
Intellectual Property (contentious and non-contentious)	34%
Property	12%
General Commercial Litigation	9%
Employment	2%
Tax	2%

CONTACTS	
Company/Commercial	David Smith
Employment	Ruth Hickling
General Commercial Litigation	Martin Russell
Intellectual Property	Gary Howes
Property	Bill Harrup
Tax	Paul Yerbury

STRONACHS 34 Albyn Place, Aberdeen, AB10 1FW *Tel:* (01224) 845845 *Fax:* (01224) 845800 *DX:* AB 41 *Ptnrs:* 23 *Asst solrs:* 15 *Other fee-earners:* 15

STUART MILLER 247 High Road, Wood Green, London, N22 4HF *Tel:* (0181) 881 7440

STUCHBERY STONE 17 Denbigh Street, London, SW1 2HF *Tel:* (0171) 233 7171 *Fax:* (0171) 233 7172 *Ptnrs:* 7 *Asst solrs:* 7 *Other fee-earners:* 7

STUDIO LEGALE SUTTI

19 PRINCES ST, LONDON, W1R 7RE
Tel: (0171) 409 1384 **Fax:** (0171) 409 1384 **Email:** SUTTI@IBM.NET

The Firm: Studio Legale Sutti has been established in Milan for more than forty years and merged with Monti & Partners in 1993. The activity of the firm is organised across three main departments: commercial and company law, intellectual property and employment.

Principal Areas of Work: The aim of Studio Legale Sutti's presence in London is that of offering a full range of prompt and efficient on-site legal services regarding Italian law and jurisdiction. In this respect, the SLS operation in the UK would like to be viewed as a barrister-like practice – fully backed by the combined resources and know-how of its Italian offices to which it is connected through a high-speed encrypted link – with the purpose of serving British law firms and corporate cousel for their clients' and employers' needs related to Italy. As a matter of fact, SLS London office targets mainly law firms, patent and trademark agents, and in-house lawyers; does not usually deal with final clients; and, far from competing with British firms, offers exclusively very specific services (i.e., everything pertaining to the Italian system of law, including litigation in Italian civil, criminal and administrative courts). This service covers the following areas of specialisation: company law, commercial contracts, international contracts, international tax law, M&A, industrial joint ventures, foreign investments, agency and franchise arrangements, EC law and competition law, financial and banking law, debt collection, insolvency, environmental law, construction law, product liability, entertainment law, commercial litigation and arbitration, white collar crime, administrative law, intellectual property advice and litigation, industrial models and design, licence negotiation, technology transfer, advertising law, pharmaceuticals, patent and trade mark agency service, labour law, employment law, employer's liability, industrial relations and pensions law.

International Associations: The practice is a member of LegIT (Specialists in Legal Information Technology), INDICAM (Institute for the Protection of Trade Marks), British Chamber of Commerce in Italy, Italian Chamber of Commerce for Great Britain.

Main Office: Via Montenapoleone 8, 20121 Milan, Italy.
Tel: (+ 39 2) 762041 *Fax:* (+ 39 2) 76204 805\76204 806.

Managing partner:	Stefano Sutti
Worldwide	
Number of Partners:	5
Other Fee-earners:	27

WORKLOADS	
Commercial/Company	45%
Intellectual property/competition	35%
Employment	20%

STURTIVANT & CO

17 BULSTRODE ST, LONDON, W1M 5FQ
Tel: (0171) 486 9524 **Fax:** (0171) 224 3164

The Firm: Established in 1985, and well-known as a specialist practice which is devoted exclusively to UK immigration law. The principal, Karen Sturtivant, is an active member of various professional associations concerned with Immigration Law and she regularly lectures and gives seminars on this subject.

Principal Areas of Work: All types of immigration work undertaken; primarily client representation for work permits, business residence, investor status and other residence categories. Also settlement; extension of stay; visitors, studies and temporary stay. Appeals to Adjudicators and Tribunals; Judicial Review and deportation and removal cases.

Additional Areas: Nationality and citizenship problems.

Clientele: Wide corporate and private client base.

Foreign Connections: Contacts with immigration lawyers in many other jurisdictions.

Number of partners:	1
Assistant solicitors:	1

WORKLOADS	
UK immigration & nationality law & work permits	
	100%

SUGARÉ & CO 36 Park Square, Leeds, LS1 2NY *Tel:* (0113) 244 6978 *Fax:* (0113) 245 5708 *Ptnrs:* 3 *Asst solrs:* 2 *Other fee-earners:* 4

SULLIVAN & CROMWELL 9A Ironmonger Lane, London, EC2V 8EY *Tel:* (0171) 710 6500 *Fax:* (0171) 710 6565 *Ptnrs:* 6

SWEPSTONE WALSH 9 Lincoln's Inn Fields, London, WC2A 3BP *Tel:* (0171) 404 1499 *Fax:* (0171) 404 1493 *DX:* 142 *Ptnrs:* 4 *Asst solrs:* 4 *Other fee-earners:* 3

SYDNEY MITCHELL Cavendish House, 39 Waterloo Street, Birmingham, B2 5PU *Tel:* (0121) 698 2200 *Fax:* (0121) 200 1513 *DX:* 13054 *Ptnrs:* 8 *Asst solrs:* 5 *Other fee-earners:* 13

TALLENTS GODFREY & CO 3 Middlegate, Newark-on-Trent, NG24 1AQ *Tel:* (01636) 671881 *Fax:* (01636) 700148 *DX:* 11801 *Ptnrs:* 8 *Asst solrs:* 4 *Other fee-earners:* 10

TARLO LYONS

WATCHMAKER COURT, 33 ST. JOHN'S LANE, LONDON, EC1M 4DB
Tel: (0171) 405 2000 **Fax:** (0171) 814 9421 **DX:** 53323 CLERKENWELL **Email:** INFO@TARLO-LYONS.COM **Internet:** WWW.TARLO-LYONS.COM

The Firm: Founded in 1927 as a general commercial practice, Tarlo Lyons has successfully pursued a strategy of developing niche areas of expertise and specialist knowledge of particular business sectors.

The firm is particularly well known for its expertise in theatre and other areas of the entertainment industry and has an excellent reputation in the IT and telecommunications sectors. Tax investigations and gaming and licensing are also specialisms. A full range of company and commercial, litigation and property services are also provided to a wide range of clients.

By offering a creative, innovative approach and a personal service, demonstrated by partner involvement with every client, the firm has expanded rapidly. Over the past two years, turnover has increased by forty percent. The firm expects to continue its dynamic expansion via organic growth and lateral hiring of specialist lawyers in niche areas. Developments in the past year include the expansion of the IT and telecommunications group, which now has 11 full-time dedicated lawyers, and the recruitment of another partner and assistant solicitor to the firm's entertainment unit.

The firm believes in developing a thorough understanding of clients' businesses and commercial priorities in order to provide the best possible advice. Clients receive regular bulletins on topical legal issues and are invited to attend in-house seminars relevant to their business. Individual lawyers contribute regularly to publications such as The Stage, Computing and Leisure Week.

Principal Areas of Work:

IT & Telecommunications: The firm acts for major insurance companies, banks, internet service providers, hardware and software vendors. It has developed a strong reputation in advising users and suppliers, particularly regarding Y2K and EMU issues, telecoms and on-line services.

Entertainment: A notable area of the firm's expertise. The Cameron Mackintosh group of companies, the leading theatrical producer, has been a client of D Michael Rose for over 20 years. The firm is also a prominent provider of legal services to the film, music and television industries. All types of contractual matters are dealt with, as well as intellectual property issues. Multi-media matters are also handled, often in conjunction with the firm's IT lawyers.

Tax Investigations: A specialism for over 30 years, the firm acts mainly for clients who are subject to criminal prosecutions by the Inland Revenue or Customs & Excise. The work involves close co-operation with accountants, with whom the firm has excellent relationships and from whom it often receives recommendations.

Company & commercial: Services include handling acquisitions and disposals, joint venture agreements and commercial contracts, and corporate finance including venture capital. Advice on employment matters, including contracts, service agreements and, in particular, outsourcing of internal functions, is also provided.

Litigation: Advice on contentious employment and intellectual property issues, as well as secured lending enforcement, are areas of particular expertise. A specialist unit provides services to the gaming and amusement industry in licensing and related matters.

Property: A wide range of commercial property transactions is handled including major acquisitions, disposals and developments, as well as landlord and tenant matters.

Recruitment & Training: Tarlo Lyons is currently one of only a handful of law firms based in central London to hold Investors in People accreditation. The firm is committed to training and developing all its members. During the coming year, it will be actively recruiting lawyers in its specialist areas. Prospective trainees should apply in writing to Robert Hails, Training Partner.

Managing partner:	Nigel McEwen
Number of partners:	22
Assistant solicitors:	9
Other fee-earners:	18

WORKLOADS	
Commercial	25%
Litigation	25%
Information technology	20%
Property	20%
Entertainment	10%

CONTACTS	
Commercial	G L Isaacs
Entertainment	D Michael Rose
Information technology	Lawrence Phillips
Litigation	M Martin
Property	P Diamond

Tarlo Lyons Solicitors

INVESTOR IN PEOPLE

TAYLOR & EMMET Norfolk Row, Sheffield, S1 1SL *Tel:* (0114) 290 2200 *Fax:* (0114) 290 2290 *DX:* 10549 *Ptnrs:* 11 *Asst solrs:* 10 *Other fee-earners:* 7

TAYLOR JOYNSON GARRETT

CARMELITE, 50 VICTORIA EMBANKMENT, BLACKFRIARS, LONDON, EC4Y 0DX
Tel: (0171) 353 1234 **Fax:** (0171) 936 2666 **DX:** 41 LONDON **Internet:** WWW.TJGUK.COM

Taylor Joynson Garrett is a major City law firm. It has an impressive UK and international client base, with strength in depth across the range of commercial disciplines enabling it to offer a full service to its corporate clients.

The Firm: Recognising that clients need advisers with specific industry knowledge, Taylor Joynson Garrett has developed various industry focus groups. The most notable of these groups is the **technology and life sciences** group which draws on its recognised expertise and reputation in Corporate, Intellectual Property, IT and Telecoms.

As well as offices in **London, Brussels and Bucharest**, the firm is affiliated with the US law firm Graham and James and Deacons Graham & James in the Pacific Rim with access to over 1400 lawyers world-wide. These affiliations are supplemented by a series of close relationships with law firms throughout Europe and elsewhere around the world.

Principal Areas of Work: The firm has a highly-regarded **Corporate** department dealing with international and domestic work. It has particular expertise in corporate and project finance, tax, mergers & acquisitions, energy, PFI and European Union law issues. It acts for a varied client base including public companies, banks and other financial institutions, management teams, private companies and venture capitalists.

The firm's **Intellectual Property** department is one of the largest in Europe and recognised as a leader in the field. It deals with contentious and non-contentious work in all aspects of intellectual property, including patent litigation, trade marks, industrial design, passing-off and trade libel. In addition, an experienced and respected team deals with IT and telecoms issues to assist clients in advances in technological fields, advising and protecting inventors, manufacturers, suppliers and users.

The **Banking** department advises on all aspects of banking and finance for a number of clearing, merchant and foreign banks (including Eastern European banks) and borrowers in relation to a broad range of industry sectors, with particular emphasis on transactional work, projects, PFI and securitisation. This department encompasses specialist teams dealing with corporate recoveries and building societies.

In the field of **Commercial Property** the firm offers a range of services incorporating specialist planning, property management and environmental teams. It is able to meet the differing needs of trading companies, developers, finance institutions and national and international investors.

Taylor Joynson Garrett's **Litigation** department handles a wide variety of commercial litigation and arbitration matters and has particular strengths in **construction, banking, property, and insurance.** In particular the specialised **Construction and Engineering** group assists clients to achieve their commercial objectives through drafting of documents to protect their interests, support and assistance in maintaining the smooth running of projects, and if necessary the pursuit or defence of claims in court or arbitration. The firm's specialist **Employment** department handles a wide variety of employment related matters including pensions and employee benefits together with increasingly complex legal relationships both domestically and internationally.

The firm also remains one of the few leading City firms with a well respected **Private Client** department, providing advice on taxation, wills and settlements (including trusts & estates) matrimonial law and residential property.

Managing partner:	Richard Marsh
Senior partner:	Michael Morrison
Number of partners:	77
Assistant solicitors:	114
Other fee-earners:	6

WORKLOADS	
Corporate & Banking	33%
Litigation	21%
Intellectual Property	18%
Commercial Property	14%
Tax and Personal Planning	8%
Employment	6%

CONTACTS	
Banking and Insolvency	Robert Gayford
Central/Eastern Europe	Philip Newhouse
Commercial Litigation	David Greig
Commercial Property	John Whitfield
Construction	Neil White, Peter Shaw
Corporate Finance	Tim Eyles
Corporate Tax	Peter Jackson
Corporate/Commercial	Declan Tarpey
Employment	Andrew Granger
Entertainment/Multimedia	Paul Mitchell
Environment & Planning	Alison Askwith, Patrick Pennal
European Union/Competition	Martin Baker
Information Technology	Glyn Morgan
Insurance/Reinsurance	Peter Kempe
Intellectual Property	Gary Moss, Richard Price
Inward Investment	David Kent
Life Sciences	Simon Cohen, David Kent
London Stock Exchange	Paul Manser
Pharmaceutical	Mark Hodgson
Project Finance	Declan Tarpey
Shipping	James Sleightholme
Tax and Personal Planning	Philippa Blake-Roberts, Michael Stanford-Tuck
Telecommunications/Broadcast	Ted Mercer

TAYLOR NICHOL 3 Station Place, London, N4 2DH *Tel:* (0171) 272 8336 *Fax:* (0171) 281 9148 *DX:* 57453 Finsbury Park. *Ptnrs:* 2 *Asst solrs:* 1 *Other fee-earners:* 2

TAYLORS Rawlings House, Exchange Street, Blackburn, BB1 7JN **Tel:** (01254) 563333 **Fax:** (01254) 682146 **DX:** 15252 Blackburn **Ptnrs:** 6 **Asst solrs:** 5 **Other fee-earners:** 2 **Contact:** Ms Elaine Hurn *Commercial firm with a reputation for problem solving providing specialist services to the geotextiles, home furnishings, textiles and wallcovering industries.*

WORKLOADS	
Intellectual property	45%
Company and commercial	25%
Commercial litigation	20%
Commercial property/ employment/ other	15%

TAYLOR VINTERS

MERLIN PLACE, MILTON RD, CAMBRIDGE, CB4 4DP
Tel: (01223) 423444 **Fax:** (01223) 423486/425446 **DX:** 122892 CAMBRIDGE 4 **Email:** INFO@TAYLOR-VINTERS.CO.UK

The Firm: As one of the largest law firms in East Anglia, Taylor Vinters has a reputation for quality legal services to the commercial sector. The University of Cambridge is just one of a number of substantial institutional clients and Taylor Vinters also has extensive experience with high-technology industries.

Principal Areas of Work:

Corporate and Commercial: Acquisitions, disposals, MBOs, joint ventures, venture capital funding, construction, employment, insolvency, intellectual property and commercial litigation.

Commercial Property: Landlord and tenant, large scale sales and purchases, development planning, agricultural and environmental law.

Rural Business Services: A new group has been established to encompass the wide range of Rural-based business activity undertaken for food processors, farmers, estates, institutions and related organisations.

Other specialisms: Personal Injury, Bloodstock, Charities and Private Client.

Managing partner:	Gerard Chadwick
Number of partners:	22
Assistant solicitors:	21
Other fee-earners:	14

CONTACTS	
Bloodstock	Christine Berry
Commercial Litigation	Edward Perrott
Commercial Property	Steven Beach
Company and Commercial	John Short
Personal injury	Paul Tapner
Private Client	Jocelyn Fox

TAYLOR WALTON

36-44 ALMA STREET, LUTON, LU1 2PL
Tel: (01582) 731161 **Fax:** (01582) 457900 **DX:** 130460 LUTON 10 **Internet:** WWW.TAYLORWALTON.CO.UK

HARPENDEN,
Tel: (01582) 765111 **Fax:** (01582) 769089 **DX:** 80450 HARPENDEN

HEMEL HEMPSTEAD,
Tel: (01442) 251411 **Fax:** (01442) 254634 **DX:** 8803 HEMEL HEMPSTEAD

ST ALBANS,
Tel: (01727) 845245 **Fax:** (01727) 864970 **DX:** 133335 ST ALBANS 14

The Firm: Taylor Walton continues to successfully expand its services to business and private clients. Its four offices in the Northern Home Counties offer specialists who advise on both national and international issues. In the past twelve months the firm has developed its services through strategic merger, by attracting partners from competing firms and by continuing its policy of recruiting staff from City or equivalent firms.

Principal Areas of Work:

Corporate & Business Services: (*Contacts:* Clive Borthwick/Mike Pettit). As an integral part of the firm's specialist commercial business unit the company/commercial team offers in-depth specialist assistance with prompt service and efficient use of IT a priority. Mergers and acquisitions work and advice upon corporate finance matters comprise a significant proportion of matters handled. Recruitment has assisted the development of further business services with particular growth in the information technology, intellectual property, construction and manufacturing sectors. High value commercial ventures including PFI projects are an increasing feature of the department's case load. The commercial business unit is structured to enable teams from all departments to be involved in complex transactions.

Commercial Property Services: (*Contacts:* Mike Kelly/Dermot Carey). The past year has seen the acquisition of a number of significant clients including national retailers and service providers who benefit from provincial fee rates and substantial expert support. Strong connections continue to be built with complementary professionals including architects, engineers and surveyors. Development and site planning, risk assessment, environmental and planning advice are provided, often to tight deadlines. Involvement in major retail and residential developments have attracted further instructions from like minded developers and professionals.

Commercial Litigation: (*Contact Partner:* Andrew Knight). Significant restructuring into specialist groups has assisted the expansion of the firm's commercial litigation team. Services range from bespoke and high volume debt recovery services to involvement in substantial business critical litigation. The department's stated policy of advising proactively upon potential settlement opportunities has found favour with clients and referring professionals, although extensive expert backup ensures that where Court proceedings are appropriate strong support is available. Main areas of work include contract disputes, shareholder and partner disputes, negligence claims and property disputes.

Managing partner:	David Fryer
Number of partners:	17
Assistant solicitors:	18
Other fee-earners:	38

WORKLOADS	
Residential property	25%
Commercial/Private Litigation	24%
Commercial Property	20%
Company Commercial	20%
Private Client	11%

CONTACTS	
Commercial property	M.P. Kelly
Company and commercial	C.O. Borthwick
Financial services	D.M. Fryer
Litigation	A.R. Knight
Private client	J. Stevens
Residential conveyancing	T.M. Shillabeer

Employment: (*Contact:* John Hobson). The Employment Unit offers advice by specialist solicitors. Representation upon contentious matters includes Employment Tribunal strategy and representation, restraint of trade, sex and race discrimination and wrongful dismissal claims. Advice upon disciplinary and health and safety issues is available to employers. Examination and drafting of employment contracts and staff handbooks provide a significant workload.

Personal Injury: (*Contact:* John Carter). Advice to plaintiffs and defendants in respect of work related, RTA and other personal injuries. Members of Personal Injury Panel offer quick assessment of claims.

Private Client/Trusts: (*Contact:* John Stevens). Additions to the private client complement have attracted increased instructions in relation to trust and tax planning (notably for business executives) together with wills and probate matters. Close liason with other professionals ensures co-ordination of personal planning activities.

Relocation Services/Residential Conveyancing: (*Contacts:* Trevor Shillabeer/Richard Atkins). In addition to traditional locally based conveyancing and remortgaging services the firm continues to expand its relocation services to employees of major companies. Increased use of IT and interactive internet instruction points have been developed with client input, and high service levels to clients have drawn corporate referrals. Employee benefit packages including fixed price conveyancing and other legal services have been successfully implemented with FTSE-100 Businesses.

Family: (*Contact:* Aileen Hartnett). A dedicated team advises upon all aspects of family affairs including divorce and separation, emergency procedures, children and financial provisions.

Foreign Connections: The firm is a member of the Euro Defi network of professional firms enabling swift access to professionals within the EU.

Value Added Services: The firm holds at least one seminar each month for clients and contacts. Specialists from with the firm and expert outside speakers provide a detailed overview and update upon legal matters of significance to varied interest groups. Bespoke newsletters are also distributed without charge to clients and contacts and networking forums form an integral part of the firm's strong base of business contacts.

TAYNTONS

CLARENCE CHAMBERS, 8-12 CLARENCE STREET, GLOUCESTER, GL1 1DZ
Tel: (01452) 522047 **Fax:** (01452) 424659 **DX:** 7560

The Firm: Established for over 140 years, Tayntons provides a prompt and integrated service across the departments, whilst maintaining its traditionally strong partner to client contact. The firm is a member of Lawgroup UK and holds a legal aid franchise.

Principal Areas of Work:

Company/ Commercial: Offers a full range of services including company formations/ acquisitions, partnership agreements, insolvency, franchising and tax.

Family: Provides specialist advice on all matters relating to child care, family, matrimonial and cohabitation problems. The firm has a member of the Law Society's Children Panel.

Litigation: Work includes consumer complaints, commercial disputes, redundancy and unfair dismissal, professional indemnity claims.

Personal Injury: It has the largest practice in Gloucestershire. Deals with all accidents with particular expertise in the recovery of damages. It has four members of APIL and two members of FOIL. One partner is a member of the Law Society's Personal Injury Panel.

Property: Work includes commercial lending, development agreements, domestic conveyancing, town and country planning.

Private Client: Offers a full range of services including wills, trusts, financial advice and tax planning.

Employment: Including acting for both employers and employees.

Managing partner:	Alan Keddie
Number of partners:	5
Assistant solicitors:	11
Other fee-earners:	13

WORKLOADS	
Personal injury	65%
General litigation	10%
Matrimonial	10%
Property/ commercial	10%
Probate/ wills	5%

CONTACTS	
Housing associations	Alan Bird
Personal injury (defendant)	Jon Fitzpatrick
Personal injury (plaintiff)	Martin Edden

TEACHER STERN SELBY

37-41 BEDFORD ROW, LONDON, WC1R 4JH
Tel: (0171) 242 3191 **Fax:** (0171) 242 1156 **DX:** 177 CH.LN. **Email:** TSS@TSSLAW.CO.UK

The Firm: Teacher Stern Selby is primarily a commercial firm which favours a close working relationship with its clients and their other professional advisers to ensure that matters are conducted with maximum speed and efficiency.

Principal Areas of Work:

Commercial Property: (*Contact Partner:* Stuart Stern). *Work includes:* acquisitions and disposals for developers, investors, landlords and tenants. Secured lending and the drafting of security documentation (acting for banks and building societies) are also handled, as is every aspect of landlord and tenant work. Shopping centres a speciality.

Company/Commercial: (*Contact Partner:* Roger Selby). The department is active in the corporate sector, handling takeovers, mergers, joint ventures, MBOs and disposals, de-mergers, reconstructions and asset sales. The firm also deals with employment law, intellectual property licences and confidentiality agreements. The firm has particular experience in computer hardware and software contracts, oil exploration agreements and financing, entertainment law (music, film, TV, cable and multimedia); and in the pharmaceutical industry.

Litigation: (*Contact Partner:* Jack Rabinowicz). Primarily in the commercial field, particularly banking, insolvency and finance house matters, together with commercial property litigation. The firm also specialises in medical negligence and personal injury cases, and has a national reputation in the field of education law. The firm has considerable experience in media and entertainment litigation, headed by Graham Shear.

Other Areas of Work: The firm gives specialist tax planning advice and has substantial experience in the formation and use of foreign trusts and offshore corporate entities to produce the most efficient tax structure to suit individual circumstances. A full range of private client services from residential conveyancing to wills, trusts, probate and estate administration is also provided. Nature of Clientele: Primarily from the finance, commercial property, corporate and entertainment fields, and also corporate and business clients from Canada, Israel and Eastern Europe. The Firm also has excellent links with accountants, banks, financial institutions, surveyors and has wide-ranging legal contacts overseas. Languages Spoken: French, German, Italian, Russian, Chinese(Mandarin), Hebrew, Arabic, Serbo-Croat, Spanish and Afrikaans.

Managing partner:	Roger Selby
Number of partners:	14
Assistant solicitors:	12
Other fee-earners:	5

WORKLOADS	
Commercial litigation	38%
Commercial property	30%
Company and commercial	14%
Secured lending	10%
Residential conveyancing/ probate	5%
Personal injury/ education/ judicial review	3%

CONTACTS	
Commercial litigation	Jack Rabinowicz
Commercial property	Stuart Stern, Nigel Fisch
Computer law	David Teacher
Education	Jack Rabinowicz
Entertainment	Roger Selby
General commercial	Roger Selby
Media companies	David Teacher
Media Litigation	Graham Shear
Medical Negligence	Jack Rabinowicz
Oil and gas	Roger Selby
Secured lending	Phil Berry

THANKI NOVY TAUBE

THE MEWS, 1A BIRKENHEAD STREET, LONDON, WC1H 8NB
Tel: (0171) 833 5800 **Fax:** (0171) 833 5805 **DX:** 37900 KINGS CROSS

The Firm: The firm specialises in the criminal litigation field with extensive exposure to the "civil liberties" area and has considerable experience in handling complex and weighty cases, often with a forensic element.

Principal Areas of Work: Criminal litigation covering a broad spectrum and including white collar crime, murder, child abuse, armed robbery and Customs & Excise cases. The firm has specialist knowledge of extradition cases. It has substantial experience of appellate work. The firm deals routinely with judicial reviews and has an ever increasing prison law work load. Recently it has set up a specialist department dealing with civil actions against the police and advises regularly in death-in-custody inquests. It has particular expertise in Police Station representations and offers 24 hours, 7-day service to detained persons. It accepts instructions for advocacy in central London Magistrates' Courts.

Nature of Clientele: Mostly legal aid but growing private client base.

Review of Clients and Matters in 1997: Extraditions to the USA, Iceland, Australia and Italy. Court of Appeal in the Appeal of Christopher Clunis in his claim for damages for negligent release into the care in the community. Defending in the Regents Canal, twins murder case. Serious frauds. Armed robberies, murders and serious assault cases. Martin Taube appears on Jimmy Young Show to advise on legal matters.

General: The firm has a strong commitment to excellence and has a quality-driven approach. Networked, computer system for file management, costing and diary systems. Provides high quality training to all its staff, both in-house and on specialist basis.

Charges: Legal Aid rates. For private clients charges vary from £130-£160 per hour.

Managing partner:	Girish Thanki
Number of partners:	3
Assistant solicitors:	5
Other fee-earners:	3

CONTACTS	
Extraditions, prison law	Girish Thanki
General crime and Appellate	Rod Novy
White collar crime	Martin Taube

THE BERKSON GLOBE PARTNERSHIP 27 Dale Street, 4th Floor, Dale House, Liverpool, L2 2HD *Tel:* (0151) 236 1234 *Fax:* (0151) 236 5678

THEODORE GODDARD

150 ALDERSGATE ST, LONDON, EC1A 4EJ
Tel: (0171) 606 8855 **Fax:** (0171) 606 4390 **DX:** 47 LONDON CHANCERY LANE WC2 **Email:** TG@THEODOREGODDARD.CO.UK
Internet: HTTP//WWW.THEOGODDARD.COM

The Firm: Theodore Goddard is a major City law firm serving the business and financial communities, with particular emphasis on the banking and finance and the media and communications sectors. Theodore Goddard's aim is to provide clients with innovative, high quality, practical and speedy advice. Although London-based, Theodore Goddard operates worldwide through an office in Brussels and a network of international associates, including Klein-Goddard in Paris and Theodore Goddard Jersey.

Principal Areas of Work:

Banking & Finance: The firm advises on the full range of corporate and finance work, including mergers and acquisitions, management buy-outs and demergers, investment capital and new issues, including Stock Exchange flotations. It has an expanding practice in the field of collective investments, insurance and financial services regulation. The firm acts for a wide range of banks, borrowers, lessors and lessees, arrangers and airlines on general banking and asset finance transactions as well as on more specialist PFI and structured and tax driven financings. It also has a recognised practice in securities and corporate trust work. Its structured finance unit is led by a banker.

Tax: The firm deals with all tax issues connected with corporate finance work, including the development of tax-related financial instruments and asset finance packages; international tax planning; the tax aspects of takeovers, corporate reconstructions and demergers, management buy-outs and buy-ins; employee share schemes and other employee benefits; personal tax planning including, together with the associated firm in Jersey, the formation and administration of off-shore trusts and companies.

Media and Communications: The firm has a leading practice in the media and communications sector, concentrating on music, film, television, theatre, and, centred on its expertise in defamation law, newspapers, advertising and publishing; it also advises extensively on the issues relating to new media and information technology including computer games and on-line publishing. The convergence of businesses and technologies in these industries results in the continuous creation of new and complex legal problems, particularly in relation to the creation and exploitation of intellectual property rights and competition and regulatory issues.

Commercial Litigation: The firm has considerable expertise in commercial litigation, particularly in relation to the banking and securities sector; fraud and asset recovery; major contractual disputes; insurance and re-insurance; product liability, especially in the healthcare industry; and in arbitration.

Property: In the property field, the emphasis is on commercial and industrial sectors. Specialist groups handle public authority work, environmental law, planning and rating, construction and development, funding and investment, secured lending, property and construction litigation, and retail and leisure transactions.

Other: Other groups have excellent reputations in the fields of EC and competition law, employment (both contentious and non-contentious) and pensions. The firm has an established practice in transport law, particularly in relation to aviation and railways.

Recruitment: The firm recruits 15-20 trainee solicitors a year. A good degree (2:1 plus), which may or may not be in law, is necessary. The firm is looking for trainees with confidence, commitment and sound commercial sense. With the firm's international focus, language skills are valuable. There is an extensive award-winning training and development programme covering all fee earners, from trainees to partners and including personal skills development, commercial management and business development training alongside legal training. The firm recruits with a view to retaining trainees who after qualification will go on to become partners with the firm. Tuition fees and a maintenance allowance are paid by the firm for both CPE and LPC. The firm runs a summer placement and open day programme. Details of summer placements and open days, as well as the firm's brochure for training contracts and application forms, are available from the Personnel Department. Applications should be made to Penny Alison (Miss), Personnel Director.

Other details:

Other offices: Brussels: 118 avenue de Cortenberg/Kortenberglaan, B-1000 Brussels, Belgium. *Tel:* (32 2) 732 27 00 *Fax:* (32 2) 735 23 52
Associated offices: Theodore Goddard Jersey, *Tel:* (01534) 876085 *Fax:* (01534) 35227; Klein Goddard, Paris *Tel:* 00 33 144 952000 *Fax:* 00 33 149 530397

Managing partner:	Peter Kavanagh
Senior partner:	Paddy Grafton Green
Number of partners:	54
Other fee-earners:	122
Total staff:	311

WORKLOADS	
Corporate/corporate finance	29%
Media/IP	17%
Property	17%
Commercial litigation	13%
Banking and Finance	12%
Corporate Tax	6%

CONTACTS	
Advertising	Rupert Earle
Arbitration	Peter Fitzpatrick
Asset finance/leasing	James Ballingall
Aviation	Rory MacCarthy
Banking	Julian Maples
Capital markets	Jayesh Patel
Collective Investment Schemes	Simon Goodworth
Commercial litigation	John Kelleher
Commercial property	David Wilkinson
Company/Commercial	Graham Stedman
Corporate finance	John Clark
Corporate tax	Tim Sanders
EC/Competition	Guy Leigh
Employment	Peter Cooke
Entertainment	Paddy Grafton Green
Environment	Douglas Evans
Film/TV	Peter Armstrong
Insolvency	Jonathan Lewis
Insurance	Jennifer Donohue
Intellectual property	Hamish Porter
IT	Arnold Segal
Media litigation	Martin Kramer
Music	Paddy Grafton Green
Pensions	Mark Catchpole
PFI	James Ballingall
Planning	Douglas Evans
Private Client	Jo Goldby
Railways	William James
Structured Finance	Nigel West
Telecommunications	John Angel
Trade	Dan Horovitz

THM TINSDILLS Chichester House, Broad Street, Hanley, Stoke-on-Trent, ST1 4EU *Tel:* (01782) 262031 *Fax:* (01782) 287571 *DX:* 20710 *Ptnrs:* 16 *Asst solrs:* 14 *Other fee-earners:* 14

THOMAS COOPER & STIBBARD

IBEX HOUSE, 42-47 MINORIES, LONDON, EC3N 1HA
Tel: (0171) 481 8851 **Fax:** (0171) 480 6097 **DX:** 548 **Email:** TCS@TCSSOLL.COM

The Firm: Thomas Cooper & Stibbard is a well established City of London firm, specialising in commercial law, with a particular emphasis towards shipping and international trade. The firm offers advice to industrial, commercial and financial clients worldwide. Thomas Cooper & Stibbard have built strong, long lasting relationships with clients, through a thorough understanding of the demands and developments of their different market places. The firm's client base is broadly international, with many of its multi-lingual lawyers travelling widely on client business. The firm has a branch office in Singapore which covers both admiralty and shipping work. It has seen a great expansion in the Spanish and South American markets, with increasing instructions from shipowners, underwriters and oil companies; the firm also has a strong presence in Greece, where it undertakes both shipping and non-contentious work for clients.

Principal Areas of Work:

Admiralty: (*Contact:* David Hebden). The firm's Admiralty specialists handle collisions at sea, salvage and towage, pollution and wreck removal and marine insurance. The firm has been instructed in connection with many of the major casualties of recent years and David Hebden is particularly well known for his work on crisis management.

Shipping: (*Contact:* Tim Kelleher). Shipping litigation expertise includes charterparty disputes, bills of lading, carriage of goods, cargo damage, storage or contamination, shipbuilding and repair contracts, management disputes and multi-modal carriage. The firm is a leading practitioner in electronic shipping and trade documentation. Apart from the mainstream shipping areas, the firm has an unusual specialisation. Stephen Swabey acts for the plaintiffs in the Factortame litigation (the Anglo-Spanish fishermen's claim against the Government).

Personal Injury: (*Contact:* John Strange). The firm is well known for marine personal injury work, acting in the main for P & I Clubs and shipowners.

Company/Commercial: (*Contact:* Stephen Swabey). The firm's Company and Commercial department advises all types of UK and international businesses including public and private companies, partnerships and individuals. Particular areas of expertise include banking, corporate finance including mergers and acquisitions, Stock Exchange listings, venture capital commercial contracts, employment law, financial services, insolvency, property and commercial litigation.

Nature of Clientele: The client base is strongly international and many of the firm's lawyers are fluent in several languages, including Spanish, French, Greek, Italian and Mandarin. Clients include a broad spectrum and include shipowners, charterers, banks, insurance companies, foreign governments and ministries, major oil companies, commodity traders and manufacturers.

Managing partner:	T.J.R. Goode
Senior partner:	D.G. Hebden
Number of partners:	15
Assistant solicitors:	8
Other fee-earners:	14

WORKLOADS	
Shipping (admiralty, maritime & carriage)	60%
Business finance & insurance	20%
Commercial litigation & international arbitration	10%
Personal injury	10%

CONTACTS	
Banking	Grant Eldred
Commercial Litigation	Nick Green
Company Law	Stephen Swabey
Construction	Tim Goode
Environment	Paul Barfield
Insurance	Tim Goode
Personal Injury	John Strange
Property	Kate Harrison
Shipping and Maritime Law	David Hebden

THOMAS EGGAR CHURCH ADAMS

5 EAST PALLANT, CHICHESTER, PO19 1TS
Tel: (01243) 786111 **Fax:** (01243) 775640 **DX:** 30300 CHICHESTER **Email:** TECA@ARGONET.CO.UK

The Firm: Formed on 1 May 1998 as a result of the merger between Thomas Eggar Verrall Bowles and Church Adams Tatham. Thomas Eggar Church Adams brings together the skills and experience of its constituent parts to form a diversified legal and financial services business with resources to build on areas of specialisation and particular industry strengths.

Principal Areas of Work: The firm has a strong commercial practice capable of handling a broad spectrum of matters covering Commercial Property, Commercial Litigation and Company & Commercial with particular expertise in providing legal services to Mortgage Lenders and the Railway and Franchising Industries. It also has a significant Private Client practice providing a service to the local community in the South East backed up by Thesis, its financial services business.

Other Offices: Chichester, Horsham, London, Reigate and Worthing.

International Connections: Thomas Eggar Church Adams is a member of AVRIO, a European Economic Interest Grouping.

Recruitment and Training: Trainee solicitors are recruited annually and a 2:1 degree, not necessarily in law, is preferred. Application forms are available from 1st June in each year, and interviews take place in September.

Managing partner:	John Stapleton
Number of partners:	43
Assistant solicitors:	41
Other fee-earners:	79

CONTACTS	
Commercial Property	Chris Bell
Company & Commercial	Tony Edwards
Financial Services	Anthony Wands
Litigation	Martin Cross
Private Client	Amanda King-Jones

THOMAS EGGAR

CHURCH ADAMS

SOLICITORS

THOMPSON & JACKSON 4 & 5 St. Lawrence Road, Plymouth, Devon, Plymouth, PL4 6HR *Tel:* (01752) 665037/221171 *Fax:* (01752) 670312 *Ptnrs:* 3 *Asst solrs:* 1 *Other fee-earners:* 2

THOMPSONS 39 Frances Street, Newtownards, BT23 7DW *Tel:* (01247) 811652 *Fax:* (01247) 819645 *Ptnrs:* 1 *Asst solrs:* 3 *Other fee-earners:* 1

THOMPSONS Congress House, Great Russell Street, London, WC1B 3LW *Tel:* (0171) 637 9761 *Fax:* (0171) 637 0000 *DX:* 35722 Bloomsbury 1 *Ptnrs:* 80 *Asst solrs:* 84 *Other fee-earners:* 92

THOMPSON SMITH & PUXON 4-5 North Hill, Colchester, CO1 1EB *Tel:* (01206) 574431 *Fax:* (01206) 563174 *DX:* 3617 Colchester *Ptnrs:* 12 *Asst solrs:* 5 *Other fee-earners:* 19

THOMSON SNELL & PASSMORE

3 LONSDALE GARDENS, TUNBRIDGE WELLS, TN1 1NX
Tel: (01892) 510000 **Fax:** (01892) 549884 **DX:** 3914 TUNBRIDGE WELLS 1 **Email:** 100673.1317@COMPUSERVE.COM

The Firm: This large, highly-regarded firm is one of the oldest legal practices in the country, tracing its roots back to 1570. It has 38 partners, 158 staff and two offices. A wide-ranging general practice, it is best known for its company/commercial, commercial property, private client, professional negligence and personal injury work. Thomson Snell & Passmore is a founder member of The Law South Group. It has a large private client base and advises business of all types and sizes, professional firms and public organisations.

Principal Areas of Work:
Company/Commercial: A wide variety of work is handled by a strong commercial team including company formations, acquisitions and disposals, corporate finance and venture capital, MBOs and MBIs, mergers and joint ventures, partnership, commercial contracts, insolvency, employment law, intellectual property, franchising, EC and general competition law, and corporate tax.
Commercial Property: The department advises tenants, investors and institutions on all aspects of commercial property including funding and tax implications. It also provides a full service to residential and commercial developers, including land acquisition and options, joint ventures, funding agreements, planning and environmental issues, unit sales/leases and estate management. The firm also advises farmers and estates on all aspects of land ownership, including agricultural holdings, tax, inheritance, development, environmental legislation and EC regulations.
Litigation: The work of the various departments includes all types of commercial disputes, insolvency, employment claims, intellectual property disputes and property related claims including landlord and tenant, building contracts and possession actions. The department dealing with personal injury and medical negligence has become a leader in the region and the professional negligence and professional conduct departments handle high volumes of work. The family department advises on all areas of matrimonial and other family problems including inheritance claims, cross border disputes and child care.
Private Client: The department handles wills, probate, trust formation and management, investment management, tax and financial planning, pensions, charities, inheritance tax, capital gains tax, income tax and tax returns. There is also a large residential property unit.
Immigration: A new immigration department services private and business clients.

Foreign Connections: The firm is a founder member of INTERLEGAL (previously EUROJURIST EEIG) with associate offices throughout Europe.

Other Offices: Lyons, East Street, Tonbridge, Kent TN9 1HL (01732) 771411 (Guy Durdant-Hollamby)

Number of partners:	38
Assistant solicitors:	20
Other fee-earners:	18

WORKLOADS	
Commercial litigation	23%
Probate & trusts	22%
Residential property	17%
PI/medical negligence	12%
Commercial property	11%
Company/commercial	10%
Family law	5%

CONTACTS	
Agriculture	Gilbert Green
Commercial litigation	Peter Radula-Scott
Commercial property	David White
Company/ commercial	Jeremy Waddell
Immigration	Richard Chalkley
Investment management	Jeremy Passmore
Matrimonial/ family	Barbara Wright
PI/ medical negligence	Andrew Watson
Probate and trusts	James Krafft
Professional conduct	Richard Chalkley
Professional negligence	Trevor May
Property development	Gilbert Green
Property litigation	Raymond Beard
Residential property	Michael Sugden
Tax planning	Jeremy Passmore
Trust management and tax returns	Kathy Larter

THORNTONS WS

50 CASTLE STREET, DUNDEE, DD1 3RU
Tel: (01382) 229111 **Fax:** (01382) 202288 **DX:** DD 28

The Firm: Thorntons WS is the largest legal firm in Tayside with offices in Dundee, Perth, Arbroath and Forfar.

Principal Areas of Work:

Employment Law Derek Reid, partner & Accredited Specialist

Commercial Leasing Stewart Brymer, partner & Accredited Specialist

Family Law Stephen Brand, partner, Accredited Specialist & qualified Mediator

Agricultural Law Michael Blair, partner & Accredited Specialist. David Laird, consultant & Accredited Specialist.

Also corporate, environmental, licensing, debt recovery, intellectual property, personal injury, estate agency network and investment services division

Nature of clientele: Private and public companies, businesses, academic institutions, housing associations, property developers, trusts, families and individuals.

Foreign connections: Member of International Jurists network.

Managing partner:	Colin Millar
Chairman:	Jack Robertson
Number of partners:	20
Assistant solicitors:	20
Other fee-earners:	20

WORKLOADS	
Residential property	27%
Commercial Property & Corporate	26%
Private client	24%
Litigation	16%
Agriculture	7%

CONTACTS	
Commercial	Graham Wilson
Litigation	Lindsay Wood
Private client	Nick Barclay
Residential property	Colin Graham

THRINGS & LONG

MIDLAND BRIDGE, BATH, BA1 2HQ
Tel: (01225) 448494 **Fax:** (01225) 319735 **DX:** 8002 BATH

2 NORTH PARADE, FROME, BA11 1AT
Tel: (01373) 465431 **Fax:** (01373) 473992 **DX:** 43803 FROME

The Firm: A West country firm with 200 years of tradition behind it. Yet it is growing fast, investing heavily in staff and systems. Over the last year the firm has increased its solicitors by 15% and now has specialists in planning and intellectual property, backing up the existing teams involved in property and company commercial work. Further qualified staff are still being sought within these departments.

On the systems side: The firm is investing heavily in modern Windows based systems in the belief that good staff and modern systems will give unbeatable value to clients.

Principal Areas of Work:

Company and Commercial: (*Contact Partner:* David Holt – Head of Department). Wide experience of company acquisitions and sales, business start-ups, company reorganisations, joint ventures, partnerships, intellectual property, information technology, charitable companies, insolvency, sports law and trading terms and conditions.

Commercial Property: All types of commercial property acquisition, sales and developments including joint venture agreements and planning and environmental law. Particular experience in French property transactions.

Charities: The Charities Department acts for a variety of charitable organisations, particularly almshouses, grant making and medical charities and churches. It provides practical and cost effective advice on all aspects of charity law and practice.

Residential Property: (*Contact Partner:* William Power – Head of Department). Extensive large volume relocation and investment purchases using computer technology.

Litigation: (*Contact Partner:* Stephen Roberts – Head of Department). The largest department and particularly known for commercial, property and planning litigation, employment law, sports law, family law, road traffic/personal injury work, medical negligence.

Private Client: (*Contact Partner:* Helen Starkie – Head of Department). Combining the skills of experienced lawyers with an in-house accountant, an ex-tax inspector and a financial services specialist together with the latest technology, the firm remains committed to providing a quality service to the private client.

The Agriculture Department: Widely recognised and respected as a specialist department providing extensive advice and representation to farmers and landowners in Somerset, Wilts, Dorset, Devon, Berks & Glos, and further afield.

Senior partner:	Jeremy Thring
Chief Executive:	Nigel Cobb
Number of partners:	12
Assistant solicitors:	18
Other fee-earners:	15

WORKLOADS	
Litigation	29%
Agriculture, probate, trusts and tax	28%
Company, commercial and charities	25%
Conveyancing	18%

CONTACTS	
Agriculture	Jonathan Cheal, David Holt
Charity	Quentin Elston
Commercial property	David Holt
Company & commercial	Jonathan Wyld
Debt recovery/credit control	Amanda Noyce
Employment law	Stephen Roberts
Family law	Meg Moss
Financial services	William Power
Litigation	Angus Halden, Stephen Roberts
Probate & trusts	Jeremy Thring, Helen Starkie
Residential property	William Power
Sports Law	Stephen Roberts
Tax	Michael Young

THURSFIELDS 14 & 27 Church Street, Kidderminster, DY10 2AJ *Tel:* (01562) 820575 *Fax:* (01562) 66783 *DX:* 16304 *Ptnrs:* 13 *Asst solrs:* 7 *Other fee-earners:* 16

TILLY BAILEY & IRVINE York Chambers, York Rd, Hartlepool, TS26 9DP *Tel:* (01429) 264101 *Fax:* (01429) 274796 *DX:* 60650 *Ptnrs:* 14 *Asst solrs:* 17 *Other fee-earners:* 26

TITMUSS SAINER DECHERT

2 SERJEANTS' INN, LONDON, EC4Y 1LT
Tel: (0171) 583 5353 **Fax:** (0171) 353 3683 **DX:** 30 LONDON **Email:** MARKETING@TITMUSS-DECHERT.COM

The Firm: Titmuss Sainer Dechert is one of the leading City of London firms, with a total complement of 315 lawyers and supporting staff. Together with Dechert Price and Rhoads, one of the largest US law firms, they form a fully integrated international legal practice, with more than 550 lawyers in ten offices located throughout the US, UK and Europe. The firms provide a full range of legal services to major industrial, property, financial and individual clients throughout the world.

Nature of Clientele: The firm's clients include substantial UK and international listed and private companies from a wide cross-section of industry and commerce.

Principal Areas of Work:

Corporate Services: (*Contact:* David Vogel). Core services include flotations, capital issues, transborder and domestic mergers, acquisitions and disposals and corporate reorganisations and recoveries.

Property: (*Contact:* Chris Edwards). A comprehensive range of property services including commercial, industrial and retail development, investment and dealing. Clients include major retailers, property developers, large corporations and public authorities.

Planning: (*Contact:* Justin True). All aspects of planning including: enquiry work; development plans; compulsory purchase; conservation; highways; infrastructure; rating and judicial review.

Construction: (*Contact:* Charles Brown). Drafting and enforcements of building contracts, collateral warranties, professional appointments, maintenance agreements, insurance and the preparation and handling of claims through negotiation, arbitration or litigation.

Environment: (*Contact:* Chris Webb). All aspects of environmental law including regulatory matters and enforcement. Dealing with the environmental implications of major multinational mergers and acquisitions under EU legislation.

Financial Services: (*Contact:* Peter Astleford). Legal, regulatory and tax advice to financial service firms and advice on the legal aspects of operating an investment management business in Europe, North America and other markets around the globe.

Insurance and Reinsurance: (*Contact:* Michael Smith). The firm serves Lloyd's and non-Lloyd's insurance and reinsurance clients and deals with mergers and acquisitions in the insurance market, insurance litigation and arbitration and advice upon the Lloyd's Act and Byelaws.

Investigations: (*Contact:* David Byrne). All civil and criminal aspects of corporate fraud, DTI inquiries, SFO investigations, Inland Revenue and Customs & Excise investigations, disciplinary proceedings, insider dealing, investigations by the SROs, money laundering and compliance.

Banking: (*Contact:* Tevor Beadle). Acting for banks, institutional lenders and capital corporations in relation to domestic and international secured lending with particular emphasis on corporate, property, trade finance and asset finance (aviation), together with related expertise in securitisation and capital markets.

Corporate Recovery: (*Contact:* Sally Unwin). Legal support and advice to lenders, insolvency practitioners and borrowers, particularly in connection with corporate rescues, debt rescheduling and workouts.

Commercial Litigation: (*Contact:* Andrew Hearn). Comprehensive commercial litigation services in a broad range of national and international disputes before courts, arbitrators, tribunals and inquiries both in the UK and overseas. The disputes concern areas as diverse as banking, insurance, intellectual property and defamation. Also provide ADR services.

Property Litigation: (*Contact:* Jeremy Grose). All forms of dispute resolution concerning landlord and tenant, lease renewals, rent reviews and possession proceedings including self-help remedies. Advice concerning boundary disputes, easements, rights of light, restrictive covenants, professional negligence relating to property, realisation of security, property related insolvency and disputes arising out of the sale of land.

Public Sector: (*Contact:* Graham McGowan). Specialist local authority consultancy for major schemes and local government finance.

Commercial Law: (*Contact:* Simon Leonard). Intellectual property, UK and EC competition law, computer law, anti-piracy, product liability, overseas joint ventures and general commercial contracts. The firm's trade mark service assists in the management and protection of trade marks, names and logos.

Employment & Pensions: (*Contact:* Charles Wynn-Evans). Acts for employers and individuals on employment and pensions disputes and all non-contentious issues particularly in relation to public list companies and flotations.

Chief Executive:	Peter Duffell
Senior Partner:	Steven Fogel
Number of partners:	42
Assistant solicitors:	81
Other fee-earners:	32

WORKLOADS	
Property	40%
Corporate	22%
Litigation	18%
Financial and insurance services	15%
Tax and private client	5%

CONTACTS	
Banking	Trevor Beadle
Commercial	Simon Leonard
Commercial litigation, IP, Defamation	Andrew Hearn
Construction	Charles Brown
Corporate	David Vogel
Corporate Recovery	Sally Unwin
Corporate Tax	Mark Stapleton
Customs & excise, VAT	Malachy Cornwell-Kelly
Employment	Charles Wynn-Evans
Environment	Chris Webb
Financial services	Peter Astleford
Insurance/ Lloyd's	Michael Smith
Investigatons	David Byrne
IT	Renzo Marchini
Pensions	Wyn Derbyshire
Planning	Justin True
Property	Chris Edwards
Property litigation	Jeremy Grose
Public sector	Graham McGowan
Tax and private client	Ian Marsh
Trade marks	Paul Kavanagh

Customs, Excise and International Trade Taxation: (*Contact:* Malachy Cornwell-Kelly). All negotiations and disputes in customs, excise, VAT, and matters arising from international trade taxation, particularly anti-dumping, origin, classification and valuation matters, especially in the area of transfer pricing.

Tax and Private Client: (*Contact:* Ian Marsh). All aspects of estate planning, both on shore and off shore for domiciles and non domiciles including drafting of wills, settlements, and all aspects of individual personal affairs (except matrimonial). UK and international tax planning of corporate & commercial transactions, tax & VAT planning of UK property transactions, personal tax planning for high net worth individuals, tax litigation.

Recruitment and Training: Trainee solicitor recruitment is organised to give the fullest attention to individual career development. Andrew Hearn, Chairman of the Trainee Solicitors Recruitment Panel, co-ordinates the training programme which embraces the CPD and which is essentially practical, but includes in-house and external seminars and courses in business development and management. *Contact:* Lynn Muncey for trainee solicitor recruitment brochure.

TODS MURRAY WS

66 QUEEN STREET, EDINBURGH, EH2 4NE
Tel: (0131) 226 4771 **Fax:** (0131) 225 3676 **DX:** ED58 **Email:** MAILDESK@TODSMURRAY.CO.UK

Tods Murray is recognised to be a leading Scottish firm offering a wide range of services with an emphasis on corporate and commercial work.

The Firm: Tods Murray is implementing a new strategy with the development of three core areas of specialism – banking, capital projects and commercial property. These core areas are of particular high quality in which the firm is seen to be highly competitive.

Tods Murray has seen significant growth in 1997 with the addition of key personnel to the firm, which has added further strength and depth of expertise, especially to the core areas of banking, capital projects and commercial property. The appointment in July 1998 of Gordon Prestige as a Banking partner will allow the firm to build on and develop further its high quality banking services.

This growth in personnel reflects the high levels of activity experienced across all areas of the firm during 1997, as demonstrated by an increase in business of 45% in one of the core areas.

At Tods Murray the focus is client-orientated, offering teams with a range of technical skills to meet clients' needs. The firm has a wide-ranging client base including listed companies, institutional investors, landowners and farmers, small businesses and private individuals.

Tods Murray has developed good working relationships with various English Law firms, for whom it conducts the Scottish aspects of cross-border transactions, and has a significant clientele based outwith Scotland. On an international level, membership of Multilaw provides Tods Murray with a network of associated law firms located in the world's major commercial centres.

The firm has invested in the latest PC network and can provide better value for money both in terms of speed of response and flexibility of working.

Principal Areas of Work: At the core of the Firm's activities are Banking, Capital Projects and Commercial Property. The Banking Team has extensive experience in corporate and public sector lending, project finance, property finance and securitisation. The Capital Projects Team deals with all capital and infrastructure projects including PFI with particular expertise in healthcare, water, waste to energy, social housing and local authority projects. The Commercial Property Team, which specialises in major developments and funding agreements, acts for a number of major insurers and pension funds in relation to their property portfolios. The Team also offers advice on planning, construction and environmental projects.

The Corporate Team is recognised for its' experience in corporate finance including public issues, acquisitions, placings and buy-outs, as well as expertise in financial services and unit trusts. The Team also has significant entertainment, leisure and travel expertise including timeshare.

The Litigation Team handles all types of commercial and civil litigation across the firm for both commercial and private clients.

The Private Client Team, with a renowned reputation, provides services to landowners and farmers undertaking all the legal work associated with landed estates and farms. The Team deals with wills, trusts and executries, charities, tax and estate planning, financial management (on behalf of both individuals and trusts) and the purchase and sale of residential property.

Managing partner:	John Biggar
Chairman:	Charles Abram
Number of partners:	29
Assistant solicitors:	39
Other fee-earners:	22

WORKLOADS	
Commercial property	33%
Corporate	31%
Tax, estates and trusts	12%
Litigation	10%
Agriculture, estates, forestry	9%
Residential property	5%

CONTACTS	
Agriculture, Landed Estates and Forestry	
	John Fulton
Banking	Hamish Patrick
Capital Projects/PFI	Ian McPake, William Simmons
Charities	David McLetchie
Commercial Property	Douglas Moffat
Construction	Ross Campbell
Corporate and Commercial	David Dunsire
Corporate Finance	William Simmons
Corporate Financial Services	Chris Athanas
Employment Law	Robert Dobie
Entertainment and Media	Richard Findlay
Hotels and Licensed Premises	Angus McIntyre
Insolvency	Robert Dobie
Intellectual Property	Richard Findlay
Leisure and Travel	David Anderson
Litigation	Michael Simpson
Pensions	Martin Thurston Smith
Planning and Environment	Ian McPake
Residential Property	Gordon Cunningham
Securitisation	Graham Burnside
Wills, Tax and Trusts	David McLetchie

TOLHURST FISHER Trafalgar Hse, 8 Nelson Street, Southend-on-Sea, SS1 1EF *Tel:* (01702) 352511 *Fax:* (01702) 348900 *DX:* 2811 *Ptnrs:* 5 *Asst solrs:* 4 *Other fee-earners:* 8

TOLLER HALES & COLLCUTT

CASTILIAN CHAMBERS, 2 CASTILIAN STREET, NORTHAMPTON, NN1 1JX
Tel: (01604) 258558 **Fax:** (01604) 258500 **DX:** 12422

The Firm: Established in 1877, Toller Hales & Collcutt is a broadly based provincial practice with four offices in Northamptonshire. It offers a full range of legal services to both commercial and private clients.

Principal Areas of Work:

Corporate/ Commercial: (*Contact Partner:* Christopher Pykett). The department undertakes all aspects of company formation, acquisition and disposal, MBOs and MBIs, joint ventures, reconstruction, franchise, agency and distribution agreements, taxation, intellectual property, EC law and insolvency.

Commercial Property: (*Contact Partner:* Andrew Rudkin). The firm offers a wide-ranging property service covering industrial, retail and offices premises, and acquisition, disposal, leasing, landlord and tenant law, building contracts, joint ventures, property taxation (VAT), investment and development work. A specialist Planning Unit deals with all planning issues. Liquor licensing is also included in this department.

Litigation: (*Contact Partner:* John Campbell). The litigation team handles all aspects of commercial and private client litigation. Specialist areas of practice include employment disputes (contracts, redundancy, wrongful dismissal and discrimination), personal injury (five PI Panel Solicitors), medical negligence, professional negligence, construction and insurance.

Family/ Child Care: (*Contact Partner:* David Eastwood). The firm has a specialist unit dealing with all aspects of family disputes which is the largest in the County.

Private Client: (*Contact Partner:* Barry Rogers). The firm offers a comprehensive service to the private client, including all types of property transfers, wills, trusts, probate and a dedicated financial planning department.

Legal Aid Franchise: Awarded during 1995 covering crime, personal injury, family, debt, employment and consumer issues.

Nature of Clientele: Clients range from insurance companies and P.L.Cs to businesses of all sizes. The firm has a strong private client base and is a member of the Conquest Network.

Other Offices: Corby, Kettering and Wellingborough.

Recruitment and Training: The firm expects to take on two trainee solicitors every year and applications should be made on the firm's own application form to Mr David Fowler.

Managing partner:	David Fowler
Senior partner:	Anthony Noone
Number of partners:	17
Assistant solicitors:	16
Other fee-earners:	27

WORKLOADS	
Litigation	36%
Private Client	28%
Family	24%
Commercial	12%

TOWNLEYS

DALBY HOUSE, 396-398 CITY ROAD, LONDON, EC1V 2QA
Tel: (0171) 713 7000 **Fax:** (0171) 713 2999 **DX:** 53303 **email:** <FIRSTNAME>@TOWNLEYS.CO.UK

The Firm: Townleys is a commercial firm specialising in every aspect of sports, sports media and sponsorship law. The firm has unparalleled experience in the domestic and international sports business, and is very much at the forefront of developments in this area. Townleys is widely regarded both at home and internationally as the pre-eminent specialist UK sports law firm.

Principal Areas of Work: The firm has particular expertise in advising on legal and commercial rights structures and strategies for sports and media clients, the drafting and negotiation of major sponsorship and broadcasting contracts, licensing, character marketing, event planning, sports governing body regulations and procedures, player contracts/endorsements/transfers, the development and protection of intellectual property rights in sports brands, international trademark programmes, personality rights, pay per view television and interactive sports rights, ambush marketing, broadcasting and sports related multi-media and IT law and regulations.

The firm has separate sports rights consultancy and international tax planning divisions.

Clients/Projects: A great deal of the firm's practice concerns the legal structuring and commercial exploitation of all types of sporting and cultural events and projects. These have included (in 1997/98 alone) Premiership and Nationwide Football League club sponsorships,

Number of partners:	5
Assistant solicitors:	15
Other fee-earners:	5

WORKLOADS	
Sports and media (including litigation)	95%
Other Commercial	5%

CONTACTS	
Broadcasting/Media	Jonathan Higton
Rules and Regulations	Darren Bailey
Sponsorship and IP	Nicholas Couchman
Sports Litigation	Jonathan Taylor
Trainee Applications	Andy Korman

the Nationwide Football League, Asian Football, Five Nations Championship broadcasting rights, Rugby World Cup 1999, the European Rugby Cup, sponsorship of the Rugby Football Union, the Davis Cup, the England and Wales Cricket Board, the English and UK Sports Councils, the UK Sports Institute, Commonwealth Games 2002, Formula One motor racing, the Brit Awards and many more.

Much of its work is international in flavour and the firm has strong overseas connections and foreign language skills. Clients include many major corporate sponsors, sponsorship consultancies, sports television distribution agencies and broadcasters, and advertising and communications agencies. In 1997, the firm produced a comprehensive legal and economic report on the European sponsorship martketplace for the European Commission.

The firm also undertakes a variety of other commercial and contentious work, including commercial and sports litigation (including high profile doping and disciplinary cases), intellectual property law, EC competition law aspects of sports agreements, company law, insolvency, and sports/leisure commercial property transactions. Fluent French, German, Spanish, Mandarin, Hokkien and Cantonese are spoken by members of the firm. Staff include former professional sports people.

TOWNSENDS

42 CRICKLADE STREET, SWINDON, SN1 3HD
Tel: (01793) 410800 **Fax:** (01793) 616294 **DX:** 6204 SWINDON 1 **Email:** SOLICITORS@TOWNSENDS.CO.UK

18 LONDON ROAD, NEWBURY, RG14 1JX
Tel: (01635) 31720 **Fax:** (01635) 32877 **DX:** 30810 NEWBURY **Email:** SOLICITORS@TOWNSENDS.CO.UK

The Firm: Townsends is a leading firm serving the M4 corridor from its offices in Swindon and Newbury. It is a progressive firm and in recent years has expanded across the broad spectrum of activities with both a growing corporate base and the growth of high quality private client services.

Quality and client care are given top priority at Townsends. Emphasis is on regular open communication with clients and client satisfaction surveys are used to evaluate service quality and improve services. In recognition of its commitment to quality and training Townsends is the first law firm in Wiltshire to receive IIP accreditation. The firm is also a Legal Aid franchise holder.

Services to business are comprehensive from cross-border acquisition work to business start ups. The employment team provides "help desk" facilities to local organisations. The property teams cover all Landlord and Tenant work as well as specialist options, development and pension fund work.

Work of the litigation division includes commercial and construction disputes, licensing, debt recovery, defamation, employment law, insurance claims, landlord and tenant, product liability and professional negligence. The construction unit continues to expand and take on high profile national and internation cases.

The firm's reputation for personal injury litigation is outstanding, handling a large volume of cases for both plaintiffs and defendants. Townsends has a national reputation in asbestosis, deafness and serious head injury cases for plaintiffs.

The personal client division provides expertise in tax and trusts, administration of estates, wills and advice for the elderly.

The family law unit is one of the largest in the south west, with seven fee earners, all of whom are members of the SFLA. The firm also has a specialist domestic violence unit and provides residential conveyancing services under the "Homes Direct" brand.

Managing partner:	Mike Sefton
Senior partner:	Julian George
Number of partners:	20
Assistant solicitors:	15
Other fee-earners:	23
Total staff:	124

WORKLOADS	
Personal Client	35%
Business Services	33%
Litigation	33%

CONTACTS	
Agriculture	Chris Goldingham
Building & Construction	John Birch
Commercial property	Tim Butler
Company/Commercial	Brian Jacomb
Employment	Jonathan Payne
Family	Richard Sharp
Head injuries	Byron Carron
Industrial diseases	Brigitte Chandler
IT and Intellectual property	Mike Sefton
Litigation	Mike Nield
Pensions related property work	Rosalind Sopel
Personal client	Sir John Sykes
Propert development	Alan Goulding

TOZERS

BROADWALK HOUSE, SOUTHERNHAY WEST, EXETER, EX1 1UA
Tel: (01392) 207020 **Fax:** (01392) 207019 **DX:** 8322

The Firm: Tozers was established in 1785 and is one of the largest law firms in Devon. The firm offers a successful blend of experience and traditional values on the one hand, and a progressive outlook and a high degree of commercial awareness on the other. All seven offices are linked on an IT network. Specialist teams have been developed to ensure expertise in niche areas.

Principal Areas of Work:

Planning & Environmental Law – including Caravan Parks & Mobile Home Law;

Charities & Schools – the specialist team advises religious, educational and other charities as well as schools both in the private and state sectors;

Commercial Lending & Recovery;

Commercial & Residential property;

Litigation – including employment, property disputes, debt recovery, criminal law and general tribunal and court work;

Family & Childcare;

Medical Negligence & Personal Injury;

Professional Negligence (including pensions mis-selling);

Wills, Probate, Tax & Trusts – including tax planning and investment management for trusts and individuals.

Agency Work: All aspects of civil and criminal litigation, licensing and personal searches.

Other Offices:

Newton Abbot Tel: (01626) 207020; Fax: (01626) 207019; DX: 59102

Teignmouth Tel: (01626) 772376; Fax: (01626) 770317; DX: 82051

Torquay Tel: (01803) 291898; Fax: (01803) 299293; DX: 59023 Torquay 1

Paignton Tel: (01803) 529101; Fax: (01803) 529201; DX: 100610

Dawlish Tel: (01626) 862323; Fax: (01626) 866851; DX: 82100

Plymouth Tel: (01752) 206460; Fax: (01752) 301662; DX 118106

Managing partner:	PW Edwards
Senior partner:	PM McMurtrie
Number of partners:	18
Assistant solicitors:	14
Other fee-earners:	10

WORKLOADS	
Litigation	32%
Commercial	30%
Property	21%
Probate	17%

CONTACTS	
Charities and schools	Richard King
Children and family	Philip Kidd
Commercial lending & property	Tim Fogarty
Litigation	Peter Edwards
Medical negligence	Laurence Vick
Planning and mobile home law	Tony Beard
Probate	Vernon Clarke

TRAVERS SMITH BRAITHWAITE

10 SNOW HILL, LONDON, EC1A 2AL
Tel: (0171) 248 9133 **Fax:** (0171) 236 3728 or 696 3500 **DX:** 79 **Email:** GRADUATE.RECRUITMENT@TRAVERSSMITH.CO.UK

The Firm: Travers Smith Braithwaite is a leading corporate, financial and commercial law firm with the expertise and capability to advise on a wide range of business activities. Today's clients include regulatory, financial, trade and industrial organisations throughout the UK and from all over the world.

Travers Smith Braithwaite prides itself on not being so large as to have an impersonal atmosphere yet enjoys a quality of work and a range of clients normally associated with larger firms. By resisting rapid growth, the firm has been able to maintain the high standards of service it provides to clients. Small, closely knit and consistent teams of lawyers will provide advice to a client year in year out, ensuring a clear understanding of the client's business and an effective working relationship. Central to the firm's approach is the philosophy that partners should be closely involved in most of the matters undertaken and that delegation should not be automatic but considered in every case in the light of both effectiveness and cost.

Principal Areas of Work: The firm's business comprises eight main areas:

Corporate Law: takeovers, mergers and acquisitions, new issues, company law, financial services and regulatory law, capital markets, private equity and venture capital.

Commercial Law: business agreements, EU and competition law, intellectual property, information technology, environment, multi-media, privatisations and broadcasting.

Banking/Insolvency: secured and unsecured lending, finance leasing, acquisition finance, trade and project finance, property finance, banking regulations, rescheduling and insolvency.

Employment: executive service agreements, restrictive covenants, health and safety, works councils and employee consultation, industrial disputes and employment litigation, employment aspects of mergers, acquisitions and reorganisations (including transfers of undertakings).

Litigation: domestic and international, commercial litigation, arbitration and ADR.

Property: acquisition, disposal and development of industrial, retail, office, residential and agricultural property, planning and construction law.

Managing partner:	Alasdair F. Douglas
Number of partners:	48
Assistant solicitors:	75
Other fee-earners:	30

WORKLOADS	
Corporate	30%
Finance	15%
Litigation	15%
Property	15%
Commercial	13%
Pensions	5%
Tax	5%
Employment	2%

CONTACTS	
Banking	Neil Murray
Commercial	Margaret Moore
Competition and EU law	Margaret Moore
Corporate	Christopher Bell
Employment	Dorothy Henderson
Environment	Christopher Carroll
Financial services	Margaret Chamberlain
Insolvency	Jeremy Walsh
Insurance/reinsurance	Stephen Paget-Brown
Litigation	John Kingston
Pensions	Paul Stannard
Property	Robert Harman
Tax	Alasdair Douglas
Venture capital	Christopher Hale

Continues overleaf

Pensions: establishment, administration and winding up of pension funds and pension litigation.

Tax: domestic and international corporate tax planning, acquisition and structured finance, employee share (and other) incentive schemes, private client tax planning.

Work Contacts:
Corporate – *Christopher Bell*
Commercial – *Margaret Moore*
Competition and EU – *Margaret Moore*
Employment – *Dorothy Henderson*
Environment – *Christopher Carroll*
Banking – *Neil Murray*
Financial Services – *Margaret Chamberlain*
Insolvency – *Jeremy Walsh*
Insurance and Reinsurance – *Stephen Paget-Brown*
Litigation – *John Kingston*
Pensions – *Paul Stannard*
Property – *Robert Harman*
Tax – *Alasdair Douglas*
Venture Capital – *Christopher Hale*

TRAVERS SMITH BRAITHWAITE

Foreign Connections: The firm enjoys a close working relationship with foreign law firms in the main legal jurisdictions and is a member of a network of European law firms.

Foreign Languages: French, German, Italian, Spanish.

Other Office: Travers Smith Braithwaite was the first City firm to open an office in Douglas to represent both Isle of Man and non-Isle of Man based corporate clients in relation to a wide range of business requirements and transactions. As Registered Legal Practitioners practising in the Isle of Man, the firm can advise on both English and Isle of Man law, including the provision of opinions to foreign lawyers as to matters of Isle of Man law. Principal areas of work include company, corporate finance, financial services, commercial, intellectual property, employment, pensions, EU and competition, insurance, shipping, banking regulations, asset and shipping finance. *Contact:* Michael Pinson: 4 Upper Church Street, Douglas, Isle of Man IM1 1EE *Tel:* (01624) 625515.

Recruitment & Training: Travers Smith Braithwaite continues to develop and is always looking to recruit, at both assistant and trainee level, people of academic excellence and sound judgement who are able to take their careers, but not themselves, seriously. The firm's training philosophy is that skill and expertise are best acquired through practical experience complemented by carefully targeted formal instruction. Great emphasis is placed on ensuring that trainees are actively involved in a broad range of work. Applications for traineeships should be made in writing to Christopher Carroll enclosing a full CV together with the names and addresses of academic and personal referees.

TRETHOWAN WOODFORD New Street, Salisbury, SP1 2LY *Tel:* (01722) 412512 *Fax:* (01722) 411300 *DX:* 58004 *Ptnrs:* 21 *Asst solrs:* 10 *Other fee-earners:* 22

TREVOR SMYTH & CO 13 Chichester Street, Belfast, BT1 4JB *Tel:* (01232) 320360 *Fax:* (01232) 325636 *Ptnrs:* 5 *Asst solrs:* 6 *Other fee-earners:* 6

TROBRIDGES 1 Ford Park Road, Mutley Plain, Plymouth, PL4 6LY **Tel:** (01752) 664022 **Fax:** (01752) 223761 **DX:** 120154 Mutley Plain **Ptnrs:** 3 **Asst solrs:** 3 **Other fee-earners:** 6 **Contact:** Mr C. Matthews *General practice with a litigation bias.*

WORKLOADS		
Personal injury litigation/ civil litigation		55%
Conveyancing/ commercial work		20%
Probate	13% Family	12%

TROWERS & HAMLINS

SCEPTRE COURT, 40 TOWER HILL, LONDON, EC3N 4DX
Tel: (0171) 423 8000 **Fax:** (0171) 423 8001 **DX:** CDE 774 LON/CITY **Internet:** HTTP://WWW.TROWERS.COM

The Firm: Trowers & Hamlins continues to flourish through successful specialisations developed across a broadly based commercial, property, litigation and private client practice. Particular strengths include housing and housing finance, local government, international and UK projects, construction, the health sector, facilities management, employment, charities, commercial property and public sector work (particularly the raising of private finance and public/private joint ventures).

Internationally and through its UK offices, the firm has developed a strong corporate and commercial practice. As leading lawyers to the housing movement, the firm's London, Manchester and Exeter offices advise government bodies, lenders and some 230 housing associations. In addition, the firm has an impressive commercial litigation reputation and a highly regarded private client practice.

Trowers & Hamlins provide practical, tailored legal solutions and is committed to achieving its clients' objectives. In all matters a client partner will call on appropriate lawyers and resources within the firm to fulfil the particular requirements of the client's brief.

Principal Areas of Work: The company/commercial department is a substantial and dynamic part of the firm with a growing City profile. It advises public and private companies and individuals operating in the financial, property, industrial and commercial sectors.

The projects and construction group advise UK and international clients in a variety of sectors, spanning innovative PFI/DBFO/BOOT project structures and joint venture/partnering initiatives.

The property department covers commercial, housing, local authority, residential, estate and institutional law. It has a substantial property team and has established a reputation for innovation and for working in the forefront of changing legislation. It provides a wide range of services to corporate clients, international businesses and individuals. Clients include investment institutions, developers, housing associations and local authorities.

The litigation department deals with a wide range of commercial civil litigation, arbitration and ADR both nationally and internationally, with a particular profile in professional and medical negligence cases. It is also involved in property, insolvency, employment and personal injury work. The department has a high reputation for its construction work including mediation and adjudication.

The private client department provides legal advice to individuals with industrial or commercial wealth, invested assets or landed estates. It is concerned particularly with tax planning, trusts, wills, probate, charities, and the administration of trusts and estates.

The firm has a strong international network, particularly in the Middle East, where it has offices in Oman, Dubai, Abu Dhabi and Bahrain. Trowers & Hamlins' considerable Anglo-German practice exemplifies its established relationships with lawyers worldwide including an associated practice in Singapore.

Nature of Clientele: The firm's clients include banks, public and private companies, national and local government departments, NHS Trusts, housing bodies, partnerships, charities and individuals.

Recruitment: The firm is always happy to hear from lawyers interested in working in a commercial environment. It recruits at least 12 trainee solicitors each year.

Other Offices: Manchester, Exeter, Oman, Dubai, Abu Dhabi, Bahrain.

Managing partner:	Ralph Picken
Senior partner:	John Clark
UK	
Number of partners:	48
Assistant solicitors:	53
Other fee-earners:	42
International	
Number of partners:	7
Assistant solicitors:	8
Other fee-earners:	6

WORKLOADS	
Property (housing, public sector, commercial property)	34%
Litigation	32%
Company/Commercial and Construction	26%
Private client	8%

CONTACTS	
Banking	Ralph Picken
Charities	Jean Dollimore
Commercial property	Elizabeth McKibbin
Company/ commercial	Donald Jones
Construction	David Mosey
Corporate finance	Jennie Gubbins
Employment	Emma Burrows
Environmental	Ian Doolittle
Facilities Management	Martin Amison
Housing (general)	Jonathan Adlington, Ian Graham
International Projects	Martin Amison
Litigation	Don Moorhouse, John Linwood
Private Client	Michael Williamson
Projects/PFI	Ian Graham, David Mosey
Public Sector	Ian Doolittle
Tax	Neil Cohen

TROWERS & HAMLINS

TRUMANS 22 Park Row, Nottingham, NG1 6GX **Tel:** (0115) 941 7275 **Fax:** (0115) 948 4272 **DX:** 10023 **Ptnrs:** 10 **Asst solrs:** 11 **Other fee-earners:** 20 **Contact:** Mr. J.M. Appleby *General practice concentrating on private client work with a strong litigation department and a growing commercial department.*

WORKLOADS			
Civil litigation	40%	Crime	15%
Matrimonial			15%
Residential conveyancing			15%
Probate	7%	Debt	5%
Company/ commercial	3%		

TRUMPS

P O BOX 8000, ONE REDCLIFF STREET, BRISTOL, BS99 2SD
Tel: (0117) 946 8200 **Fax:** (0117) 946 8201 **DX:** 7815 BRISTOL **Email:** TRUMP@TRUMPS.COM

The Firm: This expanding, substantial practice in Bristol's city-centre provides a variety of services to business and individual clients. It aims to offer clients unrivalled personal attention and is committed to providing a high quality service. Specialist teams have been developed to ensure expertise in work areas.

The firm holds a Legal Aid Franchise and was one of the first firms in Bristol to be accredited as an Investor in People.

Principal Areas of Work:

Business Client: A broad range of corporate/commercial law expertise is provided with specialisations in acquisitions and disposals, venture capital transactions, property development, employment, insolvency, intellectual property and partnership, particulary medical. There is a strong international element.

Family: The practice has notable strengths and experience in family law matters and is consistently acknowledged as the best in the region.

Litigation: Particular expertise is provided in professional indemnity and negligence, all types of insolvency, licensing, mortgage possession proceedings, personal injury and fatal accident liability and general commercial matters.

Private client: Financial services is a particular strength which enhances the traditional services of conveyancing, wills, trusts and probate.

Agency work: Agency work is undertaken in all matrimonial and civil courts in Bristol.

Recruitment and Training: Applications for training contracts should be submitted in writing with typed CV one year before commencement date, for the attention of Philip May.

Managing partner:	Robert Bourns
Senior partner:	Nicholas Pritchard
Number of partners:	8
Assistant solicitors:	15
Other fee-earners:	19

WORKLOADS	
Business client	43%
Litigation	29%
Family/ divorce	15%
Private client	13%

CONTACTS	
Commercial property	Nicholas Pritchard
Corporate/commercial	Nick Moss
Employment	Robert Bourns
Family	David Woodward
Financial services	Erica Thomas
Insolvency	Philip May
Litigation	Andrew Troup
Partnership	Nick Moss
Personal injury/medical	Jo Hillman
Private client	Erica Thomas

TUCKERS

39 WARREN STREET, LONDON, W1P 5PD
Tel: (0171) 388 8333 **Fax:** (0171) 388 7333 **DX:** 123596 REGENTS PARK 3

7 ST JOHN STREET, MANCHESTER, M3 4DN
Tel: (0161) 835 1414 **Fax:** (0161) 835 1415 **DX:** 18190 MANCHESTER

The Firm: Tuckers Solicitors, a purely criminal law firm have offices located in the North of England and Central London. The firm acts on behalf of both private and legally aided clients in all aspects of criminal law from drink driving to murder, with specialist knowledge of extradition, prison mutiny and youth cases.

We have a specialist white collar crime department which has expertise in DTI frauds, Customs & Excise cases and other business crime.

Agency Work: As the offices are staffed 24 hours a day, police station attendance is always available to clients and other firms of solicitors/accountants requiring assistance for their own clients.

Senior partner:	Franklin Sinclair
Managing partner:	Barry Tucker
Number of partners:	2
Assistant solicitors:	18
Other fee-earners:	60

WORKLOADS	
Crime (all types)	100%

CONTACTS	
Business crime/fraud	B. Craig
Crime (London)	Barry Tucker
Crime (Manchester)	Franklin Sinclair

TUCKER TURNER KINGSLEY WOOD & CO 18 Bedford Row, London, WC1R 4EB *Tel:* (0171) 242 3303 *Fax:* (0171) 831 1732 *DX:* 220 *Ptnrs:* 6 *Asst solrs:* 5 *Other fee-earners:* 8

TUGHAN & CO

MARLBOROUGH HOUSE, 30 VICTORIA STREET, BELFAST, BT1 3GS
Tel: (01232) 553300 **Fax:** (01232) 550096 **DX:** 433NR BELFAST 1 **Email:** LAW@TUGHAN.DNET.CO.UK

The Firm: Tughan & Co was established in 1896 and has developed over the years into one of the largest firms of solicitors in Northern Ireland. The firm's main priority is to provide clear sound advice to its many clients through a personal service which is supported by the latest technological developments.

Principal Areas of Work:

Litigation: *(Contact Partner:* Michael Gibson). The firm handles a broad range of litigation and arbitration and is particularly active in insurance defence work and employment disputes.

Commercial Property: *(Contact Partner:* Phyllis Agnew). The firm acts for a broad range of Irish and UK-based property developers, institutions, investors and national retail chains in connection with developments, town centre re-generation, joint ventures, PFI projects, sales and purchases and leases of commercial and industrial property in Northern Ireland.

Corporate Finance/Commercial: *(Contact Partner:* John-George Willis). The firm has been involved in a number of high profile corporate transactions in Northern Ireland in recent years, including two privatisations. Principal activities involve acquisitions, mergers, share issues in public and private companies, inward investments, joint ventures and shareholder agreements.

Construction: *(Contact Partner:* Keith Cowan). The firm is involved in both contentious and non-contentious aspects of construction projects both in Northern Ireland and further afield. Much of the work involves arbitration and ADR as well as litigation.

Insolvency: *(Contact Partner:* Keith Cowan). The firm acts for a number of receivers, administrators and liquidators and has a large insolvency practice involving, in particular, business restructuring and asset recovery.

Banking/Financial Services: *(Contact Partner:* John Mills). The banking side of the practice has grown considerably in recent years and the firm now acts for a heavyweight client list of national international banks and finance institutions requiring assets and securitisation advice. The firm also acts within Northern Ireland for the principal regulators of the UK financial services industry.

Links with other law firms: A significant number of new instructions are received on the recommendations of other law firms principally in the City of London, Glasgow/Edinburgh and Dublin, with whom Tughan & Co. has over the years developed strong links. Our knowledge of and relationship with these firms enables Tughan & Co. to react rapidly upon receipt of instructions, quite often in connection with multi-jurisdictional transations, with a Northern Ireland element.

International associations: The firm is a member of Mackrell International, an association of independent law firms throughout the world and the network is used regularly by both Tughan & Co.'s clients requiring advice from lawyers in other jurisdictions and also by other Northern Irish law firms having a close relationship with Tughan & Co.

Number of partners:	9
Assistant solicitors:	7
Other fee-earners:	5

WORKLOADS	
Litigation (including insurance and employment law)	45%
Company/ commercial (including banking, finance, M&As & insolvency	40%
Private client	10%

CONTACTS	
Banking & finance	John Mills
Commercial litigation	Keith Cowan
Commercial property	Phyllis Agnew
Construction	Keith Cowan
Conveyancing/ building estates	Noelle McKay
Corporate Finance/Commercial	John-George Willis
Debt recovery	Keith Cowan
Employment & labour law	Grahame Loughlin
Environmental law	Deirdre Magill
Insolvency	Keith Cowan
Litigation & insurance	C M H Gibson
Mergers & acquisitions	John-George Willis
Private client	Noelle McKay
Wills, trusts, estate planning	Noelle McKay

TURBERVILLES WITH NELSON CUFF

122 HIGH STREET, UXBRIDGE, UB8 1JT
Tel: (01895) 201700 **Fax:** (01895) 273519 **DX:** 45116 UXBRIDGE **Email:** SOLICITORS@TURBERVILLES.CO.UK
Internet: WWW.TURBERVILLES.CO.UK

The Firm: The firm was created in April 1998 from the merger of Turbervilles with Nelson Cuff. Its main office is in Uxbridge, with branch offices in Hillingdon and Harrow.

Principal Areas of Work: The firm handles a broad spread of work for commercial, company, private and legally-aided clients, covering commercial and domestic property; land acquisition and development; civil, family, employment and personal injury litigation; commercial litigation and debt recovery; wills, probate, estates and trusts; licensing; crime; animal welfare; immigration; County court agency.

	Sess Sigré
Senior partner:	
Number of partners:	10
Assistant solicitors:	13
Other fee-earners:	17

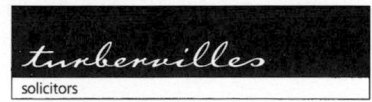

TURCAN CONNELL WS Saltire Court, 20 Castle Street, Edinburgh, Lothian *Tel:* (0131) 228 8111 *Fax:* (0131) 228 8118 *DX:* 553000 Edin 18

TURNBULL, SIMSON & STURROCK WS 26 High Street, Jedburgh, TD8 6AE **Tel:** (01835) 862391 **Fax:** (01835) 862017 **DX:** 1223 Jedburgh **Ptnrs:** 4 **Contact:** Denbeigh Kirkpatrick *Offers a broad range of services. Expertise in relation to agricultural law.*

TURNER & CO 107 Fenchurch Street, London, EC3M 5JB **Tel:** (0171) 480 7991 **Fax:** (0171) 481 0939 **Ptnrs:** 2 **Asst solrs:** 1 **Other fee-earners:** 1 **Contact:** Mr P. Turner *A specialist shipping, commodities and general commercial practice.*

TURNERS 1 Poole Rd, Bournemouth, BH2 5QQ *Tel:* (01202) 291291 *Fax:* (01202) 553606 *DX:* 7637 *Ptnrs:* 15 *Asst solrs:* 4 *Other fee-earners:* 6

T.V. EDWARDS

29 MILE END RD, LONDON, E1 4TP
Tel: (0171) 791 1050 **Fax:** (0171) 790 5101 **DX:** 300700 TOWER HAMLETS

The Firm: Established in 1929 for many years its criminal practice dominated; the firm has in the last five years substantially and successfully expanded its family and civil litigation departments.

Principal Areas of Work:
    Crime: All areas of criminal work including complex and substantial fraud. The firm has expertise in assisting professionals (bankers, solicitors, accountants) in difficulties with the police. The criminal law work of the firm has a national reputation.
    Civil Litigation: Commercial and general contract disputes; professional negligence; intellectual property.
    Personal injury and medical negligence, including industrial injury and disease, road traffic accident, Members of Personal Injury Panel and APIL.
    Housing, advice and representation of tenants and Housing Associations at all levels relating to Landlord and Tenant (public and private).
    Social Welfare law, including nationally renowned community care practice, mental health, welfare benefits, particularly judicial review.
    Employment, advice and representation on all aspects, including contracts, dismissals, discrimination, to employers and employees. Member of Employment Lawyers Association.
    Family: All areas of family law; divorce; injunctions, finance, children (public and private law) adoptions and abductions.
    Non Contentious: Wills, Probate and the administration of estates, residential and commercial conveyancing.
    Licensing: On and off licences including hotels and theatres. Agencies undertaken in local courts where knowledge of the licensing division is of great importance.

Managing partner:	Ian Duncan
Number of partners:	5
Assistant solicitors:	25
Other fee-earners:	12

WORKLOADS	
Civil	35%
Crime	35%
Family	20%
Non Contentious	10%

CONTACTS	
Civil	Alison Downie ((0171) 790 7000)
Crime	Anthony Edwards ((0171) 790 7000)
	Paul Mason ((0171) 790 7060)
Family	Tracey Parsons ((0171) 791 1050)
Licensing	Anthony Edwards ((0171) 790 7000)
Non Contentious	Ian Duncan ((0171) 791 1050)

TWEEDIE & PRIDEAUX

5 LINCOLN'S INN FIELDS, LONDON, WC2A 3BT
Tel: (0171) 242 9231 **Fax:** (0171) 831 1525 **DX:** 6 CH.LN

The Firm: A long established practice. The firm undertakes company and commercial work; commercial conveyancing; private client work including residential conveyancing, wills, trusts and probate; litigation and work for charities.

Other Office: 390 London Road, Mitcham, Surrey CR4 4EA.
Tel: (0181) 640 5124. *Fax:* (0181) 640 2695. *DX:* 88151 Mitcham South.

Foreign Languages Spoken: French and Spanish.

Foreign Connections: Zimbabwe and Albania.

Number of partners:	8
Assistant solicitors:	4
Other fee-earners:	6

WORKLOADS	
Probate & trusts	35%
Litigation	18%
Residential conveyancing	15%
Commercial conveyancing	14%
Commercial work	9%
Other private client work	5%
Charities	4%

TWITCHEN MUSTERS & KELLY

COUNTY CHAMBERS, 25-27 WESTON ROAD, SOUTHEND-ON-SEA, SS1 1BB
Tel: (01702) 339222 **Fax:** (01702) 331563 **DX:** 2821 SOUTHEND **Email:** TMKSOLS@LINK.ORG

The Firm: A firm specialising in Crime, Family and Personal Injury only. The largest criminal practice and legal aid firm in Essex and the first firm in the country to have two Higher Court Advocates conducting criminal work. The firm carries Legal Aid Franchises in eight categories. Partners are Law Society panel members in their respective fields.

Principal Areas of Work: Crime, Personal Injury and Civil Litigation, Family and Child Care. Agency work welcomed.

Contacts:
  Crime: *Patrick Musters*
  Family: *John Twitchen*
  Personal Injury: *Sean Callaghan*

Contact partner:	Patrick Musters
Number of partners:	7
Assistant solicitors:	9
Other fee-earners:	14

WORKLOADS	
Crime	50%
Family	33%
Personal Injury	17%

TYNDALLWOODS Windsor House, Temple Row, Birmingham, B2 5TS *Tel:* (0121) 624 1111 *Fax:* (0121) 624 8401 *DX:* 13039 Birmingham 1 *Ptnrs:* 10 *Asst solrs:* 12 *Other fee-earners:* 18

UNDERWOOD & CO (INCORPORATING CORBOULD RIGBY & CO)

40 WELBECK STREET, LONDON, W1M 8LN
Tel: (0171) 487 4461/(0171) 935 2821 **Fax:** (0171) 486 8974 **DX:** 9074 WEST END

The Firm: Underwood & Co is a forward-looking firm in the West End of London. Its broad client base comprises banks, public and private companies and there is a busy private client department. The firm is particularly strong in banking and professional negligence litigation, commercial property, secured lending and debt recovery. Founded in 1845, during its long history the firm has developed an impressive combination of expertise and personal service. The partnership aims to provide advice of a City standard at reasonable cost. The firm is also highly regarded for its employment and immigration work.

Principal Areas of Work:

  Banking and Commercial Litigation: The firm has strong experience in handling many sorts of commercial litigation from heavyweight banking and insolvency cases to computerised volume mortgage possession work and debt recovery.

  Professional Negligence Litigation: An early entrant into this rapidly developing growth area, the firm has successfully managed scores of cases against solicitors, surveyors, accountants and other professionals. The emphasis is on negotiating a commercially sound settlement as early as possible in proceedings and only taking an action to trial if this is really necessary to secure the best result.

  Commercial Property: The firm has wide experience in this area including the transfer of freehold and leasehold property and the grant and renewal of commercial leases. A particular speciality is acting for institutions on secured lending.

  Medical and Dental: A comprehensive service is provided for dental and medical practitioners who have long formed part of the firm's clientele. The firm also has a growing presence in the nursing home sector acting for a number of companies and home owners.

  Company/Commercial: Work includes company formation and restructuring, sale and purchase of business assets, licensing, partnership agreements and commercial contracts, intellectual property and insolvency matters.

  Employment and Immigration: The firm advises both employers and senior employees on all aspects of appointment, remuneration and termination, including transfers of undertakings and discrimination disputes. In relation to immigration, the firm advises on the issue of work permits, establishing business in the UK and residence for persons of independent means.

  Private Client: The firm provides advice on family and divorce, administration and estates, wills and probate, trusts and tax planning. Additionally this firm undertakes residential conveyancing of higher value property.

Senior partner:	Bernard Dawson
Number of partners:	9
Assistant solicitors:	10
Other fee-earners:	4

WORKLOADS	
Commercial litigation	50%
Commercial and residential property	30%
Company commercial	10%
Private client	10%

CONTACTS	
Commercial	Peter Hughes
Commercial Property	Justin Roche/Leona Mason
Employment	Roger Digby
Litigation	Bernard Dawson/Paul Redfern
Private Client	Hilary Guest

UNDERWOODS

1 HOLYWELL HILL, ST. ALBANS, AL1 1ER
Tel: (01727) 810800 **Fax:** (01727) 841293 **Email:** UNDERWOODS@COMPUSERVE.COM (ALL OFFICES)

2 BUSHFIELD ROAD, BOVINGDON, HP3 0DR
Tel: (01442) 831343 **Fax:** (01442) 831035

HAMILTON HOUSE, 111 MARLOWES, HEMEL HEMPSTEAD, HP1 1BB
Tel: (01442) 831343 **Fax:** (01442) 831035

The Firm: Founded in 1991 Underwoods is a highly-regarded firm specializing in civil litigation and local government matters and is particularly well-known for its employment, personal injury and public and administrative law work. It provides a distinctive high quality personal service and is one of the best firms. Kerry Underwood is on the Law Society's Personal Injury Panel. The firm has pioneered conditional fee work in personal injury cases and contingency fees in employment work and Kerry Underwood is probably the country's leading authority on the subject. Kerry Underwood is a Chairman of Industrial Tribunals, a Fellow of The Chartered Institute of Arbitrators, author of a book on Conditional fees – "No Win No Fee – No Worries" as well as Editor of "Employment Litigation". He also addresses seminars for the Law Society, the University of Cambridge, and others, and contributes to radio, television and legal journals. He is a member of the Law Society's Working Party on Conditional Fees. The firm undertakes agency advocacy in the Employment Appeal Tribunal as well as Industrial Tribunals.

Principal Areas of Work:

Adminstrative/Public Law: (*Contact:* Kerry Underwood). *Work includes:* judicial review, education, civil liberty matters, discrimination, human rights and considerable local authority work.

Local Government Law: (*Contact:* Robert Males/Kerry Underwood). *Work includes:* education law, judicial reviews, joint ventures, leasing and funding, transfers of undertakings.

Corporate and Commercial: (*Contact:* Robert Males). *Work includes:* business start-ups, trading agreements, venture capital, joint venture agreements, insolvency and corporate restructuring, compulsory competitive tendering and transfers of undertakings.

Employment: (*Contact:* Kerry Underwood). *Work includes:* transfer of undertakings regulations, sex and race discrimination, maternity law, EU law, Industrial Tribunal and Employment Appeal Tribunal advocacy, redundancy and contract, and severance. Clients include local authorities and major companies and employees. Kerry Underwood is a member of the Employment Law Advisers Appeal Scheme (formerly the Employment Appeal Tribunal Advice Scheme).

Litigation: (*Contact:* Sharon MacArthur). *Work includes:* personal injury, (Law Society's Personal Injury Panel), medical negligence, building disputes, intellectual property matters, debt recovery and contractual disputes.

Commercial Property: (*Contact:* Robert Males). *Work includes:* sales and acquisitions, leases, landlord and tenant law.

Private Client: (*Contact:* Robert Males). *Work includes:* residential conveyancing, probate, wills and trusts and consumer problems.

Matrimonial and Family: (*Contact:* Karen Gordon). *Work includes:* divorce, ancillary relief, child care/Children Act work and domestic violence injunctions.

Managing partner:	Kerry Underwood
Number of partners:	2
Assistant solicitors:	7
Other fee-earners:	4

WORKLOADS	
Employment	25%
Personal injury	25%
Litigation	20%
Local governt./administrative & public law	15%
Other	15%

CONTACTS	
Administrative/public law	Kerry Underwood
Commercial property	Robert Males
Corporate and commercial	Robert Males
Employment	James Lynas
	Kerry Underwood
Litigation	Sharon MacArthur
Local government	Robert Males
	Kerry Underwood
Matrimonial and family	Karen Gordon
Personal injury	Sharon MacArthur
	Tim Robinson
Private client	Karen Gordon
	Robert Males

UNGOED THOMAS & KING 6 Quay St, Carmarthen, SA31 1JT *Tel:* (01267) 237441 *Fax:* (01267) 238317 *DX:* 51400 *Ptnrs:* 3 *Asst solrs:* 2 *Other fee-earners:* 1

VARLEY HIBBS & CO

KIRBY HOUSE, LITTLE PARK ST, COVENTRY, CV1 2JZ
Tel: (01203) 631000 **Fax:** (01203) 630808 **DX:** 712341

16 HAMILTON TERRACE, LEAMINGTON SPA, CV32 4LY
Tel: (01926) 881251 **Fax:** (01926) 831900 **DX:** 11870

The Firm: Varley Hibbs and Co. is a leading Midlands firm with offices in Coventry and Leamington Spa. Established for over 60 years, the firm offers a wide range of services to a variety of businesses including public and private companies, banks, building societies and insurance companies along with company directors and private individuals. The firm is fully computerised with internal and external E-mail, Accounting and Time-Recording systems

Principal Areas of Work:

Company/Commercial Services: (*Contact Partner:* Sean Byrne). *Work includes:* all aspects of company and commercial work and commercial conveyancing, MBOs, MBIs, acquisitions, employment law, partnership law, insolvency, competition law, franchising, planning, and debt collection. Information technology services are the fastest growing of Varley Hibbs' core practice areas. Advice is provided to a variety of companies, both UK and international, on such aspects as software licensing and distribution, hardware and network supply, acquisition and sheltering of intellectual property rights, and disputes relating to both software and hardware.

Commercial Litigation: (*Contact Partner:* George Zambartas). *Work includes:* commercial and trade disputes, intellectual property, employment disputes, breach of contract, and landlord and tenant.

The firm offers full range of private client and family law services including childcare (*Contact Partner:* Susan Pearce).

Senior partner:	Edward Bayliss
Number of partners:	9
Assistant solicitors:	10
Other fee-earners:	9

WORKLOADS	
Civil and commercial litigation	24%
Company and commercial	23%
Advocacy	17%
Family	14%
Conveyancing	13%
Probate and miscellaneous	9%

VAUDREYS

13 POLICE STREET, MANCHESTER, M2 7WA
Tel: (0161) 834 6877 **Fax:** (0161) 834 2440 **DX:** 14341 MANCHESTER 1 **Email:** LEGAL@VAUDREYS.COM **Internet:** WWW.VAUDREYS.COM

The Firm: A successful law firm with a modern progressive outlook, Vaudreys is one of Manchester's leading commercial practices. Over 100 years of experience has gone into making the Vaudreys' difference – a commercial blend of understanding, knowledge and personal contact – seldom found in today's cut-throat business environment.

At Vaudreys, Clients still come first, with expert partners a first point of contact and an approach geared towards providing real and practical solutions to Clients' needs, not just textbook analysis. The 'Client first' philosophy ensures that the firm delivers the highest level of service – quickly and cost-effectively.

Vaudreys provides a comprehensive range of advice to a wide range of clients, from private companies and OMBs to large plcs and financial insitutions.

Principal Areas of Work: The workload is carried out within three departments. These handle litigation, commercial property and corporate, commercial and international work.

Clients in commerce and industry are offered a high level of commercial awareness. Through co-operation between the firm's departments, they can be assisted with every aspect of their affairs, from trading and business contracts to contracts of employment, franchising and licensing agreements. The firm's corporate lawyers provide guidance in the establishment and structure of new businesses, their incorporation and raising of finance. Acquisitions of companies and businesses, mergers, takeovers and joint ventures are also handled.

The firm acts for a wide range of insurance companies as well as other corporate concerns in relation to their self-insurance arrangements. Insurance litigation work includes on-site investigation of claims and their subsequent valuation, including industrial injury and disease claim, together with property and financial losses, and health and safety matters.

The commercial property department deals with matters such as negotiating new leases, acquisitions and disposal of premises, PFI projects, property litigation, development, planning and total facility management.

The practice also has a specialist experience in employment, construction litigation, product liability and commercial transport. Licensing, receiverships, liquidation and administrations are also handled.

Substantial experience has been gained in matters involving foreign trade, particularly with regard to western and eastern Europe, the United States and the Middle East.

The firm is committed to a radical expansion plan and an increasing investment is being made in technology to improve efficiency of service to clients.

Senior partners:	Tony Healey, Tony Martin
Number of partners:	14
Assistant solicitors:	47
Other fee-earners:	11

WORKLOADS	
Insurance litigation	35%
Commercial property	25%
Corporate	20%
Commercial litigation	15%
Private client	5%

CONTACTS	
Banking	Tony Mills
Commercial Property	Mark Pattison
Construction	Tony Healey
Corporate & Commercial	Stephen Isherwood
Employment	Sue Jenkins
Health & Safety	Sue Jenkins
	Iain Moore
Housing Association	Anne Quirk
Insurance Litigation	Mike Suddards
International & EU	Tony Martin
Licensing	Ted Quinn
Litigation	Mike Suddards
PFI	Stephen Birchall
Property Litigation	Robert Moss
Transport	Iain Moore

VEALE WASBROUGH

ORCHARD COURT, ORCHARD LANE, BRISTOL, BS1 5DS
Tel: (0117) 925 2020 **Fax:** (0117) 925 2025 **DX:** 7831 BRISTOL **Email:** CENTRAL@VEALE-WASBROUGH.CO.UK

The Firm: Veale Wasbrough is one of the leading commercial practices in the South West region with associated offices in 43 leading EU and other European cities. The firm is fully resourced and forward-looking with modern city centre offices; having on-site clients' car parking. The client base consists of high profile organisations such as major clearing banks, building societies, leading accountancy practices, local government authorities, central government departments, insurance companies, retail chain stores, construction companies, public and private utilities, plcs and private companies, professional partnerships and independent schools. It offers practical and effective advice to exacting professional standards. Overall City quality expertise at rates which reflect lower provincial overheads. Accredited as an Investor in People.

Principal Areas of Work:

Central Government: (*Contact:* Nigel Campbell). Growing national reputation for advising government departments, agencies & TECs on Public/Private partnerships, PFI, regulated procurement, partnering, judicial review and TUPE.

Company/Commercial: (*Contact:* Derek Bellew). Specialist advice to public and private companies. Particular emphasis on mergers and acquisitions, management buy outs, corporate finance, intellectual property, medical partnerships and insolvency.

Construction: (*Contact:* Roger Hoyle). National reputation in construction disputes, building and engineering contracts, professional indemnity insurance and collateral warranties.

Education: (*Contact:* Robert Boyd). Legal services to over 500 independent schools, universities and further education colleges. Including: incorporation; crisis management and all contractual issues.

Employment Law: (*Contact:* Sarah Lamont). Dedicated team with national reputation in all sectors notably local authorities, national plcs, printing and packaging industries and education. Particular expertise in industrial disputes.

Insurance Litigation: (*Contact:* David Groves). Acts for many Insurers on employers' liability, road traffic and general liability claims. Special experience in structured settlements.

Litigation: (*Contact:* Simon Pizzey). Banking, building societies, commercial disputes, judicial review, business fraud, insolvency litigation, partnership and shareholders disputes and intellectual property.

Local Government: (*Contact:* Simon Baker). Public and private sector joint ventures and financing, planning, compulsory purchase and compensation, tendering. Specialist Unit offering support to the public sector's own internal legal departments.

Personal Injury: (*Contact:* John Webster). Well regarded department acting for plaintiffs. All types of accident, product liability and criminal injury compensation claims covered. Medical Negligence Unit.

Private Client: (*Contact:* Mike Rendell). Corporate relocations, estate administration, family, residential conveyancing, re-mortgages, wills and tax planning.

Property: (*Contact:* Gary Philpott). Acquisition, financing, development, letting and disposal of all types of commercial property. Niche areas of expertise include pipelines, VAT schemes, quarrying and waste management industries.

Recruitment and Training: The firm recruits up to six trainee solicitors each year, who are law or non-law graduates with a good academic record. Applications to Paul Cottam with CV.

Specialist Interdepartmental Units: Education, Environmental, European, Finance & Banking, Insolvency, Intellectual Property, Information Technology, Local Authorities, Medical Negligence, Medical Partnerships, PFI, Public Sector, Retail, Sports.

Managing partner:	Derek Bellew
Assistant Solicitors (including Associates): 34	

WORKLOADS	
Commercial litigation	34%
Private client	20%
Company commercial	17%
Property services	15%
Personal injury	14%

CONTACTS	
Banking (non-contentious)	David Worthington
Banks & Building Soc (Litig)	Simon Pizzey
Central Government	Nigel Campbell
Commercial Litigation	Simon Pizzey
Commercial Property	Gary Philpott
Company & Commercial	Derek Bellew
Construction Law	Roger Hoyle
Corporate Finance	Stuart Whitfield
Education	Robert Boyd
Employment Law	Sarah Lamont
European & International Law	David Worthington
Insolvency	Simon Heald
Insurance Litigation	David Groves
Intellectual Property	Rosemary Collins
Local Authorities	Simon Baker
Medical Practices	Derek Bellew
Personal Tax Planning/Trusts	Mary McCartney
PFI	Gary Philpott
Pipelines	Tim Smithers
Plaintiff Personal Injury	John Webster
Public Sector & Utilities	Nigel Campbell
Regulated Procurement	Rosemary Collins
Resid & Relocat Conveyancing	Mike Rendell
Wastes Management/Environmental	Tim Smithers

INVESTOR IN PEOPLE

VEALE WASBROUGH
—— SOLICITORS ——

VEITCH PENNY

1 MANOR COURT, DIX'S FIELD, EXETER, EX1 1UP
Tel: (01392) 278381 **Fax:** (01392) 410247 **DX:** 8309 EXETER 1 **Email:** LAW@VEITCHPENNY.CO.UK **Internet:** HTTP://WWW.VEITCHPENNY.CO.UK

The Firm: Founded over 30 years ago Veitch Penny is a broad based firm offering a wide range of services to private clients and the corporate sectors. Growth has been steady over the past 10 years, and continues.

Principal Areas of Work:

Litigation: (*Contact Partner:* Michael Penny). The firm is regarded as a specialist in personal injury litigation, with one team representing plaintiffs, legal expense insurers and motoring organisations while another concentrates on defendant and insurance work. Claims arising from road and workplace accidents, and medical negligence are all catered for. The firm which additionally has a speciality in local government insurance litigation acts for various County and District Councils, Fire and Police Authorities throughout the South-West. It also conducts general litigation within both private and commercial sectors.
Company/Commercial: (*Contact Partner:* Simon Young). This is a growing department offering complete support to the smaller company. Company formation, partnership and employment law and intellectual property are among the areas covered.
Private Client: (*Contact Partner:* Charles Dowell). Private client work remains an essential part of the practice, offering conveyancing, probate and trust, taxation, agricultural property and many other topics.

Other Offices: Crediton and Tiverton.

Managing partner:	Simon Young
Number of partners:	8
Assistant solicitors:	8
Other fee-earners:	9

WORKLOADS	
Defendant Litigation	41%
Plaintiff Litigation	29%
Conveyancing	12%
General Litigation	8%
Trust & Probate	6%
Commercial	4%

CONTACTS	
Commercial	S. Young
Conveyancing	I.D. Penny, C.E.R. Dowell
Defendant insurers	M.T. Penny
Plaintiff personal injury	A.R. Harris
Probate and trusts	I.D. Penny, C.E.R. Dowell

VENTERS & CO 1-6 Camberwell Green, London, SE5 7AD *Tel:* (0171) 277 0110 *Fax:* (0171) 277 0132 *DX:* 35310 Camberwell *Ptnrs:* 1 *Asst solrs:* 7 *Other fee-earners:* 3

VICTOR LISSACK & ROSCOE 8 Bow Street, Covent Garden, London, WC2E 7AJ **Tel:** (0171) 240 2010 **Fax:** (0171) 379 4420 **DX:** 40026 Covent Garden **Ptnrs:** 2 **Asst solrs:** 3 **Other fee-earners:** 2 **Contact:** Mr Robert Roscoe or Mr Richard Almond *Specialists in white collar and all other crime including extradition and courts martial.*

WORKLOADS	
Criminal law	70%
Private client, debt collection and civil litigation	30%

VINSON & ELKINS 47 Charles Street, Berkeley Square, London, W1X 7PB *Tel:* (0171) 491 7236 *Fax:* (0171) 499 5320 *Ptnrs:* 3 *Asst solrs:* 3

VIZARDS

42 BEDFORD ROW, LONDON, WC1R 4JL
Tel: (0171) 405 6302 **Fax:** (0171) 405 6248 **DX:** 189

The Firm: Vizards is particularly noted for its expertise in the fields of insurance law, litigation, property, charities and parliamentary law acting as parliamentary and privy council agents. Over the years it has also developed a substantial commercial practice with a strong international emphasis. The firm opened a city office principally for the London market insurance community. The firm has an office in Paris and an associated office in Milan and is formally affiliated to Davis, Brown, Koehn, Shors & Roberts P.C. of Des Moines, Iowa, USA.

Principal Areas of Work:

Charities: (*Contact Partner:* Ron Perry). Vizards acts for a large national charity and other prominent private charities and has long experience in this particular field. Advice covers the establishing of new charities, the preservation of charitable status and all aspects of the administration of charities.

Commercial: (*Contact Partner:* John Hargreaves). This department offers expertise in the areas of commerce and finance to undertakings ranging from family businesses and professional partnerships to large well known corporations both in the UK and abroad. In general terms, the firm provides a complete corporate service.

Commercial Property: (*Contact Partner:* Richard Barber). The department deals with many commercial transactions involving housing associations and property developers in the UK and abroad, and it deals with all aspects of planning law.

Commercial Litigation: (*Contact Partner:* Peter Knight). A variety of work is handled for both private and corporate clients in domestic and international disputes. The department also advises on debt recovery; mortgage possession; immigration and nationality; family; employment law actions and tribunals and white collar crime.

Construction Law: (*Contact Partner:* Simon Loveday). Vizards has a well-established association with the construction industry and is able to deal with all matters of a building, architectural or engineering nature in the UK and abroad, including contractual drafting, contractual disputes and arbitration and insurance.

Environmental Law: (*Contact Partner:* Gary Hay). The firm is called upon to act and to advise in matters of health and safety regulation; contaminated land sites; company warranties and assessments and liability claims. Clients range from the individual to large companies and trusts as well as interest groups.

Insurance and Reinsurance: (*Contact Partner:* Martin Staples). The insurance department is the largest within the firm and is regarded as being one of the leading firms in this field. All areas of insurance law are covered, in particular policy drafting, construction and interpretation; litigation covering product liability and material loss, professional negligence, personal injury, transportation/ highway law and re-insurance. Clients include a wide variety of domestic and foreign insurance companies and Lloyd's syndicates. The firm's city office has been established principally to serve the London Market (Contact Partner for City office: Robert Harrison).

Medical Negligence: (*Contact Partner:* Richard Foster). The firm is one of the 18 panel firms appointed nationally to defend clinical negligence claims within the NHS.

Parliamentary: (*Contact Partner:* Ron Perry). The firm has one Roll A Agent who deals with all aspects of private and public legislation, including the Transport & Works Act 1992.

Private Client: (*Contact Partner:* Ron Perry). As well as domestic conveyancing, the department advises on trusts, wills, taxation and financial planning, and administration of estates.

Foreign Connections: (*Contact Partner:* Alex Maitland Hudson). In addition to its affiliation to the largest law firm in Iowa, USA, Vizards was a founder member of the International Grouping of Lawyers in 1980 which now consists of law firms from over 40 different countries. The firm also has an office in Paris headed by a partner who is qualified in both the English and French jurisdictions. One partner is qualified in Scotland and another in the Republic of Ireland, both of whom can deal with work in those jurisdictions.

Languages Spoken: Dutch, French, German, Gujerati, Hindi, Italian, Russian, Spanish and Urdu.

Senior partner:	Martin R. Staples
Number of partners:	29
Assistant solicitors:	28
Other fee-earners:	15

WORKLOADS	
Personal injury (Defendant)	30%
Insurance and reinsurance	20%
Company and commercial	10%
Construction and civil engineering	5%
Litigation (commercial)	5%
Medical Negligence (Defendant)	5%
Professional Indemnity	5%
Property (commercial)	5%
Public Law	5%
Transport	5%
Charities	3%
Parliamentary	2%

CONTACTS	
Charities	Ron Perry
Commercial litigation	Peter Knight
Commercial Property	Richard Barber
Company and commercial	John Hargreaves
Construction	Simon Loveday
Employment	John Livesey
Environmental Law	Gary Hay
European community	Alex Maitland Hudson
Insurance & Reinsurance	Martin Staples
Local authority liabilities	John Morrell
Medical Negligence	Richard Foster
Parliamentary/Public affairs	Ron Perry
Personal Injury (Defendant)	Martin Staples
Professional Indemnity	Robert Harrison
	Mark Whittaker
VAT/Customs & Excise	Peter Knight

WACE MORGAN 2 Belmont, Shrewsbury, SY1 1TD *Tel:* (01743) 361451 *Fax:* (01743) 231708 *DX:* 19718 *Ptnrs:* 8 *Asst solrs:* 5 *Other fee-earners:* 5

WACKS CALLER

STEAM PACKET HOUSE, 76 CROSS STREET, MANCHESTER, M2 4JU
Tel: (0161) 957 8888 **Fax:** (0161) 957 8899 **DX:** 14383 MANCHESTER 1

The Firm: Now in its twelfth year the firm has strengthened its position as a leading specialist firm in the realm of corporate finance/company/commercial work and over the past 18 months has developed a strong Biotech expertise.

Principal Areas of Work:

Company/Commercial: (*Contact:* Kevin Philbin). The firm provides vigorous expert advice and assistance for the business community on all types of corporate and commercial transactions including Stock Exchange and Takeover Panel work. It is especially renowned for its skill and pragmatic approach in negotiating merger and acquisition agreements, joint venture agreements and MBOs.

Commercial Litigation: (*Contact:* Michael Kennedy). This department has grown rapidly by providing an aggressive yet user-friendly service for the commercial client and institutional client.

Commercial Property: (*Contact:* Robert Harris). This department handles all commercial property transactions and other property related matters with the emphasis on speed (where required) in addition to skill and experience.

Employment: (*Contact:* Anthony Dempsey). Provides a commercial and practical approach to all employment and related issues for both employers and senior employees.

Intellectual Property: (*Contact:* Patricia Jones). This department was founded three years ago and has developed a full capability (both contentious and non-contentious) in this field. It now handles a significant amount of I.T. work.

Biotech: (*Contact:* Simon Wallwork). Using expertise from both the corporate and IP departments the firm has developed a strong client base in this area advising on start up, finance raising and IP strategy.

Managing partner:	Martin Caller
Senior partner:	Arran Wacks
Number of partners:	12
Assistant solicitors:	14
Other fee-earners:	8

WORKLOADS	
Company/commercial	37%
Litigation	20%
Property	20%
Intellectual property	10%
Biotech	6%
Employment	5%
Matrimonial	2%

CONTACTS	
Biotech	Simon Wallwork
Commercial property	Robert Harris
Corporate finance	Kevin Philbin
Employment	Anthony Dempsey
Gen. company/commercial	Martin Caller
Intellectual property	Patricia Jones
Litigation	Michael Kennedy

WAKE DYNE LAWTON Worley Bank House, Bolesworth Road, Tattenhall, Chester, CH3 9HL **Tel:** (01829) 773100 **Fax:** (01829) 773109 **Email:** Brian_Wake@msn.com / JB_Dyne@msn.com **Ptnrs:** 2 **Other fee-earners:** 3 **Contact:** Mr Brian Wake *Specialist practice dealing on a national basis exclusively with minerals, waste, environmental and road haulage law.*

WORKLOADS			
Minerals	40%	Waste	20%
Environmental	20%	transport	20%

WAKE SMITH

68 CLARKEHOUSE ROAD, SHEFFIELD, S10 2LJ
Tel: (0114) 266 6660 **Fax:** (0114) 267 1253 **DX:** 10534 SHEFFIELD **Email:** LEGAL@WAKE-SMITH.CO.UK

The Firm: Founded in 1802, Wake Smith is a general commercial practice providing a flexible service to companies and businesses of all sizes, as well as private clients, in the Sheffield area.

Principal Areas of Work: The main areas of work are divided into four departments: company and commercial; commercial property; commercial litigation and private client. The firm has considerable experience in the company/ commercial field, including the sale and purchase of businesses, capital structures and intellectual property rights, providing a service to quoted PLCs and major private companies, and also to smaller companies and partnerships. The firm advises in commercial disputes, insolvency and licensing and has a well developed commercial property department. In addition, the private client department provides advice on matters such as personal tax, pensions, trusts, property, family law, child care, personal injury and general litigation.

Other Offices: City Centre Office – 6 Campo Lane, Sheffield.

Number of partners:	12
Assistant solicitors:	10
Other fee-earners:	13

WORKLOADS	
Commercial	70%
Private Client	30%

CONTACTS	
Commercial Litigation	Mark Serby
Commercial Property	Neil Salter
Company Commercial	Jonathan Hunt
Domestic Conveyancing	Amanda Beacroft
Family Law	Paul Thorn
Personal Injury	Richard Lees
Private Trust Tax	Michael Tunbridge

WALKER CHARLESWORTH & FOSTER

26 PARK SQUARE, LEEDS, LS1 2PL
Tel: (0113) 245 3594 **Fax:** (0113) 244 4312 **DX:** 26415 LEEDS PARK SQUARE

The Firm: A long established practice whose Leeds office specialises in all types of advice to housing associations and whose Skipton and Settle offices specialise in building society and agricultural advice.

Managing partner:	David Butcher
Number of partners:	9
Assistant solicitors:	6
Other fee-earners:	6

WALKER LAIRD

9 GILMOUR STREET, PAISLEY, PA1 1DG
Tel: (0141) 887 5271 **Fax:** (0141) 889 3268 **DX:** 32 PAISLEY

The Firm: Walker Laird is a long established Renfrewshire firm. Its main office in Paisley is conveniently located for litigation in the Sheriff Courts of central Scotland, although legal work of all types may often be undertaken throughout Scotland. We have an established Court of Session and High Court Practice. Our partners are experienced in the enforcement of judgments, and have a particular knowledge of international child custody cases. A wide range of litigation cases is undertaken.

Principal Areas of Work:

Litigation services: *Work includes:* contract, personal injury, employment cases, employment law, divorce, child custody; specialising in international and cross border custody disputes; and all aspects of enforcing UK and foreign judgments in Scotland.
Property: All aspects of commercial or domestic conveyancing and leasing.
Criminal Law: All aspects of criminal procedure and practice in the inferior and supreme courts of Scotland.

Other offices: We have two offices in the nearby town of Renfrew.

Number of partners:	6
Assistant solicitors:	6
Other fee-earners:	4

WORKLOADS	
Civil litigation (contract, personal injury, matrimonial)	25%
Conveyancing	25%
Criminal	25%
Executries, financial services	13%
Private Client	12%

CONTACTS	
Commercial	R McGinlay
Conveyancing/ private client	R McGinlay
Criminal	P Coyle
Employment Law	H Singerman
Financial services	R McGinlay
Litigation	G Jamieson

WALKER MARTINEAU 64 Queen Street, London, EC4R 1AD *Tel:* (0171) 236 4232 *Fax:* (0171) 236 2525 *DX:* 553 *Ptnrs:* 9 *Asst solrs:* 8 *Other fee-earners:* 3

WALKER MORRIS

KINGS COURT, 12 KING STREET, LEEDS, LS1 2HL
Tel: (0113) 283 2500 **Fax:** (0113) 245 9412 **DX:** 12051 **Email:** INFO@WALKERMORRIS.CO.UK **Internet:** HTTP://WWW.WALKERMORRIS.CO.UK

The Firm: Based in Leeds, Walker Morris is one of the largest commercial law firms in the North providing a full range of legal services to industry and commerce.

Principal Areas of Work:

Corporate and Tax: (*Contact:* Peter Smart). The Company and Commercial department operates as a cohesive entity even though it comprises of a number of specialist and distinct groups, principally Corporate Finance, Banking, Insolvency, Intellectual Property, Corporate Tax and Pensions. The Intellectual Property Group also manages a trademark registration practice comprising of four trademark agents.

Commercial Property and Planning: (*Contact:* David Duckworth). The Property department (which includes a dedicated Planning Group) deals with all aspects of the acquisition of sites for development including major town centre redevelopments and large scale residential sites, town and country planning and environmental matters, property portfolios for institutional and private investors, commercial lettings and joint ventures.

Commercial Litigation: (*Contact:* Chris Caisley). The Commercial Litigation department deals with a broad scope of work both within the UK and internationally and before courts, tribunals and arbitrators. It incorporates a number of dedicated Groups headed by specialists in the areas of Construction Law, Employment, Insurance Litigation, Property Litigation and the contentious aspects of Intellectual Property Law, Banking and Secured Lending and Commercial Fraud. The department also houses the large corporate debt recovery service utilising advanced and fully integrated systems. The firm's Health Sector Group provides a full service to its health authority and trust clients and includes specific expertise in healthcare law, NHS legislation, clinical negligence, CNST and risk management, PFI work and judicial review.

Additional Areas of Work: The Walker Morris Sports Law Group acts for sports personalities, clubs and associations working within this industry, and work includes contract negotiations and disputes, personality merchandising and licensing agreements (*Contact:* Chris Caisley). The firm has also created cross-departmental practice groups focused on servicing the firm's clients in the Banking, Building Society (*Contact:* Roger Limbert) and Housing Association (*Contact:* David Duckworth) sectors.

Private Client: The firm has retained a private client department dealing with Personal Tax strategies, Probate and Trust Administration (*Contact:* Andrew Turnbull), and Family Law and related issues (*Contact:* Richard Manning).

Nature of Clientele: Clients are drawn from the whole spectrum of commerce and industry including retail, the professions, the service industries, manufacturing, construction and development, high technology, and the financial services industry.

Foreign Connections: The firm advises on European and EC issues and was a founder member of one of the first European Economic Interest Groupings amongst European law firms. The firm has a growing International practice and has developed very close and mutually beneficial relationships with law firms in the major jurisdictions worldwide. The consistent element in those relationships is a common philosophy and approach.

Office Support Services: The firm places great emphasis on the fast and accurate production and delivery of documents; its purpose-built offices in Leeds are specially networked to take the most advanced processing and communications systems.

Recruitment and Training: The firm's year-on-year expansion has resulted in its always having a continuing recruitment policy for motivated young solicitors in all major disciplines. The firm recruits around ten trainee solicitors every year. Discretionary grants are provided.

Career prospects are excellent (most of the Partners were articled with the firm). Application forms and recruitment brochures are available from Paul Emmett, Recruitment Partner. A training scheme is available to keep its lawyers up-to-date, consisting of in-house seminars, external conferences and information updates.

Managing partner:	**Philip Mudd**
Chairman:	**Chris Caisley**
Number of partners:	30
Assistant solicitors:	75
Other fee-earners:	101

WORKLOADS	
Commercial litigation	32%
Commercial property	30%
Company and commercial	20%
Building societies	12%
Private clients	4%
Tax	2%

CONTACTS	
Banking	Michael Taylor
Banking and building societies	Philip Mudd
Banking and building societies	Roger Limbert
Commercial litigation	Chris Caisley
Commercial property	David Duckworth
Commercial property devt.	Paul Walker, Mark Tordoff
Construction	Martin Scott
Corporate	Peter Smart
Corporate debt recovery	Chris Gibson
Corporate finance	Paul Emmett, Ian Gilbert
Corporate tax	Simon Concannon
EC and competition	Patrick Cantrill
Employment	David Smedley
Environment	Andrew Williamson
Family	Richard Manning
Health and public services	David Duckworth
Housing associations	David Duckworth
Insolvency	Philip Mudd
Insurance litigation	Chris Caisley
Intellectual property	Patrick Cantrill
Licensing	Patrick Whur
Pensions	Andrew Turnbull
Personal injury	Chris Caisley
PFI	David Duckworth
Private client, trust and tax	Andrew Turnbull
Professional indemnity	Roger Limbert
Property litigation	Andrew Beck
Retail	Andrew Moodie
Sports law	Chris Caisley
Town and country planning	Andrew Williamson
Trade marks	Patrick Cantrill

WALKER SMITH & WAY 26 Nicholas Street, Chester, CH1 2PQ *Tel:* (01244) 357 400 *Fax:* (01244) 357 444 *DX:* 19982 Chester 1 *Ptnrs:* 22 *Asst solrs:* 17 *Other fee-earners:* 12

WALLACE & PARTNERS

9 GREAT JAMES ST, LONDON, WC1N 3DA
Tel: (0171) 404 4422 **Fax:** (0171) 831 6850 **DX:** 377 **Email:** LAWYERS@WALLACE.CO.UK

Managing partner:	Rex Newman
Number of partners:	8
Assistant solicitors:	2
Other fee-earners:	4

The Firm: Wallace & Partners is a young and thriving central London practice which specialises in business matters, handling work often associated with large City firms. Wallace & Partners take a pro-active role in their clients' legal affairs, adopting a dynamic and professional approach at competitive prices.

Principal Areas of Work:

Company/ Commercial: (*Contact Partners:* Rex Newman and Richard Pike). *Work includes:* Stock Exchange advice including AIM, public issues, commercial contracts, venture capital, joint ventures, management buy-outs and buy-ins, mergers and acquisitions, loan arrangements, advice on the responsibilities of directors; shareholder agreements; tax planning, contracts of employment, franchising and general commercial matters.

Litigation: (*Contact Partners:* Simon Serota and Nicholas Yapp). The firm is strong in property-related litigation as well as employment, professional negligence, shareholder and boardroom disputes, and general commercial litigation.

Property: (*Contact Partners:* Adrian Wallace and Barry Shaw). *Work includes:* development, investment, acquisition and funding, planning and environmental, business leases, rent reviews, estate management and general landlord and tenant work.

Private Client: (*Contact Partners:* Barry Shaw and Adrian Wallace). This department deals with personal financial planning including wills, capital tax advice, trusts and probate.

Nature of Clientele: The firm acts for a diverse spread of clients including listed companies, family businesses, entrepreneurs, stockbrokers and foreign dignitaries.

Foreign Connections: Wallace & Partners has developed a network of contacts throughout Europe and provides advice on many aspects of international commerce. One of the partners is a member of the New York Bar.

Recruitment and Training: Contact Richard Pike for an application form.

WALL, JAMES & DAVIES 19 Hagley Road, Stourbridge, DY8 1QW *Tel:* (01384) 371622 *Fax:* (01384) 374057 *DX:* 710678 *Ptnrs:* 8 *Asst solrs:* 2 *Other fee-earners:* 4

WALSH LAWSON 54/ 62 Regent Street, London, W1R 5PJ *Tel:* (0171) 393 9393 *Fax:* (0171) 393 9303 *DX:* 37214 *Ptnrs:* 7 *Asst solrs:* 3 *Other fee-earners:* 1

WALTONS & MORSE

BIRCHIN COURT, 20 BIRCHIN LANE, LONDON, EC3V 9DJ
Tel: (0171) 623 4255 **Fax:** (0171) 626 4153 **DX:** 1065 **Email:** WALTONS@WAMLAW.CO.UK

Managing partner:	David Perry
Number of partners:	5
Assistant solicitors:	3
Other fee-earners:	5

The Firm: Waltons & Morse is a long established City firm serving the marine insurance market and with an international reputation in the areas of shipping, transport and international trade.

Principal Areas of Work:

General Description: All aspects of marine insurance, shipping and transit law including international trade.

Nature of Clientele: Lloyd's, London and overseas insurance companies, shipping and salvage companies (particularly from Japan, Korea and Australasia).

WORKLOADS	
Shipping and transit	78%
International Trade	10%
Marine Insurance	10%
Reinsurance	2%

CONTACTS	
Shipping	Michael Buckley/David Perry

WANSBROUGHS Northgate House, Devizes, SN10 1JX *Tel:* (01380) 723611 *Fax:* (01380) 728213 *DX:* 42901 Devizes *Ptnrs:* 10 *Asst solrs:* 9 *Other fee-earners:* 5

WANSBROUGHS WILLEY HARGRAVE

SOMERSET HOUSE, 37 TEMPLE STREET, BIRMINGHAM, B2 5DP
Tel: (0121) 631 4099 **Fax:** (0121) 631 3781 **DX:** 13057 BIRMINGHAM

103 TEMPLE STREET, BRISTOL, BS99 7UD
Tel: (0117) 926 8981 **Fax:** (0117) 929 1582 **DX:** 7846 BRISTOL

7 PARK SQUARE EAST, LEEDS, LS1 2LW
Tel: (0113) 244 1151 **Fax:** (0113) 243 6050 **DX:** 14099 LEEDS

30-40 EASTCHEAP, LONDON, EC3M 1HD
Tel: (0171) 456 7600 **Fax:** (0171) 456 7601 **DX:** CDE 753 LONDON

34-43 RUSSELL STREET, LONDON, WC2B 5HA
Tel: (0171) 497 3262 **Fax:** (0171) 297 1210 **DX:** 40044 COVENT GARDEN

241 GLOSSOP ROAD, SHEFFIELD, S10 2GZ
Tel: (0114) 272 7485 **Fax:** (0114) 272 8517 **DX:** 709824 SHEFFIELD 16

1A ST CROSS ROAD, WINCHESTER, SO23 9WP
Tel: (01962) 841444 **Fax:** (01962) 843133 **DX:** 2540 WINCHESTER 1

The Firm: Wansbroughs Willey Hargrave is a national partnership with a fully integrated network of 7 offices. WWH is recognised throughout the UK for its expertise in defendant litigation and as a leader in the insurance and health sectors. The firm also provides a wide range of commercial services to public sector (NHS trusts, local authorities, government departments), institutional and commercial clients.

Principal Areas of Work:

Insurance: Around 70% of the firm's lawyers handle litigation on behalf of over 100 clients, including composite insurers, Lloyd's syndicates, underwriting agencies, brokers and companies which self-insure. WWH handles a wide range of professional indemnity, employers', public and product liability and motor claims and advise on policy wording and disputes. WWH's London Market Services, based in the City, specialises in handling large cases, particularly professional negligence and property claims. It is supported by specialist lawyers in the regional offices, all of whom are fully conversant with the London Market's particular practices and procedures.

Health: WWH acts for over 100 NHS Trusts, Health Authorities, and related health sector organisations, in relation to employment, property, construction, IT/IP matters, procurement, commercial agreements/disputes, medical/clinical negligence and EL/PL cases. The NHSLA has appointed WWH to its panel. The firm's senior health lawyers are experienced in working with clients to manage high profile untoward incidents, matters relating to corporate governance and NHS law.

Property and Construction: WWH's property group act for financial institutions, public sector organisations (NHS trusts, local authorities, housing associations and educational bodies), national retail chains, and national and regional developers. Main areas of work are development; management; secured lending; investment; portfolio and landlord and tenant. Within the retail market WWH has particular knowledge of the factory outlet shopping sector.

Employment: WWH's national employment unit acts predominantly for employers in a wide range of employment disputes, Industrial Tribunal claims, and non-contentious matters. The team has considerable experience of employment law as it applies to the NHS.

Company/Commercial: WWH has a long standing reputation for its company/commercial work, acting for banks, financial institutions, quoted and larger private companies, and government departments. The firm is a substantial provider of procurement advice to the public and private sectors and has particular experience of PFI. It is also known for its IT and IP expertise.

Private Client: WWH provides advice on wills, tax, trusts, investments and family matters. A separate unit advises on the establishment and administration of charities.

Senior Partner:	Robert A. Heslett
Chief Executive:	Christopher A. Charles
Number of partners:	65
Assistant solicitors:	159
Other fee-earners:	62

WORKLOADS	
Professional Indemnity	34%
General Insurance	33%
Medical Negligence	12%
Employment and Commercial Litigation	7%
Property and Construction	7%
Company and Commercial	6%
Private Client	1%

CONTACTS	
Birmingham	Paul Murray
Bristol	John Blackwell
Leeds	Glenn Miller
London (Central and City)	Trevor Chamberlain
Sheffield	Chris Horsefield
Winchester	Valerie West

WANSBROUGHS
WILLEY HARGRAVE
SOLICITORS

WARD GETHIN 8-12 Tuesday Market Place, King's Lynn, PE30 1JT *Tel:* (01553) 773456
Fax: (01553) 766857 *DX:* 57813 *Ptnrs:* 14 *Asst solrs:* 5 *Other fee-earners:* 10

WARD HADAWAY

SANDGATE HOUSE, 102 QUAYSIDE, NEWCASTLE UPON TYNE, NE1 3DX
Tel: (0191) 204 4000 **Fax:** (0191) 204 4001 **DX:** 61265 NEWCASTLE UPON TYNE **Email:** LEGAL@WARDHADAWAY.COM **Internet:** HTTP://WWW.WARDHADAWAY.COM

TOWN HALL CHAMBERS, 7 BEACH ROAD, SOUTH SHIELDS, NE33 2QR
Tel: (0191) 204 4000 **Fax:** (0191) 456 4125 **DX:** 60755 SOUTH SHIELDS

The Firm: Ward Hadaway is one of the most progressive, commercially based firm of solicitors in the North of England. Its services are structured around client market sector groups with multi disciplined teams serving client needs.

Known for its fresh and innovative approach to the profession, WH's planned strategy for growth enables the firm to deliver a comprehensive range of legal and town planning services to ISO 9001 accredited standards. The firm continues to invest to build in-depth specialist teams with complimentary support staff and services.

WH has a substantial client base from both the public and private sectors, and has grown considerably by winning both work and reputation at local, regional and national levels.

Principal Areas of Work: Company and Commercial Services, Litigation, Property, and Private Client which are organised into specialist units.

The Company and Commercial Services department deals with corporate finance, commercial advice, banking and insolvency. Advice is given on acquisitions and disposals, joint ventures, MBOs and MBIs, venture capital, grants and business finance, inward investment, reorganisations and reconstructions, Stock Exchange, share options, employee incentive schemes, pensions, intellectual property, agency, distributorship and franchise agreements. The firm handled the largest equity funded Management Buy-Out in the North East during 1997.

The Litigation department deals with commercial litigation disputes (contracts, insolvency, product liability, debt collection, etc). The unit also has particular expertise in defamation work. The healthcare unit specialises in plaintiff and defendant personal injury. Other units specialise in employment law, family law, construction and engineering disputes, and professional disciplinary tribunal work.

The Property department deals with development work, landlord and tenant, housing associations, residential and estate development, town planning and development, and agriculture. The planning unit has 5 Chartered Town and Country Planners and associated staff making it one of the largest planning consultancies in the North East. A specialist team also advises on rural business, planning, agricultural litigation, agricultural property and environmental concerns.

The Private Client department advises on wills, administration of estates, trust planning and administration, capital tax planning, gifts and settlements, and charities.

Joint Senior Partners:	Peter Allan
	George Scott
Managing Partner:	Jamie Martin
Chief Executive:	Peter Wignall
Number of partners:	32
Assistant solicitors:	26
Other fee-earners:	34
Total staff:	190

WORKLOADS	
Litigation	35%
Property	31%
Company/Commercial	16%
Planning/Agriculture	9%
Private client services	9%

CONTACTS	
Company & Commercial	Martin A Hulls, Colin T Hewit
Litigation	Jeffrey A Keeble, Jan Collinson
Planning/Agriculture	J Neil Robson, Christopher Hewitt
Private client	Susan E Craig, Andrew Facer
Property	David Douglass, Adrian E Hill

WARD HADAWAY
——— SOLICITORS ———

WARDS 52 Broad St, Bristol, BS1 2EP *Tel:* (0117) 929 2811 *Fax:* (0117) 929 0686 *DX:* 7824 *Ptnrs:* 7 *Asst solrs:* 16 *Other fee-earners:* 7

WARNER CRANSTON

PICKFORDS WHARF, CLINK ST, LONDON, SE1 9DG
Tel: (0171) 403 2900 **Fax:** (0171) 403 4221 **DX:** 39904 LONDON BRIDGE SOUTH **Email:** WARNER_CRANSTON@COMPUSERVE.COM

This City-based Firm, which has enjoyed rapid expansion since it was founded, continues to expand its solid national and international corporate client base and is perceived as an alternative to the much larger City firms. The Firm advises many household-names who are major quoted and private companies both in the UK and overseas.

The Firm: Founded by David Warner in 1979, the Firm has now grown to a medium size. This rapid expansion has been achieved by a commitment to excel within specific fields and by an ability to adapt to the demands of a constantly changing market. In 1987, the Firm increased the size and strength of its existing litigation practice when it acquired the entire in-house litigation department of Courtaulds plc.

The philosophy of the Firm has always been that clients of national and international repute can best be served by a small, highly professional and totally committed team of lawyers. The underlying principle is one of big Firm expertise, coupled with a very personal service. From its inception, the Firm has always had a strong international practice.

Principal Areas of Work: The Firm is divided into the following departments: company commercial and finance, international commercial litigation, employment, construction, commercial property, personal injury and debt recovery.

The Firm has a strong company commercial and finance department which handles a wide variety of financial, corporate and commercial transactions, including mergers, acquisitions and disposals, asset finance and corporate finance, banking and all aspects of English and EC commercial law.

The international commercial litigation department handles substantial commercial, financial corporate and banking disputes and is well known in the area of international asset recovery. The department includes ex-barristers and provides a 'one-stop' litigation service which includes case preparation, pleadings and advocacy.

The employment department advises on service agreements, pensions, share options, unfair dismissal, redundancy, anti-discrimination and Trade Union laws. The Firm also has expertise in advising on the termination of senior executives' contracts of employment and compensation packages. A division of the employment department deals exclusively in work permits for corporate clients.

The construction law department advises on contentious and non-contentious matters for major contractors, developers, architects and insurers. The Firm is also able to offer specific expertise in the area of Alternative Dispute Resolution (ADR).

The commercial property department has grown substantially over the past year and handles transactions for corporate clients in the media, leisure, financial services and manufacturing industries, as well as for major developers and investors.

The Firm's expanding Coventry office also provides commercial litigation, personal injury and commercial property services to UK and international clients, as well as offering a highly sophisticated national computerised debt recovery service.

Warner Cranston sees itself as a totally committed, highly competitive, professional, flexible and accessible team of lawyers.

Nature of clientele: Warner Cranston acts for corporate clients, both national and international, including many household names, and both quoted and private companies. The Firm also acts for foreign governments, trade associations, chambers of commerce and insurance companies.

Foreign connections: The Firm has strong corporate and professional links in a number of countries, particularly in the United States and France which which together account for approxmately one third of the Firm's business. The Firm has set up a French team designed to service its French corporate clients. Languages other than English are spoken by partners and assistants.

Recruitment and Training: The Firm recruits candidates of the highest calibre and has an active (and continuous) recruitment programme. Considerable importance is attached to in-house training by partners and independent consultants, covering both legal and business skills. Included are regular legal updates as well as sessions on letter writing, negotiating and marketing.

Senior partner:	Ian Fagelson
Chief Executive:	Mark Dembovsky
Number of partners:	19
Assistant solicitors:	30
Other fee-earners:	21

WORKLOADS	
Company commercial and finance	37%
Commercial litigation	20%
Employment	15%
Property	14%
Construction and arbitration	7%
Personal injury	4%
Debt recovery	3%

CONTACTS	
Commercial litigation	Michael Cranston/Rachel Knapp
Commercial property	Peter Davis/Duncan Edwards/ Lawrence Radley
Commercial property (Coventry)	David Hayes
Company/commercial	Ian Fagelson/Tim Foster/ Wit Gryko
Construction litigation	Nick Speed/John Wright
Corporate immigration	Peter Alfandary
Corporate taxation	Paul Giles
Employment	David Cubitt/David Dalgarno
French Inward Investment	Peter Alfandary/ David Heard/Edward Miller
Litigation (Coventry)	Jonathan Hofstetter
Litigation/debt rec (Coventry)	Larry Coltman
Personal injury (Coventry)	Jonathan Hofstetter
US Inward investment	Ian Fagelson

WARNER GOODMAN & STREAT 66 West Street, Fareham, PO16 0JR *Tel:* (01329) 288121 *Fax:* (01329) 822714 *DX:* 40804 *Ptnrs:* 12 *Asst solrs:* 15 *Other fee-earners:* 28

WARREN & ALLEN 24 Low Pavement, Nottingham, NG1 7ED *Tel:* (0115) 955 2222 *Fax:* (0115) 948 4649 *DX:* 10030 *Ptnrs:* 10 *Asst solrs:* 12 *Other fee-earners:* 12

WATERSON HICKS

14-15 PHILPOT LANE, LONDON, EC3M 8AJ
Tel: (0171) 929 6060 **Fax:** (0171) 929 3748

The Firm: Waterson Hicks is a commercial practice specialising in all aspects of maritime law and commodity litigation. The firm's work and clientele is largely international and the firm has strong overseas connections particularly in Greece, the United States, Spanish-speaking countries and the Indian subcontinent. French, Spanish and Portuguese are spoken within the firm.

Clients include major ship owners, oil companies, charterers, commodity traders, P&I clubs, insurance companies and shipyards for whom primarily contentious work is carried out. Shipping work covers all areas of commercial and admiralty litigation and arbitration including marine insurance.

Managing partner:	M.J. Wisdom
Number of partners:	3
Assistant solicitors:	4
Other fee-earners:	2

CONTACTS	
Admiralty	Stuart Parkin
Commodities and Commercial	Martin Wisdom, Subir Karmakar
Insurance	John Hicks
Shipping	John Hicks, Brian Isola

WATMORES Chancery House, 53/66 Chancery Lane, London, WC2A 1QU *Tel:* (0171) 430 1512 *Fax:* (0171) 405 7382 *DX:* LDE 246 *Ptnrs:* 7 *Asst solrs:* 5 *Other fee-earners:* 3

WATSON BURTON

20 COLLINGWOOD STREET, NEWCASTLE UPON TYNE, NE99 1YQ
Tel: (0191) 244 4444 **Fax:** (0191) 244 4500 **DX:** 61009 NEWCASTLE **Email:** WB@DIAL.PIPEX.COM

The Firm: Watson Burton is one of the best-known firms in the North. Founded in 1820 it has been closely connected with industry and commerce in the North for many years. The firm has a corporate structure with a young management team. It is organised into four main departments; corporate, litigation, property and private client. Within each department there are a range of groupings designed to focus specialist skills on client's requirements. The firm's clients range from very substantial companies, institutions, government and statutory bodies, to individuals and small businesses.

Principal Areas of Work:

Corporate: The firm is proud of the strength and depth of its specialist expertise in its commercial group. In addition to mainstream corporate transactions and corporate finance, the corporate department has particular strengths in insolvency, intellectual property, education, competition and international issues.

Litigation: The litigation department has built a nationwide reputation on its handling of building and construction disputes and in addition to the quality case load of employment and commercial work, it has developed a particular strength in the field of insurance-related work, particularly professional negligence and its personal injury group continues to extend its client referral sources. For agency matters, contact Laura Bate or Mark Heath.

Property: The firm believes its property department to be a leading force within the region, particularly for property development and financing, institutional and investment work for industrial, commercial and retail clients, and planning and environmental matters.

Private Client: Watson Burton offers a full private client service including civil legal aid work.

Foreign/International Connections: The firm is a member of Eulex International Practice Group, an international association of lawyers, accountants and tax advisors with a network of over 60 offices around the world.

Recruitment and Training: Watson Burton continually seeks to recruit high quality solicitors with entrepreneurial flair. For the young solicitor the firm is progressive, forward-thinking and young in outlook. Management responsibilities are clearly established and the opportunity exists to acquire responsibility at a relatively early age. In addition, at least three trainee solicitors are recruited each year. A good degree (not lower than a 2(1)) is required, but not necessarily in law. Engineers and linguists are particularly welcome. Apply to Rob Langley.

Senior partner:	Andrew Hoyle
Managing partner:	John Williams
Number of partners:	20
Number of fee-earners:	78
Total Staff:	150

WORKLOADS	
Litigation	45%
Property	27%
Corporate	24%
Private client	4%

CONTACTS	
Banking/ Insolvency	Gillian Tiplady
Commercial Litigation	Allan Henderson
Commercial Property	Ken Millband/ John Williams
Construction/ Professional Negligence	Rob Langley
Corporate	Andrew Hoyle/ Gillian Hall
Education	David Foster
Employment	Chris Welch
EU	Gillian Hall
Intellectual Property	Stephen Aldred
Personal Injury	Ian Wanstall
Planning/ Environment	Bryan Riley

WATSON, FARLEY & WILLIAMS

15 APPOLD STREET, LONDON, EC2A 2HB
Tel: (0171) 814 8000 **Fax:** (0171) 814 8141 **DX:** 530 LONDON CITY EC3 **Internet:** HTTP://WWW.WFW.COM

The Firm: Watson, Farley & Williams was established in 1982. The firm has an excellent reputation in the area of banking and asset financing, particularly ship and aircraft finance, and has a number of other specialist areas. Through its spread of offices, the firm is able to offer an integrated, multi-jurisdictional service in connection with those centres where their offices are located, and worldwide through an extensive network of specialist correspondent lawyers. In each of their offices their lawyers have expertise in the laws of the local jurisdictions and a knowledge and understanding of local business customs and culture. It is a key feature of their practice, bringing together particular benefits to their clients, that the firm is divided into four international practice groups: Corporate, Finance, Litigation and Shipping. These groups are not divided by location but work together internationally.

The firm is known by its clients as providing effective, superior quality services required in specialist areas. It builds strong, long lasting relations with its clients and has a thorough understanding of the demands and developments of their different market places.

Principal Areas of Work:

International shipping group: The firm's international shipping group handles all types of domestic and international ship finance transactions acting for banks and other financial institutions and for ship owners. It advises on all aspects of their business including: new building and second hand ship financing, international cross-border lease and structured financing in many jurisdictions; sale and purchase of vessels; operating leases and other off balance sheet financings, charterparties, full pay-out lease financing, credit enhancement structures, the US Oil Pollution Act of 1990 and other environmental issues and insurance policies and their use. The group also advises on syndication methods, securitisation and asset sales, maritime legislation, Liberian law advice, French law tax-based quirat financing, IPOs private placements and high yield bond issues, lease and structured financing of drilling rigs, FPSOs and similar offshore/oil industry units.

International finance group: The firm's international finance group represents lenders, sponsors, developers, investors, vendors, output purchasers, underwriters and other project participants including government and governmental agencies. It advises on aviation and other asset finance, trade finance, cross-border tax leveraged lending and leasing, medium ticket leasing transactions, standard form lease documentation for small ticket transactions and associated agreements with suppliers and the sale and purchase of lease portfolios and leasing companies. The group also advises on derivatives and structured finance, securities and capital markets, international project finance, general banking finance, commercial property, VAT and customs duties, aviation finance, workouts and insolvencies.

International corporate group: The firm's international corporate group acts on a wide range of domestic and international transactions for both public and private companies on acquisitions, disposals and mergers, stock market flotations, IPO's and other public and private securities offerings, management buy-outs and buy-ins, business and asset sales, structuring of debt, mezzanine or equity financings, corporate restructurings and schemes of arrangement, international privatisation advice and technical assistance, UK Financial Services Act and EC compliance and EC competition law. The group in conjunction with their competition law specialists, also advises on intellectual property, outsourcing and employment matters, IP facilities management, employment, distributorship, sale, supply, purchase and agency agreements, the provision of service agreements, share option and incentive schemes and joint venture and partnership agreements, with particular experience in Europe, the USA and the CIS.

International litigation group: The firm's international litigation group is based in London and New York handling litigation and arbitration matters. Large scale litigation is often international in nature and the group is able to prosecute and defend legal proceedings on a worldwide basis. The group's lawyers have experience in a wide range of general commercial arbitration and litigation disputes including, shipping (including shipbuilding, ship sale and carriage of goods, admiralty matters), purchase, international trade, energy related matters (including offshore oil development contracts), banking, finance (including ship finance enforcement and workout), derivatives, aviation and aviation related matters, insurance (including marine insurance), real property, fraud, antitrust, competition and tax and environmental law violations and insolvency. The group is also able to advise on corporate structures having regard to potential pollution liability under environmental statutes.

Recruitment and Training: The firm is looking for about ten to twelve trainees who are likely to obtain at least a 2:1 degree, not necessarily in law. There is a generous benefits package and the firm provides financial assistance for both the Legal Practice Course and the

Managing partner:	David Warder
Senior partner:	Alastair Farley
UK	
Number of partners:	35
Assistant solicitors:	54
Other fee-earners:	22
Total staff:	229
International	
Number of partners:	28
Assistant solicitors:	53
Other fee-earners:	14
Total staff:	159

CONTACTS	
Corporate	Charles Walford
Finance	Christopher Preston
Litigation	Michael Greville
Shipping	Frank Dunne

Continues overleaf

Common Professional Examination. New trainees are introduced to the firm with a comprehensive induction course covering legal topics and practical instruction. There is also a full continuing education programme for trainees and solicitors and all trainees have the opportunity to spend time in one of the overseas offices to gain some international experience. The firm places an emphasis on training its solicitors to become good all round commercial lawyers before they are required to specialise upon qualification. For brochure and application form contact the Graduate Recruitment Officer.

Other Offices: Piraeus, Paris, New York, Moscow, Copenhagen.

WEDLAKE BELL

16 BEDFORD STREET, COVENT GARDEN, LONDON, WC2E 9HF
Tel: (0171) 395 3000 **Fax:** (0171) 836 9966 **DX:** 40009 COVENT GDN. **Email:** LEGAL@WEDLAKEBELL.CO.UK

The Firm: Wedlake Bell is a strong well established legal practice serving both the corporate and private client sectors. It acts for public and private companies, banks and financial institutions, trade associations, governmental bodies, entrepreneurs, private investors and wealthy individuals. It has particular expertise in banking, construction, food manufacturing, IT, property, telecommunications, sports and healthcare. It has significant overseas interests, acting in Europe for clients from the US, the Middle and Far Easts, Australia and Russia. Through its office on Guernsey it provides offshore services in a number of tax favourable jurisdictions. Its membership of the Trans European Law Firms Alliance enables it to offer its clients pan European legal coverage through a single contact point. It is recognised as providing legal advice of the quality of much larger firms while at the same time placing strong emphasis on the personal nature of its service to clients, the involvement of its partners and its responsive and constructive approach to legal issues.

Principal Areas of Work:

Corporate finance: (Andrew Baker). The corporate finance group advises on mergers and acquisitions (both public and private), management buy-ins and buy-outs, flotations, placings and rights issues, asset purchases and disposals, joint ventures and corporate restructuring. The group advises on all corporate regulatory and governance issues.

Commercial, IP and media: (Barry Weatherill). The commercial team advises on the protection and exploitation of intellectual property rights, competition and European law and on commercial agreements for agency, distribution, franchise, sponsorship and merchandising. It advises on data protection, information technology and internet related legal issues. It has specialist sector involvement in media, sport and food manufacturing.

Banking and Insolvency: (Philip Matthews). This group handles secured lending, syndicated and bilateral transactions for both banks and borrowers, project finance, asset finance, acquisition finance, debt restructuring and all aspects of corporate insolvency.

Commercial property: (David Earl). The firm acts in connection with all the legal aspects relevant to the trading, developing, funding and occupation of, or investment in, land and buildings for developers, investors, banks, landlords and tenants.

Employment, pensions and share schemes: (Clive Weber). This group advises on all aspects of employment law both contentious and non-contentious. It advises employers, trustees and members on a wide variety of occupational pension schemes and acts in connection with the establishment and operation of share schemes including option schemes and long term incentive plans.

Litigation: (Richard Hewitt). The firm acts in connection with disputes across a range of fields including commercial matters, banking, insurance, professional indemnity, landlord and tenant, intellectual property and defamation. It handles County Court and High Court proceedings and acts in national and international arbitrations.

Construction: (Suzanne Reeves). The construction team advises developers, contractors, sub-contractors, banks, consultants and insurers on both contentious and non-contentious issues.

Private clients: (Charles Hicks). This group covers tax planning, trusts, offshore tax jurisdictions, wills and inheritance issues, asset protection, landed estates, probate, heritage and agricultural property, charities and Lloyd's. It also advises in connection with matrimonial disputes, immigration and residential conveyancing matters.

Offshore: (Quentin Spicer). The Guernsey office handles the formation and administration of companies and trusts in a number of tax favourable jurisdictions and provides managed trust operations for financial institutions. It handles the acquisition and disposal of UK investment property for offshore investment funds and for individuals.

Managing partner:	Julian Cuppage
Senior partner:	Robert Dolman
UK	
Number of partners:	27
Assistant solicitors:	26
Other fee-earners:	17
International	
Number of partners:	3
Assistant solicitors:	1
Other fee-earners:	4

WORKLOADS	
Corporate/commercial	31%
Property/construction	27%
Litigation	24%
Private client	18%

CONTACTS	
Banking and finance	Philip Matthews
Commercial and media	Barry Weatherill
Construction	Suzanne Reeves
Corporate finance	Andrew Baker
Employment	Richard Isham
Food	Peter Whatmuff
Insolvency	Hugh Thomson
Intellectual property	Jonathan Cornthwaite
Litigation	Richard Hewitt
Pensions	Clive Weber
Private client	Charles Hicks
Property	David Earl

WEDLAKE BELL

Solicitors

Foreign connections: In Europe, Wedlake Bell is a founder member of Trans European Law Firms Alliance (TELFA), an alliance of independent commercial law firms covering all of Europe's major jurisdictions. TELFA has its central office in Brussels. In the US, the firm is associated with the Minneapolis law firm of Fredrikson & Byron and advises on commercial and investment matters involving the US and Europe.

Overseas Office: Guernsey

Recruitment and training: The firm offers both training contracts and student summer placements. CVs should be addressed to the Personnel Manager.

WEDLAKE SAINT

14 JOHN STREET, LONDON, WC1N 2EB
Tel: (0171) 405 9446 **Fax:** (0171) 242 9877 **DX:** 407 CH.LN.

The Firm: Established for over 75 years, Wedlake Saint is a progressive firm of solicitors with a relatively young partnership and a well-earned reputation for providing practical legal advice for clients – both commercial and private – with authority, imagination and efficiency.

Principal Areas of Work:

Property: (*Contact Partner:* John Woodhead). Extensive experience in both commercial and residential property. It handles all aspects of property development, town and country planning, housing associations, landlord and tenant law and compulsory purchases, as well as all aspects of offshore and international property work.

Litigation: (*Contact Partner:* Tony Usher). Litigation is an expanding area of the firm's practice and includes general commercial disputes, personal injury claims, employers' liability, health and safety, building and engineering disputes, arbitration, contentious probate, family and child law and debt collection. The department also has particular experience in the law relating to education.

Transport: (*Contact Partner:* Barry Prior). Working in liaison with other specialist divisions within the firm, the transport law department provides substantial and wide ranging legal advice on all aspects of road transport including operators' licensing, road traffic prosecutions and accidents, employment legislation, commercial contracts, the formation, purchase and disposal of business as well as management buy-outs.The firm is an associate member of the Confederation of Passenger Transport Ltd and of the Freight Transport Association. The partner heading the department is a Fellow of the Chartered Institute of Transport.

Commercial: (*Contact Partner:* Terri Corti). The department handles all aspects of company law, flotations, mergers and acquisitions, management buy-outs, reconstructions and refinance, insolvency, pension schemes, commercial contracts, intellectual property rights and EC law.It is also active in advising on the contentious and non-contentious aspects of employment law.

Tax and Probate: (*Contact Partner:* Brendan Hall). The department advises both private and corporate clients on tax planning, inheritance and estate planning, VAT and stamp duty, reliefs, allowances, claims and benefits and land transactions. The department also negotiates and deals with the Inland Revenue and conducts appeals before it. It handles trusts, wills and probate for its private clients.

Nature of Clientele: Clients include public listed and USM quoted companies, substantial private companies, national charities, housing associations, property developers, trade associations, insurance companies, road haulage and passenger undertakings, educational institutions, trade unions and banks. The firm publishes a range of brochures specifically designed to assist the business community as well as regular newsletters aimed at the employment and transport sectors and at private clients.

Recruitment: The firm recruits two trainee solicitors every year. Candidates should apply by letter and CV to Recruitment Partner. The firm has offices at 146 London Road, St Albans (01727 845515).

Number of partners:	11
Assistant solicitors:	4
Other fee-earners:	16

WORKLOADS	
Litigation	25%
Property	25%
Transport	25%
Commercial	10%
Tax and probate	10%
Charities	5%

CONTACTS	
Agency	C. Ashmore
Arbitration	A.M. Usher
Charities	N.W. Saint
Commercial	Terri Corti
Commercial property	J. Woodhead
Employment	A.M. Usher
Health and safety	N. Tomlins
Litigation	A.M. Usher
Personal injury	B.A. Prior/A.M. Usher
Residential property	D. Taylor
Road accident	A. Knott
Tax and probate	B. Hall
Transport	B.A. Prior/A. Knott

WEIGHTMANS

RICHMOND HOUSE, 1 RUMFORD PLACE, LIVERPOOL, L3 9QW
Tel: (0151) 227 2601 **Fax:** (0151) 227 3223 **DX:** 14201

Weightmans is one of the country's largest insurance based practices. It also has a thriving commercial division which enjoys an increasing national and international reputation.

The Firm: With over 330 staff in Liverpool and Birmingham, Weightmans is renowned as an approachable, unstuffy and innovative firm and is one of the country's few professionally managed legal firms.

Weightmans is committed to the development of its employees and to the highest standards of client care. This is reflected in the firm's team culture and its ability to consistently deliver cost effective premium quality services to its clients.

Client partnership agreements, flexible pricing structures, Investors in People and a progressive IT strategy are just some of the initiatives Weightmans actively promotes to ensure it remains at the forefront of the profession.

Principal Areas of Work: Weightmans has an impressive portfolio of clients. Its **defendant insurance** division acts for more than 50 insurance companies, including 8 of the top 10 insurers. Work undertaken includes personal injury, employers' and public liablility, professional indemnity and medical negligence.

In addition to general insurance work, Weightmans specialises in policy interpretation, the complex area of civil law, advice to police authorities, and claims involving uninsured motorists where it acts for the Motor Insurance Bureau.

Weightmans' key strength is its ability to work closely with its clients to avoid protracted and costly disputes by reaching rapid decisions on whether to fight – or settle. The firm has an enviable reputation for speed of settlement while maintaining the highest professional standards and was involved in the consultation process for the Woolf report. Weightmans has pioneered early dialogue and alternative dispute resolution.

The **professional indemnity division** is rated as the number 1 firm in the north west. In addition to its work for the Solicitors Indemnity Fund, the division represents architects, accountants, surveyors and other professionals. The division also has a growing reputation in the field of medical negligence.

Weightmans' **police authorities team** is probably the only specialist team in the country. Apart from EL, PL and employment work, the team advises on the complex area of civil complaints against the police and administrative law. The firm is also involved in risk management initiatives with several police forces.

Commercial

Weightmans has a long and established expertise in the licensing field which has been acknowledged by the firm's appointment to undertake licensing work throughout the country for 2 of the largest groups in the brewing and leisure industry. The team conducts town and country planning appeals and acts for several hotel chains.

The **commercial property** division handles all aspects of the acquisition, financing, development and disposal of commercial property. Clients include not only the large developers but also major institutions. The company and commercial team is well-equipped to handle the property aspects of corporate take-overs, mergers and reconstructions, as well as such issues as compulsory purchase and landlord/tenant disputes.

The **commercial litigation team** deals with corporate disputes for many names in manufacturing, shipping and construction. The firm is committed to alternative dispute resolution, arbitration, mediation and innovative legal solutions.

Its **company/commercial** division combines a niche high profile client practice with general advice to owner manged businesses which are predominant on Merseyside.

The **employment team** covers the full range of employment issues from service contracts through to unfair dismissal, redundancy, sexual/racial discrimination and trade union disputes.

Senior partner:	Mike Edge
Chief Executive:	Martin Read
Number of partners:	41
Assistant solicitors:	58
Other fee-earners:	96

CONTACTS	
Comercial Litigation	Ian Evans (Liverpool)
Commercial	David Morgan (Liverpool)
Employment	Michael Ball (Liverpool)
Insurance	Tony Pritchard (Liverpool), Nigel Dace (Birmingham)
Licensing	Mark Owen (Liverpool)
Medical Negligence	Tony Summers (Liverpool)
Professional Idemnity	Frank Maher (Liverpool)

WEIL, GOTSHAL & MANGES

ONE SOUTH PLACE, LONDON, EC2M 2WG
Tel: (0171) 903 1000 **Fax:** (0171) 903 0990 **DX:** 124402 **Email:** WEIL.LONDON@WEIL.COM

Weil, Gotshal & Manges are an international law firm recognised as offering premier US and UK law capabilities. The firm prides itself as the logical choice for international finance and corporate law clients.

The Firm: Weil, Gotshal & Manges has over 190 partners and 650 lawyers world-wide. They provide seamless US and UK capabilities of a consistently high standard across the international practice and a unique international finance and corporate practice with lawyers whose expertise bridges the traditional divides between banking, capital markets and corporate law. They have a practice which recognises the benefits for clients of sectoral and regional expertise and delivers a team of lawyers reflecting that experience. They have a team of lawyers who remain totally committed and accessible throughout the life of the deal wherever it may take place around the globe. Since opening in London in March 1996, their office has grown from twelve to seventy US and UK lawyers, picked from leading firms. The appeal of their US/UK law capabilities and their new approach to international finance and corporate law transactions – bridging the traditional divisions between banking, capital markets and corporate law – have been major factors in their success. Weil, Gotshal & Manges London was recently voted Best London Office of an Overseas Law Firm by a leading legal publication.

Principal Areas of Work: The firm's international finance and corporate law practice encompasses: – Acquisition Finance – Asset Finance & Leasing – Banking – Corporate Recovery & Insolvency – Debt & Equity Capital Markets – Derivatives – Distressed Debt Trading – Emerging Markets – High Yield Debt – International Taxation – Litigation – Mergers & Acquisitions – Project Finance – Securitisation – Structured Finance – Telecommunications & Multimedia

Other offices: Brussels, Budapest, Dallas, Houston, New York, Menlo Park, Miami, Prague, Warsaw and Washington DC.

Contacts:	Maurice Allen
Number of Partners:	16
Number of Fee-earners:	70
Total Staff:	126

WELLMAN & CO 28 West Parade, Lincoln, LN1 1JT *Tel:* (01522) 536161 *Fax:* (01522) 513007 *DX:* 11009 Lincoln 1 *Ptnrs:* 3

WENDY HOPKINS & CO 26 Windsor Place, Cardiff, CF1 3BZ *Tel:* (01222) 342233 *Ptnrs:* 2 *Other fee-earners:* 2

WESLEY GRYK 149 The Strand, London, WC2R 1JA *Tel:* (0171) 240 8485 *Fax:* (0171) 240 8486 *DX:* 51643 Covent Garden *Ptnrs:* 1 *Asst solrs:* 2 *Other fee-earners:* 3

WHATLEY, WESTON & FOX 15-16 The Tything, Worcester, WR1 1HD **Tel:** (01905) 20361 **Fax:** (01905) 22347 **DX:** 716264 **Ptnrs:** 8 **Asst solrs:** 4 **Other fee-earners:** 4 **Contact:** Nigel Horner *Niche company and commercial practice specialising in corporate and individual insolvencies. Substantial private clientele. Experienced in personal injury work.*

WORKLOADS	
Private Client	48%
Company & Commercial	37%
Insolvency	15%

WHISKERS

GATE HOUSE, THE HIGH, HARLOW, CM20 1LW
Tel: (01279) 441111 **Fax:** (01279) 444464 **DX:** 40502 HARLOW

The Firm: Founded over 125 years ago, Whiskers is a progressive firm providing a wide range of legal services for private and business clients from its well-appointed offices in Harlow [H], Epping [E].

Stephen Thirsk, the Senior Partner, is the Secretary of the West Essex Law Society, Eugene Ahern is a Member of the Law Society Personal Injury and Childrens Panels, Tim Bowles is a Solicitor Advocate (Higher Rights Civil). Stephen Thirsk and Derek King are Notaries. Kathryn Henry is a Member of The Law Society Childrens Panel.

Principal Areas of Work:
General Description:
Company and Commercial: John Roberts, [H]
Litigation: Tim Bowles [H]
Child Care: Eugene Ahern [H], Kathryn Henry [H]

Number of partners:	6
Assistant solicitors:	7
Other fee-earners:	4

CONTACTS	
Practice Manager	Steve Ray

Continues overleaf

Family and Matrimonial: Eugene Ahern [H], Tim Bowles [H], Kathryn Henry [E]
Wills, Trust and Probate: Derek King [E], Stephen Thirsk [H]
Licensing: Stephen Thirsk [H]
Conveyancing: Stephen Thirsk [H], Gerry Smith [E]
Criminal: Russell Robinson [H], Andrew Clowser [H]
Personal Injury: Eugene Ahern [H]

Other Areas of Work: The firm undertakes agency work at Epping and Harlow Magistrates Courts and at Harlow County Court (the Harlow office is in the same building as the Court).

Other Office: 265 High Street, Epping, Essex.
Tel: (01992) 561111 *Fax:* (01992) 573642. *DX:* 40400 Epping.

WHITE & BOWKER 19 St. Peter St, Winchester, SO23 8BU *Tel:* (01962) 844440 *Fax:* (01962) 842300 *DX:* 2506 Winchester *Ptnrs:* 14 *Asst solrs:* 12 *Other fee-earners:* 22

WHITE & CASE

7-11 MOORGATE, LONDON, EC2R 6HH
Tel: (0171) 726 6361 **Fax:** (0171) 726 4314

The Firm: White & Case is a global law firm which was formed in 1901. Its work encompasses corporate, capital markets and financial services transactions, litigation, arbitration and tax advice in the world's primary financial and commercial centres. The firm has over 750 lawyers based in offices around the world – in the United States, Latin America, Europe, the Middle East, Africa and Asia.

London Office: Advice is provided for corporate clients on a full range of legal issues, with particular emphasis on capital markets, corporate finance, project finance, and domestic English and international litigation.

Languages Spoken: English, French, German, Spanish.

Other Offices: New York, Washington, Los Angeles, Miami, Mexico City, São Paulo, Paris, Stockholm, Istanbul, Ankara, Brussels, Moscow, Prague, Warsaw, Budapest, Almaty, Helsinki, Johannesburg, Hong Kong, Singapore, Jakarta, Tokyo, Riyadh, Jeddah, Bangkok, Bombay, Hanoi, Ho Chi Minh City.

Executive Partner:	John Bellhouse
Administrative Partner:	Margaret R. Cole

WORKLOADS	
Capital markets	20%
Project finance	20%
Company/commercial/joint ventures	15%
Construction	15%
Corporate finance/M&A	15%
Litigation	15%

WHITEHEAD MONCKTON 72 King St, Maidstone, ME14 1BL **Tel:** (01622) 698000 **Fax:** (01622) 690050 **DX:** 4807 **Ptnrs:** 13 **Asst solrs:** 5 **Other fee-earners:** 8 **Contact:** M.W. Hardcastle *A large regional practice best known for its company/ commercial work, private client and investment services and litigation.*

WORKLOADS			
Private client	34%	Litigation	30%
Commercial	24%		

WHITELOCK & STORR 5 Bloomsbury Square, London, WC1A 2LX *Tel:* (0171) 242 8612 *Fax:* (0171) 404 4131 *DX:* 35739 *Ptnrs:* 3 *Asst solrs:* 2 *Other fee-earners:* 3

WHITTLES

PEARL ASSURANCE HOUSE, 23 PRINCESS STREET, MANCHESTER, M2 4ER
Tel: (0161) 228 2061 **Fax:** (0161) 236 1046

SUITE 9C JOSEPHS WELL, PARK LANE, LEEDS, LS3 1AB
Tel: (0113) 244 2216 **Fax:** (0113) 242 1214

Whittles is a substantial and expanding specialist Plaintiff Personal Injury and Employment Law firm.

The Firm: Founded by Preston Solicitor, John Whittle, in the 1920s the firm now has offices in Manchester and Leeds. The last decade has seen continued growth at both the Manchester and Leeds offices to enable the practice to serve an expanding Client base. Leeds office opened as recently as 1984 and expanded from one Partner on opening to the present 25 fee earners.

Whittles specialises in Plaintiff Personal Injury litigation and Employment matters and has worked closely with its Trades Union Clients for over sixty years looking after the interests of Union Members in their places of work and in their personal affairs.

Principal Areas of Work:
Personal Injury litigation: (*Contact:* Colin Mansfield) The firm specialises primarily in Personal Injury litigation, the majority of cases being workplace accidents.
Employment: (*Contact:* David Towler and Charles Hantom) Whittles do not work for employers. Cases from all over England and Wales are dealt with from the existing offices.

Managing partner:	David Towler
Senior partner:	Charles Hantom
Number of partners:	15
Assistant solicitors:	19
Other fee-earners:	33

WORKLOADS	
Personal injury litigation	90%
Employment	6%
Private Client	4%

WIGGIN AND CO

THE QUADRANGLE, IMPERIAL SQUARE, CHELTENHAM, GL50 1YX
Tel: (01242) 224114 **Fax:** (01242) 224223 **DX:** 7427 **Email:** LAW@WIGGIN.CO.UK

The Firm: Based in Cheltenham, with offices in Los Angeles and London, Wiggin and Co. has an international reputation for its specialist expertise in tax, media, communications, technology and entertainment. It is a firm with a 'city-type' practice and strong international bias.

Principal Areas of Work:
Company/ Commercial: (*Contact:* Tim Osborne, Mike Turner or Stephen Cook). The firm specialises in all aspects of media and entertainment law including satellite and cable TV, film, intellectual property, multimedia, defamation, publishing and computer technology and advice on European Community legislation. Other services include public flotations, mergers and acquisitions, MBOs, corporate reorganisations and financing, insolvency and financial services compliance and corporate tax.
Taxation: (*Contact:* Nic Stones or Michael Fullerlove). The firm offers specialist advice on UK and international tax, capital and income tax planning for individuals, including the establishment and restructuring of UK and overseas trusts, the appropriate structure for UK and overseas investment, international asset protection, and general tax advice to both public and private companies, their shareholders and executives.
Litigation: (*Contact:* Caroline Kean) The firm undertakes all aspects of commercial litigation with particular specialist expertise in media and entertainment law, defamation, copyright and commercial property.
Commercial Property: (*Contact:* Paul Wilson). The firm undertakes development structuring, sale and leaseback funding, joint venture agreements, options, secured loan transactions, sale and purchase of agricultural land and private estates and time share in the UK and EC countries.

Foreign Connections: The office in Los Angeles was opened to advise individuals and corporations on the West Coast of America wishing to do business in the UK and Europe, and to assist European clients with US investments and business activities. The firm has extensive experience in international matters and its wide range of international contacts is extended by its membership of the Wiggin Group of European Lawyers and Tax Advisers.

Managing partner:	T.W. Osborne
Number of partners:	12
Assistant solicitors:	14
Other fee-earners:	6

WORKLOADS	
Media and entertainment	40%
Private client	40%
Litigation	12%
Property	8%

CONTACTS	
Commercial property	P.M. Wilson
Company and commercial	M.W. Turner
Corporate Finance	S.S.Cook
Defamation	C.M. Kean
EC legislation	S.R. Lowde
Immigration	S.R. Lowde
International asset protection	M.R. Fullerlove
Litigation	C.M. Kean
Media and entertainment	T.W. Osborne
Private client	J.N. Stones
Tax (corporate)	P.D. Hunston

WIKBORG REIN & CO

ONE KNIGHTRIDER COURT, LONDON, EC4V 5JP
Tel: (0171) 236 4598 **Fax:** (0171) 236 4599

The Firm: Wikborg, Rein & Co is an international law firm founded in 1923. The two founding partners set the early course of the firm, establishing its reputation as a commercial firm and attracting clients from the world of shipping and other industries. Although one of the largest law firms in Norway, Wikborg, Rein & Co continues to operate on the basis of a close working relationship with each client. The firm is prepared, if required, to take on management responsibility for the detailed handling of transactions.

The London Office: The London office is staffed by three Norwegian lawyers. In addition to providing liaison services for the firm's international clients on Norwegian business and Norwegian clients on international business, the office has particular expertise in the areas of finance, shipping, mergers, acquisitions and securities.

Main Areas of Work:

Company & Corporate: *Work includes:* company formation, corporate acquisitions and disposals, demergers, finance, insolvency, joint ventures, liquidation, partnerships, registration services, share issues, voting rights.

Shipping: *Work includes:* agency, arrest, building contracts, broking, cargo claims, charters, collisions, finance, flag changes, insurance, management, mortgages, pollution, protection and indemnity claims, sales, salvage, terminals.

Oil and Gas: *Work includes:* construction contracts, drilling rigs, farm-ins, farm-outs, finance, acquisition of licence interests, offshore services, pipe-laying, pollution, R&D contracts, safety regulations, seismic surveys, supply vessels, tax, transportation and processing, unitisation.

Securities: *Work includes:* acquisitions, bonds, capital reorganisations, convertible issues, demergers, investor protection, mergers, private placings, public offers, registration services, Stock Exchange listings, trading disputes, underwriting agreements, venture capital.

Finance: *Work includes:* asset finance, debt rescheduling, guarantees, leases, loan agreements, mortgages, off-balance sheet instruments, security documentation.

Other Offices: Oslo, Bergen, Kobe.

Managing UK Partner:	Morten Lund Mathisen
Resident lawyer:	Ketil E. Bøe
Associate Lawyer:	1

WORKLOADS	
Shipping	40%
Company/ commercial	30%
Finance	30%

WILBRAHAM & CO Minerva House, East Parade, Leeds, LS1 5PS *Tel:* (0113) 243 2200 *Fax:* (0113) 244 9777 *Ptnrs:* 4 *Asst solrs:* 4 *Other fee-earners:* 1

WILDE & PARTNERS

10 JOHN STREET, LONDON, WC1N 2EB
Tel: (0171) 831 0800 **Fax:** (0171) 430 0678 **DX:** 428 LONDON **Email:** LAW@WILDES.CO.UK **Internet:** HTTP://WWW.WILDES.CO.UK

This central London firm offers a wide range of commercial services, with niche expertise factoring and invoice discounting, (in which it is recognised as the market leader), trade finance, asset based lending, insolvency and debt recovery.

The Firm: Wilde & Partners was established in 1976 and has from its beginning focused on its specialist skills. Clients include the factoring and invoice discounting subsidiaries of British and overseas banks and the majority of the members of the Factors and Discounters Association. The firm is an associate member of the Finance and Leasing Association.

The practice aims to build a relationship with clients that will be both productive and long lasting. Wilde & Partners prides itself on its ability to offer practical and cost effective solutions to legal problems and to respond promptly to requests for advice and assistance. Its objectives are to give constructive and positive advice that is consistent with the business objectives of clients.

Principal Areas of Work: Company/Commercial activities include acquisitions and disposals, company formations, setting up distributorships, agencies and franchises, employment law, management buy-ins and buy-outs, intellectual property matters and shareholder agreements.

Trade finance and banking work includes expertise in stock financing, all forms of secured and unsecured asset based lending, bills of exchange, factoring and invoice discounting, credit protection, guarantees and indemnities, letters of credit, pledges and trust receipts.

The Commercial Litigation department deals with contractual and negligence claims, shareholder disputes, fraud investigations and asset recovery, defamation and the enforcement of

Managing partner:	Simon Boon
Number of partners:	5
Assistant solicitors:	6
Other fee-earners:	10

WORKLOADS	
Trade Finance, Leasing & Banking	35%
Commercial Litigation	30%
Debt & Fraud Recovery	20%
Insolvency	10%
Commercial Property	5%

CONTACTS	
Commercial Litigation	Simon Boon
Commercial Property	Paul Burbidge
Insolvency	Abraham Ezekiel
Recoveries	Robert Weekes
Trade Finance & Commercial Law	Andrew Watson

securities, guarantees and indemnities and judgments. Alternative dispute resolution, arbitrations and appeals are undertaken where appropriate. Debt recovery is a particular specialism of the firm and annually the firm successfully collects millions of pounds of trade debts throughout the UK and overseas.

Wilde & Partners has an expanding insolvency practice acting for a number of the major insolvency practitioners, banks and corporate clients in both contentious and non-contentious situations. The firm also covers all aspects of commercial property. A range of insurance problems can be handled including policy advice and drafting, resolving claims and disputes, and fraud protection.

The firm will continue to focus on its existing specialisms and deliver a high quality professional service using the latest information technology.

WILDE SAPTE

1 FLEET PLACE, LONDON, EC4M 7WS
Tel: (0171) 246 7000 **Fax:** (0171) 246 7777 **DX:** 145 LONDON CITY EC4 **Email:** MARKETING@WILDESAPTE.COM
Internet: HTTP://WWW.WILDESAPTE.COM

LLOYD'S OFFICE, BANKSIDE HOUSE, 1ST FLOOR, 107-112 LEADENHALL STREET, LONDON, EC3A 4AA
Tel: (0171) 246 7000 **Fax:** (0171) 246 7722

27 AVENUE DES ARTS, 1040 BRUSSELS, BELGIUM
Tel: +32 2 280 1404 **Fax:** +32 2 280 1764

31ST FLOOR, ONE EXCHANGE SQUARE, HONG KONG,
Tel: +852 2 810 5081 **Fax:** +852 2 810 1295

217 RUE DU FAUBOURG ST. HONORÉ, 75008 PARIS, FRANCE
Tel: +33 1 44 95 02 70 **Fax:** +33 1 42 89 62 25

10TH FLOOR, RIVERSIDE YOMIURI BUILDING, 36-2 NIHONBASHI HAKOZAKI-CHO CHUO-KU, TOKYO, JAPAN, 103
Tel: +813 5 641 8455 **Fax:** +813 5 641 8460

The Firm: Founded in 1785, Wilde Sapte is a commercial City firm handling a wide range of work for its UK and international clients with a particular emphasis on clients in the banking and finance and insurance markets.

Wilde Sapte has a strong reputation for an innovative and commercial approach to legal problems, combining a full understanding of clients' business aims with the competitive environment in which they operate. Its long history of working with the banking and finance industry makes it particularly well placed to help banking and finance clients with all aspects of their businesses from the products that they deal in to their corporate, M&A, property and litigation needs. It has more recently been developing a similar relationship with the insurance industry.

Based at Fleet Place and at Leadenhall Street in the City of London, Wilde Sapte has offices in Brussels, Hong Kong, Paris and Tokyo to meet the needs of its clients requiring assistance with local law and business or international transactions. To complete its global capability, the firm has developed extensive connections with quality law firms in jurisdictions throughout the world and, in addition, has a number of dedicated multi-disciplinary units.

Principal Areas of Work: Wilde Sapte provides a full range of legal services to the business community with particular expertise in the banking and finance, insurance, corporate, insolvency and commercial litigation sectors.
  Banking and finance: Of an increasingly international nature, the firm has one of the largest banking practices in the UK, covering all aspects of banking and finance, including leasing, aviation, shipping and transport finance, trade finance, workouts and reconstructions, acquisition finance, capital markets, structured finance, housing association and property finance. In addition, the firm's project finance group has experienced rapid growth in recent years both in the domestic and international markets and is constantly involved in large, multi-faceted high profile transactions.
  Corporate and commercial: The corporate and commercial group handles a wide range of domestic and international corporate finance and commercial matters including mergers and acquisitions, flotations and equity issues, privatisation, venture capital, corporate restructuring, governance/regulation, commercial agreements, employment benefits, pensions, immigration and charity law.
  Insolvency: The firm's large insolvency group is pre-eminent in its field, with wide-ranging expertise in all aspects of insolvency law and practice.
  Insurance: Wilde Sapte's insurance and reinsurance practice has developed rapidly in recent years. Its 30-lawyer team, covers both contentious and non-contentious matters in all sectors of the London and international markets, operating from Fleet Place and from

Continues overleaf

Managing partner:	Steven Blakeley
Senior partner:	Mark Andrews
Worldwide	
Number of partners:	73
Assistant solcitors:	168
Trainees:	67
Other Fee-earners:	18
Total staff:	625

WORKLOADS	
Banking & Finance	36%
Litigation	34%
Company & Commercial	11%
Property	11%
Taxation	7%
Misc.	1%

CONTACTS	
Acquisition finance	James Johnson
Asset finance	Greg Kahn/Lisa Marks
Aviation	Colin Thaine
Banking	Adrian Miles
Capital markets	Martin Bartlam
Charities	Alastair Collett
Corporate and commercial	Helen Cleaveland
Corporate tax	Charlotte Sallabank
Employment	Guy Fifield
EU/Competition law	James Ashe-Taylor
Housing association finance	Richard Bethell-Jones/ James Johnson
Insolvency	Mark Andrews
Insurance	Adrian Mecz
Intellectual Property	John Hull
Leasing	Adrian Miles
Litigation	Nigel Barnett
Pensions	Alan Jarvis
Project Finance	Howard Barrie
Property/property finance	Stan Gniadkowski/ Mark Menhennet
Shipping	Giles Brand
Structured finance	Jonathan Shann
Trade finance	Elisabeth Gaunt

Lloyd's, and services every aspect of the insurance industry's legal requirements.

Litigation: The firm's commercial litigation department, renowned for its banking and finance work, has diversified in recent years to offer a wider range of specialist litigation services to its clients, including insurance, shipping, intellectual property, construction, property and regulatory matters.

Other areas of work: The firm has well-established corporate tax and property departments which work closely with, as well as independently of, each of the other departments. The firm's corporate tax practice is particularly strong as many of the banking and finance products on which the firm advises are tax led.

In addition, Wilde Sapte has developed particular areas of expertise, such as its EU/competition group, EMU group and rail group, which bring together lawyers providing specialist advice across the firm's various practice areas.

Recruitment and training: Trainee solicitors are recruited annually from a wide range of backgrounds. The Director of Training organises an extensive programme of continuing education in-house, including commercial skills and foreign language training, and there is a trainee solicitors' induction course.

Other offices: Tokyo, Hong Kong, Paris, Brussels, Lloyd's.

WILFORD MONRO 1-3 Brixton Rd, London, SW9 6DE **Tel:** (0171) 582 6002 **Fax:** (0171) 793 0538 **DX:** 33256 Kennington **Ptnrs:** 4 **Asst solrs:** 2 **Contact:** Jenny Newton *Specialist firm dealing with all legal matters affecting children including care proceedings, divorce, injunction, adoption, immigration, crime, personal injury.*

WORKLOADS			
Children (private law)	35%	Public law	35%
Adoption	15%		
Employment/ personal injury			5%
Immigration	5%	Mental health	5%

WILKIN CHAPMAN PO Box 16, Town Hall Square, Grimsby, DN31 1HE *Tel:* (01472) 358234 *Fax:* (01472) 360198 *DX:* 13511 Grimsby 1 *Ptnrs:* 14 *Asst solrs:* 15 *Other fee-earners:* 24

WILKINSON & BUTLER Peppercorn House, 8 Huntingdon Street, St Neots., PE19 1BH *Tel:* (01480) 219229 *Fax:* (01480) 472651 *DX:* 100301 St Neots *Ptnrs:* 4 *Asst solrs:* 2 *Other fee-earners:* 2

WILKINSON, WOODWARD & LUDLAM 11 Fountain St, Halifax, HX1 1LU *Tel:* (01422) 340711 *Fax:* (01422) 330417 *DX:* 16004 Halifax *Ptnrs:* 9 *Asst solrs:* 1 *Other fee-earners:* 7

WILLAN BOOTLAND WHITE Lawrence Buildings, 2 Mount Street, Manchester, M2 5WQ **Tel:** (0161) 839 1922 **Fax:** (0161) 839 1924 **DX:** 709031 MCR7 **Ptnrs:** 3 **Contact:** Mr Edward Bootland *Commercial practice specialising in Company, Commercial property, Landlord and Tenant and Rent Act, Commercial Litigation, Private Client and Conveyancing.*

WORKLOADS	
Commercial	40%
Litigation	35%
Private Client	25%

WILLANS 28/29 Imperial Square, Cheltenham, GL50 1RH *Tel:* (01242) 514707 *Fax:* (01242) 519079 *Ptnrs:* 7 *Asst solrs:* 8 *Other fee-earners:* 8

WILLCOX LANE CLUTTERBUCK WITH REES EDWARDS MADDOX

55 CHARLOTTE STREET, BIRMINGHAM, B3 1PX
Tel: (0121) 236 9441 **Fax:** (0121) 236 4733 **DX:** 712086 BIRMINGHAM 29

The Firm: Willcox Lane Clutterbuck is a modern firm with a long pedigree. Following the recent merger with Rees Edwards Maddox it has a substantial corporate finance department but still cherishes its traditional client base of private individuals and small to medium-sized businesses. It is recognised for its work in insurance litigation and tax expertise.

Principal Areas of Work:

Company/Commercial: *(3 partners). Work includes:* corporate finance, acquisitions/sales, flotations, insolvency, "management buy-ins/outs", employment contracts, computer law, intellectual property, company formations and general commercial advice to businesses, companies and individuals.

Defendant Insurance litigation: *(3 partners).* The firm handles a wide range of insurance litigation for composite insurers, underwriters and loss adjusters in connection with road traffic accidents, employers liability, public liability, personal injury and general liability.

Commercial and Agricultural Property and Construction: *(4 partners). Work includes:* the purchase and sale of all types of freehold and leasehold properties for commercial users and investors, property development, employee relocation and planning law.

Litigation and debt collection: *(3 partners). Work includes:* contract and commercial disputes, debt collection and employment and general litigation. The firm is also able to deal with all aspects of criminal work and matrimonial law.

Private client and Charities: *(2 Partners).* The firm is widely involved in the establishment, management and winding-up of trusts and charities. The firm also manages clients' financial affairs and investments as well as handling all aspects of wills and probate.

Tax: *(1 Partner).* The firm advises on tax planning and mitigation for individuals, trusts and companies.

Nature of Clientele: Clients include public and private companies, insurance companies, public utilities, local authorities, colleges, charities as well as private individuals.

Managing partner:	William M. Colacicchi
Number of partners:	13
Assistant solicitors:	9
Other fee-earners:	11

WORKLOADS	
Insurance litigation	47%
Property	20%
Private client	17%
Commercial	13%
Criminal litigation	3%

CONTACTS	
Commercial	Gareth Griffiths
Commercial/civil litigation	M. English
Criminal	J. Smitheman
Defendant personal injury	M. Asokan
Matrimonial	J. Smitheman
Private client	William Colacicchi
Property/construction	Susan Stott

WILLCOX & LEWIS The Old Coach House, Bergh Apton, Norwich, NR15 1DD *Tel:* (01508) 480 100 *Fax:* (01508) 480 001 *Ptnrs:* 2

WILLIAM HATTON

TRINITY HOUSE, TRINITY ROAD, DUDLEY, DY1 1JB
Tel: (01384) 211211 **Fax:** (01384) 456165 **DX:** 12764 DUDLEY **Email:** HATT_HO_@MSN.COM

The Firm: The practice was founded by William Hatton over 30 years ago, and in recent years has expanded rapidly to become one of the largest defendant personal injury practices in the Midlands. The firm offers competitive charging rates and a high degree of expertise with extensive knowledge of specific industrial diseases.

Principal Areas of Work:

Civil Litigation: *(Contact Partner:* A.T.R. Perry). The firm concentrates on civil litigation, primarily for insurance company clients, and with a well-established specialisation in personal injury claims arising from both road traffic and employers' liability. The practice has a long history of conducting disease litigation, with individuals specialising in claims involving particular industrial diseases, including deafness, asbestosis and R.S.I.

Other Office: The firm has an additional office in Leicester. Both offices are situated to give easy access to the motorway network and hence enable the firm to cover a wide geographical area.

Number of partners:	7
Assistant solicitors:	4
Other fee-earners:	14

WORKLOADS	
Personal injury	95%
Commercial, conveyancing and probate	5%

WILLIAMS DAVIES MELTZER

8-10 NEW FETTER LANE, LONDON, EC4A 1AP
Tel: (0171) 353 2500 **Fax:** (0171) 353 2552 **DX:** 1026 LONDON **Email:** WDM@LINK.ORG

The Firm: WDM specialises in insurance work, professional indemnity, liability claims and related commercial litigation including media and computer litigation.

Principal Areas of Work:

Professional Indemnity: WDM acts for all the property professionals (surveyors, valuers, engineers, architects, quantity surveyors etc), financial intermediaries and brokers, accountants and lawyers, insurance brokers, advertising/PR agents and media professionals, computer consultants, marine surveyors and other professionals including loss adjusters, designers and specialist contractors.

Accident and Injury Work: Employers', public and motor liability work in manufacturing, construction, transport, off-shore energy, power and retailing etc. including white collar claims and public sector work.

Insurance Disputes/Reinsurance: Disputed policy claims and inter-insurer issues, subrogation etc.

Commercial & Contract: Construction litigation, finance and property disputes.

Media: Libel and slander, entertainment and marketing industry disputes and claims.

Medical Malpractice: Defence work for hospitals and specialist clinics including novel issues in fields such as cosmetic surgery and IVF, work for professional bodies in medicine and ophthalmology etc.

Bankers: Professional Indemnity claims, recovery actions, fraud etc.

Products, Information Technology and Technical: Complex litigation involving manufactured products/computers etc., leading-edge technology and specialist marine manufacturing.

Fine Art and Antiques: Wordings, claims, investigations and recoveries.

Nature of clientele: WDM acts for Lloyd's Underwriters, UK and foreign composite insurers, brokers and adjusters, banks and financial institutions. In some cases, WDM accepts instructions from professional firms and companies direct.

Managing partner:	Hugh V. Williams
Number of partners:	5
Assistant solicitors:	10
Other fee-earners:	8

WORKLOADS	
Professional indemnity	40%
Accident & injury	20%
Insurance & policy disputes	15%
Products & technical	15%
Commercial claims	5%
Medical malpractice	5%

CONTACTS	
Accident & injury	Andrew Trott
Banking/computer	Daniel Meltzer
Employers'/ public liability	Jamie Colman
Financial Intermediaries/Reinsurance	Peter Court
Medical negligence	Sian Davies
Products & technical	Andrew Trott
Professional indemnity/Media	Hugh Williams

WILLIAMS DAVIES MELTZER
SOLICITORS

WILLIAMSON & SODEN

STANTON HOUSE, 54 STRATFORD ROAD, SHIRLEY, SOLIHULL, B90 3LS
Tel: (0121) 733 8000 **Fax:** (0121) 733 3322 **DX:** 20652

Principal Areas of Work:

Crime: (Contact: Fiona Warman-Shirley/ David Munro-Birmingham). A large and respected department deals with police matters for clients charged with anything from a motoring offence to a murder. Specialists also deal with Customs & Excise and Inland Revenue Investigations.

Company/Commercial: (Contact: John Soden). *Work includes:* new business start-ups, acquisition of commercial premises, trading agreements, mergers and acquisitions, commercial disputes and insolvencies.

Private Client: A full range of services covers all aspects of family and matrimonial law, personal injury compensation, wills, probate and trusts.

Other Office: Citadel, 190 Corporation Street, Birmingham B4 6QB. *Tel:* (0121) 212 1155 *Fax:* (0121) 212 4961.

Managing partner:	I.P. Williamson
Number of partners:	7
Assistant solicitors:	6
Other fee-earners:	6

CONTACTS	
Business clients	John Soden/Allison Scott
Disputes (general/ commercial)	Jamie Champkin
Family law	Clare Fletcher
Motor racing	David Munro/John Soden
Personal injury	GerryCusack
Planning law	Ian Williamson
Police matters (inc. motoring)	David Munro/ Fiona Warman
Property	Lynne Goldsby/Angela Beck
Telecommunications	David Munro
Wills and inheritance	Allison Scott/Angela Beck

LG WILLIAMS & PRICHARD 22 St Andrews Crescent, Cardiff, CF1 3DD *Tel:* (01222) 229716 *Fax:* (01222) 377761 *DX:* 50752 Cardiff 2 *Ptnrs:* 1 *Asst solrs:* 2 *Other fee-earners:* 4

WILLIAM STURGES & CO Alliance House, 12 Caxton St, London, SW1H 0QY *Tel:* (0171) 873 1000 *Fax:* (0171) 873 1010 *DX:* 2315 Victoria *Ptnrs:* 12 *Asst solrs:* 10 *Other fee-earners:* 10

WILLMETT & CO 27 Sheet St, Windsor, SL4 1BX *Tel:* (01753) 861381 *Fax:* (01753) 842172 *DX:* 3807 Windsor *Ptnrs:* 10 *Asst solrs:* 9 *Other fee-earners:* 6

WILLOUGHBY & PARTNERS

THE ISIS BUILDING, THAMES QUAY, 193 MARSH WALL, DOCKLANDS, LONDON, E14 9SG
Tel: (0171) 345 8888 **Fax:** (0171) 345 4555 **DX:** 42677 ISLE OF DOGS **Email:** ISIS@IPRIGHTS.COM **Internet:** WWW.IPRIGHTS.COM

PEMBROKE HOUSE, PEMBROKE STREET, OXFORD, OX1 1BL
Tel: (01865) 791 990 **Fax:** (01865) 791 772 **DX:** 82256 OXFORD

The Firm: Willoughby & Partners under its former name of Rouse & Co was founded in 1990 by Peter Rouse and was voted IP/IT firm of the year at the Legal Business Awards 1997. In December 1997, members of the non contentious intellectual property team of Dallas Brett joined the firm, together with their clients and ongoing matters. Willoughby & Partners took over Dallas Brett's offices in Oxford. Willoughby & Partners is exclusively concerned with the protection, exploitation and enforcement of intellectual property rights.

Principal Areas of Work: Advice on all aspects of the protection, exploitation and enforcement of intellectual property rights, namely trade marks, copyrights, unregistered and registered design rights, patents and all related rights.

Nature of Clientele: National and multi-national companies.

Fees: Fixed fee rate of £180 per hour (excluding VAT in a variety of industry areas and disbursements) regardless of seniority. No marking up of bills for urgency, complexity etc.

Managing partner:	Peter Rouse
Senior partner:	Tony Willoughby
Number of partners:	6
Assistant solicitors:	12
Other fee-earners:	16

WORKLOADS	
Intellectual property protection, enforcement and exploitation	100%

CONTACTS	
Intellectual property	Tony Willoughby
	Shireen Peermohamed (London)
	Anna Booy, Ben Goodger (Oxford)

WILMER, CUTLER & PICKERING

4 CARLTON GARDENS, LONDON, SW1Y 5AA
Tel: (0171) 872 1000 **Fax:** (0171) 839 3537 **Email:** LAW@WILMER.COM

The Firm: Wilmer, Cutler & Pickering is an international law firm with offices in London, Brussels, Berlin, Washington D.C., New York and Baltimore. Founded in 1962, WCP has over 200 lawyers engaged in a broadly diversified practice.

Principal Areas of Work:

International Arbitration & Litigation: (*Contact:* Gary Born). One of the world's leading international dispute resolution practices, with particular strength in international commercial arbitration. Areas of expertise include: international arbitration, under all leading institutional rules; international civil litigation, particularly in English and U.S. courts; alternative dispute resolution, including conciliation, mediation, mini-trials and negotiations; handling complex matters requiring substantive expertise in various technical fields, including construction, energy, telecommunications, ratemaking, environmental, accounting and similar matters.

Company & Commercial: (*Contact:* Andrew Parnell, Michael Holter). International commercial and corporate transactions practice, including: mergers and acquisitions; joint venture and partnership arrangements and international corporate alliances; equity and debt financing (including commercial loan transactions); subsidiary, franchise and distribution arrangements; technology and licensing matters.

Telecommunications: (*Contact:* Dieter G. Lange, Michael Holter).WCP acts on a wide range of issues, including: interconnection agreements; licences and other approvals required to implement pan-European telecommunications projects; enforcement proceedings to provide market access for new entrants; regulatory environment of individual European countries, EU, and U.S.; negotiation of national and cross-border corporate transactions and alliance; related trade, investment, and global information infrastructure issues.

Aviation: (*Contact:* Dieter G. Lange, John Kallaugher). One of WCP's main practice areas. The aviation team comprises more than 30 lawyers and experts on economic, transport and infrastructure issues. Clients include airlines, airports, governments and international agencies in the aviation sector.

Other Offices:

Brussels – Tel: +32, (2) 285 4900 (Contact: Marc Hansen)

Berlin – Tel: +49 (30) 2022 6400 (Contact: Natalie LÅbben)

Washington D.C. – Tel: +1 (202) 663 6363 (Contact: Michael Helfer)

New York – Tel: +1 (212) 230 8800 (Contact: Tom White)

Baltimore – Tel: +1 (410) 986 2800 (Contact: George Stamas)

Foreign Languages: French, German

Managing partner:	Andrew Parnell
Number of partners:	4
Assistant solicitors:	5
Other fee-earners:	2

WORKLOADS	
Company & Commercial	30%
Telecommunication	30%
International Arbitration & Litigation	25%
Aviation	15%

CONTACTS	
Aviation	Dieter G.Lange, John Kallaugher
Company & Commercial	Andrew Parnell, Michael Holter
Int. Arbitr. & Litigation	Gary Born
Telecommunication	Dieter G. Lange, Michael Holter

WILSON BROWNE PO Box No. 8, Meadow Road, Kettering, NN16 8TN *Tel:* (01536) 410041 *Fax:* (01536) 410444 *DX:* 12802 *Ptnrs:* 15 *Asst solrs:* 3 *Other fee-earners:* 72

WILSON CHALMERS & HENDRY 33A Gordon Street, Glasgow, G1 3PH *Tel:* (0141) 248 7761 *Fax:* (0141) 248 3447 *DX:* 104 Glasgow *Ptnrs:* 6 *Asst solrs:* 6 *Other fee-earners:* 2

WILSON & CO 697 High Road, London, N17 8AD **Tel:** (0181) 808 7535 **Fax:** (0181) 880 3393 **DX:** 52200 Tottenham 2 **Ptnrs:** 2 **Asst solrs:** 12 **Other fee-earners:** 8 **Contact:** Michael Hanley *Trainee Solicitors: 4. Specialist Immigration and Criminal practice.*

WORKLOADS			
Criminal	40%	Immigration	40%
Family	10%	Mental Health	5%
Personal Injury	5%		

WILSON, ELSER, MOSKOWITZ, EDELMAN & DICKER

141 FENCHURCH STREET, LONDON, EC3M 6BL
Tel: (0171) 623 6723 **Fax:** (0171) 626 9774 **DX:** 858 CITY

The Firm: The firm is one of the largest in the United States and has been serving clients for more than a quarter of a century. It has grown considerably during this period and now has offices in twelve major cities in the US, as well as in London and Tokyo. Initially the practice was insurance-related, and the firm maintains a pre-eminent position with regard to all aspects of insurance law and the insurance industry. However it has broadened its services and expertise to meet the needs of clients in the following areas: corporate organisation, negotiation, rendering business advice for both domestic and international clients on acquisitions, mergers, regulatory matters, financing, real estate and leasing transactions, contract negotiations and drafting, employment law and tax advice. The firm maintains close relationships with insurance specialist law firms in Europe.

The London Office: The London office of Wilson, Elser, Moskowitz, Edelman & Dicker is a multinational partnership associated with the US firm. The office concentrates on insurance and reinsurance work including product liability, insurance broker errors and omissions and international arbitration. Mr Cherry is both a US lawyer and a solicitor. Mr. Cherry is also a Fellow of the Chartered Institute of Arbitrators. The London office conducts litigation in English courts.

Languages Spoken: German and French (London office).

Other Offices: New York, Baltimore, Chicago, Dallas, Houston, Los Angeles, Miami, Newark, Paris, Philadelphia, San Diego, San Francisco, Washington DC, White Plains Tokyo:

Number of partners:	1
Assistant solicitors:	2

WORKLOADS	
US defence litigation	50%
Arbitration	10%
Creditors' rights	10%
D & O	10%
E & O brokers (US and UK)	10%
Insurance coverage disputes	10%

WILSON NESBITT 113 Victoria Street, Belfast, BT1 4PD *Tel:* (01232) 323864 *Fax:* (01232) 333707 *Ptnrs:* 7 *Asst solrs:* 11 *Other fee-earners:* 13

WILSONS SOLICITORS Steynings House, Fisherton St, Salisbury, SP2 7RJ *Tel:* (01722) 412412 *Fax:* (01722) 411500 *DX:* 58003 *Ptnrs:* 14 *Asst solrs:* 12 *Other fee-earners:* 24

WINCKWORTH & PEMBERTON (INCORPORATING SHERWOOD & CO)

35 GREAT PETER STREET, WESTMINSTER, LONDON, SW1P 3LR
Tel: (0171) 593 5000 **Fax:** (0171) 593 5099 **DX:** 2312 VICTORIA

The Firm: Winckworth & Pemberton is a well established Westminster firm of solicitors which incorporates the leading parliamentary agents, Sherwood & Co. The firm offers a wide range of high-quality services to private and public sector clients and has an established ecclesiastical, housing, police and private client practice. It also acts for many institutional clients with a growing educational and charitable clientele and has a thriving commercial practice.

Principal Areas of Work: The firm is structured by client sector rather than legal specialisation.

Parliamentary: (*Contact Partner:* Alison Gorlov). This department specialises in the promotion of and opposition to Private Bills in Parliament and similar legislation (Scottish Provisional Orders and Orders under the Harbours Act 1964 and the Transport and Works Act 1992) as well as charters and bye laws, and advises on all forms of primary and secondary legislation and parliamentary procedures.

Housing and Local Government: (*Contact Partner:* Andrew Murray). Winckworth & Pemberton is one of the leaders in this field of work, acting for a large number of housing associations and local authorities.

Ecclesiastical and Education: (*Contact Partner:* Paul Morris). This department provides registries for several of the Church of England's dioceses and handles church property and other work for a number of denominations. The senior ecclesiastical partner is the legal adviser to the Archbishop of Canterbury. The department also acts for schools, higher education colleges and educational charities.

Commercial Property: (*Contact Partner:* Robert Botkai). This department does all kinds of commercial property work and town & country planning, notably for public utilities, institutions and clients in the licensed trade.

Commercial and Government Services – Litigation: (*Contact Partner:* Peter Williams). A wide variety of work is handled, including injunction actions, police litigation, personal injury claims, landlord & tenant disputes and matrimonial matters. Employment law including unfair dismissal and discrimination is also practised here.

Commercial and Government Services – Tax and Commercial: (*Contact Partner:* Nicholas Owston/ George Bull). The department handles work in the public and private sectors covering contentious and non-contentious commercial and construction law and includes specialist tax services, real and intellectual property and I.T. This department also includes the firm's considerable expertise on police law and procedure and consititutional issues within and between forces.

Private Client: (*Contact Partner:* Hugh MacDougald). The firm acts for a number of landed estate owners and substantial trusts, and handles a significant amount of estate planning and probate work.

Recruitment and Training: Qualified staff should apply in the first instance to the Partnership Secretary, Mr. T.F. Vesey. The firm recruits three trainee solicitors each year – a 2:2 law or 2:1 non-law degree is usually required and applications should be made by handwritten letter (and CV) to Mr R.H.A. MacDougald.

Other Offices: Winckworth & Pemberton also has offices in Chelmsford and Oxford dealing with similar types of work.

Senior & Managing Partner:	Nick Owston
Finance Partner:	Andrew Murray
Number of Partners:	17
Assistant Solicitors:	19
Other Fee-earners:	30

WORKLOADS	
Parliamentary	20%
Housing and local government	19%
Commercial and government services	16%
Ecclesiastical, education and charities	16%
Private client	15%
Litigation	10%
Licensed property	4%

CONTACTS	
Commercial/government service	George Bull
Ecclesiastical	Paul Morris
Education	Michael Thatcher
Housing & local government	Andrew Murray
Litigation	Peter Williams
Parliamentary	Alison Gorlov
Private Client	Hugh MacDougald

WINSTANLEY-BURGESS 378 City Rd, London, EC1V 2QA *Tel:* (0171) 278 7911 *Fax:* (0171) 833 2135 *DX:* 58253 Islington *Ptnrs:* 5 *Asst solrs:* 6 *Other fee-earners:* 5

WINWARD FEARON

35 BOW ST, LONDON, WC2E 7AU
Tel: (0171) 420 2800 **Fax:** (0171) 420 2801 **DX:** 37959 KINGSWAY

This central London firm is one of the UK's top construction law practices. It has also established a significant reputation in infrastructure project work.

The Firm: Winward Fearon was founded in 1986. As a matter of policy it concentrates its development around an expanding number of niche areas rather than professing to expertise across the board. Those niche areas are carefully chosen to facilitate the creation of cross-departmental teams which specialise in industry sectors, rather than technical legal disciplines. The firm has achieved continued expansion throughout the recession by seeking in all cases to provide a top-quality and cost-effective service. It has an established and enviable client base, including large PLC's, owner-managed businesses, and developers. The firm's international links have been strengthened by its membership of Eurolegal, which is a European Economic Interest Group of law firms in several EU jurisdictions.

Types of work undertaken:

Construction: Construction law forms the bulk of the firm's practice and is carried out for national and international clients in building, civil engineering, and the professions. Typical issues may concern defective building, formation of contracts, liquidated damages, extension of time, and critical-path analysis, as well as payment. In addition, the department deals with bonds and insurance related matters, certificates, statutory obligations, variations in construction work, indemnities, and warranties, together with product liability. The work of the department is both contentious and non-contentious.

Commercial Litigation: Winward Fearon's commercial litigation team handles a wide variety of commercial claims, including employment disputes for UK and international clients. Particular expertise is provided in property and landlord and tenant litigation, including dilapidation claims, lease renewals, rent review problems, easement and right of way actions, service charge disputes, and franchises. The team often works closely with the firm's property team.

PFI and Corporate Finance: The infrastructure project, PFI and corporate finance team has handled a number of high profile transactions in the past five years. Adrian Luto has established a reputation in infrastructure projects, particularly in the independent power plant section both in the UK and overseas, while Edward Gore focuses on the purchase and sale of private companies and businesses, management buy-outs, other venture capital transactions, joint ventures and partnership agreements.

Property: The property team, headed by Guy Fearon, one of the firm's four founding partners, focuses on commercial property and residential development. Work includes the acquisition and sale of development sites, industrial estates, offices, and other commercial and investment property. The department advises on redevelopment projects, auction contracts, joint ventures, and partnership developments, including associated mortgages, taxation, property finance, and landlord and tenant work. The team also provides a service in high quality residential property.

Senior partner:	David L. Cornes
Number of ptnrs:	10
Number of fee-earners:	22
Total staff:	38

WORKLOADS	
Construction	66%
Infrastructure/PFI/corporate finance	20%
General/commercial litigation	7%
Property	7%

CONTACTS	
Construction	Richard Winward
Corporate finance	Edward Gore
General/commercial litigation	Clive Levontine
Infrastructure projects/PFI	Adrian Luto
Property	Guy Fearon

WISEMAN SOLICITORS 21 Algiers Road, Ladywell, London, SE13 7JD *Tel:* (0181) 244 5463 *Fax:* (0181) 244 5463 *Ptnrs:* 1

WITHAM WELD

70 ST GEORGE'S SQUARE, LONDON, SW1V 3RD
Tel: (0171) 821 8211 **Fax:** (0171) 630 6484 **DX:** 86164 VICTORIA 2

The Firm: Established for over 200 years, Witham Weld has a long-standing reputation in its work for every kind of client, including religious and civil institutions, charities and trusts, commercial and private clients. Today, the aim remains the same, to provide the highest quality legal services, founded on experience and expertise and supported by innovation and the use of modern working methods.

Principal Areas of Work: The firm provides advice and assistance in a wide range of areas including charity law, property, revenue and tax planning, wills and probates, company/commercial, contracts, education, employment, computer, copyright, and all forms of litigation.

Managing partner:	Nicolas Bellord
Number of partners:	6
Assistant solicitors:	4
Other fee-earners:	3

WITHERS

12 GOUGH SQUARE, LONDON, EC4A 3DE
Tel: (0171) 936 1000 **Fax:** (0171) 936 2589 **DX:** 160 **Email:** MAILTO@WITHERS.CO.UK **Internet:** WWW.WITHERS.CO.UK

The Firm: Withers is a City firm with a thriving practice serving the needs of both corporate and individual clients. The firm's practice is a broad one, embracing private client work, charities, agricultural, commercial and residential property, family law, employment, intellectual property, company and commercial law, corporate finance, banking, litigation, insolvency, commercial fraud, professional negligence and professional disciplinary work. Half of the firm's work is for corporate clients and institutions, the balance is for individuals and families. The firm has a fully staffed office in Paris, a representative office in Milan and a global network of connections with overseas lawyers.

Principal Areas of Work:

Agricultural property and estates: (*Contact:* Andrew Lane). A comprehensive service to landowners and farmers including: the acquisition, management and disposal of estates and farming businesses; agricultural land occupation; tenancies; farm partnerships and share farm agreements; property tax; development and alternative land use; planning; mineral exploitation; sporting and leisure uses; forestry; European Union legislation including quotas and set-aside; environmental law.

Banking: (*Contact:* David Dannreuther). Advice to banks and borrowers on all aspects of wholesale and retail banking, including: syndicated and conduit loans; structured finance; buyer and supplier credits; ECGD and SACE supported credits; forfeiting and trade finance; bills of exchange and letters of credit; swaps and other derivatives; securitisation and credit-enhanced transactions; capital adequacy and related regulatory issues; taxation issues relating to lending and borrowing.

Charities: (*Contact:* Alison Paines). Advice to numerous public and private charities, including companies, trusts, unincorporated associations, royal charter corporations and other not-for-profit organisations, on matters such as: formation and variation of charities; methods of charitable giving; tax efficient structures for donors and charities; appeals and fund-raising; negotiations with the charity commissioners; contracting with local authorities and the National Health Service; trustees' duties; trading arrangements; exempt charities; asset transfers between charities; contested probates and disputes between beneficiaries; cross-border giving and international charity law.

Commercial Litigation: (*Contact:* Margaret Robertson). Advice on commercial disputes of all kinds, in areas such as: commercial contracts; fraud; professional negligence; intellectual property; trade libel; emergency remedies; Companies Act remedies; banking; insolvency and asset tracing; tribunal cases; judicial review; property litigation; competition law; professional and sporting disciplinary matters.

Commercial Property: (*Contact:* Claudia D'Ambrosio). Advice to buyers and sellers, lenders and borrowers, landlords, tenants and developers on matters such as: acquisition and disposal of freehold and leasehold properties: landlord and tenant issues; property tax; collateral warranties; duty of care letters; property litigation; representation of receivers, administrators and liquidators; secured lending; planning applications, agreements and appeals; construction contracts; property aspects of corporate transactions; environmental law.

Company and Commercial: (*Contact:* Philip Durrance). Comprehensive advice for business clients, including listed and private companies, partnerships, sole traders and entrepreneurs, on matters such as: company and commercial law; sale and purchase of businesses; assets and shares; licensing; franchising and agency agreements; company secretarial services; compliance; corporate re-organisations; terms and conditions of business; shareholder agreements and joint ventures.

Corporate Finance: (*Contact:* David Gebbie). Advice on all aspects of corporate finance including: management buy-outs and buy-ins; takeovers; joint ventures; capital raising exercises; the Alternative Investment Market; Stock Exchange and Takeover Code requirements; circulars to shareholders; offer letters and agreement of initial terms; share purchase agreements; warranties and indemnities; tax implications; pension arrangements.

Employment: (*Contact:* Margaret Robertson). Advice to both employers and employees on the full range of employment issues, including: employee handbooks; service agreements; share option schemes; employee incentives; boardroom disputes; severance agreements and taxation; injunctions to restrain breach of confidence and competition; sex and race discrimination; unfair, wrongful and constructive dismissal; industrial relations.

Family Law: (*Contact:* Diana Parker). Advice on all aspects of family law, including: separation and divorce; acting as a mediator; pre-marital agreements; jurisdiction issues and forum shopping; prevention and resolution of child abduction problems; arrangements for children's residence and education; arrangements for contact with children; enforcement of foreign court orders; separation agreements; financial settlements including asset tracing; tax mitigation.

Continues overleaf

UK	
Number of partners:	43
Assistant solicitors:	48
Other fee-earners:	34
International	
Number of partners:	1
Assistant solicitors:	1

WORKLOADS	
Private Client and Charities	37%
Litigation	18%
Corporate, Company and Commercial	15%
Family	15%
Property (agricultural, commercial and residential)	
	15%

CONTACTS	
Agricultural property	Andrew Lane
Banking	David Dannreuther
Charities	Alison Paines
Commercial litigation	Margaret Robertson
Commercial property	Claudia D'Ambrosio
Company and commercial	Philip Durrance
Corporate finance	David Gebbie
Employment	Margaret Robertson
Family law	Diana Parker
France	Jonathan Eastwood
Insolvency	Jeremy Scott
Intellectual property	Stephen Digby
Italy	Anthony Indaimo
Private client	Charles Pike
Residential property	Henry Stuart
Spain	Michael Soul
Trust and probate litigation	Dawn Goodman

Insolvency: (*Contact:* Jeremy Scott). Specialist advice to major insolvency practitioners, banks and secured lenders, creditors and company directors, covering all aspects of insolvency including: liquidations and receiverships; administrations and voluntary arrangements; tracing, realisation and disposal of assets; reservation of title.

Intellectual Property: (*Contact:* Stephen Digby). Specialist advice on all aspects of the creation, ownership, protection and use of intellectual property assets, rights and resources, including: identification and evaluation of intellectual property; registration and renewal of rights; passing off and infringement actions; acquisition and assignment of agreements; agreements for use, distribution and exploitation of rights; confidentiality undertakings; licensing, merchandising and sponsorship arrangements; European law directives; international production and distribution of film and television; information technology including software licensing.

Private Client: (*Contact:* Charles Pike). A specialist and comprehensive service that focuses on the preservation and enhancement of clients' assets by advising in areas such as: estate, tax and financial planning; succession planning for individuals, landed estates and owner-managed companies; United Kingdom and international tax planning for residents and non-residents; trust formation and re-organisation in the United Kingdom and overseas; executor and trustee services including independent trusteeship for pension schemes; pension trust litigation including offshore trust disputes; international and cross-border succession issues; preparation of wills; advice to executors and beneficiaries on probate and succession law; variation of estates; Court of Protection work; heritage property including maintenance funds.

Residential Property: (*Contact:* Henry Stuart). A fast and efficient service for both United Kingdom and overseas clients in the following areas: the purchase and sale of freeholds and leaseholds; residential developments; tax efficient ownership; planning and tax advice for overseas buyers of property in England and Wales; country houses; secured lending; property transfers caused by death or family breakdown; leasehold reform; long leases; Central London leaseholds; regaining possession; managing and supervising residential investments; short term letting.

Trust and Probate Litigation: (*Contact:* Dawn Goodman). Specialist advice to trustees, executors, beneficiaries and financial institutions on all aspects of litigation affecting trusts and estates, including: applications under the Inheritance (Provision for Family and Dependants) Act 1975; construction, variation and rectification of trusts and wills; appointment and removal of trustees and executors; misapplication of assets by trustees; conflict between beneficiaries following a death; conflicting claims of co-habitees; conflict of laws involving assets in different jurisdictions.

Foreign Connections: The firm has a Paris office with a resident partner who is dually qualified as an English solicitor and French *avocat* (*Contact:* Jonathan Eastwood). The firm also has a representative office in Milan and four partners in London specialising in Italian work (*Contact:* Anthony Indaimo). Spanish work is handled in London by a partner (*Contact:* Michael Soul) who is dually qualified as an English solicitor and Spanish *abogado*, supported by a network of associate lawyers throughout Spain. The firm has strong connections with North America, the Middle East, South East Asia, and Australia.

Languages Spoken: French, Italian, German and Spanish.

WITHY KING

5 & 6 NORTHUMBERLAND BUILDINGS, QUEEN SQUARE, BATH, BA1 2JE
Tel: (01225) 425731 **Fax:** (01225) 315562 **DX:** 8014 BATH **Email:** WITHYKING.SOLICITORS@UKONLINE.CO.UK

The Firm: Withy King is one of the larger firms in the West Country and, while progressive, can trace its roots back to its foundation in 1883. It has grown from a general law practise to one which offers not only a full complement of legal services, but also particular specialisms in company, commercial property and litigation, medical negligence, and personal injury work. It is an expanding firm primarily serving clients in Bath, Somerset and West Wilts, but increasingly corporate and commercial clients elsewhere. As part of Withy King's expansion into West Wiltshire, the firm recently opened a new office in Trowbridge. Both Withy King's offices include the unusual added benefit of video conferencing facilities.

Principal Areas of Work: General Description: *Work includes:* Company sales, takeovers, reorganisations, partnerships, joint ventures, start ups, Corporate and Business finance, Employment, Intellectual property, Commercial Conveyancing, Landlord and Tenant, planning, general Civil Litigation and computerised Debt Collection, Medical negligence, Personal injury, Criminal, Family/Matrimonial, Wills, Probate, Trusts, Residential conveyancing, Licensing, Financial services and Personal tax.

Foreign Languages: French, Italian and German.

Recruitment and Training: *Contact:* Martin Powell

Managing partner:	Mike Swift
Number of partners:	11
Assistant solicitors:	9
Other fee-earners:	28

WORKLOADS	
Commercial Litigation	18%
Personal Injury/Medical Negligence	18%
Company/Commercial	17%
Financial Services	13%
Domestic Conveyancing	12%
Matrimonial	12%
Probate	10%

CONTACTS	
Contact	Mike Swift

WOLFERSTANS

DEPTFORD CHAMBERS, 60-64 NORTH HILL, PLYMOUTH, PL4 8EP
Tel: (01752) 663295 **Fax:** (01752) 672021 **DX:** 8206

The Firm: Wolferstans is a progressive and substantial regional practice with computer linked offices in Plymouth (3), Bristol and Taunton. Founded in 1812, it is a founder member of LawGroup UK with a commitment to excellence whilst providing a comprehensive personal service. Senior Partner David Gabbitass, a Higher Courts Advocate, is a member of the CICB, CICAP, an arbitrator and a member of the Discipline Committee fo the ECB. He, Jeremy Bennett, Paul Woods and Nick Roper are Chairmen of various tribunals.

Principal Areas of Work:

Company/Commercial: *Including:* company formations, acquisitions and sales, funding arrangements, management buy-outs, employment matters, licensing, commercial conveyancing and a wide range of commercial litigation. Julia Allsop is a Licensed Insolvency Practitioner. (*Contact Partner:* Nick Roper. *Partners:* 8).

Personal Injury: Led by Roy Griggs, an assessor for the PI Panel, this division of the practice operates from all major offices and acts for many major insurers as well as having a substantial plaintiff department managed by Chris Kallis. The resident partner at the Bristol office is Andrew Gibson with Mike Cummings and Simon Champion being the resident partners at Taunton. The medical specialist unit is headed by Simon Parford, an assessor and member of the Panel and a referral panel member for AVMA. The firm is involved in a number of group actions. (*Contact Partner:* Roy Griggs. *Partners:* 16).

Crime: David Teague is well known for his Courts Martial work. In addition to defence criminal work, the practice also acts for government agencies in prosecutions and provides advocates for inquests, inquiries, disciplinary hearings and tribunals. (*Contact Partner:* David Teague. *Partners:* 2).

Sport: Clients include Somerset County Cricket Club, Plymouth Argyle Football Club, Plymouth Albion Rugby Football Club and Plymouth Basketball Club. (*Contact Partner:* David Gabbitass. *Partners:* 3).

Matrimonial and Family: *Work includes:* separation and divorce, custody and access, adoption, child welfare, financial settlements and maintenance agreements. 3 partners are members of the Childrens'Panel. (*Contact Partner:* Philip Thorneycroft (Matrimonial), Jeremy Bennett (Children). *Partners:* 4).

Private Client: *Work includes:* wills, probate and trusts and residential conveyancing. (*Contact Partner:* John Chapman. *Partners:* 2).

Other Areas of Work: The firm regularly appears on behalf of accused persons at courts martial and has extensive experience in inquests and inquiries.

Languages spoken: French, Spanish, German, Greek.

Other Offices: Plymouth (3), Bristol, Taunton.

Managing partner:	David J.L. Gabbitass
Number of partners:	26
Assistant solicitors:	16
Other fee-earners:	18

WORKLOADS	
Personal injury	35%
Commercial	20%
Matrimonial and children	20%
Insurance	10%
Litigation	10%
Private	5%

CONTACTS	
Children	Jeremy Bennett
Commercial	Nick Roper
Crime	David Teague
Insurance	Roy Griggs
Litigation	Bill Duncan
Matrimonial	Phil Thorneycroft
Medical negligence	Simon Parford
Personal injury	Chris Kallis
Private	John Chapman
Probate	Gill Hollinshead
Sport	David Gabbitass

WOLLASTONS

BRIERLY PLACE, NEW LONDON ROAD, CHELMSFORD, CM2 0AP
Tel: (01245) 211211 **Fax:** (01245) 354764 **DX:** 89703 CHELMSFORD 2

The Firm: An effective team of experienced commercial lawyers offering a wide range of specialist services. Wollastons provides high levels of expertise and service to business clients based mainly in Essex, London and surrounding counties as well as foreign companies and their UK subsidiaries. It also advises private individuals and families from Essex and further afield, including some who are resident abroad. The firm is located in Chelmsford, only 35 minutes by train from central London, with easy access to the motorway network and Stansted airport. It has generous car parking for visitors. The firm is exceptionally well resourced and well organised with first rate computer and communication facilities.

Principal Areas of Work:

Company and commercial: Company sales and acquisitions (especially management buy-outs and buy-ins); insolvency and reconstructions; corporate finance; European law; intellectual property; commercial agreements; business immigration. Considerable international experience.

Employment: Employment contracts; unfair and wrongful dismissal; redundancy; race and sex discrimination; business transfers; frequent advocacy in the Industrial Tribunal.

Property: Commercial development, investment and agricultural property; securitisation for major lenders; landlord and tenant matters.

Environment and Planning: Specialist advice on all aspects of environmental law, both contentious and non contentious and on Planning Appeals; Agreements and Enforcement.

Litigation: Commercial disputes; professional negligence claims; debt recovery; insolvency; property and inheritance disputes; Alternative Dispute Resolution; personal injury; matrimonial cases.

Private Client: Wills; trusts; estate planning; probate.

Agriculture: The firm is a panel member of the NFU Legal Assistance Scheme.

Foreign Connections: Wollastons is an active member of IAG International, an association of independent professional firms represented throughout Europe and beyond.

Recruitment and Training: Wollastons welcomes enquiries from outgoing candidates with a strong academic record. The firm plans to take on one or two trainees annually.

Number of partners:	9
Assistant solicitors:	5
Consultants:	2
Other fee-earners:	11

WORKLOADS	
Company/commercial	33%
Litigation	28%
Property/planning	24%
Employment	8%
Private client	7%

CONTACTS	
Company/Commercial	Richard Wollaston
Computer law	Nigel Thompson
Employment	Kevin Palmer
Environment	Andrew Bryce
Intellectual property	Nicholas Burnett
Landlord & tenant	Nicholas Cook
Litigation	Bruce Bowler
Planning	Jim Little
Property development	Alan Wyatt
Trusts, tax etc	Kate Wollaston

WOLLASTONS
s o l i c i t o r s

WOOD & AWDRY

3 ST MARY STREET, CHIPPENHAM, SN15 3JL
Tel: (01249) 444422 **Fax:** (01249) 443666 **DX:** 34204 CHIPPENHAM

The Firm: Wood & Awdry is a long established Wiltshire practice focusing on private client work in its broadest sense: the individual, the family, the owner managed business coupled with some institutional work.

Principal Areas of Work:

Property: divided between residential/country houses/agricultural (*Contact:* Christopher Yates and Hugo Richardson),

Commercial (*Contact:* George Burges), **Succession and Inheritance** (including Trust, Court of Protection, Probate Administration, Wills and Inheritance Tax Planning) (*Contact:* Jackie Moor), **Litigation** including Personal Injury, general litigation, Employment and Crime (*Contact:* Andrew Herridge), **Family** (*Contact:* Lynda Ashworth), **Owner Managed Business** (including farms and estates) including company commercial partnership and employment together with a broad range of advice of ownership structures and related business issues (*Contact:* William Wyldbore-Smith).

Senior partner:	Christopher Yates
Partnership Secretary:	Peter Wilson
Number of partners:	6
Assistant solicitors:	7
Other fee-earners:	3

CONTACTS	
Civil Litigation	Andrew Herridge
Crime and Licensing	Andrew Watts-Jones
Family/Matrimonial	Lynda Ashworth
Owner Managed Businesses and Institutions	
	William Wyldbore-Smith
Property-commercial	George Burges
Property-residential	Christopher Yates
Succession and Inheritance	Jackie Moor

THE WOODBRIDGE PARTNERSHIP

WINDSOR HOUSE, 42 WINDSOR STREET, UXBRIDGE, UB8 1AB
Tel: (01895) 454800 **Fax:** (01895) 258649 **DX:** 45128 UXBRIDGE

The Firm: The WOODBRIDGE name has been established as Solicitors in Uxbridge for over 200 years.

Principal Areas of Work: The firm acts for Commercial, Private and Legally Aided clients. This work encompasses many categories of work including:-Commercial contracts; Computerised Debt collection; Civil, Property & Injury Litigation; Child & Family; Commercial & Residential Property; Criminal; County Court Agency.

Senior partner:	A.R. Woodbridge
Number of partners:	4
Assistant solicitors:	3
Other fee-earners:	5

WORKLOADS	
Civil litigation – personal injury/general	45%
Debt collection	25%
Family	15%
Non-contentious	15%

WOODFINE BATCHELDOR 16 St Cuthberts Street, Bedford, MK40 3JG **Tel:** (01234) 270 600 **Fax:** (01234) 210 128 **DX:** 5619 Bedford **Email:** lawful@kbnet.co.uk **Ptnrs:** 16 **Asst solrs:** 4 **Other fee-earners:** 12 **Contact:** Mr Nic Davies *A broad general practice. With three additional Local Branch offices.*

WOODFORD-ROBINSON

4 CASTILIAN TERRACE, NORTHAMPTON, NN1 1LE
Tel: (01604) 624926/231444 **Fax:** (01604) 231457 **DX:** 12424 NORTHAMPTON 1

The Firm: Established in 1908 by J.H. Woodford-Robinson, the practice is particularly noted for its work in criminal law, family and matrimonial, personal injury and mental health. Legal aid is offered and 24 hour emergency legal work is available if required.

Principal Areas of Work: Criminal court cases and attendance at police stations; civil litigation including industrial accidents; insurance claims and all personal injury including medical negligence; (one member of The Law Society Personal Injury Panel) family disputes including custody, adoption and child care cases (two solicitors are members of The Law Society Children Panel); house conveyancing and related property matters; wills, probate and trusts; independent financial advice; company and commercial; licensing law and tribunal appearances, particularly mental health review and Social Security.

Managing partner:	Neil Foster
Number of partners:	5
Other fee-earners:	2

WORKLOADS	
Crime	50%
Family	15%
Conveyancing	10%
Personal injury and medical negligence	10%
Probate	5%

WOODROFFES

36 EBURY STREET, LONDON, SW1W 0LU
Tel: (0171) 730 0001 **Fax:** (0171) 730 7900

The Firm: Founded by C.G. Woodroffe in 1877, it is a general practice with emphasis on individual attention. The office is situated in Belgravia and is close to Victoria Station.

Principal Areas of Work: Known for problem solving in the company/commercial field, charities, education and foreign work. Specialist department handling commercial conveyancing including development, hotels, nightclubs and restaurants and licensing for the same. Also transfer of works of art, residential conveyancing, probate, litigation, European Court, fraud recovery, insurance claims, insolvency and most legal matters.

Nature of Clientele: The firm acts for private clients in UK and abroad, public companies, banks and charities.

Senior partner:	P.M. Woodroffe
Number of partners:	2
Assistant solicitors:	4
Other fee-earners:	2

CONTACTS	
Banking and project finance	Sarah Taylor
Conveyancing	Roger Brown
Education and Art	Peter Woodroffe
Other matters	Peter Woodroffe

WOOLLCOMBE BEER WATTS

CHURCH HOUSE, QUEEN STREET, NEWTON ABBOT, TQ12 2QP
Tel: (01626) 202404 **Fax:** (01626) 202420 **DX:** 59100 NEWTON ABBOT

The Firm: Established in 1831, Woollcombe Beer Watts now has offices in six regional and local centres serving local businesses, private and legal aid clients.

Principal Areas of Work:

Medical Negligence and Personal Injury: (*Contact Partner:* D.S. Reed). *Work includes:* personal injury and accident compensation and specialist medical negligence work. Derek Reed is a member of the referral panel of the Association of Victims of Medical Accidents, the Law Society Medical Negligence Panel and the Law Society Personal Injury Panel.

Civil Litigation: (*Contact Partner:* F.C.Goddard). *Work includes:* consumer law, debt collection, contractual disputes and all aspects of County and High Court litigation.

Private Client: (*Contact Partner:* N.H.Rowlinson). *Work includes:* all aspects of residential conveyancing, wills, trusts & probate and tax advice.

Family: (*Contact Partner:* Catherine Strigner). *Work includes:* family and matrimonial law, residence/contact and care proceedings as well as co-habitee disputes. Two members of the department are on the Law Society Children Panel and others are members of the Solicitors Family Law Association.

Company Commercial: (*Contact Partner:* R.W. Barrett;). *Work includes:* business acquisitions, mergers and formations, trading terms and conditions, commercial contracts, planning and company & partnership matters. The firm also has a licensing and criminal law department and accepts agency instructions.

Other Offices: Torquay, Chagford, Bovey Tracey, Buckfastleigh and Exeter.

Number of partners:	21
Assistant solicitors:	14
Other fee-earners:	19

WORKLOADS	
Litigation	36%
Property	20%
Family	15%
Wills, Trust and Probate	14%
Company & Commercial	12%
Others	3%

CONTACTS	
Company and commercial	Robin Barrett
Family	Catherine Strigner
Litigation	Derek Reed
Property	Michael Setter
Wills/ trusts/ probate/ tax	Noel Rowlinson

WRAGGE & CO

55 COLMORE ROW, BIRMINGHAM, B3 2AS
Tel: (0121) 233 1000 **Fax:** (0121) 214 1099 **DX:** 13036 **Email:** POST@WRAGGE.COM

Wragge & Co is the largest single office law firm outside London. Its rapid growth and success are a result of a distinctive strategy to develop a national law firm from a single office. Wragge & Co's clients continue to appreciate the benefits of its consistent and integrated approach to client service, whilst its people enjoy working in a strong and cohesive culture.

Wragge & Co was voted Best Large Law Firm and Law Firm of the Year in the UK Legal Profession's Annual Awards (1997).

The Firm: As a full service law firm, Wragge & Co provides a comprehensive range of legal services to large companies, public authorities and financial institutions, in the UK and overseas, including over 165 listed companies. Over 20% of the firm's work is international. Quality and client care continue to be the firm's top priorities. It rigorously seeks feedback from clients on the quality of its service and develops its business in response to client demand. The firm is one of the few major firms to be accredited with the ISO 9001 standard.

Principal Areas of Work: Wragge & Co has focused on developing real strength in depth and expertise in seven core business areas (outlined below). In addition, its commitment to industry expertise and product specialisation have contributed to the firm enjoying a national reputation in areas such as pensions, IP, transport and logistics, utilities, project finance and PFI and EC/competition law.

Corporate: The corporate group advises on all aspects of a company's life from formation to flotation, through acquisitions, mergers, joint ventures and management buy-outs. The group has also built an excellent reputation for its high profile corporate finance deals – over 130 deals in 1997 with an aggregate value in excess of £2.1 billion. In 1997 the firm was voted, for the second successive year, top corporate law firm in a poll conducted by Finance Midlands.

Commercial: Through its commercial group the firm advises on intellectual property (from the largest IP group outside London), R&D agreements, competition, IT and computer law, franchising and EC law.

Dispute Resolution: Wragge & Co's dispute resolution group offers a commercial and objective assessment of clients' problems whilst maintaining a realistic approach to settlement negotiations. The firm has a number of accredited mediators.

Commercial Property: Property clients, including landlords and tenants, developers, retailers, contractors, funding institutions, investors and public authorities, are provided with a full range of specialist legal services by the rapidly growing commercial property group.

Managing partner:	**Quentin Poole**
Senior partner:	**John Crabtree**
Number of partners:	60
Assistant solicitors:	164
Other fee-earners:	97

CONTACTS	
Alternative Dispute Resolution	Paul Howard
Automotive	Bob Gilbert
Banking and Insolvency	Julian Pallett
Building Societies	Jonathan Denton
Commercial Litigation	Paul Howard
Commercial Property	Mark Dakeyne
Construction	Ashley Pigott
Corporate Finance	Richard Haywood
Debt Recovery	Ann Benzimra
Education	Philip Clissitt
Employee Benefit/Share Schemes	Peter Smith
Employment	Martin Chitty
Energy/Utilities	David Hamlett
Environmental	John Turner
EU and Competition	Guy Lougher
Executive Immigration	Nicola Mumford
Financial Services	Neil Upton/Richard Ellison
Inheritance and Estates	Louise Woodhead
Insurance	Susan Dearden
Intellectual Property	Gordon Harris/David Barron
IT/Computers	Bill Jones
Logistics	Gwyn Davies
NHS Trusts	Susan Dearden
Pensions	Vivien Cockerill
PFI	Stephen Kenny
Professional Indemnity	Mark Hick
Property Litigation	Suzanne Lloyd Holt
Public Sector	Peter Keith-Lucas
Tax	Kevin Poole
Town & Country Planning	Dan Hemming
Transport (Road/Rail)	Michael Whitehouse

Human Resources: The human resources group offers a comprehensive range of advice on employment issues (contentious and non-contentious), employee benefits, pensions schemes, personal tax, trusts and charities.

Finance and Projects: The finance and projects team includes specialists in its core areas of financial services, capital markets, insolvency, utilities, project finance and PFI, and rail and logistics.

Insurance: The insurance group provides advice on all aspects of insurance law from motor claims, general liability and product liability to professional indemnity and subrogated property claims as well as advice on policy interpretation and other non-contentious aspects.

WRIGHT HASSALL & CO

9 CLARENDON PLACE, LEAMINGTON SPA, CV32 5QP
Tel: (01926) 886688 **Fax:** (01926) 885588 **DX:** 11863 **Email:** WHASSALL@WHASSALL.DEMON.CO.UK

The Firm: Established in 1846 the firm is one of the leading Midland firms. It is organised departmentally and provides a comprehensive range of services to clients across the country.

Principal Areas of Work:

Commercial: Work includes the sale and purchase of companies and business assets, management buy-outs and joint ventures. It is also strong in intellectual property and employment law, as well as commercial contracts, partnerships and business formations.

Commercial property: The firm acts for developers and builders and work handled includes the sale and purchase of commercial property and leases, and building development work. It has a particular expertise in housing association law.

Litigation: The firm handles the whole range of litigation work, and specialises in insurance company based defendant litigation including professional indemnity, as well as matrimonial litigation.

Agricultural law: The firm has a national reputation for its expertise in dealing with all aspects of agricultural law.

Private Client: As well as conveyancing work includes advising on trusts and estates as well as investments.

Clients: The firm maintains a high level of personal contact with clients, which is partner led. It principally advises large and medium sized businesses as well as private clients. Clients include companies of all sizes, building societies, housing associations and insurance companies.

Managing partner:	Andrew Payne
Partnership Chariman:	Robin Ogg
Number of partners:	19
Assistant solicitors:	10
Other fee-earners:	16

WORKLOADS	
Litigation	43%
Commercial property	26%
Company and Commerical	13%
Private Client	13%
Agriculture	5%

CONTACTS	
Agriculture	Robin Ogg
Commercial Property	Nick Abell
Company and commercial	Peter Beddoes and Mark Lewis
Litigation	Richard Lane
Private Client	Charles McKenzie

WRIGHT, JOHNSTON & MACKENZIE 12 St Vincent Place, Glasgow, G1 2EQ *Tel:* (0141) 248 3434 *Fax:* (0141) 221 1226 *DX:* 129 Glasgow *Ptnrs:* 12 *Asst solrs:* 20 *Other fee-earners:* 10

WRIGHT SON & PEPPER

9 GRAY'S INN SQUARE, LONDON, WC1R 5JF
Tel: (0171) 242 5473 **Fax:** (0171) 831 7454 **DX:** 35

The Firm: The firm has been established in Gray's Inn Square since 1800. Its clients range from public companies and institutions through to small businesses and professional and private individuals each of whom is provided with sound practical advice quickly and efficiently on a personal basis. The firm is highly regarded for its work in advising professionals in difficulties and partnership matters.

Principal Areas of Work:

Company and Commercial: (*Contact:* Steve Alais). In addition to dealing with the normal range of commercial and company work, the firm has considerable experience in dealing with all forms of computer-related contracts and the setting up, funding and operation of private railways, and restraint of trade covenants.

Property: (*Contact:* Antony Wright). Although all aspects are covered the emphasis is on offices, shop and factory/warehouse leases and developments, planning and funding arrangements. In addition the firm has developed expertise in dealing with factory outlet centres. Antony Wright has considerable experience in acting as an expert witness in solicitors negligence in property transactions and alleged mortgage frauds.

Number of partners:	10
Assistant solicitors:	1
Other fee-earners:	4

WORKLOADS	
Solicitors' practice/partnership matters	21%
Company/commercial	16%
Family	16%
Litigation	16%
Property	16%
Trust and probate	15%

CONTACTS	
Company/commercial	S.M. Alais
Expert evidence (property)	A J Wright
Family	P L M Butner
Litigation	I Miller
Property	A J Wright
Sol. disciplinary proceedings	D T Morgan
Solicitors' practice/partnerships	N J Wright
Trust & probate	B Wates

Continues overleaf

Professional Practice and Partnership Matters: (*Contact:* Nicholas Wright or David Morgan). The firm, in addition to its general and professional partnership work, advises solicitors with regard to Solicitors Practice Rules and Solicitors Accounts Rules, solicitors and other professionals on partnership disputes, the break up of partnerships and those of them who have financial difficulties. It also represents solicitors and accountants before their Disciplinary Tribunals.

Family Law: (*Contact:* Paul Butner). All aspects of matrimonial, family, welfare and child care law are covered with special emphasis on ancillary relief in matrimonial proceedings.

Litigation: (*Contact:* Iain Miller or Derek Lavery). The firm handles general commercial and private litigation. It also provides a fully computerised debt recovery service. High Court agency work is also undertaken.

Private Client and Tax: (*Contact:* Brian Wates). *Work includes:* probates, wills, settlements, trust formation and administration, powers of attorney, Court of Protection, investment advice, personal tax and estate planning.

Other Areas of Work: The firm also handles intellectual property, building contract disputes, employment, landlord and tenant, transport law, European Union law and consumer law.

Foreign Connections: The firm has professional connections in Belgium and USA. French, German and Dutch are spoken.

WRIGLEYS

5 BUTTS COURT, LEEDS, LS1 5JS
Tel: (0113) 244 6100 **Fax:** (0113) 244 6101 **DX:** 12020 LEEDS 1

FOUNTAIN PRECINCT, LEOPOLD STREET, SHEFFIELD, S1 2GZ
Tel: (0114) 283 3306 **Fax:** (0114) 276 3176 **DX:** 12020 LEEDS 1

The Firm: Wrigleys was formed on 1 May 1996 by Matthew Wrigley and Ann Duchart following the demerger of the Dibb Lupton Broomhead (now Dibb Lupton Alsop) private client department. The firm was joined in August 1997 by the entire private client department of Hammond Suddards and now has 6 partners and a total staff of 32. Further expansion is likely in the firm's specialist areas.

Contact Partners:	Matthew Wrigley
	or Ann Duchart, Leeds;
	David Coldrick, Sheffield
Number of partners:	6
Assistant Solicitors:	9
Other fee-earners:	4

From its foundation in the mid 18th century until the early 1970's Dibb Lupton had been largely a private client firm and that tradition combined with the strength of the Hammond Suddards private client department has provided a firm basis for Wrigleys' new practice, which now operates independently of Dibb Lupton from offices in Leeds and Sheffield.

Principal Areas of Work: Wrigleys is primarily a traditional private client firm dealing in charities, capital taxes, trusts, landed estates, heritage and agricultural properties. The firm also undertakes pension work advising trustees particularly when advice independent of the employer is needed, an area in which both Tim Knight and Richard Archer are recognised specialists.

Nature of clientele: Wrigleys has inherited or acquired a number of substantial landed estates and wealthy business owning families as clients throughout the country, particularly in the North of England and also acts for a wide range of private, educational and religious charities in the North of England and elsewhere. It has a dominant position in Yorkshire in advising clients in relation to heritage properties and chattels, including some of the most important still remaining in private hands.

A.E. WYETH & CO

BRIDGE HOUSE, HIGH STREET, DARTFORD, DA1 1JR
Tel: (01322) 297000 **Fax:** (01322) 297001 **DX:** 31904 DARTFORD **Email:** IBM SCREENMAIL

8 STONE BUILDINGS, LINCOLN'S INN, LONDON, WC2A 3TA
Tel: (0171) 242 7588 **Fax:** (0171) 831 5674 **DX:** 147 CHANCERY LANE

The Firm: A.E.Wyeth & Co. have built an excellent reputation as an Insurance Litigation practice acting for Insurance Companies, Lloyds syndicates and brokers. The Firm provides specialist legal advice on a cost efficient basis. The Firm also undertakes contentious and non-contentious private client work. Legal Aid work accepted.

Principal Areas of Work:
Litigation: (*Contact:* Brian Williams). Personal Injury: Employers' liability, public liability, road traffic accidents; specialists in Health and Safety prosecutions, inquests, public health prosecutions, stress related illnesses, asbestosis and repetitive strain injury. There is a separate noise-induced hearing loss department. Commercial litigation; building and construction disputes, fire and flooding claims, product liability and professional indemnity. Local Authority litigation – personal injury and commercial.
Private client, contentious: (*Contact:* Tom Challis). Employment, family, matrimonial, debt collection and general litigation.
Private client, non-contentious: (*Contact:* Steven Ellis). Commercial and domestic conveyancing, Wills, estate planning and probate, company formation, charities.Agency work, both High Court and County Court undertaken. The office is ideally placed to deal with agency matters throughout the South East of England.

Senior partner:	Brian Williams
Number of partners:	10
Assistant solicitors:	14
Other fee-earners:	34

WORKLOADS	
Personal Injury	75%

CONTACTS	
Litigation	B. Williams
Private client: contentious	T. Challis
Private client:non-contentious	S. Ellis

WYNNE BAXTER GODFREE AND SELWOOD LEATHES HOOPER 28/29 Old Steine, Brighton, BN1 1GF *Tel:* (01273) 570 030 *Fax:* (01273) 570 756 *DX:* 2700 Brighton

YOUNG & LEE No. 6 The Wharf, Bridge Street, Birmingham, B11 2JS *Tel:* (0121) 633 3233 *Fax:* (0121) 632 5292 *DX:* 701255 Edgbaston 4 *Ptnrs:* 5 *Asst solrs:* 6 *Other fee-earners:* 3

YOUNG & PEARCE 58 Talbot Street, Nottingham, NG1 5GL *Tel:* (0115) 959 8888 *Fax:* (0115) 947 5572 *DX:* 10025 *Ptnrs:* 4 *Asst solrs:* 5 *Other fee-earners:* 3

T.C. YOUNG & SON 30 George Square, Glasgow, G2 1LH **Tel:** (0141) 221 5562 **Fax:** (0141) 221 5024 **DX:** GW 78. **Ptnrs:** 3 **Asst solrs:** 1 **Other fee-earners:** 2 **Contact:** Andrew Robertson *Specialises in acting for charities, trusts and housing associations. General private client, executry and employment work is also undertaken.*

WORKLOADS			
Housing associations	40%	General private client	30%
Charities	20%	Litigation	10%

ZAIWALLA & CO

33 CHANCERY LANE, LONDON, WC2A 1ZZ
Tel: (0171) 312 1000 **Fax:** (0171) 312 1100 **DX:** 0034 CH.LN.

The Firm: It is strong in international commercial litigation, shipping law, banking law, international arbitration, immigration, joint ventures and has a specialist Indian Law department. Commercial and domestic property conveyancing, probate and company/commercial matters are also handled. Associated firms are: Bombay and New York. International clientele, mainly from UK, South East Asia, Middle East and Greece. Languages spoken: Gujerati, Hindi and Marathi.

Senior partner:	Sarosh Zaiwalla
Number of partners:	6
Other fee-earners:	2

ZERMANSKY & PARTNERS

10 BUTTS COURT, LEEDS, LS1 5JS
Tel: (0113) 245 9766 **Fax:** (0113) 246 7465 **DX:** 12061

The Firm: The firm offers a comprehensive range of legal services and is committed to legal aid work having been awarded the Legal Aid Franchise in six areas. It is a member of Lawyers for Your Business, Solicitors' Family Law Association, Leeds Chambers of Commerce and Industry, Family Mediation and Association of Lawyers for Children.

Principal Areas of Work:

Private Client: (a) (*Fee-earners:* 7). *Work includes:* family and matrimonial law, child care, welfare, wills, probate, trusts (2 fee earners are members of the Law Society Children Panel). (b) (*Fee-earners:* 3). *Work includes:* criminal & child care.

Company and Commercial: (*Fee-earners:* 1). *Work includes:* all aspects of company/ commercial work (with particular emphasis on small to medium sized businesses and new businesses), employment matters, liquor and entertainment licensing, charities, leisure and sport.

Property: (*Fee-earners:* 3). *Work includes:* commercial conveyancing, landlord and tenant and residential conveyancing.

Litigation: (*Fee-earners:* 6). *Work includes:* commercial litigation, personal injury, medical negligence and other professional negligence, debt collection, consumer disputes, property litigation, landlord and tenant disputes, housing disrepair, immigration, injunctions.

Foreign Languages: Polish, Punjabi and Hindi.

Managing partner:	David Honeybone
Senior partner:	Russel Graham
Number of partners:	7
Assistant solicitors:	8
Other fee-earners:	4

CONTACTS	
Company & commercial	David Honeybone
Litigation	Richard Lindley
Private client, crime/care	Lynn McFadyen
Private client, matrimonial	Norman Taylor
Property	Russell Graham
Sports law	David Honeybone

IN-HOUSE LAWYERS AND COMPANY SECRETARIES

CHAMBERS & PARTNERS

IN-HOUSE LAWYERS AND COMPANY SECRETARIES

The following list represents in-house lawyers in FTSE 350 companies and major banks in the UK.

3i Smaller Quoted Companies
91 Waterloo Road, London SE1 8XP
Tel: (0171) 928 3131 **Fax:** (0171) 928 0058
David Dench, In-house Lawyer

Abbey National PLC
Abbey House, Baker Street, London NW1 6XL
Tel: (0171) 612 4000 **Fax:** (0171) 612 4010
No of lawyers in dept: 26
Gwyn Malkin, Head of Legal Services
Specialism: Handles commercial and corporate law matters and management of the legal function. Member of Legal Committee of British Bankers Association.
Career: Qualified 1975. Became Head of Legal Services at Abbey National in July 1992.
Other lawyers: Corporate (corporate and commercial/ commercial and offshore) : Philip Ramsell, Ian Wallbank, Geoffrey Pope, Alison Greene, Mike Hoye, Alan Squires, Desmond Pettit, Simon Goldburn, Mhairi Thomas. Consumer (banking, savings and lending/insurance/life) : William Johnson, John Hamilton, Carole Jones, Neil Craig, Pauline Pope, Moyra Archibald, David O'Sullivan, Jacqueline Neblett, Edward Gillibrand, Stuart Fantham, John Thurwell, Gwynedd Miller, Colin Browning, John Laing, Janine Pennel, Joanna Green.

ABN Amro Equities Holdings (UK) Limited
4 Broadgate, London EC2M 7LE
Tel: (0171) 374 1240 **Fax:** (0171) 374 7612
Email: jennystevinson@nl.abnamro.com
No of lawyers in dept: 5
Work outsourced: 25% – Litigation, property, IP, some company/commercial
Jenny Stevinson, Head of Legal/Company Secretary
Specialism: Manages Legal and Secretariat Department providing legal services to London-based equity businesses of ABN AMRO investment banking group. Specific areas include Company Law, transaction documentation for equity-related products, customer documentation, clearing and banking arrangements, supplies of goods and services, employment, property, intellectual property.
Career: King's College, London University LLB 1975. Called to the Bar, Gray's Inn, 1976. General common law, commercial, EEC, pupillages, 1976-78. Department of Trade and Industry, Solicitor's Department 1978-86: international and EEC trade, telecommunications, company and financial services law. Legal Adviser, Security Pacific Hoare Govett (Holdings) Limited 1987-1990. Group Legal Adviser and Company Secretary, Hoare Govett Limited from 1990.
Other lawyers: Helen Short, Janine Ball – product, customer, settlement documentation; Ian Spaxman, Steven Ellery – contacts for supply of goods and services, employment, IP, property.

AEA Technology PLC
Corporate Headquarters, Building 329, Harwell, Didcot OX11 0RA
Tel: (01235) 821111 **Fax:** (01235) 432149
Email: gareth.evans@aeat.co.uk
No of lawyers in dept: 1
Work outsourced: 40% – acquisitions, property, litigation
Gareth Evans, Legal Adviser and Deputy Company Secretary
Specialism: Company/Commercial, Litigation, Environmental, Employment, Competition, Acquisitions, Yellow Book Compliance, Corporate Governance.
Career: Barrister at Law, Gray's Inn, 1978. Solicitor, 1984. Contracts Officer, Post Office Data Processing Service, 1978-79. Legal Advisory/Company Secretarial positions, Vauxhall/General Motors Ltd, 1979-84. Commercial Solicitor, Central Electricity Generating Board, 1984-87. Company Secretary, UK Ninex Ltd 1987-95. Legal Adviser and Deputy Company Secretary, AEA Technology plc, 1995-present.
Personal: Married, 2 children, resides Oxon. Interests - skiing, cycling, camping, family life.

Aegis Group PLC
11a West Halkin Street, London SW1X 8JL
Tel: (0171) 470 5000 **Fax:** (0171) 470 5099
John Rowland, Company Secretary

Aggregate Industries PLC
Radcliffe House, Lode Lane, Solihull B91 2AA
Tel: (0121) 711 1717 **Fax:** (0121) 711 1505
No of lawyers in dept: 1
Work outsourced: 70% – Commercial, property, planning, litigation.
Richard Collins, Company Secretary, Solicitor
Specialism: Company/commercial, litigation, environmental, employment.
Career: St Albans School. Worcester College, Oxford. *McKenna & Co* (now *Cameron McKenna*) 1986 - 1994. Assistant Company Secretary/Solicitor, CAMAS plc 1995 - 1996. Company Secretary/Solicitor, Aggregate Industries plc.
Personal: Married with two children. Enjoys walking, reading, tennis.

Aggreko PLC
121 West Regents Street, Glasgow G2 2SD
Tel: (0141) 225 5900 **Fax:** (0141) 225 5949
Paul Allen, Company Secretary

Airtours Holidays Ltd
Wavell House, Holcombe Road, Helmshore, Lancs BB4 4NB
Tel: (01706) 240033 **Fax:** (01706) 229032
No of lawyers in dept: 2
Andrew Cooper, Company Secretary/Company Solicitor
Specialism: General legal advice to Airtours Holidays, the tour operating subsidiary of Airtours Plc, including litigation both in the UK and overseas, employment law advice and general contractual advice. Representation on travel trade bodies, including ABTA, Tour Operators Council, Code of Conduct Committee. Director of Federation of Tour Operators. Chairman of FTO Safety Committee.
Career: 1985-89: qualified, private practice, dealt with divorce and personal injury work. 1989-95: solicitor for Airtours Plc and subsequently Airtours Holidays Ltd. 1995: Company Secretary, Airtours Holidays Ltd.

Albright & Wilson plc
210-222 Hagley Road West, Oldbury B68 0NN
Tel: (0121) 429 4942 **Fax:** (0121) 420 5151
No of lawyers in dept: 2
Work outsourced: 20% – Litigation, property, overseas, major transactions, pensions.
Andrew Cree, Company Secretary
Specialism: Acquisitions and disposals, joint ventures, competition, trading matters and company secretarial. Also involved in litigation and environmental matters.
Career: Qualified 1977. Regional Solicitor, British Coal and Head of Commercial Group 1985-90. Partner, *Nabarro Nathanson* 1990-91. Deputy Group Legal Adviser, Bass plc 1991-92, then joined Albright & Wilson.
Other lawyers: Lee Callaghan.

Alliance UniChem PLC
UniChem House, Cox Lane, Chessington KT9 1SN
Tel: (0181) 391 2323 **Fax:** (0181) 974 1707
Adrian J. Goodenough, Company Secretary

Alliance & Leicester PLC
Customer Services Centre, Narborough, Leicester LE9 5XX
Tel: (01162) 004995 Fax: (01162) 004040
No of lawyers in dept: 18
Work outsourced: 20% – Treasury, tax, pensions, stock exchange, some contentious IP, employment and some IT.
Kathrine Hughes, Head of Legal
Julian Hepplewhite, Group Secretary and Chief Solicitor

Other lawyers: Jonathon Weeks – corporate, contracts, company/commercial; Debbie Brown, Mark Hepworth – employment; Felicity King – commercial; David Bowden, Lindsay Ellis – retail products, commercial; Martin Rice, David Beatty – property; John Nightingale – litigation.

Allied Domecq PLC
24 Portland Place, London W1N 4BB
Tel: (0171) 323 9000 **Fax:** (0171) 323 1742
David S. Mitchell, Company Secretary

Allied Irish Bank (GB)
Legal and Security Department, Bank Centre, Britain, Belmont Road, Uxbridge UB8 1SA
Tel: (01895) 272222 **Fax:** (01895) 239444
Tiana Peck, Head of Legal Services

American Express Bank Ltd.
60 Buckingham Palace Road, London SW1W 0RR
Tel: (0171) 824 6000 **Fax:** (0171) 730 5067
No of lawyers in dept: 4
Work outsourced: complicated transactions/litigation
Robert S.D. Sharp, Managing Counsel
Reports to: The General Counsel (New York).
Specialism: Manages the legal requirements of American Express Bank Ltd for Europe and the Middle East and Asia Pacific (Indian sub-continent region and the Far East). Principal responsibilities are providing strategic and tactical advice to senior management to assist in the fulfilment of business objectives in compliance with applicable laws and regulatory scenarios; securing appropriate legal support for transactions; and managing litigation and assistance with recoveries and "work-outs."
Career: Qualified 1972 while at *Freshfields* and solicitor in company/commercial department until 1977. Joined General Counsel's Office, American Express Bank Ltd 1977.
Other lawyers: Lawyers abroad: 95. Other lawyers in dept: J Kelloe, R Waxler, a secondee.

Amvescap PLC
11 Devonshire Square, London EC2M 4YR
Tel: (0171) 626 3434 **Fax:** (0171) 280 0642
Michael Perman, Company Secretary

Anglian Water PLC
Anglian House, Ambury Road, Huntingdon PE18 6NZ
Tel: (01480) 323000 **Fax:** (01480) 323115
John Bows, Company Solicitor

Anglo & Overseas Trust PLC
20 Finsbury Circus, London EC2M 1NB
Tel: (0171) 256 7500 **Fax:** (0171) 588 7700
K. Garvey, Head of Legal

Arab Bank Plc
PO Box 138, 15 Moorgate, London EC2R 6LP
Tel: (0171) 315 8500 **Fax:** (0171) 600 7620
Janet Bicheno, In-house Lawyer

Arcadia Group PLC
Colegrave House, 70 Berners Street, London W1P 3AE
Tel: (0171) 927 1812 **Fax:** (0171) 927 1848
Ian Jackman, Director of Legal Services and Company Secretary

Arjo Wiggins Appleton PLC
Gateway House, Basing View, Basingstoke RG21 2EE
Tel: (01256) 723000 **Fax:** (01256) 723723
No of lawyers in dept: 6
Robin P.D. Davies, Group Secretary and Solicitor
Specialism: Company secretarial, company commercial.
Career: Qualified as Solicitor in 1966. Joined Wiggins Teape Ltd in 1977. Appointed Company Secretary and Group Solicitor in Nov 1986. Appointed Company Secretary and Group

Solicitor of Wiggins Teape Appleton in June 1990 on demerger from BAT Industries. Position confirmed following merger with Arjomari in Dec 1990.
Other lawyers: A.N.Dungate – Head of Group Legal Services.

Arriva plc
Millfield House, Hylton Road, Sunderland SR4 7BA
Tel: (0191) 514 4122 **Fax:** (0191) 514 5148
Chris Applegarth, Company Solicitor

ASDA Group PLC
Asda House, Southbank, Great Wilson Street, Leeds LS11 5AD
Tel: (0113) 243 5435 **Fax:** (0113) 241 8666
No of lawyers in dept: 4
Work outsourced: 50% – Litigation, Property, Pensions, IP
Denise Jagger, Company Secretary, Corporate Counsel.
Specialism: Corporate finance, company, commercial, share schemes, pensions, public affairs.
Career: *Slaughter and May*, Solicitor 1982-1988. Scottish Heritable Trust plc – Company Solicitor 1988-1992. *Addleshaw Booth & Co* – Partner, Corporate Finance 1992-1993. ASDA Group plc – Company Secretary & Corporate Counsel 1993 – present.
Other lawyers: Nick Cooper – Commercial; Eleanor Doohan – Commercial; Gary McHale – Employment.

Ashtead Group PLC
Ashtead House, Business Park 8, Barnett Wood Lane, Leatherhead KT22 7DG
Tel: (01372) 362300 **Fax:** (01372) 376610
Internet: http://www.ashtead.group.com
No of lawyers in dept: 1
Work outsourced: 10% – Conveyancing Scotland & Eire, large company takeovers, general advice on specialist areas, litigation.
Paul Dowie Edmunds, Legal Services Manager
Specialism: Conveyancing, employment, property administration, contract negotiation. Co-ordination of all legal matters.
Career: 1970-1977 Judd School, Tonbridge, Kent. 1977-1980 St John's College, Cambridge. 1982-1986 *Ingledew Brown Bennison & Garrett*. 1984-1998 *The Reece Jones Partnership*.
Personal: Hobbies: cricket, golf, choral singing, cookery.

Associated British Foods plc
Legal Department, 3–5 Rickmansworth Road, Watford WD1 7HG
Tel: (01923) 252050 **Fax:** (01923) 223542
Paul Telford, Joint Head of Legal Department

Associated British Ports Hldgs PLC
150 Holborn, London EC1N 2LR
Tel: (0171) 430 1177 **Fax:** (0171) 430 1384
Vivian Pearce, Director of Legal Services

Associated Newspapers Ltd
Northcliffe House, 2 Derry Street, London W8 5TT
Tel: (0171) 938 6000 **Fax:** (0171) 938 4626
Harvey Kass, Legal director
Specialism: Libel (pre-publication and litigation), commercial, new media, copyright, competition law, employment and trademarks.
Career: Articled and qualified (1981) with *Wright Webb Syrett*; *Simon Olswang & Co*, associate (1982-84); legal and business adviser to several television and media companies (1984-90) including Goldcrest Films and Television, Albion Films Ltd; consultant, *Beveridge Ross & Prevezers* (1988-93); Harvey Kass & Co (1990-93) specialised in libel for national newspapers and commercial law; Associated Newspapers Ltd (1993-94); legal director since 1995.Education: Woodhouse Grammar School; LLB (1977) City of London Polytechnic, (Maxwell Law Prize); LLM (1978) Jesus College, Cambridge.
Personal: Born 1955, resides London. Leisure: family, football, tennis, golf, gardening, productions for film, TV and theatre.
Other lawyers: Edward Young, Clare Shields, John Battle; 20 freelancers.

Australia and New Zealand Banking Group
Minerva House, Montague Close, London SE1 9DH
Tel: (0171) 378 2121 **Fax:** (0171) 378 2378
Gareth Campbell, Head of Legal

Avis Europe PLC
Avis House, Park Road, Bracknell, Berks RG12 2EW
Tel: (01344) 426644 **Fax:** (01344) 485616
Judith Nicholson, Company Secretary, Director

B.A.T. Industries PLC
Windsor House, 50 Victoria Street, London SW1H 0NL
Tel: (0171) 222 7979 **Fax:** (0171) 233 1438
No of lawyers in dept: 6
Stuart P. Chalfen, The Solicitor, Legal and Secretarial Department
Reports to: Chairman & CEO
Specialism: Principal areas of work of the department in addition to advice to the Board are international M&A, general corporate & secretarial, treasury/capital markets, European and competition law. Liaison with principal operating units (which, in the UK, include Eagle Star, Allied Dunbar and British American Tobacco).
Career: 1988-present: The Solicitor, BAT Industries; 1970-1987: Associate General Counsel, Xerox Corporation; General Counsel, Rank Xerox Ltd; Managing Counsel, Xerox Corporation US Reprographic Operations, various other posts within the Xerox group; 1967-68: Articled clerk, *Bristows Cooke Carpmael*.
Other lawyers: Peter Clarke: Company Secretary; Stephen Walzer: competition and European law; Steven Hutchings: financial services; Aileen McDonald: European & M&A; Alan Porter: currently on secondment; David Williams; Sonia Page. About 570 lawyers in subsidiaries in UK and worldwide.

BAA PLC
130 Wilton Road, London SW1V 1LQ
Tel: (0171) 834 9449 **Fax:** (0171) 932 6699
Robert Herga, Head of Legal Services

Bank of America
1 Alie Street, London E1 8DE
Tel: (0171) 634 4561 **Fax:** (0171) 634 4324
Marc De Laperouse, Assistant General Counsel

Bank of Cyprus (London) Limited
27/31 Charlotte Street, London W1P 2HJ
Tel: (0171) 304 6690 **Fax:** (0171) 323 9734
Iacovos Angelides, Legal Advisor

Bank of Ireland
36 Queen Street, London EC4R 1BN
Tel: (0171) 489 8673 **Fax:** (0171) 489 9676
No of lawyers in dept: 1
Work outsourced: 20% – Litigation
Margaret W. O'Flanagan, Legal Adviser
Specialism: Provides general legal advice to Bank of Ireland on all aspects of the Bank's operations, particularly on banking law, EU law, insolvency and general commercial matters. Also advises on charity law and local government.
Career: Called to the Bar 1981. Legal Adviser to YWCA of Great Britain; in-house lawyer at Woking BC and to the Corporation of Lloyd's 1986-88 and to the Finance and Leasing Association 1988-90.

Bank of Scotland
1st Floor, Broad Street House, 55 Old Broad Street, London EC2P 2HL
Tel: (0171) 601 6711 **Fax:** (0171) 601 6713
Brian Fisher, Head of Legal

Bankers Investment Trust PLC
3 Finsbury Avenue, London EC2M 2PA
Tel: (0171) 638 5757 **Fax:** (0171) 377 5742
Wendy Taylor, Company Secretary

Bankers Trust International Plc
1 Appold Street, Broadgate, London EC2A 2HE
Tel: (0171) 982 2500 **Fax:** (0171) 982 3389
Simon H.S. Dodds, Managing Director and Counsel

Banque Paribas
10 Harewood Avenue, London NW1 6AA
Tel: (0171) 355 2000 **Fax:** (0171) 595 2555
Kevin Sowerbutts, Head of Legal

Barclays PLC
54 Lombard Street, London EC3P 3AH
Tel: (0171) 699 5000 **Fax:** (0171) 699 3414
Email: GGCO@barclays.co.uk
No of lawyers in dept: 6
Work outsourced: 50% – Litigation, Banking, Investment Management
Howard B. Trust, Group General Counsel.
Reports to: Group Finance Director.
Specialism: Provides General Counsel advice to the main Board and Senior Management on legal risk as it affects the Group and its businesses as a whole.
Career: Solicitor, *Lovell White & King* 1980-85. Solicitor, Morgan Grenfell 1985-87 and Company Secretary 1987-89. Group Legal Director, BZW 1989-95. Group General Counsel and Group Secretary Barclays plc since 1995.

Baring Asset Management (Holdings) Limited
155 Bishopsgate, London EC2M 3XY
Tel: (0171) 628 6000 **Fax:** (0171) 638 7928
Email: mala.dhillon@baring-asset.com
No of lawyers in dept: 3
Work outsourced: 15% – Special projects requiring specialist input.
M. Dhillon, Head of Legal – Compliance
Specialism: Overall responsibility for the legal and compliance functions of the Baring Asset Management group of companies. Areas of work encompass all legal issues relating to the group's investment management and investment products activities.
Career: Member of the Bar of England & Wales. BA (Hons) Law: University of Kent at Canterbury.
Other lawyers: Matthew Jackson, Michael Franey, Anne Routledge.

Barratt Developments PLC
Wingrove House, Ponteland Road, Newcastle-upon-Tyne NE5 3DP
Tel: (0191) 286 6811 **Fax:** (0191) 271 2242
Fred Brown, Company Secretary

Bass PLC
20 North Audley Street, London W1Y 1WE
Tel: (0171) 409 1919 **Fax:** (0171) 409 8503
No of lawyers in dept: 8 in UK
Work outsourced: 90% – Majority in UK; litigation, property.
Richard Winter, Director of Group Legal Affairs
Specialism: General company/commercial matters including acquisitions, disposals, joint ventures, trading agreements, general commercial contracts, regulatory affairs, marketing and intellectual property (particularly trade marks). Regularly liaises with lawyers for Bass Hotels worldwide (also owned by Bass plc). Member of Commerce and Industry Group and Competition Law Panel of CBI.
Career: Qualified 1973 and assistant solicitor with *Eversheds*, Birmingham until 1975 and between 1978 and 1994 (Partner, 1981; moved to London office 1987; appointed managing partner of London office in 1992). Solicitor with Fisons plc 1975-78. Joined Bass plc in 1994. Director of Bass Brewers Limited.
Personal: Born 1949; resides London, married with family. Leisure: tennis, sailing, skiing; member of Roehampton Club, Solway Yacht Club and Royal Corinthian SC. Education: Warwick School; Birmingham University (1970 LLB 2i).

BBA Group PLC
70 Fleet Street, London EC4Y 1EU
Tel: (0171) 842 4900 **Fax:** (0171) 353 5831
Christophe Zumstein, Director Group Services

Bear Stearns International Limited
One Canada Square, London E14 5AD
Tel: (0171) 516 6000 **Fax:** (0171) 516 6030
No of lawyers in dept: 3
Work outsourced: Documentation, production.
S. Bartlett, Head of Legal
Specialism: Responsible for all legal matters for firm's European franchise. Primarily: capital markets – new issues; OTC derivitives; structured debt & equity; regulatory; employment.
Career: 85-88 – BA Jurisprudence (Oxon); LSF 1989; 1989-1994 *Slaughter and May*; qualified as solicitor 1991. July 1994 Bear Stearns International Limited.

Beazer Group PLC
St James House, The Square, Lower Bristol Road, Bath
BA2 3EY
Tel: (01225) 428401 **Fax:** (01225) 339279
Brian Armstrong, Company Secretary

Bellway PLC
Seaton Burn House, Dudley Lane, Seaton Burn,
Newcastle-upon-Tyne NE13 6BE
Tel: (0191) 217 0717 **Fax:** (0191) 236 6230
Peter Stoker, Company Secretary

BG PLC
100 Thames Valley Park Drive, Reading RG6 1PT
Tel: (0118) 929 3367 **Fax:** (0118) 929 3327
Email: friedrick.wm@bgep.co.uk
No of lawyers in dept: 50
Work outsourced: 30% Project; regulatory; tax; property
William Friedrich, General Counsel
Specialism: Mr Friedrich has overall responsibility for advising
on all legal matters affecting BG plc. Areas of specialisation
include finance, project development and corporate.
Career: 1966-71 Union College, Schenectady, New York
(English Major BA). 1972-74 Columbia Law School, New York
(New York JD). Admitted to practice in states of New York and
California and in the District of Columbia.
Personal: Born 19 January 1949. Married, two daughters, aged
18 and 13.

BICC PLC
Devonshire House, Mayfair Place, London W1X 5FH
Tel: (0171) 629 6622 **Fax:** (0171) 409 0070
No of lawyers in dept: 2
Work outsourced: 50% – Major corporate acquisitions and
disposals, financing and property.
Christopher Pearson, Head of Legal Services
Specialism: Sole lawyer and one assistant. Deals with small
acquisitions and disposals, setting up joint ventures
(incorporated and unincorporated) worldwide, banking,
competition, employment, general corporate and some
property development work.
Career: Qualified 1972.
Other lawyers: Claire Howard – commercial property, general
corporate.

Billiton PLC
1 3 The Strand, London WC2N 5I IA
Tel: (0171) 747 3800 **Fax:** (0171) 747 3900
Hans Lim A Po, Head of Legal

Bilton PLC
Bilton House, Uxbridge Road, Ealing, London W5 2TL
Tel: (0181) 567 7777 **Fax:** (0181) 840 0249
P. Ponnaiyah, Group Solicitor & Company Secretary

Biocompatibles International PLC
Frensham House, Farnham Business Park, Weydon Lane,
Farnham GU9 8QL
Tel: (01252) 732732 **Fax:** (01252) 732777
No of lawyers in dept: 1
Work outsourced: 60% – Corporate commercial
agreements, patents, litigation, employment
Suzanne V. McLean, Legal Director and Company Secretary
Specialism: International commercial agreements, specialising
in intellectual property licences. Employment. Corporate.
Career: BA Hons: Business Law. Guildhall University 1975-78.
Barrister – Gray's Inn 1979.
Personal: Married, two children. Lives in London. Member of
Royal Thames Yacht Club.

Blue Circle Industries PLC
84 Eccleston Square, London SW1V 1PX
Tel: (0171) 828 3456 **Fax:** (0171) 245 8272
No of lawyers in dept: 5
Work outsourced: 60%
Richard F. Tapp, Company Secretary/Legal Adviser
Specialism: Responsible for provision of legal services
worldwide, in consultation with overseas subsidiaries, and for
company secretarial work in the UK. Principal areas of work are
acquisitions and disposals, contract and commercial law,
competition law and property. Responsible also for risk
management and insurance.

Career: 1981-84 National Coal Board. 1985-86 Imperial Foods
Ltd, part of Imperial Group plc. Joined Blue Circle as
Commercial Solicitor 1986, Principal Solicitor 1992, Company
Secretary and Legal Adviser 1996. LLB (Sheffield), LLM
(Leicester) FCIS, ACI Arb. MBA (Nottingham Law School).
Other lawyers: Anne C Ramsay: Senior Commercial Solicitor;
Alison Shepley: Senior Property Solicitor; Nigel Millinson:
Commercial Solicitor; Karyn Trowbridge: Property Solicitor.

BNP PLC
8-13 King William Street, London EC4P 4HS
Tel: (0171) 548 9548 **Fax:** (0171) 548 9511
M. Toubkin, Head of Legal

BOC Group PLC
Chertsey Road, Windlesham GU20 6HJ
Tel: (01276) 477222 **Fax:** (01276) 471333
Gloria Stuart, Group Director (Legal and Company Secretary)

Body Shop International PLC
Watersmead, Littlehampton BN17 6LS
Tel: (01903) 731500 **Fax:** (01903) 726250
Jane Reid, Director of Legal

Bodycote International PLC
Hulley Road, Hurdsfield, Macclesfield, Cheshire SK10 2SG
Tel: (01625) 505300 **Fax:** (01625) 505313
Email: enquiries@bodycote.com
No of lawyers in dept: 1
Work outsourced: 95% – Corporate finance, M&A, property
John R. Grime, Company Secretary
Specialism: Stock Exchange, regulatory and compliance.
Executive share option schemes. Service of board's
requirements for meetings. Investor relations.
Career: 1975-82 & 1996-97 Private practice in Manchester.
1982-95 Principal solicitor (commercial and property) Corporate
Wholesale Society Ltd. 1997-to date Bodycote International plc.
London University LLB (external via Trent Polytechnic). Qualified
1997.
Personal: Aged 45, married with 1 daughter. Lives Bramhall,
Cheshire. 3 cats. Enjoys walking and entertaining.

Booker PLC
85 Buckingham Gate, London SW1E 6PD
Tel: (0171) 411 5500 **Fax:** (0171) 411 5555
Chrissi Evans, Head of Legal Services

Boots Co PLC
1 Thanet Road West, Nottingham NG2 3AA
Tel: (0115) 950 6111 **Fax:** (0115) 959 2727
Michael John Oliver, Principal Legal Adviser
Specialism: Self-litigation employment, trading standards,
consumer protection, pharmacy.
Other lawyers: Miss P Pike – employment law. Miss H Rayner –
product liability/personal injury litigation.

Bowthorpe PLC
Gatwick Road, Crawley RH10 2RZ
Tel: (01293) 528888 **Fax:** (01293) 541905
Michael Arnaouti, Company Secretary

BPB PLC
Langley Park House, Uxbridge Road, Slough SL3 6DU
Tel: (01753) 898800 **Fax:** (01753) 898900
Robert M. Heard, Company Secretary

Bradford Property Trust PLC
69 Market Street, Bradford BD1 1NE
Tel: (01274) 723181 **Fax:** (01274) 395304
Nigel A. Denby, Finance Director

Brake Bros. PLC
Enterprise House, Godinton Road, Ashford TN23 1EU
Tel: (01233) 206000 **Fax:** (01233) 206006
Martin Purvis, Group Company Secretary

Britannic Assurance PLC
1 Wythall Green Way, Wythall, Birmingham B47 6WG
Tel: (01564) 828888 **Fax:** (01564) 828822
No of lawyers in dept: 2
Anna East, Senior Solicitor
Specialism: Commercial contracts/IT/investment management
and contracts. Property plus management of outside legal
resource.

Career: Rugby High School. Nottingham University (BA law).
Trent Polytechnic (Law Society finals). *Talbots* (articles), 1982-
84. *Eversheds*, 1984-88. British Assurance 1988 to date.
Personal: Interests: family, tennis, travel.
Other lawyers: Ruth Scott – commercial contracts, IT, some
property.

Britax International
Seton House, Warwick Technology Park, Gallows Hill,
Warwick CV34 6DE
Tel: (01926) 406309 **Fax:** (01926) 406308
Richard Marton, Chief Executive

British Aerospace PLC
Warwick House, PO Box 87, Farnborough Aerospace
Centre, Farnborough GU14 6YU
Tel: (01252) 373232 **Fax:** (01252) 383825
Philip Riley, Deputy Legal Director

British Airways PLC
Waterside (HBA3), PO Box 365, Harmondsworth UB7 0GB
Tel: (0181) 738 6870 **Fax:** (0181) 738 9964
Robert Webb QC, General Counsel

British Assets Trust PLC
One Charlotte Square, Edinburgh EH2 4DZ
Tel: (0131) 225 1357 **Fax:** (0131) 225 2375
Gordon Humphries, Company Secretary

British Energy plc
10 Lochside Place, Edinburgh EH12 9DF
Tel: (0131) 527 2000 **Fax:** (0131) 527 2277
No of lawyers in dept: 9
Work outsourced: Project support, overseas ventures,
various specialisms.
Robert M. Armour, Company Secretary
Reports to: Chairman and Chief Executive.
Specialism: Deals with corporate legal issues, corporate
governance, certain major transactions, legal and stock
exchange compliance, environmental issues, European
legislation and Scottish parliament matters. Also responsible for
estates, public relations, government relations, and private
shareholder issues.
Career: Assistant solicitor *Wright Johnston & McKenzie*,
Edinburgh 1983-85, and Partner 1986-90. Scottish Nuclear's
Company Secretary from 1990-1995. Company Secretary of
British Energy plc – 1995 to date.
Other lawyers: Dr Jean MacDonald, John Young, Beverley
Sullivan, Andrew McMillan, Sue Challenger, Kate Lewis.

British Land Co PLC
10 Cornwall Terrace, Regent's Park, London NW1 4QP
Tel: (0171) 486 4466 **Fax:** (0171) 935 5552
Anthony Braine, Company Secretary/Head of Legal

British Petroleum Co PLC
Britannic House, 1 Finsbury Circus, London EC2M 7BA
Tel: (0171) 496 4000 **Fax:** (0171) 496 4630
No of lawyers in dept: 160 worldwide
Work outsourced: 10–20% – Intellectual property litigation,
local employment and land matters, overall.
Peter B.P. Bevan, Group General Counsel
Specialism: Joined the BP Group in 1970 after qualifying as a
solicitor with a City of London firm. He worked initially in the Law
Department of BP Chemicals and then of the Parent Company.
Subsequently became Manager of the Legal function within BP
Exploration and then Assistant Company Secretary, followed by
Deputy Group Legal Adviser of the British Petroleum Company
plc. In September 1992 he became Group General Counsel.
Main areas of expertise are corporate and company law,
mergers and acquisitions, finance, and cross-jurisdictional and
cross-business issues.
Other lawyers: Assistant Group General Counsel: Peter Ling
(Singapore), John Lynch (Cleveland USA), Robert Moore, Robin
Morris, Colin Saunders, Paul Baddeley (litigation), Lesley
Stockwell (corporate), Richard Bradley (M&A).

British Sky Broadcasting Group PLC
Grant Way, Isleworth TW7 5QD
Tel: (0171) 705 3000 **Fax:** (0171) 705 3254
Internet: http://www.sky.co.uk
No of lawyers in dept: 12
Deanna Bates, Head of Legal & Business Affairs

Career: Educated at Exeter University and Guildford Law College and qualified as a Solicitor in 1987. Completed her training at *Clifford Chance*, and after qualifying joined the *Clifford Chance* commercial department where she stayed for 2 years. In 1989 joined Sky Television plc and has been Head of Legal and Business Affairs for Sky (and now BSkyB) since then.
Other lawyers: Sharon Southwell-Gray – litigation.

British Steel plc
15 Marylebone Road, London NW1 5JD
Tel: (0171) 314 5522 **Fax:** (0171) 314 5622
No of lawyers in dept: 7
Margaret O'Neill, Director – Legal Services
Reports to: Chairman/Chief Executive.
Specialism: Responsible for provision of in-house legal and intellectual property services to British Steel Group and managing external advice where required.
Other lawyers: Anthony Tallents: company/commercial; Harish Morgan: company/commercial; Freddy Maes: European law; Simon Melhuish-Hancock: company/commercial; Ian Fowler: company/commercial; Monique Bonville-Ginn: company/commercial/European law.

British Telecommunications PLC
British Telecom Centre, Room A4J, BT Group Legal Services, 81 Newgate Street, London EC1A 7AJ
Tel: (0171) 356 5000 **Fax:** (0171) 356 6135
Colin Green, Secretary and Chief Legal Adviser

British Vita PLC
Oldham Road, Middleton, Manchester M24 2DB
Tel: (0161) 643 1133 **Fax:** (0161) 653 5411
No of lawyers in dept: 2
Work outsourced: 20% – Public issues, heavyweight litigation, some M&A.
Mark Stirzaker, Company Solicitor
Specialism: Principal areas of work are mergers and acquisitions and commercial property. Also provides general commercial advice and deals with intellectual property matters.
Career: Qualified 1980.
Other lawyers: Catherine Butler.

British-Borneo Petroleum Synd PLC
8th Floor, East Wing, Bowater House, 68 Knightsbridge, London SW1X 7JZ
Tel: (0171) 581 8822 **Fax:** (0171) 584 8562
Internet: British-Borneo.co.uk
Work outsourced: 15% – Corporate finance, major M&A, some employment.
Patricia Peter, Legal Adviser and Company Secretary
Specialism: Joint ventures, acquisitions and disposals. Also equity and debt financings, general corporate, employment. Also Company Secretary.
Career: Called to the Bar 1975. Various in-house legal appointments since 1976. Joined British-Borneo 1993. Company Secretary 1994.

Brixton Estate PLC
22-24 Ely Place, London EC1N 6TQ
Tel: (0171) 400 4400 **Fax:** (0171) 405 1630
Gilbert Leversedge, Company Secretary

Brown (N.) Group PLC
53 Dale Street, Manchester M60 6ES
Tel: (0161) 236 8256 **Fax:** (0161) 238 2308
Peter Tynan, Company Secretary

Bryant Group PLC
Cranmore House, Cranmore Boulevard, Solihull B90 4SD
Tel: (0121) 711 1212 **Fax:** (0121) 711 2610
Michael Chapman, Finance Director

BTG PLC
101 Newington Causeway, London SE1 6BU
Tel: (0171) 403 6666 **Fax:** (0171) 575 1527
Andrew Popper, Director of Legal Department

BTP PLC
Hayes Road, Cadishead, Manchester M44 5BX
Tel: (0161) 775 3945 **Fax:** (0161) 775 3970
Creighton Twiggs, Company Secretary

BTR PLC
BTR House, Carlisle Place, London SW1P 1BX
Tel: (0171) 834 3848 **Fax:** (0171) 834 3879
Email: @btr.plc.uk
No of lawyers in dept: 15
Work outsourced: 50% – Litigation, larger corporate transactions, pensions, banking, real estate
David Stevens, General Counsel and Company Secretary
Specialism: Deals with legal services and negotiation of acquisitions and disposals, intellectual property, real estate management, secretarial service and pensions all on a worldwide basis.
Other lawyers: 6 in the UK : Graeme Stening, Kate Harris, Nigel Titley, John Finch, Palwinder Hare. 6 in the US, 2 in Australia, 1 in China.

Bunzl PLC
110 Park Street, London W1Y 3RB
Tel: (0171) 495 4950 **Fax:** (0171) 495 4953
No of lawyers in dept: 2
Work outsourced: 30% – Large corporate transactions, litigation, property.
Paul N. Hussey, Company Secretary
Specialism: Provides legal services and advice on company/commercial and general corporate matters, and a full company secretarial service including compliance.
Career: Qualified 1983 while with *Addleshaw Sons & Latham*. Commercial solicitor, Grand Metropolitan Retailing Division 1985-86 and Senior Solicitor, Contract Services Division 1986-87. Company Secretary and Group Legal Adviser, Compass Group 1987-88. Legal Adviser, Bunzl plc 1988-92 and then took up present position.
Personal: Educated at Woking Grammar School 1970-77, University College, Cardiff 1977-80 and College of Law 1980-81. Leisure pursuits include walking, tennis, music and golf. Born 11 January 1959. Lives in London.

Burford Holdings PLC
20 Thayer Street, London W1M 6DD
Tel: (0171) 224 2240 **Fax:** (0171) 224 1710
Katerina Angliss, Company Secretary

Burmah Castrol PLC
Burmah Castrol House, Pipers Way, Swindon SN3 1RE
Tel: (01793) 511521 **Fax:** (01793) 513506
Peter F. Goodwill, Legal Director

C Hoare & Co
37 Fleet Street, London EC4P 4DQ
Tel: (0171) 353 4522 **Fax:** (0171) 353 4521
Director of Legal Services

Cable & Wireless Communications plc
26 Red Lion Square, London WC1R 4HQ
Tel: (0171) 528 2000 **Fax:** (0171) 528 3720
No of lawyers in dept: 12
Chris Athersych, Legal Director & Company Secretary
Specialism: Member of the Senior Management Team with responsibility for all legal affairs of the Cable & Wireless Communications group, managing the legal department and providing company secretarial services to the Chairman and the Board of Directors. Member of the Law Counsel of the World Wide Group Law function of Cable & Wireless plc, which co-ordinates efforts and develops best practices of the various national legal departments within the C&W Group. Areas of work also include corporate and commercial law, financing and structuring, media contracts, telecommunications and broadcasting, regulatory, competition law and intellectual property.
Career: General Counsel and Company Secretary of Bell Cablemedia plc 1996-97, General Counsel and Assistant Company Secretary of Bell Canada International Inc 1993-1996, Vice-president Corporate Affairs and Corporate Secretary of The Canam Manac Group Inc 1986-1993, Lawyer of Stikeman, Elliott (Montreal) 1984-1986, Law Clerk of Supreme Court of Canada 1979-1980. B.LL Laval University; LL.M. Osgood Law School; M.Litt Trinity College, Oxford.
Personal: Is Canadian and an Advocate of the Quebec Bar. Married with 3 children and lives in Wimbledon. Leisure pursuits: ice hockey, skiing, swimming, squash, music, carpentry and photography. Born 1st March 1957.
Other lawyers: Mary Molyneux (Head of Legal Services), Anne Smith, Ruth Harris, Giles Pemberton, Jon Medcalf, Nicholas Bell, Wulstan Berkeley, John Whitehead, Jane McElhatton, Simon Taylor.

Cable and Wireless PLC
124 Theobalds Road, London WC1X 8RX
Tel: (0171) 315 4000 **Fax:** (0171) 315 5093
Email: www.cwplc.com
Elizabeth Wall, Group Director of Legal and Regulatory Affairs
Specialism: Has overall professional and functional responsibility for the provision of legal and regulatory services to the Cable & Wireless Group of companies worldwide. Regular conference speaker on topics concerning in-house lawyers, in-house practice management and international legal practice.
Career: Qualified: 1972, England: 1982, California, US; university: Manchester; 1973–1974, Attachee to the Court of Arbitration, International Chamber of Commerce, Paris; 1974–1977, Legal Assistant, Hawker Siddley Aviation Limited; 1985–1990, Vice President and Chief Counsel, McDonnell Douglas IS International; 1990 to date, Group Director of Legal and Regulatory Affairs, Cable and Wireless plc.
Personal: The Law Society (Commerce & Industry Group – Chairman 96/97); American Bar Association; International Bar Association; American Corporate Counsel Association, Main Board Member (USA) and European Chapter Member; Governor of the Royal College of Law; Professional awards: 'Prominent Woman in International Law Award', American Society of International Lawyers 1994; In-house Company Commercial Lawyer of the Year Award 1995; Leisure pursuits: interior decoration and design, travel, emerging technologies and the Arts.

Cadbury Schweppes PLC
PO Box 2138, Franklin House, Bourneville, Birmingham B30 2NB
Tel: (0121) 625 7000 **Fax:** (0121) 459 0383
Michael Keating, Legal Director

Cairn Energy PLC
4th Floor, 50 Lothian Road, Edinburgh EH3 9BY
Tel: (0131) 475 3000 **Fax:** (0131) 475 3031
Email: pr@cairn-energy.plc.uk
No of lawyers in dept: 6
Hew R. Dundas, General Manager, Legal

Caledonia Investments PLC
Cayzer House, 1 Thomas More Street, London E1 9AR
Tel: (0171) 481 4343 **Fax:** (0171) 488 0896
Graeme Denison, Company Secretary

Cap Gemini UK PLC
Cap Gemini House, 130 Shaftesbury Avenue, London W1V 8HH
Tel: (0171) 434 2171 **Fax:** (0171) 434 8607
Email: julie.mangan@capgemini.co.uk
No of lawyers in dept: 3
Julie Mangan, Director, Contract Services
Specialism: Responsible for the provision of in-house legal services from the drafting and negotiation of IT contracts to the provision of legal and risk management training. Other areas of responsibility include managing the Cap Gemini insurance programme, company secretarial matters and the provision of employment law advice.
Other lawyers: John Buyers – solicitor; Katie Smith – solicitor; Gavin Wakefield – barrister

Capita Group PLC
71 Victoria Street, Westminster, London SW1H 0XA
Tel: (0171) 799 1525 **Fax:** (0171) 976 0839
Ken Au, Company Secretary

Capital Radio PLC
30 Leicester Square, London WC2H 7LA
Tel: (0171) 766 6000 **Fax:** (0171) 766 6184
Email: capitalradio.co.uk
Roy Naismith, Company Secretary

Caradon PLC
Caradon House, 24 Queen's Road, Weybridge KT13 9UX
Tel: (01932) 850850 **Fax:** (01932) 823314
No of lawyers in dept: 2
Anthony Holland, Group Legal Adviser
Other lawyers: Helen Leckey – Legal adviser

Cattles PLC
Kingston House, Centre 27 Business Park,
Woodhead Road, Birstall, Batley WS17 9TD
Tel: (01924) 444466 **Fax:** (01924) 448324
Patrick Doherty, Company Secretary

Centrica PLC
117 Piccadilly, London W1V 9FJ
Tel: (0171) 647 3200 **Fax:** (0171) 647 3201
Martin Murray, Head of Legal

Chase Manhattan Bank
125 London Wall, London EC2Y 5AJ
Tel: (0171) 777 2000 **Fax:** (0171) 777 3141
Mitchell Caller, Head of Legal

Chelsfield PLC
67 Brook Street, London W1Y 2NJ
Tel: (0171) 493 3977 **Fax:** (0171) 491 9369
Robin Perrot, Company Solicitor

Christiania Bank of Kreditkasse
Lloyds Chambers, 1 Portsoken Street, London E1 8RV
Tel: (0171) 680 7000 **Fax:** (0171) 481 1860
Craig Axe, Head of Legal

Christie's International PLC
8 King Street, St James's, London SW1Y 6QT
Tel: (0171) 839 9060 **Fax:** (0171) 839 1611
Richard Aydon, Group Legal Director

Citibank NA
Hudson House, 8–10 Tavistock Street, London WC2E 7PP
Tel: (0171) 500 5000 **Fax:** (0171) 500 0188
Laurie Adams, Senior Counsel Europe

Citibank Private Bank
41 Berkeley Square, London W1X 6NA
Tel: (0171) 508 8000 **Fax:** (0171) 508 8472
Bruce Hogarth-Jones, Head of Legal

The City of London Investment Trust plc
3 Finsbury Avenue, London EC2M 2PA
Tel: (0171) 638 5757 **Fax:** (0171) 377 5742
Geoffrey Rice, Company Secretary

Close Brothers Group PLC
12 Appold Street, London EC2A 2AA
Tel: (0171) 426 4000 **Fax:** (0171) 426 4044
Robin Sellers, Group Company Secretary

Clydesdale Bank plc
Legal Services, PO Box 43, 150 Buchanan Street, Glasgow
G1 2HL
Tel: (0141) 223 2802 **Fax:** (0141) 223 2887
Jane L. Shirran, General Counsel
Specialism: Company/Commercial, Corporate Financial
Litigation and Management of the Legal function.
Career: 1980-1985 Aberdeen University. LL.B Honours (2:1);
Diploma in Legal Practice. General Counsel and Secretary,
Clydesdale Bank PLC. 1996-June 1998 Principal Solicitor with
Clydesdale Bank PLC, Legal Services, Glasgow; Responsible
for provision of legal advice to Corporate, Business Banking
and Head Office areas of Bank. 1995-1996 Senior Solicitor with
Bank of Scotland, Legal Services, Edinburgh; Provision of cor-
porate and general advice to the Bank's Head Office, Structured Finance and Investment Banking Departments. 1988-
1995 *McGrigor Donald*, Solicitors, Associate – 1992-1995; General Corporate, Banking and Insolvency; Worked in Glasgow,
London and Edinburgh offices. 1987-1988 *Tods Murray*, Edinburgh, Assistant. 1985-1987 *Allan Dawson Simpson & Hampton*,
Trainee. Other: Bank's representative on CSCB Legal Committee.

CMG PLC
Parnell House, 25 Wilton Road, London SW1V 1EJ
Tel: (0171) 592 4000 **Fax:** (0171) 592 4800
Richard Francis, Company Solicitor

Co-operative Bank Plc
PO Box 101, 1 Balloon Street, Manchester M60 4EP
Tel: (0161) 832 3456 **Fax:** (0161) 832 7849
Anne Page, Head of Legal Services

Coats Viyella PLC
28 Savile Row, London W1X 2DD
Tel: (0171) 292 9200 **Fax:** (0171) 437 2016
No of lawyers in dept: 2
Work outsourced: 20%
Sam Dow, Company Secretary
Specialism: Responsible for dealing with all areas affecting
corporate holding company and major transactions of
subsidiaries.
Career: Qualified 1983. Took up current position in 1986.
Personal: Educated at Loretto School, Musselburgh 1959-63
and University of Edinburgh 1964-68. Leisure pursuits include
golf, skiing and theatro. Born 5th January 1946. Lives in
Littleworth Common, Bucks.

Cobham PLC
Brook Road, Wimborne BH21 2BJ
Tel: (01202) 882020 **Fax:** (01202) 840523
Work outsourced: Conveyancing; M&A; Corporate
Finance; Competition.
John Pope, Company Solicitor

Colt Telecom Group PLC
15 Marylebone Road, London NW5 5JD
Tel: (0171) 390 3900 **Fax:** (0171) 390 3701
Email: colt-telecom.com
No of lawyers in dept: 1
Work outsourced: 50% – Litigation, property, employment
Mark Jenkins, Legal Services Director and Company
Secretary
Specialism: Management of all of the legal and secretarial
requirements of the group. Corporate/commercial, M&A,
Employment.
Career: Chelmer. Bar School. M.K. Electric plc/SKF (UK)
Ltd/Peek plc.
Personal: Married. 3 children.

Commercial Union PLC
St Helen's, 1 Undershaft, London EC3P 3DQ
Tel: (0171) 283 7500 **Fax:** (0171) 662 4513
Keith Grant, Head of Legal

Computacenter
Link House, 19 Colonial Way, Watford WD2 2HZ
Tel: (01923) 256040 **Fax:** (01923) 478855
Alan Pottinger, Company Secretary

Cookson Group PLC
The Adelphi, 1-11 John Adam Street, London WC2N 6HJ
Tel: (0171) 766 4500 **Fax:** (0171) 747 6600
Glen McDonnall, Assistant Company Secretary Legal
Adviser

Corporate Services Group PLC
Glaston Park, Spring Lane, Glaston LE15 9BX
Tel: (01572) 822931 **Fax:** (01572) 823510
John Abrahamson, Company Secretary

Courtaulds PLC
50 George Street, London W1A 2BB
Tel: (0171) 612 1000 **Fax:** (0171) 612 1500
Russell Miller, Head of Legal Services

Coutts Nat West Group
440 Strand, London WC2R 0QS
Tel: (0171) 753 1000 **Fax:** (0171) 753 1050
Email: webmaster@coutts.com
No of lawyers in dept: 6
Work outsourced: 50% – Litigation, Specialist advice,
Commercial transactions.
C. Carr, Group General Counsel
Career: February 1998 to date: General Counsel, Coutts Nat
West Group; 1989-1997 HSBC Holdings plc, General Manager
and Group Legal Adviser; 1983-1989 Central Electricity
Generating Board, Head of Legal Services; 1980-1983
Capsticks; 1973-1980 Bridon plc, Contracts Director; 1967-
1973 Guest Keen & Nettlefolds plc, Assistant Secretary; 1962-
1967 Elliott Automation Ltd, Deputy Legal Adviser; 1961-1962
Rolls Royce Ltd, Legal Adviser.
Personal: Married to Julia, 2 sons.

Other lawyers: Robert Stemmons (General Counsel), Saman-
tha Linsley (Assistant Counsel & Company Secretary), Sarah
Chidgey (Assistant Counsel), Russell Fairbrother (Assistant
Counsel), Gloria Glennie (Assistant Counsel).

Cox Insurance Holdings PLC
34 Leadenhall Street, London EC3A 1AT
Tel: (0171) 265 6711 **Fax:** (0171) 265 6867
C.J. Ringrose, Company Secretary

Credit Agricole Indosuez
122 Leadenhall Street, London EC3V 4QH
Tel: (0171) 971 4000 **Fax:** (0171) 971 4407
Margaret Garner, Head of Legal

Credit Lyonnais
Broadwalk House, 5 Appold Street, London EC2A 2JP
Tel: (0171) 214 7080 **Fax:** (0171) 214 7007
No of lawyers in dept: 11
E. Paget-Brown, UK General Counsel
Specialism: The entire range of legal work emanating from UK
Business activities of Credit Lyonnais includes transaction
support, drafting and negotiation of agreements, advice on
banking, capital markets, regulatory, corporate, employment
and IT matters as well as all aspects of litigation.
Career: Bristol University (LLB). Kingston University (MBA).
Barrister at law. Credit Lyonnais Rouse Ltd 1987-1997. Credit
Lyonnais 1997-.
Other lawyers: Joseph Crowley – Commodities/Derivatives.
Michael Amos – Capital Markets. Nichola Ezra – Banking.

Credit Suisse Financial Products
1 Cabot Square, London E14 4QJ
Tel: (0171) 888 8888 **Fax:** (0171) 888 4476
Eoin O'Shea, General Counsel

Creditanstalt AG
11th Floor, 125 London Wall, London EC2Y 5DD
Tel: (0171) 600 1555 **Fax:** (0171) 417 4803
No of lawyers in dept: 2
Work outsourced: 20% – Merger related, property,
employment, foreign deals.
Peter Jones, Senior Legal Counsel
Specialism: Banking, trade finance, venture capital, derivatives,
M&A, corporate finance.
Career: 1976-79 Oxford (St Catherine's College) BA Hons.
1979-81 College of Law (Chancery Lane). 1981-87 *Withers*
(articles). 1987-89 *Macfarlanes*. 1989-93 *Freshfields*. 1993 to
date Creditanstalt.
Personal: Cricket, golf, squash, sailing. Member of RAC.
Other lawyers: Michele May

Croda International PLC
Cowick Hall, Snaith, Goole DN14 9AA
Tel: (01405) 860551 **Fax:** (01405) 861767
George Bates, Company Secretary

CRT Group PLC
Eastham Hall, Eastham Village Road, Eastham L62 0AF
Tel: (0151) 328 1074 **Fax:** (0151) 328 1076
John Anthony Gittins, Finance Director

Daiwa Europe Ltd
5 King William Street, London EC4N 7AX
Tel: (0171) 548 8080 **Fax:** (0171) 548 8835
Email: daiwa.co.uk
No of lawyers in dept: 3
Work outsourced: 10% – Litigation, property, non-UK law
R. Massey, Head of Legal
Specialism: Investment banking, corporate.
Career: BA (Hons) , LLB University of Sydney. *Allen, Allen &
Hemsley, Slaughter and May.*
Personal: Lives in London.

Danka Business Systems PLC
33 Cavendish Square, London W1M 0DE
Tel: (0171) 399 3000 **Fax:** (0171) 399 3001
Paul Dumond, Company Secretary

David S Smith (Holdings) Plc
16 Great Peter Street, London SW1P 2BX
Tel: (0171) 222 8855 Fax: (0171) 222 8856
No of lawyers in dept: 2
Jillian Glover, Group Legal Adviser
Reports to: Corporate Services Director.
Specialism: Commercial, EU competition law, intellectual property and employment law. Also prepares and implements group policies on various subjects and manages external litigation.
Career: Qualified 1985, while with *Beachcroft Stanleys*. Assistant solicitor with *Alsop Wilkinson* 1986-89, then joined *McKenna & Co*. Became Group Legal Adviser to the David S Smith Group in 1992.
Other lawyers: Stephen Cook.

Davis Service Group PLC
4 Grosvenor Place, London SW1X 7DL
Tel: (0171) 259 6663 Fax: (0171) 259 6948
Malcolm Hoskin, Company secretary

De La Rue PLC
De La Rue House, Jays Close, Viables Industrial Estate, Basingstoke RG22 4BS
Tel: (01256) 329122 Fax: (01256) 467106
Louise Fluker, Senior Legal Adviser

Debenhams PLC
1 Welbeck Street, London W1A 1DF
Tel: (0171) 636 8040 Fax: (0171) 927 7806
No of lawyers in dept: 3
David Wilson, Company Secretary and General Counsel
Specialism: Born (6.7.60). Company Secretary and General Counsel (5.1.98). Corporate, commercial, employment, intellectual, property, litigation.
Career: B.A. LL.M., solicitor, chartered secretary, F.C.I.S., F.R.S.A. Admitted solicitor, 1986. B.A.T. Industries plc – solicitor – 1990-1993. Company Secretary 1993-1997. *Gouldens*, 1988-1990. *Holman Fenwick & Willan*, 1987-1988. Articled at *Farrer & Co*, 1984-1986
Personal: Interests: sport, music, collecting art.
Other lawyers: Patricia Skinner (Deputy General Counsel), Simmi Khand Pur (Legal Adviser).

Delta PLC
1 Kingsway, London WC2B 6XF
Tel: (0171) 836 3535 Fax: (0171) 836 4511
John Narciso, Company Secretary

Deutsche Morgan Grenfell
23 Great Winchester Street, London EC2P 2AX
Tel: (0171) 545 8000 Fax: (0171) 545 6155
Peter Brooks, Head of Group Legal Department

Devro PLC
Gartferry Road, Moodiesburn, Chryston, Glasgow G69 0JE
Tel: (01236) 872261 Fax: (01236) 872557
John Meredith, Company Secretary

Diageo PLC
39 Portman Square, London W1H 0EE
Tel: (0171) 486 0288 Fax: (0171) 935 5500
Kenneth Mildwaters, Director of Legal Services

Dixons Group PLC
Maylands Ave, Hemel Hempstead HP2 7TG
Tel: (01442) 353000 Fax: (01442) 233218
Geoffrey Budd, Company Secretary

Donaldson Lufkin & Jenrette International
99 Bishopsgate, London EC2M 3XD
Tel: (0171) 655 7000 Fax: (0171) 655 7204
J Harriman, Director, General Counsel

Dresdner Kleinwort Benson Ltd
PO Box 560, 20 Fenchurch Street, London EC3P 3DB
Tel: (0171) 623 8000 Fax: (0171) 929 7958
No of lawyers in dept: 6
Work outsourced: 15% – Tax structures
Simon Leifer, Director, Head of Global Markets Legal Dept
Specialism: money markets/fixed income/derivatives/securitisation.

Career: Kingston College of Law. Guilford College of Law. Admitted as a solicitor in 1985. Previously at Royal Bank of Canada and Libra Bank plc
Personal: Married. 2 children. Keen oarsman.

Edinburgh Fund Managers PLC
Donaldson House, 97 Haymarket Terrace, Edinburgh EH12 5HD
Tel: (0131) 313 1000 Fax: (0131) 313 6300
Kenneth Murray, Head of Legal

Electra Inv Tst PLC
65 Kingsway, London WC2B 6QT
Tel: (0171) 831 6464 Fax: (0171) 404 5388
Philip Dyke, Company Secretary

Electrocomponents PLC
4240 Nash Court, Oxford Business Park, Oxford OX4 2RU
Tel: (01865) 711234 Fax: (01865) 783400
Internet: http://www.electrocomponents.com
No of lawyers in dept: 2
Carmelina Carfora, Group Company Secretary
Specialism: Company secretarial – all issues; Legal; Risk Management; Corporate Benefits
Career: Essex Institute of Higher Education. Institute of Chartered Secretaries and Administrators. Now a Fellow of Institute of Chartered Secretaries and Administrators.
Other lawyers: Dr Rosemary Veale – Commercial, Intellectual, Property, Employment, Property, Company, IT. Miss Josephine Thompson – Trainee Company Secretary.

Elementis PLC
One Great Tower Street, London EC3R 5AH
Tel: (0171) 711 1400 Fax: (0171) 711 1486
Philip Brown, Company Secretary

EMAP PLC
1 Lincoln Court, Lincoln Road, Peterborough PE1 2RF
Tel: (01733) 568900 Fax: (01733) 312115
Mark Henson, Deputy Group Company Secrectary

EMI Group plc
4 Tenterden Street, Hanover Square, London W1A 2AY
Tel: (0171) 355 4848 Fax: (0171) 495 1421
Charles Ashcroft, Company Secretary and Group General Counsel

English China Clays PLC
1015 Arlington Business Park, Theale, Reading RG7 4SA
Tel: (0118) 930 4010 Fax: (0118) 930 9501
No of lawyers in dept: 2
Peter Elliott, Co Sec/Dir of Corp Services
Reports to: CEO
Specialism: Responsible for group wide legal, estates, pensions, insurance and secretariat matters.
Career: Qualified 1977, while with *Linklaters & Paines* and assistant solicitor to 1981, based in London and Brussels. Assistant solicitor and then partner with *Charles Russell & Co* 1982-87. Joined English China Clays plc in 1987 and took up current position in 1991.
Other lawyers: J.J. Jordan

European Bank for Reconstruction & Development
One Exchange Square, London EC2A 2EH
Tel: (0171) 338 6000 Fax: (0171) 338 6150
John Taylor, General Counsel

Eurotunnel PLC
Eurotunnel Administration Building, Sheraton Park, Folkestone, Kent CT19 4QS
Tel: (01303) 273300 Fax: (01303) 850360
Stephen Walker, Company Secretary

Fairey Group plc
Station Road, Egham TW20 9NP
Tel: (01784) 470470 Fax: (01784) 470848
Roger Stephens, Company Secretary

First Leisure Corporation PLC
7 Soho Street, London W1V 5FA
Tel: (0171) 437 9727 Fax: (0171) 439 0088
Gary Shillinglaw, Company Secretary

First National Bank of Chicago (The)
1 Triton Square, London NW1 3FN
Tel: (0171) 388 3456 Fax: (0171) 903 4188
J. Bestmann, Regional Counsel

FKI PLC
West House, King Cross Road, Halifax HX1 1EB
Tel: (01422) 330267 Fax: (01422) 330084
Michael J.R. Porter, Company Secretary

Flextech Television Ltd
160 Great Portland Street, London W1N 5TB
Tel: (0171) 299 5000 Fax:(0171) 299 6041
Michael Stern, Head of Legal Affairs

Fuji Capital Markets (UK) Limited
River Plate House, 7-11 Finsbury Circus, London EC2M 7DH
Tel: (0171) 972 9900 Fax:(0171) 638 3945
Sean Russell, Legal Counsel

Galen Holdings PLC
Seagoe Industrial Estate, Craigavon BT63 5UA
Tel: (01762) 334974 Fax: (01762) 350206
Stephen Campbell, Company Secretary

Gallaher Group PLC
Members Hill, Brooklands Road, Weybridge KT13 0QU
Tel: (01932) 859777 Fax: (01932) 849119
Christopher Devereux, Corporate Legal Adviser
Specialism: Responsible for provision of in-house legal service to Gallaher and related companies.
Career: Qualified 1975 and in private practice until 1978, then joined Gallaher Ltd, ultimately becoming Corporate Legal Adviser.
Other lawyers: Suzanne Wise, Simon Witham, Katy Beard.

General Accident Life Assurance plc
2 Rougier Lane, York YO90 1GA
Tel: (01904) 628982 Fax:(01904) 684684
No of lawyers in dept: 7
Work outsourced: 25% – Litigation, Acquisition
Donald Graham, Manager, Legal Services
Specialism: Insurance, IP, Litigation, Joint Ventures, Acquisitions/Disposals, General Commercial.
Career: Inns of Court Law School,1974. Exeter University 1970-1973. Radley College.
Personal: Cross country mountain bike racing.

General Cable plc
37 Old Queen St, London SW1H 9JA
Tel: (0171) 393 2828 Fax: (0171) 393 2800
John Laver, Company Secretary

General Electric Co PLC
1 Bruton Street, London W1X 8AQ
Tel: (0171) 493 8484 Fax: (0171) 493 1974
Michael Lester, Vice Chairman

GKN PLC
PO Box 55, Redditch B98 0TL
Tel: (01527) 517715 Fax: (01527) 517700
Email: information@gknplc.com
No of lawyers in dept: 8
Grey Denham, Company Secretary
Reports to: The Chairman and the Chief Executive
Specialism: Overall responsibility for all secretarial and governance services provided to the listed parent company and other central companies; and for legal and compliance services in the group worldwide. Also Director GKN (United Kingdom) plc, GKN Industries Limited, GKN Group Services Limited and President GKN North America, Inc. Member of Council, Birmingham Chamber of Commerce and Industry, Member of London Stock Exchange Regional Advisory Group.
Career: 1972 – Lecturer in Law, Leicester Polytechnic; 1974 – Senior Lecturer in Legal Philosophy, Nottingham Law School; 1977 – Company Legal Officer, Alfred Herbert Limited; 1980 – Company Lawyer, GKN plc; 1983 Deputy Head of Legal, GKN plc; 1986 – Head of Legal, GKN plc; 1995 – Chairman, GKN Group Services Limited; 1996 – Company Secretary, GKN plc.
Personal: Educated – Handsworth Grammar School; Brooklyn Technical College; Bristol College of Commerce; London

University (LL.B.); Inns of Court Law School (called 1972); Columbia University Graduate School of Business (CSEP 1995). Leisure pursuits and interests include philosophy, particle physics, Warwickshire County Cricket Club, Aston Villa Football Club, cycling and playing tennis.

Rufus Ogilvie Smals, Head of Legal Department
Specialism: M&A, joint ventures, finance, strategic contracts (automotive component supply agreements, helicopter contracts and other defence contracts), litigation management, competition law and general company and commercial work.
Career: Read law at Emmanuel College, Cambridge University. Attended Inns of Court School of Law. Called to the Bar (Middle Temple) 1973. Studied at Europa Institute, University of Amsterdam. Joined GKN in 1975, from Deputy Head of the Legal Department to Head of the Group Legal Department in 1995. Chairman of CBI Competition Panel.
Other lawyers: David Lee: Deputy Head of Legal Dept; Chris Brown: Chief Legal Adviser – strategic contracts; David Radford: Principal Legal Adviser; Sarah Eddowes: Principal Legal Adviser; Sharon Ayers: Senior Legal Adviser; Martin Elliott: Senior Legal Adviser; Mark Beardmore: Legal Adviser.

Glaxo Wellcome plc
Glaxo Wellcome House, Berkeley Avenue, Greenford UB6 0NN
Tel: (0171) 493 4060 **Fax:** (0171) 966 8330
No of lawyers in dept: 10
Work outsourced: 15% – Corporate, specialist planning, insolvency, product liability, litigation and specialist competition (litigation).
Brian Cahill, Director, Group Legal Services
Reports to: Company Secretary
Specialism: Has management responsibility for commercial legal. Manages department providing an in-house corporate legal service to Glaxo Wellcome plc and its subsidiaries. Chairman of the Legal Committee of the Association of the British Pharmaceutical Industry (ABPI).
Career: Called to the Bar, Grays Inn 1977. Legal Adviser and Manager, Legal Department of ICL plc 1979-86, then took up present position.
Personal: Educated at Southampton University (LLB).

Glynwed International PLC
Headland House, New Coventry Road, Sheldon, Birmingham B26 3AZ
Tel: (0121) 742 2366 **Fax:** (0121) 742 0403
Philip Hudson, Head of Legal

Goldman Sachs International Limited
Peterborough Court, 133 Fleet Street, London EC4A 2BB
Tel: (0171) 774 1000 **Fax:** (0171) 774 4477
Gregory K. Palm, Head of Legal

Govett Strategic Inv Tst PLC
Shackleton House, 4 Battle Bridge Lane, London SE1 2HR
Tel: (0171) 378 7979 Fax: (0171) 638 3468
Eleanor Cranmer, Corporate Secretary

Granada Group Plc
13 Cleveland Row, London SW1A 1GG
Tel: (0171) 451 3000 **Fax:** (0171) 451 3008
Work outsourced: All legal work
Graham Parrott, Company Secretary
Specialism: Acquisitions/disposals, Pensions, Property, Insurance, Share schemes, Legal and Secretarial
Personal: Born 1949. Lives in London.

Great Portland Estates PLC
Knighton House, 56 Mortimer Street, London W1N 8BD
Tel: (0171) 580 3040 **Fax:** (0171) 631 5169
Carolyn Fryer, Company Secretary

Great Universal Stores PLC
Universal House, Devonshire Street, Manchester M60 6EL
Tel: (0161) 273 8282 **Fax:** (0161) 277 4952
Philip Harland, Head of Legal

Greenalls Group PLC
Legal Department, Wilderspool House, Greenalls Avenue, Warrington WA4 6RH
Tel: (01925) 651234 **Fax:** (01925) 244957
J. Alan Farquharson, Chief Legal Adviser

Greene King PLC
Westgate Brewery, Westgate Street, Bury St Edmunds IP33 1QT
Tel: (01284) 763222 Fax: (01284) 706502
Michael St John Shallow, Finance Director

Greenwich Natwest
8th Floor, 135 Bishopsgate, London EC2M 3UR
Tel: (0171) 375 5000 **Fax:** (0171) 334 1792
Christopher Georgiou, Associate Director, Legal and Documentation

Guardian Royal Exchange Assurance Plc
Royal Exchange, London EC3V 3LS
Tel: (0171) 696 5370 **Fax:** (0171) 621 2598
A.J. McDonald, Head of Legal

Halifax plc
Trinity Road, Halifax HX1 2RG
Tel: (01422) 333333 **Fax:** (01422) 333453
Email: halifax.legal@link.org
No of lawyers in dept: 21 solicitors/1 barrister/7 legal executives
Work outsourced: 20% – Treasury/m&a/some litigation/competition
Christopher Jowett, Group Solicitor
Specialism: litigation/competition/corporate,
Career: St. Peter's School, York. Sandhurst. Harvard.
Personal: Hobbies include Golf, cycling and skiing.
Other lawyers: 3 litigation; 5 property; 2 employment; 3 retail banking; 2 financial services; 2 commercial.

Halma plc
Misbourne Court, Rectory Way, Amersham HP7 0DE
Tel: (01494) 721111 **Fax:** (01494) 728032
E.C. Tredway, Company Secretary

Hambros Bank Limited
41 Tower Hill, London EC3N 4HA
Tel: (0171) 480 5000 **Fax:** (0171) 702 4424
Kerry Thomas, Company Secretary

Hammerson PLC
100 Park Lane, London W1Y 4AR
Tel: (0171) 887 1000 **Fax:** (0171) 887 1010
Stuart Haydon, Company Secretary

Hanson Plc
1 Grosvenor Place, London SW1X 7JH
Tel: (0171) 245 1245 **Fax:** (0171) 235 3455
No of lawyers in dept: 2
Work outsourced: Property Litigation
Graham Dransfield, Legal Director
Reports to: Chairman & Chief Executive.
Specialism: Company/ Commercial, Corporate Finances. Acting for the UK head office companies and UK subsidiaries in corporate and commercial activities. Property and litigation not dealt with in-house; legal structure operates on decentralised basis.
Career: Articled *Slaughter and May* 1974-82; Joined Hanson plc 1982, Legal Director since 1992.
Other lawyers: Samantha J. Hurrell.

Hardy Oil & Gas plc
10 Great George Street, London SW1P 3AE
Tel: (0171) 470 2200 **Fax:** (0171) 470 2305
Email: hardyoil.co.uk
No of lawyers in dept: 2
Work outsourced: 20% – Some corporate, litigation, competition.
Stephen Huddle, Head of Legal Affairs
Other lawyers: Adam Dann (Legal Manager).

Hays PLC
Hays House, Millmead, Guildford GU2 5HJ
Tel: (01483) 302203 **Fax:** (01483) 455242
No of lawyers in dept: 3
Work outsourced: 60% – Acquisitions/disposals of companies/businesses, major commercial contracts, employment, litigation, property, pensions
Stephen Charnock, Group Secretary
Specialism: Legal, company secretarial, share options, pensions.

Hazlewood Foods
Rowditch, Derby DE1 1NB
Tel: (01332) 295295 **Fax:** (01332) 292300
No of lawyers in dept: 1
Work outsourced: 75% – Corporate acquisitions and disposals, employment, litigation.
Charles Oliver, Assistant Company Secretary
Specialism: Commercial property (eg *Clifford Chance* property Lawyer), employment, commercial contracts, insurance, company secretarial responsibilites, employee benefits, executive renumeration. Corporate – acquisitions/disposals. Shareholder management.
Career: University of Bristol & College of Law, London. Park House School & St Bartholomew's School, both of Newbury, Berkshire. Also ACIB-qualified.
Personal: Keen golfer and tennis player. Countryside pursuits, theatre and cinema.

Henderson Administration PLC
3 Finsbury Avenue, London EC2M 2PA
Tel: (0171) 638 5757 **Fax:** (0171) 377 5742
Mark Phythian-Adams, Head of Legal and Compliance

Henderson Smaller Cos Inv Tst PLC
3 Finsbury Avenue, London EC2M 2PA
Tel: (0171) 638 5757 **Fax:** (0171) 377 5742
Sue Dickson, Company Secretary

Hepworth PLC
2 Cavendish Square, London W1M 9HA
Tel: (0171) 307 7700 **Fax:** (0171) 631 5444
Helen Grantham, Group Company Secretary

Hewden-Stuart PLC
Blantyre Road, Bothwell, Glasgow G71 8PJ
Tel: (01698) 853585 **Fax:** (01698) 854999
Alastair W. Deakin, Finance Director

Highland Distillers PLC
West Kinfauns, Perth PH2 7XZ
Tel: (01738) 440000 *Fax* (01738) 493789
Alan Mitchelson, Director and Company Secretary

Hillsdown Holdings Plc
Hillsdown House, 32 Hampstead High Street, London NW3 1QD
Tel: (0171) 794 0677 **Fax:** (0171) 433 6402
No of lawyers in dept: 1
Work outsourced: 50% – Acquisitions and disposals, litigation, banking.
Martin Chambers, Group Legal Adviser and Company Secretary
Reports to: Chairman
Specialism: Responsible for management and co-ordination of all major legal issues at parent and operating company level, including corporate "Yellow Book" work, intellectual property, M&A, joint ventures, employment, distribution and agency contracts, competition and commercial litigation. Member of Law Society Solicitors' European Group, Commerce and Industry Group and Food Law Group.
Career: Qualified 1975, while at *Clifford Turner*. Assistant solicitor with *McKenna & Co* 1975-77. European Legal Counsel to the Eaton Corporation 1977-83 and Group Legal Controller, Guinness plc 1983-88. Chief of Staff Business and Legal Affairs, House of Fraser Holdings plc 1988-90. European Legal Controller for the Albert Fisher Group plc 1991-93, then joined Hillsdown Holdings.

House of Fraser Plc
1 Howick Place, London SW1P 1BH
Tel: (0171) 963 2000 **Fax:** (0171) 828 8885
No of lawyers in dept: 1
Work outsourced: 30% – Property, litigation, some corporate/commercial
Peter Hearsey, Company Secretary

Career block (top right)

Specialism: Company secretarial. Corporate/commercial legal. Managing legal affairs and outsourced work. Insurance. Stock exchange. Registrars.
Career: 1998 – House of Fraser plc. 1997 – Graseby plc. 1992 – 97 Southern Electric plc. 1987 – 92 *Field Fisher Waterhouse*. 1983 – 86 Manchester University. 1976 – 83 St Batholomew's School, Newbury.

HSBC Holdings plc
10 Lower Thames Street, London EC3R 6AE
Tel: (0171) 260 0926 **Fax:** (0171) 260 9838
No of lawyers in dept: 34 (5 part-time)
Work outsourced: 60% – Major transactions, litigation.
Richard E.T. Bennett, Group Legal Adviser
Specialism: Responsible for the Legal & Compliance function of the HSBC Holdings Group.
Career: Bristol University (LL.B), graduated 1973. Qualified with *Stephenson Harwood*, 1976. Assistant Solicitor with *Stephenson Harwood* until 1979 (seconded to the East Asiatic Company, Denmark 1977). Appointed Assistant Group Legal Adviser with The Hong Kong & Shanghai Banking Corporation 1979. Deputy Group Legal Adviser 1988. Head of Legal & Compliance of the Hong Kong and Shanghai Banking Corporation Ltd 1993 with responsibility for legal, compliance and secretarial functions in Asia Pacific. Appointed to present position 1 January 1998.
Personal: Born 20th September 1951. Leisure pursuits include; all sports, particularly rugby and golf. Lives in Surrey/London.
Other lawyers: D J French, D Bloom (London); N Cave (Birmingham); K S Y Ng (Asia Pacific); A C Jackson (Australia); D J W Bagley (Middle East); Dr G Bittger (Germany); P S Toohey (USA); J F Root (Brazil).

Hyder PLC
Alexandra Gate, Rover Way, Cardiff CF2 2UE
Tel: (01222) 500600 **Fax:** (01222) 585600
Geoff Williams, Company Secretary/Group Legal Adviser

IBJ International
Bracken House, 1 Friday Street, London EC4M 9JA
Tel: (0171) 236 1090 **Fax:** (0171) 489 6997
No of lawyers in dept: 5
Brian Lanaghan, Head of Legal
Specialism: Fixed income and equity new issues, derivatives, funds, custody, investment management, futures, general advisory.
Career: George Watson's College, Edinburgh. The Perse School, Cambridge. (MA) English and Law, Cambridge.
Personal: Tennis, sailing, shooting, garden design, piano, languages; French (fluent), German (reasonable).

IMI PLC
Witton, PO Box 216, Birmingham B6 7BA
Tel: (0121) 356 4848 **Fax:** (0121) 356 3526
John O'Shea, Company Secretary

Imperial Chemical Industries PLC
9 Millbank, London SW1P 3JF
Tel: (0171) 834 4444 **Fax:** (0171) 834 2042
Email: www.ici@ici.com
No of lawyers in dept: 29
Michael H.C. Herlihy, General Counsel
Specialism: Oversees the lawyers in the Group and responsible for provision of legal advice to the ICI Board and all members of the ICI Group.
Career: Qualified in 1977. University – St. Catherine's College, Oxford. Joined ICI 1979; 1985-1992 Manager of Legal Affairs Department, ICI Agrochemicals; 1992-1995 Group Taxation Controller; 1996 to date General Counsel.
Other lawyers: R.J. Peters, Deputy General Counsel; A.R. Graham, Corporate Counsel; J.C.A. Fielding, Litigation Co-ordinator; D. Jash; M.A.J. Maughan; P. Roebuck; R.W.T. Turner, Group Intellectual Property Counsel; K J Rushton, Company Secretary; N R Paton; J L Kay, Manager; R Draper; G Fish; A K Gwynne-Jones; P Snaith; C M Vaughan; G G Attrill, Deputy Manager; J R Robey; G St John Turner; S M Turner; D J Aspinall, Senior Lawyer; J Goodfellow, Litigation Manager; W Shepherd, Legal Counsel; D J Busby, Company Secretary; J H Jones, Legal Affairs Manager; P Davies, Commercial Legal Manager; A Harbert; M McLean; B Moli.

Imperial Tobacco Limited
PO Box 244, Upton Road, Southville, Bristol BS99 7UJ
Tel: (0117) 963 6636 **Fax:** (0117) 963 7207
No of lawyers in dept: 3
Work outsourced: 90% – Corporate, M&A, Litigation, IP, Commercial
Alan Porter and **Charles Hamshaw-Thomas**, General Counsel
Other lawyers: Conrad Tate.

Inchcape Plc
33 Cavendish Sq, London W1M 9HF
Tel: (0171) 546 0022 **Fax:** (0171) 546 0010
Roy Williams, Group Company Secretary

Independent Insurance Group PLC
Fifth Floor, No 2 Minster Court, Mincing Lane, London EC3R 7BB
Tel: (0171) 623 8877 Fax: (0171) 283 8275
Alison Byrne, Group Solicitor

ING Barings
60 London Wall, London EC2M 5TQ
Tel: (0171) 767 1000/7 **Fax:** (0171) 767 7780
Ian Kellow, Head of Legal & Compliance

Inspec Group
Charleston Road, Hardley, Hythe, Southampton SO45 3ZG
Tel: (01703) 894666 **Fax:** (01703) 245257
Martin Stokes, Company Secretary

Investors Capital Trust PLC
1 Charlotte Square, Edinburgh EH2 4DZ
Tel: (0131) 225 1357 **Fax:** (0131) 225 2375
M.A. Campbell, Company Secretary

J Henry Schroder & Co Ltd
120 Cheapside, London EC2V 6DS
Tel: (0171) 658 6000 **Fax:** (0171) 658 6500
Francis Neate, Group Legal Adviser

J.P. Morgan & Co Incorporated
P O Box 161, 60 Victoria Embankment, London EC4Y 0JP
Tel: (0171) 600 2300 **Fax:** (0171) 325 8150
James Wickenden, Head of Legal

Jarvis PLC
Frogmore Park, Watton-at-Stone, Hertford SG14 3RU
Tel: (01920) 832800 **Fax:** (01920) 832832
Robert Kendall, Company Secretary

JBA Holdings PLC
27-28 Calthorpe Road, Edgbaston, Birmingham B15 1RP
Tel: (0121) 627 5151 **Fax:** (0121) 627 0039
David Williams, Company Secretary and Finance Director

JJB Sports PLC
Martland Park, Challenge Way, Wigan, Lancs WN5 0LD
Tel: (01942) 221400 **Fax:** (01942) 629809
John David Greenwood, Company Secretary & Finance Director

Johnson Matthey PLC
2-4 Cockspur Street, Trafalgar Square, London SW1Y 5BQ
Tel: (0171) 269 8400 **Fax:** (0171) 269 8476
Simon Farrant, Senior Legal Adviser

Johnston Press PLC
53 Manor Place, Edinburgh EH3 7EG
Tel: (0131) 225 3361 **Fax:** (0131) 225 4580
Richard Cooper, Company Secretary

Kalon Group PLC
Ploughland House, 62 George Street, Wakefield WF1 1DL
Tel: (01924) 330100 **Fax:** (01924) 330102
Richard Burgin, Company Secretary

Kingfisher Plc
North West House, 119 Marylebone Road, London NW1 5PX
Tel: (0171) 724 7749 **Fax:** (0171) 724 1160
No of lawyers in dept: 1
Work outsourced: 95% – Company commercial, trusts, competition, M&A, contracts, property, etc.
Helen Jones, Company Secretary/Head of Legal
Specialism: Company secretarial, compliance/regulatory, management of legal areas of M&A work. Co-ordination/management of major legal matters across the group's businesses. Control/monitoring of law firms' performance/quality control/monitoring of compliance with Group Policy.
Career: Qualified Chartered Secretary 1976. Initial graduate training at Coventry Climax in finance function followed by 2½ years with Ernst & Whinney in company secretarial function. Moved to Guinness plc in October 1979 and stayed until April 1987 – working in Company Secretary, Legal and Corporate Finance Departments – principally on the legal/company secretarial work of M&A transactions. 11 years with Kingfisher plc from April 1987. Initially as Assistant Company Secretary to Kingfisher. One year in Finance working on risk management, insurance and consumer credit followed by 3½ years at Woolworths – working in marketing, buying, logistics and change management before returning to Kingfisher in May 1995, formally taking the role of Group Company Secretary on 1st June 1995.

Kwik Save Group PLC
Warren Drive, Prestatyn LL19 7HU
Tel: (01745) 887111 **Fax:** (01745) 886494
Nicholas Fairclough, Company Secretary

Kwik-Fit Hldgs PLC
17 Corstorphine Road, Murrayfield, Edinburgh EH12 6DD
Tel: (0131) 337 9200 **Fax:** (0131) 337 0062
Ken McGill, Company Secretary

Ladbroke Group Property
Maple Court, Central Park, Reeds Crescent, Watford WD1 1HZ
Tel: (01923) 434000 **Fax:** (01923) 434001
Brian Godman Wallace, Finance Director

Laird Group PLC
3 St James's Square, London SW1Y 4JU
Tel: (0171) 468 4040 **Fax:** (0171) 839 2921
Dominic Hudson, Company Secretary
Career: 1984-86 articled *Ashurst Morris Crisp*. 1986 Qualified *Ashurst Morris Crisp*. 1990 Company Secretary, The Laird Group.

Land Securities PLC
5 Strand, London WC2N 5AF
Tel: (0171) 413 9000 **Fax:** (0171) 925 0202
Clive Ashcroft, Head of Legal

Laporte PLC
Nations House, 103 Wigmore Street, W1H 9AB
Tel: (0171) 399 2400 **Fax:** (0171) 399 2401
Email: nicksmith@laporteplc.com
No of lawyers in dept: 2
Work outsourced: M & A, Property, Litigation
Nicholas Smith, Company Secretary and Director of Legal Affairs.
Specialism: Corporate Finance, Company and Commercial.
Career: 1996/97 – General Counsel, Cronos S.A. 1984-94 Legal Director, Tiphook plc, 1983-84 Company Sec and Legal Adviser, Arrow plc, 1975-83 Solicitor, Smiths Industries plc.

LASMO PLC
101 Bishopsgate, London EC2M 3XH
Tel: (0171) 892 5103 **Fax:** (0171) 892 9261
Email: lasmo.com
No of lawyers in dept: 9
Work outsourced: public financing, property, litigation, some M&A and employment work.
Anthony Golding, Group General Counsel
Reports to: Chief Executive
Specialism: Principal areas of work are corporate finance and

M&A. Work includes takeovers, rights issues, Eurobonds and convertibles, US listing and securities issues and acquisitions and disposals of assets and companies. Member of UK Energy Lawyers Group.
Career: Qualified 1977. With Courtaulds plc 1975-80, The BOC Group plc 1981-85 and then joined LASMO plc.
Personal: Educated at Highgate School 1965-70 and Clare College, Cambridge 1971-74. Leisure pursuits include bridge, golf, squash and amateur operatics. Born 2 October 1952. Lives in Letchworth, Herts.

Lazard Brothers & Co., Limited
21 Moorfields, London EC2P 2HT
Tel: (0171) 588 2721 **Fax:** (0171) 628 2485
No of lawyers in dept: 1
Will Dennis, Company Secretary and General Counsel
Specialism: Corporate Finance, banking, stock lending, asset management, capital markets.
Career: Cambridge University 1971-74, MA LLM. Foreign & Commonwealth Office 1977-86. *Clifford Chance* 1987-91. Partner *Denton Hall* 1991-93. Director N M Rothschild & Sons (Hong Kong) Ltd 1993-96. Lazard Brothers since 1996.

Legal & General Group Plc
Temple Court, 11 Queen Victoria Street, London EC4N 4TP
Tel: (0171) 528 6200 **Fax:** (0171) 528 6222
Email: Liz Tubb – gblegctj@ibmmail.com
No of lawyers in dept: 2
Work outsourced: 2 % – Large corporate transactions and litigation.
Elizabeth Tubb, Group Legal Adviser
Specialism: Main areas of responsibility: corporate, acquisitions, sales, joint ventures, insurance law and investments. Advises the Group investment and general insurance business units. Group data protection co-ordinator.
Career: Called to the Bar 1986. Legal Adviser, Edasco Ltd 1986-89, then joined Legal & General Group.
Other lawyers: David Binding (Group Secretary).

Lehman Brothers Limited
One Broadgate, London EC2M 7HA
Tel: (0171) 260 2083 **Fax:** (0171) 260 2999
No of lawyers in dept: 10
Work outsourced: 20% – Litigation, services of underwriters' counsel, occasional specialist advice.
Piers Le Marchant, European Legal Director
Specialism: Equity and fixed income capital markets. Derivatives, emerging markets. Some investment banking and litigation. Chairman of the New Products Committee.
Career: Lehman Brothers from Dec 91. Previously Nomura International plc. Qualified as Barrister 1987. Educated London University & Canford School.

Lex Service PLC
Lex House, Boston Drive, Bourne End SL8 5YS
Tel: (01628) 843888 **Fax:** (01628) 810613
No of lawyers in dept: 2
Work outsourced: 90% – Major acquisition-divestments, litigation, property.
Mark Young, Company Secretary
Specialism: Company and commercial, including acquisitions, divestments, and joint ventures. Corporate governance. Employment, non-contentious. Share schemes and long term incentives.
Career: Solicitor of the Supreme Court (Nov 83). Solicitor's panel, Chester 1981. LL.B. degree University of Hull 1977-80.
Personal: Married. 1 son. Living in Barnet. Interests: watching all forms of sport, occasionally golf, swimming, jogging, theatre, cinema, dining out and rock music from the 60's – 80's.
Other lawyers: Bob Clark – commercial contracts, commercial litigation, employment, health and safety and environmental, consumer law, and acquisitions and divestments.

Liberty International Hldgs PLC
40 Broadway, London SW1H 0BT
Tel: (0171) 887 7000 **Fax:** (0171) 222 5554
Jeremy Bottle, Company Secretary

Limit PLC
Hasilwood House, 60 Bishopsgate, London EC2N 4AJ
Tel: (0171) 650 1000 **Fax:** (0171) 650 1010
Stephen T. Clews, Company Secretary

Lloyds TSB Group PLC
71 Lombard Street, London EC3P 3BS
Tel: (0171) 626 1500 **Fax:** (0171) 398 3988
Geoffrey Johnson, Group Chief Legal Advisor

Logica PLC
Stephenson House, 75 Hampstead Road, London NW1 2PL
Tel: (0171) 637 9111 **Fax:** (0171) 446 1937
David Walker, Group Legal Adviser

Lombard Bank Limited
Lombard House, 339 Southbury Road, Enfield EN1 1TW
Tel: (0181) 805 9797 **Fax:** (0181) 344 5601
No of lawyers in dept: 3
Roger E. Stevens, Head of Legal
Other lawyers: Stephen G. Byrne: Solicitor, Deputy Company Secretary; Mayoor Patel: Barrister.

London & Manchester Group PLC
Winslade Park, Exeter EX5 1DS
Tel: (01392) 282710 **Fax:** (01392) 219939
No of lawyers in dept: 3
Work outsourced: 10% – Varies
Tony Woodward, Group Solicitor
Specialism: Company/commercial, contracts I.T., financial services.
Career: Bristol University 72-75. Admitted 1978
Personal: Director:London and Manchester (Trustees) Ltd. ABI Home Service Legal Panel.
Other lawyers: Julie Walker, Property. Duncan Eardley, Employment, Pensions.

London Clubs Management Ltd
10 Brick Street, London W1Y 8HQ
Tel: (0171) 518 0000 **Fax:** (0171) 495 6919
Sherry Hutchison, Personnel Manager

London Forfaiting Co PLC
International House, 1 St Katharine's Way, London E1 9UN
Tel: (0171) 481 3410 **Fax:** (0171) 480 7626
Martin Palmer, Company Secretary

London International Group PLC
35 New Bridge Street, London EC4V 6BJ
Tel: (0171) 489 1977 **Fax:** (0171) 489 0962
No of lawyers in dept: 1
Work outsourced: Litigation, speciality IP, franchising.
Andrew Reynolds, Group Legal Adviser
Specialism: Principal areas of work involve in-house work relevant to a consumer products and medical device company which has a medium size R&D department. Also involved in contracts, acquisitions, disposals, licensing, EC, trade marks, patents, regulatory involvement and litigation. Overseas work for group of subsidiaries throughout the world. Integration of legal matters with group tax and treasury functions and company secretarial requirements.
Career: Printer: 1960-71; *Simmons & Simmons*: 1977-82; Licensing Adviser at ITT/STC UK, Patent Department: 1982-84; London International Group plc: 1984 to present.

Lonrho PLC
4 Grosvenor Place, London SW1X 7DL
Tel: (0171) 201 6000 **Fax:** (0171) 201 6100
Michael Pearce, Company secretary

LucasVarity – Lucas Electrical and Electronic Systems
Stratford Road, Solihull B90 4GW
Tel: (0121) 627 3939 **Fax:** (0121) 627 3981
No of lawyers in dept: 2
Paul M. Almond, Legal Director
Specialism: Overall responsibility for provision of legal advice to divisional businesses worldwide, including international mergers and acquisitions, joint ventures and collaborations,

intellectual property and commercial contracts of all types. Also addresses conferences on various topics.
Career: Qualified 1979. Assistant solicitor *Foster Baxter Cooksey* 1976-82. Joined Lucas Industries 1982; Head of Legal Department 1989; appointed Legal Director Electrical & Electronic Systems Division of LucasVarity plc 1997.
Other lawyers: R A Leier (USA).

Man (E D & F) Group PLC
Sugar Quay, Lower Thames Street, London EC3R 6DU
Tel: (0171) 285 3000 **Fax:** (0171) 621 0149
Peter Clarke, Company Secretary

Manchester United PLC
Old Trafford, Manchester M16 0RA
Tel: (0161) 872 1661 **Fax:** (0161) 873 7210
David Beswitherick, Company Secretary

Marks & Spencer Plc
Michael House, 37-67 Baker Street, London W1A 1DN
Tel: (0171)268 3587 **Fax:** (0171) 487 2679
Graham Oakley, Company Secretary & Group Legal Adviser

Marley PLC
7 Oakhill Road, Sevenoaks TN13 1NQ
Tel: (01732) 455255 **Fax:** (01732) 740694
Robert Beveridge, Company Secretary & Group Solicitor

Martin Currie Investment Management
Saltire Court, 20 Castle Terrace, Edinburgh EH1 2ES
Tel: (0131) 229 5252 **Fax:** (0131) 228 5959
No of lawyers in dept:3
Julian Livingston, Group Legal Director
Specialism: Development and ongoing servicing of investment funds; compliance; company secretarial; commercial contracts; client agreements.

Mayflower Corporation PLC
Mayflower House, London Road, Loudwater, High Wycombe HP10 9RF
Tel: (01494) 450145 **Fax:** (01494) 450607
Email: rlamb@mayf.co.uk
Internet: www. mayflowercorporation.com
Robin Lamb, Company Secretary

McKechnie PLC
Leighswood Road, Aldridge, Walsall WS9 8DS
Tel: (01922) 743887 **Fax:** (01922) 451045
Ross McDonald, Company Secretary

Medeva plc
10 St James's Street, London SW1A 1EF
Tel: (0171) 839 3888 **Fax:** (0171) 930 1516
No of lawyers in dept: 2
Work outsourced: 75% – Property, litigation, commercial contracts (some), employment, IP, corporate, banking.
Mark Hardy, Corporate Development and Group Legal Director
Specialism: Litigation management – UK & US. Pensions, insurance, employment, US securities issues.
Career: Poole Grammar School. King's College London. British Railways Board 1976-79. Perrier & Labesse, Jersey, 1979-81. *Stringer Saul* 1981-82. Medeva plc 1992 to date.
Personal: Interests: rugby, cars and music.
Other lawyers: John Murphy: company commercial.

MEPC PLC
Nations House, Wigmore Street, London W1H 9AB
Tel: (0171) 911 5300 **Fax:** (0171) 499 0650
D.B.J. Price, Company Secretary

Mercury European Priv Trust PLC
33 King William Street, London EC4R 9AS
Tel: (0171) 280 2800 **Fax:** (0171) 280 2820
Amanda Marsh, Company Secretary

Merrill Lynch Europe Limited
25 Ropemaker Place, London EC2Y 9LY
Tel: (0171) 867 2000 **Fax:** (0171) 867 4456
P. Jolowicz, General Counsel

Mersey Docks & Harbour Co

Maritime Centre, Port of Liverpool, Liverpool L21 1LA
Tel: (0151) 949 6000 **Fax:** (0151) 949 6300
No of lawyers in dept: 3
Work outsourced: litgation, major corporate, joint ventures
William Bowley, Director of Legal Services
Specialism: Responsible for all the Company's legal affairs and aspects of the company secretarial, insurance, claims and share registration sections. Principal areas of work are general company/commercial matters. Also handles shipping, property and environmental law and advises on litigation. Member of Law Society Commerce and Industry Group.
Career: Articled with *J. Frodsham & Sons*, St. Helens 1971-72 and solicitor 1973-74. Joined The Mersey Docks and Harbour Company in 1974 as an assistant solicitor. Became PA to the MD 1979, Principal assistant solicitor 1981, Company Secretary and Solicitor 1982 and Director of Legal Services 1991.
Personal: Educated at Prescot Grammar School, University of Bristol (LLB) and Guildford Law School. Born 6 October 1947.
Other lawyers: Henry Hrynkiewicz; property. Janet Fallon; litigation, commercial.

Meyer International Plc

Aldwych House, 81 Aldwych, London WC2B 4HQ
Tel: (0171) 400 8888 **Fax:** (0171) 400 8700
No of lawyers in dept: 2
Work outsourced: 35% – Major corporate acquisitions, and disposals, financing, conveyancing and litigation
Amanda Burton, Company Secretary
Specialism: Legal Company Secretarial, Pensions, Insurance & Risk Management, Environmental Issues, Administration of Group Human Resources, Internal & External Relations.
Career: Queen Ethelburga's 1970-1975. Bradford Girls Grammar 1975-1977. Durham University 1978-1981. Guildford Law College 1981-1982. *Slaughter and May* 1982-1986. Tiphook plc 1986-1990. Ratners Group plc 1990-1992. Meyer International 1992-1997. Director 1997-present.
Other lawyers: Denise Wills – all major areas.

MFI Furniture Group PLC

Southon House, 333 The Hyde, Edgware Road, Colindale, London NW9 6TD
Tel: (0181) 200 8000 **Fax:** (0181) 200 8636
Hamish Thomson, Company Sec/Director of Legal Services

Millennium & Copthorne Hotels plc

Victoria House, Victoria Road, Horley, Surrey RH6 7AF
Tel: (01293) 772288 **Fax:** (01293) 772345
David Alan Hancock, Company Secretary

Mirror Group Plc

One Canada Square, Canary Wharf, London E14 5AP
Tel: (0171) 293 3000 **Fax:** (0171) 293 3360
No of lawyers in dept: 10
Work outsourced: 60% – Corporate/Commercial Property, Employment, Pensions, Competition
Paul Vickers, Secretary and Group Legal Director
Specialism: All legal/regulatory matters affecting company.
Career: Current position since 1993. Previously assistant MD TV am. Secretary and Programme Lawyer TV am 1987-92.
Other lawyers: Charles Collier Wright – Company Commercial; Martin Crudace – Litigation; Marcus Partington – Litigation; Paul Mottlam – Litigation; Roger Skelsey – Contracts; Jane Hindman – TV Programmes; Matthew Day – TV Contracts; Chris Loweth – TV Programmes

Misys plc

Burleigh House, Chapel Oak, Salford Priors, Worcs WR11 5SH
Tel: (01386) 871373 **Fax:** (01386) 871045
Ross K. Graham, Corporate Development Director & Company Secretary
Specialism: Corporate Development (acquisitions, major contracts etc). Litigation. Pensions, insurances, etc.
Career: Qualified as a Chartered Accountant in 1969. Partner in *Arthur Young*, Birmingham 1981-87, with special responsibility for corporate recovery and development. Finance Director of Misys from June 1987 shortly after flotation, with a heavy involvement in the acquisition programme and managing the risk profile of the group.

Monks Inv Tst PLC

67 Lombard Street, London EC3P 3DL
Angus MacDonald, Deputy Compliance Officer

Monument Oil & Gas PLC

Kierran Cross, 11 Strand, London WC2N 5HR
Tel: (0171) 233 1966 **Fax:** (0171) 233 3476
No of lawyers in dept: 3
Work outsourced: 20% – Stock Exchange compliance; major corporate/finance litigation; competition, EC Law.
Laurence F. Fry, Legal Manager
Specialism: Oil and gas law and practice. Mergers and acquisitions.
Career: Barrister (Middle Temple). Attorney-at-Law (California Bar). University of Nottingham.
Other lawyers: Frances Boyd, Lisa Jones (trainee solicitor).

Morgan Crucible Co PLC

Morgan House, Madeira Walk, Windsor SL4 1EP
Tel:(01753) 837000 **Fax:** (01753) 850872
Peter Wilkins, Director of Legal Affairs

Morgan Stanley & Co International Limited

25 Cabot Square, Canary Wharf, London E14 4QA
Tel: (0171) 425 8000 **Fax:** (0171) 425 8971
Richard Rosenthal, Head of Legal and European General Counsel

Morrison (Wm) Supermarkets PLC

Hilmore House, Thornton Road, Bradford BD8 9AX
Tel: (01274) 494166 **Fax:** (01274) 494831
Martin Ackroyd, Finance Director

Murray Income Trust PLC

7 West Nile Street, Glasgow G1 2PX
Tel: (0141) 226 3131 **Fax:** (0141) 248 5420
Douglas Turnbull, Company Secretary

National Express Group PLC

Worthy Park House, Abbots Worthy, Winchester SO21 1AN
Tel: (01962) 888888 **Fax:** (01962) 888898
Paula Havard, Group Solicitor

National Farmers Union (England & Wales)

Agriculture House, 164 Shaftesbury Avenue, London WC2H 8HL
Tel: (0171) 331 7200 **Fax:** (0171) 331 7230
Email: nfu.legal@nfu.org.uk
Work outsourced: 90% – Litigation on behalf of Farmers with Agricultural Disputes.
Sally Stanyer, Chief Legal Adviser
Specialism: Litigation management (for the NFU's Legal Assistance Scheme) whereby financial support is offered by the trade association to assist farmers in litigation and mediation. Regulation; competition; judicial review; professional negligence.
Other lawyers:: In HQ: Jane Adderley – European Law, CAP subsidies of quotas, agricultural tenancies. Richard Vidal – Agricultural contracts, animal health and welfare, food safety. Iona Ind – Access, rights of way, water, easements, environmental and land issues. Regina Owusu – agricultural tenancies, livestock, common law. June O'Hanlon – legal research assistant. In regions: All litigation. Michelle Rossiter (East Anglia); Julie Ballard (East Midlands); Adrienne Patterson (NE region); Fiona Foster (NW region); Amanda Alexander (Wales region); Mark Whitehouse (W.Mids region); Colin Hall and Daryl Cowan (SE region); Clare Whitlock (Central region); Alayne Addy (SW region).

National Grid Group plc

National Grid House, Kirby Corner Road, Coventry CV4 8JY
Tel: (01203) 537777 **Fax:** (01203) 423678
Fiona B. Smith, Company Secretary

National Power PLC

Windmill Hill Business Park, Whitehall Way, Swindon SN5 6PB
Tel: (01793) 892066 **Fax:** (01793) 892525
No of lawyers in dept: 25
Work outsourced: 20% – International legal advice on projects. Major High Court litigation. Overflow.
Stuart Wheeler, Company Solicitor/Head of Legal Services
Specialism: Managing provision of legal services to National Power. Major projects both international and within the UK. Oil and gas interests.
Career: Educated at Cranleigh School, Bristol University. Articled *Park Nelson & Co*. Qualified 1975. Assistant solicitor *Slaughter and May*, 1975-76. Assistant Secretary Beecham International 1976-79. Negotiator Amoco Group, 1979-88. Lawyer Sunoll 1988-91. Company Solicitor, National Power 1991 to date.
Personal: Resides Wiltshire and London. Hobbies: riding and hunting.
Other lawyers: Claire Carless – international projects. Sally Barrett Williams – UK company/commercial. Gary Chapman – litigation. Simon Wells – property.

National Westminster Bank Plc

Drapers Gardens, 12 Throgmorton Avenue, London EC2N 2DL
Tel: (0171) 920 1024 **Fax:** (0171) 920 5446
William Enderby, Group Solicitor & Chief Legal Officer

Nationsbank N A

35 New Broad Street, London EC2M 1NH
Tel: (0171) 638 3333 **Fax:** (0171) 282 2241
Leonie Brown, Head of Legal

Newsquest PLC

Newspaper House, 34-44 London Road, Morden SM4 5BR
Tel: (0181) 640 8989 **Fax:** (0181) 646 3997
John Pfeil, Finance Director

Next PLC

Desford Road, Enderby, Leicester LE9 5AT
Tel: (0116) 286 6411 **Fax:** (0116) 284 8998
Email: @next.co.uk
No of lawyers in dept: 3
Work outsourced: Major corporate deals. Specialist litigation areas.
Peter Webber, Head of Legal Department
Specialism: Corporate, Commercial, Secretarial.
Career: Oundle School, Northants. Sheffield University. Head of Legal Dept – Next since 1987.
Other lawyers: R. Clayton – Commercial Property; Mrs C. Moody – Litigation, Employment; M. Davies – Property.

NFC Plc

66 Chiltern Street, London W1M 2LT
Tel: (0171) 317 0123 **Fax:** (0171) 224 2381
No of lawyers in dept: 1
Work outsourced: 70% – M&A, litigation, property, commercial.
Timothy Fallowfield, Director of Legal Sevices and Deputy Company Secretary.
Specialism: M&A, litigation, employment, commercial, international and joint ventures, secretarial.
Career: Oxford (St Edmund Hall); *Clifford Chance* 1988-94; NFC 1994 to present.

Nikko Bank

17-21 Godliman St, London EC4V 5NB
Tel: (0171) 528 7070 **Fax:** (0171) 329 3533
Morton Hall, Head of Legal

Nikko Europe PLC

55 Victoria Street, London SW1H OEU
Tel: (0171) 799 2222 **Fax:** (0171) 222 3130
No of lawyers in dept: 7
Work outsourced: 20% – Various
Kenneth Martin, Head of Legal

Nomura International Plc
Nomura House, 1 St Martin's-Le-Grand, London EC1A 4NP
Tel: (0171) 521 2000 **Fax:** (0171) 521 3575
Mr M. Kojiro and **Mr D. Mee**, Directors, Corporate Office Legal

Northern Foods PLC
Beverley House, St Stephen's Square, Hull HU1 3XG
Tel: (01482) 325432 **Fax:** (01482) 226136
No of lawyers in dept: 4
Work outsourced: 40% – Commercial conveyancing, corporate finance, litigation, employment, intellectual property.
Carol Williams, Head of Legal
Career: Qualified, 1985. 1985-87 Booth & Co (Leeds). 1987-90 Asda plc. 1990 to date Northern Foods.
Other lawyers: Jane Parker – commercial conveyancing; Dean Savage – company commercial; Judith Wyresdale – employment/litigation.

Northern Rock
Northern Rock House, Gosforth, Newcastle upon Tyne NE3 4PL
Tel: (0191) 285 7191 **Fax:** (0191) 279 4747
No of lawyers in dept: 4
Work outsourced: All mortgage possession, some treasury, commercial litigation and commercial conveyancing.
Colin Taylor, Chief Solicitor & Group Compliance Officer
Specialism: Managing the provision of legal services to the company. Responsible for financial services and general statutory compliance. Also in charge of the company's customer relations function.
Career: Howardian High School Cardiff (1969-71). Edington Comprehensive School (1971-74). Sheffield University (1974-77). Chester Law College (1977).
Personal: Newcastle United F.C., wine and beer (in that order).
Other lawyers: Peter Milligan – litigation; Phil Broadhurst – consumer credit, conveyancing and general work; Gwilym Williams – commercial conveyancing and contracts.

Norwich Union PLC
PO Box 89, Surrey Street, Norwich NR1 3DR
Tel: (01603) 622200 **Fax:** (01603) 681307
Internet: www.norwichunion.co.uk
No of lawyers in dept: 35
Work outsourced: Major corporate work and also claims litigation.
Graham Jones, Group Secretary & Head of Legal Services
Specialism: A good deal of time is involved in company secretarial activities and in managing the activities of the legal function. Principal areas of legal interests/activity are company law (including Yellow Book), regulatory law, company commercial and major litigation.
Career: BA Hons Degree in English from Manchester University 1972, admitted as solicitor in 1977, MBA from Loughborough University 1992.
Personal: Age 47. Married with two children and lives near Norwich.
Other lawyers: Company Secretary's Dept: Annette Howlett. Company Commercial: Richard Spicker, Linda Chandler, Stephen Gidney, Donna Harris, Andrew Hawker, Mrs Susan Killeen, Amanda Nichols. Litigation: Siobhan Leslie, Emily Benson, Simon Clay, William Lingwood, Andrew Mathews. Claims Litigation: Philip Parsons. Life & Pensions: Stephen Mann, Angus Eaton, Davis Fish, Fay Gammer, Anna Holkham, Clair Marshall, Kevin Willis. Mortgage Finance: Ian Benson, Bridget Archibald, Alwin Harmer, Richard Hewitt, Ian Holden, Paul Howlett, Anne Maskell, Christine Ragan, Andrea Woodhouse. Property Legal: Fiona Page, Sandra Godfrey, Victoria Metcalf.

Nycomed Amersham PLC
Amersham Place, Little Chalfont, Amersham HP7 9NA
Tel: (01494) 544000 **Fax:** (01494) 542266
No of lawyers in dept: 5
Work outsourced: 20% – Property, litigation, corporate acquisitions, employment.
Robert Allnutt, Group Legal Adviser and Company Secretary

Specialism: Responsible for provision of legal advice on general commercial matters, intellectual property and product liability
Career: Qualified 1979.
Other lawyers: Kevin Kissane, Gillian Mitchell, Sheena Ginnings, Sara Lovick.

Ocean Group plc
Ocean House, The Ring, Bracknell RG12 1AN
Tel: (01344) 744310 **Fax:** (01344) 710031
No of lawyers in dept: 5
Work outsourced: Major acquisitions and disposals; litigation; property; overseas work; construction.
Ian Goulden, Head of Legal
Specialism: Primary responsibility for all legal affairs within Ocean Group's world-wide logistics, marine and environmental businesses. Liaising with other in-house lawyers in the subsidiary businesses and, where appropriate, external advisors. Principal area of work is the handling or supervision of major acquisitions and disposals, and contracts.
Career: Nottingham High School and Merchant Taylor School – Crosby. University of Hull. Qualified 1978. 1978-1989 with Carter Hodge, ultimately as Partner. 1989 joined Ocean Group legal department. 1993-1997 Legal Director and Company Secretary, McGregor Cory Limited. 1997-appointed to present position.
Personal: Interests include reading, golf, sailing and music.

Orange Personal Communication Services
Great Park Road, Amondsbury Park, Bradley Stoke, Bristol BS32 4QJ
Tel: (01454) 624600 **Fax:** (01454) 624700
Christopher Groves, In-house Lawyer

P & O Group
78 Pall Mall, London SW1Y 5EH
Tel: (0171) 930 4343 **Fax:** (0171) 930 6042
No of lawyers in dept: 4
Michael Gradon, Head of Legal
Reports to: Group Managing Director
Specialism: Deals with acquisitions, disposals, joint ventures, financing and other major group matters.
Career: Qualified in 1983. With Slaughter and May 1981-86. Became P&O Group Legal Director in 1991 and Company Secretary in 1996.
Personal: Educated at Haileybury 1972-76 and Downing College, Cambridge 1977-80. Leisure interests include tennis and golf. Born 7th April 1959. Lives in Oxted, Surrey.

Pearson Television Ltd
1 Stephen Street, London W1P 1PJ
Tel: (0171) 691 6000 **Fax:** (0171) 691 6100
No of lawyers in dept: 7
Work outsourced: 75% – Drafting, all litigation.
Sarah Tingay, Director of Legal & Business Affairs
Reports to: Group Chief Executive
Specialism: Acquisitions and investments, major production deals. Member of Copinger society.
Career: Qualified 1980. Joined Thames Television in 1987 as Business Affairs assistant, becoming Company Secretary to Thames TV and Pearson TV in July 1993.
Other lawyers: Alex Lee, Jocelyn Pappenheim, Samiha Zaman, Frances Kitson, Nicola Parfitt.

Peel Holdings PLC
Quay West, Trafford Wharf Road, Manchester M17 1PL
Tel: (0161) 877 4714 **Fax:** (0161) 877 4715
Peter Hosker, Legal Director

Pentland Group PLC
Pentland Centre, Lakeside, Squires Lane, Finchley, London N3 2QL
Tel: (0181) 970 2417 **Fax:** (0181) 346 2700
Richard Stevens, Company Secretary

Perpetual PLC
47-49 Station Road, Henley-on-Thames RG9 1AF
Tel: (01491) 417000 **Fax:** (01491) 416000
Peter Gardner, Company Secretary

Persimmon PLC
Persimmon House, Fulford, York YO1 4RE
Tel: (01904) 642199 **Fax:** (01904) 610014
No of lawyers in dept: 5
Work outsourced: 40% – Corporate, property, litigation.
Neil Francis, Legal Director
Specialism: Residential housing land development, planning, employment.
Career: Kingston G.S.
Personal: Interests: Cricket, hockey, golf, football.
Other lawyers: N.P. Knight, G.K.E. Hale, J.B. Brockes, H. Williams.

PIC International Group PLC
100 George Street, London W1H 5RH
Tel: (0171) 486 0200 **Fax:** (0171) 486 2005
David Baxendale, Group Legal Adviser

Pilkington PLC
Prescot Road, St Helens WA10 3TT
Tel: (01744) 28882 **Fax:** (01744) 613329
John McKenna, Group Legal Adviser & Company Secretary

Pillar Property Investments PLC
Lansdowne House, Berkeley Square, London W1X 6HQ
Tel: (0171) 915 8000 **Fax:** (0171) 915 8001
Philip Martin, Company Secretary

PizzaExpress PLC
No 7 McKay Trading Estate, Kensal Road, London W10 5BN
Tel: (0181) 960 8238 **Fax:** (0181) 960 4792
Glen Thomlinson, Company Secretary

Polypipe PLC
Broomhouse Lane, Edlington, Doncaster DN12 1ES
Tel: (01709) 770000 **Fax:** (01709) 869000
Alan Cox, Company Secretary

Powell Duffryn PLC
Powell Duffryn House, London Road, Bracknell RG12 2AQ
Tel: (01344) 666800 **Fax:** (01344) 666811
Roger Lee, Company Secretary

PowerGen PLC
53 New Broad Street, London EC2M 1JJ
Tel: (0171) 826 2742 **Fax:** (0171) 826 2716
No of lawyers in dept: 10
Work outsourced: 40% – Project work/litigation/M&A/some property and corporate.
David Jackson, Company Secretary and General Counsel
Specialism: Has wide ranging responsibilities of a legal, secretarial and corporate nature, involved in the management of PowerGen as a "Top 100" company. Provides substantial advice on new regulatory environment, including preparation of cases for MMC reference. Substantially involved in business diversification through projects in UK and abroad relating to electricity generation, gas trading and pipelines and gas field ownership. Member of Executive Committee involved with day to day running of the business.
Career: Qualified 1977. Assistant solicitor with Barlow Lyde & Gilbert 1977-79 and to the Nestlé Company Ltd 1979-81. Assistant Group Legal Adviser to Chloride Group plc 1981-87. Legal Adviser, Matthew Hall plc 1987-89, then took up current position.
Personal: Educated at Merchant Taylors' School, Northwood and University of Bristol (LLB). Born 25 January 1953. Lives in Oxfordshire.
Other lawyers: Willie Gubbins: International; Henry Loweth: Gas; Fiona Stark: Corporate; Stephanie Hammond: Property; James Jones: UKE Production & Sales; Sara Vaughan: Competition; Mark Bygraves: CHP. Chantal Thomas, Susan Kitchin.

Powerscreen International PLC
Lower Cape, Warwick CV34 5DZ
Tel: (01926) 496066 **Fax:** (01926) 496049
Andrew Harris, Group Legal Adviser and Company Secretary

Premier Farnell PLC
Farnell House, Sandbeck Way, Wetherby, West Yorks
LS22 7DH
Tel: (01937) 587241 **Fax:** (01937) 580070
Ken Mullen, Group Secretary and General Counsel

Premier Oil PLC
23 Lower Belgrave Street, London SW1W 0NR
Tel: (0171) 730 1111 **Fax:** (0171) 730 4696
Claudia Keenan, Legal Counsel and Company Secretary

Provident Financial PLC
Colonnade, Sunbridge Road, Bradford BD1 2LQ
Tel: (01274) 731111 **Fax:** (01274) 722715
David Rees, Group Legal Adviser

Prudential Corporation Plc
142 Holborn Bars, London EC1N 2NH
Tel: (0171) 548 3737 **Fax:** (0171) 548 3191
Email: prudential.co.uk
No of lawyers in dept: 5
Work outsourced: 90% – Property, employment, venture capital
Peter Maynard, Director of Legal Services
Reports to: Chief Executive
Specialism: Heads a small team of commercial lawyers providing legal services to the Corporation and its subsidiaries. **Career:** 1971-74 University of Cambridge. 1975-82 *Slaughter and May*. 1982-84 *Clifford-Turner*. 1984-98 Hong Kong Bank Group. (1984-92 Legal Adviser Europe, 1992 Compliance Director, James Capel, 1993-95 President & CEO, James Capel Inc, New York, 1996-98 Deputy Group Legal Adviser, HSBC Group). 1998 Director, Group Legal Services, Prudential Corporation plc.
Other lawyers: N.Frudd, J Parker, D Green: company/commercial; D Higgins: pensions.

Racal Electronics PLC
Western Road, Bracknell RG12 1RG
Tel: (01344) 481222 **Fax:** (01344) 454119
Email: racal.legal@pobox-quza.com
No of lawyers in dept: 12
Work outsourced: 5-25% – Overseas, litigation agency work and major M&A transactions
David Whittaker, Group Legal Director and Company Secretary
Career: Ashton-under-Lyme Grammar School, University of Leeds (LLB, 1973). Interests include: Tennis, squash, snooker, theatre.
Personal: Commercial Law/Company Law, Property Law, Litigation.
Other lawyers: Company/commercial: Paul Moffatt (Group Solicitor), Howard Castle, Mike Sullivan, Steve Dunne, Martin Pagnamenta; Pensions: Fiona Richards, Lawrence Hammond; Property: Norman Casson, Brian Cowper; Litigation: Catriona Cairns, Sarah Howlett.

Railtrack Group PLC
Railtrack House, Euston Square, London NW1 2EE
Tel: (0171) 557 8000 **Fax:** (0171) 557 9000
No of lawyers in dept: 16
Work outsourced: 90% – Corporate, commercial, litigation, conveyancing, EC competition, banking, environmental, construction, employment.
Simon Osborne, Company Secretary and Solicitor
Specialism: Company secretarial, corporate governance, corporate and general advisory.
Career: LLB (Lond) 1970; Solicitor June 1973; articled *Goodman Derrick* 1971-73; Solicitor to British Railways Board 1986-93; Company Secretary and Solicitor Railtrack PLC 1993 to present.
Other lawyers: Commercial: Nigel Dewick, Kevin Lynch, Andrew James; litigation: Andrew Litherland, Richard Smith, Helen Potton, Sheena Stark (Scotland); Property/Parliamentary: Geoffrey Kitchener, Alison Parkinson, Iain Brown (Scotland), John Vaughan-Neil, Brian Spanswick, Anne Galewski, Asheesh Mehta-Hughes.

Rank Group PLC
6 Connaught Place, London W2 2EZ
Tel: (0171) 706 1111 **Fax:** (0171) 262 9886
John Dumbleton, Controller of Legal Services

Redrow Group
Redrow House, St David's Park, CH5 3PW
Tel: (01244) 520044 **Fax:** (01244) 520564
Email: @redrow.demon.co.uk
No of lawyers in dept: 6
Work outsourced: corporate
Rhiannon E. Walker, Company Secretary
Reports to: Group Managing Director
Specialism: Company secretarial, land acquisitions, options, over seeing major company deals.
Career: Howells School Denbigh. University College of Bangor. Partner with Kerfoot Owen (Private Practice). Joined Redrow in 1996.
Other lawyers: Iain Mason (Litigation), Mike Thorne, Karen Wallis, Nigel Turner, Geoff Dean.

Reed Elsevier (UK) Ltd
Reed House, 25 Victoria Street, London SW1H 0EX
Tel: (0171) 222 8420 **Fax:** (0171) 227 5799
Mr Mellon, Head of Legal

Rentokil Initial PLC
Felcourt, East Grinstead RH19 2JY
Tel: (01342) 833022 **Fax:** (01342) 835672
Robert Ward-Jones, Company Secretary and Legal Director

Reuters Holdings PLC
85 Fleet Street, London EC4P 4AJ
Tel: (0171) 250 1122 **Fax:** (0171) 542 5896
Simon Yencken, In-house Lawyer

REXAM PLC
114 Knightsbridge, London SW1X 7NN
Tel: (0171) 584 7070 **Fax:** (0171) 581 1149
No of lawyers in dept: 2
Work outsourced: large M&A transactions, litigation, conveyancing.
David William Gibson, Company Sec/Director of Legal Affairs
Reports to: Chairman and Chief Executive
Specialism: Company and commercial, company secretarial, intellectual property, insurance, property and Head Office personnel. Member of the Law Society.
Career: Qualified as a Solicitor in 1987. Assistant Solicitor with *Alsop Wilkinson* 1987-1989. Company Solicitor with Rexam PLC (formerly Bowater plc) 1989-1995.
Other lawyers: Philip Venner.

Rio Tinto Plc
6 St James's Square, London SW1Y 4LD
Tel: (0171) 930 2399 **Fax:** (0171) 930 3249
Charles Lawton, Head of Legal

RIT Capital Partners PLC
27 St James's Place, London SW1A 1NR
Tel: (0171) 493 8111 **Fax:** (0171) 493 5765
David Wood, Company Secretary

RMC Group plc
RMC House, Coldharbour Lane, Thorpe, Egham TW20 8TD
Tel: (01932) 568833 **Fax:** (01932) 561792
No of lawyers in dept: 6
Michael Collins, Head of UK Legal Department
Reports to: Company Secretary
Specialism: Town & Country Planning, competition, transactional work.
Career: LL.B (Birmingham University), Solicitor, Prior to RMC, extensive County Council experience.
Personal: Married.
Other lawyers: Property: Ian Hoddy, Stephen Bottle, Andrew Smith, Martin Hicks; Litigation/Environmental: Andrew Jackson.

Robert Fleming & Co Limited
25 Copthall Avenue, London EC2R 7DR
Tel: (0171) 638 5858 **Fax:** (0171) 588 7219
Christopher Crouch, Head of Legal

Rolls-Royce Plc
65 Buckingham Gate, London SW1E 6AT
Tel: (0171) 222 9020 **Fax:** (0171) 227 9170
Brian Baker, General Counsel

Rothschild Asset Management Limited
Five Arrows House, St Swithins Lane, London EC4N 8NR
Tel: (0171) 280 5000 **Fax:** (0171) 634 2814
Elizabeth Horner, In-house Lawyer

Royal & Sun Alliance Property Investments
1 Bartholomew Lane London EC2N 2AB
Tel: (0171) 588 2345
David Morgan, UK Director, Legal & Compliance Services

Royal Bank of Canada
71/71A Queen Victoria Street, London EC4V 4DE
Tel: (0171) 489 1188 **Fax:** (0171) 329 6138
I. Mangat, Head of Legal

Royal Bank of Scotland Group PLC
Corporate Banking – City Unit 2, 3rd Floor,
62–63 Threadneedle Street, London EC2R 8LA
Tel: (0171) 623 4356
Derek Arnott, Group Legal Adviser

Rugby Group PLC
Crown House, Rugby CV21 2DT
Tel: (01788) 542666 **Fax:** (01788) 540256
Lyndon Hill, Director of Corporate and Legal Affairs

Safeway PLC
6 Millington Road, Hayes UB3 4AY
Tel: (0181) 848 8744 **Fax:** (0181) 756 1069
J.P. Kinch, Company Secretary

The Sage Group PLC
Sage House, Benton Park Road, Newcastle-upon-Tyne NE7 7LZ
Tel: (0191) 255 3000 **Fax:** (0191) 255 0306
Rupert Wyndam, Company Secretary

Sainsbury (J) PLC
Stamford House, Stamford Street, London SE1 9LL
Tel: (0171) 695 7468 **Fax:** (0171) 695 0011
David Thurston, Head of Group Legal Services

Salomon Smith Barney
Victoria Plaza, 111 Buckingham Palace Road, London SW1W 0SB
Tel: (0171) 721 2000 **Fax:** (0171) 222 7062
Kyra Bergin, Managing Director & Counsel

Sanwa International plc
City Place House, PO Box 245, 55 Basinghall Street, London EC2V 5DJ
Tel: (0171) 330 0300 **Fax:** (0171) 330 0420
No of lawyers in dept: 3
Work outsourced: 30% – Documentation for bond issues and securitizations.
Mark Seabrooke, Legal Director
Specialism: Banking and capital markets, fund management, corporate, commercial, employment, compliance and regulation.
Career: 1984-86 Articles, *Stephenson Harwood*. 1986-88 JP Morgan Securites Ltd. 1988 to present, Sanwa International plc.
Personal: Leeds University (1981 LLB). Magdalene College, Cambridge University (1984 LLM).
Other lawyers: Sorrel Coni, Charlotte Strickland.

Savoy Hotel PLC
1 Savoy Hill, London WC2R 0BP
Tel: (0171) 836 1533 **Fax:** (0171) 379 5421
Peter Begg, Company Secretary

Scapa Group PLC
Oakfield House, 93 Preston New Road, Blackburn BB2 6AY
Tel: (01254) 580123 **Fax:** (01254) 51764
Work outsourced: 95% – Mainly acquisitions and disposals.
Alan Wallwork, Company Secretary
Specialism: Company Commercial, Yellow Book, Compliance, Acquisitions/ Disposals, Insurance, Pensions.

Career: Formerly Company Secretary of J.Lyons & Co Ltd.1986-1996. BSc (Econ) University of London. FCIS. Married with 2 children.

Scottish & Newcastle PLC
111 Holyrood Road, Edinburgh EH8 8YS
Tel: (0131) 556 2591 **Fax:** (0131) 557 1457
No of lawyers in dept: 3
H. Andrew S. Vellani, Group Legal Adviser
Specialism: Responsible for the provision of legal services to the Scottish & Newcastle plc group of companies. Work includes company/commercial, EEC and domestic competition law (including related regulatory advocacy); joint ventures; intellectual property; acquisitions and disposals; beer supply agreements; brewing, packaging and distribution agreements; trading law (including food labelling, advertising and promotion).
Career: Kings College, Cardiff; Staffordshire University (LLB Hons); the Inns of Court School of Law, London; called to the Bar (Middle Temple) 1981. Admitted as solicitor 1991. Assistant commercial and legal adviser – Heating and Ventilating Contractors Association (Construction and Engineering Law) 1982; Assistant Group Secretary/Group Legal Adviser – The Kenneth Wilson Group (Commodity Trading Law) 1984; Group Legal Adviser – Scottish & Newcastle plc 1986 to date. Other positions held: Company Secretary – Scottish & Newcastle Breweries Ltd (re-named Scottish Courage Ltd 1995) 1990 to date. Secretary: The Fosters European Partnership.
Personal: Born 1957, resides in Edinburgh. Interests include overseas travel, music and reading.

Scottish Hydro-Electric PLC
10 Dunkeld Road, Perth PH1 5WA
Tel: (01738) 455040 **Fax:** (01738) 455045
No of lawyers in dept: 6
Work outsourced: 25% – Litigation, major projects, acquisitions, employment law, competition law.
Vincent Donnelly, Company Secretary
Specialism: Legal, insurance, company secretarial, property, administration.
Career: LLB-Glasgow University 1976. ACIS-1982. Cranfield Business School-Senior Management Programme-1996.
Personal: Married, 3 children. Resides Edinburgh.

Scottish Media Group PLC
Cowcaddens, Glasgow G2 3PR
Tel: (0141) 300 3300 **Fax:** (0141) 300 3033
Dawn Davidson, Company Secretary

Scottish Mortgage & Trust PLC
1 Rutland Court, Edinburgh EH3 8EY
Tel: (0131) 222 4000 **Fax:** (0131) 222 4488
Elizabeth Valentine, Compliance Officer

Scottish Power PLC
1 Atlantic Quay, Glasgow G2 8SP
Tel: (0141) 248 8200 **Fax:** (0141) 248 8300
James Stanley, Legal Director

Sears PLC
40 Duke Street, London W1A 2HP
Tel: (0171) 200 5999 **Fax:** (0171) 200 5850
David Drum, Company Secretary

Second Alliance Trust PLC
Meadow House, 64 Reform Street, Dundee DD1 1TJ
Tel: (01382) 201700 **Fax:** (01382) 22533
Sheila Ruckley, Company Secretary

Securicor PLC
Sutton Park House, 15 Carshalton Road, Sutton SM1 4LD
Tel: (0181) 770 7000 **Fax:** (0181) 770 1145
No of lawyers in dept: 6
Work outsourced: 15% – Litigation, property, major corporate M&A.
Nigel Griffiths, Group Legal Director
Specialism: Contract, insurance, property, employment, commercial, M & A and international.
Career: Educated at Whitgift School and Liverpool University –

LLB (Hons) 1968. Qualified as a solicitor in 1971. Securicor since 1973.
Other lawyers: Peter David: company and commercial; Angus Gribbon: company and commercial; Stephen Lyell: commercial and international; Roger Whetnell: employment.

Sedgwick Group PLC
Sedgwick House, The Sedgwick Centre, London E1 8DX
Tel: (0171) 377 3456 **Fax:** (0171) 377 3131
Alice Prosser, Senior Legal Adviser

Sema Group plc
Fulcrum House, 2 Killick Street, London N1 9AZ
Tel: (0171) 830 4213 **Fax:** (0171) 830 4206
Email: @sema.co.uk
No of lawyers in dept: 8
Work outsourced: 10% – Property, pensions, litigation, some M&A.
Andrew Vos, Group Legal Advisor
Specialism: Covering Sema Group UK, BAe Sema, Sweden, USA, Sema's worldwide Telecoms business and its Asia Pacific outsourcing business. Overall responsibility for all legal matters including major corporate legal advice, acquisitions, joint ventures and disposals. General outsourcing, systems integration and software licensing transactions. Major transactions have included international outsourcing, Telecoms contracts and UK & European acquisitions (eg BR Business Systems, Syntax Italy).
Career: Called to the Bar 1978 (Grays Inn), Barrister in Common Law Chambers, Manchester 1978-89, Legal Adviser to IBM UK Ltd 1990, then Senior Legal Adviser and Company Secretary, Integrated Systems Solutions Co Ltd. Joined Sema Group in 1995.
Other lawyers: Rachel Corder: outsourcing, employment; Mark Porter: business systems; David Wilson: telecoms; Mark Thomas: business systems; Elise Campbell: telecoms.

Senior Engineering Group PLC
Senior House, 59/61 High Street, Rickmansworth WD3 1RH
Tel: (01923) 775547 **Fax:** (01923) 896027
Frank H. Fermor, Group Company Secretary

Seton Scholl Healthcare PLC
Tubiton House, Oldham OL1 3HS
Tel: (0161) 621 2222 **Fax:** (0161) 621 2662
Work outsourced: All
Roger Gould, Company Secretary
Specialism: Stock exchange, company registration, pensions, share schemes, legal.
Career: Oxford MA in law, 1962. ACA/FCA 1966-1976. CI Management.

Severn Trent Water Ltd
2297 Coventry Road, Birmingham B26 3PU
Tel: (0121) 722 4000 **Fax:** (0121) 722 4228
No of lawyers in dept: 6
Work outsourced: 10% – M&A, some conveyancing/litigation.
Michael Knight, Head of Legal

Shell UK Limited
Shell Mex House, Strand, London WC2R 0DX
Tel: (0171) 257 1866 **Fax:** (0171) 257 3303
No of lawyers in dept: 23
Work outsourced: 15% – Litigation and major acquisitions.
Richard Wiseman, Legal Director
Specialism: Handles mainly company and commercial matters and joint ventures. Shell UK Ltd is an integrated oil company with substantial upstream interests in the North Sea as well as two refineries, a complex distribution network and some 1,500 dealer-owned and company-owned filling stations. The Legal Department is responsible for advising all of those businesses and the businesses of its subsidiary, Shell Chemicals UK Ltd.
Career: Qualified in 1974 (England) and 1984 (Victoria, Australia). Has held a number of legal posts in various companies in the Royal/Dutch Shell Group, including Shell International and Petroleum Limited and the Shell Company of Australia.
Other lawyers: Property and Planning Law: Ms Janet Batey, Mr Martin Files, Mrs Linda Bitmead, Mr Christopher Lawlor, Mrs Ali-

son Merrington, Ms Clare Reader. Refining, Distribution and Marketing Law: Mr Keith Ruddock, Mr Howard Taylor, Miss Vicki Palmer, Mr Alan Williams, Mr Adrian Dewey, Mr Mike Curless, Ms Joanne Crompton, Miss Dawn Lewendon. Upstream Oil and Gas Law: Mr Campbell, Mr Ashwin Maini, Mrs Kerrie-Lee Magill, Miss Teena Grewal, Mrs Rachel Fox, Ms Lucy Sparrow, Mrs Karin Hawkins, Mr Nanne van 't Riet, Mrs Sarah Hyde.

SIBA Specialty Chemicals
Cleckheaton Road, Low Moor, Bradford BD12 0JZ
Tel: (01274) 671267 **Fax:** (01274) 606499
Paul Wilson LL B (Hons), Company Secretary

Siebe PLC
Saxon House, 2/4 Victoria Street, Windsor SL4 1EN
Tel: (01753) 855411 **Fax:** (01753) 622030
Richard Paul Atwell Coles, Director of Legal Affairs/Co. Secretary

SIG PLC
Hillsborough Works, Langsett Road, Sheffield S6 2LW
Tel: (0114) 285 6300 **Fax:** (0114) 285 6395
Francis Prust, Company Secretary

Slough Estates PLC
234 Bath Rd, Slough SL1 4EE
Tel: (01753) 537171 **Fax:** (01753) 672662
Robert G. May, Legal Supervisor

Smith & Nephew PLC
2 Temple Place, Victoria Embankment, London WC2R 3BP
Tel: (0171) 836 7922 **Fax:** (0171) 240 7088
Email: @lo.plc.smith-nephew.com
No of lawyers in dept: 1
Work outsourced: 100% – Various
Michael G. Parson, Group Company Secretary & Legal Adviser
Reports to: Chief Executive.
Career: Qualified in 1965. Legal Department, Cunard/Trafalgar House plc 1970-75. Group Legal Director, Mass Transit Corporation, Hong Kong 1975-85. Group Secretary and Legal Adviser, Bowater plc 1987-91. Has held present position since March 1991.
Personal: Educated at Durham University (LLB) 1958-61. Born 24 October 1940.

Smith (W.H.) Group PLC
Nations House, 103 Wigmore Street, London W1H 0WH
Tel: (0171) 409 3222 **Fax:** (0171) 514 9633
Ian Haughton, Director of Legal Services

SmithKline Beecham PLC
New Horizons Court, Brentford TW8 9EP
Tel: (0181) 975 2000 **Fax:** (0181) 975 2040
No of lawyers in dept: 90
James R. Beery, Senior Vice President, General Counsel and Corporate Secretary
Reports to: Chief Executive and Chairman
Specialism: Responsible for the management of the legal function and provision of legal advice and support at all levels to SmithKline Beecham.
Career: Associate, *Cleary Gottlieb Steen & Hamilton*, New York 1971-73 and London office 1975-76. Foreign legal consultant to Nagashima & Ohno Tokyo 1973-75. Partner with *Erickson & Morrison* (London office) 1977-79 and Managing Partner, *Morrison & Foerster* (London office) 1980-92. Joined SmithKline Beecham in January 1994.

Smiths Industries PLC
765 Finchley Road, London NW11 8DS
Tel: (0181) 458 3232 **Fax:** (0181) 458 4380
Alan Smith, Head of Legal

Société Générale
Exchange House, Primrose Street, Broadgate, London EC2A 2HT
Tel: (0171) 762 4444 **Fax:** (0171) 762 4555
Mark Nimmo, Head of Legal

Somerfield Holdings Limited
Somerfield House, Whitchurch Lane, Bristol BS14 0TJ
Tel: (0117) 935 9359 **Fax:** (0117) 978 0629
No of lawyers in dept: 1
Work outsourced: Some commercial, litigation, property.
Susan Jepson, Company Solicitor
Specialism: Commercial, including some IT/IP and advertising and promotional law.
Personal: MA (Cantab).

South West Water PLC
Peninsula House, Rydon Lane, Exeter EX2 7HR
Tel: (01392) 446688 **Fax:** (01392) 434966
Email: @south-west-water.co.uk
No of lawyers in dept: 10
Work outsourced: 10% – Specialist banking and major litigation.
Kenneth D. Woodier, Group Company Secretary and Solicitor
Reports to: Group Company Secretary
Specialism: Company/commercial, litigation, competition, property, contract/procurement, environmental and employment.
Career: Management (business) prior to qualifying as a solicitor. Articles with Severn Trent Water. Legal Adviser with Investors in Industry plc (3i). Group legal manager with HP Bulmer Holdings plc and Group Legal Adviser with South West Water PLC. 15 years in legal practice.
Other lawyers: Andrew Matthews, John Jelley, Alan Roberts, Alan Podger, John Viney, Dr Buckingham, Rachael King.

Southern Electric plc
Southern Electric House, Westacott Way, Littlewick Green, Maidenhead SL6 3QB
Tel: (01628) 822166 **Fax:** (01628) 584400
No of lawyers in dept: 6
Work outsourced: 10% – Commercial, conveyancing, corporate.
Hazel Walker, Company Secretary and Director of Legal Services
Other lawyers: Tim Winson, conveyancing; Melissa Kirker, commercial/litigation.

Spirax-Sarco Engineering PLC
Charlton House, Cirencester Road, Cheltenham GL53 8ER
Tel: (01242) 521361 Fax: (01242) 581470
Peter Smith, Company Secretary

St. James's Place Capital PLC
J. Rothschild House, Dollar Street, Cirencester, Glos GL7 2AQ
Tel: (01285) 640302 **Fax:** (01285) 653993
No of lawyers in dept: 2
Work outsourced: 10% – Property, litigation, debt collection, major transactions.
Hugh Gladman, Legal & Compliance Director
Specialism: Director in charge of the legal and compliance departments, overseeing the work completed and managing the departments and, in addition, handling the following areas: corporate finance work/large commercial agreements/IT purchases/litigation/share schemes.
Career: LLB Southampton University. 1986-93 *Herbert Smith* (including articles). 1993-94 *Hammond Suddards*. 1994 to date J.Rothschild Assurance.
Personal: Hobbies include tennis and other sports, film, theatre and family.
Other lawyers: Catherine Thearle – company/commercial.

St.Ives PLC
St Ives House, Lavington Street, London SE1 0NX
Tel: (0171) 928 8844 **Fax:** (0171) 928 0617
Philip Harris, Company Secretary

Stagecoach Holdings PLC
Charlotte House, 20 Charlotte Street, Perth PH1 5LL
Tel: (01738) 442111 **Fax:** (01738) 643648
Derek Scott, Company Secretary

Stakis PLC
3 Atlantic Quay, York Street, Glasgow G2 8JH
Tel: (0141) 204 4321 **Fax:** (0141) 204 3366
No of lawyers in dept: 1
Work outsourced: 90% – All except basic contracts etc.
Simon Hodges, Company Secretary
Other lawyers: Jane Laird joined Stakis in February as Assistant Company Secretary. She came from a corporate finance background which was thought very useful for the type of work she would be doing at Stakis. Stakis prefer to use external advisers rather than have in-house lawyers.

Standard Chartered PLC
1 Aldermanbury Square, London EC2V 7SB
Tel: (0171) 280 7021 **Fax:** (0171) 280 7112
Martin Hayman, Head of Legal
Specialism: Also Company Secretary and has responsibility for Compliance. The Legal Department provides a service to the Standard Chartered Group on issues which are material in a group context, including M&A, corporate and major litigation.
Career: Cambridge University (Law) followed by private practice at The Plessey Company, ITT and Pullman Kellogg. Joined Cadbury Schweppes in 1978 first as Group Legal Adviser and then from 1985 as Secretary and Group Legal Adviser before joining Standard Chartered in May 1998.
Personal: Interested in developing client focus amongst private practice, the development of ADR and global compliance management.

Storehouse PLC
Marylebone House, 129-137 Marylebone Road, London NW1 5QD
Tel: (0171) 262 3456 **Fax:** (0171) 262 4740
Guy Johnson, Company Secretary

Stuart Ivory & Co Ltd
45 Charlotte Square, Edinburgh EH2 4HW
Tel: (0131) 226 3271 **Fax:** (0131) 226 5120
James E. Ayling, Company Secretary

Sumitomo Bank Ltd
11 Queen Victoria Street, London EC4N 4TA
Tel: (0171) 786 1000 **Fax:** (0171) 236 0049
P. Martyn, Compliance Officer

Sun Life & Provincial Holdings PLC
107 Cheapside, London EC2V 6DU
Tel: (0171) 606 7788 **Fax:** (0171) 378 1865
Phil Wiles, Group Legal Advisor

Tarmac PLC
Hilton Hall, Hilton Lane, Essington, Wolverhampton WV11 2BQ
Tel: (01902) 307407 **Fax:** (01902) 307408
Internet: http://www.tarmac.co.uk
No of lawyers in dept: 1
Work outsourced: 70% – Extensive litigation, arbitration, some conveyancing, major disposals, acquisitiions.
Dirk FitzHugh, Group Legal Adviser
Reports to: Group Chief Executive.
Specialism: Advises Tarmac plc on Group matters, monitors Business Group Legal Departments and supervises major issues including acquisitions and disposals. The legal services have been decentralised so that lawyers are allocated to the operating business groups which fall into two streams: heavy building materials and construction services.The lawyers heading the legal departments within the Business Streams and Groups are: Tarmac Heavy Building Materials: JR Stirk, Company Secretary and Solicitor. Markfield (Insurance Brokers) Ltd, D Horovitz, J Perrott (Professional Services and Social Housing), J Hobbs (UK Civils), P Collie (M&E): J Molteno (International); RA Fink (Tarmac America).
Career: Qualified 1968. Nicholas Williams & Co 1964-71 becoming partner 1969, John Mowlem & Co Legal Department 1971-73. Joined Tarmac plc 1973; Director/Secretary Tarmac International Ltd 1977-78; Secretary Tarmac Construction Ltd 1984; Group Legal Adviser 1992.

Tate & Lyle PLC
Sugar Quay, Lower Thames Street, London EC3R 6DQ
Tel: (0171) 626 6525 **Fax:** (0171) 623 5213
Robert Gibber, Senior Lawyer

Taylor Woodrow PLC
4 Dunraven Street, London W1Y 3FG
Tel: (0171) 629 1201 **Fax:** (0171) 493 1066
Richard Morbey, Company Secretary

TBI PLC
159 New Bond, London W1Y 9PA
Tel: (0171) 355 2345 **Fax:** (0171) 491 2378
Stephen Marshall, Company Secretary

Telewest Communications PLC
Genesis Business Park, Albert Drive, Woking GU21 5RW
Tel: (01483) 750900 **Fax:** (01483) 750901
Victoria Hall, Company Secretary

Templeton Emerging Markets Investment Trust PLC
Saltire Court, 20 Castle Terrace, Edinburgh EH1 2EH
Tel: (0131) 469 4000 **Fax:** (0131) 228 4506
Email: ukinfo@templeton.com
No of lawyers in dept: 5
Work outsourced: 15% – Corporate finance
Peter Arthur, In-house Lawyer
Specialism: Chief Legal Counsel, Europe. Manages delivery of European Legal Services. Company Secretary of Templeton Investment Management Ltd, Templeton Global Investors Limited and Templeton Unit Trust Managers Limited. Member of the European Management team.
Career: LLB (University of Edinburgh) 1977. Solicitor (Law Society of Scotland) 1980. F.C.I.S, Institute of Chartered Secretaries and Administrators 1990
Personal: Golf, skiing and rugby (as spectator).
Other lawyers: Nigel Austin – focus on Continental European Legal issues; Jacqueline Cave – manages Luxembourg Legal Operations; Ken Linton – delivery of European Legal Services. Sara MacIntosh – Group Company Secretarial Operations.

Tesco PLC
Tesco House, P.O.Box 18, Delamare Road, Cheshunt EN8 9SL
Tel: (01992) 632222 **Fax:** (01992) 644481
John Longworth, Head of Legal

Thames Water PLC
14 Cavendish Place, London W1M 9DJ
Tel: (0171) 636 8686 **Fax:** (0171) 436 6755
Janet M. Ravenscroft, Assistant Company Secretary

Thistle Hotels PLC
2 The Calls, Leeds LS2 7JU
Tel: (0113) 243 9111 **Fax:** (0113) 244 5555
Graham Howden, Company Secretary

Thorn PLC
Thorn House, 124 Bridge Road, Chertsey, Surrey KT16 8LZ
Tel: (01932) 573725 **Fax:** (01932) 573825
Work outsourced: 80% – Major corporate transactions
G. M. Smith, Company Secretary
Specialism: Secretarial and general corporate commercial legal advice including IT and IP.
Career: 1976-80 *Slaughter and May*, 1980-81 BOC International, 1981-88 British Olivetti Ltd, 1988-96 Thorn EMI plc, 1996 to date current position.

TI Group PLC
Lambourn Court, Abingdon OX14 1UH
Tel: (01235) 555570 **Fax:** (01235) 555818
Stephen Clarke, Director of Legal Affairs
Other lawyers: Guy Norris, David Lillicrop.

Tokai Bank Europe Ltd
1 Exchange Square, London EC2A 2JL
Tel: (0171) 638 6030 **Fax:** (0171) 588 5875
David Haig, Head of Legal & Compliance Depts.
Other lawyers: Mary Verghese–Dipple, Helleena O'Connor, Jackie Rylance.

Tomkins PLC
East Putney House, 84 Upper Richmond Road, London SW15 2ST
Tel: (0181) 871 4544 **Fax:** (0181) 877 9700
Simon Webber, Director of Corp Devel & Legal

Trinity International Holdings PLC
Kingsfield Road, Chester Business Park, Chester CH4 9RE
Tel: (01244) 687000 **Fax:** (01244) 687100
Lindy Campbell, Company Solicitor

TT Group PLC
Clive House, 12-18 Queens Road, Weybridge KT13 9XB
Tel: (01932) 841310 **Fax:** (01932) 846724
Ann Sheriff, Legal Manager

UBS AG
100 Liverpool Street, London EC2M 2RH
Tel: (0171) 901 3020 **Fax:** (0171) 901 1913
No of lawyers in dept: 30
Mark Harding, European General Counsel
Specialism: Responsible for all legal and compliance matters in the European region.
Career: Joined *Clifford Chance* 1980, partner 1987-1996. Joined UBS Sept 1996 as UK General Counsel. Became European General Counsel in 1997

Unigate PLC
Unigate House, Wood Lane, London W12 7RP
Tel: (0181) 749 8888 **Fax:** (0181) 576 6071
No of lawyers in dept: 5
Work outsourced: Major M&A; conveyancing; dedicated distribution.
P. N. Heriz-Jones, Head of Legal
Specialism: Company/commercial, IP, food, legislation, property, franchising, competition law.
Career: Cheltenham College
Other lawyers: C.F. Phillips, A.Garner – company/commercial, M&A, dedicated distribution, fleet hire; O.Skeen – company/commercial, agency, distribution, licensing; Olivia Glynn – employment.

Unilever PLC
PO Box 68, Unilever House, Blackfriars, London EC4P 4BQ
Tel: (0171) 822 5252 **Fax:** (0171) 822 5951
Email: stephen.g.williams@unilever.com
No of lawyers in dept: 27
Stephen G. Williams, General Counsel and Joint Secretary
Specialism: Responsible for all legal, intellectual property and secretarial departments in the head offices in London and Rotterdam and is also responsible for Unilever legal services worldwide.
Career: Educated at Brentwood School, Essex and King's College, University of London where gained Bachelor of Law Degree (LLB) Hons. Following Law School, joined *Slaughter and May* and spent time in their tax planning and commercial departments. In 1975 joined the department of Imperial Chemical Industries plc. In 1984 transferred to ICI's company secretary's department, becoming one of two assistant company secretaries in 1985. Appointed Joint Secretary of Unilever on 1st January 1986 and General Counsel of Unilever in 1993.
Personal: Admitted as a Solicitor and member of the Law Society in April 1972. Member of the Company Law Committee of the Law Society and of the Companies Committee of the CBI. Non-executive director of Bunzl plc.
Other lawyers: Mr A Peat – overseas legal services; Mr P Neely – UK legal services; Mr R Heath – trade mark legal services; Mr L Virelli – patents legal services; Mrs S Franklin – marketing legal services; Mr J Moolenburgh – European legal services (based in Rotterdam); Mr P Kuipers – Netherlands legal services (based in Rotterdam).

United Biscuits (Hldgs) PLC
Church Road, West Drayton UB7 7PR
Tel: (01895) 432100 **Fax:** (01895) 432028
Alan Frew, Group Company Secretary

United News & Media PLC
Ludgate House, 245 Blackfriars Road, Blackfriars, London SE1 9UY
Tel: (0171) 921 5000 **Fax:** (0171) 928 2728
Email: webmaster@unm.com
No of lawyers in dept: 5
Work outsourced: 60% – Corporate, litigation, employment
Jane Stables, Head of Legal
Career: Qualified as a lawyer in 1985 and worked in the city firm of *Freshfields* doing mainly mergers and acquisitions but always retaining an employment law specialism. Moved into industry to be company secretary and legal adviser to a retailing plc, prior to joining MAI in 1994. Took over the personnel function at MAI in 1995 and became Legal & Personnel Director on the United/MAI merger. Responsible for the United News & Media plc group legal and personnel issues.

United Utilities PLC
Birchwood Point Business Park, Birchwood Boulevard, Birchwood, Warrington WA3 7WB
Tel: (01925) 285000 **Fax:** (01925) 285199
Email: Tim.Rayner@uuil.com
No of lawyers in dept:2
Work outsourced: 75% – Major transactions, litigation, property, employment
Timothy Rayner, Group Secretary
Specialism: Company Secretarial, Company/Commercial, Corporate Finance, US Securites.
Career: Secondary School – Rossall School, Fleetwood, Lancs. Kings College, University of London, LLB (1992). Qualified 1985.
Personal: Born 4th August 1960. Leisure, travelling in France: motorsports.
Other lawyers: Joanne Bream, Group Legal Manager – Company/Commercial, Corporate Finance.

Vaux Group PLC
The Brewery, Sunderland SR1 3AN
Tel: (0191) 567 6277 **Fax:** (0191) 514 2488
No of lawyers in dept:3
Work outsourced: 5% – Unusual specialisms or short-notice large volume transactions.
Mark I. Hodgson, Company Solicitor
Specialism: Deals with conveyancing work in large pub package purchases, hotel acquisitions, including joint venture and management agreements. Also deals with commercial, landlord and tenant, employment, debt collection and some building disputes, liquor licensing.
Career: Qualified 1988. Assistant solicitor *Watson Burton* 1988-1989. Joined Vaux Group Plc as assistant Solicitor 1989.
Personal: Educated at Bede Comprehensive School 1975-1982 and Hertford College, Oxford University 1982-1985. Leisure pursuits include fell walking, attending Sunderland AFC matches and the pub. Born 6 February 1964. Lives in Wickham, Gateshead.

Vendome Luxury Group PLC
27 Knightsbridge, London SW1X 7YB
Tel: (0171) 838 8500 **Fax:** (0171) 838 8855
No of lawyers in dept: 3
Work outsourced: 20% – Corporate and financial work.
James E.K. Pyke, Group Legal Adviser
Reports to: Deputy Chairman
Specialism: Policy formulation, negotiating and drafting responsibilities in the following areas: corporate; commercial contracts; litigation; statutory and legislative compliance and lobbying. Work includes M&A; joint ventures; licensing; distribution and franchising contracts; agencies and consultancies; retail concessions and sponsorship arrangements spanning a number of prestige brands such as Alfred Dunhill, Montblanc and Hackett. Director of over 40 companies within the Group.
Career: Called to the Bar 1972. Trust Counsellor, N.M. Rothschild & Sons Ltd 1972-75. Company Lawyer to Rupert International, South Africa, advising on LP rights and brand name support 1975-77 and joined the Vendome Luxury Group (formerly Dunhill Holdings PLC) in 1978. Group Legal Adviser since 1986, Legal Director Alfred Dunhill.
Personal: Educated at Wellington 1962-67, Exeter University

1968-71 (LLB Hons) and Inns of Court School of Law. Trustee, Thorney Island Society. Leisure pursuits include sailing and water sports, travel, archaeology and food. Born 10 September 1948. Lives in London and Gloucestershire.

Vickers PLC
Vickers House, Millbank Tower, Millbank, London SW1P 4RA
Tel: (0171) 828 7777 **Fax:** (0171) 828 6585
Andrew John, In-house Lawyer

Viridian Group
120 Malone Road, Belfast BT9 5HT
Tel: (01232) 668416 **Fax:** (01232) 663579
David Flinn, Head of Legal

Vodafone Group PLC
The Courtyard, 2-4 London Road, Newbury RG13 1JL
Tel: (01635) 33251 **Fax:** (01635) 580587
Hugh Humphreys, Principal Solicitor (Property)

Wassall PLC
39 Victoria Street, London SW1H 0EE
Tel: (0171) 333 0303 **Fax:** (0171) 333 0304
Simon Pearce, Company Secretary

Weir Group PLC
149 Newlands Road, Cathcart, Glasgow G44 4EX
Tel: (0141) 637 7111 **Fax:** (0141) 637 2221
William Harkness, Company Secretary

Wessex Water PLC
Wessex House, Passage Street, Bristol BS2 0JQ
Tel: (0117) 929 0611 **Fax:** (0117) 929 3137
Andrew Phillips, Principal Solicitor

West Deutsche Landesbank
51 Moorgate, London EC2R 6AE
Tel: (0171) 638 6141 **Fax:** (0171) 457 2097
James Morris, Head of Legal

West Merchant Bank Ltd
33-36 Gracechurch Street, London EC3V 0AX
Tel: (0171) 623 8711 **Fax:** (0171) 626 1610
Email: @westmerchant.co.uk
No of lawyers in dept: 15
Work outsourced: 20% – Various
A. Allison, Head of Legal
Specialisms: Investment Banking (UK and International), Stockbroking, Regulatory Compliance (Banking and Financial Services) (UK and International) Company Law, Litigation (UK and International)
Career: Educated at Liverpool College and Wadham College, Oxford. Called to the Bar 1969. Independent practice at the Bar 1969-1987. Head of Group Compliance, Standard Chartered Bank 1987-1996. Director, Compliance and Legal Affairs, West Merchant 1996-date. Author (with others), *Banking and the Financial Services Act* (Butterworths, 1993, 2nd edition July 1998).
Personal: Fellow, Chartered Institute of Arbitrators. Chairman, Bar Association for Commerce, Finance & Industry 1995. Memberships – General Council of the Bar 1991-96, General Court Committee 1991- date, City Disputes Panel of Arbitrators & Mediators. Securities and Futures Authority's Panel of Arbitrators.
Other lawyers: Derivatives/Banking – Pauline Lawton, Kurt Krommelin, Jane Bennett, Robert Jones, Patrick Clancy. Emerging Markets – Lucian Milburn. Capital Markets – Katharine Johnson, Tim Sai Loui, Ruth Millington. General Banking Documentation – Chris Barry (Australia), Russell Grigg, Christine Schmitz (German), Rosemary McNamara. Securities – William Martin (USA).

Wetherspoon(J D) PLC
Wetherspoon House, Central Park, Reeds Crescent, Watford WD1 1QH
Tel: (01923) 477777 **Fax:** (01923) 219815
Rosalyn Schofield, Director of Legal Services and Company Secretary

Whitbread PLC
Brewery, Chiswell Street, London EC1Y 4SD
Tel: (0171) 606 4455 **Fax:** (0171) 615 1000
Simon Barratt, Legal Affairs Director and Company
Secretary

Williams PLC
Pentagon House, Sir Frank Whittle Road, Derby DE2 4XA
Tel: (01332) 202020 **Fax:** (01332) 384402
Brian Cunningham, Company Secretary

Willis Corroon Group PLC
Ten Trinity Square, London EC3P 3AX
Tel: (0171) 488 8111 **Fax:** (0171) 481 7183
Heather Thomas, Managing Director, Legal & Risk
Management

Wilson Bowden PLC
Wilson Bowden House, 207 Leicester Road, Ibstock,
Leicester LE67 5WP
Tel: (01530) 260777 **Fax:** (01530) 262805
No of lawyers in dept: 4
Work outsourced: 90% – Land acquisitions/land sales,
plot sales, litigation.
Nicolas Townsend, Group Legal Director
Specialism: Responsible for monitoring and supervision of all
major contracts for land acquisition/sale, troubleshooting,
strategic land acquisition and the provision of external legal
services for the group.
Career: Qualified in January 1970. Previously a Partner with
Gardiner & Millhouse 1976-78, *Marron Townsend* 1978-80,
Nicolas Townsend & Co 1980-87, *Staunton Townsend* 1987-89
and *Edge & Ellison* 1989-93.
Other lawyers: Owen Hill, Peter Carr, Wendy Satchwell, Lisa
Garley – planning and property.

Wimpey Homes Holdings Ltd
3 Shortlands, London W6 8EZ
Tel: (0181) 748 2000 **Fax:** (0181) 846 3121
Stefan Bort, Company Secretary

Wolseley PLC
PO Box 18, Vines Lane, Droitwich WR9 8ND
Tel: (01905) 777200 **Fax:** (01905) 777219
D.A. Branson, Head of Legal

Wolverhampton & Dudley Breweries PLC
PO Box 26, Park Brewery, Wolverhampton WV1 4NY
Tel: (01902) 711811 **Fax:** (01902) 29136
Lesley Porter, Company Secretary

Woolwich Building Society
Corporate Headquarters, Watling Street, Bexleyheath
DA6 7RR
Tel: (0181) 298 5000 **Fax:** (01322) 555708
H. Hodges, Legal Executive

WPP Group PLC
27 Farm Street, London W1X 6RD
Tel: (0171) 408 2204 **Fax:** (0171) 409 0242
David Calow, Group Legal Adviser

Yorkshire Water plc
2 The Embankment, Sovereign Street, Leeds LS1 4BG
Tel: (0113) 234 3234 **Fax:** (0113) 234 2322
No of lawyers in dept: 11
Work outsourced: 15% – Regulatory, commercial,
litigation, employment, construction litigation.
Stuart McFarlane, Head of Legal Services
Specialism: Principal areas of work for the department include
conveyancing, company/commercial, litigation (civil and
criminal) and environmental.
Career: Articled *Ian Gillis and Co* 1982-84, Solicitor 1984 to
date. Joined Yorkshire Water plc 1989, Head of Legal Services
since 1994.
Other lawyers: Mary Preston, Sarah Addison, Sapna Jedi:
company/commercial; Peter Cockburn, Dawn Carlisle, Kate
Bradshaw, Helen Lodge: property; Shona Flood, Jill Sowden,
Deborah Stirling: litigation.

Zeneca Group PLC
15 Stanhope Gate, London W1Y 6LN
Tel: (0171) 304 5000 **Fax:** (0171) 304 5151
Graeme Musker, Company Secretary/Head of Legal

LITIGATION SUPPORT

CHAMBERS & PARTNERS

INDEX TO LITIGATION SUPPORT SECTION

ALEXANDERS

SELODUCT HOUSE, STATION ROAD, REDHILL, RH1 1NF
Tel: (01737) 779500 **Fax:** (01737) 779548 **Email:** alex@alexanders.telme.com

Contact partner:	Mr J Donoghue

The Firm: For a number of years, Alexanders have been helping lawyers and their clients by providing forensic accounting, litigation support and expert witness services whenever financial issues are involved.

The firm has worked closely with insurance companies, lawyers, leading counsel and their clients, in such areas as the production of high quality reports, graphs and financial summaries of a clear, concise nature for presentation at court; litigation strategies; the examination and appraisal of documents through Discovery and assessing the quantum of claims or exposure.

Alexanders have a firm grasp of the laws of evidence and understand the necessity of providing reliable evidence. They also have first hand courtroom experience of both the Royal Courts of Justice and the Central Criminal Courts.

Computerised techniques employed by the firm ensure the accuracy of information supplied by Alexanders: databases are used for interrogation of financial information; statistical analysis checks patterns and trends and tests facts against expected values; graphics software provides simple visual interpretations of complex information.

The Partners: The Litigation Support Partners have all held senior positions within the top ten accountancy firms and have worked in public practice for a number of years. All partners are members of the Academy of Experts and are qualified accountants with a wide range of business experience.

Principal Areas of Work: Alexanders have assisted in a wide variety of cases involving loss of earnings; professional negligence; negligence of Investment Managers; fraud; conspiracy to defraud; family and marital disputes; compliance with Investor Protection regulations; insurance claims; breach of contract claims; and offences under the Companies Acts.

ARTHUR ANDERSEN

1 SURREY STREET, LONDON, WC2R 2PS
Tel: (0171) 438 3000 **Fax:** (0171) 831 1133 **Internet:** http://www.arthurandersen.com

Contacts:	David Knopf
	Richard Bolton

The Firm: Arthur Andersen has been providing litigation services to the UK legal profession since 1980. The litigation services practice combines specialists in litigation with the resources of one of the world's largest accounting and business consulting firms. We have had a significant role in many of the UK's largest commercial cases.

Arthur Andersen assists in all stages of the litigation process, from identifying, reviewing and analysing the key business issues to trial preparation, and expert evidence. We support our clients by providing accounting and economic input into their analysis of the commercial issues, and reporting our findings concisely.

The Litigation Services practice in London is part of the Business Consulting division of Arthur Andersen whose work includes valuations, competition and regulatory advice, economic consulting and business planning. We believe that the range of work we perform enhances our ability to provide expert advice in disputes. Our experienced litigation team consists of around 90 partners, managers and staff.

In a typical year we assist in numerous claims of varying size and complexity. We can offer clients a deep pool of experience in our offices throughout the UK and overseas.

Principal Areas of Work: Arthur Andersen can assist in a wide variety of financial disputes, either as a consulting expert or as an expert witness. Please call David Knopf or Richard Bolton for a copy of our brochure which expands on how we focus on your needs. Alternatively, please visit our website on http://www.arthurandersen.com to find out about our other areas of expertise.

ARTHUR ANDERSEN

ARTHUR ANDERSEN & CO, SC

BAKER TILLY

2 BLOOMSBURY STREET, LONDON, WC1B 3ST
Tel: (0171) 413 5100 **Fax:** (0171) 413 5101

The Firm: Founded over 125 years ago, Baker Tilly is a top fifteen firm of chartered accountants and business advisors in the UK. The firm has around 100 partners operating nationwide, employs some 650 staff and is an independent member of Summit International with representatives in over 100 cities worldwide.

Our specialists have acted in over 500 litigation support cases, providing expert witness and forensic accounting. They are not just experts in court – as practising accountants their evidence is based on practical and commercial experience.

For this reason, our litigation support team is active in other specialist fields including corporate finance, information technology, audit and insolvency. It is this mix of experience which makes our specialists effective expert witnesses. Our specialists have extensive experience in a wide range of cases covering loss of profits, medical negligence, loss of earnings, fraud and IT litigation.

Principal Areas of Work: Cases have included breach of contract (including computer installations and construction), other damages claims including loss of future profits, security for costs, share valuations including S459CA 1985, medical negligence, personal injury and fatal accident claims, and acting for defendants in several high profile cases brought by the SFO and as the DTI Inspector in the Barlow Clowes affair.

Number of partners	100
Number of staff:	650

Contact partners

London	Chilton Taylor	(0171) 4135100
	Michael Taub	
	Adrian Rapazzini	
	Richard Spooner	
	Peter Dickerson	
Birmingham	Ian Bond	(0121) 2332323
Bradford	Paul Byrne	(01274) 735311
Bromley	John Hudson	(0181) 2905522
Crawley	John Warner	(01293) 565165
Guildford	Martin Hoydan	(01483) 503050
Manchester	Phillip Rose	(0161) 8345777
Milton Keynes	Jim Clifford	(01908) 847474
Watford	Jim Clifford	(01923) 816400
Yeovil	Dianne Simpson-Price	(01935) 476266

BDO STOY HAYWARD

8 BAKER STREET, LONDON, W1M 1DA
Tel: (0171) 486 5888 **Fax:** (0171) 487 3686 **DX:** 9025 West End W1

The Firm: BDO Stoy Hayward established a Litigation Support Group in recognition of the need for sophisticated accountancy input into trials and potential proceedings. The firm's approach is based on partner involvement, backed by professional staff familiar with legal concepts and procedures. The firm's services include provision of letters of advice at the early stages of a matter, affidavits in support of applications, cross examination strategy and expert witness reports. Advanced computer software and graphics are used to present complex financial and quantitative data with clarity and precision.

Litigation Support Partner: Gervase MacGregor FCA (1986) specialises in international claims, partnership accounting, fraud investigation and trial support, including Legally Aided defence work. He is an expert in the application of the Solicitors Accounts Rules, on which he has lectured and written, including the Institute of Chartered Accountants book on Solicitors Accounts, and a book for accountants advising on solicitors' practices. He has also written books on professional practices and expert evidence. He has given evidence in the High Court, County Courts and Crown Courts on inter alia, fraud and solicitors accounts. He is a practising member of the Academy of Experts and a member of the Association of Certified Fraud Examiners.

Services:

Pre-trial Support: Detailed investigation and analysis of prime accounting records; advice on technical accountancy matters; evaluation of economic loss; tracing of assets.

Trial Support: Provision of expert witnesses; analysis of opposition's financial evidence; provision of detailed support during cross examination.

Settlement Support: Assistance with settlement negotiations; evaluation of taxation implications; evaluation of business implications.

Professional Negligence: Amongst the partners are current and former members of specialist committees of various professional bodies who provide guidance on technical issues, professional conduct and disciplinary matters.

Fraud: The firm has representation on the London Panel of Accountants which offers advisory support to the City and Metropolitan Fraud Squad.

Wrongful Dismissal: Assists in the preparation of claims using a computer model for evaluating loss of benefits in a damage period.

Loss of Profits and Consequential Loss

Personal Injury and Fatal Accident

Contact Partner:	Gervase MacGregor
Number of partners:	95
Number of staff:	900

CONTACTS	

Birmingham
Martin Palmer (0121) 608 6086

Bristol
Roy MacFarlane   (0117) 933 3311

Glasgow
Ken Macaldowie   (0141) 248 3761

Leeds
Bill Jenkinson   (0113) 234 1381

Manchester
Brent Wilkinson   (0161) 228 6791

Norwich
Martin Beck   (01603) 610181

Nottingham
Ian Beswick   (0115) 955 2000

Peterborough
Nick Barks   (01733) 342444

Southampton
Tim Bentall   (01703) 636 915

BDO Stoy Hayward
Chartered Accountants

BENTLEY JENNISON

HAMILTON HOUSE, 1 TEMPLE AVENUE, LONDON, EC4Y 0HA
Tel: (0171) 353 4212 **Fax:** (0171) 353 3325
Email: forensic@bentley-jennison.co.uk **Internet:** http://bentley-jennison.co.uk

The Firm: Bentley Jennison is a firm of Chartered Accountants with nine offices in England. It was established in 1984 and has since grown to be amongst the top twenty-five firms in the country. Its client focused approach has led to the development of a range of business advisory services including advanced tax specialisms, corporate finance, forensic accounting and litigation support, IT consulting, human resource and management development. It is one of the few firms committed to serving both growing businesses and public sector organisations.

A team of specialist partners and staff offer extensive experience at all stages of the litigation process from identification of key issues to preparation for trial, negotiated settlement or giving expert evidence.

The service is led by Edward Ross-McNairn who is a member of the Academy of Experts and has extensive experience across a wide spectrum of contentious matters. In addition he has given evidence in court on a number of occasions.

Litigation Support Services

- Arbitrations and determinations
- Commercial litigation
- Forensic accounting and investigations
- Medical negligence/personal injury
- Professional negligence
- Assessment of insurance claims
- Criminal litigation and fraud
- Matrimonial litigation
- Partnership disputes
- Taxation

Contact partner:	Edward Ross-McNairn
Number of partners	45
Number of staff:	235

BLICK ROTHENBERG CHARTERED ACCOUNTANTS

12 YORK GATE, REGENT'S PARK, LONDON, NW1 4QS
Tel: (0171) 486 0111 **Fax:** (0171) 935 6852

The Firm: Based in Central London, Blick Rothenberg is one of the leading independent medium sized firms of Chartered Accountants in the United Kingdom. We have been established for over 50 years and pride ourselves in providing a high quality service in a prompt and efficient manner. We have 18 partners, and around 100 staff. The firm has a developed speciality in litigation support work and 2 of our partners are members of the Academy of Experts.

Our Approach: Each assignment is controlled personally by a partner with a specialist knowledge of the litigation support process. Our reports are well researched, persuasive and noted for their clarity. Our partners carry the necessary personal authority and are both proactive and experienced in the witness box.

We are happy to meet you without cost or obligation to talk to you about the work that would be required in a particular case. We are also more than happy to provide estimates of our costs.

Principal Areas of Expertise:
The following areas are frequently handled:

- Professional negligence
- Valuations of shares and businesses
- Actions against directors
- Matrimonial disputes
- Tax investigations
- Commercial disputes, including those arising from corporate transactions.
- Shareholder and partnership disputes
- Loss of profit claims
- Personal injury and fatal accident financial claims
- Disputed probate
- Investment problems including pensions

Contact partner:	Martin G. Korn
	B Soc Sc FCA MAE
Direct Telephone	(0171) 544 8811
E-mail:	mgk@blickrothenberg.com

BURNETT SWAYNE

CHARTER COURT, THIRD AVENUE, SOUTHAMPTON, SO15 OAP
Tel: (01703) 702345 **Fax:** (01703) 702570

The Firm: Burnett Swayne is a substantial independent firm based in Southampton covering Crown Courts in Southampton, Winchester, Salisbury, Reading, Bournemouth, Portsmouth and Newport, Isle of Wight.

Happy to provide an initial assessment without fee or commitment. Legal Aid work welcomed.

Seek instructions in the following areas:-

Divorce, Partnership and Shareholder Disputes; Personal Injury and Fatal Accident; Consequential Loss; Fraud; Negligence.

Burnett Swayne Undertake:
- Valuation of businesses
- Valuation of shares in private companies
- Assessment of income or income requirement
- Fraud and other Investigations, Cash flow forecasts
- Loss of earnings, profit or capital growth

They are always mindful of the need to minimise the impact of taxation for their clients.

Litigation Support led by:

Ken Ball, FCA, ATII, Senior Partner
25 years in practice with substantial experience in tax, as well as partnership and shareholder disputes. Expert witness.

Michael Mason, FCCA
Head of Forensic Accounting Company and Fraud Investigations; Personal Injury, Matrimonial disputes. Expert witness.

Geoffrey Porter, FCA, MAE, Senior Manager
Twenty years in practice; specialist in share valuations and damages claims. Expert witness.

Contact partner:	Ken Ball
Number of partners:	8
Number of staff:	98

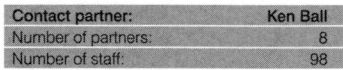

CARLTON BAKER CLARKE

GREENWOOD HOUSE, NEW LONDON ROAD, CHELMSFORD, CM2 0PP
Tel: (01245) 495588 **Fax:** (01245) 495145

The Firm: A commercially based practice with a wide range of clientele.

Mervyn Clarke FCCA: Over 25 years experience in practice. Guaranteed personal attention at Senior Partner level. Concentrating on close liaison with instructing solicitors and a very personal service. Extensive experience in commercial litigation and disputes (references available).

Litigation support services:
- Commercial Disputes
- Investigation of Fraud
- Personal Injury Claims/ Loss of Earnings/P.I.
- Matrimonial Settlements
- Share and Business Valuations
- Extensive Construction Industry Experience

Contact partner:	Mervyn Clarke

CARTER BACKER WINTER CHARTERED ACCOUNTANTS

HILL HOUSE, HIGHGATE HILL, LONDON, N19 5UU
Tel: (0171) 263 7111 **Fax:** (0171) 281 2166 **Email:** info@cbw.co.uk

The Firm: We are a long established, major independent London firm with over 70 partners and staff.

Our litigation specialists have a sound understanding of legal concepts and procedures derived from over 30 years experience of litigation work, including many leading cases. They are able to analyse complex financial data quickly and present their findings in a clear, non-technical manner, both in written form and in oral evidence.

The litigation team is led by Peter Luscombe, a CEDR accredited mediator, and Arthur Harverd, a registered arbitrator and a past Chairman of The Chartered Institute of Arbitrators. Both are members of the Academy of Experts and have given evidence as expert witnesses on numerous occasions. Their experience is wide ranging and covers both civil and criminal cases in the areas of commercial, insurance, fraud, tax, professional and medical negligence, personal injury and matrimonial disputes. Our team also includes experts in the fields of insolvency and banking.

Contacts:	Arthur D. Harverd
	Peter Luscombe

CHANTREY VELLACOTT

RUSSELL SQUARE HOUSE, 10-12 RUSSELL SQUARE, LONDON, WC1B 5LF
Tel: (0171) 509 9000 **Fax:** (0171) 436 8884 **Email:** info@cv-rsh.ftech.co.uk

The Firm: Chantrey Vellacott is a long established national top twenty firm of Chartered Accountants and a member of DFK International, an association of independent firms operating in more than 70 countries worldwide.

A team of specialist partners and staff offer extensive experience of all stages of the litigation process cases from identification of key issues to trial preparation, negotiated settlement or expert evidence.

Contact partner:	Geoff Lane
Number of partners:	53
Number of staff:	300

Principal Areas of Work:

Commercial Litigation: Business and share valuations; loss of profits/business interruption; evaluation of insurance claims, warranty and contract disputes; security for costs applications; purchase and sale disputes

Personal injury/medical negligence: Dependency claims; loss of earnings/pension rights; claims mitigation

Professional negligence: Fee disputes; claims analysis; negligent conduct; conduct prejudicial to the interests of the clients

Criminal litigation and fraud: Theft Act allegations; fraudulent/wrongful trading; concealment; false prospectus

Matrimonial litigation and partnership disputes: Asset tracing; evaluation of financial standing; division of earnings/pension rights; valuation of businesses and unquoted shares

Forensic accounting and investigations: Regulatory investigations (IMRO; SIB; DTI); Directors' Disqualification Act

Taxation: Reports on structure and effectiveness; critical analysis of advice

Insurance: Assessment of and compilation of claims

Determinations and arbitrations: Mediation; expert determination; valuations and arbitrations

COOPER LANCASTER BREWERS

ALDWYCH HOUSE, 81 ALDWYCH, LONDON, WC2B 4HP
Tel: (0171) 242 2444 **Fax:** (0171) 242 1117 **Email:** info@clb.co.uk

14 WOOD STREET, BOLTON, LANCS BL1 1DZ **Tel:** (01204) 531573 **Fax:** (01204) 361552 **Email:** info@clbinsol.u-net.com

The Firm: Cooper Lancaster Brewers has provided support to the legal profession for over 120 years.

The CLB legal support team produces reports that are clear, comprehensive, detailed and accurate. Confident in their investigative abilities, senior members of the team are comfortable appearing in court to defend a client's interests.

As one of the UK's larger firms of chartered accountants, Cooper Lancaster Brewers serves the needs of clients and legal professionals throughout the country. CLB is active in one of the top global networks of independent accountancy firms, Polaris International. CLB can, therefore, deal with disputes on an international level, drawing on the expertise of their affiliates around the world – accountants whom they know and trust.

Other offices: Lancaster, Manchester, Reigate and Sheffield.

Contact Partners:	Mark Ling (London)
	Mike Garrett (Bolton)

DELOITTE & TOUCHE

HILL HOUSE, 1 LITTLE NEW STREET, LONDON, EC4A 3TR
Tel: (0171) 936 3000 **Fax:** (0171) 936 2638 **DX:** 599 **Email:** forensic.uk@deloitte.co.uk **Internet:** http//www.deloitte.co.uk

The Firm: Deloitte & Touche has a dedicated team of forensic specialists in offices throughout the country. The firm's forensic partners have significant experience as expert witnesses, both in the UK and overseas. Where a case requires specific sector or industry expertise the firm is able to provide the appropriate expert from one of its dedicated industry or technical groups. As a leading member of Deloitte Touche Tohmatsu, the firm is also able to call upon the assistance of its 73,000 staff located in some 130 countries throughout the world.

Commercial disputes: The firm has extensive experience in general commercial disputes including claims for business interruption and loss of profits, product liability, breach of contract, intellectual property, fidelity and warranty breaches and also valuations. As one of the leading firms providing services to the public sector, Deloitte & Touche has also assisted local authorities and government bodies in a wide range of such disputes.

Determinations, Mediations and Arbitration: The firm has developed considerable expertise in the role of Expert in determinations as well as acting for clients during arbitrations and mediations.

Personal Claims: The firm has a significant reputation in personal injury, fatal accident and medical negligence claims, and in the area of structured settlements. We also provide quantum reports in matrimonial disputes and libel actions.

Professional Negligence: The firm provides expert opinion on negligence claims involving accountancy firms as well as quantum reports in claims against other professionals.

Insurance Claims: The firm provides expert accountancy services to insurance companies, loss adjusters and commercial clients and has a significant record in acting for Lloyd's Syndicates involved in disputes.

Fraud and Criminal Work: The firm conducts fraud investigations, traces and recovers assets and carries out reviews to identify the risk of fraud or money laundering in both the public and private sectors. Our investigators have access to the most advanced data recovery and computer investigation tools.

Business Intelligence Service: The firm has recently launched a new service line undertaking detailed research into individual's backgrounds, connections and other business activities, whether as part of a commercial dispute or fraud investigation or as a prelude to a new business opportunity or joint venture.

Computerised Litigation Systems: The Firm's involvement in several major liquidations has led it to develop a computerised database document management and retrieval system for large cases

Contact Partners:	John Magill
	Fergus Falk
	Mike Barford
	Will Inglis
	Mark Tantam
	George Weldon
Number of partners:	332
Number of staff:	6256

FORENSIC ACCOUNTANCY CONTACTS OUTSIDE LONDON

Belfast
Timothy Quin (01232) 531105

Birmingham/Leicester/Nottingham
Angus Pollock   (01216) 955 516

Bracknell
Ken Chalk   (01344) 727350

Cardiff/Bristol
John Reid   (01222) 2642121

Edinburgh
Roger Powdrill   (0131) 535 7229

Leeds
Chris Phillips   (0113) 292 1150

Manchester
Peter Uglow   (0161) 455 6370

Newcastle upon Tyne
Peter Smith   (0191) 202 5314

For other offices in the UK or overseas, contact
Fergus Falk
National Director of Forensic Services
London (0171) 303 5800

DOWNHAM TRAIN EPSTEIN

DTE HOUSE, HOLLINS MOUNT, BURY, BL9 8AT
Tel: (0161) 953 9510 **Fax:** (0161) 766 3685 **DX:** 711400 BURY 6

The Firm: DTE's Forensic Accounting department provides a broad range of services to the legal profession. Initial consultations will be provided free of charge.

Principal Areas Of Work:
The firm acts for plaintiffs and defendants and is able to assist solicitors and their clients with the following:
- personal injury, medical negligence and fatal accident claims
- professional negligence
- consequential loss and business interruption claims
- commercial and contractual disputes
- matrimonial disputes
- Criminal Injuries Compensation claims
- fraud and financial irregularities
- business valuation disputes
- unfair/wrongful dismissal claims
- tax investigations
- structured settlements

Litigation Support Partners:

Doug Roberts BA, FCA – Specialises in professional negligence, business interruption, contractual disputes, medical negligence and personal injury work.

Nick Fail BA (Oxon), FCA – Specialises in medical negligence and personal injury work, but is also regularly involved in consequential loss and commercial disputes.

Louise Ellison MA (Cantab), ACA – Deals with a variety of personal and commercial cases, including personal injury, fatal accident claims, business interruption and breach of contract. Specialises in personal injury claims involving injuries of the utmost severity.

Tony Gale FIPM – Ex Inland Revenue compliance officer specialising in tax investigations.

Contact Partners:	Doug Roberts
	Nick Fail
	Louise Ellison
Number of partners:	13
Number of staff:	120

ERNST & YOUNG

BECKET HOUSE, 1 LAMBETH PALACE RD, LONDON, SE1 7EU
Tel: (0171) 931 3006 **Fax:** (0171) 931 3807 **DX:** 241

The Firm: Ernst & Young is one of the leading international firms of business and financial advisers, with offices throughout the country and the world. Clients include organisations of all types and sizes, from blue-chip multinationals to governments, and from major financial institutions to private individuals.

Principal Areas of Work: Ernst & Young has extensive experience in providing the full range of forensic services in fraud and other investigations, tracing and recovery of assets, valuations, litigation, arbitrations, expert determinations and mediations.

Ernst & Young's forensic specialists are organised into core teams of experienced, dedicated professionals with specialist experience in report writing and the litigation process. For each assignment the firm assembles the best team of individuals from within Ernst & Young's worldwide organisation to provide the most comprehensive level of industry expertise to the case. Using the best team approach ensures that Ernst & Young offers an outstanding quality of service in conjunction with value for money.

Litigation Support Group
The Litigation Support Group specialises in providing expert witness and related services of the highest calibre to lawyers and their clients. The Group provides assistance at all stages of a case: from development of the statement of claim or defence through to presenting evidence at the trial. Our experience and the way we work enables us to focus at an early stage on the key issues in dispute and avoid unnecessary research and expense on unimportant matters. Our principle areas of expertise and contacts are as follows:
- Audit and accountants negligence – Robert Hughes or Nigel Macdonald
- Disputes and claims following take-overs – Tessa Sweeney or Simon de Quidt
- Business interruption and loss of profits – Frank Ilett
- Other contractual disputes – Robert Hughes
- Expert determinations and ADR – Nigel Macdonald or Robert Hughes
- Monopoly and competition enquiries – Nigel Macdonald or Frank Ilett

Contact partner:	Robert Hughes

Continues overleaf

- Intellectual property disputes – Kenny Shovell
- Computer related disputes – Kenny Shovell or Richard Indge
- Construction and projects abandonment claims – Eugene Bannon
- Personal injury and fatal accident claims – Keith Cromwell or Sara Fowler
- Divorce – Laura Snook

Fraud Investigation Group

The Fraud Investigation Group specialises in investigating allegations of fraud and the tracing and subsequent recovery of misappropriated assets. Fraud prevention is another area of expertise provided which includes risk awareness seminars and training of key staff to prevent and detect fraud.

Ernst & Young has developed bespoke software to trace funds efficiently and effectively, where they have been transferred internationally through various currencies and split into component amounts, so that they can be recovered for the client before they are dissipated.

Principal Contacts:
- Fraud investigations – David Sherwin or Sarah Evans
- Fraud risk management – David Sherwin or John Smart

Business Valuations

Ernst & Young has had a dedicated team of full time valuers for over 25 years. The Group has unparalleled experience in the field of business and share valuations, typically working on over 300 assignments each year. The Group's expertise comprises valuation for almost every business situation including: evaluating acquisition targets, independent valuations under the Companies Act, valuations for taxation purposes and negotiating values with the Inland Revenue, valuing Intellectual Property and giving evidence as a valuation expert witness in, for example, warranty claims.

Principal Contacts:
- Business and share valuations – John Allday or Jim Eales

Other Offices

Ernst & Young has offices in most major towns and cities throughout the United Kingdom and each office has a designated partner with specific responsibility for Litigation Support.

The principal regional contacts are:

Birmingham	Keith Cromwell	(0121) 232 4000
Bristol	Barbara Hadfield	(0117) 929 0808
Edinburgh	Richard Sweetman	(0131) 226 6400
Manchester	Richard Dyson	(0161) 952 1000

H.W. FISHER & COMPANY, CHARTERED ACCOUNTANTS

ACRE HOUSE, 11-15 WILLIAM ROAD, LONDON, NW1 3ER
Tel: (0171) 388 7000 **Fax:** (0171) 380 4900 **Email:** info@hwfisher.co.uk **Internet:** http://www.hwfisher.co.uk

The Firm: H W Fisher & Company is a medium sized accountancy firm comprising 20 partners and approximately 250 staff. Our forensic department offers a level of expertise rarely found outside the ranks of the largest international firms, combined with a commitment to a prompt, effective and personal service. Our effectiveness is enhanced by experience of acting for both plaintiffs and defendants.

The firm has in-depth skills in all aspects of litigation support, including personal injury and medical negligence, matrimonial, professional negligence, share and business valuations, DTI proceedings, loss of income/profits, breach of contract and fraud investigation.

The forensic department is headed by Stuart Burns who is a Member of the Academy of Experts and of the Association of Certified Fraud Examiners. He has considerable court experience and writes regularly on forensic issues for a range of professional publications.

David Selwyn, who is also a forensic partner, is UK Governor of the Association of Certified Fraud Examiners. He has particular expertise in share valuations, a subject on which he has written and lectured widely.

Contact partner:	Stuart Burns
Number of partners:	20
Number of staff:	250

GRANT THORNTON

GRANT THORNTON HOUSE, MELTON STREET, EUSTON SQUARE, LONDON, NW1 2EP
Tel: (0171) 383 5100 **Fax:** (0171) 383 4715 **DX:** 2100 EUSTON

ST JOHN'S CENTRE, 110 ALBION STREET, LEEDS, LS2 8LA
Tel: (0113) 245 5514 **Fax:** (0113) 246 5055 **DX:** 12085 LEEDS

ENTERPRISE HOUSE, 115 EDMUND STREET, BIRMINGHAM B3 2HJ
Tel: (0121) 212 4000 **Fax:** (0121) 212 4014 **DX:** 13174 BIRMINGHAM

The Firm: Grant Thornton is a leading national and international accounting and consultancy firm providing a comprehensive range of business advisory services to a wide variety of clients from private individuals to major companies. The firm operates from over 45 offices in the UK and has an international network spanning some 80 countries.

A team of specialist forensic partners and staff offer extensive experience of commercial litigation, complex insurance claims, fraud and personal injury. Investigative financial, accounting and taxation services are provided to assist in the building of a case, obtaining settlement or the giving of expert evidence in Court.

Forensic services are available from most of the firm's UK offices. The main forensic centres however are in the London office (Partner in charge: Philip Kabraji), the Leeds office (Partner in charge: Robin Hall) and the Birmingham office (Contact: Robert Kerr).

Principal Areas of Expertise: The partners in the firm have experience in a wide number of business sectors, including construction, manufacturing, motor dealers, engineering, banking, financial, oil and gas, hotel and leisure, defence and professional services.

Partners with appropriate expertise and witness box experience are available to act in contractual and commercial disputes, consequential loss of profit claims, breach of warranty, business and share valuations, fraud, computer disputes, professional negligence claims, trade disputes (including advice on EC and US anti-dumping regulations), directors' disqualification hearings, personal injury, medical negligence and fatal accident claims, structured settlements, royalty disputes, matrimonial disputes and libel claims.

Contact Partners:	Philip Kabraji (London)
	Robin Hall (Leeds)
	Robert Kerr (Birmingham)
Number of partners:	218
Number of staff:	2400

Grant Thornton

HACKER YOUNG CHARTERED ACCOUNTANTS

ST. ALPHAGE HOUSE, 2 FORE STREET, LONDON, EC2Y 5DH
Tel: (0171) 216 4600 **Fax:** (0171) 638 2159 **Email:** london@hackeryoung.co.uk **Internet:** http://www.hackeryoung.co.uk

The Firm: Hacker Young's long-established litigation support and forensic accounting group provides creative, objective and practical solutions to the financial and commercial aspects of disputes, including loss of profits; share valuations; professional negligence; fraud cases; arbitration; personal injury and medical negligence; contractual; commercial and employment disagreements; matrimonial disputes; regulatory investigations and intellectual property.

The firm has 7 UK offices and associates in over 30 countries worldwide.

Contact Partner:	D S Lazarevic
Number of partners:	42
Number of professional staff:	213

HAYS ALLAN

SOUTHAMPTON HOUSE, 317 HIGH HOLBORN, LONDON, WC1V 7NL
Tel: (0171) 969 5500 **Fax:** (0171) 969 5600 **DX:** 1005 CHANCERY LANE LONDON
Email: service@haysallan.com **Internet:** http://www.haysallan.com

The Firm: Hays Allan is a medium sized firm of Chartered Accountants with 15 partners. It has had its origins in the City for over 100 years.

Principal Areas of Expertise:
   Accountancy Disputes: Accountancy issues; ADR/arbitration; accountancy fee disputes; accountants/auditors; standards/professional negligence.
   Accounting Services/Forensic Accounting: Auditing/accounts analysis; personal accounting; divorce/matrimonial financial issues; forensic accounting; acquisitions/due diligence investigations; asset tracing; income tracking; incomplete records investigation; money laundering investigation; theft/misappropriation (financial); false accounting; fraud prevention (accounting); fraud investigation (accounting); SFA regulation; Companies Act offences/false prospectus; corporate fraud; mortgage fraud; credit card fraud; tax/subsidy fraud; common agricultural policy fraud; Customs and Excise/VAT fraud.
   Taxation: Taxation planning; business taxation/corporation tax; trust taxation; personal taxation/income tax; PAYE.

Contact Partners:	David Riley
	Neil Gillam
Number of partners:	15
Number of staff:	100

HORWATH CLARK WHITEHILL

25 NEW STREET SQUARE, LONDON, EC4A 3LN
Tel: (0171) 353 1577 **Fax:** (0171) 583 1720 **DX:** 0014 LONDON CHANCERY LANE **Email:** enquiry@horwathcw.co.uk

The Firm: Horwath Clark Whitehill's specialist litigation support unit, in conjunction with appropriate industry or business experts, handles procedures involved in the preparation and defence of claims from three major locations: London, Thames Valley and the Midlands. The unit's training programme includes the use of barristers to improve court room techniques.

Contact partner:	Mark Ladd
Number of partners:	86
Number of staff:	600

Specialist Areas of Work:

Professional Negligence: auditing, acquisitions, prospectuses, tax, VAT, Financial Services Act and directors' responsibilities.

Personal Injury and Medical Negligence: loss of earnings, pensions and fatal accident dependency claims, structured settlements and reports on discount rates for multipliers.

Valuations: businesses, matrimonial and pension funds.

General Commercial: quantum of loss, breach of contract, intellectual property, partnership disputes and employment matters.

Civil and Criminal Fraud: DTI, Crown Prosecution Service reports, mortgage fraud and PAYE and VAT.

Other Specialist in offices outside London:

Humphrey Creed	High Wycombe	(01494) 462726
	Reading	(0118) 959 7222
Chris Bicknell	Walsall	(01922) 725590
	Kidderminster	(01562) 60101
Ross MacLaverty	Leeds	(0113) 274 0404

KIDSONS IMPEY

SPECTRUM HOUSE, 20-26 CURSITOR STREET, LONDON, EC4A 1HY
Tel: (0171) 405 2088 **Fax:** (0171) 334 4734 **DX:** 458 LONDON

The Firm: Kidsons Impey is a leading UK firm of Chartered Accountants and business advisors with offices throughout the country. The firm provides advice on all litigation support matters to companies, partnerships, sole traders, trustees, private individuals, regulatory bodies and Police Authorities and acts for both plaintiffs and defendants.

In selecting a team of forensic specialists for each assignment, Kidsons Impey draws upon the wealth of technical expertise, business and court experience within the firm. Through membership of HLB International the firm can enlist the skills of experts in over 240 offices in some 90 countries worldwide.

The firm provides expert witness reports, which are clear, concise and written in plain English, avoiding jargon and technical accounting terms as far as possible. The firm's service is highly responsive; it never loses sight of the fact that it forms only one part of a team of experts working on any case.

Principal Areas of Forensic Accounting Work:

Financial Inquiry Services: Fraud and corruption investigations; Establishing benefit of crime for the Criminal Courts; Evaluating loss to the victims of crime; Compensation claims for the Criminal Courts; Confiscation issues; Acting as receivers for the Court in confiscation and litigation matters; Restraint order actions; Means enquiries conducted by Civil and Criminal Courts; Investigating money laundering; Tracing assets; Regulatory investigations conducted under the FSA; Companies Act and Charities Act.

Business Claims: Loss of profits; Commercial disputes; Civil fraud; Breach of contract; Computer related disputes; Fidelity; Intellectual property; Business interruption; Business valuations.

Personal Claims: Personal injury and fatal accident litigation; Matrimonial disputes; Compensation for loss of office; Libel.

Other Forensic Accounting Matters: Professional negligence; Insurance and reinsurance disputes; Arbitration and expert adjudication; Security for costs.

London and the South: *Richard Lewis*
Spectrum House, 20-26 Cursitor Street, London EC4A 1HY Tel: (0171) 405 2088

The Midlands: *Adrian Pym*
Bank House, 8 Cherry Street, Birmingham B2 5AD Tel: (0121) 631 2631

The North West: *Mark Blakemore*
Devonshire House, 36 George Street, Manchester M1 4HA Tel: (0161) 236 7733

The North East: *Robert Barraclough*
Barclays House, 41 Park Cross Street, Leeds LS1 2QH Tel: (0113) 242 2666

The East: *John Barnes*
Carlton House, 31-34 Railway Street, Chelmsford, Essex, CM1 1NJ Tel (01245) 269 595

The South West: *Edward Corrigan*
33 Wine Street, Bristol, BS1 2BQ Tel: (0117) 925 2255

KINGSTON SMITH

DEVONSHIRE HOUSE, 60 GOSWELL ROAD, LONDON, EC1M 7AD
Tel: (0171) 566 4000 **Fax:** (0171) 566 4010 **Email:** ks@kingsmith.co.uk

Contact partner:	Emile Woolfe
Number of partners:	37
Number of staff:	300

The Firm: The Kingston Smith litigation support facility was established in 1980, and all members of the service team have many years professional and commercial experience to complement their legal and regulatory knowledge and skills. The team undertakes a wide range of specialist assignments for lawyers, insurers, loss adjusters, professional and regulatory bodies and government agencies, acting for either defendants or plaintiffs. Civil and criminal assignments undertaken, including legally aided cases. Specialist areas include professional negligence, consequential loss and business interruption including personal injury. Matrimonial, white collar crime, fraud, regulatory and compliance matters including Directors' Disqualification. Forensic accounting including modelling in insurance and commercial cases. Inland Revenue and Customs investigations, settlements and related disputes. Business and share valuations. Sectors include financial and investment business. Specialist insolvency division.

Litigation Support Partners:

Emile Woolf FCA, FCCA, MAE, FinstM, FIIA is Chairman of the PI Requirements Committee of the Institute of Chartered Accountants in England and Wales (ICAEW) and is consulting editor of PI Quarterly, published by leading indemnity brokers, Bowrings. He lectures and writes regularly on litigation matters and is author of several leading texts including 'Professional Liability of Accountants (ICAEW)', 'Risk Management for Auditors (ICAEW)', 'Preserving Your Right to Audit (CCH Editions)', 'Auditing Today (Prentice Hall)', and 'The Legal Liabilities of Practising Accountants (Butterworths)'. He is a member of the Academy of Experts and of the ICAEW Office of Professional Standards and represents the Institute on the Joint Advisory Panel of Approved Insurers. He specialises in professional negligence and forensic accounting matters.

Benjamin Howe FCA, ATII, MAE is responsible for the consequential and material loss claims assignments arising from, e.g. medical negligence, personal injury and fire. His background includes advisory appointments and directorships in small companies giving him experience in commercial aspects of business management to complement his professional expertise. He is a member of the Academy of Experts.

Martin Muirhead FCA, MAE undertakes forensic accounting including computer modelling as well as commercial and tax related matters. Martin's extensive business and tax experience includes financial services, investment business and general commercial sectors. Recent matters include acting in relation to liability and quantum in professional negligence disputes, varied commercial litigation including business and share valuations, minority protection, Inland Revenue investigations including Special Compliance Office, PAYE Audit and Benefits compliance and advising on quantum issues. He was appointed by the Charity Commissioners, under the Charities Act 1993, to act as the first Receiver and Manager of a UK registered Charity including dispute resolution of contentious areas including fiduciary duty trustees responsibilities. He is also a Company Director and Member of the Academy of Experts.

Adrian Houstoun FCA, ACIArb is a Chartered Accountant and a member of the Chartered Institute of Arbitrators. He specialises in matters where knowledge of the law of contract, tort and evidence can be combined with his extensive business experience, including public company acquisitions and VAT services. One of his recent assignments was an appointment by the Secretary of State for Industry, as an Inspector under the Financial Services Act, to investigate alleged insider dealing in the securities of a public company. He is on the Institute of Chartered Accountants' panel of arbitrators and also undertakes investigations on their behalf into firms who are unable to obtain insurance cover. He has significant experience with business valuation cases and assisted lawyers in a number of matrimonial cases as well as advising directors following the sale of a business in connection with warranty claims.

KINGSTON
SMITH
Chartered Accountants

KPMG

20 FARRINGDON STREET, LONDON, EC4A 4PP
Tel: (0171) 311 1000 **Fax:** (0171) 311 3710 **DX:** 38050 BLACKFRIARS **Internet:** http//www.kpmg.co.uk

Legal Business's recent survey (March 1997), highlighted KPMG as 'highly recommended' and as the largest firm in the forensic accounting field.

Principal Services: KPMG's forensic accounting department has a dedicated team of more than 130 partners and professional staff throughout the UK.The firm provides specialist services in six broad areas:

Commercial disputes: Loss of profits claims; breach of contract and warranty claims; purchase and sale disputes and agreement vetting; shareholder and partnership disputes; libel and slander actions; intellectual property disputes; business and share valuations; insurance claims; security for costs applications.

Professional negligence: Accounting; auditing; corporate finance and IT implementation (liability and quantum); other professionals (quantum).

Fraud investigation: KPMG has developed particular expertise in handling investigations into fraud. Numerous assignments for government, police, companies and public bodies bear witness to the firm's reputation in this area. The firm uses a refined investigation methodology which, when combined with advanced technology, allows KPMG to investigate suspected frauds of all sizes effectively and efficiently.

Personal disputes: Personal injury claims; fatal accidents; medical negligence; family and matrimonial disputes; employment and pension disputes.

Regulatory investigations: Investigations and accounting assistance for regulatory authorities and those under investigation. Also assistance in statutory and disciplinary enquiries.

Determinations and Arbitrations: Expert determinations; arbitrations; mediations; valuations.

The provision of these services is enhanced by expert knowledge of various industry sectors including: banking, insurance, commodities, information technology, telecommunications, shipping and transportation, construction, manufacturing, infrastructure and government, leasing, retailing, healthcare and pharmaceutical, and intellectual property.

The Firm: KPMG Forensic Accounting is a leading member of the KPMG International Forensic Network providing worldwide forensic accounting services. KPMG is one of the leading professional firms in the world and provides a comprehensive range of accountancy and consulting services. The firm has experience of working with organisations of all sizes: from government to individuals, and from multinationals to privately-owned businesses. KPMG has over 85,000 personnel in 155 countries worldwide, and over 9,000 people in 33 offices in the UK.

The principal regional contacts are:

Belfast	Henry Saville	(01232) 24 3377
Birmingham	Ian Starkey	(0121) 232 3000
Bristol	Simon Pomeroy	(0117) 946 4000
Glasgow	Robin Crawford	(0141) 226 5511
Leeds	Tim Taylor	(0113) 231 3000
Manchester	Philip Ramsbottom	(0161) 838 4000
Reading	Alastair Hunter	(0118) 964 2040

Contact Partners:	Nick Andrews
	Adam Bates
	David Eastwood
	John Ellison
	Philip Haberman
	Alex Plavsic
	David Smith
	John Williams
Contact Directors:	David Davies
	Giles Williams

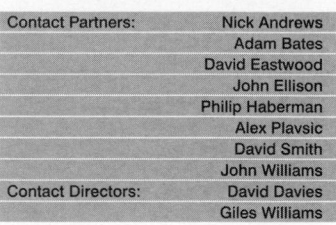

LEVY GEE

66 WIGMORE STREET, LONDON, W1H 0HQ
Tel: (0171) 467 4000 **Fax:** (0171) 467 4040 **Internet:** http://www.levygee.co.uk

The Firm: The Litigation Support department offers a comprehensive range of services including claims for consequential loss, breach of warranty, personal injury for both plaintiff and defendant, medical negligence, share valuation, matrimonial and professional negligence claims primarily for insurers.

We assist the legal profession and the public in the submission and defence of claims and help companies protect against fraud.

We provide a partner-led service, fast turnaround and access to numerous specific industry experts.

All partners are experienced Expert Witnesses.

Contact partners:	David Epstein
	David Stern
	Gail Rifkind
Number of partners:	35
Number of staff:	237

CONTACTS IN OTHER UK OFFICES	
Birmingham	
Alan R Thompson	*Tel:* (0121) 456 2525
Manchester	
Tony Freeman	*Tel:* (0161) 835 2843

Principal Areas of Work:
- Professional negligence
- Breach of contract
- Business interruption
- Breach of warranty
- Fraud Share valuation
- Due diligence
- ADR – CEDR accredited member
- Personal injury
- Matrimonial
- Medical negligence

Litigation Support led by:

David Epstein FCA ATII MBIM MAE has thirty years' experience of general practice and extensive knowledge of advising partnerships and owner-managed businesses.

David Stern FCA MAE MSPI ACIArb works extensively in the areas of contractual disputes, fraud investigations, business interruption claims and valuations, and is experienced at giving evidence in Court. He is a CEDR accredited mediator.

Gail Rifkind CA, MAE, MEWI specialises in personal injury, medical negligence and fatal accident work, for both plaintiff and defendant.

LITTLEJOHN FRAZER

1 PARK PLACE, CANARY WHARF, LONDON, E14 4HJ
Tel: (0171) 987 5030 **Fax:** (0171) 987 9707

The Firm: Littlejohn Frazer's litigation support department was founded in 1986, chiefly to provide expert opinion on liability and quantum in cases of professional negligence involving other firms of accountants but the department's work now includes most areas of litigation support. The department is led by partners who co-ordinate the provision of services from other specialist departments within the firm to ensure that appropriate technical expertise complements the firm's extensive experience of the litigation process including considerable trial experience.

The lead partner is a member of the Academy of Experts and is the co-author of "Expert Accounting Evidence – A Guide for Litigation Support" published by Accountancy Books. Partners have experience of investigations for the DTI, and the firm has undertaken a number of assignments for the Serious Fraud Office. Legally aided work is undertaken, in both civil and criminal matters. The firm has extensive experience of the insurance sector and in particular the Lloyd's market.

Contact partner:	Ian Hobbs
Number of partners:	24
Number of staff:	150

Principal Areas of Work:

Civil:
- Accountants professional negligence
- Financial consequences of:
  - personal injury
  - consequential loss, construction and fire-damage claims
  - insurance and re-insurance disputes
  - purchase and sales disputes

Criminal:
- Serious fraud
- Crime with financial motive

Companies Act offences

Investigations:
- Computer consultancy
- Forensic accounting

Regulatory:
- ICAEW
- RICS
- Lloyd's
- Law Society
- DTI, SFO

Litigation Support Partners:

I.C. Hobbs FCA: Member of Academy of Experts. Specialises in accountants' negligence, quantification of loss, share valuations, tax as a non-specialist, serious fraud, personal injury. (Direct line: 0171 369 4564)

A.H.F. Campbell FCA: Serious fraud, regulatory, Lloyd's, accountants' negligence, breach of financial warranties. (Direct line: 0171 369 4565)

J.G. Ambler ACA: Computer consultancy, software contracts. (Direct line: 0171 369 4589)

R.L. Green FCCA: Solicitors' Accounts Rules. (Direct line: 0171 369 4587)

D.R.M. Frame FCA: Serious fraud, forensic. (Direct line: 0171 369 4507)

M.T. Stenson FCA: Serious fraud, regulatory. (Direct line: 0171 369 4575)

D.W. Roberts FCA: Regulatory, Lloyd's. (Direct line: 0171 369 4551)

LONDON ECONOMICS

66 CHILTERN STREET, LONDON, W1M 1PR
Tel: 0171 446 8400 **Fax:** 0171 446 8484/5 **Internet:** http://www.londecon.co.uk

The Firm: LE is Europe's leading independent economics consultancy, with offices in Brussels, Dublin and Tokyo and fast-growing subsidiaries in Boston and Melbourne. Since its foundation in 1986, LE has provided comprehensive litigation and arbitration support in cases across the UK, the EU and Australia.

It is our business to understand the economic forces driving markets, industries and the company decision-making process. This underpins all of the work LE does across business strategy, regulation and competition policy. It is also invaluable in various aspects of litigation and arbitration. Our expertise covers:

Intrepretation of economic concepts in the context of contract or tort: litigation or arbitration can hinge on the correct definition of economic concepts such as 'demand', 'cost' or 'profit'.

Calculation of damages: combining state-of-the-art economic techniques with the latest quantitative methods and a detailed knowledge of financial and management accounting, LE specialises in the measurement of the quantum of damages for breach of contract or tort.

Competition cases under both UK competition law and Articles 85 and 86 of the EC Treaty.

Valuation of intellectual property rights: it is increasingly recognised that economists are uniquely qualified to carry out the valuation of intellectual property rights.

Tax disputes: our staff include some of the country's leading experts on economic aspects of taxation.

LE's litigation support services are based on a unique combination of skills and resources unavailable from other advisers. As specialist economic consultants, we provide a service that combines the economic expertise of the best independent academics with the professionalism and ability to deliver associated with large accounting firms.

We draft expert reports in a way that maximises the strength of the economic case: our ability to explain highly technical concepts to non-economists is second to none. LE's expert witnesses are experienced at giving evidence, appearing in court and reacting to cross-examination. We provide advice on the strengths and weaknesses of the opposition's case and expert opinions, providing ammunition for cross-examination.

Contact:	Zoltan Biro

LONDON
ECONOMICS

LUBBOCK FINE

RUSSELL BEDFORD HOUSE, CITY FORUM, 250 CITY RD, LONDON, EC1V 2QQ
Tel: (0171) 490 7766 **Fax:** (0171) 490 5102 **Email:** post@lubbockfine.co.uk **Internet:** www.lubbockfine.co.uk

The Firm: Lubbock Fine is a leading UK medium-sized practice providing a full service to personal and corporate clients on all aspects of audit, accounts, taxation and financial management. Legal support work is one of the fastest growing areas of our practice.

The team is led by Alan Cushnir who is a member of the British Academy of Experts. Partner Anthony Sober is an associate of the Chartered Institute of Arbitrators and former senior partner (now active consultant), Stanley Prashker, is an experienced arbitrator and a member of both the Institute and The Academy. Our experience extends to quantifying all financial aspects of litigation whether in formal court actions or in arbitration and mediation and complements the lawyers legal work.

Services: Services range from the provision of expert's reports and investigations to acting as expert witnesses. The firm handles substantial assignments in the following areas: matrimonial and divorce proceedings, providing independent valuations and tracing assets, arbitrating partnership disputes, claims against government bodies (e.g. Criminal Injuries Compensation Board), breach of contract, fraud and criminal work and personal injury claims.

Litigation Support Partner:
Alan M. Cushnir FCA MSPI MBAE. Member of the British Academy of Experts. Licensed insolvency practitioner. Specialises in Litigation Support and Forensic Accounting.

Contact partner:	Alan M Cushnir
Number of partners:	13

MACNAIR MASON

ST CLARE HOUSE, 30-33 MINORIES, LONDON, EC3N 1DU
Tel: (0171) 481 3022 **Fax:** (0171) 488 4458

The Firm: Macnair Mason has practised in the heart of the City for 100 years. A dedicated forensic accounting team provides expert advice in support of the legal argument to produce cost effective resolution of disputes and litigation over the following key areas of dispute:

- Loss of profits or earnings
- Share and business valuations
- Fidelity policies
- Breach of contract and warranty
- Computer system and installation
- Insurance, banking and financial services

- Personal injury and fatality claims
- Professional negligence and liability claims
- Fraud and other financial irregularities
- Intellectual property
- Property and construction
- Family and matrimonial

Contact partners:	Ken McAvoy
	Stuart Markley
	Richard Mason
Number of partners:	8

MARKS & CLERK

57-60 LINCOLN'S INN FIELDS, LONDON, WC2A 3LS
Tel: (0171) 400 3000 **Fax:** (0171) 404 4910 **Email:** admin@marks-clerk.com

The Firm: Marks & Clerk was founded in 1887. Today over 40 partners and 200 staff work for leading UK and overseas corporations worldwide as well as for start-up and private clients.

A *Managing Intellectual Property* survey of 1997 (based on over 3,000 responses to a questionnaire submitted to senior professionals from all over the world) featured separate tables for UK patent and trade mark agencies. Marks & Clerk was placed first in both these tables.

In addition to preparing and filing patent, trade mark and design applications we advise on infringement and its avoidance, reverse engineering and validity issues; we provide technical support to solicitors and barristers in litigation and perform intellectual property audits and due diligence reviews on all aspects of Intellectual Property transactions. We offer expert witnesses for proceedings in the UK and overseas and provide ancillary services such as patent, design and trade mark searching, competitor monitoring and related investigations. We also arrange appropriate documentation for global assignment and licensing transactions and assist in IP portfolio management and training services.

Contact partners:	See list below
Number of partners:	50
Number of staff:	200

Principal office contacts (or ask for duty partner):

Alicante	Aidan Clarke	Tel (00 34) 96 51 42727
Birmingham	Tony Pearce	Tel (0121) 643 5881
Cheltenham	Mike Higgins	Tel (01242) 524 520
Glasgow	Bill McCallum	Tel (0141) 221 5767
Hong Kong	Simon Speeks	Tel (00852) 526 6345
Leeds	Keith Hodkinson	Tel (0161) 236 2275
London	John Slater	Tel (0171) 400 3000
Luxembourg	Pierre Weyland	Tel (00352) 400 270
Manchester	John Allman	Tel (0161) 236 2275
Ottawa	Bob Sterling	Tel (001 613) 236 9561
Oxford	Richard Harding	Tel (01865) 397 900

MARKS & CLERK
Intellectual Property

MAZARS NEVILLE RUSSELL

24 BEVIS MARKS, LONDON, EC3A 7NR
Tel: (0171) 377 1000 **Fax:** (0171) 377 8931 **Internet:** http//www.mazarsnr.co.uk

The Firm: Mazars Neville Russell's national litigation support and forensic accounting team is regularly appointed by lawyers, commercial organisations, prosecuting authorities and regulators to investigate and advise on situations requiring independent and objective analysis and opinion from skilled and professional advisors. Extensive work has been carried out with the SFO and DTI.

The firm's technical expertise, familiarity with the litigation process, and wealth of experience in many financial and commercial sectors, combined with its ability to present financial information in an intelligible and imaginative way enables it to provide the legal profession with an extensive range of support services.

Contact Partners:	Peter Hyatt
	Glyn Williams
	Chris Makin
Number of partners:	100
Number of staff:	950

Continues overleaf

Other specialisms include:

- Professional negligence
- Contractual disputes
- Damage and loss quantification
- Reinsurance disputes
- Share and business valuations
- Personal injury, medical negligence and fatal accidents
- Structured settlements
- Fraud investigations and asset recovery
- Statutory, regulatory and corporate investigations
- Money laundering investigations
- Directors' disqualification proceedings
- Matrimonial proceedings
- Experienced expert witnesses
- Arbitration and expert determination

The Firm: Mazars Neville Russell is a leading firm of chartered accountants and consultants with 21 offices in the UK, with a fully dedicated litigation support and forensic accounting department in London, Leeds and several other of the firm's UK offices. The UK operation of Mazars is part of a true international partnership (rather than a network of independent firms) with 275 partners and approximately 3500 staff in over 30 countries around the world, with the largest concentration in Europe.

MOORES ROWLAND

CLIFFORD'S INN, FETTER LANE, LONDON, EC4A 1AS
Tel: (0171) 831 2345 **Fax:** (0171) 831 6123

The Firm: Moores Rowland Litigation Support Group assists lawyers across the country in a wide variety of cases. Specialist partners work directly with lawyers and a team of experienced professionals to provide additional support when required.

Contact partner:	Peter Miller
Number of partners:	94
Number of staff:	630

Services:

Valuation of Shares and Businesses: Experience in cases ranging from family disputes to employee share schemes and intellectual property valuations.

Damages & Negligence Claims: Provide financial and accounting expertise and expert witnesses in negotiations for settlements.

Financial Services Act/Regulatory Authorities Investigations: Have carried out numerous investigations on behalf of SRO's and others.

Fraud Investigations: Experience includes six major investigations for the DTI and working closely with the Serious Fraud Office and police authorities.

Matrimonial Disputes: Help spouses in financial divorce settlements including the investigations of hidden assets and income.

Partnership Disputes: Help resolve taxation disputes, calculate equitable adjustments and prepare remuneration packages.

Employment Matters: Advises on financial and tax implications of termination packages.

Other Areas: Trust litigation; royalty disputes: patent, copyright and trademark infringement disputes; charter party disputes.

Moores Rowland
Chartered Accountants

MOORE STEPHENS

ST PAUL'S HOUSE, WARWICK LANE, LONDON, EC4P 4BN
Tel: (0171) 334 9191 **Fax:** (0171) 248 3408

Litigation Support Partners:

Mr Gervase Hulbert OBE FCA. Experienced in criminal investigations and forensic accounting covering the various types of fraud, misappropriation, misrepresentation, and other illegal or potentially illegal activities involving money. Has undertaken many international assignments. Awarded the OBE in 1993 for services to the accountancy profession.

Contact partners:	Civil: Julian Wilkinson
	Criminal: Gervase Hulbert
Number of partners:	136
Number of staff:	990

Mr Paul Powell FCA. Member of the British Academy of Experts. Over twenty years' experience as expert witness for Arbitration and High Court proceedings covering shipping and international transportation matters, including consequential loss. Appointed by the DTI as an inspector in a major company investigation.

Mr Julian Wilkinson FCA. Member of the British Academy of Experts. Many years' experience as expert witness for Arbitration and High Court proceedings with particular experience of shipping related matters including alleged scuttling claims and joint venture disputes. Also experienced in loss of profits claims. Has given evidence in Court.

Mr Andrew Nicholl BSc, FCA. Experienced in interpretation of the application of accounting and auditing standards, including assessment of professional work by accountants. Has acted as expert accountant in major cases involving allegations of false accounting and various commercial matters. Has given evidence in Court.

Principal Areas of Work:

Loss of Profits: Business interruption; product inadequacy; infringement of intellectual property rights; breach of contract or warranties; fraud, defalcation or misappropriation; personal injury or fatal accident.

Valuations: Businesses and business assets for settlement of commercial disputes; in separation or divorce cases.

Professional Negligence: Property and information technology matters; due diligence work in business acquisitions and disputes; taxation advice; insolvency; audit and accountancy.

International Trade Claims: Particularly shipping and transport matters.

NYMAN LIBSON PAUL

REGINA HOUSE, 124 FINCHLEY ROAD, LONDON, NW3 5JS
Tel: (0171) 794 5611 **Fax:** (0171) 431 1109 **DX:** 38864 SWISS COTTAGE
Email: warrenstarr@nymanlibsonpaul.co.uk **Internet:** http//www.nymanlibsonpaul.co.uk

The Firm: Nyman Libson Paul has been established for over 65 years and has an acknowledged reputation for providing pragmatic and constructive tax and commercial advice. Partners have extensive business and commercial experience which provides a solid foundation to carry out cost-effective and perceptive investigations, prepare constructive reports and give supportive expert testimony. Partners are used to working at short notice and throughout the UK. Legal Aid work undertaken.

Contact Partners:	Warren Starr
	FCA MAE QDR
	Robert Green
	FCA MAE ACI Arb.
Number of partners:	10
Number of staff:	65

Principal areas of work:

Reports for all aspects of: auditing, tax, entertainment industry – music, film, TV and video, theatre, record. **Commercial disputes** from breach of contract and loss of profit claims to shareholder disputes;

Matrimonial issues to establish a spouse's real financial requirements or resources, including tracing assets;

Insurance claims, computing loss of earnings from issues such as personal injury and accidental damage;

Forensic accounting, untangling fraud cases or suggesting preventative measures for the future;

Assessing losses arising from professional negligence;

Tax and VAT investigations for individuals and companies, dealing with Special Compliance Office;

Mediation of commercial and financial disputes

Partners are members of The Academy of Experts and Law Society checked Experts. W. Starr is a CEDR accredited Mediator.

PANNELL KERR FORSTER

NEW GARDEN HOUSE, 78 HATTON GARDEN, LONDON, EC1N 8JA
Tel: (0171) 831 7393 **Fax:** (0171) 405 6736 **DX:** 479 CH.LN. **Email:** claxton@uk.pkf.com

The Firm: Pannell Kerr Forster's investigative accounting skills are regularly drawn upon by the legal profession. A highly skilled team acts for plaintiff and defendants, assisting solicitors or counsel in cases ranging in size from small disputes to highly complex actions.

Multi-disciplinary teams of experts can be assembled from within the firm to handle the largest corporate actions.

Contact partner:	Roger Claxton
	Nick Whitaker
	Hugh Mathew-Jones
Number of partners:	6
Number of staff:	15

An impressive track record includes cases involving
- professional negligence
- breach of contract
- corporate disputes and insurance claims

The firm also assists in
- personal injury
- fatal accident
- fraud and divorce actions

PETER LOBBENBERG & CO

74 CHANCERY LANE, LONDON, WC2A 1AA
Tel: (0171) 430 9300 **Fax:** (0171) 430 9315 **DX:** 204 LONDON/CHANCERY LANE

The Firm: A niche practice well known as specialists in matrimonial litigation support throughout the country: its clients include over 75% of the leading London family law firms listed in Chambers. Also specialises in share valuations, and operates a caring tax service for private clients and trusts. As a member of Horwath Clark Whitehill Associates, the firm has access to a wide range of facilities and specialisms.

Languages spoken: German and French.

Mr Lobbenberg is a Fellow of the Academy of Experts.

Contact partner:	Peter Lobbenberg
Number of partners:	1
Number of staff:	2

PETERS ELWORTHY & MOORE

SALISBURY HOUSE, STATION ROAD, CAMBRIDGE, CB1 2LA
Tel: (01223) 362333 **Fax:** (01223) 461424 **Email:** pem@pem.co.uk

The Firm: Peters Elworthy & Moore is a well established independent firm able to offer services over a wide area. The firm is a member of Eura-Audit International, having established contacts in all Western European countries and the USA.

Principal Areas of Expertise: The firm can offer a full range of support services for litigation. David Collison is available as an expert witness. He is a member of the Council of Chartered Institute of Taxation and the author of standard works on taxation. Roger Guthrie has experience of litigation support in the fields of commercial disputes, share valuation and partnership succession.

Contact Partners:	David Collison
	Roger Guthrie
Number of partners:	11
Number of staff:	80

PINDERS PROFESSIONAL & CONSULTANCY SERVICES

PINDER HOUSE, CENTRAL MILTON KEYNES, MK9 1DS
Tel: (01908) 350500 **Fax:** (01908) 350501 **DX:** 84752 MILTON KEYNES 3 **Email:** ellism@pinders.co.uk

The Firm: The Pinder name has become synonymous with the appraisal and valuation of businesses since 1969, providing specialist professional services to the legal and banking professions on the healthcare, retail, licensed and leisure sectors.

Particular areas of expertise include business valuations (both current and retrospective), loss of profits claims, expert witness evidence and professional negligence.

Pinders can call upon a database containing detailed trading and valuation information on over 150,000 businesses throughout the United Kingdom, together with continually updated records of sale transactions.

Mark Ellis BSc FRICS ACIArb MAE, a previous member of The RICS Skills Panel on Trading Related Valuations, heads up the professional services and litigation support team based at the head office in Milton Keynes and a team of regional valuers. Together, they combine knowledge of local values, trade sources, legislation and competition with the wider accumulation of centralised information and expertise.

Contact Director:	Mark Ellis
Associate Director:	
	Simon Bird BSc ARICS ACIArb
Consultants:	Marek Bilecki FRICS
	Chris Dallison BSc ARICS ACIArb IRRV
	Quentin Johnson FRICS

PRICEWATERHOUSECOOPERS

PLUMTREE COURT, LONDON EC4A 4HT
Tel: (0171) 583 5000 **Fax:** (0171) 212 6366

NO. 1 LONDON BRIDGE, LONDON SE1 9QL
Tel: (0171) 939 3000 **Fax:** (0171) 939 5550

Internet: http//www.pwcglobal.com

PricewaterhouseCoopers is the world's largest professional services organisation, providing authoritative and persuasive expert advice on quantum and accountancy issues arising in disputes, investigations and claims. Our dedicated team of 200 financial investigators and forensic accountants includes specialists formerly with the Inland Revenue and Customs, the police, regulators, loss adjusters and other investigative bodies.

The principal areas of work are as follows:

- Dispute resolution
- Loss of profits claims
- Breach of contract and warranty
- Professional negligence
- Construction disputes
- Ancillary relief
- Personal injury
- Intellectual property disputes
- Insurance claims services
- Fraud investigations
- Fraud risk management
- Tax investigations
- Computer forensic services

CONTACTS

London
Andrew Clark	0171 939 5761
Andrew Gordon	0171 939 4187
Rick Helsby	0171 212 2902
Gerry Lagerberg	0171 213 5912
Chris Lemar	0171 212 4832
Andrew Mainz	0171 212 4831
Andrew Palmer	0171 939 5722
Jonathan Phillips	0171 939 5657
Tony Samuel	0171 939 5746
Richard Stevens	0171 939 2616

Midlands
Tony Parton	0121 265 5073
Robert Branson	0121 200 3000

South West and Wales
Ray Burton	0117 929 2791

East Anglia
David Prior	01223 552356

Edinburgh
Bill Cleghorn	0131 260 4102

Leeds
John Nisbet	0113 289 4799

Manchester
Jeff Hunt	0161 247 4119
Mark Stansfield	0161 245 2000

REEVES & NEYLAN

CECIL SQUARE HOUSE, CECIL SQUARE, MARGATE, CT9 1BQ
Tel: (01843) 227937 **Fax:** (01843) 226326 **DX:** 30561 MARGATE **Email:** reeves.neylan@dial.pipex.com **Internet:** http://www.reeves.co.uk

The Firm: Reeves & Neylan is a corporate member of the Academy of Experts. The forensic accounting department directs considerable resources to training and attending national seminars and conferences to ensure that it is constantly at the forefront of current developments. Services are provided to Plaintiffs and Defendants throughout the UK and legal aid work is accepted.

Contact partner:	Alan Tinham
Number of partners:	23
Number of staff:	200

Forensic Accounting and Expert Evidence:
Services include:
- Calculation of quantum
- Commercial disputes, product liability claims, environmental pollution
- Loss of profit claims
- Personal injury, medical negligence/class actions and fatality claims
- Divorce
- Professional negligence
- Theft, fraud and financial irregularities
- Wrongful and fraudulent trading
- VAT and tax fraud

Other Services:
Reeves & Neylan also provides specialist services to the legal profession in the following areas:
- Estate planning, trusts and executorships
- VAT consultancy
- Solicitors' Accounts Rules audits
- Tax planning and profit improvement consultancy
- Design and implementation of practice management information systems
- Practice finance arrangements
- Investigations

REEVES & NEYLAN
CHARTERED ACCOUNTANTS

RGL INTERNATIONAL FORENSIC ACCOUNTANTS

17 DEVONSHIRE SQUARE, LONDON, EC2M 4SQ
Tel: (0171) 247 4804 **Fax:** (0171) 247 4970

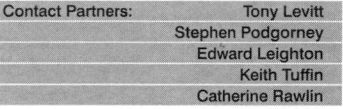

Contact Partners:	Tony Levitt
	Stephen Podgorney
	Edward Leighton
	Keith Tuffin
	Catherine Rawlin

RGL International is a market leader specialising exclusively in forensic accounting, giving dedicated support to solicitors, through the investigation and measurement of damages.

The Firm: RGL International prides itself on working quickly and efficiently, using the optimum amount of human, computer and other resources to support litigation by providing a clear picture of what happened and why. UK partners are backed by an international organisation which they can call upon as and when it is needed.

RGL International aims to present a full, unbiased report of the real circumstances behind any action. The firm helps to create the context within which clients can take the most appropriate decisions.

Types of work undertaken:

Areas of expertise include:
- Business Interruption/loss of profit
- Product Liability
- Fraud
- Personal Injury/fatal accident claims
- Reinsurance
- General quantification of damages

Once appointed by solicitors, RGL International investigates and checks the suppositions behind a claim. Highly experienced practitioners will know exactly which documents should be available for discovery, both inside and outside any company. These often include not only standard returns and records but also undisclosed management information, reports and papers from professional, trade and official bodies.

A precisely-worded request for disclosure of specific documents will indicate to the other party a client's insight into the issues involved in the claim and can often lead to negotiation of a satisfactory settlement.

Instructing solicitors are provided with a professional report for use in litigation or negotiations, highlighting any errors or omissions in the claim and its strengths or weaknesses.

Claims can often be complicated, with side issues clouding the essence of a case. When this happens, it may be valuable for the instructing solicitor to direct the RGL International team to attend meetings with the other party's experts, on a Without Prejudice basis, to resolve specific areas of disagreement or confusion. The limits to these discussions will be set by the instructing solicitor. Such meetings can greatly reduce the time spent considering a claim, thus reducing overall costs.

As a specialist firm RGL International
- never has a conflict of interest
- always dedicates a partner and team to every instruction
- ensures fees are cost effective and reasonable
- utilises experience from over 230 litigation staff worldwide

Should a claim come to court, RGL International practitioners can clearly and succinctly explain evidence included in the accounting expert's report under examination-in-chief and cross-examination. They will also be available to attend the trial, to help Counsel formulate questions based on evidence given by any opposing accounting experts.

For a copy of the firm's corporate brochure, please telephone any of the contact partners.

SAFFERY CHAMPNESS

FAIRFAX HOUSE, FULWOOD PLACE, GRAY'S INN, LONDON, WC1V 6UB
Tel: (0171) 405 2828 **Fax:** (0171) 405 7887 **DX:** 287-CHANCERY LANE, LONDON **Email:** mail@saffery.com

The Saffery Champness litigation support team works with lawyers throughout the country on a wide variety of cases. As accountants and business advisors, our expertise in and understanding of the business environment means we can offer valuable forensic accounting advice. Our team includes partners Stewart Garrard, Nick Kelsey and Ketih Weston for general financial issues, Peter Horsman and Mike Beattie for taxation and Michael Cohen for valuations.

Areas covered include:
- Personal injury and fatal accident
- Matrimonial
- Medical negligence
- Loss of profits or earnings
- Professional negligence
- Valuation of shares and businesses
- Fraud
- Inland Revenue and Customs & Excise investigations.

The Firm: Saffery Champness is a top twenty accountancy practice with nine offices in the United Kingdon and one in Guernsey. The firm has more than a century's experience of advising private clients on both their business and private affairs.

Contact partner:	Mike Beattie
	Stewart Garrard
Number of partners:	46
Number of staff:	350

Saffery Champness
CHARTERED ACCOUNTANTS

SIM KAPILA

15 BERNERS STREET, LONDON, W1P 3DE
Tel: (0171) 636 7699 **Fax:** (0171) 636 7717 **Email:** simkapila@aol.com

The Firm: Sim Kapila is a 'niche' practice known for its expertise in forensic accountancy. Its partners have acted in over 300 litigation support assignments. The firm brings together several years' experience with international accounting firms including the provision of expert evidence in court. The partners are members of the Academy of Experts and founding members of the Expert Witness Institute, contribute regularly to various legal journals and give seminars to firms of solicitors and insurers. Sim Kapila is associated with a specialist firm in the USA.

Services: Areas covered include disputes and claims involving personal injury and fatal accidents, loss of profits, business valuations, divorce, professional negligence, fraud and contractual disagreements.

The firm is happy to give an initial view without obligation on the financial and business aspects of any case.

Contact Partners:	Rakesh Kapila
	George Sim
Number of partners:	2

SIMMONS GAINSFORD

7/10 CHANDOS STREET, CAVENDISH SQUARE, LONDON, W1M 9DE
Tel: (0171) 447 9000 **Fax:** (0171) 447 9001

The Firm: Simmons Gainsford, with over 20 years experience in Forensic Accounting, are able to provide a comprehensive, commercial and pragmatic litigation support service to the legal profession.

The firm acts for both plaintiffs and defendants and deals with all types of litigation support work offering expert opinion and advice on claims relating to:
- Commercial disputes
- Business and share valuations
- Personal accident and injury claims
- Matrimonial disputes
- Professional negligence
- Loss of profits

Contact Partners:	Anthony Simmonds
	Thomas A. Lane
Number of partners:	11

THE SMITH & WILLIAMSON GROUP

NO. 1 RIDING HOUSE ST, LONDON, W1A 3AS
Tel: (0171) 637 5377 **Fax:** (0171) 631 0741 **Email:** <recipient>@smith.williamson.co.uk

Litigation Support Service: Smith & Williamson has a dedicated litigation support team whose expertise covers the full range of forensic accounting, including assistance for regulatory bodies, civil litigation and investigations of fraud.

The firm has experience in acting for either the plaintiff or the defendant and its objective is always to understand the wider implications of a case in order to provide a flexible and constructive approach to every assignment.

The Firm: Founded over 100 years ago, Smith & Williamson combines a firm of chartered accountants and an investment management house. Its full range of accountancy services covers accountancy, auditing, corporate finance, corporate recovery, corporate taxation, investigations, litigation support, management consulting and personal taxation.

Contact Partners:	Iain J. Allan
	Frank A M Akers-Douglas
	Peter G. Mills
	Peter J. Yeldon
Number of partners:	77
Number of staff:	370

Other Offices:

Birmingham	Andy Appleyard	(0121) 2362244	*Fax:* (0121) 2368035
Guildford	Graham J. Healy	(01483) 302200	*Fax:* (01483) 301232
Salisbury	Chris Appleton	(01722) 411881	*Fax:* (01722) 411438
Tunbridge Wells	Neale Jackson	(01892) 529922	*Fax:* (01892) 521225
Worcester	Neil Hickling	(01905) 610510	*Fax:* (01905) 29006
York	Tony Sleight	(01904) 640600	*Fax:* (01904) 640700

TAX INVESTIGATION SERVICES

211 PICCADILLY, LONDON, W1V 9LD
Tel: (0171) 917 9941 **Fax:** (0171) 439 0262

The Firm: Tax Investigation Services are an innovative niche firm, offering litigation support to the legal profession in fraud cases involving Customs & Excise/VAT issues.

Contact partner:	Don Mavin
Number of partners:	1

Principal Areas of Work:
Services include:
- Advising on the VAT or Duty implications of a case
- Evaluating schedules and calculations produced by Customs
- Preparing expert witness reports
- Providing expert evidence at trial

Litigation Support Partner:

Don Mavin AIIT, MAE is a former Senior Customs Investigator with several years more recent experience as a VAT and Duty Specialist in one of the top national accountancy firms. He has been instructed as an expert witness in several complex fraud trials involving VAT and fraudulent trading and also in civil actions in the High Court on a range of Customs & Excise issues. He is a member of the Institute of Indirect Taxation and the Academy of Experts, and is listed in the Law Society's Directory of Expert Witnesses.

Other Offices: The firm has an associated office in Birmingham (0121) 356 2886.

THE BAR

CHAMBERS & PARTNERS

CONTENTS BARRISTERS

Specialist Lists of Leading Sets and Barristers – London and the Regions

A–Z of Barristers' Chambers

BARRISTERS' CHARGES

The table below is a guide to the hourly rates charged by chambers for privately funded work (although the figures for the criminal Bar may also include legally aided work). In deciding how much to charge, clerks will take a number of factors into account: the barrister's seniority, experience and specialist skills, and the complexity and value of the case.

These days large commercial litigation cases are no longer charged on the basis of an hourly rate. Under pressure from their clients to cut costs, solicitors are increasingly insisting on fixed rates. In commercial sets, hourly rates are becoming a means of calculating a fixed rate for a job. Hybrid arrangements – part flat fee and part hourly rate – are also becoming common.

The emphasis on value for money also means that fewer cases now have two counsel appearing on each side. These days there is a tendency for silks to appear without juniors. There is some evidence, too, that the hourly rates for 'junior' juniors have been squeezed over the past twelve months. The top rates have not gone up, and the lowest hourly rates quoted were lower than a year ago, which means growing competition at the bottom end of the Bar.

Top rates for 'senior' juniors, by contrast, appear to have increased, as do the hourly rates for the leading commercial silks. Solicitor-advocates, seen as a threat to 'senior' commercial juniors in particular, do not seem to have made much of a dent in the work or fees of commercial sets.

HOURLY CHARGE RATES					
SENIORITY	Commercial	Tax	Chancery	Common law	Criminal
QC	£200-£800	£400-£850	£250-£500	£150-£375	£150-£350
10 yrs call	£75-£350	£175-£400	£75-£350	£75-£350	£50-£175
4-9 yrs call	£50-£250	£125-£250	£50-£250	£50-£200	£30-£125
1-3 yrs call	£25-£125	£75-£125	£25-£125	£30-£125	£10-£95

BARRISTERS' REMUNERATION

The scale of barristers' earnings has again been in the spotlight. In April the Lord Chancellor's Department published a list of the 20 barristers who received more than £190,000 in legal aid fees in 1996-97. Then in June the law lords launched an inquiry into the fees charged by four criminal silks in House of Lords appeals. That same month, Mr Justice Lightman angered former colleagues at the Bar when he expressed his concern at the fees charged by some commercial silks. "It is not unusual," he told the Chancery Bar Association, "to find briefs marked at £100,000, and a number of leaders regularly charge a brief fee of £350,000 and more . . ."

Our research suggests that such brief fees are exceedingly rare indeed. To get a brief fee of £350,000, would mean a four to six month trial with three to four months' preparation. The average commercial case – a 10 day High Court action with a couple of weeks' preparation – will earn a silk a brief fee in the region of £20-30,000. Silks are also faced with uncertainties: the unexpected settlement of a big case, for example, can leave a gaping hole in a silk's earnings.

No one disputes, however, the handsome rewards available to commercial and chancery practitioners. The elite number of silks earning around £1 million a year is small – only 15 according to our research (see the Million-A-Year-Club list on p. 1255). But it is common for commercial and chancery silks to earn around £400,000 a year. Criminal and common law silks tend to earn less – probably around £200-250,000 for reasonably successful practitioners.

Differences between practice areas are marked at the junior Bar. Our table clearly reveals the higher rewards available to successful commercial and chancery practitioners. Barristers with five years' experience in a leading commercial set can expect to earn around £100,000. They'll be doing poorly if they gross less than £50,000. In contrast, it is not unusual for a common law junior of similar standing to bill no more than £50,000.

For the first time, we have produced separate figures for the tax bar. This low-profile and highly specialist area of practice boasts some of the highest earnings at the Bar, especially at QC level. For big work solicitors and accountants generally instruct only silks. For this reason senior juniors can find their earnings reaching a plateau if they fail to take silk.

Our table, based on figures provided by chambers, provides an indication of the range of earnings, not averages. The remuneration of barristers is a reflection not only of their seniority and practice areas, but also their individual talents. Within the same sets and practice areas, there can be massive variations between barristers of similar seniority.

ANNUAL EARNINGS (THOUSANDS)					
SENIORITY	Commercial	Tax	Chancery	Common law	Criminal
QC	£200-£900	£400-£1500	£125-£700	£150-£500	£100-£500
10 yrs call	£75-£400	£175-£400	£75-£400	£75-£300	£40-£250
4-9 yrs call	£40-£300	£100-£300	£40-£250	£40-£200	£40-£100
1-3 yrs call	£25-£150	£25-£150	£20-£150	£25-£90	£20-£50

All figures represent gross earnings before deduction of expenses.

STARS AT THE BAR

This section brings together the Bar's star all-rounders – the 25 silks and 4 juniors who appear in five or more of our specialist lists. Within this group, we have selected a Top Ten. Ranking on this list is determined not only by breadth of practice, but also by level of expertise within a barrister's practice areas.

For the second year running, Gordon Pollock leads the Top Ten. He appears on nine specialist lists – one more than anyone else. The quality of Pollock's practice is also unmatched, with four 'star' rankings and three placings in the first band.

Jonathan Sumption is once again runner-up (eight lists, two 'star' rankings, four placings in band one), but this year Anthony Grabiner moves into third place by himself. Although Grabiner appears on only five lists, the quality of his practice is outstanding – three 'star' rankings (better than anyone else save Pollock) and two band ones.

All of our Top Ten have broad ranging commercial practices save one – the civil liberties/media lawyer, Geoffrey Robertson. Six of the Top Ten also appear in our Million-A-Year Club.

The Million-A-Year Club

We have again produced a list of barristers said to be earning around £1m a year. This headline figure represents earnings before the deduction of chambers expenses. These will normally account for about 20 per cent of a top silk's earnings.

The 15-strong list, based on information from our contacts at the bar, can be divided into three categories: tax silks (Aaronson, Flesch, Gardiner and Goldberg); silks with heavy commercial practices (Burton, Carr, Grabiner, Pollock, Stadlen and Sumption); and commercial chancery silks (Etherton, Oliver, Sher and Vos). The only woman on the list – Elizabeth Gloster QC – is equally at home in commercial and commercial chancery work. The inclusion of four commercial chancery silks suggests that the rewards for the top practitioners in Lincoln's Inn now match those of their colleagues in the elite commercial sets in the Temple.

All the practitioners on our list act primarily for corporate clients who regard them as good value for money. Indeed, the fees charged by the top corporate silks will often be insignificant compared to the sums which they can save or win for their clients.

THE TOP TEN STARS AT THE BAR

POLLOCK QC, GORDON	
SUMPTION QC, JONATHAN	
GRABINER QC, ANTHONY	
GLOSTER QC, ELIZABETH	CLARKE QC, CHRISTOPHER
BELOFF QC, MICHAEL	ROBERTSON QC, GEOFFREY
BURTON QC, MICHAEL	SCOTT QC, PETER
ETHERTON QC, TERENCE	

THE MILLION A YEAR CLUB

AARONSON QC, GRAHAM	GRABINER QC, ANTHONY
BURTON QC, MICHAEL	OLIVER QC, DAVID
CARR QC, CHRISTOPHER	POLLOCK QC, GORDON
ETHERTON QC, TERENCE	SHER QC, JULES
FLESCH QC, MICHAEL	STADLEN QC, NICHOLAS
GARDINER QC, JOHN	SUMPTION QC, JONATHAN
GOLDBERG QC, DAVID	VOS QC, GEOFFREY
GLOSTER QC, ELIZABETH	

9 LISTS

Gordon Pollock QC Essex Court Chambers (Gordon Pollock QC)
Administrative & Public Law, Arbitration, Banking, Commercial, Energy & Utilities, Insurance & Reinsurance, Media & Entertainment, Shipping, Sports

8 LISTS

Jonathan Sumption QC Brick Court Chambers (Christopher Clarke QC)
Administrative & Public Law, Banking, Commercial, Energy & Utilities, Financial Services, Insurance & Reinsurance, Media & Entertainment, Professional Negligence

7 LISTS

Michael Burton QC Littleton Chambers (Michael Burton QC)
Alternative Dispute Resolution, Commercial, Construction, Employment Law, Partnership, Professional Negligence, Sports Law

Christopher Clarke QC Brick Court Chambers (Christopher Clarke QC)
Arbitration, Aviation, Commercial, Insurance & Reinsurance, Media & Entertainment, Professional Negligence, Shipping

6 LISTS

Michael Briggs QC Serle Court Chambers (Charles Sparrow QC)
Commercial, Commercial Chancery, Company, Insolvency, Partnership, Property Litigation

Peter Duffy QC Essex Court Chambers (Gordon Pollock QC)
Administrative & Public Law, Civil Liberties, European Union/Competition, Media & Entertainment, Tax, Sports

Ian Glick QC One Essex Court (Anthony Grabiner QC)
Arbitration, Banking, Commercial, Energy & Utilities, Financial Services, Tax

Elizabeth Gloster QC One Essex Court (Anthony Grabiner QC)
Commercial, Commercial Chancery, Company, Financial Services, Insolvency, Professional Negligence

Jeffrey Gruder QC One Essex Court (Anthony Grabiner QC)
Arbitration, Banking, Commercial, Energy & Utilities, Insurance & Reinsurance, Shipping

Anthony Mann QC Enterprise Chambers (Anthony Mann QC)
Banking, Commercial, Commercial Chancery, Company, Insolvency, Professional Negligence

Peter Scott QC Fountain Court (Peter Scott QC)
Arbitration, Aviation, Banking, Commercial, Energy & Utilities, Professional Negligence

Andrew Smith QC Fountain Court (Peter Scott QC)
Arbitration, Aviation, Commercial, Computer Law & I.T., Insurance & Reinsurance, Parliamentary

5 LISTS

Michael Beloff QC 4-5 Gray's Inn Square (Miss Elizabeth Appleby QC & The Hon. M. Beloff QC)
Administrative & Public Law, Civil Liberties, Employment Law, Immigration, Sports

Christopher Butcher QC 7 King's Bench Walk (Stephen Tomlinson QC)
Arbitration, Commercial, Insurance & Reinsurance, Professional Negligence, Shipping

Michael Crystal QC 3/4 South Square (Michael Crystal QC)
Banking, Commercial Chancery, Company, Financial Services, Insolvency

Terence Etherton QC Wilberforce Chambers (Edward Nugee QC)
Banking, Commercial Chancery, Financial Services, Pensions, Property Litigation

Edwin Glasgow QC 39 Essex Street (Edwin Glasgow QC)
Commercial, Construction, Personal Injury, Professional Negligence, Sports

Anthony Grabiner QC One Essex Court (Anthony Grabiner QC)
Arbitration, Banking, Commercial, Energy & Utilities, Insurance & Reinsurance

Robert Hildyard QC 4 Stone Buildings (Philip Heslop QC)
Commercial Chancery, Company, Energy & Utilities, Financial Services, Insurance & Reinsurance

Ian Hunter QC Essex Court Chambers (Gordon Pollock QC)
Alternative Dispute Resolution, Arbitration, Aviation, Insurance & Reinsurance, Shipping

Linden Ife Enterprise Chambers (Anthony Mann QC)
Commercial Chancery, Company, Financial Services, Insolvency, Property Litigation

Terence Mowschenson QC One Essex Court (Anthony Grabiner QC)
Commercial, Company, Insolvency, Insurance & Reinsurance, Professional Negligence

Andrew Nicol QC Doughty Street Chambers (Geoffrey Robertson QC)
Administrative & Public Law, Civil Liberties, Defamation, Immigration & Nationality, Media & Entertainment

Lionel Read QC 1 Serjeants' Inn (Lionel Read QC)
Administrative & Public Law, Energy & Utilities, Environmental Law, Parliamentary, Planning

Geoffrey Robertson QC Doughty Street Chambers (Geoffrey Robertson QC)
Administrative & Public Law, Civil Liberties, Crime, Defamation, Media & Entertainment

Anthony Scrivener QC 2-3 Gray's Inn Square (Anthony Scrivener QC)
Administrative & Public Law, Civil Liberties, Consumer Law, Crime, Fraud

Bankim Thanki QC Fountain Court (Peter Scott QC)
Aviation, Banking, Commercial, Construction, Professional Negligence

Nigel Tozzi QC 4 Pump Court (Bruce Mauleverer QC)
Commercial, Insurance & Reinsurance, Licensing, Media & Entertainment, Professional Negligence

Geoffrey C. Vos QC 3 Stone Buildings (G.C Vos QC)
Commercial, Commercial Chancery, Insolvency, Insurance & Reinsurance, Media & Entertainment

INTERNATIONAL CONNECTIONS

A–Z set numbers are shown in square brackets

Anguilla
4-5 Gray's Inn Square [79], 8 King's Bench Walk [110]

Antigua and Barbuda
4 Breams Buildings [18], One Essex Court [45], 2 Field Court [58], 1 Mitre Court Buildings [128]

Antilles
Two Garden Court [67], 1 Gray's Inn Square [75], 8 King's Bench Walk [110], 1 Mitre Court Buildings [128]

Australia
Arbitration Chambers [1], Atkin Chambers [3], Counsels' Chambers [341], 2 Crown Office Row [34], Doughty Street Chambers [37], Enterprise Chambers [282], Enterprise Chambers [42], Essex Court Chambers [44], 4 Essex Court [47], 20 Essex Street [50], 23 Essex Street [51], Falcon Chambers [55], 2 Field Court [58], 4 Field Court [59], Francis Taylor Building [62], Godolphin Chambers [392], Gray's Inn Tax Chambers [84], 10 King's Bench Walk [114], 1 Mitre Court Buildings [128], 8 New Square [142], New Walk Chambers [299], 10 Old Square [152], 2 Paper Buildings [162], 4 Pump Court [177], 6 Pump Court [180], 3 Raymond Buildings [186], 11 Stone Buildings [206], 3 Temple Gardens [216]

Austria
Littleton Chambers [123]

Bahamas
Erskine Chambers [43], Fountain Court [61], 8 Gray's Inn Square [81], 8 King's Bench Walk [110], 12 New Square [145], 10 Old Square [152], 3 Raymond Buildings [186], 4 Stone Buildings [200]

Bangladesh
Barristers Common Law Chambers [5], Forest House Chambers [60]

Barbados
11 Old Square [154], 18 Red Lion Court [188]

Belgium
Blackstone Chambers (formerly 2 Hare Court) [15], Bracton Chambers [17], 2 Harcourt Buildings [87]

Bermuda
Erskine Chambers [43], One Essex Court [45], Two Garden Court [67], 3 Gray's Inn Square [78], 4-5 Gray's Inn Square [79], 14 Gray's Inn Square [83], 7 King's Bench Walk [109], Littleton Chambers [123], 2 Mitre Court Buildings [129], 1 New Square [137], 24 Old Buildings [149], Old Square Chambers [150], Old Square Chambers [249], 10 Old Square [152], 13 Old Square [156], 4 Stone Buildings [200], Wilberforce Chambers [226]

Botswana
1 Crown Office Row [33], Doughty Street Chambers [37], 10 King's Bench Walk [113], 1 Middle Temple Lane [125]

British Virgin Islands
24 Old Buildings [149], Thirteen Old Square [157], 4 Stone Buildings [200]

Brunei
Essex Court Chambers [44], Littleton Chambers [123]

Canada
King Charles House [357]

Cayman Islands
Bracton Chambers [17], Erskine Chambers [43], Essex Court Chambers [44], 7 King's Bench Walk [109], 1 New Square [137], 24 Old Buildings [149], 13 Old Square [156], Thirteen Old Square [157], 4 Stone Buildings [200], Wilberforce Chambers [226]

Channel Islands (see also Guernsey, Jersey)
1 Dr Johnson's Buildings [38]

China
Essex Court Chambers [44]

Cyprus
4 Essex Court [47], 2 Paper Buildings [162]

Dominican Republic
1 Gray's Inn Square [75]

Eire
Arbitration Chambers [1], Arden Chambers [2], 33 Bedford Row [9], Doughty Street Chambers [37], 1 Dr Johnson's Buildings [38], Essex Court Chambers [44], Farrar's Building [56], 9 Gough Square [72], 10-11 Gray's Inn Square [82], 2 Harcourt Buildings [89], Harcourt Chambers [90], Harcourt Chambers [360], 3 Hare Court [96], King Charles House [357], 12 King's Bench Walk [117], 8 King St [323], Littman Chambers [124], Martin's Building [310], 2 Mitre Court Buildings [130], Newport Chambers [349], 8 New Square [142], 3 Paper Buildings [163], 5 Paper Buildings [169], 3 Raymond Buildings [186], 11 South Square [195], 9 Stone Buildings [205], 11 Stone Buildings [206], Stour Chambers [254], Trinity Chambers [346], 3 Verulam Buildings [223]

Falkland Islands
13 Old Square [156]

Fiji
3 Raymond Buildings [186]

France
Bracton Chambers [17], 2 Crown Office Row [35], 1 Dr Johnson's Buildings [38], Essex Court Chambers [44], 4 Essex Court [47], 20 Essex Street [50], Francis Taylor Building [63], Keating Chambers [100]

Gambia
One Essex Court [45]

Germany
One Essex Court [45], 3 Paper Buildings [164], Pump Court Chambers [174]

Ghana
11 Old Square [154], 12 Old Square [155]

Gibraltar
29 Bedford Row Chambers [8], 2 Crown Office Row [34], Essex Court Chambers [44], 2 Field Court [58], 4 Field Court [59], Fountain Court [61], 9 Gough Square [72], 3 Hare Court [96], 1 New Square [137], 2 Paper Buildings [162], 3 Paper Buildings [163], 4 Stone Buildings [200], 7 Stone Buildings [202], 3 Verulam Buildings [223]

Greece
4 Essex Court [47]

Hong Kong

4 Breams Buildings [18], 2 Crown Office Row [35], 1 Dr Johnson's Buildings [38], Erskine Chambers [43], Essex Court Chambers [44], 4 Essex Court [47], 20 Essex Street [50], 23 Essex Street [51], Falcon Chambers [55], Fountain Court [61], 2-3 Gray's Inn Square [77], 4-5 Gray's Inn Square [79], 8 Gray's Inn Square [81], Gray's Inn Tax Chambers [84], 1 Hare Court [94], 1 Hare Court [93], Iscoed Chambers [388], Keating Chambers [100], 7 King's Bench Walk [109], Littleton Chambers [123], Littman Chambers [124], 2 Mitre Court Buildings [129], New Court Chambers [135], 1 New Square [137], Three New Square [139], 24 Old Buildings [149], Old Square Chambers [150], Old Square Chambers [249], 9 Old Square [151], 13 Old Square [156], 3 Paper Buildings [163], 5 Paper Buildings [169], 3 Raymond Buildings [186], 18 Red Lion Court [188], No. 1 Serjeants' Inn [189], 4 Stone Buildings [200], 199 Strand [207], Wilberforce Chambers [226]

India

3 Dr Johnson's Buildings [40], 2 Middle Temple Lane [126], 8 New Square [142], 2 Paper Buildings [162]

Isle of Man

8 Gray's Inn Square [81], 12 New Square [145], 22 Old Buildings [147], 24 Old Buildings [149], 13 Old Square [156]

Israel

Lamb Building [119], St. James's Chambers [334]

Italy

1 Dr Johnson's Buildings [38], 35 Essex Street [52], Goldsworth Chambers [70], 6 Gray's Inn Square [80], 11 King's Bench Walk [116], New Court [134]

Jamaica

Bracton Chambers [17], 1 Gray's Inn Square [74], 8 King's Bench Walk [110]

Jersey

1 Dr Johnson's Buildings [38], 2 Mitre Court Buildings [129], Old Square Chambers [150], Old Square Chambers [249], 2 Paper Buildings [162]

Jordan

2 Stone Buildings [198]

Kenya

Essex Court Chambers [44], 10 King's Bench Walk [113]

Lesotho

17 Carlton Crescent [380], Doughty Street Chambers [37], 4-5 Gray's Inn Square [79]

Malaysia

Erskine Chambers [43], Essex Court Chambers [44], 20 Essex Street [50], 1 Hare Court [93], 2 Middle Temple Lane [127], 1 New Square [137], 10 Old Square [152], 13 Old Square [156], 3 Raymond Buildings [186], 4 Stone Buildings [200]

Mauritius

One Essex Court [45], Gray's Inn Tax Chambers [84], 4 King's Bench Walk [104], 10 King's Bench Walk [113], Thomas More Chambers [218]

Namibia

1 Crown Office Row [33], Doughty Street Chambers [37]

Nepal

199 Strand [207]

New Zealand

17 Bedford Row [7], 9-12 Bell Yard [14], 2 Field Court [58], Francis Taylor Building [63], 1 Gray's Inn Square [75], 2 Gray's Inn Square Chambers [76], Gray's Inn Tax Chambers [84], 2 Paper Buildings [162], St. John's Chambers [250]

Nigeria

Francis Taylor Building [63], 10 King's Bench Walk [114], 12 Old Square [155], Pepys' Chambers [171], Pump Court Chambers [174]

Northern Ireland

Barnards Inn Chambers [4], Doughty Street Chambers [37], Farrar's Building [56], Two Garden Court [67], 2 Harcourt Buildings [89], 2 Hare Court [95], 8 New Square [142], 24 Old Buildings [148], Old Square Chambers [150], Old Square Chambers [249], 13 Old Square [156], Pump Court Chambers [174], 18 Red Lion Court [188], 9 Stone Buildings [205], 3 Verulam Buildings [223]

Norway

Littleton Chambers [123]

Pakistan

Forest House Chambers [60], 2 Middle Temple Lane [126], 8 New Square [142], 11 Old Square [154]

Papua New Guinea

2 Field Court [58]

Poland

35 Essex Street [52]

Scotland

33 Bedford Row [9], 20 Essex Street [50], 3 Gray's Inn Square [78], 2 Hare Court [95], Old Square Chambers [150], Old Square Chambers [249], 1 Serjeants' Inn [190], 7 Stone Buildings [202]

Singapore

4 Breams Buildings [18], Erskine Chambers [43], Essex Court Chambers [44], 20 Essex Street [50], Fountain Court [61], 2-3 Gray's Inn Square [77], Gray's Inn Tax Chambers [84], 1 Hare Court [93], Keating Chambers [100], 7 King's Bench Walk [109], Littleton Chambers [123], 1 New Square [137], Three New Square [139], 24 Old Buildings [149], 13 Old Square [156], 3 Raymond Buildings [186], 4 Stone Buildings [200], Wilberforce Chambers [226]

South Africa

1 Crown Office Row [33], Doughty Street Chambers [37], One Essex Court [45], 20 Essex Street [50], Fountain Court [61], Lamb Chambers [120], 19 Old Buildings [146], 3/4 South Square [194]

Spain

4 Essex Court [47], 24 Old Buildings [148]

Sri Lanka

2 Middle Temple Lane [126]

St. Vincent

2 Field Court [58]

Swaziland

Doughty Street Chambers [37], 4-5 Gray's Inn Square [79]

Switzerland

Essex Court Chambers [44], 8 Gray's Inn Square [81], Littleton Chambers [123]

The Grenadines

2 Field Court [58]

Trinidad & Tobago

1 Crown Office Row [33], 4-5 Gray's Inn Square [79], 4 Stone Buildings [200]

Turkey

8 Gray's Inn Square [81]

Turks & Caicos

33 Bedford Row [9], 8 Gray's Inn Square [81], 24 Old Buildings [149]

USA

Arbitration Chambers [1], Barnards Inn Chambers [4], 29 Bedford Row Chambers [8], 33 Bedford Row [9], Cloisters [30], Doughty Street Chambers [37], Enterprise Chambers [282], Enterprise Chambers [42], Erskine Chambers [43], Essex Court Chambers [44], 4 Essex Court [47], 2 Field Court [58], 4 Field Court [59], Goldsworth Chambers [70], 1 Gray's Inn Square [75], 14 Gray's Inn Square [83], Gray's Inn Tax Chambers [84], Hardwicke Building [91], Hardwicke Chambers [92], 2 Hare Court [95], 10 King's Bench Walk [114], 8 King St [323], Littleton Chambers [123], 1 Mitre Court Buildings [128], Mitre Court Chambers [131], New Court Chambers [135], 10 Old Square [152], One Paper Buildings [158], 2 Paper Buildings [160], 3 Paper Buildings [163], 18 Red Lion Court [188], St. Ive's Chambers [236], 3/4 South Square [194], 9 Stone Buildings [205], 11 Stone Buildings [206]

West Indies

3 Gray's Inn Square [78]

Yugoslavia

3 Gray's Inn Square [78]

Zimbabwe

Doughty Street Chambers [37], 1 Middle Temple Lane [125], 11 Old Square [154]

BAR
Editorial

CHAMBERS & PARTNERS

ADMINISTRATIVE & PUBLIC LAW

RESEARCH: In compiling the tables, we consider all the information available to us, paying particular regard to the market research carried out by our team of ten qualified lawyers. (The researchers' details are set out on page three.) The rankings, therefore, reflect the opinion of the market-place as revealed by systematic and objective research: see page four. (Our research is audited every year by the British Market Research Bureau.)

OVERVIEW: This is a growth area of law as judicial review continues to develop. More work will be created by the Government's plans to reform the constitution, especially the incorporation of the European Convention on Human Rights into UK law.

Barristers' profiles   p. 1509-1642

LEADING SILKS · LONDON

BELOFF Michael 4-5 Gray's Inn Square
PANNICK David Blackstone Chambers

BAXENDALE Presiley Blackstone Chambers
DRABBLE Richard 4 Breams Buildings
ELIAS Patrick 11 King's Bench Walk
GORDON Richard 39 Essex Street
GOUDIE James 11 King's Bench Walk
HOWELL John 4 Breams Buildings
LESTER OF HERNE HILL LORD Blackstone Chambers
PLEMING Nigel 39 Essex Street
ROBERTSON Geoffrey Doughty Street Chambers

APPLEBY Elizabeth 4-5 Gray's Inn Square
BOOTH Cherie 4-5 Gray's Inn Square
OUSELEY Duncan 4-5 Gray's Inn Square

ALLEN Robin Cloisters
ARDEN Andrew Arden Chambers
BLAKE Nicholas Two Garden Court
DUFFY Peter Essex Court Chambers
FITZGERALD Edward Doughty Street Chambers
FLINT Charles Blackstone Chambers
GRIFFITHS Robert 4-5 Gray's Inn Square
HAVERS Philip 1 Crown Office Row
HICKS William 1 Serjeants' Inn
KENTRIDGE Sydney Brick Court Chambers
NEWMAN Alan Cloisters
NICOL Andrew Doughty Street Chambers
OLIVER David 13 Old Square
PARKER Kenneth Monckton Chambers
POLLOCK Gordon Essex Court Chambers
PORTEN Anthony 2-3 Gray's Inn Square
PURCHAS Robin 2 Harcourt Buildings
READ Lionel 1 Serjeants' Inn
SCRIVENER Anthony 2-3 Gray's Inn Square
STEEL John 4-5 Gray's Inn Square
STRAUSS Nicholas One Essex Court
SUMPTION Jonathan Brick Court Chambers
SUPPERSTONE Michael 11 King's Bench Walk
VAUGHAN David Brick Court Chambers

NEW SILKS · 1997 AND 1998

BURNETT Ian 1 Temple Gardens
HOLGATE David 4 Breams Buildings
JAY Robert 39 Essex Street
MCCARTHY Roger Cloisters
ROTH Peter Monckton Chambers
STRAKER Timothy 2-3 Gray's Inn Square
TURNER James 4 Essex Court

FOR DETAILS OF THESE LEADING BARRISTERS
SEE PROFILES ON PAGES 1509-1642

LEADING SETS · LONDON

4-5 GRAY'S INN SQUARE (Appleby/Beloff QC)
BLACKSTONE CHAMBERS (Baxendale/Flint QC)
4 BREAMS BUILDINGS (Lockhart-Mummery QC)
11 KING'S BENCH WALK (Tabachnik/Goudle QC)

HIGHLY REGARDED · LONDON

Doughty Street Chambers (Robertson QC)
39 Essex Street (Edwin Glasgow QC)
Two Garden Court (Macdonald QC & Davies)
2-3 Gray's Inn Square (Anthony Scrivener QC)

4-5 Gray's Inn Square (Appleby & Beloff) Maintain their reputation as the leading public law set, with the focus of their expertise at the senior end. Cases include 'Antonelli v SS for Trade and Industry;' 'R v Panel of the Federation of Communication Services ex parte Kubis' and 'ex parte Help the Aged.' **Leading Barristers:** The "superb" *Michael Beloff QC* would be many people's choice for cutting edge cases. Although he is now President of Trinity College, Oxford, "he is more available than people think." *Elizabeth Appleby QC* has "the right blend of experience" and writes "spot on advice." *Cherie Booth QC* is a "hard working silk" who is "excellent on paper." *Robert Griffiths QC* does lots of mainstream commercial work which allows him to see angles other public lawyers might miss. The "outstandingly good" *Duncan Ouseley QC* is a JR specialist. *Rabinder Singh* is a rising star of the junior bar, and is described by some as the "best barrister of his generation." He has recently been involved in 'ex parte CPAG.' The "extremely bright" *Murray*

Hunt is quickly establishing a reputation in the human rights field. He is thought to be good on the academic side, and has recently written a well received book on the subject. *David Wolfe* is recommended as a junior; he is thought to be creative with good forensic skills, and was mentioned in particular in relation to his community care work. *Clive Lewis* and *Helen Mountfield* also maintain good reputations in the field.

Blackstone Chambers (Flint & Baxendale) Have an outstanding reputation in the field, acting for both applicants and respondents. Recent cases include 'R v Parliamentary Commissioner for Standards ex parte Al Fayed;' the Myra Hindley case and 'R v Legal Aid Board ex parte Kaim Todner.' **Leading Barristers:** The "exceptional" *David Pannick QC* is greatly admired. New joint heads of chambers *Charles Flint QC* and *Presiley Baxendale QC* are both recommended. She is re-establishing her practice having spent two years on the Scott Inquiry. *Lord Lester of Herne Hill QC* has a very high profile in this field, and has been actively involved in the introduction of the new Human Rights Act. The "excellent" *Michael Fordham* has a growing reputation. He is the author of a leading JR handbook, and has "that vital knowledge of caselaw." He is praised for his originality. *Dinah Rose* has a particular reputation for discrimination law, and *Pushpinder Saini* is also well thought of. *Mark Shaw* has been involved in some of the most important cases, and is considered a "good all-rounder."

4 Breams Buildings (Lockhart-Mummery) Specialise in planning and property law as well as public law. **Leading Barristers:** The first rate *Richard Drabble*

QC is a newer name on the scene than many of the more established silks, but is already considered a heavyweight in the area. He undertakes a lot of social security and mainstream public and admin law. *John Howell QC* and *David Holgate QC* are also mentioned in the tables. Recommended juniors at the set are *Christopher Katkowski* and *Nathalie Lieven*.

11 Kings Bench Walk (Tabachnik & Goudie) The set's public law work derives from their outstanding employment practice. **Leading Barristers:** *Patrick Elias QC* is a renowned employment specialist whose expertise extends to relevant judicial review work; the same can be said of *James Goudie QC*. *Nigel Giffin* is considered extremely bright and measured; he also "comes across well and is good on paper." He was junior in 'R v Brent LBC ex parte O'Malley.'

Doughty Street Chambers (Robertson) The focus of the set is civil liberties and human rights work. **Leading Barristers:** The "formidable" *Geoffrey Robertson QC* "is an effective communicator." His expertise is concentrated in certain areas such as free speech. *Andrew Nicol QC* is widely regarded as a genius. His main focus in JR work is on the immigration and nationality side. *Edward Fitzgerald QC* is known for his representation of prisoners and mental patients.He was recently involved in the Myra Hindley challenge to the Home Secretary. *Keir Starmer* is also recommended.

39 Essex Street (Glasgow) Public and administrative work is just a small part of their wide-ranging civil law practice.

Recent cases include 'R v Social Fund Inspector ex parte Taylor;' 'R v Collins ex parte MS.' **Leading Barristers:** *Richard Gordon QC* is a big name in the field, and is considered excellent on JR. *Nigel Pleming QC* is also recommended highly.

Two Garden Court (Macdonald & Davies) A set well known for their work on behalf of applicants in many areas of law, especially housing and immigration. **Leading Barristers:** The "underestimated" *Nicholas Blake QC* is said by some to be "one of the finest brains in judicial review." His particular emphasis is on immigration,

asylum and human rights issues. *Owen Davies* has a varied JR practice. The "extremely able" *Stephanie Harrison* is also recommended.

2-3 Gray's Inn Square (Scrivener) The set's work in this field has a planning and local government slant. **Leading Barristers:** *Anthony Scrivener QC* is an "extremely effective advocate" who undertakes public law, often from a civil liberties angle. *Timothy Straker QC* is seen as a "solid and reliable performer," while *Anthony Porten QC* is also recommended.

MIDLANDS AND OXFORD CIRCUIT

5 Fountain Court (Barker) A leading Birmingham set divided into six specialist groups; their recommended individuals all work within the planning and environmental group. **Leading Barristers:** *Martin Kingston QC* undertakes planning related work. *Paul Bleasdale* does planning work and is described as a "good solid junior."

Ian Dove is also recommended as is new entry to the lists *Jeremy Cahill*.

John Randall QC at **St Philip's Chambers** (Tedd) is recommended for JR cases, particularly when acting for local authorities.

In **Ropewalk Chambers** (Maxwell) the well regarded *Graham Machin* is the leading JR practitioner in Nottingham.

AGRICULTURE AND BLOODSTOCK

RESEARCH: In compiling the tables, we consider all the information available to us, paying particular regard to the market research carried out by our team of ten qualified lawyers. (The researchers' details are set out on page three.) The rankings, therefore, reflect the opinion of the marketplace as revealed by systematic and objective research: see page four. (Our research is audited every year by the British Market Research Bureau.)

Barristers' profiles   P. 1509-1642

Falcon Chambers (Gaunt & Lewison) Recognised by solicitors throughout the country as "pre-eminent," "the leader" and "well ahead." The set has a tremendous reputation. **Work Handled:** Agricultural strength comes from the set's property litigation specialism. They are particularly experienced in landlord and tenant disputes. Many of the barristers are members of the Agricultural Law Association. **Leading Barristers:** *Paul Morgan QC* ("quite excellent", "brilliant," "Rolls Royce") and *Derek Wood QC* ("real specialist", "vastly experienced," "outstanding quality") were universally acclaimed. *Jonathan Gaunt QC* is described as " very active in the area" and *Jonathan Brock QC* is "thoroughly sound." The juniors are used by many firms. *Joanne Moss* was described as "very bright indeed." *Martin Rodger* is "superb on his feet" and "knowledgeable." *Paul De La Piquerie* is "lucid."

David Vaughan QC at **Brick Court Chambers** (Clarke) was recommended for EC-related work.

David Holgate QC at **4 Breams Buildings** (Lockhart-Mummery) took silk in 1997 and remains well respected.

Peter Cranfield at **3 Verulam Buildings** (Thomas) ("thorough," "bright") has recently undertaken reported judicial reviews and has experience of EU Law.

At **Enterprise Chambers** (Mann), *Caroline Hutton* ("extremely good") and *Ann McAllister* ("first rate", "goes the extra mile") both received several recommendations.

Thomas Brudenell at **Queen Elizabeth Building** (Karsten) and *Michael Heywood* at **3 New Square** (Goodhart) both specialise in bloodstock and equine law.

The well regarded *Nigel Thomas* has recently joined **13 Old Square** (Lyndon-Stanford).

Monckton Chambers (Fowler) has a lot of involvement in agricultural issues with members regularly acting for MAFF and the NFU. *Ken Parker QC* acted in 'R v MAFF ex parte Monsanto' [1997] (pesticides), 'R v MAFF ex parte ISK Biosciences' [1997] (pesticides) and 'R v MAFF ex parte Astonquest' [1998] (fishing licences). *Peter Roth QC* handles work for the NFU and has recently been in the House of Lords in relation to live animal exports.

LEADING SET · LONDON
FALCON CHAMBERS (Gaunt QC and Lewison QC)

LEADING SILKS · LONDON
MORGAN Paul Falcon Chambers
WOOD Derek Falcon Chambers
GAUNT Jonathan Falcon Chambers
PARKER Kenneth Monckton Chambers
ROTH Peter Monckton Chambers
BROCK Jonathan Falcon Chambers
VAUGHAN David Brick Court Chambers

NEW SILKS · 1997 AND 1998
HOLGATE David 4 Breams Buildings

LEADING JUNIORS · LONDON
MOSS Joanne Falcon Chambers
RODGER Martin Falcon Chambers
BRUDENELL Thomas Queen Elizabeth Building
CRANFIELD Peter 3 Verulam Buildings
DE LA PIQUERIE Paul Falcon Chambers
HEYWOOD Michael 3 New Square
HUTTON Caroline Enterprise Chambers
MCALLISTER Ann Enterprise Chambers
THOMAS Nigel 13 Old Square

FOR DETAILS ON THESE LEADING BARRISTERS
SEE PROFILES ON PAGES 1509-1642

ALTERNATIVE DISPUTE RESOLUTION

RESEARCH: In compiling the tables, we consider all the information available to us, paying particular regard to the market research carried out by our team of ten qualified lawyers. (The researchers' details are set out on page three.) The rankings, therefore, reflect the opinion of the marketplace as revealed by systematic and objective research: see page four. (Our research is audited every year by the British Market Research Bureau.)

All those mentioned are CEDR accredited mediators.

Barristers' profiles	p. 1509 -1642

LEADING SILKS

As a Director of CEDR, *Philip Naughton QC* of **3 Serjeants' Inn** (Naughton) has a high profile in alternative dispute resolution. He is an active mediator, specialising in engineering and construction. *Michael Burton QC* has an outstanding reputation as an advocate in many areas of law, and is involved in all aspects of commercial arbitration and ADR. Also at **Littleton Chambers** (Burton) is *Michel Kallipetis QC* who is increasingly involved in ADR. *Ian Hunter QC* of **Essex Court Chambers** (Pollock) has a general commercial practice with an emphasis on shipping, insurance and banking, and at **Brick Court Chambers** (Clarke) *Hilary Heilbron QC* works in the financial services area. *Derek Wheatley QC* of **Verulam Chambers** (Edwards) has considerable experience in the banking world, and now undertakes banking mediations, including international ones.

LEADING JUNIORS

Delia Dumaresq of **Atkin Chambers** (Blackburn) brings experience of the construction and civil engineering bar to mediation, as does *Jonathan Tecks* at **Littman Chambers** (Littman). *Graham Cunningham* has a niche expertise in IT and computer based disputes. *Dr Margaret Branthwaite* of **One Paper Buildings** (Slater) has a practice which is exclusively comprised of medical negligence work, and is involved in mediation between doctors and patients and amongst doctors themselves. In **One Essex Court** (Grabiner) *Ian Grainger* has a broadly based commercial and insurance practice. *Patrick Green* of **2 Harcourt Buildings** (Henderson) is a general commercial practitioner, and has a particular interest in employment matters and computer disputes. At **Gough Square Chambers** (Philpott) *Anthony Vines* has a broad commercial and consumer law practice, and recent involvement in ADR has tended to focus on property and landlord and tenant disputes. *Elizabeth Birch* has moved from 20 Essex Street to **3 Verulam Buildings** (Thomas).

LEADING SILKS · LONDON

NAUGHTON Philip 3 Serjeants' Inn

BURTON Michael Littleton Chambers
HUNTER Ian Essex Court Chambers
KALLIPETIS Michel Littleton Chambers
KERSHEN Lawrence Cloisters
MARRIN John Keating Chambers
WHEATLEY Derek Verulam Chambers

HEILBRON Hilary Brick Court Chambers
TACKABERRY John Arbitration Chambers

LEADING JUNIORS · LONDON

AEBERLI Peter 46 Essex Street
BIRCH Elizabeth 3 Verulam Buildings
BRODIE Bruce 39 Essex Street
CUNNINGHAM Graham Francis Taylor Building

BRANTHWAITE Margaret One Paper Buildings
DUMARESQ Delia Atkin Chambers
GRAINGER Ian One Essex Court
GREEN Patrick 2 Harcourt Buildings
LOWENSTEIN Paul Littleton Chambers
MANNING Colin Littleton Chambers
STILITZ Daniel 11 King's Bench Walk
TECKS Jonathan Littman Chambers
VINES Anthony Gough Square Chambers

FOR DETAILS OF THESE LEADING BARRISTERS
SEE PROFILES ON PAGES 1509-1642

ARBITRATION

RESEARCH: Our rankings reflect the opinion of the marketplace as revealed by systematic and objective research: see page four. Our research is audited every year by the British Market Research Bureau.

LEADING SETS · LONDON

ESSEX COURT CHAMBERS (Gordon Pollock QC)

ATKIN CHAMBERS (John Blackburn QC)
ONE ESSEX COURT (Anthony Grabiner QC)
20 ESSEX STREET (David Johnson QC)
KEATING CHAMBERS (Fernyhough QC)

BRICK COURT CHAMBERS (Clarke QC)
4 ESSEX COURT (Nigel Teare QC)
FOUNTAIN COURT (Peter Scott QC)

Essex Court Chambers (Pollock) The clear leaders, with five silks and four juniors recommended. Cover the full spectrum of commercial matters. **Leading Barristers:** *V.V. Veeder QC* is still the undisputed leading silk – "a real internationalist." *Stewart Boyd QC* has a "very practical mind" and elicits universal respect as "a good technician." *Gordon Pollock QC* is recommended in this, as in other areas, as "very persuasive" and a man of "great intellect." *Michael Collins QC* is said to be "good on tricky points" and *Ian Hunter QC*, a "pure arbitration man" with "fire in his belly." Amongst the juniors, full time arbitrator *Martin Hunter* (formerly a partner at Freshfields) is very experienced and "in a class of two" with Alan Redfern at One Essex Court. The "high profile" *Toby Landau* is the leading authority on the new Act (having drafted much of it). Also recommended were *Joe Smouha* ("easy to work with") and the "tough and aggressive" *Graham Dunning*.

Atkin Chambers (Blackburn) A leading construction set with good international connections and a high profile. Strong at senior level with six silks in our table. *Anthony Butcher QC* has retired as a barrister but continues to sit as an arbitrator and receives instructions through Atkin Chambers. **Leading Barristers:** *John Blackburn QC*, dubbed by one respondent "the ideal arbitrator", now heads the set. *Colin Reese QC* was praised for being an "extremely diligent and capable arbitrator" and *Robert Akenhead QC's* skills were also much admired.

One Essex Court (Grabiner) A leading commercial set with a number of high calibre barristers. Arbitration work is a principal area of practice. Also have six silks recommended and were thought worthy of a higher ranking this year. **Leading**

Barristers: Head of Chambers *Anthony Grabiner QC* was recommended as "a good all rounder" and *Ian Glick QC* was described as "very able." Other recommended silks include *Mark Barnes QC* and *Stanley Burnton QC*. Full time arbitrator *Alan Redfern* (top junior with Martin Hunter) is "enormously well-known and respected internationally."

20 Essex Street (Johnson) Described as "one of the very few specialist arbitration sets." Handles a lot of maritime work and has former Head of Chambers *Ken Rokison QC* and a number of eminent ex-judges practising as full time arbitrators. **Leading Barristers:** The "extremely knowledgeable" *Peter Gross QC* is "very strong" as an advocate and arbitrator and is said to take "a sensible approach." A new entry to our tables is the much praised *Duncan Matthews*.

Keating Chambers (Fernyhough) A set which specialises in construction and property work. **Leading Barristers:** Include the "very practical" arbitrator *John Uff QC*. Also particularly recommended are *Richard Fernyhough QC* and the much admired *Vivian Ramsey QC*, who is also a qualified engineer. New to our list this year are *Marcus Taverner*, praised for his "quick and incisive mind" and "brilliant advocacy," *Rosemary Jackson*, a "good, sensible, practical advocate" epitomising "grace under pressure," and the highly recommended *Tim Elliott QC*.

Brick Court Chambers (Clarke) Universally respected for good quality commercial advice. Newly included in our tables this year. **Leading Barristers:** Particular mention was made of *Christopher Clarke QC* and *Mark Cran QC*. The set also has several ex-judges acting as full time arbitrators.

4 Essex Court (Teare) Handle a range of commercial work, but particularly maritime law, international trade and insurance matters. Three silks feature in our tables. **Leading Barristers:** *Belinda Bucknall QC, Nigel Teare QC* and *Jeremy Russell QC* were all recommended again this year.

Fountain Court (Scott) A leading commercial set, particularly well regarded for international arbitration work . **Leading Barristers:** *Peter Scott QC* ("always superb") and *Peter Goldsmith QC* ("top advocate") were singled out for praise.

Barristers' profiles   p. 1509-1642

LEADING SILKS · LONDON

VEEDER V.V. Essex Court Chambers

BLACKBURN John Atkin Chambers
BOYD Stewart Essex Court Chambers
BUTCHER Anthony Atkin Chambers
FERNYHOUGH Richard Keating Chambers
GLICK Ian One Essex Court
GRABINER Anthony One Essex Court
GROSS Peter 20 Essex Street
POLLOCK Gordon Essex Court Chambers
RAMSEY Vivian Keating Chambers
ROKISON Kenneth 20 Essex Street
UFF John Keating Chambers

AKENHEAD Robert Atkin Chambers
COLLINS Michael Essex Court Chambers
GOLDSMITH Peter Fountain Court
HUNTER Ian Essex Court Chambers
KNIGHT Brian Atkin Chambers
REESE Colin Atkin Chambers
SCOTT Peter Fountain Court
TACKABERRY John Arbitration Chambers

BARNES Mark One Essex Court
BUCKNALL Belinda 4 Essex Court
BURNTON Stanley One Essex Court
CLARKE Christopher Brick Court Chambers
CRAN Mark Brick Court Chambers
CROWTHER William 2 Temple Gardens
ELLIOTT Timothy Keating Chambers
GEE Steven One Essex Court
PADFIELD Nicholas One Hare Court
RUSSELL Jeremy 4 Essex Court
SMITH Andrew Fountain Court
TEARE Nigel 4 Essex Court
THOMAS Christopher Keating Chambers

NEW SILKS · 1997 AND 1998

GRUDER Jeffrey One Essex Court
MALEK Ali 3 Verulam Buildings
WHITE Andrew Atkin Chambers

LEADING JUNIORS · LONDON

HUNTER Martin Essex Court Chambers
REDFERN Alan One Essex Court

LANDAU Toby Essex Court Chambers
SMOUHA Joe Essex Court Chambers

BRODIE Bruce 39 Essex Street
BURR Andrew Atkin Chambers
BUTCHER Christopher 7 King's Bench Walk
DUNNING Graham Essex Court Chambers
HART David 1 Crown Office Row
JACKSON Rosemary Keating Chambers
MATTHEWS Duncan 20 Essex Street
PELLING Mark Monckton Chambers
TAVERNER Marcus Keating Chambers

AVIATION

RESEARCH: In compiling the tables, we consider all the information available to us, paying particular regard to the market research carried out by our team of ten qualified lawyers. (The researchers' details are set out on page three.) The rankings, therefore, reflect the opinion of the marketplace as revealed by systematic and objective research: see page four. (Our research is audited every year by the British Market Research Bureau.) In researching this section we interviewed leading solicitors, barristers, and their clerks. We also spoke to in-house lawyers at major airlines, regulatory bodies, insurers, underwriters and other clients at Lloyds.

OVERVIEW: There are minor changes to the ranking of sets following several recent moves. Most interestingly, the aviation bar was stunned by the departure from 5 Bell Yard of star name Robert Webb QC, who has appeared in all the recent major aviation cases. He has gone in-house to BA. The set has also suffered from the loss of several leading juniors and no longer occupies the pre-eminent spot on its own. It is joined this year by Fountain Court.

5 Bell Yard (Webb) A number of recent departures means that this set is no longer out on its own at the top. "The lead name in aviation" Robert Webb QC has gone in-house at BA, and Michael Crane QC and Akil Shah have moved to Fountain Court. Andrew Lydiard has also left for Brick Court Chambers. **Work Handled:** Includes: 'Kuwait Airways v Kuwait Insurance Co 1997' – acting for KA in respect of 15 aircraft lost in last Gulf War; 'Deauville v Aeroflot 1997' – anti suit injunction for Aeroflot; 'Easyjet v KLM/The BA/AA alliance' and various other proceedings before the EC; Route licence application; Article 85 proceedings. **Leading Barristers:** *Robert Lawson* has been successful in many high profile cases and is considered to be following in the footsteps of Robert Webb QC. *Giles Kavanagh* is said to be "user-friendly and good on his feet."

Fountain Court (Scott) A well respected set where the loss of Bruce Coles QC (who has been appointed a circuit judge) has been balanced by the addition of *Michael Crane QC* and *Akhil Shah* from 5 Bell Yard. **Leading Barristers:** *Michael Crane QC* is respected for being a "serious heavyweight intellectual" and is described as "a real star." *Akhil Shah,* noted as up and coming last year, is variously described as "bright," "keen" and "helpful" and he moves up a band. **Work Handled:** In the last year Michael Crane QC has been involved with

'Milor SRL v BA' and with Akhil Shah has led in 'Airbus Industrie v Patel & Ors.'

Brick Court Chambers (Clarke) Well known as a leading commercial set with an increasing presence in this field. **Leading Barristers:** *Christopher Clarke QC* is known for his work for BA. *Mark Brealey* is involved in the 'Easyjet v BA' breach of Article 86 litigation. *Andrew Lydiard* ("brilliant academic lawyer") has recently joined the set from 5 Bell Yard.

Essex Court Chambers (Pollock) **Leading Barristers:** *David Joseph* is acting for cargo interests in a large diamond theft from Brussels airport involving application of Warsaw convention. Also involved in Satellite insurance mediation for insurers.

4 Essex Court (Teare) **Leading Barristers:** The set loses David Steel QC who has been appointed a High Court Judge. Its reputation for aviation rests largely on *Charles Haddon-Cave* who has acted in all the major aviation disaster cases of recent times. Work includes the application of the Warsaw convention to a serious ballooning accident; 'Deauville v Aeroflot' – successfully defeating Aeroflot's application for an anti suit injunction; the Knight Air crash including litigation in France.

20 Essex Street (Johnson) **Leading Barristers:** *Peter Gross QC* and *Iain Milligan QC* are well regarded. New silk *Stephen Males QC* is also recommended.

Monckton Chambers (Fowler) Known

primarily as EU and competition specialists, this set also has aviation expertise. **Work Handled:** Advisory work on the BA and AA alliance. **Leading Barristers:** *Richard Fowler QC* is a pre-eminent name in the EU aspects of the aviation industry.

BANKING

Barristers' profiles   p. 1509-1642

RESEARCH: In compiling the tables, we consider all the information available to us, paying particular regard to the market research carried out by our team of ten qualified lawyers. (The researchers' details are set out on page three.) The rankings, therefore, reflect the opinion of the marketplace as revealed by systematic and objective research: see page four. (Our research is audited every year by the British Market Research Bureau.)

OVERVIEW: In researching this section we spoke to solicitors (contentious and non contentious), their clients and other professionals. Whilst good silks are still in demand amongst the leading London firms, juniors are less so. This is due to increasing specialisation among solicitors and an increasing number of litigation solicitors undertaking advocacy (where permitted) and drafting their own pleadings.

LEADING SETS · LONDON

BRICK COURT CHAMBERS (Clarke QC)
ERSKINE CHAMBERS (Richard Sykes QC)
ONE ESSEX COURT (Anthony Grabiner QC)
FOUNTAIN COURT (Peter Scott QC)
3-4 SOUTH SQUARE (Michael Crystal QC)
3 VERULAM BUILDINGS (R. Neville Thomas QC)

ESSEX COURT CHAMBERS (Gordon Pollock QC)
20 ESSEX STREET (David Johnson QC)

4-5 GRAY'S INN SQUARE (Appleby/Beloff QC)

LEADING SILKS · LONDON

GRABINER Anthony One Essex Court
POLLOCK Gordon Essex Court Chambers
SUMPTION Jonathan Brick Court Chambers

BLAIR William 3 Verulam Buildings
BRINDLE Michael Fountain Court
ETHERTON Terence Wilberforce Chambers
GLICK Ian One Essex Court
HAPGOOD Mark Brick Court Chambers
ISAACS Stuart 4-5 Gray's Inn Square
JARVIS John 3 Verulam Buildings
MALEK Ali 3 Verulam Buildings
POTTS Robin Erskine Chambers
SALTER Richard 3 Verulam Buildings
SCOTT Peter Fountain Court
SOUTHWELL Richard One Hare Court
STRAUSS Nicholas One Essex Court
SYKES Richard Erskine Chambers

ADKINS Richard 3-4 South Square
BUENO Antonio 5 Paper Buildings
CRYSTAL Michael 3-4 South Square
HIGHAM John 3-4 South Square
HOWARD Mark Brick Court Chambers
MANN Anthony Enterprise Chambers
MILLIGAN Iain 20 Essex Street
MITCHELL Gregory 3 Verulam Buildings
THOMAS Neville 3 Verulam Buildings

NEW SILKS · 1997 AND 1998

GRUDER Jeffrey One Essex Court
HACKER Richard 3-4 South Square
TODD Michael Erskine Chambers

FOR DETAILS OF THESE LEADING BARRISTERS SEE PROFILES ON PAGES 1509-1642

Brick Court Chambers (Clarke) A highly respected set with a particularly strong compliment of leading silks. **Work Handled:** Includes 'ECGD v Credit Lyonnais.' **Leading Barristers:** *Jonathan Sumption QC* ("just so good") remains one of the pre-eminent silks with a particularly strong reputation for his "outstanding" advocacy skills. *Mark Hapgood QC* ("extremely practical and good on advice") received many favourable recommendations and moves up a band in our tables. *Mark Howard QC* has made his mark as a silk. One leading litigation solicitor described him as "terrific in and out of court" and "very user friendly." Leading junior *Dominic Chambers* has joined from One Hare Court.

Erskine Chambers (Sykes) Best known for corporate law but also has a good reputation in the banking field. **Leading Barristers:** *Richard Sykes QC* has an excellent reputation for providing "clear advice" and is "good for opinion" – an "immense brain." Fellow leader *Robin Potts QC* was praised for providing "good bullish advice" and being "very impressive

all round." *Michael Todd QC* is also well regarded for banking matters. He appeared for successful defendant against Nationwide concerning allegations of cross firing cheques. Also briefed on a number of hearings in Cayman Islands regarding mandates.

One Essex Court (Grabiner) A heavyweight commercial set with high calibre barristers. **Leading Barristers:** A good compliment of leaders. Head of chambers *Anthony Grabiner QC* ("high profile and talented generally") moves to our top band. Recommended for advocacy skills and described by one litigation solicitor as "really strong in commercial and banking... difficult to fault." Junior *Rhodri Davies* is "widely used." He recently acted in 'Bhogal v Punjab National Bank' (CA, claim to equitable set off).

Fountain Court (Scott) Good reputation for banking work and have a number of silks and juniors with specialist experience. **Work Handled:** Include 'BCCI v Bank of England'; 'Sumutous, Sanwa & Arab Banks v Banque Bruxelles Lambert'; 'NM Rothschild v Bank of Ireland Mortgage Services'. **Leading Barristers:** The "good, solid" *Michael Brindle QC* and "very impressive" *Peter Scott QC* are both highly regarded. Junior and "good advocate" *Bankim Thanki* ("very bright and a delight to work with") moves up a band on recommendation from solicitors.

3-4 South Square (Crystal) Most widely known for expertise in insolvency matters but also rated for banking work. **Work Handled:** Cases handled include 'Morris v Agrichemicals;' 'Banco Exterior v Pasco (Panama);' 'Three Rivers District Council v Governor of the Bank of England.'

Leading Barristers: *Michael Crystal QC* was recognised for his vast experience on insolvency and banking related matters. *Richard Hacker QC* has taken silk and is recommended. *Robin Knowles* is seen as "extremely effective." *Mark Phillips* ("very good on banking and insolvency issues") was praised for quickly giving confidence to clients. *Robin Dicker* "gets a terrific amount of work because he is so good."

3 Verulam Buildings (Thomas) A strong commercial set – well known for their banking work. **Work Handled:** Includes 'Barclays Bank v Thomson;' 'International Credit and Investment Company (Overseas) Limited v Adham and others;' 'Camdex v Bank of Zambia and Zambia Consolidated Copper Mines.' **Leading Barristers:** *John Jarvis QC* and *Richard Salter QC* both have strong reputations for their banking work. *Ali*

Malek QC ("gives common sense advice and is liked by judges") is "making it as a silk." *Ewan McQuater* and *Jonathan Nash* were both complemented for being "sensible." *Annie Hockaday* was described as "genuinely good on banking – both on her feet and in opinions."

Essex Court Chambers (Pollock) Particularly known for commercial litigation matters including banking disputes. **Leading Barristers:** *Gordon Pollock QC* moves up a band following widespread recommendation for, among other things, his "wonderful advocacy skills."

20 Essex Street (Johnson) A commercial set which covers banking work as one of its specialisms. **Leading Barristers:** The "effective" *Iain Milligan QC* has a good reputation for his banking work.

4-5 Gray's Inn Square (Appleby and Beloff) The set covers many specialist areas including banking. **Leading Barristers:** Junior *Hodge Malek* received praise as a

"sound and careful" advocate.

Others Leading Barristers: *Richard Southwell QC* of **One Hare Court** (Neill &

Southwell) was praised as a "powerful advocate – one of the best on detail." Also felt to be good for opinions.

LEADING JUNIORS • LONDON	
DAVIES Rhodri One Essex Court	**MCQUATER Ewan** 3 Verulam Buildings
LEWIS Caroline 3 Verulam Buildings	**NASH Jonathan** 3 Verulam Buildings
MALEK Hodge 4-5 Gray's Inn Square	**THANKI Bankim** Fountain Court
CHAMBERS Dominic Brick Court Chambers	**HOCKADAY Annie** 3 Verulam Buildings
COX Raymond Fountain Court	**KNOWLES Robin** 3-4 South Square
DICKER Robin 3-4 South Square	**MILLETT Richard** Essex Court Chambers
HAVEY Peter 4-5 Gray's Inn Square	**PHILLIPS Mark** 3-4 South Square
ARDEN Peter Enterprise Chambers	**SPENCER-LEWIS Neville** 12 King's Bench Walk
BELTRAMI Adrian 3 Verulam Buildings	**STONEFROST Hilary** 3-4 South Square
BROWN Hannah 5 Bell Yard	**SULLIVAN Michael** 5 Bell Yard
LOWENSTEIN Paul Littleton Chambers	**WALTON Carolyn** 13 Old Square
OWEN David 20 Essex Street	**WOLFSON David** 3 Verulam Buildings

UP AND COMING • LONDON	
DAVIES-JONES Jonathan 3 Verulam Buildings	**STALLEBRASS Paul** 5 Paper Buildings

FOR DETAILS OF THESE LEADING BARRISTERS
SEE PROFILES ON PAGES 1509-1642

CHANCERY

RESEARCH: In compiling the tables, we consider all the information available to us, paying particular regard to the market research carried out by our team of ten qualified lawyers. (The researchers' details are set out on page three.) The rankings, therefore, reflect the opinion of the marketplace as revealed by systematic and objective research: see page four. (Our research is audited every year by the British Market Research Bureau.)

OVERVIEW: The section covers chambers and individuals with expertise in matters especially associated with the Chancery Division of the High Court (as opposed to the Queens Bench or Family Divisions). Traditionally these were mainly wills, trusts, estates and property law matters.

Nowadays the Chancery Division handles a greater range of more commercial matters, including large commercial contractual disputes, financial services, commercial disputes involving trust points and intellectual property matters. Indeed, we may be seeing the emergence of a 'Business Bar' combining the once distinct fields of commercial and chancery work. Many chancery sets already handle a great deal of commercial work as well as the traditional type of chancery work. Consequently, some sets and individuals appear in both our commercial and traditional chancery tables.

The drive towards bigger sets offering a range of specialisms – a development seen throughout the Bar – has been particularly marked in the chancery field. The result has been a turbulent year for the Chancery sets. Some have been badly hit by defections, while one long-established set – 17 Old Buildings – has been subsumed into 10 Old Square after losing several key tenants.

Sets which have strengthened their positions include Serle Court Chambers, Wilberforce Chambers and 3 Stone Buildings.

LEADING SILKS · LONDON COMMERCIAL

ALDOUS Charles 7 Stone Buildings
BRIGGS Michael Serle Court Chambers
ETHERTON Terence Wilberforce Chambers
GLOSTER Elizabeth One Essex Court
OLIVER David 13 Old Square
PATTEN Nicholas 9 Old Square
SHER Jules Wilberforce Chambers
VOS Geoffrey 3 Stone Buildings

BERRY Simon 9 Old Square
BOYLE Alan Serle Court Chambers
CRYSTAL Michael 3-4 South Square
DAVIS Nigel 7 Stone Buildings
HESLOP Philip 4 Stone Buildings
KAYE Roger 24 Old Buildings
MANN Anthony Enterprise Chambers
MCDONNELL John 1 New Square
MUNBY James 1 New Square
PURLE Charles 12 New Square
STEINFELD Alan 24 Old Buildings

ASHE Michael 9 Stone Buildings
BANNISTER Edward 3 Stone Buildings
BOMPAS Anthony 4 Stone Buildings
BRISBY John 4 Stone Buildings
HAMILTON Eben 1 New Square
HILDYARD Robert 4 Stone Buildings
MOSS Gabriel 3-4 South Square
NEWMAN Catherine 13 Old Square
ROSEN Murray 11 Stone Buildings
TALBOT Patrick Serle Court Chambers
WILLIAMSON Hazel 13 Old Square

NEW SILKS · 1997 AND 1998 COMMERCIAL

NORRIS Alastair 5 Stone Buildings
TRACE Anthony 13 Old Square

FOR DETAILS OF THESE LEADING BARRISTERS
SEE PROFILES ON PAGES 1509-1642

LEADING SETS · LONDON COMMERCIAL

13 OLD SQUARE (Lyndon-Stanford QC)
SERLE COURT CHAMBERS (Sparrow QC)
4 STONE BUILDINGS (Philip Heslop QC)

9 OLD SQUARE (Robert Reid QC)
7 STONE BUILDINGS (Charles Aldous QC)
WILBERFORCE CHAMBERS (Nugee QC)

ENTERPRISE CHAMBERS (Anthony Mann QC)
1 NEW SQUARE (Eben Hamilton QC)
24 OLD BUILDINGS (Colin Brodie QC)
3 STONE BUILDINGS (Geoffrey Vos QC)

HIGHLY REGARDED · LONDON COMMERCIAL

12 New Square (John Mowbray QC)
3-4 South Square (Michael Crystal QC)
11 Stone Buildings (Michael Beckman QC)

LONDON

COMMERCIAL CHANCERY

(Including banking, commercial contracts, companies, financial services, fraud, injunctions, insolvency, IP, media and entertainment, professional negligence and torts).

13 Old Square (Lyndon-Stanford) Still one of the strongest commercial chancery sets, with strength in depth as well as quality. **Leading Barristers:** With the elevation this year of Secretary of the Chancery Bar Association *Anthony Trace QC*, the set now has 4 silks in our table of leaders, *Hazel Williamson QC*, and the "very bright" and top band rated *David Oliver QC*. *Matthew Collings*, described as "knowledgeable, really gets to grips with a point," moves into the top band of juniors. His recent cases include 'Re Vanilla Accumulation Ltd' (insolvency) and 'R v Secretary of State ex p McCormick' (use of Companies Act transcripts).

Serle Court Chambers (Sparrow) Going from strength to strength. The recently re-named set (formerly Thirteen

Old Square) moves into the top band of our table this year. Possesses strength in depth, with 3 silks and 7 juniors among our leaders. **Leading Barristers:** There was no question that the "extraordinarily good" *Michael Briggs QC* should move into the top band of silks this year. He received much favourable comment, and is said to be a "very clever advocate – the man to choose when you want a difficult point presented clearly." He recently acted, with junior *Douglas Close*, in 'Don King Productions v Warren' (boxing partnership: rights on termination). *Alan Boyle QC* is newly included after being praised for his ability to "produce the googly point no one else has thought of." His recent work has included 'Bridge Trust Co v Attorney General of Cayman Islands' (Court of Appeal of the Cayman Islands – charitable trusts).

4 Stone Buildings (Heslop) Another set with a growing reputation – moving into the top band of our table. Good range of experience, with 4 silks and 4 juniors recommended. **Leading Barristers:** *Philip Heslop QC* ("very good, acts in lots of high profile cases"), *John Brisby QC* "a real fighter" and *Anthony Bompas QC* all feature in our company, commercial and insolvency bar sections as well.

Jonathan Crow, recently appointed Treasury Devil (Chancery), moves into the top band of juniors after several positive comments. *Robert Miles*, described by a silk from another set as "one of the best juniors I've led," is a new name this year.

9 Old Square (Reid) Also on the up for commercial chancery work. The standard of clerking was singled out for praise by a solicitor who had used a number of chancery sets. **Leading Barristers:** *Nick Patten QC,* Chairman of the Chancery Bar Association, was described as combining exceptional ability with considerable

experience, hence his position in the top band of silks. *Simon Berry QC* was praised for always preparing thoroughly before conferences and for being "imaginative, practical and extremely good at client care." The "very clever and assured" *Daniel Hochberg* remains one of the most highly rated commercial chancery juniors, and has particular expertise in heavyweight commercial trust litigation.

7 Stone Buildings (Aldous) Still one of the leading commercial chancery sets. Has two very good silks, though only one junior *Guy Newey*, was particularly recommended to us. **Leading Barristers:** *Charles Aldous QC* retains his position in the top band of our commercial chancery silks table. He recently acted in 'MMC Proceeds Inc v Lehman Brothers' (leading authority on conversion claims made by equitable owners). *Nigel Davis QC* was also recommended again this year. His recent reported cases include Priceland Ltd (company winding-up).

Wilberforce Chambers (Nugee) Preeminent for traditional chancery work, the set has been enhancing its reputation in the commercial sphere as well. **Leading Barristers:** *Jules Sher QC*, a "very persuasive advocate" with "great clarity of mind", is the only silk to appear in the top band of both our traditional and commercial chancery tables. He therefore fully justifies his description as "the outstanding silk at the Chancery Bar." He is joined in the commercial top band by *Terence Etherton QC* "a charming, persuasive and meticulous advocate," liked by judges. Jules Sher QC acted in the Lloyd's litigation ('Napier and Others v Kershaw and Others;' 'The Society of Lloyd's v Woodard'). Terence Etherton QC's recent cases include: re Park Air Services (leading Court of Appeal case on disclaimer of leases by liquidators).

Enterprise Chambers (Mann) Specialists in company and commercial work, insolvency and professional negligence in particular. **Leading Barristers:** Head of Chambers *Anthony Mann QC* and juniors *Linden Ife* and *Teresa Peacocke* are all seen as leaders for commercial chancery work.

1 New Square (Hamilton) Known for both commercial (3 silks in our tables) and traditional chancery work. Good reputation for company and insolvency work in particular, though hit by defections to other sets. **Leading Barristers:** *James Munby QC*, said to have a very large, wide-ranging practice, and *John McDonnell QC* both attracted favourable comment.

24 Old Buildings (Brodie) Have moved up in our tables this year to join the leading sets. Company, commercial and insolvency work are particular strengths. **Leading Barristers:** *Alan Steinfeld QC* and *Roger Kaye QC* both have solid reputations for commercial chancery work. Alan Steinfeld QC's recent cases include 'Chase v York Montague' (solicitors negligence/ property), Roger Kaye QC's include the Atlantic Computers case (insolvency/ directors disqualification).

3 Stone Buildings (Vos) Also join the leading sets this year. Have 2 leading silks whose strengths are company and commercial matters, insolvency and media and entertainment work. **Leading Barristers:** *Geoffrey Vos QC* Vice Chairman of the Chancery Bar Association, and "more prestigious all the time," joins the handful of silks at the very top of our table. He acted in the recently settled 'Investors Compensation Scheme v West Bromwich Building Society.' *Edward Bannister QC*, formerly at 1 New Square, is a new name on our list following numerous positive comments.

In addition to the above sets **3-4 South Square** (Crystal) (banking and insolvency specialists), **12 New Square** (Mowbray) and **11 Stone Buildings** (Beckman) are well regarded for commercial chancery work. *Stephen Smith* at **12 New Square** (Mowbray) was said to be "very inventive in developing arguments" and *Michael Ashe QC* at **9 Stone Buildings** (Ashe) to possess "great clarity of thought." *Elizabeth Gloster QC* at **One Essex Court** (Grabiner) moves up in our tables after numerous recommendations ("a thorough cross-examiner," "has natural authority and judges listen to her").

TRADITIONAL CHANCERY

(Including charities, joint ownership, mortgages, partnerships, pensions, probate, real property, revenue, trusts, settlements and wills.)

WILBERFORCE CHAMBERS (Nugee QC)

5 STONE BUILDINGS (Henry Harrod)

3 NEW SQUARE (Sir William Goodhart QC)

11 NEW SQUARE (Peter Crampin QC)

1 New Square (Eben Hamilton QC)

12 New Square (John Mowbray QC)

10 Old Square (Leolin Price QC)

11 Old Square (Crawford & Simpkiss)

13 Old Square (Michael Lyndon-Stanford QC)

Serle Court Chambers (Charles Sparrow QC)

3 Stone Buildings (Geoffrey Vos QC)

9 Stone Buildings (Michael Ashe QC)

Wilberforce Chambers (Nugee) Clearly the top traditional chancery set with ten leaders, eight of them silks. **Leading Barristers:** *Edward Nugee QC*, "still the doyen", remains at the top of our leading silks table. The 'very inventive' *Jules Sher QC*, "direct and clear", with "no false airs and graces – joins him there. Edward Nugee's recent cases include 'IRC v McGuckian' (leading House of Lords case on tax avoidance) and 'Ingram v IRC' (Court of Appeal – inheritance tax). *Nick Warren QC* – "bright, thoughtful, and good at finding ways out of problems"– and *Robert Ham QC* – "lovely to work with. Sensible, considered, thorough and good in court" – attracted favourable comment again this year. So did new silks *Brian Green QC* – "very good, especially in pensions litigation. Hard hitting. Has got that extra spark" – and *Christopher Nugee QC* – "A gutsy fighter and intellectually good. Explains clearly and will listen." His recent cases include 'Siefert v Pensions Ombudsman' (Court of Appeal – pensions – ombudsman procedure). *David Lowe QC* was recommended for trust litigation in particular, and *John Child*, who has joined the set from the now defunct 17 Old Buildings, was said to be "a very good draftsman."

5 Stone Buildings (Harrod) Second only to Wilberforce Chambers for this type of work, despite the loss of Michael Hart to the bench. Two silks and four juniors in our tables provide a range of experience. **Leading Barristers:** *Mark Herbert QC*, who has "a very good reputation in trusts

and tax," received several plaudits. He moves up in our tables. Head of Chambers *Henry Harrod* and *Shân Warnock-Smith* ("good on family provision, good all-rounder") also drew favourable comment.

3 New Square (Goodhart) Solid reputation in all areas of chancery practice, especially real property, charities, trusts and estates, equitable remedies and contested probate. Two silks and three juniors feature in our tables. **Leading Barristers:** Head of Chambers *Lord Goodhart QC* and *Bernard Weatherill QC* ("very hard working, great attention to detail") both have strong reputations. Lord Goodhart's recent successes include 'Hambro v Marlborough' (Churchill Archive – Lottery Funds). Bernard Weatherill QC recently appeared in the successful appeal of 'Marston Thompson Evershed plc v Bend.' *David Rowell*, "arguably best tax draftsman at the Bar," moves up in our table of juniors this year. *Andrew Walker* recently concluded 'Radley Kane v Kane' (contentious probate) before the Vice Chancellor in the High Court.

11 New Square (Crampin) Experienced in all areas of chancery practice, with particular strengths in trusts, charities and property law. **Leading Barristers:** The set's reputation owes a lot to head of chambers *Peter Crampin QC* and to *Sonia Proudman QC*, who was much praised and moves higher up in our tables this year. Her recent chancery matters have included breach of trust, efficacy of trust-based schemes for tax avoidance, variation of trusts and restrictive covenants in development schemes. *Dirik Jackson* also enjoys a good reputation as one of the leading juniors for traditional chancery work. His recent chancery cases include 'Frankland v IRC.'

In addition to the above, several other sets and individuals are very well regarded for traditional chancery work.

At **10 Old Square** (Price) the vastly experienced *Leolin Price QC* is still very busy. Junior *Francis Barlow*, meanwhile, is recommended as "a safe pair of hands."

At **13 Old Square** (Lyndon-Stanford) *Christopher McCall QC* is "incredibly helpful, understands what the clients want and is very pragmatic." "He could name his price and people would still beat a path to his door." The feedback we received about him merited a top ranking with Edward Nugee QC and Jules Sher QC. *Alexandra Mason*, who came to **3 Stone Buildings** (Vos) from 17 Old Buildings, is clearly very highly thought of and becomes one of our two top juniors this year. Her recent cases include 'Stone v Chataway' (distribution of estate of Lloyd's Name). *Frank Hinks* at **Serle Court Chambers** (Sparrow) was said to have a

MCCALL Christopher 13 Old Square

NUGEE Edward Wilberforce Chambers

SHER Jules Wilberforce Chambers

CRAMPIN Peter 11 New Square

HAM Robert Wilberforce Chambers

HERBERT Mark 5 Stone Buildings

MARTIN John Wilberforce Chambers

PROUDMAN Sonia 11 New Square

WARREN Nicholas Wilberforce Chambers

GOODHART Lord 3 New Square

HENDERSON Launcelot 5 Stone Buildings

LOWE David Wilberforce Chambers

MOWBRAY John 12 New Square

PRICE Leolin 10 Old Square

WEATHERILL Bernard 3 New Square

GREEN Brian Wilberforce Chambers

NUGEE Christopher Wilberforce Chambers

MASON Alexandra 3 Stone Buildings

TAUBE Simon 10 Old Square

BARLOW Francis 10 Old Square

BRIGGS John 3/4 South Square

HARROD Henry 5 Stone Buildings

HINKS Frank Serle Court Chambers

JACKSON Dirik 11 New Square

ROGERS Beverly-Ann Serle Court Chambers

ROWELL David 3 New Square

ROWLEY Keith 11 Old Square

SEMKEN Christopher 1 New Square

STEWART SMITH Rodney 1 New Square

TAUSSIG Anthony Wilberforce Chambers

TOPHAM Geoffrey 3 Stone Buildings

TUCKER Lynton 12 New Square

WARNOCK-SMITH Shân 5 Stone Buildings

ACTON Stephen 11 Old Square

AINGER David 10 Old Square

BROWNBILL David 8 Gray's Inn Square

CANT Christopher 9 Stone Buildings

CHAPMAN Vivian 9 Stone Buildings

CHILD John Wilberforce Chambers

EVANS Timothy 13 Old Square

HAYES Josephine 3 New Square

HORNE Roger 11 New Square

LONSDALE Marion 46 Essex Street

SIMMONDS Andrew 5 Stone Buildings

TIDMARSH Christopher 5 Stone Buildings

WALKER Andrew 3 New Square

"powerful offshore trusts practice" and "an incredible client list." *Keith Rowley*, a "very good draftsman" at **11 Old Square** (Crawford & Simpkiss), moves up in our tables, as does *Beverly-Ann Rogers* of Serle Court Chambers who is said to have "a very strong following." Her recent chancery work includes 'Greene v CBS' (trusts – copyright of George Bernard Shaw). At **9 Stone Buildings** (Ashe), *Vivian Chapman* was described as "an extremely polished performer" and *Christopher Cant* as "very solid."

WESTERN/WALES AND CHESTER CIRCUITS

LEADING JUNIORS · WESTERN

BAMFORD Jeremy Guildhall Chambers
BLOHM Leslie St. John's Chambers
DAVIES Stephen Guildhall Chambers
MAHER Martha Guildhall Chambers

LEADING JUNIORS
WALES & CHESTER

JARMAN Milwyn 9 Park Place
JONES Geraint 9 Park Place
KEYSER Andrew 9 Park Place

FOR DETAILS ON THESE LEADING BARRISTERS SEE PROFILES ON PAGES 1509-1642

Stephen Davies at **Guildhall Chambers** (Royce) in Bristol was described as the "finest insolvency practitioner in the West Country." Newly recommended at the same set are *Martha Maher*, "an assertive and well regarded practitioner" said to be especially strong on company work, and "rising star" *Jeremy Bamford*, who is seen as more of a generalist. *Andrew Keyser* is a new recommendation at **9 Park Place** (Murphy), Cardiff.

MIDLANDS AND OXFORD CIRCUIT

LEADING SILKS
MIDLANDS & OXFORD

RANDALL John St Philip's Chambers

LEADING JUNIORS
MIDLANDS & OXFORD

ASHWORTH Lance St Philip's Chambers
CORBETT James St Philip's Chambers
STOCKILL David 5 Fountain Court

UP AND COMING
MIDLANDS & OXFORD

CHARMAN Andrew St Philip's Chambers

FOR DETAILS ON THESE LEADING BARRISTERS SEE PROFILES ON PAGES 1509-1642

St Philip's Chambers (Tedd) Birmingham is seen as the premier set in the Midlands for chancery work. *John Randall QC* and *James Corbett* appear in our list again this year. Newly recommended are *Lance Ashworth* and the up and coming *Andrew Charman*. He is said to have "got out of the starting blocks very fast" and is building a substantial practice – "he's positive and decisive and has a practical approach to problems."

David Stockill at **5 Fountain Court** (Barker) was also recommended again as "a good combative operator." He fights hard, but isn't someone who'll spoil a settlement by being aggressive.

NORTHERN/NORTH EASTERN CIRCUITS

LEADING SILKS · NORTHERN

SMITH Peter 40 King St
ELLERAY Anthony St. James's Chambers
LEEMING Ian 9 St. John Street

NEW SILKS · 1997 AND 1998

JONES Edward Exchange Chambers

LEADING JUNIORS · NORTHERN

BERRAGAN Neil Merchant Chambers
BOOTH Michael 40 King St
CAWSON Mark St. James's Chambers
CHAISTY Paul 40 King St
DUNN Katherine 40 King St
JOHNSON Ian 14 Castle St
JOHNSON Michael 9 St. John Street
MCCARROLL John Exchange Chambers
ORR Nicholas 14 Castle St
RIDDLE Nicholas 14 Castle St
STERLING Robert St. James's Chambers

LEADING SILK · NORTH EASTERN

ALLEN James Chancery House Chambers

FOR DETAILS ON THESE LEADING BARRISTERS SEE PROFILES ON PAGES 1509-1642

Peter Smith QC (" a tough customer" and "a good person to fight your corner") at **40 King Street** (Raynor), Manchester, is seen as the premier Chancery silk in the north of England. New silk *Edward Bartley Jones QC* at **Exchange Chambers** (Waldron), Liverpool is also recommended this year. There are a number of highly regarded Northern juniors for chancery work. New to our lists this year are the "extremely hard working" *Michael Booth*, the "very thorough" *Katherine Dunn*, both at **40 King Street** (Raynor), Manchester and *Mark Cawson* at **St James's Chambers** (Sterling), Manchester. *Nicholas Orr*, meanwhile, at **14 Castle Street** (Lyon) Liverpool, continues to maintain his reputation as "a very good all-rounder".

CHARITIES

RESEARCH: In compiling the tables, we consider all the information available to us, paying particular regard to the market research carried out by our team of ten qualified lawyers. (The researchers' details are set out on page three.) The rankings, therefore, reflect the opinion of the marketplace as revealed by systematic and objective research: see page four. (Our research is audited every year by the British Market Research Bureau.)

OVERVIEW: There are no chambers which stand out as leading sets because there are few genuine specialist charity barristers. Most of the leading charity barristers are members of traditional and commercial chancery chambers.

Barristers' profiles	p. 1509-1642

LEADING SILKS · LONDON
MCCALL Christopher 13 Old Square
PICARDA Hubert 3 New Square
CRAMPIN Peter 11 New Square
HERBERT Mark 5 Stone Buildings
NUGEE Edward Wilberforce Chambers
PROUDMAN Sonia 11 New Square
UNWIN David 7 Stone Buildings
VENABLES Robert 24 Old Buildings

NEW SILKS · 1997 AND 1998
WATERS Malcolm 11 Old Square

LEADING JUNIORS · LONDON
QUINT Francesca 11 Old Square
DUMONT Thomas 11 New Square
HENDERSON William Serle Court Chambers
KESSLER James 24 Old Buildings
NEWEY Guy 7 Stone Buildings
WARNOCK-SMITH Shân 5 Stone Buildings

FOR DETAILS ON THESE LEADING BARRISTERS
SEE PROFILES ON PAGES 1509-1642

LONDON

13 Old Square (Lyndon-Stanford) One of the most respected commercial chancery practices. **Leading Barristers:** The "seriously clever" *Christopher McCall QC* is an eminent charities barrister who is nationally respected.

3 New Square (Goodhart) **Leading Barristers:** *Hubert Picarda QC's* expertise is recognised throughout the country, and he undertakes "an enormous amount of charities work." He is excellent on the academic side, and is recommended particularly "for the more esoteric stuff."

Wilberforce Chambers (Nugee) Known mainly as a traditional chancery set. **Leading Barristers:** *Edward Nugee QC* has a "very good intellect" and is a leading private client barrister.

11 New Square (Crampin) **Leading Barristers:** The "outstanding" *Peter Crampin QC* is considered "unstuffy" and a "real problem solver." *Sonia Proudman QC* is described as "good on her feet," and "sensible and commercially aware." *Thomas Dumont* has a niche in legacies for charities.

5 Stone Buildings (Harrod) Strong reputation built upon traditional chancery work. **Leading Barristers:** The "good and solid" *Mark Herbert QC* and *Shân Warnock-Smith* have respected general chancery practices which include a significant amount of charities work.

7 Stone Buildings (Aldous) Excellent reputation for commercial chancery matters. **Leading Barristers:** The "superb" *David Unwin QC* has "lots of high profile charity experience"and *Guy Newey* has a respected general chancery practice.

24 Old Buildings (Bretten) **Leading Barristers:** *Robert Venables QC* has an excellent reputation for the tax side of charities. *James Kessler* ("has a very good brain") is also a tax specialist.

11 Old Square (Crawford & Simpkiss) **Leading Barristers:** *Malcolm Waters QC* is considered "pragmatic and reliable." The "very knowledgeable and practical" *Francesca Quint* is widely regarded as the leading charities junior. She is particularly recommended for her "clear and concise" written opinions.

Serle Court Chambers (Sparrow) **Leading Barristers:** *William Henderson* recently joined chambers. He specialises in trusts, land and charities work, particularly for the Attorney General's office. He appeared in 'Varsani v Jesani'.

NORTH EASTERN CIRCUIT

Trinity Chambers (Milford) Remains the only set outside London to have established a reputation in charity law. From Newcastle they serve the entire north eastern circuit.

CIVIL LIBERTIES

RESEARCH: In compiling the tables, we consider all the information available to us, paying particular regard to the market research carried out by our team of ten qualified lawyers. (The researchers' details are set out on page three.) The rankings, therefore, reflect the opinion of the marketplace as revealed by systematic and objective research: see page four. (Our research is audited every year by the British Market Research Bureau.)

OVERVIEW: Civil liberties issues can occur in a variety of contexts, including general crime work, judicial review, housing, education, immigration, discrimination, public order cases, civil actions against the police, prisoners' rights, miscarriages of justice and Caribbean death row cases. Practitioners expect a great deal of work to be generated by the new Human Rights Act.

Barristers' profiles   p. 1509-1642

LEADING SETS · LONDON

DOUGHTY STREET CHAMBERS (Robertson QC)

TWO GARDEN COURT (Macdonald QC & Davies)

14 TOOKS COURT (Michael Mansfield QC)

HIGHLY REGARDED · LONDON

Cloisters (Laura Cox QC)

Mitre House Chambers (Francis Gilbert)

Blackstone Chambers (Flint QC/Baxendale QC)

1 Pump Court (Hoyal and Latham)

6 King's Bench Walk (Sibghat Kadri QC)

Doughty Street Chambers (Robertson) Have traditionally been the leaders, and are still considered exceptional for this type of work. Five silks and four juniors were recommended to us. Specialist areas include actions against the police, prisoners' rights, Caribbean death row cases, discrimination and judicial review. **Leading Barristers:** *Geoffrey Robertson QC,* who has particular expertise in freedom of expression matters, is still pre-eminent at the civil liberties bar. The "superb" *Edward Fitzgerald QC* is regarded as one of the best barristers in the country for prisoners' rights. He recently acted in the Myra Hindley sentencing judicial review case. *Helena Kennedy QC*, recommended for the quality of her work in this field, moves up a band in our table of silks. *Ben Emmerson,* who has a very high profile and is widely admired by both solicitors and barristers, was singled out as the top junior for civil liberties work. He and *Andrew Nicol QC* acted for the defendants in the leading Court of Appeal case on disclosure of journalist's sources 'Camelot

Group plc v Centaur Communications Ltd'. *Keir Starmer* is said to have "an analytical and incisive way of looking at things." He has particular expertise in prisoners' rights and actions against the police. *Phillippa Kaufmann* is also building an excellent niche in prisoners' rights.

Two Garden Court (Macdonald and Davies) Specialists in crime, housing, immigration and judicial review. Recommended as having a good range of people in all areas of civil liberties work. One silk and three juniors feature in our tables. **Leading Barristers:** *Nicholas Blake QC* maintains his "superb" reputation. *Henry Blaxland* acted in the Bridgewater appeal and remains highly regarded. The "very thorough" *Terry Munyard* is considered one of the best junior civil liberties barristers, and also recommended is joint head of chambers *Owen Davies.*

14 Tooks Court (Mansfield) A set with a long-standing commitment to civil liberties work. Known, among other things, for actions against the police, riot cases, appeals by alleged terrorists, judicial review and immigration. **Leading Barristers:** *Michael Mansfield QC* has an even higher profile this year after acting in the Stephen Lawrence case. He has an excellent reputation, particularly for cases where a robust approach is needed. As well as handling general criminal work *Mark Guthrie* specialises in actions against the police.

Cloisters (Cox) Has an excellent reputation in all areas of crime and civil liberties, especially racial and sexual discrimination, minority groups, and prisoners' rights. **Leading Barristers:** *Robin Allen QC* has a broad public law practice,

LEADING SILKS · LONDON

ROBERTSON Geoffrey Doughty Street Chambers

BELOFF Michael 4-5 Gray's Inn Square
BLAKE Nicholas Two Garden Court
FITZGERALD Edward Doughty Street Chambers
LESTER OF HERNE HILL Lord Blackstone Chambers
MANSFIELD Michael 14 Tooks Court
SCRIVENER Anthony 2-3 Gray's Inn Square

KENNEDY Helena Doughty Street Chambers
NICOL Andrew Doughty Street Chambers
THORNTON Peter Doughty Street Chambers

ALLEN Robin Cloisters
KADRI Sibghat 6 King's Bench Walk
MUNBY James 1 New Square
NICHOLLS Colin 3 Raymond Buildings
PLEMING Nigel 39 Essex Street
SOLLEY Stephen Cloisters

NEW SILKS · 1997 AND 1998

DUFFY Peter Essex Court Chambers
JAY Robert 39 Essex Street

LEADING JUNIORS · LONDON

EMMERSON Ben Doughty Street Chambers

CLAYTON Richard Devereux Chambers
OWEN Tim Doughty Street Chambers
STARMER Keir Doughty Street Chambers

CLOVER Anthony New Court Chambers
GILBERT Francis Mitre House Chambers
KAUFMANN Phillippa Doughty Street Chambers
LATHAM Robert 1 Pump Court

BLAXLAND Henry Two Garden Court
DAVIES Owen Two Garden Court
GOULDING Paul Blackstone Chambers
GUMBITI-ZIMUTO Andrew 6 King's Bench Walk
GUTHRIE Mark 14 Tooks Court
HIGHAM Paul 1 Pump Court
MUNYARD Terry Two Garden Court
MYLVAGANAM Tanoo 14 Tooks Court
ROSE Dinah Blackstone Chambers
SINGH Rabinder 4-5 Gray's Inn Square
TEGGIN Victoria Mitre House Chambers

UP AND COMING · LONDON

WEISSELBERG TOM Blackstone Chambers

FOR DETAILS OF THESE LEADING BARRISTERS
SEE PROFILES ON PAGES 1509-1642

with a focus on discrimination. *Stephen Solley QC* has established a reputation for acting in criminal matters with civil liberties aspects.

Mitre House Chambers (Gilbert) Particularly well known for handling public order offences and cases involving the exercise of police powers. **Leading Barristers:** Head of Chambers *Francis Gilbert* has a respected civil liberties practice on the back of his criminal work. Another recommended junior is *Victoria Teggin.*

Blackstone Chambers (Flint and Baxendale) Leading public and administrative law set. Handle a lot of judicial review work, both for and against public bodies involving issues such as equality of treatment, freedom of expression, housing, immigration and education. **Leading Barristers:** *Lord Lester of Herne Hill QC* won the Human Rights Lawyer of the Year Award. *Paul Goulding* specialises in employment law but is also respected for his civil liberties work. Also recommended

are the "extremely astute" *Dinah Rose* and *Tom Weisselberg*.

6 Kings Bench Walk (Kadri) A set with a reputation for defending the rights and liberties of individuals. Principal areas of expertise are crime, housing, immigration and discrimination. **Leading Barristers:** Head of Chambers *Sibghat Kadri QC* is experienced in this field, as is *Andrew Gumbiti-Zimuto*.

1 Pump Court (Hoyal and Latham) Best known for criminal and housing work. **Leading Barristers:** Head of Chambers *Robert Latham* has a public law and housing practice with a civil liberties element. *Paul Higham* is considered "imaginative" and is well regarded for this work.

In addition to the above, a number of individuals at other sets are worthy of mention for their civil liberties work. They include *Michael Beloff QC* of **4-5 Gray's Inn Square** (Appleby and Beloff), who has built an outstanding reputation in this as in

other fields. *Rabinder Singh* at the same set is also recommended. *Anthony Scrivener QC* of **2-3 Gray's Inn Square** (Scrivener) received many recommendations, and is admired for his great ability combined with his " human touch." *Peter Duffy QC* of **Essex Court Chambers** (Pollock) is also considered "excellent." *Richard Clayton* of **Devereux Chambers** (Burke) is said to be "very helpful."

THE NORTHERN CIRCUIT

HIGHLY REGARDED · NORTHERN

Central Chambers Manchester

Central Chambers (Khan) Manchester. A new entry to our lists this year. The only regional set to receive strong recommendations for inclusion.

COMMERCIAL (LITIGATION)

RESEARCH: In compiling the tables, we consider all the information available to us, paying particular regard to the market research carried out by our team of ten qualified lawyers. (The researchers' details are set out on page three.) The rankings, therefore, reflect the opinion of the marketplace as revealed by systematic and objective research: see page four. (Our research is audited every year by the British Market Research Bureau.)

OVERVIEW: The quality of clerking remains a big issue for practitioners, far more so than fees, and is often the decisive factor when choosing between comparable counsel. All the silks in our top band are greatly admired but, as one would expect, they are so busy that it can sometimes be difficult to get them.

In London, three other sets are now seen as being on a par with Essex Court Chambers, while 3 Verulam Buildings have also enhanced their reputation. Outside London the lists are small, reflecting a dearth of commercial barristers in the regions, although a few individuals received strong recommendations.

Barristers' profiles   p. 1509-1642

LEADING SETS · LONDON

BRICK COURT CHAMBERS (Clarke QC)
ESSEX COURT CHAMBERS (Pollock QC)
ONE ESSEX COURT (Anthony Grabiner QC)
FOUNTAIN COURT (Peter Scott QC)
3 VERULAM BUILDINGS (R. Neville Thomas QC)
7 KING'S BENCH WALK (Stephen Tomlinson QC)
LITTLETON CHAMBERS (Michael Burton QC)

HIGHLY REGARDED · LONDON

Blackstone Chambers (Baxendale QC/Flint QC)
One Hare Court (Lord Neill QC/Southwell QC)
4 Pump Court (Bruce Mauleverer QC)
Serle Court Chambers (Charles Sparrow QC)
4 Essex Court (Nigel Teare QC)
11 King's Bench Walk (Tabachnik QC/Goudie QC)

Brick Court Chambers (Clarke) Have ten silks and four juniors listed in our tables. They are the first choice for many. **Leading Barristers:** *Christopher Clarke QC*, described as "easy to work with, bright and constructive," and the "outstanding" *Jonathan Sumption QC* feature in the top band of our table of silks. *Sydney Kentridge QC* joins them there this year, as befits "an international jurist of the highest calibre." His recent cases include 'Total Gas Marketing Ltd v Arco British Ltd and Others' (HL – seller's failure to perform 'conditions precedent' terminates contract). The "wonderful intellect" of *Mark Hapgood QC* was also praised as were the "tenacity and incisiveness" of *Jonathan Hirst QC,* whose recent cases include 'Dawnay Day and Co Ltd and Another v Cantor Fitzgerald International' (1998 – permission to use corporate name revocable). A bright future is predicted for "rising stars" *Mark Howard QC* and *George Leggatt QC*. (Howard was recently involved in the Co-op take-over together with Christopher Clarke QC). Amongst the juniors the "impressive" *Charles Hollander* attracted much favourable comment.

Essex Court Chambers (Pollock) Seen as a good, solid commercial set. Once again, the clerking here received much praise. Unusually, and encouragingly for the future of the set, more juniors than silks feature in our list (seven and three respectively). **Leading Barristers:** The "fearless" *Gordon Pollock QC* is said to be "loyal to clients and a big presence in court." He led on 'Levante Establishment v Prince Jeffri.'

Andrew Hochhauser QC impressed with his "incredible talent and intelligence" and was also described as "an enthusiastic team player." *Joe Smouha* remains in our star category with work including 'Prince Al Saud v Ayas.' *Martin Griffiths* was described as "highly analytical and quite awesome." Other recommended juniors include the "tough and clear" *Geraldine Andrews*, "shrewd" *John Lockey* and *Toby Landau* (considered "user friendly").

One Essex Court (Grabiner) Seen as offering a five star service. The clerks were praised for their efficiency. Have the largest number of individuals (19) in our tables. **Leading Barristers:** *Anthony Grabiner QC* ("excellent in court") remains at the top of the field. His work in 1997 included 'National Power v Feldon and Others.' The "forceful and tenacious" *Elizabeth Gloster QC* is a popular choice, as is the "consistently good, approachable" *Christopher Carr QC. Steven Gee QC* was described as "innovative," whilst *Jeffrey Gruder QC* was praised for "incisive thinking and excellent analytical skills." *Laurence Rabinowitz* remains one of the top juniors. He has acted in most of the major DTI investigations of recent years and also appeared in the 'Total Gas Marketing' case. Also praised were "ideas man" *John McCaughran* and *Charles Graham* for being "tremendously thorough."

Fountain Court (Scott) The silks and younger juniors are highly rated. Have strength in numbers with eight silks and six juniors recommended. Much work has an international flavour. **Leading Barristers:**

Both *Peter Scott QC* and *Peter Goldsmith QC* are "absolutely first rate." Scott was instructed on 'N.R.G. v Bacon & Woodrow.' *Nicholas Stadlen QC* was seen as "bright and well organised." *David Railton QC* has been heavily involved in acting for the Manoukians (with others) in the 'Manoukian v Prince Jefri Bolkiah' litigation. New silk *Simon Browne-Wilkinson QC* was described as "impressive and approachable." Highly regarded juniors include *Bankim Thanki* and new entry *David Waksman* who is "a great all-rounder and impressive cross-examiner." His work in 1997 included 'News International v Clinger.'

3 Verulam Buildings (Thomas) With six silks and five juniors recommended, the set has established itself as a serious commercial presence. Particularly well known for banking expertise. **Work Handled:** 'D Clifton v Powergen plc' (Thomas); 'Polly Peck v Stoy Hayward' (Jarvis); 'Kuwait Finance House v BCCI' (Jarvis); 'Normaco v Lundman' (Geering). **Leading Barristers:** Head of Chambers *Neville Thomas QC* is very experienced and retains an excellent reputation. *Ian Geering QC* is "straightforward, hard-working and highly rated" while *Nicholas Merriman QC* "has a great way with judges." The popular *Ali Malek QC* was recommended as "user friendly," while *David Wolfson* and *Caroline Lewis* are also highly rated.

7 King's Bench Walk (Tomlinson) Three silks and one junior were recommended to us for their general commercial work. **Leading Barristers:** Among the silks, *Gavin Kealey QC* is "a clear advocate who

LEADING SILKS · LONDON

BURTON Michael Littleton Chambers	**GRABINER Anthony** One Essex Court	**SCOTT Peter** Fountain Court
CLARKE Christopher Brick Court Chambers	**KENTRIDGE Sydney** Brick Court Chambers	**SUMPTION Jonathan** Brick Court Chambers
GOLDSMITH Peter Fountain Court	**POLLOCK Gordon** Essex Court Chambers	
AIKENS Richard Brick Court Chambers	**BRINDLE Michael** Fountain Court	
BOSWOOD Anthony Fountain Court	**GLOSTER Elizabeth** One Essex Court	
BURNTON Stanley One Essex Court	**GLASGOW Edwin** 39 Essex Street	**LEVESON Brian** 22 Old Building
CARR Christopher One Essex Court	**GLICK Ian** One Essex Court	**MOWSCHENSON Terence** One Essex Court
DOHMANN Barbara Blackstone Chambers	**HAPGOOD Mark** Brick Court Chambers	**TALBOT Patrick** Serle Court Chambers
EDER Bernard Essex Court Chambers	**JARVIS John** 3 Verulam Buildings	**TOMLINSON Stephen** 7 King's Bench Walk
BARNES Mark One Essex Court	**HIRST Jonathan** Brick Court Chambers	**SOUTHWELL Richard** 1 Hare Court
BRATZA Nicolas 1 Hare Court	**HOWARD M. N.** 4 Essex Court	**STRAUSS Nicholas** One Essex Court
FIELD Richard 11 King's Bench Walk	**KEALEY Gavin** 7 King's Bench Walk	**TEMPLE Anthony** 4 Pump Court
FLINT Charles Blackstone Chambers	**MACGREGOR Alastair** One Essex Court	**THOMAS Neville** 3 Verulam Buildings
GEE Steven One Essex Court	**SALTER Richard** 3 Verulam Buildings	**TUGENDHAT Michael** 5 Raymond Buildings
HAMILTON Adrian 7 King's Bench Walk	**SMITH Andrew** Fountain Court	
BRIGGS Michael Serle Court Chambers	**HOWARD Mark** Brick Court Chambers	**SEYMOUR Richard** Monckton Chambers
CRAN Mark Brick Court Chambers	**LEGGATT George** Brick Court Chambers	**STADLEN Nicholas** Fountain Court
FREEDMAN Clive Littleton Chambers	**MALEK Ali** 3 Verulam Buildings	**STRACHAN Mark** 1 Crown Office Row
GEERING Ian 3 Verulam Buildings	**MANN Anthony** Enterprise Chambers	**VOS Geoffrey** 3 Stone Buildings
HEILBRON Hilary Brick Court Chambers	**MERRIMAN Nicholas** 3 Verulam Buildings	
HOCHHAUSER Andrew Essex Court Chambers	**RAILTON David** Fountain Court	

NEW SILKS · 1997 AND 1998

BOSWELL Lindsay 4 Pump Court	**CLARKE Andrew** Littleton Chambers	**JACOBS Richard** Essex Court Chambers
BROWNE-WILKINSON Simon Fountain Court	**GRUDER Jeffrey** One Essex Court	**ONIONS Jeffery** One Essex Court

FOR DETAILS OF THESE LEADING BARRISTERS SEE PROFILES ON PAGES 1509-1642

judges listen to." *Stephen Tomlinson QC* was praised for work such as Court of Appeal case 'Bouygues v Caspian.' *Christopher Butcher* is felt by some to be the best junior at the commercial bar.

Littleton Chambers (Burton) With three silks and two juniors recommended, the set is making steady progress. Leading

Barristers: Head of Chambers *Michael Burton QC* moves into our top band of silks this year with a flood of compliments: "superb intellect and courtcraft; fantastic ability to predict results; lateral thinker; gets the judge's ear; gives 110% every time." *Clive Freedman QC* is "a tenacious and hardworking litigator," known for

quickly establishing excellent rapport and empathising with his commercial clients interests. He was recently instructed on 'Yona International v La Reunion Française.'

Blackstone Chambers (Baxendale and Flint) Strong recommendations were received for *Barbara Dohmann QC, Charles Flint QC* ("first-rate in court") and *Thomas Beazley* who is "an excellent technician." Flint acted in 'British Steel plc v Customs and Excise Commissioners' [CA].

One Hare Court (Neill and Southwell) *Richard Southwell QC* is well known for his expertise in banking and insurance work. *Dominic Dowley,* who is "bright and helpful," and *James Eadie,* were also recommended.

4 Pump Court (Mauleverer) Both *Anthony Temple QC* and *Lindsay Boswell QC* were particularly recommended for "heavyweight litigation." Temple has recently been acting in 'News International Plc and Others v Michael Clinger and Others.' *Nigel Tozzi* is said to be "excellent at cross-examination."

Serle Court Chambers (Sparrow) Increasingly recognised as a commercial litigation set. *Michael Briggs QC* ("definitely a star") is a new entry to our list of leaders this year.

4 Essex Court (Teare) Handle a range of commercial matters, particularly insurance, international trade and maritime law. Both *Michael Howard QC* and *Poonam Melwani* were recommended as leaders.

LEADING JUNIORS · LONDON

RABINOWITZ Laurence One Essex Court	**SMOUHA Joe** Essex Court Chambers
BUTCHER Christopher 7 King's Bench Walk	**MORIARTY Stephen** Fountain Court
DOCTOR Brian Fountain Court	**OTTON-GOULDER Catharine** Brick Court Chambers
DOWLEY Dominic 1 Hare Court	**THANKI Bankim** Fountain Court
BEAZLEY Thomas Blackstone Chambers	**HOLLANDER Charles** Brick Court Chambers
DE GARR ROBINSON Anthony One Essex Court	**JONES Elizabeth** Serle Court Chambers
GRIFFITHS Martin Essex Court Chambers	**PHILLIPS Stephen** 3 Verulam Buildings
GRIFFITHS Alan One Essex Court	
ANDREWS Geraldine Essex Court Chambers	**MCCAUGHRAN John** One Essex Court
BLOCH Selwyn Littleton Chambers	**ORR Craig** Fountain Court
DAVIES Rhodri One Essex Court	**ROBERTSON Patricia** Fountain Court
EADIE James 1 Hare Court	**TOZZI Nigel** 4 Pump Court
LOCKEY John Essex Court Chambers	**WOLFSON David** 3 Verulam Buildings
LORD Richard Brick Court Chambers	**WYNTER Colin** Devereux Chambers
LOWENSTEIN Paul Littleton Chambers	
CAVENDER David One Essex Court	**MCQUATER Ewan** 3 Verulam Buildings
CHAMBERS Dominic Brick Court Chambers	**MELWANI Poonam** 4 Essex Court
GRAHAM Charles One Essex Court	**ONSLOW Andrew** 3 Verulam Buildings
LANDAU Toby Essex Court Chambers	**WAKSMAN David** Fountain Court
LEWIS Caroline 3 Verulam Buildings	**WHITE Antony** Cloisters

UP AND COMING · LONDON

BLANCHARD Claire Essex Court Chambers	**FLYNN Vernon** Essex Court Chambers

11 King's Bench Walk (Tabachnik and Goudie) Handle a range of commercial law and international trade matters. *Richard Field QC* was recommended as "a good team player."

WESTERN CIRCUIT

LEADING SILKS · WESTERN
PALMER Adrian Guildhall Chambers
ROYCE John Guildhall Chambers

LEADING JUNIORS · WESTERN
DAVIES Stephen Guildhall Chambers
STEAD Richard St. John's Chambers
MAHER Martha Guildhall Chambers
VIRGO John Guildhall Chambers
LEVY Neil St. John's Chambers

Guildhall Chambers (Royce) in Bristol is the leading commercial litigation set in the region, with two silks and three juniors in our tables. *Adrian Palmer QC* is felt to have "made his mark" and has risen in the tables accordingly. *Stephen Davies* received high praise – "by far the best lawyer on the circuit," he "stands out from everyone else." From the same set are *Martha Maher* who "stands her ground well" and *John Virgo*, particularly well regarded for insolvency and banking matters.

St John's Chambers (Denyer) in Bristol also have a good reputation. *Richard Stead* was recommended as tenacious. *Neil Levy* is a new entry following several recommendations, particularly for his knowledge of banking law.

MIDLANDS AND OXFORD CIRCUIT

LEADING SILKS MIDLANDS & OXFORD
RANDALL John St Philip's Chambers

LEADING JUNIORS MIDLANDS & OXFORD
ANDERSON Mark 3 Fountain Court
ASHWORTH Lance St Philip's Chambers
CAMPBELL Stephen St Philip's Chambers
CORBETT James St Philip's Chambers
CRAIG Aubrey 5 Fountain Court
STOCKILL David 5 Fountain Court

St Philip's Chambers (Tedd) (formerly 7 Fountain Court) in Birmingham is the pre-eminent commercial litigation set in the Midlands. The "incredibly busy" *John Randall QC* was the only silk recommended to us in the region. *Stephen Campbell* and *Lance Ashworth* were also recommended, as was *James Corbett*. **5 Fountain Court** is also popular with practitioners and has leading juniors *Aubrey Craig* and *David Stockill*. *Mark Anderson* at **3 Fountain Court** (Treacy) is new to our tables this year.

NORTH EASTERN CIRCUIT

LEADING JUNIORS NORTH EASTERN
GROVES Hugo Enterprise Chambers
MORGAN Charles Enterprise Chambers
MYERSON Simon Park Court Chambers
ATHERTON Ian Enterprise Chambers
JORY Hugh Enterprise Chambers

The first choice in the North East for most practitioners is **Enterprise Chambers** (Mann) in Leeds. Two juniors entered our list for the first time this year: *Ian Atherton* was recommended for general Chancery and Mercantile Court work and has been elected chairman of the North Eastern Arbitration Club by his fellow practitioners; *Hugh Jory* is "practical and capable" particularly on shareholder disputes.

Seen as a good team player, *Simon Myerson* at **Park Court Chambers** (Stewart and Smith) was also recommended by a number of practitioners.

NORTHERN CIRCUIT

LEADING SILKS · NORTHERN
LEVESON Brian Byrom Street Chambers
SMITH Peter 40 King St
WINGATE-SAUL Giles Byrom Street Chambers
EDIS Andrew 14 Castle St
JONES Edward Bartley Exchange Chambers
STEWART Stephen Byrom Street Chambers

LEADING JUNIORS · NORTHERN
ANDERSON Lesley 40 King St
COGLEY Stephen Merchant Chambers
DAVIES Stephen 8 King St
TERRY Jeffrey 8 King St
BERRAGAN Neil Merchant Chambers
CAWSON Mark St. James's Chambers
RIDDLE Nicholas 14 Castle St
SANDER Andrew Oriel Chambers

Byrom Street Chambers (Hytner) in Manchester have the most impressive collection of commercial silks in the North of England. *Brian Leveson QC* divides his time between Manchester and London and has a reputation in several areas of law. *Giles Wingate-Saul QC* has a "tremendous rounded knowledge" and is "always good value for money," while *Stephen Stewart QC* is a new entry following a number of recommendations.

Other well regarded sets include **40 King Street** (Raynor), also in Manchester, where *Lesley Anderson* was described as "impressive" and *Peter Smith QC* ("always helpful") was recommended by several solicitors. **14 Castle Street** (Lyon) in Liverpool is increasingly recognised for commercial work. *Andrew Edis QC* rose in our tables and *Nicholas Riddle* is a new entry. **8 King Street** (Armitage) had two juniors recommended including the "careful and thorough" *Jeffrey Terry*.

COMPANY

RESEARCH: In compiling the tables, we consider all the information available to us, paying particular regard to the market research carried out by our team of ten qualified lawyers. (The researchers' details are set out on page three.) The rankings, therefore, reflect the opinion of the market-place as revealed by systematic and objective research: see page four. (Our research is audited every year by the British Market Research Bureau.)

OVERVIEW: Matters dealt with include directors' duties and some forms of disqualification; the rights of shareholders including s459 petitions, take-overs, corporate reconstructions and restructurings, and corporate insolvencies. There is an overlap with insolvency and other corporate and financial areas and the leaders in company often appear in those sections too. On the whole the lists are largely unchanged. Erskine Chambers continues to dominate. Individual changes of note are the inclusion of Richard Adkins QC from 3-4 South Square. Both Lawrence Cohen QC of 24 Old Buildings and David Oliver QC of 13 Old Square were particularly praised this year. At 4 Stone Buildings Jonathan Crow is now full-time Treasury Counsel.

Barristers' profiles	p. 1509-1642

LEADING SILKS · LONDON

POTTS Robin Erskine Chambers	
SYKES Richard Erskine Chambers	

ALDOUS Charles 7 Stone Buildings	
COHEN Lawrence 24 Old Buildings	
DAVIS Nigel 7 Stone Buildings	
GLOSTER Elizabeth One Essex Court	
GOODHART Lord 3 New Square	
OLIVER David 13 Old Square	
RICHARDS David Erskine Chambers	

ADKINS Richard 3-4 South Square	
BOMPAS Anthony George 4 Stone Buildings	
BOYLE Alan Serle Court Chambers	
BRIGGS Michael Serle Court Chambers	
BRISBY John 4 Stone Buildings	
CRYSTAL Michael 3-4 South Square	
CURRY Peter 4 Stone Buildings	
HAMILTON Eben 1 New Square	
HAPGOOD Mark Brick Court Chambers	
HESLOP Philip 4 Stone Buildings	
HILDYARD Robert 4 Stone Buildings	
KOSMIN Leslie Erskine Chambers	
LYNDON-STANFORD Michael 13 Old Square	
MANN Anthony Enterprise Chambers	
MORTIMORE Simon 3-4 South Square	
MOWSCHENSON Terence One Essex Court	
PURLE Charles 12 New Square	
STEINFELD Alan 24 Old Buildings	

NEW SILKS · 1997 AND 1998

HOCHHAUSER Andrew Essex Court Chambers	
TODD Michael Erskine Chambers	

FOR DETAILS OF THESE LEADING BARRISTERS
SEE PROFILES ON PAGES 1509-1642

LEADING SETS · LONDON

ERSKINE CHAMBERS (Richard Sykes QC)	
ENTERPRISE CHAMBERS (Anthony Mann QC)	
ONE ESSEX COURT (Anthony Grabiner QC)	
13 OLD SQUARE (Michael Lyndon-Stanford QC)	
SERLE COURT CHAMBERS (Charles Sparrow QC)	
3-4 SOUTH SQUARE (Michael Crystal QC)	
4 STONE BUILDINGS (Philip Heslop QC)	
7 STONE BUILDINGS (Charles Aldous QC)	

Erskine Chambers (Sykes) "The first port of call" for company work, they continue to be "streets ahead of the rest." Especially valued on erudite and difficult points of law. Solicitors thought the clerking "brisk and efficient." Generally considered an expensive set but, as most acknowledged, "they can afford to be." **Work Handled:** Advice and litigation for Emerson against Astec Minority share-holders and for the independent directors of Astec on behalf of the company (Potts and Todd respectively). 'Banque Financiere de la Cite v Parc (Battersea) Ltd [1998]' – 'subrogation as a restitutionary remedy'. **Leading Barristers:** Heading the table are the "pro-active" *Robin Potts QC* ("a real fighter who is still active on the litigation front") and *Richard Sykes QC* ("extremely thorough"). Proving popular with instructing solicitors is *David Richards QC* ("calm, considered and user friendly"). *Michael Todd QC* has been recommended for his advice on corporate matters. A

positive wealth of skilled juniors include *David Chivers* ("excellent, bright and sensible"), *John Cone* ("cost effective for technical matters such as tricky s459s"), *Martin Moore* ("always thorough in his approach"), *Richard Snowden* ("brilliant"), and *Professor Dan Prentice* ("wonderful reputation, academic and a very fine lawyer"). The "seasoned" *Sir Thomas Stockdale* is rated for company work as well as Schemes of Arrangement.

Enterprise Chambers (Mann) "Forward thinking" commercial Chancery set recognised for its company law expertise. **Work Handled:** 'Soden v British Commonwealth' – whether company can claim in capacity of member (Mann). 'Re:Double S Printer Ltd' – whether charge in debenture over book debts fixed or floating (Ife). 'Mohans (Warehouses) Ltd v Kumar' – director's liability as accessory to misrepresentation, (Zelin and Arden). **Leading Barristers:** *Anthony Mann QC* ("thorough, analytical and approachable", "he rolls up his sleeves and gets on with it" – "a good advocate too"). Juniors include *Linden Ife* ("a punchy tough advocate").

One Essex Court (Grabiner) "A good alternative to Erskine Chambers." **Work Handled:** Scribes West – Edenote directors' disqualification case (Gloster). 'Metaloy Supplies v M.A. (CA)' (Mowchenson). **Leading Barristers:** The "first rate" *Elizabeth Gloster QC* ("very bright

and good with clients") handles a combination of insolvency and company work. *Terence Mowchenson QC* ("very practical, responsive and non-patronising"). Rated juniors include the "outstanding" *Laurence Rabinowitz* who appears in a number of sections.

13 Old Square (Lyndon-Stanford) **Work Handled:** 'UMB v Doherty [1998]' – directors' duties (Collings). 'Grand Metropolitan plc v The William Hill Group Ltd [1997]' rectification claims by companies. **Leading Barristers:** Much praised silks include *Michael Lyndon-Stanford QC* ("high quality company work") and *David Oliver QC* ("a model for the modern silk"; "easy to work with"; "pragmatic and straight talking"; "listens – doesn't preach and is also a great knockabout litigator"). Juniors include *Matthew Collings* ("a tough opponent") and *Paul Girolami* ("brilliant and charming").

Serle Court Chambers (Sparrow) Company matters are a major part of the total work handled. **Leading Barristers:** Silks include *Michael Briggs QC* ("bright and conscientious"). Rated juniors at this set include *Victor Joffe* ("intellectual and very well thought of").

3-4 South Square (Crystal) Although predominantly known as an insolvency set, the company law reputation is also good. **Work Handled:** 'Re Cosslett (Contractors) Ltd 1998 (CA)' (Mortimore); 'Galileo Group Elles v Hambros'. **Leading Barristers:** Particularly noted silks are Head of Chambers *Michael Crystal QC*, described as a wonderful advocate (more insolvency than company biased) and *Richard Adkins QC*, a new entry to the list this year. Praise for the "superb" junior *Robin Dicker* was effusive. *David Marks* was recommended this year and goes into up and coming.

4 Stone Buildings (Curry) Well thought of with a large number of individual silks and juniors recommended. **Work Handled:** Company work ranging from s459 through to complex insurance company transfer matters. Cases of interest include 'Sea Containers' litigation in Bermuda Supreme Court – legality of 'Poison Pill'; duties of directors in takeover. **Leading Barristers:** A number of highly regarded silks include the "brilliant"*Philip Heslop QC*, *Anthony Bompas QC* ("has real status", "commands respect with judges"), *John Brisby QC*

("determined, good on complex matters") and *Robert Hildyard QC* ("high calibre"). Of the juniors particularly praised were *Jonathan Crow* ("fully deserves his top ranking", now First Treasury Counsel), *Peter Griffiths* ("effective as well as being a much appreciated and refreshing wit") and *Sarah Harman* ("impressive and articulate").

7 Stone Buildings (Aldous) **Work Handled:** 'MCC Proceeds Inc v Lehman Brothers' (Aldous) 'Grandmet v William Hill [1997]' **Leading Barristers:** *Charles Aldous QC* and *Nigel Davis QC* remain highly rated, while juniors *Christopher Parker* ("confident") and *Guy Newey* ("wonderful") all received praise.

LEADING JUNIORS · LONDON	
CHIVERS David Erskine Chambers	**CROW Jonathan** 4 Stone Buildings
COLLINGS Matthew 13 Old Square	**MABB David** Erskine Chambers
CONE John Erskine Chambers	**MILES Robert** 4 Stone Buildings
DICKER Robin 3-4 South Square	**MOORE Martin** Erskine Chambers
GIROLAMI Paul 13 Old Square	**NEWEY Guy** 7 Stone Buildings
GREEN Michael 7 Stone Buildings	**PARKER Christopher** 7 Stone Buildings
HOLLINGTON Robin 1 New Square	**SNOWDEN Richard** Erskine Chambers
HOSER Philip Serle Court Chambers	**STOCKDALE BT Sir Thomas** Erskine Chambers
JOFFE Victor Serle Court Chambers	
ARDEN Peter Enterprise Chambers	**MARTEN Hedley** 3 New Square
DE GARR ROBINSON Anthony One Essex Court	**NICHOLSON Rosalind** 4 Stone Buildings
GILLYON Philip Erskine Chambers	**RABINOWITZ Laurence** One Essex Court
GIRET Jane 11 Stone Buildings	**RITCHIE Richard** 24 Old Buildings
GRIFFITHS Peter 4 Stone Buildings	**ROBERTS Catherine** Erskine Chambers
HARMAN Sarah 4 Stone Buildings	**SHEKERDEMIAN Marcia** 11 Stone Buildings
HARRISON Christopher 4 Stone Buildings	**SMITH Stephen** 12 New Square
HILL Richard 4 Stone Buildings	**STEWART Lindsey** 7 Stone Buildings
IFE Linden Enterprise Chambers	**ZELIN Geoffrey** Enterprise Chambers

UP AND COMING · LONDON	
CLOSE Douglas Serle Court Chambers	**PRENTICE Prof Dan** Erskine Chambers
CULLEN Edmund 7 Stone Buildings	**THOMPSON Andrew** Erskine Chambers
MARKS David 3-4 South Square	

FOR DETAILS OF THESE LEADING BARRISTERS SEE PROFILES ON PAGES 1509-1642

CONSTRUCTION

RESEARCH: In compiling the tables, we consider all the information available to us, paying particular regard to the market research carried out by our team of ten qualified lawyers. (The researchers' details are set out on page three.) The rankings, therefore, reflect the opinion of the marketplace as revealed by systematic and objective research: see page four. (Our research is audited every year by the British Market Research Bureau.)

OVERVIEW: Everyone we spoke to agreed that Atkin and Keating Chambers remain the two leading sets by a considerable margin. Although many interviewees expressed a preference for one, most were happy to use either, depending on availability. A majority of interviewees considered Keating Chambers their first choice, citing, among other things, a better balance of QCs and juniors. Keating also has more recommended silks and juniors than Atkin Chambers, and seems to be on the verge of establishing an overall lead, although it is too early to place the set in a band on its own.

Outside the top two sets, a frequent comment was "you have to go for a named individual" with the risk that "a passed-down brief won't necessarily go to a construction barrister." Having said that, within other sets there are some extremely popular and experienced silks and juniors. Many interviewees were happy to use non-specialist chambers, with some individuals as highly praised as almost anyone at Atkin and Keating, notably John Slater QC at 1 Paper Buildings.

Barristers' profiles   p. 1509-1642

LEADING SILKS · LONDON

AKENHEAD Robert Atkin Chambers
BLACKBURN John Atkin Chambers
FERNYHOUGH Richard Keating Chambers
FURST Stephen Keating Chambers
RAMSEY Vivian Keating Chambers
SLATER John One Paper Buildings

DENNYS Nicholas Atkin Chambers
JACKSON Rupert 2 Crown Office Row
MARRIN John Keating Chambers
TWIGG Patrick 2 Temple Gardens

GAITSKELL Robert Keating Chambers
GRAY Richard 39 Essex Street
MAULEVERER Bruce 4 Pump Court
NAUGHTON Philip 3 Serjeants' Inn
REESE Colin Atkin Chambers
SEYMOUR Richard Monckton Chambers
UFF John Keating Chambers
WHITE Andrew Atkin Chambers

BOULDING Philip Keating Chambers
TER HAAR Roger 2 Crown Office Row
THOMAS Christopher Keating Chambers
WILMOT-SMITH Richard 39 Essex Street

ACTON DAVIS Jonathan 4 Pump Court
BARTLETT Andrew One Paper Buildings
BURTON Michael Littleton Chambers
CROXFORD Ian Wilberforce Chambers
ELLIOTT Timothy Keating Chambers
FENWICK Justin 2 Crown Office Row
FRIEDMAN David 4 Pump Court
GLASGOW Edwin 39 Essex Street
KNIGHT Brian Atkin Chambers
SPEAIGHT Anthony 12 King's Bench Walk
TACKABERRY John Arbitration Chambers
WALKER Ronald 12 King's Bench Walk

NEW SILKS · 1997 AND 1998

BAATZ Nicholas Atkin Chambers
BOSWELL Lindsay 4 Pump Court
FREEDMAN Clive Littleton Chambers

FOR DETAILS ON THESE LEADING BARRISTERS
SEE PROFILES ON PAGES 1509-1642

LEADING SETS · LONDON

ATKIN CHAMBERS (John Blackburn QC)
KEATING CHAMBERS (Richard Fernyhough QC)

2 CROWN OFFICE ROW (John Powell QC)
4 PUMP COURT (Bruce Mauleverer QC)
39 ESSEX STREET (Edwin Glasgow QC)

HIGHLY REGARDED · LONDON

12 King's Bench Walk (Ronald J. Walker QC)
Monckton Chambers (Richard Fowler QC)
One Paper Buildings (John Slater QC)
3 Serjeants' Inn (Philip Naughton QC)
2 Temple Gardens (Patrick Phillips QC)

Atkin Chambers (Blackburn) The first set to specialise in construction and engineering and one of the two leading sets with great expertise at all levels. **Work Handled:** Recent cases include 'Layher v Lowe' and 'Matthew Hall & Ortech v Tarmac Roadstone.' **Leading Barristers:** Described variously as "a brilliant advocate, with great presence, speed and clarity of thought," *John Blackburn QC* "never appears fazed or misses a trick." Clients, judges and other lawyers respond to his personality and dry sense of humour. *Robert Akenhead QC* has a "powerful intellect" but is very approachable and down to earth. "Robert never makes clients feel inferior or stupid." He is also "a terrific worker with a great eye for detail." *Nicholas Dennys QC* is "forceful, incisive, impressive in court, has the knack of analysis and simple explanation – everything you need if you have to run a long case." *Colin Reese QC* moves up a band "because he's tough and brilliant" and according to one interviewee, "on his day he is more adroit at moving a tribunal in his direction than any one else at the Bar." A "hard-working, immensely likeable fellow," *Andrew White QC* is the rising star of Atkin Chambers. "You take it as read that a silk at Atkin or Keating will be phenomenally bright and totally immersed in his subject – he is that and more." *Nicholas Baatz QC* who took silk this year, is "a top choice for intellectual matters, tough, good in court, an excellent speaker." Recommended juniors include *Martin Bowdery* ("good on his feet and on the technical side"), *David Streatfield-James* ("excellent … an extremely popular junior and therefore hard to get hold of"), *Stephanie Barwise* ("a dedicated team player"), *Stephen Dennison* ("thorough … knows how to lay it on the line"), *Andrew Burr* ("user friendly … lots of empathy with the client") and *Andrew Goddard* ("one of the best juniors in Atkin, very clever").

Keating Chambers (Fernyhough) Received widespread praise for its "client friendly, efficent service" for which senior clerk, the popular Barry Bridgman, must take much of the credit. **Work Handled:** Cases include 'Co-operative Wholesale Society v Birse;' 'Tower Housing Associations v Technical & General Guarantee

Ltd;' 'British Sugar v Power Projects Ltd.' **Leading Barristers:** *Richard Fernyhough QC* is razor sharp and one of the best cross-examiners at the Bar ("he comes at a subject in a way that witnesses never expect … if a dispute rests on evidence he's your man"). *Stephen Furst QC* is seen as thoughtful rather than flamboyant – "his forte is the House of Lords where flamboyance means nothing and quality of argument everything." "Confidence oozes out of him," and he is reputed to predict outcomes with uncanny reliability. *Vivian Ramsey QC* received more recommendations for promotion to the top band than any other silk (Fernyhough came a close second). A chartered engineer, Ramsey "has his feet on the ground, knows the construction culture and is extremely good with clients." He is seen as the heir apparent to Blackburn. *John Marrin QC* "undersells himself but works his socks off for you" and "comes up with devastating arguments in court." Given his background in electrical engineering *Robert Gaitskell QC* is "a good choice for anything with an electrical element" and is liked by clients. *John Uff QC*, the "doyen of construction arbitrators world-wide," is still "a formidable advocate." *Philip Boulding QC* has "a refreshing absence of airs and graces." He has spent much of his time in Asia since taking silk and consequently has a lower profile than some of his peers. *Timothy Elliott QC* – "a great cross examiner" – is also recommended for professional negligence matters. *Christopher Thomas QC* is "good on his feet, hardworking, easy to get along with and meticulous." "Absolutely superb," *Peter Coulson* has "had a silks practice for some time" and "always does his work before a con." *Paul Darling* is "a real extrovert, who puts his heart and soul into your cause." *Rosemary Jackson* "is well prepared, sound on legal analysis, strong in argument" and "ideal for rough and tumble cases." *Finola O'Farrell* is "articulate and determined … she gives the impression of being meek but is very far from being that." She is popular with clients and instructing solicitors. *Marcus Taverner* "has a silk's practice in all but name." "Quick on his feet, he can shoot from the hip" and is "well liked and respected." With a "real knowledge of construction law and the standard forms" *Adrian Williamson* is "good for the knotty problems" and "brilliant on paperwork." He is also enthusiastic and easy to get on with. Also recommended were *Louise Randall* ("thorough and gets on well with clients"), *Alexander Nissen* ("hard working and enthusiastic"), *Simon Hargreaves* ("a personality that will take him to the top … a very good advocate") and *Richard Harding* ("impressive both in terms of advocacy and the way he treats clients"). Newly recommended, Harding

speaks Arabic and has a Middle Eastern practice.

2 Crown Office Row (Powell) A commercial and civil set that "gives a superb service." Has a reputation for professional negligence (for which it is the leading set) as well as for construction and engineering. **Work Handled:** 'McAlpine v Panatown Ltd;' 'Hopewell Project Management v Ewbank Preece Ltd;' 'Copthorne Hotels (Newcastle) Ltd v Arup;' 'Chesham Properties v Bucknall Austin Project Management Services Ltd;' 'Machin v Adams.' **Leading Barristers:** *Rupert Jackson QC* is "outstandingly bright" and "possibly the most hardworking QC of the lot." He has an excellent reputation in pure construction and professional negligence. *Justin Fenwick QC* is a "a nice fellow and a fine orator with a relaxed easy style." *Roger Stewart* is "a specialist in sorting wheat from chaff."

4 Pump Court (Mauleverer) A commercial and common law set which is "very keen to do the work." Carolyn McCombe is said to be "a truly excellent clerk." Described by some as "the third construction set that you instinctively think of after Atkin and Keating." **Work Handled:** 'George Fischer Holding Ltd v Multi Design Consultants Ltd' (Mauleverer); 'Holbeck Hall Hotel v Scarborough Borough Council and Geotechnical Engineering (Northern) Ltd' (Mauleverer); 'Panatown v McAlpine'(Friedman, Nicholson); 'Joplings Ltd v J Jarvis & Sons Plc and Others;' 'PLT v Factcase Projects Ltd and Robert Crawford.' **Leading Barristers:** *Bruce Mauleverer QC* has "what it takes – intellect, a terrific court presence and a great track record – Bruce wins cases others would lose." *David Friedman QC*, "a skilful advocate," was thought by some to be "underrated," as was *Jonathan Acton Davis QC* – "when he gets a construction brief he's very good." *Lindsay Boswell QC* has a direct manner, "clients like it." *Adrian Hughes* has "great presence and is very able indeed." *Marc Rowlands* ("terrific and incredibly user friendly") enters the table as an up and coming junior.

39 Essex Street (Glasgow) A wide ranging civil set with "some exceptionally good people." **Work Handled:** 'Re Cosslett (Contractors) Ltd;' 'Scottish Power v Britoil;' 'George Fischer GB Ltd v Multi-Design Consultants;' 'Zeneca v King Sturge;' 'Technology Partnership v Afro-Asian Satellite Communications Ltd and Chandra.' **Leading Barristers:** Those at the set with real construction experience include *Richard Gray QC* ("an excellent advocate with the rapier touch…amazingly unflappable…gets great results and is easy to deal with"), *Richard Wilmot-Smith QC* ("good at making bricks without straw"), and *Stuart Catchpole* ("safe, thorough …

gets on well with clients"). *Edwin Glasgow QC* is newly recommended ("very pleasant to work with…great gravitas … taken seriously by the higher courts").

12 King's Bench Walk (Walker) A civil and commercial set with a specialist construction group. **Work Handled:** 'Plant Contruction v Clive Adam Associates;' 'McAlpine v BAI (Run Off) Ltd;' 'Ogden v Kraemer;' 'Blue Circle v MoD;' 'J Carne v Michael Cooke Associates.' **Leading Barristers:** The best known practitioners are *Ronald Walker QC* and *Anthony Speaight QC*, the latter a skillful and inventive draftsman.

Monckton Chambers (Fowler) A popular EU and commercial set. **Leading Barristers:** *Richard Seymour QC*, recently instructed in an arbitration in Africa, is "very methodical, has nerve" and has appeared in some big cases. *Michael Patchett-Joyce* "takes his jacket off and gets on with it … user friendly."

One Paper Buildings (Slater) A common law and commercial set with some highly rated construction lawyers. **Leading Barristers:** *John Slater QC* is popular with lawyers and clients who describe him as "charming" with "an air of success about him … John rolls up his sleeves, enjoys a knockabout and inspires confidence." *Andrew Bartlett QC* likes "the technical cases" and "relates well to construction clients."

3 Sergeant's Inn (Naughton) The pre-eminent professional negligence set in the medical, dental and pharmaceutical fields is also known for the construction expertise of some of its barristers. **Work Handled:** Involved in 'Drake and Scull Engineering v Jarvis;' 'Hotel Services Ltd v Hilton International Hotels Ltd' (Naughton & McCredie); 'DCT v South West Water' (Naughton); 'London Underground Ltd v WSP South and West Ltd & Kenchington Ford' (Naughton) **Leading Barristers:** *Philip Naughton QC* is an "outstanding advocate and particularly impressive in mediation and ADR." *Mary O'Rourke* "knows her stuff" and *Fionnuala McCredie*, who joins the table as an up and coming, "will definitely make a name for herself."

2 Temple Gardens (Philips) "Quality people doing more and more construction." **Work Handled:** 'Strachan & Henshaw v GEC Alstrom;' 'George Fischer v Multi Construction;' 'Redpath Dorman Long v Wimpey;' 'Hopewell Project Management v Hopewell Energy;' 'Mackley v UK Waste.' **Leading Barristers:** *Patrick Twigg QC*, admitted to the Bars of Hong Kong, Singapore, Brunei and Gibraltar, is "outstandingly good" and "as keen as ever." *David Thomas* is "a perfect junior – hardworking, quick and responsive."

There are a number of other silks at non-specialist sets. *John Tackaberry QC* of **Arbitration Chambers** (Tackaberry) has been described as unbeatable on his day, an original thinker, one of nature's gentlemen, a top arbitrator and still an active advocate. Also recommended, but not at leading construction sets, are *Michael Burton QC* ("staggeringly effective, stupifyingly bright with an ideal lateral approach") and *Clive Freedman QC* (both at at **Littleton Chambers** (Burton)). *Rowan Planterose* of **Littman Chambers** (Littman) has an "excellent reputation for arbitration work," *Michael Stimpson* (also at **Littman Chambers**), *Ian Croxford QC* **Wilberforce Chambers** (Nugee) and *Paul Reed* **Hardwicke Building** (Aylen) for defects and loss and expense claims.

CONSUMER

RESEARCH: In compiling the tables, we consider all the information available to us, paying particular regard to the market research carried out by our team of ten qualified lawyers. (The researchers' details are set out on page three.) The rankings, therefore, reflect the opinion of the market-place as revealed by systematic and objective research: see page four. (Our research is audited every year by the British Market Research Bureau.)

OVERVIEW: This area covers consumer credit, food law, and goods-related consumer regulation such as prices or trades description. It is a growth area of law, especially on the food side. There is some high profile work, notably the beef-on-the-bone saga.

Barristers' profiles   **p. 1509-1642**

LEADING SILKS · LONDON
GOODE Roy Blackstone Chambers
SCRIVENER Anthony 2-3 Gray's Inn Square

LEADING JUNIORS · LONDON
PHILPOTT Frederick Gough Square Chambers
ANDREWS Claire Gough Square Chambers
DE HAAN Kevin 3 Raymond Buildings
HIBBERT William Gough Square Chambers
STEPHENSON Geoffrey 2-3 Gray's Inn Square
WORSLEY Daniel 2 Harcourt Buildings
SAYER Peter Gough Square Chambers
SCHOLZ Karl 3 Temple Gardens
SMITH Julia Gough Square Chambers

FOR DETAILS OF THESE LEADING BARRISTERS
SEE PROFILES ON PAGES 1509-1642

LEADING SETS · LONDON

GOUGH SQUARE CHAMBERS (Philpott)

Gough Square Chambers (Philpott) The only set of chambers with a genuine specialism in consumer law, with five members recommended. Solicitors admired the breadth of experience available, and quality of clerking. **Work Handled:** Recent cases include 'Forthright Finance v Carlyle Finance' (1997); 'Scarborough Building Society v Humberside TSD' (1997) 'Swindle v Harrison' (1997); 'Peacocks v First National Bank' (1997). **Leading Barristers:** Head of chambers *Frederick Philpott* is regarded as the outstanding junior in the field. *Claire Andrews* has recently been involved in important due diligence cases, especially

from the food law angle. *Julia Smith* does "an incredible amount of consumer credit," as does *William Hibbert*, who is known for his work on misleading prices. *Peter Sayer* also practises in consumer credit. He has in-house experience and has developed a notable niche in work relating to credit cards and advertising.

Others Leading Barristers: The "very authoritative" *Professor Roy Goode QC* at **Blackstone Chambers** (Baxendale & Flint) has an excellent academic reputation, and practises mainly in the consumer credit field. He is widely admired, although sometimes difficult to get hold of. *Anthony Scrivener QC* from **2-3 Gray's Inn Square** (Scrivener) has a broader base of regulatory work, and is considered an excellent all-round advocate. At the same set *Geoffrey Stephenson* has a general

public law and planning practice, but "does consumer law and does it well." The "very knowledgeable" *Karl Scholz* at **3 Temple Gardens** (Coffey) is a well known name in the area, and usually prosecutes. He recently prosecuted in 'MGN Ltd v Ritters'. The "active and busy" *Kevin De Haan* at **3 Raymond Buildings** (Nicholls) is known for his work on the food side. At **2 Harcourt Buildings** (Henderson), *Daniel Worsley* has a niche in consumer credit. He also works in the financial services sector, and has recently edited Halsbury's Laws on Consumer law.

CRIME

RESEARCH: In compiling the tables, we consider all the information available to us, paying particular regard to the market research carried out by our team of ten qualified lawyers. (The researchers' details are set out on page three.) The rankings, therefore, reflect the opinion of the market-place as revealed by systematic and objective research: see page four. (Our research is audited every year by the British Market Research Bureau.)

Barristers' profiles   p. 1509-1642

OVERVIEW: It is not possible to list all the barristers recommended during the course of research. Highlighted below are those with particularly strong reputations. Readers are advised to refer to the Fraud section for more information on those sets and individuals recommended for white collar crime.

LEADING SETS · LONDON

6 KING'S BENCH WALK (Michael Worsley QC)
QUEEN ELIZABETH BUILDING (Jeffreys QC & Whiteman QC)
3 RAYMOND BUILDINGS (Clive Nicholls QC)
18 RED LION COURT (Anthony Arlidge QC)

9 BEDFORD ROW (John Goldring QC)
DOUGHTY STREET CHAMBERS (Robertson QC)
TWO GARDEN COURT (Macdonald QC & Davies)
3 GRAY'S INN SQUARE (Rock Tansey QC)
1 HARE COURT (Stephen Kramer QC)
3 HARE COURT (William Clegg QC)

CROWN OFFICE ROW (Richard Ferguson QC)
FURNIVAL CHAMBERS (Andrew Mitchell QC)
2 HARCOURT BUILDINGS (Nigel Mylne QC)

HIGHLY REGARDED · LONDON

36 Bedford Row (James Hunt QC)
Cloisters (Laura Cox QC)

9-12 Bell Yard (Anthony Evans QC)
23 Essex Street (Michael Lawson QC)
3 Temple Gardens (Johnathan Goldberg QC)

Farrar's Building (Gerard Elias QC)
10 King's Bench Walk (Ronald Thwaites QC)
1 Middle Temple Lane (Dines & Trollope QC)
14 Tooks Court (Michael Mansfield QC)

6 King's Bench Walk (Worsley) The members of 6 King's Bench Walk received numerous compliments and recommendations this year. The set is particularly known for its prosecution work. **Leading Barristers:** *Roy Amlot QC* retains his position in the top band of our silks' list. *David Fisher QC* is "personable, hard working and thorough." *Ann Mallalieu QC* is considered to have had a successful year. The "tactically able" *John Ryder* is "a star" – "a real jury advocate" with "gallons of charis-

ma." *Dean Armstrong's* "controlled aggression" is helping him come to the forefront of junior courts martial work. *Mark Dennis* is admired for his "diamond cutter brain." *Anthony Leonard* "knows no bounds," chasing all points "like a terrier." The quality of *Martin Taylor's* work has led to him being added to our table of leading juniors.

Queen Elizabeth Building (Jeffreys & Whiteman) **Leading Barristers:** *Mark Ellison* is a "clear thinker" with a good reputation as an advocate. *John Kelsey-Fry* is "first class," mainly in prosecution. With a melodic, compelling voice, *Anthony Glass QC* ably fields difficult points. He is known for his common sense and integrity. *David Calvert-Smith QC*, a former First Senior Treasury Counsel, has particular expertise as a prosecutor but is regarded as an excellent all round lawyer. *William Boyce* is seen as "solid" and *Jocelyn Sparks* is "thorough and sensible."

3 Raymond Buildings (Nicholls) Have a reputation as the leading extradition set. **Leading Barristers:** *Clare Montgomery QC* has moved to the top of the table of silks since her appointment last year. She is an "enthusiastic high flier with plenty of sparkle." *Stephen Batten QC*, "the professional's professional," is an outstanding jury advocate and a superb tactician.

18 Red Lion Court (Arlidge) The set has maintained its high standards following its move from the Temple. **Leading Barristers:** The new head of chambers, *Anthony Arlidge QC*, is charismatic and effective. *David Etherington QC* is a dazzling advocate who charms juries with his "marvellous bedside manner." The "fearless" *David Lederman QC* is especially good with difficult clients, and has a shrewd tactical sense. *Linda Stern QC* is

"on a roll," with success after success in difficult cases.

9 Bedford Row (Goldring) The set is renowned for the efficiency and integrity of its clerking. Members practise in London, on the Midlands and Oxford Circuit and on the South Eastern Circuit. **Leading Barristers:** *John Goldring QC*, one of the top criminal practitioners in the capital, is regularly involved in high profile cases. Recently, he advised the Joint Disciplinary Scheme for accountants in the Maxwell case, conducted a Serious Fraud Office prosecution against a solicitors' firm accused of defrauding the Legal Aid Board and prosecuted a bank in Jersey. He is methodical and analytical with a calm, precise, compelling manner. *Nigel Rumfitt QC* is a regular at the Old Bailey. He was particularly praised for his work prosecuting and defending homicide cases. *Stephen Coward QC* and *Timothy Barnes QC* both prosecute and defend, while *David Farrer QC* has also done lengthy prosecutions.

Doughty Street Chambers (Robertson) The chambers serves London, the South East and the Midlands and Oxford Circuits. Members of chambers acted in the Canary Wharf Bombing, Iraqi Hijacking and 'Essex Range Rover Murders' trials, and in the 'Bridgewater Four' appeal. **Leading Barristers:** *Christopher Sallon QC* can "take on large matters at very short notice." New silk, *Edward Fitzgerald QC* is simply "brilliant" and his recent success in 'R v Bentley' (acting for the Bentley family) will reinforce his profile. The "tough" *James Wood* has a "clear-thinking brain." *Andrew Hall* is efficient and firm.

Two Garden Court (Macdonald & Davies) **Leading Barristers:** *Owen Davies* is "intelligent, able, experienced and human." *Kenneth MacDonald QC* has a superb reputation. New silk *Courtenay Griffiths QC* has an impressive presence backed by true ability. *Henry Blaxland* is sought after in miscarriage of justice cases and was the junior in 'R v Bentley' (successfully acting for the Bentley family). *Alastair Edie* is "experienced way beyond his call." *Adrian Eissa* is "meticulous" and "approachable."

3 Gray's Inn Square (Tansey) Leading Barristers: *Rock Tansey QC* remains one of the top criminal silks. *George Carter-Stephenson QC* is " hard-working and diligent ." *Diana Ellis* is "very experienced." The "forthright" *Jeremy Dein* rarely needs a leader. *Penny Barrett* is well respected for her work for mentally disordered clients and defendants in sexual offences cases.

1 Hare Court (Kramer) Leading Barristers: Head of Chambers *Stephen Kramer QC* is widely admired. The "charismatic" *Orlando Pownall* is one of the top juniors at the criminal Bar, as is *David Waters*. A Senior Treasury Counsel, Waters is a persuasive advocate with a "gentle but firm manner." *Kenneth Millett* is a "good defender" who "leaves no stone unturned." *Andrew Radcliffe* is is known for his excellent judgment, whether prosecuting or defending.

3 Hare Court (Clegg) Work Handled: Has a reputation for handling fraud and all other serious crime. Acted recently in the Stephen Lawrence Inquiry and also involved in War Crimes Tribunal work. Leading Barristers: Head of chambers *William Clegg QC* has "a great ability to simplify the complex." This has helped to make him a top band silk. The young *Peter Lodder*, a new addition to our tables, has "all round ability" and is "going to the top." *James Sturman* is "excellent in court." *Mark Milliken-Smith* is "great with clients," *Andrew Munday QC* has risen in stature over the past year and *Nigel Lithman QC* is a charming, punchy advocate.

Crown Office Row (Ferguson) Leading Barristers: Has many notable practitioners including head of chambers *Richard Ferguson QC*, the "razor sharp" *Peter Feinberg QC* and the "astonishingly talented" *Patrick O'Connor QC*. Popular with clients, *Stephen Leslie QC* is praised for his tremendous grasp of detail. *Stephen Winberg* is "painstaking," while *William England* is "bright and enthusiastic."

Furnival Chambers (Mitchell) Leading Barristers: Handles both prosecution and defence work and prides itself on its specialist confiscation unit. The head of chambers, *Andrew Mitchell QC*, is very experienced. *Oliver Blunt QC* is a shrewd defence silk, liked for his ability to address clients and juries in their own language. The "extremely talented" *Richard Whittam* is a top-ranked junior.

2 Harcourt Buildings (Mylne) Leading

Barristers: Headed by *Nigel Mylne QC*, this set sends criminal practitioners to courts all over London, the South East and the West. *John Bevan QC* is "as experienced as they come," *Patrick Gibbs* was described as a "young rising star" and

Nicholas Atkinson QC is brilliant in front of a jury. Treasury counsel *Aftab Jafferjee* and *Nicholas Loraine-Smith* are well respected.

36 Bedford Row (Hunt) The set covers London and the Midland and Oxford Circuit.

LEADING SILKS · LONDON

AMLOT Roy 6 King's Bench Walk	**JONES Alun** 3 Raymond Buildings
BATTEN Stephen 3 Raymond Buildings	**MONTGOMERY Clare** 3 Raymond Buildings
BLUNT Oliver Furnival Chambers	**MANSFIELD Michael** 14 Tooks Court
CLEGG William 3 Hare Court	**ROBERTS Jeremy** 9 Gough Square
FULFORD Adrian 14 Tooks Court	**TANSEY Rock** 3 Gray's Inn Square
GOLDRING John 9 Bedford Row	**THORNTON Peter** Doughty Street Chambers
ARLIDGE Anthony 18 Red Lion Court	**PITCHFORD Christopher** Farrar's Building
BEVAN Julian Queen Elizabeth Building	**PRICE Nicholas** 3 Raymond Buildings
ELIAS Gerard Farrar's Building	**ROBERTSON Geoffrey** Doughty Street
FERGUSON Richard Crown Office Row	**RUMFITT Nigel** 9 Bedford Row
GOLDSTONE Clement Crown Office Row	**SCRIVENER Anthony** 2-3 Gray's Inn Square
HESLOP Martin 1 Hare Court	**THWAITES Ronald** 10 King's Bench Walk
LAWSON Edmund 9-12 Bell Yard	**TROLLOPE Andrew** 1 Middle Temple Lane
CALVERT-SMITH David Queen Elizabeth Building	**NICHOLLS Clive** 3 Raymond Buildings
COWARD Stephen 9 Bedford Row	**MALLALIEU Ann** 6 King's Bench Walk
FEINBERG Peter Crown Office Row	**NUTTING John** 3 Raymond Buildings
FISHER David 6 King's Bench Walk	**SALLON Christopher** Doughty Street
GLASS Anthony Queen Elizabeth Building	**SEABROOK Robert** 1 Crown Office Row
GOLDBERG Jonathan 3 Temple Gardens	**TEMPLE Victor** 6 King's Bench Walk
GREENBERG Joanna 3 Temple Gardens	**WHITEHOUSE David** 3 Raymond Buildings
HILL Michael 23 Essex Street	

HIGHLY REGARDED SILKS · LONDON

ATKINSON Nicholas 2 Harcourt Buildings	**KENNEDY Helena** Doughty Street Chambers
AUSTIN-SMITH Michael 23 Essex Street	**MACDONALD Ian** Two Garden Court
BARNES Timothy 9 Bedford Row	**MACDONALD Kenneth** Two Garden Court
EVANS Anthony 9-12 Bell Yard	**O'CONNOR Patrick** Crown Office Row
FARRER David 9 Bedford Row	**SHAW Antony** 4 Brick Court
GRINDROD Helen 95A Chancery Lane	
BATE David Queen Elizabeth Building	**KAY Steven** 3 Gray's Inn Square
CASSEL Timothy 5 Paper Buildings	**LEDERMAN David** 18 Red Lion Court
COOPER Peter 2 Harcourt Buildings	**LEIGH Christopher** 1 Paper Buildings
DE SILVA Desmond 2 Paper Buildings	**MYLNE Nigel** 2 Harcourt Buildings
GREY Robin Queen Elizabeth Building	
BEVAN John 2 Harcourt Buildings	**LESLIE Stephen** Crown Office Row
CAPLAN Jonathan 5 Paper Buildings	**LISSACK Richard** 35 Essex Street
CARTER Peter 18 Red Lion Court	**LITHMAN Nigel** 3 Hare Court
COOPER John 3 Gray's Inn Square	**LOVELL-PANK Dorian** 6 King's Bench Walk
DAVIES Leighton Farrar's Building	**LYNCH Patricia** 18 Red Lion Court
EDWARDS Susan 23 Essex Street	**MUNDAY Andrew** 3 Hare Court
GODFREY Howard 3 Hare Court	**PERRY John** 3 Gray's Inn Square
HIGGS Brian 5 Paper Buildings	**SAYERS Michael** 2 King's Bench Walk
JEFFREYS David Queen Elizabeth Building	**SOLLEY Stephen** Cloisters
KHAYAT Georges 10 King's Bench Walk	**STERN Linda** 18 Red Lion Court
KRAMER Stephen 1 Hare Court	**SUTTON Richard** 18 Red Lion Court
LANGDALE Timothy Queen Elizabeth Building	**VALIOS Nicholas** Francis Taylor Building
LAWSON Michael 23 Essex Street	

NEW SILKS · 1997 AND 1998

BLACK John 18 Red Lion Court	**GRIEVE Michael** Doughty Street Chambers
CARTER-STEPHENSON George 3 Gray's Inn Square	**GRIFFITHS Courtenay** Two Garden Court
DOBBS Linda 18 Red Lion Court	**MITCHELL Andrew** Furnival Chambers
ETHERINGTON David 18 Red Lion Court	**REES Edward** Doughty Street Chambers
FITZGERALD Edward Doughty Street	

FOR DETAILS OF THESE LEADING BARRISTERS SEE PROFILES ON PAGES 1509-1642

Has annexes in Northampton and Leicester. **Leading Barristers:** The "very able" *Anesta Weekes* has acted in the Lawrence Inquiry following her move from Cloisters.

Cloisters (Cox) **Leading Barristers:** *Michael Turner* is generally regarded as the star of the set. Silks like to have him as a junior and he is "always well prepared."

9-12 Bell Yard (Evans) **Leading Barristers:** *Edmund Lawson QC* is a fraud specialist, but his general criminal practice was described as "outstanding." He is known for his work in civil rights cases. *John Harwood-Stevenson* is a good orator with "a very imposing court presence."

23 Essex Street (Lawson) **Leading Barristers:** *Michael Lawson QC* is the Leader of the South Eastern Circuit. Juries love his elegant turn of phrase.

3 Temple Gardens (Goldberg) Covers the South Eastern, Western and Midlands and Oxford Circuits. Members of the set have recently been involved in the Charles Kray drugs case, a rape case involving Fred West's cousin, the Lynn Siddons murder case and the King's Cross canal towpath rape trial. **Leading Barristers:** *Jonathan Goldberg* has a very high profile, and *Joanna Greenberg QC* has particular expertise in sexual offences cases.

Farrar's Building (Elias) Members of this set practise crime predominantly in the South Eastern and Wales and Chester Circuits, but also on the Western and Midland and Oxford Circuits. **Leading Barristers:** *Gerard Elias QC* and *Christopher Pitchford QC* received recommendations for their work on the circuit.

10 King's Bench Walk (Thwaites) **Leading Barristers:** Head of chambers *Ronald Thwaites QC* is an eminent silk, and defended in the Stephen Lawrence case. *David Nathan* was praised for his ability to quickly identify weaknesses in opponents. *Michael Wolkind* is a very well regarded junior who is "the distilled essence of a great jury advocate."

1 Middle Temple Lane (Dines & Trollope) **Leading Barristers:** The set has criminal practitioners practising throughout the country but mainly on the South Eastern Circuit. *Andrew Trollope QC* is "a tenacious, doughty fighter." *Michael Borrelli* is "outstanding in serious matters."

14 Tooks Court (Mansfield) **Leading Barristers:** The set has two silks in the top band. *Michael Mansfield QC's* high profile is an accurate reflection of his outstanding abilities. He represented the Lawrence family at the recent public inquiry. The reputation of *Adrian Fulford QC* continues to grow.

Jeremy Roberts QC of **9 Gough Square** (Roberts) is regarded as the "barrister's barrister." A consummate professional, he was praised for his integrity and his eminently sensible approach.

LEADING JUNIORS · LONDON

BORRELLI Michael 1 Middle Temple Lane	**STURMAN James** 3 Hare Court
BURKE Trevor 10 King's Bench Walk	**SWEENEY Nigel** 6 King's Bench Walk
JENNINGS Anthony Two Garden Court	**TURNER Michael** Cloisters
KELSEY-FRY John Queen Elizabeth Building	**WATERS David** 1 Hare Court
LORAINE-SMITH Nicholas 2 Harcourt Buildings	**WHITTAM Richard** Furnival Chambers
POWNALL Orlando 1 Hare Court	

ALTMAN Brian 3 Hare Court	**JENKINS Edward** 5 Paper Buildings
BOYCE William Queen Elizabeth Building	**LAIDLAW Jonathan** 1 Hare Court
CHAWLA Mukul 9-12 Bell Yard	**LEONARD Anthony** 6 King's Bench Walk
DEIN Jeremy 3 Gray's Inn Square	**MILLIKEN-SMITH Mark** 3 Hare Court
DENNIS Mark 6 King's Bench Walk	**PERRY David** 6 King's Bench Walk
ELLISON Mark Queen Elizabeth Building	**RYDER John** 6 King's Bench Walk
HILL Max 18 Red Lion Court	**TURNER Jonathan** 6 King's Bench Walk
HILLIARD Nicholas 6 King's Bench Walk	**WOLKIND Michael** 10 King's Bench Walk

BARRETT Penelope 3 Gray's Inn Square	**HACKETT Philip** 3 Hare Court
BENSON Jeremy 1 Hare Court	**HORWELL Richard** Queen Elizabeth Building
COLEMAN Nicholas 1 Hare Court	**JANNER Daniel** 23 Essex Street
CONWAY Charles 3 Hare Court	**LODDER Peter** 3 Hare Court
DAVIES Owen Two Garden Court	**LUCAS Noel** 1 Middle Temple Lane
EISSA Adrian Two Garden Court	**MARTIN-SPERRY David** Crown Office Row
EVANS Jill Doughty Street Chambers	**NATHAN David** 10 King's Bench Walk
FEDER Ami Lamb Building	**PRICE Roderick** Cloisters
GARDINER Nicholas 1 Middle Temple Lane	**RADCLIFFE Andrew** 1 Hare Court
GIBBS Patrick 2 Harcourt Buildings	**TAYLOR Martin** 6 King's Bench Walk

HIGHLY REGARDED JUNIORS · LONDON

BECK James Crown Office Row	**KHALIL Karim** 1 Paper Buildings
BLAXLAND Henry Two Garden Court	**LEWIS James** 3 Raymond Buildings
BOURNE Ian 3 Temple Gardens	**MILLETT Kenneth** 1 Hare Court
BRIGHT Andrew 4 Brick Court	**MOORE Miranda** 5 Paper Buildings
ELLIS Diana 3 Gray's Inn Square	**OWEN Tim** Doughty Street
FORTSON Rudi 3 Gray's Inn Square	**OWEN Tudor** 9-12 Bell Yard Chambers
JAFFA Ronald 3 Gray's Inn Square	**WINBERG Stephen** Crown Office Row
JAFFERJEE Aftab 2 Harcourt Buildings	

ABELL Anthony 3 Hare Court	**LYNCH Jerome** Cloisters
BANKS Robert 100E Great Portland Street	**MATTHEWS Richard** 3 Hare Court
CAUDLE John 3 Hare Court	**PEART Icah** Two Garden Court
EMMERSON Ben Doughty Street Chambers	**REES Gareth** Queen Elizabeth Building
HALL Andrew Doughty Street Chambers	**REILLY John** 14 Tooks Court
JOYCE Michael 9 Gough Square	**SAUNDERS Neil** 3 Raymond Buildings
LEIST Ian 1 Hare Court	**WEEKES Anesta** 36 Bedford Row
LEVY Michael 3 Hare Court	**WOOD James** Doughty Street Chambers
LLOYD-ELEY Andrew 1 Hare Court	

ARMSTRONG Dean 6 King's Bench Walk	**LANDSBURY Alan** 6 Gray's Inn Square
BARRACLOUGH Nicholas Francis Taylor Building	**LEWIS Raymond** 2 Paper Buildings
BARRY Joseph Mitre House Chambers	**MAIDMENT Kieran** Doughty Street Chambers
BENNETT-JENKINS Sallie 1 Hare Court	**MALCOLM Helen** 3 Raymond Buildings
BERRIMAN Trevor 10 King's Bench Walk	**MCCORMICK William** 10 King's Bench Walk
BRIMELOW Kirsty Francis Taylor Building	**OWEN-JONES David** 3 Temple Gardens
BRISCOE Constance 4 Brick Court	**REED Piers** 3 Temple Gardens
BRYANT-HERON Mark 9-12 Bell Yard	**SAUNDERS William** 3 Temple Gardens
CAUSER John 23 Essex Street	**SCOBIE James** Francis Taylor Building
CHRISTIE Richard 2 Pump Court	**SHEPHERD Nigel** 8 King's Bench Walk
EDIE Alastair Two Garden Court	**SMITH Zoe** Hardwicke Building
ENGLAND William Crown Office Row	**SPARKS Jocelyn** Queen Elizabeth Building
GUPTA Usha Furnival Chambers	**STRUDWICK Linda** Queen Elizabeth Building
HARWOOD-STEVENSON John 9-12 Bell Yard	**SWAIN Jon** Furnival Chambers
HENRY Annette 10 King's Bench Walk	**VINE James** Hardwicke Building
HUGHES David 2 Gray's Inn Square	**WASS Sasha** 6 King's Bench Walk

FOR UP AND COMING JUNIORS SEE NEXT PAGE.

SOUTH EASTERN AND EAST ANGLIAN CIRCUITS

Most work on the South Eastern Circuit is done by barristers from London. In Norwich, **Octagon House Chambers** (Lindquist and Ayers) sport three recommended juniors: *Guy Ayers, Michael Clare* and *Richard Potts*.

LEADING JUNIORS · EAST ANGLIAN

AYERS Guy Octagon House Chambers	**HAWKESWORTH Gareth** Fenners Chambers
CLARE Michael Octagon House Chambers	**POTTS Richard** Octagon House Chambers

FOR DETAILS OF THESE LEADING BARRISTERS SEE PROFILES ON PAGES 1509-1642

WESTERN CIRCUIT

Pump Court Chambers (Boney) has a well-known annexe in Winchester, and the set's *Nigel Pascoe QC* is the leader of the western circuit. In Bristol **St. John's Chambers** (Denyer) has an excellent reputation. Notable practitioners include *Roderick Denyer QC*, *Ian Dixey* and *Mark Horton*. **Albion Chambers** (Barton) fields *Charles Barton QC*, one of the premier advocates in the south-west. Also recommended were *James Tabor QC* and *Neil Ford QC*. *Julian Lambert* has "the best legal brain in Bristol." At **Guildhall Chambers** (Royce) *John Royce QC* is very well thought of by local solicitors. In Exeter, **Colleton Chambers** (Meeke) have two recommended juniors, *Martin Meeke* and *David Steele*. At **Walnut House** (Gilbert), head of chambers *Francis Gilbert QC* is well respected, as is the "very successful and able" *Paul Dunkels QC*. *Sarah Munro* is an experienced junior.

LEADING SILKS · WESTERN

BARTON Charles Albion Chambers	**ROYCE John** Guildhall Chambers
DENYER Roderick St. John's Chambers	**PASCOE Nigel** Pump Court Chambers
DUNKELS Paul Walnut House	**TABOR James** Albion Chambers
GILBERT Francis Walnut House	
BONEY Guy Pump Court Chambers	**GLEN Ian** Guildhall Chambers
FORD Neil Albion Chambers	**JENKINS Alun** All Saints Chambers

LEADING JUNIORS · WESTERN

DIXEY Ian St. John's Chambers	**MEEKE Martin** Colleton Chambers
FENNY Ian Guildhall Chambers	**MERCER Geoffrey** Walnut House
HORTON Mark St. John's Chambers	**MOONEY Stephen** Albion Chambers
LAMBERT Julian Albion Chambers	**PICTON Martin** Albion Chambers
LETT Brian South Western Chambers	
BURROWES Patrick Albion Chambers	**MATHER-LEES Michael** Albion Chambers
DUVAL Robert St. John's Chambers	**MORGAN Simon** St. John's Chambers
FITTON Michael Albion Chambers	**MUNRO Sarah** Walnut House
HART William Albion Chambers	**QURESHI Shamim** Assize Court Chambers
LANGDON Andrew Guildhall Chambers	**SMITH Richard** Guildhall Chambers
LONGMAN Michael St. John's Chambers	
BURGESS Edward St. John's Chambers	**EVANS Timothy Aylmer** Assize Court Chambers
CULLUM Michael Albion Chambers	**QUADRAT Simon** All Saints Chambers
ELDER Fiona All Saints Chambers	**STEELE David** Colleton Chambers
EVANS Susan St. John's Chambers	

FOR DETAILS OF THESE LEADING BARRISTERS SEE PROFILES ON PAGES 1509-1642

WALES AND CHESTER CIRCUIT

9 Park Place (Murphy) is the largest Cardiff chambers. *Roger Thomas QC* is considered a safe pair of hands. Juniors at the set include *Richard Twomlow, Gregg Taylor* and *Keith Thomas*. **30 Park Place** (Richards) is a well-established set with a name in white collar crime. The "absolutely brilliant" *Patrick Curran QC* "always has command of the facts and the law." He has been elevated to the highest band of leading silks. *Paul Lewis* is "excellent with clients." He has an outstanding reputation for cross-examination and pleas in mitigation. At **33**

LEADING SILKS WALES & CHESTER

CURRAN Patrick 30 Park Place
REES John Charles 33 Park Place
HARRINGTON Patrick 30 Park Place
PRICE Gerald 33 Park Place
THOMAS Roger 9 Park Place

FOR DETAILS OF THESE LEADING BARRISTERS
SEE PROFILES ON PAGES 1509-1642

Park Place (Williams) the best-known practitioner is *John Charles Rees QC*, one of the two leading silks on the circuit.

Swansea's criminal bar is considerably smaller than Cardiff's. **Iscoed Chambers** (Davies) has several well-known juniors, including *Paul Thomas*.

LEADING JUNIORS WALES & CHESTER

DAVIES Meirion 32 Park Place
DAVIES Trefor Iscoed Chambers
DAVIES Huw 30 Park Place
EVANS Elwen Mair Iscoed Chambers
LEWIS Paul 30 Park Place
QUINLAN Christopher 30 Park Place
TWOMLOW Richard 9 Park Place
BULL Gregory 33 Park Place
HOPKINS Stephen 30 Park Place
MURPHY Peter 30 Park Place
RIORDAN Kevin Iscoed Chambers
TAYLOR Gregory 9 Park Place
THOMAS Keith 9 Park Place
THOMAS Paul Huw Iscoed Chambers

THE MIDLANDS AND OXFORD CIRCUIT

The Birmingham sets dominate the circuit. Well-known practitioners at **3 Fountain Court** (Treacy) include head of chambers *Colman Treacy QC* and *Anthony Palmer QC*. *Andrew Jackson* is praised for his attention to detail, his manner with clients and his commitment. *Sybil Thomas* is "highly astute." New Birmingham superset **St Philip's Chambers** (Tedd) has *Rex Tedd QC*, *William Davis QC* and *James Burbidge* in the list of leading practitioners. At **Coleridge Chambers** (Brand) *Amjad Nawaz* is "one of the brightest criminal barristers in Birmingham." At **5 Fountain Court** (Barker), both *Anthony Barker QC* and *Stephen Linehan QC* are recommended.

In Nottingham, **No. 1 High Pavement** (Milmo) has several recommended individuals, including *Peter Joyce QC*. Other sets in Nottingham with recommendations are **King Charles House** (Everard), and **Chambers of Colin Anderson** (Anderson).

In Northampton, the **36 Bedford Row** (Hunt) annexe boasts several well-known practitioners.

LEADING SILKS • MIDLANDS & OXFORD

BARKER Anthony 5 Fountain Court	**SAUNDERS J.** 4 Fountain Court
CRIGMAN David 1 Fountain Court	**SMITH Roger** No.6 Fountain Court
JOYCE Peter No.1 High Pavement	**TEDD Rex** St Philip's Chambers
LINEHAN Stephen 5 Fountain Court	**TREACY Colman** 3 Fountain Court
PALMER Anthony 3 Fountain Court	**WAKERLEY R.** 4 Fountain Court
ESCOTT-COX Brian 36 Bedford Row	**RAGGATT Timothy** 36 Bedford Row
HUNT James 36 Bedford Row	

NEWSILKS • 1997 AND 1998

DAVIS William St Philip's Chambers	**MACUR Julia** St. Ive's Chambers
INMAN Melbourne 1 Fountain Court	

LEADING JUNIORS • MIDLANDS & OXFORD

DUCK Michael 3 Fountain Court	**NAWAZ Amjad** Coleridge Chambers
EVERARD William King Charles House	**STOBART John** King Charles House
JACKSON Andrew 3 Fountain Court	**THOMAS Sybil** 3 Fountain Court
BRAND Simon Coleridge Chambers	**MANN Paul** No.1 High Pavement
CAMPBELL-MOFFAT Audrey No.1 High Pavement	**NICHOLLS Benjamin** 1 Fountain Court
EVANS John 1 Fountain Court	**REYNOLDS Adrian** Chambers of Colin Anderson
JUCKES Robert 3 Fountain Court	(St Mary's Chambers)
BACH William 65-67 King St	**GRIFFITH-JONES Richard** 1 Fountain Court
BURBIDGE James St Philip's Chambers	**HAYNES Peter** St Philip's Chambers
CARR Peter St. Ive's Chambers	**MORRISON Howard** 36 Bedford Row
ELWICK Martin No.1 High Pavement	**SMITH Shaun** No.1 High Pavement
EVANS Michael No.1 High Pavement	**THOMAS Pat** 4 Fountain Court
FARRELL David 36 Bedford Row	**THOROGOOD Bernard** 5 Fountain Court
FARRER Paul 1 Fountain Court	**WALL Mark** 4 Fountain Court

UP AND COMING • MIDLANDS & OXFORD

EASTEAL Andrew No.1 High Pavement	**SHANT Nirmal** No.1 High Pavement

FOR DETAILS OF THESE LEADING BARRISTERS SEE PROFILES ON PAGES 1509-1642

THE NORTHERN CIRCUIT

LEADING SILKS • NORTHERN

GLOBE Henry Exchange Chambers
HENRIQUES Richard Deans Court Chambers
HOLROYDE Tim Exchange Chambers
RIORDAN Stephen 25-27 Castle Street
TURNER David Exchange Chambers
CARUS Roderick 9 St. John St
FARLEY Roger 40 King St
GARSIDE Charles 9 St. John St
GEE Anthony 28 St. John St
GOLDSTONE Clement 28 St. John St
KLEVAN Rodney 18 St. John St
MORRIS Anthony Peel Court Chambers
SHORROCK Michael Peel Court Chambers
STEER David The Corn Exchange

The Northern Circuit is particularly busy. Local solicitors expressed great confidence in the level of service provided by barristers on the Circuit, and London practitioners are becoming conspicuous by their absence.

Liverpool has a successful criminal bar. At **Exchange Chambers** (Waldron) *David Turner QC* is "very user friendly." *Simon Berkson* has "all the qualities a barrister

LEADING JUNIORS • NORTHERN

BERKSON Simon Exchange Chambers	**MCDERMOTT John** Chavasse Court Chambers
BLAKE Andrew 18 St. John St	**MEADOWCROFT Stephen** Peel Court Chambers
LEVER Bernard Peel Court Chambers	**STOUT Roger** 18 St. John Street
LLOYD Heather Peel House	**SUMNER David** Lincoln House Chambers
ATHERTON Robert India Buildings Chambers	**MCMEEKIN Ian** 58 King St
CLARKE Nicholas 9 St. John Str	**O'BYRNE Andrew** Peel Court Chambers
FORSYTH Julie Chavasse Court Chambers	**PICKUP James** Lincoln House Chambers
GREGORY James Lincoln HouseChambers	**REID Paul** Lincoln House Chambers
HARRISON Keith 24A St. John St	**WIGGLESWORTH Raymond** 18 St. John St
MARKS Richard Peel Court Chambers	**WILLIAMS David** Chavasse Court Chambers
MATTISON Andrew Chavasse Court Chambers	**WRIGHT Peter** Lincoln House Chambers
ANDREWS Philip Young Street Chambers	**HERMAN Raymond** India Buildings Chambers
BADLEY Pamela 25-27 Castle Street	**JACKSON John** 40 King St
BATRA Bunty 58 King St	**JACKSON Wayne** Manchester House Chambers
BRENNAN Timothy Manchester House Chambers	**LONG Andrew** Peel Court Chambers
CATTAN Philip 28 St. John St	**MYERS Benjamin** Young Street Chambers
DENNEY Stuart Deans Court Chambers	**WATSON David** 14 Castle St
GOODE Rowena 28 St. John St	

UP AND COMING • NORTHERN

BLACKWELL Kate Lincoln House Chambers	**SAVILL Mark** Deans Court Chambers
JUDGE Lisa Manchester House Chambers	**WHYTE Anne** 14 Castle St
ROBERTS Lisa Lincoln House Chambers	

FOR DETAILS OF THESE LEADING BARRISTERS SEE PROFILES ON PAGES 1509-1642

should have" – "formidable court presence and deep empathy for clients." *Tim Holroyde QC* has an "incisive legal mind." At **India Buildings** (Harris) *Robert Atherton* deals well with clients and "has great attention to detail." *Stephen Riordan QC* of **25-**27 **Castle Street** (Riordan) is a top-ranking silk.

Manchester too has a strong criminal bar. *Roger Stout* from **18 St John St** (Klevan) is considered "very thorough and good on detail." At **Young St Chambers** (Newton) *Benjamin Myers* has done "astonishingly well, and is never out of court." At **Peel House** (Gilmour) *Heather Lloyd* has a speciality in child cases.

NORTH EASTERN CIRCUIT

Park Court Chambers (Stewart and Smith) is the best known Leeds practice, with many recommended individuals. *Robert Smith QC* is "one of the best in the business" on the north eastern circuit. He is accomplished on his feet and technically excellent. *Michael Harrison QC's* "ability to command the court is second to none." He is "a formidable cross-examiner." The very experienced *James Chadwin QC* has a proven track record in serious crime, and is "one of the best mitigators at the bar." *Alistair MacDonald* is a "good solid performer" with an "impressive court presence." At **6 Park Square** (Spencer) *Jenny Kershaw QC's* appointment to silk was well received. *Rod Jameson* at the same chambers is known as a good jury advocate. The "dynamic" *Geoffrey Marson QC* at **Sovereign Chambers** (formerly 25 Park

LEADING SILKS • NORTH EASTERN	
CHADWIN James Park Court Chambers	**SMITH Robert** Park Court Chambers
HARRISON Michael Park Court Chambers	**STEWART James** Park Court Chambers
KERSHAW Jennifer 6 Park Square	**SWIFT Malcolm** Park Court Chambers
BOURNE-ARTON Simon Park Court Chambers	**MARSON Geoffrey** Sovereign Chambers

LEADING JUNIORS • NORTH EASTERN	
HARVEY Colin St. Paul's Chambers	**LUMLEY Gerald** 9 Woodhouse Square
BARNETT Jeremy St. Paul's Chambers	**MACDONALD Alistair** Park CourtChambers
BUBB Tim 39 Park Square	**PALMER Patrick** Sovereign Chambers
ISAACS Paul Mercury Chambers	
BATTY Christopher St. Paul's Chambers	**ROSE Jonathan** St. Paul's Chambers
JAMESON Rod 6 Park Square	**STUBBS Andrew** St. Paul's Chambers
LEES Andrew St. Paul's Chambers	

FOR DETAILS OF THESE LEADING BARRISTERS SEE PROFILES ON PAGES 1509-1642

Square) (Marson) is described as "one of the best barristers in Leeds." *Patrick Palmer* is thought "very capable," and is known for his work for the Revenue, and prosecuting and defending drugs cases. At **St. Paul's Chambers** (Sangster) *Andrew Stubbs* is liked by clients. *Jonathan Rose* "does tough cases very well." *Colin Harvey* is considered an outstanding junior on the circuit, and "always delivers." *Gerald Lumley*, one of the two top juniors on the Circuit, practises from **9 Woodhouse Square** (Collins). At **39 Park Square** (Bubb) *Tim Bubb* is a "good all-rounder."

CRIME (FRAUD)

RESEARCH: In compiling the tables, we consider all the information available to us, paying particular regard to the market research carried out by our team of ten qualified lawyers. (The researchers' details are set out on page three.) The rankings, therefore, reflect the opinion of the marketplace as revealed by systematic and objective research: see page four. (Our research is audited every year by the British Market Research Bureau.)

OVERVIEW: We have tried to include in this section only those individuals who are considered outstanding for serious fraud matters, with the emphasis on defence. Many of the individuals mentioned here also appear in the general crime section.

Barristers' profiles	p. 1509-1642

LEADING SETS · LONDON

QUEEN ELIZABETH BUILDING (Jeffreys QC & Whiteman QC)

3 RAYMOND BUILDINGS (Clive Nicholls QC)

23 ESSEX STREET (Michael Lawson QC)
3 HARE COURT (William Clegg QC)
6 KING'S BENCH WALK (Michael Worsley QC)

5 PAPER BUILDINGS (John Mathew QC)
18 RED LION COURT (Anthony Arlidge QC)

HIGHLY REGARDED · LONDON

9-12 Bell Yard (D. Anthony Evans QC)
35 Essex Street (Nigel Inglis-Jones QC)
1 Middle Temple Lane (Dines & Trollope QC)

Queen Elizabeth Building (Jeffreys & Whiteman) Possess impressive strength in depth, with eight silks and ten juniors recommended for their fraud work. Have long been recognised as one of the premier crime sets. **Leading Barristers:** *Julian Bevan QC* has "his own unique way of doing things" and appears in the highest band of leading silks. *Anthony Glass QC* is famous for his fearsome cross-examinations, and his ability to "cut the case down to the bare bones." *Vivian Robinson QC* is "great with clients, and the epitome of the modern barrister," while *Timothy Langdale QC* has impressed with his "excellent court manner." *David Calvert-Smith QC* was described as "a first class lawyer, thoroughly trusted by judges." *William Boyce* impresses solicitors with his "endless thoroughness" and *Mark Ellison* is "sensible, very relaxed, and has a good legal brain." Other recommended juniors at the set include the "upbeat and friendly" *John Kelsey-Fry, Ian Stern* (a "good all-round fraud junior" and "a good team player") and *Peter Finnigan*, described as a "conscientious worker and a clear advocate." *Gareth Rees* (ex-Cloisters) enters the up and coming list after several recommendations for his fraud work, while

Ian Winter moves from up and coming into the list of highly regarded juniors.

3 Raymond Buildings (Nicholls) Pre-eminent for extradition, this set also has a widely admired white collar crime practice. **Leading Barristers:** *Alun Jones QC* gained a high profile defending Kevin Maxwell, and is now considered a leading fraud barrister who is "very conscientious, hard working and a great battler." *Stephen Batten QC* is also highly respected for his manner in court – "there is no nonsense

LEADING SILKS · LONDON

AMLOT Roy 6 King's Bench Walk	**BEVAN Julian** Queen Elizabeth Building	**LAWSON Edmund** 9-12 Bell Yard
ARLIDGE Anthony 18 Red Lion Court	**JONES Alun** 3 Raymond Buildings	**PURNELL Nicholas** 23 Essex Street
BATTEN Stephen 3 Raymond Buildings	**LAWSON Michael** 23 Essex Street	**ROBERTS Jeremy** 9 Gough Square
CAPLAN Jonathan 5 Paper Buildings	**LISSACK Richard** 35 Essex Street	**ROBINSON Vivian** Queen Elizabeth Building
EVANS David Queen Elizabeth Building	**MATHEW John** 5 Paper Buildings	**ROOK Peter** 18 Red Lion Court
GLASS Anthony Queen Elizabeth Building	**MONTGOMERY Clare** 3 Raymond Buildings	**SCRIVENER Anthony** 2-3 Gray's Inn Square
HILL Michael 23 Essex Street	**PARROY Michael** 3 Paper Buildings	**SUCKLING Alan** Queen Elizabeth Building
CLEGG William 3 Hare Court	**LANGDALE Timothy** Queen Elizabeth Building	**SINGH Kuldip** 5 Paper Buildings
CROXFORD Ian Wilberforce Chambers	**NICHOLLS Clive** 3 Raymond Buildings	**SOLLEY Stephen** Cloisters
DE SILVA Desmond 2 Paper Buildings	**NICHOLLS Colin** 3 Raymond Buildings	**TROLLOPE Andrew** 1 Middle Temple Lane
GODFREY Howard 3 Hare Court	**RHODES Robert** 4 King's Bench Walk	**WHITEHOUSE David** 3 Raymond Buildings
GOLDBERG Jonathan 3 Temple Gardens	**SHAW Antony** 4 Brick Court	

HIGHLY REGARDED · LONDON

AUSTIN-SMITH Michael 23 Essex Street	**MOTT Philip** 35 Essex Street	
LAWSON ROGERS Stuart 23 Essex Street	**TEMPLE Victor** 6 King's Bench Walk	
COCKS David 18 Red Lion Court	**KYTE Peter** Queen Elizabeth Building	**WALKER Raymond** 1 Harcourt Buildings
DAY Douglas Farrar's Building	**RAWLEY Alan** 35 Essex Street	

NEW SILKS · LONDON 1997 AND 1998

CALVERT-SMITH David Queen Elizabeth Building	**MACDONALD Kenneth** Two Garden Court	**MITCHELL Andrew** Furnival Chambers
FISCHEL Robert 5 Paper Buildings	**MEHIGAN Simon** 5 Paper Buildings	**PETERS Nigel** 18 Red Lion Court
GRIEVE Michael Doughty Street Chambers	**MISKIN Charles** 23 Essex Street	

FOR DETAILS OF THESE LEADING BARRISTERS SEE PROFILES ON PAGES 1509-1642

about him." One solicitor described **Clare Montgomery QC** as "the closest I've found to the perfect barrister." She rises two bands in our table of silks and is widely tipped for greatness. The "subtle and clever" **Michael Bromley-Martin** is a "terrific advocate; good on the technical side and good with clients." **Alexander Cameron** is "a good all-rounder."

23 Essex Street (Lawson) Commercial fraud is a particular specialism of this long-established criminal set. Six silks and a junior appear in our tables. **Leading Barristers:** "Court wizard" **Nicholas Purnell QC** is considered a "great all-rounder," as is the "quite fearless" **Michael Lawson QC**, who is "immensely hard working and a splendid strategist." The "determined and meticulous" **Michael Hill QC** is widely respected for his "air of authority" and "knock-down cross-examinations." New silk **Charles Miskin QC** is considered "a great tactician" and juries are said to respond well to him.

3 Hare Court (Clegg) A specialist criminal set. Fraud is a key area of practice and encompasses corporate, financial services, insolvency, DTI and revenue cases. **Leading Barristers:** **William Clegg QC** is considered "very good with a jury," and has recently been involved in the 'Butte Mining' case and 'BCCI.' **Brian Altman** was described as "down to earth, organised and lucid" and **Philip Hackett** as a "very good advocate and lateral thinker." **Keith Mitchell** has impressed with his thoroughness.

6 King's Bench Walk (Worsley) Two silks and a junior were recommended for their fraud work from this specialist criminal set. **Leading Barristers:** In the top band of leading fraud silks is **Roy Amlot QC**, who has "superb style," perfect for "quiet and deft cross-examination." **David Perry** was described as "one of the brightest junior counsel involved in fraud work" and has moved up in our tables.

5 Paper Buildings (Mathew) A set specialising in criminal work with a strong bias toward commercial fraud. Five silks recommended this year. **Leading Barristers:** Leaders at the set include **Jonathan Caplan QC** ("incredibly sound, never gets ruffled") and the very experienced **John Mathew QC**, who is "top class for advice." **Kuldip Singh QC** is regarded as "very thorough and good on the technical side," as is **Simon Mehigan QC** whose experience of

civil work is regarded as a further asset.

18 Red Lion Court (Arlidge) A general common law set specialising in serious crimes. Four silks appear in our tables. **Leading Barristers:** **Anthony Arlidge QC**, co-author of a leading text on fraud, is considered a "very good all-round criminal advocate." He appears in the top band of our table of silks.

9-12 Bell Yard (Evans) A common law set covering a range of criminal and civil work. Enter the fraud tables for the first time this year, with one silk and three juniors listed as leaders. **Leading Barristers:** The "extremely subtle" **Edmund Lawson QC** has a "superb all-round legal brain," and **Mukul Chawla** has "good court presence." **Peter Doyle** is "a master of detail and a good draftsman," and **Michael Egan** "puts things in a simple way" which is very effective in court.

35 Essex Street (Rawley) Also appear in the fraud section for the first time. Have three silks noted for their work in this area. **Leading Barristers:** The "confident and bright" **Richard Lissack QC** is a well respected silk, as is **Philip Mott QC**, who is said to be "very persistent and good on detail." **Alan Rawley QC** was also recommended. He is thought to be underestimated – "not showy but a class act."

1 Middle Temple Lane (Dines & Trollope) A general common law set which had one silk and three juniors recommended for fraud work this year. **Leading Barristers:** Recommended individuals include the "diligent" **Andrew Trollope QC.**

There were several barristers at other sets who were recommended to us for their fraud work. **Jeremy Roberts QC** at **9 Gough Square** is "first class" and has a "very good way with all types of clients." **Ian Croxford QC** at **Wilberforce Chambers** is "a quick thinker, very knowledgeable and has good court presence." **Robert Rhodes QC** of **4 King's Bench Walk** is considered "good on detail," and **Stephen Solley QC** from **Cloisters** has a "good feel for a case and a nice court manner." At **Farrar's Building**, **Douglas Day QC** is "a master of detail" and possesses "tremendous courtroom presence and flair." **Simon Stafford-Michael** of **4 King's Bench Walk** has a distinctive style and is recommended for fraud work because he is a "good lateral thinker" and has "brilliant ideas." New to the list this year are **Andrew Mitchell QC** at **Furnival Chambers**, an acknowledged expert on confiscation who possesses "unquestionable ability," and **Michael Grieve QC** from **Doughty Street Chambers**, who has a "pleasant court manner."

LEADING JUNIORS · LONDON	
BOYCE William Queen Elizabeth Building	**ELLISON Mark** Queen Elizabeth Building
BROMLEY-MARTIN Michael 3 Raymond Buildings	**KELSEY-FRY John** Queen Elizabeth Building
ALTMAN Brian 3 Hare Court	**LUCAS Noel** 1 Middle Temple Lane
BOWES Michael 2 King's Bench Walk	**PERRY David** 6 King's Bench Walk
CAMERON Alexander 3 Raymond Buildings	**STAFFORD-MICHAEL Simon** 4 King's Bench Walk
CHAWLA Mukul 9-12 Bell Yard	**STEWART Neill** Queen Elizabeth Building
HACKETT Philip 3 Hare Court	**STURMAN James** 3 Hare Court
HORWELL Richard Queen Elizabeth Building	**WINBERG Stephen** Crown Office Row
INGRAM Nigel 3 Hare Court	**WOOD Michael** 23 Essex Street
KARK Thomas Queen Elizabeth Building	
DOYLE Peter 9-12 Bell Yard	**MITCHELL Keith** 3 Hare Court
EGAN Michael 9-12 Bell Yard	**STERN Ian** Queen Elizabeth Building

HIGHLY REGARDED · LONDON	
BARNES Margaret 3 Hare Court	**KING Philip** 1 Middle Temple Lane
FINNIGAN Peter Queen Elizabeth Building	**LLOYD-ELEY Andrew** 1 Hare Court
GARDINER Nicholas 1 Middle Temple Lane	**WINTER Ian** Queen Elizabeth Building

UP AND COMING · LONDON	
LLOYD-JACOB Campaspe 3 Raymond Buildings	**REES Gareth** Queen Elizabeth Building
MALCOLM Helen 3 Raymond Buildings	

FOR DETAILS OF THESE LEADING BARRISTERS SEE PROFILES ON PAGES 1509-1642

DEFAMATION

RESEARCH: In compiling the tables, we consider all the information available to us, paying particular regard to the market research carried out by our team of ten qualified lawyers. (The researchers' details are set out on page three.) The rankings, therefore, reflect the opinion of the marketplace as revealed by systematic and objective research: see page four. (Our research is audited every year by the British Market Research Bureau.)

OVERVIEW: Researching this section we spoke to many of the leading defamation solicitors, in-house counsel at major publishers and national newspapers, and a cross section of defamation barristers. Our research confirmed that 1 Brick Court and 5 Raymond Buildings are by far the most popular sets for defamation work, with most of the leading specialists based at one or the other. Although many libel actions are settled, those that do reach court will be heard in front of a jury. Skill in addressing a jury – unusual in civil law – is therefore an important attribute for practitioners in this area.

LEADING SETS · LONDON
1 BRICK COURT (Richard Hartley QC)
5 RAYMOND BUILDINGS (Patrick Milmo QC)

HIGHLY REGARDED · LONDON
DOUGHTY STREET CHAMBERS
(Geoffrey Robertson QC)

1 Brick Court (Hartley) Great strength in depth, with six silks and seven juniors in our tables. Have always specialised in libel and slander, and now cover all aspects of media and entertainment law. **Leading Barristers:** *Andrew Caldecott QC* received numerous commendations, including "thorough, good presentation and tactful with clients." He moves into our top band of silks this year. He and *Benjamin Hinchliff* acted in the recent Court of Appeal case 'Reynolds v Times Newspapers.' *Richard Rampton QC* as well as being charming is "good with juries" and "few can compete with his knowledge and understanding of the law." *Geoffrey Shaw QC* was praised for being quick to return papers, for giving advice that was "spot on" and for being a persuasive advocate. Among the juniors *Manuel Barca* is said to be easy to get on with and good with clients. *Timothy Atkinson* appeared in 'Waple v Surrey County Council', and new silk *Patrick Moloney QC* defended in 'Friend v CAA'. *Victoria Sharp* – "a very tough opponent" – moves up into the top band of juniors this year, and *Giles Crown* was identified as rapidly making a name for himself in the field.

5 Raymond Buildings (Milmo) Specialist media, entertainment and intellectual property set. With 1 Brick Court, the longstanding leaders in this type of work. Four silks and six juniors feature in our tables with three in the top band. Members of chambers appeared on both sides in 'Berezovsky and Others v Forbes Inc'. **Leading Barristers:** The set has several outstanding silks. They include *Desmond Browne QC* ("good on detail, good technician, knows his stuff backwards"); the "thorough" and "approachable" *Charles Gray QC* and *James Price QC* who received extremely high praise this year, particularly for his "superb jury speeches," and moves up to our highest band. As well as being rated for settling difficult pleadings, junior *Adrienne Page* is said to be "fast, aggressive yet charming, and analytical" and more than a match for some of the defamation silks. She and Desmond Browne QC acted in 'Shah v Standard Chartered Bank' (Court of Appeal, 2 April 1998). *Mark Warby*, meanwhile, is "good on detail, prepares well and knows his stuff." *Heather Rogers* was described as "great with clients" and "an experienced practitioner" and *David Sherborne*, though more junior, is clearly a name to watch. Clients described him as "a rising star with absolutely the right temperament for media work."

Doughty Street Chambers (Robertson) A set known for its commitment to defending freedom of speech and citizens' rights. Regularly advise TV producers, book publishers and national newspapers on media and defamation law. *Geoffrey Robertson QC* acted for 'The Guardian' in the Hamilton/Greer libel action and for 'USA Today' in one of the first actions relating to libel on the Internet.

Leading Barristers: Two leading individual practices are those of Heads of Chambers *George Carman QC* at **New Court Chambers**, well known for his success in several high profile trials and *Ronald Thwaites QC* at **10 King's Bench Walk**; "he knows how to handle a jury and he gets good results."

Barristers' profiles   p.1509-1642

LEADING SILKS · LONDON
BROWNE Desmond 5 Raymond Buildings
CALDECOTT Andrew 1 Brick Court
CARMAN George New Court Chambers
GRAY Charles 5 Raymond Buildings
PRICE James 5 Raymond Buildings

MILMO Patrick 5 Raymond Buildings
SHAW Geoffrey 1 Brick Court
SHIELDS Thomas 1 Brick Court

HARTLEY Richard 1 Brick Court
RAMPTON Richard 1 Brick Court
ROBERTSON Geoffrey Doughty Street Chambers
THWAITES Ronald 10 King's Bench Walk

NICOL Andrew Doughty Street Chambers

NEW SILK · LONDON
MOLONEY Patrick 1 Brick Court

LEADING JUNIORS · LONDON
PAGE Adrienne 5 Raymond Buildings
ROGERS Heather 5 Raymond Buildings
SHARP Victoria 1 Brick Court

BARCA Manuel 1 Brick Court
WARBY Mark 5 Raymond Buildings

ATKINSON Timothy 1 Brick Court
HINCHLIFF Benjamin 1 Brick Court
MARZEC Alexandra 5 Raymond Buildings
SHERBORNE David 5 Raymond Buildings
SUTTLE Stephen 1 Brick Court

MILLAR Gavin Doughty Street Chambers
PHILLIPS Jane 1 Brick Court
RUSHBROOKE Justin 5 Raymond Buildings

UP AND COMING · LONDON
CROWN Giles 1 Brick Court
MOORMAN Lucy Farrar's Building

FOR DETAILS OF THESE LEADING BARRISTERS
SEE PROFILES ON PAGES 1509-1642

ECCLESIASTICAL

For solicitors see under Church Law

RESEARCH: In compiling the tables, we consider all the information available to us, paying particular regard to the market research carried out by our team of ten qualified lawyers. (The researchers' details are set out on page three.) The rankings, therefore, reflect the opinion of the market-place as revealed by systematic and objective research: see page four. (Our research is audited every year by the British Market Research Bureau.)

OVERVIEW: There are few barristers who practise this esoteric area of law. They are usually instructed by the Church of England, and advise on property, employment, structures, regulation and organisation matters as well as ecclesiastical law in the strict sense. Many of those featured in the list are chancellors of various dioceses, and are actively involved in the Anglican church.

Barristers' profiles	p. 1509-1642

LEADING SILKS · LONDON

CAMERON Sheila 2 Harcourt Buildings
CLARK Christopher Pump Court Chambers
GEORGE Charles 2 Harcourt Buildings
KAYE Roger 24 Old Buildings

LEADING JUNIORS · LONDON

BRIDEN Timothy 8 Stone Buildings
SEED Nigel 3 Paper Buildings

GOULDING Paul Blackstone Chambers
HILL Mark Pump Court Chambers
MYNORS Charles 2 Harcourt Buildings
PETCHEY Philip 2 Harcourt Buildings
RODGERS June Harcourt Chambers

LEADING JUNIORS · WESTERN

NEWSOM George Guildhall Chambers

LEADING JUNIORS · NORTHERN

GARDEN Ian Derby Square Chambers

FOR DETAILS OF THESE LEADING BARRISTERS
SEE PROFILES ON PAGES 1509-1642

LEADING SETS · LONDON

2 HARCOURT BUILDINGS (Gerard Ryan QC)
PUMP COURT CHAMBERS (Guy Boney QC)

2 Harcourt Buildings (Ryan) Leading Barristers: The "outstanding" **Sheila Cameron QC** is the Vicar-General for the Archbishop of Canterbury. **Charles George QC** and **Charles Mynors** are also recommended from chambers. **Philip Petchey** is regarded as good on paper work.

Pump Court Chambers (Boney) Leading Barristers: **Christopher Clark QC** is a well-liked "practical barrister" and the "excellent" **Mark Hill** is also recommended.

Timothy Briden of **8 Stone Buildings** (Cherry) has "an excellent practice," and is regarded by many as the "number one for ecclesiastical law." He recently appeared in 'Re West Norwood Cemetery'. **Nigel Seed** of **3 Paper Buildings** (Parroy) does mainly criminal work, but is recommended as a good advocate for matters involving the church. **Paul Goulding** at **Blackstone Chambers** (Flint & Baxendale) undertakes ecclesiastical work from a public law perspective, with a focus on employment, quasi-employment, and judicial review of the church. He was recently elected chairman of the Employment Lawyers Association. The "very thorough" **June Rodgers** of **Harcourt Chambers** (Eccles) is "clearly an expert on church matters." **Roger Kaye QC** at **24 Old Buildings** (Brodie) is a leading silk in this area, as well as in insolvency.

Outside London, two juniors have a specialism in church law. **George Newsom** from **Guildhall Chambers** (Royce) in Bristol is "certainly a well known figure," and advises both the Church of England and other religious bodies, mixing this with a traditional chancery and agriculture practice. **Ian Garden** of **Derby Square Chambers** (Newton) in Liverpool is also recommended. He is actively involved in Church of England affairs as a member of the Synod.

EMPLOYMENT

RESEARCH: In compiling the tables, we consider all the information available to us, paying particular regard to the market research carried out by our team of ten qualified lawyers. (The researchers' details are set out on page three.) The rankings, therefore, reflect the opinion of the marketplace as revealed by systematic and objective research: see page four. (Our research is audited every year by the British Market Research Bureau.)

OVERVIEW: 11 King's Bench Walk and Patrick Elias QC continue to lead the field. Laura Cox QC and David Pannick QC have been promoted to join Eldred Tabachnik QC and Michael Burton QC in the second band of leading silks. Among the juniors, Thomas Linden and Dinah Rose stood out and move up into a band of their own.

LEADING FIRMS · LONDON

11 KING'S BENCH WALK (Tabachnik/Goudie QC)

BLACKSTONE CHAMBERS (Baxendale/Flint QC)
LITTLETON CHAMBERS (Michael Burton QC)
OLD SQUARE CHAMBERS (Williams QC)

DEVEREUX CHAMBERS (Jeffrey Burke QC)
4-5 GRAY'S INN SQUARE (Appleby/Beloff QC)

HIGHLY REGARDED · LONDON

Cloisters (Laura Cox QC)
Essex Court Chambers (Gordon Pollock QC)
Fountain Court (Peter Scott QC)

11 Kings Bench Walk (Tabachnik & Goudie) The set is number one, providing "high quality across the board," from experienced silks to strong juniors. Act for both individuals and employers. **Work Handled:** 'BBC v Kelly-Phillips' (CA, April 1998, unfair dismissal/fixed term contracts) and 'ECM (Vehicle Delivery Service) Ltd v Cox and Others' (EAT, 1998, transfer of undertaking/loss of contract) (Elias) the leading casual workers case 'Carmichael & Another v National Power plc (CA 1998) and in 'Polkey v AE Dayton Services Ltd' (HL, 1997) (Tabachnik) 'Crees v Royal Mutual Insurance Society Ltd' (CA, 1998, illness does not preclude return to work at end of maternity leave) (Slade and Oldham) **Leading Barristers: *Patrick Elias QC*** ("the God of employment law") is almost unanimously regarded as "THE person in the employment field." His "cachet value" does not prevent his being "occasionally available at very short notice." *Elizabeth Slade QC* is described as "incredibly incisive, giving superb written advice." *Eldred Tabachnik QC* is the elder statesman of the employment bar. His style is "thorough" and he

"has good reviews in court." The "brilliant" *Christopher Jeans QC* is widely praised for his "ability to get on with clients and understand their business" as well as his "quick, practical, thorough and accurate advice." Juniors at the set are also very much in demand. *Sean Jones* ("good at presentation and with clients") and the similarly "client-friendly" *Jonathan Swift* are highly regarded as leading juniors. *Peter Wallington* is "doing remarkably well." *Jason Coppel* receives glowing recommendations for being "able, hardworking and extremely approachable." *Adrian Lynch*, *Paul Nicholls* ("excellent") and the "client-friendly" *Daniel Stilitz* are also recommended. *Charles Bear* is a "good barrister of the old school."

Blackstone Chambers (Baxendale & Flint) Receives a high number of accolades as "one of the more intellectual sets." Tend to act mainly for respondents, but also act for applicants. **Leading Barristers: *David Pannick QC***, a major player in several other areas of law, is "quite extraordinary, one of the most important lawyers of our time." He recently appeared in 'Strathclyde Regional Council v Wallace' and 'Preston & Others v Wolverhampton Healthcare NHS Trust' (HL, pension rights of part time workers). *Anthony Lester QC* is a well known name in the general public law field and has won some of the most important cases in human rights and discrimination law. *Dinah Rose* is a "star" of the junior bar, and "presents complex matters in a straightforward manner." Her particular specialism is in discrimination cases, ('Brown v Rentokil', ECJ and 'Couch v British Board of Boxing'). *Monica Carss-Frisk* is a "solid junior – you can trust her to take a difficult case and give it a really good try." *Pushpinder*

Barristers' profiles   p. 1509-1642

LEADING SILKS · LONDON

ELIAS Patrick 11 King's Bench Walk

BURTON Michael Littleton Chambers
COX Laura Cloisters
PANNICK David Blackstone Chambers
TABACHNIK Eldred 11 King's Bench Walk

ALLEN Robin Cloisters
BELOFF Michael 4-5 Gray's Inn Square
BOOTH Cherie 4-5 Gray's Inn Square
BURKE Jeffrey Devereux Chambers
HAND John Old Square Chambers
HENDY John Old Square Chambers
LANGSTAFF Brian Cloisters
MCMULLEN Jeremy Old Square Chambers
SLADE Elizabeth 11 King's Bench Walk
UNDERHILL Nicholas Fountain Court

GOUDIE James 11 King's Bench Walk
JEANS Christopher 11 King's Bench Walk
LESTER OF HERNE HILL Lord
Blackstone Chambers
NAUGHTON Philip 3 Serjeants' Inn
PARDOE Alan Devereux Chambers

NEW SILKS · 1997 AND 1998

BEAN David Devereux Chambers
BOWERS John Littleton Chambers
CLARKE Andrew Littleton Chambers
HOCHHAUSER Andrew Essex Court Chambers
MCGREGOR Alistair 11 King's Bench Walk
MEHIGAN Simon 5 Paper Buildings

FOR DETAILS OF THESE LEADING BARRISTERS
SEE PROFILES ON PAGES 1509-1642

Saini is "a star in the making" and *Gemma White* is "very sound." *Paul Goulding* was recently elected chairman of the Employment Lawyers Association.

Littleton Chambers (Burton) Have an "enviable volume of work," done by "very good individuals." Handle all areas of employment law, and act for both applicants and respondents. **Work Handled:** 'BBC v Kelly-Phillips' (Bowers), 'William Hill Organisation v Tucker' (CA, 1998, employee's right to work his notice) (Clarke QC and Sendall). **Leading Barristers:** For difficult litigation *Michael Burton QC* is recommended; he "is incredibly incisive." The "first class" *Andrew Clarke QC* receives praise on many counts for understanding the client's business and for the "scholarly style of his written opinions." *John Bowers QC* took silk in April 1998. *Selwyn Bloch* gives "good practical advice" and is appreciated for his thorough knowledge of restrictive covenants. **Shirley Bothroyd** is "great for injunction cases." The tenacious **Antony Sendall** was recommended both by clients and instructing solicitors alike as a "great team-worker."

Old Square Chambers (Melville Williams) One of the specialist applicants' chambers. Known as an "able and friendly set" which has "good and practical juniors." **Work Handled:** 'BBC v Kelly-Phillips' (Hendy QC and Eady); 'Carmichael and Another v National Power plc' (Gill); 'Crees v Royal Mutual Insurance Society Ltd' and 'Greaves v Kwik Save Stores' (Brown). **Leading Barristers: John Hand QC** has a reputation as a good employment advocate; **John Hendy QC** has a reputation in trade union law. **Jeremy McMullen QC** is the leader of the set's Employment Law group. The leading junior at the set, **Jennifer Eady**, has a "great ability to think through problems" and is in "a large number of cutting-edge cases." The highly-rated ex-solicitor **Melanie Tether** is "very impressive, not many can match her in terms of knowledge."

Devereux Chambers (Burke) A common-law chambers recommended for its "good advocates." **Leading Barristers: David Bean QC** is a new silk and received many positive comments. He and **Ingrid Simler** acted in leading sex discrimination case 'London Underground v Edwards' (CA 1998). He has also been involved in House of Lords appeals on 'Wilson v St Helens BC/Meade v Baxendale,' with **Nick Randall** who is going to be a "big star of the future." **Bruce Carr** is generally described as "excellent." **David Griffiths-Jones** is "laid-back but good."

4-5 Grays Inn Square (Appleby & Beloff) A "quality" set which has high-profile silks and is known for its particular expertise in discrimination law. Members of chambers have recently been involved in cases relating to equal treatment and part time workers cases. Represent both applicants and respondents. **Leading Barristers: Michael Beloff QC** is seen to be undertaking less employment law, but retains "superstar quality." The "enthusiastic" **Cherie Booth QC** gets a positive rating for giving "direct, prompt and practical advice." She has recently been involved in 'Meade-Hill v British Council' (on indirect discrimination and mobility clauses) and in the House of Lords case 'Barry v Midland Bank'. "First class brain" **Tom Linden** is "absolutely charming and brilliant" and

"handles difficult cases very well." He is said to be well-liked by EAT judges.

Cloisters (Cox) The set for applicant work. "Excellent, very employee-friendly," containing "good people who look after you well." **Leading Barristers:** The "fantastic" **Laura Cox QC** is "a leading light on discrimination law." She acted for the appellants in 'Crees v Royal Mutual Insurance Society Ltd' and 'Greaves v Kwik Save Ltd'. **Brian Langstaff QC** is an "excellent applicants' lawyer with strong trade union relationships." He acted in 'Carmichael and Another v National Power plc.' **Robin Allen QC** is an "innovative and successful employment barrister." He acted for the appellant in 'London Underground v Edwards.' **Tom Kibling** is highly rated.

Essex Court Chambers (Pollock)

Known as a "good, responsive" set. **Leading Barristers:** The "robust" **Andrew Hochhauser QC** is "brilliant – the best advocate" who "gets to the detail, is strong and has a clear view of a case." The newly recommended **Claire Blanchard** is "young but gives good written advice and is good with clients." **Martin Griffiths** is also recommended. He recently appeared for the appellant in 'William Hill Organisation Ltd v Tucker' (CA 1998).

Fountain Court (Scott) A general commercial set, not primarily known for its employment work but with a couple of notable individuals. **Leading Barristers: Nicholas Underhill QC** is "extremely highly-regarded." **Brian Napier,** a former academic who is well-known at the Scottish Bar, is now making a name for himself in London.

LEADING JUNIORS · LONDON	
LINDEN Thomas 4-5 Gray's Inn Square	**ROSE Dinah** Blackstone Chambers
CARR Bruce Devereux Chambers	**JONES Sean** 11 King's Bench Walk
EADY Jennifer Old Square Chambers	**SWIFT Jonathan Mark** 11 King's Bench Walk
GOULDING Paul Blackstone Chambers	
BLOCH Selwyn Littleton Chambers	**GRIFFITH-JONES David** Devereux Chambers
BOTHROYD Shirley Littleton Chambers	**KEMPSTER Toby** Old Square Chambers
BROWN Damian Old Square Chambers	**MOOR Sarah** Old Square Chambers
CARSS-FRISK Monica Blackstone Chambers	**PITT-PAYNE Timothy** 11 King's Bench Walk
CAVANAGH John 11 King's Bench Walk	**ROSE Paul** Old Square Chambers
DEVONSHIRE Simon 5 Paper Buildings	**SENDALL Antony** Littleton Chambers
GIFFIN Nigel 11 King's Bench Walk	**SIMLER Ingrid** Devereux Chambers
GILL Tess Old Square Chambers	**TETHER Melanie** Old Square Chambers
BEAR Charles 11 King's Bench Walk	**NAPIER Brian** Fountain Court
CLARKE Gerard Blackstone Chambers	**OLDHAM Peter** 11 King's Bench Walk
DUGGAN Michael Littleton Chambers	**OMAMBALA Ijeoma** Old Square Chambers
GRIFFITHS Martin Essex Court Chambers	**PEARL David** 4 King's Bench Walk
HILLIER Andrew 5 Bell Yard	**RANDALL Nicholas** Devereux Chambers
HOGARTH Andrew 12 King's Bench Walk	**SAINI Pushpinder** Blackstone Chambers
KIBLING Thomas Cloisters	**TAYLER James** Devereux Chambers
KORN Anthony Barnards Inn Chambers	**WALLINGTON Peter** 11 King's Bench Walk
LANG Beverley Blackstone Chambers	**WHITE Antony** Cloisters
LYNCH Adrian 11 King's Bench Walk	
BRENNAN Timothy Devereux Chambers	**NEAMAN Sam** 4 Paper Buildings
DOWNING Ruth Devereux Chambers	**O'ROURKE Mary** 3 Serjeants' Inn
KERR Tim 4-5 Gray's Inn Square	**ROMNEY Daphne** 4 Field Court
LEMON Roy Devereux Chambers	**STAFFORD Andrew** 2 Crown Office Row
MCNEILL Jane Old Square Chambers	**SUTTON Mark** 4 Field Court
MILLAR Gavin Doughty Street Chambers	**THOMPSON Andrew** Francis Taylor Building

UP AND COMING · LONDON	
BLANCHARD Claire Essex Court Chambers	**STILITZ Daniel** 11 King's Bench Walk
BURNS Andrew Devereux Chambers	**WHITCOMBE Mark** Old Square Chambers
COPPEL Jason 11 King's Bench Walk	**WHITE Gemma** Blackstone Chambers
NICHOLLS Paul 11 King's Bench Walk	

FOR DETAILS OF THESE LEADING BARRISTERS SEE PROFILES ON PAGES 1509-1642

MIDLANDS AND OXFORD CIRCUIT

LEADING JUNIORS
MIDLANDS & OXFORD

JONES Jennifer 5 Fountain Court

CORBETT James St Philip's Chambers

GEORGE Sarah St Philip's Chambers

O'DONOVAN Kevin 5 Fountain Court

UP AND COMING
MIDLANDS & OXFORD

ROCHFORD Thomas St Philip's Chambers

TUCKER Katherine St Philip's Chambers

St Philip's Chambers (Tedd) Leading Barristers: *James Corbett* is a "sound and careful thinker who always works through difficult points." *Sarah George* is seen to be seriously developing her employment law work. *Thomas Rochford* appears for the first time in our up and coming category.

5 Fountain Court (Barker) Leading Barristers: *Jennifer Jones* is known as a "sensible and practical" barrister. *Kevin O'Donovan* also received praise for his work in the field.

WESTERN CIRCUIT

LEADING JUNIORS • WESTERN

KEMPSTER Toby Old Square Chambers

REDDIFORD Anthony Guildhall Chambers

UP AND COMING • WESTERN

THOMAS Robert Guildhall Chambers

WHITCOMBE Mark Old Square Chambers

Old Square Chambers (Melville Williams) Leading Barristers: *Toby Kempster* is "well-regarded and friendly to deal with," and *Mark Whitcombe* is also well respected.

NORTH EASTERN CIRCUIT

LEADING JUNIOR
NORTH EASTERN

CAPE Paul Milburn House Chambers

UP AND COMING
NORTH EASTERN

WOODWARK Jane Milburn House Chambers

Milburn House Chambers (Cape) A new specialist employment and discrimination law set in Newcastle. Leading Barristers: *Paul Cape* was a full-time union official before he was called to the Bar. He is "very impressive" and has been called "the best on Tyneside" by one instructing solicitor. *Jane Woodwark* has joined him; she is a former government legal services manager.

NORTHERN CIRCUIT

LEADING SILK • NORTHERN

HAND John 9 St. John Street

NEW SILK • NORTHERN

HORLOCK Timothy 9 St. John Street

LEADING JUNIORS • NORTHERN

GILROY Paul 9 St. John Street

BENSON John 14 Castle St

GRUNDY Nigel 9 St. John Street

HINCHCLIFFE Nick 9 St. John Street

9 St John Street (Hand) This set has the monopoly in Manchester, mainly because of its good individuals ("juniors know what they're doing and are good value") and its "commercial approach." So well respected is the set that two of our interviewees commented that they wouldn't instruct anyone else in the region. Leading Barristers: *John Hand QC*, who also practises in London, was recommended again. *Paul Gilroy* is "particularly bright, puts his clients at ease, has a down to earth manner and is receptive to others' views." The "bright and articulate" *Nigel Grundy* is recommended for straight IT work.

ENERGY & UTILITIES

See also Commercial Litigation, Construction and Planning

RESEARCH: In compiling the tables, we consider all the information available to us, paying particular regard to the market research carried out by our team of ten qualified lawyers. (The researchers' details are set out on page three.) The rankings, therefore, reflect the opinion of the market-place as revealed by systematic and objective research: see page four. (Our research is audited every year by the British Market Research Bureau.)

OVERVIEW: There is no 'Energy Bar' as such. The following tables are composed of sets and individuals specialising in commercial work (One Essex Court, Essex Court Chambers, Fountain Court and 7 King's Bench Walk), planning (2 Mitre Court and 1 Sergeant's Inn) and construction (Atkin Chambers and Keating Chambers).

Clients generally want a silk who already has a reputation in the field; someone else will already have paid for him to read and understand the Network Code, the Pooling and Settlement Agreement, the grid codes, MUCOSA, contracts for differences and the other labyrinthine licences, rules, international treaties and regulations. Very few juniors are mentioned. Because in-house departments are so strong and law firms more specialised than the Bar, counsel will be instructed only when the issues are highly complicated and the sums involved huge. When so much is at stake, energy companies tend to go straight for a silk. With such a small number of practitioners, there is an "unseemly rush to the phones" when a dispute arises, with both sides often trying to book the same team.

Barristers' profiles	p. 1509-1642

LEADING SILKS · LONDON

GRABINER Anthony One Essex Court
POLLOCK Gordon Essex Court Chambers

BOSWOOD Anthony Fountain Court
CARR Christopher One Essex Court
SCOTT Peter Fountain Court
SUMPTION Jonathan Brick Court Chambers
TOMLINSON Stephen 7 King's Bench Walk

AKENHEAD Robert Atkin Chambers
ALDOUS Charles 7 Stone Buildings
BARNES Mark One Essex Court
BOULDING Philip Keating Chambers
COOKE Jeremy 7 King's Bench Walk
CROOKENDEN Simon Essex Court Chambers
EDER Bernard Essex Court Chambers
FITZGERALD Michael 2 Mitre Court Buildings
GLICK Ian One Essex Court
HICKS William 1 Serjeants' Inn
HILDYARD Robert 4 Stone Buildings
PHILIPSON Trevor Fountain Court
RAMSEY Vivian Keating Chambers
READ Lionel 1 Serjeants' Inn
SHER Jules Wilberforce Chambers
THOMAS Christopher Keating Chambers
WHYBROW Christopher 1 Serjeants' Inn

NEW SILKS · 1997 AND 1998

GRUDER Jeffrey One Essex Court
MALES Stephen 20 Essex Street
ONIONS Jeffery One Essex Court
PERSEY Lionel 4 Field Court
WHITE Andrew Atkin Chambers

LEADING JUNIORS · LONDON

MILDON David Essex Court Chambers
RABINOWITZ Laurence One Essex Court
SCHAFF Alistair 7 King's Bench Walk

ALESBURY Alun 2 Mitre Court Buildings
CAMERON Neil 1 Serjeants' Inn
FOOKES Robert 2 Mitre Court Buildings
GRIFFITHS Alan One Essex Court

FOR DETAILS OF THESE LEADING BARRISTERS
SEE PROFILES ON PAGES 1509-1642

LEADING SETS · LONDON

ONE ESSEX COURT (Anthony Grabiner QC)

ESSEX COURT CHAMBERS (Gordon Pollock QC)
FOUNTAIN COURT (Peter Scott QC)
2 MITRE COURT BUILDINGS (FitzGerald QC)
7 KING'S BENCH WALK (Stephen Tomlinson QC)

HIGHLY REGARDED · LONDON

Atkin Chambers (John Blackburn QC)
Keating Chambers (Richard Fernyhough QC)
1 Serjeants' Inn (Lionel Read QC)

COMMERCIAL

One Essex Court (Grabiner) Seven leading individuals – more than any other set – puts them in first place. Offer specialist advice on oil and gas, electricity, telecomms, transport and water. A commercial set both in terms of the work they do and how they do it. **Work Handled:** Includes 'Scottish Power v Britoil (Exploration) Ltd.' **Leading Barristers:** *Anthony Grabiner QC* is "a class act" who "exudes confidence." He "knows how to position a case and how

to present to a judge." Having done a lot of energy work he "knows the industry well." *Christopher Carr QC* is an "enormously impressive operator" and "not someone to sit on the fence, his opinions hold a lot of weight." *Mark Barnes QC* is a "lawyer's lawyer" with a deep knowledge of energy matters. Described as "unflashy and inventive" he "sees his way through problems that don't occur to others." Definitely someone on the way up. *Ian Glick QC* ("meticulous and effective") is seen to do a lot of electricity work as well as some oil and gas. As a junior *Jeffrey Onions QC* was extremely popular with in house lawyers and is expected to retain his popularity now he has taken silk. *Jeffrey Gruder* is highly recommended. The recommended juniors are *Laurence Rabinowitz* (gives "well thought out and well directed advice") and *Alan Griffiths* ("an impressive and perceptive individual").

Essex Court Chambers (Pollock) A commercial set with considerable expertise in energy work. **Work Handled:** Includes 'Total Gas Marketing Ltd v Arco British Ltd' (Pollock); 'National Power Plc v National Grid Company Plc' (Mildon); 'National Power Plc v United Gas Compa-

ny Ltd & Utilicorp United Inc' (Mildon). **Leading Barristers:** "Formidable, fearfully independent, frightfully clever, a terrific cross examiner, an extremely attractive advocate, without equal in speed of intellect and adaptability." A description of *Gordon Pollock QC*, praised by industry lawyers and members of the Bar. *Simon Crookenden QC* is someone with a "great deal of oil and gas experience who comes at cases from a practical." Although *Bernard Eder QC* has not done a lot of energy work over the past year, he retains a reputation as a "popular clients' lawyer." Junior *David Mildon* is regarded as "the energy man" within chambers.

Fountain Court (Scott) A highly competent and efficient commercial set. **Leading Barristers:** *Anthony Boswood QC* is a formidable opponent. Clients value his judgment. *Peter Scott QC* is a relentless advocate. *Trevor Philipson QC* "likes to win cases, is interesting to listen to and gets results."

7 King's Bench Walk (Tomlinson) Oil and gas work is a particular specialism of this commercial set. **Leading Barristers:** *Stephen Tomlinson QC* is described as "a powerful advocate, excellent on technical issues and for complex science cases." He "does a fabulous job in a quiet manner … rolls up his sleeves and gets on with it." He has been involved in two ongoing disputes concerning exploitation of North Sea resources, and has been appointed sole arbitrator in the only two disputes yet submitted to arbitration under the procedures of the Electricity Arbitration Association. *Jeremy Cooke QC* recently appeared in an arbitration concerning a 20 year LNG dispute. *Alistair Schaff* is "everything a junior should be – forceful, effective, tenacious and moderate – an all round good lawyer." He has been involved in the 'Piper Alpha' litigation, still continuing in England and Scotland.

Several other silks at commercial sets were also recommended. *Jonathan Sumption QC* of **Brick Court Chambers** (Clarke) is "a major player" praised for his "brilliant advocacy and intellectual rigour." *Charles Aldous QC* of **7 Stone Buildings** (Aldous), is a "suave and persuasive advocate," and *Robert Hildyard QC* of **4 Stone Buildings** (Heslop), a diligent, sharp witted and brilliant lawyer, were also recommended for their energy work. So were *Stephen Males QC* of **20 Essex Street** (Johnson) who "grasps briefs quickly" and "understands the technical side of things as well how the industry works," and *Jules Sher QC* of **Wilberforce Chambers** (Nugee) – "a methodical intellectual."

PLANNING

2 Mitre Court (FitzGerald) A long established planning set who "go out of their way to help." Planning expertise includes minerals, utilities, infrastructure and major power projects (e.g. Sizewell B inquiry). **Leading Barristers:** *Michael Fitzgerald QC* is an "extremely perceptive and persuasive advocate," a "charming man" and a much sought-after leader.

1 Sergeant's Inn (Read) Also recommended for work in this sector. Members of the set have been involved in the promotion of power stations and in a number of overhead power line inquiries. **Leading Barristers:** *Lionel Read QC*, one of the foremost planning lawyers in the country, heads this specialist planning and local government set. He is "a brilliant, incisive thinker with not a trace of pomposity about him." *William Hicks QC* (for pipelines) and *Christopher Whybrow QC* (for his technical knowledge) were also recommended.

CONSTRUCTION

A small number of construction silks were mentioned, all at Atkin and Keating Chambers, however many others are known to undertake work in this sector. Reference should therefore be made to the Construction section of the Bar Editorial as well, where there is a more detailed list of construction silks and juniors.

Atkin Chambers (Blackburn) Experienced in acting in oil and gas industry disputes, including oil rig construction projects and pipeline disputes. Also power station projects. **Leading Barristers:** *Robert Akenhead QC* was described as "workmanlike, down to earth, approachable and, when he needs to be, aggressive without being unpleasant." *Andrew White QC* is "a lawyer with flair, who gets down to the detail and gets the work done."

Keating Chambers (Fernyhough) The set's construction work includes water, gas, power generation and transmission, offshore oil industry work and pipelines. **Leading Barristers:** *Philip Boulding QC* "listens to instructions, is never complacent or arrogant and has great attention to detail." *Vivian Ramsey QC* is "an extremely adroit advocate, both tactically and commercially." He "inspires confidence and always comes to a conclusion – after a con you feel like you got somewhere. Clients love him." "A great cross examiner," *Christopher Thomas QC* is "good on his feet, hardworking, easy to get along with and meticulous."

ENVIRONMENTAL LAW

RESEARCH: In compiling the tables, we consider all the information available to us, paying particular regard to the market research carried out by our team of ten qualified lawyers. (The researchers' details are set out on page three.) The rankings, therefore, reflect the opinion of the marketplace as revealed by systematic and objective research: see page four. (Our research is audited every year by the British Market Research Bureau.)

OVERVIEW: The table of leading environmental barristers shows few changes, although fewer silks have been included this year. It was felt that too many planning silks had been included in the past, and that the genuine environmental specialists were to be found among the juniors. Solicitors said they preferred to use the bar for advocacy skills rather than pure environmental advice. Old Square Chambers remains the leading set, and John Bates has been elevated to the top of the juniors list after many favourable comments.

Barristers' profiles p. 1509 -1642

LEADING SILKS · LONDON

GORDON Richard 39 Essex Street
HAND John Old Square Chambers
OUSELEY Duncan 4-5 Gray's Inn Square
READ Lionel 1 Serjeants' Inn
RYAN Gerard 2 Harcourt Buildings
VALLANCE Philip 1 Crown Office Row
WILLIAMS John Melville Old Square Chambers

DRABBLE Richard 4 Breams Buildings
GEORGE Charles 2 Harcourt Buildings
HAVERS Philip 1 Crown Office Row
KINGSLAND The Rt. Hon. Lord 4 Breams Buildings
STEEL John 4-5 Gray's Inn Square
STONE Gregory 4-5 Gray's Inn Square

NEW SILKS · 1997 AND 1998

BURNETT Ian 1 Temple Gardens
HOLGATE David 4 Breams Buildings
LINDBLOM Keith 2 Harcourt Buildings

FOR DETAILS OF THESE LEADING BARRISTERS
SEE PROFILES ON PAGES 1509-1642

LEADING SETS · LONDON

OLD SQUARE CHAMBERS (John Melville Williams QC)

4 BREAMS BUILDINGS (Lockhart-Mummery QC)
1 CROWN OFFICE ROW (Robert Seabrook QC)
4-5 GRAY'S INN SQUARE (Appleby/Beloff QC)
2 HARCOURT BUILDINGS (Gerard Ryan QC)
1 SERJEANTS' INN (Lionel Read QC)
3 VERULAM BUILDINGS (R. Neville Thomas QC)

HIGHLY REGARDED · LONDON

2 Mitre Court Buildings (Michael FitzGerald QC)

Old Square Chambers (Melville Williams) Tend to focus on the private law side of environmental law, particularly cases involving personal injury and nuisance. Leading Barristers: John Hand QC was recommended for "heavyweight prosecutions" and other high level cases. He also specialises in employment law and personal injury. John Melville Williams QC is recommended on the toxic torts side. The "extremely knowledgeable" John Bates is considered outstanding technically. He has a scientific training and an academic background, and is thought particularly good on written opinions. A contrasting character is the "flamboyant" Charles Pugh. He has "presence in court" and is considered an outstanding environmental law advocate, particularly for toxic torts, statutory nuisance and waste matters. William Birtles is a "good all-rounder", and is especially commended for his paper advice. Philip Mead is also rec-

ommended, particularly for his knowledge of the application of European law and for noise abatement matters.

4 Breams Buildings (Lockhart Mummery) Act predominantly for the government and local authorities. A top planning law set. Leading Barristers: Richard Drabble QC is well known on the public side of planning law, and "does tricky cases elegantly." The "very capable" Lord Kingsland QC has experience as an MEP, and is highly respected for his work on waste matters. David Holgate QC has a large planning practice, and is considered a good court advocate. The "shrewd" Christopher Katkowski was recommended for his ability over a wide range of environmental matters. David Elvin also has a broad public law practice, and is considered a "very sound advocate."

1 Crown Office Row (Seabrook) The set is best known for professional negligence, domestic commercial contract and construction law, but has several leading environmental law specialists. Leading Barristers: Philip Vallance QC has "a proven track record in environmental matters," as does Philip Havers QC. The "very user friendly" David Hart is highly thought of, both for his work on paper and his "good forensic skills." William Edis is "punchy and effective."

4-5 Grays Inn Square (Appleby & Beloff) A leading set in public and administrative law and planning. Leading Barristers: The "absolutely excellent" Duncan Ouseley QC is "astute and picks up issues quickly," he also "thinks laterally and is good on his feet." He recently

appeared in 'R v Secretary of State for Trade and Industry, Ex p Greenpeace' (Habitats Directive). John Steel QC and Gregory Stone QC are basically planners, but are sought after for environmental matters because they are considered good advocates. Among the juniors Thomas Hill is "able to manage very large and complex cases on his own," and John Hobson, experienced in public law matters, is described as "very thorough and a good advocate." David Wolfe is an up and coming name. He has a broad public law practice, and his engineering and scientific background make him an asset on cases requiring technical advice.

2 Harcourt Buildings (Ryan) Although predominantly a planning set, has a growing environmental practice. Leading Barristers: Gerard Ryan QC is one of the first barristers to specialise in environmental law, and one of the few silks in our table with a scientific training. He is considered technically good, especially on waste, utilities and EC law. Charles George QC has "fantastic attention to detail and is a good advocate." He does a lot of work on behalf of waste companies and local authorities. Robert McCracken is one of the leading juniors. He is said to have a real enthusiasm for the subject and to be "good at marshalling large and diverse cases." *Gregory Jones* is also highly rated. He does planning, regulatory work, EU law and impact assessment.

1 Serjeants Inn (Read) A planning and local government set, vastly experienced in public inquiry work. **Leading Barristers:** *Lionel Read QC* is a "wonderful character" and "superb on planning," and his opinions "always carry a great deal of weight." *Russell Harris* is "a good all-rounder," and *Rhodri Price Lewis* is "good on his feet," and "client friendly."

3 Verulam Buildings (Neville Thomas) A broadly based commercial law practice. **Leading Barristers:** The "very dynamic" *James Cameron* has an excellent reputation on the EU and international side. *Philippe Sands* was described as "more of an academic but very well known and respected." He advises specifically on international and EU matters, and in this context he is "as good as a silk." *Maurice Sheridan* is also listed, and was mentioned in particular for his "pragmatism" and "sensible approach."

2 Mitre Court Buildings (Fitzgerald) Another leading planning and local government set. **Leading Barristers:** *Neil King* is "very tuned into environmental issues" and "a good team player." He is considered good at public inquiries and on matters involving minerals.

Leading environmental lawyers at other London chambers include *Richard Gordon QC* at **39 Essex Street** (Glasgow). He is "the great man of judicial review," and is liked for his "relaxed approach" and flexibility. *Professor Richard Macrory* of **Brick Court Chambers** (Clarke) has "a very commanding presence" and is admired for his written advice, especially where EU or water law is involved. *Michael Fordham* of **Blackstone Chambers** (Baxendale and Flint) is "extremely impressive" on administrative law matters, and *John Whittaker* from **Serle Court Chambers** (Sparrow) is considered "good on detail" and "useful for academic problems." *Witold Pawlak* of **9 Bedford Row** (Goldring) has acted for the Environment Agency and local authorities on numerous environmental matters, including the recent Court of Appeal case 'R v Hertfordshire County Council, Ex p Green Environmental Industries Ltd.'

REGIONAL CIRCUITS

At **5 Fountain Court** (Barker) in Birmingham, *Martin Kingston QC* has a substantial planning practice, and is described as "a crisp and measured advocate." *Peter Goatley* is also recommended as an up and coming name, and is known for his waste management licensing work. New silk *Julia Macur QC* from **St Ives Chambers** (Coke) in Birmingham specialises in environmental health and pollution work.

At **40 King Street** (Raynor) in Manchester, *Andrew Gilbart QC* has a respected planning practice and is considered a "forceful advocate." *Stephen Sauvain QC* specialises in local government law, is "excellent at written advice," and "good in a crisis if you need things thoroughly thought out."

Andrew Moran QC at **Byrom Street Chambers** (Hytner) in Manchester, has a broad commercial and civil practice, especially in shipping. He specialises in water pollution cases, and has recently been involved in the Sea Empress case. *Charles Hyde* practises from **Albion Chambers** (Barton) in Bristol, and mixes environmental law with a matrimonial practice. He is noted for his ability in court. At **Iscoed Chambers** (Davies) in Swansea, *Wyn Richards* is "meticulous and practical, and a has a nice manner."

EUROPEAN UNION/COMPETITION

RESEARCH: Our rankings reflect the opinion of the marketplace as revealed by systematic and objective research: see page four. Our research is audited every year by the British Market Research Bureau.

LEADING SETS · LONDON

BRICK COURT CHAMBERS (Clarke QC)
MONCKTON CHAMBERS (Richard Fowler QC)

Brick Court Chambers (Clarke) A strong EU set with an annexe in Brussels. **Work Handled:** Work includes 'Heathrow Airport v Forte'; 'R v Treasury ex parte Shepherd Neame'; 'Parma Ham v Asda Stores'; 'Easy Jet Airlines v Go Airlines'. Also acted for Spanish fishermen in latest Factortame case, for Virgin Atlantic in inquiry into proposed merger of British Airways and American Airlines and for the British government in 'Grant v South West Trains'. Acted for Lunn Poly in 'R v Customs & Excise ex parte Lunn Poly'. **Leading Barristers:** *David Vaughan QC* maintains his strong reputation in EC work, especially litigation. *Gerald Barling QC* ("judges trust him") has a varied practice and was recommended again. *Nicholas Forwood QC* was described as "good on paper" and *Derrick Wyatt QC* is highly thought of but relatively low profile. *Nicholas Green QC* ("good on his feet") took silk this year, while *David Anderson* ("excellent", "easily one of the best") moves up a band to become a leading junior. *Mark Brealey* was described as "good on his feet" and *James Flynn* and *Mark Hoskins* are promoted from up and coming following recommendations from a wide range of practitioners.

Monckton Chambers (Fowler) **Work Handled:** Merger work includes Guinness-Grand Metropolitan merger and Metrocolor/Technocolor. Contentious issues include 'BRB and SNCF v Commission' (state aid and Article 85 – Channel Tunnel); 'BP v Commission' (state aid); 'Gencor v Commission' (on-going merger reference); 'Heathrow Airport Ltd v Forte' (UK) (alleged Art 86 discrimination by Heathrow Airport); 'Iberian v BPB' (package holiday reference); 'Clifton Eyewear v Dolland Aitchison'; OFT in Re Net Book Agreements; 'Lancashire Dairies v MMB and related cases' (winding up of Milk Marketing Board). **Leading Barristers:** *Richard Fowler QC* is very experienced, particularly in UK RTPA work. *Paul Lasok*

QC, former clerk to two advocates general, covers all areas of EU law and is described as "academic" and "brilliant". *Kenneth Parker QC* is "good on his feet" and "researches his subjects well". *Christopher Vajda QC* has extensive ECJ experience. The "excellent" *Nicholas Paines QC* and *Peter Roth QC* took silk in 1997. The utilities specialist *Jon Turner* ("technically good", "commercial", "hardworking") was highly recommended and moves up to the top band of leading juniors this year. *Rupert Anderson* was also praised for being "technically excellent" and *Aidan Robertson* ("concise" and "accurate") gives down to earth advice. The "impressive" *Rhodri Thompson* acts for UK government and private clients.

Blackstone Chambers (Baxendale and Flint) **Work Handled:** Acted for EBU in ECJ case involving grant of exemptions to EBU members in collective bidding rights for Olympic Games and other sport events. **Leading Barristers:** *Ian Forrester QC* now spends most of his time in Brussels working for White & Case. *Alastair Sutton* also works for White & Case. The "superb" *Adam Lewis* ("good on paper and good client contacts") was recommended again.

20 Essex Street (Johnson) **Work Handled:** 'R v Minister of Agriculture ex parte Compassion in World Farming'; 'Dekker v Caisse des Maladies'; 'Hermäs International v FHT Marketing". **Leading Barristers:** *Richard Plender QC* handles mainly competition matters and also some other EU work.

One Essex Court (Grabiner) **Work Handled:** Acted for British Gas in Transco MMC enquiry. Acted for Manchester Airport in MMC enquiry into airport charges. Acted for BT in MMC enquiry into call for mobile phones. EU work includes Eurostar v Commission. **Leading Barristers:** *Thomas Sharpe QC* ("commercial" and "forceful") has a wide-ranging UK and EC competition practice.

Essex Court Chambers (Pollock) **Work Handled:** Specialise in EU rather than domestic law, and on contentious rather than non-contentious matters. Strongest in services and distribution sectors. **Leading Barristers:** *Peter Duffy QC* is highly rated,

LEADING SILKS · LONDON

FOWLER Richard Monckton Chambers
LASOK Paul Monckton Chambers
VAUGHAN David Brick Court Chambers

BARLING Gerald Brick Court Chambers
FORRESTER Ian Blackstone Chambers
FORWOOD Nicholas Brick Court Chambers
PARKER Kenneth Monckton Chambers
PLENDER Richard 20 Essex Street
SHARPE Thomas One Essex Court
VAJDA Christopher Monckton Chambers
WYATT Derrick Brick Court Chambers

NEW SILKS · 1997 AND 1998

DUFFY Peter Essex Court Chambers
GREEN Nicholas Brick Court Chambers
PAINES Nicholas Monckton Chambers
ROTH Peter Monckton Chambers

LEADING JUNIORS · LONDON

ANDERSON David Brick Court Chambers
TURNER Jon Monckton Chambers

BREALEY Mark Brick Court Chambers
WATSON Philippa Essex Court Chambers

ANDERSON Rupert Monckton Chambers
FLYNN James Brick Court Chambers
HOSKINS Mark Brick Court Chambers
LEWIS Adam Blackstone Chambers
MERCER Hugh Essex Court Chambers
QUIGLEY Conor Brick Court Chambers
RANDOLPH Fergus Brick Court Chambers
SHARPSTON Eleanor 4 Paper Buildings
SUTTON Alastair Blackstone Chambers
THOMPSON Rhodri Monckton Chambers

UP AND COMING · LONDON

DAVIES Helen Brick Court Chambers
ROBERTSON Aidan Monckton Chambers

FOR DETAILS OF THESE LEADING BARRISTERS
SEE PROFILES ON PAGES 1509-1642

although has more of a reputation for EU human rights rather than competition work. *Philippa Watson* ("good" and "academic") has a particular reputation in EC agricultural law and energy.

4 Paper Buildings (McGregor) **Work Handled:** 'UK v Council' (the UK's unsuccessful challenge to the working time directive); 'R v Secretary of State for Transport ex parte Factortame and others'; 'Potter v Secretary of State for Employment' (the "Swan Hunter" redundancies). **Leading Barristers:** *Eleanor Sharpston* was recommended for her general EU practice.

FAMILY

RESEARCH: In compiling the tables, we consider all the information available to us, paying particular regard to the market research carried out by our team of ten qualified lawyers. (The researchers' details are set out on page three.) The rankings, therefore, reflect the opinion of the marketplace as revealed by systematic and objective research: see page four. (Our research is audited every year by the British Market Research Bureau.)

OVERVIEW: One Garden Court Family Law Chambers joins the band of leading sets this year. As in previous years, the barristers are divided into those specialising in Matrimonial Finance and those specialising in Child Care. Many barristers practise exclusively in one of these two areas, but there are some practitioners who appear in both tables.

Barristers' profiles	p. 1509-1642

LEADING SETS · LONDON
29 BEDFORD ROW CHAMBERS (Peter Ralls QC)
ONE GARDEN COURT (Platt QC & Ball QC)
ONE KING'S BENCH WALK (James Townend QC)
1 MITRE COURT BUILDINGS (Bruce Blair QC)
QUEEN ELIZABETH BUILDING (Ian Karsten QC)

HIGHLY REGARDED · LONDON
Gray's Inn Chambers (Brian Jubb)
14 Gray's Inn Square (Joanna Dodson QC)
4 Paper Buildings (Lionel Swift QC)
4 Brick Court (David Medhurst)
1 Gray's Inn Square (Scotland QC)

29 Bedford Row (Ralls) Rated by instructing solicitors, both nationwide and in London, as an ever improving set that has "matured" and now deserves its elevation into the top band. Most people interviewed felt that their true strength lay in the "quality and expertise" of the juniors. **Leading Barristers:** Recognised chiefly for his "outstanding" child care work, *Timothy Scott QC* is also respected for his matrimonial finance work. Leading juniors on the financial side, *Deborah Bangay* and *Lucy Stone* are singled out as being "exceptionally good." *Nicholas Francis* is described as a "safe pair of hands" and a "tough advocate," while *Clare Renton* and *Neil Sanders* are known as "capable practitioners" in the area of child care.

One Garden Court (Platt & Ball) With the appointment of Nicholas Martin as Chief Executive, this exclusively family law set has taken on a more corporate structure with further plans for strategic and operational development. **Work Handled:** Includes 'R v London Borough of Lambeth ex parte Caddell' (1998)(impor-

LEADING SILKS · LONDON · MATRIMONIAL FINANCE		
BARON Florence Queen Elizabeth Building	**COLERIDGE Paul** Queen Elizabeth Building	**SINGLETON Barry** One King's Bench Walk
BLAIR Bruce 1 Mitre Court Buildings	**MOSTYN Nicholas** 1 Mitre Court Buildings	
BODEY David Queen Elizabeth Building	**POSNANSKY Jeremy** 1 Mitre Court Buildings	**SEABROOK Robert** 1 Crown Office Row
POINTER Martin 1 Mitre Court Buildings		
ANELAY Richard One King's Bench Walk	**HAYWARD SMITH Rodger** One King's Bench Walk	**KUSHNER Lindsey** 14 Gray's Inn Square
BALL Alison One Garden Court	**HOROWITZ Michael** 1 Mitre Court Buildings	**PRATT Camden** One King's Bench Walk
COHEN Jonathan 4 Paper Buildings	**KARSTEN Ian** Queen Elizabeth Building	**SCOTT Timothy** 29 Bedford Row Chambers

NEW SILKS · 1997 AND 1998 · MATRIMONIAL FINANCE
TURNER James One King's Bench Walk

LEADING JUNIORS · LONDON · MATRIMONIAL FINANCE		
AMOS Tim Queen Elizabeth Building	**DYER Nigel** 1 Mitre Court Buildings	**MOOR Philip** 1 Mitre Court Buildings
BANGAY Deborah 29 Bedford Row Chambers	**FRANCIS Nicholas** 29 Bedford Row Chambers	**NATHAN Peter** One Garden Court
DAVIDSON Katharine 1 Mitre Court Buildings	**JOHNSTONE Mark** 4 Paper Buildings	**NEWTON Clive** One King's Bench Walk
DUCKWORTH Peter 29 Bedford Row Chambers	**MARKS Lewis** Queen Elizabeth Building	**STONE Lucy** 29 Bedford Row Chambers
BALCOMBE David 1 Crown Office Row	**MOYLAN Andrew** Queen Elizabeth Building	**SANDERS Neil** 29 Bedford Row Chambers
CAYFORD Philip 29 Bedford Row Chambers	**POCOCK Christopher** One King's Bench Walk	
LE GRICE Valentine 1 Mitre Court Buildings	**ROBERTS Jennifer** Queen Elizabeth Building	
ARNOT Lee 22 Old Buildings	**MITCHELL John** One Garden Court	**WILLBOURNE Caroline** One Garden Court
ATKINS Charles 29 Bedford Row Chambers	**MURFITT Catriona** 1 Mitre Court Buildings	**WINGERT Rachel** Gray's Inn Chambers
BRASSE Gillian 14 Gray's Inn Square	**SCARRATT Richard** One Garden Court	**WOOD Christopher** 1 Mitre Court Buildings
BRUDENELL Thomas Queen Elizabeth Building	**SHAW Howard** 29 Bedford Row Chambers	
HOWARD Charles New Court Chambers	**SHENTON Suzanne** One Garden Court	

UP AND COMING · LONDON · MATRIMONIAL FINANCE		
COOK Ian One King's Bench Walk	**GRICE Joanna** One King's Bench Walk	**PEEL Robert** 29 Bedford Row Chambers

FOR DETAILS OF THESE LEADING BARRISTERS SEE PROFILES ON PAGES 1509-1642

LEADING SILKS · LONDON · CHILD CARE INCLUDING ABDUCTION

DODSON Joanna 14 Gray's Inn Square	MUNBY James 1 New Square	SCOTT Timothy 29 Bedford Row Chambers
EVERALL Mark 1 Mitre Court Buildings	PARKER Judith One King's Bench Walk	
BODEY David Queen Elizabeth Building	LEVY Allan 17 Bedford Row	POSNANSKY Jeremy 1 Mitre Court Buildings
HAYWARD SMITH Rodger One King's Bench Walk	MURDOCH Gordon 4 Paper Buildings	SCOTLAND Patricia 1 Gray's Inn Square
HOROWITZ Michael 1 Mitre Court Buildings	PAUFFLEY Anna 4 Paper Buildings	SWIFT Lionel 4 Paper Buildings
HUGHES Judith 1 Mitre Court Buildings	PLATT Eleanor One Garden Court	
BALL Alison One Garden Court	KUSHNER Lindsey 14 Gray's Inn Square	PEDDIE Ian One Garden Court
KARSTEN Ian Queen Elizabeth Building	MESTON Lord Queen Elizabeth Building	

NEW SILKS · 1997 AND 1998 · CHILD CARE INCLUDING ABDUCTION

MCFARLANE Andrew One King's Bench Walk	TURNER James One King's Bench Walk

LEADING JUNIORS · LONDON · CHILD CARE INCLUDING ABDUCTION

HILDYARD Marianna 4 Brick Court	SETRIGHT Henry 1 Gray's Inn Square	
BRASSE Gillian 14 Gray's Inn Square	HOWARD Charles New Court Chambers	RENTON Clare 29 Bedford Row Chambers
BRUDENELL Thomas Queen Elizabeth Building	KIRK Anthony One King's Bench Walk	ROBERTS Jennifer Queen Elizabeth Building
BUDDEN Caroline One King's Bench Walk	LISTER Caroline One King's Bench Walk	ROWE Judith One Garden Court
COBB Stephen One Garden Court	MOOR Philip 1 Mitre Court Buildings	SLOMNICKA Barbara 14 Gray's Inn Square
CUSWORTH Nicholas 1 Mitre Court Buildings	MURFITT Catriona 1 Mitre Court Buildings	STERNBERG Michael 4 Paper Buildings
HALL Joanna 14 Gray's Inn Square	NEWTON Clive One King's Bench Walk	TAYLOR Debbie Hardwicke Building
HIGSON SMITH Gillian Gray's Inn Chambers	PLATTS Rachel 1 Mitre Court Buildings	WILLBOURNE Caroline One Garden Court
HORROCKS Peter One Garden Court	QUINN Susan 4 Brick Court	WINGERT Rachel Gray's Inn Chambers
BARDA Robin 4 Paper Buildings	JUBB Brian Gray's Inn Chambers	RODGER Caroline Gray's Inn Chambers
DASHWOOD Robert Gray's Inn Chambers	MAIDMENT Susan One King's Bench Walk	POPE Heather 1 Mitre Court Buildings
EATON Deborah One King's Bench Walk	MITCHELL Janet 4 Brick Court	SANDERS Neil 29 Bedford Row Chambers
HARDING Cherry Gray's Inn Chambers	MITCHELL John One Garden Court	SHENTON Suzanne One Garden Court
JACKSON Peter 4 Paper Buildings	NATHAN Peter One Garden Court	

FOR DETAILS OF THESE LEADING BARRISTERS SEE PROFILES ON PAGES 1509-1642

tant case dealing with the provision of services for children leaving care); 'Re B' (1997) (case decided that there was no rule of issue estoppel in family proceedings) and 'M v M' (1997) (case concerning habitual residence involving an injunction to inhibit proceedings in other jurisdictions). **Leading Barristers:** Both *Eleanor Platt QC* and *Alison Ball QC* specialise in all areas of family law, particularly child care. Leading junior *Peter Nathan* has leapt into the top band of the finance table on the strength of his "terribly good" reputation for matrimonial finance work. Others operating in this field are *Suzanne Shenton* and *Caroline Willbourne* who have been described as "reliable operators." *Stephen Cobb* and *Peter Horrocks* are respected for their child care work.

One Kings Bench Walk (Townend) Growing recognition for the quality of this set's work has justified its promotion to a higher division. Popular both in London and in the regions for their direct and efficient approach to work. **Leading Barristers:** *Barry Singleton QC* has a reputation for being a "tough, sound operator" who "shines" in court. *Camden Pratt QC* has been described as having "real flair," and new silk *James Turner QC* combines experience with talent. On the child care side *Judith Parker QC* is "one of the best operators in town." New silk, *Andrew McFarlane QC* has been particularly noted

for his handling of the most complicated cases. Leading juniors include *Christopher Pocock* and *Clive Newton* who have ever growing reputations in the field of finance, especially concerning ancillary relief. Christopher Pocock recently appeared as junior to Camden Pratt QC in 'Wicks v Wicks'.

1 Mitre Court Buildings (Blair) "Quality" and "depth of talent" are the most popular comments from both instructing solicitors and leading barristers when asked to describe 1 Mitre Court as a whole. Easily deserves its top band position. The set has lost Paul Focke to the bench and *Bruce Blair QC* is the new head of chambers. **Leading Barristers:** The elevation of *Nicholas Mostyn QC* from the new silk category straight into the top band of leading silks will come as little surprise to those familiar with his work. Described variously as first class, an excellent advocate and highly skilled and entertaining, he can also "smell blood at a hundred paces." The strong matrimonial team also includes the "thoroughly capable" *Michael Horowitz QC* and "aggressive yet skilled" *Martin Pointer QC*. Leading the child care side is the "ever professional" *Mark Everall QC* who has earned a reputation for his expertise on the Hague Convention concerning child abduction. *Rachel Platts* is held in high esteem for her child care work and *Catriona Murfitt* is noted for her "calm manner."

Queen Elizabeth Building (Karsten) Highly regarded as a specialist set, with strength in depth at all levels. **Work Handled:** Noted more for its matrimonial finance than for child care work, but handle all aspects of family law, including those with an international aspect. **Leading Barristers:** *Florence Baron QC* and *Paul Coleridge QC* both received much praise, as did the "superb" *David Bodey QC* and the "ever impressive" *Ian Karsten QC*. Leading juniors *Andrew Moylan* and *Tim Amos* were also singled out for the quality of their work. A recent addition to the band of leading child care silks is *Lord Meston QC*, particularly commended for his "clear advice and sharp adversarial skills."

Gray's Inn Chambers (Jubb) Has a growing reputation in this field. Two new juniors join the tables. **Leading Barristers:** The "adept and experienced" *Brian Jubb* and the "classy operator" *Cherry Harding* enter the tables. *Rachel Wingert* and *Robert Dashwood*, who both specialise in child care, are also well respected amongst their peers.

14 Gray's Inn Square (Dodson) Known for good quality work and experienced tenants. **Leading Barristers:** *Lindsey Kushner QC* remains highly rated and practises childcare.

4 Paper Buildings (Swift) Particularly recommended for their child care expertise. **Leading Barristers:** Silks noted for child care include the "level headed" *Anna Pauffley QC* and the "highly respected" *Gordon Murdoch QC*. Leading the matrimonial finance side is the "direct" *Jonathan Cohen QC*.

4 Brick Court (Medhurst) has three recommended juniors in *Marianna Hildyard*, *Susan Quinn* and *Janet Mitchell*. The "talented" *Allan Levy QC* at **17 Bedford Row** (Levy) is known nationally as an authority on child care, while *Patricia Scotland QC* at **1 Gray's Inn Square** (Scotland) was recommended as "brilliant on child care." **New**

Court Chambers offer the services of *Charles Howard*, who covers a wide area of family law from probate disputes to child abduction. He was involved in the litigation over the estate of Frederick West (inheritance and family provision); 'Re O' (A Minor) (1997) concerning costs orders against the Legal Aid Board, and 'Heller v Heller' (1996) – making a lump sum order against a bankrupt husband. *Robert Seabrook QC* at **1 Crown Office Row** (Seabrook) dealt with the divorce of HRH The Prince of Wales. Recently involved in 'S v S' (1997) (divorce:

staying proceedings). Handles major international matrimonial disputes. Known as a "brilliant advocate." At the same chambers is *David Balcombe* whose matrimonial finance work is said to be "technically very good."

22 Old Buildings (Hytner) is a general common law set whose family group has increased in stature over the past year. More high profile cases coupled with increased local authority work have strengthened its reputation. *Lee Arnot* has been involved in 'Re R' (1998) concerning restricting and defining the guidelines for applications.

SOUTH EASTERN AND EAST ANGLIAN CIRCUIT

The majority of instructing solicitors in the South Eastern/East Anglian circuit prefer to instruct London Counsel. However our research shows that there are pockets of talent outside the capital.

LEADING SILKS · SOUTH EASTERN

MATTHEWS Suzan Guildford Chambers

LEADING JUNIORS
SOUTH EASTERN AND EAST ANGLIAN

DAVIES Lindsay Fenners Chambers
ELLIOTT Margot Regency Chambers
ESPLEY Susan Fenners Chambers
KEFFORD Anthony East Anglian Chambers
TATTERSALL Simon Fenners Chambers

MCLOUGHLIN Timothy East Anglian Chambers
MILLER Celia East Anglian Chambers
NEWTON Roderick East Anglian Chambers
PARNELL Graham East Anglian Chambers
WAIN Peter East Anglian Chambers

East Anglian Chambers (Holt), Ipswich. The dominant set in East Anglia, boasting a strong and well thought of family team. Leading Barristers: *Anthony Kefford* was described by one practitioner as "the leading junior in the Eastern region" and according to others, there is "nobody better" for ancillary relief. *Tim McLoughlin* is considered "excellent" in his field; *Celia Miller* is extremely popular and *Roderick Newton* combines a good family practice with criminal work. *Peter Wain* is especially good on local authority work and *Graham Parnell* was described as a "very sound" practitioner.

Fenners Chambers (Davies), Cambridge. A large civil set with a first rate family group. Leading Barristers: *Lindsay Davies* and *Simon Tattersall* are experienced and well-known leaders in matrimonial finance and ancillary relief. *Susan*

Espley is known for high profile public and private cases involving children. Recent cases include Re O (1997) (abduction) and Re B (1996) (the rights of a child). Also has experience of complicated disputes over the division of the matrimonial home.

Regency Chambers (Croxon), Peterborough. Small regional set based in Peterborough. Noted mainly for her child care work, *Margot Elliott* has been described as "able to give any of the London crowd a run for their money." She is the only exclusively family law practitioner within her set.

SOUTH-WESTERN CIRCUIT

All Saints Chambers (Jenkins), Bristol. A strong provincial set offering a wide range of services. Leading Barristers: Leading silk *Mark Evans QC* is recognised for his ancillary relief practice. He has been praised for his skilful cross examination technique and is considered to have a first rate caseload.

Albion Chambers (Barton), Bristol. Has a large and well respected family group. Leading Barristers: Known mainly for his ancillary relief work, *Stephen Wildblood* has been described as a "very, very able practitioner" who "excels in all fields of family law." *Claire Wills-Goldingham* is a "hard fighter" with "good presentation skills," while the knowledgeable *Caroline Wright* is rated for her ancillary relief work. *Deborah Dinan-Hayward* has recently joined chambers from Assize Court. She has a reputation for being "very committed to her clients."

St. Johns Chambers (Denyer), Bristol. Leading Barristers: *Christopher Sharp's* elevation into the top band is long overdue according to the majority of barristers and solicitors interviewed. Described by one interviewee as "streets ahead of his rivals" in the field of ancillary relief. Recent reported cases include: 'N-v-N' 1997 concerning financial provisions in an overseas

divorce. *Richard Bromilow* was described as "a good chap" and a "sound worker." Assistant recorder *Susan Jacklin* who handles a mixed caseload, is thorough and presents a clear argument.

Assize Court Chambers (Isherwood), Bristol. Maintain their reputation for high quality work despite the loss of Deborah Dinan-Hayward to Albion Chambers. Leading Barristers: *Christopher Ferguson* is a "safe pair of hands."

Southernhay Chambers (Tyzack), Exeter. A solid set with a large number of recommended juniors. Leading Barristers: *David Tyzack* has moved up to the top band following consistent praise for his ability and his "gentle manner which should not detract from the fact that he is a top rate lawyer." He is a "real people's person." *Hugh Lewis*, who specialises in children cases is well regarded, so is *George Meredith* who recently acted in a Court of Appeal case concerning the jurisdiction of the county court in family proceedings and the

LEADING SILKS · SOUTH WESTERN

EVANS Mark All Saints Chambers

LEADING JUNIORS
SOUTH WESTERN

SHARP Christopher St. John's Chambers
TYZACK David Southernhay Chambers
WILDBLOOD Stephen Albion Chambers

NAISH Christopher Southernhay Chambers

BROMILOW Richard St. John's Chambers
CAMPBELL Susan Southernhay Chambers
CORFIELD Sheelagh Guildhall Chambers
DINAN-HAYWARD Deborah Albion Chambers
DUTHIE Catriona Guildhall Chambers
FERGUSON Christopher Assize Court Chambers
HAIG-HADDOW Alastair Eighteen Carlton Cres
JACKLIN Susan St. John's Chambers
LEWIS Hugh Southernhay Chambers
MEREDITH George Southernhay Chambers
PINE-COFFIN Margaret Ann 17 Carlton Cres
WILLS-GOLDINGHAM Claire Albion Chambers
WRIGHT Caroline Albion Chambers

FOR DETAILS OF THESE LEADING BARRISTERS SEE PROFILES ON PAGES 1509-1642

power of the court to make assessment orders in care cases. *Christopher Naish* also has a good reputation for being "solid" and "thorough." *Susan Campbell* was singled out for both her finance and children work.

17 Carlton Crescent (Gibbons), Southampton. **Leading Barristers:** *Margaret Pine-Coffin* has been rated as "a good, solid advocate."

Eighteen Carlton Crescent (Haddow),

Southampton. The oldest set in Southampton, and strong on a variety of areas including family work, enabling it to compete strongly with Bristol. **Leading Barristers:** *Alastair Haig-Haddow* is rated both as a leading practitioner and as a writer in the field of matrimonial finance. Recent reported cases include 'Hill v Hill' (CA) concerning the effect of 25 years of cohabitation after a divorce on whether further capital can be claimed.

Guildhall Chambers (Royce), Bristol. Better known for its PI practice than family, but still rated in this area. **Leading Barristers:** *Catriona Duthie* "loves nothing more than a good scrap," – "she is a real fighter in court who gets stuck in on behalf of her clients." Recently involved in the 'Dawson v Wearmouth' case. *Sheelagh Corfield* is also considered "an efficient hard worker." She was recently involved in Richardson (No 2)1996.

WALES AND CHESTER CIRCUIT

30 Park Place (Richards), Cardiff. Has an "outstanding" name in the field of family law on the Welsh circuit, with 15 practitioners. **Leading Barristers:** *Jonathan Furness's* wide spread of work has earned him high praise this year: "absolutely wonderful," "a delight with clients" and "exceedingly bright" are just some of the comments. The "proficient" *James Tillyard* is particularly recommended for finance cases and *Jane Crowley QC* is considered very experienced in children cases.

32 Park Place (Williams), Cardiff. A common law chambers with an emphasis on crime and family law. **Leading Barristers:** Leading junior *Lynne Morgan* is seen as a "sound practitioner," dealing mainly in child care work, particularly on behalf of local authorities.

Iscoed Chambers (Davies), Swansea. **Leading Barristers:** *Ruth Henke* handles cases on behalf of several local authorities. Involved in Re T, a high profile childminders case.

33 Park Place (Williams), Cardiff. **Leading Barristers:** *Jill Walters* has been singled out for her sympathetic attitude towards her clients. She also sits as a Deputy District Judge.

9 Park Place (Murphy), Cardiff. Prestigious Cardiff set with strong criminal and civil divisions. **Leading Barristers:** *Isabel Parry* received glowing reports this year; she is the first choice of many practitioners – "very bright and able."

MIDLANDS AND OXFORD CIRCUIT

5 Fountain Court (Barker), Birmingham. The largest set outside London, boasting a sizeable team of experienced family law specialists. Over recent months their numbers have grown as practitioners have either defected from other sets or been

cherry-picked. Have suffered one loss though: Estella Hindley QC to the bench. **Leading Barristers:** The "top-notch" band of barristers dealing exclusively in family law include *Robin Rowland* (a recent acquisition from 1 Fountain Court) "an excellent lawyer: very careful and works hard for his clients". *Stephanie Brown* is considered a "formidable opponent" with a particular reputation as an ancillary relief specialist. "If I was in trouble I'd go to her," said one Midlands practitioner. *Christopher James* is a "hard worker" with "an excellent courtroom manner" and "a wonderful, rich voice," while *Anne Smallwood* is said to be "popular" and "gets a lot of work."

King Charles House (Everard), Nottingham. A first rate set with a particularly good matrimonial team. **Leading Barristers:** Noted for her children work *Rowena Bridge* has been praised for her "diligence," "commitment" and "professionalism." *Amanda Cranny* pays "attention to detail" and takes a great deal of care with every case.

Chambers of Colin Anderson (Anderson), Nottingham. With an excellent reputation, the set provides strong competition for King Charles House. **Leading Barristers:** The "determined and dogged" *Mairin Casey* has won praise for her child care work, while *Nigel Page* has been described as "the man for ancillary relief in Nottingham." Leading junior *Mark Rogers* is seen as "great chap," *Beryl Gilead* has "a loyal following" and *Stuart Farquhar* has been described as "very affable and good with clients."

Other leading lights on the circuit include "the approachable and personable" *Julia Macur QC* from **St Ives Chambers** (Coke) in Birmingham. From the same set *Margaret Hodgson* was also recommended. Practising from **St Philips Chambers** (Tedd) is *David Hershman* who co-writes 'Hershman and McFarlane'. At **6 Fountain Court** (Smith) in Birmingham, *Bryce Somerville* was praised for his "controlled yet persuasive manner" in ancillary relief court work. At **3 Fountain Court** (Treacy) *Sybil Thomas* is "extremely thorough."

NORTH EASTERN CIRCUIT

26 Paradise Square (Keen), Sheffield. The chambers covers every aspect of general common law with particular strength in the family and matrimonial division. **Leading Barristers:** Leading silk *Annabel Walker QC* has an extremely "quick mind" and produces quality work.

30 Park Square (Mellor), Leeds. Though this chambers offers the full range of common law, its strengths lie in crime and family work **Leading Barristers:** Focusing on children work "the very thorough" *Jill Black QC* has a reputation for being "a red hot lawyer" who is exceptionally good at dealing with difficult or novel points of law. She also writes and lectures. In 1997 her reported cases included 'Re C and F' (adoption and removal notice).

9 Woodhouse Square (Collins), Leeds. The family law department suffered a blow this year with the loss of Paul Isaacs and Raphael Cohen to the recently formed Mercury Chambers. The focus of the work has slightly changed as a result, with more emphasis on children cases. **Leading Barristers:** The "tenacious" *Roger Bickerdike* recently handled Re C & F 1997 (adoption and removal notice) and Re W (concerning the legal position of a homosexual adopter).

37 Park Square (Sleightholme and Ferm), Leeds. A medium-sized set offering a broad range of civil and chancery law services with a strong family practice. **Leading Barristers:** The "shrewd operator" *Rodney Ferm* retains his position as a top ranking junior following praise for his quick mind and ease with clients. Both he

and "the able" *Stephen Glover* are known for their private law ancillary relief work. *Amanda Ginsburg* is recommended for her public law child care work and is considered "a real trooper."

Park Lane Chambers (Bethel), Leeds. **Leading Barristers:** *Sally Cahill* is generally thought of as "a diligent worker" and a "tough operator" who thoroughly deserves her top ranking. Recent high profile cases include 'Re JA' 1998 (concerning a child abduction to a non-convention country and whether it was the duty of the court to determine the question of a peremptory return); and 'Re W' (concerning a local authority placing a child with a lesbian couple with a view to adoption).

Sovereign Chambers (Marson), Leeds. (Formerly 25 Park Square) **Leading Barristers:** Leading junior *Jayne Pye* is well respected amongst Northern circuit barristers and instructing solicitors. Involved in 'Re S' (1996), a leading child law case concerning whether an appellant should be able to intervene in proceedings.

6 Park Square (Spencer), Leeds. Well-established general common and civil law chambers. **Leading Barristers:** *Eleanor Hamilton* has a reputation for being "an astute operator" who "is good with clients." Leading cases include 'Re C 1996' (concerning disclosure); and 'Re V 1996' CA (concerning a supervision order).

Broad Chare Chambers (Elliot), Newcastle. The only Newcastle-based chambers with a significant family department. **Leading Barristers:** *Sally Bradley* is a child care and welfare specialist, seen to prepare her cases well. *Ian Kennerley* is "straightforward and open to deal with."

Mercury Court (Nilan), Leeds. Newly formed chambers consisting of eight, pitched at the more exclusive end of the market. Deal in areas such as insolvency, civil and company disputes and private client matrimonial work. **Leading Barristers:** Both *Paul Isaacs* and *Raphael Cohen* left 9 Woodhouse Square to join this fledgling chambers. Bringing with them a "top draw" caseload they specialise exclusively in matrimonial finance. Isaacs is seen to have energy, while Cohen is a "pleasant to deal with." Child care work is handled by a visiting silk.

Others Leading Barristers: Other leading juniors include *Jane Shipley* of **6 Park Square** (Spencer), Leeds who is said to be "entertaining opposition" and "a solid operator, with a lot of common sense." Cases include 'Re O' 1996 (concerning disclosure) and 'Re V' 1996 CA (concerning supervision orders.) *Anthony Hajimitsis* has recently moved to **10 Park Square** (Campbell), Leeds and has been described as "a safe pair of hands." *Gordon Shelton* of **Broadway House** (Levine), Bradford is "delightful."

NORTHERN CIRCUIT

The Corn Exchange (Steer & Goldrein), Liverpool. General common law set dealing mainly in the fields of crime, personal injury and family. **Leading Barristers:** *Margaret de Haas QC* has recently taken silk and is universally considered an "exceptional talent."

14 Castle Street (Lyon) Liverpool. **Leading barristers:** *Michael Sellars* is noted for his child care expertise and moves into the top band on the strength of local opinion; among other things, he is a "talented advocate with first rate judgement." *Christine Johnson's* "down to earth" approach and excellent work have also earned praise from instructing solicitors.

India Buildings Chambers (Harris), Liverpool. Good reputation among barristers and solicitors in the Liverpool area. Strong child care division which regularly acts for local authorities in child care cases. *David Harris QC*, "a shining star on the Northern Circuit" was accompanied by the "tough" and "talented" *Maureen Roddy* in 'Re C,' (a House of Lords hearing involving the power of the Court under s. 38 (6) of the Children Act to order a local authority to undertake a residential assessment of a family). *Gail Owen*, who has "a great rapport with clients," and "measured" *Ross Duggan* are also recommended.

Martins Building (Fordham), Liverpool. **Leading Barristers:** *Robert Fordham QC* is "a safe pair of hands" in the field of matrimonial finance.

40 King Street (Raynor), Manchester. **Leading Barristers:** The "superb" *Philip Raynor QC* has received high praise this year with one contemporary in the Manchester area claiming that "he cannot be beaten for ancillary relief cases." The "tough" *Sonia Gal* is also recommended.

28 St. John Street (Rumbelow), Manchester. **Leading Barristers:** With the loss of Charles Bloom QC to the bench this leaves *Lindsey Kushner QC* as the main family practitioner in chambers. She has an "excellent reputation" for both the quality of her matrimonial finance and child law work.

8 King Street (Armitage), Manchester. **Leading Barristers:** *Timothy Edge* is highly rated for his ancillary relief work.

Stephen Dodds of **15 Winckley Square** (Dodds) in Preston "takes no prisoners" — "he is a real tough nut, and highly competent." *Jane Walker* of **9 St John Street** (Hand), Manchester, is said to have a good rapport with clients, while *Gillian Irving* of the same set is "able and thorough." She has recently been involved in the high profile Ashworth enquiry.

Ernest Ryder QC has recently moved to **Deans Court Chambers** (Goddard). He has a mixed family practice and an excellent reputation. "He is one of the best practitioners in town," according to several interviewees.

FINANCIAL SERVICES

RESEARCH: Our rankings reflect the opinion of the marketplace as revealed by systematic and objective research: see page four. Our research is audited every year by the British Market Research Bureau.

LEADING SETS · LONDON

ERSKINE CHAMBERS (Richard Sykes QC)

BLACKSTONE CHAMBERS (Baxendale/Flint QC)
BRICK COURT CHAMBERS (Clarke QC)
3-4 SOUTH SQUARE (Michael Crystal QC)
4 STONE BUILDINGS (Philip Heslop QC)

ONE ESSEX COURT (Anthony Grabiner QC)
3 VERULAM BUILDINGS (R. Neville Thomas QC)

Erskine Chambers (Sykes) A respected company law set with expertise in financial services law. Seen mainly on non-contentious side. Leading Barristers: *Richard Sykes QC* (the "definitive barrister") is still the most widely and highly respected silk for financial services work. Particularly respected for providing opinions. The "excellent" *Robin Potts QC* drew praise, specifically for work on collective investments. *Richard Snowden* has a good reputation and "delivers some thoughtful opinions." Described by one leading financial services solicitor as the "junior of choice." *Martin Moore* enters our tables following recommendations; he gives "good practical advice" and has been doing a lot of work advising trusts on reduction of share capital.

Blackstone Chambers (Baxendale and Flint) A set with a growing reputation for financial services work, particularly on the contentious side. "Used by regulators and poachers." Move up a band in our tables. Leading Barristers: *Barbara Dohmann QC* has a strong reputation with both solicitors and regulators and moves up a band in our tables. Described as having a "very good mind" and seen as a good advocate. The "excellent" and "impressive" *Charles Flint QC* is praised for his advocacy skills. He has a good understanding of tribunals and is felt to present the right image. *Javan Herberg* moves up a band. He

was described by one regulator as a top junior for disciplinary work.

Brick Court Chambers (Clarke) Strong set with good silks. Leading Barristers: *Jonathan Sumption QC* ("exceptionally clever") has a reputation in many fields including financial services. *Nicholas Chambers QC* is also recommended, particularly for his "good approach to tribunals."

3-4 South Square (Crystal) Main reputation is for insolvency work but also have financial services capability. Leading Barristers: *Michael Crystal QC* ("tactician and advocate") is rated for financial services matters which have an insolvency angle. The "extremely clever" *John Higham QC* is also rated. Junior *Robin Knowles* was praised by a leading financial services solicitor for being alert to commercial aspects and great for litigation or advocacy.

4 Stone Buildings (Heslop) Leading Barristers: *Anthony George Bompas QC* and *Philip Heslop QC* ("equally good on his feet and for opinions") are leading silks.

One Essex Court (Grabiner) A commercial set whose work includes financial services. Leading Barristers: *Nicholas Strauss QC* has a reputation for acting for regulators. Junior *Laurence Rabinowitz* was described as "a bit of a star generally."

3 Verulam Buildings (Thomas) Leading Barristers: *William Blair QC* is rated for his financial services work by regulators, fellow barristers and solicitors in private practice. *Richard de Lacy* was praised for his "very good" opinions.

Head of Chambers *John Powell QC* at **2 Crown Office Row** moves up in our tables following many favourable comments. He is seen as a specialist who understands the issues and "reduces the difficult to a digestible form."

HEALTH & SAFETY

See also Consumer, Environmental law and Personal Injury

RESEARCH: In compiling the tables, we consider all the information available to us, paying particular regard to the market research carried out by our team of ten qualified lawyers. (The researchers' details are set out on page three.) The rankings, therefore, reflect the opinion of the market-place as revealed by systematic and objective research: see page four. (Our research is audited every year by the British Market Research Bureau.)

OVERVIEW: There is a limited amount of work for barristers in this area, but it is growing in importance and profile. Many sets will accept instructions on health and safety issues, but only a few barristers have built up a genuine exper-tise. Health and safety work at the bar includes acting in HSE prosecutions. Many health & safety practitioners act in anti-pollution cases, and are also list-ed in the environment section. The list also includes those with a reputation on the civil tort side.

1 Temple Gardens (Carlisle) The set most frequently associated with this type of work. Leading Barristers: *Hugh Carlisle QC* undertakes a great deal of heavy pros-ecution work for the HSE, and is "the first person health & safety practitioners turn to." *Dominic Grieve* and new silk *Ian Burnett QC* are also recommended.

Old Square Chambers (Williams) Work in health and safety is more directed towards the PI side, but members also do HSE prosecution and defence. **Leading Barristers:** *John Hendy QC* has a high pro-file, and is known for his writing on the area. *John Hand QC* mixes some health and safety with environment and employ-ment law. *Philip Mead* and *Charles Pugh* are involved in health and safety work, and also appear in the environmental list.

Geoffrey Nice QC of **Farrar's Building** (Elias) defends clients in HSE prosecu-tions. *William Stevenson QC* of **One Paper Buildings** (Slater) spends about 80% of his time on this type of work, and the "fantastically busy" *Jonathan Waite* combines HSE work with his employers liability and product liability work. *Michael Ford* of **Doughty Street Cham-bers** (Robertson) works exclusively from the PI angle. From **Devereux Chambers** (Burke) *Stephen Killalea* and *Christopher Goddard* defend companies in health and safety at work prosecutions. *Tim Briden* at **8 Stone Buildings** (Cherry) was also recommended.

REGIONS

Leading Barristers: In Birmingham *Mark Eades* and *Kevin O'Donovan* at **5 Fountain Court** (Barker) and in Manchester *Andrew Long* from **Peel Court Chambers** (Shorrock) are the recommended regional practitioners.

LEADING SILKS · LONDON

CARLISLE Hugh 1 Temple Gardens

HENDY John Old Square Chambers
NICE Geoffrey Farrar's Building

HAND John Old Square Chambers
STEVENSON William One Paper Buildings

NEW SILK · 1997 AND 1998

BURNETT Ian 1 Temple Gardens

LEADING JUNIORS · LONDON

BRIDEN Timothy 8 Stone Buildings
FORD Michael Doughty Street Chambers
GODDARD Christopher Devereux Chambers
GRIEVE Dominic 1 Temple Gardens
KILLALEA Stephen Devereux Chambers
MEAD Philip Old Square Chambers
PUGH Charles Old Square Chambers
WAITE Jonathan One Paper Buildings

FOR DETAILS OF THESE LEADING BARRISTERS
SEE PROFILES ON PAGES 1509-1642

LEADING JUNIORS
MIDLANDS & OXFORD

EADES Mark 5 Fountain Court
O'DONOVAN Kevin 5 Fountain Court

LEADING JUNIORS · NORTHERN

LONG Andrew Peel Court Chambers

FOR DETAILS OF THESE LEADING BARRISTERS
SEE PROFILES ON PAGES 1509-1642

IMMIGRATION

RESEARCH: In compiling the tables, we consider all the information available to us, paying particular regard to the market research carried out by our team of ten qualified lawyers. (The researchers' details are set out on page three.) The rankings, therefore, reflect the opinion of the marketplace as revealed by systematic and objective research: see page four. (Our research is audited every year by the British Market Research Bureau.)

Barristers' profiles   p. 1509-1642

LEADING SETS · LONDON

TWO GARDEN COURT (Macdonald QC & Davies)

HIGHLY REGARDED

Blackstone Chambers (Baxendale QC/Flint QC)
Doughty Street Chambers (Robertson QC)
39 Essex Street (Edwin Glasgow QC)
6 King's Bench Walk (Sibghat Kadri QC)
14 Tooks Court (Michael Mansfield QC)

Enfield Chambers (Adrian Hall)
Plowden Buildings (William Lowe QC)

Two Garden Court (Macdonald & Davis) Undoubtedly the top immigration set, with two silks and seven juniors listed as leading in their field. **Leading Barristers:** The pre-eminent practitioner is universally accepted to be the "intellectually astute" *Nicholas Blake QC*. Joint head of chambers *Owen Davies* also undertakes respected immigration work, as does *Ian Macdonald QC* who is "liked by solicitors and clients for his common sense." The "approachable" *Laurie Fransman* is deemed to be the best nationality lawyer in the country. "Dynamic" *Richard Scannell* is thought as good as most silks on general immigration work, and also well known is the "detail conscious and unassuming" *Frances Webber*. The "combative and committed" *Stephanie Harrison* is known for her asylum work, and also in the second band of leading juniors is the "extremely thorough and knowledgeable" *Raza Husain*. He appeared for the applicant in the 'Adan' case. *Duran Seddon* has been elevated from up and coming, and is described as "thorough, good in court and with clients."

Blackstone Chambers (formerly 2 Hare Court) (Baxendale & Flint) An eminent public law set which acts predominently for the respondent. **Leading Barristers:** *David Pannick QC* performs distinguished work for the Government, and is considered an "incredibly measured and effective advocate."

Doughty Street Chambers (Robertson) Famous for their civil liberties work,

some members have respected immigration practices. **Leading Barristers:** The "enormously capable" *Andrew Nicol QC* is noted for his public law expertise. *Nadine Finch* is regarded as good on cases involving family or child issues.

39 Essex Street (Glasgow) Act for applicants and respondents, but chambers are mainly associated with judicial review work for the respondent. **Leading Barristers:** Particularly recommended were *Nigel Pleming QC* and *Alison Foster,* who has a "wonderful manner." *Robert Jay QC* has taken silk this year.

6 King's Bench Walk (Kadri) Well known for protecting the rights of ethnic minorities in the criminal and public law fields. **Leading Barristers:** Head of chambers *Sibghat Kadri QC* is a leading immigration silk. The "excellent" *Manjit Gill* is "good at novel arguments," and figured in the 'Canbolat' case. Also recommended is the "down to earth" *Harjit Grewal*, who mixes immigration work with a general family, employment and racial discrimination practice. For the first time *Rambert De Mello* enters the list. He has brought a respected immigration practice from the Midlands and is considered an excellent advocate. He recently appeared in the 'Remelien' case in the Lords.

14 Tooks Court (Mansfield) **Leading Barristers:** *Martin Soorjoo* is "thorough, and can be forceful," and, on recommendation, has moved up to the middle band of leading juniors. In the same category is *Leon Daniel*, who is considered "very good in court." He also appeared in the 'Remelien' case.

Enfield Chambers (Hall) Have four tenants who specialise in immigration. **Leading Barristers:** The "succinct" *James Gillespie* is regularly instructed on judicial review or appeal work.

Plowden Buildings (Lowe) Recently merged with 3 Paper Buildings, and have a respected young team of immigration practitioners. **Leading Barristers:** *John Walsh* has been elevated from the up and coming section, and entering the list for the

LEADING SILKS · LONDON

BLAKE Nicholas Two Garden Court

BELOFF Michael 4-5 Gray's Inn Square
KADRI Sibghat 6 King's Bench Walk
MACDONALD Ian Two Garden Court
NICOL Andrew Doughty Street Chambers
PANNICK David Blackstone Chambers
PLEMING Nigel 39 Essex Street
PLENDER Richard 20 Essex Street

NEW SILKS · 1997 AND 1998

JAY Robert 39 Essex Street

LEADING JUNIORS · LONDON

FRANSMAN Laurie Two Garden Court
GILLESPIE James Enfield Chambers
SCANNELL Richard Two Garden Court

DANIEL Leon 14 Tooks Court
HARRISON Stephanie Two Garden Court
HUSAIN Raza Two Garden Court
O'DEMPSEY Declan 4 Brick Court
SOORJOO Martin 14 Tooks Court
WEBBER Frances Two Garden Court

BEALE Judith Blackstone Chambers
COX Buster 1 Gray's Inn Square
DAVIES Owen Two Garden Court
DE MELLO Rambert 6 King's Bench Walk
DIAS Asoka 1 Gray's Inn Square
EICKE Tim Francis Taylor Building
FINCH Nadine Doughty Street Chambers
FOSTER Alison 39 Essex Street
GILL Manjit 6 King's Bench Walk
GREWAL Harjit 6 King's Bench Walk
LIVINGSTON John 3 Hare Court
SEDDON Duran Two Garden Court
SHAW Mark Blackstone Chambers
SHRIMPTON Michael Francis Taylor Building
WALSH John Plowden Buildings
WEERERATNE Aswini Doughty Street Chambers

UP AND COMING · LONDON

COX Simon Plowden Buildings
FARBEY Judith Plowden Buildings
HENDERSON Sophie Plowden Buildings

LEADING SILKS · NORTHERN

HUSSAIN Mukhtar Lincoln House Chambers

FOR DETAILS OF THESE LEADING BARRISTERS
SEE PROFILES ON PAGES 1509-1642

first time are the "excellent" *Sophie Henderson* and *Simon Cox*, and the "effective" *Judith Farbey,* who is appreciated for her "realistic advice."

INSOLVENCY

RESEARCH: Our rankings reflect the opinion of the marketplace as revealed by systematic and objective research: see page four. Our research is audited every year by the British Market Research Bureau.

LEADING SETS · LONDON

3-4 SOUTH SQUARE (Michael Crystal QC)

ERSKINE CHAMBERS (Richard Sykes QC)

13 OLD SQUARE (Michael Lyndon-Stanford QC)

4 STONE BUILDINGS (Philip Heslop QC)

ENTERPRISE CHAMBERS (Anthony Mann QC)

ONE ESSEX COURT (Anthony Grabiner QC)

1 NEW SQUARE (Eben Hamilton QC)

SERLE COURT CHAMBERS (Charles Sparrow QC)

11 STONE BUILDINGS (Michael Beckman QC)

3-4 South Square (Crystal) The "pre-eminent" insolvency set; there is "no need to go elsewhere," according to several practitioners. Some felt they were better at senior rather than junior level but generally the whole chambers are "approachable and have the respect of the Bench." **Work Handled:** 'Middle Eastern Trading v Lehman Bros.' **Leading Barristers:** *Michael Crystal QC* is acknowledged by all as "immensely knowledgeable" and "a good fighter." The "delightful" *Gabriel Moss QC* is "approachable" and "a good all-rounder." *Simon Mortimore QC* gained kudos in the Barings matters where he acted for the liquidator. *Richard Adkins QC* is a "purist" doing "big ticket restructurings," while *Richard Sheldon QC* is "thorough and good in court." New silk *Richard Hacker QC* was consistently rated ("combines technical excellence with a practical approach"). Juniors particularly praised include *John Briggs* ("down to earth," "good at partnership matters"), and *Robin Dicker*, ("phenomenally bright, concise and persuasive" – "he holds his own against heavyweight silks and judges listen to him.") *Fidelis Oditah* ("ex-don from Merton," "quick witted"), *Martin Pascoe* ("approachable and sensible"), *Mark Phillips* ("good on his feet," "always on top of the work") and *Hilary Stonefrost* ("extremely good; junior but talented") were particularly recommended.

Erskine Chambers (Sykes) One of the sets getting the important work. **Work Handled:** Advising in respect of a substantial claim for fraudulent trading against the liquidators of BCCI (Stubbs). Acting for the administrator of Barings on proposals including a scheme of arrangement designed to compromise disputes in the liquidation. 'Re: H&K (Medway) Ltd.' (1997) for the administrative receivers on the construction of s. 40 Insolvency Act. **Leading Barristers:** Include *Robin Potts QC* ("technically good" – seen as more company work oriented), *Richard Sykes QC* ("pre-eminent on company work and good on insolvency too") and a real insolvency specialist *Leslie Kosmin QC*. Particularly recommended juniors include *Sir Thomas Stockdale* who is said to have a good paper-based practice and knows everything there is to know about schemes of arrangement.

13 Old Square (Lyndon-Stanford) A general commercial set with some good insolvency expertise. **Work Handled:** 'Plant v Plant' (1998), concerning voluntary arrangements (Trace QC). 'Re Galileo Group Ltd' (1998) (Collings). 'Re Richbell Strategic Holdings Ltd' (1997) (Newman QC). **Leading Barristers:** Include *Catherine Newman QC* and *Hazel Williamson QC* ("good general expertise"). Noted juniors include the well-known *Matthew Collings* and *John Nicholls* who is said to have an excellent general practice.

4 Stone Buildings (Heslop) **Work Handled:** 'Re H&K (Medway) Ltd' (1997) (Griffiths for the liquidator; concerning priority of preferential creditors). 'MCC Proceeds Inc v Lehman Brothers' (1998) whether claim for conversion maintainable against purchaser of shares. 'Re Barton Manufacturing Co. Ltd' – misfeasance/ Insolvency Act s. 238. **Leading Barristers:** *Philip Heslop QC* is known for his involvement in the BCCI affair; *Anthony Bompas QC* commands respect with judges, while *John Brisby QC* is seen as a tough opponent. Juniors include the brilliant *Jonathan Crow* who is now First Treasury Counsel.

Enterprise Chambers (Mann) A progressive set with a good reputation for insolvency work. **Work Handled:** 'TSB v Platts' (1997), the extent to which a non-petition debt can be used to defeat a set-off claimed by a debtor in bankruptcy. 'AFC Bournemouth' – acting in sucessful CVA, and then successfully opposing creditor's challenge to CVA. 'Re: Edennote Ltd (No 2)' (1997) – acting for liquidator in part of the Sugar/Venables saga. **Leading Barristers:** Head of chambers *Anthony Mann QC* ("good to deal with") and *Linden Ife* are recommended.

One Essex Court (Grabiner) Seen as a first rate set. **Work Handled:** Continuing to act for the administrators of Barings. 'Mettalloy (Supplies) Ltd v M.A. (UK) Ltd' – costs of a liquidator in litigation conducted in the name of the company in liquidation. **Leading Barristers:** Consistently praised *Elizabeth Gloster QC* is "first rate" and a "star," while *Terence Mowschenson QC* is seen as "pragmatic." New silk *Jeffery Onions QC* is highly rated. Juniors include the well regarded *Anthony de Garr Robinson* .

General: Leading Barristers: *Eben Hamilton QC* and *Robin Hollington* of **1 New Square** (Hamilton) are highly rated, particularly for their personal insolvency expertise. The "wonderfully sound and helpful" *Michael Briggs QC* of **Serle Court Chambers** (Sparrow) was recommended again, for advocacy as well as opinions. From **11 Stone Buildings** (Beckman), three juniors were particularly recommended: the practical and knowledgeable *Marcia Shekerdemian, Jane Giret* and *Raquel Agnello.*

THE WESTERN CIRCUIT

St. John's Chambers (Denyer) Well regarded Bristol set providing good quality insolvency expertise. **Work Handled:** 'Re Atlantic Computers.' 'Re Barton Manufacturing Company Ltd.' **Leading Barristers:** *Roger Kaye QC* whose main chambers is 24 Old Buildings in London, also practises insolvency from these chambers. He is well regarded for Court of Appeal work and is often instructed by the Treasury Solicitor.

College Chambers (Belben) Well regarded by many local practitioners. **Leading Barristers:** *Derek Marshall* has a varied practice, including some good insolvency work.

Guildhall Chambers (Royce) This excellent set is particularly rated for some good insolvency juniors. **Work Handled:** 'TSB Bank plc v Platts' (No 2) (1998). 'S of S v Martin' (1998). 'Re Keenan' (1998). **Leading Barristers:** The "awesome" *Stephen Davies, Paul French* and *Jeremy Bamford* were all highly recommended.

LEADING SILKS · WESTERN
KAYE Roger St John's Chambers

LEADING JUNIORS · WESTERN
BAMFORD Jeremy Guildhall Chambers
DAVIES Stephen Guildhall Chambers
FRENCH Paul Guildhall Chambers
MARSHALL Derek College Chambers

THE MIDLANDS AND OXFORD CIRCUIT

All the recommended sets are in Birmingham. At **5 Fountain Court** (Barker), a specialist commercial and chancery group handles insolvency work. Well reputed juniors are *David Stockill, Stephen Whitaker* and *Sara Williams*. At **6 Fountain Court** (Smith) *Avtar Khangure*, new to our list this year, is praised as "very experienced with excellent technical

LEADING JUNIORS · LONDON	
ATHERTON Stephen 3-4 South Square	**MCQUATER Ewan** 3 Verulam Buildings
BRIGGS John 3-4 South Square	**ODITAH Fidelis** 3-4 South Square
CHIVERS David Erskine Chambers	**PASCOE Martin** 3-4 South Square
COLLINGS Matthew 13 Old Square	**PHILLIPS Mark** 3-4 South Square
CROW Jonathan 4 Stone Buildings	**PREVEZER Susan** Essex Court Chambers
DICKER Robin 3-4 South Square	**SNOWDEN Richard** Erskine Chambers
GIRET Jane 11 Stone Buildings	**STOCKDALE BT Sir Thomas** Erskine Chambers
GRIFFITHS Peter 4 Stone Buildings	**STONEFROST Hilary** 3-4 South Square
IFE Linden Enterprise Chambers	**TAMLYN Lloyd** 3-4 South Square
KNOWLES Robin 3-4 South Square	**TROWER William** 3-4 South Square
AGNELLO Raquel 11 Stone Buildings	**JOFFE Victor** Serle Court Chambers
ALEXANDER David 3-4 South Square	**KING Michael** 24 Old Buildings
ARDEN Peter Enterprise Chambers	**MARKS David** 3-4 South Square
ARNOLD Mark 3-4 South Square	**MILES Robert** 4 Stone Buildings
DE GARR ROBINSON Anthony One Essex Court	**MILLETT Richard** Essex Court Chambers
DE LACY Richard 3 Verulam Buildings	**NICHOLLS John** 13 Old Square
GIROLAMI Paul 13 Old Square	**RITCHIE Richard** 24 Old Buildings
GOODISON Adam 3-4 South Square	**SHEKERDEMIAN Marcia** 11 Stone Buildings
GREEN Michael Fountain Court	**TALBOT RICE Elspeth** 24 Old Buildings
HILLIARD Lexa 3-4 South Square	**TOUBE Felicity** 3-4 South Square
HOLLINGTON Robin 1 New Square	**ZACAROLI Antony** 3-4 South Square
HOSER Philip Serle Court Chambers	

knowledge." 7 Fountain Court has merged with 2 Fountain Court to become **Saint Philips Chambers** (Tedd). They have a well earned reputation for good quality insolvency work. *Anna-Rose Landes* is rated by fellow barristers and solicitors.

LEADING JUNIORS   **MIDLANDS & OXFORD**
STOCKILL David 5 Fountain Court
KHANGURE Avtar No.6 Fountain Court
LANDES Anna-Rose St Philip's Chambers
WHITAKER Stephen 5 Fountain Court
WILLIAMS Sara 5 Fountain Court

THE NORTHERN/ NORTH EASTERN CIRCUIT

40 King Street (Raynor), Manchester. A busy set good for all round Chancery matters including insolvency. **Leading Barristers:** Highly recommended and sought after by practitioners, *Peter Smith QC* can be difficult to instruct because he is so busy. *Katherine Dunn* is similarly "hard to get hold of because she is so popular." *Paul Chaisty* is seen as "commercial, practical and also extremely busy," while *Lesley Anderson* is praised for her "assertive and practical" manner.

At **Chancery House Chambers** (Allen) in Leeds *James Allen QC*, head of chambers, has years of experience and is "unquestionably a leader." *Paul Morris* is their

leading junior for insolvency work and is seen as "methodical and steady."

Mark Cawson at **St James' Chambers** (Sterling) in Manchester is praised by instructing solicitors for giving a very good service; he is "bright, good on paper and knows local judges very well."

Hugo Groves at **Enterprise Chambers** (Mann) in Leeds is "a name people don't hesitate to use." He was praised for his in-depth insolvency knowledge, his technical skills and his practical, proactive approach.

Edward Bartley Jones QC and *John McCarroll* at **Exchange Chambers** (Waldron) in Liverpool have been particularly recommended this year.

LEADING SILKS · NORTHERN
JONES Edward Exchange Chambers
SMITH Peter 40 King St

LEADING JUNIORS · NORTHERN
ANDERSON Lesley 40 King St
CAWSON Mark St. James's Chambers
CHAISTY Paul 40 King St
DUNN Katherine 40 King St
MCCARROLL John Exchange Chambers

LEADING SILKS · NORTH EASTERN
ALLEN James Chancery House Chambers

LEADING JUNIORS   **NORTH EASTERN**
GROVES Hugo Enterprise Chambers
MORRIS Paul Chancery House Chambers

INSURANCE & REINSURANCE

RESEARCH: In compiling the tables, we consider all the information available to us, paying particular regard to the market research carried out by our team of ten qualified lawyers. (The researchers' details are set out on page three.) The rankings, therefore, reflect the opinion of the marketplace as revealed by systematic and objective research: see page four. (Our research is audited every year by the British Market Research Bureau.)

OVERVIEW: In general the leading figures were well known to each other, and the only difficulty in researching the section was the nature of insurance and reinsurance work. 'Insurance' covers an extremely broad field and the tables include counsel who handle contentious and non-contentious (approval of schemes), general claims or reinsurance work. There has been little movement among the sets with Essex Court Chambers still considered pre-eminent. Those sets considered strong in insurance tend to be those which also feature prominently in commercial and banking work. The work is concentrated in London and there was only one new entry among counsel, William Wood QC of Brick Court Chambers, suggesting that instructions are increasingly concentrated on a select number of trusted individuals.

LEADING SETS · LONDON
ESSEX COURT CHAMBERS (Pollock QC)
BRICK COURT CHAMBERS (Clarke QC)
7 KING'S BENCH WALK (Tomlinson QC)
ONE ESSEX COURT (Anthony Grabiner QC)
FOUNTAIN COURT (Peter Scott QC)

HIGHLY REGARDED · LONDON
20 Essex Street (David Johnson QC)
4 Pump Court (Bruce Mauleverer QC)
3 Verulam Buildings (R. Neville Thomas QC)

Essex Court Chambers (Pollock) This well-respected set remains in a class of its own for the large number of high quality silks and juniors doing insurance work. **Leading Barristers:** Head of chambers, *Gordon Pollock QC* has long been seen as "one of the heavyweights" of the bar and a "brilliant advocate." *Stewart Boyd QC* is a top class insurance silk, and led in 'Baker v Black Sea & Baltic General Insurance.' *Bernard Eder QC*, whose recent work has included 'AIG Europe v GALT,' was praised for his "tenacity and ingenuity." *David Foxton* has risen in our rankings following many strong recommendations. He has been involved on a number of interlocutory applications in connection with the Lloyds litigation.

Brick Court Chambers (Clarke) A set which includes some of the top names at the bar, not only for insurance and reinsurance, but also for banking and commercial work. Several ranked members of the set (*Hirst QC*, *Kentridge QC*, *Popplewell QC*) were instructed on one of the major cases of the past year, 'Browne v GIO,' while the "absolutely top notch" *Christopher Clarke QC* was the leader on 'Ashton v Black Sea and Baltic' [HL]. **Leading Barristers:** *Richard Aikens QC* was described as "outstanding for his thorough and knowledgeable approach," *Sydney Kentridge QC* as "godlike." *Jonathan Sumption QC* has "a brain the size of a planet," and led *George Leggatt QC* in 'Commercial Union v NRG Victory Reinsurance.' The "red hot" *Mark Howard QC* also received considerable praise and most commentators felt he "will be a major star." New silk *William Wood QC* enters our tables for the first time on recommendation.

7 King's Bench Walk (Tomlinson) **Leading Barristers:** Among the highly regarded silks at this set are the "doughty" *Jeremy Cooke QC* and the "punchy" *Jonathan Gaisman QC.* Gaisman led in 'Eide v Lowndes Lambert.' The "D'Artagnan-like" figure of *Gavin Kealey QC* has been promoted to our second band following universal praise for his "rumbustious" style. He led on 'Den

---

Barristers' profiles   **p. 1509-1642**

LEADING SILKS · LONDON
AIKENS Richard Brick Court Chambers
BOSWOOD Anthony Fountain Court
BOYD Stewart Essex Court Chambers
CLARKE Christopher Brick Court Chambers
COOKE Jeremy 7 King's Bench Walk
CRANE Michael Fountain Court
EDER Bernard Essex Court Chambers
FLAUX Julian 7 King's Bench Walk
GRABINER Anthony One Essex Court
KENTRIDGE Sydney Brick Court Chambers
POLLOCK Gordon Essex Court Chambers
SUMPTION Jonathan Brick Court Chambers
TOMLINSON Stephen 7 King's Bench Walk
VEEDER V.V. Essex Court Chambers

EDELMAN Colin Devereux Chambers
GAISMAN Jonathan 7 King's Bench Walk
GROSS Peter 20 Essex Street
HAMILTON Adrian 7 King's Bench Walk
HUNTER Ian Essex Court Chambers
KEALEY Gavin 7 King's Bench Walk
SYMONS Christopher 3 Verulam Buildings
TEMPLE Anthony 4 Pump Court

COLLINS Michael Essex Court Chambers
CORDARA Roderick Essex Court Chambers
CRAN Mark Brick Court Chambers
DEHN Conrad Fountain Court
DOHMANN Barbara Blackstone Chambers
DONALDSON David Blackstone Chambers
FIELD Richard 11 King's Bench Walk
GEE Steven One Essex Court
GRUDER Jeffrey One Essex Court
HILDYARD Robert 4 Stone Buildings
HIRST Jonathan Brick Court Chambers
HOWARD Mark Brick Court Chambers
KENDRICK Dominic 7 King's Bench Walk
LEGGATT George Brick Court Chambers
MOWSCHENSON Terence One Essex Court
POPPLEWELL Andrew Brick Court Chambers
RAILTON David Fountain Court
ROWLAND John 4 Pump Court
RUTTLE Stephen Brick Court Chambers
SALOMAN Timothy 7 King's Bench Walk
SIMON Peregrine Brick Court Chambers
SMITH Andrew Fountain Court
VOS Geoffrey 3 Stone Buildings

NEW SILKS · 1997 AND 1998
JACOBS Richard Essex Court Chambers
ONIONS Jeffery One Essex Court
WOOD William Brick Court Chambers

FOR DETAILS OF THESE LEADING BARRISTERS
SEE PROFILES ON PAGES 1509-1642

Danske Bank and Nomura Bank v Kleinwort Benson.' The juniors receiving most frequent recommendation were *Christopher Butcher*, who appeared in the 'Yasuda Fire and Marine Insurance' case, and the "highly committed" *Stephen Hofmeyr*. The "excellent"*Alistair Schaff* is "on the way up" and recently acted on 'State of the Netherlands v Youell.'

One Essex Court (Grabiner) **Leading Barristers:** Solicitors and barristers alike recommended *Anthony Grabiner QC* who is "part of the insurance establishment." He recently led on 'Society of Lloyds v Frazer' [CA]. *Steven Gee QC* is "very strong intellectually." *Jeffrey Gruder QC* was felt to have established himself as a silk and acted on 'Proudfoot v Federal Insurance Co' and 'Euro Diam Ltd v Bathurst.' *Jeffery Onions QC* is a new silk. He received many recommendations for his work.

Fountain Court (Scott) **Leading Barristers:** *Anthony Boswood QC*, who was instructed on 'Arab Bank v Zurich Assurance,' is "highly effective," while *David Railton QC* is "an efficient

---

performer." Several people praised the "very bright" *Stephen Moriarty*.

20 Essex Street (Johnson) **Leading Barristers:** The "very sound" *Peter Gross QC* has "extremely good judgement," while *David Owen* received unanimous praise, lifting him to the top band of juniors.

4 Pump Court (Mauleverer) **Leading Barristers:** Three members were singled out for praise: *Anthony Temple QC, John

Rowland QC and *Nigel Tozzi*.

3 Verulam Buildings (Thomas) **Leading Barristers:** *Christopher Symons QC* was described as "extremely thorough," while popular junior *Rory Phillips* is seen as "a very good manager of cases" who "gets to the heart of the matter." Both were instructed on 'Hamptons v Field.'

INTELLECTUAL PROPERTY (& COMPUTER/IT)

RESEARCH: In compiling the tables, we consider all the information available to us, paying particular regard to the market research carried out by our team of ten qualified lawyers. (The researchers' details are set out on page three.) The rankings, therefore, reflect the opinion of the marketplace as revealed by systematic and objective research: see page four. (Our research is audited every year by the British Market Research Bureau.)

OVERVIEW: To research this section we interviewed solicitors, barristers, clerks, patent and trade mark agents, and pharmaceutical companies. We continue to place IP and Computer/IT in the same section because the sets and tenants recommended are similar.

Barristers' profiles   p. 1509-1642

LEADING SILKS · LONDON

FLOYD **Christopher** 11 South Square
HOBBS **Geoffrey** One Essex Court
KITCHIN **David** 8 New Square
PRESCOTT **Peter** 8 New Square
THORLEY **Simon** Three New Square
WATSON **Antony** Three New Square

BALDWIN **John** 8 New Square
MORCOM **Christopher** One Raymond Buildings
SILVERLEAF **Michael** 11 South Square
WILSON **Alastair** 19 Old Buildings
YOUNG **David** Three New Square

FYSH **Michael** 8 New Square
HOWE **Martin** 8 New Square
MILLER **Richard** Three New Square
PLATTS-MILLS **Mark** 8 New Square

NEW SILKS · 1997 AND 1998

BLOCH **Michael** One Essex Court
CARR **Henry** 11 South Square
VITORIA **Mary** 8 New Square
WAUGH **Andrew** Three New Square
WYAND **Roger** One Raymond Buildings

FOR DETAILS OF THESE LEADING BARRISTERS SEE PROFILES ON PAGES 1509-1642

LEADING SETS · LONDON

THREE NEW SQUARE (David Young QC)
8 NEW SQUARE (Michael Fysh QC)
11 SOUTH SQUARE (Christopher Floyd QC)

HIGHLY REGARDED · LONDON

One Essex Court (Anthony Grabiner QC)
19 Old Buildings (Alastair Wilson QC)
One Raymond Buildings (Morcom QC)

Three New Square (Young) Have a historical reputation for heavy patent work, but members practise in all areas of IP. **Leading Barristers:** The "outstanding" *Simon Thorley QC* is one of the leading patent silks, and is popular with clients because he is "easy to work with" and "works well in a team." The "user friendly" *Antony Watson QC* is also rated for his patent work, and has "extremely good judgment." Head of Chambers *David Young QC* is seen as a "details man," and *Richard Miller QC* is "a good performer in court." The "completely reliable" *Andrew Waugh QC* is known for his pharmaceutical work, and "gives very clear advice." *Guy Burkill* is perceived to be a good all-rounder, having command of technical matters, and being both good on paper and on his feet. *Colin Birss* has been promoted a band due to many recommendations. *Denise McFarland* is "effective and user friendly" and "particularly good with clients." *Douglas Campbell* and *Justin Turner* have both been placed in the leading juniors section for the first time.

8 New Square (Fysh) Are the largest of the three main intellectual property chambers in London. Tenants undertake a wide range of IP work, and traditionally have a more balanced spread of work than other specialist chambers. In 1997 Nick Shea retired from the bar. **Leading Barristers:** *David Kitchin QC*, regarded as one of the finest IP barristers, is "very bright." He is an "outstanding cross-examiner," and his "will to win sets him apart." The "idiosyncratic" *Peter Prescott QC* has an "unconventional" style, is "extremely clever on the law" and "devastating" in court. Head of chambers *Michael Fysh QC* practices all over the world, and has "unparalleled experience." He is described as "enthusiastic and solid." *Martin Howe QC* joins the ranks of leading silks, and is known for his work on electronics. *Mark Platts-Mills QC* is "not afraid to run difficult points," and *Mary Vitoria QC* is well regarded for her "disciplined and detailed" paperwork. *Daniel Alexander* is considered "as good as the silks." *James Mellor* is "incredibly tenacious" and "engages the judge's attention." *Richard Meade* has an excellent reputation, and *Adrian Speck* is also a recognised talent. *Michael Tappin* has been raised a band due to a general consensus that he is "very bright" and a "good all-rounder." *Fiona Clark* is "very commercial, pragmatic and forthright," and for the first time the "very solid" *George Hamer* enters the list. He has "good sound judgement."

11 South Square (Floyd) Have been elevated to the highest band of leading chambers after many recommendations from solicitors. **Leading Barristers:** Head of chambers *Christopher Floyd QC* is "a little conservative," but "judge friendly" and "effective." It is said that he has "an extraordinary strike rate in the European Patent Office." Recently involved in 'Buehler AG v Chronos Richardson.' The

"very highly rated" *Michael Silverleaf QC* has been promoted to the middle band of leading silks. He has broad experience of all IP work, but is singled out as "good on technology." *Henry Carr QC* is "devastating in cross-examination," and is regarded as a leader in the IP aspects of computers. *Richard Arnold* is "mentally quick and thorough," and a "good fighter." The "understated" *Richard Hacon* has been elevated one place, and is recognised particularly for his bio-tech work. He also acted in 'Mecklermedia v DC Congress.' *Heather Lawrence* is also a chemistry specialist. The "approachable" *Iain Purvis* is a highly recommended junior who is "crystal clear, and sees the important point straight away." The very experienced *Henry Whittle* is recommended for his "thoroughness."

One Essex Court (Grabiner) **Leading Barristers:** The "genial" *Geoffrey Hobbs QC* is described as "smooth, clever and personable." He has an "encyclopaedic knowledge of the law" on soft IP, and is "not afraid to tell you if you are wrong." *Michael Bloch QC* has been made up to silk this year, and *Emma Himsworth* is "very approachable," "a good battler and a rising star."

19 Old Buildings (Wilson) Leading Barristers: Head of chambers *Alastair Wilson QC* is described as "imaginative," and *Michael Hicks* features in the leading juniors section. *Graham Shipley* is described as a "good tactician and commercially aware."

One Raymond Buildings (Morcom) Leading Barristers: *Christopher Morcom QC* is renowned as a trademark specialist, and is admired in particular for his advisory work. *Roger Wyand QC* has "quite a presence," and "is good with solicitors, clients and judges." *Guy Tritton* was recently involved in 'Flyde Microsystems v Key Radio Systems.'

LEADING JUNIORS • LONDON

ALEXANDER Daniel 8 New Square	**BURKILL Guy** Three New Square
ARNOLD Richard 11 South Square	**MELLOR James** 8 New Square
BIRSS Colin Three New Square	**MEADE Richard** 8 New Square
HACON Richard 11 South Square	**SHIPLEY Graham** 19 Old Buildings
HAMER George 8 New Square	**SPECK Adrian** 8 New Square
HICKS Michael 19 Old Buildings	**TAPPIN Michael** 8 New Square
ASHTON Arthur One Raymond Buildings	**PURVIS Iain** 11 South Square
CAMPBELL Douglas Three New Square	**TRITTON Guy** One Raymond Buildings
CLARK Fiona 8 New Square	**TURNER Jonathan** 4 Field Court
HIMSWORTH Emma One Essex Court	**TURNER Justin** Three New Square
LAWRENCE Heather 11 South Square	**VANHEGAN Mark** 11 South Square
MCFARLAND Denise Three New Square	**WHITTLE Henry** 11 South Square
ONSLOW Robert 8 New Square	

FOR DETAILS OF THESE LEADING BARRISTERS SEE PROFILES ON PAGES 1509-1642

COMPUTER/IT

OVERVIEW: Barristers who practise in the field of IT law usually deal with cases relating to the performance of information technology systems. These cases are often contractual disputes, but require familiarity with computers. The IT bar is composed of two distinct types of individual practice: those from the IP bar, and those from the commercial sets.

LEADING SETS • LONDON

8 NEW SQUARE (Michael Fysh QC)
11 SOUTH SQUARE (Christopher Floyd QC)

THREE NEW SQUARE (David Young QC)
19 OLD BUILDINGS (Alastair Wilson QC)

ATKIN CHAMBERS (John Blackburn QC)

8 New Square (Fysh) A pre-eminent intellectual property set with four leading silks in the IT field. Leading Barristers: *John Baldwin QC* is a "clear and concise advocate who is willing to listen," and is the only IP specialist to appear in the top rankings. *David Kitchin QC* has "got it all," *Martin Howe QC* is "excellent on electronics," and *Richard Meade* also appears as a leading junior.

11 South Square (Floyd) Leading Barristers: *Michael Silverleaf QC* has an "aggressive approach," and is admired for his IT work. *Henry Carr QC* has been described as the "top IT barrister in the country," and he "understands computers and software." *Richard Arnold* is also recommended. Although she is a chemistry specialist, *Heather Lawrence* enters the list due to recommendations of her high quality IT work.

Three New Square (Young) Leading Barristers: *Guy Burkill* has been described

as a "genius at IT," particularly on advice. New silk *Andrew Waugh QC* is known for his chemicals expertise, but is also "extremely respected" for computer work. *Colin Birss* also has experience of the IT industry.

19 Old Buildings (Wilson) Leading Barristers: *Alastair Wilson QC* is described as "very clever" and "computer technically literate." *Graham Shipley* and *Rory Sullivan* also appear in the list.

Atkin Chambers (Blackburn) Leading Barristers: *John Blackburn QC* and *Andrew White QC* appear as leading IT silks. The "astute" *David Streatfield-James* appears in the top band of leading juniors, and *Dominique Rawley* is also recommended.

Other individuals that came in for particular comment this year include the "responsive and pragmatic" *Nicholas Davidson QC* at **4 Paper Buildings** (McGregor); the "very user friendly" *Patrick Twigg QC* at **2 Temple Gardens** and the "absolutely excellent" *Michael Bloch QC* at **One Essex Court** (Grabiner).

LEADING SILKS • LONDON

BALDWIN John 8 New Square
BLACKBURN John Atkin Chambers
DAVIDSON Nicholas 4 Paper Buildings
BRINDLE Michael Fountain Court
HOWE Martin 8 New Square
KITCHIN David 8 New Square
MOXON-BROWNE Robert 2 Temple Gardens
PRESCOTT Peter 8 New Square
SALTER Richard 3 Verulam Buildings
SILVERLEAF Michael 11 South Square
SMITH Andrew Fountain Court
TWIGG Patrick 2 Temple Gardens
WILSON Alastair 19 Old Buildings

NEW SILKS • 1997 AND 1998

BLOCH Michael One Essex Court
CARR Henry 11 South Square
SUSMAN Peter New Court Chambers
WAUGH Andrew Three New Square
WHITE Andrew Atkin Chambers

LEADING JUNIORS • LONDON

BLOCH Selwyn Littleton Chambers **BURKILL Guy** Three New Square	**STREATFIELD-JAMES David** Atkin Chambers
ARNOLD Richard 11 South Square	**LAWRENCE Heather** 11 South Square
BARKLEM Martyn Littleton Chambers	**MANNING Colin** Littleton Chambers
BIRSS Colin Three New Square	**MEADE Richard** 8 New Square
CUNNINGHAM Graham Francis Taylor Building	**MOSTESHAR Sa'id** Hardwicke Chambers
FOXTON David Essex Court Chambers	**SHIPLEY Graham** 19 Old Buildings
FREEDMAN Clive 3 Verulam Buildings	

UP AND COMING • LONDON

RAWLEY Dominique Atkin Chambers	**SULLIVAN Rory** 19 Old Buildings

FOR DETAILS OF THESE LEADING BARRISTERS SEE PROFILES ON PAGES 1509-1642

LICENSING

RESEARCH: Our rankings reflect the opinion of the marketplace as revealed by systematic and objective research: see page four. Our research is audited every year by the British Market Research Bureau.

3 Raymond Buildings (Nicholls) Acknowledged throughout the country as the only specialist set. Particularly recommended were their "good spread of juniors" who provide a "great service." **Leading Barristers:** *Richard Beckett QC* ("superb"), has many admirers. He has a "laid back style" with "gravitas" and is a "good all rounder." *Gilbert Gray QC* is a "magnificent orator." The juniors are much used by practitioners. *Michael Bromley-Martin* is "polished." *Kevin De Haan* has a "sharp legal brain." *Andrew Muir* is popular and *James Rankin* is "well prepared." *Stephen Walsh* is said to be the "new bright light."

Christopher Moger QC at **4 Pump Court** (Mauleverer) is retained by the Gaming Board. He is said to be "first class" and the "best there is" in the gaming field. *Nigel Tozzi* ("extremely able") at the same chambers is also used by the Gaming Board. *Martin Heslop QC* at **1 Hare Court** (Kramer) is quite new to this field but is already considered to be an expert. *Timothy Cassell QC* at **5 Paper Buildings** (Mathew) works on the gaming side but is also moving into liquor licensing matters. *Simon Mehigan QC*, at the same chambers, has recently taken silk. *Susanna Fitzgerald* at **One Essex Court** (Grabiner) is considered by some as the main alternative to 3 Raymond Buildings. She is "high profile" and "extremely effective." *Stephen Monkcom* at **Francis Taylor Building** (Thompson & Guy) is from the gaming side and co-wrote one of the most used text books.

WESTERN CIRCUIT

LEADING SILK · WESTERN
GLEN Ian Guildhall Chambers

LEADING JUNIORS · WESTERN
BARKER Kerry Guildhall Chambers
PATRICK James Guildhall Chambers
WADSLEY Peter St. John's Chambers

Guildhall Chambers (Royce), Bristol, has most of the licensing expertise. *Ian Glen QC* is very good." *Kerry Barker* ("great confidence") and *James Patrick* are rated. *Peter Wadsley* at **St John's Chambers** (Denyer), Bristol, was described by one practitioner as "the best on the western circuit."

WALES/CHESTER CIRCUIT

LEADING JUNIORS WALES & CHESTER
WALTERS Graham 33 Park Place
WALTERS Jonathan 33 Park Place

Both the above juniors are active in the area. Graham Walters is a former Clerk to the Justices and is a "true specialist."

MIDLANDS AND OXFORD CIRCUIT

LEADING SILK MIDLANDS & OXFORD
SAUNDERS John 4 Fountain Court

LEADING JUNIOR MIDLANDS & OXFORD
GOSLING John 4 Fountain Court

John Saunders QC at **4 Fountain Court** (Wakerley), Birmingham, is a national leader, being praised by practitioners up and down the country. He is a "good communicator" who "puts clients at ease." He is "good at complex affairs," has experience and his "feet are firmly on the ground." *John Gosling,* who is a junior at the same chambers, is "amenable" and "thorough." Both advocates were recently involved in 'R v CC at Stallard ex parte Shipley.'

Barristers' profiles　　　　p. 1509-1642

LEADING SET · LONDON
3 RAYMOND BUILDINGS (Clive Nicholls QC)

LEADING SILKS · LONDON
BECKETT Richard 3 Raymond Buildings
GRAY Gilbert 3 Raymond Buildings
MOGER Christopher 4 Pump Court

HIGHLY REGARDED · LONDON
HESLOP Martin 1 Hare Court
CASSEL Timothy 5 Paper Buildings

NEW SILK · 1997 AND 1998
MEHIGAN Simon 5 Paper Buildings

LEADING JUNIORS · LONDON
FITZGERALD Susanna One Essex Court
BROMLEY-MARTIN Michael 3 Raymond Bldgs
DE HAAN Kevin 3 Raymond Buildings
MUIR Andrew 3 Raymond Buildings
RANKIN James 3 Raymond Buildings
WALSH Stephen 3 Raymond Buildings
MONKCOM Stephen Francis Taylor Building
TOZZI Nigel 4 Pump Court

FOR DETAILS OF THESE LEADING BARRISTERS SEE PROFILES ON PAGES 1509-1642

NE/NORTHERN CIRCUIT

LEADING SILKS NORTH EAST AND NORTHERN
GOLDSTONE Clement 28 St. John St
GRAY Gilbert Park Court Chambers

LEADING JUNIORS NORTH EAST AND NORTHERN
WALSH Martin Peel Court Chambers
GRUNDY Clare 28 St. John St
HUMPHRY Richard 28 St. John St

28 St John Street (Rumbelow), Manchester, is the prominent set, with *Clement Goldstone QC* ("good feel for the court", "thorough"), *Clare Grundy* and *Richard Humphry* being highly thought of. *Martin Walsh* at **Peel Court Chambers** (Shorrock), Manchester, is the star junior in the north. He was described as "spectacular" and "ten out of ten."

Gilbert Gray QC, of **Park Court Chambers** (Stewart/Smith) Leeds (already mentioned as practising out of 3 Raymond Bldgs) is the best known on the NE circuit.

MEDIA & ENTERTAINMENT

RESEARCH: In compiling the tables, we consider all the information available to us, paying particular regard to the market research carried out by our team of ten qualified lawyers. (The researchers' details are set out on page three.) The rankings, therefore, reflect the opinion of the market-place as revealed by systematic and objective research: see page four. (Our research is audited every year by the British Market Research Bureau.)

| Barristers' profiles | p. 1509-1642 |

OVERVIEW: The variety of work in this field – everything from complex contractual disputes to contempt proceedings against journalists – is reflected in our list of leading chambers, a mixture of commercial, intellectual property, defamation and civil liberties sets.

LEADING SETS • LONDON

BLACKSTONE CHAMBERS (Baxendale/Flint QCs)
8 NEW SQUARE (Michael Fysh QC)

BRICK COURT CHAMBERS (Clarke QC)
ESSEX COURT CHAMBERS (Pollock QC)
5 NEW SQUARE (Jonathan Rayner James QC)
5 RAYMOND BUILDINGS (Patrick Milmo QC)

DOUGHTY STREET CHAMBERS (Robertson QC)
11 SOUTH SQUARE (Christopher Floyd QC)
3 STONE BUILDINGS (G.C Vos QC)
3 VERULAM BUILDINGS (R. Neville Thomas QC)

Blackstone Chambers (formerly 2 Hare Court) (Baxendale and Flint) Continues to be one of the leading sets in this field, with members of chambers acting for major record labels, publishing houses and individuals. **Leading Barristers:** The "excellent" *Robert Englehart QC*, one of the best-known silks in this field, remains very busy. The "practical and tough" *Ian Mill* was praised for his speed in grasping issues, and is a "first-rate" advocate. Among his cases is 'Earlmont v Marshall Cavendish,' a contractual dispute concerning the publication of a series of classical recordings. *Pushpinder Saini* is particularly well-known for music industry work. He is acting for Bob Marley's widow in a copyright dispute with former members of the 'Wailers.' *Robert Howe* is another highly-regarded junior.

8 New Square (Fysh) The set's reputation for media work – an offshoot of its specialist IP practice – continues to grow, and this year it shares top place in our rankings. **Leading Barristers:** The set boasts four leading silks. The "excellent" *David Kitchin QC* is in the top band, along with *Peter Prescott QC*. The latter is noted for his down to earth manner with clients, and

acted in 'Clark v Associated Newspapers,' the case concerning the Evening Standard's parodies of 'Alan Clark's Diaries.' *John Baldwin QC* and *Mary Vitoria QC* – the latter praised in particular for her paperwork – complete the complement of leading silks. *Daniel Alexander*, a "brilliant" and popular junior, is one to watch for the future. *James Mellor* is said to be "impressive on his feet." He also acted in the Alan Clark case.

Brick Court Chambers (Clarke) This well-known commercial set acts for a variety of clients in some high-profile cases. **Leading Barristers:** *Sydney Kentridge QC*, variously described as "top of everything," "brilliant" and "tremendous" – continues to attract lavish praise from other practitioners. *Mark Cran QC* acted for George Michael in his dispute with Sony. Head of Chambers *Christopher Clarke QC* acted successfully for Polygram in a dispute over royalties. *Jonathan Hirst QC* and the ubiquitous *Jonathan Sumption QC* are widely in demand as advocates. Both have acted for Frank Warren in his dispute with fellow boxing promoter Don King. *Charles Hollander* is a leading junior.

Essex Court Chambers (Pollock) One of the elite commercial sets, its work in this field concentrates on contractual, agency, restraint of trade and competition issues. **Leading Barristers:** *Gordon Pollock QC*, one of the best known names at the commercial Bar, is praised as a "tremendous" lawyer. He is acting for the dancer Michael Flatley in a management dispute over the 'Lord of the Dance' show. *Peter Duffy QC* acts for the 'Rolling Stones' and 'U2.' The set also has a leading junior in this field, *Richard Millett*. He acted in a dispute between the pop singer Robbie Williams and his ex-manager.

LEADING SILKS • LONDON

ENGLEHART Robert Blackstone Chambers
GRAY Charles 5 Raymond Buildings
KENTRIDGE Sydney Brick Court Chambers
KITCHIN David 8 New Square
POLLOCK Gordon Essex Court Chambers
PRESCOTT Peter 8 New Square
RAYNER JAMES Jonathan 5 New Square
ROBERTSON Geoffrey Doughty Street Chambers
SILVERLEAF Michael 11 South Square

BALDWIN John 8 New Square
BROWNE Desmond 5 Raymond Buildings
CLARKE Christopher Brick Court Chambers
CRAN Mark Brick Court Chambers
DUFFY Peter Essex Court Chambers
GARNETT Kevin 5 New Square
HIRST Jonathan Brick Court Chambers
MERRIMAN Nicholas 3 Verulam Buildings
NICOL Andrew Doughty Street Chambers
PRICE Richard Littleton Chambers
SUMPTION Jonathan Brick Court Chambers
VITORIA Mary 8 New Square
VOS Geoffrey 3 Stone Buildings

LEADING JUNIORS • LONDON

BATE Stephen 5 Raymond Buildings
MILL Ian Blackstone Chambers

ALEXANDER Daniel 8 New Square
DICKENS Paul 5 New Square
SAINI Pushpinder Blackstone Chambers
SUTCLIFFE Andrew 3 Verulam Buildings

DE FREITAS Anthony 4 Paper Buildings
HOWE Robert Blackstone Chambers
LORD David 3 Stone Buildings
MILLETT Richard Essex Court Chambers
NELSON Vincent 39 Essex Street
TOZZI Nigel 4 Pump Court

BARKER Simon 13 Old Square
DEVONSHIRE Simon 5 Paper Buildings
FLYNN Vernon Essex Court Chambers
HOLLANDER Charles Brick Court Chambers
MELLOR James 8 New Square
MICHAELS Amanda 5 New Square
WAKSMAN David Fountain Court
WARBY Mark 5 Raymond Buildings

FOR DETAILS OF THESE LEADING BARRISTERS SEE PROFILES ON PAGES 1509-1642

5 New Square (Rayner James) The set has a growing reputation in this field, derived primarily from its long-established strength in intellectual property work. There is particular emphasis on music, film and broadcasting work. Leading Barristers: *Jonathan Rayner James QC* – described as "vastly knowledgeable, thorough and helpful" – features in the list of leading silks, as does *Kevin Garnett QC*. *Paul Dickens* is the set's leading junior in this field.

5 Raymond Buildings (Milmo) The set handles a variety of work in this field, ranging from defamation to copyright disputes. Leading Barristers: *Charles Gray QC*, an outstanding advocate, is one of the top silks in this field. He is particularly known for his defamation practice. *Desmond Browne QC*, another well-known defamation silk, acted in 'Morgan v BBC,' a dispute over alleged copying of a dramatic work.

Stephen Bate is one of the two outstanding juniors in the media and entertainment field, while *Mark Warby* (excellent in defamation) is another highly-regarded junior.

Doughty Street Chambers (Robertson) The set's media and entertainment work has a strong civil liberties flavour, and tenants frequently act for the news media in freedom of speech cases. Leading Barristers: *Geoffrey Robertson QC* is one of the most high-profile silks in this field. He acted for 'USA Today' in one of the first internet libel actions, and advised the Royal Academy on its controversial 'Sensation' Exhibition. *Andrew Nicol QC* acted in 'Camelot v Centaur,' a case on the disclosure of a journalist's sources.

11 South Square (Floyd) Leading Barristers: *Michael Silverleaf QC* has built up an outstanding reputation in this field, and moves into the top band of silks on the basis of numerous recommendations from other practitioners. His recent cases include 'Martin-Smith v Williams,' a dispute between a pop singer and his former manager.

3 Stone Buildings (Vos) This set has one silk and one junior in the rankings. Head of chambers *Geoffrey Vos QC* acted for David Puttnam in a dispute over the film 'Local Hero.' *David Lord* has built up a substantial following in the music industry, acting both for pop singers and their managers.

3 Verulam Buildings (Neville Thomas) Continues to have a strong reputation in this field. Leading Barristers: *Nicholas Merriman QC* is a well-regarded silk. The "thorough" *Andrew Sutcliffe* is praised for his understanding of the music industry and his tactical awareness. His clients include Oasis, Spandau Ballet and the writers of the Spice Girls' hits.

MEDICAL NEGLIGENCE

RESEARCH: In compiling the tables, we consider all the information available to us, paying particular regard to the market research carried out by our team of ten qualified lawyers. (The researchers' details are set out on page three.) The rankings, therefore, reflect the opinion of the marketplace as revealed by systematic and objective research: see page four. (Our research is audited every year by the British Market Research Bureau.)

OVERVIEW: 3 Serjeants' Inn remains by far the leading set with four silks and ten juniors in the tables. 1 Crown Office Row (strong on silks) and 6 Pump Court (strong on juniors) stay in second position.

LEADING SETS · LONDON

3 SERJEANTS' INN (Philip Naughton QC)
1 CROWN OFFICE ROW (Robert Seabrook QC)
6 PUMP COURT (Kieran Coonan QC)

DOUGHTY STREET CHAMBERS (Robertson QC)
ONE PAPER BUILDINGS (John Slater QC)
4 PAPER BUILDINGS (Harvey McGregor QC)

HIGHLY REGARDED · LONDON

9 Bedford Row (John Goldring QC)
5 Bell Yard (Robert Webb QC)
Cloisters (Laura Cox QC)
35 Essex Street (Nigel Inglis-Jones QC)
39 Essex Street (Edwin Glasgow QC)
199 Strand (Peter Andrews QC)

3 Serjeants' Inn (Naughton) "Undoubtedly pre-eminent", "first choice", "never been let down by them" were some of the comments received about this specialist set. **Leading Barristers:** The "extremely bright" *John Grace QC* rises in our tables to join *Adrian Whitfield QC* in the top band. Both have acted on high profile cases in the last year – Grace on 'R v Bournewood' and Whitfield on the Breast Radiation Injuries litigation. Among the many juniors listed, the "amazing" *Mary O'Rourke*, the "very thorough" *James Watson*, and the "confident" *Richard Partridge* received especially high praise.

1 Crown Office Row (Seabrook) Particularly noted for its strength in depth among silks. **Work Handled:** Members of the set were instructed on several significant cases in 1997 and 1998 including 'Bolitho v City & Hackney H.A.' [HL, on liability] (Owen and Coghlan); 'Thomas v Brighton H.A.' [HL, on multipliers] (Owen and Havers). **Leading Barristers:** The involvement of the "reassuring and authoritative" *Robert Owen QC* in the above

cases has lifted him to the top rank. The "extremely knowledgeable" *Philip Havers QC* also rises in the rankings at the suggestion of a number of practitioners. *Stephen Miller QC* "can put anyone at ease or wind them up as the need arises". *Terence Coghlan QC*, ("a star"), and the "prodigiously hardworking" junior *Paul Rees* were also elevated.

6 Pump Court (Coonan) Particularly strong for juniors. **Leading Barristers:** *Kieran Coonan QC* was widely praised. He led *Christina Lambert* for the Defendant in 'Thomas v Brighton H.A.' [HL]. *Susan Burden* acted in 'West v Enfield and Haringey HA.' The "splendid" *Siobhan Goodrich* was promoted in the tables following strong recommendation.

Barristers' profiles   p. 1509-1642

LEADING SILKS · LONDON

BRENNAN Daniel 39 Essex Street
COX Laura Cloisters
GRACE John 3 Serjeants' Inn
OWEN Robert 1 Crown Office Row
RITCHIE Jean 4 Paper Buildings
SPENCER Michael One Paper Buildings
WHITFIELD Adrian 3 Serjeants' Inn

COONAN Kieran 6 Pump Court
FRANCIS Robert 3 Serjeants' Inn
HAVERS Philip 1 Crown Office Row
MASKREY Simeon 9 Bedford Row
MILLER Stephen 1 Crown Office Row
POWERS Michael One Paper Buildings

BADENOCH James 1 Crown Office Row
BRENT Michael 9 Gough Square
COGHLAN Terence 1 Crown Office Row
DAVIES Nicola 3 Serjeants' Inn
FAULKS Edward No. 1 Serjeants' Inn
GIBSON Christopher 2 Crown Office Row
IRWIN Stephen Doughty Street Chambers
UNDERHILL Nicholas Fountain Court

NEW SILKS · 1997 AND 1998

HONE Richard One Paper Buildings
SMITH Sally 1 Crown Office Row

LEADING JUNIORS · LONDON

BOWRON Margaret 1 Crown Office Row	**O'ROURKE Mary** 3 Serjeants' Inn
GOODRICH Siobhan 6 Pump Court	**OPPENHEIM Robin** Doughty Street Chambers
HOPKINS Adrian 3 Serjeants' Inn	**PRATT Duncan** New Court Chambers
JOHNSTON Christopher 3 Serjeants' Inn	**REES Paul** 1 Crown Office Row
JONES Charlotte 5 Bell Yard	**SPENCER Martin** 4 Paper Buildings
LLOYD Huw 3 Serjeants' Inn	**SPINK Andrew** 35 Essex Street
MATTHEWS Dennis 5 Bell Yard	**TAYLOR Simon** Cloisters
MOON Angus 3 Serjeants' Inn	**WATSON James** 3 Serjeants' Inn
MORRIS David 6 Pump Court	
BRANTHWAITE Margaret One Paper Buildings	**LEHAIN Philip** 199 Strand
BURDEN Susan 6 Pump Court	**NEALE Fiona** 3 Serjeants' Inn
BURNS Sue 3 Serjeants' Inn	**PARTRIDGE Richard** 3 Serjeants' Inn
FOSTER Charles 6 Pump Court	**READHEAD Simon** No. 1 Serjeants' Inn
GOODWIN Deirdre 13 King's Bench Walk	**SHAW Howard** 29 Bedford Row Chambers
GORE Allan 12 King's Bench Walk	**TRACY FORSTER Jane** 13 King's Bench Walk
HOLWILL Derek 4 Paper Buildings	**WESTCOTT David** 35 Essex Street
LAMBERT Christina 6 Pump Court	**WILLIAMS Jon** 6 Pump Court

UP AND COMING · LONDON

GARRETT Annalissa 6 Pump Court	**LANGDALE Rachel** 9 Bedford Row
HORNE Michael 3 Serjeants' Inn	

Doughty Street Chambers (Robertson) Leading Barristers: *Stephen Irwin QC* is felt to have made his mark as a new silk, particularly in his work on the Human Growth Hormone litigation. He was described as "a leader with a very good grasp of medical issues and a down-to-earth manner with clients." *Robin Oppenheim*, who acted on Brock v Frenchay NHS Trust, is "as thorough as they come, excellent."

One Paper Buildings (Slater) Leading Barristers: *Michael Spencer QC* retains his position in the top band with work such as 'Plitman v Riverside H.A.' Some found him "aggressive" but to others he is "far and away the best – a brilliant advocate." *Dr Margaret Branthwaite*, a former medical consultant, is considered "sharp as a knife" and is a new entry to the tables. The "superb" *Dr Michael Powers QC* was

some people's first choice.

4 Paper Buildings (McGregor) Leading Barristers: *Jean Ritchie QC* is seen as a real fighter and always has a thorough grasp of matters in hand. She was instructed on 'Dowdie v Camberwell H.A.' *Martin Spencer* was praised by several interviewees. His recent work has included Forbes v Wandsworth H.A. *Derek Holwill* is considered to pay good attention to detail.

9 Bedford Row (Goldring) Leading Barristers: *Simeon Maskrey QC* received glowing recommendation: "extremely personable, excellent in conference, superb in court, fights like a tiger."

5 Bell Yard (Webb) Leading Barristers: *Charlotte Jones* is "approachable", while *Dennis Matthews* has "experience and ability in court and conference."

Cloisters (Cox) Leading Barristers: The "excellent" *Laura Cox QC* remains in the top slot. Her work includes acting in Lawman v Hillingdon NHS Trust.

35 Essex Street (Inglis-Jones) Leading Barristers: *Andrew Spink* was promoted following recommendation from solicitors and praise for his "keen mind." *David Westcott* is seen as "very on the ball."

39 Essex Street (Glasgow) Leading Barristers: *Daniel Brennan QC* remains extremely highly regarded – "red hot, superb, a sensible chap" – although as Chairman of the Bar Council in the coming year he will only be taking instructions until January 1999.

199 Strand (Andrews) Leading Barristers: *Philip Lehain* was praised for his thoroughness.

WESTERN CIRCUIT

LEADING JUNIORS · WESTERN

LEWIS Charles Old Square Chambers

FOR DETAILS OF THESE LEADING BARRISTERS
SEE PROFILES ON PAGES 1509-1642

Charles Lewis of **Old Square Chambers** (Melville Williams) in London and Bristol received praise for his reliability and his practical dealings with clients.

MIDLANDS AND OXFORD CIRCUIT

LEADING SILKS
MIDLANDS & OXFORD

MAXWELL Richard Ropewalk Chambers
OLIVER-JONES Stephen 5 Fountain Court

LEADING JUNIORS
MIDLANDS & OXFORD

BRIGHT Christopher 3 Fountain Court
HUNJAN Satinder 5 Fountain Court

Particular mention went to *Stephen Oliver-Jones QC* and *Satinder Hunjan* ("very down-to-earth") both of **5 Fountain Court** (Barker) in Birmingham. *Christopher Bright* "extremely thorough and approachable" of **3 Fountain Court** (Treacy) was also praised. In Nottingham *Richard Maxwell QC* of **Ropewalk Chambers** (Maxwell) , a set

with well-known personal injury expertise, was a new entry this year. He is also attached to Doughty Street Chambers in London.

NORTHERN CIRCUIT

LEADING SILKS · NORTHERN

ARMITAGE Keith 8 King St
GILMOUR Nigel Peel House
GRIME Mark Deans Court Chambers
LEVESON Brian Byrom Street Chambers
REDFERN Michael 28 St. John St
WINGATE-SAUL Giles Byrom Street Chambers

NEW SILK · NORTHERN

GOLDREIN Iain The Corn Exchange

LEADING JUNIORS · NORTHERN

ECCLES David 8 King St
HEATON David 18 St. John Street
LYON Adrian 14 Castle St
MELTON Christopher Peel Court Chambers
ROWLEY J. James 28 St. John St

UP AND COMING · NORTHERN

SMITH Michael 8 King St

In Manchester, **8 King St** (Armitage) now has the largest number of recommended counsel. *David Eccles* and *Michael Smith* enter the tables, while *Keith Armitage QC* ("extremely thorough and very nice") was

recommended again. His recent work includes 'Marriot v West Midlands H.A.' which went to the Court of Appeal. **Byrom Street Chambers** (Hytner) has two of the leading figures on the circuit in *Brian Leveson QC* and *Giles Wingate-Saul QC*, another new entry, already highly regarded in other fields. *Christopher Melton* of **Peel Court** (Shorrock) was also ranked for the first time. Only a few individuals were singled out from Liverpool. Of these, *Iain Goldrein QC* of **Corn Exchange Chambers** (Steer/Goldrein) was praised by several interviewees as "very thorough, unstuffy and doesn't mind getting his hands dirty." He is also a full tenant at **12 King's Bench Walk** (Walker) in London.

NORTH EAST CIRCUIT

LEADING JUNIORS
NORTH EASTERN

FREEDMAN Jeremy New Court Chambers
JACKSON Simon Park Court Chambers

FOR DETAILS OF THESE LEADING BARRISTERS
SEE PROFILES ON PAGES 1509-1642

Jeremy Freedman ("a real specialist") of **New Court Chambers** (Robson) in Newcastle was a new entry this year.

In Leeds *Simon Jackson* ("thorough and well prepared") of **Park Court Chambers** (Stewart/Smith) was recommended again.

PARLIAMENTARY

RESEARCH: In compiling the tables, we consider all the information available to us, paying particular regard to the market research carried out by our team of ten qualified lawyers. (The researchers' details are set out on page three.) The rankings, therefore, reflect the opinion of the marketplace as revealed by systematic and objective research: see page four. (Our research is audited every year by the British Market Research Bureau.)

OVERVIEW: Parliamentary work traditionally consisted of promoting and opposing private bills – particularly those relating to railway construction and other major works projects – before parliamentary committees. Changes to procedure mean that this type of work is now almost defunct, with transport and works orders now subject to planning inquiry-type inspections. The practitioners who specialised in parliamentary work now act in these transport and works inspections. They also handle the remaining old-style parliamentary work; promoting and opposing bills to extend the powers of individual local authorities.

Barristers' profiles	p. 1509-1642

LEADING SILKS · LONDON

PURCHAS Robin 2 Harcourt Buildings

CLARKSON Patrick 1 Serjeants' Inn
LAURENCE George 12 New Square

CAMERON Sheila 2 Harcourt Buildings
FITZGERALD Michael 2 Mitre Court Buildings
GEORGE Charles 2 Harcourt Buildings
HENDERSON Roger 2 Harcourt Buildings
HICKS William 1 Serjeants' Inn
LOCKHART-MUMMERY Christopher
4 Breams Buildings
MACLEOD Nigel 4 Breams Buildings
READ Lionel 1 Serjeants' Inn
RYAN Gerard 2 Harcourt Buildings
STONE Gregory 4-5 Gray's Inn Square
WIDDICOMBE David 2 Mitre Court Buildings

ANDERSON Anthony 2 Mitre Court Buildings
BARTLETT George 2 Mitre Court Buildings
DEHN Conrad Fountain Court
HOWELL John 4 Breams Buildings
LINDBLOM Keith 2 Harcourt Buildings
MORIARTY Gerald 2 Mitre Court Buildings
SMITH Andrew Fountain Court
SPENCE Malcolm 2-3 Gray's Inn Square
WHYBROW Christopher 1 Serjeants' Inn
WOOLLEY David 1 Serjeants' Inn

LEADING JUNIORS · LONDON

ASPREY Nicholas Serle Court Chambers
HILL Thomas 4-5 Gray's Inn Square

HARGREAVES Sara 12 New Square
HUSKINSON Nicholas 4-5 Gray's Inn Square
PETCHEY Philip 2 Harcourt Buildings
TAIT Andrew 2 Harcourt Buildings

GLOVER Richard 2 Mitre Court Buildings
HOWELL WILLIAMS Craig 2 Harcourt Buildings
KATKOWSKI Christopher 4 Breams Buildings
LIEVEN Nathalie 4 Breams Buildings
NEWCOMBE Andrew 2 Harcourt Buildings
PUGH-SMITH John 1 Serjeants' Inn
SHANKS Murray Fountain Court
THOMAS Megan 1 Serjeants' Inn

FOR DETAILS OF THESE LEADING BARRISTERS
SEE PROFILES ON PAGES 1509-1642

LEADING SETS · LONDON

2 HARCOURT BUILDINGS (Gerard Ryan QC)
4 BREAMS BUILDINGS (Lockhart-Mummery QC)
4-5 GRAY'S INN SQUARE (Appleby/Beloff QC)
2 MITRE COURT BUILDINGS (FitzGerald QC)
1 SERJEANTS' INN (Lionel Read QC)

2 Harcourt Buildings (Ryan) The leading set in this very specialised field. *Robin Purchas QC*, who handled the Channel Tunnel Rail Link Bill, is in a league of his own in this field. He is "great if you need someone to burn the midnight oil." Other members of chambers include the "sensible and knowledgeable" *Roger Henderson QC* (admired for his involvement in Crossrail and the Jubilee Line extension), *Sheila Cameron QC* and the "prominent" *Gerard Ryan QC*. *Keith Lindblom QC* has a "flexible" approach. *Philip Petchey* is "great at ferreting details out," while *Craig Howell Williams* is "respected by tribunals."

4 Breams Buildings (Lockhart-Mummery) Highly regarded parliamentary silks include the "effective" *Christopher Lockhart-Mummery QC* and the "innovative" *John Howell QC*. Leading juniors *Christopher Katkowski* and *Nathalie Lieven* were praised for their presentation skills.

4-5 Gray's Inn Square (Appleby and Beloff) *Gregory Stone QC* is "active and efficient." *Thomas Hill* is one of the two leading juniors in this field, while *Nicholas Huskinson* also features in the rankings.

2 Mitre Court Buildings (FitzGerald) A specialist parliamentary and planning set where "you can always find someone suitable." The set has five leading silks including Head of Chambers *Michael FitzGerald QC*.

1 Serjeants' Inn (Read) One of the magic circle of sets traditionally involved in this work, its members include *Patrick Clarkson QC,* the "busy" *William Hicks QC* and the "well-known" *Lionel Read QC. Christopher Whybrow QC* is "well liked by clients."

PARTNERSHIP

RESEARCH: In compiling the tables, we consider all the information available to us, paying particular regard to the market research carried out by our team of ten qualified lawyers. (The researchers' details are set out on page three.) The rankings, therefore, reflect the opinion of the marketplace as revealed by systematic and objective research: see page four. (Our research is audited every year by the British Market Research Bureau.)

OVERVIEW: Partnership work for the bar is limited, and there are very few cases which reach court. Most chancery practitioners are competent to deal with partnership matters should they arise, but if solicitors want a full-time specialist they will usually turn to head of 48 Bedford Row, Roderick I'Anson Banks or to Serle Court Chambers. A notable new addition to the table this year is Mark Blackett-Ord of 5 Stone Buildings (Harrod).

Barristers' profiles	p. 1509-1642

LEADING SETS · LONDON

48 BEDFORD ROW	(Roderick I'Anson Banks)
SERLE COURT CHAMBERS	(Sparrow QC)

LEADING SILKS · LONDON

BRIGGS Michael	Serle Court Chambers
BURTON Michael	Littleton Chambers
DAVIS Nigel	7 Stone Buildings
ELIAS Patrick	11 King's Bench Walk

LEADING JUNIORS · LONDON

BANKS Roderick I'Anson	48 Bedford Row
BLACKETT-ORD Mark	5 Stone Buildings
GOURGEY Alan	11 Stone Buildings
HINKS Frank	Serle Court Chambers
LEVY Benjamin	Enterprise Chambers
WHITTAKER John	Serle Court Chambers

**LEADING SILKS
NORTHERN CIRCUIT**

JONES Edward Bartley	Exchange Chambers

FOR DETAILS OF THESE LEADING BARRISTERS
SEE PROFILES ON PAGES 1509-1642

48 Bedford Row (Banks) **Leading Barristers:** The "very knowledgeable" *Roderick I'Anson Banks* is one of the few dedicated partnership practitioners. He is considered an "excellent barrister," (especially from an academic perspective) and is the editor of 'Lindley & Banks on Partnership'. He is especially skilled in giving advice in conference.

Serle Court Chambers (Sparrow) **Leading Barristers:** *Michael Briggs QC*, *Frank Hinks* and *John Whittaker* are singled out as having particular expertise in relation to partnership matters.

Among other sets *Michael Burton QC* of **Littleton Chambers** (Burton) is essentially an outstanding advocate, adept in all areas of commercial law, but particularly known in employment. Panership is an offshoot from his employment practice. *Nigel Davis QC* from **7 Stone Buildings** (Aldous) has a respected chancery practice. *Patrick Elias QC* of **11 King's Bench Walk** (Tabachnik and Goudie), also known for his employment work, "knows this subject inside out." He is liked for his "common sense," for "having his feet firmly on the ground" and is considered a good tactician. *Mark Blackett-Ord* at **5 Stone Buildings** (Harrod) is a new addition to the tables this year following recommendation and the publication of a well received textbook on the subject. The "astute" *Benjamin Levy* from **Enterprise Chambers** (Mann) is considered experienced in general chancery matters.

Outside London, *Edward Bartley Jones QC* from **Exchange Chambers** (Waldron) in Liverpool is recommended.

PENSIONS

RESEARCH: In compiling the tables, we consider all the information available to us, paying particular regard to the market research carried out by our team of ten qualified lawyers. (The researchers' details are set out on page three.) The rankings, therefore, reflect the opinion of the marketplace as revealed by systematic and objective research: see page four. (Our research is audited every year by the British Market Research Bureau.)

OVERVEW: There are few changes to the pensions section this year. Many solicitors commented that their own pensions knowledge is such they rarely need to instruct a junior.

LEADING SETS · LONDON

WILBERFORCE CHAMBERS (Edward Nugee QC)

HIGHLY REGARDED · LONDON

35 Essex Street (Nigel Inglis-Jones QC)
5 Stone Buildings (Henry Harrod)

3 Stone Buildings (G.C Vos QC)
7 Stone Buildings (Charles Aldous QC)

Wilberforce Chambers (Nugee) Still "way out in front." They have a huge "concentration of skills" and most of the pensions bar work in London and nationwide. Their dominance is felt by some to be mainly due to numbers, but they also give "spot-on advice, with an eye to the commercial realities of pension schemes." They also have "the best silks." Important cases over the last year include: 'Besd v Queens Moathouses' for the Trustees; acting for the Trustees and the Pensions Committee on the South West Trains case; and involvement in 'HRTL v JAPTL,' a case on the direct liability of directors of a trust company for breach of fiduciary duties. **Leading Barristers:** *Nicholas Warren QC* is still the first choice of most solicitors. He is "a tough, knockabout silk" and possesses "a great intellect and a famously incisive manner." He is "a marvellous paperwork man but also client-friendly and gives pragmatic advice." The 'excellent' *Robert Ham QC* has tremendous presence and clients like him. *Terence Etherton QC* is "intellectually on top of the job" and "has a single-minded and tough approach." *Edward Nugee QC* has been described as "a consummate seasoned professional," although he is now seen to be winding down his practice. *Jules Sher QC* is "very robust;

quick to reach a conclusion." The "on the ball" *Brian Green QC* does about 50% pure pensions advisory work, and is admired for his pragmatism and commercial nous. He is "first rate" and "absolutely charming to deal with." New silk *Christopher Nugee QC* is "very impressive – everything his father is." He has been described as "user-friendly while coming across as cerebral, which clients like." *Paul Newman* is still relatively junior and considered likely to rise extremely quickly. He "thinks on his feet and gives crisp advice." *Charles Turnbull* "has an intellectual approach," and *Judith Bryant* is "extremely bright, organised and cost-effective." *Michael Furness* is a "very good technical pensions lawyer" involved in some quite substantial work. *Caroline Furze* and *John Martin QC* have also been recommended.

35 Essex Street (Inglis-Jones) Nigel Inglis-Jones QC, one of our leading pensions silks, is now head of chambers, re-enforcing the set's commitment to pensions work. **Leading Barristers:** *Nigel Inglis-Jones QC* is admired for his "academic" approach, but he is also described as a "consummately practical man." *John Stephens* is described as "a star among juniors" and "a powerhouse" with a "practical approach."

5 Stone Buildings (Harrod) A small chancery set with expertise in many areas of property and chancery work. **Leading Barristers:** *Mark Herbert QC* comes from a trusts and tax law background and does 20-25% pensions work, mainly for trustees or employers. He has been advising the Pensions Ombudsman on appeals against their decisions. He is "particularly good in consultation and a master of detail." *Andrew Simmonds* is "extremely tenacious in court." His recent cases include

Barristers' profiles p. 1509-1642

LEADING SILKS · LONDON

WARREN Nicholas Wilberforce Chambers
HAM Robert Wilberforce Chambers
ETHERTON Terence Wilberforce Chambers

GREEN Brian Wilberforce Chambers
HERBERT Mark 5 Stone Buildings
INGLIS-JONES Nigel 35 Essex Street
MARTIN John Wilberforce Chambers
NUGEE Edward Wilberforce Chambers
SHER Jules Wilberforce Chambers

NEW SILKS · 1997 AND 1998

NUGEE Christopher Wilberforce Chambers

LEADING JUNIORS · LONDON

CLIFFORD James 7 Stone Buildings
STEPHENS John 35 Essex Street

ASPLIN Sarah 3 Stone Buildings
FURNESS Michael Wilberforce Chambers
HITCHCOCK Richard 35 Essex Street
NEWMAN Paul Wilberforce Chambers
SIMMONDS Andrew 5 Stone Buildings
TOPHAM Geoffrey 3 Stone Buildings
TURNBULL Charles Wilberforce Chambers

BRYANT Judith Wilberforce Chambers
HAYES Josephine 3 New Square
TIDMARSH Christopher 5 Stone Buildings

UP AND COMING · LONDON

FURZE Caroline Wilberforce Chambers
LACEY Sarah 3 Stone Buildings

FOR DETAILS OF THESE LEADING BARRISTERS
SEE PROFILES ON PAGES 1509-1642

'ITN v Pensions Ombudsman' (the National Power/National Grid case) and 'Ford v Barclays Bank.' *Christopher Tidmarsh* does about 20% pensions work; he is mainly known for his advisory work.

3 Stone Buildings (Vos) A general chancery set with three recommended individuals. **Leading Barristers:** *Sarah Asplin* is a "very able and well-regarded junior." She has recently been acting for the Pensions Ombudsman defending appeals and determinations. *Geoffrey Topham* is "extremely busy with good quality work" and has a good reputation for handling "combative litigation." *Sarah Lacey* is also recommended.

7 Stone Buildings (Aldous) **Leading Barristers:** *James Clifford* appeared in the case of 'Edge v Pensions Ombudsman.'

PERSONAL INJURY

RESEARCH: In compiling the tables, we consider all the information available to us, paying particular regard to the market research carried out by our team of ten qualified lawyers. (The researchers' details are set out on page three.) The rankings, therefore, reflect the opinion of the marketplace as revealed by systematic and objective research: see page four. (Our research is audited every year by the British Market Research Bureau.)

Barristers' profiles   p. 1509-1642

LEADING SETS · LONDON

39 ESSEX STREET (Edwin Glasgow QC)
12 KING'S BENCH WALK (Ronald J. Walker QC)
OLD SQUARE CHAMBERS (Melville Williams QC)
2 TEMPLE GARDENS (Patrick Phillips QC)

2 CROWN OFFICE ROW (Graeme Hamilton QC)
FARRAR'S BUILDING (Gerard Elias QC)

DEVEREUX CHAMBERS (Jeffrey Burke QC)
9 GOUGH SQUARE (Jeremy Roberts Q.C)
PLOWDEN BUILDINGS (William Lowe QC)

9 BEDFORD ROW (John Goldring QC)
199 STRAND (Peter Andrews QC)
1 TEMPLE GARDENS (Hugh Carlisle QC)

HIGHLY REGARDED · LONDON

29 Bedford Row Chambers (Peter Ralls QC)
Cloisters (Laura Cox QC)
35 Essex Street (Nigel Inglis-Jones QC)
2 Harcourt Buildings (Roger Henderson QC)
One Paper Buildings (John Slater QC)

39 Essex Street (Glasgow) With a wealth of talent (five silks and five juniors), this is one of the pre-eminent sets. It has strength across the board, with some high powered individuals. **Leading Barristers:** Head of chambers, *Edwin Glasgow QC,* is acknowledged as one of the leading silks. *Colin Mackay QC* is "absolutely brilliant – he is measured, has a sensible approach and is good with clients." The "delightful" *Michael Tillett QC* and new entry *Richard Davies QC* ("a classy operator") also received high praise. *Daniel Brennan QC* is "hugely well regarded" and remains at the top of our tables, although his impending Chairmanship of the Bar Council means his caseload will be restricted during 1998-1999. Among the juniors, *Christian Du Cann* is considered "extremely knowledgeable." He acted on litigation arising from the MOD helicopter crash. The "straight talking" *Charles Brown* has "very good judgement." The popular *Neil Block* ("great all-rounder," "combative in court," "takes only good points") moves up the rankings this

year. By popular demand, *Charles Cory-Wright* is a new addition this year. He was instructed on 'Cutter v Eagle Star' (HL).

12 King's Bench Walk (Walker) Two silks and three juniors were recommended from this set. **Leading Barristers:** *Ronald Walker QC* is a "tenacious, vastly experienced, all rounder." He was instructed on 'Jameson v CEGB' (previous action by deceased is no bar to action by estate against different defendant over same cause of action). He is joined in the silks list by newly appointed *Frank Burton QC* whose elevation came as no surprise to those interviewed. "Dogged fighter" *Stephen Worthington* is popular, while *Allan Gore* is the "first choice on tricky cases." One of these was 'Quinn v MOD' (Crown immunity for tortious injury of armed service personnel). New entry *Hugh Hamill* is "very good on his feet and keeps the judge awake."

Old Square Chambers (Williams) Seen as good for union work and involved in some high profile cases. Two silks and four juniors appear in our list. **Leading Barristers:** Conducting some high profile litigation is head of chambers, the eminent *John Melville Williams QC.* His recent work includes 'Hill v Tomkins' (organophosphates) and infant drink litigation. *John Hendy QC* also received much praise. *Christopher Carling* is "down to earth, thorough and approachable," while *Matthias Kelly* is "clued up."

2 Temple Gardens (Phillips) Have a good spread at all levels. Many solicitors said they "would use anyone" from the set; "whoever they send will do a decent job." Five silks and two juniors are ranked. Work handled by members of the set includes: 'Amosu v Financial Times' – RSI case (Collender); 'Jolley v London Borough of Sutton' (de Navarro, Palmer); 'Dillon v M.O.D' (Browne, Porter). **Leading Barristers:** "Dogged" *Dermod O'Brien QC* is much admired and *Andrew Collender QC* "has a good grasp of detail." "Hard fighter" *Benjamin Browne QC* moves up the rankings to join the "pretty unbeatable" *Michael de Navarro QC.*

LEADING SILKS · LONDON

BRENNAN Daniel 39 Essex Street
CROWLEY John 2 Crown Office Row
GLASGOW Edwin 39 Essex Street
LANGSTAFF Brian Cloisters
MACKAY Colin 39 Essex Street
PURCHAS Christopher 2 Crown Office Row

CHERRY John 8 Stone Buildings
HENDY John Old Square Chambers
LIVESEY Bernard 2 Crown Office Row
O'BRIEN Dermod 2 Temple Gardens
STEWART Robin 199 Strand
WALKER Ronald 12 King's Bench Walk
WILLIAMS John Leighton Farrar's Building

ANDREWS Peter 199 Strand
ASHWORTH Piers 2 Harcourt Buildings
BADENOCH James 1 Crown Office Row
BAKER Nigel 9 Bedford Row
BRENT Michael 9 Gough Square
BROWNE Benjamin 2 Temple Gardens
BURKE Jeffrey Devereux Chambers
COLLENDER Andrew 2 Temple Gardens
CROWTHER William 2 Temple Gardens
DAVIES Richard 39 Essex Street
DE NAVARRO Michael 2 Temple Gardens
HENDERSON Roger 2 Harcourt Buildings
IRWIN Stephen Doughty Street Chambers
JEFFREYS Alan Farrar's Building
OWEN Robert 1 Crown Office Row
PUGH Vernon 2-3 Gray's Inn Square
PULMAN George Hardwicke Building
RITCHIE Jean 4 Paper Buildings
SPENCER Michael One Paper Buildings
STEVENSON William One Paper Buildings
STRACHAN Mark 1 Crown Office Row
TILLETT Michael 39 Essex Street
ULLSTEIN Augustus 29 Bedford Row Chambers
WALKER Raymond 1 Harcourt Buildings
WILKINSON Nigel 2 Crown Office Row
WILLIAMS John Melville Old Square Chambers

NEW SILKS · 1997 AND 1998

BURNETT Ian 1 Temple Gardens
BURTON Frank 12 King's Bench Walk
FOY John 9 Gough Square
GLANCY Robert Devereux Chambers
LOWE William Plowden Buildings
NORRIS William Farrar's Building

FOR DETAILS OF THESE LEADING BARRISTERS
SEE PROFILES ON PAGES 1509-1642

2 Crown Office Row (Hamilton) Have an "enviable" spread of talent, with two silks appearing in our top band, and another two silks and two juniors also featuring. Seen as having strength in depth. **Leading Barristers:** The top rate, all round performer *John Crowley QC* is also "brilliant with clients." *Christopher Purchas QC* is praised for "gravitas and common-sense," whilst *Thomas Saunt* is admired for his "great negotiating skills." Purchas was one of the counsel instructed in the House of Lords case of 'Wells v Wells.'

Farrar's Building (Elias) A long established common law set, particularly strong in juniors. Involved in some very high profile work. Three silks and four juniors have been strongly recommended. **Leading Barristers:** *John Leighton Williams QC* "has excellent judgement." He acted on 'Page v Sheerness Steel' and 'Wells v Wells' (HL). *William Norris QC* is a new silk. *Edward Southwell* is "highly rated, competent and sound," and *Anthony Seys Llewellyn* "pays attention to detail, and is great on complex cases." *Alan Jeffreys QC* was also felt to have made his mark. He was instructed on 'Zammitt v Stena Offshore' and 'Doughty v Stena Offshore.'

Devereux Chambers (Burke) **Leading Barristers:** *Stephen Killalea* has "style" and "only takes good points."

9 Gough Square (Roberts) **Leading Barristers:** New silk *John Foy QC* is a popular choice with excellent knowledge of occupational health and "first rate" at RSI. Recent work included the British Coal respiratory disease litigation. *Nicolas Hillier* acted on the Ford Motor Co deafness cases.

Plowden Buildings (Lowe) Praised for their willingness to travel to see solicitors and clients, for their excellent rapport with people and for the quality of the clerking. **Leading Barristers:** *William Lowe QC* is "robust and phlegmatic." *Catherine Foster* acted on 'Armstrong v British Coal.'

9 Bedford Row (Goldring) **Leading Barristers:** *Nigel Baker QC* has been involved in a number of high profile cases relating to children in care, including 'Barrat v London Borough of Enfield' and child sex abuse cases arising from the Frank Beck affair. *Simon King, Simon Wheatley* and *Jeremy Pendlebury* were also recommended.

Cloisters (Cox) **Leading Barristers:** *Brian Langstaff QC* is extremely well thought of and moves up into the top band. He is considered a persuasive advocate and has a good grasp of large cases. He was instructed on 'Amosu v Financial Times.'

One Paper Buildings (Slater) Work Handled: 'Alexander v Midland Bank;' 'Willis v Royal Doulton' (RSI) (Stevenson). 'Bates v Durox' (claim that accident triggered onset of MS) (Ferris). 'Amosu v Financial Times' (Waite). **Leading Barristers:** *William Stevenson QC* is seen as "dogged" and *Jonathan Waite* is "incisive."

199 Strand (Andrews) **Leading Barristers:** *Robin Stewart QC* and *Peter Andrews QC* are seen as thorough and careful. *Philip Lehain* is considered "a plaintiff's man" – "incredibly knowledgeable and skilful."

Other counsels receiving particular praise were the "feisty" *Frank Moat* of **Pump Court Chambers** (Boney) and *Dennis Matthews* of **5 Bell Yard** (Webb) who is "on the ball." At **1 Temple Gardens** (Carlisle), new silk, *Ian Burnett QC* is "enormously talented" and gives "reliable advice." The "silver tongued" *Roger Henderson QC*, and the "excellent" *Roger Eastman* were particularly recommended from **2 Harcourt Buildings** (Henderson). At **35 Essex Street** (Inglis-Jones), *William Coley* "gives quality advice" while the "meticulous" *David Westcott* "keeps silks on the straight and narrow."

LEADING JUNIORS · LONDON	
BLOCK Neil 39 Essex Street	**SOUTHWELL Edward** Farrar's Building
GORE Allan 12 King's Bench Walk	
BROWN Charles 39 Essex Street	**MATTHEWS Dennis** 5 Bell Yard
CRAVEN Richard Plowden Buildings	**MCINTYRE Bruce** Plowden Buildings
DU CANN Christian 39 Essex Street	**TROTTER David** Plowden Buildings
EASTMAN Roger 2 Harcourt Buildings	**WAITE Jonathan** One Paper Buildings
KILLALEA Stephen Devereux Chambers	**WHEATLEY Simon** 9 Bedford Row
KING Simon 9 Bedford Row	**WORTHINGTON Stephen** 12 King's Bench Walk
BROWN Geoffrey 39 Essex Street	**MAY Kieran** 8 Stone Buildings
BROWNE Simon Farrar's Building	**MCDERMOTT Tom** Farrar's Building
CARLING Christopher Old Square Chambers	**MOAT Frank** Pump Court Chambers
COLEY William 35 Essex Street	**PALMER Howard** 2 Temple Gardens
COOKSLEY Nigel Old Square Chambers	**PENDLEBURY Jeremy** 9 Bedford Row
FOSTER Catherine Plowden Buildings	**PORTER Martin** 2 Temple Gardens
GODDARD Christopher Devereux Chambers	**PUGH Charles** Old Square Chambers
HILLIER Nicolas 9 Gough Square	**REDDIHOUGH John** 9 Gough Square
HOLMES Jonathan Maurice Plowden Buildings	**SAUNT Thomas** 2 Crown Office Row
KELLY Matthias Old Square Chambers	**SEYS LLEWELLYN Anthony** Farrar's Building
LEHAIN Philip 199 Strand	**SNOWDEN Steven** 2 Crown Office Row
MACLEOD Duncan 9 Gough Square	**WESTCOTT David** 35 Essex Street
ASHFORD-THOM Ian 1 Temple Gardens	**FERRIS Shaun** One Paper Buildings
BISHOP Edward 1 Serjeants' Inn	**HAMILL Hugh** 12 King's Bench Walk
CORY-WRIGHT Charles 39 Essex Street	**LAMBERT Christina** 6 Pump Court

FOR DETAILS OF THESE LEADING BARRISTERS SEE PROFILES ON PAGES 1509-1642

WESTERN CIRCUIT

HIGHLY REGARDED · WESTERN
St. John's Chambers (Denyer QC) Bristol
Assize Court Chambers (Isherwood) Bristol
Guildhall Chambers (Royce QC) Bristol
Old Square Chambers (Melville Williams QC) Bristol

St John's Chambers (Denyer), Bristol. Have an enviable breadth of talent, with four juniors being highly recommended this year. **Leading Barristers:** *Glyn Edwards* "wins tricky cases," *Richard Stead* ("approachable and knowlegeable"), *Julian Ironside* and *Christopher Sharp* are all very popular.

Assize Court Chambers (Isherwood), Bristol. A favourite among practitioners and are newly ranked this year. Viewed as approachable, down to earth, responsive and quick. **Leading Barristers:** *John Isherwood* is "extremely good."

LEADING JUNIORS · WESTERN
EDWARDS Glyn St. John's Chambers
ISHERWOOD John Assize Court Chambers
IRONSIDE Julian St. John's Chambers
SHARP Christopher St. John's Chambers
STEAD Richard St. John's Chambers

FOR DETAILS OF THESE LEADING BARRISTERS SEE PROFILES ON PAGES 1509-1642

MIDLANDS AND
OXFORD CIRCUIT

HIGHLY REGARDED SETS MIDLANDS & OXFORD
5 Fountain Court (Barker QC) Birmingham
Ropewalk Chambers (Maxwell QC) Nottingham
3 Fountain Court (Treacy QC) Birmingham
St. Ive's Chambers (Coke) Birmingham
St. Philip's Chambers (Tedd QC) Birmingham

5 Fountain Court (Barker), Birmingham. Often described as "the most prestigious Birmingham set." **Leading Barristers:** Include the "outstanding" *Gareth Evans QC* and exceptional junior, *Ralph Lewis* – "he knows the law backwards, has a nice style and is a tough performer." *Satinder Hunjan* is "really good."

Ropewalk Chambers (Maxwell), Nottingham. Highly praised. Many interviewees said they would use any of the set's juniors. Work Handled: VWF cases (Maxwell and Owen); North Wales child abuse (Adams); Hillsborough (Limb). **Leading Barristers:** *Richard Maxwell QC* and *Robert Owen QC* are "first rate."

LEADING SILKS · MIDLANDS & OXFORD	
EVANS Gareth 5 Fountain Court	**OWEN Robert** Ropewalk Chambers
MAXWELL Richard Ropewalk Chambers	
OLIVER-JONES Stephen 5 Fountain Court	**WOODWARD W.C.** Ropewalk Chambers

NEW SILK · 1997 AND 1998
WOOD William 5 Fountain Court

LEADING JUNIORS · MIDLANDS & OXFORD	
BEARD Simon Ropewalk Chambers	**LEWIS Ralph** 5 Fountain Court
ADAMS Jayne Ropewalk Chambers	**GASH Simon** Ropewalk Chambers
ASHWORTH Lance St Philip's Chambers	**HUNJAN Satinder** 5 Fountain Court
BLEASDALE Paul 5 Fountain Court	**LIMB Patrick** Ropewalk Chambers
GREGORY PHILIP No.6 Fountain Court	**WORSTER David** St Philip's Chambers
KEEHAN Michael St. Ive's Chambers	

FOR DETAILS OF THESE LEADING BARRISTERS SEE PROFILES ON PAGES 1509-1642

Three juniors appear for the first time, including *Jayne Adams*. "She will go far," predicted one solicitor, she is "popular with clients, and a sensitive but devastating cross examiner." *Simon Gash* is "terrific."

St Philip's Chambers (Tedd), Birmingham. Previously 7 Fountain Court and Priory Court, the combined set is likely to be a major force in Birmingham. **Leading Barristers:** *David Worster* is "outstanding; he has a fantastic knowledge of law and a great client manner." *Lance Ashworth* is a popular entry.

WALES AND
CHESTER CIRCUIT

HIGHLY REGARDED SETS WALES & CHESTER
9 Park Place (Ian Murphy Q.C.) Cardiff
33 Park Place (Wyn Williams QC) Cardiff
Iscoed Chambers (Trefor Davies) Swansea
30 Park Place (Philip Richards) Cardiff

33 Park Place (Williams), Cardiff. **Leading Barristers:** Among the recommended counsel, *Lewis Williams QC* is a "good all rounder, liked by insurance companies;" new silk *Neil Bidder QC* is "great," while *Nicholas Jones* is "very personable with clients."

At **9 Park Place** (Murphy), Cardiff. *Nicholas Cooke QC* is a new entry. At **30 Park Place** (Richards), **Cardiff**. *Peter Grif-*

LEADING SILKS · WALES & CHESTER	
GRIFFITHS Peter 30 Park Place	**REES John** 33 Park Place
MURPHY Ian 9 Park Place	**WILLIAMS Lewis** 33 Park Place

NEW SILKS · 1997 AND 1998	
BIDDER Neil 33 Park Place	**COOKE Nicholas** 9 Park Place

LEADING JUNIORS · WALES & CHESTER	
GRIFFITHS Lawrence Iscoed Chambers	**VENMORE John** 30 Park Place
JONES Nicholas 33 Park Place	**VOSPER Christopher** Angel Chambers
MARSHALL Philip Iscoed Chambers	**WILLIAMS Lloyd** 30 Park Place
REES Philip 9 Park Place	

FOR DETAILS OF THESE LEADING BARRISTERS SEE PROFILES ON PAGES 1509-1642

fiths QC received particular praise for his thoroughness and for relating well to his clients. The "exceptional" *Philip Marshall* at **Iscoed Chambers** (Davies), Swansea. was also recommended again.

NORTH EASTERN
CIRCUIT

Park Lane Chambers (Bethel), Leeds and **Park Court Chambers** (Stewart and Smith), Leeds were recommended. Two juniors from the former, *Howard Elgot* and *Simon Thorp* and one from the latter, *Simon Jackson* were particularly highly regarded.

HIGHLY REGARDED SETS NORTH EASTERN
Park Court Chambers (Stewart/Smith QC) Leeds
Park Lane Chambers (Bethel QC) Leeds

LEADING JUNIORS NORTH EASTERN
ELGOT Howard Park Lane Chambers
JACKSON Simon Park Court Chambers
THORP Simon Park Lane Chambers

FOR DETAILS OF THESE LEADING BARRISTERS
SEE PROFILES ON PAGES 1509-1642

NORTHERN CIRCUIT

HIGHLY REGARDED SETS
NORTHERN

Deans Court Chambers (Goddard QC) Manchester

Byrom Street Chambers (Hytner QC) Manchester

9 St. John St (Hand QC) Manchester

14 Castle St (Adrian Lyon) Liverpool

Exchange Chambers (Waldron QC) Liverpool

Peel House (Gilmour QC) Liverpool

18 St. John St (Klevan QC) Manchester

28 St. John St (Rumbelow QC) Manchester

LEADING SILKS • NORTHERN

WINGATE-SAUL Giles Byrom Street Chambers

BRAITHWAITE Bill Exchange Chambers	**MORROW Graham** Exchange Chambers
GRIME Mark Deans Court Chambers	**STOCKDALE David** Deans Court Chambers
HORLOCK Timothy 9 St. John Street	**SWIFT Caroline** Byrom Street Chambers
MACHELL Raymond Deans Court Chambers	**TATTERSALL Geoffrey** Byrom Street Chambers

NEW SILKS • 1997 AND 1998

EDIS Andrew 14 Castle St	**TURNER Mark** Deans Court Chambers

LEADING JUNIORS • NORTHERN

HEATON David 18 St. John Street	**MARTIN Gerard** Exchange Chambers
HINCHLIFFE Nicholas 9 St. John Street	**RAHMAN Yaqub** Peel House
FEENY Charles Peel House, 9 St. John Street	
FEWTRELL Nick 18 St. John Street	**LAPRELL Mark** 18 St. John Street
FIELD Patrick John Deans Court Chambers	**MCDERMOTT Gerard** 8 King Street
GORTON Simon 14 Castle Street	**O'KEEFFE Darren** Derby Square Chambers
GRICE Kevin The Corn Exchange	**ROWLEY James** 28 St. John Street
HOLDER Simon India Buildings Chambers	**THOMAS Keith** New Bailey Chambers
HUNTER Winston 28 St. John Street	**WOOD Graham** India Buildings Chambers

FOR DETAILS OF THESE LEADING BARRISTERS SEE PROFILES ON PAGES ??? - ???

Deans Court Chambers (Goddard), Manchester. The set remains ahead of the field with four silks and a junior making our tables. Has an annexe in Preston. Leading Barristers: *Mark Grime QC, Raymond Machell QC* and *David Stockdale QC* were all praised, particularly for their work on behalf of defendants. Grime acted on 'Wisniewski v Central Manchester H.A.' (CA) while Machell was instructed in 'Payne v Saunders,' which at £3.2 million was the second largest ever personal injury claim. Stockdale acted on 'McCreesh v Courtaulds' (CA). New silk *Mark Turner QC is* "very bright and a good negotiator."

Byrom Street Chambers (Hytner), Manchester. Leading Barristers: "Top man" *Giles Wingate-Saul QC* is many people's first choice. He was felt to be very sound on difficult cases and has "excellent judgement." Recent work includes the Armley asbestos litigation. The "extremely able" *Caroline Swift QC* and *Geoffrey Tattersall QC* "wonderful with clients" were new entries this year.

9 St John Street (Hand), Manchester. Leading Barristers: *Timothy Horlock QC*

is considered "incisive"and is "not afraid to give an opinion" while *Nicholas Hinchliffe* was highly praised by a number of interviewees.

Exchange Chambers (Waldron), Liverpool. Leading Barristers: *Bill Braithwaite QC*, who also works out of 2 Crown Office Row (Hamilton) in London, was recommended for big claims. Recent work includes the Westmoquette litigation. *Graham Morrow QC* is a new entry following strong praise ("gets some fantastic results," "has amazing clarity of thought") while *Gerard Martin* is seen as a "heavyweight junior."

Among the recommended counsel at **India Buildings** (Gilmour), Liverpool. *Simon Holder* and *Graham Wood* were new entries. At **18 St John Street** (Klevan), Manchester. *Nick Fewtrell* is "definitely going somewhere" and *Mark Laprell* was considered particularly good at complicated matters. **28 St John Street** (Rumbelow), Manchester. is perceived to have a growing personal injury profile. Recommended individuals include *Winston Hunter,* ("very good to deal with") and the "extremely highly regarded" *James Rowley.*

PLANNING AND LOCAL GOVERNMENT

RESEARCH: In compiling the tables, we consider all the information available to us, paying particular regard to the market research carried out by our team of ten qualified lawyers. (The researchers' details are set out on page three.) The rankings, therefore, reflect the opinion of the marketplace as revealed by systematic and objective research: see page four. (Our research is audited every year by the British Market Research Bureau.)

OVERVIEW: We have made few alterations to our tables this year. None of the feedback suggested a need to change the ranking of the leading sets, though there is little to choose between the top five. There are some new names among the juniors – Paul Brown and Tom Hill at 4-5 Gray's Inn Square have been making a name for themselves, as have Russell Harris and Richard Harwood at 1 Serjeants' Inn.

LEADING SETS · LONDON

4 BREAMS BUILDINGS (Lockhart-Mummery QC)
4-5 GRAY'S INN SQUARE (Appleby/Beloff QC)

2 HARCOURT BUILDINGS (Gerard Ryan QC)
2 MITRE COURT BUILDINGS (FitzGerald QC)
1 SERJEANTS' INN (Lionel Read QC)

2-3 GRAY'S INN SQUARE (Anthony Scrivener QC)
11 KING'S BENCH WALK (Tabachnik/Goudie QC)

4 Breams Buildings (Lockhart-Mummery) Seen as the top planning set in terms of sheer brainpower. The clerking was also described as " very switched on" – a comment borne out by our dealings with the set. **Work Handled:** During the past year Nigel Macleod QC and Christopher Katkowski acted for the MOD in the inquiry into a new military training ground at Otterburn; Michael Barnes QC acted for Union Railways in the inquiry in relation to Stratford Station; Christopher Lockhart-Mummery QC acted for Sainsburys in the inquiry into a major development in Brighton, and for the developers in the inquiry into a retail development at Giants Field, Trafford Park. Recent reported cases include 'Rochester City Council v Kent County Council' (Richard Drabble QC) and 'R v Secretary of State for the Environment Ex p Camden London BC' (effect of changing local authority accounting practice – John Howell QC, Christopher Katkowski and David Elvin). **Leading Barristers:** *Christopher Lockhart-Mummery QC* was especially highly recommended for retail and leisure developments and for his swift preparation of papers and clear advice. *Nigel Macleod QC* moves up in our table, admired for his thoroughness, "incredible work rate" and "great clarity in final submissions at inquiry." *John Howell QC* gives a solid opinion, carefully researched and delivered pleasantly – "he tells it how it really is." Among the juniors *Christopher Katkowski* was described as "shrewd," with a good commercial brain. *David Elvin* received high praise from someone who had used him recently – "the other side had a silk and he turned them inside out." He is seen as a particularly good tactician who "really thinks about all the preliminary stages and ambushes people successfully." *Michael Barnes QC* is praised as being "straight down the line" with his advice. *David Holgate QC* acted for Broxbourne Borough Council in the Canada Fields development inquiry.

4-5 Gray's Inn Square (Appleby & Beloff) 4 Breams Buildings may be reputed to have the brightest planning barristers, but 4-5 Gray's Inn Square were frequently described as the leading 'commercial' planning set. **Leading Barristers:** *Brian Ash QC* had won the admiration of one solicitor for taking over and rescuing a JR case, presenting it brilliantly at the last moment. He was said to be very succinct and sharply focused. Planning solicitors liked *Clive Newberry QC's* style – "he's not one of those who just puts his case – he'll really debate things with a witness." They also unanimously agreed with our inclusion of *Duncan Ouseley QC* in the top band of silks ("he's very astute and picks up the issues quickly." "Thinks laterally and is excellent on his feet"). He has a broad-based local authority practice and is seen as straddling both areas. Apparently some clients think

LEADING SILKS · LONDON

FITZGERALD Michael 2 Mitre Court Buildings
LOCKHART-MUMMERY Christopher 4 Breams Buildings
OUSELEY Duncan 4-5 Gray's Inn Square
READ Lionel 1 Serjeants' Inn

ASH Brian 4-5 Gray's Inn Square
BARNES Michael 4 Breams Buildings
CLARKSON Patrick 1 Serjeants' Inn
HICKS William 1 Serjeants' Inn
HOWELL John 4 Breams Buildings
LINDBLOM Keith 2 Harcourt Buildings
PHILLIPS Richard 2 Harcourt Buildings
PURCHAS Robin 2 Harcourt Buildings
SILSOE Lord 2 Mitre Court Buildings
STEEL John 4-5 Gray's Inn Square
STONE Gregory 4-5 Gray's Inn Square
TAYLOR John 2 Mitre Court Buildings

ANDERSON Anthony 2 Mitre Court Buildings
ARDEN Andrew Arden Chambers
BARTLETT George 2 Mitre Court Buildings
DRABBLE Richard 4 Breams Buildings
GEORGE Charles 2 Harcourt Buildings
GOUDIE James 11 King's Bench Walk
MACLEOD Nigel 4 Breams Buildings
NEWBERRY Clive 4-5 Gray's Inn Square
PORTEN Anthony 2-3 Gray's Inn Square
PUGH Vernon 2-3 Gray's Inn Square

DINKIN Anthony 2-3 Gray's Inn Square
HOCKMAN Stephen 6 Pump Court
LOWE (Nicholas) Mark 2-3 Gray's Inn Square
MAWREY Richard 2 Harcourt Buildings
MOLE David 4-5 Gray's Inn Square
MORIARTY Gerald 2 Mitre Court Buildings
ROOTS Guy 2 Mitre Court Buildings
RYAN Gerard 2 Harcourt Buildings
SPENCE Malcolm 2-3 Gray's Inn Square
STRAKER Timothy 2-3 Gray's Inn Square
TABACHNIK Eldred 11 King's Bench Walk

NEW SILKS · 1997 AND 1998

HOLGATE David 4 Breams Buildings

so much of him that they are known to try for an adjournment if he is not available for a hearing. *Tom Hill*, new to our tables this year, was said to have "a very strong junior practice."

2 Harcourt Buildings (Ryan) Favoured by many for the diversity of experience available, as well as for the friendly and efficient clerks. Said to give excellent value for money. **Work Handled:** Heathrow

Terminal 5 inquiry (Keith Lindblom QC for Thames Water, Craig Howell Williams for a consortium of local authorities); 'Kensington & Chelsea RBC v Secretary of State' (Charles Mynors – conservation areas); Charles George QC promoted the Manchester Metro Link Extension to Ashton-under-Lyne at public inquiry; Suzanne Ornsby appeared at test cases on the Battlefields Register and demolition of unlisted buildings in a conservation area for English Heritage. **Leading Barristers:** *Keith Lindblom QC* has moved into a higher band of leading silks following glowing reports from several solicitors ("courteous and effective," "clients and inspectors love him"). *Robin Purchas QC* is said to have an incredible appetite for work, to be very good on paper and excellent in conferences. *Gerard Ryan QC* was praised for his "excellent attention to detail." "All the technically difficult stuff" goes to *Charles George QC*; "he has a razor-sharp brain," commented a number of practitioners. *Richard Phillips QC* was admired for being "the hardest working barrister I've come across" and a "very impressive advocate." *Jonathan Milner* is said by local authority practitioners to have developed a sharper edge and more commercial style.

2 Mitre Court Buildings (FitzGerald) The first choice of a number of solicitors, with seven silks and five juniors recommended to us. Again, practitioners had nothing but praise for the clerking at the set. **Work Handled:** Members of chambers have continued to be involved in the Heathrow Terminal 5 inquiry, notably Lord Silsoe QC and *Guy Roots QC*, acting for the promoters BAA plc. Michael Fitzgerald QC made several appearances upon behalf of British Airways. He also appeared at the inquiry into a new visitor centre at Gatwick with Neil King as junior. John Taylor QC has dealt with several mineral and waste inquiries over the past year, as well as acting on the redevelopment of part of Milton Keynes Shopping Centre and Merry Hill shopping centre at Dudley, both with *Robert Fookes* as junior. *George Bartlett QC* has been involved in several power-related planning and rating matters during the past year, and appeared at an inquiry in relation to a clinical waste incinerator at Bournemouth. **Leading Barristers:** *Michael FitzGerald QC* remains many solicitors' favourite planning barrister. Several also remarked on *Lord Silsoe QC's*

impressive intellect. *John Taylor QC* is said to have a strong CV on compulsory purchase and lands tribunal work; he is "a knockabout advocate with lots of presence and style." *Neil King* is "very able and nice to deal with."

1 Serjeants' Inn (Read) Have a great variety of juniors, with nine appearing in our tables. **Work Handled:** *William Hicks QC's* recent cases include acting for Fulham F.C. in 'Berkeley v Secretary of State for the Environment and Another' (CA, quashing of permission not justified). **Leading Barristers:** "Undoubtedly still top" was the comment that most succinctly sums up solicitors' views on *Lionel Read QC*. *Patrick Clarkson QC* was described as a very good advocate, who strikes the right balance in cross-examination. *Richard Harwood* was newly recommended to us this year – "he's got a really good brain – definitely the one to go to for an opinion." *Stephen Morgan* is seen as sensible and unflamboyant, while *Sasha White* is becoming a well-known name.

2-3 Gray's Inn Square (Scrivener) Another set mentioned as offering particularly good value for money and friendly, efficient clerking. **Work Handled:** Tim

Straker QC's recent cases include 'R v North Yorkshire County Council Ex p Brown & Another' (CA, conditions on old mining permission). *Mark Lowe QC* acted in 'R v Kensington & Chelsea LBC ex p Lawrie Plantation Services Ltd (CA, change of use). **Leading Barristers:** *Tim Straker QC* was recommended as a clear thinker and a sensible local government and judicial review performer. *Anthony Porten QC* is seen as an old-school local government lawyer who has been working for local authorities "since time began" – not a showman but very sound. He is known for dealing with some of the most important cases.

11 King's Bench Walk (Tabachnik & Goudie) Included primarily for local government expertise. **Leading Barristers:** *James Goudie QC* was recommended as the one to go to for local government matters; he is known to be excellent on vires points and knows local government regulations inside out.

Also well regarded for pure local authority work was **Arden Chambers**; particularly strong on vires issues.

WESTERN/WALES AND CHESTER CIRCUIT

LEADING SILKS
WALES & CHESTER

WILLIAMS Wyn Lewis 33 Park Place

LEADING JUNIORS
WALES & CHESTER

JARMAN Milwyn 9 Park Place
RICHARDS Wyn Iscoed Chambers

LEADING JUNIORS · WESTERN

WADSLEY Peter St. John's Chambers

Iscoed Chambers, Swansea (Davies) The "first class" *Wyn Richards* recently appeared at the Pembrokeshire Coast Path National Park Plan Inquiry, and in an appeal in relation to the proposed National Botanic Garden of Wales.

MIDLANDS AND OXFORD CIRCUIT

LEADING SILKS
MIDLANDS & OXFORD

KINGSTON Martin 5 Fountain Court
WOLTON Harry 5 Fountain Court

LEADING JUNIORS
MIDLANDS & OXFORD

CAHILL Jeremy 5 Fountain Court
DOVE Ian 5 Fountain Court
GOATLEY Peter 5 Fountain Court
JONES Timothy St Philip's Chambers

5 Fountain Court, Birmingham (Barker) Easily the leading planning and local government set in the Midlands. **Leading Barristers:** As well as being the leading barrister in the region, *Martin Kingston QC* enjoys a national reputation. Is seen as on a par with the top London silks.

NORTHERN CIRCUIT

LEADING SILKS · NORTHERN

GILBART Andrew 40 King St
HOGGETT John 40 King St
SAUVAIN Stephen 40 King St

NEW SILKS · 1997 AND 1998

PATTERSON Frances 40 King St

LEADING JUNIORS · NORTHERN

BARRETT John 40 King St
FRASER Vincent 40 King St
MANLEY David 40 King St

FOR DETAILS OF THESE LEADING BARRISTERS
SEE PROFILES ON PAGES 1509-1642

40 King St, Manchester (Raynor)Has no serious competition for the position of leading planning and local government set in the North. **Leading Barristers:** New silk *Frances Patterson QC* was much admired for being "tenacious and thorough, courteous but persistent." She recently acted in Modern Homes (Whitworth) Ltd v Lancashire County Council (The Times, 14 May 1998). *Andrew Gilbart QC* and *John Hoggett QC* again received several recommendations.

PRODUCT LIABILITY

RESEARCH: In compiling the tables, we consider all the information available to us, paying particular regard to the market research carried out by our team of ten qualified lawyers. (The researchers' details are set out on page three.) The rankings, therefore, reflect the opinion of the market-place as revealed by systematic and objective research: see page four. (Our research is audited every year by the British Market Research Bureau.)

OVERVIEW: Work involves multi-party litigation and regulatory advice in the pharmaceutical, engineering and medical fields. Tobacco litigation continues to provide a great deal of work for barristers.

2 Harcourt Buildings (Henderson) One of the few sets to offer an expert team in this field. **Work Handled:** Exclusively defendant work in relation to all areas of product liability, including tobacco litigation and pharmaceutical cases such as prozac and minosin. Also mine radiation cases, sheep dip cases, and mesothelioma and asbestosis claims. **Leading Barristers:** *Jonathan Playford QC* is considered an excellent advocate, and has a good deal of experience defending institutions. *Andrew Prynne QC* is described as "approachable and enthusiastic about this area" and *Charles Gibson* has a reputation in work relating to medical devices.

One Paper Buildings (Slater) An excellent reputation in the product liability field, and the expertise to handle cases which involve pharmaceutical and technical elements. **Leading Barristers:** *Michael Spencer QC* handles heavyweight group actions and is considered an expert at this type of work. He has recently been involved in tobacco and oral contraceptive litigation. *Dr Michael Powers QC* is known for his medical negligence work and is thought "first class" for product liability matters as well. *Simon Brown QC* is rated for cases with substantial technical aspects. *Jonathan Waite* has a reputation in the food products area, and has been involved in tobacco litigation.

The "superb" *Daniel Brennan QC* at **39 Essex Street** (Glasgow) is an authoritative figure praised for "sound judgment." During 1999 his availability will be temporarily limited as he assumes the Chairmanship of the Bar Council. *Justin Fenwick QC* from **2 Crown Office Row** (Powell) is a new name in the list, and is considered "solid" and a "good all-rounder." Another addition to the table is the "frighteningly bright" *Brian Langstaff QC* from **Cloisters** (Cox). He has invaluable experience of group actions and is valued for his "ability to grasp the important details." *Barry Cotter* from **Old Square Chambers** (Melville Williams) is standing counsel to several companies in relation to product liability. *Oliver Thorold* from **Doughty Street Chambers** (Robertson) is considered a highly intellectual junior. *Augustus Ullstein QC* from **29 Bedford Row** (Ralls) was also recommended as "extremely capable and familiar with the area."

Barristers' profiles   p. 1509-1642

LEADING SETS · LONDON

2 HARCOURT BUILDINGS (Roger Henderson QC)
ONE PAPER BUILDINGS (John Slater QC)

LEADING SILKS · LONDON

BRENNAN Daniel 39 Essex Street
SPENCER Michael One Paper Buildings

ASHWORTH Piers 2 Harcourt Buildings
BROWN Simon One Paper Buildings
FENWICK Justin 2 Crown Office Row
LANGSTAFF Brian Cloisters
PLAYFORD Jonathan 2 Harcourt Buildings
POWERS Michael One Paper Buildings
PRYNNE Andrew 2 Harcourt Buildings
ULLSTEIN Augustus 29 Bedford Row

LEADING JUNIORS · LONDON

COTTER Barry Old Square Chambers
GIBSON Charles 2 Harcourt Buildings
WAITE Jonathan One Paper Buildings

THOROLD Oliver Doughty Street Chambers
WEST Lawrence 2 Harcourt Buildings

FOR DETAILS OF THESE LEADING BARRISTERS
SEE PROFILES ON PAGES 1509-1642

PROFESSIONAL NEGLIGENCE

RESEARCH: In compiling the tables, we consider all the information available to us, paying particular regard to the market research carried out by our team of ten qualified lawyers. (The researchers' details are set out on page three.) The rankings, therefore, reflect the opinion of the marketplace as revealed by systematic and objective research: see page four. (Our research is audited every year by the British Market Research Bureau.)

OVERVIEW: Professional negligence overlaps with other areas to such an extent that a huge number of counsel practise it at one time or another. Consequently, for barristers to be ranked in these tables they have to be recognised as having specialist experience in the area. Competition between the sets is strong, although John Powell's chambers at 2 Crown Office Row remained the most popular choice with the majority of interviewees. Littleton Chambers (Burton) and 9 Old Square (Reid) are new entries.

Barristers' profiles	p. 1509-1642

LEADING SETS · LONDON
2 CROWN OFFICE ROW (John Powell QC)
2 CROWN OFFICE ROW (Graeme Hamilton QC)
4 PAPER BUILDINGS (Harvey McGregor QC)
4 PUMP COURT (Bruce Mauleverer QC)
2 TEMPLE GARDENS (Patrick Phillips QC)
BRICK COURT CHAMBERS (Clarke QC)
FOUNTAIN COURT (Peter Scott QC)
KEATING CHAMBERS (Richard Fernyhough QC)
ONE PAPER BUILDINGS (John Slater QC)

HIGHLY REGARDED · LONDON
39 Essex Street (Edwin Glasgow QC)
7 King's Bench Walk (Stephen Tomlinson QC)
Littleton Chambers (Michael Burton QC)
9 Old Square (Robert Reid QC)

2 Crown Office Row (Powell) Still the leading set for professional negligence with an overwhelming number of recommendations. "Front runner," "dominant," "best by far" were just a few of the comments received. Equally strong for silks and juniors. **Leading Barristers:** *John Powell QC* and *Rupert Jackson QC* have long been considered leading authorities and are consequently many people's first choice for complex cases. Recent work has included 'BCCI v Price Waterhouse and Ernst & Young' (Powell) and 'McFarlene v Wilkinson' (Jackson). Amongst the many other recommended names *Simon Russen* who ("gets to grips with big cases quickly") and "no nonsense" *Andrew Stafford* were new entries to our tables. *Bernard Livesey QC*, "a very good performer" was instructed on 'SAAMCO v Finers.'

2 Crown Office Row (Hamilton) Promoted in our tables following consistent praise as a set now doing a "broad spectrum" of work. Particularly strong in silks. **Leading Barristers:** Top silk *Michael Harvey QC* was considered "extremely thorough and detailed." He acted on 'Hornsby v K. Clark' and 'Colville Estates v Strutt & Parker.' Both *Antony Edwards-Stuart QC* and *Richard Lynagh QC* rose in our rankings with the latter particularly highly praised for his "good overall judgement."

4 Paper Buildings (McGregor) Perceived as leaders in professional indemnity, providing a "fantastic service." Recently involved in 'Re Beakman.' **Leading Barristers:** The "incredibly bright" *Nicholas Davidson QC* is a new entry at the top of the tables following overwhelm-

ing recommendations. He was instructed on such high profile matters as 'Bristol & West v Fancy and Jackson' and 'National Home Loans Association v Giffen Couch and Archer.' Among several leading juniors, the "superb" *Michael Pooles* also received strong praise. His recent work has included 'Goldcoin Joulliers v United Bank of Kuwait.'

4 Pump Court (Mauleverer) "All of the talent and none of the pretension" according to one commentator. Widely praised by a large number of solicitors. **Leading Barristers:** *Bruce Mauleverer QC*, "a popular choice," has moved to top ranking. He was instructed in relation to the collapse of Holbeck Hall Hotel into the sea in Scarborough. *Nigel Tozzi*, who has "lots of flair" and is "terrific across the board," enters the tables for the first time. His recent work includes 'DTI v Messrs Coulthard Shuttleworth and Dawes' which established the duty of care of auditors to directors personally as opposed to the company.

2 Temple Gardens (Phillips) **Leading Barristers:** Among the many leading silks, the "proficient" *Benjamin Browne QC* and *Jeremy Stuart-Smith QC* received particularly favourable comment. *Robert Moxon-Browne QC* who acted on 'The Housing Loan Corporation v William Brown' rose in the ranking following widespread praise. The "devastatingly thorough" junior, *Graham Eklund* was a new entry this year. He acted on 'Chapman Ltd and Benson Turner v Christopher' with *William Crowther QC.*

Brick Court Chambers (Clarke) Described as "the Rolls Royce of sets" with

a large number of "heavyweights" and recommended for particularly high profile cases. Noted for its commercial profile. **Work Handled:** 'Wallis Smith Trust v Coopers & Lybrand' (Hapgood, Sumption, Howard); 'NRG v Bacon & Woodrow' (Aikens, Adam, Leggatt,); 'Ernst & Young v BCCI' (Clarke) **Leading Barristers:** Include *Jonathan Sumption QC*, who is considered by some to be "the best at the bar at anything he does" and *Mark Howard QC*, "one to watch."

Fountain Court A commercial set which specialises in heavyweight, high value cases. **Leading Barristers:** Include the "first class, charming" *Peter Goldsmith QC*, whose work this year has included 'Stoy Hayward v Polly Peck,' the "solid and popular" *Raymond Cox* and the "approachable" *Bankim Thanki*. *Michael Brindle QC* ("first class, thoroughly good all rounder") was instructed on 'Bank Austria v Price Waterhouse.'

Keating Chambers (Fernyhough) A top building and construction set which deals primarily with related professional negligence claims. **Leading Barristers:** *Vivian Ramsey QC* and *Richard Fernyhough QC* were singled out for praise, as were the "excellent" *Peter Coulson* and the "smooth and clever" *Marcus Taverner.*

One Paper Buildings (Slater) Seen as a good, solid set with a broad background, the set is headed by "extremely good and hard working" *John Slater QC*. **Work Handled:** 'UCB Bank plc v Alder King & Roberts' (negligent valuation); 'Matrix Securities v Theodore Goddard and David Goldberg

LEADING SILKS · LONDON

DAVIDSON Nicholas 4 Paper Buildings	JACKSON Rupert 2 Crown Office Row	SLATER John One Paper Buildings
FENWICK Justin 2 Crown Office Row	MAULEVERER Bruce 4 Pump Court	SUMPTION Jonathan Brick Court Chambers
GIBSON Christopher 2 Crown Office Row	POWELL John 2 Crown Office Row	TER HAAR Roger 2 Crown Office Row
HARVEY Michael 2 Crown Office Row		
BRINDLE Michael Fountain Court	FLAUX Julian 7 King's Bench Walk	PATTEN Nicholas 9 Old Square
COOKE Jeremy 7 King's Bench Walk	GLASGOW Edwin 39 Essex Street	RAMSEY Vivian Keating Chambers
CROWTHER William 2 Temple Gardens	GLOSTER Elizabeth One Essex Court	SYMONS Christopher 3 Verulam Buildings
EDELMAN Colin Devereux Chambers	GOLDSMITH Peter Fountain Court	TEMPLE Anthony 4 Pump Court
EDWARDS-STUART Antony 2 Crown Office Row	MOXON-BROWNE Robert 2 Temple Gardens	
AIKENS Richard Brick Court Chambers	FERNYHOUGH Richard Keating Chambers	LYNAGH Richard 2 Crown Office Row
BROWN Simon One Paper Buildings	GAISMAN Jonathan 7 King's Bench Walk	MALEK Ali 3 Verulam Buildings
BURTON Michael Littleton Chambers	HAPGOOD Mark Brick Court Chambers	MOWSCHENSON Terence One Essex Court
CLARKE Christopher Brick Court Chambers	KEALEY Gavin 7 King's Bench Walk	SCOTT Peter Fountain Court
BARTLETT Andrew One Paper Buildings	HUGHES Iain 2 Crown Office Row	POPPLEWELL Andrew Brick Court Chambers
BERRY Simon 9 Old Square	KALLIPETIS Michel Littleton Chambers	RAILTON David Fountain Court
BROWNE Benjamin 2 Temple Gardens	LAMB Timothy 2 Temple Gardens	SEABROOK Robert 1 Crown Office Row
BURKE Jeffrey Devereux Chambers	LIVESEY Bernard 2 Crown Office Row	SEYMOUR Richard Monckton Chambers
DAVIES Richard 39 Essex Street	MANN Anthony Enterprise Chambers	STEWART Robin 199 Strand
ELLIOTT Timothy Keating Chambers	MOGER Christopher 4 Pump Court	STUART-SMITH Jeremy 2 Temple Gardens
FAULKS Edward No. 1 Serjeants' Inn	PHILIPSON Trevor Fountain Court	TURNER Janet 3 Verulam Buildings
HODGE David 9 Old Square	PHILLIPS Patrick 2 Temple Gardens	VALLANCE Philip 1 Crown Office Row
HOWARD Mark Brick Court Chambers	PLAYFORD Jonathan 2 Harcourt Buildings	

NEW SILKS · LONDON 1997 AND 1998

BOSWELL Lindsay 4 Pump Court	LEGGATT George Brick Court Chambers	PHILLIPS David 199 Strand
DOUGLAS Michael 4 Pump Court	NORRIS Alastair 5 Stone Buildings	RUTTLE Stephen Brick Court Chambers

FOR DETAILS OF THESE LEADING BARRISTERS SEE PROFILES ON PAGES 1509-1642

QC' (solicitors/ barristers) (Slater); 'BBL v Zurich Insurance' (Brown); 'Capital & Counties plc v Hampshire CC' (duties of fire brigades) (Slater, Brown). **Leading Barristers:** *Simon Brown QC* is praised for his "approachability, ability, and quick turnaround" whilst *Andrew Bartlett QC* is "shrewd, efficient and thorough."

39 Essex Street (Glasgow) **Work Handled:** 'Zeneca v Laing Management Contracting and King Sturge & Co'; 'George Fischer v Multidesign Consultants and DLE' (Manzoni). **Leading Barristers:** Particularly singled out for praise are *Charles Manzoni* and the "terrific" *Edwin Glasgow QC* who is "wonderful on his feet and gets the ear of the judge like no-one else."

7 King's Bench Walk (Tomlinson) Tend to be used mainly in heavy, commercial cases. **Leading Barristers:** Have an array of stars including the "user friendly" *Jeremy Cooke QC* and "bright and able" *Jonathan Gaisman QC*. *Julian Flaux QC* is "good in action" whilst *Christopher Butcher* has an "immense brain" and is "one to watch."

Littleton Chambers (Burton) A new addition this year, they received many recommendations from solicitors and

barristers. **Leading Barristers:** *Michel Kallipetis QC* was praised for his "tremendous presentation skills." He is joined this year by the well-known *Michael Burton QC* and the "highly competent" *Ian Gatt*.

9 Old Square (Reid) Highly regarded, particularly for their silks. **Work Handled:**

'SAAMCO' (Berry) **Leading Barristers:** *Nicholas Patten QC* is "extremely bright, on the ball and unflappable." Another popular choice is the "absolutely superb, yet modest, intellectual" *Simon Berry QC*. *David Hodge QC* "has made his mark" and "is a delight to be led by."

LEADING JUNIORS · LONDON

BUTCHER Christopher 7 King's Bench Walk	STEWART Roger 2 Crown Office Row
POOLES Michael 4 Paper Buildings	
CARR Sue 2 Crown Office Row	TAVERNER Marcus Keating Chambers
HALPERN David Enterprise Chambers	WORTHINGTON Stephen 12 King's Bench Walk
HOLWILL Derek 4 Paper Buildings	
COULSON Peter Keating Chambers	PEACOCKE Teresa Enterprise Chambers
COX Raymond Fountain Court	PHILLIPS Rory 3 Verulam Buildings
CROSS James 4 Pump Court	PITTAWAY David No. 1 Serjeants' Inn
GUGGENHEIM Anna 2 Crown Office Row	SIMMONDS Andrew 5 Stone Buildings
LAWRENCE Patrick 4 Paper Buildings	SINCLAIR Fiona 2 Crown Office Row
NEISH Andrew 4 Pump Court	TOZZI Nigel 4 Pump Court
NEWMAN Paul Wilberforce Chambers	
ADAM Tom Brick Court Chambers	PHILIPPS Guy Fountain Court
CANNON Mark 2 Crown Office Row	RUSSEN Simon 2 Crown Office Row
EKLUND Graham 2 Temple Gardens	STAFFORD Andrew 2 Crown Office Row
FERRIS Jonathan 29 Bedford Row Chambers	STITCHER Malcolm 199 Strand
GATT Ian Littleton Chambers	THANKI Bankim Fountain Court
MANZONI Charles 39 Essex Street	

PROPERTY (LITIGATION)

RESEARCH: In compiling the tables, we consider all the information available to us, paying particular regard to the market research carried out by our team of ten qualified lawyers. (The researchers' details are set out on page three.) The rankings, therefore, reflect the opinion of the marketplace as revealed by systematic and objective research: see page four. (Our research is audited every year by the British Market Research Bureau.)

OVERVIEW: The views of solicitors, clients and leading barristers, both silks and juniors, were sought to prepare this section. Interestingly the Bar's views differed noticeably from those of clients and solicitors, especially with regard to the rankings of juniors.

Sets which undertake property work can be divided into three categories. The first consists solely of Falcon Chambers – the only dedicated property litigation set. Secondly, there are the Lincoln's Inn chancery sets. Finally, there are the many common law sets which undertake this kind of work. Falcon Chambers and the chancery sets dominate the higher value commercial property market and, consequently, our rankings.

There are few changes in the leading sets this year. The strong reputation of Falcon Chambers spreads to all parts of England and Wales and it remains in first place. Indeed, many interviewees would only comment on barristers at Falcon.

Barristers' profiles   p. 1509-1642

LEADING SILKS · LONDON

LEWISON Kim Falcon Chambers
MORGAN Paul Falcon Chambers

BARNES Michael 4 Breams Buildings
BERRY Simon 9 Old Square
ETHERTON Terence Wilberforce Chambers
GAUNT Jonathan Falcon Chambers
REYNOLDS Kirk Falcon Chambers

BRIGGS Michael Serle Court Chambers
BROCK Jonathan Falcon Chambers
DOWDING Nicholas Falcon Chambers
DRISCOLL Michael 9 Old Square
WILLIAMSON Hazel 13 Old Square

ARDEN Andrew Arden Chambers
CHERRYMAN John 4 Breams Buildings
FURBER John 4 Breams Buildings
JACKSON Judith 9 Old Square
PATTEN Nicholas 9 Old Square
STEINFELD Alan 24 Old Buildings

LAURENCE George 12 New Square
MARTIN John Wilberforce Chambers
NUGEE Edward Wilberforce Chambers
REID Robert 9 Old Square

NEW SILKS · LONDON

HODGE David 9 Old Square
NUGEE Christopher Wilberforce Chambers
PYMONT Christopher 13 Old Square
TRACE Anthony 13 Old Square

FOR DETAILS OF THESE LEADING BARRISTERS
SEE PROFILES ON PAGES 1509-1642

LEADING SETS · LONDON

FALCON CHAMBERS (Gaunt QC/Lewison QC)

4 BREAMS BUILDINGS (Lockhart-Mummery QC)
9 OLD SQUARE (Robert Reid QC)
13 OLD SQUARE (Michael Lyndon-Stanford QC)

BARNARDS INN CHAMBERS (Timothy Bowles)
ENTERPRISE CHAMBERS (Anthony Mann QC)
SERLE COURT CHAMBERS (Charles Sparrow QC)
WILBERFORCE CHAMBERS (Edward Nugee QC)

Falcon Chambers (Gaunt & Lewison) By far the leading set. The clerking has improved and the service is efficient from start to finish. The silks are "without exception absolutely fantastic," and the middle ranking juniors are "solid specialists." A number of interviewees commented that the set's standing is based on landlord & tenant work, and that some rival sets are as good in other areas of property litigation. **Leading Barristers:** Interviewees fell into two groups. Those who declared **Kim Lewison QC** to be "the unchallenged king of landlord and tenant" and those who gave the accolade to **Paul Morgan QC**. Lewison described as "brilliant, quick, innovative, personable," was liked for his precision and succinctness. No one had a bad word to say about Paul Morgan who "has an incredible intellect and the person-al skills to go with it." Both solicitors and barristers commented that "you don't want Paul on the other side." Both Morgan and Lewison move into the highest band by themselves. Also moving up the rankings are **Jonathan Gaunt QC** ("really knows his papers, steady"), **Kirk Reynolds QC** ("gives forthright and confident advice ... has great charm and never panics") and **Jonathan Brock QC** ("astute, tenacious, passionate about winning.") **Nicholas Dowding QC**, who recently appeared in the Court of Appeal case 'Maryland Estates Ltd v Joseph,' was singled out for particular praise. "Nick's the closest thing to David Neuberger at the Bar today... a special combination of charm and boldness ... a superb cross examiner ... accurately assesses your chances and outcomes." Of the juniors **Timothy Fancourt** ("a lively intellect, superb with clients and frighteningly efficient") and **Stephen Jourdan** ("extremely bright and does a brilliant job") are the most popular. Jourdan was Kim Lewison's junior in the recent 'Storehouse Properties v Ocobase' case (landlord withholding consent to an assignment). Also recommended are **Wayne Clark** ("down to earth...a rising star"), **Martin Rodger** ("wins cases!"), **Caroline Shea** ("lots of energy and commitment ... comes up with good ideas"), **Edward Cole** ("reliable and steady"), **Barry Denyer-Green** ("great fun to work with"). The "bright and confident" **Jonathan Small** is up and coming.

4 Breams Buildings (Lockhart-Mummery) Received strong recommendations for the "excellent quality" of its barristers and the "helpful, receptive and eager to please" clerking service. **Leading Barristers:** Three silks were recommended: the "excellent" **Michael Barnes QC**, a greatly respected and supremely good lawyer, but less active than he was; the well-regarded **John Cherryman QC**; and **John Furber QC**, a new entrant and a "delight to deal with." **John Male** has "an extremely good reputation, is a great fighter and does the work of a leader." Also recommended were **Jonathan Karas** ("very diligent and clever"), **David Elvin** and **Nicholas Taggart** ("a team player with a great sense of humour"). "We use him alot and he's never let us down," commented one interviewee.

9 Old Square (Reid) A well established chancery set which handles real property and landlord & tenant. Known for "giving a very good service," the set is said to have excellent people and instructing solicitors "get access to them very quickly." The set has the second largest number of individuals mentioned after Falcon chambers. **Leading Barristers:** An ex solicitor, *Simon Berry QC* is "undoubtedly one of the top L&T silks and a powerful performer." He acted in 'Dukeminster Ltd v Somerfield Property Co Ltd,' a Court of Appeal case on the construction of a rent review clause. *Michael Driscoll QC* ("he's just superb and a very tough opponent") and *Nicholas Patten QC* ("a hard worker who wins cases") were recommended as "client-friendly." Others include *Judith Jackson QC* ("charming and well liked"), *Robert Reid QC* (a very senior silk whose practice ranges far wider than just property litigation), *David Hodge QC* ("punchy, inspires confidence and good at finding new ways of approaching old problems"), *Katharine Holland* ("made of the right stuff...a real fighter"), *John McGhee* ("punchy when you need someone to be punchy"), *Timothy Harry* ("a great technician, accessible and pleasant to deal with") and *Edwin Johnson* ("a good balance between a respectful approach to the judge and being forthright and getting the best for the client").

13 Old Square (Lyndon-Stanford) A wide ranging chancery set "specialising in litigation rather than paperwork." **Leading Barristers:** The set's reputation in this field is bolstered by the dedicated property litigator, *Hazel Williamson QC*. She is highly thought of for the quality and speed of her advice as well as for her "excellent personal skills." Also recommended are *Christopher Pymont QC* ("gets straight down to it ... completely unflappable") and new silk, *Anthony Trace QC* ("truly excellent and thoroughly charming").

Barnards Inn Chambers (Bowles) A fairly new set (established in 1993) covering a wide spread of work. Five juniors (including some very senior ones) specialise in landlord and tenant with three others getting involved in associated matters. **Leading Barristers:** The set has two popular property juniors. *Timothy Bowles* "should be a silk and is a tough opponent" whilst *Timothy Dutton* is "wonderful – with an incredible passion for L&T law."

Enterprise Chambers (Mann) A commercial chancery set; historically strong in property. Seven juniors specialise in property work, and nearly all tenants do some property litigation. "Provides a very client orientated service." **Leading Barristers:** *Caroline Hutton* has an excellent reputation for advisory work. Also recommended were *Benjamin Levy* ("a very senior junior"), *David Halpern*, *James Barker* (for insolvency related L&T), *Linden Ife* ("a real fighter") and *Ann McAllister* ("thoroughly grounded in property ... approachable"). *Jacqueline Baker* is newly recommended.

Serle Court Chambers (Sparrow) Advises across a broad range of work in the chancery and commercial fields. **Leading Barristers:** *Michael Briggs QC* is a strong all round chancery advocate and "very tough in court." He has a "quick and pleasant manner." The other well known name at the set, *Beverley-Ann Rogers*, is perceived to have a low profile by choice rather than ability, and "her practice could take off any time she wished."

Wilberforce Chambers (Nugee) A commercial chancery set which tends to do more real property work rather than landlord & tenant. Twenty-five of the set's 29 tenants regularly handle property matters with 12 doing it "nearly full time." **Leading Barristers:** *Terence Etherton QC* is noted for "his expertise in explaining difficult legal concepts to judges in almost any field." Immensely diligent, Etherton has the gift of making "it all look so easy." The other silks are *John Martin QC* ("has a great reputation"), *Edward Nugee QC* "an old fashioned chancery silk who is superb for a heavyweight point of law") and *Christopher Nugee QC* ("a powerful combination of a fine academic mind and a common sense advocate ... judges think highly of him") who took silk this year. He acted with Terence Etherton in 'Central London Commercial Estates Ltd v Kato Kagaku Ltd' (squatter acquired rights of leaseholder). The juniors who were recommended are *Jonathan Seitler* ("very bright and a fine draftsman"), *Anthony Taussig* (concentrates on drafting for which he is highly regarded) and *Caroline Furze*.

Recommended individuals not at leading sets include: *Alan Steinfeld QC* of **24 Old Buildings** (Brodie) and *Andrew Arden QC* of **Arden Chambers** (Arden) – an expert on the technical side of legislation, also well known in housing law. *George Laurence QC* of **12 New Square** (Mowbray) is "a charming man who believes in his cases and is very convincing." He is known for his expertise on highways and

for statute-based property law. The tenacious *Jonathan Arkush* of **11 Stone Buildings** (Beckman) was recommended again this year. He "has a good way with clients and looks after you," and often appears against silks. *Anthony Radevsky* of **5 Bell Yard** (Webb) is not only "extremely good" at L&T but has cornered the market in leasehold enfranchisement for which he is the Bar's leading expert. *James Thom* of **4 Field Court** (Brice) is a "great technical lawyer and a persuasive advocate" with "a good name in the trade" despite being at a predominantly admiralty set.

SHIPPING

RESEARCH: In compiling the tables, we consider all the information available to us, paying particular regard to the market research carried out by our team of ten qualified lawyers. (The researchers' details are set out on page three.) The rankings, therefore, reflect the opinion of the marketplace as revealed by systematic and objective research: see page four. (Our research is audited every year by the British Market Research Bureau.)

OVERVIEW: There are no changes to the leading sets this year. Interviewees agreed that the standard of the shipping bar is incredibly high, and many solicitors are happy to use anyone recommended by the clerks in the listed sets.

LEADING SETS · LONDON

BRICK COURT CHAMBERS
(Christopher Clarke QC)
4 ESSEX COURT (Nigel Teare QC)
ESSEX COURT CHAMBERS (Gordon Pollock QC)
20 ESSEX STREET (David Johnson QC)
4 FIELD COURT (Geoffrey Brice QC)
7 KING'S BENCH WALK (Stephen Tomlinson QC)

Brick Court Chambers (Clarke) **Leading Barristers:** This heavyweight commercial set boasts an array of talent, including *Christopher Clarke QC, Jonathan Hirst QC* and *Peregrine Simon QC. Richard Aikens QC* is "intellectually first rate and amazingly persuasive," while *Richard Lord* is "commercial and gets on with things."

4 Essex Court (Teare) One of the strongest sets in this field, praised for the efficiency of its clerking as well as the quality of its tenants. **Leading Barristers:** *Nigel Teare QC*, the Head of Chambers, is "quick and user friendly." *Belinda Bucknall QC* is "bright, on the ball and responds well," while *Michael Howard QC* is "a good barrister of the old school." *Jeremy Russell QC* is "fair, balanced and delivers a first class service." *Charles MacDonald QC* is "user friendly, thorough and intelligent." New silk *Timothy Brenton QC* is "an up and coming star." Of the juniors, *James Turner* "has made a good impression," *Luke Parsons* is "extremely good" and *Poonam Melwani* is "bright and independent." *Simon Rainey* is "intellectually red hot and extremely pleasant."

Essex Court Chambers (Pollock) **Leading Barristers:** *Gordon Pollock QC* is the "big gun" in this field – "head and shoulders above the rest" according to one practitioner. *Roderick Cordara QC* recent-

ly led in 'Stocznia Gdanska v Latvian Shipping.' *Michael Collins QC* is "bright and diligent", while *Stewart Boyd QC* is "academically great." *Jonathan Gilman QC* was particularly praised for his paperwork. Of the juniors, *Graham Dunning* is "amazingly cool, unflappable and has gravitas." *Joe Smouha* was described by one interviewee "one of the ablest of his generation." New entry *Claire Blanchard* is a "punchy, tenacious, advocate – a real fighter."

20 Essex Street (Johnson) A well-established shipping set with six silks and three juniors receiving recommendations. **Leading Barristers:** *Peter Gross QC*, a particular favourite among practitioners, "has a great manner with solicitors and clients and is thorough, thoughtful and considerate." Not far behind is the "dogged" and "unflappable" *Nicholas Hamblen QC*, who was praised for his "brilliant brain and convincing manner." Recently involved in 'Halki Shipping v Sopex Oil.' The "brilliant and charming" *Timothy Young QC* is considered by some to be "a future Pollock." *Michael Coburn*, a "ferocious" cross-examiner, is said to be "mature beyond his years." He won particular praise for his skill in handling technical matters. Fellow junior *Duncan Matthews* is "frighteningly bright, prepares thoroughly and has great court presence."

4 Field Court (Brice) A set commended for its "tremendous strength in depth, reasonable rates and good clerking." **Leading Barristers:** Head of Chambers *Geoffrey Brice QC* is "a delight to work with." His recent cases include 'Coltman and another v Bibby Tankers Ltd' (HL – liability for ship defect). *The* "exceptional" *Lionel Persey QC* and the "practical" *Jervis Kay QC* were also recommended. New to the lists are the "brilliant" *Chris*

Barristers' profiles   p. 1509-1642

LEADING SILKS · LONDON

POLLOCK Gordon Essex Court Chambers

AIKENS Richard Brick Court Chambers
BOYD Stewart Essex Court Chambers
BRICE Geoffrey 4 Field Court
BUCKNALL Belinda 4 Essex Court
CLARKE Christopher Brick Court Chambers
COOKE Jeremy 7 King's Bench Walk
EDER Bernard Essex Court Chambers
FLAUX Julian 7 King's Bench Walk
GAISMAN Jonathan 7 King's Bench Walk
GROSS Peter 20 Essex Street
HUNTER Ian Essex Court Chambers
MACDONALD Charles 4 Essex Court
STONE Richard 4 Field Court
TEARE Nigel 4 Essex Court
TOMLINSON Stephen 7 King's Bench Walk

COLLINS Michael Essex Court Chambers
CORDARA Roderick Essex Court Chambers
GEE Steven One Essex Court
GILMAN Jonathan Essex Court Chambers
HAMBLEN Nicholas 20 Essex Street
HAMILTON Adrian 7 King's Bench Walk
HAVELOCK-ALLAN Mark 20 Essex Street
HIRST Jonathan Brick Court Chambers
HOWARD Michael 4 Essex Court
HUNT David Blackstone Chambers
JOHNSON David 20 Essex Street
KAY Jervis 4 Field Court
LEGH-JONES Nicholas 20 Essex Street
MILLIGAN Iain 20 Essex Street
RUSSELL Jeremy 4 Essex Court
SIBERRY Richard Essex Court Chambers
SIMON Peregrine Brick Court Chambers
YOUNG Timothy 20 Essex Street

NEW SILKS · 1997 AND 1998

BLACKBURN Elizabeth 4 Field Court
BRENTON Timothy 4 Essex Court
GRUDER Jeffrey One Essex Court
JACOBS Richard Essex Court Chambers
KENDRICK Dominic 7 King's Bench Walk
PERSEY Lionel 4 Field Court

FOR DETAILS OF THESE LEADING BARRISTERS
SEE PROFILES ON PAGES 1509-1642

Smith and "potential star" *Michael Davey*. The latter is said to "have great judgment for his call." *David Goldstone*, "one of the great minds at the commercial bar," was praised for his incisiveness.

7 King's Bench Walk (Tomlinson) Universally praised for consistently high quality and strength in depth, the set delivers "a prompt, efficient service" and "knows what solicitors want." **Leading Barristers:** Amongst the silks, *Julian Flaux QC* is "pugnacious on his feet," and led in 'Ali Shipping v Shipyard Trogir.' *Jonathan Gaisman QC* is "incredibly quick and bright," *Adrian Hamilton QC* is "a wily performer" and *Jeremy Cooke QC* is "absolutely brilliant." *Stephen Tomlinson QC* was cited by many as their personal favourite for serious cases. He is "bright, commercial, easy to work with and turns papers round quickly." Of the juniors, *Alistair Schaff*, "a strong advocate," rockets to the top this year on the back of many recommendations. His recent work includes 'Effort Shipping Co Ltd v Linden Management SA' (HL – liability for infested cargo). *Stephen Hofmeyr* is "calm under pressure." Other widely praised juniors include *Robert Bright* ("keen and tenacious"), *Jawdat Khurshid*, *Rebecca Sabben-Clare* ("sensible, commercial and responsive"), and *Christopher Butcher*.

LEADING JUNIORS · LONDON

SCHAFF Alistair 7 King's Bench Walk

BAKER Andrew 20 Essex Street	**PARSONS Luke** 4 Essex Court
DUNNING Graham Essex Court Chambers	**PRIDAY Charles** 7 King's Bench Walk
MEESON Nigel 4 Field Court	**RAINEY Simon** 4 Essex Court
BERRY Steven Essex Court Chambers	**HOFMEYR Stephen** 7 King's Bench Walk
BUTCHER Christopher 7 King's Bench Walk	**LORD Richard** Brick Court Chambers
FOXTON David Essex Court Chambers	**MATTHEWS Duncan** 20 Essex Street
GOLDSTONE David 4 Field Court	**SMOUHA Joe** Essex Court Chambers
BLANCHARD Claire Essex Court Chambers	**MELWANI Poonam** 4 Essex Court
BRIGHT Robert 7 King's Bench Walk	**SABBEN-CLARE Rebecca** 7 King's Bench Walk
COBURN Michael 20 Essex Street	**SELVARATNAM Vasanti** 4 Field Court
DAVEY Michael 4 Field Court	**SMITH Christopher** 4 Field Court
HEALY Siobán 7 King's Bench Walk	**SUSSEX Charles** 4 Essex Court
JACOBS Nigel 4 Essex Court	**TURNER James** 4 Essex Court
KVERNDAL Simon 4 Essex Court	**WHITELEY Miranda** 4 Field Court

UP AND COMING

KHURSHID Jawdat 7 King's Bench Walk	**THOMAS Robert** 4 Essex Court

FOR DETAILS OF THESE LEADING BARRISTERS SEE PROFILES ON PAGES 1509-1642

At **One Essex Court** (Grabiner) *Steven Gee QC* is "first rate, brilliant and clever" and *Jeffrey Gruder QC* is "bright and tough."

SPORTS

RESEARCH: In compiling the tables, we consider all the information available to us, paying particular regard to the market research carried out by our team of ten qualified lawyers. (The researchers' details are set out on page three.) The rankings, therefore, reflect the opinion of the market-place as revealed by systematic and objective research: see page four. (Our research is audited every year by the British Market Research Bureau.)

Barristers' profiles   p. 1509-1642

OVERVIEW: We interviewed most of the leading solicitors with sports practices, as well as barristers, sports bodies and clients. Because of the nature of sports law, many of the barristers identified as leaders also practice in other fields. Only Blackstone Chambers could be genuinely said to specialise. Reputations rest otherwise on individuals, not sets.

LEADING SETS · LONDON

BLACKSTONE CHAMBERS (Baxendale/Flint QC)

Blackstone Chambers (Baxendale & Flint) Described by leading London sports lawyers as "definitely at the top" and by a regional practitioner as "streets ahead." Leading Barristers: *Charles Flint QC* and *David Pannick QC* ("brilliant – could do anything") remain extremely highly regarded. Of the juniors, *Paul Goulding* has an impressive employment law pedigree, and is considered a "good advocate." A new entry is *Robert Howe*, who is "full of common sense," and "intellectually gifted." The first choice as an advocate for one leading lawyer.

4-5 Gray's Inn Square (Appleby & Beloff) Advice to many organisations on regulations and disciplinary proceedings. Involved in high profile work in the football, rugby and boxing arenas. **Leading Barristers:** *Michael Beloff QC* has an outstanding reputation for all areas relating to public law, and is described as "a major player in sports." He is a member of the Court of Arbitration for Sport, and considered "marvellous at tribunals." *Tim Kerr* is a popular junior, and thought "extremely knowledgeable."

Essex Court Chambers (Pollock) Leading Barristers: *Gordon Pollock QC* ("brilliant, terrific") remains highly respected in this as in other fields.

11 Stone Buildings (Beckman) Leading Barristers: *Murray Rosen QC* has a history of representing high profile individuals and has been newly recommended by several practitioners this year.

Farrar's Building (Elias) Leading Barristers: *William Norris QC* has been recommended for his jockey club work and, according to one practitioner, his recent seminar on rules, regulations and disciplinary proceedings was "a model of clarity." He recently appeared in 'Jones v Welsh RFU' (change of disciplinary procedure).

Devereux Chambers (Burke) Leading Barristers: *David Griffith-Jones* is a new entry this year. He has advised on a number of PI matters in relation to sport, and was also involved in the 'Pleat v Sheffield Wednesday' dispute.

Cloisters (Cox) Leading Barristers: *Jonathan Crystal* ("good for opinions and tribunals" and "knows a lot about football") is newly recommended. He drafted the initial rules for the football Premier League. Cases include 'Thomas v QPR' (the first major footballer's claim for damages against another club and player for the loss of a career); and 'Keighley v Rugby Football League' (challenge to the proposed formation of the Rugby Super League).

Littleton Chambers (Burton) Leading Barristers: *Michael Burton QC* has a distinguished commercial and employment law practice and uses this expertise in the sports sector. He has recently been involved in the Simon Fenn ear biting case.

5 Paper Buildings (Mathew) Leading Barristers: *Kuldip Singh QC* ("extremely knowledgeable") received several glowing recommendations and moves up the table as a result. He is a member of the governing committee of the BASL.

LEADING SILKS · LONDON

BELOFF Michael 4-5 Gray's Inn Square
FLINT Charles Blackstone Chambers
PANNICK David Blackstone Chambers
BURTON Michael Littleton Chambers
GLASGOW Edwin 39 Essex Street
MACKAY Colin 39 Essex Street
POLLOCK Gordon Essex Court Chambers
REID Robert 9 Old Square
ROSEN Murray 11 Stone Buildings
SINGH Kuldip 5 Paper Buildings
BAKER Nigel 9 Bedford Row
LEVESON Brian 22 Old Buildings
NORRIS William Farrar's Buildings
STEWART Nicholas Hardwicke Building
TALBOT Patrick Serle Court Chambers

NEW SILKS · 1997 AND 1998

DUFFY Peter Essex Court Chambers
KAY Jervis 4 Field Court
PRICE Richard Littleton Chambers

LEADING JUNIORS · LONDON

GOULDING Paul Blackstone Chambers
GRIFFITH-JONES David Devereux Chambers
KERR Tim 4-5 Gray's Inn Square
CRYSTAL Jonathan Cloisters
FORDHAM Michael Blackstone Chambers
HOLLANDER Charles Brick Court Chambers
HOWE Robert Blackstone Chambers
LEWIS Adam Blackstone Chambers
BELLAMY Jonathan 39 Essex Street
DUNNING Graham Essex Court Chambers
MCQUATER Ewan 3 Verulam Buildings
NELSON Vincent 39 Essex Street
ROSE Dinah Blackstone Chambers
STONER Christopher 9 Old Square

FOR DETAILS OF THESE LEADING BARRISTERS
SEE PROFILES ON PAGES 1509-1642

TAX

RESEARCH: In compiling the tables, we consider all the information available to us, paying particular regard to the market research carried out by our team of ten qualified lawyers. (The researchers' details are set out on page three.) The rankings, therefore, reflect the opinion of the marketplace as revealed by systematic and objective research: see page four. (Our research is audited every year by the British Market Research Bureau.)

OVERVIEW: With instructions from accountants constituting up to 80% of some barristers' work, and usually at least 50-60%, comments from Big Five accountants were particularly useful.

Gray's Inn Chambers and Pump Court Tax Chambers remain the two leading sets, although Pump Court now has a marginal lead at the head of the tables. It is thought to have a little more strength in depth than Gray's Inn who have lost leading light Andrew Park to the bench. Of the others, 24 Old Buildings has been promoted. Overall the Tax Bar was said to be increasingly commercial and responsive to clients.

Banding tax silks is a difficult business. Solicitors and accountants are now more confident in their own expertise and refer to counsel far less. When they do, they want someone who "leaves you with a warm confident feeling." No one silk was capable of inspiring this emotion in every accountant and solicitor we spoke to. Each had their favoured silk or silks and consequently no individual stands out overall, save in VAT work where David Milne is the clear leader. There is a separate table of VAT silks.

There was less comment about the junior bar, although a few individuals received widespread praise, particularly Julian Ghosh. Two notable 'up & comings' are Michael Conlon (ex-head of VAT and indirect tax at Allen & Overy) and Malcolm Gammie (ex-Linklaters). Both have joined One Essex Court.

This year we have a separate table for silks and juniors regularly instructed by the Inland Revenue. Most Inland Revenue briefs go to the Chancery bar, not the Tax Bar. John Gardiner is the best-known tax silk who occasionally appears for the Revenue. Conversely, counsel instructed by the Revenue rarely act for the tax payer and almost never on corporate matters.

Barristers' profiles	p. 1509-1642

LEADING SILKS · LONDON CORPORATE TAX

AARONSON Graham One Essex Court
ALLCOCK Stephen Pump Court Tax Chambers
BRETTEN Rex 24 Old Buildings
GARDINER John 11 New Square
GOLDBERG David Gray's Inn Tax Chambers
GOY David Gray's Inn Tax Chambers
MILNE David Pump Court Tax Chambers
PROSSER Kevin Pump Court Tax Chambers

BRAMWELL Richard 3 Temple Gardens
DUFFY Peter Essex Court Chambers
FLESCH Michael Gray's Inn Tax Chambers
HERBERT Mark 5 Stone Buildings
THORNHILL Andrew Pump Court Tax Chambers
TREVETT Peter 11 New Square
VENABLES Robert 24 Old Buildings
WHITEMAN Peter Queen Elizabeth Building

LEADING SILKS · LONDON · VAT

MILNE David Pump Court Tax Chambers

CORDARA Roderick Essex Court Chambers

GOY David Gray's Inn Tax Chambers
VENABLES Robert 24 Old Buildings

NEW SILKS · 1997 AND 1998

WALTERS John Gray's Inn Tax Chambers

LEADING JUNIORS · LONDON CORPORATE TAX AND VAT

BAKER Philip Gray's Inn Tax Chambers
CULLEN Felicity Gray's Inn Tax Chambers
EWART David Pump Court Tax Chambers
GHOSH Julian 24 Old Buildings
HITCHMOUGH Andrew Pump Court Tax Chambers
PEACOCK Jonathan 11 New Square
SHIPWRIGHT Adrian Pump Court Tax Chambers

GOODFELLOW Giles Pump Court Tax Chambers
JAMES Alun 3 Temple Gardens
KESSLER James 24 Old Buildings
MATTHEWS Janek Pump Court Tax Chambers
MCCUTCHEON Barry 8 Gray's Inn Square
MCKAY Hugh Gray's Inn Tax Chambers
MEADWAY Susannah 10 Old Square
SHERRY Michael 3 Temple Gardens
SOARES Patrick 8 Gray's Inn Square
WAY Patrick 8 Gray's Inn Square

UP AND COMING · LONDON

AKIN Barrie Gray's Inn Tax Chambers
CONLON Michael One Essex Court
GAMMIE Malcolm One Essex Court
WILSON Elizabeth Pump Court Tax Chambers

FOR DETAILS OF THESE LEADING BARRISTERS
SEE PROFILES ON PAGES 1509-1642

LEADING SETS · LONDON

PUMP COURT TAX CHAMBERS (Thornhill QC)

GRAY'S INN TAX CHAMBERS (Milton Grundy)

HIGHLY REGARDED · LONDON

24 Old Buildings (G.R Bretten QC)

8 Gray's Inn Square (Patrick Soares)
11 New Square (John Gardiner QC)
3 Temple Gardens (David Braham QC)

Pump Court Tax Chambers (Thornhill) Perceived to have a slight lead in terms of depth of resources and quality of service. The set's clerking system is said to be "light years ahead of anyone else." **Work Handled:** 'Thorn Materials' (House of Lords); 'Littlewoods' (Court of Appeal); 'News International' (Court of Appeal); 'British Telecommunications' (Court of Appeal); 'Hawthorn v Smallcorn' (High Court). **Leading Barristers:** Without doubt, *David Milne QC* is *the* leader in VAT work. Praised by other silks as well as solicitors and accountants, Milne is "always immaculately prepared" and "makes the complex seem sensible and comprehensible." Others described him as easy to work with – "not into pomposity or posing." *Stephen Allcock QC* is "a fluent, commercial and gifted advocate," and a "solid, thorough and consistent performer." *Kevin Prosser QC* ("he always comes up with imaginative, commercial solutions") continues his rise through the tables. Clients like Prosser because he has "very definite ideas, but is pretty realistic too." Head of chambers, **Andrew Thornhill QC**, is "a nice man and has a brilliant brain." **David Ewart**, a "great senior junior," puts his arguments well and has "a pleasant manner" which makes him popular with clients and judges alike. He is known for VAT and private client work. At the Tax bar it is rare for a junior to be instructed in the largest matters. One of the few who does get such instructions is **Adrian Shipwright** (ex-Linklaters, Denton Hall and SJ Berwin and a Professor of Business Law at Kings College, London). **Andrew Hitchmough** ("creative and practical") was recommended for VAT and corporate work. **Elizabeth Wilson**, a new entrant as an up & coming, was described by counsel from another set as "the best pupil I have ever seen."

Gray's Inn Tax Chambers (Grundy) One of the two leading sets, dealing with all aspects of UK revenue law for companies, charities and private clients. **Work Handled:** 'British Telecom Pension Scheme Trustees' (Taxation of Underwriting Commisions) [1998] High Court; 'Girvan (Inspector of Taxes) v Orange Personal Communications Services Ltd' [1998]; 'Willoughby' [1997]; 'Kuwait Petroleum (GB) Ltd v Commrs. of Customs & Excise' ECJ; 'Vodafone Cellular Ltd v Shaw (Inspector of Taxes)' [1997]; 'Aberdeen Milk' [1998]. **Leading Barristers: David Goldberg QC** is the first choice of many leading solicitors and accountants. "You get complete value for money from David – he's thorough, throws up lots of ideas, is a great court performer and aggressive when he needs to be." Many felt **David Goy QC** had been "far too underrated for far too long." Charming and meticulous, he was recommended for VAT and property related tax as well as corporate work. Independently minded, his practice is expected to blossom. **Michael Flesch QC** is "a good commercial barrister," with "a fine eye for detail." **John Walters QC** is a sought-after silk for VAT tribunal cases. **Philip Baker** is "a well known chap for international tax treaties." He is a visiting lecturer at London University, as is **Hugh McKay** (VAT, litigation, excise duties). **Felicity Cullen** (corporate, personal and partnerships) is "thorough and clear sighted;" she gets on top of the details and is a very able team player. **Barrie Akin** is newly recommended.

24 Old Buildings (Bretten) A specialist tax set. The clerks were highly praised for their efficient service. **Work Handled:** 'Re: Schuldenfrei' (ChD); 'Man in Black' (ECJ); 'Brodie' (ChD); 'Memec' (High Court Civil Appeals); 'Dixons' (High Court Civil Appeals); 'Unigreg' (High Court Crown Office). **Leading Barristers: Rex Bretten QC** has "been there, seen it, done it." Very popular with corporate clients for advisory work, with some interviewees describing him as "head and shoulders above the rest." A very thorough lawyer, Bretten is never "grandiose or pompous." "When Rex reaches a decision he's able to articulate it clearly, unambiguously and convincingly." **Robert Venables QC** ("it's common knowledge that the man's a genius") is best known for trust and private client work but is "not afraid to take on new work." **Julian Ghosh** is "a very bright chap indeed." Fifty per cent of **James Kessler's** practice is in private client where he is instructed by many of the leading firms in that area.

8 Gray's Inn Square (Soares) **Work Handled:** 'McNulty Offshore Services v The Commissioners of Customs & Excise'; 'Manchester Tribunal Centre'; 'Parin (Hatfield) Ltd v IRC' (1998); 'Plumbly v Spencer' (1997); 'R. v CIR'. **Leading Barristers: Patrick Soares**, head of chambers, is "an impressive individual," especially in property-related matters. Also recommended were **Patrick Way** ("has a wide range of skills") and **Barry McCutcheon**.

11 New Square (Gardiner) The oldest established set to specialise exclusively in revenue law. Advise in the UK and abroad on all aspects of tax law, including consideration of European law and fiscal laws of other jurisdictions. **Work Handled:** 'Wharf Properties v CIR' [1997] (a decision of the Privy Council concerning deductibility of interest paid by a Hong Kong property developer). 'National & Provincial, Leeds Permanent and Yorkshire Building Societies v UK' [1997] (the first decision of the European Court of Human Rights on a tax related application from the UK). 'Marks & Spencer v CCE' [1997]. 'BVC' (a landmark decision on the meaning of unjust enrichment in s 80 VATA 1994 and the first case in which HM Customs & Excise led expert economic evidence). **Leading Barristers: John Gardiner QC** is a favourite with a number of leading lawyers and accountants for court work. They value his ability to "see the big picture." Technically brilliant with a marvellous litigation record – "not just for winnable cases, but the hard ones for sophisticated tax avoiders." **Peter Trevett QC** "approaches complex issues with common sense." **Jonathan Peacock** is one of the most senior members of the junior bar and regularly instructed by leading lawyers and accountants.

3 Temple Gardens (Braham) A specialist revenue law set. **Leading Barristers:** The best known names at this specialist tax set are **Richard Bramwell QC** ("the one who wrote the book"), **Alun James** (also practises in Liverpool) and **Michael Sherry** (for VAT and for advocacy; also practises in Manchester). They have also been joined by Jonathan Schwartz, an international tax specialist, formerly a partner with Paisner

& Co and the editor of the FT World Tax Report.

In addition to barristers at the specialist tax sets, a number of barristers at **One Essex Court** (one of the top commercial sets) were recommended. **Graham Aaronson QC** is, for some, "quite simply the best." Described as a "brilliant thinker who never makes assumptions". He puts people at ease and always has a view. On advisory work Aaronson is "absolutely marvellous – you can get genuinely innovative insights." This year he has been joined by two well know ex- partners from leading City firms, **Malcolm Gammie** (Linklaters) and **Michael Conlon** (A&O). Gammie, described as "a man of immense stature and huge intellect," has been "flooded with instructions" since going to the Bar. Conlon is "a good, solid, reliable source of advice and fully immersed in VAT." Peers have "immense respect for his abilities." At **Essex Court Chambers** (Pollock), another leading commercial set, two silks were recommended. **Roderick Cordara QC**, "a great VAT advocate," is the flamboyant counterpart to the methodical David Milne QC. **Peter Duffy QC** is newly recommended for indirect tax with a European angle. He "puts forward a positive argument but gives a realistic indication of your chances."

Peter Whiteman QC of **Queen Elizabeth Buildings** (Jeffreys and Whiteman) is another well known name for international corporate matters.

Of those who appear for the Inland Revenue the best known names are:

Lancelot Henderson QC of **5 Stone Buildings** is "an extremely good litigator," and "excellent in every way" (also handles personal tax matters); **Christopher McCall QC** of **13 Old Square** (Lyndon-Stanford) – "nothing other than excellent" – and **Michael Furness** of **Wilberforce Chambers** (Nugee), Standing Revenue Counsel and "a very clever chap indeed." He is described as a younger version of Christopher McCall QC. The "meticulous" **Ian Glick QC** of **Essex Court Chambers** (Pollock) is another regular in the Inland Revenue colours.

BARRISTERS' A-Z

CHAMBERS & PARTNERS

SET NUMBER
1

ARBITRATION CHAMBERS (John Tackaberry QC)

22 WILLES ROAD, LONDON, NW5 3DS
Tel: (0171) 267 2137 **Fax:** (0171) 482 1018 **DX:** 46454 LDN/KENTISH TOWN **Email:** JATQC@ATACK.DEMON.CO.UK

MEMBERS:

John Tackaberry QC (1967)   Derrick Morris (1983)
(QC-1982)

Head of Chambers:	John Tackaberry QC
Senior Clerk:	Pearl O'Brien
Tenants: 2	

The Chambers: John Tackaberry is a specialist practitioner whose principal area of expertise is international and domestic construction disputes; and related areas. Acts as advocate both in litigation and arbitration and also as arbitrator with particular experience in ICC arbitrations.

He is a Registered Arbitrator admitted to various panels of Arbitrators in this country, and a Recorder since 1988. He is also a Fellow of the Chartered Institute of Arbitrators and the Faculty of Building. He is admitted to practise at the Bars of California and the Irish Republic and as a QC in New South Wales. Ex-chairman of C.I.Arb, ex-president of Society of Construction Law & European Society of Construction Law. Member of and/or on the arbitration panels of the Chartered Institute of Arbitrators (Past Chairman), European Society of Construction Law (Past President), Faculty of Building (Fellow), UK Society of Construction Law (Past President), Inst. of Civil Engineers, Royal Inst. of British Architects, Los Angeles Center for Commercial Arbitration, American Arbitration Association; Association of Arbitrators in South Africa, Indian Council of Arbitration, Singapore International Arbitration Council and Mauritius Chamber of Commerce and Industry.

Prior to being called to the Bar, Derrick Morris had a comprehensive career in the building and civil engineering industries. Since his call to the Bar he has had substantial experience as an advocate in building and civil engineering particularly in the field of arbitrations. A great deal of Mr Morris's experience has been gained in arbitration work in South East Asia and the Far East as well as in England and Wales.

Mr Morris has written and contributed articles and papers to a number of journals and conferences – particularly on legal matters in the construction and engineering field in South East Asia and the Far East.

Additional areas of practice include planning and local government, professional negligence and international law.

Associate Members: Brendan Kilty and Karen Gough

SET NUMBER
2

ARDEN CHAMBERS (Andrew Arden QC)

ARDEN CHAMBERS, 27 JOHN STREET, LONDON, WC1N 2BL
Tel: (0171) 242 4244 **Fax:** (0171) 242 3224 **DX:** 29 (CH.LN.) **Internet:** http://www.arden-chambers.law.co.uk/arden-chambers

MEMBERS:

Andrew Arden QC (1974) (QC-1991) LLB	Caroline Hunter (1985) BA Dip Hsg Admin	Kerry Bretherton (1994) BA
David Carter (1971) LLB	Jonathan Manning (1989) MA	Arthur Moore (1992) BA DipLaw
Timothy Jones (1975)	Iain Colville (1989) LLB	Ceilidh Halloran (1992) MEd, MA, DipLaw
Linda Hayton (1975) LLB	William Okoya (1989) LLB, LLM	Scott Collins (1994) BA, LLB, LLM
Declan O'Mahony (1980) BA DipLaw FCIArb	Desmond Kilcoyne (1990) LLB, LLM	Dominic Preston (1995) BA DipLaw
Siobhan McGrath (1982) BA	Josephine Henderson (1990) BSC, DipLaw	Lydia Challen (1995) BA, MJur
Prof. Martin Partington (1984) BA LLB	Kate Jenrick (1990) LLB	Sarah Pengelly (1996) BA
Christopher Baker (1984) MA LLM	Alyson Kilpatrick (1991) LLB AdvDip (EC)	Emma Saunders (1994) BA*
Christopher Balogh (1984) MA MSC DipLaw	Andrew Dymond (1991) MA	

* Door Tenant

Head of Chambers:	Andrew Arden QC
Senior Clerk:	Barry Landa
Tenants: 26	

The Chambers: These specialist Chambers were established to provide a centre for practice which both reflected the series of works edited or written by members (see below) and promoted their corresponding expertise and experience. For up to date information on members, publications and articles, visit Chambers' web site at http: //www.arden-chambers.law.co.uk/arden-chambers. Litigation and advisory work are undertaken for a wide range of clients in the public and private sectors. All members accept instructions on the basis of direct professional access. Andrew Arden QC has also conducted five local government inquiries/reviews.

Continues overleaf

Areas of Work: Expertise is available in the following fields of law (English and European): housing, local government (finance, powers and proceedings), landlord and tenant (residential and commercial), public and administrative law, planning, environmental health and protection, competitive tendering, social security, employment, trading standards and licensing.

Publications: Members of Chambers have either written, edited or collaborated in: *Encyclopaedia of Housing Law; Housing Law Reports;* Arden & Hunter's *Local Government Finance, Law and Practice;* Arden & Partington's *Housing Law;* Arden's *Manual of Housing Law; Housing Law – Cases, Materials and Commentary; Homelessness and Allocations; Quiet Enjoyment;* Vol.3 Megarry's *The Rent Acts* (11th ed.), *Assured Tenancies;* Arden's *Housing Library: Judicial Review Proceedings; Housing Law: Pleadings in Practice;* Atkin's *Court Forms; Bibliography of Social Security Law; Claim in Time; Current Law, Journal of Housing Law, Commercial Property, Health and Housing Insight*

Foreign Languages: Fluency is available in French.

SET NUMBER

3

ATKIN CHAMBERS (John Blackburn QC)

1 ATKIN BUILDING, GRAY'S INN, LONDON, WC1R 5AT
Tel: (0171) 404 0102 **Fax:** (0171) 405 7456 **DX:** 1033 24 HOUR PAGER: (01459) 137252 **Email:** CLERKS@ATKIN-CHAMBERS.CO.UK

MEMBERS:

Ian N D Wallace QC (1948) (QC-1973)
Brian Knight QC (1964) (QC-1981)
John Blackburn QC (1969) (QC-1984)
Colin Reese QC (1973) (QC-1987)
Robert Akenhead QC (1972) (QC-1989)
Nicholas Dennys QC (1975) (QC-1991)
Andrew White QC (1980) (QC-1997)

Nicholas Baatz QC (1978) (QC-1998)
Donald Valentine (1956)
Darryl Royce (1976)
Martin Bowdery (1980)
Andrew Burr (1981)
Mark Raeside (1982)
Delia Dumaresq (1984)
Stephen Dennison (1985)
Andrew Goddard (1985)
David Streatfeild-James (1986)
William Godwin (1986)

Stephanie Barwise (1988)
Simon Lofthouse (1988)
Robert Clay (1989)
Peter D. Fraser (1989)
Dominique Rawley (1991)
Chantal-Aimee Doerries (1992)
Steven Walker (1993)
Fiona Parkin (1993)
Manus McMullan (1994)
James Howells (1995)

Head of Chambers:
John Blackburn QC

Senior Clerks:
Stuart Goldsmith
David Barnes

Tenants: 28

Main Areas of Work: Atkin Chambers has always specialised in all aspects of the law relating to construction and civil engineering. It was the first to do so, and has since 1959 provided the editors of the standard construction text, Hudson's Building and Engineering Contracts. In addition to advisory work and advocacy members also lecture and contribute to or edit law reports and other publications.

Construction is the core area of the work of members of chambers and ranges from domestic house and road-building through to the construction and commissioning of process plant and power stations and international civil engineering projects of the largest size, together with all related aspects of professional negligence. Members also act in relation to telecommunications projects, railways and rolling stock, offshore structures and pipelines and ship-building. Advice is available at every stage, from the drafting or amendment of forms of contract or warranty to the resolution of any disputes arising out of performance. Members of chambers act both for and against employers/developers, local authorities, contractors, sub-contractors and consultants, in both arbitration and litigation.

Additional Areas: In the commercial field members of chambers advise and act in relation to commercial matters generally, and in particular banking and bonds, insurance, sale of goods and landlord and tenant, both as an adjunct to construction matters and independently of them. With the PFI and as the financing and structuring of large commercial projects has become more complex, members of chambers have provided advice and acted as advocates in a wide variety of dispute often removed from the traditional core area of construction.

There has also been and continues to be rapid growth in the demand for advice and representation in connection with contract for the provision of information technology. Such contracts have considerable similarities with the traditional forms of building contract, and members of Atkin Chambers have developed and are continuing to develop new expertise in this area.

International: Members of chambers are involved in a considerable amount of international work, with both London based arbitrations of disputes which have arisen outside the jurisdiction (often involving questions of foreign law) and advisory and advocacy work overseas.

Arbitrators: Members of Chambers regularly act as either sole arbitrators or as members of panels or arbitrators. In addition, members have experience of methods of alternative dispute resolution.

Direct Access: Members of chambers are available in suitable cases for instruction directly by members of approved professional bodies, or by overseas clients, with direct professional access.

Chambers & Partners

SET NUMBER
4

BARNARDS INN CHAMBERS (Timothy Bowles)

HALTON HOUSE, 20/23 HOLBORN, LONDON, EC1N 2JD
Tel: (0171) 242 8508 **Fax:** (0171) 404 3139 **DX:** 336 CH.LN. **Email:** CLERKS@BARNARDS-INN-CHAMBERS.CO.UK

MEMBERS:

Timothy Bowles (1973)	Timothy C. Dutton (1985)	Jason Elliott (1993)
John Bryant (1976)	Craig Moore (1989)	David Thomson (1994)
Anthony Korn (1978)	Scott Sullivan (1991)	Michael Chapman (1994)
Simon Blackford (1979)	Jill Martin (1993)	Matthew Chapman (1994)
Charles Bott (1979)	Harry Potter (1993)	Zachary Bredemear (1996)
Alan Saggerson (1981)	Timothy Cowen (1993)	

Head of Chambers:
Timothy Bowles

Senior Clerk:
Andrew Flanagan

Junior Clerk:
Toby Eales

Tenants: 17

The Chambers: Barnards Inn Chambers was established in 1993 by a small group of experienced barristers with specialist practices in different fields. It operates as a professionally managed legal practice, offering the traditional services of the bar in a modern working environment with a flexible approach to meet the requirements of contemporary solicitors and their clients.

Each member of chambers has a particular area of expertise, and does not invite instructions outside that area. Overall, the chambers provide specialist advice and representation in a wide and complementary range of disciplines. The Senior Clerk will assist instructing professionals in their choice of counsel and will give a candid assessment of a member's suitability and availability for a particular case. Chambers is also an accredited Law Society external course provider with an in-house and open seminar programme. Chambers brochure is available on request.

Work Undertaken: The major areas of practice covered by members of chambers include: banking, company/commercial, consumer law, civil rights, criminal law, corporate fraud, employment law, judicial review and local government law, insolvency, landlord and tenant, property litigation, mortgages and guarantees, personal injury and professional and medical negligence, travel and tourism, pollution, trading standards, trade descriptions, health and safety matters, sports law and chancery.

SET NUMBER
5

BARRISTERS COMMON LAW CHAMBERS (Muhammad Altafur Rahman) 108 Brick Lane, London, E1 6RL **Tel:** (0171) 375 3012 **Fax:** (0171) 375 3068 **Clerk:** Hasfa Rahman Khan **Tenants:** 3 Immigration, housing, family and general common law set.

SET NUMBER
6

9 BEDFORD ROW (John Goldring QC)

9 BEDFORD ROW, LONDON, WC1R 4AZ
Tel: (0171) 242 3555 **Fax:** (0171) 242 2511 **DX:** 347 (CH.LN.)

MEMBERS:

John B. Goldring QC (1969) (QC-1987)	Philip P. Shears QC (1972) (QC-1996)	Maureen Baker (1984)
J. Stephen Coward QC (1964) (QC-1984)	Collingwood Thompson QC (1975) (QC-1998)	Barbara Connolly (1986)
David J. Farrer QC (1967) (QC-1986)	Joan Butler QC (1977) (QC-1998)	Louise J. Varty (1986)
Timothy Barnes QC (1968) (QC-1986)	Witold Pawlak (1970)	Simon King (1987)
Nigel Baker QC (1969) (QC-1988)	David H. Christie (1973)	A. David H. Matthew (1987)
Richard B. Latham QC (1971) (QC-1991)	J. Philip T. Head (1976)	Rupert C. Mayo (1987)
Christopher Hotten QC (1972) (QC-1994)	Julian D. Matthews (1979)	Stephen Baker (1989)
William Coker QC (1973) (QC-1994)	Nigel G. Godsmark (1979)	Brendan Roche (1989)
Nigel J. Rumfitt QC (1974) (QC-1994)	Simon Wheatley (1979)	Rachel Langdale (1990)
Charles T. Wide QC (1974) (QC-1995)	Jeremy Pendlebury (1980)	Cathryn McGahey (1990)
Simeon Maskrey QC (1977) (QC-1995)	John Pini (1981)	Steven Ford (1992)
	Timothy J. Spencer (1982)	Isabel Dakyns (1992)
	Kathryn M Thirlwall (1982)	Adam Weitzman (1993)
	Yvonne A. Coen (1982)	Vanessa Marshall (1994)
	Nicholas Dean (1982)	Matthew Jowitt (1994)
	Derek A. Sweeting (1983)	Bilal Rawat (1995)
	Ebraham Mooncey (1983)	William Redgrave (1995)
	Susan C. Reed (1984)	Anwar Nashashibi (1995)
		Susannah Johnson (1996)
		Simon Thomas (1995)

Head of Chambers:
John Goldring QC

Senior Clerk:
Christopher A. Owen

Tenants: 49

The Chambers: The chambers of John Goldring QC at 9 Bedford Row are a long-established set of chambers, whose members have a wide experience of advocacy and advisory work in a number of specialised fields. Instructions are accepted from lawyers and professional clients in the United Kingdom and from abroad.

Continues overleaf

In early 1995 Chambers moved from 2 Crown Office Row and acquired the freehold of two buildings at 9 Bedford Row and 9 Jockey's Fields. Chambers is now accommodated in a Grade II listed building which has been substantially renovated and stands in an elegant street.

Work Undertaken:

Civil Litigation: Members have experience and can advise upon and present cases in the following areas: - building and construction work, commercial contracts, consumer law, employment, environmental pollution (including waste disposal), financial services, information technology, insurance and reinsurance law, licensing, partnership disputes, personal injury, product liability, professional negligence, and medical negligence.

Criminal Law: Members have a great deal of experience in the provision of legal advice and advocacy in the criminal field. Chambers can provide representation at all levels of seniority and all members both prosecute and defend. There is a particular emphasis on Commercial and International Fraud.

Family Law: Members conduct all aspects of family and matrimonial work, with particular emphasis on children's work. In public law members act for parents, Guardian ad litem, the Official Solicitor and Local Authorities. In private law members advise and appear on child abduction, international disputes, residence and contact issues.

Tribunals: Chambers appear and advise in Disciplinary Tribunals of professional and other bodies, Industrial Tribunals, the Employment Appeal Tribunal, the Criminal Injuries Compensation Board, Public Inquiries, and hearings before the Traffic Commissioner. Chambers are also able to provide trained members in Alternative Dispute Resolution.

Foreign Connections and Languages Spoken: Instructions are welcomed from overseas lawyers directly. Several members of chambers speak one or more foreign languages fluently; and several members have taught and lectured on legal matters in the United States. There are practising door tenants in Bermuda, Hong Kong and Jersey.

For any further information concerning individual members of chambers and areas of practice, as well as the current level of fees and charging rates, please contact the Senior Clerk, Mr. Christopher Owen.

SET NUMBER
7

17 BEDFORD ROW (Allan Levy QC)

17 BEDFORD ROW, LONDON, WC1R 4EB
Tel: (0171) 831 7314 **Fax:** (0171) 831 0061 **Mobile:** (0831) 234861 **DX:** 370 LDN/CH **Email:** IBOARD7314@AOL.COM

MEMBERS:

Allan Levy QC (1969) (QC-1989)	Martin Howard Russell (1977)	James Chapman (1987)
Michael Gettleson (1952)	Anthony Leonard Callaway (1978)	Julian Date (1988)
Nigel Jennings (1967)	Hashim Reza (1981)	Fredric Raffray (1991)
Jane Gill (1973)	Brian Hurst (1983)	Bernard Lo (1991)
John McLinden (1991) (NZ 1975)	Richard Anthony Southall (1983)	Barry McAlinden (1993)
Dennis Sharpe (1976)	John Critchley (1985)	Christina Michalos (1994)
Brian Huyton (1977)	Miles Croally (1987)	Neville Maryon Green (1963) *

Head of Chambers:
Allan Levy QC

Senior Clerk:
Ian Boardman

Tenants: 21

* Door Tenant

The Chambers: Members are instructed by solicitors' firms throughout the country and by or on behalf of government departments, local authorities and financial institutions.

Chambers was founded in the Temple over 50 years ago by Leonard Caplan QC. Former members include Lord Justice Farquharson and Sir Laurence Verney, the Recorder of London.

Work Undertaken: Direct Professional Access Work is undertaken.
Particular areas of work in which individuals specialise are:
Asset Recovery & Preservation,(including tracing)
Banking, Building Sociey & Insurance Law
Criminal Law
Commercial Work
Entertainment and Media including defamation, music business, copyright & other intellectual property
Medical law

Human Rights
Family, Children & Divorce
Landlord & Tenant and Property Law
Personal Injury
Professional Negligence

Foreign languages: French, German, Italian

Overseas bars: New Zealand, (John McLinden)

Strong Connections with Foreign Jurisdictions: France: French law Degree: Maitrise-en-Droit. Frederic Raffray (Sorbonne, Paris); Neville Maryon Green (Paris). New Zealand: John McLinden. Western Australia: Allan Levy QC

29 BEDFORD ROW CHAMBERS (Peter Ralls QC)

29 BEDFORD ROW CHAMBERS, LONDON, WC1R 4HE
Tel: (0171) 831 2626 **Fax:** (0171) 831 0626 **DX:** 1044

MEMBERS:

Evan Stone QC (1954) (QC-1979)	Neil Sanders (1975)	Nicholas Bowen (1984)
Lord Archer QC (1952) (QC-1971)	Philip Cayford (1975)	David Holland (1986)
Augustus Ullstein QC (1970) (QC-1992)	Charles Atkins (1975)	Stephen Reynolds (1987)
	Geoffrey Ames (1976)	Rupert Butler (1988)
Timothy Scott QC (1975) (QC-1995)	Simon Gill (1977)	Nicholas Chapman (1990)
Peter Ralls QC (1972) (QC-1997)	Stephen Boyd (1977)	Robert Peel (1990)
	Simon Edwards (1978)	Nicola Gray (1990)
Ajmalul Hossain QC (1976) (QC-1998)	Michael Keane (1979)	Jonathan Southgate (1992)
	Jonathan Ferris (1979)	Stuart Hornett (1992)
Peter Duckworth (1971)	Deborah Bangay (1981)	Craig Barlow (1992)
John Zieger (1962)	Ann Hussey (1981)	Victoria Domenge (1993)
Clare Renton (1972)	Nicholas Francis (1981)	Brenton Molyneux (1994)
Howard Shaw (1973)	John Wilson (1981)	Duncan Kynoch (1994)
John Tonna (1974)	Paul Storey (1982)	Nicholas Tse (1995)
Mark Warwick (1974)	Lucy Stone (1983)	Nicholas Allen (1996)
	Timothy Walker (1983)	Peter Mitchell (1996)

Head of Chambers:
Peter Ralls QC

Clerks:
Robert Segal

Tenants: 44

Door Tenant: Professor Robert Upex.

The Chambers: Bedford Row Chambers is a progressive and growing set committed to providing its clients with an effective and efficient legal service. It works out of one of the Bar's largest and most contemporary offices, having just added a further 50% to its office space by taking over its neighbouring premises. Bedford Row Chambers resides in two Grade II listed buildings, completely modernised and wired for the latest technology and with room to expand.

Work undertaken: The work of Chambers is primarily in commercial, property, family, personal injury and general common law and extends to a wide range of litigation, advisory and drafting work.

Chancery: Breach of trust, Court of Protection, partnership, trusts, wills and probate.

Commercial: Arbitration, building and construction, commercial, companies, consumer credit, contract, economic torts, guarantees, licensing, misrepresentation, and sale of goods.

Common Law: Injunctions, employment, libel and slander, nuisance and property-related torts, personal injuries, tort, professional negligence.

Family: Family law and family provision.

Intellectual Property: Confidential information, intellectual property, copyright and passing off, trade marks and trade names.

Insolvency: Bankruptcy, insolvency, liquidations and administrations and receivership.

Property: Conveyancing, housing, land law, landlord and tenant, mortgages and securities, planning, rent reviews.

Public and Administrative Law: Judicial review, statutory appeals and tribunal work. Particularly education, special educational needs, community care and mental health work.

33 BEDFORD ROW (David Barnard)

33 BEDFORD ROW, LONDON, WC1R 4JH
Tel: (0171) 242 6476 **Fax:** (0171) 831 6065 **DX:** 75

MEMBERS:

David Barnard (1967) *
Barry Kogan (1973) +
Nigel May (1974) +
Martyn Zeidman QC (1974)
(QC-1998) +
Constance Whippman (1978)
Richard Bendall (1979)
Gary Webber (1979)
David Stanton (1979)
Keith Hanlon (1979)

Robert Carrow (1981)
Marc Galberg (1982)
Peter Gray (1983)
Michael Burke (1985)
Christopher Spratt (1986)
Francis Fitzgibbon (1986)
Susan Castle (1986)
Timothy Thorne (1987)
Smair Singh Soor (1988)
Joanne Oxlade (1988)

David Lonsdale (1988)
Jean-Paul Sinclair (1989)
Rhys Jones (1990)
Joanne Clarke (1993)
Thomas Cleeve (1993)
Timothy Pullen (1993)
Tom Boyd (1995)
Stuart Armstrong (1995)
John Law (1996)

Head of Chambers:
David Barnard

Senior Clerk:
Michael Lieberman

Tenants: 28

*Recorder
+Assistant Recorder

Chambers undertakes work in the following practice groups: (1) Property, (2) Criminal Law, (3) Family Law, (4) Commercial and Civil Litigation. Members regularly publish and lecture. Publications include *The New Civil Court in Action* (Barnard), *The Criminal Court in Action* (Barnard), *Steps to Possession* (Zeidman), *Residential Possession Proceedings* (Webber) and *Possession of Business Premises* (Webber).

David Barnard is Standing Counsel to HM Customs and Excise, and Nigel May is a part-time Judge Advocate.

36 BEDFORD ROW (James Hunt QC)

36 BEDFORD ROW, LONDON, WC1R 4JH
Tel: (0171) 421 8000 **Fax:** (0171) 421 8080 **DX:** LDE 360 **Email:** 36BEDFORDROW@LINK.ORG **Internet:** HTTP://WWW.36BEDFORDROW.CO.UK

MEMBERS:

James Hunt QC (1968)
(QC-1987) MA (Oxon) *
Brian R. Escott-Cox QC
(1954) (QC-1974) MA (Oxon)
Martin Bowley QC (1962)
(QC-1981) MA BCL (Oxon)
Michael Pert QC (1970)
(QC-1992) LLB (Manch) *
Timothy Raggatt QC (1972)
(QC-1993) LLB (Lond) *
Michael Stokes QC (1971)
(QC-1994) *
Frances Oldham QC (1977)
(QC-1994) BA (Bristol) *
Richard Benson QC (1974)
(QC-1995) *
Heather Swindells QC (1974)
(QC-1995) MA (Oxon) *
Andrew Urquhart (1963) BA
(Oxon)
Stephen Waine (1969) LLB
(Southampton) *
David Altaras (1969) BA
MA(TCD), DipCrim(Cantab)*
Christopher Metcalf (1972) *
David Lee (1973) BA/BA
(Cambridge/Harvard)
Jamie De Burgos (1973) MA
(Cambridge)
Michael Fowler (1974) LLB
(London) *
Geoffrey Solomons (1974)
LLB (Nottingham)
Michael Greaves (1976)
Sam A.G. Mainds* (1977)
LLB (B'ham)

Charles Lewis (1977) MA
(Oxford)
Andrew Neaves (1977) LLB
Howard Morrison (1977)
OBE, LLB (London) *
David Farrell (1978) LLB
(Manchester) *
Catherine Gargan (1978) LLB
(Liverpool)
Martin Beddoe (1979) MA
(Cambridge)
Martine Kushner (1980) LLB
(Cambridge)
Christopher Donnellan
(1981) BA (Oxford)
Lynn Tayton (1981) LLB
(London UCL)
Edmund Farrell (1981) LLB
(Leeds) LLM (Cantab) Dip. Eur
Law (Kings)
Anesta Weekes (1981)
Richard Wilson (1981) BA
LLM (Sussex/Cambridge)
Mercy Akman (1981) LLB
(Wales)
Christopher Plunkett (1983)
LLB (Warwick)
William Harbage (1983) MA
(Cambridge)
Simon Bull (1984) BA LLM
(Cambridge)
Joanne Ecob (1985) LLB
(Newcastle)
Robert Underwood (1986)
BA

Amjad Malik (1987) LLM
(London UCL)
Greg Pryce (1987) BA
(Wolverhampton)
Gordon Aspden (1988) LLB
(Hull)
Andrew Howarth (1988) BA
(Oxford)
Amanda Johnson (1990) LLB
(London)
John Gibson (1991) LLB
(Durham)
Matthew Lowe (1991) LLB
(Exeter)
Stuart Alford (1992) BSc
(Reading)
Sarah Gaunt (1992)
LLB/M.Phil
(Cardiff/Cambridge)
Rosa Dean (1993) BA
(Oxford)
John Lloyd-Jones (1993) BA
(Durham)
Karen Johnston (1994) MA
(Oxford)
Jeffrey Jupp (1994) BA
(Worcester)
Andrzej Bojarski (1995) LLB
(LSE)
Jonathan Kirk (1995) LLB
(Kings)
Niall Ferguson (1996) BA
(Dunelm)
Rupert Skilbeck (1996) BA
(York)
Oliver Connelly (1997)

Head of Chambers:
James Hunt QC

Practice Manager:
Peter Bennett FCCA MCIM

Senior Clerk: Martin Poulter

Silks Clerk: Graeme Logan

Senior Criminal Clerk:
Jo Pickersgill

Senior Civil/Family Clerk:
Richard Cade

Administrator: Louise Smith

Fees Clerk: Lynn Edmonds

Tenants: 55

Door Tenants: Peter Joyce QC (1991) Colman Treacy QC (1990) Elizabeth Ingham (1989)
* Recorder

Other Annexes: 24 Albion Place, Northampton, NN1 1UD Tel: (01604) 602333 Fax: (01604) 601600 DX 18544 Northampton 2;

104 New Walk, Leicester. LE1 7ND Tel: (0116) 249 2020 Fax: (0116) 255 0885 DX: 28816 Leicester 2

The Chambers: For over a century Chambers has been a London based Midland and Oxford circuit practice. Chambers operates within client orientated teams covering Crime, Fraud, Civil & Commercial and Family. Chambers has annexes in Northampton and Leicester. Chambers has a reputation for good management, innovation in client services, fairness and a very professional and friendly atmosphere. They fully comply with the Bar Practice Management Standard and Equality Code and are the only Chambers to achieve ISO 9000 quality accreditation.

Work undertaken:

Main Areas of Work: Personal injury litigation with specialists in paraplegia and brain damage; professional and medical negligence; commercial and company law; consumer law and consumer credit; planning; family law, including matrimonial finance, property and childcare; landlord and tenant; crime, including commercial fraud; contract, including sale of goods.

Additional Areas: Administrative law, agriculture, arbitration, aviation, banking, Chancery including probate, computer law, construction, boundary disputes, courts martial, defamation, discrimination, EEC, employment, environment, housing, immigration, insolvency, judicial review, licensing, animal and equestrian cases, local government, mental health, pharmaceuticals, police cases, product liability, property and sports law.

Foreign Languages: French, Spanish, Urdu, Punjabi.

Office Equipment: Fully computerised and integrated Diary and fee collection. Video conferencing facilities are available in all offices. Fully integrated computer/speech links connect all offices. E-mail and paperless office offered to clients.

Recruitment & Training: Chambers offer twelve months' pupillages. The Midland and Oxford Circuit covers a wide area and Pupils should be prepared for extensive travel and higher travel costs than those in London-based practice. Pupillage awards of £18,000 (of which £8,000 is an income guarantee) are made. Pupils regularly earn another £3,000. Mini-pupillages are available. Chambers have an excellent record of recruitment from pupils. Applications via PACH.

Registration: GB 1435

Formerly 1 King's Bench Walk

SET NUMBER
11 **48 BEDFORD ROW** (Roderick I'Anson Banks)

48 BEDFORD ROW, LONDON, WC1R 4LR
Tel: (0171) 430 2005 **Fax:** (0171) 831 4885 **DX:** 284 LDE

MEMBERS:

Roderick I'Anson Banks
(1974) LLB (London)

| Head of Chambers: |
| Roderick I'Anson Banks |
| Practice Manager: |
| Kim Pangratis |
| Tenants: 1 |

The Chambers: Specialise exclusively in partnership law and provide solicitors and other professional and trading partnerships with a full range of legal services, from the drafting of new agreements and the review of existing agreements to advice and representation in partnership disputes, arbitrations and mediations.

Chambers aim, where possible, to assist clients with the process of resolving disputes without recourse to litigation and provide constant support from the embryonic stages of a developing dispute right through to the conclusion of any litigation or until a negotiated settlement is reached.

Partnership Healthcheck (leaflet available) has been specifically developed to assist solicitors' firms in preparing and updating their agreements. Direct Professional Access work is undertaken.

Publications: Roderick I'Anson Banks is the editor of *Lindley & Banks on Partnership*, the authoritative guide to partnership law, and the author and editor of the Encyclopedia of Professional Partnerships.

SET NUMBER
12 BELL YARD CHAMBERS Bell Yard Chambers, 116-118 Chancery Lane, London, WC2A 1PP **Tel:** (0171) 306 9292 **Fax:** (0171) 404 5143 **DX:** 0075 **Clerk:** Mrs Karen Bardens **Tenants:** 29 A specialist criminal set of chambers established in 1989 which has expanded from 12 to 29 members.

SET NUMBER
13

5 BELL YARD (Robert Webb QC)

5 BELL YARD, LONDON, WC2A 2JR
Tel: (0171) 333 8811 **Fax:** (0171) 333 8831 **DX:** 400

MEMBERS:

Robert Webb QC (1971)
(QC-1988)
Robin Mathew QC (1974)
(QC-1992)
Edward Bailey (1970)
Andrew Hillier (1972)
Dennis Matthews (1973)
Kenneth Munro (1973)
Gordon Bennett (1974)

Angus Macpherson (1977)
Michael Soole (1977)
Anthony Radevsky (1978)
Paul Dean (1982)
Charlotte Jones (1982)
Michael Sullivan (1983)
Giles Kavanagh (1984)
David Fisher (1985)
Philip Reed (1985)

Matthew Reeve (1987)
Stephen Schaw-Miller (1988)
Raymond Ng (1987)
Robert Lawson (1989)
Hannah Brown (1992)
William Hansen (1992)
John Russell (1993)
Kate Vaughan-Neil (1994)
John Kimbell (1995)

Head of Chambers:
Robert Webb QC

Senior Clerk:
Kevin Moore

Tenants: 25

Door Tenants: Richard Gardiner (1969), Richard Selwyn Sharpe (1985).

Work Undertaken: Members of 5 Bell Yard practise in most areas of civil and commercial law. In particular, expertise is offered by individual members in one or more of the following:

Aviation Law: Liability – passenger and cargo; leasing; regulatory – C.A.A. and European; insurance.

Commercial Law: Banking; carriage of goods; commercial contracts; company and insolvency; insurance and reinsurance; tax.

Civil Law: Building and engineering; landlord and tenant; personal injury; professional and medical negligence; product and environmental liability; mass disasters.

Public and Employment Law: Judicial review; mental health; National Health service; pharmaceutical; coroners; town & country planning; individual and collective employment; trade union; disciplinary tribunals; public inquiries.

BELL 5 YARD

SET NUMBER
14

9-12 BELL YARD (D. Anthony Evans QC)

9-12 BELL YARD, LONDON, WC2
Tel: (0171) 400 1800 **Fax:** (0171) 404 1405 **DX:** 390

MEMBERS:

D. Anthony Evans QC (1965)
(QC-1983) BA (Cantab)
Edmund Lawson QC (1971)
(QC-1988) MA (Cantab)
Alex Carlile QC (1970)
(QC-1984)
Jeremy Carter-Manning QC
(1975) (QC-1993)
Herbert Kerrigan QC (1970)
(QC-1992)
Sonia Woodley QC (1968)
(QC-1996)
Patrick Curran QC (1972)
(QC-1995)
Michael Birnbaum QC
(1969) (QC-1992)
Peter Christopher Rouch QC
(1972) (QC-1996)
Edward Grayson (1948) MA
(Oxon)
Peter Caton (1963) MA
(Oxon)
Richard Cherrill (1967)
Martin Field (1966)

Richard Merz (1972)
Alison Barker (1973) LLB,
Harmsworth Law Scholar 1973
John Greaves (1973) LLB
(Lond)
Anthony Heaton-Armstrong
(1973)
Tudor Owen (1974) LLB
(Lond)
Alexander Cranbrook (1975)
BA
Peter Doyle (1975) LLB
Stephen John (1975)
John Harwood-Stevenson
(1975)
Timothy Spencer (1976)
Philip Katz (1976)
Peter Moss (1976)
Keith Hadrill (1977)
Michael Orsulik (1978)
Diane Chan (1979)
John Alban Williams (1979)
John McGuinness (1980)

Michael Egan (1981)
Sean Enright (1982)
Mukul Chawla (1983)
Christine Laing (1984)
Philippa McAtasney (1985)
Mohammed Khamisa (1985)
Tracey Elliott (1986)
Mark Bryant-Heron (1986)
William Hughes (1989)
Adrian Chaplin (1990)
Alexandra Healy (1992)
Mark Seymour (1992)
Richard Jory (1993)
Suzanne Reeve (1993)
Warwick Tatford (1993)
Jonathan S Kinnear (1994)
Christina Russell (1994)
Tina Davey (1993)
Jessica Gavron (1995)
Michelle Denton (1996)
Neil Griffin (1996)

Head of Chambers:
D. Anthony Evans QC

Senior Clerk:
Gary Reed

Tenants: 51

The Chambers: A common law chambers, offering a broad based expertise in all fields of Criminal and Civil law. Although the chambers' reputation is firmly vested in these areas, members are increasingly engaged in other specific fields. It has grown so that there are now nine Queen's Counsel and 43 juniors. Work has become increasingly high profile and chambers are best known for commercial fraud and white collar crime, work on behalf of the police federation and local government work.

Work Undertaken:

Civil: Professional negligence (particularly accountancy/auditing), commercial contract, building and arbitration, banking, company and general chancery, tort (including personal injury), planning, local government, family, and landlord and tenant.

Criminal: Members deal with every aspect of criminal litigation (both prosecution and defence.) The set's defence experience is broadly based, ranging from the most serious and complex commercial fraud to more common offences against the person and property. Prosecution work is undertaken for Crown Prosecution Service, Department of Trade and Industry, Serious Fraud Office, Customs and Excise, British Telecom and Local Authorities. Judicial Review in criminal matters is a particular expertise. Senior members conduct appeals from Commonwealth countries to the Privy Council.

Additional areas: Judicial review, police work (discipline, advisory and union work), licensing, aviation and sports-related problems.

Clientele: Lay clients include the solicitors and accountancy professions, City institutions, the Police Federation and its members, local government organisations, retailers, brewing and allied organisations, and a varied private clientele.

Languages Spoken: French, German, Spanish, Russian, Hindi, Urdu and Gujerati.

Recruitment & Training: Tenancy applications to D. Anthony Evans QC. On average, there are six pupils in chambers at any one time. Applications through PACH only, any other enquiries to William Hughes. Awards are currently under review. A good degree is essential.

SET NUMBERH
15 BLACKSTONE CHAMBERS (Formerly 2 Hare Court) (P Baxendale QC and C Flint QC)

BLACKSTONE HOUSE, TEMPLE, LONDON, EC4
Tel: (0171) 583 1770 **Fax:** (0171) 822 7222 **DX:** 281 **Email:** 2_HARE_COURT@LINK.ORG

MEMBERS:

Colin Ross-Munro QC (1951) (QC-1972)

Stanley Brodie QC (1954) (QC-1975)

Lord Lester of Herne Hill QC (1963) (QC-1975)

Ian Sinclair QC (1952) (QC-1979)

Ian Brownlie QC (1958) (QC-1979)

David Donaldson QC (1968) (QC-1984)

Robert Englehart QC (1969) (QC-1986)

David Hunt QC (1969) (QC-1987)

Barbara Dohmann QC (1971) (QC-1987)

Andrew Pugh QC (1961) (QC-1988)

Ian Forrester QC (1972) (QC-1988)

Roy Goode QC (1988) (QC-1990)

Maurice Mendelson QC (1965) (QC-1992)

Jonathan Harvie QC (1973) (QC-1992)

Presiley Baxendale QC (1974) (QC-1992)

David Pannick QC (1979) (QC-1992)

Jeffrey Jowell QC (1965) (QC-1993)

Stephen Nathan QC (1969) (QC-1993)

Charles Flint QC (1975) (QC-1995)

Bob Hepple QC (1966) (QC-1996)

Gerald Levy (1964)

Dawn Oliver (1965)

Alastair Sutton (1972)

Hugo Page (1977)

Judith Beale (1978)

Beverley Lang (1978)

Thomas Beazley (1979)

Ian Mill (1981)

Paul Goulding (1984)

Anthony Peto (1985)

Monica Carss-Frisk (1985)

Gerard Clarke (1986)

Adam Lewis (1985)

Robert Anderson (1986)

Mark Shaw (1987)

Andrew Green (1988)

Robert Howe (1988)

Adrian Briggs (1989)

Dinah Rose (1989)

Michael Fordham (1990)

Pushpinder Saini (1991)

Thomas Croxford (1992)

Javan Herberg (1992)

Joanna Pollard (1993)

Andrew Hunter (1993)

Gemma White (1994)

Jane Collier (1994)

Emma Dixon (1994)

Thomas de la Mare (1995)

Tom Weisselberg (1995)

Jane Mulcahy (1995)

Julia Ellins (1994)

Andrew George (1997)

Kate Gallafent (1997)

Head of Chambers:
P Baxendale QC and C Flint QC

Practice Manager:
Julia Hornor

Senior Clerk: Martin Smith

Tenants: 54

Associate Members: Judge David Edward CMG QC, The Rt. Hon. Sir Leon Brittan Kt PC QC, Anthony Steen MP, Professor Ian Kennedy, Dan Joel, Robin Morse, Maurice Fitzmaurice.

Members of chambers are recorders, arbitrators of the ICC and London Court of International Arbitration, members of the Institute of International Law, the ICSID Panel of Arbitrators and Conciliators and the INTELSAT Panel of Experts. Chambers has amongst its members the Panel Chairman of Appeals under the Consumer Credit Act, who also sits on the DTI Advisory Committee on Arbitration, and a former legal adviser to the Foreign and Commonwealth Office.

The Chambers: The chambers' main reputation is for its work in the fields of commercial, employment and public law; however, the specialisations of individual members within these categories are diverse. The chambers are fully computerized, using Microsoft Product software – and aim to offer an efficient and cost-effective service.

Continues overleaf

Publications: Works include: *Principles of Public International Law; Commercial Law; Legal Problems of Credit and Security; Hire Purchase Law and Practice; Principles of Corporate Insolvency Law; Consumer Credit Legislation; Constitutional and Administrative Law; de Smith Woolf & Jowell Judicial Review of Administrative Action* (1995); *Vienna Convention on the Law of Treaties; International Law Commission; Halsbury on Aliens, Arbitration and the European Convention on Human Rights.*

Work Undertaken:

Commercial: *Work includes:* international trade, banking, insurance, carriage of goods, conflict of laws, corporate fraud, financial services, regulatory tribunals, defamation, media and entertainment and intellectual property.

Public: *Work includes:* judicial review both for and against public bodies arising from decisions in areas such as freedom of expression, equality of treatment, immigration, education, social security, housing, planning and local government. The combined expertise of members in commercial and public law proves particularly valuable in City regulation and financial services cases.

Employment: Chambers also specialises extensively in employment law, ranging from enforcement of contractual terms to sex, race and disability discrimination.

Additional Areas: International and European law.

Foreign Connections: The chambers has close links with a network of lawyers across Europe, and members have a wide-ranging experience of advocacy before English, European and Commonwealth courts and tribunals. Members of chambers appear before the European Court of Justice and the European Court of Human Rights, with two senior members practising in European Community law from Brussels.

Languages Spoken: French, German, Italian, Spanish, Finnish, Swedish, Urdu, Hindi, Punjabi, Japanese.

Recruitment & Training: Chambers has its own applications procedure. The application form is available on request. A first or upper second class degree is usually required, although not necessarily in law. Pupillage awards of up to £23,000 are available. Mini-pupillages for a week in the year preceding pupillage are strongly encouraged for potential pupils of the chambers.

SET NUMBER

16 11 BOLT COURT (Richard Mandel) 11 Bolt Court, London, EC4A 3DQ **Tel:** (0171) 353 2300 **Fax:** (0171) 353 1878 **DX:** 0022 **Clerk:** John Bowker **Tenants:** 25 A general common law set, with several members also practising in criminal, family, planning and employment law. Also at Redhill Chambers.

SET NUMBER

17 BRACTON CHAMBERS (Ian McCulloch) Bracton Chambers, 95a Chancery Lane, London, WC2A 1DT **Tel:** (0171) 242 4248 **Fax:** (0171) 242 4232 **DX:** LDE 416 Chancery Lane **Clerk:** Ian Hogg **Tenants:** 16 A specialist civil set of chambers with a particular emphasis on chancery and commercial work.

SET NMBER
18

4 BREAMS BUILDINGS (Christopher Lockhart-Mummery QC)

4 BREAMS BUILDINGS, LONDON, EC4A 1AQ
Tel: (0171) 430 1221/353 5835 **Fax:** (0171) 430 1677 **DX:** 1042 **Internet:** HTTP: //WWW.4BREAMSBUILDINGS.LAW.CO.UK

MEMBERS:

Christopher Lockhart-Mummery QC (1971) (QC-1986)

Nigel Macleod QC (1961) (QC-1979)

Michael Barnes QC (1965) (QC-1981)

John Cherryman QC (1955) (QC-1982) LLB

Michael Howard QC MP (1964) (QC-1982) *

David Hands QC (1965) (QC-1988)

The Rt. Hon. Lord Kingsland QC (1972) (QC-1988)

Joseph Harper QC (1970) (QC-1992)

John Howell QC (1979) (QC-1993)

John Furber QC (1973) (QC-1995)

Richard Drabble QC (1975) (QC-1995)

David QC Holgate QC (1978) (QC-1997)

Colin Sydenham (1963) MA (Cantab)

Stephen Bickford-Smith (1972)

Eian Caws (1974)

Robert Bailey-King (1975)

Anne Seifert (1975)

Christopher Lewsley (1976)

John Male (1976)

Viscount Dilhorne (1979)

David Smith (1980)

Anne Williams (1980)

Christopher Katkowski (1982)

Alice Robinson (1983)

David Elvin (1983)

Jonathan Karas (1986)

Timothy Mould (1987)

Nathalie Lieven (1989)

John Litton (1989)

Nicholas Taggart (1991)

Karen McHugh (1992)

David Forsdick (1993)

Timothy Morshead (1995)

Graeme Keen (1995)

James Maurici (1996)

Alison Oakes (1996)

Head of Chambers:
Christopher Lockhart-Mummery QC

Senior Clerk:
Stephen Graham

Junior Clerk: Jay Fullilove

Tenants: 36

The Chambers: A specialist planning, property and public law set housed in spacious, self contained, air conditioned chambers, just off Chancery Lane. The accommodation has six floors, of which one is for administration and one dedicated to conference facilities.

Members of Chambers belong to both the Planning and Environmental Bar Association, of which Nigel Macleod is Vice-Chairman and Anne Williams is Treasurer, and the Administrative Law Bar Association of which Richard Drabble is Vice-chairman. Chambers has a general membership of the Chancery Bar Association. Stephen Bickford-Smith sits as arbitrator and The Viscount Dilhorne sat as a part-time chairman of Value Added Tax tribunals. Christopher Katkowski and David Elvin are members of the Panel of Junior Counsel to the Crown and six other members of Chambers are on the Supplementary Panel. Prior to taking Silk last year, David Holgate was Junior Counsel to the Inland Revenue on Rating and Valuation matters, he was succeded by Timothy Mould. In addition five members of chambers are recorders and one is an assistant recorder.

Publications: *Works include: Hill's Law of Town and Country Planning (4th Edition); Town Planning Law Handbook and Casebook; Atkin's Court Forms – Town and Country Planning* (editor); *Hill and Redman's Law of Landlord and Tenant* (several members are editors); *Halsbury's Laws – Landlord and Tenant* (4th Edition) (contributory editors); *Halsbury's Laws – Town & Country Planning* (edited entirely within chambers); *Encyclopaedia of Rating and Local Taxation* (editor); *Atkin's Court Forms – Rating and Community Charge* and *Journal of Planning Law* (members of the Editorial Boards); *Corfield and Carnwath's Compulsory Acquisition and Compensation; Halsbury's Laws – European Communities* (contributory editors); *Emden's Building Contracts and Practice* (editor); *Unlawful Interference with Land* by David Elvin and Jonathan Karas; *Party Walls: The New Law* by Stephen Bickford-Smith and Colin Sydenham; *Halsbury's Laws – Compulsory Acquisition* (edited entirely within chambers).

Work Undertaken:
Main Areas of Work: Administrative law; construction; environment; housing; judicial review; landlord and tenant; local government; parliamentary; planning and property.
Additional Areas: Agriculture; arbitration; Education; European Community Law, international law, energy, consumer credit, financial services, revenue and tax law and welfare.

Clientele: Developers, property companies, local authorities and government regulatory bodies. Members accept Direct Professional Access from the approved professions.

Foreign Connections: Michael Barnes QC is a member of the Singapore Bar and the Hong Kong Bar; Joseph Harper QC is a member of the Antigua Bar.

Associated Chambers: 40 King Street, Manchester.

Recruitment and Training: Tenancy and mini-pupillage applications should be addressed to David Elvin. Pupillage applications should be made through the Bar PACH scheme directly to Chambers. Three funded pupillages are awarded annually each of £19,000 for 12 months (although applications for six month pupillages are still considered). Space for mini-pupillages is limited and, during the summer months in particular, preference is given to final year students.

* Rt. Hon. Michael Howard QC is the Member of Parliament for Folkestone.

BRICK COURT CHAMBERS (Christopher Clarke QC) formerly 15/19 Devereux Street, London WC2R 3JJ

7-8 ESSEX STREET, LONDON, WC2R 3LD
Tel: (0171) 583 0777 **Fax:** (0171) 583 9401 **DX:** 302

MEMBERS:

Christopher Clarke QC (1969) (QC-1984)	Timothy Charlton QC (1974) (QC-1993)	David Anderson (1985)
Nicholas Lyell QC (1965) (QC-1980) MP	Mark Hapgood QC (1979) (QC-1994)	Michael Swainston (1985)
Philip Owen QC (1949) (QC-1963)	Mark Howard QC (1980) (QC-1996)	Fergus Randolph (1985)
Sydney Kentridge QC (1977) (QC-1984)	Stephen Ruttle QC (1976) (QC-1997)	Conor Quigley (1985)
David Vaughan QC (1962) (QC-1981)	Andrew Popplewell QC (1981) (QC-1997)	David Garland (1986)
Nicholas Chambers QC (1966) (QC-1985)	George Leggatt QC (1983) (QC-1997)	Neil Calver (1987)
Richard Aikens QC (1973) (QC-1986)	William Wood QC (1980) (QC-1998)	Dominic Chambers (1987)
Jonathan Sumption QC (1975) (QC-1986)	Nicholas Green QC (1986) (QC-1998)	Richard Slade (1987)
Hilary Heilbron QC (1971) (QC-1987)	Peter Irvin (1972)	Harry Matovu (1988)
Nicholas Forwood QC (1970) (QC-1987)	Peter Brunner (1971)	Cyril Kinsky (1988)
Mark Cran QC (1973) (QC-1988)	David Lloyd-Jones (1975)	Paul Wright (1990)
	Charles Hollander (1978)	Sarah Lee (1990)
Jonathan Hirst QC (1975) (QC-1990)	James Flynn (1978)	Helen Davies (1990)
Gerald Barling QC (1972) (QC-1991)	Paul Walker (1979)	Mark Hoskins (1991)
	Andrew Lydiard (1980)	Tom Adam (1991)
Peregrine Simon QC (1973) (QC-1991)	Richard Lord (1981)	Michael Bools (1991)
	Catharine Otton-Goulder (1983)	Alan Roxburgh (1992)
		Jemima Stratford (1993)
	Mark Brealey (1984)	Alec Haydon (1993)
		Roger Masefield (1994)
		Simon Salzedo (1995)
		Andrew Thomas (1996)

Head of Chambers: Christopher Clarke QC
Senior Clerks: Ian Moyler, Julian Hawes
Administrator: Nancy Lockwood
Tenants: 53

The Chambers: Brick Court Chambers have been established for over 75 years. Members of Chambers practice predominately Commercial/European Community Law (which includes Banking, Insurance, Financial Services, Sale of Goods, Contract Shipping, Administrative and Public Law, Media and Entertainment, Sports Law, Competition and Regulatory).

Members of chambers appear regularly in County Court, all High Court divisions, Court of Appeal, House of Lords, Privy Council European Court of Justice and The European Court of Human Rights in Strasbourg.

Members of Chambers have extensive experience of Industrial Tribunals, VAT Tribunals, DTI inquiry, public inquiries and disciplinary tribunals.

Chambers have an annexe in Brussels.

Further details are available from the Clerks to Chambers.

BRICK COURT CHAMBERS

B A R R I S T E R S

1 BRICK COURT (Richard Hartley QC)

1 BRICK COURT, TEMPLE, LONDON, EC4Y 9BY
Tel: (0171) 353 8845 **Fax:** (0171) 583 9144 **DX:** 468

MEMBERS:

Richard Hartley QC (1956) (QC-1976)	Andrew Caldecott QC (1975) (QC-1994)	Manuel Barca (1986)
Richard Rampton QC (1965) (QC-1987)	Edward Garnier QC (1976) (QC-1995)	Timothy Atkinson (1988)
		Rupert Elliott (1988)
Geoffrey Shaw QC (1968) (QC-1991)	Patrick Moloney QC (1976) (QC-1998)	Jane Phillips (1989)
Thomas Shields QC (1973) (QC-1993)	Stephen Suttle (1980)	Caroline Addy (1991)
	Victoria Sharp (1979)	Benjamin Hinchliff (1992)
Harry Boggis-Rolfe (1969)	Harvey Starte (1985)	Giles Crown (1993)
		Catrin Evans (1994)
		Lorna Skinner (1996)

Head of Chambers: Richard Hartley QC
Senior Clerk: John Woodcock
Tenants: 20

The Chambers: These chambers have specialised in the law of libel and slander for over 75 years. The work of chambers now also covers all aspects of media and information law, including contempt of court, breach of confidence, and broadcasting law; some general common law and commercial work and judicial review is undertaken.

Members of chambers are experienced in the pre-publication review of newspapers, books, radio and television programmes and have written or contributed to most of the leading works on defamation and contempt of court including Duncan and Neill on *Defamation*, Carter-Ruck on *Libel and Slander*, Arlidge and Eady on *Contempt of Court*, Halsbury's Laws of England, Bullen & Leake & Jacob's Precedents of Pleading and Atkin's Forms and Precedents. Members of chambers frequently receive instructions from Commonwealth and foreign jurisdictions and frequently conduct cases in such jurisdictions.

SET NUMBER 21

4 BRICK COURT (David Medhurst)

4 BRICK COURT, TEMPLE, LONDON, EC4Y 9AD
Tel: (0171) 797 8910 **Fax:** (0171) 797 8929 **DX:** 491

MEMBERS:

Edward Lyons QC (1952) (QC-1974)	Susan Quinn (1983)	Annabel Wentworth (1990)
David Medhurst (1969)	Marc Roberts (1984)	Michael Simon (1992)
Mira Chatterjee (1973)	Peter Lynch (1985)	Edward Knapp (1992)
Nicholas Easterman (1975)	Anthony Bell (1985)	Gwynneth Knowles (1993)
David Burgess (1975)	Simon Molyneux (1986)	Levi Peter (1993)
Robert Colover (1975)	Michael Mylonas-Widdall (1988)	Caroline Sumeray (1993)
Marianna Hildyard (1977)	Tobias Long (1988)	Stan Gallagher (1994)
Janet Mitchell (1978)	Colin Ishmael (1989)	Sue Piyadasa (1994)
Michael Haynes (1979)	Deborah Archer (1989)	Jolyon Perks (1994)
Richard St Clair-Gainer (1983)	Alexa Storcy-Rca (1990)	Teresa Pritchard (1994)
	Abigail Sheppard (1990)	Rachael Morton (1994)
		Sarah Morris (1996)

Head of Chambers: David Medhurst
Senior Clerk: Michael Corrigan
Tenants: 33

SET NUMBER 22

4 BRICK COURT (Anne Rafferty QC) 4 Brick Court, Temple, London, EC4Y 9AD Tel: (0171) 583 8455 Fax: (0171) 353 1699 DX: 453 Clerk: Michael Eves Tenants: 37

SET NUMBER 23

4 BRICK COURT (Antony Shaw QC)

4 BRICK COURT, TEMPLE, LONDON, EC4Y 9AD
Tel: (0171) 797 7766 **Fax:** (0171) 797 7700 **DX:** 404 (CH.LN.) **Email:** CHAMBERS@4BRICK.CO.UK

MEMBERS:

Antony Shaw QC (1975) (QC-1994)	David Boyd (1977)	Anthea Parker (1990)
Laxmi Devi Reilly (1972)	Constance Briscoe (1983)	Julia Krish (1992)
Adrian Taylor (1977)	John Lyons (1986)	Susan Belgrave (1989) BA MSc (Econ) LLB
Jane Drew (1976)	Anne Gibberd (1985)	
Catherine Nicholes (1977)	William Evans (1988)	Jillian Brown (1991)
Aditya Kumar Sen (1977)	Mark Mullins (1988)	Michael Horton (1993)
Anthony Wadling (1977)	Michael Magarian (1988)	Helen Curtis (1992)
Vera Mayer (1978)	Declan O'Dempsey (1987)	Rajeev Thacker (1993)
Anne Spratling (1980)	Peter Rowlands (1990)	Dermot Casey (1994)
Melanie Lewis (1980)	Michael Conning (1990)	Rebecca Trowler (1995)
Martin Seaward (1978)	Piers Mostyn (1989)	Andrew Allen (1995)
Meena Gill (1982)	Frances Orchover (1989)	Lesley-Anne Cull (1995)
Andrew Cohen (1982)	Fenella Morris (1990)	Jerry Fitzpatrick (1996)
Martha Cover (1979)	Michael Baker (1990)	Sarah Elliott (1996)
Roderick Jones (1983)	Edgar Prais QC (1990) (QC-1993)	
Nicholas O'Brien (1985)	Andrew Short (1990)	

Head of Chambers: Antony Shaw QC
Chambers Manager: Gloria Zimmerman
Senior Clerk: Paul Sampson
Ist Junior Clerk: George Mo
Clerks: Danny Norman Samantha Gibbs
Fees Clerk: Chamira Athauda
Tenants: 45

The Chambers: Chambers undertake a wide range of work which falls into three main fields: civil, crime and family.

Work Undertaken:

Civil: Housing, landlord and tenant, personal injury, employment (including discrimination and trade union law), professional negligence (including medical negligence), judicial review, inquests, mental health, chancery, contract and consumer protection, European law, immigration, Education.

Crime: Including serious fraud and drugs.

Family: Including divorce, matrimonial finance, public and private Children Act proceedings, child abduction, domestic violence, adoption, wardship, inheritance and cohabitees.

Languages: French, Italian, Spanish, Bengali, Punjabi, Hindi, Hebrew and Slovak.

BRIDEWELL CHAMBERS (Colin Challenger)

BRIDEWELL CHAMBERS, 2 BRIDEWELL PLACE, LONDON, EC4V 6AP
Tel: (0171) 797 8800 **Fax:** (0171) 797 8801 **DX:** 383 **Email:** NBROOKS@BRIDEWELL.LAW.CO.UK

MEMBERS:

Colin Challenger (1970)
Jo Boothby (1972)
Gordon Pringle (1973)
Juliet Oliver (1974)
Deborah Jefferson (1975)
Neville Willard (1976)
Ernest James (1977)
Adrienne Knight (1981)
James Thomson (1983)
Peter Gray (1984)

Vincent Williams (1985)
Ian Lawrie (1985)
David Josse (1985)
Dafydd Enoch (1985)
Adam Clemens (1985)
James Doyle (1985)
Simon Walsh (1987)
Patricia Roberts (1987)
Sally Atherton (1987)
Mark Graffius (1990)

Paul Michell (1991)
Carolyn Rothwell (1991)
Alan Walmsley (1991)
Brian Cummins (1992)
Andrew Slaughter (1993)
Lloyd Sefton-Smith (1993)
Paul Walker (1993)
Maria Scotland (1995)

Head of Chambers:
Colin Challenger
Senior Clerk:
Norman Brooks
Tenants: 28

The Chambers: Chambers covers most significant areas of criminal, civil and family law. Specialist teams deal with serious crime, housing, landlord and tenant, family and children, personal injury and cases for and against police forces. Individual tenants specialise in commercial law, judicial review, licensing, wills and probate, professional negligence, Official Referee work and marine accidents.

A detailed guide to the full services we provide, including the Bridewell Conditional Fee Agreement, can be found on the Chambers website at //www.bridewell.law.co.uk, or by contacting the clerks.

Languages spoken: French and German

Recruitment and Training: Pupillage applications to PACH. Tenancy applications may be sent to Ian Laurie.

BRITTON STREET CHAMBERS (Marvin Gederon) First Floor, 20 Britton Street, London, EC1M 5NQ **Tel:** (0171) 608 3765 **Fax:** (0171) 608 3746 **DX:** 53329 Clerkenwell EC1 **Clerk:** Mr R. Phillips **Tenants:** 13 General Common Law set handling both civil and criminal work. Immigration, Family, Landlord and Tenant.

CHAMBERS OF MARTIN BURR (Martin Burr) Eldon Chambers, 30-32 Fleet Street, London, EC4Y 1AA **Tel:** (0171) 353 4636 **Fax:** (0171) 353 4637 **DX:** 146 (Ch.Ln.) **Clerk:** Colin Middleton **Tenants:** 15 The areas of law covered include: chancery (especially trusts, wills etc.), charities, common law, company, crime, ecclesiastical, employment, family and child welfare, landlord and tenant, personal injury, planning and local government, and revenue.

CHANCERY CHAMBERS (Lawrence St. Ville) 70/72 Chancery Lane, London, WC2A 1AB **Tel:** (0171) 405 6879 **Fax:** (0171) 430 0502 **Clerk:** Angela Harris **Tenants:** 22 Broadly-based common law chambers with the majority of the work being in the criminal sector. Also specialise in immigration, family law and housing.

95A CHANCERY LANE (Helen Grindrod QC) First Floor, 95a Chancery Lane, London, WC2A 2JG **Tel:** (0171) 404 4777 **Fax:** (0171) 404 8777 **DX:** 425 (Ch.Ln.) **Clerk:** Mark Auger **Tenants:** 15 A set of specialist criminal practitioners with expertise in all aspects of criminal law.

95A CHANCERY LANE (Ms Marie-Claire Sparrow) 2nd Floor, 95A Chancery Lane, London, WC2A 1DT **Tel:** (0171) 405 3101 **Fax:** (0171) 405 3112 **DX:** 53657 W. Hampstead

SET NUMBER
30
CLOISTERS (Laura Cox QC)

CLOISTERS, 1 PUMP COURT, TEMPLE, LONDON, EC4Y 7AA
Tel: (0171) 827 4000 **Fax:** (0171) 827 4100 **DX:** LDE 452

MEMBERS:

Laura Cox QC (1975)
(QC-1994)
John Platts-Mills QC (1932)
(QC-1964)
Anna Worrall QC (1959)
(QC-1989)
Alan Newman QC (1968)
(QC-1989)
Elizabeth Lawson QC (1969)
(QC-1989)
Stephen Solley QC (1969)
(QC-1989)
Lawrence Kershen QC
(1967) (QC-1992)
Brian Langstaff QC (1971)
(QC-1994)
Arthur Davidson QC (1953)
(QC-1976)
Robin Allen QC (1974)
(QC-1995)

Roger McCarthy QC (1975)
(QC-1996)
Roderick Price (1971)
Stuart Montrose (1972)
Jonathan Crystal (1972)
Peter Guest (1975)
Thomas Culver (1976)
Philip Engelman (1979)
Jacques Algazy (1980)
Andrew Buchan (1981)
Michael Turner (1984)
Antony White (1983)
Timothy Horgan (1983)
Jerome Lynch (1983)
Dr. Simon W. Taylor (1984)
Pauline Hendy (1985)
Anthony Bradley (1989)
Patricia Hitchcock (1988)

Paul Epstein (1988)
Paul Spencer (1988)
Thomas Kibling (1990)
Lewis Power (1990)
Jason Galbraith-Marten
(1991)
Christopher Quinn (1992)
Matthew Ryder (1992)
Peter Shaw (1992)
Caspar Glyn (1992)
Rufus D'Cruz (1993)
Navjot Sidhu (1993)
Louise Brooks (1994)
Rachel Crasnow (1994)
Sally Robertson (1995)
James Laddie (1995)
Ulele Burnham (1997)

| Head of Chambers: |
| Laura Cox QC |
| **Senior Clerk:** |
| Michael Martin |
| **Tenants:** 43 |

Associate Members: David Thomas QC, Peter Pimm, John Whitmore, Amir Majid.

The Chambers: Founded in 1952 by D.N. Pritt QC, one of the most distinguished silks of his day, Cloisters is a progressive and expanding set of chambers fully equipped to meet the wide and growing demands of modern practice. Pritt was a passionate champion of civil liberties, both in the United Kingdom and around the world. The law has changed dramatically since Pritt's day, but the principles established by Cloisters' founder are as relevant now as they ever have been. Concern for our clients has always been, and remains, our guiding philosophy and, where necessary, we are prepared to risk unpopularity for the sake of principle.

From its inception, Cloisters has provided a broad range of expertise, while maintaining its specialist reputation in specific fields. The breadth of practice is one of Cloisters' strengths and, perhaps, its most striking feature. Members of Chambers continue to act in landmark cases in many areas of the Law, civil and criminal, and we undertake the whole range of court, tribunal and appellate work, from the smallest claims to the House of Lords and the European Courts. Expansion in recent years into areas such as commercial work and media law has not reduced Chambers' traditional conern for the rights of the individual.

Cloisters welcomes direct access instructions from overseas lawyers and from those professions both in the UK and abroad who are entitled under the Bar Rules to use this facility.

Work Undertaken: Administrative/Public/Local Government Law; Civil Liberties; Contract and Commercial Law; Criminal Law; EC Law; Employment/Industrial/Discrimination Law; Personal Injury/Medical Negligence; Family Law; Fraud (Criminal & Civil); Media/Defamation; Sports Law; International Law; International Human Rights.

SET NUMBER
31

CROWN OFFICE ROW (Richard Ferguson QC)

1 CROWN OFFICE ROW, LONDON, EC4Y 7HH
Tel: (0171) 797 7111 **Fax:** (0171) 797 7120 **DX:** 226

MEMBERS:

Richard Ferguson QC (1956) (QC-1973)
Paul Purnell QC (1962) (QC-1982)
Richard Henriques QC (1967) (QC-1986)
Peter Feinberg QC (1972) (QC-1992)
Stephen Leslie QC (1971) (QC-1993)
Patrick O'Connor QC (1970) (QC-1993)
Clement Goldstone QC (1971) (QC-1993)
Roger Farley QC (1974) (QC-1993)
Lionel Lassman (1955)
Alan Greenwood (1970)
David Martin-Sperry (1971)
Henry C. Grunwald (1972)

Michael Cousens (1973)
Nigel Lambert (1974)
Stephen Winberg (1974)
Peter McGrail (1977)
Sonja Shields (1977)
Andrew Turton (1977)
David Hislop (1979)
Robert Hunter (1979)
Isabelle Gillard (1980)
Preston Dass (1983)
Charles Ward-Jackson (1985)
Sandy Canavan (1987)
Peter Clarke (1988)
James Montgomery (1989)
Christopher Henley (1989)
James Beck (1989)
Sangita Modgil (1990)
Eamonn M. Sherry (1990)

Benjamin Squirrell (1990)
Peter Binder (1991)
William England (1991)
Julie-Anne Kincade (1991)
Anthony Orchard (1991)
Ann Tayo (1991)
Anthony Ventham (1991)
Simon Gruchy (1993)
Gerard Doran (1993)
David McGrath (1993)
Louise Sweet (1994)
Alphege Bell (1995)
Martin Watts (1995)
Jacqueline Slee (1995)
Victoria Wootton (1995)
David Haeems (1996)

Head of Chambers:
Richard Ferguson QC

Senior Clerk:
John Phipps

Tenants: 46

The Chambers: This forward looking set aims to provide a complete service within the areas of criminal law, libel, licensing and actions against the police.

Main areas of work: Much of chambers' work involves criminal cases, and members have been involved in political and terrorist matters, in those raising issues of public and media importance, and in human rights cases. Chambers take particular pride in their willingness to defend unpopular individual positions; but members also take very seriously their obligation to prosecute cases fairly and effectively. Ten members of the set have completed professional courses on fraud trial practice, and many have acted in complex trials involving VAT, company and commercial fraud.

Additional areas of work: Individual members also practise in the fields of libel, licensing law, and actions against the police.

Languages: French, Italian and Spanish, Portuguese, Hebrew.

SET NUMBER
32

1 CROWN OFFICE ROW (Robert Seabrook QC)

1 CROWN OFFICE ROW (GROUND FLOOR), TEMPLE, LONDON, EC4Y 7HH
Tel: (0171) 797 7500 **Fax:** (0171) 797 7550 **DX:** 1020

MEMBERS:

Robert Seabrook QC (1964) (QC-1983)
Robert Owen QC (1968) (QC-1988)
Duncan Matheson QC (1965) (QC-1989)
Philip Vallance QC (1968) (QC-1989)
James Badenoch QC (1968) (QC-1989)
Stephen Miller QC (1971) (QC-1990)
David Foskett QC (1972) (QC-1991)
Terence Coghlan QC (1968) (QC-1993)
Guy Mansfield QC (1972) (QC-1994)
Philip Havers QC (1974) (QC-1995)

Sally Smith QC (1977) (QC-1997)
Gregory Chambers (1973)
Christopher Smyth (1972)
Anthony Niblett (1976) *
Margaret Bowron (1978)
Paul Rees (1980)
David Balcombe (1980)
James King-Smith (1980) *
David Hart (1982)
Neil S. Garnham (1982)
Martin Forde (1984)
William Edis (1985)
Janet Waddicor (1985) *
Keith Freeman (1985)
John Gimlette (1986)
David L. Evans (1988)
Amanda Grant (1988)

Paul Rogers (1989) *
Angus McCullough (1990)
Keeley Bishop (1990) *
John Whitting (1991)
Martin Downs (1990) *
Jeremy Cave (1992) *
Richard Booth (1993)
Philippa Whipple (1994)
Sydney Chawatama (1994)
Sarah Lambert (1994)
Owain Thomas (1995)
Jeremy Hyam (1995)
Katharine Hogg (1996)
Ben Collins (1996)
Shaheen Rahman (1996)

Head of Chambers:
Robert Seabrook QC

Senior Clerk:
Alan Smith

Tenants: 42

The Chambers: A long-established set of chambers which aims to offer a comprehensive service of advisory work and advocacy and whose members have a wide experience in a number of specialist fields principally professional negligence, domestic commercial contract, administrative and construction law. Chambers accept Direct Professional Access. A number of tenants (*) practise mainly from an annexe at Blenheim House, 120 Church Street, Brighton BN1 1WH Tel: (01273) 625625 which is available for local conferences.

Work Undertaken: Professional negligence in particular medical and solicitors' negligence, domestic commercial contract, adminstrative law and judicial review, construction law, planning, personal injury, representation at public inquiries and before professional disciplinary tribunals, human rights and European Community law, matrimonial and family law, landlord and tenant and employment. Criminal work is undertaken, in particular fraud and other serious crime. Individual members specialise in different fields which are set out in detail in a brochure which is available upon request.

Chambers Facilities: Three large conference rooms are available but members of chambers are willing, in appropriate cases, to travel to clients/solicitors for conferences. Chambers use WordPerfect 6.0 software.

Recruitment & Training: There are on average three pupils preferably for 12 months. Generous awards for at least two pupils are available for the first six months of at least 8,000 with a guaranteed level of earnings of at least 8,000 in the second six months. Normally a first or upper second degree is required. Applications for 1998 are closed. This Chambers is a member of the Pupillage Application Clearing House Scheme (PACH) whereby a single application is made to all participating chambers, who will select and interview from the pool of applicants pursuant to commonly agreed rules. For details of the scheme and an application form, write to The General Council of the Bar.

SET NUMBER 33

1 CROWN OFFICE ROW (Mark Strachan QC)

1 CROWN OFFICE ROW (3RD FLOOR), TEMPLE, LONDON, EC4Y 7HH
Tel: (0171) 583 9292 **Fax:** (0171) 353 9292 **DX:** 212

MEMBERS:

Mark Strachan QC (1969) (QC-1987)	Sebastian Neville-Clarke (1973)	Aedeen Boadita-Cormican (1990)
Sir Godfray Le Quesne QC (1947) (QC-1962)	William Hewitson (1975)	Paul Marshall (1991)
James Guthrie QC (1975) (QC-1993)	Andrew Young (1977) Pierre Janusz (1979)	Aidan Casey (1992)
Richard Jones QC (1972) (QC-1996)	Peter Knox (1983) James Dingemans (1987)	Farzana Aslam (1993)
Michael Irvine (1964)	Michael Lazarus (1987) Peter Dean (1987)	Bertha Cooper-Rousseau (1993)
Iain McLeod (1969)	Joseph O'Neill (1987)	Marcus Dignum (1994)
Terence Walker (1973)	Howard Stevens (1990)	Ian Rogers (1995) Umesh Kumar (1995)

Head of Chambers: Mark Strachan QC

Senior Clerk: James Donovan (mobile 0956 498217)

Tenants: 25

The Chambers: The chambers are a long-established set, having been founded by Sir Frank Soskice in 1945, upon his appointment as Solicitor-General. A comprehensive service is offered in all areas of law, with the exception of the well-recognised specialist fields, such as revenue. It has always had a strong connection with the work of the Privy Council.

Work Undertaken:
  General Description: Commercial and common law, although individual practices differ significantly.
  Main Areas of Work:
  General Commercial: Both domestic and international, (including I.C.C. and other arbitrations), banking, negotiable instruments, agency, insurance, sale and carriage of goods, building and engineering disputes, employment and industrial relations and professional negligence.
  Appellate Work: In the Privy Council from overseas, covering most fields of law and in particular commercial and general common law work, cases dealing with the written constitutions of Commonwealth countries and criminal law.
  Common Law: Most forms of non-specialist civil litigation including personal injury, medical negligence and landlord and tenant work.

Foreign Languages: French, Italian, Spanish, Dutch, German, Irish.

SET NUMBER
34 **2 CROWN OFFICE ROW** (Graeme Hamilton QC)

2 CROWN OFFICE ROW, TEMPLE, LONDON, EC4Y 7HJ
Tel: (0171) 797 8100 **Fax:** (0171) 797 8101 **DX:** 344 LONDON LIX: LON 144 **Email:** MAIL@2COR.CO.UK

MEMBERS:

Graeme Hamilton QC (1959) (QC-1978)
John Archer QC (1950) (QC-1975)
John Crowley QC (1962) (QC-1982)
Michael Harvey QC (1966) (QC-1982)
Christopher Purchas QC (1966) (QC-1990)
Nigel Wilkinson QC (1972) (QC-1990)
Antony Edwards-Stuart QC (1976) (QC-1991)
Roger ter Haar QC (1974) (QC-1992)
Richard Lynagh QC (1975) (QC-1996)

Michael Kent QC (1975) (QC-1996)
Jonathan Woods (1965)
David Tucker (1973)
Thomas Saunt (1974)
George Gadney (1974)
John Stevenson (1975)
James Holdsworth (1977)
Andrew Phillips (1978)
John Greenbourne (1978)
Anna Guggenheim (1982)
Michael Curtis (1982)
Deborah Taylor (1983)
Ian Swan (1985)
Ben Patten (1986)
Jane DeCamp (1987)

Steven Snowden (1989)
Susan Hodgson (1989)
Jason Evans-Tovey (1990)
Rohan Pershad (1991)
Simon Howarth (1991)
Andrew Rigney (1992)
Leigh-Ann Mulcahy (1993)
Clive Weston (1993)
Patrick Blakesley (1993)
James Maxwell Scott (1995)
Robert Stokell (1995)
Suzanne Chalmers (1995)
Andrew O'Connor (1996)
Andrew Davis (1996)

Head of Chambers:
Graeme Hamilton QC
Clerk: David Newcomb
Tenants: 38

The Chambers: Established over 50 years, chambers now have 39 members including 10 QCs. Present and former members have been involved in many of the leading cases in the development of the common law. Individuals or teams of counsel are available to undertake a wide variety of litigation, arbitration, and advisory work both within the UK and internationally.

Work Undertaken:

Insurance and reinsurance: contract disputes;
Professional negligence: including that of architects, engineers, surveyors, lawyers, accountants and doctors;
Construction and engineering disputes: both in the Official Referee's court and in domestic and international arbitrations;
General commercial: litigation and arbitration (including ICC arbitrations) involving contractual disputes of all kinds;
Product liability claims of all types: including large scale co-ordinated actions;
Personal injury claims: including disaster litigation and cases of severe and permanent disablement.
General common law: including claims in negligence, nuisance and other torts;

Other Areas of Expertise: Include administrative law and judicial review cases, environmental law, planning inquiries and appeals, employment law and commercial fraud, both civil and criminal.

Languages Spoken: French; German; Italian.

Clientele: Chambers have developed strong links with the insurance market and many of their clients are insurance companies, underwriting syndicates and brokers.

TWO CROWN
OFFICE ROW

SET NUMBER
35 **2 CROWN OFFICE ROW** (John Powell QC)

2 CROWN OFFICE ROW, SECOND FLOOR, TEMPLE, LONDON, EC4Y 7HJ
Tel: (0171) 797 8000 **Fax:** (0171) 797 8001 **DX:** 1041

MEMBERS:

John L. Powell QC (1974) (QC-1990)	Charles Douthwaite (1977)	Nicholas Brown (1989)
Rupert Jackson QC (1972) (QC-1987)	Glen Tyrell (1977)	Andrew Nicol (1991)
Bernard Livesey QC (1969) (QC-1990)	Gavin Hamilton (1979)	Ben Hubble (1992)
Justin Fenwick QC (1980) (QC-1993)	Andrew Stafford (1980)	Charles Phipps (1992)
Michael Brooke QC (1969) (QC-1994)	Barbara Kaplan (1980)	Paul Sutherland (1992)
Christopher Gibson QC (1976) (QC-1995)	Simon Monty (1982)	Graeme McPherson (1993)
Iain Hughes QC (1974) (QC-1996)	Martin Fodder (1983)	Aisha Bijlani (1993)
Christopher Critchlow (1972)	Mark Cannon (1985)	Nicola Shaldon (1994)
Prof. Eva Lomnicka (1974)	Ian Holtum (1985)	Charlotte Goldberg (1995)
Simon Russen (1976)	Paul Parker (1986)	Jamie Smith (1995)
	Roger Stewart (1986)	Alison Millar (1995)
	Sue Carr (1987)	Anneliese Day (1996)
	Hugh Evans (1987)	Ben Elkington (1996)
	Jalil Asif (1988)	Seánin Gilmore (1996)
	Fiona Sinclair (1989)	

Head of Chambers: John Powell QC
Senior Clerk: Annie Hopkins
Practice Manager: Lizzy Wiseman
Tenants: 39

General: A commercial and civil set with a particular reputation for claims involving professionals and other service providers. Members of chambers are editors of the leading text, *Jackson & Powell on Professional Negligence.*

The Set: The set has been established for over 50 years and has premises at both 2 Crown Office Row and at 1 Crane Court. Heads of chambers are elected for three year terms. Previous heads have been Roger Toulson Q.C. (now Toulson J.) and Rupert Jackson Q.C. who continues in practice. The chambers seeks to provide an efficient and friendly service at reasonable rates for commercial and other clients. The range of expertise within chambers is reflected in several leading publications (see below) and an annual programme of lectures by members of chambers, to which professional clients are invited.

Types of Work Undertaken: Advocacy, advice and drafting in the main fields of commercial and civil law for UK and overseas clients. Members of chambers regularly appear in all divisions of the High Court, the Court of Appeal, the House of Lords and the Privy Council as well as in arbitrations and various tribunals. Senior members appear in overseas jurisdictions.

Professional liability: The particular expertise in this field extends well beyond professional negligence. It includes claims based on fraud and breach of fiduciary duty, appearing on misconduct complaints before disciplinary tribunals and insurance and reinsurance disputes involving professionals. Main professions covered are accountants and auditors, architects and engineers, barristers and solicitors, bankers, financial advisers (including appointed representatives), insurance intermediaries, Lloyd's agents, medical practitioners, surveyors and valuers.

Other specialisations: Groups and individuals in chambers have particular expertise in the following areas of law: banking and consumer credit, confidentiality, construction and engineering, employment, insurance and reinsurance, financial services and securities regulation (U.K., E.C. and international), environment and planning, judicial review, land contamination, personal injury and privatisation disputes.

The chambers have considerable experience in multi-party litigation in fraud recovery, disaster, medical, pharmaceutical and product liability contexts.

Publications: *Jackson & Powell on Professional Negligence*, now in its 4th edition, is edited by Rupert Jackson Q.C., John Powell Q.C., Iain Hughes Q.C., Mark Cannon, Roger Stewart, Hugh Evans, Fiona Sinclair and Jalil Asif. Hugh Evans is author of *Lawyer's Liabilities*. Charles Phipps is co-author (with Toulson J.) of *Confidentiality*. Professor Eva Lomnicka is co-editor of *The Encyclopedia of Financial Services Law* along with John L. Powell Q.C and also co-edits *The Encyclopedia of Consumer Credit*. Members of chambers regularly contribute to professional journals and other publications as well as delivering papers at academic and other conferences.

Foreign connections: Michael Brooke Q.C. is a practising avocat at the Paris Bar. Barbara Kaplan is a member of the Hong Kong Bar and also practises from Des Voeux Chambers, Hong Kong.

Languages spoken: There are members of chambers fluent in the major European languages.

SET NUMBER
36
DEVEREUX CHAMBERS (Jeffrey Burke QC)

DEVEREUX CHAMBERS, DEVEREUX COURT, LONDON, WC2R 3JJ
Tel: (0171) 353 7534 **Fax:** (0171) 353 1724 **DX:** 349 (CH.LN.) **Email:** ELTON@DEVCHAMBERS.CO.UK
Internet: HTTP: //WWW.DEVCHAMBERS.CO.UK/

MEMBERS:

Jeffrey Burke QC (1964)
(QC-1984)

Peter Weitzman QC (1952)
(QC-1973)

Diana Cotton QC (1964)
(QC-1983)

Alan Pardoe QC (1971)
(QC-1988)

Colin Edelman QC (1977)
(QC-1995)

Robert Glancy QC (1972)
(QC-1997)

David Bean QC (1976)
(QC-1997)

Roy Lemon (1970)

Peter Wulwik (1972)
Professor Ian Smith (1972)
Gerald Rabie (1973)
Christopher Goddard (1973)
Ian Lee (1973)
Elizabeth Andrew (1974)
Richard Greening (1975)
David Griffith-Jones (1975)
Richard Clayton (1977)
Ruth Downing (1978)
Nicholas Bard (1979)
Timothy Brennan (1981)
Stephen Killalea (1981)
Graham Read (1981)

Colin Wynter (1984)
Bruce Carr (1986)
Ingrid Simler (1987)
Joanna Heal (1988)
Philip Thornton (1988)
James Tayler (1989)
Nicholas Randall (1990)
Keith Bryant (1991)
Richard Harrison (1991)
Natasha Joffe (1992)
Peter Edwards (1992)
Andrew Burns (1993)
Dijen Basu (1994)
Patricia Haitink (1995)

Head of Chambers:
Jeffrey Burke QC

Senior Clerk:
Elton Maryon

Practice Managers: Clifford
Holland, Nicholas Wise

Practice Development Manager:
Angela Griffiths

Tenants: 36

The Chambers: Devereux Chambers offers a comprehensive inter-disciplinary service to its clients. Areas of special expertise include administrative and local government law, commercial litigation, employment law, insurance and reinsurance, professional negligence, personal injury and medical negligence.

Chambers has a wide client base ranging from public companies, underwriters and brokers to local authorities, government departments, trades unions and individual litigants. All members of Chambers are advocates making regular appearances before Judges, Tribunals and Arbitrators.

Appointments: A number of senior members of Chambers serve as Deputy High Court Judges, Recorders and Assistant Recorders. Members of Chambers sit on the Criminal Injuries Compensation Board, Criminal Injuries Compensation Appeals Panel and Mental Health Independent Review Tribunal and also chair Tribunals and Inquiries.

The junior members of Chambers include the Junior Counsel to the Inland Revenue, Common Law and members of the Supplementary Panel of Treasury Counsel, Common Law. Members of Chambers play a prominent role in the Bar's professional bodies and associations and Chambers includes members of the Bar Council and its Professional Conduct Committee and other Bar Council committees.

Chambers also includes founders, committee members and members of COMBAR, the London Common Law and Commercial Bar Association, the Employment Law Bar Association, the Employment Lawyers Association, the Administrative Law Bar Association, the Personal Injuries Bar Association, the Association of Personal Injuries Lawyers, the Industrial Law Society, The British Association for Sport and Law, the Revenue Bar Association, London Maritime Association and CENTREBAR.

Members of Chambers regularly appear in leading cases and have written or co-written prominent text and practitioners' books in their specialist fields.

Publications: Three Members of Chambers, Professor Ian Smith, Christopher Goddard and Nicholas Randall, co-wrote *Health and Safety – the New Legal Framework* published by Butterworths. Ian Smith also co-wrote *Smith and Wood on Industrial Law* and is the author of the Employment Law and Social Security titles in Halsbury's Laws. He and Nicholas Randall are editors of *Harvey on Industrial Relations and Employment Law*. David Bean is the author of *Injunctions* (Longmans), co-author of *Injunctions and Undertakings* (Jordans) and editor of *Law Reform for All* (Blackstones). Richard Clayton is the author of *Practice and Procedure in Industrial Tribunals* (LAG, 1986) and the co-author of *Civil Actions against the Police* (Sweet and Maxwell, 2nd edition 1992), *Judicial Review Procedure* (Wiley, 2nd edition 1997) and, in preparation, co-author *The Bill of Rights in English Law* (Oxford University Press) *Judicial Review of Local Government Decisions* (Wiley) and *Commercial Judicial Review* (Wiley). David Griffith-Jones is the author of *Law and the Business of Sport* (Butterworths 1998). Bruce Carr is a contributing author to FT Law and Tax, *Litigation Practice* (Emergency Procedures). Ingrid Simler is a contributing author to Tolley's *Employment Law* (1994). James Tayler is a contributor to *Dix on Employment Law* (Butterworths) and Nicholas Randall is the author of the Pensions title in Halsbury's Laws.

Seminars: Members of Chambers are available to give lectures and seminars both externally and as part of Chambers own Law Society accredited seminar programme.

DEVEREUX
CHAMBERS

Pupillage: Great emphasis is placed on the calibre of pupils recruited to ensure that the high standards are maintained and generous pupillage awards are offered.

Types of work undertaken: The major areas of practice are *commercial and common law* especially: *administrative and local government; commercial; construction; consumer and business credit; discrimination; education; employment; environment; Europe; health and safety; mortgage and guarantee litigation; industrial injury and disease; insurance and reinsurance; judicial review; medical negligence; landlord and tenant; pensions; personal injury; police complaints, civil liberties and human rights; product liability; professional negligence; property; public interest immunity; revenue; telecomunications; tribunals and inquiries; VAT/customs and excise.*

In addition, individual members of Chambers offer expertise in the following areas of law: *community care; contempt; crime (including white collar crime); defamation; electoral & parliamentary; family; housing and sport.*

Other matters: Devereux Chambers aims to offer competitive rates which the Senior Clerk will be happy to discuss. Estimates of fees will be given on request.
• Instructions by Professional Direct Access are accepted by agreement.
• Chambers is fully computerised to ensure maximum efficiency and compatibility.
• Members of Chambers are available to give lectures and present seminars in their specialist fields.
• A programme of seminars accredited by the Law Society is planned for 1998/99.
• Conferences and consultations may be conducted outside Chambers (including out of London) upon request.
• A brochure is available on request and the Senior Clerk and Practice Managers will be happy to give more detailed information about members of Chambers and areas of expertise.

DEVEREUX CHAMBERS

SET NUMBER
37 DOUGHTY STREET CHAMBERS (Geoffrey Robertson QC)

DOUGHTY STREET CHAMBERS, 11 DOUGHTY STREET, LONDON, WC1N 2PG
Tel: (0171) 404 1313 **Fax:** (0171) 404 2283 **DX:** 223 (CH.LN.)

MEMBERS:

Geoffrey Robertson QC (1973) (QC-1988)
Louis Blom-Cooper QC (1952) (QC-1970)
Richard Maxwell QC (1968) (QC-1988)
Helena Kennedy QC (1972) (QC-1991)
Peter Thornton QC (1969) (QC-1992)
Christopher Sallon QC (1973) (QC-1994)
Andrew Nicol QC (1978) (QC-1995)
Edward Fitzgerald QC (1978) (QC-1995)
Stephen Irwin QC (1976) (QC-1997)
Edward Rees QC (1973) (QC-1998)
Michael Grieve QC (1975) (QC-1998)
Jonah Walker-Smith (1963)
Oliver Thorold (1971)
Frank Panford (1972)
Richard Allfrey (1974)
James Wood (1975)

Nicholas Paul (1980)
Gavin Millar (1981)
Kate Markus (1981)
Isabella Forshall (1982)
Paul Bogan (1983)
Tim Owen (1983)
David Bentley (1984)
Heather Williams (1985)
Martin Westgate (1985)
Ben Emmerson (1986)
Aswini Weereratne (1986)
Jill Evans (1986)
Anthony Metzer (1987)
Keir Starmer (1987)
Sally Hatfield (1989)
Robin Oppenheim (1988)
Michelle Strange (1989)
Kieran Maidment (1989)
Paul Taylor (1989)
Hugh Barton (1989)
Sadakat Kadri (1989)
Paul Brooks (1989)
Andrew Hall (1991)
Phillippa Kaufmann (1991)

Quincy Whitaker (1991)
Nadine Finch (1991)
Michael Ford (1992)
Ian Wise (1992)
Richard Hermer (1993)
Althea Brown (1995)
Jonathan Glasson (1996)
Anthony Hudson (1996)
Justice Ismail Mahommed (1984) (1956, South African Bar) SC (1974)*
Guy Ollivry QC (1957) (QC-1987) *
Fenton Ramsahoye (1953) SC (1971)*
Adrian Hardiman (1988) (1974 Ireland) SC (1989)*
Prof. Kevin Boyle (1992) (1971 N. Ireland)*
Christine Booker (1977) *
Julian Fulbrook (1977) *
Geraldine Van Bueren (1980) *
Dr Jill Peay (1991) *
Jonathan Cooper (1992) *

Head of Chambers:
Geoffrey Robertson QC
Practice Manager:
Christine Kings
Senior Clerk: Michelle Simpson
Tenants: 48

* Associate Tenants

The Chambers: Chambers offers a wide range of experience and specialisations, notably in the advocacy of civil liberties and human rights. Counsel are engaged in crown court trials of all kinds, judicial review proceedings, and actions in the High Court and the county courts. They appear regularly at inquests and a variety of tribunals. Many have taken leading cases to the European Commission and the European Court of Human Rights.

Continues overleaf

Individual practitioners specialise in criminal law, media law and defamation, public and administrative law, prisoners' rights and cases involving issues of mental health, discrimination, immigration, employment and housing, personal injury and medical negligence. Members of chambers have written or contributed to numerous books and publications in their specialist areas. The emphasis in chambers is on customer care and a friendly but professional service. Our offices have been recently expanded and refurbished providing dedicated reception and conference rooms with disability access and two fully equipped libraries. Doughty Street Chambers was awarded Barristers Chambers of the Year in 1995, 1996, and was runner-up in 1998, and was the Bronze winner of the Law Firm Management Award in 1997.

Details of specialist teams are available on request.

SET NUMBER
38 1 DR JOHNSON'S BUILDINGS (Martin Thomas QC)

1 DR JOHNSON'S BUILDINGS, TEMPLE, LONDON, EC4Y 7AX
Tel: (0171) 353 9328 **Fax:** (0171) 353 4410 **DX:** 297

MEMBERS:

Martin Thomas QC (1967) (QC-1979)	Jennifer Oldland (1978)	Pamilla Gill (1989)
Lord Hooson QC (1949) (QC-1960)	Alexander Granville (1978)	Graham Brodie (1989)
John Mortimer QC (1948) (QC-1966)	Nicholas Hamblin (1981)	Claire Hickman (1994)
	Dingle Clark (1981)	Hilary Pollock (1993)
Peter Digney (1968)	Stewart Wernham (1984)	Adam Kane (1993)
Robert Britton (1973)	Brendan Anderson (1985)	Justin Levinson (1994)
John Sabido (1976)	Sylvester McIlwain (1985)	Jeannie Mackie (1995)
James Dean (1977)	Gordon Wignall (1987)	Emma Nott (1995)
	Clifford Mailer (1987)	Elizabeth Jay (1996)
	Camille Habboo (1987)	

Head of Chambers:
Martin Thomas QC

Senior Clerk:
John Francis

Tenants: 26

The Chambers: 1 Dr Johnson's Buildings are a broadly-based common law set. In addition to their practices in this jurisdiction the senior silks have substantial experience in Hong Kong, Singapore and South Africa. Juniors have complementary practices. There are associated chambers in Chester (Sedan House) and Lewes (Westgate Chambers).

Work Undertaken: Administrative law, arbitration, substantial criminal cases (including serious fraud), courts martial, and police cases, extradition, foreign laws, immigration, judicial review, licensing, matrimonial, mental health, personal injury and professional negligence. Chambers accept direct access from the approved professions.

Foreign Connections and Languages Spoken: One member (Donald Von Landauer) practises solely in Paris and St. Helier, Channel Islands; door tenants have connections in Hong Kong, Ireland and Rome.

SET NUMBER
39
TWO DR JOHNSON'S BUILDINGS (David Batcup) Two Dr Johnson's Buildings, Temple, London, EC4Y 7AY **Tel:** (0171) 353 4716 **Fax:** (0171) 334 0242 **DX:** 429 Ch.Ln **Clerk:** Patrick Duane **Tenants:** 50 Mixed set with a varied common law practice covering criminal law (defence and prosecution), matrimonial, personal injury, and landlord and tenant cases.

SET NUMBER
40
3 DR JOHNSON'S BUILDINGS (J.A. Hodgson) 3 Dr Johnson's Buildings, Temple, London, EC4Y 7BA **Tel:** (0171) 353 4854 **Fax:** (0171) 583 8784 **DX:** LDE 1009 **Clerk:** John E. Hubbard **Tenants:** 24 Specialising in family law and general common law.

SET NUMBER
41
2 DYERS BUILDING (Nadine Radford QC) 2 Dyers Buildings, Holborn, London, EC1N 2JT **Tel:** 0171 404 1881 **Fax:** 0171 404 1991 **Clerk:** Graham Islin **Tenants:** 11 **DX:** 175 London Chancery Lane

---

ENTERPRISE CHAMBERS (Anthony Mann QC)

9 OLD SQUARE, LINCOLN'S INN, LONDON, WC2A 3SR
Tel: (0171) 405 9471 **Fax:** (0171) 242 1447 **DX:** LDE 301

MEMBERS:

Anthony Mann QC (1974) (QC-1992)	Ann McAllister (1982)	Laura Garcia-Miller (1989)
Benjamin Levy (1956)	Peter Arden (1983)	Zia Bhaloo (1990)
Timothy Jennings (1962)	Geoffrey Zelin (1984)	James Pickering (1991)
David Halpern (1978)	Jacqueline Baker (1985)	Soraya McKinnell (1991)
Charles Morgan (1978)	Adrian Jack (1986)	Hugh Jory (1992)
Caroline Hutton (1979)	Nigel Gerald (1985)	Bridget Williamson* (1993)
Michael James* (1976)	James Barker (1984)	Matthew Hardwick (1994)
Teresa Rosen Peacocke (1982)	Hugo Groves* (1980)	Sarah Richardson (1993)
Linden Ife (1982)	Ian Atherton (1988)	Edward Francis (1995)
	Alistair Henry* (1998)	Shanti Mauger (1996)

Head of Chambers:
Anthony Mann QC

Clerks:
Barry Clayton, Tony Armstrong

Tenants: 29

* practised as a solicitor before joining Chambers.

The Chambers: Enterprise Chambers is a forward thinking Commercial Chancery set, based in Lincoln's Inn with an established branch in Leeds and Newcastle. Members specialise in insolvency, company and commercial, property, landlord and tenant, professional negligence and general chancery work. Members act for a wide range of clients, from multinational public companies to private individuals.

Chambers approach: Our emphasis is on providing a commercial, practical and prompt service tailored to the requirements of each client. Members of chambers recognise the importance of working as a team and being approachable and accessible to solicitors and clients. Chambers was the first set to publish charge out rates for all members and we are happy to provide estimates of fees before any work is undertaken. We also have the unique advantage of Chambers facilities in London, Leeds, and Newcastle.

Members of chambers regularly speak at seminars and conferences and the chambers is authorised by The Law Society as a course provider. A list of workshop and seminar topics is available from Rozi Premji.

ERSKINE CHAMBERS (Richard Sykes QC)

ERSKINE CHAMBERS, 30 LINCOLN'S INN FIELDS, LONDON, WC2A 3PF
Tel: (0171) 242 5532 **Fax:** (0171) 831 0125 **DX:** 308 **Email:** CLERKS@ERSKINE-CHAMBERS.LAW.CO.UK

MEMBERS:

Richard Sykes QC (1958) (QC-1981) MA (Cantab)	Michael Todd QC (1977) (QC-1997) BA (Keele)	Mary Stokes (1989) MA (Oxon), LLM (Harvard)
R.A.K. Wright QC (1949) (QC-1973) MA (Oxon)	David Mabb (1979) MA (Cantab)	Andrew Thompson (1991) MA, LLM (Cantab)
W.F. Stubbs QC (1957) (QC-1978) MA, LLB (Cantab)	Martin Moore (1982) BA (Oxon)	Prof Dan Prentice (1982) LLB (Belfast) JD (Chicago), MA (Oxon)
Sir Thomas Stockdale Bt (1966) MA (Oxon)	David Chivers (1983) BA (Cantab)	Nigel Dougherty (1993) BA, LLM (Cantab)
Robin Potts QC (1968) (QC-1982) BA, BCL (Oxon)	Ceri Bryant (1984) MA, LLM (Cantab)	Leon Kuschke (1993) BCOM, LLB
David Richards QC (1974) (QC-1992) MA (Cantab)	Richard Snowden (1986) MA (Cantab), LLM (Harvard)	James Potts (1994) BA (Oxon)
John Cone (1975) LLB	Catherine Roberts (1986) MA, LLM (Cantab)	Andrew Thornton (1994) LLB (Hull)
Leslie Kosmin QC (1976) (QC-1994) MA, LLM (Cantab), LLM (Harvard)	Philip Gillyon (1988) BA (Cantab)	

Head of Chambers:
Richard Sykes QC

Senior Clerk: Mike Hannibal

Tenants: 23

The Chambers: Erskine chambers has a long established reputation as a company law set and provides specialists at all levels of experience in the fields of English and Commonwealth company law, corporate insolvency, financial services and related commercial and professional negligence matters. There are 23 members of Chambers including seven QC's. The practices of the majority of the individual members of Chambers are litigation based although we also continue to maintain our traditionl strength in technical, advisory and drafting matters. The clerks are always happy to discuss the practices of individual members of Chambers and to make appropriate recommendations. It is Chambers' aim to provide a professional and efficient service in a personal and approachable manner.

Continues overleaf

Work Undertaken: The work regularly undertaken in Chambers ranges from the largest and most complicated pieces of corporate litigation to the smallest advisory or drafting matter. The breadth of experience and expertise within Chambers allows a flexible response to meet the differing levels of complexity and urgency in both large and small matters. As specialists in company law, members of Chambers undertake work in all areas in which issues of company law arise, including in particular, directors' duties, shareholders' disputes, corporate insolvencies, takeovers, corporate reconstructions, loan capital and banking securities, financial services, accounting and auditing, professional negligence, corporate fraud, and other commercial matters. Members of Chambers regularly advise and appear as advocates and expert witnesses in a number of Commonwealth and other jurisdictions, including Hong Kong, Singapore, Malaysia, the Bahamas, Bermuda and the Cayman Islands.

Other Services Offered: Direct Professional Access is accepted from members of recognised professional institutions.

Recruitment & Training: Erskine Chambers is subscribing to the PACH scheme. All applications for pupillage in 1999/2000 should be made through the scheme.

SET NUMBER
44 **ESSEX COURT CHAMBERS** (Gordon Pollock QC)

24 LINCOLN'S INN FIELDS, LONDON, WC2A 3ED
Tel: (0171) 813 8000 **Fax:** (0171) 813 8080 **DX:** 320 **Email:** CLERKSROOM@ESSEXCOURT-CHAMBERS.CO.UK
Internet: HTTP: //WWW.ESSEXCOURT-CHAMBERS.CO.UK **Office hours:** 7.45 am – 7.00 pm

MEMBERS:

Gordon Pollock QC (1968) (QC-1979)	Jack Beatson QC (1973) (QC-1998)	Sara Cockerill (1990)
Michael Thomas QC (1955) (QC-1973)	Richard Jacobs QC (1979) (QC-1998)	John Snider (1982)
Ian Hunter QC (1967) (QC-1980)	Christopher Greenwood (1978)	Vernon Flynn (1991)
Stewart Boyd QC (1967) (QC-1981)	David Mildon (1980)	Brian Dye (1991)
V.V. Veeder QC (1971) (QC-1986)	Victor Lyon (1980)	Nigel Eaton (1991)
Michael Collins QC (1971) (QC-1988)	Mark Smith (1981)	Claire Blanchard (1992)
Richard Siberry QC (1974) (QC-1989)	Geraldine Andrews (1981)	Perdita Cargill-Thompson (1993)
Jonathan Gilman QC (1965) (QC-1990)	Graham Dunning (1982)	Vaughan Lowe (1993)
Bernard Eder QC (1975) (QC-1990)	Mark Templeman (1981)	Toby Landau (1993)
Roderick Cordara QC (1975) (QC-1994)	Susan Prevezer (1983)	Paul Stanley (1993)
Simon Crookenden QC (1975) (QC-1996)	Steven Berry (1984)	Martin Hunter (1994)
Andrew Hochhauser QC (1977) (QC-1997)	David Joseph (1984)	Philippa Hopkins (1994)
Peter Duffy QC (1978) (QC-1997)	Richard Millett (1985)	Paul McGrath (1994)
Anthony Dicks QC (Hong Kong) (1961) (QC-1994)	Huw Davies (1985)	James Collins (1995)
	Joe Smouha (1986)	Stephen Houseman (1995)
	Philippa Watson (1988)	Paul Key (1997)
	Hugh Mercer (1985)	David Scorey (1997)
	Martin Griffiths (1986)	Sam Wordsworth (1997)
	Karen Troy-Davies (1981)	Nathan Pillow (1997)
	John Lockey (1987)	James O'Reilly SC (1983)
	Simon Bryan (1988)	Martin Lau (1996)
	David Foxton (1989)	
	Malcolm Shaw (1988)	

Head of Chambers:
Gordon Pollock QC

Senior Clerk:
David Grief

Clerks: Joe Ferrigno and Nigel Jones

Office Manager: Jo Morris

Tenants: 58

A full-service commercial set, acting for clients ranging from major institutions and multi-national corporations to private companies and individuals. Members advise across the whole spectrum of international, commercial and European law, and act as advocates in litigation and commercial arbitration worldwide.

The Set: Essex Court Chambers, called Four Essex Court until its relocation to Lincoln's Inn Fields in 1994, was formed as a separate chambers in 1961, when the set at Three Essex Court split into two sets. The founding members of Four Essex Court were Michael Kerr (later Lord Justice Kerr), Robert MacCrindle, Michael Mustill (later Lord Mustill), Anthony Evans (later Lord Justice Evans), and Anthony Diamond (later Judge Diamond). Chambers grew rapidly in the late 1960s and 1970s, developing a reputation as one of the leading sets of commercial barristers in England, during which time Mark Saville (later Lord Saville), Johan Steyn (later Lord Steyn), Anthony Colman (later Mr Justice Colman) and John Thomas (later Mr Justice Thomas) joined.

Types of Work Undertaken: The work of chambers covers the entire range of international and commercial litigation and arbitration. The fields of work for which chambers are best known are: Administrative Law & Judicial Review, Agriculture & Farming, Arbitration,

Aviation, Banking, Chinese Law, Company Law and Insolvency, Conflict of Laws, Construction & Engineering, Commodity Transactions, Computer Law, Employment Law, Energy & Utilities Law, Entertainment & Sports Law, Environmental Law, European Law, Financial Services, Human Rights, Injunctions & Arrests, Insurance & Reinsurance, International Commercial Fraud, International Trade & Transport, Professional Negligence, Public International Law, Public Law, Sale of Goods & Product Liability, Shipping, South Asian Law, VAT & Excise.

Also, members act as arbitrators and mediators in domestic and international disputes when invited to do so by the parties concerned, or by the person or body named in the contract.

Publications: Several members have written or co-operated on legal works. These include: *Arnould on Marine Insurance* (co-editor: Jonathan Gilman QC); *Mustill & Boyd on Commercial Arbitration* (co-author: Stewart Boyd QC); *Scrutton on Charterparties* (co-editors: Stewart Boyd QC and David Foxton); *Chitty on Contracts* (co-editor: Jack Beatson); *International Law* (Professor Malcolm Shaw); *The Law of Guarantees* (Geraldine Andrews and Richard Millett) and *International Commercial Arbitration* (co-author: Martin Hunter); *The Law of the Sea* (co-author: Vaughan Lowe); *Commercial Debt in Europe: Recovery & Remedies* (Hugh Mercer); *Cross Border Litigation within ASEAN: The Prospects for Harmonization of Civil and Commercialisation Litigation*, by Kluwer Law Intl. (1997); Malek & Ong, *Various Legal complexities of syndicated loans.*

Foreign Connections: The international nature of chambers' practice is underlined by the fact that French, German, Italian, Spanish and Chinese are spoken within chambers. Members have appeared as advocates in the European Commission, European Court of Justice, and European Court of Human Rights; in the courts of jurisdictions including Hong Kong, Malaysia, Australia, Belfast, Dublin, Gibraltar, St Vincent, Brunei, Kenya and the Cayman Islands; and in arbitrations in places such as Paris, Geneva, Singapore, New Orleans and Beijing.

SET NUMBER
45 **ONE ESSEX COURT** (Anthony Grabiner QC)

ONE ESSEX COURT, TEMPLE, LONDON, EC4Y 9AR
Tel: (0171) 583 2000 **Fax:** (0171) 583 0118 **DX:** 430 (CH.LN.) **Email:** CLERKS@ONEESSEXCOURT.CO.UK
Internet: WWW.ONEESSEXCOURT.CO.UK

MEMBERS:

Anthony Grabiner QC (1968) (QC-1981)	Thomas Sharpe QC (1976) (QC-1994)	Kenneth MacLean (1985)
Gerald Butler QC (1955) (QC-1975)	Terence Mowschenson QC (1977) (QC-1995)	Charles Graham (1986)
Stanley Burnton QC (1965) (QC-1982)	Jeffrey Gruder QC (1977) (QC-1997)	Anthony de Garr Robinson (1987)
Graham Aaronson QC (1966) (QC-1982)	Thomas Ivory QC (1978) (QC-1998)	Laurence Rabinowitz (1987)
Christopher Carr QC (1968) (QC-1983)	Michael Bloch QC (1979) (QC-1998)	Neil Kitchener (1991)
Nicholas Strauss QC (1965) (QC-1984)	Jeffery Onions QC (1981) (QC-1998)	Joseph Hage (1991)
Roydon Thomas QC (1960) (QC-1985)	Susanna FitzGerald (1973)	Alain Choo Choy (1991)
Peter Leaver QC (1967) (QC-1987)	Alan Redfern (1995)	Michael Rollason (1992)
Ian Glick QC (1970) (QC-1987)	Richard Behar (1965)	David Cavender (1993)
Elizabeth Gloster QC (1971) (QC-1989)	Michael Conlon (1974)	Daniel Toledano (1993)
Geoffrey Hobbs QC (1977) (QC-1991)	Malcolm Gammie (1997)	Zoe O'Sullivan (1993)
Mark Barnes QC (1974) (QC-1992)	Michael Malone (1975)	Emma Himsworth (1993)
Steven Gee QC (1975) (QC-1993)	Ian Grainger (1978)	Jacob Grierson (1993)
Alastair R. MacGregor QC (1974) (QC-1994)	Rhodri Davies (1979)	Lisa Lake (1994)
	Stephen Auld (1979)	Edmund Nourse (1994)
	Alan Griffiths (1981)	Graeme Halkerston (1994)
	Clare Reffin (1981)	Sa'ad Hossain (1995)
	John McCaughran (1982)	Daniel Jowell (1995)
	Richard Gillis (1982)	Camilla Bingham (1996)
	Andrew Lenon (1982)	Philip Roberts (1996)
		Michael Fealy (1997)
		Anushka Rosen (1997)

Head of Chambers:
Anthony Grabiner QC

Clerks: Robert Ralphs
Paul Shrubsall

Tenants: 56

The Chambers: One Essex Court was founded in 1966, at that time there were 4 members. There are now 54 members of Chambers, of whom 20 are Queen's Counsel. The set occupies 1, 2, and 3 Essex Court, a site historically synonymous with commercial law.

Clerks: Robert Ralphs (Home (0181) 449 8472)
Paul Shrubsall (Home (01474) 872 590)

Continues overleaf

Work Undertaken: The range of work carried out embraces every aspect of domestic and international commerce and finance. The principal areas of practice are; arbitration, commercial law, company and insolvency, European Union law, intellectual property and revenue law.

Recruitment & Training: Chambers offer 4 x 12 month pupillages each year. Chambers operate an award scheme which offers to each pupil the sum of £27,500 in his or her year of pupillage. Part of the award may, at the discretion of chambers, be advanced during a prospective pupil's year of vocational training. Applicants for pupillage should (save in exceptional circumstances) have at least an upper second class degree. Chambers participates in the Pupillage Applications Clearing House (PACH), and all applications for pupillage should be made through PACH.

SET NUMBER
46 **ONE ESSEX COURT** (Sir Ivan Lawrence QC)

1 ESSEX COURT, TEMPLE, LONDON, EC4Y 9AR
Tel: (0171) 936 3030 **Fax:** (0171) 583 1606 **DX:** LDE 371 **Email:** ONE.ESSEX_COURT@VIRGIN.NET

MEMBERS:

Sir Ivan Lawrence QC (1962) (QC-1981)	Norman Joss (1982)	Jane Farquharson (1993)
Paul H. Norris (1963)	Grace Ong (1985)	Nicholas Grundy (1993)
Patrick Mullen (1967)	Barry Coulter (1985)	Sean Brannigan (1994)
Roger Bull (1974)	Peter John (1989)	Simon Mills (1994)
Mark Lyne (1981)	Julian Benson (1991)	Rachel Sleeman (1996)
	Rachel Lawrence (1992)	

Head of Chambers:
Sir Ivan Lawrence QC
Senior Clerk:
Chris Doe
Tenants: 16

Door Tenants: Graeme Mew (1982) (Attorney, Toronto, Canada)

The Chambers: A common law and commercial group offering advisory and advocacy skills from specialist barristers. We aim to provide an efficient, friendly and value-for-money service at all times, a commitment which is formalised in our Client Charter. We offer standard fees in many areas of work.

Work undertaken: Arbitration, agency and franchising, contractual disputes including sale of goods and services, company law, conflict of laws, construction, banking and consumer credit, crime, family, housing, immigration, insolvency, insurance, judicial review, landlord and tenant, partnership, personal injuries, professional negligence and property law.

Foreign Languages: French, Italian, Spanish, German and Cantonese.

SET NUMBER
47 **4 ESSEX COURT** (Nigel Teare QC)

4 ESSEX COURT, TEMPLE, LONDON, EC4Y 9AJ
Tel: (0171) 797 7970 **Fax:** (0171) 353 0998 **DX:** 292 LONDON (CHANCERY LANE) **Email:** CLERKS@4ESSEXCOURT.LAW.CO.UK

MEMBERS:

Nigel Teare QC (1974) (QC-1991)	John Ferry (1956)	Nigel Jacobs (1983)
M. N. Howard QC (1971) (QC-1986)	George Economou (1965)	Luke Parsons (1985)
Belinda Bucknall QC (1974) (QC-1988)	Simon Gault (1970)	Simon Croall (1986)
Charles Macdonald QC (1972) (QC-1992)	Geoffrey Kinley (1970)	Nigel Cooper (1987)
Jeremy Russell QC (1975) (QC-1994)	Giles Caldin (1974)	Poonam Melwani (1989)
Timothy Brenton QC (1981) (QC-1998)	Charles Sussex (1982)	James M. Turner (1990)
John de Cotta (1955)	Charles Haddon-Cave (1978)	Robert Thomas (1992)
	Paul Griffin (1979)	Nevil Phillips (1992)
	Michael Nolan (1981)	Thomas Macey-Dare (1994)
	Marion Smith (1981)	Jonathan Chambers (1996)
	Simon Rainey (1982)	Stewart Buckingham (1996)
	Simon Kverndal (1982)	

Head of Chambers:
Nigel Teare QC
Senior Clerk:
Gordon Armstrong
Tenants: 30

Door Tenants: Ronny Tong QC (1974)(QC-1990), Robert Ribeiro QC (1978)(QC-1990), Prof. Nicholas Gaskell (1976), Michel Koenig (1953), Prof. Francis D. Rose (1983).

The Chambers: Members of Chambers at 4 Essex Court (formerly situated at 2 Essex Court) are available to give specialist advice (including direct advice to foreign lawyers and members of certain other professional bodies) and to undertake advocacy work in their respective fields. They conduct all types of commercial litigation in London and abroad, together with arbitrations and marine, aviation and other inquiries.

Information on the specialist fields of practice of particular members can be obtained from chambers' staff.

Work Undertaken:

General Description: Members of Chambers specialise in a wide spectrum of commercial law, with a particular emphasis on maritime law, international trade, insurance.

Main Areas of Work: *Commercial Law, Shipping and International Trade:* including banking, carriage of goods by sea, land and air, marine and non-marine casualties, marine and general insurance and reinsurance, salvage, collision and oil-pollution, domestic and international sale of goods; ship and civil construction and financing.

Business Law and Financial Services: including insurance and reinsurance, banking, securities and commodities trading, company law and insolvency.

Disaster and Multi party litigation, Air Law.

EC Law: including competition law, intellectual property, public procurement, mergers and acquisitions and the business law aspects of 1992 and the Single European Market.

Entertainment and Media Law.

Employment Law.

Judicial Review: in related areas.

Foreign Connections: There are members of the French, Spanish, Greek, Cyprus, New South Wales, Hong Kong and New York Bars in chambers. There is a close association with Temple Chambers in Hong Kong.

SET NUMBER
48 **5 ESSEX COURT** (Jeremy Gompertz QC)

5 ESSEX COURT, TEMPLE, LONDON, EC4Y 9AH
Tel: (0171) 410 2000 **Fax:** (0171) 410 2010 **DX:** 1048

MEMBERS:

Jeremy Gompertz QC (1962) (QC-1988)	Charles Apthorp (1983)	Lyn Hayhow (1990)
Mervyn Roberts (1963)	John Butcher (1984)	Evelyn Pollock (1991)
Marie Catterson (1972)	Fiona Barton (1986)	Sarah Buckingham (1991)
Christopher Moss QC (1972) (QC-1994)	Simon Davenport (1987)	Jason Beer (1992)
Nicholas Ainley (1973)	Andrew Waters (1987)	Samantha Leek (1993)
John Bassett (1975)	Stephanie Farrimond (1987)	Jeremy Johnson (1994)
Simon Freeland (1978)	David Walbank (1987)	Prabjot Virdi (1995)
Peter Spink (1979)	Anne Studd (1988)	Stephen Rose (1995)
Nicholas Wilcox (1977)	Christopher Kerr (1988)	Nadeem Ahmed (1996)
Gerard Pounder (1980)	Georgina Kent (1989)	Mandy McClean (1996)
	Giles Powell (1990)	

Head of Chambers:
Jeremy Gompertz QC

Senior Clerk:
Michael Dean

Tenants: 31

The Chambers: General common law chambers which were established over 40 years ago. Several members of chambers are recorders and assistant recorders.

Work Undertaken: Chambers are an established common law set. The principal areas of practice are professional negligence, personal injuries (including group litigation), civil jury actions for false imprisonment and malicious prosecution (mainly for defendants), judicial review, general commercial common law (including sale of goods, restraint of trade, confidentiality, consumer credit and employment), family (especially matrimonial finance) and all aspects of criminal law (including serious fraud) both for prosecution and defence. Members of chambers also have expertise in probate, company and partnership, landlord and tenant, EC law, licensing, police law and public interest immunity in civil and criminal litigation.

Languages Spoken: French, German and Mandarin.

Recruitment & Training: Tenancy applications should be sent to Mervyn Roberts. All applications from established practitioners will be treated in confidence. Applications for pupillage should be made via the PACH scheme. Up to two pupillage awards are offered of £10,000 for 12 months commencing in October.

ESSEX
5
COURT

SET NUMBER
49 ESSEX HOUSE CHAMBERS (Yosefaly Serugo-Lugo) 1st Floor, 76 The Broadway, Stratford, London, E15 1NG **Tel:** (0181) 536 1077 **Fax:** (0181) 555 7135 **Clerk:** Judith Nankoude **Tenants:** 14 Chambers undertakes work on immigration, judicial review, civil, landlord and tenant, medical negligence, crime, international law, personal injury, child care/family, European law.

SET NUMBER
50

20 ESSEX STREET (David Johnson QC)

20 ESSEX STREET, LONDON, WC2R 3AL
Tel: (0171) 583 9294 **Fax:** (0171) 583 1341 **DX:** 0009 (CH.LN.) **Email:** CLERKS@20ESSEXST.COM **Internet:** WWW.20ESSEXST.COM

MEMBERS:

David Johnson QC (1967) (QC-1978)
Elihu Lauterpacht QC (1950) (QC-1970)
Murray Pickering QC (1963) (QC-1985)
Nicholas Legh-Jones QC (1968) (QC-1987)
Sir Arthur Watts QC (1957) (QC-1988)
Richard Plender QC (1972) (QC-1989)
Iain Milligan QC (1973) (QC-1991)
Angus Glennie QC (1974) (QC-1991)
Peter Gross QC (1977) (QC-1992)

Mark Havelock-Allan QC (1974) (QC-1993)
Timothy Young QC (1977) (QC-1996)
Nicholas Hamblen QC (1981) (QC-1997)
Stephen Males QC (1978) (QC-1998)
Julian Cooke (1965)
Richard Wood (1975)
Michael Tselentis SC (1995) (SC – South Africa – 1989)
Edmund Broadbent (1980)
Stephen Morris (1981)
David Owen (1983)
Christopher Hancock (1983)
Duncan Matthews (1986)

Geraldine Clark (1988)
Andrew Baker (1988)
Daniel Bethlehem (1988)
Michael Coburn (1990)
Lawrence Akka (1991)
Clare Ambrose (1992)
Karen Maxwell (1992)
Graham Charkham (1993)
Guy Morpuss (1991)
Sarah Masters (1993)
Philip Edey (1994)
Charles Kimmins (1994)
Michael Collett (1995)
Michael Ashcroft (1997)

Head of Chambers:
David Johnson QC
Senior Clerk:
Neil Palmer
Tenants: 35

Work Undertaken: Barristers at 20 Essex Street advise on a wide range of domestic and international commercial law and finance, and appear as counsel in litigation and commercial arbitration worldwide; work includes (but is not limited to):

Commercial: Admiralty, agency, arbitration, aviation, bailment, banking and financial services; carriage by land, sea and air, commodities and futures, company law and partnership, conflicts of laws, construction; disciplinary proceedings, entertainment law, insurance and reinsurance; international sales and commodity trading; oil and gas; professional negligence; sale of goods; shipping; all types of domestic and international commercial agreements.

European Community: Some members practise in both London and Brussels specialising in the substantive law of the European Community including harmonisation, competition law and trade regulations, free movement of goods, persons and services, agriculture, intellectual property and environmental law and policy. All members advise on such areas as the Brussels Convention and the Rome Convention.

International: Members of chambers engaged in this field appear before the International Court of Justice and other international tribunals.

Senior members, including Kenneth Rokison QC, Lord Donaldson, Sir Christopher Staughton, Lord Bridge, Lord Griffiths and Sir Brian Neill, act as arbitrators in both domestic and international arbitrations. Some members also act as mediators.

Languages Spoken: French, German, Italian and Spanish.

Subject to admission to local bars, instructions are accepted to appear in the courts of Hong Kong, Singapore, Malaysia, South Africa, Australia and other foreign jurisdictions.

Administration: *Office Hours:* 8.15 a.m. – 6.45 p.m. weekdays.
Out of Office Hours: Neil Palmer: (0181) 660 2633 Mobile 0831 505863
Brian Lee: (0181) 642 5865.

20 Essex Street

SET NUMBER
51
23 ESSEX STREET (Michael Lawson Q.C.)

23 ESSEX STREET, LONDON, WC2R 3AS
Tel: (0171) 413 0353 **Fax:** (0171) 413 0374 **DX:** 148 (LDE) **Email:** CLERKS@ESSEXSTREET23.DEMON.CO.UK

MEMBERS:

Michael Lawson QC (1969) (QC-1991) *
Michael Hill QC (1958) (QC-1979)
Nicholas Purnell QC (1968) (QC-1985) *
Heather Hallett QC (1972) (QC-1989) *
Michael Austin-Smith QC (1969) (QC-1990) *
Susan Edwards QC (1972) (QC-1993) *
Stuart Lawson Rogers QC (1969) (QC-1994) *
Charles Miskin QC (1975) (QC-1998) **
Charles Byers (1973) *
P. James Richardson (1975)
Michael Wood (1976) **
Brendan Finucane (1976)
Christopher Kinch (1976) **

Simon Davis (1978) **
Roderick James (1979)
John Causer (1979)
Daniel Janner (1980)
Simon Russell Flint (1980) **
John Price (1982)
Oscar Del Fabbro (1982)
Graham Cooke (1983)
Joanna Glynn (1983) **
Elroy Claxton (1983) **
Rupert Pardoe (1984)
Andrew Carnes (1984)
Alan Kent (1986)
Johannah Cutts (1986)
Wayne Cranston-Morris (1986)
Garrett Byrne (1986)
Paul Ozin (1987)
Heather Norton (1988)

Iain Morley (1988)
William Carter (1989)
Keith Hotten (1990)
Isobel Ascherson (1990)
Simon Medland (1991)
Ian Acheson (1992)
Mark Fenhalls (1992)
Andrew Hurst (1992)
Richard Milne (1992)
Fiona Horlick (1992)
Eloise Marshall (1994)
Hannah Swain (1994)
Rufus Stilgoe (1994)
Alexia Durran (1995)
Clare Strickland (1995)
Alan May (1995)

Head of Chambers:
Michael Lawson Q.C.

Chambers Manager:
David Burt

Practice Manager:
Nicholas Hopgood

Deputy Practice Manager:
Daren Milton

Tenants: 47

*Recorder
** Assistant Recorder

Door Tenants: Ian Goldsworthy QC, Alison Jones.

The Chambers:

Work Undertaken:

   Criminal: Mainstream crime, both defending and prosecuting. Silks and Juniors have established reputations in child abuse/sexual abuse cases. Chambers specialise, in commercial fraud/white collar crime on a national and international level. Expertise is avilable in third party disclosure, mutual assistance and ECHR implications. Teams available.

   Civil: Members are instructed in areas of common-law, particularly where they are crime related: civil fraud, actions against the police for malicious prosecution, false imprisonment etc.

Additional Areas of Work: Advice and representation available for DTI investigations, director's disqualification proceedings, regulatory hearings, disciplinary proceedings, (Lloyd's of London, police, medical) extradition hearings and inquests. Individuals also specialise in public and administrative, employment, personal injury, planning, matrimonial, defamation and environmental law.

Publications: James Richardson is editor of *Archbold* and *Criminal Law Week*. Joanna Glynn and William Carter are contributing editors to *Archbold*. Daniel Janner is one of the two editors to the *Criminal Appeal Reports*.

Recruitment:

   Tenancy Applications: To Michael Wood.

   Pupillage: Chambers offers two twelve month (funded) and three first six month (unfunded) pupillages. Travel allowances are available. Sponsored pupils are accepted additionally. Chambers is a member of PACH. Full details are published in the Bar Council's Chambers' Pupillages and Awards Handbook. Applications to John Price.

   Mini-pupillages: A limited number are available. Applications to John Price.

Training: Chambers has an internal continuing education programme for members and pupils. Members of Chambers devise and conduct external programmes.

Video Conferencing: Chambers has video conferencing equipment and arbitration rooms available for hire.

35 ESSEX STREET (Nigel Inglis-Jones QC)

35 ESSEX STREET, TEMPLE, LONDON, WC2R 3AR
Tel: (0171) 353 6381 **Fax:** (0171) 583 1786 **DX:** 351 LONDON

MEMBERS:

Nigel J. Inglis-Jones QC (1959) (QC-1982) BA (Oxon)

David C. Calcutt QC (1955) (QC-1972) MA, LLB, MuSB (Cantab)

Alan D. Rawley QC (1958) (QC-1977) MA (Oxon)

Dominik Lasok QC (1954) (QC-1982) LLM, PhD, Dr Juris, LLD

Christopher Wilson-Smith QC (1965) (QC-1986)

Philip C. Mott QC (1970) (QC-1991) MA (Oxon)

Linda E. Sullivan QC (1973) (QC-1994) BA (Hons)

Richard Lissack QC (1978) (QC-1994)

Richard E.R.S. Rains (1963) LLB *

Hywel I. Jenkins (1974) LLB (Hons)

John L. Stephens (1975) BA (Oxon)

Richard M. Mawhinney (1977) BA (Oxon)

William L. Coley (1980) MA (Cantab)

Robin S. Tolson (1980) BA (Cantab)

Stephen Climie (1982) BA (Lincoln)

David G. Westcott (1982) BA (Oxon), BCL

Christopher M. Kemp (1984) BA (Oxon), Dip Law

Harry Trusted (1985) MA (Cantab)

Andrew J.M. Spink (1985) BA (Cantab)

Alison McCormick (1988) BA (Oxon)

Susan C. Freeborn (1989) BA (Cantab)

Richard G. Hitchcock (1989) BA (Oxon)

Jonathan E.S. Hand (1990) BA(Oxon)

Thomas R.G. Leeper (1993) BA (Hons)

Nathan W. Tavares (1992) BSE (Hons)(Eng)

Grace Malden (1993) (Cantab)

Matthew J. Phillips (1993) (Oxon)

Nicholas Stallworthy (1993) (Oxon)

Rachel Willmot (1994) (Oxon)

Robert-Jan Temmink (1996) B.A (Hons) (Cantab)

Head of Chambers:
Nigel Inglis-Jones QC
Senior Clerk:
Derek Jenkins
Tenants: 30

* Door Tenant

The Chambers: Located within a short walk of the Royal Courts of Justice, our premises have been designed specifically to meet the needs of our clients. Priority has been given to the provision of dedicated and spacious conference and arbitration rooms. These are air-conditioned and fully wheelchair accessible. With advance notice, we are usually able to arrange parking facilities for severely disabled clients. Parking is also available in Essex Street.

Advocacy and Advice: The barristers of 35 Essex Street provide advocacy and advice covering a wide range of specialist areas of commercial and common law practice. In addition to appearing as advocates in the English Appellate Courts, the High Court, the County Court and a wide variety of tribunals, and undertaking arbitration work, we place particular emphasis on providing focused and practical advice both on paper and in conference on litigious and non-litigious matters. We also undertake work in foreign jurisdictions.

Responding to Change: The range of services both lay and professional clients expect from the Bar have changed dramatically in recent years. 35 Essex Street has developed and grown to meet these demands, whilst retaining and refining our skills as advocates in the broadest sense.

Our successful relocation to Essex Street in January 1995 from our former premises in Lamb Building has provided us with the opportunity both to expand our numbers to meet the increasing level of demand for our services and to improve the facilities we are able to make available to our clients.

Expertise, Flexibility and Accessibility: Our underlying approach is to provide genuine expertise at each level of call, both individually and in teams, with fee structures and response times which can be adapted to match our clients' needs. At the same time, we seek to make ourselves as accessible as possible, whilst actively seeking to establish constructive and open working relationships with our clients.We believe that the quality of service offered by our barristers is enhanced by the flexibility of our clerking and administrative team and our willingness to implement and exploit developments in information technology.

Clerks, Working Practices and Information Technology: Our highly capable clerking and administrative staff, led by Derek Jenkins, benefit from ten years' experience of working for us as a team. They are always happy to discuss clients' particular requirements and to identify the member or members of chambers with the specialist skills needed to meet those requirements and, where necessary, to provide suitable cover. Work in progress is actively monitored, using the latest computer technology to ensure the setting and meeting of realistic deadlines and the efficient organisation of trial and conference commitments. Advance fee quotations will gladly be provided upon request, as will information about the terms upon which members of chambers are willing to undertake work on a conditional fee basis.

Our computer systems enable us to send and receive documents by most forms of electronic mail or to provide copies on computer disk of any work produced. We can be contacted by e-mail via Link or over the Internet.

Contact Details: The clerks can be contacted between 9am and 6pm Monday to Friday by telephone on (0171) 353 6381 or (0171) 583 2997, by fax on (0171) 583 1786 and by e mail on Link. After hours, a Duty Clerk can be reached on 07771 714295.

Categories of Work
Commercial Fraud
Contract
Child Care
Intellectual Property
Local Government Law
Medical Negligence
Occupational Pension Schemes & Trusts
Personal Injury
Property Law
Professional Negligence

Foreign Connections: Dominick Lasok QC can advise on Polish law and chambers have an Italian affiliate practising in Milan, Avv. Mauto Rubino-Sammartano

Languages Spoken: French, German, Italian, and Polish

SET NUMBER
53 39 ESSEX STREET (Edwin Glasgow QC)

39 ESSEX STREET, LONDON, WC2R 3AT
Tel: (0171) 832 1111 **Fax:** (0171) 353 3978 **DX:** 298 **Email:** 39ESSEXSTREET@MSN.COM / 106433.752@COMPUSERVE.COM

MEMBERS:

Edwin Glasgow QC (1969) (QC-1987)
Colin Mackay QC (1967) (QC-1989)
Simon Goldblatt QC (1953) (QC-1972)
Daniel Brennan QC (1967) (QC-1985)
Nigel Pleming QC (1971) (QC-1992)
Richard Gray QC (1970) (QC-1993)
Richard Gordon QC (1972) (QC-1994)
Richard Davies QC (1973) (QC-1994)
Richard Wilmot-Smith QC (1978) (QC-1994)

Michael Tillett QC QC (1965) (QC-1996)
Robert Jay QC (1981) (QC-1998)
Alan Cooper (1969)
David Melville (1975)
Charles Brown (1976)
Roderick Noble (1977)
Colin McCaul (1978)
Neil Block (1980)
Geoffrey B. Brown (1981)
Christian Du Cann (1982)
Charles Cory-Wright (1984)
Alison Foster (1984)
Jonathan Bellamy (1986)
Stuart Catchpole (1987)

David Bradly (1987)
Charles Manzoni (1988)
Steven Kovats (1989)
Eleanor Grey (1990)
Bernard Doherty (1990)
Vincent Nelson (1980)
Jennifer Richards (1991)
Sean Wilken (1991)
Bruce Brodie (1993)
Alan Maclean (1993)
Matthew Seligman (1994)
Tim Ward (1994)
Adam Robb (1995)
Sam Grodzinski (1996)
Parishil Patel (1996)
Kristina Stern (1996)

Head of Chambers:
Edwin Glasgow QC

Senior Clerk:
Nigel Connor

Tenants: 39

Members of Chambers have wide experience of all courts and tribunals from the House of Lords, Privy Council, Court of Appeal and International and Domestic Arbitrations, through to Public Enquiries, Industrial and VAT tribunals. They have also participated in significant investigations before Parliamentary Select Committees. Several Members of Chambers are on the Main and Supplementary Treasury Panels of Counsel instructed on behalf of the Crown. Members also undertake pro bono work for public interest organisations.

The Chambers: 39 Essex Street is a long established set whose barristers have widespread expertise and experience in almost every aspect of commercial, public and common law. The chambers is fully computerised to ensure an efficient and effective service. The size of Chambers ensures that there is a critical mass of expertise in each specialist area, and co-operation and collaboration among members of different practice areas is common place and actively encouraged. The barristers at 39 Essex Street see themselves as part of a legal team, working closely with the professional and lay client in a complementary and strategic way.

Work Undertaken: Chambers' particular expertise is in the fields of insurance law, personal injury, construction, public law and judicial review, commercial law, and professional negligence. Within this broad range members of chambers have developed specialisms in the following areas:

Commercial: Insurance and reinsurance, commodities and derivatives (in particular oil and gas law), media and entertainment, sports law, banking, sale and carriage of goods, insolvency and company law and international commercial arbitration.

Public: All aspects of judicial review for both applicants and respondents. Areas of expertise include local authorities (especially their powers and financing) and other public bodies; environmental law; health trusts; education; commercial, civil liberties and human rights; community care; mental health; housing and housing associations and immigration. With

Continues overleaf

expertise in both public and commercial law, members of chambers are uniquely placed to advise and represent clients in cases dealing with the powers and duties of regulatory bodies.

Professional Indemnity: Act for both plaintiffs and defendants in matters involving solicitors and barristers, doctors and other medical practitioners, surveyors, architects, engineers, accountants, insurers and insurance brokers and other professionals.

Personal Injury: Multi-Plaintiff group actions, disaster litigation and injuries of maximum severity.

Additional Areas: VAT, Customs & Excise, European Law.

Publications: *Judicial Review: Law and Procedure* (Gordon); *Local Authority Powers* (Gordon); *Waiver, Variation and Estoppel* (Wilken).

Languages Spoken: French, Italian, Spanish, German

Recruitment and Training: Chambers are a member of PACH. We offer up to four pupillages each year with scholarship awards of £18,500. The decision as to offers of pupillage depends in particular upon: academic record (a first or upper second class degree is usually required), performance at interview, performance in any mini-pupillages and references.

SET NUMBER 54 — 46 ESSEX STREET (Geoffrey Hawker)

46 ESSEX STREET, LONDON, WC2R 3GH
Tel: (0171) 583 8899 **Fax:** (0171) 583 8800 **DX:** 1014 LONDON/CHANCERY LANE

MEMBERS:

Geoffrey Hawker BSc(Eng), Ceng FICE FIStructE, MsoclS (France), MconsE, FCIArb
Jonathan Sofer
John Nicholas William Bridges-Adams MA (Oxon), DipED FCIArb
Philip Storr
Ivan Clarke
Allan Goh
Marion Lonsdale BSc, LLB, A.T.I.I
Alan Turner MSc, LLB, FICE

David Ryan
Michael Milne BA, FRICS, FCIArb
Deborah Toussaint
Georgia Mitropoulos
Albert Cheah
Peter Aeberli BA (Oxon), M.A.Edin
Robert Sliwinski BSc LLB
James Candlin BSc
Richard Keogh
Peter Chapman BSc, LLB, FICE, FCIArb

Medina Marks
Andrew Copeland
Annie Walshe
Mathew Bagnall
Michael Peglow DPhil (Oxon), DR.IUR, MSc.Econ
Karl Volz
Mary Hughes BA, MPhil, PhD
Daniel Tobin
Sally Cowen
Richard Bentwood

Head of Chambers: Geoffrey Hawker
Senior Clerk: Stephen English (0171) 583 8899 mobile (0850) 828177
Junior Clerk: Gawin Cole
Fees Clerk: Elizabeth Wolfe
Tenants: 28

Specialisations: Arbitration; Building & Civil Engineering; Commercial law; Common Law; Contruction; Education; European Law; Family; German Law; Landlord & Tenant; Personal Injury; Planning; Professional Negligence; VAT, Tax & Chancery.

Direct Professional Access , Conditional Fee arrangements accepted.

Languages: French; German; Chinese; Greek; Malay.

SET NUMBER 55 — FALCON CHAMBERS (Jonathan Gaunt QC & Kim Lewison QC)

FALCON COURT, LONDON, EC4Y 1AA
Tel: (0171) 353 2484 **Fax:** (0171) 353 1261 **DX:** 408

MEMBERS:

Derek Wood QC CBE (1964) (QC-1978) MA, BCL
Jonathan Gaunt QC (1972) (QC-1991) BA
Kim Lewison QC (1975) (QC-1991) MA
Paul Morgan QC (1975) (QC-1992) MA
Kirk Reynolds QC (1974) (QC-1993) MA
Jonathan Brock QC (1977) (QC-1997) MA
Nicholas Dowding QC (1979) (QC-1997) MA

Edwin Prince (1955) BA
Paul de la Piquerie (1966) LLB
Joanne R. Moss (1976) MA LLM (EC Law)
Edward Cole (1980) MA
Wayne Clark (1982) LLB, BCL
Guy Fetherstonhaugh (1983) BSc
Martin Rodger (1986) BA
Timothy Fancourt (1987) MA
Barry Denyer-Green (1972) LLM, PhD

Stephen Jourdan (1989) MA
Gary Cowen (1990) LLB
Jonathan Small (1990) BA
Janet Bignell (1992) MA, BCL
Martin Dray (1992) LLB
Caroline Shea (1994) MA
Anthony Tanney (1994) BA M.Jur
Catherine Taskis (1995) BA BCL
Emily Windsor (1995) BA DSU (E.C. Law)

Head of Chambers: Jonathan Gaunt QC & Kim Lewison QC
Senior Clerk: Mark Clewley
Tenants: 25

The Chambers: Falcon Chambers is a set of 25 barristers, 7 QCs and 18 juniors, all of whom specialise in litigation and property law. Work is principally undertaken in the litigation of all aspects of real property and property-related law, and also in advisory and drafting work in the same fields.

Work Undertaken: Chambers is best known for its expertise in landlord and tenant, including commercial property, rent review, residential landlord and tenant, and agricultural holdings, tenancies and production controls. Members are also specialists in the more general areas of property law including easements, restrictive covenants, mortgages, conveyancing, co-ownership and trusts of land, and options and rights of pre-emption. The economic recession of the 1990s has resulted in Chambers being frequently involved in cases where property rights and principles of insolvency law meet, and where claims against solicitors and surveyors for negligence arise.

Even in the specialist fields, a good deal of work is concerned with contract law and statutory interpretation.

Work in the commercial property field means that chambers have considerable experience in arbitration law and practice, and with any work involving valuers and the principles of valuation.

Some members are specialists in the fields of town and country planning, compulsory purchase, EU competition law and building and engineering disputes.

Litigation is the core of chambers work, but chambers has always had a substantial volume of advisory work. Many members have developed particular skills in drafting, especially leases and other conveyancing documents.

Direct Professional Access work is accepted in appropriate cases, and members are frequently engaged in advising arbitrators or experts, or sitting as legal assessors.

Publications: Many members are the authors or editors of the leading textbooks and other publications in our specialist fields, for example *Woodfall on Landlord and Tenant*; *Megarry on the Rent Acts*; *Muir Watt on Agricultural Holdings*; and *Gale on Easements*.

Other: Chambers enjoys strong links with the Royal Institution of Chartered Surveyors and with the Chartered Insitute of Arbitrators. Senior Members of Chambers organise the Blundell Memorial Lectures every year, which are given in association with the R.I.C.S., the Bar Council and the Law Society. They are founder members of COMBAR, and are all members of the Chancery Bar Association and the London Common Law and Commercial Bar Association. Joanne Moss is Chairman of the Agricultural Law Association, and Kim Lewison Q.C. is a Governor of the Anglo-American Real Property Association.

SET NUMBER
56 FARRAR'S BUILDING (Gerard Elias QC)

FARRAR'S BUILDING, TEMPLE, LONDON, EC4Y 7BD
Tel: (0171) 583 9241 **Fax:** (0171) 583 0090 **DX:** 406

MEMBERS:

Gerard Elias QC (1968) (QC-1984) *

Michael Lewer QC (1958) (QC-1983) *

John Leighton Williams QC (1964) (QC-1986) *

Christopher Pitchford QC (1969) (QC-1987) *

Douglas Day QC (1967) (QC-1989) *

Peter Birts QC (1968) (QC-1990) *

Geoffrey Nice QC (1971) (QC-1990) *

Patrick Harrington QC (1973) (QC-1993) *

Leighton Davies QC (1975) (QC-1994) *

Alan Jeffreys QC (1970) (QC-1996) *

William Norris QC (1974) (QC-1997)

Tim Dutton QC (1979) (QC-1998)

Edward Southwell (1970) *

Anthony Webb (1970) *

Richard Nussey (1971)

Anthony Seys Llewellyn (1972) *

Stephen Rubin (1977)

Gregory Treverton-Jones (1977)

Stephen Jones (1978)

Tom McDermott (1980)

Simon Browne (1982)

Tracy Ayling (1983)

Daniel Matovu (1985)

Nigel Spencer Ley (1985)

Jonathan Watt-Pringle (1987)

Andrew Peebles (1987)

David Wicks (1989)

James Todd (1990)

Helen Hobhouse (1990)

Lucy Moorman (1992)

Joanne Cash (1994)

Melissa Pack (1995)

Darryl Allen (1995)

Lee Evans (1996)

Head of Chambers:
Gerard Elias QC

Senior Clerk/Practice Manager:
Alan Kilbey

Chambers Manager:
Janet Eades

Tenants: 34

* Recorder

The Chambers: A long-established common law set undertaking a wide range of London civil work as well as retaining strong links with the South Eastern and Wales and Chester Circuits. Specialist expertise in particular areas (such as general commercial, personal injury, professional negligence, medical negligence, landlord and tenant, building work, employment, sports and competition, solicitors costs and taxation, and crime) exists at all levels of seniority, thus ensuring excellent back-up facilities. Chambers' administration is fully computerised. Three silks are members of the Criminal Injuries Compensation Board, and the Head of Chambers is Chairman of the ECB Disciplinary Committee and former leader of the Wales and Chester Circuit. Other members serve on the Bar Council and specialist Bar Association committees.

Continues overleaf

Work Undertaken:

Main Areas: Professional negligence, medical negligence, personal injury, employment and industrial relations, commercial, landlord and tenant and property law, insurance, building, defamation, betting and licensing.

Additional Areas: Administrative and Judicial review, civil rights of prisoners, trespass, rights of way and countryside law, planning and agricultural work (including milk quotas), taxation & costs.

Criminal Law: Heavy crime, especially fraud. Prosecution and defence work of all kinds and on all circuits.

Foreign Connections: Thomas McDermott is a member of the Bar of Ireland.

SET NUMBER

57 FIELD COURT CHAMBERS (Melanie Spencer) Field Court Chambers, Grays Inn, London, WC1R 5EP **Tel:** (0171) 404 7474 **Fax:** (0171) 404 7475 **DX:** 136 (Ch.Ln.) **Email:** clerks@fieldcourt-chambers.law.co.uk **Clerk:** Paul Mellor **Tenants:** 9 A civil set emphasising company and commercial although individuals' specialisations include professional negligence, family and personal injury.

SET NUMBER

58 2 FIELD COURT (Norman Palmer) 2 Field Court, Gray's Inn, London, WC1 **Tel:** (0171) 405 6114 **Fax:** (0171) 831 6112 **DX:** 457 **Clerk:** Michael Clark **Tenants:** 27 Main areas of work general common law, land law, administrative and local government, family law, insolvency, company, employment and licensing.

SET NUMBER
59

4 FIELD COURT (Geoffrey Brice QC)

GRAY'S INN, LONDON, WC1R 5EA
Tel: (0171) 440 6900 **Fax:** (0171) 242 0197 **DX:** 483 LONDON/CHANCERY LANE **Email:** CHAMBERS@4FIELDCOURT.CO.UK

MEMBERS:

Geoffrey Brice QC (1960) (QC-1979)	Sarah Miller (1971)	David Goldstone (1986)
Andrew Rankin QC (1950) (QC-1968)	Lloyd Lloyd (1973)	Colin Wright (1987)
Richard Stone QC (1952) (QC-1968)	Alison Green (1974)	Nicholas Saunders (1989)
	James Thom (1974)	Christopher Smith (1989)
John Reeder QC (1971) (QC-1989)	William Whitehouse-Vaux (1977)	Stephen Wilson (1990)
R Jervis Kay QC (1972) (QC-1996)	Robert Bourne (1978)	Michael Davey (1990)
	Daphne Romney (1979)	Timothy Hill (1990)
Lionel Persey QC (1981) (QC-1997)	Nigel Meeson (1982)	Arshad Ghaffar (1991)
	Mark Sutton (1982)	Nicholas Dugdale (1992)
Elizabeth Blackburn QC (1978) (QC-1998)	Yvonne Green (1982)	Julian Taylor (1994)
	Jonathan D C Turner (1982)	Charles Davis (1995)
Allan Myers (1988) (QC Aus.)	Vasanti Selvaratnam (1983)	Madeleine Heal (1996)
	Miranda Whiteley (1985)	Eoin O'Shea (1996)

Head of Chambers:
Geoffrey Brice QC

Senior Clerk:
Christopher James

Clerks: Paul Coveney, Venetia Jeffcock, Jean-Pierre Schulz

Tenants: 34

The Chambers: Established in the 1920s, 4 Field Court is a commercial set. Barristers at 4 Field Court offer advocacy and advisory expertise and experience in many aspects of commercial, chancery/commercial and civil law.

Members appear before all courts and tribunals in England and Wales, as well as in the European court and range of overseas courts and tribunals. Members of Chambers also act as arbitrators, as mediators in Alternative Dispute Resolution and as expert witnesses.

Work Undertaken: The breadth of expertise and experience within Chambers is such that Members are able to deal with a very wide range of civil litigation and other matters. Principle areas of practice include: Shipping and Maritime law; Commercial Contracts; Insurance and Reinsurance; Banking and Financial Services; Road, Rail and Air Law; Professional Negligence; Employment Law; Property Law; Intellectual Property; EC, Free Trade and Competition; Public, Administrative and Local Government; Licensing.

Foreign Connections: Barristers at 4 Field Court are members of the Bars of Antigua and Barbuda, California, Gibraltar, New South Wales, New Zealand, Papua New Guinea, St. Vincent and The Grenadines and Victoria. Languages spoken include French, German, Italian and Urdu.

SET NUMBER
60
FOREST HOUSE CHAMBERS (David Singer) Forest House, 15 Granville Road, Walthamstow, London, E17 9BS **Tel:** (0181) 925 2240 **Fax:** (0181) 556 6125 **Clerk:** David Singer **Tenants:** 4 General common law set handling criminal, immigration and family law matters.

SET NUMBER
61

FOUNTAIN COURT (Peter Scott QC)

FOUNTAIN COURT, TEMPLE, LONDON, EC4Y 9DH
Tel: (0171) 583 3335 **Fax:** (0171) 353 0329 **DX:** LDE 5

MEMBERS:

Peter Scott QC (1960) (QC-1978)	Nicholas Underhill QC (1976) (QC-1992)	Timothy Howe (1987)
Conrad Dehn QC (1952) (QC-1968)	Nicholas Stadlen QC (1976) (QC-1991)	Michael A. Green (1987)
Christopher Bathurst QC (1959) (QC-1978)	Timothy Wormington (1977)	Bankim Thanki (1988)
Anthony Boswood QC (1970) (QC-1986)	David Railton QC (1979) (QC-1996)	Patricia Robertson (1988)
Peter Goldsmith QC (1972) (QC-1987)	Simon Browne-Wilkinson QC (1981) (QC-1998)	Jeffrey Chapman (1989)
Trevor Philipson QC (1972) (QC-1989)	Brian Doctor (1991)	Brian Napier (1990)
Michael Lerego QC (1972) (QC-1995)	Gillian Keene (1980)	Derrick Dale (1990)
Andrew Smith QC (1974) (QC-1990)	Michael McLaren (1981)	Akhil Shah (1990)
Lord Falconer of Thoroton QC (1974) (QC-1991)	Philip Brook Smith (1982)	Marcus Smith (1991)
Michael Brindle QC (1975) (QC-1992)	Raymond Cox (1982)	Paul Gott (1991)
Michael Crane QC (1975) (QC-1994)	David Waksman (1982)	Veronique Buehrlen (1991)
	Anthony Martino (1982)	Andrew Mitchell (1992)
	Thomas Keith (1984)	Richard Handyside (1993)
	Murray Shanks (1984)	John Taylor (1993)
	Guy Philipps (1986)	Richard Coleman (1994)
	Stephen Moriarty (1986)	James Butters (1994)
	Craig Orr (1986)	Adam Tolley (1994)
		Louise Merrett (1995)
		Philippa Hamilton (1996)

Head of Chambers:
Peter Scott QC

Chambers Director:
Ric Martin

Head of Clerking: Mark Watson

Chambers Administrator:
Prue Woodbridge

Tenants: 47

Hours: 8.00am to 9.00pm Monday to Friday and from 9.00am to 1.00pm on Saturdays. After hours 0831 465305.

Associated tenants: Peter Carter QC (1947, QC-1990) (Emeritus Fellow and Tutor in Law, Wadham College, Oxford), Richard Hooley (1984) (Fellow and Tutor in Law, Fitzwilliam College, Cambridge), Andrew Burrows (1985) (Professor of English Law, University College, London, Law Commissioner for England and Wales), Gladys Li (1971), Izzet Sinan (1981) (Brussels).

The Chambers: Fountain Court is a substantial and long established commercial and civil set of chambers in London, with a modern, client-focused approach.

The core work of most members of Chambers is commercial, with particular specialities in aviation; banking and financial services; chancery; entertainment; mergers and acquisitions; insurance and reinsurance; City regulatory work; financial services; oil and gas law; intellectual property; employment law; administrative law; professional negligence; insolvency and shipping.

Fountain Court also retains a strong "generalist" tradition and is notable for the wide range of other civil work undertaken including administrative law and judicial review; engineering and building disputes; restrictive trade practices; computers and information law; Parliamentary; European law (including competition law) and tax. Civil work of almost any character is likely to be within the experience of one or more members of Chambers.

The size of Chambers and the range of experience of its members enable it, at short notice if necessary, to provide services right across the spectrum, from fielding teams of Counsel at all levels for large scale litigation to providing junior Counsel for small scale civil litigation, such as Industrial Tribunal work and County Court trials. Several members have experience in sitting as arbitrators internationally and domestically. Members of chambers regularly work abroad, not only in international arbitrations but also as advocates in overseas jurisdictions, including Hong Kong, Singapore, Gibraltar, Bahamas and in the European Court of Justice.

Languages spoken: French, German, Italian, Greek, Russian and Afrikaans.

Publications: *The Law of Bank Payments* (editors Michael Brindle Q.C. and Raymond Cox, with contributions from members of Chambers); *Chitty on Contracts* (Co-editor Stephen Moriarty); *Laundering and Tracing* (contributor Stephen Moriarty); *Confidentiality and the Law* (Contributor Jeffrey Chapman); *Harvey on Industrial Relations and Employment Law* (co-editor Brian Napier); *Butterworths Employment Law* (contributor Brian Napier).

FOUNTAIN

COURT

CHAMBERS

SET NUMBER

62 FRANCIS TAYLOR BUILDING (D.A. Pears) Francis Taylor Building (2nd Floor), Temple, London, EC4Y 7BY **Tel:** (0171) 353 9942 **Fax:** (0171) 353 9924 **DX:** LDE 211 London/Chancery Lane **Tenants:** 32 Members of Chambers practice within a number of specialist teams, covering: crime; family; landlord & tenant/real property; personal injury/medical negligence; professional negligence; mercantile and consumer credit; employment and insolvency.

SET NUMBER

63 FRANCIS TAYLOR BUILDING (Andrew Thompson & David Guy) Francis Taylor Building (3rd Floor), Temple, London, EC4Y 7BY **Tel:** (0171) 797 7250 **Fax:** (0171) 797 7299 **DX:** 46 London Chancery Lane **Tenants:** 26 A civil set, practising across the field of common law litigation. Individual members' specialities also include employment law, and commercial and EC work.

SET NUMBER

64 FRANCIS TAYLOR BUILDING (N.P. Valios QC) Francis Taylor Building, Temple, London, EC4Y 7BY **Tel:** (0171) 353 7768 **Fax:** (0171) 353 0659 **DX:** 441 London/Chancery Lane **Clerk:** Janet Clark, David Green **Tenants:** 36 A general common law set of chambers.

SET NUMBER

65 FURNIVAL CHAMBERS (Andrew Mitchell) 32 Furnival Street, London, EC4A 1JQ **Tel:** (0171) 405 3232 **Fax:** (0171) 405 3322 **DX:** 72 **Clerk:** John Gutteridge **Tenants:** 41 A set of specialist criminal practitioners with additional expertise in confiscation, commercial fraud, and all other aspects of criminal law.

SET NUMBER

66 # ONE GARDEN COURT FAMILY LAW CHAMBERS (Miss Eleanor F. Platt QC & Miss Alison Ball QC)

ONE GARDEN COURT, TEMPLE, LONDON, EC4Y 9BJ
Tel: (0171) 797 7900 **Fax:** (0171) 797 7929 **DX:** 1034 (CH.LN.)

MEMBERS:

Eleanor F. Platt QC (1960) (QC-1982)
Alison Ball QC (1972) (QC-1995)
Ian Peddie QC (1971) (QC-1992)
Jane Crowley QC (1976) (QC-1998) *
Ellen B. Solomons (1964)
Caroline Willbourne (1970)
John Mitchell (1972)
Bruce Coleman (1972)
Peter Nathan (1973)
Jennifer Beckhough (1973)
Suzanne H. Shenton (1973)
Elizabeth Szwed (1974)

Peter Horrocks (1977)
Sheron Bedell-Pearce (1978)
Martin O'Dwyer (1978)
Ann Marie Wicherek (1978)
Richard Scarratt (1979)
Judith Rowe (1979)
Kay Halkyard (1980)
Veronica Lachkovic (1982)
Susannah Walker (1985)
Paul Rippon (1985)
Caroline Hely Hutchinson (1983)
Stephen Cobb (1985)
John Stocker (1985)
Gary Crawley (1988)
Gillian Cleave (1988)

Alan Inglis (1989)
Andrew Bagchi (1989)
Michael Liebrecht (1989)
Catherine Jenkins (1990)
Ariff Rozhan (1990)
Ian Robbins (1991)
Nora O'Flaherty (1991)
Joanna Geddes (1992)
Andrew Norton (1992)
Emma Hudson (1995)
Susan Budaly (1994)
Alexander Chandler (1995)
Nicola Fox (1996)
Sassa Ann Amaouche (1996)

Head of Chambers:
Miss Eleanor F. Platt QC & Miss Alison Ball QC

Senior Clerk:
Howard Rayner

Chief Executive:
Nicholas Martin

Other Clerks: Chris Ferrison and junior staff.

Fees Clerk: Dennis Davies

Tenants: 41

Academic Associate: Prof. Michael Freeman
Door Tenant: Carolyn Hamilton
* Practises mainly from 30 Park Place, Cardiff. *Tel:* (01222) 398421.

The Chambers: Formed as a specialist family set in January 1989 by a group of well-established family law practitioners and in 1997 became the largest chambers where all members specialise in family law.

Work Undertaken: One Garden Court offers a comprehensive service to solicitors, local authorities, child care professionals and their clients. Members practise at all levels in the law relating to marriage, divorce, the Children Act 1989, wardship, cohabitation, inheritance, child abduction, judicial review, surrogacy, matrimonial professional negligence and all other aspects of family law. All are members of the Family Law Bar Association. Direct Professional Access work may be accepted by individual members of chambers if appropriate.

Mediation: In January 1997 One Garden Court was the first chambers to set up a full mediation service, offering fully trained and qualified FMA/BALM mediators.

Additional Areas: Personal injuries, professional and medical negligence, mental health, education, local authority housing and administration, family-related crime, human rights issues.

Associated Chambers: Miss Bedell-Pearce practises from Denton, North Yorks, LS29 0HE, *Tel:* (01943) 817230. Mrs Jane Crowley QC also practises from 30 Park Place, Cardiff *Tel:* (01222) 398421

Tenancy applications: Heads of Chambers.

Pupillage Co-ordinator: Andrew Bagchi

Mini-pupillages: Alexander Chandler.

Chambers is a member of PACH.

SET NUMBER 67 — TWO GARDEN COURT (I. Macdonald QC & O. Davies)

2 GARDEN COURT, TEMPLE, LONDON, EC4Y 9BL
Tel: (0171) 353 1633 **Fax:** (0171) 353 4621 **DX:** 34 (CH.LN.) **Email:** BARRISTERS@2GARDENCT.LAW.CO.UK

MEMBERS:

Ian Macdonald QC (1963) (QC-1988)
Owen Davies (1973)
Nicholas Blake QC (1974) (QC-1994)
Kenneth Macdonald QC (1978) (QC-1997)
Courtenay Griffiths QC (1980) (QC-1998)
Michael House (1972)
Marguerite Russell (1972)
David Watkinson (1972)
Terry Munyard (1972)
Mark George (1976)
Henry Blaxland (1978)
Lalith De Kauwe (1978)
Frances Webber (1978)
Icah Peart (1978)
Laurie Fransman (1979)
Jan Luba (1980)

Anne Jessup (1981)
Celia Graves (1981)
Markanza Cudby (1983)
Simon Farrell (1983)
Michael Hall (1983)
Anthony Jennings (1983)
Ravinder Rahal (1983)
Stephen Cottle (1984)
Nerida Harford-Bell (1984)
Debra Gold (1985)
Beatrice Prevatt (1985)
Elizabeth Veats (1986)
Richard Scannell (1986)
Mary McKeone (1986)
Amanda Meusz (1986)
Dexter Dias (1988)
Adrian Eissa (1988)
Leslie Thomas (1988)
Judy Khan (1989)
Alison Grief (1990)

Colin Hutchinson (1990)
Jasbinder Chahal (1991)
Yvette Genn (1991)
Stephanie Harrison (1991)
Maggie Jones (1991)
Joanne Harris (1991)
Jon Holbrook (1991)
Stephen Simblett (1991)
Valerie Easty (1992)
Alastair Edie (1992)
Peter Weatherby (1992)
Raza Husain (1993)
Rajiv Menon (1993)
Rob Littlewood (1993)
Duran Seddon (1994)
Liz Davies (1994) (Solicitor 1989-1993)
Stephen Cragg (1996) (Solicitor 1989-1996)
Daniel Friedman (1996)

Head of Chambers: I. Macdonald QC & O. Davies
Senior Clerk: Colin Cook
Tenants: 54

A general common law set specialising in criminal defence work, family and child care law, housing, immigration and judicial review.

SET NUMBER 68 — GOLDSMITH BUILDING (John Griffith Williams QC)

GOLDSMITH BUILDING, TEMPLE, LONDON, EC4Y 7BL
Tel: (0171) 353 7881 **Fax:** (0171) 353 5319 **DX:** 435 **Email:** CLERKS@GOLDSMITH-BUILDING.LAW.CO.UK

MEMBERS:

John Griffith Williams QC (1968) (QC-1985)
Michael Maguire QC (1949) (QC-1967)
Eric Somerset Jones QC (1952) (QC-1978)
Christopher Llewellyn-Jones QC (1965) (QC-1990)
Merfyn Hughes QC (1971) (QC-1994)
Michael Farmer QC (1972) (QC-1995)
Robin Hay (1964)

Harry Martineau (1966)
Martin Hall-Smith (1972)
Christopher Morris-Coole (1974)
John Gallagher (1974)
John Friel (1974)
Charles Calvert (1975)
Robert Leonard (1976)
Patrick Routley (1979)
Anthony Higgins (1978)
Mark Maitland-Jones (1986)
Gordon Dawes (1989)

David Burles (1984)
Julie Browne (1989)
Deborah Hay (1991)
Claire Newton (1992)
Daniel Lawson (1994)
Sadie Wright (1994)
Clive Rawlings (1994)
Thomas Roe (1993)
Jerome Mayhew (1995)
Angela Fane (1992)

Head of Chambers: John Griffith Williams QC
Senior Clerk: Edith A. Robertson
Tenants: 28

The Chambers: Goldsmith Building is an established set of chambers with members at all levels of seniority. Chambers is able to provide individuals or teams of counsel to undertake a wide variety of litigation, arbitration and advisory work. The traditional strength of chambers has been its high standard of advocacy. Chambers' work is centred on London and the South eastern Circuit, with strong senior connections on the Wales and Chester and Northern Circuits. We provide an efficient, flexible and comprehensive legal service with established specialist practice groups.

Continues overleaf

Chambers has eight Practice Groups, namely, Personal Injury, Professional Negligence, Crime, Family, Business Law, Landlord and Tenant, Public and Administrative Law and Employment. These groups form the core of the infrastructure of chambers. The groups meet on a regular basis and continuing education is one of their objectives. In addition to the practice groups chambers also have specialists in the areas of environmental law, insolvency, and commercial fraud.

Goldsmith Building has developed a programme to provide seminars on a range of legal topics, and as authorised providers of continuing education by the Law Society all seminars carry a CPD rating. Chambers publishes a range of Newsletters, which contain news and information about chambers and comments on current developments in the law.

Chambers has an experienced clerking team and the clerks are always ready to advise on suitable counsel and fee levels along with liaising with courts on the listing of cases. Members of Chambers and the Clerks are aware of the needs of clients and strive to give the highest quality of service. A Chambers charter has been adopted which details the level of service you can expect when you instruct a member of chambers or deal with the clerks. More specific information, fee levels, Chambers brochure and other Chambers publications are available from the clerks.

SET NUMBER 69

GOLDSMITH CHAMBERS (Philip Sapsford QC) Goldsmith Building, Temple, London, EC4Y 7BL **Tel:** (0171) 353 6802 **Fax:** (0171) 583 5255 **DX:** 376 **Clerk:** Mrs Celia Monksfield **Tenants:** 35 A common law set of chambers with an emphasis on criminal, family and Civil work.

SET NUMBER 70

GOLDSWORTH CHAMBERS

11 GRAY'S INN SQUARE, FIRST FLOOR, LONDON, WC1R 5JD
Tel: (0171) 405 7117 **Fax:** (0171) 831 8308 **DX:** 1057 CHANCERY LANE

MEMBERS:

John Goldsworth (1965)	Sean Middleton (1991)	Paulene Gandhi (1995)
Feliks Kwiatkowski (1977)	Jane Harvey (1992)	Tim Scrantom (1995)
Romasa Butt (1985)	Mary Malecka (1994)	
Peter Marks (1987)	Kemi Ogun (1994)	

Head of Chambers:
The Management Committee

Consultants: Mr Geoffrey Pimm, Mr John Goldsworth

Tenants: 10

Door Tenants: Gaetano Sardo (Advocato, Milan Bar, Italy), Timothy O. Scranton (Member, Georgia & South Carolina Bar).

Work Undertaken: Arbitration, chancery work, company law, commercial, contract, immigration, insurance, revenue, succession and VAT, medical negligence, personal injury, Human Rights, education, employment, judicial review.

SET NUMBER 71

GOUGH SQUARE CHAMBERS (Frederick Philpott)

6-7 GOUGH SQUARE, LONDON, EC4A 3DE
Tel: (0171) 353 0924 **Fax:** (0171) 353 2221 **DX:** 476 LINK: BOB WEEKES **Email:** GSC@GOUGHSQ.CO.UK **Internet:** WWW.GOUGHSQ.CO.UK

MEMBERS:

Frederick Philpott (1974)	Jonathan Goulding (1984)	Cyrus Katrak (1991)
Peter Sayer (1975)	Stephen Neville (1986)	Anthony Vines (1993)
Claire Andrews (1979)	Julia Smith (1988)	Frederica Cogswell (1995)
William Hibbert (1979)	Julian Gun Cuninghame (1989)	Iain MacDonald (1996)
Barry Stancombe (1983)		

Head of Chambers:
Frederick Philpott

Senior Clerk:
Bob Weekes

Chambers Administrator:
Elizabeth Owen-Ward

Tenants: 13

The Chambers: Gough Square Chambers is a commercial and common law set with a particular specialisation in consumer law. Chambers aims to provide an efficient, friendly and flexible service at competitive rates.

Areas of Practice:

Consumer Law: Consumer credit (agreements, licensing and advertising), trade descriptions and trademarks, food safety, pricing, weights and measures, consumer contracts, mortgages, shops, timeshare, product safety. Chambers is instructed in this specialist area by in-house lawyers and solicitors acting for banks, building societies and other lenders, supermarkets, retailers of electrical, white and brown goods, food retailers and other manufacturers and distributors of a wide range of products. Chambers publishes a free quarterly Trading Law Bulletin which charts the recent developments in this area of law. This can be viewed at our website. Please contact the Senior Clerk to join our mailing list to receive this.

Business and Commercial Law: Banking, secured lending, financial services, company and partnership, insolvency, employment, sale and supply contracts.
Property: Mortgages, landlord and tenant, land.
Commercial fraud: Criminal and civil frauds.
Additional Areas: Professional negligence, medical negligence, personal injury.

Facilities: Chambers is able to accept instructions via CD Rom, and the Internet. Outside normal working hours the Senior Clerk can be contacted on 0860 219162.

SET NUMBER
72

9 GOUGH SQUARE (Jeremy Roberts QC)

9 GOUGH SQUARE, LONDON, EC4A 3DE
Tel: (0171) 353 5371 **Fax:** (0171) 353 1344 **DX:** 439

MEMBERS:

Jeremy Roberts QC (1965) (QC-1982) *	Trevor Davies (1978)	Andrew Wheeler (1988)
Michael Brent QC (1961) (QC-1983) *	Frederick Ferguson (1978)	Sally-Ann Hales (1988)
John Rogers QC (1963) (QC-1979)	Grahame Aldous (1979)	Stephen Glynn (1990)
	Duncan Macleod (1980)	Jane Sinclair (1990)
Patrick Upward QC (1972) (QC-1996)	Christopher Wilson (1980)	Philip Jones (1990)
Gary Burrell QC (1977) (QC-1996) *	Nicolas Hillier (1982)	Clare Padley (1991)
	Roger Hiorns (1983)	John Tughan (1991)
John Foy QC (1969) (QC-1998)	Simon Carr (1984)	Jeremy Crowther (1991)
John Reddihough (1969) *	Gaurang Naik (1985)	Aileen Downey (1991)
Andrew Baillie (1970) *	Andrew Ritchie (1985)	Laura Begley (1993)
David Gerrey (1975)	Jacob Levy (1986)	Timothy Ashmole (1993)
Michael Joyce (1976)	Jonathan Loades (1986)	Louise Neilson (1994)
	Alexander Verdan (1987)	Christopher Stephenson (1994)
	Edwin Buckett (1988)	

Head of Chambers:
Jeremy Roberts QC

Practice Director:
Joanna Poulton MBA LLB

Tenants: 37

* Recorder

The Chambers: A well-established common law set specialising in particular in Personal Injury, Medical Negligence, Professional Negligence, Serious Fraud and Family.

We are noted for our friendly yet commercial approach which we believe enhances our ability to provide realistic advice to our clients. Focused along the lines of specialist teams we draw upon the considerable depth of knowledge and expertise held in Chambers through regular team meetings.

Our facilities are modern and up-to-date including disabled facilities, large dedicated conference rooms and full computerisation. We are professionally managed by a qualified Practice Director who is happy to discuss any aspect of our service and in particular to recommend suitable counsel. A brochure is available on request.

Work Undertaken:

Personal Injury: We can offer experts on complex multi-party actions, industrial disease, RSI, deafness, lifting, marine accidents, PTSD etc. representing either plaintiffs or defendants. Special payment terms are negotiable for union or insurance backed claims. All members of chambers have agreed to accept conditional fee work and where appropriate single agreements covering individual firms can be negotiated.

Medical Negligence: We can offer true experts who are renowned for being sensitive to the issues in these cases yet tenacious advocates and negotiators. Our experience for both plaintiffs and defendants includes brain injuries, birth defects, failed sterilisations, surgical and non-surgical maltreatment.

Professional Negligence: Members of our Professional Negligence team regularly advise on and appear in cases involving all aspects of professional negligence but in particular actions involving solicitors, accountants , insurance brokers and surveyors.

Serious Fraud: Chambers has some of the country's leading fraud practitioners. Ten members of chambers regularly prosecute for the SFO and for CPS HQ as well as defending some of the most complex fraud cases such as Blue Arrow and Nissan. We can provide experts on advance fee frauds, city frauds, pension frauds, mortgage frauds etc.

General Crime: The crime team has established an enviable reputation in both prosecuting and defending general crime on the M & O Circuit and in particular at Northampton, Luton, St Albans, Aylesbury, Birmingham Crown Courts. In addition members of chambers regularly appear in the major London Crown Courts.

Family: Our specialist family team undertake a full range of family law work including care proceedings, adoption, residence & contract applications and ancillary relief.

SET NUMBER
73 GRAY'S INN CHAMBERS (Brian Jubb)

GRAY'S INN CHAMBERS, GRAY'S INN, LONDON, WC1R 5JA
Tel: (0171) 404 1111 **Fax:** (0171) 430 1522 **DX:** 0074 (CH.LN.)

MEMBERS:

Brian Jubb (1971)	Rachel Wingert (1980)	Alistair Perkins (1986)
Caroline Rodger (1968)	Gillian Marks (1981)	Nigel Cox (1986)
Elisabeth Brann (1970)	Heather MacGregor (1982)	Ian Lewis (1989)
Richard Clough (1971)	Geoffrey Mott (1982)	Judit Seymour (1990)
Gillian Higson Smith (1973)	Jonathan Cowen (1983)	Joanna Clarke (1993)
Rozanna Malcolm (1974)	Timothy Compton (1984)	Justin Gray (1993)
David Houston (1976)	Melanie Nazareth (1984)	Amina Ahmed (1995)
Janette Haywood (1977)	Noah Weiniger (1984)	William Metaxa (1995)
Cherry Harding (1978)	Robert Dashwood (1984)	Charlotte Bayati (1995)

Head of Chambers:
Brian Jubb
Senior Clerk:
The Senior Clerk
Clerks: John Rugg (Practice Manager), Mark Darvell
Tenants: 27

Door Tenants: Sir Charles Fletcher-Cooke QC (1936), Dr Doreen Hinchliffe (1953), Melanie Den Brinker (1984), Marilyn Freeman (1986), Nicholas Stonor (1993).

SET NUMBER
74 1 GRAY'S INN SQUARE (Carl Teper) 1 Gray's Inn Square, Gray's Inn, London, WC1R 5AA **Tel:** (0171) 405 8946 **Fax:** (0171) 405 1617 **DX:** 1013 Chancery Lane **Practice Manager:** Jacqueline Chase **Tenants:** 45 The chambers are a common law set, with individual barristers specialising in a variety of areas.

SET NUMBER
75 1 GRAY'S INN SQUARE (The Baroness Scotland of Asthal QC) 1 Gray's Inn Square, Gray's Inn, London, WC1R 5AG **Tel:** (0171) 405 3000 **Fax:** (0171) 405 9942 **DX:** LDE 238 **Email:** onegrays.demon.co.uk **Clerks:** Steven Ashton **Tenants:** 34 Commercial, international law, arbitration, serious crime, general civil, family, children, international child abduction, public law and judicial review.

SET NUMBER
76 2 GRAY'S INN SQUARE CHAMBERS (Giles Eyre)

2 GRAY'S INN SQUARE, LONDON, WC1R 5AA
Tel: (0171) 242 0328 **Fax:** (0171) 405 3082 **DX:** 43 LONDON CHANCERY LANE **Email:** CLERKS@2GIS.CO.UK
Internet: HTTP: //WWW.2GIS.CO.UK

MEMBERS:

Giles Eyre (1974)	Kevin Haven (1982)	Terence Woods (1989)
Peter Leighton (1966)	Anthony Moore (1984)	Rebecca Priestley (1989)
Keith Knight (1969)	Jacqueline Marks (1984)	Myles Watkins (1990)
John Robson (1974) FCIA	John Church (1984)	Joanne Brown (1990)
Edward Cross (1975)	Gabrielle Jan Posner (1984)	Andrea Rivers (1990)
Richard Robinson (1977)	Fawzia King (1985)	Christopher Rice (1991)
Peter Fortune (1978)	Francis Collaco Moraes (1985)	James Arney (1992)
Christopher McConnell (1979)	Surinder Bhakar (1986)	Henry Drayton (1993)
David Hughes (1980)	Sorrel Dixon (1987)	Daniel Barnett (1993)
Nergis-Anne Matthew (1981)	Susan Baldock (1988)	Judith Parr (1994)
Jane Rayson (1982)	Adrian Roberts (1988)	(1985 – New Zealand)
Milan Dulovic (1982)	Mark Whalan (1988)	

Head of Chambers:
Giles Eyre
Practice Manager:
Paul Simpson
Senior Clerk: Bill Harris
Tenants: 34

The Chambers: The Chambers provides a responsive, courteous and efficient service in all areas of common law practice. Through the use of modern administrative systems, a management committee and a spirit of teamwork, chambers is able to meet the varied requirements of solicitors. Specialisation is achieved through the use of practice groups, which enable members to pool their specialist knowledge and expertise and to offer a full and professional service to clients. Chambers, as part of the service it provides holds a minimum of six 2 hour Law Society accredited seminars every year.

Publications: Peter Fortune is a contributor to Blackstone's *Criminal Practice (Road Traffic and Evidence)*. Gabrielle Jan Posner is author of *The Teenager's Guide to The Law* (Cavendish 1995). Jane Rayson is co-author of *How to make Applications in the Family Proceedings Court* and *Blackstone's Guide to the Family Law Act 1996*.

Work Undertaken:

Family: Matters covered encompass child law including public and private Children Act proceedings, care work (including representing guardians ad litem), adoption, wardship and child abduction, matrimonial and related proceedings (including property and financial disputes and disputes between co-habitees).

Criminal: Members practise in all areas of crime, receiving instructions on behalf of the prosecution and defence. Particular emphasis is placed upon defence work. Members have particular experience in areas of fraud, child abuse, drug trafficking, sexual offence, public order licensing, actions against the police.

Personal Injury and Medical Negligence: Members act for individuals, trade unions and insurance company clients, for both plaintiff and defendant, in claims arising from accidents at work, medical negligence, road traffic accidents, occupiers' liability and defective products. Conditional Fee Agreements are undertaken.

Employment: Chambers undertakes advisory and advocacy work in Employment Tribunals, EAT, High Court and internal disciplinary hearings. Specific areas of expertise are unfair dismissal, redundancy, discrimination and the provision of advice to employers prior to the dismissal of employees and directors.

Property: Chambers offers representation and advice on all property matters including public and private sector housing, business tenancies and all aspects of landlord and tenant law, trusts, claims to possession of land, easement and mortgage disputes, conveyancing, and disputes involving joint owners and co-habitees.

Contract and commercial: Areas of law covered include contract and tort, partnership disputes, professional negligence, sale of goods, agency, bills of exchange, banking, insolvency, building and engineering contracts, consumer credit, insurance, guarantee and suretyship and disqualification of directors.

Foreign Languages: French, Serbo-Croat, Malay and Punjabi.

Information Technology: The Chambers and a majority of members are contactable via Email. Written work can also be provided on disk in a variety of formats.

Charges: Comprehensive details of chambers' fee structures are available from the Senior Clerk.

Recruitment and Training: Pupillage applications through PACH. Mini-pupillages and student visits are available. Sponsored pupils are accepted.

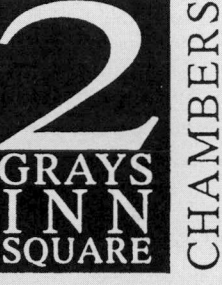

2-3 GRAY'S INN SQUARE (Anthony Scrivener QC)

2-3 GRAY'S INN SQUARE, GRAY'S INN, LONDON, WC1R 5JH
Tel: (0171) 242 4986 **Fax:** (0171) 405 1166 **DX:** 316 (CH.LN.) **Email:** CHAMBERS@2-3GRAYSINNSQUARE.CO.UK

MEMBERS:

Anthony Scrivener QC (1958) (QC-1975)

Sir Graham Eyre QC (1954) (QC-1970)

Malcolm Spence QC (1958) (QC-1979)

Patrick Ground QC (1960) (QC-1981)

Harry Wolton QC (1969) (QC-1982)

Christopher Cochrane QC (1965) (QC-1988)

Anthony Porten QC (1969) (QC-1988)

Anthony Dinkin QC (1968) (QC-1991)

Vernon Pugh QC (1969) (QC-1986)

(Nicholas) Mark Lowe QC (1972) (QC-1996)

Timothy Straker QC (1977) (QC-1996)

John Haines (1967)

Richard Rundell (1971)

Geoffrey Stephenson (1971)

David Lamming (1972)

Adrian Trevelyan Thomas (1974)

Nicholas Nardecchia (1974)

Tobias Davey (1977)

Graham Stoker (1977)

Ian Albutt (1981)

Steven Gasztowicz (1981)

Mary Cook (1982)

Morag Ellis (1984)

James Findlay (1984)

Katie Astaniotis (1985)

Michael Bedford (1985)

Philip Kolvin (1985)

Simon Bird (1987)

Ranjit Bhose (1989)

Gillian Carrington (1990)

Robin Green (1992)

Harriet Murray (1992)

Peter Miller (1993)

Ian Ponter (1993)

Philip Coppel (1994)

Thomas Cosgrove (1994)

Richard Ground (1994)

David Lintott (1995)

Jonathon Easton (1995)

Wayne Beglan (1995)

Head of Chambers:
Anthony Scrivener QC

Chambers Director:
Douglas Lewis CBE

Senior Clerk: Martin Hart

Tenants: 40

The Chambers: A long-established set, now based in Gray's Inn. Former members of chambers include Sir Edward Marshall Hall KC, Lord Birkett, Lord Chief Justice Widgery, Lord Bridge of Harwich, Mr Justice Hidden, and Mr Justice Penry-Davey. Current members of Chambers include Anthony Scrivener QC, a former Chairman of the Bar, Sir Graham Eyre QC, who was the Inspector for the Airport Inquiries, and Malcolm Spence QC who is the Chairman of the Planning and Environment Bar Association.

Over the last 40 years and with increasing size, chambers have widened their original common law base to develop substantial practices in administrative law, local government law and town and country planning law. They have, however, retained a strong common law practice, covering both general and large commercial disputes, and continue to enjoy a solid criminal practice.

Continues overleaf

Work Undertaken:

General Description: The principal areas of work undertaken by chambers are listed below. Details of the specialities of each member are available on request form the senior clerk. Various members also practice or are admitted in other jurisdictions, including Hong Kong, Singapore, Malaysia, Jamaica, Trinidad, the Cayman Islands, the British Virgin Islands and certain Australian jurisdictions.

Counsel are available at any level of experience required. The junior tenants are available at short notice for all Magistrates' Court, County Court and tribunal hearings, as well as for any procedural applications. Members of chambers will work in any part of England and Wales, Scotland (planning matters only) and Ireland.

Main Areas of Work:

Town and Country Planning, Administrative and Local Government law (including judicial review; housing law; public and local government finance; compulsory purchase; rating; highways; environmental law).

Commercial law (including building and engineering disputes; company law; commercial arbitrations; banking law; insolvency, corporate and individual; agency law; restraint of trade; computer contracts).

Common law (including personal injuries; professional negligence, including medical, accountants and solicitors; employment law, including industrial tribunal work).

Consumer law (including sale of goods; trade descriptions; trading law; food safety; data protection).

Criminal law (including white collar crime; serious fraud; capital cases).

Property law (including landlord and tenant; mortgages; housing associations).

Foreign Languages: French, Italian, Greek and German.

Recruitment & Training: Pupils are received each year; pupillage funds are available.

SET NUMBER
78

3 GRAY'S INN SQUARE (Rock Tansey QC)

3 GRAY'S INN SQUARE, GRAY'S INN, LONDON, WC1R 5AH
Tel: (0171) 520 5600 **Fax:** (0171) 520 5607 **DX:** 1043 (CH.LN.)

MEMBERS:

Rock Tansey QC (1966) (QC-1990)	Ronald Jaffa (1974)	Bill Maley (1982)
John Perry QC (1975) (QC-1989)	Brendan Keany (1974)	Leroy Redhead (1982)
Steven Kay QC (1977) (QC-1997)	Jonathan Mitchell (1974)	Colin Wells (1987)
George Carter-Stephenson QC (1975) (QC-1998)	Philip Statman (1975)	Alison Levitt (1988)
William Taylor QC (Scotland QC 1986) (1990) (English QC-1998)	Rudi Fortson (1976)	Sarah Harris (1989)
	Diana Ellis (1978)	Adrian Kayne (1989)
	Roger Offenbach (1978)	Helen Valley (1990)
John Cooper QC (1983) (QC-1998)	Chester Beyts (1978)	Arlette Piercy (1990)
David Hooper (1971)	Robert Anthony (1979)	Emma Akuwudike (1992)
Colin Allan (1971)	Paul Keleher (1980)	Richard Furlong (1994)
David Farrington (1972)	Paul Mendelle (1981)	Sylvia de Bertodano (1993)
	Penelope Barrett (1982)	Tyrone Smith (1993)
	Jeremy Dein (1982)	Aisling Byrnes (1994)
	Simon Pentol (1982)	Nichola Howard (1995)

Head of Chambers:
Rock Tansey QC

Senior Clerk:
Guy Williams

First Junior Clerks: Marc King and Steven Lucas

Tenants: 37

The Chambers: Established in 1975, 3 Gray's Inn Square is a specialist Criminal Defence Set which aims to ensure that everyone has equal access to the best representation. Chambers has earned a reputation as a leader in its field by maintaining the highest standards of professionalism, integrity, commitment and both accessibility and approachability.

Work Undertaken: First-class representation is provided at every level of seniority by Practitioners who appear regularly in "high-profile cases" and who offer experience in the conduct of all categories of criminal case including European Human Rights, International Criminal Tribunal, (International) Terrorism and War Crimes, Murder, Serious Fraud, Organised Crime, International Drugs Trafficking/allied Money Laundering and offences of Extreme/Sexual Violence.

Within this framework there is a positive commitment to legally-aided Clients and, where appropriate, pro-bono work is undertaken.

Particular expertise is provided in all aspects of Appellate Work, including Judicial Review and Privy Council. Further, there is experience in the conduct of Civil Cases, especially Actions against the Police and allied issues and Mental Health Review Tribunals.

In recent years Chambers has presented lectures to Solicitors and Practitioners generally, concerning the effect of significant changes in Criminal Legislation. Some Members have also lectured nationally and internationally to and on behalf of Legal/Human Rights organisations on Drug Trafficking and International War Crimes.

Publications: Rudi Fortson: *Law on the Misuse of Drugs*; Gary Summers: designer of Marshall computer program for criminal trial lawyers.

Foreign Connections: Rock Tansey QC & Steven Kay QC have founded the European Criminal Bar Association in order to advance issues of mutual concern for European Criminal Defence Lawyers. Rock Tansey QC is the First Chairman of the ECBA and organised its inaugural conference at the European Commission for Human Rights cases. Steven Kay QC, Defence Counsel in the first International Criminal Tribunal for the former Yugoslavia undertakes European Human Rights cases. John Perry QC also practises in Bermuda and is a member of the West Indian Bar.

Services: Conference Rooms, Video Conferences, E-Mail, Disks accepted, Voice Mail for all Members of Chambers. A 24-hour Clerking service for emergencies and overnight cases is provided. Chambers is fully computerised as is our Crown Court List Checking System.

SET NUMBER
79

4-5 GRAY'S INN SQUARE (Miss Elizabeth Appleby QC & The Hon. M. Beloff QC)

4-5 GRAY'S INN SQUARE, GRAY'S INN, LONDON, WC1R 5AY
Tel: (0171) 404 5252 **Fax:** (0171) 242 7803 **DX:** 1029 **Email:** CHAMBERS@4-5GRAYSINNSQUARE.CO.UK

MEMBERS:

Elizabeth Appleby QC (1965) (QC-1979)	Lady Hazel Fox QC (1950) (QC-1993)	Richard Humphreys (1986)
Michael Beloff QC (1967) (QC-1981)	Gregory Stone QC (1976) (QC-1994)	Clive Lewis (1987)
William Wade QC (1946) (QC-1968)	Cherie Booth QC (1976) (QC-1995)	James Ramsden (1987)
Gary Flather QC (1962) (QC-1984)	Richard Spearman QC (1977) (QC-1996) MA (Cantab)	Thomas Hill (1988)
David Mole QC (1970) (QC-1990)	Sam Aaron (1986)	Rabinder Singh (1989)
Brian Ash QC (1975) (QC-1990)	Robin Campbell (1969)	Thomas Linden (1990)
Stuart Isaacs QC (1975) (QC-1991)	Nicholas Huskinson (1971)	Sarah Moore (1990)
Duncan Ouseley QC (1973) (QC-1992)	Julian Chichester (1977)	Helen Mountfield (1991)
W. Robert Griffiths QC (1974) (QC-1993)	John Hobson (1980)	Paul Brown (1991)
John Steel QC (1978) (QC-1993)	Timothy Corner (1981)	Andrew Tabachnik (1991)
Clive Newberry QC (1978) (QC-1993)	Richard McManus (1982)	David Wolfe (1992)
	Peter M. Village (1983)	Murray Hunt (1992)
	Hodge M. Malek (1983)	Andrew Fraser-Urquhart (1993)
	Tim Kerr (1983)	Ami Barav (1993)
	Peter Havey (1984)	Karen Steyn (1995)
	Jane Oldham (1985)	Marie Demetriou (1995)
	Paul Stinchcombe (1985)	Sarah-Jane Davies (1996)
	Kishore Sharma (1986)	Jonathan Moffett (1996)
		Andrew Sharland (1996)
		James Strachan (1996)

Head of Chambers:
Miss Elizabeth Appleby QC & The Hon. M. Beloff QC

Senior Clerk:
Michael Kaplan

Tenants: 48

One Head of Chambers (Elizabeth Appleby QC) is a recorder and a Deputy High Court Judge. The other (Michael Beloff QC) is a Judge of the Court of Appeal of Jersey and Guernsey and a Member of the Court of Arbitration for Sport and President of Trinity College, Oxford. Several members are also recorders. Chambers also have two officers of the Local Government and Planning Bar Association and had the first two Chairmen of the Administrative Law Bar Association. One member is a former Junior, two are present Junior Counsel to the Crown on Common Law. Two practitioners are international arbitrators.

The Chambers: A large commercial set which favours an interdisciplinary approach, particularly where public and commercial law meet; and with expertise in EC and ECHR law.

Publications: Members of chambers have written or contributed to: *The Sex Discrimination Act; Halsbury's Laws 4th Ed., Vol.45; Judicial Review, Butterworths* (contributing editor); *Public Law; Current Legal Problems; Irish Jurist;* revised notes to sections of *The Town and Country Planning Act 1971, (Encyclopaedia of Planning); EC Banking Law; Banking and the Competition Law of the EC, (consultant editor); EC Case Citator; Paget's Law of Banking; Journal of International Banking Law; Crown Office Digest,* (co-editors). Clive Lewis is author of *Judicial Remedies in Public Law.* Murray Hunt is author of Human Rights Law in English Courts: Rabinder Sing is author of the Future of Human Rights in the United Kingdom.

Former Members: The Right Honourable Lord Justice Schiemann; The Honourable Mr Justice Keene; The Honourable Mr Justice Collins; The Honourable Mr Justice Moses; The Honourable Mr Justice Sullivan; Richard Yorke QC (1956)(QC-1971); Sir Douglas Frank QC, former President of the Lands Tribunal; His Honour Judge Bernard Marder QC, President of the Lands Tribunal; his Honour Judge Bernard Marder QC [Victor Wellings QC, former President of the Lands Tribunal];

Continues overleaf

Door Tenants: Professor G.H. Treitel QC; Professor E.P. Ellinger; Lord Borrie QC; Sir John Freeland QC (1952, QC-1987); Marc Dassesse (Brussels Bar); Professor Sir D.G.T. Williams; Patrick Patelin (Juriste d'Entreprise, Paris); Edmond McGovern (also in Brussels); Narinder Hargun (Bermuda); Brian Harris QC; Jeremy Gauntlett (SC) (South Africa); John Sackar QC (NSW); Mansoor Jamal Malik (Oman).

Work Undertaken:

General Description: The Chambers cover a wide range of specialist areas, inparticular administrative and planning law, comercial law, EC and Human Rights Law.

Main Areas of Work:

Public Law/Town and Country Planning Law: *Work includes:* local government, town and country planning, highways, rating, environmental, markets, constitutional, parliamentary, human rights, public health, welfare and social security, licensing, education, immigration, extradition, nationality, elections, air, public inquiries and all areas of judicial review.

Commercial Law: *Work includes:* banking, financial services, accounting, negotiable instruments, insurance and reinsurance, shipping, sale of goods, company and insolvency, partnership, building and engineering disputes, commercial fraud, domestic, international and ICC arbitrations.

General Common Law (Civil): *Work includes:* landlord and tenant, libel, confidentiality and contempt, professional negligence, road traffic (operators' licensing), domestic associations.

Employment Law: *Work includes:* industrial relations, trade unions, sex and racial discrimination.

Additional Areas of Work: European Community/Convention law and competition and restrictive practices. Sport.

Foreign Connections: Members of Chambers have appeared at the Privy Council, the European Court of Justice and of Human Rights, international arbitration tribunals and other courts worldwide, including Hong Kong, the Far East, Bermuda, Anguilla and Trinidad. One member is a former Judge of the Court of Appeal in Swaziland and a current Judge of the Court of Appeal in Lesotho.

Other Matters: The chambers have been the first set to appoint an academic panel as a research and advisory facility. Its members are Professor Craig (Administrative), Professor M. Grant (Local government and planning), Professor P Davies (Employment), Professor J Usher (EC), Professor E Barendt (Media, Human Rights, Welfare), Professor A Arnull (Birmingham). The Chambers now publishes a journal covering areas of work in which members practice and recent developments in the law.

SET NUMBER
80 6 GRAY'S INN SQUARE (Michael Boardman) 6 Gray's Inn Square, Gray's Inn, London, WC1R 5AZ **Tel:** (0171) 242 1052 **Fax:** (0171) 405 4934 **DX:** 224 **Clerk:** Mr Russell Kinsley **Tenants:** 29 A common law practice, with criminal work, prosecution and defence, and expertise in family, industrial tribunal, employment and personal injury law. Email by arrangement.

SET NUMBER
81 **8 GRAY'S INN SQUARE** (Patrick C. Soares)

8 GRAY'S INN SQUARE, GRAY'S INN, LONDON, WC1R 5AZ
Tel: (0171) 242 3529 **Fax:** (0171) 404 0395 **DX:** 411 (CH.LN.)

MEMBERS:

Patrick C. Soares (1983) LLB, LLM, FTII	David J. Brownbill (1989) LLB	Ian Ferrier (1976) MA (Oxon)
Barry McCutcheon (1975) BA, LLM, FTII	Patrick Way (1994)	Denzil Davies (1965)
	Christopher Whitehouse (1997)	

Head of Chambers:
Patrick C. Soares

Senior Clerk:
Marie Burke

Tenants: 7

All categories of law including stamp duty, international estate planning, property, trusts, ESOPs.

10-11 GRAY'S INN SQUARE (Alan Masters)

10-11 GRAY'S INN SQUARE, GRAY'S INN, LONDON, WC1R 5JD
Tel: (0171) 405 2576 **Fax:** (0171) 831 2430 **DX:** 484

MEMBERS:

Alan Masters (1979)	Mark Muller (1991)	Peter Morel (1993)
Jean McCreath (1978)	Michael Ivers (1991)	Henrietta Marriage (1993)
John Donnelly (1983)	Edmund Eldergill (1991)	Stephen Field (1993)
Harriette Black (1986)	Annie Dixon (1991)	Ian Painter (1993)
Terence Boulter (1986)	Yolanda Solari (1991)	Rima Baruah (1994)
Ciarân Magill (1988)	Kate McCrimmon (1992)	Alison Moore (1994)
Robert Trevis (1990)	Matthew Pardoe (1992)	Katie Thorne (1994)

Head of Chambers:
Alan Masters

Senior Clerk:
Richard Loasby

Tenants: 21

Some members are dually called to the Irish Bar.

Door Tenants: Sally Mitchell, Tom Davidson, Alexis Mina.

We pride ourselves on being a progressive and innovative set, with a blend of youth and experience ideally suited to the challenges of practising law in a modern society.

We have an established reputation as campaigners and pioneers and have been involved in several landmark cases.

In 1986 we discarded the traditional chambers structure in favour of a more business-like policy, setting up as a limited company with a board of directors responsible for management finance and strategy.

Members of chambers specialise within one of our three teams, Civil, Crime and Family. Within each team are practice working groups which concentrate on a particular field of law such as medical negligence and personal injury.

We understand that solicitors and their clients need to feel they are working in partnership with us on cases, and have developed an infrastructure to support and facilitate their requirements.

14 GRAY'S INN SQUARE (Joanna Dodson QC)

14 GRAY'S INN SQUARE, GRAY'S INN, LONDON, WC1R 5JP
Tel: (0171) 242 0858 **Fax:** (0171) 242 5434 **DX:** 399 (CH.LN.)

MEMBERS:

Joanna Dodson QC (1971) (QC-1993)	David G P Turner (1976)	Stephen Lyon (1987)
Louise S. Godfrey QC (1972) (QC-1991)	Sarah Forster (1976)	Michelle Corbett (1987)
	Gillian Brasse (1977)	Mark Jarman (1989)
Lindsey Kushner QC (1974) (QC-1992)	Brenda Morris (1978)	Rebecca Brown (1989)
	Kate Hudson (1981)	Samantha King (1990)
Patricia Dangor (1970)	Caroline Reid (1982)	Richard Alomo (1990)
Norman Patterson (1971)	Karen McLaughlin (1982)	David Bedingfield (1991)
Joanna Hall (1973)	Monica Ford (1984)	David Vavrecka (1992)
Mhairi McNab (1974)	Mark Emanuel (1985)	Jane De Zonie (1994)
Barbara Slomnicka (1976)	Pamela Warner (1985)	Dominic Brazil (1995)
	Karoline Sutton (1986)	Samantha Whittam (1995)

Head of Chambers:
Joanna Dodson QC

Senior Clerk:
Stephen Lavell

Tenants: 30

Members of chambers belong to the Family Law Bar Association.

The Chambers: A family and civil set with particular expertise in children's cases and financial matters, with a strong general common law side.

Work Undertaken:
Main Areas of Work: Family and matrimonial, including wardship, adoption, care, children and ancillary relief; personal injury, including running-down accidents; employment and labour law; landlord and tenant and housing; licensing work; building and construction and contract cases.
Additional Areas of Work: Civil liberties, crime, company, discrimination, ecclesiastical, judicial review, police cases, product liability, professional negligence, sale of goods and welfare.

Clientele: Individuals, companies, local authorities, guardians ad litem, the Official Solicitor.

Foreign Connections: Patricia Dangor is a member of the Bermuda Bar and David Bedingfield is a member of the Georgia Bar.

Recruitment & Training: Tenancy applications should be sent to Joanna Dodson QC; pupillage applications to Jane De Zonie. Two first six and one second six months pupils are taken each year. Awards of £4,000 are offered for the first six months of pupillage and minimum earnings are guaranteed at that level for the second six. Mini-pupillages are available.

GRAY'S INN TAX CHAMBERS (Milton Grundy)

THIRD FLOOR, GRAY'S INN CHAMBERS, GRAY'S INN, LONDON, WC1R 5JA
Tel: (0171) 242 2642 **Fax:** (0171) 405 4078 (GROUP 4) **DX:** 352 LONDON CHANCERY LANE FAX: (0171) 831 9017 (GROUPS 2 & 3)
Out of Hours number: 0956 144 042 **Email:** CLERKS@TAXBAR.COM **Internet:** HTTP: //WWW.TAXBAR.COM

MEMBERS:

Milton Grundy (1954)	David Goy QC (1973) (QC-1991)	Hugh McKay (1990)
Michael Flesch QC (1963) (QC-1983)	John Walters QC (1977) (QC-1997)	Aparna Nathan (1994)
David Goldberg QC (1971) (QC-1987)	Felicity Cullen (1985)	Conrad McDonnell (1994)
	Philip Baker (1979)	Barrie Akin (1976)
		Nicola Shaw (1995)

Head of Chambers:
Milton Grundy
Senior Clerk:
Chris Broom
Tenants: 12

Door Tenants: Graham Wilson and Abraham Swersky.

The Chambers: Gray's Inn Tax Chambers is a leading set of specialist tax practitioners. Its members deal with all aspects of United Kingdom revenue law and cover the whole gamut of work dealt with by tax practitioners from accumulation and maintenance settlements to zero-coupon bonds. They have established expertise in litigation before the Special Commissioners, General Commissioners, the VAT and Duties Tribunals, the Supreme Court, the House of Lords, the Privy Council, the Court of Justice of the European Communities and the courts of certain colonies, commonwealth and foreign jurisdictions. They give advice to taxpayers who are in dispute with the Inland Revenue or Customs and advise clients on the planning of their business and personal affairs. Members of Chambers advise on corporate tax planning including acquisitions, mergers, takeovers and methods of financing; property transactions; international business; cross-border transactions; offshire and domestic trusts; estate planning and all the direct and indirect taxes, including VAT. Work is accepted from (amongst others) local authorities, companies, charities and private clients. Direct professional access is accepted from members of the appropriate professional bodies.

Appointments and Memberships: All members of Chambers belong to the Revenue Bar Association of which Michael Flesch is a former chairman and Hugh McKay is presently secretary. Milton Grundy is President of the International Tax Planning Association and a Fellow of the Chartered Institute of Taxation; he is the draftsman of the Trusts Law of the Cayman Islands and (with Philip Baker) of the IBC Act and the Trusts Act of Belize. John Walters QC and Barrie Akin are chartered accountants and Philip Baker and Aparna Nathan are visiting lecturers at London University. Hugh McKay and Aparna Nathan are on the Customs and Excise VAT Tribunal advocates list.

Publications: Members have written, contributed to or edited the following: *Whiteman on Income tax; VAT and Property; British Tax Review; Asset Protection Trusts; Double Taxation Conventions and International Tax Law; Value Added Tax Encyclopedia; Offshore Business Centres; The Law of Partnership Taxation; International Fiscal Strategy; The Laws of the Internet; The Offshore Financial Law Reports* and various articles on international tax developments.

Foreign Connections: Members of Chambers advise clients in Hong Kong, Singapore, Australia, New Zealand, the USA and Mauritius. The chambers also advise the revenue departments of Commonwealth countries and ex-colonies on the interpretation of their statutes.

Languages Spoken: French, German, Italian, Chinese (Mandarin and some Cantonese), Hebrew, Hindi and Tamil.

Office Equipment: The Chambers are fully computerised using Windows 95, Microsoft Word 7, Microsoft Excel, Wordperfect 6.1, Visio 3.2 for drawing diagrams, Microsoft Powerpoint and email. The chambers maintains a popular website, which offers a rapid reporting of tax cases. The address is www.taxbar.com.

100E GREAT PORTLAND STREET 100E Great Portland Street, London, WIN 5PD **Tel:** (0171) 636 6323 **Fax:** (0171) 436 3544 **DX:** 94252 Marylebone

ONE HARCOURT BUILDINGS (Simon Buckhaven) 1 Harcourt Buildings, Temple, London, EC4Y 9DA **Tel:** (0171) 353 9421/0375 **Fax:** (0171) 353 4170 **DX:** 417 London/Chancery Lane **Clerk:** William Lavell **Tenants:** 34 General Common Law. Also practise in chancery, commercial law, contract and tort.

SET NUMBER
87

2 HARCOURT BUILDINGS (Roger Henderson QC)

2 HARCOURT BUILDINGS (GROUND FLOOR), TEMPLE, LONDON, EC4Y 9DB
Tel: (0171) 583 9020 **Fax:** (0171) 583 2686 **DX:** 1039 **Email:** CLERKS@HARCOURT.CO.UK

MEMBERS:

Roger Henderson QC (1964)
(QC-1980) *
Piers Ashworth QC (1956)
(QC-1973) *
Jonathan Playford QC (1962)
(QC-1982) *
Richard Mawrey QC (1964)
(QC-1986) *
Adrian Brunner QC (1968)
(QC-1994) *
Stephen Powles QC (1972)
(QC-1995) *
Andrew Prynne QC (1975)
(QC-1995)
Quintin Iwi (1956)
Prof Alan Dashwood (1969)
Adrian Cooper (1970) *

Daniel Worsley (1971) *
Bernard O'Sullivan (1971)
Gavin Gore-Andrews (1972)
Andrew Jordan (1974)
Jonathan Harvey (1974)
Kenneth Hamer (1975) *
Lawrence West (1979) *
Roger Eastman (1978)
Sara Staite (1979) *
Barbara Cameron (1979)
James Palmer (1983)
Charles Gibson (1984)
George Alliott (1981)
Conrad Griffiths (1986)
Benjamin Battcock (1987)
Marina Wheeler (1987)

Wendy Outhwaite (1990)
Averil Harrison (1990)
Patrick Green (1990)
Charles Bourne (1991)
Prashant Popat (1992)
Oliver Campbell (1992)
Isabella Zornoza (1993)
Malcolm Sheehan (1993)
Felicia Fenston (1994)
Geraint Webb (1995)
Toby Riley-Smith (1995)
Julianna Mitchell (1994)
Andrew Kinnier (1996)
Lance Ashworth (1987) +
Frank Schoneveld (1992) +

Head of Chambers:
Roger Henderson QC

Senior Clerk:
John White

Tenants: 39

Recorder/Assistant Recorder.
+*Door Tenant.*

Work Undertaken: Commercial and common law, particularly product liability; personal injury; medical and other professional negligence; insurance; local government; public procurement; public law; judicial review; environmental law; health and safety; railways; telecommunications; information technology; intellectual property; education; food; sport; employment and discrimination; construction and engineering; consumer credit; financial services; EC law; competition; land; housing; landlord and tenant; and family and inheritance.

Members of chambers also practise at the above address in association with the English barristers of the firm of Stanbrook & Hooper, 2 Rue de Taciturne, B-1000 Brussels under the name **Stanbrook and Henderson.**

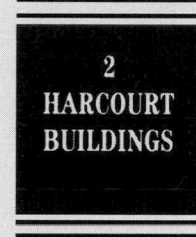

2 HARCOURT BUILDINGS

SET NUMBER
88

2 HARCOURT BUILDINGS (Nigel Mylne QC)

2 HARCOURT BUILDINGS, TEMPLE, LONDON, EC4Y 9DB
Tel: (0171) 353 2112 **Fax:** (0171) 353 8339 **DX:** 489

MEMBERS:

Nigel Mylne QC (1963)
(QC-1984)
John Bevan QC (1970)
(QC-1997) MA (Cantab)
Nicholas Atkinson QC
(1971) (QC-1991)
Peter Cooper QC (1974)
(QC-1993) LLB
John Williams (1973) LLB
Stephen Clayton (1973)
Stephen Smyth (1974)
Nicholas Loraine-Smith
(1977) BA (Oxon)
William Adlard (1978)
Philip Shorrock (1978) BA
(Cantab)
Robin Leach (1979) MA
(St Andrews)
Mark Gadsden (1980) BA
(Oxon)

Aftab Jafferjee (1980) BA
(Dunelm)
Timothy Probert-Wood
(1983) LLB (Hull)
Rhyddian Willis (1984) LLB
(Nottingham)
Ian Darling (1985) LLB
(London)
Lucia Whittle-Martin (1985)
BSc (London)
Patrick Gibbs (1986) BA
(Oxon)
Jonathan Rees (1987) BA
(Oxon)
Matthew Farmer (1987) BA
(London)
Peter Clement (1988) LLM
LLB (London)
Marina Churchill (1989) LLB
(Buckingham)
Laura Cobbs (1989) LLB
(Buckingham)

Stewart Hamblin (1990) BA
(Leicester)
Toby Fitzgerald (1993) BSc
(Bristol)
Thomas Wilkins (1993) BSc
(Bristol)
James Dawes (1993) BSc
(Dunelm)
Lisa Wilding (1993) MA
(Cantab)
Peter Coombe (1994) BA
(Oxon)
Sally Halkerston (1994) BA
(Kingston)
Sally Thompson (1994)
AGSM
Benedict Kelleher (1994)
LLB MSc (Bristol)
William Emlyn Jones (1996)
(Soton) LLB

Head of Chambers:
Nigel Mylne QC

Senior Clerk:
Michael Watts

Tenants: 33

The Chambers: A substantial and long established set with 4 QCs and two Junior Treasury Counsel which concentrates exclusively on criminal work.

Work Undertaken: Members of Chambers cover all criminal work for both prosecution and defence, practising on the South Eastern and Western Circuits. In addition to handling cases from murder to shoplifting, members specialise in commercial, revenue and VAT frauds, drugs

Continues overleaf

cases, extradition, defences under the Food and Drugs Act, Courts Martial and ecclesiastical jurisdiction.

Clientele: Both individuals and public and private companies.

Pupillage: Applicants for pupillage to Mr. Ian Darling. Applications can be sent at any time. Chambers have four to five pupils completing six and twelve month pupillages at any one time.

SET NUMBER 89

2 HARCOURT BUILDINGS (Mr Gerard Ryan QC)

2 HARCOURT BUILDINGS, TEMPLE, LONDON, EC4Y 9DB
Tel: (0171) 353 8415 **Fax:** (0171) 353 7622 **DX:** 402 LDE **Email:** CLERKS@TWOHARCOURTBLDGS.DEMON.CO.UK

MEMBERS:

Gerard Ryan QC (1955) (QC-1981)
Sheila Cameron QC (1957) (QC-1983)
Robin Purchas QC (1968) (QC-1987)
Richard Phillips QC (1970) (QC-1990)
Charles George QC (1974) (QC-1992)
Keith Lindblom QC (1980) (QC-1996)

Christopher Beaumont (1950)
Robert McCracken (1973)
Philip Petchey (1976)
Jonathan Milner (1977)
Andrew Kelly (1978)
Timothy Comyn (1980)
Andrew Tait (1981)
Craig Howell Williams (1983)
Suzanne Ornsby (1986)

Meyric Lewis (1986)
Andrew Newcombe (1987)
Charles Mynors (1988)
Gregory Jones (1991)
Douglas Edwards (1992)
Euan Burrows (1995)
Joanna Clayton (1995)
James Pereira (1996)

Head of Chambers:
Mr Gerard Ryan QC
Senior Clerk:
Allen Collier
First Junior Clerk: Paul Munday
Second Junior Clerk: Andrew Briton
Tenants: 23

The Chambers: A specialist Chambers for more than half a century with particular expertise in planning, environmental, property, and administrative law. Disabled conference facilities are available by prior arrangement. Members accept Direct Professional Access from the approved professions. A Chambers brochure is available on request.

All members of Chambers belong to the Planning and Environment Bar Association of which Douglas Edwards is Secretary. Members of Chambers also belong to the Administrative Law Bar Association, the Bar European Group, the Association for Regulated Procurement, the United Kingdom Environmental Law Association, the Ecclesiastical Law Society, The Education Law Society and the Parliamentary Bar.

Two members of Chambers are Deputy High Court Judges, four are Recorders of the Crown Court and three are Diocesan Chancellors. Craig Howell Williams and Meyric Lewis are members of the Supplementary Panel of Junior Counsel to the Crown. Gerard Ryan QC chaired the Tribunal of Inquiry into the gas explosion at Loscoe, Derbyshire. Charles George QC conducted the Independent Inquiry into Planning Decisions in the London Borough of Brent. Robert McCracken was Chairman of the United Kingdom Environmental Law Association. Christopher Beaumont is a Chairman of the Agricultural Land Tribunal. Sheila Cameron QC is Vicar General of the Province of Canterbury and was a Parliamentary Boundary Commissioner for England. Richard Phillips QC is an assistant Parliamentary Boundary Commissioner for England.

Publications include: *Education Case Reports* (editor-in-chief), *Journal of Planning and Environment Law* (editorial board), *Journal of Architectural Conservation* (editorial board), *Planning Appeal Decisions* (joint editor), and *Planning and Environmental Law Bulletin* (joint editor). Charles Mynors is the author of *'Planning Applications and Appeals'* (1987), *'Planning Control and the Display of Advertisements'* (1992) and *'Listed Buildings and Conservation Areas'* (1995).

Main Areas of Work: planning, environmental, compulsory purchase, administrative, local government finance, public procurement, parliamentary, transport and works, energy, utilities, education, highways, licensing, housing, human rights (European Convention) and EC Law.

Additional Areas: ecclesiastical law, landlord and tenant, the law of commons and that relating to easements, agricultural tenancies, rating and restrictive covenants.

Foreign Connections: Chambers include members called to the Dublin and Northern Ireland Bars.

Former Members of Chambers include: Roy Vandermeer QC, currently Inspector at the Heathrow Terminal Five inquiry; Peter Boydell QC, former Leader of the Parliamentary Bar and first Chairman of what is now the Planning and Environment Bar Association; Michael Harrison QC, now Mr Justice Harrison and Sir John Drinkwater QC.

SET NUMBER
90 # HARCOURT CHAMBERS (Patrick Eccles QC)

2 HARCOURT BUILDINGS, TEMPLE, LONDON, EC4Y 9DB
Tel: (0171) 353 6961 **Fax:** (0171) 353 6968 **DX:** 373

MEMBERS:

Hugh Eccles QC (1968) (QC-1990) MA (Oxon)

Roger Evans (1970) MA (Cantab)

June Rodgers (1971) MA (Dublin), MA(Oxon), Chancellor Diocese of Gloucester

Benedict Sefi (1972) BA (Oxon)

John Dixon (1975) MA (Oxon)

Gavyn Arthur (1975) MA (Oxon)

Stephen Barstow (1976) MA (Cantab)

Jonathan Baker (1978) MA (Cantab)

Alicia Collinson (1982) MA, MPhil (Oxon)

Christopher Frazer (1983) MA, LLM (Cantab)

Frances Judd (1984) BA (Cantab)

Edward Hess (1985) MA (Cantab)

Clive Blackwood (1986) BA (Cantab)

Matthew Brett (1987) BA (Oxon)

Napier Miles (1989) BA (Oxon)

Camilla De Sousa Turner (1989) BA (Cantab)

Piers Pressdee (1991) BA (Cantab)

Sara Granshaw (1991) BA (Oxon)

Sally Max (1991) BA(Cantab)

Rohan Auld (1992) BA(Cantab)

Richard Gregory (1993) BA (Cantab)

John Vater (1995) BA (Oxon)

Nicholas Goodwin (1995) BA (Oxon)

Aidan Vine (1995) BA (Oxon) MA (Cornell)

Door Tenant: Peter Clarke (1970) BA, BCL (Oxon)

Head of Chambers:
Patrick Eccles QC

Senior Clerk:
Brain Wheeler

Tenants: 25

The Chambers: A Long-established set of common law chambers with a history dating back to the mid-nineteenth century. Many former members of chambers have attained high judicial office, including one Lord Chancellor.

Harcourt Chambers offers an advisory and advocacy service, principally in the areas of Family Law, and Commercial, Property, Personal Injury and Professional Liability Law.

Harcourt Chambers comprises leading and junior counsel who practice from the Temple and, for the convenience of circuit solicitors, from premises in Oxford. Members of chambers seek to provide an efficient and friendly service for solicitors in London, the Home Counties and the Thames Valley, the Midland and Oxford Circuit and Gloucestershire.

HARCOURT CHAMBERS
London & Oxford

SET NUMBER
91 # HARDWICKE BUILDING (Walter Aylen QC)

HARDWICKE BUILDING, NEW SQUARE, LINCOLN'S INN, LONDON, WC2A 3SB
Tel: (0171) 242 2523 **Fax:** (0171) 691 1234 **DX:** LDE393 **Email:** CLERKS@HARDWICKE.CO.UK **Internet:** WWW.HARDWICKE.CO.UK

MEMBERS:

Walter Aylen QC (1962) (QC-1983)

Nicholas Stewart QC (1971) (QC-1987)

George F. Pulman QC (1971) (QC-1989)

Romie Tager QC (1970) (QC-1995)

Philip Raynor QC (1973) (QC-1994)

Zoe Smith (1970)

Robert Willer (1970)

Michael Hopmeier (1974)

Kenneth Craig (1975)

Philip Kremen (1975)

Nigel Jones (1976)

Stephen Lennard (1976)

Stephen Warner (1976)

John Landaw (1976)

James Vine (1977)

Steven Weddle (1977)

Michael Oliver (1977)

Philip Wakeham (1978)

Nicholas Baker (1980)

Rory Field (1980)

David Matthias (1980)

Indira Ramsahoye (1980)

David Aaronberg (1981)

Hugh Jackson (1981)

Alan Smith (1981)

Neil Mendoza (1982)

Daniel Flahive (1982)

William Bojczuk (1983)

Ian Brook (1983)

Timothy Banks (1983)

Gerard Forlin (1984)

John Greenan (1984)

Debbie Taylor (1984)

Charles Briefel (1984)

Lindsey MacDonald (1985)

Karl King (1985)

Justin Webster (1985)

Montague Palfrey (1985)

Jonathan Whitfield (1985)

Dr Richard Ough (1985)

Michelle Stevens-Hoare (1986)

Tom Nicholson Pratt (1986)

James Mulholland (1986)

Francis Lloyd (1987)

Judith Spooner (1987)

Paul Reed (1988)

Peter Kirby (1989)

Ann Mulligan (1989)

Steven Woolf (1989)

Caroline Hallissey (1990)

Alexis Campbell (1990)

Sara Benbow (1990)

Rachel Baker (1990)

Eithne Ryan (1990)

Ian Clarke (1990)

Kyriakos Argyropoulos (1991)

Kevin McCartney (1991)

Tony Horspool (1991)

Ingrid Newman (1992)

Colm Nugent (1992)

Richard Bates (1992)

David Preston (1993)

Julia Jarzabkowski (1993)

Emily Formby (1993)

Roshi Amiraftabi (1993)

Sabuhi Chaudhry (1993)

Niki Langridge (1993)

Brian St. Louis (1994)

John Clargo (1994)

Alexander Goold (1994)

David Leckie (1994)

Deanna Heer (1994)

Lynn Freeston (1996)

Philip Grey (1996)

Sa'id Mosteshar *

Jennet Treharne *

Stephen Joelson *

Pauline Gray *

* Door Tenant

Head of Chambers:
Walter Aylen QC

Clerks: Kevin Mitchell, Greg Piner, Gary Brown, Jason Housden

Tenants: 74

Continues overleaf

The Chambers: This large set has 74 members and practices mainly civil and commercial law, crime and family law. Notable specialisms include professional negligence, landlord and tenant and international child abduction. Hardwicke Building is a modern progressive set with a strong business culture. It is committed to providing a specialist, high quality service to all its solicitors. Members act for corporate and non-corporate clients as well as local authorities, government agencies and other professionals with direct access to the Bar.

Walter Aylen Q.C became head of chambers in 1991, as a result of its continued expansion, its premises became too small and chambers moved into its current, modern premises in August 1996.

Membership of chambers is regulated to suit the changing demands of the legal marketplace so that appropriately qualified specialist counsel are available for all classes of cases, at all levels, including publicly funded litigation and conditional fee work. Developments in the past year include the recruitment of Daniel Flahive, James Mulholland, Gerard Forlin and Philip Grey to strengthen the specialist criminal group in chambers.

Technology has an important role in chambers as a whole and it has this year appointed an I.T manager. Tenants practice individually and in groups using the latest networked computer technology from research and conference facilities. As part of its technology development, chambers are installing video conferencing facilities to improve its communication with clients, both in the UK and overseas.

Work Undertaken:

General Description: The Main groups in chambers are civil, crime and family. Within the civil group, which undertakes a broad spectrum of commercial work, there are also a number of specialist teams covering professional negligence, landlord and tenant, personal injury and medical negligence. Hardwicke Building is one of the foremost sets in the area of professional negligence and has represented clients in many leading cases, both at first instance and in the Court of Appeal. Both the civil and family groups are able to provide arbitration and mediation facilities as well as trained arbitrators and mediators.

The Criminal Group is 32 strong and carries out the entire range of both defence and prosecution work (including CPS, SFO, FIG and Customs and Excise). Some members of the group have particular specialisation in the conduct of cases of serious fraud.

The Family Team of 15 members undertakes all aspects of family and matrimonial work and is especially strong in the field of financial and international child abduction.

Chambers has a strong commitment to providing a range of specialist barristers whose individual skills appropriately reflect the demands of specialist solicitors. It is anticipated that chambers will continue to grow to meet the increasing demand for its specialist skills.

Main Areas of Work:

Arbitration	Defamation	Matrimonial and Family
Administration	Employment	Media & Entertainment
Banking	Energy	Partnership
Bankruptcy	Equity, Wills & Trusts	Personal Injury & Medical
Building and Construction	Financial Services	Negligence
Chancery	Fraud	Planning
Care/Children	Housing	Probate
Common Law	Insolvency	Professional Negligence
Commercial	Insurance	Property
Company	Intellectual Property	Public Law and Public
Contract	International Law	Utilities
Conveyancing	Judicial Review	Sale of Goods
Corporate Fraud	Landlord and Tenant	Satellite &
Criminal	Licensing	Telecommunications
		Sports Law

Languages Spoken: English, French, Farsi, German, Greek, Hindi, Italian, Portuguese, Russian, Spanish, Urdu.

SET NUMBER

92 HARDWICKE CHAMBERS (Sa'id Mosteshar) Hardwicke Building, Lincoln's Inn, London, WC2A 3SB **Tel:** (0171) 402 2010 **Fax:** (0171) 402 3231 **DX:** 393 **Email:** Info@Mosteshar.com **Clerk:** Lesley Richardson **Tenants:** 1 Specialist practitioner with expertise in communications and broadcasting law, information technology law and space law.

SET NUMBER
93 **1 HARE COURT** (Lord Neill of Bladen QC & Richard Southwell QC)

1 HARE COURT, TEMPLE, LONDON, EC4Y 7BE
Tel: (0171) 353 3171 **Fax:** (0171) 583 9127 **DX:** 0065 (CH.LN.) **Email:** ADMIN-ONEHARECOURT@BTINTERNET.COM

MEMBERS:

Lord Neill of Bladen QC (1951) (QC-1966)

Richard Southwell QC (1959) (QC-1977)

Howard Page QC (1967) (QC-1987)

Nicolas Bratza QC (1969) (QC-1988) *

Nicholas Padfield QC (1972) (QC-1991)

Julian Malins QC (1972) (QC-1991)

William Ballantyne (1977)

Paul Smith (1978)

Dominic Dowley (1983)

James Eadie (1984)

Andrew J. Moran (1989)

Nicholas Lavender (1989)

Khawar M. Qureshi (1990)

Alison Padfield (1992)

Jonathan Adkin (1997)

* Member of the European Commission of Human Rights.

Joint Heads of Chambers:
Lord Neill of Bladen QC &
Richard Southwell QC

Senior Clerks: Barry C. Ellis
Paul Ballard

Tenants: 15

Door Tenant: Professor Ingrid De Lupis Frankopan (1977).

The Chambers: A long-established set of chambers specialising in commercial, international, and related fields of litigation, arbitration and legal advice. Richard Southwell QC is President of Lloyd's Appeal Tribunal and Howard Page QC is Deputy President of Lloyd's Appeal Tribunal. The chambers are members of the Commercial Bar Association (COMBAR). James R. Eadie (Junior Counsel to the Crown, Common Law).

Work Undertaken:

General Description: All aspects of commercial practice, with an emphasis on international work.

Main Areas of Work: Arbitration; commercial contracts; banking; international trade; insurance and reinsurance; construction and engineering; commercial fraud; negotiable instruments; documentary credits; commercial aspects of company and insolvency law; partnerships; Privy Council appeals; professional negligence; constitutional and administrative law; financial markets and services; public international law; conflict of laws.

Additional Areas: Scandinavian and environmental law (Professor De Lupis Frankopan); and Arab laws (Professor Ballantyne).

Arbitrators: Certain members of Chambers are highly experienced in the field of arbitration (international, commercial and construction: ICC, LCIA, Lloyds, UNCITRAL, amongst others).

Clientele: Brochure available on request. Chambers operate the Direct Professional Access scheme.

Foreign Connections: A high proportion of work originates overseas. Subject to admission to local bars, instructions are accepted to appear in the courts of Hong Kong, Singapore, Malaysia and other foreign jurisdictions. The chambers are members of the London Court of International Arbitration.

Former Members: Sir Henry Fisher, President of Wolfson College, Oxford 1975-85, Arbitrator; Lord Slynn of Hadley, Lord of Appeal in Ordinary (former Judge of the Court of Justice of the European Communities); Sir Roger Parker, former Lord Justice of Appeal, Arbitrator; Sir Mark Waller, a Lord Justice of the High Court; H.H. Judge Raymond Jack QC, Circuit Mercantile Judge of the Bristol Mercantile Court.

1 HARE COURT (Stephen Kramer QC)

1 HARE COURT, TEMPLE, LONDON, EC4Y 7BE
Tel: (0171) 353 5324 **Fax:** (0171) 353 0667 **DX:** 444 (CH.LN.)

MEMBERS:

Stephen Kramer QC (1970) (QC-1995)	Paul Dodgson (1975)	Brian O'Neill (1987)
Sir Allan Green QC KCB (1959) (QC-1987)	Orlando Pownall (1975)	Kenneth Millett (1988)
Paul Worsley QC (1970) (QC-1990)	Andrew Radcliffe (1975)	Michael Logsdon (1988)
Martin S Heslop QC (1972) (QC-1995)	Martin Hicks (1977)	Brendan Kelly (1988)
	Jeremy Benson (1978)	Parmjit-Kaur Cheema (1989)
Charles Salmon QC (1972) (QC-1996)	Andrew Lloyd-Eley (1979)	Christopher Hehir (1990)
	Andrew Colman (1980)	Alex Lewis (1990)
Brian Warner (1969)	Ian Leist (1981)	Craig Ferguson (1992)
Nicholas Coleman (1970)	David Howker (1982)	Kate Bex (1992)
Jacqueline Samuel (1971)	Jonathan Laidlaw (1982)	Nina Grahame (1993)
John Jones (1972)	Sally Howes (1983)	Christopher Foulkes (1994)
David Waters (1973)	James Dawson (1984)	Matthew Johnson (1995)
Louise Kamill (1974)	Sallie Bennett-Jenkins (1984)	Oliver Glasgow (1995)
	Michael Holland (1984)	Riel Karmy-Jones (1995)
	Shani Barnes (1986)	

Head of Chambers:
Stephen Kramer QC

Senior Clerk:
Deryk Butler

First Junior Clerk: Ian Fitzgerald

Chambers Administrator:
Stephen Wall

Tenants: 40

The Chambers: Chambers has long been established as a set specialising in criminal law and ancillary matters. Members prosecute and defend at all levels and act for many firms of solicitors, both large and small, throughout England and Wales.

Specialisations include commercial fraud and corruption cases, financial services work, trade descriptions, and extradition.

2 HARE COURT (P Baxendale QC and C Flint QC) 2 Hare Court, Temple, London, EC4Y 7BH **Tel:** (0171) 583 1770 **Fax:** (0171) 822 7222 **DX:** 281 **Clerk:** Martin Smith **Tenants:** 54 See entry for Blackstone Chambers, Blackstone House, Temple, London, EC4.

3 HARE COURT (William Clegg QC)

3 HARE COURT, TEMPLE, LONDON, EC4Y 7BJ
Tel: (0171) 353 7561 **Fax:** (0171) 353 7741 **DX:** 17

MEMBERS:

William Clegg QC (1972) (QC-1991) *.	Nigel Ingram (1972) ++	Gelaga King (1985)
The Rt. Hon. John Morris QC (1954) (QC-1973) *	Mark Halsey (1974)	Timothy Kendal (1985)
	Robert Neill (1975)	Mark Milliken-Smith (1986)
Michael Lewis QC (1956) (QC-1975) *	Andrew Williams (1975)	Christopher Campbell-Clyne (1988)
Howard Godfrey QC (1970) (QC-1991) *	Margaret Barnes (1976)	
	John Caudle (1976)	Richard Matthews (1989)
Andrew Munday QC (1973) (QC-1996)	Anthony Abell (1977)	Thomas Derbyshire (1989)
	Philip Hackett (1978)	Jonathan Ashley Norman (1989)
T. Alun Jenkins QC (1972) (QC-1996) *	John Dodd (1979)	
	Michael Levy (1979)	Craig Rush (1989)
Peter Griffiths QC (1970) (QC-1995) *	Margaret Dodd (1979) +	James Ageros (1990)
	John Livingston (1980)	Christine Agnew (1992)
Nigel Lithman QC (1976) (QC-1997)	Maura McGowan (1980)	Michael Epstein (1992)
	Brian Altman (1981) **	Valerie Charbit (1992)
Robert Flach (1950)	Peter Lodder (1981)	Adam Budworth (1992)
Ronald Trott (1956) +	Keith Mitchell (1981)	John Hurlock (1993)
Charles Conway (1969)	James Sturman (1982)	Alison Pople (1993)
Deborah Champion (1970) *	Jane McIvor (1983)	Christine Henson (1994)

+Door Tenant
*Recorder
++Standing Counsel to the Department of Trade & Industry
**Junior Treasury Counsel at CCC

Head of Chambers:
William Clegg QC

Senior Clerk:
John Grimmer

Tenants: 44

The Chambers: 3 Hare Court is a leading set of specialist criminal practitioners at the forefront of Defence and Prosecution work in the South East and throughout the country, as well as abroad. The seven Silks and body of active juniors spread across the call range are well respected and frequently involved in high profile cases. Fraud remains an important part of chambers' practice embracing corporate, financial services, insolvency, D.T.I., revenue and

V.A.T. Some members of Chambers specialise in Divisional and Appellate Courts proceedings and undertake regulatory and supervisory bodies tribunal advocacy. All aspects of pre-trial advice and representation are competently provided and Chambers is able to offer a 24 hour clerking service for emergencies and overnight cases.

Additional Areas of Work: Immigration, extradition, licensing.

Languages: Dutch, French, German, Hebrew and Welsh, Italian, Serbo-Croat and Krio (Sierra Leone).

SET NUMBER
97 HOLBORN CHAMBERS (Stuart Stevens) 6 Gate Street, Lincoln's Inn Fields, London, WC2A 3HP **Tel:** (0171) 242 6060 **Fax:** (0171) 242 2777 **DX:** 159 **Clerk:** Anthony Halls **Tenants:** 34 Varied practice including work in the areas of crime, civil, matrimonial, landlord and tenant, industrial and land tribunals and chancery.

SET NUMBER
98 INTERNATIONAL LAW CHAMBERS (Sami D. El-Falahi) ILC House, 77-79 Chepstow Road, Bayswater, London, W2 5QR **Tel:** (0171) 221 5684 **Fax:** (0171) 221 5685 **Clerk:** Mrs Christine Lanscombe **Tenants:** 2

SET NUMBER
99 JOHN STREET CHAMBERS 2 John Street, London, WC1N 2HJ **Tel:** (0171) 242 1911 **Fax:** (0171) 242 2515 **DX:** 1000 Chancery Lane **Tenants:** 11 Chambers established in 1997. Specialisms in crime, civil & commercial, immigration (including judicial review), family, personal injury, employment, human rights and mental health (including judicial review).

SET NUMBER
100 KEATING CHAMBERS (Richard Fernyhough QC)

10 ESSEX STREET, OUTER TEMPLE, LONDON, WC2R 3AA
Tel: (0171) 544 2600 **Fax:** (0171) 240 7722 **DX:** 1045

MEMBERS:

Richard Fernyhough QC (1970) (QC-1986)	Vivian Ramsey QC (1979) (QC-1992)	Michael Bowsher (1985)
John Uff QC (1970) (QC-1983)	Robert Gaitskell QC (1978) (QC-1994)	Alexander Nissen (1985)
Martin Collins QC (1952) (QC-1972)	Philip Boulding QC (1979) (QC-1996)	Nerys Jefford (1986)
Christopher Thomas QC (1973) (QC-1989)	Alan Steynor (1975)	Louise Randall (1988)
John Marrin QC (1974) (QC-1990)	Rosemary Jackson (1981)	Robert Evans (1989)
Stephen Furst QC (1975) (QC-1991)	Marcus Taverner (1981)	Sarah Hannaford (1989)
Timothy Elliott QC (1975) (QC-1992)	Peter Coulson (1982)	Simon Hargreaves (1991)
	Ian Pennicott (1982)	Richard Harding (1992)
	Paul Darling (1983)	Jane Lemon (1993)
	Finola O'Farrell (1983)	Piers Stansfield (1993)
	Adrian Williamson (1983)	Jonathan Lee (1993)
		Simon Hughes (1995)
		Abdul-Lateef Jinadu (1995)
		Sandip Jobanputra (1996)

Head of Chambers:
Richard Fernyhough QC
Senior Clerk:
Barry Bridgman
Tenants: 32

The Chambers: Keating Chambers is active in all aspects of construction and engineering law, disputes involving professional negligence, information technology and other property-related matters. Members of Chambers are involved in litigation and arbitration in the United Kingdom and abroad as advocates, arbitrators, legal assessors, adjudicators and mediators.

Members of Keating Chambers are involved in building disputes, disputes relating to civil, mechanical and electrical engineering projects, computers, process plant, the oil and gas industry and dredging. Chambers is also active in environmental law, EU procurement law and Information Technology (including Year 2000 problems).

Work Undertaken:
General Description: All aspects of construction and engineering law, landlord and tenant and other property-related work.
Main Areas of Work: Building and engineering contracts, in the UK and abroad, litigation and arbitration (including ICC and FIDIC arbitration), development contracts, contractual claims under construction contracts, claims in respect of defective buildings, professional negligence in building and construction matters. Local authority work (including building control work). European community law in particular public procurement.
Appointments as Arbitrator: Senior members of chambers act as arbitrators and legal assessors, through the ICC, internationally and in the UK, ranging from very substantial

Continues overleaf

construction and commercial matters to the smaller arbitrations.

Additional Areas of Work: Mechanical and chemical engineering cases – most types of commercial and insurance contracts – general professional negligence – performance bonds and warranties – Mareva and other types of injunctions. Some members also practise in information technology law, aviation law, landlord and tenant, planning and other property-related matters.

Nature of Clientele: Building contractors; property developers and owners; specialist contractors; government departments and agencies; local authorities; architects; engineers; quantity surveyors; surveyors; insurance companies and professional indemnity insurers.

Foreign Connections: Many members of chambers act and advise in litigation or arbitration abroad, in particular in Hong Kong, Singapore, the Middle East and in Paris (the headquarters of the ICC).

Recruitment: Both six and twelve month pupillages are offered. Awards of up to £20,000 over a twelve month period are available to pupils.

ONE KING'S BENCH WALK (James Townend QC)

1 KING'S BENCH WALK, TEMPLE, LONDON, EC4Y 7DB
Tel: (0171) 936 1500 **Fax:** (0171) 936 1590 **DX:** L.D.E. 20 DELIVERY ONLY **Email:** DDEAR@1KBW.CO.UK **Internet:** WWW.1KBW.CO.UK

MEMBERS:

James Townend QC (1962) (QC-1978) MA (Oxon)

Anthony Hacking QC (1965) (QC-1983) MA (Oxon)

Rodger Hayward Smith QC (1967) (QC-1988) MA (Oxon)

Barry Singleton QC (1968) (QC-1989) MA (Cantab)

Judith Parker QC (1973) (QC-1991) BA (Oxon)

Camden Pratt QC (1970) (QC-1992) MA (Oxon)

Pamela Scriven QC (1970) (QC-1992) LLB (London)

Richard Anelay QC (1970) (QC-1993) BA (Bristol)

Roderic Wood QC (1974) (QC-1993) BA (Oxon)

Stephen Bellamy QC (1974) (QC-1996) MA (Cantab)

Michael Gale QC (1957) (QC-1989) BA (Cantab)

Gordon Jackson QC (1979) (QC-1989) LLB (St. Andrews)

James Turner QC (1976) (QC-1998) LLB (Hull)

Andrew McFarlane QC (1977) (QC-1998) **

Clive Newton (1968) MA (Oxon), BCL (Oxon)

Michael Warren (1971) MA (Oxon)

Andrew McDowall (1972) MA (Oxon), BCL (Lond)

John Reddish (1973) MA (Oxon)

Charles Kemp (1973) LLB (Lond)

John Tanzer (1975) BA

David Rennie (1976) BA

Caroline Budden (1977)

Caroline Lister (1980)

Anthony Kirk (1981) LLB (Lond), AKC

Susan R Maidment (1968) LLB, LLM (LSE), LLD (Keele)

Julian Woodbridge (1981)

Christopher Pocock (1984) BA (Oxon)

Stephen Shay (1984) BA (Oxon)

Deborah Eaton (1985)

Sarah O'Connor (1986) LLB

Deiniol Cellan-Jones (1988) BA (Oxon)

Philip Marshall (1989) LLB

Elizabeth Selman (1989) LLB (Lond)

Richard Barton (1990)

Marcus Fletcher (1990)

Caroline Gibson (1990)

Joanna Grice (1991)

Rebecca James (1992)

James Roberts (1993)

Richard Harrison (1993)

Ian Cook (1994)

Shona Mulholland (1994)

Graham Crosthwaite (1995)

Adam Jay (1995)

Benedick Rayment (1996)

Sean Esprit (1996)

Head of Chambers:
James Townend QC

Senior Clerk:
David Dear

Tenants: 46

The Chambers: These chambers are a large, long established set, specialising in family and criminal law, with strength at all levels of seniority. Teams of counsel are provided for more protracted, complex and important cases. The work of chambers is principally in London and on the South Eastern Circuit, but work is also undertaken throughout the country.

Work Undertaken:

Main Areas of Work: The chambers specialise in all aspects of family law, including matrimonial finance and child care litigation, and in criminal law, both prosecution and defence, including serious fraud work.

Other Areas of Work: The chambers have varied common law expertise. *Work includes:* personal injury, professional and medical negligence, contracts (including sale of goods), planning, landlord and tenant, judicial review, insolvency, employment and industrial disputes, tribunals, inquiries and Official Referees' business, police cases and human rights cases in the UK and at the European Court.

Memberships: Institute of Chartered Arbitrators, British Institute of International & Comparative Law, Family Law Bar Association and International Academy of Matrimonial Lawyers.

Publications: R. Hayward Smith QC & Clive Newton are the editors of Jackson's *Matrimonial Finance & Taxation*. James Turner QC and Stephen Shay are editors of Archbold: *Criminal Pleading Evidence & Practice*. Andrew McFarlane QC is co-author of Hershman and McFarlane: *Children Law and Practice*.

Also At: Kings Bench Chambers, 174 High Street, Lewes, BN7 1YE
Tel: (01273) 402600; *Fax:* (01273) 402609

2 KING'S BENCH WALK (Lord Campbell of Alloway QC)

2 KING'S BENCH WALK, TEMPLE, LONDON, EC4Y 7DE
Tel: (0171) 353 9276 **Fax:** (0171) 353 9949 **DX:** 477 CHANCERY LANE **Email:** CHAMBERS@2KBW.CO.UK

MEMBERS:

Lord Campbell of Alloway ERD QC (1939) (QC-1965)
George Papageorgis (1981)
Philip Rueff (1969)
Anthony Dalgleish (1971)
Alun Evans (1971)
Rene Yee Lock Wong (1973)
Jefferson Colgate-Stone (1974)
Ian Slack (1974)
David Mendes da Costa (1976)

Robert Gifford (1977)
Patricia Lloyd (1979)
Sheila Gaylord (1983)
Anthony Levy (1983)
Jeremy Lynn (1983) B.Sc.
David Markham (1983)
Sarah Davies (1984)
Deepak Kapur (1984)
Simon Livesey (1987)
Stephen Perian (1987)
Nan Alban-Lloyd (1988)
Vishnu Gokhool (1989)

Gregory Meadowcroft (1990) LLB (Leic) LLM (Lond) (M July 1990)
Claudia Lorenzo (1991)
Brian Kennedy (1992)
Tanya Callman (1993)
Arun Katyar (1993)
David Sandeman (1993)
Lee Freeman (1994)
Janice Johnson (1994)
Abigail Dean (1995)
Lachlan Wilson (1996)

Head of Chambers:
George Papageorgis
Titular Head of Chambers:
Lord Campbell of Alloway ERD QC
Senior Clerk: Brenda Anderson
Tenants: 31

These Chambers are located on the first and second floors of one of the oldest buildings in the Temple, built by Christopher Wren.

A wide range of work is undertaken in the field of General Common Law as well as Criminal Law, Family Law, Administrative Law, work before Tribunals, Education Law, Employment Law and Human Rights.

Constant review is kept on the changing needs of solicitors and the public, while at the same time the Bar's traditional values are maintained and fostered by members who present a welcoming attitude to lay and professional clients.

2 KING'S BENCH WALK (Anthony Donne QC) 2 King's Bench Walk, Temple, London, EC4Y 7DE **Tel:** (0171) 353 1746 **Fax:** (0171) 583 2051 **DX:** 1032 **Clerk:** Mr R.L.D. Plager **Tenants:** 63 The chambers have an annexe in Plymouth, Devon.

4 KING'S BENCH WALK (Nicholas Jarman QC)

4 KING'S BENCH WALK, TEMPLE, LONDON, EC4Y 7DL
Tel: (0171) 353 3581 **Fax:** (0171) 583 2257 **DX:** 1050

MEMBERS:

Nicholas Jarman QC (1965) (QC-1985)
Basil Hillman (1968)
Robert Spencer Bernard (1969)
Christopher Cousins (1969)
John Gilbert Harvey (1973)
Moira Pooley (1974)
John Denniss (1974)
David A. Pearl (1977)
Barnaby Evans (1978)
John Riley (1983)
Reginald Arkhurst (1984)

Jane Alt (1984)
Philip Goddard (1985)
Peter Nightingale (1986) *
Benjamin Gumpert (1987)
Andrew Granville Stafford (1987)
Rhodri Williams (1987)
Adrienne Morgan (1988) *
Satvinder Juss (1989)
Claire Jacobs (1989)
John Metcalf (1990) *
Kevin Higgins (1990)
Paul Wakerley (1990)

Kate Mather (1990)
Fiona McCreath (1991)
Cressida Murphy (1991)
Michael Skelley (1991)
Kim Preston (1991)
Suki Johal (1991)
Giles Curtis-Raleigh (1992)
Hefin Rees (1992)
Brendan Davis (1994)
Benn Maguire (1994)
Amanda Drane (1996)

Head of Chambers:
Nicholas Jarman QC
Clerks: Lee Cook, Philip Burnell Jayne Barnes, Simon Morris
Tenants: 34

*Formerly a solicitor

Chambers provides expertise in almost every area of common law. Notable specialisims include contract, crime, employment, european community, family, immigration, personal injury, property, planning and professional negligence.

Contract and commercial work includes experience in the sale of goods, supply of services, consumer credit, partnership, mortgages, insolvency and bankruptcy, as well as passing off, commercial fraud, insurance, banking and guarantee, building and construction.

A wide range of criminal work is undertaken at all levels on behalf of both defendants and prosecuting authorities. Specialities include serious violent and sexual crime, fraud and drug related offences among others.

There is expertise within chambers in european community law, in particular the free movement of goods and services and EC public procurement law.

Continues overleaf

All aspects of employment law are handled including wrongful and unfair dismissal, discrimination and trade union law. Immigration expertise covers rights of asylum seekers, family members, visitors and applicants for work permits.

Family law is also a specialism, including ancillary relief and all child related matters. Members have experience in the related field of inheritance claims as well as wills and probate generally.

Personal injury work includes catastrophic injuries, industrial accidents and product liability. Professional negligence is regarded as a separate specialist area and includes medical negligence as well as claims against auditors, architects, engineers, lawyers and surveyors.

Comprehensive expertise is provided in all types of planning, environmental and local government law as well as related areas such as highways and compulsory purchase. Members have wide experience of judical review in these and other fields. Advice is given across a broad spectrum of land related matters, including business and residential tenencies, housing association matters, real property issues and general housing and land use disputes.

SET NUMBER 105 — 4 KING'S BENCH WALK (Robert Rhodes QC)

4 KING'S BENCH WALK, TEMPLE, LONDON, EC4Y 7DL
Tel: (0171) 822 8822 **Fax:** (0171) 822 8844 **DX:** 422 **Email:** 4KBW@BARRISTERSATLAW.COM / LAW@BARRISTERSATLAW.COM
Internet: WWW.BARRISTERSATLAW.COM

MEMBERS:

Robert Rhodes QC (1968) (QC-1989)
John Toogood (1957)
Keith Evans (1962)
Kenneth Cameron (1969)
William Rees (1973)
David Cattle (1975)
Greville Davis (1976)
Clive Anderson (1976)
Bruce Stuart (1977)
Graham Hulme (1977)
Margaret Howard (1977)
Chris Van Hagen (1980)

Alison Watts (1981)
Andrew Gordon-Saker (1981)
Justin Shale (1982)
Simon Stafford-Michael (1982)
David Harounoff (1984)
Martin Hurst (1985)
David Stern (1989)
Samuel Jarman (1989)
Graham Huston (1991)
Anne Crossfield (1993)
Nigel Hood (1993)

Emma Edhem (1993)
Katherine Dunn (1993)
Adrian Maxwell (1993)
Paul Bowen (1993)
Peter Shaw (1995)
Oliver Mishcon (1993)
Yutaka Yazawa (1994)
Nicola Murphy (1995)
Michael Nelson (1992)
Lawrence Power (1995)
Kimberley Aiken (1995)
Kimberley Farmer (1997)

Head of Chambers:
Robert Rhodes QC

Senior Clerk:
Ian Lee

Tenants: 35

Door Tenants: HHJ Heppel QC, Michel Y. Horton, Walter Rudeloff, Phillip Henry, Anika Khan.

The Chambers: Common law set specialising in commercial fraud, financial services, serious criminal fraud, commercial litigation, environmental law, and insurance and reinsurance. Also at King's Bench Chambers, 175 Holdenhurst Rd, Bournemouth, BN8 8DQ.

SET NUMBER 106

5 KING'S BENCH WALK (David Cocks QC) 18 Red Lion Court, London, EC4A 3EB **Tel:** (0171) 520 6000 Chambers have moved – please see entry under 18 Red Lion Court.

SET NUMBER 107 — 6 KING'S BENCH WALK (Sibghat Kadri QC)

6 KING'S BENCH WALK, TEMPLE, LONDON, EC4Y 7DR
Tel: (0171) 353 4931 / 583 0695 **Fax:** (0171) 353 1726 **DX:** 471 (CH.LN.)

MEMBERS:

Sibghat Kadri QC (1969) (QC-1989)
Tariq Rafiq (1961)
William Geldart (1975)
James Bowen (1979)
Harjit Grewal (1980)
Sylvester Carrott (1980)
Terence Gallivan (1981)
Linda Pearce (1982)
Manjit Singh Gill (1982)

Rambert De Mello (1983)
Andrew Gumbiti-Zimuto (1983)
Elizabeth Joseph (1983)
Michael Cogan (1986)
Robin Howat (1986)
Helen Clarke (1988)
Emily Driver (1988)
Martin Taylor (1988)
Alev Giz (1988)

Lorna Tagliavini (1989)
Manjit Singh Panesar (1989)
Rona Neathey (1991)
Malek Wan Daud (1991)
Stephen Knafler (1993)
Maryam Najand (1994)
Shahram Taghavi (1994)
Shereener Browne (1996)

Head of Chambers:
Sibghat Kadri QC

Senior Clerk:
Gary Jeffery

Tenants: 26

The Chambers: Established 25 years ago, this was the first multi-racial chambers at the Bar. The principle of equal access to the profession is of great importance hence the high representation of non-white and female members within chambers. The head of chambers S Kadri QC, recently elected a bencher of Inner Temple, has been at the forefront of fighting on race issues for many years including several racial violence trials. The set remains commited to criminal defence work. Members of chambers were responsible for setting up the Society of Black Lawyers in the 1970s.

The set does a range of civil and human rights work principally in areas of judicial review, immigration, housing, employment, race discrimination, local government and family. Several members of chambers are on the CRE's list of approved counsel. Over the years members of chambers have appeared in numerous reported cases.

SET NUMBER
108

6 KING'S BENCH WALK (Michael Worsley QC)

6 KING'S BENCH WALK, TEMPLE, LONDON, EC4Y 7DR
Tel: (0171) 583 0410 **Fax:** (0171) 353 8791 **DX:** 26 (CH.LN.)

MEMBERS:

Michael Worsley QC (1955) (QC-1985)
Ann Curnow QC (1957) (QC-1985)
Roy Amlot QC (1963) (QC-1989)
Ann Mallalieu QC (1970) (QC-1988)
James Curtis QC (1970) (QC-1993)
Victor Temple QC (1971) (QC-1993)
Dorian Lovell-Pank QC (1971) (QC-1993)
Joanna Korner QC (1974) (QC-1993)
Bruce Houlder QC (1969) (QC-1994)

David Spens QC (1973) (QC-1995)
David Fisher QC (1973) (QC-1996)
Wendy Joseph QC (1975) (QC-1998)
Howard Vagg (1974)
Jonathan Turner (1974)
Nigel Sweeney (1976)
Mark Dennis (1977)
Anthony Leonard (1978)
Philippa Jessel (1978)
Marks Moore (1979)
David Perry (1980)
John Ryder (1980)
Nicholas Hilliard (1981)
Sasha Wass (1981)

Andrew Brierley (1984)
Martyn Bowyer (1984)
Simon Denison (1984)
Emma Broadbent (1986)
Irena Ray-Crosby (1990)
Dean Armstrong (1985)
Peter Grieves-Smith (1989)
Timothy Cray (1989)
Simon Laws (1991)
Duncan Penny (1992)
Jason Dunn-Shaw (1992)
Annabel Darlow (1993)
Sarah Whitehouse (1993)
Duncan Atkinson (1995)
Annabel Pilling (1996)

Head of Chambers:
Michael Worsley QC

Senior Clerk:
David Garstang

Tenants: 38

The Chambers: A specialist criminal set with twelve QCs and one Senior and three Junior Treasury Counsel. Chambers have particular experience in advocacy in the higher courts. Members also handle civil work with individual specialisations.

Nine members of chambers are recorders and one is a D.T.I. Inspector. Additionally, members belong to the Criminal Bar Association and the Bar Senate. Mr. Dennis is an editor on *Archbold*.

Work Undertaken:

Main Areas of Work: *Criminal:* For both prosecution and defence mainly in London and the South Eastern Circuit specialising in commercial crime, fraud, VAT cases and regulatory work.
Civil: Libel, police law, false imprisonment/malicious prosecutions, some commercial, defamation and professional tribunals.
Other specialities: Members appear before coroners' courts, inquiries, disciplinary and industrial tribunals; also work is undertaken involving trade descriptions, extradition, licensing matters and human rights.

Foreign Languages: French, German, Italian and Spanish.

Recruitment & Training: Applications for tenancy should be sent to the Head of Chambers; those for pupillage to Duncan Penny. There are eight pupils in chambers at any one time. Awards and mini-pupillages are available.

SET NUMBER
109

7 KING'S BENCH WALK (Stephen Tomlinson QC)

7 KING'S BENCH WALK, TEMPLE, LONDON, EC4Y 7DS
Tel: (0171) 583 0404 **Fax:** (0171) 583 0950/353 2455 **DX:** 239 (CH.LN.) **Email:** CLERKS@7KBW.LAW.CO.UK

MEMBERS:

Stephen Tomlinson QC
(1974) (QC-1988) *
Adrian Hamilton QC (1949)
(QC-1973)
John Willmer QC (1955)
(QC-1967)
Jeremy Cooke QC (1976)
(QC-1990) +
Timothy Saloman QC (1975)
(QC-1993) +
Francis Reynolds QC (1960)
(QC-1993)
Gavin Kealey QC (1977)
(QC-1994)
Julian Flaux QC (1978)
(QC-1994)

Jonathan Gaisman QC
(1979) (QC-1995)
Dominic Kendrick QC
(1981) (QC-1997)
Charles Priday (1982)
Alistair Schaff (1983)
Adam Fenton (1984)
Stephen Hofmeyr (1982)
Christopher Butcher (1986)
Stephen Kenny (1987)
Richard Southern (1987)
Robert Bright (1987)
Gavin Geary (1989)
David Bailey (1989)

David Edwards (1989)
David Allen (1990)
Simon Picken (1989)
Andrew Wales (1992)
Siobán Healy (1993)
Stephen Phillips (1993)
Rebecca Sabben-Clare
(1993)
Jawdat Khurshid (1994)
Richard Waller (1994)
Leigh Williams (1996)
Timothy Kenefick (1996)
John Bignall (1997)

Head of Chambers:
Stephen Tomlinson QC

Clerks:
Linda Stinton, Bernie Hyatt,
Greg Leyden

Tenants: 32

*Recorder
+Assistant Recorder

Work Undertaken: Established in 1883, this set of chambers has had a successful and prestigious history. All members of Chambers specialise in commercial law. Much of the set's work is international in character.

Principal fields of practice include international trade and transport, insurance/reinsurance, shipping, professional negligence and banking. Other areas of specialisation include conflicts of law, financial services, oil and gas, and commodity transactions.

Most of Chambers' work is in the Commercial Court or in commercial arbitration in London; however, members of Chambers also appear in the European Courts of Justice, the Privy Council, and in jurisdictions such as Hong Kong, Singapore, Bermuda and the Cayman Islands.

Languages: Dutch, Flemish, French, German, Italian and Russian.

SET NUMBER
110

8 KING'S BENCH WALK (L.G. Woodley QC) 8 King's Bench Walk, Temple, London, EC4Y 7DU
Tel: (0171) 797 8888 **Fax:** (0171) 797 8880 **DX:** 195 **Clerk:** Mr Marc Foss **Tenants:** 54 General common law set undertaking both criminal and civil work.

SET NUMBER
111

9 KING'S BENCH WALK (Ali Mohammed Azhar) 9 King's Bench Walk, Temple, London, EC4Y 7DX **Tel:** (0171) 353 9564 **Fax:** (0171) 353 7943 **DX:** 118 Chancery Lane **Clerk:** John Lee **Tenants:** 18 Has practitioners in criminal, civil, family, immigration and industrial law. A mixed set with Asian, African and English barristers, two of whom are experts in Islamic and Hindu law.

SET NUMBER
112

9 KING'S BENCH WALK (F. Ashe Lincoln QC)

9 KING'S BENCH WALK, TEMPLE, LONDON, EC4Y 7DX
Tel: (0171) 353 7202 **Fax:** (0171) 583 2030 **DX:** 472 CHANCERY LANE

MEMBERS:

F. Ashe Lincoln QC (1929)
(QC-1947)
Surendra Popat (1969) *
Peter Gribble (1972)
Peter Marsh (1975)
Keith Stones (1975)
Alice Deschampsneufs
(1976)
Henry Michael Greenslade
(1982)

Amir Sultan (1983)
Isabel Delamere (1985)
Miles Trigg (1987)
William McGivern (1987)
Susan Brown (1989)
Zacharias Miah (1990)
Bosmath Sheffi (1991)
Gwen Bankole-Jones (1991)
Peter St John Howe (1992)

Michael Murhpy (1992)
Obi Obuka (1993)
Paul Pavlou (1993)
Elaine Sneller (1994)
Christopher Jacobs (1994)
Annunziata Villarosa (1995)
Richard Ladmore (1995)
Anne-Marie Lowey (1995)
Benjamin Burgher (1995)

Head of Chambers:
F. Ashe Lincoln QC

Senior Clerk:
Gary Morgan

Junior Clerks:
Gary Nichols/Alex McBlain

Tenants: 25

* Assistant Recorder

A long established common law set providing a high standard of service. Languages spoken include: French, German, Greek, Hebrew, Bengali, Punjabi, Urdu, Hindi. Areas of specialist practice include: commercial and general, civil, employment, housing, immigration, licensing, landlord and tenant, personal injury, professional negligence, sale of goods, crime, defence and prosecution at all levels, family law – all areas undertaken, chancery, trusts, insolvency land law and probate.

SET NUMBER
113 10 KING'S BENCH WALK (Jan Paulusz) 10 King's Bench Walk, Temple, London, EC4Y 7EB **Tel:** (0171) 353 7742 **Fax:** (0171) 583 0579 **DX:** 24 **Clerk:** Lee Kyprian **Tenants:** 26

SET NUMBER
114

10 KING'S BENCH WALK (Ronald Thwaites QC)

10 KING'S BENCH WALK, TEMPLE, LONDON, EC4Y 7EB
Tel: (0171) 353 2501 **Fax:** (0171) 353 0658 **DX:** 294 (CH.LN.)

MEMBERS:

Ronald Thwaites QC (1970) (QC-1987)	Robin Miric (1978) LLB	Michael Lee (1987) BA (UCLA), JD (Hons Suffolk Univ)
Winston Roddick QC (1968) (QC-1986)	Jonathan Woodcock (1981) LLB LSE LLM (Lon)	Trevor Berriman (1988) LLB Hons
Alper Riza QC (1973) (QC-1991)	Trevor Burke (1981)	Nigel Daniel (1988) LLB Hons
Georges M Khayat QC (1967) (QC-1992)	John Evan Jones (1982)	
Louis Schaffer (1955) MA (Cantab) LLB (Cantab)	Marc Brittain (1983)	James Shaw (1988) LLB Hons
	Nicholas Doherty (1983) LLB	Dina Karallis (1989) BA Hons, LLM (Lond)
Richard Akinjide (1956)	Julie O'Malley (1983) LLB (Sheff)	Simon Cheetham (1990)
David Nathan (1971) LLB Hons (Manchester)	Jollyon Robertson (1983)	Russell Stone (1992) MA (Oxon)
Jonathan Lurie (1972)	Annette Henry (1984) LLB Hons	Iain Daniels (1992) LLB Hons (Sheff)
Sheilagh Davies (1974) LLB Hons (Lond)	William McCormick (1985) LLB Hons	Christopher Harding (1992) LLB Hons (Lond)
Esther Kayman (1974)	Bibiana Ihuomah (1986) LLB Hons	Mary Ruck (1993) LLB (Cardiff)
Laura Brickman (1976)		
Timothy Sewell (1976)	Kevin Leigh (1986) LLB Hons (Leicester)	Siza Agha (1993) LLB
Michael Wolkind (1976)		Gary Herbert (1996)
Barry Gilbert (1978) LLB, Dip. Arabic	Helen McCormack (1986) LLB Hons	Francesca Wiloy (1996)

Head of Chambers:
Ronald Thwaites QC

Senior Clerk:
C. Drury

Tenants: 40

The Chambers: A powerful, long established leading set which has offered strong representation in common law matters over many years. Members of chambers appear in civil and criminal courts at every level and in arbitrations and tribunals. Chambers has an acknowledged reputation in commercial "white collar" fraud, which has been reinforced by the addition to chambers of leading and junior counsel who specialise in civil law. Chambers offers spacious conference rooms and a computerised administration centre. Practitioners are able to offer written work in a wide variety of formats for the convenience of clients.

Work Undertaken:

Criminal: Work embraces all aspects of crime, especially commercial crime, serious fraud, drugs and DTOA confiscation orders, money laundering, computer crime, licensing and firearms. Many members defend in major trials and undertake cases on behalf of the prosecuting authorities.

Civil: There is specialisation at junior and leading counsel level in all aspects of common law and especially personal injuries, medical negligence, libel, landlord and tenant, local government, environment, planning, compulsory purchase, building disputes, employment, chancery, insolvency, company law and law relating to the Internet.

Defamation: A small number of practitioners have advised and appeared in major libel trials and act for both plaintiffs and defendants.

Valuers Negligence: A number of practitioners at all levels of seniority handle a large number of such cases for insurers and have also acted for plaintiffs.

Actions Against the Police: Chambers receives instructions in many cases of this kind.

Family: All aspects of matrimonial law, including wardship and local authority work.

International: International arbitration, EC law, USA law, cases in Trinidad & Tobago, African law, Privy Council appeals, cases in The Gambia, Singapore and Hong Kong are all within the experience of members of chambers.

Languages: Arabic, French, German, Italian, Spanish and Welsh.

Recruitment & Training: Chambers is a member of the PACH pupillage scheme administered by the Bar Council. Awards are available. No third six month pupils or squatters are taken. Suitably qualified practitioners of more than eight years' call (civil) and ten years' call (criminal) are invited to submit tenancy application to head of chambers with full CV and copy references. Chambers is an equal opportunities organisation.

SET NUMBER
115

11 KING'S BENCH WALK (F.J. Muller QC)

11 KING'S BENCH WALK, TEMPLE, LONDON, EC4Y 7EQ
Tel: (0171) 353 3337 **Fax:** (0171) 583 2190 **Email:** clerks@11kbw.co.uk

MEMBERS:

F.J. Muller QC (1961) (QC-1978)	Nicholas Campbell (1979)	Simon Mallett (1987)
James Spencer QC (1975) (QC-1991)	Jeremy Richardson (1980)	Adrian Waterman (1988)
Andrew Robertson QC (1975) (QC-1996)	Christopher Attwooll (1980)	David Brooke (1990)
	Toby Wynn (1982)	Robert Toone (1993)
Francis Radcliffe (1962)	Rebecca Caswell (1983)	Ian Skelt (1994)
Matthew Caswell (1968)	Fiona P. Swain (1983)	Simon Antrobus (1995)
Richard Barlow (1970)	Graham Reeds (1984)	Sarah Margee (1996)
	John Cooper (1985)	Tina Dempster (1997)

Head of Chambers:
F.J. Muller QC

Clerks:
A. Blaney (London – QCs)
A. Dunstone (Leeds – Juniors)

Tenants: 22

Leeds Annexe: 3 Park Court, Park Cross Street, Leeds LS1 2QH.
Tel: (0113) 297 1200 Fax: (0113) 297 1201

Clerk: A.P. Dunstone

The Chambers: 11 King's Bench Walk is a long-established London set with distinguished history. Former members include the Rt Hon Sir George Waller, the former Lord Chief Justice: Lord Taylor of Gosforth, and the current Vice President of the Queen's Bench division: Lord Justice Kennedy. Chambers has an extensive practice on the North Eastern Circuit, and remains a true circuit set in the sense that members live, practice and are available for conferences and consultations throughout the entire circuit (Bradford, Durham, Hull, Leeds, Newcastle-upon-Tyne, Sheffield, Teeside, and York).

SET NUMBER
116

11 KING'S BENCH WALK (Eldred Tabachnik QC and James Goudie QC)

11 KING'S BENCH WALK, TEMPLE, LONDON, EC4Y 7EQ
Tel: (0171) 632 8500 **Fax:** (0171) 583 9123/ 3690 **DX:** 368 (CH.LN.)

MEMBERS:

Eldred Tabachnik QC (1970) (QC-1982) BA, LLB (Capetown), LLM (Lond)	Elisabeth Mary Caroline Laing (1980) BA (Cantab)	Akhlaq Choudhury (1992) BSc (Glas), LL.B (Lond)
James Goudie QC (1970) (QC-1984) LLB (Lond)	Adrian Charles Edmund Lynch (1983) LLB (Lond)	Paul Nicholls (1992) LL.B (Sheff), BCL (Oxon)
Richard Alan Field QC (1977) (QC-1987) LLB(Bris), LLM(Lond)	Siobhan Marie Lucia Ward (1984) MA, LŁM (Cantab)	Daniel Stilitz (1992) BA (Oxon), MA (City)
Patrick Elias QC (1973) (QC-1990) LLB (Exon), MA, PhD (Cantab)	John Patrick Cavanagh (1985) MA (Oxon), LLM (Cantab)	Clive Sheldon (1991) BA (Cantab) LLM (U.Penn)
Michael Alan Supperstone QC (1973) (QC-1991) MA, BCL (Oxon)	Nigel Giffin (1986) MA (Oxon)	Nigel Porter (1994) MA LLM (Cantab)
Elizabeth Ann Slade QC (1972) (QC-1992) MA (Oxon)	Charles Bear (1986) BA (Oxon)	Jason Coppel (1994) BA (Oxon), LLM, EUI (Florence)
Alistair John McGregor QC (1974) (QC-1997) LLB (Lond)	Peter Wallington (1987) MA, LL.M (Cantab)	Cecilia Ivimy (1995) BA (Oxon)
Christopher James Marwood Jeans QC (1980) (QC-1997) LLB (Lond), BCL (Oxon)	Jonathan Mark Swift (1989) BA (Oxon), LLM (Cantab)	Tom Restrick (1995) BA (Oxon)
Philip James Sales (1985) MA (Cantab), BCL (Oxon) First Treasury Junior, Common Law	Timothy Sheridan Pitt-Payne (1989) BA, BCL (Oxon)	Richard Leiper (1996) LLB, MJur
	Peter Oldham (1990) BA (Cantab) Dip Law (City)	Julian Wilson (1997) BA (Oxon)
	Seán Jones (1991) BA, BCL (Oxon)	

Head of Chambers:
Eldred Tabachnik QC and James Goudie QC

Senior Clerk:
Philip Monham

Tenants: 30

Work Undertaken: The 30 members of these chambers (eight of whom are Queen's Counsel) provide specialist legal advice and advocacy services covering the following three principal areas:

Commercial Law/International Trade: Arbitration (domestic and international); insurance and reinsurance; banking (especially letters of credit, guarantees and performance bonds); carriage of goods; international and domestic sales of goods; Stock Exchange, commodities and futures transactions; financial services; mergers and acquisitions; corporate and insolvency law; professional negligence (particularly accountants' negligence); music and film agreements; intellectual property.

Public and Administrative Law: Local authorities, especially their powers and financing; judicial review of central and local government and other public bodies, including financial services institutions; competitive tendering and public authority contracts; education; sex and race discrimination; elections; civil liberties; immigration; EC public law; housing and housing associations; environmental law.

Employment Law: Company directors; share options; incentive bonuses and pension rights; wrongful and unfair dismissal; the protection of confidential information; restrictive covenants; transfers of undertakings; sex and race discrimination and equal pay; strikes and other trade disputes; trade union membership; EC employment law.

Publications: Members of chambers have written or contributed to *Halsbury's Laws (Administrative Law Title); Goudie & Supperstone on Judicial Review; Harvey on Industrial Relations and Employment Law; Butterworths Employment Law Handbook; Tolley's Employment Handbook; Immigration Law and Practice; Butterworths Local Government Law* (forthcoming).

Office hours: 8.00am to 7.00pm Monday to Friday.

Out of office hours: Tel: 0831 304714 (mobile); Philip Monham (0181) 658 1034

Full brochure available upon request.

SET NUMBER
117

12 KING'S BENCH WALK (Ronald J. Walker QC)

12 KING'S BENCH WALK, TEMPLE, LONDON, EC4Y 7EL
Tel: (0171) 583 0811 **Fax:** (0171) 583 7228 **DX:** 1037 (CH.LN.) **Email:** CHAMBERS@12KBW.CO.UK

MEMBERS:

Ronald Walker QC (1962) (QC-1983)	Neville Spencer-Lewis (1970)	Andrew Pickering (1987)
Charles Whitby QC (1952) (QC-1970)	Toby Hooper (1973)	Hugh Hamill (1988)
Timothy Stow QC (1965) (QC-1989)	John King (1973)	Nicholas Vineall (1988)
Anthony Goldstaub QC (1972) (QC-1992)	Andrew Hogarth (1974)	Adam Chambers (1989)
Anthony Speaight QC (1973) (QC-1995)	Brian Gallagher (1975)	Catherine Brown (1990)
Richard Methuen QC (1972) (QC-1997)	Stephen Worthington (1976)	Kate Chandler (1990)
Iain Goldrein QC (1975) (QC-1997)	Nicholas Heathcote Williams (1976)	Caroline Evans (1991)
Margaret de Haas QC (1977) (QC-1998)	Allan Gore (1977)	Vincent Moran (1991)
Frank Burton QC (1982) (QC-1998)	Lincoln Crawford (1977)	Patrick Vincent (1992)
Peter Grobel (1967)	Alexander Hill-Smith (1978)	Willliam Audland (1992)
Peter Dedman (1968)	William Featherby (1978)	Joel Kendall (1993)
	Susan Rodway (1981)	Richard Viney (1994)
	Jonathan Howard (1983)	Carolyn D'Souza (1994)
	Paul Russell (1984)	Michael Ginn (1994)
	Nigel Lewers (1986)	Catherine Peck (1995)
	Freya Newbery (1986)	Timothy Petts (1996)

Head of Chambers:
Ronald J. Walker QC

Clerks:
Tony Day and John Cooper

Practice Manager:
Lisa Pavlovsky

Tenants: 43

The Chambers: This is an established set providing in depth expertise in a range of civil and commercial work. Chambers has specialist groups of barristers with particular expertise in the fields of Construction and Employment law. Chambers has a progressive outlook: it has modern staffing arrangements and is equipped with the latest computerisation, thus ensuring that work is dealt with quickly and efficiently with the needs of each individual client in mind.

Work Undertaken:

Commercial: includes banking and credit transactions; sale of goods; carriage of goods; accountants' and bankers' negligence.

Construction: includes all standard form building contracts; engineering, mining and computer contracts; architects', engineers' and surveyor's negligence.

Employment: includes race relations; equal opportunity; trade union work; restrictive covenants; transfers of undertakings; wrongful and unfair dismissal; equal pay; bonus and pension schemes. Chambers also has expertise in EC employment law.

Insurance and Reinsurance: includes drafting and construction of policies; material damage.

Personal Injury and Medical Negligence: includes all industrial disease claims particularly asbestos and RSI; brain damage; spinal injuries; all other employers', public, and product liability claims.

Professional Negligence: includes solicitors' and barristers' negligence in addition to those above-mentioned.

Property Law: includes landlord and tenant; housing..

Public Law: includes environmental; judicial review; local governmental law.

Continues overleaf

Publications: Members of chambers have written, edited or contributed to various publications, including: *Walker & Walker: The English Legal System; Bullen & Leake & Jacob's Precedents of Pleadings; Master and Servant* in *Halsbury's Laws of England,* 3rd Edition; *Master and Servant,* (in *Atkins Encylopaedia of Court Forms – 2nd Edition); Law of Defective Premises; Architects Journal Legal Handbook; Construction Disputes: Liability and the Expert Witness; Odgers: Pleading and Practice; Consumer Credit Law and Practice; Medical Negligence: Case Law; Architect's Legal Handbook; Butterworths Personal Injury Litigation Service; Commercial Litigation: Pre-emptive Remedies; Personal Injury Litigation Law; Cordery on Solicitors.*

Recruitment & Training: Chambers is a member of PACH to which all applications for pupillage should be made. Pupils are offered terminable 12-month pupillages with a guaranteed income of £15,000.

Clientele: The chambers' Construction Group receives an increasing volume of Direct Professional Access instructions from construction professionals such as chartered surveyors, engineers and architects.

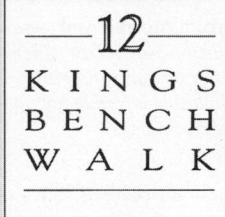

SET NUMBER 118   13 KING'S BENCH WALK (Graeme Williams QC)

13 KING'S BENCH WALK, TEMPLE, LONDON, EC4Y 7EN
Tel: (0171) 353 7204 **Fax:** (0171) 583 0252 **DX:** 359 LONDON LIX: LON 066 **Email:** CLERKS@13KBW.LAW.CO.UK

MEMBERS:

Graeme Williams QC (1959) (QC-1983) M.A. (Oxon).
Julian Baughan QC (1967) (QC-1990) B.A. (Oxon).
Roger Ellis QC (1962) (QC-1996) LLB. BSc (Lond).
David Ashton (1962) M.A. (Oxon).
Alexander Dawson (1969) M.A. (Oxon).
Anthony McGeorge (1969) M.A. (Cantab).
Robert Lamb (1973) M.A. (Cantab).
David Richardson (1973) M.A. LLB (Cantab).
James Gibbons (1974)
Deirdre Goodwin (1974) LLB. (Lond).
David Grant (1975) M.A. LLB. (Cantab).
Jane Tracy Forster (1975) LLB. (Liverpool).
Paul W. Reid (1975) M.A. (Cantab).
David Bright (1976)

Simon Hughes M.P. (1974) B.A. (Cantab).
Simon Draycott (1977)
Donald Lambie (1978) LLB. (London).
Alasdair Brough (1979) M.A. (Cantab).
Nigel Daly (1979) LLB. (London).
Nicholas Syfret (1979) M.A. (Cantab).
Andrew Glennie (1982) M.A. (Oxon).
A. John Williams (1983) M.A. (Cantab).
Jonathan Coode (1984) B.A. (East Anglia).
Neil Vickery (1985) M.A. (Cantab).
Neil Moore (1986) LLB. (Nottingham).
Sarah Gibbons (1987) B.A. (Birmingham).
Arthur Blake (1988) LLB. (Lond).

Sinclair Cramsie (1988) LLB. (Leeds).
Gerard Quirke (1988) B.A. (Hull).
Fiona Hay (1989) BSc. B.A. (Exeter).
Adrian Higgins (1990) M.A. (Oxon).
Edmund Walters (1991) B.A. (Bristol).
Heather Wenlock (1991) M.Phil D.Phil (Oxon).
Vivian Walters (1991) B.A. (Leic).
Shantanu Majumdar (1992) B.A. (Oxon).
Deshpal Singh Panesar (1993) LLB. (Lond).
Susan Chan (1994) B.A. (Oxon).
Paul Mitchell (1994) B.A. (York).
Andrew Pote (1983) LLB. (East Anglia).

Head of Chambers:
Graeme Williams QC

Senior Clerk:
Stephen Buckingham,
Kevin Kelly

Chambers Administrator:
Penny McFall

Tenants: 39

The Chambers: These chambers were founded as a separate set in 1971, although the origin of Chambers goes back many years ealier. In 1988 this set were the first to open separate premises in Oxford. They have wide and varied experience in all fields of general Civil Litigation and provide a comprehensive service in the Criminal Law on the Midland and Oxford Circuit. Chambers has an expanding Famliy Practice, based in Oxford.

Work Undertaken:

Common Law/Civil Practice:
1. Administrative, especially judicial review
2. Building and Construction
3. (All aspects of) Business Law including contract, Sale of Goods, Banking, Company and Partnership
4. Clubs and Unincorporated Associations
5. Employment
6. Insolvency
7. Landlord & Tenant
8. Medical negligence
9. Personal injury

Criminal Practice (London and Oxford): Both prosecution and defence work. Standing Counsel to Customs and Excise on M & O Circuit.

Family Practice (based in Oxford)

Specialist Practices: While the range of expertise covered by KBC as a whole is broad, individual members are regarded as specialists in their own fields.

Silks' expertise is in:

- Personal Injury/Medical Negligence
- Criminal Law
- Business Law and Landlord & Tenant

Among the Senior Juniors are specialists in each of the categories of work described.

Administration: A key factor in the service Chambers offers is flexibility:

- Excellent conference facilities in both London and Oxford;
- All members of Chambers are available for conferences at either location;
- Members of Chambers increasingly provide documents, whether advices or drafts, which are transmitted electronically (e.g. by e-mail or LIX).

SET NUMBER
119 **LAMB BUILDING** (Ami Feder)

LAMB BUILDING, GROUND FLOOR, TEMPLE, LONDON, EC4Y 7AS
Tel: (0171) 797 7788 **Fax:** (0171) 353 0535 **DX:** 1038 (CH.LN.)

MEMBERS:

Ami Feder (1965) LLB	Spenser R. Hilliard (1975) LLB (Lond)	Bernard Richmond (1988)
Kenneth Wheeler (1956)	Jaqueline A. Perry (1975) MA (Oxon)	M. Jane Terry (1988)
Maureen V. Mullally (1957) LLB (Lond)	Angela E. Hodes (1979) BA (Lond)	Jeremy Haughty (1989)
Ivan Krolick (1966) LLB (Dunhelm)	Michael Hartman (1975)	David Brounger (1990)
David M.T. Edlin (1971) MA (Oxon)	Michael Phillips (1980) LLB (Lond)	R. Frances Hindle (1990)
John Fox (1973) LLB, BDS, LDSRCS	Christa Fielden (1982)	J.M. Seamus Kearney (1992)
Anthony T.K. Edie (1974) LLB	J. David Cook (1982) BA (Keele)	Lindsay Weinstein (1992)
Jeremy Gordon (1974) LLB (Lond)	Richard Roberts (1983) BA (Cantab)	Paul Crampin (1992)
John C. Waters (1974)	Deborah Sawhney (1987) BA (Keele)	Anita Geser (1992)
Alan Barton (1975) LLM (Lond)	Susannah Cotterill (1988)	Joanne Rothwell (1994)
		Martin Cole (1994)
		Joy Dykers (1995)
		Paul Bitmead (1996)

Head of Chambers:
Ami Feder

Senior Clerk:
Gary Goodger

Tenants: 33

Types of work undertaken: The work of chambers covers all aspects of English common law and some general Chancery, predominantly on the South Eastern and Western Circuits.

The principal areas of practice are civil and criminal commercial fraud; professional and particularly medical negligence; personal injury; family and childcare including wardship and property; landlord and tenant and housing law; insolvency and bankruptcy; contractual disputes including partnership and sale of goods; all criminal law; disciplinary hearings and the armed forces; consumer credit, hiring, and leasing transaction; building law; employment, immigration specialists.

Additional specialisations: Individual members offer expertise in licensing, food and drugs, mental health, computer law, and Israeli law (Ami Feder is qualified as an advocate in Israel). Ivan Krolick belongs to the Chartered Institute of Arbitrators. A brochure is available on request.

SET NUMBER
120

LAMB CHAMBERS (Christopher Gardner QC)

LAMB BUILDING, ELM COURT, TEMPLE, LONDON, EC4Y 7AS
Tel: (0171) 797 8300 **Fax:** (0171) 797 8308 **DX:** 418 LONDON

MEMBERS:

Christopher Gardner QC (1968) (QC-1994)
Michael Burke-Gaffney QC (1959) (QC-1977)
Julian Priest QC (1954) (QC-1974)
Ian Leeming QC (1970) (QC-1988)
Jonathan Cole (1964)
J.A.L. Sterling (1953)
Donald Anderson (1969)
Anthony McNeile (1970)

Mark West (1973)
David di Mambro (1973)
Jeremy Carey (1974)
Anthony Connerty (1974)
Stephen Shaw (1975)
Simon Brilliant (1976)
Robert Thoresby (1978)
Bruce Silvester (1983)
Colin Mendoza (1983)
Paul M. Emerson (1984)
Kim Franklin (1984)
Thomas Graham (1985)

Gerwyn Samuel (1986)
Simon Wood (1987)
James Stuart (1990)
Katherine Gough (1990)
Elizabeth F. Haggerty (1994)
Rhiannon Jones (1993)
Richard Hayes (1995)
Timothy Firth (1996)
Annette Prandzioch (1995)
Alexandra Stagi (1996)
Susan Lindsey (1997)

Head of Chambers:
Christopher Gardner QC

Senior Clerk:
John Kelly

Tenants: 30

The Chambers: Lamb Chambers is a long-established set, specialising in mainstream civil litigation and structured in three specialist groups:

Commercial Group: This group specialises in all commercial litigation, including commercial contracts, sale & carriage of goods, supply of goods & services, companies, partnerships, corporate & personal insolvency, service contracts, guarantees, credit & security, banking, bills of exchange, passing off, intellectual property and confidentiality, competition, franchising, insurance, economic and other commercial torts, and professional negligence connected with the above. Members undertake commercial arbitrations, both LCIA and ICC, Alternative Dispute Resolution and Direct Professional Access work.

Personal Injury & Professional Negligence Group: This group specialises in tortious litigation, including personal injury, fatal accidents, medical negligence and associated professional negligence claims, and all matters relating to the assessment of damages, structured and infant settlements and insurance. We handle claims relating to product liability, toxins, infectious diseases, factory, construction site, road traffic and other transport accidents, claims relating to the liability of employers, independent contractors, public authorities (including the Police), occupiers, clubs, owners of animals and claims for compensation for occupational diseases and criminal injuries.

Property Group: This group specialises in all property-related work and construction litigation, including all aspects of landlord and tenant law – commercial, residential and agricultural; leasehold enfranchisement; construction disputes before the Official Referee and in arbitration, together with the professional negligence of architects and engineers; mortgages; housing options; easements and restrictive covenants; torts relating to land; professional negligence of surveyors, solicitors and others concerning property; and the drafting, construction and enforcement of contracts. Members of the Group also undertake arbitrations, Alternative Dispute Resolution and Direct Professional Access work.

Certain members of chambers also have additional personal specialisms in the following areas of law beyond the ambit of the three chambers groups: EC, restrictive trade practice, rating, civil fraud, family & wardship, and costs.

Publications: Professor Adrian Sterling (Professorial Fellow, Queen Mary and Westfield College, and visiting Senior Research Fellow, King's College, University of London) is author of *The Data Protection Act 1984, Copyright Law in the United Kingdom and the Rights of Performers, Authors and Composers in Europe, Encyclopaedia of Data Protection* (co-editor), and *Intellectual Property Rights in Sound Recordings, Film and Video*.Kim Franklin is joint editor of the *Construction Law Journal*, and a contributing author of *Construction Disputes – Liability and the Expert Witness, Architect's Journal Legal Handbook* and *The Legal Obligations of the Architect*. David di Mambro is General Editor of Butterworth's Supreme Court Manual.

A chambers brochure, featuring detailed individual CVs, is available on request.

SET NUMBER
121

LIBRARY CHAMBERS First Floor, Gray's Inn Chambers, Gray's Inn, London, WC1R 5JA **Tel:** (0171) 404 6500 **Fax:** (0171) 404 6394 **DX:** 78 Chancery Lane

SET NUMBER
122 LION COURT (Steven Jacobs)

CHANCERY HOUSE, 53-64 CHANCERY LANE, LONDON, WC2A 1SJ
Tel: (0171) 404 6565 **Fax:** (0171) 404 6659 **DX:** 98 (CH.LN.)

MEMBERS:

Steven Jacobs (1974)	Georgina Nicholas (1983)	Louise McCullough (1991)
Neil Taylor QC (1949) (QC-1975)	Steve Hosking (1988)	Philippa Mendel (1992)
Gerard Boyd (1967)	Paul Brinkworth (1990)	Paul Kaffel (1993)
Laraine Kaye (1971)	David Newberry (1990)	Victoria Myerson (1995)
Shini Cooksley (1975)	John Honey (1990)	Alexander Krikler (1995)
	Stephen Bailey (1991)	

Head of Chambers:
Steven Jacobs

Practice Manager:
Kim Brown

Administration Clerk:
Brian Newton

Tenants: 16

The Chambers: Lion Court is a common law set offering a wide range of experience and expertise.

Work Undertaken: Crime, general common law, probate, commercial law, insolvency, insurance, banking, employment, personal injury, criminal injuries, matrimonial, family, childcare, licensing, local authority, planning, landlord and tenant, immigration, media and judicial review.

Languages Spoken: French.

SET NUMBER
123 LITTLETON CHAMBERS (Michael Burton QC)

3 KING'S BENCH WALK NORTH, TEMPLE, LONDON, EC4Y 7HR
Tel: (0171) 797 8600 **Fax:** (0171) 797 8699/8699 **DX:** 1047 **Email:** LITTLETONCHAMBERS@COMPUSERVE.COM

MEMBERS:

Michael Burton QC (1970) (QC-1984)	John Bowers QC (1979) (QC-1998)	Michael Duggan (1984)
Michel Kallipetis QC (1968) (QC-1989)	Colin Manning (1970)	Peter Trepte (1987)
	Richard Perkoff (1971)	Paul Lowenstein (1988)
Daniel Serota QC (1969) (QC-1989)	Philip Bartle (1976)	Raoul Downey (1988)
Ian Mayes QC (1974) (QC-1993)	Mark Lomas (1977)	Martyn Barklem (1989)
	Timothy Higginson (1977)	Charles Samek (1989)
Richard Price OBE QC (1969) (QC-1996)	Caroline Harry Thomas (1981)	Jeffrey Bacon (1989)
Clive Freedman QC (1978) (QC-1997)	John Davies (1981)	Jeremy Lewis (1992)
	Shirley Bothroyd (1982)	Naomi Ellenbogen (1992)
	Selwyn Bloch (1982)	Daniel Tatton-Brown (1994)
Andrew Clarke QC (1980) (QC-1997)	Antony Sendall (1984)	Victoria Bather (1995)
	Ian Gatt (1985)	Stuart Ritchie (1995)
		Carol Davis (1996)

Head of Chambers:
Michael Burton QC

Chief Executive:
David Douglas

Clerks: Deborah Anderson
Alistair Coyne, Tim Tarring.

Fees Clerk: Tony Shaddock

A/C's Receivable Manager:
Nita Johnston

Tenants: 32

Door Tenants: Donald Harris (1958), Prof. Neil MacCormick (1971)

Work Undertaken:

General Description: A set practising in all areas of civil and commercial law with a wide spread of work including all aspects of business and employment law, intellectual property and commercial fraud. Chambers are members of COMBAR and a number of members are accredited mediators.

Main Areas of Work: There are 9 main specialities in Chambers with the following specialist groups:
Employment Law, Banking, Financial Services and Insurance, Entertainment and Media; Construction; Commercial Fraud; Professional Negligence; ADR; Public and European; Insolvency

Additional Areas:
• ADR; Arbitration; Carriage of Goods; Company Law; Consumer Credit Law; Corporate Finance; Insolvency; International Trade; Letters of Request.
• Competition Law; Computer Law; EC; Environment; Family; Pharmaceuticals; Telecommunications; Transport; Sale of Goods.
• Administrative Law; Civil Liberties; Charities; Discrimination; Education; Election law; Housing; Immigration; Judicial Review; Landlord and Tenant; Local Government; Mental Health; Parliamentary; Planning.
• Construction; Sports and Entertainment Law; Matrimonial Finance and Children; Pensions.

Languages Spoken: French, German, Italian and Cantonese.

Recruitment & Training: Members of Chambers fund 2 pupils per year. Chambers are members of PACH.

Publications and Lectures: A number of Members regularly publish books and contribute articles to professional publications. Members of Chambers provide lectures on a wide range of subjects and Chambers are accredited by the Law Society and Bar Council.

SET NUMBER
124 LITTMAN CHAMBERS (Mark Littman QC)

12 GRAY'S INN SQUARE, GRAY'S INN, LONDON, WC1R 5JP
Tel: (0171) 404 4866 **Fax:** (0171) 404 4812 **DX:** 0055 (CH.LN.) **Email:** ADMIN@LITTMANCHAMBERS.COM
Internet: www.littmanchambers.com

MEMBERS:

Mark Littman QC (1947) (QC-1961)	Jonathan Tecks (1978)	Julie Anderson (1993)
Michael Stimpson (1969)	Barbara Hewson (1985)	Damian Falkowski (1994)
Robert Kirk (1972)	Monique Allan (1986)	Alexander Hickey (1995)
Brian McClure (1976)	Seán Naidoo (1990)	James Roberts (1996)
Rowan Planterose (1978)	Martin Gibson (1990)	Philip Lewis (1958)
Andrzej Kolodziej (1978)	Rupert Higgins (1991)	John Finnis (1970)
	Niamh McCarthy (1991)	

Head of Chambers:
Mark Littman QC

Senior Clerk:
Lee Cutler

Junior Clerk:
Stephen Lawrence

Chambers Administrator:
Karen Raymond

Tenants: 19

Members of Chambers offer specialist advocacy, advisory, drafting and arbitration services to solicitors and to those with direct access to the Bar. They belong to the Commercial Bar Association.

Work undertaken:

Commercial: *Work includes:* banking, shipping, insurance, negotiable instruments, sale of goods, consumer credit, commodities, competition, international trade and financial services

European Community: *Work includes:* agriculture, competition, free movement, environmental law, financial services, regulatory aspects of the internal market (food, consumer law), jurisdiction and foreign judgements, public procurement and sex discrimination.

Commercial Property: *Work includes:* contracts and conveyancing, drafting, easements, landlord and tenant, rating, rent reviews and restrictive covenants.

Chancery: *Work includes:* company, insolvency, partnerships, passing off, suretyship and wills and intestacy.

Planning and Environmental Law: *Work includes:* compulsory purchase, enforcement, planning and pollution.

Construction Law: *Work includes:* building and engineering.

Additional Areas: Commercial conciliation and arbitration (ICC and LMAA), administrative law, computers, defamation, electronics, employment law, judicial review, professional negligence, human rights, mental health, and discrimination law.

Clientele: Public and private companies, institutions and private clients.

Foreign Languages: Afrikaans, French, German, Italian, Polish, Russian and Spanish.

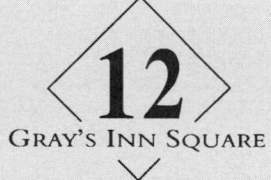

SET NUMBER
125 1 MIDDLE TEMPLE LANE (Colin Dines & Andrew Trollope QC)

1 MIDDLE TEMPLE LANE, TEMPLE, LONDON, EC4Y 9AA
Tel: (0171) 583 0659 (12 lines) **Fax:** (0171) 353 0652 **DX:** 464

MEMBERS:

Colin Dines (1970)	Gopal Hooper (1973)	Richard Butcher (1985)
Andrew Trollope QC (1971) (QC-1991)	Philip King (1974)	Barbara Strachan (1986)
Roger Backhouse QC (1965) (QC-1984)	Brian Reece (1974)	James Lachkovic (1987)
David Ashby (1963)	John Plumstead (1975)	Harry Bowyer (1989)
Nicholas Gardiner (1967)	Michael Borrelli (1977)	Anthony Korda (1988)
Tony Docking (1969)	Ian Copeman (1977)	Andrew Newton (1989)
Graham Arran (1969)	Bernard Eaton (1978)	Avirup Chaudhuri (1990)
Godfree Browne (1971)	Noel Lucas (1979)	Rachel Bright (1991)
Jonathan Davies (1971)	Christopher Amor (1984)	Richard Beynon (1990)
Brian Argyle (1972)	Emma Gluckstein (1985)	Philomena Murphy (1992)
Andrew Campbell (1972)	Simon Mayo (1985)	Natasha Wong (1993)
	Mark Rainsford (1985)	Robert Jones (1993)
	Andrew Marshall (1986)	

Head of Chambers:
Colin Dines & Andrew Trollope QC

Senior Clerk:
J. Pyne

Tenants: 36

Most members belong to the Criminal Bar Association, and several serve on various committees connected with criminal law. In addition, two members are on the Immigration Panel for the Home Office. Four members are recorders and two are assistant recorders. One member is standing counsel to H.M. Customs & Excise.

The Chambers: Chambers were established in December 1976 by Mr. Ronald Grey QC, and since then have flourished, growing both in size and in the quality and range of work undertaken. Members practise mainly in London, the South East and the Home Counties, but have accepted cases all over the country. Outside office hours, the senior clerk can be contacted on (01708) 641 671. Mobile (0976) 281902.

Work Undertaken:

Main Areas of Work: *Criminal:* For both prosecution and defence, with an increasing amount of serious white-collar crime. Members have recently acted in major VAT, company and mortgage fraud cases. The whole range of crime is also handled from murder, drugs and sexual offences to motoring offences and juvenile crime.

Additional Areas of Work: Courts martial; employment law; immigration, for applicants and the government; licensing; extradition and medical negligence.

Foreign Connections: Godfree Browne is a member of the Zimbabwe and Botswana Bars and an advocate in the High Court of Zimbabwe.

Languages Spoken: French and German.

Recruitment & Training: Tenancy applications to Colin Dines/Noel Lucas; pupillage applications to Rachel Bright. Chambers usually have between seven and ten pupils and applications are welcome at any time. Pupillage awards and mini-pupillages are available at chambers' discretion.

SET NUMBER
126 2 MIDDLE TEMPLE LANE (Satya Dhama) 2 Middle Temple Lane, 3rd Floor, Temple, London, EC4Y 9AA **Tel:** (0171) 583 4540 **Fax:** (0171) 583 9178 **Clerk:** Barry Leach **Tenants:** 14 General common law set with specialist practitioners in French, EC, Mohammedan and Hindu law. Also undertake criminal cases (mainly defence) and family law matters.

SET NUMBER
127 2 MIDDLE TEMPLE LANE (Harjit Singh) 2 Middle Temple Lane, Ground Floor, London, EC4Y 9AA **Tel:** (0171) 353 1356 **Fax:** (0171) 583 4928 **DX:** 0072 **Clerk:** Mr Matthew Jones **Tenants:** 13 Common law set with emphasis on: crime, civil litigation, chancery, company, employment, immigration, industrial tribunals, judicial review, landlord and tenant, matrimonial, personal injury, professional negligence.

SET NUMBER
128 **1 MITRE COURT BUILDINGS** (Bruce Blair QC)

1 MITRE COURT BUILDINGS, TEMPLE, LONDON, EC4Y 7BS
Tel: (0171) 797 7070 **Fax:** (0171) 797 7435 **DX:** LDE 342 CHANCERY LANE

MEMBERS:

Bruce Blair QC (1969) (QC-1989)	John Elvidge (1968)	Katharine Davidson (1987)
Michael Horowitz QC (1968) (QC-1990)	Michael Nicholls (1975)	Richard Todd (1988)
	Robin Spon-Smith (1976)	Rachel Platts (1989)
Jeremy Posnansky QC (1972) (QC-1994)	Valentine Le Grice (1977)	Gavin Smith (1981)
	Heather Pope (1977)	Timothy Bishop (1991)
Judith Hughes QC (1974) (QC-1994)	Nicholas Carden (1981)	Elisabeth Todd (1990)
	Catriona Murfitt (1981)	Geoffrey Kingscote (1993)
Mark Everall QC (1975) (QC-1994)	Nigel Dyer (1982)	Louise Potter (1993)
Martin Pointer QC (1976) (QC-1996)	Philip Moor (1982)	Stephen Trowell (1995)
	Charles Todd (1983)	Justin Warshaw (1995)
Nicholas Mostyn QC (1980) (QC-1997)	Christopher Wood (1986)	Nicholas Yates (1996)
	Nicholas Cusworth (1986)	

Head of Chambers:
Bruce Blair QC

Senior Clerk:
R. Beams

Tenants: 29

The Chambers: 1 Mitre Court Buildings is the longest established Chambers practising exclusively in the area of family law. Chambers offers advocacy, advisory and drafting expertise over the entire range of family and matrimonial law, whether child or finance oriented, and undertakes work at all levels of Court. Together with its service to privately paying clients, 1 Mitre Court Buildings has a strong commitment to and involvement in legally aided family work. Chambers is regularly instructed by the Official Solicitor and local authorities as well as on behalf of individual clients. 1 Mitre Court Buildings frequently handles cases with an international dimension. All members of Chambers belong to the Family Law Bar Association.

MITRE COVRT
BVILDINGS

SET NUMBER
129 2 MITRE COURT BUILDINGS (Michael FitzGerald QC)

2 MITRE COURT BUILDINGS, TEMPLE, LONDON, EC4Y 7BX
Tel: (0171) 583 1380 **Fax:** (0171) 353 7772 **Mobile:** 0802 776533 **DX:** 0032 CHANCERY LANE

MEMBERS:

Michael FitzGerald QC (1961) (QC-1980)
David Widdicombe QC (1950) (QC-1965)
Lord Silsoe QC (1951) (QC-1972)
Gerald Moriarty QC (1951) (QC-1974)
Anthony Anderson QC (1964) (QC-1982)

John Taylor QC (1958) (QC-1983)
George Bartlett QC (1966) (QC-1986)
Matthew Horton QC (1969) (QC-1989)
Guy Roots QC (1969) (QC-1989)
Alun Alesbury (1974)
Robert Fookes (1975)
Nicholas Burton (1979)

Neil King (1980)
Michael Humphries (1982)
Richard Glover (1984)
Mary Macpherson (1984)
Michael Druce (1988)
Reuben Taylor (1990)
Victor Moore (1992)
Rupert Warren (1994)
Christopher Boyle (1994)

Head of Chambers:
Michael FitzGerald QC
Clerks:
Robert Woods, Frances Kaliszewska, Kirstie Conway, Errol McKenzie, Joan Matthewson (Administrator)
Tenants: 21

The Chambers: A long-established and well known set currently comprising 21 members of whom 9 are QCs. All members specialise in Planning and Local Government Law.

Work Undertaken: The main specialist area practised by all members comprises Planning and Local Government which includes town and country planning, environmental law, compulsory purchase and compensation, rating and council tax, utilities and infrastructure, local government, public and administrative, Parliamentary bills and Transport and Works Act. All members appear at public inquiries, the Lands Tribunal and the Courts

Clientele: A wide range including companies, corporations, public and private utilities, local authorities, government departments and foreign governments, individuals and residents associations. Instructions are accepted under the Direct Access Scheme.

Foreign Connections: Members have appeared or advised in relation to a number of jurisdictions including Hong Kong, Jersey and Bermuda.

Recruitment & Training: Applications for tenancy should be addressed to Michael FitzGerald QC. Applications for pupillage should be addressed to Joan Matthewson. Chambers have two to three pupils at any one time and substantial awards are available for pupils; details will be provided on application. Mini-pupillages are also available.

SET NUMBER
130 2 MITRE COURT BUILDINGS (Roger Gray)

2 MITRE COURT BUILDINGS, (FIRST FLOOR), TEMPLE, LONDON, EC4Y 7BX
Tel: (0171) 353 1353 **Fax:** (0171) 353 8188 **DX:** 0023 LONDON CHANCERY LANE

MEMBERS:

Roger Gray (1984) MA DipLaw
Michael Pearson (1952) BCL, MA (Oxon)
Florence O'Donoghue (1959) MA (Trinity College, Dublin), FCIArb
John Parker (1975) BSc (Lond)
Barry Forward (1981) BSc (Econ)

Simon O'Toole (1984) BA DipLaw
Anthony Bell (1985) BA Hons
James Holmes-Milner (1989) MA (Cantab) DipLaw
Delyth Evans (1991) LLB Hons (Lond)
Sarah Clover (1993) MA(Oxon) LLM
Philip McCormack (1994) LLB Hons

Teresa Pritchard (1994) MA Hons (St.And) DipLaw
Michael Shaw (1994) LLB Hons
Timothy Parker (1995) BA Hons DipLaw
Peter Hunt (1964) * MA (Cantab)
Alison Throp (1992)* BA Hons DipLaw

Head of Chambers:
Roger Gray
Senior Clerk:
John Markham
Tenants: 14

* Door Tenant

The Chambers: A long-established set that offers an efficient, comprehensive and friendly service. All members practise from London on the South Eastern circuit and several have strong connections with the Western and Midland & Oxford circuits.

Work Undertaken: General common law. Members of chambers practise in one or more of the following areas: crime, family, general civil and chancery litigation.

In addition individual members of chambers undertake work in the following specific fields of practice: administrative law, building law, conveyancing, child abduction, defamation, ecclesiastical law, employment, landlord & tenant, licensing, personal injury, planning, professional negligence and wardship.

Pupillage: Applications for 1999 pupillages on Chambers' own application form available from Philip McCormack.

2 MITRE COURT BUILDINGS
Barristers' Chambers

SETNUMBER
131 ## MITRE COURT CHAMBERS (John Burton)

MITRE COURT CHAMBERS, TEMPLE, LONDON, EC4Y 7BP
Tel: (0171) 353 9394 **Fax:** (0171) 353 1488 **DX:** 449 CH.LN. **Mobile:** 0411 139587 **Email:** MITRECOURT.COM

MEMBERS:

John M. Burton (1979)	Roger Turner (1982)	Julia Goring (1991)
Peter Shier (1952)	Leslie Wise (1985)	Philip Brown (1991)
Graeme Ford (1972)	Pieter Briegel (1986)	Mukhtiar S. Otwal (1991)
Gillian Frost (1979)	Ian C. Bridge (1988)	Andrew Espley (1993)
Peter J. Hofford (1979)	Neil Mercer (1988)	Lucy Bolton (1994)
Bartholomew V. O'Toole (1980)	Andrew Forsyth (1989)	Adam Glass (1994)
Alexander Laban (1981)	Christopher Blake (1990)	Charlotte Newell (1994)
	Carl Hackman (1990)	Max Thorowgood (1995)

Head of Chambers:
John Burton
Practice Manager:
Alistair Adams
Senior Clerk:
William Ingleton
Clerks:
Tiffany McBlain,
David Harrison
Tenants: 23

An established set with members practising in civil, personal injury, crime and family law.

Work Undertaken:

Civil work includes banking, insolvency, commercial, general contract, insurance, employment, landlord and tenant, and professional negligence.

Personal injury work includes accidents at work, industrial diseases and medical negligence. Conditional fee agreements.

Crime work incorporates all areas of defence work including serious fraud. Members of chambers also prosecute on behalf of statutory agencies in addition to the CPS in matters such as food, planning and environment.

Family work includes matrimonial finance, children and divorce.

In addition to individual specialisations, each member of Chambers is dedicated to one of three teams covering personal injury, crime and family. Members undertake direct professional access work and contribute to specialist publications and seminars.

Foreign Languages: German, French, Punjabi.

SET NUMBER
132 MITRE HOUSE CHAMBERS (Francis P. Gilbert) Mitre House, 44 Fleet St, London, EC4Y 1BN
Tel: (0171) 583 8233 **Fax:** (0171) 583 2692 **DX:** 0005 **Practice Manager:** Mr Osman Avdji
Tenants: 30 **Out of hours emergency number:** 0956 316 404 Undertake a wide range of work including crime, family, licensing, landlord and tenant, social security, industrial tribunals, mental health work, immigration, personal injury, actions against the Police and judicial review.

SET NUMBER
133 ## MONCKTON CHAMBERS (Richard Fowler QC)

4 RAYMOND BUILDINGS, GRAY'S INN, LONDON, WC1R 5BP
Tel: (0171) 405 7211 **Fax:** (0171) 405 2084 **DX:** 257 **Email:** CHAMBERS@MONCKTON.CO.UK

MEMBERS:

Richard Fowler QC (1969) (QC-1989)	Christopher Vajda QC (1979) (QC-1997)	Jennifer Skilbeck (1991)
Richard Seymour QC (1972) (QC-1991)	Mark Pelling (1979)	Raymond Hill (1992)
Kenneth Parker QC (1975) (QC-1992)	Rupert Anderson (1981)	Jessica Simor (1992)
Paul Lasok QC (1977) (QC-1994)	Michael Patchett-Joyce (1981)	Paul Harris (1994)
Peter M. Roth QC (1976) (QC-1997)	Melanie Hall (1982)	Rebecca Haynes (1994)
Nicholas Paines QC (1978) (QC-1997)	Andrew Macnab (1986)	Aidan Robertson (1995)
	Jon Turner (1988)	Kassie Smith (1995)
	Peter Mantle (1989)	Daniel Beard (1996)
	Rhodri Thompson (1989)	George Peretz (1990)

Head of Chambers:
Richard Fowler QC
Senior Clerk:
Graham Lister
Practice Manager:
Milly Ayliffe
Tenants: 24

The Chambers: A leading commercial set providing specialised advocacy and advice in European Community law, commercial litigation, competition law, public law and judicial review. High quality work, promptness, value for money and efficiency are regarded by Chambers as essential to its success.

Work Undertaken:

European Law: Chambers specialises in all aspects of European law, particularly in litigation. Members of Chambers appear regularly before the ECJ on cases involving agriculture, competition, equal pay, pensions, sex discrimination, state aids, VAT and customs. Recent cases include: *Factortame, R v MAFF ex p British Agro Chemicals [1997], R v MAFF ex p Hedley – Lomas [1997], R v HM Treasury ex p BT [1996], R v CCE ex Lunn Poly [1997]*,

Continues overleaf

Redrow v CCE [1997] and *Midland Bank v CCE* [1998]. Members of Chambers have also been involved in numerous high profile European cases in the UK courts including *Preston & Others v Wolverhampton Healthcare NHS Trust and Fletcher v Midland Bank PLC* [1998] *R v MAFF ex p Anastasiou (No 2)* [1998], *R v MAFF ex p First City Trading* [1997], *Three Rivers District Council v Bank of England* [1996], *Society of Lloyds v Clementson* [1996], *and Iberian v BPB* [1996]. In addition Bellamy and Child's the Common Market Law of Competition is edited by Peter Roth QC and The European Court of Justice: Practice and Procedure is written by Paul Lasok QC.

Commercial Law: Expertise includes international and domestic arbitration, banking, international and domestic commercial fraud recovery and tracing, consumer credit, construction law, insurance and re-insurance and professional negligence. In the last year members of Chambers have appeared in international arbitrations in the Middle East, Africa and Eastern Europe as well as in London. Recent cases include *North Atlantic Insurance Co Ltd v Bishopsgate Insurance Ltd* [1998], *Gold Coin Joailliers v United Bank of Kuwait* [1996], *Coban v Allen* [1996], *Regia Autonoma de Electriciate Renel v Gulf Petroleum International Ltd.* [1996], *Re BCCI (No 10)* [1995], *and Crown Estates Commissioners v John Mowlem* [1994].

Competition Law: Members of Chambers regularly appear in and advise on MMC references, OFT inquiries, RTPA investigations and ECJ cases. Both Ken Parker QC and Peter Roth QC recently appeared for the respective parties in the House of Lords *MD Foods v Baines* concerning the application of RTPA. In the last year Richard Fowler QC has acted in the Guinness/Grand Met Merger. Teams from Chambers continue to act for the various parties in the RPC reference in relation to the televising of Premier League football and the RPC reference in relation to the resale price maintenance of medicaments. Paul Lasok QC appeared in *Gencor v Commission* [1998] and *Coca Cola v Commission* [1998]. Members of Chambers also acted in the package holidays reference to the MMC and *re Net Book Agreements* [1997]. Jon Turner is standing counsel to the Director General of Fair Trading. Members of Chambers are also extensively involved in competition and related regulatory matters concerning the utilities; acting both for the regulators (including Oftel, Ofwat and Offer) and the regulated companies.

Juducial Review: Chambers is also a major centre of expertise in judicial review, recent major cases include: *R v Chief Constable of Sussex ex p ITF* [1998] [HL], *R v Home Office ex p Mc Avoy* [1998], *R v Home Office ex p Launder* [1997], *R v Home Office ex p Camden City Council* [1997], *R v Secretary of State for Employment exp Seymour-Smith* [1997] and various judicial reviews arising out of litigation in connection with the ban on British Beef.

MONCKTON
MCHAMBER^{S}
4 RAYMOND BUILDINGS

---

134 NEW COURT (John Gilmartin)

NEW COURT, TEMPLE, LONDON, EC4Y 9BE
Tel: (0171) 583 5123 **Fax:** (0171) 353 3383 **DX:** 0018

MEMBERS:

John Gilmartin (1972)	Stuart Whitehouse (1987)	Deborah Todman (1991)
Paul Randolph (1971)	Ann Courtney (1987)	Judith Charlton (1991)
John Gordon (1970)	Christopher Maynard (1988)	Juliette Levy (1992)
Giuseppe Cala (1971) Italian Bar	Douglas Livingstone (1989)	James Hasslacher (1993)
Robert Arnold (1974)	Oliver Hyams (1989)	Nigel Taylor (1993)
Simon Kumalo (1974)	Stuart Nichols (1989)	Giles Bain (1993)
Richard Kingsley (1977)	John Lamb (1990)	Robin Powell (1993)
Michael Harrison (1979)	Norma Laming (1990)	Judith Murray (1994)
Susan Shackleford (1980)	Helen Soffa (1990)	Caitlin Ferris (1996)
Alun Jenkins (1981)	Jane Humphreys (1990)	Jeremy Garrood (1996)
Andrew Dickins (1983)	Doushka Krish (1991)	Christopher Poole (1996)

Head of Chambers:
John Gilmartin

Senior Clerk:
Paul Bloomfield

Tenants: 34

The Chambers: The chambers have a general practice with a wide range of work. Members of chambers have their own specialities and the chambers aim to provide a choice of counsel in any area of work undertaken.

Work Undertaken:
Company/Commercial: Business-related law, credit and security, contract related disputes of all kinds, insolvency, employment and place-of-work related disputes, financial services, unincorporated associations, partnerships and related matters.
Property: Land law, landlord and tenant, and related matters.
Criminal Law: All areas of prosecution and defence work, including fraud, white collar crime and custom offences.

Torts and negligence: Actions of all kinds including medical negligence (anaesthesia and cardio-thoracic surgery, childbirth and cerebral damage).

Family: All aspects of Family Law including ancillary relief, child care, public and private law, Children Act proceedings, acting for Guardians, local Authorities and Parents.

Civil: Company/Commercial, Personal Injury (including Conditional Fee Agreements), Medical and other Professional Negligence, Landlord and Tenant, Licensing, Employment, Education Law, Judicial Review, Immigration and Mental Health.

Additional Work Undertaken: Penalties in civil law.

Languages Spoken: Fluent German; French, Russian, Italian and Hebrew

Telephone Numbers: Residence: London (0171) 603 5028 (and fax); Voicebank 042 691 1997; Mobile 0831 220445.

SET NUMBER
135 NEW COURT CHAMBERS (George Carman QC)

5 VERULAM BUILDINGS, GRAY'S INN, LONDON, WC1R 5LY
Tel: (0171) 831 9500 **Fax:** (0171) 269 5700 **DX:** 363 CHANCERY LANE **Email:** MAIL@NEWCOURTCHAMBERS.COM
Internet: WWW.NEWCOURTCHAMBERS.COM

MEMBERS:

George Carman QC (1953) (QC-1971)	Charles Howard (1975)	Daniel Gatty (1990)
Frederic Reynold QC (1960) (QC-1982)	Paul Stewart (1975)	Joël Donovan (1991)
	Gail Carrodus (1978)	Adam Korn (1992)
Peter Susman QC (1966) (QC-1997)	John Wardell (1979)	Christopher Wagstaffe (1992)
	Michael McParland (1983)	Thomas Grant (1993)
Neville Sarony (1964) (QC Hong Kong 1992)	Hugh Tomlinson (1983)	Estelle Overs (1994)
Malcolm Knott (1968)	Terence Bergin (1985)	
Anthony Clover (1971)	Jonathan Steinert (1986)	Alexander Pelling (1995)
Duncan Pratt (1971)	Andrew Davies (1988)	Nichola Warrender (1995)
Michael Brompton (1973)	Georgina Middleton (1989)	David Pliener (1996)
	Tejina Mangat (1990)	

Head of Chambers:
George Carman QC

Senior Clerk:
Bill Conner

Tenants: 28

The Chambers: New Court Chambers is a common law set offering particular expertise in commercial litigation, property litigation, professional negligence, defamation, computer supply litigation, employment, discrimination, civil liberties, medical negligence & personal injury, family, travel and sports law.

A number of barristers at New Court Chambers are regarded as specialists in these fields, and Chambers' litigation experience in other jurisdictions includes the Far East, United Sates and Caribbean.

New Court Chambers places emphasis not only on providing a high standard of advocacy and advice, but also on the need to deliver a friendly and efficient service. Barristers are notably approachable and the experienced clerks understand the requirements of modern practice.

Chambers maintains extensive databases of case law and throughout the year circulates updates to solicitors and provides training seminars on a variety of topics. Seminars are Law Society accredited and can be adapted to meet the needs of the audience.

New Court Chambers offers spacious and attractive conference rooms. Facilities for the disabled are also provided. Foreign languages spoken include French, German, Hindi, Nepali and Hebrew.

SET NUMBER
136 NEW COURT (John Fitzgerald)

NEW COURT, TEMPLE, LONDON, EC4Y 9BE
Tel: (0171) 797 8999 **Fax:** (0171) 583 5885 **DX:** 420

MEMBERS:

J.V. Fitzgerald (1971)	Matthew Kime (1988)	Gary Fern (1992)
Alison Firth (1980)	Alan Coulthard (1987)	

Head of Chambers:
John Fitzgerald

Senior Clerk:
Simon Coomber

Tenants: 5

The Chambers: Each tenant specialises in intellectual property law.

Work Undertaken: All areas of intellectual property law, including copyright and design right, passing off, confidential information, trademarks and service marks, registered designs, patents (UK and European), computer and telecommunications law and practice, entertainment and media law, plant breeders' rights, and semiconductor chip protection. As a result of their work in the field of intellectual property, several tenants also have experience with

Continues overleaf

commercial contracts and licensing, music and character merchandising, malicious/injurious falsehood and trade libel, engineering and technical litigation, and UK and EC law governing restraint of trade and competition.

Additional experience: Members of chambers have a broad range of scientific qualifications, both academic and vocational. John Fitzgerald has wide experience of highly technical commercial contract matters. Alison Firth is joint author of the *Introduction to Intellectual Property Law* (3rd ed. 1995), and is the author of *Trade Marks the New Law*. Members of chambers also carry out prosecution/defence work in relation to intellectual property matters and are available on short notice to make applications for urgent injunctions or other urgently needed interlocutory relief.

Recruitment & Training: Applications for pupillages and tenancies should be sent to Mr. John Fitzgerald. Discretionary awards are available to pupils. Most successful applicants have a science degree, or some equivalent practical experience.

SET NUMBER 137

1 NEW SQUARE (Eben Hamilton QC)

1 NEW SQUARE, LINCOLN'S INN, LONDON, WC2A 3SA
Tel: (0171) 405 0884 **Fax:** (0171) 831 6109 **DX:** 295 LONDON/CHANCERY LANE **Email:** 1NEWSQUARE@COMPUSERVE.COM

MEMBERS:

Eben W. Hamilton QC (1962) (QC-1981)	James Munby QC (1971) (QC-1988)	David Eaton Turner (1984)
Rodney Stewart Smith (1964)	Christopher Semken (1977)	Sandra Corbett (1988)
	Michael Roberts (1978)	Colette Wilkins (1989)
Michael K.I. Kennedy (1967)	Robin Hollington (1979)	Mark Hubbard (1991)
John B.W. McDonnell QC (1968) (QC-1984)	Clive Hugh Jones (1981)	John Samuel Eidinow (1992)
	Kathryn Lampard (1984)	Sebastian Prentis (1996)
		David Warner (1996)

Head of Chambers:
Eben Hamilton QC

Senior Clerk:
Warren Lee

Tenants: 17

The Chambers: A general chancery and commercial set, in spacious chambers with modern facilities.

Work Undertaken:
Main Areas of Work: General chancery and commercial litigation, including companies, insolvency, banking, corporate finance and financial services, property, trusts, landlord and tenant, charities and professional negligence.
Additional Areas of Work: Most other areas are handled, including arbitration, securities, partnership, family law, intellectual property, entertainment, fraud, housing, judicial review, pensions, private international law, sale of goods, sports law and wills.

Clientele: Individuals, public and private companies. Most members accept Direct Professional Access; apply to the clerk for further details.

Foreign Connections: Some members appear before the courts in Hong Kong, Singapore, Malaysia, Bermuda, the Cayman Islands and Gibraltar.

Languages Spoken: French.

Robin Hollington is the author of *Minority Shareholders' Rights*.

Recruitment & Training: Pupillage applications to Sandra Corbett. Awards are available.

NEW
1
SQUARE

SET NUMBER 138

3 NEW SQUARE (Lord Goodhart QC)

3 NEW SQUARE, LINCOLN'S INN, LONDON, WC2A 3RS
Tel: (0171) 405 5577 **Fax:** (0171) 404 5032 **DX:** 384 (CH.LN.) **Email:** LAW@THREENEWSQUARE.DEMON.CO.UK

MEMBERS:

Lord Goodhart QC (1957) (QC-1979)	Bernard Weatherill QC QC (1974) (QC-1996)	Charles Marquand (1987)
Hubert Picarda QC (1962) (QC-1992)	Andrew Walker (1975)	Adam Deacock (1991)
	Michael Heywood (1975)	Justin Holmes (1993)
Hedley Marten (1966)	Josephine Hayes (1980)	Mary Hughes (1995)
David Rowell (1972)	Thomas Jefferies (1981)	Dov Ohrenstein (1995)
David Parry (1972)	Roger Mullis (1987)	Camilla Lamont (1995)

Head of Chambers:
Lord Goodhart QC

Senior Clerk:
Richard Bayliss

Tenants: 17

The Chambers: 3 New Square is a modern commercial chancery set committed to a vigorous tradition of excellence. Advocacy, advice and drafting are available in all areas, with efficient administration.

Work Undertaken:

Commercial: Banking, credit and security, competition, contracts, consumer credit, economic torts, finance, franchising, fraud, forgery and misrepresentation, guarantees, partnerships, title retention, restitution and tracing.

Company: Companies Court, capital, charges, directors' disqualification, directors' duties, liquidation, receiverships, securities, shareholder disputes.

European Law: All aspects relating to other work undertaken.

Financial services: City regulation, tribunals; derivative instruments.

Insolvency: Corporate and personal, including international.

Judicial review

Professional negligence: Legal, financial, surveyors & valuers.

Pension Schemes: All aspects of occupational and personal pension schemes; fraud and insolvency.

Property: Commercial, agricultural and residential; constructive trusts, conveyancing, easements, highways, landlord and tenant, Lands Tribunal, licences, mortgages and securities, planning, property-related torts, restrictive covenants.

Traditional Chancery: Charities, Court of Protection, equitable remedies, fiduciary duties, probate, tax & tax planning (including VAT), trusts & settlements, wills.

Publications:

* *Specific Performance* (2nd ed 1996) – Lord Goodhart QC (with Prof Gareth Jones QC);
* *The Law & Practice Relating to Charities* (2nd ed 1995) – Hubert Picarda QC;
* *The Law Relating to Receivers, Managers & Administrators* – Hubert Picarda QC;
* Halsbury's Laws of England (4th ed), titles on: *Corporations*, Lord Goodhart QC;
* *Money*, Charles Marquand & Dov Ohrenstein;
* *Mortgages*, Thomas Jefferies (assisted by Camilla Lamont);
* *Specific Performance*, Lord Goodhart QC;
* *Receivers*, Hubert Picarda QC.

Direct Professional Access (inc overseas). Fees negotiated with clerk, fixed or hourly basis.

SET NUMBER
139 THREE NEW SQUARE (David E.M. Young QC)

3 NEW SQUARE, LINCOLN'S INN, LONDON, WC2A 3RS
Tel: (0171) 405 1111 **Fax:** (0171) 405 7800 **DX:** 454 **Email:** THREENEWIP@AOL.COM

MEMBERS:

David Young QC (1966) (QC-1980)	Richard Miller QC (1976) (QC-1995)	Colin Birss (1990)
Antony Watson QC (1968) (QC-1986)	Guy Burkill (1981)	Justin Turner (1992)
Simon Thorley QC (1972) (QC-1989)	Andrew Waugh QC (1982) (QC-1998)	Douglas James Campbell (1993)
	Denise McFarland (1987)	Thomas Mitcheson (1996)

Head of Chambers:
David E.M. Young QC

Senior Clerk:
Ian Bowie

Tenants: 11

Members belong to the Intellectual Property and Chancery Bar Associations. David Young is the author of *Passing Off*, Chairman of the Plant Seeds Varieties Tribunal, a recorder on the South Eastern Circuit and Deputy Judge of the Patent County Court. David Young, Anthony Watson and Simon Thorley are deputy High Court Judges in Chancery and Queens' Bench Division. Simon Thorley is a part-time Chairman of the Copyright Tribunal and is Chairman of the Intellectual Property Bar Association. In addition, for many years, members have edited *Terrell on the Law of Patents*.

The Chambers: A specialist intellectual property set. The Chambers' clientele are mostly companies – Direct Professional Access is accepted.

Word Processing: The chambers use Word for Windows and discs will be provided on request using Word for Windows, WordPerfect 5.1 and other formats.

Work Undertaken:

Intellectual Property: Covering a wide range of subject areas, particularly science, technology, biotechnology, entertainment and media, including patents (UK and European), copyright, designs (registered and unregistered), service marks, plantbreeders rights, trade marks (registered and unregistered), passing off, trade libel and malicious falsehood, confidential information, franchising and licensing (including licences of right and product licensing) and information technology. Members also handle related aspects of EC law and general litigation with a significant technical content.

Additional Areas of Work: Arbitration and professional negligence.

Clientele: Mainly companies.

Foreign Connections: Chambers' QCs have appeared in Singapore and Hong Kong.

Continues overleaf

Former Members: Sir Douglas Falconer, Lord Justice Aldous.

Languages Spoken: French, German and Japanese.

Recruitment & Training: Tenancy and pupillage applications should be made via the PACH scheme. Awards of £7,500 per six months are available (currently under review). Mini-pupillages are offered throughout the year. A science degree is preferred.

SET NUMBER
140

5 NEW SQUARE (Jonathan Rayner James QC)

5 NEW SQUARE, LINCOLN'S INN, LONDON, WC2A 3RJ
Tel: (0171) 404 0404 **Fax:** (0171) 831 6016 **Pager:** (01426) 109206 **DX:** 272 LONDON
Email: CHAMBERS@FIVENEWSQUARE.CITYSCAPE.CO.UK **Internet:** WWW.CITYSCAPE.CO.UK/USERS/FK40

MEMBERS:

Jonathan Rayner James QC (1971) (QC-1988)
Kevin Garnett QC (1975) (QC-1991)
James Sunnucks (1950) DL
Ernest H Scamell (1949) + Recorder

Sir Patrick Sinclair (1961)
John Ross Martyn (1969) +
Alexander Stewart (1975)
Edward Bragiel (1977)
Paul Dickens (1978)
Amanda Michaels (1981)

Julia Clark (1984)
Nicholas Caddick (1986)
Gwilym Harbottle (1987)
Simon Sugar (1990)
Andrew Norris (1995)
Alistair Abbott (1996)

Head of Chambers:
Jonathan Rayner James QC

Senior Clerk:
Ian Duggan

Tenants: 16

The Chambers: A progressive set that continues to adapt to meet the needs of modern practice, providing a cost-effective service that is suited to the problems involved. Chambers specialise in two core areas:

Intellectual Property & Entertainment:
Copyright, Designs, Moral Rights, Performers' Rights, Trade Marks, Passing Off, Patents, Criminal Remedies, Copyright Tribunal, Entertainment Contracts, Confidential Information, Related EC Aspects.

Chancery/Commercial:
Company, Partnership, Insolvency, Charities, Wills & Administration, Inheritance Act, Trusts & Fiduciaries, Banking & Securities, Land Law & Conveyancing, Landlord & Tenant, Capital Taxes, Professional Negligence.

SET NUMBER
141

7 NEW SQUARE (Nicholas Storey)

7 NEW SQUARE, LINCOLN'S INN, LONDON, WC2A 3QS
Tel: (0171) 430 1660 **Fax:** (0171) 430 1531 **DX:** 106 (CH.LN.)

MEMBERS:

Margaret Puxon QC (1954) (QC-1982)
Philip Proghoulis (1963)
Martin Burr (1978)
Nicholas Storey (1982)
Andrew Gifford (1988)

Andrew Baker (1990)
Linda Goldman (1990)
John Suddaby (1990)
Farah Amin (1991)
Paul Taylor (1991)
Lisa Sinclair (1993)

Margaret Bloom (1994)
Fiona Darroch (1994)
Katherine Howells (1994)
Sally Bullock (1995)
Timothy Ludbrook (1996)

Head of Chambers:
Nicholas Storey

Senior Clerk:
John Collins

Tenants: 16

SET NUMBER
142

8 NEW SQUARE (Michael Fysh QC)

8 NEW SQUARE, LINCOLN'S INN, LONDON, WC2A 3QP
Tel: (0171) 405 4321 **Pager** (24 Hours): 01459 115439 **Fax:** (0171) 405 9955 **DX:** 379 (CH.LN)

MEMBERS:

Michael Fysh QC SC (1994) (1965) (QC-1989)
Alun Kynric Lewis QC (1954) (QC-1978)
Peter Prescott QC (1970) (QC-1990)
John Baldwin QC (1977) (QC-1991)
David Kitchin QC (1977) (QC-1994)

Mark Platts-Mills QC (1974) (QC-1995)
Martin Howe QC (1978) (QC-1996)
Mary Vitoria QC (1975) (QC-1997)
George Hamer (1974)
Fiona Clark (1982)
James Mellor (1986)
Daniel Alexander (1988)

Robert Onslow (1991)
Michael Tappin (1991)
Richard Meade (1991)
Adrian Speck (1993)
James St. Ville (1995)
Charlotte May (1995)
Thomas Moody-Stuart (1995)
Lindsay Lane (1996)

Head of Chambers:
Michael Fysh QC

Senior Clerk:
John F. Call

Deputy Senior Clerk:
Tony Liddon

Assistant Clerk: Susan Harding

Tenants: 20

The Chambers: The chambers specialise in intellectual property law of all kinds, and are the largest set in the country practising in this area. Many members of chambers are authors of, or contributors to, the leading books and encyclopaedias on intellectual property law. All are members of the Patent and Chancery Bar Associations.

A brochure giving further information and individual biographies of all members of chambers is available upon request. Our clerks, John Call, Tony Liddon and Sue Harding have each been with chambers for over 18 years and have considerable experience of the work undertaken by Chambers. They will be happy to assist in choice of Counsel.

Former Members: Mr Justice Jacob, Mr Justice Laddie

Work Undertaken: Intellectual property, including patents, copyright, passing off, trade and service marks, designs and registered designs, counterfeiting, data protection, franchising, hallmarks, plant breeders' rights, publishing, telecommunications, trade libel, trade descriptions, trade secrets and confidential information. Members also specialise in European law, competition and restrictive trade practices, entertainment and media law, advertising law, computer law, licensing and administrative law (principally where these are ancillary to intellectual property cases). Commercial, environmental and other work with a significant scientific or technical content is also handled.

Foreign Connections: Several members of chambers conduct cases in the Far East, Australia, India and Ireland.

Languages Spoken: French, German, Spanish and Welsh.

Recruitment & Training: Up to two pupillages are offered each year, usually for twelve months. Pupils with scientific or technical backgrounds are strongly encouraged, although others will be considered in exceptional circumstances. Awards of £20,000 are offered. Chambers are members of PACH (Pupillage Applications Clearing House).

SET NUMBER
143 | 11 NEW SQUARE (Peter Crampin QC)

11 NEW SQUARE, LINCOLN'S INN, LONDON, WC2A 3QB
Tel: (0171) 831 0081 **Fax:** (0171) 405 0798/2560 **DX:** 319

MEMBERS:

Peter Crampin QC (1976) (QC-1993)	Stephen Lloyd (1971)	Alistair Craig (1983)
Sonia Proudman QC (1972) (QC-1994)	Jill Gibson (1972)	Gilead Cooper (1983)
	Michael Jefferis (1976)	Ulick Staunton (1984)
Miles Shillingford (1964)	Mark Studer (1976)	Piers Feltham (1985)
Roger Horne (1967)	Robert Pearce (1977)	Howard Smith (1986)
Dirik Jackson (1969)	Andrew Francis (1977)	Marie-Claire Bleasdale (1993)
Peter Castle (1970)	Thomas Dumont (1979)	Daniel Margolin (1995)

Head of Chambers:
Peter Crampin QC

Senior Clerk:
Michael Gibbs

Asst. Senior Clerk: Gary Ventura

Tenants: 20

11 New Square is a leading and progressive set of chambers specialising in Chancery work. Its members – two silks and eighteen juniors – possess notable expertise in both traditional and evolving areas of chancery practice.

The aims of chambers are:
To provide first class advocacy, advice and drafting in the areas of member's expertise.
To develop constructive and lasting working relationships between members and their clients.
To be approachable, and responsive to the needs of clients.

Work Undertaken:
Property: All aspects of land law and conveyancing, and landlord and tenant work. Chambers contains specialists in restrictive covenants, easements (including rights of light) and mines and minerals.
Trusts and Estates: All aspects of the administration of trusts and estates, including probate and family provision litigation. Members offer specialist expertise in the field of the taxation of trusts.
Professional Negligence: Members of Chambers at all levels have wide experience in the conduct and defence of claims for professional negligence, particularly of solicitors, accountants and surveyors.
Charities and Pensions: Chambers contains groups of members with particular expertise in both these areas.
Commercial Law: Particularly in areas such as banking and security, partnerships and joint ventures.
Company and Corporate and individual insolvency: In the corporate field, members have particular experience in areas such as minority shareholders' rights and directors' conduct, winding up, administration and receivership.

Additional Specialisations: Individual members of Chambers have developed particular expertise in a wide variety of other fields such as planning, environmental waste, judicial review, intellectual property, Court of Protection work and the taxation of costs.

Members of chambers are members of the Chancery Bar Association, the Professional Negligence Bar Association, PEBA, STEP, the Charity Law Association and ACTAPS.

11 NEW SQUARE (John Gardiner QC)

11 NEW SQUARE, LINCOLN'S INN, LONDON, WC2A 3QB
Tel: (0171) 242 4017 **Fax:** (0171) 831 2391 **DX:** 315 **Email:** JOHNMOORE@11NEWSQUARE.COM **Internet:** WWW.11NEWSQUARE.COM

MEMBERS:

John Gardiner QC (1968) (QC-1982)	Peter Rees QC (1953) (QC-1969)	Jonathan Peacock (1987)
Barry Pinson QC (1949) (QC-1973)	Peter Trevett QC (1971) (QC-1992)	Francis Fitzpatrick (1990)
		Grania Lyster (1992)
		Jolyon Maugham (1997)

Head of Chambers:
John Gardiner QC

Senior Clerk:
J. Moore

Tenants: 8

Areas of Practice: This is the oldest established set to specialise exclusively in revenue law. Members advise in the UK and abroad on all aspects of tax law including all personal and corporate taxes, VAT and customs and stamp duties. Tax planning and advocacy services are provided for clients ranging from large multinational corporations to private individuals including those of modest means. The set also advises in relation to professional negligence actions.

The chambers offer a considerable range of experience in litigation before tribunals of first instance including the Commissioners of Inland Revenue and VAT Tribunals through the High Court to the House of Lords and the European Court of Human Rights and the courts of certain colonies and Commonwealth jurisdictions.

Languages: French, Luxembourgeoise.

Internet: The chambers maintain pages on the world wide web, displaying the latest information about chambers and including tax law articles and other information. The web pages can be found at www.11newsquare.com on the Internet.

12 NEW SQUARE (John Mowbray QC)

12 NEW SQUARE, LINCOLN'S INN, LONDON, WC2A 3SW
Tel: (0171) 419 1212 **Fax:** (0171) 419 1313 **DX:** 366 LONDON/CHANCERY LANE LIX: LON 057 **Email:** 12NEWSQUARE@COMPUSERVE.COM **Internet:** HTTP://OURWORLD.COMPUSERVE.COM/HOMEPAGES/12NEWSQUARE

MEMBERS:

John Mowbray QC (1953) (QC-1974)	Nicholas Le Poidevin (1975)	Nicholas Terras (1993)
John Macdonald QC (1955) (QC-1976)	Stuart Barber (1979)	Louise Davies (1995)
Charles Purle QC (1970) (QC-1989)	Sara Hargreaves (1979)	Edwin Simpson (1990)
George Laurence QC (1972) (QC-1991)	Stephen Smith (1983)	Richard Buckley (1969)
	Leigh Sagar (1983)	John Muir (1968) +
Lynton Tucker (1971)	Claire Staddon (1985)	Robert Sterling (1970) +
Colin Braham (1971)	Ross Crail (1986)	Anthony Elleray QC (1977) (QC-1993) +
Christopher Russell (1971)	Ian Peacock (1990)	Roger Birch (1979) +
	Simon Adamyk (1991)	Mark Cawson (1982) +
	Jane Evans-Gordon (1992)	

+ Door Tenant

Head of Chambers:
John Mowbray QC

Senior Clerk:
Clive Petchey

Tenants: 21

Work Undertaken: 12 New Square undertakes litigation and advisory work, both in the UK and internationally, including Direct Professional Access and legal aid work. The work done by members of Chambers covers three broad areas: Company and commercial – including individual and corporate insolvency, receivership, partnership, Mareva injunctions, Anton Piller orders and fraud; Property – including landlord and tenant, mortgages and conveyancing; Trusts – equity, probate, pension schemes and capital taxation. Members of Chambers also cover public/administrative law aspects of these areas including parliamentary, public inquiries, local government and planning law, judicial review and constitutional law. Our practice extends to the above areas as well as negligence on the part of professionals in those fields.

John Mowbray Q.C. is a member if the Bahamian Bar and has also been called to the Eastern Caribbean Bar, as have John Macdonald Q.C., Charles Purle Q.C., Stephen Smith and Nicholas Terras. Nicholas Le Poidevin is a member of the Isle of Man Bar.

A brochure, containing a more detailed profile of Chambers, with some of our reported cases, is available on request, or via our Web site at:
http://ourworld.compuserve.com/homepages/12newsquare

Languages: French and German.

Pupillage: Applications via PACH.

19 OLD BUILDINGS (Alastair Wilson QC)

19 OLD BUILDINGS, LINCOLN'S INN, LONDON, WC2A 3UP
Tel: (0171) 405 2001 **Fax:** (0171) 405 0001 **DX:** 397 (CH.LN.) **Email:** CLERKS@OLDBUILDINGSIP.COM

MEMBERS:

Alastair Wilson QC (1968)
(QC-1987) MA (Cantab)

Brian Reid (1971) MA
(Cantab), LLM (Lond)

Graham Shipley (1973) MA
(Cantab), Dip Comp Sci (Cantab)

Michael Hicks (1976) BA
(Cantab)

Peter McLean Colley (1989)
BSc (Lond), PhD (Lond), LLB
(Lond)

Cedric Puckrin (1990) BA,
LLB (Cape Town)

Rory Sullivan (1992) MA
(Oxon)

Tamsin Holman (1995) MA
(Oxon)

Head of Chambers:	Alastair Wilson QC
Senior Clerk:	Barbara Harris
Tenants: 8	

The Chambers: This set – founded by Sir Duncan Kerly – has specialised for over a century in intellectual property law. Chambers also offer expertise in cases relating to computers and other technical subject matter, competition, media and entertainment. Publications written or contributed to by members of chambers include: *European Patent Office Reports, The Future of Legal Protection for Industrial Design, The CIPA Black Book, Melville's Forms and Agreements on Intellectual Property and International Licensing.*

Direct Professional Access work is undertaken. A chambers brochure is available on request.

Work Undertaken:

Intellectual Property: Patents, copyright, designs, trade marks, passing off, plant varieties, confidential information (including ex-employee cases).

Computers and other technical subject-matter: Advocacy requiring technical or scientific ability.

Media and Entertainment: Public performance, film, recording and performers' rights; merchandising; broadcasting, cable and satellite distribution.

Competition Law: UK and EC monopolies and restrictive practices law, in particular relating to r and d, licensing, distribution and franchising.

Additional areas: Pharmaceutical registration.

Languages: French.

22 OLD BUILDINGS (Benet Hytner QC)

22 OLD BUILDINGS, LINCOLN'S INN, LONDON, WC2A 3UJ
Tel: (0171) 831 0222 **Fax:** (0171) 831 2239 **DX:** 201 LDE

MEMBERS:

Benet Hytner QC (1952)
(QC-1970)

John Price QC (1961)
(QC-1980)

Giles Wingate-Saul QC
(1967) (QC-1983)

Brian Leveson QC (1970)
(QC-1986)

Rodney Scholes QC (1968)
(QC-1987)

Timothy King QC (1973)
(QC-1991)

Geoffrey Tattersall QC
(1970) (QC-1992)

Caroline Swift QC (1977)
(QC-1993)

Andrew Moran QC (1976)
(QC-1994)

David Allan QC (1974)
(QC-1995)

Michael Black QC (1978)
(QC-1995)

Stephen Stewart QC (1975)
(QC-1996)

Patrick Hamlin (1970)

Mark Batchelor (1971)

Susan Cooper (1976)

Michael Daiches (1977)

Anne Ralphs (1977)

Charles Utley (1979)

Jane Hill (1980)

Howard Lederman (1982)

Rehna Azim (1984)

Jonathan Bennett (1985)

Rajinder Sahonte (1986)

Tina Cook (1988)

Simon Chapman (1988)

Frank Feehan (1988)

Gemma Taylor (1988)

Ronald Coster (1989)

Anthony Jerman (1989)

Lee Arnot (1990)

Richard Furniss (1991)

Mary Lazarus (1991)

Paul Lonergan (1991)

Emma Romer (1992)

Marcia Hyde (1992)

Daniel Oudkerk (1992)

John Horan (1993)

Matthew Hutchings (1993)

Philip Rogers (1994)

Sarah Kewley (1994)

Naomi Hawkes (1994)

Stefano Nuvoloni (1994)

Damian Woodward-Carlton
(1995)

Anna Thomas (1995)

Angus Withington (1995)

Henry Pitchers (1996)

Gareth Compton (1997)

Head of Chambers:	Benet Hytner QC
Senior Clerk:	Alan Brewer (London) Peter Collison (Manchester)
Tenants: 47	

All the Silks are based at 25, Byrom Street, Manchester and all the juniors at 22 Old Buildings, Lincoln's Inn.

24 OLD BUILDINGS (G.R Bretten QC) 24 Old Buildings (First Floor), Lincoln's Inn, London, WC2A 3UJ **Tel:** (0171) 242 2744 **Fax:** (0171) 831 8095 **DX:** 386 **Clerk:** Mr Anthony Hall **Tenants:** 9 A specialist revenue law set, dealing with all tax matters and revenue litigation.

SET NUMBER
149 **24 OLD BUILDINGS** (C.A. Brodie QC)

24 OLD BUILDINGS, LINCOLN'S INN, LONDON, WC2A 3UJ
Tel: (0171) 404 0946 **Fax:** (0171) 405 1360 **DX:** 307 (CH.LN.) **Email:** CLERKS@24OLDBUILDINGS.LAW.CO.UK

Internet: HTTP://WWW.24OLDBUILDINGS.LAW.CO.UK

MEMBERS:

Colin Brodie QC (1954)
(QC-1980)
Martin Mann QC (1968)
(QC-1983)
Alan Steinfeld QC (1968)
(QC-1987)
Roger Kaye QC (1970)
(QC-1989)
Lawrence Cohen QC (1974)
(QC-1993)
Thomas Baxendale (1962)
Philip Shepherd (1975)

Michael King (1971)
Paul Teverson (1976)
John Davies (1977)
Richard Ritchie (1978)
Francis Tregear (1980)
Daniel Gerrans (1981)
Michael Gadd (1981)
Elizabeth Weaver (1982)
Stephen Moverley Smith (1985)
Helen Galley (1987)
Adrian Francis (1988)

Amanda Harington (1989)
Elspeth Talbot Rice (1990)
Nicholas Cherryman (1991)
Christopher Young (1988)
Clare Stanley (1994)
Stuart Adair (1995)
Bajul Shah (1996)
Steven Thompson (1996)
Graham Virgo MA BCL
(academic) (Door Tenant)

Head of Chambers:
C.A. Brodie QC

Senior Clerk:
Nicholas Luckman

First Junior Clerk:
Jeremy Hopkins

Listing:
Daniel Wilson

Fees Administration:
Tony Steeden

Tenants: 26

24 Old Buildings with 21 juniors and 5 Queen's Counsel is a large commercial Chancery litigation Chambers, specialising in litigation arising from most areas of commercial dispute.

The Chambers: 24 Old Buildings was established as a result of a merger of two eminent Chancery sets over thirty years ago. Since then Chambers has developed to reflect the changes that have taken place in the Chancery field and now offers the specialist expertise required for a wide range of commercial and equity disputes and problems. Although Chambers specialises principally in litigation, members also provide specialist advice on specific points of law and construction, and generally in relation to situations involving legal or factual difficulties. Members have been involved in some of the most widely reported cases of the last ten years, involving such well known names as BCCI, Maxwell, Barings, Barlow Clowes, B & C, The Lloyds litigation and Tottenham Hotspur.

Martin Mann QC, Alan Steinfeld QC and Roger Kaye QC sit as Deputy Judges in the Chancery Division of the High Court; Richard Ritchie is Standing Counsel to the Department of Trade and Industry (Insolvency) and Junior Counsel to the Crown (Chancery), Stephen Moverley Smith is Junior Counsel to the Crown (Chancery).

Members appear in the civil courts (particularly the High Court and county courts throughout the UK), tribunals (including Insolvency Practitioners' and the Institute of Chartered Accountants) and overseas courts (including the Cayman Islands, the British Virgin Islands, Bermuda, Hong Kong, Singapore, the Turks & Caicos, and the Isle of Man). Chambers has strong connections with law firms in New York and Geneva. All members undertake Direct Professional Access instructions from members of recognised professional institutions, particularly accountants and surveyors. Members of Chambers belong to the following specialist associations: Chancery Bar, Professional Negligence, Insolvency Lawyers, Pension Lawyers, and Contentious Trust and Probate Specialists. Members include the Consultant editor and expert contributors to the publication "Tolley's Insolvency Law".

Chambers continues to invest heavily in information technology both as a research tool and in the interest of administrative efficiency. Considerable importance is placed on recruitment in order to attract high calibre barristers, and consolidate Chambers strength in the key areas of work.

Members work in specialist groups within Chambers covering the following areas of law:
Civil Fraud: Including the tracing, recovery and freezing of assets.
Company law: Including mergers and acquisitions, reductions of capital, shareholders' rights, directors' duties and liability, directors' disqualification.
Commercial Law: Comprising a wide range of general contract and business law including commercial contracts, banking, mortgages, guarantees, securities and bills of exchange.
Contract Disputes: Advice and litigation concerning all sorts of contractual issues, including such specialist areas as computers, entertainment and restraint of trade.
Financial Services: Advice and litigation in relation to the Financial Services Act 1986 and ancillary regulations. Acting for investors, financial services providers and regulatory bodies such as the FSA and the PIA.
Insolvency: *Both individual and corporate*, including liquidations, administration and receivership.
Pensions: Advice and litigation for employers, pension fund trustees receivers and liquidators, and members of occupational pension schemes. Categories include breach of trust and employers' and trustees' duties in administration and winding up processes.

Property: Including landlord and tenant (residential and commercial- including rent reviews and valuations disputes), conveyancing, easements, restrictive covenants, vendor and purchaser disputes.

Professional Negligence: Particularly in matters involving solicitors, accountants and surveyors.

Trusts: Including breach of trust claims, constructive trusts, appointment and removal of trustees.

Probate: including Inheritance Act claims.

SET NUMBER
150 OLD SQUARE CHAMBERS (Hon. John Melville Williams QC)

1 VERULAM BUILDINGS, GRAY'S INN, LONDON, WC1R 5LQ
Tel: (0171) 269 0300 **Fax:** (0171) 405 1387 **DX:** 1046 CHANCERY LANE/LONDON

MEMBERS:

John Melville Williams QC (1955) (QC-1977)	John H. Bates (1973)	Jonathan Clarke (1990)
John Hendy QC (1972) (QC-1987)	Christopher Makey (1975)	Christopher Walker (1990)
John Hand QC (1972) (QC-1988)	Nigel Cooksley (1975)	Nicholas Booth (1991)
	Charles Pugh (1975)	Sarah Moor (1991)
Lord Wedderburn QC (1953) (QC-1990)	Matthias Kelly (1979)	Ian Scott (1991)
	Toby Kempster (1980)	Oliver Segal (1992)
Jeremy McMullen QC (1971) (QC-1994)	Paul Rose (1981)	Helen Gower (1992)
	Jane McNeill (1982)	Roy Lewis (1992)
Ian Truscott QC (1995) (QC-1997)	Barry Cotter (1985)	Mark Whitcombe (1994)
	Louise Chudleigh (1987)	Elizabeth Melville (1994)
Charles Lewis (1963)	Ijeoma Omambala (1988)	Melanie Tether (1995)
Christopher Carling (1969)	Jennifer Eady (1989)	Emma Smith (1995)
William Birtles (1970)	Philip Mead (1989)	Rohan Pirani (1995)
Diana Brahams (1972)	Damian Brown (1989)	
	Tess Gill (1990)	

Head of Chambers:
Hon. John Melville Williams QC

Senior Clerk:
John Taylor

Administrator:
Brenda Brown

Tenants: 38

Old Square Chambers, Hanover House 47 Corn Street, Bristol BS1 1HT
Tel: (0117) 927 7111 Fax: (0117) 927 3478 DX: 78229 Bristol.

Work Undertaken: Employment law, personal injury and product liability, medical negligence, environmental law and sports law.

Languages Spoken: French, German, Spanish, Italian, Dutch, Ibo.

Foreign Connections: There are door tenants practising at the Hong Kong, Bermuda, Scotland, Northern Ireland and Jersey Bars.

SET NUMBER
151 9 OLD SQUARE (Robert Reid QC)

9 OLD SQUARE, LINCOLN'S INN, LONDON, WC2A 3SR
Tel: (0171) 405 4682 **Fax:** (0171) 831 7107 **DX:** 305 LX: LON 069 **Email:** CHAMBERS@9OLDSQUARE.CO.UK

MEMBERS:

Robert Reid QC (1965) (QC-1980)	David Hodge QC (1979) (QC-1997)	Christopher Stoner (1991)
Michael Driscoll QC (1970) (QC-1992)	Daniel Hochberg (1982)	Andrew P.D. Walker (1991)
	John Dagnall (1983)	Simon Burrell (1988)
Nicholas Patten QC (1974) (QC-1988)	John McGhee (1984)	Michael Pryor (1992)
	Timothy Harry (1983)	Alan Johns (1994)
Judith Jackson QC (1975) (QC-1994)	Edwin Johnson (1987)	Stephanie Tozer (1996)
Simon Berry QC (1977) (QC-1990)	Thomas Leech (1988)	William V.W Norris (1997)
	Katharine Holland (1989)	

Head of Chambers:
Robert Reid QC

Senior Clerk:
Christopher McSweeney

Tenants: 20

The Chambers: A well-established chancery set. The practice of chambers extends to all aspects of landlord and tenant and real property, company, partnership, insolvency, mortgages and professional negligence with a strong emphasis on litigation. The Chambers does a substantial amount of sports related work.

Work Undertaken:

Real Property: Including vendor and purchaser, mortgages, restrictive covenants, easements, conveyancing, possessory title, licences and estoppel interests, nuisance and other property related torts.

Professional Negligence: Including solicitors, surveyors, accountants and other finance and property related professional negligence, professional disciplinary proceedings and wasted costs orders.

Continues overleaf

Landlord and Tenant: Including rent reviews, dilapidations claims and other Official Referees Business, leasehold enfranchisement, business, residential and agricultural tenancies.

Commercial: Loans, guarantees, mortgages, partnerships, personal property, including retention of title, sale of goods and consumer credit, confidential information, passing off, covenants restricting trade or employment, fraud, misrepresentation, conspiracy and other economic torts, Mareva and Anton Piller Orders.

Insolvency: Personal and corporate insolvency, receivers and administrators.

Company: Including minority shareholder protection, shares sale disputes, directors' duties and directors' disqualification.

Trusts and Related Areas: Constructive trusts, offshore trusts, tracing claims, settlements and wills, probate, administration of estates and family provision, charities, unincorporated associations and clubs.

Sports law: Disciplinary and constitutional matters, commercial exploitation of sporting events, advising governing bodies.

Individual Specialisations: Individual members have additional fields of specialisation which include building societies, compulsory purchase, computer law, judicial review, local government, the law of markets and fairs and shops, oil and mining law, parliamentary work, planning law, environmental law and trading standards.

Client Base: Chambers act for a broad range of commercial and private clients; legal aid work is undertaken. Most members accept Direct Professional Access work (contact clerk for details). Members are instructed by lawyers in the Far East, the Bahamas, Bermuda, the Cayman Islands, Gibraltar, Jersey and other jurisdictions.

Languages: French, German, Spanish.

Information Technology: Most IBM compatible word-processing software can be accommodated. Electronic transfer of documents is available (LIX) or E-mail. Contact clerks for details.

9
OLD SQUARE

---

10 OLD SQUARE (Leolin Price CBE QC)

10 OLD SQUARE, LINCOLN'S INN, LONDON, WC2A 3SU
Tel: (0171) 405 0758 **Fax:** (0171) 831 8237 **DX:** 306

MEMBERS:

Leolin Price QC (1949) (QC-1968) CBE	Richard Wallington (1972)	David Partington (1987)
James Bonney QC (1975) (QC-1995)	George Newsom (1973)	Susannah Meadway (1988)
	Andrew Lloyd-Davies (1975)	Eason Rajah (1989)
Michael Mello QC (Bermuda)	Rt. Hon. James Arbuthnot M.P (1975)	Rupert D'Cruz (1989)
Philip Rossdale (1948)	Jeffrey Price (1975)	Jeremy Callman (1991)
David Ainger (1961)	David Schmitz (1976)	Jonathan Gavaghan (1992)
Michael Mark (1964)	Owen Rhys (1976)	Samuel Laughton (1993)
Francis Barlow (1965)	Geraint Thomas (1976)	Kevin Farrelly (1993)
David Ritchie (1970)	Simon Taube (1980)	Michael Waterworth (1994)
Frances Burton (1972)	Andrew De La Rosa (1981)	Luke Norbury (1995)
Gregory Hill (1972)	Michael Michell (1984)	Nicholas Harries (1995)
	Dr. Paul Stafford (1987)	Robert Arnfield (1996)

Head of Chambers:
Leolin Price CBE QC

Senior Clerk:
Keith Plowman

Tenants: 34

The Chambers: 10 Old Square is a large Chancery set with barristers specialising in every area within the broad spectrum of Chancery Law.

Principal Areas of Work: Trusts, Charities, Probate, Administration of Estates, Wills Receivership, Insolvency, Taxation, Landlord and Tenant, Company, Property, Building, Commercial, Professional Negligence, and Partnership are all comprehensively covered.

Additional Specialisations: Commercial and Financial Regulation, Litigation in Foreign Courts and all Commonwealth jurisdictions, Privy Council Appeals, Water & Sewerage, Sale of Goods, Navigation, Fisheries, Employment, Construction and Arbitrations.

Detailed information is available from the Senior Clerk who is happy to provide advice on the availability of suitable counsel.

10 OLD SQUARE

SET NUMBER
153 **11 OLD SQUARE** (Grant Crawford & Jonathan Simpkiss)

11 OLD SQUARE, LINCOLN'S INN, LONDON, WC2A 3TS
Tel: (0171) 430 0341 **Fax:** (0171) 831 2469 **DX:** 1031 **Email:** CLERKS@11OLDSQUARE.CO.UK

MEMBERS:

Carol Ellis CBE QC (1951) (QC-1980)

Edward Davidson QC (1966) (QC-1994)

Gordon Nurse (1973)

Grant Crawford (1974)

Jonathan Simpkiss (1975) FCI Arb

Peter Smith QC (1975) (QC-1992)

Reziya Harrison (1975) FCI Arb

Malcolm Waters QC (1977) (QC-1997)

Stephen Acton (1977)

Elizabeth Ovey (1978)

Keith Rowley (1979)

Sián Thomas (1981)

Glenn Campbell (1985)

Mark West (1987)

Katherine McQuail (1989)

Nigel Burroughs (1991)

Peter Dodge (1992)

Tony Oakley (1994)

Benjamin Davey (1994)

Nicole Sandells (1994)

Kate Selway (1995)

Alex Hall Taylor (1996)

Head of Chambers:
Grant Crawford & Jonathan Simpkiss

Senior Clerk:
Keith Nagle

Tenants: 22

Work Undertaken: General Description: The work undertaken by members of chambers is primarily in the chancery and commercial fields, and extends to a wide range of litigation, advisory and drafting work.

Property: Conveyancing, land law, landlord and tenant, (business, residential, leasehold enfranchisement and agricultural), mortgages and securities, rent reviews, nuisance and property-related torts.

Commercial: Commercial agreements, sale of goods, economic torts, guarantees, joint ventures, partnerships, restraint of trade and consumer credit.

Company: Minority shareholder protection and other intra-company disputes, directors' fiduciary duties, take-overs, mergers and acquisitions.

Insolvency: Corporate and individual insolvency, receiverships, liquidations, administrations and voluntary arrangements.

Professional Negligence: Claims involving solicitors, barristers, accountants, surveyors and others.

Chancery: Trusts, breach of trust, charities, clubs and friendly societies, Court of Protection, wills, probate, administration of estates and family provision.

Pension Schemes: Advice and litigation.

Building Societies: Constitution and powers, relations with members and third parties, mergers, take-overs and conversion, standard documentation.

Finance: Banking (including security documentation) and financial services.

Additional areas: Confidential information, copyright and passing off, conflict of laws, judicial review.

Clientele: Chambers operate the Direct Professional Access scheme. Instructions are also accepted from lawyers abroad, in particular the Far East, but also from jurisdictions in Europe and elsewhere.

Languages: French and Spanish.

Word Processing System: Microsoft Word, IBM compatible, 3.5" disks. Please speak to the clerks if you wish to deliver or receive text on disk or by electronic communication.

Publications: *'Swaps and Local Authorities: A Mistake?'* in *Swaps and Off-Exchange Derivatives Trading: Law and Regulation* (pub. FT Law & Tax, 1996), Mark West (co-author); *Good Faith in Sales* (pub. Sweet & Maxwell, 1997), Reziya Harrison; *Wurtzburg and Mills on Building Society Law* (pub. Sweet and Maxwell) eds. Malcolm Waters QC, Elizabeth Ovey, Kate Selway.

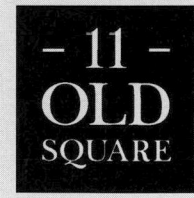

11 OLD SQUARE (Simeon Thrower)

11 OLD SQUARE, LINCOLN'S INN, LONDON, WC2A 3TS
Tel: (0171) 242 5022 **Fax:** (0171) 404 0445 **DX:** 164 LONDON CHANCERY LANE

MEMBERS:

J. Simeon Thrower (1973)	Patrice Wellesley-Cole (1975)	John Lloyd (1988)
Francesca Quint (1970)	Gordon Apsion (1977)	Jennifer Gray (1992)
Christopher H. Cutting (1973)	Nicholas Macleod-James (1986)	Gabriel Buttimore (1993)
K. Mydeen (1973)	Marc C. Maitland (1988)	Steven Ball (1995)
Malcolm D. Sinclair (1978)		Manjeet Kaler (1993)

Head of Chambers:
Simeon Thrower

Senior Clerk:
Christopher Watts

Tenants: 13

The Chambers: An established set of Chambers with a broad practice covering Chancery, common law and criminal matters.

Work undertaken: Arbitration, banking, chancery, charities, company and commercial, construction, criminal, family, fraud – both civil and criminal, housing, immigration, insolvency, insurance and reinsurance, judicial review, landlord and tenant, licensing, local government, personal injury, planning, probate, product liability, professional negligence, property, sale of goods, trusts and wills.

Clientele: Members of Chambers act for individuals, public and private companies, charities, local authorities, banks and financial institutions. Chambers operate the Direct Professional Access scheme.

Foreign Languages: German, French.

12 OLD SQUARE (Charlotte Boaitey) 12 Old Square, Lincoln's Inn, London, WC2A 3TX **Tel:** (0171) 404 0875 **Fax:** (0171) 404 8377 **Clerk:** Mr Steven Russell **Tenants:** 29 A common law set undertaking a range of work including Landlord & Tenant, Employment, Immigration, Family, Personal Injury and Crime (Prosecution & Defence).

13 OLD SQUARE (Mr Michael Lyndon-Stanford QC)

13 OLD SQUARE, LINCOLN'S INN, LONDON, WC2A 3UA
Tel: (0171) 404 4800 **Fax:** (0171) 405 4267 **DX:** 326 LONDON/CHANCERY LANE

MEMBERS:

Michael Lyndon-Stanford QC (1962) (QC-1979)	Christopher Pymont QC (1979) (QC-1996)	Carolyn Walton (1980)
Christopher H. McCall QC (1966) (QC-1987)	Catherine Newman QC (1979) (QC-1995)	Jonathan Russen (1986)
		Richard Morgan (1988)
David Oliver QC (1972) (QC-1986)	Timothy Evans (1979)	Nicholas Peacock (1989)
	Simon Barker (1979)	Gregory Banner (1989)
Hazel Williamson QC (1972) (QC-1988)	Mark Cunningham (1980)	Amanda Tipples (1991)
	Anthony Trace QC (1981) (QC-1998)	Michael Gibbon (1993)
Richard McCombe QC (1975) (QC-1989)	Paul Girolami (1983)	Rebecca Stubbs (1994)
	Matthew Collings (1985)	James Aldridge (1994)
Nigel M. Thomas (1976)	John Nicholls (1986)	Andrew Ayres (1996)
		Robert Sterling (1996)

Head of Chambers:
Mr Michael Lyndon-Stanford QC

Senior Clerk:
John C. Moore

Tenants: 26

The Chambers: This is a long established set and believes it has maintained its position at the forefront of Chancery litigators, providing high quality, well researched advice and excellent advocacy skills across a broad range of legal expertise. The vast majority of work involves litigation, actual or potential. Urgent cases are dealt with at short notice and matters requiring expertise in a number of different specialist areas are also routinely handled.

Work Undertaken:

Company Law: *Work includes:* shareholders' rights, breach of fiduciary duty, corporate insolvency, financial regulation, monopolies and mergers Members also appear in applications under the Company Directors Disqualification Act and before the tribunals which regulate the provision of financial and insolvency services.

Commercial Law: *Work includes:* judicial review, commercial contracts, banking, guarantees and securities, insurance, consumer credit, restraint of trade, partnership, personal insolvency/bankruptcy, and pre-trial remedies (urgent or otherwise).

Property: *Work includes:* landlord and tenant, vendor and purchaser, conveyancing, mortgages and securities on land, easements and covenants, boundaries, trespass and nuisance.

Professional Negligence: *Work includes:* claims against solicitors, barristers, accountants, actuaries, surveyors, valuers and architects in a company, property or commercial context.

Trusts and Related Areas: *Work includes:* wills and probate, administration of estates, family provision, charities, building and friendly societies, trusts, unincorporated associations and revenue/tax.

Intellectual Property: *Work includes:* copyright, performers' rights, design rights, moral rights, trademarks, passing off, breach of confidence, music, publishing, television and film industry work.

Additional Areas of Work: In addition to the above main areas above, practitioners have experience in diverse specialist fields, including private international law, competition law, highways, markets and commons, telecommunications, matrimonial finance and property, mental health, pensions and superannuations and lotteries.

Clientele: Many of chambers' clients come from the corporate business community, but individual clients are as welcome as the large organisations and legal aid matters are regularly undertaken.

On top of their work in London, members of Chambers appear in court and give advice throughout the UK and abroad. QCs in chambers have appeared in courts in Hong Kong, Bermuda, the Cayman Islands and elsewhere.

Several members are called to the bars of the Isle of Man, Singapore and Hong Kong. David Oliver has a License Speciale en Droit Europeen (Brussels). Hazel Williamson is a fellow of the Chartered Institue of Arbitrators. Richard McCombe is the present Attorney-General to the Duchy of Lancaster. Mark Cunningham and Paul Girolami are junior counsel to the Crown, Chancery.

13 OLD SQUARE
LINCOLN'S INN

LONDON WC2A 3UA

SET NUMBER

157 THIRTEEN OLD SQUARE (Charles Sparrow QC) Thirteen Old Square, Lincoln's Inn, London, WC2A 3UA **Tel:** (0171) 242 6105 **Fax:** (0171) 405 4004 **DX:** LDE 1025 **Email:** clerks@thirteenoldsquare.co.uk **Clerks:** Mr Terry Buck, Mr Stephen Whitaker **Tenants:** 30 Thirteen Old Square (the Chambers of Charles Sparrow QC) – see Serle Court Chambers.

SET NUMBER

158 ## ONE PAPER BUILDINGS (John Slater QC)

1 PAPER BUILDINGS, TEMPLE, LONDON, EC4Y 7EP
Tel: (0171) 583 7355 **Fax:** (0171) 353 2144 **DX:** 80

MEMBERS:

John Slater QC (1969) (QC-1987)	Martyn Berkin (1966)	Shaun Ferris (1985)
Michael Spencer QC (1970) (QC-1989)	Margaret Bickford-Smith (1973)	David Platt (1987)
Andrew Bartlett QC (1974) (QC-1993)	Colin Nixon (1973)	William Vandyck (1988)
	John Powles (1975)	Marion Egan (1988)
Simon Brown QC (1976) (QC-1995)	Nicholas Davies (1975)	Erica Power (1990)
Dr Michael Powers QC (1979) (QC-1995)	Jonathan Waite (1978)	Benedict Newman (1991)
William Stevenson QC (1968) (QC-1996)	Gordon Catford (1980)	Toby Gee (1992)
	Julian Field (1980)	Alexander Antelme (1993)
Richard Hone QC (1970) (QC-1997)	Jane Davies (1981)	Dr Margaret Branthwaite (1993)
	Steven Coles (1983)	
	James Medd (1985)	Claire Toogood (1995)

Head of Chambers:
John Slater QC

Senior Clerk:
Julian Campbell

Tenants: 28

The Chambers: A long established common law chambers, which in recent years has become more specialist. Now one of the leading sets in product liability. Past matters handled include the Sellafield leukaemia litigation, the Opren claims, the Benzodiazepine cases, cavity wall insulation the Dunlop tyre case and other substantial product liability disputes.

Work Undertaken: The principal areas of practice include: professional negligence, particularly in the subject areas of solicitors, medical, insurance, and building: Product liability, both generally and in pharmaceutical cases: Insurance, including policy disputes and reinsurance; personal injury, with in-depth expertise in industrial disease; and construction work which includes all types of building and engineering cases.

In addition, general commercial and common law work is undertaken, and individual members offer some further specialities.

Many members of One Paper Buildings are contributors to *Medical Negligence* (joint editor, Dr Michael Powers QC) or to *Emden's Construction Law* (general editor, Andrew Bartlett QC).

Direct professional access work and conditional fee work is accepted.

Brochures and CV's are available on request.

SET NUMBER
159 1 PAPER BUILDINGS (Roger Titheridge QC) 1 Paper Buildings (1st Floor), Temple, London, EC4Y 7EP **Tel:** (0171) 353 3728 **Fax:** (0171) 353 2911 **DX:** 332 **Clerk:** Mr Nigel Witchell **Tenants:** 35 Common law set with particular emphasis on crime, civil and matrimonial work.

SET NUMBER
160 ## 2 PAPER BUILDINGS (Robin Griffiths)

2 PAPER BUILDINGS, TEMPLE, LONDON, EC4Y 7ET
Tel: (0171) 936 2613 **Fax:** (0171) 353 9439 **DX:** 210 (CH.LN.)

MEMBERS:

Robin Griffiths (1970)	James Dennison (1986)	Rachael James (1992)
Richard Hayden (1964)	Mark Stern (1988)	Jennifer Dempster (1993)
Peta Gee (1973)	Sandra Briggs-Watson (1985)	Maryam Syed (1993)
Mark Love (1979)	Jamal Sapsard (1987)	
Mark Wyeth (1983)	Joseph Stone (1989)	Caroline Whysall (1993)
Eric Ogden (1983)	Polly-Anne Comfort (1988)	Fay Baker (1994)
Wendy Fisher-Gordon (1983)	John Talbot-Bagnall (1988)	John Crosfill (1995)
Quentin Purdy (1983)	Kevin Dent (1991)	Peter Dahlsen (1996)
Neil Petersen (1983)	Simon Tolkien (1994)	
Penelope Rector (1980)	Pankaj Pathak (1992)	Sally Hancox (1996)

Head of Chambers:
Robin Griffiths

Clerks:
Joanne Thomas, Marc Newson

Tenants: 28

The Chambers: We are an established common law set offering a wide range of services with particular emphasis upon all aspects of criminal law. Chambers have strong connections with the American Bar and legal academia. One member is currently an annual lecturer at the University of Iowa, College of Law.

Work Undertaken: Criminal Law, Family Law, Personal Injury, Judicial Review, Intellectual Property (with special emphasis on the music industry), Landlord and Tenant and Courts Martial.

Foreign Languages: Certain members of Chambers are fluent in foreign languages such as Urdu, Hindi, Punjabi and French.

Recruitment & Training: Chambers will always consider applications from experienced and well qualified barristers who wish to develop and specialise their practices. Four pupillages will be offered: – two 1st six pupillages (to commence in October 1999) and two 2nd six pupillages to commence in April 2000.

SET NUMBER
161 2 PAPER BUILDINGS (Steven Hadley) 2 Paper Buildings, Temple, London, EC4Y 7ET **Tel:** (0171) 353 0933 **Fax:** (0171) 353 0937 **DX:** 286 LDE **Clerk:** Ms Lynn Pilkington **Tenants:** 20 A common law set with an emphasis on criminal defence work.

SET NUMBER
162 ## 2 PAPER BUILDINGS (Desmond de Silva QC)

FIRST AND SECOND FLOORS, 2 PAPER BUILDINGS, LONDON, EC4Y 7ET
Tel: (0171) 936 2611 **Out of Hours:** 0860 416061 **Fax:** (0171) 583 3423 **DX:** LDE 494 **Email:** CLERKS@2PBBARRISTERS.CO.UK
Internet: HTTP://WWW.2PBBARRISTERS.CO.UK

MEMBERS:

Desmond de Silva QC (1964) (QC-1984)	Paul G. O'Donovan (1975)	Sharon Baxter (1987)
Lord Richard QC (1955) (QC-1971)	Christopher Sutton-Mattocks (1975)	Sandra Folkes (1989)
Nigel T. Salts QC (1961) (QC-1983)	Christopher Strachan (1975)	Marios P. Lambis (1989)
Harendra de Silva QC (1970) (QC-1995)	Jerry Hayes (1977)	Charles Benson (1990)
	Patrick Cahill (1979)	Zöe Martin (1990)
Vasant Kothari (1960)	Kim Hollis (1979)	Catherine M. Hill (1991)
Panos C. Zorbas (1964)	Michel G.A. Massih (1979)	Morag Duff (1991)
Peter J. Martin (1969)	Colin Campbell (1979)	Daren Samat (1992)
Raymond Lewis (1971)	Janina Pasiuk (1983)	Fiona Henderson (1993)
Robin Pearse Wheatley (1971)	David J. Brock (1984)	Paul Mylvaganam (1993)
Lady Ponsonby (1971)	Simon K. Ward (1984)	Stephen Brassington (1994)
Peter A. Corrigan (1972)	Lee Karu (1985)	John Kearney (1994)
Notu Hoon (1975)	John Femi-Ola (1985)	Pavlos Panayi (1995)
Roderick Johnson (1975)	Aruna Chandran (1985)	James Tilbury (1996)
	Gerard McCoy (1986)	Mark Summers (1996)
	Steven Berrick (1986)	

Head of Chambers:
Desmond de Silva QC

Senior Clerk:
Robin Driscoll

1st Junior:
Stephen Ball

2nd Junior:
John Gillespie

Fees Clerk:
Marc Jennings

Tenants: 44

The Set: 2 Paper Buildings is one of the longest established sets in the Temple. Chambers has historically had extensive political connections; former Heads of Chambers include the Rt. Hon. Sir Dingle Foot QC MP (Solicitor General), a minister in Churchill's government and Sir Charles Fletcher-Cooke QC MP, a minister in Macmillan's government. The Rt. Hon. Lord Richard of Ammanford QC, the Lord Privy Seal, is the leader of the House of Lords and a Cabinet minister.

2 Paper Buildings is a specialist defence set providing a complete service from the Magistrates Court upwards. It has a very longstanding Commonwealth connection and this is reflected in Chambers' diverse membership. In the past year the total number of members has increased by seven, including one QC.

Types of work undertaken: Members practice principally in white collar fraud, terrorist, major drugs, extradition and murder cases as well as all other criminal work. Several members of Chambers practise in the civil, family and immigration fields. Chambers has always had a strong civil liberties tradition, a number of members deal with civil actions against the police. Desmond de Silva QC has saved the lives of 35 people in Privy Council or Commonwealth cases, more than any other Barrister currently practising in England and Wales.

Various members of Chambers prosecute for different authorities. For example Desmond de Silva QC led the successful prosecution team in the extradition of Roderick Newall from Gibraltar to Jersey.

Chambers aims to continue to improve the efficiency of our service for both lay and professional clients. Though a traditional set we consider ourselves at the forefront of the modernisation and technological changes that the Bar has experienced in recent times.

2 PAPER BUILDINGS
BARRISTERS

---

163   3 PAPER BUILDINGS (Isaac Jacob)

3 PAPER BUILDINGS, TEMPLE, LONDON, EC4Y 7EU
Tel: (0171) 797 7000 **Fax:** (0171) 797 7100 **DX:** 0071 (LDE) **Email:** CLERKS@3PB.CO.UK **Internet:** WWW.3PB.CO.UK

MEMBERS:

Isaac E. Jacob (1963)	Peter McMaster (1981)	Angus Piper (1991)
Gerald Owen QC (1949) (QC-1969)	Edward Denehan (1981)	Anthony Bingham (1992)
	David Marshall (1981)	Andrew Bruce (1992)
Fenton Bresler (1951)	Martin Young (1984)	Lana Wood (1993)
Susan Solomon (1967)	Sheila Foley (1988)	Jonathan Lewis (1996)
Christopher Aylwin (1970)	Geoffrey Killen (1990)	James Hanham (1996)

Head of Chambers:
Isaac Jacob

Clerk to Chambers:
Matthew Curness

Tenants: 17

The Chambers: A modern, well-equipped set with specialists in a broad range of business and commercial activities.

Work Undertaken: Administrative law, banking and bills of exchange, contracts of carriage, company and corporate law, computer law and data protection, construction and engineering contracts, employment, financial services, guarantee and indemnity, injunctions and pre-emptive remedies, insolvency, intellectual property, landlord and tenant, matrimonial finance and property, partnership, personal injury, planning and local government, professional negligence, real property, sale of goods.

Clientele: In addition to English solicitors (in private practice and employed), clients include law firms in the USA and Europe, and professionals entitled to direct access.

Recruitment & Training: There are normally 3 pupillage vacancies (each of 6 months) per year. Further information from the pupillage secretary.

---

164 3 PAPER BUILDINGS (Samuel Parrish) 3 Paper Buildings, Temple, London, EC4Y 7EU **Tel:** (0171) 353 6208 **Fax:** (0171) 353 5435 **DX:** 337 **Clerk:** Dawn Jago **Tenants:** 27 An established general common law set offering specialist expertise in company law, venture capital, crime (including corporate fraud), immigration and handling a wide range of private client work.

---

165 3 PAPER BUILDINGS (Michael Parroy QC) 3 Paper Buildings, Temple, London, EC4Y 7EU **Tel:** (0171) 583 8055 **Fax:** (0171) 353 6271 (Two lines) **DX:** 1024 **Email:** 3paper.lond@bogo.co.uk **Chief Clerk:** John Charles Charlick **Tenants:** 67 General common law set handling civil and criminal matters.

SET NUMBER
166

4 PAPER BUILDINGS (Harvey McGregor QC)

4 PAPER BUILDINGS (GROUND FLOOR), TEMPLE, LONDON, EC4Y 7EX
Tel: (0171) 353 3366 **Fax:** (0171) 353 5778 **DX:** 1036 LONDON/CHANCERY LANE **Email:** CLERKS@4PAPERBUILDINGS.COM

MEMBERS:

Harvey McGregor QC (1955) (QC-1978)
James Wadsworth QC (1963) (QC-1981)
Harold Burnett QC (1962) (QC-1982)
R.G. Marshall-Andrews QC MP (1967) (QC-1987)
Douglas Hogg QC MP (1968) (QC-1990)
Jean Ritchie QC (1970) (QC-1992)
Nicholas Davidson QC (1974) (QC-1993)

Christina Gorna (1960)
Michael Keane (1963)
Anthony De Freitas (1971)
L.J. West-Knights (1977)
Michael Pooles (1978)
Jane Mishcon (1979)
Martin Spencer (1979)
Eleanor Sharpston (1980)
Derek Holwill (1982)
Patrick Lawrence (1985)
Matthew Jackson (1986)
Julian Picton (1988)

Francis Bacon (1988)
William Flenley (1988)
Clare Price (1988)
Alison Gulliver (1989)
Mark Simpson (1992)
Philip Moser (1992)
Graham Reid (1993)
Simon Wilton (1993)
Sarah Christie-Brown (1994)
Spike Charlwood (1994)
Kieron Beal (1995)
Catherine Ewins (1995)

Head of Chambers:
Harvey McGregor QC

Senior Clerk:
Stephen Smith

Tenants: 31

The Chambers: This is an established set with members specialising in a number of different areas of commercial and common law. Further details are set out in the Chambers brochure.

Work Undertaken:

Main Areas of Work: This is a specialist set in the areas of professional negligence and medical negligence. Members of Chambers act for both plaintiffs and defendants. In the field of professional negligence, they appear in cases concerning all the various professions particularly solicitors, accountants, surveyors and insurance brokers, and in the area of medical negligence represent patients, the NHSLA, NHS Trusts and individual doctors, midwives and nurses. Chambers has a long tradition of expertise in the personal injury field, the Head of Chambers, Harvey McGregor QC, having acted in a number of the leading cases in this area and being the author of McGregor on Damages.

Additional Areas: Chambers also specialise in European law, computer law, agricultural law, commercial fraud, urgent interlocutory relief, building and construction and judicial review.

Services to clients Chambers aim to provide a flexible, practical and commercial approach to litigation which is driven by the needs, budget and convenience of our clients.

4 Paper Buildings

SET NUMBER
167

4 PAPER BUILDINGS (Lionel Swift QC)

4 PAPER BUILDINGS, TEMPLE, LONDON, EC4Y 7EX
Tel: (0171) 583 0816 **Fax:** (0171) 353 4979 **DX:** 1035 **Email:** CLERKS@4PAPERBUILDINGS.CO.UK

MEMBERS:

Lionel Swift QC (1959) (QC-1975)
Gordon Murdoch QC (1970) (QC-1995)
Anna Pauffley QC (1979) (QC-1995)
Jonathan Cohen QC (1974) (QC-1997)
Harry Turcan (1965)
Roger Smith (1968)
Amanda Barrington-Smyth (1972)
Ian Ridd (1975)

Robin Barda (1975)
Michael Sternberg (1975)
Peter Jackson (1978)
Christopher Coney (1979)
Marcus Scott-Manderson (1980)
Charles Joseph (1980)
Michael Stern (1983)
David Reade (1983)
Mark Johnstone (1984)
Elizabeth Coleman (1985)
Catherine Wood (1985)

Jeremy Rosenblatt (1985)
Sam Neaman (1988)
Barbara Mills (1990)
Christopher Cope (1990)
Joy Brereton (1990)
Gavin Mansfield (1992)
Cyrus Larizadeh (1992)
Justin Ageros (1993)
Sarah Lowe (1995)
Alexander Schofield (1997)

Head of Chambers:
Lionel Swift QC

Senior Clerk:
Michael Reeves

1st Junior Clerk: Mike Lay

Chambers Manager: Kay May

Tenants: 29

The Chambers: A leading family law set with a strong civil side.

Work Undertaken:

Family Law: Adoption care proceedings (for local authorities, families and guardians ad litem), child abduction, Children Act cases, cohabitees, divorce, inheritance and family provision, judicial review, matrimonial finance and wardship.
Civil: Arbitration, banking and securities, construction, contract (commercial and general), employment and industrial tribunals, judicial review, landlord and tenant, personal injury, professional negligence, sale of goods and consumer credit, tort.

Recruitment and Training: Chambers is a member of PACH.

4
PAPER
BUILDINGS

SET NUMBER
168 **5 PAPER BUILDINGS** (Incorporating European Law Chambers) (Antonio Bueno QC)

5 PAPER BUILDINGS (GROUND FLOOR), TEMPLE, LONDON, EC4Y 7HB
Tel: (0171) 583 9275 / 4555 **Fax:** (0171) 583 1926 / 2031 **DX:** 415 **Email:** 5PAPER@LINK.ORG

MEMBERS:

Antonio Bueno QC (1964) (QC-1989)	Robert Percival (1971)	Jonathan Rich (1989)
Angus Nicol (1963)	Richard King (1978)	Satinder Gill (1991)
Steven Walsh (1965)	Adrian Iles (1980)	Paul Stallebrass (1991)
Robert Denman (1970)	Paul Infield (1980)	Richard Evans (1993)
Graham Platford (1970)	Ian Wright (1983)	Nicola Rushton (1993)
Nicholas Wood (1970)	Ann Brownlow (1984)	Cyril Adjei (1995)
Donald Broatch (1971)	Lawrence Jacobson (1985)	Klaus Reichert (1996)
	Simon Devonshire (1988)	

Head of Chambers:
Antonio Bueno QC

Senior Clerk:
Alan Stammers

Tenants: 22

Work Undertaken: The Chambers' principal fields of specialisation in both advocacy and advisory work are as follows: commercial law (including banking, international and domestic sales of goods, carriage of goods, sales of business, financial services, companies, partnerships and insolvency), employment (including wrongful and unfair dismissal, discrimination and confidential information), entertainment, European and international law, judicial review/social regulation (including health and safety, immigration, public housing, shipping and trade descriptions), matrimonial finance and child welfare, professional negligence (including negligence in the fields of legal, accountancy, surveying, valuation and medical practice), property (including landlord and tenant), tort and personal injury.

Recruitment & Training: Pupillage applications via PACH. Awards are available, details on application. Mini-pupillage applications to Nicola Rushton.

5 PAPER BUILDINGS

SET NUMBER
169 5 PAPER BUILDINGS (Brian Higgs QC) 5 Paper Buildings, Temple, London, EC4Y 7HB **Tel:** (0171) 353 5638 **Fax:** (0171) 353 6166 **DX:** 367 Chancery Lane **Email:** 101722,633@compuserve.com **Clerk:** Russell Ayles **Tenants:** 25 Primarily a common law set which deals mainly with criminal, matrimonial and personal injury matters.

SET NUMBER
170 **5 PAPER BUILDINGS** (John Mathew QC)

5 PAPER BUILDINGS, TEMPLE, LONDON, EC4Y 7HB
Tel: (0171) 583 6117 **Fax:** (0171) 353 0075 **DX:** 365 **Email:** CLERKS@5-PAPERBUILDINGS.LAW.CO.UK

MEMBERS:

John Mathew QC (1949) (QC-1977)	Simon Mehigan QC (1980) (QC-1998)	Julian Christopher (1988)
Michael Corkery QC (1949) (QC-1981)	Stanley Hughes (1971)	Martin Evans (1989)
Timothy Cassel QC (1965) (QC-1988)	Edward Jenkins (1977)	Anuja Dhir (1989)
David Stokes QC (1968) (QC-1989)	Ian Wade (1977)	Lynn Griffin (1991)
	Graham Trembath (1978)	Justin Cole (1991)
Godfrey Carey QC (1969) (QC-1991)	Nicholas Fooks (1978)	Nicholas Griffin (1992)
Jonathan Caplan QC (1973) (QC-1991)	Charles Judge (1981)	David Mpanga (1993)
	Maurice Aston (1982)	Emma Deacon (1993)
Kuldip Singh QC (1975) (QC-1993)	Miranda Moore (1983)	Tom Allen (1994)
	Amanda Pinto (1983)	Michael Hick (1995)
Oliver Sells QC (1972) (QC-1995)	Miles Bennett (1986)	Alex Bailin (1995)
	David Groome (1987)	
	Robert O'Sullivan (1988)	

Head of Chambers:
John Mathew QC

Senior Clerk:
Stuart Bryant

Tenants: 32

Door Tenants: Charles Barton QC (1960)(QC-1982), James Tabor QC (1974)(QC-1995), Gareth Hawkesworth (1972) and Stephen Franklin (1974).

The Chambers: For more than a century these chambers have been recognised as one of the leading sets specialising in litigation. The work of these chambers consists primarily of criminal law and general common law and certain other areas of civil law.

Work Undertaken: This set deals with all aspects of criminal law, including commercial fraud (members of these chambers have been involved in almost every major fraud case in the past decade and the set is recognised as one of the leading sets in this area), financial services, licensing, environmental law, food and drugs, health and safety, trade descriptions, copyright theft and extradition. The common law and civil law work of chambers includes commercial

Continues overleaf

litigation (including commercial fraud), defamation, contempt, media law, judicial review, arbitration, tribunals and inquiries, professional disciplinary work, sports law, torts, professional negligence, actions against the police, personal injury, restraint of trade, breach of confidence, employment law, human rights, sale of goods, passing off, competition law, entertainment law and immigration.

SET NUMBER

171 PEPYS' CHAMBERS (Terence de Lury) 17 Fleet Street, London, EC4Y 1AA **Tel:** (0171) 936 2710 **Fax:** (0171) 936 2501 **DX:** 463 Ch.Ln. **Clerk:** Wanda Bogucka **Tenants:** 10 Specialist, civil law chambers with corporate conference facilities, clerk and administration at 17 Fleet Street.

SET NUMBER

172 PHOENIX CHAMBERS (The Hon. Bruce Pitt) First Floor, Gray's Inn Chambers, Gray's Inn, London, WC1R 5JA **Tel:** (0171) 404 7888 **Fax:** (0171) 404 7897 **DX:** 78 Lond/Chancery Lane **Email:** clerks@phoenix-chambers.co.uk **Internet:** http: //www.phoenix-chambers.co.uk **Clerk:** Laurie Gallogly **Tenants:** 24 A recently formed general Common Law Chambers with a wide range of litigation experience.

SET NUMBER

173 PLOWDEN BUILDINGS (William Lowe QC)

2 PLOWDEN BUILDINGS, TEMPLE, LONDON, EC4Y 9BU
Tel: (0171) 583 0808 **Fax:** (0171) 583 5106 **DX:** 0020 (CH.LN.) **Email:** BAR@PLOWDENBUILDINGS.CO.UK

MEMBERS:

William Lowe QC (1972) (QC-1997)	Fiona Moore-Graham (1986)	Christina Anthony (1990)
Bruce McIntyre (1969)	Andrew Collings (1987)	Graeme Gaston (1991)
Arnold Cooper (1969)	David Lyons (1987)	Claire Lindsay (1991)
Charlotte Buckhaven (1969)	Simon Dyer (1987)	Peter Freeman (1992)
Elizabeth Hindmarsh (1974)	Kate Gordon (1988)	Jeffrey Lamb (1992)
David Trotter (1975)	Peter Morton (1988) LLB, LLM	Simon Cox (1992)
Richard Craven (1976)	Lawrence Jones (1988)	Judith Farbey (1992)
Simon Sandford (1979)	Paul Orton (1988)	John Walsh (1993)
Javed Azam (1981)	Camilla Quigley (1988)	Ali Bajwa (1993)
R James Shrimpton (1981)	David Brook (1988)	Frances Zammit (1993)
Susan Holdham (1983)	Sarah Dines (1988)	Anthony Potter (1994)
Mark Dacey (1985)	Michael James (1989)	Diane Cade (1994)
Jonathan Holmes (1985)	Martin Haukeland (1989)	Anna McKenzie (1994)
Lawrence McNulty (1985)	Jonathan de Rohan (1989)	Alistair Speirs (1995)
Ian West (1985)	Kerry Cox (1990)	Jamie Clarke (1995)
Catherine Foster (1986)	Mark Watson-Gandy (1990)	Edward Broome (1996)
Michael Bailey (1986)	Sophie Henderson (1990)	Catherine McKenzie Smith*

Head of Chambers:
William Lowe QC

Senior Clerk:
Paul Hurst

Practice Manager:
Stephen Evers

Tenants: 50

* Door Tenant

The Chambers: Established in 1980, Plowden Buildings is a Common Law set based in the heart of the Temple, London. Chambers have grown rapidly in recent years and, with 50 members, are now one of the larger sets in the country. Chambers have a well established reputation, particularly in London, the South East and the North East where members regularly appear in court. As a result of Chambers strength in depth, Plowden Buildings are able to field several specialist teams of experienced practitioners, of varying years call, to service Instructing Solicitors' requirements.

Work Undertaken: Chambers have long specialised in a wide range of personal injury, professional negligence and commercial work since being established in 1980 but as Chambers have grown in size, so too has the range of expertise Chambers are able to provide to Instructing Solicitors. Chambers have a particularly strong reputation in personal injury, occupational disease, professional and medical negligence, and a wide variety of commercial and contractual dispute work. Chambers has a number of specialist teams covering such areas as personal injury, medical and professional negligence, occupational disease, commercial, employment, landlord and tenant, professional indemnity, immigration, crime and family and matrimonial work, incorporating child care.

Languages: French, German, Italian, Hindi, Punjabi, Urdu.

Recruitment and Training: Tenancy applications to Stephen Evers, Practice Manager. Pupilage applications to PACH.

PUMP COURT CHAMBERS (Guy Boney QC)

3 PUMP COURT, TEMPLE, LONDON, EC4Y 7AJ
Tel: (0171) 353 0711 **Fax:** (0171) 353 3319 **DX:** 362

MEMBERS:

Guy Boney QC (1968) (QC-1990)	Charles Gabb (1975)	Leslie Samuels (1989)
Nigel Pascoe QC (1966) (QC-1988)	Andrew Barnett (1977)	Anthony Akiwumi (1989)
	Michael Dineen (1977)	Justin Gau (1989)
Christopher Clark QC (1969) (QC-1984)	Timothy O'Flynn (1979)	Sean Brunton (1990)
	Jane Miller (1979)	Helen Khan (1990)
Paul Garlick QC (1974) (QC-1996)	Robert Hill (1980)	Penelope Howe (1991)
Geoffrey Still (1966)	Miranda Allardice (1982)	Geoffrey Kelly (1992)
Stewart Patterson (1967)	Damien Lochrane (1983)	Patricia Poyer-Sleeman (1992)
Adam Pearson (1969)	Oba Nsugbe (1985)	
Frank Moat (1970)	Matthew Scott (1985)	James Newton-Price (1992)
Giles Harrap (1971)	Desmond Bloom-Davies (1986)	Elizabeth Gunther (1993)
Frank Abbott (1972)		Oliver Peirson (1993)
Michael Montgomery (1972)	Mark Hill (1987)	Helen Fields (1993)
Charles Parry (1973)	Graham Howard (1987)	Mark Ashley (1993)
John Ker-Reid (1974)	Anne Waddington (1988)	Luke Blackburn (1993)
Michael Butt (1974)	Hugh Travers (1988)	Robert Pawson (1994)
Philip Gillibrand (1975)	Philip Warren (1988)	Mark Dubbery (1996)
	Edward Boydell (1989)	

Head of Chambers:
Guy Boney QC

Senior Clerk:
David Barber

Tenants: 48

The Chambers: An established set undertaking a wide variety of work, with individual members working in specialist teams. Direct Professional Access work is accepted.

Members: Nine members of chambers are recorders. Michael Montgomery is Standing Counsel to the D.T.I. (SE Circuit). Nigel Pascoe QC is leader of the Western Circuit.

Work Undertaken:
Main Areas of Work: Family and Matrimonial; Employment; Inheritance and Property Law; Personal Injury; All aspects of Criminal Law.
Specialisations include: Childcare Work & Matrimonial Finance; Criminal Law (including Customs & Excise; Serious Fraud; Drugs; Sexual Offences; Extradition Proceedings and Criminal Appeals); Professional and Medical Negligence; Contract; Ecclesiastical Law; Inheritance Act; Nigerian Law.
Additional Areas of Work: Agricultural; Aviation; Boundaries, Rights of way; I.T.; Courts Martial; Coroner's Court; EC and Environment Law; Judicial Review; Landlord and Tenant; Motor racing litigation; Police and general Disciplinary Tribunals; Road Traffic; Yachting.

International Connections: Oba Nsugbe is a barrister and solicitor of the Supreme Court of Nigeria and advises on all aspects of Nigerian law. He has direct access to established chambers in Lagos. Dr. Gerhard Dannemann is a member of the German Bar and is a door-tenant of chambers.

Languages: French, German.

Associated Chambers: Chambers are also at Pump Court Chambers, 31 Southgate Street, in Winchester and Pump Court Chambers, Temple Street, Swindon SN1 1SQ.

Recruitment & Training: Tenancy applications should be sent to Head of the Tenancy Committee. All pupillage applications should be made via the PACH Scheme.

1 PUMP COURT (Jane Hoyal and Robert Latham) 1 Pump Court, Temple, London, EC4Y 7AB
Tel: (0171) 583 2012 **Fax:** (0171) 353 4944 **DX:** LDE 109 **Email:** name@1pumpcourt.co.uk
Internet: http://www.1pumpcourt.co.uk **Clerk:** Ian burrow **Tenants:** 39 1 Pump Court is a radical and progressive set of Chambers providing a specialist service to legally-aided and private clients, and which seeks to secure equality of access to justice.

2 PUMP COURT (Philip Singer QC) 2 Pump Court, Temple, London, EC4Y 7AH **Tel:** (0171) 353 5597 **Fax:** (0171) 583 2122 **DX:** 290 (Ch.Ln.) **Clerk:** John Arter **Tenants:** 29 A long-established common law set, offering advocates and draftsmen of great experience in a wide variety of fields.

SET NUMBER
177 ## 4 PUMP COURT (Bruce Mauleverer QC)

4 PUMP COURT, TEMPLE, LONDON, EC4Y 7AN
Tel: (0171) 353 2656 **Fax:** (0171) 583 2036 **DX:** 303 **Email:** 4_PUMP_COURT@COMPUSERVE.COM

MEMBERS:

Bruce Mauleverer QC (1969) (QC-1985)
Anthony Temple QC (1968) (QC-1986)
David Friedman QC (1968) (QC-1990)
David Blunt QC (1967) (QC-1991)
Christopher Moger QC (1972) (QC-1992)
Jeremy Storey QC (1974) (QC-1994)
Jonathan Marks QC (1975) (QC-1995)
Jonathan Acton Davis QC (1977) (QC-1996)

John Rowland QC (1979) (QC-1996)
Michael Douglas QC (1974) (QC-1997)
Lindsay Boswell QC (1982) (QC-1997)
Laurence Marsh (1975)
Allen Dyer (1976)
Jeremy Nicholson (1977)
Oliver Ticciati (1979)
Nigel Tozzi (1980)
Andrew Fletcher (1980)
Peter Hamilton (1968)
Alexander Charlton (1983)
David Sears (1984)

Adrian Hughes (1984)
James Cross (1985)
Duncan McCall (1988)
Aidan Christie (1988)
Andrew Neish (1988)
Kirsten Houghton (1989)
Marc Rowlands (1990)
Dominic McCahill (1991)
Phyllida Cheync (1992)
Simon Henderson (1993)
Michael Davie (1993)
Alexander Gunning (1994)
Rachel Ansell (1995)
Claire Packman (1996)

Head of Chambers:
Bruce Mauleverer QC
Senior Clerk:
Carolyn McCombe
Tenants: 34

Work Undertaken: The Work of Chambers covers a wide spectrum of commercial and common law. Specialist areas include insurance and reinsurance; professional negligence; all aspects of construction, engineering and property disputes; information technology and computer law; international and domestic arbitrations (both as counsel and arbitrator); banking, financial services and stock exchange work; employment and restraint of trade; professional disciplinary tribunals; gaming, lotteries and licensing and personal injury work.

Some members of Chambers also have expertise in matrimonial finance; entertainment and advertising; shipping; environmental law and judicial review.

SET NUMBER
178 ## 5 PUMP COURT (Rex Bryan)

5 PUMP COURT, TEMPLE, LONDON, EC4Y 7AP
Tel: (0171) 353 2532 **Fax:** (0171) 353 5321 **DX:** 497 LDE **Email:** FIVEPUMP@NETCOMUK.CO.UK

MEMBERS:

Rex Bryan (1971)
Norman Primost (1954)
Anthony Hunter (1962)
Simeon Hopkins (1968)
Kenneth Dow (1970)
Helen Christodoulou (1972)
John Evison (1974)
Alistair Keith (1974)
Crispian Cartwright (1976)
Tristan Chaize (1977)

Hugo Charlton (1978)
Graham Campbell (1979)
Anne Ratcliffe (1981)
Tristram Hodgkinson (1982)
Christina Morris (1983)
Michael Collard (1986)
Mark James (1987)
Tazeen Hasan (1988)
Sebastian Gooch (1989)
Corinna Schiffer (1989)

Derek O'Sullivan (1990)
Allister Walker (1990)
Jane Humphreys (1990)
Jack Nicholls (1991)
Anthony Ross (1991)
Stephen Ellis-Jones (1992)
Bradley Say (1993)
Emma Smith (1994)
Sarah Marley (1995)
Laura Elfield (1996)

Head of Chambers:
Rex Bryan
Senior Clerk:
Tim Markham
First Junior:
Jayne Goodrham
Tenants: 30

Work Undertaken: Five Pump Court Chambers is a long established common law set of 30 members of chambers in three specialised practice groups focusing on Civil, Criminal and Family law. A guide to our practices is available upon request.

Fees for paperwork can be agreed in advance upon sight of the papers, or guidance can be given as to the appropriate hourly rates. Direct Professional Access and Conditional Fee work is undertaken. Chambers has dedicated conference rooms with video facilities, and free parking can be arranged.

Chambers is open from 8.30 am to 7.00 pm and the Clerks can be contacted in the evenings or at weekends.

Principal areas of Practice:

Civil: Landlord and Tenant, Real Property, Contract/Commercial, Professional Negligence, Personal Injury, Construction, Partnership. Trusts, Trade Description, Industrial Deafness, Insolvency, Judicial Review, Employment, Arbitration, Consumer Credit and Licensing.
Criminal: Fraud, Sexual Offences, DTI, Serious Violence, Car Ringing and Importation of Drugs.
Family: Financial Provision and Children, Private and Public law, Inheritance Act claims, Trusts.

Languages Spoken: French, German, Italian, Greek, Urdu and Hindi.

For further information please contact the Senior Clerk.

SET NUMBER
179 **6 PUMP COURT** (Kieran Coonan QC)

6 PUMP COURT, GROUND AND LOWER GROUND, LONDON, EC4Y 7AR
Tel: (0171) 583 6013 **Fax:** (0171) 353 0464 **DX:** 409

MEMBERS:

Kieran Coonan QC (1971) (QC-1990)	Alan Jenkins (1984)	Annalissa Garrett (1991)
Michael Curwen (1966)	Andrew Hockton (1984)	Alexander Hutton (1992)
Jon Williams (1970)	Susan Burden (1985)	Nicholas Peacock (1992)
David Morris (1976)	Christina Lambert (1988)	Katharine Gollop (1993)
Jeremy Morgan (1989) FCI Arb	Andrew Post (1988)	Janet Jenkins (1996)
	Charles Foster (1988)	Emma Brown (1995)
Siobhan Goodrich (1980)	John Gordon (1989)	Alice Robertson (1996)
Richard Power (1983)	Andrew Kennedy (1989)	John Davies (1955)
	Róisín Lacey (1991)	Richard Craven (1976)

Head of Chambers:
Kieran Coonan QC

Senior Clerk:
Adrian Barrow

Tenants: 25·

The Chambers: These Chambers have enjoyed a reputation over the past 25 years for providing specialist advice and advocacy on behalf of Plaintiffs and Defendants in the field of Healthcare Law.

Work Undertaken: Most members of Chambers specialise in the major areas of medical negligence, mental health law and the regulation of the conduct of care professionals.

Members of Chambers appear before Inquests, Inquiries (both public and private) and various Judicial/Administrative Tribunals. Individuals also undertake criminal cases which frequently incorporate medico-legal issues.

Personal injury and professional negligence work (particularly affecting solicitors), housing, family, and employment law, are strongly represented in Chambers. A small group practises in the developing and specialist area of the law relating to Costs.

Many of the leading cases in these fields have featured members of this set. Some members of Chambers have previously practised in the professions of solicitor, medical practitioner and veterinary surgeon.

SET NUMBER
180 **6 PUMP COURT** (Stephen Hockman QC)

6 PUMP COURT, TEMPLE, LONDON, EC4Y 7AR
Tel: (0171) 797 8400 **Fax:** (0171) 797 8401 **DX:** 293 CHANCERY LANE

MEMBERS:

Stephen Hockman QC (1970) (QC-1990)	Caroline Topping (1984)	Paul Mee (1992)
Andrew Goymer (1970)	David Walden-Smith (1985)	Mark Watson (1994)
Adèle Williams (1972)	Peter Gower (1985)	Edward Grant (1994)
Michael Harington (1974)	Peter Harrison (1987)	Nina Ellin (1994)
Richard Barraclough (1980)	Peter Forbes (1990)	Clare Wright (1995)
Nicholas Baldock (1983)	Oliver Saxby (1992)	Mark Beard (1996)
Mark Bailey (1984)	Patrick Chamberlayne (1992)	Deborah Charles (1996)
	Judith Butler (1993)	

Head of Chambers:
Stephen Hockman QC

Senior Clerk:
Richard Constable

Tenants: 22

ADDRESS FOR ANNEXE: 6/8 MILL STREET, MAIDSTONE, KENT ME15 6XH

Work Undertaken: The work of chambers includes a wide range of common law work in London and on the South Eastern Circuit. The set has specialists in criminal law, personal injury, planning, environmental, local government and administrative law and family law.

181   PUMP COURT TAX CHAMBERS (Andrew Thornhill QC)

16 BEDFORD ROW, LONDON, WC1R 4EB
Tel: (0171) 414 8080   **Fax:** (0171) 414 8099   **DX:** LONDON 312

MEMBERS:

Donald C. Potter QC (1948) (QC-1972)	Ian Richards (1971)	Giles W.J. Goodfellow (1983)	**Head of Chambers:** Andrew Thornhill QC
Andrew R. Thornhill QC (1969) (QC-1985)	Janek Matthews (1972)	Jeremy Woolf (1986)	**Senior Clerk:** Graham Kettle
David C. Milne QC (1970) (QC-1987)	John M. Tallon (1975) William G.S. Massey QC (1977) (QC-1996)	David Ewart (1987) Andrew Hitchmough (1991)	**Tenants:** 17
Stephen J Allcock QC (1975) (QC-1993)	Roger Thomas (1979) Kevin J. Prosser QC (1982) (QC-1996)	Rupert Baldry (1987) Adrian J. Shipwright (1993) Elizabeth Wilson (1995)	

Areas of Work: We are a specialist set of chambers who undertake litigation and advisory work on all aspects of tax law, both corporate and personal. The corporate tax issues covered include company reconstructions and demergers, transfer pricing, capital allowances, and the use of losses. Advice is also given to non-residents conducting business in the UK. The personal tax issues include the creation and operation of trusts and close companies both on and off shore, issues relating to residence and domicile, the making of gifts and matters affected by the reserved benefit rules.

A wide range of drafting is undertaken.

Personal and corporate tax matters come together in relation to employee remuneration, including share options and pension schemes, employee share ownership plans, profit sharing schemes and National Insurance contributions. Direct tax litigation is conducted in the General and Special Commissioners as well as in the Higher Courts.

A significant proportion of the work undertaken by Chambers now involves VAT and Customs Duty, which has led to an increase in the volume of litigation in all Courts including the VAT and Duties Tribunal, the High Court, the House of Lords and the European Court of Justice.

182   QUEEN ELIZABETH BUILDING (Lindsay Burn)

QUEEN ELIZABETH BUILDING, TEMPLE, LONDON, EC4Y 9BS
Tel: (0171) 353 7181 (12 lines)   **Fax:** (0171) 353 3929 (2 lines)   **DX:** 340 (CH.LN.)

MEMBERS:

Lindsay Burn (1972)	Anthony Haycroft (1982)	Neil Fry (1992)	**Head of Chambers:** Lindsay Burn
Richard Guy (1970)	Fiona Gibb (1983)	Stephanie Jackson (1992)	**Senior Clerk:** Michael Price
Shelagh Farror (1970)	Carol Atkinson (1985)	Amanda-Jane Field (1992)	**Tenants:** 46
Claire Miskin (1970)	Philip St. John-Stevens (1985)	Sharon Sawyerr (1992)	
Peter Stage (1971)	Tim Devlin (1985)	Janet Weeks (1993)	
Jonathan Lowen (1972)	Divya Bhatia (1986)	Susan Gore (1993)	
Peter Prideaux-Brune (1972)	Fiona Munro (1986)	Anna McKenna (1994)	
James Pavry (1974)	Debora Price (1987)	Richard Cartwright (1994)	
Keith Salvesen (1974)	Karen Holt (1987)	Alison Easton (1994)	
Simon Wild (1977)	Jane Probyn (1988)	Gerald Browne (1995)	
David Jeremy (1977)	Barbara Philcox (1988)	Emma Gardiner (1995)	
Laura Harris (1977)	Kate Purkiss (1988)	Lawrence Aiolfi (1996)	
Peter Walsh (1978)	Jennifer Driscoll (1989)	Marcus Thompson (1996)	
Walton Hornsby (1980)	Tayo Adebayo (1989)	Suzanne Fine (1976)	
Graham Blower (1980)	David Scutt (1989)	(Door Tenant)	
Nicola Simpson (1982)	Lawrence Henderson (1990)		
Charles Digby (1982)			

Work Undertaken:

General Description: General criminal practice, undertaking both prosecution and defence, with 21 barristers specialising in this area, primarily in London and the South Eastern Circuit. We also have a very strong team of family practitioners (18 barristers) who deal with all areas of family law including matrimonial finance, child care, (both public law and private law) and education (including special educational needs, admissions and exclusions and Judicial Review). There are also a number of trained family mediators in Chambers.

Other Areas of Work: *Includes:* common law, contract law, courts martial, employment, fraud, landlord and tenant, personal injury litigation, sale of goods, licensing and tribunals.

SET NUMBER 183 QUEEN ELIZABETH BUILDING (David Jeffreys QC & Peter Whiteman QC)

HOLLIS WHITEMAN CHAMBERS (QEB), QUEEN ELIZABETH BUILDING, TEMPLE, LONDON, EC4Y 9BS
Tel: (0171) 583 5766 **Fax:** (0171) 353 0339 **DX:** 482 **Email:** HOLLIS.WHITEMAN@BTINTERNET.COM

MEMBERS:

David A. Jeffreys QC (1958) (QC-1981)
Peter Whiteman QC (1967) (QC-1977)
Rt. Hon. Lord Carlisle QC (1954) (QC-1971)
Robin D. Grey QC (1957) (QC-1979)
Alan B. Suckling QC (1963) (QC-1983)
Anthony T. Glass QC (1965) (QC-1986)
Vivian Robinson QC (1967) (QC-1986)
John Hilton QC (1964) (QC-1990)
Brian J. Barker QC (1969) (QC-1990)
Julian Bevan QC (1962) (QC-1991)
David H. Evans QC (1972) (QC-1991)
Timothy Langdale QC (1966) (QC-1992)
David Bate QC (1969) (QC-1994)

Rebecca M. Poulet QC (1975) (QC-1995)
Peter E. Kyte QC (1970) (QC-1996)
David Calvert-Smith QC (1969) (QC-1997)
Peter Clarke QC (1972) (QC-1997)
Anthony Wilcken (1966)
Anthony G. Longden (1967)
Christopher R. Mitchell (1968)
Neill A. Stewart (1973)
Linda D. Strudwick (1973)
Ian F. Paton (1975)
William Boyce (1976)
Richard E. Horwell (1976)
Jeremy Donne (1978)
John Kelsey-Fry (1978)
Mark Ellison (1979)
Peter Finnigan (1978)
Nick Wood (1980)
Gareth Rees (1981)
Thomas V.W. Kark (1982)

Edward F.T. Brown (1983)
Ian M. Stern (1983)
Jane Sullivan (1984)
Phillip Bennetts (1986)
Sean Larkin (1987)
Jocelyn Sparks (1987)
Edward Henry (1988)
Sarah Plaschkes (1988)
Ian Winter (1988)
Zoe Johnson (1990)
Emma Lowry (1991)
Lydia Barnfather (1992)
Victoria Coward (1992)
William Wastie (1993)
Peter Warne (1993)
Selva Ramasamy (1992)
Adrian Darbishire (1993)
Benjamin Summers (1994)
Leah Saffian (1992)
Mark Aldred (1996)

Head of Chambers:
David Jeffreys QC & Peter Whiteman QC

Senior Clerk:
Michael Greenaway

Tenants: 52

The Chambers: Hollis Whiteman Chambers (QEB) is a long-established specialist criminal set, providing advocacy and advice of the highest quality. Chambers is dedicated to giving an effective and individual service whenever needed, and at short notice. The 52 Members have expertise at all levels of seniority: 17 QCs and 4 Treasury Counsel are matched with a strong middle order and 20 tenants of less than 15 years' call. 20 tenants sit as Recorders in the Crown Court.

Chambers defend and prosecute from the Magistrates' Court to the House of Lords. Members of Chambers are regularly involved in complex, high profile and grave cases. There is also daily representation in courts of all levels, at every stage of proceedings.

In addition to "pure crime", Members specialise in Judicial Review, Food Law, Health and Safety Act and Trading Standards cases, Licensing and Extradition. Members of Chambers also appear in other tribunals including: Public Inquiries, the General Medical Council, the General Optical Council, Courts-Martial and Police Disciplinary Proceedings.

Peter Whiteman QC, a deputy High Court Judge, provides specialist revenue advice, particularly on corporate and international tax law, and representation at both national and international levels.

SET NUMBER 184 QUEEN ELIZABETH BUILDING (Ian Karsten QC)

QUEEN ELIZABETH BUILDING, TEMPLE, LONDON, EC4Y 9BS
Tel: (0171) 797 7837 **Fax:** (0171) 353 5422 **DX:** LONDON 339

MEMBERS:

Ian Karsten QC (1967) (QC-1990)
David Bodey QC (1970) (QC-1991)
Paul Coleridge QC (1970) (QC-1993)
Florence Baron QC (1976) (QC-1995)
Lord Phillimore (1972)
Lord Meston QC (1973) (QC-1996)
Peter Wright (1974)

Michael Hosford-Tanner (1974)
Andrew Tidbury (1976)
Thomas Brudenell (1977)
Andrew Moylan (1978)
Roderick Blyth (1981)
Oliver Wise (1981)
Lewis Marks (1984) BA (Oxon)
Rowena Corbett (1984)
Tim Amos (1987)

Jennifer Roberts (1988)
Sarah Edwards (1990)
Matthew Firth (1991)
Elizabeth Clarke (1991)
Camilla Henderson (1992)
Stewart Leech (1992)
Alexander Thorpe (1995)
Catherine Cowton (1995)
Victoria Hunt (1995)
James Ewins (1994)

Head of Chambers:
Ian Karsten QC

Senior Clerk:
Ivor Treherne

Tenants: 26

Continues overleaf

Work Undertaken: A set covering a range of specialist fields of the common law, with some members specialising in family law, and others concentrating on a range of work including commercial law, criminal law, disciplinary tribunals, employment law, equine and animal law, EC law, insolvency, judicial review, landlord and tenant, medical negligence, partnership law, personal injuries, private international and foreign law, probate, professional negligence and sports law.

Languages Spoken: French, German and Italian.

SET NUMBER
185 **ONE RAYMOND BUILDINGS** (Christopher Morcom QC)

1 RAYMOND BUILDINGS, GRAY'S INN, LONDON, WC1R 5BH
Tel: (0171) 430 1234 **Fax:** (0171) 430 1004 **DX:** 16 **Email:** CHAMBERS@IPBAR1RB.COM

MEMBERS:

Christopher Morcom QC (1963) (QC-1991)

David Micklethwait (1970) MA (Cantab)

Roger Wyand QC (1973) (QC-1997) MA (Cantab)

Malcolm Chapple (1975) BSc (City)

Arthur Ashton (1988) South Africa (1975) BA LLB (Rhodes)

Peter Farmery (1979) BA (Dunelm) LLM (London) *

John Adams (1984) LLB (Dumelm)

Paul Diamond (1985) BA (Exon) LLM (Cantab) *

Guy Tritton (1987) BSc (Dunelm)

Jessica Jones (1991) BSc (Soton)

Ashley Roughton (1993) BSc (Lond) PhD (Oxon)

Michael Edenborough (1992) MA (Cantab) PhD (Oxon)

James Graham (1994) MSc

Head of Chambers:
Christopher Morcom QC

Senior Clerk:
Geoffrey C.B. Maw

Tenants: 16

Door Tenants: Amedee Turner QC (1954) (QC 1976) MA (Oxon), David Kay (1979) (USA-1990) BA (Kingston); Philip Zornoza

Work Undertaken: Chambers comprises of a specialist group of intellectual property practitioners, whose areas of expertise include patents, trademarks and passing off, copyright and designs, entertainment law, confidential information, franchising, information technology and EC competition law relating to IP and whose members all have degrees in science or engineering.

***Peter Farmery** specialises in banking, financial services, insolvency and commercial litigation.

***Paul Diamond** specialises in commercial litigation, judicial review, administrative housing law.

SET NUMBER
186 **3 RAYMOND BUILDINGS** (Clive Nicholls QC)

3 RAYMOND BUILDINGS, GRAY'S INN, LONDON, WC1R 5BH
Tel: (0171) 831 3833 **Fax:** (0171) 242 4221 **DX:** 237 LONDON **Email:** CHAMBERS@THREERAYMOND.DEMON.CO.UK

MEMBERS:

Clive Nicholls QC (1957) (QC-1982)

Colin Nicholls QC (1957) (QC-1981)

Gilbert Gray QC (1953) (QC-1971) *

Richard Beckett QC (1965) (QC-1987)

John Nutting QC (1968) (QC-1995)

Stephen Batten QC (1968) (QC-1989)

Alun Jones QC (1972) (QC-1989)

David Whitehouse QC (1969) (QC-1990)

Nicholas Price QC (1968) (QC-1992)

Montague Sherborne QC (1960) (QC-1993)

Francis Evans QC (1977) (QC-1994)

Clare Montgomery QC (1980) (QC-1996)

Colin Pitt (1968)

John Blair-Gould (1970)

Andrew Muir (1975)

Kevin de Haan (1976)

Richard Atchley (1977)

Michael Bromley-Martin (1979)

Mark Harris (1980)

James Hines (1982)

James Rankin (1983)

Jane Humphryes (1983)

Neil Saunders (1983)

Stephen Walsh (1983)

Crispin Aylett (1985)

Alexander Cameron (1986)

Helen Malcolm (1986)

James Lewis (1987)

John Hardy (1988)

Hugo Keith (1989)

Hugh Davies (1990)

Campaspe Lloyd-Jacob (1990)

Tania Bromley-Martin (1983)

Richard Wormald (1993)

Alisdair Williamson (1994)

Julian Knowles (1994)

Head of Chambers:
Clive Nicholls QC

Senior Clerk:
Ian Collins

Tenants: 36

The Chambers: Established in the early 1920s, chambers now have thirty-six members (including 12 QCs) who practise in a broad area of criminal, licensing and administrative law, ranging from appearances in Magistrates' Courts and Crown Courts to the special demands of disciplinary, regulatory and appellate tribunals and international courts. Chambers' practice has developed extensively in recent years, and members advise and appear in cases throughout the world.

3 Raymond Buildings have been completely refurbished. They provide large conference rooms and are equipped with the latest computer and communications facilities.

Work Undertaken:

Criminal Law: Cases are handled at all levels of gravity, both for the prosecution and the defence. Chambers specialise in complex commercial crime including cases in the Far East. Several members are on the panel of DTI Inspectors.

Extradition: Extradition proceedings are handled for foreign governments and defendants, both in the United Kingdom and elsewhere.

Licensing: Some members practise exclusively in licensing law, with particular specialisations in betting, gaming and lotteries and in liquor and public entertainment.

Tribunals and Administrative Law: Tribunal work includes coroners' inquests, regulatory and disciplinary tribunals. Associated with this, and with other areas of practice, is an expanding volume of work in Administrative law and Judicial Review.

Human Rights Law: Members handle cases before the European Commission and the Court of Human Rights.

Privy Council Cases: Members present constitutional, criminal and common law appeals from Commonwealth countries to the Privy Council.

Environmental Law and Consumer Law: Pollution control and statutory nuisances, consumer protection and trading law, regulation under the Health and Safety at Work Act 1974 and associated legislation.

Other Areas: Individual members specialise in all aspects of common law, matrimonial law and VAT.

SET NUMBER
187

5 RAYMOND BUILDINGS (Patrick Milmo QC)

5 RAYMOND BUILDINGS, GRAY'S INN, LONDON, WC1R 5BP
Tel: (0171) 242 2902 **Fax:** (0171) 831 2686 **DX:** 1054 LDE **Email:** CLERKS@MEDIA-ENT-LAW.CO.UK
Internet: HTTP: //WWW.MEDIA-ENT-LAW.CO.UK

MEMBERS:

Patrick Milmo QC (1962) (QC-1985) MA (Cantab)	Richard Parkes (1977) MA (Cantab)	Justin Rushbrooke (1992) MA(Oxon)
Charles Gray QC (1966) (QC-1984) BA (Oxon)	Mark Warby (1981) MA (Oxon)	Matthew Nicklin (1993) LLB (Newcastle)
Gordon Bishop (1968) MA (Cantab)	Stephen Bate (1981) MA (Cantab) Dip Law	Godwin Busuttil (1994) MA, MPhil(Cantab)
Michael Tugendhat QC (1969) (QC-1986) MA (Cantab)	Andrew Monson (1983) BA (Oxon)	Adam Wolanski (1995) MA(Cantab)
Desmond Browne QC (1969) (QC-1990) BA (Oxon)	Heather Rogers (1983) LLB	William Bennett (1994) BA (Liverpool)
Adrienne Page (1974) BA	Alexandra Marzec (1990) LLB	Jacob Dean (1995) BA (Oxon)
James Price QC (1974) (QC-1995) BA (Oxon)	David Sherborne (1992) BA(Oxon)	Anna Coppola BA (London) Dip Law (1996)

Head of Chambers:
Patrick Milmo QC

Senior Clerk:
Kim Janes

Tenants: 21

The Chambers: An established set specialising in media and entertainment law and intellectual property; also undertaking work in a wide range of commercial matters. Members appear before courts at all levels, including all divisions of the High Court and the European Court of Human Rights. They frequently represent clients before professional tribunals, in arbitrations and in disciplinary proceedings, and advise on and appear in overseas litigation.

Work undertaken: Media, entertainment and sports law together with a broad range of commercial litigation.

The areas of practice in the field of media, entertainment and sports law include, but are not limited to, defamation, breach of confidence, contempt, malicious falsehood and slander of goods/title, copyright and contractual disputes of all kinds (e.g. books, music, film, video and television), Copyright Tribunal applications, judicial review applications, restraint of trade disputes (in sport and pop), other sports disputes, EU/competition matters, multimedia and telecommunications law.

In addition, members of chambers carry out substantial work in the wider commercial field, covering such subjects as insurance and reinsurance, sale of goods, shipping, professional negligence, employment law, international law, company law, administrative law and landlord and tenant.

18 RED LION COURT (Anthony Arlidge QC)

18 RED LION COURT, LONDON, EC4A 3EB
Tel: (0171) 520 6000 **Fax:** (0171) 520 6248/49 **DX:** 478 LDE

MEMBERS:

Sir Derek Spencer QC (1961) (QC-1980)
Anthony Arlidge QC (1962) (QC-1981)
David Cocks QC (1961) (QC-1982)
James Stewart QC (1966) (QC-1982)
Henry Green QC (1962) (QC-1988)
David Lederman QC (1966) (QC-1990)
Graham Parkins QC (1972) (QC-1990)
Linda Stern QC (1971) (QC-1991)
Peter Rook QC (1973) (QC-1991)
Richard Sutton QC (1969) (QC-1993)
Christopher Ball QC (1972) (QC-1993)
Peter Carter QC (1974) (QC-1995)
Rosamund Horwood-Smart QC (1974) (QC-1996)

Nigel Peters QC (1976) (QC-1997)
John Black QC (1975) (QC-1998)
Patricia Lynch QC (1979) (QC-1998)
David Etherington QC (1979) (QC-1998)
Linda Dobbs QC (1981) (QC-1998)
David Radcliffe (1966)
Carey Johnston (1977)
David Green (1979)
Stephen Harvey (1979)
Peter Fenn (1979)
Jonathan Fisher (1980)
Alexander Milne (1981)
Janine Sheff (1983)
Richard Kovalevsky (1983)
Mark Lucraft (1984)
Angela Morris (1984)
Rupert Overbury (1984)
David Marshall (1985)
Brendan Morris (1985)
Simon Spence (1985)

Robert Boyle (1985)
Robin Du Preez (1985)
Jane Bewsey (1986)
Max Hill (1987)
Shane Collery (1988)
David Huw Williams (1988) GRSC, Dip LL
John Anderson (1989)
Candida Hill (1989)
Sara Lawson (1990)
David Holborn (1991)
Sean Hammond (1991)
Allison Clare (1992)
Matthew Gowan (1992)
Paul Hardy (1992)
Tom Forster (1993)
Barnaby Jameson (1993)
Claudia Mortimore (1994)
Michelle Nelson (1994)
Jacqueline Hall (1994)
Adam Wiseman (1994)
Elizabeth Webster (1995)
Gillian Jones (1996)

Head of Chambers:
Anthony Arlidge QC

Senior Clerk:
Kenneth Darvill

First Junior:
Mark Bennett

Tenants: 54

The Chambers: With 18 QCs, specialises in criminal law dealing with serious crimes in particular. Some members offer general common law. Members practise in London and on the South East Circuit, which is served by our annexe in Chelmsford. Chambers have standing counsel to the Inland Revenue, DTI Inspectors, recorders and assistant recorders.

Publications: Arlidge and Parry on *Fraud;* Arlidge and Eady on *Contempt; Journal of International Banking Law* (UK Correspondent); Dobbs and Lucraft, *Road Traffic Law and Practice* (Sweet & Maxwell 1994); Rook and Ward, *Sexual Offences* (Waterlows 1990); Carter and Harrison *Offences of Violence* (Waterlows 1991); Fisher and Merrills *Pharmacy Law and Practices* (Blackwells 1995); Fisher and Bewsey, *The Law of Investor Protection*, Mortimore on *Immigration and Adoption* (Hammicks 1994).

Work Undertaken:

Main Areas of Work: Criminal: Commercial fraud, Inland Revenue and Customs and Excise offences, drugs and problems arising from the Drug Trafficking Offences Act, money laundering, extradition, child abuse, obscene publications, road traffic, licensing, judicial review, privy council, health and safety at work, personal injury, medical negligence, professional negligence, disciplinary and tribunal work, contract, tort, immigration, peerage, civil liberties and family.

Clientele: Individuals, public and private companies, HM Customs and Excise, local authorities, Serious Fraud Office and CPS government departments.

Foreign Connections: Nigel Peters is a member of the Northern Ireland Bar and Barbados Bar. David Marshall is a member of the Hong Kong Bar and the New York Bar.

Recruitment & Training: Applications for tenancy should be sent to David Green; pupillage applications to Barnaby Jameson.

Chambers have up to seven pupils at any one time, four of whom are guaranteed £10,000 for the year. Mini-pupillages are available.

*Chambers annexe at: Thornwood House, 102 New London Road, Chelmsford CM2 0RG *Tel:* (01245) 280880 *Fax:* (01245) 280882 *DX:* 89706 Chelmsford 2

NO. 1 SERJEANTS' INN (Edward Faulks QC)

NO.1 SERJEANTS' INN, FLEET STREET, LONDON, EC4Y 1LL
Tel: (0171) 415 6666 **Fax:** (0171) 583 2033 **DX:** 364

MEMBERS:

Edward Faulks QC (1973) (QC-1996)+	Antony Baldry (1975) M.P.	Mary Pinder (1989)
Martin Wilson QC (1963) (QC-1982) *	Veronica Hammerton (1977) + David Pittaway (1977)	Selena Marris (1991)
Crawford Lindsay QC (1961) (QC-1987) *	Simon Readhead (1979) + Nicholas Yell (1979)	Gerard Boyle (1992)
Adrian Redgrave QC (1968) (QC-1992) *	John Norman (1979) Alastair Hammerton (1983)	Wendy Herring (1993)
Nicholas Browne QC (1971) (QC-1995) *	Edward Bishop (1985) Sarah Paneth (1985)	Andrew Warnock (1993)
Brian Leech (1967) *	Julian Waters (1986)	Alison Clarke (1994)
John Ross (1971) *	Marc Rivalland (1987)	Paul Stagg (1994)
William Hunter (1972)	Justin Althaus (1988)	Ivor Collett (1995)

Associate Members: W.P.Andreae-Jones QC (1965) (QC-1984)*, Jonathan Foster QC (1970) (QC-1989)*.

* Recorder
+ Assistant Recorder

The Chambers: No. 1 Serjeants' Inn is an established common law/commercial set with a forward thinking and client-focused approach, committed to providing a service of the highest quality.

Work Undertaken: Chambers main reputation is for its work in the fields of professional negligence (including medical negligence), claims against public authorities, commercial and insurance disputes, personal injury claims (including disaster litigation) and commercial fraud. Members of Chambers have written 'Pittaway and Hammerton: Professional Negligence Cases' recently published by Butterworths.

The Service: In key areas of practice, members of Chambers have been involved in leading cases and offer expertise at all levels rivalling that of the best known specialist sets. Whilst being in independent practice, they are accustomed to working with one another in teams, providing complementary skills and levels of experience. They also recognise the importance of working in teams with clients, are sympathetic to the pressures on a solicitor's time, and seek to provide a cost effective and efficient litigation team or advisory service.

Head of Chambers:
Edward Faulks QC

Senior Clerk:
Clark Chessis

Practice Development Manager:
Rosemary Thorpe

Tenants: 28

NO. 1 SERJEANTS' INN

1 SERJEANTS' INN (Lionel Read QC)

1 SERJEANTS' INN, LONDON, EC4 1NH
Tel: (0171) 583 1355 **Fax:** (0171) 583 1672 **DX:** 440 **Email:** SERJEANTS.INN@VIRGIN.NET

MEMBERS:

Lionel Read QC (1954) (QC-1973) MA (Cantab)*	John Pugh-Smith (1977) MA (Oxon)	Roy Martin (1990) (QC-Scotland), LLB (Glasgow)
David Woolley QC (1962) (QC-1980) MA (Cantab)	Simon Pickles (1978) MA (Cantab)	William Upton (1990) MA, LLM (Cantab)
Anthony Rumbelow QC (1967) (QC-1990)	John Dagg (1980) BSC (Dunelm), LLB (London)	Sasha White (1991) MA (Cantab)
Patrick Clarkson QC (1972) (QC-1991) *	Neil Cameron (1982) BA (Dunelm)	Robert Douglas White (1993) LLB (LSE)
Christopher Whybrow QC (1965) (QC-1992) LLB (London)	Stephen Morgan (1983) LLB (Warw), MA (Nott)	Richard Harwood (1993) MA, LLM (Cantab)
William Hicks QC (1975) (QC-1995) MA (Cantab)	Richard Langham (1986) BA (Oxon)	Martin Edwards (1995) BA, MA LMRTPI
Martin Wood (1972) LLB (London)	Russell Harris (1986) MA (Cantab)	Matthew Reed (1995) MA (Cantab) MA (City)
Rhodri Price Lewis (1975) MA (Oxon) DipCrim (Cantab)+	Megan Thomas (1987) BA (Sheff)	Scott Lyness (1996) LLB (Hull)
	Yousef Bassa (1989) LLB (Essex)	

*Recorder
+Assistant recorder.

Head of Chambers:
Lionel Read QC

Senior Clerk:
William King

Tenants: 25

Continues overleaf

The Chambers: A specialist planning and local government set, in modern and spacious accommodation. Members undertake both advocacy and advisory work and accept Direct Professional Access from the approved professions. There is an emphasis on public inquiry work.

Work Undertaken: Town and country planning; environmental protection; integrated pollution control; waste disposal; hazardous substances; compulsory purchase and compensation; highways; public health; local government; statutory undertakers; administrative law and judicial review; parliamentary work; landlord and tenant; rating

Foreign Connections: Members of chambers have been involved in arbitrations abroad and practise in Scotland.

Recruitment & Training: Pupillage applications via PACH. Chambers offer up to two first six months' and up to two second six months' pupillages each year. Chambers may offer a twelve months' pupillage. Awards of up to £8,000 are available.

SET NUMBER
191 **3 SERJEANTS' INN** (Philip Naughton QC)

3 SERJEANTS' INN, LONDON, EC4Y 1BQ
Tel: (0171) 353 5537 **Fax:** (0171) 353 0425 **Mobile:** 0385 736844 **DX:** 421

MEMBERS:

Philip Naughton QC (1970) (QC-1988)	Huw Lloyd (1975)	Jonathan Holl-Allen (1990)
Adrian Whitfield QC (1964) (QC-1983)	Anthony Cottle (1978)	Christopher Johnston (1990)
	James Watson (1979)	Michael Horne (1992)
Robert Francis QC (1973) (QC-1992)	Sue Burns (1979)	Fionnuala McCredie (1992)
	Andrew Grubb (1980)	Richard Partridge (1994)
Nicola Davies QC (1976) (QC-1992)	Fiona Neale (1981)	Mark Ley-Morgan (1994)
	Mary O'Rourke (1981)	Anthony Jackson (1995)
John Grace QC (1973) (QC-1994)	George Hugh-Jones (1983)	Debra Powell (1995)
	Adrian Hopkins (1984)	George Thomas (1995)
Philip Gaisford (1969)	Angus Moon (1986)	Clodagh Bradley (1996)
Malcolm Fortune (1972)	Ian Wright (1989)	Orla Ward (1996)
Geoffrey D. Conlin (1973)	John Beggs (1989)	Ranald Davidson (1996)

Head of Chambers:
Philip Naughton QC

Senior Clerk:
Nick Salt

Junior Clerks:
Lee Johnson, Tracy Barker

Administrator:
Helen Ensor

Tenants: 32

Types of Work Undertaken:

Professional Negligence: In the medical, dental, and pharmaceutical fields tenants act for plaintiffs and defendants, including health authorities throughout the country and all the medical defence organisations. Tenants have appeared in many of the major cases in this field including *Sidaway, Hotson, Roberts v Johnstone, Howard v Essex RHA, Sion v Hampstead HA, Hopkins v Mackenzie, Rance,* Burton, and the pertussis vaccine litigation. Tenants also deal with a wide range of other forms of professional liability, including that of architects, surveyors, engineers and lawyers and matters governed by the Health & Safety at Work Act.

Medical Ethics: Tenants act in cases concerning treatment decisions, caesarean sections and other ethical issues and are available at very short notice for urgent applications. Cases in which tenants have appeared include *Bland, re F (sterilisation), re S (Hospital Patient: Court's Jurisdiction), B v Croydon HA, Robb, ex p Martin, re S (Adult: Refusal of Treatment), re T (Wardship: Medical Treatment), and re MB.*

Professional Discipline and Review: Tenants appear in disciplinary cases before bodies such as the General Medical and Dental Councils, and the NHS Tribunal and handle judicial review and Privy Council appeals. They also appear at internal hospital and public inquiries such as Cleveland.

Construction and Engineering: The principal areas of work undertaken concern standard form and other contracts for building and civil, mechanical, electrical, chemical and process engineering projects; defects in design and workmanship; performance obligations; loss and expense claims; and warranties. Associated areas of work include the professional negligence of architects, engineers, surveyors and valuers; nuisance; matters governed by the Health & Safety at Work regulations; and environmental matters.

Police Work: Tenants specialising in this field act for over a dozen police forces in civil claims for false imprisonment, assault, malicious prosecution, and negligence; and in disciplinary and employment matters. Tenants regularly present risk management seminars in specialist areas including public order and firearms.

Employment: Work undertaken includes advising and acting in wrongful dismissal claims, industrial tribunal cases, the drafting of employment contracts, race and sex discrimination claims and European law.

Crime: Both defence and prosecutions are undertaken. Tenants who specialise in crime have particular experience in proceedings relating to professional practice, fraud, Health and Safety at Work and medical and ethical issues. In addition, a wide range of personal injuries, commercial contract and common law work is undertaken.

Languages: French.

Recruitment and Training: Chambers offer two to three 12 month pupillages starting each October.

Awards: Chambers offer each of the candidates an award of £7,500 and guarantee minimum earnings of £7,500 during the second 6 months.

Applications: 3 Serjeants' Inn is a member of the Pupillage Applications Clearing House Scheme (PACH), and all applications should be made in accordance with the rules of the scheme.

THREE
SERJEANTS'
INN

SET NUMBER
192 **SERLE COURT CHAMBERS** (Charles Sparrow QC)

THIRTEEN OLD SQUARE, LINCOLN'S INN, LONDON, WC2A 3UA
Tel: (0171) 242 6105 **Fax:** (0171) 405 4004 **DX:** LDE 1025 **Email:** CLERKS@SERLECOURT.CO.UK
Internet: HTTP://WWW.SERLECOURT.CO.UK

MEMBERS:

Charles Sparrow QC (1950)
(QC-1966) LLB (Lond) DL
Patrick Talbot QC (1969)
(QC-1990) MA (Oxon)
Alan Boyle QC (1972)
(QC-1991) BA (Oxon)
Michael Briggs QC (1978)
(QC-1994) MA (Oxon)
Kenneth Farrow (1966) MA
BCL (Oxon)
John Whittaker (1969) MA
BCL (Oxon)
Nicholas Asprey (1969) LLB
(Edin)
Frank Hinks (1973) MA BCL
(Oxon)
Victor Joffe (1975)
MA(Cantab) LLB (Cantab)
Beverly-Ann Rogers (1978)
LLB (Lond)

William Henderson (1978)
BA (Cantab)
James Behrens (1979) MA
(Cantab)
Philip Hoser (1982) MA
(Cantab)
Elizabeth Jones (1984) BA
(Cantab)
Richard Walford (1984) LLB
Philip Jones (1985) MA BCL
(Oxon) LLM (Dal)
Philip Marshall (1987) MA
(Cantab) LLM (Harvard)
Nicholas Harrison (1988) BA
(Oxon)
Bridget Lucas (1989) BA
(Oxon)
Clare Hoffmann (1990) BA
Jill Johnston (1990) MA
(Cantab)

Douglas Close (1991) MA
BCL(Oxon)
Kathryn Purkis (1991) BA
(Hons) (Cape Town) BA (Oxon)
David Blayney (1992)
BA(Oxon)
John Machell (1993)
LLB(Soton)
David Drake (1994) BA
BCL(Oxon)
Justin Higgo (1995)
BA(Oxon)
Daniel Lightman (1995)
BA(Oxon)
Hugh Norbury (1995)
BA(Oxon) LLM
Timothy Collingwood (1996)
BA BCL(Oxon)

Head of Chambers:
Charles Sparrow QC
Senior Clerks:
Terry Buck
Steven Whitaker
Tenants: 30

The Chambers: Serle Court Chambers (formerly Thirteen Old Square) is a well established set of chambers in Lincoln's Inn which provides effective litigation expertise and a practical creative approach across a broad range of work in the chancery and commercial fields.

Work Undertaken:

Business and Commercial: This area, which accounts for a significant proportion of the work of Chambers, encompasses all types of contractual dispute, guarantees and securities, sale of goods, agency, restraint of trade and, in particular, commercial fraud (including tracing remedies and restitution, Mareva and other interlocutory relief, and constructive trusts).

Property: The practice of Chambers covers all aspects of real and personal property, including landlord and tenant disputes, mortgages, easements and covenants, and development contracts, as well as environmental matters and nuisance.

Company and Insolvency: Many members of Chambers have significant expertise and experience in the fields of company law and insolvency (both corporate and personal): particular specialisations include shareholders' and directors' disputes, breach of fiduciary duty, the disqualification of directors, liquidation, administration and receivership, voluntary arrangements and bankruptcy.

Trusts and Estates: Including the administration of estates and family provision.

Professional Negligence: Especially relating to accountants, financial advisers, solicitors and surveyors.

Partnerships: Both contentious and non-contentious issues.

Within each of these areas of practice Serle Court Chambers can provide a full team of barristers at all levels.

Other areas in which individual members of Chambers have particular expertise include Financial Services, Entertainment Law, Intellectual Property, Sports Law, Charities, Commons Registration and Parliamentary work. In addition to appearing in the English Courts, members of Chambers also frequently appear in overseas courts and in arbitrations.

SERLE COURT
CHAMBERS

193 SOMERSETT CHAMBERS (Lanre Oke) 52 Bedford Row, London, WC1R 4LR **Tel:** (0171) 404 6701 **Fax:** (0171) 404 6702 **DX:** 44 LDE **Clerk:** Ms Rosemarie Phillips **Tenants:** 15 Crime, Common Law, Family and Landlord & Tenant.

194

3/4 SOUTH SQUARE (Michael Crystal QC)

3-4 SOUTH SQUARE, GRAY'S INN, LONDON, WC1R 5HP
Tel: (0171) 696 9900 **Fax:** (0171) 696 9911 **DX:** 338 (CH.LN.) **Email:** CLERKS@SOUTHSQUARE.COM

MEMBERS:

Michael Crystal QC (1970) (QC-1984) LLB (Lond), BCL (Oxon)
Muir Hunter QC (1938) (QC-1965) MA (Oxon)
Christopher Brougham QC (1969) (QC-1988) BA (Oxon)
Gabriel Moss QC (1974) (QC-1989) MA, BCL (Oxon)
Simon Mortimore QC (1972) (QC-1991) LLB (Exon)
John Higham QC (1976) (QC-1992) MA, LLM (Cantab)
Marion Simmons QC (1970) (QC-1994) LLB, LLM (Lond)
Richard Adkins QC (1982) (QC-1995) MA (Oxon)
Richard Sheldon QC (1979) (QC-1996) MA (Cantab)
Richard Hacker QC (1977) (QC-1998) MA (Cantab) Lic sp Dr Eur (Bruxelles)
Clive Cohen (1989) (SC 1975) BA, LLB (Witwatersrand)
John Briggs (1973) LLB, (Lond) Ex, Du D d'U (Nancy)

David Marks (1974) MA, BCL (Oxon)
Martin Pascoe (1977) BA, BCL (Oxon)
Robin Knowles (1982) MA (Cantab)
William Trower (1983) MA (Oxon)
Mark Phillips (1984) LLB, LLM (Bristol)
Robin Dicker (1986) BA, BCL (Oxon)
David Alexander (1987) MA (Cantab)
Antony Zacaroli (1987) BA, BCL (Oxon)
Mark Arnold (1988) BA (Cantab)
Lexa Hilliard (1987) LLB, (Lond)
Stephen Atherton (1989) LLB,(Lancaster) LLM (Cantab)
Sandra Bristoll (1989) BA (Cantab)
Adam Goodison (1990) BA(Dunelm)

Hilary Stonefrost (1991) MSC (Lond)
Lloyd Tamlyn (1991) BA(Cantab)
Glen Davis (1992) MA(Oxon)
Andreas Gledhill (1992) MA(Cantab)
Fidelis Oditah (1992) MA BCL D Phil (Oxon)
Roxanne Ismail (1993) LLB (Lond)
Barry Isaacs (1994) MA(Oxon) MA(HARV) ASA
Ben Valentin (1995) BA BCL(Oxon) LLM(Cornell)
Felicity Toube (1995) BA BCL(Oxon)
Jeremy Goldring (1996) BA (Oxon) MA (York)
Samantha Knight (1996) BA (Oxon)
Lucy Frazer (1996) BA (Cantab)

Head of Chambers:
Michael Crystal QC

Senior Clerk:
Jason Pithers

Clerks:
Michael Killick
Jim Costa

Administrator:
Lynne Isaacs

Tenants: 37

The Chambers: Members of these chambers practice primarily in business, financial and commercial law and have particular experience in insolvency law. Other areas of specialisation are detailed below.

Members of chambers practise regularly in the Companies Court, Commercial Court, Queen's Bench and Chancery Divisions of the High Court, the Court of Appeal, the House of Lords and the Privy Council and the provincial Courts in England and Wales.

Members of chambers have experience of advocacy in foreign Courts and tribunals, of acting as arbitrators or examiners in connection with English and overseas litigation and disputes, and of acting as expert witnesses on English law in cases proceeding in other jurisdictions. They are able to accept instructions direct from overseas lawyers and from members of professional bodies authorised by the General Council of the Bar to instruct counsel without the intervention of a solicitor.

Work Undertaken includes:

Corporate and International Insolvency: Receivership; Administration; Liquidation; Arrangements with creditors; Insolvent Partnerships.

Company Law: Mergers and Acquisitions; Shareholders and Directors disputes; Partnership Disputes.

Banking: Credit and Security; Factoring; Mortgages; Finance Leasing; Guarantees; Bills of Exchange; Bonds relating to Construction Contracts and International Trade.

Personal Insolvency.

Financial Services: City, Market and Banking Regulation; Stock Exchange, Commodity and Currency Transactions, Derivatives.

Commercial and Business Law: Civil aspects of Commercial Fraud; Breach of Contract; Sale of Goods; Retention of Title; International Trade; Insurance and Reinsurance; Tax-related litigation; Tracing Remedies; Pre-trial Remedies and Enforcement of Foreign and Domestic Judgements; Obtaining Evidence for Foreign Proceedings.

Professional Negligence and disciplinary proceedings: particularly concerning Accountants, Financial Advisers and Solicitors.

Languages Spoken: French, German, Italian, Spanish, Chinese (Mandarin) and Afrikaans.

195 11 SOUTH SQUARE (Christopher Floyd QC)

11 SOUTH SQUARE (2ND FLOOR), GRAY'S INN, LONDON, WC1R 5EU
Tel: (0171) 405 1222 **Fax:** (0171) 242 4282 **DX:** 433

MEMBERS:

Christopher Floyd QC (1975) (QC-1992) +	Henry Carr QC (1982) (QC-1998)	Richard Arnold (1985)
	C.D. (Henry) Whittle (1975)	Heather Lawrence (1990)
Michael Silverleaf QC (1980) (QC-1996)	Richard Hacon (1979)	Mark Vanhegan (1990)
	Iain Purvis (1986)	Jacqueline Reid (1992)
		Hugo Cuddigan (1995)

+ *Assistant Recorder at the Patents County Court.*

Head of Chambers:
Christopher Floyd QC

Clerks:
Rochelle Haring
Martyn Nicholls

Tenants: 11

Work Undertaken: The chambers specialise principally in patent and other intellectual property matters and related EC and domestic competition law. The majority of members of chambers have academic or practical technical and scientific backgrounds to the equivalent of at least degree level. They also act in matters with a high technical content outside the field of intellectual property and are happy to accept instructions in commercial and other disputes in this category, such as computer, pharmaceutical, engineering and similar matters.

196 STANBROOK & HENDERSON (Clive Stanbrook QC & Roger Henderson QC)

2 HARCOURT BUILDINGS, TEMPLE, LONDON, EC4Y 9DB
Tel: (0171) 353 0101 **Fax:** (0171) 583 2686

Stanbrook and Henderson is an asssociation between the chambers of Roger Henderson QC at 2 Harcourt Buildings (see other reference for a full list) and the members of the European law firm of Stanbrook and Hooper in Brussels who are also members of the English bar, namely:

Clive Stanbrook QC (1972) (QC1989)

Philip Bentley QC (1970) (QC 1991)

John Ratliff (1980)

Debra Holland (1996)

Head of Chambers:
Clive Stanbrook QC & Roger Henderson QC

Senior Clerk:
John White

Tenants: 4

197

STAPLE INN CHAMBERS (Veronica Ramsden) 9 Staple Inn, London, WC1V 7QH **Tel:** (0171) 242 5240 **Fax:** (0171) 405 9495 **DX:** 132 **Clerk:** Brian Monument **Tenants:** 25 A general common law chambers.

198

2 STONE BUILDINGS (Jamal Nasir) 1st Floor, 2 Stone Buildings, Lincoln's Inn, London, WC2A 3RH **Tel:** (0171) 405 3818 **Fax:** (0171) 831 1971 **Clerk:** Adrienne Bianchet Specialises in foreign laws, private and public international law and Islamic law. Membership of the Jordan and other Arab Bars.

199 3 STONE BUILDINGS (G.C Vos QC)

3 STONE BUILDINGS, LINCOLN'S INN, LONDON, WC2A 3XL
Tel: (0171) 242 4937 **Fax:** (0171) 405 3896 **DX:** 317

MEMBERS:

Geoffrey C. Vos QC (1977) (QC-1993) MA (Cantab)	David da Silva (1978) MA (Oxon)	Carlos A.L.de S. Pimentel (1990) LLB, LLM(Exon)
Edward Alexander Bannister QC (1973) (QC-1991)	Alexandra Mason (1981) BA (Hons) (London)	Asaf Kayani (1991) LLB (Leeds), BCL (Oxon)
David R. Stanford (1951) LLB, MA (Cantab)	Robert A. Hantusch (1982) MA (Cantab)	Sarah H. Lacey (1991) BA (Cantab)
Geoffrey J. Topham (1964) MA (Cantab)	Sarah J. Asplin (1984) MA (Cantab), BCL (Oxon)	Marian Conroy (1991) LLB (Hull)
Andrew J. Cosedge (1972) LLB (Exon)	Sarah E. Girling (1986) MA (Cantab)	Andrew M. Twigger (1994) BA (Oxon)
Alan M. Tunkel (1976) BA (Oxon)	David W. Lord (1987) LLB (Bristol)	Fenner Moeran (1996) BSc (Bristol)

Head of Chambers:
G.C. Vos QC

Senior Clerk:
Andrew Palmer

Tenants: 18

Continues overleaf

The Chambers: 3 Stone Buildings is an established and expanding set of general chancery chambers with a considerable breadth of expertise. Individual attention is combined with professional efficiency. The chambers have experienced practitioners in most areas of financial litigation and advisory work.

Work Undertaken: Particular specialisations include company and commercial litigation, revenue law, trusts and property, insolvency, and partnership formation and disputes. Tax planning and pension matters, and the drafting of settlement, conveyancing and commercial documentation are extensively undertaken.

Nature of Clientele: Companies, banks, trustees and private clients. Direct access instructions are accepted from accountants and other professionals, and from overseas lawyers. Chambers have founder membership of C.E.D.R. (alternative dispute resolution).

Foreign Languages Spoken: French, Portuguese and Spanish.

Recruitment & Training: Chambers are participating in the PACH scheme for the pupillage year 1998/9 and offer 2 first six month pupillages and 2 second six each year. At least 2 (and normally all) of these pupillages are funded with awards, of which details are available on request, as is a full statement of Chambers' policy on pupillage.

Publications: Alexandra Mason & Marian Conroy are the co-authors of *Spencer Maurice's Family Provision on Death* (7th Edition).

4 STONE BUILDINGS (Philip Heslop QC)

4 STONE BUILDINGS, LINCOLN'S INN, LONDON, WC2A 3XT
Tel: (0171) 242 5524 **Fax:** (0171) 831 7907 **DX:** 385 **Email:** D.GODDARD@4STONEBUILDINGS.LAW.CO.UK

MEMBERS:

Philip Heslop QC (1970) (QC-1985)	John Brisby QC (1978) (QC-1996)	Jonathan Brettler (1988)
Peter Curry QC (1953) (QC-1973)	Jonathan Crow (1981)	Paul Greenwood (1991)
Stephen Hunt (1968)	John Scott (1982) (QC Hong Kong 1996)	Andrew Clutterbuck (1992)
Anthony George Bompas QC (1975) (QC-1994)	Malcolm Davis-White (1984)	Nicholas Cox (1992)
Robert Hildyard QC (1977) (QC-1994)	Robert Miles (1987)	Richard. G Hill (1993)
Peter Griffiths (1977)	Rosalind Nicholson (1987)	Orlando Fraser (1994)
	Sarah Harman (1987)	Anna Markham (1996)
	Christopher Harrison (1988)	Hermann Boeddinghaus (1996)

Head of Chambers:
Philip Heslop QC

Senior Clerk:
David Goddard

Tenants: 22

The Chambers: There are 22 members of Chambers, including 5 silks and one Hong Kong QC. One of the juniors in Chambers is the first Junior Counsel to the Treasury in Chancery (the "Treasury Devil"), and another is on the main Chancery Panel. Chambers belong to the Commercial Bar Association, the Chancery Bar Association and the Insolvency Lawyers Association. 4 Stone Buildings specialises in company/commercial law, covering all aspects of company law, commercial and general business law, corporate insolvency, and financial services and regulatory work, with a particular emphasis on litigation.

Work Undertaken:

Company law: Areas of work covered include the formation and acquisition of companies, corporate finance, mergers and acquisitions, reductions and reorganisations of share capital, schemes of arrangement, shareholder and boardroom disputes, Stock Exchange and related regulatory matters, securities and corporate banking. There is also a strong emphasis on commercial fraud and asset recovery, often involving urgent applications to Court.

Insolvency: Chambers deals with receiverships, administrations and liquidations, as well as all aspects of individual insolvency, and the satellite litigation that arises out of insolvencies. Members of Chambers are also regularly involved in applications to disqualify company directors, either for the DTI or for the directors themselves.

Financial services and regulatory work: This is varied and includes litigation, inquiries and investigations under the Companies Act and the Financial Services Act, disciplinary hearings before the various SROs and SIB work. Members of Chambers regularly act for the DTI and other regulatory bodies, as well as advising corporate and institutional clients and individuals.

Commercial and business law: Members of Chambers regularly conduct a variety of litigation in the Commercial Court and in the Chancery Division. Particular specialisations have been developed by individual members of Chambers including oil & gas and mineral rights, banking, insurance and media law.

Foreign Connections: These have enabled members of Chambers to appear over the last few years in the Bahamas, Bermuda, the British Virgin Islands, the Cayman Islands, Hong Kong, Gibraltar, Malaysia, Singapore and Trinidad.

Significant cases: Cases in which various members of Chambers have been instructed include Maxwell, Polly Peck, BCCI, Lloyd's, Blue Arrow and Guinness, together with a number of insurance transfer schemes and building society demutualisations.

Recruitment and Training: Candidates for pupillage are expected to have good degrees but a successful candidate must also have the confidence and ambition to succeed, the common sense to recognise the practical advice that a client really needs, and the ability to get on well with clients and Solicitors. Awards of up to £10,000 are offered per six months. Chambers are a member of PACH.

SET NUMBER 201

5 STONE BUILDINGS (Henry Harrod)

5 STONE BUILDINGS, LINCOLN'S INN, LONDON, WC2A 3XT
Tel: (0171) 242 6201 **Fax:** (0171) 831 8102 **DX:** 304 LONDON/CHANCERY LANE **Email:** CLERKS@5-STONEBUILDINGS.LAW.CO.UK

MEMBERS:

Henry Harrod (1963) *	Martin Farber (1976)	Karen Walden-Smith (1990)
Shân Warnock-Smith (1971)	Launcelot Henderson QC (1977) (QC-1995)	Tracey Angus (1991)
Alastair Norris QC (1973) (QC-1997) +	Andrew Simmonds (1980)	Henry Legge (1993)
Richard Fawls (1973)	Christopher Tidmarsh (1985)	David Rees (1994)
Mark Herbert QC (1974) (QC-1995)	Michael O'Sullivan (1986)	Anna Clarke (1994)
Mark Blackett-Ord (1974)	Patrick Rolfe (1987)	Leon Sartin (1997)
	Barbara Rich (1990)	

Head of Chambers:
Henry Harrod

Senior Clerk:
Paul Jennings

Tenants: 19

*Recorder
+Assistant recorder

The Chambers: 5 Stone Buildings is a Chancery set known for specialist expertise in the fields of property litigation, professional negligence and occupational pensions. Two former members are now in the Court of Appeal and a third has recently been appointed to the Chancery bench. Members have been involved in the Polly Peck and Maxwell litigation and in the leading cases on tax avoidance, undue influence, right to buy, ethical investment, pension surplus and duties of pension trustees. All members advise on trusts, wills, administration of estates and land law. A number of members specialise in private client and estate planning and partnership. Commercial litigation and insolvency work is also undertaken. An efficient modern service of the highest standard is provided.

SET NUMBER 202

7 STONE BUILDINGS (Charles Aldous QC)

7 STONE BUILDINGS, LINCOLN'S INN, LONDON, WC2A 3SZ
Tel: (0171) 405 3886 **Fax:** (0171) 242 8502 **DX:** 335 **Email:** CHALDOUS@VOSSNET.CO.UK

MEMBERS:

Charles Aldous QC (1967) (QC-1985)	Alastair Walton (1977)	Lindsey Stewart (1983)
Michael Nield (1969)	John Randall QC (1978) (QC-1995)	Edmund Cullen (1991)
David Unwin QC (1971) (QC-1995)	Guy Newey (1982)	Patricia Carswell (1993)
Nigel Davis QC (1975) (QC-1992)	Christopher R. Parker (1984)	Tom Bannister (1993)
	James Clifford (1984)	Andrew Westwood (1994)
		Siward Atkins (1995)

Head of Chambers:
Charles Aldous QC

Senior Clerk:
Tony Marsh

Practice Manager:
Shona Kelly B.A.

Tenants: 15

The Chambers: A specialist chancery set, founded in the 1870s, handling all aspects of chancery and commercial practice other than shipping. Much of the work is contentious. All members accept Direct Professional Access.

Work Undertaken: Company and commercial law; corporate finance; credit and security and banking; entertainment law; equitable remedies; mistake and misrepresentation; fiduciary duties; constructive trusts; tracing; financial services; fraud; freezing and recovery of assets; insolvency; insurance; intellectual property; pre-trial remedies; Anton Piller and Mareva Orders; landlord and tenant; pensions; professional negligence and regulation; property; trusts and charities; wills, probate and administration of estates.

Associated Chambers: John Randall practises principally at Priory Court, Birmingham.

Clientele: Mainly businesses and professions, particularly accountants in various capacities.

Recruitment & Training: Chambers offer awards during pupillage, and are members of PACH. Mini-pupillages are encouraged.

7 STONE BUILDINGS

SET NUMBER
203 **7 STONE BUILDINGS** (John Bishop)

7 STONE BUILDINGS, LINCOLN'S INN, LONDON, WC2A 3SZ
Tel: (0171) 242 0961 **Fax:** (0171) 405 7028 **DX:** 1007

MEMBERS:

John Bishop (1970)	Susan Pyle (1985)	Richard Burrington (1993)
Godfrey Ashmore (1961)	Matthew Owens (1988)	Catherine Le Quesne (1993)
Gay Martin (1970)	Patricia Cave (1989)	Sarah Clarke (1994)
Robert Conway (1974)	Adam Swirsky (1989)	Noel Casey (1995)
Julian Lynch (1976)	Shabbir Lakha (1989)	Jonathan Ellis (1995)
Philip Mobedji (1977)	Linda Goldman (1990)	Iain Simkin (1995)
Gillian Temple-Bone (1978)	Johnathon Tod (1990)	Tony Badenoch (1996)
Simon Birks (1981)	Charles Chadwick (1992)	
Cheryl Williams (1982)	Simon Gerrish (1993)	

Mr. G. Ashmore sits on the Rent Assessment Tribunal.

Work Undertaken: General common law, including crime, family, commercial, landlord and tenant, personal injuries, town and country planning, local government and environment, tribunals and licensing work, professional negligence and sale of goods, education.

Languages spoken: French, German, Swahili, Gujerati, Punjabi, Maltese.

Recruitment & Training: There are, on average, 3 pupils in chambers at any one time. Pupillage applications should be sent to PACH. Mini pupillages and student visits available. On application to Pupillage Committee enclose SAE. Tenancy applications to Mrs Gay Martin.

Head of Chambers:
John Bishop
Senior Clerk:
T. Grant
Tenants: 25

SET NUMBER
204 **8 STONE BUILDINGS** (John Cherry QC)

8 STONE BUILDING'S, LINCOLNS INN,, LONDON, WC2A 3TA
Tel: (0171) 831 9881 **Fax:** (0171) 831 9392 **DX:** 216

MEMBERS:

John M. Cherry QC (1961) (QC-1988)	Keiran May (1971)	Richard Menzies (1993)
	Stewart Room (1991)	Marcus Baldwin (1994)
Timothy J. Briden (1976)	Nigel Waddington (1992)	Sarah Howard-Jones (1994)

Work Undertaken: Members of Chambers practise principally in the areas of personal injury, professional negligence and medical negligence. Individual specialisations include: ecclesiastical law, health and safety, Inheritance Act claims, immigration, insurance and Employment law.

Head of Chambers:
John Cherry QC
Senior Clerk:
Alan Luff
Mobile: 0802 411348
Junior Clerk: Paul Eeles
Tenants: 7

SET NUMBER
205 **9 STONE BUILDINGS** (Michael Ashe QC)

LINCOLN'S INN, LONDON, WC2A 3TG
Tel: (0171) 404 5055 **Fax:** (0171) 405 1551 **DX:** 314 CHANCERY LANE **Email:** 9STONEB@COMPUSERVE.COM

MEMBERS:

T. Michael Ashe QC (1971) (QC-1994) (QC Northern Ireland 1998)*	Penelope Jane Reed (1983)	Philip Flower (1979)
	Araba Taylor (1984)	Helene Pines Richman (1992)
David Iwi (1961)	Lynne M. Counsell (1986)	
Cenydd I. Howells (1964) +	Robert S. Levy (1988)	Mel Nebhrajani (1994)
Vivian R. Chapman (1970) +	Timothy Sisley (1989)	Daniel Bromilow (1996)
Christopher I. Cant (1973)	John A.C. Smart (1989)	

+ Full Recorder

* Assistant Recorder

Door Tenants: Graeme C. Wood (1968), Mr. W.H. Ruffin (1972) (North Carolina Bar USA), Mr. Peter Clayton (1977)(Hong Kong Bar), Mr. N. Critelli (1991) (Iowa and New York Bar USA).

The Chambers: A general chancery set undertaking litigation, advisory work and drafting over a whole range of subjects including: tax and tax planning (including stamp duties), wills and trusts, landlord and tenant, business agreements, companies and insolvency, financial services and securities regulations, charities, commons registration, employment law, and professional negligence. (Some members are practitioners in US and Ireland).

Fuller details and information can be obtained from the Chambers Information Booklet, which is available on request.

Head of Chambers:
Michael Ashe QC
Senior Clerk:
Alan Austin
Tenants: 15

9 STONE
BUILDINGS

11 STONE BUILDINGS (Michael Beckman QC)

11 STONE BUILDINGS, LINCOLN'S INN, LONDON, WC2A 3TG
Tel: +44 (0)171 831 6381 **Fax:** +44 (0)171 831 2575 **DX:** 1022 CHANCERY LANE **Email:** CLERKS@11STONEBUILDINGS.LAW.CO.UK
Internet: WWW.11STONEBUILDINGS.LAW.CO.UK

MEMBERS:

Michael Beckman QC (1954) (QC-1976)
Peter Sheridan QC (1956) (QC-1977)
Murray Rosen QC (1976) (QC-1993)
Edward Cousins (1971)
Edward Cohen (1972)
Alan Bishop (1973)
Adrian Salter (1973)
Donald McCue (1974)
John Phillips (1975)
Nigel Meares (1975)
Robert Deacon (1976)
Jonathan Arkush (1977)

Jane Giret (1981)
Sidney Ross (1983)
Roland Higgs (1984)
Marc Dight (1984)
Alan Gourgey (1984)
Tina Kyriakides (1984)
Raquel Agnello (1986)
Marcia Shekerdemian (1987)
Charles Holbech (1988)
Tim Penny (1988)
Sally Barber (1988)
Marilyn Kennedy-McGregor (1989)
Jonathan Middleburgh (1990)

Birgitta Meyer (1992)
Sheila Macdonald (1993)
Christopher Wilkins (1993)
Max Mallin (1993)
James Barnard (1993)
Nick Parfitt (1993)
Jonathan Lopian (1994)
Denis Daly (1995)
Christopher Boardman (1995)
Tom Weekes (1995)
Jamie Riley (1995)

Head of Chambers:
Michael Beckman QC

Senior Clerk:
Christopher Berry

Clerks: Gareth Davies, Caron Levy, Will Sheldon (Listing)

Communications & Client Care: Nicholas Ozga

Emergency overnight & week end service:
Christopher Berry
Home: +44 (0)181 946 9139
Mobile: 0836 566251
Gareth Davies
Home: +44 (0)181 542 1211
Mobile: 0467 443519

Tenants: 36

The Chambers: 11 Stone Buildings is a busy **Commercial** and **Chancery** set specialising in business litigation, arbitration and private client work. The Chambers has been praised in the press for its responsiveness, flexibility in working practices and approach to fee levels. In 1997 the set won *The Lawyer* award for Barristers' Chambers of the year.

There are 36 barristers including 3 QCs occupying the whole of 11 Stone Buildings organised into specialist groups that offer a service to in-house lawyers, DPA clients and London, provincial and international law firms.

The Chambers is particularly well known for its expertise in the following specialist bar categories:

Contract & Commercial
Company & Insolvency
Fraud (Civil & Criminal)
Intellectual Property
Media & Entertainment
Sports Law – *Murray Rosen QC is the chairman of the Bar Sports Law Group*
Property & Land – *Edward Cousins is the author of 'Cousins on Mortgages' and 'Pease and Chitty's Law of Markets and Fairs', the fifth edition of which has just been published*
Public Law & Tribunals
Succession & Trusts – *Sidney Ross is the author of 'Inheritance Act Claims, Law and Practice' that has been recently updated by way of a supplement*
Professional Negligence

Fee Levels are carefully monitored by Christopher Berry, our senior clerk, and a flexible approach is maintained, as we believe that each case has its own special requirements. This flexibility allows our lay clients greater access to experienced lawyers. However, hourly rates can be quoted to assist the client in budgeting for our services. As a general guide, they are as follows:

Pupils	£25-£150 per instruction	Senior Barristers	£100-£175 per hour
Junior Barristers	£25-£100 per hour	Silks	£175+ per hour

Conditional fee work is being continually developed and we will respond to government initiatives as they arise.

Languages Spoken: French, German, Italian, Portuguese, Spanish and Swedish.

199 STRAND (Peter Andrews QC)

199 STRAND, LONDON, WC2R 1DR
Tel: (0171) 379 9779 **Fax:** (0171) 379 9481 **DX:** 322 CH.LN. **Email:** CHAMBERS@199STRAND.CO.UK

MEMBERS:

Peter Andrews QC
QC (1970) (QC-1991)
Robin Stewart QC (1963)
(QC-1979) *
Simon Hawkesworth QC
(1967) (QC-1982) *
Robin De Wilde QC (1971)
(QC-1993)
David Phillips QC (1976)
(QC-1997)
David C. Wilby QC (1974)
(QC-1998)
Charles Welchman (1966)
Malcolm Stitcher (1971)
Alan Green (1973)
Keith Walmsley (1973)

Steven Whitaker (1973)
Elizabeth-Anne Gumbel
(1974)
Simon Levene (1977)
Quintin Tudor-Evans (1977)
Andrew Goodman (1978)
Philip Lehain (1978)
Francis Treasure (1980)
Christopher Hough (1981)
Martin Kurrein (1981)
Jacqueline Beech (1981)
Patrick Sadd (1984)
Philomena Harrison (1985)
Martin Hutchings (1986)
Michael Harrison (1986)

Henry Charles (1987)
James Aldridge (1987)
Richard Serlin (1987)
Henry Witcomb (1989)
Mark Wonnacott (1989)
Sophie Garner (1990)
Timothy Nesbitt (1991)
Rachel Vickers (1992)
Portia Spears (1992)
Eliot Woolf (1993)
Nicholas Isaac (1993)
Louise Davies (1996)
Mark Sefton (1996)

Head of Chambers:
Peter Andrews QC

Senior Clerk:
Martin Griffiiths

Tenants: 37

*Recorder

Associate Tenants: Stephen Guest (1980), Clive Coleman (1986), Keith Northrop (1989).

Work Undertaken: Chambers undertakes work for clients in London, throughout the country and abroad and offers its services in the following areas:

Personal injury: Accidents including employers, public and occupiers liability, road traffic accidents, occupational diseases, medical accidents, health and safety, product liability, disaster litigation.

Medical Negligence: Negligence of doctors, dentists and nurses. Inquests. Hospital Inquiries. Criminal cases in repect of medical malpractice. Disciplinary proceedings.

Property: Conveyancing, boundary disputes, commercial developments of land, mortgages.

Landlord and Tenant: Housing, residential and commercial leases, rent reviews, dilapidation, agricultural tenancies.

Professional Indemnity: Negligence claims for and against lawyers, architects, engineers, surveyors, valuers, accountants, financial intermediaries, and insurance brokers. Proceedings before professional and other regulatory bodies.

Commercial: Contract, sale of goods, carriage of goods, insolvency, partnership, insurance, consumer credit, company law, competition law, passing off, financial services, fraud, franchising, building disputes.

Employment: Wrongful and unfair dismissal, protection of confidential information, restrictive covenants, sex and race discrimination, transfer of undertakings.

Transport: Operators' licensing and construction and use, including the application of tachograph legislation in the road haulage and coach industries. Public Inquiries. Disputes in respect of the carriage of goods by road rail and air.

Direct Professional Access: Chambers accepts instructions from members of the professional bodies recognised by the Bar Council.

Languages: French, German, Hebrew, Japanese, Mandarin.

Recruitment and Training: Two funded 12-month pupillages are available; and applications from students for mini-pupillages are welcomed throughout the year. All enquiries and applications should be addressed to Philomena Harrison.

169 TEMPLE CHAMBERS (Evan Ashfield) 2nd Floor, 169 Temple Chambers, Temple Avenue, London, EC4Y 0DA **Tel:** (0171) 583 7644 **Fax:** (0171) 353 8554 **DX:** 348 **Practice Manager:** Mrs Sylvia Tucker **Tenants:** 14 General common law and commercial set.

TEMPLE FIELDS CHAMBERS (Carol Churchill) Hamilton House, 1 Temple Avenue, London, EC4Y 0HA **Tel:** (0171) 353 6336 **Fax:** (0171) 353 6556 **DX:** 129 Chancery Lane **Tenants:** 2 Temple Fields specialises in international commercial and civil litigation. We undertake work throughout Europe, the Caribbean and America.

1 TEMPLE GARDENS (Hugh Carlisle QC)

1 TEMPLE GARDENS, TEMPLE, LONDON, EC4Y 9BB
Tel: (0171) 583 1315 **Fax:** (0171) 353 3969 **DX:** 382 LONDON **Email:** CLERKS@1TEMPLEGARDENS.CO.UK

MEMBERS:

Hugh B.H. Carlisle QC (1961) (QC-1978) MA (Cantab)

Lord Mayhew of Twysden QC (1955) (QC-1972) MA (Oxon)

Norman A. Miscampbell QC (1952) (QC-1974) MA (Oxon)

Guy R. Sankey QC (1966) (QC-1991) MA (Oxon)

John R.A. Bate-Williams (1976) LLB (Wales)

Ian Ashford-Thom (1977) LLB (Exon)

Ian D. Burnett QC (1980) (QC-1998) MA (Oxon)

William G. Hoskins (1980) MA (Oxon)

Dominic C.R. Grieve (1980) MA (Oxon)

Mark A. Bishop (1981) MA (Cantab)

Alison B. Hewitt (1984) LLB (London)

Robin B-K Tam (1986) MA (Cantab)

Paul A.J. Kilcoyne (1985) LLB (B'ham)

James Bell (1987) LLB (Wales)

Simon G.J. Brown (1988) LLB (London)

Jane R. Llewelyn (1989) MA (Cantab)

Philip D.P. Astor (1989) MA (Oxon)

Keith F. Morton (1990) BSc (Hull)

James R. Laughland (1991) BA (Kent)

Charles Ciumei (1991) BA (Hons) (Oxon)

Charles Curtis (1992) BA (Dunelm)

Richard Wilkinson (1992) LLB (Bristol)

Nicholas Bacon (1992) LLB (Hons) (Essex)

Marcus Grant (1993) BA (Reading)

David Barr (1993) MA (Cantab)

Alexandra Issa (1993) MA (Oxon)

Alexander Glassbrook (1995) BA (Bristol)

Nicholas Moss (1995) MA (Cantab)

Timothy Kevan (1996) BA (Cantab)

Julia Smyth (1996) LLB (London)

Emma-Jane Hobbs (1996) BA (Bristol)

Head of Chambers:
Hugh Carlisle QC

Senior Clerk:
Dean Norton

Tenants: 31

Main Areas of Work: General common law, in particular personal injury, professional negligence and product liability claims and claims in nuisance and other torts; insurance and other contractual disputes; public and administrative law and judicial review; immigration law; employment law; public inquiries and inquests; health and safety; VAT; fraud both civil and criminal.

Languages: French, German and Spanish.

TEMPLE (1) GARDENS

2 TEMPLE GARDENS (Patrick Phillips QC)

2 TEMPLE GARDENS, LONDON, EC4Y 9AY
Tel: (0171) 583 6041 **Fax:** (0171) 583 2094 **DX:** 134 (CH.LN.) **Email:** CLERKS@2TEMPLEGARDENS.CO.UK
Internet: WWW.2TEMPLEGARDENS.CO.UK

MEMBERS:

Patrick Phillips QC (1964) (QC-1980)

William Crowther QC (1963) (QC-1980)

Timothy Preston QC (1964) (QC-1982)

Dermod O'Brien QC (1962) (QC-1983)

Patrick Twigg QC (1967) (QC-1985)

Michael de Navarro QC (1968) (QC-1990)

Andrew Collender QC (1969) (QC-1991)

Robert Moxon-Browne QC (1969) (QC-1990)

Timothy Lamb QC (1974) (QC-1995)

Alexander Layton QC (1976) (QC-1995)

Benjamin Browne QC (1976) (QC-1996)

Jeremy Stuart-Smith QC (1978) (QC-1997)

Daniel Pearce-Higgins QC (1973) (QC-1998)

Henry de Lotbiniere (1968)

Rosalind Foster (1969)

Roger Hetherington (1973)

Howard Palmer (1977)

Stephen Archer (1979)

Monya Anyadike-Danes (1980)

John McDonald (1981)

David Thomas (1982)

Christopher Russell (1982)

Sarah Vaughan-Jones (1983)

Graham Eklund (1984)

Martin Porter (1986)

Catherine Rabey (1987)

Andrew Miller (1989)

Neil Moody (1989)

Jennifer Gray (1988)

Bradley Martin (1990)

Timothy Otty (1990)

Daniel Crowley (1990)

John Snell (1991)

Paul Downes (1991)

Tim Lord (1992)

Marie Louise Kinsler (1993)

Rupert Reece (1993)

David Turner (1993)

Clare Brown (1993)

Done Green (1994)

Lucy Wyles (1994)

Justin Mort (1994)

Bruce Gardiner (1994)

Nina Goolamali (1995)

Adam Constable (1995)

Neil Hext (1995)

Roger Harris (1996)

Head of Chambers:
Patrick Phillips QC

Senior Clerk:
Christopher Willans

Deputy Senior Clerk:
Tom Grove

Administrator:
Louise Jennings

Tenants: 47

The Chambers: This set occupies some of the finest rooms in the Temple offering outstanding facilities for conferences, comfortably accommodating up to 20. Chambers' main areas of work cover a wide range of common law and commercial practice. Members carry out advocacy and advisory work in the UK (both in London and on circuit) and internationally.

Continues overleaf

Work Undertaken: The major areas of practice are general commercial law (including sale and carriage of goods, restraint of trade, confidentiality, product liability, mergers and acquisitions, company and employment law, and arbitrations), commercial and civil fraud, insurance and reinsurance, all areas of professional negligence, disaster litigation, environmental law (including cases concerning fire, flood, electricity, gas, water, highways and health and safety at work), personal injuries (including employers' liability and occupational diseases), and building construction and engineering cases. Disputes involving conflicts of law and jurisdiction and EC problems are regularly handled. This list is not exhaustive and individual members of chambers offer expertise in administrative law and judicial review, criminal law, landlord and tenant and professional disciplinary tribunals.

Recruitment & Training: Pupillages and mini-pupillages by arrangement. Apply to the Secretary of the Pupillage Committee.

Nature of Clientele: Insurance companies; UK and international construction companies; UK and international businesses of all sizes and across a wide field of activity; private clients.

Foreign Languages: French, German, Italian, Spanish.

Charges: The senior clerk will be happy to provide details on request.

Office Equipment: Chambers makes full use of modern technology. Chambers and members of chambers use WordPerfect 5.1 on IBM compatible computers for word processing. Documents can be converted to other word processing formats, can be sent and received electronically on LIX (Legal Information Exchange), and will be sent on disc when required.

SET NUMBER
212

3 TEMPLE GARDENS (David Braham QC)

3 TEMPLE GARDENS, TEMPLE, LONDON, EC4Y 9AU
Tel: (0171) 353 7884 **Fax:** (0171) 583 2044

MEMBERS:

David Braham QC (1957) (QC-1979)

Richard Bramwell QC (1967) (QC-1989)

John Dick (1974)

Michael Sherry (1978)

Alun James (1986)

Eamon McNicholas (1994)

David Southern (1982)

Jonathan Schwarz (1998) *

*formerly a solicitor.

Head of Chambers:
David Braham QC

Senior Clerk:
Frank Skelton

Tenants: 8

One member of chambers belongs to the Institute of Taxation and Chartered Accountants in England and Wales, and all are members of the Revenue Bar Association.

The Chambers: A specialist revenue law set, handling all aspects of tax law and company law generally. The Chambers accept Direct Professional Access from the approved professions.

Publications: Members have written, edited or contributed to the following: *The Taxation of Companies and Company Reconstructions; Inheritance Tax on Lifetime Gifts; The Offshore Tax Planning Review; Weinberg and Blank on Takeovers and Mergers; Practical Tax Planning and Precedents; Whiteman on Income Tax; F.T. World Tax Report; Bulletin for Fiscal Documentation; European Company Law.*

Work Undertaken: All areas of tax law: corporate and business tax, including company reconstructions and demergers; personal tax, including Capital Gains Tax, trusts and inheritance tax planning; employee remuneration, pension schemes and share option schemes; back duty investigations; tax litigation and VAT; associated drafting.

Associated Chambers: Michael Sherry also practises in Manchester, in the Chambers of Michael Shorrock QC at Peel Court Chambers, 45 Hardman Street. Alun James also practises in Liverpool, in the Chambers of John Kay QC at Exchange Chambers, Pearl Assurance House, Derby Square.

Recruitment & Training: Mini pupillages are available.

3 TEMPLE GARDENS (John Coffey QC)

3 TEMPLE GARDENS, TEMPLE, LONDON, EC4Y 9AU
Tel: (0171) 353 3102 **Fax:** (0171) 353 0960 **DX:** 485

MEMBERS:

John Coffey QC (1970)
(QC-1996)
Jeffrey Pegden QC (1973)
(QC-1996)
Geoffrey Birch (1972)
Peter Ader (1973)
Karl Scholz (1973)
Richard Crabtree (1974)
Piers Reed (1974)
Jayne Gilbert (1976)
Robert Whittaker (1977)
Andrew Campbell-Tiech
(1978)

Ann Cotcher (1979)
William Saunders (1980)
Simon Connolly (1981)
Simon Smith (1981)
Alasdair Smith (1981)
Kim Halsall (1982)
Dee Connolly (1982)
Stella Reynolds (1983)
Martin Lahiffe (1984)
Charles Geekie (1985)
Catherine Popert (1987)
Benjamin Aina (1987)
Susan Krikler (1988)

Nicholas Bleaney (1988)
Frances McKeever (1988)
Martin Rutherford (1990)
Carolyn Pearson (1990)
Clemency Firth (1992)
Astra Emir (1992)
Evan Nuttall (1993)
Nicholas Corsellis (1993)
Alexander Williams (1995)
Gareth Patterson (1995)
Amanda Hamilton (1997)

Head of Chambers:
John Coffey QC

Senior Clerk:
Kevin Aldridge

Tenants: 34

The Chambers: A well-established set of chambers specialising in all areas of criminal law, family law and several other areas of common law. Members appear as advocates in the Magistrates Court, Crown Court, High Court, Queen's Bench Divisional Court, the Court of Appeal and the House of Lords. Other tribunals include Police Disciplinary Tribunals, Professional Tribunals, Mental Health Tribunals, Industrial Tribunals, Inquests and other Judicial Inquiries.

Work Undertaken:

Crime: Chambers specialise in all areas of criminal law and have an extensive group of practitioners available at all levels of call. Commercial and corporate fraud is an important specialisation of a number of members and the field of sexual abuse is also a speciality.

Family Law: The expanding matrimonial work of chambers extends to all aspects of this field. Matrimonial property disputes and all sections of the law relating to children are the province of a number of members. Advice is given to both Local Authorities and to individual clients.

Common Law: A broad range of common law work is handled including actions for false imprisonment and malicious prosecution, personal injury matters, employment law, professional negligence claims and contractual disputes.

Memberships: Criminal Bar Association, Family Law Bar Association.

Recruitment & Training: Training and pupillage applications should be sent to Nicholas Corsellis, including a detailed CV and references. Chambers currently offer pupillage awards.

3 TEMPLE GARDENS (Wilfred Jenner Emanuel Forster-Jones) Fifth Floor North, Temple, London, EC4Y 9AU **Tel:** (0171) 353 0853 **Fax:** (0171) 583 2823 **DX:** 0008 Chancery Lane **Email:** 100106.1577@compuserve.com **Clerk:** Brian Peters **Tenants:** 14 General common law set handling crime, discrimination, employment, fraud, housing, immigration, judicial review, police cases, landlord and tenant and family.

3 TEMPLE GARDENS (Jonathan Goldberg QC)

THREE TEMPLE GARDENS, TEMPLE, LONDON, EC4Y 9AU
Tel: (0171) 583 1155 **Fax:** (0171) 353 5446 **DX:** 0064

MEMBERS:

Jonathan Goldberg QC
(1971) (QC-1989)
Robert Watson (1963)
Joanna Greenberg QC (1972)
(QC-1994)
Philip G. Levy (1968)
David Owen-Jones (1972)
Roger Graham (1973)
Kenneth Hind CBE (1973)
Ian Bourne (1977)

Mio Sylvester (1980)
Grace Amakye (1983)
Jonathan Dunne (1986)
Lauren Soertsz (1987)
Paul Addison (1987)
Neil Guest (1989)
Andrew Rutter (1990)
Caroline Kennedy-Morrison
(1990)
Dominic McGinn (1990)

Christopher Gillespie (1991)
James Buchanan (1993)
Robert Tolhurst (1992)
Ed Vickers (1993)
Pascal Bates (1994)
Gary Grant (1995)
Kim Whittlestone (1995)
Helen Guest (1996)

Head of Chambers:
Jonathan Goldberg QC

Senior Clerk:
Adrian Duncan Esq.

Tenants: 25

Continues overleaf

The Chambers: This is a relatively small but strong and well-established set specialising in criminal work. Head of Chambers Jonathan Goldberg QC is a noted defender who has been briefed in many of the best known criminal trials of the past 2 decades at the Old Bailey and elsewhere. Second Silk Joanna Greenberg QC is likewise establishing a leading reputation as a defender.

Practising from elegant rooms once occupied by Marshall Hall QC, this set prides itself on a professional but friendly and unpompous approach to its clients.

Other areas of work: Members of Chambers also regularly undertake commercial fraud, extradition, licensing and road traffic cases, and civil cases where contentious issues of fact are involved and expert cross-examination of witnesses required.

Jonathan Goldberg QC and Joanna Greenberg QC also sit as Recorders and Ian Bourne as Assistant Recorder.

SET NUMBER

216 3 TEMPLE GARDENS (D.C. Gordon) 3 Temple Gardens, Temple, London, EC4Y 9AU **Tel:** (0171) 353 0832 **Fax:** (0171) 353 4929 **DX:** 427 **Clerk:** Mr James Edmiston MA (Oxon) **Tenants:** 24 Members of Chambers have experience in a broad range of common law matters and specialise in Crime, Immigration, Family, Judicial Review, Landlord & Tenant, Commercial, Company and Insolvency.

SET NUMBER

217 3 TEMPLE GARDENS (Dermot Wright) 3 Temple Gardens, Temple, London, EC4Y 9AU **Tel:** (0171) 583 0010 **Fax:** (0171) 353 3361 **DX:** 0073 **Clerk:** Richard Deller **Tenants:** 22 Broad-based common law chambers with particular experience in criminal, family, landlord and tenant and personal injury work.

SET NUMBER

218 THOMAS MORE CHAMBERS More House, 51-52 Carey Street, Lincoln's Inn, London, WC2A 2JB **Tel:** (0171) 404 7000 **Fax:** (0171) 831 4606 **DX:** 90 (Ch.Ln.) **Clerk:** Christopher Hallett **Tenants:** 17 Common law chambers with particular expertise in Fraud and Customs cases, also strong teams in Employment, Commercial, Family Law, Personal Injury and Professional Negligence.

SET NUMBER

219 TINDAL CHAMBERS (A.T.C. Nicholson) Francis Taylor Building, Lower Ground Floor, Temple, London, EC4Y 7BY **Tel:** (0171) 353 5352 **Fax:** (0171) 353 0659 **Clerk:** Paul Green **Tenants:** 0 See under Tindal Chambers, Chelmsford.

SET NUMBER

220 14 TOOKS COURT (Michael Mansfield QC) 14 Tooks Court, Cursitor St, London, EC4A 1LB **Tel:** (0171) 405 8828 **Fax:** (0171) 405 6680 **DX:** 68 (Ch.Ln.) **Clerk:** Carol Thomas **Tenants:** 35 General common law practice with particular expertise in civil liberties, crime, matrimonial law, personal injury, and fraud.

SET NUMBER

221 TOWER HAMLETS BARRISTERS' CHAMBERS (Mohammed Hasmot Ullah) 45 Brick Lane, Second Floor, London, E1 GRL **Tel:** (0171) **Fax:** (0171) 247 9825 **Clerk:** A.R. Khan **Tenants:** 10 A Common Law Chambers.

SET NUMBER

222 TRAFALGAR CHAMBERS (Christopher Cleverly) 53 Fleet Street, Temple, London, EC4Y 1BE **Tel:** (0171) 583 5858 **Fax:** (0171) 353 5302 **DX:** 89 **Clerk:** Michael Sweeney **Tenants:** 20 A common law set with a varied practice including civil, criminal, chancery and family law.

SET NUMBER
223 **3 VERULAM BUILDINGS** (R. Neville Thomas QC)

3 VERULAM BUILDINGS, GRAYS INN, LONDON, WC1R 5NT
Tel: (0171) 831 8441 **Fax:** (0171) 831 8479 **DX:** LDE 331 **Email:** CLERKS@3VERULAM.CO.UK **Internet:** HTTP: //WWW.3VERULAM.CO.UK

MEMBERS:

R. Neville Thomas QC (1962) (QC-1975)	S. Clive Freedman (1975)	Adrian Beltrami (1989)
Nicholas Merriman QC (1969) (QC-1988)	Richard de Lacy (1976)	Amanda Green (1990)
John Jarvis QC (1970) (QC-1989)	Elizabeth Birch (1978)	Annie Hockaday (1990)
Christopher Symons QC (1972) (QC-1989)	Michael Kay (1981)	John Odgers (1990)
	Andrew Onslow (1982)	Jonathan Mark Phillips (1991)
Ian Geering QC (1974) (QC-1991)	Peter Cranfield (1982)	James Evans (1991)
William Blair QC (1972) (QC-1994)	Andrew Sutcliffe (1983)	David Wolfson (1992)
Nicholas Elliott QC (1972) (QC-1995)	Stephen Phillips (1984)	Jonathan Harold Marks (1992)
	Rory Phillips (1984)	David Quest (1993)
Richard Salter QC (1975) (QC-1995)	Tom Weitzman (1984)	Richard Edwards (1993)
Janet Turner QC (1979) (QC-1996)	Ewan McQuater (1985)	Jonathan Davies-Jones (1994)
Ali Malek QC (1980) (QC-1996)	Anne Wakefield (1968)	David Pope (1995)
	Philippe Sands (1985)	Richard Brent (1995)
Gregory Mitchell QC (1979) (QC-1997)	Jonathan Nash (1986)	Sonia Tolaney (1995)
	James Cameron (1987)	Ian Wilson (1995)
	Ross Cranston M.P. (1976)	Catherine Gibaud (1996)
	Caroline Lewis (1988)	Natalie Baylis (1996)
	Juliet May (1988)	
	Maurice Sheridan (1984)	
	Angharad Start (1988)	

Head of Chambers:
R. Neville Thomas QC

Senior Practice Manager:
Roger Merry-Price

Tenants: 48

The Chambers: 3 Verulam Buildings is a leading commercial set of chambers in Gray's Inn, formerly at 3, Gray's Inn Place.

Work Undertaken: Members of Chambers deal with a wide range of commercial work. They are all specialist advocates. As well as representing clients in Court, in arbitrations and before tribunals, they undertake advisory work, settle pleadings and draft contracts and other documentation to meet the needs of clients. They accept direct access work from other professions and regularly accept instructions from overseas lawyers.

Members of Chambers are recognised as specialists in the fields of commercial law, banking, insurance and reinsurance, professional negligence, media and entertainment, public, international and environmental law. In addition, 3 Verulam Buildings has recognised specialists in many other areas of law. This diversity enables 3 Verulam Buildings to offer advice and representation to clients in the huge variety of business contexts in which legal issues arise. It also provides clients with the opportunity to seek specialised assistance on different legal aspects of the same problem.

Door Tenants: Michael Blair QC (Deputy Chief Executive and General Counsel to the Securities and Investments Board), Stephen Silber QC (Law Commissioner), Prof Alan Boyle (University of Edinburgh), Prof James Crawford SC(NSW) (Whewell Professor of International Law, Cambridge), Prof Mark Freedland (University of Oxford), Prof Andreas Lowenfeld (University of New York), Prof Graham Zellick (Principal, Queen Mary College, University of London), Alaric Dalziel, Louise Edwards, Baroness Elles, Paul Heim CMG, Volker Heinz, Jane Owen, Aarif Barma (HK), Arjan Sakhrani SC (HK), Ronny Wong SC (HK), Thomas J Schoenbaum.

Recruitment: Chambers offers 4 pupillages of 12 months, each with an award of not less than £20,000. Candidates should have a first-class or 2.1 degree (which need not be in law). Applications will be received only through the PACH scheme of the Bar Council (telephone (0171) 440 4000).

SET NUMBER
224 VERULAM CHAMBERS (Michael Edwards QC) Peer House, 8-14 Verulam Street, London, WC1X 8LX **Tel:** (0171) 813 2400 **Fax:** (0171) 405 3870 **DX:** 436 Chancery Lane **Clerk:** Trevor Austin **Tenants:** 39 Commercial, chancery, private international law, interlocutory applications, arbitration, general common law (including crime and family/matrimonial), planning, French law, environmental and fire precautions law, and shipping.

SET NUMBER
225 WARWICK HOUSE CHAMBERS (Christopher & Cheryl Drew) Warwick House Chambers, 8 Warwick Court, Gray's Inn, London, WC1R 5DJ **Tel:** (0171) 430 2323 **Fax:** (0171) 430 9171 **DX:** 1001 **Practice Manager:** Mr Neil Calver **Tenants:** 16 A general, criminal, family and commercial set.

WILBERFORCE CHAMBERS (Edward Nugee QC)

8 NEW SQUARE, LINCOLN'S INN, LONDON, WC2A 3QP
Tel: (0171) 306 0102 **Fax:** (0171) 306 0095 **DX:** 311 LONDON CHANCERY LANE WC2 **Email:** CHAMBERS@WILBERFORCE.CO.UK

MEMBERS:

Edward Nugee QC (1955) (QC-1977)	Robert Ham QC (1973) (QC-1994)	Jonathan Seitler (1985)
Jules Sher QC (1968) (QC-1981)	Brian Green QC (1980) (QC-1997)	Thomas Lowe (1985)
David Lowe QC (1965) (QC-1984)	Christopher Nugee QC (1983) (QC-1998)	James Ayliffe (1987)
Terence Etherton QC (1974) (QC-1990)	Anthony Taussig (1966)	Judith Bryant (1987)
John Martin QC (1972) (QC-1991)	John Child (1966)	Joanna Smith (1990)
Nicholas Warren QC (1972) (QC-1993)	Charles Turnbull (1975)	Joanne Wicks (1990)
Ian Croxford QC (1976) (QC-1993)	Thomas Seymour (1975)	Paul Newman (1991)
	Gabriel Hughes (1978)	Gabriel Fadipe (1991)
	Michael Furness (1982)	Caroline Furze (1992)
	Michael Tennet (1985)	Jonathan Evans (1994)
		Emily Campbell (1995)
		Rupert Reed (1996)

Head of Chambers:
Edward Nugee QC

Senior Clerk:
Declan Redmond

Chambers Director:
Suzanne Cosgrave

Tenants: 29

The Chambers: Wilberforce Chambers is a commercial/chancery set comprising 29 barristers including 10 QCs. It has a well-established reputation for its ability to combine imagination and intellectual rigour with practical advice and effective conduct of litigation over a wide range of work. The Chambers has introduced a new staffing structure to ensure that it follows best practice in its business operations and makes extensive use of the new information technology tools now available to aid legal research and communication with all its clients.

Work Undertaken: Litigation, advice and drafting in all areas of modern commercial and chancery practice. The main categories are listed below, but are not intended to be exhaustive, please contact Declan Redmond, Senior Clerk, or Suzanne Cosgrave, Chambers Director for more information and a brochure.

    Commercial: Commercial and other contracts, banking and securities, financial services, Lloyds drafting and litigation, economic torts, breach of confidence, oil and gas law, sports law and white-collar crime e.g. breaches of health and safety legislation.

    Company: Shareholders' disputes, directors' disqualification proceedings, merger and acquisitions, corporate insolvency, partnerships and joint ventures.

    Employment: Wrongful dismisssal and all forms of discrimination.

    Equitable remedies: Injunctions, breach of fiduciary duties, tracing.

    Local government and administrative law.

    Pensions: All aspects of occupational and personal pension schemes.

    Professional Negligence: Accountants, actuaries, auditors, barristers, solicitors, surveyors, trustees and others.

    Property: All matters relating to land, commercial property transactions, landlord and tenant, property finance negligence and fraud, mortgages and other securities, nuisance and trespass, commons, highways, school sites, heritage property and church property.

    Trusts: Trusts, settlements, wills, charities, estate planning and associated tax advice.

Overseas: Members appear for clients outside the UK, in Singapore, Bermuda, Hong Kong and the Cayman Islands.

Direct Professional Access: Members are regularly instructed by recognised professional institutions.

Appointments: Members of Chambers serve as Deputy High Court Judges, as Recorders and as the First Standing Junior Counsel in Chancery matters. Members of chambers belong to the Chancery Bar Association, the Commercial Bar Association, the Association of Pension Lawyers and the Revenue Bar Association.

Recruitment: Pupillage applications should be made via PACH. Applications from students for mini-pupillages are encouraged. The mini-pupillage is a structured week with a formal assessment.

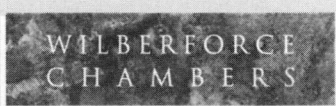

BIRMINGHAM

SET NUMBER
227
COLERIDGE CHAMBERS (Simon D. Brand) Coleridge Chambers, 190 Corporation Street, Birmingham, B4 6QD **Tel:** (0121) 233 3303 **Fax:** (0121) 236 6966 **DX:** 23503 **Clerk:** W.B. Maynard **Tenants:** 17 General common law practice. Bias towards crime, expertise in PI and matrimonial law.

SETNUMBER
228
1 FOUNTAIN COURT (David Crigman QC)

1 FOUNTAIN COURT, STEELHOUSE LANE, BIRMINGHAM, B4 6DR
Tel: (0121) 236 5721 **Fax:** (0121) 236 3639 **DX:** 16077

MEMBERS:

David Crigman QC (1969) (QC-1989)	Giles Harrison-Hall (1977)	Richard Atkins (1989)
Melbourne Inman QC (1979) (QC-1998)	Benjamin Nicholls (1978)	James Puzey (1990)
Malcolm Morse (1967)	Michael Conry (1979)	Gary Thornett (1991)
Robert Hodgkinson (1968)	Stephen Eyre (1981)	Paul Considine (1992)
Michael Dudley (1972)	Thomas Dillon (1983)	Anthony Johnston (1993)
Richard Griffith-Jones (1974)	John Evans (1983)	Nicholas Smith (1994)
Thomas Busby (1975)	Neal Williams (1984)	Thomas Williams (1995)
Christopher Millington (1976)	Simon Ward (1986)	Stuart Baker (1995)
	Jonathan Salmon (1987)	Simon Phillips (1996)
	Sarah Buxton (1988)	Andrew Smith (1997)
	Paul Farrer (1988)	

Head of Chambers:
David Crigman QC

Senior Clerk:
C.T. Hayfield

Tenants: 29

The Chambers: Broadly based chambers covering crime, personal injuries, medical negligence, commercial law and other contracts, sale of goods and consumer credit, chancery, landlord and tenant, family law and wardship, employment, defamation, licensing, planning, copyright, EC competition law, intellectual property. The set also has experience in internal, domestic, disciplinary and professional tribunals.

SETNUMBER
229
3 FOUNTAIN COURT (Colman Treacy QC)

3 FOUNTAIN COURT, STEELHOUSE LANE, BIRMINGHAM, B4 6DR
Tel: (0121) 236 5854 **Fax:** (0121) 236 7008 **DX:** 16079

MEMBERS:

Colman Treacy QC (1971) (QC-1990)	Philip Parker (1976)	William Wall (1985)
Anthony Palmer QC (1962) (QC-1979)	Colin Mackintosh (1976)	Michael Duck (1988)
Peter Andrews QC (1970) (QC-1991)	Anthony Engel (1965)	Andrew Wallace (1988)
David Jones (1967)	Ann Chavasse (1971)	Adrian Keeling (1990)
Donald McConville (1963)	Patrick Darby (1978)	Carolyn Hilder (1991)
Jayne Calderwood (1964)	Michael Burrows (1979)	Justine Lattimer (1991)
Trevor Faber (1970)	Bernard Linnemann (1980)	Steven Bailey (1992)
Peter Arnold (1972)	David Travers (1981)	Matthew Barnes (1992)
Robert Juckes (1974)	Mark Anderson (1983)	Heidi Kubik (1993)
Sybil Thomas (1976)	Christopher Bright (1985)	Simon Harvey (1995)
	Andrew Jackson (1986)	John Butterfield (1995)
	Francis Laird (1986)	Jonathan Jones (1995)
	David Mason (1986)	Adreeja Chatterjee (1997)

Head of Chambers:
Colman Treacy QC

Senior Clerk:
Jonathan Maskew

Tenants: 36

The Chambers: A long-established set, handling a broad range of civil matters and able to provide counsel at all levels of seniority for criminal cases. A chambers brochure is available on request.

Work Undertaken:

Crime: Prosecution and defence work at all levels (including the Court of Appeal). There is a large team of specialists which can deal with the most complex cases. The work covers armed robbery, rape, child abuse, complicated commercial fraud, consumer protection and trade description, police disciplinary tribunals and road traffic.

Civil: Building contracts, chancery, commercial litigation, company law, consumer credit, criminal injuries compensation, defamation, divorce, employment and industrial relations, family provision, insolvency, intellectual property, judicial review, landlord and tenant, licensing, local government, matrimonial finance and property, family and child welfare, mental health tribunals, personal injury compensation, planning, probate and wills, professional and medical negligence, professional disciplinary tribunals, real property and trusts.

SET NUMBER
230 4 FOUNTAIN COURT (Richard Wakerley QC) 4 Fountain Court, Steelhouse Lane, Birmingham, B4 6DR **Tel:** (0121) 236 3476 **Fax:** (0121) 200 1214 **DX:** 16074 Clerk **Tenants:** 30 The principal areas of work undertaken by chambers are: commercial, criminal, personal injury, family and licensing.

SETNUMBER
231 # 5 FOUNTAIN COURT (Anthony Barker QC)

5 FOUNTAIN COURT, STEELHOUSE LANE, BIRMINGHAM, B4 6DR
Tel: (0121) 606 0500 **Fax:** (0121) 606 1501 **DX:** 16075 FOUNTAIN CT. BIRMINGHAM

MEMBERS:

Anthony Barker QC (1966) (QC-1985)	Jean Draycott (1980)	Michele Friel (1991)
Harry Wolton QC (1969) (QC-1982)	Timothy Newman (1981)	Jennifer Jones (1991)
David Stembridge QC (1955) (QC-1990)	Stephanie Brown (1982)	Marion Wilson (1991)
Martin Kingston QC (1972) (QC-1992)	Neil Thompson (1982)	Hugh O'Brien-Quinn (1992)
Stephen Linehan QC (1970) (QC-1993)	Michael Stephens (1983)	David Park (1992)
Gareth Evans QC (1973) (QC-1994)	Andrew McGrath (1983)	Peter Goatley (1992)
Stephen Oliver-Jones QC (1970) (QC-1996)	Satinder Hunjan (1984)	Nicholas Xydias (1992)
William Wood QC (1970) (QC-1997)	David Stockill (1985)	Marc Wilkinson (1992)
Nicholas Budgen (1962)	Richard Lee (1985)	Nicola Preston (1992)
John West (1965)	Richard Moat (1985)	Hugh Richards (1992)
Stephen Whitaker (1970)	Ian Dove (1986)	Isabel Hitching (1992)
Michael Elsom (1972)	Lorna Meyer (1986)	Jonathan Down (1993)
Mark Eades (1974)	Bernard Thorogood (1986)	David Taylor (1993)
Jeremy Cahill (1975)	Mark Heywood (1986)	Nageena Khalique (1994)
Roger Giles (1976)	Simon Drew (1987)	Rachael Price (1994)
Walter Bealby (1976)	Aubrey Craig (1987)	Robert Smallwood (1994)
Anne Smallwood (1977)	Adam Oyebanji (1987)	Rachel Cotter (1994)
Robin Rowland (1977)	Eugene Hickey (1988)	Joanne Duffy (1994)
Christopher James (1977)	Caroline Baker (1988)	Anthony Potter (1994)
David Iles (1977)	Joanna Chadwick (1988)	Anna Diamond (1996)
Kevin O'Donovan (1978)	Sara Williams (1989)	David Mitchell (1995)
Paul Bleasdale (1978)	Malcolm Duthie (1989)	Naomi Gilchrist (1996)
Ralph Lewis (1978)	Martin Liddiard (1989)	Matthew Taylor (1996)
Rosalind Bush (1978)	Becket Bedford (1989)	Jeremy Wright (1996)
	Michael Anning (1990)	Emma Hogan (1996)
	Melanie McDonald (1990)	
	Ashley Wynne (1990)	
	Mary Bennett (1990)	
	Allan Dooley (1991)	
	Mark Radburn (1991)	

Head of Chambers:
Anthony Barker QC

Practice Director:
Tony McDaid

Tenants: 79

The Chambers: Within Chambers we have six specialist practice groups, each with its own membership, group identity and Head of Group. This enables us to offer genuine expertise in all main areas of work. The younger tenants usually gain experience from several disciplines until their particular field of expertise is ascertained, at which point they will join one of the established specialist groups. The six specialist groups are Personal Injury & Medical Negligence, Crime & Licensing, Commercial & Chancery, Planning & Environment, Family and Employment.

5 Fountain Court offers unrivalled facilities for its clients, including: -
- 11 purpose built dedicated conference rooms.
- A video conference studio capable of providing both national and international video conference links.
- A large Arbitration room.
- Seminar Suite capable of seating 40 delegates.

SET NUMBER
232 NO.6 FOUNTAIN COURT (Roger Smith QC)

6 FOUNTAIN COURT, STEELHOUSE LANE, BIRMINGHAM, B4 6DR
Tel: (0121) 233 3282 **Fax:** (0121) 236 3600 **DX:** 16076

MEMBERS:

Roger Smith QC (1972) (QC-1992)
Michael Hutt (1968)
John Mason (1971)
Dorothy Seddon (1974)
Denis Desmond (1974)
James Quirke (1974)
Philip Bown (1974)
Philip Gregory (1975)
Anthony Lowe (1976)
Bryce Somerville (1980)

Amanda Pittaway (1980)
Jonathan Davis (1983)
Andrew Tucker (1977)
Avtar Khangure (1985)
John Stenhouse (1986)
Peter Cooke (1985)
William Rickarby (1975)
Nicholas Tarbitt (1988)
Robert Price (1990)
John Attwood (1989)
Janet Pitt-Lewis (1976)

Simon Davis (1990)
Tariq Bin Shakoor (1992)
Stephen Cadwaladr (1992)
Lee Marklew (1992)
Caroline Egan (1993)
James Dunstan (1995)
David Watson (1994)
David Swinnerton (1995)
Terence Bushell (1982)

Head of Chambers:
Roger Smith QC
Senior Clerk:
Mike Harris
Clerks:
Clive Ridley & Georgina Jones
Tenants: 30

Door Tenant: Miss Jane Walker (1974).

The Chambers: Traditionally strong in crime this established yet progressive set of chambers continues to expand steadily and now offers expertise over a large range of work. The clerks, whilst ensuring efficient and helpful administration, remember the importance of being friendly and approachable.

Work Undertaken: Criminal work, tribunals and inquiries, Water Authority cases, police civil litigation and discipline, personal injury, landlord and tenant, planning, building, general chancery, partnerships, licensing, family law, minors (Children Act, wardship etc), commercial, probate and inheritance, companies, insolvency and bankruptcy, wrongful dismissal, building and construction, consumer credit and trading standards, local government law, housing and environmental health.

SET NUMBER
233 8 FOUNTAIN COURT (Ian Strongman TD)

8 FOUNTAIN COURT, STEELHOUSE LANE, BIRMINGHAM, B4 6DR
Tel: (0121) 236 5514 **Fax:** (0121) 236 8225 **DX:** 16078 **Email:** CLERKS@NO8CHAMBERS.CO.UK

MEMBERS:

Keith Vaughan (1968)
Amanda White (1976)
Monica Pirotta (1976)
Jonathan Perkins (1980)
Derek Hickman (1982)
Ian Strongman (1981)
Stephen Murray (1986)

Sally Hickman (1987)
Nicholas Starks (1989)
Anthony Hartley (1991)
Robert Cowley (1992)
Julie Sparrow (1992)
Kristina Montgomery (1993)
Abid Mahmood (1992)

Nandini Dutta (1993)
Richard Ace (1993)
Timothy Clarke (1992)
Deni Matthews (1996)
Lord Archer* QC (1952) (QC-1971)
Richard Jones* (1979)

Head of Chambers:
Ian Strongman TD
Senior Clerk:
Christine Maloney
Rosemarie Maloney
Tenants: 18

* Door Tenant

The Chambers: A forward-looking set, broadly based with an emphasis on providing a friendly and efficient service.

Work undertaken: Common Law Chambers with emphasis on crime, family/children, personal injury, employment, building disputes, planning, company/commercial and landlord & tenant.

SET NUMBER
234 NEW COURT CHAMBERS (Christopher Morris) Suite 200, Gazette Buildings, 168 Corporation Street, Birmingham, B4 6TZ **Tel:** (0121) 693 6656 **Fax:** (0121) 693 6657 **DX:** 23533 Birmingham 3 **Clerk:** Paul McNab **Tenants:** 13 General common law, criminal law, family, housing, immigration, landlord and tenant, matrimonial, professional negligence, wardship and childcare, civil actions against the police.

SET NUMBER
235 ROWCHESTER CHAMBERS (Wilbert A. Harris) Rowchester Chambers, 4 Rowchester Court, Whitall St, Birmingham, B4 6DH **Tel:** (0121) 233 2327 **Fax:** (0121) 236 7645 **DX:** 16080 **Clerk:** Steven Wilson **Tenants:** 15 Common law and criminal practice. Main areas are civil litigation, immigration, employment, matrimonial, crime and personal injury.

SETNUMBER
236 ## ST. IVE'S CHAMBERS (Edward Coke)

ST. IVE'S CHAMBERS, FOUNTAIN COURT, STEELHOUSE LANE, BIRMINGHAM, B4 6DR
Tel: (0121) 236 0863 (6 LINES) **Fax:** (0121) 236 6961 **DX:** 16072

MEMBERS:

Edward Coke (1976)	Edward Dismorr (1983)	Matthew Haynes (1991)
Julia Macur QC (1979) (QC-1998) *	Peter Grice (1984)	Gregory Rogers (1992)
Margaret Hodgson (1975)	David Jackson (1986)	Richard Dewsbery (1992)
Peter Carr (1976)	Stuart Clarkson (1987)	Barbara Schenkenberg (1993)
Roderick Henderson (1978)	Michael Singleton (1987)	Nicholas Cole (1993)
Kenneth Bladon (1980)	Catherine Preen (1988)	Ian Thomas (1993)
Peter Anthony (1981)	Jayne Mullen (1989)	Lucy Hawkins (1994)
Barry Berlin (1981)	Andrew Maguire (1988)	Peter Cooper (1996)
Michael Keehan (1982)	Janet Newman (1990)	Michael Walsh (1996)
Paul Lopez (1982)	Jeremy Weston (1991)	

Head of Chambers:
Edward Coke

Senior Clerks:
Linda Butler, Craig Jeavons

Tenants: 29

* Assistant Recorder

The Chambers: A forward looking set offering a depth of experience in advocacy and advisory work across a broad spectrum including Family/Childcare, Crime, Personal injury, Housing, Landlord and Tenant, Commercial Litigation and Employment. Individual Tenants specialise in trading standards, environmental and pollution law, licensing and Chancery work.

Languages: German.

SETNUMBER
237 ## ST PHILIP'S CHAMBERS (Rex Tedd QC)

FOUNTAIN COURT, STEELHOUSE LANE, BIRMINGHAM, B4 6DR
Tel: (0121) 246 7000 **Fax:** (0121) 246 7001 **DX:** 16073

MEMBERS:

Rex Tedd QC (1970) (QC-1993)	Stephen Campbell (1982)	Robin Lewis (1991)
John Randall QC (1978) (QC-1995)	Kevin Hegarty (1982)	Glyn Samuel (1991)
John Rogers QC (1963) (QC-1979)	Lawrence Messling (1983) **	Claire Starkie (1991)
Michael Stokes QC (1971) (QC-1994) *	John Edwards (1983)	Hugh Williams (1992) *
Patrick McCahill QC (1975) (QC-1996)	Peter Haynes (1983)	John de Waal (1992) **
William Davis QC (1975) (QC-1998)	Petar Starcevic (1983)	Philip Le Cornu (1992)
Ronald Newbold (1965)	Peter McCartney (1983)	Julie Moseley (1992)
Michael Garrett (1967)	Thomas Rochford (1984)	Katherine Tucker (1993)
Brian Healy (1967)	Samantha Powis (1985)	Anthony Verduyn (1993)
John Price (1969)	Christopher Adams (1986)	Jane Owens (1994) *
Peter Clarke (1970)	Nicholas Cartwright (1986)	Andrew Charman (1994) *
Douglas Readings (1972)	Anna-Rose Landes (1986)	Devan Rampersad (1994)
Graham Cliff (1973)	Gareth Walters (1986)	Elizabeth Walker (1994)
James Corbett (1975)	Lorna Findlay (1987)	Angus Burden (1994)
Timothy Jones (1975)	Lance Ashworth (1987) +	Rosalyn Carter (1994)
Guy Spollon (1976)	Elizabeth McGrath (1987)	David Tyack (1994)
Richard Perks (1977)	Alastair Smail (1987)	Brian Dean (1994)
William Pusey (1977)	Conrad Rumney (1988)	Anthony Fryer (1995) *
Morris Cooper (1979)	Lawrence Watts (1988)	Alistair Macdonald (1995)
James Burbidge (1979)	Alison Cook (1989)	Catherine McCahey (1996)
Stephen Thomas (1980)	Ailsa Cox (1989)	James Morgan (1996)
Roger Dyer (1980)	Timothy Hanson (1989)	Claire Cunningham (1996)
David Worster (1980)	Edward Pepperall (1989)	Louise McCabe (1996)
Makhan Shoker (1981)	Amarjit Rai (1989)	Martin Wilson QC (1963) (QC-1982) **
David Hershman (1981)	Edmund Beever (1990)	Christopher Hotten QC (1972) (QC-1994) **
	Philip Capon (1990)	Andrew McFarlane QC (1977) (QC-1998) **
	Vanessa Meachin (1990)	David Lock M.P. (1985) **
	Andrew Lockhart (1991)	
	Lisa Evans (1991)	
	Sarah George (1991)	

Head of Chambers:
Rex Tedd QC

Deputy Head of Chambers:
John Randall QC

Practice Managers:
Robin Butchard, Clive Witcomb

Senior Clerks:
Matthew Fleming, Richard Fowler, David Partridge

Clerks:
Su Gilbert, Charles Jones, Marguerite Lawrence

Tenants: 82

* Formerly a practising solicitor

** Door Tenant

The Chambers: St. Philip's Chambers was formed 1st June 1998, by the merger of two of Birmingham's established sets of Chambers, Priory Chambers and No. 7 Fountain Court.

The merged set offers strength in depth with five major practice groups providing specialist services, supported by a clerking team of exceptional experience, dedicated to providing a very friendly high quality service with a commitment to meeting the needs of each client. Chambers has been extended and refurbished to provide the best of modern facilities.

Work Undertaken: Our Specialist Practice Groups are: Chancery and Commercial, Criminal Law, Family Law, Personal Injury and Medical Negligence, Property, Planning and Public Law.

Chambers also provide expertise in a very wide range of other subjects including Employment, Licensing and General Common Law.

SET NUMBER
238 VICTORIA CHAMBERS (Lee Masters) Victoria Chambers, 177 Corporation St, Birmingham, B4 6RG **Tel:** (0121) 236 9900 **Fax:** (0121) 233 0675 **DX:** 23520 Birmingham 3 **Clerk:** Lisa Clarke **Tenants:** 16 Common law chambers with expertise in crime, family law, and all civil litigation. Also specialise in public and administrative law together with immigration and actions against the police.

BOURNEMOUTH

SET NUMBER
239 KING'S BENCH CHAMBERS BOURNEMOUTH (Peter Heppel QC) Wellington House, 175 Holdenhurst Road, Bournemouth, BN8 8DQ **Tel:** (01202) 250025 **Fax:** (01202) 250026 **DX:** 7617 Bournemouth **Clerk:** Alan Conner **Tenants:** 14

SET NUMBER
240 LORNE PARK CHAMBERS (Michael Parroy QC) Lorne Park Chambers, 20 Lorne Park Road, Bournemouth, BH1 1JN **Tel:** (01202) 292102 **Fax:** (01202) 298498 **DX:** 7612 **Email:** 3paper.lond@bogo.co.uk **Clerk:** Stephen Clark **Tenants:** 67 Annexe of 3 Paper Buildings in London.

BRADFORD

SET NUMBER
241 BROADWAY HOUSE (Sydney Levine) Broadway House, 9 Bank St, Bradford, BD1 1TW **Tel:** (01274) 722560 **Fax:** (01274) 370708 **DX:** 11746 **Email:** name@broadwayhouse.co.uk **Internet:** www.broadwayhouse.co.uk **Clerk:** Neil Appleyard **Tenants:** 30 A general common law set which also has specialists in civil, family, commercial, and chancery.

BRIGHTON

SET NUMBER
242 ## CROWN OFFICE ROW CHAMBERS (Mr Robert Seabrook QC)

BLENHEIM HOUSE, 120 CHURCH STREET, BRIGHTON, BN1 1WH
Tel: (01273) 625625 **Fax:** (01273) 698888 **DX:** 36670 BRIGHTON 2

MEMBERS:

Anthony Niblett (1976)	Timothy Bergin (1987)	Ian Bugg (1992)
James King-Smith (1980)	Paul Rogers (1989)	Giles Colin (1994)
Janet Waddicor (1985)	Keeley Bishop (1990)	Simon Sinatt (1993)
Jacqueline Ross (1985)	Martin Downs (1990)	
Adam Smith (1987)	Jeremy Cave (1992)	Sally Ann Smith (1996)

Head of Chambers: Mr Robert Seabrook QC
Senior Clerk: Alan G. Smith
Clerk (Brighton): Jenny Lewis
Tenants: 14

The Chambers: Chambers have been in Brighton for some 20 years as an Annexe of 1 Crown Office Row, a long-established common law set in the Temple which has maintained strong Sussex connections for nearly half a century. Brighton-based members practise from centrally located modern premises on one floor with the benefit of a lift. The Brighton County and Magistrates' Courts are a few minutes' walk away. Chambers are equipped with modern computer technology and direct telephone and computer links to 1 Crown Office Row. Conference facilities are excellent.

Continues overleaf

Work Undertaken: Chambers undertake all types of general common law work – civil, criminal and family. Particular expertise can be offered in the areas of professional negligence, personal injury, landlord and tenant, building, employment, licensing and all types of family proceedings.

Recruitment & Training: Please apply to James King-Smith for pupillages in Brighton.

SUSSEX CHAMBERS (Paul Ashwell)

SUSSEX CHAMBERS, 9 OLD STEINE, BRIGHTON, BN1 1FJ
Tel: (01273) 607953 **Fax:** (01273) 571839 **DX:** 2724 BRIGHTON 1

MEMBERS:

Paul Ashwell (1977)	Emma Clout (1989)	Joanne Briggs (1993)
Stuart Lambert (1965)	Dominic Dudkowski (1986)	Suvi Wheeler (1994)
Michael Jones (1972)	Anne Cranfield (1992)	John Marsden-Lynch (1988)
Nicholas Hall (1973)	Richard Lovegrove (1986)	Louise Inward (1995)
Michael Fullerton (1990)	Darren Howe (1992)	Derville Rowland (1996)

Head of Chambers:
Paul Ashwell

Senior Clerk:
Stewart Dewar
Elizabeth Blunden

Tenants: 15

Chambers: Established in Brighton for over 30 years, Chambers is situated a few minutes walk from Brighton County and Magistrates' Courts. Members practise in London and on the South Eastern Circuit.

Work undertaken:
Main Areas of Work:
Civil: Bankruptcy and insolvency, building, contract, education, employment, land, companies, judicial review, landlord and tenant, licensing, local government, mental health and social welfare, mortgages, personal injury, planning, professional negligence, property and commercial. Direct Professional Access is available.
Crime: All areas of criminal law.
Family: All aspects of private and public law including ancillary relief, children, and emergency remedies including domestic violence. All issues and children only mediation is also available.

BRISTOL

ALBION CHAMBERS (J.C.T. Barton QC)

ALBION CHAMBERS, BROAD ST, BRISTOL, BS1 1DR
Tel: (0117) 927 2144 **Fax:** (0117) 926 2569 **DX:** 7822

MEMBERS:

Charles Barton QC (1969) (QC-1989)	Tacey Cronin (1982)	Simon Burns (1992)
James Tabor QC (1974) (QC-1995)	Julian Lambert (1983)	Paul Cook (1992)
Neil Ford QC (1976) (QC-1997)	Caroline Wright (1983)	Allan Fuller (1993)
Elizabeth Hailstone (1962)	Ignatius Hughes (1986)	Rebecca Curtis (1993)
Christopher Jervis (1966)	Stephen Mooney (1987)	Jason Taylor (1995)
Timothy Hills (1968)	Charles Hyde (1988)	Elizabeth Cunningham (1995)
Nicholas O'Brien (1968)	Deborah Dinan-Hayward (1988)	Daniel Leafe (1996)
David Fletcher (1971)	Patrick Burrowes (1988)	
David Spens (1972)	Claire Wills-Goldingham (1988)	Andrew Thornhill QC (1969) (QC-1985) *
Michael Roach (1975)	Myles Watkins (1990)	Christopher Wilson-Smith QC (1965) (QC-1986) *
Martin Steen (1976)	John Livesey (1990)	David Bodey QC (1970) (QC-1991) *
Gavin Chalmers (1979)	Alexander Ralton (1990)	
William Hart (1979)	Nkumbe Ekaney (1990)	Paul Dunkels QC (1972) (QC-1993) *
Stephen Wildblood (1981)	Claire Rowsell (1991)	Simon Mehigan QC (1980) (QC-1998) *
John Geraint-Norris (1980)	Michael Cullum (1991)	
Michael Mather-Lees (1981)	Michael Fitton (1991)	
Martin Picton (1981)	Nicholas Sproull (1992)	

Head of Chambers:
J.C.T. Barton QC

Senior Clerk:
D.H. Milsom

Junior Clerks:
Bonnie Colbeck (Criminal), Michael Harding, Paul Taylor (Civil/family)

Fees Clerks:
Rosemarie Blanshard/ Lesley Carpenter

Tenants: 41

* Door Tenants

The Chambers: A large and still expanding set, the members of which handle a wide variety of specialist legal areas. Chambers accommodation now includes three boardroom-style rooms for major conferences.

Work Undertaken:

Individual members practise across a broad range of legal areas, including agriculture, arbitration, banking and securities, general chancery work, commercial and company law, crime (including Courts Martial), employment law, family law, housing, inheritance, insolvency, judicial review, landlord and tenant, local government, Official Referee's business (business contracts etc), personal injury, planning, professional negligence, property, tribunal work (including employment, disciplinary and mental health tribunals), and trusts, wills and probate law. Members work predominantly on the Western Circuit. A chambers' information booklet is available on request.

Recruitment and Training: Applications for pupillage to W. Hart, with CV. There are usually three or four pupils in chambers, and six- and twelve-month pupillages are available. Interviews are held in November and December, or subsequently, by special appointment.

SET NUMBER
245 ALL SAINTS CHAMBERS (T. Alun Jenkins QC) All Saints Chambers, 9-11 Broad Street, Bristol, BS1 2HP **Tel:** (0117) 921 1966 **Fax:** (0117) 927 6493 **DX:** 7870 Bristol **Clerk:** Steve Freeman **Tenants:** 36 A strong provincial set offering a specialist and efficient service to solicitors and lay clients in most areas of law.

SET NUMBER
246 ASSIZE COURT CHAMBERS (John Isherwood) Assize Court Chambers, 14 Small St, Bristol, BS1 1DE **Tel:** (0117) 926 4587 **Fax:** (0117) 922 6835 **DX:** 78134 **Clerk:** Peter Nixon **Tenants:** 27 A general common law set which handles chancery, crime, common law, landlord and tenant, family, commercial law, construction law, mental health law and employment law.

SET NUMBER
247 FREDERICK PLACE CHAMBERS (Robert Spicer) 9 Frederick Place, Clifton, Bristol, BS8 1AS **Tel:** (0117) 973 8667 **Fax:** (0117) 973 8667 **Clerk:** Lin Spicer **Tenants:** 2 Prompt advice and opinions in general civil law; particularly employment law, health and safety at work and succession.

SET NUMBER
248 GUILDHALL CHAMBERS (John Royce QC) Guildhall Chambers, Broad Street, Bristol, BS1 2HG **Tel:** (0117) 927 3366 **Fax:** (0117) 929 8941 **DX:** 7823 **Clerk:** Mrs Dorothy Hewitt **Tenants:** 40 Details of specialist teams available on request.

SET NUMBER
249 OLD SQUARE CHAMBERS (Hon. John Melville Williams QC)

HANOVER HOUSE, 47 CORN STREET, BRISTOL, BS1 1HT
Tel: (0117) 927 7111 **Fax:** (0117) 927 3478 **DX:** 78229 BRISTOL

MEMBERS:

John Melville Williams QC (1955) (QC-1977)	John H. Bates (1973)	Jonathan Clarke (1990)
John Hendy QC (1972) (QC-1987)	Christopher Makey (1975)	Christopher Walker (1990)
John Hand QC (1972) (QC-1988)	Nigel Cooksley (1975)	Nicholas Booth (1991)
Lord Wedderburn QC (1953) (QC-1990)	Charles Pugh (1975)	Sarah Moor (1991)
	Matthias Kelly (1979)	Ian Scott (1991)
Jeremy McMullen QC (1971) (QC-1994)	Toby Kempster (1980)	Oliver Segal (1992)
Charles Lewis (1963)	Paul Rose (1981)	Helen Gower (1992)
Ian Truscott QC (1995) (QC-1997)	Jane McNeill (1982)	Roy Lewis (1992)
	Barry Cotter (1985)	Mark Whitcombe (1994)
Christopher Carling (1969)	Louise Chudleigh (1987)	Elizabeth Melville (1994)
William Birtles (1970)	Ijeoma Omambala (1988)	Melanie Tether (1995)
Diana Brahams (1972)	Jennifer Eady (1989)	Emma Smith (1995)
	Philip Mead (1989)	Rohan Pirani (1995)
	Damian Brown (1989)	
	Tess Gill (1990)	

Head of Chambers:
Hon. John Melville Williams QC

Senior Clerk:
John Taylor

Administrator:
Brenda Brown

Tenants: 38

Old Square Chambers, 1 Verulam Buildings, Gray's Inn, London WC1R 5LQ DX: 1046 Chancery Lane/London. Tel: (0171) 269 0300 Fax: (0171) 405 1387

Work Undertaken: Employment law, personal injury and product liability, medical negligence, environmental law and sports law.

Languages Spoken: French, German, Spanish, Italian, Dutch, Ibo.

Foreign Connections: There are door tenants practising at the Hong Kong, Bermuda, Scotland, Northern Ireland and Jersey Bars.

SETNUMBER
250 **ST. JOHN'S CHAMBERS** (Roderick Denyer QC)

ST. JOHN'S CHAMBERS, SMALL ST, BRISTOL, BS1 1DW
Tel: (0117) 921 3456 **Fax:** (0117) 929 4821 **DX:** 78138 VIDEO CONFERENCE 01179 221 586 **Email:** CLERKS@STJOHNS.UK.COM

MEMBERS:

Roderick Denyer QC (1970) (QC-1990)	Robert Duval (1979)	Andrea Hopkins (1992)
Nigel Hamilton QC (1965) (QC-1981)	Ralph Dixon (1980)	John Sharples (1992)
	Susan Jacklin (1980)	Dianne Martin (1992)
Martin Mann QC (1968) (QC-1983)	Charles Auld (1980)	Christine Bateman (1992)
	Peter Wadsley (1984)	Edward Burgess (1993)
Roger Kaye QC (1970) (QC-1989)	Ian Dixey (1984)	Kathryn Skellorn (1993)
	Richard Bromilow (1977)	David Maunder (1993)
Paul Grumbar (1974)	Leslie Blohm (1982)	Andrew McLaughlin (1993)
Christopher Sharp (1975)	Susan Hunter (1985)	Jacqueline Humphreys (1994)
Ian Bullock (1975)	Glyn Edwards (1987)	
Nicholas Marston (1975)	Simon Morgan (1988)	Bruce Walker (1994)
Timothy Grice (1975)	Louise O'Neill (1989)	Jetsun Lebasci (1995)
Mark Horton (1976)	Jean Corston (1991)	Gavin Doig (1995)
John Blackmore (1983)	Neil Levy (1986)	John Dickinson (1995)
Michael Longman (1978)	Guy Adams (1989)	Judi Evans (1996)
Richard Stead (1979)	Susan Evans (1989)	Simon Goodman (1996)

Head of Chambers:
Roderick Denyer QC

Clerk to Chambers:
Richard Hyde

Tenants: 44

Associate Members: Professor Nigel Lowe (1972), Professor Roy Light (1992), Kamala Das (1975).

CAMBRIDGE

SETNUMBER
251 **FENNERS CHAMBERS** (Lindsay Davies)

FENNERS CHAMBERS, 3 MADINGLEY ROAD, CAMBRIDGE, CB3 0EE
Tel: (01223) 368761 **Fax:** (01223) 313007 **DX:** 5809 CAMBRIDGE 1 **Email:** CLERKSROOM@FENNERS.FLEXNET.CO.UK
Internet: HTTP://WWW.FLEXNET.CO.UK/~FENNERS

MEMBERS:

Lindsay Davies (1975)**	Caroline Pointon (1976)	Alasdair Wilson (1988)
Kenneth Wheeler (1956)+	Oliver Heald (1977)	Caroline Beasley-Murray (1988)
David Stokes QC (1968) (QC-1989) *+	Simon Tattersall (1977)	
	Paul Leigh-Morgan (1978)	Clive Pithers (1989)
Peter King (1970)	Tim Brown (1980)	Timothy Meakin (1989)
Michael Yelton (1972) *	Paul Hollow (1981)	Andrew Taylor (1989)
Gareth Hawkesworth (1972)*	Stuart Bridge (1981)	Hazel Clark (1990)
Geraint Jones (1972)	Martin Collier (1982)	James Wilson (1991)
Oliver Sells QC (1972) (QC-1995) *+	Liza Gordon-Saker (1982)	Caroline Horton (1993)
	Rebecca Litherland (1987)	Charles Myatt (1993)
Andrew Gore (1973)	Meryl Hughes (1987)	Katharine Ferguson (1995)
Stephen Franklin (1974)	George Foxwell (1987)	William Josling (1995)
Susan Espley (1976)		

+Door Tenant
*Recorder
** Assistant Recorder

The Chambers: Undertake all common law and most chancery work. In the main areas of work, chambers are organised on the basis of groups, consisting of those tenants who practise extensively in that particular field. Identified specialists undertake work in the additional areas of practice. Chambers occupy extensive premises with ample on-site parking and easy access for the disabled. Also at 8-12 Priestgate, Peterborough.

Work Undertaken:
   Main Areas of Work: Contract and commercial, personal injury, property, crime, matrimonial and family, employment, planning, local government and environmental law.
   Additional Areas: Company and partnership, building contracts, agricultural work, licensing, professional negligence, conveyancing, contentious and non-contentious probate.

Nature of Clientele: Includes local government, public utilities, Inland Revenue and Customs and Excise.

Recruitment & Training: Tenancy and pupillage applications to Susan Espley: awards of £8,000 for 12 months pupillage. Contact William Josling for student visits/mini-pupillage.

Head of Chambers:
Lindsay Davies

Senior Clerk:
Mark Springham

Tenants: 34

SET NUMBER
252 REGENCY CHAMBERS (Raymond Croxon QC) Sheraton House, Castle Park, Cambridge, CB3 0AX **Tel:** (01223) 301517 **Fax:** (01223) 359267 **DX:** 12349 Peterborough 1 **Clerk:** Mr Paul Wright **Tenants:** 12 Also at Peterborough.

CANTERBURY

SETNUMBER 253 BECKET CHAMBERS

17 NEW DOVER ROAD, CANTERBURY, CT1 3AS
Tel: (01227) 786331 **Fax:** (01227) 786329 **DX:** 5330 CANTERBURY

MEMBERS:

Philip Newton (1984)	Corey Mills (1987)	Paul Tapsell (1991)
Ronald Edginton (1984)	Jeremy Hall (1988)	Louisa Adamson (1994)
Kevin Jackson (1984)	Gregory Dowell (1990)	Nicholas Fairbank (1996)
Christopher Wall (1987)	Clive Styles (1990)	

Senior Clerk:
Julie Lewis-MacKay

Tenants: 11

The Chambers: Becket Chambers are located only a few minutes walk from the local courts and the city centre. There is a dedicated conference facility, and a large private car park.

Work Undertaken: Chambers undertake all aspects of general common law and criminal work. Members specialise in the following areas: children and family proceedings, matrimonial finance and family provision, medical and professional negligence, personal injury, bankruptcy and insolvency, employment, sale of goods, consumer credit, housing, landlord and tenant, local government and crime. The Senior Clerk will be happy to provide further details on any aspect upon request.

SET NUMBER
254 STOUR CHAMBERS (Roy Warne) Stour Chambers, Barton Mill House, Barton Mill Road, Canterbury, CT1 1BP **Tel:** (01227) 764899 **Fax:** (01227) 764941 **DX:** 5342 Canterbury **Clerk:** Neil Terry **Tenants:** 9 Mainly matrimonial practice also specialising in criminal, personal injury, chancery, medical and professional negligence, landlord and tenant and child law.

CARDIFF

SETNUMBER 255 9 PARK PLACE (Ian Murphy QC)

9 PARK PLACE, CARDIFF, CF1 3DP
Tel: (01222) 382731 **Fax:** (01222) 222542 **DX:** 50751 CARDIFF 2

MEMBERS:

Ian Murphy QC (1972) (QC-1992)	Richard Twomlow (1976)	Peter Brooks (1986)
Roger Thomas QC (1969) (QC-1994)	Keith Thomas (1977)	Sarah Jones (1989)
Nicholas Cooke QC (1977) (QC-1998)	Philip Davies (1978)	Julian Reed (1991)
	Isabel Parry (1979)	Brian Jones (1992)
Philip Rees (1965)	Ieuan Morris (1979)	Steven Donoghue (1992)
Martyn Kelly (1972)	Milwyn Jarman (1980)	John McGlyne (1993)
Gregg Taylor (1974)	Karl Williams (1982)	Hugh Wallace (1993)
Richard Francis (1974)	Janet McDonald (1985)	David Elias (1994)
David Essex Williams (1975)	Paul Hopkins (1985)	Juliet Gibbon (1994)
Geraint Jones (1976)	Owen Prys Lewis (1985)	Owen Thomas (1994)
	Susan Ferrier (1985)	Gwydion Hughes (1994)
	Andrew Keyser (1986)	

Head of Chambers:
Ian Murphy QC

Senior Clerk:
James Williams

Clerks:
Nigel East, Lesley Haikney

Tenants: 32

The Chambers: A long established set of chambers, offering varied legal services. Members undertake a broad range of work, although each has particular areas of specialisation. Former members of chambers include a Lord Justice of Appeal, and several circuit judges. Specialisations include: criminal, personal injury, professional negligence, chancery, planning, commercial, family and employment.

Members and Work Undertaken: Several members of chambers are fluent in Welsh.

Associated Chambers: Several members of chambers also practise from Farrar's Building, Temple.

SET NUMBER
256 30 PARK PLACE (Philip Richards) 30 Park Place, Cardiff, CF1 3BA **Tel:** (01222) 398421 **Fax:** (01222) 398725 **DX:** 50756 Cardiff 2 **Clerk:** Mr Huw Davies **Email:** 100757.1456@compuserve.com **Tenants:** 40 General common law set practising in a wide range of civil work, family law and crime.

SET NUMBER
257 32 PARK PLACE (Christopher Williams) 32 Park Place, Cardiff, CF1 3BA **Tel:** (01222) 397364 **Fax:** (01222) 238423 **DX:** 50769 **Clerk:** Mr Daivd Brimming **Tenants:** 24 Common law chambers with emphasis on crime and family law. Some commercial and landlord and tenant work.

SET NUMBER
258 33 PARK PLACE (Wyn Williams QC) 33 Park Place, Cardiff, CF1 3BA **Tel:** (01222) 233313 **Fax:** (01222) 228294 **DX:** 50755 **Clerk:** Graham Barrett **Tenants:** 37 Senior long established common law and criminal chambers. Specialists in planning, personal injury, local government, employment, licensing and criminal law.

CHELMSFORD

SET NUMBER
259 18 RED LION COURT (Anthony Arlidge QC) Thornwood House, 102 New London Road, Chelmsford, CM2 0RG **Tel:** (01245) 280 880 **Fax:** (01245) 280 882 **DX:** 89706 Chelmsford 2

SET NUMBER
260 THORNWOOD HOUSE (Anthony Arlidge QC) 102 New London Road, Chelmsford, CM2 0RG **Tel:** (01245) 280880 **Fax:** (01245) 280882 **DX:** 89706 Chelmsford 2 **Clerk:** Ken Darvill Annexe of 18 Red Lion Court, Anthony Arlidge QC. The set practices predominantly in the field of crime.

SET NUMBER
261 TINDAL CHAMBERS (Gareth J Nixon-Moss)) 3 New Street, Chelmsford, CM1 1NT **Tel:** (01245) 267742 **Fax:** (01245) 359766 **DX:** 3358 Chelmsford 2 **Clerk:** Barry Madden **Tenants:** 16

SET NUMBER
262 TRINITY CHAMBERS (Tina Harringdon/Robin Howard) 140 New London Road, Chelmsford, CM2 0AW **Tel:** 01245 605040 **Fax:** 01245 605041 **DX:** 89725 Chelmsford 2

CHESTER

SET NUMBER
263 40 KING ST (Philip Hughes QC) 40 King St, Chester, CH1 2AH **Tel:** (01244) 323886 **Fax:** (01244) 347732 **DX:** 22154 **Clerk:** Mr Robert King **Tenants:** 25 Largest set of common law chambers in Chester.

SET NUMBER
264 SEDAN HOUSE (Meirion Lewis-Jones) Sedan House, Stanley Place, Chester, CH1 2LU **Tel:** (01244) 348282 **Fax:** (01244) 342336 **DX:** 19984 **Clerk:** Royce V. Parsons **Tenants:** 19 Common law and criminal chambers with some members specialising in planning, chancery, landlord and tenant, agricultural holdings, trade descriptions, local government, licensing, matrimonial, employment, personal injury, commercial contract and civil.

SET NUMBER
265 WHITE FRIARS CHAMBERS (J.P. Hedgecoe) 21 White Friars, Chester, CH1 1NZ **Tel:** (01244) 323070 **Fax:** (01244) 342930 **DX:** 19979 **Clerk:** Mr Robin Whinnett **Tenants:** 19 This set offers an efficient service in all mainstream areas of practice including in particular Criminal, Family, and Common Law. Full brochure on request.

CHICHESTER

SET NUMBER

266 CHICHESTER CHAMBERS (Michael Bechman QC) 3 East Pallant, Chichester, PO19 1TR **Tel:** (01243) 784538 **Fax:** (01243) 780861 **DX:** 30303 **Clerk:** Mr Jonathan Kay **Tenants:** 13 General common law practice with bias towards crime. Have expertise in personal injury and matrimonial law.

COLCHESTER

SET NUMBER

267 EAST ANGLIAN CHAMBERS 52 North Hill, Colchester, CO1 1PY **Tel:** (01206) 572756 **Fax:** (01206) 562447 **DX:** 3611 **Clerk:** Mr Fraser McLaren **Tenants:** 50 Established in three centres in East Anglia (Also Norwich and Ipswich), chambers have a general common law practice well represented in crime, civil and family.

COVENTRY

SET NUMBER

268 3 CASTLE YARD (Roy Ashton) Hay Lane, Coventry, CV1 5RF **Tel:** (01203) 553554 **Fax:** (01203) 559848 **Clerk:** Andrew Hutchins **Tenants:** 20 An annexe of 22 Albion Place, Northampton.

DURHAM

SET NUMBER

269 DURHAM BARRISTERS' CHAMBERS (Mr Christopher Roy-Toole) 27 Old Elvet, Durham, DH1 3HN **Tel:** (0191) 386 9199 **Fax:** (0191) 384 6020 **DX:** 60229 Durham 1 **Email:** christopher_roy-toole@link.org

EASTBOURNE

SET NUMBER

270 EASTBOURNE CHAMBERS (William Khan) 15 Hyde Gardens, Eastbourne, BN21 4PR **Tel:** (01323) 642102 **Fax:** (01323) 642402 **DX:** 6925 Eastbourne **Clerk:** Peter Farrow **Tenants:** 8 A common law set, specialising in criminal, family, immigration, landlord and tenant, sale of goods and personal injury law.

SET NUMBER

271 KING'S CHAMBERS (Piers Doggart) 5A Gildredge Road, Eastbourne, BN21 4RB **Tel:** (01323) 416053 **Fax:** (01323) 416110 **DX:** 6931 Eastbourne 1 **Clerk:** Sharon Longhurst **Tenants:** 5 Established in December 1992, this set's main areas of practice are company/commercial, chancery, crime, general common law, family, employment and personal injury.

ENFIELD

SET NUMBER

272 ENFIELD CHAMBERS (Adrian Hall) First Floor, 9-10 River Front, Enfield, EN1 3SZ **Tel:** (0181) 364 5627 **Fax:** (0181) 364 5973 **Email:** enfieldchambers@compuserve.com **DX:** 90638 Enfield 1 **Clerk:** Kevin Tarrant **Tenants:** 11 Common law chambers with expertise in: Crime, Family, Immigration, Landlord and Tenant and general Civil.

EXETER

CATHEDRAL CHAMBERS

15 CASTLE STREET, EXETER, EX4 3PT
Tel: (01392)210 900 **Fax:** (01392) 210 901 **DX:** 122699 EXETER **Email:** CATHEDRAL.CHAMBERS@:ECLIPSE.CO.UK

MEMBERS:

Christina Gorna (1960)	Laurence Vaughan-Williams (1988)	Darren White (1996)	**Senior Clerk:** Jan Wood
James Leckie (1964)		The Rt Hon Douglas Hogg M.P QC (1968) (QC-1990)	**Tenants:** 9
Richard Wood (1975)	Jennifer Moore (1992)		
James Hayward (1985)	Annie Ives (1994)		

COLLETON CHAMBERS (Martin Meeke)

COLLETON CRESCENT, EXETER, EX2 4DG
Tel: (01392) 274898 **Fax:** (01392) 412368 **DX:** 8330 EXETER

MEMBERS:

Martin Meeke (1973)	David Steele (1975)	Peter M. Ashman (1985)	**Head of Chambers:** Martin Meeke
Richard Merrett (1959)	Richard Crabb (1975)	Jonathan Farquharson (1988)	**Senior Clerk:** Philip Alden
Stephen Lowry (1960)	Julie MacKenzie (1978)	Melissa Barlow (1991)	**Tenants:** 17
Richard Rains (1963)	Mark V. Horton (1981)	Philip Drinkwater (1995)	
Michael Brabin (1976)	Mark Whitehall (1983)	Ruth Vincent (1995)	
David Puttick (1971)	Terence Holder (1984)		

Also at: 22 The Crescent, Taunton, Somerset, TA1 40B
Tel: (01823) 324252 **Fax:** (01823) 327489, **DX:** 96100 Taunton 1

SOUTHERNHAY CHAMBERS (David Tyzack)

33 SOUTHERNHAY EAST, EXETER, EX1 1NX
Tel: (01392) 255777 **Fax:** (01392) 412021 **DX:** 8353 EXETER

MEMBERS:

David Tyzack (1970)	Hugh Lewis (1970)	Nicholas Berry (1988)	**Head of Chambers:** David Tyzack
Jeremy Posnansky QC (1972) (QC-1994)	Robert Alford (1970)	Rebecca Ogle (1989)	**Senior Clerk:** Joy Daniell
Alastair Norris QC (1973) (QC-1997)	Michael Templeman (1973)	Jacqueline Ahmed (1988)	**Tenants:** 16
	Valentine Le Grice (1977)	Juliet Foster (1989)	
George Meredith (1969)	Christopher Naish (1980)	Emma Crawforth (1992)	
	Susan Campbell (1986)	James Hassall (1995)	

General Information: Established in 1976, Chambers has 16 members. Door Tenants (Jeremy Posnansky QC, Alastair Norris QC, and Valentine Le Grice) are happy to attend conferences in Exeter, where modern facilities are provided.

Work Undertaken: Civil, with emphasis on Family, Landlord & Tenant, Personal Injury, Planning, Licensing, Professional Negligence, CICB, Chancery, Commercial Litigation/Property, Housing, Equity Trusts & Wills.

The Senior Clerk will provide detailed information on request.

SET NUMBER
276
WALNUT HOUSE (Francis Gilbert QC)

WALNUT HOUSE, 63 ST. DAVID'S HILL, EXETER, EX4 4DW
Tel: (01392) 279751 **Fax:** (01392) 412080 **DX:** 115582 EXETER ST. DAVIDS **Email:** 106627.2451@COMPUSERVE.COM

MEMBERS:

Francis Gilbert QC (1970) (QC-1992)	Iain Leadbetter (1975)	Elizabeth Ingham (1989)
Paul Dunkels QC (1972) (QC-1993)	Corinne Searle (1982)	Robert MacRae (1990)
	Sarah Munro (1984)	Andrew Oldland (1990)
Francis Burkett (1969)	Martin Edmunds (1983)	Shane Lyon (1976)
Jonathan Barnes (1970)	Michael Melville-Shreeve (1986)	Mary McCarthy (1994)
Geoffrey Mercer (1975)	Mark Treneer (1987)	David Evans (1996)
Andrew Chubb (1975)	Andrew Eaton Hart (1989)	Adam Vaitilingam (1987)

Head of Chambers:
Francis Gilbert QC

Senior Clerk:
Chris Doe

Tenants: 20

The Chambers: Established in 1972 the chambers now have 20 members including four who sit as recorders and two who sit as assistant recorders. Formerly an annexe of 4 Pump Court, the chambers are now independent although close links remain.

Work Undertaken:

General Description: The work of Chambers covers the full range of civil and criminal matters in the South West. Brochures are available on request detailing the areas of expertise of members in Chambers, particularly in the fields of Family Law, Personal Injury, Medical Negligence and Crime.

Main Areas of Work: Work undertaken includes construction, courts martial, criminal law, discrimination, employment, family, children, general common law, general chancery, housing, judicial review, landlord and tenant, licensing, matrimonial, mental health, personal injury, planning, police cases, probate, professional negligence, sale of goods, trusts and wills.

GUILDFORD

SET NUMBER
277
GUILDFORD CHAMBERS (Jeffrey Widdup)

STOKE HOUSE, LEAPALE LANE, GUILDFORD, GU1 4LY
Tel: (01483) 539131 **Fax:** (01483) 300542 **DX:** 97863 GUILDFORD 5 **Email:** GUILDFORD.BARRISTERS@BTINTERNET.COM

MEMBERS:

Jeffrey Widdup (1973)	Matthew Pascall (1984)	Ghislaine Watson-Hopkinson (1991)
Suzan Matthews QC (1974) (QC-1993)	Paula Clements (1985)	Richard Button (1993)
Selwyn Shapiro (1979)	Janet Haywood (1985)	Robin Sellers (1994)
Jonathan Davies (1981)	Laura Smallwood (1987)	Nichola Hatcher (1995)
Simon Oliver (1981)	Francesca Blatch (1987)	Jonathan Page (1996)
Claire Shrimpton (1983)	Jerome Wilcox (1988)	
	George Coates (1990)	

Head of Chambers:
Jeffrey Widdup

Senior Clerk:
Richard Moore

Tenants: 18

The Chambers: In recent years these chambers have expanded rapidly and they now offer a comprehensive and friendly service across a broad range of family, criminal and civil matters. Members attend conferences at any venue convenient to the client, and appear in courts and tribunals across the country. Several members have lectured at the University of Surrey, and one of the Door Tenants is the Professor of Competition Law at University College, London.

Work Undertaken:

Common Law and Civil Work: Including landlord and tenant, contract, tort (including professional negligence), personal injuries, building disputes and official referee work, sale of goods, licensing, employment and industrial tribunals, mental health tribunals, inquests and arbitrations.

Family: Including divorce, financial applications including the Inheritance Act and Children Act, care proceedings, residence and contact applications, adoption, cohabitees, injunctions and international child disputes.

Chancery: Including property disputes, rights of way, covenants and boundary disputes, company and partnerships, and insolvency.

Local Government and Public Law: Including planning appeals, enforcement of planning control, pollution, highways, public authority prosecution and defence work, housing law and judicial review.

Crime: All areas including fraud. Chambers has developed a specialisation in cases involving illegal radio stations.

HARROW-ON-THE-HILL

SET NUMBER
278
HARROW ON THE HILL CHAMBERS (Marc Beaumont)

60 HIGH STREET, HARROW-ON-THE-HILL, HA1 3LL
Tel: (0181) 423 7444 **Fax:** (0181) 423 7368 **DX:** 130112 SLOUGH 6

MEMBERS:

Marc Beaumont (1985)	Mark Kimsey (1990)	Graeme Simpson (1994)
Guy Boney QC (1968) (QC-1990)	Andrew Dowden (1991)	Anu Gopinathan (1994)
Christopher Clark QC (1969) (QC-1984)	Justin Bearman (1992)	Andrew Wilkins (1995)
	Victoria Green (1994)	Rajeev Shetty (1993)
Paul Bridges (1984)	Peter Nugent (1994)	Jonathan Whitley (1993)
Terence Bergin (1985)	Anthony Swift (1984)	Khalid Sheikh (1993)

Head of Chambers:
Marc Beaumont

Chambers Manager:
Michele Acton

Tenants: 13

The Chambers: A broadly-based set with members offering expertise in five main areas of work: commercial, general civil litigation, property, matrimonial, and criminal litigation. The set welcomes direct professional access work.

Main Areas of Work:

Commercial: Company/commercial disputes, partnership, consumer transactions and sale of goods disputes, insurance disputes, building actions, claims arising from employment, insolvency matters and banking transactions.

General Civil Litigation: All types of personal injury work, professional negligence of solicitors, surveyors, valuers, accountants and doctors, industrial accidents, nuisance and trespass to land, defamation, and interlocutory procedural and injunctive disputes.

Property: Mortgages, possession actions, consumer credit, conveyancing, landlord and tenant (including Rent Act and Housing Act possession actions), planning, public sector housing, boundaries and easements, licences and claims under the Inheritance (provision for Family and Dependants) Act 1975.

Matrimonial: All aspects of family and matrimonial law including ancillary relief disputes, and matters arising under The Children Act 1989.

Criminal Litigation: Chambers is instructed by several branches of the Crown Prosecution Service, and undertakes prosecution and defence work in the local courts in North London and Hertfordshire.

HASTINGS

SET NUMBER
279
WESTGATE CHAMBERS (John Collins) 16-17 Wellington Square, Hastings, TN34 1PB **Tel:** (01424) 432105 **Fax:** (01424) 717850 **DX:** 7062 Hastings **Clerk:** Sean Gould **Tenants:** 4 Annexe of Westgate Chambers in Lewes

HULL

SET NUMBER
280
WILBERFORCE CHAMBERS (Bernard Gateshill) Wilberforce Chambers, 171 High St, Hull, HU1 1NE **Tel:** (01482) 323264 **Fax:** (01482) 325533 **DX:** 11940 **Clerk:** John Kennedy **Tenants:** 21 Although a general common law set, these chambers specialise in family law and civil litigation. Other areas covered include criminal, personal injury, and medical negligence.

IPSWICH

SET NUMBER
281
EAST ANGLIAN CHAMBERS (John Holt) 5 Museum St, Ipswich, IP1 1HQ **Tel:** (01473) 214481 **Fax:** (01473) 231388 **DX:** 3227 **Tenants:** 50 Also at 57, London Street Norwich (01603 617351) and 52, North Hill Colchester (01206 572756).

LEEDS

SETNUMBER 282 · ENTERPRISE CHAMBERS (Anthony Mann QC)

38 PARK SQUARE, LEEDS, LS1 2PA
Tel: (0113) 246 0391 **Fax:** (0113) 242 4802 **DX:** 26448 (LEEDS PARK SQUARE)

MEMBERS:

Anthony Mann QC (1974) (QC-1992)	Linden Ife (1982)	Laura Garcia-Miller (1989)
Nigel Gerald (1985)	Ann McAllister (1982)	Zia Bhaloo (1990)
Benjamin Levy (1956)	Peter Arden (1983)	James Pickering (1991)
Timothy Jennings (1962)	Geoffrey Zelin (1984)	Soraya McKinnell (1991)
David Halpern (1978)	Jacqueline Baker (1985)	Hugh Jory (1992)
Charles Morgan (1978)	Nigel Gerald (1985)	Bridget Williamson* (1993)
Caroline Hutton (1979)	James Barker (1984)	Matthew Hardwick (1994)
Michael James* (1976)	Adrian Jack (1986)	Sarah Richardson (1993)
Teresa Rosen Peacocke (1982)	Hugo Groves* (1980)	Edward Francis (1995)
	Ian Atherton (1988)	Shanti Mauger (1996)
	Alistair Henry* (1998)	

Head of Chambers:
Anthony Mann QC

Clerks:
Barry Clayton, Tony Armstrong and Joanne Glew.

Tenants: 29

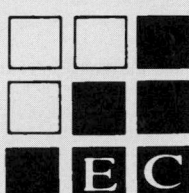

* practised as a solicitor before joining Chambers.

For further information about the set please see London entry.

SETNUMBER 283 · 11 KING'S BENCH WALK (Mr F.J Muller QC)

LEEDS ANNEXE, 3 PARK COURT, PARK CROSS STREET, LEEDS, LS1 2QH
Tel: (0113) 297 1200 **Fax:** (0113) 297 1201 **Email:** clerks@11kbw.co.uk **Internet:** http://www.11kbw.co.uk

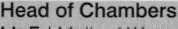

See London entry for members of Chambers.

London set with extensive North East Circuit practice split between Civil and Criminal teams.

The Chambers: The civil team offers experience at all levels, including Queen's Counsel, and practice is specifically focused upon:

Professional Negligence: in particular medical negligence;

Personal Injury: with extensive experience in health & safety and industrial diseases litigation. Members of Chambers have been involved from the outset on behalf of the Defendant in the British Coal Respiratory Disease Litigation – the largest personal injury action ever brought in England.

Chancery and Commercial law: members of Chambers practice in Leeds Mercantile Court;

Family Law (including children and property disputes);

In addition, individuals specialise in employment, V.A.T, landlord & Tenant, Local Government, contractual disputes, consumer credit, civil torts.
The criminal team also offers expertise at every level both in Prosecution and Defence work. Chambers specialises in major crime: including commercial fraud, serious sexual offences and offences against the person.

Members of Chambers undertake Conditional Fees work and Direct Professional Access. Pleadings and paperwork returned within 7 working days. A brochure is available on request and Chambers' website is located at www.11kbw.co.uk

Head of Chambers:
Mr F.J Muller QC

Senior Clerk:
A. Blaney (London – QCs)
A. Dunstone (Leeds – Juniors)

Tenants: 22

SET NUMBER 284

MERCURY CHAMBERS Mercury House, 33-35 Clarendon Road, Leeds, LS2 9NZ **Tel:** (0113) 234 2265 **Fax:** (0113) 244 4243 **Clerk:** Carole Dexter New specialised civil and commercial law chambers.

SETNUMBER
285 **PARK COURT CHAMBERS** (James Stewart QC, Robert Smith QC)

PARK COURT CHAMBERS, 40 PARK CROSS ST, LEEDS, LS1 2QH
Tel: (0113) 243 3277 **Fax:** (0113) 242 1285 **DX:** 26401

MEMBERS:

Wilfred Steer QC (1950)
(QC-1972)
James Chadwin QC (1958)
(QC-1976)
James Stewart QC (1966)
(QC-1982)
Robert Smith QC (1971)
(QC-1986)
Michael Harrison QC (1969)
(QC-1987)
Malcolm Swift QC (1970)
(QC-1988)
Anton Lodge QC (1966)
(QC-1989)
Paul Worsley QC (1970)
(QC-1990)
Louise S. Godfrey QC (1972)
(QC-1991)

Simon Bourne-Arton QC
(1975) (QC-1994)
David Hatton QC (1976)
(QC-1996)
Henry Prosser (1969)
Tim Hirst (1970)
Timothy Hartley (1970)
Andrea Addleman (1977)
Tom Bayliss (1977)
Jonathan Devlin (1978)
Adrian Robinson (1981)
John Lodge (1980)
Michael Taylor (1980)
Simon Jackson (1982)
Alistair MacDonald (1983)
Caroline Wigin (1984)
Simon Phillips (1985)

Sharon Beattie (1986)
Simon Myerson (1986)
Nadim Bashir (1988)
Taryn Turner (1990)
Andrew Thompson (1989)
Maria Davies (1988)
Elyas Patel (1991)
Ashley Tucker (1990)
Scott Wilson (1993)
Paul Greaney (1993)
Nicholas Johnson (1994)
Jenny Kent (1993)
Jason Pitter (1994)
Gilbert Gray * QC (1953)
(QC-1971)
Joanna Dodson* QC (1971)
(QC-1993)

Head of Chambers:
James Stewart QC
Robert Smith QC

Senior Clerk:
Roy Kemp

Tenants: 37

* Door Tenant

The Chambers: Park Court Chambers is one of the largest sets of chambers outside London. It is a long established but modern and expanding set based in the thriving commercial centre Leeds. It offers a wide range of services.

Principal Areas of Practice: Crime, corporate fraud, personal injury, general commercial, family, landlord and tenant, licensing and medical negligence.

SETNUMBER
286 **PARK LANE CHAMBERS** (Martin Bethel QC)

PEARL CHAMBERS, 19 WESTGATE, LEEDS, LS1 2RD
Tel: (0113) 228 5000 **Fax:** (0113) 228 1500 **DX:** 26404 LEEDS PARK SQUARE

MEMBERS:

Martin Bethel QC (1965)
(QC-1983) MA, LLM (Cantab)
Stuart Brown QC (1974)
(QC-1991) BA, BCL (Oxon)
Christopher Storey QC
(1979) (QC-1995)
David Wilby QC (1974)
(QC-1998)
Alaric Dalziel (1967)
Howard Elgot (1974) BA,
BCL (Oxon)
Angela Finnerty (1976) LLB
Sally Cahill (1978) LLB
(Hons)

Elizabeth O'Hare (1980) LLB
(Hons)
George Sigsworth (1977) MA
(Cantab)
Lindy Armitage (1985) LLB
David Zucker (1986) LLB
(Hons)
William Hanbury (1985) LLB
Simon Thorp (1988) BA
Joanne Astbury (1989) LLB
Hons
Richard Copnall (1990) BSc
Kaiser Nazir (1991) LLB

Andrew Axon (1992) BA
Adam Korn (1992) MA
James Murphy (1993) BA
Hons
Corin Furness (1994) LLB
(Hons)
Steven Turner (1993) BA
(Hons)
Dornier Whittaker (1994) BA
(Hons)
Sara Anning (1995)
Stephen Friday (1996)

Head of Chambers:
Martin Bethel QC

Senior Clerk:
John Payne

Tenants: 25

The Chambers: The set aims to provide a service to clients across the North Eastern Circuit. Members practise in all areas of the general common law and the criminal law, but as chambers continue to expand, the range of individual specialisations is increasing.

Main Areas of Work: Personal injury (including industrial disease claims), professional negligence (including claims against architects, surveyors, accountants and solicitors), medical negligence and drug-related injury claims, crime, family law (including all aspects of ancillary financial relief and custody disputes), contractual disputes, sale of goods claims, carriage of goods and misrepresentation claims, employment (both at common law and before tribunals), real property (including landlord and tenant), general chancery and company law, injunctions and all other aspects of interlocutory relief, planning, licensing, and taxation both direct and indirect.

Additional Areas: Insurance, business and commercial litigation, housing, local government, building and engineering disputes, fraud, partnership disputes, defamation, aviation claims and arbitration.

SET NUMBER
287

5 PARK PLACE (Philip Raynor QC)

LEEDS, LS1 2RU
Tel: (0113) 242 1123 **Fax:** (0113) 242 1124 **DX:** 713113 (LEEDS PKSQ)

MEMBERS:

Philip Raynor QC (1973) (QC-1994)	John Jackson (1970)	Ruth Stockley (1988)
Nigel Macleod QC (1961) (QC-1979)	Harold Halliday (1972)	Fiona Ashworth (1988)
John Hoggett QC (1969) (QC-1986)	Alan Evans (1978)	Paul Tucker (1990)
	Shokat Khan (1979)	Geoffrey Pass (1975)
Andrew Gilbart QC (1972) (QC-1991)	Vincent Fraser (1981)	Andrew Singer (1990)
Peter Smith QC (1975) (QC-1992)	David Manley (1981)	Stephen Pritchett (1990)
	Michael Booth (1981)	Lesley Anderson (1989)
Roger Farley QC (1974) (QC-1993)	John Barrett (1982)	Matthew Smith (1991)
	Sonia Gal (1983)	Sally Harrison (1992)
Stephen Sauvain QC (1977) (QC-1995)	Nicholas Braslavsky (1983)	Martin Carter (1992)
	Paul Chaisty (1982)	Wilson Horne (1992)
Frances Patterson QC (1977) (QC-1998)	Mark Halliwell (1985)	Lucy Powis (1992)
	Anthony Crean (1987)	Amanda Johnson (1992)
Eric Owen (1969)	Simon Hilton (1987)	Mark Harper (1993)
	Katherine Dunn (1987)	Sarah Pritchard (1993)

Arbitrator: Sir Iain Glidewell

Associate Members: John Tackaberry QC (1967) (QC-1982), John Campbell (1981), Julian Ghosh (1993)

The Chambers: A large and well-established set, the members of which appear before the full range of courts and statutory tribunals. Counsel are available at all ranks of seniority, including seven silks, and the breadth of individual specialities and aptitudes available in chambers means that it offers a wide range of specialist advisory and advocacy services.

Members have written, edited or contributed to a large number of legal journals, most notably in the fields of planning, local government, and highway law.

Main Areas of Work: Town and country planning, local government law and finance, administrative law, parliamentary law, compulsory purchase and compensation, highways law, environmental protection, public health, commercial chancery litigation, landlord and tenant law, law of trusts, partnerships, intellectual property, insolvency (corporate and individual), banking, wills and intestacy, civil liability, personal injury, professional liability, employment and industrial law, building disputes, consumer credit, sale of goods, family and matrimonial law, hire purchase, licensing, and criminal law.

Additional Areas: Markets and fairs, trading standards, EC law, housing, data protection, company law, immigration and defamation.

Members accept Direct Professional Access from the approved professions.

Languages: French, German, Hungarian, Norwegian, Punjabi, Romanian, Urdu.

Head of Chambers:
Philip Raynor QC

Senior Clerk:
William Brown

Clerking:
Bar Management Services

Partners: William Brown, Colin Griffin & Michael Stubbs

Tenants: 44

SET NUMBER
288

6 PARK SQUARE (Shaun M. Spencer QC) No. 6 Park Square, Leeds, LS1 2LW **Tel:** (0113) 245 9763 **Fax:** (0113) 242 4395 **DX:** 26402 **Email:** chambers@no6.co.uk **Internet:** http://www.no6.co.uk **Practice Director:** Tim Collins **Tenants:** 32 Chambers operates in 4 teams specialising in the following areas: Criminal, Personal Injury, family, chancery and Commercial.

SETNUMBER
289
10 PARK SQUARE (A.N. Campbell QC)

10 PARK SQUARE, LEEDS, LS1 2LH
Tel: (0113) 245 5438 **Fax:** (0113) 242 3515 **DX:** 26412

MEMBERS:

A.N. Campbell QC (1972) (QC-1994)
John Henry Munkman (1948) LLB
Charles Brian Kealy (1965) LLB
Richard William Wallace Sutton (1968) BA
Andrew Paul Lander Woolman (1973) MA
David Lawrence Bradshaw (1975) LLB
Martin William Rudland (1977) LLB

Andrew Thomas Alastair Dallas (1978) BA
Felicity Anne Davies (1980) BA
William James Clappison (1981) BA
Julian Nicholas Goose (1984) LLB
John Raymond Guy Worrall (1984) LLB, BA
Simon Roger Greenwood Hickey (1985) LLB
S.T. Kealey (1991)
G. Exall (1991)

Peter Moulson (1992)
Clive Heaton (1992)
John Hayes (1993)
T.S. Storey (1993)
Edward Bindloss (1993)
Abdul Iqbal (1994)
Philippa Wordsworth (1995)
Louis Doyle (1996)
Geraldine Kelly (1996)
Anthony Hajimitsis (1984)
Sarah Clarke* (1994)

Head of Chambers:
A.N. Campbell QC

Senior Clerk:
Craig Place

Practice Director:
Vicky Thompson

Tenants: 24

*Door Tenant

The Chambers: A general common law set, handling a broad range of legal matters.

Work undertaken: Bankruptcy, chancery, commercial law, company law, crime, employment, family, landlord and tenant, licensing, medical negligence, personal injury, probate, property, wardship, wills and trusts.

SETNUMBER
290
30 PARK SQUARE (J.W. Mellor)

30 PARK SQUARE, LEEDS, LS1 2PF
Tel: (0113) 243 6388 **Fax:** (0113) 242 3510 **DX:** 26411

MEMBERS:

J.W. Mellor (1953)
P. Collier QC (1970) (QC-1992)
J.M. Black QC (1976) (QC-1994)
A. Kershaw (1975)
D.A. McGonigal (1982)
M. Haigh (1970) (formerly a solicitor)
S.N. Haring (1982)

M.S. Rodger (1983)
R.M.L. Hallam (1984)
K. Buckingham (1986)
C.L. Hill (1988)
C. Burn (1985)
M. Pearson (1984)
A. Granville-Fall (1990)
J. Hargan (1990)
R. Cole (1991)

N. Frith (1992)
M. Teeman (1993) (formerly a solicitor)
T. White (1993)
I. Shiels (1992)
N. Barker (1994)
E. Auckland (1995)
I. Gilmore (1996)
W. Tyler (1996)

Head of Chambers:
J.W. Mellor

Senior Clerk:
Jennifer Thompson

Tenants: 24

The Chambers: Specialists in criminal and family law. Also undertake work (including non-contentious and advisory) in a wide range of common law subjects. Advocates with experience in all courts, tribunals and inquiries.

Work Undertaken: All aspects of family law; divorce, child care, injunctions, criminal defence and prosecution: common law expertise in personal injury, contract, property disputes, professional negligence, licensing and insolvency.

SETNUMBER
291   37 PARK SQUARE (John Sleightholme, Rodney Ferm)

37 PARK SQUARE, LEEDS, LS1 2NY
Tel: (0113) 243 9422 **Fax:** (0113) 242 4229 **DX:** 26405 LEEDS

MEMBERS:

John Sleightholme (1982)	Paul Fleming (1983)	Caroline Ford (1993)
Rodney Ferm (1972)	Freddy Apfel (1986)	Mark Gore (1994)
Rt Hon Douglas Hogg QC	Jeremy Lindsay (1986)	David Taylor (1995)
MP (1968) (QC-1990)	Amanda Ginsburg (1985)	Joanne Holroyd (1994)
John Graham (1955)	Dawn Tighe (1989)	Stuart Roberts (1994)
Barbara Wootliff (1956)	Linda Caines (1990)	Taryn Lee (1992)
John Dunning (1973)	Tony Kelbrick (1992)	Jason Macadam (1990)
Stephen Glover (1978)	Steven Crossley (1992)	Michael Burden (1993)
Paul Kirtley (1982)	Piers Hill (1987)	

Head of Chambers:
John Sleightholme, Rodney Ferm

Senior Clerk:
Ann Fothergill

Tenants: 23

Work undertaken: General common law including criminal law, licensing, family law, personal injury, contract, employment law, company and commercial, landlord and tenant, real property disputes, planning and local government law.

SET NUMBER
292   39 PARK SQUARE (T.M.A. Bubb) 39 Park Square, Leeds, LS1 2NU **Tel:** (0113) 245 6633 **Fax:** (0113) 242 1567 **DX:** 26407 **Clerk:** Mark Heald **Tenants:** 14 Crime, Family [both private and public law]. Personal injury, Licensing, Landlord & Tenant, Civil Litigation.

SETNUMBER
293   ST. PAUL'S CHAMBERS (Nigel Sangster QC)

5TH FLOOR, ST. PAUL'S HOUSE, 23 PARK SQUARE SOUTH, LEEDS, LS1 2ND
Tel: (0113) 245 5866 **Fax:** (0113) 245 5807 **DX:** 26410 LEEDS (PARK SQUARE)

MEMBERS:

Nigel Sangster QC (1976)	Alison J. Hunt (1986)	Michael S. Burdon (1993)
(QC-1998)	Fiona Dix-Dyer (1986)	Sukhbir S. Bassra (1993)
Timothy R. Newcombe	Howard K. Crowson (1987)	Sarah H. Barlow (1993)
(1972)	Andrew J. Stubbs (1988)	Michael J. Harrison (1994)
Peter C. Benson (1975)	Simon Bickler (1988)	Alex Bates (1994)
Colin T. Harvey (1975)	David De Jehan (1988)	John Harrison (1994)
Jeremy V. Barnett (1980)	Christopher M. Batty (1989)	Nigel R. Edwards (1995)
Philip A. Standfast (1980)	Jonathan S. Godfrey (1990)	Kirstie A Watson (1995)
Jonathan L. Rose (1981)	Alex Foster (1990)	Nick Dry (1996)
Guy A. Kearl (1982)	Jonathan Sandiford (1992)	Derek J. Duffy (1997)
Andrew J. Lees (1984)	Nicola Saxton (1992)	Natasha Gordon-Dean (1997)

Head of Chambers:
Nigel Sangster QC

Senior Clerk:
Catherine J. Grimshaw

Tenants: 31

Nigel Sangster QC is elected Member of the Bar Council and sits as an Assistant Recorder. Peter Benson sits as a Recorder. Members of Chambers belong to the Family Law Bar Association and the Criminal Bar Association.

The Chambers: Founded in 1982, St. Paul's Chambers have expanded to 31 practitioners. Members have complementary areas of expertise with the specific intention of providing a service in most areas of legal work.

Work Undertaken:

Criminal: *Work includes:* the traditional areas of crime with members acting for both prosecution and defence. In addition there are specialists in fraud, serious crime (including violence and sexual offences), breathalyser cases, licensing, Courts Martial, and Firearms Act offences.

Civil: Chambers have particular expertise in personal injury claims, employment, landlord and tenant, Trading Standards cases, family and child care work, matrimonial, professional negligence and police disciplinary cases.

SETNUMBER 294 SOVEREIGN CHAMBERS (Formerly known as 25 Park Square) (Geoffrey C. Marson QC)

25 PARK SQUARE, LEEDS, LS1 2PW
Tel: (0113) 245 1841 **Fax:** (0113) 242 0194 **DX:** 26408 LEEDS PARK SQUARE **Email:** SOVEREIGNCHAMBERS@BTINTERNET.COM
Internet: HTTP: //WWW.SOVEREIGNCHAMBERS.CO.UK

MEMBERS:

Geoffrey C. Marson QC (1975) (QC-1997)
John H. Muir (1969)
Richard L. Newbury (1976)
Patrick J.S. Palmer (1978)
Charles W. Ekins (1980)
Mushtaq A. Khokhar (1982)
Steven D. Garth (1983)
David M. Gordon (1984)
Marilyn A. Fricker (1969)
Lynn Driscoll (1981)
Gerard M. Heap (1985)
Andrew W. Lewis (1985)
Mark D. McKone (1988)
Stephen Bedeau (1980)
Denise L. Gresty (1990)
Andrew P. Haslam (1991)

Roger A. Birch (1979)
David S. Dixon (1992)
Nicholas J H Lumley (1992)
Charity E. Rigby (1993)
Andrew B. Semple (1993)
M Jayne Pye (1995) (formerly a solicitor)
Darren Finlay (1994)
Matthew R. Smith (1996)
Christopher Dunn (1996)
James F. Keeley (1993)
Peter J. Wilson (1995)
Diana Maudslay (1997)
John Mowbray QC (1953) *
John MacDonald QC (1955) *
Charles Purle QC (1970) *
George S Laurence QC (1972) *

Lynton Tucker (1971) *
Colin Braham (1971) *
Christopher Russell (1971) *
Nicholas Le Poidevin (1975)*
Stuart Barber (1979) *
Sara Hargreaves (1979) *
Jane Bridge (1981) *
Margaret McCabe (1981) *
Stephen J Smith (1983) *
Leigh Sagar (1983) *
Claire Staddon (1985) *
Ross Crail (1986) *
Ian Peacock (1990) *
Jane Evans-Gordon (1992) *
Nicholas Terras (1993) *
Louise Davis (1995) *

* Door Tenants

Head of Chambers:
Geoffrey C. Marson QC

Practice and Finance Manager:
Paul Slater

Chambers Administrator:
Chris Dixon

Tenants: 28

The Chambers: Teams of Members have developed considerable expertise forming specialist groups which among others include Family/Matrimonial, Crime, (both Prosecution and Defence), Commercial/Chancery, Intellectual Property, Planning, Employment, Personal Injury, Fraud. The new trading name and logo mark the profound changes and restructuring that Chambers has recently undertaken and represents a new approach, a new structure and a new strategy.

Reorganising the traditional clerking arrangements combined with the recent implementation of the very latest computer technology, Chambers feels well placed to continue its policy of expansion and to maintain its position as one of the leading sets in the rapidly expanding commercial City of Leeds.

Work Undertaken: Building disputes, commercial and civil litigation, company law, criminal law, employment law, environmental/pollution law, family law (including childcare and matrimonial finance), housing, immigration, inheritance disputes, insolvency, insurance, judicial review, landlord and tenant, licensing, local authority work, partnership law, personal injury, medical negligence, planning, property law, professional negligence, public law, race relations cases and intellectual property law.

Languages: French, German, Hindi, Punjabi, Urdu, Czech.

SOVEREIGN
C H A M B E R S

SETNUMBER 295 9 WOODHOUSE SQUARE (John Morris Collins)

9 WOODHOUSE SQUARE, LEEDS, LS3 1AD
Tel: (0113) 245 1986 **Fax:** (0113) 244 8623 **DX:** 26406 **Email:** WOODHOUSE9@AOL.COM

MEMBERS:

John M. Collins (1956)
Sarwar Saleem (1960)
Charles R. Sinclair-Morris (1966)
Gerald Lumley (1972)
Simon Jack (1974)
Rebecca Thornton (1976)
Jeffrey Lewis (1978)
Bryan Cox (1979)
David Hall (1980)

Helen Hendry (1983)
Christopher Dodd (1984)
Sarah Greenan (1987)
Austin Newman (1987)
Roger Bickerdike (1986)
Jane Hodgson (1989)
John Holroyd (1989)
Mavis Pilkington (1990)
Steven Lunt (1991)

Joanna Cross (1992)
Eimear McAllister (1992)
Justin Crossley (1993)
Anesh Pema (1994)
Mark Henley (1994)
Andrew Wilson (1995)
Heather Humpage (1996)
John Brodwell (1998)

Head of Chambers:
John Morris Collins

Senior Clerk:
The Senior Clerk

Clerks:
Civil – Samantha Ashford (Qualified Solicitor)
Crime – Helen Dring

Tenants: 26

The Chambers: Founded in 1928, Chambers is, and always has been, committed to providing a comprehensive, flexible and user-friendly service comprising advocacy and advisory work. The latest information technology has recently been installed to enable effective communication and the clerks are always available to discuss solicitors' particular requirements. In anticipation of the proposed Legal Aid changes, Chambers already operates a successful block contracting system with efficient adminstration and a speedy return of papers. This is achieved by the distribution of work within agreed teams, all with relevant expertise. Chambers additionally offers 6 specialist groups, each with their own Head, who meet regularly to ensure that a cohesive service is provided with the required expertise. Members of the groups regularly lecture at national and local levels and other individuals include a qualified doctor and a civil engineer. Chambers has ample car parking and is within easy walking distance of the Leeds Courts.

Work Undertaken: Administrative law, chancery, commercial, construction litigation and arbitration, crime, family, housing, landlord and tenant, licensing, medical negligence, personal injury, planning, probate, professional negligence, property, taxation, trusts.

Specialist Departments: chancery and commercial, housing, crime, family, personal injury, property.

Languages: French, German, Spanish, Gujerati, Urdu

LEICESTER

SET NUMBER
296

36 BEDFORD ROW (James Hunt QC)

104 NEW WALK, LEICESTER, LE1 7ND
Tel: (0116) 249 2020 **Fax:** (0116) 255 0885 **DX:** 28816 LEICESTER 2 **Email:** 36BEDFORDROW@LINK.ORG **Internet:** HTTP: //WWW.36BED-FORDROW.CO.UK

MEMBERS:

James Hunt QC (1968) (QC-1987) MA (Oxon) *
Brian R. Escott-Cox QC (1954) (QC-1974) MA (Oxon)
Martin Bowley QC (1962) (QC-1981) MA BCL (Oxon)
Michael Pert QC (1970) (QC-1992) LLB (Manch) *
Timothy Raggatt QC (1972) (QC-1993) LLB (Lond) *
Michael Stokes QC (1971) (QC-1994) *
Frances Oldham QC (1977) (QC-1994) BA (Bristol) *
Richard Benson QC (1974) (QC-1995) *
Heather Swindells QC (1974) (QC-1995) MA (Oxon) *
Andrew Urquhart (1963) BA (Oxon)
Stephen Waine (1969) LLB (Southampton) *
David Altaras (1969) BA MA(TCD), DipCrim(Cantab)*
Christopher Metcalf (1972) *
David Lee (1973) BA/BA (Cambridge/Harvard)
Jamie De Burgos (1973) MA (Cambridge)
Michael Fowler (1974) LLB (London) *
Geoffrey Solomons (1974) LLB (Nottingham)
Michael Greaves LLB (B'ham) (1976)
Sam A.G. Mainds* (1977)

Charles Lewis (1977) MA (Oxford)
Andrew Neaves (1977) LLB
Howard Morrison (1977) OBE, LLB (London) *
David Farrell (1978) LLB (Manchester) *
Catherine Gargan (1978) LLB (Liverpool)
Martin Beddoe (1979) MA (Cambridge)
Martine Kushner (1980) LLB (Cambridge)
Christopher Donnellan (1981) BA (Oxford)
Lynn Tayton (1981) LLB (London UCL)
Edmund Farrell (1981) LLB (Leeds) LLM (Cantab) Dip. Eur Law (Kings)
Anesta Weekes (1981)
Richard Wilson (1981) BA LLM (Sussex/Cambridge)
Mercy Akman (1981) LLB (Wales)
Christopher Plunkett (1983) LLB (Warwick)
William Harbage (1983) MA (Cambridge)
Simon Bull (1984) BA LLM (Cambridge)
Joanne Ecob (1985) LLB (Newcastle)
Robert Underwood (1986) BA

Amjad Malik (1987) LLM (London UCL)
Greg Pryce (1987) BA (Wolverhampton)
Gordon Aspden (1988) LLB (Hull)
Andrew Howarth (1988) BA (Oxford)
Amanda Johnson (1990) LLB (London)
John Gibson (1991) LLB (Durham)
Matthew Lowe (1991) LLB (Exeter)
Stuart Alford (1992) BSc (Reading)
Sarah Gaunt (1992) LLB/M.Phil (Cardiff/Cambridge)
Rosa Dean (1993) BA (Oxford)
John Lloyd-Jones (1993) BA (Durham)
Karen Johnston (1994) MA (Oxford)
Jeffrey Jupp (1994) BA (Worcester)
Andrzej Bojarski (1995) LLB (LSE)
Jonathan Kirk (1995) LLB (Kings)
Niall Ferguson (1996) BA (Dunelm)
Rupert Skilbeck (1996) BA (York)
Oliver Connelly (1997)

Head of Chambers:	James Hunt QC
Practice Manager:	Peter Bennett FCCA MCIM
Senior Clerk:	Martin Poulter
Silks Clerk:	Graeme Logan
Senior Criminal Clerk:	Jo Pickersgill
Senior Civil Family Clerk:	Richard Cade
Administrator:	Louise Smith
Fees Clerk:	Lynn Edmonds
Tenants: 55	

• Recorder

SET NUMBER
297 65-67 KING ST (William Bach) 65-67 King St, Leicester, LE1 6RP **Tel:** (0116) 254 7710 **Fax:** (0116) 247 0145 **DX:** 10873 **Clerk:** Ms Jeanette Petty **Tenants:** 17 General common law set covering broad range of law, including all civil litigation, planning, personal injury, medical negligence, matrimonial, crime, and employment.

SET NUMBER

298   2 NEW ST (Paul Spencer) 2 New St, Leicester, LE1 5NA **Tel:** (0116) 262 5906 **Fax:** (0116) 251 2023 **DX:** 10849 Leicester 1 **Clerk:** Carey Hutt **Tenants:** 26 The Chambers are situated in the old 'legal quarter' of Leicester and undertake a variety of work. A general common law set with specialists in most fields including crime, civil, commercial, matrimonial, Chancery and immigration.

SET NUMBER

299   NEW WALK CHAMBERS (John Snell) 27 New Walk, Leicester, LE1 6TE **Tel:** (0116) 255 9144 **Fax:** (0116) 255 9084 **DX:** 10872 Leicester 1 **Clerk:** Michael J. Ryan BSc, MBA, ACIARB **Tenants:** 19 New Walk Chambers is a long established set situated in a large Georgian property close to the Crown Court, County Court and Industrial Tribunal building.

SET NUMBER

300   21 PORTLAND RD (John Whitmore) 21 Portland Road, Leicester, LE2 3AB **Tel:** (0116) 270 6235 **Fax:** (0116) 270 5532 **Clerk:** Mrs Whitmore **Tenants:** 1 Expertise in civil liberties and equal opportunities on both a litigation and advisory basis.

LEWES

SET NUMBER

301   WESTGATE CHAMBERS (John Collins)

WESTGATE CHAMBERS, 144 HIGH ST, LEWES, BN7 1XT
Tel: (01273) 480510 **Fax:** (01273) 483179 **DX:** 50250 LEWES 2

WESTGATE CHAMBERS. 16/17 WELLINGTON SQUARE, HASTINGS, EAST SUSSEX, TN34 1PB.
Tel: 01424 432 105. **Fax:** 01424 717 850 **DX:** 7062 HASTINGS. Also at Chichester.

MEMBERS:

John Collins (1967)	Andrew Judge (1986)	Colm Davis-Lyons (1990)
Maureen Mullally (1957)	John Mannion (1987)	Alexandra Frith (1993)
Henry Spooner (1971)	Claire Jakens (1988)	Louisa Morelli (1993)
Jeremy Gold (1977)	Pierce Power (1989)	Sarah Howe (1993)
Gavin Argent (1978)	Ronald Lindsay (1975)	Brian Aldred (1994)
Philip Meredith (1979)	Helena Szumowska (1989)	Jonathan Edwards (1994)
Nicholas Hamblin (1981)	Paul Cregan (1990)	Maria Hancock (1995)
Christopher De Havas (1984)	Aviva Le Prevost (1990)	Sarah Thorne (1996)
Guy Russell (1985)	Jeremy Wainwright (1990)	Adele White (1996)

Head of Chambers:
John Collins
Clerks:
Julie Haggar/ Sharon Prevett/
Lucy Ashton
Fees Clerk:
Bruce Margrett/John Sadler
Tenants: 19

The Chambers: Westgate Chambers are located in a 17th Century listed building in the High Street of Lewes and are only a few minutes away from the local Courts. Members primarily practise on the South Eastern circuit but are prepared to travel.

Work Undertaken:
    Crime: Work embraces all areas including homicide, fraud, drug conspiracies and offences of violence (including sexual) against the person.
    Family: Children (Private and Public), Divorce, Inheritance/Family Provision, Emergency Procedures, Injunctive Relief, International Abduction, Inherent Jurisdiction.
    Civil: Personal Injury, General Torts & Civil Injunctions, Property & Landlord & Tenant, contract & Consumer, Planning & Environmental, Licensing, Arbitration, Tribunals & Inquries.

WESTGATE
CHAMBERS

LIVERPOOL

SET NUMBER

302   14 CASTLE ST (Adrian Lyon) 14 Castle St, Liverpool, L2 0NE **Tel:** (0151) 236 4421/8240/6759/6757 **Fax:** (0151) 236 1559/227 3005 **DX:** 14176 **Tenants:** 39 **Clerk:** Mr Stuart Jones **Other Clerks:** David Blunsden (Common Law), Neil Grinsdale and Gary Quinn (Chancery Law). Specialists in both General Common Law and all aspects of Chancery work.

SET NUMBER
303 25-27 CASTLE STREET (Stephen Riordan QC)

25-27 CASTLE STREET, 1ST FLOOR, LIVERPOOL, L2 4TA
Tel: (0151) 236 5072 **Fax:** (0151) 236 4054 **DX:** 14224

MEMBERS:

Stephen Riordan QC (1972) (QC-1992) *	Brendan Carville (1980)	Lesley Carter (1990)
Gerard Wright QC (1954) (QC-1973)	David Owen (1981)	Ian Harris (1990) +
	Wendy-Jane Lloyd (1983)	Simon Driver (1991)
Gerald Baxter (1971)	Desmond Lennon (1986)	Anya Horwood (1991)
Pamela Badley (1974) *	Nicholas Johnson (1987)	Nigel Power (1992)
Neville Biddle (1974) **	Tim Kenward (1987)	Charles Lander (1993)
Anthony Barraclough (1978)	Edmund Haygarth (1988)	Damian Nolan (1994)
Anthony Goff (1978)	Jason Smith (1989)	Teresa Loftus (1995)

*recorder
**assistant recorder
+ former solicitor

Head of Chambers:
Stephen Riordan QC

Senior Clerk:
Joanne Stapley

Tenants: 23

The Chambers: A general common law set.

Work Undertaken: Criminal law (defence and prosecution), Family law (including financial relief and applications involving children) and Civil law (the principal areas undertaken by Chambers are personal injury litigation, contractual claims, employment law, local authority work and housing cases). Individual members of Chambers also specialise in discrimination law, judicial review, civil liberties, police law, education law, medical negligence, professional negligence, company law, commercial law, arbitration, landlord and tenant, equine law and licensing. For information about the specialised areas of practice contact one of the clerks.

Recruitment & Training: Please contact Tim Kenward.

SET NUMBER
304
CHAVASSE COURT CHAMBERS (Andrew Mattison) 2nd Floor, Chavasse Court, 24 Lord Street, Liverpool, L2 1TA **Tel:** (0151) 707 1191 **Fax:** (0151) 707 1189 **DX:** 14223 Liverpool **Clerk:** Mr Colin Cubley **Tenants:** 30 A long-established set with a particular emphasis on criminal law, but also with a wide range of civil work and family work (including child care).

SET NUMBER
305
THE CORN EXCHANGE (David Steer QC & I. Goldrein QC) The Corn Exchange Chambers, The Corn Exchange (5th Floor), Fenwick St, Liverpool, L2 7QS **Tel:** (0151) 227 1081/5009 **Fax:** (0151) 236 1120 **DX:** 14221 **Clerk:** Ms alex Keith **Tenants:** 31 General Common Law including Crime, Family (including child care) and Personal Inujry (including Medical Negligence).

SET NUMBER
306 DERBY SQUARE CHAMBERS (Simon Newton)

MERCHANTS COURT, DERBY SQUARE, LIVERPOOL, L2 1TS
Tel: (0151) 709 4222 **Fax:** (0151) 708 6311 **DX:** 14213 LIVERPOOL 1

MEMBERS:

Simon Newton (1970)	Darren O'Keeffe (1984)	Amanda Howard (1994)
Scott Donovan (1975)	James Prowse (1986)	John de Bono (1995)
David Brunnen (1976)	Catherine Ellis (1987)	Ivan Cartwright (1993)
Thomas Ryan (1979)	Ann Beattie (1989)	James Benson (1995)
Graham Wells (1982)	Ian Garden (1989)	Kenneth Delaney (1996)
James Byrne (1983)	Simon Dawes (1990)	Joanna Mallon (1996)
Ruth Howe (1983)	Francis Ledwidge (1990)	
Bernadette Goodman (1983)	Timothy Holloway (1991)	

Head of Chambers:
Simon Newton

Senior Clerk:
Allan Weston

Tenants: 22

The Chambers: An established set with members specialising in industrial accident and personal injuries, medical and professional negligence, contract, employment, matrimonial and crime.

Members offer a wide range of advocacy and advisory skills.

Members belong to the Family Law Bar Association, Professional Negligence Bar Association, the Personal Injuries Bar Association, the Association of Personal Injury Lawyers, the Ecclesiastical Law Society and the Criminal Bar Association.

SET NUMBER
307

EXCHANGE CHAMBERS (William Waldron QC)

PEARL ASSURANCE HOUSE, DERBY SQUARE, LIVERPOOL, L2 9XX
Tel: (0151) 236 7747 **Fax:** (0151) 236 3433 **DX:** 14207 **Email:** EXCHANGECHAMBERS@BTINTERNET.COM
Internet: HTTP: //WWW.EXCHANGECHAMBERS.CO.UK

Members and Work Undertaken: Chambers undertake all aspects of general common law work, with members specialising in the following areas:

William Waldron QC (Silk 1982) – Crime
David Turner QC (Silk 1991) – Crime
Bill Braithwaite QC (Silk 1992) – Personal injury litigation, particularly injuries to the brain and spine
Henry Globe QC (Silk 1994) – Crime
Graham Morrow QC (Silk 1996) – Personal injury litigation, crime, trespass to the person
Tim Holroyde QC (Silk 1996) – Crime, personal injury litigation, licensing law
Edward Bartley Jones QC (Silk 1997) – Chancery, commercial, professional negligence
Peter Smith (1954) – Crime, general common law
Frank Nance (1970) – Crime and general civil litigation
Simon Earlam (1975) – Civil litigation, in particular personal injury and medical negligence
Christopher Cornwall (1975) – General common law, crime and personal injury
Eric Lamb (1975) – Crime
James Rae (1976) – Crime
Gerard Martin (1978) – Personal injury litigation
Judith Fordham (1991) – Family law
Gordon Cole (1979) – Crime
Tania Griffiths (1982) – Personal injury, housing, crime.
Roger Hillman (1983) – Family law, personal injury, general civil law
Neil Cadwallader (1984) – General Chancery, Commercial, professional negligence
Karen Gregory (1985) – Family law
Dennis Talbot (1985) – Crime
Paul Clark (1994) – Personal injury litigation
Gerald Jones (1995) – Criminal law and licensing
Simon Berkson (1986) – Crime and personal injury
Alun James (1986) – Tax and VAT
William F. Waldron (1986) – Crime and personal injury, trespass to the person
Mark Mulrooney (1988) – Family law and civil law
Brian Cummings (1988) – Crime
John McCarroll (1988) – General Chancery & commercial
Rebecca Clark (1989) – Crime, family law, general common law
Catherine Howells (1989) – Family law, general civil law, landlord and tenant
Michael Wood (1989) – Commercial law (including shipping law, construction contracts, company and EEC law)
Christopher Stables (1990) – Crime, general common law (including personal injury litigation)
Julie Case (1990) – General Chancery and commercial law
John Philpotts (1990) – Crime
Amanda Yip (1991) – Crime, family law, general common law
Paul Timothy Evans (1992) – Crime, general common law, copyright, intellectual property and insurance law.
David Casement (1992) – Commercial law, EC law, general civil law.
Charlotte Kenny (1993) – Crime, general common law, employment law
Robert Dudley (1993) – Crime, general common law
Simon Fox (1994) – Personal injury litigation and general common law
Kelly Pennifer (1994) – Commercial law, EC law, general civil law
Rachel Silverbeck (1997) – Crime, Family, Personal Injury.
Clair Gourley (1997) – Family, Personal Injury, Common law.

Recruitment and Training: One or two pupillages with financial support are offered each year. Applications to Mr C. Cornwall, with CV and names of two referees.

Head of Chambers:
William Waldron QC

Senior Clerk:
Roy Finney

Practice Manager
Tom Handley

Tenants: 43

EXCHANGE
CHAMBERS

SET NUMBER
308

FIRST NATIONAL CHAMBERS (John Leach) 2nd Floor, 24 Fenwick Street, Liverpool, L2 7NE **Tel:** (0151) 236 2098 **Fax:** (0151) 255 0484 **DX:** 14167 Liverpool 1 **Clerk:** Mark Bloor **Tenants:** 12 A small set (founded 1982) which practises the full range of general common law. Individual specialities include personal injury, crime, family, employment, local authority and civil liberties work.

SETNUMBER
309
INDIA BUILDINGS CHAMBERS (David Harris QC)

INDIA BUILDINGS, WATER STREET, LIVERPOOL, L2 0XG
Tel: 0151 243 6000 **Fax:** 0151 243 6040 **DX:** 14227

MEMBERS:

David Harris QC (1969)
(QC-1989)
John Briggs (1953)
Michael Wolff (1964)
Robert Atherton (1970)
Michael Byrne (1971)
Raymond Herman (1972)
Richard Brittain (1971)
Stephen Bedford (1974)
Geoffrey Lowe (1975)
Maureen Roddy (1977)
Ross Duggan (1978)
Graham Wood (1979)

Gail Owen (1980)
Gareth Jones (1984)
Michael Kennedy (1985)
Jacqueline Wall (1986)
Jean France-Hayhurst (1987)
Charles Davey (1989)
Damian Sanders (1988)
Simon Holder (1989)
Rachel Andrews (1989)
Louis Browne (1988)
Zia Chaudhry (1991)
Jonathan Taylor (1991)

Patricia Pratt (1991)
Steven Swift (1991)
Jonathan Butler (1992)
John Gibson (1993)
Ben Jones (1993)
David Flood (1993)
Leona Harrison (1993)
Sara Mann (1994)
Michael Scholes (1996)
John Dixon (1995)
John Chukwuemeka (1994)

Head of Chambers:
David Harris QC
Practice Manager:
J. Robert Moss
Clerk:
Helen Southworth
Junior Clerks:
Alastair Webster, Gail Curran
Neil McHugh
Tenants: 35

The Chambers: There are currently 35 members, comprising 1 Queen's Counsel and 34 Juniors.

Work Undertaken:

Main Areas of Work: Chambers practise in the following fields (i) crime, both prosecution and defence, including fraud work; (ii) all aspects of family work, including disputes about children and ancillary relief claims; (iii) personal injury litigation; (iv) commercial disputes; (v) professional negligence claims; (vi) employment law; and (vii) general common law.
Additional Areas: Certain members of chambers have experience in (i) building disputes, (ii) administrative law, (iii) insurance disputes, (iv) landlord and tenant, (v) licensing, (vi) financial services, (vii) company law, partnership disputes, and (viii) contract law.

Recruitment & Training: Normally one pupillage each year. Financial support on merit and subject to negotiation. All pupils stand a good chance of tenancy.

SETNUMBER
310
MARTIN'S BUILDING (R.A. Fordham QC)

2ND FLOOR, MARTIN'S BUILDING, 4 WATER ST, LIVERPOOL, L2 3SP
Tel: (0151) 236 4919 **Fax:** (0151) 236 2800 **DX:** 14232

MEMBERS:

R.A. Fordham QC (1967)
(QC-1993)
D.J. Boulton (1970)
David Geey (1970) LLB
A. McDonald (1971)
D.M. Kerr (1971)
Jack Cowan (1971)
R.L. Halligan (1972)
M. Compton-Rickett (1972)
Antonis Georges (1972)
M.I. Davis (1979)

A.G. Menary (1982)
K.M. Reade (1983)
M. Chatterton (1983)
D.M. McGuire (1987)
S.J. Knapp (1986)
Peter Kidd (1987)
N.S. Lawrence (1988)
Andrew Downie (1990)
Kate Symms (1990)
Timothy Grover (1991)
Steven Seed (1991)

Jonathan Dale (1991)
Charan Romain (1991)
Nicola Shaw (1992)
Gregory Hoare (1992)
David Edwards (1994)
Helen Wren (1994)
Malcolm Dutchman-Smith (1995)
Jeremy Greenfield (1995)
Andrew Carney (1995)
Daniel Rogers (1998)

Head of Chambers:
R.A. Fordham QC
Senior Clerk:
J. Kilgallon
Tenants: 31

The Chambers: A long-established set of chambers handling the full range of general common law work, with a rapidly developing commercial law practice. Situated in Martin's Building since 1971, chambers have excellent conference facilities and make full use of computer technology. Current members include four Recorders and one Assistant Recorder. Members belong to The Family Law Bar Association, The Bar European Group, The Commercial Bar Association, The Northern Bar Association, The Association of Personal Injuries Lawyers and the Irish Bar.

Members and Work Undertaken: All members have a general common law practice with the following specialities:
Robert Fordham QC (1968) Family law, Planning, Licensing, Personal Injury, Crime
David Boulton (1970) Crime, Fraud, Police Discipline
David Geey (1970) Personal Injury, Professional Negligence, Employment, Crime, Commercial, Licensing
Andrew McDonald (1971) Crime, Personal Injury, Professional Negligence, Employment law

David Kerr (1971) Crime, Sale of Goods, Personal Injury, Negligence
Jack Cowan (1971) Crime
Rodney Halligan (1972) Crime
Mary Compton-Rickett (1972) Crime, Family law, Landlord and Tenant, Mental Health Tribunal work, Personal Injury, Financial Ancillary Relief, Child Law
Jonathan Dale (1991) Sale of Goods, Employment, general Commercial work, Personal Injury.
Gregory Hoare (1992) Crime.
Malcolm Dutchman-Smith Crime.

SETNUMBER 311 ORIEL CHAMBERS (Andrew T. Sander)

ORIEL CHAMBERS, 14 WATER STREET, LIVERPOOL, L2 8TD
Tel: (0151) 236 7191 **Fax:** (0151) 227 5909 **DX:** 14106 LIVERPOOL LIX: LIV001

MEMBERS:

A.T. Sander (1970) *	G. Bundred (1982)	P. Brant (1993)
B.S. Joynes (1957)	S. Evans (1985)	H. Brandon (1993)
A. Edwards (1972) *	G. Thomas (1977)	J. Dawson (1994)
W. Rankin (1972)	A. Fox (1986)	F. Somerset-Jones (1994)
A. Murray (1974) **	P. Goodbody (1986)	M. Cottrell (1996)
N.A. Wright (1974) **	J. Nicholls (1989)	A. M. Frodsham (1996)
R. Bradley (1978)	J. Baldwin (1990)	J. Sawyer (1978)
P. Cowan (1980)	J. Gruffydd (1992) +	
P. Fogarty (1982)	H. Belbin (1992)	

*Recorder
+Former solicitor
**Assistant Recorder

Head of Chambers:
Andrew T. Sander
Chamber's Director:
Sarah Cavanagh
Tenants: 25

The Chambers: A broadly based set, the members of which have experience in a number of specialised areas of the law.

Work Undertaken: Arbitration, banking, building, childcare, commercial and company law, general common law, consumer credit, consumer law, criminal law, defamation, disaster litigation, employment law, environmental law, family law, housing, insurance, international trade, landlord and tenant, leasing and factoring agreements, licensing, local government, matrimonial ancillary relief, medical law, partnerships and business arrangements, personal injury, planning, professional negligence, tribunals and inquiries.

SETNUMBER 312 PEEL HOUSE (Nigel Gilmour QC)

GROUND FLOOR, PEEL HOUSE, 5-7 HARRINGTON ST, LIVERPOOL, L2 9QA
Tel: (0151) 236 4321 **Fax:** (0151) 236 3332 **DX:** 14225

MEMBERS:

Nigel Gilmour QC (1970) (QC-1990)	James McKeon (1982)	Yaqub Rahman (1991)
Arthur Noble (1965)	Gwynn Price Rowlands (1985)	Fiona McNeill (1992)
Martyn Bennett (1969)	Michael Connolly (1985)	Peter Foster (1992)
Christopher Alldis (1970)	Mark Breheny (1986)	Rory Mates (1993)
Philip J. Hall (1973)	Simon Christie (1988)	William K. Rankin (1994)
Charles Feeny (1977)	Margaret Hickland (1988)	Stephen Kemp (1995)
Heather Lloyd (1979)	Deborah Gould (1990)	Rachel Hughes (1995)
Thomas Somerville (1979)	Joanne Lewthwaite (1990)	Susan Clarke (1996)
Titus Gibson (1981)	Paul A Becker (1990)	
Peter Gregory (1982)	Alan Sellers (1991)	

Head of Chambers:
Nigel Gilmour QC
Senior Clerk:
Michael R. Gray
Tenants: 28

Three members of chambers are Recorders of the Crown Court.

The Chambers: A general common law chambers dealing with all aspects of the laws of tort, contract, crime and family.

Work Undertaken: Includes building and construction law, child care law, consumer credit, contract law, work in the Coroner's Court, criminal law (including fraud), divorce and ancillary relief, employment and industrial relations, family and childcare law (including divorce, custody and matrimonial finance), health and safety at work, injunctive and other equitable remedies, judicial review, landlord and tenant, licensing, medical negligence and other professional negligence, personal injury, planning, road traffic, and sale of goods.

PEEL HOUSE CHAMBERS

SET NUMBER
313 VICTORIA CHAMBERS (Vincent Deane) 19 Castle Street, Liverpool, L2 4SX **Tel:** (0151) 236 9402 **Fax:** (0151) 231 1296 **DX:** 14193 Liverpool Clerk: Jenny Connor **Tenants:** 13 General common law chambers with emphasis on crime, family law and civil litigation. Some chancery work.

MAIDSTONE

SET NUMBER
314 MAIDSTONE CHAMBERS 33 Earl St, Maidstone, ME14 1PF **Tel:** (01622) 688592 **Fax:** (01622) 683305 **DX:** 51982 Maidstone 2 **Clerk:** Robert Davis **Tenants:** 13 Maidstone Chambers is a general common law set.

SET NUMBER
315 6-8 MILL STREET (Stephen Hockman QC) 6-8 Mill Street, Maidstone, ME5 6XH **Tel:** (01622) 688094 **Fax:** (01622) 688096 **DX:** 51967 Maidstone 2 **Clerk:** John Rugg **Tenants:** 23 A general common law set and annexe of 6 Pump Court.

MANCHESTER

SET NUMBER
316 **BYROM STREET CHAMBERS** (B.A. Hytner QC)

25 BYROM ST, MANCHESTER, M3 4PF
Tel: (0161) 829 2100 **Fax:** (0161) 829 2101 **DX:** 718156

MEMBERS:

Benet Hytner QC (1952) (QC-1970)	Rodney Scholes QC (1968) (QC-1987)	Andrew Moran QC (1976) (QC-1994)
John Price QC (1961) (QC-1980)	Timothy King QC (1973) (QC-1991)	David Allan QC (1974) (QC-1995)
Giles Wingate-Saul QC (1967) (QC-1983) LLB	Geoffrey Tattersall QC (1970) (QC-1992)	Michael Black QC (1978) (QC-1995)
Brian Leveson QC (1970) (QC-1986)	Caroline Swift QC (1977) (QC-1993)	Stephen Stewart QC (1975) (QC-1996)

Head of Chambers:
B.A. Hytner QC

Senior Clerk:
Peter Collison

Tenants: 12

The Chambers: Byrom Street Chambers is a set of chambers consisting wholly of Silks who practise from Manchester and London. Each member offers advice and advocacy in the specialist fields of law in which he or she practises. The specialisms of members overlap and include:

Administrative Law and Judicial Review, Local Government and Public Inquiries.
Commercial Law and in particular Banking, Financial Services, Intellectual Property and Sale of Goods.
Company Law.
Crime, with an emphasis on Homicide, Sexual Offences, Commercial Fraud and Conspiracy.
Computers and Information Technology.
Construction, Building and Engineering and associated matters of Procurement, Insurance, Funding and Professional Liabilities.
Domestic and International Commercial Arbitration and ADR.
Environmental Law.
General Common Law.
Insurance and Reinsurance.
Personal Injury Claims, especially Disaster Litigation, Severe and Permanent Disablement, Industrial Diseases and Class Actions.
Product Liability.
Professional Negligence including that of Doctors, Lawyers, Architects, Engineers, Surveyors, Accountants and Financial Intermediaries.
Shipping and International Trade.
Sports Law.
Tribunal and Inquiries.
Members of Chambers accept references as Arbitrators, Mediators, Adjudicators and Legal Assessors.
All Silks hold, or have held, part-time judicial office. Giles Wingate-Saul QC and Brian Leveson QC sit as Deputy High Court Judges as did Benet Hytner QC until 1997. Geoffrey Tattersall QC sits as Judge of Appeal in the Isle of Man having succeeded Benet Hytner QC who held the appointment from 1980-1997.
Further information regarding individual expertise and fee structure can be obtained from Peter Collison, the Senior Clerk.

SETNUMBER
317 CENTRAL CHAMBERS

GREG'S BUILDINGS, NO1 BOOTH STREET, MANCHESTER, M2 4DU
Tel: (0161) 833 1774 **Fax:** (0161) 835 1405 **DX:** 14467 MANCHESTER 2

MEMBERS:

Fauz Mohammad Khan (1988)	Tonia Grace (1992)	Bob Sastry (1996)
Stella M. Massey (1990)	Nazmun Nisha Ismail (1992)	Peter Ward (1996)
	M. Ayaz Qazi (1993)	James Collins (1997)

Clerks:
Jayne Lever, Neil Vickers

Tenants: 10

A modern, approachable, forward thinking set with an emphasis on civil liberties. Chambers specialise in serving the disadvantaged and putting at the forefront the interests of clients in a manner consistent with the very high duty owed to them. Specialist practitioners in Criminal Defence, Housing, Family, Immigration, Personal Injury, Employment, Judicial Review, Civil Police Actions and Prison Law.

Chambers operates an Equal Opportunities Policy and opposes discrimination on the grounds of sex, race, disability, age or sexuality.

Year established – 1996 (Formerly known as Garden Court North)

SET NUMBER
318 CHAMBERS OF IAN MACDONALD (Ian MacDonald QC) Waldorf House, 5 Cooper Street, Manchester, M2 2FW **Tel:** (0161) 236 1840 **Fax:** (0161) 236 0929 **Tenants:** 11

SETNUMBER
319 COBDEN HOUSE CHAMBERS (Howard Baisden & Peter Keenan)

19 QUAY STREET, MANCHESTER, M3 3HN
Tel: (0161) 833 6000 **Fax:** (0161) 833 6001 **DX:** 14327 MANCHESTER 3 **Email:** CLERKS@COBDEN.CO.UK
Internet: HTTP://WWW.COBDEN.CO.UK

MEMBERS:

Howard Baisden (1972)	Ian Metcalfe (1985)	David Riddell (1993)
Peter Keenan (1962)	Richard Hartley (1985)	Richard Gee (1993)
Peter Watkins (1952)	Mark Monaghan (1987)	James Hilsdon (1993)
Harry Narayan (1970)	Joanne Woodward (1989)	Simon Nichol (1994)
John Broadley (1973)	Robin Kitching (1989)	Susan Gilmour (1994)
Charles Machin (1973)	Timothy Willitts (1989)	Julian Orr (1995)
Nigel Fieldhouse (1976)	Martin Littler (1989)	Christopher Oakes (1996)
Stuart Neale (1976)	Sarah Harrison (1989)	Hilary Manley (1996)
Michael Goldwater (1977)	William Gregg (1990)	Martin Callery (1997)
Richard Oughton (1978)	Sean Kelly (1990)	Michael Heywood (1975) *
Mary Fallows (1981)	Julia Cheetham (1990)	James Morris (1977) *
David Uff (1981)	Marc Willems (1990)	Deanna Hymanson (1988) *
Colin Green (1982)	Rajen Dalal (1991)	Matthew Kime (1988) *
Leonard Webster (1984)	Jonathan Smith (1991)	
Louise Blackwell (1985)	Alison Woodward (1992)	

* Door Tenants

Head of Chambers:
Howard Baisden & Peter Keenan

Senior Clerk/Practice Manager:
Trevor Doyle

Assistant Clerks:
David Hewitt, Scott Baldwin, Daniel Monaghan.

Administrator:
Jackie Morton

Tenants: 40

The Chambers: Cobden House Chambers is comprised of the members of the former Hollins and Bridge Street Chambers and occupies the recently renovated premises of the old Manchester County Court. Chambers is able to offer a wide range of expertise by means of specialist departments. In addition, Chambers provides a fast and efficient service and a timetable for the completion of instructions can be given on delivery. A new brochure is available on request or for further information visit our website.

Areas of specialisation:

Administrative; Agriculture; Arbitration; Banking; Bankruptcy; Care proceedings; Chancery (general); Chancery land law; Charities; Commercial; Commercial litigation; Commercial property; Common land; Common law (general); Company & Commercial; Competition; Consumer Law; Conveyancing; Copyright; Courts martial; Crime; Crime-corporate fraud; Defamation; Employment; Equity, Wills & Trusts; Family; Family provision; Housing; Information technology; Insolvency; Intellectual property; Landlord & Tenant; Licensing; Medical negligence; Partnerships; Patents; Pensions; Personal injury; Planning; Probate & Administration; Professional negligence; Sale & Carriage of goods; Tax-captial & Income; Trademarks.

Chambers' facilities: Conference Rooms, Facilities for Seminars and Arbitrations, Disabled access, disks accepted.

Cobden House
CHAMBERS

SETNUMBER
320

DEANS COURT CHAMBERS (H.K. Goddard QC)

DEANS COURT CHAMBERS, CUMBERLAND HOUSE, CROWN SQUARE, MANCHESTER, M3 3HA
Tel: (0161) 834 4097 **Fax:** (0161) 834 4805 **DX:** 718155 MANCHESTER 3

MEMBERS:

Harold Keith Goddard QC
(1959) (QC-1979)
Richard Henriques QC
(1967) (QC-1986)
Mark Stephen Eastburn·
Grime QC (1970) (QC-1987)
Raymond Donatus Machell
QC (1973) (QC-1988)
David Andrew Stockdale
QC (1975) (QC-1995)
David Thomas Fish QC
(1973) (QC-1997)
Ernest Ryder TD QC (1981)
(QC-1997)
Mark George Turner QC
(1981) (QC-1998)
Richard Kevin Kent Talbot
(1970)
John Duncan (1971)
John Bromley-Davenport
(1972)

John Raymond Gregory
(1972)
Peter Atherton (1975)
Alan James Booth (1978)
Ruth Trippier (1978)
Philip Andrew Butler (1979)
Craig Gardner Sephton
(1981)
Patrick John Field (1981)
Stuart Henry McDonald
Denney (1982)
Timothy Oliver Trotman
(1983)
Warwick Timothy Cresswell
Smith (1982)
Russell Davies (1983)
Anna Louise Bancroft (1985)
Frances Margaret Heaton
(1985)

Paul Benedict Humphries
(1986)
Karen Rachel Brody (1986)
Christopher John Hudson
(1987)
Jonathan Robert Grace
(1989)
Nicholas Edward Grimshaw
(1989)
Edward P. Morgan (1989)
Andrew Timothy Grantham
(1991)
Seamus Ronald Andrew
(1991)
Janet Ironfield (1992)
Peter Richard Burns (1993)
Mark Savill (1993)
Sebastian Clegg (1994)
David Stuart Boyle (1996)
Simon McCann (1996)

Head of Chambers:
H.K. Goddard QC
Senior Clerk:
Terry Creathorn
Tenants: 37

The Chambers: A well-established set, numbering among its tenants seven silks and 30 juniors. Members appear before courts and tribunals across England and Wales, including London. Some accept direct access from the approved professions. Enquiries should be addressed to the Clerk of chambers.

Work Undertaken:

Civil work: Including all personal injury matters, professional negligence (particularly solicitors, accountants, doctors, architects, surveyors, civil engineers and insurance brokers), environmental law and pollution, and consumer credit.

Criminal work: Including homicide and sexual offences, commercial fraud, conspiracy, drug importation and supply, and excise and revenue offences.

Family work: Including the financial consequences of divorce and separation, preservation of assets and injunctive relief, emergency protection for spouses and children, inter-jurisdictional disputes, disputes concerning children and all aspects of the Children Act 1989.

Commercial and Chancery work: Including commercial disputes (including international litigation), supply and sale of goods and services, product liability, banking and financial services, insurance law, construction and building disputes, arbitration, intellectual property, partnership, bankruptcy and insolvency.

Associated Chambers: Chambers has an annexe in Preston, and some members have chambers in London.

SET NUMBER
321

334 DEANSGATE CHAMBERS (Ian Walker McIvor) 334 Deansgate, Manchester, M3 4LY **Tel:** (0161) 834 3767 **Fax:** (0161) 839 6868 **Clerk:** Mr Rachel Campbell **Tenants:** 1 A general common law set of chambers.

SET NUMBER
322

KENWORTHY'S CHAMBERS (Frank Burns) Kenworthy's Chambers, 83 Bridge St, Manchester, M3 2RF **Tel:** (0161) 832 4036 **Fax:** (0161) 832 0370 **Clerk:** Mr Stuart Johnson **Tenants:** 16 General common law chambers, with expertise in civil litigation, criminal and C.I.C.B. work, family law and Children's Act, employment, defamation, landlord and tenant, housing, licensing and personal injury.

SETNUMBER
323
8 KING ST (Keith Armitage QC)

8 KING ST, MANCHESTER, M2 6AQ
Tel: (0161) 834 9560 **Fax:** (0161) 834 2733 **DX:** 14354 MANCHESTER 1 **ISDN:** 0161 835 1402 X2

MEMBERS:

Keith Armitage QC (1970) (QC-1994) LLB (Hons)

J.J. Rowe QC (1960) (QC-1982) (Oxon)

Elizabeth Rylands (1973) LLB (Hons)

David Eccles (1976) BA (Cantab)

Jeffrey Terry (1976) LLB, MA, FACIArb

Gerard McDermott (1978) LLB

Digby C. Jess (1978) BSc (Hons), LLM, ACIArb

Philip Holmes (1980) MA (Cantab)

Peter Main (1981) LLB, DipPetLaw

Kim Frances Foudy (1982) LLB

Farooq Tahir Ahmed (1983) LLB

Stephen Davies (1985) MA (Cantab)

Shirley Worrall (1987) LLB

Michael Joseph Smith (1989) MA (Oxon), BCL

Ian Wood (1990) BA

Jonathan Thompson (1990) (Cantab) LLM, MA

Mark Forte (1989) LLB

Christopher Scorah (1991) MA (Oxon)

Timothy Hodgson (1991) BA D.Phil (Oxon)

Joanne Connolly (1992) LLB

Timothy Edge (1992) MA (Oxon)

Kevin Naylor MB (1992) CHB LLB LLM

Kirsten Barry (1993) LLB

John Parr (1989) LLB

James Boyd (1994) LLB, LLM

David Sandiford (1995) BA (Oxon)

Head of Chambers:
Keith Armitage QC

Senior Clerk:
Peter Whitman

Clerk:
David Lea

Tenants: 27

The Chambers: Chambers have had a long and distinguished history and from an original bias towards common law a wide range of services has been developed.

Work Undertaken: General common law, commercial and chancery, criminal law, personal injury, medical and professional negligence, employment (including race and sex discrimination), commercial fraud, matrimonial and child care law, landlord and tenant, contract (including building), administrative law, Anglo-American disputes, insurance law, arbitration, environmental law, company law, licensing, construction, sale of goods and consumer credit. Video conferencing is available within chambers.

SETNUMBER
324
40 KING ST (Philip Raynor QC)

40 KING ST, MANCHESTER, M2 6BA
Tel: (0161) 832 9082 **Fax:** (0161) 835 2139 **DX:** 718188

MEMBERS:

Philip Raynor QC (1973) (QC-1994)

Nigel Macleod QC (1961) (QC-1979)

John Hoggett QC (1969) (QC-1986)

Andrew Gilbart QC (1972) (QC-1991)

Peter Smith QC (1975) (QC-1992)

Roger Farley QC (1974) (QC-1993)

Stephen Sauvain QC (1977) (QC-1995)

Frances Patterson QC (1977) (QC-1998)

Eric Owen (1969)

John Jackson (1970)

Harold Halliday (1972)

Alan Evans (1978)

Shokat Khan (1979)

Vincent Fraser (1981)

David Manley (1981)

Michael Booth (1981)

John Barrett (1982)

Sonia Gal (1983)

Nicholas Braslavsky (1983)

Paul Chaisty (1982)

Mark Halliwell (1985)

Anthony Crean (1987)

Simon Hilton (1987)

Katherine Dunn (1987)

Ruth Stockley (1988)

Fiona Ashworth (1988)

Paul Tucker (1990)

Geoffrey Pass (1975)

Andrew Singer (1990)

Stephen Pritchett (1990)

Lesley Anderson (1989)

Matthew Smith (1991)

Sally Harrison (1992)

Martin Carter (1992)

Wilson Horne (1992)

Lucy Powis (1992)

Mark Harper (1993)

Sarah Pritchard (1993)

Richard Lander (1993)

Andrew Latimer (1995)

Elizabeth Berridge (1996)

Adrian Farrow (1997)

Katie Nowell (1996)

Head of Chambers:
Philip Raynor QC

Senior Clerk:
William Brown

Clerking:
Bar Management Services (Partners: William Brown, Colin Griffin & Michael Stubbs)

Tenants: 44

Arbitrator: Sir Iain Glidewell

Associate Members: John Tackaberry QC (1967) (QC-1982), John Campbell (1981), Julian Ghosh (1993)

The Chambers: A large and well-established set, the members of which appear before the full range of courts and statutory tribunals. Counsel are available at all ranks of seniority, including seven silks, and the breadth of individual specialities and aptitudes available in chambers means that it offers a wide range of specialist advisory and advocacy services.

Members have written, edited or contributed to a large number of legal journals, most notably in the fields of planning, local government, and highway law.

Main Areas of Work: Town and country planning, local government law and finance, administrative law, parliamentary law, compulsory purchase and compensation, highways law, environmental protection, public health, commercial chancery litigation, landlord and tenant law, law of trusts, partnerships, intellectual property, insolvency (corporate and individual), banking, wills and intestacy, civil liability, personal injury, professional liability, employment and industrial law, building disputes, consumer credit, sale of goods, family and matrimonial law, hire purchase, licensing, and criminal law.

Additional Areas: Markets and fairs, trading standards, EC law, housing, data protection, company law, immigration and defamation.

Members accept Direct Professional Access from the approved professions.

Languages: French, German, Hungarian, Norwegian, Punjabi, Romanian, Urdu.

40 KING STREET
MANCHESTER

5 PARK PLACE
LEEDS

SET NUMBER
325

58 KING ST (Beverly Lunt) 58 King St, First Floor Kingsgate House, 51-53 South King St, Manchester, M2 6DE **Tel:** (0161) 831 7477 **Fax:** (0161) 832 5645 **Tenants:** 17 **Clerk:** Mr F. Greene General common law chambers.

SET NUMBER
326

LINCOLN HOUSE CHAMBERS (Mukhtar Hussain QC) 5th Floor Lincoln House, 1 Brazennose Street, Manchester, M2 5EL **Tel:** (0161) 832 5701 **Fax:** (0161) 832 0839 **DX:** 14338 Manches 1 **Clerk:** Andrew Weaver **Tenants:** 32 A common law set with an extensive practice both prosecuting and defending all areas of criminal work. Particular expertise in immigration law.

SET NUMBER
327

LLOYDS HOUSE CHAMBERS (Paul Marshall) 3rd Floor, Lloyds House Chambers, 18 Lloyd Street, Manchester, M2 5WA **Tel:** (0161) 839 3371 **Fax:** (0161) 832 3371 **DX:** 14388 Manchester 1 **Clerk:** Hilary Smith **Tenants:** 6 Mainly criminal law set, specialising in defence work. Also handles some civil work.

SET NUMBER
328

MANCHESTER HOUSE CHAMBERS (J.D.S. Wishart) Manchester House Chambers, 18-22 Bridge St, Manchester, M3 3BZ **Tel:** (0161) 834 7007 **Fax:** (0161) 834 3462 **DX:** 718153 Manchester 3 **Clerk:** Teresa Thiele **Tenants:** 21 General common law set. Practice includes personal injury, matrimonial law, crime and civil litigation. Including Commercial and Chancery Law.

SET NUMBER
329

MERCHANT CHAMBERS (David Berkley)

NUMBER ONE, NORTH PARADE, PARSONAGE GARDENS, MANCHESTER, M3 2NH
Tel: (0161) 839 7070 **Fax:** (0161) 839 7111 **DX:** 14319 MANCHESTER 1

MEMBERS:

David Berkley (1979)	Catherine Fisher (1990)	Daniel Feetham (1994)
Neil Berragan (1982)	Andrew Noble (1992) FRICS	Stefan Brochwicz-Lewinski
Stephen Cogley (1984)	Jonathan Rule (1993)	(1995)

Head of Chambers:
David Berkley

Chambers Administrator:
Alastair Campbell

Tenants: 8

The Chambers: Manchester has a proud tradition as a city of innovation. It boasts Courts specialising in Chancery, Mercantile, and Official Referee's Business. Merchant Chambers was launched in November 1996 as a specialised group of practitioners that concentrates exclusively upon satisfying the needs of the local commercial and business communities.

The Chambers attempts to satisfy the requirements of commercial lawyers and their clients and to provide a service which is subject to objective quality assessment.

The Chambers Administrator is on hand to deal personally with all inquiries and to elicit the individual requirements of each instructing solicitor. By careful recruitment and planned growth the dynamic needs of a changing legal landscape will be met.

The Chambers offers seminars to solicitors and other professionals and participates in the fast-growing field of continuing education.

MERCHANT CHAMBERS
C O M M E R C I A L ◆ B A R R I S T E R S

SET NUMBER
330

OLD COLONY HOUSE (Paul McDonald) South King Street, Manchester, M2 6DQ **Tel:** (0161) 834 4364 **Fax:** (0161) 832 9149 **DX:** 18160 Manchester 3 **Clerk:** L.F. Dooley **Tenants:** 17 A common law set undertaking a broad range of work, with a particular expertise in criminal work.

SET NUMBER
331

PARSONAGE CHAMBERS (M.J. Holt) 5th Floor, Parsonage Chambers, 3 The Parsonage, Manchester, M3 2HW **Tel:** (0161) 833 1996 **Fax:** (0161) 833 2001 **DX:** 718183 Manchester 3 **Clerk:** Mr Louise Cuttle **Tenants:** 9 Criminal, Common law, Personal injury, and Matrimonial work undertaken.

SET NUMBER
332 PEEL COURT CHAMBERS (Michael Shorrock QC) Peel Court Chambers, 45 Hardman Street, Manchester, M3 3HA **Tel:** (0161) 832 3791 **Fax:** (0161) 835 3054 **DX:** 14320 **Clerk:** Shell Edmunds **Tenants:** 32 The members of Chambers offer expertise in a wide variety of fields, notably commercial law, including commercial fraud, common law, family law, licensing and medical negligence.

SETNUMBER
333 QUEENS CHAMBERS (Mark Lamberty)

5 JOHN DALTON ST, MANCHESTER, M2 6ET
Tel: (0161) 834 6875/4738 **Fax:** (0161) 834 8557 **DX:** 718182 MANCHESTER 3

MEMBERS:

Mark Lamberty (1970)	David Mercer (1980)	Charles Brown (1982)
John Bailey (1966)	Robert Osman (1974)	Peter Rothery (1994)
Monica Stalker (1967)	Gordon Hennell (1982)	Nicholas Courtney (1990)
Roger Green (1972)	Steven Barker (1983)	Judith McCullough (1991)
Peter Buckley (1972)	Susan Grocott (1986)	Timothy Prudhoe (1994)
Eric Shannon (1974)	Heather Hobson (1987)	Warren Potts (1995)
Timothy Ryder (1977)	Patrick Thompson (1990)	Peter Horgan (1993)
Howard Bradshaw (1977)	Christopher Godfrey (1993)	Wendy Pearson (1996)
Paul Holmes (1979)	Michael Hayton (1993)	

Head of Chambers: Mark Lamberty
Senior Clerk: Terence Mylchreest
Tenants: 26

General common law set with specialist practitioners in crime, family, civil and commercial work.

Members also practise from 4 Camden Place, Preston.

SETNUMBER
334 ST. JAMES'S CHAMBERS (R.A. Sterling)

ST. JAMES'S CHAMBERS, 68 QUAY ST, MANCHESTER, M3 3EJ
Tel: (0161) 834 7000 **Fax:** (0161) 834 2341 **DX:** 14350 M1

MEMBERS:

Robert Sterling (1970)	Mark Cawson (1982)	Christopher Cook (1990)
Anthony Elleray QC (1977) (QC-1993) *	Michael Mulholland (1976)	Giles Maynard-Connor (1992)
	David Binns (1983)	Janice Wills (1991)
Percy Wood (1961)	Ian Foster (1988)	James Hurd (1994)
Robert Mundy (1966)	Lucy Wilson-Barnes (1989)	David Calvert (1995)
Barrie Searle (1975)	Jonathan Cannan (1989)	James Fryer-Spedding (1994)
David Porter (1980)	Sarah Wheeldon (1990)	Anthony Rubin (1960)
Timothy Lyons (1980)	Ruth Tankel (1990)	Joseph Jaconelli (1972)

Head of Chambers: R.A. Sterling
Senior Clerk: Stephen J. Diggles
Tenants: 21

* Assistant Recorder

Door Tenants: Anthony Rubin (1960), Joseph Jaconelli (1972).

The Chambers: A chancery and general common law set of chambers.

Work Undertaken:
Chancery: All aspects of property law, including land law, mortgages, nuisance and trespass, rights of way, landlord and tenant, joint property, agricultural holdings work, trusts, settlements and wills; pension schemes; charities; personal property and intellectual property. Business and commercial law, including business agreements and breach of contract; injunctions and other equitable remedies; fraud; professional negligence and indemnity insurance; loans and securities; companies and partnerships; associations; receivers; bankruptcy and insolvency; confidential information; taxation; and tribunals.
Common Law: Including building and construction law; sale of goods; contract law; consumer and consumer credit law; crime; employment law; employer's liability and health and safety at work; environmental law; family (divorce, children, matrimonial finance and property); licensing; personal injuries; professional and medical negligence; police disciplinary hearings; road traffic cases; and tribunals.

Other expertise: Timothy Lyons has written works on inheritance tax and insolvency, and sits on the editorial board of the *Law and Tax Review*. Jonathan Cannan has written works on corporation tax and articles on tax matters generally.

Languages: French, German, Hebrew, Russian, and Spanish.

SETNUMBER 335 — 9 ST. JOHN STREET (John Hand QC)

9 ST. JOHN STREET, MANCHESTER, M3 4DN
Tel: (0161) 955 9000 **Fax:** (0161) 955 9001 **DX:** 14326 **Email:** NINESJS@GCONNECT.COM

MEMBERS:

John Hand QC (1972) (QC-1988)	Christine Riley (1974)	David Gilchrist (1987)
Ian Leeming QC (1970) (QC-1988)	John Dowse (1973)	Simon James (1988)
Roderick Carus QC (1971) (QC-1990)	Peter Cadwallader (1973)	David Friesner (1988)
Charles Garside QC (1971) (QC-1993)	Simon Temple (1977)	Ian Little (1989)
Timothy Horlock QC (1981) (QC-1997)	Jonathan Parkin (1978)	Christopher L.P. Kennedy (1989)
Leslie Portnoy (1961)	Michael Murray (1979)	Nigel Bird (1991)
Christopher St. John Knight (1966)	Nicholas Hinchliffe (1980)	Anthony Howard (1992)
Terence Rigby (1971)	Nicholas Clarke (1981)	Hannah Spencer (1993)
Michael Johnson (1972)	Nigel Grundy (1983)	Rachel Wedderspoon (1993)
Leslie Hull (1972)	Michael P.G. Leeming (1983)	Jaime Hamilton (1993)
	Gillian Irving (1984)	Tariq Sadiq (1993)
	Steven Johnson (1984)	Robert Darbyshire (1995)
	Paul Gilroy (1985)	Brian McCluggage (1995)
	Jane Walker (1987)	
	Carlo Breen (1987)	

Head of Chambers:
John Hand QC

Chief Clerk:
Graham Rogers

Senior Clerk – Crime, Family:
Graham Livesey.

Senior Clerk – Civil, Employment, Commercial/ Chancery:
Tony Morrissey

First Assistant Clerk:
Paul Morecroft

Tenants: 38

Long established in Manchester, in 1993 we moved to our present premises which provide modern well equipped and comfortable accommodation. 9 St John Street Chambers are determined to meet the requirements and expectations of clients and to provide modern, accessible and efficient service whilst maintaining the reputation for excellence and integrity which the Bar has always enjoyed.

In order to meet the increasing demands for specialisation members of Chambers have formed themselves in groups practising in the following areas:

Employment, Industrial Relations and Discrimination, Personal Injury, Environment and Medical Negligence, Commercial and Property with General Chancery, Crime, Trading Standards work, Family, and Mental Health.

Special Interest Group Brochures are available from any of the clerking teams.

SETNUMBER 336 — 18 ST. JOHN STREET (Rodney C. Klevan QC)

18 ST. JOHN STREET, MANCHESTER, M3 4EA
Tel: (0161) 278 1800 **Fax:** (0161) 835 2051 **DX:** 728854 MANCHESTER 4

MEMBERS:

Rodney C. Klevan QC (1966) (QC-1984)	Jennifer Caldwell (1973)	Samantha Birtles (1989)
Martin Steiger QC (1969) (QC-1994)	Raymond Wigglesworth (1974)	Nigel Poole (1989)
Jonathan Foster QC (1970) (QC-1989)	Paul O'Brien (1974)	Elisabeth Tythcott (1989)
Peter Birkett QC (1972) (QC-1989)	Christopher Diamond (1975)	Raquel Simpson (1990)
Andrew Edis QC (1980) (QC-1997)	Roger Stout (1976)	Joy Booth (1992)
Andrew Blake (1971)	Malcolm McEwan (1976)	Mark Benson (1992)
Roger Hedgeland (1972)	N.A. Fewtrell (1977)	Susan Harrison (1993)
Alastair Forrest (1972)	Mark Laprell (1979)	Simon Broadhurst (1994)
Paul Dockery (1973)	David Heaton (1983)	Michael Garvin (1994)
	Richard Vardon (1985)	Sarah Williams (1995)
	Brian Williams (1986)	Simon Kilvington (1995)
	Mandy Brown (1987)	Andrew Moore (1996)
	Toby Sasse (1988)	Saul Brody (1996)

Head of Chambers:
Rodney C. Klevan QC

Clerk:
Michael Farrell

Chambers Administrator:
Jo Kelly

Tenants: 35

We are general common law Chambers with distinct Civil, Family and Criminal Departments, together with 3 Chancery Practitioners, and with expertise at all levels.

SET NUMBER 337

24A ST. JOHN STREET (Paul Chambers) 24A St. John Street, Manchester, M3 4DF **Tel:** (0161) 833 9628 **Fax:** (0161) 834 0243 **Clerk:** Lynn Wallwork **Tenants:** 27 General common law chambers with emphasis on crime, civil litigation, employment, and family law including wardship.

SET NUMBER
338

28 ST. JOHN ST (Anthony Rumbelow QC)

28 ST. JOHN ST, MANCHESTER, M3 4DJ
Tel: (0161) 834 8418 **Fax:** (0161) 835 3929 **DX:** 728861 MANCHESTER 4 **Email:** CLERK@28STJOHN.CO.UK

MEMBERS:

Anthony Rumbelow QC (1967) (QC-1990)	Andrew C. Lowcock (1973)	Charles Eastwood (1988)
Anthony Gee QC (1972) (QC-1990)	Rowena Goode (1974)	Jeffrey K. Samuels (1986)
Charles Chruszcz QC (1973) (QC-1992)	John Phillips (1976)	Clare Grundy (1989)
Lindsey Kushner QC (1974) (QC-1992)	Bernard Wallwork (1976)	Sally-Ann Ross (1990)
	Stephen J. Rothwell (1977)	Paul Taylor (1985)
Michael Redfern QC (1970) (QC-1993)	Graham Platts (1978)	Michael Rawlinson (1991)
L. Clement Goldstone QC (1971) (QC-1993)	Philip M.D. Grundy (1980)	Alastair Wright (1991)
	John R. Jones (1981)	Diana Kloss (1986)
	Sarah Singleton (1983)	Richard Norton (1992)
	Winston Hunter (1985)	Magdalen Case (1992)
Clive Freedman QC (1978) (QC-1997)	Guy Vickers (1986)	Richard Tyrrell (1993)
	J. James Rowley (1987)	Guy Mathieson (1993)
Philip D. Cattan (1970)	Nigel G. Clayton (1987)	Alexander Kloss (1993)
Richard Humphry (1972)	Anthony P. Hayden (1987)	Annette Gumbs (1994)
	David Humphries (1988)	Darrel Crilley (1996)

Head of Chambers:
Anthony Rumbelow QC

Clerks:
Jack Pickles
Christopher Ronan

Manager:
Bridget Knight

Tenants: 39

The Chambers: We are a long-established general common law set offering a broad, comprehensive service combined with the availability of in-depth specialist knowledge. Members of chambers are organised into practice groups and teams of barristers at all levels can be provided where appropriate. Fee quotations are available from the Clerks.

Recognised as both a friendly and professional set, Chambers has a history of involvement in the activities of the specialist Bar Associations, Medical Appeal Tribunals and voluntary and legal advice centres. A number of members sit as Recorders and Assistant Recorders. Disabled access is available.

Work Undertaken: A broad spectrum involving civil, commercial and criminal litigation and family law. Individual members of chambers have also developed particular areas of specialisation such as personal injury, professional negligence, planning, environmental law, public health, fraud, licensing, official referee work, construction, employment, industrial relations, landlord and tenant and chancery law.

Recruitment & Training: Tenancy applications to Graham Platts; pupillage through PACH and mini pupillage applications to Clare Grundy.

SET NUMBER
339

YOUNG STREET CHAMBERS (Lesley Newton) 38 Young Street, Manchester, M3 3FT **Tel:** (0161) 833 0489 **Fax:** (0161) 835 3938 **DX:** 25583 M5 **Clerk:** Peter Wright **Email:** clerks@young-st-chambers.com **Internet:** http://www.clerks 25 Young Street chambers is a progressive common law set. Members of chambers are organised in civil, criminal and family teams, although individual practitioners have particular specialisations within each team.

MIDDLESBROUGH

SET NUMBER
340

CLEVELAND CHAMBERS (George B. Stewart) 63-65 Borough Rd, Middlesbrough, TS1 3AA **Tel:** (01642) 226036 **Fax:** (01642) 245987 **DX:** 60549 **Clerk:** Sean Flaherty **Tenants:** 30 General common law set strong in both criminal and civil litigation. Several members specialise in family and employment law.

SET NUMBER
341

COUNSELS' CHAMBERS (Stuart Lightwing) York House, Borough Road, Middlesbrough, TS1 2HJ **Tel:** (01642) 213000 **Fax:** (01642) 213003 **DX:** 60524 (Middlesbrough) **Clerk:** Pam Haw **Tenants:** 4

SET NUMBER
342

FOUNTAIN CHAMBERS (Peter J.B. Armstrong) Cleveland Business Centre, 1 Watson Street, Middlesbrough, TS1 2RQ **Tel:** (01642) 217037 **Fax:** (01642) 232275 **DX:** 711700 **Clerk:** Robert F. Minns **Tenants:** 19 Broadly-based general chambers with specialists in most areas of the law.

NEWCASTLE UPON TYNE

343 BROAD CHARE CHAMBERS (Eric A Elliott)

BROAD CHARE CHAMBERS, 33 BROAD CHARE, NEWCASTLE UPON TYNE, NE1 3DQ
Tel: (0191) 232 0541 **Fax:** (0191) 261 0043 **DX:** 61001

MEMBERS:

Eric Elliott (1974)	Anthony Hawks (1975)	Anne Richardson (1986)
Paul Batty QC (1975) (QC-1995)	Robin Horner (1975)	David Rowlands (1988)
Patrick Cosgrove QC (1976) (QC-1994)	Roger Elsey (1977)	Mark Styles (1988)
	Judith Moir (1978)	Carl Gumsley (1989)
James Harper (1957)	Sally Bradley (1978)	James Brown (1990)
Frederick Such (1960)	Christopher Dorman O'Gowan (1979)	Julie Clemitson (1991)
Euan Duff (1973)	Kester Armstrong (1982)	Michelle Temple (1991)
Timothy Hewitt (1973)	Lesley McKenzie (1983)	Rachel Smith (1992)
Christine Harmer (1973)	Ian Kennerley (1983)	S. Anderson (1993)
J. Ronald Mitchell (1973)	Pauline Moulder (1983)	Elizabeth Lugg (1994)
Beatrice Bolton (1975)	John O'Sullivan (1984)	Sara Robinson (1994)

Head of Chambers:
Eric A Elliott

Senior Clerk:
Brian Bell

Tenants: 32

The Chambers: A large and long-established set, with an increasing range of specialists.

Seven members of chambers are Recorders, one is an Assistant Recorder and one is a Deputy Chancery Master.

Work Undertaken:
Criminal work: All aspects.
Family law: Including all aspects of child law, financial disputes, divorce, Inheritance Act cases and emergency protection.
Civil work: Including personal injury, professional negligence, general contract, building disputes, employment law, licensing, planning and some commercial.
Chancery work: Most aspects.

344 ENTERPRISE CHAMBERS (Anthony Mann QC)

65 QUAYSIDE, NEWCASTLE UPON TYNE, NE1 3DS
Tel: (0191) 222 3344 **Fax:** (0191) 222 3340 **DX:** 61134 NEWCASTLE UPON TYNE 1

MEMBERS:

Anthony Mann QC (1974) (QC-1992)	Ann McAllister (1982)	Laura Garcia – Miller (1989)
Benjamin Levy (1956)	Peter Arden (1983)	Zia Bhaloo (1990)
Timothy Jennings (1962)	Geoffrey Zelin (1984)	Soraya McKinnell (1991)
David Halpern (1978)	Jacqueline Baker (1985)	James Pickering (1991)
Charles Morgan (1978)	Nigel Gerald (1985)	Hugh Jory (1992)
Caroline Hutton (1979)	James Barker (1984)	Bridget Williamson (1993)
Michael James (1976)	Adrian Jack (1986)	Matthew Hardwick (1994)
Teresa Rosen Peacocke (1982)	Hugo Groves* (1980)	Sarah Richardson (1993)
Linden Ife (1982)	Ian Atherton (1988)	Edward Francis (1995)
	Alistair Henry* (1998)	Shanti Mauger (1996)

Head of Chambers:
Anthony Mann QC

Clerks:
Barry Clayton, Tony Armstrong and Dennis Peck

Newcastle receptionists:
Elaine Browne and Emma Sutherland

Tenants: 29

* Practised as a solictor before joining the Bar.

For further information about the set please see the London entry.

345 NEW COURT CHAMBERS 3 Broad Chare, Newcastle Upon Tyne, NE1 3DQ **Tel:** (0191) 232 1980 **Fax:** (0191) 232 3730 **DX:** 61012 **Clerk:** Brian Dickson **Tenants:** 36 Undertakes most general common law work with a special emphasis on crime, family law and civil litigation.

346   TRINITY CHAMBERS (J.T. Milford QC)

TRINITY CHAMBERS, 9-12 TRINITY CHARE, QUAYSIDE, NEWCASTLE UPON TYNE, NE1 3DF
Tel: (0191) 232 1927 **Fax:** (0191) 232 7975 **DX:** 61185

MEMBERS:

J.T. Milford QC (1969) (QC-1989)	D. Smith (1979)	R.G.S Adams (1993)
A.T. Hedworth QC (1975) (QC-1996)	P.K. Sloan (1981)	A.M. Ditchfield (1993)
C.L. Kelly (1965)	J.A. Smart (1981)	R. Scott-Bell (1993)
S.M. Duffield (1969)	S.E. Wood (1981)	N. Stonor (1993)
J.J.L. Hargrove (1970)	J.D. Richardson (1982)	J.J. Gilbert (1994)
C.J. Knox (1974)	T.H. Spain (1983)	S. Pryke (1994)
J. Lowe (1976)	R.S.M. Hudson (1985)	C. Holland (1994)
C.J.F. Vane (1976)	C.T. Goodwin (1988)	S. Woolrich (1994)
B.C. Forster (1977)	R.B. Cooper (1989)	P Caulfield (1996)
M.J. Wilkinson (1979)	T. Gittins (1990)	S. Routledge (1998)
	F. McCrae (1987)	
	C.A. Oliver (1990)	

Head of Chambers:
J.T. Milford QC

Senior Clerk:
Colin Hands

Tenants: 32

4 members of chambers are Recorders and 2 are Assistant Recorders.

The Chambers: A long-established chambers, located opposite the new Law Courts on the Quayside. Trinity Chambers provides a broadly-based common law, criminal law and family law service together with a specialist chancery, construction and commercial service for most leading local solicitors and local authorities. Several members will accept instructions under the Direct Professional Access scheme, particularly from accountants, arbitrators, chartered surveyors and architects. Enquiries to Clerk.

Work Undertaken:

Main Areas of Work: Administrative law; chancery, including land law, administration of estates, trusts, charities and Court of Protection; commercial law, including banking, insurance, sale of goods, carriage of goods, shipping, commercial credit, company and insolvency law; company law; competition law and restraint of trade; construction and engineering law and related professional negligence matters; consumer credit law; contractual disputes; criminal law; employment disputes, particularly Industrial Tribunal work; environmental and public utilities law; family law; insolvency law; landlord and tenant law; licensing law; local government law; matrimonial law; medical negligence; partnership law; personal injury; professional negligence; rating; and tax and EC law relating to all the preceding fields.

Additional Areas of Work: There are groups of practitioners specialising solely in chancery law, construction and commercial law, family law, personal injuries and criminal law, who are thus able to offer a specialist service not ordinarily found on circuit.

347   WESTGATE CHAMBERS (Ian Dawson)

67A WESTGATE RD, NEWCASTLE UPON TYNE, NE1 1SG
Tel: (0191) 261 4407 **Fax:** (0191) 222 1845 **DX:** 61044

MEMBERS:

Ian Dawson (1971)	Brian Mark (1981)	Joseph O'Brien (1989)
Antony Braithwaite (1971)	David Mason (1984)	Susan Boothroyd (1990)
Stephen Rich (1972)	Richard Selwyn-Sharpe (1985)	Stephanie Jarron (1990)
Giles Pinkney (1978)	Anthony Davis (1986)	Claire Middleton (1991)
Geoffrey Hunter (1979)	Philip Walling (1986)	William Hare (1994)
Thomas Finch (1981)	Sarah Mallett (1988)	Nicholas Peacock (1996)

Head of Chambers:
Ian Dawson

Senior Clerk:
Shaun Murtagh

Criminal Clerk:
Lynn Davis

Practice Manager:
Stan Zych

Tenants: 18

The Chambers: Mixed civil and criminal, with an emphasis on specialisation.

Specialist groups:
Chancery/Commercial
Personal Injury/Medical Negligence
General common law/Crime and Family

348   MILBURN HOUSE CHAMBERS (Paul Cape) A Floor, Milburn House, Dean Street, Newcastle-upon-Tyne, NE1 1LE **Tel:** (0191) 230 5511 **Fax:** (0191) 230 5544 **DX:** 716640 Newcastle 20

NEWPORT

SET NUMBER
349 NEWPORT CHAMBERS (Hilary Roberts) 12 Clytha Park Rd, Newport, NP9 4PB **Tel:** (01633) 255855 **Fax:** (01633) 253441 **DX:** 33208 Newport **Clerk:** Antony Naylon **Tenants:** 13 General common law set with particular emphasis on crime, personal injury, employment, family work and civil law.

NORTHAMPTON

SET NUMBER
350 22 AND 23 ALBION PLACE (Peter Hollingworth) 22 and 23 Albion Place, Northampton, NN1 1UD **Tel:** (01604) 636271 **Fax:** (01604) 232931 **DX:** 12464 **Clerk:** Russell Burton **Tenants:** 20 Busy and expanding set undertaking a variety of work, especially family, and criminal and civil litigation.

SET NUMBER
351 ## 36 BEDFORD ROW (James Hunt QC)

24 ALBION PLACE, NORTHAMPTON, NN1 1UD
Tel: (01604) 602333 **Fax:** (01604) 601600 **DX:** 18544 NORTHAMPTON 2 **Email:** 36BEDFORDROW@LINK.ORG **Internet:** HTTP: //36BEDFORDROW.CO.UK

MEMBERS:

James Hunt QC (1968) (QC-1987) MA (Oxon) *
Brian R. Escott-Cox QC (1954) (QC-1974) MA (Oxon)
Martin Bowley QC (1962) (QC-1981) MA BCL (Oxon)
Michael Pert QC (1970) (QC-1992) LLB (Manch) *
Timothy Raggatt QC (1972) (QC-1993) LLB (Lond) *
Michael Stokes QC (1971) (QC-1994) *
Frances Oldham QC (1977) (QC-1994) BA (Bristol) *
Richard Benson QC (1974) (QC-1995) *
Heather Swindells QC (1974) (QC-1995) MA (Oxon) *
Andrew Urquhart (1963) BA (Oxon)
Stephen Waine (1969) LLB (Southampton) *
David Altaras (1969) BA MA(TCD), DipCrim(Cantab)*
Christopher Metcalf (1972) *
David Lee (1973) BA/BA (Cambridge/Harvard)
Jamie De Burgos (1973) MA (Cambridge)
Michael Fowler (1974) LLB (London) *
Geoffrey Solomons (1974) LLB (Nottingham)
Michael Greaves LLB (B'ham) (1976)

Sam A.G. Mainds* (1977)
Charles Lewis (1977) MA (Oxford)
Andrew Neaves (1977) LLB
Howard Morrison (1977) OBE, LLB (London) *
David Farrell (1978) LLB (Manchester) *
Catherine Gargan (1978) LLB (Liverpool)
Martin Beddoe (1979) MA (Cambridge)
Martine Kushner (1980) LLB (Cambridge)
Christopher Donnellan (1981) BA (Oxford)
Lynn Tayton (1981) LLB (London UCL)
Edmund Farrell (1981) LLB (Leeds) LLM (Cantab) Dip. Eur Law (Kings)
Anesta Weekes (1981)
Richard Wilson (1981) BA LLM (Sussex/Cambridge)
Mercy Akman (1981) LLB (Wales)
Christopher Plunkett (1983) LLB (Warwick)
William Harbage (1983) MA (Cambridge)
Simon Bull (1984) BA LLM (Cambridge)
Joanne Ecob (1985) LLB (Newcastle)
Robert Underwood (1986) BA

Amjad Malik (1987) LLM (London UCL)
Greg Pryce (1987) BA (Wolverhampton)
Gordon Aspden (1988) LLB (Hull)
Andrew Howarth (1988) BA (Oxford)
Amanda Johnson (1990) LLB (London)
John Gibson (1991) LLB (Durham)
Matthew Lowe (1991) LLB (Exeter)
Stuart Alford (1992) BSc (Reading)
Sarah Gaunt (1992) LLB/M.Phil (Cardiff/Cambridge)
Rosa Dean (1993) BA (Oxford)
John Lloyd-Jones (1993) BA (Durham)
Karen Johnston (1994) MA (Oxford)
Jeffrey Jupp (1994) BA (Worcester)
Andrzej Bojarski (1995) LLB (LSE)
Jonathan Kirk (1995) LLB (Kings)
Niall Ferguson (1996) BA (Dunelm)
Rupert Skilbeck (1996) BA (York)
Oliver Connelly (1997)

Head of Chambers:
James Hunt QC

Practice Manager:
Peter Bennett FCCA MCIM

Senior Clerk:
Martin Poulter

Silks Clerk:
Graeme Logan

Senior Criminal Clerk:
Jo Pickersgill

Senior Civil Family Clerk:
Richard Cade

Administrator:
Louise Smith

Fees Clerk:
Lynn Edmonds

Tenants: 55

*Recorder

SET NUMBER

352 CHARTLANDS CHAMBERS (Mrs Jane Page) 3 St Giles Terrace, Northampton, NN1 2BN **Tel:** (01604) 603322 **Fax:** (01604) 603388 **DX:** 12408 Northampton **Clerk:** Mr Andrew Davies **Tenants:** 8 Specialist family and general common law service including matrimonial finance, cohabitation disputes, children, domestic violence, personal injury, employment, tort, contract.

NORWICH

SET NUMBER

353 EAST ANGLIAN CHAMBERS East Anglian Chambers, 57 London Street, Norwich, NR2 1HL **Tel:** (01603) 617351 **Fax:** (01603) 633589 **DX:** 5213 **Clerk:** Stephen Collis **Tenants:** 50 Established in three centres in East Anglia (also in Colchester and Ipswich). Chambers have a general common law practice well represented in crime, civil, and family.

SET NUMBER

354 OCTAGON HOUSE CHAMBERS (Andrew Lindqvist & Guy Ayers) Octagon House Chambers, 19 Colegate, Norwich, NR3 1AT **Tel:** (01603) 623186 **Fax:** (01603) 760519 **DX:** 5249 Norwich-1 **Email:** octagon@netmatters.co.uk **Clerk:** Corinne Ashton **Tenants:** 13 A mixed common law set, handling criminal, family, fraud, landlord and tenant, matrimonial, medical negligence, personal injury, professional negligence, wardship and childcare.

NOTTINGHAM

SET NUMBER
355 ## CHAMBERS OF COLIN ANDERSON (St. Mary's Chambers) (Colin Anderson)

50 HIGH PAVEMENT, NOTTINGHAM, NG1 1HW
Tel: (0115) 950 3503 **Fax:** (0115) 958 3060 **DX:** 10036

MEMBERS:

Colin J.D. Anderson (1973)	Hilary Watson (1979)	Maria Mulrennan (1990)
Andrew N.R. Hamilton (1970)	Mark N. Rogers (1980)	James Hett (1991)
R. Calder Jose (1971)	Victoria Hodges (1980)	Judith Claxton (1991)
Christopher M. Butler (1972)	Adrian Reynolds (1982)	Stuart Lody (1992)
Andrew Lloyd-Davies (1973)	Richard Hedley (1983)	Andrew McNamara (1992)
Noel P. Philo (1975)	Michael Michell (1984)	Alison Friar (1993)
Owen Rhys (1976)	Stuart A. Farquhar (1985)	Patrick Wainwright (1994)
Nigel B. Page (1976)	Sean Hale (1988)	Anna Soubry (1995)
David P.R. Smart (1977)	Robert Egbuna (1988)	Simon Eckersley (1995)
Jeremy H.C. Lea (1978)	Beryl Gilead (1989)	Sarah Knight (1996)
	Mairin Casey (1989)	Rachel Rowley (1997)

Head of Chambers:
Colin Anderson

Senior Clerk:
David Wilson

Tenants: 32

The Chambers: Work undertaken by chambers covers a broad spectrum. Particular strengths are in Criminal Law, General Common Law including Personal Injuries, Medical and Professional Negligence, Matrimonial and Children's cases. Specialists are available in all these areas. A full Chancery and Commercial Law service is also available.

SET NUMBER
356

NO.1 HIGH PAVEMENT (John B. Milmo QC)

NO.1 HIGH PAVEMENT, NOTTINGHAM, NG1 1HF
Tel: (0115) 941 8218 **Fax:** (0115) 941 8240 **DX:** 10168 NOTTINGHAM

MEMBERS:

John B. Milmo QC (1966)
(QC-1984)
Peter Joyce QC (1968)
(QC-1991)
John Warren QC (1968)
(QC-1994)
Peter Walmsley (1964)
Michael Pearce (1975)
Stuart Rafferty (1975)
John Burgess (1978)
Guy Napthine (1979)
Paul Mann (1980)
Gregory Dickinson (1981)
Shaun Smith (1981)

Balraj Bhatia (1982)
Timothy Palmer (1982)
Godfrey Napthine (1983)
Errol Ballentyne (1983)
Audrey Campbell-Moffat
(1987)
Clive Stockwell (1988)
Michael Evans (1988)
Christopher Geeson (1989)
Richard Thatcher (1989)
James McNamara (1990)
Michael Auty (1990)
Andrew Easteal (1990)

Avik Mukherjee (1990)
Kate Hargreaves (1991)
Dawn Pritchard (1992)
Paul King (1992)
Sarah Munro (1990)
Steven Coupland (1993)
Nirmal K. Shant (1984) LLB
Martin Elwick (1981)
Justin Wigoder (1977)
Jonathan Eley (1987) BA
Steven Gosnell (1995)
Sonal Ahya (1995)

Head of Chambers:
John B. Milmo QC

Senior Clerk:
David Duric

Tenants: 35

The Chambers: This specialist criminal set of chambers was established on the 1st of January 1990 to provide a comprehensive service to both prosecution and defence in all aspects of criminal work including serious fraud. For details of areas of expertise of individual barristers please contact the Senior Clerk.

SET NUMBER
357

KING CHARLES HOUSE (William Everard)

KING CHARLES HOUSE, STANDARD HILL, NOTTINGHAM, NG1 6FX
Tel: (0115) 941 8851 **Fax:** (0115) 941 4169 **DX:** 10042

MEMBERS:

William Everard (1973)
Michael O'Connell (1966)
Eric Dumbill (1971)
Ross Fitzpatrick (1972)
John Stobart (1974)
James Howlett (1980)
Vivien Buchanan (1981)
Stephen Lowne (1981)
Richard Toombs (1983)
Amanda Cranny (1984)
Pami Dhadli (1984)
Kevin Salmon (1984)

Patrick Gallagher (1984)
Caroline Bradley (1985)
Mohammed Zaman (1985)
Rowena Bridge (1975)
Michael Cranmer-Brown
(1986)
Mark Van der Zwart (1988)
Ian Way (1988)
Jonathon Dee (1989)
Alastair Munt (1989)
Sharron McNeilis (1990)
Adrian Jackson (1990)

Margo Ford (1991)
Jane Morris (1991)
Richard Jones (1991)
Jonathan Straw (1992)
Edna Leonard (1992)
Libby Grimshaw (1993)
Jeremy Janes (1992)
Julie Warburton (1993)
Tracey Kirwin (1995)
Neil Wylie (1996)

Head of Chambers:
William Everard

Senior Clerk:
Geoff Rotherham

Tenants: 33

The Chambers: King Charles House has been established for more than 20 years providing specialist barrister services, both advocacy and advisory, throughout the East Midlands, South Yorkshire, Lincolnshire and Humberside. It covers the whole range of common law work, chambers being divided into teams (criminal, civil, family) to provide the appropriate high levels of expertise required to meet the demands of modern legal practice. The clerking team is experienced, friendly and approachable. Chambers can provide a wide range of expertise and experience across the whole price range. It has a modern and flexible approach to work designed to accommodate solicitors' and clients' needs for an efficient and competitive service from the Bar.

Work Undertaken: Criminal law including fraud. A broad range of civil work including building, chancery, commercial, company, consumer law, employment, family and childcare, intellectual property, lanlord and tenant, licensing, professional and medical negligence, personal injury, and town and country planning.

Training and Recruitment: Tenancy applications to the Head of Chambers. Chambers has no pupillage vacancies before Autumn 2000.

SET NUMBER
358

ROPEWALK CHAMBERS (Richard Maxwell QC)

24 THE ROPEWALK, NOTTINGHAM, NG1 5EF
Tel: (0115) 947 2581/2/3/4 **Fax:** (0115) 947 6532 **DX:** 10060 NOTTINGHAM 17 **Email:** CLERK@ROPEWALK.CO.UK **Internet:** HTTP://WWW.ROPEWALK.CO.UK

MEMBERS:

Richard Maxwell QC (1968) (QC-1988)
W.C. Woodward QC (1964) (QC-1985)
Anthony Goldstaub QC (1972) (QC-1992)
Ian McLaren QC (1962) (QC-1993)
R.F. Owen QC (1977) (QC-1996)
Richard Payne (1964)
G.M. Jarand (1965)
Graham Machin (1965)
Richard H. Burns (1967)
Richard Swain (1969)

Antony Berrisford (1972)
Douglas Herbert (1973)
Stephen Beresford (1976)
Simon Gash (1977)
Alison Hampton (1977)
Simon Beard (1980)
Jayne Adams (1982)
Rosalind Coe (1983)
Soofi Din (1984)
Dominic Nolan (1985)
Bryony Clark (1985)
Andrew Prestwich (1986)
Patrick Limb (1987)
Richard Seabrook (1987)

Philip Turton (1989)
Toby Stewart (1989)
Jinder Boora (1990)
Jonathan Mitchell (1992)
Jason Cox (1992)
Deborah Davies (1993)
Elizabeth Hodgson (1993)
Richard Gregory (1993)
Helen Mulvein (1993)
Andrew Hogan (1996)
Mark Diggle (1996)
Prof. Michael Bridge (1994)

Head of Chambers:
Richard Maxwell QC
Senior Clerk:
David Austin
Tenants: 36

The Chambers: Ropewalk Chambers provide a comprehensive and specialised, largely civil advocacy service, together with all the necessary advice and paperwork for proceedings in most courts, inquiries and tribunals throughout the country. The administration and clerking provide an efficient infrastructure. Chambers are open from 8.00am to 6.00pm and provide conference rooms (up to 20 people) (with full facilities for the disabled) and client car parking.

Work Undertaken:

1. **Personal Injury** – including industrial and insidious disease, (asbestos induced, asthma, cancer, dermatitis, poisoning, radiation, stress, RSI and VWF), road traffic and industrial disaster, medical accidents, product liability, health and safety at work, medical negligence.

2. **Business and Property** – including commercial, (banking, corporate finance, sale of goods, consumer credit and protection, competition) company, professional negligence (legal, financial and negligence within the building, engineering and surveying professions), building, construction, engineering, landlord and tenant (commercial, residential, agricultural and housing), chancery (boundaries, conveyancing, easements, inheritance, probate, wills and trusts), intellectual property.

3. **Employment** – Wrongful and unfair dismissal, restrictive covenants, trade secrets discrimination).

4. **Planning and Environment** – including administrative, compulsory purchase heritage, judicial review, local government, lands tribunal, pollution, nature conservation, rating.

5. **Family Law** – Matrimonial, finance and property, wardship and children.

6. **Also Full Arbitration** – including alternative dispute resolution facilities.

Clientele: All clients, without discrimination, insurance company, trade union, corporate, local government, privately funded or otherwise. Direct Professional Access is available.

Charges and further information: Please contact David Austin, Chambers Clerk on 0115 947 2581

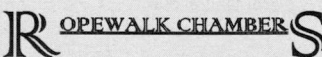

OXFORD

SET NUMBER
359

1 ALFRED STREET (Michael Parroy QC) 1 Alfred Street, High Street, Oxford, OX1 4EH **Tel:** (01865) 793736 **Fax:** (01865) 790760 **DX:** 4302 **Email:** 3paper.lond@bogo.co.uk **Clerk:** Russell Porter **Tenants:** 67 Annexe of 3 Paper Buildings in London. For conference facilities contact London chambers.

SETNUMBER
360 HARCOURT CHAMBERS (Patrick Eccles QC)

HARCOURT CHAMBERS, CHURCHILL HOUSE, 38 ST. ALDATES, OXFORD, OX1 1BA
Tel: (01865) 791559 **Fax:** (01865) 791585 **DX:** 4371

MEMBERS:

Hugh Eccles QC (1968)
(QC-1990) MA (Oxon)

Roger Evans (1970) MA
(Cantab)

June Rodgers (1971) MA
(Dublin), MA(Oxon),
Chancellor Diocese of
Gloucester

Benedict Sefi (1972) BA
(Oxon)

John Dixon (1975) MA
(Oxon)

Gavyn Arthur (1975) MA
(Oxon)

Stephen Barstow (1976) MA
(Cantab)

Jonathan Baker (1978) MA
(Cantab)

Alicia Collinson (1982) MA,
MPhil (Oxon)

Christopher Frazer (1983)
MA, LLM (Cantab)

Frances Judd (1984) BA
(Cantab)

Edward Hess (1985) MA
(Cantab)

Clive Blackwood (1986) BA
(Cantab)

Matthew Brett (1987) BA
(Oxon)

Napier Miles (1989) BA
(Oxon)

Camilla De Sousa Turner
(1989) BA (Cantab)

Piers Pressdee (1991) BA
(Cantab)

Sara Granshaw (1991) BA
(Oxon)

Sally Max (1991) BA(Cantab)

Rohan Auld (1992)
BA(Cantab)

Richard Gregory (1993) BA
(Cantab)

John Vater (1995) BA (Oxon)

Nicholas Goodwin (1995) BA
(Oxon)

Aidan Vine (1995) BA (Oxon)
MA (Cornell)

Head of Chambers:
Patrick Eccles QC

Senior Clerk:
Brian Wheeler

Tenants: 24

Door Tenant: Peter Clarke (1970) BA, BCL (Oxon)

The Chambers: A long-established set of common law chambers with a history dating back to the mid-nineteenth century. Many former members of chambers have attained high judicial office, including one Lord Chancellor.

Harcourt Chambers offers an advisory and advocacy service, principally in the areas of Family Law, and Commercial, Property, Personal Injury and Professional Liability Law.

Harcourt Chambers comprises leading and junior counsel who practice from the Temple and, for the convenience of circuit solicitors, from premises in Oxford. Members of chambers seek to provide an efficient and friendly service for solicitors in London, the Home Counties and the Thames Valley, the Midland and Oxford Circuit and Gloucestershire.

SETNUMBER
361 KING'S BENCH CHAMBERS (Graeme Williams QC)

KING'S BENCH CHAMBERS, 32 BEAUMONT ST., OXFORD, OX1 2NP
Tel: (01865) 311066 **Fax:** (01865) 311077 **DX:** 4318 OXFORD LIX: OXF 003 **Email:** CLERKS@KBC-OXFORD.LAW.CO.UK

MEMBERS:

Graeme Williams QC (1959)
(QC-1983) M.A. (Oxon).

Julian Baughan QC (1967)
(QC-1990) B.A. (Oxon).

Roger Ellis QC (1962)
(QC-1996) LLB. BSc (Lond).

David Ashton (1962) M.A.
(Oxon).

Alexander Dawson (1969)
M.A. (Oxon).

Anthony McGeorge (1969)
M.A. (Cantab).

Robert Lamb (1973) M.A.
(Cantab).

David Richardson (1973)
M.A. LLB (Cantab).

James Gibbons (1974)

Deirdre Goodwin (1974)
LLB. (Lond).

David Grant (1975) M.A.
LLB. (Cantab).

Jane Tracy Forster (1975)
LLB. (Liverpool).

Paul W. Reid (1975) M.A.
(Cantab).

David Bright (1976)

Simon Hughes M.P. (1974)
B.A. (Cantab).

Simon Draycott (1977)

Donald Lambie (1978) LLB.
(London).

Alasdair Brough (1979) M.A.
(Cantab).

Nigel Daly (1979) LLB.
(London).

Nicholas Syfret (1979) M.A.
(Cantab).

Andrew Glennie (1982) M.A.
(Oxon).

A. John Williams (1983)
M.A. (Cantab).

Jonathan Coode (1984) B.A.
(East Anglia).

Neil Vickery (1985) M.A.
(Cantab).

Neil Moore (1986) LLB.
(Nottingham).

Sarah Gibbons (1987) B.A.
(Birmingham).

Arthur Blake (1988) LLB.
(Lond).

Sinclair Cramsie (1988) LLB.
(Leeds).

Gerard Quirke (1988) B.A.
(Hull).

Fiona Hay (1989) BSc. B.A.
(Exeter).

Adrian Higgins (1990) M.A.
(Oxon).

Edmund Walters (1991) B.A.
(Bristol).

Heather Wenlock (1991)
M.Phil D.Phil (Oxon).

Vivian Walters (1991) B.A.
(Leic).

Deshpal Singh Panesar
(1993) LLB. (Lond).

Shantanu Majumdar (1992)
B.A. (Oxon).

Susan Chan (1994) B.A.
(Oxon).

Paul Mitchell (1994) B.A.
(York).

Andrew Pote (1983) LLB.
(East Anglia).

Head of Chambers:
Graeme Williams QC

Senior Clerk:
Stephen Buckingham,
Kevin Kelly

Chambers Administrator:
Penny McFall

Tenants: 38

The Chambers: These Chambers were founded as a seperate set in 1971, although the origin of Chambers goes back many years earlier. In 1988 this set were the first to open separate premises in Oxford. They have wide and varied experience in all fields of general Civil

Continues overleaf

Litigation and provide a comprehensive service in the Criminal Law on the Midland and Oxford circuit. Chambers has an expanding Family Practice, based in Oxford.

Work undertaken:

Common Law/Civil Practice:
Administrative, especially judicial review
Building and Construction
(All aspects of) Business Law including Contract, Sale of Goods, Banking, Company and Partnership
Clubs and Unincorporated Asssociations
Employment
Insolvency
Landlord & Tenant
Medical negligence
Personal injury

Criminal Practice (Oxford and London): both prosecution and defence work. Standing Counsel to Customs & Excise on M & O circuit.

Family Practice, based in Oxford

Specialist Practices: While the range of expertise covered by 13 KBW as a whole is broad, individual members are regarded as specialists in their own fields.

Silks' expertise is in:
Personal Injury/Medical Negligence
Criminal Law
Business Law and Landlord & Tenant

Among the Senior Juniors are specialists in each of the categories of work described.

Administration:
A key factor in the service Chambers offers is flexibility:
Excellent conference facilities in both Oxford and London.
All members of Chambers are available for conferences at either location.
Members of Chambers increasingly provide documents, whether advices or drafts, which are transmitted electronically (e.g. by e-mail or LIX).

PETERBOROUGH

SET NUMBER 362 | FENNERS CHAMBERS (Lindsay Davies)

FENNERS CHAMBERS, 8-12 PRIESTGATE, PETERBOROUGH, PE1 1JA
Tel: (01733) 562030 **Fax:** (01733) 343660 **DX:** 12314 PETERBOROUGH 1 **Email:** CLERKSROOM@FENNERS.FLEXNET.CO.UK
Internet: HTTP://WWW.FLEXNET.CO.UK/~FENNERS

MEMBERS:

Lindsay Davies (1975) #	Simon Tattersall (1977)	Caroline Beasley-Murray (1988)
Kenneth Wheeler (1956) +	Paul Leigh-Morgan (1978)	Clive Pithers (1989)
Peter King (1970)	Tim Brown (1980)	Timothy Meakin (1989)
Michael Yelton (1972) *	Paul Hollow (1981)	Andrew Taylor (1989)
Gareth Hawkesworth (1972)*	Stuart Bridge (1981)	Hazel Clark (1990)
Geraint Jones (1972)	Martin Collier (1982)	James Wilson (1991)
Andrew Gore (1973)	Liza Gordon-Saker (1982)	Caroline Horton (1993)
Stephen Franklin (1974)	Meryl Hughes (1987)	Charles Myatt (1993)
Susan Espley (1976)	Rebecca Litherland (1987)	Katharine Ferguson (1995)
Caroline Pointon (1976)	George Foxwell (1987)	William Josling (1995)
Oliver Heald (1977)	Alasdair Wilson (1988)	

Head of Chambers:
Lindsay Davies

Senior Clerk:
Mark Springham

Tenants: 32

+ Door Tenant

* Recorder

Assistant Recorder

Also at 3 Madingley Road, Cambridge. Please see the Cambridge entry.

SET NUMBER

363 REGENCY CHAMBERS (Raymond Croxon QC) Cathedral Square, Peterborough, PE1 1XW **Tel:** (01733) 315215 **Fax:** (01733) 315851 **DX:** 12349 Peterborough 1 **Clerk:** Paul Wright **Tenants:** 12 General common law to include family, personal injury, medical negligence, landlord and tenant, employment and crime. Also at Cambridge.

PINNER

SET NUMBER

364 WESTGATE CHAMBERS (Henry B. Hograve & John Collins) Paramount House, 8a Elm Park Road, Pinner, HA5 3LA **Tel:** (0181) 429 4833 **Fax:** (0181) 868 2676 **DX:** 35605 Pinner **Clerk:** Maureen Flanagan **Tenants:** 25 A general common law practice.

PLYMOUTH

SET NUMBER

365 DEVON CHAMBERS (Richard Hough) 3 St. Andrew Street, Plymouth, PL1 2AH **Tel:** (01752) 661659 **Fax:** (01752) 601346 **DX:** 8290 Plymouth 2 **Clerk:** Mr Kerslake **Tenants:** 10 General common law set undertaking civil, matrimonial and criminal cases (defence and prosecution).

SET NUMBER

366 KING'S BENCH CHAMBERS (Anthony Donne QC) King's Bench Chambers, 115 North Hill, Plymouth, PL4 8JY **Tel:** (01752) 221551 **Fax:** (01752) 664379 **DX:** 8237 Plymouth 1 **Clerk:** Mr R. L.D. Plager **Tenants:** 70 Annexe of 2 King's Bench Walk, London.

POOLE

SET NUMBER

367 EATON HOUSE (Rupert Massey) First Floor, 4 Eaton Road, Branksome Park, Poole, BH13 6DG **Tel:** (01202) 766301 **Fax:** (01202) 766301 **Clerk:** Jean alexander-Brown **Tenants:** 2 Chambers handle criminal and civil matters in France as liaising advocates with rights of audience. Rupert Massey is adviser to the Federation of Small Businesses (UK) one of the largest pressure-groups of its kind in Western Europe.

PORTSMOUTH

SET NUMBER

368 ## GUILDHALL CHAMBERS PORTSMOUTH (Edo de Vries)

PRUDENTIAL BUILDINGS, 16 GUILDHALL WALK, PORTSMOUTH, PO1 2DE
Tel: (01705) 752400 **Fax:** (01705) 753100 **DX:** 2225 PORTSMOUTH 1

MEMBERS:

Edo de Vries Ret. (1969)	Lee Young (1991)	Lisa England (1992)	
Peter Fortune (1978)	Tom Garnham (1995)	(Squatter)	
Richard Colbey (1984)		Roderick Jones (1983)	
Stuart Ellacott (1989)	Timothy Dunn (1996)	(Door Tenant)	

An established common law set of chambers handling a wide range of law including landlord and tenant, tax, personal injury, professional negligence, family and crime.

Head of Chambers:
Edo de Vries

Senior Clerk:
Tristan Thwaites

Junior Clerk:
Miss Jodie McGuire

Tenants: 9

SET NUMBER
369
PORTSMOUTH BARRISTERS' CHAMBERS (Andrew Parsons)

PORTSMOUTH BARRISTERS' CHAMBERS, VICTORY HOUSE, 7 BELLEVUE TERRACE, PORTSMOUTH, PO5 3AT
Tel: (01705) 831292 **Fax:** (01705) 291262 **DX:** 2239 PORTSMOUTH **Email:** CLERKS@PORTSMOUTHBAR.COM

MEMBERS:

Andrew Parsons (1985) LLB (Hons)

Lincoln Brookes (1992) LLB (Hons)

Timothy Concannon (1993) Former Solicitor

Simon McGrath (1995) MA (Hons)

Sasha Warren (1996) BA (Hons) (UWCC), LLB (Hons) (City)

Martyn Booth (1996) LLB (Hons) (Southampton)

Guy J Russell (1985) BA (Hons) – Door Tenant

Head of Chambers:
Andrew Parsons

Senior Clerk:
Jackie Morrison

Tenants: 6

Door Tenant: Guy J. Russell (1985)

General Description: Chambers undertakes predominantly civil work and aims to provide a modern, high quality, fast, friendly and efficient service.

Main Areas of Work:

Business & Commerce: Contract, company, construction (official referee's work), partnership, carriage of goods and shipping.

Matrimonial & Children: Ancillary relief, care and Children Act matters.

Negligence: Professional negligence (principally medical, solicitor's and financial adviser's negligence) and personal injury.

Property and Finance: Mortgages, land law, wills, trusts, probate, Inheritance Act, landlord and tenant, banking, consumer credit, insolvency, pensions, SFA related work.

By prior arrangement work may be sent to us without obligation to be considered by a member of chambers and if no fee can be agreed will be returned without charge.

A brochure is available on request.

PRESTON

SET NUMBER
370
4 CAMDEN PLACE (Mark Lamberty) 4 Camden Place, Preston, PR1 3JL **Tel:** (01772) 828300 **Fax:** (01772) 825380 **DX:** 17156 Preston 1 **Clerk:** Terence Mylchreest **Tenants:** 26 Annexe of Queens Chambers, Manchester. See under Queens Chambers for full listing.

SET NUMBER
371
DEANS COURT CHAMBERS (Harold Goddard QC) 41-43 Market Place, Preston, PR1 1AH **Tel:** (01772) 555163 **Fax:** (01772) 555941 **Clerk:** Terry Creathorn **Tenants:** 37 Deans Court Chambers offer a wide range of specialist and advocacy services. Please see expanded entry, Deans Court Chambers, Manchester.

SET NUMBER
372
NEW BAILEY CHAMBERS (Pat Bailey) 10 Lawson Street, Preston, PR1 2QT **Tel:** (01772) 258087 **Fax:** (01772) 880100 **DX:** 710050 Preston 10 **Clerk:** Savannah Biswas **Tenants:** 16 A common law set with expertise in chancery, personal injury, family, commercial and crime.

SET NUMBER
373

15 WINCKLEY SQUARE (R.S. Dodds)

15 WINCKLEY SQUARE, PRESTON, PR1 3JJ
Tel: (01772) 252828 **Fax:** (01772) 258520 **DX:** 17110 PRESTON 1 **Email:** CLERKS@WINCKLEYSQ.DEMON.CO.UK
Internet: WWW.WINCKLEYSQ.DEMON.CO.UK

MEMBERS:

R.Stephen Dodds (1976)	Paul Hart (1982)	Louise Harvey (1991)
Roger M. Baldwin (1969)	Paul Hague (1983)	Marie Mitchell (1991)
Barbara J. Watson (1973)	John Woodward (1984)	Julie Taylor (1992)
Simon Newell (1973)	Richard M. Hunt (1985)	Emma Cornah (1992)
Robert Crawford (1976)	D. Mark Stuart (1985)	Fraser Livesey (1992)
P. Nicholas D. Kennedy (1977)	Richard J. Bennett (1986)	Jonathan Buchan (1994)
Timothy G. White (1978)	P. Bruce Henry (1988)	Martin Hackett (1994)
Richard A. Haworth (1978)	Peter J. Anderson (1988)	Lee Blakey (1995)
Glyn Williams (1981)	Kathryn Johnson (1989)	Paul Davis (1996)
David J. Kenny (1982)	Samantha Bowcock (1990)	Jacob Dyer (1995)
Jane E. Cross (1982)	Simon Burrows (1990)	Paul Gillott (1996)
Anthony Cross (1982)	Paul Creaner (1990)	
	Michael Whyatt (1992)	

Head of Chambers:
R.S. Dodds

Senior Clerk:
Michael Jones

Tenants: 36

The Chambers: A medium sized set, seeking to provide a comprehensive service to solicitor clients both in private and institutional practice throughout the town, the county and beyond into Cumbria, Manchester and Merseyside.

Membership: Several tenants are members of the Family Law Bar Association.

Work Undertaken: All common law work with particular emphasis and experience in all areas of family work, crime, contract, personal and industrial injury, licensing, planning, landlord and tenant and employment law. Work on a Direct Access basis is accepted. Expanding chancery and associated case types.

READING

SET NUMBER
374

WESSEX CHAMBERS 48 Queen's Road, Reading, RG1 4BD **Tel:** (0118) 956 8856 **Fax:** (0118) 956 8857 **DX:** 4012 Reading 1 **Email:** wessexchambers@compuserve.com **Tenants:** 8 General common law, civil litigation, crime, family, personal injury, company, commercial, landlord & tenant, employment, professional negligence, licensing, IP, immigration, arbitrations.

REDHILL

SET NUMBER
375

REDHILL CHAMBERS (Richard Mandel) Seloduct House, 30 Station Road, Redhill, RH1 1NF **Tel:** (01737) 780781 **Fax:** (01737) 761760 **DX:** 100203 Redhill 1 **Clerk:** Jan Rogers **Tenants:** 25 General common law set, with several members also practising chancery, employment, family, insolvency, planning and criminal law especially fraud. Also at 11 Bolt Court, London.

SHEFFIELD

SET NUMBER
376

BANK HOUSE CHAMBERS (Mr J. Durham Hall QC) Old Bank House, Hartshead, Sheffield, S1 2EL **Tel:** (0114) 275 1223 **Fax:** (0114) 276 8439 **DX:** 10522 **Clerk:** Miss D. Peat **Tenants:** 25

SET NUMBER
377

FIGTREE LANE CHAMBERS (D. Gothorp) 19 Figtree Lane, Sheffield, S1 2DJ **Tel:** (0114) 275 9708 **Fax:** (0114) 272 4915 **DX:** 10629 Sheffield 1 **Clerk:** Mr P. Bromage **Tenants:** 12 General common law with expertise in crime, personal injury, planning, labour law, landlord and tenant, licensing, matrimonial, professional negligence and chancery.

SET NUMBER
378   26 PARADISE SQUARE (Roger Keen QC) 26 Paradise Square, Sheffield, S1 2DE **Tel:** (0114) 273 8951 **Fax:** (0114) 276 0848 **DX:** 10565 **Clerk:** Tim Booth **Tenants:** 29 General common Law set of chambers, with expertise in all aspects of crime, Civil and family law.

SOLIHULL

SET NUMBER
379   BERKELEY CHAMBERS (Anthony Smith QC) 321 Stratford Road, Shirley, Solihull, B90 3BL **Tel:** (0121) 733 6925 **Fax:** (0121) 733 6926 **Clerk:** Elizabeth Box **Tenants:** 3 A small set specialising in planning and building work.

SOUTHAMPTON

SET NUMBER
380

17 CARLTON CRESCENT (Mr Jeremy Gibbons QC)

17 CARLTON CRESCENT, SOUTHAMPTON, SO15 2XR
Tel: (01703) 320320 **Fax:** (01703) 320321 **DX:** 96875 SOUTHAMPTON CARLTON CRESCENT **Email:** KM@BAR-17CC.DEMON.CO.UK
Internet: HTTP://WWW.BAR-17CC.DEMON.CO.UK

MEMBERS:

Jeremy S. Gibbons QC (1973) (QC-1995)
Linda E. Sullivan QC (1973) (QC-1994)
Jonathan M. Fulthorpe (1970)
Peter J.H. Towler (1974)
Michael P. Kolanko (1975)
William H. Webster (1975)
Nicholas Somerset Haggan (1977)
Hugh Merry (1979)

Margaret Ann Pine-Coffin (1981)
Malcolm T.P. Gibney (1981)
Timothy D. Howard (1981)
Philip A. Glen (1983)
Michael W. Forster (1984)
Gary Grant (1995)
Dylan R. Morgan (1986)
Timothy K. Moores (1987)
Peter Doughty (1988)

Roberta Holland (1989)
Adam Hiddleston (1990)
Hayley Griffiths (1990)
Trevor Ward (1991)
Catherine Burrett (1992)
Sarah Ferrari (1993)
Frida Hussain (1995)
Peter Savill (1995)
Jeremy Burns (1996)

Head of Chambers:
Mr Jeremy Gibbons QC
Senior Clerk:
Gregory P. Townsend
Administrator:
Sue Benoke
Tenants: 26

The Chambers: Full details can be found at our website: http://www.bar-17cc.demon.co.uk

SET NUMBER
381

EIGHTEEN CARLTON CRESCENT (Alastair Haig Haddow)

EIGHTEEN CARLTON CRESCENT, SOUTHAMPTON, SO15 2XR
Tel: (01703) 639001 **Fax:** (01703) 339625 **DX:** 96877 SOUTHAMPTON

MEMBERS:

Andrew Massey (1969)
Alastair Haig-Haddow (1972)
Ashley Ailes (1975)
Gary Fawcett (1975)
Keith Wylie (1976)
Charles Cochand (1978)
Angus Robertson (1978)

Richard Egleton (1981)
Martin Blount (1982)
Christopher Wing (1985)
Elizabeth Manuel (1987)
Andrew Houston (1989)
Omar Malik (1990)
Christine Munks (1991)

Imogen Robins (1991)
Peter Glenser (1993)
Sally Carter (1994)
Michael Thom (1994)
Richard Hall (1995)
Toby Case (1996)
Peter Asteris (1996)

Head of Chambers:
Alastair Haig Haddow
Senior Clerks:
Lynda Knight
Paul Cooke
Tenants: 21

Door Tenants: Guy Boney QC, Michael Ollerenshaw and Jonathan Speck.

Work Undertaken: *Work includes:* general common law including personal injury; criminal law; family and matrimonial law including child care law, wardship and matrimonial property; landlord and tenant; planning; employment; commercial law; licensing; professional negligence and chancery.

SET NUMBER
382

COLLEGE CHAMBERS (Robin Belben)

COLLEGE CHAMBERS, 19 CARLTON CRESCENT, SOUTHAMPTON, SOUTHAMPTON, SO1 2ET
Tel: (01703) 230338 **Fax:** (01703) 230376 **DX:** 38533 (SOUTHAMPTON 3)

MEMBERS:

Robin Belben (1969)	Mark Courtney Stewart (1989)	Daniel Nother (1994)
Kenneth Pain (1969)	Anthony Hand (1989)	Arabella Grundy (1995)
Jonathan Swift (1977)	Jessica Habel (1991)	Andrew Lorie (1996)
John Sabine (1979)	Gary Self (1991)	Baljinder Uppal (1996)
Derek Marshall (1980)	Catherine Breslin (1990)	
Douglas Taylor (1981)	Andrew Kinghorn (1991)	

Head of Chambers:
Robin Belben
Senior Clerk:
Wayne Effeny
Tenants: 16

Work Undertaken: *Work includes:* general common law including family and matrimonial, child care law, wardship and matrimonial property (including cohabitee desputes); personal injury; contract; tort; landlord and tenant; employment; licensing; professional and medical negligence; commercial law; chancery; land law (including boundary disputes) and criminal law.

Instructing solicitors are always welcome to have an informal discussion with the clerks.

SOUTHSEA

SET NUMBER
383

SOUTHSEA CHAMBERS (G.H. Garner) PO Box 148, Southsea, PO5 2TV **Tel:** (01705) 291261 **Fax:** (01705) 826685 **DX:** 2266 **Clerk:** Mrs Babette Lodge **Tenants:** 2 Handles general common law, personal injury, professional negligence, matrimonial and family and landlord and tenant.

ST. ALBANS

SET NUMBER
384

TINDAL CHAMBERS (Gareth J Nixon-Moss) 3 Waxhouse Gate, St. Albans, AL5 4DU **Tel:** (01727) 843383 **Fax:** (01727) 842820 **DX:** 6116 St Albans **Clerk:** Riuchard Gilbert **Tenants:** 16 Work undertaken includes Town & Country Planning; Trading Standards; Family, European Law; Negligence; Personal Injury; Insolvency; Civil, Crime & Commercial; Local Government; Employment; Building Disputes; Licensing; Consumer Credit; Environment; and Landlord & Tenant. Including Direct Professional Access.

STOKE ON TRENT

SET NUMBER
385

REGENT CHAMBERS (Peter Rank) 29 Regent Street, Stoke on Trent, ST1 3BT **Tel:** (01782) 286666 **Fax:** (01782) 201866 **DX:** 20720 (Hanley) **Clerk:** Patricia Lancaster **Tenants:** 8 General civil law including matrimonial, landlord and tenant, equity and trusts, land law, housing, personal injury, and arbitration, planning and construction law and criminal law, contract law, professional negligence, company and insolvency, consumer credit, sale of goods, law of tourism, welfare and benefits law, licensing law, employment, immigration, family.

SWANSEA

SET NUMBER
386

ANGEL CHAMBERS (T. Glanville Jones) Angel Chambers, 94 Walter Rd, Swansea, SA1 5QA **Tel:** (01792) 464623 **Fax:** (01792) 648501 **DX:** 39566 **Clerk:** Crispin Cormack **Tenants:** 19 Chambers handle all areas of general common law.

SET NUMBER
387

GOWER CHAMBERS (Bryan Thomas) 57 Walter Road, Swansea, SA1 5PZ **Tel:** (01792) 644466 **Fax:** (01792) 644321 **DX:** 52956 Swansea **Email:** clerk@gowerchambers.co.uk **Clerk:** Jeremy Thorne **Tenants:** 12 Chambers undertake a wide variety of work including criminal, matrimonial, general common law, construction, planning and chancery matters.

SETNUMBER 388 · ISCOED CHAMBERS (Trefor Davies)

ISCOED CHAMBERS, 86 ST HELEN'S RD, SWANSEA, SA1 4BQ
Tel: (01792) 652988/9 **Fax:** (01792) 458089 **DX:** 39554 SWANSEA

MEMBERS:

Wyn Richards (1968)
Lawrence Griffiths (1957)
Kenneth Lloyd Thomas (1966)
Trevor Lawton Tucker (1971)
Trefor Davies (1972)
Peter Christopher Rouch QC (1972) (QC-1996)
Kevin Riordan (1972)
Frank Phillips (1972)
Patrick Thomas John Griffiths (1973)
John James Jenkins (1974)

Philip Derek Marshall (1975)
Paul Huw Thomas (1979)
Robert Michael Craven (1979)
Stephen Robert Tristram Rees (1979)
Elwen Mair Evans (1980)
Stewart Karl Anthony Sandbrook-Hughes (1980)
Francis Jones (1980)
Owen Huw Rees (1983)
Mark Spackman (1986)

Ruth Henke (1987)
John Hipkin (1989)
David Andrew Harris (1990)
Robert James Buckland (1991)
Catherine Louise Heyworth (1991)
William Peters (1992)
Kate Hughes (1992)
Ian Wright (1994)
Iwan Davies (1995)
Elizabeth Gow (1995)

Head of Chambers:
Trefor Davies

Senior Clerk:
Wally Rainbird

1st Junior: Jeff Evans
2nd Junior: Kris Thorne

Practice Manager:
Sheila Budge

Tenants: 29

Work Undertaken: This well established set of chambers offers an all round service to solicitors and others with the right of Direct Professional Access. The principal fields of work are civil, criminal and family law but with specialised expertise in a variety of areas including personal injury, planning, local government, environment, highways, fraud, trade descriptions, licensing, family, child law, chancery and housing.

SWINDON

SETNUMBER 389 · PUMP COURT CHAMBERS (Guy Boney QC)

TEMPLE CHAMBERS, TEMPLE STREET, SWINDON, SN1 1SQ
Tel: (01793) 539899 **Fax:** (01793) 539866 **DX:** 38639 SWINDON 2

MEMBERS:

Guy Boney QC (1968) (QC-1990)
Nigel Pascoe QC (1966) (QC-1988)
Christopher Clark QC (1969) (QC-1984)
Paul Garlick QC (1974) (QC-1996)
Geoffrey Still (1966)
Stewart Patterson (1967)
Adam Pearson (1969)
Frank Moat (1970)
Giles Harrap (1971)
Frank Abbott (1972)
Michael Montgomery (1972)
Charles Parry (1973)
John Ker-Reid (1974)
Michael Butt (1974)
Philip Gillibrand (1975)

Charles Gabb (1975)
Andrew Barnett (1977)
Michael Dineen (1977)
Timothy O'Flynn (1979)
Jane Miller (1979)
Robert Hill (1980)
Miranda Allardice (1982)
Damien Lochrane (1983)
Oba Nsugbe (1985)
Matthew Scott (1985)
Desmond Bloom-Davies (1986)
Mark Hill (1987)
Graham Howard (1987)
Anne Waddington (1988)
Hugh Travers (1988)
Philip Warren (1988)
Edward Boydell (1989)
Leslie Samuels (1989)

Anthony Akiwumi (1989)
Justin Gau (1989)
Sean Brunton (1990)
Helen Khan (1990)
Penelope Howe (1991)
Geoffrey Kelly (1992)
Patricia Poyer-Sleeman (1992)
James Newton-Price (1992)
Elizabeth Gunther (1993)
Helen Fields (1993)
Oliver Peirson (1993)
Mark Ashley (1993)
Luke Blackburn (1993)
Robert Pawson (1994)
Mark Dubbery (1996)

Head of Chambers:
Guy Boney QC

Senior Clerk:
David Barber

Tenants: 48

The Chambers: An established set undertaking a wide variety of work, with individual members working in specialist teams. Direct Professional Access work is accepted.

Members: Nine members of chambers are recorders. Michael Montgomery is Standing Counsel to the D.T.I. (SE Circuit). Nigel Pascoe QC is leader of the Western Circuit.

Work Undertaken:
Main Areas of Work: Family and Matrimonial; Employment; Inheritance and Property Law; Personal Injury; All aspects of Criminal Law.
Specialisations include: Childcare & Matrimonial Finance; Criminal Law (including Customs & Excise; Serious Fraud; Drugs; Sexual Offences; extradition proceedings and Criminal Appeals); Professional and Medical Negligence; Contract; Consumer Law; Ecclesiastical Law, Inheritance Act.

Associated Chambers: Pump Court Chambers 3 Pump Court, Temple EC4Y 7AJ and Pump Court Chambers, 31 Southgate Street Winchester SO23 9EE.

Recruitment & Training: Tenancy applications should be sent to Head of the Tenancy Committee. All pupillage applications should be made via the PACH Scheme.

TAUNTON

COLLETON CHAMBERS (Martin Meeke)

POWLETT HOUSE, 34 HIGH ST, TAUNTON, TA1 4PN
Tel: (01823) 324252 **Fax:** (01823) 327489 **DX:** 96100 TAUNTON 1

MEMBERS:

Martin Meeke (1973)	David Steele (1975)	Peter M. Ashman (1985)
Richard Merrett (1959)	Richard Crabb (1975)	Jonathan Farquharson (1988)
Stephen Lowry (1960)	Julie Mackenzie (1978)	Melissa Barlow (1991)
Richard Rains (1963)	Mark V. Horton (1981)	
Michael Brabin (1976)	Mark Whitehall (1983)	Philip Drinkwater (1995)
Anthony Puttick (1971)	Terence Holder (1984)	Ruth Vincent (1995)

Head of Chambers:
Martin Meeke
Senior Clerk:
Philip Alden
Tenants: 17

Also at: Colleton Chambers, Colleton Crescent, Exeter, Devon, EX1 1RR.
Tel: (01392) 274898, **Fax:** (01392) 412368, **DX:** 8330 Exeter.

SOUTH WESTERN CHAMBERS (Brian Lett) 12 Middle Street, Taunton, TA1 1SH **Tel:** (01823) 331919 **Fax:** (01823) 330553 **DX:** 32146 (Taunton) **Email:** barclerk@clara.net **Internet:** www.southwesternchambers.co.uk **Clerk:** Stephen Ward **Tenants:** 15 General common law, family, criminal, employment, personal injury, civil litigation, landlord and tenant, licensing, planning, serious fraud.

TRURO

GODOLPHIN CHAMBERS (Barrie Van Den Berg) 50 Castle Street, Truro, TR1 3AF **Tel:** (01872) 276312 **Fax:** (01872) 271920 **DX:** 81233 Truro **Clerk:** Julian Coia **Tenants:** 12 Common law set handling civil, family, and criminal work.

WATFORD

WATFORD CHAMBERS (Aisha Henthorn) 74 Mildred Avenue, Watford, WD1 7DX **Tel:** (01923) 220553 **Fax:** (01923) 222618 **DX:** 42551 BUSHEY **Clerk:** Barry Henderson **Tenants:** 10 General common law set handling a wide range of matters including civil, crime and family.

WINCHESTER

PUMP COURT CHAMBERS (Guy Boney QC)

31 SOUTHGATE STREET, WINCHESTER, SO23 9EE
Tel: (01962) 868161 **Fax:** (01962) 867645 **DX:** 2514

MEMBERS:

Guy Boney QC (1968) (QC-1990)	Charles Gabb (1975)	Anthony Akiwumi (1989)
Nigel Pascoe QC (1966) (QC-1988)	Andrew Barnett (1977)	Justin Gau (1989)
	Michael Dineen (1977)	Sean Brunton (1990)
Christopher Clark QC (1969) (QC-1984)	Timothy O'Flynn (1979)	Helen Khan (1990)
Paul Garlick QC (1974) (QC-1996)	Jane Miller (1979)	Penelope Howe (1991)
	Robert Hill (1980)	Geoffrey Kelly (1992)
Geoffrey Still (1966)	Miranda Allardice (1982)	
Stewart Patterson (1967)	Damien Lochrane (1983)	Patricia Poyer-Sleeman (1992)
Adam Pearson (1969)	Oba Nsugbe (1985)	James Newton-Price (1992)
Frank Moat (1970)	Matthew Scott (1985)	Elizabeth Gunther (1993)
Giles Harrap (1971)	Desmond Bloom-Davies (1986)	Helen Fields (1993)
Frank Abbott (1972)	Mark Hill (1987)	Oliver Peirson (1993)
Michael Montgomery (1972)	Graham Howard (1987)	Mark Ashley (1993)
Charles Parry (1973)	Anne Waddington (1988)	
John Ker-Reid (1974)	Hugh Travers (1988)	Luke Blackburn (1993)
Michael Butt (1974)	Philip Warren (1988)	Robert Pawson (1994)
Philip Gillibrand (1975)	Edward Boydell (1989)	Mark Dubbery (1996)
	Leslie Samuels (1989)	

Head of Chambers:
Guy Boney QC

Senior Clerk:
David Barber

Tenants: 48

The Chambers: An established set undertaking a wide variety of work, with individual members working in specialist teams. Direct Professional Access work is accepted.

Members: Nine members of chambers are recorders. Michael Montgomery is Standing Counsel to the D.T.I. (SE Circuit). Nigel Pascoe QC is leader of the Western Circuit.

Work Undertaken:

Main Areas of Work: Family and Matrimonial; Employment; Inheritance and Property Law; Personal Injury; All aspects of Criminal Law.

Specialisations include: Childcare & Matrimonial Finance; Criminal Law (including Customs & Excise; Serious Fraud; Drugs; Sexual Offences; extradition proceedings and Criminal Appeals); Professional and Medical Negligence; Contract; Consumer Law; Ecclesiastical Law, Inheritance Act.

Associated Chambers: Pump Court Chambers 3 Pump Court, Temple EC4Y 7AJ and Pump Court Chambers, Temple St, Swindon SN1 1SQ.

Recruitment & Training: Tenancy applications should be sent to Head of the Tenancy Committee. All pupillage applications should be made via the PACH Scheme.

4 ST. PETER STREET (Michael Parroy QC) 4 St. Peter Street, Winchester, SO23 8BW **Tel:** (01962) 868884 **Fax:** (01962) 868644 **DX:** 2507 **Email:** 3paper.lond@bogo.co.uk **Tenants:** 67 **Clerk:** Stuart Pringle

WOLVERHAMPTON

SETNUMBER
396 ## CLAREMONT CHAMBERS (Ian McCulloch)

26 WATERLOO ROAD, WOLVERHAMPTON, WV1 4BL
Tel: (01902) 426222 **Fax:** (01902) 426333 **DX:** 722200 WOLVERHAMPTON 15

MEMBERS:

Ian McCulloch (1951)	Mark Garside (1993)	Anthony Thorndike (1994)
Desmond Keane QC (1964)	Naomi Hobbs (1993)	George Fairburn (1995)
(QC-1981)	Ruth Tonge (1993)	Rashpal Mondair (1995)
Jonathan Gidney (1991)	David Maxwell (1994)	Fiona Harding * (1993)
Mohammed Khan (1983)	Jain Brown (1994)	

Head of Chambers:
Ian McCulloch

Senior Clerk:
Meriel Acton

Tenants: 12

* Door Tenant

The Chambers: An established set offering a wide range of experience and expertise. Particular specialisation's include Criminal, Family, Immigration, Commercial, Employment, Contract, Landlord & Tenant, Planning, Professional Negligence and Personal Injury.

Administration: Out of office Hours: Meriel Acton 0976 805643

SET NUMBER
397 CLOCK CHAMBERS (Prof. J. Ritson) 78 Darlington Street, Wolverhampton, WV1 4LY **Tel:** (01902) 313444 **Fax:** (01902) 421110 **DX:** 10423 Wolverhampton **Clerk:** Henry Soulsby **Tenants:** 15 Established 1993. Handles civil, commercial and criminal matters. Work includes family law, personal injury, professional negligence, landlord and tenant, employment, race and sex discrimination.

SET NUMBER
398 TRAFALGAR CHAMBERS Trafalgar House, Market Street, Wolverhampton, WV1 3AB **Tel:** (01902) 713121 **Fax:** (01902) 713353

YORK

SETNUMBER
399 ## YORK CHAMBERS (Simon Hawkesworth QC)

14 TOFT GREEN, YORK, YO1 6JT
Tel: (01904) 620048 **Fax:** (01904) 610056 **DX:** 65517 YORK 7 **Email:** YORKCHAMBERS.CO.UK

MEMBERS:

Simon Hawkesworth QC (1967) (QC-1982) *	Christopher Williams (1981)	John Elvidge (1988)
Aidan Marron QC (1973)	Gillian Matthews (1986)	Charity Norman (1988)
(QC-1993)	Phillip Crayton (1986)	Daniel Cordey (1990)
David Gripton (1969)	Helen Proops (1986)	Martin Todd (1991)
Mark Grenyer (1969)	Peter Johnson (1986)	James Robinson (1992)
Michael Bowerman (1970)	Robert Terry (1986)	Richard Scott (1992)
J. Raymond Priest (1973)	Rosslyn Lee (1987)	Daniel Edwards (1993)
Martin Lindsay (1977)	Nicholas Price (1987)	Diane Campbell (1995)
Michael O'Neill (1979)	David Lamb (1987)	Ravinder Randhawa (1995)
Stephen Twist (1979)	Peter Makepeace (1988)	Edward Legard (1996)

Head of Chambers:
Simon Hawkesworth QC

Senior Clerk:
Kevin Beaumont

Tenants: 29

The Chambers: With its Central position on the North Eastern Circuit, York has proved an ideal base for chambers providing a comprehensive advocacy and advisory service to solicitors throughout the North of England.

Along with modern accommodation including three conference rooms and facilities for the disabled, Chambers has a modern computer system which includes the diary and the abililty for members to acccess to the library where law reports arc held on compact disc.

Work Undertaken:
   Main Areas of Work: Personal Injury including medical negligence, industrial disease and accidents at sea. Child care and ancillary relief. Crime including computer fraud and Courts Martial.

Other Areas of Work: Members of Chambers also work regularly in the following areas: professional negligence, contract, commercial, employment, landlord and tenant, consumer credit, education, actions involving the Police and Police discipline, licensing, trading standards Tribunals (including CICB and Mental Health), Planning Building and Boundary Disputes, Equine, Immigration and Wills.

BARRISTERS'
Profiles

CHAMBERS & PARTNERS

AARONSON, Graham QC
One Essex Court (Anthony Grabiner QC),
London (0171) 583 2000
Recommended in Tax
Specialisation: Principal area of practice is commercial taxation, covering all aspects, in particular: mergers and acquisitions, structured finance, corporate reorganisations, insurance taxation, oil taxation, capital allowances and transfer pricing. Acted in Scorer v. Olin Energy Systems, Elliss v. BP Oil, BMI (No. 3) v. Melluish, Unigate v. McGregor, Nuclear Electric v Bradley. Clients include major companies; the leading city solicitors and the 'Big 5' accountancy firms.
Prof. Memberships: Chairman Revenue Bar Association 1994; Chairman, Tax Law Review Committee 1994-1998. Bencher of Middle Temple since 1991.
Career: Educated at City of London School and Trinity Hall, Cambridge 1963-66 (Waraker Law Scholar). Called to the Bar 1966 and practised commercial law before joining 4 Pump Court to specialise in taxation, 1968-73. Managing Director of Worldwide Plastics Development Ltd 1973-77. Director Bridgend Group Plc 1973-92. Tenant at Queen Elizabeth Building 1978-1991. Took Silk 1982. Joined current Chambers in 1991. Advisor on tax reform to Israel Treasury 1986-89 as part of the team brought in to tackle Israel's hyper-inflation.
Personal: Founder, Standford Grange Rehabilitation Centre for Offenders. Born 31st December 1944. Lives in Stanmore, Middlesex.

ABELL, Anthony
3 Hare Court (William Clegg QC), London
(0171) 353 7561
Recommended in Crime
Specialisation: Specialist in cases of serious crime with an emphasis on fraud. Also regularly acts in cases of murder, manslaughter, rape, armed robbery and drugs manufacture, importation and supply. Interesting cases include R v Pearlberg & Others (Bank Fraud and corruption); R v Paris & Others (International Bank Fraud); R v Feld (Fraud upon shareholders of a PLC, prosecution brought by SFO); R v Bailey & Cooke (Paedophile ring, child abduction and murders); R v Thompson & Others (Barking double murder and torture); R v Virgo (Child destruction and torture); R v Guerrellor (Child manslaughter); R v Varathadasan (Tamil Tigers murder); R v Hall & Others (Drugs manufacture). Important reported cases in the Court of Appeal include: R v McKechnie & Others (94Cr. App. R.51) Manslaughter, inconsistent verdicts; R v C (Times 4/2/93) Rape (Number of counts on indictment).
Prof. Memberships: Criminal Bar Association, South Eastern Circuit.
Career: Called to the Bar in 1977 and joined present chambers in 1978.
Personal: Educated at Kings School Rochester and London University (LL.B Hons). Leisure pursuits include opera, theatre, walking and windsurfing. Born 31st October 1953, lives in London.

ACTON, Stephen
11 Old Square (Grant Crawford & Jonathan Simpkiss), London (0171) 430 0341
Recommended in Traditional Chancery
Specialisation: Specialises in general Chancery work with a particular emphasis on 'commercial Chancery' and company law. Practice includes company and insolvency work; partnership; real property and securities (especially institutional lending); conveyancing disputes; equitable remedies and trusts; probate and estates; landlord and tenant (particularly commercial leases); contractual disputes and commercial Chancery litigation generally; professional negligence in the above fields. Recent reported cases include Parker-Tweedale v Dunbar Bank (No.1) (mortgagee's duty of care) and (No.2) (mortgagee's right to costs); Norwich & Peterborough BS v Steed (No.1) (leave to appeal out of time) and (No.2) (rectification of land

registry). Re Dennis (severance of joint tenancy by act of bankruptcy). Articles include 'Creditors and Administration Orders' in Palmer's 'In Company' (March 1993).
Prof. Memberships: Chancery Bar Association; Professional Negligence Bar Association.
Career: Called to the Bar 1977, Joined present Chambers 1978. Lectured in company and partnership law at Holborn Law Tutors 1977-1979 and wrote the HLT Company Law Handbook.
Personal: Educated at Ilford County High School for Boys 1964-1971 and at Trinity College, Cambridge 1972-1976 (double first; starred 1st in Law Part II). Leisure pursuits include golf, tennis, skiing, theatre, cinema and supporting Tottenham Hotspur. Born 27th April 1953. Lives in London.

ACTON DAVIS, Jonathan QC
4 Pump Court (Bruce Mauleverer QC), London
(0171) 353 2656
Recommended in Construction
Email: jjactondavis@msn.com
Specialisation: Practice covers construction law work and professional negligence, also general common law matters. Clients include most large construction companies, insurers and other commercial bodies.
Prof. Memberships: Official Referees' Bar Association, Professional Negligence Bar Association, COMBAR, London Common Law Bar Association, Association des Juristes-Franco-Brittaniques.
Career: Called to the Bar 1977 and joined 4 Pump Court 1978, Member of Bar Council 1993 to date, Bencher of Inner Temple 1995; Queen's Counsel,1996. Assistant Recorder 1997.
Personal: Born 15th January 1953. Educated at Harrow School and P.C.L. LLB (Lond.) Leisure pursuits include cricket and South Western France.

ADAM, Tom
Brick Court Chambers (Christopher Clarke QC),
London (0171) 583 0777
Recommended in Professional Negligence
Specialisation: Professional negligence, NRG v. Bacon & Woodrow (Court of Appeal – successfully mediated) led by Sydney Kentridge QC on two day appeal from Hong Kong in the Privy Council re: tax recoveries. Led by Jonathan Sumption QC on a six week underwriters indemnity action, case settled before Trial.
Career: Norwich Cathedral School, Trinity College Cambridge, Solicitor (Macfarlanes) 1990-1991, called to the Bar 1991, Tenant Brick Court Chambers 1992.
Personal: Married, two children.

ADAMS, Jayne
Ropewalk Chambers (Richard Maxwell QC),
Nottingham (0115) 947 2581/2/3/4
Recommended in Personal Injury

ADKINS, Richard QC
3/4 South Square (Michael Crystal QC), London
(0171) 696 9900
Recommended in the following lists: Banking, Company, Insolvency

AEBERLI, Peter
46 Essex Street (Geoffrey Hawker), London
(0171) 583 8899
Recommended in Alternative Dispute Resolution
Specialisation: Peter Aerbili MA (Edin.) BA (Oxon.) Dip. Arch. RIBA ARIAS FCIArb. Arbitrator, mediator and practising barrister specialising in construction and environmental law. Prior to reading law as a Scholar of Hertford College, Oxford, worked with a national multi-disciplinary design consultancy and was the project architect for a range of medium and large scale developments. For a time was a lecturer at Edinburgh University. Listed on the Chartered Institute of Arbitrators' panel of arbitrators. Accredited CEDR mediator. Member of the RIBA contracts committee and represents the RIBA on various JCT sub-committees. Member and vice-chairman of the RIBA London Region

panel of conciliators. Sub-editor on the Arbitration and Dispute Resolution Law Journal. Course director for the Chartered Institute of Arbitrators. Tutor on the Kings College Centre of Construction Law MSc/Diploma in Construction Law. Has extensive lecturing experience and is a contributor to the architectural and the legal press.

AGNELLO, Raquel
11 Stone Buildings (Michael Beckman QC),
London +44 (0)171 831 6381
Recommended in Insolvency
Specialisation: Specialist in corporate and personal insolvency and general company law. Involved recently in defending the DTI public interest petition against the Ostrich Farming Corporation and acting for the administrators of Polly Peck International v Forsyth. Other cases of interest include: RE Cranley Mansions Limited – creditors voluntary arrangements; Re Witney Town Football Club – unregistered companies.
Personal: Languages: Portuguese, French and Swedish. Educated in the United Kingdom, Sweden and France. For information on fee levels please refer to the Chambers entry.

AIKENS, Richard QC
Brick Court Chambers (Christopher Clarke QC),
London (0171) 583 0777
Recommended in the following lists: Commercial (litigation), Insurance & Reinsurance, Professional Negligence, Shipping
Specialisation: Commercial law (including insurance and reinsurance, shipping, banking, commodities, oil and gas, arbitration etc). Recent Cases: Marc Rich v Bishop Rock Marine (duty of care contract) (HL); NRG v Bacon & Woodrow (professional's advice in company purchase); The 'MAKHUTAI' (privity of contract; bailment on terms) (PC); The 'STAR SEA' (marine insurance: duty of utmost good faith per contract) (CA); Royal Boskalis Westminster NV v Irevor Rex Mountain (marine insurance; illegality; conflict of laws) (CA); Reeman v Department of Transport (duty of care; economic loss) (CA); Banque Worms v Owners of 'MAULE' (mortgagee's rights of sale) (PC).
Career: Called 1973; QC 1986; Recorder 1993. Deputy High Court Judge, Director, Bar Mutual Indemnity Fund 1988.
Personal: Born 28.8.48. Married 1979.

AINGER, David
10 Old Square (Leolin Price CBE QC), London
(0171) 405 0758
Recommended in Traditional Chancery

AKENHEAD, Robert QC
Atkin Chambers (John Blackburn QC), London
(0171) 404 0102
Recommended in the following lists: Arbitration, Construction, Energy & Utilities
Specialisation: Practising Barrister specialising in the field of Construction law – Arbitration and Litigation. Has practised continually and exclusively since 1972 in Construction Law. Practice has been in the English Courts and in British and international arbitrations. International work has involved arbitrations and contracts inter alia in Europe, Africa, Middle East, Asia, Australia, Fiji, W. Indies and USA. Work has frequently included claims relating to final account, defects, delay and disruption and measurement. Has lectured and given seminars on all legal aspects of building and civil engineering. Recent publication: 'Site Investigation and the Law' (Thomas Telford Ltd – 1984).
Career: Called to Bar July 1972; Queen's Counsel 1989; Assistant Recorder 1990; Recorder 1994.
Personal: Born 15th September 1949. Educated Exeter University (LL.B. Hons.). Bar Final 1972 (8th out of 700).

AKIN, Barrie
Gray's Inn Tax Chambers (Milton Grundy), London (0171) 242 2642
Recommended in Tax
Specialisation: All aspects of revenue law, with particular emphasis on corporate, financial and cross border issues (including banking, leasing and asset finance) and on investment management.
Prof. Memberships: Fellow, Institute of Chartered Accountants in England and Wales. Committee member, Revenue Bar Association.
Career: Bury Grammar School and Sheffield University (LLB); called 1976; ACA 1982; Tax Partner at Ernst & Young London 1986-1996. Joined Gray's Inn Tax Chambers July 1996.
Personal: Born 7/1/54.

ALDOUS, Charles QC
7 Stone Buildings (Charles Aldous QC), London (0171) 405 3886
Recommended in the following lists: Chancery, Company, Energy & Utilities
Specialisation: Specialist in company law, insolvency, and contract and commercial disputes. Practice also covers professional negligence and general Chancery work. Recent notable cases include: MCC Proceeds Inc. v. Lehman Brothers [1998], Grandmet v. William Hill [1997], Amoco (UK) Exploration Company v. Teesside Gas and Transportation Ltd. [1997], Macmillan Inc. v. Bishopsgate Investment Trust [1996], Macmillan Inc. v. Bishopsgate Investment Trust [1995], Mirror Group Newspapers Pension Trustees v. Lehman Brothers [1994], Re: Bishopsgate Investment Management Ltd. (No. 2) [1994], GE Capital v. Bankers Trusts & Ors [1994], Supreme Travels Ltd. v. Little Olympian Each-Ways Ltd. [1994], Macmillan Inc. v. Bishopsgate Investment Trust [1993], Re: BSB Holdings (BSkyB) [1993].
Career: Called to the Bar 1967 and joined present Chambers in the same year. Took silk 1985. Appointed Junior Counsel to the Department of Trade and Industry.
Personal: Educated at Harrow and University College, London (LL.B). Born 3rd June 1943. Lives in London and Suffolk.

ALESBURY, Alun
2 Mitre Court Buildings (Michael FitzGerald QC), London (0171) 583 1380
Recommended in the following lists: Energy & Utilities, Planning
Specialisation: Practice encompasses public and administrative law, town and country planning, parliamentary and local government work (including highways, compulsory purchase and rating). Involved in Windscale Inquiry, Vale of Belvoir Inquiry, Stansted/Heathrow Terminal 5 Inquiry (all as advocate) and Windermere Inquiry (as Inspector). Clients include individuals, developers, landowners, local and other public authorities and the Government.
Prof. Memberships: Planning and Environment Bar Association (Founder Member 1986, Hon. Sec. 1986-88), Parliamentary Bar Mess.
Career: Called to the Bar 1974, Junior Treasury Counsel (Planning).
Personal: Educated at Cambridge University 1967-70 (MA). Leisure pursuits include walking, travel and sailing. Born 14th May 1949.

ALEXANDER, Daniel
8 New Square (Michael Fysh QC), London (0171) 405 4321
Recommended in the following lists: Intellectual Property, Media & Entertainment
Specialisation: Specialises principally in intellectual property, competition, EC and scientific commercial law. Also environmental and administrative law. Practice includes advocacy and advisory work in a wide variety of cases, many with EC and international aspects. Cases include Apple Corps v Apple Computer (trade marks – contract – Article 85/EC – foreign competition law), Chiron v

Organon (genetic engineeering patent – Patents Act, section 44 – conflict of laws), Greenpeace v Plant Genetic Systems (genetic engineering – plant varieties and environmental law – European Patent Office), ICI v Montedison (chemical patent), Great Lakes v Texaco (commercial contracts), Portman v MAFF (judicial review, EC Law), BSkyB v PRS (copyright tribunal). Joint editor of 'Clark & Lindsell on Torts' and the 'Encyclopedia of UK and European Patent Law'. Joint author (with Mr Justice Jacob) of 'Guidebook to Intellectual Property Law'. Author of articles on legal and scientific topics and a regular lecturer and speaker at seminars. Speaks fluent German and good French.
Prof. Memberships: Bar European Group, Chancery Bar Association, Environmental Law Foundation, Patent Bar Association.
Career: Called to the Bar and admitted to the New York Bar in 1988. Joined current chambers in 1989. Junior Counsel to the Crown in Patent Cases (from Spring 1997).
Personal: Educated at University College, Oxford (BA, Physics and Philosophy, 1985), Central London Polytechnic (Dip.Law 1986) and Harvard Law School (LLM, 1987). Born 4th October 1963.

ALEXANDER, David
3/4 South Square (Michael Crystal QC), London (0171) 696 9900
Recommended in Insolvency
Specialisation: Company, commercial, financial and insolvency.
Career: BA Cantab, call to Bar 1987. In practice since 1988, call to Bermuda Bar (Ad hoc) 1998.

ALLCOCK, Stephen J QC
Pump Court Tax Chambers (Andrew Thornhill QC), London (0171) 414 8080
Recommended in Tax
Specialisation: Principal area of practice is Revenue Law advisory work.
Career: Called to the Bar 1975, joined present chambers 1977. Lecturer in law London University (Queen Mary College) 1975-77.
Personal: Educated Bristol Grammar School 1963-70 and Cambridge (Jesus College) 1971-74.

ALLEN, James H. QC
Chancery House Chambers (James H. Allen QC), Leeds (0113) 244 6691
Recommended in the following lists: Chancery, Insolvency

ALLEN, Robin QC
Cloisters (Laura Cox QC), London (0171) 827 4000
Recommended in the following lists: Administrative & Public Law, Civil Liberties, Employment
Specialisation: Discrimination, European, Human Rights, Employment and Administrative Law.
Prof. Memberships: Chair of the Employment Law Bar Association and committee member of the Discrimination Law Association.
Career: Most important cases include: London Underground v Edwards (Single Mothers and Shiftwork); Bossa v Ansett (EC Article 48 and Race Relations Act); ex parte Martin (ECHR Article 8 and Access to Medical Records); Balfour v The Foreign and Commonwealth Office (PII and National Security); ex parte Seymour Smith (EC challenge to the two year qualifying period for unfair dismissal); ex parte Gerry Adams (EC challenge exclusion order); Polkey v A E Dayton Services (unfair dismissal); Delaney v Staples (Wages Act); ex parte Puhlhofer (homeless persons in judicial review); ex parte Hammell (interlocutory relief in judicial review); Alexander v Home Office (damages for discrimination); Hampson v Department of Education (Justification for indirect discrimination); ex parte Gallagher (damages for breach of EC law); Jones v Tower Boot (Employer's liability for harassment). Has worked for the CRE, EOC and Fair Employment Commission for Northern Ireland. Counsel for the "Great Ape Trial" on Channel 4 in December 1995. In 1990, acted for PC Singh in the longest ever race discrimination

claim, later the subject of a Channel 4 reconstruction. Has co-ordinated the Employment Law Advisers Appeal Scheme at the EAT and is vice chair of the Bar Pro Bono Unit. In 1992 appointed an expert to the European Commission on UK Law. Represents Bar Council on the Royal Courts of Justice Citizens Advice Bureau, Assistant Recorder, writes and lectures widely in his areas of law; has contributed chapters to three books forthcoming in 1998: A Practitioners Guide to the Human Rights Act – Hart; The Legal Framework and Social Consequences of Free Movement of Persons in the European Union – Kluwer; Women, Work and Inequality – MacMillan.

ALTMAN, Brian
3 Hare Court (William Clegg QC), London (0171) 353 7561
Recommended in the following lists: Crime, Crime: Fraud
Junior Treasury Counsel at the Central Criminal Court.

AMLOT, Roy QC
6 King's Bench Walk (Michael Worsley QC), London (0171) 583 0410
Recommended in the following lists: Crime, Crime: Fraud
Specialisation: Principal area of practice is criminal law with an emphasis on high profile, serious crime cases and commercial fraud. Defence work includes Barlow Clowes, Blue Arrow, Brent Walker and Polly Peck (for the Liquidator). Prosecution work includes the Brighton bombing, Guildford Four (on appeal) and Clive Ponting cases. Editor, 'Phipson on Evidence' (11th Edition).
Prof. Memberships: Chairman of Criminal Bar Association.
Career: Called to the Bar 1963 and became a tenant of King's Bench Walk in 1964. Treasury Counsel 1977-89. Took Silk 1989.
Personal: Educated at Dulwich College 1953-60. School Governor, Dulwich College. Leisure pursuits include skiing, music, squash, and windsurfing. Born 22nd September 1942. Lives in London.

AMOS, Tim
Queen Elizabeth Building (Ian Karsten QC), London (0171) 797 7837
Recommended in the following lists: Family: Matrimonial Finance
Specialisation: All aspects of family law and related professional negligence, but predominantly family finance, married or unmarried, alive or dead. Specially interested in Anglo-German cases and those with a foreign or international element. Fluent in German (including legal German). Work experience in German Courts and German law firms. Articles include "Financial Injunctive Relief under the 1989 Act" [1994] Fam Law 445.
Prof. Memberships: Family Law Bar Association and British German Jurists Association.

ANDERSON, Anthony QC
2 Mitre Court Buildings (Michael FitzGerald QC), London (0171) 583 1380
Recommended in the following lists: Parliamentary, Planning
Specialisation: Practice encompasses planning, rating, compulsory purchase, parliamentary and local government law. Involved in Stansted Airport Inquiry, Manchester Regional Shopping Inquiry, Exeter Sub-Regional Shopping Inquiry and Crawley Business Parks Inquiry amongst others. Joint Editor 'Ryde on Rating' (12th and 13th Editions).
Prof. Memberships: Planning and Environment Bar Association. Chairman of Tribunals, the Securities and Futures Authority.
Career: Called to the Bar 1964 and joined current chambers 1965. Took Silk 1982. Appointed Recorder 1995.
Personal: Educated at Harrow School and Magdalen College, Oxford. Born 12th September 1938.

ANDERSON, David
Brick Court Chambers (Christopher Clarke QC), London (0171) 583 0777
Recommended in European Union/Competition
Specialisation: European Union Law, Competition Law, Public/Administrative Law, Human Rights Law. Over 50 cases in the European Court of Justice and 15 before the European Commission/Court of Human Rights. Involved at all stages of Factortame and Sunday Trading litigaton; various cases ICI v Commission (cartel law); ex p Rees Mogg [1994] Q.B. 552 (Maastricht Treaty); Care C-448/93 ex p Scotia (pharmaceutical licensing); Case C-302/94 ex p BT (telecoms regulation); Iberian Trading [1996] 2 C.M.L.R. 601 (effect of Commission decision); Case C-180/96R UK v Commision (BSE); Case C-249/96 Grant v SW Trains (sexual orientation discrimination); Building Societies v UK [1997] (retrospective legislation; human rights); Easyjet v BA [1998] (Article 86). Publications include References to the European Court (Sweet & Maxwell Litigation Library, 1995).
Career: Called 1985; Lawyer from Abroad, Covington & Burling, Washington DC, 1985-86; Stage in Cabinet of Lord Cockfield, EC Commission, 1987-88; Visiting Lecturer then Visiting Fellow, King's College London, from 1989 to date; Junior Counsel to the Crown, Common Law, since 1995.

ANDERSON, Lesley
40 King St (Philip Raynor QC), Manchester (0161) 832 9082
Recommended in the following lists: Commercial (litigation), Insolvency
Specialisation: Corporate and personal insolvency including directors' disqualifications, Banking, Commercial Landlord and Tenant. Professional Negligence and Commercial Litigation.
Prof. Memberships: Chancery Bar Association, Northern Chancery Bar Association, Northern Circuit Commercial Bar Association. On DTI Panel for Directors' Disqualifications.
Career: Lecturer in law at University of Manchester 1984-1989; Training Manager, Norton Rose M5 Group of Solicitors 1989-1991.

ANDERSON, Mark
3 Fountain Court (Colman Treacy QC), Birmingham (0121) 236 5854
Recommended in Commercial (litigation)
Specialisation: Professional negligence, general commercial law including credit and securities, personal injury and medical negligence.
Prof. Memberships: Midland Chancery & Commercial Bar Association. Personal Injuries Bar Association
Career: Educated at King Edward's School, Birmingham and Exeter College Oxford.

ANDERSON, Rupert
Monckton Chambers (Richard Fowler QC), London (0171) 405 7211
Recommended in European Union/Competition
Specialisation: Practice includes all aspects of EU and domestic competition law including OFT, MMC and Commission investigations, EU law generally, VAT and customs and excise, utilities regulation. Recent cases include MMC inquiries into Electrical Retailing, Technicolor/Metrocolor and Mobile Telephones; the Supply of Sugar, Ready Mixed Concrete, Freight Forwarding Services, Ceiling Tiles and Rugby Union Football in the RP Court; Endtotal v SP Radio A/S (judgement 30 April 1997, High Court) and News International v Customs & Excise (Court of Appeal judgement 30 March 1998) Contributor to Bellamy and Child, 'Common Market Law of Competition', Weinberg and Blank on Take-Overs and Mergers, Copinger on Copyright.
Prof. Memberships: Member of the Bar European Group.
Career: Called 1981.

ANDREWS, Claire
Gough Square Chambers (Frederick Philpott), London (0171) 353 0924
Recommended in Consumer Law
Specialisation: Consumer law – experienced in civil litigation prosecuting and defending regulatory offences, and advising on interpretation of statutes. Cases include: R v. Warwickshire CC [1993] AC 583 (misleading prices); LB Bexley v. Gardner Merchant [1991] COD (improvement notices). Clients have included food and other wholesalers and retailers and enforcement authorities. Other main areas of practice include landlord and tenant, employment and commercial fraud.
Prof. Memberships: Food Law Group, ALBA, EBA, London Common Law and Commercial Bar Association.

ANDREWS, Geraldine
Essex Court Chambers (Gordon Pollock QC), London (0171) 813 8000
Recommended in Commercial (litigation)
Specialisation: Broad-based practice. In particular shipping, insurance and reinsurance, banking law, asset tracing and preservation, international commodity transactions, company law, EC law, entertainment, intellectual property (excluding patents) and general commercial and Chancery matters.
Prof. Memberships: Member of COMBAR, the London Common Law and Commercial Bar Association, and the Bar European Group; supporting member of the London Maritime Arbitrators' Association.
Career: King's College, University of London: LLB (First Class Hons), 1980.
Personal: Born 1959.

ANDREWS, Philip B.
Young Street Chambers (Lesley Newton), Manchester (0161) 833 0489
Recommended in Crime
Specialisation: Practice encompasses all aspects of criminal law.
Prof. Memberships: Criminal Bar Association.
Career: Called to Bar (Inner Temple) February 1977 thereafter practising on Northern Circuit. Visiting lecturer law, University of Manchester 1979-1982.
Personal: Born 24.7.50. Educated at Blackpool Grammar School and University of Hull (LLB) (Hons).

ANDREWS, Peter QC
199 Strand (Peter Andrews QC), London (0171) 379 9779
Recommended in Personal Injury
Specialisation: Catastrophic injury litigation including major spinal cord injury, brain damage and peri-natal birth trauma claims. Recent reported cases: Oksuzoglu v. Kay (medical negligence, causation and costs); Smoldon v Nolan (spinally injured rugby player's successful action against the match referee); Mansfield v Weetabix (hypoglycaemia as a defence to negligent driving).
Prof. Memberships: Professional Negligence Bar Association; Personal Injury Bar Association; Midland & Oxford Circuit; AVMA.
Career: Christ's College Cambridge and Bristol Universities (Undergraduate Scholar). Lincoln's Inn: Hardwicke Scholar. Junior practice in personal injury and medical negligence. Recorder of the Crown Court. Silk: 1991. Recent Publications: Catastrophic Injuries – A Practical Guide to Compensation (Sweet & Maxwell 1997); Personal Injury Handbook (contributor) (Sweet & Maxwell 1997); Kemp & Kemp: the Quality of Damages (Sweet & Maxwell 1998): chapter on structured settlements.

ANELAY, Richard QC
One King's Bench Walk (James Townend QC), London (0171) 936 1500
Recommended in Family: Matrimonial Finance
Specialisation: All areas of family and criminal law. Has undertaken leading work in matrimonial finance, child care, Inheritance Act provision, international child abduction, serious fraud, murder, manslaughter and rape. Election law: acted in Tower Hamlets Election. Case (1990) – 22 day hearing before Commissioner. In public law children case has undertaken leading work for local authorities, parents and guardians ad litem in complex medical, Munchaussen syndrome, proxy, sexual, physical and emotional abuse cases. Reported cases: Re KDT (Minor) Court of Appeal [1994] 2 FCR 721; Re G FCR [1994] 2 FCR 216.
Career: Called in 1970. Took silk in 1993. Recorder in 1992.
Personal: Born 1946. Educated at Queen Elizabeth Grammar School, Darlington and Bristol University (BA Hons Classics and Philosophy). Enjoys golf.

APPLEBY, Elizabeth QC
4-5 Gray's Inn Square (Miss Elizabeth Appleby QC & The Hon. M. Beloff QC), London (0171) 404 5252
Recommended in Administrative & Public Law
Specialisation: Public and Administrative Law; Local Government.
Career: Called 1965, QC 1979, Bencher Lincoln's Inn 1986, Recorder Crown Court. Chaired the enquiry into the affairs of Lambeth Council, Appointed Inspector of Department of Trade inquiries, appeared in Westdeutsche Landesbank Firm Zentrich v. Litigation BC; Morgan Grenfell v. London Borough of Sutton, Graham Jones v Ronald Hellard, R v Hereford & Worcester.
Career: Deputy High Court Judge.

ARDEN, Andrew QC
Arden Chambers (Andrew Arden QC), London (0171) 242 4244
Recommended in the following lists: Administrative & Public Law, Planning, Property Litigation
Specialisation: Principal areas of practice are housing and landlord and tenant law (including homelessness, right to buy/acquire and enfranchisement, leases and service charges, rents and security of tenure, disrepair and environmental health, business tenancies), housing association law (including finance, disposals, status, powers and procedures, committee membership, mixed-funding arrangements, stock acquisition) local government (including finance, asset disposals, local authority companies, powers and procedures, committee structures, access to information, competitive tendering [English and European], mixed-funding arrangements, superannuation, waste disposal), and miscellaneous aspects of public and administrative law. Has conducted five local government inquiries/reviews; appeared for the Objectors at the Westminster Audit Hearing (1994). Author/Co-Author: Housing Law, Local Government Finance Law, Assured Tenancies (Vol. 3, The Rent Acts, 11th ed.), Manual of Housing Law, Homelessness and Allocation, Annotated Statutes (including Housing Acts 1980, 1985, 1988, 1996, Local Government and Housing Act 1989, Housing Grants, Construction and Urban Renewal Act 1996). General Editor/Joint Editor: Housing Encyclopaedia, Housing Law Reports, Journal of Housing Law, Arden's Housing Library. Editorial Board Member: Journal of Local Government Law.
Prof. Memberships: Administrative Law Bar Association; Local Government, Planning and Environmental Bar Association; Bar European Group.
Career: Called to the Bar 1974. Director, Small Heath Community Law Centre 1976-78. Silk 1991. Founded Arden Chambers in 1993.
Personal: Educated at University College London 1969-72 (LLB). Writes novels and thrillers. Born 20th April 1948. Lives in London.

ARDEN, Peter
Enterprise Chambers (Anthony Mann QC), London (0171) 405 9471
Recommended in the following lists: Banking, Company, Insolvency
Specialisation: Areas of practice: Business and financial law, in particular banking, bank and other securities, insolvency (corporate and individual) and related areas. Regularly instructed by clearing banks, other financial institutions and their appointees. Acted in many of the large insolvencies in recent years. Cases include Re Dallhold Estates (appointment of administrators over foreign companies), Leyland DAF Ltd v Lipe Ltd (interlocutory injunctions against administrative receivers), Re Leyland DAF Ltd (whether administrative receivers bound by exclusive jurisdiction clause), William Gaskell Group Ltd v Highley (whether charge fixed or floating and automatic crystallisation), Re Thomas Christy Ltd (effect of disqualification judgement on proceedings by liquidation), Re Ellis Son & Vidler Ltd (sale of goods and storage contract and equitable interests/remedies), Re WAL Holdings Ltd (contest between debenture holder and finance companies), Walker v Hocking (bankrupt seeking to interfere with exercise of powers by trustee), Re Business City Express Ltd (application for recognition of Eire scheme of arrangement), Re Edennote Ltd (sanction for exercise of powers by liquidator) and Re West Park Gold & Country Club (dismissal of partnership administration petition as an abuse).

ARKUSH, Jonathan
11 Stone Buildings (Michael Beckman QC), London +44 (0)171 831 6381
Recommended in Property Litigation
Specialisation: Conducts commercial and Chancery litigation, including contract, partnership, company, insolvency, probate and real property, with a broad advisory and drafting practice covering those areas. He also has an interest in international law, in particular relating to human rights.

ARLIDGE, Anthony QC
18 Red Lion Court (Anthony Arlidge QC), London (0171) 520 6000
Recommended in the following lists: Crime, Crime: Fraud
Specialisation: Serious fraud from Griffiths and Others in 1965 to Blue Arrow. Author of Arlidge and Parry on Fraud 2nd edn. Revenue cases including Carmel College. Prosecuted Jeremy Bamber and defended Baroness De Stempel. In the past year clients include Michael Allcock defended for corruption in relation to the Revenue, Terence Ramsden, Dr. Crockett (alleged purchase of kidneys for transplant) and Dr Bichan (Butte Mining). Appeared in Graham and Ords, the post-Preddy appeals. Disciplinary tribunals including General Medical Council, Stock Exchange, Lloyds, Fimbra.
Career: Double first class degree in law, Cambridge.

ARMITAGE, Keith QC
8 King St (Keith Armitage QC), Manchester (0161) 834 9560
Recommended in Medical Negligence

ARMSTRONG, Dean
6 King's Bench Walk (Michael Worsley QC), London (0171) 583 0410
Recommended in Crime
Specialisation: Prosecutes and defends in all forms of crime and commercial fraud.
Career: MA (Cantab.).

ARNOLD, Mark
3/4 South Square (Michael Crystal QC), London (0171) 696 9900
Recommended in Insolvency
Specialisation: Business and financial law, including in particular insolvency (corporate and individual), banking, company, chancery and professional negligence.
Prof. Memberships: COMBAR, Chancery Bar Association.
Career: M.A. Cantab. (Downing College, Cambridge).

ARNOLD, Richard
11 South Square (Christopher Floyd QC), London (0171) 405 1222
Recommended in the following lists: Computer & I.T., Intellectual Property

ARNOT, Lee
22 Old Buildings (Benet Hytner QC), London (0171) 831 0222
Recommended in Family: Matrimonial Finance
Specialisation: Family law including matrimonial finance, public and private law aspects of the Children Act 1989, adoption, child abduction and applications under the Inheritance (Provision for Family and Dependants) Act 1975. Property disputes between cohabitees and family members.
Prof. Memberships: F.L.B.A.
Career: Called to the Bar in 1990.

ASH, Brian QC
4-5 Gray's Inn Square (Miss Elizabeth Appleby QC & The Hon. M. Beloff QC), London (0171) 404 5252
Recommended in Planning

ASHE, T. Michael QC
9 Stone Buildings (Michael Ashe QC), London (0171) 404 5055
Recommended in the following lists: Chancery, Financial Services
Specialisation: Practice focuses on business and finance litigation and advice. Work includes contract, company law, tax, financial services, securities regulation and civil and criminal aspects of commercial fraud. Also handles Chancery work, judicial review and conflicts of laws. Regularly instructed outside the United Kingdom, particularly in South East Asia, North America and Europe. Practising member of both Bars of Ireland. Publications include 'Money' (4th Edition Halsbury's Laws of England, Butterworths 1980); 'Injunctions' (4th Edition Halsbury's Laws of England, Butterworths 1991); 'Insider Dealing' (2nd Edition Tolley 1993); 'Insider Crime' (Jordans 1993); CCH Guide to Financial Services Regulation (1997). Editor of The Company Lawyer since 1983 and of International Tracing of Assets (FT Law and Tax 1997). Has also contributed numerous articles to various periodicals. Regularly addresses conferences both in the United Kingdom and overseas and broadcasts frequently on both TV and radio on commercial law issues.
Prof. Memberships: Chancery Bar Association, Revenue Bar Association, Commercial Bar Association, International Association of Irish Lawyers.
Career: Civil Service 1967-1970. Called to the Bar 1971. Merchant banker, 1971-1976. Called to the Bar of Ireland 1975. Joined chambers in 1978. Honorary Consultant to the Commercial Crime Unit, Commonwealth Secretariat 1980-1984. Special Counsel, Commercial Affairs Department Singapore. 1988-1991. Called to the Bar of Northern Ireland 1993. Took Silk England and Wales 1994. Took Silk Northern Ireland 1998.

ASHFORD-THOM, Ian
1 Temple Gardens (Hugh Carlisle QC), London (0171) 583 1315
Recommended in Personal Injury
Specialisation: Practice covers common law and public law work, primarily personal injuries and disaster litigation, including inquests, professional negligence, judicial review and employment law.
Prof. Memberships: Common Law and Commercial Bar Association, Administrative Law Bar Association.
Career: Called to the Bar 1977 and joined current chambers in 1979.

Personal: Educated at Exeter University 1972-6 (LL.B). Bracton Law Prize. Born 13th October 1953. Lives in London.

ASHTON, Arthur
One Raymond Buildings (Christopher Morcom QC), London (0171) 430 1234
Recommended in Intellectual Property
Specialisation: Principal area of practice is trade marks, trade secrets and copyright. Other main areas of practice include Industrial Designs, Patents and Passing Off. Practice covers advice and the conduct of litigation. Clients have included major corporations from Europe, the United States and Japan.
Career: Called to the Bar; England and Wales 1988; South Africa 1975.
Prof. Memberships: Educated at Rhodes University and University of Louvain. Practises solely in London.

ASHWORTH, Fiona
40 King St (Philip Raynor QC), Manchester (0161) 832 9082
Recommended in Family/Matrimonial
Specialisation: Personal Injury (Employer's and Public liability, Disease, Road Traffic). Medical & PI related professional negligence. Family and matrimonial provision.
Prof. Memberships: P.I.B.A., F.L.B.A.
Career: Bolton School (Girl's Division). Leeds University.

ASHWORTH, Lance
St Philip's Chambers (Rex Tedd QC), Birmingham (0121) 246 7000
Recommended in the following lists: Chancery, Commercial (litigation), Personal Injury
Specialisation: Commercial Law. Group Actions. Insolvency and Directors Disqualification – Panel Counsel. Personal Injury.
Prof. Memberships: P.I.B.A. Midland Chancery and Commercial Bar Association.
Career: Oundle School. Pembroke College Cambridge. M.A (Cantab).
Personal: Married, 3 children. Desperately seeking sleep.

ASHWORTH, Piers QC
2 Harcourt Buildings (Roger Henderson QC), London (0171) 583 9020
Recommended in the following lists: Personal Injury, Product Liability
Specialisation: General commercial and contract; insurance and reinsurance; personal injuries; product liability; professional negligence and torts. One of Chambers' most distinguished practitioners. Has an extensive range of experience and expertise, particularly in the fields of negligence and other torts, and insurance. Recent reported cases include Harris v. Wyre Forest DC [1990] (surveyor's negligence); Murphy v. Brentwood PC [1991] (local authority duty of care); Thomas v. Burn [1991] (judgment Act; Gillingham BC v. Medway Dock Co [1993] (nuisance/public highways); Cambridge Water Co Ltd v. Eastern Counties Water Plc [1994] and Roebuck v. Mungovin [1994] (dismissal for want of prosecution).
Prof. Memberships: Chairman, Bar Mutual Indemnity Fund Ltd.
Career: Called to the Bar in 1956 and joined 2 Fountain Court, Birmingham. Took Silk and joined present chambers 1973. Appointed Recorder 1974. Became Deputy High Court Judge, 1980.
Personal: Educated at Christ's Hospital 1943-50 and Pembroke College, Cambridge 1952-55. Governor of Christ's Hospital. Leisure pursuits include sailing, bridge and chess. Born 27th May 1931. Lives in Berkshire.

ASPLIN, Sarah J.
3 Stone Buildings (G.C Vos QC), London (0171) 242 4937
Recommended in Pensions
Specialisation: Principal area of practice is

pensions litigation, advice and drafting. Acts for beneficiaries, principal employers and trustees in relation to questions of construction, winding up, merger, general administration and appeals from the Pensions Ombudsman. Also general chancery matters including trusts, probate and partnership advice and litigation. Cases include Imperial Tobacco, British Coal and Hillsdown Holdings Plc.
Prof. Memberships: Chancery Bar Association, Revenue Bar Association, Association of Pension Lawyers, ACTAPS.
Career: Called 1984. Joined 3 Stone Buildings 1985.
Personal: Educated at Southampton College for Girls 1976-8; Fitzwilliam College, Cambridge 1979-82 (MA Law); St Edmund Hall, Oxford 1982-83 (BCL) and College of Legal Education 1983-4.

ASPREY, Nicholas
Serle Court Chambers (Charles Sparrow QC), London (0171) 242 6105
Recommended in Parliamentary
Specialisation: Areas of practice include general chancery and commercial law, property law, probate, partnership, professional negligence, insolvency and parliamentary work.
Prof. Memberships: Chancery Bar Association, Parliamentary Bar Association, The Thomas More Society.
Career: Called 1969 and in practice at Thirteen Old Square (Charles Sparrow QC) since 1972.

ATHERTON, Ian
Enterprise Chambers (Anthony Mann QC), Newcastle upon Tyne (0191) 222 3344, London (0171) 405 9471, Leeds (0113) 246 0391
Recommended in Commercial (litigation)
Specialisation: All aspects of Commercial Chancery work with an emphasis on property litigation, professional negligence in property related fields, construction and engineering litigation and arbitration. Sits as an arbitrator in property, commercial and construction matters.
Prof. Memberships: Royal Institution of Chartered Surveyors – Associate, Chartered Institute of Arbitrators – Fellow and Panel Member, Chancery bar Association, Northern Chancery Bar Association, Professional Negligence Bar Association, Society of Construction Law, The Arbitration Club.
Career: Graduated in 1977 with BSc Quantity Surveying. From 1977 to 1987 worked as a Chartered Quantity Surveyor in the public and private sector. Read Law part-time 1983-1987. Called to the Bar 1988.
Personal: Gardening. Married to a solicitor.

ATHERTON, Peter
Deans Court Chambers (H.K. Goddard QC), Manchester (0161) 834 4097
Recommended in Environmental Law
Specialisation: Common law practice and in particular in areas of environmental law in cases involving civil or criminal liability, major accidents involving personal injury and property damage, product liability, professional negligence. Appeared for manufacturers of gas compression equipment at Piper Alpha Disaster Inquiry and in multi party actions arising from noise and dust pollution and water contamination. Experience of issues concerning clinical waste disposal and of claims for defective animal foodstuffs.
Prof. Memberships: UKELA; Environmental Law Foundation; Personal Injury Bar Association; Professional Negligence Bar Association; American Bar Association.
Career: Former Chairman of Young Barristers Committee Bar Council. Founder Member of Northern Circuit Free Representation and Advice Scheme. Called 1975 – Assistant Recorder 1994. Educated Mount St. Mary's College and Birmingham University.
Personal: Married, 2 children. Leisure pursuits include soccer, golf and walking.

ATHERTON, Robert
India Buildings Chambers (David Harris QC), Liverpool 0151 243 6000
Recommended in Crime
Specialisation: Knowledge and experience covers a wide variety of criminal cases, including murder/manslaughter, robbery, rape and other sexual offences (particularly including those involving children and children's evidence). Also handles lengthy and serious fraud cases.
Career: Called 1970.

ATHERTON, Stephen
3/4 South Square (Michael Crystal QC), London (0171) 696 9900
Recommended in Insolvency

ATKINS, Charles
29 Bedford Row Chambers (Peter Ralls QC), London (0171) 831 2626
Recommended in Family: Matrimonial Finance
Specialisation: Principal area of practice encompasses all areas of matrimonial finance and Inheritance Act claims. Also specialises in chidren cases including child abduction. Appeared in numerous high-profile and complex big-money cases.
Prof. Memberships: FLBA
Career: Called to the Bar in 1975 and joined present Chambers 1987. Assistant Recorder 1997.
Personal: MA Cantab. Secretary of Bar Cricket Club "The Refreshers".

ATKINSON, Nicholas QC
2 Harcourt Buildings (Nigel Mylne QC), London (0171) 353 2112
Recommended in Crime

ATKINSON, Timothy
1 Brick Court (Richard Hartley QC), London (0171) 353 8845
Recommended in Defamation
Specialisation: Libel and slander, breach of confidence, contempt, reporting restrictions and media law generally. Recent reported cases: Mc Donalds v Steel and Morris, Waple v Surrey County Council.
Career: Called to the Bar 1988.
Personal: Educated at St. Paul's School and Balliol College, Oxford. Lives in London.

AUSTIN-SMITH, Michael QC
23 Essex Street (Michael Lawson QC), London (0171) 413 0353
Recommended in the following lists: Crime, Crime: Fraud
Specialisation: Fraud, major crime, homicide. Also crime related civil and police law.
Prof. Memberships: C.B.A. South Eastern Circuit.
Career: Educated at Hampton Grammar School and Exeter University. Called to Bar 1969. Recorder 1986. D.T.I. Inspector 1988 & 1989. Silk 1990.
Personal: Leisure interests include sailing & rugby football.

AYERS, Guy
Octagon House Chambers (Andrew Lindqvist & Guy Ayers), Norwich (01603) 623186
Recommended in Crime

AYLIFFE, James
Wilberforce Chambers (Edward Nugee QC), London (0171) 306 0102
Recommended in Chancery
Specialisation: Specialises in Commercial/Chancery litigation including asset finance, banking, company financial services, insolvency, professional negligence, property.
Prof. Memberships: COMBAR, Chancery Bar Association.
Career: BA (Hons) Politics, Philosophy and Economics from New College, Oxford (1985). Diploma in Law from City University, London (1986) (Distinction).

BAATZ, Nicholas QC
Atkin Chambers (John Blackburn QC), London (0171) 404 0102
Recommended in Construction
Specialisation: At English Bar since 1979 specialising in construction law. Extensive experience as advocate in the Supreme Court and in Arbitration. Experience of legal and technical disputes involving commercial, industrial, residential and institutional buildings, process plant, mining, tunnels, bridges, railways, landfill and land reclamation projects, offshore structures, ships, motorways, telecommunications and computer hardware and software. Advised in relation to principal standard form building and engineering contracts; Acted as arbitrator, as legal assessor to lay arbitrators and commissioner for evidence. Advised arbitrators on arbitration law and practice. Acted as party's representative in conciliation proceedings. Advised upon drafting of industry standard form contract. Lectured and written on Building and Engineering Law.
Career: Barrister-at-Law 1978; Called to Bar Gray's Inn 1978. Editor 'Building Law Reports' since 1986 (senior editor since 1994). Editor 'Current Law' since 1980; Legal Correspondent for 'Building Technical File' 1983-90. F.C.I. Arb. 1994. QC 1998.
Personal: Educated Christ Church, Oxford 1973-77 (M.A., B.C.L.); Inns of Court School of Law 1977-78.

BACH, OF LUTTERWORTH, Lord
65-67 King St (William Bach), Leicester (0116) 254 7710
Recommended in Crime

BADENOCH, James QC
1 Crown Office Row (Robert Seabrook QC), London (0171) 797 7500
Recommended in the following lists: Medical Negligence, Personal Injury
Specialisation: Principal area of practice is medical negligence and medically-related work. Also handles personal injury matters. Major cases include Wilsher v Essex Area Health Authority (House of Lords); the Wendy Savage enquiry; and Dobbie v Medway Health Authority (Court of Appeal). Contributor to 'Medical Negligence' (Powers and Harris, Butterworths 1990 and 2nd Edn. 1994).
Prof. Memberships: Professional Negligence Bar Association, London Common Law Bar Association.
Career: Called to the Bar in 1967 and joined current chambers in 1968. Appointed Recorder 1987. Took silk 1989. Deputy High Court Judge 1994.
Personal: Educated at Dragon School, Oxford; Rugby School 1959-63 and Magdalen College, Oxford (MA) 1964-67. Born 24th July 1945. Lives in London.

BADLEY, Pamela
25-27 Castle Street (Stephen Riordan QC), Liverpool (0151) 236 5072
Recommended in Crime
Specialisation: Criminal bar, including sexual offences and cases with child witnesses, homicide, drugs and fraud.
Prof. Memberships: CBA.
Career: Warwick University LLB, Leicester University LLM, Recorder.

BAKER, Andrew
20 Essex Street (David Johnson QC), London (0171) 583 9294
Recommended in Shipping
Specialisation: Main areas of practice are dry shipping, arbitration, banking (principally international trade financing and foreign exchange trading/derivatives), international trade/commodities, conflict of laws, insurance and reinsurance (including in particular marine, mortgage indemnity insurance and LMX reinsurance). Experience as arbitrator. Reported cases include Honam Jade [1991] 1 Lloyd's Rep 38 (C/A), PNB v de Boinville

[1992] 1 Lloyd's Rep 7 (C/A), Banque Paribas v Cargill [1992] 2 Lloyd's Rep 19 (C/A), Nissho Iwai v Cargill [1993] 1 Lloyd's Rep 80 (Comm Ct), Angelic Grace [1995] 1 Lloyd's Rep 87 (C/A), Orjula [1995] 2 Lloyd's Rep 395 (Comm Ct), Nicholas H [1995] 2 Lloyd's Rep 299 (H/L), Atlas [1996] 1 Lloyd's Rep 642 (Comm Ct), Roar Marine v Bimeh Iran [1998] 1 Lloyd's Rep 423 (Comm Ct).
Prof. Memberships: Lincoln's Inn, COMBAR.
Career: Born 21.12.65. Educated at Lenzie Academy, Merton College, Oxford (reading Mathematics 1983-1986) and The City University (Diploma in Law, 1987). Called to the Bar 1988. Joined 3 Essex Court (now 20 Essex Street) in 1989.
Personal: Married with two sons. Keen golfer.

BAKER, Jacqueline
Enterprise Chambers (Anthony Mann QC), London (0171) 405 9471
Recommended in Property Litigation

BAKER, Nigel QC
9 Bedford Row (John Goldring QC), London (0171) 242 3555
Recommended in the following lists: Personal Injury, Sports Law
Specialisation: Principal area of practice is personal injury with an emphasis on maximum severity claims, sports injuries, medical negligence cases and local authority child abuse cases. Also involved in serious crime cases, both prosecuting and defending. Clients include leading insurance companies. Addresses medico-legal societies and participates in personal injury and medical negligence seminars.
Prof. Memberships: Common Law Bar Association. Founder Member, Hertfordshire Medico-legal Society. Personal Injury Bar Association, Bar Sports Law Group.
Career: Called to the Bar 1969 and joined present chambers 1973 (when located at 2 Crown Office Row). Appointed Recorder 1985. (Chairman Fulbourn Hospital Enquiry). (Member of Bar Council 1985). Took Silk 1988. Sits as Deputy High Court Judge, 1994. Bencher (Middle Temple) 1997.
Personal: Educated at Norwich School, Southampton University 1961-64 (BA Law 1st Class) and Queens' College, Cambridge 1964-66 (LLM). Leisure pursuits include football, fell-walking, gardening and music. Born 21st December 1942. Lives in Letchworth.

BAKER, Philip
Gray's Inn Tax Chambers (Milton Grundy), London (0171) 242 2642
Recommended in Tax
Specialisation: All forms of Revenue Law, with particular specialisation in international taxation (issues of residence and domicile, double taxation agreements, foreign tax credit and transfer pricing).
Prof. Memberships: Barrister, Grays Inn (1979); Visiting Professional fellow, Queen Mary and Westfield College. Committee Member, International Tax Planning Association; Member, Addington Society; Committee Member, International Fiscal Association (UK Branch); Member, Expert Panel, Fiscal Affairs Department, International Monetary Fund.
Career: 1979-1987, Lecturer in Law, School of Oriental and African Studies, London University. 1987 – present, Barrister, Grays Inn Tax Chambers.
Personal: Educated: Emmanuel College, Cambridge (MA); Balliol College, Oxford (BCL); University College, London (LLM); SOAS, London (PhD); London Business School (MBA). Married, two children. Awarded OBE, July 1997.

BALCOMBE, David
1 Crown Office Row (Robert Seabrook QC), London (0171) 797 7500
Recommended in Family: Matrimonial Finance

BALDWIN, John QC
8 New Square (Michael Fysh QC), London (0171) 405 4321
Recommended in the following lists: Computer & I.T., Intellectual Property, Media & Entertainment
Specialisation: Specialises in all aspects of intellectual property law, including patents, trade marks, copyrights, confidential information, computer law, entertainment law, passing off, trade libel, EC law, data protection, restrictive covenants and restraint of trade. Co-editor of 'Patent Law of Europe and the United Kingdom' (Butterworths). Has contributed numerous articles to scientific journals. Recent reported cases include Hoechst UK Ltd v Chemiculture Ltd (1993) FSR 270 (confidential information, information obtained under statutory power); Vodafone v Orange (Trade Marks, Malicious falsehood); MCA v Charly Records (copyright infringement); Dimplex v DeLonghi 1996 FSR 622 (patents, threats), Polylima v Finch 1995 FSR 751 (breach of confidence, restrictive covenants), Harrods v Harrods (Buenos Aires) Ltd. 1997 FSR 538 (implied licence, fiduciary duty, passing off).
Career: Called to the Bar 1977 (Gray's Inn). Took Silk 1991.
Personal: Educated at Nelson Grammar School 1958-1965, Leeds University (BSc 1st Class Hons Agricultural Chemistry) 1965-1968 and St Johns College, Oxford (D.Phil) 1968-1972. Oxford University Research Fellow (computer modelling) 1972-1975. British Council Fellowship for research in Holland 1975. Soil Science Society of Great Britain Prize 1975. Born 15th August 1947.

BALL, Alison QC
One Garden Court Family Law Chambers (Miss Eleanor F. Platt QC & Miss Alison Ball QC), London (0171) 797 7900
Recommended in the following lists: Family: Child Care including child abduction, Family: Matrimonial Finance
Specialisation: All aspects of family law.
Prof. Memberships: Family Law Bar Association, South Eastern Circuit.
Career: Called to the Bar in 1972. Founder member of One Garden Court (Family Law Chambers) 1989. Assistant Recorder 1992. Mediator (FMA) 1993. Took Silk in 1995.
Personal: Educated at Bedales School, 1955-1966 and Kings College, London University 1967-1971. Lives in London.

BAMFORD, Jeremy
Guildhall Chambers (John Royce QC), Bristol (0117) 927 3366
Recommended in the following lists: Chancery, Insolvency

BANGAY, Deborah
29 Bedford Row Chambers (Peter Ralls QC), London (0171) 831 2626
Recommended in Family: Matrimonial Finance
Specialisation: Family Law especially: Matrimonial Finance (Re P CA 1991 FLR 1 286 – wordship contempt); Private Children (GV J CA 1993 FLR 1 1008 – ouster); Public Law Children Work (Re H CAA 1994 1 FLR CA 3).
Prof. Memberships: Family Law Bar Association.
Career: 1972-6, Wycombe High School; 1976-9, Exeter University LL.B Hons; 1970-80, Council of Legal Education; 1982-92, 13 Kings Bench Walk/Hardwicke Building – 1992, 29 Bedford Row.
Personal: Football, swimming and cooking.

BANKS, Robert
100E Gt Portland Street, London (0171) 636 6323
Recommended in Crime

BANKS, Roderick l'Anson
48 Bedford Row (Roderick l'Anson Banks), London (0171) 430 2005
Recommended in Partnership
Specialisation: Exclusively partnership law. Has specialised in this area since 1977. Handles all

aspects of partnership law from the drafting and review of agreements to advice and representation in partnership disputes, arbitrations and mediations. Acts for solicitors, doctors, accountants, and other professional firms, as well as various financial and commercial institutions. Editor of 'Lindley & Banks on Partnership', Author and Editor of 'The Encyclopedia of Professional Partnerships'. Contributor of articles to 'Legal Business', 'Solicitors' Journal', 'Commercial Lawyer' and 'The Lawyer'. Has conducted seminars for NIS Group, Lawnet, CLT, National Law Tutors, Jordans and various solicitors' firms and has appeared in two videos for Legal Network TV.
Prof. Memberships: Lincoln's Inn.
Career: Called to the Bar 1974 and joined Stone Buildings, (Chambers of D.R. Stanford). Set up 48 Bedford Row in 1991, as the only chambers specialising exclusively in partnership law. CEDR Accredited Mediator, 1993. Hon. Associate of British Veterinary Association. Founder member of the Association of Partnership Practitioners.
Personal: Educated at Westminster School 1965-69 and University College London 1970-73. Leisure pursuits include reading and films. Born 5 December 1951. Lives in Beare Green, Surrey.

BANNISTER, Edward Alexander QC
3 Stone Buildings (G.C Vos QC), London (0171) 242 4937
Recommended in the following lists: Chancery, Insolvency
Specialisation: Specialises in company/insolvency and commercial litigation and all related matters, including property and contract; extensive professional negligence litigation practice. Recent cases include; Stein v Blake [1996] AC 243 (set off in insolvency); Re Senator Hanseatische Verwaltungsgesselschaft mbh [1997] 1 WLR 515 (lottery legislation – public interest winding up); Re Richborough Furniture Ltd [1996] 1 BCLC 507 (disqualification – de facto directors); Re Duckwari plc [1997] Ch 201 (now reversed – measure of compensation on breach of s 320 Companies Act 1985).
Career: Called to the Bar 1974, Silk 1991.

BARCA, Manuel
1 Brick Court (Richard Hartley QC), London (0171) 353 8845
Recommended in Defamation
Specialisation: Practises in media law; defamation; malicious falsehood; contempt of court; breach of confidence; media/literary copyright; passing off.
Career: Graduate Trainee, Reuters 1984-5. Called to the Bar 1986 (Lincoln's Inn, Levitt Scholar). Joined 1 Brick Court in 1987. Cases include: Major v New Statesman, Upjohn v BBC, Cumming v Scottish Daily Record, Watts v Times Newspapers, Bottomley v Express Newspapers, Howarth v Guardian Newspapers, British Coal v NUM, Berkoff v Times Newspapers, Stern v Piper, Home Secretary v BBC, Venables v Bose, Marks & Spencer v Granada TV, ITN v Living Marxism.
Personal: Born 1962. Educated at Wimbledon College and Churchill College, Cambridge (MA). Lives in London.

BARDA, Robin
4 Paper Buildings (Lionel Swift QC), London (0171) 583 0816
Recommended in the following lists: Family: Child Care including child abduction
Specialisation: All aspects of matrimonial, family and childcare law.
Prof. Memberships: Family Law Bar Association.
Career: B.A. Oxon 1970 (PPE). Called to the Bar 1975.

BARKER, Anthony QC
5 Fountain Court (Anthony Barker QC), Birmingham (0121) 606 0500
Recommended in Crime

BARKER, James
Enterprise Chambers (Anthony Mann QC), London (0171) 405 9471
Recommended in Property Litigation

BARKER, Kerry
Guildhall Chambers (John Royce QC), Bristol (0117) 927 3366
Recommended in Licensing
Specialisation: All aspects of licensing law including: Liquor licensing, public entertainment and local authority licensing (acting for applicants, objectors, police authorities, licensing justices and local authorities). Has expertise in Betting, Gaming and Lotteries Licensing. Former Justices' Clerk and contributor to Paterson's Licensing Acts. Publications include "Betting Gaming and Lotteries" (Fourmat Publishing 1992).

BARKER, Simon
13 Old Square (Mr Michael Lyndon-Stanford QC), London (0171) 404 4800
Recommended in Media & Entertainment
Specialisation: Media and Entertainment Litigation especially music, broadcasting and Copyright Tribunal. Commercial litigation and arbitration especially takeovers, warranty claims, company and partnership law, disputes concerning accounting and valuations, accountants' negligence. Reported cases: Copyright Tribunal, copyright infringment and remedies, breach of confidence, performers' rights, trust law, company law, contempt, accountants' negligence, insolvency, costs.
Prof. Memberships: Fellow of Institute of Chartered Accountants. Member of Chartered Institute of Arbitrators.
Career: 1976 – Qualified as chartered accountant. 1979 – Barrister, Lincoln's Inn. 1982 – Fellow ICAEW. 1995 – Assistant Recorder.

BARKLEM, Martyn
Littleton Chambers (Michael Burton QC), London (0171) 797 8600
Recommended in Computer & I.T.

BARLING, Gerald QC
Brick Court Chambers (Christopher Clarke QC), London (0171) 583 0777
Recommended in European Union/Competition
Specialisation: EC Law, UK Competition and Administrative Law.
Prof. Memberships: Vice Chairman Bar European Group (1993-94); Chairman Bar European Group (1994-96) Chairman EC Sub-Ctee, IPC Bar Council (1991-92).
Career: Called 1972, took silk 1991, Assistant Recorder 1989, Recorder 1993. Silk, Northern Ireland 1991. Important cases: R v Secretary of State for Transport ex parte: Factortame I, II, III & IV Sunday Trading cases acting for B&Q; R v MAFF ex parte RSPCA; R v SS for Trade & Industry ex parte Greenpeace; R v Customs & Excise ex parte Lunn Poly; R v IRC ex parte Commerzbank. Numerous pharmaceutical licencing cases including R v Licensing Authority ex parte Generics & R v MAFF ex parte Monsanto; R v Treasury ex parte BT; numerous appearances in ECJ Luxembourg.
Personal: Born 18 September 1949 in Preston. Educated at St. Mary's College, Blackburn and New College, Oxford. Degree in Law (First Class Hons). Scholarships include Peel Foundation (USA), Burnett Open Exhibition (Oxford), Harmsworth Entrance Exhibition (Middle Temple) and Astbury Law Scholarship (Middle Temple). Languages: French

BARLOW, Craig
29 Bedford Row Chambers (Peter Ralls QC), London (0171) 831 2626
Recommended in Administrative & Public Law
Specialisation: Specialist in public and administrative law with particular expertise in judicial review in a wide range of areas including coroners, human rights, mental health, community care, immigration, local authorities, inferior courts and tribunals. Assistant editor of specialist administrative law publications including: Crown Office Practice (Sweet & Maxwell) and Crown Office Digest (Sweet & Maxwell). Interesting cases include R v Norwich Stipendiary Magistrate Exp. Keeble [1998] The Times, Feb 5th (statutory Construction), R v Sedgemoor District Council, ex parte McCarthy [1996] 28 HLR 607 (Housing law – medical condition adequacy of authorities inquiries); R v Chippenham Magistrates Court, ex parte Thompson [1996] 160 JP 207 (Magistrate's Court – power to make hospital order); R v Wilson and Another, ex parte Williamson [1995] The Independent, 19 April (Mental Health – legality of detention); Re C [1994] 1 WLR 290 (Medical treatment – whether advance directive binding); Re C (A Minor) [1994] 1 FLR 111 (Statutory construction).
Prof. Memberships: Administrative Law Bar Association, Bar European Group.
Career: Writes and lectures on judicial review. Sometime contributor to legal journals: 'Falling at the last fence' (1993) NLJ at 158-9, 'Competence and the right to die' (1993) 143 NLJ 1719; 'Reasons for life: Solving the Sphinx's riddle' (1993) 143 NLJ 1005; 'The Black Hole Theory' (1993) 143 NLJ 322, 'When is a defence not a defence?' (1992) 142 NLJ 1765.
Personal: Educated at Nottingham Trent University (Law: 1st Class Hons). Winner of the 1991 Nottingham Law Journal Prize. Born 18th April 1969.

BARLOW, Francis
10 Old Square (Leolin Price CBE QC), London (0171) 405 0758
Recommended in Traditional Chancery
Specialisation: Specialising in the full range of Chancery matters, contentious and non-contentious, with particular emphasis on probate, breach of trust and property and advisory work and drafting relating to UK and foreign trusts and estates with associated tax advice.
Prof. Memberships: STEP, Charity Law Association, Chancery Bar Association.
Career: Dauntsey School; Christ Church, Oxford; 1962 BA; 1966 MA. Called 1965 Inner Temple; Bencher, Lincoln's Inn; Deputy Social Security Commissioner 1996; Joint editor of 'Williams on Wills', 4th, 5th, 6th and 7th editions (1974, 1980, 1987, 1996), Wills title in Halsbury's Laws 4th ed., vol 50 (reissue) and Executors title (to be published shortly).

BARNES, Margaret
3 Hare Court (William Clegg QC), London (0171) 353 7561
Recommended in Crime: Fraud
Specialisation: Principal area of practice is criminal law, particularly fraud cases, including mortgage and VAT fraud and fraud on the Legal Aid Fund. Major cases include R v. Linskill, R v. Reece (solicitors' fraud), R v. Harding and others (VAT fraud), R v. Trevelyan (corruption by Ministry of Defence official), R v. Griffiths (child abduction), R v. Impact Industries (conspiracy to defraud). R v. Cogolato (murder).
Prof. Memberships: Criminal Bar Association.
Career: Former solicitor. Articles with Ingham Clegg & Crowther, Blackpool 1968-71 and assistant solicitor 1971-73. Solicitor with Davis Hanson 1975-76. Called to the Bar and joined current chambers 1976.
Personal: Educated at Haslingden Grammar School, Rossendale, Lancashire 1955-63 and University of Sheffield 1963-67 (B. Jur). Leisure pursuits include a house in France, walking and theatre. Born 24th October 1944. Lives in London.

BARNES, Mark QC
One Essex Court (Anthony Grabiner QC), London (0171) 583 2000
Recommended in the following lists: Arbitration, Commercial (litigation), Energy & Utilities
Specialisation: Commercial law and litigation, with experience of company and insolvency law, European Community Law and administrative law, where these touch upon commercial disputes. In the commercial field, practice includes banking (and international banking), commodities, gas and electricity supply contracts, sale of commercial goods, share sales and professional negligence. Has acted and advised in arbitrations (under ICC and LME rules, and ad hoc) and in or in connection with expert determinations and redeterminations in the gas and construction industries.

BARNES, Michael QC
4 Breams Buildings (Christopher Lockhart-Mummery QC), London (0171) 430 1221/353 5835
Recommended in the following lists: Planning, Property Litigation
Specialisation: Property, local government and public law with particular emphasis on landlord and tenant, planning and judicial review. He is an editor (formerly general editor) of Hill and Redman on the Law of Landlord and Tenant and a Contributory Editor of Halsbury's Law of England, Landlord and Tenant. Sat as Inspector on the Public Inquiry into the Hinkley Point C Nuclear Power Station.
Prof. Memberships: Member of the Hong Kong Bar. Chancery Bar Association. Member of the Planning and Envrionment Bar Association and a Bencher of the Middle Temple.
Career: Called to the Bar in 1965. Took silk in 1981.

BARNES, Timothy QC
9 Bedford Row (John Goldring QC), London (0171) 242 3555
Recommended in Crime
Specialisation: Commercial fraud and other serious criminal work. Clients include SFO, CPS, HQ and CPS areas on Midland and Oxford Circuit, and major defence solicitors in London and on Circuit. Acted for the prosecution in Wallace Smith and Durnford Ford cases (SFO) and in the de Stempel fraud (CPS West Mercia). Prosecuted 'R v Kellard and others (Britannia Park Ltd)' (1990). Acted for the defence in Swithland Motors (Howes Percival, Northampton) and in Pearce (Lloyds Re-Insurance Fraud) (Kingsley Napley). Assists in teaching at seminars for accountants and lawyers on techniques of expert evidence and advocacy.
Prof. Memberships: Criminal Bar Association.
Career: Called to Bar, Gray's Inn 1968. Queen's Counsel 1986. Recorder 1987.
Personal: Educated at Bradfield College and Christ's College, Cambridge. Married with 4 children. Interests include music and gardening.

BARNETT, Jeremy V.
St. Paul's Chambers (Nigel Sangster QC), Leeds (0113) 245 5866
Recommended in Crime

BARON, Florence QC
Queen Elizabeth Building (Ian Karsten QC), London (0171) 797 7837
Recommended in Family: Matrimonial Finance

BARRACLOUGH, Nicholas
Francis Taylor Building (D.A. Pears), London (0171) 353 9942
Recommended in Crime
Specialisation: Specialist criminal law practitioner with a general practice. Recent cases include R v Frost (1998) (rape and murder), R v Costaine (1997) (hit man case).
Prof. Memberships: Criminal Bar Association.
Career: LLB (Hons). Called 1990 Inner Temple.
Personal: Born 12th March 1967.

BARRETT, John

40 King St (Philip Raynor QC), Manchester
(0161) 832 9082

Recommended in Planning

Specialisation: Town and country planning, environment, compulsory purchase, highways, local government, judicial review, waste disposal, retail, minerals and housing.
Prof. Memberships: Planning and Environment Bar Association. Member of Northern Circuit.
Career: Called 1982; elected member of Northern Circuit 1983. Former assistant editor of the Encyclopaedia of Environmental Health. Occasional lecturer at University of Newcastle-upon-Tyne.
Personal: Married with two children.

BARRETT, Penelope

3 Gray's Inn Square (Rock Tansey QC), London
(0171) 520 5600

Recommended in Crime

Specialisation: Criminal defence specialist, who promarily conducts serious criminal cases: large-scale drugs importations, fraud, serious sexual offences, murder and other violent crime. Substantial experience in representing mentally disordered offenders. Contributor to the Practical Guide to Forensic Psychotherapy. Lectures on mentally disordered offenders, disclosure and other aspects of criminal law evidence.
Prof. Memberships: Criminal Bar Association, Liberty, British Academy of Forensic Sciences, Association of Women Barristers.
Career: Called to the Bar 1982.
Personal: Educated at Haygrove Comprehensive School, Bridgwater College and Trinity Hall, Cambridge (BA Hons 1981). Born 23rd September 1959. Lives in London.

BARRY, Joseph

Mitre House Chambers (Francis P. Gilbert), London (0171) 583 8233

Recommended in Crime

BARTLETT, Andrew QC

One Paper Buildings (John Slater QC), London
(0171) 583 7355

Recommended in the following lists: Construction, Professional Negligence

Specialisation: Professional negligence, insurance/reinsurance construction, product liability. Acts for major insurance companies and Lloyds syndicates in insurance and reinsurance disputes. Recent cases include Group Josi Re v. Walbrook. Negligence practice includes engineers, architects, surveyors and solicitors. Particularly enjoys civil engineering cases with technical issues such as slope stability, foundation capacity, stiffness of superstructures, causes of flooding. Also enjoys legal issues (such as contract interpretation, as in Community Housing Assn v. Finnegan). Practises as an arbitrator in insurance, financial services and other fields.
Prof. Memberships: PNBA, London Common Law and Commercial Bar Association, ORBA, FCIArb. On panel of Chartered Institute of Arbitrators.
Career: Called to the Bar 1974, took silk 1993.
Personal: Born 1952. Educated at Whitgift School and Jesus College Oxford. Lives in Dulwich.

BARTLETT, George QC

2 Mitre Court Buildings (Michael FitzGerald QC), London (0171) 583 1380

Recommended in the following lists: Parliamentary, Planning

Specialisation: Planning, public and administrative law, including in particular energy matters; compulsory purchase and compensation; rating. Assistant Parliamentary Boundary Commissioner.
Prof. Memberships: Planning and Environmental Bar Association; Parliamentary Bar Mess.
Career: MA (Oxon).Called 1966; silk 1986 A Recorder and Deputy High Court Judge.

BARTON, Charles QC

Albion Chambers (J.C.T. Barton QC), Bristol
(0117) 927 2144

Recommended in Crime

BARWISE, Stephanie

Atkin Chambers (John Blackburn QC), London
(0171) 404 0102

Recommended in Construction

Specialisation: General commercial including all aspects of the law relating to the construction and civil engineering industry both in litigation and arbitration, including misconduct of and appeals from arbitrators: Mooney v Boot 80 BLR 66. Practice also involves professional negligence in general and in particular of architects, engineers and surveyors. A further area of specialisation is rights appurtenant to land and property: party wall disputes, easements including interference with rights of support, e.g. acted in Midland Bank plc v. Bardgrove Property Services 60 BLR 1 (Court of Appeal 1992).
Prof. Memberships: Secretary of Official Referees' Bar Association. London Common Law and Commercial Bar Association.
Career: Called to the Bar 1988. Joined Atkin Building in 1989.
Personal: Educated at Bolton School and Cambridge University (Downing College). Fluent in French and German.

BATE, David QC

Queen Elizabeth Building (David Jeffreys QC & Peter Whiteman QC), London (0171) 583 5766

Recommended in Crime

Specialisation: All aspects of criminal law with a particular emphasis on commercial fraud, white collar crime, organised crime and drugs importations. Appears primarily for the defence since taking silk
Prof. Memberships: Criminal Bar Association
Career: Called 1969. Crown Court Recorder. Took Silk 1994.
Personal: Educated at Hendon Grammar School and Manchester University (LL.B). Leisure pursuits: running, tennis, singing and wine.

BATE, Stephen

5 Raymond Buildings (Patrick Milmo QC), London (0171) 242 2902

Recommended in Media & Entertainment

Specialisation: Television, music, film, video, new media and telecommunications, dealing with contractual, intellectual property (including Copyright Tribunal), regulatory, judicial review and competition matters. Also defamation and breach of confidence. Major cases, etc. include BBC Enterprises v Hi-Tech Xtravision (rights in encrypted transmissions) Island Records v Tring (election between remedies), A&M records v VCI (copyright in sound recordings), R v ITC ex p TVNI (judicial review of Channel 3 licences), MMC Report on Channel 3 Networking, MMC Report on Cinemas, Candy Rock v PPL (Copyright Tribunal), BBC World Service TV v. Star TV (termination of television service), Enigma v Goldcrest (film rights), Nicholl v Ryder (Manager/artist dispute).
Career: Called 1981.

BATES, John H.

Old Square Chambers (Hon. John Melville Williams QC), London (0171) 269 0300

Recommended in Environmental Law

Specialisation: An experienced environmental law practitioner in both civil and criminal courts and in statutory inquiries. Has particular expertise in water pollution and waste management cases and has been involved in a number of appeals against noise related abatement notices. In addition has acted in judicial review actions on environmental matters, advised in such areas as nature conservation, contaminated land, transfrontier shipment of waste, water abstraction licensing, land drainage disputes and fishing rights.
Prof. Memberships: Chairman UK Environment Law Association 1991-1993.

Career: Author: 'Water and Drainage Law', 'Marine Environment Law', 'UK Waste Law'.

BATRA, B.L.

58 King St (Beverly Lunt), Manchester
(0161) 831 7477

Recommended in Crime

BATTEN, Stephen QC

3 Raymond Buildings (Clive Nicholls QC), London (0171) 831 3833

Recommended in the following lists: Crime, Crime: Fraud

Specialisation: All forms of Crime: White Collar (First Defendant R v Blackspur Leasing; R Szjraber for SFO); Murder (First Defendant in private prosecution for murder of Stephen Lawrence); Dishonesty (Brinks Matt); Professional Tribunals: Health & Safety (Port Ramsgate Walkway Collapse).
Career: BA (Oxon). Call 1968. QC 1989. Recorder of the Crown Court.

BATTY, Christopher M.

St. Paul's Chambers (Nigel Sangster QC), Leeds (0113) 245 5866

Recommended in Crime

BAXENDALE, Presiley QC

Blackstone Chambers (formerly 2 Hare Court) (P Baxendale QC and C Flint QC), London (0171) 583 1770

Recommended in Administrative & Public Law

Specialisation: Principal area of practice is public and administrative law. Also deals with local government, education, employment, financial services and general commercial law matters. Counsel to the Inquiry into Exports of Defence Equipment and Dual Use of Goods to Iraq.
Prof. Memberships: London Common Law and Commercial Bar Association, Administrative Law Bar Association.
Career: Called to the Bar and joined Hare Court in 1974. Appointed Junior Counsel to Crown (Common Law). Took silk in 1992.
Personal: Educated at Oxford University (MA). Governor of the LSE. Executive Committee: Justice.

BEALE, Judith

Blackstone Chambers (formerly 2 Hare Court) (P Baxendale QC and C Flint QC), London (0171) 583 1770

Recommended in Immigration & Nationality

Specialisation: Judicial Review; race and sex discrimination, immigration and nationality, employment law and education, European Convention on Human Rights.
Prof. Memberships: Administrative Law Bar Association; ELA.
Personal: Halsbury's Laws 4th ed. Vol 4(2): British Nationality title.

BEAN, David QC

Devereux Chambers (Jeffrey Burke QC), London (0171) 353 7534

Recommended in Employment

Specialisation: Principal area of practice is employment and trade union law. Also deals with commercial and general common law, administrative and education law. Major cases include Lemenda Trading v African Middle East Petroleum (conflict of laws – public policy); Kleinwort Benson v South Tyneside (local authority interest rate swaps); Ticehurst v British Telecommunications (industrial action – withdrawal of goodwill); Wandsworth LBC v NASUWT (teachers' boycott of school tests); Re Leyland DAF (employees' rights in insolvency); Clayton v Hereford & Worcester Fire Brigade (direct discrimination); London Underground v Edwards (indirect discrimination); Meade v British Fuels (transfer of undertakings). Clients include several major employers and trade unions. Author of 'Enforcement of Injunctions and Undertakings' (Jordans 1991) and 'Injunctions' (FT Law & Tax 7th Edn. 1997). Editor 'Law Reform for All' (Blackstone

1996). Lectures regularly on injunctions and on employment law.
Prof. Memberships: Employment Law Bar Association (Vice-Chairman), Employment Lawyers' Association, London Common Law Bar Association, Administrative Law Bar Association, COMBAR.
Career: Called to the Bar 1976. Recorder 1996. QC 1997. Member, Bar Council 1995-8.

BEAR, Charles
11 King's Bench Walk (Eldred Tabachnik QC and James Goudie QC), London
(0171) 632 8500
Recommended in the following lists: Employment, Planning

BEARD, Simon
Ropewalk Chambers (Richard Maxwell QC), Nottingham (0115) 947 2581/2/3/4
Recommended in Personal Injury
Specialisation: All aspects of personal injury, work with particular emphasis on defendant industrial disease (NIHL, RSI, Lung Disease) and plaintiff medical negligence counsel for defendants in Hurditch v Sheffield Health Authority. Provisional damages.
Prof. Memberships: Personal Injuries Bar Association. Professional Negligence Bar Association. Nottinghamshire Medico Legal Society, Committee Member.
Career: Call 1980. MA Jurisprudence Jesus College, Oxford.
Personal: Married, 2 children. Gardening, walking, cricket.

BEAZLEY, Thomas
Blackstone Chambers (formerly 2 Hare Court) (P Baxendale QC and C Flint QC), London
(0171) 583 1770
Recommended in the following lists: Commercial (litigation), Financial Services, Insurance & Reinsurance
Specialisation: Practice encompasses commercial law (including fraud, insurance and reinsurance), private international law and financial services. Commercial fraud work includes acting for and against insurers/reinsurers, acting in claims relating to takeovers and general international commercial and banking disputes and numerous jurisdictional disputes (eg Kleinwort Benson Ltd v Glasgow City Council [1996] 2 ALLE.R. 257 C.A.; 1997 3WLR 923 HOL); Re: Polly Peck International PLC Independent 13/05/98; Marinari v. Lloyds Bank [1993] ALL ER (EC) 84 Ausbacher v Binks Stem Times 26/06/97 C.A. Financial services work includes acting for and against regulatory bodies (permanently SFA, IMRO and SIB) and for clients under DTI investigations. Has acted for and against a number of foreign states in commercial litigation.
Prof. Memberships: COMBAR.
Career: Called to the Bar 1979 and since 1980 practised as a commercial barrister. Has acted as Arbitrator for the London Court of International Arbitration.
Personal: Working knowledge of Dutch, French and German.

BECK, James
Crown Office Row (Richard Ferguson QC), London (0171) 797 7111
Recommended in Crime

BECKETT, Richard QC
3 Raymond Buildings (Clive Nicholls QC), London (0171) 831 3833
Recommended in Licensing
Specialisation: Licensing. Work includes preparation and advice relating to applications and objections in all licensing matters, such as liquor, gaming, betting and amusement centres, representing parties at all levels from local committees to Divisional Court. Advises on lotteries and other related activities. Clients include the Rank Organisation, Ladbrokes and the J.D. Wetherspoon Organisation.

Career: Called to the Bar 1965 and joined present chambers 1967. Took silk 1987.

BELLAMY, Jonathan
39 Essex Street (Edwin Glasgow QC), London (0171) 832 1111
Recommended in Sports Law
Specialisation: General commercial law, professional negligence and insurance work, including personal injuries.
Prof. Memberships: London Common Law & Commercial Bar Association; Bar Sports Law Group.
Career: Called 1986. MA (Oxon) Jurisprudence 1985.
Personal: Fluent French. Sporting interests include tennis, golf and skiing.

BELOFF, Michael QC
4-5 Gray's Inn Square (Miss Elizabeth Appleby QC & The Hon. M. Beloff QC), London (0171) 404 5252
Recommended in the following lists: Administrative & Public Law, Civil Liberties, Employment, Immigration & Nationality, Sports Law

BELTRAMI, Adrian
3 Verulam Buildings (R. Neville Thomas QC), London (0171) 831 8441
Recommended in Banking
Specialisation: Banking, insolvency, commercial litigation, professional negligence.
Prof. Memberships: COMBAR.
Career: Educated at Stonyhurst, Downing College Cambridge and Harvard Law School. Called to the Bar 1989.
Personal: Married with one son.

BENNETT-JENKINS, Sallie
1 Hare Court (Stephen Kramer QC), London (0171) 353 5324
Recommended in Crime

BENSON, Jeremy
1 Hare Court (Stephen Kramer QC), London (0171) 353 5324
Recommended in Crime

BENSON, John
14 Castle St (Adrian Lyon), Liverpool (0151) 236 4421/8240/6759/6757
Recommended in Employment
Specialisation: Specialist practitioner in all aspects of employment law inc interlocutory relief, restrictive covenants, personal injuries, professional negligence.
Prof. Memberships: Employment Law Bar Association, Personal Injuries Bar Association.
Career: LL.B (Hons). Called to the Bar in 1978. Part-time chairman of industrial tribunals.
Personal: Age 43.

BERKSON, Simon
Exchange Chambers (William Waldron QC), Liverpool (0151) 236 7747
Recommended in Crime

BERRAGAN, Neil
Merchant Chambers (David Berkley), Manchester (0161) 839 7070
Recommended in the following lists: Chancery, Commercial (litigation)
Specialisation: Commercial and property litigation; general commercial disputes, banking, corporate insolvency and related professional indemnity work. Recent major cases and clients include: (commercial) Shell UK, Rolls Royce, UNCL, CWS, Pendragon Group, Nightfreight, TNT, UPS; (banking) RBS, Co-Operative Bank; several national insurers; (property) Ladbrokes, P & O, Whitbread; (corporate insolvency) IP clients include KPMG, Andersens; directors' disqualification for Insolvency Unit and for respondents. Commercial chancery: shareholder disputes, emergency and other restraint injunctions.
Career: Educated Pocklington School, York and Pembroke College, Oxford. Call 1982. London

chambers at 22 Old Buildings, Lincoln's Inn (Ben Hytner QC).
Personal: Lives in Alderley Edge. Married, 3 children & vasectomy. Travels in Ireland.

BERRIMAN, Trevor
10 King's Bench Walk (Ronald Thwaites QC), London (0171) 353 2501
Recommended in Crime
Specialisation: Fraud and all serious crime, R v Barrett (commercial fraud), R v Leslie (gang rape), R v Yilmar Hussan (political assasination).
Prof. Memberships: CBA; South Eastern Circuit.
Personal: Skiing, climbing and wood carving.

BERRY, Simon QC
9 Old Square (Robert Reid QC), London (0171) 405 4682
Recommended in the following lists: Chancery, Professional Negligence, Property Litigation
Specialisation: Property and Commercial Litigation.
Prof. Memberships: Chancery Bar Association, Professional Negligence Bar Association.
Career: Called to Bar 1977. Silk 1990. Assistant Recorder 1996.

BERRY, Steven
Essex Court Chambers (Gordon Pollock QC), London (0171) 813 8000
Recommended in the following lists: Insurance & Reinsurance, Shipping
Specialisation: Broad based practice, in particular the associated fields of insurance and reinsurance, shipping, international banking, international sale of goods and arbitration.
Career: Exeter College, Oxford BA (Jurisprudence) (First Class Hons); BCL (First Class Hons) 1983. Astbury Scholar, Middle Temple. Eldon Law Scholar. Called to the Bar 1984.
Personal: Born 1961.

BEVAN, John QC
2 Harcourt Buildings (Nigel Mylne QC), London (0171) 353 2112
Recommended in Crime
Specialisation: General criminal law, emphasis on high-profile serious cases. Prosecutions include: Child Abuse – Jasmine Beckford, Heidi Koseda; Terrorism – Sidhu and others (1994: 98 Criminal Appeal Reports 59); Hayes and Taylor (Harrods bombing); Patrick Kelly; McArdle and McKinley (South Quay bombing 1996); Murder – Kenneth Erskine (Stockwell Strangler), Morss and Tyler (Child Victim Daniel Handley), Miah and others (Victim, Richard Everitt), Chindamo (Headmaster, Philip Lawrence), Eades and others (Police Sergeant Robertson); Also – McLean (Notting Hill Rapist), Evans, Whitby and Burrell (death of illegal immigrant, Joy Gardner).
Prof. Memberships: Criminal Bar Association. South-Eastern Circuit.
Career: Called 1970. Treasury Counsel 1983-1997. Took Silk 1997.

BEVAN, Julian QC
Queen Elizabeth Building (David Jeffreys QC & Peter Whiteman QC), London (0171) 583 5766
Recommended in the following lists: Crime, Crime: Fraud
Specialisation: High profile general crime with emphasis on white collar fraud. Recently involved in Maxwell case; Gokal; Sanction busting cases.
Career: Former 1st Senior Treasury Counsel.

BICKERDIKE, Roger
9 Woodhouse Square (John Morris Collins), Leeds (0113) 245 1986
Recommended in Family/Matrimonial
Specialisation: Highly noted junior specialising in family/matrimonial work with particular emphasis on public law children cases and ancillary relief work. Considerable experience in appellate work both in the High Court and in the Court of Appeal. Involved in numerous reported cases, some of them landmark. Busy matrimonial practice, with an

increasing emphasis on cases where there are substantial assets.
Prof. Memberships: Member of the Family Bar Association, and Association of Lawyers for Children.
Career: Called to the Bar in 1986.

BIDDER, Neil
33 Park Place (Wyn Williams QC), Cardiff
(01222) 233313
Recommended in Personal Injury
Specialisation: Personal Injury, Criminal Law.
Prof. Memberships: Personal Injury Bar Association, Criminal Bar Association.
Career: M.A (Cantab), LLM (Dalhousie University Canada). Recorder since 1994.

BIRCH, Elizabeth
3 Verulam Buildings (R Neville Thomas QC), London (0171) 831 8441
Recommended in Alternative Dispute Resolution
Specialisation: Specialist in arbitration, mediation, commercial and maritime law including banking, commodities, conflict of laws and disputes as to jurisdiction, injunctions (anti-suit, mareva and other), insurance (marine, non-marine and Lloyd's Market), international sale of goods, oil and gas, shipping, transportation and all types of contractual and professional disputes. Receives appointments to sit as arbitrator and mediator in commercial and shipping disputes. Sat as arbitrator in numerous Lloyd's market disputes determining claims by Names against Members' Agents and Managing Agents. Founder and Director of ACI (Arbitration for Commerce and Industry), an arbitration group offering lawyer arbitrators to determine business and professional disputes in fields such as banking, insurance and financial services. Sits on the Court of Appeal Panel of mediators and has successfully mediated a number of commercial disputes.
Prof. Memberships: Fellow fo the Chartered Institute of Arbitrators (FCIArb), supporting member of the London Maritime Arbitrator's Association (LMAA), Qualified Mediator ('QDR') accredited by the Centre for Dispute Resolution (CEDR) and The Academy of Experts. Appointed to the Panels of the Lloyd's Arbitration Schemes ('LAS') Tiers 1 and 2 from 1992 to date. On the ACI Panel of Arbitrators and on the list of supporting members of LMAA available to sit as arbitrator and mediator. Sits on the part of the Commercial Court Committee which considers ADR and its role in the Commercial Court. Member of the Commercial Bar Association (COMBAR) - secretary 1993 to 1996. Member of the London Common Law and Commercial Bar Association (LCLCBA). Supporting member of the London Maritime Arbitrators' Association (LMAA).
Career: Called to Gray's Inn 1978; joined 3 Essex Court in 1980; the Chambers moved in 1994 becoming known as 20 Essex Street; joined 3 Verulam Buildings in 1998.
Personal: Leisure interests include family, skiing, tennis, gardening and community interests. Lives in London.

BIRSS, Colin
Three New Square (David E.M. Young QC), London (0171) 405 1111
Recommended in the following lists: Computer & I.T., Intellectual Property
Specialisation: Intellectual property, computer contract law. Cases before United Kingdom courts include: Merrell Dow v Norton (terfenadine – Patents Court, CA and HL), Harrods v Harrodian School (passing off – High Court and CA), Kirin – Amgen v Boehringer Mannheim (erythropoietin – Patents Court and CA), Fujitsu (Computer Software Patent – CA), NAD Electronics v NAD Computer Systems (trade mark and passing off – High Court). Chocosuisse v Cadbury (passing off Swiss chocolate). Cases before the European Patent Office include: Eli Lilly (fluoxetine), Berlex Biosciences (E. Coli inclusion bodies), Biogen

(lambda promoter), Net 1 Corp. (smart cards).
Career: Called 1990; joined chambers 1991.
Personal: Educated at Downing College, Cambridge 1983-86 (MA 1st Class Natural Sciences); City University 1988-89 (Dip Law). Born 28th December 1964.

BIRTLES, William
Old Square Chambers (Hon. John Melville Williams QC), London (0171) 269 0300
Recommended in Environmental Law
Specialisation: Principal areas of practice are environmental, planning and local government law. Has had considerable experience in both civil and criminal aspects of pollution claims including land contamination (arising from oil, toxic waste and industrial waste disposal), water (e.g. Barry Docks, Cardiff), air (particularly industrial smells and noise). Major inquiries include the Sizewell B Nuclear Power Station Inquiry (1984-1986), the second Part I Environmental Protection Act Inquiry (Cumbria 1994), the Westminster Council District Audit Inquiry (1994-1995) and various internal inquiries for local authorities.
Prof. Memberships: Planning and Local Government Bar Association; Administrative Law Bar Association; Council Member United Kingdom Environmental Law Association; Environmental Law Foundation. Senior Associate Member St. Antony's College Oxford.
Career: Academic lawyer 1968-1974. Called to the Bar 1970. Joined Old Square Chambers 1986. Recorder 1993. Publications etc: Co-author of 'Planning and Environmental Law' (Longman 1994 with Richard Stein); co-author of 'Local Government Finance Law' (Butterworths 1998 with Anna Forge). Numerous articles and chapters in books. Frequent speaker at legal conferences.

BISHOP, Edward
No. 1 Serjeants' Inn (Edward Faulks QC), London (0171) 415 6666
Recommended in Personal Injury
Specialisation: His practice falls into four main areas of specialisation: personal injury, medical negligence, police cases and general professional negligence. Represents both plaintiffs and defendants and has particluar experience in back pain cases, sports injuries and psychological damage caused by police arrest. Has also been instructed or appeared in the following notable cases: successful judicial review of a vaccine damage tribunal decision; alleged negligent mis-diagnosis of epilepsy; structured settlement for Jersey resident tetraplegic. Recent cases include Limb v Union Jack Removals (CA) (1998) The Times February 17 (striking out of claims in personal injury cases where no judgement has been entered).
Prof. Memberships: Professional Negligence Bar Association, Personal Injury Bar Association.
Career: Called to the Bar in 1985. Educated at Kings School, Canterbury and Pembroke College, Oxford.

BLACK, J.M. QC
30 Park Square (J.W. Mellor), Leeds
(0113) 243 6388
Recommended in Family/Matrimonial
Specialisation: Family Law: Re B (Parentage) [1996] 2 FLR 15 (Human Fertilisation and Embryology Act 1990); Re V (Declaration Against Parents) [1995] 2 FLR 1003 (first instance report, subsequently appealed); Re C and F (adoption, removal notice) [1997] 1 FLR 190.
Career: Called 1976, QC 1994. Co-author 'The Family Court Practice' (Family Law); 'A Practical Approach to Family Law' (Blackstone).

BLACK, John QC
18 Red Lion Court (Anthony Arlidge QC), London (0171) 520 6000
Recommended in Crime

BLACKBURN, Elizabeth QC
4 Field Court (Geoffrey Brice QC), London (0171) 440 6900
Recommended in Shipping
Specialisation: All aspects of maritime law including carriage of goods, international trade, collision, salvage, towage, general average, marine pollution, insurance, arbitration, jurisdictional disputes, offshore structures/pipeline work. Also sits as a commercial arbitrator. Major cases: The Abidin Daver; The Goring; The Sea Prince; The Nakhodka; The Iron Baron; Higham v Stena Sealink.
Prof. Memberships: London Maritime Arbitrators Association (supporting member), Environmental Law Association, British Insurance Law Association, London Common Law and Commercial Bar Association, Commercial Bar Association, British Maritime Law Association.
Career: Educated City of London School for Girls; Manchester University BA Hons 1976 Class II Div. 1. Bar Part 1 and Finals. Called to Bar of Middle Temple 1978. QC 1998.
Personal: Gardening, art, family life, France.

BLACKBURN, John QC
Atkin Chambers (John Blackburn QC), London (0171) 404 0102
Recommended in the following lists: Arbitration, Computer & I.T., Construction
Specialisation: In the fields of building and civil engineering disputes, professional negligence actions involving contractors and engineers and arbitration, including international arbitration. Has conducted several heavy disputes under rules of the International Chamber of Commerce in Paris. Has been appointed Arbitrator in disputes arising out of construction contracts under the International Chamber of Commerce, also acts as arbitrator over disputes arising in England. Has been admitted to the bar in Hong Kong and Singapore to conduct cases arising out of building and civil engineering contracts. Construction Law Experience has involved him in advising upon, presenting and defending all kinds of building and civil engineering claims Worldwide. Advises and acts for numerous Public Corporations. Advises on and drafts various kinds of building and different types of engineering contracts. Work undertaken generally involves substantial projects involving sophisticated plan, and building and engineering structures including tunnels, dams and hydro-electric schemes.
Career: Called to the Bar 1969. Took silk 1984.

BLACKETT-ORD, Mark
5 Stone Buildings (Henry Harrod), London (0171) 242 6201
Recommended in Partnership
Specialisation: Well-known for his experience in advice and litigation concerning partnerships and other quasi-corporate bodies, from unincorporated associations to bodies alleged to be carrying on the business of insurance (Re a company No. 007816 of 1994) (1997) 2 BCLC 685. Has appeared in cases at all levels to the House of Lords and European Court (Webb v Webb (1994) QB 696). Co-edited the original 4th edition of 'Partnership' in Halsbury Laws of England, and wrote the major new book 'Partnership' (Butterworth, 1997).

BLACKWELL, Kate
Lincoln House Chambers (Mukhtar Hussain QC), Manchester (0161) 832 5701
Recommended in Crime

BLAIR, Bruce QC
1 Mitre Court Buildings (Bruce Blair QC), London (0171) 797 7070
Recommended in Family: Matrimonial Finance

BLAIR, William QC
3 Verulam Buildings (R. Neville Thomas QC), London (0171) 831 8441
Recommended in the following lists: Banking, Financial Services
Specialisation: Commercial work, domestic and international banking, arbitration, business law, commercial fraud, company law, financial services, international trade, insolvency, private international law. Cases include: Esal v Oriental Credit 1985; LAFB v Bankers Trust 1988; LAFB v Manufacturers Hanover 1989; IE Contractors v Lloyds Bank 1990; Barclays Bank v O'Brien 1993; Macmillan v Bishopsgate 1994; Polly Peck v Citibank 1994; TSB v Camfield 1995; Wahda Bank v Arab Bank 1998.
Career: Called to the Bar 1972, Silk 1994. Visiting professor of law (London School of Economics), member of the International Monetary Law committee of the International Law Association, member of FLP working party on Single European Currency, assistant recorder. Co-editor 'Encyclopaedia of Banking Law', co-author 'Banking and Financial Services Regulation'.

BLAKE, Andrew
18 St. John Street (Rodney C. Klevan QC), Manchester (0161) 278 1800
Recommended in Crime

BLAKE, Nicholas QC
Two Garden Court (I. Macdonald QC & O. Davies), London (0171) 353 1633
Recommended in the following lists: Administrative & Public Law, Civil Liberties, Immigration & Nationality
Specialisation: Practises in the field of public and adminstrative law with particular emphasis on immigration and asylum and human rights issues connected with public officials. Recent cases: Asylum and immigration: Onibiyo (CA) T (HL), Adan (HL), Islam and Shah (CA). Public law: ex p JCWI and B (CA), ex p Avraam (CA), ex p Castelli. Actions for damages: Makanjuola (CA), Oluto (CA), W (CA). ECJ: Radiom, Surinder Singh. ECHR: Chahal, XYZ, D v. UK. Crime: Judith Ward (CA), ex p Hickey and Davis (DC). Privy Council: Guerra v. Trinidad. Principal publications: Macdonald and Blake 'Immigration Law and Practice' 3rd, 4th editions and Supplement.
Prof. Memberships: ALBA, ILPA (Chair 1993-1997), JUSTICE Member of Council 1996 – .
Career: Called MT 1974, in present chambers since 1975; QC (1994).
Personal: Educated at Cranleigh School, Magdalene College, Cambridge. Married with 3 children.

BLANCHARD, Claire
Essex Court Chambers (Gordon Pollock QC), London (0171) 813 8000
Recommended in the following lists: Commercial (litigation), Employment, Shipping
Specialisation: Broad-based commercial practice. In particular Shipping, Insurance, Banking, Conflicts and Employment.
Career: Liverpool Polytechnic LLB (Hons) 1991. Inns of Court School of Law. Called to the Bar 1992.
Personal: Born 1969.

BLAXLAND, Henry
Two Garden Court (I. Macdonald QC & O. Davies), London (0171) 353 1633
Recommended in the following lists: Civil Liberties, Crime
Specialisation: Criminal law at Crown Court and appellate level. Some leading work. Junior counsel in appeals of Colin Wallace, Michael Hickey (the Carl Bridgewater murder), and Derek Bentley.
Prof. Memberships: CBA. Justice, Amnesty International Lawyers Group.
Career: BA in English Literature.

BLEASDALE, Paul
5 Fountain Court (Anthony Barker QC), Birmingham (0121) 606 0500
Recommended in the following lists: Administrative & Public Law, Personal Injury
Specialisation: Personal Injury Litigation; Plaintiff and Defendants. In particular industrial disease claims and also medical negligence. Planning and Environment; Developers and Local Authorities. Appeals and Local Plan, UDP and Compulsory Purchase Inquiries.
Prof. Memberships: Personal Injuries Bar Association, Planning Environment Bar Association.
Career: London University, Recorder of the Crown Court, Deputy Chairman of the Agricultural Lands Tribunal.

BLOCH, Michael QC
One Essex Court (Anthony Grabiner QC), London (0171) 583 2000
Recommended in the following lists: Computer & I.T., Intellectual Property

BLOCH, Selwyn
Littleton Chambers (Michael Burton QC), London (0171) 797 8600
Recommended in the following lists: Commercial (litigation), Computer & I.T., Employment
Specialisation: Practice encompasses business law and employment law. Work includes general commercial litigation, restraint of trade, garden leave and other interlocutory injunctions, confidential information, wrongful and unfair dismissal, discrimination, entertainment and sports law. Co-author, 'Employment Covenants and Confidential Information' (Butterworths, 1993). Contributor to conferences on employment law.
Prof. Memberships: ELBA, COMBAR, ELA.
Career: Attorney, South Africa 1976. Called to the Bar 1982 and joined current chambers in the same year.
Personal: Educated at Stellenbosch and Witwatersrand Universities, South Africa. (BA, LL.B). Born 23rd February 1952. Lives in London.

BLOCK, Neil
39 Essex Street (Edwin Glasgow QC), London (0171) 832 1111
Recommended in Personal Injury
Specialisation: A contract and tort based practice. Insurance (including policy avoidance/fraud and material loss claims eg McGregor v Prudential Assurance Co 1998 Lloyds). Personal injury (including sporting cases eg Smolden v Whitworth & Nolan, O'Neill v Wimbledon & Fashanu), catastrophic injury claims, medical negligence (in particular paediatric brain damage), professional negligence (including solicitors, accountants, surveyors and valuers, architects, stockbrokers and insurance brokers) and product liability.
Prof. Memberships: Professional Negligence Bar Association, Personal Injury Bar Association, London Common Law and Commercial Bar Association, Bar Sports Law Group.
Career: Called to the Bar in 1980.
Personal: B.A. (Hons), LLM (Exon).

BLOHM, Leslie
St. John's Chambers (Roderick Denyer QC), Bristol (0117) 921 3456
Recommended in Chancery

BLUNT, Oliver QC
Furnival Chambers (Andrew Mitchell), London (0171) 405 3232
Recommended in Crime
Specialisation: Entirely defence-based practice with a substantial emphasis on murder, terrorism, fraud & drugs cases. Represented such clients as Maria Hnatiuk (Murder – Norwich Crown Court 1996), Michael Boyle (ex I.R.A. contract gunman – CCC 1996), Maria O'Sullivan V.A.T. fraud – (CCC 1995) Pornography (Southwark Crown Court 1996), Ngarimu (female contract killer – CCC 1995), Celia Becket (Infanticide – Nottingham Crown Court

1995) & Michael Sams (Kidnapping, blackmail, false imprisonment & murder – Nottingham Crown Court 1993). Acted on behalf of the Iranian Embassy and defended two members of the consulate staff in separate terrorist trials (Regina -v- Tabari-Abcou & Regina -v- Fouladi). Appeared for the second defendant in Regina v Canning and Lamb (I.R.A. Trial CCC 1993). Conducted the trial and successful appeal of the leaders of the Chelsea 'Headhunters' (Regina -v- Drake and others), the first major football hooligan case. Appointed by the Registrar of Court of Criminal Appeals to conduct two Home Secretary's references relating to murder cases involving a discredited forensic scientist (Clift). In 1992 represented the only two defendants (Cahill and Bussutil) to be acquitted in a £90 million amphetamine sulphate product in case (Regina v Butler and others Wood Green Crown Court). In 1993 successfully defended the first defendant in £150 million cocaine importation on the Foxtrot Five (Regina v Hillier and others – Southwark Crown Court) the largest recorded drug importation ever into the UK at the time. Acted for Syd Owen, 'Ricky' of Eastenders (acquitted of wounding – Snaresbrook Crown Court 1995). In 1997 appeared for the only defendant (Casey) to be acquitted in a multi-million pound arson/insurance fraud (Regina v Ellis and others CCC).
Prof. Memberships: S.E. Circuit. Criminal Bar Association.
Career: Called to Bar 1974. Queen's Counsel 1994. Recorder 1995.
Personal: Born 8/3/51. Married with 4 children. Member of Roehampton Club and Barnes Cricket Club.

BODEY, David QC
Queen Elizabeth Building (Ian Karsten QC), London (0171) 797 7837
Recommended in the following lists: Family: Child Care including child abduction, Family: Matrimonial Finance
Specialisation: Family. Matrimonial finance/child care including child abduction both private and public law. Acted for Official Solicitor in his role as guardian ad litem in S. Pembrokeshire paedophile trial. M:D & Ors 1996 3FCR 581. Gave evidence to the House of Lords Committee on the Domestic Violence and Family Homes Bill 1995 now part of the Family Law Act 1996. Has acted in numerous Family Law leading cases.
Prof. Memberships: Chairman of Family Law Bar Association.
Career: Called 1970. QC 1991. Recorder 1993; Deputy High Court Judge 1995.

BOMPAS, Anthony George QC
4 Stone Buildings (Philip Heslop QC), London (0171) 242 5524
Recommended in the following lists: Chancery, Company, Financial Services, Insolvency
Specialisation: Principal area of practice is company law (all aspects, including minority shareholders proceedings and insolvency) and financial services. Other main area of practice is professional negligence work. Has been instructed in many of the major, widely publicised, company matters in recent years, including the Guinness affair, the Blue Arrow, the Barlow Clowes, and the Brent Walker and BCCI affairs. Author of 'Investigations by the DTI' in Tolley's 'Company Law' (3rd Ed.).
Prof. Memberships: Chancery Bar Association, Insolvency Lawyers' Association and Commercial Bar Association (COMBAR).
Career: Called to the Bar 1975 and joined present chambers in 1976. Junior Counsel to the DTI 1989-94. Took Silk in 1994.
Personal: Educated at Merchant Taylors' School, Northwood 1964-69 and Oriel College, Oxford 1970-74. Born 6th November 1951.

BONEY, Guy QC
Pump Court Chambers (Guy Boney QC), Winchester (01962) 868161
Recommended in Crime
Specialisation: All aspects of serious criminal work, principally on Western Circuit but also London. Also handles personal injury and family cases.
Prof. Memberships: Criminal Bar Association, London Common Law Bar Association.
Career: Called to the Bar 1968; Silk 1990. Assistant Recorder 1982; Recorder 1985; Deputy High Court Judge 1994; authorised to sit at Old Bailey 1995. Educated Winchester; New College, Oxford.
Personal: Married to QC, 2 children. Hobbies; Music, antiques. Born 28/12/44.

BOOTH, Alan James
Deans Court Chambers (H.K. Goddard QC), Manchester (0161) 834 4097
Recommended in Family/Matrimonial
Specialisation: Ancillary relief and professional negligence arising out of ancillary relief.
Prof. Memberships: FLBA, PNBA.
Career: Bolton School (Boy's Division). Selwyn College Cambridge.
Personal: Married, 2 children.

BOOTH, Cherie QC
4-5 Gray's Inn Square (Miss Elizabeth Appleby QC & The Hon. M. Beloff QC), London (0171) 404 5252
Recommended in the following lists: Administrative & Public Law, Employment
Specialisation: Specialist in all aspects of employment law including trade union rights and discrimination law. Also specialises in public administrative law. Notable public law includes E v Dorset County Council and others [1995]. Notable employment cases this year are Grant v SW Trains (sexual orientation discrimination). Preston v Wolverhampton NHS Trust [1997] IRLR 233 Barry v Midland Bank [1998] IRLR 138 (both sex discrimination cases) and Wilson v St Helens Borough Council [1997] IRLR 505. Phelps v LB of Hillingdon (dyslexia), White and others v Ealing LBC (SEN) R v Treasury ex parte Shepherd Neame (VAT).
Prof. Memberships: Employment Law Bar Association, Administrative Law Bar Association, COMBAR, Industrial Law Society, ELA.
Career: Called to the Bar 1976. Tenant at New Court Chambers 1977-91, before joining present chambers in 1991. Former Chair of Bar Information Technology Committee. Took Silk in 1995. Chair of the Bar Conference 1997. The Lawyers Magazine Legal Personality of the Year 1997. Vice Chair of the Equal Opportunities Committee to Bar Council.
Personal: Educated at Seafield Grammar School 1965-72, and at the London School of Economics (LL.B) 1972-75. Former Parliamentary candidate for Thanet North in 1983. School governor, governor of LSE. Leisure pursuits include keep fit, theatre, reading and spending time with her children. Born 23rd September 1954. Lives in Downing Street.

BOOTH, Michael
40 King St (Philip Raynor QC), Manchester (0161) 832 9082
Recommended in Chancery
Specialisation: Chancery and commercial, including company, insolvency, property, computer related litigation (hardware and software including copyright ownership), commercial contracts, banking, professional negligence and competition aspects relating to the above.
Career: Scholarship to Manchester Grammar School. Open scholarship to Trinity College Cambridge. President Cambridge Union Society, Michaelmas 1979.
Personal: Married, three young children. Hobbies include walking, swimming, tennis, reading (literature and history), theatre, wine and antiques. Avid football fan.

BORRELLI, Michael
1 Middle Temple Lane (Colin Dines & Andrew Trollope QC), London (0171) 583 0659 (12 lines)
Recommended in Crime

BOSWELL, Lindsay QC
4 Pump Court (Bruce Mauleverer QC), London (0171) 353 2656
Recommended in the following lists: Commercial (litigation), Construction, Professional Negligence
Specialisation: Specialises in professional negligence (solicitors, accountants, insurance brokers, architects, surveyors, valuers, local authorities), construction, employment, aviation, administrative law and art litigation.
Prof. Memberships: PNBA, COMBAR, ELBA, LCLCBA, ORBA.
Career: BSc (London) Econ (Hons) Economics and Social Anthropology. Diploma in Law (City University).

BOSWOOD, Anthony QC
Fountain Court (Peter Scott QC), London (0171) 583 3335
Recommended in the following lists: Commercial (litigation), Energy & Utilities, Insurance & Reinsurance

BOTHROYD, Shirley
Littleton Chambers (Michael Burton QC), London (0171) 797 8600
Recommended in Employment

BOULDING, Philip QC
Keating Chambers (Richard Fernyhough QC), London (0171) 544 2600
Recommended in the following lists: Construction, Energy & Utilities
Specialisation: Construction and civil engineering law, including arbitration and professional negligence.
Career: Qualified 1979; Gray's Inn; Queen's Counsel 1996. Admitted to Hong Kong Bar 1997.
Personal: Downing College, Cambridge (1976) BA Law 1st class Hons, (1977) postgraduate LLB (now LLM), 1979 MA; 1976 elected to title of Scholar of Downing College, 1976 Harris Scholar, 1976 Pilley Scholar, 1977 Senior Harris Scholar, 1976 Rebecca Flowers Squire Scholar. Gray's Inn Holken Entrance Award (1978) and Gray's Inn Senior Holken Award (1979). Born 1954. Clients in this field include local authorities, major PLCs, international joint ventures, governments and professionals from all the construction and engineering disciplines. Current instructions involve many of the largest Hong Kong airport core contracts.

BOURNE, Ian
3 Temple Gardens (Jonathan Goldberg QC), London (0171) 583 1155
Recommended in Crime

BOURNE-ARTON, Simon QC
Park Court Chambers (James Stewart QC, Robert Smith QC), Leeds (0113) 243 3277
Recommended in Crime

BOWDERY, Martin
Atkin Chambers (John Blackburn QC), London (0171) 404 0102
Recommended in Construction
Specialisation: Barrister specialising in construction and civil engineering.
Career: Called 1980, Inner Temple.

BOWERS, John QC
Littleton Chambers (Michael Burton QC), London (0171) 797 8600
Recommended in Employment
Specialisation: Employment law, pensions, judicial review, discrimination. Recent cases have included Associated British Ports v TGWU (injunctions to prevent national dock strike); McLaren v Home Office (role of judicial review in employment); News Group Newspapers Ltd v SOGAT and Others ("the Wapping cases"); Porter & Nanayakkara v Queens

Medical Centre (dismissal of Consultant Paediatricians following Allitt murders); Saatchi & Saatchi plc v M. Saatchi and C. Saatchi and Others (garden leave case); Sibson v UK (application to European Court of Human Rights on remedies for disadvantages caused to employees who are not members of trade unions in "closed shops"). Author of many publications including 'Bowers on Employment Law', 'Textbook of Labour Law', 'Transfer of Undertakings', 'Industrial Tribunal Practice', The Employment Act 1988, 'The Employment Law Manual' (chapter on Tribunals) and 'Basic Procedure in Courts and Tribunals'
Prof. Memberships: ELBA, ALBA, ELA

BOWES, Michael
2 King's Bench Walk (Anthony Donne QC), London (0171) 353 1746
Recommended in Crime: Fraud
Specialisation: Main area of practice is criminal law, specialising in commercial fraud. Has also prosecuted and defended across the range of serious crime. Other areas of practice are financial regulatory work and licensing.
Prof. Memberships: Criminal Bar Association, Western Circuit.
Career: Called to the Bar in 1980. Joined 2 King's Bench Walk in 1996.
Personal: Educated at St George's College, Weybridge (1969-75), Manchester University (LL.B) 1976-79. Born on 22nd December 1956.

BOWLES, Timothy
Barnards Inn Chambers (Timothy Bowles), London (0171) 242 8508
Recommended in Property Litigation
Specialisation: Landlord and Tenant, Real Property Litigation, Chancery Litigation. Leading cases include Lloyds Bank v Rosset 1991 1AC 107 (Leading House of Lords case on constructive trusts; in Court of Appeal also on Land registration – contracts for the sale of land – equitable priorities); New England Properties v Portsmouth News Shops 1993 EGLR 84 (Repairing Covenants); Cordon Bleu Freezer Foods v Marbleace Ltd 1987 1 EGLR 143 (Rent Review). Funnell v Stewart 1996 1 WLR 288 (Charities). Prudential Assurance Co v Waterloo Real Estate Times May 13 1998 (adverse possession).
Prof. Memberships: Deputy Master of the Chancery division – Chancery Bar Association; Fellow of the Chartered Institute of Arbitrators; Deputy Chairman – Agricultural Land Tribunal; Chairman – London and South Eastern Rent Assessment Panels and Leasehold Valuation Tribunals.
Career: Called 1973 Gray's Inn. Senior (Mold) Scholar.
Personal: Born March 1951. Lives in Guildford, Surrey. Enjoys sailing.

BOWRON, Margaret
1 Crown Office Row (Robert Seabrook QC), London (0171) 797 7500
Recommended in Medical Negligence

BOYCE, William
Queen Elizabeth Building (David Jeffreys QC & Peter Whiteman QC), London (0171) 583 5766
Recommended in the following lists: Crime, Crime: Fraud
Specialisation: Crime and linked regulatory and disciplinary proceedings – especially high profile, grave and complex criminal matters from homicide to serious fraud.
Prof. Memberships: Criminal Bar Assocation.
Career: Called to the Bar in 1976. Senior Treasury Counsel at the Central Criminal Court. Recorder.

BOYD, Stewart QC
Essex Court Chambers (Gordon Pollock QC), London (0171) 813 8000
Recommended in the following lists: Arbitration, Insurance & Reinsurance, Shipping
Specialisation: Arbitration, banking, commodity contracts, company law and insolvency,

competition and restrictive practices, construction, copyright, EEC law, employment, financial services, industrial relations, insurance and reinsurance, oil and gas, private international law, shipping and aviation. Has been appointed an arbitrator in numerous international commercial disputes in many fields, such as advertising, banking, commercial agency, computer software, construction, electricity generation and transmission, insurance and reinsurance, intellectual property, oil and gas, shipping. **Career:** Trinity College, Cambridge: MA. Called to the Bar 1967. Queen's Counsel 1981. **Personal:** Born 1943.

BOYLE, Alan QC
Serle Court Chambers (Charles Sparrow QC), London (0171) 242 6105
Recommended in the following lists: Chancery, Company
Specialisation: Commercial and chancery litigation, financial services and entertainment. Cases during the last year include: Thyssen-Bornemisza v Thyssen Bornemisza (undue influence, waiver of legal profession privilege, Court of Appeal, Bermuda); Goose v Wilson Sandford (delay in delivering judgement, miscarriage of justice, order for new trial, Court of Appeal). Atlantic litigation (claims by British and Commonwealth arising out of takeover of failed computer leasing company).
Prof. Memberships: Member Supreme Court Rules Committee. Deputy High Court Judge. Editor and contributor, The Practice and Procedure in the Companies Court, Lloyds of London Press.
Career: Royal Shrewsbury School, St Catherine's College Oxford (MA). Called to the Bar 1972. Silk 1991.
Personal: Married, two daughters.

BRADLEY, Anthony
Cloisters (Laura Cox QC), London (0171) 827 4000
Recommended in Administrative & Public Law
Specialisation: Public law, representing applicants for judicial review and public authorities, and advising on constitutional issues. Important cases include M v Home Office [1994] and R v Devon County Council ex p. Baker [1995]. Publications include Bradley and Ewing, 'Constitutional and Administrative Law' (12th ed. 1997 – with K.D. Ewing) and 'European Human Rights Law: Text and Materials' (1995 – with M. Janis and R. Kay). Consultant on administrative law to the Commonwealth Secretariat.
Prof. Memberships: Administrative Law Bar Association, Education Law Association.
Career: Formerly a solicitor (1960-89). Fellow of Trinity Hall, Cambridge 1960-68. Professor of Constitutional Law, University of Edinburgh 1968-89. Called to the Bar in 1989.
Personal: Hon LLD, Staffordshire University (1993) and Edinburgh University (1998).

BRADLEY, Sally
Broad Chare Chambers (Eric A Elliott), Newcastle upon Tyne (0191) 232 0541
Recommended in Family/Matrimonial

BRAITHWAITE, Bill QC
Exchange Chambers (William Waldron QC), Liverpool (0151) 236 7747
2 Crown Office Row (Graeme Hamilton QC), London (0171) 797 8100
Recommended in Personal Injury
Specialisation: Personal injury litigation, including medical negligence, with a particular interest in injury to the brain and spine. The Consultant Editor of Kemp & Kemp on ' The Quantum of Damages'. Joint Editor of 'Medical Aspects of Personal Injury Litigation' (1997).
Prof. Memberships: European Brain Injury Society; International Medical Society of Paraplegia; Spinal Injuries Association; Association of Personal Injury Lawyers.
Career: Called 1970, QC 1992.

Personal: Gordonstoun School, Liverpool University. Class 1 Heavy Goods Vehicle Licence. Motor Racing Competition Licence.

BRAMWELL, Richard QC
3 Temple Gardens (David Braham QC), London (0171) 353 7884
Recommended in Tax
Specialisation: Principal areas of practice are corporate and personal tax planning and tax disputes. Well-known within the football industry. Guest speaker at the Inland Revenue's 1996 Technical Conference on Tax Appeals. Co-Author of 'Taxation of Companies and Company Reconstructions' (7th Edition, 1998). Member of the Editorial Boards of 'Taxation' and 'The Offshore Taxation Review'.
Career: Took silk in 1989.

BRAND, Simon
Coleridge Chambers (Simon D. Brand), Birmingham (0121) 233 3303
Recommended in Crime

BRANTHWAITE, Margaret
One Paper Buildings (John Slater QC), London (0171) 583 7355
Recommended in the following lists: Alternative Dispute Resolution, Medical Negligence

BRASSE, Gillian
14 Gray's Inn Square (Joanna Dodson QC), London (0171) 242 0858
Recommended in the following lists: Family: Child Care including child abduction, Family: Matrimonial Finance
Specialisation: Practice covers all aspects of Family work including public and private law cases under the Children Act, wardship, adoption and child abduction, as well as ancillary relief matters, and Inheritance Act cases. Reported cases include O v Berkshire C.C. (Education Procedure)(1992)2FLR7, Re B Contact (1994) 2FLR1, Re W (arrangements to place for adoption) (1995) 1FLR163. Conran v Conran [1997] 2 FLR 615 (Money – wife's contribution).
Prof. Memberships: Family Law Bar Association, Association of Lawyers for Children, committee member, Bar Benevolent Association.
Career: Called 1977. Appointed Deputy District Judge September 1995.
Personal: Educated at Varndean School for Girls, Brighton, and Liverpool University. Leisure pursuits include: travel, concerts, theatre, eating out, keep fit, my two daughters.

BRATZA, Nicolas QC
1 Hare Court (Lord Neill of Bladen QC & Richard Southwell QC), London (0171) 353 3171
Recommended in Commercial (litigation)

BREALEY, Mark
Brick Court Chambers (Christopher Clarke QC), London (0171) 583 0777
Recommended in the following lists: Aviation, European Union/Competition

BRENNAN, Daniel QC
39 Essex Street (Edwin Glasgow QC), London (0171) 832 1111
Recommended in the following lists: Medical Negligence, Product Liability

BRENNAN, Timothy
Devereux Chambers (Jeffrey Burke QC), London (0171) 353 7534
Recommended in the following lists: Employment, Tax

BRENNAND, T.W.
Manchester House Chambers (J.D.S. Wishart), Manchester (0161) 834 7007
Recommended in Crime

BRENT, Michael QC
9 Gough Square (Jeremy Roberts QC), London

(0171) 353 5371
Recommended in the following lists: Medical Negligence, Personal Injury
Specialisation: Plaintiff personal injury (particularly injuries of maximum severity), fatal accident and medical negligence cases, often involving structured settlements. Cases include: Arnold v CEGB, Loveday v Renton, Almond v Leeds WHA, Wilson v Graham, Hayden v Hayden, Boocock v Hilton International, Allen v Bloomsbury HA, Smith v Glennon, Robinson v Jacklin and Fitzgerald v Ford.
Prof. Memberships: Personal Injuries Bar Association, Professional Negligence Bar Association, London Common Law & Commercial Bar Association, APIL and AVMA.
Career: Called 1961, took silk in 1983. Recorder 1990. Deputy High Court Judge in 1994.
Personal: Educated at Manchester Grammar School and Manchester University.

BRENTON, Timothy QC
4 Essex Court (Nigel Teare QC), London (0171) 797 7970
Recommended in Shipping
Specialisation: Principal areas of practice are shipping (including Admiralty), international trade, commercial contracts, insurance (marine and non-marine), reinsurance, sale and carriage of goods (international and domestic) and commercial fraud. On editorial board of 'International Maritime Law' (Law Text Publishing Ltd). Appointed QC 1998.
Prof. Memberships: COMBAR, supporting member of London Maritime Arbitration Association.
Career: Royal Navy 1975-79. Lecturer in law at King's College, London 1979-80. Called to the Bar 1981 and joined 4 Essex Court.
Personal: Educated at King's School, Rochester to 1975; Bristol University 1976-79 (LLB) and Bar School 1980-81. Born 4th November 1957.

BRETTEN, Rex QC
24 Old Buildings (G.R Bretten QC), London (0171) 242 2744
Recommended in Tax
Specialisation: All aspects of United Kingdom taxation, with special emphasis on multi-national corporate work, the interaction of United Kingdom and foreign taxes, and the operation of Double Taxation Treaties; Tax Litigation.
Career: Commenced practice at the Bar in 1971. Appointed Queen's Counsel in 1980. Appointed a Bencher of Lincoln's Inn in 1989.

BRICE, Geoffrey QC
4 Field Court (Geoffrey Brice QC), London (0171) 440 6900
Recommended in Shipping
Specialisation: Principal areas of practice are admiralty and commercial law (including arbitration). Author of 'Maritime Law of Salvage' (2nd ed. 1993, 3rd edition with publishers) and numerous articles in periodicals in the UK, USA and Europe.
Career: Called to the Bar and joined present chambers in 1960. Lloyd's Salvage Arbitrator 1978, Wreck Commissioner 1978. Took Silk 1979. Appointed Recorder 1980 and Bencher of Middle Temple 1986. Visiting Professor of Maritime Law, Tulane University, USA since 1989 and University of Natal, South Africa, since 1996. Deputy High Court Judge since 1996.
Personal: Educated at University College, London (LL.B 1959). Born 21st April 1938. Lives in London.

BRIDEN, Timothy J.
8 Stone Buildings (John Cherry QC), London (0171) 831 9881
Recommended in the following lists: Ecclesiastical, Health & Safety
Specialisation: Principal area of practice is ecclesiastical law. Editor, 'Macmorran's Handbook for Churchwardens and Parochial Church Councillors' and 'Moore's Introduction to English Canon Law'. Also handles personal injury and

Health & Safety cases.
Prof. Memberships: Inner Temple, Ecclesiastical Law Society.
Career: Called to the Bar 1976; joined 1 Temple Gardens 1977 and moved to 8 Stone Buildings 1996. Appointed Chancellor of the Diocese of Bath and Wells 1993 and Chancellor of the Diocese of Truro 1998. Secretary of Ecclesiastical Judges Association since 1996.
Personal: Educated at Ipswich School 1958-70 and Downing College Cambridge (BA 1974; LL.B 1975; MA 1978). Born 29th October 1951. Lives in South London.

BRIDGE, Rowena
King Charles House (William Everard), Nottingham (0115) 941 8851
Recommended in Family/Matrimonial

BRIGGS, John
3/4 South Square (Michael Crystal QC), London (0171) 696 9900
Recommended in the following lists: Insolvency, Traditional Chancery
Specialisation: All personal and corporate insolvency related work, including representing insolvency practitioners before Recognised Professional Bodies and Insolvency Practitioners Tribunal.
Prof. Memberships: Insolvency Lawyers Association. British Italian Law Association (Committee Member).
Career: LLB (London). Ex. Du Doc d'Univ (Nancy, France). 1973: Called to the Bar. 1973-75: Jurist Linguist, European Court of Justice. Deputy Bankruptcy Registrar of the High Court. Joint Senior Author, Muir Hunter on Personal Insolvency (Stevens, 1987). Joint Author, Asset Protection Trusts (Keyhaven, 1997).

BRIGGS, Michael QC
Serle Court Chambers (Charles Sparrow QC), London (0171) 242 6105
Recommended in the following lists: Commercial (litigation), Chancery, Company, Insolvency, Partnership, Property Litigation
Specialisation: Main fields of chancery and commercial litigation including corporate insolvency, property, commercial fraud, professional negligence and regulation and international jurisdiction disputes (including Brussels and Lugano conventions).
Career: Called to Bar in 1978, Lincolns Inn. Pupil to Patrick Talbot and John Jarvis. Joined Serle Court in 1979. One of the junior counsel to the Crown, Chancery (1990-94). Took silk in 1994.
Personal: Married with 4 children. Leisure activities include sailing, solo and choral singing, member of Bar Yacht Club and Emsworth sailing club.

BRIGHT, Andrew
4 Brick Court (Anne Rafferty QC), London (0171) 583 8455
Recommended in Crime
Specialisation: Specialist Criminal Junior. Regularly appearing in cases of murder, sexual offences, drug trafficking, armed robbery and fraud in London and the Midlands. Has frequently appeared as leading junior, particularly in fraud cases in which he mostly defends. Notable cases have included R v. Grantham, the leading case on fraudulent trading, several solicitor, mortgage and V.A.T. frauds lasting 3 months or more and the last two spy cases of the Cold War.
Prof. Memberships: The Criminal Bar Association (Co-opted to the committee 1993 – 1995).
Career: Called to the Bar 1973.
Personal: Educated at Wells Cathedral School and University College, London. Governor of two schools in Hertfordshire where he lives with his wife and four children.

BRIGHT, Christopher
3 Fountain Court (Colman Treacy QC), Birmingham (0121) 236 5854
Recommended in Medical Negligence
Specialisation: All aspects of Medical Negligence, particularly for the plaintiff.
Prof. Memberships: AVMA/APIL. Birmingham and Warwickshire Medico-Legal societies.
Career: Durham University BA Hons. Malcolm Hilberry Award, Gray's Inn. Medical Negligence Litigation Pilot Group; Birmingham. Lecturer upon AVMA regional and national courses and to health service professionals/clinicians.
Personal: Interests: Wine, Tuscany and Gloucester RFC.

BRIGHT, Robert
7 King's Bench Walk (Stephen Tomlinson QC), London (0171) 583 0404
Recommended in Shipping
Specialisation: Principal area of practice encompasses shipping, insurance and reinsurance work. Also deals with more general commercial work. Clients include P & I Clubs and insurance companies.
Prof. Memberships: Commercial Bar Association.
Career: Called to the Bar 1987 and became a tenant of current chambers 1988.
Personal: Educated at Oxford University 1982-86 (BA, BCL). Born 22nd August 1964. Lives in London.

BRIMELOW, Kirsty
Francis Taylor Building (D.A. Pears), London (0171) 353 9942
Recommended in Crime

BRINDLE, Michael QC
Fountain Court (Peter Scott QC), London (0171) 583 3335
Recommended in the following lists: Banking, Commercial (litigation), Computer & I.T., Professional Negligence
Specialisation: Practice encompasses a variety of work in the commercial and corporate sphere as well as employment law. Emphasis on banking and financial services, company law, professional negligence in financial and commercial matters, insurance and international trade. Experienced in City-related matters, including litigation arising out of audits, take-overs and rights issues. Practises in chancery as well as commercial and common law courts. Important cases include Evening Standard & Henderson [1987] (employment injunction); Caparo v Dickman [1989] (auditors' negligence); Morgan Crucible v Hill Samuel [1990] (merchant banker's and auditor's negligence and take-over code); G & H Montage v Irvani [1990] (bills of exchange); Rome & Bathurst v Punjab National Bank [1990-92] (insurance); Re Bishopsgate Investment Management [1993] (constructive trust); Deposit Protection Board v Dalia [1993] (depositor compensation); Shah v Bank of England [1994] (banking supervision); Philip Brothers v European Commission [1994] (garnishee order); and Camdex v Bank of Zambia (1997) and BCCI v Price Waterhouse (Banking Act 1987). Author of journal articles and of 'Law of Bank Payment' [1996] (with Raymond Cox).
Prof. Memberships: Midland & Oxford Circuit.
Career: Called to the Bar in 1975 and joined Fountain Court Chambers in 1976. Took silk in 1992.
Personal: Educated at Westminster School 1965-69 and New College, Oxford (Double First in Classics and Jurisprudence). Part-time lecturer in Jurisprudence at New College, Oxford 1976-82. Chairman of Trustees: Public Concern at Work. Born 23rd June 1952. Lives in London.

BRISBY, John QC
4 Stone Buildings (Philip Heslop QC), London (0171) 242 5524
Recommended in the following lists: Chancery, Company, Insolvency
Specialisation: Litigation and advice in the fields

of company law, corporate insolvency and financial services. Emphasis on heavy corporate litigation in the Chancery Division. Cases: Instructed in a number of actions resulting out of the Maxwell affair with a view to locating and recovering assets on behalf of the Maxwell pensioners, and in other high profile fraud or asset recovery situations such as DPR Futures, Barlow Clowes and BCCI. Has also acted for and against various regulatory bodies such as SIB, IMRO and LAUTRO. Has appeared in well over 60 reported cases, well-known recent examples being Re Cloverbay [1991] Ch 90, Re Bishopsgate Investment Management [1993] Ch 1 and Re British & Commonwealth Holdings plc [1993] AC 426. Publications: Former Contributor: Encyclopaedia of Forms and Precedents (4th edn) Vol 9 Companies.
Prof. Memberships: Member of the Commercial Bar Association (COMBAR) and Chancery Bar Association.
Career: Call 1978. QC 1996.
Personal: Educated at Westminster School 1969-73 and Scholar of Christ Church, Oxford 1974-77. Born 8th May 1956. Lives in London and Northamptonshire.

BRISCOE, Constance
4 Brick Court (Antony Shaw QC), London (0171) 797 7766
Recommended in Crime
Specialisation: Crime; organized crime, white collar crime. Special interest mental health and nanny offenders.
Career: Assistant recorder 1996. President MHRT 1994.

BROCK, Jonathan QC
Falcon Chambers (Jonathan Gaunt QC & Kim Lewison QC), London (0171) 353 2484
Recommended in the following lists: Agriculture & Bloodstock, Property Litigation
Specialisation: Barrister specialising in commercial property litigation and advice; overseas work particularly in commonwealth jurisdictions; agriculture; ecclesiastical law.
Prof. Memberships: Fellow of the Chartered Institute of Arbitrators; an Assistant Recorder; member Bar Council 1992 to date; chairman commonwealth subcommittee of International Relations Committee; Bar permanent representative UK Inter-Professional Group; member of working parties on the Structure of the Bar, reform of the Court of Appeal and ADR.
Career: St Pauls School; Corpus Christi College, Cambridge (MA 1974); called 1977; silk 1997; editor Woodfall on Landlord and Tenant.
Personal: Football, cricket, skiing. Married with five children.

BRODIE, Bruce
39 Essex Street (Edwin Glasgow QC), London (0171) 832 1111
Recommended in the following lists: Alternative Dispute Resolution, Arbitration
Specialisation: Practises as arbitrator and advocate in arbitration with emphasis on international commercial disputes. Also serves as mediator (CEDR accredited mediator). Before transfer to Bar in 1993 was Frere Cholmeley senior litigation partner.
Personal: Called 1993.

BROMILOW, Richard
St. John's Chambers (Roderick Denyer QC), Bristol (0117) 921 3456
Recommended in Family/Matrimonial

BROMLEY-MARTIN, Michael
3 Raymond Buildings (Clive Nicholls QC), London (0171) 831 3833
Recommended in the following lists: Crime: Fraud, Licensing
Specialisation: Criminal Law, particularly commercial fraud, both prosecuting and defending. Cases include Blue Arrow, BCCI and advising in Nissan and Maxwell. All forms of

licensing, including liquor, public entertainment, betting, gaming and lotteries. B.Sc. (Civil Engineering).
Career: Called to the Bar in 1979. Department of Trade and Industry Inspector 1989, 1990.

BROUGHAM, Christopher QC
3/4 South Square (Michael Crystal QC), London (0171) 696 9900
Recommended in Insolvency

BROWN, Charles
39 Essex Street (Edwin Glasgow QC), London (0171) 832 1111
Recommended in Personal Injury

BROWN, Damian
Old Square Chambers (Hon. John Melville Williams QC), London (0171) 269 0300
Recommended in Employment
Specialisation: Leading cases: Wise v USDAW [1996] IRLR 609, Greaves v Kwiksave [1998] IRLR 245, RJB Mining v NUM [1997] IRLR 621, Safeways v Burell [1997]IRLR 200, PLA v Payne [1994] IRLRG. All employment areas: discrimination, restraint of trade, wrongful dismissal, Trade Union law and strikes. International Labour Law (including EU and ILO) and human rights.
Prof. Memberships: Employment Law Bar Association; Industrial Law Society; Employment Lawyers Association; Contributor to Industrial Law Journal, The Guardian. Publications: Tolleys Employment Law – Contributor; Employment Tribunal Practice and Procedure – Co-Author; Employment Law Precedents – Co-Author; Numerous pamphlets.
Career: Called to Bar 1989; Lecturer in International Labour Law. LL.M course at King's College.
Personal: Interests include Politics, Trade Union history, Arsenal Football Club and cinema.

BROWN, Geoffrey B.
39 Essex Street (Edwin Glasgow QC), London (0171) 832 1111
Recommended in Personal Injury
Specialisation: General commercial work (including damage to property/businesses and insurance contract disputes, but also commercial contract and property disputes generally. Personal injury and related work (including health insurance and medical negligence). Professional negligence
Career: MA Cantab.

BROWN, Hannah
5 Bell Yard (Robert Webb QC), London (0171) 333 8811
Recommended in Banking
Specialisation: Principal areas of practice are banking law and general commercial litigation including insurance and reinsurance.

BROWN, Paul
4-5 Gray's Inn Square (Miss Elizabeth Appleby QC & The Hon. M. Beloff QC), London (0171) 404 5252
Recommended in Planning
Specialisation: Town and Country Planning, Environmental Law, Local Government and Employment.
Prof. Memberships: PEBA, ALBA
Career: LL.B (Hons) (N.Z) Ph.D. (Cantab).

BROWN, Simon QC
One Paper Buildings (John Slater QC), London (0171) 583 7355
Recommended in the following lists: Product Liability, Professional Negligence
Specialisation: Principal areas of practice are professional negligence (valuers, accountants, surveyors, architects, engineers and solicitors) product liability and insurance claims. Recent notable cases include Arab Bank v Zurich & Lloyds: fraud; Eagle Star v John D. Wood (Commercial) & Allied Appeals: 'fall in property market'; Capital & Counties and Digital Equipment Corporation v Hampshire County Council 'liability

of Fire Brigades'; and Carroll & others v Fearon & Dunlop Plc; car tyre product liability.
Prof. Memberships: Professional Negligence Bar Association, Official Referees Bar Association, London Common Law and Commercial Bar Association. Currently updating and editing the section on `Architects Engineers and Surveyors' in Emdens Construction Law.
Career: Called to the Bar in 1976 and joined 1 Paper Buildings in 1977.
Personal: Educated at Harrow School and Queens' College, Cambridge. Leisure pursuits include gardening, cricket and golf. Born 23rd August 1952.

BROWN, Stephanie
5 Fountain Court (Anthony Barker QC), Birmingham (0121) 606 0500
Recommended in Family/Matrimonial

BROWNBILL, David J.
8 Gray's Inn Square (Patrick C. Soares), London (0171) 242 3529
Recommended in Traditional Chancery
Email: 100102.2362@compuserve.com
Specialisation: Chancery law, including the creation, administration and taxation of domestic and offshore trusts and companies; structuring of international estates of high net worth individuals; international estate planning and asset protection (including capital taxation, political risks, forced heirship and insolvency); company law (especially the use and operation of companies in international transactions); wills, probate and administration of international estates; advice and representation regarding litigation on all related matters in the English and Commonwealth courts. Editor of the 'Journal of International Trust and Corporate Planning'. Drafted the Antigua International Companies Bill.
Prof. Memberships: An attorney of the Supreme Court of theTurks & Caicos Islands. A member of the Society of Trust and Estate Practitioners (STEP), serving on the International and Technical Committees. Academician of the International Academy of Estate and Trust Law.
Career: Called to the Bar 1989, joining 8 Gray's Inn Square in the same year. Formerly a solicitor, admitted 1980.

BROWNE, Benjamin QC
2 Temple Gardens (Patrick Phillips QC), London (0171) 583 6041
Recommended in the following lists: Personal Injury, Professional Negligence
Specialisation: Personal Injury and Disaster Litigation: (Clapham Junction Inquiry and Litigation. M1 Aircrash Litigation) Professional Indemnity, especially solicitors. Barristers, Surveyors, (FNB v Key & Taylor). Fire Claims (Digital Equipment v Hampshire County Council & Others.) Insurance related litigation. General Commercial Litigation. Farming related cases.
Prof. Memberships: Commercial and Common Law Bar Association. APIL.
Career: Called to Bar 1976. Tenancy 2 Temple Gardens since 1977. QC 1996.
Personal: Married two children.

BROWNE, Desmond QC
5 Raymond Buildings (Patrick Milmo QC), London (0171) 242 2902
Recommended in the following lists: Defamation, Media & Entertainment
Specialisation: Defamation and media law. Recent reported libel cases include: Elton John v Mirror (1996) 3 WLR 593: (Quantum and exemplary damages); BDM v Boxer Commercial (1996) EMLR 349: (Interlocutory injunction in libel); Watts v Times Newspapers (1996) 2 WLR 427: (Qualified privilege); Allason v Haines (1996) EMLR 143: (Parliamentary privilege); Oyston v Blaker (1996) 1 WLR 1326: (Limitation Act); Derbyshire CC v Times Newspapers HL (1993) AC 534: (Local government right to sue); Telnikoff v Matusevitch HL: (1992) 2 AC 343: (Fair comment); Joyce v Sengupta CA

(1993) 1 WLR 337: (Malicious falsehood). Acted for Defendants throughout Spycatcher litigation in London and Strasbourg. Confidentiality cases include Barrymore v News Group (1997) FSR 600; "Kiss and Tell" injuction. Also acted for successful Defendants in Graham v Rechem (a 15-month toxic nuisance action).
Prof. Memberships: Western Circuit.
Career: Called to the Bar 1969. Legal correspondent for 'British Medical Journal' 1970-79. Silk 1990. Recorder 1994.
Personal: Educated: Eton and New College, Oxford (Scholar). Born 5th April 1947.

BROWNE, Simon Peter Buchanan
Farrar's Building (Gerard Elias QC), London (0171) 583 9241
Recommended in Personal Injury
Specialisation: Practice covers general common law with particular specialisation in personal injury, health and safety, medical negligence and taxation of costs (is a contributing author "Greenslade on Costs").
Prof. Memberships: South Eastern Circuit.
Career: Called to the Bar in 1982.
Personal: Born 5th November 1959.

BROWNE-WILKINSON, Simon QC
Fountain Court (Peter Scott QC), London (0171) 583 3335
Recommended in Commercial (litigation)
Specialisation: Has a general commercial practice, including shipping, banking, insurance, professional negligence and fraud.
Career: Called to the Bar in 1981 and joined Fountain Court in 1982. QC 1998
Personal: Educated at Oxford University. Born in August 1957.

BRUDENELL, Thomas
Queen Elizabeth Building (Ian Karsten QC), London (0171) 797 7837
Recommended in the following lists: Agriculture & Bloodstock, Family: Child Care including child abduction, Family: Matrimonial Finance
Specialisation: Principal areas of practice are family law and equine litigation.
Prof. Memberships: Family Law Bar Association.
Career: Called to the Bar 1977 and joined current chambers in 1978.
Personal: Educated at Eton College 1969-74. Born 12th August 1956. Lives in London.

BRYAN, Simon
Essex Court Chambers (Gordon Pollock QC), London (0171) 813 8000
Recommended in Insurance & Reinsurance
Specialisation: Specialist in insurance and reinsurance, shipping, commercial law and arbitration. Has experience acting for Lloyd's syndicates, members and managing agents. Practice also covers professional negligence.
Prof. Memberships: Commercial Bar Association
Personal: Called to the Bar 1988.
Career: Educated at Arnold School 1977-1984 and at Magdalene College, Cambridge 1984-87. Born 23rd November 1965.

BRYANT, Judith
Wilberforce Chambers (Edward Nugee QC), London (0171) 306 0102
Recommended in Pensions
Specialisation: Practice covers a wide range of advisory and litigation work in chancery/commercial matters, with particular emphasis on: trusts and their taxation, including advice on the creation and administration of trusts, the duties of trustees and breaches of trust, overseas trusts and their taxation, conflicts of laws, the variation of trusts, and the drafting of trust deeds and related instruments; pension schemes, including advice in relation to the construction of trust deeds and rules of pension schemes, the duties of pension scheme trustees and breaches of those duties, applications to Court in relation to pension schemes, and complaints to the Pensions

Ombudsman; wills and probate, including advice on the construction of wills, conflicts of laws, the variation of wills, the administration of estates, the duties of executor, and contentious probate matters; professional negligence relating to trusts and pension schemes.
Prof. Memberships: Society of Trust and Estate Practitioners (STEP).
Career: Called to the Bar: 1987. Jesus College, Cambridge 1982-1986. BA 1st Class Hons (1985), LLM (1986).

BRYANT-HERON, Mark
9-12 Bell Yard (D. Anthony Evans QC), London (0171) 400 1800
Recommended in Crime
Specialisation: Specialist in criminal law, with an emphasis on drug trafficking and fraud. Practice is evenly divided between prosecution and defence work.
Prof. Memberships: Criminal Bar Association, South-Eastern Circuit.
Career: Called to the Bar in 1986.
Personal: Educated at Cambridge University 1981-84.

BUBB, T.M.A.
39 Park Square (T.M.A. Bubb), Leeds (0113) 245 6633
Recommended in Crime

BUCHANAN, Vivien
King Charles House (William Everard), Nottingham (0115) 941 8851
Recommended in Family/Matrimonial

BUCKNALL, Belinda QC
4 Essex Court (Nigel Teare QC), London (0171) 797 7970
Recommended in the following lists: Arbitration, Shipping
Specialisation: Admiralty practitioner specialising in marine insurance (hull and yacht), P.I. and fatal accident claims (arising from shipboard incidents), ships' collision, salvage, maritime pollution and dry shipping work. Also land based building and construction disputes and air law (in particular limitation of liability).
Prof. Memberships: Western Circuit; Combar.
Career: Education: The School of St. Helen and St. Katherine (Abingdon); Oxford University (MA). Appointments: QC – 1988; Lloyd's panel of Salvage Arbitrators; Master of Middle Temple – 1996; Recorder – 1997. Languages: French and Italian.
Personal: A longstanding interest in the RNLI. Ice skating and canoeing.

BUDDEN, Caroline
One King's Bench Walk (James Townend QC), London (0171) 936 1500
Recommended in the following lists: Family: Child Care including child abduction
Specialisation: Principal area of practice is family law, including public and private law aspects of the Children Act, adoption, wardship and related social services law, child abduction, matrimonial finance, solicitors' negligence relating to family law matters. Public interest immunity.
Prof. Memberships: Family Law Bar Association, Professional Negligence Bar Association; FLBA representative on the Bar Council.
Career: Called to the Bar 1977.
Personal: Educated at Alfred Colfox School, Bridport, Dorset, and Bristol University (LL.B 1976). Born 30 July 1954. Lives in London.

BUENO, Antonio QC
5 Paper Buildings (Antonio Bueno QC), London (0171) 583 9275 /4555
Recommended in Banking
Fax: (0171) 583 1926
Specialisation: Principal area of practice is commercial law. With emphasis on banking and commercial fraud. Overseas work and member of various overseas bars.

Prof. Memberships: S.E. Circuit. Member LCLCBA. JT Editor Atkins Court Forms (1976). Asst. Editor Paget's Law of Banking (1982). JT Editor Byles on Bills of Exchange.
Career: Called 1964. Silk 1989. Recorder 1989.

BULL, Gregory
33 Park Place (Wyn Williams QC), Cardiff (01222) 233313
Recommended in Crime

BURBIDGE, James
St Philip's Chambers (Rex Tedd QC), Birmingham (0121) 246 7000
Recommended in Crime

BURDEN, Susan
6 Pump Court (Kieran Coonan QC), London (0171) 583 6013
Recommended in Medical Negligence
Specialisation: General personal injury work, medical/dental negligence actions (including high value birth trauma cases) for Plaintiffs and Defendants; disciplinary hearings. Drafted British Medical Association's green paper response on 'Competition'. Lectures given: IBC/Hempsons' 'Reducing NHS Medical Negligence Liabilities'; Euroforums's 'Claims by Injured Children'; chaired Euroforum's 'Spinal Injuries'. Instructed in benzodiazepine litigation. Cases reported in Medical Law Reports: Scott v Bloomsbury HA [1990] 1MedLR 214; Walker v Huntingdon HA [1994] 5 MedLR 356.
Prof. Memberships: Bar Professional Negligence Association.
Career: Guildford County School for Girls, Charterhouse, New College Oxford BA. Hons (Jurisprudence) 1984; MA.
Personal: Born 15.7.61. Classical music, especially opera, singing.

BURGESS, Edward
St. John's Chambers (Roderick Denyer QC), Bristol (0117) 921 3456
Recommended in Crime

BURKE, Jeffrey QC
Devereux Chambers (Jeffrey Burke QC), London (0171) 353 7534
Recommended in the following lists: Employment, Personal Injury, Professional Negligence
Specialisation: Principal areas of practice are: Commercial and Common Law, Employment Law, Discrimination, Personal Injury, Medical Negligence, Professional Negligence, Insurance, Public and Administrative Law. Recent cases include: Green v. British Aerospace (1995) CA – discovery in mass redundancy case; Burgess v. Bass Taverns (1995) CA – dismissal for trade union reasons. A substantial number of cases involving brain damage or other serious injuries in excess of £1 million. Blue Circle v West Midlands CC (1995) CA - Lands Tribunal award of compensation for compulsory purchase; Wandsworth BC v NAS/UWT (1993) CA – industrial action - teachers; R. v Hull University ex p Page (1992) CA, HL – security of tenure, university lecturers; BT v Ticehurst (1992) CA – deductions from pay during industrial action; London Underground v RMT (1995) CA industrial action – underground workers; Palmer v Associated British Ports (1994) HL – action short of dismissal – dock workers; Hunt v Douglas (1991) HL – interest on costs.
Prof. Memberships: Committee Member Personal Injuries Bar Association. Employment Law Bar Association.
Career: Called, 1964 (Major Scholarship: Middle Temple). QC: 1984. Recorder: 1983. Legal Member Mental Health Independent Review Tribunal (1993). Since 1993 appointed by Lord Chancellor to sit as a Deputy High Court Judge.
Personal: Educated Shrewsbury School. Open Exhibition in Classics to Brasenose College, Oxford MJA (Oxon) Jurisprudence. Interests, football, cricket and wine.

BURKE, Trevor
10 King's Bench Walk (Ronald Thwaites QC), London (0171) 353 2501
Recommended in Crime
Specialisation: In the last 12 months successfully defended John Fashanu in the football corruption trial at Winchester, Nigel Benn on a serious assault at Middlesex, Terry Marsh on a student grant fraud. Currently briefed and defended Gary Glitter.
Prof. Memberships: CBA, Member of South Eastern Circuit.
Career: Recently returned to 10KBW, where I was a pupil and tenant for the first 5 years of my career.

BURKILL, Guy
Three New Square (David E.M. Young QC), London (0171) 405 1111
Recommended in the following lists: Computer & I.T., Intellectual Property
Specialisation: All Intellectual Property aspects, mainly patent with particular interest in computer hardware and software and electronics. Has acted for many leading multinational companies in the computer, electronics, paper, chemical, pharmaceutical, aviation and other fields. Most recent notable cases include: Pavel v Sony (Walkman case in Patent County Court & CT of Appeal); Lubrizol v Exxon (oil additives); Hoechst v British Petroleum; Discovision v Disctronics (compact disc mastering).
Prof. Memberships: Intellectual Property Bar Assn; Chancery Bar Assn.
Career: Winchester College; Corpus Christi College Cambridge – MA Degree, First Class Hons. in Engineering (Electrical Option); Called to Bar 1981.
Personal: Leisure interests include music, opera and travel.

BURNETT, Ian D. QC
1 Temple Gardens (Hugh Carlisle QC), London (0171) 583 1315
Recommended in the following lists: Administrative & Public Law, Environmental Law, Health & Safety, Personal Injury
Specialisation: Public Law, Judicial Review, Coroners, Professional Negligence, Personal Injury. Public inquiries (King's Cross, Clapham Junction, Guildford Four, Southall Rail); Ex Parte Richmond Borough Council (Nos 1, 2 and 4) [1994] 1 WLR 74, [1995] Env LR 390, [1995] Env LR 409 and [1996] 1 WLR 1460 (Environmental JR); Ex Parte Jamieson [1995] QB 1 (Coroners); Elguzouli-Daf v Commissioner & others [1995] QB 335, Mulcahy v MoD [1996] QB 732 (Duty of Care); R v Associated Octel [1996] 1 WLR 1543 (Health & Safety); Boddington v British Transport Police [1998] 2 WLR 639 (JR).
Prof. Memberships: ALBA, COMBAR, PIBA.
Career: MA (Oxon). Called M.T. 1980. Junior Counsel to the Crown (Common Law) 1992-1998; QC 1998.

BURNS, Andrew
Devereux Chambers (Jeffrey Burke QC), London (0171) 353 7534
Recommended in Employment
Email: burns@devchambers.co.uk
Website: www.devchambers.co.uk
Specialisation: Principal areas of practice are: Employment including sex, race and disability discrimination, commercial and common law, insurance litigation and professional negligence, employer's liability and personal injury. Recent cases: Carter v Reiner Moritz [1997] ICR, 881, EAT; Anson v Trump (The Times) May 8 1998, CA.
Prof. Memberships: Employment Law Bar Assocation. London Common Law & Commercial Bar Association.
Career: Called 1993.
Personal: Educated at Dover Grammar School and Downing College, Cambridge, MA (Law). Astbury Scholar, Middle Temple.

BURNS, Sue
3 Serjeants' Inn (Philip Naughton QC), London
(0171) 353 5537
Recommended in Medical Negligence
Specialisation: Principal areas of practice are
Medical Law, including Medical Negligence and
matters relating to Coroners Courts, also
Construction Law.
Prof. Memberships: Professional Negligence Bar
Association. Official Referees' Bar Association.
Career: Called to Bar in 1979, joined 3 Serjeants'
Inn in 1995.
Personal: Educated at Merchant Taylors' Girls
School and Liverpool University.

BURNTON, Stanley QC
One Essex Court (Anthony Grabiner QC),
London (0171) 583 2000
*Recommended in the following lists: Arbitration,
Commercial*
Specialisation: Commercial legal advice and
litigation; international arbitration; jurisdiction and
conflicts of law issues; accounting and auditing
issues and professional negligence; banking;
insurance and reinsurance; oil and gas cases,
contractual and technical, including unitisation
disputes; joint ventures and partnership; corporate
and business acquisitions and breach of warranty
claims; computers; data protection.
Career: Called to the Bar 1965; QC 1982;
Recorder; Deputy High Court Judge in the
Chancery Division; Bencher of Middle Temple.

BURR, Andrew
Atkin Chambers (John Blackburn QC), London
(0171) 404 0102
*Recommended in the following lists: Arbitration,
Construction*
Specialisation: Practises primarily in domestic and
international construction disputes. Acts as
advocate in litigation and arbitration and in an
advisory capacity regarding ADR. Experienced in
all aspects of construction law and professional
negligence, particularly of architects, engineers
and surveyors. General and articles editor
'Construction Law Journal' (Sweet and Maxwell);
general editor 'Arbitration and Dispute Resolution
Law Journal' (Lloyds of London Press); editor
'European Construction Contracts' (Wiley
Chancery Law).
Prof. Memberships: ACI Arb. (Committee member
European Branch), ABA international associate,
Swiss Arbitration Association, ORBA, COMBAR,
BILA.
Career: Called November 1981. Joined chambers
in 1983. Speaks Italian and French.
Personal: Educated at Barclay School, Stevenage
and Trinity Hall, Cambridge. Lives in London.

BURROWES, Patrick
Albion Chambers (J.C.T. Barton QC), Bristol
(0117) 927 2144
Recommended in Crime

BURTON, Frank QC
12 King's Bench Walk (Ronald J. Walker QC),
London (0171) 583 0811
Recommended in Personal Injury
Specialisation: Principal area of practice is
personal injury work with an emphasis on industrial
diseases and medical negligence. Co-author of
'Medical Negligence Case Law' and 'Personal
Injury Limitation Law', both published by
Butterworths.
Prof. Memberships: Personal Injury Bar
Association, Member of Executive.
Career: University lecturer 1974-83. Called to the
Bar and joined present chambers 1982. QC 1998.
Personal: B.A. Hons 1st Class and PhD. Born 19th
June 1950. Lives in London.

BURTON, Michael QC
Littleton Chambers (Michael Burton QC),
London (0171) 797 8600
*Recommended in the following lists: Alternative
Dispute Resolution, Commercial (litigation),
Construction, Employment, Partnership,
Professional Negligence, Sports Law*
Specialisation: Wide range of practice in general
commercial litigation in the Commercial, Q.B. and
Chancery Divisions and arbitration. Has had
reported cases in the fields of employment and
trade unions, intellectual property, defamation and
entertainment, Mareva injunctions, European and
public law, Convention and P.I.L., insurance,
banking and insolvency, professional negligence,
letters of request, extradition and elections.
Prof. Memberships: COMBAR; London Common
Law and Commercial Bar Association; ELBA; ELA;
ORBA; Bar Sports Law Group.
Career: Called Grays Inn 1970. Joined 2 Crown
Office Row (now Littleton Chambers) 1971, Head
of Chambers 1991; Recorder, Deputy High Court
Judge. Bencher of Grays Inn.
Personal: Educated at Eton College and Balliol
College, Oxford. Lives in London with 4 daughters.

BUTCHER, Anthony QC
c/o Atkin Chambers (John Blackburn QC),
London (0171) 404 0102
Recommended in Arbitration

BUTCHER, Christopher
7 King's Bench Walk (Stephen Tomlinson QC),
London (0171) 583 0404
*Recommended in the following lists: Arbitration,
Commercial, Insurance & Reinsurance,
Professional Negligence, Shipping*
Specialisation: Insurance and reinsurance,
commercial agreements, banking, agency,
shipping, international trade, arbitration, and
professional negligence.
Career: Called to the Bar 1986. Recent cases
include: Henderson v Merrett Syndicates Ltd
[1995] 2 A.C. 145 (Negligence – duty of care –
duty of agents at Lloyd's), Barclays Bank plc and
Others v British and Commonwealth Holdings plc
[1996] WLR.1 (Banking – company law),
Commercial Union v Mander [1996] 2 Lloyd's Re
640 (Practice – Discovery). Barings Plc v Coopers
& Lybrand [1997] 1 BCLC 427 (Auditors – Duty of
Care).
Personal: Born 1962. M.A. (Oxon). Has a working
knowledge of French and Italian.

BYRNE, Garrett
23 Essex Street (Michael Lawson QC), London
(0171) 413 0353
Recommended in Environmental Law
Specialisation: Environmental law and planning,
particularly criminal aspects of environmental law.
Instructed by major city solicitors to advise and
represent substantial industrial concerns and major
developers. Regular speaker at conferences.
Prof. Memberships: United Kingdom
Environmental Law Association; Environmental
Law Foundation, founding member of
'EarthRights', environmental law and resource
centre.
Career: Called to the Bar in 1986, Masters degree
in Environmental Law in 1993.

CAHILL, Jeremy
5 Fountain Court (Anthony Barker QC),
Birmingham (0121) 606 0500
*Recommended in the following lists: Administrative
& Public Law, Planning*
Specialisation: Planning (Housing, minerals,
waste, retail, CPO), Personal Injury. Town and
Country Planning including: Section 78 Planning
Appeals; Local Plan Inquiries for Local Authorities
and on behalf of Objectors; Enforcement Notice
Appeals; Section 288 Appeals; High Court
Challenge to adoption of Local Plans; Judicial
Review of Planning Authority decisions; Breach of
Planning Control Criminal Proceedings; Mineral
Plan Appearances and Minerals Appeals; Waste

Appeals; Retail Appeals; Golf Course Appeals;
Leisure/Licensing Appeals; Certificate of Alternative
Development Hearings. Compulsory Purchase:
Roads and wider statutory powers; Promotion of
and objection to schemes. Other Local
Government Powers and Duties: Pollution Control;
Waste Management and Licensing; Animal
rendering processes; Noise abatement and
statutory nuisance. Other Public and Administrative
Law Proceedings: Lands Tribunal. Practice
examples: Merry Hill Shopping Centre Inquiry
(1996); Peddimore Major Investment Site Inquiry
(1996); Birmingham Northern Relief Road Inquiry
(1994-95); Channel Tunnel Rail Freight Terminal
Inquiry: Hams Hall; M42 Business Park Inquiry;
Junction 28 M1 Call In Inquiry (1997); South
Loughborough Call In Inquiry (1997) 650 houses;
Successful application to quash (in part) Sandwell
UDP (1996); Successful challenge by Judicial
Review of the decision of two mineral planning
authorities to classify quarries as "dormant" (1996);
Resisting application to quash Tamworth Local
Plan (1995); Quashing Noise Abatement Notice
issued against Kart Club (1996).
Prof. Memberships: PEBA, APIL.
Career: M42 Business Park inquiry, Cambridge
New Settlement Aid, Channel Tunnel Rail Link
Hams Hall, Birmingham Northern Relief Road,
Merry Hill Retail inquiry.

CAHILL, Sally
Park Lane Chambers (Martin Bethel QC), Leeds
(0113) 228 5000
Recommended in Family/Matrimonial

CALDECOTT, Andrew QC
1 Brick Court (Richard Hartley QC), London
(0171) 353 8845
Recommended in Defamation
Specialisation: Defamation, confidence,
contempt of court and media related law generally.
Career: Called to the Bar 1975.
Personal: Educated Eton College and New
College, Oxford. Lives in London.

CALVERT-SMITH, David QC
Queen Elizabeth Building (David Jeffreys QC &
Peter Whiteman QC), London (0171) 583 5766
*Recommended in the following lists: Crime,
Crime: Fraud*
Specialisation: Crime. Terrorism: Hindawi, 'Peep-
Show' and Syrian Embassy bombing, 1981 IRA
bombing campaign, Israeli Embassy bombing.
Corporate Homicide: Herald of Free Enterprise.
Serious Fraud: Polly Peck. Corruption: Allegations
of bribery in professional football. Last 12 months:
Iraq, hi-jacking, RHCE. Alleged murder by arson for
insurance.
Prof. Memberships: Bar Council Member. Vice
Chairman Education & Training of General
Management. Chairman Criminal Bar Association
Committee.
Career: Eton, King's Cambridge, called 1969,
Treasury Counsel 1986-1997.
Personal: Married. Keen sportsman and singer.
Fluent Greek and French speaker.

CAMERON, Alexander
3 Raymond Buildings (Clive Nicholls QC),
London (0171) 831 3833
Recommended in Crime: Fraud
Specialisation: Has substantial experience in
commercial fraud cases. Larger trials include R v
Cohen and others [1992] (Blue Arrow); R v Thomas
and Others [1994] (Blackspur Leasing) R v Aspin
and others [1988] (Arms to Iran Fraud). Other main
areas of work are crime, extradition and licensing,
both advisory and court work.
Prof. Memberships: Criminal Bar Association,
International Bar Association.
Career: Called to the Bar 1986 and joined 3
Raymond Buildings in 1987.
Personal: Educated at Bristol University (LL.B
Hons). Born 27th August 1963.

CAMERON, James
3 Verulam Buildings (R. Neville Thomas QC), London (0171) 831 8441

Recommended in Environmental Law
Specialisation: Principal area of practice encompasses international, EC and UK environmental law. Work includes the enforcement of environmental standards, international (and EC) trade law, environmental assessments, environmental warranties, "toxic tort" litigation and conflict of laws. Other main area of work is public law and judicial review of ministerial (and other public) decisions, and the application of European law in that context. Important recent cases include R v Secretary of State for the Environment, ex parte Greenpeace (THORP) [1994]; R v Secretary of State for Trade and Industry ex parte Duddridge [1994]. Involved in several international negotiations, including the UN Climate Change Convention and the Earth Summit (1992). Clients include intergovernmental organisations (EC, UN) environmental organisations, plaintiffs injured in environmental incidents, banks, local authorities, waste companies, multi-national corporations and industrial concerns and developing countries. Editor 'Review of European Community and International Environmental Law' (RECIEL) and member of Advisory Board, 'Environmental Judicial Review Bulletin'. Editor, 'International Trade Law Reports'. Author of several books including 'Trade and the Environment, the Search for Balance' (1994) and 'EC Legal Systems: An Introductory Guide' (1992) and contributor of many chapters to publications on international environmental and public international law topics.
Prof. Memberships: UK Environmental Law Association, Environmental Law Foundation (Advisory Board), World Trade Law Association (WTLA) Council Member. UCN Environmental Law Commission.
Career: Called to the Bar and joined current chambers 1987.
Personal: Educated at Stowe School, Buckinghamshire. University of Western Australia 1981-1982. University College, London (LL.B, 1985). Queens' College, Cambridge (LL.M, 1986). Dual British/Australian National. Director, Foundation for International Environmental Law and Development (FIELD), School of Oriental and African Studies, University of London. Fellow of Royal Society of Arts and Royal Geographical Society.

CAMERON, Neil
1 Serjeants' Inn (Lionel Read QC), London (0171) 583 1355

Recommended in the following lists: Energy & Utilities, Planning
Specialisation: Planning and environmental. Recent work includes: UK Nirex RCF appeal, Barnsley MBC CPO Special Parliamentary Procedure.
Prof. Memberships: Planning and Environment Bar Association.
Career: Called 1982.
Personal: Educated at Eton College and Durham University.

CAMERON, Sheila QC
2 Harcourt Buildings (Mr Gerard Ryan QC), London (0171) 353 8415

Recommended in the following lists: Ecclesiastical, Parliamentary

CAMPBELL, Douglas James
Three New Square (David E.M. Young QC), London (0171) 405 1111

Recommended in Intellectual Property
Specialisation: All intellectual property matters – Chemistry (biotechnology) computers. Notable Cases: Union Carbide v BP (1998) RPC 1, Conran (Sir Terence Orby) v Mean Fiddler Holdings (1997) FSR 856; Lubrizol v Exxon 1997 RPC 195; Roadtech Computer Systems v Unison Software 1996 FSR 805; Johnson v Mabuchi 1995 RPC 387; Valeo Vision v Flexible Lamps 1995 RPC 205.

Prof. Memberships: Intellectual Property Bar Assn; Chancery Bar Assn; AIPPI.
Career: Dollar Academy, Scotland 1976-1984; (Scholarship to) Hertford College, Oxford 1984 – 1988 1st Class Hons, Chemistry with Distinction in Quantum Chemistry. 1989/90 Employed by Andersen Consulting in Information Technology 1990/91 Teaching English in Kagoshima, Japan. Fluent in Japanese. Called to Bar 1993, Pegasus Scholarship to Melbourne, Australia 1997.
Personal: Athletics, Karate, Equestrian pursuits.

CAMPBELL, Stephen
St Philip's Chambers (Rex Tedd QC), Birmingham (0121) 246 7000

Recommended in Commercial (litigation)
Specialisation: Commercial law, building, personal injury.
Prof. Memberships: Midland Chancery and Commercial Bar Association. Personal Injury Bar Association. Birmingham Official Referee Users Group.
Career: King Edward VI School, Birmingham. Liverpool University.
Personal: Married, 3 children. Tennis.

CAMPBELL, Susan
Southernhay Chambers (David Tyzack), Exeter (01392) 255777

Recommended in Family/Matrimonial
Specialisation: Family Law. Practice covers all areas of family law: Ancillary Relief and all aspects of law relating to children, particularly Care proceedings.
Prof. Memberships: Family Law Bar Association.
Career: Called 1986. Spent 7 years as an employed barrister in local government, specialising in care proceedings.
Personal: Born 29-4-64. Two children. Enjoys swimming and walking.

CAMPBELL-MOFFAT, Audrey
No.1 High Pavement (John B. Milmo QC), Nottingham (0115) 941 8218

Recommended in Crime

CANNON, Mark
2 Crown Office Row (John Powell QC), London (0171) 797 8000

Recommended in Professional Negligence
Specialisation: Professional negligence (lawyers, accountants, insurance brokers, Lloyd's members and managing agents, financial advisers, valuers, architects and engineers); general commercial law; building and construction; insurance and reinsurance. Editor 'Jackson and Powell on Professional Negligence' (3rd ed, 1992: chapter 7, Insurance Brokers; 4th ed, 1997, chapters 7, Insurance Brokers, and 9, Members' and Managing Agents at Lloyd's). Recent interesting cases include ICS v. West Bromwich Building Society and Others [1998] 1 W.L.R. 896.
Prof. Memberships: COMBAR; London Common Law and Commercial Bar Association; Professional Negligence Bar Association.
Career: Educated at Lincoln College, Oxford 1980-3 (BA in Modern History) and Robinson College, Cambridge 1983-4 (Part 1B of Law Tripos). Called to the Bar 1985.

CANT, Christopher I.
9 Stone Buildings (Michael Ashe QC), London (0171) 404 5055

Recommended in Traditional Chancery

CAPE, Paul
Milburn House Chambers (Paul Cape), Newcastle-upon-Tyne (0191) 230 5511

Recommended in Employment
Specialisation: Almost exclusively Employment and Discrimination Law, acting for both employers and employees with a particular interest in local authority work.
Prof. Memberships: Employment Law Bar Association.
Career: Obtained a 'first' in Law at Newcastle

Polytechnic following a career as a trade union official. Co-founder and Head of Chambers, Milburn House Chambers, a set specialising in all aspects of Employment and Discrimination Law.
Personal: Interests include theatre, reading and watching cricket. Born 5 March 1955.

CAPLAN, Jonathan QC
5 Paper Buildings (John Mathew QC), London (0171) 583 6117

Recommended in the following lists: Crime, Crime: Fraud

CARLING, Christopher
Old Square Chambers (Hon. John Melville Williams QC), London (0171) 269 0300

Recommended in Personal Injury
Specialisation: Multi-Party actions involving transport disasters, pharmaceutical products, health and safety at work, in particular industrial injuries and diseases 64 VWF; industrial deafness, asbestosis; Sports Injuries: Head injuries; back injuries (including chronic pain syndrome)
Prof. Memberships: Association of Personal Injury Lawyers (APIL) (Executive Committee member for 5 years), Personal Injury Bar Association (PIBA) (Executive Committee Member).
Career: Founder Member of APIL and PIBA. Former Consultant to European Commission on Health-Safety in the UK.
Personal: Fell-walking, gardening, opera, golf and cricket.

CARLISLE, Hugh B.H. QC
1 Temple Gardens (Hugh Carlisle QC), London (0171) 583 1315

Recommended in Health & Safety
Specialisation: Health and Safety at Work. R v Board of Trustees of Science Museum (1993 IWLR 1171 CA); R v Associated Octel Co Ltd (1996 4 All ER 846, 1996 1 WLR 1543 HL); R v British Steel plc (1995 I WLR 1356 CA); R v Nuclear Electric plc (Sept 1995); R v Coalite Products Ltd (Feb. 1996); HSE v Howletts Zoo (Oct '95); R v Port Ramsgate and others (Jan – Feb 1997) etc. Personal Injuries (Fields v. Hereford Health Authority: 1992) etc.
Career: Called to Bar Middle Temple 1961; Junior Treasury Counsel, Personal injuries cases, 1975-78; QC 1978; DTI Inspector into Ramor Investments Ltd 1979-85 and into Milbury Plc 1982-5; Bencher, Middle Temple 1985. Recorder of the Crown Court (since 1983).
Personal: Married with 2 children. Interests include fly fishing, wordworking and croquet.

CARMAN, George QC
New Court Chambers (George Carman QC), London (0171) 831 9500

Recommended in Defamation
Specialisation: Has appeared in major trials in defamation, contract and commercial and copyright cases as well as certain areas of the criminal law in recent years. Appeared in trials in Malaysia, Hong Kong, Singapore and Bermuda and advisory work in the United States.
Career: Called to the Bar 1953. QC 1971. Bencher Lincoln's Inn 1978.
Personal: Educated at Balliol College, Oxford; 1st Class Honours Law.

CARR, Bruce
Devereux Chambers (Jeffrey Burke QC), London (0171) 353 7534

Recommended in Employment
Specialisation: Employment Law, Commercial Law, Personal Injury. Regularly instructed on behalf of both employers and Trade Unions, in particular in the EAT. Also frequently appears in interlocutory injunction applications, ranging from restrictive covenants to trade disputes. Substantial practice in descrimination, Transfer of Undertakings and large scale redundancy matters. Member – Supplementary Panel of Treasury Counsel (Common Law). Leading reported cases – Employment Law. Recent cases include: Robb v LB Hammersmith (1991) IRLR 72. Green v British

Aerospace (1995) CA. Tyldesley v TML Plastics (1996) ICR 356. Cast v Croydon College CA (1998). Sirdar v M.O.D. (1997).
Prof. Memberships: Employment Law Bar Association; Member – EAT User Group.
Career: Called 1986. Inner Temple. Publications: author 'Emergency procedures', Litigation Practice (Longmans), author 'High Court Procedure', (Longmans).
Personal: Cambs High School for Boys, Cambridge. Hills Road Sixth Form College, Cambridge. LSE (BSc Economics) 1983, Central London Polytechnic (Dip Law) 1985

CARR, Christopher QC
One Essex Court (Anthony Grabiner QC), London (0171) 583 2000
Recommended in the following lists: Commercial (litigation), Energy & Utilities

CARR, Henry QC
11 South Square (Christopher Floyd QC), London (0171) 405 1222
Recommended in the following lists: Computer & I.T., Intellectual Property
Specialisation: Principal areas of practice are patents, copyrights, designs and trade marks. Leading cases include R v Registrar of Designs ex parte Ford Motor Company (House of Lords) R v Licensing Authority ex parte Smith Kline & French (House of Lords) and Scotia v Norgine (European Court). Also has a substantial practice in computer contracts (including negligence claims); and judicial review relating to the grant of product licences. In addition, has appeared in numerous cases in the Data Protection Tribunal on behalf of the Registrar.
Career: Called to the Bar 1982. Joined South Square in 1983. Educated at Hertford College, Oxford and the University of British Columbia. Lives in London.

CARR, Peter
St. Ive's Chambers (Edward Coke), Birmingham (0121) 236 0863 (6 lines)
Recommended in Crime

CARR, Sue
2 Crown Office Row (John Powell QC), London (0171) 797 8000
Recommended in Professional Negligence
Specialisation: Principal area of practice is professional negligence: solicitors, medical, surveyors, barristers, architects, and engineers. Also handles employment, general contract and insurance work. Important cases include Broadley v Guy Clapham [1993], Hopkins & MacKenzie [1995] (both concerning limitation); Interdesco S.A v Nullifire Ltd [1992] (registration of foreign judgement) and Morley v Heritage Plc [1993] (employment), Hipwood v Gloucestershire HA [1995] (Discovery). Fluent in French and German.
Prof. Memberships: Committee Member Professional Negligence Bar Association, Commercial and Common Law Bar Association. Member of New South Wales Bar.
Career: Called to the Bar 1987 and joined Crown Office Row in 1988.
Personal: Born 1st September 1964. Educated at Wycombe Abbey School 1976-82 and Trinity College, Cambridge 1983-86 (MA). Leisure pursuits include sports, music and acting.

CARSS-FRISK, Monica
Blackstone Chambers (formerly 2 Hare Court) (P Baxendale QC and C Flint QC), London (0171) 583 1770
Recommended in the following lists: Administrative & Public Law, Employment
Specialisation: Judicial review, Employment law, with a particular emphasis on discrimination in both domestic and EU law, and the European Convention on Human Rights (particularly in the commercial context). Also handles general commercial contract disputes (including conflict of laws issues) and commercial fraud.

Prof. Memberships: Administrative Law Bar Association, Employment Lawyers Association, COMBAR.
Career: Called to the Bar 1985 and joined current chambers in 1986.
Personal: Educated at London University (LL.B, 1983) and Oxford University (BCL, 1984). Speaks Swedish and Finnish. Member of Board of Interrights. Contributor to Halsbury's Laws on Constitutional Law and Human Rights.

CARTER, Peter QC
18 Red Lion Court (Anthony Arlidge QC), London (0171) 520 6000
Recommended in Crime
Specialisation: Principal area of practice is criminal law, both prosecution and defence work. Particular focus on fraud cases, but also handles drugs cases, offences of violence and sexual offences. Acted in BCCI and DPR litigation and has defended in a number of murder cases. Also deals with local authority and pollution cases. Clients include CPS headquarters, SFO and Customs and Excise. Author of 'Offences of Violence' and regular seminar speaker.
Prof. Memberships: Criminal Bar Association, South Eastern Circuit.
Career: Called to the Bar 1974 and joined current chambers in 1975. Secretary of Criminal Bar Association 1987-90. Took Silk 1995.
Personal: Educated at University College, London 1970-73 (LL.B). Governor of British Institute of Human Rights. Leisure pursuits include poetry, cricket and walking. Born 8th August 1952. Lives in Enfield, Middlesex.

CARTER-STEPHENSON, George QC
3 Gray's Inn Square (Rock Tansey QC), London (0171) 520 5600
Recommended in Crime
Specialisation: Experience in the conduct of the most serious and complex Criminal Cases including Murder, Serious Fraud, "Organised Crime" and Drug Trafficking. A specialist in the field of Criminal Defence.
Prof. Memberships: South Eastern Circuit, Criminal Bar Association.
Career: Called to the Bar in 1975 and joined current Chambers in 1977.
Personal: Leeds University 1971 to 1974 (LLB Honours).

CARUS, Roderick QC
9 St. John Street (John Hand QC), Manchester (0161) 955 9000
Recommended in Crime

CASEY, Mairin
Chambers of Colin Anderson (St. Mary's Chambers) (Colin Anderson), Nottingham (0115) 950 3503
Recommended in Family/Matrimonial

CASSEL, Timothy QC
5 Paper Buildings (John Mathew QC), London (0171) 583 6117
Recommended in the following lists: Crime, Licensing
Specialisation: Principal area of practice is serious crime cases, both prosecuting and defending. Major cases include major corruption case in Hong Kong and a major murder case in Trinidad & Tobago, defending (in retrial) the Master of the Bowbelle in criminal proceedings concerning sinking of 'The Marchioness', defence work in the Guiness case, prosecuting John Tyndall of the BNP under the Public Order Act; and other serious cases including murder and bullion robbery. Also handles licensing law, particularly gaming licensing for companies such as Aspinall's and Napoleons, also liquor and betting shop licences. Author of extradition section of 'Atkins Court Forms'. Also handles food hygiene cases: successfully defended Le Gavroche.
Prof. Memberships: Criminal Bar Association, Bar Council. Bencher, Lincoln's Inn 1994.

Career: Called to the Bar in 1965 and joined 1 Hare Court. Joined 5 Paper Buildings 1969. Junior Treasury Counsel, Central Criminal Court 1978-86 and Senior Treasury Counsel 1986-88. Assistant Boundary Commissioner 1981. Took Silk 1988.
Personal: Educated at Eton College 1955-60. Patron of Cassell Hospital for Nervous Disorders. Leisure pursuits include hunting, shooting, tennis, skiing and opera. Born 30th April 1942. Lives in Stokenchurch.

CATCHPOLE, Stuart
39 Essex Street (Edwin Glasgow QC), London (0171) 832 1111
Recommended in Construction
Specialisation: Construction and civil engineering. Professional negligence. Public law. Commercial law. Cases: currently counsel to the Ministry of Agriculture Fisheries and Food at the BSE inquiry; counsel for Sheffield Wednesday FC at the public inquiry and inquests. Details of reported cases and experience in any of areas of practice can be provided on request.
Prof. Memberships: Official Referees Bar Assocation. Administrative Law Bar Association. Appointed to the Supplementary Panel of Treasury Counsel Common Law in May 1992.
Career: Durham University 1983-1986: First Class Honours Degree in Law (Maxwell Law Prize). Colchester Royal Grammar School 1975-1982: A-Level History, English & Classical Civilisation (all Grade A).
Personal: Married. 2 year old son. Speaks French. Enjoys theatre, cinema, wine.

CATTAN, Philip D.
28 St. John St (Anthony Rumbelow QC), Manchester (0161) 834 8418
Recommended in Crime

CAUDLE, John
3 Hare Court (William Clegg QC), London (0171) 353 7561
Recommended in Crime

CAUSER, John
23 Essex Street (Michael Lawson QC), London (0171) 413 0353
Recommended in Crime
Specialisation: Commercial fraud and related areas of civil and criminal law including disqualification of directors, actions against the police etc. Recent clients include Lord Brocket and Roger Levitt. Legal and other disciplinary proceedings.
Prof. Memberships: Gambian Bar [1982].
Career: BA English Literature 1977. Called (Inner Temple) 1979.
Personal: Puzzle setting and solving, toy making, bicycling, photography, stamp collecting.

CAVANAGH, John Patrick
11 King's Bench Walk (Eldred Tabachnik QC and James Goudie QC), London (0171) 632 8500
Recommended in Employment
Specialisation: Principal areas of practice are employment law, local government law and judicial review. In employment law particular emphasis on discrimination and equal pay, TUPE (including CCT), the European aspects of employment law, restraint of trade, wrongful dismissal, industrial disputes and large-scale redundancies. Has recently acted in Preston v.Wolverhampton Healthcare (part-time pensions), Gregory v Wallace (breach of contract), Jepson v Labour Party (all-women shortlists), Clark v Secretary of State (scope of Article 119) and R v Portsmouth CC, ex parte Coles (public procurement).
Prof. Memberships: Treasurer of Employment Law Bar Association, member of Employment Lawyers Association, ALBA and COMBAR. Member of Supplementary Panel of Treasury Counsel for Employment Work.
Career: Called 1985. Joined 11 King's Bench Walk 1985.
Personal: Educated: Warwick School; New

College, Oxford (MA); Clare College, Cambridge (LLM) and University of Illinois.

CAVENDER, David
One Essex Court (Anthony Grabiner QC), London (0171) 583 2000
Recommended in Commercial
Specialisation: Commercial Litigation.
Prof. Memberships: COMBAR.
Career: Called to Bar and joined 1 Essex Court in 1993.
Personal: Educated at Kings College, London 1986-89 (LL.B 1st class Hons). Born 1964.

CAWS, Eian
4 Breams Buildings (Christopher Lockhart-Mummery QC), London
(0171) 430 1221/353 5835
Recommended in Planning
Specialisation: Planning and related work. Editor of Halsbury's Laws of England on Compulsory Acquisition, Chairman of the Berkshire Structure Plan.
Prof. Memberships: Committee member of the Planning and Environment Bar Association.
Career: Called to the Bar 1974.

CAWSON, Mark
St. James's Chambers (R.A. Sterling), Manchester (0161) 834 7000
Recommended in the following lists: Chancery, Commercial (litigation), Insolvency
Specialisation: General Chancery/Commercial with emphasis on contentious insolvency and company work, and professional negligence. Recent cases include A.F Budge directors' disqualification, Home Income Scheme litigation, Secretary of State for Trade and Industry v Ashcroft [1998] Ch 71, Barakot v Epiette [1998] 1BCLC 283.
Prof. Memberships: Northern Circuit, Chancery Bar Association, Northern Chancery Bar Association, Northern Circuit Commercial Bar Association, Professional Negligence Bar Association.
Career: Wrekin College. Liverpool University. Called 1982 (Lincoln's Inn). Junior Counsel to Treasury (Charity/Manchester) Dti's Panel of Counsel for Directors' Disqualification work.

CAYFORD, Philip
29 Bedford Row Chambers (Peter Ralls QC), London (0171) 831 2626
Recommended in Family: Matrimonial Finance
Specialisation: Family practice, heavily biased towards ancillary relief and matters with a commercial bias including company and entertainment law contracts. Also handles a wide range of common law, commercial, entertainment and other family law matters. Reported Court of Appeal decisions on Hague Convention and jurisdiction issues, on a derivative shareholder action arising from breakdown of family owned company, and on setting aside consent orders. Other reported decisions on children cases, professional negligence actions, inquests, etc.
Prof. Memberships: Middle Temple
Career: Called to the Bar 1975 and joined 29 Bedford Row 1978.

CHADWIN, James QC
Park Court Chambers (James Stewart QC, Robert Smith QC), Leeds (0113) 243 3277
Recommended in Crime

CHAISTY, Paul
40 King St (Philip Raynor QC), Manchester (0161) 832 9082
Recommended in the following lists: Chancery, Insolvency
Specialisation: Insolvency, Administration, Receivership, Director Disqualification, Banking, Commercial Landlord and Tenant.
Prof. Memberships: Northern Chancery Bar Association, Chancery Bar.
Career: CIS v Argyll, House of Lords 1997. Re Sankey. On DTI Panel re Directors Disqualification.

Re Sutton.

CHAMBERS, Dominic
Brick Court Chambers (Christopher Clarke QC), London (0171) 583 0777
Recommended in the following lists: Banking, Commercial (litigation)
Specialisation: Principal area of practice is commercial law, including banking, conflicts, negotiable instruments, insurance & reinsurance, guarantees and indemnities. Also handles commercial fraud, partnership and professional negligence. Professional clients predominantly major City law firms and law firms in the Channel Islands. Extensive experience of impact of US Banking and commercial law in England.
Prof. Memberships: COMBAR.
Career: Called to the Bar and joined 1 Hare Court in 1987. Joined the Chambers of Christopher Clarke QC in September 1997.
Personal: Educated at Harrow School 1976-81 and King's College, London 1983-86. Born 28th February 1963. Lives in London.

CHAMBERS, Nicholas QC
Brick Court Chambers (Christopher Clarke QC), London (0171) 583 0777
Recommended in Financial Services
Specialisation: Practitioner in the High Court, the Court of Appeal, the House of Lords and the Privy Council, arbitrations, disciplinary and regulatory tribunals. Specialises in Banking: Acted for all the clearing banks as well as other major and central banks, Commercial Law: wide variety of commercial cases including: Derby v Weldon, Shearson Lehman v McClaine Watson, Seaconsar v Bank Markazi. Regulatory: retained by large insurance companies in regulatory matters as well as representing individual associations and regulators. Media: acted for a number of television companies. Construction and similar work: Cases included ICC arbitrations, work for British Coal and valuation of large part of Italian Power Generating Industry.
Career: Called to Bar 1966. Queen's Counsel 1985. Recorder 1987. Deputy High Court Judge 1994. Bencher – Gray's Inn 1994. Director – The Incorporated Council of Law Reporting for England and Wales 1994. ICC and SIF Arbitrator. Publications include Editorial Board – Handbook of International Trade (Macmillan Publishers Ltd) 1988.
Personal: Born 25 February 1944. Educated King's School, Worcester and Hertford College, Oxford (MA). Scholarships and prizes: Meeke Scholar, Lee Essay Prize. Holker Senior Exhibition. Has working knowledge of French.

CHAPMAN, Vivian R.
9 Stone Buildings (Michael Ashe QC), London (0171) 404 5055
Recommended in Traditional Chancery
Specialisation: Property litigation with particular interest in Law of Commons and Greens. Recent reported cases; TSB Bank Plc v Botham [1995] EGCS3 (Fixtures); R. v Suffolk County Council Ex Parte Steed [1997] 1 EGLR 131 (Greens); Fitzpatrick v Sterling Housing Association Ltd [1998] 2 WLR (Landlord and Tenant).
Prof. Memberships: Lincoln's Inn: Middle Temple.

CHARMAN, Andrew
St Philip's Chambers (Rex Tedd QC), Birmingham (0121) 246 7000
Recommended in Chancery
Specialisation: Company law, commercial law, insolvency, financial services, professional negligence, real property, trusts, litigation, advisory and drafting.
Prof. Memberships: Member of the Chancery Bar Association and the Midland Chancery and Commercial Bar Association. Associate of the Chartered Institute of Arbitrators.
Career: Educated at Imberhorne School, East Grinstead and Clare College, Cambridge. Worked as a researcher at The House of Commons then

articles with Freshfields in London and Tokyo followed by practice as a solicitor in Freshfields' corporate department.

CHAWLA, Mukul
9-12 Bell Yard (D. Anthony Evans QC), London (0171) 400 1800
Recommended in Crime

CHERRY, John M. QC
8 Stone Buildings (John Cherry QC), London (0171) 831 9881
Recommended in Personal Injury
Specialisation: Main areas of practice are personal injury, medical negligence, professional negligence. Involved in number of structured settlement cases.
Prof. Memberships: Gray's Inn.
Career: Cheshunt Grammar School and Council of Legal Education. Called to Bar in 1961. Recorder 1987. QC 1988. Member of Criminal Injuries Compensation Board since 1988.

CHERRYMAN, John QC
4 Breams Buildings (Christopher Lockhart-Mummery QC), London
(0171) 430 1221/353 5835
Recommended in Property Litigation
Specialisation: Moved from Lincolns Inn to Breams Buildings in 1992 to concentrate on property related litigation and advice, including mining, professional negligence, mortgage securities, contaminated land and rating as well as mainstream landlord and tenant and vendor and purchaser work. A Bencher at Grays Inn and a member of the Chancery Bar Association. Recent cases include TSB Bank v Camfield 1995 CA and Dunbar Bank v Nadeem 1998 CA (variants of O'Brien), Bentley v Gaisford 1996 CA (solicitors undertaking), Mannai Investment Co. v Eagle Star 1997 HL (validity of break notice) and Shimizu (U.K.) v Westminster City Council 1997 HL (listed building: demolition or alteration).

CHILD, John
Wilberforce Chambers (Edward Nugee QC), London (0171) 306 0102
Recommended in Traditional Chancery
Specialisation: Heavy trust work – advice and drafting and some litigation. In part this is private client work dealing with family trusts and landed estates. The remaining part is commercial trust work, mostly relating to the Society of Lloyd's. Cases include Re Hampden's Settlement Trusts [1977] TR177; Re Hay's Settlement Trusts [1982] 1WLR202 and Napier v Kershaw [1997] L Re LR1.
Prof. Memberships: Chancery Bar Association; Revenue Bar Association; and Society of Trust and Estate Practitioners. Books – main contributor vol 19 (Sale of land) Encyclopaedia of Forms and Precedents (4th ed.). Forms of accumulation and maintenance Settlements for Encyclopaedia of Forms and Precedents (5th ed.) Vol 40.
Career: Firsts in Law at University of Southampton and Sidney Sussex College Cambridge. BA Scholar Sidney Sussex College. Droop Scholar and Tancred Common Law Student, Hon Soc of Lincoln's Inn. Supervisor in Law at Sidney Sussex and other Cambridge colleges 1966-78.
Personal: Married to a GP in Epsom. Two sons Andrew (24) and Jeremy (21). Interests include education and languages. Enjoys tennis and badminton.

CHIVERS, David
Erskine Chambers (Richard Sykes QC), London (0171) 242 5532
Recommended in the following lists: Company, Insolvency
Specialisation: Principal area of practice is company law, including corporate insolvency. Contributor to 'Gore-Brown on Companies', 'Practice and Procedure in the Companies Court' and 'Co-Operatives That Work'.
Prof. Memberships: Chancery Bar Association, COMBAR, Insolvency Lawyers Association.

Member of Chancery Working Group reporting to Lord Woolf.
Career: Called to the Bar 1983 and joined Erskine Chambers 1984.
Personal: Born 1960. Educated at Downing College, Cambridge 1979-82.

CHRISTIE, Richard
2 Pump Court (Philip Singer QC), London (0171) 353 5597
Recommended in Crime
Specialisation: All areas of criminal work but especially fraud and cases requiring substantial client care. (i) R v Johnson (Aldin) [1995] 2 Cr. App. R. I (Albi and severance); (ii) Martin v Watson [1994] Q.B.425 and A.C.74 (malicious prosecution); (iii) R v MIAN [1997] (1.5m. cannabis importation by high ranking Pakistani, said to have been framed by Pakistani Regime); (iv) R v PARR [1997] (Money laundering following Eurobond fraud in and out of the jurisdiction); (v) R v Hewett [1997] (serious sexual offences: severance and similar facts); (vi) R v Phipps [1998] (Murder: educationally subnormal defendant, cut-throat defences).
Career: Clifton College; Manchester University; Touche Ross & Co (Accountants).
Personal: Cinema and Reading. Wife (solicitor) and 3 children.

CLARE, Michael
Octagon House Chambers (Andrew Lindqvist & Guy Ayers), Norwich (01603) 623186
Recommended in Crime

CLARK, Christopher QC
Pump Court Chambers (Guy Boney QC), London (0171) 353 0711
Recommended in Ecclesiastical

CLARK, Fiona
8 New Square (Michael Fysh QC), London (0171) 405 4321
Recommended in Intellectual Property
Specialisation: Specialises in all aspects of intellectual property law including related contractual and EC matters, breach of confidence and trade libel. Has a particular interest in copyright, designs (both registered and unregistered) and trade marks. Also has extensive experience of product branding and in media and entertainment law. Practice embraces a wide range of cases with a high technical content covering areas such as mechanical and construction engineering, computer software, electronics, architectural design and textiles. Publications include 'Encyclopedia of United Kingdom and European Patent Law' (co-author). Reported cases: Johnstone Safety v Peter Cook, Southco v Dzus Fasteners, Consorzio del Prosciutto di Parma v Marks and Spencer, Dalgetty v Food Brokers, McDonald v Graham, Coil Controls v Suzo, Norowzian v Arks.
Prof. Memberships: Intellectual Property Bar Association; Chancery Bar Association.
Career: Called to the Bar 1982.
Personal: Educated at Trinity College, Cambridge. Competent in French and German.

CLARK, Wayne
Falcon Chambers (Jonathan Gaunt QC & Kim Lewison QC), London (0171) 353 2484
Recommended in Property Litigation
Specialisation: Property litigation, including commercial leases, vendor and purchaser disputes, easements, restrictive covenants, mortgages and property related professional negligence.
Prof. Memberships: Chancery Bar Association, COMBAR.
Career: L.L.B. (Lon), BCL (Oxon), former lecturer in law at QMC, London University. Contributor to Halsbury's Laws of England, Vol 27 (i), 4th ed., Landlord and Tenant. Contributor to Hill and Redman, Law of Landlord and Tenant, Standing Counsel (civil) to Attorney General, Co-Author,

Renewal of Business Tenancies Law Practice (Sweet & Maxwell 1997).
Personal: Keen chess player.

CLARKE, Andrew QC
Littleton Chambers (Michael Burton QC), London (0171) 797 8600
Recommended in the following lists: Commercial (litigation), Employment
Specialisation: Experienced employment lawyer, having appeared in this area before all relevant courts and tribunals. Particular specialism in disputes relating to restrictive covenants and confidential information. Also handles commercial and company law matters, both relating to employment (including directors' duties) and generally. Acted for PLA in docks dispute, in relation to industrial action and the two year Industrial Tribunal. Appeared in numerous important cases on individual employment rights, sex and race discrimination, restrictive covenants and "garden leave" injunctions. Clients include major UK companies, solicitors' firms and senior employees.
Prof. Memberships: Employment Law Bar Association; Employment Lawyers Association; COMBAR (Committee Member).
Career: Called to the Bar 1980, QC 1997, joined Littleton Chambers in 1981.
Personal: Educated at Crewe County Grammar School, King's College London 1974-77 (LL.B) and Lincoln College, Oxford 1977-79 (BCL). Leisure pursuits include playing and watching cricket and football, and collecting modern prints and porcelain. Lives in Cheshunt. Born 23rd August 1956.

CLARKE, Christopher QC
Brick Court Chambers (Christopher Clarke QC), London (0171) 583 0777
Recommended in the following lists: Arbitration, Aviation, Commercial (litigation), Insurance & Reinsurance, Media & Entertainment, Professional Negligence, Shipping
Specialisation: General commercial law, including banking, shipping, insurance and financial services, oil and gas law, international trade, sale of goods, share sale agreements, takeovers and mergers, defamation and entertainment law, administrative law, disciplinary tribunals and employment law. Attorney of the Supreme Court of the Turks and Caicos Islands. Recent Cases: Arab Monetary Fund v Hashim; R v ITC ex parte Referendum Party; Gruppo Torras v Sheikh Fahad; Credit Suisse v Allerdale; LDC Trustees v Barings Plc, BCCI v E&Y, Royal Boskalis v Trevor Rex Mountain. Rowland v Bock. Counsel to the 'Bloody Sunday' Inquiry, Société Anonyme D'Intermédiare. Luxembourgois v Farex, Ashton v Black Sea and Baltic General Insurance, Henderson v Merret and Ernst Young.
Career: Called to Bar 1969; Silk 1984. Recorder. Deputy High Court Judge.
Personal: MA (Cantab).

CLARKE, Gerard
Blackstone Chambers (formerly 2 Hare Court) (P Baxendale QC and C Flint QC), London (0171) 583 1770
Recommended in Employment
Specialisation: Commercial, employment and public law, with an emphasis on employment work, particularly in injunctive proceedings concerning confidential information, restrictive covenants and employee competition, terminations of senior employees, and TUPE cases. Commercial work covers a wide range of business disputes including commercial fraud and financial services. Public law work in a variety of fields including Education, NHS, Mental Health, media and sports regulation. Also practises in defamation and media law. Recent interesting cases include Scully UK v Lee 1998 IRLR, Wallace v Gregory 1998 IRLR, R v Riverside Mental Health NHS Trust ex parte Huzzey, Times April 1998, Holly v Smyth 1998

IWLR, R v Cobham Hall School ex parte G [1997] ELR, Credit Suisse v Armstrong [1996] IRLR 450, Spring v Guardian Assurance PLC [1995] 2 AC 296 and Meade Hill v British Council [1995] 1CR 847.
Prof. Memberships: Employment Lawyers' Association, Employment Law Bar Association, Administrative Law Bar Association.
Career: Called to the Bar 1986. Legal Assistant to Comptroller and City Solicitor, Corporation of London, advising on employment law, 1986. Voluntary work for the Free Representation Unit and several Citizens Advice Bureaux and other advice centres since 1985. Member of ELAAS scheme of EAT. Occasional Spokesman for the National Council for Civil Liberties from 1989-90. Joined present chambers 1987.
Personal: Born 1962. Educated in Solihull and at Wadham College, Oxford (MA).

CLARKE, Nicholas
9 St. John Street (John Hand QC), Manchester (0161) 955 9000
Recommended in Crime

CLARKSON, Patrick QC
1 Serjeants' Inn (Lionel Read QC), London (0171) 583 1355
Recommended in the following lists: Parliamentary, Planning
Specialisation: Planning, Local Government, Environmental, Parliamentary.
Prof. Memberships: Planning & Environmental Bar Association.
Career: Called 1972, Silk 1991, Recorder 1996.

CLAYTON, Richard
Devereux Chambers (Jeffrey Burke QC), London (0171) 353 7534
Recommended in the following lists: Administrative & Public Law, Civil Liberties
Specialisation: Principal areas of practice are public law and civil liberties/human rights. Public law embraces education, health care, prisoners' rights, regulatory and disciplinary matters as well as local government law eg community care, homelessness and local government finance. Also handles civil actions against the police, employment law (both individual and collective), discrimination law and European law. Acted in R v Chief Constable of South Wales ex p Merrick [1994] 1 WLR 663 (the right to legal advice); R v Governors of Hasmonean High School ex p N and E [1994] ELR 343 (school admissions and special educational needs); Philip Hodge v Kell [1994] ICR 656 (maternity rights); Home Secretary v Barnes *The Times* 19th December 1994 (the legality of the Prison strike); R v Chief Constable of West Midlands Police ex p Wiley [1995] 1 AC 274 (public interest immunity); R v Home Secretary ex p Hickey No 2 [1995] 1 WLR 734 (prisoners' rights); R v Northern & Yorkshire RHA ex p Trivedi, [1995] 1 WLR 961 (the disciplinary procedure for General Practitioners); R v Home Secretary ex p Goswell, [1995] COD 223 (Brooke J) [1995] COD 438 (CA) (police complaints procedure); Hellewell v Chief Constable of Derbyshire [1995] 1 WLR 804 (breach of confidence); Rai v United Kingdom (1995) EHRLR 92 (freedom of assembly under European Convention); R v Metropolitan Police Commissioner ex p P. (1996) 8 Admin LR 6 (judicial review to quash caution); London Borough of Harrow v Cunningham [1996] IRLR 256 (unfair dismissal); Elliott v Chief Constable of Wiltshire, *The Times* 5th December 1996 (misfeasance in a public office); R v Southwestern Magistrates ex p Cofie [1997] 1 WLR 585 (judicial review of search warrant); R v Lincolnshire Crown Court ex p Jude [1997] 3 All ER 737 (breach of peace); R v Press Complaints Commission ex p Stewart Brady (1997) 9 Admin LR 274 (privacy rights); Bamber v United Kingdom [1998] EHRLR 110 (freedom of expression under Article 10); R v Northampton CC ex p W [1998] COD 110 (school admissions); R v Legal Aid Board ex p Owners Abroad [1998] PIQR 116. Clients include numerous victims of the West

Midlands Serious Crime Squad; Save Guy's Hospital Campaign; local authorities. Author of *Practice and Procedure at Industrial Tribunals* (LAG) (1986); *Civil Actions against the Police* (Sweet & Maxwell) (2nd edition 1992); *Judicial Review Procedure* (Wiley) (2nd edition 1997). Contributor to legal periodicals, radio and television. Regularly lectures on public law and human rights.
Prof. Memberships: Administrative Law Bar Association (Committee since 1996); Employment Law Bar Association; Liberty; Society of Labour Lawyers; Legal Action Group (Committee since 1985).
Career: Called to Bar 1977; South Islington Law Centre 1980-82; *Osler, Hoskin Harcourt* (Toronto) 1983; Returned to practice 1984; joined Devereux Chambers 1996.
Personal: Educated New College, Oxford. Leisure pursuits include reading, cinema, theatre and travel. Born 25th May 1954. Lives in London.

CLEGG, William QC
3 Hare Court (William Clegg QC), London (0171) 353 7561
Recommended in the following lists: Crime, Crime: Fraud
Specialisation: Specialist in defending cases of alleged fraud. Cases include Brent Walker, Butte Mining Ltd, R v Smith (£100m bank fraud), R v Smithson (The Arrows fraud), R v De Vandiere (VAT fraud), R v Alder (international bank fraud), R v Vanderval (letter of credit fraud), R v Morley (fraudulent trading), R v Hales (solicitors legal aid fraud). Cases of a more general nature include R v Serafinowicz (War Crimes), R v Wardell (Nuneaton Building Society murder) and R v Stagg (Wimbledon Common murder), R v Varathadasan (Tamil Tigers), R v McMahon (UDA terrorists). Has also been instructed in a lengthy public enquiry by the Medical Protection Society and many cases in the Court of Appeal Criminal Division and Divisional Court. Was a member of the standing committee of Justice on fraud trials and prepared submissions to the Fraud Trials Committee chaired by Roskill (HMSO 1986).
Prof. Memberships: Criminal Bar Association (Committee members); South Eastern Circuit (Committee member).
Career: Called to the Bar 1972 and joined present chambers in 1973. Took silk 1991. Appointed Recorder 1992. Head of Chambers 1995.
Personal: Educated at Bristol University (LL.B). Leisure pursuits include squash, cricket and wine. Born 5th September 1949.

CLIFFORD, James
7 Stone Buildings (Charles Aldous QC), London (0171) 405 3886
Recommended in Pensions
Specialisation: Specialises in pensions and trusts and has general commercial chancery litigation practice. Recent cases handled include Edge v The Pensions Ombudsman, Hood Sailmakers Ltd v Axford, Miller v Scorey, Process Developments Ltd v Hogg, Coloroll Pension Trustees Limited v Russell, Thrells Ltd v Lomas and Nestle v National Westminster Bank, Mettoy Pensions Trustees v Evans. Contributor to Trust Law International, British Pensions Lawyer, and author of Pensions Title, Atkins Court Forms.
Prof. Memberships: Association of Pension Lawyers, Chancery Bar Association.
Career: Called to the Bar in 1984.
Personal: Educated at Oxford University.

CLOSE, Douglas
Serle Court Chambers (Charles Sparrow QC QC), London (0171) 242 6105
Recommended in the following lists: Chancery, Company
Specialisation: General commercial chancery litigation, in particular commercial fraud (domestic and international), business agreements, trusts litigation and insolvency. Recent cases include: Don King Productions Inc v Frank Warren & Ors, the Palumbo litigation, and the Wahr-Hansen

litigation in the Cayman Islands.
Prof. Memberships: Chancery Bar Association; Insolvency Lawyers Association.
Career: Called 1991.
Personal: Born 1966. Educated at Berkhamsted School; Jesus College, Oxford (MA, BCL). Interests include theatre, restaurants, abstract art.

CLOVER, Anthony
New Court Chambers (George Carman QC), London (0171) 831 9500
Recommended in Civil Liberties
Specialisation: Professional negligence (medical; solicitors; etc). Contract and commercial. Civil liberties: Junior counsel for members of the Maguire family at Sir John May's Inquiry concerning the Guilford and Woolwich Bombings, and in Court of Appeal (1992) 1 QB 936. Represented the Headteacher of Highbury Grove Comprehensive School at the Disciplinary Inquiry into running of the school (1993). Considerable experience of appearing (for plaintiffs and defendants) in civil actions against the police; has represented prisoners in actions against the Home Office. Criminal law: defence; and prosecuting, instructed by Customs and Excise.
Prof. Memberships: Professional Negligence Bar Association.
Career: Called (Middle Temple) 1971. (Astbury Scholarship). Recorder: 1995.
Personal: Educated at Stowe; and Exeter College, Oxford (Exhibitioner).

COBB, Stephen
One Garden Court Family Law Chambers (Miss Eleanor F. Platt QC & Miss Alison Ball QC), London (0171) 797 7900
Recommended in Family: Child Care including child abduction
Specialisation: Family law, including public and private law aspects of the Children Act 1989, adoption, child abduction and children cases with an international element, matrimonial finance, judicial review (mainly family law related), applications/appeals under Part X Children Act 1989 (registration of Childminding and day care services for children).
Prof. Memberships: F.L.B.A.
Career: Called to the Bar in 1985.
Personal: Winchester College. Liverpool University (LL.B Hons. 1984) Born 12.4.1962. Lives in London. Married. 3 children.

COBURN, Michael
20 Essex Street (David Johnson QC), London (0171) 583 9294
Recommended in Shipping
Specialisation: Commercial law, including in particular carriage at sea, international sales of goods and insurance.
Career: Called 1990.
Personal: Educated at Charterhouse; Worcester College, Oxford; City University.

COCKS, David QC
18 Red Lion Court (Anthony Arlidge QC), London (0171) 520 6000
Recommended in Crime: Fraud

COGHLAN, Terence QC
1 Crown Office Row (Robert Seabrook QC), London (0171) 797 7500
Recommended in Medical Negligence
Specialisation: Covers all aspects of medical work including medical negligence. Has appeared for both plaintiffs and defendants in numerous medical negligence actions and arbitrations as well as regularly appearing in the GMC, GDC and other disciplinary bodies. Represented all the health authorities involved in the "Myodil" litigation and the defendant in Bolitho v City & Hackney HA (House of Lords). Clients have included the Medical Defence Union, Medical Protection Society, MDDUS, the Welsh Office and leading medical negligence solicitors. Has lectured at various seminars on personal injury and medical

negligence matters and also on television.
Prof. Memberships: Professional Negligence Bar Association.
Career: Called in 1968. Recorder of the Crown Court 1989. QC 1993.
Personal: Education: New College, Oxford (BA, MA).

COGLEY, Stephen
Merchant Chambers (David Berkley), Manchester (0161) 839 7070
Recommended in Commercial (litigation)
Specialisation: Commercial. Seven reported cases in the fields of Insolvency, Shareholder disputes, Banking, Consumer Credit/Licensing in last year. Instructed frequently in Banking and Finance Leasing cases by Banks and Finance Houses and Building Societies. Clients include RBS, Rothchilds, Dew Group, Cheshire Building Society. Acted in Exchange Travel at first instance and in Court of Appeal (x2).
Prof. Memberships: Founder member of Northern Circuit Commercial Bar Association. COMBAR member.
Career: Also at 22 Old Buildings Lincolns London. Tel: (0171) 831 0222. Fax: (0171) 831 2239.
Personal: Lives Lancashire and Scotland. Hobbies: fell running, mountaineering and rock climbing.

COHEN, Jonathan QC
4 Paper Buildings (Lionel Swift QC), London (0171) 583 0816
Recommended in Family: Matrimonial Finance
Specialisation: Practice encompasses all areas of family law, in particular matrimonial finance, professional negligence arising out of family law matters and childcare.
Prof. Memberships: Family Law Bar Association, Professional Negligence Bar Association.
Career: Called to the Bar 1974 and joined present chambers in 1975. Recorder and Silk 1997.
Personal: School Governor. Born 1951.

COHEN, Lawrence QC
24 Old Buildings (C.A. Brodie QC), London (0171) 404 0946
Recommended in the following lists: Company, Insolvency
Specialisation: The main areas of Business Law including: Insolvency (personal & corporate); Civil Fraud; Company Law; Contract Disputes; Financial Services; Partnership Law; Professional Negligence; Property Law; Landlord and Tenant.
Prof. Memberships: Associate Member, Chartered Institute of Arbitrators; Member of the Financial Panel of Chartered Institute of Arbitrators; Member of the Chancery Bar Association; Member of the Insolvency Lawyers Association.
Career: Birmingham University (LLB); Queens Counsel (1993); Assistant Recorder (1995).

COHEN, Raphael
Mercury chambers, Leeds (0113) 234 2265
Recommended in Family/Matrimonial
Specialisation: Specialist in matrimonial property work. Involved in cases with substantial assets and with a commercial bias including company accounts and contracts.
Career: Called to the Bar in 1981. A founder member of Mercury Chambers which is a specialist civil and commercial set.

COLE, Edward
Falcon Chambers (Jonathan Gaunt QC & Kim Lewison QC), London (0171) 353 2484
Recommended in Property Litigation
Specialisation: Real property.
Prof. Memberships: Gray's Inn.
Career: Called to the Bar in 1980.
Personal: Contributor to Megarry on the Rents Act 11th Edition; Specialist Editor Hill & Redman Law of Landlord and Tenant. Contributor Halsbury's Laws, vol 27, title Landlord and Tenant. Atkin's Court Forms: title Agriculture.

COLEMAN, Nicholas
1 Hare Court (Stephen Kramer QC), London
(0171) 353 5324
Recommended in Crime

COLERIDGE, Paul QC
Queen Elizabeth Building (Ian Karsten QC),
London (0171) 797 7837
Recommended in Family: Matrimonial Finance

COLEY, William L.
35 Essex Street (Nigel Inglis-Jones QC),
London (0171) 353 6381
Recommended in Personal Injury
Specialisation: Principal area of practice is
personal injury, both plaintiff and defendant work.
Also handles professional negligence.
Prof. Memberships: Western Circuit, London
Common Law & Commercial Bar Association;
Personal Injury Bar Association (PIBA);
Professional Negligence Bar Association (PNBA);
Association of Personal Injury Lawyers (APIL);
Association for Victims of Medical Accidents
(AVMA).
Career: Called to the Bar in 1980 and joined Essex
Street in 1981.
Personal: Educated at Radley College 1971-75
and Downing College, Cambridge 1976-79. Born
20th September 1957.

COLLENDER, Andrew QC
2 Temple Gardens (Patrick Phillips QC), London
(0171) 583 6041
Recommended in Personal Injury
Specialisation: Wide experience of substantial
personal injury actions with specialisations in
medical negligence, occupational claims, repetitive
strain injuries, post traumatic stress disorder and
disaster litigation. Recent high profile cases include
Mughal v Reuters [1993], Frost v South Yorkshire
Police [1997], Amosu v Financial Times [1998].
Prof. Memberships: London Common Law Bar
Association. Professional Negligence Bar
Association. Personal Injuries Bar Association.
Career: University of Bristol – LLB (Hons) 1968.
Called Lincoln's Inn July 1969. Silk April 1991.
Recorder January 1993.
Personal: Married – 2 sons. Sailing, Violin,
Member of Bar Human Rights Committee.

COLLINGS, Matthew
13 Old Square (Mr Michael Lyndon-Stanford
QC), London (0171) 404 4800
*Recommended in the following lists: Chancery,
Company, Insolvency*
Specialisation: Company law (litigation and
advisory work) including corporate reconstructions,
takeovers and mergers, shareholders disputes,
directors duties and disqualification. Reported
cases include: British & Commonwealth, Leeds
United, Carecraft, Manlon, Barings, UMB v
Doherty, and Legal Costs Negotiators.
Corporate insolvency. Reported cases include:
Arrows, BCCI, Harris Simons, Wallace Smith,
Charnley Davies, Galileo Group, Vanilla
Accumulation, Hamlet International and Atlantic
Computers.
Personal insolvency and bankruptcy. Reported
cases include: Naeem, Murjani. Financial services
(including regulatory and tribunal work). Reported
cases include: SIB v Lancashire & Yorkshire.
Commercial Chancery including: guarantees and
securities, share sale warranties and professional
negligence.
Prof. Memberships: Chancery Bar Association.
Member, Insolvency Rules Advisory Committee.

COLLINS, Michael QC
Essex Court Chambers (Gordon Pollock QC),
London (0171) 813 8000
*Recommended in the following lists: Arbitration,
Insurance & Reinsurance, Shipping*
Specialisation: Insurance, Shipping, Conflict of
laws, Commercial and Technical Contract and Tort
disputes generally, Arbitration.
Prof. Memberships: American Bar Association,

International Bar Association, Commercial Bar
Association
Career: University of Exeter LLB (First Class
Hons). Called to the Bar 1971. Queen's Counsel
1988. Recorder 1997.
Personal: Born 1948.

COMYN, Timothy
2 Harcourt Buildings (Mr Gerard Ryan QC),
London (0171) 353 8415
Recommended in Planning
Specialisation: Planning, Local Government,
Compulsory Purchase, Environmental,
Parliamentary and Administrative Law.
Prof. Memberships: Planning and Environmental
Bar Association, Administrative Law Association,
Parliamentary Bar Mess, Member of S.E. Circuit.
Career: Called to the Bar 1980. Joined 2 Harcourt
Buildings in 1981. Educated at Ampleforth College
and Hull University.

CONE, John
Erskine Chambers (Richard Sykes QC), London
(0171) 242 5532
Recommended in Company
Specialisation: Corporate reorganisations and
reconstructions including reduction of capital and
schemes of arrangement. Takeovers and mergers.
Schemes of arrangement in insolvencies.
Prof. Memberships: Chancery Bar Association.
COMBAR. A Bar Representative on the Law
Society Company Law Committee, Member of the
Law Reform Committee of the Bar Council.

CONLON, Michael
One Essex Court (Anthony Grabiner QC),
London (0171) 583 2000
Recommended in Tax
Specialisation: VAT, customs and excise duties
and other indirect taxes, including investigations
and litigation; European Community law;
commercial litigation.
Prof. Memberships: Fellow of The Chartered
Institute of Taxation (FTII); Fellow of The Institute of
Advanced Legal Studies (FIALS); RBA; COMBAR;
President of the VAT Practitioners Group; Institute
of Indirect Tax; Customs Practitioners Group;
Fellow of the Institute of Continuing Professional
Development (FICPD); Member British Industry in
Sport (BISL); Guild of Tax Advisers; Tax Law Review
Committee; Editor "VAT Intelligence".
Career: Enfield Grammar School; Queens'
College, Cambridge; Called to Bar 1974 (Inner
Temple); mixed common law practice; Senior Legal
Adviser, HM Customs & Excise (1977-86); KPMG
(1986-88); Partner, Coopers & Lybrand (1988-91);
Freshfields (1991-93); Solicitor (1992); Partner
Allen & Overy (1993-97); returned to Bar.
Personal: Married; two children; recreations
include music, literature, badminton; lives in East
Sussex.

CONWAY, Charles
3 Hare Court (William Clegg QC), London
(0171) 353 7561
Recommended in Crime

COOK, Ian
One King's Bench Walk (James Townend QC),
London (0171) 936 1500
Recommended in Family: Matrimonial Finance
Specialisation: Main areas of practice:
matrimonial finance, public law children cases,
child abduction, crime. Reported cases: Re H
(Abduction: Acquiesence) [1997] 1 FLR 872, HL.
Re S (Care Proceedings: Split Hearing) [1996] 2
FLR 773, FD.
Prof. Memberships: FLBA
Career: BA (Hons) 1st Class Philosophy, King's
College London. CPE City of London Polytechnic.

COOK, Mary
2-3 Gray's Inn Square (Anthony Scrivener QC),
London (0171) 242 4986
Recommended in Planning
Specialisation: Planning and Local Government
work. Wide Planning Enquiry experience extending
to all fields, both promoting and resisting
development including enforcement, called-in
applications and Local Plan appearances, the
promotion of CPO particularly town centre and
development corporation schemes, footpath and
road closures. Extensive recent experience of non-
food and food retail schemes, green belt and
Conservation/Listed Building issues. Court
experience includes judicial review and high court
challenges, Lands Tribunal claims, and
proceedings involving inforcement of
environmental/planning/trade description
legislation.
Prof. Memberships: Planning and Environmental
Bar Association.
Career: Called 1982, commenced practice form
these chambers in 1985.
Personal: Educated at the Royal School, Bath and
University College Cardiff. Married with 3 children
and living in London.

COOKE, Jeremy QC
7 King's Bench Walk (Stephen Tomlinson QC),
London (0171) 583 0404
*Recommended in the following lists: Energy &
Utilities, Insurance & Reinsurance, Professional
Negligence, Shipping*
Specialisation: Specialises in all aspects of
commercial law including insurance and
reinsurance, shipping, professional negligence,
international sale of goods (oil and gas in
particular) and banking. Important litigation
includes the Feltrim names action against Lloyd's
agents.
Prof. Memberships: Commercial Bar Association;
London Maritime Arbitrators Association.
Career: Called to the Bar 1976 and joined present
chambers in the same year. Took Silk 1990.
Appointed Assistant Recorder 1994.
Prof. Memberships: (MA Jurisprudence 1st class).
Oxford University rugby Blue 1968 and 1969.
Director of Christian Youth and Schools Charitable
company, Christian Impact Ltd. Leisure pursuits
include golf. Born 28.9.1949. Lives in London.

COOKE, Nicholas QC
9 Park Place (Ian Murphy QC), Cardiff
(01222) 382731
Recommended in Personal Injury
Prof. Memberships: Wales and Chester circuit,
Planning and Environmental Bar Association,
Bristol and Cardiff Chancery Bar Association.
Career: King Edward's School, Birmingham.
U.C.W. Aberystwyth (1st Class Honours LL.B).
Personal: Hockey, Theatre.

COOKSLEY, Nigel
Old Square Chambers (Hon. John Melville
Williams QC), London (0171) 269 0300
Recommended in Personal Injury
Specialisation: Principal area of practice for many
years has been personal injury litigation and has a
widespread practice throughout the country. Other
areas of practice include professional negligence,
contract, product liability and sporting injuries.
Prof. Memberships: Personal Injury Bar
Association, Association of Personal Injury
Lawyers, London Common Law and Commercial
Bar Association.
Career: Called to the Bar in 1975.
Personal: Educated at Felsted School and
Cambridge University. Lives in North Hertfordshire.
Outside interests include sport.

COONAN, Kieran QC
6 Pump Court (Kieran Coonan QC), London
(0171) 583 6013
Recommended in Medical Negligence
Specialisation: Practises across a wide medico-
legal spectrum, with particular emphasis on

medical negligence, personal injury and mental health matters. Also practises in the criminal law and in the professional conduct field.
Prof. Memberships: Professional Negligence Bar Association; Personal Injury Bar Association; Criminal Bar Association.
Career: Called 1971; Commenced practice in 1974; Silk 1990; Head of Chambers 1991; Recorder 1996.

COOPER, John
3 Gray's Inn Square (Rock Tansey QC), London (0171) 520 5600
Recommended in Crime
Specialisation: Specialist in serious criminal law. Also deals with general common law.
Career: Called to the Bar in 1983. Member New South Wales Bar. Represented the British employees in the BCCI litigation. Butterworths' Law Prizeman. Successfully represented the Defendant in the 'Leah Betts' Ecstasy drug trials. Leading authority in Master of the Rolls court on the criminality of wheel clamping (Arthur v. Anker) and indictment rules (R v Wrench). Instructed for Louise Woodward by campaign committee. Commended by 'The Lawyer' in the category "Barrister of the Year 1998". Publications include Code E PACE (Sweet & Maxwell) and Judicial Review from the Magistrates Court (Sweet & Maxwell). Advisor to the emerging democracies in Eastern Europe upon criminal law and justice. Entry in Debrett's "People of Today" page 414.

COOPER, Peter QC
2 Harcourt Buildings (Nigel Mylne QC), London (0171) 353 2112
Recommended in Crime

COPPEL, Jason
11 King's Bench Walk (Eldred Tabachnik QC and James Goudie QC), London (0171) 632 8500
Recommended in Employment
Specialisation: European employment law issues including sex discrimination, transfer of undertakings and free movement. Junior counsel in Fletcher v Midland Bank (test cases on pension rights for part-time workers), Adams v Lancashire CC (leading case on transfer of pension rights under TUPE), Mann v Secretary of State for Employment (validity under EC law of artificial ceiling on a week's pay and deductions from a protective award), Page v CST (leading case on compensation under the Commercial Agents Regulations) and Spencer v UK (rights to privacy under the ECHR).
Career: Co-author of Butterworths' 'EC Law for UK Lawyers' (1994); author of 'The Human Rights Act: enforcing the European Convention in the Domestic Courts' (John Wiley 1998).

CORBETT, James
St Philip's Chambers (Rex Tedd QC), Birmingham (0121) 246 7000
Recommended in Chancery, Commercial (litigation), Employment
Specialisation: Practice covers broad range of commercial, company and insolvency work. Regularly instructed for DTI in cases under Company Director's Disqualification Act. Work also includes Official Referee's Business.
Prof. Memberships: Fellow of Chartered Institute of Arbitrators. Member of Chancery Bar Association. International Bar Association and Employment Law Bar Association and Professional Negligence Bar Association.
Career: LLB and LLM (European Legal Studies), University of Exeter. Called in 1975. Irish Bar (1981) and Northern Irish Bar (1994). Joined present chambers in 1983. Lecturer in European and commercial law, 1975-1977 (Leicester University).

CORDARA, Roderick QC
Essex Court Chambers (Gordon Pollock QC), London (0171) 813 8000
Recommended in the following lists: Insurance & Reinsurance, Shipping, Tax
Specialisation: Insurance and reinsurance litigation; Lloyd's disciplinary hearings; Shipping and shipbuilding work; Banking; Film industry litigation; Oil and gas disputes; Far Eastern family disputes and related estate matters; General business litigation; Indirect tax work – advising on all aspects of VAT law and VAT planning.
Career: Trinity Hall, Cambridge: BA (Law) (First class) 1974. Called to the Bar 1975. Queen's Counsel 1994.
Personal: Born 1953.

CORFIELD, Sheelagh
Guildhall Chambers (John Royce QC), Bristol (0117) 927 3366
Recommended in Family/Matrimonial

CORNER, Timothy
4-5 Gray's Inn Square (Miss Elizabeth Appleby QC & The Hon. M. Beloff QC), London (0171) 404 5252
Recommended in the following lists: Administrative & Public Law, Planning
Specialisation: Major part of practice is in the fields of town and country planning, public law including education, local government and environmental law. Planning work includes appeals throughout the country relating to retail, housing, offices, listed buildings and conservation areas, waste, and minerals. Interesting recent cases include R v Secretary of State for the Environment ex p. Slot [1997] The Times, 11th December (Court of Appeal, Judicial Review, natural justice), R v Teesside Development Corporation ex p. William Morrison Supermarket PLC [1998] JPL 23 (Judicial Review, bias), Ex p. Scott [1998] 1 WLR 226 (whether a charity can be judicially reviewed), Shepherd v Secretary of State [1998] JPL 215 (Court of Appeal, interpretation of General Development Order). Recent public inquiries include appearances for Land Securities PLC, Tesco, B&Q, and Westminster City Council. Also acted for Leeds City Council at its UDP inquiry. Publications include article at [1998] JPL 301, 'Planning, Environment, and the European Convention on Human Rights'.
Prof. Memberships: Member of Planning & Environment Bar Association (Committee member and Chairman of the continuing education sub-committee) and Administrative Law Bar Association.
Career: Called to the Bar 1981. Appointed a member of the Attorney General's Supplementary Panel of Counsel (land and planning) 1995. Admitted to the Bar of Gibraltar 1996.
Personal: Educated at Bolton School 1966 to1976 and Magdalen College, Oxford (Demy, MA Jurisprudence and BCL) 1976 to1980. Languages include French and some Italian. Leisure pursuits include opera singing, walking, gardens and comparative philology. Born 25th July 1958. Lives in London.

CORY-WRIGHT, Charles
39 Essex Street (Edwin Glasgow QC), London (0171) 832 1111
Recommended in Personal Injury
Specialisation: Main areas of Practice: Professional Negligence, Personal Injury, Insurance, Construction. Major Cases: Personal Injury: Nicholls v. Rushton (no recovery of damages for shock); Giles v. Thompson (CA, HL) (legality of credit hire agreements); Campbell v. Mylchreest; Sharp v. Pereira (jurisdiction re interim payments); Construction: Barclays v. Fairclough (contributory negligence); SAS v John Laing (retention of title clauses); Insurance: Banque Financiere v Skandia (insurers duty of utmost good faith).

Prof. Memberships: PIBA, Professional Negligence Bar Association, COMBAR.
Career: Balliol College, Oxford 1977-80; City University 1981-82; Called to the Bar 1984; chambers of Crawford Lindsay QC 1984-88; Chambers of John Dyson QC, Colin Mackay QC, Edwin Glasgow QC (39 Essex Street) 1988-98
Personal: Married, 2 children. Interests: Music, reading, sport.

COTTER, Barry
Old Square Chambers (Hon. John Melville Williams QC), London (0171) 269 0300
Recommended in Product Liability
Specialisation: All aspects of product liability law, personal injury and medical negligence, public inquiries and multi-party actions.
Prof. Memberships: Personal Injury Bar Association, Committee Member.
Career: LLB Called to Bar in 1985
Personal: LLB University College, Lincoln's Inn Scholarship. Based in Bristol and London. Author: Defective and Unsafe Products: Law and Practice (Butterworths 1996). Appeared in Clapham Junction Rail Inquiry, Strangeways (Woolf) inquiry, Severn Tunnel inquiry, Ashworth Hospital inquiry.

COULSON, Peter
Keating Chambers (Richard Fernyhough QC), London (0171) 544 2600
Recommended in the following lists: Construction, Professional Negligence
Specialisation: Involved in all types of engineering, construction and related disputes, in the High Court and in arbitration both in the UK and abroad; reported cases include: Ashville v Elmer; Ben Barrett v Boot; Barker v Leyden; British Airways v PDP and McAlpine; Copthorne v Boris; Design 5 v Keniston; McAlpine Humbrook v McDermott; Marston v Barnard; Regalian v LDDC; Wates v Bredero; Wessex v HLM; Woodspring v Venn.
Career: Qualified 1982; Gray's Inn; Member of Keating Chambers since 1984; associate of the Chartered Institute of Arbitrators 1990; editor 'Construction Law Yearbook'; contributor to 'The Cricketer'.
Personal: Lord Wandsworth College; University of Keele (BA Hons Law, English 2.1). Born 1958; resides London. Interests: British art, architecture, music, comedy, cricket. Working knowledge of French.

COWARD, J. Stephen QC
9 Bedford Row (John Goldring QC), London (0171) 242 3555
Recommended in Crime
Specialisation: Specialist in all aspects of serious crime from murder to fraud. Appeared in the following cases: 1. R v Stanley – assistant bosun Herald of Free Enterprise. 2. R v Nedrick and R v Slack – the liability of secondary parties in murder. 3. R v Ivor Jones and others – the leading authority on section 16 Firearms Act 1968. 4. R v Prime – espionage. 5. R v John Tanner – the murder of Rachel McLean, the Oxford undergraduate. 6. R v Leslie Jones – murder allegation turning on the cooling rate of dead bodies. 7. R v Hayes and others – acted for the SFO. 8. R v Cheung - acted for the SFO. 9. R v Robinson – the 'Yardie' trial. 10. R v Baroness de Stempel – acted for the Defendant.
Career: Educated at King James Grammar School, Huddersfield and University College, London (LL.B). 1962: Lecturer in Law and Constitutional History, University College, London and Bramshill Police College. 1964: Called to the Bar (Inner Temple). 1980: Appointed Recorder. 1984: Took Silk. 1997: High Court Examiner (The State of New York v Don King Boxing Promotions).
Personal: Born 1937, lives in Northampton. Leisure pursuits: Gardening, wine, singing.

COX, Buster
1 Gray's Inn Square (Carl Teper), London
(0171) 405 8946
Recommended in Immigration & Nationality

COX, Laura QC
Cloisters (Laura Cox QC), London
(0171) 827 4000
Recommended in the following lists: Employment, Medical Negligence, Personal Injury
Specialisation: Practice is divided evenly between employment law, discrimination and professional (principally medical) negligence. Employment work includes sex and race discrimination and equal pay, and is predominantly Industrial Tribunal, Employment Appeal Tribunal and further appellate advisory work and representation, with some judicial review. Medical negligence work involves claims of the utmost severity, such as cerebral palsy. Recent cases include: Webb v EMO Air Cargo (UK) Ltd (European Court of Justice and HL – pregnancy discrimination); Tredget v Bexley H.A. (nervous shock in medical negligence); R v MoD ex parte Smith and Others (armed forces homosexuals); R v Registrar of Births and Deaths ex parte P and G (transsexuals birth certificates) Burton & Rhule v De Vere Hotels (discrimination by third parties (Bernard Manning), employer's liability), Harrods v Remick & Ors (contract workers-discrimination), P v S and Somerset County Council (discrimination against transsexuals), Crees v Royal London Insurance (maternity rights) and FBU v Knowles & Johnson (meaning of 'industrial action'). Clients include trade unions and individual members, applicants and respondents in employment and discrimination cases and plaintiffs and defendants in medical negligence cases. Regular conference and seminar speaker or chair in her fields of practice.
Prof. Memberships: Employment Law Bar Association (Committee). Professional Negligence Bar Association. Association of Personal Injury Lawyers, Administrative Law Bar Association, Personal Injuries Bar Association, Association of Women Barristers, Legal Action Group, American Trial Lawyers' Association, Liberty. Member of the Council, Justice.
Career: Appointed Recorder 1995. Elected Head of Chambers at Cloisters 1995. Chairman of Bar Council Sex Discrimination Committee 1997. British member of the International Labour Organisation.
Personal: Educated at Wolverhampton High School for Girls 1963-70 and Queen Mary College, London University 1970-73 (LL.B) and L.S.E.1973-75 (LL.M). Leisure pursuits (work and three children permitting) include music, cooking, theatre, cinema, swimming, watching football.

COX, Raymond
Fountain Court (Peter Scott QC), London
(0171) 583 3335
Recommended in the following lists: Banking, Insurance & Reinsurance, Professional Negligence
Specialisation: Principal areas of practice are all aspects of reinsurance and insurance, banking (including documentary credits, bills, financial services and credit security) professional negligence (including valuers, accountants, solicitors and banks) and commercial law generally.
Career: Raymond Cox is co-editor of 'Law of Bank Payments', Brindle and Cox, (FT Law and Tax, 1996) and has lectured on insurance and banking.

COX, Simon
Plowden Buildings (William Lowe QC), London
(0171) 583 0808
Recommended in Immigration & Nationality
Specialisation: All aspects of immigration and social security, also child support. All levels from judicial review and appeals to Court of Appeal to advice and representation on appeals to appellate authorities. Reported cases in last 12 months include: *R v Immigration Appeal Tribunal ex parte*

Jeyeanthan, Times, 23 April 1998 (Secretary of State's appeal to IAT invalid unless in proper form); *R v Chief Adjudicator ex parte Akpre* [1998] Imm AR 205 (adjudicator who disbelieved appellant can deal consider further material referred by Secretary of State).
Prof. Memberships: Immigration Law Practitioners Association.
Career: Called to Bar 1992. Publications: *Child Support Handbook* (co-author), Child Poverty Action Group ('CPAG'), annually since 1996; *Migration and Social Security Handbook* (co-author), CPAG, 1997.

CRAIG, Aubrey
5 Fountain Court (Anthony Barker QC), Birmingham (0121) 606 0500
Recommended in Commercial (litigation)
Specialisation: Intellectual property, partnership, insolvency, principal and surety and general commercial.
Prof. Memberships: Member of New York and US Federal Bars (1982). Society of Insolvency Practitioners. Chancery Bar Association. Midland Chancery & Commercial Bar Association.
Career: LLB (Sheffield) 1970. CLE: 1971-1972. New York – 1977-1987.

CRAMPIN, Peter QC
11 New Square (Peter Crampin QC), London
(0171) 831 0081
Recommended in the following lists: Charities, Traditional Chancery
Specialisation: Chancery:- property litigation and advice, trusts, charities, pensions, insolvency, prof. neg., Court of Protection.
Career: Called 1976. 2nd Junior Counsel to the A-G in charity matters 1988-93. Took silk 1993. Recorder.
Personal: Born 7 July 1946.

CRAN, Mark QC
Brick Court Chambers (Christopher Clarke QC), London (0171) 583 0777
Recommended in the following lists: Arbitration, Commercial (litigation), Insurance & Reinsurance, Media & Entertainment
Specialisation: Commercial advocacy and advisory work; some areas of EC work; general civil litigation. Specialist knowlege of the gaming industry, most fields of the entertainment industry, and some areas of audit and accountancy. Recent Cases: George Michael v Sony; Williams Grand Prix v Newey; R v Gaming Board ex parte Kingsley; Ritz Casino transfer to 50 St James's; Wrightson Syndicates v Winchester Bowring; Eagle Star v BBL.
Career: 2 years articles in Chartered Accountancy. Called to Bar 1973; Silk 1988.
Personal: Educated Gordonstoun School (scholarship) and Bristol University LLB (Hons, Second) 1970.

CRANE, Michael QC
Fountain Court (Peter Scott QC), London
(0171) 583 3335
Recommended in the following lists: Aviation, Insurance & Reinsurance

CRANFIELD, Peter
3 Verulam Buildings (R. Neville Thomas QC), London (0171) 831 8441
Recommended in Agriculture & Bloodstock
Specialisation: Barrister specialising in professional indemnity (including claims against accountants, architects, brokers, financial advisers, solicitors, surveyors and valuers). European Union law, judicial review, the law relating to pensions and pension schemes, banking and building society law, company law and corporate insolvency, changes and other security documents, asset protection and recovery, financial services, partnerships, agricultural law (including EU aspects), general Chancery and commercial litigation and advisory work. Cases include: Barclays Bank v Layton Lougher & Co (1996 and 1998); Meat and Livestock Commission v

Manchester Wholesale Meat and Poultry Ltd (1996); R v Secretary of State for the Environment and Ministry of Agriculture Fisheries and Food, ex p Standley: R v Same, ex p Metson (1997); Mercantile Credit Co Ltd v Fenwick (1997): Adams v Lancashire County Council and Bet Catering Services Ltd (1997); UCB Bank Plc v David J Pinder Plc and Lovell White Durrant (1997).
Career: Qualified 1982; publications: Encyclopaedia of Forms and Precedents, 5th edition, vol 6: Building Societies (with Timothy Lloyd QC, now Lloyd J).

CRANNY, Amanda
King Charles House (William Everard), Nottingham (0115) 941 8851
Recommended in Family/Matrimonial

CRAVEN, Richard
Plowden Buildings (William Lowe QC), London
(0171) 583 0808
Recommended in Personal Injury

CRIGMAN, David QC
1 Fountain Court (David Crigman QC), Birmingham (0121) 236 5721
Recommended in Crime

CROOKENDEN, Simon QC
Essex Court Chambers (Gordon Pollock QC), London (0171) 813 8000
Recommended in Energy & Utilities
Specialisation: Shipping. Insurance and Reinsurance: policies; proportional and excess of loss involving both Lloyds of London and the company market. Building/Engineering. Commodity sales. Arbitration. Energy & Utilities.
Prof. Memberships: Fellow of the Chartered Institute of Arbitrators. Panel member, Lloyds of London Arbitration Panel.
Career: Corpus Christi College, Cambridge MA (Mechanical Sciences). Called to the Bar 1975. Queen's Counsel 1996.
Personal: Born 1946.

CROSS, James
4 Pump Court (Bruce Mauleverer QC), London (0171) 353 2656
Recommended in Professional Negligence
Specialisation: A general and varied practice in common law and commercial litigation/arbitration, but with particular emphasis on professional negligence (whether of architects, engineers, the medical profession, solicitors, surveyors or valuers), construction and civil engineering, insurance and reinsurance, banking, product liability, sale of goods and commodities and contractual disputes (both domestic and international).
Prof. Memberships: COMBAR, London Common Law and Commercial Bar Association, Official Referees Bar Association.
Career: Called to the Bar in 1985 and joined 4 Pump Court in 1986.
Personal: Educated at Shrewsbury and Magdalen College, Oxford.

CROW, Jonathan
4 Stone Buildings (Philip Heslop QC), London
(0171) 242 5524
Recommended in the following lists: Chancery, Company, Financial Services, Insolvency

CROWLEY, Jane QC
30 Park Place (Philip Richards), Cardiff
(01222) 398421
Recommended in Family/Matrimonial
(also One Garden Court Family Law Chambers (Miss Eleanor F Platt QC & Miss Alison Ball QC))
Specialisation: Child care and other Children Act applications, ancillary relief, Public Law including education, Family related crime eg Child abuse, rape etc.
Prof. Memberships: Family Law Bar Association (regional representative).
Career: LL.B (Hons) London. Graduated 1976.

Practised 1976-1980 at 34 Park Place. 1980 to date at 30 Park Place. Recorder 1996. QC 1998. **Personal:** Married, 2 children.

CROWLEY, John QC
2 Crown Office Row (Graeme Hamilton QC), London (0171) 797 8100
Recommended in Personal Injury

CROWN, Giles
1 Brick Court (Richard Hartley QC), London (0171) 353 8845
Recommended in Defamation
Specialisation: All aspects of media law, including defamation, malicious falsehood, passing off, copyright and related rights, breach of confidence, advertising regulation, press and broadcasting complaints, judicial review, contempt of court and reporting restrictions. Member of the Bar Pro Bono Unit and the Free Representation Unit. Junior counsel in David Ashby v Times Newspapers Limited (1995), Andy McNab v Associated Newspapers Limited (CA) [1996] 9 C.L. 207, Bruce Grobbelaar v News Group Newspapers Limited. **Career:** MA (Cantab.), LLM (London).

CROWTHER, William QC
2 Temple Gardens (Patrick Phillips QC), London (0171) 583 6041
Recommended in the following lists: Arbitration, Personal Injury, Professional Negligence

CROXFORD, Ian QC
Wilberforce Chambers (Edward Nugee QC), London (0171) 306 0102
Recommended in the following lists: Construction, Crime: Fraud
Specialisation: Professional negligence (in particular accountants). Construction and civil engineering. Crime ("white collar" and consumer protection). Called to the Bar 1976.

CRYSTAL, Jonathan
Cloisters (Laura Cox QC), London (0171) 827 4000
Recommended in Sports Law
Specialisation: Specialist sports lawyer. Notable cases include: McCord v. Cornforth and Swansea City, Thomas v. QPR, Watson & Bradford City v. Gray & Huddersfield Town, Redman v. British Lions; Wheeler v. Leicester City Council; Sarfraz Nawaz v. Alan Lamb; Keighley Cougars v. RFL, ARL v. RFL, Bonetti v. Laws and Grimsby Town. Advisory work including England Rugby Union Squad, Team Scotland World Cup 1998, Liverpool FC, Alan Shearer, Stan Collymore, Naseem Hamed and Jimmy White. Drafting experience includes the Premier League Rules. Further specialism in defamation and business law. Notable cases include Richard Branson/Virgin Atlantic v. British Airways; Dr Smith v. Dr Houston; Jason Donovan v. The Face and Rantzen v. The People. George Best v Clydesdale Bank plc. **Prof. Memberships:** Bar Sports Law Group, British Association for Sport and Law and Combar. **Career:** Called to the Bar 1972. 2 Harcourt Buildings 1973-1992. Cloisters 1992- the present. Legal Reader Associated Newspapers until 1985. **Personal:** Educated Leeds Grammar School and Queen Mary College, University of London 1968-1971. Director, Tottenham Hotspur FC 1991-1993. Married with young children living in Central London.

CRYSTAL, Michael QC
3/4 South Square (Michael Crystal QC), London (0171) 696 9900
Recommended in the following lists: Banking, Chancery, Company, Financial Services, Insolvency
Specialisation: Commercial and financial law. **Career:** Called to the Bar, Middle Temple, 1970; Queen's Counsel 1984; Bencher Middle Temple 1993; Senior Visiting Fellow Centre for Commercial Law Studies, University of London since 1987; DTI Inspector 1988-89, 1992; Member Insolvency Rules Committee 1993-1997; Deputy High Court

Judge, since 1995; Member Financial Law Panel since 1996.

CULLEN, Edmund
7 Stone Buildings (Charles Aldous QC), London (0171) 405 3886
Recommended in Company
Specialisation: Bankruptcy and insolvency, company law, equity and trusts, landlord & tenant, partnership, professional negligence, property, easements, commercial litigation. Cases include: Re: MTI Trading Systems Ltd [1997], One Life v. Roy & Anor [1996], British Racing Drivers' Club Ltd. v. Hexstall Erskine & Co. [1996], ADT v. BDO Binder Hamlyn [1995], Langton v. Langton & Anor [1995], Re: Thundercrest [1994], Busby & Anor v. Co-operative Insurance Society Ltd. [1993] Barclays Mercantile Business Finance Ltd. & Anor v. SIBEC Developments & Ors [1992]. **Prof. Memberships:** Chancery Bar Association. **Career:** Called to the Bar 1990. Joined present chambers 1991. **Personal:** Educated at Winchester, University of Bristol.

CULLEN, Felicity
Gray's Inn Tax Chambers (Milton Grundy), London (0171) 242 2642
Recommended in Tax
Specialisation: All aspects of Revenue Law including in particular commercial and corporate tax, capital gains tax, stamp duty, taxation of individuals and tax litigation. **Prof. Memberships:** Revenue Bar Association. Chancery Bar Association. Called to the Bar 1985. Joined Gray's Inn Tax Chambers 1986. **Career:** LL.B Birmingham (Class 1 Hons), LLM Cantab.

CULLUM, Michael
Albion Chambers (J.C.T. Barton QC), Bristol (0117) 927 2144
Recommended in Crime

CUNNINGHAM, Graham
Francis Taylor Building (N.P. Valios QC), London (0171) 353 7768
Recommended in the following lists: Alternative Dispute Resolution, Computer & I.T.
Specialisation: Contentious and non-contentious computer, information technology and telecommunications work, including national and international regulatory telecommunications issues; technology transfer; all types of commercial trading relationships, intellectual property law and competition law. Former legal director, company secretary and management team member with computer company Wang, and intellectual property and technology transfer legal adviser with ITT Corporation. Accredited mediator with CEDR for alternative dispute resolution. **Career:** Called 1976. Joined Francis Taylor Building in 1994. **Personal:** Educated at Cranleigh School and Brunel University.

CUNNINGHAM, Mark
13 Old Square (Mr Michael Lyndon-Stanford QC), London (0171) 404 4800
Recommended in Chancery
Specialisation: General chancery practitioner, with a bias towards commercially orientated litigation and particular specialisms in the disqualification of directors and intellectual property. He has appeared in reported cases concerning; company law, directors' disqualification, personal insolvency, sale of land, landlord and tenant, rent reviews, easements, land registration, copyright, passing off, entertainment law and the Inheritance Act. **Prof. Memberships:** Chancery Bar Association. Patent Bar Association. **Career:** Called 1980. Appointed Junior Counsel to the Crown (Chancery), February 1992. **Personal:** Educated at Stonyhurst College and Magdalen College Oxford (B.A. History). Born 6/6/1956. Lives in Buckinghamshire. 4 children.

CURRAN, Patrick QC
30 Park Place (Philip Richards), Cardiff (01222) 398421
Recommended in Crime

CURRY, Peter QC
4 Stone Buildings (Philip Heslop QC), London (0171) 242 5524
Recommended in Company

CUSWORTH, Nicholas
1 Mitre Court Buildings (Bruce Blair QC), London (0171) 797 7070
Recommended in Family: Child Care including child abduction
Specialisation: Ancillary relief. Child abduction. Child care, both public and private law. **Prof. Memberships:** Family Law Bar Association. **Career:** MA (Oxon). Called to the Bar 1986. **Personal:** Married (to Rachel Platts of Counsel), one daughter.

DAGNALL, John
9 Old Square (Robert Reid QC), London (0171) 405 4682
Recommended in Chancery
Specialisation: Specialisations are chancery, commercial and property litigation; including: banking, trusts, civil fraud, insolvency, property (including mortgages and landlord and tenant) and professional negligence. **Prof. Memberships:** Member of Chancery Bar Association, Professional Negligence Bar Association and Parliamentary Bar Mess. **Career:** Bristol Grammar School, St John's College, Oxford (BA (Jurisprudence – 1st Class), BCL). Called Nov 1983, tenant Mar 1985. **Personal:** Family, church, real tennis, bridge. Further details on application.

DANIEL, Leon
14 Tooks Court (Michael Mansfield QC), London (0171) 405 8828
Recommended in Immigration & Nationality

DARLING, Paul
Keating Chambers (Richard Fernyhough QC), London (0171) 544 2600
Recommended in Construction
Specialisation: Building and engineering cases, important cases include: Temloc v Errill; Richard Roberts v Douglas Smith; Wyatt v Gleeson; Yeandle v Wynn Realisations; Vascroft v Seeboard; Mooney v Boot; PLC v McAlpine; McAlpine v Unex; Hunt v Paul Sykes; Chatbrown v McAlpine; Barking & Dagenham v Stanford Asphalt; Holbeck Hall Hotel v Scarborough. **Career:** Qualified 1983. Middle Temple; director Family Pharmaceutical Company; Editor 'Construction Law Newsletter'; member of editorial team ' Keating on Building Contracts'. **Personal:** Winchester College; St Edmund Hall, Oxford (1981 BA, 1982 BCL). Horseracing, Newcastle United.

DASHWOOD, Robert
Gray's Inn Chambers (Brian Jubb), London (0171) 404 1111
Recommended in Family: Child Care including child abduction

DAVEY, Michael
4 Field Court (Geoffrey Brice QC), London (0171) 440 6900
Recommended in Shipping

DAVIDSON, Katharine
1 Mitre Court Buildings (Bruce Blair QC), London (0171) 797 7070
Recommended in Family: Matrimonial Finance
Specialisation: Handles all types of family law, but principally financial relief claims. **Prof. Memberships:** Family Law Bar Association. **Career:** Educated at Epsom College 1978-80 and the University of Oxford 1981-84. Born 19th June 1962. Called to the Bar in 1987 and joined 1 Mitre Court Buildings in 1988.

DAVIDSON, Nicholas QC
4 Paper Buildings (Harvey McGregor QC),
London (0171) 353 3366
*Recommended in the following lists: Computer
& I.T., Professional Negligence*
Specialisation: Solicitors' and financial negligence.
Other main areas of work cover general commercial
cases, including computer litigation.
Prof. Memberships: Professional Negligence Bar
Association (Chairman), Bar European Group,
COMBAR, Society for Computers and Law.
Career: Called 1974; joined present Chambers
1975. Silk 1993.
Personal: Educated at Winchester 1964-69
(Scholar) and Trinity College Cambridge
(Exhibitioner in Economics) 1969-72. Certificate of
Honour, Bar Finals.

DAVIES, Helen
Brick Court Chambers (Christopher Clarke QC),
London (0171) 583 0777
Recommended in European Union/Competition
Specialisation: All aspects of EC law generally.
Philip Alexander Securities v Bamberger [1997] EU
LR 63; R v Treasury ex p British Telecommunications
plc (Case C392/93) [1996] QB 615.
Career: Called November 1991, Brick Court
Chambers (1992-present), Stage in DGIV (October
1993).

DAVIES, Huw
30 Park Place (Philip Richards), Cardiff
(01222) 398421
Recommended in Crime
Specialisation: Criminal law, particularly Customs
and Excise work and fraud.
Prof. Memberships: C.B.A.
Career: LL.B. M.Phil. An Assistant Recorder.
Standing Counsel to HM Customs and Excise.

DAVIES, Huw
Essex Court Chambers (Gordon Pollock QC),
London (0171) 813 8000
Recommended in Aviation
Specialisation: All types of commercial work,
domestic and international, in the context of
litigation (principally in the Commercial Court) and
arbitration. In the areas of international sale of
goods; construction (including ship construction);
shipping; commodities (principally oil and gas);
insurance, reinsurance; aviation. Professional
negligence, general chancery work including
corporate takeovers; insolvency; corporate fraud;
conspiracy and constructive trust claims.
Considerable experience of appearing in the Privy
Council in relation to appeals to the Privy Council
from Commonwealth countries.
Career: University College, Cardiff (LLB Hons),
1984. Called to the Bar 1985.
Personal: Born 1962.

DAVIES, J. Meirion
32 Park Place (Christopher Williams), Cardiff
(01222) 397364
Recommended in Crime
Specialisation: Crime and general common law.
Prof. Memberships: Criminal Bar Association.
Career: Joined Chambers Aug 1976.

DAVIES, Jane
One Paper Buildings (John Slater QC), London
(0171) 583 7355
Recommended in Construction
Prof. Memberships: Professional negligence in a
building context (architects, engineers, quantity
surveyors, project administrators) as well as
accountants and solicitors; insurance policy
disputes, contract and commercial disputes.
Numerous large claims in the building industry.
Career: Read English at Lady Margaret Hall,
Oxford, entrance scholarship; diploma in Arts
Administration, Arts Council of Great Britain,
worked as arts administrator and stage designer
before coming to the Bar. Jules Thorn Scholar
(Middle Temple).
Personal: Second home in France: fluent French.

DAVIES, Leighton QC
Farrar's Building (Gerard Elias QC), London
(0171) 583 9241
Recommended in Crime
Specialisation: All areas of major crime, both
Prosecution and Defence. Has appeared in several
high profile cases, mainly in Wales, over past 10
years.
Prof. Memberships: Criminal Bar Association.
Career: Educated at Rhondda County Grammar
School, Porth (1961-68). Corpus Christi College,
Oxford (1968-72): – MA, BCL. Inns of Court School
of Law (1973-4). Called 1975. QC 1994, Appointed
Recorder 1994.
Personal: Fly fishing, watching most sport
(particularly rugby). Married (1979), 3 children 2
sons, 1 daughter.

DAVIES, Nicola QC
3 Serjeants' Inn (Philip Naughton QC), London
(0171) 353 5537
Recommended in Medical Negligence
Specialisation: Practice covers all aspects of
medical law, including medically related crime.
Career: Called to the Bar in 1976. Member of the
Supplementary Treasury Panel (common law)
1988-92. QC 1992. Assistant Recorder 1995.
Personal: Educated at Bridgend Girls Grammar
1964-71 and Birmingham University 1971-74.

DAVIES, Owen
Two Garden Court (I. Macdonald QC & O.
Davies), London (0171) 353 1633
*Recommended in the following lists: Administrative
& Public Law, Civil Liberties, Crime, Immigration &
Nationality*
Specialisation: Administrative and public law:
Judicial review in fields including immigration,
environment, mental health, prisoners, civil liberties
and public policy. Criminal Law: Defence work in
all areas, especially related to public order, drugs,
immigration, fraud and extradition.
Prof. Memberships: Executive member of ALBA.
Member Bar Council. Privy Council cases for
appellants on Death Row.
Career: Cases include Thorp, Pergau Dam, Save
our Railways. Standing counsel to Greenpeace.
Joint head of Chambers.
Personal: Fluent speaker of German.

DAVIES, Rhodri
One Essex Court (Anthony Grabiner QC),
London (0171) 583 2000
*Recommended in the following lists: Banking,
Commercial (litigation)*
Specialisation: Principal area of practice is
banking and general commercial work including
swaps, letters of credit, negotiable instruments,
mandates, facility letters, loan agreements and
other financial disputes with or between banks.
Acted in recent swaps litigation, representing
various banks in Hazell v London Borough of
Hammersmith & Fulham and in restitution claims in
Kleinwort Benson v Sandwell and Kleinwort
Benson v Birmingham. Also handles general
commercial work, encompassing contractual
disputes, sale of goods, arbitration, insurance,
reinsurance and professional negligence.
Prof. Memberships: South Eastern Circuit,
LCLCBA.
Career: Called to the Bar in 1979 and joined 1
Essex Court in 1980.
Personal: Educated at Winchester College 1970-
74 and Downing College, Cambridge 1975-78.
Leisure pursuits include running, walking and
sailing. Born 29th January 1957. Lives in
Harpenden, Herts.

DAVIES, Richard QC
39 Essex Street (Edwin Glasgow QC), London
(0171) 832 1111
*Recommended in the following lists: Personal
Injury, Professional Negligence*

DAVIES, Stephen
Guildhall Chambers (John Royce QC), Bristol
(0117) 927 3366
*Recommended in the following lists: Chancery,
Commercial (litigation), Insolvency*

DAVIES, Stephen
8 King St (Keith Armitage QC), Manchester
(0161) 834 9560
Recommended in Commercial (litigation)
Specialisation: Deals with general commercial
and insurance litigation, construction work
including arbitration, professional negligence
cases (including solicitors, architects, engineers
and surveyors) and banking disputes.
Prof. Memberships: Northern Circuit Commercial
Bar Association; Official Referees' Bar Association;
Professional Negligence Bar Association.
Career: Educated at Baines' School, Poulton-le-
Fylde and Downing College, Cambridge. Called to
the Bar in 1985 and joined current chambers in
1986 after 12 months' pupillage in London.

DAVIES, Trefor
Iscoed Chambers (Trefor Davies), Swansea
(01792) 652988/9
Recommended in Crime
Specialisation: Crime

DAVIES-JONES, Jonathan
3 Verulam Buildings (R. Neville Thomas QC),
London (0171) 831 8441
Recommended in Banking
Specialisation: General commercial work,
including banking, insurance and reinsurance,
fraud, professional negligence and sale of goods.
Career: MA (Cantab).

DAVIS, Nigel QC
7 Stone Buildings (Charles Aldous QC), London
(0171) 405 3886
*Recommended in the following lists: Chancery,
Company, Insolvency, Partnership*
Specialisation: Principal area of practice is
chancery, with emphasis on company, insolvency,
banking and property litigation and also general
commercial litigation. Has acted for banks and
institutions (both UK and overseas) and for a range
of licensed insolvency practitioners and
professional practices. Has appeared in a number
of reported cases, on subjects extending to
company meetings; constructive trusts; insurance;
world-wide mareva injunctions; insolvency; and
real property. Acted as counsel to the inquiry of the
Board of Banking Supervision into the collapse of
Barings Bank. Other areas of practice include
professional negligence (solicitors); partnership;
and media and entertainment.
Personal: Education: Charterhouse; University
College, Oxford (MA).

DAVIS, William QC
St Philip's Chambers (Rex Tedd QC),
Birmingham (0121) 246 7000
Recommended in Crime

DAVIS-WHITE, Malcolm
4 Stone Buildings (Philip Heslop QC), London
(0171) 242 5524
Recommended in Financial Services

DAY, Douglas QC
Farrar's Building (Gerard Elias QC), London
(0171) 583 9241
Recommended in Crime: Fraud
Specialisation: Specialist criminal practice, with a
particular emphasis on commercial fraud. Acts for
both prosecution and defence. Practice also
covers personal injury and professional
negligence. Important cases include R v Kellard
(the Britannia Park trial), the longest jury trial in
English legal history. Defence counsel R v Harris
and R v Kitchin. Has undertaken several Serious
Fraud Office prosecutions.
Prof. Memberships: Criminal Bar Association;
Commercial and Common Law Bar Association;

Society for Computers and Law; Professional Conduct Committee of the Bar Council 1989-92. Chairman Legal Services Committee, Bar Council. **Career:** Called to the Bar 1967. Joined present chambers 1980, after twelve years at 2 Pump Court (J Thomas QC MP). Appointed Recorder of the Crown Court 1987. Took silk 1989. Assistant Parliamentary Boundary Commissioner 1992. Deputy High Court Judge 1994.
Personal: Educated at Bec School 1955-62, and at Selwyn College, Cambridge 1963-66. Highly computer literate with a keen interest on the use of computers in court.

DE FREITAS, Anthony
4 Paper Buildings (Harvey McGregor QC), London (0171) 353 3366
Recommended in Media & Entertainment
Specialisation: Sporting and entertainment contracts, professional negligence. Agricultural holdings. Warren v Mendy 1989 IWLR 853, Featherston v Staples 1986 IWLR 861, John v George 1996 EGLR 1 .
Prof. Memberships: Professional Negligence Bar Association. Agricultural Law Association.
Career: Stonyhurst College, St. John's College Oxford. MA Oxon, Assistant Recorder.

DE GARR ROBINSON, Anthony
One Essex Court (Anthony Grabiner QC), London (0171) 583 2000
Recommended in the following lists: Commercial (litigation), Company, Insolvency
Specialisation: Practice includes a broad range of substantial commercial and chancery litigation, with an emphasis on international fraud, company law, insolvency, share/business sale agreements and banking.
Prof. Memberships: Commercial Bar Association, Chancery Bar Association and Insolvency Practitioners Association.
Career: Called to the Bar in 1987.
Personal: Born in 1963. Educated at University College, Oxford 1981-5 and Harvard University 1985-6.

DE HAAN, Kevin
3 Raymond Buildings (Clive Nicholls QC), London (0171) 831 3833
Recommended in the following lists: Consumer Law, Licensing
Specialisation: Specialises in all areas of environmental law, consumer protection and licensing. Environmental practice includes all relevant aspects of EC law and covers pollution control, waste regulation, statutory nuisances and environmental issues arising in road transport licensing and health and safety regulation. Experience includes conducting proceedings before various regulatory bodies, associated judicial reviews, defending criminal prosecutions. Contributor to 'Pollution in the UK' (Sweet & Maxwell 1995). Clients have included a number of public corporations and institutions. Consumer protection practice includes all aspects of regulation under the Trade Description Act 1968, the Medicines Act 1968, the Consumer Credit Act, the Consumer Protection Act 1987, the Weights and Measures Act 1985, the Food Safety Act 1990 and the relevant EC law. Contributor to 'Food Safety, Law and Practice'(Sweet & Maxwell 1994). Clients have included a number of major public companies, former nationalised industries, banks, building societies and other institutions. Licensing practice includes all aspects, particularly betting, gaming and lotteries. Has considerable experience of proceedings before various reglatory bodies, appeals and associated judicial reviews. Clients have included major casino operators, bookmaking concerns and promoters of lotteries and competitions. Other areas of practice include some extradition and commercial fraud work.
Prof. Memberships: Local Government, Environmental and Planning Bar Association.
Career: Called to the Bar 1976.
Personal: Educated at the Universities of London and Brussels (VUB).

DE HAAS, Margaret
The Corn Exchange (David Steer QC & I. Goldrein QC), Liverpool (0151) 227 1081/5009
Recommended in Family/Matrimonial
Specialisation: Ancillary relief; child care; medical negligence, personal injury.
Prof. Memberships: Family Law Bar Association; Professional Negligence Bar Association.
Career: LL.B (Hons) (Bristol). Author of several books on personal injury litigation and ancillary relief.
Personal: Theatre; reading; my children.

DE LA PIQUERIE, Paul
Falcon Chambers (Jonathan Gaunt QC & Kim Lewison QC), London (0171) 353 2484
Recommended in Agriculture & Bloodstock
Specialisation: Agricultural Law. Landlord and Tenant. Property. Business Tenancies. Professional Negligence (property).
Prof. Memberships: Gray's Inn.
Career: LLB (Hons) Birmingham University. Recorder. Chairman Agricultural Lands Tribunal. SE area.
Personal: Married. Golf.

DE LACY, Richard
3 Verulam Buildings (R. Neville Thomas QC), London (0171) 831 8441
Recommended in the following lists: Financial Services, Insolvency
Specialisation: Principal area of practice is commercial law, particularly banking, finance, financial services, accountants', solicitors' and barristers' professional indemnity. Also deals with insolvency, company law, property law and arbitration. Acts for clearing banks, major accountancy firms and leading insolvency practitioners. Specialist editor 'Bullen & Leake & Jacob: Precedents of Pleading' (13th Edn).
Prof. Memberships: Fellow of The Chartered Institute of Arbitrators, COMBAR, Chancery Bar Association; Institute of Chartered Accountants Practice Regulation Review Committee.
Career: Called to the Bar 1976. Harmsworth Scholar, Middle Temple.
Personal: Educated at Hymers College, Hull (1965-71) and Clare College, Cambridge 1972-75 (MA 1979). Born 4th December 1954.

DE MELLO, Rambert
6 King's Bench Walk (Sibghat Kadri QC), London (0171) 353 4931 /583 0695
Recommended in Immigration & Nationality
Specialisation: Judicial Review; Education; Discrimination; Social Security; Local Government; Civil Actions Against the Police; Housing; Prison; Employment; Extradition; Human Rights. Cases: 1. Remihen v Secretary of State for Social Security [1998] INLR 238 HL; 2. R v Sec of State for the Home Dept Ex Parte Khan [1998] INLR 206.
Prof. Memberships: Barrister-at-law.
Career: LLM; MA.
Personal: Hill-walking; cycling; reading; music.

DE NAVARRO, Michael QC
2 Temple Gardens (Patrick Phillips QC), London (0171) 583 6041
Recommended in Personal Injury
Specialisation: Personal injury forms a significant part of a wide common law and commercial practice. Reported personal injury cases include Adams v SEB [1993] (CA), Green v Building Scene [1994] (CA), O'Shea v Kingston-upon-Thames [1995] (CA), Hunter v Butler [1995] (CA), Jolly v LB of Sutton [1998] (CA). Other reported cases include Wentworth v Wiltshire CC [1992] (CA), Nykredit Mortgage Bank v Edward Erdman [1996] (HL), John Monroe (Acrylics) v LFCDA [1997] (CA).
Prof. Memberships: PIBA (Chairman). Western Circuit.
Career: Called 1968, QC 1990, Recorder 1990.

DE SILVA, Desmond QC
2 Paper Buildings (Desmond de Silva QC), London (0171) 936 2611
Recommended in the following lists: Crime, Crime: Fraud
Specialisation: Crime, commercial fraud, extradition, constitutional law. R v Levitt and others (City Fraud); R v Jaqui Oliver (Fraud – Britain's foremost female National Hunt Jockey); R v Lord Brocket (Insurance Fraud); R v Ghizzelli (EEC Fraud); R v Segers (Football match fixing/corruption). R v Ron Atkinson (road rage).
Prof. Memberships: Criminal Bar Association; British Academy of Forensic Sciences.
Career: Middle Temple – called to the Bar of England and Wales 1964. QC 1984. Deputy Circuit Judge 1976-1984. Apart from the UK, has practised in many other countries and is a member of many foreign Bars.
Personal: Married, one daughter. Leisure interests: travelling, politics.

DEHN, Conrad QC
Fountain Court (Peter Scott QC), London (0171) 583 3335
Recommended in the following lists: Insurance & Reinsurance, Parliamentary
Specialisation: Litigation and arbitration. Cases include National Company for Cooperative Insurers v St Paul Reinsurance Co & ORS (1997-8), St Albans v International Computers (1996) 4 All ER 481, CA; Office of Fair Trading v RMC & ORS (1996) Tr.L.R.78; Alpina, Zurich & Bavarian Re v Clarksons (1989) NLJ 256 (1995) 1 LLR 64; Arbitration over dispute between two Lloyds syndicates (1990); Chaired Lloyds Disciplinary Tribunal, 1986. Parliamentary work includes (i) Statutory construction, (ii) Private Bills. Cases include; (i) R v British Coal Corporation ex p. Vardy (1993) ICR 720; R v Devon C.C. exp. George (1989) A.C. 573; A-G ex Rel. Yorkshire Derwent Trust (1992) 1 A.C. 425; Royco Homes v Southern Water Authority (1979)IWLR 1366 H.L; (ii) Cross Rail, 1994; Redbridge LB, 1989; Dartford-Thurrock Crossing, 1986; Ginns & Gutteridge Leicester (Crematorium) 1983; London Dockland Development Corporation Order 1981.
Prof. Memberships: Committee of Commercial Bar Association 1990- ; Director, Bar Mutual Indemnity Fund 1988- ; Bar European Group. Member of Council of Statute Law Society, 1996 – ; Member of Parliamentary Bar Mess; Governor, Inns of Court School of Law, 1996-.
Career: Called to Bar 1952; QC 1968; Recorder 1974; Deputy High Court Judge 1988; Bencher, Gray's Inn 1977; Treasurer 1986.
Personal: 1st Class Hons. P.P.E., Oxford, 1950; Holt Scholar, Gray's Inn, 1951.

DEIN, Jeremy
3 Gray's Inn Square (Rock Tansey QC), London (0171) 520 5600
Recommended in Crime
Specialisation: Specialises in defence crime, now regularly instructed in leading work. Particular interest in appellate work having conducted many appeals for 'Justice'. Happy to undertake appelate work on pro bono basis. Appeared in R v Tarrant [1997], leading ECA decision on jury selection.
Prof. Memberships: Middle Temple.
Career: 2.1 Hons, University of London. Former Lecturer in the Law of Evidence and Criminal Procedure.
Personal: Married with three children. Leisure interests include sport, reading and travel.

DENNEY, Stuart Henry McDonald
Deans Court Chambers (H.K. Goddard QC), Manchester (0161) 834 4097
Recommended in Crime
Specialisation: Crime, including fraud. Actions against the Police.
Prof. Memberships: Criminal Bar Association
Career: St. Johns School, Leatherhead. Gonville & Caius College Cambridge, 77-80. M.A.
Personal: Married, 1 son. Interests: Rugby Union, Malt Whisky.

DENNIS, Mark
6 King's Bench Walk (Michael Worsley QC), London (0171) 583 0410
Recommended in Crime
Fax: (0171) 353 8791
Prof. Memberships: C.B.A.
Career: Senior Treasury Counsel.

DENNISON, Stephen
Atkin Chambers (John Blackburn QC), London (0171) 404 0102
Recommended in Construction
Specialisation: Practice covers the whole spectrum of construction activity. Extensive experience of conducting trials in the Official Referees' Courts and in arbitration.
Career: Called to Bar 1985.
Personal: Born 26 February 1958. Educated Manchester University (LL.B.).

DENNYS, Nicholas QC
Atkin Chambers (John Blackburn QC), London (0171) 404 0102
Recommended in Construction
Specialisation: Building and Civil Engineering disputes and related matters including Planning & Local Government, Landlord & Tenant, Judicial Review, Conflict of Laws and general commercial work. Extensive arbitration experience as advocate, before both international and domestic tribunals. International disputes usually involving large multinational corporations or Governmental Agencies in many parts of the world. Appointed to act as sole arbitrator under the Common and Commercial Bar Association Scheme and as Chairman by the London Court of International arbitration.
Career: Admitted to Middle Temple August 1973; Called to the Bar November 1975; Queen's Counsel May 1991.
Personal: Born 14th July 1951. Educated Eton College and Brasenose College, Oxford (P.P.E.).

DENYER, Roderick QC
St. John's Chambers (Roderick Denyer QC), Bristol (0117) 921 3456
Recommended in Crime
Specialisation: Personal Injury, Crime, Public Family Law.
Career: QC 1990; Recorder 1990; Deputy High Court Judge 1994; Bencher Inner Temple 1997.

DENYER-GREEN, Barry
Falcon Chambers (Jonathan Gaunt QC & Kim Lewison QC), London (0171) 353 2484
Recommended in Property Litigation
Specialisation: Compulsory purchase and compensation; planning; agricultural tenancies.
Prof. Memberships: Royal Institution of Chartered Surveyors.

DEVONSHIRE, Simon
5 Paper Buildings (Antonio Bueno QC), London (0171) 583 9275 /4555
Recommended in the following lists: Employment, Media & Entertainment
Specialisation: All aspects of employment and entertainment law, including dismissal, discrimination, restrictive covenants and confidential information, agency, recording, publishing and management disputes, copyright and intellectual property.
Prof. Memberships: Employment Law Bar Association. LCLCBA.
Career: Called 1988.

DIAS, Asoka
1 Gray's Inn Square (Carl Teper), London (0171) 405 8946
Recommended in Immigration & Nationality

DICKENS, Paul
5 New Square (Jonathan Rayner James QC), London (0171) 404 0404
Recommended in Media & Entertainment
Specialisation: Principal areas are copyright and design rights, moral rights, performers' rights, trade marks, passing off, confidential information, media and entertainment law and computer law. Particular interest in musical copyright infringement, information technology, multimedia and Internet. Clients include leading companies and artistes in the entertainment field and national newspapers. Joint Consulting Editor for Intellectual Property matters, Butterworths' Encyclopaedia of Forms and Precedents. Contributor to new edition of Copinger & Skone James on Copyright.
Prof. Memberships: Intellectual Property Bar Association, Chancery Bar Association
Career: M.A. (Cantab), A.R.C.O., former Organ Scholar (Cantab).
Personal: Recitalist/accompanist at local concerts, school governor, skiing, tennis.

DICKER, Robin
3/4 South Square (Michael Crystal QC), London (0171) 696 9900
Recommended in the following lists: Banking, Company, Insolvency
Specialisation: Specialises in business, commercial and financial law, in particular banking, corporate restructuring and insolvency. Has acted in relation to almost all of the recent major corporate collapses including BCCI (for the Liquidators), MCC (For the Administrators) and Olympia & York (for the Administrators). Reported cases in the last year include Morris v. Agrichemicals; BCCI (No.8) [1998] AC 214 (House of Lords) the leading decision on charge-backs and flawed assets; Re Oasis Merchandising Services Ltd [1998] Ch 170 (Court of Appeal) liquidator's power to sell statutory causes of action; Re Mid East Training Ltd [1998] 1 All ER 557 (Court of Appeal) cross-border insolvency; BCCI v Al-Saud [1997] 1 BCLC 457 (Court of Appeal) insolvency set-off. Recently acted for the plaintiffs in Phillips Petroleum v Enron in relation to the purported termination of a long term Gas Sales Agreement. Also advises in relation to securities, debt discounting and factoring, debt issues, securitisations and general corporate issues instructured both by English and United States law firms. Contributing Editor to Totty & Moss on Insolvency.
Career: Called to the Bar (Middle Temple) in 1986 and was a Harmsworth Exhibitioner. Now a practising barrister at 3/4 South Square, Gray's Inn and specialises in business and financial law, in particular banking, corporate restructuring, insolvency, acquisitions and mergers. Was an Exhibitioner at Brasenose College, Oxford, where he was awarded a BA (Jurisprudence) and BCL.

DINAN-HAYWARD, Deborah
Albion Chambers (J.C.T. Barton QC), Bristol (0117) 927 2144
Recommended in Family/Matrimonial
Specialisation: Solely practising in matrimonial, child care and family law which includes any aspect of this area.
Prof. Memberships: F.L.B.A. and Bristol F.L.B.A. where is the Treasurer.
Career: Wykeham House, Fareham. Sheffield University; LLB. Called 1988.
Personal: Dressage. Law reporting for Family Law Reports.

DINKIN, Anthony QC
2-3 Gray's Inn Square (Anthony Scrivener QC), London (0171) 242 4986
Recommended in Planning
Specialisation: Specialises in Town and Country Planning, Local Government, Valuation and Compensation, Landlord & Tenant, Restrictive Covenants. With extensive experience in conducting Planning Inquiries concerning all aspects of Planning including major Food & Non-Food Retailing Developments, Local Plans, CPO's and Enforcement. Court experience includes Legal Challenges/Judicial Review of Secretary of State/Inspector and Local Government Decisions and appearances in the Lands Tribunal.

Career: College of Estate Management (Bsc.Est. Management) 1966; Called to the Bar 1968; QC 1991; Crown Court recorder 1989; past Lecturer and External Examiner in Law, Reading University. Legal Member of Lands Tribunal 1998-.

DIXEY, Ian
St. John's Chambers (Roderick Denyer QC), Bristol (0117) 921 3456
Recommended in Crime

DOBBS, Linda QC
18 Red Lion Court (Anthony Arlidge QC), London (0171) 520 6000
Recommended in Crime
Specialisation: Crime – Customs and Excise Offences, Fraud, Sexual Offences. Tribunals – Disciplinary and Professional Conduct. Other areas of practice – General Crime, Licensing and some media work.

DOCTOR, Brian
Fountain Court (Peter Scott QC), London (0171) 583 3335
Recommended in Commercial (litigation)
Specialisation: Practice encompasses common law and general commercial work, including insurance, professional negligence and jurisdiction matters.
Prof. Memberships: Commercial Bar Association.
Career: Solicitor in London 1978-1980; South African Bar 1980-1992 (took silk in SA 1990); joined Fountain Court Chambers 1992.
Personal: B.A., LL.B (Witwatersrand) B.C.L. (Balliol College, Oxford), Born 8 December 1949.

DODDS, R.Stephen
15 Winckley Square (R.S. Dodds), Preston (01772) 252828
Recommended in Family/Matrimonial

DODSON, Joanna QC
14 Gray's Inn Square (Joanna Dodson QC), London (0171) 242 0858
Recommended in the following lists: Family: Child Care including child abduction
Specialisation: Practice encompasses all aspects of family law.
Prof. Memberships: Family Law Bar Association.
Career: Called to the Bar 1971. Joined Gray's Inn Square in 1991 and took silk in 1993.
Personal: Educated at James Allen's Girls School 1956-63 and Newnham College, Cambridge (BA 1967, MA 1971). Born 5th September 1945. Lives in London.

DOERRIES, Chantal-Aimée
Atkin Chambers (John Blackburn QC), London (0171) 404 0102
Recommended in Construction
Specialisation: Principal areas of practice are building and engineering disputes, advising on non-litigious building and engineering matters, all types of professional negligence disputes (in particular regarding architects, surveyors and engineers), power station and utility disputes and arbitrations. Also covers general commercial work. Recent cases include David Flood v Shand Construction (assignment of damages claims under FCEC contract, Court of Appeal), R v Chester and North Wales Legal Aid Area Office (availability of legal aid to limited company, Court of Appeal).
Prof. Memberships: Secretary of Official Referees' Bar Association (1997 to date). Bar Pro Bono Unit. Bar European Group. Society for Computers and Law.
Career: Called to the Bar 1992. Major Harmsworth Entrance Exhibition and Diplock Scholar, Middle Temple. Gertrude de Gallaix Achievement Award for Study of Law, FAWCO.
Personal: Educated at Roedean School (1982-86) and New Hall, Cambridge (1987-91). Fluent in German and working knowledge of French.

DOHMANN, Barbara QC
Blackstone Chambers (formerly 2 Hare Court)
(P Baxendale QC and C Flint QC), London
(0171) 583 1770
*Recommended in the following lists: Commercial
(litigation), Financial Services, Insurance &
Reinsurance*
Specialisation: Insurance and Reinsurance;
Financial Services; Banking; Private International
Law; Commercial Fraud (civil); Commercial
Arbitration; Disciplinary Tribunals; Regulatory
Tribunals.
Prof. Memberships: Treasurer of COMBAR;
London Common Law and Commercial Bar
Association, Learned Society for International Civil
Procedure Law.
Career: Called to the Bar in 1971; Queen's
Counsel 1987; Recorder 1990. Sits as a Deputy
High Court Judge.
Personal: Educated in German and American
schools, Universities of Erlangen, Mainz and Paris.
Languages: German, French, Spanish, Italian.

DONALDSON, David QC
Blackstone Chambers (formerly 2 Hare Court)
(P Baxendale QC and C Flint QC), London
(0171) 583 1770
*Recommended in the following lists: Financial
Services, Insurance & Reinsurance*
Specialisation: All aspects of commercial law,
particularly of an international nature, including
related areas of public, regulatory and European
law. Fluent in French and German.
Career: M.A. (Cantab); Dr.iur (Freiburg i.Br.);
former Fellow of Gonville and Caius College,
Cambridge; former DTI Inspector into Guinness
plc; Deputy High Court Judge; called 1968, took
silk 1984.

DOUGLAS, Michael QC
4 Pump Court (Bruce Mauleverer QC), London
(0171) 353 2656
Recommended in Professional Negligence
Specialisation: Professional Negligence, Contract
disputes, insurance, construstion, judicial review,
landlord and tenant, casements.
Prof. Memberships: COMBAR, Professional
Negligence Bar Association, Personal Injuries Bar
Association, ORBA.
Career: Called to the Bar in 1974. Previous
chambers at 2 Harcourt Buildings and 9 Devereux
Court. Joined present chambers in October 1992.
Queen's Counsel 1997.
Personal: Educated at Westminster School and
Balliol College, Oxford 1970-1973.

DOVE, Ian
5 Fountain Court (Anthony Barker QC),
Birmingham (0121) 606 0500
*Recommended in the following lists: Administrative
& Public Law, Planning*
Specialisation: Planning and Local Government,
Personal Injury.
Prof. Memberships: Planning and Environment
Bar Association. Personal Injury Bar Association.
Association of Personal Injury Lawyers.

DOWDING, Nicholas QC
Falcon Chambers (Jonathan Gaunt QC & Kim
Lewison QC), London (0171) 353 2484
Recommended in Property Litigation

DOWLEY, Dominic
1 Hare Court (Lord Neill of Bladen QC &
Richard Southwell QC), London
(0171) 353 3171
Recommended in Commercial (litigation)
Specialisation: Insurance/reinsurance, banking
and financial services/regulation specialist.
Career: Called to the Bar and joined One Hare
Court in 1983.
Personal: Educated at Oxford university 1977-80.
Bacon Scholar of Gray's Inn: Barstow Law Scholar.
Born 25th March 1958. Lives in London.

DOWNING, Ruth
Devereux Chambers (Jeffrey Burke QC),
London (0171) 353 7534
Recommended in Employment
Specialisation: Specialist in common law;
employment law including sex and race
discrimination, unfair dismissal and equal pay.
Practice also covers all types of medical
negligence and personal injury law and in
particular industrial injuries, deafness, RSI and
other diseases.
Prof. Memberships: Employment Law Bar
Asssociation.
Career: Called to the Bar 1978. Joined present
chambers 1979.
Personal: Educated at the Mary Datchelor Girls
School 1966-1973, and at New Hall, Cambridge
(BA Hons) 1974-1977. Leisure pursuits include
fellwalking, theatre, cooking, collecting modern
ceramics. Born 19th September 1954. Lives in
London.

DOYLE, Peter
9-12 Bell Yard (D. Anthony Evans QC), London
(0171) 400 1800
Recommended in Crime: Fraud
Specialisation: Principally serious crime (but with
a combined general common law practice),
commercial fraud and revenue offences. Advice
given in connection with the exercise by the
Serious Fraud Office of its statutory powers,
compliance with regulatory provisions and
requests for international judicial assistance.
Criminal appeals to the Privy Council undertaken,
as well as Tribunal work (discipline and
employment). Cases include – the Maxwell trial (for
Ian Maxwell), the defence of the Surrey Police
Officers (the "Guildford Four" case) and the
Stephen Lawrence Inquiry (instructed by the
Superintendents' Association).
Prof. Memberships: Criminal Bar Association.
South Eastern Circuit.
Career: Called to the Bar 1975.

DRABBLE, Richard QC
4 Breams Buildings (Christopher Lockhart-
Mummery QC), London
(0171) 430 1221/353 5835
*Recommended in the following lists: Administrative
& Public Law, Environmental Law, Planning*
Specialisation: Specialises in public law, planning,
local government and social security.
Prof. Memberships: Vice Chairman of the
Administrative Law Bar Association, member of the
Planning and Environmental Bar Association.
Career: Member of the Panel of Junior Counsel to
the Crown (Common Law) 1992-1995, took Silk
1995, contributor to Goudie and Supperstone
Judicial Review.

DRISCOLL, Michael QC
9 Old Square (Robert Reid QC), London
(0171) 405 4682
Recommended in Property Litigation

DRUCE, Michael
2 Mitre Court Buildings (Michael FitzGerald
QC), London (0171) 583 1380
Recommended in Planning
Specialisation: Main areas of practice are town
and country planning, compulsory purchase and
compensation, rating, local government,
environmental and administrative law. Major
inquiries include the Runnymede Local Plan; and
TAG McLaren HQ inquiry. Has recently appeared
before the Grand Court of the Cayman Islands.
Prof. Memberships: Planning and Environment
Bar Association. Justice.
Career: Called to Bar 1988 and joined current
chambers 1990.
Personal: Educated at Repton School and Sidney
Sussex College, Cambridge. Born 23rd March
1964. Married with 2 children. Lives in London.

DU CANN, Christian
39 Essex Street (Edwin Glasgow QC), London
(0171) 832 1111
Email: cdc@39Essex.co.uk
Recommended in Personal Injury
Specialisation: Catastrophic injury. Occupational
disease (especially asbestos ULD and stress
claims). Disaster claims. Health and Safety law
(including criminal prosecution). Sports injury
claims. Also specialises in medical and
professional negligence.
Prof. Memberships: Member of Grays Inn
(member of its Continuing Education Committee
and Advocacy teacher). Member of Personal Injury
Bar Association. Member of London Common Law
and Commercial Bar Association. Member of
Professional Negligence Bar Association.
Career: Called to the Bar 1982. Practiced at 39
Essex Street since 1991.
Personal: Speaks French and Spanish.

DUCK, Michael
3 Fountain Court (Colman Treacy QC),
Birmingham (0121) 236 5854
Recommended in Crime
Specialisation: Principal area of practice is crime.
R v Sara Thornton, (authority on provocation), R v
Christie, Bell, Francis (custody time limits).
Career: Called to the Bar in 1988. Practised at 3
Fountain Court, from April 1989.
Personal: Born 1965. Leisure interests include
travel, golf and water-skiing.

DUCKWORTH, Peter
29 Bedford Row Chambers (Peter Ralls QC),
London (0171) 831 2626
Recommended in Family: Matrimonial Finance
Specialisation: Specialist in matrimonial finance,
inheritance and professional negligence. Works:
'Matrimonial Property & Finance', 6th Edn (1998)
FT Law & Tax, 'Family Finance Toolkit' software, 3rd
Edn (1998) with Graham Reeds. Reported cases
include: Hepburn (1989) 1 FLR 373 (nominal
orders), Happé (1990) 2 ELR 212 (Army pensions),
Bishop v Plumley (1991) 1 FLR 121 (inheritance
claims by mistresses), Hildebrand (1992) 1 FLR
244 (discovery), Pounds (1994) 1FLR 775 (consent
orders), Thomas (1995) 2 FLR 668 (companies),
Ward (1996) 2 FLR 480 (pensions adjustment
orders) and Harris v Scholfield Roberts & Hill
(1998) (exceptions to Kelley v Corston immunity).
Prof. Memberships: FLBA (Treasurer since 1995).
Lawyers Christian Fellowship.
Career: LLB (Manchester), LRAM, called 1971.
Personal: Interests: piano, computing, people,
Alpha courses.

DUFFY, Peter QC
Essex Court Chambers (Gordon Pollock QC),
London (0171) 813 8000
*Recommended in the following lists: Administrative
& Public Law, Civil Liberties, European
Union/Competition, Media & Entertainment, Tax,
Sports Law*
Specialisation: Has a broadly based practice
mainly in the fields of judicial review, European
Community Law (all aspects) and public
international law including particularly cases under
the European Convention on Human Rights.
During past year, cases in the English courts
included ex p. Diane Blood; R v Lord Chancellor ex
p. Witham (court fees); R v MOD ex p. Perkins (EC
rights of homosexual armed forces personnel), ex
p. Seymour Smith (part time workers) and R v
Radio Authority ex p. Bull (advertising by Amnesty
International); in the European Court of Human
Rights, cases included Buckley v UK, Akdivar v
Turkey, Philis v Greece and Halford v UK; in the
European Court of Justice, cases included
Eurotunnel (the duty free regime), R v MAFF ex p.
NFU (IACS penalties) and R v MAFF ex p
Compassion in World Farming (veal crates). Editor
of European Human Rights Reports since 1982.
Monthly columnist on European law for the
Solicitor's Journal.

Prof. Memberships: Member of Irish and Northern Irish Bars. Whilst a junior, was a Member of Supplementary Panel of Treasury Counsel (Common Law). Vice Chairman of the Bar European Group. A past International Chairman of Amnesty International.
Personal: Educated at Cambridge and Brussels Universities: (licence spéciale en droit européen: la plus grande distinction; LLB: 1st class hons.). Fluent in French.

DUGGAN, Michael
Littleton Chambers (Michael Burton QC), London (0171) 797 8600
Recommended in Employment Law
Specialisation: Principal areas of practice are: Employment; all areas including discrimination, transfer of undertakings, wrongful and unfair dismissal, business re-organisations and redundancies, restrictive covenants and trade union law especially labour disputes. Also substantial experience of disability discrimination cases. Also substantial practice in building and construction law. Other areas: Health and Safety, Professional negligence especially construction related, contract and commercial disputes including interlocutory injunctions (Marevas/Anton Pillers).
Career: Called to the Bar 1984. Author: Modern Law of Strikes. Business Re-Organisations and Employment Law (FT Law & Tax). Termination of Employment of Directors (FT Law & Tax June 1997). Employment Agencies (forthcoming). Regular Lecturer on Race, Sex and Disability Discrimination; handling Strikes, handling redundancies, TUPE and wrongful dismissal.
Personal: BA. BCL. LLM (First Class, Sidney Sussex College, Cambridge University). Holt Scholar of Gray's Inn. Lives in Gray's Inn, London and Coton, Cambridgeshire.

DUGGAN, Ross
India Buildings Chambers (David Harris QC), Liverpool 0151 243 6000
Recommended in Family/Matrimonial
Specialisation: A specialist in all aspects of Family Law especially public law children's work for local authorities, parents and Guardians ad Litem. Also experienced in personal injury work.
Prof. Memberships: FLBA/PIBA.
Career: Called 1978. Recorder 1997.

DUMARESQ, Delia
Atkin Chambers (John Blackburn QC), London (0171) 404 0102
Recommended in Alternative Dispute Resolution
Specialisation: All aspects of construction, building and engineering disputes, including International and Domestic Arbitrations and Professional negligence. Aspects of insolvency, landlords and tenants, insurance work.
Prof. Memberships: Official Referees Bar Association (ORBA) Panel of adjudicators, New South Wales Bar (Australia). CEDR Mediator and panel of adjudicators. Fellow of Chartered Institute of Arbitrators.
Career: 1967 – BA – Australia. Prior to reading law, worked and travelled extensively in Southeast Asia (as an archaeologist) and Europe. 1973 – MA (Hons) – London (Work and research on disadvantaged groups and communities) 1983 – Dip Law (Hons); 1984 – called; Inner Temple.
Personal: One son. Interests include music, modern art, Italian culture and Language.

DUMONT, Thomas
11 New Square (Peter Crampin QC), London (0171) 831 0081
Recommended in Charities
Specialisation: Professional Negligence principally solicitors and accountants: Bristol & West v Christie, Acland & Lensum 3rd Parties (1996). Private Client advice and litigation, including wills and probate, trusts and charities: Re Tepper's Will Trusts (1987), Wood v Smith (1993), Crowden v Aldridge (1993). Commercial Property: Landlord &

Tenant, Restrictive Covenants and Mortgages: Mortgage Corporation v Nationwide Credit Corporation (1994).
Prof. Memberships: Charity Law Association; Society of Trust & Estate Practitioners; Professional Negligence Bar Association; Bar Council Nominated Spokesman on Solicitors' Negligence; Legal Network T.V. Broadcaster on Probate and Tax matters.
Career: MA (Cantab) Exhibitioner in Law, Trinity Hall. Called 1979, Gray's Inn, Master Tapp Memorial Prizewinner. Lecturer in Trusts and Revenue, University of Westminster 1981-85. Examiner in Revenue, Inns of Court School of Law.
Personal: Married with two young children. Fellow of the Zoological Society of London. Plays Cricket whenever possible.

DUNKELS, Paul QC
Walnut House (Francis Gilbert QC), Exeter (01392) 279751
Recommended in Crime

DUNN, Katherine
40 King St (Philip Raynor QC), Manchester (0161) 832 9082
Recommended in the following lists: Chancery, Insolvency
Specialisation: General Chancery both litigation and non-litigious including personal and corporate insolvency, company law, landlord and tenant, professional negligence, mortgages and land law generally, trusts and wills and probate.
Prof. Memberships: Northern Circuit, Northern Chancery Bar Association, Chancery Bar Association, Northern Circuit Commercial Bar Association.
Career: On DTI Panel for Directors' Disqualifications.

DUNN-SHAW, Jason David
6 King's Bench Walk (Michael Worsley QC), London (0171) 583 0410
Recommended in Crime
Specialisation: Defending and prosecuting in all criminal matters but with a particular enthusiasm for fraud.
Prof. Memberships: Committee of the Central London Courts Bar Mess.
Career: Malvern College, Manchester University, University of Westminster.

DUNNING, Graham
Essex Court Chambers (Gordon Pollock QC), London (0171) 813 8000
Recommended in the following lists: Arbitration, Shipping, Sports Law
Specialisation: Specialist in all aspects of international and commercial law, particularly arbitration, banking and finance, commodities and trade, insurance and reinsurance, professional negligence and shipping and transport. In the international field practice covers jurisdictional and private disputes, arbitrations, injunctions, forum conveniens and applicable law. Commodities and trade work covers cases involving oil, metals, foodstuffs and futures. Practice encompasses all aspects of insurance and reinsurance litigation involving Lloyd's syndicates. Professional negligence experience covers cases involving insurance brokers, actuaries, accountants and solicitors. Broad based shipping and transport practice covers charterparty diputes and bill of lading claims, ship sale and shipbuiding, aviation.
Prof. Memberships: Commercial Bar Association; British Insurance Law Authority; British Maritime Law Association; London Maritime Arbitrators Association.
Career: Called to the Bar 1982. Joined present chambers the following year.
Personal: Educated at Cambridge University (BA Hons. 1st class) 1977-1980, and at Harvard Law School (LL.M) 1980-1981. Scholarships: Emmanuel College Entrance Scholarship (1977), University of Cambridge Squire Law Scholarship (1978 and 1979), Lincoln's Inn Hardwicke

Scholarship (1979), Kennedy Scholar, Harvard Law School (1980), Lincoln's Inn Denning Scholarship (1981). Born 13th March 1958. Lives in London.

DUTHIE, Catriona
Guildhall Chambers (John Royce QC), Bristol (0117) 927 3366
Recommended in Family/Matrimonial

DUTTON, Timothy C.
Barnards Inn Chambers (Timothy Bowles), London (0171) 242 8508
Recommended in Property Litigation
Specialisation: Property-related litigation, with a strong landlord and tenant bias: rent reviews and lease renewals; breaches of covenant and other disputes in respect of commercial property; long leases of residential property (including leasehold enfranchisement); Rent Act and Housing Act tenancies.
Prof. Memberships: Chancery Bar Association.
Career: Called to the Bar in 1985. Employed for several years (post-call) in the property litigation departments of Speechly Bircham and Lovell White Durrant.
Personal: Born 1962. Educated at Godalming Grammar School (1972-1980) and Durham University (1981-1984).

DUVAL, Robert
St. John's Chambers (Roderick Denyer QC), Bristol (0117) 921 3456
Recommended in Crime

DYER, Nigel
1 Mitre Court Buildings (Bruce Blair QC), London (0171) 797 7070
Recommended in Family: Matrimonial Finance
Specialisation: Family Law, principally ancillary relief often involving 'big money cases' where assets are held in companies, trusts and farms in the U.K. and abroad.
Prof. Memberships: Family Law Bar Association.
Career: Called to the Bar by Inner Temple 1982.
Personal: Married with 2 children and lives in London.

EADES, Mark
5 Fountain Court (Anthony Barker QC), Birmingham (0121) 606 0500
Recommended in Health & Safety

EADIE, James
1 Hare Court (Lord Neill of Bladen QC & Richard Southwell QC), London (0171) 353 3171
Recommended in Commercial (litigation)
Specialisation: Junior Counsel to the Crown – Common Law.

EADY, Jennifer
Old Square Chambers (Hon. John Melville Williams QC), London (0171) 269 0300
Recommended in Employment
E-mail address: JEady@compuserve.com
Specialisation: All aspects of employment and discrimination law. Cases of significance: R v BCC ex p Vardy 1993 (pit-closures JR), Associated Newspapers v Wilson 1995 HL (trade union), RJB v NUM 1995 CA (strike ballot), MRS v Marsh 1996 CA (TUPE), RMT v Intercity 1996 CA (strike ballot), Smith v BCC 1996 HL (equal pay), BRS v Loughran 1997 NICA (equal pay), Tuck v BSG 1996 EAT (TUPE), NACODS v Gluchowski 1996 EAT (trade union), Wilson v St Helens 1996 EAT (TUPE), Halford v UK 1997 ECHR (Human Rights), BBC v Kelly-Phillips 1998 CA (employment contracts), Okoye v Nicol and ors 1997 CA (race discrimination); England v Magill (1997) (the Westminster "gerrymandering" case); Inquiries: The UCATT Inquiry (1992). Publications: 'Discrimination: Remedies and Quantum' (Sweet & Maxwell) (1998), 'Employment Tribunal Procedure' (LAG) (1996), 'Employment Law Review' (IER), Contributor ICSL 'Employment Law Manual' (Blackstone), Contributor 'Employment Law

Precedents' (Sweet & Maxwell), occasional contributor ILJ, 'The Guardian', etc.
Prof. Memberships: Vice-Chair Industrial Law Society, Secretary of the Employment Law Bar Association, Bar representative for London IT consultative committee, member of the EAT users' group, ELA member.
Career: 1986 BA Hons PPE (Oxon), 1988 Dip Law. Called 1989, Northern Ireland Bar 1994. Standing junior counsel to NUJ and NUM, appointed to the Treasury panel. ICSL Employment law assessor.

EASTEAL, Andrew
No.1 High Pavement (John B. Milmo QC), Nottingham (0115) 941 8218
Recommended in Crime

EASTMAN, Roger
2 Harcourt Buildings (Roger Henderson QC), London (0171) 583 9020
Recommended in Personal Injury
Specialisation: Predominantly common law practice with a particular emphasis on personal injury matters, health and safety (civil and criminal prosecution and defence work) and professional negligence (especially medical negligence). Also deals with the law relating to markets.
Prof. Memberships: Criminal Bar Association, COMBAR, Professional Negligence Bar Association, Official Referees' Bar Association, Personal Injury Bar Association.
Career: Called to the Bar 1978 and joined current chambers in 1981.
Personal: Educated at Maidstone Grammar School 1964-72; St. John's College, Durham 1972-75; and Council of Legal Education 1976-78. Born 23rd May 1953. Lives in London.

EATON, Deborah
One King's Bench Walk (James Townend QC), London (0171) 936 1500
Recommended in the following lists: Family: Child Care including child abduction
Specialisation: All aspects of family law including matrimonial finance and children (private and public law), inter country adoption and professional negligence. Co-Author: Wildblood and Eaton: Financial Provision In Family Matters published by Sweet and Maxwell 1998. Author: Sweet and Maxwell Practical Research Papers. Regular lecturer on ancillary relief and children matters. Contributor to Family Law.
Prof. Memberships: Family Law Bar Association. Intercountry Adoption Lawyers Association.
Career: Called to the Bar in 1985.
Personal: Born 28th March 1962, BSc (Hons) Psychology and Anthropology, Diploma in Law. Leisure pursuits include travel, opera, theatre and cinema.

ECCLES, David
8 King St (Keith Armitage QC), Manchester (0161) 834 9560
Recommended in Medical Negligence
Specialisation: Medical Negligence, Personal Injury, Civil actions for malicious prosecution and wrongful arrest. Ancillary Relief. Cases include: Smith v West Lanes Health A [1995] PIQP P514; Wagstaffe v Wagstaffe [1992] IWLR 320; Wilding v Chief Constable of Lancashire (March); Hyland v Chief Constable of Lancs – Times 7/2/96.
Prof. Memberships: PIBA, PMBA.
Career: Wilmslow Grammar School and Clare College, Cambridge.
Personal: Theatre, cinema, playing bridge, reading & travel.

EDELMAN, Colin QC
Devereux Chambers (Jeffrey Burke QC), London (0171) 353 7534
Recommended in the following lists: Insurance & Reinsurance, Professional Negligence
Specialisation: Principal areas of practice are insurance and reinsurance, professional negligence and commercial law. Recent reported cases include Youell v Bland Welch

(The 'Superhulls Cover' case) [1992] (reinsurance/reinsurance brokers' negligence), Eagle Star v Provincial Insurance [1993] (contribution between insurers), Shell v P&O [1995] (Carriage by road), O'Connell v Eagle Star [1995] (Bloodstock Insurance), Mercury v DGT [1996] (telecommunications) and Hamptons Residential v Field [1997] (professional indemnity insurance). Was involved for E&O insurers in a number of the Lloyd's Names actions and reported decisions arising from that litigation. Has written articles for 'International Insurance Law Review' and the 'British Insurance Law Association Journal'. Contributor to "Insurance Disputes" (LLP). Regular speaker/chairman at EuroForum and other conferences on insurance and reinsurance topics.
Prof. Memberships: Commercial Bar Association, member of Middle Temple and Midlands & Oxford Circuit.
Career: Called to the Bar in 1977 and has been a tenant at Devereux Chambers since 1979. Appointed Assistant Recorder in 1993. Took Silk in 1995. Appointed Recorder 1996.
Personal: Educated at Haberdashers' Aske's School, Elstree 1961-72 and Clare College, Cambridge 1973-76. Leisure pursuits include skiing, walking, badminton. Born 2nd March 1954. Lives in London.

EDER, Bernard QC
Essex Court Chambers (Gordon Pollock QC), London (0171) 813 8000
Recommended in the following lists: Commercial (litigation), Energy & Utilities, Insurance & Reinsurance, Shipping
Specialisation: Most work of a litigious nature involving appearances in arbitration and the Commercial Court, Court of Appeal and House of Lords. All aspects of commercial law, including insurance and reinsurance, shipping and banking, international sale of goods, oil and gas.
Career: Downing College, Cambridge BA (Law) (First Class Hons); Called to the Bar 1975; Queen's Counsel 1990.
Personal: Born 1952.

EDGE, Timothy
8 King St (Keith Armitage QC), Manchester (0161) 834 9560
Recommended in Family/Matrimonial
Specialisation: Ancillary Relief. Childrens Law – Public Law – International abduction. Associate counsel at North Wales tribunal inquiry.
Prof. Memberships: FLBA
Career: MA (Oxon)
Personal: Sport – including rugby, soccer and tennis. Travel. Jazz Music.

EDIE, Alastair
Two Garden Court (I. Macdonald QC & O. Davies), London (0171) 353 1633
Recommended in Crime

EDIS, Andrew QC
14 Castle St (Adrian Lyon), Liverpool (0151) 236 4421/8240/6759/6757
Recommended in the following lists: Commercial (litigation), Personal Injury

EDIS, William
1 Crown Office Row (Robert Seabrook QC), London (0171) 797 7500
Recommended in Environmental Law
Specialisation: Environmental litigation, both civil and criminal. Particular expertise in relation to contaminated land, particulate emission, water and air pollution and nuclear installations. Professional negligence, particularly medical, legal and surveyors'.
Prof. Memberships: PNBA, UKELA

EDWARDS, David
7 King's Bench Walk (Stephen Tomlinson QC), London (0171) 583 0404
Recommended in Insurance & Reinsurance
Specialisation: Commercial law predominantly

insurance and reinsurance, international sale of goods, banking and finance, shipping.
Career: Called to the Bar 1989. Recent cases include: Marc Rich v Bishop Rock The "Nicholas H" [1996] AC 211 (shipping – duty of care owed by Classification Society); New Hampshire v MGN [1997] 1 LRLR 24 (fidelity insurance – joint or composite); Glencore v Portman [1996] 1 Lloyd's Rep. 430 and [1997] 1 Lloyd's Rep. 225 (insurance – non-disclosure); The "Bergen" [1997] 1 Lloyd's Rep. 380 (Clarke J) (jurisdiction – Brussels Convention); The "Lendoudis Evangelos II" [1997] 1 Lloyd's Rep. 404 (charterparty – duration expressed "without guarantee"); The Sumitomo Bank, Limited v Banque Bruxelles Lambert SA [1997] 1 Lloyd's Rep. 487 (syndicated lending – duty owed by arranger to syndicate members); Source v TUV [1997] 3 WLR 364 (jurisdiction – Brussels Convention).
Personal: Born 1966. King's School, Chester and Peterhouse, Cambridge, M.A. (Cantab). Member of Commercial Bar Association.

EDWARDS, Glyn
St. John's Chambers (Roderick Denyer QC), Bristol (0117) 921 3456
Recommended in Personal Injury

EDWARDS, Martin
1 Serjeants' Inn (Lionel Read QC), London (0171) 583 1355
Recommended in Planning
Specialisation: Principal areas of practice are town and country planning and environmental law including judicial review, public inquiries and prosecutions.
Prof. Memberships: Planning and Environmental Bar Association and Legal Member of RTPI.
Career: Admitted as a Solicitor 1981, called to the Bar 1995. BA (Hons) Law, MA (Environmental Law).

EDWARDS, Susan QC
23 Essex Street (Michael Lawson QC), London (0171) 413 0353
Recommended in Crime
Specialisation: Crime, Fraud, Corporate Crime, Child Abuse.
Prof. Memberships: C.B.A.
Career: Parkstone Grammar School, Poole. Southampton University – LL.B (1971), Recorder. QC 1993.
Personal: Tennis.

EDWARDS-STUART, Antony QC
2 Crown Office Row (Graeme Hamilton QC), London (0171) 797 8100
Recommended in Professional Negligence
Specialisation: Principal area of practice is insurance, reinsurance and general commercial litigation and advice. Considerable experience of major insurance and reinsurance disputes, both marine and non-marine, together with highly complicated technical commercial cases including radioactive contamination (Merlins v BNFL, Blue Circle Industries plc v MOD, leading test cases), microbiology and chemistry (AKZO v Cyprus, contaminated paint) and electron beam welding (Burnley Engineering v Cambridge Vacuum Engineering). Other main areas of practice involve professional negligence work particularly concerning architects and engineers, but also insurance brokers, Lloyd's agents, solicitors, accountants and surveyors, both for plaintiffs and defendants. Also involved in several major construction cases and arbitrations. Clients have included major insurance companies, BNFL, leading professional practices and large construction firms.
Prof. Memberships: COMBAR, London Common Law and Commercial Bar Association.
Career: Called to the Bar 1976 and joined Crown Office Row in 1977. Took Silk in 1991. Appointed Recorder in 1997. Chairman, Home Office Advisory Committee on Service Candidates, 1995 -.
Personal: Education: Sherborne School, Dorset 1960-64, RMA Sandhurst 1965-66, St. Catharine's

College, Cambridge 1969-72. Married with 4 children. Leisure pursuits include restoring property in France, theatre, fishing and shooting. Born 2nd November 1946. Lives in London.

EGAN, Marion
One Paper Buildings (John Slater QC), London (0171) 583 7355
Recommended in Insurance & Reinsurance
Specialisation: Insurance/reinsurance: Deutsche Rückversicherung v Walbrook Insurance [1995] 1 WLR 1017. Groupe Josi Re v Walbrook Insurance [1996] 1 WLR 1152. Professional negligence: South Australia Asset Management Corp v York Montague [1996] 3 WLR 87.
Prof. Memberships: Commercial Bar Association. O.R. Bar Association. Professional Negligence Bar Association.
Career: Cambridge Law Degree. MA (Cantab). Called to Bar 1988. 1 year at a Canadian law firm. Taught commercial law at Inns of Court School of Law.

EGAN, Michael
9-12 Bell Yard (D. Anthony Evans QC), London (0171) 400 1800
Recommended in Crime: Fraud
Specialisation: Criminal law; Serious Fraud, additionally representing solicitors, accountants and other professionals. Advising the Police Federation and Police Authorities, representing police officers in crime, Discipline and Inquests. Notable cases: The 'Wapping' police cases, R v Attwell & others (The 'Guildford 4' officers), R v Melvin & Dingle (the 'Tottenham 3' officers), DPP v Clegg (in the H. of L. only), SFO v Crawford & others (the European Leisure Plc case), R v Walker (The Hare Brother's excise fraud), SFO v Falkovsky and others. Most recently appeared for the Police Federation in the Stephen Lawrence Inquiry.
Prof. Memberships: Criminal Bar Association.
Career: 5 years' articles 1971-1976 - included extensive experience of conveyancing, company and probate. Practised as a solicitor 1976-1981. Called to the Bar in 1981.

EICKE, Tim
Francis Taylor Building (Andrew Thompson & David Guy), London (0171) 797 7250
Recommended in Immigration & Nationality
Specialisation: EC law, including European Immigration Law and the EC Association Agreements, Free Movement and Equal Treatment (Cases: C-75/94 Gallagher [1995] ECR I-4253 (ECJ) and [1996] 2 CMLR 951 (CA); C-416/96 El Yassini; Sahota [1998] 2 WLR 626; Boukssid, Times, 6/3/98; Yiadom, Times 1/5/98); Judicial Review (Cases: R v Legal Aid Board ex p. Eccleston, Times 6/5/98); Human Rights (Cases: Court of Human Rights in Sheffield and Horsham and European Commission of Human Rights in Laskey et al. (1997) 24 EHRR 39 and National & Provincial et al (1998) 25 EHRR 127; Amicus submissions to the European Court of Human Rights in Chahal (1997) 23 EHRR 413, Akdivar v Turkey (1997) 23 EHRR 143, Ahmed and McGinley); Employment Law; Education Law, Discrimination (Race and Sex); Private International Law; General Commercial and Civil.
Prof. Memberships: ILPA (Executive Committee), Bar European Group, Employment Law Bar Association, Administrative Law Bar Association, British German Jurists Association.
Career: Called 1993; LLB (Hons) Dundee University.
Personal: Bi-lingual German-English, advanced French; Assistant Editor, 'European Human Rights Reports'. Member of the Justice Expert Panel on Human Rights in the EU.

EISSA, Adrian
Two Garden Court (I. Macdonald QC & O. Davies), London (0171) 353 1633
Recommended in Crime

EKLUND, Graham
2 Temple Gardens (Patrick Phillips QC), London (0171) 583 6041
Recommended in Professional Negligence
Specialisation: Professional negligence – particularly Surveyors, Solicitors, Accountants and Insurance Brokers. Insurance related matters – particularly fraudulent claims, policy construction points, fire and disaster claims, including pollution and contamination claims. Personal injury – particularly serious injuries (including tetraplegic and paraplegic cases). Computer and IT. Reported cases include: Jones & Marsh McLennan v Crowley Colosso (1996); Yorkshire Water v Sun Alliance (1996); John Munroe (Acrylics) Limited v London Fire and Civil Defence Authority (1997); Chapman v Christopher (1998).
Prof. Memberships: PNBA, PIBA.
Career: Educated at Auckland University (1969-1974) BA; LLB (Hons). Barrister and Solicitor of the High Court of New Zealand (1975-1978). Solicitor of the Supreme Court of England and Wales (1979-1984). Called 1984.
Personal: Married – 2 children. Interests include music, particularly opera and piano, cricket, wine.

ELDER, Fiona
All Saints Chambers (T. Alun Jenkins QC), Bristol (0117) 921 1966
Recommended in Crime

ELGOT, Howard
Park Lane Chambers (Martin Bethel QC), Leeds (0113) 228 5000
Recommended in Personal Injury
Specialisation: Personal Injury, industrial disease litigation, medical and professional negligence, insurance and commercial litigation. Counsel in benzodiazepine and other group litigation. Many reported cases at first instance, in Court of Appeal and House of Lords. Highlights of past year include appearances in I louse of Lords in Clarke v Kato; Cutter v Eagle Star conjoined appeals, several appearances in the Court of Appeal and many High Court trials on North Eastern, Northern and Midland and Oxford Circuits, including personal injury claims of maximum severity.
Prof. Memberships: PIBA; PNBA
Career: BA BCL New College, Oxford. 3 Paper Buildings, Temple 1974-86, present chambers since 1986. Chairman, North Eastern Circuit Remuneration and Terms of Work Committee Member, Bar Council Remuneration and Terms of Work Committee.
Personal: Married, 3 children. Ski-ing. Italy. Music. Football.

ELIAS, Gerard QC
Farrar's Building (Gerard Elias QC), London (0171) 583 9241
Recommended in Crime

ELIAS, Patrick QC
11 King's Bench Walk (Eldred Tabachnik QC and James Goudie QC), London (0171) 632 8500
Recommended in the following lists: Administrative & Public Law, Employment, Partnership

ELLERAY, Anthony QC
St. James's Chambers (R.A. Sterling), Manchester (0161) 834 7000
Recommended in Chancery
Specialisation: Chancery and General Commercial Litigation; Professional Negligence; Landlord and Tenant. Recent cases include Walker v Turpin (1994) (payment in); Jervis v Harris (1996) (Landlord and Tenant repairs and 1938 Act); Bass v Latham Crossley and Davies (1996) (partnership/holding out); Shaikh v Bolton MBC (1996) (statutory interest on compulsory purchase). Pearce Deceased (1998) (Inheritance Act).
Prof. Memberships: Chancery Bar Association; Northern Chancery Bar Association; Professional Negligence Bar Association.
Career: Called to the Bar 1977; took Silk 1993.

Prof. Memberships: Educated: Bishop Stortford College 1967-1972. Trinity College Cambridge 1973-1976. Born 19th August 1954.

ELLIOTT, Margot
Regency Chambers (Raymond Croxon QC), Cambridge (01223) 301517
Regency Chambers (Raymond Croxon QC), Peterborough (01733) 315215
Recommended in Family/Matrimonial
Also at Cambridge (01223) 301517
Specialisation: Sole area of practice is family law, with particular emphasis on child law, public and private, including care proceedings, adoption, wardship and residence and contact disputes.
Prof. Memberships: Family Law Bar Association.
Career: Educated at Wakefield Girl's High School and University of Newcastle Upon Tyne (LL.B. 1987). Called to the Bar in 1989; member of current chambers since 1991.
Personal: Born 29th July 1966. Lives in Cambridgeshire with husband and one child.

ELLIOTT, Timothy QC
Keating Chambers (Richard Fernyhough QC), London (0171) 544 2600
Recommended in the following lists: Arbitration, Construction, Professional Negligence
Specialisation: Building and civil engineering; professional negligence; bonds and guarantees; computer software. Clients include national and international contractors and developers, professional, national and local government. Also acts as Arbitrator and legal assessor.
Career: Qualified 1975. Middle Temple QC 1992.
Personal: Marlborough College and Trinity College, Oxford (1973 MA Oxon). Born 1950; resides London.

ELLIS, Diana
3 Gray's Inn Square (Rock Tansey QC), London (0171) 520 5600
Recommended in Crime

ELLISON, Mark
Queen Elizabeth Building (David Jeffreys QC & Peter Whiteman QC), London (0171) 583 5766
Recommended in the following lists: Crime, Crime: Fraud
Specialisation: Criminal practice specialising in commercial fraud and Treasury Counsel work. Interesting cases include both the Guinness trial and appeal.
Career: Called 1979. Appointed Junior Treasury Counsel to the Crown at the Central Criminal Court 1994.
Personal: Educated at Pocklington School, Skinners School and the University of Wales.

ELVIN, David
4 Breams Buildings (Christopher Lockhart-Mummery QC), London (0171) 430 1221/353 5835
Recommended in the following lists: Environmental Law, Planning, Property Litigation
Specialisation: real property, landlord and tenant, agriculture, trespass, judicial review, compulsory purchase, compensation, planning, environmental law (including nature conservation), nuisance, highways, local government, education and professional negligence.
Career: Called to the Bar by the Middle Temple in 1983 and is member of the Administrative Law Bar Association, Chancery Bar Association and the Planning and Environmental Bar Association. Educated at the A.J. Dawson Grammar School, Co. Durham and at Hertford College, Oxford obtaining a B.A. (First Class Honours) in Jurisprudence and a B.C.L. In 1983 he won the Bar Association for Finance Commerce and Industry Prize. He is one of the Junior Counsel to the Crown (Common Law) having served as a Supplementary Panellist from 1991 to 1995. He is co-author of Unlawful Interference with Land (1995).

ELWICK, Martin
No.1 High Pavement (John B. Milmo QC), Nottingham (0115) 941 8218
Recommended in Crime

EMMERSON, Ben
Doughty Street Chambers (Geoffrey Robertson QC), London (0171) 404 1313
Recommended in the following lists: Civil Liberties, Crime
Specialisation: Civil liberties and international human rights law, including representation of applicants before the European Court of Justice in Luxemberg and the European Court and Commission of Human Rights in Strasbourg; civil actions against police and public law, particularly prisoners' rights. Also criminal law, especially political offences and cases involving police malpractice; Commonwealth capital appeals, extradition, deportation and international enforcement of asset confiscation. Editor of European Human Rights Law Review (Sweet & Maxwell). Human rights Editor of Archbold Criminal Pleading, Evidence and Practice. Author Butterworth's Guide to the Police Act 1997. Council of Europe Representative on Human Rights Courses in Central and Eastern Europe.
Career: Called to the Bar 1986.
Personal: Bristol University 1982-85. Born 30th August 1963.

ENGLAND, William
Crown Office Row (Richard Ferguson QC), London (0171) 797 7111
Recommended in Crime

ENGLEHART, Robert QC
Blackstone Chambers (formerly 2 Hare Court) (P Baxendale QC and C Flint QC), London (0171) 583 1770
Recommended in Media & Entertainment
Specialisation: Both commercial and copyright aspects of music business and media, especially broadcasting, disputes; also practices in general commercial law, including commercial judicial review, and intellectual property.
Career: Called 1969, QC 1986, Recorder and Deputy High Court Judge.

ESCOTT-COX, Brian R. QC
36 Bedford Row (James Hunt QC), Northampton (01604) 602333
Recommended in Crime
Specialisation: Achieved the first ever Murder Conviction using 'DNA fingerprinting' and is an acknowledged leading Counsel in this field. (R v Pitch fork). Defended Newbury in the Civil and Criminal action Revill v Newbury went to Court of Appeal (elderly man shot burglar to defend allotment shed). Prosecution of Sara Thornton from original Murder, through the re-trial to Manslaughter (1996).
Career: MA Oxford. Called to the Bar 1954. Took Silk 1974. Bencher of Lincoln's Inn. Member of 3 Fountain Court Birmingham (still a door Tenant) now a member of 36 Bedford Row WC1 London.
Personal: Plays in Jazz Band.

ESPLEY, Susan
Fenners Chambers (Lindsay Davies), Cambridge (01223) 368761
Recommended in Family/Matrimonial
Specialisation: Children cases, both public and private law. Representing Guardian ad litem, Local Authorities and parents.
Prof. Memberships: FLBA. Part-time Chairman: Mental Health Review Tribunals.
Personal: Antiques, music, theatre.

ETHERINGTON, David QC
18 Red Lion Court (Anthony Arlidge QC), London (0171) 520 6000
Recommended in Crime
Specialisation: Criminal practitioner. Experienced in wide range of criminal work including commercial fraud, VAT, drugs and serious professional crime. Also experienced in civil jury

actions such as Malicious Prosecution. Adviser to television companies on documentary and dramatic work including Kavanagh QC, Wing and a Prayer and The Bill.
Prof. Memberships: Elected member General Council of the Bar and Committee of the Eastern Circuit. Appointed member of the Criminal Bar Association Committee and Professional Conduct Committee. Chambers 18 Red Lion Court (Anthony Arlidge QC).
Career: Call 1979 (Middle Temple), Assistant Recorder of the Crown Court 1997, Queen's Counsel 1998.

ETHERTON, Terence QC
Wilberforce Chambers (Edward Nugee QC), London (0171) 306 0102
Recommended in the following lists: Banking, Chancery, Financial Services, Pensions, Property Litigation
Specialisation: Chancery and Commercial litigation and advice. Particular areas are commercial property and landlord and tenant; Financial Services including Unit Trusts, and Property Enterprise Trusts; Banking issues, particularly related to property backed and syndicated loans; The Lloyd's Insurance Market; international fraud and asset tracing; company law; professional negligence; trust and pensions litigation. Delivered a 1996 Blundell Memorial Lecture on Property Law and has also lectured on duties of care in syndicated loan transactions.
Career: Called 1974. Took silk 1990.
Prof. Memberships: FCIArb, Combar, Chancery Bar Association.

EVANS, D. Anthony QC
9-12 Bell Yard (D. Anthony Evans QC), London (0171) 400 1800
Recommended in Crime
Specialisation: Prinicpal area of practice is criminal work (both defence and prosecution) encompassing both commercial fraud and general criminal matters. Has acted in DTI Inspections, including Report on James Neill Holdings plc and other companies. Also handles some licensing work. Appeared for the SFO in part of the BCCI litigation in the Resort Hotels (Feld) case and in the Johnson Matthey litigation; for one of the Guildford 4 policemen and for one of the policemen prosecuted as a result of the Wapping riots.
Prof. Memberships: Criminal Bar Association.
Career: Called to the Bar 1965. Tenant at Iscoed Chambers, Swansea 1965-83. Appointed Recorder 1980. Took silk 1983. Tenant at 3 Paper Buildings 1983-90, then joined current chambers.
Personal: Educated at Clifton College, Bristol and Corpus Christi College, Cambridge. Leisure pursuits include rugby football (committee member of Swansea RFC) and horse racing. Born 15th March 1939. Lives in Neath, West Glamorgan and London.

EVANS, David H. QC
Queen Elizabeth Building (David Jeffreys QC & Peter Whiteman QC), London (0171) 583 5766
Recommended in Crime: Fraud
Specialisation: Principal area of specialisation within criminal law is criminal fraud. Before taking silk in 1991 appeared in several high profile cases as Junior. Acted for Ian Posgate in the Howden trial, for Morgan Grenfel in the Guinness enquiry, and for UBS Phillips & Drew in the Blue Arrow trial. Since 1991 has appeared both for the prosecution and defence in a series of major fraud trials including defendants in the BCCI enquiry, the collapse of the Swithland motor group, the Aveling Barford pension fund fraud and several high profile mortgage frauds including acting for the solicitor defendant in the Harrovian case. Has prosecuted for the SFO and the Fraud Investigation Group.
Prof. Memberships: Criminal Bar Association
Career: Educated at the London School of Economics BSc. Econ, MSc 1962-67, Wadham College Oxford B.A. Oxon 1968-70. QC 1991.

EVANS, Elwen Mair
Iscoed Chambers (Trefor Davies), Swansea (01792) 652988/9
Recommended in Crime

EVANS, Gareth QC
5 Fountain Court (Anthony Barker QC), Birmingham (0121) 606 0500
Recommended in Personal Injury

EVANS, Jill
Doughty Street Chambers (Geoffrey Robertson QC), London (0171) 404 1313
Recommended in Crime
Specialisation: Serious Crime, Drugs, Conspiracy to Pervert the course of Justice. Special Expertise:- Offences involving children and Young Persons both as defendants and victims of crime. R v Henry & others (Kings Cross Canalside rape). R v Cross & others. (Allegations of False imprisonment and Child Abuse at special Educational Needs School). Mentally ill offenders.
Prof. Memberships: C.B.A., Haldane Society.
Career: Former Solicitor, Partner Saunders & Co W9. Called to Bar 1986.

EVANS, John
1 Fountain Court (David Crigman QC), Birmingham (0121) 236 5721
Recommended in Crime

EVANS, Mark QC
All Saints Chambers (T. Alun Jenkins QC), Bristol (0117) 921 1966
Recommended in Family/Matrimonial

EVANS, Michael
No.1 High Pavement (John B. Milmo QC), Nottingham (0115) 941 8218
Recommended in Crime

EVANS, Susan
St. John's Chambers (Roderick Denyer QC), Bristol (0117) 921 3456
Recommended in Crime

EVANS, Timothy
13 Old Square (Mr Michael Lyndon-Stanford QC), London (0171) 404 4800
Recommended in Traditional Chancery
Specialisation: Trusts and contentious probate, charities, insolvency.
Prof. Memberships: Chancery Bar Association; COMBAR.
Career: Marlborough College, Pembroke College, Oxford MA (History), Called to the Bar 1979.
Personal: Born 15/12/1955.

EVANS, Timothy Aylmer
Assize Court Chambers (John Isherwood), Bristol (0117) 926 4587
Recommended in Crime
Specialisation: All aspects of Criminal Law including fraud, homicide, sex offences, prison riots (Cardiff and Pucklechurch 1990), public disorder and drugs.
Prof. Memberships: Criminal Bar Association, member of Western Circuit.
Career: LLB (London). Called to the bar 1982. Magistrates Court Clerk. Present Chambers since 1984. Standing Counsel for Western Circuit to Department of Social Security and Department of Health.
Personal: Wildlife photographer, travel, walking, music, supporter of Welsh Rugby Team.

EVERALL, Mark QC
1 Mitre Court Buildings (Bruce Blair QC), London (0171) 797 7070
Recommended in the following lists: Family: Child Care including child abduction
Specialisation: Work includes matrimonial finance, public and private law children cases, international child abduction, adoption, and cases with an international aspect. Editor, Rayden & Jackson on Divorce & Family Matters.
Prof. Memberships: Family Law Bar Association;

Bar European Group; International Academy of Matrimonial Lawyers: Administrative Law Bar Association.
Career: Took silk in 1994.

EVERARD, William
King Charles House (William Everard), Nottingham (0115) 941 8851
Recommended in Crime

EWART, David
Pump Court Tax Chambers (Andrew Thornhill QC), London (0171) 414 8080
Recommended in Tax
Specialisation: Revenue, trusts, professional negligence, Customs & Excise v Ferrero (UK) (1997), Customs & Excise v Kilroy Television Company (1997), Garner v Pounds (1997), Customs & Excise v Leightons Ltd (1995).
Prof. Memberships: Revenue Bar Association.
Career: Hamilton Grammar School; Trinity College, Oxford.
Personal: Bridge, golf.

FANCOURT, Timothy
Falcon Chambers (Jonathan Gaunt QC & Kim Lewison QC), London (0171) 353 2484
Recommended in Property Litigation
Specialisation: Principal area of practice is real property based chancery work (litigation). This includes commercial property, landlord and tenant, surveyors' and solicitors' professional negligence, conveyancing, building contracts, mortgages, easements and restrictive covenants, equity and trusts and commercial contracts. Other main area is bankruptcy and insolvency. General Editor of 'Megarry: The Rent Acts'; author of 'Enforceability of Landlord and Tenant Covenants' (1997).
Prof. Memberships: Lincoln's Inn, Chancery Bar Association.
Career: Called to the Bar in 1987 and joined Falcon Chambers in 1989.
Personal: Educated at Whitgift School 1974-82 and Gonville & Caius College, Cambridge 1983-86. Born 30th August 1964.

FARBEY, Judith
Plowden Buildings (William Lowe QC), London (0171) 583 0808
Recommended in Immigration & Nationality
Specialisation: Immigration; public and administrative law.
Prof. Memberships: Includes JCWI; 12 PA; ALBA; member, Council of Justice.
Career: Called to Bar 1992. Winner, 1997 Bar Pro Bono Award.

FARLEY, Roger QC
40 King St (Philip Raynor QC), Manchester (0161) 832 9082
Recommended in Crime

FARQUHAR, Stuart A.
Chambers of Colin Anderson (St. Mary's Chambers) (Colin Anderson), Nottingham (0115) 950 3503
Recommended in Family/Matrimonial

FARRELL, David
36 Bedford Row (James Hunt QC), Northampton (01604) 602333
Recommended in Crime
Specialisation: Fraud and serious crime. Child cases. R v Neave: Murder of a child; Defence Junior counsel. Operations Neath: Serious Fraud involving motor vehicles, £6 million+. Prosecution counsel (leader).
Prof. Memberships: C.B.A.
Career: LLB Hons Manchester. Ashby-de-la-Zouch Grammar School. Assistant Recorder M&O Circuit.
Personal: Married, 5 children. Interests; Tennis, Sailing.

FARRER, David J. QC
9 Bedford Row (John Goldring QC), London (0171) 242 3555
Recommended in Crime
Specialisation: All areas of serious crime – murder and commercial fraud, both Prosecution and Defence, often with International dimension. Clients include S.F.O., F.I.G., D.T.I., C.P.S., (HQ and regionally on SE and Midlands and Oxford Circuits), as well as range of large and medium firms. Variety of non-criminal work in Q.B.D. and Chancery Divisions involving fraud, undue influence and accounting issues – partnership, insolvency. Civil clients include former England football coach. Prosecuted SFO "Blackspur" and "Norton" cases and R.v.Morgan (Celine Figard murder). Defended first "DNA profiling" murder (R .v. Pitchfork). Regularly train and organise seminars for accountants on investigation, reporting and giving evidence in court.
Prof. Memberships: European Bar Group; Criminal Bar Association.
Career: Teaching modern languages 1965-1967. Called to bar in 1967; Appointed Recorder 1983; Took silk 1986; Member of Bar Council 1987-1989; Chairman Bar services committee 1989-1992; Edited current Bar action pack (Good practice guide). Educated at Queen Elizabeth's Grammar school, Barnet and Downing College Cambridge. Took LLB in Public and Private International Law. Leisure Pursuits include tennis, Rugby (watching only), local history, music and cricket (playing and watching).

FARRER, Paul
1 Fountain Court (David Crigman QC), Birmingham (0121) 236 5721
Recommended in Crime

FAULKS, Edward QC
No. 1 Serjeants' Inn (Edward Faulks QC), London (0171) 415 6666
Recommended in the following lists: Medical Negligence, Professional Negligence
Specialisation: Principal area of practice is professional negligence (particularly medical, veterinary, barristers, solicitors, literary agents, publishers), local authority cases (including child abuse) and education cases. Also handles general common law work including personal injury and media related work. Appeared in W v Essex County Council (1997) 2 FLR 535, Beasley v Bucks, County Council (1997) PIQR 473, Slevin v South West Hampshire HA (1997) 8 Med LR 175, Phelps v London Borough of Hillingdon The Times October 10, 1997, Capital & Counties plc v Hampshire County Council and Others [1997] The Times 20/3/97 (CA), Lonrho v Fayed [1994] 1A ER 188 (CA), M v Newham London Borough [1994] 2 WLR 544, T v Surrey County Council [1994] 4 AER, De Martell v Merton and Surrey HA (1995) 6 Med. LR 234, X v Bedfordshire CC HLE (1995) 3 WLR 152, and Crawford v Dalley and Royal Marsden Hospital (1995) 6 Med. LR 343. Clients include hospitals, local authorities, police authorities, insurance companies and individual plaintiffs. Has been involved in litigation arising out of radiotherapy and HIV haemophilia cases. Media clients include publishers, literary agents and advertising agencies. Author of articles on medical and veterinary negligence and has addressed these topics and local authority negligence at conferences and seminars.
Prof. Memberships: Fellow of Chartered Institute of Arbitrators, Common Law & Commercial Bar Association, Professional Negligence Bar Association.
Career: Called to the Bar 1973 and became a member of present Chambers in 1974.
Personal: Educated at Wellington College, 1963-68 and Jesus College, Oxford 1969-72. Former literary agent. Leisure pursuits include cricket. Born 19th August 1950. Lives in London.

FEDER, Ami
Lamb Building (Ami Feder), London (0171) 797 7788
Recommended in Crime
Specialisation: Principal area of practice is fraud work in both the criminal and civil fields and general commercial and international work. Also practices at 9 Malchei, Israel Square, Tel-Aviv 64163. Tel: 03-5243381 Fax: 03-5243387
Prof. Memberships: Criminal Bar Association; Common Law and Commercial Bar Association; European Bar Association.
Career: Called to the Bar 1965; Member of the Israel Bar.
Personal: Educated in Israel (Hebrew University of Jerusalem, the branch in Tel Aviv) and in England (London LSE).

FEENY, Charles
Peel House (Nigel Gilmour QC), Liverpool (0151) 236 4321
Recommended in Personal Injury
Specialisation: Specialises in personal injury, with particular reference to medical negligence and industrial disease. In medical negligence, appeared in Lybert v Warrington HA [1996] PIQR, P45. Jones v Liverpool HA [1996] PIQR P251. Acts for major employers and insurers in range of industrial disease claims, including Ford, Vauxhall, ICI. Recently appeared for British Gas in VWF litigation.
Prof. Memberships: PIBA
Career: Birkenhead School 1965-72. Corpus Christi College, Cambridge 1973-76. BA Hons Law. Called Inner Temple Nov 1977. Practised at Peel House since. Assistant Recorder 1996.
Personal: Married with five children. Involved in voluntary sector, Director of Liverpool Council for Voluntary Service. Interests – theatre, walking and football. Supports Everton and Whitby Town.

FEINBERG, Peter QC
Crown Office Row (Richard Ferguson QC), London (0171) 797 7111
Recommended in Crime

FENNY, Ian Charles
Guildhall Chambers (John Royce QC), Bristol (0117) 927 3366
Recommended in Crime
Specialisation: All serious crimes of violence with a particular specialisation in offences against women, children and vulnerable victims. Serious fraud and large-scale conspiracies. Drugs importation and large-scale possession with intent to supply. Category 4 Prosecutor. Lectures to legal practitioners, medical practitioners and police officers on issues involving child abuse both physical and sexual.
Prof. Memberships: Membership Criminal Bar Association. Western Circuit.
Career: LL.B (Reading) 1977. Called to Bar (Gray's Inn) 1978. Married to a member of the Bar, 3 children. Hobbies: Motor racing, equestrian sports.

FENTON, Adam
7 King's Bench Walk (Stephen Tomlinson QC), London (0171) 583 0404
Recommended in Insurance & Reinsurance
Specialisation: Insurance (including Lloyd's matters), reinsurance, shipping.
Career: Called to the Bar, 1984. Recent cases include: North Atlantic v. Bishopsgate [1998] 1 Lloyd's Rep. 459 (Basis on which excess to be applied); Johnston v. Leslie & Godwin [1995] L.R.L.R. 472 (Duty of broker to retain documentation/collect claims); Aiken v. Wrightson [1995] 1 W.L.R. 1281 (Insurance – duty of Managing Agent).
Personal: Born 1961.

FENWICK, Justin QC
2 Crown Office Row (John Powell QC), London
(0171) 797 8000
*Recommended in the following lists: Construction,
Product Liability, Professional Negligence*
Specialisation: Professional Negligence;
Construction; Pharmaceutical product liability.
Prof. Memberships: Combar; PNBA; LCLBA;
ORBA.
Career: MA (Cantab) 1971 (Modern Languages
and Architectural History). Grenadier Guards 1968-
81; called to the Bar November 1980. Pupillage
Lamb Building – July 81 – July 82. Tenancy July 82
– July 89. 2 Crown office Row July 1989 – present.
QC 1993.

FERGUSON, Christopher
Assize Court Chambers (John Isherwood),
Bristol (0117) 926 4587
Recommended in Family/Matrimonial

FERGUSON, Richard QC
Crown Office Row (Richard Ferguson QC),
London (0171) 797 7111
Recommended in Crime

FERM, Rodney
37 Park Square (John Sleightholme, Rodney
Ferm), Leeds (0113) 243 9422
Recommended in Family/Matrimonial

FERNYHOUGH, Richard QC
Keating Chambers (Richard Fernyhough QC),
London (0171) 544 2600
*Recommended in the following lists: Arbitration,
Construction, Professional Negligence*
Specialisation: Construction and engineering law;
arbitration both international and domestic.
Career: Qualified 1970; Middle Temple; QC 1986;
FCI Arb 1992; Recorder of the Crown Court 1986.
Personal: Merchant Taylors School; University
College, London (1966 LLB Hons). Born 1943;
resides Rottingdean. Tennis, flying, opera.
Languages: French.

FERRIS, Jonathan
29 Bedford Row Chambers (Peter Ralls QC),
London (0171) 831 2626
Recommended in Professional Negligence
Specialisation: Professional negligence; landlord
and tenant. SAAMCO v York Montague Ltd [1997]
AC 191 HL; Nykredit v Erdman (No 2) [1997] 1
WLR 1627 HL; EPIC v Goddard & Smith [1992] 2
EGLR 155 CA: no summary judgment in
professional opinion negligence claims; Mortgage
Corporation v Sandoes [1997] 2 PNLR CA
procedural guidelines in professional negligence
(and other) trials; UCB v Pinders [1998] 2 PNLR
contributory negligence post – Platform Home
Loans v Oyston; City of Westminster v Clarke
[1993] 90 LGR 210 HL: local authority occupation
agreement lease or licence; Belvedere Court
Management Ltd v Frogmore Developments
[1996] 1 AER 312 CA: tenants' right of first refusal
LTA 1987; Richardson v Leathbond "Chiswick
Village" April, May, June 1997 at Brentford County
Court: over 100 witnesses called in trial of tenants'
right of first refusal; Safeland v Vitaria The Times
2/12/98: Landlord's right to peaceably re-enter for
rent arrears; Cheese v Thomas [1994] 1 AER 35
CA: undue influence; Great House at Sonning v
Berkshire County Council The Times 23/3/96 CA:
injunction to restrain public nuisance.
Prof. Memberships: Chancery Bar Association,
Professional Negligence Bar Association, ORBA.
Career: Latymer Upper Grammar School; Durham
University; Central London Poly; called 1979
Middle Temple; Assistant Recorder 1996.
Personal: Married Deborah Bangay, barrister,
1985; twin sons born 20/5/93; member of the
Garrick Club; Leander Club.

FERRIS, Shaun
One Paper Buildings (John Slater QC), London
(0171) 583 7355
Recommended in Personal Injury
Specialisation: All types of personal injury, in
particular industrial disease cases. Medical
negligence. Professional negligence. Product
liability. Cases: Hall v Clarke [CA] – analysis of
principles behind awards for handicap on the
labour market and costs award where Plaintiff has
failed to beat a payment into court. Bates v Durox –
Claim that injury triggered onset of Multiple
Sclerosis. Hauser v Sunderland Football Club –
claim by professional footballer arising out of
treatment by club physiotherapist. Presently
involved in: – a number of cases involving one
major industrial employer defending claims arising
out of asbestos exposure in the electrical and
mining industries; – organo phosphate litigation
defending manufacturers of commercial sheep dip.
Prof. Memberships: South Eastern Circuit.
London Common Law and Commercial Bar
Association. PIBA.
Career: Trinity College Oxford. Bar Exams 1995.
Editor: Current Law.
Personal: Football, music, cricket.

FEWTRELL, N.A.
18 St. John Street (Rodney C. Klevan QC),
Manchester (0161) 278 1800
Recommended in Personal Injury

FIELD, Patrick John
Deans Court Chambers (H.K. Goddard QC),
Manchester (0161) 834 4097
Recommended in Personal Injury
Specialisation: General Common Law particularly
personal injury and professional negligence.
Prof. Memberships: Northern Circuit; Personal
Injuries Bar Asociation; Professional Negligence
Bar Associaton.
Career: Called 1981. Educated at Wilmslow
Grammar School and Kings College, London.

FIELD, Richard Alan QC
11 King's Bench Walk (Eldred Tabachnik QC
and James Goudie QC), London
(0171) 632 8500
*Recommended in the following lists: Commercial
(litigation), Insurance & Reinsurance*
Specialisation: Principal area of practice is
Commercial Law. Has appeared in a wide range of
matters in this area including insurance, banking
and E.C Competition law. Other areas of practice
include professional negligence, especially
auditors' negligence, and public law in a
commercial context.
Prof. Memberships: COMBAR; London Common
Law and Commercial Bar Asociation, British
Insurance Law Association; ALBA.
Career: 1969-1977 taught in the law faculties of
the Universities of British Columbia; Hong Kong;
and McGill; called to the Bar 1977; appointed
Queen's Counsel 1987; Assistant Recorder 1995;
Deputy High Court Judge 1998; Master of the
Bench of Inner Temple 1998.
Personal: Educated: Bristol University (LLB) and
London University (LLM).

FINCH, Nadine
Doughty Street Chambers (Geoffrey Robertson
QC), London (0171) 404 1313
Recommended in Immigration & Nationality
Specialisation: Predominantly civil liberties
practice, specialising in all areas of immigration
law. Particular experience of cases involving
asylum, the interaction between immigration and
family law, applications by gay and lesbian
appellants, the use of European Convention on
Human Rights and European law and deportation.
Recent cases include R v. Secretary of State for the
Home Department ex parte Meftah Zighem [1996]
Imm AR 194, R v. Secretary of State for the Home
Department ex parte Toprak [1996] Imm AR 332,
and R v. SSHD ex p. Lucy Ouma [1997] Imm AR
606.

Prof. Memberships: Executive Member of
Immigration Law Practitioners Association,
member of Stonewall Immigration Group,
Administrative Law Bar Association, Family Law
Bar Association.
Career: Called to the Bar 1991. Joined present
chambers in 1997. Prior to 1989 employed in legal
research and community work.

FINNIGAN, Peter
Queen Elizabeth Building (David Jeffreys QC &
Peter Whiteman QC), London (0171) 583 5766
Recommended in Crime: Fraud
Specialisation: Principal area of practice is
criminal law with a particular emphasis on
commercial and professional/City fraud cases.
Also deals with Revenue offences and V.A.T.
frauds. Major cases include Blue Arrow, Iraqi
Supergun, Brinks Mat handling (R v Noye and
others) and the Guppy case. Clients include the
S.F.O., H.M. Customs and Excise and the Fraud
Investigation Group of the C.P.S.
Prof. Memberships: Lincoln's Inn.
Career: Called to the Bar 1979 and joined current
chambers in 1981. Standing Counsel to H.M.
Customs & Excise.
Personal: Educated at Sevenoaks School 1967-74
and University of Newcastle-upon-Tyne 1975-78.
Lives in Twickenham, Middlesex.

FISCHEL, Robert QC
5 Paper Buildings (Brian Higgs QC), London
(0171) 353 5638
Recommended in Crime: Fraud
Specialisation: Mortgage (commercial &
residential), advance fee, solicitors' accounts &
general accounting frauds.
Prof. Memberships: C.B.A.
Career: Prosecuting and defending in fraud cases
regularly over the past 10 years. Presently engaged
to lead for the crown in England's largest mortgage
fraud.
Personal: Good knowledge of French & German,
and computer literate.

FISHER, David QC
6 King's Bench Walk (Michael Worsley QC),
London (0171) 583 0410
Recommended in Crime
Specialisation: Criminal law specialist, including
drugs, sexual allegations and fraud.
Prof. Memberships: General Council of the Bar
since 1997. Advocacy Studies Board since 1997.
Criminal Bar Association. South Eastern Circuit.
Career: Called to the Bar in 1973. Tenant of current
chambers since 1974. Recorder since 1991. QC in
1996.

FITTON, Michael
Albion Chambers (J.C.T. Barton QC), Bristol
(0117) 927 2144
Recommended in Crime

FITZGERALD, Edward QC
Doughty Street Chambers (Geoffrey Robertson
QC), London (0171) 404 1313
*Recommended in the following lists: Administrative
& Public Law, Civil Liberties, Crime*
Specialisation: Specialises in public law, criminal
law, and mental health and European human rights
law. Has represented prisoners and mental
patients both in the English courts and in
Strasbourg. Criminal law experience includes
cases involving specialist issues of mental health,
extradition and European Community law. Recent
cases include Venables & Thompson and Ex parte
Pierson in the House of Lords involving the rights
of H.M.P detainees and mandatory lifers, the Myra
Hindley case, and the Bridgewater Three case in
both the Divisional Court and Court of Appeal (on
the reference back). Was counsel for Derek Bentley
on his recent posthumous appeal. Has also
represented defendants in many Caribbean death
penalty cases in the Privy Council. Published work
includes articles on psychological defences, and
the rights of prisoners and mental patients. Has

also lectured in both the United States and the Caribbean on comparative criminal procedure. Advises local authorities on mental health law and has worked for the Official Solicitor in numerous cases involving minors and mental patients.
Career: Called to the Bar 1978. Took silk 1995.
Personal: Education: BA (Hons) (Congratulatory First), M.Phil, criminology. Qualified in both New York and American law. Languages: French and Italian. Born 1953. Winner of Times/Justice Human Rights Award 1998.

FITZGERALD, Michael QC
2 Mitre Court Buildings (Michael FitzGerald QC), London (0171) 583 1380
Recommended in the following lists: Energy & Utilities, Parliamentary, Planning
Specialisation: All aspects of Planning and Local Government law. Major Infastructure cases include; Channel Tunnel, Sizewell nuclear power station, Wynch farm oilfield and pipeline, Maidenhead, Windsor and Eton flood relief scheme, Terminals 4 and 5 Heathrow, Birmingham Northern Relief Road and M20. Major Contentious cases include: Green Belt – HQ for British Airways, HQ for RMC, HQ and manufacturing for TAG/McLaren; Research laboratories for Amersham International; AONB – Holiday villages at Longleat and Sellindge, Major land valuation, compensation and rating cases in UK and Hong Kong.
Prof. Memberships: Leader of the Parliamentary Bar. Planning and Environment Bar Association. Chairman of the Advisory Panel on Standards for the Planning Inspectorate Executive Agency. 21 years as a Committee Member of the Joint Oxford Planning Conference.
Career: Called to the Bar in 1961. Appointed QC 1980.
Personal: Educated at Downside and Cambridge. Leisure pursuits include opera, music, shooting, fishing.

FITZGERALD, Susanna
One Essex Court (Anthony Grabiner QC), London (0171) 583 2000
Recommended in Licensing
Specialisation: Specialises in liquor, gaming, betting and public entertainment licensing and lotteries law. Has represented or advised major leisure and gaming operators, concert promoters, retail liquor companies, breweries and petrol companies. Professional clients include major Licensing Solicitors, City and West End firms and the CPS. Author of articles published in 'Licensing Review' and 'The Solicitors Journal' and the 'Consumer Policy Review'. Contributor to 'Gambling and Public Policy' (1991). Has drafted submissions to the government on changes in Liquor and Public Entertainment Licensing Law and on amendments to the Gaming Act 1968 for Business in Sport and Leisure. Has lectured at conferences and spoken at seminars in the UK and abroad. Has also appeared on radio.
Prof. Memberships: Director of Business in Sport & Leisure, CLCBA, South Eastern Circuit, Commercial Women in Law, Society for the Study of Gambling (Committee Member), Mediator accredited by CEDR.
Career: Called to the Bar in 1973 and joined present chambers in 1975.

FLAUX, Julian QC
7 King's Bench Walk (Stephen Tomlinson QC), London (0171) 583 0404
Recommended in the following lists: Insurance & Reinsurance, Professional Negligence, Shipping
Specialisation: General commercial law including insurance and reinsurance, shipping, international sale of goods, banking and professional negligence.
Career: Called to the Bar 1978. Took Silk 1994.
Personal: Born 1955. B.C.L., M.A. (Oxon). Has a working knowledge of French.

FLESCH, Michael QC
Gray's Inn Tax Chambers (Milton Grundy), London (0171) 242 2642
Recommended in Tax
Specialisation: Advises on all aspects of revenue law, and appears before the Commissioners, High Court, Court of Appeal, House of Lords and Privy Council in revenue cases. Regular lecturer on tax-related topics.
Prof. Memberships: Revenue Bar Association, immediate past Chairman.
Career: Called to the Bar 1963. Teaching Fellow, University of Chicago 1963-64. Part-time lecturer in Revenue law, University College London 1964-82. Joined present chambers 1965. Took Silk 1983. Bencher of Grays Inn 1993.
Personal: Educated at Gordonstoun School 1953-58 and University College, London 1959-62 (LL.B Class 1, Hons). Governor of Gordonstoun School 1976-1996. Leisure pursuits include all forms of sport. Keen Arsenal and Middlesex supporter, member of MCC, Twickenham and Wimbledon debenture holder. Born 11th March 1940. Lives in London.

FLINT, Charles QC
Blackstone Chambers (formerly 2 Hare Court) (P Baxendale QC and C Flint QC), London (0171) 583 1770
Recommended in the following lists: Administrative & Public Law, Commercial (litigation), Financial Services, Sports Law
Specialisation: Commercial law specialist. Practice covers substantial corporate litigation in all divisions of the High Court, and financial services litigation, including disciplinary tribunals. Has a particular interest in commercial fraud and sports law. Practice also covers judicial review in a commercial context, including judicial review of Inland Revenue decisions. Interesting cases include R v. Inland Revenue ex p. Matrix Securities [1994] I WLR 334 (judicial review/tax). Also acted for the plaintiff in Arab Monetary Fund v. Hashim [1991] 2 AC 114, and International Tennis Federation in Wilander v Tobin [1997] 2 Lloyds 293.
Prof. Memberships: Fellow of the Chartered Institute of Arbitrators, Commercial Bar Association, Administrative Law Bar Association, British Association for Sport and Law.
Career: Called to the Bar 1975, joining present chambers in the same year. Appointed Junior Counsel to the Crown (Common Law) 1991-1995 and took Silk 1995.

FLOYD, Christopher QC
11 South Square (Christopher Floyd QC), London (0171) 405 1222
Recommended in Intellectual Property

FLYNN, James
Brick Court Chambers (Christopher Clarke QC), London (0171) 583 0777
Recommended in European Union/Competition
Specialisation: European Community/Competition Law. R v Customs and Excise export re: Lunn Poly. Advised on the implementation of 'Windfall Tax'.
Career: Partner of Linklaters (Brussels Office 1993-1996). Tenant Brick Court Chambers (1996-).
Personal: Fluent French (written and spoken).

FLYNN, Vernon
Essex Court Chambers (Gordon Pollock QC), London (0171) 813 8000
Recommended in the following lists: Commercial (litigation), Media & Entertainment
Specialisation: Broad-based practice in international and commercial law. In particular Media & Entertainment, Commercial, Banking and Finance, Shipping and Employment.
Career: Trinity College, Cambridge: Law (First Class Hons). Called to the Bar 1991.
Personal: Born 1966.

FOOKES, Robert
2 Mitre Court Buildings (Michael FitzGerald QC), London (0171) 583 1380
Recommended in the following lists: Energy & Utilities, Environmental Law, Planning
Specialisation: Specialises in Planning and Local Government Law. Member of the Planning and Environment Bar Association. Recent Reported Cases include: the Howletts Zoo 'tigers' case (Health and Safety at Work); Camden LBC v SSE and Barker (estoppel); J.L. Engineering v SSE (lawful use); Knott v SSE and Bannister v SSE (s.73A and planning conditions); R v Berkshire CC ex p Wokingham (county matters).
Career: Has advised or appeared at Inquiry in a wide range of topical planning proposals including: Development Corporation: CPOs; Energy: Hinkley Point 'C', Sizewell 'C' power stations, North Yorks overhead line; Transport and Works Act orders: Greater Manchester, Central Railways, Portsmouth Harbour, Canary Wharf and Millennium Tower; Hungerford Bridge. Roads: M4, M40 and A1M motorway service area multiple inquiries; Minerals: old mineral permission judicial reviews; opencast inquiries and mineral plan omissions; Aviation: airfield and heliport inquiries, Thames Heliport (Court of Appeal); Retail: Merry Hill extension. Environmental; Surrey Waste Local Plan (incineration); Discharge Licence appeals; STW CPO; enforcement against hospital incinerator; Lands Tribunal: restrictive covenants and disturbance compensation.
Personal: Educated at St Edwards School, Oxford and Christ Church, Oxford.

FORD, Michael
Doughty Street Chambers (Geoffrey Robertson QC), London (0171) 404 1313
Recommended in Health & Safety
Specialisation: Principal areas of practice are employment law, public law, tort, civil liberties and health and safety.
Prof. Memberships: Member of the Industrial Law Society, Institute for Employment Rights.
Career: Qualified as solicitor (1989). Lecturer in Law at University of Manchester (1990-92). Called to Bar 1992.
Personal: Co-author of 'Redgrave's Health and Safety and Munkman's Employer's Liability. Numerous other publications, especially on employment law. Keen cyclist.

FORD, Neil QC
Albion Chambers (J.C.T. Barton QC), Bristol (0117) 927 2144
Recommended in Crime

FORDHAM, Michael
Blackstone Chambers (formerly 2 Hare Court) (P Baxendale QC and C Flint QC), London (0171) 583 1770
Recommended in the following lists: Administrative & Public Law, Environmental Law, Sports Law
Specialisation: Specialist in public and administrative law, and particularly judicial review. Member of Attorney-General's Supplementary Panel. Cases include Diane Blood [1997] 2 WLR 806 (posthumous use of sperm), Fayed (1998) 1 All ER 93 (review of Parliamentary Commissioner for Standards), Evans [1997] QB 443 (prisoner release dates), Dockgrange [1997] Env LR 575 (EC waste control) and Bhaugeerutty Times 1.5.98 (majority tribunal decision following chairman's death). Also environmental law and sports law. Author of 'Judicial Review Handbook'. Editor of journal 'Judicial Review'. Lectures in administrative law at Hertford College, Oxford. Called to the Bar 1990.
Personal: Educated at Spalding Grammar School, Hertford College, Oxford (BA & BCL), and University of Virginia (LL.M). Oxford Hockey Blue (1986). Awarded Karmel, Mould and Prince of Wales Scholarships at Gray's Inn.

FORDHAM, R.A. QC
Martin's Building (R.A. Fordham QC), Liverpool
(0151) 236 4919
Recommended in Family/Matrimonial
Specialisation: All aspects of family/matrimonial
property law.
Prof. Memberships: F.L.B.A.

FORRESTER, Ian QC
Blackstone Chambers (formerly 2 Hare Court)
(P Baxendale QC and C Flint QC), London
(0171) 583 1770
Recommended in European Union/Competition
Has practised from Brussels since 1972.
Specialisation: European Community Law:
competition, distribution, joint ventures,
discriminatory pricing, trade, customs, dumping,
affecting, inter alia, fisheries, sport, steel,
pharmaceuticals, semiconductors, gaming,
automotive parts, professional practices,
agriculture, sugar, dangerous substances and
software. Clients include international companies,
trade associations and governments. Practice
before European Commission, Parliament,
European Court of Justice, European Court of First
Instance, Strasbourg Institutions, House of Lords,
Court of Session, GATT/WTO. Appeared before the
European Court of Justice in, inter alia, DCL v.
Commission and Bulloch, Bethell v. Commission,
Control Data v. Commission (I and II), Du Pont v.
Customs & Excise, Government of Gibraltar v.
Commission, Canon v. Council, Liberal Democrats
v. European Parliament, BBC et al v. Commission
(the Magill case), Bosman v. UEFA. Author and co-
author of numerous articles on EC law and policy;
translations of the German Civil Code, Commercial
Code and Introductory Law.
Prof. Memberships: Faculty of Advocates; New
York Bar; European Trade Law Association
(Chairman), visiting Professor in European Law,
Glasgow University, Member British Invisibles
European Committee.
Career: Called to the Scots Bar 1972, English Bar
1996. Took Silk 1988 and joined current chambers
1989.

FORSYTH, Julie
Chavasse Court Chambers (Andrew Mattison),
Liverpool (0151) 707 1191
Recommended in Crime

FORTSON, Rudi
3 Gray's Inn Square (Rock Tansey QC), London
(0171) 520 5600
Recommended in Crime
Specialisation: Extensive criminal law experience,
with specialist knowledge on law relating to misuse
of drugs, drug-trafficking offences, money-
laundering and fraud. Author of `The Criminal
Justice Act 1993' and `Law on the Misuse of Drugs
and Drug Trafficking Offences'. Annotator for
`Current Law Statutes' on Criminal Justice Acts
1991 and 1993, Police and Magistrates Courts Act
1994 and Drug Trafficking Act 1994. Former
contributing editor of `Archbold Criminal Pleading,
Evidence and Practice'. Addresses conferences
and seminars.
Prof. Memberships: Criminal Bar Association,
International Bar Association, American Bar
Association, Forensic Science Society.
Career: Called to the Bar 1976 (pupillage at 1
Crown Office Row) and joined current chambers in
1978.
Personal: Educated at University College, London
1972-75 (LL.B Hons). Leisure pursuits include
yachting, chess and cooking. Born 2nd March
1952.

FORWOOD, Nicholas QC
Brick Court Chambers (Christopher Clarke QC),
London (0171) 583 0777
Recommended in European Union/Competition
Specialisation: EEC Law, UK Competition Law
and Administrative Law.
Prof. Memberships: Member, CCBE Permanent
Delegation to the European Courts; Bar Council

International Relations Committee; British Institute
for International and Comparative Law;
International Bar Association; International Law
Association; Society for Computers and the Law;
UK Association for European Law.
Career: Called to Bar 1970, Middle Temple. Irish
Bar 1991. Queen's Counsel 1987.
Personal: Born 22 June 1948 in Scarborough.
Educated at Stowe School and St. John's College,
Cambridge (1966-69): B.A., M.A. (1973).
Mechanical Sciences 1968 (1st Class Hons), Law
(Part II) 1969. McMahon, Haarwork and Astbury
Scholarships.

FOSTER, Alison
39 Essex Street (Edwin Glasgow QC), London
(0171) 832 1111
Recommended in Immigration & Nationality
Specialisation: Public law; human rights; medical
law, including medical negligence. Also tax.
Practice predominantly in Judicial Review, some
statutory tribunals.
Prof. Memberships: Membership: Supplementary
Treasury Panel. Committee member Administrative
Law Bar Association.
Personal: BA (Oxon). M Phil (London). Dips in Law
(City). Chambers of Edwin Glasgow QC from 1986
to present.

FOSTER, Catherine
Plowden Buildings (William Lowe QC), London
(0171) 583 0808
Recommended in Personal Injury

FOSTER, Charles
6 Pump Court (Kieran Coonan QC), London
(0171) 583 6013
Recommended in Medical Negligence
Specialisation: Medical and other professional
negligence. Reported cases include Fallows v.
Randle [1997] 8 Med LR 160, Bancroft v. Harrogate
HA [1997] 8 Med LR 398, Hind v. York HA [1997] 8
Med LR 377, Ogden v. Airedale HA [1996] 7 Med
LR 153, Kahl v. Freistaat Bayern [1995] PIQR P401.
Prof. Memberships: PNBA, Medico-Legal Society.
Career: Educated at Shrewsbury School & St
John's College, Cambridge (MA, Vet MB, MRCVS).
Research in wild animal anaesthesia in Saudi
Arabia and comparative anatomy at RCS, Research
Fellow at Hebrew University, Jerusalem. Also a
member of the Irish Bar. Numerous publications.

FOWLER, Richard QC
Monckton Chambers (Richard Fowler QC),
London (0171) 405 7211
*Recommended in the following lists: Aviation,
European Union/Competition*
Specialisation: EC and UK competition law.
Prof. Memberships: Committee member
COMBAR; member Competition Law Association;
member Legal Services Committee of Bar Council.
Career: Specialised since 1973 (including working
from 1977 to 1984 on Case No.IV/29.479 – IBM) in
the preparation, drafting and presentation of
submissions on behalf of clients to the European
Commission (also OFT and MMC) and in High
Court and European Court proceedings, and
advising a wide range of national and international
clients on competition law matters. Recent cases
include Guinness/Grand Met merger; Re Premier
League Football (RP Court).

FOXTON, David
Essex Court Chambers (Gordon Pollock QC),
London (0171) 813 8000
*Recommended in the following lists: Computer
& I.T., Insurance & Reinsurance, Shipping*
Specialisation: Commercial practice, in particular
international insurance and reinsurance; shipping
and the international carriage of goods;
professional negligence; Lloyd's litigation (LMX
and US Casualty underwriting). Banking, sale of
goods, company sales, computer supply disputes
and professional negligence actions. Has
appeared on numerous occasions in commercial
arbitration.

Career: Magdalen College, Oxford 1983-86 BA
(First Class Hons) in Jurisprudence, 1986.
Bachelor of Civil Law (First Class Hons). Called to
the Bar 1989.
Personal: Born 1965.

FOY, John QC
9 Gough Square (Jeremy Roberts Q.C), London
(0171) 353 5371
Recommended in Personal Injury
Specialisation: Practice encompasses plaintiff
and defendant personal injury and medical
negligence work, with a particular emphasis on
occupational disease. Appeared in Mountenay v.
Bernard Matthews [1994], Mughal v. Reuters Ltd
[1993]; Hunt v. Douglas Roofing [1990] and Arnold
v. CEGB [1988], British Coal Respiration Disease
Litigation (1998) inter alia. Clients include all major
trade unions. Frequently chairs and addresses
conferences and seminars, and has appeared on
BBC TV and radio.
Prof. Memberships: Association of Personal Injury
Lawyers, Personal Injury Bar Association.
Career: Called to the Bar and joined 9 Gough
Square in 1969.
Personal: LL.B (Hons) Birmingham University,
1967. Leisure pursuits include sports. Born 1st
June 1946. Lives in Suffolk.

FRANCIS, Nicholas
29 Bedford Row Chambers (Peter Ralls QC),
London (0171) 831 2626
Recommended in Family: Matrimonial Finance
Specialisation: Principal area of practice is
matrimonial ancillary relief work, with a particular
interest in pension issues and foreign asset cases.
Other main areas within practice are professional
negligence; and residence, contact, education and
child abduction cases. Major cases include Re P
(A Minor) [1992] (Education); Re D (minors) [1993]
(conciliation: Privilege); C v C [1994] (wasted costs
order); S v S (reserved costs order) [1995] B v
Miller & Co [1996] and H v H [1997]. Several
articles on ancillary relief for Family Law with
particular emphasis on the issue of costs and
discovery. Regular lecturer on costs and discovery
and on international aspects of family proceedings;
and contributor to Legal Network T.V.
Prof. Memberships: Family Law Bar Association.
Career: Called to the Bar in 1981 and joined 29
Bedford Row in 1983. Elected to Bar Council in
November 1994.
Personal: Educated at Radley College 1971-76
and Downing College, Cambridge 1977-80 (BA
Law 1980, MA 1984). Leisure pursuits include
racing dinghies. Born 1958. Lives in London.

FRANCIS, Robert QC
3 Serjeants' Inn (Philip Naughton QC), London
(0171) 353 5537
Recommended in Medical Negligence
Specialisation: Principal area of practice is
medical law, including medical negligence actions
for plaintiffs and defendants, ethical cases
concerning treatment of patients (particularly
termination of treatment), and disciplinary
proceedings (General Medical Council, General
Dental Council etc.). Leading cases include: Re F
(Mental Patient: Sterilization), Airedale NHS Trust v.
Bland, Roy v Kensington etc FPC, B v Croydon HA,
Re T (Wardship: Medical Treatment); Re MB. Other
areas of practice include administrative law,
employment, crime.
Prof. Memberships: Professional Negligence Bar
Association, LCLCBA, CBA.
Career: Called to the Bar 1973; Queen's Counsel
1992. Assistant Recorder 1996.
Personal: Uppingham School, Exeter University.
Born 4th April 1950.

FRANSMAN, Laurie
Two Garden Court (I. Macdonald QC & O.
Davies), London (0171) 353 1633
Recommended in Immigration & Nationality
Specialisation: All immigration, but particularly
employment and self-employment, company

relocations, investors, European Community law. All British nationality law.
Prof. Memberships: Administrative Law Bar Association; Immigration Law Practitioners' Association (co-founder, executive committee member).
Career: Member of the editorial board of 'Immigration and Nationality Law and Practice' (Tolleys). Nationality law consultant to Halsbury's Laws of England (4th ed.). Books: 'British Nationality Law and the 1981 Act' (1982); 'Tribunals Practice and Procedure' (jointly 1985); 'Immigration Emergency Procedures' (jointly, 1986); 'Fransman's British Nationality Law' (1989); 'The Constitution of the United Kingdom' (contrib., 1991); 'Strangers and Citizens' (contrib., 1994); 'Citizenship and Nationality Status in the New Europe' (contrib., 1998); 'Fransman's British Nationality Law' (1998) 2nd ed.

FRASER, Peter D.
Atkin Chambers (John Blackburn QC), London (0171) 404 0102
Recommended in Construction
Specialisation: Construction and engineering disputes; multi-party contractual disputes and commercial litigation. Insurance litigation, professional negligence of architects, surveyors and engineers. Arbitration proceedings. Recent cases include arbitrations concerning Harbour Exchange on the Isle of Dogs, the West Yorkshire Playhouse in Leeds; international arbitration in South Africa regarding Bokaa Dam project in Botswana. High Court proceedings in England in relation to Euro Disney; Canary Wharf and the Copthorne Hotel in Newcastle. Delta Civil Engineering Co. Ltd v LDDC (CA) 81 BLR 19; Copthorne Hotel (Newcastle) Ltd. v Arup Associates (CA) 85 BLR 22.
Career: Called to Bar by Middle Temple 1989. Editor of the Building Law Reports. Author of 'How to Pass Law Exams' (HLT Publications 1991).
Personal: Born 1963. Educated Harrogate Grammar School and St John's College Cambridge. BA in Law, Cambridge University; LL.M Cambridge University; MA in Law, Cambridge University. Open exhibitioner and MacMahon Law Scholar of St. John's College, Cambridge. Astbury Scholar of the Middle Temple.

FRASER, Vincent
40 King St (Philip Raynor QC), Manchester (0161) 832 9082
Recommended in Planning
Specialisation: Town and Country Planning, environment, compulsory purchase, highways, local government and judicial review. Co-author of 'Planning Decisions Digest'.
Prof. Memberships: Planning and Environment Bar Association. Member of Northern Circuit.

FREEDMAN, Clive QC
Littleton Chambers (Michael Burton QC), London (0171) 797 8600
Recommended in the following lists: Commercial (litigation), Construction

FREEDMAN, Jeremy
New Court Chambers (David Robson QC), Newcastle Upon Tyne (0191) 232 1980
Recommended in Medical Negligence
Specialisation: Practises exclusively in Personal Injury work. Specialises in medical negligence. Regularly instructed on behalf of several Health Authorities/NHS Trusts as well as acting on behalf of Plaintiffs. Conducted a number of large claims, in particular, brain damage cases, both on behalf of Plaintiffs and Defendants.
Prof. Memberships: North Eastern Circuit, Professional Negligence Bar Association and Personal Injury Bar Association. Assistant Recorder.
Career: Called to the Bar, 1982 and joined present set of Chambers in same year.
Personal: Educated at Oundle, Manchester University and City University of London. Born 1959. Married, two children.

FREEDMAN, S. Clive
3 Verulam Buildings (R. Neville Thomas QC), London (0171) 831 8441
Recommended in Computer & I.T.
Specialisation: General commercial litigation, in particular cases involving technical issues, large quantities of documents and/or computer support. CEDR Accredited Mediator.
Career: Called to the Bar in 1975.
Personal: Educated at Harrow School and Trinity College, Cambridge.

FRENCH, Paul
Guildhall Chambers (John Royce QC), Bristol (0117) 927 3366
Recommended in Insolvency
Specialisation: Main areas of practice are: Insolvency (all aspects of corporate, personal and partnership insolvency, including directors disqualification); Bank Recovery (including mortgages, receiverships, guarantees and indemnities); Company Law and Partnership (including shareholder and partnership disputes and fiduciary duties); Property litigation.
Prof. Memberships: Chancery Bar Association. Bristol and Cardiff Chancery Bar Association. Society for Practitioners of Insolvency. Bar Sports Law Group. Society for Computers and Law.
Career: Called 1989.

FRIEDMAN, David QC
4 Pump Court (Bruce Mauleverer QC), London (0171) 353 2656
Recommended in Construction
Specialisation: Principal area of practice covers all stages and all aspects of construction and engineering litigation and arbitration, both domestic and international. Also deals with professional negligence, particularly in relation to claims relating to professionals in the construction field.
Prof. Memberships: Chairman Official Referees' Bar Association.
Career: Called to the Bar 1968. Tenant at 3 Paper Buildings 1970-92. Took Silk and appointed Assistant Recorder 1990. Joined Pump Court 1992.
Personal: Educated at Tiffin Boys' School, Kingston-upon-Thames and Lincoln College, Oxford 1963-67 (MA, BCL). Born 1st June 1944.

FULFORD, Adrian QC
14 Tooks Court (Michael Mansfield QC), London (0171) 405 8828
Recommended in Crime
Specialisation: Crime generally including White Collar fraud and Court of Appeal and Divisional court work.
Prof. Memberships: Criminal Bar Association, South Eastern Circuit, Member Legal Aid Board (Chairman), Member Professional Conduct Committee.
Career: Former contributor Atkins Court Forms. Former Editor of Archibold. Current lecturer in Criminal Law at Middle Temple. Assistant Recorder.
Personal: Keen horseman and motorcyclist. Leisure pursuits also include golf, tennis and scuba diving.

FURBER, John QC
4 Breams Buildings (Christopher Lockhart-Mummery QC), London (0171) 430 1221/353 5835
Recommended in Property Litigation
Specialisation: Principally law of Landlord and Tenant but also covers property litigation, planning and compulsory purchase of land.
Prof. Memberships: Member of Chancery Bar Association and Planning and Environmental Bar Association.
Career: Contributor to Halsbury's Laws of England, Landlord and Tenant (1981 edition) and Compulsory Acquisition and now general editor of Hill and Redman's law of Landlord and Tenant.
Personal: Called to Bar in 1973, took silk in 1995.

FURNESS, Jonathan
30 Park Place (Philip Richards), Cardiff (01222) 398421
Recommended in Family/Matrimonial

FURNESS, Michael
Wilberforce Chambers (Edward Nugee QC), London (0171) 306 0102
Recommended in the following lists: Tax, Pensions
Specialisation: Trusts, both private and commercial, especially pensions (advisory work, ombudsman appeals and other litigation, including the ongoing National Grid v Mayes litigation) and charities (on behalf of HM Attorney General and others, particularly in relation to the making of charitable schemes). Regularly appears in the High Court and Court of Appeal, with 6 reported cases in the Court of Appeal in the last year, including Parinv v IRC (stamp duty) Frankland v IRC (inheritance tax) Centaur v IRC (corporation tax) and Dixons v Sarsfield (industrial buildings). As standing counsel he cannot act against the Revenue, but does undertake tax-related (and other) professional negligence litigation.
Prof. Memberships: Chancery Bar Association, Revenue Bar Association, Association of Pension Lawyers.
Career: Called 1982, First Standing Junior Counsel to the Inland Revenue in Chancery Matters, Junior Counsel to the Crown (Chancery Panel).
Personal: Secretary, Bar Theatrical Society.

FURST, Stephen QC
Keating Chambers (Richard Fernyhough QC), London (0171) 544 2600
Recommended in Construction
Specialisation: Building and civil engineering; professional negligence including valuation; computers including software; important cases include Darlington v Wiltshire; Bank of East Asia v SDA; Tesco Stores Ltd v Ward Investments; Strachan & Henshaw v Stein Industrial.
Career: Qualified 1975; Middle Temple; QC 1991; assistant recorder; editor of 'Construction Law Yearbook'; 'Keating on Building Contracts'; arbitrator.
Personal: The Edinburgh Academy, St Edmund Hall, Oxford, Leeds University (1972 BA Hons, 1974 LLB Hons). Born 1951; resides London.

FURZE, Caroline
Wilberforce Chambers (Edward Nugee QC), London (0171) 306 0102
Recommended in the following lists: Pensions, Property Litigation
Specialisation: Practice covers most aspects of chancery/commercial litigation and advice, including landlord and tenant, professional negligence, insolvency, pension funds, partnership, contentious probate and the administration of estates. Interest in ecclesiastical law. Co-editor (with E Nugee QC) of the Fourth Edition (Reissue) of the title "Real Property" in Halsbury's Law.
Career: BA (Cantab) (1st class honours in Chemistry). Called to the Bar 1992.

FYSH, Michael QC, SC
8 New Square (Michael Fysh QC, SC), London (0171) 405 4321
Recommended in Intellectual Property
Specialisation: Specialist in all aspects of intellectual property and European Community law. Experienced in litigation and advisory work both in the English courts and in overseas jurisdictions. Publications include 'Russell-Clarke on Registered Designs' 5th edition (Sweet & Maxwell 1974); 'The Industrial property Citator'(European Law Centre 1982 and supplements); 'Spycatcher Cases' (Sweet & Maxwell 1989); 'Breach of Confidence' (with F. Gurry) 2nd edition (Oxford University Press, in preparation). Also editor of 'Reports of Patent Cases' (The Patent Office) and 'Fleet Street Reports' (London, Sweet & Maxwell) 1974-1995.
Prof. Memberships: Member, Bar Council of England and Wales; Vice-Chairman, Central Asia

and Transcaucasian Law Association.
Career: Called to the Bar 1965. Took silk 1989. Head of chambers since 1993. Calls to overseas Bars: Northern Ireland 1974 (QC 1990), Ireland 1975 (Senior Counsel 1994), New South Wales 1975, Bombay and Supreme Court of India 1982, Pakistan 1987, Trinidad and Tobago 1990 (Senior Counsel 1990). Has also practised at the Malaysian and Singapore Bars and before the European Patent Office, Munich. Lecturer, WIPO, Geneva.
Personal: Born USA, 1940. Educated at Downside School, Grenoble University, France 1958-1959 and at Oxford University (BA natural sciences) 1959-1962, MA 1969. Languages include French and some knowledge of Russian.

GAISMAN, Jonathan QC
7 King's Bench Walk (Stephen Tomlinson QC), London (0171) 583 0404
Recommended in the following lists: Insurance & Reinsurance, Professional Negligence, Shipping

GAITSKELL, Robert QC
Keating Chambers (Richard Fernyhough QC), London (0171) 544 2600
Recommended in Construction
Specialisation: Construction law, including particularly electrical, mechanical and process engineering; instructed in numerous international and UK major engineering/building disputes, both litigation and arbitration (including appointments as an arbitrator and mediator) concerning, inter alia, complex engineering projects (especially power stations), defence, computer facilities, chemical processing, food and drink production, oil and gas rigs, hospitals, motorways, bridges, tunnels, dredging, water treatment, airports abattoirs, nuclear fuel processing and commercial property; cases include University of Glasgow v Whitefield; ICI v Bovis; Lamacrest v Case; Cameron v Mowlem; Surrey Heath v Lovell.
Career: Qualified 1978; Gray's Inn; QC 1994; practising Queen's Counsel; arbitrator, mediator, and adjudicator; Assistant Recorder, Vice President of the IEE; Senator of the Engineering Council, Past Chairman Management and Design Division of Institution of Electrical Engineers; IEE Council; practised in UK and abroad as professional electrical engineer, employed by, inter alia, GEC (South Africa); Reyrolle Parsons, Matthew Hall and Rendell Palmer & Tritton, lectured widely in UK and abroad on legal and engineering matters, particularly international construction contracts; lecturer, King's College, London: MSc in Construction Law under Far Eastern Legal Systems; participated in Legal Network TV programmes on engineers' professional negligence, arbitration, and Official Referees' practice; committee member of London Common Law & Commercial Bar Association, IEE/IMechE Model Form Contracts committee; former member of ORBA Committee, Bar Council Public Affairs Committee and Centre for Dispute Resolution (CEDR) Committee; former examiner in contract law, RICS; regular legal columnist 'Engineering Management Journal'; numerous publications on legal and engineering topics published in journals in both UK and abroad, including the journals of most of the major professional engineering institutions; contributor to 'Construction Law Yearbook'.
Personal: Hamilton High School, Zimbabwe, University of Cape Town (1971) BSc Eng, Ph.D. (King's College, London), FIEE, C Eng, FCI Arb). Born 1948; resides London. Reading, theatre, walking; Methodist local preacher, Worshipful Company of Engineers, Past Chairman IEE Professional Group on Engineering and Law.

GAL, Sonia
40 King St (Philip Raynor QC), Manchester (0161) 832 9082
Recommended in Family/Matrimonial
Specialisation: Matrimonial finance, care

abduction. Assistant recorder.
Prof. Memberships: F.L.B.A., I.B.A., E.L.B.A.
Career: French, German, Rumanian, Hungarian, Norwegian. Worked in Eastern Europe on joint ventures.
Personal: Bridge, travel.

GAMMIE, Malcolm
One Essex Court (Anthony Grabiner QC), London (0171) 583 2000
Recommended in Tax
Specialisation: All commercial taxation and related administrative law, including international and European taxation, corporate and employee taxation, property taxation and value added tax. Consultant Editor of Butterworths Tax Handbooks and of Land Taxation; consultant to Fiscal Affairs Directorate of OECD; Director of Research of Tax Law Review Committee; 1998 Unilever Professor of International Business Law at Leiden University, The Netherlands.
Prof. Memberships: Chartered Institute of Taxation (President 1993-94); Association of Taxation Technicians, International Fiscal Association (Member, Permanent Scientific Committee), European Bar Group.
Career: Sidney Sussex College, Cambridge; qualified 1975 as solicitor with Linklaters & Paines; subsequently with CBI and as Director of National Tax Services at KMG Thomson McLintock (now KPMG); tax partner at Linklaters & Paines 1987-97; Called to the Bar 1997.
Personal: Married with 4 children. Interests include music and church architecture.

GARDEN, Ian
Derby Square Chambers (Simon Newton), Liverpool (0151) 709 4222
Recommended in Ecclesiastical

GARDINER, John QC
11 New Square (John Gardiner QC), London (0171) 242 4017
Recommended in Tax
Specialisation: Revenue law. Involved in the two Woolwich cases, Pattison v Marine Midland, Ensign Tankers (Leasing) v. Stokes, International Commercial Bank v Willingale, Glaxo Group Ltd v. IRC and Nuclear Electric v Bradley.
Prof. Memberships: Revenue Bar Association.
Career: Called to the Bar 1968 and joined New Square in 1970. Took Silk 1982. Treasurer of Senate of Inns of Court and Bar Council, 1985-86; Bencher, Middle Temple.
Personal: Educated at Bancroft's School, Woodford 1957-63 and Fitzwilliam College, Cambridge 1964-68 (M.A, LL.M) Born 28th February 1946. Lives in London.

GARDINER, Nicholas
1 Middle Temple Lane (Colin Dines & Andrew Trollope QC), London (0171) 583 0659 (12 lines)
Recommended in the following lists: Crime, Crime: Fraud

GARNETT, Kevin QC
5 New Square (Jonathan Rayner James QC), London (0171) 404 0404
Recommended in Media & Entertainment
Specialisation: Practises extensively in the field of media and entertainment with a particular leaning to music, film and publishing work. Also practises widely in the Intellectual Property field. Is Senior Editor of Copinger and Skone James on Copyright. Other main area of practice is general Chancery litigation.
Prof. Memberships: Chancery Bar Association; Intellectual Property Bar Association; Common Law Bar Association.

GARNHAM, Neil S.
1 Crown Office Row (Robert Seabrook QC), London (0171) 797 7500
Recommended in Administrative & Public Law
Specialisation: Principal areas of practice are Administrative and Public Law, Professional

Negligence including Medical Negligence, and Personal Injury. Public Law work includes mental health, extradition, education, immigration and human rights. Cases include Thomas v Bunn [1991] (HL – interest in PI cases); Racz v Home Office [1994] (HL – misfeasance in public office); Re K [1994] (CA – adoption of foreign national); Ex parte McQuillan [1995] (Exclusion orders); Ex parte Onibiyo [1996] (CA – fresh claims for political asylum); T v Home Office [1996] (HL – political offences in asylum law); Gregory v UK [1994] (ECHR – bias in jury trials); D v UK [1997] (ECHR – Article 3).
Prof. Memberships: ALBA, PNBA, PIBA.
Career: Called 1982; Junior Counsel to the Crown 1995.
Personal: Educated Ipswich School and Peterhouse Cambridge.

GARRETT, Annalissa
6 Pump Court (Kieran Coonan QC), London (0171) 583 6013
Recommended in Medical Negligence
Specialisation: Specialises in all aspects of medical negligence and medically related work including representing families and Doctors at inquests and disciplinary tribunals. Also handles mental health, physiotherapy negligence, dental negligence and product liability cases. Also serious personal injury and fatal accident cases. Acts for both Plaintiffs and Defendants. Special interest in limitation issues and birth trauma cases. Recent cases include: Ex parte Dennis Feard Stevens (long running inquest into prison death); Kirwan v Barking, Havering & Brentwood HA (obstetric medical negligence); Haigh v Pinderfields NHS Trust (physiotherapy negligence); Mallia v Hinchingbrooke NHS Trust (blindness in one eye following contact lens use). Also involved in toxic shock litigation.
Prof. Memberships: PNBA, AVMA, PIBA & APIL.
Career: Called to the Bar in 1991. Joined Chambers in 1992. Standing Counsel to HM Customs & Excise.
Personal: Educated at Durham University (BA (Hons)). Born 21st June 1966. Lives in London.

GARSIDE, Charles QC
9 St. John Street (John Hand QC), Manchester (0161) 955 9000
Recommended in Crime
Specialisation: Crime, including fraud; employment including discrimination; judicial Review; other Crown office work; Personal Injury.
Prof. Memberships: Employment Law Association.
Career: Called 1971. QC 1993.

GASH, Simon
Ropewalk Chambers (Richard Maxwell QC), Nottingham (0115) 947 2581/2/3/4
Recommended in Personal Injury

GATT, Ian
Littleton Chambers (Michael Burton QC), London (0171) 797 8600
Recommended in Professional Negligence
Specialisation: Professional negligence (principally solicitors and surveyors). Nationwide Managed Litigation (1997-1998); Birmingham Midshires v. David Parry. Employment: Member of the Attorney-General's Supplementary Panel of Treasury Counsel; Commercial Fraud: Guinness Trial 1990; numerous SFO prosecutions
Prof. Memberships: COMBAR, Professional Negligence Bar Association, Employment Law Bar Association, Criminal Bar Association.
Career: Hutton GS, Preston (1974-1981); Hertford College, Oxford (1981-1984) BA Jurisprudence (1st). Called to the Bar 1985. Joined 2 Crown Office Row (now Littleton Chambers) 1986. CEDR Accredited Mediator. Co-Author "Arlidge and Parry on Fraud" 2nd edn.
Personal: Married with 3 children. Interests: rugby, cars, wine. Lives Dorking, Surrey.

GAUNT, Jonathan QC
Falcon Chambers (Jonathan Gaunt QC & Kim Lewison QC), London (0171) 353 2484
Recommended in the following lists: Agriculture & Bloodstock, Property Litigation
Specialisation: The joint Head of Falcon Chambers, the members of which specialise in landlord and tenant and property law. Called to the Bar in 1972 and took silk in 1991. An Editor of the landlord and tenant and property volume of Halsbury's Laws', having recently re-written the chapters on repairing covenants, rent and rent review. Also joint editor of the new edition of Gale on Easements.

GEE, Anthony QC
28 St. John St (Anthony Rumbelow QC), Manchester (0161) 834 8418
Recommended in Crime

GEE, Steven QC
One Essex Court (Anthony Grabiner QC), London (0171) 583 2000
Recommended in the following lists: Arbitration, Commercial (litigation), Insurance & Reinsurance, Shipping
Specialisation: Commercial law and litigation, insurance/reinsurance, contracts, banking, arbitration, shipping, aviation, computer law. Author: 'Mareva Injunctions and Anton Piller relief' (4th ed: 1998).
Prof. Memberships: COMBAR.
Career: QC (1993); formerly standing junior Counsel to DTI (ECGD). Foreign Jurisdictions: Antigua.

GEERING, Ian QC
3 Verulam Buildings (R. Neville Thomas QC), London (0171) 831 8441
Recommended in Commercial (litigation)
Specialisation: Commercial law, specialising in civil claims based on international and domestic commercial fraud and claims for restitution. Banking, insurance and professional negligence.
Prof. Memberships: COMBAR, London Common Law and Commercial Association.
Career: Queen's Counsel 1991. Recorder 1995.

GEORGE, Charles QC
2 Harcourt Buildings (Mr Gerard Ryan QC), London (0171) 353 8415
Recommended in the following lists: Ecclesiastical, Environmental Law, Parliamentary, Planning
Specialisation: Principal area of practice is planning and environmental law, administrative and parliamentary matters. Has advised and represented applicants and local planning authorities in relation to major development schemes, particularly those involving public infrastructure provision, housing, minerals, listed buildings and local government finance. Involved in promoting the King's Cross Railways Bill and Transport and Works Orders for extensions to the Manchester and Leeds Light Rail systems. Counsel in, inter alia, Pioneer Aggregates (UK) Ltd v Secretary of State for the Environment [1985], Save Britain's Heritage v Number 1 Poultry Ltd [1991], R. v Parliamentary Commissioner for Administration ex p. Balchin [1996]. Clients include Railtrack, BG plc, the Audit Commission, Manchester City Council, Greater Manchester, West Yorkshire and Merseyside Passenger Transport Executives, RMC Group plc and Laing Homes Ltd. Has frequently represented applicants in judicial review proceedings involving planning and environmental law challenges. Other main area of practice is ecclesiastical law and commons.
Prof. Memberships: Inner Temple; King's Inns, Dublin.
Career: Called to the Bar 1974 and joined 2 Harcourt Buildings in 1975. Conducted Independent Inquiry into Planning decisions in the London Borough of Brent 1991. Took Silk 1992. Called to the Irish Bar 1995. Appointed Recorder 1997. Appointed Chancellor of the Diocese of Southwark 1996
Personal: Educated at Bradfield College 1958-63, Magdalen College, Oxford 1963-66 (1st Class

Hons Modern History) and Corpus Christi, Cambridge 1966-7. Author of 'The Stuarts: A Century of Experiment' (1973). Leisure pursuits include tennis, architecture and travel. Born 8th June 1945. Lives in Sevenoaks, Kent.

GEORGE, Sarah
St Philip's Chambers (Rex Tedd QC), Birmingham (0121) 246 7000
Recommended in Employment
Specialisation: Employment law including both wrongful and unfair dismissal, sexual, racial and disability discrimination. Restrictive covenants and directors' duties. Complementary field of practice in company law (including disqualification of company directors) and related Chancery Division Work.
Prof. Memberships: Employment Lawyers Association, Employment Law Bar Association.
Career: MA (Cantab); Member of Middle Temple; Recipient of the Jules Thorne Scholarship; Called October 1991.

GHOSH, I.J.
24 Old Buildings (G.R Bretten QC), London (0171) 242 2744
Recommended in Tax
Specialisation: Unusually for a Junior, advises primarily on City-based, corporate tax (both Advisory and Litigation). Corporate Tax: Structured Finance and Banking Tax; Mergers and Acquisitions, EC tax, International Tax. VAT; Customs duties. Co-author of 'Taxation of Loan Relationships, Financial Instruments and Foreign Exchange' (Butterworths). Cases within the previous year: Norbury Developments Ltd v CEC (whether building land should be mandatorily standard rated – recently heard by the European Court of Justice), Memec v. IRC; Unigreg Ltd v CEC. Advised the OECD on Controlled Foreign Company issues. Drafted the legislation for the new fiscal regime in Malta.
Prof. Memberships: Revenue Bar Association; Bar European Group; VAT Practitioner's Group; Lawyer's Share Shemes Group; International Tax Planning Association.
Career: Also a Fellow of Queen Mary and Westfield College, University of London.

GIBBS, Patrick
2 Harcourt Buildings (Nigel Mylne QC), London (0171) 353 2112
Recommended in Crime
Specialisation: Defence Advocacy. Practises in all areas of crime. Since 1990 has been pricipally engaged in defending cases of professional fraud, sex crime and controlled drugs.
Prof. Memberships: Criminal Bar Association.
Career: Called 1986.
Personal: Born 24.4.1962. Educated at Eton College, Christ Church, Oxford and The City University.

GIBSON, Charles
2 Harcourt Buildings (Roger Henderson QC), London (0171) 583 9020
Recommended in Product Liability
Specialisation: Common Law/Commercial with an emphasis on product liability (in particular Group Actions), professional negligence, personal injury, insurance. Notable cases include Connelly v RTZ; Hodgson v Imperial Tobacco (the tobacco lung cancer litigation); the Opren Litigation; the Benzodiazepine litigation; the interest rate swap litigation; asbestos claims; Mine Radiation Injury claims; other product liability cases for various manufacturers; the Kings Cross and Clapham Inquiries for the London Fire Brigade; the Severn Tunnel Inquiry.
Prof. Memberships: PNBA. Common Law and Commercial Bar Association.
Career: Educated Wellington College; BA Hons Durham; Dip Law. Called to the Bar 1984. Author: Group Action in Product Liability Law and Insurance.
Personal: Born 1960. Married; 3 children.

GIBSON, Christopher QC
2 Crown Office Row (John Powell QC), London (0171) 797 8000
Recommended in the following lists: Medical Negligence, Professional Negligence
Specialisation: Professional negligence (lawyers, medical practitioners, accountants, valuers and building professionals); general commercial law, insurance, and building and construction. Cases include Mortgage Express v. Bowerman, the consolidated appeal in the BBL litigation, Abbey National v. Key Surveyors (Court appointed expert), and Thorman v. New Hampshire (professional indemnity insurance).
Prof. Memberships: COMBAR, Professional Negligence Bar Association, Fellow of the Chartered Institute of Arbitrators.
Career: Educated at St Paul's School, and Brasenose College, Oxford; called to the Bar Middle Temple 1976; silk in 1995.
Personal: Married with 2 daughters; interests include Whitstable and motor-cycles.

GIFFIN, Nigel
11 King's Bench Walk (Eldred Tabachnik QC and James Goudie QC), London (0171) 632 8500
Recommended in the following lists: Administrative & Public Law, Employment
Specialisation: Specialises principally in most aspects of public and administrative law including education, local authority powers, local government finance, housing, social services, travellers, elections, competitive tendering and commercial judicial review. Also undertakes advisory work in all these fields. Practice also covers employment law, especially public sector work, and general commercial law. Employment work includes transfer of undertakings, dismissals, discrimination and restrictive covenants. Commercial work includes general contract, professional negligence and CMR (carriage by road). Important cases include Hazell v Hammersmith & Fulham LBC (House of Lords; local authority interest rate swaps); Palmer v A.B.P. (House of Lords; personal contracts and union membership); R v A.B.P. ex parte Plymouth CC (judicial review of animal exports); R v Institute of Chartered Accountants ex parte Brindle (Court of Appeal; stay of disciplinary proceedings pending litigation); R v Warwickshire CC ex parte Collymore (discretionary awards, judicial review). R v Hammersmith & Fulham LBC ex p.M (asylum seeker's rights under National Assistance Act); Hillsdown Holdings plc v Pensions Ombudsman (use of pension fund surplus). Contributor to the Administrative Law title of 'Halsbury's Laws of England'; contributor of education law chapter to forthcoming 'Butterworth's Local Government Law'.
Prof. Memberships: Administrative Law Bar Association (committee member); Education Law Association; Planning and Environmental Bar Association; Employment Law Bar Association.
Career: Called to the Bar 1986. Joined present chambers 1987.
Personal: Educated at Worcester College, Oxford (BA Hons 1st class) 1982-1985. Born 1963.

GILBART, Andrew QC
40 King St (Philip Raynor QC), Manchester (0161) 832 9082
Recommended in the following lists: Environmental Law, Planning
Specialisation: Town planning, compulsory purchase, highways, environment law and judicial review. Particularly experienced in major development projects involving airport expansion, roads, incineration, waste disposal, retailing, minerals, housing and motorway services. Contributor of articles to Journal of Planning and Environment Law.
Prof. Memberships: Member of Northern Circuit, Planning and Environment Bar Association, Associate member American Bar Association.
Career: Called 1972, elected member of Northern

Circuit 1973; Appointed Queens Counsel 1991: Recorder of The Crown Court.
Personal: Read Law at Trinity Hall, Cambridge. Married with two children. Enjoys tramping in the hills of the Peak District when time permits.

GILBERT, Francis
Mitre House Chambers (Francis P. Gilbert), London (0171) 583 8233
Recommended in Civil Liberties

GILBERT, Francis QC
Walnut House (Francis Gilbert QC), Exeter (01392) 279751
Recommended in Crime

GILEAD, Beryl
Chambers of Colin Anderson (St. Mary's Chambers) (Colin Anderson), Nottingham (0115) 950 3503
Recommended in Family/Matrimonial

GILL, Manjit Singh
6 King's Bench Walk (Sibghat Kadri QC), London (0171) 353 4931 /583 0695
Recommended in Immigration & Nationality
Specialisation: Specialises in all aspects of public law (with a particular emphasis on human rights, immigration, education, housing, local government, welfare benefits, community care, mental health and European law). Also specialises in employment, discrimination, civil actions against the police and landlord and tenant as well as being involved in common law fields generally. Numerous reported cases particularly in the immigration and education fields. Has appeared as leading counsel in several cases.
Prof. Memberships: Member of Administrative Law Bar Association, Discrimination Law Association, Education Law Association, Immigration Law Practitioners Association. Bar European Group.
Career: Called 1982. He is on the Commission for Racial Equality's list of approved counsel. Appointed by Attorney General to list of approved counsel to the Crown in Common Law matters (1992). Editor of the Immigration and Nationality Law Reports (from 1997).
Personal: He has spoken at national and international conferences, appeared before UN committees on human rights issues, convened training sessions on international human rights, immigration, racial harassment and related areas. Languages: Punjabi/Urdu.

GILL, Tess
Old Square Chambers (Hon. John Melville Williams QC), London (0171) 269 0300
Recommended in the following lists: Employment, Environmental Law
Specialisation: Principal areas of practice are employment and industrial law, health and safety and environment. She specialises in particular in sex and race discrimination, equal pay and European law including public law aspects. Cases include Strathclyde Regional Council v Wallace [1998] ICR 205, HL (Sc.) (equal pay); Carmichael v National Power plc [1998] IRLR 301, CA (casual workers); Halfpenny v IGE Medical Systems Ltd [1997] ICR 1007, EAT, (maternity); British Coal Corporation v Keeble [1997] IRLR 336 (sex discrimination – time limits); Scullard v (1) Knowles (2) Southern Regional Council for Education and Training [1996] CR 399, EAT, (equal pay and Article 119); Stewart v Cleveland Guest (Engineering) Ltd [1994] IRLR 440; EAT (sexual harassment); Roscoe v Hargreaves [1991] ICR (pension claim under Article 119); Hewcastle Catering Ltd v Ahmed [1991] IRLR 473,CA (illegal employment contracts); London Borough of Newham v Nalgo [1992] IRLR (labour injunctions) and Reay and Hope v BFNL (claim on behalf of children of nuclear power workers who contracted leukaemia).
Prof. Memberships: Management Committee member of Public Law Project, and member Environmental Law Foundation. Member of

Lawyers for Liberty; Personal Injury Bar Association, Employment Law Bar Association, Employment Law Association.
Career: Prior to transferring to the Bar in 1989, was solicitor with trade union and private practice experience. Appointed as part-time industrial tribunal chairman in 1995, has published work on equality law and is co-author and editor of 'Health and Safety Liabiity and Litigation' FT Law & Tax published 1995.

GILLESPIE, James
Enfield Chambers (Adrian Hall), Enfield (0181) 364 5627
Recommended in Immigration & Nationality
Specialisation: Offers specialist advice and representation in all aspects of immigration and nationality law, including asylum. Considerable experience of conducting cases before immigration Adjudicators and the Immigration Appeal Tribunal, judicial review and appeals to the Court of Appeal. Acts for a wide range of immigration clients, including prominent Middle East dissidents. Conducts training courses in immigration law for solicitors. Managing Editor of 'Tolley's Immigration and Nationality Law and Practice'.
Prof. Memberships: Founder member of the Immigration Law Practitioners Association and member of executive committee 1985-1992.
Career: Before being called to the Bar in 1991 worked for the Joint Council for the Welfare of Immigrants representing clients in the Immigration Appeal Tribunal.

GILLYON, Philip
Erskine Chambers (Richard Sykes QC), London (0171) 242 5532
Recommended in Company
Specialisation: Company law, corporate insolvency, financial services. Cases include: Re BSB Holdings Ltd [1996] 1 BCLC 155. Possfund Custodian Trustee Ltd. v Diamond [1996] 1 WLR 1351. Re Exchange Travel (Holdings) Ltd [1996] 2 BCLC 524. Represented Guinness Peat Group PLC in its minority shareholder's action against the British Land Company PLC re Stanhope Properties PLC/Broadgate Properties PLC.
Prof. Memberships: Commercial Bar Association; Chancery Bar Association; Insolvency Lawyers Association; Middle Temple.
Career: Hymers College, (1974-1984); Downing College, Cambridge (1984-1987); Called 1988; Joined Erskine Chambers 1989.
Personal: Born: 1965. Lives in London.

GILMAN, Jonathan QC
Essex Court Chambers (Gordon Pollock QC), London (0171) 813 8000
Recommended in Shipping
Specialisation: Insurance, reinsurance and shipping cases. Appears as counsel in very many London arbitrations. Regularly acts as umpire or arbitrator in London arbitrations. Has been retained as expert witness on English law in foreign proceedings on many occasions (mostly insurance or reinsurance cases).
Career: Called to the Bar 1965. Silk 1990.
Personal: Born 1942.

GILMOUR, Nigel QC
Peel House (Nigel Gilmour QC), Liverpool (0151) 236 4321
Recommended in Medical Negligence
Specialisation: All areas of medical negligence with particular experience of cases of brain damage following birth negligence. Cases relating to General Practitioners.
Prof. Memberships: Personal Injury Bar Association; Liverpool Medical – Legal Society; Northern Arbitration Association.
Career: LLB Hons Liverpool University. Recorder 1990.

GILROY, Paul
9 St. John Street (John Hand QC), Manchester (0161) 955 9000
Recommended in Employment
Specialisation: Has extensive experience of advisory/drafting work and advocacy in field of Employment Law. As well as advising on non-contentious matters and acting for employers and employees in all forms of employment litigation in the Industrial Tribunals, the County Court and High Court, he has also appeared before NHS Tribunals, Internal Police Disciplinary Inquiries and Internal hearings conducted by Professional Sports Bodies. Has recently acted in the Public Inquiry into the Personality Disorder Unit at Ashworth High Security Hospital. Acts for and against local and public authorities, trade unions and plcs. In the High Court he specialises in injunctive work and wrongful dismissal. In the Industrial Tribunal he has much experience of Transfers of Undertakings, Discrimination and Redundancy work, dealing regularly with multiple Applicant cases. He acted for numerous Applicants in the armed forces pregnancy dismissal litigation conducted in Industrial Tribunals across the UK in 1994 and 1995. Is approved by the Commission for Racial Equality and the Equal Opportunities Commission to act in discrimination cases. In addition to the traditional areas of Employment Law practice, deals with general commercial work and quasi-employment matters such as litigation concerning the Commercial Agents Regulations. Contributes to professional publications, annotates employment legislation for Current Law Statutes, and is a frequent speaker on Employment Law. Notable cases: Provident v Hayward (1989) 3 All ER 298 (Garden Leave). YKK v Ely (1993) IRLR 500 (Equivocal Resignation).
Prof. Memberships: Employment Lawyers Association; Employment Law Bar Association; NCFRAS.
Career: Called 1985 (Gray's Inn) Door Tenant: Farrar's Building, Temple, London EC4Y 7BD.

GINSBURG, Amanda
37 Park Square (John Sleightholme, Rodney Ferm), Leeds (0113) 243 9422
Recommended in Family/Matrimonial

GIRET, Jane
11 Stone Buildings (Michael Beckman QC), London +44 (0)171 831 6381
Recommended in the following lists: Chancery, Company, Insolvency
Specialisation: Specialises in company Law, corporate and personal insolvency, partnership and general Chancery and commercial litigation. Has particular expertise in disputes between shareholders or involving directors and complex receiverships and administrations, often involving drafting and advisory work in the company field. Acted for Macmillan Inc (a subsidiary of MCC) as part of the litigation involving the late Robert Maxwell. Other cases of interest include: Bjijmji & Others v Chatwani & Others, Chancery Division [1991] – shareholders dispute Virdi v Abbey Leisure & Others, Court of Appeal – shareholders dispute Martin Coulter Enterprises Limited, Chancery Division – shareholders dispute.

GIROLAMI, Paul
13 Old Square (Mr Michael Lyndon-Stanford QC), London (0171) 404 4800
Recommended in the following lists: Company, Insolvency
Specialisation: Practice principally concerns Chancery matters of the commercial type, with an emphasis on litigation, including matters involving company, insolvency (corporate and personal), landlord and tenant, property and trust questions.
Prof. Memberships: Chancery Bar Association and COMBAR.
Career: Called to the Bar, 1983. Joined 13 Old Square 1985. Junior Counsel to the Crown (Chancery).

Personal: Born 5th December 1959. Educated St Paul's School London and Corpus Christi College, Cambridge. Lives in London.

GLANCY QC, Robert QC
Devereux Chambers (Jeffrey Burke QC), London (0171) 353 7534
Recommended in Personal Injury
Specialisation: Principal areas of practice are personal injury and medical negligence cases, professional negligence generally (architects, engineers, surveyors and solicitors), construction law and employment law. Considerable experience of industrial disease cases such as repetitive strain injury, asbestos related conditions and welder's fume cases. Appeared in case of D.F. Estates v Church Commisioners for England on economic loss in tort and whether builder is liable for sub-contractor. Also appeared in a number of medical negligence cases such as Newell v Goldenberg concerned with warnings and sterilisation operations. One of the joint authors of the P.I.B.A. Personal Injury Handbook
Prof. Memberships: Personal Injury Bar Association.
Career: Called to the Bar 1972. Assistant Recorder 1993. Queen's Counsel 1997.
Personal: Educated at Manchester Grammar School and St. John's College, Cambridge. Lives in London.

GLASGOW, Edwin QC
39 Essex Street (Edwin Glasgow QC), London (0171) 832 1111
Recommended in the following lists: Commercial (litigation), Construction, Personal Injury, Professional Negligence, Sports Law
Specialisation: All areas of commercial and common law litigation including insurance, professional negligence and major personal injury cases. Has been involved in most of the public inquiries and litigation associated with disasters over the past ten years. Has extensive experience of litigation, arbitration and human rights work overseas including USA; Australia; Hong Kong; Singapore; France and Africa. Recent cases include: Svenska Bank v Sun Alliance; Trafalgar House v Davy Offshore; Capital and Counties v Planned Maintenance; BBL; Sun Valley Poultry; Kuwait Investment Office.
Prof. Memberships: London Common Law and Commercial Bar Association.
Career: LLB (Hons); Called to the Bar 1969; Silk 1987. Chairman Financial Reporting Review Panel 1992-1998.

GLASS, Anthony T. QC
Queen Elizabeth Building (David Jeffreys QC & Peter Whiteman QC), London (0171) 583 5766
Recommended in the following lists: Crime, Crime: Fraud
Specialisation: Practice encompasses all aspects of criminal law, with a specialisation in commercial fraud, V.A.T. fraud and drugs importations since taking silk. Recently involved in Barlow Clowes, BCCI, Guildford police cases, Reg Ellis arson/fraud and Abbey National Fraud.
Prof. Memberships: Criminal Bar Association, South Eastern Circuit.
Career: Called to the Bar 1965 and joined current chambers in 1982. Appointed Recorder 1985. Took silk 1986. Bencher of Inner Temple.
Personal: Educated at Royal Masonic Schools 1948-58 and Lincoln College, Oxford 1960-63. Born 6th June 1940. Lives in London.

GLEN, Ian QC
Guildhall Chambers (John Royce QC), Bristol (0117) 927 3366
Recommended in the following lists: Crime, Licensing
Specialisation: Over twenty years experience acting for all sides in all aspects of liquor, betting, gaming, lotteries and public entertainment. Licensing work complemented by broad judicial review practice. Also experienced in the law of

clubs, including meetings and litigation over discipline. In criminal cases has frequently prosecuted and defended licensees, bookmakers and the organisers of lotteries and public entertainments. Has particular experience of noise nuisance cases.

GLENNIE, Angus QC
20 Essex Street (David Johnson QC), London (0171) 583 9294
Recommended in Aviation
Specialisation: Shipping. Insurance. Arbitration. Recent cases include: Ultisol litigation concerning forum non conveniens, anti-suit injunctions and limitation: reported [1996] 2 Lloyd's Rep 140, [1997] 2 Lloyd's Rep 485, 493, 507, 533; Stocznia Gdanska v Latvian Shipping Co (HL), Shipbuilding, [1998] 1 WLR 574; Baker v Black Sea Baltic General Insurance Co Ltd (HL) re-insurance [1998] 1 WLR 974.
Career: MA (Cantab), Trinity Hall. Called 1974, QC 1991. Also practising member of Scots bar, Member of Gibraltar Bar.

GLICK, Ian QC
One Essex Court (Anthony Grabiner QC), London (0171) 583 2000
Recommended in the following lists: Arbitration, Banking, Commercial (litigation), Energy & Utilities, Financial Services, Tax
Specialisation: Principal areas of practice are banking, commercial law, financial services, insurance, accountants' negligence, revenue litigation and arbitration. Important cases include PCW litigation; Tin Council litigation; Crown Agent Enquiry; Woolwich BS v CIR (restitution); Smith New Court v Citibank (measure of damages in fraud); Gallagher v Jones (application of accepted principles of commercial accountancy to computation of profits for tax purposes), Shah v Bank of England (banking regulation); Deeny v Gooda Walker (taxability of damages recovered in Lloyds' litigation); R v CIR ex p. Warburgs (judicial review of Revenue decisions) and Fuji Finance v Aetna (nature of a contract of insurance). Conference speaker.
Prof. Memberships: Chairman, Commercial Bar Association, 1997-.
Career: Called to the Bar in 1970. At Lamb Building 1970-80. Joined 1 Essex Court in 1980. Junior Counsel to the Crown, Common Law 1985-87. Standing Counsel to the DTI in export credit cases 1985-87. Took Silk in 1987.
Personal: Educated at Bradford Grammar School and Balliol College, Oxford. Born 18th July 1948. Lives in London.

GLOBE, Henry QC
Exchange Chambers (William Waldron QC), Liverpool (0151) 236 7747
Recommended in Crime

GLOSTER, Elizabeth QC
One Essex Court (Anthony Grabiner QC), London (0171) 583 2000
Recommended in the following lists: Commercial (litigation), Chancery, Corporate Finance/ Company, Financial Services, Insolvency, Professional Negligence
Specialisation: Principal areas of expertise are company law, banking, insurance and insolvency. Also covers commercial fraud, financial services, media and telecommunications and professional negligence. Recent major cases include: acting for the D.T.I. in the disqualification proceedings arising out of the collapse of Barings (1998); acting for EMLICO and its liquidators in the litigation arising out of EMLICO's redomestication to Bermuda (1996-1998); acting for Charterhouse Development (France) in its recent action against Lloyd's underwriters (1996); acting for the administrators of Barings in the action against ING (1996); acting for the banks in the interest rate swaps litigation; representing the liquidators of Barlow Clowes in litigation against various directors and third party professionals (1992-1995); acting for

banks/administrators of Olympia & York, Canary Wharf (1993-1994); acting for the Society of Lloyd's in a case involving the question of priority between the Society and various Names (1993); representing recently-appointed trustees of Maxwell Pension Funds in relation to the Maxwell collapse (1992-1995); acting for the D.T.I in the case of Sher v The Policy Holders Protection Board (1993); Hazell v Hammersmith & Fulham Borough Council (1992) (House of Lords); prosecuting in the criminal trials arising out of the Guinness bid for Distillers (1990) and (1991). Called to the Bars of Bermuda, Gibraltar and the Isle of Man for specific cases. Working knowledge of French.
Prof. Memberships: Chancery Bar Association, COMBAR, Insolvency Lawyers' Association, INSOL.
Career: Called to the Bar in 1971. Member of the panel of junior counsel representing the DTI in company matters 1982-89. Took Silk in 1989. Bencher of the Inner Temple and Deputy High Court Judge of the Chancery Division in 1992, Judge of the Courts of Appeal of Jersey & Guernsey (part-time) in 1994 and Recorder 1995.
Personal: Educated at Roedean School 1962-67 and Girton College, Cambridge 1967-70. Born 5th June 1949.

GLOVER, Richard
2 Mitre Court Buildings (Michael FitzGerald QC), London (0171) 583 1380
Recommended in the following lists: Parliamentary, Planning
Specialisation: Specialises in all areas of Planning and Local Government Law.
Prof. Memberships: Member of the Planning and Environment Bar Association and The Parliamentary Bar.
Career: Called in 1984. Has acted in a wide range of inquiries including the Toyota Factory in Derbyshire, Centre Parcs Holiday Village at Longleat, Oasis Holiday Village near Folkestone and Mizens Farm (new HQ for McLaren Racing). Parliamentary Bills include Channel Tunnel, Dartford River Crossing and Heathrow Express. Rating Bases include Mosanto Chemical works, Port Talbot Steelworks, Shall Haven Oil refinery, B.P. Oilfield at Welton, Bristol Airport and BT. Editor of Ryde on Rating and the Council Tax.
Personal: Educated at Harrow and Cambridge.

GLOVER, Stephen
37 Park Square (John Sleightholme, Rodney Ferm), Leeds (0113) 243 9422
Recommended in Family/Matrimonial

GOATLEY, Peter
5 Fountain Court (Anthony Barker QC), Birmingham (0121) 606 0500
Recommended in the following lists: Environmental Law, Planning
Specialisation: Undertakes a wide range of planning work including appeals, local plan and unitary development plan inquiries, enforcement appeals, High Court challenges (both statutory and judicial review) and section 187B injunctions.
Prof. Memberships: Planning and Environment Bar Association.
Career: Previously a solicitor and partner in a medium sized commercial firm who specialised in commercial and residential property development. Called 1992.
Personal: Educated at Whitefriars Cheltenham and Worcester College, Oxford. Married with two children. Lives near Cheltenham, Gloucestershire.

GODDARD, Andrew
Atkin Chambers (John Blackburn QC), London (0171) 404 0102
Recommended in Construction
Specialisation: Principal areas of practice are building and engineering litigation and arbitration. Particular interests include professional negligence, management contracts, extension of time claims and highways works. Has also been involved in various disputes involving NHS

Hospitals, NHS Trusts, etc. Allied work includes bonds, guarantees and insurance.
Prof. Memberships: ORBA (Committee Member)
Career: Called to the Bar 1985.
Personal: Independent Schools Association Whitbread Memorial Trophy; BA Hons. Law (First Class) Sussex 1984; Inner Temple Queen Elizabeth II Scholarship 1985; Poland Prize 1985.

GODDARD, Christopher
Devereux Chambers (Jeffrey Burke QC), London (0171) 353 7534
Recommended in the following lists: Health & Safety, Personal Injury
Specialisation: Principal area of practice is plaintiff and defendant personal injury with a special interest in occupational disease. Also medical and legal professional negligence. Regularly speaks at conferences and seminars in these fields. Co-author 'Health and Safety: The New Legal Framework' Butterworths and contributor to Butterworths 'Personal Injury Handbook'.
Prof. Memberships: Personal Injury Bar Association.
Career: Manchester University 1969-1972. Called to Bar in 1973.

GODFREY, Howard QC
3 Hare Court (William Clegg QC), London (0171) 353 7561
Recommended in the following lists: Crime, Crime: Fraud
Specialisation: Serious crime especially fraud, both corporate and personal, including some work overseas. Experienced in VAT and Tax Frauds, Insider Dealing, Stock Exchange, Banking, Accounting, Insurance, Corruption and Extradition. Practice also includes General Crime especially drugs cases and civil fraud.
Prof. Memberships: South Eastern Circuit, Criminal Bar Association.
Career: Called 1970. Took silk in 1991. Recorder 1992.
Personal: Born 17th August 1946. Educated University of London – London School of Economics (LL.B.). Lives in Berkshire.

GOLDBERG, David QC
Gray's Inn Tax Chambers (Milton Grundy), London (0171) 242 2642
Recommended in Tax
Specialisation: Practice concentrates on revenue law and commercial litigation with a tax or financial aspect. Clients include solicitors, accountants and corporations. Co-author of 'Introduction to Company Law' (1971, 3rd Edn 1987) and 'The Law of Partnership Taxation' (1976, 2nd Edn 1979). Author of various articles and notes for legal periodicals, mainly concerning tax and company law.
Prof. Memberships: Revenue Bar Association, Chancery Bar Association.
Career: Called to the Bar and joined current chambers in 1971. Took Silk 1987. Bencher of Lincoln's Inn 1998.
Personal: Educated at Plymouth college and London School of Economics 1966-70 (LL.B, LL.M). Chairman of Trustees of the Skills Workshop for Anatomical Techniques. Leisure pursuits include reading, writing letters and thinking. Born 12th August 1947. Lives in London.

GOLDBERG, Jonathan QC
3 Temple Gardens (Jonathan Goldberg QC), London (0171) 583 1155
Recommended in the following lists: Crime, Crime: Fraud
Fax: (0171) 353 5446
Specialisation: Has defended in many of the most notable jury trials at the Old Bailey and elsewhere over the past two decades. These include Roger Levitt (white collar fraud), Brinksmat, R v Rosenthal (The Stamford Hill child sex abuse case involving Orthodox Jews), R v Laming (The Sonic Binoculars horse nobbling case), R v Charlie Kray and many others. He is qualified at the New York Bar and has

worked in Malaysia, Singapore and Gibraltar. He has had successes in libel and commercial cases requiring strong cross-examination also, and is not limited to crime. He is noted for battling and winning against seemingly overwhelming odds.
Career: Called in 1971; appointed a QC in 1989; a Recorder in 1992.
Personal: Educated at Manchester Grammar and Trinity Hall Cambridge.

GOLDREIN, Iain QC
The Corn Exchange (David Steer QC & I. Goldrein QC), Liverpool (0151) 227 1081/5009
12 King's Bench Walk (Ronald J. Walker QC), London (0171) 583 0811
Recommended in Medical Negligence
Mobile: 0831 703 156
Email: goldhaas@netcomuk.co.uk
Specialisation: Complex Professional (including Medical) Negligence (with particular expertise in brain damage at birth); Catastrophic Injury Claims; General Commercial including Insurance coverage; Pre-Emptive Commercial Remedies; Product Liability. Cases of Interest: Rayeware v TGWU; Sion v Hampstead Health Authority. Publications: 'Property Distribution on Divorce' [FT Law and Tax] [1st and 2nd editions with Margaret de Haas QC]; 'Personal Injury Litigation: Practice and Precedents' [Butterworths]; Ship Sale and Purchase, Law and Technique [Lloyds of London Press] with Clifford Chance; 'Commercial Litigation: Pre-emptive Remedies' [Sweet and Maxwell] with Judges Wilkinson and Kershaw QC; 'Butterworths Personal Injury Litigation Service' with Margaret de Haas QC; 'Bullen and Leake and Jacob's Precedents of Pleadings' [Sweet and Maxwell], with Sir Jack Jacob; 'Pleadings, Principles and Practice' [Sweet and Maxwell], with Sir Jack Jacob; 'Structured Settlements' [Butterworths], Editor-in-Chief with Margaret de Haas QC [1st Edition 1993. 2nd Edition May 1997]; 'Medical Negligence: Cost Effective Case Management' [Butterworths] with Margaret de Haas QC, [May, 1997].
Prof. Memberships: Professional Negligence Bar Association; Personal Injury Bar Association; London Common Law & Commercial Bar Association. Companion of the Academy of Experts; Fellow of the Royal Society of Arts; Associate of the Chartered Institute of Arbitrators; Nominated Counsel: Environmental Law Foundation; Mediator, registered with the Academy of Experts. Awards: University of Cambridge Squire Scholarship for Law; Exhibitioner and Ziegler Prize, Pembroke College Cambridge; Inner Temple Duke of Edinburgh Scholarship.
Career: Appointments: Queen's Counsel; Assistant Recorder; Visiting Professor (The Sir Jack Jacob Chair in Litigation) Nottingham Law School.
Personal: New ideas, classical Hebrew, English Legal History and classic motor vehicles. Educated at Merchant Taylors' School, Crosby (Harrison Scholar), Hebrew University, Jerusalem (1971), Pembroke College, Cambridge (1971-1974).

GOLDRING, John B. QC
9 Bedford Row (John Goldring QC), London (0171) 242 3555
Recommended in Crime
Specialisation: Serious criminal work of all kinds. Civil and criminal fraud. Professional disciplinary work. Prosecuted Beverley Allitt. Represented one of the consultants in the case concerning payment for organ transplants (kidneys). Appeared and advised in many serious tax and fraud cases, both for the defence and the prosecution. Recently involved in the Jersey currency futures case, involving Cantrade Bank.
Prof. Memberships: Criminal Bar Association, involved in United States with National Institute of Trial Advocacy and the Council for Court Excellence Washington.
Career: Called to the Bar 1969. Counsel to Inland Revenue (crime, Midland and Oxford Circuit) for 2 years before taking silk in 1987. Recorder. Deputy

High Court Judge. A Deputy Senior Judge in Cyprus. Bencher of Lincoln's Inn. Currently head of chambers.
Personal: Born 9.11.44. Educated at Wyggeston Grammar School, Leicester. Exeter University. Lives in London and Rutland.

GOLDSMITH, Peter QC
Fountain Court (Peter Scott QC), London (0171) 583 3335
Recommended in the following lists: Arbitration, Commercial (litigation), Professional Negligence

GOLDSTONE, David
4 Field Court (Geoffrey Brice QC), London (0171) 440 6900
Recommended in Shipping

GOLDSTONE, L. Clement QC
Crown Office Row (Richard Ferguson QC), London (0171) 797 7111
28 St. John St (Anthony Rumbelow QC), Manchester (0161) 834 8418
Recommended in the following lists: Crime, Licensing
Specialisation: Crime, Licensing.
Prof. Memberships: Criminal Bar Association.
Career: B.A. (Cantab.) 1970. Called (Middle Temple) 1971. Recorder 1992. Queen's Counsel 1993. Treasurer, Northern Circuit 1998.

GOODE, Rowena
28 St. John St (Anthony Rumbelow QC), Manchester (0161) 834 8418
Recommended in the following lists: Crime
Specialisation: Crime.
Prof. Memberships: Criminal Bar Association.
Career: Recorder 1997.

GOODE, Roy QC
Blackstone Chambers (formerly 2 Hare Court) (P Baxendale QC and C Flint QC), London (0171) 583 1770
Recommended in Consumer Law
Specialisation: Commercial law; banking; credit and security; international trade law; consumer credit Author of Commercial Law (2nd edn. 1995) and other leading textbooks in the above fields which are widely cited in the courts.
Prof. Memberships: Norton Rose Professor of English Law in the University of Oxford, Fellow of St. John's College, Oxford. Former Chairman of Executive Committee of JUSTICE. Panel Chairman of appeal under Consumer Credit Act 1974. Member of Board of London Court of International Arbitration. Former Chairman of the Commission on International Commercial Practice of the International Chamber of Commerce.
Career: Admitted as solicitor 1955; partner, Victor Mishcon & Co., solicitors, 1963-1971. Appointed Professor Law, Queen Mary College, University of London 1971, and Crowther Professor of Credit and Commercial Law 1973. Founder and first Director of Centre for Commercial Law Studies, QMC. Transferred to Bar 1988. Took silk 1990. Hon. Bencher, Inner Temple, 1992. Appointed Norton Rose Professor of English Law. University of Oxford, 1990. Member of Department of Trade and Industry Advisory Committee on Arbitration 1985-. Chairman of Pension Law Review Committee 1992-93. LL.B. (Lond.) 1954; LLD (Lond. 1976); OBE 1972, CBE 1994; Hon. DSc Econ (Lond.) 1996; Elected Fellow of the British Academy 1988; Fellow of the Royal Society of Arts 1990.

GOODFELLOW, Giles W.J.
Pump Court Tax Chambers (Andrew Thornhill QC), London (0171) 414 8080
Recommended in Tax
Specialisation: Revenue Law including all aspects of direct and indirect tax and tax related aspects of commercial disputes including finance leasing and professional negligence and variation of trusts. Areas of particular interests include all forms of litigation, and advisory work on cover managed businesses and offshore trusts. Co-author of

Inheritance Tax Planning (Longman) and Finance Provision and Taxation on Divorce.
Career: Called to the Bar 1983. Joined present Chambers in 1985.

GOODHART, Lord QC
3 New Square (Lord Goodhart QC), London (0171) 405 5577
Recommended in the following lists: Company, Traditional Chancery
Specialisation: Principal area of practice is Chancery work, encompassing pension funds, trusts and estates, property, consumer credit and personal taxation. Other main area of work is company law and insolvency. Recent cases include Forward Trust v Whymark [1990] (consumer credit), Davis v Richards & Wallington Industries [1990] (pensions) and Hambro v Duke of Marlborough [1994] (trusts). Co-author of 'Specific Performance' (the leading modern authority on this subject), (2nd Edn, 1996) and section of Halsbury's Laws on corporations.
Prof. Memberships: Chancery Bar Association, International Commission of Jurists, Institute for Fiscal Studies.
Career: Called to the Bar 1957. In practice at the Chancery Bar since 1960. Took Silk 1979. Knighted 1989. Member Committee on Standards in Public Life 1997.
Personal: Educated at Eton College 1946-51, Trinity College, Cambridge 1953-57 (BA, MA) and Harvard Law School 1957-58 (LL.M). Chairman, Court of Discipline of Cambridge University since 1993. Life Peer, 1997. Born 18th January 1933.

GOODISON, Adam
3/4 South Square (Michael Crystal QC), London (0171) 696 9900
Recommended in Insolvency

GOODRICH, Siobhan
6 Pump Court (Kieran Coonan QC), London (0171) 583 6013
Recommended in Medical Negligence
Specialisation: Medical negligence and related work; professional misconduct, disciplinary tribunals, inquests, and inquiries. Acts for Plaintiff and Defendant. Other areas of practice include professional negligence, personal injury and some crime.
Prof. Memberships: Professional Negligence Bar Association, LCLBA, CBA.
Career: Called to the Bar in 1980. Joined chambers in 1981. Born 15.3.57.
Personal: Educated at King's College London (LLB). Lives in London. Formerly a member of Great Ormond St Ethics Committee.

GOODWIN, Deirdre
13 King's Bench Walk (Graeme Williams QC), London (0171) 353 7204
Recommended in Medical Negligence

GORDON, Richard QC
39 Essex Street (Edwin Glasgow QC), London (0171) 832 1111
Recommended in the following lists: Administrative & Public Law, Environmental Law
Specialisation: Specialist in public and administrative law with particular expertise in judicial review for both respondent and applicants, especially in the areas of local authority, commercial environmental, civil liberties and health and social services. Author of 'Judicial Review: Law and Procedure', 'Crown Office Proceedings', 'Local Authority Powers' and 'Community Care Assessments.' Co-Editor of 'Local Authority Law;' Editor in chief of 'Crown Office Digest.' Visiting Professor of Law, University College, London.
Prof. Memberships: Administrative Law Bar Association.
Career: Called to the Bar 1972. Took silk 1994.
Personal: Educated at Oxford University (Open Scholar).

GORE, Allan
12 King's Bench Walk (Ronald J. Walker QC), London (0171) 583 0811
Recommended in the following lists: Medical Negligence, Personal Injury
Specialisation: Professional negligence, encompassing medical, dental and legal cases both contentious and non-contentious. Personal injury work. Special interest and experience in transport mass accidents and disasters, and industrial disease, particularly concerning asbestos cases. Contributing author to 'Butterworths County Court Precedents and Pleadings: Divisions P on Professional Negligence and Q on Personal Injury'; and to 'Cordery on Solicitors: Division J on Negligence' and to Butterworths Personal Injury Litigation Service' Division VIII on Pleadings. Regular conference and seminar speaker.
Prof. Memberships: Executive of Association of Personal Injury Lawyers and Personal Injury Bar Association. Professional Negligence Bar Association, AVMA, ATLA, APLA.
Career: Called 1977. Joined current chambers 1991.
Personal: Educated Purley Grammar School, Croydon 1962-69; Trinity Hall, Cambridge 1970-74. Born 25th August 1951. Lives in London.

GORTON, Simon
14 Castle St (Adrian Lyon), Liverpool (0151) 236 4421/8240/6759/6757
Recommended in Personal Injury

GOSLING, J.
4 Fountain Court (Richard Wakerley QC), Birmingham (0121) 236 3476
Recommended in Licensing

GOUDIE, James QC
11 King's Bench Walk (Eldred Tabachnik QC and James Goudie QC), London (0171) 632 8500
Recommended in the following lists: Administrative & Public Law, Employment, Planning
Specialisation: Specialises in all aspects of employment law, with particular emphasis on TUPE, Restrictive Covenants and European Law relating to employment matters. Other main areas of practice include: Public Law (Capital Finance) and Commercial (Contractual disputes, insurance).
Career: Solicitor 1966 to 1970. Called to the Bar Inner Temple 1970. Bencher, Recorder, Deputy High Court Judge, Queen's Bench Division, Past Chairman Law Reform Committee, General Council of the Bar, Past Chairman Administrative Law Bar Association, Chairman Society of Labour Lawyers.
Personal: Educated at Dean Close School, Cheltenham and L.S.E. (LL.B Hons). F.C.I. Arb.

GOULDING, Paul
Blackstone Chambers (formerly 2 Hare Court) (P Baxendale QC and C Flint QC), London (0171) 583 1770
Recommended in the following lists: Civil Liberties, Ecclesiastical, Employment, Sports Law
Specialisation: Specialist in employment law, (particularly restraint of trade, transfer of undertakings, discrimination, industrial action, Europe; Credit Suisse v Armstrong; Biggs v Somerset CC) sports law (Modahl v BAF, Formula 1, football and rugby cases), judicial review (R v BBC, ex p. Referendum Party) and financial services (SFA and IMRO disciplinary proceedings).
Prof. Memberships: Employment Lawyers' Association (Chairman), European Employment Lawyers Association, British Association for Sport and Law, Administrative Law Bar Association.
Career: St Edmund Hall, Oxford. Call 1984.

GOURGEY, Alan
11 Stone Buildings (Michael Beckman QC), London +44 (0)171 831 6381
Recommended in Partnership
Specialisation: Has a practice covering most areas of commercial work, including contract, company disputes and insolvency, commercial fraud, professional negligence, entertainment law, intellectual property and product liability. Has also developed particular specialities in all aspects of distribution agreements, pre-emptive remedies and partnership disputes.

GOY, David QC
Gray's Inn Tax Chambers (Milton Grundy), London (0171) 242 2642
Recommended in Tax
Specialisation: Specialist in all aspects of revenue law. Has particular expertise in the tax aspects of real property transactions, and in all types of tax litigation. Important cases include Lubbock Fine v. H.M. Customs & Excise [1994] (VAT on the surrender of tenancies); LASMO (TNS) Ltd v. IRC [1994] (oil taxation); IRC v Willoughby [1997] (taxation under s.739 ICTA). Publications include 'VAT on Property' (co-author) (Sweet & Maxwell 2nd Edition 1993), and Butterworths Tax Planning (consultant editor). Regular speaker on the subject of revenue law.
Prof. Memberships: Revenue Bar Association.
Career: Called to the Bar 1973. Joined present chambers 1974. Took Silk 1991.
Personal: Educated at Haberdashers' Askes School and King's College, London. Born 11th May 1949. Lives in Guildford.

GRABINER, Anthony QC
One Essex Court (Anthony Grabiner QC), London (0171) 583 2000
Recommended in the following lists: Arbitration, Banking, Commercial (litigation), Energy & Utilities, Insurance & Reinsurance

GRACE, John QC
3 Serjeants' Inn (Philip Naughton QC), London (0171) 353 5537
Recommended in Medical Negligence

GRAHAM, Charles
One Essex Court (Anthony Grabiner QC), London (0171) 583 2000
Recommended in the following lists: Commercial (litigation), Insurance & Reinsurance
Specialisation: Principal area of practice is general/chancery commercial work including heavyweight litigation relating to take-overs and the role of merchant banks (qua corporate financiers) and accountants in that connection. Specialises in professional negligence, construction of documents, bank guarantees and facilities etc., share sale agreements, accountancy issues, computer-related disputes and issues of private international law.
Prof. Memberships: South Eastern Circuit, Commercial Bar Association.
Career: Called to the Bar in 1986 and joined Essex Court in 1987.
Personal: Educated at Wellington College 1974-79 and University College, Oxford 1980-84 MA Classics (First Class Honours). Born 1st April 1961. Lives in London.

GRAINGER, Ian
One Essex Court (Anthony Grabiner QC), London (0171) 583 2000
Recommended in Alternative Dispute Resolution
Specialisation: A broad based commercial lawyer, with particular emphasis on professional negligence, insurance and conflicts/jurisdictional issues. Often sits as an examiner under RSC O.70. CEDR Accredited Mediator.
Prof. Memberships: South Eastern Circuit, COMBAR, London Common Law and Commercial Bar Association, Bar European Group, British Italian Law Association.
Career: Called to the Bar in 1978. In 1 Essex Court since 1979.
Personal: Educated at University College, Oxford, 1974-77. Speaks fluent Italian and is a passionate Italophile.

GRAY, Charles QC
5 Raymond Buildings (Patrick Milmo QC), London (0171) 242 2902
Recommended in the following lists: Defamation, Media & Entertainment
Specialisation: Defamation, media and entertainment law. Recent libel cases include Elton John v Mirror; Rantzen v Mirror; Charleston v News Group; Derbyshire CC v Times; Aldington v Tolstoy; Botham and Lamb v Imran Khan; Aitken v Guardian; al Fayed v Condé Nast; Marks & Spencer v Granada. Media and entertainment experience includes confidence (Spycatcher litigation); copyright (A&M Records v VCI; Thatcher memoirs); contempt and passing off.
Career: Called to the Bar 1966. QC 1984; Recorder 1991; Bencher, Lincolns Inn 1992; Deputy High Court Judge.
Personal: Educated at Winchester and Trinity College Oxford.

GRAY, Gilbert QC
Park Court Chambers (James Stewart QC, Robert Smith QC), Leeds (0113) 243 3277
3 Raymond Buildings (Clive Nicholls QC), London (0171) 831 3833
Recommended in Licensing

GRAY, Richard QC
39 Essex Street (Edwin Glasgow QC), London (0171) 832 1111
Recommended in Construction
Specialisation: Principal area of practice is Construction and Engineering litigation or arbitration in UK and abroad. Acts as Arbitrator in such disputes, both domestic and international.
Prof. Memberships: ORBA (Offical Referees Bar Assocation).
Career: Called to the Bar in 1970. Took silk in 1993.

GREEN, Brian QC
Wilberforce Chambers (Edward Nugee QC), London (0171) 306 0102
Recommended in the following lists: Pensions, Traditional Chancery
Specialisation: Pensions and Private Client specialist having wide ranging experience of contentious and non-contentious general chancery work. Has acted for the sponsoring companies or the trustees of major pension schemes, and for the trustees and/or the beneficiaries of the largest trusts (private and commercial).
Prof. Memberships: APL, Revenue Bar Association, STEP.
Career: Called to the Bar 1980. Member of Revenue Law Committee of the Law Society since 1994. (1978-85 tenured lectureship in Law at LSE).
Personal: Educated at Ilford County High School and St Edmund Hall Oxford (BA, BCL: double first).

GREEN, Michael A.
Fountain Court (Peter Scott QC), London (0171) 583 3335
Recommended in the following lists: Company, Insolvency
Specialisation: Principal areas of work are company and insolvency law. Also handles large scale commercial actions, having been involved for 3 years in Maxwell litigation (acting for Lehman Brothers), and then Lloyds litigation (acting on behalf of auditors). Cases include Derby v. Weldon, Macmillan Inc. v. Bishopsgate Investment Trust Plc, Re Barings Plc
Career: Called to the bar in 1987. Joined 7 Stone Buildings in 1988. Joined present chambers in 1998. Appointed Junior Counsel to the Crown, Chancery in 1997 and a DTI Inspector in 1997.
Personal: Educated at University College School 1971-82, and Jesus College Cambridge 1983-86. Leisure pursuits include skiing, squash and tennis. Born 23rd October 1964.

GREEN, Nicholas QC
Brick Court Chambers (Christopher Clarke QC), London (0171) 583 0777
Recommended in European Union/Competition
Specialisation: Litigation, advisory and representational work in relation to United Kingdom competition law; all aspects of EC law generally; EC competition law; competition law aspects of merger's and takeovers; intellectual property licensing including software licensing; media law; telecommunications; environmental law; public procurement; conflicts of laws; public law. Has been instructed in over 30 cases before the European Court of Justice. Recent cases include: Coloroll, Francovich II, Sunag, Factortame, Eurotunnel, R v MCA ex parte Generics; matters re the beef ban; acting for brewers in disputes with tenant over Article 85; companies in broadcast, telecommunications and transport sectors, in disputes with regulators and competitors.
Career: Called to Bar 1986; Barrrister of the Inner Temple, Brick Court Chambers both in London and Brussels. 1981-85: Lecturer in Law, University of Southampton; Vice Chairman Bar European Group 1998 -.
Personal: Born 15 October 1958. LL.B (1980), LL.M (1981), Ph.d (1985). Has over 50 publications in journals world wide in relation largely to EC law. Two principal publications are 'Commercial Agreements and Competition law: Practice and Procedure in the UK and EEC (1986) (second edition being prepared); and 'Legal Foundations of the Single European Market' (1991).

GREEN, Patrick
2 Harcourt Buildings (Roger Henderson QC), London (0171) 583 9020
Recommended in Alternative Dispute Resolution

GREENBERG, Joanna QC
3 Temple Gardens (Jonathan Goldberg QC), London (0171) 583 1155
Recommended in Crime
Specialisation: Defending in all types of serious criminal cases.
Prof. Memberships: Bar Council, Criminal Bar Association, Justice, Liberty.
Career: Called to the Bar 1972, took Silk 1994, Assistant Recorder 1992, Recorder 1995, Chairman of Police Discipline Appeals Tribunals 1997.
Personal: Educated University of London, King's College. Lives in London.

GREENWOOD, Celestine
Chavasse Court Chambers (Andrew Mattison), Liverpool (0151) 707 1191
Recommended in Family/Matrimonial

GREGORY, James
Lincoln House Chambers (Mukhtar Hussain QC), Manchester (0161) 832 5701
Recommended in Crime

GREGORY, Philip
No.6 Fountain Court (Roger Smith QC), Birmingham (0121) 233 3282
Recommended in Personal Injury

GREWAL, Harjit
6 King's Bench Walk (Sibghat Kadri QC), London (0171) 353 4931 /583 0695
Recommended in Immigration & Nationality

GREY, Robin D. QC
Queen Elizabeth Building (David Jeffreys QC & Peter Whiteman QC), London (0171) 583 5766
Recommended in Crime
Specialisation: Criminal law. Defends and prosecutes in all areas of criminal law, with a particular emphasis on large-scale fraud in recent years. Has also defended in over thirty high-profile murder cases during the course of his career. Successfully defended in the Richardson Gang case of 1970s, in the "Nasty Tales" case at the time of the Oz trial, in the "King Squealer" robberies in

the late 1970s, and in the Brinks Matt case in the early 1990s. Fraud trials include a successful defence in the Eagle Trust case (1993). In the past three years has defended solicitors, accountants and bank managers in relation to white collar offences. Has considerable experience lecturing on professional conduct, jury trials and criminal procedure. Has also written articles for the Centre for Policy Studies and the Criminal Bar Association newsletter. Practice also includes civil matters arising out of criminal cases.
Prof. Memberships: Bar Council, Society of Forensic Medicine, Criminal Bar Association, International Bar Association, Eastern Europe Forum and the Council of Russian and UK Cooperation.
Career: Called to the Bar 1957 and worked as Crown Counsel in Aden 1959-63, before joining present chambers in 1963. Took Silk in 1979 and was appointed Recorder in the same year. Chairman of Police Appeals Tribunals 1988. Adviser to the Foreign Office in Russian Federation jury trials in 1993. Legal Assessor to General Medical Council, 1995.

GRICE, Joanna
One King's Bench Walk (James Townend QC), London (0171) 936 1500
Recommended in Family: Matrimonial Finance
Specialisation: All areas of family law including ancillary relief, care and private law matters.
Prof. Memberships: FLBA.

GRICE, Kevin
The Corn Exchange (David Steer QC & I. Goldrein QC), Liverpool (0151) 227 1081/5009
Recommended in Personal Injury
Specialisation: Personal injury, in particular industrial accidents and disease, medical negligence and other professional negligence. Environmental torts.
Prof. Memberships: PIBA, PNBA, APIL.
Career: LLB, Liverpool University 1976. Called to Bar 1977. University lecturer 1977-1985. Assistant Recorder 1996.

GRIEVE, Dominic C.R.
1 Temple Gardens (Hugh Carlisle QC), London (0171) 583 1315
Recommended in Health & Safety
Specialisation: Health and safety at work and pollution cases (criminal and civil). Junior prosecution counsel in: R v Nuclear electric plc (Mold Sept. 1995 incident at Wylfa Power Station) R v Coalite Ltd (Leicester Feb. 1996 Pollution by Dioxins); R v Port Ramsgate, Old Bailey January - March 1997. Personal injury. Insurance/negligence work. Local Government (enforcement work).
Prof. Memberships: Common Law Bar Association and Criminal Bar Association.
Career: Hon. Degree Modern History Oxford 1978. Called to Bar 1980. 1982-90 Chamber of Anthony Cripps QC: 1, Harcourt Buildings (General Common Law). 1990 - date: 1, Temple Gardens.

GRIEVE, Michael QC
Doughty Street Chambers (Geoffrey Robertson QC), London (0171) 404 1313
Recommended in the following lists: Crime, Crime: Fraud

GRIFFITH-JONES, David
Devereux Chambers (Jeffrey Burke QC), London (0171) 353 7534
Recommended in the following lists: Employment, Sports Law
Specialisation: General common lawyer. Specialist in Employment (including dismissal, discrimination, TUPE, industrial disputes, restraint of trade and injunctions) and Sport (including personal injury, discipline and regulation, sport as a profession, competition and the commercial exploitation of sport). Author of 'Law and the Business of Sport' (Butterworths, 1997).
Prof. Memberships: London Common Law and Commercial Bar Association; Employment

Lawyers' Association; Employment Law Bar Association; British Association of Sport and the Law; Bar Sports Law Group; Industrial Law Society.
Career: Called to the Bar 1975. FCIArb 1991. Recorder 1992.

GRIFFITH-JONES, Richard
1 Fountain Court (David Crigman QC), Birmingham (0121) 236 5721
Recommended in Crime

GRIFFITHS, Alan
One Essex Court (Anthony Grabiner QC), London (0171) 583 2000
Recommended in the following lists: Administrative & Public Law, Commercial (litigation), Energy & Utilities
Specialisation: Administrative and public law (especially commercial judicial review), general commercial law (including insurance, company law, conflict of laws), utility regulation and environmental law. For Milk Marque defeating the JR challenge to the reorganisation of the UK milk industry. For Lloyd's defeating the JR challenge to Lloyd's reconstruction and renewal. For Scottish Power in the successful JR challenge to OFFER's price control decisions. For pharmaceutical, agrochemical, TV and radio, and telecommunications companies in judicial reviews of licensing and planning decisions. For EMLICO (General Electric's main insurer) in insolvency and JR actions in Bermuda. For the ABI in the Policyholders Protection Board litigation (insurance). Advises major insurance companies on the restructuring of life funds and on legal accounting issues. For the banks in the Hammersmith & Fulham interest rate swaps litigation, and in subsequent restitution cases. In the environmental field, clients include British Nuclear Fuels, National Grid, NORWEB and Powergen. For BNFL defeating the Greenpeace JR challenges to the Sellafield THORP plant.
Prof. Memberships: Administrative Law Bar Association, Commercial Bar Association (Committee).
Career: Called 1981. (Called to Bermuda Bar for EMLICO litigation).
Personal: Born 1953. Educated Jesus College, Oxford (MA, BCL). Formerly Fellow and Tutor in Law, Exeter College, Oxford.

GRIFFITHS, Courtenay QC
Two Garden Court (I. Macdonald QC & O. Davies), London (0171) 353 1633
Recommended in Crime

GRIFFITHS, Lawrence
Iscoed Chambers (Trefor Davies), Swansea (01792) 652988/9
Recommended in Personal Injury
Specialisation: High Court Personal Injury. Medical Negligence.
Prof. Memberships: Wales and Chester Circuit. Personal Injury Bar Association.
Career: Gowerton Grammar School, Christ College Cambridge (MA). Numerous appointments including Recorder of the Crown Court 1972-1993, Circuit Prosecuting Counsel to the Inland Revenue 1969-1993, Circuit Standing Counsel to HM Customs and Excise 1989-1993, Head of Iscoed Chambers 1983-1993.
Personal: Married 1959, 2 daughters 1 son. Travel by sea, wine and food, walking, snooker.

GRIFFITHS, Martin
Essex Court Chambers (Gordon Pollock QC), London (0171) 813 8000
Recommended in the following lists: Commercial (litigation), Employment
Specialisation: Appears as an advocate in Courts and tribunals including domestic arbitrations, the County Court (including Mercantile and Business Lists), the Queen's Bench Division of the High Court (including the Commercial Court), the Chancery Division of the High Court, the Court of Appeal and the Privy Council. Employment law

practice including domestic disciplinary tribunals, the Industrial Tribunal, the Employment Appeal Tribunal.
Prof. Memberships: Member of COMBAR; Member of ELBA.
Career: New College, Oxford: BA (First Class Hons with Distinction) 1984; MA 1988; City University, London: Postgraduate Diploma in Law 1985. Called to the Bar 1986.
Personal: Born 1962.

GRIFFITHS, Peter QC
30 Park Place (Philip Richards), Cardiff (01222) 398421
Recommended in Personal Injury

GRIFFITHS, Peter
4 Stone Buildings (Philip Heslop QC), London (0171) 242 5524
Recommended in the following lists: Chancery, Company, Insolvency
Specialisation: Principal area of practice is company law, focusing on insolvency and minority shareholder disputes. Other main areas of work include partnership, civil fraud, bankruptcy and professional negligence. Contributor to 'Atkins Court Forms' Vol 10 (Companies Winding Up) 1988 and 'Encyclopaedia of Forms and Precedents' 5th Ed Vol 11 (Companies) 1992.
Prof. Memberships: Chancery Bar Association, Insolvency Lawyers' Association and COMBAR..
Career: Called to the Bar in 1977 and joined present chambers in 1978.
Personal: Educated at Repton 1966-71 and St Catharine's College, Cambridge, 1972-75.

GRIFFITHS, W. Robert QC
4-5 Gray's Inn Square (Miss Elizabeth Appleby QC & The Hon. M. Beloff QC), London (0171) 404 5252
Recommended in Administrative & Public Law
Specialisation: Has an inter-disciplinary practice with an emphasis on public law. Main areas of practice are administrative and public law, planning, commercial law and employment law. Acted in numerous appellate cases for Government Departments as Junior Counsel to the Crown, inter alia Delaney v Staples and Mclaren v The Home Office (civil service contracts). Junior Counsel for the Home Office in the Strangeways Inquiry. As a leader has represented the Sultan of Brunei in the Court of Appeal and the Privy Council (Marsel v Apong 1998 1 WLR 674) and is retained by the Sabah Foundation in two appeal cases before the Court of Appeal of Malaysia.
Prof. Memberships: Administrative Law Bar Association, COMBAR, Local Government Planning and Environmental Bar Association.
Career: Called to the Bar 1974. Junior Counsel to the Crown (common law) 1989-93. Took Silk 1993. Called to the Brunei Bar 1996.
Prof. Memberships: Educated at Haverfordwest Grammar School and St Edmund Hall, Oxford. Leisure pursuits include reading, collecting modern first editions, and cricket. Born 24th September 1948.

GRIME, Mark Stephen Eastburn QC
Deans Court Chambers (H.K. Goddard QC), Manchester (0161) 834 4097
Recommended in the following lists: Medical Negligence, Personal Injury
Specialisation: Personal Injury including Disease Litigation; Insurance related litigation; Construction; Medical Negligence; Professional Negligence – other than medical; Commercial; Arbitration. Significant reported cases: Bence Graphics International v Fasson [1997] 1All ER 979; Wisniewski v Central Manchester HA [1996] 7 Med LR 248; Cruden Construction v Commission for the New Towns [1995] 2 Lloyd's Rep 387; Crocker v British Coal Corporation [1995] 29 BMLR 159; Fairhurst v St Helens & Knowsley HA [1995] PIQR Q1; Khan v Armaguard [1994] 3 All ER 545; Wood v Gahlings [1993] PIQR P76; Family Housing Association (Manchester) Ltd v Michael Hyde

[1993] 1 All ER 567; Bradley v Eagle Star Insurance Co Ltd [1989] 1 AC 957; Wilkinson v Ancliff (BLT) Ltd [1986] 3 All ER 427, [1986] 1 WLR 1352.
Prof. Memberships: Past Chairman of Northern Arbitration Association; Fellow – Chartered Institute of Arbitrators. Member – Northern Circuit Commercial Bar Association; Society for Computers and Law; United Kingdom Environmental Law Association; Professional Negligence Bar Association; Personal Injury Bar Association.
Career: Trinity College, Oxford (Scholar). Called (Middle Temple) – 1970. Queen's Counsel – 1907. Recorder – 1990. Official Referee Recorder – 1996. Fellow – Chartered Institute of Arbitrators – 1996. Bencher of Middle Temple – 1997.

GRINDROD, Helen QC
95A Chancery Lane (Helen Grindrod QC), London (0171) 404 4777
Recommended in Crime

GROSS, Peter QC
20 Essex Street (David Johnson QC), London (0171) 583 9294
Recommended in the following lists: Arbitration, Aviation, Insurance & Reinsurance, Shipping
Specialisation: Arbitration (ICC; LCIA; UNCITRAL; LMAA), aviation, banking, carriage of goods, commodities, conflict, energy, financial services, insurance and reinsurance, shipping (wet and dry).
Prof. Memberships: Deputy Chairman SFA Consumer Arbitration Scheme Panel. Member of the Board of The London Court of International Arbitration. New South Wales Bar.
Career: Cape Town and Oxford Universities; called 1977 Queen's Counsel 1992.

GROVES, Hugo
Enterprise Chambers (Anthony Mann QC), Leeds (0113) 246 0391
Recommended in Commercial (litigation), Insolvency

GRUDER, Jeffrey QC
One Essex Court (Anthony Grabiner QC), London (0171) 583 2000
Recommended in the following lists: Arbitration, Banking, Commercial (litigation), Energy & Utilities, Insurance & Reinsurance, Shipping
Specialisation: Principal areas of practice are commercial disputes, insurance and reinsurance, banking, oil and gas disputes. Other areas of practice are shipping and transport, financial services and commodity disputes. Recently appeared in Investors Compensation Scheme v West Bromwich Building Society, Vitol Energy v Pisco, Indian Grace (No 2) (1997), Chevron v Total (1996), Autocar v Motemtronic (1996), British Gas v Eastern Electricity (1996). Other important cases have included Sheldon v Outhwaite (1995), Standard Bank v Bank of Tokyo (1995), Indian Grace (1993), Euro-diam v Bathurst (1990), Miss Jay Jay (1987) and Nai Genova (1984). Has appeared frequently in arbitrations. Clients include major banks, insurance companies and corporations. Supervisor at Cambridge University 1977-79. Previously part time lecturer at Central London Polytechnic on International Trade.
Prof. Memberships: COMBAR.
Career: Called to the Bar in 1977. QC 1997. At 4 Essex Court (now Essex Court Chambers) 1978-93. Joined current chambers in 1993.
Personal: Educated at City of London School 1966-72 and Trinity Hall, Cambridge 1973-76. Born 18th September 1954. Interests include tennis, theatre, cinema and reading. Lives in Radlett.

GRUNDY, Clare
28 St. John St (Anthony Rumbelow QC), Manchester (0161) 834 8418
Recommended in Licensing

GRUNDY, Nigel
9 St. John Street (John Hand QC), Manchester
(0161) 955 9000
Recommended in Employment
Specialisation: Recent cases:- Parkinson v March
Consulting Ltd CA 1997 IRLR 519. Boys and Girls
Welfare Society v McDonald 1996 IRLR 129.
Mennell v Newell and Wright (Transport
Contractors) Ltd 1996 ICR 607. Specialising in
Employment, Discrimination and Trade Union Law.
Prof. Memberships: Employment Law Bar
Association; Professional Negligence Bar
Association. Northern Circuit Commercial Bar
Association.
Career: MA (Hons) Oxon Jurisprudence.
Personal: Golf, tennis.

GUGGENHEIM, Anna
2 Crown Office Row (Graeme Hamilton QC),
London (0171) 797 8100
Recommended in Professional Negligence
Specialisation: Specialises in insurance litigation
(particularly professional indemnity), construction,
product liability, general commercial and common
law, personal injury.
Prof. Memberships: London Common Law &
Commercial Bar Association; COMBAR; Official
Referees Bar Association.
Career: Called to the Bar 1982.
Personal: Educated at Somerville College, Oxford
(BA Jurisprudence) 1978-1981. Born 2nd
September 1959. Lives in London. Speaks French.
Interests: sailing.

GUMBITI-ZIMUTO, Andrew
6 King's Bench Walk (Sibghat Kadri QC),
London (0171) 353 4931 /583 0695
Recommended in Civil Liberties
Specialisation: Race Discrimination Law.
Prof. Memberships: Discrimination Law
Association. Employment Law Bar Association.
Career: Practises from London Chambers but
undertakes work throughout England and Wales.
Personal: Has been an active member and
supporter of organisations whose objects are to
fight against discrimination on the grounds of race,
religion, sex or sexual orientation. Practice consists
of advising and representing applicants and
respondents in all areas of Discrimnation law.

GUPTA, Usha
Furnival Chambers (Andrew Mitchell), London
(0171) 405 3232
Recommended in Crime

GUTHRIE, Mark J.
14 Tooks Court (Michael Mansfield QC), London
(0171) 405 8828
Recommended in Civil Liberties
Specialisation: Criminal defence, especially
serious violent offences, drug offences, and public
order cases, and cases involving civil liberties. Civil
actions against the police.
Prof. Memberships: Middle Temple, South
Eastern Circuit, Criminal Bar Association.
Career: Called 1984. Has made numerous media
appearances speaking on legal issues. Occasional
election observer abroad.
Personal: Born Cape Town 17/12/1960. LL.B
(Hons) Manchester University. Long history of
involvement in anti-apartheid struggle. Interests
include Third World travel

HACKER, Richard QC
3/4 South Square (Michael Crystal QC), London
(0171) 696 9900
*Recommended in the following lists: Banking,
Insolvency*

HACKETT, Philip
3 Hare Court (William Clegg QC), London
(0171) 353 7561
*Recommended in the following lists: Crime,
Crime: Fraud*
Specialisation: Practice is principally in the area of
commercial fraud and related issues such as

restraint, confiscation, money laundering and
directors disqualification. Also has experience of a
broad range of commercial work including banking
and insurance. Other areas of specialisation
include Health & Safety prosecutions and the
application of European Law to criminal, regulatory
and disciplinary matters. He has acted in relation to
a number of well known cases including Maxwell,
three BCCI trials (including Gokal), Gooda Walker,
Arrows Finance and Polly Peck.

HACON, Richard
11 South Square (Christopher Floyd QC),
London (0171) 405 1222
Recommended in Intellectual Property

HADDON-CAVE, Charles
4 Essex Court (Nigel Teare QC), London
(0171) 797 7970
Recommended in Aviation
Specialisation: Has a broad commercial practice
which includes a wide variety of cases in the
aviation field. He has been instructed in many of
the major aviation disasters of recent times
including the Knight Air crash at Dunkeswick, the
Thai Air crash at Kathmandu, the British Midland
crash at Kegworth and the British Airtours disaster
at Manchester. He appears regularly as an
advocate in the High Court in London and Hong
Kong.
Prof. Memberships: Member of the Executive
Committee of COMBAR, the Personal Injury Bar
Association, the Hong Kong Bar and the Royal
Aeronautical Society Air Law Committee.

HAIG-HADDOW, Alastair
Eighteen Carlton Crescent (Alastair Haig
Haddow), Southampton (01703) 639001
Recommended in Family/Matrimonial

HAJIMITSIS, Anthony
10 Park Square (A. Campbell QC), Leeds
(0113) 245 5438
Recommended in Family/Matrimonial
Specialisation: Matrimonial Finance, Public Law
Children Cases.
Prof. Memberships: FLBA.
Career: Leeds Grammar School; Oxford
University; Inner Temple (1984 Call).
Personal: Married.

HALL, Andrew
Doughty Street Chambers (Geoffrey Robertson
QC), London (0171) 404 1313
Recommended in Crime
Specialisation: Practice predominantly serious
crime, including leading work. Substantial
experience of homicide and other serious violence,
firearms, explosives, and large drug conspiracies.
Growing fraud practice including VAT, mortgage
and insolvent trading cases. Has regularly written,
lectured and broadcast on a wide range of issues
within the criminal justice sphere.
Prof. Memberships: Criminal Bar Association, Bar
Overseas Advocacy Committee.
Career: Educated at Marist College, University of
Birmingham (LL.B 1974), University of Sheffield
(MA [Criminology] 1976). Admitted as solicitor
1980. Partner and head of criminal law department,
Hodge Jones & Allen London before transfer to the
Bar in 1991. Director of Legal Action Group,
Member of Editorial Board of International Journal
of Evidence and Proof.

HALL, Joanna
14 Gray's Inn Square (Joanna Dodson QC),
London (0171) 242 0858
*Recommended in the following lists: Family:
Child Care including child abduction*

HALPERN, David
Enterprise Chambers (Anthony Mann QC),
London (0171) 405 9471
*Recommended in the following lists: Professional
Negligence, Property Litigation*
Specialisation: Property litigation and advisory

work and professional negligence (especially in
relation to solicitors).
Career: Educated at St Paul's School; won an
Open Exhibition to Magdalen College, Oxford,
where he read law. Has practised at the Chancery
Bar as a member of Enterprise Chambers since
1979. Practises in all areas of commercial
Chancery work but with an emphasis on property
litigation and professional negligence. Has an
interest in human rights in the countries of the
former Soviet Union.

HAM, Robert QC
Wilberforce Chambers (Edward Nugee QC),
London (0171) 306 0102
*Recommended in the following lists: Pensions,
Traditional Chancery*
Specialisation: Practice largely in the fields of
trusts and tax law, industry occupational pension
schemes, but extends to other areas of property
law.
Prof. Memberships: Association of Pension
Lawyers. Chancery Bar Association, Revenue Bar
Association, Society of Trust and Estate
Practioners, Wales and Chester Circuit.
Career: BA & BCL (Oxon); Called to the Bar 1973;
QC 1994.

HAMBLEN, Nicholas QC
20 Essex Street (David Johnson QC), London
(0171) 583 9294
Recommended in Shipping
Specialisation: Principal areas of practice are
shipping, international sale of goods, commodities,
insurance and re-insurance, conflicts of laws and
arbitration. Acts as arbitrator in maritime, insurance
and international commercial arbitrations. LAS and
ACI arbitrator.
Career: Called to the Bar 1981. Took Silk 1997.
Personal: Educated at St. John's College, Oxford
(MA) and Harvard Law School (LL.M). Born 1957.

HAMER, George
8 New Square (Michael Fysh QC), London
(0171) 405 4321
Recommended in Intellectual Property
Specialisation: Specialises in all aspects of
intellectual property and media law, including
patents, copyright, passing off, trade marks,
service marks and confidential information.
Important cases include: (patents) Catnic
Components v. Hill & Smith; SKM v. Wagner
Hsiung's Patent; (trade marks/passing off) Rolls
Royce v. Dodd; Neutrogena v. Golden; (copyright)
Baroness Thatcher v. Assoc. Newspapers and v.
Mirror Group; Sillitoe v. McGraw Hill; (registered
designs) Goodyear (tyre treads); Amper S.A;
(other) Estate of Bob Marley (PC). Has also given
expert evidence in cases in Israel (LEGO) and for
proceedings in the United States (Apple
Computer).
Career: Called to the Bar 1974.
Personal: Educated at Sedbergh School 1962-
1968 and Imperial College, London (BSc
chemistry; A.R.C.S.) 1968-1971. Semi-fluent in
German and a good knowledge of French and
Spanish. Leisure pursuits include tennis, golf,
skiing and gardening. Born 26th February 1949.

HAMILL, Hugh
12 King's Bench Walk (Ronald J. Walker QC),
London (0171) 583 0811
Recommended in Personal Injury
Specialisation: Personal injury; employers' liabilty
and public liability claims; employment law –
professional negligence, consumer credit/credit
hire.
Prof. Memberships: PIDA. London and Common
Law Bar Association. Personal Injury Bar
Association.
Career: BA Hons (Dublin). Dip. law (City
University). Called to Bar 1988.

HAMILTON, Adrian QC
7 King's Bench Walk (Stephen Tomlinson QC), London (0171) 583 0404

Recommended in the following lists: Commercial (litigation), Insurance & Reinsurance, Shipping
Specialisation: Specialises in commercial and arbitration work, including insurance (marine and non-marine), shipping, private international law, banking and professional negligence.
Career: Called to the Bar and joined current chambers in 1949. Took Silk in 1973. Appointed Recorder 1974 and Deputy High Court Judge 1982.

HAMILTON, Eben W. QC
1 New Square (Eben Hamilton QC), London (0171) 405 0884

Recommended in the following lists: Chancery, Company, Insolvency
Specialisation: Specialises in company and corporate finance, commercial chancery and insolvency.
Career: Called to the Bar, 1962. QC 1981. Bencher, Inner Temple 1985. DTI Inspector, Atlantic Computers plc 1990-1994, Deputy High Court Judge, Chancery division since 1991. Admitted regularly to appear in courts of Hong Kong and Singapore in company and insolvency matters.

HAMILTON, Eleanor W.
6 Park Square (Shaun M. Spencer QC), Leeds (0113) 245 9763

Recommended in Family/Matrimonial
Specialisation: Substantial Asset Matrimonial Finance. Public Law. Child cases particularly with medical or ethical issues. Education Law.
Prof. Memberships: Inner Temple, FLBA.
Career: Assistant Recorder of North Eastern Circuit.
Personal: Married, 4 daughters.

HAMILTON, Peter
4 Pump Court (Bruce Mauleverer QC), London (0171) 353 2656

Recommended in the following lists: Financial Services
Specialisation: Principal area of practice is financial services work, covering all contentious and non-contentious aspects of life assurance, including selling practices, administration of policies, claims, agency, regulatory and disciplinary aspects relating to insurance companies; also interpretation and application of the Insurance Companies Act 1982 and regulations. Author of 'Life Assurance Law and Practice' (1995 FT, Law and Tax).
Prof. Memberships: Life Assurance Legal Society, Professional Negligence Bar Association, Bar Association for Commerce, Finance and Industry, Official Referees Bar Association.
Career: Called to the Bar 1968. Tenant at 2 Dr. Johnson's Buildings, 1968-77. Company Secretary and head of legal department, Allied Dunbar Assurance plc (formerly Hambro Life Assurance) 1977-1991. Member, Lautro Disciplinary Panel, 1990-95. Joined present chambers 1991.
Personal: Educated at Rhodes University (South Africa) 1960-62, (BA) and Cambridge University 1963-65 (MA). Born 20th April 1941.

HAMLIN, Patrick
22 Old Buildings (Benet Hytner QC), London (0171) 831 0222

Recommended in Administrative & Public Law
Specialisation: Principal area of practice is local government law, particularly in the fields of public health/environmental protection matters, licensing, planning and listed buildings and judicial review. Cases include Orchard Leigh Properties (fixtures and fittings in listed buildings), The Time Life Building and Eaves v. Mendip B.C. (Glastonbury Festival licensing), National Provincial Building Society v Lloyd. Also handles professional negligence and general commercial work. Wide range of local authority clients.
Prof. Memberships: Administrative Law Bar

Association.
Career: Called to the Bar 1970. Appointed Recorder 1994.
Personal: Educated at Birkenhead School and Inns of Court School of Law (McCaskie Scholarship). Assistant Parliamentary Boundary Commissioner. Leisure pursuits include skiing, listed buildings and English furniture. Born 4th August 1947. Lives in London.

HAND, John QC
Old Square Chambers (Hon. John Melville Williams QC), London (0171) 269 0300

Recommended in the following lists: Employment, Environmental Law, Health & Safety
Specialisation: Is experienced in most areas of common law litigation (including appearing at and conducting inquiries), concentrates on employment law, personal injury litigation and environmental law and is familiar with EC law principles. In employment law recent cases have included RMT v London Underground (CA), Brown v Rentokil (HL), NUT v Others v St Mary's C of E School (CA) and Church v W. Lancs NHS Trust. In Environmental Law has represented the defence in R v Coalite and R v Associated Octel (No 2) and the plaintiff in Clifton v Powergen, as well as appearing in environment related health and safety cases.
Prof. Memberships: Employment Law Association, Employment Law Bar Association, Personal Injury Bar Association, Association of Personal Injury Lawyers, Professional Negligence Bar Association, UKELA, Bar European Group, Society for Computer and Law.
Career: Called 1972 Bencher 1996 (Gray's Inn); Queen's Counsel (1988); Recorder 1991.

HAPGOOD, Mark QC
Brick Court Chambers (Christopher Clarke QC), London (0171) 583 0777

Recommended in the following lists: Banking, Commercial (litigation), Company, Professional Negligence
Specialisation: Litigation, advisory and drafting work in the whole field of commercial law, including agency; banking; commodities and futures; insurance; international trade, jurisdictional disputes; mortgages; reservation of title; sale of goods; security interests. Cases of note: NRG v Bacon & Woodrow, BBL v Eagle Star, ESSO v Milton, Derby v Welldon, Seaconsar v Bank Markazi.
Career: Member of Gray's Inn. Called to the Bar in February 1979; Appointed to Silk in April 1994.
Personal: Editor of 'Paget's Law of Banking' 11th Ed. 1996. Sole Contributor to 'Halsbury's Law of England', Title 'Banking'. Joint Contributor to 'Halsbury's Law of England', Title 'Bills of Exchange'. Contributor of two Chapters in 'Using set-off as Security' (IBA 1990). The following leading textbooks contain an acknowledgement of assistance received from Mark Hapgood: 'Mustill & Boyd on Commercial Arbitration'; 'Wood on English and International Set-Off'.

HARDING, Cherry
Gray's Inn Chambers (Brian Jubb), London (0171) 404 1111

Recommended in the following lists: Family: Child Care including child abduction
Specialisation: Family: children, abduction, adoption, private/public law. Matrimonial, all aspects, education.
Prof. Memberships: Family Law Bar Association, Bar European Group, Justice, Legal Action Group, Inter Country Adoption Association, Association of Lawyers for Children
Career: LLB (Hons) Kings College, London. Called to the Bar 1978, Gray's Inn. Married, three children.

HARDING, Richard
Keating Chambers (Richard Fernyhough QC), London (0171) 544 2600

Recommended in the following lists: Construction

Specialisation: Construction; engineering, Middle East arbitration.
Career: Qualified 1992; Middle Temple.
Personal: Latymer Upper School; Pembroke College, Oxford; University of Alexandria, Egypt (1990 MA Oriental Studies (Arabic, Persian), 1991 Common Professional Examination). Born 1967; resides London. Cricket, rugby, travel. Languages: Arabic, French, German, Persian, Spanish.

HARDY, John
3 Raymond Buildings (Clive Nicholls QC), London (0171) 831 3833

Recommended in Environmental Law
Specialisation: Environmental crime. Defended in largest ever meat fraud prosecuted by a local authority. Experienced in cases under The Food Safety Act 1990, Environmental Protection Act 1990 etc. Has prosecuted and defended in a large variety of 'environmental crime'.
Prof. Memberships: Criminal Bar Association.
Career: Called 1988.
Personal: BA (hons) Magdalen Oxford.

HARGREAVES, Sara
12 New Square (John Mowbray QC), London (0171) 419 1212

Recommended in Parliamentary
Specialisation: General chancery with litigation bias. Recent cases include Inverugie v Hackett; Long v London Borough of Tower Hamlets. Parliamentary: 1997 conducted Barnsley M.B.C. (Oakwell Regeneration Area) CPO 1994 through SPP for promoter.
Prof. Memberships: Chancery Bar Association.
Career: LLB (Hons) King's College, London University. Called 1979.

HARGREAVES, Simon
Keating Chambers (Richard Fernyhough QC), London (0171) 544 2600

Recommended in Construction
Specialisation: All aspects of litigation and arbitration concerning general construction, engineering, power and utilities contracts. Related negligence and professional negligence claims. ICC Arbitrations. Cases include: DMD v Toyo.
Prof. Memberships: Inner Temple; Official Referees' Bar Association; COMBAR.
Career: Called to Bar, October 1991 (and called to the Bar of Gibraltar, May 1997). Member of editorial team of Construction Law Yearbook. Case reporter for Construction Law Journal.
Personal: Shrewsbury School (scholar), Worcester College, Oxford (1989 BA Law 2(1)). Born 1968. Resides London.

HARMAN, Sarah
4 Stone Buildings (Philip Heslop QC), London (0171) 242 5524

Recommended in Company
Specialisation: Specialises in company and commercial litigation and advice, bankruptcy and insolvency, directors disqualification. Recent reported cases include: Re Farmizer (Products) Ltd [1995] BCC 926 (wrongful trading), re Sutton Glass Ltd [1996] BCC 174 (directors disqualification), BRDC v. Hextall Erskine & Co.[1996] 3 All ER 667 (solicitors' negligence), Re Dawes & Henderson (Agencies) Ltd [1997] 1 BCLC 329, Re Leeds United [1996] 2 BCLC 545, SOS v. Laing & Ors [1996] 2 BCLC 326.
Prof. Memberships: Member of the Chancery Bar Association, Insolvency Lawyers Association and COMBAR, Member of Bar Council 1989-95, Chairman Young Barristers' Committee 1992.
Career: Called to Bar 1987.
Personal: Educated at Wycombe Abbey School and Trinity College, Oxford.

HARRINGTON, Patrick QC
30 Park Place (Philip Richards), Cardiff (01222) 398421

Recommended in Crime

HARRIS, David QC
India Buildings Chambers (David Harris QC), Liverpool 0151 243 6000
Recommended in Family/Matrimonial
Specialisation: All civil, in particular professional negligence, personal injury (including injuries of the utmost severity such as cerebral palsy caused by obstetric mismanagement and traumatic brain and spinal damage cases), commercial and construction disputes; family, including children work (especially abuse cases) and financial disputes; serious crime (especially fraud, sexual offences and murder); administrative and public law.
Prof. Memberships: Committee member – Family Law Bar Association.
Career: Called 1969. QC 1989.

HARRIS, Russell
1 Serjeants' Inn (Lionel Read QC), London (0171) 583 1355
Recommended in the following lists: Environmental Law, Planning
Specialisation: Public Law aspects of Environmental law including Public Inquiry advocacy, Judicial Review, Injunctions, Integrated Pollution Control, Town and Country Planning and Environmental Crime.
Prof. Memberships: Committee member of PEBA, member of UKELA, IPC working party.
Personal: Co-author of Environmental Law and Practice O.U.P.(in progress).

HARRISON, Christopher
4 Stone Buildings (Philip Heslop QC), London (0171) 242 5524
Recommended in the following lists: Chancery, Company
Specialisation: Company and Commercial Litigation, Insolvency, Financial Servies, Regulatory Work, Professional Negligence.
Career: Called to the Bar 1988.
Personal: Trinity Hall, Cambridge.

HARRISON, Keith
24A St. John Street (Paul Chambers), Manchester (0161) 833 9628
Recommended in Crime
Specialisation: Serious crime especially sexual offences, homicide, fraud and police actions.
Prof. Memberships: Lincoln's Inn.

HARRISON, Michael QC
Park Court Chambers (James Stewart QC, Robert Smith QC), Leeds (0113) 243 3277
Recommended in Crime
Specialisation: Commercial fraud; crime (general). Family (children); professional negligence. In RE A (A minor) (abduction) (1997) (CA). In RE W (minors) (disclosure) (1998) (CA). In RE 8 (minor) (adoption; immigration) (1998) (CA).
Prof. Memberships: CLBA. FLBA.
Career: LLB. Gray's Inn (1969); QC 1987.

HARRISON, Peter
6 Pump Court (Stephen Hockman QC), London (0171) 797 8400
Recommended in Planning
Specialisation: Most aspects of planning and local government law. Public inquiry, court and advisory work. In particular deals with planning and environmental matters – appeared for London Borough of Camden at its UDP inquiry, regulatory offence prosecution and defence work including ancient monuments, hackney carriage and private hire law.
Prof. Memberships: Planning and Environment Bar Association, Criminal Bar Association, South Eastern Circuit (Committee member).
Career: Called to the Bar 1987.
Personal: Educated at St John's College, Durham University 1983-86. Born 1965. Lives in Islington, London.

HARRISON, Stephanie
Two Garden Court (I. Macdonald QC & O. Davies), London (0171) 353 1633
Recommended in the following lists: Administrative & Public Law, Immigration & Nationality
Specialisation: Practising in all fields of public and adminstrative law with a specialisation in immigration and asylum law. Expertise in European Community law. Also has experience in discrimination law in all courts and tribunals. Work with other lawyers in the field of sexual orientation discrimination was recognised in 1997 with the Stonewall Equality Award. Has experience in European human rights cases and civil actions against the police and public authorities primarily arising from immigration related detention.
Prof. Memberships: Immigration Law Practitioners Association.
Career: Called to the Bar in Nov 1991. Important recent cases include R .v. MOD ex parte Smith and Others, CA and ECHR, R v SSHD ex parte Danie, CA, R v SSHD ex parte Obi, QBD, R v SSHD exparte Salem, CA. Islam v SSHD CA and HL.

HARROD, Henry
5 Stone Buildings (Henry Harrod), London (0171) 242 6201
Recommended in Traditional Chancery
Specialisation: Specialises in all areas of Chancery work.
Prof. Memberships: Chancery Bar Association; Society of Trust and Estate Practitioners. Association of Contentious Trust and Probate Specialists.
Career: Called to the Bar 1963. Tenant at 46 Grainger Street, Newcastle-upon-Tyne 1964-1968 before joining 4 Paper Buildings in 1968. Member of present chambers since 1969 and head since 1990. Conveyancing Counsel of the Court 1991. Bencher of Lincoln's Inn 1991. Appointed Recorder 1993.

HARRY, Timothy
9 Old Square (Robert Reid QC), London (0171) 405 4682
Recommended in Property Litigation
Specialisation: Property litigation, professional negligence and Chancery work.
Prof. Memberships: PNBA
Career: Called 1983. Lecturer, Hertford College, Oxford, 1983-1988. An Editor, Hill & Redman's 'Landlord & Tenant'. Called to the Bar, Hong Kong 1982.
Personal: Educated Monmouth School; MA, BCL (Oxford).

HART, David
1 Crown Office Row (Robert Seabrook QC), London (0171) 797 7500
Recommended in the following lists: Arbitration, Environmental Law
Specialisation: Has conducted a wide range of environmental litigation, including water (Cambridge Water & Bowden on enforceability of EC Directives), particulate emissions (Coalite and Orimulsion), methane (Loscoe) and claims against consultants arising out of land decontamination surveys and assessment of methane risks. Is also frequently instructed in professional negligence cases, (particularly medical, surveyors and engineers) contract claims, and arbitrations (construction, engineering and general contract), as well as flood and fire claims.
Prof. Memberships: Member of UKELA and ALBA.
Career: Called 1982.

HART, William
Albion Chambers (J.C.T. Barton QC), Bristol (0117) 927 2144
Recommended in Crime

HARTLEY, Richard QC
1 Brick Court (Richard Hartley QC), London (0171) 353 8845
Recommended in Defamation

HARVEY, Colin T.
St. Paul's Chambers (Nigel Sangster QC), Leeds (0113) 245 5866
Recommended in Crime

HARVEY, Michael QC
2 Crown Office Row (Graeme Hamilton QC), London (0171) 797 8100
Recommended in Professional Negligence
Specialisation: Predominantly civil and commercial matters, including but not limited to: commercial and contractual disputes, professional negligence, international arbitration, construction and engineering contracts, insurance and reinsurance law, conflict of laws, sale of goods, carriage of goods, agency, product liability. Sits as arbitrator.
Prof. Memberships: Legal Services Committee of Bar Council 1994-; COMBAR; LCCLBA; ORBA.
Career: Called 1966. QC 1982. Recorder 1986. Authorised to sit as a Deputy High Court Judge and Deputy Official Referee. Bencher Gray's Inn 1991. Review Board, Council of Legal Education 1993-94; Speaker at Conferences; Joint author of title 'Damages' in Halsbury's Laws of England.
Personal: Born 22 May 1943. Educated at St. John's School, Leatherhead and Christ's College, Cambridge. Married with two children.

HARWOOD, Richard
1 Serjeants' Inn (Lionel Read QC), London (0171) 583 1355
Recommended in Planning
Specialisation: Specialist in planning, environmental, Parliamentary and public affairs and administrative law. Major cases include William Cook (reasons), Tesco Stores v North Norfolk (implementation of planning permission), Searle (enabling development). Public inquiries include Manchester Airport second runway, M40 MSA, retail, UDP, highways and commons. Acted on Channel Tunnel Rail Link Bill and drafted amendments to various Public Bills. Author: Planning Enforcement. Contributor: Archaeology in Law, the Planning Factbook.
Prof. Memberships: Planning and Environment Bar Association.
Career: Jesus College, Cambridge MA (1st Class) and LLM. Called to the Bar 1993.
Personal: Born 1970. London Borough Councillor.

HARWOOD-STEVENSON, John
9-12 Bell Yard (D. Anthony Evans QC), London (0171) 400 1800
Recommended in Crime

HAVELOCK-ALLAN, Mark QC
20 Essex Street (David Johnson QC), London (0171) 583 9294
Recommended in Shipping
Specialisation: Shipping (shipbuilding contracts, charterparty disputes and all aspects of carriage of goods by sea), insurance, international sale of goods, banking and arbitration law. Has appeared as counsel in arbitrations under the rules of the ICC, LMAA, GAFTA, FOSFA, Refined Sugar Association etc. Has also acted as arbitrator in arbitrations under the rules of the LCIA, LMAA and Lloyd's Arbitration Scheme.
Prof. Memberships: Fellow of the Chartered Institute of Arbitrators, COMBAR, London Maritime Arbitrators' Association (Supporting Member and Chairman, Supporting Members' Liaison Committee 1991-1996).
Career: Called to the Bar July 1974. Joined present chambers (then 3 Essex Court) August 1975. Queen's Counsel 1993. Bencher of Inner Temple 1995. Recorder 1997.
Personal: Born 4th April 1951. Educated at Eton College 1963-1968, Durham University 1969-1971 (BA), Trinity College, Cambridge 1972-74 (LLB). Lives in Central London.

HAVERS, Philip QC
1 Crown Office Row (Robert Seabrook QC),
London (0171) 797 7500
*Recommended in the following lists: Administrative
& Public Law, Environmental Law, Medical
Negligence*

HAVEY, Peter
4-5 Gray's Inn Square (Miss Elizabeth Appleby
QC & The Hon. M. Beloff QC), London
(0171) 404 5252
Recommended in Banking

HAWKESWORTH, Gareth
Fenners Chambers (Lindsay Davies),
Cambridge (01223) 368761
Recommended in Crime
Specialisation: Fraud, sexual offences, serious
crime.
Prof. Memberships: Criminal Bar Association.
Career: Rugby School. Open classical scholar
Magdalene College Cambridge. Called to Bar
1972. Recorder.

HAYES, Josephine
3 New Square (Lord Goodhart QC), London
(0171) 405 5577
*Recommended in the following lists: Pensions,
Traditional Chancery*
Specialisation: Pension schemes; property
litigation. Particular experience in fraud, breach of
fiduciary duty and asset recovery. Recent reported
cases include: Penn v Bristol & West BS; Hambros
Bank v BHBT; Miller v Stapleton; Miller v Scorey;
Seifert v Pensions Ombudsman; Lloyds Bank v
Carrick.
Prof. Memberships: Chancery Bar Association;
Association of Women Barristers (Chairwoman
1996-8; Vice President 1998-).
Career: MA (Oxon). Called 1980. Alumni Fellow,
Yale Law School; LLM (Yale).

HAYNES, Peter
St Philip's Chambers (Rex Tedd QC),
Birmingham (0121) 246 7000
Recommended in Crime
Specialisation: Principally a crown court advocate
dealing with frauds, sexual and drug trafficking
offences, practice includes all aspects of criminal
law including the prosecution and defence of
proceedings brought by Local Authorities and
other public bodies.

HAYWARD SMITH, Rodger QC
One King's Bench Walk (James Townend QC),
London (0171) 936 1500
*Recommended in the following lists: Family:
Child Care including child abduction, Family:
Matrimonial Finance*
Specialisation: Specialises in family law and
criminal law. Editor of 'Jackson's Matrimonial
Finance and Taxation' (5th and 6th edns) and
Practitioners Child Law Bulletin.
Prof. Memberships: South Eastern Circuit, Family
Law Bar Association, Criminal Bar Association.
Career: Called to the Bar in 1967 and joined 1
King's Bench Walk in 1968. Appointed Recorder in
1986. Took Silk 1988.
Personal: Educated at Brentwood School and St.
Edmund Hall, Oxford.

HEALY, Siobán
7 King's Bench Walk (Stephen Tomlinson QC),
London (0171) 583 0404
Recommended in Shipping
Specialisation: General commercial and contract
(including sale of goods), insurance and
reinsurance; shipping, international trade and
commodities. Professional negligence; banking;
conflicts of law; commercial arbitration.
Career: Call 1993, Inner Temple. Formerly Solicitor
at Richards Butler, admitted 1990. BA Hons
(Oxon); LL.M Northwestern, Chicago.
Personal: Born 6 August 1965. Education:
Brasenose College, Oxford; Northwestern
University, Chicago. Member: Combar, BILA,

LMMA supporting member. Director, Bar Mutual
Indemnity Fund Limited.

HEATON, David
18 St. John Street (Rodney C. Klevan QC),
Manchester (0161) 278 1800
*Recommended in the following lists: Medical
Negligence, Personal Injury*
Specialisation: Medical Negligence. Personal
Injury.
Prof. Memberships: PIBA, PNBA.
Career: Educated at William Hulme's Grammar
School, Manchester and Corpus Christi College,
Cambridge.
Personal: Enjoys walking, reading, music, good
food and wine. Married, 3 children.

HEILBRON, Hilary QC
Brick Court Chambers (Christopher Clarke QC),
London (0171) 583 0777
*Recommended in the following lists: Alternative
Dispute Resolution, Commercial (litigation)*
Specialisation: General commercial law, including
financial services, corporate law, insurance,
banking, conflict of laws, shipping, international
trade and commerce, arbitration, sale of goods;
administrative law and some common law
including professional negligence and defamation
law. Department of Trade & Industry Inspector into
Blue Arrow Plc. 1989 – 91.
Prof. Memberships: Chairman of the London
Common law and Commercial Bar Association
(1991-93); Chairman of the independent working
party into Civil Justice; Director of The City
Disputes Panel Limited; Member of the Bar Council
(1991-); Member of the Commercial Court
Committee; Member of the Marshall Aid
Commemoration Commission (March 1996-).
Member of the Advisory Council of CEDR 1996,
Member of Civil Justice Council (1998-).
Career: Called to the Bar 1971; Silk 1987; Member
of the Bar of NSW, Australia (1 May 1996). Bencher
of Gray's Inn (July 1995). Senior Counsel Bar of
NSW, Australia Nov. 1997. Deputy High Court
Judge.
Personal: MA (Oxon).

HENDERSON, Launcelot QC
5 Stone Buildings (Henry Harrod), London
(0171) 242 6201
*Recommended in the following lists: Tax, Traditional
Chancery*
Specialisation: General chancery work, mainly
concentrating on trusts, tax and private client work,
pensions, charities, Court of Protection, and all
aspects of Revenue Law (apart from VAT). Recent
reported cases: Deeny v Gooda Walker (taxation of
damages); IRC v Willoughby and McGuckian v IRC
(tax avoidance); Bricom Holdings v IRC (controlled
foreign companies); Steele v European Vinyls and
Memec Plc v IRC (double tax treaties); LM
Tenancies 1 Plc v IRC (stamp duty and the
contingency principle); National Westminster Bank
v IRC (date of issue of shares for BES relief);
Harries v Church Commissioners (ethical
investment of church funds); R v IRC, ex parte
Roux Waterside Inn Ltd (withdrawal of Revenue
approval from pension scheme); and numerous
other cases appearing for the Inland Revenue.
Prof. Memberships: Chancery Bar Association;
Revenue Bar Association; Hong Kong Bar
Association (1998).
Career: Called 1977; Standing Junior Counsel to
the Inland Revenue (chancery) 1987-1991;
standing Junior Counsel to the Inland Revenue
1991-5. Took Silk in 1995.
Personal: Born 1951. Educated at Westminster
School and Balliol College, Oxford. Fellow of All
Souls College, Oxford, 1974-81 and 1982-89.
Married with 3 young children.

HENDERSON, Roger QC
2 Harcourt Buildings (Roger Henderson QC),
London (0171) 583 9020
*Recommended in the following lists: Financial
Services, Parliamentary, Personal Injury*
Specialisation: Specialises in common law and
public law. Work covers professional negligence,
product liability, contract, personal injuries, judicial
review, local government, parliamentary and
finance, especially local government finance and
public transport. Cases handled include R v Sec of
State for Environment ex.p. Brent, and re
Westminster City Council. Counsel for British Rail in
Clapham Inquiry,counsel to Kings Cross Enquiry.
Has acted for British Rail, Railtrack, GMC, British
Telecom and London Regional Transport, Stock
Exchange and many local authorities. Promoted
numerous Parliamentary Bills. Involved in three
Lloyds' names' actions.
Prof. Memberships: Bencher of Inner Temple
1985. Member of St Kitts & Nevis Bar.
Career: Called to the bar in 1964. Joined 2
Harcourt Buildings in 1966. Took silk in 1980.
Recorder from 1983, Deputy High Court Judge
from 1987. Chairman of Civil Service Arbitration
Tribunal 1994.
Personal: Educated at Radley College 1956-61.
First Class Honours in Law at St. Catharine's
College Cambridge. Positions held include
Chairman Council of Governors of London Hospital
Medical College, former president of British
Academy of Forensic Sciences. Leisure pursuits
include fly fishing, gardening, shooting and travel.
Born 21st April 1943.

HENDERSON, Sophie
Plowden Buildings (William Lowe QC), London
(0171) 583 0808
Recommended in Immigration & Nationality

HENDERSON, William
Serle Court Chambers (Charles Sparrow QC),
London (0171) 242 6105
Recommended in Charities
Specialisation: Charity, Trust and Land Law. Re
Basham (1986) 1WLR 1498; Boscawen v Bajwa
(1996) 1 WLR 328; Fennell v Stewart (1996) 1 WLR
288; Re Segelman Deed (1996) Ch 171; Gaudiya
Mission v Brahmachary (1998) 2 WLR 175.
Prof. Memberships: Chancery Bar Association.
ACTAPs.
Career: 1968-72 St Paul's School London; 1973-77
Trinity College Cambridge – BA in Natural Sciences
(Pt I) and Law (Pt I).
Personal: Married with 3 children. Enjoys sailing.

HENDY, John QC
Old Square Chambers (Hon. John Melville
Williams QC), London (0171) 269 0300
*Recommended in the following
lists: Employment, Health & Safety, Personal Injury*
Specialisation: Primarily trade union and industrial
relations cases. Has appeared in most of the
leading cases over the last 15 years. Also deals
with employment law more generally. Extensive
practice also in P.I. and medical negligence.
Standing counsel to NUM, NUJ and POA; co-
author of: 'Redgrave's Health and Safety',
'Munkman's Employer's Liability' and 'Personal
Injury Practice'. Member of Editorial Board of
Encyclopaedia of Employment Law; Journal of
Personal Injury Litigation; The Litigator.
Prof. Memberships: ILS, ELA, ELBA (Exec Cttee
1998-), APIL, PIBA, ATLA, CLBA, ABA, SE. Circuit,
W. Circuit, Chair Institute of Employment Rights
1989-.
Career: Called 1972 Gray's; Director Newham
Rights Centre 1973-76; practice 1977-; silk 1987;
Bencher of Grays Inn 1995.
Personal: LLB London (external); LLM (Queens,
Belfast).

HENKE, Ruth
Iscoed Chambers (Trefor Davies), Swansea
(01792) 652988/9
Recommended in Family/Matrimonial
Specialisation: Family law – particularly child law.
Recent reported cases include G+R (1995) FLR
(proof of risk of harm under S31); Re H (1995) FLR
(disclosure of adoption files).
Prof. Memberships: FLBA.
Career: Worcester College, Oxford. Tenant Iscoed
Chambers. Substantial family law practice
emphasis on child care work.

HENRIQUES, Richard QC
Deans Court Chambers (H.K. Goddard QC),
Manchester (0161) 834 4097
Recommended in Crime
Specialisation: Serious crime.
Prof. Memberships: Leader Northern Circuit,
Bencher Inner Temple, Criminal Bar Association.
Career: Bradfield College, Worcester College
Oxford. Recorder of Crown Court Since 1984.

HENRY, Annette
10 King's Bench Walk (Ronald Thwaites QC),
London (0171) 353 2501
Recommended in Crime
Specialisation: Mental Health Law. Author of the
Mental Health Law Referencer [Sweet & Maxwell].
Mental Health Act Commissioner. Press reported
cases within last 12 months: Stokes (large scale
DSS fraud) and Nolan & Hurford (professional
blackmail racket of prostitute and Rampton officials
exposed by undercover reporters).
Career: Merchant Taylors 9 O'Levels, 4 A Levels,
University of Manchester II LLB Hons in Law. Inns
of Court School of Law.

HERBERG, Javan
Blackstone Chambers (formerly 2 Hare Court)
(P Baxendale QC and C Flint QC), London
(0171) 583 1770
*Recommended in the following lists: Administrative
& Public Law, Financial Services*
Specialisation: Specialist in public and
administrative law, with an emphasis on judicial
review, and financial services law. Practice also
covers regulatory/disciplinary tribunals and general
commercial law. Interesting cases include R v
Higher Education Funding Council ex parte
Institute of Dental Surgery [1994] 1WLR 242 (right
to reasons); R v BCC ex parte BBC [1995] 7 Admin
LR 575 (right to complain to Broadcasting
Complaints Commission); British Steel v Customs
& Excise [1997] 2 All ER 366 (restitution of
overpaid duties; public/private law); Shocked v
Goldschmidt [1998] 1 All ER 372 (C.A., judgment
in default after trial). Ming Pao Newspapers v A-G
of Hong Kong [1996] AC 907, PC (Freedom of
Expression); Tan Te Lam v A-G of Hong Kong
[1997] AC 97, PC (Legality of Detention). Has
conducted regulatory proceedings for SIB and
IMRO (including Morgan Grenfell/Peter Young Unit
Trusts affair). Publications include Constitutional
and Administrative Law (Cavandish, 1995, co-
author); de Smith Woolf and Jowell, Judicial
Review of Administrative Action (assistant editor,
5th ed. supplement, 1998); case notes in Public
Law and in Judicial Review.
Prof. Memberships: Administrative Law Bar Assn,
COMBAR.
Career: Called 1992.
Personal: Educated at University College School,
University College London (LL.B), and Merton
College, Oxford (BCL).

HERBERT, Mark QC
5 Stone Buildings (Henry Harrod), London
(0171) 242 6201
*Recommended in the following lists: Charities,
Pensions, Tax, Traditional Chancery*
Specialisation: Principal area of practice is
general chancery work, including trusts, capital
taxation, taxation of trusts, probate, family
provision, charities and off-shore trusts. Also
handles pensions work, both advisory and

litigation. Important cases include Mettoy Pension
Trustees v Evans [1990]; Re Christy Hunt Pension
Fund [1991]; Fitzwilliam v IRC [1993]. Hamar v
Pensions Ombudsman, R v Opra ex parte
Littlewoods (1997). Co-Editor of 'Whiteman on
Capital Gains Tax'. Other publications include 'The
Drafting and Variation of Wills'.
Prof. Memberships: Chancery Bar Association;
Revenue Bar Association; Association of Pension
Lawyers.
Career: Called to the Bar 1974. Tenant at 17 Old
Buildings 1975-1977 before joining Queen
Elizabeth Building in 1977. At present chambers
since 1991. Took Silk 1995.
Personal: Educated at Lancing College 1962-1966
and King's College, London 1967-1970. Born 12th
November 1948. Lives in London

HERMAN, Raymond C.
India Buildings Chambers (David Harris QC),
Liverpool 0151 243 6000
Recommended in Crime
Specialisation: Deals with substantial criminal
cases for both the defence and prosecution in the
court at all levels. This includes the most serious
offences, such as murder/manslaughter, rape,
serious fraud, drugs offences, robbery and crimes
of violence.
Prof. Memberships: Criminal Bar Association.
Career: Called 1972.

HERSHMAN, David
St Philip's Chambers (Rex Tedd QC),
Birmingham (0121) 246 7000
*Recommended in the following lists: Family/
Matrimonial, Family: Child Care including child
abduction*
Specialisation: Family Law. Particular expertise in
the law relating to children, international child
abduction and adoption. Also criminal cases
concerning child abuse and Registered Homes
Tribunal work.
Prof. Memberships: Family Law Bar Association,
The British Agencies for Adoption and Fostering,
the Intercountry Adoption Lawyers' Association and
the Association of Lawyers for Children. Public and
administrative law concerning children.
Career: Called to the Bar in 1981. Appointed part-
time Chairman of the Registered Homes Tribunal in
1995. Co-Author of Children: Law and Practice,
contributor to Family Court Practice and Child
Protection Training and Resource Pack (National
Childrens Bureau). Member of Sweet and Maxwell
Research Paper Editorial Board. Lecturer for the
Law Society Children Panel and accredited course
provider for the Law Society. Lecturer for Judicial
Conferences and Justices Family Panel Training.
Personal: Educated at The Kings School
Worcester, Kings College London. Married with
four daughters. Lives near Worcester.

HESLOP, Martin S QC
1 Hare Court (Stephen Kramer QC), London
(0171) 353 5324
*Recommended in the following lists: Crime,
Licensing*
Specialisation: Serious crime (both prosecution
and defence), commercial fraud, gaming, licensing
generally, health & safety, food & drugs.
Career: Called 1972 (Lincoln's Inn), Junior
Treasury Counsel 1987, First Junior Treasury
Counsel 1991, Senior Treasury Counsel 1992,
Queens Counsel 1995 – Recorder of the Crown
Court.
Personal: Sailing, travel, photography, wine and
good food.

HESLOP, Philip QC
4 Stone Buildings (Philip Heslop QC), London
(0171) 242 5524
*Recommended in the following lists: Chancery,
Company, Financial Services, Insolvency*
Specialisation: Principal areas of practice are
company and financial services law, regulatory,
corporate insolvency and corporate banking.
Prof. Memberships: Commercial Bar Association

(COMBAR), Chancery Bar Association and
Insolvency Lawyer's Association.
Career: Called to the Bar 1970 and joined present
chambers in 1972. Joint Junior Counsel (Chancery)
DTI 1980-85. Took Silk in 1985. Deputy Chairman,
IMRO Membership Tribunal since 1988. Joint DTI
Inspector, Consolidated Goldfields Plc 1988.
Bencher Lincoln's Inn, 1993. Called to the Hong
Kong, Bermuda and Gibraltar Bars for specific
cases.
Personal: Educated at Haileybury 1961-66 and
Christ's College, Cambridge 1967-71 (B.A. Hons
1970, LL.M 1971). President, Cambridge Union
Society 1971. Born 24 April 1948.

HEYWOOD, Michael
3 New Square (Lord Goodhart QC), London
(0171) 405 5577
Recommended in Agriculture & Bloodstock
Specialisation: General Chancery and
Commercial Practice. Principal areas of practice
are property law and professional negligence. Has
a particular interest in and experience of
agricultural and rural matters, including
bloodstock.
Prof. Memberships: Chancery Bar Association;
Professional Negligence Bar Association.
Career: B.Sc (Lond) 1973; Called 1975; Member
N.E. circuit.
Personal: Lives in Yorkshire and London; member
NFU, CLA and NSA.

HIBBERT, William
Gough Square Chambers (Frederick Philpott),
London (0171) 353 0924
Recommended in Consumer Law
Specialisation: Consumer Law – in particular
consumer credit licensing (particulary Minded to
Revoke Notices), advising on credit and loan
agreements, defending regulatory prosecutions,
and acting in civil litigation. Clients include finance
houses, product manufacturers, food producers
and multiple retailers. Other main areas of practice
include corporate, commercial, insolvency and
fraud matters.
Prof. Memberships: Food Law Group and London
Common and Commercial Bar Association.
Career: Called to the Bar 1979.
Personal: Charterhouse and Worcester College,
Oxford. Lives in London.

HICKS, Michael
19 Old Buildings (Alastair Wilson QC), London
(0171) 405 2001
Recommended in Intellectual Property
Specialisation: All aspects of intellectual property
including patents, designs, copyrights, trade marks
and confidential information. Commercial cases
with a scientific or technical subject matter
including computers and electronics. EC cases
with an intellectual property content.
Prof. Memberships: Inner Temple, Intellectual
Property Bar Association. Chancery Bar
Association.
Career: Called to the Bar in November 1976.
Joined present chambers in 1979.
Personal: Educated at Brighton College school
and Trinity College, Cambridge (BA Natural
Sciences). Races dinghies and small keel boats.

HICKS, William QC
1 Serjeants' Inn (Lionel Read QC), London
(0171) 583 1355
*Recommended in the following lists: Administrative
& Public Law, Energy & Utilities, Parliamentary,
Planning*
Specialisation: Planning, Environment,
Administrative & Public Law, Parliamentary,
Highways and Transportation, Energy.
Prof. Memberships: Planning and Environmental
Bar Association, Parliamentary Bar Mess,
Administrative Law Bar Association.
Career: Magdalene College Cambridge MA
(Economics). Called to the Bar 1975. Joined
present chambers in 1976. Took silk in 1995.

HIGGS, Brian QC
5 Paper Buildings (Brian Higgs QC), London
(0171) 353 5638
Recommended in Crime
Specialisation: Deals with murder, serious organised crime, armed robbery, rape, offences against the State (e.g. official secrets), terrorism, computer crime.
Career: Called to the Bar in 1955. Took silk in 1974. Operates on all Crown Prosecution Circuits in the South East. Is briefed regularly in all Level 1 Crown Courts. Appears in trials, pleas, Court of Appeal and House of Lords, European Court of Human Rights. Queen's Counsel. Acting only with a junior except in exceptional cases. Recorder.

HIGHAM, John QC
3/4 South Square (Michael Crystal QC), London
(0171) 696 9900
Recommended in the following lists: Banking, Financial Services, Insolvency
Specialisation: Called 1976, silk 1992. Broad commercial practice with particular interests in financial services, banking and professional negligence, as well as insolvency. Has acted in virtually all the major corporate insolvencies of the last ten years. Joint editor of 'The Law and Practice of Corporate Administrations'. Assistant Recorder.
Prof. Memberships: Member of Chancery Bar Association. Former Executive Committee Member of COMBAR. Former Chairman of Combar North American Liaison Committee.

HIGHAM, Paul
1 Pump Court (Jane Hoyal and Robert Latham), London (0171) 583 2012
Recommended in Civil Liberties

HIGSON SMITH, Gillian
Gray's Inn Chambers (Brian Jubb), London
(0171) 404 1111
Recommended in the following lists: Family: Child Care including child abduction

HILDYARD, Marianna
4 Brick Court (David Medhurst), London
(0171) 797 8910
Recommended in the following lists: Family: Child Care including child abduction

HILDYARD, Robert QC
4 Stone Buildings (Philip Heslop QC), London
(0171) 242 5524
Recommended in the following lists: Chancery, Company, Energy & Utilities, Financial Services, Insurance & Reinsurance
Specialisation: Principally, company law, financial services, company/commercial litigation and corporate insolvency. Specialist in insurance company transfer schemes. Other specialist work areas include insurance/reinsurance litigation and oil and gas litigation. Recent court cases include Macmillan v BIT (Maxwell litigation/conflicts of laws), NRG Victory (insurance company transfer scheme), LDDC v Regalian (restitution), Kurz v Stella Musical (choice of jurisdiction clause), Phillips Petroleum v Enron (take or pay gas sales agreement) and Charter Re ('pay to be paid' reinsurance clause). Contributor: Butterworth's Encyclopaedia of Forms and Precedents (company volume); Tolley's Company Law.
Prof. Memberships: Chancery Bar Association, Insolvency Lawyers' Association, Commercial Bar Association (COMBAR).
Career: Called to the Bar in 1977, Junior Counsel to the Crown (Chancery) 1992-94, appointed Queen's Counsel 1994.
Personal: Educated at Eton College; Christ Church Oxford. Languages: Spanish.

HILL, Mark
Pump Court Chambers (Guy Boney QC), London (0171) 353 0711
Recommended in Ecclesiastical
Specialisation: Personal injury, professional and medical negligence and ecclesiastical law. Leading cases include NEM v Jones [1990] 1 AC 24 (HL); Pacific Associates v Baxter [1990] 1 QB 993 (CA); Tribe v Tribe [1996] Ch 107 (CA); Re St Peter's Oundle [1997] 4 Ecc LJ 163.
Prof. Memberships: Professional Negligence Bar Association; Personal Injury Bar Association; Western Circuit Wine Committee; Ecclesiastical Law Society; General Synod's Legal Aid Commision.
Career: Deputy Chancellor of the Diocese of Winchester [since 1994]; Case Notes Editor, Ecclesiastical Law Journal [since 1996]; Visiting Fellow, Emmanuel College, Cambridge [1998]. Publications include 'Ecclesiastical Law' (Butterworths, 1995) and 'English Canon Law' (University of Wales Press, 1998). Has lectured on various subjects including church law and religious human rights at Oxford University, Inns of Court School of Law, Cardiff Law School and Columbus Law School, Washington DC.

HILL, Max
18 Red Lion Court (Anthony Arlidge QC), London (0171) 520 6000
Recommended in Crime

HILL, Michael QC
23 Essex Street (Michael Lawson QC), London
(0171) 413 0353
Recommended in the following lists: Crime, Crime: Fraud
Specialisation: Principal area of practices are commercial fraud, international crime, homicide and professional crime.
Prof. Memberships: Criminal Bar Association (Chairman 1982-1986); Society for the Reform of Criminal Law; Board of Directors 1988 – date, Management Committee 1992 – 1995; Inns of Court Advocacy Training Committee (chairman, 1994 – date).
Career: Treasury Counsel (Inner London Sessions/Crown Court) from 1969 to 1974; Treasury counsel (Central Criminal Court) from 1974 to 1979; Queen's Counsel 1979; Queen's Counsel (N.S.W.) 1991; Recorder 1977 – 1997; called, Gray's Inn, 1958; Bencher, Gray's Inn, 1986; Director, Bar Mutual Indemnity Fund Ltd (Chairman, Investment Committee – 1992 – date).

HILL, Richard. G
4 Stone Buildings (Philip Heslop QC), London
(0171) 242 5524
Recommended in Company
Specialisation: Company and commercial litigation; corporate insolvency litigation and advice, financial services, banking. Leading recent cases: Dawnay Day & Co Ltd v. D'Alphen & Ors [1997] IRLR 442, Ispahani v. Bank Melli Iran (The Times) 29 December 1997.
Prof. Memberships: Chancery Bar Association, COMBAR.
Career: 1993 call. Educated at Gonville & Caius College, Cambridge (BA Hons – 1st Class).

HILL, Thomas
4-5 Gray's Inn Square (Miss Elizabeth Appleby QC & The Hon. M. Beloff QC), London
(0171) 404 5252
Recommended in the following lists: Environmental Law, Parliamentary, Planning
Specialisation: Principal area of practice is planning and environmental law, in particular public inquiry work involving detailed investigation of environmental and other impacts. Recent instructions have involved proposals for major retail, housing and business development, works to listed buildings, minerals, waste and airport-related development (including successfully promoting Manchester Airport's Second Runway). Also judicial review and advisory work involving the interpretation and application of the Town and Country Planning Act 1990, the Environmental Protection Act 1990 and subordinate legislation; prosecutions under EPA. Has also appeared in Parliament for promoters of private legislation with environmental implications.
Prof. Memberships: Planning and Environmental Bar Association (Committee Member 1990-95); Administrative Law Bar Association.
Career: Called to the Bar 1988.

HILLIARD, Lexa
3/4 South Square (Michael Crystal QC), London
(0171) 696 9900
Recommended in Insolvency

HILLIARD, Nicholas
6 King's Bench Walk (Michael Worsley QC), London (0171) 583 0410
Recommended in Crime
Specialisation: Criminal Law
Career: Treasury Counsel at the Central Criminal Court. Contributing editor to Archbold and editor of the Criminal Appeal Reports.

HILLIER, Andrew
5 Bell Yard (Robert Webb QC), London
(0171) 333 8811
Recommended in Employment
Specialisation: Principal area of practice is employment law including employer/employee disputes (wrongful/unfair dismissal); protection of confidential information, non-solicitation of customers, board-room disputes, partnership disputes, strikes and collective disputes, trade union law and race and sex discrimination. Particular emphasis on local government and health service law, including employment and public law issues. Other main areas of work are mental health law, including psychiatric damage and medical negligence cases and disciplinary tribunals.

HILLIER, Nicolas
9 Gough Square (Jeremy Roberts Q.C), London
(0171) 353 5371
Recommended in Personal Injury

HIMSWORTH, Emma
One Essex Court (Anthony Grabiner QC), London (0171) 583 2000
Recommended in Intellectual Property
Specialisation: All aspects of Intellectual Property Law.
Prof. Memberships: The Intellectual Property Lawyers Organisation, The Intellectual Property Bar, Chancery and Commercial Bar Associations.
Career: Called 1993.
Personal: BSc in Biological Sciences with Honours in Biochemistry, Dip Law (City), Dip EC Law (Kings).

HINCHLIFF, Benjamin
1 Brick Court (Richard Hartley QC), London
(0171) 353 8845
Recommended in Defamation
Specialisation: Defamation, contempt of court, reporting restrictions and media-related law generally.
Career: Called to the Bar 1992.
Personal: Educated Radley College and St John's College Oxford. Lives in London and Yorkshire.

HINCHLIFFE, Nicholas
9 St. John Street (John Hand QC), Manchester
(0161) 955 9000
Recommended in the following lists: Employment, Personal Injury
Specialisation: Personal injury, industrial disease, catastrophe injury claims, medical negligence.
Prof. Memberships: PIBA. PNBA.
Career: LLB. Manchester, Middle Temple 1980.
Personal: Championship rifle shooting.

HINKS, Frank
Serle Court Chambers (Charles Sparrow QC QC), London (0171) 242 6105
Recommended in the following lists: Partnership, Traditional Chancery
Specialisation: Domestic and International trusts including taxation: Re Ojjeh Trusts [1993] (Cayman Islands) Re Hampstead Trusts [1995] (Cayman Islands). Real property including landlord and

tenant and commons: Reed v Madon [1989] (rights of burial); Westminster C.C. v Duke of Westminster [1991] (landlord and tenant) Mid-Glamorgan C.C. v Ogwr B.C. [1995] (commons). Dugan – Chapman v Grosvenor Estate Belgravia [1997] (leasehold enfranchisement), National Trust v. Ashbrook [1997] (commons). Chancery and commercial litigation: Finers v Miro [1991] (Constructive trusts). Professional negligence and regulation. Partnership Law: Kerr v Morris [1987]. Charities.
Prof. Memberships: Chancery Bar Association.
Career: Called to Bar in 1973. Joined present chamber in 1974.
Personal: Educated at Bromley Grammar School 1961-1967; St Catherine's College,Oxford 1968-1972. BA 1st Class Hons; B.C.L. 1st Class Hons.

HIRST, Jonathan QC
Brick Court Chambers (Christopher Clarke QC), London (0171) 583 0777
Recommended in the following lists: Commercial (litigation), Insurance & Reinsurance, Media & Entertainment, Shipping
Specialisation: General Commercial Law including Shipping, banking, insurance, re-insurance, sale of goods, professional negligence and defamation. Recent Important Cases: Ernst & Young v Butte Mining (1996) 2 All E.R. 623; Credit Lyonnais v ECGD (1996) 1 Lloyd's 200; Apple v EMI (C.A.); Berriman v Rose Thompson Young. Acting for auditors in Maxwell affair. Mother Bertha Music Ltd. v Bourne Music (acting for Phil Spector).
Prof. Memberships: Member of the General Council of the Bar 1985-; Chairman Law Reform Committee 1992-94; Chairman Professional Standard Committee 1995-; Queens Counsel 1990.
Career: Call to Bar July 1975, Inner Temple. Pupillages with John Phillips, Nicholas Phillips (now Lord Justice Phillips). Started practicing July 1976: Brick Court Chambers. Bencher, Inner Temple 1994.
Personal: Born 2 July 1953, London. Educated at Eton College and Trinity College, Cambridge (M.A. Law).

HITCHCOCK, Richard G.
35 Essex Street (Nigel Inglis-Jones QC), London (0171) 353 6381
Recommended in Pensions
Specialisation: Principal area of practice is pensions, encompassing both UK and international pension schemes and advice on contentious and non-contentious matters relating thereto. In particular specialises in professional negligence and employment law aspects of pension disputes.
Prof. Memberships: Chancery Bar Association, Association of Penisons Lawyers. Regular speaker at legal conferences.
Career: Called to the Bar 1989.
Personal: Educated at King Edwards School, Birmingham (1977-1984) and Magdalen College, Oxford (1985-1988).

HITCHMOUGH, Andrew
Pump Court Tax Chambers (Andrew Thornhill QC), London (0171) 414 8080
Recommended in Tax
Specialisation: Practices in all areas of revenue law, both advisory and litigation.
Prof. Memberships: Revenue Bar Association; VAT Practitioners Group. Publications: Co-editor of Potter Monroe's Tax Planning. Ray's Practical Inheritance Tax Planning.

HOBBS, Geoffrey QC
One Essex Court (Anthony Grabiner QC), London (0171) 583 2000
Recommended in Intellectual Property

HOBSON, John
4-5 Gray's Inn Square (Miss Elizabeth Appleby QC & The Hon. M. Beloff QC), London (0171) 404 5252
Recommended in the following lists: Administrative & Public Law, Environmental Law, Planning
Specialisation: Public law, local government, planning and environmental law. Member of the Supplementary Panel of Treasury Counsel Standing Counsel to the Rent Assessment Panel. Extensive experience of planning and administrative law cases in the High Court. Such cases include Tesco Stores Ltd v Secretary of State (House of Lords) on planning gain, and R v Leeds Development Corporation ex p Kirkstall Valley Campaign on bias. Environmental law cases include judicial review proceedings relating to the Environmental Protection Act, the Environmental Information Regulations 1992 and EC Directives in relation to Environmental Assessment, Birds and Habitats. Public inquiry work includes Stansted and Heathrow (T5) inquiries, compulsory purchase orders, and development plans including promoting mineral and waste subject plans and several UDP's.
Prof. Memberships: Admininstrative Law Bar Association; Planning and Environmental Bar Association.
Career: Former Solicitor, Called to Bar 1980. Specialist Adviser to the Northern Ireland Affairs Committee of the House of Commons for its enquiry into the planning system in Northern Ireland.
Personal: LLM (St John's College, Cambridge).

HOCHBERG, Daniel
9 Old Square (Robert Reid QC), London (0171) 405 4682
Recommended in Chancery
Specialisation: "Commercial Chancery" and a wide range of general chancery litigation including offshore trust litigation, real property, business agreements, professional negligence, succession, securities and loans, insolvency and landlord and tenant. Cases include West v Lazards (Jersey breach of trust), Blampied v Ram (Jersey trust application), Midland Bank v Federated Pension Fund (breach of trust and exemption clauses), Co-Operative v Tesco (restrictive covenants), Hammersmith & Fulham v Tops Shop Centre (relief from forfeiture), Wates v Citygate Properties (section 25 notice).
Prof. Memberships: Chancery Bar Association; Association of Contentious Trust and Probate Specialists.

HOCHHAUSER, Andrew QC
Essex Court Chambers (Gordon Pollock QC), London (0171) 813 8000
Recommended in the following lists: Commercial (litigation), Company, Employment
Specialisation: Areas of practice include arbitration, banking, breach of contract, company law, commercial fraud, entertainment cases, employment, partnership disputes, professional negligence, takeovers, mergers and share sale disputes.
Prof. Memberships: Fellow of the Chartered Institute of Arbitrators; Member of Gibraltan Bar.
Career: University of Bristol (LLB), University of London (LLM). Called to the English Bar 1977. Harmsworth Scholar of Middle Temple. Queen's Counsel 1997.
Personal: Born 1955.

HOCKADAY, Annie
3 Verulam Buildings (R. Neville Thomas QC), London (0171) 831 8441
Recommended in Banking
Specialisation: Commercial work, particularly banking, civil claims arising out of fraud, company, corporate and personal insolvency, guarantees, mortgages and other securities.
Career: Tutor in company law at Cambridge University 1988-89, and in banking law at London

University 1989-90. Called to the Bar 1990. Tenant at 3 Verulam Buildings (formerly 3 Gray's Inn Place) 1991 to date.
Personal: MA from Trinity Hall Cambridge 1988, LLM in Commercial Law from London University 1989. Born 12 November 1966.

HOCKMAN, Stephen QC
6 Pump Court (Stephen Hockman QC), London (0171) 797 8400
Recommended in Planning
Specialisation: Principal area of practice is local government, planning and administrative law.
Prof. Memberships: Planning and Environment Bar Association, Administrative Law Bar Association.
Career: Called to the Bar in 1970 and joined Pump Court in 1971. Appointed Recorder 1987. Took Silk 1990. Elected to Bar Council 1995.
Personal: Educated at Eltham College, London (1955-65) and Jesus College, Cambridge (1966-69). Born 4th January 1947. Lives in London and Peterborough.

HODGE, David QC
9 Old Square (Robert Reid QC), London (0171) 405 4682
Recommended in the following lists: Professional Negligence, Property Litigation
Specialisation: Principal areas of practice are general Chancery and Property Litigation and related professional negligence, particularly solicitors, barristers and valuers. Important cases include Graham v Philcox [1984] (Easements); TCB v Gray [1986-8] (guarantees); Sharma v Knight [1986] (landlord and tenant); Bank of Baroda v Shah [1988] (undue influence); Sen v Headley [1991] (equity), HIT Finance v Lewis & Tucker [1993] (professional negligence); Mortgage Corporation v Nationwide Credit [1994] (registered land); Ridehalgh v Horsefield [1994] (wasted costs); Allied Maples v Simmons & Simmons [1995] (Professional negligence) and Garston v Scottish Widows [1996] (Landlord & Tenant). Contributed chapter on Chancery Matters to the 4th Edition of 'The Law and Practice of Compromise' by David Foskett QC.
Prof. Memberships: Chancery Bar Association. Professional Negligence Bar Association.
Career: Called to bar in 1979. Joined 9 Old Square in 1980. QC 1997.
Personal: Born 1956. Educated at University College, Oxford 1974-8 (BA, BCL). Author of 'Secret Trusts: The Fraud Theory Revisited'(1980) Conveyancer. Chairman, Lincoln's Inn Bar Representation Committee 1997-8.

HODGSON, Margaret
St. Ive's Chambers (Edward Coke), Birmingham (0121) 236 0863 (6 lines)
Recommended in Family/Matrimonial
Specialisation: Private matrimonial: residence/contact; financial ancillary relief; adoption. Public family law: child care; freeing; adoption. Representation of parents, local authorities and guardians ad litem. Cases: G and others (minors) and R (A minor) ex parte, R v Birmingham Juvenile Court [1989] CA 2 FLR 454. Re P (Minors) (Breakdown of Adoption Placement) F.D. (1996) 3 FCR 657.
Prof. Memberships: Family Law Bar Association.
Career: Warwick University LL.B. (Hons). Deputy Head of Chambers.

HOFMEYR, Stephen
7 King's Bench Walk (Stephen Tomlinson QC), London (0171) 583 0404
Recommended in the following lists: Insurance & Reinsurance, Shipping
Specialisation: Practice encompasses insurance and reinsurance (both marine and non-marine) and international trade and shipping. Most recent cases include Brown v KMR (Lloyd's litigation); Royal Boskalis v Mountain and Manifest Shipping & Co Ltd v Uni-Polaris Insurance Co Ltd ('Starsea') (both marine insurance). Other specialisations

include banking and professional malpractice (especially accountant's negligence).
Prof. Memberships: COMBAR.
Career: Called to the Bar 1982. Attorney and Conveyancer of the Supreme Court of South Africa 1982-85. Joined current chambers 1987. Also Advocate of the Supreme Court of South Africa.
Personal: Educated at Diocesan College, Rondebosch, Cape Town, University of Cape Town (B. Com 1974-76; LL.B 1977-79) and University College, Oxford (MA, Jurisprudence, 1979-81). Leisure pursuits include walking, birdwatching, tennis and skiing. Born 10th February 1956. Lives in Walton on Thames.

HOGARTH, Andrew
12 King's Bench Walk (Ronald J. Walker QC), London (0171) 583 0811
Recommended in Employment
Specialisation: All aspects of employment and trade union law. Has had particular experience of wrongful dismissal claims, Transfer of Undertakings cases, sex discrimination claims and employment disputes connected with insolvent companies and their receivers.
Career: MA (Cantab). Called to the Bar 1974. Joined 12 King's Bench Walk in 1975.

HOGGETT, John QC
40 King St (Philip Raynor QC), Manchester (0161) 832 9082
Recommended in Planning
Specialisation: Town Planning, Compulsory Purchase, Highways, Environment Law & Judicial Review.
Prof. Memberships: Northern Circuit; Planning & Environment Bar Association.
Career: Called 1969, Queen's Counsel 1986, Recorder of the Crown Court.

HOLDER, Simon M.
India Buildings Chambers (David Harris QC), Liverpool 0151 243 6000
Recommended in Personal Injury
Specialisation: Personal injury litigation, procedure, employers liabilities cases and professional negligence actions, especially medical negligence. Recent reported case: Bannister v SGB Plc and others [1997] 4AER 129.
Prof. Memberships: The Personal Injury Bar Association. Professional Negligence Bar Association. A.P.I.L.

HOLGATE, David QC
4 Breams Buildings (Christopher Lockhart-Mummery QC), London (0171) 430 1221/353 5835
Recommended in the following lists: Administrative & Public Law, Agriculture & Bloodstock, Environmental Law, Planning
Specialisation: Judicial review, planning, compulsory purchase, rating local government and environment law. Reported cases covering a wide field include Bushell v Secretary of State, Shimizu v Westminster City Council, R v Secretary of State for Social Services ex p. AMA, R v Somerset C.C. ex p. Fewings, IJT Securities v Secretary of State and Chesterfield Properties v Secretary of State, and, in the Lands Tribunal, Glasshouse Properties v DTp and Fennessy v London City Airport. Has appeared for government bodies, local authorities, developers and local objectors in a broad range of public inquiries including Sizewell B, Canvey Island, Piper Alpha, and Point of Ayr Gas Terminal.
Career: Called to Bar in 1978. Formerly a member of the panel of Junior Counsel to the Crown (1986-97) and Junior Counsel to the Inland Revenue in Rating and Valuation matters (1990-7). Queen's Counsel (1997).
Personal: Graduated in Law from Exeter College, Oxford.

HOLLAND, Katharine
9 Old Square (Robert Reid QC), London (0171) 405 4682
Recommended in Property Litigation
Specialisation: All aspects of property litigation, including commercial and residential property disputes, surveyors' and solicitors' professional negligence, mortgages, landlord and tenant, conveyancing, easements, restrictive covenants, property rights, insolvency and commercial contracts.
Prof. Memberships: Chancery Bar Association and Professional Negligence Bar Association.
Career: Called to the Bar in 1989 and joined 9 Old Square in 1990.
Personal: Educated at Lady Manners School, Bakewell and Hertford College, Oxford (BA, BCL).

HOLLANDER, Charles
Brick Court Chambers (Christopher Clarke QC), London (0171) 583 0777
Recommended in the following lists: Commercial (litigation), Media & Entertainment, Sports Law
Specialisation: Commercial practice in High Court, Arbitrations and Regulatory Tribunals. Banking; insurance and reinsurance; shipping and international carriage and sale of goods; oil and gas; financial services law; professional negligence; other contractual disputes. Defamation, entertainment and sport law. Cases involving law of discovery and documents. Some appointments as Arbitrator. Recent Cases: NRG v Bacon & Woodrow; Sarrio v Kuwait Investment Office. Acted for Katrina Krabbe in IAAF tribunal and also for Sandra Gasser. Acted for Ron Baker (Director of Barings) in SFA hearing.
Career: Called to the Bar 1978. Regular lecturing on the law of documents, discovery evidence.
Personal: Born 1 December 1955. Married, 2 children. Educated University College School, Hampstead, London and King's College Cambridge. M.A.; First Class Hons. in Classics. Publications: Style & Hollander 'Documentary Evidence'. Treasurer of Bar Sports Law Association.

HOLLINGTON, Robin
1 New Square (Eben Hamilton QC), London (0171) 405 0884
Recommended in the following lists: Company, Insolvency
Specialisation: Principal areas of work are Company Law and Insolvency. Author of 'Minority Shareholders' Rights' (Sweet & Maxwell, 2nd Ed. 1994).
Prof. Memberships: Chancery Bar Association.
Career: Called to the Bar 1979 and joined 1 New Square 1981.
Personal: Educated at Oxford University 1974-77 (MA) and University of Pennsylvania 1977-78 (LL.M). Born 30th June 1955.

HOLMES, Jonathan Maurice
Plowden Buildings (William Lowe QC), London (0171) 583 0808
Recommended in Personal Injury
Specialisation: Principal areas of practice are personal injury/industrial disease litigation and company directors disqualification. Group action experience in acting for both plaintiffs and defendants: VWF, NCB action; PPA; RSI action. Asbestos NE Shipyards, Metro Cammell and Craven Tasker actions.
Prof. Memberships: ACI ARB; Northern Chancery Bar Association; Official Referees Bar Association; Society of Practitioners of Insolvency.
Career: Called 1985.

HOLROYDE, Tim QC
Exchange Chambers (William Waldron QC), Liverpool (0151) 236 7747
Recommended in Crime
Specialisation: Crime. Personal injuries.
Prof. Memberships: Criminal Bar Association. Personal Injuries Bar Association.
Career: Called 1977. QC 1996. Recorder 1997. Educated Bristol GS; Wadham College, Oxford.

HOLWILL, Derek
4 Paper Buildings (Harvey McGregor QC), London (0171) 353 3366
Recommended in the following lists: Medical Negligence, Professional Negligence
Specialisation: Principal area of practice is professional negligence including medical negligence cases. Acts primarily for defendant insurance companies, Solicitors Indemnity Fund and Health Authorities, but also some work for plaintiffs. Also handles commercial litigation and general common law work, including personal injury cases. Reported cases include Landall v Dennis Faulkner and Alsop; Saddington v Colleys Professional Services.
Prof. Memberships: Professional Negligence Bar Association
Career: Called to the Bar 1982 and joined present chambers 1983.
Personal: Leisure pursuits include Lindy Hop, scuba diving and travel. Born on 25th September 1959. Lives in London.

HONE, Richard QC
One Paper Buildings (John Slater QC), London (0171) 583 7355
Recommended in Medical Negligence
Specialisation: Medical negligence, solicitors and professional negligence, insurance litigation: Stovin v Wise H.L. (1996 3 WLR 388); Dhak v N. American Ins (1996 1 WLR 936); Dobson v N. Tyneside HA (1996 33 BMLR 146); Jones v Liverpool HA (1995 30 BMLR 1); Robinson v Salford HA (1992 3 MLR 270), Parrish v ICI (1991).
Personal: LCLFBA, PNBA, PIBA.
Career: St Paul's School (Scholar), Univ. College Oxford (MA), Recorder Crown Court 1991-, Master of the Bench Middle Temple 1994. QC 1997.

HOPKINS, Adrian
3 Serjeants' Inn (Philip Naughton QC), London (0171) 353 5537
Recommended in Medical Negligence
Specialisation: Deals with all aspects of medical law, including medical negligence, professional ethics and discipline. Recent cases include Re F (A mental patient – sterilisation); Re C (refusal of medical treatment), Re G and Re S (PVS cases) and Ratcliffe v Plymouth & Torbay Health Authority (res ipsa). Also handles matters relating to coroners courts.
Prof. Memberships: Western Circuit, Professional Negligence Bar Association.
Career: Called to the Bar and joined 3 Serjeants' Inn in 1984. Appointed to supplementary panel of Treasury Counsel, Common Law, in 1995.
Personal: Educated at Warwick School and St. Peter's College, Oxford. Leisure interests include travel. Born 16th May 1961. Lives in London.

HOPKINS, Stephen
30 Park Place (Philip Richards), Cardiff (01222) 398421
Recommended in Crime

HORLOCK, Timothy QC
9 St. John Street (John Hand QC), Manchester (0161) 955 9000
Recommended in Personal Injury
Specialisation: Personal Injury, Industrial Disease, Medical Negligence.
Prof. Memberships: PIBA, PNBA, APIL.
Career: Called 1981, Silk 1997. Manchester Grammar School and St John's College, Cambridge. Assistant Recorder 1997.
Personal: Football, tennis, cricket. 3 sons.

HORNE, Michael
3 Serjeants' Inn (Philip Naughton QC), London (0171) 353 5537
Recommended in Medical Negligence
Specialisation: Medical and dental negligence (plaintiff and defendant), medical and dental disciplinary hearings, coroners' inquests.
Prof. Memberships: Professional Negligence Bar Association.

Career: Royal Grammar School, Newcastle-upon-Tyne (1977-87), Trinity Hall, Cambridge (1988-1991), Called to the Bar October 1992 (Gray's Inn).
Personal: Leisure interests: rugby, football, skiing and walking. Born: 24th November 1969.

HORNE, Roger
11 New Square (Peter Crampin QC), London (0171) 831 0081
Recommended in Traditional Chancery
Email: roger@number7.demon.co.uk
Internet: http://www.number7.demon.co.uk/
Specialisation: Trusts, tax, pensions, conveyancing, mines and minerals.
Career: Has for a number of years been a member of the Bar Council's IT Committee and of other Committees dealing with IT, the law and the Courts. His web site which contains a commentary on the Trusts of Land and Appointment of Trustees Act 1996 and indexes to recent House of Lords' cases, has been widely praised.

HOROWITZ, Michael QC
1 Mitre Court Buildings (Bruce Blair QC), London (0171) 797 7070
Recommended in the following lists: Family: Child Care including child abduction, Family: Matrimonial Finance
Specialisation: Family law, including ancillary relief, childcare and child abduction. Contributing Editor Rayden & Jackson on Divorce 17th edition.
Prof. Memberships: Professional Conduct Committee, Director Bar Mutual Indemnity Fund Ltd.

HORROCKS, Peter
One Garden Court Family Law Chambers (Miss Eleanor F. Platt QC & Miss Alison Ball QC), London (0171) 797 7900
Recommended in Family: Child Care including child abduction
Specialisation: Principal area of practice is child law, both public and private, including disputes as to residence and contact, care proceedings, wardship, adoption and abduction cases under the Hague and European Conventions. Frequently advises and represents local authorities and guardians-ad-litem as well as private clients. Other areas of work include child-related criminal cases, probate, boundaries and easements.
Prof. Memberships: Family Law Bar Association.
Career: Called to the Bar in 1977; joined present chambers in 1996.
Personal: Educated at Winchester 1968-72, Trinity Hall, Cambridge 1973-76 and College of Law 1976-77. Leisure pursuits include real tennis, cricket and opera. Born 31st January 1955. Lives in London.

HORTON, Mark
St. John's Chambers (Roderick Denyer QC), Bristol (0117) 921 3456
Recommended in Crime

HORWELL, Richard E.
Queen Elizabeth Building (David Jeffreys QC & Peter Whiteman QC), London (0171) 583 5766
Recommended in the following lists: Crime, Crime: Fraud
Specialisation: General Crime. Counsel for the Serious Fraud Office in Lloyds and Guinness. Defended in MTM. Much of this year spent in prosecuting an IRA case.
Career: Senior Treasury Counsel.
Personal: Works Porsche driver in last year's Panama Alaska Rally.

HOSER, Philip
Serle Court Chambers (Charles Sparrow QC QC), London (0171) 242 6105
Recommended in the following lists: Chancery, Company, Insolvency
Specialisation: Company Law: Re Bermuda Cablevision Ltd [1998] BCLC 1 (P.C) and ongoing petition in Bermuda. Re Duckwari (Nos. 1 & 2) [1995] BCC 89 (CA); [1997] 1WLR 48 (H.Ct); The

Times 18/5/98 (CA) (to be reported). Insolvency: Re Richbell Strategic Holdings Ltd. [1997] 2BCLC 429. Guarantees: Kova Establishment v Sasco Investments, The Times 1998.
Prof. Memberships: Chancery Bar Association. Insolvency Lawyers' Association.
Career: M.A. (Cantab), Called 1982. Joined Serle Court Chambers 1997.

HOSKINS, Mark
Brick Court Chambers (Christopher Clarke QC), London (0171) 583 0777
Recommended in European Union/Competition
Specialisation: Principal area of practice is European law. Cases before EC Courts include Case T – 595/93 and Case C-321/95P Stichling Greenpeace v Council [1995] ECR II-2205 and [1998] ECR I-### (environmental law/standing); Case T-228/95 Lehrfreund v Council and Commission [1996] ECR II-III (interim relief); Case C 265/95 Commission v France judgment of 9.12.97 (free movement of goods): Case C-3/97 R v Goodwin and Unstead, judgment of 28.5.98 (VAT). Cases before domestic courts include Oakdale v Nat West [1997]ECC 130 (competition law/banking); R v Comptroller of Patents, Designs and Trade Marks, ex parte Lenzig [1997] Eulr 237 (TRIPs); R v Department of the Environment, ex parte Watson, judgment of 21.7.98 (CA) (regulation of genetically modified organisms). Publications include 'Remedies in EC Law' (2nd ed, Sweet & Maxwell).
Career: Called to Bar 1991. Legal Secretary to Judge David Edward, European Court of Justice of the European Communities, Luxembourg, 1994-95. Member of the Common Law Supplementary Panel to the Crown (for the EC law matters), 1997-.

HOWARD, Charles
New Court Chambers (George Carman QC), London (0171) 831 9500
Recommended in the following lists: Family: Child Care including child abduction, Family: Matrimonial Finance
Specialisation: Family Law . Not only conventional areas but also related matters including Inheritance Act and Probate disputes, constructive trust issues, family-oriented judicial review and solicitor's negligence in relation to family work. Also handles a considerable amount of personal injury litigation, medical negligence cases, judicial review and actions against the police. Senior member of well-organised and expanding family practice group.
Prof. Memberships: FLBA
Career: Called to the Bar in 1975. In full-time practice since 1976.
Personal: Education: St. John's College, Cambridge 1969-72 and St. Antony's College, Oxford 1972-73.

HOWARD, M. N. QC
4 Essex Court (Nigel Teare QC), London (0171) 797 7970
Recommended in the following lists: Commercial (litigation), Shipping
Specialisation: Principal areas of practice are international commercial and shipping law, including insurance, international trade and sale of goods. Extensive experience of Arbitrations both as Counsel and as Arbitrator in many International Arbitrations connected with International Trade, Shipping or Insurance. Acts for Shipowners, Charterers, Insurers, P&I Clubs and Salvage companies.
Prof. Memberships: COMBAR, London Common Law and Commercial Bar Association.
Career: Called to the Bar Gray's Inn 1971 (Bencher 1995). Tenant at Queen Elizabeth Building 1972-89. Took Silk 1986. Member of the Panel of Salvage Arbitrators appointed by the Committee of Lloyd's since 1989. Joined Essex Court in 1990. Appointed Recorder 1993.
Personal: Educated at Clifton College, 1960-64 and Magdalen College, Oxford 1965-70 (MA BCL). Leisure pursuits include books, music and sport.

Born 10th June 1947. Lives in London. Other: Senior editor, 'Phipson on Evidence' (14th Ed 1990), Contributor of 'Frustration and Shipping Law' in 'Frustration and Force Majeure' (ed McKendrick, 2nd Edn 1995), 'Foreign Currency Judgments in Contract Claims' in 'Consensus Ad Idem: Essays for Guenter Treitel' (ed Rose, 1996) and author of articles in legal periodicals. Visiting Professor of Law, Essex University 1987-92, Visiting Professor of Maritime Law, University College, London. Member, Editorial Board, Lloyd's Maritime Commercial Law Quarterly.

HOWARD, Mark QC
Brick Court Chambers (Christopher Clarke QC), London (0171) 583 0777
Recommended in the following lists: Banking, Commercial (litigation), Insurance & Reinsurance, Professional Negligence
Specialisation: All areas of commercial law, particularly City disputes and takeovers, insurance, reinsurance, banking and financial services, arbitration, major contract disputes, accountants', brokers' and lawyers' negligence, commercial fraud, international trade and arbitration, DTI and similar investigations.
Prof. Memberships: Combar, LCLCBA
Career: Called to Bar in 1980, took silk in 1996. Recent important reported cases in which involved include: Axa v Field; Commercial Union v Mander; Henderson v Merrett and Ernst & Whinney; Deeny v Walker, Willis Corroon and others; CNW v Girozentrale; Kuwait Airways Corporation v Kuwait Insurance Company; B&C v Samuel Montagu v BZW; Sudwestdeutsche Landesbank v Bank of Tokyo; Jones v Sherwood; AMF v Hashim; Channel Tunnel Group v Balfour Beatty. Has advised and acted for various parties in relation to a number of DTI and similar inquiries, including Atlantic Computers, Barlow Clowes and Matrix Churchill.
Personal: Born 1st April 1958. Educated at University of London – Queen Mary and Westfield College (LL.B, 1978; LL.M,1979).

HOWE, Martin QC
8 New Square (Michael Fysh QC), London (0171) 405 4321
Recommended in the following lists: Computer & I.T., Intellectual Property
Specialisation: Specialist in all aspects of intellectual property, including patents, trade marks and copyrights. Also specialises in European Community law mainly but not exclusively relating to intellectual property. Practice emphasises 'heavy' technology cases, particularly those involving computers, and commercial cases with a heavy technical content. Regularly appears before the European Patent Office in Munich. Publications include 'Halsbury's Laws on Trade Marks, Trade Names and Designs' 1984 and 1995 editions (joint editor with Mr Justice Jacob); and 'Europe and the Constitution after Maastricht' (Nelson & Pollard, Oxford 1993). Important recent cases include: Biogen v Medeva (1996)(H.L.: patents; genetic engineering); Pioneer v Warner [1995] (patents: direct product of process); Ibcos v Barclays [1994] (copyright: computer programmes); Robin Ray v Classic FM (1998) (copyright; joint authorship; implied licence).
Career: Called to the Bar 1978; QC 1996.
Personal: Educated at Winchester College 1968-72 and at Trinity Hall, Cambridge BA 1973-1977, MA 1979. Baker Prize for Engineering 1974. Tripos Part I (Engineering) 1975, 1st class. Tripos Part II (Law) 1977, class 2:1. Everard ver Heyden Prize (for advocacy) 1978.

HOWE, Robert
Blackstone Chambers (formerly 2 Hare Court) (P Baxendale QC and C Flint QC), London (0171) 583 1770
Recommended in the following lists: Media & Entertainment, Sports Law
Specialisation: Principal areas of practice are general domestic & international commercial law,

entertainment/copyright, and employment/disciplinary law. Handles a wide range of cases within these fields, including disputes involving conflicts of law, sale of goods & international trade, financial services, commercial fraud, copyright/media. Examples of interesting recent cases: Sundt Wrigley v Wrigley (marevas & legal costs/financial services/foreign exchange trading/investment mandates), Baldock v Addison [1995] 1 WLR 158 (copyright/discovery), MOD v Foxley (secret commissions/trust/tracing), "The Jam" litigation (partnership/copyright), Gibson Gas Tankers v Allen Engineering (shipbuilding contract/misrepresentation/sale of goods), BETA v London Commodities Exchange (commodity trading/financial services/disciplinary), "The Smiths" litigation (partnership), Chief Rabbi v Jewish Chronicle (confidentiality/copyright), Edwards v The International Amateur Athletic Federation, The Times, June 1997 (restraint of trade/EU law -Arts.59/60).
Prof. Memberships: COMBAR, Employment Lawyers Association, Employment Law Bar Association.
Career: Called to the Bar 1988. Joined present chambers 1990.
Personal: Educated at Trinity Hall, Cambridge 1983-86 (MA) and at St. Edmund Hall, Oxford 1988-89 (BCL). Middle Temple Fox Scholar 1988-89 (one year fellowship in the litigation department of Frazer & Beatty, Toronto, Canada 1987-88. Born 10th June 1964.

HOWELL, John QC
4 Breams Buildings (Christopher Lockhart-Mummery QC), London
(0171) 430 1221/353 5835
Recommended in the following lists: Administrative & Public Law, Parliamentary, Planning
Specialisation: Public law, local government law including local government finance, planning, compulsory purchase and compensation, social security and environment law.
Prof. Memberships: Committee member of the Administrative Law Bar Association and a member of the Planning and Environment Bar Association.
Career: Queen's College, Oxford. Called 1979, Queen's Counsel (1993).

HOWELL WILLIAMS, Craig
2 Harcourt Buildings (Mr Gerard Ryan QC), London (0171) 353 8415
Recommended in the following lists: Parliamentary, Planning
Specialisation: Town and country planning and environment law. Member of the Supplementary Panel of Junior Treasury Counsel (Planning).
Personal: Local Government Planning and Environment Bar Association (Secretary 1994-1996). Parliamentary Bar Mess.

HUGHES, Adrian
4 Pump Court (Bruce Mauleverer QC), London
(0171) 353 2656
Recommended in Construction
Specialisation: Broad commercial practice which includes insurance and reinsurance, shipping, commodities, and construction and engineering. He has a particular interest in international law and in marine pollution and environmental work.
Prof. Memberships: Lloyd's Tier One Arbitrator; Member Vice Chancellor's Practice Directions Working Party; Chairman of the China Working Party of the Bar and Law Society; Bar Council International Relations Committee; Council Member Society of Construction Law.
Career: Royal Naval Officer (1977-1984). Called to the Bar 1984; Practising from 4 Pump Court.
Personal: Educated at Warwick School and Wadham College, Oxford.

HUGHES, David
2 Gray's Inn Square Chambers (Giles Eyre), London (0171) 242 0328
Recommended in Crime

HUGHES, Iain QC
2 Crown Office Row (John Powell QC), London
(0171) 797 8000
Recommended in Professional Negligence
Specialisation: Principal area of practice is professional negligence and general common law. Work covers all aspects of professional negligence (solicitors, surveyors and valuers, architects, barristers, accountants and engineers). Editor: Jackson and Powell on Professional Negligence.
Prof. Memberships: Professional Negligence Bar Association. Personal Injury Bar Association.
Career: Called to the Bar 1974 and joined current chambers in 1977. Silk in 1996. Vice-chairman Professional Negligence Bar Association.

HUGHES, Judith QC
1 Mitre Court Buildings (Bruce Blair QC), London (0171) 797 7070
Recommended in the following lists: Family: Child Care including child abduction
Specialisation: Family Law, dealing with childrens cases and ancillary relief. Became a QC in 1994 and a bencher of the Inner Temple 1994 and Recorder 1995.

HUMPHREYS, Richard
4-5 Gray's Inn Square (Miss Elizabeth Appleby QC & The Hon. M. Beloff QC), London
(0171) 404 5252
Recommended in Planning

HUMPHRY, Richard
28 St. John St (Anthony Rumbelow QC), Manchester (0161) 834 8418
Recommended in Licensing

HUNJAN, Satinder
5 Fountain Court (Anthony Barker QC), Birmingham (0121) 606 0500
Recommended in the following lists: Medical Negligence, Personal Injury
Specialisation: Medical negligence and catastrophic personal injury cases.
Prof. Memberships: Professional Negligence Bar Association and Personal Injuries Bar Association.
Career: LLB (Honours).

HUNT, David QC
Blackstone Chambers (formerly 2 Hare Court) (P Baxendale QC and C Flint QC), London (0171) 583 1770
Recommended in Shipping
Specialisation: Specialist in all aspects of commercial law, with a particular emphasis on arbitration, civil fraud, shipping (dry work), shipbuilding and ship repairing. Practice also covers general contract and tort, and private international law. Interesting recent cases include Standard Bank v Bank of Tokyo 1995 (banking); Pertamina v Thahir [1992-94] Singapore (bribery); Dubai Bank Ltd. v Galadari [1989-92] (fraud); Derby & Co. Ltd. v Weldon [1990-91] (fraud); Publications include articles for the Solicitors' Journal.
Prof. Memberships: COMBAR
Career: Called to the Bar 1969. Took Silk 1987. Appointed Recorder of the Crown Court 1991. Chairman of Gray's Inn Continuing Education Committee.
Personal: Educated at Charterhouse School 1960-65 and Trinity College, Cambridge 1965-68. Working knowledge of French. Leisure pursuits include sailing, golf and skiing. Born 22nd June 1947. Lives in Tunbridge Wells.

HUNT, James QC
36 Bedford Row (James Hunt QC), Northampton (01604) 602333
Recommended in Crime
Leader of the Midland and Oxford Circuit.
Specialisation: Crime. Personal Injury, Professional Negligence. Defence Counsel to Beverly Allitt and Matrix Churchill.
Career: Called to the Bar in 1968, became Circuit Junior in 1976, Deputy Circuit Judge in 1979 and

Crown Court Recorder in 1982. Took Silk in 1987 and was a member of the General Council of the Bar from 1988 to 1991 and from 1996 to date. He was elected Head of Chambers at 1 Kings Bench Walk (now 36 Bedford Row) in 1990 and a Master of the Bench at Gray's Inn in 1994. Became a deputy High Court Judge in 1995.

HUNT, Murray
4-5 Gray's Inn Square (Miss Elizabeth Appleby QC & The Hon. M. Beloff QC), London
(0171) 404 5252
Recommended in the following lists: Administrative & Public Law
Specialisation: Principal area of practice is public law, including judicial review, local government and human rights. Notable cases include Good v Epping Forest DC (Planning Obligations); R v City of London exp. Matson (duty to give reasons); R v Greater Manchester Police Authority, exp. Century Motors (contracting out police functions); Warren v Uttlesford DC (challenge to Local Plan); Saunder v UK (right to silence); Stran v Greece (expropriation). Britton v SSE (planning and international obligation).
Prof. Memberships: Administrative Law Bar Association.
Career: Called 1992; Stagiaire at European Commission of Human Rights 1993; former lecturer in constitutional and administrative law, Oxford University. Executive Editor European Human Rights Law Review. Author of 'Using Human Rights Law in English Courts' (1997). Co-editor of 'A Practitioner's Guide to the Impact of the Human Rights Act 1998'.
Personal: Educated Oxford University (BA & BCL) and Harvard Law School (LL.M.). Born 29.9.65.

HUNTER, Ian QC
Essex Court Chambers (Gordon Pollock QC), London (0171) 813 8000
Recommended in the following lists: Arbitration, Aviation, Insurance & Reinsurance, Shipping
Specialisation: Broad-based commercial practice. More particularly Arbitration, Aviation, Banking, Conflict of laws, European law, Financial Services, Insurance & Reinsurance, International Commercial Fraud, Professional Negligence & Shipping.
Career: Pembroke College, Cambridge MA (Law; double first) 1966; LL.B 1967; Harvard Law School, Cambridge, USA LL.M 1968. Called to the English Bar 1967; Called to the Bar of New South Wales 1993; Queen's Counsel 1980; Bencher 1986; Recorder 1986; Deputy High Court Judge 1993.
Personal: Born 1944. Fluent French.

HUNTER, Martin
Essex Court Chambers (Gordon Pollock QC), London (0171) 813 8000
Recommended in the following lists: Alternative Dispute Resolution, Arbitration
Specialisation: Specialist in arbitration, particularly international arbitration, since 1967. Has acted as advocate, sole arbitrator or as a member of tribunals of three arbitrators on many occasions in both the UK and abroad. Has also represented parties in conciliations, mediations and other ADR procedures and has acted as both conciliator and mediator. Publications include 'Law and Practice of International Commercial Arbitration' (Sweet & Maxwell, 2nd edition 1991) co-author; 'The Freshfields Guide to Arbitration and ADR Clauses in International Contracts' (Kluwer 1992) co-author; 'The Internationalisation of International Arbitration' (Kluwer 1995) joint editor. Has also written numerous articles for various national and international professional journals, and has often addressed conferences and seminars on arbitration related subjects.
Prof. Memberships: International Council for Commercial Arbitration; ICC's International Court of Arbitration; ICC's Commission on International Commercial Arbitration; Panel of Judicial Chairmen, City Disputes Panel; World Intellectual

Property Organisation's Arbitration Consultative Committee; International Council for Commercial Arbitration's delegation to UNCITRAL in relation to arbitration matters; Institute of Business Law and Practice Working Party on ADR; Editorial Board of Arbitration International; Board of Advisors of American Review of International Arbitration.
Career: Assistant solicitor, Freshfields, 1964-67. Litigation partner, Freshfields, 1967-94. Called to the Bar 1994. Appointed Sweet & Maxwell Professor of International Dispute Resolution, Nottingham Law School in 1995.
Personal: Educated at Shrewsbury School 1950-55 and Pembroke College, Cambridge 1957-60. Further academic appointments: Honorary Dean of Post graduate Studies, Asser Instituut, The Hague since 1991; Honorary Fellow, Faculty of Law, University of Edinburgh since 1992; Senior Visiting Fellow, Centre for Commercial Law Studies, Queen Mary and Westfield College, London University since 1988. Leisure pursuits include cruising under sail and golf. Born 23rd March 1937. Lives in Weybridge.

HUNTER, Winston
28 St. John St (Anthony Rumbelow QC), Manchester (0161) 834 8418
Recommended in Personal Injury
Specialisation: Medical Negligence, Industrial Diseases.
Prof. Memberships: PIBA, PNBA.

HUSAIN, Raza
Two Garden Court (I. Macdonald QC & O. Davies), London (0171) 353 1633
Recommended in Immigration & Nationality

HUSKINSON, Nicholas
4-5 Gray's Inn Square (Miss Elizabeth Appleby QC & The Hon. M. Beloff QC), London (0171) 404 5252
Recommended in the following lists: Parliamentary, Property Litigation
Specialist in Local Government, Town and Country Planning and Property Litigation.
Specialisation: Practice encompasses local government, including compulsory purchase and compensation, town and country planning, administrative and parliamentary law, landlord and tenant matters and professional negligence. Recently involved in the River Usk Barrage Order Inquiry [1994], Channel Tunnel Rail Link Bill and acted in British Railways Board v Secretary of State for the Environment [1994]. Clients include local authorities and urban development corporations. Former Assistant Editor, 'Woodfall: Landlord and Tenant'.
Prof. Memberships: Planning and Environment Bar Association, Parliamentary Bar Association, Assistant Recorder (civil) 1995.
Career: Called to the Bar 1971 and joined present chambers in 1972.
Personal: Educated at Eton (1962-66) and King's College, Cambridge (1967-70). Born 7th December 1948. Lives in London.

HUSSAIN, Mukhtar QC
Lincoln House Chambers (Mukhtar Hussain QC), Manchester (0161) 832 5701
Recommended in Immigration & Nationality

HUTTON, Caroline
Enterprise Chambers (Anthony Mann QC), London (0171) 405 9471
Recommended in the following lists: Agriculture & Bloodstock, Property Litigation

HYDE, Charles
Albion Chambers (J.C.T. Barton QC), Bristol (0117) 927 2144
Recommended in Environmental Law

IFE, Linden
Enterprise Chambers (Anthony Mann QC), London (0171) 405 9471
Recommended in the following lists: Chancery, Company, Financial Services, Insolvency, Property Litigation
Specialisation: Principal area of practice is commercial chancery, including insolvency, company, commercial agreements, property, professional negligence, banking and securities and financial services. Regularly receives instructions from major clearing banks and other financial institutions, and from insolvency practitioners. Notable recent cases include Sterling Estates v Pickard [1997] (lease disclaimer by liquidator), TSB v Platts [1997] (cross-claims in bankruptcy), Nottingham Building Society v Peter Bennett & Co [1997] (service), Re Double S. Printers Limited [1998] (fixed and floating charges).

INGLIS-JONES, Nigel J. QC
35 Essex Street (Nigel Inglis-Jones QC), London (0171) 353 6381
Recommended in Pensions
Specialisation: Has 35 years' experience as an occupational pensions schemes specialist. Also deals with other trusts, contract, tort and criminal fraud. Major cases handled include Re Imperial Foods Pension Scheme; Re Courage Group's Pension Schemes [1987]; Mettoy Pension Trustee v Evans [1990]; Davis v Richards & Wallington Industries Ltd [1990]; LRT Pension Fund Trustee Co Ltd v Hatt & others [1993]; British Coal Corporation v British Coal Staff Superannuation Scheme [1994]; Re Prudential Assurance Pension Scheme; Century Life and Britannia Life v Pensions Ombudsman [1995]; Hillsdown Holdings plc v Pensions Ombudsman [1996] and Re National Grid Group of the Electricity Supply Pension Scheme [1997]. Author of 'The Law of Occupational Pension Schemes' (Sweet & Maxwell). Has spoken at and chaired many conferences and seminars.
Prof. Memberships: Chancery Bar Association, Association of Pensions Lawyers, Western Circuit. Bencher of the Inner Temple since 1982.
Career: National Service with the Grenadier Guards (subaltern) 1953-55. Called to the Bar in 1959 and joined chambers at Essex Street in 1960. Took Silk in 1982. Recorder 1978-93. Deputy Social Security Commissioner since 1993.
Personal: Educated at Eton College 1948-53 and Trinity College, Oxford 1955-58. Leisure pursuits include fishing, collecting English drinking glass and English miniature glass, gardening and travelling. A member of the congregation of St.Paul's church, Onslow Square. Born 7th May 1935. Lives in London.

INGRAM, Nigel
3 Hare Court (William Clegg QC), London (0171) 353 7561
Recommended in Crime: Fraud

INMAN, Melbourne QC
1 Fountain Court (David Crigman QC), Birmingham (0121) 236 5721
Recommended in the following lists: Crime

IRVING, Gillian
9 St. John Street (John Hand QC), Manchester (0161) 955 9000
Recommended in Family/Matrimonial
Specialisation: She practices in all aspects of Public and Private law but confesses a preference for child care law, and specifically, non-accidental injury cases. Recent years have seen a growth in judicial review applications and Hague Convention work. She represented the Patients in the Public Inquiry into the Personality Disorder Unit at Ashworth Hospital. She has appeared in the following reported cases: Manchester City Council v S [1991] 2 FLR 370; Stockport M.B.C. v D [1995] 1 FLR 370; RE: B [1996] 2 FLR 693; RE: C [1997] 1FLR HL; A Metropolitan Borough Council v DB [1997] 2FLR 388, and RE: CH [1998] 1FLR 402.

Prof. Memberships: Child Concern, Family Law Bar Association.
Career: 1979 BA (Hons) Law. 1984 Called to the Bar: Inner Temple, Door Tenancy at 1 Mitre Court, London.
Personal: Married. No children. Interests include travel, wine and politics.

IRWIN, Stephen QC
Doughty Street Chambers (Geoffrey Robertson QC), London (0171) 404 1313
Recommended in the following lists: Medical Negligence, Personal Injury
Specialisation: Principal area of practice is medical negligence covering a broad range of serious medical accidents including cerebral palsy, surgical and other medical cases. Other main areas of work are major personal injury cases, legal negligence arising out of public law cases with a medical or health content. Major cases include the Hormone Growth Hormone/Creutzfeldt – Jacob disease, BSE – linked CJD litigation, Clunis v Camden & Islington HA; Birmingham Orthopaedic Hospital Bone Tumour Service; and the Clapham Rail disaster enquiry. Author of "Practitioner's Guide to Medical Negligence" (Legal Action Group, 1995). Regularly lectures and writes on medico-legal issues. Vice-chairman, Legal Aid & Fees Committee of Bar Council.
Prof. Memberships: Professional Negligence Bar Association, Association of Personal Injury Lawyers, Action for the Victims of Medical Accidents, Personal Injury Bar Association, Justice.
Career: Called to the Bar 1976 and tenant of No.1 Dr. Johnson's Buildings, founder member of Doughty Street Chambers. Called to the Bar of Northern Ireland 1997. QC 1997.
Personal: Educated at Methodist College, Belfast 1961-71 and Jesus College, Cambridge 1972-75. Leisure pursuits include reading prose and verse, Irish history and hillwalking. Born 5th February 1953. Lives in Radlett, Herts.

ISAACS, Paul
Mercury Chambers, Leeds (0113) 234 2265
Recommended in the following lists: Crime, Family/Matrimonial
Specialisation: Highly regarded specialist in matrimonial property work. The Counsel of choice of the leading firms of solicitors in cases involving substantial assets and complex accountancy/valuation evidence. Recent cases have involved assets of £10-40 million. Principal area of criminal practice, commercial fraud.
Personal: Read Law at Trinity College, Cambridge (Lizette Bentwich Prize Winner). Called to the Bar in 1974. Recorder of the Crown Court approved to try family cases.

ISAACS, Stuart QC
4-5 Gray's Inn Square (Miss Elizabeth Appleby QC & The Hon. M. Beloff QC), London (0171) 404 5252
Recommended in Banking
Specialisation: Principal area of practice is commercial law, including arbitration, banking, insurance/reinsurance and shipping. Other main area of work is EC law, covering free movement of goods, services, persons and capital, common agricultural policy, common commercial policy and competition law. Involved in Sunday trading cases, the BSE litigation, tin litigation, Iranian assets litigation, insurance brokers' duties of care and many European Court cases. Clients include major banks and other financial institutions, insurers/reinsurers (both corporate and in the Lloyd's market) trade organisations and multinational corporate clients. LCIA and ICC Arbitrator. Author, 'EC Banking Law' (2nd Ed, 1994) and Consultant Editor, Butterworths' EC Case Citator. Has addressed many seminars on commercial and EC law topics both in the UK and Singapore.
Prof. Memberships: COMBAR, IBA, Member of the New York and Brussels Bars.

Career: Called to the Bar 1975 and joined current chambers in 1978. Took silk 1991. Appointed Recorder 1997.
Personal: Educated at The Haberdashers' Aske's School, Elstree 1963-70; Downing College Cambridge, Cambridge 1971-74 (MA Law, Double First); and Universite Libre de Bruxelles 1975-76 (Licence Special en Droit Europeen: Grande Distinction). Speaks French, German and Spanish. Leisure pursuits include travel and languages. Born 8th April 1952. Lives in London.

ISHERWOOD, John
Assize Court Chambers (John Isherwood), Bristol (0117) 926 4587
Recommended in Personal Injury

JACKLIN, Susan
St. John's Chambers (Roderick Denyer QC), Bristol (0117) 921 3456
Recommended in Family/Matrimonial

JACKSON, Andrew
3 Fountain Court (Colman Treacy QC), Birmingham (0121) 236 5854
Recommended in Crime
Specialisation: Crime: Prosecution and Defence work.
Prof. Memberships: Criminal Bar Association.
Career: Manchester University: [1981-1984] BA (Hons). The City University: (1984-1985). Diploma in law.

JACKSON, Dirik
11 New Square (Peter Crampin QC), London (0171) 831 0081
Recommended in Traditional Chancery
Specialisation: Practice covers broad range of Chancery work – in particular trusts, probate, administration of estates, family provision, Court of Protection, conveyancing, commercial and agricultural landlord and tenant, partnership, insolvency, solicitors' negligence. Recent interesting cases include: Hastingwood Property Ltd. v Saunders Bearman Anselm (1991, liability of vendor's solicitors for deposit), Gran Gelato Ltd. v Richcliff (Group) Ltd. (1992, liability of vendor's solicitors to purchaser for negligent mis-statement), Aspen Property Investment PLC v Ratcliffe (1993, director's liability for company's breach of contract), Re Brook Martin (Nominees) Ltd. (1993, disclosure of confidential documents belonging to solicitors' nominee company in liquidation), Murphy v Sawyer-Hoare (1993, liability of assignee's guarantor on disclaimer of lease), Hannaford v Smallacombe (1994, validity of notice to quit agricultural holding), Walton v Walton (1994, proprietary estoppel), Re Duxbury (1995, validity of sole trusteeship of Public Trustee), Frankland v I.R.C. (1997, IHT on distribution out of discretionary trust within 3 months of settlor's death), Duncan Investments Ltd. v Underwoods (1998, liability of vendor's estate agent to purchaser for negligent mis-statement).
Prof. Memberships: Chancery Bar Association, Professional Negligence Bar Association.
Career: Called to the Bar 1969. Tenant at 7 New Square 1970-94. Joined present chambers 1994. Recorder since 1992.
Personal: Born 1946. Educated at Tonbridge School and Trinity College, Cambridge. Married with three children. Lives in London. Recreation: music (cellist).

JACKSON, John
40 King St (Philip Raynor QC), Manchester (0161) 832 9082
Recommended in Crime
Specialisation: Commercial Fraud.
Personal: Criminal Bar Association.
Personal: Interests include sport and sailing.

JACKSON, Judith QC
9 Old Square (Robert Reid QC), London (0171) 405 4682
Recommended in Property Litigation
Specialisation: Commercial property particularly landlord and tenant, chancery and professional negligence. Cases include: Prudential Assurance Co Ltd v Newman Industries Ltd (minority shareholders' rights), Re Bond Worth (retention of title), Mosley v Hickman (Leasehold Reform Act 1967), Abbey National v Moss (trusts for sale), UCB Bank plc v Beasley (s70 (1)(g) Land Registration Act 1925), Amsprop Trading Ltd v Harris Distribution Ltd (s56 Law of Property Act 1925), Scott v National Trust (Judicial Review of Charity).
Prof. Memberships: Chancery Bar Association; Professional Negligence Bar Association.
Career: Queen Mary College, London (1970-73) (LL.B); (1973-74) (LL.M). Called to Bar in 1975. Took silk in 1994. Contributor to Megarry's Rent Acts (11th ed.)

JACKSON, Peter
4 Paper Buildings (Lionel Swift QC), London (0171) 583 0816
Recommended in the following lists: Family: Child Care including child abduction
Specialisation: Deals with all aspects of the law relating to children. Clients include children (by guardians ad litem), parents and local authorities.
Prof. Memberships: Family Law Bar Association.
Career: Called to the Bar 1978 and joined present chambers 1979. Assistant Recorder 1998.
Personal: Educated at Marlborough College 1969-73 and Brasenose College, Oxford 1974-77. Born 9th December 1955. Lives in London.

JACKSON, Rosemary
Keating Chambers (Richard Fernyhough QC), London (0171) 544 2600
Recommended in the following lists: Arbitration, Construction
Specialisation: Construction and engineering litigation and arbitration, including professional negligence; party wall disputes.
Career: Qualified 1981; Middle Temple.
Personal: Born 1958, resides London.

JACKSON, Rupert QC
2 Crown Office Row (John Powell QC), London (0171) 797 8000
Recommended in the following lists: Construction, Professional Negligence
Specialisation: Practice encompasses professional negligence (including medical negligence) and construction. Co-author of 'Jackson and Powell on Professional Negligence'.
Prof. Memberships: Professional Negligence Bar Association, Official Referees' Bar Association.
Career: Called to the Bar 1972 and joined Crown Office Row 1973. Took Silk 1987. Appointed Recorder 1991.
Personal: Educated at Jesus College, Cambridge 1967-71. Born 7th March 1948.

JACKSON, Simon
Park Court Chambers (James Stewart QC, Robert Smith QC), Leeds (0113) 243 3277
Recommended in the following lists: Medical Negligence, Personal Injury
Specialisation: Personal Injury/Medical Negligence. Crime.
Prof. Memberships: P.N.B.A. and P.I.B.A.
Career: Leeds University [LL.B (Hons)]. Called 1982.

JACKSON, W.T.
Manchester House Chambers (J.D.S. Wishart), Manchester (0161) 834 7007
Recommended in Crime

JACOBS, Nigel
4 Essex Court (Nigel Teare QC), London (0171) 797 7970
Recommended in Shipping

JACOBS, Richard QC
Essex Court Chambers (Gordon Pollock QC), London (0171) 813 8000
Recommended in the following lists: Commercial (litigation), Insurance & Reinsurance, Shipping
Specialisation: All types of commercial work – shipping, insurance, reinsurance, professional negligence, commodities, banking, Lloyd's disciplinary proceedings, disputes arising from sales of businesses (warranty claims etc.).
Career: Pembroke College, Cambridge MA (1st Class Hons), 1978. Called to the Bar, 1979.
Personal: Born 1956.

JAFFA, Ronald
3 Gray's Inn Square (Rock Tansey QC), London (0171) 520 5600
Recommended in Crime
Fax: (0171) 520 5607
Specialisation: Long term experience of defending those charged with serious crime including murder, robbery, rape, drugs trafficking, importation and serious assaults. Often instructed in cases where the defendant is difficult, has psychiatric problems or where the allegation revolves around sexual abuse of children. Has conducted many fraud cases involving companies, company VAT, charities, Local Authority employees, advanced fee and mortgages.
Prof. Memberships: Criminal Bar Association.
Career: LLB Nottingham University. One of the founder members who set up the Bar Pro Bono Unit. A member of the management committee solely responsible for considering all applications relating to criminal work.
Personal: Married with two children. An elected trustee of the Rett Syndrome Association UK, a national charity helping families, carers and sufferers of this neurological disorder which only affects females.

JAFFERJEE, Aftab
2 Harcourt Buildings (Nigel Mylne QC), London (0171) 353 2112
Recommended in Crime
Specialisation: Junior Treasury Counsel at the Central Criminal Court.
Prof. Memberships: Criminal Bar Association.
Career: Past Member of the Criminal Bar Association Committee. Past Member of the Professional Conduct Committee of the Bar.

JAMES, Alun
3 Temple Gardens (David Braham QC), London (0171) 353 7884
Recommended in Tax
Specialisation: Specialises in tax and VAT. Business tax includes corporate work; advice for owner-managed businesses and employee-related issues. Also advises on personal tax matters for private clients. Co-author of 'Taxation of Companies and Company Reconstructions' (Sweet & Maxwell, 6th Ed 1994 and 7th Ed 1998). Handles an increasing amount of litigation, notably before the VAT Tribunals and in the professional negligence context.
Prof. Memberships: Revenue Bar Association.
Career: Called to the Bar 1986 and joined 3 Temple Gardens 1988. Also a member of Exchange Chambers (William Waldron QC), Liverpool.
Personal: Scholar of St. John's College, Oxford (BA, Hons 1st Class, Jurisprudence, BCL). Born 15th January 1964. Lives in Coventry.

JAMES, Christopher
5 Fountain Court (Anthony Barker QC), Birmingham (0121) 606 0500
Recommended in Family/Matrimonial

JAMESON, R.M.M.
6 Park Square (Shaun M. Spencer QC), Leeds (0113) 245 9763
Recommended in Crime

JANNER, Daniel
23 Essex Street (Michael Lawson QC), London (0171) 413 0353
Recommended in Crime
Specialisation: Crime (general); Police Law; Employment law; Sex and Race discrimination.
Prof. Memberships: 23 Essex Street.
Career: Called to Bar in 1980 (Jules Thorn Scholar, Middle Temple); Editor Criminal Appeal Reports since 1994.
Personal: President Cambridge Union Society (1978).

JARMAN, Milwyn
9 Park Place (Ian Murphy QC), Cardiff (01222) 382731
Recommended in the following lists: Chancery, Planning
Specialisation: Chancery, Planning and Local Government, Personal Injury. Reported cases include: BP Properties Ltd v Buckler [1987] 2 EGLR 168 (adverse possession); R v Port Talbot Borough Council ex p Jones [1988] 2 ACL ER 207 (judicial review: housing); R v Dairy Produce Quota Tribunal for England and Wales ex parte Davies [1987] 2 EGLR 7 (judicial review: agriculture); R v West Glamorgan County Council ex p Morris and Hood-Williams [1992] JPL 374 (judicial review planning), Huish v Ellis [1995] BCC 462 (professional negligence).
Prof. Memberships: Chancery Bar Association, Bristol and Cardiff Chancery Bar Association.
Career: Called 1980.
Personal: Born 1957. LLB (Wales) 1st Class. LLM (Cantab).

JARVIS, John QC
3 Verulam Buildings (R. Neville Thomas QC), London (0171) 831 8441
Recommended in the following lists: Banking, Commercial (litigation)
Specialisation: Principal areas of practice are banking (both litigation and transactional work) and commercial law. Specialist experience in banking and financing work, insolvency and professional negligence. Practice covers law and practice of international finance, project development and finance, trade disputes, professional liability, insolvency, constructive trusts and arbitration. Has drafted all the major security documentation for a new bank, and appeared in a number of banking cases such as Tai Hing Cotton Ltd v Lin Chong Bank Ltd [1986] AC 80 in the Privy Council. Other recent reported cases include Barclays Bank v O'Brien [1993] (priority in equity of wife's interest against creditor); Deposit Protection Board v Dalia [1993] (validity of equitable assignments to enable claim on fund); Wadha Bank v Arab Bank [1993] (legality of performance bonds and counter guarantees); Re Arrows Ltd Nos 1-4 [1992-93]; Brink Mat Ltd v Noye [1991] (bank as constructive trustee) and Barclays Bank Plc v Taylor, TSB v Taylor [1989] (extent of bank's duty of confidentiality). International Editor of the 'Journal of Banking and Finance Law and Practice'. Author of a number of articles in banking law. Co-author of 'Lender Liability' (1993), and contributing author to 'Banks; Liability and Risk'(1995).
Prof. Memberships: COMBAR, London Common Law and Commercial Bar Association (Chairman 1995/1997).
Career: Called to the Bar and joined present Chambers 1970. Took Silk 1989. Appointed Recorder 1992. Sits as a Deputy High Court Judge.
Personal: Educated at King's College School, Wimbledon 1955-65. Open Exhibitioner and Senior Scholar of Emmanuel College (and Cambridge University Scholar) 1966-69 (MA Hons). Governor of King's College School. Leisure pursuits include rugby, tennis, sailing, skiing, cycling, collecting modern British paintings, opera and gardening. Born 20th November 1947. Lives in Wimbledon and Eyeworth.

JAY, Robert QC
39 Essex Street (Edwin Glasgow QC), London (0171) 832 1111
Recommended in the following lists: Administrative & Public Law, Civil Liberties, Immigration & Nationality

JEANS, Christopher James Marwood QC
11 King's Bench Walk (Eldred Tabachnik QC and James Goudie QC), London (0171) 632 8500
Recommended in Employment
Specialisation: Specialises in Employment law.
Prof. Memberships: Employment Lawyers Association, Employment Law Bar Association.
Career: 1974-1977: LLB degree at King's College, London. 1977-79: BCL degree at St. John's College, Oxford. 1980: called to the Bar (Gray's Inn). Since 1983 has practised full time at the Bar, specialising in Employment law, at chambers of Lord Irvine QC (now chambers of Eldred Tabachnik QC and James Goudie QC).
Personal: Main interests: sport (especially football and cricket), travel, theatre, cinema.

JEFFORD, Nerys
Keating Chambers (Richard Fernyhough QC), London (0171) 544 2600
Recommended in the following lists: Construction
Specialisation: Construction and civil engineering.
Career: Qualified 1986; Grays Inn; member of editorial team 'Keating on Building Contracts'.
Personal: Lady Margaret Hall, Oxford (1984, MA); University of Virginia (1985 Ll.M). Born 1962. London Welsh Chorale.

JEFFREYS, Alan QC
Farrar's Building (Gerard Elias QC), London (0171) 583 9241
Recommended in Personal Injury
Specialisation: Principal area of practice is personal injury litigation, both plaintiff and defendant. Work includes motor, employment and public liability claims. Other main areas of practice are medical and solicitors negligence, general insurance, and Health and Safety.
Career: Called to the Bar in 1970 (Gray's Inn) and joined Farrar's Building in 1971. Recorder since 1993. Took Silk April 1996.
Personal: Born 27th September 1947. Educated at Llandaff Cathedral School (to 1961), Ellesmere College 1961-66 and King's College, London 1966-69. Lives in London.

JEFFREYS, David A. QC
Queen Elizabeth Building (David Jeffreys QC & Peter Whiteman QC), London (0171) 583 5766
Recommended in Crime
Specialisation: Specialist criminal practice, including commercial fraud and related work such as Law Society disciplinary tribunals. Has prosecuted for the SFO, also the (ill-fated) Herald of Free Enterprise case, appeared for the CPS in the Court of Appeal (1995) in Cowan and Others ('right to silence' at trial); defended in the Alexander Howden reinsurance case (Grob and Others) as well as in other serious cases of alleged murder, drugs importation, blackmail, forgery and fraud.
Prof. Memberships: Criminal Bar Association (with particular involvement in law reform), Crown Court and Magistrates' Courts Rule Committees. Has lectured on Corporate criminal liability.
Career: Called 1958, Treasury Counsel CCC 1975-81, Recorder 1979, silk 1981, joint head of chambers 1995.
Personal: Educated Cambridge University, worked one year in the City before call to the Bar.

JENKINS, Edward
5 Paper Buildings (John Mathew QC), London (0171) 583 6117
Recommended in Crime
Specialisation: Commercial fraud (tax evasion, corruption, city banking fraud); Health and Safety, Trading Standards, Control of Pollution.
Prof. Memberships: S.E. Circuit, C.B.A.

JENKINS, T. Alun QC
All Saints Chambers (T. Alun Jenkins QC), Bristol (0117) 921 1966
Recommended in Crime

JENNINGS, Anthony
Two Garden Court (I. Macdonald QC & O. Davies), London (0171) 353 1633
Recommended in Crime
Specialisation: Involved in major Crown Court criminal cases including terrorism, animal rights, drugs, prison disturbances, armed robbery, murder and fraud. Cases include disturbances at Risley Remand Centre (1990), Dartmoor Prison (1991), Manchester United supporters riot on ferry, dolphin interference case; IRA cases: MacFlhoinn and Hayes and Taylor; Sehan (largest ever police seizure of heroin); Ronnie Lee (animal rights bombing), Whitemoor prison egress, North Wales sex abuse inquiry, Brownbill v M.P.C. (£150,000 damages against the police), Michael Smith v Police (largest damages in W.Midlands), Keith Birchall (murder conviction quashed on appeal). Editor of 'Justice under Fire: The Abuse of Civil Liberties in Northern Ireland' (1990). Written articles on criminal justice for The Times, Independent, Guardian and The New Law Journal. Contributing editor of Archbold.
Prof. Memberships: Criminal Bar Association
Career: Called to the Bar 1983 and Northern Ireland Bar in 1987, joined current chambers in 1986.
Personal: Educated at St. Patrick's College, Belfast 1971-78, Warwick University 1978-81 and Inns of Court School of Law 1981-82. Leisure pursuits include theatre, Italy, Liverpool F.C. and Irish literature. Born 11th May 1960. Lives in London.

JOFFE, Victor
Serle Court Chambers (Charles Sparrow QC QC), London (0171) 242 6105
Recommended in the following lists: Chancery, Company, Insolvency
Specialisation: Main areas of practice are company law (especially shareholders' disputes and minority rights; directors' duties and directors' disqualification) and corporate insolvency, with emphasis on litigation. Other ares of practice include partnership, commercial chancery and banking (including tracing and proprietary claims). Advises in many litigious matters from overseas, particularly the United States, Jersey, Malaysia and Gibraltar. Publications include 'Companies Act 1980 – A Practitioners Guide'; 'Buckley on the Companies Acts' (joint editor, forthcoming edition); 'Mithani on Disqualifiaction of Directors' (joint editor forthcoming edition).
Prof. Memberships: Chancery Bar Association; Insolvency Practitioners Association; International Bar Association.
Career: MA, LL.B (Cantab); Called to the Bar 1975. Lecturer in law, LSE 1974-1980; Attorney, New York State Bar (1998).

JOHNSON, Christine
14 Castle St (Adrian Lyon), Liverpool (0151) 236 4421/8240/6759/6757
Recommended in Family/Matrimonial

JOHNSON, David QC
20 Essex Street (David Johnson QC), London (0171) 583 9294
Recommended in Shipping
Specialisation: Specialises in commercial matters including all aspects of carriage of goods by sea, charterparty disputes, international sale of goods especially commodity disputes (wide experience of arbitration under trade rules such as GAFTA, FOSFA, RSA, LME etc as well as ICC, LCIA, LMAA and ad hoc arbitration), insurance (marine and non-marine, disciplinary proceedings under Lloyd's by-laws and several of the "Lloyd's cases"), reinsurance, banking, professional indemnity/negligence, oil industry disputes and a very wide spread of commercial arbitration

including building disputes. Appears in original or appellate courts abroad (e.g. Hong Kong, Singapore and Dublin) as well as English courts at all levels. Acts as arbitrator (both sole and as a member of panels) or umpire in a variety of domestic and international commercial arbitrations including ICC, LCIA, LMAA and ad hoc.
Prof. Memberships: LMAA (Supporting Member); COMBAR; Western Circuit.
Career: Solicitor and Notary Public 1952; Called to the Bar 1967; Queen's Counsel 1978; Recorder of the Crown Court 1984; Bencher of the Inner Temple 1985.
Personal: Travelling, sailing, skiing, shooting, music (especially opera), keeping roof on old house. Married with four children (determined non-lawyers).

JOHNSON, Edwin
9 Old Square (Robert Reid QC), London (0171) 405 4682
Recommended in Property Litigation
Specialisation: Property, chancery and commercial litigation and advisory work. In particular commercial and residential property disputes, professional negligence, mortgages, landlord and tenant, conveyancing, easements, restrictive covenants, property rights, insolvency and commercial contracts. Recent cases include Church Commissioners v Ibrahim [1997] 03 EG 136, (right to indemnity costs in leases); Gardner v Marsh & Parsons (mitigation of damages for professional negligence)[1997] 1 WLR 489; Crown Estate Commissioners v. Aberdeen Steak Houses Group plc (Break notices and termination of business tenancies) [1997] EGCS 14.
Prof. Memberships: Chancery Bar Association.
Career: Called to the Bar in 1987 and joined 9 Old Square in 1988. educated at Lancing College and Christ Church College, Oxford (BA).

JOHNSON, Ian
14 Castle St (Adrian Lyon), Liverpool (0151) 236 4421/8240/6759/6757
Recommended in Chancery
Specialisation: General chancery with particular emphasis on: probate and administration of estates, landlord and tenant, conveyancing and real property, trusts, partnerships.
Prof. Memberships: Chancery Bar Association. Northern Chancery Bar Association.
Career: Tenant at 20 North John Street, October 1983 to July 1997. Tenant at 14 Castle Street, August 1997 to date. July 1998 appointed senior lecturer in law at Manchester Metropolitan University, a full-time appointment. Continues to practise on a part-time basis only.
Personal: Married Elizabeth eldest daughter Lord and Lady Evans of Claughton (1989). Two daughters (1995 and 1998).

JOHNSON, Michael
9 St. John Street (John Hand QC), Manchester (0161) 955 9000
Recommended in Chancery
Specialisation: General Chancery, with emphasis on traditional chancery fields, and on revenue matters, professional negligence and High Court Litigation.
Prof. Memberships: Chancery Bar Association, Northern Chancery Bar Assiiation (Chairman) Professional Negligence Bar Association.
Career: Chancery Practitioner since 1972, Assistant Recorder (Civil and Crime), part-time Chairman, VAT and Duties Tribunals.
Personal: Fluent in Spanish, good knowledge of French, educated in North and South America, and at Trinity College, Cambridge University.

JOHNSTON, Christopher
3 Serjeants' Inn (Philip Naughton QC), London (0171) 353 5537
Recommended in Medical Negligence
Specialisation: Principal areas of practice are medical and dental negligence, medical ethics employment and civil actions involving the police.

Considerable experience acting for both plaintiff and defendant in all aspects of medico-legal work, including high value claims (brain damage, blindness, serious physical injury) and class actions. Experience in medical ethics work (B v Croydon Health Authority, [1995] 1 All E R 683, CA: force feeding of mental patient, A NHS Trust v D: persistent vegetative case. Re V.S. (Adult: Mental Disorder) [1995] 3 Med Law Rev 292 Ret (A Minor) (Liver Transplant : Consent) at first instance). Acting for defendant in first dental negligence class action (Appleton v Garrett (1996) PIQR). Professional disciplinary work (General Dental Council). Experience acting for the Police in unlawful arrest and false imprisonment cases. Employment experience comprises: industrial tribunal claims including unfair dismissal and race and sex discrimination (particularly in health context). Co-author of Bar Council's submission on Small Personal Injury claims.
Prof. Memberships: Professional Negligence Bar Association.
Career: Called to the Bar in 1990. Joined Serjeants' Inn in 1991.
Personal: School: Ballymena Academy. University: Trinity Hall, Cambridge (Law, 1st class). Interests: cinema and history.

JOHNSTONE, Mark
4 Paper Buildings (Lionel Swift QC), London (0171) 583 0816
Recommended in Family: Matrimonial Finance
Specialisation: Financial provision on divorce. Practice includes family provision under the Inheritance Act 1975. Reported cases: Lloyds Bank v Egremont & Egremont [1990]; Re N [1992]; Hampshire County Council v S [1993]. Wrote three chapters in 'Brown on Divorce'.
Prof. Memberships: Family Law Bar Association.
Career: Called to the Bar 1984.
Personal: Lives in London.

JONES, Alun QC
3 Raymond Buildings (Clive Nicholls QC), London (0171) 831 3833
Recommended in the following lists: Crime, Crime: Fraud
Specialisation: Principal areas of practice are commercial crime and extradition. Acts in cases of serious and complex fraud, both trials and advisory work, primarily for the defence. Undertakes extradition and advisory work for foreign governments and fugitives. Appears frequently on appeal or review in criminal cases and associated matters such as coroners' cases. Notable cases include the Alexander Howden reinsurance trials (appearing for Kenneth Grob in the first SFO trial, 1989-90); the Blue Arrow Trial 1990-91 (defending Stephen Clark); the defence of Andrew Kent in an alleged fraud against The Securities Association (1993) and the Maxwell Criminal Trial (defending Kevin Maxwell, 1995). Involved in eight full House of Lords appeals in extradition cases, acting in six of them for foreign governments. Author of 'Jones on Extradition' (Sweet & Maxwell, 1995).
Prof. Memberships: Bar Council, Criminal Bar Association.
Career: Called to the Bar in 1972 and joined current chambers in 1973. Took silk 1989. Appointed Recorder 1992.
Personal: Educated at Oldershaw Grammar School, Wallasey 1960-67 and Bristol University 1967-70. Leisure pursuits include bridge, cricket, gardening and writing (currently working on book concerning the law of conspiracy). Born 19th March 1949. Lives in Greenwich, London.

JONES, Charlotte
5 Bell Yard (Robert Webb QC), London (0171) 333 8811
Recommended in Medical Negligence
Specialisation: Main area of practice is medical negligence, acting for Plaintiffs and Defendant health authorities and trusts, in all types of medical cases, in particular brain damaged baby claims,

other obstetric, paediatric, gynaecological, cancer and orthopaedic cases. Other substantial areas of practice are employment, appearing in industrial tribunals and the employment appeal tribunal, often for healthcare clients, and personal injuries, particularly in the context of aviation/mass disasters.
Prof. Memberships: Professional Negligence Bar Association; COMBAR. South Eastern Circuit.
Career: Educated Trinity Hall Cambridge (BA Hons) 1978-81. Called to the Bar by Middle Temple (1982).
Personal: Married with 2 children and lives in Kent.

JONES, Edward Bartley QC
Exchange Chambers (William Waldron QC), Liverpool (0151) 236 7747
Recommended in the following lists: Chancery, Commercial (litigation), Insolvency, Partnership
Specialisation: Commercial, Professional Negligence, Insolvency, Banking, Chancery Companies, Commercial Property and Landlord and Tenant, Commercial Arbitration, Intellectual Property, Planning.
Prof. Memberships: Northern Circuit Chancery Bar Association; Chancery Bar Association; Northern Circuit Commercial Bar Association.
Career: B.A. (Oxon.) 1973 called 1975. Practised in Liverpool from 1976. Joined Exchange Chambers as Head of Commercial Department 1994. Formerly part-time Tutor in Law at Liverpool University. Assistant Recorder. QC (1997)

JONES, Elizabeth
Serle Court Chambers (Charles Sparrow QC QC), London (0171) 242 6105
Recommended in the following lists: Commercial (litigation), Chancery
Specialisation: Broad range of commercial Chancery and property litigation, with particular emphasis on civil fraud (both in commercial and trust contexts) and entertainment (especially music industry and publishing).
Career: Called to the Bar 1984. Joined Thirteen Old Square 1985. Member ACTAPS.

JONES, Geraint
9 Park Place (Ian Murphy QC), Cardiff (01222) 382731
Recommended in Chancery

JONES, Gregory
2 Harcourt Buildings (Mr Gerard Ryan QC), London (0171) 353 8415
Recommended in Environmental Law
Specialisation: Principal areas of practice: planning, environmental, compulsory purchase, all aspects of local government, education, administrative, parliamentary, European (EC and European Convention). Gave expert evidence before House of Commons Environment Committee's report into the burning of Secondary Liquid Fuel in Cement Kilns (1997). Reported Cases: R v Essex CC ex p Jackson Projects (HC) [1995] COD 155 (compulsory purchase); Torbay v Mills & Cross [1995] 159 JP 682 (DC) (highways); Houghton v SSE (1995) P & CR 178; [1996] PLR 6 (green belt s.54A); Harper v SSE (HC) [1994] JPL B 107 (planning); Charles Church Developments v Hart DC (HC) (local plan) [1995] JPL B133; R v SSE ex p Slot (HC) (natural justice, European Convention, footpaths) [1997] JPL B14; R v Sandhu (CA) (listed buildings/relevence of evidence) The Times (1997) 2 January; [1997] Crim L.R.288 [1997] JPL 853 [1998] PLR 17; R v Somerset CC ex p Harcombe [1998] COD 71 (national assistance, exercise of local authority's discretion to recover nursing home costs); R v Elmbridge BC ex p Active Office (DC) The Times (1997) 29 December (judicial review of decision by local authority to commence listed building prosecution); R v Local Government Ombudsman ex p Turpin (HC) [1998] EGCS 18; Berkeley v SSE & FFC (CA) (planning, s.54A, environmental assessment, European law) (1998) The Times2 March. Berkeley v SSE & FFC (No.2) (Costs)

(1998) The Times 7 April. O'Brien v Hertsmere BC [No1] (1997) 74 P+ CR 264 (advertisement law, burden of proof). O'Brien v Hertsmere BC [No.2] [1998] JPL B73 (whether defendent could be convicted of continuing offence pending appeal to High Court on original offence). R v SSETR ex p Marson (environmental assessment, European duty to give reasons) The Times (1998) 18 May. R v Greenwich LBC ex p Glen International [1998] EGCS 102 (Housing, renovation grant).
Prof. Memberships: Member of the National Council of the United Kingdom Environmental Law Association. Jean Pierre Warner Scholar to the European Court of Justice (Cabinet of Advocate General Jacobs) [1995] Planning and Environment Bar Association, Bar European Group, Association of Regulated Procurement, UK European Law Association, Administrative Bar Association, Education Law Society, Ecclesiastical Law Society.
Career: Called to the Bar, Lincoln's Inn (1991). King's Inns, Dublin (1997). Joined 2 Harcourt Buildings June 1993.
Personal: Educated Colfe's School. New College, Oxford (MA), University College, London (LL.M). Born 4th January 1968.

JONES, Jennifer
5 Fountain Court (Anthony Barker QC), Birmingham (0121) 606 0500
Recommended in Employment Law

JONES, Nicholas David
33 Park Place (Wyn Williams QC), Cardiff (01222) 233313
Recommended in Personal Injury

JONES, Seán
11 King's Bench Walk (Eldred Tabachnik QC and James Goudie QC), London (0171) 632 8500
Recommended in Employment
Specialisation: Principal area of practice is employment law, including discrimination. Acts for both applicants and respondents. Has been instructed by individuals, unions, multi-national businesses, small firms, local authorities and employer's federations. Has lectured/tutored at Nottingham University, Worcester College, Oxford and King's College, London and given seminars,including addressing the Employment Lawyers' Association.
Prof. Memberships: ELBA, COMBAR, Discrimination Law Association, Industrial Law Society.
Career: Called to the Bar and joined present chambers in 1991.
Personal: Educated at Colchester Royal Grammar School 1977-84 and Worcester College, Oxford 1985-89 (BA Hons in Jurisprudence, BCL). Born 9th July 1966. Lives in London.

JONES, Timothy
St Philip's Chambers (Rex Tedd QC), Birmingham (0121) 246 7000
Arden Chambers (Andrew Arden QC), London (0171) 242 4244
Recommended in Planning
Specialisation: Town and Country Planning, representing local authorities and developers in development plan inquiries, development control appeals, compulsory-purchase inquiries and High Court applications. Public and Administrative Law, representing local authorities and applicants in judicial reviews related to planning, housing, caravan sites, rating and disabled persons. Important cases include: Buckley v United Kingdom [1994 & 1996] (complaint to European Commission and Court of Human Rights about the effect of planning and criminal law on the traditional lifestyle of Romanies); R v Secretary of State for the Environment ex parte T. Smith [1988] (declaration that county council in breach of its duty re caravan sites); Wychavon D.C. v Secretary of State for the Environment [1994] (local authority did not have standing to bring proceedings for non-implementation of a European Union

Directive); Wyre Forest D.C. v Secretary of State for the Environment and Allens [1990] (House of Lords held planning permission should be interpreted in accordance with extended definition in a related statute rather than normal English usage).
Prof. Memberships: Planning & Environment Bar Association, Administrative Law Bar Association (Committee).
Career: Called to the Bar 1975. Practises from both St Philip's Chambers, Fountain Court, Birmingham (0121 246 7000) and Arden Chambers, London (0171 242 4244).
Personal: Educated at Christ's Hospital, Jesus College Cambridge and the London School of Economics. Called to the Bar of Ireland 1990 and to the Bar of Northern Ireland 1998. Fellow Royal Geographical Society.

JORY, Hugh
Enterprise Chambers (Anthony Mann QC), Leeds (0113) 246 0391
Recommended in Commercial (litigation)

JOSEPH, David
Essex Court Chambers (Gordon Pollock QC), London (0171) 813 8000
Recommended in Aviation
Specialisation: Experienced in arbitration. Advocate in many ad hoc arbitrations in London involving a wide variety of commercial disputes particularly charterparty, aviation, insurance, reinsurance and commodities. Many of these disputes are governed by foreign law. Litigation experience: all types of commercial work including insurance, reinsurance, aviation, shipping, sale of goods, letters of credit, commercial fraud.
Career: Law Society Finals 1983, Called to Bar – 1984; began practice – 1985, in commercial chambers at Essex Court.
Personal: Born 22 April 1961. Educated at Pembroke College, Cambridge (B.A (law – 2nd class Hons.)); Good working French and basic Italian.

JOURDAN, Stephen
Falcon Chambers (Jonathan Gaunt QC & Kim Lewison QC), London (0171) 353 2484
Recommended in Property Litigation
Specialisation: Commercial, agricultural and residential landlord and tenant, conveyancing, mortgages, solicitors' and surveyors' professional negligence, real property, insolvency aspects of real property.
Prof. Memberships: Professional Negligence Bar Association, Chancery Bar Association.
Career: Formerly a practising solicitor. Contributor to Halsbury's Laws (4th Edition) volume 27 (Landlord and Tenant).

JOYCE, Michael
9 Gough Square (Jeremy Roberts Q.C), London (0171) 353 5371
Recommended in Crime

JOYCE, Peter QC
No.1 High Pavement (John B. Milmo QC), Nottingham (0115) 941 8218
Recommended in Crime

JUBB, Brian
Gray's Inn Chambers (Brian Jubb), London (0171) 404 1111
Recommended in the following lists: Family: Child Care including child abduction

JUCKES, Robert
3 Fountain Court (Colman Treacy QC), Birmingham (0121) 236 5854
Recommended in Crime
Specialisation: Crime: equally for prosecution and defence. 1997: junior for prosecution in R v Tracey Andrews; four other murder cases, three for defence. C of A; respondent in R v Kendrick Hopkins and R v Callender; most kinds of criminal work but increasing rape and child abuse; fraud.
Prof. Memberships: CBA.

Career: Marlborough College 1963-68. Exeter University 1969-72 (BA Hon Soc/Law). Extensive travel and variety of work in Australia, America and Europe prior to starting at Bar 1975. Nose to grindstone since. Recorder 1995.
Personal: As much sport as time allows especially tennis, golf,cricket, skiing. Current reading obsession; Patrick O'Brien. Culturing three sons 18, 15 and 11.

JUDGE, Lisa
Manchester House Chambers (J.D.S. Wishart), Manchester (0161) 834 7007
Recommended in Crime

KADRI, Sibghat QC
6 King's Bench Walk (Sibghat Kadri QC), London (0171) 353 4931 /583 0695
Recommended in the following lists: Civil Liberties, Immigration & Nationality

KALLIPETIS, Michel QC
Littleton Chambers (Michael Burton QC), London (0171) 797 8600
Recommended in the following lists: Alternative Dispute Resolution, Professional Negligence
Specialisation: Professional negligence, employment law, entertainment and media law, building and construction, general commercial and business law. Other areas of practice include health and safety.
Prof. Memberships: Professional Negligence Bar Association, COMBAR, Employment Law Bar Association, ORBA.
Career: Called 1968 Gray's Inn; QC 1989; Recorder 1989, Deputy High Court Judge, Deputy Official Referee.
Personal: Cardinal Vaughan School. University College London. Exchequer & Audit Department (now National Audit Office) 1960 to 1968.

KARAS, Jonathan
4 Breams Buildings (Christopher Lockhart-Mummery QC), London (0171) 430 1221/353 5835
Recommended in Property Litigation
Specialisation: Practises in the fields of real property and planning (with a particular emphasis on landlord and tenant). Co-author of 'Unlawful Interference with Land' (1996) and a contributing editor to the 'Compulsory Purchase' title of Halsbury's Laws of England (1996) and to Hill and Redman's 'Law of Landlord and Tenant'.
Prof. Memberships: Planning and Environment Bar Association, Chancery Bar Association.
Career: Member of Supplementary Panel of Junior Counsel to the Crown (Common Law).

KARK, Thomas V.W.
Queen Elizabeth Building (David Jeffreys QC & Peter Whiteman QC), London (0171) 583 5766
Recommended in Crime: Fraud
Specialisation: Practice principally involves cases of commercial fraud including: fraudulent trading; VAT fraud; duty diversion; mortgage fraud; bankruptcy offences. Has also been involved in cases of alleged insider dealing, prosecuting for the DTI and defending. Also defends and prosecutes cases concerning computer misuse and data protection (see DPP v Brown – House of Lords). Landmark cases have included defending as junior several SFO and Special Casework prosecutions (eg. second defendant in the Levitt case; Terry Ramsden; Swithland Motors). Criminal Law (General): Prosecutes and defends in all areas of criminal law. Member of 'Justice'.
Personal: Born 12th December 1960. Educated at Eton, Buckingham University and Ronnie Scotts.

KARSTEN, Ian QC
Queen Elizabeth Building (Ian Karsten QC), London (0171) 797 7837
Recommended in the following lists: Family: Child Care including child abduction, Family: Matrimonial Finance
Specialisation: Family, including finance, children,

child abduction, choice of forum, adoption, judicial review. Specially interested in cases with foreign or international element. Also civil work (especially medical negligence). Fluent French and German. Numerous reported cases, including foreign divorces, finance, child abduction, adoption, care proceedings, judicial review, medical negligence, etc.
Prof. Memberships: Family Law Bar Association, Professional Negligence Bar Association, International Academy of Matrimonial Lawyers.
Career: Called 1967, commenced practice 1970, QC 1990. Formerly Lecturer in Law, LSE.

KATKOWSKI, Christopher
4 Breams Buildings (Christopher Lockhart-Mummery QC), London
(0171) 430 1221/353 5835
Recommended in the following
lists: *Administrative & Public Law, Environmental Law, Parliamentary, Planning*
Specialisation: Planning inquiry experience extends to all fields including acting for all the leading retailers in a large number of shopping inquiries; substantial experience of conservation cases (e.g. the Mappin & Webb inquiry for English Heritage, and obtaining planning permission to develop over an Anglo-Saxon cemetery in Croydon); promoting a major development for the Army (Otterburn in the Northumberland National Park) and conducting Local Plan inquiries. Leading planning court cases include: Tesco Witney (planning gain); Bolton (reasons); Mitchell (affordable housing); Edwards (alternative sites); Walton (implementation of old planning permissions); Porter (issue estoppel). Environmental law experience includes: FOE v SSE (quality of drinking water litigation) and Ennerdale Water (abstraction inquiry). Leading public law cases include: Spycatcher (Contempt of court); Foster (jurisdiction of Social Security commissions); Balfour (national security); Save Our Railways (privatisation); Camden (housing revenue account subsidy); Warren (subpoena of judges). Public affairs experience includes advising various serving and former Cabinet ministers during the Scott inquiry.
Career: Lectured in law at the City of London Polytechnic, 1979-83. Called to the Bar, February 1982. Began practice at the Bar in January 1984.
Personal: Born 16th January 1957 in Sussex, Polish parents. Educated at Cardinal Newman School, Hove, Sussex and Fitzwilliam College, Cambridge M.A; LL.B (First Class Honours). Elected senior Scholar of College and University prize in law.

KAUFMANN, Phillippa
Doughty Street Chambers (Geoffrey Robertson QC), London (0171) 404 1313
Recommended in Civil Liberties
Specialisation: Civil practitioner specialising in prisoners' rights, constitutional and administrative law, human rights including applications under the European Convention and ICCPR, actions against the police, mental health, employment and discrimination. Also undertakes death row appeals from the Commonwealth to the Privy Council.
Prof. Memberships: Member of ALBA; Council Member of Justice.
Career: Called to the Bar 1991. Education: LL.B (Hons) 1st class, LL.M distinction, Scarman Scholar. Born 1966.

KAVANAGH, Giles
5 Bell Yard (Robert Webb QC), London
(0171) 333 8811
Recommended in Aviation
Specialisation: Commecial litigation with emphasis on aviation (including aviation finance, leasing and insurance) and professional negligence.
Prof. Memberships: COMBAR.
Career: Appeared in Philcox v CAA (extent of CAA's duty of care), Perrett v P.F.A (extent of Regulator's duty to passengers) and a number of

M1 British Midland disaster cases.
Personal: M.A., LL.M (Cantab). President Cambridge Union Society, Michaelmas 1981, Member Middle Temple Hall Committee.

KAY, R Jervis QC
4 Field Court (Geoffrey Brice QC), London
(0171) 440 6900
Recommended in the following lists: Shipping, Sports Law
Specialisation: Admiralty and all areas of shipping including international trade and commercial law, arbitration, marine insurance, carriage of goods, salvage, collision, marine pollution, towage, personal injury arising out of marine incidents. Practice also includes contractual and personal injuries cases arising out of sporting events, particularly yachting, rugby football.
Prof. Memberships: London Maritime Arbitration Association (supporting member), London Common Law and Commercial Bar Association (Committee), COMBAR, British Maritime Law Association, Bar Sports Law Group.
Career: Called to Bar 1972, joined current chambers in 1974. Called to the Bar of New South Wales 1984. Called to the Bar of Antigua and Barbuda 1998. Took silk 1996.
Personal: Educated Wellington College and Nottingham University (LL.B), Editor Atkins Court Forms – vol 3 Admiralty, 1979, 1990, 1994 Editions. Leisure pursuits: Books, racing, skiing and sailing (member of R.O.R.C and R.Y.A). Resides in Suffolk and London.

KAY, Steven QC
3 Gray's Inn Square (Rock Tansey QC), London
(0171) 520 5600
Recommended in Crime
Specialisation: Wide experience in all areas of UK criminal law, with regular appearances in domestic Murder, Fraud and Drug Trafficking trials. International criminal law now a speciality. Defence counsel for Tadic the first defendant to be tried before the UN war crimes tribunal for Yugoslavia and the first international criminal trial since the Nuremberg and Tokyo trials. Also representing Musema a defendant before the UN international criminal tribunal for Rwanda. Expertise in European agricultural fraud (in Lomas v The Commission 1992). Lectures at conferences throughout the world on specialist subjects.
Prof. Memberships: Criminal Bar Association, European Criminal Bar Association (founder member and Treasurer), International Bar Association, Forensic Science Society.
Career: Called to the Bar 1977, QC 1997, Secretary CBA 1993-1996.
Personal: Born 4/8/54, lives in London.

KAYE, Roger QC
24 Old Buildings (C.A. Brodie QC), London
(0171) 404 0946 St John's Chambers (Roderick Denyer QC), Bristol (0117) 921 3456
Recommended in the following lists: Chancery, Ecclesiastical, Insolvency
Specialisation: The main areas of Business and Commercial Law including: Insolvency (personal & corporate); Civil Fraud; Company Law; Contract Disputes; Banking and Financial Services; Partnership Law; Professional Negligence; Land and Property Law; Landlord and Tenant; Directors Disqualification and other regulatory work.
Prof. Memberships: Member of the Chancery Bar Association, Member of the Insolvency Lawyers Association.
Career: Birmingham University (LLB); Queen's Counsel 1989; Recorder 1994; Deputy High Court Bankruptcy Registrar 1985; Deputy High Court Judge (Chancery Division) 1990; Junior Treasury Counsel (Insolvency) (from 1978-1989). Deputy Chancellor of the Dioceses of Southwark, St Albans and Hereford. Judicial Chairman City Disputes Panel 1997.

KEALEY, Gavin QC
7 King's Bench Walk (Stephen Tomlinson QC), London (0171) 583 0404
Recommended in the following lists: Commercial (litigation), Insurance & Reinsurance, Professional Negligence
Specialisation: Specialises in all aspects of commercial law for mainly international clients. Particular emphasis on insurance, reinsurance, banking, financial services, professional negligence, conflicts of laws, shipping and contracts of all kinds. Recent cases include Den Danske A/S, Normura Bank and others v Kleinwort Benson, Skipton BS and Economic Insurance (Dec. 1997, Thomas J, Loan Portfolio Transfers, lending criteria, insurance construction); Denby v Marchant & Yasuda v Llyods's Underwriters (16 March 1998. CA. Aggregate Extension Clauses); Sumitomo Bank Ltd, Sanwa Bank Ltd & Arab Bank Ltd v Banque Bruxelles Lambert [1997] 1 Lloyd's Rep 487 (duties of care owed to syndicate of banks by Agent bank), Tharros Shipping v Bias Shipping [1997] 1 Lloyd's Rep 246 and Pendennis Shipyard v Magrathea [1998] 1 Lloyd's Rep 315 (costs payable by a non-party); Glencore v Portman [1997] 1 Lloyd's Rep 225 (insurance, non-disclosure, waiver); DR Insurance v Central Nat. Ins. [1996] 1 Lloyd's Rep 74 (conflicts of laws, proper law, illegality); 'Marinor' [1996] 1 Lloyd's Rep 301 (charterparty incorporation terms); Excess Insurance v Mander [1997] 2 Lloyd's Rep 119 (reinsurance, incorporation, arbitration clause); Also has experience appearing before foreign courts as both advocate and expert. Speaks very good French.
Career: Called to the Bar 1977. Joined present chambers 1978. Took Silk 1994.
Personal: Educated at University College, Oxford (BA Hons Jurisprudence 1st class). Lecturer in law, King's College, London 1976-77.

KEEHAN, Michael
St. Ive's Chambers (Edward Coke), Birmingham
(0121) 236 0863 (6 lines)
Recommended in Personal Injury

KEFFORD, Anthony
East Anglian Chambers (John Holt), Norwich
(01603) 617351
Recommended in Family/Matrimonial
Specialisation: Divorce, Matrimonial Finance, all aspects of Child Law including care proceedings. Local Authority work undertaken.
Prof. Memberships: Family Law Bar Association.
Career: Called to the Bar in 1980.

KELLY, Matthias
Old Square Chambers (Hon. John Melville Williams QC), London (0171) 269 0300
Recommended in Personal Injury
Specialisation: Personal injuries. Has dealt with all types of PI for both Plaintiff and Defendants. Particular specialisation in catastrophic injuries including brain injuries. Experienced in complicated litigation including radioactive pollution: (Merlin v BNFL (1990) 3 WLR 383). Other cases: H v MOD (1991) 2 QB 103, Rastin v British Steel (1994) 1 WLR 732. Page v Sheeness Steel (1997) P1QR Q1. Member editorial panel Sweet and Maxwell Special Research papers in Personal Injuries Law.
Prof. Memberships: Environmental Law Foundation; Secretary, Personal Injury Bar Association.
Career: Called to the bar 1979. Member Irish Bar (Belfast and Dublin). Member New York State Bar and US Federal Bar. Former Consultant to the European Commission on UK Health and Safety Law. Editor, Sweet & Maxwell Personal Injuries Manual.

KELSEY-FRY, John
Queen Elizabeth Building (David Jeffreys QC & Peter Whiteman QC), London (0171) 583 5766
Recommended in the following lists: Crime, Crime: Fraud
Specialisation: Practice equally divided between high profile prosecution and defence. Recent cases: Serafinowicz (war crimes); Donald & Cressey (largest police corruption case since 1960's); Charlie Kray.
Career: Senior Treasury Counsel.

KEMPSTER, Toby
Old Square Chambers (Hon. John Melville Williams QC), Bristol (0117) 927 7111
London (0171) 269 0300
Recommended in Employment
Specialisation: Concentrates primarily on employment law and personal injury law. His employment practice covers both individual and collective rights, dealing with contractual and statutory remedies. His personal injury practice is mainly work or industry related, but he has been involved in multi-plaintiff product liability, disease and 'disaster' cases. (Notable cases Alexander v STC, Isle of Scilly v Brintel; Johnson v British Midland Airways).
Prof. Memberships: APIL, ILS, ELA and PIBA.
Career: Member of chambers since 1982.

KENDRICK, Dominic QC
7 King's Bench Walk (Stephen Tomlinson QC), London (0171) 583 0404
Recommended in the following lists: Insurance & Reinsurance, Shipping
Specialisation: Specialist in commercial litigation, including shipping, insurance/reinsurance, overseas sales, letters of credit, jurisdiction disputes and agency disputes. Recent reported cases include Bates v. Barrow [1995] 1 LLRep (stop loss insurance; effect of illegality); Glencore v Bank of China (CA) [1996] 1 LLRep 135 (letters of credit); Monarch Airlines v London Luton [1998] 1 LLRep 403 (aviation); Laconian Confidence [1997] 1 LLRep 39 (shipping); Commercial Union v NRG Victory ('Exxon Valdez') (CA) [1998] 1 LLRep 80 (reinsurance).
Career: Called to the Bar 1981. Joined present chambers 1982. QC 1997.
Personal: Educated at Cambridge University (MA) 1973-1976. Born 22nd February 1955.

KENNEDY, Helena QC
Doughty Street Chambers (Geoffrey Robertson QC), London (0171) 404 1313
Recommended in the following lists: Civil Liberties, Crime

KENNEDY, Michael J.
India Buildings Chambers (David Harris QC), Liverpool 0151 243 6000
Recommended in Family/Matrimonial
Specialisation: Family Law specialist dealing with public law Children Act work, including the representation of Local Authorities, parents and Guardians ad Litem in cases involving, inter alia, issues of physical, sexual and emotional abuse of children.
Prof. Memberships: Family Law Bar Association.
Career: Called 1985.

KENNERLEY, Ian
Broad Chare Chambers (Eric A Elliott), Newcastle upon Tyne (0191) 232 0541
Recommended in Family/Matrimonial

KENTRIDGE, Sydney QC
Brick Court Chambers (Christopher Clarke QC), London (0171) 583 0777
Recommended in the following lists: Administrative & Public Law, Commercial (litigation), Insurance & Reinsurance, Media & Entertainment
Specialisation: General commercial and common law, constitutional law and law relating to newspapers.
Career: Called to Bar 1977, Lincoln's Inn.

Practising barrister, England, 1977 to date. Silk 1984. Admitted as Advocate of the Supreme Court of South Africa, 1949. Appointed Senior Counsel, South Aftica 1965. Former Judge of the Courts of Appeal of Jersey and Guernsey and Constitutional Court of South Africa.
Personal: Born Johannesburg, South Africa, 1922. Educated University of Witwatersrand (B.A. 1941) and Oxford University (B.A. Hons. in Jurisprudence, 1948; M.A. 1955).

KERR, Tim
4-5 Gray's Inn Square (Miss Elizabeth Appleby QC & The Hon. M. Beloff QC), London (0171) 404 5252
Recommended in the following lists: Administrative & Public Law, Employment, Sports Law
Specialisation: Judicial review, sports law, education law, local government, employment law, professional negligence, disciplinary tribunals, defamation, European, human rights and commercial. Sports law clients include Tottenham Hotspur FC (gaining readmission to FA Cup and six restored points); Chelsea FC; Middlesbrough FC; AEK Athens FC (gaining readmission to UEFA Cup); Slavia Prague FC; the Football League (Stevenage FC v Football League, CA, 1996); the Rugby Football League; the Rugby Football Union; the Welsh Rugby Union; Lennox Lewis (Lewis v Bruno and WBC, 1995). Co-author of forthcoming book on Sports Law. Judicial reviews include Bart's hospital closure cases (including R v Health Secretary ex p. Hackney LBC, CA, 1995); challenges to disciplinary investigations into audits of Maxwell and Polly Peck companies (including R v Chance ex p. Smith, DC, 1995); and Camelot's challenge to the "Big Three" bookmakers' competing product (R v DPP ex p. Camelot Group plc, DC, 1997). Education cases include X v Bedfordshire CC (HL, 1995), Christmas v Hampshire County Council (1997, successful defence in first ever educational negligence High Court trial), Richardson v Solihull MBC (CA, 1998) and R v East Sussex ex p. Tandy (1998, HL). Employment cases include: Snowball v Gardner Merchant (1987); Associated British Ports v TGWU (1987, HL); Doughty v Rolls-Royce (1992: CA); Duffy v Yeomans & Partners (1995, CA) and Preston v Wolverhampton MBC (HL, 1998, part timers' claim for equal access to pension schemes, pending in ECJ).
Prof. Memberships: Administrative Law Bar Association; Employment Law Bar Association; Secretary of the Bar Sports Law Group.
Personal: Runner of four marathons and keen Chelsea supporter.

KERSHAW, Jennifer Christine QC
6 Park Square (Shaun M. Spencer QC), Leeds (0113) 245 9763
Recommended in Crime
Specialisation: Violent and/or sexual offending; mentally disordered offenders; children and young persons; controlled drugs; public family law.
Prof. Memberships: Lincoln's Inn.
Career: LL.B Hons. London 1973; Call 1974; Assistant Recorder 1996; Silk 1998.

KERSHEN, Lawrence QC
Cloisters (Laura Cox QC), London (0171) 827 4000
Recommended in Alternative Dispute Resolution

KESSLER, James
24 Old Buildings (G.R Bretten QC), London (0171) 242 2744
Recommended in the following lists: Charities, Tax
Specialisation: Revenue law, more particularly CGT, IHT, and what is loosely described as 'private client' work; offshore trusts; also taxation of charities. Has a particular fondness for trust drafting (having written the leading textbook on the subject).
Career: Called to the bar 1984.

KEYSER, Andrew
9 Park Place (Ian Murphy QC), Cardiff (01222) 382731
Recommended in Chancery
Specialisation: Contract litigation; principal and surety; banking; partnership; landlord and tenant; professional negligence.
Prof. Memberships: Chancery Bar Association. Bristol and Cardiff Chancery Bar Association.
Career: Education; Cardiff High School, Balliol College, Oxford (MA). Called to Bar 1986.

KHALIL, Karim S.
1 Paper Buildings (Roger Titheridge QC), London (0171) 353 3728
Recommended in Crime
Specialisation: Defence and prosecution, with particular experience in serious violence (including murder), rape and other sexual offences. Represented the principal masochist in R v Brown (HL decision on consent in cases of assault). Criminal and civil litigation relating to company fraud. Represented the Appellant in Hannan v. DTI (CA decision on the Company Directors' Disqualification Act). Civil claims against the police.
Prof. Memberships: South Eastern Circuit; SE Circuit Liaison Committee (Secretary); Criminal Bar Association; Professional Conduct and Complaints Committee; Bar Disciplinary Tribunal.
Career: Queens' College, Cambridge; call – 1984; Assistant Recorder – 1997.
Personal: Married with two sons; tennis and golf; saxophonist in Jazz band.

KHANGURE, Avtar
No.6 Fountain Court (Roger Smith QC), Birmingham (0121) 233 3282
Recommended in Insolvency

KHAYAT, Georges M QC
10 King's Bench Walk (Ronald Thwaites QC), London (0171) 353 2501
Recommended in Crime
Specialisation: Fraud – (White Collar Cases, Banking, Mortgage, Insurance, V.A.T etc).
Prof. Memberships: Chairman Surrey and South London Bar Mess 1995-1998, Member South Eastern Circuit, Deputy Head of Chambers.
Career: Called to the Bar 1967, Lincoln's Inn. Recorder of the Crown Court 1987. QC 1992.
Personal: Reading, music, boating, travel and horse riding.

KHURSHID, Jawdat
7 King's Bench Walk (Stephen Tomlinson QC), London (0171) 583 0404
Recommended in Shipping
Specialisation: General Commercial law, including international trade and sale of goods, carriage of goods by sea and road, shipping, insurance and reinsurance. Involved in State of the Netherlands v Youell [1997] 2 Lloyd's Rep 440 (QB); [1998] 1 Lloyd's Rep 236 (CA).
Prof. Memberships: COMBAR
Career: Educated at Cranleigh School and St. Catherine's College, Oxford.
Personal: Enjoys a wide variety of sports, including hockey, and travelling.

KIBLING, Thomas
Cloisters (Laura Cox QC), London (0171) 827 4000
Recommended in Employment
Specialisation: Specialises in employment law with a particular emphasis on discrimination law, local government issues and individual employment rights. In recent years he has been involved in a number of the leading discrimination cases. Lectures widely on all aspects of employment law and publications include 'the Employment Law Handbook' (LAG).
Career: Called to the Bar 1990. Joined present chambers 1991.
Personal: Born 19th August 1957.

KILLALEA, Stephen
Devereux Chambers (Jeffrey Burke QC),
London (0171) 353 7534
*Recommended in the following lists: Health &
Safety, Personal Injury*
Specialisation: Principal areas of practice are
personal injury and Health & Safety. Predominantly
plaintiff but some defence work. Emphasis on
accidents in industry and accidents involving
death, brain damage and spinal injury. Also
handles specialised crime, including health and
safety prosecutions and medical negligence.
Prof. Memberships: Personal Injuries Bar
Association; Association of Personal Injury
Lawyers.
Career: Called to the Bar in 1981.
Personal: Born 25th January 1959. LL.B (Hons)
Sheffield. Lives in Sussex.

KING, Michael
24 Old Buildings (C.A. Brodie QC), London
(0171) 404 0946
Recommended in Insolvency
Specialisation: The main areas of Business Law
including: Insolvency (personal & corporate); Civil
Fraud; Company Law; Contract Disputes;
Partnership Law; Professional Negligence;
Property Law; Landlord and Tenant; Trusts;
Settlements; Probate and Wills.
Prof. Memberships: Member of the Chancery Bar
Association, Member of the Insolvency Lawyers
Association.
Career: Christ's College Cambridge (MA).

KING, Neil
2 Mitre Court Buildings (Michael FitzGerald
QC), London (0171) 583 1380
*Recommended in the following lists: Environmental
Law, Planning*
Specialisation: Practice encompasses town and
country planning, compulsory purchase and
compensation, rating, local government,
environmental and public and administrative law.
Joint Editor, 'Ryde on Rating and the Council Tax'.
Prof. Memberships: Planning and Environment
Bar Assocation.
Career: Called to the Bar 1980 and joined current
chambers 1982.
Personal: Educated at Harrow School 1970-74
and New College, Oxford 1975-78. Married with 4
children. Leisure pursuits include music, golf and
real tennis. Born 14th November 1956. Lives in
Whitchurch-on-Thames.

KING, Philip
1 Middle Temple Lane (Colin Dines & Andrew
Trollope QC), London (0171) 583 0659 (12 lines)
Recommended in Crime: Fraud

KING, Simon
9 Bedford Row (John Goldring QC), London
(0171) 242 3555
Recommended in Personal Injury
Specialisation: Personal injury and professional
negligence practice acting for both Plaintiffs and
Defendants but with emphasis on defence work.
Regular clients are principally insurers and
corporate bodies, including professional indemnity
insurers for solicitors, architects and surveyors.
Experience includes professional and insurance
fraud cases.
Personal: Professional Negligence Bar
Association, International Bar Association.
Career: Called to the Bar in 1987, joined current
chambers in 1988. Early practice in crime and
general common law; subsequent specialisation
as above.
Personal: Educated at Haberdashers' Aske's
School, Elstree and St. John's College, Oxford (MA
Jurisprudence). Leisure pursuits include music,
walking, motor cycling.

KINGSLAND, The Rt. Hon. Lord QC
4 Breams Buildings (Christopher Lockhart-
Mummery QC), London
(0171) 430 1221/353 5835
Recommended in Environmental Law
Specialisation: Waste & Waste Disposal;
Contaminated Land; Integrated Pollution Control;
Water Resources; Pollution and Planning;
European Community Environmental Law; Judicial
Review.
Prof. Memberships: PEBA; UKELA; Bar European
Group.
Career: Call to the Bar, 1972; Queen's Counsel,
1988; Member of the European Parliament 1979-
94; Privy Counsellor 1994; Bencher of the Middle
Temple since 1996 and a contributor to Halsbury's
Laws on Compulsory Acquisition and on the
European Communities.

KINGSTON, Martin QC
5 Fountain Court (Anthony Barker QC),
Birmingham (0121) 606 0500
*Recommended in the following lists: Administrative
& Public Law, Environmental Law, Planning*
Specialisation: All aspects of Planning,
Environmental and CPO law including minerals and
waste disposal matters.
Prof. Memberships: Planning and Environment
Bar Association.
Career: Called 1972, Silk 1992, Recorder of the
Crown Court, Assistant Parliamentary Boundary
Commissioner, Assistant Chairman Agricultural
Land Tribunal.

KINLEY, Geoffrey
4 Essex Court (Nigel Teare QC), London
(0171) 797 7970
Recommended in Aviation

KIRK, Anthony
One King's Bench Walk (James Townend QC),
London (0171) 936 1600
*Recommended in the following lists: Family:
Child Care including child abduction*
Specialisation: Family (including Divorce and
Children), Child Care, Family Provision,
International Child Abduction.
Career: Recent cases include: Re B (Wardship:
Abortion) 1991 2 FLR 426; Re H (A Minor) (Role of
Official Solicitor) 1993 2 FLR 552; Essex County
Council v B (Education Supervision Order) 1993 1
FLR 866; Re B (Child Sex Abuse: Standard of
Proof) 1995 1 FLR 904; Re C (Adoption: Parties)
1995 2 FLR 483; Re B (Contempt Evidence) 1996 1
FLR 239. Re W (Minor) (Unmarried Father: Child
Abduction) Re B (A Minor) (Unmarried father: Child
Abduction) 1998 2 FLR 146.
Prof. Memberships: Committee member of the
General Council of the Bar, the Family Law Bar
Association and the South Eastern Circuit. Wrote
the chapter in Jackson's Matrimonial Finance and
Taxation (6th edition) on 'Enforcement'.
Personal: Ipswich School and King Edward VII
School, Lytham; Kings College London (LLB Hons
AKC).

KITCHIN, David QC
8 New Square (Michael Fysh QC), London
(0171) 405 4321
*Recommended in the following lists: Computer
& I.T., Intellectual Property, Media & Entertainment*
Specialisation: All areas of intellectual property
including patents, trade marks, passing off,
copyright, designs, malicious falsehood,
confidential information, media and entertainment
law, computer law and EC and other competition
law with an intellectual property element. Also
handles some technical commercial work.
Publications include 'The Trade Marks Act 1994'
(Sweet & Maxwell) co-author; 'Kerly's Law of Trade
Marks and Trade Names' (Sweet & Maxwell) co-
editor; 'Patent Law of Europe and the United
Kingdom' (Butterworths) co-editor.
Prof. Memberships: Chancery Bar Association,
Intellectual Property Bar Association.
Career: Called to the Bar 1977 and joined

chambers 1979. Took Silk 1994. Chairman, Code
of Practice Committee, National Office of Animal
Health (1995).
Personal: Educated at Oundle School 1968-72
and Fitzwilliam College, Cambridge 1973-76. Born
30th April 1955.

KLEVAN, Rodney C. QC
18 St. John Street (Rodney C. Klevan QC),
Manchester (0161) 278 1800
Recommended in Crime

KNIGHT, Brian QC
Atkin Chambers (John Blackburn QC), London
(0171) 404 0102
*Recommended in the following lists: Arbitration,
Construction*
Specialisation: Practices in the field of
construction law in United Kingdom and English
speaking tribunals worldwide. In 1991 Appointed
Recorder of the Crown Court to sit as an Official
Referee in the UK High Court specialising in the
trial of all kinds of construction law.
Career: Called to the Bar November 1964, also
called to the Bar of Northern Ireland and Hong
Kong. Practising Barrister since 1966. Silk 1981.
Recorder 1991. F.C.I. Arb 1995.
Personal: Educated Colbayn's High School,
University College London. LL.B. (Hons) 1959;
LL.M. 1961. Pupillage with Sir Graham Eyre QC,
A.L. Price QC and K.F. Goodfellow QC.

KNOWLES, Robin
3/4 South Square (Michael Crystal QC), London
(0171) 696 9900
*Recommended in the following lists: Banking,
Financial Services, Insolvency*
Specialisation: Practice covers a wide aspect of
general commercial, business and financial
litigation, and legal advice, including banking and
financial services, professional negligence and
disciplinary proceedings, commercial fraud,
corporate insolvency and reconstruction, corporate
and partnership disputes, pensions and charities,
insurance and reinsurance.
Prof. Memberships: Assistant Recorder;
Commercial Bar Association (Committee and
North American Liaison Committtee); Bar Pro Bono
Unit (Management Committee); Chancery Bar
Association. Talks have included 'Resolving
disputes involving serious commercial fraud',
'Multi-party commercial disputes', 'Alternative
dispute resolution' and 'Co-operation between
Courts in international insolvency'.
Career: Called to the Bar in 1982; Middle Temple;
Gray's Inn; South Eastern Circuit.
Personal: MA in Law.

KORN, Anthony
Barnards Inn Chambers (Timothy Bowles),
London (0171) 242 8508
Recommended in Employment
Specialisation: Specialises in all aspects of
employment law, including sex, race, and disability
discrimination, equal pay, TUPE, contracts of
employment, restrictive covenants, unlawful
deductions, redundancy and unfair dismissal.
Appeared for the Respondent in Smith v Gardner
Merchant (1998) – sex discrimination and sexual
orientation.
Prof. Memberships: Employment Lawyers
Association: member of management committee.
Member of Employment Law Bar Association.
Career: Magdalen College, Oxford. Researcher on
industrial relations legal information bulletin and
editor of intellectual property in business.
Previously employed as 'in house' counsel with
Paisner & Co and Dibb Lupton Broomhead.

KOSMIN, Leslie QC
Erskine Chambers (Richard Sykes QC), London
(0171) 242 5532
*Recommended in the following lists: Company,
Insolvency*
Specialisation: Practice encompasses Company
law and corporate insolvency; especially litigation

involving directors' duties, shareholders rights and remedies, internal company disputes and claims of professional negligence against Accountants and Solicitors.
Prof. Memberships: COMBAR, Chancery Bar Association. Insolvency Lawyers Association.
Career: Called to the Bar 1976 and joined Erskine Chambers 1977. Took Silk: 1994.
Personal: MA, LL.M (Cantab), LL.M Harvard Law School. Born 12th August 1952. Lives in London.

KRAMER, Stephen QC
1 Hare Court (Stephen Kramer QC), London (0171) 353 5324
Recommended in Crime
Specialisation: Criminal law specialist.
Prof. Memberships: Criminal Bar Association.
Career: Called to the Bar in 1970. Joined 1 Hare Court, Temple in 1988 from 10 King's Bench Walk. Assistant Recorder 1987-91. Recorder since 1991. Standing Counsel (Criminal Law) to Customs & Excise 1989-1995. Appointed QC 1995. Head of Chambers 1996 -
Personal: Educated at Keble College, Oxford and the University of Nancy (France). Born 12th September 1947.

KUSHNER, Lindsey QC
28 St. John St (Anthony Rumbelow QC), Manchester (0161) 834 8418
Recommended in the following lists: Family/Matrimonial, Family: Child Care including child abduction, Family: Matrimonial Finance

KUSHNER, Martine
36 Bedford Row (James Hunt QC), London (0171) 421 8000, Northampton (01604) 602 333
Recommended in Family/Matrimonial
Specialisation: All aspects of Family Law both public and private. Public Law – care proceedings representing parents, children, guardians ad litem and local authorities; Public Interest Immunity; Wardship. Private Law: divorce, residence and contact, ancillary relief including 'Big Money' cases. Financial claims between cohabitees. Child Abduction/Hague convention. Judicial Review. Legal consultant.
Prof. Memberships: FLBA. Criminal Bar Association. Board Member Northampton Family Mediation Service.
Career: Mancester High School for Girls; Birmingham University LLB Hons; City Polytechnic MA Business Law; Middle Temple – Entrance Award; Jules Thorne Prize Winner. Also presented a number of seminars covering the new Family Law Act and the Trustee Act.
Personal: Married with two children.

KVERNDAL, Simon
4 Essex Court (Nigel Teare QC), London (0171) 797 7970
Recommended in Shipping

KYTE, Peter E. QC
Queen Elizabeth Building (David Jeffreys QC & Peter Whiteman QC), London (0171) 583 5766
Recommended in Crime: Fraud
Specialisation: All aspects of crime, particularly commercial fraud, though recent practice has included murders, robberies and major drugs cases.
Prof. Memberships: Criminal Bar Association.
Career: Five years in mining finance and investment banking before practising at Bar. Called 1990, Recorder 1992, Silk 1996.
Personal: Trinity Hall Cambridge (MA Law). Ex-member NY Stock Exchange and Chicago Board of Trade. Married. Two children.

LACEY, Sarah H.
3 Stone Buildings (G.C Vos QC), London (0171) 242 4937
Recommended in Pensions
Specialisation: Pensions litigation and advice, acting for beneficiaries, employers, administrators and trustees, including trustees and administrators

of public sector schemes. Also covers other Chancery areas including commercial, partnership, trusts, tax and probate.
Prof. Memberships: Chancery Bar Association, Association of Pensions Lawyers, Association of Contentious Trust and Probate Specialists. Sits on the Bar Council. Member of the Careers Advice network.
Career: Called to the Bar 1991, and joined 3 Stone Buildings in 1993.
Personal: Educated at Prince William School, Oundle (1982 – 7) and Downing College, Cambridge (1987-90). Enjoys walking, travelling and playing the piano.

LAIDLAW, Jonathan
1 Hare Court (Stephen Kramer QC), London (0171) 353 5324
Recommended in Crime

LAMB, Timothy QC
2 Temple Gardens (Patrick Phillips QC), London (0171) 583 6041
Recommended in Professional Negligence
Specialisation: Professional negligence cases have concerned; accountants, architects, building management systems engineers, civil engineers, contractor's design, doctors, electrical engineers, forensic experts, geotechnicians, mechanical engineers, solicitors, structural engineers, surveyors, teachers, valuers. Reported cases include: Lambert v Lewis (1982) AC 225, Ronex Properties v Laing (John) Construction (1983) QB 398, Kaliszewska v Claque (1984) 5 Con. LR 62, Wimpey v Poole (1984) 2 LL Rep 499, Imperial College of Science and Technology v Norman and Dawbarn (a firm) (1986) 2 Const. LJ 280, Driscoll v NYE Saunders 17 Con. LR 73, BBL v Eagle Star (1994) 2 EGLR 108 (first instance), Nycklen Finance Ltd v Edwards Symmons & Partners (1996) 5 CL. 83.
Prof. Memberships: ORBA, LCLCBA.
Career: Call: 1974. Appointed: Queen's Counsel 1995, Assistant Recorder 1998. Educated: Brentwood School, Lincoln College, Oxford. Born: 27th November 1951.

LAMBERT, Christina
6 Pump Court (Kieran Coonan QC), London (0171) 583 6013
Recommended in the following lists: Medical Negligence, Personal Injury
Specialisation: Medical and dental law: negligence actions, disciplinary work, health service administrative law, pharmaceutical and product liability. Also criminal work, particularly involving medical disputes. Interesting cases include Thomas v Brighton Health Authority; Johnstone v Camden & Islington Health Authority; Myodil litigation and HCV litigation.
Prof. Memberships: Professional Negligence Bar Association, Criminal Bar Association, Personal Injury Bar Association.
Career: MA (Hons) Cantab, 1985, Diploma in Law, City University, 1987, called to the Bar in 1988.

LAMBERT, Julian
Albion Chambers (J.C.T. Barton QC), Bristol (0117) 927 2144
Recommended in Crime

LANDAU, Toby
Essex Court Chambers (Gordon Pollock QC), London (0171) 813 8000
Recommended in the following lists: Arbitration, Commercial (litigation)
Specialisation: International and commercial arbitration. All aspects of international and commercial litigation.
Prof. Memberships: New York Bar Association, COMBAR, London Court of International Arbitration, Swiss Arbitration Association.
Career: Merton College, Oxford BA (Law) (First Class Hons) 1990 (MA: 1994); Bachelor of Civil Law (BCL) (First Class Hons) 1991. Harvard Law School, Cambridge, Massachusetts LL.M (1993).

Called to the Bar 1993. New York State Bar: Admitted as an Attorney and Counselor-at-Law by the state of New York 1994.
Personal: Born 1967.

LANDES, Anna-Rose
St Philip's Chambers (Rex Tedd QC), Birmingham (0121) 246 7000
Recommended in Insolvency

LANDSBURY, Alan
6 Gray's Inn Square (Michael Boardman), London (0171) 242 1052
Recommended in Crime

LANG, Beverley
Blackstone Chambers (formerly 2 Hare Court) (P Baxendale QC and C Flint QC), London (0171) 583 1770
Recommended in the following lists: Administrative & Public Law, Employment
Specialisation: Public law, civil liberties, employment and discrimination law. Interesting cases include DPP v Hutchinson (Greenham Common Byelaws held unlawful by the House of Lords.); Lloyd v McMahon (surcharged Liverpool Labour Councillors); Thomas v NUM (right of striking miners to picket); Halford v Sharples (acted for Assistant Chief Constable Alison Halford in her sex discrimination claim against Merseyside Police); Christmas v Hampshire County Council (duty of care owed by teachers to children with special education needs); ex parte S (admission to mental hospital and Caesarean section against patient's wishes). Publications include articles for the Modern Law Review, Industrial Law Journal and Legal Action and co-author of Public Law Project's 'Applicant's Guide to Judicial Review'.
Career: Called to the Bar 1978. Appointed part-time chairman of Industrial Tribunal 1995. Former lecturer in law at the University of East Anglia.
Personal: Born 13th October 1955.

LANGDALE, Rachel
9 Bedford Row (John Goldring QC), London (0171) 242 3555
Recommended in Medical Negligence
Specialisation: All aspects of medical negligence work, but with a particular emphasis on Gynaecological, Obstetric and Paediatric cases. Children Act Proceedings and Public Inquiries (1997-8 involved in the North Wales Tribunal of Inquiry).
Prof. Memberships: Action for Victims of Medical Accidents (Lawyers Group). Family Law Bar Association.
Career: LL.B. (Hons) (1983-1986) M.PHIL. (Cantab) (1986-1987). A.G.'s department, Sydney, Australia 1988-1989. Called to the Bar: 1990.

LANGDALE, Timothy QC
Queen Elizabeth Building (David Jeffreys QC & Peter Whiteman QC), London (0171) 583 5766
Recommended in the following lists: Crime, Crime: Fraud
Specialisation: Principal area of practice is all aspects of criminal law with an emphasis on high profile, serious crime cases and commercial fraud.
Prof. Memberships: Criminal Bar Association.
Career: Called to the Bar 1966. Treasury Counsel 1979-1992. QC 1992.

LANGDON, Andrew
Guildhall Chambers (John Royce QC), Bristol (0117) 927 3366
Recommended in Crime
Specialisation: All aspects of defending crime. Particular interest in cases concerning civil liberties. Has recently been involved in defending in SFO prosecution and large scale drugs importations.
Prof. Memberships: CBA
Career: Bristol University, call 1986.

LANGSTAFF, Brian QC
Cloisters (Laura Cox QC), London
(0171) 827 4000
Recommended in the following
lists: Employment, Personal Injury, Product Liability
Specialisation: Principal area of practice is personal injury, collective employment and Trade Union cases. Has been instructed in most major industrial disputes (eg ambulancemen's strike, coal strike, Wapping) since the early 1980s and many important collective employment and Trade Union cases, although majority of practice has been in cases of serious personal injury (usually caused at work). Other area of practice is medical negligence and product liability, including actions against drug producers. Important cases include Page v Hull University (employment), Walker v Northumberland C.C. (personal injury: stress at work), Reay & Hope v BNFL (The 'Sellafield' case), Peach v Metropolitan Police (Fatal assault by police/discovery issues), Ratcliffe v North Yorkshire C.C. (Equal Pay), News International v SOGAT (picketing: the 'Wapping' dispute), Clarke & Others v NUM (Miners' strike), Milligan & Securicor (TUPE; employment); R v Employment Secretary ex parte Unison (Judicial Review, employment). Adams v Lancs CC (Transfers of Undertaking); Clark v BET (the largest award yet for wrongful dismissal); Carmichael v National Power (contracts of employment); Jesuthasan v Hammersmith (discrimination); MOD v Wheeler (compensation); Quinn v MOD (mesothelioma) and the 'tobacco' cases. Major lay clients include most Trade Unions and their members as well as legally aided victims of accidents (both factory and medical). Professional clients include Trade Union solicitors (in private practice and in-house), law centres, medical and environmental practices and the Medical Defence Union. Author of 'Health & Safety at Work' in Vol. 20 of Halsbury's Laws (4th edn) and of various articles in journals. Former senior lecturer in law. Conference speaker on equal pay and employment issues, and employers' liability for work-related illnesses.
Prof. Memberships: LCLCBA; ELBA; ALBA; APIL; ILS (Committee Member); PIBA (Committee Member).
Career: Called to the Bar in 1971. Lecturer in law 1971-75. Joined present Chambers in 1977. Appointed Assistant Recorder in 1991, Recorder 1995. Took Silk in 1994.
Personal: Educated at George Heriot's School, Edinburgh 1953-66 and St. Catharine's College, Cambridge 1967-70. Chairman of Governors of local primary school. Enjoys sport, theatre and TV, politics, mowing the lawn, his family and travel. Born 30th April 1948.

LAPRELL, Mark
18 St. John Street (Rodney C. Klevan QC), Manchester (0161) 278 1800
Recommended in Personal Injury

LASOK, Paul QC
Monckton Chambers (Richard Fowler QC), London (0171) 405 7211
Recommended in European Union/Competition
Specialisation: Specialist in all aspects of European Community law. Main areas of work include agriculture, competition, trade law and VAT. Publications include 'The European Court of Justice: Practice and Procedure' (Butterworths 2nd edition 1994). European editor of 'Weinberg & Blank on Take-Overs and Mergers' (Sweet & Maxwell). Joint editor of the Common Market Law Reports and CMLR Antitrust Reports. Cases include Mercury v Director General of Telecommunications (1996, HL; telecommunications regulation); Marchant & Eliot v Higgins (1996, CA: Article 85); Three Rivers District Council v Bank of England (1996, liability of banking regulator); R v HM Treasury, ex parte British Telecommunications (1996, CA and ECJ: public procurement, interlocutory injunction, state liability); Hopkins v National Power and Powergen

(1996, High Court and ECJ: ECSC/EC competition law). R v CCE ex parte Kays (1996: VAT capping); Commission v United Kingdom (1997, ECJ; prduct liability); United Kingdom v Commission (1998, ECJ; BSG).
Prof. Memberships: Bar European Group.
Career: Called to the Bar 1977. Legal secretary (law clerk) to Advocate-General J.P Warner and Advocate-General Sir Gordon Slynn, Court of Justice of the European Communities 1980-84. Private practice in Brussels, specialising in European Community law 1985-87.
Personal: Educated at Jesus College, Cambridge 1972-75 (MA) and at Exeter University 1975-77 (LL.M). PhD Exeter University 1986.

LATHAM, Robert
1 Pump Court (Jane Hoyal and Robert Latham), London (0171) 583 2012
Recommended in Civil Liberties
Specialisation: Housing, Administrative Law and Civil Liberties. Involved in a number of group actions including the 'Kingshold Estate' (see Legal Action, October 1995). Recent judicial review applications have related to the housing duty owed to asylum seekers, unfair and irrational allocation policies, abuse of power by councillors, renewed applications for accommodation.
Career: Founder members of chambers (1978) which won the 1997 Times Award for the law firm contributing most to equal opportunities. Former councillor and health authority member. Victim Support Chair.

LAURENCE, George QC
12 New Square (John Mowbray QC), London (0171) 419 1212
Recommended in the following
lists: Parliamentary, Property Litigation
Specialisation: Practice encompasses property litigation (including landlord and tenant, planning and judicial review), parliamentary and countryside law (rights of way, commons). Has appeared frequently as counsel before opposed Bill Committees in both Houses of Parliament. Promoted Wye Navigation Order for Environment Agency under TWA 1992 [1997]. Acted in numerous reported cases, many on rights of way, including Celsteel v Alton House [1986]; R v Secretary of State for Environment ex parte Stewart [1987], Riley [1988], Rubinstein [1990], Burrows [1991], O'Keefe [1993, 1996], Cowell [1993, CA], Bagshaw [1994], Emery [1997, CA], Billson [1998].
Prof. Memberships: Chancery Bar Association, Administrative Law Bar Association, Planning and Environment Bar Association, Parliamentary Bar Association.
Career: Called to the Bar 1972. Joined 9 Old Square 1973; current chambers January 1991. Took Silk April 1991. Appointed Assistant Recorder 1993. Appointed Deputy High Court Judge (Chancery) 1997.
Personal: Educated at University of Cape Town 1966-68 (BA) and University College, Oxford 1969-71 (MA). Rhodes Scholar. Leisure pursuits include sport and theatre. Born 15th January 1947. Lives in London.

LAWRENCE, Heather
11 South Square (Christopher Floyd QC), London (0171) 405 1222
Recommended in the following lists: Computer
& I.T., Intellectual Property
Specialisation: All aspects of intellectual property: patents, trade marks, copyright, registered and unregistered design right, passing off and breach of confidence; other matters with a technical content such as computer contract disputes, pharmaceutical licensing and data protection; media and entertainment law.
Prof. Memberships: Intellectual Property Bar Association (formerly patent Bar Association) (Hon. Lec, 1992-1997) Royal Society of Chemistry (Associate Member).
Career: BA Hons (1st Class) Oxon (Chemistry).

MA, DPHIL Oxon (Chemistry). Called to the Bar October 1991 (Middle Temple).

LAWRENCE, Patrick
4 Paper Buildings (Harvey McGregor QC), London (0171) 353 3366
Recommended in Professional Negligence
Specialisation: Principal area of practice is professional negligence. Cases include Bristol & West BS v May, May & Merrimans [1996] 2 All ER 801; Penn v Bristol & West BS [1997] 1 WLR 1356; Bristol & West BS v Fancy & Jackson [1997] 4 All ER 582; Platform Home Loans Ltd v Oyston Shipways Ltd, The Times 15th January 1998.
Prof. Memberships: PNBA.
Career: B.A. (Oxon). Called 1985.

LAWSON, Edmund QC
9-12 Bell Yard (D. Anthony Evans QC), London (0171) 400 1800
Recommended in the following lists: Crime,
Crime: Fraud
Specialisation: Specialist in commercial crime and accounting/auditing negligence. Acts mainly for defendants in large fraud cases as well as advising government departments in relation to insider dealing and regulatory affairs. Has considerable experience in advising on accounting and auditing matters. Practice also covers general crime, particularly the defence of police officers, and judicial review. Interesting cases include 'Blue Arrow' (defended UBS Phillips & Drew); 'Maxwell' (defence of Ian Maxwell); the 'Pan-El' case in Singapore, and the 'Wallace Smith' Chancery case against auditors. Also defended police officers in the prosecutions following the 'Guildford Four' and 'Birmingham Six' cases. 1998: Leading Counsel to Stephen Lawrence Inquiry.
Prof. Memberships: Criminal Bar Association.
Career: Called to the Bar 1971. Pupil then tenant at King's Bench Walk 1971-1976. Joined present chambers 1976. Took silk 1988.
Personal: Educated at the City of Norwich School and at Trinity Hall, Cambridge 1967-1970. Leisure pursuits include music and rugby. Born 17th April 1948. Lives in London.

LAWSON, Michael QC
23 Essex Street (Michael Lawson QC), London (0171) 413 0353
Recommended in the following lists: Crime,
Crime: Fraud
Specialisation: Criminal law specialist. Practice covers general crime, serious organized crime, drugs, child sexual abuse and commercial fraud. Contributor to the Inns of Court School of Law Manual of Professional Conduct and author of 'Refocus on Child abuse'(1994). Experience of advocacy teaching. Governing Committee IATC.
Prof. Memberships: Criminal Bar Association.
Career: Called to the Bar in 1969 and joined present chambers in 1971. Appointed Assistant Recorder in 1983 and Recorder in 1987. Took Silk in 1991. Leader of the South Eastern Circuit Nov 1997.
Personal: Educated at Monkton Combe School 1959-64 and London University 1966-69. Born 3rd February 1946.

LAWSON, Robert
5 Bell Yard (Robert Webb QC), London (0171) 333 8811
Recommended in Aviation
Specialisation: All aspects of aviation litigation and advisory work. In particular: aviation insurance; liability of carriers, manufacturers, maintainers and tour operators; aircraft leases and finance; and, arrest of aircraft.
Prof. Memberships: COMBAR
Career: BA (Oxon). Dip Law (City). Called 1989.

LAWSON ROGERS, Stuart QC
23 Essex Street (Michael Lawson QC), London (0171) 413 0353
Recommended in Crime: Fraud
Specialisation: Handles all areas of criminal law,

particularly commercial fraud and Customs & Excise. Has acted in major VAT and other tax and company frauds and drugs importation cases. Professional clients include H.M. Customs & Excise, The Serious Fraud Office and Inland Revenue. Also disciplinary tribunals work. Department of Trade Inspectorate 1987.
Prof. Memberships: Criminal Bar Association, CCLBA.
Career: Called to the Bar in 1969. Joined present chambers in 1990. Previously at Lamb Building, Temple 1969-89. Standing Counsel to H.M.Customs & Excise (S.E. Circuit Crime) 1989-1994. Recorder since 1990. Legal Assessor to General Medical and Dental Councils ince 1989.
Personal: Educated at Buckingham College 1959-64 and London University (LSE) 1965-68. Past Director of Watford A.F.C. Ltd. Leisure interests include reading, music, theatre and gardening. Born 23rd March 1946.

LE GRICE, Valentine
1 Mitre Court Buildings (Bruce Blair QC), London (0171) 797 7070
Recommended in Family: Matrimonial Finance

LEA, Jeremy H.C.
Chambers of Colin Anderson (St. Mary's Chambers) (Colin Anderson), Nottingham (0115) 950 3503
Recommended in Family/Matrimonial

LEDERMAN, David QC
18 Red Lion Court (Anthony Arlidge QC), London (0171) 520 6000
Recommended in Crime
Specialisation: Crime in all its aspects from fraud to robbery to murder to Brinks Gold Bullion Robbery.
Prof. Memberships: C.B.A.
Career: Cambridge M.A.
Personal: Eating, drinking, sport, theatre, cinema, opera, history, reading.

LEEMING, Ian QC
9 St. John Street (John Hand QC), Manchester (0161) 955 9000
Recommended in Chancery
Specialisation: Chancery and Commercial Litigation, with some Official Referees' work. Insolvency, contentious company work, banking, professional negligence and civil fraud are emphasised. Reported cases include Williams v Burlington (1977) (Company Charges) Brady v Brady (1988) (Financial assistance for purchase of shares). Re: Abbey Leisure (1990) (Unfair prejudice petitions) P&C&R&T Ltd (1991) (Administrators and Section 11 of Insolvency Act 1986). Sen v. Headly (1991) (death-bed gifts of land). Connaught Restaurants (1992) (Indemnity costs in forfeiture proceedings). Morse v Barratt (1993) (exception to Murphy v Brentwood principles). Re Jennings (1994) (Family provisions claims). Kershaw v Whelan (1996) (Discovery and waiver of Professional Privilege).
Prof. Memberships: Chancery Bar Association. Northern Chancery Bar Association. Official Referees Bar Association. Professional Negligence Bar Association.
Career: Called 1970. Silk 1988. Recorder of the Crown Court 1989. Practised at Northern Chancery and Commercial Bar until taking silk. Since has divided time between London and Manchester. Joined Lamb Chambers 1992.
Personal: Born 10 April 1948. Manchester University LL.B. (1970). Sometime lecturer in Law Manchester University. Hobby – Squash.

LEES, Andrew J.
St. Paul's Chambers (Nigel Sangster QC), Leeds (0113) 245 5866
Recommended in Crime

LEGGATT, George QC
Brick Court Chambers (Christopher Clarke QC), London (0171) 583 0777
Recommended in the following lists: Commercial (litigation), Insurance & Reinsurance, Professional Negligence
Specialisation: Commercial Law: including insurance and reinsurance, banking, professional negligence (involving accountants, actuaries, insurance brokers, solicitors and barristers), shipping, company acquisitions and international trade. Other areas of practice include defamation, broadcasting law and judicial review.
Career: Took silk 1997; cases of note: Westdeutsche Landesbank v London Borough of Islington; NRG v Bacon & Woodrow.

LEGH-JONES, Nicholas QC
20 Essex Street (David Johnson QC), London (0171) 583 9294
Recommended in Shipping
Specialisation: Insurance, marine insurance, commercial arbitration and maritime contracts of carriage, international trade. Recent reported cases included Ackman v Policyholders Protection Board [1994] 2 AC 57, HL (scope of protection under Policyholders' Protection Act 1975) and Zeeland Navigation Co v Bank Worms [1995] 1 Lloyd's Rep 251 (rights of foreclosure under ship mortgage). Highlight was publication of 9th ed. of Macgillivray on Insurance Law in Dec 1997, of which I am the General Editor.
Prof. Memberships: London Maritime Arbitrators' Association, Supporting Member Commercial Bar Association, Common Law and Commercial Bar Association.
Career: M.A. History, Oxon. 1964; M.A. Jurisprudence Oxon. 1966. Lecturer-in-Law New College Oxford 1967-1971; called to the Bar 1968; appointed Queen's Counsel 1987; Visiting Professor in Commercial Law King's College London 1998-2001.
Personal: Leisure interests – modern history, vintage motor cars.

LEHAIN, Philip
199 Strand (Peter Andrews QC), London (0171) 379 9779
Recommended in the following lists: Medical Negligence, Personal Injury
Specialisation: Specialist in the areas of medical negligence and personal injury, with a particular emphasis on sports injuries. Practice also covers Professional Negligence and Misconduct, Employment, Construction and General Commercial. Recent reported cases include Joyce v Merton Sutton & Wandsworth H.A. (1996) PIQR 121 (secondary causation in a lock-in syndrome patient with a misplaced suture following a brachial catheterisation) and Smoldon v Nolan (1997) P.I.Q.R. 133 (duty and standard of care of a rugby referee to a player injured after repeated scrummage collapses).
Prof. Memberships: Professional Negligence Bar Association (Treasurer), Action for Victims of Medical Accidents, Personal Injuries Bar Association.
Career: Called to the Bar 1978. Joined present chambers 1990.
Personal: Educated at Queen Mary College, London (LL.B). Working knowledge of French. Leisure pursuits include rugby, cricket, skiing, music cinema, and flying. Born 1st September 1955. Lives in London.

LEIGH, Christopher H. de V. QC
1 Paper Buildings (Roger Titheridge QC), London (0171) 353 3728
Recommended in Crime

LEIST, Ian
1 Hare Court (Stephen Kramer QC), London (0171) 353 5324
Recommended in Crime
Specialisation: General crime including fraud and drugs, prosecuting and defending. Some medical

and professional negligence work, and Human Rights.
Prof. Memberships: Criminal Bar Association. Administrative Law Bar Association.
Career: Call 1981. 1983-1996 5 Kings Bench Walk (David Cocks QC). 1996-1998 1 Hare Court (Stephen Kramer QC).
Personal: Sport and travel.

LEMON, Roy
Devereux Chambers (Jeffrey Burke QC), London (0171) 353 7534
Recommended in Employment
Specialisation: Main areas of practice are employment, business law and injunctions. Reported cases include London Underground v NUR [1989] IRLR 341 & 343; Post Office v Marney [1990] IRLR 170; BT v Ticehurst [1992] ICR 383; Lee v GEC Plessey [1993] IRLR 383 and Nagarajan v Agnew & LRT [1994] IRLR 61. RMT v London Underground Ltd [1995] IRLR 636.
Career: Called to the Bar in 1970 and joined present chambers in 1972.
Personal: Born 31st March 1946. London University (LL.B, 1968). Leisure interests include flying, sailing, skiing and driving. Lives in Fetcham.

LEONARD, Anthony
6 King's Bench Walk (Michael Worsley QC), London (0171) 583 0410
Recommended in Crime
Specialisation: General criminal practice with a concentration on fraud.
Prof. Memberships: Inner Temple, South Eastern Circuit, Criminal Bar Association.
Career: Called to the Bar in 1978 and joined current chambers in 1979. Standing Counsel to the Inland Revenue, South Eastern Circuit.
Personal: Leisure interests include music and theatre. Born 21st April 1956. Lives in London.

LESLIE, Stephen QC
Crown Office Row (Richard Ferguson QC), London (0171) 797 7111
Recommended in Crime
Specialisation: General and Commerical/White Collar crime (including overseas) Criminal Taxation Appeals. Privy Council Commonwealth Appeals.
Prof. Memberships: Criminal Bar Association. South Eastern though practise on other circuits.
Career: Call 1971. Silk 1993.

LESTER OF HERNE HILL, Lord QC
Blackstone Chambers (formerly 2 Hare Court) (P Baxendale QC and C Flint QC), London (0171) 583 1770
Recommended in the following lists: Administrative & Public Law, Civil Liberties, Employment
Specialisation: Public law, employment, media law, European law.
Prof. Memberships: English, Northern Irish and Irish Bars.
Career: Called to English Bar 1963: QC 1975; Bencher Lincoln's Inn 1985; Former Recorder South Eastern Circuit; Deputy High Court Judge.
Personal: Married with two children.

LETT, Brian
South Western Chambers (Brian Lett), Taunton (01823) 331919
Recommended in Crime
Specialisation: H.Brian G.Lett Born 9/8/1949. Called Inner Temple 1971. Practiced exclusively at the London Bar until 1992 when he moved to the West of England and joined the Western Circuit. Now practises mainly in London and the West. Specialises in serious crime and in particular serious fraud. Equally happy prosecuting or defending. Has prosecuted all types of crime as a leading junior, including murders and serious fraud [instructed by the S.F.O]. Led the defence team in many cases involving professional defendants [solicitors, accountants and policemen]. Has particular experience in defending United States

citizens. Defends regularly before disciplinary tribunals.

Prof. Memberships: Criminal Bar Association. Central Criminal Court Bar Mess.

Personal: Married with 4 children of school age. R.F.U. youth coach. Chairman- Monte San Martino Trust.

LEVER, B.L.
Peel Court Chambers (Michael Shorrock QC), Manchester (0161) 832 3791
Recommended in Crime

LEVESON, Brian QC
22 Old Buildings (Benet Hytner QC), London (0171) 831 0222
Byrom Street Chambers (B.A. Hytner QC), Manchester (0161) 829 2100
Recommended in the following lists: Commercial (litigation), Medical Negligence, Sports Law

LEVY, Allan QC
17 Bedford Row (Allan Levy QC), London (0171) 831 7314
Recommended in the following lists: Family: Child Care including child abduction

LEVY, Benjamin
Enterprise Chambers (Anthony Mann QC), London (0171) 405 9471
Recommended in the following lists: Partnership, Property Litigation

Specialisation: Landlord and Tenant; General Chancery; Partnership; Land Law. Cases include United Scientific Holdings Ltd. v Burnley [1987] AC 904 (L&T); Hayim v Citibank [1987] AC 730 (Trusts); Walters v Bingham [1988] FTLR 260 (Partnership); Lehmann v Herman [1993] 1 EGLR 172 (Party Wall).

Prof. Memberships: Lincoln's Inn.

Career: M.A., LL.B. Cambridge. Called 1956; Head of Chambers 1986; Bencher 1989; Chairman Disipline and Appeals Committee: Council for Licensed Conveyancers.

LEVY, Michael
3 Hare Court (William Clegg QC), London (0171) 353 7561
Recommended in Crime

Specialisation: Wholly criminal practice – mostly defence, but not exclusively. General crime and fraud. Some leading work. Recent cases include R v Serafinowicz (The first ever prosecution under the War Crimes Act); R v Murphy & Others (Importation of £125 million of cocaine); R v Nicolson & Others ('Operation Comfort' – Gas Oil Fraud); R v Khaliq & Others (Nigerian Advance fee Fraud). R v Jeans & OR5. (Drug Importation Case).

Prof. Memberships: South Eastern Circuit. Member of Criminal Bar Association. British Academy of Forensic Science.

Career: Called to Bar in 1979 – Gray's Inn. Joined 3 Hare Court in January 1992. (formerly at Francis Taylor Building).

LEVY, Neil
St. John's Chambers (Roderick Denyer QC), Bristol (0117) 921 3456
Recommended in Commercial (litigation)

LEVY, Robert S.
9 Stone Buildings (Michael Ashe QC), London (0171) 404 5055
Recommended in Property Litigation

Specialisation: All aspects of property litigation (including associated professional negligence) with an emphasis on commercial tenancies, housing and conveyancing. Recently reported in Bristol City Council v Lovell [1998] 1 WLR 446 H of L and Farrer v Copley Singleton [1998] 1 PNLR 22.

Prof. Memberships: Chancery Bar Association.

Career: Called 1988 LLB LLM (Cantab). Contributed several title to Atkins' Court Forms including Easements, Trespass to Land, Commons.

Personal: Born 1964. Married with 1 child. Leisure

activities: skiing, piano, banjo, ukelele. Also a member of Assize Court Chambers, Bristol, 14 Small Street, Bristol BS1 1DE.

LEWIS, Adam
Blackstone Chambers (formerly 2 Hare Court) (P Baxendale QC and C Flint QC), London (0171) 583 1770
Recommended in the following lists: European Union/Competition, Sports Law

Specialisation: European Community law within a public, commercial, competition and sports law practice

Career: Call 1985. Professional experience with Wilmer Cutler & Pickering in Washington D.C. and London and McCutcheon Doyle Brown & Enersen in San Francisco between 1985-88, and in the Cabinet of Sir Leon Brittan, European Commissioner responsible for competition and financial institutions, in Brussels in 1991-1992.

Personal: Fluent in French and a working knowledge of German and Norwegian.

LEWIS, Caroline
3 Verulam Buildings (R. Neville Thomas QC), London (0171) 831 8441
Recommended in the following lists: Banking, Commercial (litigation), Financial Services

Specialisation: Commercial litigation; in particular, claims based on international and domestic commercial fraud, professional negligence, banking, financial services and insolvency.

Prof. Memberships: COMBAR, London Common Law and Commercial Bar Association.

Career: Called to the Bar 1988.

LEWIS, Charles
Old Square Chambers (Hon. John Melville Williams QC), London (0171) 269 0300
Recommended in Medical Negligence

Specialisation: Medical negligence on behalf of patients. Also personal injuries. Wrote the first textbook on the medical negligence action. Now in its fourth edition: 'Medical Negligence, a Practitioner's Guide' (published by Butterworths) [May 1998]. Has lectured extensively and published numerous articles. Consultant Editor: 'Medical Litigation.'

Prof. Memberships: Bar Professional Negligence Association; Bar Personal Injuries Group.

Career: Called to the Bar 1963. Joined Old Square Chambers 1991.

Personal: Educated at Charterhouse and Oriel College, Oxford. Interests include opera, singing, golf, languages, cycling and the English countryside.

LEWIS, Clive
4-5 Gray's Inn Square (Miss Elizabeth Appleby QC & The Hon. M. Beloff QC), London (0171) 404 5252
Recommended in Administrative & Public Law

Specialisation: Main areas of practice are public law and judicial review, EC law, education, local government, discrimination and environmental law. Interesting cases include R v HM Treasury ex p. Shepherd Neame Ltd (1998) (compatability of budget increases on beer duty with European law) Richardson v Solihull MBC (special educational needs) Preston v Wolverhampton NHS Trust (1998) (compatibility of time limits for equal pay claims with European law) Barry v Midland Bank plc (1997) (sex discrimination in calculation of redundancy payments) R v Secretary of State ex p. RSPB (1996) (Birds Directive) R v Powys Council ex p. Hambridge (1998) (power to charge for provision of community care services) R v Maldon DC ex p. Pattini (1998) (lawfulness of provision of pharmaceutical services in a supermarket) R v Secretary of State ex p. Lancashire CC (1994) (local government reorganisation). Publications include 'Judicial Remedies in Public Law' (1992) and 'Remedies and the Enforcement of European Community Law' (1996).

Prof. Memberships: Administrative Law Bar Association; Local Government Planning and

Environmental Bar Association, Bar European Group.

Career: Fellow, Selwyn College, Cambridge 1986-1993, Lecturer in Law, University of Cambridge 1989-1993. Called to the Bar 1987. Joined present chambers in 1992.

LEWIS, Hugh
Southernhay Chambers (David Tyzack), Exeter (01392) 255777
Recommended in Family/Matrimonial

Specialisation: Principally Children Act Care proceedings and adoption. Some Private Law child cases.

Prof. Memberships: Family Law Bar Association.

Career: Educated Clifton College and Birmingham University. T.A. Called 1970. Family law specialist throughout career.

Personal: Born 1946. Married with 4 children. Leisure pursuits – hill-walking, skiing, fishing, study of history and archaeology.

LEWIS, James
3 Raymond Buildings (Clive Nicholls QC), London (0171) 831 3833
Recommended in Crime

Specialisation: Extradition; fraud: judicial review of criminal matters and especially review of warrants; case stated; restraint orders; election work. Notable cases in the last year; R v Governor of Brixton Prison ex parte Levin [1997] AC 741 (HL); R v Secretary of State for the Home Department ex parte Launder [1997] 1 WLR 839 (HL); R v Secretary of State for the Home Department ex parte Gilmore [1997] 2 Cr App R 374. R v Bow Street Magistrates Court [1998] 2 WLR 498; R v Staines Magistrates Court ex parte Westfallen [1998] 1 WLR 652; Government of Switzerland v Rev [1998] 3 WLRI (PC). R v Governor of Belmarsh Prison ex parte Gilligan (No 2) [1998] COD 195.

LEWIS, Paul
30 Park Place (Philip Richards), Cardiff (01222) 398421
Recommended in Crime

LEWIS, Ralph
5 Fountain Court (Anthony Barker QC), Birmingham (0121) 606 0500
Recommended in Personal Injury

Specialisation: Catastrophic Injury Claims; Industrial Diseases; Medical Negligence; Professional Negligence.

Prof. Memberships: Personal Injury Bar Association; Professional Negligence Bar Association.

Career: Jesus College, Oxford BA (Oxon). Called to Bar 1978. Middle Temple. Assistant Recorder of the Crown Court.

Personal: Wine, antiques, shooting, skiing.

LEWIS, Raymond
2 Paper Buildings (Desmond de Silva QC), London (0171) 936 2611
Recommended in Crime

Personal: Commercial/company fraud and appeared in a number of high profile cases over past few years. Firearms expert.

Career: 6 years working for merchant bank in corporate finance.

Personal: First novel published 1991.

LEWIS, Rhodri Price
1 Serjeants' Inn (Lionel Read QC), London (0171) 583 1355
Recommended in the following lists: Environmental Law, Planning

LEWISON, Kim QC
Falcon Chambers (Jonathan Gaunt QC & Kim Lewison QC), London (0171) 353 2484
Recommended in Property Litigation

Specialisation: Specialises in Chancery and real property law. Practice covers landlord and tenant, rent review, interpretation of contracts, agricultural holdings, conveyancing, easements, restrictive

covenants, compulsory acquisitions, suretyship and professional negligence in connection with real property. Publications include 'Woodfall on Landlord and Tenant' (General Editor since 1990); 'The Interpretation of Contracts' (1997); 'Lease or Licence' (1985); 'Development Land Tax' (1976); 'Drafting Business Leases' (1996). Consultant Editor of Property & Compensation Reports since 1990. Recent reported cases include Hindcastle v Barbara Attenborough Associates (disclaimer on insolvency); Jervis v Harris (entry to repair); Co-operative Wholesale Society v National Westminster Bank (the headline rent cases); Garston v Scottish Widows (business tenancies) Curtis v London Rent Assessment Committee (fair rent). In 1988 appointed by the Department of the Environment as a member of the Study Team investigating professional negligence and insurance against professional liability. Blundell lecturer three times.
Prof. Memberships: COMBAR; London Common Law & Commercial Bar Association; Chancery Bar Association. Governor of Anglo-American Real Property Institute 1995-1997.
Career: Called to the Bar in 1975. Member of Falcon Chambers since 1976. Took Silk 1991. Appointed Assistant Recorder in 1993. Recorder 1997
Personal: Educated at St. Paul's School 1965-70 and Downing College, Cambridge (1st Class Hons in English Tripos) 1970-73. Fluent French speaker. Council Member of the Liberal Jewish Synagogue 1989-1995; Council Member Leo Baeck College.

LIEVEN, Nathalie
4 Breams Buildings (Christopher Lockhart-Mummery QC), London
(0171) 430 1221/353 5835
Recommended in the following lists: Administrative & Public Law, Parliamentary, Planning
Specialisation: Specialises in local government, planning, social security and judicial review (including education, health and mental health).
Career: Has promoted a number of Parliamentary Bills. Contributes to Halsbury's Laws of England, Town and Country Planning and is a member of the Planning and Environment Bar Association. Called to Bar in 1989. Appointed to the Supplementary Panel of Junior Counsel to the Crown (Common Law) in 1995.

LIGHTWING, Stuart
Counsels' Chambers (Stuart Lightwing), Middlesbrough (01642) 213000
Recommended in Family: Matrimonial Finance
Specialisation: Family/Matrimonial Finance, Employment, Professional Negligence, Personal Injury and Partnership.
Prof. Memberships: Professional Negligence Bar Association.
Career: LL.B., FCIS., FRSA., FCIArb. Called 1972 (M.T.). Harmsworth Law Scholar. Also Barrister in NSW, Australia. Chairman of Medical Appeal Tribunals.

LIMB, Patrick
Ropewalk Chambers (Richard Maxwell QC), Nottingham (0115) 947 2581/2/3/4
Recommended in Personal Injury
Specialisation: All personal injuries actions including tort claims for psychiatric harm and industrial diseases litigation. Hicks v Chief Constable of South Yorkshire Police [1992] 2 AER 63, Alcock v Chief Constable of South Yorkshire Police [1992] 1 AC 310, Frost v Chief Constable of South Yorkshire Police [1997] 3 WLR 1195, Bannister v SGB plc [1997] 4 AER 129, VSEL v Cape [1998] PIQR 207, Tranmore v Scudder (CAT April 28, 1998).
Prof. Memberships: Personal Injuries Bar Association; Nottinghamshire Medico-Legal Society.
Career: The Edinburgh Academy; Pembroke College, Cambridge.

LINDBLOM, Keith QC
2 Harcourt Buildings (Mr Gerard Ryan QC), London (0171) 353 8415
Recommended in the following lists: Environmental Law, Parliamentary, Planning
Specialisation: Planning, Local Government, Parliamentary, Compulsory Purchase and Compensation Law. Work for both private and public sector clients.
Prof. Memberships: Planning and Environment Bar Association; Parliamentary Bar Mess.
Career: Called to the Bar 1980. Joined Harcourt Buildings (Peter Boydell QC) in 1981. QC 1996.

LINDEN, Thomas
4-5 Gray's Inn Square (Miss Elizabeth Appleby QC & The Hon. M. Beloff QC), London (0171) 404 5252
Recommended in Employment
Specialisation: Employment law, particularly appellate work; cases with a European dimension, restraint of trade and wrongful dismissal; well known for transfer of undertakings matters. Discrimination law, including disability discrimination and equal pay. Local government and administrative law. Human Rights Law. General commercial.
Prof. Memberships: Member of the Management Committee of the Employment Lawyers Association, Administrative Law Bar Association.
Career: BA Jurisprudence (First Class) and BCL at Keble College, Oxford 1984-89; called to the Bar 1989. Awarded Council of Legal Educational Studentship, and Prince of Wales, Atkin and Karmel Scholarships at Gray's Inn.

LINEHAN, Stephen QC
5 Fountain Court (Anthony Barker QC), Birmingham (0121) 606 0500
Recommended in Crime

LISSACK, Richard QC
35 Essex Street (Nigel Inglis-Jones QC), London (0171) 353 6381
Recommended in the following lists: Crime, Crime: Fraud
Specialisation: Crime, commercial fraud, financial services, professional negligence, personal injury, medical negligence. Cases include: R v Maxwell, Lyme Bay Canoe Disaster (Corporate Manslaughter), Pescado (Corporate Manslaughter). R v Litchfield (Maria Assumpta), re Southall Rail Disaster (Corporate Manslaughter).
Career: QC (1994 – aged 37), Assistant Recorder 1993.

LISTER, Caroline
One King's Bench Walk (James Townend QC), London (0171) 936 1500
Recommended in the following lists: Family: Child Care including child abduction
Specialisation: Child abduction, public law and private law cases involving children and their families, representing parents, local authorities, guardians and the official solicitor. Ancillary relief.
Prof. Memberships: FLBA.
Career: B.Sc. London University in Comparative Physiology and Microbiology.
Personal: Endurance riding, walking. Two children who require endless ferrying!

LITHMAN, Nigel QC
3 Hare Court (William Clegg QC), London (0171) 353 7561
Recommended in Crime
Specialisation: Serious crime, both heavy defence and prosecutions. Cases include: R v Paton – murder by battered wife; R v Ngai – murder by mother of 4 children; R v Linford – death in custody. Fraud: R v Ghiselli & Others – E.E.C. Fraud and many other white collar frauds. Drugs: Operation Wimpole, Operation Max. Defended serial rapists and Prosecuted or Defended major robbery conspiracies. Private Prosecutions for campaign against Death by Dangerous Driving and Association T.V. appearances. Appeared in the

British Indian Ocean Territories. Since taking Silk has continued to be instructed in the heaviest fraud, murder, rape and other criminal cases.
Prof. Memberships: Assistant Recorder. Member of the C.B.A.
Personal: Committee Member of South Eastern Circuit and Essex Bar Mess and Liaison Committees. Personal interests include 'Fresh Air', travel and the Arts.

LIVESEY, Bernard QC
2 Crown Office Row (John Powell QC), London (0171) 797 8000
Recommended in the following lists: Personal Injury, Professional Negligence
Specialisation: Principal specialisation is litigation in the following fields: general common & commercial law, personal injuries, professional negligence (architects, doctors, engineers, solicitors, surveyors and valuers) and insurance. Leading cases include Spring v. Guardian Assurance (negligent references); Ancell v. Chief Constable of Bedfordshire (liability of police); Halford v. Brookes (limitation); Kumar v. AGF Insurance Ltd (Construction of Insurance Contract); Wood v. Bentall Simplex Ltd (Fatal Accidents Act damages).
Prof. Memberships: COMBAR, Bar European Group; Personal Injuries Bar Association, Professional Negligence Bar Association.
Career: Called to the Bar 1969. Appointed Recorder 1987. Silk in 1990.
Personal: Educated at Peterhouse, Cambridge (MA, LLB).

LIVINGSTON, John
3 Hare Court (William Clegg QC), London (0171) 353 7561
Recommended in Immigration & Nationality
Specialisation: Political asylum work especially with reference to the former Yugoslavia. Undertakes work for refugees from whatever former Republic, and regardless of ethnic origin i.e. Serb, Croat, Muslim or other minority. Fully conversant with all draft evasion and citizenship problems that arise.
Career: Called to the Bar 1980. Member of Grays Inn. Member of Committee of British South Slav States Law Association.
Personal: Learning Serb – Croat. Married to a Serb.

LLOYD, Heather
Peel House (Nigel Gilmour QC), Liverpool (0151) 236 4321
Recommended in Crime
Specialisation: Crime, particularly allegations of sexual abuse.
Prof. Memberships: Criminal Bar Association.
Career: Liverpool University 2:1 LLB 1979.
Personal: Married, 2 children.

LLOYD, Huw
3 Serjeants' Inn (Philip Naughton QC), London (0171) 353 5537
Recommended in Medical Negligence
Specialisation: Specialises in medical law medical negligence and medical ethics work. Recent interesting cases include Re J (A minor) (1992) 3 WLR 5c7; Res S [1993] Fam 123; R v Mid Glamorgan FHSA, South Glamorgan H.A. ex p. Martin; Re S (1995) 1 WLR 110; Secretary of State for Home Dept. v Robb (1995) 2 WLR 722; Re S (hospital patient: court's jurisdiction) (1995) 2 WLR 38; Re J (hospital patient: foreign curator) [1995] 3 WLR 596; Re CH [1996] 1 FLR; Re R (adult: medical treatment) [1996] 2 FLR 99; Re C (adult patient: publicity) [1996] 2 FLR 25; Re T (wardship: medical treatment) [1997] 1 FLR 502; Re D (Medical Treatment) [1998] 1 FLR 411.
Prof. Memberships: London Common Law and Commercial Bar Association. Professional Negligence Bar Association.
Career: Called to the Bar 1975. Middle Temple, Blackstone Entrance Exhibition and Benefactors Senior Law Scholar.

Personal: Educated at City of London School and Leicester University (LL.B). Born 10th May 1952.

LLOYD-ELEY, Andrew
1 Hare Court (Stephen Kramer QC), London (0171) 353 5324
Recommended in the following lists: Crime, Crime: Fraud

LLOYD-JACOB, Campaspe
3 Raymond Buildings (Clive Nicholls QC), London (0171) 831 3833
Recommended in the following lists: Crime, Crime: Fraud
Specialisation: Fraud: Doyle and others (C.C.C.) (Abbey National Corruption Case). Extradition: Examples of successful applications against the Italian Government include Barone and Cavallo. IRA: Gannon and others (C.C.C.); Nicholas Mullen (Court of Appeal).
Career: MA (Oxon).
Personal: The Arts.

LOCKEY, John
Essex Court Chambers (Gordon Pollock QC), London (0171) 813 8000
Recommended in Commercial (litigation)
Specialisation: Insurance and Reinsurance. International trade. Shipping law.
Career: Downing College, Cambridge BA (Law) (starred First) 1985. Harvard Law School LLM 1986. Called to the Bar 1987.
Personal: Born 1963.

LOCKHART-MUMMERY, Christopher QC
4 Breams Buildings (Christopher Lockhart-Mummery QC), London (0171) 430 1221/353 5835
Recommended in the following lists: Parliamentary, Planning
Specialisation: Advises and appears for developers and local authorities at public inquiries and in the High Court. Planning inquiries include the Channel Tunnel Terminal (Waterloo), National Gallery Extension, Mansion House Square Development and Heathrow T.5. Planning cases in the House of Lords include Westminster City Council v British Waterways Board, Westminster City Council v Great Portland Estates, Tesco Stores Ltd v Secretary of State for the Environment. Recent multi-million compensation cases heard in the Lands Tribunal are County & District Properties v London Borough of Harrow, Glasshouse Properties v Secretary of State for Transport, and Carmarthen District Council v Land Authority for Wales.
Career: Called to the Bar July 1971. Took Silk 1986; Bencher Inner Temple 1993; Head of Chambers April 1993; Recorder May 1994; Deputy High Court Judge 1995.
Personal: Born 7th August 1947. Educated at Stowe School and Trinity College, Cambridge (BA Hons).

LODDER, Peter
3 Hare Court (William Clegg QC), London (0171) 353 7561
Recommended in Crime
Specialisation: Fraud and General Crime, Leading and Junior work. Recent reported cases include R v Gray & Ors 1995 2 Cr App R100: Insider Dealing case, authority on question of what evidence in a conspiracy may be relied upon after Crown has elected to proceed on substantives. R v Hancock & Ors 1996 2 Cr App R 554 on whether particulars in a conspiracy to defraud are ingredients of the offence. R v Comerford 1998 1 Cr App R 235 on the circumstances under which a Judge may swear a jury anonymously and order its protection. Occasional prosecutor for Customs & Excise and the Serious Fraud Office.
Prof. Memberships: Elected member of General Council of the Bar since 1994, committee member of Criminal Bar Association, member International Bar Association.
Career: Awarded Jules Thorn (Major) scholarship by Middle Temple 1982.

LOFTHOUSE, Simon
Atkin Chambers (John Blackburn QC), London (0171) 404 0102
Recommended in Construction
Specialisation: Construction and civil engineering, professional negligence (architects, surveyors, engineers and quantity surveyors), energy, oil and gas. Contentious (litigation and arbitration) and non-contentious. Instructed in relation to large commercial and residential developments, airport terminals, hospitals, computer installations and engineering projects onshore and offshore. Cases include Vickery v Modern Securities [1988] 1 BCLC 428 (CA); Cadmus v Amec 51 ConLR 105; Crittal Windows v TJ Evers 54 Con LR 66; Humber Oil Terminals Trustees v Harbour and General 59 BLR 1 (CA); King v McKenna [1991] 2 QB 480.
Prof. Memberships: Official Referees Bar Association. Common Law and Commercial Bar Association.
Career: LL.B (Hons) (Lond); Called 1988. Articles Editor for Current Law 1990-1995.
Personal: Married. Main leisure interest: squash.

LOMNICKA, Prof. Eva
2 Crown Office Row (John Powell QC), London (0171) 797 8000
Recommended in the following lists: Financial Services
Specialisation: Advisory work in consumer credit, securities regulation and financial services, reflecting publications: (1) 'Encyclopedia of Consumer Credit Law'; (2) 'Lomnicka and Powell, Encyclopedia of Financial Services Law'; (3) 'Palmer's Company Law' (Part 11); (4) 'Ellinger and Lomnicka, Modern Banking Law'.
Career: Professor of Law, King's College London. Called to the Bar 1974.
Personal: Born 17 May 1951; 1969-73 Girton College, Cambridge (MA, LLB; Chancellor's Medal). Married with 3 children.

LONG, A.P.
Peel Court Chambers (Michael Shorrock QC), Manchester (0161) 832 3791
Recommended in the following lists: Crime, Health & Safety

LONGMAN, Michael
St. John's Chambers (Roderick Denyer QC), Bristol (0117) 921 3456
Recommended in Crime

LONSDALE, Marion
46 Essex Street (Geoffrey Hawker), London (0171) 583 8899
Recommended in Traditional Chancery
Specialisation: Chancery and tax, especially VAT, practice with particular emphasis on contentious matters (including back duty, judicial review and professional negligence) and litigation at all levels.
Prof. Memberships: Revenue Bar Association. Chancery Bar Association. Chartered Institute of Taxation (ATII).
Career: In practice since 1987. Called to the Bar 1984 following obtaining LLB (hons) London University as external student and passing Bar finals (in top 100) whilst employed full-time by the Chamber of Shipping. Nottingham University 1973-76. B.Sc (Hons) Geography.
Personal: Interests: cycling, sport, upholstery, countryside stewardship.

LORAINE-SMITH, Nicholas
2 Harcourt Buildings (Nigel Mylne QC), London (0171) 353 2112
Recommended in Crime

LORD, David W.
3 Stone Buildings (G.C Vos QC), London (0171) 242 4937
Recommended in the following lists: Insurance & Reinsurance, Media & Entertainment
Specialisation: Principal area of practice is chancery and commercial law. Work includes media and entertainment, insurance and reinsurance, company law, insolvency and bankruptcy. Acted in Deeny and Others v Gooda Walker Ltd and Others on behalf of the Gooda Walker Action Group (Lloyd's Names).
Prof. Memberships: Middle Temple, Lincoln's Inn, Chancery Bar Association.
Career: Called to the Bar in 1987 and became a tenant at Stone Buildings in 1988.
Personal: Educated at King's School Rochester 1971-81 and Bristol University 1982-86 (LL.B Hons). Leisure pursuits include most sports, especially skiing, tennis and hockey. Born 28th September 1964. Lives in London.

LORD, Richard
Brick Court Chambers (Christopher Clarke QC), London (0171) 583 0777
Recommended in the following lists: Commercial (litigation), Shipping
Specialisation: General Commercial and Common Law, including Shipping, Insurance, Professional Negligence and Employment Law. Recent important Cases: 'Houda', Kuwait Petroleum Corp. v I.D. Oil, 'Aditya Vaibhav', 'Subro Valour', 'DELFINI'. NRG v Bacon & Woodrow, "APOSTOLIS" A Meredith Jones v Vangemar.
Prof. Memberships: Heilbron Committee (Joint Working Party of the Civil Courts).
Career: Called to Bar 24 November 1981, Inner Temple.
Personal: Born 2 Jaunuary 1959 in Leamington. Educated at Stowe School and Cambridge – M.A. 1 year Scholarship at Cambridge (1979-80). Publication: Controlled Drugs – Law and Practice (Butterworths Nov 1984). Guide to the Arbitration Act 1996 (with Simon Salzedo (Cavendish 1996).

LOVELL-PANK, Dorian QC
6 King's Bench Walk (Michael Worsley QC), London (0171) 583 0410
Recommended in Crime

LOWE, David QC
Wilberforce Chambers (Edward Nugee QC), London (0171) 306 0102
Recommended in Traditional Chancery
Specialisation: Wide advisory and litigation practice, both in England and abroad, covering all aspects of property law and the law of trusts. English and offshore trust litigation. Comprehensive range of private client advisory work: related applications to Court covering directions by Trustees, variation of trusts, and compromises of family disputes and problems arising as a result of professional negligence or breach of duty. Inheritance tax planning in relation to settled landed estates with an emphasis on heritage property – collections, historic houses and their contents, including the sale of high value chattels. Involved in trust aspects of the sale of the Thyssen-Bornemisza Collection to the Kingdom of Spain. Trust aspects of commercial transactions, including takeover of Wellcome by Glaxo, Forte by Granada and the Savoy Group by Blackstone: incentive and other funds or schemes for employees: trust matters relating to Lloyds. Pension matters including litigation. Charity law and practice including litigation.
Career: Called to the Bar July 1965. In practice, in Wilberforce Chambers 1966 to date. QC 1984. Master of the Bench of the Middle Temple 1992. Harmsworth Scholar, Middle Temple.
Personal: Born 1st November 1942. Read Law at Cambridge 1961-64. M.A. (First Class). Scholar and MacMahon Law Student at St. John's College, Cambridge.

LOWE, (Nicholas) Mark QC
2-3 Gray's Inn Square (Anthony Scrivener QC), London (0171) 242 4986
Recommended in Planning
Specialisation: Town and Country Planning (all areas and with particular experience of shopping, housing, B use class, listed buildings and major energy, waste and incineration projects). Local government and administrative law (including local

government finance, vires and employment and TUPE), environmental and property related litigation and all tribunal work including Lands Tribunal.
Prof. Memberships: P.E.B.A. A.L.B.A.
Career: Colchester Royal Grammar. Leicester University LLB 1969. Called to Bar 1972. Same Chambers since 1973. QC 1996.

LOWE, William QC
Plowden Buildings (William Lowe QC), London (0171) 583 0808
Recommended in Personal Injury
Specialisation: Personal injury, including Medical Negligence and Industrial Disease. Crime. Licensing.
Prof. Memberships: PIBA
Career: Educated at Sedburgh School, Yorkshire. Newcastle University. Call 1972.

LOWENSTEIN, Paul
Littleton Chambers (Michael Burton QC), London (0171) 797 8600
Recommended in the following lists: Alternative Dispute Resolution, Banking, Commercial (litigation)
Specialisation: Principal area of practice is commercial and business law, covering all aspects of commercial litigation, in particular: multinational disputes and conflict of laws; professional negligence (especially of solicitors, surveyors and valuers); 'boardroom bust-ups'; domestic and international trade disputes; entertainment & media; claims concerning defective plant and machinery and employment covenants. Other main areas of practice are banking, building societies, financial transactions and security documentation and insolvency. Recent notable cases include The Evia Luck (No.2) [1992]; Mont v Mills [1993]; Hanover Insurance Brokers v Schapiro [1994]; Re: Shoe Lace Ltd (in liquidation) [1994]; Nicholls v Kinsey [1994]; Halifax B.S. v Brown (No.1) & (No.2) [1995] and Bristol & West B.S. v May, May & Merrimans [1996]; Bristol & West B.S v. Daniels [1997]; Bristol & West B.S. v Bhadresa [1997] and Bristol & West B.S. v Fancy Jackson [1997]. Accredited as a Mediator by CEDR.
Prof. Memberships: COMBAR; PNBA; LCLCBA; Centre for Dispute Resolution.
Career: Called to the Bar 1988 and joined current chambers 1989 (when located at 2 Crown Office Row). **Personal:** Educated at Westminster School 1977-81, Manchester University 1983-86 (LL.B Hons) and Cambridge University 1986-87 (LL.M). Leisure pursuits include sailing and skiing. Born 31st December 1963. Lives in London.

LUBA, Jan
Two Garden Court (I. Macdonald QC & O. Davies), London (0171) 353 1633
Recommended in Administrative & Public Law

LUCAS, Noel
1 Middle Temple Lane (Colin Dines & Andrew Trollope QC), London (0171) 583 0659 (12 lines)
Recommended in the following lists: Crime, Crime: Fraud

LUMLEY, Gerald
9 Woodhouse Square (John Morris Collins), Leeds (0113) 245 1986
Recommended in Crime
Specialisation: Respected Criminal specialist who has appeared in many high profile cases. Practice includes homicide, sexual offences, child abuse, drugs and fraud. Has a keen interest in psychiatry and often acts for mentally disturbed defendants. Also has substantial experience of Licensing law.
Career: Called to the Bar in 1972.

LYDIARD, Andrew
Brick Court Chambers (Christopher Clarke QC), London (0171) 583 0777
Recommended in Aviation
Specialisation: Commercial litigation insurance, reinsurance and aviation.
Career: BA (Hons) LLM (Harvard).

LYNAGH, Richard QC
2 Crown Office Row (Graeme Hamilton QC), London (0171) 797 8100
Recommended in Professional Negligence
Specialisation: Principal areas of practice are professional negligence, insurance, personal injury and general common law. Work includes many aspects of profession negligence (surveyors, valuers, lawyers, accountants and doctors). Interesting recent cases include McCullagh v Lane Fox [1994] 1 EGLR 48, [1996] 1 EGLR 35, Headford v Bristol and District Health Authority [1995] 6 Med LR 1; Craneheath v York Montague [1994] 1 EGLR 154, [1996] 1 EGLR 130.
Prof. Memberships: COMBAR.
Career: Called to Bar 1975, Took Silk 1996. Gray's Inn.
Personal: Born 14th November 1952. LLB London.

LYNCH, Adrian Charles Edmund
11 King's Bench Walk (Eldred Tabachnik QC and James Goudie QC), London (0171) 632 8500
Recommended in Employment
Specialisation: Principal area of practice is employment law, covering unfair and wrongful dismissal, sex and race discrimination, trade union law and restrictive covenants. Other main areas of practice are commercial and public law.
Prof. Memberships: Gray's Inn, COMBAR
Career: Called to the Bar in 1983 and joined present chambers in 1984.
Personal: Educated at King's College, London.

LYNCH, Jerome
Cloisters (Laura Cox QC), London (0171) 827 4000
Recommended in Crime

LYNCH, Patricia QC
18 Red Lion Court (Anthony Arlidge QC), London (0171) 520 6000
Recommended in Crime

LYNDON-STANFORD, Michael QC
13 Old Square (Mr Michael Lyndon-Stanford QC), London (0171) 404 4800
Recommended in Company
Specialisation: Principal fields of practice consist of company and commercial litigation, including minority shareholders proceedings, insolvency, business law, commercial fraud, professional negligence, equity, insurance and reinsurance. Recent cases include Senate Electrical Wholesalers Ltd v Alcatel Submarine Networks Ltd. (Court of Appeal 22/6/98) concerning share purchase agreements.
Prof. Memberships: Chancery Bar Association, Commercial Bar Association, Insolvency Lawyers' Association.
Career: QC 1979. Has practised in foreign jurisdictions and has been called (ad hoc) for cases in Hong Kong, Singapore and the Isle of Man.
Personal: M.A. (Cantab). Member of the Inner Temple and of Lincoln's Inn.

LYON, Adrian
14 Castle St (Adrian Lyon), Liverpool (0151) 236 4421/8240/6759/6757
Recommended in Medical Negligence
Specialisation: Medical negligence and personal injury work. Conducted the case of Lybert a lead authority on informed consent in the Court of Appeal. Junior Counsel in a number of Cervical Cancer Radiotherapy cases at Christie. Was Junior Counsel on the Generic Legal Aid Certificate for the Manchester 'Selection' Radiotherapy Cases. Junior Counsel in a Class Action involving over 100 clients suing the North Staffordshire HA in request of a Radiotherapy accident. Handling over 50 cerebal palsy cases.
Prof. Memberships: Personal Injury Bar Association. Employment Bar Association. FLBA member.
Career: Pursued a general common law practice in Liverpool, since call in 1975. Recorder. Latterly,

practice has been more concentrated on professional negligence, commercial law, personal injury and employment law.
Personal: Married to Professor Christina Lyon, Dean of the Faculty of Law at Liverpool, 2 children. Hobbies include, travel, music and reading but most importantly walking the two dogs.

LYON, Victor
Essex Court Chambers (Gordon Pollock QC), London (0171) 813 8000
Recommended in Insurance & Reinsurance
Specialisation: Insurance-related litigation and advocacy roles. General litigation and commercial law.
Career: Trinity College, Cambridge MA (Junior Scholar). Called to the Bar 1980.
Personal: Born 1956.

MABB, David
Erskine Chambers (Richard Sykes QC), London (0171) 242 5532
Recommended in Company

MACDONALD, Alistair
Park Court Chambers (James Stewart QC, Robert Smith QC), Leeds (0113) 243 3277
Recommended in Crime
Specialisation: Principally, drug cases and those in which a scientific or medical element plays a large part. These often involve DNA analysis as an important part and forensic pathological evidence is frequently of considerable significance. Commercial fraud is a growing area of practice.
Prof. Memberships: Criminal Bar Association.
Career: Wigan Grammar School followed by an honours degree in biochemistry. I conducted toxicological analyses and immunological research as a student. Once qualified, I spent two years as a toxicologist in the Department of Forensic Medicine, Charing Cross Hospital Medical School using sophisticated analytical equipment of the sort used by the Government Forensic Science Service. I then researched liver transplantation and the development of liver disease in cystic fibrosis patients after I converted to law.
Prof. Memberships: I sing second bass with the Leeds Festival Chorus and enjoy music. I also ski, ride, play tennis and enjoy all sports.

MACDONALD, Charles QC
4 Essex Court (Nigel Teare QC), London (0171) 797 7970
Recommended in Shipping
Specialisation: Admiralty and Commercial shipping, Carriage of Goods, International Trade, Commercial and International Arbitration, Insurance and Reinsurance, Private International law, Marine/Environmental law, Transport. Has extensive experience of all types of marine litigation including upwards of 100 salvage arbitration disputes. Among his recent cases concerning road transport, collision, pilotage, damages, charterparty war risks, international arbitration, conflict of laws and commercial fraud are: Spectra v Hayesoak. CA, 30497 'The Common Venture' [1995] 2 LLR 230; Oceangas (Gibraltar) Limited v PLA [1993] 2 LLR 292; The Botany Triad v Lu Shan [1993] 2 LLR 259; 'The Product Star (No 2)' [1993] 1 LLR 397; 'The Paula D'Alesio' [1994] 2 LLR 366; 'The Polessk and Akademik Oisif Orbeli' [1996] 2 LLR 40; Standard Chartered Bank v PNSC et al [1996] 2 LLR 365. Also regularly appears in City of London commercial arbitrations. Publications: General Editor, 'International Maritime Law' (Lawtext Publishing Limited).
Career: Glasgow Academy, New College Oxford (MA Hons Jurisprudence 1971). Called to Bar, Lincoln's Inn, 1972. Appointments: Queen's Counsel, 1992. Assistant Recorder of the Crown Court, 1996.
Personal: DOB 31.8.49, Glasgow. Married with three daughters and lives in East Sussex.

MACDONALD, Ian QC
Two Garden Court (I. Macdonald QC & O. Davies), London (0171) 353 1633
Recommended in the following lists: Crime, Immigration & Nationality
Specialisation: Administrative law: particularly immigration and education law, criminal law, civil law, including actions, involving the police, coroners' inquests, employment and trade union law, race and sex discrimination law. British Representative on Commission Speciale pour l'etude les lois anti-trust (1963-65). Member of legal committee of inquiry into student sit-ins at Manchester University (1971). Member of independent trade union committee of inquiry into events on rights- to-work march on Friday 19 March 1976. Chairman of Inquiry into death of Ahmed Ullah and racial violence in Manchester schools (1987-88). Chair of inquiry into recruitment fraud in London Borough of Hackney (1995-96). Publications: Resale Price Maintenance (1964); The Land Commission Act 1967 (Co-author); Race Relations and Immigration Law (1969); Race Relations; The New Law (1977); Macdonald's Immigration Law and Practice (1983), 4th edition (1995) with Nicholas Blake QC; The New Nationality Law with Nicholas Blake QC (1984); Murder in the playground (Co-author) (1990); Consultant Editor Butterworth's Encyclopaedia of Forms and Precedents – Nationality and Immigration (1994). Has written numerous articles on (inter alia) immigration, race, employment law etc. for New Law Journal. IDS Brief. IDS Brief Supplements, Oxford Economic Law Review, Race & Class, Race Today, Immigration & Nationality Law and Practice and for journals in the US. Is on editorial board of Immigration & Nationality Law and Practice.
Prof. Memberships: Immigration Law Practitioners Association (President since 1984). Criminal Bar Association. Administrative Law Bar Association. Bar European Group.
Personal: Fluent French.

MACDONALD, Kenneth QC
Two Garden Court (I. Macdonald QC & O. Davies), London (0171) 353 1633
Recommended in the following lists: Crime, Crime: Fraud
Specialisation: A criminal defence specialist. Complex Frauds (including SFO work, deposit-taking frauds, advance fee frauds, solicitor frauds etc). Sanctions-busting cases (all aspects, including the illegal export of arms and weapons-making equipment, computers, high technology, pharmaceuticals etc. Clients in this area include major foreign defence corporations). Terrorism (Irish, Sikh, Palestinian and Algerian). Bombings, murders and possession of arms and explosives). Major drugs conspiracies (importation, manufacture and supply) Murders (including multiple murders and child killings). Obscene publications (books, videos, lyrics, artwork. Clients include major record companies and video producers. Has a substantial advice-based practice in this area). Cases include: Matrix Churchill; The Ordtech Appeal; R v McKane (an IRA trial involving bombings and multiple murders); R v Kinsella (the Warrington bombing case – again the IRA); R v Sakaria (a sikh terrorist case involving explosives and conspiracies to murder); R v Zekra (the alleged car-bombings of the Israeli Embassy and a Jewish charity building in London).

MACGREGOR, Alastair R. QC
One Essex Court (Anthony Grabiner QC), London (0171) 583 2000
Recommended in Commercial (litigation)
Specialisation: Practice covers a wide range of commercial litigation including, in particular, disputes relating to takeovers, share sale agreements, newspaper and other distributorships, the oil and gas industry, partnerships and joint ventures, banking transactions and securities, professional negligence and conflict of laws.

Recent important cases include Hytec v Coventry C.C. [1997] 1WLR 1666- ('unless' orders – striking out); Wahda Bank v Arab Bank [1996] 1 Lloyds 470 (proper law of counter-guarantees – UN and EU sanctions legislation); Gamlestaden v Casa de Suecia SA [1994] 1 Lloyds 433 (Brussels Convention); Aiglon Limited v Gau Shan Co Limited [1993] 1 Lloyds 164 (Mareva injunction – Insolvency Act ss 238 and 423 – jurisdiction); Korso Finance v Wedge (guarantees and indemnities – jurisdiction); Bailey v News International (termination of distributorships); Hallett v British Board of Boxing Control (refusal of manager's licence); Re British & Commonwealth Holdings PLC.
Prof. Memberships: South Eastern Circuit, COMBAR.
Career: Called to the Bar in 1974 and joined One Essex Court in 1975. Took Silk in 1994.
Personal: Educated at Glasgow Academy (to 1968), Edinburgh University 1969-70 and Oxford University 1970-73 (MA, 1st Class Hons). Born 23rd December 1951.

MACHELL, Raymond Donatus QC
Deans Court Chambers (H.K. Goddard QC), Manchester (0161) 834 4097
Recommended in Personal Injury

MACHIN, Graham
Ropewalk Chambers (Richard Maxwell QC), Nottingham (0115) 947 2581/2/3/4
Recommended in Administrative & Public Law
Specialisation: Planning, Local Government, Environmental Law and Real Property, including professional negligence claims and criminal cases relating to these areas. Major tasks in recent years have included the representation of planning authorities at UDP and Local Plan inquiries.
Prof. Memberships: Planning and Environment, Administrative Law and Professional Negligence Bar Associations; Legal Associate (and former Council member) of the RTPI; Member and East Midlands Regional Chair of UK Environmental Law Association.
Career: Educated at Nottingham High School and Lincoln College, Oxford; BCL, MA. Called 1965 by Gray's Inn. In practice at Ropewalk Chambers since 1965.
Personal: Married since 1966 to Judith Machin; 4 children, 2 grandchildren. Leisure interests numerous but unremarkable.

MACKAY, Colin QC
39 Essex Street (Edwin Glasgow QC), London (0171) 832 1111
Recommended in the following lists: Personal Injury, Sports Law
Specialisation: Personal injury; medical and solicitors negligence; insurance. Page v. Smith [1996] AC 155 HL; Elliott v. Saunders & Liverpool FC (1994); O'Neil v. Fashanu & Wimbledon FC (1995); Brady v. Sunderland FC (1998); Knight v. Chester City FC (1997).
Prof. Memberships: LCLCBA (Past Vice-Chairman). PIBA.
Career: M.A. Oxford.

MACLEOD, Duncan
9 Gough Square (Jeremy Roberts Q.C), London (0171) 353 5371
Recommended in Personal Injury
Specialisation: Principal area of practice is medical negligence and personal injury work. Other main areas of work cover police civil actions and the law and practice of food safety. Co-author of 'Food Safety: Law and Practice' (1994).
Career: Called to the Bar 1980. Tenant at 4 King's Bench Walk 1981-89 before joining present chambers. Visiting lecturer at Hong Kong University, University of Malaya, Kuala Lumpur and University of Mauritius.
Personal: BA (Hons) University of London 1974-77 and LLB (Hons) 1978-80 University of Wales. Born 21st March 1955. Lives in London.

MACLEOD, Nigel QC
4 Breams Buildings (Christopher Lockhart-Mummery QC), London (0171) 430 1221/353 5835
Recommended in the following lists: Parliamentary, Planning
Specialisation: Planning, local government, environmental, parliamentary, public, and administrative law. Has appeared in many major public inquiries, including highways, shopping, nuclear power stations, airports, housing, and waste development proposal inquiries, as well as in Parliamentary Bill proceedings concerning major development projects. Clients have included Government Departments, local authorities, and major organisations and companies. Promoted a major development for the Ministry of Defence (Otterburn in Northumberland National Park).
Prof. Memberships: Chairman Planning and Environment Bar Association; member of Administrative Law Bar Association and the Parliamentary Bar Mess.
Career: Called to Bar 1961; QC 1979; Recorder 1981; Deputy High Court Judge sitting on Planning Cases, since 1992; Bencher Gray's Inn 1993.
Personal: M.A., B.C.L., Christ Church Oxford. Lives in London and Derbyshire.

MACRORY, Richard
Brick Court Chambers (Christopher Clarke QC), London (0171) 583 0777
Recommended in Environmental Law
Specialisation: Environmental law, EC law.
Prof. Memberships: UK Environmental Law Association (first chairman).
Career: Called to Bar in 1974. Professor of Environmental Law at Imperial College, London, 1991. 1997- Specialist Advisor House of Commons Select Committee on Environment, Transport and Regions. Member Royal Commission on Environmental pollution. Author of "Bibliography of European Environmental Law" (Oxford University Press 1995). Editor Journal of Environmental Law.

MACUR, Julia QC
St. Ive's Chambers (Edward Coke), Birmingham (0121) 236 0863 (6 lines)
Recommended in the following lists: Crime, Environmental Law, Family/Matrimonial

MAHER, Martha
Guildhall Chambers (John Royce QC), Bristol (0117) 927 3366
Recommended in the following lists: Chancery, Commercial (litigation)
Specialisation: Commercial contracts and fraud, company especially shareholder actions, insolvency (company and individual), partnership disputes especially involving professional partnerships; banking; director disqualifications; professional negligence involving Solicitors, Accountants, Vets in particular. Growing equestrian practice. Recent cases include Bristol and West Building Society v Back and Melinek and Secretary of State for Trade and Industry v Griffiths (RE West Mid Packaging Services Limited) (CA).
Prof. Memberships: Chancery Bar Association, Society of Practitioners in Insolvency.
Career: BCL, LLB (Cork) LLM (Cantab). Call 1987 Inner Temple. Cork Examiner Scholarship, Inner Temple Major Scholarship.
Personal: Very keen on all equestrian sports.

MAIDMENT, Kieran
Doughty Street Chambers (Geoffrey Robertson QC), London (0171) 404 1313
Recommended in Crime

MAIDMENT, Susan R
One King's Bench Walk (James Townend QC), London (0171) 936 1500
Recommended in the following lists: Family: Child Care including child abduction
Specialisation: Principal area of practice is family law including private and public law relating to children, ancillary relief and divorce, Inheritance Act

claims and property disputes between unmarried partners. Author of numerous articles on all aspects of family law in a variety of legal journals and books of essays. Author of Judicial Separation Research Study commissioned by Law Commission and published by SSRC Socio-Legal Research Centre, Wolfson College, Oxford, 1982 and 'Child Custody and Divorce: The Law in Social Context' (Croom Helm 1984). Lectures frequently to lawyers and social workers on all areas of family law.
Career: Called 1968. Lecturer in Law, University of Bristol 1967-70, and University of Keele 1970-76. Senior Lecturer in Law, specialising in family law, University of Keele 1976-84. General Secretary International Society on Family Law 1979-85. Nuffield Foundation Social Science Research Fellow, studying child-custody decision making, 1982-83. Pupil at 1 Mitre Court 1984-85, then tenant at 4 Brick Court 1985-89. Joined 1 Kings Bench Walk in 1989.
Personal: Educated at South Hampstead High School 1955-62 and London School of Economics 1962-65 (LL.B) and 1965-66 (LL.M). Awarded LLD at University of Keele and Fellowship in 1984 for publications in Family law. Born 15th February 1944. Lives in London.

MALCOLM, Helen
3 Raymond Buildings (Clive Nicholls QC), London (0171) 831 3833
Recommended in the following lists: Crime, Crime: Fraud
Specialisation: Has substantial experience in commercial fraud and corruption cases (prosecuted in R v Gee). Also specialises in extradition (Hagan & Croft, Kiriakos, Allison (on computer misuse)).
Prof. Memberships: International Bar Association, Criminal Bar Association.
Career: MA (Oxon) Oriental Studies (Persian with Arabic), Qualified 1996. Tutor, Inns of Court and Bar Educational Trust. Advocacy Trainer, Gray's Inn. Archbold Editor (Chapter 30 – Company/Commercial Crime).

MALE, John
4 Breams Buildings (Christopher Lockhart-Mummery QC), London
(0171) 430 1221/353 5835
Recommended in the following lists: Planning, Property Litigation
Specialisation: Landlord and tenant, town and country planning, compulsory purchase and compensation.
Prof. Memberships: Called to the Bar by Lincolns Inn in 1976 and is a member of the Chancery Bar Association and the Planning and Environment Bar Association.
Career: Educated at Minchenden Grammar School, London and Sidney Sussex College, Cambridge obtaining a B.A. in law. One of the contributors to Halsbury's Laws on Town and Country Planning. An editor of Hill & Redman's Law of Landlord and Tenant.

MALEK, Ali QC
3 Verulam Buildings (R. Neville Thomas QC), London (0171) 831 8441
Recommended in the following lists: Arbitration, Banking, Commercial (litigation), Professional Negligence
Specialisation: All aspects of commercial law with an emphasis on banking including bank secrecy, regulatory issues, auditing of banks (acting in negligence cases against auditors), securities, letters of credit, bills of exchange, performance bonds, sovereign debt and state immunity problems, domestic banking cases, syndicated loans, insolvencies, white collar crime and banking frauds, tracing, constructive trusts and injunctions. Also handles financial professional negligence cases, international and domestic arbitrations, insurance disputes and conflict of laws. Cases include Cryne v Barclays (1987) (bank's rights in

making demands for repayment); Re Rafidain (1992) (bank accounts/sovereign immunity); Barclays v Khaira (1992) (bank's duties on taking security); A and others (1994) (Banking Act 1987); Robertson v CIBC (1994) (Privy Council case on bank's duties when served with a subpoena). National Provincial Building Society v Lloyd (1996) (mortgagees rights); Barclays v Thompson (1996) (undue influence); Glencore v Bank of China (1996) (letters of credit); BCCI v PW (1997) (Banking Act 1987). Ispahani v Bank Melli (1998) (conflict of laws; Box v Barclays Bank (1998) (constructive trust). Frequent speaker on these topics to conferences and seminars. Presented joint paper at Creaton Conference on Banks, Fraud and Crime entitled 'Cross-Border Fraudulent Activity' (Pub. Lloyd's of London Press, 1994).
Prof. Memberships: International Bar Association, COMBAR, London Common Law and Commercial Bar Association.
Career: Called to the Bar 1980 and joined current chambers 1981.
Personal: Educated at Bedford School and Keble College, Oxford (MA, BCL). Leisure pursuits include family life. Born 1956.

MALEK, Hodge M.
4-5 Gray's Inn Square (Miss Elizabeth Appleby QC & The Hon. M. Beloff QC), London (0171) 404 5252
Recommended in the following lists: Banking, Financial Services
Specialisation: Specialises in commercial law, including accountancy, banking, company, financial services, fraud, insurance, securities, professional negligence and shipping. Instructed in complex commercial litigation in the commercial court and in arbitrations, including Banque Financiere v Westgate [1990] (banking and insurance fraud), Johnson Matthey v Arthur Young (collapse of Johnson Matthey Bank), Ocean v Bimeh Iran Insurance Company [1990] (reinsurance), Trafalgar Tours v Henry (jurisdiction), Gucci v Gucci [1991] (passing-off), Lombard Finance v Brookplain [1991] (banking), Westdeutsche Landesbank v Islington [1994] (interest rate swaps), NPRT v Allen, Allen and Hemsley [1996] (banking), R v Secretary of State ex p.Greenpeace [1997] (judicial review) and AEI v PPL [1997] (copyright). Instructed in fraud cases by Serious Fraud Office. Acted for SRO's in disciplinary proceedings and judicial review. Acts in French criminal proceedings, including investigation into Alma crash [1998]. Counsel for Customs & Excise (European) and on Supplemental Panel for Treasury (common law). Joint author of `Discovery' (Sweet & Maxwell, 1992) Lectures on civil procedure.
Prof. Memberships: COMBAR.
Personal: Educated at Bedford School 1968-77, University of the Sorbonne, 1978 and Keble College, Oxford 1978-82 (MA,BCL). Fellow of the Royal Numismatic Society (Council 1991-4); Shamma Prize (1997).

MALES, Stephen QC
20 Essex Street (David Johnson QC), London (0171) 583 9294
Recommended in the following lists: Aviation, Energy & Utilities
Specialisation: International trade and commercial law; shipping; sale of goods and commodity trading; letters of credit, performance bonds and bills of exchange; arbitration; energy law; insurance; conflict of laws; breach of confidence. Appointed as arbitrator; evidence of English law for overseas courts. Principal cases: The Lutetian [1982] 2 Lloyd's Rep 140 (time charter withdrawal); The Playa Larga [1983] 2 Lloyd's Rep 171 (diversion of Cuban sugar sold to Chile); The Golden Anne [1984] 2 Lloyd's Rep 489 (anti-suit injunction); K/S A/S Bani v Korea Shipbuilding [1987] 2 Lloyd's Rep 445 (security for arbitration costs); The Naxos [1990] 1 WLR 1337 (sale of sugar); The Bazias 3 [1993] QB 673 (arbitration

security); Amoco v Amerada Hess [1994] 1 Lloyd's Rep 330 (North Sea oilfield redetermination); The Griparion (No 1) [1994] 1 Lloyd's Rep 578 (inquiry as to damages); The Fanis [1994] 1 Lloyd's Rep 633 (damages for breach of charterparty); Gill & Duffus v Rionda Futures [1994] 2 Lloyd's Rep 67 (sale contract demurrage); The Andreas P [1994] 2 Lloyd's Rep 183 (ship sale); Far Eastern Shipping v Sovcomflot [1995] 1 Lloyd's Rep 520, Potter J (enforcement of arbitration award); The Niobe [1995] 1 Lloyd's Rep 579 (ship sale); Petromin v Sencav [1995] 1 Lloyd's Rep 603 (security for costs, permament stay); The Xing Su Hai [1995] 2 Lloyd's Rep 15 (Brussels Convention and Order 11); Toepfer v Molino Boschi [1996] 1 Lloyd's Rep 510 (anti-suit injunction); Grogan v Robin Meredith Plant Hire [1996] CLC 1127 (incorporation of standard conditions); Lexmar v Nordisk [1997] 1 Lloyd's Rep 289 (Brussels Convention); Ocular Sciences v Aspect Vision Care [1997] RPC 289 (breach of confidence, duties of directors); The Selda [1998] 1 Lloyd's Rep 416 (GAFTA default clause); Cargill v Bangladesh Sugar [1996] 2 Lloyd's Rep 524 [1998] 1 WLR 461 (performance bonds); Scottish Power v Britoil, CA, Nov 1997 (sale of gas from North Sea gas field; whether injunction to be granted to restrain future breaches of long term contract); Rafsanjan Pistachio Producers v Kauffmanns, Rix J, Dec 1997 (whether binding contract at prices to be agreed); Huyton v Jakil, CA March 1998 (appeal from arbitrators and order for remission struck out for want of prosecution). Casenotes and articles: Fundamental breach – burden of proof – reasonableness [1978] CLJ 24; Notice of contract terms – a common law requirement of reasonableness? [1996] LMCLQ 334; Confidence in arbitration [1998] LMCLQ 245.
Prof. Memberships: Member of Commercial Court Committee, Combar, LCLCBA, IBA Energy Lawyers Group.
Career: St John's College, Cambridge 1974-7. Called 1978. Queens Counsel 1998.

MALINS, Julian QC
1 Hare Court (Lord Neill of Bladen QC & Richard Southwell QC), London (0171) 353 3171
Recommended in the following lists: Financial Services
Specialisation: General commercial work especially civil fraud shipping, insurance, sale of goods, financial services, professional disciplinary and defamation [junior counsel in Jeffrey Archer-v-The Star and Elton John-v-The Sun].
Prof. Memberships: Member of The Commercial Bar Association. Member of The Corporation of London since 1981. Disciplinary Tribunal Chairman of SFA. Governor of the Museum of London.
Career: Read law at Brasenose College, Oxford. Called to the Bar in 1972. Took silk in 1991. Appointed a Disciplinary Tribunal Chairman for The Securities and Futures Authority Ltd in 1994. Elected to the Bar Council in 1986. Elected to the City Council in 1981.
Personal: Born 1st May 1950. Married with 3 daughters. Boxing Blue 1968, 1969 and 1970. Played first class rugby [Springboks 1969, Fiji 1970]. Member of the Editorial Board of Counsel Magazine. Member of the Policy Committee of the London Chamber of Commerce and Industry.

MALLALIEU, Ann QC
6 King's Bench Walk (Michael Worsley QC), London (0171) 583 0410
Recommended in Crime

MANLEY, David
40 King St (Philip Raynor QC), Manchester (0161) 832 9082
Recommended in the following lists: Environmental Law, Planning
Specialisation: Planning Appeals, Conduct of Local Plans, UDP's (7 in 3 years), Highways, CPO's, Environmental Law, Judicial Review.

Prof. Memberships: PEBA
Career: Called to bar in 1981. General Common Law Practice 1981-1988. Specialised exclusively in above areas 1988 to date.

MANN, Anthony QC
Enterprise Chambers (Anthony Mann QC), London (0171) 405 9471
Recommended in the following lists: Banking, Commercial (litigation), Chancery, Company, Insolvency, Professional Negligence
Specialisation: Broad commercial chancery practice with an emphasis on Insolvency and banking law. Recent reported cases include Re MC Bacon [1990] (insolvency, transaction at undervalue); Re David Meek Plant Ltd [1993] (Proceedings for recovery of leased equipment); National Westminster Bank v Skelton [1993] (cross-claims in mortgage possession actions) Smith New Court v Citibank [1996] (damages for fraud); Kleinwort Benson v South Tyneside [1993] and South Tyneside v Svenska [1994] (local authority swaps; ultra vires transactions; interest; Re Secure & Provide Plc [1992] (public interest winding up petitions); Nestle v National Westminster Bank [1993] (principles for assessing losses arising from breach of trust) and Target Holdings v Redfern [1995] (solicitors' negligence and breach of trust); Barclays Bank v Eustice [1995] (discovery; privilege; transactions at an undervalue); Barrow v Bankside Agency Ltd [1996] (issue estoppel; Lloyds litigation); Fitch v Official Receiver [1996] (bankruptcy – rescinding bankruptcy order); Gold Coin Joailliers v UBK [1996] (duty of care in bank references); London Borough of Sutton v Wellesley Housing Assoc [1996] (Local authority ultra vires).

MANN, Paul
No.1 High Pavement (John B. Milmo QC), Nottingham (0115) 941 8218
Recommended in Crime

MANNING, Colin
Littleton Chambers (Michael Burton QC), London (0171) 797 8600
Recommended in the following lists: Alternative Dispute Resolution, Computer & I.T.
Specialisation: Principal areas of practice are general commercial and business law specialising in commercial contract disputes including computer litigation (involving the supply and implementation of computer systems, networking and associated intellectual property rights) and also professional negligence (primarily solicitors and valuers).
Prof. Memberships: COMBAR London Common Law and Commercial Bar Association. CEDR Accredited Mediator.
Career: Called, Gray's Inn, 1970.
Personal: Educated at Christ's College School, Finchley, London and at University College London.

MANSFIELD, Michael QC
14 Tooks Court (Michael Mansfield QC), London (0171) 405 8828
Recommended in the following lists: Civil Liberties, Crime

MANZONI, Charles
39 Essex Street (Edwin Glasgow QC), London (0171) 832 1111
Recommended in the following lists: Construction, Professional Negligence
Specialisation: All areas of professional negligence, including Accountants, Solicitors, Architects, Engineers and Surveyors. Practice emphasises construction/engineering and computer industry cases, and encompasses litigation, arbitration and mediation. Also practises in general construction/engineering and computer industry cases and the associated insurance law. Recent cases include Black Country Development Corporation v Kier, Multi Design Consultants v George Fischer, Zeneca v LMC, Balfour Beatty v Docklands Light Railway.

Prof. Memberships: Institution of Mechanical Engineers. Official Referees Bar Association. Society of Computers and Law. London Common Law and Commercial Bar Association.
Career: Qualified and practised as a Mechanical Engineer before qualifying for the Bar in 1988.

MARKS, David
3/4 South Square (Michael Crystal QC), London (0171) 696 9900
Recommended in the following lists: Company, Insolvency
Specialisation: Insolvency, company, commercial. 1997/8 cases include: John Dee Group v WMH. Re A & C Supplies Ltd. Re Datadeck Ltd.
Prof. Memberships: Chancery Bar Association. Insolvency Lawyers Association. Society of Practitioners of Insolvency (legal member). International Bar Association. Justice. Joint Editor: Rowlatt on Principal and Surety. General Editor: Tolley's Insolvency Service. Editor: Encyclopaedia of Forms and Precedents (Guarantees). Contributor to Lightman & Moss: Law of Receivers of Companies and Totty & Moss: Insolvency.
Career: Oxford University: MA, BCL. Member, Illinois and Federal Bars, United States. Bilingual: French. Deputy Registrar in Bankruptcy. Data Appeal tribunal, Deputy Chairman.

MARKS, Lewis
Queen Elizabeth Building (Ian Karsten QC), London (0171) 797 7837
Recommended in Family: Matrimonial Finance
Career: Recent cases include: F v F (Ancillary Relief: Substantial Assets) [1995] 2 FLR 45. Dart v Dart [1996] 2 FLR 286 C/A; H v H (Child Abduction: Acquiescence) [1996] 2 FLR 570 C/A, [1997] 1 FLR 872 H/L; S v S (Child Abduction: Non-Convention Country) [1994] 2 FLR 681.
Prof. Memberships: Family Law Bar Association; DPA Accepted.
Personal: Born 1961. Called 1984. Educated Oxford University (BA Juris)

MARKS, R.L.
Peel Court Chambers (Michael Shorrock QC), Manchester (0161) 832 3791
Recommended in Crime

MARQUAND, Charles
3 New Square (Lord Goodhart QC), London (0171) 405 5577
Recommended in Financial Services
Specialisation: Principal area of practice: financial services, UK and EC. Also company/commercial. Engaged as adviser to Polish and Estonian govts. on harmonisation of financial services legislation with EC standards by EC Commision (PHARE), and by Know-How Fund (Foreign Office) to advise Romanian officials. Author of various articles on financial services topics. Lectures on financial services (incl. law of derivatives) to universities, solicitors and conferences.
Prof. Memberships: Chancery Bar Association, Bar European Group.
Career: Called 1987: Practised at chambers of J.J.Rowe QC. 1993-1996: Legal Adviser at HM Treasury dealing with a wide range of financial services issues and related areas (company/commercial), drafting legislation, implementing and negotiating EC Directives. Closely involved inter alia with legal framework for CREST, Public Offers of Securities regulations and investment advertisement exemptions, 1996: Joined 3 New Square.
Personal: MA Oxon.

MARRIN, John QC
Keating Chambers (Richard Fernyhough QC), London (0171) 544 2600
Recommended in the following lists: Alternative Dispute Resolution, Construction
Specialisation: Barrister practising also as arbitrator, legal assessor, mediator and lecturer in the field of building and civil engineering; professional negligence; contaminated land;

bonds and guarantees; computer software disputes; clients include national and international contractors, professionals, and national and local government.
Career: Qualified 1974; Inner Temple; QC 1990; recorder 1997; CEDR accredited mediator 1993.
Personal: Sherborne School and Magdalene College, Cambridge (1973 MA Catab). Born 1951; resides London.

MARSHALL, Derek
College Chambers (Robin Belben), Southampton (01703) 230338
Recommended in Insolvency
Specialisation: General civic practice with particular interest in professional negligence and insolvency.
Prof. Memberships: Professional Negligence Bar Association.
Career: Southampton University LL.B.

MARSHALL, Philip
Serle Court Chambers (Charles Sparrow QC QC), London (0171) 242 6105
Recommended in Chancery
Specialisation: Commercial fraud (Cala Cristal v Al-Borno; Canada Trust v Stolzenberg); insolvency (BIM v Maxwell; Re: Murjahi); banking (Wahda Bank v Arab Bank); company; commercial litigation; professional negligence (Brown v GRE; Peach Publishing v Slater).
Prof. Memberships: Chancery Bar Association.
Career: Queens' Cambridge; Harvard Law School. Former Fellow of Queens' Cambridge. Joint editor of "The Practice and Procedure of the Companies Court".

MARSHALL, Philip Derek
Iscoed Chambers (Trefor Davies), Swansea (01792) 652988/9
Recommended in Personal Injury

MARSON, Geoffrey C. QC
Sovereign Chambers (Formerly known as 25 Park Square) (Geoffrey C. Marson QC), Leeds (0113) 245 1841
Recommended in Crime

MARTEN, Hedley
3 New Square (Lord Goodhart QC), London (0171) 405 5577
Recommended in the following lists: Chancery, Company
Specialisation: Specialist in a broad area of Chancery work including company law, (particularly minority shareholders' disputes and directors' disqualification proceedings), contract, insolvency, landlord & tenant, and trusts, (particularly contested probate); Judicial review. Also acts for Solicitors in proceedings brought by the Law Society under the Solicitors Act 1974. Important cases include Cowan v Department of Health [1991] (landlord & tenant, trusts); Vestey v Clifton-Brown [1991] (Variation of Trusts Act 1958); Re Packaging Direct Ltd [1993] (Director's Disqualification); re: a Solicitor [1996] (judicial review).
Career: Called to the Bar 1966. Chancery Bar representative on the Bar Council 1989-95. Executive head of chambers since 1995.
Personal: Born 1943. Educated at Winchester College and Magdalene College, Cambridge (MA 1966). Lives in London. Three children.

MARTIN, Gerard
Exchange Chambers (William Waldron QC), Liverpool (0151) 236 7747
Recommended in Personal Injury
Specialisation: Personal Injury including medical negligence; catastrophic injuries including – brain, spine, amputees and cerebral palsy; PI claims against M.O.D.
Prof. Memberships: PIBA, PNBA, APIL.
Career: St Joseph's College Blackpool. Cambridge University. Called 1978. Assistant Recorder 1997.

MARTIN, John QC
Wilberforce Chambers (Edward Nugee QC),
London (0171) 306 0102
*Recommended in the following lists: Pensions,
Property Litigation, Traditional Chancery*
Specialisation: Advocate specialising in chancery
and commercial Supreme Court litigation. Also
advises in contentious matters, covering the wide
range of topics comprising modern commercial
chancery practice, Since 1993 he has been a
Deputy High Court Judge in the Chancery Division.
Judicial experience: Deputy High Court Judge,
Chancery Division since 1993: cases include
matters relating to director's disqualification;
passing off; undue influence in relation to
mortgages; receivers' rights to possession.
Assistant recorder. Arbitrator in solicitors'
partnership dispute.
Career: Called to the Bar in July 1972. Practised at
the Chancery Bar in Liverpool joining Wilberforce
Chambers in 1981. Took silk in 1991.

MARTIN, Roy
1 Serjeants' Inn (Lionel Read QC), London
(0171) 583 1355
Recommended in Planning
Specialisation: Planning, environmental, Queen's
Counsel Scotland (1988).
Prof. Memberships: Planning and Environmental
Bar Association, Affiliate of the Royal Incorporation
of Architects in Scotland.
Prof. Memberships: Harris Superquarry inquiry for
applicants (1994-95). Gartcosh Powerstation
inquiry for applicants (1997). City of Edinburgh v
Secretary of State for Scotland (House of Lords
1997).

MARTIN-SPERRY, David
Crown Office Row (Richard Ferguson QC),
London (0171) 797 7111
Recommended in Crime

MARZEC, Alexandra
5 Raymond Buildings (Patrick Milmo QC),
London (0171) 242 2902
Recommended in Defamation

MASKREY, Simeon QC
9 Bedford Row (John Goldring QC), London
(0171) 242 3555
Recommended in Medical Negligence
Specialisation: Principal area of practice is
professional negligence with an emphasis on
medical negligence. Also involved in disciplinary
cases and all forms of litigation with a medical
element (including public law child care
proceedings). Member of the Education Faculty of
the Royal College of Surgeons. Regular contributor
to AVMA conferences. Leading counsel in R v
Dixon (1995), Poynter v Hillingdon Health Authority
(1997), Spargo v Essex Health Authority (1998),
Fleming v Lincolnshire Police (1998).
Prof. Memberships: Professional Negligence Bar
Association. Member of the Midland and Oxford
Circuit. Member of AVMA Bar group.
Career: Called to the Bar in 1977. Appointed
Recorder in 1997. Took silk in 1995.
Personal: Educated at King's School, Grantham
and Leicester University. Born 17th May 1955.

MASON, Alexandra
3 Stone Buildings (G.C Vos QC), London
(0171) 242 4937
Recommended in Traditional Chancery
Specialisation: Wills, trusts, capital taxation and
related professional negligence. Includes non-
contentious drafting of wills, settlements and
related documentation, charities, construction of
documents, variation of trusts applications,
contentious probate, breach of trust actions, and
applications under the Inheritance (Provision for
Family and Dependants) Act 1975. Also Court of
Protection Applications. Recent work includes
acting for the representative beneficiary in the pilot
application concerning deceased Lloyd's names
(Re Yorke) and making applications for leave to

distribute under the later Practice Direction.
Prof. Memberships: Chancery Bar Association,
Revenue Bar Association, STEP.
Career: BA Hons, History, UCL 1979. Diploma in
Law, City University 1980. Joint Author of 7th Ed.
'Spencer Maurice's Family Provision on Death'.

MATHER-LEES, Michael
Albion Chambers (J.C.T. Barton QC), Bristol
(0117) 927 2144
Recommended in Crime

MATHEW, John QC
5 Paper Buildings (John Mathew QC), London
(0171) 583 6117
Recommended in Crime: Fraud

MATTHEWS, Dennis
5 Bell Yard (Robert Webb QC), London
(0171) 333 8811
*Recommended in the following lists: Medical
Negligence, Personal Injury*
Specialisation: Principal areas of practice are
medical and other professional negligence work,
insurance and major personal injury litigation (both
group and individual). Also handles general
commercial litigation. Clients include health
authorities and trusts, medical defence
organisations, professional indemnity insurers,
corporate insurers and Lloyd's syndicates.
Prof. Memberships: London Common Law and
Commercial Bar Association, Professional
Negligence Bar Association.
Career: Called to the Bar 1973.
Personal: Born 16th March 1950.

MATTHEWS, Duncan
20 Essex Street (David Johnson QC), London
(0171) 583 9294
*Recommended in the following lists: Arbitration,
Aviation, Shipping*
Specialisation: Principally, all types of international
and domestic commercial matters including in
particular international trade and carriage of goods,
oil and gas, construction, conflict of laws,
insurance and reinsurance, banking, financial
services, professional negligence. Advocacy:
Counsel appearing before the High Court, Court of
Appeal and House of Lords in England and a
variety of legal and commercial arbitration tribunals
both in England and abroad including international
bodies such as UNCITRAL and ICC and other
domestic organisations such as the LMAA. Have
also been appointed and sat as arbitrator.
Reported cases: House of Lords – 'The Maria D'
[1992] 1 AC 21; 'The Naxos' [1990] 1 WLR 1337.
Privy Council – 'The Mahkutai' [1996] AC 650.
Court of Appeal 'The Berge Sund' [1993] 2 L1 Rep
453; Soules v Intertradex [1991] 1 L1 Rep 378;
Dole Dried Fruit v Trustin Kerwood [1990] 1 L1 Rep
309; Medway v Meurer [1990] 2 L1 Rep 112. Ist
Instance – 'The Visvliet' [1997] 1 Int ML 5; Toepfer v
Molino Boschi [1996] 1 L1 Rep 510; Aratra v Taylor
Joynson Garrett [1995] 4 AER 695; Swiss Bank
Corporation v Premier League The Times 9
February 1995; Kaufmann v Credit Lyonnais Bank
The Times 1 February 1995; 'The Andreas P'
[1994] 2 L1 Rep 183; 'The Giannis NK' [1994] 2 L1
Rep 171; 'The Cebu (No 2)' [1993] QB 1.
Prof. Memberships: COMBAR; LCLCBA.
Supporting Member LMAA; Franco British Lawyers
Society; British Italian Law Association; British
German Jurists Association.
Career: Westminster School. Magdalen College,
Oxford. BA (Hons) Oxon 1984. MA 1996.

MATTHEWS, Janek
Pump Court Tax Chambers (Andrew Thornhill
QC), London (0171) 414 8080
Recommended in Tax
Specialisation: Tax related advice and litigation.
Prof. Memberships: Chartered Accountant.
Career: Co-author: Self Assessment (Tolleys).

MATTHEWS, Richard
3 Hare Court (William Clegg QC), London
(0171) 353 7561
Recommended in Crime
Specialisation: Criminal Law Specialist including
Fraud. Cases include: R v Schultz (Supermarket
Manager kidnap/robbery); R v Trevelyan
(Corruption by Ministry of Defence official); R v
Martin (Child sexual abuse/murder); R v Davis
(D.T.I. Fraudulent trading); R v Smith & Palk (D.T. I.
Fraudulent trading); R v Wilson (Kidnap and rape);
R v Langley (V.A.T./Inland Revenue fraud).
Prof. Memberships: Criminal Bar Association
South Eastern Circuit
Career: Principal Legal Advisor Parliamentary War
Crimes Group 1988-1989. Called to the Bar 1989.
Joined Chambers 1989.
Personal: Born 5th April 1966. Educated at Girton
College, Cambridge University. (M.A. Cantab).
Lives in London.

MATTHEWS, Suzan QC
Guildford Chambers (Jeffrey Widdup), Guildford
(01483) 539131
Recommended in Family/Matrimonial
Specialisation: All areas of Family Law, particularly
ancillary relief involving substantial assets, private
companies, complex financial structures. Child
Care (Public Law), s.8 Applications, Adoption,
Surrogacy, Abduction. Recent cases Hellyer v
Hellyer, Atkinson v Atkinson, Re W (A
Minor)(Residence Order). Criminal Law.
Murder/attempt murder, rape, kidnapping and
serious sexual offences against children, and those
involving young or vulnerable clients/witnesses.
Abuse of Process issues particularly in delayed
reporting of sexual offences.
Prof. Memberships: Family Law Bar Association;
Criminal Bar Association; British Agency for
Adoption and Fostering; Family Rights Group.
Career: BSc. (Hons) Business Administration
1972. Middle Temple 1974. Bradford Chambers
1974. Guildford Chambers 1979. Gas Consumer
Council 1987-1996. Assistant Boundary
Commissioner 1992. Queen's Counsel 1993.
Chairman, Committee of Special Inquiry, MAFF
1993. Recorder 1995. Criminal Inquiries
Compensation Appeals Panel 1996. Lord
Chancellor's Advisory Board on Family Law 1997.
Personal: Married, one son.

MATTISON, Andrew
Chavasse Court Chambers (Andrew Mattison),
Liverpool (0151) 707 1191
Recommended in Crime

MAULEVERER, Bruce QC
4 Pump Court (Bruce Mauleverer QC), London
(0171) 353 2656
*Recommended in the following lists: Construction,
Professional Negligence*
Specialisation: Principal areas of practice are
construction and other commercial contracts and
professional negligence work, covering all aspects
of litigation and arbitration, both domestic and
international. Has acted for insurers, contractors,
building owners, engineers, accountants and
solicitors. International arbitrations in Hong Kong,
Dubai, Egypt and Switzerland. Also sits as an
arbitrator.
Prof. Memberships: Official Referees' Bar
Association, Commercial Bar Association,
Professional Negligence Bar Association, Member
of Executive Committee of Combar.
Career: Called to the Bar in 1969, took silk in 1985.
Recorder 1985. Deputy Official Referee 1989.
Deputy High Court Judge 1992. Head of
Chambers 1992. Bencher Inner Temple 1993. Vice
Chairman International Law Association 1994.
Member of Executive Committee of the
International Social Science Council (UNESCO)
1994. FCIArb.
Personal: Born 22nd November 1946. Educated at
Sherborne School and Durham University.

MAWREY, Richard QC
2 Harcourt Buildings (Roger Henderson QC), London (0171) 583 9020
Recommended in the following lists: Financial Services, Planning
Specialisation: Main areas of practice are commercial law and local authority work. Commercial work includes contracts, leasing, finance and credit law, financial services, computer law and commercial drafting. Local authority work covers contracts, public procurement, public liability, finance, employment and all aspects of passenger transport. Advising on local taxation, land development, housing, community services and computer problems. Author of 'Computers and the Law'. Specialist Editor: Butterworths 'County Court Precedents and Pleadings' and 'Bullen & Leake & Jacob's Precedents of Pleadings'.
Prof. Memberships: London Common Law and Commercial Bar Association, Local Government Planning and Environmental Bar Association.
Career: Called to the Bar 1964 and joined present chambers 1965. Appointed Assistant Recorder 1981. Took Silk 1986. Appointed Recorder 1986 and Deputy High Court Judge 1994.
Personal: Scholar of Rossall School and Exhibitioner of Magdalen College, Oxford (BA Jurisprudence 1963, First Class Honours, and Eldon Scholar of Oxford University 1964, MA 1967.) Born 20th August 1942. Lives in London.

MAXWELL, Richard QC
Ropewalk Chambers (Richard Maxwell QC), Nottingham (0115) 947 2581/2/3/4
Recommended in the following lists: Medical Negligence, Personal Injury

MAY, Kieran
8 Stone Buildings (John Cherry QC), London (0171) 831 9881
Recommended in Personal Injury
Specialisation: Principal area of practice is personal injury work, particularly asbestos-related diseases, industrial deafness and serious accident work. Also handles professional negligence matters, particularly in the medical and legal fields.
Prof. Memberships: Professional Negligence Bar Association and Personal Injuries Bar Association
Career: Called to the Bar 1971.
Personal: Educated at Oxford University (BA).

MCALLISTER, Ann
Enterprise Chambers (Anthony Mann QC), London (0171) 405 9471
Recommended in the following lists: Agriculture & Bloodstock, Property Litigation
Specialisation: Principal area of practice is landlord and tenant, property law and agricultural tenancies, although practice also includes all aspects of general chancery law (mortgages, partnerships, guarantees, insolvency) and, increasingly, professional negligence work.
Career: Called to the Bar in 1982.
Personal: Read law and languages at Newnham College, Cambridge. After graduating in 1975 went to LSE and gained an LL.M in law. Taught law for three years at the University of London (School of Oriental and African Studies).

MCCALL, Christopher H. QC
13 Old Square (Mr Michael Lyndon-Stanford QC), London (0171) 404 4800
Recommended in the following lists: Charities, Tax, Traditional Chancery
Specialisation: Specialises in trust, revenue and charity law. Has appeared in numerous appeals in the House of Lords, Privy Council and Court of Appeal; has regularly addressed specialist associations and seminars.
Prof. Memberships: Member of Bar Council 1973-1976. Committee Member, Chancery Bar Association 1990-92.
Career: Called to Bar Lincolns Inn, November 1966. Took silk, April 1987. Benches 1993. 2nd Junior Counsel to the Inland Revenue in Chancery

Matters 1977-1987. Junior Counsel to the Attorney-General in Charity Matters 1981-1987. Practised at 7 New Square Lincolns Inn 1967-1994, subsequently 13 Old Square.
Personal: Born 3 March 1944. Married 1981, no children. Educated Winchester College (Scholar), Magdalen College, Oxford (Demy): 1st class, Mathematical Moderations 1962 and Schools 1964. Eldon Scholarship: 1966.

MCCARROLL, John J.
Exchange Chambers (William Waldron QC), Liverpool (0151) 236 7747
Recommended in the following lists: Chancery, Insolvency

MCCARTHY, Roger QC
Cloisters (Laura Cox QC), London (0171) 827 4000
Recommended in Administrative & Public Law
Specialisation: Wide ranging public and administrative law practice including the span of local authority, health authority/trust functions. Extensive practice in regulation of private and public nursing and residential homes for adults and children, also tribunals, inquiries and inquests. Advisory work and representation for private individuals, public bodies and commercial bodies, families, Official Solicitor. Has appeared in over 50 reported cases at all court levels in the past which include the following subjects areas:- (in alphabetical order) children, community care services, crime, disabled persons, discrimination, education, hospital and health services, housing, judicial review, local government finance, licensing and registration, mental health, nursing and residential care, planning, social security, social services, and trade descriptions. Has appeared in a large number of reported Registered Homes Tribunal decisions setting significant criteria on a wide range of topics. Other main area of practice apart from public and administrative law lies in family law including all aspects of the law relating to children. Consulting editor of community care publication "Registered Homes".
Prof. Memberships: Member of Administrative Law Bar Association and Family Law Bar Association.
Career: Called to the Bar 1975. Took silk 1996. Joined Cloisters Jan 1997.
Personal: Lives in London. Enjoys family, company, countryside and culture.

MCCAUGHRAN, John
One Essex Court (Anthony Grabiner QC), London (0171) 583 2000
Recommended in Commercial (litigation)
Specialisation: Principal area of practice is commercial litigation.
Prof. Memberships: Commercial Bar Association
Career: Called to the Bar in 1982.
Personal: Educated at Methodist College, Belfast 1969-76 and Trinity Hall, Cambridge 1977-80. Born 24th April 1958. Lives in London.

MCCOMBE, Richard QC
13 Old Square (Mr Michael Lyndon-Stanford QC), London (0171) 404 4800
Recommended in Insolvency
Specialisation: Commercial Chancery, including insolvency. Has worked since starting practice in a set of Chambers dealing with all aspects of Chancery practice. This has involved a good deal of insolvency work for office holders and those on the receiving end of the claims. Work continues to include company law, property, commercial contracts, including commercial fraud and international asset tracing cases. Heavily involved in the litigation following the collapse of the International Tin Council in the early 1990's, including advising all claimant creditors upon the mechanics of the settlement of the claims. Worked for a major merchant bank in claims made against it uder the Financial Services Act in respect of listing particulars. Has also worked upon the BCCI litigation in the Cayman Islands and upon a large

partnership/trust dispute and other Chancery matters in Singapore; admitted ad hoc to the Bars of both those countries. Speaks French and German. Has experience of dealing with German court documents, interviewing witnesses and conducting correspondence in German, obtained during the course of an appointment as Companies Act Inspector (with JK Heywood FCA of Price Waterhouse) into the affairs of Norton Group Plc (1991-92). Also works in various cases involving the inter-play of legal and accountancy skills. Recently involved in ART. 86 case involving traffic at a major British Port.
Prof. Memberships: Chancery Bar Association, COMBAR, Criminal Bar Association, Singapore Academy of Law.
Career: Called to the Bar 1975, Silk 1989. Junior Council to the Director General of Fair Trading 1982-89. Recorder of the Crown Court (1996). Deputy High Court Judge. Attorney-General of the Duchy of Lancaster. Leader of the UK delegation (comprising solicitors and barristers from all the UK jurisdictions) to the CCBE (Council of the Bars and Law Societies of the European Union).
Personal: Educated at Sedbergh School, Graf Stauffenberg Gymnasium Osnabrück and Downing College, Cambridge. Lives in Kew and has a "bolt hole" (with telephone!) in rural France. Hobbies include cricket and rugby football, karate with the children and flying small aircraft.

MCCORMICK, William
10 King's Bench Walk (Ronald Thwaites QC), London (0171) 353 2501
Recommended in Crime
Specialisation: Experienced in cases of large scale corporate fraud and serial offences. Cases include R v Robert Black (child abductions and murders); R v Moss and others (franchise underwriting fraud); R v Brittain (allegations of murders by warden of home for elderly). He is also regularly involved in allied litigation including restraint and confiscation proceedings. He recently appeared in Francisco v Diedrick (claim for damages for alleged murder).
Prof. Memberships: APIL. Bar Sports Law Group. CBA.
Career: LLB (Wales). Called 1985. Gray's Inn.

MCCRACKEN, Robert
2 Harcourt Buildings (Mr Gerard Ryan QC), London (0171) 353 8415
Recommended in Environmental Law
Specialisation: Principal area of practice is environmental law, especially land use and planning aspects. Acted in Heathrow Terminal 5 Inquiry, Windermere Speed Limit Inquiry/Otterburn MOD Inquiry, Newham LBC v. E.L.H.A. [1986] JPEL 60, City of London Building Society v Flegg [1988] AC 54 and R v Northumbria Water Authority ex p Able [1996] COD p187. Clients include National Grid, BP, Elf, Tesco, Bryant Homes, Greenpeace, and the Treasury Solicitor. Author of various articles for legal periodicals including 'Liability of Funding Institutions for Contaminated Land' (JPF,1992).
Prof. Memberships: Local Government Planning and Environmental Bar Association (Secretary 1992-94), United Kingdom Environmental Law Association (Chairman 1995-1997). Member Legal Advisory Panel to Council for the Protection of Rural England. Honorary Counsel to Council for National Parks.
Career: Called to the Bar 1973 and joined 2 Harcourt Buildings 1974.
Personal: Educated at Worcester College, Oxford 1968-71 (MA). Former educational missionary in East Africa. Leisure pursuits include fell walking, natural science and painting. Born 15th March 1950.

MCCREDIE, Fionnuala
3 Serjeants' Inn (Philip Naughton QC), London
(0171) 353 5537
Recommended in Construction
Specialisation: Principal areas of practice are construction and engineering litigation and arbitration, including professional negligence. Experienced in high value, multiparty litigation acting for employers, contractors and sub-contractors. Important cases include Christiani & Nielsen v Birmingham City Council, Norwich Union v Schal, Hilton v Hotel Services Limited. Other main area of practice is employment: industrial tribunal claims including unfair dismissal and race and sex discrimination.
Prof. Memberships: Official Referees Bar Association, Professional Negligence Bar Association.
Career: First career in property development for a Housing Association. Called to the Bar in 1992; Middle Temple.
Personal: Born 1 January 1965, Educated: School North London Collegiate School; Manchester University (BSc Hons 1986), Brunel University (MA 1990), Middlesex Polytechnic (CPE 1991). Interests include skiing and hill walking.

MCCULLOUGH, Angus
1 Crown Office Row (Robert Seabrook QC), London (0171) 797 7500
Recommended in Environmental Law
Specialisation: Environmental Litigation – especially Contaminated Land, Water Pollution, Particulate Emissions, & Environmental claims involving personal injury.
Prof. Memberships: UKELA, Professional Negligence Bar Association
Career: BA (Hons) Oxon in Zoology.

MCCUTCHEON, Barry
8 Gray's Inn Square (Patrick C. Soares), London (0171) 242 3529
Recommended in Tax
Specialisation: Revenue law, including capital taxation, trusts, foreign domiciliaries, offshore and international planning, insurance based planning and employee share schemes. Author of 'McCutcheon on Inheritance Tax'. Founder and Editor of 'Private Client Business' and co-editor of 'Euro-Trusts: The New European Dimension for Trusts' and 'Death and Taxes in Europe'. Well-known as lecturer and conference organiser in the UK and internationally.
Prof. Memberships: Chartered Institute of Taxation (Ex-Chairman, Capital Taxes Sub-Committee), Society of Trust and Estate Practitioners.
Career: Called to the Bar 1975. Tax consultant to Ernst & Young (as is now known) 1978-85. Joined present chambers in 1985.

MCDERMOTT, Gerard
8 King St (Keith Armitage QC), Manchester (0161) 834 9560
Recommended in Personal Injury
Specialisation: Personal Injury, including spinal injury and brain damage cases. Medical negligence. Employment – Recent notable cases: instructed as Junior Counsel for Rentokil in Brown v Rentokil – House of Lords (Scotland) – Times Law Reports 3rd July 1998 – a sex discrimination case involving maternity rights and the interpretation of the Equal Treatment Directive. Presently the subject of an Article 177 reference to the European Court of Justice.
Prof. Memberships: Personal Injury Bar Association; Bar European Group.
Career: Manchester University 1974 – 1977 (LLB Hons). Called to the Bar 1978 (Middle Temple). Admitted to the New York State Bar 1990.
Personal: Member of the Bar Council 1983 – 1988 and 1990 – 1996. Chariman of the Young Barristers Comittee 1987. Currently Chairman of the American Bar Association Working Party of the Bar Council – responsible for maintaining and developing links between the ABA and the Bar

Council and Vice Chairman of International Relations Committee.

MCDERMOTT, John
Chavasse Court Chambers (Andrew Mattison), Liverpool (0151) 707 1191
Recommended in Crime

MCDERMOTT, Tom
Farrar's Building (Gerard Elias QC), London (0171) 583 9241
Recommended in Personal Injury
Specialisation: Practice covers general common law matters with an emphasis on personal injury. Also handles professional and medical negligence and employment.
Prof. Memberships: South Eastern Circuit.
Career: Called to the Bar and joined Farrar's Building in 1980.
Personal: Educated at University College, London (LL.B, 1978) and Queens' College, Cambridge (Institute of Criminology) (M.Phil, 1979). Called to the Irish Bar, King's Inns, Dublin in 1991. Born 11th September 1955. Lives in Hertfordshire.

MCDONNELL, John B.W. QC
1 New Square (Eben Hamilton QC), London (0171) 405 0884
Recommended in Chancery
Specialisation: Practice has a strong bias towards litigation. Regularly instructed in trials both in the Chancery Division and in the Queen's Bench Division. Matters include securities for borrowing, company or insolvency matters, judicial review, human rights, questions concerning trusts (especially charities) or constructive trusts, commercial fraud, professional negligence, copyright and intellectual property, real property, landlord and tenant and partnership. Has regularly advised two of the Clearing Banks on banking and security matters. Frequently involved in cases with an international element. Has appeared frequently in the Supreme Court of Hong Kong, the High Court of the Isle of Man and the Grand Court of the Cayman Islands.
Career: Called to the Bar, 1968. Took Silk 1984. Elected a Bencher of Lincoln's Inn, 1993. Before commencing practice at the Bar had worked in the United States Congress, Conservative Research Dept, H.M. Diplomatic Service (as Assistant Private Secretary to the Foreign Secretary). Sits as a Deputy High Court Judge attached to the Chancery Division.
Prof. Memberships: Governor of the Inns of Court School of Law.

MCFARLAND, Denise
Three New Square (David E.M. Young QC), London (0171) 405 1111
Recommended in Intellectual Property
Specialisation: All aspects of Intellectual Property. Recent Cases include: Ray v Classic FM, BA v PRS, (Copyright Tribunal) Cinpres v Melea (CA), PLG v Ardon, Cala v McAlpine, British Diabetic Association v The Diabetic Society, Lancs Fires v SA Lyons, Novamedix v NDM, Norsk Hydro's As Patent, Carflow v Linwood (second trial), as well as numerous decisions from the Trade Marks Registry, and copyright tribunal.
Prof. Memberships: British Council Member of AIPPI; Committee member of T.I.PL.O; Women's Bar Assn; Intellectual Property Bar Assn; Chancery Bar Assn. Former Examiner for Chartered Institute of Trade Mark Agents professional examination.
Career: Cambridge University (MA).
Personal: Riding and all country pursuits, music and theatre.

MCFARLANE, Andrew QC
One King's Bench Walk (James Townend QC), London (0171) 936 1500
Recommended in Family: Child Care including child abduction
Specialisation: Principal area of practice is family law. Handles all aspects with particular expertise in the law relating to children (both public and private

law), international child abduction and adoption. Has appeared before the House of Lords and before the European Court of Human Rights. Co-author with David Hershman of 'Children: Law & Practice' (Family Law 1991), contributor to 'Family Court Practice' (Family Law 1998) and Editorial Board: Sweet & Maxwell, 'Practical Research Papers'. Regular lecturer at nationally organised conferences and seminars.
Prof. Memberships: Midlands & Oxford Circuit, Family Law Bar Association, Association of Lawyers for Children, British Agencies for Adoption and Fostering.
Career: Called to the Bar in 1977. At Priory Chambers, Birmingham 1978-93 and remains a door tenant at St Philip's Chambers, Birmingham. Joined 1 King's Bench Walk in 1993. Appointed Assistant Recorder in 1994. QC 1998.
Personal: Educated at Shrewsbury School 1968-72, Durham University 1972-76, University of Wales (LLM (Canon Law)) 1994-98. Leisure interests include theatre, conjuring, walking and his children. Born 20th June 1954. Lives in Malvern.

MCGHEE, John
9 Old Square (Robert Reid QC), London (0171) 405 4682
Recommended in Property Litigation
Specialisation: Property, chancery and commercial litigation. Recent cases include Escalus Properties v Robinson [1996] QB 231 (forfeiture); Barrett v Morgan [1997] 12 EG 155 (notice to quit); and Bankers Trust v Namdar [1997] EGCS 20 (subrogation).
Career: University College Oxford 1980-83 (MA).

MCGREGOR, Alistair John QC
11 King's Bench Walk (Eldred Tabachnik QC and James Goudie QC), London (0171) 632 8500
Recommended in Employment
Specialisation: Principal area of practice is intellectual property, encompassing trade secrets, confidential information (particularly in relation to employment contracts and commercial transactions), restraint of trade (in all areas of application but especially employment law), copyright, trade marks and passing off (especially anti-piracy work). Other main area is commercial and company law including sale of goods, entertainment contracts, agency, partnership and fiduciary duties (especially of directors). Lecturer for London University External LLB (1974-77) and for solicitors and accountant's professional examinations. Has written journal articles.
Prof. Memberships: COMBAR, ELBA.
Career: Called to the Bar in 1974. At Crown Office Row from 1975 until joining present chambers in 1981.
Personal: Educated at Haberdasher's Aske's School, Elstree 1963-70 and Queen Mary College, London University (LLB Hons, 1973). Leisure interests include orchestral music. Professional musician (trombone) and teacher (1968-78). Born 11th March 1950. Lives in Stamford, Lincs.

MCINTYRE, Bruce
Plowden Buildings (William Lowe QC), London (0171) 583 0808
Recommended in Personal Injury

MCKAY, Hugh
Gray's Inn Tax Chambers (Milton Grundy), London (0171) 242 2642
Recommended in Tax
Specialisation: Revenue Law especially concentrating upon litigation, commercial/corporate tax issues and VAT.
Prof. Memberships: Secretary, Revenue Bar Association, Member – Chancery Bar Association, Chartered Institute of Taxation, VAT Practitioners Group, Law Society VAT and Duties Sub-committee (co-opted) and Institute of Indirect Taxation.
Career: Called to the Bar 1990, joined present chambers 1991. Visiting Fellow (Tax), London School of Economics 1993 to date.
Personal: Born 26th June 1966. Lives in

Marylebone. Educated at King's College, London (LL.M. Tax) and Leeds University (MA), FTII, AIIT.

MCLAREN, Michael
Fountain Court (Peter Scott QC), London (0171) 583 3335
Recommended in Aviation
Specialisation: Practice includes a broad spread of commercial and common law work, specialising in aviation, shipping, banking and professional negligence. Other areas covered include employment, insurance, building and parliamentary work. Notable cases include Morgan Crucible Co Plc v. Hill Samuel [1991] (professional negligence); Bibby Bulk Carriers Ltd v. Cansulex Ltd [1989] and The Stolt Loyalty [1993] (both shipping); Irish Aerospace (Belgium NV v. European Organisation for the Safety of Air Navigation [1992] (aviation/judicial review) and Morris v. London Iron & Steel Co Ltd [1988] (employment).
Prof. Memberships: Wales & Chester Circuit, COMBAR.
Career: Called to the Bar in 1981 and joined Fountain Court Chambers in 1982.
Personal: Educated at Eton College and Cambridge University (MA Law, 1st Class Hons). Born 29th November 1958.

MCLOUGHLIN, Timothy
East Anglian Chambers (John Holt), Norwich (01603) 617351
Recommended in Family/Matrimonial
Specialisation: Specialises in Divorce, Matrimonial Finance, all aspects of Child Law (including care proceedings). Local Authority work undertaken.
Prof. Memberships: Family Law Bar Association.
Career: Called to the Bar in 1978.

MCMANUS, Richard
4-5 Gray's Inn Square (Miss Elizabeth Appleby QC & The Hon. M. Beloff QC), London (0171) 404 5252
Recommended in the following lists: Administrative & Public Law, Aviation, Financial Services
Specialisation: Contempt of Court, Discrimination, Education, Employment, European Community Law, Extradition, Financial Services Act and Social Security. Recent cases: Homosexuality and Directive 76/207 ('Perkins'); R v ICS ex parte Taylor (Financial Services and Damages); Closure of Hackney Downs School; R v Commissioners of Customs and Excise ex parte Kay & Co (Suspension VAT refunds contrary to Bill of Rights); Author 'Education and the Courts'.
Prof. Memberships: Administrative Law Bar Association.
Career: Called 1982. Junior Counsel to the Crown (Common Law) 1992 to date.
Personal: Educated at Downing College, Cambridge.

MCMEEKIN, I.
58 King St (Beverly Lunt), Manchester (0161) 831 7477
Recommended in Crime

MCMULLEN, Jeremy QC
Old Square Chambers (Hon. John Melville Williams QC), London (0171) 269 0300
Recommended in Employment
Specialisation: Employment, public law, sport law. Includes discrimination, contracts, restrictive covenants, industrial action, directorships, dismissal, injunctions, inquiries eg Clapham Junction, Westminster Auditor. Part-time Employment Tribunal Chairman. Assistant Recorder.
Prof. Memberships: Vice-President ILS and ELBA; former ACAS equal pay expert. Publications: Employment Tribunal Procedure; Employment Precedents; Labour Law Review.
Career: Called 1971, worked in New York and for GMB before practising in 1985. Silk 1994; N. Ireland 1996.
Personal: Educated at Oxford and LSE.

MCNEILL, Jane
Old Square Chambers (Hon. John Melville Williams QC), London (0171) 269 0300
Recommended in Employment
Specialisation: Employment including discrimination under domestic and European law; wrongful and unfair dismissal; redundancy; restraint of trade. Cases include Kapur v. Barclays; Preston v. Wolverhampton Healthcare NHS Trustee; Fletcher v. Midland Bank plc. Also personal injury and medical negligence.
Prof. Memberships: Employment Law Bar Association; COMBAR; PIBA.
Personal: B.A. Hons (Oxon); Dip. Law (City University); Fluent Italian and French. Called 1982.

MCQUATER, Ewan
3 Verulam Buildings (R. Neville Thomas QC), London (0171) 831 8441
Recommended in the following lists: Banking, Commercial (litigation), Insolvency, Sports Law
Specialisation: Has specialised in international and domestic banking law since starting in practice. Range of banking work covers the entire spectrum, including guarantees, charges, securities, letters of credit, performance bonds, banker/customer relationship questions, negligent security valuations and Mareva Injunctions. Also has substantial practices in professional negligence (principally accountants, bankers, solicitors and valuers) and insolvency (all aspects, acting for liquidators, receivers, administrators, trustees in bankruptcy and other parties affected by insolvency). Successfully defended rugby player accused of causing broken neck, referee found liable. Assistant Editor of the 'Encyclopaedia of Banking Law' since 1987.
Prof. Memberships: COMBAR.
Career: Called to the Bar 1985 and joined current Chambers 1986. Admitted to the Bar of the Cayman Islands on a series of individual cases.
Personal: Educated at Merchiston Castle School, Edinburgh (1975-80) and Cambridge University 1981-84 (MA Hons in Law, First Class). Born 30th October 1962. Lives in London.

MEAD, Philip
Old Square Chambers (Hon. John Melville Williams QC), London (0171) 269 0300
Recommended in the following lists: Environmental Law, Health & Safety
1, Verulam Buildings, Gray's Inn, London. (0171) 831 0801 and 47 Corn Street, Bristol. BS1 1HT. (0117) 9277111.
Specialisation: Environmental law, personal injury law including toxic torts and product liability, employment and discrimination law. Has particular knowledge of the application of European law to the above areas. Acts for both plaintiffs/applicants and defendants/respondants, and is familiar with multi-plaintiff actions. Regularly lectures and writes on European Law. Consultant to the European Commission on Health and Safety. Author of litigation manual for the Environmental Law Foundation on European Environmental Law.
Prof. Memberships: Association of Personal Injury Lawyers, Employment Law Bar Association, Environmental Law Foundation, United Kingdom Environmental Law Association and Bar European Group.
Career: Called to the Bar 1989; member Western Circuit, and practises from chambers' annexe in Bristol.
Personal: Visiting fellow and occasional lecturer, Durham University; LLM, European University Institute, Florence.

MEADE, Richard
8 New Square (Michael Fysh QC), London (0171) 405 4321
Recommended in the following lists: Computer & I.T., Intellectual Property
Specialisation: Specialises in all aspects of intellectual property, with particular experience in biotechnology and electronics patent litigation, trade mark litigation including comparative advertising cases, music copyright, 'Euro' defences, and jurisdiction under the Brussels Convention. Notable cases include Chiron v Organon and Murex (genetic engineering and HCV blood tests), Chiron v Evans (protein chemistry and pertussis vaccines), Vodafone v Orange and BT v AT&T (both comparative advertising), Elvis Presley Trade Mark, Beloit v Valmet, Chocosuisse v Cadburys (passing off). Publications: Atkins' Court Forms section on Trade Marks and Trade Names (editor); Supreme Court Practice (Trade Marks and Patents sections – assistant editor); Kerly's Law of Trade Marks (co-author, in preparation).
Prof. Memberships: Lincoln's Inn.
Career: With Andersen Consulting (information technology management consultancy) 1988-90. First in year on Bar Vocational Course (1990-91) and winner of Scarman Scholarship, Ede & Ravenscroft and Wilfred Parker Prizes. Called to the Bar in 1991.
Personal: Educated at William Ellis School, Gospel Oak, North London 1978-84 and University College, Oxford 1985-88 (BA). Born 14th November 1966.

MEADOWCROFT, S.C.
Peel Court Chambers (Michael Shorrock QC), Manchester (0161) 832 3791
Recommended in Crime

MEADWAY, Susannah
10 Old Square (Leolin Price CBE QC), London (0171) 405 0758
Recommended in Tax
Specialisation: Advisory, drafting and litigation work in the fields of trusts and associated taxation, pensions, wills, probate and the administration of estates, family provision. Court of Protection matters, charities, professional negligence and all areas of real property law. A contributor to Foster's Inheritance Tax, assistant editor of Williams on Wills, and co-editor of the new edition of Halsbury's Laws of England: Wills. Counsel in Re Segelman [1996] ch 171.
Prof. Memberships: STEP (Society of Trust and Estate Practitioners). Chancery Bar Association; Revenue Bar Association.

MEEKE, Martin
Colleton Chambers (Martin Meeke), Exeter (01392) 274898
Recommended in Crime

MEESON, Nigel
4 Field Court (Geoffrey Brice QC), London (0171) 440 6900
Recommended in Shipping
Specialisation: Practice covers all areas of Commercial law and Shipping including admiralty, arbitration, aviation, banking, carriage of goods, conflict of laws, insurance and reinsurance, international trade and sale of goods.
Prof. Memberships: LMAA (Supporting Member), COMBAR, BMLA, ABA, Forum on Air and Space Law.
Career: Called to the Bar 1982 and joined current chambers 1983. Admitted to California Bar 1990. Accredited Mediator by CEDR 1993. Visiting lecturer University College, London since 1994. Admiralty Court Committee. Member of Admiralty working group for Lord Woolf's Access to Justice Inquiry.
Personal: Magdalen College, Oxford (1st class hons Jurisprudence). Author of Admiralty Jurisdiction & Practice (1993), Ship & Aircraft Mortgages (1989), contributor to Ship Sale & Purchase (2nd edition 1993). Various articles and conference papers.

MEHIGAN, Simon QC
5 Paper Buildings (John Mathew QC), London (0171) 583 6117
Recommended in the following lists: Crime: Fraud, Employment, Licensing
Specialisation: Complex criminal (and civil) fraud of all types including associated regulatory, DTI directors disqualification and disciplinary proceedings. Advice to victims of fraud, particularly in relation to investigations. Restraint of Trade, Breach of Confidence (both in relation to employment and the commercial law generally). Licensing of all types but particularly concerning casinos.
Career: Appeared for the defence in the Blue Arrow and Nissan Tax trials as well as many other commercial fraud and corruption cases. Advised and appeared also in the Guinness and Maxwell cases. Frequent involvement for companies and banks seeking to resist witness summonses. Formerly worked in corporate finance department of a merchant bank. Co-author Mehigan and Griffiths, 'Restraint of Trade and Business Secrets' (FT Law and Tax) Third Edition, 1996; Co-author 'The Law of Confidential Information' (Butterworths) 1999, Editor 'Paterson's Licensing Acts' (current and previous 4 editions). Has appeared in many leading cases including Provident Financial Group Plc v. Hayward (1989) (garden leave), Clarke v. Newland (1991) (Construction of restrictive covenants), Hanover Insurance Brokers Ltd v. Schapiro (non-poaching of employees).
Personal: Called 1980. QC 1998.

MELLOR, James
8 New Square (Michael Fysh QC), London (0171) 405 4321
Recommended in the following lists: Intellectual Property, Media & Entertainment
Specialisation: Has a wide-ranging intellectual property practice in patents (electronics/chemical/mechanical devices/biotech), copyright and designs (engineering drawings/databases/computer software/literary works), trade marks and passing off (Levi's) and confidential information (chemical formulae/business information). Important cases handled include Fyffes v Chiquita (1991 – trade marks – Articles 85/86 EEC), Rediffusion v Link-Miles (1992 – flight simulator patent), Levi's v BTC (1993 – international counterfeiting of Levi's 501 jeans) and Boots v Superdrug (1993 – get-up of sun protection products), GEC Alsthom v FKI Engineering (1996 patent, copyright, confidential information) Vodafone v Orange (1996 malicious falsehood, trade marks), Harrods v Harrods (Buenos Aires) Limited (1997 – trade marks, passing off, contract, licence); Prince v Prince Sports Group (1997 – internet domain name, trade mark threats); Marks & Spencer v One in a Million (1998 – internet domain names); Alan Clark v Associated Newspapers (1998 – passing off); Budweiser Trade Mark (1998). Further experience in arbitrations with intellectual property or technical elements and in the Copyright Tribunal. Work experience in a variety of engineering disciplines in the UK, France, Germany, Somalia, the Congo and Iraq. Co-editor of 'Kerly on Trade Marks', editor of 'Computers – Atkin's Court Forms', co-author of The Trade Marks Act 1994 – Text and Commentary. Member of the Disability Panel of the Bar Council. Committee Member of Chancery Bar Association.
Prof. Memberships: Intellectual Property Bar Association, Chancery Bar Association.
Career: Called to the Bar in 1986 and joined current chambers in 1987.
Personal: Educated at Rugby School and King's College, Cambridge (MA, Eng). Leisure activities include windsurfing, skiing, cycling, running, sailing, reading and music. Born 16th May 1961.

MELTON, Christopher
Peel Court Chambers (Michael Shorrock QC), Manchester (0161) 832 3791
Recommended in Medical Negligence

MELWANI, Poonam
4 Essex Court (Nigel Teare QC), London (0171) 797 7970
Recommended in the following lists: Commercial (litigation), Shipping
Specialisation: Specialises in all aspects of commercial law, international trade and shipping. Practice also covers professional negligence.
Prof. Memberships: COMBAR
Career: Called to the Bar 1988. Joined present chambers 1990.
Personal: Educated at Wycombe Abbey 1980-1985 and Sidney Sussex College, Cambridge 1985-1988. Leisure pursuits include theatre and restaurants. Born 20th May 1967. Lives in London.

MERCER, Geoffrey
Walnut House (Francis Gilbert QC), Exeter (01392) 279751
Recommended in Crime

MERCER, Hugh
Essex Court Chambers (Gordon Pollock QC), London (0171) 813 8000
Recommended in European Union/Competition
Specialisation: Specialist in commercial and European Community law, with a particular emphasis on cross-frontier litigation involving issues of EC Law, jurisdiction and comparative law. Experience of EC litigation before national courts covers competition and agriculture, social security, employment and freedom of movement. Also has experience before the European Commission in the area of competition law. Important cases include litigation on complex distribution agreements for large automobile manufacturers and a mandatory injunction to prevent breach of EC competition rules. Publications include 'Commercial Debt in Europe, Recovery & Remedies' (Longmans 1991). Since 1989, co-editor of 'The European Advocate'.
Prof. Memberships: Bar European Group, Union Internationale Des Avocats, Agriculture Law Association, International Relations Committee of the Bar Council.
Career: Called to the Bar 1985. Former lecturer at London School of Economics, and at Kings College, London (summer courses on European Law).
Personal: Educated at Downing College, Cambridge 1981-84 and at Université Libre de Bruxelles (Licence Spéciale en Droit Européen avec Grande Distinction) 1985-86. Fluent in French, German, and reasonably fluent in Spanish and Italian. Leisure pursuits include squash, mountain walking, and photography.

MEREDITH, George
Southernhay Chambers (David Tyzack), Exeter (01392) 255777
Recommended in Family/Matrimonial
Specialisation: Care proceedings and private law children act applications, wardship and inherent jurisdiction cases. Recent cases in court of appeal concerning jurisdiction of county court in family proceedings and power of court to make assessment orders in care cases.
Prof. Memberships: Family Law Bar Association. Christian Mediation and Arbitration Service.
Career: Called to Bar 1969. Wardship and care cases from 1975.
Personal: Married with 3 children. Enjoys walking and computers.

MERRIMAN, Nicholas QC
3 Verulam Buildings (R. Neville Thomas QC), London (0171) 831 8441
Recommended in the following lists: Commercial (litigation), Financial Services, Media & Entertainment
Specialisation: Barrister specialising in commercial work; banking; insurance; international trade, financial services, shipping and related aspects of company and insolvency work. Maritime, commodity and international arbitration. Intellectual property, entertainment law and

gaming, and professional negligence. Cases: Creation Records v News Group 1997; Macmillan v Bishopsgate Investment Trust 1995; Re: Paramount Holdings 1993; Barclays Bank v Homan 1993: Baytur V Finagro Holdings 1992; Crockfords v Mehta 1992.
Career: Qualified 1969; QC 1988; recorder; Master of the Bench, Inner Temple

MESTON, Lord QC
Queen Elizabeth Building (Ian Karsten QC), London (0171) 797 7837
Recommended in the following lists: Family: Child Care including child abduction

MICHAELS, Amanda
5 New Square (Jonathan Rayner James QC), London (0171) 404 0404
Recommended in Media & Entertainment
Specialisation: Intellectual property, with an emphasis on copyright, trade marks and passing off. Entertainment law, including music industry, performing rights, publishing, advertising, film and television disputes. General Chancery and commercial litigation.
Career: Call: 1981.
Personal: BA in law from Durham, MA in Advanced European Studies from College of Europe, Bruges. Fluent French. Author of 'A Practical Guide to Trade Mark Law' (2nd ed. 1996) Sweet & Maxwell.

MIFFLIN, Helen
30 Park Place (Philip Richards), Cardiff (01222) 398421
Recommended in Family/Matrimonial
Specialisation: Family, Care Proceedings, Ancillary Relief.
Prof. Memberships: Family Bar Association.
Career: LLB (Hons) Leicester.

MILDON, David
Essex Court Chambers (Gordon Pollock QC), London (0171) 813 8000
Recommended in Energy & Utilities
Specialisation: All types of commercial litigation including gas and electricity litigation, insurance, banking, shipping, international sale of goods and international commercial arbitration; also Lloyd's and LIFFE disciplinary proceedings.
Career: Emmanuel College, Cambridge, MA (1st Class Honours); LL.B (1st Class Honours). Called to the Bar: 1980. Called to Bar of Antigua and Barbuda: 1990.

MILES, Robert
4 Stone Buildings (Philip Heslop QC), London (0171) 242 5524
Recommended in the following lists: Chancery, Company, Insolvency
Specialisation: Company and Commercial Litigation, Corporate Insolvency; Oil and gas; Amongst reported cases are: Derby v Weldon (worldwide Marevas); Re Atlantic Computers (corporate insolvency); acting for the liquidators of the pension fund trustee company in the Maxwell affair; BCCI (corporate insolvency) Phillips v Euron (oil and gas).
Prof. Memberships: Committee of the Chancery Bar Association; COMBAR.
Career: Called to the Bar 1987.
Personal: 1984 BA (Hons) in PPE (1st Class) Christ Church, Oxford. 1985 Diploma in Law (with distinction) City University, London. 1986 Bar Finals (Denning Prize; Megarry Prize). 1987 BCL (1st Class) Christ Church, Oxford.

MILL, Ian
Blackstone Chambers (formerly 2 Hare Court) (P Baxendale QC and C Flint QC), London (0171) 583 1770
Recommended in Media & Entertainment
Specialisation: Principal areas of practice are commercial law and intellectual property (copyright, passing off and confidential information) with specialist knowledge and

experience in the music industry and other entertainment fields including sport. Major cases include Panayiotou v Sony Music (the George Michael case) and Silvertone v Mountfield (the Stone Roses case). Clients have included all the major record and music publishing companies, film production companies, television broadcasters, recording artists, songwriters and leading sports figures.
Career: Called to the Bar 1981 and joined current chambers 1982.
Personal: Educated at Epsom College 1971-75 and Trinity Hall, Cambridge 1976-80 (MA in Classics and Law). Leisure pursuits include good food and wine, theatre and opera. Born 9th April 1958. Lives in London.

MILLAR, Gavin
Doughty Street Chambers (Geoffrey Robertson QC), London (0171) 404 1313
Recommended in the following lists: Defamation, Employment
Specialisation: Specialises in public/employment law, defamation/media and medical work. Election law is a particular speciality. Mostly appears in QBD, the Divisional Court and employment tribunals, although has undertaken a number of high profile public inquiries and has reported cases in the Court of Appeal and House of Lords. Also undertakes related criminal work and pro bono work for Liberty.
Prof. Memberships: Member of ELBA, ALBA, APIL and AVMA. Member of Westminister City Council 1985 to 1994 and served on its Social Services, Policy and Resources, Contracts, Education and Housing Committees. Currently a member of the Public Affairs committee of the Bar Council.
Personal: Born 1959.

MILLER, Celia
East Anglian Chambers (John Holt), Ipswich (01473) 214481
Recommended in Family/Matrimonial
Specialisation: Divorce, Matrimonial Finance all aspects of Child Law (including care proceedings). Local Authority work undertaken.
Prof. Memberships: Family Law Bar Association.
Career: Called to the Bar in 1978.

MILLER, Richard QC
Three New Square (David E.M. Young QC), London (0171) 405 1111
Recommended in Intellectual Property

MILLER, Stephen QC
1 Crown Office Row (Robert Seabrook QC), London (0171) 797 7500
Recommended in Medical Negligence
Specialisation: Professional Negligence, particularly medical negligence and medically related disciplinary and Inquiry work. Interesting cases include: Wilsher v Essex Health Authority; Gold v Haringey Health Authority; Aboul Hosn v The Trustees of the Italian Hospital; AB v Wyeth and others (Benzodiazepine litigation); Rage (Breast Radiation Injury Group Action); OCP (oral contraceptive pill) Group Action; Johnstone v Camden & Islington Heath Authority; Al-Kandari v J R Brown & Co; Talbot v Berkshire County Council; Zeebrugge Ferry Inquiry and criminal proceedings. Publications include a chapter in 'Medical Negligence' (contributor) Powers & Harris (Butterworths 1994 2nd Edition). Regular speaker at conferences and seminars on the subject of medical negligence and damages.
Prof. Memberships: Professional Negligence Bar Association; London Common Law & Commercial Bar Association; Personal Injury Bar Association.
Career: Called to the Bar 1971; Silk 1990. Appointed Recorder of the Crown Court 1993.
Personal: Educated at Oxford University (BA).

MILLETT, Kenneth
1 Hare Court (Stephen Kramer QC), London (0171) 353 5324
Recommended in Crime
Specialisation: Criminal defence; civil liberties; civil actions against the police.

MILLETT, Richard
Essex Court Chambers (Gordon Pollock QC), London (0171) 813 8000
Recommended in the following lists: Banking, Insolvency, Media & Entertainment
Specialisation: Main areas of practice cover banking, insolvency, commercial litigation, reinsurance, company law, and media and entertainment. Major litigation includes the Maxwell, Polly Peck, Barings and BCCI cases. Co-author of 'The Law of Guarantees' (Longmans 1995) and regularly addresses conferences and seminars.
Prof. Memberships: Commercial Bar Association.
Career: Called to the Bar 1985. Joined present chambers 1990.

MILLIGAN, Iain QC
20 Essex Street (David Johnson QC), London (0171) 583 9294
Recommended in the following lists: Aviation, Banking, Shipping
Specialisation: Arbitration, aviation, banking, carriage of goods, commodities, conflict, energy, financial services, insurance, shipping. Recent cases include: Bankers Trust v Dharmala [1995] 4 Bank LR 381, BCCI v Price Waterhouse (4.3.98 The Times), Fraser Shipping v Colton [1997] 1 Lloyd's Rep 586, Morgan Stanley v Puglisi [1998] CLC 481, New Hampshire v MGN [1996] CLC 1692, Niobe Maritime v Tradax [1995] 1 Lloyd's Rep 579.
Prof. Memberships: Commercial Bar Association London & Common Law Bar Association.
Career: Cambridge (1st) 1972 Queen's Counsel 1991.

MILLIKEN-SMITH, Mark
3 Hare Court (William Clegg QC), London (0171) 353 7561
Recommended in Crime
Specialisation: Criminal Law specialist involving serious cases of wide compass.
Prof. Memberships: South Eastern Circuit, Criminal Bar Association.
Career: Called in 1986.

MILMO, Patrick QC
5 Raymond Buildings (Patrick Milmo QC), London (0171) 242 2902
Recommended in Defamation
Specialisation: Defamation, copyright, and all other areas of law concerned with the media; judicial review; sporting regulations, especially horseracing.
Career: Recent cases. R v Disciplinary Committee of Jockey Club. Exp. Aga Khan [1993] I W.L.R. 909 (judicial review); Time Warner v Channel 4 TV [1994] EMLR 1. [Copyright – film]; McDonald's Corporation v Steel [1995] 3 ALLE.R. 615 [defamation]; Godfrey v Lees [1995] EMLR 307 (Copyright – musical work); Broxton v McClelland [1997] EMLR 157; Ramsden v MGN [1998].
Publication: Joint Editor of 'Gatley on Libel & Slander' (9th Edition).

MILNE, David C. QC
Pump Court Tax Chambers (Andrew Thornhill QC), London (0171) 414 8080
Recommended in Tax
Specialisation: Specialist in revenue law, especially tax litigation, fighting and settling appeals and dispute resolution.
Prof. Memberships: Institute of Chartered Accountants in England and Wales.
Career: Accountant, articled to Whinney Murray & Co 1966-69. Called to the Bar 1970 and joined current chambers in 1972. Took Silk 1987. Appointed Recorder 1994.
Personal: Educated at Harrow 1958-63 and Oxford 1963-66. Born 22nd September 1945. Lives in London.

MILNER, Jonathan
2 Harcourt Buildings (Mr Gerard Ryan QC), London (0171) 353 8415
Recommended in Planning

MISKIN, Charles QC
23 Essex Street (Michael Lawson QC), London (0171) 413 0353
Recommended in Crime: Fraud
Specialisation: Fraud and regulatory cases including those concerning banking, insurance, letters of credit and guarantees, trade, corruption, money laundering, advance fees, loan churning and public revenue. Other main areas of practice include general crime, disciplinary cases and civil cases involving both fraud and police law.
Prof. Memberships: Criminal Bar Association.
Career: Called to the Bar 1975 (Gray's). Joined what is now Essex Street in 1977. Assistant Recorder of the Crown Court, 1992. Standing Counsel to the Inland Revenue (Crime), 1993-1998. Queen's Counsel 1998.
Personal: Educated at Charterhouse School and Worcester College, Oxford. Lives in London.

MITCHELL, Andrew QC
Furnival Chambers (Andrew Mitchell QC), London (0171) 405 3232
Recommended in the following lists: Crime, Crime: Fraud
Specialisation: Defence work: Money Laundering, Asset forfeiture, Fraud as Leading and Junior counsel (VAT/SFO prosecutions) – represented a 'Guinness defendant', a European Leisure Plc defendant, a 'Blue Arrow' defendant and advised in BCCI overseas. Further, has acted in cases involving murder/manslaughter, drugs, rape and other sexual offences as Leading and Junior counsel. Prosecution Work: Fraud for CPS Headquarters as Leading and Junior Counsel including handling the transfer of serious complex fraud, drafting statements of evidence and case statements; drugs cases as Leading Counsel – prosecuted a number of significant drug cases involving the use of resident informants; rape and child abuse; murder as Junior Counsel; attempted murder as Leading Counsel. Appearance in the Court of Appeal on points of law relating to confiscation for the Central Confiscation Branch of CPS and in the House of Lords for CPS Headquarters. Preferred type of work is fraud, drugs, confiscation, money laundering. Has handled as Leading Counsel very involved and sensitive issues of disclosure and public interest immunity. Specialises in asset forfeiture (confiscation) and has written a leading book on the subject published by Sweet & Maxwell. Represents the Crown Prosecution Service, Customs & Excise, Inland Revenue, receivers, defendants and third parties in High Court proceedings in relation to the confiscation legislation. Has acted for the Gibraltar government on matters relating to money laundering and confiscation, and advised the Jamaican and Trinidad and Tobagan governments. Acted on behalf of South Yorkshire Police in matters relating to production orders and the extent of police powers under the Police Criminal Evidence Act, 1984.
Career: Called to Bar 1976, Gray's Inn. Ireland and Gibraltar Assistant Recorder 1995. Queens Counsel 1998.
Personal: Born 6 August 1954.

MITCHELL, Gregory QC
3 Verulam Buildings (R. Neville Thomas QC), London (0171) 831 8441
Recommended in Banking
Specialisation: Principal area of practice is commercial law, specialising in banking law, corporate insolvency law, solicitors' and accountants' negligence, breach of warranty claims arising on the sale of businesses,

confidential information claims and commercial fraud. Clients include domestic retail and merchant banks, foreign banks, professional indemnity insurers, and a wide range of large and small businesses, both UK and international. Reported cases include OSI v. AVCL & Others, Boomtime Holdings v Goldman Sachs, Spindler & Verity v. Lloyds Bank, Barclays Bank PLC v Estates and Commercial Ltd., Produce Marketing Consortium Ltd., Bank of Baroda v. Panessar, Royal Trust Bank v. National Westminster Bank PLC, TSB Private Bank v. Chabra, Femis Bank (Anguilla) v. Lazar, Samuel Sherman PLC.
Prof. Memberships: COMBAR, London Common Law and Commercial Bar Association.
Career: Called to the Bar in 1979, joined present chambers in 1981 and appointed Queen's Counsel in 1997.
Personal: Educated at King's College, London (BA Hons) 1977, Diploma in Law 1978, Ph.D 1981. Born 27th July 1954. Lives in London.

MITCHELL, Janet
4 Brick Court (David Medhurst), London (0171) 797 8910
Recommended in the following lists: Family: Child Care including child abduction
Specialisation: Child Car Law, Public Law Cases, Family Law – Litigation. Provided procedure guidelines to local authorities on setting up Care in the Community Programme. Particular areas include: child sexual abuse, child protection issues, female and male paedophiles, public interest immunity. Latest case 5 week representing a local authority in respect of incest, child sexual abuse, sexual abuse by mother, father, stepfather and inter-sibling abuse. Abuse in which question of 13 year old under represented was raised.
Prof. Memberships: Family Law Bar Association. Lawyers for children.
Career: Called to the Bar in 1997. Lecturing on Advocacy, Litigation and Public Law Cases particularly in the area of child sexual and physical abuse.
Personal: Travel, reading, swimming, tennis, Times crossword. Widow – 2 daughters. Husband also a Barrister died in 1989.

MITCHELL, John
One Garden Court Family Law Chambers (Miss Eleanor F. Platt QC & Miss Alison Ball QC), London (0171) 797 7900
Recommended in the following lists: Family: Child Care including child abduction, Family: Matrimonial Finance
Specialisation: Practices in all areas of family law with special emphasis on Children's cases and social services law. Acted for the local authority in the South Pembrokeshire Paedophile ring cases in 1994/5. Reported cases include Re G & R (1995) 2 FLR 867; Re S (discharge of Court Order) (1995) 2 FLR 639. Recent experience includes advising in two cases involving lottery winners.
Prof. Memberships: F.L.B.A.; British Agencies for Adoption and Fostering.
Career: Peterhouse, Cambridge. Deputy District Judge (South Eastern Circuit); Contributes to 'Principals and Practice of Forensic Psychiatry' (ed. Burgess and Bouden). Contributes to Sweet and Maxwell's 'Practical Research Papers'.
Personal: Theatre, Riding.

MITCHELL, Keith
3 Hare Court (William Clegg QC), London (0171) 353 7561
Recommended in Crime: Fraud
Specialisation: Principal area of practice is serious defence crime and fraud, including Inland Revenue, VAT, (including VAT tribunal) and Company fraud, have defended in a number of high profile drug and murder cases. Defence Advocate specialist in serious crime, including fraud. Has been involved in a number of high profile cases including R v Samarashinha (contract killing), R v West (contract killing millionaire Donald

Urquart), R v Nelson (shooting of Police officers), Broadwater Farm riots. Has also been involved in a number of notable appeal cases, including R v Watson (1988) Q.B. (removal of Walhein direction) and R v Aziz, Yorganci and Tosun 1995 (House of Lords decision on character).
Prof. Memberships: South Eastern Circuit, Criminal Bar Association.
Career: Purbeck Upper School, East London University (BA Hons LAW).
Personal: Married with three children. Interests: Sport (football, rugby, sailing, water-skiing). Music (guitar), Bath Society of Recital Artists.

MOAT, Frank
Pump Court Chambers (Guy Boney QC), London (0171) 353 0711
Recommended in Personal Injury
Specialisation: Called 1970. Personal injury specialist, with a particular emphasis on industrial accidents and diseases, including claims for asbestos related conditions. Practice also covers professional negligence and family law.

MOGER, Christopher QC
4 Pump Court (Bruce Mauleverer QC), London (0171) 353 2656
Recommended in the following lists: Licensing, Professional Negligence
Specialisation: General commercial and common law, especially insurance, construction matters; professional negligence, and regulatory and disciplinary proceedings.
Prof. Memberships: ORBA; LCLBA; COMBAR; PNBA; Barristers' Overseas Advocacy Committee.
Career: Called 1972: joined 4 Pump Court 1973: Assistant Recorder 1990: Silk 1992: Recorder 1993: FCIA 1997.
Personal: Educated Sherborne School 1963-68 and Bristol University 1969-71 (LL.B Hons). Born 28th July 1949.

MOLE, David QC
4-5 Gray's Inn Square (Miss Elizabeth Appleby QC & The Hon. M. Beloff QC), London (0171) 404 5252
Recommended in Planning
Specialisation: Principal area of practice is local government and administrative law and judicial review, planning, environmental and rating law. Clients include major developers including retailers, housebuilders and other service providers. Also acts for government departments, development corporations and local authorities.
Prof. Memberships: Administrative Law Bar Association, Planning and Environment Bar Association.
Career: Called to the Bar and joined present chambers 1970. Treasury Solicitors Panel 1980. Junior Counsel to Inland Revenue in rating and valuation matters 1984. Took Silk in 1990. Appointed Recorder 1995.
Personal: Educated at Trinity College, Dublin (MA 1966) and London School of Economics (LL.M 1969). Born 1st April 1943. Lives in London and Somerset.

MOLONEY, Patrick QC
1 Brick Court (Richard Hartley QC), London (0171) 353 8845
Recommended in Defamation
Specialisation: Media law, (libel, slander, malicious falsehood, passing off, breach of confidence, contempt of court, reporting restrictions, judicial review).
Career: BA BCL (Oxon); Asst. Prof. Univ. of British Columbia (1974-75); 1 Brick Court (1978 to present). QC (1998).

MONKCOM, Stephen
Francis Taylor Building (Andrew Thompson & David Guy), London (0171) 797 7250
Recommended in Licensing
Specialisation: Common law practice, with a particular emphasis on licensing law. Practice also covers betting, gaming and lotteries. Publications

include 'Smith & Monkcom: The Law of Betting, Gaming and Lotteries' (Butterworths 1987) (second edition in preparation). Contributor to Halsbury's Laws of England vol 4 (1) (reissue) Title 'Betting'. Joint Editor 'Encyclopaedia of Forms and Precedents' 5 ed. reissue Title 'Gaming, Betting and Lotteries.'
Career: Called 1974. Joined present chambers 1976.
Personal: Born 9th June 1949.

MONTGOMERY, Clare QC
3 Raymond Buildings (Clive Nicholls QC), London (0171) 831 3833
Recommended in the following lists: Crime, Crime: Fraud
Specialisation: Criminal law, particularly commercial fraud and extradition. Counsel in Guinness, Brent Walker, Maxwell and Morgan Grenfell insider dealing ring trials. Counsel in leading extradition cases; Osman and Schmidt, Practitioner editor 'Archbold Criminal Pleading, Evidence and Practice'.
Career: Called to the Bar 1980. 1992 – 1996 Supplementary Panel (Common Law). Queen's Counsel 1996.

MOON, Angus
3 Serjeants' Inn (Philip Naughton QC), London (0171) 353 5537
Recommended in Medical Negligence
Specialisation: Specialist in medical negligence and medically related litigation. Particular interest in judicial review in the medical context and medical ethical decisions. Instructed by both Plaintiffs and Defendants in medical negligence actions and for parties involved in medical disciplinary tribunals and inquests. Additional areas of practice include commercial contract and employment law. Major reported cases in the medical and commercial fields include Walford v Miles [1992] 2 AC 128 (House of Lords); Gregory v Ferro (GB) Ltd and ors [1995] 6 Med LR 321 (Court of Appeal) Mahmood v Siggins [1996] 7 Med LR 76. R v Milling (Medical Referee), Ex Parte West Yorkshire Police Authority [1997] 8 Med. LR 392 and Re C (A Minor) (Medical Treatment) [1998] 1 Lloyd's Rep Med 1.
Career: Called to the Bar 1986.
Personal: Educated at King's College, Taunton and Christ's College, Cambridge (MA, Law). Born 17th September 1962.

MOONEY, Stephen
Albion Chambers (J.C.T. Barton QC), Bristol (0117) 927 2144
Recommended in Crime

MOOR, Philip
1 Mitre Court Buildings (Bruce Blair QC), London (0171) 797 7070
Recommended in the following lists: Family: Child Care including child abduction, Family: Matrimonial Finance
Specialisation: Family law, with particular emphasis on the financial aspects of marital breakdown. Regular lecturer and contributor (with Nicholas Mostyn QC as co-author) to 'Family Law' magazine.
Prof. Memberships: Family Law Bar Association (Committee Member since 1987 and current Head of Education & Training).
Career: Called to the Bar in 1982 and joined Mitre Court Buildings in 1983. Member of General Council of the Bar 1987-89. Council of Legal Education 1988-91 (Board of Examiners 1989-92). Phillips Committee on Financing Pupillage (1989).
Personal: Educated at Canford School 1972-77 and Pembroke College, Oxford 1978-81. Leisure pursuits include cricket, football and rugby union. Lives in Bromley.

MOOR, Sarah
Old Square Chambers (Hon. John Melville Williams QC), London (0171) 269 0300
Recommended in Employment
Specialisation: Principal area of practice is

Employment Law, including sex and race discrimination, equal pay, restrictive covenant and industrial action. Also rapidly developing environmental law practice.
Prof. Memberships: Employment Law Bar Association, Industrial Law Society and Employment Lawyers Association.
Career: Queen's College, Cambridge BA Law (1989), Kennedy Memorial Scholar at Harvard Law School (1990), Council of Legal Education (1991). Called 1991. Joined Old Square Chambers 1992. Cases of note include Pink v Stockport Heath Authority with John Hendy QC, South Durham Health Authority v UNISON, Hunter v Canary Wharf and Hunter v London Dockland Development Corporation. Contributor to 'Employment Precedents and Company Documents' (FT Law and Tax).

MOORE, Martin
Erskine Chambers (Richard Sykes QC), London (0171) 242 5532
Recommended in the following lists: Company, Financial Services
Specialisation: Company Law (contentious and non-contentious). Schemes of Arrangement. Reduction of Capital. Schemes for transfer of long term insurance business. Recent cases: Re BSB Holdings Ltd (1996) 1 BCLC 155; Possfund Custodian Trustee Ltd v Diamond (1996) 1 WLR 1351.
Career: BA (Oxon). Year Qualified: 1982. Lincoln's Inn.
Personal: Born: 1960.

MOORE, Miranda
5 Paper Buildings (John Mathew QC), London (0171) 583 6117
Recommended in Crime

MOORMAN, Lucy
Farrar's Building (Gerard Elias QC), London (0171) 583 9241
Recommended in Defamation
Career: Cambs. LLM.

MORAN, Andrew G. QC
Byrom Street Chambers (B.A. Hytner QC), Manchester (0161) 829 2100
Fax (0161) 829 2100
22 Old Buildings (Benet Hytner QC), London (0171) 831 0222 Fax (0171) 831 2239
Recommended in Environmental Law
Email: byromst25@ad.com
Specialisation: General commercial litigation, shipping, professional negligence, environmental law (civil and criminal). Counsel for defence in 'Sea Empress' prosecution.
Prof. Memberships: COMBAR
Career: Educated at West Park G.S., St Helens, Balliol College Oxford, Britannia Royal Naval College Dartmouth. Royal and Merchant Navy Officer.
Personal: Married, 7 children. Hobbies: family, sport, travel.

MORCOM, Christopher QC
One Raymond Buildings (Christopher Morcom QC), London (0171) 430 1234
Recommended in Intellectual Property
Specialisation: Intellectual Property including in particular trademarks; also copyright, designs, patents, confidential information.
Prof. Memberships: Member of S.A.C.I.P., Council Member of AIPPI (British Group), Associate Member of: ITMA, CIPA, INTA, President of LIDC; Chairman of Competition Law Association; A Director of the Intellectual Property Institute; Member of Board of International Trademark Association (INTA).
Career: Called to the Bar 1963 (Middle Temple); Bencher (1996); Certificate of Honour; Astbury Scholarship; Took Silk 1991.
Personal: Interests include music & walking.

MORGAN, Charles
Enterprise Chambers (Anthony Mann QC), Leeds (0113) 246 0391
Recommended in Commercial (litigation)
Specialisation: General commercial Chancery litigation, particularly commercial property law, construction and engineering law, utilities and environmental law.
Prof. Memberships: Fellow of the Chartered Institute of Arbitrators (Chairman of Northumbria Branch); member of North Eastern Circuit, Northern Chancery Bar Association, Bar European Group, Franco-British Lawyers Society, Society for Computers and Law.
Career: Called to the Bar 1978. Practises principally on the North Eastern Circuit from Chambers' branches in Leeds and Newcastle. Lectures regularly in England and abroad on commercial law and arbitration.
Personal: Born 1954. Educated at Newcastle Royal Grammar School and Clare College Cambridge (BA 1977; MA 1981). Father of 4. Interests: sound recording and production, computing, gardening, the South of France. Website address: http://ourworld.compuserve. com/homepages/charlesjamorgan.

MORGAN, Lynne
32 Park Place (Christopher Williams), Cardiff (01222) 397364
Recommended in Family/Matrimonial

MORGAN, Paul QC
Falcon Chambers (Jonathan Gaunt QC & Kim Lewison QC), London (0171) 353 2484
Recommended in the following lists: Agriculture & Bloodstock, Property Litigation
Specialisation: All aspects of real property, commercial property litigation and agricultural holdings.
Prof. Memberships: Chancery Bar Association, COMBAR, London Commercial and Common Law Bar Association, Professional Negligence Bar Association, Agricultural Law Association.
Career: Called to the Bar in 1975, Silk 1992. Joint Editor Woodfall on Landlord and Tenant, looseleaf edition. Joint Editor Gale on Easements, 16th Edition.

MORGAN, Simon
St. John's Chambers (Roderick Denyer QC), Bristol (0117) 921 3456
Recommended in Crime

MORGAN, Stephen
1 Serjeants' Inn (Lionel Read QC), London (0171) 583 1355
Recommended in Planning
Specialisation: Local Government; Town and Country Planning; Environmental Law and Public Law. Compulsory Purchase and Compensation; Highways; Advertisements.
Prof. Memberships: PEBA
Career: Law degree, followed by MA in Town and Country Planning. Always been in local government Chambers.
Personal: Family; walking; bird watching; Football

MORIARTY, Gerald QC
2 Mitre Court Buildings (Michael FitzGerald QC), London (0171) 583 1380
Recommended in the following lists: Parliamentary, Planning
Specialisation: Local Government, Administrative/Public Law, Planning, Parliamentary, Environment (water, waste disposal).
Prof. Memberships: Administrative Law Bar Association, Planning and Environment Bar Association.

MORIARTY, Stephen
Fountain Court (Peter Scott QC), London (0171) 583 3335
Recommended in the following lists: Commercial (litigation), Insurance & Reinsurance
Specialisation: Practice encompasses common law and all kinds of commercial work, including

insurance and reinsurance, professional negligence and banking. Major cases include Re State of Norway's Application [1990]; Caparo Industries v Dickman [1990]; Lord Napier and Ettrick v R. F. Kershaw Ltd [1993]; Henderson v Merrett Syndicates Ltd [1994] and Feltrim Underwriting v Arbuthnott [1994]. Editor, Insurance Section, 'Chitty on Contracts' (26th and 27th Editions). Contributor to 'Laundering & Tracing' (O.U.P. 1995).
Prof. Memberships: Society of Public Teachers of Law, London Common Law and Commercial Bar Association, COMBAR.
Career: Fellow and Tutor in Law, Exeter College, Oxford 1979-86. Called to the Bar 1986 and joined current chambers in the same year.
Personal: Educated at Brasenose College, Oxford, 1974-78 (BA 1977, BCL 1978 and Vinerian Scholar). Born 14th April 1955.

MORRIS, Anthony QC
Peel Court Chambers (Michael Shorrock QC), Manchester (0161) 832 3791
Recommended in Crime
Specialisation: Crime, commercial fraud (recent cases include R v Smith and others – the Butte Mining case), medical negligence, civil liberties and human rights law, including prisoners' rights. Was junior counsel to Woolf Inquiry on Prisons 1990-91.
Prof. Memberships: CBA
Personal: Called to the Bar 1970. Assistant Recorder 1983. Recorder 1988. QC 1991.
Personal: Educated at Manchester Grammar School and Keble College Oxford (1966-69).

MORRIS, David
6 Pump Court (Kieran Coonan QC), London (0171) 583 6013
Recommended in Medical Negligence
Specialisation: Specialises in medical law, including medical negligence, medical disciplinary work, inquests and criminal cases involving medical disputes.
Prof. Memberships: Professional Negligence Bar Association.
Career: Called to the Bar 1976. Joined present chambers 1977.
Personal: Educated at Bristol University (LL.B) 1971-1974. Born 4th September 1953. Lives in London.

MORRIS, Paul Howard
Chancery House Chambers (James H. Allen QC), Leeds (0113) 244 6691
Recommended in Insolvency

MORRISON, Howard
36 Bedford Row (James Hunt QC), London WC1R 4JH
Recommended in Crime
Specialisation: Criminal law, especially fraud, serious violence and drugs. Experienced in prosecuting and defending child sex cases. Prosecute for C.PS., Customs and Excise 'A', Serious Fraud Office. D.T.I. Experienced in courts martial defence. Recent high profile defence cases include defending Zejnal Delalic at the International War Crimes Tribunal in The Hague.
Prof. Memberships: Criminal Bar Association, Commonwealth Judges and Magistrates Association, Justice. Sits on Inns of Court Disciplinary Tribunal. Member of Race Relations Committee, Bar Council, Member of Fijian and Caribbean Bars. European Criminal Bar Association.
Career: LL.B. (London). Called to Bar, Grays Inn 1977. Practice on Midland and Oxford Circuit. Former Infantry Officer (Airborne). Former experience of voluntary work in West and Central Africa, former Chief Magistrate of Fiji and Attorney General of Anguilla. Recorder (Crime and Civil). Legal advisor to Department of International Development. OBE (1988). Fellow of Royal Geographical Society. Advocacy Teacher, Grays Inn.

Personal: Married, one daughter, one son. Active private pilot and yachtsman. Qualified scuba diver.

MORROW, Graham QC
Exchange Chambers (William Waldron QC), Liverpool (0151) 236 7747
Recommended in Personal Injury

MORTIMORE, Simon QC
3/4 South Square (Michael Crystal QC), London (0171) 696 9900
Recommended in the following lists: Company, Insolvency
Specialisation: Practice covers business and financial law with a particular specialisation in insolvency law. Has had substantial involvement in almost all of the major insolvencies of recent years: BCCI, Olympia & York, Maxwell, Polly Peck and Facia. Counsel for the administrators and liquidators of Barings on the making of the administration orders, the sale to ING, the bond holders litigation and the implementation of the CDP settlement plan. Important reported cases include: Re Cosslett Contractors [1997] (charge in building contract). Re BCCI (No 10) [1997] (cross-border set-off issues), Macmillan v Bishopsgate [1996] (priorities in shares in foreign company), Re ILG [1995] (status of "pipeline" monies), Re Butler's Wharf [1995] (subrogation rights of guarantor). In the company law field, he has particular experience in shareholders' disputes; eg Re Leeds United Holdings [1996].
Career: Called to the Bar (Inner Temple) in 1972; QC in 1991. Called to the BVI Bar 1991. Admitted ad hoc to the Bermuda and Cayman Islands Bars. Accredited CEDR mediator.

MOSS, Gabriel QC
3/4 South Square (Michael Crystal QC), London (0171) 696 9900
Recommended in the following lists: Chancery, Insolvency

MOSS, Joanne R.
Falcon Chambers (Jonathan Gaunt QC & Kim Lewison QC), London (0171) 353 2484
Recommended in Agriculture & Bloodstock
Specialisation: Agricultural land, partnerships, quotas. E.C. law, general and agricultural.
Prof. Memberships: Chairman Agricultural Law Association. Fellow Chartered Institute of Arbitrators. Legal Advisor RICS milk quotas committee.
Career: Publications: Hill & Redman 'Agricultural Holdings', 'Milk Quotas: Law & Practice', 'Handbook of milk quota compensation'; Muir Watt and Moss 'Agricultural Holdings' (14th edition). Handbook of EC law for Bench and Bar, co editor 'Agriculture.'
Personal: MA (Cantab); called 1976; LLM (London) European Law.

MOSTESHAR, Sa'id
Hardwicke Chambers (Sa'id Mosteshar), London (0171) 402 2010
Recommended in Computer & I.T.
Fax: (0171) 402 3231.
E-Mail: SM@mofeshar.com
Specialisation: Principal practice in all regulatory and transactional aspects of communications law, ranging from telecommunications to computer networking and broadcasting; leading practitioner in outer space law covering transactions, regulations and public international law of outer space, with considerable experience in matters such as rights to orbital positions and frequencies ('Telenor v. British Sky Broadcasting Group Plc', 'National Transcommunications Limited', 'Nordiska Satellitaktiebolaget' and 'Swedish Space Corporation'). Other main areas of practice cover intellectual property rights and licensing, including those arising in multimedia projects and the use of the Internet.
Prof. Memberships: FCA; IBA Past Chairman of Satellite Communications Sub-Committee, Past

Chairman Outer Space Committee; ABA Past Chairman European Communication Committee; FCBA; IISL.
Career: Called to the English Bar 1975, California Bar 1980. Author of EC Regulation of Telecommunications; Satellite Communications; Research and Inventions in Outer Space; Co-author Satellite and Cable Television; and many other books and articles. Visiting Fellow and Professor at UCL and UCSD. Education: Southampton, LSE and Oxford.

MOSTYN, Nicholas QC
1 Mitre Court Buildings (Bruce Blair QC), London (0171) 797 7070
Recommended in Family: Matrimonial Finance

MOTT, Philip C. QC
35 Essex Street (Nigel Inglis-Jones QC), London (0171) 353 6381
Recommended in Crime: Fraud
Specialisation: Main areas of practice are crime, particularly commercial fraud, personal injuries, medical and professional negligence. Previous cases include R v Wharton, successful SFO prosecution involving experimental use of computer technology for court presentation; R v Graham & Others, guideline case on convictions for obtaining property by deception after R v Preddy; Welton v North Cornwall DC, duty of care owed by environmental health officer.
Prof. Memberships: Western Circuit.
Career: Called to the Bar in 1970 and joined chambers at Essex Street in 1971. Recorder of the Crown Court since 1987. Took Silk in 1991. Deputy High Court Judge since 1998.
Personal: Educated at King's College, Taunton 1955-65 and Worcester College, Oxford 1966-69 (BA, MA). Enjoys sailing and the countryside. Born 20th April 1948.

MOULD, Timothy
4 Breams Buildings (Christopher Lockhart-Mummery QC), London (0171) 430 1221/353 5835
Recommended in Planning
Specialisation: Specialises in local government and planning law and related areas of public law. Currently on the supplementary Panel of Junior Counsel to the Crown, Junior Counsel to the Inland Revenue on Rating and Valuation matters, and contributor to Halsbury's Laws of England, Town and Country Planning and the Encyclopaedia of Rating and Local Taxation.
Prof. Memberships: Member of the Planning and Environment Bar Association and the Administrative Law Bar Association.

MOUNTFIELD, Helen
4-5 Gray's Inn Square (Miss Elizabeth Appleby QC & The Hon. M. Beloff QC), London (0171) 404 5252
Recommended in Administrative & Public Law
Specialisation: Principal areas of practice are public and administrative law, employment law (particularly discrimination), European Community and human rights work. Joint editor of "European Human Rights Law Review". Publications include "The Blackstone Guide to the Human Rights Act 1998" with John Wadham. Leading cases include acting for the Law Society in R v Lord Chancellor ex parte The Law Society (Nos 1 & 2) (changes to legal aid), for students in the Bar School entrance procedure cases, for Friends of the Earth in R v Secretary of State for the Environment ex parte Friends of the Earth (drinking water standards litigation), for the applicants in Meade Hill v The British Council (indirect discrimination and mobility clauses), and in Adams v Lancashire County Council and BET (transfers of undertakings and pensions), for the applicants in R v Lancashire MBC ex parte RADAR, and R v Sefton MBC ex parte Help the Aged (Community Care), Brown v CAO (casual workers and sick pay) and, in the ECJ in Snares v CAO (free movement of workers in the EC).

Career: Called to the Bar 1991. Called to the Bar of Gibraltar 1994.
Personal: Educated at Magdalen College, Oxford (BA (Hons) Modern History (1st Class)), City University 1989-1990 (Diploma in Law) and King's College, London 1994 (Postgraduate Diploma in EC Law).

MOWBRAY, John QC
12 New Square (John Mowbray QC), London (0171) 419 1212
Recommended in Traditional Chancery
Specialisation: Litigation, with some advisory work, mediating and arbitrating, mainly in the following fields: Trusts, including related taxes, pension funds and Caribbean and other offshore trusts; Contract disputes, mainly international; Conflict of laws in connection with the above and generally; Property, including landlord and tenant, mortgages and insolvency aspects. Representative reported cases include: Arlen Bahamas Management v Trust Corporation of Bahamas (1971-6) 1 Law Reports of Bahamas 456 (power of modification of trust instrument); Security Trust v Royal Bank [1976] A.C. 503 P.C. (priority of charges on land); Tito v Waddell [1977] Ch. 106 (governmental trusts); Borden U.K. v Scottish Timber Products [1981] Ch. 25 C.A. (retention of this clause); Official Custodian v Parway Estates [1985] Ch. 151 C.A. (insolvency of tenant-equitable relief from forfeiture-mortgagee's rights – and see the next case in the volume); News Group v SOGAT [1986] I.C.R. 716 C.A. (trust of trade union branch funds – sequestration); Basingstoke and Deane BC v Host Group [1988] 1 W.L.R. 348 C.A. (rent review clause); Alghussein v Eton College [1988] 1 W.L.R. 587 H.L. (breach of contract – not profiting from one's own wrong); Australian Commercial Research and Development v ANZ [1989] 3 All E.R. 65 (plaintiff with same action in two jurisdictions); Dubai Bank v Galadari [1990] Ch. 98 C.A. (privilege for copy documents); Imperial Group Pension Trust v Imperial Tobacco [1991] 1 W.L.R. 589 (employment principles applied to pension fund trusts); Lemos v Coutts & Co. (Cayman) 1992-93 CILR 460 Cayman Islands C.A. (cross-border trust litigation – discovery and Mareva orders against trustees); Inverugie Investments v Hackett [1995] 1 W.L.R. 713 P.C. (assessment of damages for trespass in letting property); Re T.C. Pagarani (1998/99) 2 D.F.L.R. 1 British Virgin Islands C.A (incompletely constituted trust).
Prof. Memberships: Chancery Bar Association; Centre for Dispute Resolution (Accredited Mediator); Step International Committee.
Career: Former Chairman Chancery Bar Association, Member of Bar Council and Deputy High Court Judge. A permanent member of the Bars of The Bahamas (1971) and of The Eastern Caribbean (1992) and appears in the Cayman Islands. An Editor of Lewin on Trusts 16th Ed. (17th in preparation) and of the Chase Journal.

MOWSCHENSON, Terence QC
One Essex Court (Anthony Grabiner QC), London (0171) 583 2000
Recommended in the following lists: Commercial (litigation), Company, Insolvency, Insurance & Reinsurance, Professional Negligence
Specialisation: Principal areas of practice: company/commercial matters including matters involving the law relating to banking (including bills of exchange, letters of credit, syndicated loan agreements), breach of trust, conflict of laws, contract (including conditions of sale, share and business sale agreements, licensing and franchising, restraint of trade, retention of title, and sale of goods), companies (including shareholder disputes, shareholder agreements, technical aspects of company law, takeovers, Stock Exchange regulations, broking and dealing), equitable remedies, financial services (including matters relating to the various self regulatory organisations), insolvency, insurance, partnership,

and professional negligence. Reported cases including Derby v Weldon, Sharneyford Supplies v Edge, Elliss v BP Oil Northern Ireland Refinery Ltd, Re Westock Realisations Ltd, Dept of Environment v Bates, Investment and Pensions Services v Gray, Acatos v Watson Crimpfil Ltd v Barclays Bank plc, Eastglen ltd v Grafton, Metalloy (Supplies) Limited v M.A. (U.K.) Limited (CA), Wake v Renault (UK) Ltd, BCCI v Prince Fahd Bin Salman Al Saud, Arbuthnot Latham Bank v Trafalgar Holdings, and Board of Governors of National Heart and Chest Hospital v Chettle.
Prof. Memberships: Chancery and Commercial Bar and Insolvency Lawyers Associations.
Career: Called to the bar in 1977. Queen's Counsel 1995.
Personal: Educated at Eagle School and Peterhouse. London University (LLB (Hons)) and Oxford BCL (Hons). FCIArb 1989.

MOXON-BROWNE, Robert QC
2 Temple Gardens (Patrick Phillips QC), London (0171) 583 6041
Recommended in the following lists: Computer & I.T., Professional Negligence
Specialisation: Professional Negligence, including especially accountants, solicitors and surveyors, and cases arising in the field of building and construction. Also very experienced in all matters relating to insurance law and practise.
Prof. Memberships: ORBA, Professional Negligence Bar Association, C.L.B.A., COMBAR.
Career: Called to the Bar 1969, QC 1990, Recorder 1992. Deputy Official Referee 1993.
Personal: Born 1946. Educated Gordonstan School, University College Oxford (BA).

MOYLAN, Andrew
Queen Elizabeth Building (Ian Karsten QC), London (0171) 797 7837
Recommended in Family: Matrimonial Finance

MUIR, Andrew
3 Raymond Buildings (Clive Nicholls QC), London (0171) 831 3833
Recommended in the following lists: Licensing
Specialisation: Extensive experience of licensing work encompassing liquor, gaming, betting, lotteries and public entertainment. Has addressed Law Society on 'rave' parties.
Prof. Memberships: South Eastern Circuit.
Career: Called to the Bar 1975, and joined 3 Raymond Buildings in 1976. BA (Hons)
Personal: Educated at Stonyhurst College 1965-70, Ealing Technical College 1970-73 and Council of Legal Education 1974-75. Leisure pursuits include horse racing, cricket and rugby. Born 25th December 1951. Lives in Lodsworth.

MUNBY, James QC
1 New Square (Eben Hamilton QC), London (0171) 405 0884
Recommended in the following lists: Civil Liberties, Chancery, Family: Child Care including child abduction

MUNDAY, Andrew QC
3 Hare Court (William Clegg QC), London (0171) 353 7561
Recommended in Crime

MUNRO, Sarah
Walnut House (Francis Gilbert QC), Exeter (01392) 279751
Recommended in Crime

MUNYARD, Terry
Two Garden Court (I. Macdonald QC & O. Davies), London (0171) 353 1633
Recommended in Civil Liberties

MURDOCH, Gordon QC
4 Paper Buildings (Lionel Swift QC), London (0171) 583 0816
Recommended in the following lists: Family: Child Care including child abduction
Specialisation: All types of family litigation,

including public and private law Children Act matters, divorce, matrimonial finance, international child abduction, Inheritance Act applications, medico-legal issues, adoption, wardship, disputes between unmarried couples and mental health issues.
Prof. Memberships: Family Law Bar Association (Committee), London Common Law and Commercial Bar Association.
Career: Called 1970. Recorder and Silk 1995.
Personal: Born 1947. Educated Falkirk High School and Sidney Sussex College, Cambridge (MA, LL.B).

MURFITT, Catriona
1 Mitre Court Buildings (Bruce Blair QC), London (0171) 797 7070
Recommended in the following lists: Family: Child Care including child abduction, Family: Matrimonial Finance
Specialisation: Family Law: Child Care (Public and Private Law) and Hague Convention Child Abduction Proceedings; Matrimonial Finance (and financial proceedings under The Children Act and Inheritance Acts)
Prof. Memberships: Family Law Bar Association; Grays Inn.
Career: St. Mary's Ascot 1968-1976. Leicester Polytechnic School of Law 1977-80. Called to the Bar 1981. From 1981 in Practice at 1 Mitre Court.
Personal: Art and Architecture, Travel, amateur Artist & Mosaicist, Skiing, Gardening and Sacred Choral Music.

MURPHY, Ian QC
9 Park Place (Ian Murphy QC), Cardiff (01222) 382731
Recommended in Personal Injury
Specialisation: Queen's Bench Division work, in particular personal injury litigation. Medical Negligence, Criminal Law, Childrens Act, Public and Private Law.
Prof. Memberships: Personal Injury Bar Association.
Career: St.Illtyd's College Cardiff. L.S.E. (LLB), Baltic Exchange.
Personal: Married Penelope 1974. Two daughters – Anna 3/4/82 and Charlotte 3/12/84. Golf, Cricket, Skiing.

MURPHY, Peter
30 Park Place (Philip Richards), Cardiff (01222) 398421
Recommended in Crime

MYERS, Benjamin J.
Young Street Chambers (Lesley Newton), Manchester (0161) 833 0489
Recommended in Crime

MYERSON, Simon
Park Court Chambers (James Stewart QC, Robert Smith QC), Leeds (0113) 243 3277
Recommended in Commercial (litigation)
Specialisation: All areas of commercial law, including Company Directors disqualification and corporate fraud (civil and criminal) working knowledge of Jewish (Talmudic) law, and computing.
Prof. Memberships: CBA.
Career: Downing College, Cambridge (MA).
Personal: Married, 4 children. Interests – computing, sport, securing a moment to myself.

MYLNE, Nigel QC
2 Harcourt Buildings (Nigel Mylne QC), London (0171) 353 2112
Recommended in Crime

MYLVAGANAM, Tanoo
14 Tooks Court (Michael Mansfield QC), London (0171) 405 8828
Recommended in Civil Liberties

MYNORS, Charles
2 Harcourt Buildings (Mr Gerard Ryan QC), London (0171) 353 8415

Recommended in the following lists: Ecclesiastical, Planning
Specialisation: Specialises in planning, ecclesiastical and environmental law, and compulsory purchase; particular expertise in listed buildings. Author of 'Planning Applications and Appeals', 'Planning Control and the Display of Advertisements' and 'Listed Buildings and Conservation Areas' (2nd edn, 1995); Member, Editorial Board, Journal of Planning and Environment Law; Consultant Editor, Planning and Environmental Law Bulletin. Appears at planning inquiries for and against planning authorities (including a number of significant cases for English Heritage), at consistory court hearings, and in the Lands Tribunal.
Prof. Memberships: Planning and Environment Bar Association; Member of General Committee, Ecclesiastical Law Society; Fellow, Royal Town Planning Institute; Associate, Royal Institution of Chartered Surveyors; Member, Institute of Historic Building Conservation.
Career: Local authority planning officer 1977-86; called to the Bar 1988; Deputy Chancellor, Diocese of Worcester, 1998.
Personal: Degrees in architecture (Cambridge) and town planning (Sheffield). Currently starting next book (on trees and forestry).

NAISH, Christopher
Southernhay Chambers (David Tyzack), Exeter (01392) 255777
Recommended in Family/Matrimonial
Specialisation: Family Law. All aspects of the law relating to children (acting for Local Authorities, guardians and family members); ancillary relief. Personal Injuries. Acting mainly for Plaintiffs but also for Defendants' insurers.
Prof. Memberships: Family Law Bar Association. Personal Injuries Bar Association.
Career: Call 1980. Joined chambers in 1981.
Personal: Born 21st December 1957. Married with three children.

NAPIER, Brian
Fountain Court (Peter Scott QC), London (0171) 583 3335
Recommended in Employment
Specialisation: Transfer of Undertakings – Meade and Baxendale v British Fuels [1998] House of Lords; Discrimination (sex, race, disability) and equal pay; General employment law, stautory and common law.
Prof. Memberships: Member, Faculty of Advocates, Edinburgh, (Clerk: Susan Hastie), Member ACAS Panel of arbitrators.
Career: Academic lawyer 1975-1994. Practising barrister/advocate, 1994-. Joint editor: 1. Harvey on Industrial Relations (chapters on European law, equal opportunities, equal pay); 2. Transfer of Undertakings (Sweet & Maxwell, 1998-).

NARDECCHIA, Nicholas
2-3 Gray's Inn Square (Anthony Scrivener QC), London (0171) 242 4986
Recommended in Planning
Specialisation: Principal areas of practice are town and country planning, compulsory purchase and compensation, administrative law, environmental law, other areas of local government law and landlord and tenant law.
Prof. Memberships: Planning and Environment Bar Association.
Career: Called to the Bar in 1974. Member of Middle Temple and Lincoln's Inn.
Personal: Educated at Downside School and St Catharine's College, Cambridge University (MA).

NASH, Jonathan
3 Verulam Buildings (R. Neville Thomas QC), London (0171) 831 8441
Recommended in Banking
Specialisation: Principal area of work is banking and commercial work, including domestic and international banking matters, security and sale of goods, insurance and reinsurance. Other main

areas of work are corporate insolvency, arbitration and professional negligence (particularly of accountants, solicitors and surveyors). Acted in Al Saudi Bank v Clarke Pixley (auditors negligence) and Deposit Protection Board v Dahlia (obligations of deposit protection board).
Prof. Memberships: COMBAR.
Career: Called to the Bar in 1986 and joined 3 Verulam Buildings in 1987.
Personal: BA (Oxon).

NATHAN, David
10 King's Bench Walk (Ronald Thwaites QC), London (0171) 353 2501
Recommended in Crime
Specialisation: All areas of major criminal defence within London and throughout the UK. In recent years bulk of cases has involved fraud, corruption, serious violence, large scale importation and supply of drugs and armed robbery.
Prof. Memberships: Bar Council, Criminal Bar Association.
Career: City of London School and Manchester University.

NATHAN, Peter
One Garden Court Family Law Chambers (Miss Eleanor F. Platt QC & Miss Alison Ball QC), London (0171) 797 7900
Recommended in the following lists: Family: Child Care including child abduction, Family: Matrimonial Finance
Specialisation: Family
Prof. Memberships: F.L.B.A.
Career: Called 1973. Spent 15 months as solicitor. Deputy D.J. since 1993. Mediator (trained 1996).
Personal: Married, 3 children.

NAUGHTON, Philip QC
3 Serjeants' Inn (Philip Naughton QC), London (0171) 353 5537
Recommended in the following lists: Alternative Dispute Resolution, Construction, Employment
Specialisation: Specialist in construction and engineering law, including domestic and international contract disputes, often of a highly technical nature. Commercial and manufacturing contracts. Professional negligence, particularly in relation to surveyors, engineers, architects and lawyers. Long experience in all aspects of employment Law. Also medical law. A recognised expert in the field of Alternative Dispute Resolution. (Experienced and accredited).
Prof. Memberships: Centre for Dispute Resolution (Director); Bar Mutual Indemnity Fund (Director); London Common Law and Commercial Bar Association (Committee Member). ORBA, ELBA, COMBAR, IBA, LCIA.
Career: Held various positions in the chemical and chemical engineering industry 1964-71. Called to the Bar 1970. Joined present chambers 1973. Took Silk 1988. Bencher Gray's Inn (1996).
Personal: Educated at Nottingham University (LL.B) 1961-64.

NAWAZ, Amjad
Coleridge Chambers (Simon D. Brand), Birmingham (0121) 233 3303
Recommended in Crime

NEALE, Fiona
3 Serjeants' Inn (Philip Naughton QC), London (0171) 353 5537
Recommended in Medical Negligence
Specialisation: Practice is almost exclusively medical negligence, keeping a balance between Plaintiff and Defendant.
Prof. Memberships: PNBA, PIBA, Western Circuit.
Career: Called to the Bar 1981.

NEAMAN, Sam
4 Paper Buildings (Lionel Swift QC), London (0171) 583 0816
Recommended in Employment
Specialisation: Principal area of practice is employment law including unfair dismissal, redundancy, sex, race and disability discrimination, primarily in the banking, insurance, finance and computer industries. Other main areas of work are banking, securities and consumer credit, specialising in cheque and credit card law, in particular under S.75 of The Consumer Credit Act. Has conducted a wide range of general litigation in all courts and tribunals. Reported cases include Jarrett and Ors v Barclays Bank and Ors, First Sport Ltd v Barclays Bank Plc, Winchester Cigarette Co Ltd v Payne (No's 1 and 2), at the Court of Appeal. Clients include major banks, insurance companies and computer companies.
Prof. Memberships: Industrial Law Society, Employment Law Bar Association, Employment Lawyers' Association, British Association for Sport and the Law. Sam Neaman is Legal Adviser to the Amateur Boxing Association of England.
Career: Called to the Bar 1988 and joined present chambers in the same year.
Personal: Educated at Oxford University 1983-86 (MA Hons) and City University 1986-1987 (Dip.Law). Leisure pursuits include boxing (member Angel ABC since 1986 and active boxer since 1980), and playing drums in jazz and rhythm and blues bands. Born 28th April 1964. Lives in London.

NEISH, Andrew
4 Pump Court (Bruce Mauleverer QC), London (0171) 353 2656
Recommended in Professional Negligence
Specialisation: General commercial & common law. Principal areas of practice are insurance and reinsurance (including Lloyd's litigation) and professional negligence (especially brokers, lawyers, accountants and surveyors).
Prof. Memberships: COMBAR, London Common Law and Commercial Bar Association.
Career: Called 1988.
Personal: MA (St. Andrews), Dip Law (City).

NELSON, Vincent
39 Essex Street (Edwin Glasgow QC), London (0171) 832 1111
Recommended in the following lists: Media & Entertainment, Sports Law

NEWBERRY, Clive QC
4-5 Gray's Inn Square (Miss Elizabeth Appleby QC & The Hon. M. Beloff QC), London (0171) 404 5252
Recommended in Planning

NEWCOMBE, Andrew
2 Harcourt Buildings (Mr Gerard Ryan QC), London (0171) 353 8415
Recommended in Parliamentary
Specialisation: Principal areas of practice are parliamentary and planning work. Also including compulsory purchase, local government, environmental and general public law.
Prof. Memberships: Planning & Environment Bar Association; Parliamentary Bar Mess; Equine Lawyers Association.
Career: Called to the Bar in 1987; also member of the Irish Bar.
Personal: Born 6th February 1953.

NEWEY, Guy
7 Stone Buildings (Charles Aldous QC), London (0171) 405 3886
Recommended in the following lists: Charities, Chancery, Company
Specialisation: General Chancery practice includes charities, company, financial services, insolvency, property, solicitors' negligence and trusts.
Career: Called to the Bar 1982. Joined present Chambers 1983. One of the Junior Counsel to the Crown (Chancery). Junior Counsel to the Charity Commissioners.
Personal: Educated at Tonbridge School and Queens' College, Cambridge (BA 1st class, LL.M 1st class, MA). Bar Exams 1st class, 1982. Born 21st January 1959. Lives in Sevenoaks, Kent.

NEWMAN, Alan QC
Cloisters (Laura Cox QC), London (0171) 827 4000
Recommended in Administrative & Public Law
Specialisation: Main areas of practice are commercial law, general international law (including EC law), constitutional and administrative law, defamation. Recent interesting commercial cases include Brinks Limited v Trustee in Bankruptcy of Noye & others (an extensive commercial action involving tracing the proceeds of the Brink's Mat robbery). References before the European Court of Justice include Reading BC v Payless DIY Limited (1993) 1 CMLR 426 (legality of Sunday trading legislation), and Overseas Union Insurance Limited v New Hampshire Company (1992) QB 434 (Reinsurance. Article 21 of the Brussels Convention). Recent constitutional and administrative cases include R v Horseferry Magistrates' Court ex parte Bennet (1994) 1 AC 42 (House of Lords. Circumvention of proper extradition procedure into UK. Abuse of process jurisdiction). Defamation cases include Derbyshire County Council v Times Newspapers Limited (1992) QB 770 (Court of Appeal. Impact of European Convention on Human Rights on defamation law. Right of local authority to sue in libel).
Prof. Memberships: Administrative Law Bar Association; Bar European Group; International Bar Association.
Career: Called to the Bar 1968. Attorney-at-law, State Bar of California, USA 1976. Took Silk 1989. Appointed Recorder 1991.
Personal: Educated at City of London School and Trinity Hall, Cambridge MA (Law 1st Class Hons) and LL.B (International law). Foundation Scholar (Trinity Hall) and Astbury Law Scholar (Middle Temple). Fluent in French with a working knowledge of Spanish. Leisure pursuits include Scuba diving, cinema, theatre, food and wine. Born 30th April 1946.

NEWMAN, Catherine QC
13 Old Square (Mr Michael Lyndon-Stanford QC), London (0171) 404 4800
Recommended in the following lists: Chancery, Insolvency
Specialisation: Principal area of work encompasses business and commercial chancery work, including corporate insolvency, business agreements and breach of contract, loans and security, partnership and professional negligence. Involved in large insolvencies: Maxwell, BCCI. Other main area of work is land law and equity. Acted (for the London Borough of Hammersmith and Fulham) at all stages of the swaps litigation: capacity, restitution and successive claims.
Prof. Memberships: Chancery Bar Association.
Career: Called to the Bar 1979 and joined present chambers in 1980. Appointed Deputy Registrar in Bankruptcy 1991. Assistant Recorder 1998. Took silk in 1995. Acts as an arbitrator.
Personal: Educated at Convent of the Sacred Heart High School 1965-72 and University College, London. (LL.B 1st Class Hons 1978). Harmsworth Scholar of the Middle Temple 1979-80. Born 7th February 1954. Lives in London.

NEWMAN, Paul
Wilberforce Chambers (Edward Nugee QC), London (0171) 306 0102
Recommended in the following lists: Pensions, Professional Negligence
Specialisation: Specialises in personal and occupational pension schemes, with a particular interest in the pensions aspects of corporate and personal insolvency. Acts for trustees, beneficiaries

and employers across the spectrum of pensions litigation and advisory work and acts both for and against the Pensions Ombudsman in appeals against his determinations. Also deals with general chancery/commercial matters (with an emphasis on litigation) and with disputes relating to the Lloyd's market and the provision of financial services. Major pensions cases include Melton Medes; Belling; Simpson Curtis Pension Trustee Ltd; Cocking v Prudential Insurance. Contributor to Ellison on Pensions Law and Practice and to Lightman & Moss, Law of Corporate Receivers. SWT v Wightman and National Grid.
Prof. Memberships: Association of Pension Lawyers.
Career: BA (Cantab); LLM (Harvard Law School); Called to the Bar in 1991.

NEWSOM, George
Guildhall Chambers (John Royce QC), Bristol (0117) 927 3366
Recommended in Ecclesiastical
Specialisation: Restrictive Covenants, title, easements, agricultural holdings, farming partnerships, wills, trusts, charities, churches and burial grounds. Current publications: Preston & Newsom's Covenants affecting Freehold Land, Newsom's Faculty Jurisdiction of the Church of England.
Prof. Memberships: Fellow of the Chartered Institute of Arbitrators, Chancery Bar Association, Bristol & Cardiff Chancery Bar Association.
Career: Called to the Bar in 1973, Chairman of the Agricultural Land Tribunal for the South West Area since 1988.
Personal: Born 1948, MA (Oxon: Eng & Econ), continuing interest in technology and computing, gn@guildhallchambers.co.uk

NEWTON, Clive
One King's Bench Walk (James Townend QC), London (0171) 936 1500
Recommended in the following lists: Family: Child Care including child abduction, Family: Matrimonial Finance
Specialisation: General Common law, Commercial Fraud (civil), Family (including divorce and children), Child care, Matrimonial Finance and Property.
Career: Recent cases include: Re W (Minors) (sexual abuse, standard of proof) 1994 1 FLR 419 (represented local authority in C.A case as to standard of proof); Re B (Child Sexual abuse; Standard of proof) – 1995 1 FLR 904 (represented local authority in a High Court case involving inter alia the admissibility of expert evidence); Re C (a Minor) Adoption 1994 2 FLR 513 (represented GAL in adoption case in C.A); Re M and R (Child Abuse: Evidence) 1996 2FLR 195 (represented local authority in important case under the Children Act 1989). Re N (Residence: Hopeless Appeals) 1995 2FLR 230 (represented Official Solicitor) FNCB v Humberts 1995 2 AELR 673 (important CA decision on limitation in professional negligence cases).
Personal: Born 1944. Call 1968 Middle Temple. Oxford University MA (Oxon) Jurisprudence (1st Class Honours), B.C.L. (Oxon); Lecturer in Law, Oriel College, Oxford; Co-Editor of Jackson's` Matrimonial Finance and Taxation, 6th Edn.; Editor of 'Practitioners Child Law Bulletin' F.T. Law and Tax.

NEWTON, Roderick
East Anglian Chambers (John Holt), Ipswich (01473) 214481
Recommended in Family/Matrimonial
Specialisation: Matrimonial finance, all aspects of Child Law (including care proceedings). Local Authority work undertaken. Also specialising in crime, both prosecution and defence particularly offences involving sexual abuse of both children and adults.
Prof. Memberships: Family Law Bar Association. Criminal Law Bar Association.
Career: Called to the Bar in 1982.

NICE, Geoffrey QC
Farrar's Building (Gerard Elias QC), London (0171) 583 9241
Recommended in Health & Safety

NICHOLLS, Benjamin
1 Fountain Court (David Crigman QC), Birmingham (0121) 236 5721
Recommended in Crime

NICHOLLS, Clive QC
3 Raymond Buildings (Clive Nicholls QC), London (0171) 831 3833
Recommended in the following lists: Crime, Crime: Fraud
Specialisation: Principal area of practice is extradition, which he practises worldwide, being a member of the Bar of the Australian Capital Territories and having been specially called and admitted to the Bars of Hong Kong, The Bahamas, Cayman Islands, Malaysia, Ireland and Fiji. The factual complex of his extradition practice includes commercial crime, as well as terrorism and drug trafficking. He is particularly experienced (with teams drawn from his own Chambers) in preparing and presenting extradition requests for foreign governments, both in the UK and abroad. These have included the Bank Bumiputra fraud (the Osman case) in which he represented the Attorney General of Hong Kong in the UK, Hong Kong and Malaysia and the Werner Rey case (the largest corporate fraud in Swiss history) in which he successfully represented the Government of Switzerland in the Bahamas. He has advised and represented some 28 countries and many prominent fugitives and appeared in most of the leading extradition cases in England, including 13 in the House of Lords and Privy Council. Much of his practice is outside the UK and includes mutual assistance and human rights.
Prof. Memberships: British delegate to the International Law Association Committee on Extradition and Human Rights, member of the British Institute of International and Comparative Law, Bar European Group, Criminal Bar Association, European Criminal Bar Association, Franco British Lawyers Society.
Career: Educated at Brighton College, Trinity College Dublin, Sidney Sussex College Cambridge, MA LLM. Call 1957. QC 1982. Head of Chambers since 1994.

NICHOLLS, Colin QC
3 Raymond Buildings (Clive Nicholls QC), London (0171) 831 3833
Recommended in the following lists: Civil Liberties, Crime: Fraud
Specialisation: Principal areas of practice are commercial crime, extradition and civil liberties. Specialises in cases having an international element. Notable trials include 'Guinness' 1990 (defending the stockbroker, Anthony Parnes); 'Brent Walker' 1994 (defending George Walker), and 'BCCI' 1997 (defending the shipping magnate, Abbas Gokal). Significant reported cases include the 'Soering Case', 1989 in the European Court of Human Rights (death row in the US); and R v Horseferry Road Magistrate, ex parte Bennett 1994 (disguised extradition and abuse of power). Advised in the Bhopal, Greenpeace, Marcos litigations and in the *mani puliti* trials in Italy.
Prof. Memberships: Admitted ad hoc to the Bar of Hong Kong. Commonwealth Lawyers Association, Vice-President (1985-1996), Hon. Treasurer (1997), Bar European Group, British Institute of International and Comparative Law, Criminal Bar Association.
Career: Called to the Bar 1957, QC in 1981 and elected a Bencher of Gray's Inn in 1990. Recorder of Crown Courts.
Personal: Educated at Brighton College, M.A., LL.B, Dublin.

NICHOLLS, John
13 Old Square (Mr Michael Lyndon-Stanford QC), London (0171) 404 4800
Recommended in the following lists: Chancery, Insolvency

NICHOLLS, Paul
11 King's Bench Walk (Eldred Tabachnik QC and James Goudie QC), London (0171) 632 8500
Recommended in Employment
Specialisation: Specialises in employment law (including unfair and wrongful dismissal, discrimination and restraint of trade and confidential information), commercial law (including sale, insurance and contract disputes) and public law.
Prof. Memberships: ALBA, COMBAR, ELBA, ILS.
Career: Called to the Bar and joined present Chambers 1992.
Personal: Educated at Sheffield University (LLB First Class) 1986-1989 and at Oxford University (BCL 1st Class, Vinerian Scholar) 1989-1990.

NICHOLSON, Jeremy
4 Pump Court (Bruce Mauleverer QC), London (0171) 353 2656
Recommended in Construction
Specialisation: Principal areas of practice are construction and professional negligence work, covering all aspects of litigation, arbitration and advisory matters. Also deals with general commercial and contract law. Clients include insurers, contractors, building owners, engineers, architects, surveyors and solicitors. Has acted in a number of international arbitrations. Speaker at various seminars for solicitors.
Prof. Memberships: Official Referees' Bar Association, Professional Negligence Bar Association, COMBAR, London Common Law and Commercial Bar Association.
Career: Called to the Bar 1977 and joined Pump Court 1978.
Personal: Educated at Rugby School 1968-73, Trinity Hall, Cambridge 1973-76 (MA) and College of Law 1976-77 (Harmsworth Scholar). Born 21st March 1955.

NICHOLSON, Rosalind
4 Stone Buildings (Philip Heslop QC), London (0171) 242 5524
Recommended in Company
Specialisation: Company and commercial and corporate reconstruction and financial services; amongst reported cases: Hockerill Athletic Club Ltd; Burford Midland Properties v Marley Extrusions; Derby v Weldon; BSB Holdings Ltd; Anthony & Ors v Wright & Ors; Lightning Electrical Contractors Ltd.
Prof. Memberships: COMBAR; Chancery Bar Association; BACFI.
Career: Called 1987. Author 'Table A Articles of Association' (Sweet & Maxwell 1997).
Personal: Magdalen College, Oxford (Hons Modern History) MA. The City University (Dip Law).

NICOL, Andrew QC
Doughty Street Chambers (Geoffrey Robertson QC), London (0171) 404 1313
Recommended in the following lists: Administrative & Public Law, Civil Liberties, Defamation, Immigration & Nationality, Media & Entertainment
Specialisation: Media law in all its aspects including defamation, confidence, copyright, contempt, restrictions on court reporting, publicity injunctions and rights of access to information. Administrative law especially immigration and nationality but extending to all situations where decisions of public bodies are subject to judicial review. Civil Liberties especially concerning freedom of expression and privacy. Diverse range of other civil work including (non-medical) professional negligence, race and sex discrimination, contract and tort. Appellate crime including Divisional Court, Court of Appeal and Privy Council.

Prof. Memberships: Chair of Immigration Law Practitioners' Association. Member of Council of Europe delegations to advise on media law to Croatia, Albania, Slovakia, Belarus, Moldova. Presented papers to international conferences on Media and the Judiciary (Justice, Madrid 1993) and National Security and Freedom of Expression (Article 19, Johannesburg 1995). Chaired conference on Family and Immigration (Oxford University Continuing Education 1997) and presented seminars to ILPA,. solicitors and university groups.
Career: Called to the Bar in 1978. QC 1995. Taught law at London School of Economics for 10 years.
Personal: Born 1951. Degrees: BA 1st Class; LL.B 1st Class, LLM (Harvard), Harkness Fellow 1973-6. Has published 'Media Law' (1992), 'Subjects, Citizens, Aliens and Others' (1990) and contributes an annual survey on Reporting Restrictions to OUP's 'Yearbook of Media Law'.

NISSEN, Alexander
Keating Chambers (Richard Fernyhough QC), London (0171) 544 2600
Recommended in Construction
Specialisation: Construction and civil engineering law including arbitration and professional negligence; reported cases include Darlington Borough Council v Wiltshier.
Career: Qualified 1985; Middle Temple; treasurer and committee member of Official Referees' Bar Association; member of editorial team 'Keating on Building Contracts' and Construction Law Yearbook.
Personal: Mill Hill School; Manchester University (1984 LLB Hons.) Born 1963; resides London.

NORRIS, Alastair QC
5 Stone Buildings (Henry Harrod), London (0171) 242 6201
Recommended in the following lists: Chancery, Professional Negligence
Specialisation: Chancery and business related litigation; professional negligence.
Prof. Memberships: Chancery Bar Association, Professional Negligence Bar.
Career: Called to the Bar 1973. Joined Chambers in 1974, QC 1997. F.C.I. Arb. Concentrates on Chancery and business related litigation, with particular specialisation in professional negligence (solicitors, barristers, accountants and surveyors). Instructed by most of the major London and regional specialist firms. Acts as arbitrator. Also practises from Exeter.
Personal: Educated at Pates Grammar School, Cheltenham and St. John's College, Cambridge. Born 17th December 1950.

NORRIS, William QC
Farrar's Building (Gerard Elias QC), London (0171) 583 9241
Recommended in the following lists: Personal Injury, Sports Law
Specialisation: Personal Injury (Farrant v Thanet DC, Jefferson v Royal Ordnance. Kent v BRB.) Professional negligence, sports and competition law, licensing (Jones & Ebbw Vale v WRU, Cardiff RFC v WRU).
Career: Benefactors Scholarship, Middle Temple, QC 1997.
Personal: Lecturer to Judicial Studies Board (Damages). Advocacy Teaching UK & USA.

NUGEE, Christopher QC
Wilberforce Chambers (Edward Nugee QC), London (0171) 306 0102
Recommended in the following lists: Pensions, Property Litigation, Traditional Chancery
Specialisation: Practice a broad spread of chancery and commercial litigation including property, landlord and tenant, professional negligence, pensions (including pensions ombudsman appeals) and trusts. Recent and current cases include Phillips v British Gas (sale of North Sea Gas); Republic of Panama v Noriega (tracing assets); Central London Commercial

Estates v Kato Kagaku (adverse possession of registered leashold land); SWT v Wightman (Railway Pension Scheme); Department of Health v Moss (index linking of public sector pensions).
Career: Called 1983; practised in chambers since 1984; QC 1998.

NUGEE, Edward QC
Wilberforce Chambers (Edward Nugee QC), London (0171) 306 0102
Recommended in the following lists: Charities, Pensions, Property Litigation, Traditional Chancery
Specialisation: Mainstream Chancery practice, with emphasis on trusts, occupational pension schemes, revenue law, landlord and tenant and property law generally. Has appeared in a substantial number of landlord and tenant, revenue and other appeals in the House of Lords, and in many of the leading cases on trusts, land law and pension schemes.
Career: Called 1955, Inner Temple (Bencher 1976, Treasurer 1996); QC 1977.
Personal: Educated Radley College; Worcester College, Oxford (Eldon Law Scholar). T.D. 1964.

NUTTING, John QC
3 Raymond Buildings (Clive Nicholls QC), London (0171) 831 3833
Recommended in Crime
Specialisation: Extensive experience in Criminal law: Many IRA trials, R v Bailey & Others (paedophile murders), Michael Smith (the GEC Spy) the Taylor Sisters murder trial, Seymon Serafimovich and Andrei Sawoniuk (War Crimes), the Rachel Nickell murder, Donald & Cressey (police corruption), R v Ireland (multiple murder of homosexuals), R v Greenway (Parliamentary corruption). Also specialises in Commercial crime, Disciplinary tribunals, Inquests and Inquiries (the Falkland Islands War Crimes Inquiry).
Prof. Memberships: Member of the Bar Council (1976-1980, 1986-1987). Chairman of the Young Bar (1978-1979). Vice Chairman of the Criminal Bar Association (1995-1997). Member of the Lord Chancellor's Advisory Committee on Legal Education and Conduct (1997-).
Career: Called 1968. Recorder of the Crown Court (1986-). Bencher of the Middle Temple (1991-). Treasury Counsel at the Central Criminal (1987-1995) (First Junior Treasury Counsel 1987-88; First Senior Treasury Counsel 1993-95) QC 1995-. A Judge of the Courts of Appeal of Jersey and Guernsey (1995-). Deputy High Court Judge attached to the Queen's Bench and Chancery Divisions (1998-).
Personal: Educated at Eton and McGill University BA 1964.

O'BRIEN, Dermod QC
2 Temple Gardens (Patrick Phillips QC), London (0171) 583 6041
Recommended in Personal Injury
Specialisation: Insurance claims, policy issues, fires, floods, explosions. Electrical and mechanical engineering. Personal injury. Restitution. Practice and procedure. Local authorities liabilities. Major reported cases include: Hurst v Hampshire CC [1997], Silverton v Goodall [1997], Evans v MIB [1997], Vernon v Bosley [1997], Hippolyte v Bexley LB [1995], Talbot v Berkshire CC [1993], Lipkin Gorman v Karpnale (Playboy Club) [1991], Legal Aid Board v Russell [1991], Wharf v Eric Cumine Associates [1991 HK], Swatees v Kingston upon Thames BC [1991], Rigby v Chief Constable of Northamptonshire [1985], Russell v Barnet LB [1984], Hobbs v Marlowe [1978], Taylor v Hepworths [1977], Heath v Drown [1972].
Prof. Memberships: London Common Law Bar Association. Western Circuit.
Career: Oxford BA (Law) 1961 MA. Called: Inner Temple 1962. Crown Court Recorder 1978 (and OR's business). QC 1983. Bencher Inner Temple 1993.
Personal: Farming, forestry.

O'BYRNE, A.J.M.
Peel Court Chambers (Michael Shorrock QC), Manchester (0161) 832 3791
Recommended in Crime

O'CONNOR, Patrick QC
Crown Office Row (Richard Ferguson QC), London (0171) 797 7111
Recommended in Crime

O'DEMPSEY, Declan
4 Brick Court (Antony Shaw QC), London (0171) 797 7766
Recommended in Immigration & Nationality
E-mail: Declan@odempsey.compulink.co.uk
Specialisation: Principal areas of practice are employment, immigration, administrative law, and professional negligence (solicitors and medical). Has particular expertise in discrimination, as well as immigration, asylum and human rights cases. Other areas of specialism include public enquiries, judicial review, administrative and employment tribunals and employment law relating to senior employees. With Michael Supperstone QC he is the author of Supperstone & O'Dempsey on Immigration and Asylum (4th Edition FT Law & Tax 1996), and writes with Andrew Allen, two of the Unfair Dismissal chapters in Tolley's Employment Law (Looseleaf and CD-Rom). With Andrew Short of 4 Brick Court, he is author of Disability Discrimination: the Law and Practice (1st Edition, FT Law and Tax 1996). Briefed the Labour front bench Peers on clauses in the pensions Act 1995, the Asylum and Immigration Appeals Act 1993 and the Asylum and Immigration Act 1996. Instructed on the Inquiry into the Personality disorder Inti Ashworth special Hospital in 1997-1998. Lectures on the International Diploma in Humanitarian Assistance.
Prof. Memberships: Immigration Law Practitioners Association, London Commercial and Common Law Bar Association, Administrative Law Bar Association. Called to the Bar 1987; first full time Employment Law Caseworker for the FRU 1987-88.
Prof. Memberships: Immigration Law Practitioners Association. Employment Law Bar Association, London Common Law and Commercial Bar Association, and the Administrative Law Bar Association and the Immigration Law Practitioners' Association.
Career: Called to the Bar in 1987, full-time Employment Law caseworker for the Free Representation Unit 1987-88.

O'DONOVAN, Kevin
5 Fountain Court (Anthony Barker QC), Birmingham (0121) 606 0500
Recommended in the following lists: Employment, Health & Safety

O'FARRELL, Finola
Keating Chambers (Richard Fernyhough QC), London (0171) 544 2600
Recommended in Construction
Specialisation: Construction law in general, including, in particular loss and expense claims (lectures regularly on various aspects); shipbuilding and dredging litigation, noise pollution cases.
Prof. Memberships: Member Bar/IBC Committee; member of editorial team 'Keating on Building Contracts'; member of Official Referees Bar Association.
Career: Qualified 1983; Inner Temple; Council of Legal Education 1983.
Personal: St Philomena's School; Durham University (1982 BA Hons Dunelm).

O'KEEFFE, Darren
Derby Square Chambers (Simon Newton), Liverpool (0151) 709 4222
Recommended in Personal Injury

O'ROURKE, Mary
3 Serjeants' Inn (Philip Naughton QC), London
(0171) 353 5537
Recommended in the following lists: Construction, Employment, Medical Negligence

ODITAH, Fidelis
3/4 South Square (Michael Crystal QC), London
(0171) 696 9900
Recommended in Insolvency

OLDHAM, Peter
11 King's Bench Walk (Eldred Tabachnik QC and James Goudie QC), London
(0171) 632 8500
Recommended in Employment

OLIVER, David QC
13 Old Square (Mr Michael Lyndon-Stanford QC), London (0171) 404 4800
Recommended in the following lists: Administrative & Public Law, Chancery, Company, Financial Services
Specialisation: Principally Commercial/Chancery, with some insolvency.
Career: Called to the Bar 1972. Took silk 1986. (Lincoln's Inn: Hardwick Scholar) Standing Junior Counsel to the Director General of Fair Trading. Acted for Guinness in connection with the aftermath of the Distillers takeover, Price Waterhouse in claims arising after the collapse of BCCI, Macmillan Inc. and Swiss Bank with claims arising out of the collapse of Robert Maxwell's corporate empire, Granada plc in connection with the financing of BSB and subsequently B Sky B, and the Princess of Wales.
Personal: Born 4 June 1949. Educated Westminster School; Trinity Hall Cambridge; Institut d'Etudes Europeanes, Brussels. BA Cantab (2/1), Licence Special en droit European. Fluent Spanish and working knowledge of French.

OLIVER-JONES, Stephen QC
5 Fountain Court (Anthony Barker QC), Birmingham (0121) 606 0500
Recommended in the following lists: Medical Negligence, Personal Injury
Specialisation: Personal Injury & Medical Negligence.
Prof. Memberships: Medical Negligence: Plaintiff and Defendant Litigation in General Surgery, Obstetrics and Gynaecology, Paediatrics, Vascular & Respiratory medicine, Orthopaedics, Neurology, Drug-related injury and Toxicology, Surgical, Nursing, Midwifery & General Practitioners Practice; Personal Injury: Tetraplegic & Paraplegic Claims and other claims involving brain damage, major spinal injury and 'injuries of the utmost severity'. Fatal and non-fatal accident claims generally.
Career: Year of call 1970. Silk 1996. Recorder of the Crown Court. Member of the Professional Negligence Bar Association. Member of the Personal Injuries Bar Association.

OMAMBALA, Ijeoma
Old Square Chambers (Hon. John Melville Williams QC), London (0171) 269 0300
Recommended in Employment
Specialisation: Employment law, discrimination law – race, sex and disability, trade union law.
Prof. Memberships: ELBA, DLA, APIL, ILS.

ONIONS, Jeffery QC
One Essex Court (Anthony Grabiner QC), London (0171) 583 2000
Recommended in the following lists: Commercial (litigation), Energy & Utilities, Insolvency, Insurance & Reinsurance
Specialisation: Undertakes a wide range of complex commercial work. He has a particular experience in arbitration, banking, insolvency, insurance, oil and gas and media related cases.
Prof. Memberships: Insolvency Lawyers Association, London Common Law and Commercial Bar Association, Administrative Law Bar Association.

ONSLOW, Andrew
3 Verulam Buildings (R. Neville Thomas QC), London (0171) 831 8441
Recommended in Commercial (litigation)
Specialisation: Banking and finance; financial services; commercial fraud; solicitors', auditors' and valuers' negligence. Major recent cases include Wallace Smith Trust Co. v Deloittes Haskins and Sells.
Prof. Memberships: COMBAR
Career: 1970-74 Lancing College. 1975 -79 Corpus Christi College, Oxford. BA Hons Literae Humaniores (1st Class).
Personal: Married. 5 Children.

ONSLOW, Robert
8 New Square (Michael Fysh QC), London (0171) 405 4321
Recommended in Intellectual Property
Specialisation: Principal areas of practice are intellectual property including trade marks, musical and literary copyright, industrial designs and patents as well as computer law and contract disputes with a technical element. Also specialises in advising on legal issues relating to Internet commerce, Data Protection and commercial uses of data.
Prof. Memberships: Lincoln's Inn.
Career: Technical Assistant at Mewburn Ellis, Chartered Patent Agents 1987-89. Called to the Bar and joined current chambers in 1991.
Personal: Educated at Eton College 1978-83 and Magdalen College, Oxford 1984-87 (BA Hons in Physics). Leisure interests include music (piano and violin). Born 31st May 1965.

OPPENHEIM, Robin
Doughty Street Chambers (Geoffrey Robertson QC), London (0171) 404 1313
Recommended in Medical Negligence
Specialisation: Specialist in the areas of medico-legal work, personal injury, and employment law. Personal injury and medico-legal practice includes medical negligence and serious personal injury (has developed a specialisation in cerebral palsy, spinal and head injuries claims), multi plaintiff group actions, medical inquests, mental health law and health related public law. He is currently generic counsel in the tobacco and organophosphate group actions and two child abuse group actions. He also practises in public law and media and entertainment law. Notable reported cases: Dole Chadee, Privy Council (Constitutional challenge to fairness of trial following prejudicial press coverage); ex p Taylor (review of the refusal of the Attorney General to prosecute for contempt); Nelson v Rye (fiduciary's liability) and Hodgson v Imperial Tobacco (liability of lawyers under conditional fee agreements). Contributor to Personal Injury manual (Sweet and Maxwell 1997), Liberty's Rights Guide and to forthcoming Personal Injury Practical Research Papers to be published by Sweet and Maxwell. Regular lecturer to solicitors.
Prof. Memberships: Action for Victims of Medical Accidents; Association of Personal Injury Lawyers; Administrative Law Bar Association; Professional Negligence Bar Association and Personal Injury Bar Association.
Career: Called to the Bar 1988.
Personal: Born 1962. Lives in London.

ORNSBY, Suzanne
2 Harcourt Buildings (Mr Gerard Ryan QC), London (0171) 353 8415
Recommended in Planning
Specialisation: Specialist fields are planning and environmental law (civil and criminal jurisdictions) for both the private and public sector.
Prof. Memberships: Secretary of the Planning and Environment Bar Association; Member of the United Kingdom Environmental Law Association.

Career: Called to the Bar in 1986. Joined present Chambers in 1990, previously practised at the Criminal Bar and employed in the electricity supply industry.
Personal: Educated at St Georges College, Weybridge and University College London (LLB Hons 1985).

ORR, Craig
Fountain Court (Peter Scott QC), London (0171) 583 3335
Recommended in Commercial (litigation)
Specialisation: Practice covers all areas of commercial law, including city related litigation (especially merchant banking-related matters), accountants' negligence actions, commercial fraud (civil actions), banking and insurance litigation. Important cases include British & Commonwealth v Quadrex and Samuel Montagu, Caparo v Dickman [1990]; Eagle Trust v Cowan de Groot [1992]; Society of Lloyd's v Mason and Clementson [1995]; and AMF v Hashim [1996].
Prof. Memberships: COMBAR.
Career: Called to the Bar in 1986 and joined Fountain Court in 1988.
Personal: Educated at Cambridge University 1981-84 (MA) and Oxford University (BCL, Vinerian Scholar). Born 8th January 1962.

ORR, Nicholas
14 Castle St (Adrian Lyon), Liverpool (0151) 236 4421/8240/6759/6757
Recommended in Chancery
Specialisation: General chancery, particularly property litigation, family provision, landlord and tenant and partnerships. Also commercial litigation and drafting and professional negligence.
Prof. Memberships: Northern Circuit, Chancery Bar Association, Northern Chancery Bar Association, Northern circuit Commercial Bar Association.

OTTON-GOULDER, Catharine
Brick Court Chambers (Christopher Clarke QC), London (0171) 583 0777
Recommended in Commercial (litigation)
Specialisation: General Commercial Law.
Career: Called to Bar 22 November 1983, Lincoln's Inn. Pupillages with John Thomas QC (4 Essex Court) and Jonathan Sumption QC (1 Brick Court). Practised at Brick Court Chambers 21 December 1984 to date. Cases of note: Credit Suisse v Allersale D.C., Arab Monetary Fund v Hashim, Hazell v London Borough of Hammersmith & Fulham.
Personal: Born 9 April 1955 in Chester. Educated at King George V School, Hong Kong; King Edward VI High School for Girls and Somerville College, Oxford (1973-77) – Literae Humaniores without Viva Voce Examination, First Class. Qualified as Solicitor of Supreme Court 1980. Gained Seymour Scholarship (on entry to Oxford) and Hardwicke Scholarship at Lincoln's Inn.

OUSELEY, Duncan QC
4-5 Gray's Inn Square (Miss Elizabeth Appleby QC & The Hon. M. Beloff QC), London (0171) 404 5252
Recommended in the following lists: Administrative & Public Law, Environmental Law, Planning
Specialisation: Planning and environmental law work undertaken covers Court, Inquiry, Lands Tribunal and advisory work of all types for and against authorities, also including compulsory purchase and compensation, highways and waste disposal. Public law work undertaken includes Court and advisory work covering all aspects of judicial review affecting central and local government, regulatory bodies and utilities; particularly local government organisation and finance, competitive tendering, social security and social services, health, medicine and pharmacies, utilities and financial services regulation, planning and environmental law.
Prof. Memberships: Planning and Environment Bar Association. Administrative Law Bar

Association.
Career: QC 1992. Recorder 1994. Chairman of EIPs in1985 and 1991. Appeared in Hong Kong and in Northern Ireland. QC Northern Ireland 1997.

OWEN, David
20 Essex Street (David Johnson QC), London
(0171) 583 9294
Recommended in the following lists: Banking, Insurance & Reinsurance
Specialisation: Main areas of practice are commercial law, arbitration, banking, insurance and reinsurance, sale of goods, professional negligence, contracts of carriage, shipping and commodities. Joint editor 'MacGillivray on Insurance Law'.
Prof. Memberships: London Court of International Arbitration, International Bar Association, COMBAR.
Career: At H.M. Treasury 1979-81. Called to the Bar and joined chambers at Essex Street in 1983.
Personal: Educated at Marlborough College 1971-75 and Merton College, Oxford 1976-79 (BA, 1st Class Hons). Born 21st June 1958.

OWEN, Eric
40 King St (Philip Raynor QC), Manchester
(0161) 832 9082
Recommended in Environmental Law
Specialisation: Works exclusively in the spheres of planning environmental and local government with a particular interest in European aspects and mineral planning, waste disposal and authorisations. Appears regularly as an advocate before tribunals and courts with jurisdiction in these areas, whether civil or criminal. Undertakes advisory work and deals regularly with experts in environmental fields, including pollution, water, noise, electricity and conservation.
Prof. Memberships: Member of the Planning Environmental and Local Goverment Bar Association, and of its Committee. Member of the Bar European Group.
Career: Graduated LLB (Hons) Liverpool University 1968. Called to the Bar 1969. Former Lecturer at Liverpool University. Specialism in Environmental and related fields developed after standing for election to the U.K. and the European Parliaments. Represented Highways Agency in Manchester Airport Second Runway application and North Yorkshire Local Authority in Electricity Act Inquiry Vale of York. Promoted various Local Plans, UDP's, Minerals Local Plans and highway schemes and appeared for objectors in such cases. Major cases include Bryan v U.K [1996] 1 P.L.R. 47 (European Court of Human Rights). Addressed Annual Conference of Planning Inspectorate (1996) and Mineral Planning Conferences in York 1998 (RTPI) and Solihull 1998 (QPA).
Personal: Ordained June 1997.

OWEN, Gail
India Buildings Chambers (David Harris QC), Liverpool 0151 243 6000
Recommended in Family/Matrimonial
Specialisation: All aspects of public law Children Act work, including the representation of Local Authorities, parents and Guardians ad Litem. This work involves, inter alia, issues of physical, sexual and emotional abuse of children. Also practices in all areas of private law Children Act work, divorce proceedings, adoption proceedngs and all aspects of finance and property disputes ancillary relief proceedings and disputes between unmarried couples).
Career: Called 1980.

OWEN, R.F. QC
Ropewalk Chambers (Richard Maxwell QC), Nottingham (0115) 947 2581/2/3/4
Recommended in Personal Injury

OWEN, Robert QC
1 Crown Office Row (Robert Seabrook QC), London (0171) 797 7500
Recommended in the following lists: Medical Negligence, Personal Injury
Specialisation: Profesional negligence, medical negligence, product liability, multi-party actions, disaster litigation, commercial fraud.
Prof. Memberships: London Common Law and Commercial Bar Association, Chairman 1994-95, Professionál Negligence Bar Association.
Career: Called 1968, QC 1988, Recorder 1987, DTI Inspector 1990, Deputy High Court Judge 1994. Chairman General Council of the Bar 1997.

OWEN, Tim
Doughty Street Chambers (Geoffrey Robertson QC), London (0171) 404 1313
Recommended in the following lists: Civil Liberties, Crime
Specialisation: Main areas of practice are public law (especially prison, police and inquest law), civil actions against the police and prisoners' private law actions (assault, negligence and misfeance). Other areas include criminal law with experience in terrorist cases and cases involving prison law element, public order and appellate work. Privy Council (pro bono) and ECHR work. Co-author of 'Prison Law', OUP 1998 (second edition).
Prof. Memberships: Haldane Society, ALBA, INQUEST Lawyers' Group.
Career: Called 1983.
Personal: Educated at Atlantic College and London School of Economics. Lives in London.

OWEN, Tudor
9-12 Bell Yard (D. Anthony Evans QC), London
(0171) 400 1800
Recommended in Crime

OWEN-JONES, David Roderic
3 Temple Gardens (Jonathan Goldberg QC), London (0171) 583 1155
Recommended in Crime
Specialisation: Drugs and Fraud cases – Prosecution and Defence. Environmental Law cases – practice on South Eastern Circuit and Midland Circuit.
Prof. Memberships: CBA.
Career: University of London LLB, LLM. Council of Europe, Commission of Human Rights.

PADFIELD, Nicholas QC
1 Hare Court (Lord Neill of Bladen QC & Richard Southwell QC), London
(0171) 353 3171
Recommended in Arbitration
Specialisation: Specialises in cases with an international dimension involving the conflict of laws, particularly banking, financial instruments and securities. Also, construction, accountants' negligence, extradition, universities/students and bloodstock. Generally, where the background is commercial, and dispute involves domestic or international law.
Prof. Memberships: Fellow of Chartered Institute of Arbitrators. Panel of Lloyd's Arbitrators. Member of LCIA, IBA and Bar European Group. Executive Committee of COMBAR. Vice-Chairman, Joint Regulations Committee of Bar Council.
Career: MA (Oxon), LLB (Cantab) International Law. Silk (1991). Recorder. Master of the Bench, Inner Temple. Hockey Blue (Oxford) and International.

PAGE, Adrienne
5 Raymond Buildings (Patrick Milmo QC), London (0171) 242 2902
Recommended in Defamation
Plaintiffs who have in recent years achieved good settlements for whom I have acted include the model and actress Liz Hurley, Dusko Doder, the former Washington Post journalist, who settled against Time Magazine for damages of £175,000 plus indemnity costs; Lord Spencer; Clare Short MP; Kevin McNamara MP; and Michael Hurley, a

retired US drugs enforcement agent who successfully complained of an allegation in a book that he had permitted a breach of security that enabled terrorists to blow up Pan Am flight 103 over Lockerbie. Led by Desmond Browne QC, I acted as junior for the BBC, the New Statesman and Duncan Campbell in consolidated actions for malicious falsehood arising out a BBC Watchdog broadcast concerning a clinic providing private medical treatment for AIDS patients. The outcome was that two Plaintiffs abandoned their claims (one at an early stage of the trial, the other after four months), and the claim against the third of the Plaintiffs was dismissed. Again, led by Desmond Browne QC, I acted as junior for Channel 4 and Duncan Campbell in Nixon v Channel 4 which ended four weeks into the trial when the Plaintiff abandoned his claim and paid the Defendants costs.

PAGE, Nigel B.
Chambers of Colin Anderson (St. Mary's Chambers) (Colin Anderson), Nottingham
(0115) 950 3503
Recommended in Family/Matrimonial

PAINES, Nicholas QC
Monckton Chambers (Richard Fowler QC), London (0171) 405 7211
Recommended in European Union/Competition
Specialisation: Administrative and public law and EC law. All areas of administrative and public law, challenges to central and local government and other administrative decision-making, particularly but not exclusively on EC law grounds. Areas of EC practice include agriculture, competition, customs, employment, free movement of goods, free movement of persons, pensions, public procurement, sex discrimination, social security, state aid, VAT. Also handles UK competition law and general commercial litigation. Numerous ECJ appearances include: The Sunday Trading cases; Coloroll and the subsequent cases on pensions; R v Secretary of State for Employment ex p Seymour-Smith; Card Protection Plan v Cmmrs for Customs & Excise (VAT). Reported cases in English courts include Kirklees MBC v B & Q (Sunday trading injunctions); R v MAFF ex p Hamble Fisheries; In re Ready Mixed Concrete Agreements (restrictive trade practices); Iberian v BPB [1996] (competition, effect in national court of EC Commission decision); U v W (freedom to provide services, human fertilisation). Contributor to Bellamy & Child 'Common Market Law of Competition'; Halsbury's Laws of England; Vaughan 'Law of the European Communities'. Joint editor (with Paul Lasok QC) Common Market Law Reports.
Prof. Memberships: Administrative Law Bar Association, Bar European Group (former Chairman), Competition Law Association, UK Association for European Law.
Career: Called to the Bar 1978. QC 1997.
Personal: Educated at Oxford University 1973-76 (MA, jurisprudence) and Université libre de Bruxelles (Licence spéciale en droit Européen).

PALMER, Adrian QC
Guildhall Chambers (John Royce QC), Bristol
(0117) 927 3366
Recommended in Commercial (litigation)

PALMER, Anthony QC
3 Fountain Court (Colman Treacy QC), Birmingham (0121) 236 5854
Recommended in Crime

PALMER, Howard
2 Temple Gardens (Patrick Phillips QC), London
(0171) 583 6041
Recommended in Personal Injury
Specialisation: Insurance and Reinsurance: insurance policy disputes; repudiation for fraud/non-disclosure/breach of condition. Personal Injury: local authority and employers' liability. Professional Indemnity: engineers; insurance brokers; surveyors; accountants; architects; solicitors. Construction: contract disputes; building

regulations on spread of fire. Commercial Arbitration: International fraud; commercial disputes.
Career: Lecturer at King's College, London 1977-8. Tenant at 2 Temple Gardens 1978 – date.
Personal: Cricket; Fieldsports; Theatre. Married, four children. Lives in Fulham, London.

PALMER, Patrick J.S.
Sovereign Chambers (Formerly known as 25 Park Square) (Geoffrey C. Marson QC), Leeds (0113) 245 1841
Recommended in Crime

PANNICK, David QC
Blackstone Chambers (formerly 2 Hare Court) (P Baxendale QC and C Flint QC), London (0171) 583 1770
Recommended in the following lists: Administrative & Public Law, Employment, Immigration & Nationality, Sports Law
Specialisation: Practices mainly in the fields of public and administrative law, employment law, immigration law, European law and sports law. He has appeared in more than 40 cases in the House of Lords, over 20 cases in the European Court of Justice, and over a dozen cases in the European Court of Human Rights. He is a Fellow of All Souls College, Oxford, and a member of the Editorial Committee of 'Public Law'. He writes a fortnightly column on the law for 'The Times'. His recent cases include ex parte Thompson and Venables, ex parte the Revd Moon, ex parte Diane Blood, McDermott v The Princess of Wales, Diane Modahl v The British Athletics Federation, and R v BBC ex parte The Referendum Party.

PARDOE, Alan QC
Devereux Chambers (Jeffrey Burke QC), London (0171) 353 7534
Recommended in Employment
Specialisation: Practises in employment law, local government law, commercial law. Many reported cases eg. recently: (employment) Port of London Authority v Payne [1993] ICR 447, [1994] ICR 555 (CA); (local government) West Wilts D.C. v Garland [1995] Ch. 297; (commercial) Transthene Packaging v Royal Insurance LL. Reins. L.R. 32.
Prof. Memberships: Supporting member, London Maritime Arbitrators' Association; Member of the Committee of COMBAR; Administrative Law Bar Association; Underwriting Member of Lloyds 1990-1997.
Career: Full-time University Teacher of Law 1965-72 (Universities of Exeter, Auckland, New Zealand and Sussex). Called to the Bar 1971. Tenant at 7 Kings Bench Walk 1973-80 and at 12 Gray's Inn Square 1980-89. Joined Devereux Chambers in 1989. Took Silk 1988. Appointed Recorder 1990. Elected Bencher of Lincoln's Inn 1998.
Personal: Educated at Oldbury Grammar School 1954-61 and St. Catharine's College, Cambridge 1961-65. Born 16th August 1943. Lives in Notting Hill, London.

PARKER, Christopher R.
7 Stone Buildings (Charles Aldous QC), London (0171) 405 3886
Recommended in Company
Specialisation: Main areas of practice are company and insolvency law. Also undertakes general Chancery work. Recent reported cases: MTI Trading Systems Ltd. v. Winter [1997], Re: A Company (No.002015 of 1996) [1996], Watkins v. A.J. Wright (Electrical) Ltd. [1996], R & H Electrical Ltd. and Anor v. Haden Bill Electrical Ltd.: Re: Haden Bill Electrical Ltd. [1995], Securum Finance PLC v. Camswell Ltd. [1994], Aeroworld Ltd. v. Connaught Leisure Ltd. [1994], S.N. Group PLC v. Barclays Bank PLC [1993], W.G. Clark (Properties) Ltd. v. Dupre Properties Ltd. [1992], Re: Kirby's Coaches Ltd. [1990] Re: Welfab Engineering Ltd. [1990], Re Gorman (A Bankrupt), ex parte the Trustee of the Bankrupt v. The Bankrupt and Anor [1989].
Career: Called to the Bar 1984. Joined present

Chambers 1986.
Personal: Educated at Keble College, Oxford BA Jurisprudence, 1st class, (1977-80) and BCL (1980-81), University of Illinois LL.M (1981-82), Harvard Law School LLM (1982-83). Born 13th October 1958. Lives in London.

PARKER, Judith QC
One King's Bench Walk (James Townend QC), London (0171) 936 1500
Recommended in Family: Child Care including child abduction

PARKER, Kenneth QC
Monckton Chambers (Richard Fowler QC), London (0171) 405 7211
Recommended in the following lists: Administrative & Public Law, Agriculture & Bloodstock, European Union/Competition
Specialisation: Specialises in EC law, public law and judicial review. Recent reported cases include: R v Secretary of State for the Environment ex p Greenpeace [1994] (challenge to decision to authorise testing at Sellafield), R v Home Secretary ex p Hagan and Croft [1994] (challenge to decision to extradite British women to Oregon), R v MAFF ex p NFFO [1995] ECJ (challenge to fish conservation policy), R v Home Secretary ex p Norney [1995] (challenge to policy on referring IRA lifers to Parole Board), R v Secretary of State for Trade and Industry ex p Consumer's Association [1996] (challenge to implementation of Unfair Contract Terms Directive), BRB/SNCF v Commission [1996] ECJ (challenge to decision affecting operation of Channel Tunnel), R v Home Secretary ex p O'Dhunbuir [1997] (challenge to closed visits in high security prisons), MD Foods v Baines [1997] HL (application of RTPA to supply agreements) and R v Home Secretary ex p Launder [1997] CA, and HL (challenge to decision to extradite ex MD of Wardley Merchant Bank to Hong Kong). Also regularly instructed by the Commissioners of Customs and Excise on appeals in VAT cases. Recent cases include Elida Gibibs v CCE [1996] ECJ, Argos v CCE [1996] ECJ and CCE v Wellington Hospital [1997] CA.
Prof. Memberships: Called to the Bar in 1975 and took silk in 1992. Fellow in Law at Exeter College Oxford between 1973 and 1976. He is on the executive of COMBAR.

PARNELL, Graham
East Anglian Chambers (John Holt), Ipswich (01473) 214481
Recommended in Family/Matrimonial
Specialisation: Childcare law; private law family cases; ancillary relief. General common law (including personal injury and medical negligence). Acted for the local authority in Re B (Children Act Proceedings) (Issue Estoppel) [1997] 1 FLR 285.
Prof. Memberships: Family Law Bar Association.
Career: MA (Oxon).

PARROY, Michael QC
3 Paper Buildings (Michael Parroy QC), London (0171) 583 8055
Recommended in Crime: Fraud

PARRY, Isabel
9 Park Place (Ian Murphy QC), Cardiff (01222) 382731
Recommended in Family/Matrimonial

PARSONS, Luke
4 Essex Court (Nigel Teare QC), London (0171) 797 7970
Recommended in Shipping

PARTRIDGE, Richard
3 Serjeants' Inn (Philip Naughton QC), London (0171) 353 5537
Recommended in Medical Negligence
Specialisation: Medical Negligence and related areas of medical law; disciplinary tribunals, mental health, inquests.
Career: Qualified in Medicine at the Welsh School of Medicine 1988. Called to the Bar 1994.

PASCOE, Martin
3/4 South Square (Michael Crystal QC), London (0171) 696 9900
Recommended in Insolvency
Specialisation: Martin Pascoe was called to the Bar in 1977 and joined 3/4 South Square in 1989 when chambers moved to Gray's Inn from the Temple. His practice includes a broad range of commercial and chancery litigation, with particular emphasis on corporate insolvency, often with substantial international elements, as well as more than 100 cases acting for defendant solicitors in professional negligence actions. He acted for the English administrators of the Olympia and York group, and has since 1991 acted for the English liquidators of BCCI SA and the Cayman Islands liquidators of BCCI Overseas. Recent reported cases include Re BCCI SA (No 11) [1997] 1 BCLC 80, which has restated the law relating to the scope of English ancillary liquidations, and Hughes v Hannover Re [1997] 1BCLC 497, which is the first Court of Appeal case on s.426 Insolvency Act 1986. He has substantial experience of insurance insolvencies, including acting for US-based reinsurers of EMLICO in the winding-up proceedings before the Supreme Court of Bermuda and in judicial review proceedings in the Supreme Court, Court of Appeal for Bermuda and Privy Council seeking the quashing of decisions permitting EMLICO's redomestication to Bermuda: Kemper Re v Minister of Finance (Bermuda) Times 18 May 1998 (PC).
Prof. Memberships: COMBAR, Chancery Bar Association.

PASCOE, Nigel QC
Pump Court Chambers (Guy Boney QC), Winchester (01962) 868161
Recommended in Crime
Specialisation: Serious crime, including fraud. Also defamation and Courts Martial work.
Prof. Memberships: Leader of the Western Circuit.
Career: Called in 1964, joining 3 Pump Court. Recorder: 1979. Silk: 1988.
Personal: Presents 'The Trial of Penn & Mead'.

PATCHETT-JOYCE, Michael
Monckton Chambers (Richard Fowler QC), London (0171) 405 7211
Recommended in Construction
Specialisation: Principal area of practice is commercial litigation. Work includes professional negligence (principally of surveyors and solicitors); construction work and other Official Referees' business; and commercial contract-orientated work ranging from sale and supply agreements to employment contracts. Reported cases include Dorrell v Dorrell [1985]; R v Clerk to Croydon JJ, ex p. Chief Constable of Kent [1989]; Kerridge v James Abbott & Partners [1992]; G. Percy Trentham Ltd v Archital Luxfer and others [1993]; and Lexair Ltd (in Administrative Receivership) v Edgar W. Taylor Ltd [1994]; Coban v Allen [1996] (CA); Gold Coin Joailliers v United Bank of Kuwait [1996] (CA).
Prof. Memberships: Official Referees' Bar Association, Administrative Law Bar Association.
Career: Called to the Bar 1981. Tenant at 22 Old Buildings (formerly 3 Hare Court) until 1988, then joined current chambers.
Personal: Educated at Manchester Grammar School to 1975; Trinity Hall, Cambridge 1976-79 and Inns of Court Law School 1980-81.

PATRICK, James
Guildhall Chambers (John Royce QC), Bristol (0117) 927 3366
Recommended in Licensing

PATTEN, Nicholas QC
9 Old Square (Robert Reid QC), London (0171) 405 4682
Recommended in the following lists: Chancery, Professional Negligence, Property Litigation
Specialisation: General commercial/chancery: professional negligence. Cases include: Target

Holdings Ltd v Redferns [1996] AC 421; Mortgage Express Ltd v Bowermans [1996] 2AER 836; Bristol & West Building Society v Mothew [1996] 4AER 698; Mannai Investment Co. Ltd v Eagle Star Life Assurance Co [1997] HL.
Prof. Memberships: Chancery Bar Association (Chairman); Professional Negligence Bar Association.

PATTERSON, Frances QC
40 King St (Philip Raynor QC), Manchester (0161) 832 9082
Recommended in Planning
Specialisation: Specialist in Town Planning, Compulsory Purchase, Highways, Environmental Law and Judicial Review. Experience in projects involving airport expansion, roads, incineration, waste disposal, retailing, minuals and housing.
Prof. Memberships: Member of Northern Circuit; Committee member Planning and Environment Bar Association.
Career: Called 1977. Assistant Recorder 1996. Appointed Queen's Council 1998.

PAUFFLEY, Anna QC
4 Paper Buildings (Lionel Swift QC), London (0171) 583 0816
Recommended in the following lists: Family: Child Care including child abduction

PAWLAK, Witold
9 Bedford Row (John Goldring QC), London (0171) 242 3555
Recommended in Environmental Law
Specialisation: Environmental pollution (R v Hertfordshire C.C. ex parte Green Environmental Industries (1997) Env. LR, Shanks McEwan Ltd v Environment Agency (1997)), R v Leighton & Town and Country Refuse Collection Ltd (1997) Env. LR. Financial services (Spring v Guardian Assurance HL (1994) R v Lautro ex parte Butters CA (1994) Legal & General v Ferrari CA (1995)). Family (S (Hospital Patient: Foreign Curator CA and FD (1995)). Wells v First National Bank (1998) PNLR. Carlton v Fulchers (1997) PNLR.
Prof. Memberships: FLBA, PIBA, British Polish Legal Association.
Career: MA (Cantab). Called in 1970. Recorder 1995.
Personal: Skiing, Art, Auctions.

PEACOCK, Jonathan
11 New Square (John Gardiner QC), London (0171) 242 4017
Recommended in Tax
Specialisation: Revenue law. Work encompasses advice on all aspects of UK tax, including VAT, Customs and Excise duties and EC levies administered by HM Customs and Excise; tax litigation in all tribunals (including tax-related aspects of commercial disputes, judicial review and professional negligence). Involved in the Woolwich Building Society litigation resulting in the recovery of over £100 million from the Inland Revenue.
Prof. Memberships: Revenue Bar Association, Chancery Bar Association, VAT Practitioners Group.
Career: Called to the Bar 1987; joined current chambers 1988.
Personal: Educated at King's School, Macclesfield 1975-79, Nunthorpe Grammar School, York 1979-82 and Corpus Christi College, Oxford 1983-86 (1st Class Degree in Jurisprudence). Born 21st April 1964.

PEACOCKE, Teresa Rosen
Enterprise Chambers (Anthony Mann QC), London (0171) 405 9471
Recommended in the following lists: Chancery, Professional Negligence
Specialisation: Principal area of practice is litigation in all areas of commercial/chancery law, particularly professional negligence, partnership law, property, landlord and tenant, company law, insolvency and bankruptcy, and banking.

Professional negligence cases include White v Jones (solicitors' negligence, House of Lords) and Roberts v J. Hampson & Co. Other areas of professional negligence handled include accountants, tax consultants, barristers, architects, engineers and surveyors.
Prof. Memberships: Professional Negligence Bar Association, Anglo-American Real Property Institute, Association of Women Barristers, American Women Lawyers in London Group.
Career: Called to the Bar 1982: tenant at 7 New Square 1982-89, then joined Enterprise Chambers.
Personal: Educated at University of Michigan (Analytical Philosophy and Logic BA 1977, MA 1979). Lives in London.

PEARCE, Ivan
Furnival Chambers (Andrew Mitchell), London (0171) 405 3232
Recommended in Crime
Specialisation: Cases including asset forfeiture and confiscation. The appointment of receivers and the general enforcement of confiscation orders in both the High Court and the Magistrates Court.
Prof. Memberships: Criminal Bar Association. Administrative Bar Association.
Career: Priestlands School, Lymington, Merristwood Agricultural College, Exeter University, LLB.
Personal: Rowing, sailing.

PEARL, David A.
4 King's Bench Walk (Nicholas Jarman QC), London (0171) 353 3581
Recommended in Employment
Specialisation: Specialises in employment law. Practice also covers personal injury and professional negligence work.
Prof. Memberships: Employment Law Bar Association, Personal Injuries Bar Association, Professional Negligence Bar Association.
Career: Called to the Bar 1977. Joined present chambers 1986. Part-time Industrial Tribunal Chairman since September 1994.
Personal: Educated at Ilford County High School 1965-1972 and Pembroke College, Cambridge 1972-1975. Born 19th March 1954.

PEART, Icah
Two Garden Court (I. Macdonald QC & O. Davies), London (0171) 353 1633
Recommended in Crime
Specialisation: All major criminal work, including leading work. Areas of particular expertise include public order offences, armed robbery, conspiracy to defraud, terrorism, murder and large-scale drugs conspiracy/importation.
Prof. Memberships: S.E. Circuit; CBA; LSE Lawyers Group.
Career: 9 Stone Buildings 1978-82; 76B Chancery Lane 1982-87; 2 Garden Court, Temple, 1987 to date. Assistant Recorder 1997 to date.
Personal: Interests include sports, cinema, reading, music and my children (not necessarily in that order!).

PEDDIE, Ian QC
One Garden Court Family Law Chambers (Miss Eleanor F. Platt QC & Miss Alison Ball QC), London (0171) 797 7900
Recommended in the following lists: Family: Child Care including child abduction
Specialisation: Child Care Law: includes numerous cases involving 'Munchhausen' allegations; physical and sexual abuse. Many reported cases. Criminal Law: especially cases involving children as witnesses. Recent cases include R v Campbell [1996] (machete attack on Wolverhampton Primary School); R v Evans [1995] (Pembrokshire Paedophile case – 8 months).
Prof. Memberships: Committee Member. FLBA since 1990.
Career: Gordonstoun School, LLB (Hons) University College London. Called to the Bar in 1971, QC in 1991, Assistant Recorder 1993, Recorder of Crown Court 1996.

PEEL, Robert
29 Bedford Row Chambers (Peter Ralls QC), London (0171) 831 2626
Recommended in the following lists: Family: Matrimonial Finance
Specialisation: Principal areas of practice are ancillary relief, child abduction and personal injury.
Prof. Memberships: Member of Bar Council since 1996. Committee member of Family Law Bar Association.
Career: Oxford University (BA Hons). City University (DIP Law). Called to the Bar 1990.
Personal: Fluent in French and Spanish.

PELLING, Mark
Monckton Chambers (Richard Fowler QC), London (0171) 405 7211
Recommended in Arbitration
Specialisation: Specialises in domestic and international arbitration, banking, corporate fraud and tracing, insurance and re-insurance, commercial litigation and competition litigation. Recent reported cases include: North Atlantic Insurance Co Ltd v. Bishopsgate Insurance Ltd [1998], Turner v. Stevenage Borough Council [1997], Regia Autonoma de Electricitate Renel v Gulf Petroleum International Ltd [1996], Re BCCI (No 10) [1995], Deeney & Others v Walker & Others [1995], Re The Net Book Agreements v EC Commission [1994].
Prof. Memberships: COMBAR; ORBAR.

PENDLEBURY, Jeremy
9 Bedford Row (John Goldring QC), London (0171) 242 3555
Recommended in Personal Injury
Specialisation: Specialises in the areas of professional negligence, personal injury and contract law. Within the field of professional negligence, practice concentrates mainly on medical negligence, solicitor's negligence and surveyor's negligence. Personal injury work includes industrial accident, fatal accident and industrial disease claims. Contract work covers general contract and consumer claims. Recent reported cases include Singh v Duport Harper Foundries Ltd (1994) 2 All ER 889; Hoskins v Wiggins Teape (1994) PIQR P337.
Prof. Memberships: Inner Temple.
Career: Called to the Bar 1980. Harcourt Buildings, Temple 1982-1994. Joined present Chambers 1994.
Personal: Educated at Eastbourne College 1970-1975, Kent University 1976-1979 and the Inns of Court Law School 1979-1980. Born 23rd September 1957.

PENNICOTT, Ian
Keating Chambers (Richard Fernyhough QC), London (0171) 544 2600
Recommended in Construction
Specialisation: Building and engineering contracts.
Career: Qualified 1982; Middle Temple.
Personal: Born 1958. Leisure, Golf.

PERRY, David
6 King's Bench Walk (Michael Worsley QC), London (0171) 583 0410
Recommended in the following lists: Crime, Crime: Fraud

PERRY, John QC
3 Gray's Inn Square (Rock Tansey QC), London (0171) 520 5600
Recommended in Crime
Specialisation: Practice encompasses all areas of criminal law. Contributor of articles to Criminal Law Review.
Prof. Memberships: Criminal Bar Association.
Career: Called to the Bar 1975 and joined 2 Crown Office Row. Part-time lecturer, LSE 1975-79 and later Senior Lecturer, City of London Polytechnic (now Guildhall University). Joined current chambers in 1988. Took Silk 1989. Appointed Assistant Recorder 1989, and Recorder 1991.

Personal: Educated at LSE 1967-70 (LL.B, LL.M 1974) and Warwick University (MA Industrial Relations, 1974).

PERSEY, Lionel QC
4 Field Court (Geoffrey Brice QC), London (0171) 440 6900
Recommended in the following lists: Energy & Utilities, Shipping
Specialisation: Commercial litigation and arbitration, with particular emphasis upon shipping and maritime law, insurance, international trade, commodities, product liability, construction, oil and gas and conflict of laws. Has sat as arbitrator in commercial disputes.
Prof. Memberships: COMBAR, LCLCBA, LMAA (supporting member).
Career: Called to the Bar in 1981, took silk in 1997. Supplementary Panel of Treasury Counsel 1992-1997.
Personal: Born 1958. Educated at Haberdashers' Aske's School, Birmingham University 1976-1980 (LL.B.) and UniversitE de Limoges 1978-1979.

PETCHEY, Philip
2 Harcourt Buildings (Mr Gerard Ryan QC), London (0171) 353 8415
Recommended in the following lists: Ecclesiastical, Parliamentary

PETERS, Nigel QC
18 Red Lion Court (Anthony Arlidge QC), London (0171) 520 6000
Recommended in Crime: Fraud
Specialisation: Main areas of practice are criminal law and judicial review. Criminal law: specialising in serious fraud, revenue offences, money laundering and allied financial investigations. Other main areas of practice include obscene publications, licensing and public entertainment law. Judicial review: specialising in disputes in connection with the criminal process, licensing and public entertainment law. This often involves aspects of international and European law.
Career: Called to the Bar 1976. Silk 1997, Assistant Recorder, formerly Standing Counsel to HM Counsel and Excise.

PHILIPPS, Guy
Fountain Court (Peter Scott QC), London (0171) 583 3335
Recommended in the following lists: Insurance & Reinsurance, Professional Negligence
Specialisation: All areas of commercial litigation (including arbitration), particularly insurance and reinsurance, banking and financial services, and professional negligence.
Career: Called 1986. Member of Supplementary Panel of Treasury Counsel, Common Law. Member of California Bar.
Personal: Born 1961. Educated Magdalen College, Oxford and City University.

PHILIPSON, Trevor QC
Fountain Court (Peter Scott QC), London (0171) 583 3335
Recommended in the following lists: Aviation, Energy & Utilities, Professional Negligence
Specialisation: General commercial litigation with recent reported cases in the fields of aviation, commercial fraud and restitution. Practice has recently included a number of lengthy professional negligence actions in London and Hong Kong.

PHILLIPS, David QC
199 Strand (Peter Andrews QC), London (0171) 379 9779
Recommended in Professional Negligence
Specialisation: General commercial and common law practice, specialising in professional negligence relating to property/land and finance.
Prof. Memberships: Professional Negligence Bar Association, Chancery Bar Association, Bristol & Cardiff Chancery Bar Association.
Career: Called 1976. 3 New Square, Lincoln's Inn 1978-1990. Present chambers since 1990. Door

tenant 30 Park Place, Cardiff since 1995. Assistant Recorder since 1994. Took Silk in 1997.
Personal: Born 4th May 1953. Educated Rugby School & Balliol College, Oxford.

PHILLIPS, Jane
1 Brick Court (Richard Hartley QC), London (0171) 353 8845
Recommended in Defamation
Specialisation: Libel & slander, malicious falsehood, contempt, passing-off, breach of confidence, reporting restrictions and all forms of media law, including pre-publicaton advice. Cases include: Adams v Associated Newspapers Limited (CA); Allason v BBC and Hat Trick Productions; Ashby v Times Newspapers Limited; C v MGN Limited, South West Wales Newspapers Limited and others (CA); Lloyd v Express Newspapers Limited (CA); Marks and Spencer PLC v Granada; Upjohn v BBC and Professor Oswald.
Career: Called to the Bar in July 1989.
Personal: Educated at St. Paul's Girls' School and Worcester College, Oxford.

PHILLIPS, Mark
3/4 South Square (Michael Crystal QC), London (0171) 696 9900
Recommended in the following lists: Banking, Financial Services, Insolvency
Specialisation: Area of practice: insolvency – administration, insurance, banking – regulatory work for the Bank of England. Commercial work arising out of insolvencies. Notable cases: Three Rivers District Council + ORS v The Governor and Company of the Bank of England. (July 1997 – unreported). Galileo Group Limited – William Jason Hughes E v Hambros Bank Limited (1798 2 VOLR 364).
Career: Education: LLB LLM (commercial) Bristol University. Appointed Assistant Recorder – July 1998.
Personal: Motorsport enthusiast.

PHILLIPS, Patrick QC
2 Temple Gardens (Patrick Phillips QC), London (0171) 583 6041
Recommended in Professional Negligence

PHILLIPS, Richard QC
2 Harcourt Buildings (Mr Gerard Ryan QC), London (0171) 353 8415
Recommended in Planning

PHILLIPS, Rory
3 Verulam Buildings (R. Neville Thomas QC), London (0171) 831 8441
Recommended in the following lists: Insurance & Reinsurance, Professional Negligence
Specialisation: Principal areas of practice are insurance and reinsurance and professional negligence.
Career: Called 1984. Member, Supplementary Panel of Junior Treasury Counsel, Common Law.

PHILLIPS, Stephen
3 Verulam Buildings (R. Neville Thomas QC), London (0171) 831 8441
Recommended in Commercial (litigation)
Specialisation: Principal area of practice is commercial and business law. Work includes general contractual disputes, banking and finance, company law and insolvency, international and domestic trade, commercial fraud, professional negligence and gaming contracts. Clients include banks and other financial institutions, insurance companies and funds and casinos. Contributor to 'The Encyclopaedia of Banking Law.'
Prof. Memberships: Wales and Chester Circuit, COMBAR, London Common Law and Commercial Bar Association.
Career: Called to the Bar 1984 and joined present chambers 1985.
Personal: Educated at King's School, Chester 1973-80 and University College, Oxford 1980-83. Born 10th October 1961.

PHILPOTT, Frederick
Gough Square Chambers (Frederick Philpott), London (0171) 353 0924
Recommended in Consumer Law
Specialisation: Consumer Law – consumer credit (drafting of regulated credit and hire agreements), advising on consumer credit advertising, consumer credit licensing, acting in civil litigation e.g. extortionate credit bargains – Ketley v. Scott [1981] ICR 241 and connected lender claims – Jarrett v. Barclays Bank [1997] 2 All ER 484) and in criminal prosecutions (e.g. Carrington Carr v Leicester [1993] Crim LR 938), food safety (criminal proceedings), pollution (Empress Car Co (Abertillery) Ltd v National Rivers Authority [1998] 1 All ER 481), misleading prices (e.g. R v Warwickshire CC [1993] AC 583), trade descriptions, weights and measures, Fair Trading Act, Trading Schemes Act. Clients include banks, finance houses, food producers and supermarkets.
Prof. Memberships: Food Law Group.
Career: Called 1974.

PICARDA, Hubert QC
3 New Square (Lord Goodhart QC), London (0171) 405 5577
Recommended in Charities
Specialisation: Chancery law generally but particular expertise in all aspects of law relating to charities, banking, corporate insolvency and derivative trading. Recent cases include: Wellcome Plc v Glaxo Holdings (disputed take over); Oldham BC v AG (-sale of recreation ground) R v Lord President of Council (judicial review of university visitor); Bridge Trust Ld v AG of Caymans; Jyske Bank (Gibraltor) Ltd v Spieldnaes. Clients include: Wellcome Trust, Garfield Weston Foundation, Wolfson Foundation, many leading and medium range charities, housing associations, universities and local authorities. Advisory work and appearances in receiverships of Gomba Holdings, BCCI and Royal Masonic Hospital. Advisory work in Singapore, Hong Kong and Caymans.
Prof. Memberships: Chancery Bar Association, Insolvency Lawyers Association, Charity Law Association (President).
Career: Called 1962. QC 1992. Visiting lecturer in banking and derivative trading law 1995-1996; Malaysia, Sarawak, Singapore. Editorial Board: Journal of International Banking and Finance Law, Trust Law International.
Personal: Author of Picarda Law relating to Receivers Managers Administrators (2nd ed 1990) Picarda Law and practice relating to Charities (2nd ed 1995). Halsbury Title on Receivers (1998). Managing Editor: Receivers Administrators and Liquidators Quarterly 1993-.

PICKUP, James
Lincoln House Chambers (Mukhtar Hussain QC), Manchester (0161) 832 5701
Recommended in Crime
Specialisation: 1. Commercial Fraud. R v Clive Smith and others (Butte Mining Trial) before Newman J. at Old Bailey, March 1997 - June 1998. 2. Murder. 1996 R v Po Ming Li and others - Triad murder tried by Recorder of Manchester. 1996 R v Buffy and others - 12 week trial before Mitchell J in Manchester. 3. Professional Negligence.
Prof. Memberships: Criminal Bar Assocation. Personal Injury Bar Association.
Career: Kings School Macclesfield 1961-71. Lincoln College Oxford MA Jurisprudence 1975, BCL 1976. Crown Court Recorder 1997.
Personal: Married, 2 children. Wife pharmaceutical lawyer Zeneca plc. Cricket (Member Lancs CCC, MCC).

PICTON, Martin
Albion Chambers (J.C.T. Barton QC), Bristol (0117) 927 2144
Recommended in Crime

PINE-COFFIN, Margaret Ann
17 Carlton Crescent (Mr Jeremy Gibbons QC), Southampton (01703) 320320
Recommended in Family/Matrimonial
Specialisation: Practice covers all areas of family law with a special emphasis on child care. Particular expertise in physical injuries to children. Has good working knowledge of French and Italian.
Prof. Memberships: Western Circuit; Family Law Bar Association.
Career: Called to the Bar 1981.
Personal: Born 1956. Married, 2 children. Special interests: travel abroad.

PITCHFORD, Christopher QC
Farrar's Building (Gerard Elias QC), London (0171) 583 9241
Recommended in Crime
Specialisation: General common law practitioner, with a particular emphasis on personal injury and crime.
Career: Called to the Bar 1969. Tenant at 30 Park Place, Cardiff before joining present chambers in 1987. Took silk 1987, and was appointed Recorder of the Crown Court in the same year. Motor Insurers Bureau Arbitrator since 1994.
Personal: Born 28th March 1947. Lives in Bedlinog, Mid Glam.

PITT-PAYNE, Timothy Sheridan
11 King's Bench Walk (Eldred Tabachnik QC and James Goudie QC), London (0171) 632 8500
Recommended in Employment
Specialisation: Principal areas of practice are employment law (especially race and sex discrimination, wrongful and unfair dismissal, transfer of undertakings and industrial action) and public and local government law (including education law). Also handles commercial law matters including professional negligence, sale of goods and general contractual disputes. Contributer to 'Supperstone and Goudie on Judicial Review' (Butterworths, 1992).
Prof. Memberships: Employment Law Bar Association.
Career: Lecturer in Law, University of Melbourne 1986-87. Lecturer in Law, University of Auckland 1988. Called to the Bar in 1989 and joined present chambers in 1990. Member of the Attorney General's Supplementary Panel of Counsel from 1994.
Personal: Educated at St. Augustine's College, Westgate-on-Sea, Kent 1976-82 and Worcester College, Oxford 1982-86 (BA (Hons) Jurisprudence 1985, BCL 1986). Born 18th November 1964. Lives in London.

PITTAWAY, David
No. 1 Serjeants' Inn (Edward Faulks QC), London (0171) 415 6666
Recommended in Professional Negligence
Specialisation: Professional negligence work for plaintiffs and defendants, including medical cases, solicitors, accountants, insurance brokers and financial advisers. Has been instructed in cases involving misdiagnosis of cancer, obstetrics and gynaecology, paediatrics (including renal failure), and negligent treatment of a mental patient. He has particular experience in cerebral palsy cases. Also, negligent conduct by solicitors of medical negligence and personal injury litigation, and negligent advice by accountants on the sale of companies, including a major football club. Other main area of practice is general commercial and contract work, including carriage of goods and employment. Cases include Dhak v Insurance Company of North America (UK) Ltd (1996) 1 WLR 936; Chamberlain v Vinyl Products v Patel (1996) ICR 113; Betts v London Borough of Newham (1996) PIQR 301 (CA); Nash v Kingston & Richmond Health Authority (1996) MLR. Co-editor of 'Atkins Court Forms' (Professional Negligence/Personal Injury). General Editor of

"Pittaway & Hammerton: Professional Negligence Cases" (June 1998).
Prof. Memberships: Bencher of the Inner Temple; Executive Committee, Professional Negligence Bar Association, Chairman of Bar Liaison Committee of the Inner Temple, Midland & Oxford Circuit.
Career: Called to the Bar in 1977 and joined No.1 Serjeants' Inn in 1979. Appointed an Assistant Recorder in 1998.
Personal: Educated at Uppingham School 1968-72 and Sidney Sussex College, Cambridge 1973-77. Born 29th June 1955. Lives in London.

PLANTEROSE, Rowan
Littman Chambers (Mark Littman QC), London (0171) 404 4866
Recommended in Construction
Specialisation: Principal areas of practice are building and engineering and general commercial litigation. Other areas include more general professional negligence and practice and procedural matters in litigation and arbitration. Engineering related work has ranged widely and included train building and computer and telephone technology.
Prof. Memberships: ORBA (Committee Member); COMBAR; Chartered Institute of Arbitrators (Council Member).
Career: Called to the Bar in 1978.
Personal: Educated at Eastbourne College and Downing College, Cambridge University. Lives in London and Gloucestershire.

PLATT, Eleanor F. QC
One Garden Court Family Law Chambers (Miss Eleanor F. Platt QC & Miss Alison Ball QC), London (0171) 797 7900
Recommended in the following lists: Family: Child Care including child abduction
Specialisation: All aspects of Family Law with particular emphasis upon children and cases involving medical issues. Has been involved in sterilisation and surrogacy mattters and was instructed on behalf of the Northern Region in the Cleveland Enquiry.
Prof. Memberships: Family Law Bar Association; S.E. circuit; Gene Therapy Advisory Committee; Deputy Chairman National Health Service Tribunal; Legal Assessor General Medical/Dental Councils. Called to the Bar 1960, Recorder 1982, Silk 1982. Deputy Judge, High Court Family Division since 1987.
Personal: LL.B. London. Married with two children. Many interests including music, travel and skiing.

PLATTS-MILLS, Mark QC
8 New Square (Michael Fysh QC), London (0171) 405 4321
Recommended in Intellectual Property
Specialisation: Specialist in all aspects of intellectual property, including patents, trade marks, passing off, registered designs, copyright and design right. Also handles commercial work with a technical content. Recent interesting cases include [1998] Ladney & Hendry: Appln (Patent – Inventors kits) [1998] IPC magazines v MGN Ltd (Copyright, comparative advertising, incidental use) [1998] George Harrison v Lingasong (performers' rights – early Beatles performances), [1997] Brain v Ingledew Brown (patent threats) [1997] Waterford v Nagli (Trade Mark – importation) [1996] Electronic Techniques v Critchley Components (Design Right – Must Fit defence – Copyright – Transformers and brochures for transformers) Hutchison Telecommunications v Hook [1994] (copyright, secondary infringement – "Rabbit" logo); Apple Corps v Cooper [1993] (copyright – "Sergeant Pepper's Lonely Hearts Club band" photographs); Universal Thermosensors v Hibben [1992] (Breach of confidence, Anton Piller practice – design of thermosensors, competition by ex-employees).
Career: Called to the Bar 1974. Joined present chambers 1975. Took silk 1995.
Personal: Educated at Bryanston School 1963-1969 and at Balliol College, Oxford (BA

Engineering Science and Economics) 1969-1972. Born 17th January 1951.

PLAYFORD, Jonathan QC
2 Harcourt Buildings (Roger Henderson QC), London (0171) 583 9020
Recommended in the following lists: Product Liability, Professional Negligence
Specialisation: Many professional negligence and product liablility cases in recent years. Currently involved in the tobacco lung cancer litigation. Also involved in a substantial amount of insurance recovery litigation of various kinds.
Career: Called 1962, Silk 1982. Bencher of Inner Temple; Recorder Midland and Oxford Circuit.

PLEMING, Nigel QC
39 Essex Street (Edwin Glasgow QC), London (0171) 832 1111
Recommended in the following lists: Administrative & Public Law, Civil Liberties, Immigration & Nationality
Specialisation: Administrative and public law; environmental law and related regulatory work; local government law; and construction law.
Career: Called 1971, Junior Counsel to the Crown (Common Law) – 1985 to 1992, Queen's Counsel – 1992.

PLENDER, Richard QC
20 Essex Street (David Johnson QC), London (0171) 583 9294
Recommended in the following lists: European Union/Competition, Immigration & Nationality
Specialisation: European Community, Immigration and Nationality. Also experienced in public and private international law and adminstrative law.
Career: Dulwich College, LCC scholar, 1957-64; Queens' College Cambridge, open exhibitioner, BA 1967, LLB 1968 (Rebecca Squire Prize) LLD 1993; University of Illinois, LLM 1970 (summa cum laude), JSD 1971 (College of Law Prize); called to the Bar 1972 (Berridale Keith Prize); Legal Adviser, UNHCR, 1974-76; Référendaire Court of Justice of the European Communities. 1980-83; QC 1989; Bencher Inner Temple 1996; Recorder 1998. Principal publications; *International Migration Law*, 1972, 2nd ed, 1988; *Cases and Materials on the Law of the European Communities*, with J A Usher, 1979, 2nd ed 1988, 3rd ed 1993; *The European Contracts Convention: The Rome Convention on the Choice of Law for Contracts*, 1991; *European Courts Practice and Precedents*, 1996; contributions to encyclopedias, periodicals and books in English, French and German.
Personal: Born 1945.

POCOCK, Christopher
One King's Bench Walk (James Townend QC), London (0171) 936 1500
Recommended in Family: Matrimonial Finance
Specialisation: Family, (including divorce and children) matrimonial finance and property. Financial disputes between unmarried couples, inheritance and family provision..
Prof. Memberships: S.E. Circuit; Family Law Bar Association.
Personal: Born 1960. Call 1984 Inner Temple. Education, St Dunstan's College; Pembroke College Oxford (BA Juris). Working knowledge of French; DPA Accepted.

POINTER QC, Martin QC
1 Mitre Court Buildings (Bruce Blair QC), London (0171) 797 7070
Recommended in Family: Matrimonial Finance
Specialisation: Handles all types of family law, but principally financial relief claims. Pioneer of pension-splitting in ancillary relief.
Prof. Memberships: Family Law Association, International Academy of Matrimonial Lawyers.
Career: Called to the Bar in 1976 and joined Mitre Court Buildings in 1978. Silk 1996.
Personal: Educated at The King's School, Grantham 1964-71 and the University of Leicester 1972-75. Born 17th July 1953. Lives in London.

POLLOCK, Gordon QC
Essex Court Chambers (Gordon Pollock QC), London (0171) 813 8000
Recommended in the following lists: Administrative & Public Law, Arbitration, Banking, Commercial (litigation), Energy & Utilities, Insurance & Reinsurance, Media & Entertainment, Shipping, Sports Law
Specialisation: Broad-based commercial lawyer with a substantial court and advisory practice dealing with the major commercial issues of the day. He has been instructed in most of the major commercial litigation of recent years. Areas of practice include: arbitration, banking, commodity disputes, conflict of laws, employment law, entertainment and sports law, financial services, insurance & reinsurance, judicial review, monopolies and mergers, oil and gas cases, professional negligence, shipping, takeovers.
Career: Trinity College, Cambridge: MA, LLB. Called to the Bar 1968. Queen's Counsel 1979. Bencher: Gray's Inn. Sits as Deputy High Court Judge of the Chancery and Queen's Bench Divisions.
Personal: Born 1943.

POOLES, Michael
4 Paper Buildings (Harvey McGregor QC), London (0171) 353 3366
Recommended in Professional Negligence
Specialisation: Principal area of practice is professional negligence, particularly concerning solicitors. Also acts for and against members of the Bar, accountants, surveyors, architects, engineers and doctors. Other main areas of practice are personal injury and general insurance matters, on behalf of a large number of insurance companies.
Prof. Memberships: Professional Negligence Bar Association.
Career: Called to the Bar 1978 and joined present chambers in 1980.
Personal: Educated at Perse School, Cambridge, 1967-74 and University of London 1974-7. Born 14th December 1955. Lives in Cambridge.

POPE, Heather
1 Mitre Court Buildings (Bruce Blair QC), London (0171) 797 7070
Recommended in the following lists: Family: Child Care including child abduction
Specialisation: Family: Matrimonial Finance. Family: Children: Private and Public Law, Child Abduction.
Prof. Memberships: Family Law Bar Association. Bar representative for FLBA on Family Court Business Committee in Luton. Member of the Western Circuit.
Career: B.A. (Hons) (Wales) Diploma of Education (Wales). Called to the Bar 1977. Member of Inner Temple.
Personal: Theatre, music, reading, tennis, travel.

POPLE, Alison
3 Hare Court (William Clegg QC), London (0171) 353 7561
Recommended in Crime
Specialisation: Criminal Law Specialist with a recent emphasis on fraud. Recent cases include R v Clews and others (Bute Mining, prosecution brought by SFO), R v Lloyd and others (ATM fraud).
Prof. Memberships: Criminal Bar Association, South Eastern Circuit.
Career: Called to Bar 1993. Fox Scholar (Middle Temple) 1993-1994. Joined present chambers in 1995.
Personal: Educated at Ulverston Victoria High School, and Huddersfield Polytechnic. Born 8th November 1968.

POPPLEWELL, Andrew QC
Brick Court Chambers (Christopher Clarke QC), London (0171) 583 0777
Recommended in the following lists: Insurance & Reinsurance, Professional Negligence
Specialisation: General commercial, including shipping, banking, insurance and reinsurance, international trade, financial services, arbitration, professional disciplinary, telecommunications and some employment and defamation.
Prof. Memberships: Supplementary Panel of Treasury Counsel (1988).
Career: Called to Bar of England and Wales 1981. Has been appointed as ICC Arbitrator. Cases of note: Gruppo Torras v Sheikh Fahad, Hill v Mercantile & General, Vitol v Norelf.
Personal: Born 14 January 1959. Educated at Radley College and Downing College, Cambridge (B.A. Hons (Cantab) in Law Class: First).

PORTEN, Anthony QC
2-3 Gray's Inn Square (Anthony Scrivener QC), London (0171) 242 4986
Recommended in the following lists: Administrative & Public Law, Planning
Specialisation: Planning and Local Government work, especially public inquiries and High Court; judicial review.
Prof. Memberships: PEBA, ALBA.
Career: Called 1969. Silk 1988. Recorder 1993.
Personal: Epsom College; Emmanuel College, Cambridge.

PORTER, Martin
2 Temple Gardens (Patrick Phillips QC), London (0171) 583 6041
Recommended in Personal Injury
Specialisation: Common law (principally personal injury and professional negligence claims), Judicial Review (especially liabilities of local authorities exercising statutory functions), Commercial (particularly insurance related work). Cases include Young v Church April 1997 (Liability for psychiatric injury); ex p Steed [1996] 71P + CR 463; Thompson v Wickens [1996] 1 WLR 561; Vasey v Surrey Free Inns [1996] PIQR P373; Yates v Thakenham Tiles [1995] PIQR P135; Oliver v Monk [1995] PIQR P465.
Prof. Memberships: Inner Temple, Western Circuit, LCCBA, PIBA.
Career: Born 1962. Call 1986. Educated St John's College, Cambridge: MA (Law) LLM (Public Law).
Personal: Married, two daughters. PPL (1989); Skiing.

POSNANSKY, Jeremy QC
1 Mitre Court Buildings (Bruce Blair QC), London (0171) 797 7070
Recommended in the following lists: Family: Child Care including child abduction, Family: Matrimonial Finance
Specialisation: Family Law. Practice covers all areas of family law: ancillary relief and all aspects of the law relating to children. Appeared in many reported cases, including W v W (refusal of decree absolute) 1998, S v S (forum non conveniens) 1997, Re W (lesbian adoption) 1997, Phillips v Peace (financial provision for children) 1996, Baker v Baker (standard of proof in ancillary relief applications) 1995, Cornick v Cornick, Nos. 1 and 2, (leave to appeal out of time, and variation of maintenance principles) 1995. Articles in International Family Law and Family Law.
Prof. Memberships: Family Law Bar Association; Fellow of International Academy of Matrimonial Lawyers; Medico-Legal Society.
Career: Call 1972; Silk 1994. Deputy High Court Judge, 1997; Admitted to the Bar of Antigua.
Personal: Born 8th March 1951. Married with two daughters. Lives in London. Enjoys travel, scuba diving and computers.

POTTS, Richard
Octagon House Chambers (Andrew Lindqvist & Guy Ayers), Norwich (01603) 623186
Recommended in Crime

POTTS, Robin QC
Erskine Chambers (Richard Sykes QC), London (0171) 242 5532
Recommended in the following lists: Banking, Company, Financial Services, Insolvency
Specialisation: Specialist in all aspects of company law including insolvency and financing and banking transactions. Experience extends to practice in overseas courts such as Bermuda, Hong Kong, Bahamas, Cayman Islands and Gibraltar. Interesting cases include the Paramount Case [1995] Court of Appeal and House of Lords (acting for the successful airline pilots); Macmillan IZNC v BIT [1994] (arising out of the Maxwell affair). Also represented British Land Plc in litigation brought by Stanhope Properties. Has fought several section 459 petitions including three major trials in the past year.
Prof. Memberships: Commercial Bar Association; Insolvency Lawyers Association; Society of Practitioners of Insolvency.
Career: Called to the Bar 1968. Joined present chambers 1969. Took silk 1982.
Personal: Educated at Wolstanton Grammar School, Newcastle-under-Lyme, and at Magdalen College, Oxford (BA and BCL) 1963-1967. Bigelow Fellow, University of Chicago Law School 1967-1968. Leisure pursuits include history, gardening, travel and wine. Born 2nd July 1944. Lives in London.

POWELL, John L. QC
2 Crown Office Row (John Powell QC), London (0171) 797 8000
Recommended in the following lists: Financial Services, Professional Negligence
Specialisation: Commercial law, especially professional negligence, accountancy, financial services and securities law (UK, EC and international), investment fraud, insurance, judicial review, arbitration, confidentiality and construction. Leading counsel for plaintiff liquidators in BCCI audit litigation. Reported cases include BCCI Overseas v Price Waterhouse (1998) (audit negligence), Mond v Hyde and DTI (1998) (immunity and liability of insolvency service); Fawkes-Underwood v Hamiltons (1997) (accountants negligence), Swinney v Chief Constable of Northumbria (1996) (confidentiality and immunity), Kaufmann v Credit Lyonnais (1995) (disclosure in regulatory context) R v PIA ex parte Lucas Fettes (pension miselling judicial review). Major involvements in Barlow Clowes, Lloyds, pension-miselling and Maxwell litigation as well as several recovery actions arising from U.K. and overseas frauds. Practice reflects main publications: (1) 'Jackson & Powell on Professional Negligence' and (2) 'Lomnicka & Powell, Encyclopedia of Financial Services Law' (Sweet & Maxwell). Chairman Bar Law Reform Committee (1997-).
Prof. Memberships: COMBAR, PNBA, Bar European Group, Society of Construction Law (President 1991-93).
Career: Called 1974. Silk 1990. Attorney of the Turks and Caicos Islands. Asst. Recorder. Bencher, Middle Temple.
Personal: Educated at Christ College, Brecon, Amman Valley Grammar School and Trinity Hall, Cambridge 1969-73 (MA, LLB). Welsh speaker. Born 14th September 1950.

POWERS, Dr Michael QC
One Paper Buildings (John Slater QC), London (0171) 583 7355
Recommended in the following lists: Medical Negligence, Product Liability
Specialisation: Medical negligence (plaintiff and defendant). Co-editor of the leading textbook 'Medical Negligence' (Butterworths 1990, 1994). Pharmaceutical law and all areas of common law touching upon medical and scientific matters. Group litigation for plaintiffs and defendants. Clients include McKenna & Co, Linklaters & Paines, Kennedys, Wedlake Bell, Irwin Mitchell, Hart Brown,

Russell Jones & Walker and many other leading firms. Pharmaceutical clients include: John Wyeth & Brother, Duphar Laboratories, Merrell Dow, 3M RIKER, Schering.

Prof. Memberships: Professional Negligence Bar Association; London Common Law and Commercial Bar Association; Fellow Royal Society of Medicine, British Medical Association, Association of Anaesthetists, Medico-Legal Society.

Career: Medical Practice (1972-1980): Obstetrics, Medicine, Anaesthesia, ITU and GP. Called to the Bar (Lincoln's Inn) 1979; QC 1995. President of the South of England Coroners' Society (1987/88). Founder member of Society of Doctors in Law. Chapters in many books; writes and lectures widely. Recent Cases reported include: Powell v Boladz and others [1998] Lloyd's Rep Med 111 (CA); Robertson v Nottingham Health Authority [1997] Med LR 1 (CA); AB & Others v Roche Products [1997] 8 Med LR 57 (CA).

Personal: Enthusiasm for advocacy and training of trial skills. Recreations: technology, sailing, walking, music and photography.

POWNALL, Orlando
1 Hare Court (Stephen Kramer QC), London (0171) 353 5324
Recommended in Crime

PRATT, Camden QC
One King's Bench Walk (James Townend QC), London (0171) 936 1500
Recommended in Family: Matrimonial Finance
Specialisation: Medical negligence, Medical Law, Environment, General common law, personal injuries, Matrimonial Finance and Property, Family (including Divorce and Children), Child care, Crime, Commercial Fraud (criminal), Commercial Fraud (civil). Interesting cases: Southern Water Authority v. Nature Conservancy Council [1992] 3 AER 481, HL (environmental damage/The Wildlife & Countryside Act); Re P [1995] 1 FLR 831 (International Child Abduction); Wicks v Wicks (C.A) [1998] 1 FLR 470 (Matrimonial financial relief: interim lump sum and transfer of property orders); R v Curtis Howard (the Gatwick Airport 'Body in Boot case'); Prosecution Counsel case of Regina v Sion Jenkins (the murder of 'Billie Jo') [1998]; R v Ron Brown (case of the MP's mistress's knickers).
Prof. Memberships: South Eastern Circuit (Committee Member); Chairman, Sussex Sessions Bar Mess; Chairman, Sussex Courts Liaison Committee 1993; Member Area Criminal Justice Liaison Committee 16.
Career: Call 1970, Silk 1992. Recorder 1993. Deputy High Court Judge, Family Division.
Personal: Educated at Lincoln College, Oxford (MA Juris).

PRATT, Duncan
New Court Chambers (George Carman QC), London (0171) 831 9500
Recommended in Medical Negligence
Specialisation: Principally practises in medical negligence and substantial personal injury claims. Considerable experience of claims involving birth and brain injuries of the utmost severity and has conducted medical negligence claims involving most medical and surgical specialities. Lectures on topics related to medical negligence. Other areas of practice solicitors' negligence, product liability, employment and related contractual claims. Professional clients include both specialised medical negligence departments and general litigation departments.
Prof. Memberships: Professional Negligence Bar Association, AVMA, APIL, Employment Law Bar Association, Medico-Legal Society.
Career: Called to the Bar 1971. Joined chambers 1972.
Personal: Educated RGS Newcastle and University College, Oxford. Lives in London. Leisure pursuits include choral singing, local amenity societies, theatre, concert and opera.

PRENTICE, Prof Dan
Erskine Chambers (Richard Sykes QC), London (0171) 242 5532
Recommended in Company

PRESCOTT, Peter QC
8 New Square (Michael Fysh QC), London (0171) 405 4321
Recommended in the following lists: Computer & I.T., Intellectual Property, Media & Entertainment
Specialisation: Specialist in all aspects of intellectual property law. Has been involved in numerous reported cases, recent examples of which include: Biogen v Medeva; Aztech Systems Pte v Creative Technology Ltd; Chiron v Murex; Imperial Chemical Industries v Montedison; Strix v Otter; Consorzio del Prosciutto di Parma v Marks & Spencer. Publications include 'Modern Law of Copyright' Butterworths 1980 1994 and 'Data Processing and the Law' (chapter in) Sweet & Maxwell 1984. Notes in Law Quarterly Review: 'Finding out who to sue' (1973) 89 LQR 482 and 'American Cyanamid v. Ethicon' (1975) 91 LQR 168. Contributions to European Intellectual Property Review include 'Towards a small claims patent court' 10 EIPR 246; 'Trade marks invisible at point of sale: some corking cases' 12 EIPR 241; 'Was AutoCad wrongly decided?' (1992) 6 EIPR 191.
Prof. Memberships: Intellectual Property Bar Association; Chancery Bar Association.
Career: Called to the Bar 1970. Took Silk 1990.
Personal: Educated at St George's College (Argentina), Dulwich College, University College London (BSc Physics) and Queen Mary College London (MSc Nuclear Engineering). Fluent in Spanish. Leisure pursuits include flying, music, reading and, formerly, programming in assembler language. Born 23rd January 1943.

PREVEZER, Susan
Essex Court Chambers (Gordon Pollock QC), London (0171) 813 8000
Recommended in Insolvency
Specialisation: Main area of practice covers insolvency, commercial litigation, property law, company law. Major litigation includes BCCI. Millwall FC, Levitt, Emlico, KWELM, contributor to Lightman and Moss on Receivers
Prof. Memberships: Commercial Bar Association. Chancery Bar Association.
Career: Called to Bar 1983. 7 years at Michael Crystal QC's Chambers. Joined Present Chambers 1997 (December)

PRICE, Gerald QC
33 Park Place (Wyn Williams QC), Cardiff (01222) 233313
Recommended in Crime

PRICE, James QC
5 Raymond Buildings (Patrick Milmo QC), London (0171) 242 2902
Recommended in Defamation

PRICE, Leolin QC
10 Old Square (Leolin Price CBE QC), London (0171) 405 0758
Recommended in Traditional Chancery
Specialisation: Principal areas of practice are chancery and commercial work, trusts, land, charities and partnership. Other main areas are taxation, constitutional and administrative law. Important cases include Pickin v British Railways Board (1974); Harman v Home Office (1983); R v. HM Treasury ex p. Smedley [1985]; Craven v. White [1989]; Brady v. Brady [1989]; Thomas v. University of Bradford [1987]; National Westminster Bank v. Morgan [1985]; Lloyd's Bank v. Rosset [1990]; CIBC v. Pitt [1994]; Baden v. Societe Generale [1993] and Harvela v. Royal Trust [1986]. Inverugie v Hackett (1995); Taylor v SFO (1998); Nadeem v Dunbar Bank(1998). Lectures to various bodies on legal, trust and tax matters.
Prof. Memberships: Chancery Bar Association, Chartered Institute of Arbitrators. Bencher of the Middle Temple since 1970. New South Wales Bar Association.
Career: Called to the Bar in 1949 and joined chambers at 10 Old Square in 1952. Took Silk in 1968. Called to the Bahamas Bar (QC 1969) and the Bar of New South Wales (QC 1987) (chambers at Selborne Chambers, 174 Phillip Street, Sydney, NSW. Tel: 612 233 51888 Fax: 612 233 1137). Treasurer of Middle Temple, 1990. Called to the British Virgin Islands Bar 1994.
Personal: Educated at the Judd School, Tonbridge and Keble College, Oxford (MA). Chairman, Institute of Child Health since 1976; Governor and Trustee of Great Ormond Street Hospital for Sick Children since 1972; Chancellor of the Diocese of Swansea & Brecon since 1982. Interests include politics. Born 11th May 1924. Lives in Hampstead and Llanbedr, near Crickhowell, Powys.

PRICE, Nicholas QC
3 Raymond Buildings (Clive Nicholls QC), London (0171) 831 3833
Recommended in Crime
Specialisation: Criminal law, commercial crime, licensing, disciplinary tribunals, inquests and inquiries.
Career: Called to the Bar in November 1968. Took silk in 1992. Recorder of the Crown Court since 1987. Member of Grays Inn Continuing Education/Advocacy Training Committee.

PRICE, Richard OBE QC
Littleton Chambers (Michael Burton QC), London (0171) 797 8600
Recommended in the following lists: Media & Entertainment, Sports Law
Specialisation: Principal areas of entertainment and media law experience include film, video and music rights and financing disputes, copyright infringement and piracy, the 'fair dealing' provisions of copyright law (BBC v British Sky Broadcasting Ltd. 1991 re: World Cup Football broadcasts), Anton Piller and Mareva injunctions, and corporate/partnership disputes within the entertainment industry. Clients have included major film and music production and distribution companies and broadcasters, and leading artists, directors and producers. Also specialises in election and administrative law, and professional negligence work.
Prof. Memberships: COMBAR, London Common Law and Commercial Bar Association, PNBA.
Career: Called to the Bar in 1969. Joined present Chambers in 1987, having previously been a member of Chambers of the late Lewis Hawser QC. Appointed QC 1996. Accredited CEDR mediator 1997.
Personal: Educated at King Edward VII School, Sheffield, and King's College London.

PRICE, Roderick
Cloisters (Laura Cox QC), London (0171) 827 4000
Recommended in Crime
Specialisation: Criminal defence, principally acting as a leading junior. Most often concerned in fraud, drug trafficking and murder cases. Consistently appeared in leading reported cases which have established important principles in complex areas of the criminal law. More recent cases include: R v Preston [1994] H.L. (interception of telecommunications); R v Gray and Liggins [1995] (insider dealing); R v Jones and Barham [1997] (conditional admissability rule in conspiracy and joint enterprise cases); R v Avis [1997] (sentencing guidelines in firearms cases).
Prof. Memberships: Criminal Bar Association.
Career: Called to the Bar 1971, Inner Temple.
Personal: Interests include sailing, badminton and cricket.

PRIDAY, Charles
7 King's Bench Walk (Stephen Tomlinson QC), London (0171) 583 0404
Recommended in Shipping
Specialisation: Principal areas of practice are shipping, banking, insurance and general commercial work, acting for shipowners, charterers, oil traders, other commodity traders, banks, insurance companies and brokers. Reported cases include The "Deichland" [1990] (jurisdiction); The "Maciej Rataj" [1991] (jurisdiction – has been to the European Court of Justice); The "Kyzicos" [1989] (chartorparty – laytime), The "Ulyanovsk" [1990] and the "European Enterprise" [1989] (construction of Hague-Visby rules).
Prof. Memberships: London Maritime Arbitration Association.
Career: Called to the Bar and joined Seven King's Bench Walk in 1982.

PROSSER, Kevin J. QC
Pump Court Tax Chambers (Andrew Thornhill QC), London (0171) 414 8080
Recommended in Tax
Specialisation: Principal area of practice is Revenue law, including litigation. Co-author of Potter and Prosser, 'Tax Appeals' (Sweet & Maxwell).
Career: Called to the Bar 1982 and joined present chambers in 1983.
Personal: Was once expelled from Tanzania for spying.

PROUDMAN, Sonia QC
11 New Square (Peter Crampin QC), London (0171) 831 0081
Recommended in the following lists: Charities, Traditional Chancery
Specialisation: Area of work: general chancery litigation and advice, with particular emphasis on trusts, charities, bankers' securities and all aspects of property law. Considerable experience in pursuing and in defending breach of trust claims, involving private, charitable and commercial trusts. Also professional negligence.
Prof. Memberships: Chancery Bar Association, STEP, Charity Law Association.
Career: Called to the Bar (Lincoln's Inn) 1972. (Kennedy Scholar, Buchanan Prize). Joined Chambers at 11 New Square in 1974. Took silk in 1994. Bencher 1996. Assistant Recorder 1997.
Personal: Born 1949; Married 1987, 1 daughter. Educated at St Paul's Girls' School and Lady Margaret Hall Oxford. BA 1st Class Hons 1971, Eldon Law Scholar 1973, MA 1973.

PRYNNE, Andrew QC
2 Harcourt Buildings (Roger Henderson QC), London (0171) 583 9020
Recommended in Product Liability
Specialisation: General common law practice with an emphasis on product liability (principally pharmaceuticals), insurance disputes, medical negligence, personal injury, railway law and employment matters. Notable cases include the Opren litigation for Eli Lilly from 1986, the Clapham Accident Enquiry for British Railways Board (BRB) 1989, the Benzodiazepine litigation for Roche Products Ltd 1990-92, the Severn Tunnel Accident Enquiry for BRB 1992 and Crizzle v Board of Governors of St. Matthias School (EAT, 1993 – race discrimination). Recently advised BRB and Railtrack on safety implications and legal duties arising from privatisation. Currently instructed for the defendants in the Lariam litigation and the tobacco lung cancer litigation. Member of the Lord Chancellor's Working Group on Multi-Party Actions.
Prof. Memberships: South Eastern Circuit.
Career: Called to the Bar 1975 and tenant at King's Bench Walk 1976-78, then joined current chambers.
Personal: Educated at Marlborough College and Southampton University (LL.B, Hons). Born 28th May 1953.

PUGH, Charles
Old Square Chambers (Hon. John Melville Williams QC), London (0171) 269 0300
Recommended in the following lists: Environmental Law, Health & Safety, Personal Injury
Specialisation: Principal areas of practice are accident claims (road traffic, rail, aviation, workplace, particularly toxic exposure) and pollution/nuisance claims. Has had considerable experience with major accidents, i.e. Kings Cross, Clapham Junction, Manchester Airport, Kegworth; with pollution claims involving personal injury (Camelford water) and alleged injury to livestock and contamination of land arising from toxic waste incineration (Rockley v Coalite; Graham v Re-chem). Nuisance litigation includes water (e.g. fishfarms) noise, dust, and the leading cases of Hunter v LDDC and Hunter v Canary Wharf Limited.
Prof. Memberships: Personal Injury Bar Association; Environmental Law Foundation.
Career: Called to the Bar 1975. Joined Old Square Chambers in 1989.
Personal: Co-author of Toxic Torts (Cameron May, 2nd ed. 1995, with Martyn Day). Member of the editorial board of the Journal of Personal Injury Litigation. Course tutor in the Summer School on Environmental Law organised by the Foundation for International Law & Development (FIELD). Invited speaker at numerous conferences including the American Trial Lawyers Association Annual Convention.

PUGH, Vernon QC
2-3 Gray's Inn Square (Anthony Scrivener QC), London (0171) 242 4986
Recommended in the following lists: Personal Injury, Planning
Specialisation: Town & Country Planning; Local Government Law; Common Law – Professional Negligence & Personal Injury; International Law/Extradition.
Prof. Memberships: Local Government & Planning Bar.
Career: LL.B (UCW); LLM (Cantab); University Lecturer in Property, Commercial & Planning; Hardwicke Scholar; Sir Thomas Moore Bursary; Bencher Lincoln's Inn; Crown Court Recorder.
Personal: Married, 3 daughters. Chairman, International Rugby Football Board. Director Rugby World Cup. I.O.C. Federation Member.

PUGH-SMITH, John
1 Serjeants' Inn (Lionel Read QC), London (0171) 583 1355
Recommended in the following lists: Environmental Law, Parliamentary, Planning
Specialisation: Planning, Local Government, Environmental and Parliamentary matters. Involved in numerous public inquiries for both private and public sectors with continuing emphases on housing, minerals, retailing, contaminated land, waste and related environmental issues.
Prof. Memberships: Planning and Environment Bar Association (Committee Member), United Kingdom Environmental Law Association, Environmental Law Foundation.
Career: Called to the Bar 1977. Joined Serjeants' Inn 1984. Publications include 'Neighbours and the Law' (1st & 2nd Editions: 1988 & 1993), 'Archaeology at Law' (1st Edition: 1996), contributions to the 'Journal of Planning and Environmental Law'. Joint Editorial Adviser for 'Property and Compensation Reports' and 'Planning Law Case Reports'.
Personal: Born 1954. Lives, mainly, in Norfolk.

PULMAN, George F. QC
Hardwicke Building (Walter Aylen QC), London (0171) 242 2523
Recommended in Personal Injury
Specialisation: Personal injuries: esp. multi-party actions, radiation-induced injuries (cancers), Myalgic Encephelomyelitis (post viral fatigue syndrome). Related professional negligence:

solicitors and doctors. Amicus Curiae in Opren; Ldg Col. for MAFF in L.S.A. litigation; Molinari v. Min. of Defence; Sellafield & Dounreay Radiation cancers; Kegworth 'Kings Cross' and 'Herald of Free Enterprise' disasters. 'McDonnell' costs order (plaintiff's payment into court).
Prof. Memberships: Legal action group – author of paper on multi-party actions (Book published 1995). Public Law: Judicial Review (esp. Repts) Dairy produce quotas, transport, roads and vehicles.
Career: Junior Counsel to crown (common law) 1982-89. QC: 1989. Recorder: 1996. Lecturer: Judicial Studies Board. Formerly member: Legal Aid Board (Chairman of Multi-Party Action Committee). Deputy Chancellor: Diocese of Peterborough.

PURCHAS, Christopher QC
2 Crown Office Row (Graeme Hamilton QC), London (0171) 797 8100
Recommended in Personal Injury
Specialisation: Practice encompasses personal injury, product liability and professional negligence.
Prof. Memberships: COMBAR.
Career: Called to the Bar 1966 and joined Crown Office Row 1967. Appointed Recorder 1986 and took Silk in 1990.
Personal: Educated at Marlborough College 1957-61 and Trinity College, Cambridge 1962-65. Leisure pursuits include shooting, tennis and golf. 20th June 1943. Lives in Surrey.

PURCHAS, Robin QC
2 Harcourt Buildings (Mr Gerard Ryan QC), London (0171) 353 8415
Recommended in the following lists: Administrative & Public Law, Parliamentary, Planning
Specialisation: Principal areas of practice are parliamentary, planning and local government work, compulsory purchase (including Hong Kong and Privy Council), compensation, public and administrative and environmental law; recent cases include Bolton MBC 1995, H.L.; Kettering BC 1996 CA; Blue Circle 1995 CA; Wards v Barclays Bank 1994 CA.; Batchelor 1989 C.A.; Heatherington (UK) Ltd 1995 DC; Fletcher Estate 1997 DC; Chieveley P.C.1997 DC; Fox 1993 DC; Braintree D.C. 1995 DC; Lambeth LBC CA 1992; Mid Essex G.C. 1993.
Prof. Memberships: Parliamentary Bar Mess; Planning and Environment Bar Association; Administrative Law Bar Association; South Eastern Circuit.
Career: Called to the Bar in 1968 and joined Harcourt Buildings in 1969. Took silk in 1987. Appointed Recorder in 1989; Deputy High Court Judge 1994; Master of Bench Inner Temple 1996.
Personal: Educated at Marlborough College and Trinity College, Cambridge (Senior Exhibitioner). Born 12th June 1946.

PURLE, Charles QC
12 New Square (John Mowbray QC), London (0171) 419 1212
Recommended in the following lists: Chancery, Company
Specialisation: Leading litigator in cases covering a wide sphere, from computers through breach of trust to VAT. Recent cases have had their emphasis on fraud, including a fraudulent trading and misrepresentation appeal in Hong Kong and an important procedural ruling in the BCCI liquidation on the proper elements of a fraudulent trading claim against a foreign state bank.
Prof. Memberships: Gray's Inn, Lincoln's Inn.
Career: LLB (Nottingham), BCL (Oxon). FICPD.
Personal: Married twice, with 6 children. Now awaiting grandchildren. Opera, music, fine wine and food help to relax.

PURNELL, Nicholas QC
23 Essex Street (Michael Lawson QC), London (0171) 413 0353
Recommended in Crime: Fraud
Specialisation: Principal area of practice is criminal law, particularly commercial fraud. Work includes

financial regulatory and professional disciplinary tribunals. Member of the Lord Chancellor's Advisory Committee on Legal Education and Conduct 1991-97. Member of the Criminal Committee Judicial Studies Board 1991-96.
Prof. Memberships: South Eastern Circuit.
Career: Called to the Bar 1968. Prosecuting Counsel, Inland Revenue 1977-79. Treasury Counsel 1979-85. Took Silk in 1985. Recorder since 1986. Bencher of the Middle Temple since 1990.
Personal: Educated at the Oratory School 1958-62 and King's College, Cambridge 1963-66(MA). Governor of the Oratory School. Born 29th January 1944.

PURVIS, Iain
11 South Square (Christopher Floyd QC), London (0171) 405 1222
Recommended in Intellectual Property
Specialisation: All aspects of intellectual property. Recent reported cases include Gerber v Lectra (patent damages); United Biscuits v ASDA (Penguin/Puffin 'own brand' dispute); Milliken v Walk Off Mats (prior use of invention); Electrolux v Black & Decker and Honeywell v ACL (patent actions – disclosure of experiments).
Prof. Memberships: IPBA member.
Career: MA Cantab; BCL Oxon. Ten years practice in this field, including sitting as arbitrator.
Personal: Married. Two children. Skiing, sailing, watching football and exploring prehistoric monuments.

PYE, M Jayne
Sovereign Chambers (Formerly known as 25 Park Square) (Geoffrey C. Marson QC), Leeds (0113) 245 1841
Recommended in Family/Matrimonial

PYMONT, Christopher QC
13 Old Square (Mr Michael Lyndon-Stanford QC), London (0171) 404 4800
Recommended in Property Litigation
Specialisation: Practice encompasses company law, landlord and tenant matters, chancery and commercial work and insolvency.
Prof. Memberships: Chancery Bar Association.
Career: Called to the Bar 1979 and joined Old Square in 1980. Appointed QC 1996.
Personal: Educated at Marlborough College and Christ Church, Oxford (MA). Born 16th March 1956.

QUADRAT, Simon
All Saints Chambers (T. Alun Jenkins QC), Bristol (0117) 921 1966
Recommended in Crime

QUIGLEY, Conor
Brick Court Chambers (Christopher Clarke QC), London (0171) 583 0777
Recommended in European Union/Competition
Specialisation: Specialist in all aspects of European Community law, esp. free movement of goods, excise duties, tax, state aids and agriculture. Recent cases include: R v MAFF, ex p. Hedley Lomas (Ireland) Ltd., European Court of Justice, 23 May 1996; right of damages against public bodies for administrative breach of EC law; Publishers Association v European Commission (1995) I-ECR 23: Net Book Agreement.
Prof. Memberships: Bar European Group, COMBAR.
Career: Called to the Bar in 1985. Pennington Fellow of EC Law, Lady Margaret Hall, Oxford 1991-6. Chairman Bar European Group 1992-1994, Editor, EC section of Current Law. Author, European Community Contract Law (1997). Cases of note: R v MAFF ex p. Hedley Lomas, Publishers Association v The European Commission [Net Book Agreement].
Personal: Born 21st February 1958. Educated at King's College, London; Europa Institut, University of Amsterdam.

QUINLAN, Christopher
30 Park Place (Philip Richards), Cardiff (01222) 398421
Recommended in Crime

QUINN, Susan
4 Brick Court (David Medhurst), London (0171) 797 8910
Recommended in the following lists: Family: Child Care including child abduction
Specialisation: Childcare law. Work includes public law aspects of childcare, residence, contact and adoption.
Prof. Memberships: Family Law Bar Association.
Career: Called to the Bar 1983 and joined current chambers in 1988.
Personal: Educated at London University (LL.B). Born 17th May 1960.

QUINT, Francesca
11 Old Square (Simeon Thrower), London (0171) 242 5022
Recommended in Charities
Specialisation: Principal area of practice is chancery, with a focus on charities. Work includes advice on setting up charities, amending constitutions, negotiating with Charity Commission, schemes, arrangements with other charities or trading companies and dispute resolution. Other main areas of practice are trusts, land, probate and capital taxation, particularly deeds of variation, Inheritance Act applications, advice and litigation relating to land or trusts. Recent cases include Gunning v. Buckfast Abbey Trustees (dispute between parents and charity school); Re WHVS Higby Will Trust (contest between Oxford College and next of kin as beneficiary of substantial bequest); Re MJK Kay Deceased (partition of estate), Henrietta Barnett School Governors v. Hampstead Garden Suburb Institute (dispute between voluntary school and landlord charity) and Gray v Taylor CA (status of almshouse resident). Clients include educational establishments and charities and city livery companies. Publications include 'Running a Charity' (Jordans); 'Charities: The Law & Practice' (FT Law & Tax, co-author); Butterworth's Encyclopedia of Forms and Precedents – Charities and Charitable Giving; Charity Law Association model governing documents for charities.
Prof. Memberships: Founder Member, Charities Unit of CEDR (Centre for Dispute Resolution). Chancery Bar Association, Charity Law Association (executive committee member), Society of Trust and Estate Practitioners, Statute Law Society (council member).
Career: Called to the Bar 1970. Law Reporter, All England Law Reports, 1970-71. Charity Commission Legal Assistant 1972-74, Assistant Commissioner 1974-84 and Deputy Commissioner 1984-89. Joined present Chambers 1990. Qualified mediator (1997).
Personal: Educated at St. Paul's Girls' School and King's College, London (LLB, AKC). Trustee/adviser to various charities and kindred institutions.

QURESHI, Khawar M.
1 Hare Court (Lord Neill of Bladen QC & Richard Southwell QC), London (0171) 353 3171
Recommended in Administrative & Public Law
Specialisation: The areas of law in which extensive advice has been given and court appearances made are commercial, public international law, adminstrative and public law.
Prof. Memberships: ALBA, BIICL, COMBAR.
Career: LLB, LLM (Cantab). Queen Mother's Scholar 1990 (Middle Temple). (1990 call). Guest lecturer/supervisor Cambridge University (1990-1993). Visiting lecturer in international law, King's College, London (1994-). Legal adviser to Bosnian Government in Dayton peace talks (November 1995). Has advised several foreign governments on constitutional matters.
Personal: Interests include cricket and squash. Pro-bono legal adviser to several charities and Chairman of Trustees of War Child.

QURESHI, Shamim
Assize Court Chambers (John Isherwood), Bristol (0117) 926 4587
Recommended in Crime

RABINOWITZ, Laurence
One Essex Court (Anthony Grabiner QC), London (0171) 583 2000
Recommended in the following lists: Commercial (litigation), Company, Energy & Utilities, Financial Services
Specialisation: Regulatory matters, professional negligence, financial services, oil and gas, computer, and other commercial disputes. Recent cases include: Conoco & Ors v Phillips, Amoco (UK) Exploration Co v Teesside Gas Transportation Limited and Enron Corp; Total Gas Marketing Ltd v ARCO British Ltd & Ors; Bank Austria v. Price Waterhouse; IBM v. Sagem; B & C v. Atlantic and others.
Prof. Memberships: Member of Middle Temple.
Career: 1 Essex Court 1987. Junior Counsel for the Crown, Chancery (1995).
Personal: BA LLB (Wits). BA BCL (Oxon). Rhodes Scholar (1983, South Africa).

RADCLIFFE, Andrew
1 Hare Court (Stephen Kramer QC), London (0171) 353 5324
Recommended in Crime
Specialisation: General Criminal Law, prosecuting and defending, with particular emphasis on commercial fraud. Recent cases include R v Cowan, Gayle, Ricciardi (1996) 1 Cr App R 1; R v Sec. State for Home Dept. and Director of Serious Fraud Office ex p. Fininvest s.p.a. (1997) 1 Cr App R 257; R v Graham (H.K.) and others (1997) 1 Cr App R 302.
Prof. Memberships: Criminal Bar Association.
Career: Called 1975. Joined present Chambers 1990.
Personal: Educated St. Edmund Hall, Oxford.

RADEVSKY, Anthony
5 Bell Yard (Robert Webb QC), London (0171) 333 8811
Recommended in Property Litigation
Specialisation: Landlord and tenant law relating to commercial and residential property, leasehold enfranchisement, rent review, dilapidations and service charges. Also handles mortgages, specific performance of contracts for the sale of land, restrictive covenants and professional negligence claims against solicitors and surveyors. Author of 'Service of Documents' (Longman, 2nd Edn, 1989); 'Drafting Pleadings' (Tolley, 2nd Edn 1995).
Prof. Memberships: Chancery Bar Association.
Career: Called to the Bar 1978 and joined Temple Gardens. Joined current chambers in 1993.
Personal: Educated at Alleyn's School, Dulwich 1966-73 and Southampton University 1974-77 (LL.B, Hons). Born 22nd August 1955.

RAESIDE, Mark
Atkin Chambers (John Blackburn QC), London (0171) 404 0102
Recommended in Construction
Specialisation: Clients include Statutory and other Authorities; Developers; Contractors; Receivers, Liquidators; Insurers; Foreign companies; Numerous professionals including architects, engineers, quantity and chartered surveyors. Represents clients in all divisions of High Court and commercial arbitration and has been engaged for protracted trials, inter-county work and making appeals to Higher Courts. Type of work engaged includes fraud, professional negligence, nuisance, JCT of the ICE type disputes including defects, loss and expense claims and points of construction and providing legal advice on procedure, evidence, tactics. In addition drafting Standard Form Contracts in particular direct warranties.
Career: Called to Middle Temple 1982.
Personal: B.A., M.Phil, (Cantab.).

RAGGATT, Timothy QC
36 Bedford Row (James Hunt QC),
Northampton (01604) 602333
Recommended in Crime
Specialisation: Undertakes Crime and Fraud.
Regina v Bartlet. Defence of the managing director
of computer leasing company in £30 million fraud
1995/6. The client was granted bail as the largest
surety ever fixed by an English Court. R v Canon
(murder of Shirley Banks). Regina v Richards 54
day bank fraud defence. Dartmoor Prison Riots,
"Sleepwalker" murder in Stafford. Prosecuted R v
Myles and others: The Largest Murder Trial in the
West Midlands since the Birmingham bombings.
Career: Called to the Bar, 1972. Took silk 1993.
Member of 3 Fountain Court Chambers
Birmingham until 1994 (still door tenant) now
member of One KBW – now 36 Bedford Row
London WC1. Criminal Bar Association.
Personal: Golf.

RAHMAN, Yaqub
Peel House (Nigel Gilmour QC), Liverpool
(0151) 236 4321
Recommended in Personal Injury

RAILTON, David QC
Fountain Court (Peter Scott QC), London
(0171) 583 3335
Recommended in the following lists:
Commercial (litigation), Insurance & Reinsurance,
Professional Negligence

RAINEY, Simon
4 Essex Court (Nigel Teare QC), London
(0171) 797 7970
Recommended in Shipping

RAMPTON, Richard QC
1 Brick Court (Richard Hartley QC), London
(0171) 353 8845
Recommended in Defamation

RAMSEY, Vivian QC
Keating Chambers (Richard Fernyhough QC),
London (0171) 544 2600
Recommended in the following lists: Arbitration,
Construction, Energy & Utilities, Professional
Negligence
Specialisation: Building and construction law;
professional negligence.
Career: Qualified 1979; Middle Temple; QC 1992;
chartered engineer; member of Institution of Civil
Engineers 1976; graduate engineer Ove Arup &
Partners, London Middle East 1972-1977; arbitrator
(domestic and international, including ICC) 1988 to
date; special professor, department of Civil
Engineering, University of Nottingham 1990 to
date; joint editor 'Construction Law Journal'.
Personal: Harley School, Rochester, USA;
Abingdon School; Oriel College Oxford; City
University (1972 MA, 1978 Dip Law, C Eng MICE).
Born 1950; resides Swanley Village.

RANDALL, John QC
St Philip's Chambers (Rex Tedd QC),
Birmingham (0121) 246 7000
Recommended in the following lists:
Administrative & Public Law, Chancery, Commercial
(litigation)
Specialisation: Principal areas of practice are:
Chancery and commercial law, companies,
corporate insolvency, judicial review, professional
negligence, real property, town and country
planning.
Prof. Memberships: Midland and Oxford Circuit;
Chancery Bar Association, Chairman, Midland
Chancery & Commercial Bar Association.
Career: Called Lincoln's Inn 1978; Bar of New
South Wales 1979; Silk 1995; Assistant Recorder
1995; Deputy Head of Chambers 1998. London
chambers: 7 Stone Buildings (Charles Aldous QC)
– Lincoln's Inn, London (0171) 242 3546.
Personal: Born 1956. Educated at Rugby School,
Loomis Institute, Conn. USA and Jesus College,
Cambridge (MA).

RANDALL, Louise
Keating Chambers (Richard Fernyhough QC),
London (0171) 544 2600
Recommended in Construction
Specialisation: Construction, engineering and
professional negligence.
Career: Qualified 1988; Middle Temple.
Personal: Keele University (BA Hons). Born 1964;
resides London.

RANDALL, Nicholas
Devereux Chambers (Jeffrey Burke QC),
London (0171) 353 7534
Recommended in Employment
Specialisation: Broad range of employment work
undertaken for both employers and trade unions.
Reported cases include Wilson v St. Helens [1998]
ICR 387. A contributing editor of Harvey on
Industrial Relations and Employment Law and
author of Halsbury's Laws Pensions Volume.
Prof. Memberships: Employment Law Bar
Association.
Career: General secretary of the L.S.E Students
Union (1988). Part time lecturer in labour law at
L.S.E (1990-1993).
Personal: Football, cricket and jazz.

RANDOLPH, Fergus
Brick Court Chambers (Christopher Clarke QC),
London (0171) 583 0777
Recommended in European Union/Competition
Specialisation: All aspects of EC law, including
trade, competition, commercial agency,
shipping and agriculture/fisheries. Recent
reputed case: Chequepoint Sarl v McClelland –
Security for costs – discrimination on grounds
of nationality. [1996] 3 WLR 341. R v MAFF ex
parte: Factortame.
Career: Harrow School: 1975-79. Buckingham
University/Aix en Provence. Called to the Bar 1985.
Stagaire Commission legal service: 1988.

RANKIN, James
3 Raymond Buildings (Clive Nicholls QC),
London (0171) 831 3833
Recommended in Licensing
Specialisation: All aspects of licensing law
including liquor, public entertainment, betting and
gaming and bingo. Has had considerable
experience in applying and opposing. Has
appeared for most of the major companies,
including Wetherspoons, Whitbread, Greenalls,
Regent Inns, Morlands and Everards. Was briefed
by the respondent in the Court of Appeal case of
SITKI. Also specialises in Judicial Review, and
appears regularly in the Divisional Court. Advises in
lotteries and competitions.
Career: Called to the Bar 1983. Joined Raymond
Buildings (Formerly Queen Elizabeth Building) in 1984.
Personal: Educated at Eton and Buckingham
University LLB (Hons) 1982.

RAWLEY, Alan D. QC
35 Essex Street (Nigel Inglis-Jones QC),
London (0171) 353 6381
Recommended in Crime: Fraud
Specialisation: Commercial Fraud (Guinness;
Blue Arrow et al); Contempt of Court (In Re Lonrho
HL 1989; OFT v Norris (1995); Civil liability of the
Police (Hill v Chief Constable of West Yorkshire;
Rogers v Chief Constable of Dorset; and many
cases involving issues of false imprisonment and
malicious prosecution); Medical Negligence
(Aboul-Hosn).
Prof. Memberships: Western Circuit; Commercial
and Common Law Bar Association; Criminal Bar
Association.
Career: Middle Temple; called June 1958; Bencher
1985; Silk 1977; Bar Council and Senate; Deputy
Chairman Cornwall Quarter Sessions 1971; A
Recorder of the Crown Court since 1972; Fellow
Commoner, Magdalene College, Cambridge, since
1991.
Personal: Educated at Wimbledon College and
Brasenose College, Oxford (MA). Served with RTR
(Nat. Serv.) 1956-1958.

RAWLEY, Dominique
Atkin Chambers (John Blackburn QC), London
(0171) 404 0102
Recommended in Computer & I.T.
Specialisation: All areas of construction and civil
engineering disputes in arbitration and litigation.
Contractual disputes regarding the design and
supply of computer networks.
General commercial disputes. Private International
Law aspects of contractual disputes.
Professional Negligence.
Career: Called 1991.

RAYNER JAMES, Jonathan QC
5 New Square (Jonathan Rayner James QC),
London (0171) 404 0404
Recommended in Media & Entertainment
Specialisation: Principal areas of practice are
media and entertainment law and intellectual
property law, in particular contract, licensing,
confidence, copyright, design rights, performers'
rights, trade marks and passing off. Advisory and
litigation. Specialisation in EC aspects.
Co-editor of 'Copinger and Skone James' on
copyright since 1980. Joint Consulting
Editor for 'The Encyclopaedia of Forms and
Precedents' (Entertainment). Member
of Editorial Board of `Entertainment
Law Review'.
Career: Commenced practice in 1975, having
been called to the Bar in 1971. Appointed Silk in
1988. Member of the Chancery Bar Association,
Intellectual Property Bar Association and the
International Association of Entertainment
Lawyers. Assistant Recorder since 1994.
Personal: Born 26th July 1950. Educated
at King's College School, Wimbledon 1961-68,
Christ's College, Cambridge 1968-72
(M.A.; LL.B.) and Brussels University 1972-73 (Lic.
spéc. Droit Européen). Fluent in French.
Lives in London.

RAYNOR, Philip QC
40 King St (Philip Raynor QC), Manchester
(0161) 832 9082
Recommended in Family/Matrimonial
Specialisation: Commercial, professional
negligence and matrimonial finance litigation. CTN
Cash & Carry v Gallaher (1994): economic duress.
Walkin v. South Manchester Health Authority
(1995): limitation; Healds Foods v. Hyde Dairies
(1996): expert determination.
Prof. Memberships: Family Law Bar Association;
Professional Negligence Bar Association; Northern
Circuit Commercial Bar Association.
Career: Lecturer in law, Manchester University
1971-4. Recorder.

READ, Graham
Devereux Chambers (Jeffrey Burke QC),
London (0171) 353 7534
Recommended in Environmental Law
Specialisation: Commercial, Professional
Negligence, property (including construction) and
environmental law. More recently reported
decisions include: Sonardyne Limited v Firth
[1997] EGCS 84 (professional
negligence/property); Agrafax Public Relations v
USS Inc Times 22nd May 1995, Ngcobo v Thor
Chemicals Times 10th November 1995, Connelly v
RTZ [1997] 3
WLR 373 (forum non conveniens and commercial
or environmental law); Reay v British Nuclear
Fuels [1994] 1 MLR 1, R v Sec State for
Trade and Industry ex p. Dudridge Times 26th
October 1995, R v Greenwich LBC ex p.
Williams Times 29th December 1995 and (C.A.)
[1996] 8CL 448 (environmental law).
Prof. Memberships: Professional Negligence Bar
Association.
Career: MA Trinity Hall, Cambridge; Arden Scholar
Gray's Inn; called 1981.

READ, Lionel QC
1 Serjeants' Inn (Lionel Read QC), London
(0171) 583 1355
Recommended in the following lists:
Administrative & Public Law, Energy & Utilities,
Environmental Law, Parliamentary, Planning
Specialisation: M40 inquiry 1973. Stanstead/T5
inquiry for BAA 1981-83. Lakeside Regional
shopping centre inquiry for Capital and Counties
1984. Runnymede shopping centre inquiry for
applicants 1988. Cambridge sub-regional
shopping centre inquiry for Capital and Counties
1990. Various superstore inquiries for Tesco and
Sainsbury. Rock chacterisation facility inquiry 1995
for NIREX.
Prof. Memberships: Planning and Environmental
Bar Association. Administrative Law Bar
Association.
Career: Smith v Skinner 1986 for Camden
Councellors.

READHEAD, Simon
No. 1 Serjeants' Inn (Edward Faulks QC),
London (0171) 415 6666
Recommended in Medical Negligence
Specialisation: Principal area of practice is
medical work including defendant work for Health
Authorities and professional negligence work for
plaintiffs and defendants. Other main areas of
practice include personal injury work. He has
expertise in public and administrative law, including
judicial review, and is experienced in the Divisional
Court. On the commercial side, his practice
includes contract based commercial disputes. He
appeared in the cases of: Riverside Mental Health
NHS Trust v Fox (1994) 1 FLR 614 (application to
force feed an anorexic), R v HM Coroner for East
Berkshire ex parte Buckley (unreported) D.C.
referred to in R v HM Coroner for North
Humberside and Scunthorpe ex parte Jamieson
(1994) 2 WLR 82 at page 96 (following a death in
Broadmoor Hospital). He regularly addresses
seminars and conferences on professional
negligence and related matters.
Prof. Memberships: Professional Negligence Bar
Associaton, Personal Injury Bar Associaton,
Administrative Law Bar Association and London
Commercial and Common Law Bar Association.
Career: Called to the Bar in 1979. Appointed
Assistant Recorder in 1995.
Personal: Educated at Lincoln College, Oxford.

REDDIFORD, Anthony
Guildhall Chambers (John Royce QC), Bristol
(0117) 927 3366
Recommended in Employment

REDDIHOUGH, John
9 Gough Square (Jeremy Roberts Q.C), London
(0171) 353 5371
Recommended in Personal Injury
Specialisation: Principal areas of practice are
personal injury, medical and professional
negligence. Over 20 years' experience of all
aspects of such work including cases involving
injuries of utmost severity resulting from accident
or medical negligence, fatal accidents claims and
industrial disease. Acted in cases involving severe
brain damage, paraplegia, loss of limbs etc. Also
handles matters of general commercial law (sale
and carriage of goods, insurance and reinsurance,
contract and tort) and criminal advocacy. Clients
include trade unions, insurance companies, health
authorities and NHS Trusts.
Prof. Memberships: Midland and Oxford Circuit.
Personal Injury Bar Association.
Career: Called to the Bar 1969 and joined current
chambers in 1972. Standing Counsel, H.M.
Customs & Excise 1989. Appointed Recorder
1994.
Personal: Educated at Manchester Grammar
School 1959-65 and Birmingham University 1965-
68 (LL.B Hons). Leisure pursuits include skiing,
gardening, running, music and reading. Born 6th
December 1947.

REDFERN, Alan
One Essex Court (Anthony Grabiner QC),
London (0171) 583 2000
Recommended in Arbitration
Specialisation: Main area of practice is as an
Arbitrator and adviser on international dispute
resolution, including mediation and conciliation.
Has over 30 years experience of complex
international commercial arbitration cases. Before
transferring to the Bar in May 1995, was the senior
litigaton partner of the international law firm
Freshfields. He is the co-author of a leading text
book on 'Law and Practice of International
Commercial Arbitration' and has written extensively
on Arbitration issues in professional journals.
Prof. Memberships: Fellow of Chartered Institute
of Arbitrators, member of the ICC's International
Commission on Arbitration and the Swiss
Arbitration Association.
Career: Became a litigation partner in 1963,
transferred to the Bar in 1995.

REDFERN, Michael QC
28 St. John St (Anthony Rumbelow QC),
Manchester (0161) 834 8418
Recommended in Medical Negligence

REED, Paul
Hardwicke Building (Walter Aylen QC), London
(0171) 242 2523
Recommended in Construction
Specialisation: Principal areas of practice are
Construction, Civil Engineering arbitration and
litigation especially defects and loss and expense
claims. Professional Negligence including
surveyors, architects and engineers. Reported
cases in 1997-1998: Holbeck Hall Hotel Ltd v
Scarborough Borough Council – the rights of
adjoining land owners. The case centered on the
catastrophic collapse of the hotel into the sea in
1993. General Construction v Aegon – the
enforcement in the UK of a Mauritian arbitration
award against a UK bondsman. South Coast
Shipping v Havant Borough Council – the
interpretation of the 'CEG' Gdn contract and the
right of appeal from an arbitrators award.
Prof. Memberships: London Common Law and
Commercial Bar Association, Chartered Institute of
Arbitrators, Professional Negligence Bar
Association.
Career: Called to the Bar in 1988. LLB (Hons),
MSc.

REED, Philip
5 Bell Yard (Robert Webb QC), London
(0171) 333 8811
Recommended in Aviation
Specialisation: General Commercial and Civil
Litigation. Aviation Law (in particular aviation
finance), insurance and reinsurance, employment
law, professional negligence.
Prof. Memberships: COMBAR. L.C.L.C.B.A.
Career: M.A. (Oxon.)

REED, Piers
3 Temple Gardens (John Coffey QC), London
(0171) 353 3102
Recommended in Crime
Specialisation: Consumer/Regulatory work (e.g)
Trading Standards, Food Safety, Health & Safety at
Work, defended Birse Construction Re fatal
accident prosecution; defended SAPPI (UK) Ltd
Re: environmental pollution prosecution; general
defence work for MARS (UK) Ltd. Defence work
generally from murder to fraud.
Prof. Memberships: Criminal Bar Association.
Assistant Junior Herts & Beds Bar Mess. Bar
Liason Member St Albans TIG Group.
Career: Called 1974. Member Lincoln's Inn and
Northern Ireland Inns of Court. Approved Tutor for
Lincoln's Inn continuing education programme.
Personal: Married with two daughters. Fanatic
sports follower.

REES, Edward QC
Doughty Street Chambers (Geoffrey Robertson
QC), London (0171) 404 1313
Recommended in Crime
Specialisation: Notable cases in which he has
appeared include: the trial, appeal, civil litigation
and Judicial Review proceedings of Winston
Silcott; the Whitemoor Prison breakout trial; the
Orgreave Miners trial; the St. Paul's, Bristol riot trial;
the 'Bradford Twelve' trial; the trial of Ron Brown
M.P.; R v Ben & others – a serious VAT fraud; R v
Howes & others – a serious gold fraud.

REES, Gareth
Queen Elizabeth Building (David Jeffreys QC &
Peter Whiteman QC), London (0171) 583 5766
Recommended in the following lists: Crime,
Crime: Fraud
Specialisation: Practice mainly concerned with
company and commercial fraud including cases
alleging market manipulation, fraudulent trading,
mortgage fraud, company director offences
(allegations relating to collapse of Johnson Mathey
Bank in 1998), Customs diversion fraud (R v Hare
1997) and corruption. Frequently in cases
prosecuted by the Serious Fraud Office. Has
continued to defend in murder cases (recently
representing a profoundly deaf client) and sexual
offences including rape of Austrian tourist at Kings
Cross and the allegation of rape by 10 year old
boys of a girl in their class. Junior counsel acting
for Craig Charles ('Red Dwarf') in rape allegations.
Has advised and has presented seminars to
accountants, bankers and solicitors on Money
Laundering, giving expert evidence and Inland
Revenue practice on Search and Seizure
prosecutions. Has spoken and written on deaf
people and the court process.
Prof. Memberships: Criminal Bar Association.
Association International Jeune Advocats (AIJA).
Career: Reading University BA. Bar exams 1979.
Worked for Canadian Law firm and as Journalist
before beginning practice in 1981.

REES, John Charles QC
33 Park Place (Wyn Williams QC), Cardiff
(01222) 233313
Recommended in the following lists: Crime,
Personal Injury

REES, Paul
1 Crown Office Row (Robert Seabrook QC),
London (0171) 797 7500
Recommended in the following lists:
Environmental Law, Medical Negligence

REES, Philip
9 Park Place (Ian Murphy QC), Cardiff
(01222) 382731
Recommended in Personal Injury
Specialisation: Personal Injury. Medical
Negligence. Trusts. Commercial. Landlord and
Tenant.
Career: LL.B. (Hons) Bristol. Called 1965 (Middle
Temple). Recorder of the Crown Court since 1983.
Assistant Boundary Commissioner.
Personal: Music, Sport.

REESE, Colin QC
Atkin Chambers (John Blackburn QC), London
(0171) 404 0102
Recommended in the following lists: Arbitration,
Construction
Specialisation: All aspects of arbitration law but
mainly concerned with domestic or international;
building, civil engineering, and associated
professional negligence disputes as Counsel and
Arbitrator.
Career: So far as landmark reported decisions are
concerned, can claim his share of the credit (or
should accept his share of the responsibility) for
the recognition of "Minter" interest (see: F.G. Minter
Ltd. v Welsh Health Mechanical Services
Organisation (1980) 13 BLR 1); the recognition of
the different powers of judges and arbitrators and
the development of jurisprudence concerning sub-

contractors name-borrowing arbitrations (see: Northern Regional Health Authority v Derek Crouch Construction Co. Ltd. [1984] QB 644 and Gordon Durham & Co. v Haden Young Ltd. (1990) 52 BLR 61) and, more recently, for the recognition of the extent of availability of Court ordered security for costs in international arbitrations (i.e. CoppEe Lavalinv. Ken-Ren [1995] 1 AC 38).
Personal: Born 28 March 1950. Called to the Bar 1973. Silk 1987. A Recorder authorised to deal with High Court Official Referees' business.

REID, Paul Campbell
Lincoln House Chambers (Mukhtar Hussain QC), Manchester (0161) 832 5701
Recommended in Crime
Prof. Memberships: Criminal Bar Association.
Career: M.A. (Cantab.) (Engineering). Called to Bar 1973. Recorder 1993.
Personal: D.o.b. 27 March 1949. Educated at Merchant Taylors School, Crosby and Christ's College Cambridge (1968-72). Married with 2 children. Leisure interests include tennis, acoustic guitar and amateur dramatics.

REID, Robert QC
9 Old Square (Robert Reid QC), London (0171) 405 4682
Recommended in the following lists: Property Litigation, Sports Law

REILLY, John
14 Tooks Court (Michael Mansfield QC), London (0171) 405 8828
Recommended in Crime

RENTON, Clare
29 Bedford Row Chambers (Peter Ralls QC), London (0171) 831 2626
Recommended in the following lists: Family: Child Care including child abduction
Specialisation: Principal area of practice is family law, including child abduction, public and private law children work, matrimonial finance, pensions, and the law as it affects cohabitees. Other areas of practice include personal injury and professional negligence. Recent cases: Re W [1995] 2 FLR 159, K v K (Financial Relief: Widow's pension) 1 FLR 35 and Re R (Abduction: Hague and European Conventions) 1 FLR 663. K v D [1998] 1 F.L.R 700.
Prof. Memberships: Family Law Bar Association; Statute Law Society; Board of Family Mediation Association. Association of Personal Injury Lawyers.
Career: Called to the Bar 1972. Joined chambers at Bedford Row in 1980.

REYNOLDS, Adrian
Chambers of Colin Anderson (St. Mary's Chambers) (Colin Anderson), Nottingham (0115) 950 3503
Recommended in Crime

REYNOLDS, Kirk QC
Falcon Chambers (Jonathan Gaunt QC & Kim Lewison QC), London (0171) 353 2484
Recommended in Property Litigation
Specialisation: Called to the Bar 1974. Queen's Counsel 1993. Full time practice as landlord and tenant specialist at Falcon Chambers since 1975. Co-author 'The Handbook of Rent Review', 'The Renewal of Business Tenancies' and 'Dilapidations: the Modern Law and Practice'. Blundell Memorial Lecturer 1982, 1987 and 1993. Advisor to Royal Institution of Chartered Surveyors on arbitration practice and Course Tutor on official R.I.C.S. training courses for arbitrators.
Prof. Memberships: Member of R.I.C.S. Committee producing and revising official Guidance Notes for Arbitrators and Independent Experts. Appointed on a number of occasions by President of R.I.C.S. and President of Law Society as arbitrator, and by arbitrators as Legal Assessor. Elected an Honorary Associate of R.I.C.S. in 1997.

RHODES, Robert QC
4 King's Bench Walk (Robert Rhodes QC), London (0171) 822 8822
Recommended in the following lists: Crime: Fraud, Financial Services
Specialisation: Civil and criminal fraud, Revenue and Customs & Excise investigations, financial services, judicial review.
Career: Called 1968. Standing Revenue counsel 1979-89. Queen's Counsel 1989. Deputy Chairman IMRO Membership Appeal Tribunal since 1992. Member KASW Appeal Tribunal. Published and lectured extensively (in England and abroad) on white collar crime.
Personal: Born 2.8.45. Educated St Paul's School (foundation scholar) and Pembroke College, Oxford. Former international fencer. Interests: opera, theatre, art, reading, real tennis and watching cricket.

RHYS, Owen
10 Old Square (Leolin Price CBE QC), London (0171) 405 0758
Recommended in Property Litigation
Specialisation: Property litigation, including commercial landlord and tenant, restrictive covenants (also in the Lands Tribunal), easements, disputes concerning contracts for the sale of land, mortgages and related professional negligence.
Prof. Memberships: Chancery Bar Association.
Career: Called 1976. Practised in Chancery Chambers since 1977. Representative cases: Westway Homes v Moores (1991) 31 EG 578 (CA) relating to land options. Balabel v Mehmet (1990) 1 EGLR 220 (CA) contract for sale of land. Yorkshire Metropolitan Properties Ltd v CRS Ltd [1997] NPC 60 (rectification of commercial lease).
Personal: Interests include skiing, sailing and mountain walking.

RICHARDS, David QC
Erskine Chambers (Richard Sykes QC), London (0171) 242 5532
Recommended in Company

RICHARDS, Jennifer
39 Essex Street (Edwin Glasgow QC), London (0171) 832 1111
Recommended in Administrative & Public Law
Specialisation: Specialises in most aspects of public and administrative law, including local government, mental health, community care, health services, education and human rights. Practice also covers general commercial law (general contract, professional negligence and insurance). Editor of 'Crown Office Digest', co-author to the Social Services title of 'Halisbury's Laws of England' and contributor to R Gordon's 'Judicial Review: Practice and Procedure'.
Prof. Memberships: Administrative Law Bar Association, London Commercial and Common Law Bar Association.
Career: Called to the Bar 1991 and joined present chambers in 1992.
Personal: Educated at Clare College, Cambridge (BA (Hons) Law, 1st class) and at University of Toronto (Masters in Laws, specialist thesis on Canadian Charter of Rights and Freedoms).

RICHARDS, Wyn
Iscoed Chambers (Trefor Davies), Swansea (01792) 652988/9
Recommended in the following lists: Environmental Law, Planning
Specialisation: Main areas of practice are planning, highway and environmental law acting, at inquiries and in Court, for clients in both the public and private sectors.
Prof. Memberships: Planning and Environmental Bar Association. Wales and Chester Circuit.
Career: Call 1968. Recorder 1985. Assistant Commissioner of the Boundary Commission in Wales 1982 and 1992. Head of Chambers 1993.
Personal: Educated at Trinity Hall, Cambridge. Welsh Speaker.

RIDDLE, Nicholas
14 Castle St (Adrian Lyon), Liverpool (0151) 236 4421/8240/6759
Recommended in the following lists: Chancery, Commercial (litigation)
Specialisation: General Chancery, recent cases: Cadogan v. McCarthy & Stone [1996] EGCS 94, concerning landlord's intention to redevelop on termination of business tenancy. The Mortgage Business Ltd v. Barclays Bank (1996, unreported) concerning negligent bank referencing. Birtwistle v Lilley (1996, unreported) concerning the ownership of a newspaper. Brooks v Baynard [1998] T.L.R 269 (concerning security for costs).
Prof. Memberships: Chancery Bar Association. Northern Chancery Bar Association. Society for Computers and Law.
Career: Educated at The King's School, Canterbury; Gonville and Caius College. Practice in Liverpool chancery chambers, from 1972. Head of chambers from 1977, until merger with present chambers in 1996.
Personal: Leisure interests: reading, music, food, wine, travel.

RIORDAN, Kevin
Iscoed Chambers (Trefor Davies), Swansea (01792) 652988/9
Recommended in Crime
Specialisation: Crime.
Prof. Memberships: CBA. Hong Kong Bar. Gray's Inn. Wales and Chester Circuit.
Career: BCL National University Ireland, Cork.

RIORDAN, Stephen QC
25-27 Castle Street (Stephen Riordan QC), Liverpool (0151) 236 5072
Recommended in Crime

RITCHIE, Jean QC
4 Paper Buildings (Harvey McGregor QC), London (0171) 353 3366
Recommended in the following lists: Medical Negligence, Personal Injury
Specialisation: All aspects of medical negligence and medical work, and personal injury work. Acts for plaintiffs Trusts and authorities. Cases include Re F [1990]; De Martell v Merton and Sutton Health Authority [1993] and [1995], Ritchie v Chichester Health Authority [1994]; Joyce v Merton, Sutton and Wandsworth Health Authority [1995] and [1996]; Waters v West Sussex Health Authority [1995]; Corley v North West Hertfordshire Health Authority [1997]. Contributor to 'Safe Practice in Obstetrics and Gynaecology' (Ed. Clements) 1994. Legal update lecture at AVMA Conference 1997.
Prof. Memberships: Professional Negligence Bar Association.
Career: Called to the Bar 1970. Silk 1992. Recorder 1993. Member of Supreme Court Rules Committee 1993-1997. Chairman of Inquiry into care of Christopher Clunis 1993-94. Member of Judicial Studies Board 1998-.
Personal: Kings College London (LL.B) and McGill University, Montreal (LL.M).

RITCHIE, Richard
24 Old Buildings (C.A. Brodie QC), London (0171) 404 0946
Recommended in the following lists: Company, Insolvency
Specialisation: The main areas of Business Law including: Insolvency (personal & corporate); Civil Fraud; Company Law; Contract Disputes; Financial Services; Partnership Law; Property Law; Landlord and Tenant; Directors Disqualification.
Prof. Memberships: Member of the Chancery Bar Association, Member of the Insolvency Lawyers Association.
Career: St. Catherine's College Oxford (BA), Standing Counsel to the DTI, Junior Counsel to the Crown (Chancery).

ROBERTS, Catherine
Erskine Chambers (Richard Sykes QC), London (0171) 242 5532
Recommended in Company

ROBERTS, Jennifer
Queen Elizabeth Building (Ian Karsten QC), London (0171) 797 7837
Recommended in the following lists: Family: Child Care including child abduction, Family: Matrimonial Finance
Specialisation: All aspects of family law with an emphasis on financial cases. Special interest in pensions/cases with a pensions aspect. Inheritance Act claims. Professional negligence arising out of matrimonial litigation.
Prof. Memberships: Family Law Bar Association. Member of the Western Circuit.
Career: LL.B (Hons). Called 1988.

ROBERTS, Jeremy QC
9 Gough Square (Jeremy Roberts Q.C), London (0171) 353 5371
Recommended in the following lists: Crime, Crime: Fraud
Specialisation: Principal area of practice covers criminal cases, particularly criminal fraud, both prosecuting and defending. Also handles other serious crime cases such as murders, robberies and drugs cases. Other area of work is personal injury and general common law. Appeared in R v Grantham (fraudulent trading), Home Secretary's reference re Hickey and Others (1989-the Carl Bridgwater murder case), various cases of cruelty to patients (R v Spencer, R v Smails eg); and in R v Cohen and others (the Blue Arrow case, 1991). Chaired two Bar Council working parties producing reports on the problems of criminal fraud cases. Author of 'Some Procedural Problems in Criminal Fraud Cases' (OUP 1995). Chaired several conferences and seminars on topics related to commercial fraud.
Prof. Memberships: Bar Council, Midland and Oxford Circuit, Criminal Bar Association.
Career: Called to the Bar and joined 9 Gough Square in 1965. Appointed Recorder 1981. Took Silk 1982.
Personal: Educated at Winchester College 1954-59 and Brasenose College, Oxford 1959-63. Leisure pursuits include horse racing, canals, opera and theatre. Born 26th April 1941. Lives in Brentford Middlesex.

ROBERTS, Lisa
Lincoln House Chambers (Mukhtar Hussain QC), Manchester (0161) 832 5701
Recommended in Crime

ROBERTSON, Aidan
Brick Court Chambers (Christopher Clarke QC), London (0171) 583 0777
Recommended in European Union/Competition
Specialisation: Competition Law, European Union Law, Judicial Review and Utility Regulation. Principal cases include R v Customs & Excise ex p Littlewoods [Court of Appeal 1998, reported The Times, 3 March 1998], Banks v Coal Authority [Court of Appeal 1998, High Court 1996, reported [1997] EuLR 610], R v Customs & Excise ex p Lunn Poly [Divisional Court 1998, reported The Times, 8 April 1998], AG v Blake [Court of Appeal 1997, reported The Times, 22 December 1997], Norbain v Dedicated Micros [High Court 1997] and R v OFTEL ex p BT [Divisional Court 1996]. Also various European Commission proceedings including British Digital Broadcasting Plc [1998] and Anglo- American/Lonrho [1997]. Co-author of Green & Robertson's Commercial Agreements & Competition Law (2nd edition 1997).
Prof. Memberships: Bar European Group (Committee Member). Solicitors European Group. Member Editorial Board, European Law Reports. Administrative Law Bar Association. Competition Law Association. Society of Public Teachers of Law.
Career: 1990-99 Fellow & tutor in law at Wadham College, Oxford. 1990-96 University Lecturer in Law, Oxford University. 1988-90 Solicitor, Eversheds, Leeds. 1986-88 Articled Clerk, Bootle Hatfield, London. 1985-86 Law Society Finals, Newcastle upon Tyne Polytechnic. 1984-85 LLM, Jesus College, Cambridge. 1981-84 BA Hons in Law, Jesus College, Cambridge.

ROBERTSON, Geoffrey QC
Doughty Street Chambers (Geoffrey Robertson QC), London (0171) 404 1313
Recommended in the following lists: Administrative & Public Law, Civil Liberties, Crime, Defamation, Media & Entertainment
Specialisation: Has appeared in many landmark cases involving public, media and criminal law, both at trial and on appeal, and has argued human rights causes in Commonwealth Courts, the Privy Council and the European Court in Strasbourg. His memoir, 'The Justice Game', was published in 1998.
Career: Called to Bar 1973; Silk 1988. He is an Assistant Recorder.
Personal: Born 1946. BA, LLB, BCL, Rhodes Scholar. Author of three current textbooks, 'Freedom, the Individual and the Law', 'Obscenity' and 'Media Law'. Currently visiting Professor in Human Rights at Birkbeck College. His play, 'The Trials of Oz', won a BAFTA 'Best Play' nomination for 1991, and he was the recipient of a 1993 Freedom of Information Award. He has conducted a number of missions on behalf of Amnesty International to South Africa and Vietnam, and led the 1992 Bar Council/Law Society Human Rights Mission to Malawi. In 1990 he served as councel to the Royal Commission investigating traffick in arms and mercenaries to the Colombian drugs cartels.

ROBERTSON, Patricia
Fountain Court (Peter Scott QC), London (0171) 583 3335
Recommended in Commercial (litigation)

ROBINSON, Vivian QC
Queen Elizabeth Building (David Jeffreys QC & Peter Whiteman QC), London (0171) 583 5766
Recommended in Crime: Fraud
Specialisation: All aspects of crime, particularly Commercial Fraud. Was involved for the Defence in the Blue Arrow trial and the Blackspur Leasing trial and has prosecuted cases on behalf of the Serious Fraud Office. 1998 will spend 6 months defending in 'Thompson' Fraud in Hong Kong.
Prof. Memberships: Criminal Bar Association.
Career: Educated at Queen Elizabeth Grammar School, Wakefield. The Legs School, Cambridge and Sidney Sussex College, Cambridge. Called to the Bar in 1967. Took Silk 1986. A Recorder of the Crown Court since 1986.
Personal: Married with 3 teenage children. Lives in Oxfordshire.

ROCHFORD, Thomas
St Philip's Chambers (Rex Tedd QC), Birmingham (0121) 246 7000
Recommended in Employment
Specialisation: Employment (including unfair and wrongful dismissal and discrimination). Commercial and general civil, including personal injury.
Prof. Memberships: Employment Law Bar Assocation, Personal Injury Bar Association, Midland & Oxford Circuit.
Career: Called 1984. Member of St Philip's Chambers, a large and thriving Birmingham set, with a number of practitioners well established in employment law.
Personal: Born 1961. Educated: Ampleforth College; Gonville and Caius College, Cambridge (MA).

RODDY, Maureen
India Buildings Chambers (David Harris QC), Liverpool 0151 243 6000
Recommended in Family/Matrimonial
Specialisation: Practises solely in the field of family law. Specialises in dealing with public law Children Act work, including representation of Local Authorities, parents and Guardians ad Litem in cases involving inter alia, issues of physical, sexual and emotional abuse of children.
Prof. Memberships: Committee member – Family Law Bar Association; Chairwoman – Liverpool Medico-Legal Society.
Career: Called in 1977.

RODGER, Caroline
Gray's Inn Chambers (Brian Jubb), London (0171) 404 1111
Recommended in the following lists: Family: Child Care including child abduction

RODGER, Martin
Falcon Chambers (Jonathan Gaunt QC & Kim Lewison QC), London (0171) 353 2484
Recommended in the following lists: Agriculture & Bloodstock, Property Litigation
Specialisation: Handles a range of commercial and agricultural property work, including landlord and tenant, rent review, milk quota, agricultural holdings and real property. Important cases include Little v. Courage (Court of Appeal, 1994 – options in leases), Pennel v Payne (Court of Appeal, 1994 – agricultural holdings) and Rous v Mitchell (Court of Appeal, 1990 – Fraud). Editor of 'Woodfall on Landlord & Tenant and former editor of 'Bernstein & Reynolds Handbook of Rent Review'.
Prof. Memberships: Chancery Bar Association, Agricultural Law Association, Professional Negligence Bar Association.
Career: Called to the Bar in 1985 and joined Falcon Chambers in 1986.
Personal: Educated at St. Aloysius College, Glasgow 1973-79 and University College, Oxford 1979-83. Born 1962. Lives in London.

RODGERS, June
Harcourt Chambers (Patrick Eccles QC), London (0171) 353 6961
Recommended in Ecclesiastical
Specialisation: Family and ecclesiastical.
Prof. Memberships: Family Law Bar Association. Ecclesiastical Law Society.
Career: MA Trinity College Dublin. MA Lady Margaret Hall Oxford. Called: 1971: Middle Temple. Midland and Oxford Circuit. Chancellor of the Diocese of Gloucester.
Personal: Architectural history.

ROGERS, Beverly-Ann
Serle Court Chambers (Charles Sparrow QC QC), London (0171) 242 6105
Recommended in the following lists: Property Litigation, Traditional Chancery
Specialisation: Chancery and commercial litigation and advice. All aspects of property litigation including commercial and residential property disputes, professional negligence, landlord and tenant, mortgages, conveyancing, easements, restrictive covenants, boundary disputes, equitable rights and trusts of land: Commercial and business agreements; Partnerships; Company and Insolvency law.
Career: Called to Bar in 1978. Joined 13 Old Square in 1980.

ROGERS, Heather
5 Raymond Buildings (Patrick Milmo QC), London (0171) 242 2902
Recommended in Defamation

ROGERS, Mark N.
Chambers of Colin Anderson (St. Mary's Chambers) (Colin Anderson), Nottingham (0115) 950 3503
Recommended in Family/Matrimonial

ROMNEY, Daphne
4 Field Court (Geoffrey Brice QC), London (0171) 440 6900
Recommended in Employment
Specialisation: Employment law, particularly in the

fields of wrongful and unfair dismissal, restrictive covenants and discrimination. Clients include insurance companies, PLCs, health authorities and NHS trusts. Also practises in the field of defamation and media law.
Prof. Memberships: Employment Law Bar Association.
Career: Called to the Bar in 1979. Libel reader for The Observer since 1982.
Personal: Born 29 July 1955. BA (Cantab).

ROOK, Peter QC
18 Red Lion Court (Anthony Arlidge QC), London (0171) 520 6000
Recommended in Crime: Fraud
Specialisation: Commercial and tax fraud. Major cases include Lester Pigott, Barlow Clowes, 'Nissan', Maxwell, 'Africar'.
Prof. Memberships: Committee, Criminal Bar Association. QC 1991.
Career: Publication. Rook and Ward on 'Sexual Offences' 2nd Ed. 1997. Sweet & Maxwell.

ROOTS, Guy QC
2 Mitre Court Buildings (Michael FitzGerald QC), London (0171) 583 1380
Recommended in Planning
Specialisation: Main areas of practice are town and country planning, environmental law, compulsory purchase and compensation, rating, local government, parliamentary and administrative law. Has been involved in many leading cases acting for a wide cross section of clients in the public and private sectors. Has spoken at and chaired numerous conferences and seminars. General Editor of 'Ryde on Rating and the Council Tax'.
Prof. Memberships: Planning and Environment Bar Association, Administrative Law Bar Association.
Career: Called to the Bar in 1969. Joined 2 Mitre Court Buildings in 1972. Took Silk in 1989. Appointed Assistant Recorder in 1992.
Personal: Educated at Winchester College and Brasenose College, Oxford (MA in Jurisprudence).

ROSE, Dinah
Blackstone Chambers (formerly 2 Hare Court) (P Baxendale QC and C Flint QC), London (0171) 583 1770
Recommended in the following lists: Administrative & Public Law, Civil Liberties, Employment, Sports Law
Specialisation: Discrimination, employment, public law, human rights.
Prof. Memberships: ALBA, ELBA, member Council of JUSTICE.
Career: Called to Bar 1989. Member of supplementary panel of treasury counsel (Common Law). Co-editor: Halsbury's Laws 4th ed. re-issue: Race Relations; Contributor: Halsbury's Laws 4th ed. re-issue: Constitutional Law & Human Rights. Contributor to "Human Rights Law: Practice & Procedure" – Butterworths, 1998.

ROSE, Jonathan L.
St. Paul's Chambers (Nigel Sangster QC), Leeds (0113) 245 5866
Recommended in Crime

ROSE, Paul
Old Square Chambers (Hon. John Melville Williams QC), London (0171) 269 0300
Recommended in Employment
Specialisation: Discrimination, Unfair Dismissal, Wrongful Dismissal and Restraint of Trade. Personal Injury/Medical Negligence.
Prof. Memberships: Industrial Law Society, Employment Law Bar Association, Personal Injury Bar Association, APIL.
Career: Called to Bar 1981. Acted in a number of leading cases in employment law involving allegations of discrimination and harassment and unfair dismissal. Undertaken injunctive litigation in fields of breach of confidence and restraint of

Trade. Personal Injury: Acted on behalf of Plaintiffs in: Opren litigation, Benzodiazepine litigation, British Midland Air crash, Camelford Water Pollution, Mull of Kintyre Helicopter Crash.

ROSEN, Murray QC
11 Stone Buildings (Michael Beckman QC), London +44 (0)171 831 6381
Recommended in the following lists: Chancery, Sports Law
Specialisation: An incisive and creative tactitian and advocate, he has guided and executed a wide range of cases, often multi-jurisdictional, in commercial and media law. His work covers complex fraud and insolvency including asset-tracing, intellectual property and entertainment disputes, financial services, and lawyers' and accountants negligence. Recent high-profile examples have involved the affairs of the late Robert Maxwell, Crazy Eddie Inc, Lambeth Council, Robbie Williams, assorted football clubs and several thousand ostriches. He acts variously both for institutions, authorities and enforcement agencies, and for corporate, professional and individual clients. As founding Chairman of the Bar Sports Law Group, he has a special interest in sports-related cases, and is also available to sit as an arbitrator or assist in ADR.

ROTH, Peter M. QC
Monckton Chambers (Richard Fowler QC), London (0171) 405 7211
Recommended in the following lists: Administrative & Public Law, Agriculture & Bloodstock, European Union/Competition
Fax: (0171) 405 2084. LDE: 257.
Specialisation: Public law (e.g. R v. Chief Constable of Sussex ex p. International Trader's Ferry [1998] (HL: export of livestock)); EC law and UK competition law (e.g. Associated Dairies v Baines [1997] (HL: RTPA); Case C-432/92 Anastasiou and Others; Case C-60/92 Otto BV v Postbank NV); Commercial litigation and ADR; Professional negligence (e.g. Hemmens v Wilson Browne).
Career: Publications: General Editor, 'Bellamy & Child's Common Market Law of Competition' (Supplement to 4th ed.).
Personal: MA (Oxon), LL.M. Called to the Bar, 1976. QC, 1997. Harmsworth Scholar, Middle Temple. Visiting Associate Professor, Univ. of Pennsylvania Law School, 1987. Co-chairman, UJIA Bench and Bar Committee.

ROWE, Judith
One Garden Court Family Law Chambers (Miss Eleanor F. Platt QC & Miss Alison Ball QC), London (0171) 797 7900
Recommended in Family: Child Care including child abduction
Specialisation: All aspects of family law including public and private law aspects of the Children Act, adoption, child abduction and children cases with an international element. Judicial review and professional negligence (family law related).
Prof. Memberships: FLBA.
Career: Called to the Bar in 1979. Moved to 1, Garden Court in 1996 to specialise wholly in family law.
Personal: Born 7 August 1957. Educated at Rednock School, Gloucestershire. University College London (LL.B Hons 1978). Lives in London. Married with one young child. Interests include travel, theatre and watersports.

ROWELL, David
3 New Square (Lord Goodhart QC), London (0171) 405 5577
Recommended in Traditional Chancery
Specialisation: Land law, trusts, succession, personal taxation, landlord and tenant.
Prof. Memberships: Chancery Bar Association. Charity Bar Association.
Career: BA (Oxon) called 1972. Cases: Hambro v Duke of Marlborough (1994) Ch. 158. Robin v Gerson Berger Association (1986) 1 All E.R. 374.

Challock P.C. v Shirley (1995) 42E.G. 137. Prepared Law Pack's "Last Will and Testament Kit".

ROWLAND, John QC
4 Pump Court (Bruce Mauleverer QC), London (0171) 353 2656
Recommended in Insurance & Reinsurance
Specialisation: Principal area of practice is insurance disputes and general advisory work related to the industry, predominantly reinsurance, but also direct insurance. Recent work has included close involvement in Lloyd's names litigation representing Members Agents, Managing Agents and Lloyd's Auditors. Other areas of practice include general commercial disputes including a number of major ICC Arbitrations, inter alia, for Total Oil Company in relation to worldwide uranium sales and for Sogex Construction Group. Has a significant professional negligence practice involving claims against lawyers, accountants and brokers. Also carries out gaming and casino licensing work and provides commercial law advice direct to overseas lawyers.
Prof. Memberships: COMBAR.
Career: Called to the Bar in 1979 and joined 4 Pump Court in 1980. Took Silk in 1996.
Personal: Educated at Aquinas College, Perth, Western Australia; University of Western Australia (B.Econs, Hons) and King's College, University of London LL.B (Hons).

ROWLAND, Robin
5 Fountain Court (Anthony Barker QC), Birmingham (0121) 606 0500
Recommended in Family/Matrimonial

ROWLANDS, Marc
4 Pump Court (Bruce Mauleverer QC), London (0171) 353 2656
Recommended in Construction
Specialisation: Construction, Civil Engineering, Arbitration Law & Practice.
Prof. Memberships: ORBA, COMBAR.
Career: Magdalen, Oxford (Law).

ROWLEY, J. James
28 St. John St (Anthony Rumbelow QC), Manchester (0161) 834 8418
Recommended in the following lists: Medical Negligence, Personal Injury
Specialisation: Brain and spinal injuries; all aspects of medical negligence and in particular cerebral palsy, iatrogenic injury and late diagnosis in cancers; asbestos-related disease and Hand Arm Vibration Syndrome. Contributor of chapter on Pension Loss to Personal Injury Handbook.
Prof. Memberships: PIBA (Publications Committee).
Career: Stonyhurst and Emmanuel, Cambridge.
Personal: Armchair sportsman and gardener; married, 3 boys.

ROWLEY, Keith
11 Old Square (Grant Crawford & Jonathan Simpkiss), London (0171) 430 0341
Recommended in Traditional Chancery
Specialisation: Principal area of work is general chancery. Work includes company law and insolvency, real property (including landlord and tenant), pension schemes, and professional negligence work in these areas. Important cases handled include Re Thompson's Settlement, R v Panel on Take-Overs and Mergers, Re I.L.G Travel Ltd, Re William Makin & Sons, Collins v. Tipton & Coseley BS, Bogg v Raper and Gillett v Holt. Clients include banks, building societies, insolvency practitioners and insurers.
Prof. Memberships: Chancery Bar Association, Professional Negligence Association.
Career: Called to the bar 1979 and joined 11 Old Square in 1981.
Personal: Educated at Woking Grammar School for Boys 1968-75 and King's College London 1975-78. Lives in London. Born 20th August 1957.

ROYCE, Darryl
Atkin Chambers (John Blackburn QC), London
(0171) 404 0102
Recommended in Construction
Specialisation: Advising upon and acting for parties involved in construction projects, including regular appearances before Official Referees and lay arbitrators. Previous experience as an arbitrator.
Prof. Memberships: Founder Member, Society of Construction Law.

ROYCE, John QC
Guildhall Chambers (John Royce QC), Bristol
(0117) 927 3366
Recommended in the following lists:
Commercial (litigation), Crime
Specialisation: Personal Injuries. Industrial Deafness. Commercial Fraud. Cryptosporidiosis Litigation against Yorkshire Water & Thames Water. Lead contaminated cattle feed actions for N.F.U. Counsel to Inquiry into Ashworth High Security Hospital.
Prof. Memberships: Personal Injury Bar Association; Sports Law Bar Association.
Career: QC 1987; Recorder 1986; Deputy High Court Judge Q.B.D. 1993.
Personal: Austrian qualified ski instructor.

RUMFITT, Nigel J. QC
9 Bedford Row (John Goldring QC), London
(0171) 242 3555
Recommended in Crime
Specialisation: Crime of all types, prosecuting and defending. Extensive experience of medical issues (Junior, Beverley Allitt case). Since taking Silk has done a number of high profile cases. Successfully defended Ruth Neave, helped expose massive police/Home Office dishonesty in R v Robinson & Ors at Leicester (Yardie case). Prosecuted Bedford Hotel murder and Celice Beckett (child prisoner)
Career: Educated at Leeds Modern School; Pembroke College, Oxford; Northweston University School of Law, Chicago Illinois. MA (Oxon) in Jurisprudence; BCL (Oxon); 2:2 in Bar Finals; Harmsworth Law Scholar (Middle Temple). Called to Bar (Middle Temple) 1974. Assistant Recorder 1991, Recorder 1995. Chambers of D. Draycott QC, 1 Essex Court 1975-1988. Present chambers 1988 to date. QC 1994.
Personal: Born 6.3.1950, Leeds. Married. Interests include skiing, windsurfing and sailing. Speaks fluent French and has studied French law, holds consultations in French without interpreter.

RUSHBROOKE, Justin
5 Raymond Buildings (Patrick Milmo QC), London (0171) 242 2902
Recommended in Defamation
Specialisation: Defamation including Internet libel; entertainment and media law, including copyright, passing off, trademarks, confidence, contempt; general chancery and commercial litigation including banking and sale of goods. Recent cases include: Aitken v Pressdram (1997) EMLR 415, *The Times*, 21 May 1997 (CA). Botham v Khan *The Times*, 15 July 1996 (CA). Attorney General v Newspaper Publishing (1997) 1 WLR 926 (CCA). Re: Austintel (1997) 1WLR 616 (CA), (1997) 1 BCLC 233.
Career: MA (Oxon). Worked for Morgan Grenfell & Co Ltd, 1986-88.

RUSSELL, Jeremy QC
4 Essex Court (Nigel Teare QC), London
(0171) 797 7970
Recommended in the following lists: Arbitration, Shipping
Specialisation: Specialist in shipping law and international trade. Practice covers shipping, Admiralty, insurance (marine and non-marine), sale and carriage of goods (domestic and international). Also handles commercial arbitrations both as advocate and occasionally as arbitrator. Has addressed a number of conferences in London and Singapore on shipping matters.

Prof. Memberships: COMBAR; London Common Law and Commercial Bar Association; London Maritime Arbitrators Association (supporting member).
Career: Called to the Bar 1975. Joined present chambers 1977. Took silk 1994.

RUSSEN, Simon
2 Crown Office Row (John Powell QC), London
(0171) 797 8000
Recommended in Professional Negligence
Specialisation: Principal area of practice is professional negligence – Solicitors, Barristers, accountants, surveyors and valuers, architects and engineers.
Prof. Memberships: FCIArb; Professional Negligence Bar Association; COMBAR.
Career: Called to the Bar 1976. Fellow of Chartered Institute of Arbitrators 1991.

RUTTLE, Stephen QC
Brick Court Chambers (Christopher Clarke QC), London (0171) 583 0777
Recommended in the following lists: Insurance & Reinsurance, Professional Negligence
Specialisation: Reinsurance, Insurance, Lloyds, Shipping, General Commercial and Professional Negligence.
Prof. Memberships: Member: British Insurance Law Association: LMAA; Lloyds Arbitrator Tier 1 and Tier 2.
Career: Called to Bar 1976, Gray's Inn. Pupillage with Sir Nicholas Lyell QC MP. Practised at Brick Court Chambers since 1976.
Personal: Educated Westminster School (Queen's Scholar) and Queens' College, Cambridge (Exhibitioner). B.A. Honours Degree in English/Law. Lecturer at numerous Insurance and Reinsurance Seminars. CEDR Appointed Mediator.

RYAN, Gerard QC
2 Harcourt Buildings (Mr Gerard Ryan QC), London (0171) 353 8415
Recommended in the following lists: Environmental Law, Parliamentary, Planning
Specialisation: Environmental and Planning Law including countryside matters commons and village greens. Environmental work includes minerals and planning and waste disposal problems with their common law incidents and water resources and engineering.
Prof. Memberships: Parliamentary Bar. Planning and Environmental Bar Association.
Career: First degree was in Natural Sciences (Cambridge, M.A.); Harmsworth Scholar of Middle Temple; QC 1981; a Recorder of the Crown Court since 1986. Has promoted or opposed many major public works including harbours, railways and reservoirs.

RYDER, Ernest TD QC
Deans Court Chambers (H.K. Goddard QC) Manchester (0161) 834 4097
Recommended in Family/Matrimonial
Specialisation: Public and Administrative law with an emphasis on family litigation; providing a specialist service in matrimonial finance and all disputes relating to children, public authorities, health care and professsional negligence.
Prof. Memberships: FLBA. PIBA. Child Concern.
Career: MA (Cantab). Call 1981 Gray's Inn. Assistant Recorder 1996. QC 1997. Counsel to the Tribunal (North Wales) 1996.
Personal: TA Commission 1982. TD 1996.

RYDER, John
6 King's Bench Walk (Michael Worsley QC), London (0171) 583 0410
Recommended in Crime

RYDER, Matthew
Cloisters (Laura Cox QC), London
(0171) 827 4000
Recommended in Crime

SABBEN-CLARE, Rebecca
7 King's Bench Walk (Stephen Tomlinson QC), London (0171) 583 0404
Recommended in Shipping
Specialisation: Barrister specialising in all areas of commercial law, including insurance and reinsurance, professional negligence, shipping, banking and conflict of laws. Recent Cases: The 'Starsea' (marine insurance); American Centennial – INSCO (reinsurance); the 'Happy Fellow' (conflicts of law); The 'Hill Harmony" (charterparty dispute); Prentis Donegan v Leeds & Leeds (insurance brokers).
Prof. Memberships: COMBAR.

SAINI, Pushpinder
Blackstone Chambers (formerly 2 Hare Court) (P Baxendale QC and C Flint QC), London (0171) 583 1770
Recommended in the following lists: Administrative & Public Law, Employment, Media & Entertainment
Specialisation: Commercial law (including copyright and entertainment law) public law (including human rights). Cases include George Michael v Sony, A&M Records v VCI Ltd, ZYX Music v King, Wailer v Island Records, R v Radio Authority ex p. Guardian Media Group, Tony Bland, Banks v CBS, R v Secretary of State ex parte O'Dhiuibir, A-G v Blake, Lisa Stansfield v Sovereign, Rees v Apollo Watches, R v Secretary of State ex parte RP Scherer, R v Secretary of State ex parte Monsanto; Called to the Bar 1991. Co-author, Halsbury's Laws, European Convention on Human Rights.
Prof. Memberships: JUSTICE, ELA, ALBA, BEG
Personal: Educated at Corpus Christi College, Oxford (BA and BCL, both First Class) Atkin Scholar of Gray's Inn. Languages: Punjabi, Hindi, French, Urdu.

SALLON, Christopher QC
Doughty Street Chambers (Geoffrey Robertson QC), London (0171) 404 1313
Recommended in Crime

SALOMAN, Timothy QC
7 King's Bench Walk (Stephen Tomlinson QC), London (0171) 583 0404
Recommended in Insurance & Reinsurance
Specialisation: General commercial law, including shipping, insurance and reinsurance, international sale of goods, banking and State immunity.
Career: Called to the Bar 1975; took Silk 1993. Appointed Assistant Recorder 1996.
Personal: B.A. (Oxon).Working knowledge of French. Leisure pursuits include golf.

SALTER, Richard QC
3 Verulam Buildings (R. Neville Thomas QC), London (0171) 831 8441
Recommended in the following lists: Banking, Commercial (litigation), Computer & I.T., Financial Services
Specialisation: Principal areas of practice are banking, commercial law, financial services, insolvency, professional negligence and building. Clients include most major UK and international banks. Contributor to 'Banks – Liability and Risk' (2nd ed 1995) and 'Banks and Remedies' (2nd ed 1998) for Lloyd's of London Press; and to Vol. 20 'Halsbury's Laws' (4th ed 1993 – Re-issue 'Guarantees'). Lecturer to the Chartered Institute of Arbitrators 1979-93. Lectures frequently on banking and other commercial law topics.
Prof. Memberships: London Common Law and Commercial Bar Association, COMBAR, Chartered Institute of Arbitrators.
Career: Called to the Bar 1975. Tenant at Hare Court, 1977-82, then joined current chambers. Bencher of the Inner Temple 1991. Member of the Council of Legal Education 1990-1996. Chairman of the Board of Examiners, Bar Vocational Course, 1992-93. Governor of the Inns of Court School of Law 1996-. Took Silk in 1995.
Personal: Educated at Harrow County School for

Boys 1963-70, Balliol College, Oxford 1970-73 and Inns of Court School of Law 1973-75. Chairman, Shoscombe Village Cricket Club.

SANDER, A.T.
Oriel Chambers (Andrew T. Sander), Liverpool (0151) 236 7191
Recommended in Commercial (litigation)

SANDERS, Neil
29 Bedford Row Chambers (Peter Ralls QC), London (0171) 831 2626
Recommended in the following lists: Family: Child Care including child abduction, Family: Matrimonial Finance
Specialisation: Principal area of practice encompasses all areas of matrimonial finance and the law relating to children including child abduction cases. Other main areas of practice cover work relating to the Inheritance (Provision for Family and Dependents) Act 1975.
Prof. Memberships: Family Law Bar Association.
Career: Called to the Bar 1975 and joined present chambers in 1976.
Personal: Educated at Fettes College, Edinburgh 1966-71, Pembroke College, Cambridge 1971-74 and the College of Law 1974-75. Leisure pursuits include tennis, sailing, skiing, music and theatre. Born 17th April 1953. Lives in London.

SANDS, Philippe
3 Verulam Buildings (R. Neville Thomas QC), London (0171) 831 8441
Recommended in Environmental Law
Specialisation: Barrister specialising in advisory work to governments, international organisations, corporations and individuals on public international law (including ICJ and Arbitration), EU and public law, environmental law. Cases include: R v Secretary of State ex p (High Court) Hungary/Slovakia (International Court of Justice); Greenpeace and others v European Commission (ECJ); Tradex v Republic of Albania (International Centre for the Settlement of Investment Disputes – arbitration); St Vincent v Guinea (International Tribunal for the Law of the Sea); numerous intergovernmental negotiations and consultancies (EC, World Bank, Asia Development Bank).
Career: Qualified 1985; reader in international law at the University of London (SOAS); global professor of law, New York University; director of studies, foundation for international development. Publications: Bowett's law of international Institutions 1999; Principles of International Environmental Law, 1995, editor in chief, review of European community and International Environmental Law.

SAUNDERS, J. QC
4 Fountain Court (Richard Wakerley QC), Birmingham (0121) 236 3476
Recommended in the following lists: Crime, Licensing
Specialisation: Licensing: Represented a number of breweries in Crown Courts, Divisional Court and Court of Appeal. Cases include: R v Stafford Crown Court ex parte Shipley (CA) and R v Stafford Crown Court ex parte Shipley (Divisional Court). Crime: general crime and fraud.
Career: Magdelen College, Oxford.
Personal: Music. Sailing.

SAUNDERS, Neil
3 Raymond Buildings (Clive Nicholls QC), London (0171) 831 3833
Recommended in Crime
Specialisation: General crime – Prosecuting and Defending – including R v Donald & Cressey – police corruption. Commercial and company fraud – (mainly defending solicitors or valuers in mortgage frauds including defence of His Honour Judge Gee). Police Disciplinary Tribunals (both in London Metropolitan Police and in provinces). Inquests (acting for police officers or company employees) before the Coroners Court. Licensing – mainly liquor.

Prof. Memberships: Bar Council, Criminal Bar Association.
Career: BA (Hons) Law 1982; called to the Bar 1983.

SAUNDERS, Nicholas
4 Field Court (Geoffrey Brice QC), London (0171) 440 6900
Recommended in Aviation
Specialisation: Aviation law. Practice covers all aspects including air accidents, pilot/aircrew negligence, aviation insurance, carriage of goods by air, and licensing. General commercial work also undertaken, including Admiralty, international trade, insurance and sports/entertainment law.
Career: Former RAF pilot. Joined present chambers 1990.
Personal: Educated at Radley College 1967-72, Hull University LL.B (1987) and Cambridge University LL.M (1988). Governor of Woodleigh Preparatory School, Malton, N.Yorks. Leisure pursuits include shooting, fly fishing and golf. Born 20th July 1954. Lives in Cambridgeshire.

SAUNDERS, William
3 Temple Gardens (John Coffey QC), London (0171) 353 3102
Recommended in Crime
Specialisation: Defending in serious crime in particular crimes of violence, drug offences and fraud. Junior Counsel for defence in the Sussex murder case.
Prof. Memberships: Criminal Bar Association. South Eastern Circuit.
Career: Called 1980.
Personal: Aged 43. Married, two children. One-time member of Antartic expedition.

SAUNT, Thomas
2 Crown Office Row (Graeme Hamilton QC), London (0171) 797 8100
Recommended in Personal Injury

SAUVAIN, Stephen QC
40 King St (Philip Raynor QC), Manchester (0161) 832 9082
Recommended in the following lists: Environmental Law, Planning
Specialisation: Town Planning, Compulsory Purchase, Highways, Environment Law, Judicial Review.
Prof. Memberships: Northern Circuit, Planning and Environment Bar Association. Editor Encyclopedia of Highway Law and Practice. Author of Sauvain's 'Highway Law'.
Career: Called 1977. Queen's Counsel 1995.

SAVILL, Mark
Deans Court Chambers (H.K. Goddard QC), Manchester (0161) 834 4097
Recommended in Crime
Specialisation: Specialises in all areas of criminal law.
Prof. Memberships: Criminal Bar Association.
Career: Called to the Bar – November 1993 (Inner Temple).
Personal: Born 17th May 1969. Educated at Eton College and Durham University BA (Hons). Interests include sport and cooking.

SAYER, Peter
Gough Square Chambers (Frederick Philpott), London (0171) 353 0924
Recommended in Consumer Law
Specialisation: Consumer Law – consumer credit, credit and charge cards, trades descriptions and fair trading. Also Financial Services Act work and fraud (criminal and civil). Clients include banks, finance houses, card issuers and retailers. Has written 'Credit Cards and the Law' (Fourmat) and articles in legal journals.
Career: Called to the Bar 1975. Formerly in-house Counsel to Access, the Joint Credit Card Company Ltd and American Express Europe Ltd.

SAYERS, Michael QC
2 King's Bench Walk (Anthony Donne QC), London (0171) 353 1746
Recommended in Crime

SCANNELL, Richard
Two Garden Court (I. Macdonald QC & O. Davies), London (0171) 353 1633
Recommended in Immigration & Nationality
Specialisation: Principally judicial review and appeals to the Court of Appeal, although all immigration appellate work. Major recent cases include T v Secretary of State for the Home Department [1996] 1 All ER 865 (House of Lords, Junior to Nicholas Blake QC); Secretary of State for the Home Department v Savchenkov [1996] Imm AR 28 (Court of Appeal, junior to Nicholas Blake QC) and MAR v United Kingdom [1997] (European Commission of Human Rights).
Prof. Memberships: Member Immigration Law Practitioners Association.
Career: Editor of Butterworths Immigration Law Service; Co-author Immigration – recent developments in Legal Action (since 1985).

SCARRATT, Richard
One Garden Court Family Law Chambers (Miss Eleanor F. Platt QC & Miss Alison Ball QC), London (0171) 797 7900
Recommended in Family: Matrimonial Finance
Specialisation: All aspects of family law with particular emphasis on the financial aspects of marital breakdown and family provision generally. Considerable experience of both public and private law matters in relation to the Children Act 1979 and international child abduction. Recent cases: Re T & E (Proceedings: Conflicting Interests) FD [1995] 1 FLR 581 and SW v H (Abduction: Access Rights) FD [1997] 1 FLR 971
Prof. Memberships: Family Law Bar Association.
Career: Called to the Bar in 1979 (Lincoln's Inn) and joined Garden Court in 1996.
Personal: Born in 1955 and educated at Ryde School, Isle of Wight and Birmingham University (LLB Hons). Married with three sons. Lives in London and Cornwall. Apart from family, leisure pursuits include piano, gardening, walking and skiing.

SCHAFF, Alistair
7 King's Bench Walk (Stephen Tomlinson QC), London (0171) 583 0404
Recommended in the following lists: Energy & Utilities, Insurance & Reinsurance, Shipping
Specialisation: All aspects of international commercial law; specifically, conflict of laws/jurisdiction disputes, shipping, insurance (marine and non-marine), reinsurance, banking, international sale of goods, oil disputes and commercial negligence. Leading cases: "The Maciej Rataj" [1995] 1 LLR 302 (ECJ; Art.21&22 of Brussels Convention); Effort v Linden [1998] 2 WLR 206 (HL; dangerous goods); Royal Boskalis v Mountain [1997] 2 ALL ER 929 (CA; illegality/marine insurance); McFarlane/Hegarty v Caledonia [1994] 1 LLR 16; [1997] 2 LLR 259 (CA; "Piper Alpha"/negligence).
Career: Called to the Bar 1983.
Personal: Born 1959. M.A. (Cantab).

SCHOLZ, Karl
3 Temple Gardens (John Coffey QC), London (0171) 353 3102
Recommended in Consumer Law
Specialisation: 1. Advising on regulated consumer credit agreements and on matters affecting the enforceability of legal charges on the home; 2. Prosecuting and defending in criminal proceedings brought under consumer protection legislation; frequently instructed by Trading Standards Authorities to appear in the Divisional Court in cases concerning the scope of liability under such legislation – eg in relation to misleading price indications in AG Stanley Ltd v Surrey County Council; MGN Ltd v Ritters and Denard v Burton Retail Ltd.; 3. Appearing before the Director General of Fair Trading (fitness to hold a licence).

SCOBIE, James T.N.
Francis Taylor Building (N.P. Valios QC), London
(0171) 353 7768
Recommended in Crime
Specialisation: Specialist in all areas of criminal law. Exclusively defence work. Acted in high profile cases including offences of murder, sexual offences and cases involving the supplying and/or importation of drugs on a large scale.
Career: Educated at Eton College 1974-78. Exeter University 79-81. Dip Law City Universtiy 1983. Called 1982.
Personal: Secretary Old Etonian Football Club. Interested in playing and watching all sports, especially football and cricket. MCC member since 1979.

SCOTLAND, Patricia QC
1 Gray's Inn Square (The Baroness Scotland of Asthal QC), London (0171) 405 3000
Recommended in Family: Child Care including child abduction

SCOTT, Peter QC
Fountain Court (Peter Scott QC), London
(0171) 583 3335
Recommended in the following lists: Arbitration, Aviation, Banking, Commercial (litigation), Energy & Utilities, Professional Negligence
Specialisation: Commerical Law. Practice covers a broad spread of commercial and civil work. Particular specialities include banking, financial services, professional negligence, insurance, City regulatory and public administration matters. Much of his work is international in character and European Community Law is an integral part of it. Important cases include Hazell v. Hammersmith & Fulham Borough Council (HL) [1991] (swaps/local authorities/banking); National Westminster Bank v. Morgan (HL) [1985] (banking/undue influence); Bank Leumi v. British National Insurance Co Ltd [1988] (insurance); Devis v. Atkins (HL)(employment); Arab Monetary Fund v. Hashim (banking, commercial fraud) [1994]; Defrenne v. Sabena (ECJ) (European Law and employment) and Re BICC (insolvency/sovereign immunity). Has acted both for and against the Bank of England and many other banks including all the London Clearing Banks and a variety of foreign banks, merchant banks and other financial institutions both in the UK and abroad. Has appeared in the courts of Hong Kong and Bermuda, as well as the European Court of Justice and the European Court of Human Rights. Involved in international arbitrations both as Counsel and Arbitrator.
Prof. Memberships: COMBAR, Midland & Oxford Circuit, London Common Law & Commercial Bar Association (Chairman 1983-85), Chairman of Appeal Board of Institute of Actuaries. Judicial Chairman of City Disputes Panel.
Career: Called to the Bar and joined Fountain Court Chambers in 1960. Took silk in 1978. Chairman of the Bar Council 1987. Member of Interception of Communications Tribunal. Bencher of the Middle Temple.
Personal: Educated at Monroe High School, Rochester, New York and Balliol College, Oxford. Born 19th April 1935. Lives in London

SCOTT, Timothy QC
29 Bedford Row Chambers (Peter Ralls QC), London (0171) 831 2626
Recommended in the following lists: Family: Child Care including child abduction, Family: Matrimonial Finance
Specialisation: Principal area of practice is Family law. Works in all areas, including ancillary relief, child abduction, private and public law children's cases. Involved in a large amount of international work including jursidictional disputes, recognition of foreign decrees and transnational enforcement. Other main area of practice is solicitors' negligence, both arising out of family law matters and generally. Clients include leading Family law solicitors firms in and outside London. Contributor

of articles to Family Law magazine and of chapter on Matrimonial Law in 'International Tracing of Assets' (FT Law & Tax 1997). Regular speaker at seminars on various family law topics.
Prof. Memberships: Family Law Bar Association, Professional Negligence Bar Association.
Career: Called to the Bar in 1975 and joined present Chambers in 1976. Appointed QC and Assistant Recorder in 1995.
Personal: Queen's Scholar, Westminster School 1962-66, Open Exhibitioner New College, Oxford 1967-70. Born 19th July 1949. Lives in London.

SCRIVENER, Anthony QC
2-3 Gray's Inn Square (Anthony Scrivener QC), London (0171) 242 4986
Recommended in the following lists: Administrative & Public Law, Civil Liberties, Consumer Law, Crime, Crime: Fraud
Specialisation: Administrative and Public Law, Consumer Law, Crime, Serious Fraud, civil liberties, Environmental law, Personal injury, Local Government and City regulatory. Monopolies work and Food Law. Also specialises in appeal work (over 30 appearances in house of Lords). Has appeared in courts Hong Kong, Malaysia, Singapore, Trinidad, Jamaica, British Virgin Islands as well as European Court of Justice. Also called to Bar in Jamaica.
Career: Practice 1961. Took Silk 1975. Chairman of the Bar 1991. Bencher of Lincoln's Inn.
Personal: Leisure: Walking, opera, Chess.

SEABROOK, Robert QC
1 Crown Office Row (Robert Seabrook QC), London (0171) 797 7500
Recommended in the following lists: Crime, Family: Matrimonial Finance, Professional Negligence
Specialisation: Extensive experience includes notably professional negligence (medical, solicitors, surveyors, accountants), civil jury actions, matrimonial finance and property, commercial fraud and major crimes. Cases include Al Kandari v Brown [1987], Smith v Bush [1990], Baker v Kaye (1997), Kapkunde v Abbey National Building Society (1998), Professor Nicolaises (MC) (1998) Lady Foster v H M Customs and Excise [1993], Silcott v Metropolitan Police Commission [1996], HRH The Prince of Wales (Royal Divorce) (1996), Tombolis [1991], Flick [re-appeal 1995] and the Charing Cross Lynn Rogers murder case [1992].
Career: Called to Bar in 1964. Took silk in 1983. Recorder since 1985. Deputy High Court Judge since 1992. Leader of the South Eastern Circuit 1989-1992. Chairman of the Bar, 1994.
Personal: Educated at St Georges's College, Harare, Zimbabwe and University College, London (LL.B). Member of the court of the University of Sussex 1988-93. Governor of Brighton College since 1993. Interests include travel, listening to music and wine. Lives in London and Brighton.

SEDDON, Duran
Two Garden Court (I. Macdonald QC & O. Davies), London (0171) 353 1633
Recommended in Immigration & Nationality
Specialisation: All aspects of immigration law including deportation, family reunion and asylum. Also specialises in social security law. Important cases include Onibiyu v SSHD [1996] Imm AR 379 CA and Radion Shingara ECJ (both led by N. Blake QC).
Prof. Memberships: Immigration Law Practitioners Association.
Career: Member of editorial board of 'Immigration and Nationality Law and Practice' (Tolleys). Publications: Migration and Social Security Handbook (jointly) CPAG 1997.

SEED, Nigel
3 Paper Buildings (Michael Parroy QC), London (0171) 583 8055
Recommended in Ecclesiastical
Specialisation: Member of the London Diocesan

Synod and Bishop's Council since 1985. Vice-chairman of the diocesan finance committee. In addition to ecclesiastical law, undertakes judicial review, planning, criminal and general common law cases.
Prof. Memberships: Chancellor of the Diocese of Leicester 1989. Special Adjudicator in Immigration and Asylum Appeals. Member of the Inner Temple, Western Circuit (assistant recorder) and Ecclesiastical Law Society. Born 30.01.51.

SEITLER, Jonathan
Wilberforce Chambers (Edward Nugee QC), London (0171) 306 0102
Recommended in Property Litigation
Specialisation: Property litigation and professional negligence arising out of it, including: landlord and tenant, bank securitisation and negligence claims against solicitors and valuers. Acts for both landlords and tenants, banks and their customers and, in professional negligence actions, Plaintiffs and insurers. Co-author of 'Property Finance Negligence: Claims Against Solicitors and Valuers' published by Sweet & Maxwell. Lectures widely both for lecture companies and in-house.
Prof. Memberships: Professional Negligence Bar Association, Commercial Bar Association.
Career: Called to the Bar 1985
Personal: Educated Pembroke College, Oxford, City University (Dip. Law).

SELLARS, Michael
14 Castle St (Adrian Lyon), Liverpool
(0151) 236 4421/8240/6759/6757
Recommended in Family/Matrimonial
Specialisation: Care cases: Represents local authorities, G.A.L's and parents. Recent substantial cases have involved complex medical issues arising from infant deaths and Munchausen's Syndrome by Proxy. Private law children's cases: all areas but particularly interested in (a) international aspects, including child abduction and emergency remedies; and (b) paternity disputes: see K v M [1996] 1 FLR 312. Privately or legally ancillary relief cases.
Prof. Memberships: Family Law Bar Association.
Career: B.A. (Hons) Durham in Law (1979). Called to the Bar in 1980. Since 1981 practised on the North Circuit and in Cheshire and North Wales.

SELVARATNAM, Vasanti
4 Field Court (Geoffrey Brice QC), London (0171) 440 6900
Recommended in Shipping
Specialisation: All aspects of international commercial and shipping law, including Admiralty. Clients include the major P & I Clubs, shipowners, charterers and salvors.
Prof. Memberships: COMBAR; European Bar Association.
Career: Called to the Bar 1983: joined current chambers (formerly located at Queen Elizabeth Building) in 1985.
Personal: Born 9.4.61. Educated at St. Augustine's Priory, Ealing and King's College, London (LL.B (Hons.) 1982, LL.M 1984).

SEMKEN, Christopher
1 New Square (Eben Hamilton QC), London (0171) 405 0884
Recommended in Traditional Chancery
Specialisation: General Chancery, especially property including landord and tenant, partnership, wills and trusts, professional negligence in such areas, both for and against solicitors, barristers, and surveyors.
Prof. Memberships: Chancery Bar Association, Professional Negligence Bar Association.
Personal: MA Oxon 1976, called to the Bar 1977, in practice at 1 New Square, Lincoln's Inn 1978 to date.

...ocial ...h) volume on ...e Primary Purpose ...pose' (co-author, Justice, ...service ...Halsb... ...rths, 1998). Member of the ...oard of, and contributor to, 'JR'. Notable cases include: R v SSHD ex parte Thompson and Venables [1997] 3 WLR 23 (HL); R v SSHD ex parte Fayed [1997] 1 All ER 228 (CA); SSHD v Adan [1998] 1 WLR (HL); R v SSHD and IAT, ex parte Robinson [1997] 4 All ER 210 (CA); R v SSHD, ex parte Cambolat [1997] Imm AR 442 (CA); and R v SSHD, ex parte Rahman [1997] Imm AR 197 (CA).

Prof. Memberships: Administrative Law Bar Association (Committee Member), Immigration Law Practitioners Association, Justice.

Career: Member of Borough Solicitor's Department, Bournemouth Borough Council 1985-86. Stagiaire at the European Parliament (Human Rights Unit) 1986. Called to the Bar 1987 and joined current chambers in 1988. Pegasus scholarship to Melbourne law firm 1991. Junior Counsel to the Crown (Common Law) 1995.

Personal: Educated at Durham University (BA) and Cambridge University (LL.M). Born 6th June 1962.

SHEA, Caroline
Falcon Chambers (Jonathan Gaunt QC & Kim Lewison QC), London (0171) 353 2484
Recommended in Property Litigation
Specialisation: Landlord and Tenant. Property Litigation.
Prof. Memberships: Chancery Bar Association. COMBAR. Contributor of legal articles to Property Week. Contributor to Woodfall CD Service.
Career: MA Cantab. Called to Bar 1994. Joined Falcon Chambers 1995.

SHEKERDEMIAN, Marcia
11 Stone Buildings (Michael Beckman QC), London +44 (0)171 831 6381
Recommended in the following lists: Company, Insolvency
Specialisation: Specialises in company law and all aspects of personal and corporate insolvency, including administrations, bankruptcy, voluntary arrangements, shareholders' disputes and wrongful trading. Practice also includes partnerships, banking and other areas of commercial litigation, drafting and advice. Cases of interest include: Re Campbell (whether a Criminal Injuries Compensation Award vests in a trustee a bankruptcy); Re Kumar (set aside a transaction at an undervalue); Re Living Images Ltd (directors disqualification, directors liability for a voidable preference, wrongful trading, diversion of assets); Re Carecraft Construction Ltd (approval of 'plea bargaining' between a director and the Secretary of State); Re Hamlet International PLC (whether a contractual lien is a charge registrable under section 395 Companies Act 1985).

SHELDON, Richard QC
3/4 South Square (Michael Crystal QC), London (0171) 696 9900
Recommended in Insolvency
Specialisation: Banking, bank securities, bankruptcy and insolvency. Corporate insolvency, general commercial and fraud (civil), company law, mergers, acquisitions and disposal of companies, financial services, international trade, finance of international trade, mortgages, partnership, solicitors' negligence, accountants' negligence. Contributed to Halsbury's Laws (4th ed vol 7).
Prof. Memberships: Chancery Bar Association, Commercial Bar Association.
Career: Called to the Bar 1979. Queens Counsel 1996. Cambridge MA.

SHELTON, Gordon E.
Broadway House (Sydney Levine), Bradford (01274) 722560
Recommended in Family/Matrimonial
Specialisation: Principal area of practice family law.

Prof. Memberships: Family Law Bar Association.
Career: Educated Ashville College, Harrogate. Leicester University. Called 1981.

SHENTON, Suzanne H.
One Garden Court Family Law Chambers (Miss Eleanor F. Platt QC & Miss Alison Ball QC), London (0171) 797 7900
Recommended in the following lists: Family: Child Care including child abduction, Family: Matrimonial Finance
Specialisation: Family Law – all aspects of The Children Act 1989, Wardship – Financial Ancilliary Relief – Professional Negligence (Matrimonial). Mediator B.A.L.M.
Prof. Memberships: Family Law Bar Association.
Career: 1973 Called to the Bar – Middle Temple. In continuous practice 1973-96.
Personal: Born 14 February 1951. Malvern Girls College 1962-69, Manchester University LL.B. Hons. 1972.

SHEPHERD, N.
8 King's Bench Walk (L.G. Woodley QC), London (0171) 797 8888
Recommended in Crime

SHEPHERD, Philip
24 Old Buildings (C.A. Brodie QC), London (0171) 404 0946
Recommended in Aviation
Specialisation: International Aviation litigation including aviation insurance, carriers liability for passengers and cargo, product liability of manufacturers and maintainers, aircraft leasing and finance, arrest of aircraft; law relating to travel agents and tour operators; regulatory work; arbitration. Junior Counsel for British Airways in the leading case on carriers liability – Sidhu v British Airways in the House of Lords. Thos. Cook v Air Malta 1997 2 Lloyd's LR p399. H5 Air Service v CAA 1998 1 Lloyds LR p364.
Prof. Memberships: European Air Law Association, Lawyers Flying Association, Royal Aeronautical Society, Air Law Group, Grays Inn, COMBAR.
Career: St George's College, London School of Economics, Monash University Melbourne (Aus). Inns of Court Law School.
Personal: Flying light aircraft. Married to Amanda (a solicitor with Reynolds Porter Chamberlain). 2 sons.

SHER, Jules QC
Wilberforce Chambers (Edward Nugee QC), London (0171) 306 0102
Recommended in the following lists: Chancery, Energy & Utilities, Pensions, Traditional Chancery
Specialisation: Chancery & Commercial Litigation and Advice. Covers the wide range of work comprised in a modern commercial chancery practice including Lloyd's litigation and advice, instructed by Freshfields (Guy Moreton) and Simmons & Simmons (Christopher Braithwaite), North Sea Oil and Gas tract participation disputes (acting for British Gas and major oil companies in litigation in the Commercial Court and Chancery Division), Trust litigation in the U.K. and abroad (Singapore, Cayman Islands, Bahamas, Hong Kong), Trust aspects of takeovers (acted in Glaxo takeover of Wellcome and Granada takeover of Forte), Professional Negligence (Accountants, Solicitors), Pensions litigation (Imperial Group v Imperial Tobacco, London Regional Transport Pension Fund Trustee Co. Ltd v Hatt, MacDonald v Horn).
Career: B.Comm., LL.B. (Rand), B.C.L. (Oxon).Called to the Bar of England and Wales in 1968. Took Silk 1981. Recorder. Advocate of the Supreme Court of South Africa; Deputy High Court Judge (Chancery Division); Member of the Commercial Bar Association & Chancery Bar Association.

SHERBORNE, David
5 Raymond Buildings (Patrick Milmo QC), London (0171) 242 2902
Recommended in Defamation
Specialisation: Defamation, Malicious Falsehood, Contempt of Court, Freedom of the Press, Breach

of Confidence, Copyright, Criminal, Media and Entertainment, General Commercial/Contract, Employment, Professional Negligence, Criminal and Sports Law.
Career: Called to the Bar 1992. Senior Scholar, Gray's Inn.
Personal: Educated at University College School, London and New College, Oxford.

SHERIDAN, Maurice
3 Verulam Buildings (R. Neville Thomas QC), London (0171) 831 8441
Recommended in Environmental Law
Specialisation: EC environmental, especially regarding direct effect of Directives; nuisance and negligence, including regarding professional negligence; waste management.
Prof. Memberships: Bar European Group; British Italian Law Association; British Bulgarian Law Association; COMBAR.
Career: Sorbonne 1980; Stage with EC Commission 1985; LLB Bristol; LLM (International law) Cantab 1985-6; assisting in approximation programmes regarding EC environmental *Acquis* in Central and Eastern Europe – 1992 to date.
Personal: Travelling, theatre, cinema, contemporary dance.

SHERRY, Michael
3 Temple Gardens (David Braham QC), London (0171) 353 7884
Recommended in Tax
email: sherry@taxlawchambers.demon.co.uk
Specialisation: Revenue law, covering all aspects of direct and indirect taxation for commercial and substantial private clients. Co-author 'Whiteman on Income Tax' (Sweet & Maxwell, 3rd Edn 1988) and author of 'Tax Planning for Family Company Shareholders' (Key Haven 1993). Annual supplements to 'Whiteman on Income Tax' and 'Whiteman on Capital Gains Tax'; sole editor since 1988.
Prof. Memberships: Institute of Chartered Accountants (Faculty of Taxation; Deputy Chairman 1998, also Technical Committee), Institute of Taxation, Institute of Indirect Taxation (President 1995-1998), Gray's Inn.
Career: Called to the Bar in 1978. With Ernst & Young 1978-83, then with specialist Tax Chambers at 3 Temple Gardens since 1983.
Personal: Scholar of Lincoln College, Oxford 1974-77. Inns of Court School of Law 1977-78. Leisure pursuits include swimming, bridge and croquet. Born 8th May 1956. Lives near Battle.

SHIELDS, Thomas QC
1 Brick Court (Richard Hartley QC), London (0171) 353 8845
Recommended in Defamation

SHIPLEY, Graham
19 Old Buildings (Alastair Wilson QC), London (0171) 405 2001
Recommended in the following lists: Computer & I.T., Intellectual Property
Specialisation: Principal area of practice encompasses intellectual property and technology work, including electronic and computer cases and EC aspects. Regular seminar speaker, and has appeared on radio and television ('Science Now') broadcasts.
Prof. Memberships: Intellectual Property Bar Association, Chancery Bar Association.
Career: Called to the Bar 1973 and joined present chambers in 1975, when located at Pump Court.
Personal: Educated at King's School, Chester 1959-66, Trinity College, Cambridge 1966-71 (B.A. Mathematics 1969, Diploma in Computer Science, Distinction 1970) and Inns of Court School of Law 1971-73. Former Director of 'Trinity 69 Foundation' charity. Leisure pursuits include electronics, house restoring, woodwork, Japanese cookery and motor cycle riding. Born 10th January 1948. Lives in Saffron Walden.

...essional Discipline; Tribunals
...icial Review; Torts; Sports Law;

...erships: London Common Law and
...cial Bar Association; International Bar
...tion; Criminal Bar Association; Bar Sports
Law Group; British Association for Sport and Law.
Career: Called 1975. Queen's Counsel 1993.
Member of the governing committee of the British
Association for Sport and Law. Vice Chairman of
the Bar Sports Law Group. Former member of the
Bar's Professional Conduct Committee (3 years)
and of its Law Reform Committee (6 years).
Personal: Born 1954 in London.

SINGH, Rabinder
4-5 Gray's Inn Square (Miss Elizabeth Appleby
QC & The Hon. M. Beloff QC), London
(0171) 404 5252
*Recommended in the following lists: Administrative
& Public Law, Civil Liberties, Planning*
Specialisation: All aspects of public law,
employment law and European Community and
human rights law.
Prof. Memberships: Administrative Law Bar
Association (Secretary), Planning and Environment
Bar Association, Employment Law Bar Association;
Bar European Group.
Career: Called:1989. Appointed to supplementary
panel of junior counsel to the Crown: 1992.
Additional Junior Counsel to the Inland Revenue:
1997.
Personal: B.A. (Law) 1985: Trinity College,
Cambridge LL.M. 1986: University of California,
Berkeley. Visiting fellow, Queen Mary and Westfield
College, London since 1995.

SINGLETON, Barry QC
One King's Bench Walk (James Townend QC),
London (0171) 936 1500
Recommended in Family: Matrimonial Finance

SLADE, Elizabeth Ann QC
11 King's Bench Walk (Eldred Tabachnik QC
and James Goudie QC), London
(0171) 632 8500
Recommended in Employment
Specialisation: Specialises in all aspects of
employment law with particular emphasis on
European aspects of Employment Law; Transfer of
Undertakings; Sex and Race Discrimination; Equal
Pay; Employment aspects of pensions. Leading
cases include: Foster & Others v British Gas; Reed
Executive plc v Sommers; Shepherd v Jerrom;
Westminster City Council v Pensions Ombudsman
and Haywood, CREES v The Royal London
Insurance Society.
Prof. Memberships: Employment Law Bar
Association; Employment Lawyers Association;
ALBA; Bar European Group.
Career: Called to the Bar in 1972; original author
'Tolley's Employment Handbook'; Assistant
Recorder 1995-; Deputy High Court Judge 1998-;
1990 Bencher of the Inner Temple; 1992 Appointed
QC; 1994 Master of the Staff, Inner Temple; Chair
of Employment Law Bar Association 1995-97; Hon
Vice President 1998-.
Personal: Education: Lady Margaret Hall, Oxford.
Exhibitioner.

SLADE, Richard
Brick Court Chambers (Christopher Clarke QC),
London (0171) 583 0777
Recommended in Insurance & Reinsurance
Specialisation: Banking,insurance and sale of
goods.
Career: Called to Bar 1984, Lincoln's Inn.
Pupillage at Brick Court Chambers. Practised at
Brick Court Chambers, 1988 to date.
Personal: Born 1963, London. Educated at Eton
and Trinity, Cambridge. B.A. History/Law. One
Senior Scholarship at Trinity. Contributor to Paget,
Law of Banking.

SLATER, John QC
One Paper Buildings (John Slater QC), London
(0171) 583 7355
*Recommended in the following
lists: Construction, Professional Negligence*
Specialisation: Construction & Civil Engineering,
Professional Negligence (architects, engineers,
surveyors, accountants, solicitors, trade mark
agents), insurance/reinsurance, product liability.
Recent cases include: Capital & Counties v
Hampshire County Council (first leader for
claimants); Alzal v Ford, Wessex Regional Health
Authority v HLM; Alliance & Leicester v Edgestop;
Team Services v Kier Management; Kier
Construction v Royal Insurance. Mainly briefed by
insurers and major corporations. Much used for
lengthy complex trials with large volumes of paper.
Reputation as an effective cross examiner.
Previously used in interrelated insurance policy and
project disputes eg. in fire, flood, building collapse,
product failure cases. Enjoys Court work of all
types.
Personal: Born 1946. Educated Sedbergh School,
University College, Oxford. Called to the Bar 1969,
QC 1987 (Aged 40), sits as domestic and
international arbitrator (LCIA, ICC). Lives in
Highgate with wife and three offspring.

SLOMNICKA, Barbara
14 Gray's Inn Square (Joanna Dodson QC),
London (0171) 242 0858
*Recommended in Family: Child Care including
child abduction*

SMALL, Jonathan
Falcon Chambers (Jonathan Gaunt QC & Kim
Lewison QC), London (0171) 353 2484
Recommended in Property Litigation
Specialisation: Property Litigation.
Prof. Memberships: Chancery Bar Association,
COMBAR and LCCBA (Committee Member).
Career: Nottingham University 1988 BA (History);
City University 1989 Diploma in Law; Inns of Court
Studentship; Wolfson & Kennedy Scholarships;
Elected member of The Bar Council (1994-97).

SMALLWOOD, Anne
5 Fountain Court (Anthony Barker QC),
Birmingham (0121) 606 0500
Recommended in Family/Matrimonial

SMITH, Andrew QC
Fountain Court (Peter Scott QC), London
(0171) 583 3335
*Recommended in the following lists: Arbitration,
Aviation, Commercial (litigation), Computer & I.T.,
Insurance & Reinsurance, Parliamentary*
Specialisation: Principal area of work is
commercial law, especially insurance, reinsurance,
banking and dry shipping law. Also handles
professional negligence work relating to
accountants, solicitors, brokers, surveyors and
doctors, employment, computer and parliamentary
work. Acts for major banks, insurance companies,
syndicates and professional firms. Sits as an
Arbitrator.
Prof. Memberships: London Common Law and
Commercial Bar Association (Secretary 1983-
1991), South Eastern Circuit.
Career: Called to the Bar 1974. Joined Fountain
Court 1975. County Court Rules Committee 1979-
1983 and Queen's Bench Procedural Committee
1986-1990. Took silk in 1990. Vice-Chairman of Bar
Standards Review Body 1994. Assistant Recorder
1991. Assistant Parliamentary Boundary
Commissioner 1993. Recorder 1996.
Personal: Educated at Wyggeston Grammar
School for Boys. Graduated from Wadham
College, Oxford with BA Literae Humaniores and
BA Jurisprudence (First Class). Astbury Scholar at
Middle Temple 1974. Born 31st December 1947.

SMITH, Christopher
4 Field Court (Geoffrey Brice QC), London
(0171) 440 6900
Recommended in Shipping
Specialisation: All areas of commercial practice
including Admiralty and other shipping work,
professional negligence, insurance, international
trade and carriage of goods by road and sea.
Particular interest in yacht related litigation
including collisions and ownership disputes.
Notable cases include BBL v Eagle Star [1993]
(measure of damages for negligent valuation); The
"Shizelle" [1992] (mortgages of unregistered ships
or yachts); The "River Gurara" [1997] (package
limitation under Hague Rules). Publications include
contributing to volume 3 (Admiralty) of Atkin's
Court Forms.
Prof. Memberships: COMBAR; LCLCBA.
Career: Called to the Bar in 1989, joined
Chambers in 1990.
Personal: Educated at Oundle School and
Southampton University. Interests include sailing
and riding.

SMITH, Julia
Gough Square Chambers (Frederick Philpott),
London (0171) 353 0924
Recommended in Consumer Law
Specialisation: Consumer Law – in particular
consumer credit and mortgage actions (eg First
National Bank v Syed [1991] 2 All ER 250 and
Jarrett v Barclays Bank [1997] 2 All ER 484)
including consumer credit drafting, extortionate
credit bargains, and licensing. Clients include
banks, finance houses, leasing companies and
retailers.
Prof. Memberships: London Common Law and
Commercial Bar Association.
Career: Called to the Bar 1988
Personal: Cheltenham Ladies College and
Liverpool University.

SMITH, Michael Joseph
8 King St (Keith Armitage QC), Manchester
(0161) 834 9560
Recommended in Medical Negligence
Specialisation: Main areas of practice include
personal injury, medical negligence, other
professional negligence, civil actions involving the
police. Also construction, commercial and
insurance litigation.
Prof. Memberships: Personal Injury Bar
Association. Northern Circuit Commercial Bar
Association.
Career: Educated at St Mary's High School,
Astley; Christ Church, Oxford (BCL, MA). Called to
the Bar 1989.

SMITH, Peter QC
40 King St (Philip Raynor QC), Manchester
(0161) 832 9082
*Recommended in the following lists: Chancery,
Commercial (litigation), Insolvency*
Specialisation: Insolvency, Landlord and tenant,
Professional negligence. Recent cases: Re:
Exchange Travel 1996 BCLC 524, Norglen v Reeds
Rains 1998 HL 1 AER 218; CIS v Argyll Stores, HL
1997.
Prof. Memberships: Professional Negligence Bar
Association, Northern Chancery Bar Association,
Northern Commercial Bar Association, Chancery
Bar Association.
Career: Called to Bar in 1975. Lecturer at
Manchester University 1977-1983. Northern Circuit
1979-1996. Took Silk in 1994. Assistant Recorder
1994. Deputy High Court Judge 1996.

SMITH, Richard
Guildhall Chambers (John Royce QC), Bristol
(0117) 927 3366
Recommended in Crime

SMITH, Robert QC
Park Court Chambers (James Stewart QC, Robert Smith QC), Leeds (0113) 243 3277
Recommended in Crime
Specialisation: A balanced practice involving prosecution and defence work. Defence instructions include a large proportion of professional defendants such as medical practitioners, accountants, police officers. Has a particular interest in medico-legal matters and scientific evidence. Recent cases of importance: Attorney General's Reference (No 3 of 1994): Criminal Liability for pre-natal injuries: Court of Appeal Criminal Division: [1996] 2WLR 412 /House of Lords: [1997] 3 WLR 42; R v Beedie Court of Appeal Criminal Division: The Double Jeopardy Rule in Criminal Proceedings. [1997] 2 Cr.App.R. 167; R v Woolin: Foresight of consequences as proof of intent in murder: House of Lords 15.6.98 reversing Court of Appeal [1997] I Cr.App.R 97.
Career: Common Law Practitioner specialising in Criminal and Civil litigation from commencing practice in Leeds in 1971. Appointed Queen's Counsel and a Recorder in 1986. Served for 3 years as a Member of the Criminal Injuries Compensation Board. Joined London chambers at 3 Serjeants' Inn [Adrian Whitfield QC] as a door tenant in 1994. Member of the International Bar Association.

SMITH, Roger QC
No.6 Fountain Court (Roger Smith QC), Birmingham (0121) 233 3282
Recommended in Crime

SMITH, Sally QC
1 Crown Office Row (Robert Seabrook QC), London (0171) 797 7500
Recommended in Medical Negligence

SMITH, Shaun
No.1 High Pavement (John B. Milmo QC), Nottingham (0115) 941 8218
Recommended in Crime

SMITH, Stephen
12 New Square (John Mowbray QC), London (0171) 419 1212
Recommended in the following lists: Chancery, Company
Specialisation: Complex and heavy commercial litigation, often with a Chancery or jurisdictional element (especially issues arising under the Brussels/Lugano convention) and involving restraints on disposals of assets; also professional negligence, civil fraud, insurance, property disputes and insolvency. Conducted numerous witness examinations, including several in the USA and in New Zealand. Called to the Bar of the Eastern Caribbean States Supreme Court and conducted several hearings on Tortola BVI at first instance (including at trial) and on appeal to the Court of Appeal of the Eastern Caribbean, and appeared on a further appeal to the Privy Council. Previous cases: Derby v Weldon (acted for Salomon Inc.); DSQ Property Company (formerly DeLorean Motor Company) v Lotus Cars (acted for John Z. DeLorean); Morris v Mahfouz (BCCI; acted for Khalid Bin Mahfouz and others); FTIT Ltd. v Morgan Stanley and Coopers & Lybrand (Maxwell; acted for liquidators (Deloitte Touche) appointed by Swiss Bank Corporation); Senate Electrical Wholesalers v Alcatel Submarines Networks (acted for Northern Telecom); Village Cay Marina v Acland (Privy Council decision about share registration and receivership in the BVI).
Prof. Memberships: Middle Temple (Jules Thorn Scholar).
Career: Scholar, University College Oxford 1979-1982, First class hons. degree in Jurisprudence, Oxford University 1982 (Wronker and Jurisprudence Prizes winner). Called to the Bar in England and Wales, August 1983.
Personal: Married to Lorraine, 5 children. Principal leisure interests: family, deer and deer stalking, wildfowling, alpaca farming.

SMITH, Zoe
Hardwicke Building (Walter Aylen QC), London (0171) 242 2523
Recommended in Crime
Specialisation: Criminal advocate with particular interest in complex fraud litigation. Also has substantial experience in drug and rape cases.
Career: Called in 1970. Recorder.

SMOUHA, Joe
Essex Court Chambers (Gordon Pollock QC), London (0171) 813 8000
Recommended in the following lists: Arbitration, Commercial (litigation), Shipping
Specialisation: Litigation involving appearances in arbitration, the Commercial Court, Court of Appeal and other courts hearing civil claims. All aspects of commercial law including shipping, banking, insurance and reinsurance, international sale of goods, oil and gas, public international law and other related areas. Art litigation including title, dealer commission, purchasing syndicate disputes. VAT: includes both substantial High Court and Tribunal work and general advisory work on non-contentious matters, schemes etc.
Career: Magdalene College, Cambridge, BA Law (Hons) 1984; MA 1988; New York University School of Law, 1984-85: LL.M in International Trade Law: Called to the Bar 1986 (Middle Temple).
Personal: Born 1963.

SNOWDEN, Richard
Erskine Chambers (Richard Sykes QC), London (0171) 242 5532
Recommended in the following lists: Company, Financial Services, Insolvency
Specialisation: Handles mainly company law and corporate insolvency with an emphasis on litigation. Has been involved in a number of reported company and insolvency cases. Is the junior counsel who advised the successful employees in the Paramount Airways case, (Powdrill v Watson) and represented them at all stages of the litigation, including in the House of Lords. Also deals with financial services matters. Assistant editor of 'Lightman & Moss on the Law of Receivers of Companies' and joint editor of 'Company Directors: Law and Liability'. Regularly lectures/speaks at conferences on insolvency and corporate matters.
Prof. Memberships: Chancery Bar Association, COMBAR, Insolvency Lawyers Association, Society of Practitioners of Insolvency. Member of one of the Financial Law Panel's working groups on Director's Duties.
Career: Called to the Bar in 1986 and joined Erskine Chambers in 1987.
Personal: Educated at Downing College, Cambridge 1981-84 (MA, 1st Class Hons.) and Harvard Law School 1984-85 (LL.M). Leisure pursuits include golf, cricket and music. Born 22nd March 1962. Lives in Rotherfield, E.Sussex.

SNOWDEN, Steven
2 Crown Office Row (Graeme Hamilton QC), London (0171) 797 8100
Recommended in Personal Injury
Specialisation: Wide range of personal injury (including Health & Safety) and medical negligence for both plaintiffs and defendants; professional indemnity (accountants, brokers, surveyors, solicitors); insurance and insurance-related work.
Prof. Memberships: PIBA (committee member) and COMBAR.
Career: Called 1989. Joined chambers in 1991.
Personal: Born 1967. Educated at Boroughmuir High School (Edinburgh) and Nottingham University.

SOARES, Patrick C.
8 Gray's Inn Square (Patrick C. Soares), London (0171) 242 3529
Recommended in Tax
Specialisation: Specialist in all aspects of revenue law, including structuring land transactions for the optimum tax position, value added tax and stamp duty on land transactions, taxation of overseas trusts and international estate and trust planning. Also conducts tax appeals at all levels. Publications include 'Vat Planning for Property Transactions', 'Land and Tax Planning', 'Trusts and Tax Planning', 'Taxation of Non-Resident Trusts', 'Taxation of Land Development', 'Offshore Investment in UK Property' and 'Tax Strategy for Conveyancing Transactions'. Tax editor of the 'Property Law Bulletin' and co-editor of 'Trusts for Europe'.
Prof. Memberships: Fellow of the Institute of Taxation.
Career: Called to the Bar 1983. Previously a tax partner in a leading firm of London solicitors, having been admitted a solicitor in 1972.
Personal: Educated at University College, London (MA Taxation).

SOLLEY, Stephen QC
Cloisters (Laura Cox QC), London (0171) 827 4000
Recommended in the following lists: Civil Liberties, Crime, Crime: Fraud

SOMERVILLE, Bryce
No.6 Fountain Court (Roger Smith QC), Birmingham (0121) 233 3282
Recommended in Family/Matrimonial

SOORJOO, Martin
14 Tooks Court (Michael Mansfield QC), London (0171) 405 8828
Recommended in Immigration & Nationality

SOUTHWELL, Edward
Farrar's Building (Gerard Elias QC), London (0171) 583 9241
Recommended in Personal Injury
Specialisation: Wide ranging personal injury practice, both plaintiff and defendant, with emphasis in recent years on industrial disease/injury (including deafness, lung disorders, RSI etc). Also handles medical and solicitors' negligence. Lay clients have included the Ford Motor Company, British Rail, the M.O.D. and ICI.
Prof. Memberships: London Common Law Bar Association, South Eastern Circuit and Personal Injury Bar Association.
Career: Called to the Bar in 1970 and joined Farrar's Building in 1971. Recorder since 1987.
Personal: Educated at Charterhouse School 1959-64. Assistant Boundary Commissioner. Chairman of NHS Trust Disciplinary Inquiry Panels.

SOUTHWELL, Richard QC
1 Hare Court (Lord Neill of Bladen QC & Richard Southwell QC), London (0171) 353 3171
Recommended in the following lists: Banking, Commercial (litigation)
Specialisation: Banking, insurance, major commercial litigation and arbitration, both domestic and international, arbitrator.
Prof. Memberships: Chairman, Legal Services Committee, Bar Council 1990-91. Chairman, Professional Standards Committee, Bar Council 1988-90. Member of Executive of COMBAR.
Career: Bencher Inner Temple. President, Lloyd's Appeal Tribunal. Judge of the Courts of Appeal of Jersey and Guernsey. Deputy Judge of the High Court, Queen's Bench Division.

SPARKS, Jocelyn
Queen Elizabeth Building (David Jeffreys QC & Peter Whiteman QC), London (0171) 583 5766
Recommended in Crime

SPEAIGHT, Anthony QC
12 King's Bench Walk (Ronald J. Walker QC), London (0171) 583 0811
Recommended in Construction
Specialisation: Construction; professional negligence; other contractual, tort and property related work; public law.
Prof. Memberships: Official Referee Bar

Association (past committee member), Member of the Council of the Society of Construction Law; London Common Law and Commercial Bar Association; Professional Negligence Bar Association; Personal Injury Bar Association.
Career: Called to the Bar in 1973, took Silk in 1995. Chairman of the Editorial Board of "Counsel" journal of the Bar of England and Wales (1990-4).

SPECK, Adrian
8 New Square (Michael Fysh QC), London (0171) 405 4321
Recommended in Intellectual Property
Specialisation: Specialises in all aspects of intellectual property, including patents trade marks and passing off, confidential information, designs, copyright and performers' rights. Also specialises in jurisdiction disputes under the CJJA 1982/Brussels Convention and entertainment litigation. Cases include Biogen v Medeva (biotechnology patent); Chiron v Evans (biotechnology patent); Wagamama v City Centre Restaurants (Trade Mark and passing off; EC directive); Pearce v Ove Arup Partnership (jurisdiction of English Court over infringement of foreign intellectual property under Brussels Convention); Fort Dodge v Azko (jurisdictional dispute over proceedings for infringement of patent); Lancashire Fires v S.A. Lyons (breach of confidence; trade secrets; ex employer/employee dispute); Cobra v Rata (Anton Pillers; use of documents in other proceedings; use for contempt); Baywatch v Home Video Channel (Trade Mark and passing off; EC directive); Trebor Bassett v Football Association (Trade Mark infringement; photographs of footballers on football cards); Scandecor Development v Scandecor Marketing (trade mark and passing off; international group of companies fragmented).
Prof. Memberships: Intellectual Property Bar Association, Gray's Inn and Lincoln's Inn.
Career: Called to the Bar 1993 (Wilfred Parker Prize).
Personal: Born 1969. Educated at Seaford Head Comprehensive School, East Sussex 1980-87 and King's College, Cambridge 1988-91 (Scholar, 1st Class Honours in Physics and Theoretical Physics).

SPENCE, Malcolm QC
2-3 Gray's Inn Square (Anthony Scrivener QC), London (0171) 242 4986
Recommended in the following lists: Parliamentary, Planning
Specialisation: Specialises in planning and parliamentary work. Many years experience of attending planning inquiries and appearing before the Lands Tribunal in compensation for compulsory purchase cases. Also many appearances in the High Court and Court of Appeal in planning, compensation and local government cases. Parliamentary work includes appearances before Select Committee in relation to the Channel Tunnel Bill and the Channel Tunnel Rail Link Bill.
Prof. Memberships: Chairman of Planning and Environment Bar Association 1994-1998.
Career: Called to the Bar (Gray's Inn) in 1958. Took Silk in 1979. Recorder of the Crown Court. Deputy High Court Judge since 1988.

SPENCER, Martin
4 Paper Buildings (Harvey McGregor QC), London (0171) 353 3366
Recommended in Medical Negligence
Specialisation: Medical Negligence and P.I. especially back injury cases for the Royal College of Nursing (has been dealing with such cases since 1987). Recent cases include: De Martell, Smith v Tunbridge Wells H.A., Forbes (now a leading case on limitation) and Figgett v Davies.
Prof. Memberships: PNBA. London Common Law Bar Association. Personal Injury Bar Association.
Career: BA (Oxon) 1977, BCL (Oxon) 1978, Bar Finals 1979, Danish Government Scholar, Copenhagen University 1979-1980, Pupil, Fountain Court 1980-81. Joined present chambers 1981.

Personal: Married with three Children. Fluent Danish speaker. Interests include music, sport and bridge.

SPENCER, Michael QC
One Paper Buildings (John Slater QC), London (0171) 583 7355
Recommended in the following lists: Medical Negligence, Personal Injury, Product Liability
Specialisation: Disaster Litigation, most particularly pharmaceutical claims. Has represented manufacturers in claims involving Eraldin, Opren, Whooping cough vaccine, Benzodiazepines sex hormones including pregnancy tests, OC's and HRT, and many other products. Other specialist areas are general consumer PI claims, such as tobacco related disease, medical negligence and more general professional negligence and personal injury.
Prof. Memberships: Midland and Oxford circuit, London Common Law and Commercial Bar Association, Professional Negligence Bar Association and Medico-Legal Society.
Career: Called to Bar 1970; Recorder 1987; QC 1989; Bencher Inner Temple 1996.
Personal: Born 1 December 1947. Educated Ampleforth College and Hertford College, Oxford (MA).

SPENCER-LEWIS, Neville
12 King's Bench Walk (Ronald J. Walker QC), London (0171) 583 0811
Recommended in Banking
Specialisation: Principal area of specialisation is Banking Act work on behalf of the Bank of England in respect of unauthorised deposit-taking. Also deals with general banking work such as the banker's duty to advise and general civil work, including professional negligence, contract, misrepresentation (eg Royscot Trust Ltd v Rogerson) etc.
Prof. Memberships: London Common Law and Commercial Bar Association.
Career: Called to Bar 1970. Joined Kings Bench Walk in 1980.
Personal: Educated at Radley College and Pembroke College, Oxford. Lives in London.

SPINK, Andrew J.M.
35 Essex Street (Nigel Inglis-Jones QC), London (0171) 353 6381
Recommended in Medical Negligence
Specialisation: Handles all aspects of High Court and County Court medical negligence litigation on behalf of plaintiffs (particular experience in cases involving brain damage at birth resulting in cerebral palsy). Also experienced in all aspects of personal injury, acting for plaintiffs and defendants (particular interest in brain and spinal injury claims and claims involving environmental and occupational exposure to asbestos and other harmful substances). Other main area of practice is professional negligence, acting for plaintiffs and defendants in cases involving negligence of actuaries, accountants, surveyors and lawyers. Lectures at conferences for lawyers on structured settlements and asbestos-related litigation.
Prof. Memberships: AVMA, APIL, London Common Law & Commercial Bar Association.
Career: Called to the Bar in 1985 and joined chambers at Essex Street in 1986.
Personal: Educated at Sherborne School, Dorset 1975-80 and Queens' College, Cambridge 1981-84. Interests include mountain and hill walking, skiing, France, travel in Asia, computers and opera. Born 21st April 1962. Lives in London and Devizes.

SPOLLON, Guy
St Philip's Chambers (Rex Tedd QC), Birmingham (0121) 246 7000
Recommended in Family/Matrimonial
Specialisation: Specialises in all forms of family law with particular emphasis towards ancillary relief.
Prof. Memberships: F.L.B.A.

Career: Called to the Bar 1976.
Personal: Married. 2 children. Historic motor racing – as both competitor and spectator.

STADLEN, Nicholas QC
Fountain Court (Peter Scott QC), London (0171) 583 3335
Recommended in Commercial (litigation)
Specialisation: General Commercial Law including banking, insurance, city takeovers and professional negligence. Currently acting for Bank of England against BCCI and for British & Commonwealth against Atlantic Computers, BZW, NM Rothschild and Spicer and Oppenheim. Acted for British Airways against Virgin, British & Commonwealth against Samuel Montagu & Quadrex, ACLI against M&R, Savoy against THF, CE Heath against Gooda Walker Syndicates. Pro Bono: Privy Council Capital Punishment Appeal from Jamaica; successful appeal by President of Oxford Union against dismissal from office.
Prof. Memberships: Former member: Combar North American Committee; Bar Council Public Affairs Committee. Assistant Recorder, South Eastern Circuit.
Career: Classical Scholar at St. Paul's and Trinity College, Cambridge. English Speaking Union Scholar, Hackley School, New York. President Cambridge Union Society. Winner Observer Mace Debating Championship. 1st in Order of Merit, Part 1 Bar Exams.

STAFFORD, Andrew
2 Crown Office Row (John Powell QC), London (0171) 797 8000
Recommended in the following lists: Employment, Professional Negligence
Specialisation: Employment law, professional negligence, construction law, commercial litigation. Rock Refrigeration v Jones (covenants in restraint of trade, Court of Appeal); Malik v BCCI (measure of damages for employer's breach of contract, House of Lords); Flood v Shand Construction (assignment of damages claims under JCT Form, Court of Appeal); Ermis Skai v Banque Indosuez (validity of demand under performance bond, Commercial Court); Brostoff v CKL (Liability of accountants' association for fraud of employee, Court of Appeal); Bennett v Greenland Houchen (Limitation in sols/negligence, Court of Appeal).
Career: Call 1980.

STAFFORD-MICHAEL, Simon
4 King's Bench Walk (Robert Rhodes QC), London (0171) 822 8822
Recommended in Crime: Fraud
Specialisation: Fraud, Insurance and Reinsurance. Fraud: Regulation, compliance and money laundering; serious fraud investigations conducted by the SFO, CPS, Inland Revenue, C&E, DTI and SIB; and criminal and commercial litigation. Major trials include: Jyske Bank, Guinness, Arrows and Wallace Duncan Smith. Notable recent matters include R v W & Another (Court of Appeal), R v EPA ex p Green Environmental Industries (in respect of which the House of Lords has granted leave to appeal from the Court of Appeal) and preparing the pending appeal in R v Hayes [the Swithland Motors case] . Insurance and Reinsurance: Marine and Non-marine; Regulation and Insolvency; London Market/Lloyd's of London law and practice; construction of complex policy language; Equitas; international litigation and arbitration; long tail-environmental/mass tort/product's liability; CAT claims; professional indemnity claims; D&O claims; settlement counsel and mediator. Notable recent matters include: Lasmo plc v London Market Insurers et al (Court of Appeal) and settlement counsel retained on behalf of US corporate assureds to advise on settlement of certain environmental claims brought against London Market Insurers.
Prof. Memberships: Criminal Bar Association, American Bar Association, International Bar

Association and Federation of Insurance and Corporate Counsel.
Career: West Bridgeford Comprehensive School, University of Bristol and Gray's Inn. Co-Chair of the International Insurance Coverage Litigation Committee of the ABA. Journal of Money Laundering, Advisory Board 1998.
Personal: Simon Stafford-Michael is married to Johanna and they have four children. They live in Gloucestershire.

STALLEBRASS, Paul
5 Paper Buildings (Antonio Bueno QC), London (0171) 583 9275
Recommended in Banking
Specialisation: Principal areas of practice are commercial and banking law including securities, negotiable instruments, payment methods, conflicts, commercial fraud and asset tracing. Other areas of work include professional negligence, entertainment and European Law.

STARMER, Keir
Doughty Street Chambers (Geoffrey Robertson QC), London (0171) 404 1313
Recommended in the following lists: Administrative & Public Law, Civil Liberties, Crime

STEAD, Richard
St. John's Chambers (Roderick Denyer QC), Bristol (0117) 921 3456
Recommended in the following lists: Commercial (litigation), Personal Injury

STEEL, John QC
4-5 Gray's Inn Square (Miss Elizabeth Appleby QC & The Hon. M. Beloff QC), London (0171) 404 5252 Fax: (0171) 242 7803
DX: 1029 London
Recommended in the following lists: Administrative & Public Law, Environmental Law, Planning
E-mail: jbs@4-5graysinnsquare.co.uk
Specialisation: Has worked for many national and international clients in both the public and private sectors at the highest level in public, administrative, planning and environmental law. Practices in judicial review and public inquiry work. Specialities include retail, leisure, housing, minerals, waste disposal, highways, aviation, compulsory purchase and licensing. Particularly experienced in cases involving scientific, engineering and technically complex issues.
Prof. Memberships: Planning and Environment Bar Association; Administrative Law Bar Association.
Career: Called to the Bar 1978. Silk 1993. Assistant Recorder.
Personal: Educated: Harrow School 1967-1972; Durham University (BSc Hons chemistry) 1973-1976; President Durham University Athletic Union 1975; Gray's Inn Moot Prize 1978, Member Attorney General's panel (planning etc) 1979-1993; PPL (Helicopters and Fixed Wing); Director; Kandahar Ski Club. Director, The Busoga Trust (water relief in Uganda). Lives near Chipping Norton, Oxon.

STEELE, David
Colleton Chambers (Martin Meeke), Exeter (01392) 274898
Recommended in Crime

STEER, David QC
The Corn Exchange (David Steer QC & I. Goldrein QC), Liverpool (0151) 227 1081/5009
Recommended in Crime

STEINFELD, Alan QC
24 Old Buildings (C.A. Brodie QC), London (0171) 404 0946
Recommended in the following lists: Chancery, Company, Insolvency, Property Litigation
Specialisation: The main areas of business law including: insolvency (personal and corporate), civil fraud, company law, contract disputes, financial services, partnership law, professional

negligence, property law, landlord and tenant, pensions.
Prof. Memberships: Chancery Bar Association, Insolvency Lawyers Association.
Career: Downing College, Cambridge (BA Hons, LLB). Year of Call 1968. Year of Silk 1987. Deputy High Court Judge 1994 (Chancery Division).

STEPHENS, John L.
35 Essex Street (Nigel Inglis-Jones QC), London (0171) 353 6381
Recommended in Pensions
Specialisation: Principal area of practice is pensions, covering all aspects of UK and international occupational pension schemes and claims associated therewith (eg. professional negligence, executive severance etc.). Also deals with offshore trusts and claims to ownership of antiquities (i.e claims by nations, museums, temples, etc to ownership of ancient works of art). Frequently addresses both commercial and legal conferences.
Prof. Memberships: Association of Pensions Lawyers, Chancery Bar Association, IPEBLA.
Career: Called to the Bar in 1975. Joined present chambers in 1977.
Personal: Educated at Oxford University (BA, 1974). Born 30th March 1953. Leisure pursuits include travel. Lives in London.

STEPHENSON, Geoffrey
2-3 Gray's Inn Square (Anthony Scrivener QC), London (0171) 242 4986
Recommended in the following lists: Consumer Law, Planning
Specialisation: Local government and public law with particular emphasis on planning local government finance and administration, housing and consumer and environmental law.
Prof. Memberships: Planning and Environment Bar Association. Administrative Law Bar Association. Parliamentary Bar Association Fellow of the Chartered Insurance Institute.

STERLING, Robert
St. James's Chambers (R.A. Sterling), Manchester (0161) 834 7000
Recommended in Chancery
Specialisation: Chancery with emphasis on commercial litigation, corporate and personal insolvency and professional negligence. Recently reported cases: White v Richards (1993) 68 P & C.R. 105; Griffiths v Yorkshire Bank Plc (1994) I.W.L.R. 1427; Alsop Wilkinson v Neary (1996) I.W.L.R. 1220; Ross v. Telford The Times July 4th 1997 C.A.
Prof. Memberships: Chancery Bar Association, Northern Chancery Bar Association, Professional Negligence Bar Association, Northern Circuit Commercial Bar Association.
Career: Head of Chambers, Chairman of Northern Chancery Bar Association 1994-1997. Acts as arbitrator in commercial disputes.

STERN, Ian M.
Queen Elizabeth Building (David Jeffreys QC & Peter Whiteman QC), London (0171) 583 5766
Recommended in Crime: Fraud
Specialisation: Fraud: involved in a number of large fraud cases. Disciplinary Tribunals: appeared at a number of professional bodies – most regularly at the General Optical Council. Serious Crime: Murder; attempted murder; rape, drugs and firearms offences.
Prof. Memberships: Member of the Criminal Bar Association, South East Circuit and a number of local Bar Messes. Called to the New South Wales Bar, Australia in 1989.
Personal: Married to a G.P. and has three daughters. Runs on a fairly regular basis and completed the London Marathon in 1992.

STERN, Linda QC
18 Red Lion Court (Anthony Arlidge QC), London (0171) 520 6000
Recommended in Crime
Specialisation: Criminal Law, particularly sexual offences and child abuse.
Prof. Memberships: Fellow of the Royal Society for the Encouragement of Arts, Manufacturers and Commerce. Member of the Forensic Science Society.
Career: Called to the Bar by Gray's Inn, July 1971: Recorder 1990: Queen's Counsel 1991. D.T.I. Inspector: Chairman of Police Appeals Tribunals.

STERNBERG, Michael
4 Paper Buildings (Lionel Swift QC), London (0171) 583 0816
Recommended in Family: Child Care including child abduction
Specialisation: All aspects of family and family-related law including matrimonial, finance, Children Act applications, international abduction, wardship, disputes between unmarried persons, Inheritance Act claims, applications to remove children from jurisdiction, and child law with specific reference to sexual abuse and contested adoptions. Matrimonial finance work includes investigation of overseas trusts and companies and all aspects of membership of Lloyd's in divorce settlements. Recent cases include the highly publicised residence case concerning a Zulu boy where the official solicitor instructed, ancillary relief cases where assets were substantial, and cases of murder of one parent by another. Clients have included entertainers, publishers, politicians, industrialists, and the Official Solicitor to the Supreme Court.
Prof. Memberships: Family Law Bar Association. Assistant Secretary Family Law Bar Association 1986-1988.
Career: Called to the Bar 1975 and joined 3 Dr. Johnson's Buildings. Moved to present chambers in 1994.
Personal: Educated at Carmel College, Wallingford 1962-70, Queen's College, Cambridge 1970-74. (MA, LL.M). Governor of North London Collegiate School, Trustee of Sternberg Charitable Settlement. Freeman of the City of London and Member of the Worshipful Company of Horners. Member of Reform Club and City Livery Club. Born 12th September 1951.

STEVENSON, William QC
One Paper Buildings (John Slater QC), London (0171) 583 7355
Recommended in the following lists: Health & Safety, Personal Injury
Specialisation: Principal area of practice involves product, public and employers' liability, occupation-related diseases and disorders including legionella pneumophilia, asthmas, asbestos-related diseases and disorders, upper limb disorders, cancers and noise induced hearing loss. Has acted in RSI claims by ceramic, banking and electronics industry employees and toxic shock syndrome claims against sanitary protection manufacturers. Has chaired and addressed conferences and seminars on occupational diseases. Other reported personal injury cases include Cox v HCB Angus [1991] ICR 687 (construction of s. 29 Factories Act 1961), Kenning v Eve Construction [1989] 1 WLR 118 (disclosure of expert report) and Gaskill v Preston [1981] 3 All ER 427 (deductibility of Family Income Supplement from claim for loss of earnings) and Hunter v Butler (1995) Kemp Vol. 1 25-008/1 (black economy earnings in Fatal Accidents claims). Other major cases encompass air handling and ventilation problems and product liability claims including Aswan Engineering v Lupdine [1987] WLR 1 (C.A) (plastic containers).
Prof. Memberships: London Common Law and Commercial Bar Association.
Career: Called to the Bar 1968 and joined present chambers in 1969. Appointed Recorder in 1992.

Personal: Educated at Marlborough College 1957-61. Evan Williams Exhibitioner at Trinity College Oxford 1962-65 (MA 1969). Admitted Lincoln's Inn 1962 – Hardwicke and Droop Scholarships. Honourable Artillery Company 1965-81 (TD 1980). Leisure pursuits include country sports, skiing and sailing. Born 17th October 1943. Lives in London.

STEWART, James QC
Park Court Chambers (James Stewart QC, Robert Smith QC), Leeds (0113) 243 3277
Recommended in Crime
Specialisation: Crime, commercial fraud. Representative cases; R v Cheshire 93 W App R 251 (causation in murder). R v Tandy 87 Cr. App. R 45 (alcoholism as a basis of diminished responsibility). R v Ali 1993 2 ALLER 409 (bugged cell confessions) R v Camplin 1978 AC 705 (provocation).
Career: Call 1966; Bencher Inner Temple 1993. Head of Chambers. Appointments – Recorder 1982. Deputy High Court Judge 1993. Approved to sit at Central Criminal Court 1990. QC 1982.

STEWART, Lindsey
7 Stone Buildings (Charles Aldous QC), London (0171) 405 3886
Recommended in Company
Specialisation: Specialises in Chancery and commercial litigation. Practice covers company law, corporate and personal insolvency, banking, civil fraud, credit and security, professional negligence and trusts.Cases include: Alsop Wilkinson & Ors v. Neary & Ors [1995]; Fuji Finance Inc v. Aetna Insurance Co Ltd & Anor [1995]; Re: SN Group plc [1993]; Dubai Bank Ltd v. Galadari [1992]; Derby & Co Ltd & Ors v. Weldon & Ors [1991]; Re K (QB) (Restraint Order) [1989]; Montagu Trust Co (Jersey) Ltd & Ors v. Inland Revenue Commissioners [1989]; Attorney-General of the Bahamas v. Royal Trust Co & Anor [1986].
Prof. Memberships: Chancery Bar Association; Faculty of Advocates.
Career: Called to the Bar 1983. Tenant at Queen Elizabeth Building 1985-1990. Called to the Scottish Bar 1990. Joined present chambers 1991.
Personal: Educated at Harris Academy, Dundee 1973-1979 and University College, Oxford 1979-1982. Born 24th April 1961. Lives in London.

STEWART, Neill A.
Queen Elizabeth Building (David Jeffreys QC & Peter Whiteman QC), London (0171) 583 5766
Recommended in Crime: Fraud
Specialisation: All crime, in particular Fraud, both for the prosecution and the defence. Cases include Savings and Investment Bank (Isle of Man) and Eagle Trust.
Prof. Memberships: Criminal Bar Association.
Career: Educated at Clare College, Cambridge BA (Mechanical Sciences Tripos) 1968. Employed by Sir Alexander Gibb and Partners, consulting civil engineers 1968 – 1970. Called to the Bar 1973.

STEWART, Nicholas QC
Hardwicke Building (Walter Aylen QC), London (0171) 242 2523
Recommended in Sports Law
E-mail: nstewart@hardwicke.co.uk
Specialisation: Most areas of civil litigation, with emphasis on Chancery and business litigation. Sports law: acted for Newport AFC and other Welsh clubs against FA of Wales [1995], Slough FC in arbitration over promotion to GM Vauxhall Conference [1995], Stevenage Borough FC against Football League [1996], Vinny Jones against Premier League [1997]. Cross-border disputes. White-collar and environmental crime. Arbitration and mediation. European Court of Human Rights.
Prof. Memberships: Chancery Bar Association; Professional Negligence Bar Association; Bar Sports Law Group; CEDR Accredited Mediator; Associate Member, Chartered Institute of Arbitrators; Certified Diploma, Chartered Association of Certified Accountants.

Career: Called 1971. Silk 1987. Deputy High Court Judge since 1991. Chairman Bar Human Rights Committee 1994-8.

STEWART, Robin QC
199 Strand (Peter Andrews QC), London (0171) 379 9779
Recommended in the following lists: Personal Injury, Professional Negligence

STEWART, Roger
2 Crown Office Row (John Powell QC), London (0171) 797 8000
Recommended in the following lists: Construction, Professional Negligence
Specialisation: Sorting wheat from chaff.
Prof. Memberships: ORBA, PNBA, COMBAR, LCLCBA
Career: MA LLM, Editor Chapter 2 of Jackson and Powell on Professional Negligence (Architects and Engineers)

STEWART, Stephen QC
Byrom Street Chambers (B.A. Hytner QC), Manchester (0161) 829 2100
Recommended in Commercial (litigation)
Specialisation: Insurance, Professional Negligence, Sales of Goods, General Contractual Disputes.
Prof. Memberships: Northern Circuit Commercial Bar Association – Treasurer and Founder member. Professional Negligence Bar Association.
Career: Assistant Recorder.

STEWART SMITH, Rodney
1 New Square (Eben Hamilton QC), London (0171) 405 0884
Recommended in Traditional Chancery

STEYNOR, Alan
Keating Chambers (Richard Fernyhough QC), London (0171) 544 2600
Recommended in Construction
Specialisation: Building and engineering disputes including arbitrations; also property work including landlord and tenant; recent cases include Rotherham Metropolitan District Council v Frank Haslam Milan; Smith & Gordon Limited v John Lewis Partnership.
Career: Qualified 1975; Gray's Inn; Assistant Recorder 1991; Recorder 1996.
Personal: Brentwood School; Corpus Christi College, Cambridge (1967 BA, 1971 MA, 1992 FCI Arb). Born 1945; resides Norwich.

STILITZ, Daniel
11 King's Bench Walk (Eldred Tabachnik QC and James Goudie QC), London (0171) 632 8500
Recommended in the following lists: Alternative Dispute Resolution, Employment
Specialisation: Employment law. Other main areas of practice are public law, commercial law and environmental law.
Prof. Memberships: Employment Law Bar Associaton. Administrative Law Bar Associaton. Former COMBAR Committee Member.
Career: Called to the bar in 1992.
Personal: New College Oxford, BA (1st Class Hons). City University, MA. Born 1 August 1968.

STIMPSON, Michael
Littman Chambers (Mark Littman QC), London (0171) 404 4866
Recommended in Construction
Specialisation: All construction matters with emphasis on mechanical and civil engineering disputes, particularly in relation to public utility industries and statutory undertakers. Non-contentious drafting for developers and employers. The law relating to residential care and nursing homes. Cases: South Coast Shipping Co. Ltd. v Havant Borough Council (effect of method statements bound into contracts); Kimbell Construction Ltd. v National Rivers Authority (inaccurate quantities in contracts). Family

Management v Gray (damage to reversions of leases).
Prof. Memberships: ORBA Committee Member, External Tutor to Centre of Construction, Law and Management Kings College London, Lecturer to Water Training International.
Career: Queens College Nassau, Inns of Court School of Law. Legal Director to Federation of Civil Engineering Contractors. Many and varied cases at arbitration and in the Official Referees' Courts.
Personal: Folk, blues, country and blue grass singer/player.

STITCHER, Malcolm
199 Strand (Peter Andrews QC), London (0171) 379 9779
Recommended in Professional Negligence

STOBART, John
King Charles House (William Everard), Nottingham (0115) 941 8851
Recommended in Crime
Specialisation: CRIME including complex frauds e.g Britannia Park, R v Charlton & Ors. R v Hancock and Local Authority prosecutions (for defence). Practice also has a preponderance of sexual/violence cases.

STOCKDALE, David Andrew QC
Deans Court Chambers (H.K. Goddard QC), Manchester (0161) 834 4097
9 Bedford row, London (0171) 242 3555
Recommended in Personal Injury
Specialisation: All aspects of personal injury work, including accident, industrial disease and multi-plaintiff litigation; employer's liability; health and safety; professional negligence (in particular, medical and solicitors).
Prof. Memberships: Northern Circuit, Personal Injuries Bar Association, Professional Negligence Bar Association.
Career: Called 1975. Assistant Recorder 1990. Recorder 1993. Queen's Counsel 1995.
Personal: Educated at Giggleswick School and Pembroke College, Oxford.

STOCKDALE BT, Sir Thomas
Erskine Chambers (Richard Sykes QC), London (0171) 242 5532
Recommended in the following lists: Company, Insolvency
Specialisation: Corporate reorganisation and reconstructions including reduction of capital and schemes of arrangement. Takeovers and mergers. Schemes of arrangement in insolvency, including insolvent insurance companies.
Prof. Memberships: COMBAR. Chancery Bar Association. Law Society's Company Law Committee.
Career: Worcester College, Oxford MA. Bencher, Lincoln's Inn.

STOCKILL, David
5 Fountain Court (Anthony Barker QC), Birmingham (0121) 606 0500
Recommended in the following lists: Chancery, Commercial (litigation), Insolvency
Specialisation: Commercial and Chancery, Property, Company, Insolvency.
Prof. Memberships: Chancery Bar Association, Midland Chancery and Commercial Bar Association.
Career: Called to Bar in 1985. Door tenant at 11 New Square, Lincoln's Inn. Recent cases: Re Coca Cola v Gilbey; Secretary of State for Trade and Indusrty v Banister; Snell & Prideaux Limited v Dutton Mirrors Limited; Fisher and Gimson (Builders) Limited Application; Chaggar v Chaggar; Cooke v Cooke; Wilson Bowden v Milner.
Personal: Educated at St John's College, Cambridge (MA Cantab).

STONE, Gregory QC
4-5 Gray's Inn Square (Miss Elizabeth Appleby QC & The Hon. M. Beloff QC), London (0171) 404 5252
Recommended in the following lists: Environmental Law, Parliamentary, Planning
Specialisation: Specialises in planning, environmental and parliamentary law. Practice also covers local government, highways and administrative law. Important work includes the Channel Tunnel Rail Link Bill; Terminal 5, Heathrow; Belvedere Waste to Energy plant; M25 MSA Inquiry; M40 MSA Inquiry; British Rail (No3) Bill; Toxic Waste Incinerator Inquiries; Mucking Landfill Inquiry; Blue Water Park Regional Shopping Centre Inquiry; Hewitt's Farm Regional Shopping Centre Inquiry.
Prof. Memberships: Planning and Environment Bar Association; Parliamentary Bar Association.
Career: Called to the Bar 1976. Joined present chambers 1991. Took Silk 1994. Standing Counsel to Department of Trade and Industry for South Eastern Circuit (1989-1990).
Personal: Educated at L'Université de Rennes, France 1965, The Queen's College, Oxford 1966-1969, and Manchester University 1970-1972. Born 12th December 1946. Lives in London.

STONE, Lucy
29 Bedford Row Chambers (Peter Ralls QC), London (0171) 831 2626
Recommended in Family: Matrimonial Finance
Specialisation: Specialises in family law, principally "big money" ancillary relief cases. Has acted on behalf of a number of high-profile media clients.
Prof. Memberships: Member of Bar Council Law Reform Committee 1994 -7; and Family Law Bar Association Committee 1998-6; F v F [1996] 1 FLR 833.
Career: MA Cantab; called to the Bar in 1983.
Personal: Born 1959. Married with one child. Lives in London.

STONE, Richard QC
4 Field Court (Geoffrey Brice QC), London (0171) 440 6900
Recommended in Shipping

STONEFROST, Hilary
3/4 South Square (Michael Crystal QC), London (0171) 696 9900
Recommended in the following lists: Banking, Insolvency

STONER, Christopher
9 Old Square (Robert Reid QC), London (0171) 405 4682
Recommended in Sports Law

STOUT, Roger
18 St. John Street (Rodney C. Klevan QC), Manchester (0161) 278 1800
Recommended in Crime

STRACHAN, Mark QC
1 Crown Office Row (Mark Strachan QC), London (0171) 583 9292
Recommended in the following lists: Commercial (litigation), Personal Injury

STRAKER, Timothy QC
2-3 Gray's Inn Square (Anthony Scrivener QC), London (0171) 242 4986
Recommended in the following lists: Administrative & Public Law, Planning
Specialisation: Principal areas of practice are local government, public law and town and country planning. Has acted in many leading public law cases concerning, inter alia, compulsory purchase, planning, housing and housing benefits, Sunday trading, caravan sites and 'new age travellers', free speech, professional advertising, discrimination and professional conduct. Appeared in many Privy Council Appeals. Represented the returning officers in the first challenge to a European election

result and in the first challenge to a Parliamentary result for 70 years. Acts for many local authorities and regulatory bodies.
Prof. Memberships: Administrative Law Bar Association, Planning Bar Association, Crown Office Users' Committee.
Career: Called to the Bar 1977. Silk 1996.
Personal: Educated at Malvern College and Downing College, Cambridge (1st Class Hons). Senior Harris Scholar, Downing College Prize for Law, Holt Scholar of Gray's Inn, awarded Lord Justice Holker Senior Award. Born 25th May 1955.

STRAUSS, Nicholas QC
One Essex Court (Anthony Grabiner QC), London (0171) 583 2000
Recommended in the following lists: Administrative & Public Law, Banking, Commercial (litigation), Financial Services
Specialisation: Main areas of practice are banking, commercial, arbitration (as advocate and as arbitrator), insurance, professional negligence, financial services and regulatory work.
Prof. Memberships: South Eastern Circuit, COMBAR.
Career: Called to the Bar in 1965. Took Silk in 1984. Sits as deputy High Court Judge.
Personal: Born 29th July 1942. Educated at Highgate School and Jesus College, M.A. Cambridge (1st class Honours), B.A., LL.M.

STREATFEILD-JAMES, David
Atkin Chambers (John Blackburn QC), London (0171) 404 0102
Recommended in the following lists: Computer & I.T., Construction
Specialisation: Building and civil engineering. Experience of all the main standard forms of contract and subcontracts, together with contracts for the petrochemical industry, Process engineering, the utilities (water and electricity), Power Stations, telecommunications and computer software supply and development. In addition, general commercial related matters – financing arrangements, guarantees and bonds, sale of goods, service agreements and commercial leases. Professional Negligence. Engineers, Architects, Quantity Surveyors and surveyors and valuers. International commercial Arbitration.
Career: BA (Oxon). Called 1986

STRUDWICK, Linda D.
Queen Elizabeth Building (David Jeffreys QC & Peter Whiteman QC), London (0171) 583 5766
Recommended in Crime
Specialisation: Specialises in defence work but also handles prosecution. 24 years covering all areas of serious crime including Murder, Manslaughter, Fraud, Sexual Offences, Drug Offences.
Career: Called 1973.
Personal: Educated Manchester University.

STUART-SMITH, Jeremy QC
2 Temple Gardens (Patrick Phillips QC), London (0171) 583 6041
Recommended in Professional Negligence
Specialisation: Insurance and Insurance Related Disputes; Professional Negligence; Product Liability; General Commercial and Common Law.
Prof. Memberships: L.C.L.C.B.A., P.I.B.A.
Career: M.A. Cantab.
Personal: Playing the french horn, skiing, history, keeping sheep.

STUBBS, Andrew J.
St. Paul's Chambers (Nigel Sangster QC), Leeds (0113) 245 5866
Recommended in Crime

STUBBS, W.F. QC
Erskine Chambers (Richard Sykes QC), London (0171) 242 5532
Recommended in Insolvency

STURMAN, James
3 Hare Court (William Clegg QC), London (0171) 353 7561
Recommended in the following lists: Crime, Crime: Fraud
Specialisation: Specialist criminal defence advocate involved in many major cases. Particular expertise in fraud, also advisory work to banks on criminal matters and in "quasi criminal" tribunals. Extensive experience in the Court of Appeal criminal division particularly in cases in which did not appear in the Lower Court. Major cases include Stagg – Wimbledon Common murder. Sivalingham-Tamil Tigers. Vanduvall – financial instrument fraud. Richardson – fraud on revenue of an E.U. State. Reilly- disclosure. Callan – D.T.A. Woodward – effect of drink in reckless driving. McGovern – S76 P.A.C.E. Griffiths – abuse of process. Coswell – Timeshare fraud. Extensive experience in mortgage and diversion frauds.
Prof. Memberships: Member of Gibralter Bar. C.B.A I.B.A. B.A.F.S.
Career: Called 1982, joined Chambers 1983.
Personal: Secretary Gray's Inn F.C. Cricket.

SUCKLING, Alan B. QC
Queen Elizabeth Building (David Jeffreys QC & Peter Whiteman QC), London (0171) 583 5766
Recommended in Crime: Fraud
Specialisation: Crime and Fraud. Clowes. Maxwell. Shivpuri 1987 AC 1, Howe & Others 1987 AC 417.
Prof. Memberships: Middle Temple, Bencher. CBA.
Career: Queens' College, Cambridge MA LL.M. Harmsworth Law Scholar, Middle Temple.
Personal: b. Hong Kong 1938.

SULLIVAN, Michael
5 Bell Yard (Robert Webb QC), London (0171) 333 8811
Recommended in Banking
Specialisation: Banking, aviation finance and commercial litigation. Also professional negligence.

SULLIVAN, Rory
19 Old Buildings (Alastair Wilson QC), London (0171) 405 2001
Recommended in Computer & I.T.
Specialisation: All aspects of intellectual property law including patents, copyrights, design rights, trade marks, passing off and confidential information; matters relating to computers and other scientific and technical subject-matter, entertainment and media law; co-editor of European patent office reports; news editor of European Intellectual Property Review; languages include French and some German.
Prof. Memberships: Intellectual Property Bar Association; Chancery Bar Association.
Career: IBM UK Limited 1989-1991; called to Bar 1992.
Personal: Educated at Repton School, Derbyshire and St John's College, Oxford.

SUMNER, David
Lincoln House Chambers (Mukhtar Hussain QC), Manchester (0161) 832 5701
Recommended in Crime

SUMPTION, Jonathan QC
Brick Court Chambers (Christopher Clarke QC), London (0171) 583 0777
Recommended in the following lists: Administrative & Public Law, Banking, Commercial (litigation), Energy & Utilities, Financial Services, Insurance & Reinsurance, Media & Entertainment, Professional Negligence
Specialisation: Specialist in all areas of commercial law, including banking, corporate finance, financial services, insolvency, oil and gas, insurance and sale of goods. Practice also covers administrative law and intellectual property. Recent Cases: ADT v Binder Hamlyn; Digital Corp v Hampshire C.C.; R v ITC ex parte Virgin Television; Smith New Court v Scrimgeour Vickers.

Career: Called to the Bar 1975. Joined present chambers 1977. Took silk 1986. Appointed Recorder 1994.
Personal: Educated at Eton 1961-1966 and Magdalen College, Oxford 1967-1970. Fellow, Magdalen College, Oxford 1971-1975. Interests include history and music.

SUPPERSTONE, Michael Alan QC
11 King's Bench Walk (Eldred Tabachnik QC and James Goudie QC), London
(0171) 632 8500
Recommended in Administrative & Public Law
Specialisation: All aspects of Administrative and Public law. Other main areas of practice include employment law.
Career: Called to the Bar in 1973. Appointed Queen's Counsel 1991. Recorder 1996; Deputy High Court Judge; Chairman of Administrative Law Bar Association; Principal editor of latest edition of the administrative law title of 'Halsbury's Laws of England'; co-editor of Supperstone and Goudie on Judicial Review; consulting editor of Supperstone and O'Dempsey on Immigration and Asylum. Member of editorial committee of Public Law.
Personal: Educated at St. Paul's School and Lincoln College, Oxford (MA; BCL).

SUSMAN, Peter QC
New Court Chambers (George Carman QC), London (0171) 831 9500
Recommended in Computer & I.T.
Specialisation: Specialises in commercial contract disputes (with particular experience of computer contract disputes) and professional negligence claims (against solicitors, surveyors and valuers, mortgage brokers, accountants and architects). His versatile previous experience of common law and chancery cases, together with 18 months working as an associate with the leading New York law firm of Debevoise & Plimpton (he also has a law degree from the University of Chicago), leads to him being instructed in cases which cover more than one area of expertise.
Prof. Memberships: Professional Negligence Bar Association (PNBA). London Common Law Bar Association, Society for Computers and Law.
Career: Called 1966, took silk 1997. Associate with Debevoise & Plimpton, Attorneys, New York City, USA 1970-72. Joined current Chambers 1967. Appointed Recorder 1993.
Personal: Educated Dulwich College 1953-61, Lincoln College, Oxford 1961-64 (Oldfield Scholar and BA 1964, MA 1969) and University of Chicago Law School, 1964-65 (British Commonwealth Fellow and Fulbright Scholar, JD 1965). Leisure pursuits include clarinet, squash, windsurfing and skiing. Born 20th February 1943.

SUSSEX, Charles
4 Essex Court (Nigel Teare QC), London
(0171) 797 7970
Recommended in Shipping
Specialisation: Practice encompasses Shipping, Insurance, Banking and International Trade. Includes advisory work and advocacy both in the Commercial and Admiralty Courts, arbitration, and on appeal. Other main area of work is Hong Kong Law, appearing in the Hong Kong High Court, Court of Final Appeal and in arbitrations in Hong Kong and elsewhere overseas.
Prof. Memberships: Western Circuit; COMBAR; Hong Kong Bar Association.
Career: Admitted as a solicitor 1976 and in practice 1976-82. Called to the Bar 1982. Called to the Hong Kong Bar 1983, and in full-time practice at the Bar of Hong Kong 1983-89. Called to the New South Wales Bar 1989. Joined 4 Essex Court 1989.
Personal: Educated at St. Peter's School, Southborne 1962-1969, King's College, London 1970-73 (LL.B 1973) and College of Law, Lancaster Gate 1974. Born 9th July 1951. Lives in Binley, Hampshire.

SUTCLIFFE, Andrew
3 Verulam Buildings (R. Neville Thomas QC), London (0171) 831 8441
Recommended in Media & Entertainment
Fax: (0171) 831 8479.
Specialisation: Commercial and chancery litigation; in particular media and entertainment law (appeared in leading cases Elton John v Dick James and Zang Tumb Tuum v Holly Johnson), intellectual property, banking and professional negligence. Clients include artistes, producers, major record and publishing companies, clearing and merchant banks. Also acts as arbitrator in commercial and IP matters.
Prof. Memberships: COMBAR, London Common Law and Commercial Bar Association, Chancery Bar Association.
Career: Called to the Bar 1983. Joined Verulam Buildings 1984.
Personal: Educated at Winchester College and Worcester College Oxford. Born 7th September 1960. Lives in London and Yorkshire.

SUTTLE, Stephen
1 Brick Court (Richard Hartley QC), London
(0171) 353 8845
Recommended in Defamation

SUTTON, Alastair
Blackstone Chambers (formerly 2 Hare Court) (P Baxendale QC and C Flint QC), London
(0171) 583 1770
Recommended in European Union/Competition
Specialisation: Specialist in all aspects of European Community law and international trade law. Current practice can be divided into advisory work and litigation. Undertakes advisory work for governments, companies and trade associations on all areas of EC Law and on external relations with other countries, in particular Japan, Central and Eastern Europe, the EFTA states and North America. Also advises on the internal market, trade policy, competition and state aids, intellectual property, telecommunications, financial services, audiovisual policy, environmental protection and social policy. Also covers advisory work on international trade law within GATT/WTO. Contentious work includes representing clients in the European Court of Justice. Acted for the applicants in the following cases: Liberal Democrats v European Parliament (action for failure to act); Ferchimex S.A. v Commission (antidumping); and Titan Cement v Commission (state aids). Also acted for the applicants in the EFTA Court in Scottish Salmon Growers Association v EFTA (state aids). Publications include 'Trends in the Regulation of International Trade in Textiles', 'Yearbook of World Affairs', 1977; 'Relations between the European Community and Japan in 1982 & 1983', 'Oxford Yearbook of European Law', 1983; 'Financial Services and Competition Policy' Butterworth's Competition Law, 1998; Butterworth's European Law Service, 1992 (co-editor); 'EC Insurance Law', Butterworth, 1992; Commentary on EC legal developments in 1992 in Butterworth's Annual European Review, 1993; and 'European Union and the Rule of Law in Maastricht and Beyond' (The Federal Trust, 1994).
Career: Called to the Bar 1972. Lecturer in EC and Public International Law, University College, London 1967-73. Commission of the European Communities 1973-89. EC negotiator for textiles agreements 1973-77. First Secretary, Commission Delegation in Japan 1979-84. Principal administrator for international trade policy in the Directorate-General for External Relations, 1984-85. Member of Cabinet of Lord Cockfield, Vice-President of the European Commission, 1985-88. Head of Division for Insurance, EC Commission, 1989. Since 1990, partner in the firm White & Case, Brussels, and a barrister at current chambers. Visiting Fellow, Centre for European Legal Studies, Faculty of Law, University of Cambridge, 1993-94. Visiting Fellow (Parsons Fellowship), Faculty of Law, University of Sydney, Australia.

Personal: Educated at Aberdeen University (LL.B) 1963-66, and at University College, London (LL.M & Diploma in International and Comparative Air and Space Law) 1966-67. Languages include French, Spanish and Japanese. Leisure pursuits include golf, squash and rugby. Born 6th January 1945. Lives in Brussels and London.

SUTTON, Mark
4 Field Court (Geoffrey Brice QC), London (0171) 440 6900
Recommended in Employment
Specialisation: Practice covers all aspects of employment law, particularly in connection with financial services, airlines and universities. Also undertakes professional negligence cases.
Career: Called to the Bar 1982
Personal: BA Hons, Dip Law. Born 25th June 1958.

SUTTON, Richard QC
18 Red Lion Court (Anthony Arlidge QC), London (0171) 520 6000
Recommended in Crime

SWAIN, Jon
Furnival Chambers (Andrew Mitchell), London (0171) 405 3232
Recommended in Crime

SWAINSTON, Michael
Brick Court Chambers (Christopher Clarke QC), London (0171) 583 0777
Recommended in Financial Services
Specialisation: California Bar 1988. MA (Cantab) BCL (Oxon). General commercial practice including financial services (litigation and disciplinary tribunals). Banking insurance and international trade, shipping.
Career: Called in 1985. Tenant Brick Court Chambers [1991]. Cases of note: Axa v Field, Cox v Bankside; Giles v Thompson; Chairman v Woc, BROWN v GIO; Golden Eagle Refinery v Associated International Insurance.

SWEENEY, Nigel
6 King's Bench Walk (Michael Worsley QC), London (0171) 583 0410
Recommended in Crime

SWIFT, Caroline QC
Byrom Street Chambers (B.A. Hytner QC), Manchester (0161) 829 2100
Recommended in Personal Injury

SWIFT, Jonathan Mark
11 King's Bench Walk (Eldred Tabachnik QC and James Goudie QC), London
(0171) 632 8500
Recommended in Employment
Specialisation: Specialises in all aspects of employment and trade union law including dismissal, discrimination, collective disputes and European law appearing both for applicants and respondents. Employment practice also includes restraint of trade, confidential information and interlocutory injunctions. Other practice areas include public and adminstrative law, and local government law with a particular emphasis on education law matters.
Prof. Memberships: Employment Law Bar Association; Employment Lawyers Association; Industrial Law Society; Discrimination Law Association; COMBAR; Administrative Law Bar Association.
Career: Called to the Bar in 1989; joined present chambers in the same year.
Personal: Educated at New College, Oxford (BA(Hons) Jurisprudence) and Emmanuel College, Cambridge (LLM). Born 11th September 1964. Lives in London.

SWIFT, Lionel QC

4 Paper Buildings (Lionel Swift QC), London
(0171) 583 0816

*Recommended in the following lists: Family:
Child Care including child abduction*

Specialisation: Practice encompasses all areas of
family law, commercial crime, and he does general
common law work.

Prof. Memberships: Bencher, Inner Temple since
1984.

Career: Solicitor, Natal, South Africa, 1954. Called
to the Bar 1959 and joined present chambers in
1961. Took Silk in 1975. Appointed Recorder in
1979.

Personal: Educated at University College, London
(LL.B 1951), Brasenose College, Oxford (BCL
1959) and University of Chicago Law School (J.D.
1960). Born Bristol, 3rd October 1931.

SWIFT QC, Malcolm QC

Park Court Chambers (James Stewart QC,
Robert Smith QC), Leeds (0113) 243 3277
Fax (0113) 243 1285
DX 26401 Leeds Park Square

Recommended in Crime

E-mail: malswiftqc@aol.com
Also at: 6 Gray's Inn Square (Michael Boardman)
London (0171) 242 1052 Fax: (0171) 405 4934
DX: LDE 224 Chancery Lane

Prof. Memberships: Leader of the North Eastern
Circuit (January 1998-) Member of the Bar Council
(January 1997-)

Career: LLB; AKC (Kings College London). Called
to the Bar Trinity 1970 – Grays Inn. Recorder of the
Crown Court (1987-). Queens Counsel (1988).

SYKES, Richard QC

Erskine Chambers (Richard Sykes QC), London
(0171) 242 5532

*Recommended in the following lists: Banking,
Company, Financial Services, Insolvency*

SYMONS, Christopher QC

3 Verulam Buildings (R. Neville Thomas QC),
London (0171) 831 8441

*Recommended in the following lists: Insurance
& Reinsurance, Professional Negligence*

Specialisation: Commercial work with emphasis
on Insurance and Reinsurance and Professional
Negligence. Appeared in many commercial court
cases and arbitrations for and against insurance
companies, reinsurers, Lloyd's syndicates, brokers
and other professionals. Recent cases include
acting for Willis Corroon in their successful defence
of claim brought by Kuwait Airways; acting for
Ernst and Young in their successful defence of
action brought against them by NRG concerning
the acquisition of Victory Re, acting for John D.
Wood in BBL at first instance advancing the
argument, accepted by Phillips J. and later by the
House of Lords, that valuers should not be liable
for losses arising from a fall in the property market.
Increasingly involved in Environmental Law
particularly environmental warranty claims and
landfill problems. Aviation. Town & Country
Planning. Carved out small niche in acting in rugby
accident cases successfully defending Bedford
School in the Van Oppen case and successfully
defending the front row prop in the Smoldon case.

Career: Called to the Bar in 1972; Junior Counsel
to the Crown (Common Law) 1985-1989; Took silk
1989; Recorder 1993. Deputy High Court Judge
1998.

TABACHNIK, Eldred QC

11 King's Bench Walk (Eldred Tabachnik Q.C.
and James Goudie Q.C.), London
(0171) 632 8500

*Recommended in the following lists:
Employment, Planning*

Specialisation: Principal area of practice is
employment law. Has appeared in numerous
matters for individuals, trade unions, multi-national
businesses, local authorities and employer's
federations in the areas of unfair dismissal,
wrongful dismissal, discrimination, collective
disputes, restraint of trade, European law relating
to employment.

Prof. Memberships: ALBA; COMBAR: London
Common Law and Commercial Bar Association.

Career: Called to the Bar 1970; Appointed
Queen's Counsel 1982; Assistant Recorder 1995;
Master of the Bench, Inner Temple 1998.

Personal: Educated at University of Cape Town
and London University (LLM).

TABOR, James QC

Albion Chambers (J.C.T. Barton QC), Bristol
(0117) 927 2144

Recommended in Crime

TACKABERRY, John QC

Arbitration Chambers (John Tackaberry QC),
London (0171) 267 2137

*Recommended in the following lists: Alternative
Dispute Resolution, Arbitration, Construction*

Specialisation: QC (England and Wales, New
South Wales, United Nation Commissioner chairing
Gulf War Compensation Dispute Panel. Building
and Civil Engineering Litigation and arbitration,
both in the UK and internationally. Increasingly
involved in arbitration and was first QC to appear
on List of Arbitrators of all three of the following
organisations: Institute of Civil Engineers, Royal
Institute of British Architects and the Chartered
Institute of Arbitrators. Arbitrations are primarily in
construction field but also include commodity and
shipping disputes and arbitrations under French
and Swiss law. Co-author of 'Construction Contract
Dictionary', contributor to 'Liability of Contractors'
(1986); specialist editor for the first and second
edition of the 'Handbook of Arbitration Practice'
(1987, 1993), and a principal editor for the third
edition (1998). Author of articles for specialist legal
publications. Frequent contributor to conferences
and courses run by, inter alia, the Chartered
Institute of Arbitrators, National Federation of
Building Trades Employers and Federation of Civil
Engineering Contractors, as well as other
conferences for individual companies and
management organisations.

Prof. Memberships: Fellow of Chartered Institute
of Arbitrators (Chairman), Society of Construction
Arbitrators, Society of Construction Law (first
President), European Society of Construction law
(President 1985-87), American Arbitration
Association, Supporting Member of London
Maritime Arbitrators' Association.

Career: Called to the Bar 1967. Took silk 1982.
Admitted to the Irish Bar 1987. Appointed Recorder
1988. Admitted to practice at the Bar of California
1988. Admitted to practice at the New South Wales
Bar 1989, and took silk 1990. Admitted to Panel of
International Arbitrators, Indian Council of
Arbitration 1991. Appointed member of Panel of
Accredited Arbitrators, Singapore International
Arbitration 1992. Elected UK Jurisdiction Council
member of the Interpacific Bar Association (Tokyo)
1993. 1997-2000 appointed as an arbitrator on
panel of China International Economic and Trade
Arbitration Commission. 1998 appointed – United
Nations Commissioner – Chairman of.

Personal: Educated at Downside School,
Somerset 1952-58; Trinity College, Dublin 1958-59
(Economics/French) and Downing College,
Cambridge 1959-63 (BA Law 1963, MA 1969).
Born 13th November 1939.

TAGGART, Nicholas

4 Breams Buildings (Christopher Lockhart-
Mummery QC), London
(0171) 430 1221/353 5835

Recommended in Property Litigation

Specialisation: All aspects of property law,
including landlord and tenant, conveyancing on
property related professional negligence matters.
Also specialist editor of Hill and Redman's Law of
Landlord and Tenant.

Prof. Memberships: Member of Chancery Bar
Association.

Career: Called to the Bar 1991.

TAIT, Andrew

2 Harcourt Buildings (Mr Gerard Ryan QC),
London (0171) 353 8415

Recommended in Parliamentary

Specialisation: Main areas of practice are
parliamentary, planning, environmental,
administrative and local government work.

Prof. Memberships: Parliamentary Bar; Planning &
Environment Bar Association. Administrative Law
Bar Association.

Career: Called to the Bar in 1981 and joined 2
Harcourt Buildings in 1982.

Personal: Educated at Hertford College, Oxford.
Born 18th May 1957.

TALBOT, Patrick QC

Serle Court Chambers (Charles Sparrow QC
QC), London (0171) 242 6105

*Recommended in the following lists:
Commercial (litigation), Chancery, Sports Law*

Specialisation: Chancery/Commercial Litigation
and advice, including commercial fraud,
commercial and agricultural property, banking and
credit, professional negligence, sports law,
charities, computer law, insolvency, trusts and
probate.

Prof. Memberships: Chancery Bar Association,
British Association for Sport and Law.

Career: Joined Serle Court Chambers 1970, QC
1990. Recorder.

TALBOT RICE, Elspeth

24 Old Buildings (C.A. Brodie QC), London
(0171) 404 0946

Recommended in Insolvency

Specialisation: Commercial Chancery Litigation,
including in particular: insolvency (both corporate
and personal); company; property, including
commercial landlord and tenant, mortgages and
other securities; professional negligence; trusts;
probate; partnership; financial services and
general business based disputes including fraud
and tracing. Notable cases: Arab bank Plc v
Mercantile Holdings Ltd [1994] Ch 71 (Financial
assisitance in a company's purchase of shares).
Re Oasis Merchandising Services Ltd (Ward v
Aitken and ORS) [1995] BCC 911 [1997] BCC 282
CA (Liquidator's wrongful trading claim funded by
champertous agreement). Hocking v Walker [1997]
BPIR 712 (Power of trustee in bankruptcy required
production of privileged documents). Rey v
Government of Switzerland [1998] 3 WLR 1, PC
(extradition on charges of corporate fraud and
bankruptcy offences).

Prof. Memberships: Chancery Bar Association,
Insolvency Lawyers Association.

Career: Durham University (BA Hons). Call 1990.

Personal: Married with two ponies. Active
sportswoman.

TAMLYN, Lloyd

3/4 South Square (Michael Crystal QC), London
(0171) 696 9900

Recommended in Insolvency

Specialisation: Insolvency; company; professional
negligence; instructed on KWELM insurance
insolvencies and professional negligence actions;
Kempe v Ambassador Insurance (Privy Council)
[1998] BCC 311B (insurance insolveny and
schemes of arrangement); Tam Wing Chuen v
BCCI (Privy Council) [1996] 2 BCLC 69 (insolvency
set-off); Mutual Reinsurance v Peat Marwick [1997]
1 BCLC 1 (Court of Appeal: auditor's negligence);
Re Structures and Computers Limited [1998] BCC
348. Contributor to Halsbury's Laws of England,
Volumes 7(2) and (3); Lightman and Moss, Law of
Receivers of Companies; Insolvency of Banks (Ed.
Opitah).

Career: Scholarship to Pembroke College,
Cambridge; Double first; Prizes for best results in
finals year, including two individual Best Script
Prizes in Commercial Law and Contract & Tort II
Papers; employed by Law Commission 1987.

TANSEY, Rock QC
3 Gray's Inn Square (Rock Tansey QC), London
(0171) 520 5600
Recommended in Crime
Specialisation: Specialist Criminal Defence Silk with considerable expertise and experience in the conduct of the gravest cases in particular, Human Rights, Terrorism, Espionage, Murder, Serious Fraud, Drug Trafficking and 'Organised Crime'. Most notable cases include the Attempted Assassination of the Israeli Ambassador, the Tottenham Riots which concerned the murder of PC Blakelock, the Blackmail of Heinz Plc, a Conspiracy to post incendiary devices to Ministers of State, numerous Terrorist Cases (eg. the Brighton and Warrington 'Bombings') and uniquely the trading of State Secrets by a KGB Spy. Appeared in the recently concluded trial of a Palestinian Group charged with bombing the Israeli Embassy in London. Accomplishments in the sphere of Human Rights comprise inter alia; the representation of the Directorate of Human Rights of the Council of Europe at a Conference in St Petersburg, Russia 1994; and very recently the formation, chairmanship and organisation of the inaugural Conference (at the E.H.C.R., Strasbourg in May 1997) of the European Criminal Bar Association in order to advance major legal issues of mutual concern among European Defence Lawyers.
Prof. Memberships: South Eastern Circuit, Criminal Bar Association (Committee member 1990-96), IBA, Chairman of the European Criminal Bar Association 1997.
Career: Called to the Bar 1966 and Head of Chambers 1988.
Personal: Educated at Bristol University – LL.B and Diploma in Social Studies

TAPPIN, Michael
8 New Square (Michael Fysh QC), London
(0171) 405 4321
Recommended in Intellectual Property
Specialisation: Specialises in all aspects of intellectual property law, but with a particular interest in chemical, pharmaceutical and biotechnological work. Co-editor of 'Encyclopaedia of United Kingdom and European Patent Law'. Recent cases include: 'Boehringer v Amgen' (Biotechnology patents, Issue estoppel); 'Microsoft v Electro-wide' (Copyright, summary judgment); 'Norton v 3M' (patents, metered dose inhaler; 'Harrison v Lingasong' (performer's rights); 'Petrolite v Dyas' (patent, summary judgment), 'Allied Colloids v Cytec' (Patent, flocculating agent); 'Kitechnology v Unicor' (Confidential information, Brussels Convention); 'BSkyB v Lyons' (Unauthorised decoders, EC Law); 'Coca Cola v Gilbey' (Counterfeiting, contempt of Court).
Prof. Memberships: Intellectual Property Bar Association.
Career: Called to the Bar and joined current chambers in 1991.
Personal: Educated at Cheltenham Grammar School 1975-82; St. John's College, Oxford 1982-87; Merton College, Oxford 1987-89; BA 1st Class Hons in Chemistry, D.Phil in Biochemistry. Born 11th November 1964.

TATTERSALL, Geoffrey QC
Byrom Street Chambers (B.A. Hytner QC), Manchester (0161) 829 2100
22 Old Buildings Lincoln's Inn, London
(0171) 831 0222
Recommended in Personal Injury
Specialisation: Principal areas of practice are personal injury claims involving severe and permanent disablement and professional negligence. Other areas include commercial litigation, insurance, administrative law and judicial review, civil claims against the police and general common law.
Prof. Memberships: Personal Injury Bar Association.
Career: Recorder 1989. Queen's Counsel 1992.

Senior Counsel New South Wales 1995. Bencher of Lincoln's Inn 1997. The Judge of Appeal of the Isle of Man 1997.
Personal: Born 1947. Educated Manchester Grammar School and Christ Church Oxford.

TATTERSALL, Simon
Fenners Chambers (Lindsay Davies), Cambridge (01223) 368761
Recommended in Family/Matrimonial

TAUBE, Simon
10 Old Square (Leolin Price CBE QC), London
(0171) 405 0758
Recommended in Traditional Chancery
Specialisation: Specialising in Chancery work (both litigation and advisory work) with special expertise in the fields of trusts, estates and tax, professional negligence, charity, real property, Inheritance Act claims; important cases include Berill v IRC (1981), Re: Trafford (1985), Moore v IRC (1985), Re: Bunning (1984), Sinclair v Lee (1993), Re: Hobley (1997), Keane v Martin (1997).
Prof. Memberships: Member Chancery Bar Association, STEP and Working Party Trust Law Committee.
Career: Westminster School; Merton College, Oxford (1978 Modern History 1st class), Called 1980, Middle Temple and Lincoln's Inn.
Personal: Choral singing, tennis.

TAUSSIG, Anthony
Wilberforce Chambers (Edward Nugee QC), London (0171) 306 0102
Recommended in the following lists: Property Litigation, Traditional Chancery
Specialisation: Equity and trusts, land/conveyancing, revenue, pensions, financial services, charities, housing associations.
Career: Called to the Bar 1966. Conveyancing Counsel of the Court since 1991. Publication: 'Housing associations and their committees'. A guide to the legal framework. 1992.
Personal: Educated at Winchester College and Magdalen College, Oxford.

TAVERNER, Marcus
Keating Chambers (Richard Fernyhough QC), London (0171) 544 2600
Recommended in the following lists: Arbitration, Construction, Professional Negligence
Specialisation: Construction and engineering; professional negligence; bonds and securities; sits as arbitrator in domestic and international disputes.
Career: Qualified 1981; Gray's Inn.
Personal: Monmouth School; Leicester University; King's College, London (1979 LLB Hons, 1980 LLM). Interests, music, drama, literature, sport, trees. Born 1958; resides Benington.

TAYLER, James
Devereux Chambers (Jeffrey Burke QC), London (0171) 353 7534
Recommended in Employment
Specialisation: Employment; Discrimination; Administrative and Local Government. Cases of interest include; ECM v Cox; the Times 10/10/98 Thompson v Walon and BRS Automotive [1997] IRLR 343 EAT; BSG Property Services v Tuck [1996] IRLR 134 EAT (transfers of undertakings) and Allen v Redbridge LBC [1994] 1 WLR 139 DC (Trading Standards).
Prof. Memberships: ELBA (Committee member); ILS; ELA; ALBA; LCLCBA (Committee member)
Career: Wadham College Oxford; BA (Hons) Biology (1983-1986): PCL (1987-1988); CPE: ICSL Bar Finals (1988-1989). [Qeen Mother Scholarship; CLE Studentship]. Contributor to Dix on Contracts of Employment (Butterworths 1997). Currently writing for Butterworths Discrimination Law. Regular journal articles and conference appearances.

TAYLOR, Debbie
Hardwicke Building (Walter Aylen QC), London
(0171) 242 2523
Recommended in Family: Child Care including child abduction
Specialisation: International family law; disputes including child abduction, divorce and the cross-jurisdiction enforcement of financial orders. Australian and Indian family law matters. Mental Health related private and public law applications and child protection.
Career: Called 1984. Solicitor and Barrister Western Australia – 1990. Legal Member, Mental Health Review. Tribunals – 1994.

TAYLOR, Gregg
9 Park Place (Ian Murphy QC), Cardiff
(01222) 382731
Recommended in Crime

TAYLOR, John QC
2 Mitre Court Buildings (Michael FitzGerald QC), London (0171) 583 1380
Recommended in Planning
Specialisation: Practice includes Town and Country Planning, compulsory purchase and compensation, environmental, and public and administrative law – high profile cases include: extension to Whately Quarry, Coin Street, Merry Hill Shopping Centre and Howlett Zoo (Tigers Case).
Career: Called to the Bar 1958. QC 1983. MA, LL.B (Cantab) LL.M. (Harvard).
Personal: Married, 1 daughter. Lives at Clifton, Beds.

TAYLOR, Martin
6 King's Bench Walk (Sibghat Kadri QC), London (0171) 353 4931 /583 0695
Recommended in Crime

TAYLOR, Simon W.
Cloisters (Laura Cox QC), London
(0171) 827 4000
Recommended in Medical Negligence
Specialisation: Specialises in medical law, including medical negligence, medical disciplinary work, mental health work, health service administrative law, inquests and defamation and criminal cases involving medical disputes.
Prof. Memberships: Professional Negligence Bar Association; British Academy of Forensic Sciences; Society of Doctors In Law; British Medical Association.
Career: Qualified doctor. Called to the Bar 1984. Joined present chambers 1998.
Personal: Educated at Cambridge (BA Hons) 1983. MB BChir 1987. Born 4th July 1962. Lives in Sussex.

TEARE, Nigel QC
4 Essex Court (Nigel Teare QC), London
(0171) 797 7970
Recommended in the following lists: Arbitration, Shipping
Specialisation: General Commercial work with particular emphasis on Carriage of Goods, Sale of Goods, Ship Finance and all aspects of Shipping law.
Prof. Memberships: COMBAR.
Career: Junior Counsel to Treasury in Admiralty Matters 1987-91. Queen's Counsel 1991. Recorder (Crown Court) 1997. Lloyd's Salvage Arbitrator 1995.
Personal: Educated: King William's College, Isle of Man. St. Peter's College, Oxford.

TECKS, Jonathan
Littman Chambers (Mark Littman QC), London
(0171) 404 4866
Recommended in Alternative Dispute Resolution
Specialisation: Practice covers commercial and construction disputes as counsel, arbitrator and mediator. Counsel in cross-border litigation 'Kleinmort Benson v City of Glasgow' (ECJ/HL). Co-author of 'The Arbitration Act 1996 – A Commentary' published by Blackwell Science in September 1996. Lecturer and speaker on

arbitration and alternative dispute resolution topics. Conducts community mediations with Mediation Somerset.
Prof. Memberships: Fellow, Panel Member and Professional Committee Member of Chartered Institute of Arbitrators. Member of Financial Services and ABTA Scheme Panels. Member of European Network for Dispute Resolution. Member of LCIA. Founder Member of City Disputes Panel. CEDR Accredited Mediator.
Career: Haberdashers' Aske's School and Selwyn College, Cambridge. Called 1978 and practising since then. Littman Chambers from 1995.
Personal: Located in London and Somerset. Married with two children. Fluent French and German, basic Italian and Hebrew. Interests include horse riding, cycling and the guitar.

TEDD, Rex QC
St Philip's Chambers (Rex Tedd QC), Birmingham (0121) 246 7000
Recommended in Crime

TEGGIN, Victoria
Mitre House Chambers (Francis P. Gilbert), London (0171) 583 8233
Recommended in Civil Liberties

TEMPLE, Anthony QC
4 Pump Court (Bruce Mauleverer QC), London (0171) 353 2656
Recommended in the following lists: Commercial (litigation), Insurance & Reinsurance, Professional Negligence
Specialisation: Principal areas of practice are insurance and reinsurance, commercial finance, stock exchange and Lloyd's disciplinary enquiries, banking, gaming lotteries and licensing. Also, common law cases of all sorts particularly professional negligence and construction.
Prof. Memberships: COMBAR, London Common Law and Commercial Bar Association, ORBA, Professional Negligence Bar Association.
Career: Called to the Bar in 1968; took silk in 1986. Recorder 1986. Deputy High Court Judge 1994.
Personal: MA (Oxon) Jurisprudence.

TEMPLE, Victor QC
6 King's Bench Walk (Michael Worsley QC), London (0171) 583 0410
Recommended in the following lists: Crime, Crime: Fraud
Specialisation: Company Fraud.
Career: Senior Treasury Counsel at the Central Criminal Court 1989-1992. A D.T.I. Inspector into the Affairs of National Westminster Bank, 1992. A Chairman of Police Disciplinary Tribunals 1993 on. Recorder of the Crown Court. Elected a master of the Bench, Inner Temple, 1996.

TEMPLEMAN, Mark
Essex Court Chambers (Gordon Pollock QC), London (0171) 813 8000
Recommended in Insurance & Reinsurance
Specialisation: Insurance and reinsurance, shipping, international sale of goods and international trade finance, in the context of both domestic and international litigation and arbitration. Also general commercial litigation of all types.
Career: Keble College, Oxford MA (Jurisprudence); BCL (1980). Inns of Court, 1979. Called to the Bar 1981.
Personal: Born 1958.

TER HAAR, Roger QC
2 Crown Office Row (Graeme Hamilton QC), London (0171) 797 8100
Recommended in the following lists: Construction, Professional Negligence
Specialisation: Practice encompasses professional negligence, construction law and insurance and reinsurance work.
Prof. Memberships: Official Referee's Bar Association, Administrative Law Bar Association, London and Commercial Bar Association, COMBAR.

Career: Called to the Bar and joined Crown Office Row 1974. Took Silk 1992. Bencher of the Inner Temple.
Personal: Educated at Magdalen College, Oxford 1970-73. Born 14th June 1952.

TERRY, Jeffrey
8 King St (Keith Armitage QC), Manchester (0161) 834 9560
Recommended in Commercial (litigation)
Specialisation: Commercial and Chancery. Notable Cases: Snapes v Aram [1998], The Times, 8th May (CA); Sheil v St Helens MBC [1997] 2 CL 412 (ChD); Co-op Bank v Tipper [1996] 4 All ER 366 (ChD); Bank of Baroda v Reyarel [1995] 2 FLR 376 (CA); Transthene v Royal Ins [1996] LRLR 32 (QB:Merc); Jones v Roberts [1995] 2 FLR 422 (ChD); Carlton v Halestrap (1988) 4 BCC 538 (ChD); Re Windward Islands [1983] BCLC 293 (Companies Ct). Papers and Publications: Service Out of the Jurisdiction Under the Brussels Convention (NCCBA); Global Exposures – Are Directors and Officers Covered? (American Bar Association); Shares Buy-Back & Financial Assistance (Manchester University Centre for Law and Business); Arbitration Act 1996 (Law Society – NW Commerce and Industry Group); Party Walls Act 1996 (Manchester University Centre for Law and Business); Insider Dealing (Firm of Stockbrokers); Landlord's Intention To Demolish and Reconstruct Under the 1954 Act [1998] RRLR.
Prof. Memberships: Founder Member, Northern Circuit Commercial Bar Association; Nothern Circuit Mercantile List Liason Group; International Associate of the American Bar Association and member of the International Committee of the Dispute Resolution Section; Northern Chancery Bar Association and member of the Standing Committee; COMBAR; Northern Arbitration Association; Union Internationale des Avocats; Bar European Group.
Career: LLB (Lond) [1975]; Called to the Bar [1976]; MA (Business Law), with Distinction, [1981]; Fellow of the Chartered Institute of Arbitrators, awarded President's Prize in Award Writing Examination, [1996]; Fellow of the Society for Advanced Legal Studies [1998].
Personal: Life Member, King's College (London) Theology and Religious Studies Society; St Mary's, Todmorden, member of Parochial Church Council and Finance Committee; New Testament Greek; Smallholding Husbandry; Married, 2 children b 1983, 1987.

TETHER, Melanie
Old Square Chambers (Hon. John Melville Williams QC), London (0171) 269 0300
Recommended in Employment
Specialisation: Employment law, education, public law. Significant cases include: Preston and others v Wolverhampton Healthcare NHS Trust and others (1998) ICR 227; Addison and others v Denholm Ship Management (UK) Ltd (1997) ICR 770; Omar v Worldwide News Inc (1998) IRLR 291. Writes Equal Pay section in Tolley's Employment Law. Employment law adviser to Association of Colleges.
Prof. Memberships: Vice-President and former Chair, Industrial Law Society. Editorial Board, Industrial Law Journal; Employment Law Bar Association; Employment Lawyers' Association.
Career: Partner in Norton Rose until 1995.

THANKI, Bankim
Fountain Court (Peter Scott QC), London (0171) 583 3335
Recommended in the following lists: Aviation, Banking, Commercial (litigation), Construction, Professional Negligence
Specialisation: Commercial and civil including banking, aviation, professional negligence, arbitration, insurance, international trade, employment, disciplinary tribunals and sports law. Noteworthy cases include Deposit Protection Board v Barclays Bank and Dalia (banking/banking

supervision), Bank of England- BCCI claims (tort/banking supervision), Football Association v Tottenham Hotspur (arbitration/contract/disciplinary), Gurtner v Beaton (aviation/agency), Southampton CC v Academy Cleaning (local authority/contract tenders), Re a firm of solicitors (solicitors/conflicts), British Coal v Smith (employment/equal pay), Kecskemeti v Rubens Rabin (solicitors' negligence/wills), BCCI v Price Waterhouse (auditors' negligence), HIV haemophilia litigation, NRG v Swiss Bank Corporation & others (reinsurance/professional negligence), Shannon v Country Casuals (Subpoena). Involved in civil and disciplinary aspects of Barlow Clowes and Polly Peck affairs. Lay clients include the Bank of England and major clearing and merchant banks as well as the BBC, British Coal and The Football Association. Professional clients include most of the major City law firms. Author of the forthcoming 'Carriage by Air' (Butterworths). Lectures on aviation law to international airlines.
Prof. Memberships: Commercial Bar Association, Common Law & Commercial Bar Association.
Career: Called to the Bar 1988.
Personal: Educated at Balliol College, Oxford (MA, 1st Class Hons 1986). Harmsworth Scholar, Middle Temple 1988.

THOM, James
4 Field Court (Geoffrey Brice QC), London (0171) 440 6900
Recommended in Property Litigation
Specialisation: Principal area of work is commercial property litigation, including disputes arising out of commercial conveyancing transactions, dilapidations cases, service charge disputes, rent reviews and lease renewals. Other main areas of work are: professional negligence (for both claimants and defendants) in claims against solicitors, surveyors and valuers, often in cases with a commercial property aspect and also in claims against architects, engineers and others (not medical); commercial law (with emphasis on commercial contracts, banking and commercial lending). Joint author of "Handbook of Dilapidations" (Sweet & Maxwell, 1992). Regular speaker at conferences and seminars on the law of landlord and tenant.
Prof. Memberships: Professional Negligence Bar Association, COMBAR. Bar Sports Law Group.
Career: Called to the Bar 1974. Called to the Bar of St. Vincent and the Grenadines 1997.
Personal: Educated at Felsted School 1965-68 and Corpus Christi College, Oxford 1969-73 (BA 1972, BCL 1973). Born 19th October 1951. Lives in Hampstead, London.

THOMAS, Christopher QC
Keating Chambers (Richard Fernyhough QC), London (0171) 544 2600
Recommended in the following lists: Arbitration, Construction, Energy & Utilities
Specialisation: Construction and engineering; professional negligence; bonds and guarantees; oil, power and transport projects in UK and overseas; arbitration and mediation – domestic and international; cases include Croudace Ltd v Lambeth BC; Int'l Press Centre v Norwich Union Life Insurance Society; McAlpine Humberoak v McDermott Int'l.
Career: Qualified 1973; Lincoln's Inn, Queen's Counsel 1989, admitted to the Bar of Gibraltar 1990; Assistant Recorder; lecturer; Fellow of the Chartered Institute of Arbitrators.
Personal: University of Kent, Canterbury (BA Law 1st class); Faculté International de Droit Compare (Diplôme de Droit Comparé); King's College, London (PhD. Law). Born 1950; resides London.

THOMAS, David
2 Temple Gardens (Patrick Phillips QC), London (0171) 583 6041
Recommended in Construction
Specialisation: Construction and civil engineering

litigation and arbitration. Recent reported cases: Drury Offshore v Emerald Field Contracting, GPT Realisations v Panatown. Soundcraft v Padmanor, Balfour Beatty v DLR, Chesham Properties v Bucknall Austin.
Prof. Memberships: ORBA, BEG.
Career: Oxford: 1st Class Honours in Law 1981. Called to Bar 1982; Called to Bar of Gibraltar 1996.

THOMAS, Keith
New Bailey Chambers (Pat Bailey), Preston (01772) 258087
Recommended in Personal Injury
Specialisation: Professional negligence and personal injury work including in particular animal welfare, equine and equestrian litigation.
Prof. Memberships: Personal Injury Bar Association. Equine Lawyers Association. Member of Northern Circuit.
Career: King Edward VII School. Lytham. Merton College, Oxford. Called to the Bar – 1969.
Personal: Joint Master of Vale Lune Harriers. Member of Racehorse Owners Association.

THOMAS, Keith
9 Park Place (Ian Murphy QC), Cardiff (01222) 382731
Recommended in Crime

THOMAS, Megan
1 Serjeants' Inn (Lionel Read QC), London (0171) 583 1355
Recommended in Parliamentary
Specialisation: Principal areas of Practice are: Planning – dealing with planning applications and appeals, retail, major infrastructure, numerous local plans enforcements and section 106 agreements. Environmental law – statutory nuisances, waste and landfill, minerals. Local governments and public law – housing homeless persons, highways, housing and landlord & tenant, local government finance rating and judicial review. General property matters – easements, restrictive covenants and nuisance.
Career: Called 1987.

THOMAS, Nigel M.
13 Old Square (Mr Michael Lyndon-Stanford QC), London (0171) 404 4800
Recommended in Agriculture & Bloodstock
Specialisation: Agricultural Law: Davies v. H & R Eckroyd Ltd (1996) EGCS 77; Law of Commons and Village Green: R v Suffolk C.C. ex Parte Steed (1995) 2EGLR 232, Lord Dynevor v Richardson [1995] Ch.D. 173.
Prof. Memberships: Chancery Bar Association, Bristol and Cardiff Chancery Bar Association Wales and Chester Circuit.
Career: Called to the Bar 1976 (Gray's Inn). Lecturer in Agricultural Law, Central Law Training.

THOMAS, Pat A.
4 Fountain Court (Richard Wakerley QC), Birmingham (0121) 236 3476
Recommended in Crime
Specialisation: Crime, both prosecution and defence. Junior Council for defence of Sheila Bower, Central Criminal Court Jan – Feb 1998.
Prof. Memberships: CBA
Career: Lincoln College Oxford, Grays Inn, Recorder.
Personal: Reading, Theatre, Walking.

THOMAS, Paul Huw
Iscoed Chambers (Trefor Davies), Swansea (01792) 652988/9
Recommended in Crime

THOMAS, R. Neville QC
3 Verulam Buildings (R. Neville Thomas QC), London (0171) 831 8441
Recommended in the following lists: Banking, Commercial (litigation), Insolvency
Specialisation: Principal area of practice encompasses all aspects of commercial contracts, especially for banks, shipping companies, trading

companies, commodity dealers and property companies.
Prof. Memberships: Commercial Bar Association, London Common Law Bar Association.
Career: Called to the Bar and joined present chambers 1962. Took Silk 1975. Recorder 1975-81. Master of the Bench, Inner Temple 1985.
Personal: Educated at Oxford University (MA 1960, BCL 1961). Born 31st March 1936. Lives in London and Wales.

THOMAS, Robert
Guildhall Chambers (John Royce QC), Bristol (0117) 927 3366
Recommended in Employment

THOMAS, Robert
4 Essex Court (Nigel Teare QC), London (0171) 797 7970
Recommended in Shipping
Specialisation: All aspects of shipping and related areas, including insurance; International Sale of Goods; Jurisdiction Disputes, etc. Salvage & Collisions.
Prof. Memberships: Commercial Bar Association, LCIA and supporting member of LMAA.
Career: M.A. (Hons), Trinity College, Cambridge. Licence Spéciale en Droit Européen, Université Libre de Bruxelles. BCL, St Catherine's College, Oxford. Fluent French, working knowledge of German.

THOMAS, Roger QC
9 Park Place (Ian Murphy QC), Cardiff (01222) 382731
Recommended in Crime

THOMAS, Sybil
3 Fountain Court (Colman Treacy QC), Birmingham (0121) 236 5854
Recommended in the following lists: Crime, Family/Matrimonial
Specialisation: All aspects of criminal and family law, with a particular interest in cases involving the disabled and mentally ill.
Prof. Memberships: Midland and Oxford Circuit, Family Law Bar Association (Chairman, Birmingham branch), Criminal Bar Association.
Career: Called to the Bar 1976. Recorder 1997.

THOMPSON, Andrew
Francis Taylor Building (Andrew Thompson & David Guy), London (0171) 797 7250
Recommended in Employment
Specialisation: Specialises in all areas of employment law including dismissal, discrimination, TUPE, restrictive covenants, business reorganisations, and EU law relating to employment matters. Other areas of practice include public and administrative law, education law, trade union law, professional negligence and general common law. Joint editor 'Harvey on Industrial Relations and Employment Law' since 1976, and contributor to Halsbury's Laws Vol 47 (Trade and Labour).
Prof. Memberships: Administrative Law Bar Association, Employment Law Bar Association.
Career: Called to the Bar in 1969. Joined present chambers 1970.
Personal: Educated at Trinity College, Dublin 1963-67. Governor of St Mary's University College, Strawberry Hill. Lives in London.

THOMPSON, Andrew
Erskine Chambers (Richard Sykes QC), London (0171) 242 5532
Recommended in Company
Specialisation: Specialist in commercial litigation, particularly involving issues of company law, corporate insolvency, partnership disputes and professional negligence; advisory work in the same fields; cases include Re BSB Holdings Ltd (No 2) (1996 1 BCLC 155), Re H & K (Medway) Ltd (1997 1 WLR 1422), Re Sentinel Securities plc (1996 1 WLR 316), Re SH & Co (Realizations) 1990 Ltd (1993 BCC 60), Re CSTC Ltd (1995 BCC 173),

Banque Financiére de la Cité v Parc (Battersea) Ltd (1998 2 WLR 475).
Career: Merchant Taylor's School; St Catharine's College, Cambridge (1989 BA; 1990 LLM; 1992 MA); Called to Inner Temple 1991.
Personal: Leisure: gardening, hill walking, birding.

THOMPSON, Rhodri
Monckton Chambers (Richard Fowler QC), London (0171) 405 7211
Recommended in European Union/Competition
Specialisation: European Community law including administrative law and competition. Treasury Supplementary Panel (EC Law). Appears regularly in High Court, ECJ and CFI for UK government departments and private clients. Cases include BCCI et al. v Bank of England (misfeasance in public office); R v Chief Constable of Sussex ex parte ITF (exports of livestock); Advisor to FA Premier League on implications of Bosman judgement. Acting for BBC in RPC reference of Premier League TV contract. Contributor to 'Bellamy & Child, Common Market Law of Competition', (4th Edn 1993, Supplement 1997); 'Weinberg & Blank on Takeovers and Mergers', Vaughan Law of the European Communities Service, 'Rights of Establishment and Freedom to Provide Services' (Butterworths looseleaf) and author of 'The Single Market for Pharmaceuticals' (Butterworths, 1994). Regular speaker at conferences/in house seminars on EC law.

THORLEY, Simon QC
Three New Square (David E.M. Young QC), London (0171) 405 1111
Recommended in Intellectual Property
Specialisation: Extensive Intellectual Property Practice particularly in field of Chemical and Biotechnical Patents and expanding to passing off, trade marks, copyright, designs and breach of confidence. Advises on EC law relating to I.P. Experience in arbitrations. Recent Cases: Biogen v Medeva, Biotech Patents, House of Lords; Canon v Green Cartridge, Patent/copyright, Hong Kong Privy Council; Harrods v Harrodian School – Passing Off; Phillips v Remington – Trade Marks; Lubrizol v Exxon – Patents.
Prof. Memberships: Chairman Intellectual Property Bar Assn; Member Chancery Bar Assn; AIPPI; Member of Bar Council (1995 -)
Career: Rugby School 1963 – 67. Keble College Oxford – MA Jurisprudence 1968 – 71. Called to Bar 1972. Appointed person to hear Trade Mark Appeals 1996. Deputy High Court Judge 1998. Deputy Chairman Copyright Tribunal 1998.

THORNHILL, Andrew R. QC
Pump Court Tax Chambers (Andrew Thornhill QC), London (0171) 414 8080
Recommended in Tax
Specialisation: Principal area of practice is revenue law, both advisory and litigation.
Prof. Memberships: Revenue Bar Association.
Career: Called to the Bar 1969. Took Silk 1985. Appointed Assistant Recorder 1995. Currently Head of Chambers.
Personal: Born 4th August 1943.

THORNTON, Peter QC
Doughty Street Chambers (Geoffrey Robertson QC), London (0171) 404 1313
Recommended in the following lists: Civil Liberties, Crime
Specialisation: Principal area of practice is criminal defence work including commercial fraud; appellate work, notably Privy Council appeals (Caribbean, Mauritius, Hong Kong, New Zealand) often in capital cases; and all forms of serious crime including murder, terrorism, Official Secrets Act, corruption and drugs cases. Other main area of work is civil rights cases including actions against the police or government, suspects' and prisoners' rights and international human rights. Recent reported cases include R v Christou [1992] (undercover police); Walker v R [1994] (Privy

Council jurisdiction: appeal against death sentence); R v Basford and Lawless (witness too ill to continue); R v Aroyewumi [1994] (sentencing in Class A drugs cases); Freemantle v R [1994] (the proviso in identification cases), Re W [1994] (rights of children), Lobban [1995] (editing co-defendant's statement) and R v Kelly and Lindsay [1998] (stealing body parts). Author of 'Public Order Law' (Blackstone Press 1987) and 'Decade of Decline:Civil Liberties in the Thatcher Years' (Liberty 1989). Editor of the Penguin Civil Liberty Guide (1989); currently contributing editor to Archbold and member of editorial board of the Criminal Law Review. Regular broadcaster on legal and civil liberty topics. Teaches advocacy and criminal evidence to solicitors and barristers. Has lectured and chaired seminars, on trial by jury, PACE, police powers, the CPS, evidence, white collar crime, emergency powers, miscarriages of justice, and the right of silence.
Prof. Memberships: Midland and Oxford Circuit, Criminal Bar Association, Administrative Law Bar Association, formerly Chairman of the National Council for Civil Liberties and of the Civil Liberties Trust. Member of the Just Television Advisory Group.
Career: Called to the Bar 1969. Also called to the Bars of Trinidad, Northern Ireland, Isle of Man. Tenant at 1 King's Bench Walk 1971-78 and at 1 Dr. Johnson's Buildings 1978-90. Founder member of Doughty Street Chambers in 1990 and currently deputy head of chambers. Took Silk 1992. Recorder of the Crown Court 1997.

THOROGOOD, Bernard
5 Fountain Court (Anthony Barker QC), Birmingham (0121) 606 0500
Recommended in Crime
Specialisation: Criminal Law - all areas covered but very extensive experience of the most serious categories of offenced, including commercial fraud. Very significant experience of video-link and Appellate work. Particular interest in matters involving claims of public interest immunity and matters involving expert evidence. Trading Standards, Health and Safety, Road Traffic.
Prof. Memberships: Criminal Bar Association. Forensic Science Society.
Career: 1981-85 Short Service Commission (Army). 1986 Called to the Bar.
Personal: Married, 3 children.

THOROLD, Oliver
Doughty Street Chambers (Geoffrey Robertson QC), London (0171) 404 1313
Recommended in Product Liability

THORP, Simon
Park Lane Chambers (Martin Bethel QC), Leeds (0113) 228 5000
Recommended in Personal Injury
Specialisation: Personal Injury (including claims of maximum severity); Industrial diseases; Medical Negligence.
Prof. Memberships: PIBA.
Career: Called 1988.

THWAITES, Ronald QC
10 King's Bench Walk (Ronald Thwaites QC), London (0171) 353 2501
Recommended in the following lists: Crime, Defamation
Specialisation: Principal area of practice is major high-profile first division criminal trials of all kinds including corporate frauds. In addition does some civil actions (mainly involving the police) and some professional disciplinary tribunals. The expanding area of work is in defamation of which details are set out below. Cases in defamation (acting both for plaintiffs and defendants): Cooper v Roger Cook & Central Television (1993) (trial); Dr. Osagie v Doncaster Health Authority & Others (1995) (trial); Wright and Callaghan v BBC (1995) (trial); Kelvin Mackenzie v Business Magazines (UK) Ltd & Others (1996) (reported); Basham v Martyn Gregory & Little Brown (1996) (trial); Morgan v

MGN (1997) (unreported); Harris v Three Valleys Water (1997).
Prof. Memberships: South Eastern Circuit; Criminal Bar Association; British Association of Sport and Law.
Career: Called to the Bar in 1970; Appointed Queen's Counsel 1987. Began career developing mixed common law practice until crime took over, making a return in recent years to more varied court and advisory work including defamation, money laundering, and lecturing on advocacy and ethics. Called to the Bar of Trinidad and Tobago.
Personal: Educated at Grangefield Grammar (Stockton-on-Tees) and Kingston College of Technology LLB (Lon).

TIDMARSH, Christopher
5 Stone Buildings (Henry Harrod), London (0171) 242 6201
Recommended in the following lists: Pensions, Traditional Chancery
Specialisation: Chancery practitioner, with a particular emphasis on trusts and probate, pension schemes, property litigation and professional negligence. Standing junior counsel to the Inland Revenue (Chancery). Important cases include Bridge Trust v AG of Cayman Islands (charities); British Coal v British Coal Staff Superannuation Scheme Trustees [1994]; Stannard v Fisons [1991]; Electricity Supply Nominees litigation, (all pensions). The Pointwest litigation (solicitors negligence). Hughes v Greenwich LBC (1994) (right to buy). Re a Debtor (415 of 1993) [1994]; Re a Debtor (6349 of 1994) (bankruptcy). Spectros v Maddon (1996); Vodafone v Shaw (1996); Hall v I.R.C. (1997), IRC v Lloyds Private Banking (all tax).
Prof. Memberships: Chancery Bar Association, STEP.
Career: Called 1985.
Personal: Educated at Merton College, Oxford (BA) 1980-83.

TILLETT QC, Michael
39 Essex Street (Edwin Glasgow QC), London (0171) 832 1111
Recommended in Personal Injury
Specialisation: Common Law practice with emphasis on personal injury. Particular experience of air and sea disaster cases including the Herald, Lauda Air and Marchioness litigation, occupational diseases, medical negligence and insurance work.
Prof. Memberships: PIBA and LCLCBA.
Career: Called July 1965. Silk: April 1996.

TILLYARD, James
30 Park Place (Philip Richards), Cardiff (01222) 398421
Recommended in Family/Matrimonial
Specialisation: Family/Matrimonial, Personal Injury with an emphasis on medical negligence, Environmental Law.
Prof. Memberships: F.L.B.A.
Career: Sherbourne School, Leeds University BSc (Chem. Eng).

TODD, Michael QC
Erskine Chambers (Richard Sykes QC), London (0171) 242 5532
Recommended in the following lists: Banking, Company
Specialisation: Principal area of practice is company law including corporate insolvency and banking securities work, with an emphasis on litigation both in the UK and abroad.
Prof. Memberships: COMBAR, Chancery Bar Association, Insolvency Lawyers Association.
Career: Called to the Bar in 1977 and joined Erskine Chambers. QC year 1997.
Personal: Educated at Keele University (BA). Born 16th February 1953.

TOMLINSON, Stephen QC
7 King's Bench Walk (Stephen Tomlinson QC), London (0171) 583 0404
Recommended in the following lists: Commercial (litigation), Energy & Utilities, Insurance & Reinsurance, Shipping

TOPHAM, Geoffrey J.
3 Stone Buildings (G.C Vos QC), London (0171) 242 4937
Recommended in the following lists: Pensions, Traditional Chancery
Specialisation: Main field of practice is occupational pension schemes, acting both in Litigation and Advisory work for members, pensioners, trustees and employers (cases include Imperial Tobacco, Courage, Brooks v Brooks, Lloyds Bank, National Grid). Other main areas are trusts and estates, and capital taxes.
Prof. Memberships: Chancery Bar Association, Association of Pensions Lawyers, Associate of Pensions Management Institute, Revenue Bar Association.
Career: Called June, 1964. Member of Lincoln's Inn. Joined Stone Buildings in 1965.
Personal: Educated at Haileybury and Trinity Hall, Cambridge.

TOUBE, Felicity
3/4 South Square (Michael Crystal QC), London (0171) 696 9900
Recommended in Insolvency
Specialisation: Insolvency, banking, general commercial, restitution. 1997/8 cases include Secretary of State for Trade and Industry v Anderson and others, Njie v Corn. Publications: Rose (ed.) Restitution and Banking Law; Failure of Contracts; various articles for Insolvency Intelligence, case editor for Totty and Moss CD-ROM; Contributor to Totty and Moss.
Prof. Memberships: COMBAR, Chancery Bar Association.
Career: BA, BCL (Oxon).

TOZZI, Nigel
4 Pump Court (Bruce Mauleverer QC), London (0171) 353 2656
Recommended in the following lists: Commercial (litigation), Insurance & Reinsurance, Licensing, Media & Entertainment, Professional Negligence
Specialisation: General commercial and common law practice covering all areas, including contract disputes, professional negligence, insurance & reinsurance, media and entertainment, employment, agency, construction, professional disciplinary hearings and gaming.
Prof. Memberships: COMBAR, Professional Negligence Bar Association.
Career: Called to the Bar and joined present chambers 1980.
Personal: Educated at Exeter University (LL.B Hons first class) 1976-79. Bar Finals 1980 (first class). Leisure pursuits include hockey, theatre and cinema. Born 31st August 1957.

TRACE, Anthony QC
13 Old Square (Mr Michael Lyndon-Stanford QC), London (0171) 404 4800
Recommended in the following lists: Chancery, Insolvency, Property Litigation
Specialisation: Principal area of practice encompasses insolvency, property, trusts, chancery and general commercial work, including a number of cases outside the UK. Recent cases include: Re Jeffrey S. Levitt Ltd [1992] (privilege against self-incrimination); Re Mirror Group (Holdings) Ltd [1993] (liability of assignees on liquidation); Gomba Holdings (UK) Ltd v Minories Finance Ltd (No.2) [1993] (mortgagee's costs); Lotteryking Ltd v AMEC Properties Ltd [1995] (set – off against assignees); Re BCCI SA (No.10) [1996] (insolvency set – off); Slough Estates Plc v Welwyn Hatfield DC [1996] (measure of damages for fraudulent misrepresentation); Grand Metropolitan plc v The William Hill Group Ltd [1997]

(rectification); Jordan Grand Prix Ltd v Baltic Insurance Group [1998] (Brussels Convention); Bogg v Raper [1998] (will drafting and exclusion clause; Plant v Plant [1998] (individual voluntary arrangements). Contributor to Butterworths European Law Service (company law). Deputy Managing Editor: 'Receivers, Administrators and Liquidators Quarterly'. Has sat as an Arbitrator. Honorary Secretary, Chancery Bar Association.
Prof. Memberships: Chancery Bar Association; COMBAR; Bar Sports Law Group; ACTAPS (Association of Contentious Trust and Probate Specialists).
Career: Called to the Bar 1981.
Personal: Educated at Magdalene College, Cambridge (MA, 1st Class Honours).

TRACY FORSTER, Jane
13 King's Bench Walk (Graeme Williams QC), London (0171) 353 7204
Recommended in Medical Negligence

TREACY, Colman QC
3 Fountain Court (Colman Treacy QC), Birmingham (0121) 236 5854
Recommended in Crime
Specialisation: Criminal Law. All types of serious crime cases including commercial fraud. Equal split between prosecution and defence work. Recent reported cases: Fellows (computer pornography) : Callender (res gestae) : Kendrick & Hopkins (theft and gifts inter vivos). Regulatory Law of all types, representing businesses and local authorities.
Career: Jesus College Cambridge (open scholar) : Call 1971 : Silk 1990 : Recorder. Head of Chambers.

TREVELYAN THOMAS, Adrian
2-3 Gray's Inn Square (Anthony Scrivener QC), London (0171) 242 4986
Recommended in Planning
Specialisation: Planning, Local Government, Compulsory Purchase, Compensation and Judicial Review. Wide range of experience in all types of Planning Inquiry.
Prof. Memberships: Planning and Environment Bar Association.
Career: MA (Cantab). Called to Bar 1974. Joined present chambers in 1975.

TREVETT, Peter QC
11 New Square (John Gardiner QC), London (0171) 242 4017
Recommended in Tax
Specialisation: Revenue Law. Practice covers all aspects of commercial, private client and trust taxation in the UK, including stamp duty, VAT, unit trusts, insurance company taxation and offshore trusts. Hong Kong profits tax, stamp duty and estate duty planning. Regular lecturer on revenue law.
Prof. Memberships: Revenue Bar Association, Chancery Bar Association and Society of Trust and Estate Practitioners (Committee Member).
Career: Called to Bar 1971. Joined present Chambers 1973. Took Silk 1992.
Personal: Educated Kingston Grammar School. Queens' College, Cambridge (1966-71) (MA. LL.M). Born 25th November 1947.

TRITTON, Guy
One Raymond Buildings (Christopher Morcom QC), London (0171) 430 1234
Recommended in Intellectual Property
Specialisation: Intellectual Property – emphasis on trade mark and passing-off although substantial practice in patent and design rights. Also, has a large amount of franchise litigation and computer/I.T. experience. Mead Corporation v Riverwood International; Hodgkinson & Corby v Wards; Hazelgrove Superleague Business Machines; Chiron v Organon. Book: 'Intellectual Property in Europe Sweet & Maxwell' 800 pages 1996.
Prof. Memberships: Patent Bar Association.

Career: Eton College, Durham BSC Natural Sciences (Computing, Physics & Psychology). Pegasus Scholar. Computer Programmes.
Personal: Married – 1 child. Piano, computers, shooting.

TROLLOPE, Andrew QC
1 Middle Temple Lane (Colin Dines & Andrew Trollope QC), London (0171) 583 0659 (12 lines)
Recommended in the following lists: Crime, Crime: Fraud
Specialisation: Practice has predominantly consisted of City, commercial and other fraud cases for more than 15 years.
Prof. Memberships: Criminal Bar Association Committee Member.
Career: A Recorder of the Crown Court since 1989.

TROTTER, David
Plowden Buildings (William Lowe QC), London (0171) 583 0808
Recommended in Personal Injury

TROWER, William
3/4 South Square (Michael Crystal QC), London (0171) 696 9900
Recommended in Insolvency

TUCKER, Katherine
St Philip's Chambers (Rex Tedd QC), Birmingham (0121) 246 7000
Recommended in Employment
Specialisation: Employment Law, European Law and Commercial Law.
Prof. Memberships: Employment Lawyers Association. Bar European Group. Employment Law Bar Association.
Career: Hardwicke, Mansfield and J.P. Warner Scholarships, Lincoln's Inn. Sometime Stagiäre to Advocate General Jacobs, European Court of Justice. Visiting Lecturer at Birmingham University. Contributor to CCH Employment Lawyer and Employment Law Service.

TUCKER, Lynton
12 New Square (John Mowbray QC), London (0171) 419 1212
Recommended in Traditional Chancery

TUGENDHAT, Michael QC
5 Raymond Buildings (Patrick Milmo QC), London (0171) 242 2902
Recommended in Commercial (litigation)
Specialisation: Wide range of domestic and international commercial law, in particular banking, insurance, commercial fraud, international sales, professional negligence and intellectual property, and defamation, media law and contempt of court – including experience as an arbitrator.
Prof. Memberships: Member of the Bar Council 1992-4. Member of Commercial Bar Association – member of Executive 1992-4. Member of the London Court of International Arbitration.
Career: Born 21 October 1944. 1963-7 Gonville & Caius College Cambridge, Scholar and MA; 1967-8 Yale University, Henry Fellowship; 1969 called to the Bar, Inner Temple; 1986 Queen's Counsel; 1988 Master of the Bench of the Inner Temple. Recorder of the Crown Court since 1994, authorised to sit as a Deputy Judge of the High Court; 1998 trained as a Mediator with World Intellectual Property Organisation, Geneva. Publications: contributions to 'Restitution and Banking Law' ed Francis Rose Mansfield Press 1998 and to various legal journals.

TURNBULL, Charles
Wilberforce Chambers (Edward Nugee QC), London (0171) 306 0102
Recommended in Pensions

TURNER, David QC
Exchange Chambers (William Waldron QC), Liverpool (0151) 236 7747
Recommended in Crime
Specialisation: Criminal advocacy and licensing. Leading counsel for "Boy A" in the James Bulger case.
Prof. Memberships: Northern Circuit. Criminal Bar Association.
Career: King George V Grammar School, Southport. MA, LL.M, Queens' College, Cambridge. Called 1971. Recorder since 1990. Appointed QC 1991.

TURNER, James QC
One King's Bench Walk (James Townend QC), London (0171) 936 1500
Recommended in the following lists: Family: Child Care including child abduction, Family: Matrimonial Finance
Specialisation: Principal areas of practice encompass all areas of criminal law, family law and administrative law. Criminal work includes both prosecution and defence and regular instructions to represent medical practitioners in connection with both criminal and disciplinary matters. Considerable knowledge and experience of technical and procedural points of law. Is an editor of 'Archbold: Criminal Pleading, Evidence and Practice'. Within family law, has particular expertise in financial matters and international child abduction work and has appeared in finance cases in the Grand Court of the Cayman Islands. Speaker at criminal and family law conferences. Administrative law includes work as a member of the supplementary panel of Treasury Counsel (Common Law) and extradition work in England and abroad.
Prof. Memberships: Called to the Bar and joined current Chambers, 1976. Appointed Queen's counsel 1998. Member of Criminal Bar Association, Family Law Bar Association and Administrative Law Bar Association.
Personal: Educated at Robertsbridge Secondary Modern School, Bexhill Grammar School and the University of Hull (LLB (Hons) 1975). Born 23rd November 1952. Lives in London.

TURNER, James M. QC
4 Essex Court (Nigel Teare QC), London (0171) 797 7970
Recommended in the following lists: Administrative & Public Law, Shipping
Specialisation: Shipping, commercial and related private international law: Red Sea Insurance v Bouygues [1995] 1AC 190; Citi-March Ltd v Neptune Orient Lines [1997] 1 Lloyd's Rep. 72; Colonia Versicherug AG v Amoco [1997] 1 Lloyd's Rep. 261; Netherlands v Youell [1998] 1 Lloyd's Rep 236; "Giuseppe di Vittorio" [1998] 1 Lloyd's Rep 136. Fluent German and Dutch.
Prof. Memberships: COMBAR; Institute of Linguists; LCLCBA.
Career: B.A. (Dunelm), LL.M (Tübingen). Call 1990.
Personal: Cycling, languages, walking.

TURNER, Janet QC
3 Verulam Buildings (R. Neville Thomas QC), London (0171) 831 8441
Recommended in Professional Negligence
Specialisation: Principal areas of practice are i) insurance/reinsurance – particularly actions by or against insurers brokers and other intermediaries; and ii) professional negligence in particular accountants, brokers and commercial surveyors/valuers.
Prof. Memberships: LCLCBA, COMBAR, ORBA.
Career: Called 1979. Joined current chambers 1988. Took Silk 1996.
Personal: Educated at Wycombe Abbey School and Bristol University (1975-1978) LL.B. 1st Class Hons. Harmsworth Scholar. Sachs Law of Evidence prize 1979.

TURNER, Jon
Monckton Chambers (Richard Fowler QC),
London (0171) 405 7211
Recommended in European Union/Competition
Specialisation: Specialisms include European
Community law, competition law at both national
and EC levels, public law (especially environmental
law) and judicial review. Practice also includes
utility regulation work in the water, electricity and
telecommunications sectors (9 months working as
legal adviser to the Telecommunications and Posts
division of the DTI) and commercial litigation.
Competition law litigation includes the ready mixed
concrete contempt case [1996], the Net Book
Agreement review [1997], the reference of the
agreement relating to freight forwarding services
[1997], the reference of arrangements for televising
Premier League football [1997] and the review of
resale price maintenance of medicaments [1997]
(all in the Restrictive Practices Court); Clover Leaf
Cars v BMW (CA and High Court).
Environmental/judicial review cases include R v
Secretary of State for the Environment ex parte
Greenpeace [1994] (the "THORP" nuclear
reprocessing plant litigation); R v Secretary of State
for the Environment ex parte Standley [1997]
(concerning the EC Nitrates Directive and nitrate
levels in certain East Anglian rivers), R v
Environment Agency ex parte Leam [1997]
(concerning the use of substitute liquid fuel in lime
and cement kilns), Bowden v South West water
(pollution of shellfish by sewage). Acted in
numerous MMC inquiries, including Plasterboard,
National Newspapers, Carlsberg-Tetley, South West
Water and Number Portability.
Prof. Memberships: Member of the New York Bar.
Career: Standing Counsel to the Director General
of Fair Trading since August 1997. Member of the
Crown Supplementary Panel on the common law
side.

TURNER, Jonathan
6 King's Bench Walk (Michael Worsley QC),
London (0171) 583 0410
Recommended in Crime
Specialisation: All and any criminal matters.
Prof. Memberships: C.B.A.
Career: Hindley & Abram Grammar School.
University College, London.
Personal: Golf, cricket, rugby league.

TURNER, Jonathan D C
4 Field Court (Geoffrey Brice QC), London
(0171) 440 6900
Recommended in Intellectual Property
Specialisation: Intellectual property; competition
and free trade; IT litigation; tax aspects of IP.
Significant cases include PLG v Ardon (patent –
European Patent Convention), Jif Lemon (passing
off), C&H v Klucznik (design right – pig fender).
Publications include chapters in Halsbury's Laws
and Vaughan's Law of the EC on the application of
EC competition law to IP, franchising, exclusive
dealing and selective distribution; European Patent
Office Reports; Countdown to 2000 – a guide to
the legal issues; Association between Acute
Glaucoma, the Weather and Sunspot Activity.
Prof. Memberships: Chartered Institute of
Arbitrators (fellow); Chartered Institute of Patent
Agents (associate); TIPLO; IP Bar Association; Bar
European Group; Society for Computers and the
Law.
Career: Educated at Rugby School (A levels in
maths, physics and chemistry), Cambridge
University (MA, law), Brussels University (Diploma
in European law), London University (electronics
and biochemistry). Law clerk at Sughrue et al, IP
and antitrust attorneys, Washington DC. Chambers
of Alastair Wilson QC 1983-1995. Head of IP and IT
law, Coopers & Lybrand 1995-7. Joined present
Chambers in 1997.
Personal: Married, 3 children; cyclist; guitar player.

TURNER, Justin
Three New Square (David E.M. Young QC),
London (0171) 405 1111
Recommended in Intellectual Property
Specialisation: Intellectual Property especially
those areas relating to Biotechnology,
Pharmacology and medicine. Leading cases
include: Biogen v Medeva (House of Lords); SKB v
Norton (Clavulanic Acid – patents and confidential
information in a strain of Bacteria). Appears in
European Patent office in Munich.
Prof. Memberships: Intellectual Property Bar
Assn; Chancery Bar Assn; Royal College of
Veterinary Surgeons.
Career: Royal Veterinary College, London
University (1981 – 86). Emmanual College,
Cambridge – PHD on immunology/virology. Called
to the Bar in 1991. Contributor to Terrell on Law of
Patents (14th Edn).

TURNER, Mark George QC
Deans Court Chambers (H.K. Goddard QC),
Manchester (0161) 834 4097
Recommended in Personal Injury
Specialisation: Industrial disease litigation; Group
actions; Insurance law; Professional negligence.
Prof. Memberships: Personal Injury Bar
Association; Northern Commercial Bar Association.
Career: Sedbergh School 1972-77. The Queen's
College, Oxford 1977-80. Dean's Court Chambers
1981. Assistant Recorder 1997-. Queens Counsel
1998.

TURNER, Michael
Cloisters (Laura Cox QC), London
(0171) 827 4000
Recommended in Crime
Specialisation: Criminal Law. Specialising in all
aspects of criminal work. Considerable experience
in all areas of serious criminal work including
serious fraud and appellate work in the Court of
Appeal. More recent cases include the M50 murder
appeal R v Browning, the Greens Wine Inquiry, R v
Burraway and Others, R. v. Caruz and Others,
Connelly v Dale (a Divisional Court case TLR July
13, 1995), (the first known case of its kind,
committing a police officer for contempt for
interfering with a Solicitor's lawful enquiry on behalf
of her client), R v X CA 1994 C.L.R 827, R v Hickey
and Others (Bridgewater Appeal).
Prof. Memberships: Criminal Bar Association.
Career: Called to Bar 1981. Law Centre worker
until 1985. Started at Cloisters with a mixed
practice including Employment and personal injury
work as well as general common law.
Personal: D.O.B. 20.12.57. Educated at Mill Hill
School and Sussex University LL.B Hons. Founder
member of Sussex F.R.U. Working knowledge of
French. Laptop friendly.

TWIGG, Patrick QC
2 Temple Gardens (Patrick Phillips QC), London
(0171) 583 6041
*Recommended in the following lists: Computer
& I.T., Construction*
Specialisation: Building and engineering disputes
and insurance matters. Appointed as arbitrator for
disputes both in the U.K. and overseas. Counsel in
many arbitrations in the U.K. and overseas (in
particular I.C.C. arbitrations).
Prof. Memberships: Admitted to the Bars of Hong
Kong, Singapore, Brunei (as a specialist in building
and civil engineering disputes) and Gibraltar.
Career: LLB; LLM; called to the Bar 1967;
appointed by the A.G. to deal with common law
matters for the Crown 1983; QC 1986; Recorder
1987; Official Referee Recorder 1991; Deputy High
Court Judge QBD 1993; panel of Mediators,
Singapore Academy of Law 1997; International
panel of Arbitrators, SIAC 1997; FCI ANG 1998.

TWOMLOW, Richard
9 Park Place (Ian Murphy QC), Cardiff
(01222) 382731
Recommended in Crime

TYZACK, David
Southernhay Chambers (David Tyzack), Exeter
(01392) 255777
Recommended in Family/Matrimonial
Specialisation: All aspects of Family Law,
including Private and Public Law children work,
Ancillary Relief, Adoption, and Inheritance. Some
P.I. and general common law.
Prof. Memberships: Inner Temple. Western Circuit.
Family Law Bar Association.
Career: Called 1970. Head of Chambers 1988.
Chairman of Devon & Cornwall Branch, Family Law
Bar Association 1990. Assistant Recorder July
1996.
Personal: Married with 2 children. Enjoys
gardening, skiing, walking and cycling.

UFF, John QC
Keating Chambers (Richard Fernyhough QC),
London (0171) 544 2600
*Recommended in the following lists: Arbitration,
Construction*
Specialisation: Construction and engineering;
international arbitration; appointed arbitrator in
many substantial disputes in most parts of the
world.
Career: Qualified 1970. Gray's Inn; assistant
engineer 1966-1970; Barrister in construction
chambers 1970; arbitrator in various disputes
1977; QC 1983; assistant recorder 1993; Professor
of Engineering Law, King's College, London 1991;
chairman of Commission of Inquiry into Yorkshire
Water 1996; Chairman of Public Enquiry into rail
accident at Southall (1997); FICE, FCI Arb, Fellow
Royal Academy of Engineering; publications of
note: 'Construction Law'; Construction Industry
Model Arbitration Rules; contributor to 'Keating on
Building Contracts'.
Personal: King's College, London (BSc
Engineering PhD).

ULLSTEIN, Augustus QC
29 Bedford Row Chambers (Peter Ralls QC),
London (0171) 831 2626
*Recommended in the following lists: Personal
Injury, Product Liability*
Specialisation: Principal area of practice is
professional negligence for all professions, both for
Plaintiffs and Defendants. Has had considerable
experience of multi-party litigation including Opren
(Nash v Ely Lilly) and Myodil (Chrzanowska v Glaxo
Laboratories Limited). Other main areas of practice
are personal injuries, which has included
appointment by the Federal District Court in Ohio,
USA to the Foreign Fracture Panel in the Shiley
Heart Valve litigation. Also practises substantially in
the Family Division.
Prof. Memberships: ORBA, FLBA, A.T.L.A. (US)
Member Gibraltar Bar.
Career: Called to the Bar 1970. QC 1992. Joined
Bedford Row 1991.
Personal: Educated at Bradfield College and LSE.
Lives in London.

UNDERHILL, Nicholas QC
Fountain Court (Peter Scott QC), London
(0171) 583 3335
*Recommended in the following lists:
Employment, Medical Negligence*
Specialisation: Specialist in commercial,
employment and medical/pharmaceutical law.
Recent cases include Kleinwort Benson v.
Birmingham, Associated Newspapers v. Wilson,
Meade v. British Fuels, Grant v. South West Trains;
also the haemophilia/HIV, hepatitis C and other
multi-party actions; experience both as Chairman
and as advocate in HC (90)9 cases.
Prof. Memberships: COMBAR; Employment
Lawyers Association; Employment Law Bar
Association; Industrial Law Society.
Career: Called to the Bar 1976. Joined present
chambers 1977. Took silk 1992. Recorder 1994.
Deputy High Court Judge 1998. Appointed
Attorney-General to Prince of Wales 1998.
Personal: Born 12th May 1952.

UNWIN, David QC
7 Stone Buildings (Charles Aldous QC), London
(0171) 405 3886
Recommended in Charities
Specialisation: A wide range of Chancery and
Commercial work, including Company Law and
insolvency, Charity cases, professional negligence,
and entertainment. Barlow Clowes International Ltd
v Vaughan; Oldham Borough Council v Attorney-
General; Harries v Church Commissioners for
England; ADT v BDO Binder Hamlyn;
entertainment cases have included the dispute
between George Michael and Sony (Panayiotou v
Sony Music).
Career: Educated at Clifton College and Trinity
College, Oxford (BA Hons. 1st Class). Called to bar
1971. Silk 1995. Appointed Junior Counsel to the
Crown, Chancery, 1982-1995. Treasury Junior
Counsel in Charity Matters 1987-1995.

UPTON, William
1 Serjeants' Inn (Lionel Read QC), London
(0171) 583 1355
Recommended in Environmental Law
Specialisation: Main area of practice is
environmental, planning and local government law.
Clients include local authorities, developers and
local amenity groups. Assistant author 'Neighbours
& the Law' (Sweet & Maxwell, 2nd edn, 1994).
Experienced lecturer.
Prof. Memberships: Planning & Environment Bar
Association.
Career: Called to the Bar in 1990.
Personal: Educated at Trinity College, Cambridge
1985-89 (MA & LL.M). Chair, Planning Aid for
London. Fellow of the Royal Society of Arts.

VAJDA, Christopher QC
Monckton Chambers (Richard Fowler QC),
London (0171) 405 7211
Recommended in European Union/Competition
Specialisation: All aspects of EC law.
Career: Has appeared in over 40 cases before the
Court of Justice of the European Communities and
Court of First Instance acting for companies,
private individuals and the UK Government. Cases
include Ford v Commission (1982 and 1984), Bulk
Oil v Sun Oil (1986), Sharp v Council (1988), the
Factortame cases, Saeger v Dennemeyer (1991),
Werner (1993), Air France v Commission (1994),
Alpine Investments (1995), the Ladbroke cases,
Cartonboard (1998). Domestic EC reported cases
include three House of Lords cases: Garden
Cottage Foods v Milk Marketing Board (1984),
Factortame (1989), and ICI v Colmer (HM Inspector
of Taxes) (1996). Other cases include Bourgoin v
MAFF (1986) (CA), Shearson Lehman Hutton v
Maclaine Watson & Co (1989) (Commercial Ct),
Apple Corps Ltd v Apple Computer (1992) (Ch. D).
R v OFTEL ex parte BT (1996). Numerous
publications including the state aid chapter in
Bellamy & Child, Common Market Law of
Competition.

VALIOS, Nicholas P. QC
Francis Taylor Building (N.P. Valios QC), London
(0171) 353 7768
Recommended in Crime
Specialisation: Specialist in commercial fraud,
Custom & Excise fraud (VAT/diversion), money
laudering, sexual offences, crimes of violence. R v
Nash & ors (mortgage fraud), R v Hawley & ors
(company fraud and asset stripping), R v Walsh &
ors (diversion fraud), MOD v Farquhar (loss of Gulf
War Computer), R v Denton ('Yardie' informant –
murder).
Prof. Memberships: CBA, CCC Bar Mess, London
Common Law and Commercial Bar Association.
Career: Stonyhurst College. Call: 1964. Assistant
Recorder 1981. Recorder 1986. Silk 1991.
Personal: Computer related matters, windsurfing,
tennis.

VALLANCE, Philip QC
1 Crown Office Row (Robert Seabrook QC),
London (0171) 797 7500
Recommended in the following lists:
Environmental Law, Professional Negligence
Specialisation: Principal area of practice is
professional negligence and indemnity/liability
insurance, especially in the construction and
environmental context. Cases range from Anns v
Merton (1978) to Cambridge Water v E. Counties
Leather (1994). Also advises extensively on
environmental law (contaminated land, "waste",
pollution exclusion clauses, nuisance etc), where
clients include major insurance companies, water
companies, local authorities and waste
disposal/landfill operators.
Prof. Memberships: Official Referees' Bar
Association, London Common Law and
Commercial Bar Association.
Career: Called to the Bar 1968 and joined 1 Crown
Office Row. Took Silk in 1989.
Personal: Educated at Bryanston School and New
College, Oxford (Scholar; BA Modern History).
Born 20th December 1943. Lives in London.

VANHEGAN, Mark
11 South Square (Christopher Floyd QC),
London (0171) 405 1222
Recommended in Intellectual Property

VAUGHAN, David QC
Brick Court Chambers (Christopher Clarke QC),
London (0171) 583 0777
Recommended in the following
lists: Administrative & Public Law, Agriculture &
Bloodstock, European Union/Competition
Specialisation: EC law generally, and EC
related public law cases.
Prof. Memberships: Honorary Vice-President of
the Bar European Group.
Career: QC (1981) QC (NI) 1981. Appeared
regularly in the European Court of Justice since
1975 in a wide range of cases and in major EC
related public law cases, in particular Factortame;
Stoke City Council v B&Q. R v Customs & Excise
ex parte Emu Tabac S.A.R.L.; Brewing Industry
Disputes.

VAUGHAN, Kieran
Francis Taylor Building (N.P. Valios QC), London
(0171) 353 7768
Recommended in Crime
Specialisation: Specialist in all areas of criminal
law. Exclusively defence work. Acted in prominent
political cases: R v Gannon, and R v McHugh (IRA
conspiracies to causes explosions). Serious crimes
of violence and drugs. (Murder; large scale
importation and supplying).
Career: Educated at St. Patrick's College, Armagh,
N. Ireland. Universtiy of Kent at Canterbury. Call:
1993.
Personal: All motor sports, jet-skiing and gaelic
football.

VEEDER, V.V. QC
Essex Court Chambers (Gordon Pollock QC),
London (0171) 813 8000
Recommended in Arbitration, Insurance &
Reinsurance
Specialisation: Practised at the Commercial Bar to
date, principally as advocate and arbitrator in the
field of international trade.
Prof. Memberships: Chairman of ARIAS (UK).
Member of the United Kingdom's Department of
Trade and Industry Advisory Committee on the Law
of Arbitration 1990-1996.
Career: Jesus College, Cambridge MA 1970
(Modern Languages & Law). Called to the English
Bar 1971. Queen's Counsel 1986.
Personal: Born 1948.

VENABLES, Robert QC
24 Old Buildings (G.R Bretten QC), London
(0171) 242 2744
Recommended in the following lists: Charities,
Tax
Specialisation: All types of tax, including VAT,
Customs and Excise Duties and NI contributions.
Trusts, whether or not tax-related. Specialities:
Offshore, EC and International Taxation,
Challenging Cases. Recent and current cases:
Lady Ingram's Executors v IRC (HL November
1998 – inheritance tax – reservation of benefits); R
v Dimsey (CA, Crim. Div., autumn 1998 – alleged
international tax fraud); Parker Hale v
Commissioners of Customs & Excise (VAT Tribunal
autumn 1998 – compensation for arms dealers); R
v Customs and Excise Commissioners ex parte
Emu Tabac SARL (European Court of Justice
'Death cigarettes' – EC Excise Directive – Judicial
Review – Injunction); Unigreg v Comissioners of
Customs of Customs & Excise (QBD Customs
duties – International Harmonised Convention -EC
legislation); Memec plc v IRC (CA – Anglo-German
convention – transparency of foreign partnerships);
Re Katz Will Trusts (Privy Council – breach of trust);
Steele v EVC International NV (CA – Anglo-Dutch
convention – corporate joint ventures – connected
persons); R v IRC ex parte Unilever PLC (CA
judicial review – group relief revenue abuse of
power); N Ltd v Inspector of Taxes (SC – group
relief – £50,000,000 allowable loss); In re Nissan
(UK) Limited (Companies Court – Revenue
winding-up petition – alleged international tax fraud
involving several £100,000,000's); Marshall v Kerr
(HL – Offshore trusts – deeds of variation).
Prof. Memberships: Fellow of the Chartered
Institute of Taxation.
Career: MA (Oxon). LLM (LSE). Tutorial Fellow of
St. Edmund Hall, Oxford 1975-80. Currents
publications: 'Control of Companies' (forthcoming
1998), 'Non-Resident Trusts' – 7th edition
(forthcoming 1998), 'Inheritance Tax Planning' – 3rd
edition 1997, 'Tax Planning and Fundraising for
Charities' – 3rd edition (forthcoming 1998),
'National Insurance Contributions Planning 1990.
Consulting Editor of the Corporate Taxation Review,
The EC Tax Journal, The Offshore Taxation Review,
The Personal Tax Planning Review. Taxation Editor
of The Charity Law and Practice Review.

VENMORE, John
30 Park Place (Philip Richards), Cardiff
(01222) 398421
Recommended in Personal Injury
Specialisation: Personal injury including industrial
disease litigation. Some medical negligence.
Professional negligence claims arising out of the
conduct of personal injury and medical accident
litigation.
Prof. Memberships: Wales and Chester Circuit. PIBA.
Career: Called 1971.

VILLAGE, Peter M.
4-5 Gray's Inn Square (Miss Elizabeth Appleby
QC & The Hon. M. Beloff QC), London
(0171) 404 5252
Recommended in Planning
Specialisation: Specialist in all aspects of
planning and environmental law, particularly High
Court challenges to the grant of planning
permission (statutory and judicial review) and local
plans; retail, housing and minerals/waste inquiries;
Major infrastructure projects, including electricity
(especially way leaves). Compulsory purchase and
compensation and rating (Lands Tribunal and
Arbitrations). Environmental liability issues. Notable
cases: Ex parte Rose Theatre [1990] 2 WLR 186 on
behalf of the Rose Theatre Trust Co; Ex parte Sister
Frost [1997] 73 P & CR 199 on behalf of the
owners of Canary Wharf; Costco [1993] 3 PLR 114
on behalf of Safeway; British Railways Board v
Slough BC [1993] 2 PLR 42 (Local Plan challenge);
R v Teeside Development Corporation ex parte
Redcar and Cleveland BC [1998] JPL 23 (quashing
a retail permission).

Prof. Memberships: Planning and Environmental Bar Association; Administrative Law Bar Association.
Career: Called to the Bar 1983 and the Bar of Northern Ireland 1997.
Personal: Lives in Wimbledon; married with 3 children; Governor of Repton School; Leisure pursuits: fly fishing.

VINE, James
Hardwicke Building (Walter Aylen QC), London (0171) 242 2523
Recommended in Crime
Specialisation: Both prosecution & defence of: drugs importation, VAT fraud, confiscation proceedings and computer fraud. Customs & Excise list 'A'. Extensive experience of P.I.I. proceedings. Appears regularly as a leading junior. In last year successfully prosecuted a serving metropolitan police officer for conspiracy to import four lorry loads of drugs. Successful prosecution and defence of large scale VAT frauds.
Prof. Memberships: S.E. Circuit. C.B.A. Kent & Inner London Bar Messes. Society for computers and the law.
Career: He has developed and used a computer database program which has been used successfuly in the preparation and presentation of numerous cases.
Personal: Travels when possible, and speaks a few foreign languages badly.

VINES, Anthony
Gough Square Chambers (Frederick Philpott), London (0171) 353 0924
Recommended in Alternative Dispute Resolution
Specialisation: Consumer law: consumer credit, trade descriptions, food and product safety. Other main areas of practice include contract, landlord and tenant, insolvency, fraud and crime. ADR: CEDR-accredited mediator; commercial, landlord and tenant, property and consumer disputes.
Prof. Memberships: Midland and Oxford Circuit, London Common Law and Commercial Bar Association, Centre for Dispute Resolution.
Career: St John's College, Cambridge, Called 1993.
Personal: Lives in London.

VIRGO, John A.
Guildhall Chambers (John Royce QC), Bristol (0117) 927 3366
Recommended in Commercial (litigation)
Specialisation: Professional Negligence of surveyors, solicitors and financial advisers; lead counsel in mis-sold pensions litigation, Bristol Mercantile Court; author of 'Surveyors' Liability, Law & Practice', Jordans (Feb.1998).
Prof. Memberships: Bristol & Cardiff Chancery Bar Association.
Career: Reported cases include Bell v McCubbin 1990.1.AER 54; Rhone v Stevens 1994.2.W.L.R.429; Cocking v Prudential CCH Commercial Law Cases 692.
Personal: Regularly lectures and contributes articles to leading law journals on all aspects of Professional Negligence.

VITORIA, Mary QC
8 New Square (Michael Fysh QC), London (0171) 405 4321
Recommended in the following lists: Intellectual Property, Media & Entertainment
Specialisation: Specialises in intellectual property law and media law, covering patents, copyright, trade marks, passing off, performers' rights, design rights, confidential information and contracts relating to the above. Co-author of 'Modern Law of Copyright and Designs'; Editor of 'Fleet Street Reports' and 'Reports of Patent Cases'; Chief Editor of 'Encyclopedia of UK and European Patent Law'; Author of sections on copyright and patents in 'Halsbury's Laws' (Vols 9 & 35); and Editor of 'European Intellectual Property Review'.
Prof. Memberships: Chancery Bar Association, Intellectual Bar Association.

Career: Called to the Bar in 1975. QC 1997. Lecturer in Law at Queen Mary College, London University 1975-78. Joined 8 New Square in 1978.
Personal: Educated at London University (BSc and PhD in Chemistry, LL.B). Leisure interests include opera, travel and bird watching.

VOS, Geoffrey C. QC
3 Stone Buildings (G.C Vos QC), London (0171) 242 4937
Recommended in the following lists: Commercial (litigation), Chancery, Insolvency, Insurance & Reinsurance, Media & Entertainment
Specialisation: Principal area of practice is chancery and commercial litigation, including particularly company, insurance and reinsurance, financial services, media and pensions. Acted in Investors Compensation Scheme v West Bromwich Building Society, Deeny v Gooda Walker, Global Container Lines v Bonyal Shipping Co, Cox v Bankside, LDC Trustees Ltd v Barings Plc, MGN Pension Trustees Limited v Credit Suisse, Scher v Policyholder Protection Board, R v Independent Television Commission ex p. TSW and Re M.C. Bacon Limited amongst others.
Prof. Memberships: Vice-Chairman of Chancery Bar Association, Inner Temple, Lincoln's Inn.
Career: Called to the Bar 1977 and joined current chambers in 1979. Took Silk in 1993.
Personal: Educated at University College School, and Gonville and Caius College, Cambridge.

VOSPER, Christopher
Angel Chambers (T. Glanville Jones), Swansea (01792) 464623
Recommended in Personal Injury

WADSLEY, Peter
St. John's Chambers (Roderick Denyer QC), Bristol (0117) 921 3456
Recommended in the following lists: Licensing, Planning
Specialisation: Town & Country Planning; Environmental Law; Practice covers advice and public inquiries; judicial review. Also deals with solicitors' negligence.
Prof. Memberships: Planning & Environment Bar Association.
Career: MA., LL.M (Cantab.); Post-Graduate certificate in environmental law (Bristol University); formerly a solicitor.

WAIN, Peter
East Anglian Chambers (John Holt), Ipswich (01473) 214481
Recommended in Family/Matrimonial
Specialisation: Family/Matrimonial specialising particularly in child care law.
Prof. Memberships: Family Law Bar Association, Criminal Law Bar Association.
Career: Stamford School, Lincolnshire; Leeds University 1966-69; Clerk to the Felixstowe, Ipswich and Woodridge Justices 1978-1987; Part Time President of Mental Health Review Tribunal.

WAITE, Jonathan
One Paper Buildings (John Slater QC), London (0171) 583 7355
Recommended in the following lists: Health & Safety, Personal Injury, Product Liability
Specialisation: Product Liability, Personal Injury, Health & Safety, Professional Negligence. Important Cases: Bourne v Colodense [1987] ICR 291 (costs in relation to Trade Union backed Plaintiff); McFarlane v EE Caledonia (No 2) [1995] IWLR 366 (costs – maintenance/champerty); Hegarty v EE Caledonia [1996] 1 LIR 413 (Piper Alpha – psychiatric injury); R v Trustees of Science Museum [1993] 3 AER 853 (legionnaires disease – s.3 Health & Safety at Work Act 1974).
Prof. Memberships: Personal Injury Bar Association; London Common Law and Commercial Bar Association.
Career: Sherborne, Trinity College, Cambridge. Called to the Bar 1978.
Personal: Golf, skiing, bridge.

WAKERLEY, R.M. QC
4 Fountain Court (Richard Wakerley QC), Birmingham (0121) 236 3476
Recommended in Crime

WAKSMAN, David
Fountain Court (Peter Scott QC), London (0171) 583 3335
Recommended in the following lists: Commercial (litigation), Media & Entertainment
Specialisation: Entertainment law. Has had considerable experience of contentious and advisory work in this field, concerning both contractual and intellectual property aspects. Clients include major record and publishing companies, artistes, managers and producers. Other main areas of practice are banking, insolvency and general commercial litigation. Clients here include clearing and international banks, other financial institutions and substantial corporations. He has lectured extensively on commercial law topics.
Prof. Memberships: Commercial Bar Association.
Career: Called to the Bar 1982.
Personal: Educated at Manchester and Oxford Universities. Leisure pursuits include music, sailing and running. Lives in London and the Lake District.

WALFORD, Richard
Serle Court Chambers (Charles Sparrow QC), London (0171) 242 6105
Recommended in the following lists: Chancery
Specialisation: Commercial Disputes (including share and asset sale agreements, loans and security, commercial fraud, cross-border contracts, financing of international trade, and financial services); Company Law (especially shareholders' disputes, directors' duties, directors' disqualification, and corporate insolvency/rescue); Professional Negligence work in these and related fields. Speaks French and German, and acts for clients based in those and other countries. Particular strengths include "plain English" pleading, striking out and other interlocutory applications, and cross examination.
Prof. Memberships: COMBAR, Franco-British Lawyers' Society; Chancery Bar Association; Clarity; Professional Negligence Bar Association.

WALKER, Andrew
3 New Square (Lord Goodhart QC), London (0171) 405 5577
Recommended in Traditional Chancery
Specialisation: Property litigation (all aspects); insolvency; restitutionary remedies; commercial and traditional chancery litigation. Recent cases include Elliott v Safeway Stores plc (1995) (commercial property); the 'Churchill Papers' case (1996) (ownership of Cabinet papers); Kane v Radley-Kane (1998) (administrators' duties).
Prof. Memberships: CBA.
Career: Harry A. Bigelow Fellow, University of Chicago Law School, 1973. Called to Bar 1975.
Personal: Educated at Westminster and Trinity College, Cambridge (scholar). Born 27.5.51.

WALKER, E.A. QC
26 Paradise Square (Roger Keen QC), Sheffield (0114) 273 8951
Recommended in Family/Matrimonial

WALKER, Jane
9 St. John Street (John Hand QC), Manchester (0161) 955 9000
Recommended in Family/Matrimonial
Specialisation: Principal area of practice is family law, particularly public law child care cases, regularly representing local authorities and guardians ad litem as well as parents. Other areas of practice include personal injury and professional and medical negligence work.
Prof. Memberships: Family Law Bar Association, Personal Injury Bar Association, Professional Negligence Bar Association, Child Concern (vice chair).

Career: Called to the Bar 1987 and joined current chambers in 1988.
Personal: Born 21st May 1965. Educated at Failsworth School and Balliol College, Oxford. Leisure pursuits include football, travel, photography and reading.

WALKER, Raymond QC
1 Harcourt Buildings (Simon Buckhaven), London (0171) 353 9421/0375
Recommended in the following lists: Crime: Fraud, Personal Injury

WALKER, Ronald QC
12 King's Bench Walk (Ronald J. Walker QC), London (0171) 583 0811
Recommended in the following lists: Construction, Personal Injury

WALL, Mark
4 Fountain Court (Richard Wakerley QC), Birmingham (0121) 236 3476
Recommended in Crime
Specialisation: All types of criminal work undertaken, mostly on the Midland and Oxford Circuit. In particular much of his time has been spent recently dealing with fraud work including defending in one of the largest excise frauds yet tried (R v Carlton + ors – Birmingham Crown Court). Prosecutes for the CPS and the DSS for whom he is their chief crown court prosecutor in Birmingham. Prosecutes and defends in equal measure.
Career: Junior of the Midland and Oxford Circuit.

WALLINGTON, Peter
11 King's Bench Walk (Eldred Tabachnik QC and James Goudie QC), London (0171) 632 8500
Recommended in the following lists: Administrative & Public Law, Employment
Specialisation: Principal area of practice is employment law. Deals with all types of work in Industrial Tribunals and Employment Appeal Tribunal, High Court and County Court litigation on all aspects of employment disputes including injunctions, wrongful dismissal, discrimination, health and safety and European social legislation. Advises and lectures on all these areas. Regular conference speaker for IPD. Also has extensive industrial consultancy experience. Other main area of practice is public law, including judicial review, especially in relation to local authorities and education. Editor 'Butterworth's Employment Law Handbook' and contributor to 'Supperstone and Goudie on Judicial Review' and 'Tolley's Employment Law Handbook'.
Prof. Memberships: Employment Lawyers Association, Employment Law Bar Association, Industrial Law Society.
Career: Fellow of Trinity Hall, Cambridge, and University Lecturer in Law 1973-79. Professor of Law, Lancaster University 1979-88, Professor of Law, Brunel University 1988-91. Called to the Bar in 1987 and joined present chambers in 1990.
Personal: Educated Hemel Hempstead Grammar School 1957-64 and Trinity Hall, Cambridge 1965-69 (MA and LLM, both 1st Class Hons). Past Area Chairman NACAB. Enjoys hill walking, music and reading. Born 25th March 1947. Lives in Wadhurst, E Sussex.

WALSH, John
Plowden Buildings (William Lowe QC), London (0171) 583 0808
Recommended in Immigration & Nationality
Specialisation: Specialist in immigration law, having appeared before numerous immigration adjudicators and tribunals. Has an expanding judicial review practice and is particularly interested in European law cases. Reported cases include: R v SSHD ex parte Yennin [1995] Imm AR 93; M v SSHD [1996] 1 ALL ER 870; R v SSHD ex parte Gnanavarathan [1995] Imm AR 64; Munchula v SSHD [1996] Imm AR 344. Has a leading case on the EEC-Turkey Association Agreement pending

before the European Court of Justice: R v SSHD ex parte Savas C – 37/98.
Prof. Memberships: ILPA, ALBA, ELAS, Bar European Group.
Career: BA, MA, LLB. Called to the Bar in 1993, having changed career from a school Headmaster. Former Fellow of Trinity College, Dublin.

WALSH, M.
Peel Court Chambers (Michael Shorrock QC), Manchester (0161) 832 3791
Recommended in Licensing

WALSH, Stephen
3 Raymond Buildings (Clive Nicholls QC), London (0171) 831 3833
Recommended in Licensing
Specialisation: All aspects of licensing. Clients include public companies, private individuals, local authorities, licensing justices and the Metropolitan Police. Practice also includes criminal law and civil liberties.

WALTERS, Graham
33 Park Place (Wyn Williams QC), Cardiff (01222) 233313
Recommended in Licensing

WALTERS, Jill
33 Park Place (Wyn Williams QC), Cardiff (01222) 233313
Recommended in Family/Matrimonial

WALTERS, John QC
Gray's Inn Tax Chambers (Milton Grundy), London (0171) 242 2642
Recommended in Tax
Specialisation: All aspects of commercial taxation including judicial review in tax-related cases. A special emphasis in litigation at all levels.
Prof. Memberships: Revenue Bar Association, Institute of Chartered Accountants, Chartered Institute of Taxation.
Career: FCA. Called to the Bar 1977, joined present Chambers 1978. Took Silk 1997.
Personal: Educated at Rugby School and Balliol College Oxford. Born 15 September 1948. Lives in London and Suffolk.

WALTERS, Jonathan
33 Park Place (Wyn Williams QC), Cardiff (01222) 233313
Recommended in Licensing

WALTON, Carolyn
13 Old Square (Mr Michael Lyndon-Stanford QC), London (0171) 404 4800
Recommended in Banking
Specialisation: Principal areas of practice are company, insolvency, banking and property. Reported cases include: Re Sumito Bank Ltd. v Rabo Bank Nederland (CA) (1988), Polly Peck International v Nadir (CA) (1992), Hind castle v Barbara Attenborough (HL) (1996)
Prof. Memberships: Chancery Bar Association; Insolvency Lawyers Association; Society of Practitioners in Insolvency.
Career: Called to Bar in 1980. 1981-1984 Assistant Legal Advisor, Williams & Glyn's Bank plc; 1984-1987 Legal Advisor, SociEtE GEnErale in London. Joined 13 Old Square in 1987.
Personal: Educated at St. Paul's Girls' School and Queen Mary College, London University (LL.M)

WARBY, Mark
5 Raymond Buildings (Patrick Milmo QC), London (0171) 242 2902
Recommended in the following lists: Defamation, Media & Entertainment
Specialisation: Libel, slander and malicious falsehood. Other media and entertainment work includes breach of confidence, literary and artistic copyright and management contract disputes. Libel cases include Brent Walker v. Time Out, CA [1991], Frank Warren v. Terry Marsh [1992], Ex p Coventry Newspapers, CA [1993], Upjohn v. BBC [1994], Jones v. Pollard, CA [1996], Aitken v.

Guardian & Granada [1997]. Breach of confidence: Paddy Ashdown v. News Group [1992] and John Bryan v. Mirror Group [1993] (photographs of Duchess of York). Newspaper night lawyer 1981-86. Legal Correspondent 'Small Business Outlook' 1984-85.
Prof. Memberships: Gray's Inn.
Career: Called to the Bar 1981 and joined current chambers 1983.
Personal: Educated at Bristol Grammar School and St. John's College, Oxford. Born 1958.

WARNOCK-SMITH, Shân
5 Stone Buildings (Henry Harrod), London (0171) 242 6201
Recommended in the following lists: Charities, Traditional Chancery
Specialisation: Principal area of practice encompasses all aspects of trusts, estates and associated taxation and charities. Handles both advisory and contentious work in connection with on and off shore trusts and estates, variations of trusts, construction and rectification of settlements and wills; probate actions; Court of Protection applications; and professional negligence in those areas. Instructed by private client departments on behalf of individuals, lay and professional trustees and executors in the U.K. and abroad and by accountants. Recent cases include Midland Bank v. Wyatt (the first case on 'sham' trusts in the U.K.), Weatherhill v. Pearce (execution of wills), Re Segelman (rectification of wills and trusts for the poor and needy) and Re Yorke (distribution of Lloyd's estates). Lecturer, writer and broadcaster on trust and estate matters.
Prof. Memberships: Society of Trust and Estate Practitioners, Charity Law Association, Chancery Bar Association, member of the Professional Conduct Committee of the Bar.
Career: Called to the Bar 1971. Joined 10 Old Square in 1979 following an academic career. Moved to 5 Stone Buildings in January 1996.
Personal: Educated at Westlake High School (Auckland, New Zealand), Portsmouth High School and King's College London.

WARREN, Nicholas QC
Wilberforce Chambers (Edward Nugee QC), London (0171) 306 0102
Recommended in the following lists: Financial Services, Pensions, Traditional Chancery
Specialisation: Main areas of practice are in the fields of pensions and private client business, both advisory and litigation. Has appeared in many of the leading pensions cases including Imperial Foods, Courage, Thrells, LRT, Coloroll, Chloride, National Grid/National Power and South West Trains. Also has wide experience of revenue litigation having formerly been standing junior counsel to the Inland Revenue in Chancery matters.
Prof. Memberships: Association of Pensions Lawyers (Main Committee member); STEP; Revenue Bar Association.
Career: BA (Oxon) 1970. Called to the Bar in 1972; QC 1993. Assistant Recorder 1995.

WASS, Sasha
6 King's Bench Walk (Michael Worsley QC), London (0171) 583 0410
Recommended in Crime
Specialisation: Criminal Law.
Prof. Memberships: Elected member of the Committee of the Criminal Bar Association: 1992-1995; 1995-1998 and the South Eastern Circuit Committee, 1989-1992; 1993-1996. Treasurer of the CBA since 1997.
Career: Called 1981. Specialising in serious fraud, environmental law and complex criminal cases. Defence and prosecution practice. Serious Fraud: wide experience of financial fraud involving work in the City, for example the defence of Roger Levitt; professional fraud cases defending lawyers and other professionals and commercial fraud such as in the gambling industry. Environmental Law: for

example: defence specialist on the criminal aspects of the Sea Empress grounding 1996. Serious Crime work has focused on high level police corruption, drug importation, money laundering and complex trials such as the defence of Rosemary West.

WATERS, David
1 Hare Court (Stephen Kramer QC), London (0171) 353 5324
Recommended in Crime

WATERS, Malcolm QC
11 Old Square (Grant Crawford & Jonathan Simpkiss), London (0171) 430 0341
Recommended in Charities
Specialisation: Principal specialist areas are mortgage lending, building societies and charities. Also covers other areas of general chancery practice, including land law, trusts and professional negligence. Acted in C.&G. v B.S.C. and B.S.C. v Halifax B.S. and Leeds P.B.S. (building society conversions), C.&G. v Norgan (mortgages) and Peggs v Lamb (charities). Joint editor of 'Wurtzburg & Mills – Building Society Law', and 'Current Law Commentary on the Building Societies Act 1986'. Member of working party involved in drafting Standard Conditions of Sale.
Prof. Memberships: Chancery Bar Association, Charity Law Association, Professional Negligence Bar Association.
Career: Called to Bar 1977. Joined 11 Old Square 1978. Took silk 1997.
Personal: Educated at Whitgift School 1963-71 and St. Catherine's College Oxford 1972-76 (B.A. and B.C.L.). Lives in London.

WATSON, Antony QC
Three New Square (David E.M. Young QC), London (0171) 405 1111
Recommended in Intellectual Property

WATSON, David
14 Castle St (Adrian Lyon), Liverpool (0151) 236 4421/8240/6759/6757
Recommended in Crime

WATSON, James
3 Serjeants' Inn (Philip Naughton QC), London (0171) 353 5537
Recommended in Medical Negligence
Specialisation: Principally litigation relating to the medical profession and other areas of professional negligence. Also personal injury, employment and general commercial work.
Prof. Memberships: Professional Negligence Bar Association, CEDR Accredited Mediator.
Personal: MA (Cantab). Called to the Bar 1979.

WATSON, Philippa
Essex Court Chambers (Gordon Pollock QC), London (0171) 813 8000
Recommended in European Union/Competition
Specialisation: Most work is in the area of EU law and is both of an advisory and litigious nature; EC agricultural law; Energy.
Career: Trinity College, Dublin: MA (Legal Science) 1973; King's Inn, Dublin; Called to Bar of Ireland: 1973; University of Cambridge: LLB 1974: PhD in Law 1977; Called to the Bar of England and Wales 1988.
Personal: Born 1951.

WAUGH, Andrew QC
Three New Square (David E.M. Young QC), London (0171) 405 1111
Recommended in the following lists: Computer & I.T., Intellectual Property
Specialisation: All aspects of Intellectual Property with particular emphasis on Chemical, Pharmaceutical and Biotechnical/Generic Engineering matters, as well as a broader commercial practice. Appears regularly at European Patent Office in Munich for clients which have included Eli Lilly, Amgen and Biogen. Notable UK cases have included: 3M v Rennicks – Patents

(Thermoformed Laminates); Bonzel v Intervention (Cardiac Catheters); Optical Recording v Hayden Labs (Compact Discs); Biogen v Medeva (Recombinant Hepatitis B Vaccine); Rediffusion Simulation v Singer Link Miles (flight simulators); Amgen v Boehringher Mannheim (Erythropoietin); SKB v Norton (Augmentin); Merrell Dow v Norton (Terfenadine); Optical Sciences v Aspect Vision Care (Contact Lenses); Hoechst v B.P (Purification of acetic acid); UCC v BP (Polyethylene production); Palmaz v Boston Scientific (cardiac stents).
Prof. Memberships: Intellectual Property Bar Assn; Chancery Bar Assn; AIPPI.
Career: 1980 City University First Class Hons in Chemical and Administrative Studies; 1981 Dip-Law; 1982 Called to the Bar. QC 1998, 6 Month Pupillage at Chambers of Kenneth Rokison. 1983 joined Chambers of William Aldous at 6 Pump Court (now headed by David Young at 3 New Square).
Personal: Tennis, rugby, Association Football, cycling.

WAY, Patrick
8 Gray's Inn Square (Patrick C. Soares), London (0171) 242 3529
Recommended in Tax
Specialisation: All forms of taxation both as an adviser and as an advocate. Publications include: 'Tax advice for company transactions' (Gee); 'The Enterprise Investment Scheme: A Practical Guide' (Longmans); Co-author 'Death and Taxes' (Longmans); Contributor Tolley's Tax Planning 1998-9 ('The Enterprise Investment Scheme' and 'Stamp Duty in Property Transactions'). Recent High Court cases: Wannell v Rothwell (share dealing); Barnett v Brabyn (SchD/Sch E); 'Continental Shipping' (judicial review and s20 TMA), Templeton v Jacobs (benefits in kind) 'Archon Shipping' (judicial review and s20 TMA).
Prof. Memberships: Revenue Bar Association and Law Society's Stamp Duty Committee.
Career: Admitted as a solicitor (1979). Head of tax at Gouldens (1987-94). Called to the Bar 1994.

WEATHERILL, Bernard QC
3 New Square (Lord Goodhart QC), London (0171) 405 5577
Recommended in Traditional Chancery
Specialisation: Practises in most areas of traditional and commercial chancery litigation and company law and insolvency, but principal areas of work are in property litigation (including landlord and tenant, mortgages and securities), breach of trust cases, equitable remedies, contested probate, directors' duties and minority shareholders' rights, business and commercial contract disputes and (not least) solicitors' negligence work. Clients include lending institutions, property companies, directors, liquidators and administrative receivers, and private clients.
Prof. Memberships: Chancery Bar Association, Professional Negligence Bar Association, Society of Practitioners of Insolvency.
Career: Called 1974. Bar Council 1989-95. Queens's Counsel 1996.

WEBBER, Frances
Two Garden Court (I. Macdonald QC & O. Davies), London (0171) 353 1633
Recommended in Immigration & Nationality

WEEKES, Anesta
36 Bedford Row (James Hunt QC), London (0171) 421 8000
Recommended in Crime
Specialisation: Criminal law; including capital murder cases before the Privy Council, fraud, train crash cases (Maidstone East Railway Station and Tattenham Corner). All other areas of criminal work. Employment law; [general employment law & discrimination, acting for a number of local authorities]. Highlights of 1998 – the Stephen Lawrence inquiry [Counsel to the inquiry].

Prof. Memberships: Professional Standards Committee of the Bar Council. Employment Law Bar Association. Industrial Society.
Career: Advocacy teacher for the Inter Inn Advocacy Commitee – teaching pupils, judges and training advocates for Gray's Inn and the circuits. April 1998 took part in an advocay training video sponsored by the Bar Council. 1996 – Member of a team of advocates from UK involved in a 3 week course in advocacy skills teaching South African lawyers and judges. Appeared on television and radio dealing with legal issues and sometimes representing the Bar. A speaker on more than one occasion at the Woman lawyer conference and the Bar Counsel over the last 3 years.

WEERERATNE, Aswini
Doughty Street Chambers (Geoffrey Robertson QC), London (0171) 404 1313
Recommended in Immigration & Nationality

WEISSELBERG, Tom
Blackstone Chambers (formerly 2 Hare Court) (P Baxendale QC and C Flint QC), London (0171) 583 1770
Recommended in the following lists: Administrative & Public Law, Civil Liberties
Specialisation: Judicial review, general commercial law (with an emphasis on fraud), employment law and discrimination law. Recent cases include R v Legal aid Board, ex parte Floods of Queensferry (availability of legal aid to companies purporting to act in a fiduciary capacity), News International v Clinger and Jyske Bank v Spieldnaes (both involving allegations of fraud and breach of fiduciary duty).
Prof. Memberships: Member of ALBA and ELA. Pegasus Scholar in Bermuda and the United States during 1997.
Career: Educated at Merton College, Oxford (BA – 1st Class) and City University. Called to the Bar in 1995.

WEITZMAN, Tom
3 Verulam Buildings (R. Neville Thomas QC), London (0171) 831 8441
Recommended in Insurance & Reinsurance
Specialisation: Clients include major UK insurers (for example the Royal, Sun Alliance, CU), various Lloyd's syndicates, major UK brokers (for example Sedgwicks, Jardines), major UK plcs, the trustees of the Maxwell Pension Funds, a major UK tobacco Manufacturer and many others.
Prof. Memberships: COMBAR.
Career: BA (Oxon), 1984 Call, Gray's Inn.

WEST, Lawrence
2 Harcourt Buildings (Roger Henderson QC), London (0171) 583 9020
Recommended in Product Liability
Specialisation: Personal Injury, including Medical Negligence. Commercial, including Intellectual and Industrial Property and Competition. Local Authority and Governmental Agency Law. Environmental law. Expertise in Professional Negligence of all kinds and Insurance. He has a general common law practice, specialising in tort and general commercial law, in which fields he has practised in both Canada and England.
Career: Called to Bar in Ontario in 1973. Practised in Toronto as an advocate with the leading Canadian law firm, McCarthy, Tetrault, where he was involved with a substantial number of commercial litigation and medical negligence actions. Called to Bar in Gray's Inn 1979. Since then has practised from 2 Harcourt Buildings.
Personal: Born Toronto, 1946. LLM (London); LLB, BA (Toronto).

WESTCOTT, David G.
35 Essex Street (Nigel Inglis-Jones QC), London (0171) 353 6381
Recommended in the following lists: Medical Negligence, Personal Injury
Specialisation: Principal areas of practice are cases of severe personal injury, especially head

and spinal (including sporting) injuries and medical negligence. Other main areas of practice are solicitors' negligence, contract and sale of goods. Significant cases include Van Oppen v Harpur Trust (CA) (schoolboy breaking neck playing rugby), Linden Gardens v Lenesta Sludge (HL) (principles of recovery of damages – contract assigned) and King v. E. Cambridgeshire District Council and Thompson v Wickens Building Group (sub nom Gardner v Southwark LBC) (CA) (automatic strike-out/abuse of process)
Prof. Memberships: Western Circuit, PIBA, PNBA, London Common Law & Commercial Bar Association.
Career: Called to the Bar in 1982 and joined Essex Street in 1983.
Personal: Educated at Cranleigh School 1965-75 and Brasenose College, Oxford 1976-79, 80-81 (BA, BCL). Born 14th May 1957. Lives in London with medical wife and 2 young children.

WHEATLEY, Derek QC
Verulam Chambers (Michael Edwards QC), London (0171) 813 2400
Recommended in Alternative Dispute Resolution
Specialisation: Resolution of banking and related commercial disputes. This year has resolved disputes including one between a major clearing bank and its customer and given expert evidence on the winning side in a banking case in Hong Kong on behalf of a major Japanese bank.
Prof. Memberships: Member of CEDR, Barrister (QC), FRSA, member of the Joint Bar Council/Law Society Committee on Banking Law.
Career: At the Bar was a Recorder of the Crown Court doing banking and commercial cases, then Chief Legal Adviser at Lloyd's Bank and the Banking Representative of the Commercial Court Committee, Vice-President of the Bar Assocation for Commerce, Finance and Industry.

WHEATLEY, Simon
9 Bedford Row (John Goldring QC), London (0171) 242 3555
Recommended in Personal Injury
Specialisation: Professional negligence, personal injury, disciplinary tribunals, industrial tribunals. Recent cases include Royal College of Veterinary Surgeons v Marshal Dale (1995) – Disciplinary action against vet for allegedly unlawfully docking dogs tails. Harris v Harris (1996) – Claim for damages by school boy who sustained amputation of leg when he fell off his father's lawn mower. RBS v Etridge (1998) – Undue Influence. Whether Bank had notice when instructing negligent solicitor to give advice to wife in mortgage transaction.
Prof. Memberships: Personal Injuries Bar Association; London Common Law and Commercial Bar Association.
Career: Called to the Bar 1979. Practised in the chambers of Raymond Walker QC at Harcourt Buildings until 1994 when joined present chambers.
Personal: Born 8th August 1956. Educated Marlborough College 1969-1973; Brunel University 1974-1978. Inns of Court School of Law 1979. Sits as part-time judge advocate on court martials (from 1994).

WHITAKER, Stephen
5 Fountain Court (Anthony Barker QC), Birmingham (0121) 606 0500
Recommended in Insolvency

WHITCOMBE, Mark
Old Square Chambers (Hon. John Melville Williams QC), Bristol (0117) 927 7111
Old Square Chambers (Hon. John Melville Williams QC), London (0171) 269 0300
Recommended in Employment
Specialisation: Employment Law, Discrimination Law, Personal Injury.
Prof. Memberships: Employment Law Bar Association. Industrial Law Society. Personal Injury Bar Association. Bar Pro Bono Unit.
Career: Wadham College, Oxford (BA, BCL).

Middle Temple Scholarship. Called to the Bar 1994. Based in Bristol and London.
Personal: Born 22nd August 1971. Lives in Bristol.

WHITE, Andrew QC
Atkin Chambers (John Blackburn QC), London (0171) 404 0102
Recommended in the following lists: Arbitration, Computer & I.T., Construction, Energy & Utilities
Specialisation: Domestic and international civil engineering and building disputes. Also specialises in computer litigation. Major projects include the Channel Tunnel: Counsel for TML in main and sub-contract disputes; Harbour City Hong Kong: Counsel for the contractors in disputes with the employer; Oil Rigs: Counsel for contractors in connection with several oil rig construction projects (High Court). Accountants' negligence actions. Solicitors' negligence actions. Publication: 'Contributor Forms & Precedents: Building Contracts'.
Career: Called to the Bar Lincoln's Inn 1980. Queen's Counsel (1997). Megarry Scholar and Hardwicke Scholar.
Personal: Born 25th January 1958. LL.B. (Hons.) Wales (1979) 2:1. Interests include music, farming and gardening.

WHITE, Antony
Cloisters (Laura Cox QC), London (0171) 827 4000
Recommended in the following lists: Commercial (litigation), Employment
Specialisation: Employment Law, Public Law, Judicial Review and Commercial Law.
Prof. Memberships: Administrative Law Bar Association.
Career: Called to bar in 1983 (Middle Temple); awarded Middle Temple Scholarship 1983-4 and the Middle Temple Prize for administrative law. Concerned largely in commercial and public law with particular emphases on public sector collective employment work and fraud involving directors and other fiduciaries. Recent interesting cases include: AG for Hong Kong v Reid [1994] (remedial constructive trusts and dishonest fiduciaries); ex parte Matson [1997] (reason giving in Administrative Law); Harrison v Kent CC [1995] (discrimination against trade union member); HRH Princess of Wales v Taylor [1995] (Privacy).
Personal: MA (Cantab) First Class Honours (Parts I and II).

WHITE, Gemma
Blackstone Chambers (formerly 2 Hare Court) (P Baxendale QC and C Flint QC), London (0171) 583 1770
Recommended in Employment
Specialisation: Employment law, in particular discrimination (sex, race and disability) and restrictive covenants. Also handles immigration and public law disputes as well as general commercial.
Prof. Memberships: Employment Law Association, Administrative Law Bar Association.
Career: Educated at King's College London and the University of Paris I-Panthéon-Sorbonne (LL.B and Maîtrise en Droit Français 1992); Oxford University (BCL 1993). Called to the Bar in 1994.
Personal: Fluent in French.

WHITE, Sasha
1 Serjeants' Inn (Lionel Read QC), London (0171) 583 1355
Recommended in Planning
Specialisation: Principal areas of practice is planning, environmental and local government law.
Prof. Memberships: Planning and Environmental Bar Association.
Career: Called to Bar in 1991. Pupil to William Hicks QC joined Chambers as tenant 1993.
Personal: Educated Bedales and Trinity College, Cambridge. Born 1967. Author of 'Planning Law Appeals' (Central Law Publishing) March 1997.

WHITEHOUSE, David QC
3 Raymond Buildings (Clive Nicholls QC), London (0171) 831 3833
Recommended in the following lists: Crime, Crime: Fraud
Specialisation: Principal specialist areas are Crime, from Mafia and Colombian Cartel drugs importing trials to the Bob Monkhouse joke books case; Fraud including City Fraud (Barlow Clowes – Investment fraud, Landhurst Leasing Plc – Leasing fraud and corruption, Abbey National plc – Corruption and Norton Plc – Rights Issue); Local Authority Fraud (West Wiltshire Privatisation case, Brent Housing); Mortgage Fraud (R v Annen and others) and Licensing – liquor, casino and bingo. Also specialises in Disciplinary Tribunals and has appeared before the Institute of Chartered Accountants, Securities and Futures Authority, LIFFE, General Medical Council, UK British Boxing Board of Control, Institute of Chartered Engineers.
Prof. Memberships: Criminal Bar Association, International Bar Association.
Career: Called to the Bar 1969 and joined current chambers in 1970 after pupillage in defamation Chambers. Libel read The Sun 1969-1975. Appointed Recorder 1987. Took silk 1990.
Personal: Educated at Trinity College, Cambridge 1964-67 (MA).

WHITELEY, Miranda
4 Field Court (Geoffrey Brice QC), London (0171) 440 6900
Recommended in Shipping
Specialisation: Commercial contract litigation with an emphasis on shipping and international trade. Principal areas of practice include arbitration, Admiralty, carriage of goods by sea and road (both domestic and CMR), international and domestic sale of goods, conflict of laws and jurisdiction disputes, insurance, personal injury and fatal accidents at sea (including public inquiries and inquests) and professional negligence.
Career: Called to the Bar in 1985. CEDR Accredited Mediator 1998.
Prof. Memberships: COMBAR and London Common Law and Commercial Bar Association.

WHITEMAN, Peter QC
Queen Elizabeth Building (David Jeffreys QC & Peter Whiteman QC), London (0171) 583 5766
Recommended in Tax
Specialisation: All areas of corporate and commercial taxation with special emphasis on mergers and acquisitions, structured financing arrangements, oil company taxation, insurance company taxation, international corporate taxation, cross-border transactions, transfer pricing and capital allowances. Appeared in BP Oil Development Ltd v IRC, Esso Petroleum Ltd v IRC, Girobank plc v Clarke, ICI plc v Colmer, Bradley v London Electricity plc, Padmore v IRC, Post Office Counters Ltd v Customs & Excise, Johnson v Prudential Assurance Co Ltd, J. Sainsbury plc v O'Connor. Also appeared in Exxon Corporation v Internal Revenue Commissioner in the US Tax Court as the UK tax expert witness. Clients include major international companies, solicitors and accountancy firms.
Prof. Memberships: Revenue Bar Association; Honorary Adviser to the Unitary Tax Campaign 1982.
Career: Lecturer London School of Economics 1965-1970. Called to the Bar 1967; Queen's Counsel 1977. Founded Chambers of Peter Whiteman QC in 1977, becoming Joint Head of Hollis Whiteman Chambers on merger in 1991. Bencher of Lincoln's Inn 1985. Author "Whiteman on Income Tax", "Whiteman on Capital Gains Tax", "British Tax Encyclopedia". Professor of International Tax Law, University of Florida and University of Virginia 1980. Attorney-at-Law, State of New York 1982. Recorder 1986; Deputy High Court Judge 1994.
Personal: Educated Leyton County High School and London School of Economics (LLB Hons; LLM Distinction).

WHITFIELD, Adrian QC
3 Serjeants' Inn (Philip Naughton QC), London
(0171) 353 5537
Recommended in Medical Negligence
Specialisation: Principal area of practice is medical negligence and other medical law, including treatment decisions. Cases include Sidaway, Hotson, in Re F (Sterilisation) and de Martell. Has extensive G.M.C. and other tribunal experience. Acts for plaintiffs and defendants. Visiting Research Fellow at Centre of Medical Law and Ethics, King's College, London. Writes and lectures regularly on medico-legal subjects.
Prof. Memberships: London Common Law and Commercial Bar Association, Professional Negligence Bar Association, Medico-Legal Society.
Career: Call 1964: Recorder 1981: Queen's Counsel 1983: Chairman of NHS Tribunal 1993.
Personal: Educated Ampleforth College and Magdalen College Oxford: Demy (Open Scholar). Lives in London.

WHITTAKER, John
Serle Court Chambers (Charles Sparrow QC), London (0171) 242 6105
Recommended in the following lists: Chancery, Environmental Law, Partnership
Specialisation: Principal area of practice is chancery including related commerce and property. More specialised areas include partnerships and environmental law (waste).
Career: Called 1969, joined Thirteen Old Square (Serle Court Chambers) in 1970.
Personal: Magdalen College, Oxford (MA, BCL).

WHITTAM, Richard
Furnival Chambers (Andrew Mitchell), London (0171) 405 3232
Recommended in Crime
Specialisation: Junior Treasury Cousel to the Crown at the Central Criminal Court. Specialist Criminal practitioner with considerable experience in complex cases. Serious fraud experience in advance fee, leasing, Certificate of Deposit, mortgage and DSS frauds. Defended in substantial Customs and Excise cases. Public Interest Immunity. Information Technology.
Prof. Memberships: Criminal Bar Association; S E Circuit.
Personal: Educated at Marple Hall School and University College London. Formerly active in sport, now golf and occasional cricket.

WHITTLE, C.D. (Henry)
11 South Square (Christopher Floyd QC), London (0171) 405 1222
Recommended in Intellectual Property

WHYBROW, Christopher QC
1 Serjeants' Inn (Lionel Read QC), London (0171) 583 1355
Recommended in the following lists: Energy & Utilities, Parliamentary

WHYTE, Anne
14 Castle St (Adrian Lyon), Liverpool (0151) 236 4421/8240/6759/6757
Recommended in Crime

WIDDICOMBE, David QC
2 Mitre Court Buildings (Michael FitzGerald QC), London (0171) 583 1380
Recommended in Parliamentary
Specialisation: Local Government, Planning and Environmental, Parliamentary, Judicial Review, Compensation etc.
Prof. Memberships: Parliamentary Bar, California Bar, Hong Kong Bar.
Career: Includes Editor Ryde on Rating, 1968 – 83; Chairman Government Committee on Conduct of Local Government Business 1986; "Fares Fair" Case House of Lords, 1982; Westminster Audit Case 1993-.
Personal: Clubs – Athanaeum, Garrick.

WIGGLESWORTH, Raymond
18 St. John Street (Rodney C. Klevan QC), Manchester (0161) 278 1800
Recommended in Crime

WILDBLOOD, Stephen
Albion Chambers (J.C.T. Barton QC), Bristol (0117) 927 2144
Recommended in Family/Matrimonial

WILKINSON, Nigel QC
2 Crown Office Row (Graeme Hamilton QC), London (0171) 797 8100
Recommended in Personal Injury

WILLBOURNE, Caroline
One Garden Court Family Law Chambers (Miss Eleanor F. Platt QC & Miss Alison Ball QC), London (0171) 797 7900
Recommended in the following lists: Family: Child Care including child abduction, Family: Matrimonial Finance
Specialisation: All aspects of family law with particular emphasis on ancillary relief, questions of jurisdiction and child abduction matters. She has been involved in many "big money" cases, most notable of which recently was Dart.
Prof. Memberships: Sits on the committee of the Family Law Bar Association and on the Bar Council with particular reference to Legal Services.
Career: Called to Bar 1970. Bencher of Inner Temple. Sits as a Deputy District Judge of the Family Division, appointed 1990.
Personal: BA Joint Honours: Philosophy and Ancient Greek, University of London. Qualified as a Mediator in 1993.

WILLIAMS, David H.
Chavasse Court Chambers (Andrew Mattison), Liverpool (0151) 707 1191
Recommended in Crime

WILLIAMS, John Leighton QC
Farrar's Building (Gerard Elias QC), London (0171) 583 9241
Recommended in Personal Injury
Specialisation: General common law, with emphasis on personal injuries and medical negligence work.
Career: Called to the Bar 1964. Appointed Recorder 1985. Took silk 1986. Member of the Criminal Injuries Compensation Board since 1987. Master of the Bench, Grays Inn 1994.

WILLIAMS, John Melville QC
Old Square Chambers (Hon. John Melville Williams QC), London (0171) 269 0300
Recommended in Environmental Law, Personal Injury
Specialisation: Environmental toxic torts; agricultural environmental damages claims; waste-incineration; environmental insurance; some planning; particular interest in scientific aspects of environmental issues. Notable cases: Graham v Rechem; Camelford Water Claims, organophosphate sheep dip cases.
Prof. Memberships: Environmental Law Foundation – Member of Advisory Council; Association of Personal Injury Lawyers (1st President 1990-1994), Association of Trial Lawyers of America (Chair International Practice Section 1991), Personal Injury Bar Association.
Career: Called 1955; QC 1977; Recorder 1985-1993; Legal Assessor to the General Medical Council and General Dental Council 1984 -. Member CICB 1998 -.

WILLIAMS, Jon
6 Pump Court (Kieran Coonan QC), London (0171) 583 6013
Recommended in Medical Negligence

WILLIAMS, Lloyd
30 Park Place (Philip Richards), Cardiff (01222) 398421
Recommended in Personal Injury

WILLIAMS, Sara
5 Fountain Court (Anthony Barker QC), Birmingham (0121) 606 0500
Recommended in Insolvency

WILLIAMS, Wyn Lewis QC
33 Park Place (Wyn Williams QC), Cardiff (01222) 233313
Recommended in the following lists: Personal Injury, Planning

WILLIAMSON, Adrian
Keating Chambers (Richard Fernyhough QC), London (0171) 544 2600
Recommended in Construction
Specialisation: Construction and engineering law; professional negligence; disputes concerning substantial commercial and technical projects; cases include Aughton v Kent; Damond Lock v Laing Investments; Barclays Bank v Fairclough Building Ltd; West Faulkner Associates v LB Newham; Birse v Haiste; Hytec v Coventry C.C.
Career: Qualified 1983; Middle Temple; tenant in chambers of John Loyd QC 2 Crown Office Row 1985-1989; tenant at Keating Chambers 1989 to date; wrote chapters on JCT and NSC Forms of Contract for 'Keating on Building Contracts'. (5th 1991 and 6th 1995 editions).
Personal: Highgate School, Trinity Hall, Cambridge (1982 BA 1st Class Hons 1985 MA). Born 1959. Married with 3 children.

WILLIAMSON, Hazel QC
13 Old Square (Mr Michael Lyndon-Stanford QC), London (0171) 404 4800
Recommended in the following lists: Chancery, Insolvency, Property Litigation
Specialisation: Chancery Litigation including company and insolvency aspects. Emphasis on commercial property aspects. National Westminster Bank v Arthur Young series of cases on rent review, arbitration procedure and appeals. BCCI v Aboody 1988: undue influence and bank mortgages.
Career: Qualified 1972, Gray's and Lincoln's Inn. Silk 1988. Recorder 1996, Deputy High Court Judge 1994. Chairman of the Chancery Bar Association 1994 – 97. Member of the DETR, Property Advisory Group. Publications: 'Law and Valuation of Leisure Property' (Estates Gazette) Joint Editor and Contributor.
Personal: Educated Wimbledon High School and St Hilda's College, Oxford. BA 1969, MA 1982, FCIArb 1992.

WILLS-GOLDINGHAM, Claire
Albion Chambers (J.C.T. Barton QC), Bristol (0117) 927 2144
Recommended in Family/Matrimonial

WILMOT-SMITH, Richard QC
39 Essex Street (Edwin Glasgow QC), London (0171) 832 1111
Recommended in Construction
Specialisation: Law relating to construction contracts, including insurance and guarantees, professional negligence and insolvency.
Prof. Memberships: ORBA, London Common Law and Commercial Bar Association.
Career: Called to Bar in 1978, took silk 1994.

WILSON, Alastair QC
19 Old Buildings (Alastair Wilson QC), London (0171) 405 2001
Recommended in the following lists: Computer & I.T., Intellectual Property
Specialisation: Principal area of practice is intellectual property and technology cases, including EC aspects. Other areas of work include lotteries and setting aside Anton Piller orders. Cases of importance include, inter alia, Chelsea Man v Chelsea Girl, Intergraph v SSI, PLG (Netlon) v Ardon and Chiron v Murex. Clients include British Railways Board, Ford Motor Company, Associated Newspapers, Irish Dairy Board and Netlon. Has presented numerous seminars on intellectual

property and computer law. Recently made a video on trade mark law for Legal Network Television.
Prof. Memberships: Society for Computers and Law, Intellectual Property Bar Association, Chancery Bar Association.
Career: Called to the Bar 1968 and joined current chambers when located at 3 Pump Court in 1970. Took Silk in 1987. Appointed Recorder in 1996.
Personal: Educated at Wellington College and Pembroke College. Leisure pursuits include gardening and building. Born 26th May 1946. Lives in Norwich.

WILSON, Elizabeth
Pump Court Tax Chambers (Andrew Thornhill QC), London (0171) 414 8080
Recommended in Tax
Specialisation: Revenue Law. Litigation in all courts.
Prof. Memberships: Revenue Bar Association. Called to the Bar in 1995.
Career: Assistant managing editor of Personal Tax Planning Review. Assistant editor of Ray's Practical IHT Planning. Educated at Cambridge University.
Personal: Martial Arts, travel.

WINBERG, Stephen
Crown Office Row (Richard Ferguson QC), London (0171) 797 7111
Recommended in the following lists: Crime, Crime: Fraud

WINGATE-SAUL, Giles QC
Byrom Street Chambers (B.A. Hytner QC), Manchester (0161) 829 2100
Recommended in the following lists: Commercial (litigation), Medical Negligence, Personal Injury

WINGERT, Rachel
Gray's Inn Chambers (Brian Jubb), London (0171) 404 1111
Recommended in the following lists: Family: Child Care including child abduction, Family: Matrimonial Finance
Specialisation: Principal area of practice is family law including public and private law children cases, ancillary relief and property disputes between unmarried couples. Author of "Capital Provision for Children of Unmarried Parents" in Family Law.
Prof. Memberships: Family Law Bar Association.
Career: Called to the Bar 1980 and joined chambers in Lincoln's Inn. Moved to present chambers in 1990.
Personal: Educated at London University (LL.B 1979, LL.M 1986). Lives in London.

WINTER, Ian
Queen Elizabeth Building (David Jeffreys QC & Peter Whiteman QC), London (0171) 583 5766
Recommended in Crime: Fraud
Specialisation: Specialist in criminal law with a particular emphasis on fraud and white collar crime. Acted for the defence in the Lady Aberdour and Swindon Town FC frauds. Practice also covers police powers and civil liberties law. Even split between prosecution and defence work.
Prof. Memberships: Bar Council Legal Services Committee.
Career: Called to the Bar in 1988. Joined present chambers in 1990.
Personal: Educated at Bristol University 1984-87. Leisure pursuits include international rally driving and playing the saxophone and piano. Born 25th March 1966. Lives in Fulham.

WOLFE, David
4-5 Gray's Inn Square (Miss Elizabeth Appleby QC & The Hon. M. Beloff QC), London (0171) 404 5252
Recommended in the following lists: Administrative & Public Law, Environmental Law
Specialisation: Public law, including judicial review, local government, town and country planning and environmental law (including cases involving substantial scientific and technical evidence), discrimination, education, employment,

social security.
Prof. Memberships: Administrative Law Bar Association, Planning and Environmental Bar Association, Employment Law Bar Association, UK Environmental Law Association, Discrimination Law Association.
Career: BSc MEng (Manchester) 1987, PhD (Engineering, Cambridge) 1991, Called to the Bar 1992, Middle Temple (Harmsworth and Queen Mother's scholarships).

WOLFSON, David
3 Verulam Buildings (R. Neville Thomas QC), London (0171) 831 8441
Recommended in the following lists: Banking, Commercial (litigation)
Specialisation: Practice encompasses all areas of commercial law (particularly banking, insolvency and domestic and international sale of goods), professional negligence and entertainment law. Recent cases include Ghana Commercial Bank v C&L [tracing proceeds of fraud], Barclays Bank v Zaroovabli [mortgages and registrable interests], Re Schuppan (a bankrupt) [conflict of interest in insolvency], Art Corporation v Schuppan [duty of disclosure on Mareva injunctions], Art Corporation v Schuppan [international sale of goods], Blackspur Leasing [negligent audit claim], Investors Compensation Scheme v West Bromwich Building Society [acted for solicitor third parties in major action re home income plans]. Advised about the recovery of gold and other assets from Second World War. Clients include banks and other lenders, insurers and professional indemnity insurers, Solicitors' Indemnity Fund, liquidators and insolvency practitioners, general commercial clients. Contributing author to Bank Liability and Risk, (2nd ed) several articles in various legal journals including New Law Journal, Commercial Lawyer and International Insurance Law Review. Articles for in-house magazines of various firms of solicitors. Contributor to Law Commision Consultation Paper on the Third Party (Rights against Insurers) Act 1930. Lecturer at legal seminars and conferences.
Prof. Memberships: COMBAR
Career: MA (Cantab) (Oriental Studies and Law). Exhibitioner and Scholar of Selwyn College. Stuart of Rannoch award. Squire scholarship. Inner Temple Major scholarship. Council of Legal Education scholarship. Called to the Bar in 1992.
Personal: Married to Louise. Interests include country walks and mobile telephones (seperately).

WOLKIND, Michael
10 King's Bench Walk (Ronald Thwaites QC), London (0171) 353 2501
Recommended in Crime
Specialisation: Criminal defence, acting as a Leading Junior in all types of cases. Led in many notorious murders from R v Boyce (a dismemberment 'nagging wife' provocation) 1984, to R v Morss (the paedophile killing of Daniel Handley) 1996. Also led in Turkish and Libyan terrorist trials and advised on the Lockerbie bombing. Has acted many times for top target criminals charged with murder, armed robbery or drug offences. Appeared for the first defendant in the Foxtrot 5 importation of cocaine worth £125 million. Reported Court of Appeal cases and has also appeared in Privy Council capital cases. In fraud has acted for lawyers, bankers and accountants and is currently instructed in several multi-million £ VAT frauds.

WOLTON, Harry QC
5 Fountain Court (Anthony Barker QC), Birmingham (0121) 606 0500
Recommended in Planning
Specialisation: Town & Country Planning; Residential, Employment, Retail, Recreation, minerals, waste, Personal Injuries & Medical Negligence.
Prof. Memberships: Planning & Environment Bar Association; Personal Injury Bar Association.
Career: Called 1969. Silk 1982. Recorder 1985.

Attorney sent to sit as Deputy High Court Judge 1990.
Personal: Cattle Breeding & Dendrology.

WONNACOTT, Mark
199 Strand (Peter Andrews QC), London (0171) 379 9779
Recommended in Property Litigation

WOOD, Christopher
1 Mitre Court Buildings (Bruce Blair QC), London (0171) 797 7070
Recommended in Family: Matrimonial Finance
Specialisation: Principally ancillary relief.
Prof. Memberships: F.L.B.A.
Career: Oxford University (MA). Université d'Aix-Marseilles III (Diplôme d'Etudes Supérieures d'Université).
Personal: Single. Interests: history, politics, Norway, France.

WOOD, Derek QC
Falcon Chambers (Jonathan Gaunt QC & Kim Lewison QC), London (0171) 353 2484
Recommended in Agriculture & Bloodstock
Specialisation: Specialises in all aspects of property law, including commercial and agricultural landlord and tenant disputes, rent review, housing, easements and boundaries, compulsory purchase, tax and planning, building and engineering disputes, joint development agreements and professional negligence in connection with real property. Experienced in the conduct of cases in the courts, before public inquiries and tribunals, and also in arbitrations. Has made numerous appearances as advocate before arbitrators in England and Hong Kong, including two engineering disputes as leading counsel for the Government of Hong Kong. Many appointments as both arbitrator in England (mostly as sole arbitrator) and independent expert across a whole range of property related matters. Consulting Editor (with Bernstein, Marriott and Tackaberry) and contributor to 3rd Edition of the 'Handbook of Arbitration Practice' 1997 (Sweet & Maxwell and Chartered Institute of Arbitrators). Public appointments include Property Advisory Group 1975-1994; Chairman of Expert Committees on the Rating of Plant and Machinery 1991-1992 & 1997-1998 (both Department of the Environment); Chairman of Standing Advisory Committee on Trunk Road Assessment (SACTRA) (Department of Transport). 1986-1994. Chaired working party which produced Code of Practice on Commercial Leases in England and Wales 1995.
Prof. Memberships: Honorary Fellow of Central Association of Agricultural Valuers (FAAV) 1988; Honorary Associate of Royal Institute of Chartered Surveyors (Hon ARICS) 1991; Fellow of Chartered Institute of Arbitrators (FCIArb) by examination 1993.
Career: Called to the Bar 1964. Took Silk 1978. Recorder to the Crown Court 1985. Bencher of the Middle Temple 1986. Deputy Official Referee and Deputy High Court Judge (Chancery Division).
Personal: Educated at the University of Oxford (MA, BCL). Principal of St Hugh's College, Oxford (since 1991). Awarded CBE in New Year's Honours List 1995 for services to property law. Born 14th October 1937.

WOOD, Graham N.
India Buildings Chambers (David Harris QC), Liverpool 0151 243 6000
Recommended in Personal Injury
Specialisation: Personal injury, including health and safety and industrial disease, medical and other professional negligence. Commercial and construction disputes. Administrative law, especially education and local government cases. Employment, including race and sex discrimination. Recent work has involved test litigation for 85 dBA liability against Fords and other major industry in industrial deafness cases and solicitor negligence in handling large scale scheme settlements for industrial disease.

Particular interest in catastrophic injury.
Prof. Memberships: PIBA PNBA
Career: Assisstant Recorder 1995. Co-founder Northern Circuit Free Representation and Advice Scheme. Co-author Binghams Negligence Cases.
Personal: Sailing. Married with 3 children.

WOOD, James
Doughty Street Chambers (Geoffrey Robertson QC), London (0171) 404 1313
Recommended in Crime
Specialisation: Specialist in civil liberties and criminal appellate work including the Bridgewater and Birmingham Six appeals. Practice also includes a large amount of leading criminal defence work, particularly cases which raise political, policing and public order issues. Has also handled numerous civil actions against the police, inquests and prisoners' rights work. Advisor to Liberty and author of 'The Right to Silence: The Case for Retention' (1991).
Prof. Memberships: Liberty.

WOOD, Michael
23 Essex Street (Michael Lawson QC), London (0171) 413 0353
Recommended in Crime: Fraud
Specialisation: All aspects of criminal work both prosecuting and defending, with an emphasis on commercial fraud, including advising those concerned or interested in fraud litigation such as solicitors and accountants.
Prof. Memberships: Criminal Bar Association; Bar Human Rights Committee.
Career: Called to the Bar 1976; Assistant Recorder 1994.
Personal: Born 22nd October 1953. Attended Rugby School and Southampton University.

WOOD, Richard
20 Essex Street (David Johnson QC), London (0171) 583 9294
Recommended in the following lists: Aviation, Financial Services
Specialisation: Specialises in commercial disputes, including aviation, shipping, insurance and reinsurance, commodities and banking. Represented Names in Lloyd's litigation. Court Examiner 1988-97.
Prof. Memberships: Supporting Member of LMAA.
Career: Called 1975.

WOOD, William QC
5 Fountain Court (Anthony Barker QC), Birmingham (0121) 606 0500
Recommended in Personal Injury

WOOD, William QC
Brick Court Chambers (Christopher Clarke QC), London (0171) 583 0777
Recommended in Insurance & Reinsurance
Specialisation: Insurance/reinsurance, aviation. Acted for Ernst and Young in Lloyds related actions.
Career: Took Silk 1998.

WOODWARD, W.C. QC
Ropewalk Chambers (Richard Maxwell QC), Nottingham (0115) 947 2581/2/3/4
Recommended in Personal Injury
Specialisation: Embraces common law, personal injury, employer's liability, insurance, disaster, insidious disease, poisoning, medical and professional negligence, throughout the land. Involvement in consequences of Markham mine, Flixborough, Hillsborough disasters and in asbestos, noise induced hearing loss, white finger, mucous membrane, fire and explosion litigation for example.
Career: St. John's College Oxford. Inner Temple. Called 1964. Head of Ropewalk Chambers 1985-1994. Silk 1985. Recorder. Deputy High Court Judge. Founder member Notts Medico-Legal Society and East Midlands Business and Property Bar Association. Special Professor Nottingham University Law Department.

Personal: Married, 3 children. Ponds. Serendipity.

WOODWARK, Jane
Milburn House Chambers (Paul Cape), Newcastle-upon-Tyne (0191) 230 5511
Recommended in Employment
Specialisation: Almost exclusively employment and discrimination law, acting for both employers and employees.
Prof. Memberships: Employment Law Bar Association; Industrial Law Society.
Career: Has a Master's degree in Industrial Relations, London School of Economics. Prior to the Bar, worked for a national employers' organisation. Specialised in employment law advice and had particular responsibility for advising on equalities issues and transfers of undertakings. Fulfilled a central role in advising employers during three national industrial disputes in 1986, 1989 and 1992. Contributor to Employment Law for Local Authority Employers published by Croner Publications Ltd. Co-founder Milburn House Chambers.
Personal: Born 18 June 1956. Cinema, contemporary literature and hill-walking.

WOOLLEY, David QC
1 Serjeants' Inn (Lionel Read QC), London (0171) 583 1355
Recommended in Parliamentary

WORSLEY, Daniel
2 Harcourt Buildings (Roger Henderson QC), London (0171) 583 9020
Recommended in the following lists: Consumer Law, Financial Services
Specialisation: Finance house, banking, leasing, consumer credit litigation and drafting (e.g. longstanding litigation adviser and advocate for many of the major banks and finance houses; drafting of stocking agreements for financing motor imports trade; editor of contentious forms in Butterworths' Consumer Credit Legislation and Goode and senior editor of new [1998] Consumer Credit volume of Halsbury's Laws). Disciplinary, regulatory and other professional and financial quasi-criminal work (including major disciplinary prosecutions for one of the City regulatory bodies and redrafting of its disciplinary rules). Contract, sale of goods and commercial litigation and drafting. Other areas include general common law including personal injury and official referee work. Widely experienced advocate.
Career: Called May 1971, Gray's Inn. Recorder (sitting in civil and crime). Assessor UKCC Nursing.
Personal: Born 1948. BA (Cambridge).

WORSTER, David
St Philip's Chambers (Rex Tedd QC), Birmingham (0121) 246 7000
Recommended in Personal Injury
Specialisation: Personal Injury; Chancery and Commercial; Directors Disqualification. (Panel Counsel)
Prof. Memberships: PIBA. Chancery Bar Association, Midland Chancery and Commercial Bar Association.
Career: Called 1980.
Personal: Educated at Pembroke College, Cambridge, MA (Cantab).

WORTHINGTON, Stephen
12 King's Bench Walk (Ronald J. Walker QC), London (0171) 583 0811
Recommended in the following lists: Personal Injury, Professional Negligence
Specialisation: Professional negligence, personal injury, environmental law. Blue Circle v Ministry of Defence, Nuclear Pollution, [1998] 3 All ER 385.
Prof. Memberships: PIBA, LCLCBA, ORBA.
Career: Trinity College, Cambridge.

WRIGHT, Caroline
Albion Chambers (J.C.T. Barton QC), Bristol (0117) 927 2144
Recommended in Family/Matrimonial

WRIGHT, Peter
Lincoln House Chambers (Mukhtar Hussain QC), Manchester (0161) 832 5701
Recommended in Crime

WYAND, Roger QC
One Raymond Buildings (Christopher Morcom QC), London (0171) 430 1234
Recommended in Intellectual Property
Specialisation: All aspects of Intellectual Property law including the effect of EU competition law. Important cases: Twentieth Century Fox v Tryrare, Chanel v Triton, Assidoman v Mead Nokia Mobile Phones Limited's Application, Biotrading and Financing v Biohit, Ladney's Application, Philips v Remington.
Prof. Memberships: Bar European Group, Intellectual Property Bar Association Vice-Chairman, Chancery Bar Association.
Career: MA (Natural Sciences) Downing College, Cambridge. Assistant Recorder, Patents County Court 1994. QC 1997.

WYATT, Derrick QC
Brick Court Chambers (Christopher Clarke QC), London (0171) 583 0777
Recommended in European Union/Competition
Specialisation: European Community Law.
Career: Called to Bar 1972; Silk 1993. Professor of Law, Oxford University, 1996. At Brick Court Chambers since Oct. 1985. Has had numerous publications in the field of European Community Law. Lectures and conference addresses by invitation in various universities in the UK and abroad. Appearances in English Courts and Irish Courts. Advice to public bodies and business enterprises. Legal practice mainly consists of litigation before the Court of Justice of the European Communities in Luxembourg. Cases of note: Government of Gibraltar v The Council, United Kingdom; R v Inland Revenue ex parte: Commerzbank; Webb v Emo.

WYNTER, Colin
Devereux Chambers (Jeffrey Burke QC), London (0171) 353 7534
Recommended in Commercial (litigation)
Specialisation: Insurance and Re-insurance, litigation and arbitration, carriage of goods. Professional negligence.
Prof. Memberships: COMBAR.
Career: Junior Counsel for Defendant Lloyd's Managing Agents in Stockwell v Outhwaite (1991-1992); Agnew – Somerville v Wellington (1994-1996). Also, Caudle v Sharp; Pacific & General Insurance v Baltica Insurance (1996) LRLR, 8; Cicatiello v Anglo European (1994) 1 LLR 678. Home Insurance Co. v M.E. Rutty (1996) LRLR, 415, Virdee v National Grid Co. Plc (1992) IRLR 555, Lambert v West Devon Borough Council, 27/3/97 TLR.
Personal: LLB (First Class) (London), 1982, M.Phil (Cantab) 1983; fluent in French.

YOUNG, David QC
Three New Square (David E.M. Young QC), London (0171) 405 1111
Recommended in Intellectual Property
Specialisation: All aspects of Intellectual Property, Patent (especially Chemical Patent cases), and Passing Off, Trade Marks, Copyright, Franchising, Restrictive Practices, Designs, Breach of Confidence and Computer Law. Appears in Hong Kong and Singapore. Notable Cases include: American Cyanamid v Ethicon (Interloc Injuntion); 3M v Rennicks (Patent); Windsurfing International v Tabur Marine (GB) Ltd (patent); Willemijn v Madge Networks (Patent/Computers); Germinal Holdings (Plant Variety); Allied Signal v Sundstrand (Patent County Court – Electronics); Glaverbel v British Coal; Hoechst v BP (High Court – Patent). Lubrizol

Corpn v. Exxon.

Prof. Memberships: Intellectual Property Bar Assn; Chancery Bar Assn; AIPPI.

Career: Monckton Combe School, Hertford College Oxford – MA. Called to Bar 1966, appointed QC 1980. Master of Lincolns Inn; Recorder of Crown Court (1987 -); Chairman Plant Seeds and Varieties Tribunal (1987 -); Deputy High Court Judge Chancery Division 1993; Deputy Patent County Court Judge 1990. Co-author Terrell on Law of Patents; Young on Passing Off.

Personal: Tennis, skiing, country pursuits.

YOUNG, Timothy QC
20 Essex Street (David Johnson QC), London (0171) 583 9294
Recommended in Shipping

Specialisation: Main area of practice is commercial law and international trade and related areas including arbitration and judicial review. Author of 'Voyage Charters' (1993, LLP). Sometime lecturer in law at St. Edmund Hall, Oxford. Significant recent reported cases: (i) Glencore Grain Rotterdam v Lorico [1997] 2 Lloyd's Rep 386 (FOB Sale Letter of credit waiver) CA; (ii) The Kriti Rex [1996] 2 Lloyd's Rep 171 (COA, unseaworthiness, damages); (iii) AG of New Zealand v Anderson [1995] 2 Lloyd's Rep 264 (Due diligence); (iv) Gill & Duffus v Rionda Futures

[1994] 2 Lloyd's Rep 67 (Sale of goods, demurrage, counter guarantee); (v) The Island Archon [1994] 2 Lloyd's Rep 227 (Implied indemnities).

Prof. Memberships: COMBAR, London Common Law & Commercial Bar Association.

Career: Called to the Bar in 1977 and joined present chambers in 1978. Took Silk 1996.

Personal: Educated at Malvern College 1967-71 and Magdalen College, Oxford 1972-76 (BA, BCL). Born 1st December 1953. Lives in London.

ZACAROLI, Antony
3/4 South Square (Michael Crystal QC), London (0171) 696 9900
Recommended in Insolvency

Specialisation: Practice covers a wide area of business and commercial law, including all aspects of corporate and personal insolvency, litigation relating to property, commercial fraud, constructive trusts, banking, securities, insurance, pensions and professional negligence. Recent reported cases include Cosslett (contractors) Ltd [1998] 2 WLR l3l, Doorbar v Alltime Securities [1996] 1WLR456, Don King Productions v Warren [1998] AllER.608, Natwest Bank v Royal Trust Bank [1996] BCC613.

Career: Called to the Bar (Middle Temple) November 1987 and awarded a Middle Temple

Queen Mother's Scholarship. Lecturer in Law at Pembroke College, Oxford, from 1987-91. Has contributed to Lightman & Moss: The Law of Receivers of Companies; Totty & Jordan: Insolvency (Statutory powers of investigation, Antecedent transactions, Associaties); and Gore-Browne on Companies (Financial Markets & Insolvency).

ZELIN, Geoffrey
Enterprise Chambers (Anthony Mann QC), Leeds (0113) 246 0391
Recommended in Company
London (0171) 405 9471
Newcastle (0191) 222 3344
Leeds (0113) 246 0391

Specialisation: Practises in all areas of company and partnership law including shareholder and partnership disputes, insolvency, enforcement of directors' duties and disqualification. Apart from company law his practice encompasses all areas of commercial Chancery work including property disputes and professional negligence.

Prof. Memberships: Chancery Bar Association

Career: Called to the Bar 1984. Practising in these Chambers since December 1986.

Personal: Interests include skiing, cricket.

INDEX TO THE BAR (including PROFILES)